ENCYCLOPEDIA
OF
AMERICAN QUAKER GENEALOGY

WILLIAM WADE HINSHAW, Washington, D.C.
Author and Publisher

THOMAS WORTH MARSHALL, Washington, D. C.
Editor and Compiler

DR. HARLOW LINDLEY, Columbus, Ohio
(Collaborator and Historian for Ohio)

THE OHIO QUAKER GENEALOGICAL RECORDS
(Now to be Published)

LISTING: Marriages, Births, Deaths, Certificates, Disownments, etc., and Much Collateral Information of Interest to Genealogy, History, Biology, and Social Conditions.

VOLUME IV

(NOTE: This book is one of a two-vol-set, designated as Volumes IV & V, and contains about one-half of the Ohio Quaker Genealogical Records; the other half will be found in Volume V.)

CONTENTS: Volume IV contains the genealogical records found in all original books (known to exist of the 30 Monthly Meetings listed below and now belonging to and under the jurisdiction of the two presently established Ohio Yearly Meetings, viz: the Wilbur and Gurney Branches of the Society of Friends in Ohio; 25 of the said Monthly Meetings are in Ohio, 4 are in western Pa., and 1 in Michigan. (See Volume V for the records of 21 Monthly Meetings in Ohio belonging to Wilmington and Indiana Yearly Meetings.)

N. B.: The records of all Branches are included: Orthodox, Hicksite, Wilbur and Gurney Friends. The Genealogical Records of Meetings of All Types are kept by Monthly (Business) Meetings. Each monthly meeting is attended by Delegates from its sub-ordinate meetings, viz: Meetings for Worship and their Preparative Meetings, under its jurisdiction. Although hundreds of Meetings for Worship have been established in Ohio, their genealogical records are found in the books of the monthly meetings to which they were attached.

Names of the 30 Mo. Mtgs., whose records are contained in this book, and dates of organization:

1.	Westland, Washington Co., Pa.	1785	16.	Sandy Spring, Columbiana Co., O.	1820
2.	Redstone, Fayette Co., Pa.	1793	17.	Goshen (Darby Creek), Logan Co., O.	1824
3.	Sewickley, Westmoreland Co., Pa.	1799	18.	Upper Springfield, Columbiana Co., O.	1825
4.	Concord, Belmont Co., O.	1801	19.	Deerfield (Pennsville), Morgan Co., O.	1827
5.	Plymouth-Smithfield, Jeff. Co., O.	1802	20.	Plainfield, Belmont Co., O.	1828
6.	Middleton, Columbiana Co., O.	1803	21.	Marlborough, Stark Co., O.	1828
7.	Short Creek (Mt. Pleasant) Jeff. Co., O.	1804	22.	Chesterfield, Athens Co., O.	1837
8.	Salem, Columbiana Co., O.	1805	23.	Gilead, Morrow Co., O.	1838
9.	New Garden, Columbiana Co., O.	1808	24.	West, Mahoning Co., O.	1845
10.	Stillwater, Belmont Co., O.	1808	25.	Greenwich, Morrow Co., O.	1848
11.	Providence, Fayette Co., Pa.	1817	26.	Plymouth, Washington Co., O.	1850
12.	Carmel, Columbiana Co., O.	1817	27.	East Goshen, Mahoning Co., O.	1870
13.	Alum Creek, Delaware Co., O.	1817	28.	Columbus, Franklin Co., O.	1874
14.	Flushing, Belmont Co., O.	1818	29.	Cleveland, Cuyahoga Co., O.	1883
15.	Somerset, Belmont Co., O.	1820	30.	Adrian, Michigan (joined O.Y.M. 1869)	1831

Data extracted from original Books of Minutes and Records by:
Cleo F. Thornburgh, Dorothy H. (THORNBURGH) Fausey,
Mrs. J. E. McMullan and Margaret S. Norris,
under the personal direction of
Dr. Harlow Lindley, of Columbus, Ohio

Data edited, compiled and tabulated by
Thomas Worth Marshall, of Washington, D. C.

Mrs. J. E. McMullan, of Huntington, Indiana,
Special Assistant Compiler

All work under the personal supervision of
William Wade Hinshaw, Washington, D. C.

Originally published: Ann Arbor, Michigan, 1946
Reprinted: Genealogical Publishing Co., Inc.
Baltimore, 1973, 1994
Library of Congress Catalogue Card Number 68-31728
International Standard Book Number 0-8063-0548-7
Made in the United States of America

AFFECTIONATELY AND FILIALLY
DEDICATED TO
THE MEMORY OF ALL OUR QUAKER ANCESTORS
WHOSE METICULOUSLY KEPT RECORDS
FURNISH THE DATA FOR THIS
ENCYCLOPEDIA OF AMERICAN QUAKER GENEALOGY

FOREWORD

This book, Volume IV, containing about one-half of the genealogical records extracted from original books of Friends' Meetings in Ohio, combined with the records of four meetings in Pennsylvania, and of one in Michigan, is published simultaneously with Volume V, containing the other half of the Ohio records, the two books having a total of about 2,600 pages of closely tabulated data,-an exact count not yet made. (For full details see Thomas W. Marshall's INTRODUCTION to this book.)

The credit for the successful completion of these two books is principally due to our Editor and Compiler, Thomas W. Marshall, of Washington, D. C., whose untiring interest and personal labor and care, over the past thirteen years, have brought this project to a successful close. Mr. Marshall is not a professional genealogist; but for many years he has devoted much time to Historical and Genealogical research in the Records of early Quaker meetings, doing this as a Hobby. Son of Quaker parents, Swain and Cynthia (Swain) Marshall, Thomas Worth Marshall was born and reared at Economy, Indiana; graduated with a degree of Civil Engineer, at Purdue University (1894), and, after engaging in Engineering work in Indianapolis, Chicago and Anaconda (Mont.) for nine years, he engaged in private practice as a civil engineer in Washington, D. C. (1904), where he has designed the engineering work for many prominent public and private buildings. All of his American ancestors came to America during the early Colonial period, including his ancestors, John Tilly and John Howland, who came over on the Mayflower; several of his ancestors were among those who bought Nantucket Island and settled there about 1660. He is now the head of his own engineering firm, with offices at 1147 Connecticut Avenue, Washington, D. C. In these offices he has set apart a space where our collections of Quaker records are stored and where with his assistant genealogist, Margaret S. Norris, he compiles and edits all of our books during his spare time. When, about 15 years ago, he learned that my wife, Mabel Clyde Hinshaw, and I, were engaged in the copying of Quaker genealogical records in order to preserve them, he volunteered to help us without any kind of remuneration; his offer was gratefully accepted, and he has been working with us on that basis continually since. It is certain that we could not have accumulated such a vast amount of records without his expert aid. We, as well as our subscribers, owe him a deep debt of gratitude.

Another great man to whom much of the success of our Ohio project is due is Dr. Harlow Lindley, Curator of History for the Ohio State Museum, Columbus, Ohio, who, when he learned of our plan to start the copying of Ohio Quaker records in 1933, graciously volunteered to team up with Mr. Marshall, Mrs. Hinshaw and myself, in that he would personally superintend the work of our genealogists in their labors, and would arrange with custodians of the several vaults where books were stored to cordially co-operate with us and give our copyists free access to all books. Needless to say, his deeply appreciated offer was promptly accepted, and the work of extracting the genealogical data from hundreds of original books got under way at once. Dr. Lindley is so well known and so highly regarded everywhere as a historian that there is no need to introduce him further to our subscribers. He has worked with us constantly on this Ohio project during the past thirteen years, giving freely of his time, energies and knowledge of Quaker history to the end that our compilations of Ohio records might be made as perfect as possible. Under his direction, our genealogists made a clean sweep from West to East, of the entire State, spending several months at each vault where original books were known to Dr. Lindley to be stored, extracting the genealogical records from thousands of hand-written pages of hundreds of old musty books whose ink was often so faded that the script could only be read with the aid of a strong magnifying glass. From these books our genealogists extracted:-(a) Marriage Certificates; (b) Births, Deaths and Burials; (c) Certificates of Removal; (d) Disownments and Reception of new members by convincement and on request, to do which they had to read every word contained in both Men's and Women's Minutes. It was a stupendous task, which must be done with meticulous care. The first genealogists whom we sent to work in Ohio under the direction of Dr. Lindley were the Misses Cleo F. and Dorothy H. Thornburg, of Richmond, Indiana, both of whom had been working for us previously in the copying of Indiana Quaker records. They started working on Ohio records in 1933; in something over two years they extracted the genealogical data found in original books which had by that time been deposited in the several fire-proof vaults. Many books were still in the care of clerks and recorders of meetings, as well as in public and private libraries scattered over the State. Dr. Lindley's wide acquaintance enabled him to locate almost all of these books and make them accessible to our copyists. Mrs. J. E. McMullan, of Huntington, Indiana, and Margaret S. Norris, of Washington, D. C., were detailed to finish the Ohio project. Mrs. McMullan compiled the Ohio data into chronological and alphabetical order in about five years; her work was so well done that when her compilations reached Mr. Marshall, he found

FOREWORD

little editing to do on them. Mrs. McMullan is now compiling our Indiana material, much of which she had copied herself from Indiana books.

As Mrs. McMullan's compilations reached Mr. Marshall, he edited them and then turned them over to Margaret S. Norris, who typed them and made the "Master" copies for the printer. She has also made the Indexes to Family Names for both volumes of Ohio records, a huge job in itself, requiring excessive care and more than a year of intensive labor. The vast amount of labor entailed in the preparation of our two volumes of Ohio records will be appreciated when it is realized that these records cover, perhaps, more than a million individuals. This is merely an estimate; an accurate accounting is impossible.

Although a few books have been lost or destroyed by fires, etc., we now feel well satisfied that our two huge volumes of Ohio Quaker records contain all essential genealogical data found in the original books of all Ohio Monthly Meetings which were organized prior to 1890. The genealogical records of all classes of Friends' Meetings have always been kept by the Monthly Meetings.

Almost 300 years ago, Quaker immigrants began settling all along our Eastern Shores from Rhode Island to Georgia; they were at first barred from Massachusetts, but were later allowed to enter that Colony and set up meetings. Their arrivals preceded William Penn by almost 30 years. Although the Quakers earliest to arrive were, for some years, persecuted in all Colonies except Rhode Island, they managed, somehow, to preserve most of their records of marriages, births, deaths, etc. Not until comparatively recent times were Quakers required by laws to obtain Civil marriage licenses in order to marry; nor were they required to send marriage certificates to County Recorders' offices for record. Their meetings required them, however, to appear before them, "hand in hand", declare their intentions to marry and obtain permission. For over 200 years Quaker marriage certificates were recorded only in the books of Quaker meetings. Thus, hundreds of thousands of Quaker marriages cannot be found without examination of Quaker records.

When it is recognized that many millions of present-day Americans are descendants of American Quaker ancestors, even though they may not have been connected with the Society of Friends for several generations, the great importance of American Quaker records to genealogy and history, will be clearly seen.

An ancient philosopher once said: "KNOW THYSELF". Each one of us holds a "spark" of every ancestor he ever had. In the tenth generation back (which is within the period which has elapsed since the Society of Friends was organized) each of us has 1024 different ancestors. No matter what names these ancestors bore, one is as important to us as another. They all are units belonging to our own characters. In tracing our ancestral lineages, we should not stop with merely tracing the line of the name under which we were born; we should trace all lines if we desire to know ourselves. Ancestor seekers who are Quaker descendants are, indeed, fortunate. No other American genealogical records are as complete as the Quaker records.

Many prominent men and women of Ohio have aided us in collecting the Ohio Quaker material, to all of whom we are deeply indebted. A few among these are:-Mr. Edward F. Stratton, of Salem, Ohio; Mr. Ralph S. Coppock, of Alliance, Ohio; Mr. Edward Escolme, of Tecumseh, Mich.; Mr. H. O. Reeder, of Kensington, Ohio; Judge Homer W. Hammond, of Lisbon, Ohio; and Mildred M. Jones, of Mt. Pleasant, Ohio. Many other names should be added, but they are too numerous to be listed here. We are grateful to them all; they deserve the gratitude, too, of all Americans.

It is our hope that our compilations of Ohio Quaker genealogical records may aid millions of American ancestor seekers.

                                                    WILLIAM WADE HINSHAW

The Mayflower Hotel
Washington, D. C.

FRIENDS IN OHIO

Churches, like individuals, have a genealogical record. The first meeting of Friends established within the limits of Ohio (Concord, near Colerain, in 1801) descended directly from Westland Monthly Meeting, located near Brownsville, Pennsylvania, which was established in 1782. Westland Monthly Meeting was set off from Hopewell (Winchester, Virginia). Hopewell Monthly Meeting was set off from Nottingham. Nottingham was set off from New Garden, Pennsylvania. New Garden was set off from Kennett, Pennsylvania. Kennett was set off from Chester, Pennsylvania. Chester was set off from Burlington Monthly Meeting and Burlington was set off from Salem, New Jersey Monthly Meeting, which was established the last day of May in 1676.

Ohio Yearly Meeting was established by Baltimore Yearly Meeting in 1813 and Baltimore Yearly Meeting was organized in 1672. Indiana Yearly Meeting, embracing the Friends of western and southwestern Ohio, was established by Ohio Yearly Meeting in 1813 and in 1892 that part of Indiana Yearly Meeting in southwestern Ohio was organized into a Yearly Meeting distinguished as Wilmington Yearly Meeting.

THE PLANTING

The first direct contact of Friends with the Old Northwest so far as we have positive proof was in 1773, just ten years after Great Britain had secured title to the territory from France. Two Friends, members of the Philadelphia Yearly Meeting, Zebulon Heston and John Parrish, prompted by a desire to make a religious visit to the Delaware Indians who had moved westward into the eastern part of what is now the state of Ohio, spent about ten weeks making a trip in order to express their interest in the welfare of these first Americans.

The first Friends minister of record to cross the Ohio River and preach in the limits of the Northwest Territory was Thomas Beals who was born in Chester County, Pennsylvania, in March 1719, the son of John and Sarah Bowater Beals. From John and Sarah descended a very large number of members of the now widely extended Yearly Meetings of Indiana, Western, Iowa and Wilmington, as well as those west of the Mississippi River and to the Pacific coast. Among them are to be found a large number of outstanding ministers in the Society of Friends. The Beals family moved from Pennsylvania and Maryland and later to Hopewell, near Winchester, Virginia. Thomas Beals moved with this family to North Carolina in 1748 or 1749 being then about twenty-nine years old, and first stopped at Cane Creek. Then, with his family, he moved to New Garden, North Carolina, which was frontier territory. In a very short time he was joined by some other families, and in the year 1753, being then about thirty-four years of age, he came forth in the ministry. How long he lived at New Garden we do not know but presume it was for several years. The next move he made was to Westfield, Surry County, North Carolina. Here he was instrumental in the development of a large meeting. He must have lived at New Garden and Westfield about thirty years, during which time he paid several lengthy visits to the Indians.

In the year 1775, twenty years before Wayne's Treaty with the Indians at Greenville, Ohio, Beals, accompanied by four Friends, started to pay a visit to the Shawnee Indians and some other tribes and, after passing a fort not far from Clinch Mountain in Virginia, they were arrested and carried back to the fort to be tried for their lives on the charge of being confederates with the hostile Indians. The officers, understanding that one of them was a preacher, required a sermon before they went in for trial. Beals thought it right to hold a meeting with the soldiers, which proved to be a highly favored season. A young man then in the fort was converted and, some time after, moved among Friends and became a member and, at a very advanced age, bore public testimony to the truth of the principles of which he was convinced at the fort. After this meeting was over the Friends were kindly entertained and were free and at liberty to go on their journey. They crossed the Ohio River into what is now the state of Ohio and held many meetings with the Indians with satisfaction and returned home with much peace of mind. Thomas Beals told his friends that he saw with his spiritual eye the seed of Friends scattered all over that good land and that one day there would be the greatest gathering of Friends there of any place in the world and that his faith was strong in the belief that he would live to see Friends settle north of the Ohio River.

In 1781, Beals moved from Westfield, North Carolina, to Blue Stone, Giles County, Virginia, where he lived but a few years. While there, their sufferings were very great in many ways, not only from lack of the necessities of life, but their son-in-law, James Horton, was taken prisoner by the Indians and, from the most reliable information that could be obtained, was carried to old Chillicothe, near Frankfort, Ohio, and there put to death. This move to Blue Stone does not appear to have had the approval of Beals' friends, for Nathan Hunt states that they sent a committee to send him back to Westfield, North Carolina. The little meeting of twenty or thirty families was entirely broken up at Blue Stone.

In the year 1785, he moved to Lost Creek, Tennessee, and in 1793 he moved to Grayson County, Virginia, at which several places Nathan Hunt states that Thomas Beals set up meetings and says that he was very zealous for the support of the testimonies of Friends. In 1799, Beals, who had visited this country twenty four years before, now moved to Quaker Bottom, Ohio, along with other members of his family and in the spring of 1801 he moved to Salt Creek, near the present town of Adelphia.

On August 29, 1801, he died and was buried near Richmondale, Ross County, Ohio, in a coffin of regular shape, hollowed out of a solid white walnut tree by his ever faithful friend, Jesse Baldwin, and assisted by Enoch Cox and others, and covered by a part of the same tree, which was selected for the purpose by the deceased while living. The grave of Thomas Beals was recently located and local Friends have erected an appropriate monument to his memory.

In planting Quakerism in the old Northwest, the story of Thomas Beals and his faithful wife and devoted family is but one illustration of the hundreds that might be given, nor was he the only one buried in a log coffin. Many were buried in nothing but boards laid around them among the lone mountains, never to be seen or marked by loved ones, but to Thomas Beals belongs the credit of having been the first friend to carry the message of Christ into the vast region north and west of the Ohio, which, in a few years, was to become the great center of life not only of the Society of Friends, but of our Nation.

Any attempt to sketch the early history of the Quakers in the Old Northwest must begin at the Atlantic seaboard. Not until disastrous Indian wars had forced the tribes to reservations or driven them toward the Mississippi was there any pronounced movement of the Friends to The West.

Explaining the movement, and the original settlements of Friends, the first established meeting of friends west of the Alleghany Mountains was at Westland Meeting in southwestern Pennsylvania. This was provided for by the action of Hopewell Monthly Meeting, Virginia, November 11, 1782. In 1776, it had been reported that eighteen families had moved west of the mountains.

On the other side of the Monongahela River,

at Redstone, in Fayette County, another Friends settlement was made. Hopewell Monthly Meeting gave sanction to other changes in 1785 and Westland became a monthly meeting and Redstone a preparative meeting and this condition continued until April 26, 1793, when Redstone Monthly Meeting was established. By 1797 a quarterly meeting was established to be called Redstone. This quarterly meeting held its first session March 5, 1798 with Baltimore Yearly Meeting as the parent body. The later history of Redstone Quarterly Meeting is an illustration of what happened to the several Friends organizations in the shifting of population. Called into existence in the midst of the eighteenth century, as just explained, it had an honorable and useful existence of sixty-four years. Its membership, in turn, was depleted by removals farther west, and the meeting was laid down in 1862.

Groups of Friends from Pennsylvania, Maryland, and Virginia were augmented by a large movement from the Carolinas and Georgia. Probably the greatest contributing factor in this movement was the slavery issue, and after the passage of the famous Ordinance of 1787 Friends knew that the territory north and west of the Ohio would be forever free from slavery, although there were doubtless other contributing reasons.

In the year 1796, George Harlan and family, members of the Society of Friends, moved to the Ohio region stopping first at Columbia (Cincinnati) and the next year located on the Little Miami River within the present limits of Warren County, becoming the first sheriff of the county and later a member of the General Assembly of the state. So far as is known this was the first Quaker family to locate in Ohio. In 1796, James Baldwin and Phineas Hunt, with their families, members of the Society of Friends, from Westfield, North Carolina, moved to the Virginia shore of the Ohio River. In February, 1797, the Baldwins and Hunts crossed the Ohio River and settled opposite Green Bottom near each other. Two families of Friends were now settled together in the Northwest Territory with one before mentioned (the Harlans) quite remote from them.

On May 8th of the same year, 1797, a group of Friends moved from Westland, Pennsylvania, and settled at High Bank on the east side of the Scioto River below Chillicothe. In the latter part of this same year, Jesse Baldwin moved from his first location opposite Green Bottom, some eighteen miles down the Ohio, and settled in what was called Quaker Bottom, in Lawrence County, opposite the mouth of the Guyandot River, and the present town of Guyandot. So far as can be ascertained, this was where Friends in the Northwest Territory first sat down to hold a meeting for divine worship.

John Warner, son of Isaac and Mary, was born at High Bank, Ross County, Ohio, on July

12, 1798. So far as we know, he was the first child born as a birthright member of the Society of Friends northwest of the Ohio River, and, on November 11 of the same year, Rebecca Chandler, daughter of William and Hannah Chandler, was born near the same place.

In 1798, a group of Friends from Hopewell, Virginia, settled at High Bank and another group from North Carolina settled at Salt Creek, near Richmondale, Ross County, Ohio, In 1799 Obediah Overman and his family from Grayson County, Virginia, arrived with Thomas Beals and his family, already mentioned. On their arrival, they opened a meeting for worship in the dwelling of Jesse Baldwin which was regularly held during their residence at that place. The nearest meeting to them was Westland, Pennsylvania, about two hundred miles away. Sometime during the year 1799, Taylor Webster and family from Redstone, Pennsylvania, settled at Grassy Prairies, five miles northeast of Chillicothe.

The intensified movement began around 1800. By 1800, settlements were being made west of the Ohio River, some miles out from Wheeling, Virginia. Just about the same time, Friends from the south were migrating into southern and southwestern, Ohio, and soon the eastern and New England states were making their contributions. They constituted a meeting-going population. Those people, who, in the long march through the wilderness had rested on First-days and at the accustomed hour, had gathered around their campfires for silent worship or listened to vocal ministry from some of their own number, were not likely to neglect their religious duties when their travels were ended. There is a tradition which probably is true that at Concord (Colerain) a group assembled first on the trunk of a fallen tree, then were invited to the newly erected cabin of Jonathan Taylor and later moved to the log meeting house which was one of the earliest structures.

The first Friends moved into eastern Ohio in September, 1800. In less than one year Friends so increased that two preparative meetings were established and on December 19, 1801, Concord Monthly Meeting was opened, consisting of the two preparative meetings at Concord and Short Creek. These first preparative meetings were branches of Westland Monthly Meeting, Pa., and the first monthly meeting was a branch of Redstone QM, Pennsylvania. The stream of emigrants seemed unending and soon there were Friends communities in Belmont, Jefferson, Harrison, Columbiana, Morgan and Washington Counties. Early in 1804 these meetings began to look to the establishment of a quarterly meeting. Their request was granted by the yearly meeting in 1806 and Short Creek QM convened for the first time on June 6, 1807.

In the latter part of 1799 some families of friends from Bush River MM, South Carolina, settled near the present site of Waynesville.

Some months later a group of Friends arrived from Hopewell MM, Va., and during the same year, a few from North Carolina. Other Friends continued to arrive and a volunteer meeting for worship was established April 26, 1801, at Waynesville. Twelve families were represented in the meeting. All of these members were certified to Westland Monthly Meeting, Western Pennsylvania. This meeting was recognized by Westland MM, December 26, 1801, and Miami MM was established October 13, 1803. From this nucleus developed the meetings of Ohio west of the Hocking River, including what later became West Branch QM to the north and Whitewater QM in eastern Indiana, as well as all the friends meetings in Indiana and farther west.

The rapid settlement of Friends in the valleys of the Miamis is shown by the fact that in three years, from the middle of 1804 to the middle of 1807, there were received at Miami MM 367 removal certificates conveying to that meeting the membership of 1697 persons. These did not all settle in the vicinity of Waynesville nor even in Warren County, but were scattered through what are now Clinton, Highland, Greene, Montgomery, Miami and Preble counties in Ohio, and Wayne County, Indiana.

EARLY HISTORY OF OHIO YEARLY MEETING.

Late in the 18th Century when the tide of emigration was turning from the southern and eastern states to the new Northwest, it embraced among its number many Friends who for various reasons were seeking homes amid the wooded hills of eastern Ohio. Some had become dissatisfied with the conditions of slavery about them, while others saw possibilities for themselves and their children that they could never realize in the older communities. As they settled in this new country, they soon established meetings for worship and discipline under the care and authority of Baltimore YM, to which body reports were made and delegates sent year by year.

After several years had passed and the number of meetings increased, the Friends felt the need of a YM within reach of more Friends who wished to attend. Accordingly, in the 10th month of 1810, the quarterly meetings of Redstone and Salem sent a request to Baltimore YM for the establishment of a YM for Friends west of the Alleghany Mountains. In the minutes of the Baltimore YM for that year we find the following recorded:

At the YM of Friends held in Baltimore for the western shore of Maryland and by adjournments from the 15th of 10th Mo. to the 19th of the same inclusive 1810. The seventh of the month and fourth of the week.

Redstone and Salem QM having forwarded for the consideration of this meeting propositions for a division thereof so as to establish another yearly meeting on the western side of the Alleghany, which being weightily considered, a tender sympathy was felt for friends in this remote situation to the westward and the exercise into which the meeting was introduced on the subject resulting in a conclusion that it be referred for further consideration.

In 1811, 10th Mo. 15th of the Mo. and 3rd of the week, this record is made:

The request from four quarterly meetings was brought before the yearly meeting. The very important subject relative to a division of this yearly meeting, referred for further consideration from the meeting last year, being resumed and the four quarters west of the Alleghany Mountains having in their reports expressed their united judgment in favor of establishing a yearly meeting north west of the Ohio River, a weighty deliberation thereon engaged the attention of the meeting, and much tender feeling being witnessed thereon engaged the attention of the meeting for Friends in their remote situation, it was concluded that a committee be appointed to unite with a committee of women friends in deliberating further of the proposition, and to report to a future setting. The following Friends were accordingly appointed to the service, viz.: Evan Thomas, Thomas More, Isaac Balderston, Gerard T. Hopkins, Joseph Griest, Thomas Wood, Solomon Shepherd, Abel Thomas, James Mendenhall, Asa Moore, John McPherson, Israel Janney, Thomas Farquhar, Henry Mills, William Wood, Samuel Potts, Horton Howard, Carmon Thomas, Abraham Warrington, William Heald, Elisha Schooley, Robert Hannah, John Hunt, James Hadley, Thomas Shreve, George Ellicott, and Goldsmith Chandlee. Seventh of the Month and fifth of the week.

The following report from the Committee appointed on the subject of a division of this yearly meeting was read and considered, viz.:

The Committee appointed to take into consideration the proposal of a division of the yearly meeting as brought forward from the quarterly meetings west of the Alleghany Mountains having met in company with women Friends by a free communication of sentiment, are united in believing (it) to be a right one, but are most easy to propose that the weighty subject may continue under consideration of Friends another year and the yearly meetings with which this corresponds may also be informed thereof. Which is submitted to the yearly meeting.
Signed on behalf of the Committee.
Evan Thomas
James Mendenhall
Mary Mifflin
Sarah Janney

Again in 1812 the same request was considered as follows:

At the yearly meeting held in Baltimore for the Western Shore of Maryland and by adjournments from the 12th day of 10th month to the 16th of the same inclusive, 1812.

The consideration of the important subject of a division of the yearly meeting, as continued from the meeting last year, being resumed, copies of minutes were produced from the yearly meetings of Friends in Philadelphia and Virginia informing that each of the said meetings had appointed a committee (most of whom were present) to unite with us in deliberating thereon. It was concluded to refer the subject to the consideration of a committee in conjunction with those Friends now attending by the appointment of the above yearly meetings, and such committee of women friends as may be appointed by their meeting, and to report to a future sitting. The following friends were appointed to that service: Isiah Balderston, Evan Thomas, George Ellicott, William Riley, Thomas Wood, Joseph Griest, John Talbott, Abel Thomas, James Mendenhall, Israel Janney, Asa Moore, Thomas Shreve, David Grave, Joseph Thomas, Henry Mills, John Haines, Joseph Steere, Jonathan Taylor, Isaac Parker, Horton Howard, Thomas French, Thomas Grissell, Samuel Davis, Nathan Galbreath, John Furnace, Mordecai Walker, Ennion Williams, John Stall and Gerard T. Hopkins. Thirteenth of the month and third of the week.

The committee appointed on the important subject of a division of this yearly meeting brought in the following report:
To the Yearly Meeting now sitting:

The committee appointed to unite with women Friends in a further consideration of the interesting subject of a yearly meeting to be held in the state of Ohio, report we have several times met and have had the company of several brethren of the yearly meetings of Philadelphia and Virginia, and believe that in our deliberation with a degree of solemnity under which we are free to propose that the quarterly meetings west of the Alleghany Mountains within the verge of this yearly meeting be at full liberty to convene together at Short Creek on the third first day in 8th month next, in the capacity of a yearly meeting, agreeable to their prospect and to desire as expressed in the report to the meeting last year. All of which we submit to the yearly meeting.
Signed on behalf of the committee by
James Mendenhall
Gerard T. Hopkins
Rachel Neave
Sarah Brown

Which was united with, and the quarterly meetings to the westward of the Alleghany Mountains, which hitherto belonged to this yearly meeting, were left at liberty to send representative thereunto accordingly.

And so it came about that according to this liberty granted by Baltimore YM, Ohio YM opened with the reading of the following minute:

At Ohio Yearly Meeting for the State of Ohio, Indiana Territory and the adjacent parts of Pennsylvania and Virginia; first opened and held at Short Creek the 14th of 8th month 1813. In the minutes of this first year of the Yearly Meeting we find this record, the following named Friends are appointed to propose the name of a Friend for Treasurer of this meeting and what sum they believe necessary to be raised the ensuing year for the benefit of the Society, and what proportion thereof they apprehend each Quarter should pay; viz.: Jacob Griffith, Samuel Jones (of Redstone), Charles Dinjee, Isaac Parker, Joseph Steere, Abner Grigg, Tacheers Test, William Heald, Abraham Warrington, Richard Garrett, Robert Whittaker, Noah Harris, Samuel Jones (of West Branch), Samuel Brown and Henry Yout. Enoch Harris was appointed Treasurer of the Yearly Meeting.

For some reason Friends were interested in naming their meetings for streams. Among the principal Friends meetings contributing directly to the making of Ohio Quakerism are Hopewell and South River in Virginia; Redstone in Pennsylvania; Cane Creek, Spring, Deep River, Deep Creek, Symons Creek, Suttons Creek, Core Sound, Neuse, Woodland, Back Creek, South Fork, New Garden, Holly Springs and Piney Woods in North Carolina; Bush River and Cane Creek in South Carolina; and Lost Creek in Tennessee. And in Ohio we find Short Creek, Cross Creek, Stillwater, Dry Run, New Garden, Alum Creek, Sandy Spring, Miami, Lee's Creek, Fairfield, Clear Creek, Green Plains, Tod's Fork, Turtle Creek, Caesar's Creek, South Fork, Mill Creek, Lick Branch, Walnut Creek, Last Fork, Grassy Run, Lytle's Creek and West Branch. The same type of names are found in Indiana, Iowa and Kansas.

When Ohio Yearly Meeting was organized in 1813, it consisted of the following Monthly Meetings: Westland and Redstone in southwestern Pennsylvania and Short Creek, Concord, Plymouth, Plainfield, Stillwater, Middleton, Salem, New Garden, West Branch, Mill Creek, Elk, Miami, Caesar's Creek, Fall Creek, Fairfield, Center, Darby Creek and Clear Creek in Ohio. In 1815 all these Monthly Meetings were still in existence with the addition of Union, Marlborough and Cincinnati. In 1822 we find Providence Monthly Meeting in addition to the two southwestern Pennsylvania. In Ohio, the following Monthly Meetings, in addition to the ones already named, had been established; Carmel, Sandy Spring, Smithfield, Flushing, Somerset, Lee's Creek, Newberry, Springfield, Green Plain, Alum Creek, and Westfield. These were all in existence before the opening of Indiana Yearly Meeting in 1821 after which those in western and southern Ohio were attached to Indiana Yearly Meeting. However, they were all located within the limits of the state of Ohio. Beginning with 1809 (White Water) several monthly meetings were established in Indiana by Baltimore and Ohio

Yearly Meetings. These meetings were transferred to Indiana Yearly Meeting in 1821.

In 1826, two years before the Separation (Hicksite), the names of Monthly Meetings belonging to Ohio Yearly Meeting were, Westland, Redstone, Smithfield, Short Creek, Mount Pleasant, Concord, Flushing, Middleton, Salem, Upper Springfield, Marlborough, Stillwater, Plainfield, Somerset, Ridge, New Garden, Elk Run and Carmel. In the same year the names of the Monthly Meetings in Ohio belonging to Indiana Yearly Meeting were Miami, West Branch, Center, Fairfield, Elk, Caesar's Creek, Mill Creek, Fall Creek, Goshen (name changed from Darby Creek in 1824), Clear Creek, Union, Cincinnati, Newberry, Lee's Creek, Springfield, Alum Creek, Green Plain, Westfield, Springboro and Dover.

At the time of the two major separations in Ohio, the Hicksite in 1828 and the Wilburite or Conservative in 1854, some monthly meetings were divided, each claiming to be the legal Friends meeting and in some instances the meeting as a whole joined in the separation movement. This was true for the state as a whole in 1828, but the Conservative separation only included the territory within the field of Ohio Yearly Meeting. In 1832 the following Hicksite Monthly Meetings were in existence in the state: Short Creek, Concord, Smithfield, Flushing, Salem, Middleton, Stillwater, Plainfield, Deerfield, Somerset, New Garden, Carmel and Marlborough in Ohio Yearly Meeting, and Miami, Springborough, Cincinnati, Green Plain, Goshen, Center, Fall Creek, Alum Creek, Westfield and Elk in Indiana Yearly Meeting.

As a result of this separation, the meeting records were scattered. In many cases, the original meeting obtained the records and in other cases the separated body obtained them. When the meeting as a whole joined the separatists movement, that meeting carried on with the former records. All this makes the problem of Friends Monthly Meeting records in Ohio a difficult one. As an aid to those interested in these records, we give as much data as is available concerning their whereabouts.

DEPOSITORIES OF FRIENDS MEETING RECORDS IN OHIO

The records of Ohio Yearly Meeting are much scattered. The greater number are preserved in the vault of the People's Bank in Mt. Pleasant; in the Friends Yearly Meeting House in Damascus, Harris Stanley in charge; in the vault of the Conservative Friends Meeting House in Salem, Edward F. Stratton in charge; and in the vault of the Friends Boarding School near Barnesville. The largest collection of Hicksite Quaker records is in the Friends Historical Library at Swarthmore College, Swarthmore, Pennsylvania. The records of the Ohio Yearly Meeting, Conservative, are to be found chiefly at Salem, Ohio, and Friends Boarding School at Barnesville as mentioned above.

The Library of the Ohio State Archealogical and Historical Society, Columbus, and Western Reserve Historical Society Library each have a few books. Others are in the custody of individuals and of local meetings.

The largest collection of meeting records within the limits of Ohio is to be found in the library of Wilmington College. These are records of meetings belonging to Wilmington Yearly Meeting. Some are still held within the limits of their respective monthly meetings. The Library of the Ohio State Archealogical and Historical Society has a few books of records of meetings in Wilmington Yearly Meeting.

The minutes of the monthly meetings in Ohio belonging to Indiana Yearly Meeting (Orthodox) are to be found in their respective meetings or in the Yearly Meeting vault at Richmond, Indiana.

The minutes of the meetings in Ohio belonging to Indiana Yearly Meeting (Hicksite or General Conference) are preserved in the vault of the Friends Home, Waynesville, and at the Laura-moore, Richmond, Indiana.

QUAKER "FIRSTS" in OHIO

The following data covering the beginning of activities of Friends in Ohio is accurate so far as available information is concerned.

1773 Zebulon Heston and John Parrish made a visit to the Delaware Indians in Ohio

1775 Thomas Beals, first Friends minister to preach in the Old Northwest Territory. He moved to Ohio in 1799 and died in 1801 and was buried at Richmondale, Ohio.

1795 George Harlan and family, members of the Society of Friends, settled on the Little Miami River at Deerfield, about four miles from the present town of Morrow.

1797 First meeting for worship held at Quaker Bottom in Lawrence County.

1798 John Warner, son of Isaac and Mary Warner was born 7 Mo. 12, 1798, and Rebecca Chandler, daughter of William and Hannah Chandler, was born 11 Mo. 11, 1798. Both were born in Ross County.

1801 First Monthly Meeting established at Concord (Colerain) 12 Mo. 19, 1801. Volunteer meeting for worship established at Waynesville 4 Mo. 26, 1801. It was recognized as a meeting for worship by Westland Monthly Meeting (Pa.) 12 Mo. 26, 1801, and Redstone Quarterly Meeting (Pa.) granted a monthly meeting 9 Mo. 5, 1803 which was officially opened 10 Mo. 13, 1803 as Miami Monthly Meeting.

1807 Short Creek Quarterly Meeting (Mt. Pleasant) met 6 Mo. 6, 1807.

1813 Ohio Yearly Meeting met at Short Creek (Mt. Pleasant) 8 Mo. 14, 1813

1813-
1814 Yearly Meeting house at Mt. Pleasant erected (still standing).

1837 Ohio Yearly Meeting Boarding School (Mt. Pleasant) 1 Mo. 23, 1837.

HARLOW LINDLEY

Columbus, Ohio

INTRODUCTION

When the Quakers began settlements in Ohio and Indiana, their meetings were established by and attached to Redstone, (Pa.) Quarterly Meeting in Baltimore Yearly Meeting. This condition continued until 1813, when Ohio Yearly Meeting was established by Baltimore Yearly Meeting and took jurisdiction over all meetings in Ohio, western Pennsylvania and Indiana. Indiana Yearly Meeting was established in 1821 and took jurisdiction over western Ohio and all of Indiana. With the Hicksite separation, separate Yearly Meetings were established to serve the Hicksite Monthly Meetings in the territory of Ohio Yearly Meeting and those in the territory of Indiana Yearly Meeting. About 1854 Ohio Yearly Meeting was divided into the Gurney and Wilbur branches. The Gurney branch holds its Yearly Meeting at Damascus--the Wilbur branch at Stillwater, near Barnesville. About 1892, Wilmington Yearly Meeting was organized and took jurisdiction over the meetings in south-central Ohio which had previously belonged to Indiana Yearly Meeting. Indiana Yearly Meeting still has jurisdiction over meetings in west-central and south-western Ohio.

The Monthly Meetings whose records are abstracted in this volume are those in the areas of Ohio Yearly Meeting held at Damascus and Ohio Yearly Meeting held at Stillwater near Barnesville. Records of meetings formerly held in these areas, but now laid down (including Hicksite), are included. The Yearly Meeting held at Damascus includes Monthly Meetings in northern Ohio, as far south as Columbus, a few meetings in southeastern Michigan and (formerly) a few meetings in western Pennsylvania. The Yearly Meeting held near Barnesville includes Monthly Meetings in east-central and southeastern Ohio and meetings (now laid down) in western Pennsylvania. It will be noted that the areas of the two branches overlap in east-central Ohio and in western Pennsylvania. Attempt has been made to designate the Gurney and Wilbur records by the letters G and W, respectively. Similarly, Hicksite records are designated by the letter H.

Records of Monthly Meetings in south-central Ohio (Wilmington Yearly Meeting) and west-central and southwestern Ohio (Indiana Yearly Meeting) may be found in Volume V of this Encyclopedia.

The first Friends migrating to Ohio became members of Hopewell Monthly Meeting, Virginia, and a little later of Westland or Redstone Monthly Meetings, Pennsylvania until they could establish meetings of their own. As Monthly Meetings were established in Ohio these Friends automatically became members of the new meetings within whose territories they happened to reside. No certificates of transfer were issued and no list of names was entered in the records of either meeting. Similarly, when an Ohio Meeting was divided to set up a new Monthly Meeting, the membership was divided according to place of residence and no list of members of the new meeting was entered in the records of either meeting. The names of persons who became members of new meetings in this way will disappear from the records of the parent meeting but may be followed to the records of any new meeting in which they may appear by reference to the family name index at the end of the book.

Washington, D. C.   THOMAS WORTH MARSHALL

CONTENTS

ABBREVIATIONS

b	born
bur	buried
cert	certificate
ch	child, children
co	chosen overseer (s)
com	complained, complained of
con	condemned
d	died
dec	deceased
dis	disowned, disowned for
dt	daughter, daughters
fam	family
form	formerly
gc	granted certificate
gct	granted certificate to
gl	granted letter
h	husband
jas	joined another society
ltm	liberated to marry, left at liberty to marry
m	marry, married, marrying, marriage
mbr	member
mbrp	membership
mcd	married contrary to discipline
MH	meeting house
MM	monthly meeting
mos	married out of society
mou	married out of unity
mtg	meeting
prc	produced a certificate
prcf	produced a certificate from
QM	quarterly meeting
rec	receive, received
recrq	received by request
relfc	released from care for
relrq	released by request
rem	remove, removed
rm	reported married
rmt	reported married to
roc	received on certificate
rocf	received on certificate from
rol	received on letter
rolf	received on letter from
rpd	reported
rq	request, requests, requested
rqc	requested certificate
rqct	requested certificate to
rqcuc	requested to come under care (of mtg)
rst	reinstate, reinstated
s	son, sons
uc	under care (of mtg)
w	wife
YM	yearly meeting

WESTLAND MONTHLY MEETING

Westland Monthly Meeting, located in Washington County, Pennsylvania, was opened the 12th of 11th month, 1785, by direction of Warrington and Fairfax Quarterly Meeting. The verge of the meeting included Washington, Allegheny, Westmoreland, Fayette and Greene Counties, Pa., and adjoining counties in Virginia (now West Virginia) and Ohio.

Local meetings subordinate to Westland Monthly Meeting included Westland, Redstone, Little Redstone, Fallowfield, Sandy Creek, (Va.), Pike Run, Richland (Va.), Plymouth, Sandhill and Wheeling.

Early members included Eleazar Brown, Joseph Brown, Nathan Brown, Elizabeth Brown, John Cadwallader, Rees Cadwallader, Ruth Cadwallader, Septimus Cadwallader, Sarah Cadwallader, Thomas Cook, John Coope, Mary Coope, John Couzens, Sarah Couzens, James Crawford, Josiah Crawford, Henry Dixon, Josiah Dixon, Dinah Dixon, Elizabeth Dixon, David England, Mary England, Obed Garwood, Aaron Hackney, John Heald, Elizabeth Hewes, Amos Hough, clerk, Samuel Jackson, Rebecca Jackson, Isaac Jenkinson, John Jenkinson, Barnabas McNamee, Aaron Newport, Isaac Pedan, John Raley, Frances Raley, Mary Raley, Sarah Rigg, Ann Schooley, Abraham Smith, Henry Smith, Martha Smith, clerk, Sarah Smith, Benjamin Townsend, John Townsend, Ebenezer Walker, William Wilson and Elizabeth Wilson.

The meeting was divided by the Hicksite movement in 1828 and again by the Wilburite movement in 1854. The Orthodox and Hicksite branches were laid down in 1864. Members of the Orthodox branch were transferred to Redstone Monthly Meeting; members of the Hicksite branch to Salem Monthly Meeting. The Wilburite (or Conservative) branch was laid down in 1865.

RECORDS

ADAMSON
1787, 9, 8. James dis
1789, 4, 25. Hannah (form Heald) dis mou
1792, 1, 28. Hannah rst by rq
1806, 5, 24. Hannah gct Middleton MM
1808, 2, 27. Margaret (form Smith) dis mcd
1811, 9, 28. Middleton MM was given permission
    to rst James

ADBERT
1849, 2, 21. Beulah (form Crawford) dis mcd

AILES
1804, 6, 7. Mary [Ayles] m Nathan GAUSE

1786, 5, 13. Amos con mcd
1786, 5, 13. Ann (form Brown) con mcd
1806, 11, 22. Joseph gct Redstone MM, to m
    Sarah Ball
1807, 5, 23. Sarah, w Joseph, rocf Redstone
    MM, dtd 1807,4,3
1813, 9, 25. Aaron con mou
1814, 9, 29. Amos dis mou
1815, 11, 30. Stephen dis mou
1815, 11, 30. Sarah Waits (form Ailes) dis mou
1819, 1, 28. James dis mcd
1821, 11, 22. Aaron dis jas
1824, 9, 23. Isaac dis mcd
1832, 6, 20. Joseph dis mou

AIRY
1802, 3, 27. Mary [Ary] rocf Redstone MM, dtd
    1802,3,5
1803, 3, 26. Mary gct Redstone MM

ALDERSON
1843, 6, 21. Cert rec for Harrison & w, Emma,
    & ch, William Charles, Agness & Anna Mary,
    from Preston MM, England, endorsed to Cin-
    cinnati MM
1843, 6, 21. Cert rec for Elizabeth, sister of
    Harrison, from Preston MM, England, endors-
    ed to Cincinnati MM

ALLEN
1792, 10, 31. William, s Joseph & Deborah,
    Washington Co., Pa.; m at Fallowfield,
    Sarah ENGLAND, dt David & Mary, Washing-
    ton Co., Pa.
1799, 3, 27. Deborah m James WINDER
1800, 12, 31. Joseph, Washington Co., Pa.; m
    at Westland, Hannah Beirson

1793, 8, 24. William & w, Sarah, dis
1793, 8, 24. Amy Stockdale (form Allen) dis
    mou
1796, 2, 27. Samuel dis disunity
1797, 2, 25. Joshua dis mou
1799, 6, 22. Orpha, w James, rocf Kennet MM,
    dtd 1798,12,13
1799, 10, 26. Isaac & w, Sarah, & ch, Emmor &

David, rocf London Grove MM, dtd 1799,5,1
1803, 12, 24. John rocf London Grove MM, dtd
    1803,8,13
1804, 8, 25. John con mou
1806, 7, 26. John gct Middleton MM
1807, 6, 27. Joseph & w, Hannah, dis disunity
1817, 1, 23. David gct Salem MM, O.
1818, 1, 22. New Garden MM was given per-
    mission to rst Hannah

ALMAN
1791, 3, 26. John & three ch recrq
1793, 3, 23. Hannah [Almond] rocf Hopewell
    MM, dtd 1792,12,3
1804, 4, 28. John [Almon] & w, Hannah, & ch,
    William, Ebeneezer, Thomas, John, Jesse &
    Hannah, gct Middleton MM

ALSTON
1792, 7, 28. Thomas [Alstone] rocf Duck Creek
    MM, dtd 1791,11,12
1793, 7, 27. Thomas gct Concord MM

ANDERSON
1788, 5, 1. Margaret m Benjamin GILBERT

1787, 4, 14. Margaret rocf Newgarden MM, dtd
    1783,9,6

ANDREWS
1792, 10, 27. Mary (form Shepherd) dis

ANTRIM
1801, 12, 26. John & w, Elizabeth, & gr dt,
    Esther, rocf Hopewell MM, dtd 1801,7,6,
    endorsed by Red Stone MM, 1801,12,4
1809, 11, 25. Esther Heacock (form Antrim) dis
    mou
1818, 2, 19. John & w, Elizabeth, gct Red-
    stone MM

ARNOLD
1800, 5, 24. Joseph & s, Joseph, rocf Con-
    tentnea MM, dtd 1800,3,8
1800, 7, 26. Sarah & dt, Mary, Sarah & Penina
    rocf Contentney MM, dtd 1800,3,8

ASHMEAD
1824, 12, 23. Abigail (form Carver) dis mcd

ATHERTON
1812, 4, 2. Boaz, s Richard & Ann, Washing-
    ton Co., Pa.; m at Westland, Mary ROSS, dt
    Reuben & Elizabeth, Washington Co., Pa.

1790, 12, 25. Richard rocf Warrington MM, dtd
    1790,11,13
1794, 1, 26. Cert rec for Mary, Thomas, Fran-
    ces & Ann, ch Henry, from Warrington MM,
    dtd 1792,11,12, endorsed to Redstone MM
1804, 9, 22. Richard rocf Concord MM
1811, 11, 23. Boaz recrq
1814, 4, 23. Boaz & w, Mary, gct Plainfield

ATHERTON, continued
    MM

AYRES
1812, 10, 24. Rebecca (form Heaton) rpd mcd

BACKMAN
1864, 4, 21. Ruth transferred to Salem MM;
    this mtg being laid down (H)

BAILY
1796, 6, 25. Ellis rocf New Garden MM, dtd
    1796,4,2
1806, 4, 26. Ellis [Bailey] con mou
1806, 9, 27. Hannah (form Johnson) con mou
1806, 9, 27. Ellis gct Redstone MM

BAKER
1861, 3, 28. Philena G. (form Griffith) con
    mcd (H)
1864, 4, 21. Philena G. transferred to Salem
    MM; this mtg being laid down (H)

BALL
1788, 7, 26. Joseph rocf Richland MM, dtd
    1788,3,20
1797, 5, 27. Thomas rocf Richland MM, dtd
    1797,4,20
1797, 10, 28. Jesse rocf Richland MM, dtd
    1797,8,17
1797, 10, 28. John & w, Ann, & ch, Joel, Jo-
    seph, Margaret, Jesse, Sarah, James, Su-
    sanna & Iden, rocf Richland MM, dtd 1797,
    8,17
1798, 3, 24. Cert rec some time ago for
    Jesse & John & fam endorsed to Redstone MM
1798, 7, 28. Thomas dis mou
1799, 8, 24. Jesse rocf Redstone MM, dtd
    1799,5,31
1801, 10, 24. Jesse gct Redstone MM
1806, 11, 22. Joseph Ailes gct Redstone MM, to
    m Sarah Ball
1808, 4, 23. Jesse rocf Redstone MM, dtd
    1808,4,1
1809, 12, 23. Jesse gct Redstone MM, to m Mercy
    Vail
1810, 3, 24. Mercy rocf Redstone MM, dtd
    1810,3,2
1831, 8, 24. David dis mou

BANGHAM
1801, 11, 28. Elizabeth rocf South River MM,
    Va., dtd 1801,10,10

BARNETT
1823, 12, 4. Mary m Charles DINGEE

BARRETT
1811, 5, 25. Mary & Rachel rocf Redstone MM
    dtd 1811,3,1
1814, 12, 1. Nathan Walton & w, Mary, & Ra-
    chel Barrett, a minor in their care, gct
    New Garden MM

BATTIN
1793, 5, 2. John, s Richard & Elizabeth,
    Washington Co., Pa.; m at Westland, Ann
    RELY, dt Robert & Ann, Washington Co., Pa.

1792, 1, 28. John rocf Kennet MM, dtd 1791,
    12,15
1792, 11, 24. Sarah rocf Kennet MM, dtd 1792,
    9,13
1793, 1, 26. Elizabeth rocf Warrington MM,
    dtd 1792,11,10
1795, 8, 22. Sarah (form Rigg) dis mou
1801, 7, 25. Abigail rocf Bradford MM, dtd
    1801,5,15
1805, 1, 26. Sarah rst by rq
1805, 2, 23. Sarah gct Short Creek MM
1806, 10, 25. Sarah gct Middleton MM
1811, 5, 25. John & w, Ann, & ch, Eli, Rob-
    ert, Elizabeth, Lydia, John, Fanny, David,
    Ann, Joshua & Ezra, gct Salem MM, O.

BEAL
1793, 5, 25. Margaret (form Crawford) dis mou

BECK
1804, 10, 4. Phebe m Mahlon WHITACRE
1804, 11, 14. Edward, s Preston, Harrison Co.,
    Va.; m at Richland, Ruth YATES, dt Benja-
    min & Phebe, Harrison Co., Va.

1798, 5, 26. Preston & w, Sarah, & ch, Ann,
    Edward, Phebe, Paul, Rachel, Mary & Pres-
    ton, recrq
1801, 2, 28. Ann Yates (form Beck) con mou
1802, 6, 26. Lydia (form Brown) dis mou
1806, 10, 15. Preston & w, Sarah, & ch, Paul,
    Rachel, Mary, Preston, Richard, John &
    Sarah, gct Salem MM
1806, 11, 22. Edward & w, Ruth, & unnamed in-
    fant gct Salem MM

BEESON
1803, 3, 31. Hannah m Jonas HARRIS

1803, 1, 22. Hannah recrq
1803, 5, 28. Amaziah [Beason] & w, Isabel, &
    ch, Rachel, Igal, Darius, Rosanna & Ama-
    ziah, rocf Lost Creek MM, Tenn., dtd 1802,
    9,18
1803, 10, 22. John recrq

BELL
1793, 5, 25. Margaret (form Crawford) dis mou
1826, 7, 27. Elma (form Vernon) dis mcd

BENNETT
1864, 4, 21. Elisha transferred to Salem MM,
    this mtg being laid down (H)
1864, 4, 21. Elizabeth transferred to Salem
    MM, this mtg being laid down (H)

BENTLEY
1820, 2, 24. Hannah H. (form Kenworthy) dis

BENTLEY, continued
    mou

BERRY
1799, 4, 27. Phebe rocf Hopewell MM, dtd
    1799,3,4
1799, 8, 24. Samuel rocf Crooked Run MM, dtd
    1799,6,13
1799, 12, 28. David & w, Hannah, & ch, Thomas,
    Samuel, Hannah & Beulah, rocf Hopewell MM,
    dtd 1799,11,4
1801, 8, 22. Samuel gct Redstone MM
1804, 2, 25. Phebe dis

BETTLE
1795, 3, 28. Everhard dis mou & disunity

BETTS
1790, 4, 24. Ann, w Enoch, & ch, Margaret,
    Sarah, Ann & Lydia, rocf New Garden MM,
    dtd 1788,9,6
1791, 12, 24. Margaret Stratton (form Betts)
    dis mou
1794, 9, 27. Ann Lewis (form Betts) dis mcd
1794, 9, 27. Sarah Murry (form Betts) dis
    mcd
1801, 8, 22. Lydia Smith (form Betts) dis mou

BINNS
1821, 7, 26. Jonathan rocf Marsden MM, Eng-
    land, dtd 1820,5,4, endorsed by Providence
    MM, 1821,6,19
1822, 5, 23. Jonathan dis mcd

BISHOP
1790, 2, 27. Stephen dis mcd
1790, 2, 27. Naomi (form Smith) dis mcd
1800, 5, 24. Joseph rocf Core Sound MM, dtd
    1800,1,25

BLACKBURN
1817, 12, --. William, s Thomas & Elizabeth,
    Washington Co., Pa.; m at Pike Run, Rachel
    McKENNAN, dt James & Rachel
1827, 5, 3. Ruth m Abraham SMITH

1787, 4, 14. Anthony rocf Monallen MM, dtd
    1783,11,10
1787, 5, 12. Joseph & w, Deborah, & ch, John,
    James, Thomas, Anthony, Joseph, Zachariah,
    Deborah, Finley & Rachel, rocf Monallin
    MM, dtd 1786,11,10
1787, 8, 11. John B. dis mou
1788, 11, 22. James dis mou
1790, 3, 27. Thomas dis
1791, 3, 26. Joseph dis mou
1791, 10, 22. Anthony, s Joseph, dis mou
1810, 12, 23. Plymouth MM was given permission
    to rst James
1816, 5, 23. William & w, Amy, & ch, Samuel,
    Jesse, William, Ruth, Amy, Isaac & John,
    rocf Dunnings Creek MM, dtd 1816,5,15
1818, 6, 25. Samuel dis mcd

1824, 8, 26. Jesse dis mcd
1825, 1, 27. William Jr. gct Providence MM,
    to m Ann Hewitt
1825, 6, 23. Ann rocf Providence MM, dtd
    1825,4,19
1833, 9, 25. Amy Miller (form Blackburn) dis
    mcd
1833, 10, 23. William & w, Rachel, & ch, John,
    Thomas, Ann, Rachel & Joseph, gct Spring-
    borough MM, O.
1833, 10, 23. Isaac gct Springborough MM, O.
1834, 8, 28. Ann Vore (form Blackburn) con
    mcd (H)
1846, 7, 22. Elizabeth (form Vore) dis mcd &
    jas
1847, 2, 25. Elizabeth (form Vore) dis jas (H)
1850, 7, 24. David dis mcd
1853, 5, 25. Nathan, minor, gct Providence MM
1858, 11, 24. Abel H. gct Muncy MM, Pa., to m
    Caroline Hoagland (W)
1859, 1, 27. Elizabeth (form Cleaver) dis
    mcd (H)
1862, 4, 23. Abel H. gct Muncy MM, Pa. (W)
1862, 4, 23. Rachel H. rmt Thomas Y. French
    (W)
1863, 1, 1. William & w, Ann, & ch, Abel,
    Lydia, Martha, Amy Hannah, William,
    George, Jonathan, Charles, Thomas & Daniel,
    dis joining Wilburite Separatists in 1854
1863, 1, 1. Rachel French (form Blackburn)
    dis joining Wilburite Separatists in 1854
1863, 3, 25. Nathan W. & w, Rebecca, rocf
    Providence MM, dtd 1863,3,5 (W)

BLACKLEDGE
1798, 3, 29. Martha [Blacklege] m Uriah WHITE

1797, 5, 27. Joseph rocf Buckingham MM, dtd
    1797,4,3
1797, 8, 26. Thomas con mou
1799, 6, 22. William & w, Elizabeth, & ch,
    Robert & Sarah, rocf Buckingham MM, dtd
    1798,9,3
1799, 8, 24. Isaac dis mou
1804, 2, 25. Levi [Blacklege] dis mou
1804, 9, 22. Joseph [Blacklege] gct Middleton
    MM
1809, 6, 24. William & w, Elizabeth, & ch,
    Robert, Sarah, Elizabeth, Samuel & John,
    gct Short Creek MM
1815, 11, 30. Cert rec for Mary from Goshen
    MM, dtd 1815,2,8, endorsed to Plainfield
    MM
1819, 5, 21. Abraham [Blacklege] dis disunity
1818, 7, 23. James [Blacklege] dis disunity
1818, 7, 23. William [Blacklege] dis disunity

BOGUE
1800, 5, 24. Malachi Jolly & w, Mary, & ch,
    John, Philip & Malachi, & Mary's ch, Cath-
    erine, Miriam & Huldy Bogue, rocf Trent
    MM, N. C., dtd 1800,1,12
1800, 5, 24. Job rocf Trent MM, N. C., dtd

BOGUE, continued
    1800,1,12

BOOTH
1788, 12, 27. Mary Horton (form Booth) rocf
    Concord MM, dtd 1787,10,3
1789, 1, 24. Mary Horton (form Booth) dis mou
1807, 6, 27. Elizabeth rst by rq
1814, 6, 2. Elizabeth gct Short Creek MM
1836, 3, 24. Mary Ann (form Pusey) con mcd
    (H)
1844, 4, 25. Mary Ann dis jas (H)

BORAM
1813, 4, 8. Ann m Abel JOHN

1800, 11, 22. Aron & w, Elizabeth, & dt, Ann,
    rocf Deer Creek MM, dtd 1800,9,25
1821, 11, 22. John dis mcd
1822, 1, 24. Mary (form Crawford) dis mcd
1826, 8, 24. Aaron & w, Elizabeth, & ch,
    Richard, Nathan, Elizabeth, Frances, Cas-
    sandra & Mary, gct Carmel MM, O.

BORDEN
1799, 8, 24. Mary rocf Evesham MM, dtd 1799,
    2,8
1802, 6, 26. Mary gct Redstone MM

BOSTICK
1789, 4, 25. Mary & ch, Lardner, Mary, John &
    Keziah, rocf Wilmington MM, dtd 1788,11,12

BOSWELL
1801, 12, 26. Ezra & w, Elizabeth, & s, Jesse,
    rocf Back Creek MM, N. C., dtd 1801,9,26

BOTTOMLEY
1806, 9, 27. Hannah (form Finch) con mou
1812, 11, 28. Hannah gct Redstone MM

BOYD
1800, 4, 26. Jane (form White) dis mou

BRACKEN
1808, 8, 29. Rebecca m Caleb WHITACRE
1818, 10, 29. Rachel m Shaidlock NEGUS
1819, 7, 1. Sarah m Isaac BRANSON

1806, 6, 28. Rebecca & ch, Rachel, Solomon,
    Elisha, Sarah & Caleb, rocf Gunpowder MM,
    dtd 1806,4,23
1813, 3, 27. Solomon [Brackin] dis
1821, 7, 26. Elisha gct Short Creek MM, O.
1822, 7, 25. Caleb, minor, gct Short Creek MM,
    O.

BRADFIELD
1803, 3, 26. Cynthia & ch, John &.Mary, rocf
    Mt. Pleasant MM, dtd 1802,8,28

BRADFORD
1802, 8, 28. Thomas, minor, rocf South River

MM, dtd 1801,10,10

BRANNEN
1787, 6, 9. Mary rocf Monallin MM, dtd
    1783,11,10
1790, 2, 27. Mary dis

BRANSON
1819, 7, 1. Isaac, s Abraham & Sarah, Bel-
    mont Co., O.; m at Westland, Sarah BRACK-
    IN, dt Caleb & Rebecca, Washington Co.,Pa.
1837, 5, 11. Aaron, s Jacob & Rebecca, Fay-
    ette Co., Pa.; m at Pike Run, Frances
    CRAWFORD, dt Richard & Priscilla, Washing-
    ton Co., Pa.

1819, 8, 26. Sarah M. gct Concord MM, O.
1837, 11, 22. Frances gct Redstone MM

BREWER
1790, 9, 29. Elias, widower, Fayette Co.,
    Pa.; m at Redstone, Mary CADWALLADER, dt
    John & Sarah, Fayette Co., Pa.

1790, 6, 26. Elias recrq

BRIGHT
1800, 11, 27. Henrietta m John GARRETSON

1799, 7, 27. Henrietta recrq

BROCK
1796, 1, 23. John Nathan rocf Hopewell MM,
    dtd 1795,11,2
1796, 1, 23. Oddy rocf Hopewell MM, dtd
    1795,11,2
1796, 4, 23. John & w, Jane, rocf Hopewell
    MM, dtd 1795,8,3
1806, 7, 26. John gct Concord MM

BROOKS
1818, 7, 1. William, s James & Martha,
    Washington Co., Pa.; m at Wheeling, Mary
    ENGLAND, dt Samuel & Tacy, Washington Co.,
    Pa.

1818, 3, 26. William recrq
1822, 4, 25. William & w, Mary, & ch, Esther,
    Martha & Tacy, gct Stillwater MM

BROWN
1793, 9, 4. Mary m Moses VOTAW
1825, 11, 9. Eleazer, s Eleazer & Sarah, Fay-
    ette Co., Pa.; m at Wheeling, Elizabeth
    ENGLAND, dt Samuel & Tacey, Washington
    Co., Pa.

1786, 1, 14. Ann (form Jenkinson) dis mcd
1786, 5, 13. Ann Ailes (form Brown) con mcd
1787, 8, 11. Rachel Powell (form Brown) dis
    mou
1791, 8, 27. Leah Hayes (form Brown) dis mou
1791, 10, 22. Elizabeth (form Gregg) dis mou

BROWN, continued
1792, 10, 27. Joseph dis mou
1794, 9, 27. Samuel dis mou
1795, 4, 25. Isaiah dis
1800, 5, 24. Miriam & ch, Sarah, Jane, Moses
       & Mary (Moses had d since dte of cert)
       rocf Trent MM, N. C., dtd 1800,1,12
1800, 6, 28. Reuben Ross & w, Elizabeth, &
       her dt, Rebecca Brown, & their ch, Mary &
       Anna, rocf Trent MM, N. C., dtd 1800,1,12
1800, 9, 27. Aaron & w, Anna, & s, Horton,
       rocf Trent MM, dtd 1800,1,12
1800, 12, 27. Lydia rocf Goose Creek MM, dtd
       1800,8,25
1802, 6, 26. Lydia Beck (form Brown) dis
       mou
1803, 4, 23. Rebecca Hill (form Brown) dis
       mou
1804, 5, 26. Samuel Smith gct Baltimore MM,
       to m Ann Brown
1808, 5, 28. Miami MM was given permission
       to rst Joseph
1825, 12, 22. Elizabeth gct Providence MM

BUCKLES
1795, 3, 28. Mary (form Hoge) dis mou

BUFFINGTON
1799, 4, 29. Sarah (form Milleson) dis mcd

BUNDY
1799, 11, 23. Cert rec for Josiah & s, Benja-
       min, Moses & Stanton, from Core Sound MM,
       dtd 1799,9,1, endorsed to Redstone MM
1799, 11, 23. Cert rec for Bathia, w Josiah,
       & dt, Susanna, Abigail & Ruth, from Core
       Sound MM, dtd 1799,9,1, endorsed to Red-
       stone MM
1800, 5, 24. Joseph rocf Contentney MM, dtd
       1800,3,8
1800, 6, 28. Mary rocf Trent MM, N. C., dtd
       1800,1,12
1801, 4, 25. Cert rec for Mary some time ago
       endorsed to Redstone MM
1801, 9, 26. Jacob Lewis gct Redstone MM, to
       m Mary Bundy
1801, 12, 26. Cert rec for Josiah & w,
       Bathia, & ch, Benjamin, Moses, Stanton,
       Susanna, Abigail & Ruth, from Redstone MM,
       dtd 1801,12,4, endorsed to Concord MM
1802, 9, 25. Cert rec for Joshua & w, Nelly,
       from Trent MM, dtd 1802,1,12, endorsed to
       Simons Creek MM .

BURDEN
1804, 8, 25. Job & w, Mary, rocf Redstone MM,
       dtd 1804,6,1
1805, 1, 26. Sarah, Levi, Reuben, Hannah,
       Job, Mary & Lydia, ch Job, recrq
1806, 1, 25. Levi, minor s Job, gct Redstone
       MM
1808, 4, 23. Job & w, Mary, & ch, Reuben,
       Hannah, Job, Joel, Mary, Lydia, David &

Ann, gct Salem MM
1809, 7, 22. Sarah gct Salem MM

BURGE
1801, 4, 25. Judith m John HANK
1806, 5, 28. Miriam m John NEGUS

1798, 5, 26. Judith & dt, Meriam, rocf
       Shrewsbury MM, dtd 1797,11,6
1812, 8, 22. Jacob & w, Miriam, & s, Albert,
       rocf Redstone MM, dtd 1812,7,31
1829, 6, 24. Jacob [Burdg] & w, Miriam, &
       ch, William, Hannah, Lewis, Oliver & Mary,
       gct Providence MM

BURGESS
1861, 2, 28. Charles, minor, rocf Chester-
       field MM, O.
1863, 4, 30. Charles, minor, gct Chester-
       field MM, O.

BURNETT
1793, 9, 28. Cert rec for John from Flushing
       MM, endorsed to Redstone MM

BURNS
1803, 2, 26. Mary & ch, Rachel, Elizabeth,
       Mary Jane & John, rocf Goose Creek MM,
       Va., dtd 1802,3,6

BURSON
1796, 11, 26. Edward recrq
1797, 2, 25. James, Thomas, David, Sarah,
       Levi, Joseph, Isaac, Abraham & Margaret,
       ch Edward, recrq
1800, 2, 22. Hannah & s, Silas, rocf Goose
       Creek MM, dtd 1799,12,30
1800, 12, 31. Hannah [Beirson] m at Westland
       Joseph ALLEN
1806, 5, 24. Sarah (form Burson) dis mou
1808, 1, 23. James dis mcd
1809, 9, 23. David gct New Garden MM
1810, 3, 24. Silas gct New Garden MM, O.
1811, 8, 24. Thomas dis mou
1815, 8, 31. David & w, Jane, rocf New Gar-
       den MM, O., dtd 1814,9,15
1815, 11, 30. Joseph dis mou
1815, 11, 30. Levi dis mcu
1816, 1, 25. Isaac dis
1818, 9, 24. David & w, Jane, gct Smithfield
       MM, O.
1819, 7, 22. Elizabeth Wise (form Burson) dis
       mcd
1821, 12, 27. Margaret (form Burson) dis mcd
1823, 1, 23. Abraham dis mcd

CADWALLADER
1787, 1, 24. Mary m Aaron NEWPORT
1789, 4, 1. Marah m Francis TOWNSEND
1790, 9, 1. Rees, widower, Fayette Co., Pa.;
       m at Redstone, Elizabeth SHARPLES, wd,
       Fayette Co., Pa.
1790, 9, 29. Mary m Elias BREWER

CADWALLADER, continued
1796, 3, 2. Asa, s Rees & Ruth, Fayette
     Co., Pa.; m at mtg in Fayette Co., Jane
     MEVAY, dt Josiah Haines, Washington Co.,
     Pa.
1812, 1, 29. Agnes m Abner PARSON

1787, 8, 11. Marah rocf Crooked Run MM, dtd
     1787,6,2
1790, 11, 27. Sarah recrq
1793, 10, 26. Jesse Townsend gct Redstone MM,
     to m Edith Cadwallader
1793, 10, 26. Israel Wilson gct Redstone MM,
     to m Martha Cadwallader
1796, 8, 27. Jane gct Redstone MM
1803, 8, 27. Elizabeth rocf Redstone MM, dtd
     1803,6,3
1808, 9, 24. David Grave gct Horsham MM, to
     m Ruth Cadwallader
1811, 8, 24. Agness rocf Horsham MM, dtd
     1811,5,1

CALL
1820, 8, 24. Sarah (form Hoge) dis mcd

CAMPBELL
1790, 10, 6. Abel, s William & Mary, Fayette
     Co., Pa.; m at Redstone, Susanna DIXON, dt
     William & Rebecca, Fayette Co., Pa.
1791, 1, 12. William, s William & Mary, Fay-
     ette Co., Pa.; m at Redstone, Ruth CRAW-
     FORD, dt James & Margaret, Fayette Co.,Pa.

1789, 5, 16. William recrq
1790, 3, 27. Abel, Margaret, Mary & Eliza-
     beth, recrq
1803, 8, 27. · Esther, w John, rocf Cane Creek
     MM, S. C., dtd 1803,4,23
1807, 12, 26. Mary dis
1815, 6, 29. William & w, Ruth, & ch, James,
     Ephraim, William, Margaret, Ruth, Rachel,
     Dugal, Abel & Benjamin, gct Marlborough
     MM, O.
1863, 4, 22. Lewis dis joining Orthodox in
     1854 (W)
1863, 4, 22. Deborah dis joining Orthodox in
     1854 (W)

CARLETON   •
1824, 3, 25. Nathan Crawford gct Plainfield
     MM, to m Mary Carleton

CARR
1793, 4, 27. William & w, Sarah, & s, Jesse,
     rocf Gunpowder MM, dtd 1792,11,24
1793, 8, 24. Priscilla rocf Gunpowder MM,
     dtd 1792,11,24
1794, 8, 23. James & w, Elizabeth, & ch, Ann
     & Samuel, rocf Gunpowder MM, dtd 1793,10,
     26
1802, 8, 28. James & w, Elizabeth, & ch,
     Ann, Samuel, Kinsey, Catherine & Aletta,
     gct Concord MM

1802, 8, 28. William & w, Sarah, & ch, Jesse,
     Ann, Joshua, Thomas & Susanna, gct Con-
     cord MM
1805, 1, 26. Priscilla gct Short Creek MM

CARROL
1801, 8, 22. Edward & w, Elizabeth, & ch, Jo-
     seph, Sarah, Edward, Margery, Deborah,
     Thomas, Elizabeth & Isaac, rocf Lisburn
     MM, Ire., dtd 1800,9,18; Isaac had d since
     cert was issued
1807, 11, 28. Sarah recrq
1810, 3, 24. Sarah [Carrel] gct Plymouth MM,
     O.
1816, 10, 24. Susanna recrq
1821, 7, 26. Susanna gct Providence MM

CARSON
1832, 1, 25. Mary (form McCall) dis mcd

CARTER
1787, 12, 22. Mary & ch, Joseph, Mary & James,
     rocf Mount Holly MM, dtd 1787,9,6
1792, 2, 25. Mary Stephenson (form Carter)
     dis mou
1794, 4, 26. Joseph Jr. dis disunity
1796, 5, 28. James gct Redstone MM
1796, 5, 28. Mary, w Joseph, gct Redstone MM
1801, 10, 24. Richard rocf Baltimore MM, dtd
     1801,3,12
1802, 9, 25. Mary & s, James, rocf Redstone
     MM, dtd 1802,7,30

CARVER
1816, 4, 4. John, s Henry & Tabitha, Harri-
     son Co., O.; m at Westland, Abigail MILLI-
     SON, dt James & Abigail, Washington Co.,
     Pa.

1801, 3, 28. Henry rocf Trent MM, dtd 1800,1,
     12, endorsed by Redstone MM, 1801,1,6
1816, 5, 23. Abigail gct Plainfield MM
1821, 4, 26. Abigail & ch, Betsy Ann, Henry &
     Millison, rocf Flushing MM, O., dtd 1821,3,
     23
1824, 12, 23. Abigail Ashmead (form Carver)
     dis mcd
1837, 9, 20. Betsy Ann dis jas
1839, 9, 25. James dis jas
1839, 9, 25. Henry dis jas

CATTELL
1812, 9, 3. Enoch, s Jonas & Elizabeth, Fay-
     ette Co., Pa.; m at Westland, Martha DIN-
     GEE, dt Charles & Martha, Washington Co.,
     Pa.

1788, 6, 28. Jonas & w, Elizabeth, & ch, Ra-
     chel, Ann, Esther, Enoch, Hannah & David,
     rocf Evesham MM, dtd 1788,3,7
1812, 11, 28. Martha gct Redstone MM
1863, 4, 22. William dis joining Orthodox in
     1854 (W)

CATTELL, continued
1863, 4, 22. Mary dis joining Orthodox in 1854 (W)

CHADWICK
1800, 7, 26. Mitty [Chadwicks] rocf Core Sound MM, dtd 1800,5,14
1801, 10, 24. Cert rec for Mitty some time ago endorsed to Core Sound MM

CHANDLER
1791, 9, 28. Jonathan, s Isaac & Esther, Fayette Co., Pa.; m at Redstone, Martha COULSON, dt Samuel & Tamar, Fayette Co., Pa.
1797, 3, 29. William, s William, Washington Co., Pa.; m at Fallowfield, Hannah WINDER, dt John, Washington Co., Pa.

1788, 11, 22. Jonathan rocf Kennet MM, dtd 1788,8,14
1789, 4, 25. William Jr. rocf New Garden MM, dtd 1789,3,7
1789, 4, 25. Swithin rocf Kennet MM, dtd 1787,8,16, endorsed by Hopewell MM, dtd 1787,11,3
1789, 7, 25. Swithin dis mcd
1789, 7, 25. Rachel (form Hoge), w Swithin, dis mcd
1791, 4, 23. Enoch rocf Kennet MM, dtd 1791, 2,17
1793, 4, 27. Hannah, w Enoch, & ch, Rache, Sarah, Margaret, Joshua, Ann, Phebe, Esther, Swithin, Hannah & Eli, recrq
1793, 5, 25. Hannah, w Enoch, & ch, Rachel, Sarah, Margaret, Joshua, Anne, Phebe, Esther, Swithen, Hannah & Eli, gct Redstone MM
1814, 5, 2. Enoch rocf Redstone MM, dtd 1814,4,29
1814, 9, 1. Elisha Milleson gct Redstone MM, to m Hannah Chandler
1817, 4, 24. Enoch Jr. gct Plainfield MM

CHASE
1807, 9, 26. Abigail, w Abner, rocf Dartmouth MM, Mass., dtd 1806,10,20
1807, 12, 26. Abigail dis jas

CLARK
1804, 10, 27. Samuel Clark & w, Ruth, & Abel Thomas, an apprentice, rocf Redstone MM, dtd 1804,8,31
1807, 7, 25. Samuel Clark & w, Ruth, & their apprentice, Abel Thomas, gct Redstone MM

CLEAVER
1821, 2, 7. Peter, s John & Susanna, York Co., Pa.; m at Pike Run, Jane TAYLOR, dt Benjamin & Elizabeth, Washington Co., Pa.
1831, 4, 28. Isaac, s John & Susanna, Washington Co., Pa.; m at Westland, Susanna SHAW, dt Samuel & Elizabeth, Washington Co., Pa. (H)
1832, 3, 1. Nathan, s John & Susanna, Washington Co., Pa.; m at Westland, Sarah LINTON, dt Mahlon & Ann, Washington Co., Pa. (H)
1837, 11, 30. Alice G. m Ezra COMLY (H)

1803, 1, 22. Abigail, w Ezekiel, & ch, Mary, Abigail, Ezekiel, Peter & David, rocf Crooked Run MM, dtd 1801,5,2
1815, 11, 2. John & w, Ann, rocf Warrington MM, dtd 1815,8,23
1820, 5, 25. Isaac & w, Elizabeth, & ch, Samuel, John, Eli, Alice & Jane, rocf Warrington MM, dtd 1820,4,19
1821, 3, 22. Jane, w Peter, gct Warrington MM
1829, 1, 21. John & Ann dis jH
1829, 4, 23. Nathan rocf Warrington MM, dtd 1828,6,18 (H)
1829, 6, 24. Isaac dis jH
1830, 2, 25. Peter & w, Jane, & ch, Susanna, Elizabeth, John & Maria, rocf Warrington MM, dtd 1829,9,24 (H)
1833, 12, 25. Sarah (form Linton) dis mcd & jH
1837, 6, 21. Amos G. dis mcd & jH
1837, 7, 26. Samuel G. dis mcd
1837, 9, 20. Betsy Ann dis jas
1837, 9, 21. Amos G. con mcd (H)
1838, 10, 24. Alice Comley (form Cleaver) dis mcd & jH
1839, 5, 22. Eli, s John, dis jH
1839, 7, 24. John W. dis jH
1839, 7, 25. Samuel G. dis mcd (H)
1839, 12, 26. Eli con mcd (H)
1840, 2, 19. Isaac, s John, dis jH
1840, 10, 22. Eli U. gct Short Creek MM (H)
1841, 2, 25. Eli T. con mcd (H)
1841, 9, 22. Eli dis mcd
1841, 9, 23. John W. dis jas (H)
1841, 11, 24. Eliza Garretson (form Cleaver) dis mcd & jas
1842, 1, 27. Eli T. gct New Garden MM, O. (H)
1842, 8, 25. Jane C. Jr. dis jas (H)
1842, 10, 27. Amelia & ch, Lewis K. & Mary Ann recrq (H)
1844, 5, 23. Eliza Garretson (form Cleaver) dis jas (H)
1844, 6, 27. Rebecca & dt, Mary Ann, recrq (H)
1845, 1, 23. Eli rocf Short Creek MM, dtd 1844,11,21 (H)
1845, 1, 23. Hiram T. gct New Garden MM, O.(H)
1846, 7, 23. Rachel Ann Shipley (form Cleaver) dis jas (H)
1847, 8, 25. Rachel Ann Shipley (form Cleaver) dis mcd & jas
1848, 1, 27. Philena & Isaac Jefferson, minors, rocf New Garden MM, dtd 1847,10,21 (H)
1849, 7, 26. Bentley con mcd (H)
1849, 10, 24. Bentley dis mcd
1850, 6, 27. Elizabeth rocf Carmel MM, O., dtd 1849,12,15
1857, 1, 22. John Ira con mcd (H)

CLEAVER, continued

1859, 1, 27. Elizabeth Blackburn (form
    Cleaver) dis mcd (H)
1859, 8, 25. Benjamin con mcd (H)
1864, 4, 21. Amos G. & ram & John Ira trans-
    ferred to Salem MM, this mtg being laid
    down (H)
1864, 4, 21. Hiram, Isaac N., Eli V., Lesh
    B., Philena & Jefferson transferred to
    Salem MM, this mtg being laid down (H)
1864, 4, 21. Isaac, Susanna S., Ann, Peter,
    Jane, Nathan, Sarah L. & Martha trans-
    ferred to Salem MM, this mtg being laid
    down (H)
1864, 4, 21. Isaac A. transferred to Salem
    MM, this mtg being laid down (H)
1864, 4, 21. John, Benjamin, Elizabeth &
    Mary Eliza transferred to Salem MM, this
    mtg being laid down (H)

COFFIN

1832, 7, 26. Mary (form Forgerson) dis mcd
    (H)

COGEL

1799, 5, 25. Sarah, w Isaac, rocf Goose Creek
    MM, dtd 1797,11,27

COLCLASER

1787, 8, 11. Abigail (form Dinnen) dis mou
1787, 8, 11. Eleanor (form Dinnen) dis mou

COLE

1825, 2, 24. Ann rocf Baltimore MM for Western
    District, dtd 1825,1,7
1825, 6, 23. Ann gct Baltimore MM for Western
    District

COLVIN

1797, 2, 25. Sarah (form Shepherd) dis mou

COMELY

1837, 11, 30. Ezra [Comly], s Samuel & Susanna,
    Washington Co., Pa.; m at Westland, Alice
    G. CLEAVER, dt Isaac & Elizabeth, Wash.
    Co., Pa. (H)

1837, 4, 27. Samuel & w, Susanna, & ch,
    Lydia & Isaac W., rocf Monalan MM, dtd
    1837,3,22 (H)
1837, 5, 25. Phebe rocf Monalan MM, dtd 1837,
    3,22 (H)
1837, 9, 21. Ezra rocf Gunpowder MM, dtd
    1837,5,3 (H)
1838, 10, 24. Alice [Comley] (form Cleaver) dis
    mcd & jH
1842, 4, 21. Samuel [Comley] & w, Susanna, &
    s, Isaac, gct Clear Creek MM, Ill. (H)
1842, 4, 21. Phebe & Lydia (Comley] gct Clear
    Creek MM, Ill.(H)

COMMONS

1802, 12, 25. Cert rec for William, minor, from

London Grove MM, dtd 1801,12,3, endorsed
to Hopewell MM

CONNER

1790, 8, 28. Elizabeth (form Foreman) dis mcd

COOK

1786, 9, 27. Thomas, s John & Rebecca, Wash-
    ington Co., Pa.; m at Redstone, Elizabeth
    COOPE, dt John & Mary, Fayette Co., Pa.

1787, 11, 24. Jeremiah & w, Rachel, & s, Al-
    len, rocf Pipe Creek MM, dtd 1787,10,15
1799, 4, 27. Rebecca, dt Thomas, gct London
    Grove MM
1803, 5, 28. Amos Cook & w, Elizabeth, & ch,
    John, Dinah, Amos, Stephen, Abraham &
    Ruth, also Sarah Pennel, their cousin,
    rocf Cane Creek MM, S. C., dtd 1803,2,19
1803, 5, 28. Levi & w, Ann, & ch, Betty &
    Isaac, rocf Cane Creek MM, S. C., dtd
    1803,2,19
1806, 11, 22. Jeremiah & w, Rachel, & ch, Al-
    len, Hannah, Ellis, Sarah & Mary, gct Con-
    cord MM
1864, 7, 27. Mary Ann (form Rogers) dis mcd
    (W)

COOPER

1846, 12, 24. Ruth (form Grave) dis mcd (H)
1851, 12, 24. Ruth (form Grave) dis mcd

COPE

1786, 9, 27. Elizabeth [Coope] m Thomas COOK
1789, 12, 10. Isaac, s John, Fayette Co., Pa.;
    m at Little Redstone, Sarah KIRK, dt Jo-
    seph, Fayette Co., Pa.
1792, 12, 12. John [Coope], s John, Fayette
    Co., Pa.; m at Fallowfield, Ruth DIXON,
    dt Henry, Washington Co., Pa.
1796, 12, 7. Caleb, s John, Washington Co.,
    Pa.; m at Fallowfield, Amy DIXON, dt Henry,
    Washington Co., Pa.
1801, 11, 4. Jesse [Coope], s John & Mary,
    Fayette Co., Pa.; m at Fallowfield, Marga-
    ret DIXSON, dt Henry & Elizabeth, Washing-
    ton Co., Pa.
1819, 9, 2. John, s Isaac & Sarah, Fayette
    Co., Pa.; m at Westland, Sarah SMITH, dt
    George & Hannah, Washington Co., Pa.
1854, 3, 29. Ruth m Jonathan KNIGHT Jr.
1796, 11, 28. Caleb prcf Redstone MM, to m Amy
1797, 3, 25. Amy gct Redstone MM [Dixon
1802, 4, 24. Margaret gct Redstone MM

1803, 1, 22. Alice gct Redstone MM
1803, 3, 26. Caleb & w, Amy, & ch, Henry,
    John & Samuel, rocf Redstone MM, dtd
    1803,3,4
1803, 3, 26. Jesse & w, Margaret, & dt,
    Elizabeth, rocf Redstone MM, dtd 1803,3,4
1819, 9, 23. Joseph & w, Elizabeth, & ch,

COPE, continued

Ruth & Elihu, rocf Providence MM, dtd 1819,8,24

1819, 10, 28. Sarah gct Providence MM

1822, 6, 27. Joseph & w, Elizabeth, & ch, Ruth, Elihu & Uriah, gct Providence MM

1823, 10, 23. John Raley gct Providence MM, to m Sarah Cope

1824, 4, 22. Sarah Raley & ch, Ruth & Jesse Cope, rocf Providence MM, dtd 1824,3,23

1826, 5, 25. John Raley & w, Sarah, & ch, Ruth & Jesse Cope, gct Providence MM

1826, 5, 25. Elihu & Uriah rocf Providence MM, dtd 1826,2,21

1827, 7, 26. Aaron Vansciock gct Providence MM, to m Ruth Cope

1827, 8, 23. Uriah, minor, gct Providence MM

1832, 8, 22. Elihu gct Providence MM, O.

1843, 9, 20. George & w, Elmira, rocf Providence MM

1846, 4, 22. Isaac Perkins rocf Providence MM, dtd 1846,4,2

1846, 5, 27. Mary Ann, Dawsey, Ruth, Henry, Sarah Jane, John Cousins & Charles Binns, ch John & Sarah S., rocf Providence MM, dtd 1846,4,30

1847, 1, 27. Oliver rocf Providence MM, dtd 1846,12,31

1847, 3, 24. Oliver gct Marlborough MM, O., to m Mary H. Enlows

1848, 3, 22. Mary H. rocf Marlborough MM, O., dtd 1848,1,25

1848, 6, 21. John rocf Providence MM, dtd 1848,6,21

1849, 12, 26. Sarah S. rst by rq with consent of Providence MM

1850, 1, 23. Isaac P. dis mcd

1852, 2, 25. Mary Ann Hutchin (form Cope) dis mcd

1857, 7, 22. Henry rmt Sarah Gray (W)

1860, 2, 2. Mary H. gct Marlborough MM, O.

1860, 4, 25. Dawsey dis mcd (W)

1862, 4, 23. Sarah Jane Lohnes (form Cope) dis mcd (W)

1863, 1, 1. George & w, Elmire, dis joining Wilburite Separatist in 1854

1863, 1, 1. Henry & w, Sarah, dis joining the Wilburite Separatist in 1854

1863, 1, 1. John Cozens & Charles Binns dis joining the Wilburite Separatist in 1854

1863, 3, 5. Dawsey dis mou

1863, 4, 22. Mary H. dis joining Orthodox in 1854 (W)

1865, 2, 22. John H. gct Upper Springfield MM, O. (W)

1865, 2, 22. Sarah G. & s, Allison, gct Coal Creek MM, Ia. (W)

1865, 7, 26. Henry dis joining Army (W)

COPELAND
1821, 6, 27. Ann m Miles DAVIES

1821, 4, 26. Ann recrq

1855, 7, 26. Ann Eliza (form Morgan) dis mcd (H)

COULSON
1789, 2, 4. Jehu, s Samuel & Tamar, Fayette Co., Pa.; m at Redstone, Jane HARVEY, wd, Fayette Co., Pa.

1791, 9, 28. Martha m Jonathan CHANDLER

1786, 8, 12. Thomas & Jabez, ch Tamar, recrq

1787, 2, 10. Martha recrq

1787, 4, 14. Tamar rocf Nottingham MM, dtd 1783,11,29

1787, 8, 11. Jehu recrq

COURTNEY
1815, 3, 2. Martha rocf New Garden MM, dtd 1815,1,19

1820, 7, 27. Martha gct New Garden MM, O.

COUZENS
1791, 5, 28. Ann m Bradways THOMPSON

1799, 3, 28. Hannah m George SMITH

1793, 10, 26. Mary Hill (form Couzens) dis mou

1811, 5, 25. John & w, Sarah, gct Short Creek MM

COX
1794, 2, 22. Cert rec for Sarah, w Jacob, & ch, Thomas, Robert, Jacob, Rebecca, Rachel & John, from Warrington MM, dtd 1792,11,12, endorsed to Redstone MM

1800, 5, 24. Sarah rocf Trent MM, N. C., dtd 1800,1,12

1803, 8, 27. Thomas & w, Tamer, & dt, Hannah, rocf Cain Creek MM, S. C., dtd 1803,5,21

CRAWFORD
1791, 1, 12. Ruth m William CAMPBELL

1810, 5, 2. William, s John & Ann, Fayette Co., Pa.; m at Pike Run, Hannah Griffith, dt Jacob & Lydia, Washington Co., Pa.

1813, 9, 29. Elizabeth m Arthur McGIRR

1828, 10, 1. Sarah m Samuel ROGERS

1837, 5, 11. Frances m Aaron BRANSON

1787, 4, 14. John con mcd

1788, 3, 22. Sarah Garwood (form Crawford) dis mcd

1788, 11, 22. Ann, w John, rocf Deer Creek MM, dtd 1788,10,9

1788, 12, 27. William, s John, recrq

1792, 12, 22. Josiah Jr. dis mou

1793, 5, 25. Margaret Beal (or Bell) (form Crawford) dis mou

1793, 8, 24. Joseph dis mou

1796, 1, 23. John dis

1796, 2, 27. James dis disunity

1797, 7, 22. Ephraim gct Redstone MM, to m Susanna Nichols

1798, 8, 25. Susanna [Crafford] (form Nichols) rocf Kennet MM, dtd 1796,11,17, endorsed

CRAWFORD, continued
       by Redstone MM, 1797,9,29
1799, 6, 22. Elizabeth, w John, rocf Red-
    stone MM, dtd 1798,11,28
1800, 11, 22. William dis mcd
1805, 12, 28. Frances rocf Deer Creek MM, dtd
    1805,11,28
1811, 7, 27. Ann Fleming (form Crawford) dis
    mou
1811, 8, 24. Richard recrq
1811, 8, 24. Elizabeth recrq
1816, 3, 28. Mary, Nathan & Sarah, ch Fran-
    ces, recrq

1822, 1, 24. Mary Boram (form Crawford) dis
    mcd
1823, 8, 28. Mary (form Finch) dis mcd
1824, 3, 25. Nathan gct Plainfield MM, to m
    Mary Carleton
1824, 9, 23. Mary rocf Plainfield MM, dtd
    1824,7,22
1825, 5, 26. William dis disunity
1825, 6, 23. Hannah (form Crawford) dis mcd
1830, 4, 22. Ann (form Crawford) con mcd (H)
1830, 7, 21. Ann (form Crawford) dis mou
1834, 10, 22. John dis
1834, 12, 24. Benjamin dis disunity
1838, 9, 26. Israel dis mcd
1838, 12, 26. Lydia dis jas
1838, 12, 26. Margaret dis jH
1838, 12, 26. Margaret Jr. dis jH
1839, 6, 26. Ann Sharp (form Crawford) dis
    mcd
1847, 4, 21. James Robinet dis mcd
1847, 5, 26. Seaborn gct Redstone MM
1849, 2, 21. Beulah Adbert (form Crawford)
    dis mou
1849, 8, 22. Mark, minor, gct Redstone MM
1851, 8, 27. Henry M. dis mcd
1856, 6, 25. Richard Jr. dis mcd (W)
1857, 12, 23. Sarah Frances Rogers (form Craw-
    ford) dis mcd (W)
1858, 3, 24. Seaborn dis mcd (W)
1859, 1, 26. Nathan Jr. dis mcd (W)
1863, 1, 1. Richard & w, Priscilla, & dt,
    Elizabeth, dis joining Wilburite Separa-
    tists in 1854
1863, 1, 1. Nathan dis joining Wilburite
    Separatists in 1854
1864, 4, 21. Ann transferred to Salem MM,
    this mtg being laid down (H)
1865, 1, 25. Thomas F. dis mcd (W)

CROASDALE
1851, 9, 25. Joseph C. rocf Wilmington MM,
    Del., dtd 1851,5,23 (H)
1864, 4, 21. Joseph S. transferred to Salem
    MM, this mtg being laid down (H)

CROSS
1813, 8, 28. Hannah (form Hartley) con mcd

CROUCH
1860, 12, 26. Priscilla (form Rogers) dis mcd
    (W)

CUMMINS
1806, 8, 23. Elizabeth (form Finch) dis mou
1816, 8, 22. Ruth (form Finch) dis mou

CURL
1802, 10, 23. Sarah & step-ch, Elizabeth, Su-
    sanna & Samuel, rocf South River MM, dtd
    1801,10,14
1804, 8, 25. Elizabeth Low (form Curl) dis
    mou
1807, 11, 28. Sarah recrq
1810, 3, 24. Sarah gct Plymouth MM

CUSTARD
1841, 7, 21. Hannah (form Jenkins) rpd mcd

DANIEL
1802, 8, 28. James & w, Hannah, & ch, Re-
    becca, William, Jasper, Hannah, Mary, John
    (Jonathan in women's minutes) & Tacy, rocf
    Goose Creek MM, dtd 1801,10,3

DAVIS
1821, 6, 27. Miles [Davies], s Joshua & Jane,
    Washington Co., Pa.; m at Pike Run, Ann
    COPELAND, dt John & Jane, Westmoreland
    Co., Pa.

1790, 11, 27. Samuel & w, Mary, & ch, Rebecca
    & Samuel, recrq
1794, 2, 22. Hannah (form Rees) dis mou
1798, 9, 22. Joshua & w, Jane, & ch, Jacob,
    Daniel, Joshua, Miles & Hannah, rocf Red-
    stone MM, dtd 1798,8,31
1801, 4, 25. Joshua Jr. gct Redstone MM
1801, 4, 25. Joshua [Davies] gct Redstone MM
1801, 9, 26. Abraham Davis & w, Hannah, & ch,
    Phebe, Edward, Ellis & Rachel, also Tacy
    McCann, rocf Fairfax MM, dtd 1800,11,22,
    endorsed by Redstone MM, 1801,7,31
1802, 6, 26. Jacob dis mou
1808, 8, 27. Daniel dis
1808, 11, 26. Hannah Moor (form Davis) dis
1817, 7, 24. Joshua [Davies] gct Middleton
    MM, O.
1819, 8, 26. Joshua rocf Carmel MM, dtd 1819,
    1,16
1820, 7, 27. Joshua gct Stillwater MM
1825, 4, 21. Miles & s, Hiram C., gct Plane-
    field MM
1848, 10, 26. John Horton & w, Rachel, & Cin-
    thia Horton Davis, a minor, rocf Plain-
    field MM, dtd 1848,8,17

DEEMS
1811, 5, 30. Mark, s Mark & Elizabeth, Wash-
    ington Co., Pa.; m at Westland, Ann RELEY,
    dt John & Mary, Washington Co., Pa.

DEEMS, continued
1845, 8, 27. Peter dis mcd
1845, 8, 27. John R. dis mcd
1849, 10, 24. Albert dis mcd
1856, 9, 24. Harrison dis mcd (W)

DEMSEY
1798, 5, 26. Sarah rocf London Grove MM, dtd
1798,1,3

DEW
1800, 6, 28. Joseph Dew & s, Joseph & Elias,
& gr s, Joseph HALl, rocf Core Sound MM,
dtd 1800,5,14
1800, 7, 26. Cherry rocf Core Sound MM, dtd
1800,5,14
1800, 7, 26. Susanna rocf Core Sound MM, dtd
1800,5,14
1800, 8, 23. Viley & dt, Abigail, rocf Core
Sound MM, dtd 1800,5,14

DICKINSON
1787, 11, 24. Jesse rocf Gwynedd MM, dtd
1787,5,29
1787, 12, 22. Jesse dis mou

DILHORN
1794, 6, 28. Nathaniel [Dillhorn] rocf Crooked Run MM, dtd 1794,5,3, endorsed by Redstone MM, 1794,6,27
1816, 6, 27. Nathaniel con mcd
1817, 10, 23. Nathaniel gct Phila. MM

DILLON
1799, 5, 25. James & w, Ann, & ch, William,
Rachel, John, Agness & Elizabeth Ann, rocf
Goose Creek MM, dtd 1797,10,30

DINGEE
1803, 12, 8. Rachel m Abel HEWIT
1811, 1, 31. Hannah m David HILLES
1812, 9, 3. Martha m Enoch CATTELL
1823, 12, 4. Charles, s Charles & Martha,
Washington Co., Pa.; m at Westland, Mary
BARNETT, dt David & Rachel, Washington
Co., Pa.
1824, 3, 4. Ann m Thomas FARQUHAR

1802, 6, 26. Charles & w, Martha, & ch, John,
Hannah, Martha, Sarah, Ann & Charles, rocf
Concord MM, Pa., dtd 1802,5,5
1802, 6, 26. Rachel rocf Concord MM, dtd
1802,5,5
1808, 12, 24. John gct New Garden MM, O., to m
Bathsheba Walton
1809, 6, 24. Bathsheba rocf New Garden MM,
dtd 1809,3,16
1819, 4, 22. John & w, Bathsheba, & ch, Ruth,
Martha, Nathan & Mary, gct Short Creek MM
1830, 4, 21. Charles & w, Mary, & ch, William,
Samuel, John & Hannah, gct Carmel MM, O.
1844, 1, 24. Sarah gct Salem MM, Ia.
1846, 11, 25. David, minor, s Charles & Mary,

rocf Marlborough MM, dtd 1846,9,9
1850, 2, 20. Uriah, minor, rocf Marlborough
MM, dtd 1850,1,29
1855, 3, 22. William gct Spring Creek MM, Ia.
1855, 3, 22. David, minor, gct Spring Creek
MM, Ia.
1853, 10, 26. William rocf Marlborough MM, O.,
dtd 1853,9,27
1860, 2, 22. Adaline rocf Upper Springfield
MM, dtd 1859,11,25 (W)
1863, 5, 27. David dis active part in war (W)
1864, 2, 24. William dis mcd & joining Orthodox (W)

DINNEN
1787, 6, 9. Andrew & w, Rachel, & ch, Abigail, William, Susanna, Eleanor, Rachel,
John, Anthony & Joseph, rocf Monallin MM,
dtd 1783,11,10
1787, 8, 11. Abigail Colclaser (form Dinnen)
dis mou
1787, 8, 11. Eleanor Colclaser (form Dinnen)
dis mou
1788, 8, 23. Rachel May (form Dinnen) dis mou

DIXON
1790, 10, 6. Susanna m Abel CAMPBELL
1792, 9, 26. Hannah m Joseph Pennock
1795, 12, 2. Rebecca m John WOODS
1796, 12, 7. Amy m Caleb COPE
1801, 11, 4. Margaret [Dixson] m Jesse COOPE

1786, 4, 8. Hannah & Immanuel, ch Joshua,
recrq
1787, 4, 14. Rebecca rocf Kennet MM, dtd 1786
10,12
1787, 11, 24. John & w, Mary, & ch, Rebecca,
Elizabeth & Susanna, rocf Wilmington MM,
dtd 1787,9,12
1788, 11, 22. Susanna rocf New Garden MM, dtd
1788,10,4
1788, 12, 27. William & w, Rebecca, & ch, Joseph & William, rocf New Garden MM, dtd
1788,10,4
1790, 9, 25. Samuel rocf Kennet MM, dtd
1790,4,15
1795, 10, 24. John & w, Mary, & ch, Rebecca,
Elizabeth, Susanna, John, Samuel, Edith
& Mary, gct Redstone MM
1804, 5, 26. Henry & w, Elizabeth, & ch,
Simon, Elizabeth & Mary, gct Middleton MM
1804, 5, 26. Henry Jr. gct Middleton MM
1807, 4, 25. Emanuel rocf Middleton MM, dtd
1807,2,14
1816, 9, 26. Thomas Raley gct Centre MM,
Del., to m Ann Dixon
1824, 1, 22. Immanuel con mcd

DODSON
1827, 7, 26. Emala (form Lewis) dis mcd

DUGAN
1808, 3, 26. Hannah rst by rq

DULY
1816, 3, 29. Rebecca [Deulea] m Moses ELLIOTT

1789, 12, 26. Avis, w Joshua, rocf Shrewsbury
    MM, dtd 1789,9,7
1792, 8, 5. Joshua & ch recrq
1815, 9, 28. Rebecca [Dulea] rocf Redstone
    MM, dtd 1815,9,1

DUNCAN
1791, 5, 28. Margaret rocf Fairfax MM, dtd
    1791,2,12
1796, 11, 26. Sarah (form Hough) dis mcd
1796, 12, 24. Margaret dis disunity

DUVALL
1801, 12, 26. Lydia (form Milleson) dis mcd

EAKEY
1810, 8, 23. Sarah (form McCall) dis mou

EASTON
1791, 2, 26. Redwood rocf Creek MM, N. Y.,
    endorsed to ND MM, Phila., Pa., 1790,11,23

EDMUNDSON
1819, 8, 26. Phebe (form Vale) dis mcd

ELLIOTT
1803, 9, 1. Joseph [Eliot], s Isaac & Alice,
    Washington Co., Pa.; m at Pike Run, Eliza-
    beth JOHN, dt Joseph & Mary, Washington
    Co., Pa.
1805, 11, 6. Isaac Jr., s Isaac & Alice,
    Washington Co., Pa.; m at Pike Run, Ruth
    McCALL, dt John & Sarah, Washington Co.,
    Pa.
1816, 3, 29. Moses, s Isaac & Alice, Washing-
    ton Co., Pa.; m at Pike Run, Rebecca Deu-
    lea DULY, dt John & Aves, Fayette Co.,Pa.

1796, 9, 24. Isaac & w, Alice, & ch, Benja-
    min, Joseph, Elizabeth, Isaac, Alice, Mary,
    Moses & Francis, rocf Warrington MM, dtd
    1796,2,13
1802, 12, 25. Benjamin [Elliot] dis mou
1810, 3, 24. Joseph & w, Elizabeth, & ch,
    Mary, Isaac & John, gct Salem MM, O.
1813, 2, 27. Alice McCall (form Elliott) dis
    mcd
1815, 11, 30. Francis [Elliot] gct Marl-
    borough MM, O.
1816, 4, 25. Isaac & w, Alice, gct West Marl-
    borough MM
1816, 4, 25. Isaac Jr. & w, Ruth, & ch, John,
    Sarah, Phebe, Joseph & James, gct West
    Marlborough MM
1816, 4, 25. Mary gct West Marlborough MM
1816, 5, 23. Moses & w, Rebecca, gct Marl-
    borough MM, O.
1846, 2, 19. Abraham Vanscioc gct Marlborough
    MM, to m Rachel Elliott (H)

ELLIS
1792, 6, 23. Rowland rocf Hopewell MM, dtd
    1792,11,7
1801, 12, 26. Mary & ch, Gainer, Elizabeth,
    Enos & Mary, rocf Southland MM, dtd 1801,
    9,30

ELLYSON
1797, 1, 28. Zachariah & w, Mary, & ch, Isaac,
    Gideon, Zachariah & Robert, rocf Goose
    Creek MM, dtd 1796,9,26
1811, 8, 24. Isaac [Ellison] gct Salem MM, O.
1815, 12, 28. Gideon gct Salem MM; returned
    1816,6,27 because of his not living there
1816, 9, 26. Zechariah & w, Mary, & ch,
    Robert, William, Margery, Anna, John &
    Mary, gct Salem MM, O.
1816, 10, 24. Gideon dis mcd
1816, 10, 24. Zechariah Jr. dis mcd

ENGLAND
1792, 10, 31. Sarah m William ALLEN
1803, 2, 3. Joseph, s Joseph & Elizabeth,
    Washington Co., Pa.; m at Westland, Mary
    HUTTON, dt Thomas & Mary, Washington Co.,
    Pa.
1808, 10, 6. Hannah m Abraham VANSCOYOC
1808, 10, 27. Hannah m Jacob SMITH
1818, 7, 1. Mary m William BROOKS
1825, 11, 9. Elizabeth m Eleazer BROWN

1787, 3, 10. Samuel rocf Gunpowder MM, dtd
    1786,12,30
1787, 5, 12. Hannah rocf Gunpowder MM, dtd
    1786,12,30
1789, 1, 24. Robert & Joseph rocf Gunpowder
    MM, dtd 1787,11,24
1789, 1, 24. Samuel con mou
1790, 5, 22. David dis disunity
1792, 10, 27. Elizabeth Kimberley (form Eng-
    land) dis mou
1796, 9, 24. Israel dis disunity
1798, 1, 27. Ann (form Winders) dis mcd
1799, 5, 25. Susanna dis
1799, 8, 24. Tacy & ch, Joseph, Hannah,
    Elizabeth, Esther, Tacy & Mary, recrq
1799, 12, 28. Isaac dis disunity
1800, 5, 24. David dis disunity
1800, 8, 23. Mary Icehouer (form England)
    dis mou
1805, 3, 23. John gct Short Creek MM
1808, 8, 27. John gct Gunpowder MM
1809, 5, 27. John rocf Gunpowder MM, dtd
    1809,2,22
1819, 4, 22. Joseph Jr. & w, Hannah, & ch,
    Sarah, Josiah & Mary, gct Salem MM, O.
1821, 11, 22. Tacy gct Salem MM, O.
1822, 9, 26. Esther gct Stillwater MM
1824, 6, 24. Esther rocf Stillwater MM, dtd
    1824,1,24
1826, 7, 27. Tacy rocf Salem MM, O., dtd
    1826,4,19
1830, 7, 21. Tacy Jr. & Jane Jr. dis jH

ENGLAND, continued
1830, 8, 25. George & Tacy dis jH
1830, 9, 22. Samuel & Samuel Jr. dis jH
1830, 10, 27. Jane gct Salem MM, O.
1831, 10, 27. George con mcd (H)
1833, 3, 28. Samuel gct Concord MM, O., to m
    Emma Given (H)
1833, 11, 21. Emma rocf Concord MM, dtd 1833,
    7,24 (H)
1838, 7, 26. George dis mcd (H)
1864, 4, 21. Samuel & fam transferred to
    Salem MM, this mtg being laid down (H)
1864, 4, 21. Tacy transferred to Salem MM,
    this mtg being laid down (H)

ENLOWS
1810, 4, 4. James, s Luke & Susanna, Wash-
    ington Co., Pa.; m at Pike Run, Sarah JOHN
    dt Joseph & Mary, Washington Co., Pa.

1809, 12, 23. James recrq
1811, 5, 25. James gct Redstone MM
1818, 6, 25. John, minor s James, gct Provi-
    dence MM
1847, 3, 24. Oliver Cope gct Marlborough MM,
    O., to m Mary H. Enlows

ERWIN
1801, 12, 26. James & w, Mary, & dt, Susannah,
    rocf Goose Creek MM, dtd 1801,10,3
1802, 8, 28. Samuel & M, Sarah, & ch, Wil-
    liam, James, Mary, John & Mahlon, rocf
    Goose Creek MM, dtd 1801,10,3

EVANS
1791, 1, 22. Cadwallader & w, Sarah, & ch,
    Mary, Evan, James & John, rocf Warrington
    MM, dtd 1790,11,13
1791, 1, 22. Eleanor, dt Cadwallader, rocf
    Warrington MM, dtd 1790,11,13
1791, 5, 28. Mary recrq
1799, 8, 24. Eleanor (form Lester) dis mou
1801, 11, 28. Mary rocf Crooked Run MM, dtd
    1801,5,2
1802, 3, 27. Cadwallader & w, Sarah, & ch,
    Evan, James, John, Asher, Sarah, Benoni
    & Pamela, gct Concord MM, N. W. of Ohio
    River
1802, 3, 27. Mary gct Concord MM
1803, 7, 23. Thomas rocf Cester (Chester?)
    MM, dtd 1800,11,24
1804, 11, 24. Elenor gct Short Creek MM

EVERITT
1837, 11, 2. George W., s Isaac & Rebecca,
    Adams Co., Pa.; m at Westland, Ann SMITH,
    dt Henry & Rebecca, Washington Co., Pa.(H)

1837, 8, 24. John & w, Susanna, rocf
    Monallen MM, dtd 1837,6,22 (H)
1837, 8, 24. George W. rocf Monallen MM, dtd
    1837,6,22 (H)
1839, 3, 27. Ann (form Smith) dis mcd & jH

1844, 3, 28. George W. & w, Ann, & s, John,
    gct Clear Creek MM, Ill. (H)
1853, 4, 21. John & w, Susanna, gct Warring-
    ton MM (H)

FARQUHAR
1824, 3, 4. Thomas, s Thomas & Hannah, Wash-
    ington Co., Pa.; m at Westland, Ann DINGEE
    dt Charles & Martha, Wash. Co., Pa.
1830, 11, 30. Ann m Jeremiah ROGERS
1790, 11, 27. Thomas & w, Hannah, & s, Jo-
    seph, rocf Pipe Creek MM, dtd 1790,6,19

1790, 11, 27. William & w, Elizabeth, rocf
    Pipe Creek MM, dtd 1790,6,19
1790, 11, 27. Sarah, w Allen, & s, Samuel,
    rocf Pipe Creek MM, dtd 1790,9,18
1810, 2, 24. Joseph gct Plymouth MM, O.[Thomas
1810, 6, 23. Alan gct Plymouth MM, O.(s of
1812, 11, 28. Alan rocf Plymouth MM, dtd 1812,
    5,16
1814, 3, 26. Alan gct Concord MM
1816, 6, 27. William gct Plainfield MM, O.
1826, 5, 25. David dis mcd
1831, 4, 20. David rst by rq
1831, 4, 20. Hannah recrq
1835, 2, 18. John gct Smithfield MM, O.
1839, 10, 23. Mary, Joseph & William, ch Da-
    vid & Hannah, recrq
1849, 2, 21. Mary Thistlethwaite (form Far-
    quhar) dis mou
1853, 10, 26. Joseph dis mcd
1856, 6, 26. Hannah Ann rocf Short Creek MM,
    dtd 1855,7,26 (H)
1861, 7, 21. Caroline West (form Farquhar)
    dis mcd (W)
1863, 4, 22. Hannah dis joining Orthodox in
    1854 (W)
1863, 6, 4 Caroline West (form Farquhar)
    dis mcd
1863, 7, 22. Hannah Greenlee (form Farquhar)
    dis mcd (W)
1864, 4, 21. Hannah Ann transferred to Salem
    MM, this mtg being laid down (H)
1865, 7, 26. Thomas dis mcd & joining Army
    (W)

FARRINGTON
1802, 2, 27. Cert rec for Abraham & w, Debo-
    rah, & s, Moses, from Redstone MM, dtd
    1801,10,30, endorsed to Concord MM

FAULKNER
1786, 7, 8. Robert & w, Elizabeth, & dt,
    Susanna, rocf Hopewell MM, dtd 1786,3,6
1788, 3, 22. Hannah rocf Hopewell MM, dtd
    1788,2,4
1789, 10, 24. Hannah gct Hopewell MM
1794, 1, 26. Robert [Falkner] dis
1798, 2, 24. David & Elizabeth [Falconer],
    ch Robert, gct Crooked Run MM
1798, 2, 24. Thomas & Susanna [Falconer], ch
    Robert, gct Hopewell MM

FAULKNER, continued
1800, 6,   28. David & w, Judith, & ch, Jesse,
    Phebe, Thomas, Mary, Judith & Solomon,
    rocf Hopewell MM, dtd 1800,3,3

FELL
1791, 2, 26. Rachel, w Mahlon, & ch, Ezra,
    Ann, Aaron, Elizabeth, Moses & Mahlon,
    rocf Wrightstown MM, dtd 1790,4,6

FERRALL
1802, 5, 22. James rocf South River MM, Va.,
    dtd 1801,10,10
1802, 5, 22. Mary rocf South River MM, Va.,
    dtd 1801,10,10

FIELDS
1826, 6, 22. Rachel (form Finch) dis mcd

FINCH
1802, 11, 27. Samuel & w, Peninah, & ch,
    Lydia, Rachel, Sarah, Ruth & Mary, rocf
    Hopewell MM, dtd 1802,1,4, endorsed by
    Redstone MM, 1802,10,29
1802, 11, 27. Hannah & Elizabeth, dt Samuel &
    Peninah, rocf Hopewell MM, dtd 1802,2,1,
    endorsed by Redstone MM, 1802,10,29
1802, 12, 25. David rocf Hopewell MM, dtd
    1802,4,1, endorsed by Redstone MM, 1802,10,
    29
1806, 4, 26. David dis mou
1806, 8, 23. Elizabeth Cummins (form Finch)
    dis mou
1806, 9, 27. Hannah Bottomley (form Finch)
    con mcd
1816, 8, 22. Ruth Cummins (form Finch) dis mou
1817, 3, 27. Sarah Hopton (form Finch) dis
    mcd
1823, 8, 28. Mary Crawford (form Finch) dis
    mcd
1826, 6, 22. Rachel Fields (form Finch) dis
    mcd
1834, 5, 21. Samuel gct Providence MM

FISHER
1802, 11, 4. Alice m Joshua COPE
1834, 2, 26. Mary m Obed GARWOOD
1836, 12, 7. Hannah m William KNIGHT

1792, 1, 28. Abel recrq
1798, 5, 26. Cert rec for Samuel & w, Ruth,
    & ch, Rachel, Mary, Elizabeth & Frances,
    from Monallen MM, dtd 1797,8,24, endorsed
    to Redstone MM
1800, 10, 25. Abel John & w, Mary, & two minor
    ch in their care, Alice & Ruth Fisher,
    rocf Monallen MM, dtd 1800,9,27
1804, 9, 22. Ruth gct Dunings Creek MM
1815, 4, 27. John & w, Lydia, & ch, Mary &
    Rebecca, rocf Dunnings Creek MM, dtd 1815,
    3,15
1821, 2, 22. Elizabeth rocf Short Creek MM,
    dtd 1820,12,19

1823, 6, 26. Elizabeth gct Short Creek MM
1841, 5, 26. Rebecca Harrison (form Fisher)
    dis mou
1842, 11, 23. Rebecca Harrison (form Fisher)
    rst by rq
1850, 11, 20. William dis mcd

FITZ RANDOLPH
1796, 4, 23. James & w, Elizabeth, & ch,
    Jonah, Jacob, Anna, Israel, Richard,
    Phebe, Edward, Margaret & Joel, rocf
    Rahway MM, dtd 1795,9,17
1803, 10, 22. Israel, s James, gct Redstone MM
1808, 3, 26. Jonah dis mou
1809, 5, 27. Jacob dis mou
1810, 5, 26. Margaret Wood (form Fitz Ran-
    dolph) dis mou
1812, 7, 25. Richard gct Middleton MM, O.
1812, 7, 25. Edward gct Middleton MM, O.
1814, 6, 30. Anna Wood (form Fitz Randolph)
    dis mou
1822, 10, 24. Phebe Hoge (form Fitz Randolph)
    dis mcd
1829, 6, 24. Isaac dis mou
1833, 1, 23. Joel dis mou
1834, 4, 23. Abraham dis mou

FLEMING
1811, 7, 27. Ann (form Crawford) dis mou

FLOWER
1844, 4, 25. Phebe (form Hartley) dis jas (H)

FORMAN
1793, 5, 16. John, s Robert & Mary, Mononga-
    gela Co., Pa.; m at Sandy Creek, Sarah
    MORTON, dt Samuel & Hannah, Monongahela
    Co., Pa.

1789, 3, 28. Robert & w, Mary, & ch, Joseph,
    Richard, Samuel, Rachel, Jane, Mary,
    Isaac & Rebecca, rocf Nottingham MM, dtd
    1788,10,11
1789, 8, 22. Elizabeth rocf Nottingham MM,
    dtd 1788,10,11
1789, 12, 26. John rocf Nottingham MM, dtd
    1788,10,11
1790, 8, 28. Elizabeth Conner (form Foreman)
    dis mcd
1792, 9, 22. Joseph [Foreman] dis mou

FOWLER
1847, 12, 25. Sally m Joseph RALEY

1831, 11, 23. Sally rocf Short Creek MM, dtd
    1831,10,18
1831, 11, 23. Anna M. rocf Short Creek MM, dtd
    1831,10,18
1836, 11, 23. Anna M. Thistlethwaite (form
    Fowler) dis mcd

FRAZIER
1800, 5, 24. Daniel & w, Nelly, & ch, William

FRAZIER, continued
    & Nelly, rocf Trent MM, N. C., dtd 1800,1,
    12

FREEMAN
1799, 8, 24. Lydia (form Grant) dis mou

FRENCH
1790, 10, 23. Joshua Hunt & w, Esther, & ch,
    Esther, Enoch, Nathan, Caleb & Stacy, &
    Thomas French, an apprentice, rocf Evesham
    MM, dtd 1790,8,6
1862, 4, 23. Thomas Y. rmt Rachel H. Black-
    burn (W)
1862, 6, 26. Rachel H. gct Salem MM, O. (H)
1863, 1, 1. Rachel (form Blackburn) dis join-
    ing the Wilburite Separatists in 1854

FURGASON
1825, 10, 27. Mary rocf Redstone MM, dtd 1825,
    8,31
1830, 10, 27. Mary [Ferguson] dis jH
1832, 7, 26. Mary Coffin (form Forgerson) dis
    mcd (H)

FURNIS
1803, 8, 27. Robert & w, Hannah, & ch, Mary,
    Esther, John & Seth, rocf Cane Creek MM,
    S. C., dtd 1803,4,23

GAMBLE
1796, 6, 25. Cert rec for Joseph & w, Eliza-
    beth, from Pipe Creek MM, dtd 1795,12,19,
    endorsed to Redstone MM
1801, 9, 26. Joseph & w, Elizabeth, rocf Red-
    stone MM, dtd 1801,8,28

GAPEN
1789, 8, 22. Zachariah recrq

GARRETSON
1796, 3, 10. Anna m George WALKER
1800, 11, 27. John, s William & Mary, Washing-
    ton Co., Pa.; m at Pike Run, Henrietta
    BRIGHT, dt William & Rebecca

1794, 12, 27. Anna rocf Warrington MM, dtd
    1794,10,11
1795, 1, 24. William & w, Mary, & ch, Cas-
    pares, John, Mary, Joseph, Sarah, Armel .&
    Patience, rocf Warrington MM, dtd 1794,10,
    11
1821, 5, 24. Joanna (form Johnston) dis mcd
1825, 1, 27. Rachel rocf Warrington MM, dtd
    1824,8,18
1828, 7, 24. Rachel gct Warrington MM
1841, 11, 24. Eliza (form Cleaver) dis mcd &
    jas
1844, 5, 23. Eliza (form Cleaver) dis jas (H)

GARRETT
1819, 4, 22. Ann (form Gregg) dis mcd

GARWOOD
1834, 2, 26. Obed, s Jesse & Lydia, Washing-
    ton Co., Pa.; m at Westland, Mary FISHER,
    dt John & Lydia, Washington Co., Pa.
1837, 5, 26. Mary m Elon HOLE

1787, 6, 9. Charity, w William, rocf Evesham
    MM, N. J., dtd 1787,4,6
1787, 12, 22. Samuel dis mcd
1788, 3, 22. Sarah (form Crawford) dis mcd
1788, 4, 26. Joseph dis mou
1802, 11, 27. Charity Jenkins (form Garwood)
    dis mou
1803, 11, 26. Cert rec for Isaiah & w, Mary,
    & ch, Thomas, Mary, Esther, Sarah, Hope,
    Hannah & Isaiah, from Southland MM, dtd
    1803,9,29, endorsed to Middleton MM
1803, 11, 26. Cert rec for Daniel from South-
    land MM, dtd 1803,9,29, endorsed to Middle
    ton MM
1834, 5, 21. Mary gct Redstone MM
1835, 6, 24. Mary rocf Redstone MM, dtd
    1835,6,3
1856, 12, 25. Joseph H. Miller gct Redstone
    MM, to m Rebecca Garwood
1863, 4, 22. Abraham dis joining Orthodox in
    1854 (W)
1863, 4, 22. Jesse R. dis joining Orthodox
    in 1854 (W)
1863, 4, 22. Mariam dis joining Orthodox in
    1854 (W)
1863, 4, 22. Miri C. dis joining Orthodox in
    1854 (W)
1863, 4, 22. Rebecca Miller (form Garwood)
    dis joining Orthodox in 1854 (W)
1863, 4, 22. William dis joining Orthodox in
    1854 (W)

GASKILL
1825, 7, 28. Hannah (form Smith) con mcd
1826, 4, 27. Hannah gct Center MM, O.

GAUSE
1804, 6, 7. Nathan, s Solomon & Ruth, Fay-
    ette Co., Pa.; m at Westland, Mary AYLES,
    dt Amos & Ann, Washington Co., Pa.

1804, 7, 28. Mary gct Redstone MM

GIBSON
1793, 7, 27. John & w, Mary, & ch, Joshua,
    Joseph, Betty & James, rocf Kennet MM, dtd
    1792,9,13
1795, 3, 28. Cert rec for John some time ago
    endorsed to Redstone MM

GILBERT
1788, 5, 1. Benjamin, s Benjamin & Sarah,
    Westmoreland Co., Pa.; m at Little Red-
    stone, Margaret ANDERSON, dt William &
    Elizabeth, Westmoreland Co., Pa.

1788, 2, 23. Benjamin rocf ND MM, Phila., Pa.

GILBERT, continued
    dtd 1787,5,22

GIVEN
1833, 3, 28. Samuel England gct Concord MM,
    O., to m Emma Given (H)

GRANT
1795, 8, 22. Margery, w James, & ch, John,
    Anthony, Lydia, Annzube & Judith, rocf
    Shrewsbury MM, dtd 1794,10,6
1799, 8, 24. Lydia Freeman (form Grant) dis
    mou
1802, 5, 22. John dis mou
1803, 7, 23. Anthony dis disunity
1803, 7, 23. Mary & dt, Catharine & Sarah,
    rocf Back Creek MM, N. C., dtd 1802,8,28
1804, 8, 25. Ann Hook (form Grant) dis mou
1811, 6, 22. Judith Stronn (form Grant) dis
    mou

GRAVE
1796, 4, 29. Enos [Greave], s Jacob & Rebeccah
    New Castle Co., Pa.; m at Pike Run, Betty
    JONES, dt John & Betty, York Co., Pa.
1823, 1, 1. Albina m Josiah JOHN

1790, 2, 27. Jesse [Greave] & w, Elizabeth,
    & ch, Tacy & Hannah, rocf New Garden MM,
    dtd 1789,10,3
1792, 10, 27. David & w, Rachel, rocf Kennet
    MM, dtd 1792,9,13
1794, 6, 28. Enos rocf Kennet MM, dtd 1794,
    2,13
1796, 6, 25. Enos & w, Betty, gct Redstone MM
1808, 9, 24. David gct Horsham MM, to m Ruth
    Cadwallader
1809, 6, 24. Ruth rocf Horsham MM, dtd 1808,
    12,23, endorsed by Center MM, 1809,5,1
1810, 11, 24. Ann rocf Kennet MM, dtd 1810,11,
    6
1817, 1, 23. Albina, Samuel, Jehu, Mary-Ann,
    David, Maris-Taylor & Ruthanna, ch Ann,
    recrq
1829, 7, 22. Ann dis jH
1833, 3, 28. Samuel [Graves] dis disunity (H)
1834, 10, 22. Jehu dis disunity
1834, 10, 22. Samuel dis disunity
1836, 1, 28. Jehu dis disunity (H)
1837, 1, 25. Mary Ann Johnson (form Grave)
    dis mou
1838, 4, 26. Mary Ann Johnston (form Graves)
    dis mcd (H)
1844, 4, 24. Maris Taylor dis disunity
1846. 12, 24. Ruth Cooper (form Grave) dis
    mcd (H)
1851, 12, 24. R..n Cooper (form Grave) dis mcd

GRAY
1801, 7, 25. Cert rec for Elijah & w, Mary, &
    ch, Esther & Samuel, from Bradford MM, dtd
    1801,5,15, endorsed to Redstone MM
1857, 7, 22. Sarah rmt Henry Cope (W)

1859, 9, 29. Mary E. dis jas
1863, 2, 5. Spring Creek MM, Ia., was given
    permission to rst Mary E.
1863, 3, 25. Nathan gct Upper Springfield MM,
    O. (W)
1863, 3, 25. Ann gct Upper Springfield MM,
    O. (W)
1864, 3, 23. Mary Michener (form Gray) dis
    mcd (W)

GREEN
1795, 6, 27. Joseph & w, Lydia, rocf Warring-
    ton MM, dtd 1795,3,7
1798, 9, 22. Joseph dis
1804, 4, 28. Lydia gct Middleton MM

GREENLEE
1863, 7, 22. Hannah (form Farquhar) dis mcd
    (W)

GREGG
1792, 10, 4. Joseph, Fayette Co., Pa.; m at
    Sandy Creek, Mary SMITH, Monongohela
    Co., Pa.
1810, 11, 1. Nathaniel, s Abner & Sarah, Bel-
    mont Co., O.; m at Westland, Elizabeth
    MILLS, dt Henry & Elizabeth, Washington
    Co., Pa.

1787, 5, 12. Thomas & w, Amy, & ch, Nimrod,
    Elizabeth, Dinah, Samuel, Ruth & John,
    rocf Fairfax MM, dtd 1783,3,8
1789, 3, 28. Daniel rocf Nottingham MM, dtd
    1788,2,23
1790, 3, 27. Daniel dis mcd
1790, 11, 27. Isaac rocf Wilmington MM, dtd
    1789,8,12
1791, 10, 22. Joseph rocf Goose Creek MM,
    dtd 1791,9,26
1791, 10, 22. Elizabeth Brown (form Gregg)
    dis mou
1798, 12, 22. Elizabeth (form Hough) dis mcd
1799, 5, 25. Elizabeth, Thomas, George, Mar-
    tha, William, Levi & Samuel, ch George &
    Mary, rocf Fairfax MM, dtd 1798,7,28
1801, 3, 28. Mary, w George, rocf Fairfax
    MM, dtd 1801,2,28
1807, 10, 24. John & w, Orpha, & ch, Joseph,
    Caiphas, Orpha, Ruth, John, George, Ann
    & Mary, rocf Redstone MM, dtd 1807,7,31
1809, 9, 23. Cephas dis mou
1809, 11, 25. Orpha Mires (form Gregg) dis
    mou
1811, 1, 26. Elizabeth gct Plainfield MM
1811, 2, 23. Ruth South (form Gregg) con mcd
1811, 4, 27. Joseph dis mou
1811, 8, 24. Joseph rst by rq
1813, 8, 28. Nathaniel & w, Elizabeth, & s,
    Henry, rocf Plainfield MM, dtd 1813,6,26
1814, 2, 26. George gct London Grove MM
1815, 3, 2. Nathaniel & w, Elizabeth, & s,
    Henry, gct Plainfield MM, O.
1816, 12, 26. George rocf London Grove MM,

GREGG, continued
    dtd 1816,6,5
1818, 12, 24. Mary Myars (form Gregg) dis mcd
1819, 4, 22. Ann Garrett (form Gregg) dis mcd
1819, 8, 26. George dis mcd
1829, 3, 26. Nathaniel & w, Elizabeth, & ch,
    Ruthanna, Jonas, Martin & Nathan Pusey,
    rocf Summerset MM, O., endorsed by Duck
    Creek MM, 1828,9,25, endorsed by Short
    Creek MM, 1829,1,22 (H)
1830, 5, 27. Nathaniel & w, Elizabeth, & ch,
    Ruthanna, Jonas, Martin, Nathan, Pusey &
    Nimrod, gct Plainfield MM, O. (H)
1840, 1, 23. Charles Lewis gct Plainfield MM,
    to m Lydia Ann Gregg (H)

GREWELL
1807, 8, 22. John rocf Duck Creek MM, Del.,
    dtd 1807,2,7
1808, 7, 23. John dis
1817, 7, 24. John recrq

GRIEST
1787, 2, 10. Deborah [Grist] rocf East Noting-
    ham MM, dtd 1786,7,29
1788, 2, 23. William [Ghrist] & ch, Joseph &
    John, recrq
1863, 3, 5. Ruth M. gct Sugar River MM, Ind.

GRIFFITH
1802, 3, 4. Rebecca m Isaac MARTIN
1806, 11, 27. Israel, s Jacob & Lydia, Wash-
    ington Co., Pa.; m Latitia SHAW, dt Samuel
    & Susanna, Washington Co., Pa.
1810, 5, 2. Hannah m William CRAWFORD
1813, 12, 1. Isaac, s Jacob & Lydia, Washing-
    ton Co., Pa.; m at Pike Run, Rebecca JOHN,
    dt Joseph & Mary, Washington Co., Pa.
1814, 4, 27. Esther m Curtis PYLE
1818, 5, 6. Rebecca m William McGIRR
1833, 12, 28. Eliza m Milton MARSH (H)
1847, 12, 23. Elizabeth P. m Joshua MILLHOUSE

1791, 5, 28. Jacob & w, Lydia, & ch, Isaac,
    Rebecca Israel, Hannah & Allan, rocf
    Warrington MM, dtd 1791,2,12
1800, 4, 26. Cert rec for Benjamin from War-
    rington MM, endorsed to Red Stone MM
1808, 3, 26. Benjamin forfeited his right of
    mbrp
1820, 10, 26. Amos gct Gunpowder MM, to m
    Edith Price
1821, 4, 26. Edith, w Amos, rocf Gunpowder
    MM, dtd 1821,2,7
1822, 8, 22. David dis mcd
1825, 8, 25. Mary (form Shepherd) dis mcd
1825, 6, 23. Jason dis mcd
1829, 2, 18. Israel dis jH
1829, 6, 24. Lydia dis jH
1829, 7, 22. Letitia dis jH
1829, 11, 25. Jacob dis jH
1833, 7, 25. Eli R. gct Carmel MM, O., to m
    Mary Ann Marsh (H)

1833, 11, 21. Mary Ann rocf Carmel MM, dtd
    1833,10,19 (H)
1836, 5, 25. Mary dis jH
1837, 6, 21. Eli dis mcd & jH
1837, 9, 20. Eliza Marsh (form Griffith) dis
    mcd & jH
1839, 10, 23. Joel dis mcd
1839, 10, 24. Lavenia & ch, Oliver Francis &
    Joel Emlin, rocf Short Creek MM, dtd
    1839,7,25 (H)
1840, 2, 19. Samuel dis jH
1840, 3, 26. Samuel con mcd (H)
1840, 8, 27. Eliza Jane recrq (H)
1841, 6, 23. Daniel P. gct Redstone MM
1843, 11, 22. Israel Jr. dis jH
1851, 2, 20. Joel dis mcd (H)
1854, 9, 20. Amos & w, Edith, & ch, George,
    Mary R., Amos & Edith A., gct Redstone MM
1854, 9, 20. Esther P. gct Redstone MM
1856, 4, 23. Emmor H. gct Middleton MM, to m
    Cynthia Heald (W)
1861, 3, 28. Philena G. Baker (form Griffith)
    con mcd (H)
1862, 8, 27. Cynthia rocf Middleton MM, O.,
    dtd 1862,5,17 (W)
1863, 1, 1. Emor dis joining the Wilburite
    Separatists in 1854
1863, 3, 25. Amos dis joining Orthodox in
    1854 (W)
1863, 3, 25. Edith dis joining Orthodox in
    1854 (W)
1863, 4, 22. Amos Jr. dis joining Orthodox
    in 1854 (W)
1863, 4, 22. Esther Patterson (form Grif-
    fith) dis joining Orthodox in 1854 (W)
1863, 4, 22. Mary dis joining Orthodox in
    1854 (W)
1864, 4, 21. Eli R. transferred to Salem
    MM, this mtg being laid down (H)
1864, 4, 21. Eliza Jane & Samuel transferred
    to Salem MM, this mtg being laid down (H)
1864, 4, 21. Israel L. transferred to Salem
    MM, this mtg being laid down (H)
1864, 4, 21. Letitia & A. Rebecca trans-
    ferred to Salem MM, this mtg being laid
    down (H)
1864, 4, 21. Oliver R. transferred to Salem
    MM, this mtg being laid down (H)
1864, 4, 21. Oscar transferred to Salem MM,
    this mtg being laid down (H)
1864, 10, 26. Daniel P. dis joining Orthodox
    (W)
1864, 10, 26. Sarah Louiza dis joining Ortho-
    dox in 1854 (W)

GRISELL
1804, 4, 5. Agnes m Samuel VAIL

1786, 7, 8. Joseph & w, Priscilla, & ch,
    Agness & Thomas, rocf Uwchland MM, dtd
    1786,5,4
1791, 6, 25. Agnes, minor, gct Hopewell MM
1796, 4, 23. Thomas & ch, Joseph, Rachel,

38

GRISELL, continued
Ann, Samuel & Thomas, recrq
1796, 7, 23. Martha [Grissel] rocf Concord
    MM, dtd 1795,12,9
1802, 6, 26. Margaret [Grissel] rocf Concord
    MM, dtd 1802,5,5
1802, 6, 26. Agnes [Grissel] rocf Concord MM,
    dtd 1802,4,7
1803, 12, 24. Thomas & w, Martha, & ch, Jo-
    seph, Rachel, Ann, Samuel, Thomas, Martha,
    Charles, Margaret & Hannah, gct Middleton
    MM

HAGAMAN
1821, 11, 22. Michael & w, Sarah, rocf Provi-
    dence MM, dtd 1821,7,24
1822, 4, 25. Michael & w, Sarah, gct Provi-
    dence MM

HAINES
1832, 4, 25. Nathan J. Rogers gct Redstone
    MM, to m Atlantic Haines
1863, 3, 25. Eli dis joining Orthodox in 1854
    (W)

HALL
1818, 1, 1. Joseph D., s Abner & Lavina,
    Washington Co., Pa.; m at Westland, Mary
    HILLES, dt William & Rebecca, Washington
    Co., Pa.

1800, 5, 24. Joseph rocf Contentney MM, dtd
    1800,3,8
1800, 6, 28. Lavina & dt, Susanna, Sarah,
    Lany & Rachel, rocf Core Sound MM, dtd
    1800,5,14
1800, 6, 28. Joseph Dew & s, Joseph & Elias,
    & gr s, Joseph Hall, rocf Core Sound MM,
    dtd 1800,5,14
1802, 5, 22. Cert rec for Jesse & s, Joseph,
    from Contentney MM, N. C., dtd 1802,3,13,
    endorsed to Concord MM
1817, 8, 28. Joseph D. rocf Short Creek MM,
    dtd 1817,6,24   [1818,2,24
1818, 8, 27. Rachel rocf Short Creek MM, dtd
1819, 10, 28. Rachel gct Short Creek MM
1823, 2, 20. Joseph D. & w, Mary, & s, Joseph
    Hilles, gct Flushing MM, O., returned
    1823,8,27, because of their not moving
1829, 2, 18. Mary dis JH
1829, 6, 24. Joseph D. dis JH
1844, 4, 24. Joseph Hilles dis JH

HAMMET
1803, 3, 26. Sarah rocf Concord MM, dtd 1803,
    2,19
1806, 8, 23. Sarah gct Miami MM

HAMMOND
1789, 3, 28. Daniel & w, Elizabeth, recrq

HANCOCK
1853, 6, 23. William, s Joel & Mary, Washing-

ton Co., Pa.; m at Westland, Sabina
UNDERWOOD, dt Mary, Washington Co., Pa.

1824, 5, 27. Joel & w, Mary, & ch, Mary &
    Hannah, rocf Dunnings Creek MM, dtd 1824,
    4,14
1824, 5, 27. William rocf Dunnings Creek MM,
    dtd 1824,4,14
1824, 5, 27. Elizabeth rocf Dunnings Creek
    MM, dtd 1824,4,14
1830, 7, 21. John rocf Deer Creek MM, Md.,
    dtd 1830,6,10; w, Hannah, d before cert
    was rec
1863, 1, 1. Hannah dis joining Wilburite
    Separatists in 1854
1863, 1, 1. William & w, Sabina, & ch,
    Jesse, Joel, Mary & George, dis joining
    Wilburite Separatists in 1854

HANK
1801, 4, 25. John, widower, Greene Co., Pa.;
    m at Westland, Judith BURGE, wd, Greene
    Co., Pa.

1801, 1, 24. John rocf Crooked Run MM, dtd
    1792,5,5
1829, 6, 24. Judith gct Providence MM

HANNA
1802, 1, 23. Benjamin rocf South River MM,
    dtd 1801,9,12
1802, 1, 23. Thomas rocf South River MM,
    dtd 1801,9,12
1801, 12, 26. Robert & w, Catherine, & ch,
    Robert, Esther, Catherine & Ann, rocf
    South River MM, dtd 1801,9,12

HARLAN
1788, 6, 28. Joshua dis jas
1792, 1, 28. George Jr. dis
1792, 3, 24. Elizabeth dis

HARRIS
1803, 3, 31. Jonas, Jefferson Co., O.; m at
    Sandhill, Hannah BEESON, dt Henry, Fayette
    Co., Pa.

1789, 12, 26. Amy & ch, Sarah, Jemimah & Ja-
    cob, rocf Rahway MM, N. J., dtd 1789,3,19
1790, 3, 27. Sarah Parime (form Harris) dis
    mou
1791, 9, 24. Jacob dis mou
1800, 7, 26. Cert rec for George from Core
    Sound MM, dtd 1800,5,14, endorsed back to
    Core Sound MM
1800, 7, 26. Cert rec for Mary & ch, Mary,
    Esther, Sarah, Josiah, George & Daniel,
    from Core Sound MM, dtd 1800,5,14, endors-
    ed to Redstone MM
1802, 1, 23. Jonas rocf South River MM, dtd
    1801,9,12

HARRISON
1841, 5, 26. Rebecca (form Fisher) dis mou
1842, 11, 23. Rebecca (form Fisher) rst by rq
1855, 5, 24. William recrq
1855, 8, 23. Elizabeth, John F., Lydia Ann,
    Emma, Mary & William Henry, ch William &
    Rebecca, recrq
1863, 3, 25. Rebecca dis joining Orthodox in
    1854 (W)

HARRY
1795, 11, 30. George & w, Phebe, & ch, Hannah,
    John, Thomas, Cyrus & Mary, rocf Kennet
    MM, dtd 1795,9,17
1796, 4, 23. Cert rec for George & fam some
    time ago endorsed to Redstone MM
1809, 9, 23. Jacob rocf Kennet MM, dtd 1809,
    7,4
1822, 8, 22. Jacob dis mcd
1838, 8, 23. Lewis & w, Sarah, & ch, Naomi,
    William G., Lewis C. & Susanna, rocf Mo-
    nallen MM, dtd 1838,7,18 (H)
1847, 4, 22. Naomi Linton (form Harry) con
    mcd (H)
1851, 2, 20. William G. dis mcd (H)
1853, 6, 23. Eliza Jane (form Reid) con mcd
    (H)
1864, 4, 21. Comley, Jesse & John transferred
    to Salem MM, this mtg being laid down (H)
1864, 4, 21. Lewis & Sarah transferred to
    Salem MM, this mtg being laid down (H)
1864, 4, 21. Mary transferred to Salem MM,
    this mtg being laid down (H)

HARTLEY
1819, 9, 2. Elias P. (or Ellis), s Roger &
    Hannah, Washington Co., Pa.; m at Westland,
    Meribah SMITH, Washington Co., Pa.

1797, 5, 27. Mahlon & w, Hannah, & ch, Edward,
    Mahlon, Roger & Hannah, rocf Falls MM,
    dtd 1796,10,5
1797, 5, 27. Thomas [Hartly] rocf Falls MM,
    dtd 1796,10,5
1804, 2, 25. Edward dis mou
1808, 5, 28. Roger dis
1813, 8, 28. Hannah Cross (form Hartley) con
    mcd
1816, 7, 25. Roger & w, Hannah, & ch, Eliza-
    beth, Agness, Peter Vickers, Harriett West
    & Hannah, recrq
1818, 12, 24. Ellis Pugh recrq
1823, 12, 25. Roger M. rst by rq
1827, 7, 26. Mary (form Waits) dis mcd
1829, 6, 25. Peter dis disunity (H)
1829, 12, 23. Roger M. dis disunity
1832, 5, 23. Peter V. dis mou
1833, 9, 25. Meribah dis jH
1834, 6, 25. Elizabeth Morris (form Hartley)
    dis mou
1838, 9, 26. Harriet Ruble (form Hartley)
    dis mcd
1842, 4, 20. Phebe & Ann dis jH

1843, 6, 22. Meribah & dt, Lydia, gct Clear
    Creek MM, Ill. (H)
1843, 8, 24. Ann gct Clear Creek MM, Ill. (H)
1843, 8, 24. Elizabeth gct Clear Creek MM,
    Ill. (H)
1844, 4, 25. Phebe Flower (form Hartley)
    dis jas (H)
1845, 5, 21. Lydia Mills (form Hartley) dis
    mcd & jH
1846, 4, 22. Elizabeth H. Smith (form Hart-
    ley) dis mcd
1863, 4, 22. Agness & Hannah dis joining
    Orthodox in 1854 (W)

HARVEY
1789, 2, 4. Jane m Jehu COULSON
1790, 10, 27. Job, s Amos & Keziah, Fayette
    Co., Pa.; m at Redstone, Hannah JOURDAN,
    dt James & Charity, Fayette Co., Pa.

1788, 10, 25. Jane recrq
1789, 9, 26. Amos & Catherine Harvy, ch Jane
    Coulson, recrq
1790, 6, 26. Job rocf Kennet MM, dtd 1790,
    3,11
1793, 11, 23. Job gct Hopewell MM, Va.
1795, 6, 27. Job & w, Eleanor, rocf Hopewell
    MM, dtd 1794,7,7
1821, 10, 29. Amos gct Smithfield MM, O.
1821, 10, 29. Mary gct Smithfield MM, O.
1836, 5, 26. Margaret & dt, Gulielma Maria
    Minican, rocf Plainfield MM, O., dtd
    1836,1,14 (H)

HATCHER
1798, 3, 24. William & w, Mary, & ch, Rachel,
    Sarah, Thomas & John, rocf Goose Creek MM,
    dtd 1797,11,27
1801, 3, 28. Joshua & w, Jane, & ch, John,
    Mahlon, William, Sarah & Mary, rocf Goose
    Creek MM, dtd 1799,9,30

HATFIELD
1786, 9, 9. Martha rocf Richland MM, dtd
    1786,6,15
1788, 9, 27. Jonas recrq
1789, 1, 24. Rachel rocf Fairfax MM, dtd
    1788,10,25
1789, 3, 28. Abel Janney, Deborah & Thomas,
    ch Jonas & Rachel, recrq
1797, 4, 22. Lydia (form Long) dis mou
1806, 7, 26. Jonas & w, Rachel, & ch, Abel,
    Deborah, Thomas, Martha, Rachel, Mary,
    Jonas, Ann, John & Nathan, gct Miami MM

HAVILAND
1863, 4, 22. Lydia K. (form Stanley) dis
    joining Orthodox in 1854 (W)

HAWLEY
1801, 6, 27. Caleb & w, Hannah, & ch, Nathan,
    David, Amos, Caleb, Benjamin, Mary, Rich-
    ard, Jesse, Elisha & Hannah, rocf Brad-

HAWLEY, continued
        ford MM, dtd 1801,5,15
1802, 4, 24. Nathan dis disunity

HAYES
1791, 8, 27. Leah (form Brown) dis mou

HAYHURST
1790, 9, 25. Mary, w James, & ch, Sarah, Ra-
        chel, Job, Eli & Hannah, rocf Gunpowder
        MM, dtd 1790,4,24

HEACOCK

1806, 11, 26. Nathan [Haycock], s John & Es-
        ther, Washington Co., Pa.; m at Pike Run,
        Hannah JOHN, dt Joseph & Mary, Washington
        Co., Pa.

1806, 2, 22. Nathan recrq
1809, 11, 25. Esther (form Antrim) dis mou
1811, 10, 26. Nathan & w, Hannah, & ch, Phebe
        & Joseph, gct Salem MM, O.
1816, 7, 25. Esther rst by rq
1822, 3, 28. Samuel & ch, John G., Larkin,
        Caleb, Eliza, Meriam & Martha, recrq
1827, 8, 23. Esther Strawn (form Haycock) dis
        mcd
1833, 9, 25. John G. dis mcd
1833, 10, 23. Caleb dis mcd
1833, 10, 23. Larkin A. gct Short Creek MM
1841, 10, 27. Benjamin gct Short Creek MM
1841, 11, 24. Mariam [Haycock] gct Short Creek
        MM, O.

HEALD
1786, 4, 13. John, s Nathan & Rebecca, Wash-
        ington Co., Pa.; m at Westland, Phebe
        HUTTON, dt Thomas & Mary, Washington Co.,
        Pa.
1792, 11, 1. William, s Nathan & Rebecca,
        Washington Co., Pa.; m at Westland, Sarah
        WILSON, dt William & Elizabeth, Washington
        Co., Pa.
1798, 3, 29. Nathan Jr., s Nathan & Rebecca,
        Washington Co., Pa.; m at Westland, Rachel
        SMITH, dt Thomas & Rachel, Allegany Co.,
        Pa.

1787, 11, 24. William dis
1789, 4, 25. Hannah Adamson (form Heald) dis
        mou
1790, 5, 22. William rst by rq
1802, 11, 27. Rachel dis
1805, 8, 24. Rachel rst by rq
1805, 9, 28. Rachel gct Middleton MM
1856, 4, 23. Emmor H. Griffith gct Middleton
        MM, to m Cynthia Heald (W)

HEATON
1805, 10, 26. John rocf Kingwood MM, dtd 1805,
        9,12
1809, 2, 25. Sarah & Rebecca recrq

1811, 9, 28. Sarah Johnson (form Heaton) dis
        mou
1812, 10, 24. Rebecca Ayres (form Heaton) rpd
        mcd
1815, 8, 31. John dis disunity

HERBERT
1793, 4, 27. Ann rocf Gunpowder MM, dtd
        1792,11,24
1802, 8, 28. Ann gct Concord MM

HESTON
1809, 6, 29. Ann m Jonathan KNIGHT
1810, 11, 29. Abraham, s Eber & Ann, Washing-
        ton Co., Pa.; m at Westland, Deborah JACK-
        SON, dt Isaac & Elizabeth, Washington
        Co., Pa.
1824, 7, 1. Sarah m George PUSEY

1796, 4, 23. John & w, Elizabeth, & ch, Mar-
        garet, rocf Wrightstown MM, dtd 1795,10,6,
        endorsed by Redstone MM, 1796,4,22
1796, 7, 23. Titus & w, Sarah, & dt, Uphimea,
        rocf Wrightstown MM, dtd 1795,10,6, en-
        dorsed by Redstone MM, 1796,7,1
1796, 10, 22. Zebulon & w, Sarah, rocf Wrights-
        town MM, dtd 1796,9,6
1796, 10, 22. Eber & w, Ann, & ch, Abraham,
        Letitia, Ann, Mary & Sarah, rocf Wrights-
        town MM, dtd 1796,9,6
1799, 11, 23. Elizabeth rocf Wrightstown MM,
        dtd 1799,1,8
1801, 2, 28. Elizabeth dis
1802, 3, 27. Titus dis disunity
1802, 10, 23. John & w, Elizabeth, & ch, Mar-
        garet, Anna, Tacy, Rebecca, John & Zebu-
        lon, gct Concord MM
1806, 11, 22. Letitia Powel (form Heston) dis
        mou
1813, 2, 27. Sarah, w Titus, & dt, Euphemia,
        gct New Garden MM
1815, 11, 2. Abraham & w, Deborah, & ch, Ma-
        ria Ann, Elizabeth & David, gct New Garden
        MM, O.
1835, 11, 25. Eber Jr. dis disunity

HEWITT
1803, 12, 8. Abel [Hewit], s Jonathan & Ann,
        Washington Co., Pa.; m at Westland, Rachel
        DINGEE, dt Charles & Martha, Washington
        Co., Pa.

1787, 5, 12. Jonathan & w, Ann, & ch, Abel,
        Sarah & Joseph, & Elizabeth, b since dte
        of cert, rocf Monallin MM, dtd 1786,12,11
1803, 2, 26. Abel rocf Redstone MM, dtd
        1802,12,31
1806, 8, 23. Abel & w, Rachel, & ch, Ann &
        Charles, gct Redstone MM
1808, 5, 28. Rebecca [Hewit] rocf Redstone
        MM, dtd 1808,4,29
1817, 9, 25. Rebecca gct Providence MM
1825, 1, 27. William Blackburn, Jr. gct

HEWITT, continued
Providence MM, to m Ann Hewitt
1826, 8, 24. Sarah, minor, rocf Providence MM,
dtd 1826,6,20
1829, 6, 24. Sarah [Hewit], minor, gct Providence MM
1843, 6, 21. Rachel [Hewit] rocf Providence
MM, dtd 1843,6,1

HILL
1793, 10, 26. Mary (form Couzens) dis mou
1800, 4, 26. Mary rst by rq
1803, 4, 23. Rebecca (form Brown) dis mou
1804, 6, 23. Cert rec for Robert from Back
Creek MM, N. C., dtd 1803,8,27, endorsed
to Miami MM
1804, 6, 23. Cert rec for Susanna & dt, Martha, from Back Creek MM, N. C., dtd 1803,
8,27, endorsed to Miami MM
1846, 3, 26. Almira (form John) dis mcd (H)
1848, 8, 23. Almira (form John) dis mou
1848, 8, 23. Elizabeth (form Rogers) dis
mou

HILLES
1801, 3, 12. Hugh, s William & Rebecca, Washington Co., Pa.; m at Westland, Elizabeth
WILSON, dt William & Elizabeth
1803, 3, 31. Ann m Mahlon LINTON
1811, 1, 31. David, s William & Rebecca, Washington Co., Pa.; m at Westland, Hannah
DINGEE, dt Charles & Martha, Washington
Co., Pa.
1814, 7, 27. Rebecca d
1818, 1, 1. Mary n Joseph D. HALL

1795, 10, 24. William & w, Rebecca, & ch, Hugh,
Mary, Ann, Eli, David & Samuel, rocf Uwchland MM, dtd 1795,8,6
1806, 12, 27. Eli gct Goshen MM
1808, 12, 24. Samuel gct Goshen MM
1810, 5, 26. Hugh & w, Elizabeth, & ch, Rebecca, Sarah, Ann & William, gct New Garden MM, O.
1829, 9, 23. David dis JH
1831, 10, 27. David dis disunity (H)
1834, 3, 26. Charles dis disunity
1842, 8, 24. Edmund dis disunity
1844, 1, 24. Ann Eliza, Martha & Mary gct
Salem MM, Ia.
1844, 2, 21. William D. gct Salem MM, Ia.
1844, 2, 21. Eli & David Pugh, minors, gct
Salem MM, Ia.

HOAGLAND
1858, 11, 24. Abel H. Blackburn gct Muncy MM,
Pa., to m Caroline Hoagland (W)

HOCKET
1842, 8, 26. Moses Jr., s Moses & Olive,
Tippecanoe Co., Ind.; m at Westland, Ruth
SOPHER, dt Joseph & Phebe

1842, 10, 26. Ruth gct Sugar River MM, Ind.

HOGE
1787, 12, 22. Leah Lazader (form Hoge) dis mou
1788, 6, 28. Mary, Lavina, Rachel & Elizabeth, ch Solomon & Esther, rocf Richland
MM, dtd 1788,1,17
1789, 4, 25. John & w, Mary, & ch, William,
Jonathan & Jacob, rocf Hopewell MM, dtd
1788,11,3
1789, 7, 25. Rachel Chandler (form Hoge), w
Swithin, dis mcd
1789, 8, 22. Isaiah dis joining militia
1792, 3, 24. Thomas dis mou
1795, 3, 28. Mary Buckles (form Hoge) dis
mou
1796, 3, 26. Rachel dis
1796, 5, 28. Cert rec for Esther from Hopewell MM, dtd 1796,1,4, endorsed to Redstone MM
1796, 8, 27. Solomon & w, Mary, rocf Hopewell MM, dtd 1795,4,6
1797, 3, 25. Jesse rocf Hopewell MM, dtd
1797,2,6
1798, 5, 26. Ann Smith (form Hoge) dis mou
1803, 1, 22. Jonathan rocf Redstone MM, dtd
1802,12,21
1803, 5, 28. William dis disunity
1804, 5, 26. Jonathan [Hogue] gct Redstone
MM
1820, 8, 24. Sarah Call (form Hoge) dis mcd
1820, 8, 24. Esther (form Hoge) dis mcd
1820, 9, 21. Mary dis jas
1822, 8, 22. Barak dis mcd
1822, 8, 22. William dis mcd
1822, 10, 24. Phebe (form Fitz Randolph) dis
mcd
1830, 11, 29. Solomon dis mou

HOLE
1837, 5, 26. Elon, s David & Ann, Columbia
Co., O.; m at Westland, Mary GARWOOD, dt
John & Lydia Fisher, Washington Co., Pa.

1837, 7, 26. Mary gct Carmel MM, O.
1841, 5, 26. Elon & w, Mary, & ch, Catherine, & Beulah Ann, rocf Carmel MM, dtd
1841,3,20
1851, 4, 23. Elon & ch, Beulah Ann, Lydia,
David & Anne, gct Carmel MM, O.
1851, 4, 23. Catherine gct Carmel MM, O.

HOLLOWAY
1800, 11, 22. David & w, Hannah, & ch, Daten,
Lydia & Margaret, rocf Crooked Run MM,
dtd 1800,10,1
1802, 8, 28. Asa & w, Mary, & ch, Stanton,
Mary, Sarah, Isaac, Hannah, Eli & James,
rocf South River MM, dtd 1801,9,12

HOOK
1804, 8, 25. Ann (form Grant) dis mou

HOOPS
1804, 3, 24.   Cert rec for Jesse & w, Sarah,
       & ch, Esther, John, Wilson & Isaac, from
       New Garden MM, dtd 1803,6,8, endorsed to
       Middleton MM

HOOVER
1801, 12, 26.   John rocf Back Creek MM, N. C.,
       dtd 1801,9,26
1803, 5, 28.   Andrew [Hover] & ch, Frederick
       Henry & Andrew, rocf Back Creek MM, N. C.,
       dtd 1802,8,12
1803, 5, 28.   Elizabeth [Hover] & dt, Su-
       sanna, Rebecca, Catherine & Sarah, rocf
       Back Creek MM, N. C., dtd 1802,8,12

HOPKINS
1826, 9, 21.   Anne rst by rq with consent of
       Redstone MM
1829, 3, 26.   Ann gct Redstone MM (H)
1833, 4, 24.   Ann dis jH

HOPTON
1817, 3, 27.   Sarah (form Finch) dis mcd

HORNER
1802, 12, 25.   Ann, w Thomas, rocf Bush River
       MM, S. C., dtd 1802,9,25; settled at Little
       Miami

HORTON
1788, 12, 27.   Mary (form Booth) rocf Concord
       MM, dtd 1787,10,3
1789, 1, 24.   Mary (form Booth) dis mou
1818, 8, 27.   Rachel (form John) dis mou
1820, 7, 27.   Rachel rst by rq
1830, 6, 23.   Rachel dis jH
1830, 8, 26.   John [Horten] recrq (H)
1832, 4, 26.   Mary, minor dt Rachel, recrq (H)
1834, 8, 28.   John & w, Rachel, & dt, Mary,
       gct Marlborough MM (H)
1848, 10, 26.   John Horton & w, Rachel, &
       Cynthia Horton Davis, a minor, rocf Plain-
       field MM, dtd 1848,8,17 (H)
1856, 12, 25.   John relrq (H)

HOUGH
1800, 5, 28.   Ann m John JACKSON

1790, 10, 23.   Amos & w, Elizabeth, & ch, Sa-
       rah, Benjamin, Thomas, Elizabeth, Ann,
       John, James (Joseph in women's minutes),
       Ruth & Mary, rocf Fairfax MM, dtd 1790,
       7,24
1794, 5, 24.   Sarah, dt Elizabeth, gct Fair-
       fax MM
1795, 5, 23.   Sarah rocf Fairfax MM, dtd 1795,
       1,24
1796, 11, 26.   Sarah Duncan (form Hough) dis
       mcd
1798, 10, 25.   Ann con mou
1798, 12, 22.   Benjamin rst by rq
1798, 12, 22.   Elizabeth Gregg (form Hough) dis

mcd
1799, 2, 23.   Thomas dis disunity
1801, 2, 28.   Joseph, Mary, Ruth & Susanna,
       ch Amos & Elizabeth, gct Redstone MM
1801, 8, 22.   Catherine & ch, Elizabeth, Ra-
       chel & Amos, recrq
1802, 3, 27.   Benjamin & w, Catherine, & ch,
       Elizabeth, Rachel & Amos, gct Concord MM

HOWARD
1799, 10, 26.   Horton & s, Henry & Joseph,
       rocf Core Sound MM, N. C., dtd 1799,9,1
1799, 12, 28.   Mary, w Horton, rocf Core Sound
       MM, dtd 1799,9,1

HULL
1804, 8, 25.   Hannah (form Rees) dis mou

HUNT
1790, 10, 23.   Joshua Hunt & w, Esther, & ch,
       Elisha, Enoch, Nathan, Caleb & Stacy, &
       Thomas French, an apprentice, rocf Eve-
       sham MM, dtd 1790,8,6
1800, 5, 24.   Robert & w, Abigail, & s, Seth,
       rocf Crooked Run MM, dtd 1800,1,4
1802, 4, 24.   Robert & w, Abigail, & s, Seth,
       gct Redstone MM
1803, 6, 25.   Cert rec for John from Crooked
       Run MM, dtd 1802,12,4, endorsed to Red-
       stone MM
1858, 4, 22.   Jonathan T. Rogers gct Spiceland
       MM, Ind., to m Mary Hunt

HUNTER
1803, 8, 27.   Cert rec for Hugh & w, Elizabeth
       from Goose Creek MM, dtd 1800,10,27, en-
       dorsed to Concord MM

HUPP
1821, 5, 24.   Phebe (form Johnson) con mcd
1834, 5, 21.   Phebe dis jas

HUTCHIN
1852, 2, 25.   Mary Ann (form Cope) dis mcd

HUTTON
1786, 4, 13.   Phebe m John HEALD
1794, 5, 8.   John, s Thomas & Mary, Washing-
       ton Co., Pa.; m at Westland, Jane PENNEL,
       dt Joshua & Susanna, Washington Co., Pa.
1803, 2, 3.   Mary m Joseph ENGLAND
1814, 1, 6.   Margaret m Isaac JACKSON

1787, 3, 10.   Joseph & w, Sarah, & ch, Abel,
       Sarah, Elizabeth, Amos, John & Asabel,
       rocf Fairfax MM, dtd 1785,12,24
1788, 2, 23.   John recrq
1788, 6, 28.   Margaret recrq
1789, 8, 22.   Sarah dis
1789, 11, 28.   Elizabeth Powell (form Hutton)
       dis mou
1791, 5, 28.   Thomas rocf Goshen MM, dtd
       1791,3,11

HUTTON, continued

1792, 1, 28. Abel dis mou
1794, 10, 2. Amos & w, Beulah, dis
1798, 4, 28. Joseph dis mou
1800, 6, 28. John, s Joseph, dis mcd
1803, 10, 22. Joseph & w, Sarah, gct Concord MM
1806, 11, 22. Amos & w, Beulah, rst by rq
1807, 1, 24. Amos & Beulah gct Short Creek MM
1815, 6, 1. Lavina rocf Plymouth MM, dtd 1815,2,18
1815, 6, 29. Thomas dis mou
1815, 11, 2. Thomas, Jr., minor, gct Redstone MM
1817, 1, 23. John Jr., minor, gct Middleton MM
1817, 4, 24. Fairfield MM was given permission to rst John
1817, 10, 23. Levina gct Plymouth MM, O.
1818, 8, 27. Susanna [Huton] gct Middleton MM, O.
1819, 3, 25. John gct Middleton MM, O.
1829, 9, 24. William rocf Smithfield MM, dtd 1829,6,23 (H)

ICENHOUR

1800, 8, 23. Mary [Icehouer] (form England) dis mou
1803, 11, 26. Mary rst by rq
1804, 4, 28. Mary gct Middleton MM

IREY

1799, 6, 22. Hannah recrq
1807, 1, 24. Hannah gct Salem MM

JACKMAN

1855, 3, 22. Ruth (form Lilly) con mcd (H)

JACKSON

1810, 11, 29. Deborah m Abraham HESTON
1814, 1, 6. Isaac, s Joseph & Esther, Washington Co., Pa.; m at Westland, Margaret HUTTON, dt Thomas & Mary, Washington Co., Pa.

1787, 4, 14. William rocf Bradford MM, dtd 1786,11,17
1789, 8, 22. William gct New Garden MM
1792, 10, 27. Isaac & w, Elizabeth, & ch, Sarah, Sydney, Mercy & Deborah, rocf Uwchland MM, dtd 1792,9,6
1801, 9, 26. Isaac & w, Elizabeth, & ch, Sarah, Sidney, Mercy, Deborah, Ann, Samuel & Jesse, rocf Redstone MM, dtd 1801,8,28 (Jesse had d since dte of issue)
1801, 10, 24. Ann gct Redstone
1814, 12, 1. Sarah, Sydney, Mercy & Ann gct New Garden MM
1815, 6, 29. Isaac & w, Margaret, gct New Garden MM
1815, 11, 2. Samuel, minor, gct New Garden MM, O.

JAMES

1794, 1, 26. Samuel rocf Haverford MM, dtd

1793,8,9
1795, 6, 27. Hannah rocf Fairfax MM, dtd 1795,3,28
1795, 8, 22. Joshua, Evan, George, Samuel, Anne & Margaret, ch Samuel & Hannah, recrq
1801, 11, 28. Isaac & w, Sarah, & ch, John, Elizabeth, Joseph (Josiah in women's minutes)), Mary, Catherine, Sarah & Isaac, rocf South River MM, Va., dtd 1801,6,13
1801, 11, 28. John & w, Martha, & ch, Benjamin & Elizabeth, rocf South River MM, Va., dtd 1801,7,11
1801, 12, 26. Cert rec for Hannah, w Thomas, from Warrington MM, dtd 1801,10,10, endorsed to Redstone MM

JAY

1802, 12, 25. Layton & w, Elizabeth, & ch, Patience, Charlotte, William, John, James & Abigail, rocf Bush River MM, S. C., dtd 1802,9,25 (settled at Little Miami)

JEFFERIES

1809, 5, 27. Caleb & w, Phebe, & ch, Amos & Rhoda, recrq
1820, 7, 27. Caleb [Jeffers] & w, Phebe, & ch, Emmor & Rhoda, gct Plainfield MM, O.

JELKS

1801, 10, 24. Richard & w, Mary, rocf Trent MM, dtd 1800,1,12, endorsed by Redstone MM, 1801,10,2
1801, 10, 24. Priscilla rocf Trent MM, dtd 1800,1,12, endorsed by Redstone MM, 1801, 10,2

JENKINS

1802, 11, 27. Charity (form Garwood) dis mou
1835, 10, 21. Mary rocf Short Creek MM, dtd 1835,5,18
1835, 10, 21. Hannah rocf Short Creek MM, dtd 1835,5,18
1841, 5, 26. Mary White (form Jenkins) rpd mou
1841, 7, 21. Hannah Custard (form Jenkins) rpd mcd
1786, 1, 14. Ann Brown (form Jenkinson) dis mcd
1786, 7, 8. Isaac con mou
1787, 11, 24. Mary Porter (form Jenkinson) dis mou
1792, 10, 27. Rebecca & ch, Ann, Elizabeth & Mary, recrq
1798, 9, 22. Isaac dis disunity
1803, 12, 24. Rebecca & ch, Ann, Elizabeth, Mary, John, Sarah & Rebecca, gct Redstone MM
1838, 9, 26. Smithfield MM, O. was given permission to rst Isaac

JEWEL

1795, 8, 22. Cert rec for Patience from Shrewbury MM, dtd 1795,3,2, endorsed to

JEWEL, continued
    Redstone MM

JOHN
1803, 9, 1. Elizabeth m Joseph ELIOT
1806, 11, 26. Hannah m Nathan HAYCOCK
1810, 4, 4. Sarah m James ENLOWS
1812, 12, 30. Sarah [Johns] m Amasa LIPSEY
1813, 4, 8. Abel, s Joseph & Mary, Washington
    Co., Pa.; m at Pike Run, Ann BORAM, dt
    Aaron & Elizabeth, Washington Co., Pa.
1813, 12, 1. Rebecca m Isaac GRIFFITH
1817, 11, 5. Joseph Jr., s Joseph & Mary,
    Washington Co., Pa.; m at Pike Run, Eliza-
    beth ROBINETT, dt James & Priscilla, Wash-
    ington Co., Pa.
1818, 7, 30. Joseph, s Abel & Mary, Washing-
    ton Co., Pa.; m at Westland, Martha WALTON,
    dt Benjamin & Ruth, Washington Co., Pa.
1821, 5, 31. Ann m Abraham WALTON
1823, 1, 1. Josiah, s Joseph & Mary, Wash-
    ington Co., Pa.; m at Pike Run, Albina
    GRAVE, dt Joshua & Ann, Washington Co.,
    Pa.

1792, 12, 22. Gideon rocf Uwchland MM, dtd
    1792,5,10
1800, 1, 25. Nathan [Johns] Jr. rocf Balti-
    more MM, dtd 1799,11,14
1800, 10, 25. Abel John & w, Mary, & two min-
    or ch in their care, Alice & Ruth Fisher,
    rocf Monallen MM, dtd 1800,9,27
1800, 11, 22. Nathan [Johns] & w, Elizabeth,
    & dt, Ann & Mary, rocf Baltimore MM, dtd
    1800,10,9
1801, 1, 24. Nathan [Johns] Jr. gct Redstone
    MM
1801, 5, 23. Joseph & w, Mary, & ch, Eliza-
    beth, Hannah, Sarah, Rebecca, Abel, Ra-
    chel, Joseph & Josiah, rocf Monallin MM,
    dtd 1801,4,23
1801, 5, 23. Rachel [Johns] rocf Redstone MM,
    dtd 1801,4,3
1802, 12, 25. Mary [Johns] gct Deer Creek MM
1803, 11, 26. Ann Mitchel (form Johns) dis
    mou
1813, 1, 23. Nathan [Johns] & w, Rachel, &
    ch, Elizabeth, John, Richard, Samuel &
    Sarah, gct Middleton MM
1818, 7, 23. Rachel Horton (form John) dis
    mcd
1821, 8, 23. Ann J. Walton & dt, Mary John,
    gct New Garden MM, O.
1829, 7, 22. Joseph dis jH
1829, 11, 25. Albina & Josiah dis jH
1836, 9, 21. Elizabeth Rogers (form John)
    dis mou
1839, 4, 24. Joseph Jr. gct Redstone MM
1840, 2, 19. Jeremiah gct Redstone MM
1841, 11, 24. Joseph Jr. rocf Redstone MM, dtd
    1841,11,3
1846, 3, 26. Almira Hill (form John) dis mcd
    (H)

1846, 11, 26. Mary Ann Tomelson (form John)
    dis mcd (H)
1848, 4, 26. Joseph dis mcd & jas
1848, 8, 23. Almira Hill (form John) dis mou
1850, 7, 24. Mary Ann Tumbleson (form John)
    dis mcd
1862, 2, 20. Josiah con mcd (H)
1862, 10, 23. Phebe rocf Middleton MM, O.,
    dtd 1862,9,17 (H)
1864, 4, 21. David, Asenath, Taylor, Ellen,
    Emma & Joseph transferred to Salem MM,
    this mtg being laid down (H)
1864, 4, 21. Josiah & Phebe transferred to
    Salem MM, this mtg being laid down (H)

JOHNSON
1791, 10, 12. Catherine m Nimrod GREGG

1788, 12, 27. Isaac [Johnston] & w, Lydia, &
    ch, Catherine, Reuben, Isaac, Hadley,
    Lydia, Reuel & Zillah, rocf New Garden MM,
    dtd 1788,10,4
1792, 9, 22. Betty, w Caleb, rocf Wilmington
    MM, dtd 1792,4,11
1796, 6, 25. Jonathan, rocf New Garden MM,
    dtd 1795,11,7
1796, 6, 25. William rocf New Garden MM, dtd
    1795,11,7
1799, 8, 24. Hannah rocf New Garden MM, dtd
    1798,11,4
1800, 1, 25. Richard & w, Sarah, rocf Deer
    Creek MM, dtd 1799,9,29
1800, 4, 26. Cert rec for Sarah from Hopewell
    MM, endorsed to Redstone MM
1801, 5, 23. Rachel rocf Redstone MM, dtd
    1801,4,3
1802, 5, 22. Elizabeth & ch, Hadley, Isaac,
    Lewis, Robert & Richard, rocf New Garden
    MM, dtd 1797,11,4
1806, 5, 24. Sarah (form Burson) dis mou
1806, 9, 27. Isaac con mou
1806, 9, 27. Hannah Baily (form Johnson) con
    mou
1806, 9, 27. Lydia Ramsey (form Johnson) con
    mou
1808, 8, 27. Zillah gct Redstone MM
1811, 9, 28. Sarah (form Heaton) dis mou
1816, 10, 24. Isaac Jr. gct White Water MM,
    Ind.
1821, 3, 22. William [Johnston] con mcd
1821, 4, 26. Jonathan [Johnston] dis mcd
1821, 4, 26. Ruel [Johnston] dis mcd
1821, 5, 24. Joanna Garretson (form Johnston)
    dis mcd
1821, 5, 24. Phebe Hupp (form Johnson) con
    mcd
1823, 12, 25. Isaac Jr. dis mcd
1824, 6, 24. Richards dis
1826, 3, 23. New Garden MM was given per-
    mission to rst Sarah
1826, 5, 25. Robert dis mcd
1837, 1, 25. Mary Ann (form Grave) dis mou
1838, 4, 26. Mary Ann [Johnston] (form

JOHNSON, continued
    Graves) dis mcd

JOLLY
1800, 5, 24. Malachi Jolly & w, Mary, & ch,
    John, Philip & Malachi, & Mary's ch,
    Catherine, Miriam & Huldy Bogue, rocf
    Trent MM, N. C., dtd 1800,1,12

JONES
1796, 4, 29. Betty m Enos GREAVE

1788, 4, 26. Thomas recrq
1790,, 5,22. Martha rocf Pipe Creek MM, dtd
    1789,8,15
1792, 11, 24. Mary, w Thomas, recrq
1795, 9, 26. Betty rocf York MM, dtd 1795,6,
    10
1796, 3, 26. Samuel rocf York MM, dtd 1795,
    6,10
1798, 4, 28. Samuel gct Redstone MM

1806, 3, 22. Mary (form Milleson) con mou
1809, 2, 25. Ann (form Milleson) dis mou
1809, 10, 28. Mary gct Plymouth MM
1829, 6, 24. John rocf Evesham MM
1843, 4, 26. John gct Salem MM, Ia.
1853, 4, 21. Maria P. con mcd (H)
1863, 6, 24. Mary (form Rogers) dis mcd (W)

JORDAN
1790, 10, 27. Hannah [Jourdan] m Job HARVEY

1788, 6, 28. Hannah [Jourdan] rocf Kennet
    MM, dtd 1788,5,28
1841, 6, 24. Maria con mcd (H)
1864, 4, 21. Maria transferred to Salem MM,
    this mtg being laid down (H)

KELLY
1802, 12, 25. Robert & w, Sarah, & ch, Mary
    & Charles Paty, rocf Bush River MM, S. C.,
    dtd 1802,9,25 (settled at Little Miami)
1802, 12, 25. Samuel & w, Hannah, & ch, Mary,
    Isaac, John, Timothy, Samuel & Moses,
    rocf Bush River MM, S. C., dtd 1802,9,25
    (settled at Little Miami)
1863, 4, 22. Jane (form Miller) dis joining
    Orthodox in 1854 (W)

KENWORTHY
1815, 5, 4. Ruth m George SMITH
1841, 11, 3. Mary m Joseph H. MILLER

1814, 9, 29. Amos rocf Dunnings Creek MM,
    dtd 1814,7,13
1814, 9, 29. Ruth rocf Dunnings Creek MM, dtd
    1814,7,13
1814, 9, 29. Jesse & w, Hannah, rocf Dunning
    Creek MM, dtd 1814,7,13
1814, 9, 29. Isaac & w, Hannah, rocf Dunning
    Creek MM, dtd 1814,7,13

1814, 9, 29. William rocf Dunnings Creek
    MM, dtd 1814,8,10
1815, 3, 2. Amos gct Redstone MM, to m
    Mary Miller
1815, 8, 3. Mary rocf Redstone MM, dtd
    1815,6,2
1820, 2, 24. Hannah H. Bentley (form Ken-
    worthy) dis mou
1821, 3, 22. Amos & w, Mary, & ch, William &
    Robert, gct Miami MM, O.
1863, 4, 22. Rachel dis joining Orthodox in
    1854

KERBY
1808, 3, 26. Mary (form McNamee) dis mou
1821, 1, 25. Short Creek MM was given per-
    mission to rst Mary

KIMBERLEY
1792, 10, 27. Elizabeth (form England) dis mou

KINLEY
1801, 12, 26. Edward & w, Margaret, & ch, John
    Frederick, Isaac, Dan, Davis & Rebecca,
    rocf Back Creek MM, N. C., dtd 1801,8,29

KINSEY
1801, 2, 28. Richard & w, Rhoda, & s, Jesse,
    rocf Trent MM, dtd 1800,1,21, endorsed by
    Redstone MM, 1801,1,30
1814, 12, 29. Joseph & w, Elizabeth, & ch,
    William, Robert Cooper, Eliza Ann, Maria
    & Thomas, rocf Little Britain MM, dtd
    1814,11,12
1821, 3, 22. William dis mcd
1824, 1, 22. Robert Cooper dis mcd
1829, 5, 27. Maria Maple (form Kinsey) dis
    mcd
1832, 6, 20. Thomas dis mou
1833, 4, 30. Joseph gct Milford MM, Ind.
1833, 4, 30. Eliza Ann gct Milford MM, Ind.

KIRK
1789, 12, 10. Sarah m Isaac COOPE

1787, 12, 22. Joseph & w, Judith, & ch, Eliza-
    beth, Mary, Sarah, Judith, Ann, Deborah,
    William & Susanna, rocf Nottingham MM,
    dtd 1787,10,27
1788, 6, 28. William & w, Rachel, & ch, Ca-
    leb, Betty, Sarah, William & Timothy, rocf
    Goose Creek MM, dtd 1788,5,26
1791, 2, 26. Elizabeth dis
1802, 11, 27. Caleb gct Concord MM
1807, 12, 26. Esther, w Adam, & dt, Phebe,
    rocf Redstone MM, dtd 1807,7,31
1809, 12, 23. Esther & dt, Phebe, gct Plain-
    field MM

KNIGHT
1809, 6, 29. Jonathan, s Abel & Ann, Wash-
    ington Co., Pa.; m at Westland, Ann HESTON
    dt Eber & Ann, Washington Co., Pa.

KNIGHT, continued

1815, 2, 9. Dorothy m James MILLISON

1825, 4, 22. Ann m Nathan WHEALDON

1836, 12, 7. William, s Jonathan & Ann, Washington Co., Pa.; m at Westland, Hannah FISHER, dt John & Lydia, Washington Co., Pa.

1854, 3, 29. Jonathan Jr., s Jonathan & Ann, Washington Co., Pa.; m at Westland, Ruth COPE, dt John & Sarah S., Washington Co., Pa.

1801, 10, 24. Abel & w, Ann, & ch, Jonathan, Ann & Dorothy, rocf Buckingham MM, dtd 1801,9,7

1843, 4, 26. Henry dis mcd

1843, 4, 26. David dis mcd

1844, 10, 23. Oliver dis mou

1854, 8, 23. Jonathan Jr. & w, Ruth C., gct Spring Creek MM, Ia.

1857, 5, 27. Abel dis mcd (W)

1857, 9, 25. Elizabeth (form Linton) dis mcd (H)

1857, 12, 24. Abel con mcd

1859, 9, 29. Abel con mou

1863, 3, 5. Zephaniah Z. dis mou

1863, 3, 25. Jonathan dis mcd (W)

1863, 3, 25. Hannah dis joining Orthodox in 1854 (W)

1863, 3, 25. William dis joining Orthodox in 1854 (W)

1863, 4, 22. Lydia dis joining Orthodox in 1854 (W)

1863, 4, 22. Ann Sr. dis joining Orthodox in 1854 (W)

1863, 11, 5. Jonathan con mcd

LAMBERT

1801, 3, 28. Abner & w, Winnifred, & ch, Mary, Joseph, Benjamin, Albert, Elizabeth, Abner, Daniel & Anna, rocf Trent MM, dtd 1800,1,12, endorsed by Redstone 1801,3,6

LAMBORN

1826, 5, 25. Elizabeth rocf Upper Springfield MM, O., dtd 1826,3,25

1831, 1, 26. Elizabeth dis jH

1831, 3, 24. Elizabeth gct New Garden MM, O. (H)

LANE

1835, 12, 23. Hannah & Mary Dix, minor, rocf Baltimore MM for Eastern & Western Districts, dtd 1835,11,5

1836, 3, 23. Cert rec for Hannah & Mary Dix 1835,12,23, endorsed to Redstone MM

LANING

1845, 7, 23. Martha (form McGirr) dis mcd

1846, 6, 25. Martha (alias McGirr) dis mcd (H)

LAWTON

1799, 9, 28. James & w, Susanna, & ch, Jesse, Rebecca & Simeon, rocf Newport MM, R. I., dtd 1796,7,6

1829, 2, 18. James & w, Susanna, & ch, Jesse, Rebecca & Simeon, gct Deerfield MM, O.

1829, 9, 23. James dis mcd

LAZADER

1787, 12, 22. Leah (form Hoge) dis mou

LEE

1800, 6, 28. Thomas rocf Gunpowder MM, dtd 1800,11,20

LESTER

1791, 1, 22. Hannah, w John, & ch, Mary, Eleanor & Elizabeth, rocf Richland MM, dtd 1790,8,19

1799, 8, 24. Eleanor Evans (form Lester) dis mou

1801, 9, 26. Mary dis

1806, 10, 25. Elizabeth dis

LEWELLIN

1786, 6, 22. Margaret [Lawallan] m Isaac McNAMEE

1786, 5, 13. Isaac rocf Fairfax MM, dtd 1785,12,24

1786, 5, 13. Deborah & ch, Deborah, Mary, Hannah, Shadrach & Sarah, rocf Fairfax MM, dtd 1785,12,24

1787, 1, 15. Ann rocf Fairfax MM, dtd 1785,8, 27

1787, 5, 12. Margaret McNamee (form Lewellin) rocf Fairfax MM, dtd 1785,8,27

1787, 11, 24. Ann dis

1791, 5, 28. Deborah [Lewallen] Jr. dis

1792, 5, 26. Mary & Hannah dis

1806, 11, 22. Sarah Vantruce (form Lewellen) rpd mou

LEWIS

1794, 10, 2. Beulah m Amos HUTTON

1814, 3, 3. Beaulah m Benjamin UNDERWOOD

1814, 11, 10. Jehu, s Samuel & Catherine, Washington Co., Pa.; m at Westland, Rachel MILLS, dt Henry & Elizabeth, Washington Co., Pa.

1816, 8, 1. Sarah m John MILLISON

1849, 11, 29. Joseph, s Jehu & Rachel, Putnam Co., Ill.; m at Westland, Mary H. SRIVER, dt John & Rachel Horton, Washington Co., Pa. (H)

1792, 1, 28. Samuel & w, Catherine, & ch, Isaac, Beulah & Jehu, rocf Hopewell MM, dtd 1791,12,5

1792, 6, 23. Jacob rocf Hopewell MM, dtd 1792,5,7

1792, 6, 23. Elizabeth rocf Hopewell MM, dtd 1792,5,7

LEWIS, continued

1794, 4, 26. Henry & w, Susanna, & ch, William
    Mary, Lewis & Esther, rocf Hopewell MM,
    dtd 1794,1,6

1794, 8, 23. Elizabeth Morris (form Lewis)
    con mou

1794, 9, 27. Ann (form Betts) dis mcd

1795, 11, 30. John rocf Hopewell MM, dtd
    1795,11,2

1799, 10, 26. John gct Redstone MM, to m Han-
    nah Roberts

1800, 1, 25. Hannah, w John, rocf Redstone
    MM, dtd 1800,1,3

1801, 7, 25. Sarah & ch, Rachel, Catherine,
    Elizabeth, Beulah, David & Sarah, recrq

1801, 9, 26. Jacob gct Redstone MM, to m
    Mary Bundy

1801, 11, 28. Samuel rocf Hopewell MM, dtd
    1801,9,7

1801, 12, 26. Jesse & w, Jane, & ch, Jason &
    Susannah, rocf Goose Creek MM, dtd 1801,
    10,3

1802, 3, 27. Mary rocf Redstone MM, dtd 1802,
    1,29

1802, 7, 24. Jehu gct Sadsbury MM, to m Su-
    sanna Way

1802, 7, 24. Elizabeth gct Hopewell MM

1803, 4, 23. Henry & w, Susanna, & ch, Wil-
    liam, Mary, Lewis, Esther, Catherine,
    Anna, Samuel & Susannah, gct Concord MM

1803, 4, 23. Jacob & w, Mary, & dt, Hannah,
    gct Concord MM

1803, 8, 27. Susanna rocf Sadsbury MM, dtd
    1802,12,7 [da, gct Short Creek MM

1804, 4, 28. Jehu & w, Susanna, & dt, Matil-

1804, 11, 24. Eleanor gct Short Creek MM

1807, 2, 28. Jehu & ch, Matilda Way & Emily,
    rocf Short Creek MM, dtd 1807,2,21

1808, 11, 26. Mary rocf Short Creek MM, dtd
    1808,10,18

1810, 3, 24. John & w, Hannah, & ch, Rachel,
    Jehu, Adoni, Cynthia & Griffith, gct Short
    Creek MM, O.

1812, 5, 23. Beulah rocf Short Creek MM, dtd
    1811,12,24

1812, 12, 26. Matilda, minor, gct Radnor MM

1816, 6, 27. Sarah rocf Short Creek MM, dtd
    1816,2,20

1816, 10, 24. Isaac con mcd

1816, 11, 21. Mary recrq

1820, 9, 21. Matilda rocf Radnor MM, dtd
    1820,4,13

1827, 7, 26. Emala Dodson (form Lewis) dis
    mcd

1829, 1, 21. Jehu & Rachel dis jH

1829, 6, 24. Isaac dis jH

1833, 3, 28. Jehu & w, Rachel, & ch, Samuel,
    Joseph & Elizabeth, gct Friends in Ill.
    (H)

1834, 4, 23. Mary dis jH

1840, 1, 23. Charles gct Plainfield MM, to
    m Lydia Ann Gregg (H)

1840, 12, 23. Charles dis mcd & jH

1850, 1, 23. Joseph dis mcd & jH

1850, 1, 24. Joseph rocf Clay Creek MM, Ill.
    (H)

1851, 9, 25. Mary S. gct Plainfield MM, O.
    (H)

1855, 10, 25. Charles W. & w, Lydia Ann, &
    ch, Isaac, John Ira & William Harvey, gct
    Planefield MM (H)

1864, 4, 21. Jehu F., Rachel O., John F.,
    Mary L. & Helen M. transferred to Salem
    MM, this mtg being laid down (H)

1864, 4, 21. Joseph & Mary H. transferred to
    Salem MM, this mtg being laid down (H)

LILLY

1805, 4, 27. Ruth rocf Londongrove MM, dtd
    1804,10,3

1811, 9, 28. Robert, Jane, Ellis, Hannah &
    Phebe, ch Thomas, recrq

1817, 7, 24. Robert con mcd

1818, 3, 26. Robert gct Plainfield MM, O.

1818, 5, 28. Thomas & w, Ruth, & ch, Jane,
    Ellis, Hannah, Phebe, Ruth & Thomas, gct
    Redstone MM

1855, 3, 22. Ruth Jackman (form Lilly) con
    mcd (H)

1855, 6, 21. Solomon P. [Lilley] con mcd (H)

1855, 12, 27. Solomon P. [Lilley] gct West
    MM, O. (H)

1864, 4, 21. Ellis & Homer C. [Lilley] trans-
    ferred to Salem MM, this mtg being laid
    down (H)

1864, 4, 21. Ellis N. & Phebe Ann [Lilley]
    transferred to Salem MM, this mtg being
    laid down (H)

1864, 4, 21. Thomas W. transferred to Salem
    MM, this mtg being laid down (H)

LINTON

1803, 3, 31. Mahlon, s Joshua & Hannah, Wash-
    ington Co., Pa.; m at Westland, Ann HILLES
    dt William & Rebecca, Washington Co., Pa.

1832, 3, 1. Sarah m Nathan CLEAVER (H)

1832, 10, 31. William H., s Mahlon & Ann,
    Washington Co., Pa.; m at Pike Run, Matil-
    da TAYLOR, dt Benjamin & Elizabeth,
    Washington Co., Pa. (H)

1796, 10, 22. Daniel rocf Wrightstown MM, dtd
    1796,9,6

1801, 11, 28. Mahlon rocf Wrightstown MM, dtd
    1801,9,8

1802, 5, 22. David rocf Falls MM, dtd 1802,
    4,7

1802, 5, 22. Nathan rocf Falls MM, dtd 1802,
    4,7

1802, 5, 22. Samuel & ch, Jane, Elizabeth &
    James, rocf Falls MM, dtd 1802,4,7

1802, 6, 26. Joshua rocf Falls MM, dtd 1802,5,
    5

1803, 4, 23. Hannah rocf Falls MM, dtd 1802,
    6,9

1803, 7, 23. Benjamin rocf Falls MM, dtd

LINTON, continued
    1803,8,4
1803, 10, 22. Joshua dis
1806, 5, 24. Benjamin dis
1807, 4, 25. Daniel gct Center MM, O.
1825, 10, 27. Benjamin rst by rq
1829, 6, 24. Benjamin & Mahlon dis jH
1829, 7, 22. Ann dis jH
1833, 12, 25. Sarah Cleaver (form Linton) dis
    mcd & jH
1835, 8, 26. Matilda [Lynton] (form Taylor)
    dis mcd & jH
1835, 10, 21. William H. dis mcd & jH
1835, 10, 21. Mary Ann Thistlethwaite (form
    Linton) dis mou & jH
1837, 9, 21. Mary Anne Thistlethwaite (form
    Linton) dis mcd (H)
1839, 5, 22. Samuel dis mcd
1840, 9, 23. Isaiah dis mcd
1840, 12, 23. Joseph dis jH
1846, 7, 23. Margaret Packer (form Linton)
    con mcd (H)
1846, 9, 24. Margaret Packer (alias Linton)
    gct Short Creek MM, O. (H)
1847, 4, 22. Naomi (form Harry) con mcd (H)
1851, 1, 22. Margaret Packer (form Linton)
    dis mcd
1851, 2, 20. Joseph dis mcd (H)
1857, 9, 25. Elizabeth Knight (form Linton)
    dis mcd (H)
1859, 4, 21. Caroline L. Maxwell (form Linton)
    con mcd (H)
1864, 4, 21. Hilles & Oliver M. transferred
    to Salem MM, this mtg being laid down (H)
1864, 4, 21. Matilda & Benjamin L. transferred
    to Salem MM, this mtg being laid down (H)

LIPSEY
1801, 3, 5. Amasa, s Rasco & Tamar, Washing-
    ton Co., Pa.; m at Westland, Rachel WIL-
    SON, dt Wm. & Elizabeth
1812, 12, 30. Amasa, s Rasco & Tamer, Jeffer-
    son Co., O.; m at Pike Run, Sarah JOHNS,
    dt Benjamin & Elizabeth WILSON, Washing-
    ton Co., Pa.

1800, 6, 28. Amasa rocf Trent MM, dtd 1800,1,
    12
1800, 6, 28. Sarah & Mary, dt Amasa, rocf
    Trent MM, dtd 1800,1,12, endorsed by Con-
    tentney MM, 1800,3,8
1813, 2, 27. Sarah gct Short Creek MM

LLOYD
1863, 7, 22. Eliza Merrit (form Lloyd) dis mcd
    (W)

LOBBS
1808, 11, 26. James rocf Daiby MM, dtd 1807,
    4,22, endorsed by Redstone MM, 1808,4,1

LOHNES
1862, 4, 23. Sarah Jane (form Cope) dis mcd

LONG
1787, 10, 13. Lydia, minor, rocf Hopewell MM,
    dtd 1787,7,2
1797, 4, 22. Lydia Hatfield (form Long) dis
    mou

LONSDALE
1823, 9, 25. John rocf Providence MM, dtd
    1823,6,24

LOW
1804, 8, 25. Elizabeth (form Curl) dis mou

LUPTON
1801, 11, 28. Rachel rocf Crooked Run MM, dtd
    1801,5,30

McCADDON
1790, 12, 1. John, Fayette Co., Pa.; m at
    Redstone, Elizabeth SILVERTHORN, dt Wm. &
    JANE, Fayette Co., Pa.

1786, 5, 13. John recrq

McCALL
1805, 2, 7. William, s John & Sarah, Wash-
    ington Co., Pa.; m at Wheeling, Elizabeth
    ELLIOTT, dt Isaac & Alice, Washington
    Co., Pa.
1805, 11, 6. Ruth m Isaac ELLIOTT

1789, 5, 16. Sarah & ch, Thomas, William,
    Mary, Ruth & John, recrq
1791, 11, 26. Sarah, minor, dt Sarah, recrq
1803, 1, 22. Thomas dis mou
1810, 8, 23. Sarah Eakey (form McCall) dis
    mou
1813, 2, 27. Alice (form Elliott) dis mcd
1823, 8, 28. Alice, minor, gct Marlborough MM
1828, 3, 27. William dis disunity
1828, 4, 24. Elizabeth, w William, & ch, Sa-
    rah, Thomas, George, Matilda, Eleanor
    (Eliza Ann in men's minutes), Jane, Solo-
    mon & William Elliott, gct Marlborough MM
1832, 1, 25. Mary Carson (form McCall) dis
    mcd
1832, 9, 26. Thomas rocf Marlborough MM, dtd
    1832,7,31
1833, 1, 23. Thomas gct Marlborough MM, O.
1847, 10, 27. Mary gct Chesterfield MM, O.

McCANN
1801, 9, 26. Abraham Davis & w, Hannah, & ch,
    Phebe, Edward, Ellis & Rachel, also Tacy
    McCann, rocf Fairfield, dtd 1800,11,22,
    endorsed by Redstone MM, 1801,7,31

McCLAY
1820, 1, 27. Sarah (form Young) dis mcd

McCLURE
1825, 8, 25. Robert recrq
1829, 9, 23. Robert dis mou

McCONNEL

1802, 1, 23. James & w, Rachel, & ch, Jesse, Edward, Levi, Daniel, Ann & Sarah, rocf Southland MM, dtd 1801,9,2

McGIRR

1813, 9, 29. Arthur, s Arthur & Ann, Washington Co., Pa.; m at Pike Run, Elizabeth CRAWFORD, dt Seaborn & Frances, Washington Co., Pa.
1818, 5, 6. William, s Arthur & Nancy, Washington Co., Pa.; m at Pike Run, Rebecca GRIFFITH, dt Joseph & Mary John, Washington Co., Pa.

1809, 2, 25. William [McGarr] recrq
1810, 11, 24. Arthur [McGarr] rec in mbrp
1811, 9, 28. James [McGerr] recrq
1815, 3, 30. James gct Marlborough MM, O.
1823, 4, 24. Arthur & w, Elizabeth, & ch, Frances, Nancy & Sarah, gct Plainfield MM, O.
1829, 5, 27. William dis jH
1829, 11, 25. Rebecca dis jH
1845, 7, 23. Martha Laning (form McGirr) dis mcd
1845, 8, 27. Ann [McGerr] dis jH
1846, 6, 25. Martha Laning (alias McGirr) dis mcd (H)
1851, 4, 24. Joseph con mcd (H)
1864, 4, 21. Ann transferred to Salem MM, this mtg being laid down (H)
1864, 4, 21. Isaac transferred to Salem MM, this mtg being laid down (H)
1864, 4, 21. William & Rebecca [McGerr] transferred to Salem MM, this mtg being laid down (H)

McGREW

1787, 4, 14. James & w, Jane, rocf Monallen MM, dtd 1783,12,15, with ch, Isabel & Thomas, b since cert was issued
1787, 10, 13. Elizabeth, Mary, James & Finley, ch James & Jane, recrq
1788, 6, 28. Finley & w, Dinah, & ch, Jacob & Margaret, rocf Monallen MM, dtd 1787,10, 15
1791, 5, 28. James Jr. rocf Warrington MM, dtd 1791,3,12
1793, 2, 23. Margaret Wilson (form McGrew) dis mcd

McJUNKIN

1847, 5, 26. Mary Ann (form Rogers) dis mou

McKENNAN

1817, 12, --. Rachel m William BLACKBURN

1816, 1, 25. Rachel [McKanan] recrq

McMILLAN

1803, 8, 27. Elizabeth [McMILLEN] (form White) dis mou

1808, 6, 25. Thomas & w, Jane, & ch, Taylor & Jane, rocf Warrington MM, dtd 1808,3,24
1811, 11, 23. Thomas & w, Jane, & ch, Taylor & Jane, gct Middleton MM, O.

McNAMEE

1786, 4, 20. Sarah m John TOWNSEND
1786, 6, 22. Isaac, s Barnabas & Mary, Washington Co., Pa.; m at Westland, Margaret LAWALLAN, dt Shadrach & Deborah

1787, 5, 12. Margaret (form Lewellin) rocf Fairfax MM, dtd 1785,8,27
1791, 7, 23. Isaac dis
1801, 11, 28. Elias dis mou
1802, 5, 22. Reuben dis mou
1807, 9, 26. Margaret & ch, Barnabas, Mary, Sarah, Mashack, Elias, Reuben, William, Cyrus & Helena, gct Short Creek MM
1808, 3, 26. Mary Kerby (form McNamee) dis mou
1818, 2, 19. Plainfield MM was given permission to rst Isaac

McNEELY

1818, 1, 22. Sarah rocf New Garden MM, dtd 1817,5,15
1818, 11, 26. Sarah gct New Garden MM, O.

McVAY

1796, 3, 2. Jane [Mevay] m Asa CADWALLADER

1795, 11, 30. Jane rocf Goshen MM, dtd 1795, 5,8
1797, 4, 22. Elizabeth (form Smith) dis mou

MACE

1800, 7, 26. Cert rec for Francis & w, Pharaba, & ch, David, Jonas & Alice, from Core Sound MM, dtd 1800,5,14, endorsed back to Core Sound MM
1800, 7, 26. Cert rec for James & w, Sarah, & ch, Joseph, Benjamin, John, Enoch, Mary & Anna, from Core Sound MM, dtd 1800,5,14, endorsed back to Core Sound MM
1800, 9, 27. Cert rec for John & w, Hannah, & s, John, from Core Sound MM, dtd 1800,5, 14, endorsed back to Core Sound or Contentney MM

MAPLE

1829, 5, 27. Maria (form Kinsey) dis mcd

MARSH

1833, 12, 28. Milton, s James & Edith, Columbiana Co., O.; m at Westland, Eliza GRIFFITH, dt Israel & Laetitia, Washington Co., Pa. (H)

1833, 7, 25. Eli R. Griffith gct Carmel MM, O., to m Mary Ann Marsh (H)
1834, 3, 27. Eliza G. gct Carmel MM, O. (H)
1837, 8, 24. Emmor B. & w, Rebecca W., & ch,

MARSH, continued
    Henry, Amanda & Mary, rocf Bradford MM,
    dtd 1837,6,6
1837, 9, 20. Eliza (form Griffith) dis mcd &
    JH
1837, 9, 21. Milton & w, Eliza, rocf Carmel
    MM, dtd 1837,5,20 (H)
1838, 2, 22. Nathan Pusey gct Baltimore MM
    for Western District to m Mary H. Marsh
    (H)
1864, 4, 21. Hannah G. transferred to Salem
    MM, this mtg being laid down (H)
1864, 4, 21. Milton & Eliza G. transferred to
    Salem MM, this mtg being laid down (H)

MARSHALL
1795, 1, 24. Pemela rocf New Garden MM, dtd
    1794,3,2, endorsed by ND MM, Phila., Pa.
1795, 2, 28. Permelia Townsend (form Marshall)
    dis mcd

MARTIN
1802, 3, 4. Isaac, s Thomas & Elizabeth,
    Washington Co., Pa.; m at Pike Run, Re-
    becca GRIFFITH, dt Jacob & Lydia, Washing-
    ton Co., Pa.
1809, 11, 1. Isaac, s Thomas & Elizabeth,
    Washington Co., Pa.; m at Pike Run, Martha
    WILSON, dt Benjamin & Elizabeth, Washing-
    ton Co., Pa.
1827, 9, 29. Edith m Joel PRICE

1801, 8, 22. Isaac recrq
1808, 4, 23. Edith, dt Isaac, gct Redstone MM
1812, 5, 23. Isaac & w, Martha, & ch, Rebecca
    & Thomas, gct Short Creek MM
1812, 12, 26. Edith, minor, rocf Redstone MM,
    dtd 1811,10,20
1821, 4, 26. Edith dis
1825, 9, 22. Edith rst by rq

MATHEWS
1802, 1, 23. Mary rocf Gun Powder MM, dtd
    1801,10,31
1802, 10, 23. Elizabeth & Miriam rocf Balti-
    more MM, dtd 1802,8,12
1803, 7, 23. Mary gct Gunpowder MM
1803, 7, 23. Elizabeth Robinson (form Mathews)
    dis mou
1807, 7, 25. Miriam gct Redstone MM
1858, 5, 27. Gunpowder MM was given permis-
    sion to rst Ann Eliza Mathews (form Mor-
    gan)

MATTOCK
1798, 7, 28. Jane (form Shepherd) dis mou

MAXSON
1789, 10, 24. Stephen rocf Shrewsbury MM,
    N. J., dtd 1789,9,7
1792, 2, 25. Tacy [Maxon] rocf Shrewsbury MM,
    dtd 1791,10,3

MAXWELL
1859, 4, 21. Caroline L. (form Linton) con
    mcd (H)
1864, 4, 21. Caroline transferred to Salem
    MM, this mtg being laid down (H)

MAY
1788, 8, 23. Rachel (form Dinnen) dis mou

MAINS
1787, 4, 14. Elizabeth rocf Monallin MM, dtd
    1783,11,10

MELTON
1800, 5, 24. Stafford rocf Trent MM, N. C.,
    dtd 1800,1,12
1800, 5, 24. Esther rocf Trent MM, N. C., dtd
    1800,1,12
1803, 2, 26. Stafford gct Concord MM

MENDENHALL
1803, 7, 23. Caleb & s, Susanna, & ch, Miri-
    am, Griffith, William, Caleb, Susanna &
    Grace, rocf Deep River MM, N. C., dtd
    1802,7,5
1809, 2, 25. Cert rec for Aaron & w, Lydia,
    & ch, William, Abigail & Hannah, from
    Bradford MM, dtd 1808,9,7, endorsed to
    New Garden MM, O.

MERCER
1799, 6, 22. John rocf Kennet MM, dtd 1799,
    5,10
1800, 12, 27. John gct Kennet MM
1810, 3, 24. John & w, Hepsibah, & ch,
    Matthias, Solomon, Joseph & Daniel, rocf
    Redstone MM, dtd 1809,12,29
1826, 3, 23. Matthias dis mou
1832, 9, 26. Joseph rpd mcd
1833, 4, 30. Elizabeth Snider (form Mercer)
    dis mou

MERIDETH
1849, 6, 21. James M. gct Birmingham MM (H)

MERRIT
1863, 7, 22. Eliza (form Lloyd) dis mcd (W)

MICHENER
1803, 11, 26. Esther [Michiner] & ch, Hannah,
    Mordecai & Jonathan, rocf Redstone MM, dtd
    1803,9,30
1804, 8, 25. Thomas [Michiner] rocf Redstone
    MM, dtd 1804,5,4
1805, 2, 23. Rachel rocf Redstone MM, dtd
    1804,11,2
1807, 7, 25. Esther & ch, Mordecai & Jonathan,
    gct Short Creek MM
1807, 9, 26. Hannah Powel (form Michener) dis
    mou
1810, 1, 27. Esther & s, Mordecai & Jonathan,
    rocf Short Creek MM, dtd 1809,10,24
1810, 3, 24. Rachel dis

MICHENER, continued

1810, 8, 25. John & w, Naomi, rocf Redstone
MM, dtd 1810,6,26

1811, 6, 22. John & w, Naomi, gct Short Creek
MM

1811, 11, 23. Mordecai [Michiner] dis mou

1813, 10, 23. William [Michiner] rocf Fairfax
MM, dtd 1813,7,23

1822, 1, 24. Jonathan [Michiner] dis mcd

1825, 8, 25. William [Michiner] dis disunity

1834, 7, 24. William recrq (H)

1864, 3, 23. Mary (form Gray) dis mcd (W)

MILBOURN

1802, 1, 23. Sarah & ch, Zenis, Samuel, Jonathan, William, Jacob, Lot, Anna & David,
rocf South River MM, dtd 1801,6,13

MILLER

1841, 11, 3. Joseph H., s Solomon & Ruth,
Montgomery Co., Ind.; m at Westland, Mary
KENWORTHY, dt Jesse & Hannah, Washington
Co., Pa.

1789, 4, 25. Mary rocf New Garden MM, dtd
1788,10,4

1790, 8, 28. Tacy rocf Rahway MM, dtd 1790,4,
21

1792, 6, 23. Peter & ch, David, Joseph, Ann,
Margaret, Mary & Tacy, recrq

1795, 6, 27. Caleb rocf Kennet MM, dtd 1793,
6,13

1797, 1, 28. Cert rec for Caleb some time
ago endorsed to Kennet MM

1800, 5, 24. Mason & w, Ruth, rocf Trent MM,
N. C., dtd 1800,1,12

1808, 6, 25. Levi & w, Deborah, & ch, Morris,
Robert, Isaac, Hannah & Mary, recrq

1808, 10, 22. Susanna rocf Middleton MM, dtd
1808,4,9

1810, 9, 22. Susanna gct New Garden MM, O.

1811, 1, 26. Levi & w, Deborah, & ch, Morris,
Robert, Isaac, Hannah, Mary & Levi, gct
New Garden MM, O.

1815, 3, 2. Amos Kenworthy gct Redstone MM,
to m Mary Miller

1833, 9, 25. Amy (form Blackburn) dis mcd

1836, 3, 23. Sugar River MM, Ind. was given
permission to rst Amy

1840, 3, 25. Maria & ch, William B., Franklin, Hezekiah P., Mary Ann & James Madison, rocf Sandy Spring MM, O.

1842, 6, 22. Joseph H. rocf Sugar River MM,
Ind., dtd 1842,1,29

1843, 9, 20. MariaP.& ch, William B., Franklin,
Hezekiah P., Mary Ann, James Madison, Mordicai & Frances P., gct Sandy Spring MM,O.

1856, 12, 25. Joseph H. gct Redstone MM, to m
Rebecca Garwood

1857, 4, 23. Rebecca G. rocf Redstone MM, dtd
1857,4,1

1857, 6, 24. William Henry dis mcd & jas (W)

1858, 1, 27. Oliver H. dis mcd (W)

1863, 3, 25. David dis joining Orthodox in
1854 (W)

1863, 3, 25. Elizabeth & Anna dis joining
Orthodox in 1854 (W)

1863, 3, 25. William dis joining Orthodox in
1854 (W)

1863, 4, 22. Jane Kelly (form Miller) dis
joining Orthodox in 1854 (W)

1863, 4, 22. Joseph H. dis joining Orthodox
in 1854 (W)

1863, 4, 22. Rebecca (form Garwood) dis
joining Orthodox in 1854 (W)

1863, 4, 22. Sabina, Rachel J. & Ruth Ann dis
joining Orthodox in 1854 (W)

MILLESON

1815, 2, 9. James [Millison] Jr., s James &
Abigail, Washington Co., Pa.; m at Westland, Dorothy KNIGHT, dt Abel & Ann, Washington Co., Pa.

1816, 4, 4. Abigail [Millison] m John CARVER

1816, 8, 1. John, s James & Abigail, Washington Co., Pa.; m at Westland, Sarah
LEWIS, dt Samuel & Sarah, Jefferson Co.,O.

1795, 1, 24. William & w, Elizabeth, & ch,
Elisha, rocf London Grove MM, dtd 1794,
10,29

1796, 9, 24. James & w, Abigail, & ch, Sarah,
Mary, Lydia, James, Ann & John, rocf Bradford MM, dtd 1795,4,17, endorsed by Redstone MM, 1796,9,2

1799, 4, 29. Sarah Buffington (form Milleson)
dis mcd

1801, 12, 26. Lydia Duvall (form Milleson) dis
mcd

1806, 3, 22. Mary Jones (form Milleson) con
mou

1809, 2, 25. Ann Jones (form Milleson) dis
mou

1814, 9, 1. Elisha gct Redstone MM, to m
Hannah Chandler

1815, 3, 30. Hannah rocf Redstone MM, dtd
1814,12,30

1816, 6, 27. James [Millison] Jr. & w, Dorothy, dis

1817, 2, 20. James Jr. & w, Dorothy, rst by
rq

1817, 3, 27. Ann, dt James & Dorothy, recrq

1817, 4, 24. Elisha & w, Hannah, gct Plainfield MM

1817, 6, 26. James Jr. & w, Dorothy, & ch,
Jonathan & Ann, gct Plainfield MM, O.

1817, 6, 26. William & w, Elizabeth, gct
Plainfield MM, O.

1817, 7, 24. Rachel Scott (form Milleson)
dis mcd

1822, 5, 23. John dis mcd

MILLHOUSE

1848, 5, 24. Elizabeth P. [Millhous] gct
Short Creek MM, O.

MILLIGAN
1806, 5, 1. John, s James & Ann, Washington
Co., Pa.; m at Westland, Abigail RIGG, dt
Clement & Sarah, Washington Co., Pa.

1813, 3, 27. John [Millegan] & w, Abigail, &
ch, Ann, Clement, James, John, Joseph &
William, gct Salem MM

MILLS
1810, 11, 1. Elizabeth m Nathaniel GREGG
1813, 6, 3. Joseph, s Henry & Elizabeth,
Washington Co., Pa.; m at Westland, Sarah
RALEY, dt Eli & Mary, Washington Co., Pa.
1814, 11, 10. Rachel m Jehu LEWIS
1815, 1, 5. Martha m Nathan PUSEY

1788, 1, 26. Henry & w, Elizabeth, & dt,
Mary, rocf Hopewell MM, dtd 1787,11,5 (ch
had d since cert was issued)
1802, 12, 25. Alexander & w, Enice, & ch, John,
Sally, Hepzibah, & Sidney, rocf Bush River
MM, S. C., dtd 1802,9,25 (settled at Little
Miami)
1802, 12, 25. James & w, Lydia, & ch, William,
John, Isaac, James, Sarah, David, Curtis,
Elisha & Abijah, rocf Bush River MM, S. C.,
dtd 1802,9,25 (settled at Little Miami)
1802, 12, 25. Mary (late Richards or Richardson) con mcd
1813, 1, 23. James recrq
1814, 7, 28. James dis
1817, 3, 27. Henry dis disunity
1820, 4, 27. Abel dis mcd
1823, 10, 23. Henry M. recrq
1829, 4, 22. Joseph dis jH
1829, 7, 22. Sarah dis jH
1830, 3, 24. Henry dis jH
1830, 6, 23. Elizabeth dis jH
1836, 8, 25. Eli R. con mcd (H)
1837, 2, 22. Eli dis mou
1838, 3, 22. Eli R. gct Redstone MM (H)
1839, 8, 21. Henry dis jH
1839, 8, 22. Henry gct Plainfield MM, to m
Esther Rhodes (H)
1840, 3, 26. Joseph & w, Sarah, & ch, Joshua
L., Pusey, Abel, Sarah Elizabeth & Martha,
gct Honey Creek MM, Ind. (H)
1840, 3, 26. Henry gct Honey Creek MM, Ind.
(H)
1840, 3, 26. Mary Ann gct Honey Creek MM, Ind.
(H)
1845, 5, 21. Lydia (form Hartley) dis mcd &
jH
1845, 6, 25. Pusey dis mcd & jH

MINIKEN
1815, 8, 3. William & w, Margaret, & ch,
Mary, John, Ann & Sarah Simpson, rocf
Redstone MM, dtd 1815,6,2
1818, 2, 19. William & w, Margaret, & ch,
Mary, John, Ann, Sarah Simpson & Hannah,
gct Redstone MM

1836, 5, 26. Margaret Harvey & dt, Gulielma
Maria Minican, rocf Plainfield MM, O.,
dtd 1836,1,14 (H)

MITCHEL
1787, 8, 11. Susanna & ch, Thomas, Mary &
Samuel, rocf Buckingham MM, dtd 1785,9,5,
also dt, Sarah, b since dte of cert
1803, 11, 26. Ann (form Johns) dis mou

MOORE
1787, 12, 22. John & w, Bathsheba, rocf Evesham MM, dtd 1787,9,7
1789, 6, 27. Elizabeth, David, Joshua, Mordecai, Cyrus & Joseph, ch John & Bathsheba, recrq
1793, 1, 26. Mary rocf Rahway MM, dtd 1792,
9,20
1808, 11, 26. Hannah [Moor] (form Davis) dis

MORGAN
1794, 6, 28. Esther (form Townsend) dis mou
1801, 11, 28. Hannah rocf Baltimore MM, dtd
1801,10,8
1802, 4, 24. William rocf Baltimore MM, dtd
1802,1,14
1802, 6, 26. John & w, Ann, & ch, Mary &
Hannah, rocf Baltimore MM, dtd 1802,5,13
1806, 1, 25. John & w, Ann, & ch, Mary, Hannah & Elizabeth, gct Redstone MM
1809, 2, 25. Salem MM was given permission
to rst Esther
1813, 4, 24. William & ch, Oliver, Ann, Rachel, Miriam, William, George & Mary,
recrq
1817, 7, 24. Ann (form Peden) con mou
1819, 5, 27. Oliver gct Redstone MM
1820, 3, 23. Oliver rocf Redstone MM, dtd
1820,2,2
1821, 8, 23. Ann Pyle (form Morgan) dis mcd
1822, 9, 26. Oliver dis disunity
1825, 1, 27. Ann, w Elijah, gct Smithfield
MM, O.
1829, 6, 24. Miriam dis jas
1830, 6, 23. William M. dis mcd
1830, 7, 21. George gct New Garden MM, O.
1830, 9, 22. Rachel Thomas (form Morgan) dis
mou
1832, 10, 24. George rocf New Garden MM, O.,
dtd 1832,6,21
1834, 3, 26. Esther dis jas
1837, 7, 26. Ruth dis jas
1841, 1, 27. Hannah dis jas
1855, 7, 26. Ann Eliza Copeland (form Morgan) dis mcd (H)
1858, 5, 27. Gunpowder MM was given permission to rst Ann Eliza Mathews (form Morgan) (H)

MORLAND
1801, 11, 28. Jason [Morelan] & w, Mary, &
ch, Elizabeth & Mary, rocf Goose Creek
MM, Va., dtd 1801,10,3

MORLAND, continued
1803, 10, 22.   Cert rec for Jonas from Goose
    Creek MM, dtd 1802,9,4, endorsed to Middle
    ton MM

MORRIS
1793, 10, 17.   Eliza m Thomas TOWNSEND

1792, 1, 28.   Elizabeth recrq
1794, 8, 23.   Elizabeth (form Lewis) con mou
1798, 4, 28.   Mary recrq
1804, 11, 24.   Richard rocf Shrewsbury MM,
    dtd 1802,12,6, endorsed by Redstone MM,
    1804,6,29
1808, 11, 26.   Lydia rst by rq with consent of
    Shrewsbury MM
1823, 6, 26.   Jonathan recrq
1827, 7, 26.   Lydia gct Stillwater MM, O.
1829, 3, 25.   Elizabeth dis jH
1829, 4, 22.   Jonathan dis jH
1831, 4, 21.   Jonathan gct Carmel MM, O. (H)
1832, 5, 24.   Susan recrq (H)
1834, 6, 25.   Elizabeth (form Hartley) dis
    mou
1835, 4, 23.   Amanda, Ruthanna, Sarah Jane &
    Henry C., ch Susan, recrq (H)
1835, 5, 28.   Susan & ch gct Richmond MM,
    Ind. (White Water) (H)
1837, 6, 22.   Mary S. rocf Baltimore MM for
    Western District, dtd 1837,3,3 (H)
1844, 11, 21.   Mary S. gct Baltimore MM (H)

MORTON
1793, 5, 16.   Sarah m John FORMAN

1789, 9, 26.   Hannah [Moreton], w Samuel, &
    ch, Thomas, William, Hannah, Elizabeth,
    Sarah, Ann, Mary, Susanna, Rebecca, Phebe
    & Edith, rocf Concord MM, dtd 1788,12,3
1790, 8, 28.   Samuel rocf Concord MM, dtd
    1790,6,9
1796, 11, 25.   Hannah & ch, Ann, Mary, Benjamin,
    John & Hannah, rocf Monallen MM, dtd
    1796,8,18
1802, 7, 24.   Hannah & ch, Ann, Mary, Benjamin,
    John & Hannah, gct Concord MM

MULLEN
1801, 2, 28.   John & w, Lydia, & ch, Jane,
    Hannah, Sarah, John, Rachel, Isaiah &
    Samuel, rocf Crooked Run MM, dtd 1801,1,31

MURRY
1794, 9, 27.   Sarah (form Betts) dis mcd

MYRES
1787, 7, 14.   Phebe rocf Fairfax MM, dtd
    1784,5,22
1797, 9, 23.   Isaiah & w, Alice, & ch, David,
    William & Elizabeth, rocf Fairfax MM, dtd
    1797,3,25
1805, 3, 23.   Isaiah & w, Alice, & ch, William
    & Elizabeth, gct Middleton MM

1805, 3, 23.   David gct Middleton MM
1809, 11, 25.   Orpha [Mires] (form Gregg) dis
    mou
1818, 12, 24.   Mary [Myars] (form Gregg) dis
    mcd

NEALINS
1788, 6, 28.   Rachel rocf Abington MM, dtd
    1787,11,26

NEGUS
1806, 5, 28.   John, s Shaidlock & Sarah, Wash-
    ington Co., Pa.; m at house of John Hank
    in Green Co., Miriam BURDG, dt Jacob &
    Judith, Green Co., Pa.
1818, 10, 29.   Shaidlock, s Shaidlock & Sarah,
    Green Co., Pa.; m at Westland, Rachel
    BRACKIN, dt Caleb & Rebecca, Washington
    Co., Pa.

1789, 6, 27.   Sarah, w Shedlock, & ch, Levina,
    John, Rebecca, Joshua & Sarah, rocf Burl-
    ington MM, dtd 1788,2,24, also ch, West,
    b since dte of cert
1806, 8, 23.   Miriam gct Redstone MM
1814, 6, 30.   Shaidlock rocf Redstone MM, dtd
    1814,4,29
1832, 5, 23.   Shaidlock & w, Rachel, & ch,
    Caleb Bracken, Rebecca Miller, Sarah
    Smith, Elisha, Maria Whitacre, Albert
    Burdg & Elwood, gct Upper Springfield MM,
    O.

NEWBURN
1817, 10, 29.   George [Newbourn], s David &
    Thamer, Washington Co., Pa.; m at Wheel-
    ing, Lydia VANSCOYOC, dt Enoch & Lydia,
    Washington Co., Pa.

1790, 8, 28.   Tamer [Newbourn] & ch, John,
    Rachel, Sarah, Dorothy, Hannah & Jacob,
    rocf Wrightstown MM, dtd 1790,5,4
1815, 12, 28.   Jacob [Newbern] rocf Redstone
    MM, dtd 1815,12,1
1817, 8, 28.   George rocf Redstone MM, dtd
    1817,7,23
1827, 2, 22.   Ann rocf Redstone MM, dtd 1827,
    1,28
1830, 8, 25.   George & Lydia dis jH
1830, 12, 27.   Ann dis jH
1837, 4, 26.   Jacob & w, Mary, & dt, Lydia,
    gct Upper Springfield MM, O.

NEWBY
1799, 10, 26.   Henry & w, Susanna, & ch, Job &
    James, rocf Trent MM, N. C., dtd 1799,9,7

NEWPORT
1787, 1, 24.   Aaron, s Jesse & Elizabeth,
    Fayette Co., Pa.; m at Redstone, Mary CAD-
    WALLADER, dt Rees & Ruth, Fayette Co.,Pa.

1786, 12, 16.   Rebecca, w Thomas, rocf Duck

NEWPORT, continued
    Creek MM, dtd 1786,2,25, also s, John, b
    since dte of cert
1787, 1, 15. Thomas rocf Duck Creek MM, dtd
    1786,7,22
1794, 7, 26. Jesse & ch, Richard, Lydia &
    Mary, rocf Abington MM, dtd 1794,5,26
1794, 7, 26. Elizabeth, w Jesse, rocf Duck
    Creek (or Deer Creek) MM, dtd 1794,6,7
1795, 7, 25. Elizabeth dis disunity
1796, 1, 23. Lydia Powel (form Newport) dis
    mou
1798, 5, 26. Mary, w Aaron, & ch, Elizabeth,
    Jesse, Ruth, Joseph, Rees & Nathan, rocf
    Redstone MM, dtd 1797,6,30
1805, 9, 28. Mary & ch, Elizabeth, Jesse,
    Ruth, Joseph, Reece, Nathan, Noble, Edith,
    Abigail & Jonah, gct Concord MM

NICHOLS
1793, 8, 24. Elizabeth rocf Kennet MM, dtd
    1793,6,13
1797, 7, 22. Ephraim Crawford gct Redstone
    MM, to m Susanna Nichols
1798, 8, 25. Susanna Crafford (form Nichols)
    rocf Kennet MM, dtd 1796,11,17, endorsed by
    Redstone MM, 1797,9,29

NICHOLSON
1793, 6, 22. Joseph & ch recrq
1793, 7, 27. Joseph & ch, James & Elizabeth,
    gct Redstone MM
1793, 7, 27. Cert rec for Sarah from Rahway
    MM, dtd 1793,6,19, endorsed to Redstone
    MM

NIXON
1804, 6, 23. Cert rec for Thomas from Back
    Creek MM, N. C., dtd 1803,8,27, endorsed
    to Miami MM

NUTT
1812, 10, 24. Hannah rocf Fairfax MM, dtd
    1810,6,27, endorsed by Middleton & Red-
    stone MM, 1811,10,29
1815, 8, 3. Hannah Smith (form Nutt) dis
    mcd

OLIPHANT
1802, 2, 27. Samuel & w, Elizabeth, & ch,
    Rachel, Ann, Rebecca, Samuel & Ephraim,
    rocf Goose Creek MM, Va., dtd 1802,9,5

OMAN
1791, 9, 24. Eli recrq

O'NEAL
1802, 12, 25. Abijah & w, Anna, & ch, Maryann,
    Sarah, John Kelly, William, Rebecca, Abi-
    jah & Rhoda, rocf Bush River MM, S. C.,
    dtd 1802,9,25 (settled at Little Miami)

ONG
1792, 2, 25. Jacob & w, Mary, & ch, Rebecca,
    Finley & Jacob, rocf Hopewell MM, dtd
    1791,6,6

PACKER
1801, 9, 26. Moses rocf Redstone MM, dtd
    1801,7,31
1846, 7, 23. Margaret (form Linton) con mcd
    (H)
1846, 9, 24. Margaret (alias Linton) gct
    Short Creek MM, O. (H)
1851, 1, 22. Margaret (form Linton) dis mcd

PAINTER
1800, 6, 28. David & w, Martha, & ch, Hannah,
    Jesse, Jacob & Thomas, rocf Hopewell MM,
    dtd 1800,3,3
1803, 10, 22. Cert rec for Jacob & w, Mary,
    & ch, David, Samuel, Robert, Abigail & Jo-
    seph, from Crooked Run MM, dtd 1802,10,2,
    endorsed to Middleton MM

PARIME
1790, 3, 27. Sarah (form Harris) dis mou

PARNEL
1803, 5, 28. George & brother, James, & sis-
    ters, Esther & Ruth, rocf Cane Creek MM,
    dtd 1803,3,19

PARKER
1800, 5, 24. Nathan rocf Contentney MM, dtd
    1800,3,8

PARSON
1812, 1, 29. Abner, s Vincent & Miriam, Wash-
    ington Co., Pa.; m at Pike Run, Agness
    CADWALADER, dt Abram & Oner, Montgomery
    Co., Pa.

1801, 8, 22. Abner recrq
1804, 2, 25. Ann (form Smith) dis mou
1807, 10, 24. Joshua recrq
1810, 10, 27. Joshua gct Fairfield MM, O.
1817, 9, 25. Fairfield MM, O. was given per-
    mission to rst Ann [Parsons]
1829, 11, 25. Abner dis jH
1839, 8, 21. Abraham dis disunity
1840, 7, 22. Joel [Parsons] dis disunity

PARVIANCE
1786, 6, 17. James & w, Elizabeth, & ch, Na-
    thaniel, John, James, David, Thomas, Jo-
    seph, George, William & Richard, rocf
    Hopewell MM, dtd 1786,5,1

PATE
1801, 12, 2. Charlotte m Bordon STANTON

1801, 10, 24. Charlotte rocf Trent MM, dtd
    1800,1,10, endorsed by Redstone MM, 1801,
    10,2

PATTERSON

1802, 6, 26. Rebecca (form Vanscoyoc) dis mou

1863, 4, 22. Esther (form Griffith) dis joining Orthodox in 1854 (W)

PATTY

1802, 12, 25. Mary, w Charles, rocf Bush River MM, S. C., dtd 1802,9,25 (settled at Little Miami)

PAXSON

1803, 9, 24. Cert rec for Benjamin & w, Ruth, & ch, William, Mary, John & Rachel, from Goose Creek MM, Va., dtd 1802,10,16, endorsed to Middleton MM

PECK

1787, 4, 14. Hannah rocf Sadsbury MM, dtd 1784,8,21

1792, 2, 25. John rocf Sadsbury MM, dtd 1791, 3,23

PEDEN

1797, 1, 5. Alexander, s Samuel & Lydia, Washington Co., Pa.; m at Pike Run, Abigail WALTON, dt Abraham & Rachel, Washington Co., Pa.

1789, 5, 16. Alexander rocf Warrington MM, dtd 1788,12,13

1789, 5, 16. Lydia Sr., w Samuel, rocf Warrington MM, dtd 1788,12,13

1789, 5, 16. Lydia Jr. rocf Warrington MM, dtd 1788,12,13

1790, 11, 27. Alexander gct Warrington MM, to m Lydia Thomas

1791, 5, 28. Lydia, w Alexander, rocf Warrington MM, dtd 1791,2,12

1814, 12, 29. Thomas gct Red Stone MM

1817, 7, 24. Ann Morgan (form Peden) con mou

1818, 1, 22. Alexander dis

1819, 10, 28. Thomas [Payton] rocf Red Stone MM

1821, 3, 22. Thomas dis mcd

1822, 9, 26. Jesse dis disunity

1824, 2, 26. Lydia Sr. dis

1824, 4, 22. Darius dis

1824, 9, 23. Obadiah dis disunity

1825, 5, 26. Lydia [Pedan] & minor sisters, Rachel & Margaret, gct Short Creek MM

1825, 12, 22. Joseph [Pedan] & minor brother, Alexander, gct Short Creek MM, O.

1829, 11, 26. Blue River MM was given permission to rst Derias [Paden] (H)

PELLET

1800, 4, 26. Francis & w, Mary, rocf Warrington MM, dtd 1800,3,8

1807, 6, 27. Francis & w, Mary, & ch, Eleanor, Abel, John, Mary & Elizabeth, gct Middleton MM

PENNEL

1794, 5, 8. Jane m John HUTTON

1805, 3, 28. Sarah m Jesse RIGG

1793, 3, 23. Jane recrq

1795, 9, 26. Sarah recrq

1803, 5, 28. Amos Cook & w, Elizabeth, & ch, John Dinah Amos Stephen Abraham & Ruth, also Sarah Pennel, their cousin, rocf Cane Creek MM, dtd 1803,2,19

PENNOCK

1792, 9, 26. Joseph, Washington Co., Pa.; m at Fallowfield, Hannah DIXON, Washington Co., Pa.

1792, 1, 28. Joseph [Pinnock] rocf Kennett MM, dtd 1791,12,15

1808, 7, 23. Priscilla (form Rigg) dis mou

PERKINS

1795, 12, 26. Ann (form Smith) dis mou

1798, 6, 23. Ann rst by rq

1804, 6, 23. Cert rec for Isaac & w, Penninah, & ch, Caleb, Ann, Abigail, Lydia, Sabinah & John, from New Garden MM, N. C., dtd 1803,8,27, endorsed to Miami MM

1804, 6, 23. Cert rec for Thomas from New Garden MM, N. C., dtd 1803,8,27, endorsed to Miami MM

1809, 5, 27. Ann, w Robert, gct Salem MM, O.

PERRY

1800, 5, 24. Daniel & w, Lydia, rocf Trent MM, N. C., dtd 1800,1,12

PHILIPS

1789, 3, 28. Solomon & w, Martha, rocf Wilmington MM, dtd 1788,11,12

1789, 3, 28. Eli rocf Kennet MM, dtd 1788,10, 16

1792, 2, 25. Eli dis mou

1813, 10, 23. Samuel gct Redstone MM

1813, 10, 23. Solomon [Phillips] & w, Martha, & ch, Solomon, Ruth, Ellis, Elizabeth & Jonathan, gct Redstone MM

1813, 10, 23. James gct Redstone MM

1860, 4, 26. Elma Swan (form Philips) dis mcd (H)

1864, 4, 21. Ellis transferred to Salem MM, this mtg being laid down (H)

1864, 4, 21. Mary transferred to Salem MM, this mtg being laid down (H)

1864, 4, 21. Solomon, Thomas, Elizabeth, James, Ellis & Martha Jane, transferred to Salem MM, this mtg being laid down (H)

1864, 4, 21. William transferred to Salem MM, this mtg being laid down (H)

PICKLE

1794, 5, 24. Sarah (form Rees) dis mou

PIDGEON
1803, 2, 26. William Jr. & w, Alice, & ch,
    Mary, Rachel, Elizabeth & Benjamin, rocf
    Goose Creek MM, Va., dtd 1802,4.3

PLUMMER
1818, 7, 23. Rebecca, minor, rocf Smithfield
    MM, dtd 1818,5,15
1821, 5, 24. Rebecca gct Smithfield MM, O.

PORTER
1787, 11, 24. Mary (form Jenkinson) dis mou

POUTS
1801, 12, 26. Jacob & w, Leanor, & ch, Jacob,
    Levi & Elizabeth, rocf Back Creek MM, N.C.,
    dtd 1801,9,16

POWEL
1787, 8, 11. Rachel (form Brown) dis mou
1789, 11, 28. Elizabeth (form Hutton) dis mou
1796, 1, 23. Lydia (form Newport) dis mou
1806, 11, 22. Letitia (form Heston) dis mou
1807, 9, 26. Hannah (form Michener) dis mou
1838, 10, 25. Martha (form Pyle) dis mcd (H)

PRICE
1827, 9, 29. Joel, s Daniel & Elizabeth,
    Baltimore Co., Md.; m at Pike Run, Edith
    MARTIN, dt Isaac & Rebecca, Belmont Co.,O.

1820, 10, 26. Amos Griffith gct Gunpowder MM,
    to m Edith Price
1827, 12, 27. Edith gct Gunpowder MM
1834, 4, 23. Edith M. recrq
1838, 11, 21. Mary rst by rq with consent of
    Redstone MM
1841, 7, 21. Mary gct Providence MM
1842, 3, 23. Edith Mary dis jas

PUGH
1802, 12, 25. Ellis & w, Phebe, rocf Bush
    River MM, S. C., dtd 1802,9,25 (settled at
    Little Miami)

PUSEY
1815, 1, 5. Nathan, s Nathan & Mary, Wash-
    ington Co., Pa.; m at Westland, Martha
    MILLS, dt Henry & Elizabeth, Washington
    Co., Pa.
1824, 7, 1. George, s Nathan & Mary, Wash-
    ington Co., Pa.; m at Westland, Sarah HES-
    TON, dt Eber & Ann, Washington Co., Pa.

1813, 11, 27. Nathan rocf Clear Creek MM, dtd
    1813,9,23
1815, 3, 2. Nathan & w, Martha, gct Plain-
    field MM, O.
1816, 11, 21. Nathan & w, Martha, & s, Joseph,
    rocf Plainfield MM, dtd 1816,5,24
1817, 8, 28. William rocf Clear Creek MM,
    dtd 1817,10,12
1819, 5, 21. George rocf Hopewell MM, dtd

1819,2,4
1821, 11, 22. William dis disunity
1824, 12, 23. George dis
1824, 12, 23. Sarah dis
1834, 10, 22. Nathan dis jH
1834, 10, 22. Martha dis jH
1836, 3, 24. Mary Ann Booth (form Pusey) con
    mcd (H)
1838, 2, 22. Nathan gct Baltimore MM for
    Western District, to m Mary H. Marsh (H)
1838, 8, 23. Mary M. rocf Baltimore MM for
    Western District, dtd 1838,6,8 (H)
1839, 5, 22. Joseph M. dis jH
1840, 1, 23. Mary G. con mcd (H)
1843, 4, 27. Joseph con mcd (H)
1847, 9, 23. Elizabeth M. relrq (H)
1850, 6, 27. Nathan & w, Mary M., & ch, John
    Marsh & Nathan, gct Baltimore MM for Wes-
    tern District (H)
1853, 12, 21. Joshua con mcd
1864, 4, 21. Joseph M. & fam transferred to
    Salem MM, this mtg being laid down (H)

PYLE
1814, 4, 27. Curtis, s Nathan & Martha, Wash-
    ington Co., Pa.; m at Pike Run, Esther
    GRIFFITH, dt Jacob & Lydia, Washington Co.,
    Pa.

1790, 2, 27. John & w, Susanna, & ch, Jesse
    & Sarah, rocf New Garden MM, dtd 1789,7,4
1809, 8, 26. Nathan recrq
1811, 12, 23. Palmer, William & Nathan, ch
    Nathan, recrq (also ch, Phebe)
1812, 2, 22. Martha rocf Concord MM, dtd
    1811,12,4
1813, 6, 26. Curtis recrq
1820, 10, 26. George Palmer dis mcd
1821, 8, 23. Ann (form Morgan) dis mcd
1825, 7, 28. William dis
1829, 4, 22. Curtis dis jH
1829, 6, 24. Nathan dis jH
1830, 12, 27. Martha dis jH
1834, 3, 26. Maria Taylor (form Pyle) dis mcd
1834, 12, 25. Maria Taylor (form Pyle) con mcd
    (H)

1838, 10, 25. Martha Powel (form Pyle) dis mcd
    (H)
1842, 5, 26. Curtice dis disunity (H)
1843, 7, 26. Esther & Ruth dis jH
1857, 5, 28. Rebecca (form Taylor) gct
    Middleton MM, O. (H)
1864, 4, 21. Esther & ch transferred to Salem
    MM, this mtg being laid down (H)

RALEY
1788, 5, 8. Robert, s Robert & Ann, Washing-
    ton Co., Pa.; m at Westland, Sarah TOWN-
    SEND, dt Thomas & Sarah, Washington Co.,Pa.
1793, 5, 2. Ann [Rely] m John BATTIN
1798, 5, 3. Jane m John WHITE
1811, 5, 30. Ann [Reley] m Mark DEEMS

RALEY, continued
1813, 6, 3. Sarah m Joseph MILLS
1847, 12, 25. Joseph, s James & Rachel, Bel-
    mont Co., O.; m at Westland, Sally FOWLER,
    dt Eli & Sarah, Belmont, O.

1787, 1, 13. Robert dis
1787, 8, 11. Frances & brother, James, gct
    Crooked Run MM, Va.
1787, 10, 13. Eli rocf Crooked Run MM, dtd
    1787,9,7
1788, 4, 26. Cert rec for Eli, 1787,10,13,
    endorsed to Crooked Run MM
1790, 5, 22. Frances rocf Crooked Run MM, dtd
    1790,1,30
1798, 2, 24. Robert Sr. rst by rq
1801, 6, 7. James & w, Rachel, & ch, Joshua,
    Hannah, Abigail, Asa & Ann, rocf Hopewell
    MM, dtd 1801,5,4
1802, 12, 25. Eli & w, Mary, & ch, John, Sarah,
    David, Joseph & Ann, rocf Hopewell MM, dtd
    1802,2,1
1814, 11, 3. David gct Short Creek MM
1815, 3, 30. Michael dis mou
1815, 6, 29. John Jr. dis mou
1816, 9, 26. Thomas gct Centre MM, Del., to
    m Ann Dixon
1817, 5, 22. Ann, w Thomas, rocf Center MM,
    Del., dtd 1817,1,6
1821, 10, 29. Ann Sweney (form Raley) dis mcd
1823, 1, 23. Joseph dis mcd
1823, 10, 23. John gct Providence MM, to m
    Sarah Cope
1824, 4, 22. Sarah Raley & ch, Ruth & Jesse
    Cope, rocf Providence MM, dtd 1824,3,23
1825, 7, 28. James dis
1826, 5, 25. John Raley & w, Sarah, & ch,
    Ruth & Jesse Cope, gct Providence MM
1829, 5, 27. Thomas dis jH
1829, 7, 22. Ann dis jH
1829, 12, 23. Mary, Elizabeth & Eli dis jH
1830, 1, 27. Robert dis mou
1831, 1, 26. Eli, Jr. gct Short Creek MM, O.
1832, 9, 27. Thomas [Railey] & w, Ann, & ch,
    Mary, Phebe, Jehu, John & Kersey, gct Car-
    mel MM, O. (H)
1837, 9, 20. Mary, Phebe, Jehu & John, ch
    Thomas, gct Carmel MM
1840, 8, 27. Elizabeth gct Honey Creek MM,
    Ind. (H)
1840, 9, 24. Eli [Railey] gct Honey Creek MM,
    Ind. (H)
1848, 2, 23. Sally gct Short Creek MM, O.
1851, 2, 19. Short Creek MM was given per-
    mission to rst Elizabeth

RAMSEY
1806, 9, 27. Lydia (form Johnson) con mou

RATCLIFF
1831, 11, 23. Harrison & w, Mildred, rocf
    Short Creek MM, dtd 1831,10,18

READER
1799, 12, 28. John recrq
1810, 9, 22. John dis

REES
1794, 2, 22. Hannah Davis (form Rees) dis
    mou
1794, 5, 24. Sarah Pickle (form Rees) dis
    mou
1802, 11, 27. Joel dis disunity
1804, 8, 25. Jacob dis mou
1804, 8, 25. Morris dis mou
1804, 8, 25. Nathan dis mou
1804, 8, 25. Hannah Hull (form Rees) dis
    mou

REGISTER
1802, 11, 27. William & w, Abigail, & ch,
    Robert & Thomas, rocf Chester MM, dtd
    1802,9,27
1805, 2, 23. Thomas con mou
1807, 12, 26. Robert dis mou
1822, 4, 25. Thomas dis jas
1823, 12, 25. Sandy Spring MM was given per-
    mission to rst Robert

REID
1834, 8, 28. John [Read] & w, Rebecca, & ch,
    Eliza Jane, Priscilla C. & Joseph Durose,
    rocf Bradford MM, Pa., dtd 1834,5,6, en-
    dorsed by Concord MM, 1834,8,20 (H)
1842, 9, 21. George rocf Carmel MM, dtd
    1842,6,18
1853, 5, 26. Rebecca C. & ch, William Penn,
    Mary Ellen, John Hall & George Washington,
    gct Bradford MM (H)
1853, 6, 23. Eliza Jane Harry (form Reid)
    con mcd (H)
1853, 8, 25. Joseph D. gct Bradford MM (re-
    turned by him 1855,5,5) (H)
1858, 1, 28. Joseph D. gct Birmingham MM, Pa.
    (H)

REYNOLDS
1788, 11, 22. James & w, Hannah, & ch, Henry
    & Sarah Way, rocf Wilmington MM, dtd
    1788,10,15
1801, 6, 27. James dis disunity
1804, 10, 27. Hannah & ch, Henry, Sarah, Re-
    becca, Elizabeth, John, Ann, Maria & Han-
    nah, gct Middleton MM

RHODES
1839, 8, 22. Henry Mills gct Plainfield MM,
    to m Esther Rhodes (H)

RICHARDS
1800, 11, 22. Rowland & w, Lydia, & ch, Sarah,
    Catharine & Sidney, rocf Crooked Run MM,
    dtd 1800,10,1
1800, 11, 22. Mary rocf Crooked Run MM, dtd
    1800,10,1
1801, 11, 28. Abijah & w, Esther, & ch, Sam-

RICHARDS, continued
      uel, Esther, Edith, Abijah & Mary, rocf
      Goose Creek MM, Va., dtd 1801,10,3
1802, 12, 25. Mary Mills (late Richards or
      Richardson) con mcd

RICHARDSON
1787, 11, 24. John & w, Lydia, & ch, Nehemiah,
      Joseph, Mary, Samuel, Lydia, Hannah &
      Faithful, rocf Nottingham MM, dtd 1787,10,
      27
1798, 5, 26. Joseph dis mou
1802, 12, 25. Mary Mills (late Richards or
      Richardson) con mou
1804, 4, 28. Lydia Jr. gct Middleton MM
1804, 4, 28. Mary gct Middleton MM
1842, 5, 26. Hannah B. con mcd (H)
1842, 6, 23. Hannah B. gct Carmel MM, O.

RIDGWAY
1795, 7, 25. Timothy & w, Michal, & ch, Paul,
      Daniel, Job, Thomas, Laviner & John, rocf
      Little Eggharbour MM, dtd 1794,5,8, en-
      dorsed by Redstone MM, 1794,12,26
1801, 12, 26. Paul dis mou
1802, 7, 24. Francis Townsend & w, Marah, &
      Job Ridgway, his apprentice, gct Concord
      MM
1803, 2, 26. Daniel dis mou
1812, 3, 28. Timothy & w, Michel, & ch, John,
      Richard & Kezia, gct Plainfield MM, O.
1812, 3, 28. Thomas gct Plainfield MM, O.
1812, 4, 25. Lavina dis
1816, 5, 23. Plainfield MM was given per-
      mission to rst Levina [Ridgeway]

RIGG
1805, 3, 28. Jesse, s Clement & Sarah, Wash-
      ington Co., Pa.; m at Westland, Sarah PEN-
      NEL, dt Joshua & Susannah, Washington Co.,
      Pa.
1806, 5, 1. Abigail m John MILLIGAN
1807, 11, 5. Miriam m Aaron WALKER

1786, 9, 9. Clement & ch, Ephraim, Sarah,
      Clement, Abigail, Jesse, Priscilla &
      Merium, recrq
1795, 8, 22. Sarah Battin (form Rigg) dis mou
1797, 4, 22. Clement Jr. dis disunity
1802, 5, 22. Ephraim dis mcd
1808, 7, 23. Priscilla Pennock (form Rigg)
      dis mou
1816, 2, 22. Jesse & w, Sarah, & ch, Nathan-
      iel, Hiram, Miriam & Sarah, gct Short
      Creek MM
1842, 7, 28. Matilda recrq (H)

ROBERTS
1799, 10, 26. John Lewis gct Redstone MM, to
      m Hannah Roberts

ROBINETT
1816, 7, 5. Priscilla [Robinette] m Richard

CRAWFORD
1817, 11, 5. Elizabeth m Joseph JOHN Jr.

1814, 6, 30. Priscilla recrq
1816, 8, 22. Elizabeth recrq

ROBINSON
1803, 7, 23. Elizabeth (form Mathews) dis
      mou
1804, 2, 25. Jacob rocf Wilmington MM, dtd
      1802,8,5
1807, 5, 23. Jacob dis

ROGERS
1828, 10, 1. Samuel, s Jeremiah & Priscilla,
      Washington Co., Pa.; m at Pike Run, Sarah
      CRAWFORD, dt Seaborn & Frances, Washing-
      ton Co., Pa.
1836, 11, 30. Jeremiah, s Samuel & Susanna,
      Washington Co., Pa.; m at Westland, Ann
      FARQUHAR, dt Charles & Martha DINGEE,
      Washington Co., Pa.
1838, 7, 8. Mary d ae 52y (an elder)

1791, 12, 24. Ruth (form Smith) dis mou
1797, 10, 28. Ruth rocf Warrington MM, dtd
      1797,7,8
1797, 12, 23. Lewis recrq
1798, 5, 26. Mary & Levi, ch Lewis & Ruth,
      recrq
1799, 12, 28. Josiah & w, Alice, & ch, Jane,
      Evan, John & Josiah, rocf Hopewell MM,
      dtd 1798,8,6
1802, 9, 25. Lewes dis disunity
1802, 11, 27. Ruth & ch, Mary, Levi & Ann,
      gct Monallan MM
1806, 10, 25. Josiah & w, Alice, & ch, Jane,
      Evan, John, Josiah, Sarah & Alice, gct
      Concord MM
1810, 5, 26. Philip recrq
1810, 11, 24. Mary rst by rq with consent of
      Deer Creek MM
1814, 1, 22. Priscilla [Rodgers] rocf Deer
      Creek MM, dtd 1813,9,23
1814, 3, 26. Ruth & ch returned cert granted
      to Monallin MM several yrs ago, without
      having used it
1814, 4, 23. Ruth & ch, Mary, Levi & Ann,
      gct New Garden MM, O.
1815, 2, 2. Nathan & Samuel, ch Philip,
      recrq
1817, 8, 28. Jeremiah recrq
1820, 2, 24. James, Marian, Samuel & Ann
      Cassandra, ch Jeremiah & Priscilla, recrq
1831, 1, 26. Samuel dis mou
1831, 5, 25. James R. dis mou
1832, 4, 25. Nathan J. gct Redstone MM, to m
      Atlantic Haines
1832, 8, 22. Atlantic rocf Redstone MM, dtd
      1832,8,1
1836, 9, 21. Elizabeth (form John) dis mou
1840, 7, 22. Nathan & w, Atlantic, & ch, Eli,
      Jonathan, Lindley & Mary, gct Redstone MM

ROGERS, continued

1841, 8, 25. Samuel W. dis disunity
1841, 8, 25. David G. dis disunity
1842, 1, 26. Philip Sr. dis mcd
1842, 6, 22. Winston D. gct Redstone MM
1843, 7, 26. Nathan & w, Atlantic, & ch, Eli, Jonathan, Linley, Mary, Edith & Elizabeth L., rocf Redstone MM, dtd 1843,6,28
1843, 7, 26. Winston D. rocf Redstone MM, dtd 1843,6,28
1845, 2, 19. Sarah dis jas
1847, 1, 27. Philip Jr. dis mcd
1847, 5, 26. Mary Ann McJunkin (form Rogers) dis mou
1848, 8, 23. Elizabeth Hill (form Rogers) dis mou
1850, 1, 23. Winston dis mcd
1857, 5, 28. Atlantic & ch, Lindley M., Mary & Edith G., gct Redstone MM
1857, 12, 23. Sarah Frances (form Crawford) dis mcd (W)
1858, 4, 22. Jonathan T. gct Spiceland MM, Ind., to m Mary Hunt
1859, 3, 3. Jonathan T. gct Upper Springfield MM, O.
1860, 12, 26. Priscilla Crouch (form Rogers) dis mcd (W)
1863, 1, 1. Jeremiah & w, Ann, dis joining Wilburite Separatists in 1854
1863, 4, 22. Eli, Jonathan & Lindley dis joining Orthodox in 1854 (W)
1863, 4, 22. Atlantic & Edith dis joining Orthodox in 1854 (W)
1863, 6, 24. Mary Jones (form Rogers) dis mcd (W)
1864, 7, 27. Mary Ann Cook (form Rogers) dis mcd (W)
1865, 9, 20. Joseph H. dis joining Army (W)

ROSS

1800, 6, 28. Reuben Ross & w, Elizabeth, & her dt, Rebecca Brown, & their ch, Mary & Anna, rocf Trent MM, N. C., dtd 1800,1, 12
1815, 3, 30. Reuben & w, Elizabeth, & ch, Anna, Elizabeth & Phebe, gct Plainfield MM, O.

RUBLE

1838, 9, 26. Harriet (form Hartley) dis mcd.

RUSSEL

1793, 4, 27. Cert rec for Esther from Crooked Run MM, endorsed to Redstone MM

SAMMS

1788, 11, 22. Nathaniel & w, Sarah, rocf Chester MM, dtd 1788,8,25
1794, 2, 22. John & w, Sarah, & ch, Ann, John, Benjamin & Jesse, rocf Abington MM, dtd 1793,10,28
1803, 10, 22. Samuel Shaw gct Middleton MM, to m Sarah Samms

SAUNDERS

1791, 10, 22. Paul rocf Duck Creek MM, endorsed by SD MM, Phila., Pa., 1791,9,21

SCHOOLEY

1792, 10, 27. Isaac gct Goose Creek MM
1803, 2, 26. Elisha & w, Rachel, & ch, John, Mary, Sarah, Deborah, Israel, William, Rachel & Elizabeth, rocf Goose Creek MM, dtd 1802,4,3

SCOTT

1817, 7, 24. Rachel (form Milleson) dis mcd

SEXTON

1801, 8, 22. Cert rec for Hannah, w Masheck, & dt, Catherine, Hannah & Mary from Hopewell MM, dtd 1801,5,4, endorsed to Redstone MM

SHARP

1839, 6, 26. Ann (form Crawford) dis mcd

SHARPLESS

1790, 9, 1. Elizabeth [Sharples] m Rees CADWALLADER

1789, 2, 28. Elizabeth rocf Concord MM, dtd 1788,11,5
1791, 8, 27. Benjamin [Sharples], minor, rocf Chester MM, dtd 1791,6,27
1801, 4, 25. Benjamin gct Redstone MM

SHARPNECK

1820, 1, 27. Hannah (form Vernon) dis mcd

SHAW

1806, 11, 27. Latitia m Israel GRIFFITH
1828, 9, 3. Thomas, s Samuel & Susanna, Columbiana Co., O.; m at Wheeling, Ann VANSCOYOC, dt Enoch & Lydia, Washington Co., Pa.
1831, 4, 28. Susanna m Isaac CLEAVER (H)

1797, 10, 28. Samuel & w, Elizabeth, & ch, John, Thomas, Letitia, Susanna & Margaret, rocf Richland MM, dtd 1797,8,17
1800, 5, 24. Samuel Jr. dis
1803, 10, 22. Samuel gct Middleton MM, to m Sarah Samms
1805, 12, 28. Sarah rocf Middleton MM, dtd 1805,12,14
1808, 3, 26. Samuel & w, Sarah, & dt, Margaret, gct Salem MM
1808, 3, 26. Thomas gct Salem MM
1813, 12, 25. John gct Miami MM, O.
1815, 6, 29. Benjamin Vore gct New Garden MM, to m Margaret Shaw
1816, 8, 22. Susanna gct New Garden MM, O.
1818, 6, 25. Susanna rocf New Garden MM, dtd 1818,3,19
1829, 5, 28. Ann gct New Garden MM, O. (H)
1829, 8, 20. Susanna dis jH

SHAW, continued
1831, 1, 26. Ann dis JH

SHEPHERD
1787, 11, 24. Solomon & w, Margaret, & ch,
     Jane, John, Solomon, Elizabeth, Mary, Jo-
     seph, Sarah, Benjamin & Thomas, rocf Mo-
     nallin MM, dtd 1783,11,10
1790, 1, 23. John dis
1791, 10, 22. Solomon Jr. dis mou
1792, 6, 23. Joseph dis disunity
1792, 10, 27. Mary Andrews (form Shepherd) dis
1794, 10, 25. Elizabeth dis
1797, 2, 25. Sarah Colvin (form Shepherd)
     dis mou
1798, 7, 28. Jane Mattock (form Shepherd) dis
     mou
1799, 12, 28. Benjamin dis mcd
1804, 2, 25. William dis mou
1805, 4, 27. Solomon & w, Margaret, gct Red-
     stone MM
1806, 5, 24. Cert granted Solomon & w, Marga-
     ret, a short time ago, was returned, en-
     dorsed by Redstone MM
1810, 11, 24. Solomon gct Redstone MM
1812, 11, 28. Thomas dis mou
1816, 3, 28. Solomon rocf Redstone MM, dtd
     1815,10,27
1817, 5, 22. Redstone MM was given permission
     to rst Joseph
1823, 9, 25. Joseph & w, Elizabeth, & ch,
     Mary, Solomon, Rachel, Jacob, Louisa, Wil-
     son, Margaret Jane & Emily, rocf Provi-
     dence MM, dtd 1823,6,24
1825, 4, 21. John rocf Providence MM, dtd
     1825,3,22
1825, 8, 25. Mary Griffith (form Shepherd)
     dis mcd
1826, 1, 26. John dis mcd
1828, 7, 24. Joseph & w, Elizabeth, & ch,
     Solomon, Rachel, Jacob, Louisa, William
     Wilson, Margaret Jane, Emily & Joseph,
     gct Providence MM

SHERRICK
1821, 9, 27. Joanna (form Vanscioc) dis mcd
1825, 10, 27. Rachel [Sherick] (form Vansciock)
     dis mcd

SHINN
1803, 9, 24. Cert rec for Caleb & w, Mary,
     from Springfield MM, N. J., dtd 1803,8,3,
     endorsed to Middleton MM
1803, 9, 24. Cert rec for Thomas & w, Abi-
     gail, & ch, Mary & Joshua, from Mt. Holly
     MM, dtd 1803,7,7, endorsed to Middleton MM

SHIPLEY
1846, 7, 23. Rachel Ann (form Cleaver) dis
     jas (H)
1847, 8, 25. Rachel Ann (form Cleaver) dis
     mcd & jas

SHORES
1803, 2, 26. James & ch, James, Rebecca,
     Alice & Rachel, recrq
1804, 3, 24. Cert rec for Sarah from Goose
     Creek MM, dtd 1803,12,26, endorsed to
     Middleton MM
1804, 4, 28. James & ch, James, Rebecca,
     Alice & Rachel, gct Middleton MM

SHOTWELL
1792, 10, 27. Titus & w, Deborah, & ch, Dan-
     iel, Hope, Edward, Titus & Miriam, rocf
     Rahway MM, dtd 1792,9,20

SHREVE
1789, 2, 28. Abigail & s, Joseph, rocf Upper
     Springfield MM, N. J., dtd 1788,9,3
1789, 8, 22. John rocf Haddonfield MM, N.J.,
     dtd 1788,10,13
1790, 4, 24. Kezia rocf Upper Springfield MM,
     N. J., dtd 1789,11,4
1791, 10, 22. Kezia Stevens (form Shreve) dis
     mou

SIDWELL
1788, 6, 28. Hugh & w, Mary, & dt, Charity,
     rocf Hopewell MM, dtd 1787,9,3
1806, 9, 27. Margaret rocf Nottingham MM,
     dtd 1806,1,10

SILVERTHORN
1790, 12, 1. Elizabeth m John McCADDON

1790, 7, 24. William & w, Jane, & ch, Eliza-
     beth, Thomas, James, Abraham & Isaac,
     rocf Kingwood MM, dtd 1790,6,10 (cert re-
     turned 1791,9,24 because it was not origi-
     nal one issued)
1793, 3, 23. William & w, Jane, dis disunity

SINCLEAR
1803, 9, 24. Cert rec for George from Goose
     Creek MM, dtd 1803,4,2, endorsed to
     Middleton MM

SINK
1803, 7, 23. George & s, Andrew, rocf Back
     Creek MM, N. C., dtd 1802,8,28
1803, 7, 23. Mary & dt, Eve, Ann & Sarah,
     rocf Back Creek MM, N. C., dtd 1802,8,28

SMALL
1800, 6, 28. Jonas & s, Timothy, John, Silas
     & Edmund, rocf Core Sound MM, dtd 1800,5,
     14 (returned to Core Sound 1800,9,27)
1800, 7, 26. Comfort rocf Core Sound MM, dtd
     1800,5,14
1800, 9, 27. Cert rec for Sarah, w Jonas,
     & dt, Hannah & Anna, from Sore Sound MM,
     dtd 1800,5,14, endorsed to Contentney MM

SMITH
1792, 10, 4. Mary m Joseph GREGG

SMITH, continued
1797, 4, 22. Hannah m Jonathan WILSON
1798, 3, 29. Rachel m Nathan HEALD Jr.
1799, 3, 28. George, s Abraham & Sarah, Washington Co., Pa.; m at Westland, Hannah
COUZENS, dt John & Sarah, Washington Co.,
Pa.
1807, 8, 6. Henry Jr., Washington Co., Pa.;
m at Westland, Rebecca SMITH, Washington
Co., Pa.
1807, 8, 6. Rebecca, Washington Co., Pa.; m
at Westland, Henry Smith, Jr.
1808, 10, 27. Jacob, s Thomas & Elizabeth,
Washington Co., Pa.; m at Wheeling, Hannah
ENGLAND, dt Joseph & Elizabeth, Washington
Co., Pa.
1815, 5, 4. George, s Abraham & Sarah, Washington Co., Pa.; m at Westland, Ruth KEN-
WORTHY, dt William & Sarah, Washington
Co., Pa.
1819, 9, 2. Meribah m Ellis P. HARTLEY
1819, 9, 2. Sarah m John COPE
1827, 5, 3. Abraham, s George & Hannah,
Washington Co., Pa.; m at Westland, Ruth
BLACKBURN, dt William & Amy, Washington
Co., Pa.
1837, 11, 2. Ann m George W. EVERITT (H)

1787, 7, 14. Mary rocf Fairfax MM, dtd 1786,
7,22
1787, 10, 13. John & w, Sarah, & ch, Joseph,
Jonah, Samuel, Phebe, Aaron, Ann & Sarah,
rocf Fairfax MM, dtd 1786,7,22
1789, 2, 28. John & w, Jane, & s, John, rocf
Concord MM, dtd 1788,10,8
1789, 7, 25. George con mcd
1789, 12, 26. Sarah, w Timothy, rocf Upper
Springfield MM, N. J., dtd 1788,7,9
1790, 2, 27. Naomi Bishop (form Smith) dis
mcd
1790, 10, 23. Ritchard, s Timothy, recrq
1790, 10, 23. Timothy & ch, Micajah, Anthony,
Timothy, Daniel, Sarah & James, recrq
1791, 12, 24. Ruth Rogers (form Smith) dis
mou
1792, 9, 22. Jacob & ch, Samuel, Thomas, Jonathan, Elizabeth, Ann, Israel, William,
Ephraim & Deborah, rocf Kingwood MM, dtd
1792,6,14
1793, 8, 24. Cert rec for Randal from
Wrightstown MM, endorsed to Redstone MM
1795, 8, 22. Anthony & w, Lydia, rocf Little
Eggharbour MM, dtd 1794,8,14, endorsed by
Redstone MM, 1795,7,24
1795, 8, 22. Samuel rocf Hopewell MM, dtd
1794,9,1, endorsed by Redstone MM, 1795,8,
21
1795, 12, 26. Ann Perkins (form Smith) dis
mou
1796, 5, 28. Thomas & w, Rachel, & ch, Jesse,
Rachel, Samuel, Thomas, Phebe & Sarah,
rocf Fairfax MM, dtd 1796,3,26
1796, 5, 28. Hannah rocf Fairfax MM, dtd

1796,3,26
1797, 4, 22. Elizabeth McVay (form Smith) dis
mou
1797, 6, 24. Benjamin dis mou
1798, 5, 26. Ann (form Hoge) dis mou
1798, 5, 26. Mary Underwood (form Smith) dis
mcd
1798, 7, 28. Jonathan dis disunity
1799, 5, 25. Samuel, s Jacob, dis disunity
1799, 11, 23. Mary, w George, & ch, George &
Tamer, rocf Crooked Run MM, dtd 1798,12,1
1799, 11, 23. William, Samuel & Amos, ch
George & Mary, recrq
1799, 11, 23. Randal rocf Redstone MM, dtd
1799,5,3
1800, 3, 22. Randal dis disunity
1801, 8, 22. Lydia (form Betts) dis mou
1801, 11, 28. Samuel dis disunity
1802, 5, 22. Jesse dis disunity
1803, 5, 28. Thomas & w, Deborah, & ch,
Coperthwite, John, Margaret, Elizabeth,
Judith & James, rocf Redstone MM, dtd
1802,12,31
1803, 7, 23. Thomas, s Jacob, dis disunity
1804, 2, 25. Jonathan rst by rq
1804, 2, 25. Ann Parson (form Smith) dis mou
1804, 5, 26. Samuel gct Baltimore MM, to m
Ann Brown
1804, 6, 23. Cert rec for John & s, Nathan &
John, from Back Creek MM, N. C., dtd 1803,
8,27, endorsed to Miami MM
1804, 6, 23. Cert rec for Letitia & dt, Rachel, Sarah, Elizabeth, Peninah & Gulielma
from Back Creek MM, N. C., dtd 1803,8,27,
endorsed back to Miami MM
1804, 11, 24. Thomas & w, Rachel, & ch, Samuel,
Thomas, Phebe & Sarah, gct Middleton MM
1804, 11, 24. Israel dis disunity
1805, 1, 26. Rebecca recrq
1805, 5, 25. Samuel rst by rq
1805, 6, 22. Samuel gct Middleton MM
1806, 2, 22. Naomy & dt, Mary, gct Short
Creek MM
1806, 5, 24. Jonathan gct Short Creek MM
1806, 11, 22. George & w, Mary, & ch, William,
Samuel, Amos, George, Tamer, Tacy & Benjamin, gct Concord MM
1807, 10, 24. Samuel gct Pine Street MM,
Southern District, Phila., Pa.
1808, 2, 27. Copperthwait dis disunity
1808, 2, 27. Margaret Adamson (form Smith)
dis mcd
1808, 9, 24. Samuel & w, Ann, & dt, Eliza
Ann, rocf SD MM, Phila., Pa., dtd 1808,6,
22
1810, 2, 24. Henry & w, Martha, gct Baltimore MM for Eastern District
1810, 2, 24. Samuel & w, Ann, & ch, Eliza
Ann & William Brown, gct Baltimore MM for
Eastern District
1810, 7, 28. William dis mou
1810, 11, 24. Jacob & w, Hannah, gct Fairfield MM, O.

SMITH, continued
1810, 11, 24. Ephraim gct Fairfield MM, O.
1810, 12, 23. John dis disunity
1811, 8, 24. Elizabeth (form Smith) dis mcd
1813, 8, 28. Timothy & w, Hannah, rocf Red-
    stone MM, dtd 1813,4,30
1815, 8, 3. Hannah (form Nutt) dis mcd
1816, 12, 26. William recrq
1816, 12, 26. Prudence rst with consent of
    Goose Creek MM
1816, 12, 26. Levina & William, ch William &
    Prudence, recrq
1817, 2, 20. Hannah recrq
1817, 6, 26. Meribah recrq
1817, 12, 25. Benjamin gct New Garden MM
1818, 9, 24. John rst by rq with consent of
    Gunpowder MM
1821, 1, 25. Ann (form Vernon) dis mcd
1822, 8, 22. James dis mcd
1823, 12, 25. Thomas dis mcd
1825, 7, 28. Hannah Gaskill (form Smith) con
    mcd
1825, 9, 22. Joseph recrq   [Timothy]
1825, 12, 22. Hannah gct Providence MM (wd of
1826, 11, 23. William dis mcd
1826, 12, 28. Lavina, dt Prudence, gct Centre
    MM, O.
1826, 12, 28. Prudence gct Centre MM, O.
1829, 1, 21. Rebecca dis jH
1829, 3, 25. Henry dis jH
1829, 6, 25. Sarah Thistlethwaite (form
    Smith) con mcd (H)
1829, 12, 23. Sarah Thistlethwaite (form
    Smith) dis mou & jH
1830, 1, 27. Joseph gct Providence MM
1831, 1, 26. Cousins dis mou
1833, 11, 20. Abraham & w, Ruth, & ch, Hannah
    & Amy, gct Springborough MM, O.
1838, 5, 24. Jesse con mcd (H)
1839, 2, 20. Jesse dis mcd & jH
1839, 3, 27. Ann Everett (form Smith) dis
    mcd & jH
1842, 3, 24. Rebecca gct Clear Creek MM, Ill.
    (H)
1842, 3, 24. Rachel gct Clear Creek MM, Ill.
    (H)
1842, 4, 20. Rachel dis jH
1843, 7, 27. Jesse gct Clear Creek MM (H)
1846, 4, 22. Elizabeth H. (form Hartley) dis
    mcd
1853, 4, 20. George gct Somerset MM, O., to
    m Christiana Young
1853, 8, 24. Christian & ch, Mary, Nathan,
    Sarah & Ann Gray, rocf Sommerset MM, O.,
    dtd 1853,6,26
1863, 1, 1. Christiana & ch, Nathan & Ann
    Gray, dis joining Wilburite Separatists
    in 1854
1863, 3, 25. Christiana gct Upper Springfield
    MM, O. (W)

SNIDER
1833, 4, 30. Elizabeth (form Mercer) dis mou

SOPHER
1842, 8, 26. Ruth m Moses HOCKETT Jr.

1814, 11, 3. Joseph & w, Phebe, rocf Dunning
    Creek MM, dtd 1814,9,14
1829, 7, 22. Joseph Sopher gct Providence MM,
    to m Sarah Wayts
1829, 11, 25. Sarah Sopher & dt, Susanna
    Wayts, minor, rocf Providence MM, dtd
    1829,10,1
1832, 4, 25. Mary dis
1835, 3, 25. William, minor s Joseph, gct
    Sugar River MM, Ind.
1836, 11, 23. Joseph & w, Sarah, & ch, Hannah
    & Lydia, gct Redstone MM

SOUTH
1811, 2, 23. Ruth (form Gregg) con mcd

SPRAY
1803, 8, 27. Samuel & w, Mary, & ch, Dinah,
    John, James, Samuel, Mary & Jesse, rocf
    Cane Creek MM, S. C., dtd 1803,4,23
1803, 8, 27. Naomi rocf Cane Creek MM, S. C.,
    dtd 1803,4,23

SRIVER
1849, 11, 29. Mary H. m Joseph LEWIS (H)

1848, 10, 26. Mary H. & s, William Henry,
    rocf Plainfield MM, dtd 1848,8,19 (H)
1864, 4, 21. William H. transferred to Salem
    MM, this mtg being laid down (H)

STAATS
1815, 6, 29. Margaret rst by rq with consent
    of Redstone MM
1815, 8, 3. Margaret gct Plainfield MM, O.

STANDSBURY
1790, 8, 28. Mary rocf Rahway MM, dtd 1790,4,
    21

STANLEY
1863, 4, 22. Lydia K. Haviland (form Stanley)
    dis joining Orthodox in 1854 (W)

STANTON
1801, 12, 2. Bordon, Bellmont Co., N. W.
    Territory; m at Plymouth, N. W. Territory,
    Charlotte PATE, dt Mary JELKS, Jefferson
    Co., N. W. Territory

1800, 5, 24. Joseph & w, Hannah, & dt,
    Elizabeth, rocf Trent MM, N. C., dtd
    1800,1,12
1800, 5, 24. Borden & w, Susanna, rocf Trent
    MM, N. C., dtd 1800,1,12
1800, 6, 28. Lydia & ch, Abigale, Borden,
    Enoch, William & Job, rocf Trent MM, N.C.,
    dtd 1800,1,12
1800, 9, 27. Abigail & ch, Abigail, Lydia,
    Henry, David, Benjamin & Joseph, rocf Core

STANTON, continued
     Sound MM, dtd 1800,5,14
1801, 2, 28. Benjamin & w, Mary, & ch, Elias,
     Benjamin, Sarah & Dorcas, rocf Trent MM,
     dtd 1800,1,12, endorsed by Redstone MM,
     1801,1,30 (Benjamin, a minister. Dorcas
     had d before cert was rec)
STAPLETON
1806, 4, 26. Joshua & w, Susannah, & dt,
     Susannah, rocf Baltimore MM, dtd 1805,11,
     14
1807, 5, 23. Samuel rocf Baltimore MM, dtd
     1806,12,11
1807, 9, 26. Samuel dis disunity
1812, 5, 23. Samuel recrq
1814, 4, 23. Susanna gct Middleton MM
1814, 9, 1. Joshua gct Middleton MM
1815, 3, 30. Samuel con mou
1816, 5, 23. Samuel gct Middleton MM, O.

STEEL
1800, 5, 24. Benajah & w, Sarah, & ch, Mary,
     Peter & Elijah, rocf Trent MM, N. C., dtd
     1800,1,12

STERN
1838, 5, 25. Ann rocf Dunings Creek MM, dtd
     1838,2,22, endorsed by Providence MM,
     1838,4,5
1852, 9, 22. Ann gct Redstone MM
1863, 5, 27. Ann dis joining Orthodox in 1854
     (W)

STEVENS
1791, 10, 22. Kezia (form Shreve) dis mou

STEVENSON
1792, 2, 25. Mary (form Carter) dis mou

STICKLE
1811, 4, 27. George [Steigle] & w recrq
1811, 4, 27. Jane recrq
1814, 4, 23. George & w, Jane, gct Redstone
     MM

STOCKDALE
1793, 8, 24. Amy (form Allen) dis mou
1822, 7, 25. Amy rst by rq
1843, 7, 26. Amy gct Carmel MM, O.

STOKES
1796, 5, 28. Elizabeth rocf Fairfax MM, dtd
     1796,3,26

STONE
1835, 9, 23. Mary (form Walker) dis mou
1835, 12, 24. Mary (form Walker) con mcd (H)

STRATTON
1791, 12, 24. Margaret (form Betts) dis mou
1801, 12, 26. Cert rec for Benjamin & w, Amy,
     & ch, Rebecca, Naomi & Levi, from South
     River MM, dtd 1801,10,10, endorsed to

Redstone MM
1802, 1, 23. Daniel & w, Shady, & ch, John,
     Margaret, Mary, Daniel & Elias, rocf South
     River MM, dtd 1801,10,10
1803, 12, 24. Cert rec for Joseph & w, Naomy,
     & ch, Hannah & Joel, from South River MM,
     Va., dtd 1802,9,11, endorsed to Middleton
     MM
1803, 12, 24. Cert rec for Jacob & w, Rebecca,
     from South River MM, Va., dtd 1802,9,11,
     endorsed to Middleton MM

STRAWN
1800, 9, 25. Cert rec for Thomas [Strawhen]
     from Richland MM, dtd 1797,4,20, endorsed
     to Redstone MM
1811, 6, 22. Judith [Stronn] (form Grant)
     dis mou
1827, 8, 23. Esther (form Haycock) dis mcd

STUART
1786, 9, 9. Ruth rocf Warrington MM, dtd
     1786,2,11

STURGEON
1792, 9, 22. Phebe (form Webster) dis mou

SWAN
1860, 4, 26. Elma (form Philips) dis mcd (H)
1864, 4, 21. Ruth transferred to Salem MM,
     this mtg being laid down (H)

SWENEY
1821, 10, 29. Ann (form Raley) dis mcd

TALBOTT
1792, 9, 22. Benjamin & w, Susanna, & ch,
     Mary, Beulah & John, rocf Monallin MM, dtd
     1792,6,11
1793, 8, 24. Cert rec for Joseph [Talbot] &
     w, Mary, & four ch from Pipe Creek MM, en-
     dorsed to Redstone MM
1809, 4, 22. Samuel & w, Rachel, & ch, Jo-
     seph, Nathan, John, Rebecca & Samuel, rocf
     Hopewell MM, dtd 1809,3,6
1815, 8, 3. Joseph [Talbot] dis disunity
1817, 8, 28. Samuel & w, Rachel, & ch, Nathan
     Rebecca, John, Samuel & David, gct Short
     Creek MM

TAYLOR
1821, 2, 7. Jane m Peter CLEAVER
1832, 10, 31. Matilda m William H. LINTON (H)

1793, 9, 28. Ambrose & w, Mary, & ch, Jacob,
     Mordecai, Stephen, Abijah, Peter & Mary,
     rocf Chester MM, dtd 1793,2,25
1795, 5, 23. Ambrose & ch, Jacob, Mordecai,
     Stephen, Abijah, Peter & Mary, gct Hope-
     well MM

TAYLOR, continued

1801, 2, 28. Jonathan & w, Ann, & dt, Re-
    becca, rocf Crooked Run MM, dtd 1800,3,1,
    endorsed by Redstone MM, 1801,1,30
1809, 6, 24. Benjamin & w, Elizabeth, & ch,
    Jane, William, Griffith & Joseph, also
    Jonah, b since issuing of cert, rocf War-
    rington MM, dtd 1809,1,19
1820, 1, 27. Hannah recrq
1823, 2, 20. William gct Warrington MM
1825, 1, 27. William rocf Warrington MM, dtd
    1824,12,22
1828, 6, 26. Griffith dis disunity
1829, 4, 23. William dis mcd (H)
1829, 5, 27. Benjamin & Elizabeth dis jH
1831, 6, 22. William dis mou
1833, 10, 24. Joseph dis disunity (H)
1834, 2, 19. Joseph dis mcd
1834, 3, 26. Maria (form Pyle) dis mcd
1834, 12, 25. Maria (form Pyle) con mcd (H)
1835, 6, 24. Jonah dis disunity
1835, 8, 26. Matilda Lynton (form Taylor) dis
    mcd & jH
1836, 6, 23. Maria dis jH
1836, 8, 25. Joseph rst by rq
1837, 12, 27. Eliza dis jH
1842, 10, 27. Rebecca recrq (H)
1845, 7, 24. Mary Ann con mcd (H)
1850, 10, 23. Mary (form Taylor) dis mcd
1851, 6, 26. Elmira con' mcd (H)
1851, 7, 23. Elmira (form Taylor) dis mcd
1857, 5, 28. Rebecca Pyle (form Taylor) gct
    Middleton MM
1864, 4, 21. Mary Ann transferred to Salem
    MM, this mtg being laid down (H)
1864, 4, 21. Elizabeth transferred to Salem
    MM, this being laid down (H)

TEMPLE
1806, 12, 27. Nathaniel recrq

THISTLETHWAITE
1829, 6, 25. Sarah (form Smith) con mcd (H)
1829, 12, 23. Sarah (form Smith) dis mou & jH
1835, 7, 23. Sarah gct Redstone MM (H)
1835, 10, 21. Mary Ann (form Linton) dis mou
    & jH
1836, 11, 23. Anna M. (form Fowler) dis mcd
1837, 9, 21. Mary Anne (form Linton) dis mcd
    (H)
1845, 4, 23. Anna M. rst by rq
1849, 2, 21. Mary (form Farquhar) dis mou
1863, 1, 1. Anne M. dis joining the Wilburite
    Separatists in 1854

THOMAS
1790, 11, 27. Alexander Peden gct Warrington
    MM, to m Lydia Thomas
1800, 5, 24. David & s, Abel, rocf.Trent MM,
    N. C., dtd 1800,1,12
1800, 9, 27. Huldy rocf Core Sound MM, dtd
    1800,5,14
1803, 12, 24. David & s, Abel, gct Redstone

MM
1804, 10, 27. Samuel Clark & w, Ruth, & Abel
    Thomas, an apprentice, rocf Redstone MM,
    dtd 1804,8,31
1807, 7, 25. Samuel Clark & w, Ruth, & their
    apprentice, Abel Thomas, gct Redstone MM
1830, 9, 22. Rachel (form Morgan) dis mou

THOMPSON
1791, 5, 28. Bradways, s Nathaniel & Hannah,
    Washington Co., Pa.; m at Westland, Ann
    COUZENS, dt John & Sarah, Washington Co.,
    Pa.

1790, 3, 27. Bradway recrq
1803, 5, 28. Bradway & w, Ann, & ch, Mary,
    John Couzens, Sarah, Hannah, Samuel &
    Rezan, gct Concord MM

THORN
1792, 7, 28. Isaac & w, Hannah, & ch, Anna,
    Catherine, Margaret, William, Sarah, Thom-
    as & Elizabeth, rocf Rahway MM, dtd 1792,
    5,17

THORNBURG
1797, 2, 25. Benjamin dis disunity
1797, 9, 23. Edward dis disunity
1798, 9, 22. Mary dis disunity
1821, 2, 22. Albena [Thornburgh] dis jas

TILTON
1813, 3, 27. Enoch recrq
1813, 7, 24. Elizabeth, w Enoch, & ch, James,
    Mary, Sarah, Matthias, Enoch & Joseph,
    recrq
1816, 4, 25. Enoch & w, Elizabeth, & ch,
    James, Mary, Sarah, Matthias, Enoch, Jo-
    seph, John & Charles, gct Redstone MM

TOMLINSON
1845, 7, 24. Mary Ann (form John) dis mcd (H)
1850, 6, 26. Mary Ann [Tumbleson] (form
    John) dis mcd

TOWNSEND
1786, 4, 20. John, s Thomas & Sarah, Wash-
    ington Co., Pa.; m at Westland, Sarah
    McNAMEE, dt Barnabas & Mary, Washington
    Co., Pa.
1786, 6, 21. Rebecca m John WILDMAN
1788, 5, 8. Sarah m Robert RELEY
1789, 4, 1. Francis, widower, Fayette Co.,
    Pa.; m at Redstone, Marah CADWALLADER, dt
    Joseph & Mary, Fayette Co., Pa.
1790, 12, 9. David, s Francis & Rachel, Fay-
    ette Co., Pa.; m at Westland, Mary WALTON,
    dt Benjamin & Ruth, Fayette Co., Pa.
1793, 10, 17. Thomas, s Thomas & Sarah, Wash-
    ington Co., Pa.; m at Westland, Eliza
    MORRIS, dt Jonathan & Mary, Washington
    Co., Pa.

TOWNSEND, continued

1786, 6, 17. Benjamin & w, Jemima, & ch,
Benjamin, Mary & Martha, rocf Concord MM,
dtd 1786,5,3

1786, 6, 17. Joseph rocf Concord MM, dtd
1786,5,3

1787, 7, 14. Francis & ch, Benjamin, Jacob,
Isaac & Rachel, rocf Concord MM, dtd 1786,
11,8

1787, 7, 14. Lydia, dt Francis, rocf Concord
MM, dtd 1786,11,8

1788, 3, 22. Joseph gct Hopewell MM, to m
Sinah Walker

1788, 4, 26. Jesse rocf Hopewell MM, dtd
1788,4,7

1788, 6, 28. Sinah rocf Hopewell MM, dtd
1788,6,2

1789, 2, 28. David rocf Wilmington MM, dtd
1788,9,10

1790, 3, 27. Hannah rocf Bradford MM, dtd
1789,12,18

1790, 6, 26. Lydia gct Uwchland MM

1792, 7, 28. Esther rocf New Garden MM, dtd
1792,2,4

1792, 11, 24. Hannah, dt Francis, dis

1793, 10, 26. Jesse gct Redstone MM, to m
Edith Cadwallader

1794, 4, 26. Edith rocf Redstone MM, dtd
1794,4,25

1794, 6, 28. Esther Morgan (form Townsend)
dis mou

1795, 2, 28. Benjamin, s Francis, dis mcd

1795, 2, 28. Permelia (form Marshall) dis mcd

1796, 3, 26. Cert rec for Hannah, w Joseph,
& ch, Elizabeth, Sarah & John Ferris,
from Wilmington MM, dtd 1796,12,16, endorsed to Redstone MM

1796, 7, 23. Sarah rocf Concord MM, dtd
1795,12,9

1797, 4, 22. Benjamin Jr. dis mou

1800, 6, 28. Hannah & s, John, rocf Redstone
MM, dtd 1800,5,30

1800, 9, 25. Isaac, minor, rocf Core Sound
MM, dtd 1799,9,4, endorsed by Redstone
MM, 1800,8,29

1800, 11, 22. Elizabeth rocf Redstone MM, dtd
1800,10,31

1801, 6, 27. Sarah Jr. gct Uwchland MM

1801, 9, 26. Mary Walton (form Townsend) dis
mou

1802, 7, 24. Aaron dis mou

1802, 7, 24. Francis Townsend & w, Marah, &
Job Ridgway, his apprentice, gct Concord
MM

1803, 4, 23. Talbert rocf New Garden MM, dtd
1801,12,5

1803, 5, 28. John & w, Elvi, &·ch, Selah,
James, Rachel, Jonathan (Jane in women's
minutes), Mary, William, Esther, Sarah &
Elizabeth, rocf Cane Creek MM, S. C., dtd
1803,3,19

1803, 6, 25. Benjamin & w, Jemima, & ch, Martha, Aaron, Robert, Edith & Eli, gct Concord MM

1803, 6, 25. Moses, s Benjamin, gct Redstone
MM

1805, 9, 28. Mary Walton (form Townsend) con
mou

1805, 10, 26. Jesse & w, Edith, & ch, Sabina,
Rees Cadwallader, Ruth & Ann, gct Redstone
MM

1806, 6, 28. Francis & w, Marah, rocf Concord
MM, dtd 1806,1,21

1808, 10, 22. Abel rocf Middleton MM, dtd 1808
8,13

1808, 10, 22. Hannah rocf Middleton MM, dtd
1808,8,13

1809, 5, 27. Sina & ch, Rachel, Martha &
Francis, rocf Middleton MM, dtd 1808,11,12

1809, 10, 28. Aaron rocf Plymouth MM, dtd 1809,
8,19

1810, 10, 27. Francis & w, Marah, gct Plymouth
MM, 0.

1811, 5, 25. Sina & dt, Rachel, gct Hopewell
MM

1812, 7, 25. Francis, minor, gct Middleton MM

1812, 7, 25. Martha gct Middleton MM

1812, 7, 25. Abel gct Middleton MM

1813, 2, 27. Aaron gct Plymouth MM

1813, 3, 27. Thomas & w, Eliza, & ch, Amelia,
Mary, Morris & Harriet, gct Plainfield MM,
0.

1817, 10, 23. Hannah gct Middleton MM

1830, 6, 23. Phebe dis jH

TRUMAN

1864, 4, 21. Morris transferred to Salem MM,
this mtg being laid down (H)

TULLIS

1803, 11, 26. Cert rec for John & w, Sarah, &
ch, Rebecca, Richard, Jane & Nancy, from
South River MM, Va., dtd 1802,11,9, endorsed to Middleton MM

1804, 7, 28. Cert rec for Richard [Tollis]
& w, Ann, & ch, William, Jason & Ann, from
Goose Creek MM, Va., dtd 1802,2,6, endorsed to Middleton MM

UNDERWOOD

1814, 3, 3. Benjamin, s Willin & Sarah,
Washington Co., Pa.; m at Westland; Beau-
lah LEWIS, dt Samuel & Sarah, Jefferson
Co., 0.

1853, 6, 23. Sabina m William HANCOCK

1787, 5, 12. Sarah rocf New Garden MM, dtd
1781,12,2

1791, 5, 28. Willing & w, Sarah, & ch, John,
Susanna & Sarah, rocf Warrington MM, dtd
1791,2,12

1798, 5, 26. Mary (form Smith) dis mcd

1798, 5, 26. Willin & w, Sarah, & ch, John,
Susanna, Sarah, Benjamin, Willin, Joseph
& Betty, gct Redstone MM

1800, 5, 24. Willin & w, Sarah, & ch, John,

UNDERWOOD, continued
    Susanna, Sarah, Benjamin, Joseph, Betty &
    Willin, rocf Redstone MM, dtd 1800,5,2
1803, 7, 23. John, s Willin, gct Redstone MM
1804, 6, 23. Cert granted John to Redstone
    MM, 1803,7,23, returned with an endorse-
    ment by that mtg, 1804,5,4
1805, 4, 27. Deborah, w Alexander, rocf War-
    rington MM, dtd 1804,9,8
1806, 4, 26. John & Sarah, ch Willin, gct
    Middleton MM
1806, 9, 27. Cert granted to Middleton MM
    for Sarah a short time ago, returned with
    an endorsement by that mtg, 1806,8,9
1807, 4, 25. Susannah gct Middleton MM
1807, 11, 28. Willin & w, Sarah, & ch, Sarah,
    Benjamin, Joseph, Betty, Willin & Amos,
    gct Middleton MM
1811, 5, 25. Deborah gct Middleton MM
1814, 2, 26. Benjamin rocf Middleton MM, dtd
    1814,1,6
1815, 4, 27. Benjamin dis
1815, 6, 1. Beulah dis
1853, 1, 26. Sabina recrq

UPDEGRAFT
1792, 4, 28. Betty rocf York MM, dtd 1791,11,
    9
1795, 9, 26. Cert rec for Ann & ch, Eli,
    Edith & Ann, from York MM, endorsed to
    Redstone MM
1801, 11, 28. Nathan & w, Ann, & ch, Joseph
    (Josiah in women's minutes), David, Rachel,
    Hannah, Nathan & Ann, rocf Crooked Run MM,
    dtd 1801,5,2

VAIL
1804, 4, 5. Samuel, s Abraham & Margaret,
    Fayette Co., Pa.; m at Westland, Agness
    GRISELL, dt Joseph & Priscilla, Washing-
    ton Co., Pa.

1790, 12, 25. Rebecca rocf Rahway (or Plain-
    field) MM, dtd 1790,6,16
1790, 12, 25. Stephen & w, Mary, rocf Rahway
    MM, dtd 1790,9,16
1791, 11, 26. Shubel, Aaron, Sarah, Randall,
    Mary, Hugh & Catherine, ch Stephen &
    Mary, recrq
1793, 7, 27. Cert rec for Abraham & w, Marga-
    ret, & ch, Benjamin, Mercy, Robert, Samuel,
    Stephen, Catherine & Taylor, from Rahway
    MM, dtd 1793,4,17, endorsed to Redstone MM
1804, 5, 26. Agnes gct Redstone MM
1809, 12, 23. Jesse Ball gct Redstone MM, to
    m Mercy Vail
1815, 11, 30. Robert & w, Martha, & ch, Eliza
    & Isaac, rocf Warrington MM, dtd 1815,8,23
1818, 3, 26. Phebe [Vale] rocf Carmel MM, dtd
    1818,2,21
1819, 8, 26. Phebe Edmundson (form Vale) dis
    mcd
1820, 5, 25. Robert [Vale] & w, Martha, & ch,

    Eliza & Isaac, gct Warrington MM
1838, 7, 26. Isaac & w, Mary Ann, rocf War-
    rington MM, dtd 1838,6,20 (H)
1839, 4, 25. Martha rocf Warrington MM, dtd
    1839,2,20 (H)
1858, 1, 28. Isaac [Vale] & w, Mary Ann, &
    ch, John C., Eli, Elizabeth A., Ezeal W.,
    Robert A., Nathan C. & Isaac E., gct Clear
    Creek MM, Ill (H)

1858, 1, 28. Martha [Vale] gct Clear Creek
    MM, Ill. (H)

VANSCOYOC
1808, 10, 6. Abraham, s Enoch & Lydia, Wash-
    ington Co., Pa.; m at Wheeling, Hannah
    ENGLAND, dt Samuel & Tacy, Washington Co.,
    Pa.
1816, 5, 1. Mary m Jacob NEWBOURN
1817, 10, 29. Lydia m George NEWBOURN
1828, 9, 3. Ann m Thomas SHAW

1799, 7, 27. Enoch [Vanschihoc] & w, Lydia,
    & ch, Ann, Rebecca, Abraham, Enoch, Mary,
    Moses, Lydia & Joanna, recrq
1802, 6, 26. Rebecca Patterson (form Vanscoy-
    oc) dis mou
1813, 5, 22. Enoch [Vanschiock]dis mou
1817, 7, 24. Moses [Vanscioch] dis mcd
1821, 9, 27. Joanna Sherrick (form Vanscioc)
    dis mcd
1825, 10, 27. Rachel Sherick (form Vansciock)
    dis mcd
1827, 7, 26. Aaron [Vansciock] gct Providence
    MM, to m Ruth Cope
1830, 8, 25. Aaron & Ruth dis jH
1830, 9, 22. Enoch, Abraham & Hannah dis jH
1844, 6, 27. Aron & w, Ruth, & ch, Isaac,
    Enoch, Jesse, Abraham, Sarah, Jane Anna,
    Harrison & Simeon, gct Marlborough MM (H)
1846, 2, 19. Abraham [Vanscioc] gct Marlbor-
    ough MM, to m Rachel Elliott (H)
1852, 3, 24. Enoch gct Marlborough MM, O.
1852, 3, 24. Isaac gct Marlborough MM, O.

VANTRUCE
1806, 11, 22. Sarah (form Lewellen) rpd mou

VERNON
1808, 8, 27. Sarah rocf Redstone MM, dtd
    1807,7,31
1812, 3, 28. Ann, Hannah, Elmy, Jacob & Ben-
    jamin, ch Sarah, recrq
1820, 1, 27. Hannah Sharpneck (form Vernon)
    dis mcd
1821, 1, 25. Ann Smith (form Vernon) dis mcd
1826, 7, 27. Elma Bell (form Vernon) dis mcd
1830, 10, 27. Jacob dis mou
1832, 2, 22. Benjamin dis mou

VIA

1803, 5, 28. Cert rec for Mary from South River MM, dtd 1802,9,11, endorsed to Redstone MM

VICKERS

1796, 10, 22. Rachel rocf Bradford MM, dtd 1796,6,16

VORE

1809, 3, 25. Benjamin rocf Baltimore MM for Western District, dtd 1808,9,7, endorsed by Redstone MM, 1809,2,3
1815, 6, 29. Benjamin gct New Garden MM, to m Margaret Shaw
1815, 11, 2. Margaret rocf New Garden MM, O., dtd 1815,9,14
1817, 3, 27. Jacob rocf Baltimore MM for Western District, dtd 1816,12,6
1820, 4, 27. Isaac rocf Baltimore MM for Western District, dtd 1820,1,7
1825, 8, 25. Isaac gct Baltimore MM for Western District
1826, 3, 23. Jacob dis mou
1829, 7, 22. Benjamin dis jH
1833, 1, 24. Benjamin con mcd (H)
1834, 8, 28. Ann (form Blackburn) con mcd (H)
1840, 4, 22. Isaac dis jas
1841, 5, 27. Isaac dis jas (H)
1846, 2, 19. Edmund gct Clear Creek MM, Ill. (H)
1846, 7, 22. Elizabeth Blackburn (form Vore) dis mcd & jas
1847, 2, 25. Elizabeth Blackburn (form Vore) dis jas (H)

VOTAW

1793, 9, 4. Moses, s Isaac, Washington Co., Pa.; m at Fallowfield, Mary BROWN, dt Joseph, Washington Co., Pa.
1801, 7, 9. Joseph, s Isaac & Ann, Harrison Co., Va.; m at Richland, Va., Phebe YEATES dt Benjamin & Phebe, Harrison Co., Va.

1793, 1, 26. Isaac & w, Ann, & ch, Moses, Isaac, Joseph, Thomas, Daniel & Samuel, rocf Goose Creek MM, dtd 1792,11,26
1796, 8, 27. John & w, Rebeccah, & ch, Ann & Mary, rocf Goose Creek MM, dtd 1796,3,28
1798, 5, 26. Isaac Jr. con mcd
1798, 5, 26. Sarah (form Yates) con mcd
1804, 12, 22. Joseph & w, Phebe, & s, Benjamin, gct Middleton MM
1805, 3, 23. John & w, Rebecca, & ch, Ann, Mary, James, Lydia, Leah & Rachel, gct Middleton MM
1805, 6, 22. Moses & w, Mary, & ch, Elizabeth, Isaac, Sarah, Ann, Joseph, Mary & Daniel, gct Middleton MM
1805, 6, 22. Thomas gct Middleton MM
1805, 8, 24. Isaac & w, Anne, gct Middleton MM
1806, 4, 26. Samuel, a minor, gct Salem MM
1806, 5, 24. Isaac Jr. & w, Sarah, & ch,

Phebe, Mary, Benjamin & Jemima, gct Salem MM
1806, 9, 27. Daniel con mou
1807, 7, 25. Daniel gct Salem MM

WADE

1800, 12, 27. Royal & w, Phebe, & ch, Owen, Nathan, Elizabeth, Mary, Sarah & Rhoda, rocf Core Sound MM, dtd 1800,5,14

WALKER

1796, 3, 10. George, s Ebenezer & Mary, Westmoreland Co., Pa.; m at Westland, Anna GARRETSON, dt William & Mary, Washington Co., Pa.
1807, 11, 5. Aaron, s Ebenezer & Dianna, Washington Co., Pa.; m at Westland, Miriam RIGG, dt Clement & Sarah, Washington Co., Pa.

1788, 3, 22. Joseph Townsend gct Hopewell MM, to m Sinah Walker
1796, 4, 23. Anna gct Redstone MM
1799, 11, 23. Dianna rocf Richland MM, dtd 1799,10,17
1802, 6, 26. William & w, Martha, & s, Mordecai, rocf Hopewell MM, dtd 1801,11,2
1803, 8, 27. Isaac & w, Mary, & dt, Jane, rocf Hopewell MM, dtd 1803,8,1
1807, 7, 25. Aaron recrq
1810, 7, 28. Cert rec for Lewis from Hopewell MM, dtd 1810,7,2, endorsed to Short Creek MM
1812, 1, 25. Aaron dis
1820, 7, 27. Jesse, minor, gct Flushing MM,O.
1825, 5, 26. Flushing MM was given permission to rst Aaron
1829, 7, 22. Isaac dis jH
1831, 9, 22. Isaac con mcd (H)
1835, 9, 23. Mary Stone (form Walker) dis mou
1835, 12, 24. Mary Stone (form Walker) con mcd (H)
1840, 2, 19. William dis jH
1847, 4, 22. William con mcd (H)

WALTER

1799, 9, 28. Thomas Jr. rocf Concord MM, dtd 1799,3,4
1799, 12, 28. Cert rec for Thomas Jr. in 9th mo, endorsed to Redstone MM

WALTON

1790, 12, 9. Mary m David TOWNSEND
1797, 1, 5. Abigail m Alexander PEDEN
1818, 7, 30. Martha m Joseph JOHN
1821, 5, 31. Abraham, s Abraham & Rachel, Washington Co., Pa.; m at Westland, Ann JOHN, wd, dt Aaron & Elizabeth BORAM, Washington Co., Pa.

1787, 11, 24. Benjamin & w, Ruth, & ch, Joseph, Mary, Abraham, David, Martha, Gabriel, Bathsheba, Amos & John, rocf Richland MM,

WALTON, continued
    dtd 1787,8,16
1796, 9, 24. Abigail rocf Richland MM, dtd
    1796,5,19
1796, 10, 22. Abraham & w, Rachel, & ch, Jona-
    than, Margaret, Ruth & Abraham, rocf Rich-
    land MM, dtd 1796,5,19
1796, 10, 22. Nathan & w, Mary, rocf Richland
    MM, dtd 1796,5,19
1801, 9, 26. Mary (late Townsend) dis mou
1805, 9, 28. Benjamin gct Middleton MM
1805, 9, 28. John gct Middleton MM
1806, 1, 25. Mary rst by rq
1806, 2, 22. Mary gct Salem MM
1807, 3, 28. Bathsheba gct Salem MM
1807, 3, 28. Martha gct Salem MM
1808, 5, 28. Ruth Wealdon (form Walton) dis
    mou
1808, 12, 24. John Dingee gct New Garden MM,
    O., to m Bathsheba Walton
1811, 12, 28. Martha rocf Middleton MM, dtd
    1810,12,8, endorsed by New Garden MM, dtd
    1811,10,17
1814, 6, 30. Mary rocf WD MM, Phila., Pa., dtd
    1814,5,18
1814, 9, 29. Cert rec for Mary 1814,6,30, en-
    dorsed to New Garden MM
1814, 12, 1. Nathan Walton & w, Mary, & Ra-
    ch Barrett, a minor in their care, gct
    New Garden MM
1815, 6, 1. Margaret gct New Garden MM, O.
1815, 6, 29. Abraham & w, Rachel, gct New
    Garden MM, O.
1815, 6, 29. Jonathan & Abraham Jr. gct New
    Garden MM, O.
1815, 11, 2. David gct New Garden MM, O.
1821, 8, 23. Ann J. Walton & dt, Mary John,
    gct New Garden MM, O.

WARNER
1796, 4, 23. Mary, w Isaac, rocf Kennet MM,
    dtd 1796,1,14, endorsed by Redstone MM,
    1796,4,22

WAY
1802, 7, 24. Jehu Lewis gct Sadsbury MM, to
    m Susanna Way

WAYNE
1788, 6, 28. Patience rocf Evesham MM, dtd
    1787,11,9

WAYTS
1815, 11, 30. Sarah [Waits] (form Ailes) dis
    mou
1824, 7, 22. Mary [Waytes], minor, rocf
    Providence MM, dtd 1824,2,24
1827, 7, 26. Mary Hartley (form Waits) dis
    mcd
1829, 7, 22. Joseph Sopher gct Providence
    MM, to m Sarah Wayts
1829, 11, 25. Sarah Sopher & dt, Susanna
    Wayts, a minor, rocf Providence MM, dtd

    1829,10,1
1831, 3, 23. Shaidlock N. rocf Providence MM,
    dtd 1831,3,3
1834, 9, 24. Susanna dis jas
1836, 7, 27. Shaidlock N. gct Providence MM

WEAVER
1789, 10, 24. Sarah, w Isaac, & ch, William,
    Abraham & Sarah, rocf Chester MM, dtd
    1788,5,26
1790, 2, 27. Isaac Jr. rocf Phila. MM, dtd
    1788,10,31
1790, 10, 23. James rocf Chester MM, dtd 1788,
    6,30
1799, 9, 28. Isaac dis disunity

WEBSTER
1791, 2, 26. Taylor & w, Hannah, & ch, Wil-
    liam, Phebe, Rebecca, Susanna & John, rocf
    Rahway MM, dtd 1790,11,18
1792, 9, 22. Phebe Sturgeon (form Webster)
    dis mou

WEST
1795, 10, 24. Elizabeth recrq
1798, 7, 28. George rocf Deer Creek MM, dtd
    1797,10,26
1861, 7, 21. Caroline (form Farquhar) dis
    mcd (W)
1863, 6, 4. Caroline (form Farquhar) dis mcd

WHEALDON
1825, 4, 22. Nathan, Jefferson Co., O.; m at
    Westland, Ann KNIGHT, dt Abel & Ann, Wash-
    ington Co., Pa.

1808, 5, 28. Ruth [Wealdon] (form Walton) dis
    mou
1815, 9, 28. Short Creek MM was given per-
    mission to rst Ruth
1822, 8, 22. Rebecca, Rachel & Martha Smith,
    minors, rocf Short Creek MM, dtd 1822,5,21
1824, 5, 27. Rachel gct Short Creek MM
1825, 7, 28. Ann gct Short Creek MM
1840, 2, 19. Martha gct Short Creek MM
1844, 7, 24. Martha rocf Short Creek MM, dtd
    1843,10,24
1847, 7, 21. Martha Smith gct Springfield MM,
    O.

WHEELER
1819, 10, 28. Gould rocf Short Creek MM, dtd
    1819,7,20
1821, 4, 26. Gould gct Cincinnati MM

WHINERY
1803, 6, 25. Robert & w, Phebe, & dt, Abi-
    gail, rocf Warrington MM, dtd 1803,2,12
1804, 8, 25. Robert [Whinnery] & w, Phebe,
    & ch, Abigail & Phebe, gct Middleton MM

WHITACRE
1804, 10, 4. Mahlon, s Edward & Martha, Co-

WHITACRE, continued
lumbiana Co., O.; m at Richland, Va.,
Phebe BECK, dt Preston & Sarah, Harrison
Co., Va.
1808, 8, 29. Caleb, s John & Naomi, Columbi-
ana Co., O.; m at Westland, Rebecca BRACK-
EN, dt Solomon & Sarah MILLER, Washington
Co., Pa.

1799, 6, 22. Edward [Whitaker] rocf Goose
Creek MM, dtd 1797,1,30
1799, 6, 22. Martha [Whitaker] & ch, Mahlon,
Thomas, John, Isaac, Martha, Edward &
Kesiah, recrq
1802, 2, 27. Mary [Whitiker] rocf Goose Creek
MM, Va., dtd 1801,9,5
1803, 8, 27. Thomas con mou
1804, 12, 22. Phebe gct Middleton MM
1805, 1, 26. Edward & w, Martha, & ch, Mahlon, John, Isaac, Martha, Edward, Keziah,
Phebe & Asahel, gct Middleton MM
1805, 11, 23. Thomas gct Salem MM
1815, 6, 1. Caleb rocf New Garden MM, O.,
dtd 1815,4,13
1822, 8, 22. Maria gct Concord MM
1831, 3, 23. Maria rocf Short Creek MM, dtd
1830,11,23
1832, 5, 23. Maria gct Upper Springfield MM,
O. (rem with Shaidlock Negus & w)

WHITE
1798, 3, 29. Uriah, s Jesse & Mary, Green
Co., Pa.; m at Westland, Martha BLACKLEGE,
dt Thomas & Margaret, Green Co., Pa.
1798, 5, 3. John, s James & Elizabeth, Washington Co., Pa.; m at Westland, Jane RALEY
dt Robert & Ann, Washington Co., Pa.

1796, 4, 23. Uriah rocf Hopewell MM, dtd
1796,2,1
1796, 4, 23. Mary, w Jesse, & ch, Jane,
James, Rachel, Jesse & Israel, rocf Hopewell MM, dtd 1796,2,1
1796, 8, 27. Elizabeth rocf Hopewell MM, dtd
1796,2,1
1797, 5, 27. John recrq
1799, 6, 22. Jesse rocf Goose Creek MM, dtd
1798,12,24
1800, 4, 26. Jane Boyd (form White) dis mou
1802, 4, 24. Jesse & w, Mary, & ch, Rachel,
Jesse, Israel & Mary, gct Concord MM
1802, 4, 24. John & w, Jane, & ch, Ann &
Phebe, gct Concord MM
1802, 5, 22. James dis mou
1803, 8, 27. Elizabeth McMillen (form White)
dis mou
1807, 2, 28. Uriah & w, Martha, & ch, Jesse,
Thomas, James, Isaac & Margaret, gct Salem
MM
1841, 5, 26. Mary (form Jenkins) rpd mou

WHITEMORE
1839, 10, 24. Francis W. recrq (H)

1840, 10, 22. Francis W. gct Honey Creek
MM, Ind. (H)

WHITESIDES
1786, 10, 14. Hannah rocf New Garden MM, dtd
1786,3,4

WICKERSHAM
1802, 6, 26. Cert rec for Isaac & w, Elizabeth, from Hopewell MM, dtd 1802,3,1, endorsed to Concord MM

WILDMAN
1786, 6, 21. John, s William & Deborah, Fayette Co., Pa.; m at Redstone, Rebecca
TOWNSEND, dt Thomas & Sarah, Washington
Co., Pa.

1786, 5, 13. John rocf Fairfax MM, dtd
1786,3,25

WILKINS
1804, 6, 23. Amos rocf Cedar Creek MM, Va.,
dtd 1804,1,14, endorsed by Redstone MM,
1804,5,4
1811, 1, 26. Amos gct Waynoak MM, Va.

WILLETS
1793, 4, 27. Cert rec for Rachel & ch from
Pipe Creek MM, endorsed to Redstone MM

WILLIAMS
1799, 8, 24. Isaiah & w, Dinah, & ch, Benjamin, Mary, Tacy, Martha, Abraham, Susanna & Ann, rocf Goose Creek MM, dtd
1799,4,29
1800, 7, 26. Anna & ch, Elizabeth, Samuel &
John, rocf Core Sound MM, dtd 1800,5,14
1804, 4, 28. Benjamin gct Middleton MM
1804, 10, 27. Isaiah & w, Dinah, & ch, Mary,
Tacy, Martha, Abraham, Susanna, Ann, Hannah, John & Elizabeth, gct Middleton MM

WILLIS
1843, 9, 20. Joel rocf Redstone MM
1855, 6, 21. Joel gct Spring Creek MM, Ia.

WILSON
1792, 11, 1. Sarah m William HEALD
1797, 4, 22. Jonathan, s William & Elizabeth, Washington Co., Pa.; m at Westland,
Hannah SMITH, dt Thomas & Rachel, Alle-
gany Co., Pa.
1801, 3, 5. Rachel m Amasa LIPSEY
1801, 3, 12. Elizabeth m Hugh HILLES
1809, 11, 1. Martha m Isaac MARTIN

1791, 6, 25. Israel gct Duck Creek MM
1792, 7, 23. Israel roc endorsed by Duck
Creek MM, 1791,11,12
1793, 2, 23. Margaret (form McGrew) dis mcd
1793, 10, 26. Israel gct Redstone MM, to m
Martha Cadwallader

WILSON, continued

1794, 1, 25. Martha rocf Redstone MM, dtd 1794,1,24

1794, 4, 26. Cert rec for Jeremiah & w, Joanna, from Kingwood MM, dtd 1793,5,9, endorsed to Redstone MM

1800, 1, 25. Benjamin & ch, Henry, Benjamin Kid & Martha, rocf Deer Creek MM, dtd 1799,9,29

1800, 1, 25. Joseph rocf Baltimore MM, dtd 1799,11,14

1803, 8, 27. Christopher & w, Mary, & s, John, rocf Cane Creek MM, S. C., dtd 1803,5,21

1803, 8, 27. Jehu & w, Sarah, & ch, Dinah, John, Isaac, Seth, Amos & Betty, rocf Cane Creek MM, S. C., dtd 1803,5,21

1806, 5, 24. Henry con mou

1807, 4, 26. Martha Jr. gct Short Creek MM

1807, 11, 28. Benjamin Kid dis mou

1808, 4, 23. Joseph dis disunity

1810, 10, 27. Israel & w, Martha, & ch, Ruth, William, Edith, John, Hannah, David, Rachel, Israel & Jonathan, gct Plainfield MM, O.

1820, 3, 23. Henry gct Plainfield MM, O.

WINDER

1797, 3, 29. Hannah m William CHANDLER

1799, 3, 27. James, s John & Margaret, Fayette Co., Pa.; m at Fallowfield, Deborah ALLEN, dt Joseph, Fayette Co., Pa.

1796, 4, 23. John & w, Margaret, & ch, Ann, Abner, Marcy & Elizabeth, rocf Kennet MM, dtd 1795,11,12

1796, 6, 25. Hannah [Winders] rocf Kennet MM, dtd 1795,10,15, endorsed by Redstone MM, 1796,6,3

1798, 1, 27. Ann England (form Winder) dis mcd

WISE

1819, 7, 22. Elizabeth (form Burson) dis mcd

WOOD

1788, 11, 22. Jacob [Woods] & w, Isabel, & ch, Joseph, John, Elizabeth, Jacob, Joshua, Enos & Lewis, rocf New Garden MM, dtd 1788, 9,6

1797, 6, 24. Elizabeth dis

1798, 1, 27. Joseph [Woods] dis mou

1801, 12, 26. Cert rec for Rachel from Crooked Run MM, dtd 1801,5,30, endorsed to Concord MM

1804, 4, 28. Jacob [Woods] gct Middleton MM

1805, 10, 26. Enos [Woods] gct Middleton MM

1807, 1, 24. Joshua [Woods] dis

1809, 1, 28. Ruth rocf Hopewell MM, dtd 1808,11,7

1810, 5, 26. Margaret (form Fitz Randolph) dis mou

1814, 6, 30. Anna (form Fitz Randolph) dis mou

1815, 6, 1. Ruth gct Hopewell MM

1816, 6, 27. Middleton MM was given permission to rst Joshua

1816, 11, 21. Ruth rocf Pipe Creek MM, dtd 1816,9,14

1823, 4, 24. Ruth gct Miami MM

WOODROW

1801, 12, 26. Cert rec for Mary from Southland MM, dtd 1801,9,30, endorsed to Concord MM

WOODWARD

1861, 10, 23. David C. rocf Bradford MM, dtd 1861,7,3 (W)

1864, 2, 24. David C. gct Bradford MM (W)

WORLEY

1792, 2, 25. John rocf York MM, dtd 1791,9,7

1796, 4, 23. Cert rec for John from York MM, dtd 1796,1,6, endorsed to Redstone MM

WORREL

1801, 12, 26. Eleanor rocf Robinson MM, dtd 1798,11,27, endorsed by Redstone MM, 1801, 7,31

1803, 3, 26. Cert rec some time ago for Eleanor endorsed to Concord MM

1845, 2, 19. Isaac R. [Worral] rocf Short Creek MM, dtd 1845,1,21

1850, 1, 23. Isaac R. dis mcd

WRAY

1853, 5, 26. Thomas rocf Clear Creek MM, Ill., dtd 1853,4,7 (H)

1860, 4, 26. Thomas gct Clear Creek MM, Ill. (H)

WRIGHT

1802, 5, 22. Schooley & w, Levina, & ch, Mary, Elizabeth, Hannah, Amos, Sarah & Aaron, also Rebecca, b since dte of cert, rocf Crooked Run MM, dtd 1799,11,2

1803, 7, 28. Hannah rocf Lost Creek MM, Tenn., dtd 1802,9,18

1803, 9, 24. Cert rec for Joseph & w, Elizabeth, & ch, John, Benjamin, Martha, Charity & Judith, from Goose Creek MM, Va., dtd 1802,8,7, endorsed to Middleton MM

1803, 10, 22. Schooley & w, Lavina, & ch, Mary, Elizabeth, Hannah, Amos, Sarah & Aaron, also Rebecca, b since dte of cert, rocf Crooked Run MM, dtd 1797,11,2

1803, 11, 26. Cert rec for Jemima & ch, Jane, Joshua, Jemimah, Joab & Job from Bush River MM, dtd 1803,4,30, endorsed to Miami MM

1809, 7, 22. Schooley & w, Levina, & ch, Mary, Elizabeth, Hannah, Amos, Sarah, Aaron, Rebecca, William & Fanny, gct Plainfield MM

YARNAL
1794, 9, 27. Cert rec for ch of George from
    Gunpowder MM, endorsed to Redstone MM
1802, 6, 26. Phebe rocf Crooked Run MM, dtd
    1801,8,1

YATES
1801, 7, 9. Phebe m Joseph VOTAW
1804, 11, 14. Futh m Edward BECK

1796, 2, 27. Benjamin & w, Phebe, & ch, Sa-
    rah, Phebe, James, Ruth, Mary, Jemima &
    Benjamin, rocf Goose Creek MM, dtd 1795,
    11,30
1798, 5, 26. Sarah Votaw (form Yates) con mcd
1801, 2, 28. Ann (form Beck) con mou
1805, 10, 26. Benjamin & w, Phebe, & ch, Mary,
    Jemima & Benjamin, gct Salem MM
1806, 1, 25. James gct Salem MM
1822, 12, 26. New Garden MM was given per-
    mission to rst Ann

*   *   *   *   *   *   *

COPE
1802, 11, 4. Joshua, s John & Mary, Washington
    Co., Pa.; m at Pike Run, Alice FISHER, dt
    Isaac & Elizabeth, Bedford Co., Pa.

CRAWFORD
1816, 7, 5. Richard, s Seaborn & Frances,
    Washington Co., Pa.; m at Pike Run, Pris-
    cilla ROBINETTE, dt James & Priscilla
1848, 8, 7. Thomas d ae 98y (an elder)
1850, 1, 23. Frances d ae 84y (an elder)

DIXON
1792, 12, 12. Ruth m John COOPE

ELLIOTT
1805, 2, 7. Elizabeth m William McCALL

ENGLAND
1812, 5, 28. Joseph, Wash. Co., Pa., s Samuel
    & Tacy; m at Westland, Hannah RELEY, dt
    John, County aforesaid, & Mary

GRAVE
1855, 4, 24. Ruth d ae 90y (a minister)

GREGG
1791, 10, 12. Nimrod, s Thomas & Amy, Fayette
    Co., Pa.; m at Redstone, Catharine JOHNSON,
    dt Isaac & Lydia, Fayette Co., Pa.

1810, 10, 27. Nathaniel prc of clearness from
    Plainfield MM, O., to m Elizabeth Mills

HUTTON
1794, 10, 2. Amos, s Joseph & Sarah, Washing-
    ton Co., Pa.; m at Westland, Beulah LEWIS,
    dt Samuel & Catharine, Washington Co., Pa.

YEATMAN
1789, 9, 26. John recrq

YOUNG
1786, 2, 11. Silas dis
1787, 4, 14. John dis
1801, 3, 28. James & w, Dinah, rocf Fairfax
    MM, dtd 1800,12,27
1801, 10, 24. Four youngest ch of James recrq
1812, 6, 27. James Jr. dis mou
1819, 8, 26. Evan dis mcd
1820, 1, 27. Sarah McClay (form Young) dis
    mcd
1845, 8, 28. Susanna con mcd (H)
1845, 11, 27. Susanna gct Carmel MM (H)
1853, 4, 20. George Smith gct Somerset MM, O.,
    to m Christiana Young

YUNT
1803, 7, 23. Henry & s, Andrew, rocf Back
    Creek MM, N. C., dtd 1802,8,28
1803, 7, 23. Mary & dt, Catharine & Sarah,
    rocf Back Creek MM, N. C., dtd 1802,8,28

*   *   *   *   *   *   *

JACKSON
1800, 5, 28. John, s Samuel & Rebecca, Fay-
    ette Co., Pa.; m at Fallowfield, Ann
    HOUGH, dt Amos & Elizabeth, Washington
    Co., Pa.

JENKINSON
1804, 4, 28. Mary gct Middleton MM

JOHNS
1800, 1, 25. Richard & w, Sarah, rocf Deer
    Creek, dtd 1799,9,29

JOHNSON
----, --, --. Joshua, mbr London Grove MM,
    rpd mcd

NEWBURN
1816, 5, 1. Jacob [Newbourn], s David &
    Thamer, Washington Co., Pa.; m at Wheel-
    ing, Mary VANSCOYOCK, dt Enoch & Lydia,
    Washington Co., Pa.

OLDHAM
1791, 5, 28. William, mbr Monellen MM, com
    enlisting in military service

RALEY
1812, 5, 28. Hannah [Reley] m Joseph ENGLAND

ROSS
1812, 4, 2. Mary m Boaz ATHERTON

WALTON
1794, 5, 29. Abraham, s Benjamin & Ruth,
    Washington Co., Pa.; m at Westland, Mary
    HEALD, dt Nathan & Rebecca, Washington
    Co., Pa.

WILSON
1803, 8, 27. Dinah rocf Cane Creek, S. C.,
     dtd 1803,5,21

HEALD
1794, 5, 29. Mary m Abraham WALTON

WOOD
1795, 12, 2. John [Woods], s Jacob, Fayette
     Co., Pa.; m at Fallowfield, Rebecca DIXON,
     dt Henry, Washington Co., Pa.

MILLHOUSE
1847, 12, 23. Joshua V., s William & Martha,
     Belmont Co., O.; m at Pike Run, Elizabeth
     P. GRIFFITH, dt Amos & Edith, Washington
     Co., Pa.

REDSTONE MONTHLY MEETING

Redstone Monthly Meeting, located in Fayette County, Pennsylvania, was set off from Westland Monthly Meeting, 26th of 4th month, 1793, by order of Fairfax Quarterly Meeting. Besides Fayette County, the verge of the meeting probably included part of Westmoreland County, Pa., and of Monongalia County, Virginia (now West Virginia). The first settlement of Friends in this section appears to have been at Uniontown about 1769. In 1776 Warrington and Fairfax Quarterly Meeting reported that eighteen families of Friends were then residing about Redstone, Uniontown and Brownsville.

Local meetings are mentioned at Redstone, Uniontown, Sandy Hill, Spring Hill, Providence, Sandy Creek (Va.), Center, Sewickley, and Brownsville.

Early members included Jacob Beason, Mary Brewer, Eleazer Brown, Nathan Brown, Asa Cadwalader, John Cadwallader, Rees Cadwallader, Septimus Cadwallader, Elizabeth Cadwallader, Sarah Cadwallader, Elizabeth Campbell, Margaret Campbell, Enoch Chandler, Jonas Chattle, Elizabeth Cattell, Rachel Cattell, John Coope, Samuel Coope, Mary Cope, Josiah Crawford, William Dixon, Rebeckah Dixon, Obed Garwood, Amy Gragg, Jonathan Hewitt, John Hoge, Mary Hogue, Esther Hunt, Samuel Jackson, Rebecca Jackson, Finley McGrew, James McGrew, Sr., clerk, John Moore, Samuel Morten, Thomas Newport, Jacob Ong, Mary Ong, James Perviance, Elizabeth Perviance, Ann Schoolly, John Shreve, Timothy Smith, Jane Smith, Sarah Smith, Benjamin Talbott, Isaac Thorn, Ebeneezer Walker and Taylor Webster.

The meeting was divided by the Hicksite movement in 1828 and again by the Wilburite movement in 1854. The Hicksite branch was laid down in 1852; the Orthodox branch in 1866. No Wilburite records have been found, so the period of existence of that branch is unknown.

RECORDS

ADAMS
1804, 3, 2. Hannah (form Townsend) dis mou

AILES
1806, 12, 10. Joseph [Ales], s Amos & Ann,
    Washington Co., Pa.; m at Redstone, Sarah
    BALL, dt John & Ann, Washington Co., Pa.

1804, 3, 30. Nathan Gause gct Westland MM, to
    m Mary Ailes
1807, 4, 3. Sarah, w Joseph, gct Westland MM

AIRY
1807, 10, 7. Mary, wd, m William PRAY

1798, 8, 3. Mary (form Jones) con mou
1802, 3, 5. Mary, w John, gct Westland MM
1803, 4, 29. Mary rocf Westland MM, dtd 1803,
    3,26
1805, 10, 4. Elizabeth & John, ch Mary,
    recrq
1818, 8, 26. Elizabeth Swindler (form Airy)
    con mcd
1818, 10, 21. John, minor, gct White Water MM,
    Ind.

ALLEN
1852, 9, 30. Phebe J. m Caspar WILLIAMS

1852, 8, 4. Phebe J. rocf Limington MM,
    Maine, dtd 1852,6,26

ALLIBONE
1794, 7, 25. Phebe rocf Indian Spring MM,
    Md., dtd 1794,2,21
1795, 6, 26. Elias, s Benjamin, rocf Indian
    Spring MM, Md., dtd 1794,12,19
1796, 6, 3. Phebe gct Baltimore MM
1796, 6, 3. Elias, stepson of Phebe, gct
    Baltimore MM

ANTRIM
----, --, --. Caleb & Martha [Antram]
    Ch: Mary   b 1797, 8, 31
        Deborah   " 1801, 1, 18
        Joshua   " 1803, 1, 26
        Caleb   " 1805, 9, 5
1819, 5, 3. John d ae 80y bur Sandy Hill
1823, 4, 10. Deborah m Lewis CAMPBELL
1826, 1, 25. Elizabeth d ae 90y bur Sandy Hill
1834, 7, 20. Martha d ae 60y bur Sandy Hill
1837, 11, 30. Caleb [Antram], s John & Eliza-
    beth, Fayette Co., Pa.; m at Redstone, Sa-
    rah BARTLETT, Fayette Co., Pa.
1842, 2, 24. Caleb d ae 86y bur Sandy Hill
1853, 7, 6. Sarah d bur Sandy Hill

1800, 1, 3. Caleb & w, Martha, & ch, Jesse
    & Mary, rocf Hopewell MM, dtd 1799,6,3
1801, 12, 4. Cert rec for John & w, Elizabeth,
    & gr dt, Esther, from Hopewell MM, dtd

1801,5,6, endorsed to Westland MM
1808, 7, 29. Jesse dis mou
1818, 3, 25. John & w, Elizabeth, rocf West-
    land MM, dtd 1818,2,19
1829, 7, 29. Caleb, Jr. dis mcd
1843, 11, 1. Maria [Antram] (form Holloway)
    dis mcd
1854, 8, 2. Joshua [Antram] dis mcd

ARNOLD
1794, 6, 27. Lydia (form Hackney) dis mou

ATHERTON
1794, 11, 21. Mary, Thomas, Francis & Ann, ch
    Henry, rocf Warrington MM, dtd 1791,11,12,
    endorsed by Westland MM, 1794,2,22
1800, 2, 28. Mary Neal (form Atherton) dis
    mou
1800, 5, 30. Thomas dis mou

BAIN
1819, 11, 3. John rocf Aberdeen MM, Scotland,
    dtd 1819,4,15
1820, 5, 31. Cert rec for John some time ago
    endorsed to White Water MM, Ind.

BAILEY
1832, 2, 29. Reuben d ae 60y bur Sandy Hill
1834, 12, 12. Margaret d ae 59y bur Sandy Hill
1853, 9, 10. Ellis d ae 79y bur Sandy Hill

1807, 5, 29. Ellis rocf Westland MM, dtd 1806,
    9,27
1813, 3, 5. Margaret [Baily] rocf Pipe Creek
    MM, dtd 1812,5,16
1814, 4, 29. Reuben [Baily] rocf Indian
    Spring MM, dtd 1797,1,4
1823, 10, 29. Rebecca (form Jackson) dis mcd
1846, 2, 4. Mary C. (form Cock) dis mcd

BALL
1800, 3, 12. Margaret m Samuel GREGG
1806, 12, 10. Sarah m Joseph ALES
1810, 1, 4. Jesse, s Joseph & Sarah, Wash-
    ington Co., Pa.; m at Sandy Hill, Mercy
    VAIL, dt Abraham & Margaret, Fayette Co.,
    Pa.

1798, 5, 4. John & w, Ann, & ch, Joel, Jo-
    seph, Margaret, Jesse, Sarah, James, Su-
    sannah & Iden, rocf Richland MM, dtd 1797,
    8,17, endorsed by Westland MM, 1798,3,24
1798, 5, 4. Jesse rocf Richland MM, dtd
    1797,8,17, endorsed by Westland MM, 1798,
    3,24
1799, 5, 31. Jesse gct Westland MM
1802, 1, 1. Jesse rocf Westland MM, dtd
    1801,10,24
1805, 2, 1. Joel dis mou
1808, 4, 1. Jesse gct Westland MM
1810, 3, 2. Jesse Jr. dis mou
1810, 3, 2. Mercy gct Westland MM
1810, 8, 31. Joseph dis mou

BALL, continued
1812, 10, 30. James dis mou
1813, 3, 5. Susannah dis
1824, 6, 2. Eliza Vail (form Ball) dis mcd

BARBER
1799, 3, 1. Samuel & w, Ann, & ch, Sarah,
    Cornelius, Abraham & Dorothy, rocf Indian
    Spring MM, dtd 1798,9,21
1805, 5, 3. Isaac & w, Mary, & ch, Abraham,
    Isaac, Jacob, Maryann & Jane, rocf Piles
    Grove MM, N. J., dtd 1805,3,21
1805, 5, 3. Rebecca rocf Piles Grove MM,
    N. J., dtd 1805,3,21
1805, 5, 3. Samuel & w, Ann, & ch, Sarah,
    Cornelius, Abraham, Dorothy & Elizabeth,
    gct Short Creek MM
1805, 8, 2. Cert rec for Isaac & fam some
    time ago endorsed to Middleton MM
1805, 8, 2. Cert rec for Rebecca some time
    ago endorsed to Middleton MM

BARNET
1814, 12, 2. Stephen recrq
1815, 10, 27. Samson [Barnett] dis disunity

BARRETT
1802, 3, 5. David & w, Rachel, & ch, Mary,
    Hannah & Rachel, rocf Hopewell MM, dtd
    1801,12,7
1810, 8, 23. Sarah, minor, gct Short Creek MM
1811, 3, 1. Mary & Rachel, minors, gct West-
    land MM
1812, 7, 31. David dis disunity

BARTLETT
1837, 11, 30. Sarah m Caleb ANTRAM

1800, 2, 28. Sarah recrq
1816, 3, 27. Caleb Hunt gct Gunpowder MM, to
    m Rhoda M. Bartlett
1816, 9, 25. Rhoda Hunt & s, Joseph Bart-
    lett, rocf Gunpowder MM, dtd 1816,7,24
1829, 9, 2. Joseph gct Baltimore MM (H)
1830, 3, 31. Joseph gct Baltimore MM
1832, 10, 3. Joseph gct Baltimore MM (the
    first cert was lost)

BEESON
1796, 12, 15. Jesse, s Henry & Mary, Fayette
    Co., Pa.; m at Sandy Hill, Mary CAMPBELL,
    dt William & Mary, Fayette Co., Pa.

1796, 1, 22. Jesse recrq
1807, 8, 28. Jesse dis

BENNETT
1815, 12, 13. Elizabeth m David MILLER
1823, 7, 9. Isaac, s William & Grace, Fay-
    ette Co., Pa.; m at Redstone, Maria JONES,
    dt Samuel & Ruth, Fayette Co., Pa.
        Ch: Louisa   b 1824, 3, 29
            Emla

1812, 7, 3. William & w, Grace, & ch,
    James, William & Elisha, rocf New Garden
    MM, dtd 1812,4,21
1812, 7, 3. Amos rocf New Garden MM, dtd
    1812,4,21
1812, 7, 3. Elizabeth rocf New Garden MM,
    dtd 1812,4,21
1812, 7, 3. Isaac rocf New Garden MM, dtd
    1812,4,21
1824, 8, 4. William [Bennet] Jr. dis dis-
    unity
1829, 4, 29. Maria dis jH
1829, 6, 3. William dis jH
1829, 7, 1. Grace dis jH
1830, 2, 3. Isaac dis jH
1830, 9, 1. Elisha dis mcd
1832, 7, 4. Elisha con mcd (H)
1835, 9, 30. Isaac & fam gct White Water MM,
    Ind. (H)
1835, 9, 30. Maria J. & ch gct White Water
    MM, Ind. (H)
1836, 2, 3. Louisa & Emily, minor ch Isaac
    & Maria, gct White Water MM, Ind.
1840, 12, 2. Elizabeth recrq (H)
1841, 2, 3. Elizabeth & ch, Margaret C.,
    William C., Henry S., Mary L. & Sarah Ann,
    recrq (H)
1843, 6, 28. Isaac & w, Mariah, & ch, Emily,
    Ruthanna, Lloyd D., Edith J., William &
    Linden, rocf White Water MM, Ind., dtd
    1843,4,26 (H)
1843, 6, 28. Louisa rocf White Water MM,
    Ind., dtd 1843,4,26 (H)
1844, 12, 4. Louiza & Emily rocf White Water
    MM, Ind., dtd 1844,11,23
1844, 12, 25. Elisha & w, Elizabeth, & ch,
    Margaret C., William C., Henry S., Mary L.
    Sarah Ann & Cephas J., gct Cincinnati MM
    (H)
1846, 2, 17. Elisha & w, Elizabeth, & ch,
    Margaret C., Henry C., William, Sarah &
    Mary, rocf Cincinnati MM, dtd 1846,1,22
    (H)
1848, 1, 26. Louisa Crocker (form Bennett)
    con mcd (H)
1848, 5, 31. Louiza Crocker (form Bennett)
    dis mcd
1849, 10, 3. Emly dis disunity
1852, 2, 25. Margaret C. Jones (form Bennett)
    dis mcd (H)

BENTLEY
1798, 9, 28. John & w, Susanna, rocf Warring-
    ton MM, dtd 1798,5,12
1819, 4, 21. John & w, Susanna, gct White
    Water MM, Ind.

BERRY
1801, 8, 28. Samuel rocf Westland MM, dtd
    1801,8,22
1803, 7, 1. Patience rocf Hopewell MM, dtd
    1802,9,6
1809, 6, 2. Samuel dis mcd

BINNS
1818, 12, 6. Alice d ae 44y bur Redstone
----, --, --. Jonathan & Eliza
     Ch: Mary   b 1830, 7, 22
         Edward   " 1840, 6, 8
1830, 3, 10. Wm., s David & Margaret, Fayette
     Co., Pa.; m at Redstone, Ruth GIBSON, dt
     Amos & Hannah, Fayette Co., Pa.
     Ch: Gibson   b 1830, 12, 10
         Charles   " 1832, 2, 19
1832, 7, 2. John d bur Redstone
1833, 6, 30. Richard d bur Redstone
1834, 11, 15. Eliza d bur Redstone
1836, 3, 9. Sarah m Charles KINSEY
1838, 4, 5. Ann m Nathan COOK

1819, 8, 4. David & s, John, rocf Knase-
     barrowe MM, Eng., dtd 1818,8,10, endorsed
     by Short Creek MM, O.
1827, 1, 31. William, Richard & David, ch
     David, recrq
1827, 1, 31. Jonathan recrq
1827, 2, 28. Margaret & dt, Sarah & Ann, rec-
     rq
1827, 5, 30. Jonathan gct Salem MM, O.
1830, 4, 28. Eliza (form Pennell) dis mcd
1830, 11, 3. Jonathan rocf Salem MM, O., dtd
     1830,8,25
1832, 8, 1. William & w, Ruth, & ch, Gibson
     & Charles, gct Providence MM
1834, 2, 26. Eliza rst by rq
1836, 11, 2. Jonathan gct Short Creek MM, to
     m Eliza M. Hussey
1837, 6, 28. Eliza M. rocf Short Creek MM, O.,
     dated 1837,4,8
1839, 7, 31. David Jr. gct Short Creek MM, O.
1841, 6, 30. William & w, Ruth, & ch, Gibson,
     Richard, David, Mary & Amos, rocf Provi-
     dence MM, dtd 1841,6,3
1842, 6, 29. William & w, Ruth, & ch, Gibson,
     Richard, David, Mary & Amos, gct Short
     Creek MM, O.
1847, 6, 30. David & w, Margaret, gct Short
     Creek MM, O.
1847, 12, 1. Jonathan & w, Eliza, & s, Ed-
     ward, gct Short Creek MM, O.
1849, 2, 28. Mary, minor dt Jonathan, gct
     Short Creek MM, O.
1862, 4, 30. Gibson rocf Short Creek MM, O.

BLACKBURN
1803, 8, 10. Deborah m Finley McGREW

1794, 12, 26. Zachariah dis mou
1798, 3, 2. Deborah McGrew (form Blackburn)
     dis mcd
1798, 3, 2. Rachel Maricle (form Blackburn)
     dis mou
1803, 6, 3. Moses & w, Mary, & ch, Deborah,
     Thomas & Ann, rocf Monallin MM, dtd 1802,11,
     17
1805, 11, 29. Thomas dis mou
1806, 5, 30. Ann Ong (form Blackburn) con mou

1809, 3, 3. Thomas rst by rq
1812, 5, 29. Finley gct Plymouth MM, O.
1812, 7, 3. Deborah gct Plymouth MM, O.
1815, 3, 21. Plymouth MM refused to accept
     cert granted some time ago for Finley
     [Blackburne]; they returned it to this
     mtg
1843, 3, 29. Lydia (form Wood) dis mcd
1862, 12, 31. Nathan & w, Rebecca, dis join-
     ing Wilburite Separatists

BLAIR
1801, 1, 2. Rebekah rocf York MM, dtd 1800,
     9,10
1816, 11, 20. Rebecca gct Cincinnati MM, O.

BLOOMFIELD
1807, 12, 4. Susanna (form Kirk) dis mou
1810, 11, 2. Rachel (form Kirk) dis mcd

BOGUE
1801, 3, 13. Ruth m John CADWALLADER

1800, 5, 30. William Melton & w, Sarah, &
     ch, Jonathan Bogue, her s by a form m, &
     Fanny & Moses Melton, rocf Trent MM,
     N. C., dtd 1800,1,12
1800, 7, 4. Ruth rocf Trent MM, N. C., dtd
     1800,1,12

BOOTH
1801, 8, 28. Robert rocf Wilmington MM, dtd
     1801,2,11
1803, 12, 30. Robert dis mou
1812, 1, 3. Benjamin [Boothe] rocf Wrights-
     town MM, dtd 1811,6,4
1813, 1, 1. Benjamin dis mou

BORDEN
1801, 10, 30. Elizabeth & ch, Archibald &
     Mary, rocf Pyles Grove MM, N. J., dtd
     1801,7,23
1802, 7, 2. Mary rocf Westland MM, dtd
     1802,6,26
1803, 10, 28. Job [Burden] recrq
1804, 6, 1. Job & w, Mary, gct Westland MM
1806, 2, 28. Levi [Burden] rocf Westland
     MM, dtd 1806,1,25
1810, 12, 28. Elizabeth [Burden] & ch gct
     Miami MM
1811, 11, 29. Levi gct Salem MM, O., to m
     Rhoda Holloway
1812, 2, 28. Rhoda rocf Salem MM, O.
1815, 6, 30. Joel [Burden] rocf Marlborough
     MM, O., dtd 1814,12,14
1815, 9, 29. Mary gct Miami MM
1822, 9, 4. Levi [Burden] & w, Rhoda, & ch,
     Charlotte, Amos, Reuben, Mary Ann & Joel,
     gct Marlborough MM, O.

BOSS
1807, 1, 11. Lydia (form Gibson) dis mou

BOSTICK
1800, 10, 3. Mary Morris (form Bostick) dis
    mou

BOTTOMLEY
1813, 1, 1. Hannah rocf Westland MM, dtd
    1812,11,28
1829, 4, 1. Hannah gct Providence MM

BOUVIER
1815, 9, 1. Elizabeth & dt, Hannah, rocf
    SD MM, Pa., dtd 1815,1,25
1825, 2, 2. Elizabeth & dt, Hannah Mary, gct
    WD MM, Phila., Pa.

BOYD
1814, 6, 3. Sarah rocf Middleton MM, O., dtd
    1813,11,11
1862, 12, 31. Ruth dis joining Wilburite
    Separatists

BRACKEN
1830, 9, 1. Mary [Brackin] recrq
1836, 6, 1. Caleb & w, Mary, gct Upper
    Springfield MM, O.
1840, 6, 3. Caleb & w, Mary, rocf Upper
    Springfield MM, O., dtd 1840,4,25
1842, 2, 2. Caleb & w, Mary, gct Flushing
    MM, Ohio

BRANDON
1794, 2, 21. Ann (form Morten) dis mcd

BRANSON
1836, 8, 3. Aaron rocf Flushing MM, O., dtd
    1836,4,21
1837, 3, 29. Aaron gct Westland MM, to m
    Frances Crawford
1838, 1, 3. Frances rocf Westland MM, dtd
    1837,11,22
1839, 4, 3. Samuel rocf Flushing MM, O., dtd
    1839,1,24
1841, 11, 3. Samuel gct Flushing MM, O.
1860, 4, 4. Aaron dis disunity
1862, 12, 31. Frances & ch, Rebecca Ann,
    Oliver, Richard, Susan, Thomas & Elma,
    dis joining Wilburite Separatists

BREWER
1807, 7, 31. Mary, w Elias, & ch, Sarah, Ra-
    chel, John, Richard, Mary, Martha, Ann &
    Hannah, gct Short Creek MM
1807, 8, 28. Elias dis disunity

BRIGGS
1801, 7, 3. William & w, Esther, recrq
1801, 8, 28. Israel Shreve, Samuel Miller,
    George Green & Maria, ch William, recrq
1802, 12, 3. William & w, Esther, & ch, Is-
    rael Shreve, Samuel Miller, George Green &
    Maria, gct Concord MM, N. W. Territory

BROOK
1794, 9, 26. Ann (form Dillon) dis mou
1795, 5, 22. Mary (form Garwood) dis mcd

BROOMHALL
1824, 12, 16. Mahlon, s James & Hannah, Pres-
    ton Co., Va.; m at Sandy Creek, Ann SMITH,
    dt John & Sarah
1847, 1, 30. Ann d ae 70y bur Sandy Creek

1824, 3, 31. Mahlon recrq
1831, 6, 29. Mahlon dis disunity

BROWN
1801, 10, 8. Thomas, s Eleazer, Fayette Co.,
    Pa.; m at Prividence, Elizabeth FAUSTER,
    wd, dt Timothy Kirk, Chester Co., Pa.
1802, 4, 8. Joseph, s Eleazer & Sarah,
    Fayette Co., Pa.; m at Providence, Sarah
    HEWITT, dt Jonathan & Ann, Fayette Co.,
    Pa.
----, --, --. Isaac & Rebekah
    Ch: Elizabeth b 1803, 4, 9
        Wm.   " 1804, 11, 11
        Joseph   " 1807, 5, 18
1806, 12, 9. Margaret d ae 86y bur Providence
1806, 12, 12. Margaret Jr. d bur Providence

1797, 6, 30. Eleazer gct Deer Creek MM, to m
    Mary Miflin
1799, 2, 1. Eleazer dis disunity
1800, 8, 1. Ann White (form Brown) con mou
1802, 12, 31. Isaac & w, Rebecca, rocf Hope-
    well MM, dtd 1802,9,6
1806, 3, 28. Nathan gct Salem MM, O.
1808, 7, 1. Eleazer Jr. dis mou
1808, 9, 2. Joseph & w, Sarah, & ch, Ann,
    Ruth, Alice & Margaret, gct Salem MM, O.
1808, 10, 28. Isaac & w, Rebekah, & ch, Eliza-
    beth, William & Joseph, gct Short Creek
    MM, O.
1813, 3, 5. Ann recrq
1813, 3, 5. Phebe recrq
1813, 3, 5. Prophet recrq
1816, 4, 24. Thomas & w, Elizabeth, & her s,
    Francis Foster, & their ch, Samuel, Sarah,
    Margaret, Ebanor, Joshua, Timothy & Esther
    Brown, gct Newgarden MM, O.
1818, 3, 25. Prophet gct Carmel MM, O.
1818, 4, 22. Ann gct Carmel MM, O.
1818, 4, 22. Phebe gct Carmel MM, O.

BUCK
1846, 5, 27. Phebe (form Hendrix) con mcd (H)
1846, 11, 25. Phebe gct New Garden MM, O. (H)

BUNDY
1801, 10, 7. Mary m Jacob LEWIS

1799, 11, 29. Josiah & s, Benjamin, Moses &
    Stanton, rocf Core Sound MM, N. C., dtd
    1799,9,1, endorsed by Westland MM

BUNDY, continued
1800, 7, 4. Bathia & dt, Susanna, Abigail &
    Ruth, rocf Core Sound MM, N. C., dtd 1799,
    9,1, endorsed by Westland MM 1799,11,23
1801, 5, 29. Mary rocf Trent MM, dtd 1800,1,
    12,, endorsed by Westland MM, 1801,3,28
1801, 12, 4. Josiah & w, Bathia, & ch, Benja-
    min, Moses, Stanton, Susannah, Abigail &
    Ruth, gct Westland MM
1862, 12, 31. Sarah Ann dis joining Wilburite
    Separatists

BURDEN
1805, 2, 25. Peter, s Peter & Elizabeth, b
----, --, --. Levi & Rhoda
    Ch: Charlotte b 1813, 8, 15
        Amos   " 1815, 8, 26
        Reuben   " 1817, 10, 21
        Mary Ann   " 1819, 9, 10
        Joel   " 1821, 9, 25

BURGE
1807, 12, 9. Jacob [Burdg], s Jacob & Judith,
    Fayette Co., Pa.; m at Redstone, Miriam
    MATHEWS, dt Wm. & Ann, Fayette Co., Pa.
1810, 4, 22. Peter [Burdg], s Jacob & Miriam,
    b
1798, 2, 2. Sarah (form Vail) dis mcd
1802, 1, 1. Jacob rocf Shrewsbury MM, dtd
    1801,7,6
1806, 5, 2. John Negus gct Westland MM, to
    m Miriam [Burdge]
1812, 7, 31. Jacob [Burdge] & w, Miriam, & s,
    Albert, gct Westland MM

BURNET
1799, 5, 10. Robert, s Stephen & Annable,
    Fayette Co., Pa.; m at Center, Ann SMITH,
    dt Thomas & Deborah, Fayette Co., Pa.
    Ch: John   b 1800, 3, 25
        David   " 1803, 2, 4
        Rebecca   " 1805, 1, 24
        Rachel   " 1808, 2, 21
        Deborah   " 1810, 12, 23
1800, 3, 6. Rebecca m Job JEFRIS
1805, 1, 9. Daniel, s Stephen & Anabell,
    Fayette Co., Pa.; m at Redstone, Ann GAUSE,
    dt Solomon & Ruth, Fayette Co., Pa.

1793, 10, 25. John rocf Flushing MM, dtd 1793,
    8,1, endorsed by Westland MM, 1793,9,28
1796, 4, 22. Stephen & w, Annable, & ch, Rob-
    ert & Daniel, rocf Plainfield & Rahway MM,
    dtd 1795,11,19
1796, 7, 29. Thomas rocf Rahway & Plainfield
    MM, dtd 1795.11.19

1805, 3, 1. Job Jeffries & ch, Darlington &
    Catherine, & step-ch, Rachel & Mary Bur-
    nett, gct Miami MM
1811, 3, 29. Stephen & w, Annibal, gct Short
    Creek MM
1811, 3, 29. Robert & w, Anna, & ch, John,

David, Rebecca, Rachel & Deborah, gct
    Short Creek MM
1812, 7, 3. Stephen & w, Annable, rocf Short
    Creek MM, dtd 1812,4,21
1813, 1, 29. Stephen gct Stillwater MM, O.
1814, 3, 4. Daniel & w, Ann, & ch, Anabel
    & Stephen, gct Miami MM

BURWELL
1799, 8, 30. Hannah (form Peden) dis mou

CADWALADER
1798, 12, 19. Jonah [Cadwallader], s Rees &
    Ruth, Fayette Co., Pa.; m at Redstone, Ann
    CATTELL, dt Jonas & Elizabeth, Fayette
    Co., Pa.
    Ch: Elma   b 1800, 1, 7
        Allen   " 1801, 10, 8
        Mifflin   " 1803, 7, 17
        Evalen   " 1805, 9, 7
        Edith   " 1807, 8, 30
        Lea   " 1809, 6, 8
        Jonah   " 1811, 8, 29
1799, 3, 30. Ruth [Cadwallader] m William
    DAWSON
1799, 9, 4. Ruth [Cadwallader] m Samuel
    JONES
1801, 3, 13. John [Cadwallader], s John &
    Sarah, Fayette Co., Pa.; m at Center,
    Ruth BOGUE, dt Mark & Sarah, Fayette Co.,
    Pa.
1801, 5, 13. Amy [Cadwallader] m Benjamin
    SHARPLESS
1807, 5, 8. Isaac [Cadwallader], s John &
    Sarah, Fayette Co., Pa.; m at Center,
    Elizabeth DAWSON, dt William & Sarah, Fay-
    ette Co., Pa.
1811, 8, 29. Ann d ae 32y bur Redstone
1812, 7, --. Jonah Jr. d bur Redstone
1815, 5, 22. Jonah Sr. d ae 41y bur Redstone
1815, 9, 6. Lea d bur Redstone

1796, 2, 26. Asa gct Westland MM, to m Jane
    McVay
1796, 9, 2. Jane rocf Westland MM, dtd 1796,
    8,27
1801, 12, 4. Rachel Vernon (form Cadwalader)
    dis mou
1802, 10, 1. Ann Fry (form Cadwalader) dis
    mou
1803, 6, 3. Elizabeth gct Westland MM
1805, 5, 3. Septimus & w, Sarah, & ch, Sam -
    uel, Septimus, Joseph, Eli & Lydia, gct
    Middleton MM
1805, 5, 3. Mary [Cadwallader] gct Middleton
    MM
1805, 5, 3. Elizabeth gct Middleton MM
1805, 5, 3. Sarah gct Middleton MM
1805, 8, 2. Asa & w, Jane, & ch, Abigail,
    William, Reece & Harmon, gct Short Creek
    MM, O.
1806, 3, 28. John Jr. & w, Ruth, & ch, Anna &
    Sarah, gct Short Creek MM

CADWALADER, continued
1807, 12, 4. Isaac & w, Elizabeth, gct Concord MM, O.
1808, 9, 30. Rees gct Gunpowder MM, to m Hannah Dillon
1809, 2, 3. John & w, Sarah, gct Plainfield MM
1809, 6, 2. Joseph gct Plainfield MM, O.
1809, 6, 2. Hannah, w Rees, rocf Gunpowder MM, dtd 1809,2,22
1809, 9, 29. David gct Plainfield MM, O.
1811, 11, 1. Hannah Irish (form Cadwalader) dis mcd
1813, 10, 1. Rees & w, Hannah, & s, Dillon & Alfred, gct Plainfield MM, O.
1815, 2, 3. Jonah dis mou
1819, 5, 26. Edith, minor, gct Salem MM, O.
1827, 4, 4. Elma gct Salem MM, O.
1829, 7, 29. Mifflin gct Middleton MM, O.(H)
1829, 9, 6. William B. Irish gct Middleton MM, to m Lydia Cadwalader (H)
1829, 9, 30. Mifflin dis JH
1830, 2, 3. Allen dis mcd
1830, 3, 3. Emlin gct Stillwater MM, O.

CAMPBELL
----, --, --. Abel & Susannah
    Ch: Lewis   b 1794, 12, 27
        Wm.   " 1797, 4, 19
        James   " 1799, 10, 22
        Mary   " 1802, 3, 1
        Susanna " 1806, 9, 16
        Abel   " 1809, 11, 27
        Ellis   " 1812, 5, 30
1823, 4, 10. Lewis, s Abel & Susanna, Fayette Co., Pa.; m at Sandy Hill, Deborah ANTRIM, dt Caleb & Martha, Fayette Co., Pa.
    Ch: James   b 1831, 3, 5
        Milton   " 1833, 6, 22
        Mary Ann " 1837, 12, 5
        Joseph M. " 1841, 4, 11
1824, 2, 12. William, s William & Ruth, Fayette Co., Pa.; m at Sandy Hill, Mary ANTRAM dt Caleb & Martha, Fayette Co., Pa.
1834, 8, 16. Elizabeth d bur Sandy Hill
1834, 8, 14. Milton d bur Sandy Hill
1846, 12, 5. Abel d ae 83y bur Sandy Hill
1847, 8, 31. Susanna d ae 79y bur Sandy Hill

1797, 2, 3. Elizabeth Crawford (form Campbell) con mou
1802, 9, 3. Alexander rocf Nottingham MM, dtd 1802,2,27
1811, 2, 1. Elizabeth Mitchel (form Campbell) dis mcd
1811, 8, 2. Alexander dis disunity
1823, 12, 31. William rocf Marlborough MM, O., dtd 1823,12,27
1824, 12, 1. William, s Abel, dis mcd
1827, 5, 30. Mary Price (form Campbell) dis mcd
1829, 7, 29. William & w, Mary, & ch, Morgan, Robert & Ruth, gct Providence MM

1829, 7, 29. James dis mcd
1830, 3, 31. Susanna Jr. dis
1836, 9, 28. Abel Jr, dis mou
1837, 2, 1. Ellis dis disunity
1847, 12, 29. Martha Coldren (form Campbell) dis mcd
1849, 11, 28. Susan Gray (form Campbell) dis mcd
1858, 11, 3. Mary Ann Hibbs (form Campbell) dis mcd
1862, 12, 31. Morgan & w, Priscilla, & ch, Mary Margaret, Elizabeth & Ruth Ann, dis joining Wilburite Separatists
1862, 12, 31. William & ch, Robert, Ruth, Joseph, Eliza Ann, Samuel & Clark, dis joining Wilburite Separatists
1863, 2, 4. Caleb dis mcd

CANADA
1822, 2, 27. Rebecca (form Peden) dis mcd

CAREY
1843, 4, 5. Abel, s Lewis & Rachel, Columbiana Co., O.; m at Redstone, Maria P. MILLER, dt David & Elizabeth, Fayette Co., Pa.

1843, 6, 28. Maria P. gct Salem MM, O.

CARR
1808, 9, 2. Caleb rocf Mount Holly MM, N.J., dtd 1808,8,4
1810, 5, 4. Caleb dis
1833, 12, 4. Upper Springfield MM was given permission to rst Caleb

CARTER
1796, 7, 1. James rocf Westland MM, dtd 1796,5,28
1796, 9, 2. Mary rocf Westland MM, dtd 1796,5,28
1802, 7, 30. James gct Westland MM
1802, 7, 30. Mary gct Westland MM

CARVER
1800, 7, 4. Henry rocf Trent MM, N. C., dtd 1800,1,12
1801, 3, 6. Cert rec for Henry some time ago endorsed to Westland MM

CATTELL
1790, 10, 12. Jonas, s Jonas & Elizabeth, b
1798, 5, 9. Esther m Thomas FRENCH
1798, 12, 19. Ann m Jonah CADWALLADER
1802, 11, 10. Rachel m Stephen DARLINGTON
1814, 11, 2. Hannah m William YEATES
----, --, --. David & Margaret
    Ch: Myra   b 1816, 1, 22
        Ezra   " 1817, 8, 18
        Hannah
        Wright   " 1818, 10, 11
        Jonathan
        Wright   " 1820, 6, 25

CATTELL, David & Margaret, continued
    Ch: William   b 1822, 1, 7
        Elma   " 1823, 11, 12
        Esther   " 1826, 4, 13
        George   " 1828, 2, 22
1828, 2, 3. Jonas d ae 87y bur Redstone (an elder)
1837, 1, 15. David d ae 49y bur Redstone (an elder)
1837, 5, 30. Elizabeth d ae 90y bur Redstone (an elder)
1838, 3, 23. Elma d bur Redstone
1840, 10, 1. James Jr., s James & Deborah, Columbiana Co., O.; m at Redstone, Hannah W. CATTELL, dt David & Margaret, Fayette Co., Pa.
1840, 10, 1. Hannah W. m James CATTELL Jr.
1841, 10, 6. Myra m Jesse R. GARWOOD
1842, 9, 5. Marianna, dt Ezra & Ruthanna, b
1843, 11, 8. James, s James & Deborah, Columbiana Co., O.; m at Redstone, Ann DARLINGTON, dt Stephen & Rachel, Fayette Co., Pa.
----, --, --. Wm. & Mary
    Ch: Albert   b 1847, 7, 20
        Elmina   " 1849, 11, 25
        Sarah
        Elizabeth " 1854, 6, 18
        Esther Beu-
        lah   " 1858, 5, 28
1853, 3, 25. Margaret d ae 67y bur Redstone
1860, 6, 6. Beulah m Ezra ELLYSON

1806, 8, 1. Jonas Jr. gct Abington MM
1812, 5, 29. Jonas rocf Upper Evesham MM, N. J., dtd 1812,3,7
1812, 7, 31. Enoch gct Westland MM, to m Martha Dingee, Jr.
1812, 12, 4. Martha rocf Westland MM, dtd 1812,11,28
1813, 4, 2. Enoch & w, Martha, gct Salem MM, O.
1813, 5, 28. Jonas Jr. dis mou
1813, 9, 3. David gct Hopewell MM, to m Margaret Wright
1814, 1, 28. Margaret rocf Hopewell MM, dtd 1813,12,9
1840, 12, 2. Hannah W. gct Upper Springfield MM, O.
1841, 3, 31. Ezra gct Short Creek MM, to m Ruthanna Patterson
1841, 12, 1. Ruthanna P. rocf Short Creek MM, dtd 1841,10,19
1842, 3, 2. Jonathan W. gct Upper Springfield MM, O., to m Deborah Ellyson
1842, 6, 1. Jonathan W. gct Upper Springfield MM, O.
1842, 9, 28. Ezra & w, Ruthanna P., gct Short Creek MM
1843, 10, 4. William gct Upper Springfield MM, to m Mary Ellyson
1844, 4, 3. Mary rocf Upper Springfield MM, O., dtd 1844,3,23
1844, 7, 31. Ann D. gct Salem MM, O.

1844, 9, 4. Maryanne, minor, dt Ezra & Ruthanna, gct Short Creek MM, O.
1849, 10, 3. George gct Short Creek MM, to m Jane H. Patterson
1850, 1, 30. George gct Short Creek MM
1853, 6, 29. Esther gct Short Creek MM, O.
1855, 5, 2. Beulah gct Short Creek MM, O.
1860, 5, 2. Beulah rocf Short Creek MM, O.
1864, 8, 31. William & w, Mary, & ch, Albert, Almina, Sarah, Elizabeth & Esther B., gct Springfield MM, O.

CHALFANT
1830, 1, 6. Eliza Ann m Joseph NEGUS

1812, 1, 3. Evan & w, Ruth, & ch, Joshua, Evan, Thomas & Elizabeth, rocf London Grove MM, dtd 1811,10,9
1812, 1, 3. Sarah rocf London Grove MM, dtd 1811,10,9
1812, 1, 3. Lydia rocf London Grove MM, dtd 1811,10,9
1812, 5, 29. Mary rocf London Grove MM, dtd 1812,3,4
1813, 10, 1. Lydia Johnson (form Chalfont) dis mou
1815, 4, 28. Sarah Philips (form Chalfant) dis
1815, 6, 2. Mary gct London Grove MM
1816, 6, 26. Ann & ch, Eli & Amos, rocf Fallowfield MM, dtd 1816,5,13
1816, 6, 26. Annanias rocf Sadsbury MM, dtd 1816,5,7
1816, 11, 20. Cert granted 6mo.1816 for Mary Kenaday (form Chalfant) to London-grove MM, returned because of her mcd; dis 1817, 2,19
1817, 12, 24. Thomas dis disunity
1819, 12, 1. Evan Jr. dis mcd
1820, 3, 1. Elizabeth Shurn (form Chalfant) dis mou
1821, 8, 1. Evan & w, Ruth, gct White Water MM, Ind.
1823, 1, 1. Hannah recrq
1823, 4, 2. Able recrq
1823, 12, 31. Eliza & Rachel, ch Abel & Hannah, recrq
1829, 4, 29. Hannah dis jH
1829, 6, 3. Abel dis jH
1830, 4, 28. Rachel dis jH
1844, 12, 25. Abel & w, Hannah, gct Plainfield MM, O. (H)

CHANDLER
----, --, --. Enoch & Hannah
    Ch: Enoch   b 1795, 4, 9
        Mary   " 1797, 7, 22
        Martha   " 1797, 7, 22
1796, 12, 7. Rachel m John COCK
1814, 9, 14. Hannah m Elisha MILLISON

1793, 6, 21. Hannah, w Enoch, & ch, Rachel, Sarah, Margaret, Joshua, Ann, Phebe, Es-

CHANDLER, continued
    ther, Swithen, Hannah & Eli, rocf West-
    land MM, dtd 1793,5,25
1796, 10, 28. Sarah Golden (form Chandler)
    dis mou
1800, 1, 3. Jonathan dis disunity
1800, 7, 4. Margaret Staats (form Chandler)
    dis
1805, 11, 1. Phebe Gummere (form Chandler) con
    mcd
1806, 1, 3. Ann Young (form Chandler) con
    mcd
1807, 1, 11. Miriam, w David, & s, Aaron, rocf
    Wilmington MM, dtd 1807,1,6
1807, 5, 1. Joshua dis mou
1807, 7, 3. Esther Golden (form Chandler)
    dis mcd
1812, 5, 29. Swithin con mou
1812, 7, 3. Eli, minor, gct Plainfield MM
1814, 3, 4. Miriam & s, Aaron, gct Miami MM
1814, 4, 29. Enoch Jr., minor, gct Westland
    MM
1816, 4, 24. Enoch & w, Hannah, gct Plain-
    field MM, O.
1816, 6, 26. Martha dis
1816, 6, 26. Mary gct Plainfield MM, O.
1818, 11, 25. Martha James (form Chandler) dis
    mcd
1819, 9, 29. Spencer dis mou
1820, 6, 28. Martha & ch, Esther, Rachel,
    Jane, Mary & Jason, gct Flushing MM, O.
1820, 8, 2. Tabitha Norris (form Chandler)
    dis
1823, 7, 2. Swithin gct Flushing MM, O.
1826, 5, 31. Flushing MM was given permission
    to rst Martha

CHANY
1794, 4, 25. Tacy (form Greave) dis mou
1814, 10, 28. Thirza (form Christ) dis mcd

CHANTRY
1818, 10, 21. Thomas rocf Goshen MM, dtd
    1818,7,1
1821, 4, 4. Thomas gct Pine St. MM, Phila.

CLARK
1802, 3, 5. Samuel & w, Ruth, rocf York MM,
    dtd 1801,12,9
1804, 8, 31. Samuel Clark & w, Ruth, & ap-
    prentice, Abel Thomas, gct Westland MM
1807, 12, 4. Samuel Clark & w, Ruth, & ap-
    prentice, Abel Thomas, rocf Westland MM,
    dtd 1807,7,25
1845, 7, 30. Anna Maria [Clarke] rocf Totten-
    ham MM, England, dtd 1844,9,5
1845, 7, 30. Catherine [Clarke] rocf Eden-
    derry MM, Ire., dtd 1844,11,14
1848, 3, 29. Catharine Eves (form Clark) dis
    mcd & jas
1848, 5, 3. Anna Maria dis jas

CLELLAND
1808, 4, 1. Mercy (form Wilson) dis mou

COATS
1814, 12, 2. Sidney rocf York MM, dtd 1814,9,
    7
1815, 7, 28. Mary rocf York MM, dtd 1815,6,7
1815, 9, 1. Rachel rocf York MM, dtd 1815,6,
    7

1823, 12, 3. Hannah S. gct Marlborough MM,O.

COBB
1844, 10, 14. Wm. d bur Redstone

1838, 10, 3. Eli Haines gct Falmouth MM,
    Maine, to m Phebe Cobb
1839, 7, 3. Mary rocf Falmouth MM, Maine,
    dtd 1839,5,23
1844, 4, 3. William rocf Falmouth MM, Maine,
    dtd 1843,10,26
1854, 3, 1. Mary gct Salem MM, Mass.

COCK
1796, 12, 7. John, Fayette Co., Pa.; m at
    Redstone, Rachel CHANDLER, dt Enoch & Han-
    nah, Fayette Co., Pa.
    Ch: James   b 1797, 9, 10
        John   " 1799, 9, 15 d 1803,10,19
        Margaret " 1802, 3, 7 " 1803,10,21
        Robert   " 1804, 6, 18 " 1805, 7,15
        William   " 1806, 7, 5
        Benson   " 1808, 9, 24
        Elizabeth " 1811, 2, 18
        Mary   " 1813, 7, 30
        John   " 1818, 3, 30
        Sarah Ann " 1820, 7, 21
1821, 10, 6. Sarah Ann d bur Redstone
1824, 6, 27. John Jr. d bur Redstone

1796, 3, 25. John rocf Hardshaw MM, Great
    Britain, dtd 1794,7,15, endorsed by ND MM,
    Phila. 1796,2,9
1799, 10, 4. Elizabeth (form Moore) dis mou
1808, 9, 30. Elizabeth rst by rq
1820, 11, 29. James dis
1829, 6, 3. John dis jH
1830, 2, 3. Elizabeth dis jH
1836, 3, 30. William dis mou
1838, 4, 4. Benson dis mcd
1838, 8, 29. Maria (form Wood) dis mcd
1846, 2, 4. Mary C. Bailey (form Cock) dis
    mcd
1848, 1, 26. George D. & w, Susan W., & dt,
    Ada, rocf Little Falls MM, dtd 1847,12,7
    (H)
1851, 11, 26. George D. & w, Susan W., & ch,
    Ada & Laviner, gct Baltimore MM (H)

COLDREN
1847, 12, 29. Martha (form Campbell) dis mcd

COLLINS

1807, 6, 3. John, s Francis & Ann, Burlington Co., N. J.; m at Redstone, Esther HUNT, wd, dt Enoch & Rachel Roberts, Fayette Co., Pa.

1807, 7, 31. Esther & dt, Rachel Hunt, gct Chester MM, N. J.

CONNER

1839, 1, 24. Wm. d ae 73y bur Sandy Creek
1845, 2, 27. Elizabeth d ae 76y bur Sandy Creek

1807, 5, 29. Elizabeth rst by rq
1810, 9, 28. Phebe (form Penrose) dis mcd
1819, 6, 30. William recrq

COOK

1803, 10, 28. Rebecca rocf New Garden MM, dtd 1803,4,2
1803, 12, 2. Rebecca Cope (form Cook) dis mcd
1807, 8, 28. Susanna Sharp (form Cook) con mou
1813, 1, 1. Mary Lloyd (form Cook) dis mcd
1813, 3, 5. John dis mcd
1814, 6, 3. Sarah Sparks (form Cook) dis

1839, 1, 2. Ann H. gct Upper Springfield MM, O.

COOPER

1807, 10, 2. William rocf Baltimore MM, dtd 1807,8,12
1808, 12, 2. William dis mou

COPE

----, --, --. Isaac & Sarah
    Ch: Mary   b 1791, 4, 30
        Joseph   " 1793, 1, 6
        John   " 1795, 9, 8
        Judith   " 1798, 1, 15
        Sarah   " 1800, 8, 2
        Anna   " 1802, 12, 4
        Isaac   " 1804, 12, 23
        Ruth   " 1809, 4, 30
        Jesse   " 1812, 3, 10
1797, 12, 14. Samuel, s John & Mary, Fayette Co., Pa.; m at Sandy Creek, Sarah WILLETS, dt John & Rachel, Monongalia Co., Pa.
    Ch: Rachel   b 1799, 7, 11
        Joseph   " 1801, 3, 15
        Samuel   " 1803, 9, 3
        Willis   " 1805, 10, 22
        Lydia   " 1808, 3, 12
        Demsey   " 1810, 2, 1
        Eliza   " 1812, 8, 27
        Elma   " 1816, 7, 23
----, --, --. Joshua & Alice
    Ch: Elizabeth b 1803, 9, 8
        Hannah   " 1805, 2, 26
        John   " 1806, 11, 14

    Ch: Evan   b 1809, 1, 19
        Amos   " 1811, 1, 23
        Hiram   " 1813, 10, 25
        Martha   " 1816, 2, 13
1805, 5, 6. Mary d ae 64y bur Providence
1805, 5, 8. Joseph, s John & Mary, Fayette Co., Pa.; m at Redstone, Elizabeth DIXON, dt John & Mary, Fayette Co., Pa.
1812, 7, 3. John d ae 82y bur Providence
1814, 7, 7. Mary m Thomas Priece
1816, 10, 31. Joseph, s Isaac & Sarah, Fayette Co., Pa.; m at Providence, Elizabeth FISHER, dt Isaac & Elizabeth, Bedford Co., Pa.

1794, 8, 22. Samuel [Coope] dis
1796, 10, 28. Caleb gct Westland MM, to m Amy Dixon
1797, 3, 31. Amy rocf Westland MM, dtd 1797, 3,25
1797, 7, 28. Samuel rst rq
1801, 10, 2. Jesse gct Westland MM, to m Margaret Dixon
1802, 5, 28. Margaret rocf Westland MM, dtd 1802,4,24
1802, 10, 1. Joshua gct Westland MM, to m Alice Fisher
1803, 3, 4. Caleb & w, Amy, & ch, Henry, John & Samuel, gct Westland MM
1803, 3, 4. Jesse & w, Margaret, & dt, Elizabeth, gct Westland MM
1803, 4, 1. Alice rocf Westland MM, dtd 1803,1,22
1803, 12, 2. James D. dis mcd
1803, 12, 2. Rebecca (form Cook) dis mcd
1804, 3, 2. John Jr. & w, Ruth, & ch, Caleb, Simon & Mary, gct Middleton MM, O.
1804, 5, 4. Israel gct Middleton MM, O.
1805, 8, 30. Joseph & w, Elizabeth, gct Middleton MM, O.
1815, 12, 1. Rachel, minor, gct Concord MM, Pa.
1817, 6, 25. Cert rec for Rachel from Concord MM, Pa., dtd 1817,5,1, endorsed to Providence MM
1862, 12, 31. Amos & w, Rachel, & ch, William, Joshua, Thomas, Margaret, Mary Ann & Calvin, dis joining Wilburite Separatists
1862, 12, 31. Jesse & w, Elizabeth, & ch, Caroline, Emily, Mary, Jane A., Mercy, Albert, Allen, Lydia & Almira, dis joining Wilburite Separatists
1862, 12, 31. Lewis & Elma dis joining Wilburite Separatists
1862, 12, 31. Sarah & dt, Eliza, dis joining Wilburite Separatists
1862, 12, 31. Sarah Ann & ch, Rachel W., Mary, Melissa & Lucinda, dis joining Wilburite Separatists
1863, 2, 4. Emmor dis mcd

COPPOCK

1801, 7, 3. John & w, Catherine, rocf Nottingham MM, dtd 1801,3,28

COPPOCK, continued
1802, 1, 1. Cert rec for John & w, Catharine,
    endorsed to Concord MM, N. W. Territory

COULSON
1794, 9, 26. Thomas [Colston] dis mou
1802, 12, 3. Jabez dis mou
1804, 6, 1. Jehu Coulson & w, Jane, & ch,
    Amos & Catherine Harvey, & Uriah, Jehu,
    David, Jabez, Rachel & Jesse Coulson, gct
    Middleton MM

COX
1794, 11, 21. Sarah, w Jacob, & ch, Thomas,
    Robert, Jacob, Rebecca, Rachel & John,
    rocf Warrington MM, dtd 1790,11,12, en-
    dorsed by Westland MM, 1794,2,22
1800, 2, 28. Jacob dis mou
1800, 5, 30. Thomas dis mou

CRAWFORD
1797, 8, 2. Ephraim, s James & Margaret, Fay-
    ette Co., Pa.; m Susanna NICHOLS, dt Sam-
    uel & Elizabeth
1817, 2, 11. Cassandra, dt Elijah & Christine,
    b

1795, 5, 22. Elijah dis
1796, 4, 22. Cassandra Davis (form Crawford)
    dis mou
1796, 9, 2. Able dis mou
1797, 2, 3. Elizabeth (form Campbell) con
    mou
1797, 9, 29. Cert rec for Susanna Nichols
    (now Crawford) some time ago endorsed to
    Westland MM
1798, 9, 28. Elizabeth, w John, gct Westland
    MM
1801, 7, 3. Levi dis mou
1801, 8, 28. Ephraim Jr. dis mou
1802, 10, 29. Ruth Shaw (form Crawford) dis
    mou
1807, 10, 2. Elijah rst by rq
1808, 9, 2. Christianna recrq
1808, 12, 2. Josiah dis mou
1810, 6, 1. Jacob, Levi, Abel & Joseph, ch
    Elijah, recrq
1818, 9, 23. Elijah dis disunity
1819, 11, 3. Christiana dis
1820, 3, 1. Jacob dis
1821, 11, 28. Levi dis disunity
1824, 2, 4. Abel Lee & Josiah, minor ch Eli-
    jah, gct Carmel MM, O.
1832, 5, 30. James Sidwill dis disunity
1837, 3, 29. Aaron Branson gct Westland MM,
    to m Frances Crawford
1845, 7, 2. Cassandra dis jas
1849, 8, 29. Mark, minor, rocf Westland MM,
    dtd 1849,8,22
1851, 6, 4. Mark dis jas
1855, 4, 4. Seaborn dis mcd

CROCKER
1848, 1, 26. Louisa (form Bennett) con mou
    (H)
1848, 5, 31. Louisa (form Bennett) dis mcd

DARLINGTON
1802, 11, 10. Stephen, s Thomas & Hannah,
    Chester Co., Pa.; m at Redstone, Rachel
    CATTELL, dt Jonas & Elizabeth, Fayette
    Co., Pa.
    Ch: Brinton   b 1804, 12, 3
        Israel   " 1807, 1, 5
        Hannah   " 1808, 3, 2
        Thomas   " 1809, 11, 25
        Ann   " 1811, 7, 30
        Jess   " 1813, 3, 4
        William   " 1815, 3, 9
1843, 11, 8. Anna m James CATTELL
1848, 2, 22. Rachel d ae 72y
----, --, --. Brinton & Martha
    Ch: Wm. T.
        Mary
        Elma C.

1801, 7, 3. Stephen rocf Concord MM, dtd
    1801,4,8
1826, 8, 2. Brinton gct Salem MM, O.
1836, 3, 2. Israel gct Adrian MM, Mich.
1836, 3, 2. Ann gct Adrian MM, Mich.
1836, 6, 29. Jesse gct Adrian MM, Mich.
1836, 6, 29. Thomas gct Salem MM, O.
1841, 2, 3. Ann rocf Adrian MM, Mich., dtd
    1841,1,14
1846, 12, 2. William gct Salem MM, to m
    Catherine Williams
1847, 12, 1. Catharine W. rocf Salem MM, O.,
    dtd 1847,11,10
1849, 4, 4. William T., Mary & Elma C. rocf
    Salem MM, Ia., dtd 1849,2,14
1853, 6, 29. William, minor s Brinton, gct
    Red Cedar MM, Ia.
1857, 6, 3. Elma C. gct Bloomington MM, Ia.
1862, 12, 31. Mary gct Bloomington MM, Ia.
1862, 12, 31. William & w, Catherine, dis
    joining Wilburite Separatists
1862, 12, 31. Hannah dis joining Wilburite
    Separatists

DAVIS
1796, 4, 22. Cassandra (form Crawford) dis
    mou
1796, 9, 2. Joshua & w, Jane, & ch, William,
    Jacob, Daniel, Joshua, Miles, Hannah &
    Josias, rocf Indian Spring MM, dtd 1796,1,
    15
1798, 2, 2. William dis mou
1798, 8, 31. Joshua & w, Jane, & ch, Jacob,
    Daniel, Joshua, Miles & Hannah, gct West-
    land MM
1801, 5, 29. Joshua Jr. rocf Westland MM, dtd
    1801,4,25
1801, 7, 31. Cert rec for Abraham & w, Han-
    nah, & ch, Edward, Ellis & Rachel, from

DAVIS, continued
    Fairfax MM, dtd 1800,11,22, endorsed to
    Westland MM
1801, 7, 3. Cert rec for Phebe from Fairfax
    MM, dtd 1800,11,22, endorsed to Westland
    MM
1804, 3, 2. Samuel & w, Mary, & ch, Mary,
    William, Elizabeth, Rachel & Joshua, gct
    Middleton MM
1804, 3, 2. Rebecca gct Middleton MM
1805, 6, 28. Joshua dis mcd
1822, 5, 1. Catharine (form Vail) dis mcd

DAVISON
1816, 10, 23. Elizabeth (form Mathiet) dis mou

DAWSON
1799, 3, 30. William, s Benjamin & Elizabeth,
    Fayette Co., Pa.; m at Center, Ruth CAD-
    WALADER, dt John & Sarah, Fayette Co., Pa.
1807, 5, 8. Elizabeth m Isaac CADWALLADER

1796, 4, 22. William rocf Cecil MM, dtd
    1795,11,14
1805, 8, 2. Elizabeth & George, minor ch of
    William, rocf Cecil MM, Md., dtd 1800,11,
    15; original cert was lost
1808, 10, 28. Ruth & ch, Lydia, Isaac, Susan
    & Sinah, gct Plainfield MM

DENNIS
1795, 12, 25. John & w, Deborah, & ch, Aaron,
    Edith, Asenath, John, Kesiah, Mary & Ra-
    chel, rocf Kingwood MM, dtd 1795,10,8
1804, 5, 4. Aaron dis mou
1808, 9, 2. Keziah dis
1809, 3, 3. Asenith Quail (form Dennis) dis
    mou
1809, 3, 31. Edith dis
1813, 1, 1. John Jr. gct Hardwick MM, N. J.;
    returned 1813,7,2
1814, 4, 1. John Jr. gct Hardwick & Randolph
    MM, N. J.
1816, 11, 20. Mary Richards (form Denis) dis
    mcd

DICKINSON
1802, 9, 3. Joseph & w, Elizabeth, & ch,
    Gains, Elizabeth, Thomas, Joseph, Richard
    Nuzum, Hannah & Rebecca, rocf Robinson MM,
    dtd 1802,4,29
1808, 4, 1. Gains dis mou
1808, 4, 1. Elizabeth Ray (form Dickinson)
    dis mcd
1814, 7, 29. Thomas con mcd
1814, 7, 29. Joseph & w, Elizabeth, & ch,
    Richard, Hannah & Rebecca, gct Darby Creek
    MM, O.
1814, 7, 29. Joseph Jr. gct Darby Creek MM, O.
1815, 4, 28. Thomas gct Darby Creek MM, O.
1816, 2, 21. Cadwalader rocf Phila. MM, dtd
    1815,9,28
1817, 1, 22. Cadwalader dis disunity

DILHORN
1824, 8, 18. Mary d ae 75y bur Redstone

1794, 6, 27. Cert rec for Nathaniel from
    Crooked Run MM, dtd 1794,5,3, endorsed to
    Westland MM
1795, 6, 26. George & w, Mary, & ch, Robert
    Milnor & Mary, rocf Crooked Run MM, dtd
    1795,4,4
1804, 8, 31. Robert Milnor con mou
1819, 12, 29. Robert Milnor gct White Water
    MM, Ind.
1829, 6, 3. George dis jH

DILLON
1794, 3, 21. Moses & w, Hannah, & ch, Ann,
    John, Mary, Rebecca, Moses, Hannah, Martha
    & Lloyd, rocf Gunpowder MM, Md., dtd 1793,
    9,28
1794, 9, 26. Ann Brook (form Dillon) dis mou
1795, 8, 21. Moses [Dillin] & w, Hannah, & ch,
    John, Mary, Rebekah, Moses, Hannah, Mar-
    tha & Isaac, gct Gunpowder MM
1808, 9, 30. Rees Cadwalader gct Gunpowder
    MM, to m Hannah Dillon

DINGEE
1812, 7, 31. Enoch Cattell gct Westland MM,
    to m Martha Dingee, Jr.
1850, 2, 27. Charles Hillis [Dingy] rocf Marl-
    borough MM, dtd 1850,1,29
1857, 4, 1. Charles H., minor, gct Spring
    Creek MM, Ia.

DIXON
----, --, --. John & Mary
    Ch: Nathan   b 1796, 7, 10
        Ruth   " 1798, 10, 28
        Isaac   " 1801, 3, 29
1798, 1, 11. Wm., s Wm. & Rebecca, Fayette
    Co., Pa.; m at Sandy Hill, Jane MORRISON,
    dt Wm. & Hannah, Fayette Co., Pa.
    Ch: Sarah   b 1798, 9, 23
        Samuel   " 1800, 6, 23
        Thomas   " 1802, 2, 25
        Hannah   " 1803, 11, 18
        Susanna   " 1806, 2, 12
        William   " 1809, 5, 25
1802, 8, 27. Rebecca [Dixson] Jr. d bur Red-
    stone
1805, 8, 15. Rebecca [Dixson] d ae 83y bur
    Redstone
1805, 5, 8. Elizabeth m Joseph COPE
1816, 10, 30. Susanna m Samuel HICKLIN
1821, 1, 3. Thomas d bur Sandy Hill
1822, 6, 5. Ruth m Abner HEALD
----, --, --. Isaac & Jane
    Ch: Lydia   b 1824, 9, 22
        John   " 1826, 2, 17
        Rebecca
        Samuel
        Eliza
        Nathan

DIXON, Isaac & Jane, continued
    Ch: Isabella
1833, 11, 20. Wm. d ae 92y bur Sandy Hill
1834, 5, 3. Mary d ae 72y bur Redstone
1835, 7, 14. Rebecca d ae 88y bur Sandy Hill
    (an elder)
1838, 7, 26. John d ae 84y bur Redstone
1841, 9, 26. John d

1795, 11, 27. John & w, Mary, & ch, Rebekah,
    Elizabeth, Susanna, John, Samuel, Edith &
    Mary, rocf Westland MM, dtd 1795,10,24,
    endorsed by Westland MM, 1795,8,23
1796, 10, 28. Caleb Cope gct Westland MM, to
    m Amy Dixon
1801, 10, 2. Jesse Cope gct Westland MM, to
    m Margaret Dixon
1808, 12, 30. Ruth (form Jackson) dis mcd
1809, 6, 2. William Jr. & w, Jane, & ch, Sa-
    rah, Samuel, Hannah & Susannah, gct Short
    Creek MM
1817, 9, 24. Edith Philips (form Dixon) dis
    mcd
1819, 9, 1. Thomas, minor, gct Flushing MM,
    O.
1820, 3, 1. Samuel [Dixen] gct Middleton MM,
    to m Hannah Hatcher
1820, 3, 1. Cert.granted Thomas [Dixen]
    1819,9,1, to Flushing MM, returned unused
1820, 8, 2. Hannah rocf Middleton MM, dtd
    1820,5,22
1821, 5, 30. Samuel & w, Hannah, & s, John
    N., gct Middleton MM
1823, 4, 30. Sarah rocf Flushing MM, O., dtd
    1823,2,21
1823, 9, 3. Nathan dis mcd
1823, 10, 1. Isaac gct Middleton MM, to m
    Jane Hicklan
1823, 10, 1. Mary Hatcher (form Dixon) dis
    mcd
1823, 10, 29. Sarah Johnson (form Dixon) dis
    mcd
1824, 12, 1. Jane rocf Middleton MM, dtd
    1824,3,22
1827, 5, 30. Jane & ch, William & Joseph,
    rocf Flushing MM, O., dtd 1827,1,26
1833, 5, 1. Isaac dis disunity
1834, 1, 29. William dis mcd
1834, 4, 30. Joseph dis jas
1836, 8, 3. John Jr. gct Middleton MM, O.
1847, 2, 3. Jane, w Isaac, & ch, Lydia, Re-
    becca, Samuel, Eliza, Nathan & Isabella,
    gct Salem MM, O.

DOWNARD
1835, 9, 2. Eliza (late Wiggins) dis mou

DOWNS
1802, 9, 3. Ann [Down] (form Duly) con
    mcd
1803, 7, 1. Lydia (form Grist) dis mcd
1810, 12, 28. Mary (form Miller) dis mou
1816, 6, 26. Jeremiah recrq

1816, 10, 23. Jeremiah & w, Ann, gct Plain-
    field MM, O.

DUGDALE
1833, 7, ·3. Ruth gct New Garden MM, O. (H)

DULY
1802, 9, 3. Ann Down (form Duly) con mou
1804, 3, 2. Joshua [Dooley] dis disunity
1807, 7, 31. Lydia [Deuly] gct Short Creek MM
1807, 8, 28. Phebe Rossel (form Duly) dis mou
1807, 8, 28. Sarah Wetsel (form Duly) dis mcd
1815, 9, 1. Rebecca gct Westland MM

EDWARDS
1814, 10, 28. Elizabeth (form Trayer) dis mcd

ELLIOT
1819, 3, 24. Martha (form Miller) dis mcd

ELLIS
1805, 3, 1. Rowland gct Miami MM; rem about
    1800

ELLYSON
1860, 6, 6. Ezra, s Isaac & Elizabeth, Fay-
    ette Co., Pa.; m at Redstone, Beulah CAT-
    TELL, dt David & Margaret, Fayette Co., Pa.

1842, 3, 2. Jonathan W. Cattell gct Upper
    Springfield MM, O., to m Deborah Ellyson
1843, 10, 4. William Cattell gct Upper Spring-
    field MM, to m Mary Ellyson
1852, 2, 4. Daniel & Sarah, minor ch Eliza-
    beth, rocf Upper Springfield MM, O., dtd
    1851,12,27
1856, 12, 3. Elizabeth rocf Upper Springfield
    MM, O., dtd 1856,10,25
1860, 5, 2. Ezra rocf Upper Springfield MM,
    O.
1861, 4, 3. Daniel con mcd
1861, 5, 29. Ezra & w, Beulah C., gct Short
    Creek MM, O.
1864, 8, 31. Elizabeth gct Upper Springfield
    MM

ELWOOD
1848, 8, 2. Ruth (form Lilley) dis mou
1850, 2, 20. Ruth (form Lilley) dis mcd (H)

ENLOW
1812, 10, 8. James, s Luke & Susanna, Fayette
    Co., Pa.; m at Providence, Ruth HEWIT, dt
    Jonathan & Ann, Fayette Co., Pa.
    Ch: Oman   b 1814, 5, 14
        Emily   " 1815, 8, 11
1817, 2, 2. Oman d bur Providence

1811, 6, 28. James [Enlows] rocf Westland MM,
    dtd 1811,5,25

ENOS
1809, 6, 2. Robert & w recrq

ENOS, continued
1809, 6, 2. Mary recrq

EVANS
1793, 9, 27. Mary Newport (form Evans), w
   Thomas, dis mcd
1803, 10, 28. Sarah (form Townsend) dis mcd
1807, 1, 2. Joanna recrq
1811, 8, 2. Joanna gct Concord MM, O.

EVES
1848, 3, 29. Catharine (form Clark) dis mcd &
   jas

EXLINE
1835, 9, 30. Jane (form Smith) dis mou

EYRE
1842, 8, 31. Miller Gibson gct Short Creek
   MM, O., to m Ann P. Eyre

FALLIS
1796, 12, 30. John & w, Mary, & ch, Miriam,
   Rachel, Elizabeth, Mary, Jonathan & Isaiah,
   rocf Hopewell MM, dtd 1796,5,2
1806, 5, 30. Richard & w, Phebe, & ch, Mary,
   Lydia & Rachel, rocf Hopewell MM, dtd
   1805,3,4
1806, 8, 1. Mary rocf Hopewell MM, dtd 1805,
   12,2
1808, 1, 29. Rachel Grabel (form Follis) con
   mcd
1809, 11, 3. Jonathan dis mou
1814, 3, 4. Isaiah dis mou
1814, 3, 4. Richard & w, Phebe, & ch, Mary,
   Lydia, Rachel, Eliza, John & Thomas, gct
   Centre MM, O.
1814, 7, 1. John & w, Mary, & ch, Esther,
   Ann & Sarah, gct Center MM, O.
1814, 7, 1. Mary Jr. gct Centre MM, O.
1816, 9, 25. Center MM, O. was given permission
   to rst Isaiah
1821, 1, 3. Springfield MM, O. was given permission to rst Jonathan

FARQUHAR
1797, 6, 30. Samuel con mou
1802, 7, 2. William & w, Elizabeth, gct Concord MM, N. W. Territory
1803, 7, 1. Samuel dis disunity
1813, 5, 28. Sarah gct Plymouth MM, O.

FARRINGTON
1799, 8, 9. Abraham, s Joseph & Phebe, Fayette Co., Pa.; m at Center, Deborah KIRK,
   dt Joseph & Judith, Fayette Co., Pa.

1797, 2, 3. Abraham rocf Third Haven MM, dtd
   1796,11,17
1801, 10, 30. Abraham & w, Deborah, & s,
   Moses, gct Westland MM
1805, 3, 1. Abraham & w, Deborah, & ch,
   Moses & Judith, rocf Short Creek MM, dtd

1805,1,19
1815, 6, 2. Abraham & w, Deborah, & ch,
   Moses, Judith, Jesse Kirk, Phebe, Billion
   & John, gct Salem MM, O.

FAWCETT
1838, 10, 4. Abner, s William & Abigail, Co-
   lumbiana Co., O.; m at Redstone, Elizabeth
   GARWOOD, dt Jesse & Lydia, Fayette Co.,
   Pa.
1853, 6, 2. Emmir, s William F. & Elizabeth,
   Columbiana Co., O.; m at Redstone, Lydia
   W. MILLER, dt David & Elizabeth, Fayette
   Co., Pa.

1838, 11, 28. Elizabeth G. gct Upper Springfield MM, O.
1854, 5, 3. Lydia M. gct Salem MM, O.

FEAR
1845, 7, 2. Elizabeth (form Smith) dis mou

FELL
1801, 12, 4. Ezra dis mou
1803, 4, 1. Ann dis
1803, 6, 3. Aaron gct Concord MM, O.
1803, 7, 1. Rachel & ch, Rachel & Joseph,
   gct Concord MM, O.
1810, 9, 28. Moses dis mou
1811, 8, 30. Mahlon dis mou

FINCH
1802, 10, 29. Cert rec for Samuel & w, Peninah
   & ch, Lydia, Rachel, Sarah, Ruth & Mary,
   from Hopewell MM, dtd 1802,1,4, endorsed
   to Westland MM
1802, 10, 29. Cert rec for David from Hopewell
   MM, dtd 1802,1,4, endorsed to Westland MM
1802, 10, 29. Cert rec for Elizabeth from Hopewell MM, dtd 1802,1,4, endorsed to Westland MM
1802, 10, 29. Cert rec for Hannah from Hopewell MM, dtd 1802,1,4, endorsed to Westland MM

FISHER
1813, 11, 4. Ruth m Joseph HEWITT
1816, 10, 31. Elizabeth m Joseph COPE

1798, 6, 29. Samuel & w, Ruth, & ch, Rachel,
   Mary, Elizabeth & Francis, rocf Monallin
   MM, dtd 1797,8,24, endorsed by Westland
   MM, 1798,5,26
1802, 10, 1. Joshua Cope gct Westland MM, to
   m Alice Fisher
1802, 10, 1. Samuel & w, Ruth, & ch, Rachel,
   Mary, Frances, Joel & Cassander, gct Concord MM, N. W. Territory
1813, 3, 5. Ruth rocf Dennings Creek MM, dtd
   1812,12,16
1815, 2, 3. Abel dis jas
1815, 4, 28. Elizabeth rocf Dennings Creek
   MM, dtd 1815,3,15

FISHER, continued
1825, 8, 3. Isaac & w, Elizabeth, & ch,
    James, John & David, rocf Providence MM,
    dtd 1825,6,21
1829, 4, 29. Isaac & w, Elizabeth, & ch,
    James, John & David, gct Providence MM
1834, 1, 29. Obed Garwood gct Westland MM, to
    m Mary Fisher

FITZ RANDOLPH
1796, 7, 1. Abigail rocf Plainfield & Rah-
    way MM, dtd 1795,10,21
1804, 3, 2. Israel rocf Westland MM, dtd
    1803,10,22

FOREMAN
----, --, --. Samuel & Elizabeth [Forman]
    Ch: Jesse   b 1805, 6, 2
        Deborah " 1807, 1, 10
        Ann   " 1809, 3, 4
        Rhoda   " 1811, 3, 1
        Hannah   " 1813, 5, 23
        Abner   " 1815, 4, 7
        Ellis   " 1816, 10, 9
        Richard " 1818, 7, 4
        James   " 1822, 2, 16
1805, 1, 24. Samuel, s Robert & Mary, Monon-
    galia Co., Pa.; m at Sandy Creek, Eliza-
    beth WILLETS, dt John & Rachel, Monongalia
    Co., Pa.
1809, 6, 8. Rebecca [Forman] m Jesse WILLITS
1812, 2, 4. Robert [Forman] d ae 75y bur
    Sandy Creek
1822, 5, 14. Mary [Forman] d ae 76y bur Sandy
    Creek
1832, 10, 21. Jane [Forman] d ae 53y bur Sandy
    Creek
1838, 4, 24. Sarah [Forman] d ae 53y bur San-
    dy Creek
1841, 8, 20. Elizabeth [Forman] d ae 60y bur
    Sandy Creek
1841, 8, 21. James [Forman] d bur Sandy Creek
1846, 11, 29. John [Forman] d ae 79y bur Sandy
    Creek
1847, 10, 7. Samuel d ae 72y bur Sandy Creek

1795, 5, 22. Richard dis mou
1808, 6, 3. Isaac dis mou
1813, 7, 2. Rachel gct Plymouth MM, O.
1822, 7, 3. Jane gct Smithfield MM, O.
1826, 11, 1. Jane rocf Smithfield MM, O., dtd
    1826,9,18
1832, 5, 30. Deborah Harvey (form Foreman)
    dis mcd
1833, 1, 30. Jesse [Forman] dis mcd
1834, 7, 30. Ann Harvey (form Foreman) dis
    mcd
1834, 10, 29. Rhoda dis disunity
1839, 12, 4. Hannah Spurgen (form Forman) dis
    mcd
1842, 2, 2. Ellis [Forman] dis mcd
1844, 4, 3. Richard [Forman] dis mcd
1845, 7, 30. Abner [Forman] dis

FORRESTER
1838, 5, 30. Hannah (form Lane) dis mcd
1841, 12, 1. Hannah dis mcd

FOSTER
1801, 10, 8. Elizabeth [Fauster] m Thomas
    BROWN

1801, 5, 29. Elizabeth, wd, & ch, Rachel &
    Francis, rocf Nottingham MM, dtd 1801,3,28
1814, 7, 29. Rachel dis
1816, 4, 24. Thomas Brown & w, Elizabeth, &
    her s, Francis Foster, & their ch, Samuel,
    Sarah, Margaret, Ebanor, Joshua, Timothy
    & Esther Brown, gct Newgarden MM, O.

FRANKHOUSER
1837, 2, 1. Ruth (form Willets) dis mou
1839, 7, 31. Ruth rst by rq

FREEMAN
1815, 9, 14. Mahala m Joseph SMITH

1814, 4, 1. Mahala recrq

FRENCH
1798, 5, 9. Thomas, s Thomas & Marcy, Fay-
    ette Co., Pa.; m at Redstone, Esther CAT-
    TELL, dt Jonas & Elizabeth, Fayette Co.,
    Pa.

1794, 12, 26. James Jr. rocf Evesham MM, N. J.
    dtd 1794,10,10
1798, 6, 1. Robert rocf Haddonfield MM, dtd
    1797,12,11
1799, 8, 2. James gct Mountholly MM
1804, 6, 29. Robert gct Abington MM
1808, 7, 1. Thomas French & w, Esther, & two
    apprentices, Moses Townsend & Patience
    Thomas, gct Salem MM

FRY
1802, 10, 1. Ann (form Cadwalader) dis mcd

FURGUSON
1818, 11, 25. Mary recrq
1825, 8, 31. Mary [Furgason] gct Westland MM

GAMBLE
1796, 9, 2. Joseph & w, Elizabeth, rocf Pipe
    Creek MM, dtd 1795,12,19, endorsed by West
    land MM 1796,6,25
1801, 8, 28. Joseph & w, Elizabeth, gct West-
    land MM

GAREE
1806, 10, 3. Sarah (form Smith) dis mou

GARNER
1849, 11, 28. Rebecca (form Smith) dis mcd

GARRISON
1796, 2, 26. George Walker gct Westland MM,

GARRISON, continued
   to m Anna Garrison

GARWOOD
1800, 11, 5. Jesse, s Obed & Mary, Fayette Co.,
  Pa.; m at Redstone, Lydia ROBERTS, dt
  Griffith & Rachel, Fayette Co., Pa.
  Ch: Mary   b 1802, 3, 31
      Griffith   " 1804, 4, 25
      Rachel   " 1806, 12, 22
      Obed   " 1808, 5, 2
      Joseph   " 1810, 1, 30
      Elizabeth " 1811, 4, 9
      Lydia   " 1813, 4, 4
      Rebecca   " 1815, 3, 11
      Jesse
       Roberts " 1819, 3, 10
      Abraham   " 1819, 3, 10
      David   " 1820, 8, 25
1821, 2, 2. David d bur Redstone
1834, 1, 28. Obed d bur Redstone
1836, 3, 31. Lydia m Israel NEGUS
1838, 10, 4. Elizabeth m Abner FAWCETT
1840, 12, 9. Abraham, s Jesse & Lydia, Fayette
  Co., Pa.; m at Redstone, Mary Ann MILLER
  dt Wm. & Rebecca, Fayette Co., Pa.
  Ch: Lydia Ann b 1841, 8, 28
      Wm. Miller " 1843, 8, 24
      Obed   " 1845, 6, 26
      Rebecca
      Jane   " 1847, 9, 19
      Eli H.   " 1849, 10, 29
      Allice   " 1852, 4, 20
      Jason H. " 1855, 1, 17
      Oliver J. " 1857, 5, 20
      Edith G. " 1860, 1, 19
1841, 10, 6. Jesse R., s Jesse & Lydia, Fayette Co., Pa.; m at Redstone, Myra CATTELL
  dt David & Margaret, Fayette Co., Pa.
  Ch: David
      Cattell   b 1842, 11, 2
      Benjamin V." 1852, 11, 4
      Lydia Mar-
      garet   " 1858, 9, 10
1847, 1, 7. Rebecca m Joseph H. MILLER
1851, 9, --. Lydia Ann d bur Redstone
1853, 10, 5. Lydia d ae 71y bur Redstone
1854, 2, 1. Jesse d ae 75y bur Redstone

1793, 4, 26. Obed, Jr. dis mou
1794, 6, 27. Elizabeth Mason (form Garwood)
  dis mou
1795, 5, 22. Mary Brook (form Garwood) dis
  mcd
1814, 9, 2. Sidney (form Gregg) dis mcd
1820, 8, 30. Mary Vernon (form Garwood) dis
  mcd
1821, 8, 29. Lydia (form Gregg) con mcd
1822, 7, 31. Mary Sr. gct Middleton MM, O.
1822, 7, 31. Darby Creek MM, O. was given
  permission to rst Sidney
1824, 12, 1. Lydia gct Darby Creek MM, O.
1830, 8, 4. Griffith dis mcd

1834, 1, 29. Obed gct Westland MM, to m Mary
  Fisher
1834, 6, 4. Mary rocf Westland MM, dtd
  1834,5,21
1835, 6, 3. Mary gct Westland MM
1835, 11, 4. Joseph dis mcd
1866, 2, 28. William M. dis mcd

GAUSE
----, --, --. Nathan & Mary
  Ch: Amos   b 1805, 8, 30
     Eli   " 1807, 12, 30
1805, 1, 9. Ann m Daniel BURNET
1808, 1, 21. Amos d bur Redstone
1808, 3, 16. Samuel, s Solomon & Ruth, Fayette Co., Pa.; m at Redstone, Mary PEARCE,
  dt James & Mariam
  Ch: Solomon b 1808, 11, 28
     Miriam   " 1811, 1, 7
     Ruthanna " 1812, 8, 27
1809, 11, 8. Eli, s Solomon & Ruth, Fayette
  Co., Pa.; m at Redstone, Martha PEARCE,
  dt James & Mariam
  Ch: James
     Pearce   b 1810, 5, 30
     Jesse   " 1811, 12, 31
     Ann   " 1814, 1, 8
----, --, --. Isaac & Patience
  Ch: Israel   b 1812, 4, 13
     John   " 1814, 7, 10

1795, 6, 26. Ruth recrq
1798, 3, 2. Sarah rocf Kennet MM, dtd 1798,
  1,11
1798, 8, 31. Charles rocf Hopewell MM, dtd
  1798,7,2
1799, 5, 3. Solomon rocf Kennet MM, dtd
  1799,2,14
1799, 6, 28. Samuel, Eli, Isaac, Abraham &
  Ruth, minor ch Solomon & Ruth, recrq
1799, 10, 4. Nathan recrq
1799, 10, 4. Ann recrq
1802, 4, 2. Sarah, w Enoch, gct Concord MM,
  N. W. Territory
1802, 12, 31. Sarah returned cert endorsed by
  Concord MM, N. W. Territory, 1802,11,30,
  endorsed to Westland MM
1804, 3, 30. Nathan gct Westland MM, to m
  Mary Ailes
1804, 9, 28. Mary, w Nathan, rocf Westland
  MM, dtd 1804,7,28
1806, 5, 2. Sarah, w Enoch, gct Salem MM, O.
1808, 4, 1. Jesse rocf London Grove MM, dtd
  1808,3,9
1810, 12, 28. Jesse gct Kennet MM
1814, 3, 4. Solomon & w, Ruth, & dt, Ruth,
  gct Miami MM
1814, 3, 4. Eli & w, Martha, & ch, James
  Pearse, Jesse & Ann, gct Miami MM
1814, 3, 4. Samuel & w, Mary, & ch, Solomon,
  Miriam & Ruthanna, gct Miami MM
1814, 3, 4. Abraham gct Miami MM
1815, 9, 29. Isaac & w, Patience, & ch, Is-

GAUSE, continued
    rael & John, gct Miami MM
1817, 5, 21. Nathan & w, Mary, & ch, Eli, Ann,
    Solomon & Ruth, gct Elk MM, O.
1828, 10, 1. Sarah (form Moore) dis mcd

GIBBONS
1812, 8, 28. Joshua rocf Concord MM, dtd
    1812,1,8
1826, 8, 30. Joshua dis mcd

GIBSON
1797, 3, 4. Hannah m John LAMB
1809, 7, 23. Phebe d ae 38y bur Connelsville
1810, 9, 29. Amos, s John & Ruth, Loudon Co.,
    Va.; m at Redstone, Hannah MILLER, dt
    Robert & Casandra, Fayette Co., Pa.
1830, 3, 10. Ruth m William BINNS
1837, 5, 10. John, s Amos & Hannah, Fayette
    Co., Pa.; m at Redstone, Rebecca GLOVER,
    dt Wm. & Hannah, late of Burlington Co.,
    N. J.
        Ch: Hannah   b 1839, 5, 7
            Lydia S.   " 1841, 2, 8
            Mary Ann   " 1843, 3, 4
            Amos E.   " 1844, 9, 15
            Wm. Stanley " 1846, 8, 6
1842, 2, 18. Amos d ae 62y bur Redstone
1843, 12, 9. Robert E., s Miller & Ann P., b
1844, 11, 8. Hannah Gibson d ae 58y bur Red-
    stone (an elder)

1795, 4, 24. Thomas & w, Hannah, rocf Kennet
    MM, dtd 1795,3,12
1795, 4, 24. Phebe rocf Kennet MM, dtd 1794,
    10,16
1795, 6, 26. John & w, Mary, & ch, Joshua,
    Joseph, Betty & James, rocf Kennet MM, dtd
    1792,9,13, endorsed by Westland MM, 1795,
    3,28
1795, 7, 24. Joshua & w, Lydia, & ch, Hannah,
    John, Lydia, Susanna, Eliza & Mary, rocf
    Gunpowder MM, dtd 1795,4,24
1795, 7, 24. Hannah rocf Kennet MM, dtd 1795,
    3,12
1796, 9, 30. Hannah, w Nathaniel, rocf Uwch-
    land MM, dtd 1795,10,8
1796, 10, 28. Christiana rocf Kennet MM, dtd
    1796,5,12
1796, 12, 2. Christiana Griffith (form Gibson)
    dis mou
1800, 2, 28. Samuel rocf Wilmington MM, dtd
    1798,8,15
1800, 10, 31. Thomas Jr. rocf Wilmington MM,
    dtd 1798,8,15
1804, 11, 30. Samuel dis
1805, 3, 29. Elizabeth Rogers (form Gibson)
    dis mou
1805, 3, 29. Thomas, s John, con mou
1807, 1, 11. Lydia Boss (form Gibson) dis mou
1808, 7, 1. Nathaniel rst by rq with consent
    of Kennet MM
1809, 6, 2. Joseph dis mou

1809, 6, 2. Susanna Shaeffer (form Gibson)
    dis mcd
1810, 11, 30. Hannah gct Goose Creek MM
1811, 5, 31. Thomas Jr. dis
1813, 1, 29. John dis disunity
1813, 3, 5. John Jr. dis mcd
1815, 4, 28. Joshua & w, Lydia, gct Cincin-
    nati MM
1815, 4, 28. Mary gct Cincinnati MM
1815, 4, 28. Eliza gct Cincinnati MM
1826, 6, 28. Amos & w, Hannah, & ch, Ruth,
    John, Mary, Miller & Sarah, rocf Goose
    Creek MM
1842, 8, 31. Miller gct Short Creek MM, O.,
    to m Ann P. Eyre
1843, 8, 2. Ann P. rocf Short Creek MM, O.,
    dtd 1843,5,23
1844, 9, 4. Miller & w, Ann P., & s, Robert
    E., gct Short Creek MM, O.
1848, 5, 3. Mary gct Short Creek MM, O.
1848, 8, 2. John & w, Rebecca, & ch, Hannah,
    Lydia S., Mary Ann, Amos E. & William Stan
    ley, gct Upper Springfield MM, O.
1849, 10, 31. Sarah gct Upper Springfield MM,
    O.

GILBERT
----, --, --. Abner & Ann
        Ch: Elizabeth   b 1799, 11, 4
            Benjamin   " 1800, 12, 13
            George   " 1802, 4, 10
            Susanna   " 1804, 3, 12
            Ann   " 1807, 11, 1
            Jesse   " 1810, 8, 26

1798, 8, 31. Abner rocf Bradford MM, dtd
    1798,4,13
1799, 5, 31. Abner con mcd
1802, 10, 1. Ann rocf Sadsbury MM, dtd 1801,
    10,6
1861, 8, 28. Abner gct Driftwood MM, Ind.,
    to m Anzanetta Walton
1862, 12, 31. Benjamin & w, Lydia, & ch, Sa-
    rah Ann, Mary, Eliza C. & Susan M., dis
    joining Wilburite Separatists
1862, 12, 31. George & w, Hannah, & ch, Rebec-
    ca McGrail, Alice Cope, Ann Eliza, Gil-
    bert, Joshua, Sarah, Edith M. & Ellen C.,
    dis joining Wilburite Separatists
1862, 12, 31. Samuel C. dis joining Wilburite
    Separatists
1862, 12, 31. Ann Hutton & ch, Addison, Mary,
    Finley, Annie, Rebecca, Susan, Linneus &
    Deborah Gilbert (form Hutton) dis joining
    Wilburite Separatists
1863, 2, 4. Abner gct Grove MM, Ind.

GILLILAN
1822, 2, 27. Susannah (form Peden) dis mcd

GLOVER
1837, 5, 10. Rebecca m John GIBSON

GLOVER, continued
1836, 3, 30. Rebecca rocf Evesham MM, N. J.,
    dtd 1835,12,11
1838, 8, 29. William rocf Chester MM, N. J.
1842, 3, 2. William, minor, gct Miami MM, O.

GOLDEN
1796, 10, 28. Sarah (form Chandler) dis mou
1807, 7, 3. Esther (form Chandler) dis mcd

GOMERY
1805, 11, 1. Phebe [Gummere] (form Chandler)
    con mcd
1811, 8, 2. Phebe gct Short Creek MM

GRABEL
1808, 1, 29. Rachel (form Follis) con mcd

GRAVE
----, --, --. Enos & Betty
    Ch: Jesse   b 1799, 7, 29
        Sarah   " 1801, 9, 6
        David   " 1803, 8, 11
        Jonathan " 1806, 5, 22 d 1808, 6,13
        Susanna   " 1808, 11, 22
        Rebecca   " 1811, 4, 30
        Kersey   " 1813, 11, 20
        Enos   " 1816, 8, 15
1808, 6, 13. Jonathan d bur Redstone

1794, 4, 25. Tacy Chany (form Greave) dis mou
1796, 7, 1. Enos & w, Betty, rocf Westland
    MM, dtd 1796,6,25
1798, 8, 31. Hannah Medheart (form Grave) dis
    mou
1816, 6, 26. Jonathan L. & w, Lydia, & ch,
    Israel, Sarahann, Allen, David & Warner,
    rocf Center MM, Del., dtd 1816,5,6
1816, 6, 26. Nathan & w, Hannah, & ch, Stephen,
    John L., Pusey & Elwood, rocf Center MM,
    Del., dtd 1816,5,6
1816, 8, 21. Cert rec for Jonathan & fam some
    time ago endorsed to White Water MM, Ind.
1816, 8, 21. Cert rec for Nathan & fam some
    time ago endorsed to White Water MM, Ind.
1816, 11, 20. Enos & w, Betty, & ch, Jesse,
    Sarah, David, Susanna, Rebecca J., Kersey
    & Enos, gct White Water MM, Ind.

GRAY
1801, 7, 31. Elijah & w, Mary, & ch, Esther &
    Samuel, rocf Bradford MM, dtd 1801,5,15,
    endorsed by Westland MM, 1801,7,25
1803, 4, 29. Elijah & w, Mary, & ch, Esther,
    Samuel & David, gct Concord MM, N. W.
    Territory
1849, 11, 28. Susan (form Campbell) dis mcd

GREEN
1816, 10, 23. Lot rocf Concord MM, Del., dtd
    1815,12,23
1825, 9, 28. Lott dis disunity
1827, 1, 31. Mary (form Morgan) dis mcd

GREGG
1800, 3, 12. Samuel, s Thomas & Ann, Fayette
    Co., Pa.; m at Redstone, Margaret BALL,
    dt John & Ann, Fayette Co., Pa.
----, --, --. Jehu d

1793, 11, 22. Joseph & w, Mary, gct Goose Creek
    MM
1797, 3, 31. Thomas dis disunity
1797, 6, 30. Dinah dis mcd
1797, 6, 30. Israel rocf Goose Creek MM, dtd
    1797,5,29
1798, 2, 2. Samuel & w, Ann, & ch, Mary,
    Abel, Phebe, Eli, Gulielma & Jesse, rocf
    Goose Creek MM, dtd 1797,10,30
1798, 9, 28. Israel dis mcd
1799, 8, 30. John & w, Orpha, & ch, Joseph,
    Cephas, Orpha, Ruth & John, rocf Kennet
    MM, dtd 1794,11,13; two ch b since cert
    was issued, namely, George & Ann, recrq
1801, 5, 1. Samuel & w, Margaret, dis
1802, 4, 2. Samuel & w, Ann, & ch, Mary,
    Abel, Phebe, Eli, Gulielma & Phineas, gct
    Concord MM, N. W. Territory
1804, 9, 28. Thomas Jr. rocf Kennet MM, dtd
    1803,8,11
1804, 12, 28. Ruth Wood (form Gregg) con mou
1806, 2, 28. Thomas dis
1807, 7, 31. John & w, Orpah, & ch, Joseph,
    Cephas, Orpah, Ruth, John, George, Ann &
    Mary, gct Westland MM
1809, 4, 28. John dis
1813, 9, 3. Thomas Jr. dis
1813, 10, 1. Catherine dis disunity
1814, 9, 2. Sidney Garwood (form Gregg) dis
    mcd
1817, 4, 23. Bani dis mou
1817, 11, 26. Amy McCortney (form Gregg) dis
    mou
1821, 8, 29. Lydia Garwood (form Gregg) con
    mcd
1823, 9, 3. Nimrod dis
1826, 1, 4. Zillah gct Darby Creek MM, O.
1828, 6, 4. Amy gct Elk MM, O.
1841, 6, 30. Elihu dis disunity

GRIFFITH
1845, 9, 4. Daniel P. (or David P.), s Amos
    & Edith, Washington Co., Pa.; m at Red-
    stone, Sarah Louisa HOUGH, dt Washington
    & Maria, Fayette Co., Pa.
    Ch: Jonathan   b 1846, 9, 23
        Anna Mary " 1848, 7, 14
1860, 10, 10. Esther P. m Asahel H. PATTERSON
1863, 12, 9. Mary R. m Thomas PENROSE
1866, 4, 11. Edith Ann m Samuel GRUBB

1796, 9, 2. William & w, Sarah, rocf Warring
    ton MM, dtd 1796,6,11
1796, 9, 2. Eli & Samuel, ch William & Sa-
    rah, recrq
1796, 12, 2. Christiana (form Gibson) dis
    mou

GRIFFITH, continued
1805, 6, 28. Christiana rst by rq
1806, 1, 31. Christianna gct Kennet MM
1818, 5, 27. Eli gct Stillwater MM, O.
1820, 3, 1. Abraham gct Plainfield MM, O.
1821, 2, 28. Ruth gct Providence MM
1821, 2, 28. Sarah Jr. gct Providence MM
1821, 4, 4. William & w, Sarah, & ch, Wil-
       liam Mode, Elisha, Milton, Newton, Emlin &
       Elma, gct Providence MM
1841, 6, 30. Daniel P. rocf Westland MM, dtd
       1841,6,23
1844, 10, 30. Martha (form Wiggins) dis mou
1854, 10, 4. Amos & w, Edith, & ch, George,
       Mary R., Amos & Edith A., rocf Westland
       MM, dtd 1854,9,20
1854, 10, 4. Esther P. rocf Westland MM, dtd
       1854,9,20
1857, 7, 29. Daniel P. & w, Sarah, & ch,
       Jonathan & Anna Mary, gct Honey Creek MM,
       Ia.
1858, 2, 3. George P. gct Honey Creek MM,Ia.
1864, 9, 28. Amos T. gct Smithfield MM, O.,
       to m Mary E. Wood
1865, 3, 29. Oscar recrq
1865, 6, 28. Oscar J. gct Short Creek MM, O.,
       to m Mary Elma Pettit

GRISSELL
1813, 4, 2. Elizabeth recrq
1819, 5, 26. Elizabeth gct Short Creek MM, O.

GRIST
1796, 12, 26. Margaret [Ghrist], dt Joseph &
       Margaret, b
1811, 8, 4. Deborah [Ghrist] d ae 62y bur
       Providence

1794, 5, 23. Joseph [Griest] & w, Margaret,
       & ch, William, Phebe, George, Lydia, Re-
       becca, Joseph, Therza & Ohpha, recrq
1801, 3, 6. Phebe New (form Grist) dis mou
1803, 7, 1. Lydia Downs (form Grist) dis mcd
1807, 4, 3. John gct Salem MM, O.
1808, 10, 28. Joseph dis mou
1809, 11, 3. Joseph Jr. dis mou
1814, 12, 2. Rebecca dis
1814, 10, 28. Thirza Chany (form Ghrist) dis
       mcd
1865, 8, 30. Ruth M. [Griest] gct Sugar River
       MM, Ind.

GRISWALD
1804, 3, 2. Samuel Vail gct Westland MM, to
       m Agness Griswald

GRUBBS
1817, 4, 11. Susanna d bur Redstone
1866, 4, 11. Samuel, s Curtis & Ann, Jeffer-
       son Co., O.; m at Brownsville, Edith Ann
       GRIFFITH

1811, 5, 3. Susanna [Grubb] rocf Hopewell

NM, dtd 1811,1,10

GUTHRY
1849, 11, 28. Anna (form Smith) dis mcd

HACKNEY
1806, 8, 8. Aaron d ae 67y bur Redstone
1832, 2, 3. Joseph d ae 61y bur Redstone
1834, 6, 7. Hannah d ae 90y bur Redstone

1794, 6, 27. Lydia Arnold (form Hackney) dis
       mou
1802, 12, 31. John dis disunity
1804, 2, 3. Aaron Jr. dis mou
1806, 7, 4. George dis mcd
1814, 1, 28. Mary Jenkinson (form Hackney)
       dis mou (also Jenkins)
1814, 1, 28. Lydia (form Sidwell) dis mcd
1816, 4, 24. John dis

HAINES
----, --, --. Eli & Ruth
       Ch: Chalkley   b 1803, 7, 8
           Miller   " 1804, 9, 29
           Atlantic   " 1806, 1, 7
           Hiram   " 1807, 4, 2
           Mary   " 1808, 6, 14
           Tamson   " 1810, 1, 31
           Lydia   " 1811, 7, 12
           Sarah   " 1814, 2, 17
           John   " 1817, 9, 4
1812, 4, 13. Mary d ae 62y bur Redstone
1818, 2, 12. John d bur Redstone
1823, 4, 28. Hiram d bur Redstone
----, --, --. Chalkley & Sarah
       Ch: Esther   b 1825, 3, 17
           Ruth   " 1826, 10, 20
           Eliza Ann " 1828, 9, 27
           Joseph W. " 1830, 11, 10
           Lydia M.   " 1832, 11, 15
1828, 10, 2. Tamson m Lewis B. WALKER
1829, 6, 20. Ruth d ae 48y bur Redstone
1831, 8, 29. Mary d bur Redstone
1832, 5, 3. Atlantic m Nathan ROGERS
1833, 4, 9. John d ae 79y bur Redstone
1833, 7, 1. Ruth d bur Redstone
1833, 8, 1. Sarah m Edmund LIPSEY
1838, 1, 10. Lydia m Abraham STANLEY
1853, 6, 2. Phebe D. d ae 77y

1809, 4, 28. Eli & w, Ruth, & ch, Chalkley,
       Miller, Atlantick, Hiram & Mary, rocf Hope-
       well MM, dtd 1809,1,2
1810, 12, 28. John & w, Mary, rocf Hopewell
       MM, dtd 1809,1,2
1823, 4, 30. Chalkley gct New Garden MM, O.
1826, 5, 31. Miller dis
1828, 2, 27. Atlantick gct Smithfield MM, O.
1828, 10, 29. Tamson Walker (form Haines) gct
       Flushing MM, O.
1829, 11, 4. Atlantic rocf Smithfield MM, O.,
       dtd 1829,10,19
1830, 2, 3. Chalkley & w, Sarah, & ch, Es-

HAINES, continued
ther, Ruth & Eliza Ann, rocf Marlboro MM,
O., dtd 1830,1,29
1833, 10, 30. Chalkley & w, Sarah, & ch, Esther, Eliza Ann, Joseph W. & Lydia M.,
gct Upper Springfield MM, O.
1838, 10, 3. Eli gct Falmouth MM, Maine, to m
Phebe Cobb
1839, 7, 3. Phebe C. rocf Falmouth MM,
Maine, dtd 1839,5,23

HALL
1801, 12, 4. Sarah (form Hayhurst) dis mou

HAMMIT
1802, 3, 5. Cert rec for Sarah from Salem
MM, N. J., dtd 1801,2,23, endorsed to Concord MM, N. W. Territory

HAMMOND
1801, 7, 3. George & w, Deborah, & ch, Margaret, Sarah, James, William, Deborah,
Mary, Ruth & Benjamin, rocf Monallin MM,
dtd 1801,4,23
1802, 7, 30. Cert rec for George & w, Deborah, some time ago endorsed to Concord MM,
N. W. Territory
1806, 2, 28. Joseph McGrew gct Short Creek MM
to m Margaret Hammond
1820, 11, 1. Sarah (form Townsend) dis mcd
1844, 12, 4. Ammi Willets gct Smithfield MM,
O., to m Maria Hammond

HANEY
1841, 6, 30. Cassandra (form Miller) dis mcd

HARLAN
1793, 8, 23. Sarah Lackey (late Harlan) dis
mou
1805, 3, 1. George & w, Margery, & ch, Aaron,
Samuel & Moses, gct Miami MM; rem about
1793

HARRIS
1854, 9, 23. Susanna d ae 62y bur Sandy Hill

1794, 2, 21. Jemima dis jas
1800, 8, 1. Mary & Ann, ch Zemeriah, rocf
Trent MM, N. C., dtd 1800,1,12
1800, 10, 31. Josiah, George & Daniel, s Nehemiah, rocf Core Sound MM, N. C., dtd 1800,
5,14
1800, 10, 31. Mary, w Nehemiah, & dt, Mary,
Esther & Sarah, rocf Core Sound MM, N. C.,
dtd 1800,5,14, endorsed by Westland MM,
1800,7,26
1801, 3, 6. Cert rec for Mary & Ann some time
ago endorsed to Contentney MM, N. C.
1802, 5, 28. Mary & ch, George, Daniel, Mary,
Esther & Sarah, gct Core Sound MM, N. C.
1802, 5, 28. Josiah gct Core Sound MM, N. C.
1802, 7, 30. George gct Core Sound MM, N. C.
1807, 7, 31. Susanna rocf Hopewell MM, Va.,

dtd 1806,8,4

HARRISON
1796, 9, 30. Sarah, w Peter, rocf Pipe Creek
MM, dtd 1796,5,14
1798, 8, 3. William & ch, Elizabeth & Rachel,
rocf Pipe Creek MM, dtd 1798,5,19
1800, 1, 3. William dis mcd
1806, 5, 30. Elizabeth & Rachel, minor ch
William, gct Middleton MM
1813, 1, 1. Sarah gct Short Creek MM

HARRY
1796, 9, 2. George & w, Phebe, & ch, Hannah,
John, Thomas, Cyrus & Mary, rocf Kennet
MM, dtd 1795,9,17, endorsed by Westland MM
1796,4,23
1798, 11, 2. George dis mou
1798, 11, 2. Hannah rocf Kennet MM, dtd 1798,
8,16
1799, 2, 1. Cert rec for Hannah some time
ago endorsed back to Kennet MM
1815, 9, 1. John dis mou

HARTLEY
1807, 7, 31. Thomas rocf Buckingham MM, Pa.,
dtd 1806,9,1, endorsed by Short Creek MM,
dtd 1807,3,21
1808, 4, 1. Charity (form Sidwell) dis mou
1809, 3, 31. Thomas dis mcd
1809, 11, 3. Mary (form Sidwell) dis mou
1811, 3, 1. Thomas rst by rq
1812, 10, 2. Barbara recrq
1812, 12, 4. Elizabeth & Leah, ch Thomas &
Barbara, recrq

HARVEY
1804, 6, 1. Jehu Coulson & w, Jane, & ch,
Amos & Catherine Harvey, & Uriah, Jehu,
David, Jabez, Rachel & Jesse Coulson, gct
Middleton MM
1806, 10, 3. Samuel Smith gct Middleton MM,
to m Catharine Harvey
1822, 2, 27. Rachel (form Peden) dis mcd
1832, 5, 30. Deborah (form Foreman) dis mcd
1834, 7, 30. Ann (form Foreman) dis mcd

HATCHER
1820, 3, 1. Samuel Dixen gct Middleton MM,
to m Hannah Hatcher
1823, 10, 1. Mary (form Dixon) dis mcd

HAVILAND
1860, 5, 23. Joseph, s Isaac & Lydia, Duchess
Co., N. Y.; m at Brownsville, Lydia H.
STANLEY, dt Eli & Ruth HAINS

1861, 1, 2. Joseph rocf Nine Partners MM,
N. Y., dtd 1860,11,18
1862, 4, 2. Joseph & w, Lydia H., gct Nine
Partners MM, N. Y.

HAYHURST
1801, 12, 4. Sarah Hall (form Hayhurst) dis
        mou
1805, 3, 29. Rachel Young (form Hayhurst) dis
        mou
1807, 8, 28. Job dis mou
1813, 4, 2. Eli dis mou
1813, 4, 2. John dis mou

HEACOCK
1847, 3, 3. Jesse rocf Muncy MM, dtd 1846,9,
        23
1853, 3, 2. Jesse gct Driftwood MM, Ind.

HEALD
1822, 6, 5. Abner, s William & Sarah, Colum-
        biana Co., O.; m at Redstone, Ruth DIXON,
        dt John & Mary, Fayette Co., Pa.

HEMPSON
1798, 3, 2. John [Hampson] rocf Phila. MM,
        dtd 1797,10,27
1802, 12, 3. John dis mcd
1803, 1, 28. Sarah (form Shotwell) dis mcd

HENDRIX
1811, 8, 30. Isaac rocf Monallin MM, dtd
        1811,1,23
1811, 8, 30. Stephen rocf Monallin MM, dtd
        1811,1,23
1811, 5, 31. Mary, Martha & Ann, minors, rocf
        Monallin MM, dtd 1811,3,20
1813, 12, 31. Stephen dis disunity
1814, 3, 4. Jacob dis mcd
1814, 6, 3. Mary (form Mains) dis mcd
1814, 6, 3. Martha Townsend (form Hendrix)
        dis
1815, 6, 2. Mary gct Salem MM, O.
1840, 3, 4. Phebe [Hendricks] rocf Monallen
        MM, dtd 1839,12,17 (H)
1840, 4, 29. Samuel [Hendricks] rocf Monallen
        MM, dtd 1840,1,20 (H)
1846, 5, 27. Phebe Buck (form Hendrix) con
        mcd (H)

HESTON
1794, 4, 25. William & w, Mercy, & ch,
        Phinehas, Mercy & Amos, rocf Goose Creek
        MM, Va., dtd 1793,10,28
1796, 4, 22. Cert rec for John & w, Elizabeth,
        & dt, Margaret, from Wrightstown MM, dtd
        1795,10,6, endorsed to Westland MM
1796, 7, 1. Cert rec for Titus & w, Sarah,
        & dt, Uphemia, from Wrightstown MM, dtd
        1795,10,6, endorsed to Westland MM
1805, 3, 29. Amos & w, Ann (form Kirk) dis
        mcd
1806, 3, 28. William & w, Mercy, & dt, Mercy,
        gct Miami MM
1810, 12, 28. Miami MM was given permission to
        rst Ann

HEWES
1817, 5, 12. Elizabeth d ae 80y bur Providence

HEWES
1817, 5, 12. Elizabeth d ae 80y bur Provi-
        dence

HEWITT
1802, 4, 8. Sarah [Hewit] m Joseph BROWN
1812, 10, 8. Ruth [Hewit] m James ENLOWS
----, --, --. Able & Rachel
        Ch: Jonathan b 1807, 10, 13
            Martha   " 1809, 7, 31
            Sarah   " 1812, 4, 4
            Joseph   " 1814, 4, 17
1813, 11, 4. Joseph, s Jonathan & Ann, Fay-
        ette Co., Pa.; m at Providence, Ruth
        FISHER, dt Isaac & Elizabeth, Bedford Co.,
        Pa.
        Ch: Cyrus   b 1814, 8, 12
            Amos   " 1816, 6, 24

1802, 12, 31. Able gct Westland MM
1806, 10, 3. Abel & w, Rachel, & ch, Ann &
        Charles, rocf Westland MM, dtd 1806,8,23
1808, 4, 29. Rebecca gct Westland MM
1814, 4, 1. Susanna gct Salem MM, O.
1815, 12, 1. Abel dis
1862, 12, 31. Ruth dis joining Wilburite
        Separatists

HIBBS
1858, 11, 3. Maru Ann (form Campbell) dis mcd

HICKLIN
1816, 10, 30. Samuel, s William & Jane, Stark
        Co., O.; m at Redstone, Susanna DIXSON,
        dt John & Mary

1817, 3, 26. Susannah gct Marlborough MM, O.
1823, 10, 1. Isaac Dixon gct Middleton MM, to
        m Jane Hicklan.

HILL
1796, 9, 2. Susannah (form Yarnel) dis mou
1822, 2, 27. Ruth (form Peden) dis mcd
1822, 5, 29. Ruth rst by rq
1822, 7, 31. Ruth gct Middleton MM, O.

HOBERT
1823, 12, 3. Nancy (form Townsend) dis mou
        (also Hubert)

HOBSON
1795, 9, 25. John recrq
1795, 9, 25. Ann & ch, Francis, Mary, Agness,
        Joseph, Jane, Esther, Phebe & William, rec-
        rq
1796, 9, 30. Joseph rocf Warrington MM, dtd
        1796,2,13
1802, 4, 30. Joseph & w, Ann, & ch, Francis,
        Mary, Ann, Joseph, Jane, William, Esther,
        Phebe & James, gct Concord MM, N. W.
        Territory
1803, 7, 1. John con mou
1804, 6, 29. John gct Short Creek MM, O.

HOGE

----, --, --. John & Mary
    Ch: Sarah   b 1790, 10, 17
        John   " 1793, 9, 6
1806, 10, 10. Jonathan, s John & Mary, Fayette
    Co., Pa.; m at Center, Ann MILLER, dt
    Peter & Isaac, Fayette Co., Pa.
    Ch: David   b 1807, 7, 12
        Jacob Jen-
         kins   " 1810, 8, 8
        Charlotta " 1813, 10, 16
        Wm.   " 1816, 4, 22
        Tacy   " 1818, 6, 8
        Peter
         Miller " 1825, 6, 8

1796, 6, 3. Esther [Hogue] rocf Hopewell MM,
    dtd 1796,1,4, endorsed by Westland MM,
    1796,5,28
1802, 12, 31. Jonathan [Hogue] gct Westland MM
1804, 6, 1. Jonathan [Hogue] rocf Westland
    MM, dtd 1804,5,26
1807, 12, 4. William gct Concord MM, O.
1808, 7, 1. Jonathan dis
1815, 4, 28. John [Hogue] Jr. dis
1830, 11, 3. David [Hogue] dis mou
1835, 6, 3. Anna & s, Peter Miller, gct
    Flushing MM, O.
1835, 7, 1. Tacy gct Providence MM
1835, 12, 30. Charlotte dis jas
1840, 6, 3. Jacob dis mcd
1840, 6, 3. William dis mcd
1840, 11, 4. Rachel (form Roberts) dis mcd

HOLLEN
1835, 9, 30. Susanna (form Smith) dis mou

HOLLINGSWORTH
1808, 9, 2. Isaac rocf Hopewell MM, dtd
    1807,12,7
1816, 4, 24. Isaac gct Hopewell MM

HOLLOWAY
1822, 9, 5. Job, s Amos & Hepsibah, Stark
    Co., O.; m at Sandy Hill, Ann WOOD, dt
    John & Catherine, Fayette Co., Pa.

1811, 11, 29. Levi Borden gct Salem MM, O.,
    to m Rhoda Holloway
1822, 10, 30. Ann gct Marlborough MM, O.
1825, 6, 1. Ann & ch, Maria & Nathan, rocf
    Marlborough MM, O., dtd 1825,2,26
1843, 11, 1. Maria Antram (form Holloway) dis
    mcd
1852, 4, 28. Nathan dis mcd

HOPKINS
1825, 9, 28. Ann (form Townsend) dis mcd
1826, 8, 30. Westland MM was given permission
    to rst Ann
1829, 4, 29. Ann rocf Westland MM, dtd 1829,
    3,26 (H)
1839, 5, 1. Ann dis jas (H)

HOUGH
1818, 6, 3. Washington, s Joseph & Ruth,
    Fayette Co., Pa.; m at Redstone, Maria G.
    PENNELL, dt Jesse & Hannah, Fayette Co.,
    Pa.
    Ch: Anna Maria b 1820, 5, 13
        Sarah Lou-
         iza   " 1822, 10, 24
        Eliza P. " 1825, 7, 25
        Joseph
         William " 1827, 12, 29
1845, 4, 3. Eliza P. m William LLOYD
1845, 9, 4. Sarah Louisa m David P. GRIFFITH

1800, 5, 2. John Jackson gct Westland MM, to
    m Ann Hough
1801, 3, 6. Joseph, Mary, Ruth & Susannah,
    ch Amos, dec, rocf Westland MM, dtd 1801,
    2,28
1806, 1, 31. Mary Jackson (form Hough) dis
    mcd
1806, 8, 29. Joseph gct Miami MM
1807, 8, 28. Susanna, minor, gct Short Creek
    MM
1807, 10, 2. Ruth Ross (form Hough) dis mcd
1808, 12, 30. Susanna returned cert granted
    some time ago, due to her returning
1814, 9, 30. Susan Kimber (form Hough) dis
    mcd
1818, 4, 22. Washington rocf Fairfax MM, dtd
    1818,4,1
1829, 4, 1. Washington dis jH
1829, 4, 29. Maria dis jH
1838, 5, 2. Anna Maria [Hugh] gct Salem MM,
    O.
1840, 7, 1. Sarah Louisa gct Salem MM, O.
1843, 8, 2. Sarah Louisa rocf Salem MM, O.,
    dtd 1843,6,21

HUBERT
1823, 12, 3. Nancy (form Townsend) dis mcd
    (also Hobert)

HUNT
1802, 7, 4. Enoch d bur Redstone
1807, 10, 30. Emmor, s Elisha & Mary, b
----, --, --. Caleb & Rhoda
    Ch: Alfred   b 1817, 4, 5
        Eliza   " 1818, 10, 10
        Ruth Ann " 1819, 11, 25
        Mary   " 1821, 3, 7
        Emund   " 1822, 11, 4
        Elisha F. " 1824, 9, 14
        Mordecai M." 1828, 8, 13
----, --, --. Stacy & Rebecca
    Ch: George
        Dillwyn b 1819, 3, 13
        Milton " 1821, 3, 23

1798, 5, 4. Joshua & w, Rachel, & ch, Mary &
    David, rocf Crooked Run MM, dtd 1797,12,30
1800, 1, 3. William rocf Crooked Run MM, dtd
    1799,8,3

HUNT, continued

1800, 1, 3. Phebe rocf Crooked Run MM, Va.,
   dtd 1799,8,3
1802, 4, 30. Robert & w, Abigail, & s, Seth,
   rocf Westland MM, dtd 1802,4,24
1803, 7, 1. Abigail Jr. rocf Crooked Run
   MM, dtd 1801,5,2
1804, 3, 2. William & w, Phebe, & s, Robert,
   gct Middleton MM, O.
1804, 3, 30. Robert & w, Abigail, & ch, John
   & Seth, gct Middleton MM, O.
1805, 5, 3. Abigail Jr. dis disunity
1806, 10, 31. Elisha gct Baltimore MM, to m
   Mary Hussey
1807, 3, 6. Mary, w Elisha, rocf Baltimore
   MM, dtd 1807,1,8

1807, 7, 31. Esther Collins & dt, Rachel
   Hunt, gct Chester MM, N. J.
1807, 8, 28. Nathan & minor brother, Stacy,
   gct Salem MM, O.
1811, 6, 28. Joshua & w, Rachel, & ch, Mary,
   David, Samuel, Joshua & Jonathan, gct
   Short Creek MM
1811, 8, 30. Stacy rocf Salem MM, dtd 1811,4,
   16
1811, 11, 1. Caleb gct Phila. MM
1812, 12, 4. Caleb returned cert granted some
   time ago, without having used it
1816, 3, 27. Caleb gct Gunpowder MM, to m
   Rohda M. Bartlett
1816, 4, 24. Stacy gct Middleton MM, to m
   Rebecca Mercer
1816, 9, 25. Rhoda & s, Joseph Bartlett, rocf
   Gunpowder MM, dtd 1816,7,24
1816, 9, 25. Rebecca rocf Middleton MM, dtd
   1816,8,12
1820, 6, 28. Cert rec for Nathan & w, Ann, &
   ch, Ira, Esther, Enoch, Caleb & Rachel,
   from Marlborough MM, O., dtd 1820,3,25, endorsed to Providence MM
1822, 5, 1. Stacy & w, Rebecca, & ch, George
   Dillwyn & Milton, gct Providence MM
1823, 10, 1. Esther, Enoch & Rachel, ch Nathan, rocf Salem MM, O., dtd 1823,6,25
1823, 12, 31. Esther, minor, gct Chester MM,
   N. J.
1827, 4, 4. Elisha & w, Mary, & s, Emmor, gct
   Salem MM, O.
1829, 7, 29. Rhoda dis jH
1830, 3, 3. Enoch, minor, gct Salem MM, O.
1830, 3, 31. Rachel, minor, gct Salem MM, O.
1830, 4,28. Caleb dis
1831, 9, 28. Elisha & w, Mary, rocf Salem MM,
   O. (H)
1834, 12, 31. Alfred, Eliza, Ruth Ann & Edmund, ch Caleb & Rhoda M., gct Chester MM,
   N. J.
1835, 11, 4. Elisha & Mary & minor ch of Caleb, gct Chester MM, N. J. (H)
1835, 12, 2. Mary, Elisha & Mordecai M., ch
   Caleb & Rhoda M., gct Chester MM, N. J.
1838, 7, 4. Ruth Ann gct Chester MM (H)

1842, 2, 11. Eliza gct Chester MM, N. J.(H)

HUSSEY

1806, 10, 31. Elisha Hunt gct Baltimore MM, to
   m Mary Hussey
1808, 12, 30. Miriam rst by rq with consent of
   Baltimore MM
1824, 6, 2. Miriam gct Baltimore MM for
   Western District
1836, 11, 2. Jonathan Binns gct Short Creek
   MM, to m Eliza M. Hussey

HUTTON

1798, 11, 30. Joel & w, Mary, rocf Monallin
   MM, dtd 1798,6,21
1798, 11, 30. Elizabeth & Mary, ch Joel &
   Mary, recrq
1801, 7, 3. Rebecca & ch, Susanna, Rachel,
   Nathan, William, James & Deborah, rocf
   Monallin MM, dtd 1801,3,18
1805, 5, 31. Joel & w, Mary, & ch, Elizabeth,
   Mary, Deborah & James, gct Short Creek MM,
   O.
1815, 7, 28. William dis disunity
1815, 12, 27. Thomas Jr. rocf Westland MM, dtd
   1815,11,2
1816, 11, 20. Thomas, an apprentice, gct White
   Water MM, Ind.
1862, 12, 31. Ann & ch, Addison, Mary, Finley,
   Annie, Rebecca, Susan, Linneus & Deborah
   Gilbert (form Hutton) dis joining Wilburite Separatists

INNES

1813, 9, 3. Robert gct Concord MM, Pa.
1822, 2, 27. Mary rocf Providence MM, dtd
   1821,12,25
1828, 12, 31. Mary [Innis] gct Salem MM, O.

IRISH

1811, 11, 1. Hannah (form Cadwalader) dis
   mcd
1826, 2, 1. William B. recrq
1827, 1, 3. Washington & Franklin, ch William B., recrq
1829, 9, 2. William B. dis jH
1829, 9, 6. William B. gct Middleton MM, to
   m Lydia Cadwalader (H)
1832, 2, 29. William B. & ch, Nathaniel &
   Franklin, gct Middleton MM, O. (H)
1833, 1, 30. Franklin, minor, gct New Garden
   MM, O.

JACKSON

1796, 7, 1. Phebe rocf Rahway & Plainfield
   MM, dtd 1795,12,16
1797, 12, 1. Phebe gct Rahway MM
1800, 5, 2. John gct Westland MM, to m Ann
   Hough
1801, 8, 28. Isaac & fam gct Westland MM
1802, 12, 3. Ann, w John, rocf Westland MM,
   dtd 1801,10,24
1804, 6, 1. Susanna Updegraff (form Jackson)

JACKSON, continued
      dis
1804, 12, 28. Samuel dis disunity
1806, 1, 31. Mary (form Hough) dis mcd
1806, 7, 4. Joseph dis mcd
1808, 12, 30. Ruth Dixon (form Jackson) dis
      mcd
1810, 2, 2. Josiah dis mou
1816, 3, 27. Jesse con mcd
1816, 3, 27. Elizabeth (form Sharpless) con
      mcd
1820, 8, 2. John & w, Ann, & ch, Amos,
      Elizabeth, Rebecca, Samuel, Joseph, Thom-
      as, Mary & Amanda, gct Cincinnati MM
1823, 10, 29. Rebecca Bailey (form Jackson)
      dis mcd
1824, 4, 28. Jesse & w, Elizabeth, & ch,
      Elma, Samuel, Mary L. & Jonathan Sharp-
      less, rocf Providence MM, dtd 1824,3,23
1826, 6, 28. Jesse & w, Elizabeth, & ch,
      Elma, Samuel, Mary S., Jonathan & Joseph,
      gct Providence MM
1830, 3, 3. Samuel dis

JACOBS
1801, 7, 3. Hannah rocf Hopewell MM, dtd
      1801,3,3
1804, 3, 30. Hannah Smith (form Jacobs) dis
      mou

JAMES
1818, 11, 25. Martha (form Chandler) dis mcd

JEFFRIES
1800, 3, 6. Job [Jefris], widower, Fayette
      Co., Pa.; m at Sandy Hill, Rebecca BURNET,
      wd, Fayette Co., Pa.

1797, 4, 24. Job & w, Rebecca, & s, Darling-
      ton, rocf Hopewell MM, dtd 1797,2,6
1805, 3, 1. Job & ch, Darlington & Cathe-
      rine, & step-ch, Rachel & Mary Burnett,
      gct Miami MM; rem about 1804
1835, 6, 3. Sarah (form Miller) dis mcd
1836, 11, 2. Jane (form Smith) dis mou

JELKS
1800, 8, 29. Richard & w, Mary, rocf Trent
      MM, N. C., dtd 1800,1,12
1800, 8, 29. Priscilla rocf Trent MM, N. C.,
      dtd 1800,1,12
1801, 10, 2. Cert rec for Richard Jelks & w &
      dt, Charlotte Pate & Priscilla Jelks, some
      time ago endorsed to Westland MM

JENKINS
1832, 11, 1. Israel, s Jonathan & Ann, Hamp-
      shire Co., Va.; m at Redstone, Lydia WILLIS
      dt Robert & Casandra MILLER, Fayette Co.,
      Pa.
1848, 3, 30. William, s Joshua & Sibbel, Co-
      lumbiana Co., O.; m at Redstone, Lydia [Pa.
      MILLER, dt William & Rebecca, Fayette Co.,

1813, 10, 1. Mary (form Hackney) dis mou
1833, 1, 2. Lydia Jenkins & ch, Joel & Susan
      Willis, gct Short Creek MM, O.
1848, 5, 31. Lydia M. gct New Garden MM, O.

JENKINSON
1804, 6, 29. Rebecca [Jenkenson], w Isaac,
      & ch, Ann, Elizabeth, Mary, John, Sarah &
      Rebecca, rocf Westland MM, dtd 1803,12,24
1807, 10, 2. Rebecca & ch, Ann, Elizabeth,
      Mary, John, Sarah & Rebecca, gct Short
      Creek MM
1814, 1, 28. Mary (form Hackney) dis mou

JEWEL
1795, 11, 27. Patience rocf Shrewsbury MM, dtd
      1795,3,2, endorsed by Westland MM, 1795,
      8,22
1806, 7, 4. Patience gct Middleton MM, O.

JOHN
1801, 2, 4. Nathan, s Nathan & Elizabeth,
      Washington Co., Pa.; m at Redstone, Rachel
      JONES, dt John & Betty, Wash. Co., Pa.

1794, 5, 23. Sarah & ch, Mordecai, Susanna,
      Elizabeth, Mary, Jane, Samuel & Daniel,
      recrq
1801, 4, 3. Rachel [Johns] gct Westland MM
1807, 10, 2. Elizabeth dis
1812, 4, 3. Mary Tate (form John) dis mcd
1812, 4, 3. Susannah Tate (form John) dis
      mcd
1815, 10, 27. Jane dis
1817, 1, 22. Margaret Weymore (form Johns)
      dis mcd
1839, 5, 1. Joseph Jr. rocf Westland MM, dtd
      1839,4,24
1840, 3, 4. Jeremiah [Johns] rocf Westland
      MM
1841, 11, 3. Joseph Jr. gct Westland MM
1842, 3, 30. Jeremiah dis disunity

JOHNSON
1796, 4, 22. Caleb rocf London Grove MM, dtd
      1795,4,24
1800, 5, 2. Sarah rocf Hopewell MM, dtd
      1799,5,6, endorsed by Westland MM
1804, 6, 1. Sarah gct Short Creek MM
1808, 10, 28. Zillah rocf Westland MM, dtd
      1808,8,27
1813, 4, 30. Zillah dis
1813, 10, 1. Lydia (form Chalfont) dis mou
1815, 6, 30. Catherine (form Wood) dis mcd
1823, 10, 29. Sarah (form Dixon) dis mcd

JONES
1799, 9, 4. Samuel, s John & Betty, Fayette
      Co., Pa.; m at Redstone, Ruth CADWALADER,
      dt Rees & Ruth, Fayette Co., Pa.
      Ch: Maria   b 1800, 8, 13
          Rees   " 1802, 6, 20
          Susan   " 1804, 5, 7

JONES, Samuel & Ruth, continued
        Ch: Edith   b 1806, 3, 11
            Eleanor   " 1808, 3, 31
            Ruthanna   " 1810, 5, 13
            Clarkson   " 1812, 8, 11
            Samuel
              Howard   " 1815, 7, 22
            Alfred   " 1817, 8, 4
            Franklin   " 1822, 3, 1
1801, 2, 4. Rachel m Nathan JOHNS
1810, 4, 21. John d ae 7ly bur Redstone
1818, 9, --. Alfred d bur Redstone
1823, 7, 9. Maria m Isaac BENNETT

1794, 5, 23. Aquilla & w, Elizabeth, & ch,
    Susanna Buffington & Hannah, rocf Balti-
    more MM, dtd 1793,11,29
1795, 7, 24. Elizabeth & two ch, Susanna
    Buffington & Hannah, gct Gunpowder MM
1797, 11, 3. John & w, Betty, & ch, Rachel &
    John, rocf York MM, dtd 1797,5,10
1797, 11, 3. Mary rocf York MM, dtd 1797,5,10
1798, 5, 4. Samuel rocf Westland MM, dtd
    1798,4,28
1798, 8, 3. Mary Airy (form Jones) con mou
1799, 5, 31. Kersey, son Samuel, recrq
1802, 7, 2. Amy, w Jonathan, rocf Hopewell
    MM, dtd 1802,4,5
1809, 11, 3. Amy, w Jonathan, gct Plymouth
    MM, O.
1810, 9, 28. Martha gct Sadsbury MM
1812, 12, 4. Kersey, minor s Samuel, gct Uwch-
    land MM
1815, 10, 27. Maria, minor, gct Uwchland MM
1816, 10, 23. Deborah gct Baltimore MM for
    Eastern District
1817, 9, 24. John dis mcd
1817, 9, 24. Maria rocf Uwchland MM, dtd
    1817,5,8
1826, 10, 4. Susanna Morris (form Jones) dis
    mcd
1827, 5, 30. Reese dis mcd
1829, 4, 1. Samuel dis jH
1829, 6, 3. Ruth dis jH
1830, 3, 31. Edith, Eleanor & Ruthanna dis jH
1835, 11, 4. Edith T., Eleanor & Ruthanna
    gct White Water MM, Ind. (H)
1835, 11, 4. Ruth & s, Franklin, gct White
    Water MM, Ind. (H)
1835, 12, 2. Clarkson gct White Water MM (H)
1836, 2, 3. Clarkson gct White Water MM,
    Ind.
1836, 2, 3. Franklin, minor, gct White Water
    MM, Ind.
1837, 6, 28. Howard gct White Water MM, Ind.
    (H)
1844, 5, 29. M. Oliver rocf Short Creek MM,
    O., dtd 1843,9,19, endorsed by Dover MM,
    O.
1851, 12, 3. Mathew Oliver con mcd
1852, 2, 25. Margaret C. (form Bennett) dis
    mcd (H)
1861, 7, 31. Mary C. (form Rogers) dis

JOYCE
1807, 1, 30. Deborah, w Thomas, rocf Balti-
    more MM, dtd 1806,12,11

KENNEDY
1816, 11, 20. Cert granted 6 mo. 1816 to Mary
    [Kenaday] (form Chalfant) to London-grove
    MM, returned because of her mcd; dis
    1817,2,19

KENT
1819, 6, 30. Joseph recrq

KENWORTHY
1815, 3, 15. Amos, s William & Mary, Washing-
    ton Co., Pa.; m at Redstone, Mary MILLER,
    dt Robert & Cassandra, Fayette Co., Pa.

1815, 6, 2. Mary gct Westland MM
1865, 6, 28. Rachel gct Springboro MM, O.

KERWOO (also KEVODE and KERVODE)
1803, 10, 28. Ann (form Updegraff) dis mou

KILLE
1858, 4, 1. John, s Clayton & Rebecca, Stark
    Co., O.; m at Redstone, Jane MILLER, dt
    Wm. & Rebecca, Fayette Co., Pa.

1858, 6, 30. Jane M. gct Marlborough MM, O.

KIMBER
1814, 9, 30. Susan (form Hough) dis mcd

KINSEY
1836, 3, 9. Charles, s Aaron & Sarah, Harri-
    son Co., O.; m at Redstone, Sarah BINNS,
    dt David & Margaret, Fayette Co., O.

1800, 7, 4. Christopher & w, Mary, & ch, Sa-
    rah & John, rocf Trent MM, N. C., dtd
    1800,1,12
1800, 8, 29. Richard & w, Rhoda, & s, Jesse,
    Benjamin & Stephen, rocf Trent MM, N. C.,
    dtd 1800,1,12
1801, 1, 30. Cert rec for Richard & fam some
    time ago endorsed to Westland MM
1803, 9, 2. Benjamin & Stephen gct Concord
    MM, O.
1804, 8, 3. Christopher & w, Mary, & ch, Sa-
    rah, John, Absolom & Nathan, gct Short
    Creek MM
1836, 6, 1. Sarah B. gct Short Creek MM, O.

KIRK
1799, 6, 7. Judith m David SMITH
1799, 8, 9. Deborah m Abraham FARRINGTON

1794, 8, 22. Mary dis
1796, 4, 22. Esther, w Adam, & ch, Isaiah,
    Hannah, Rebecca, Benjamin & Ann, rocf Ken-
    net MM, dtd 1783,5,15, endorsed by Fairfax
    MM, 1795,12,26

KIRK, continued
1798, 8, 3. Hannah Webb (form Kirk) dis mou
1798, 12, 28. Rebecca dis
1800, 11, 28. Benjamin dis mou
1800, 11, 28. Mary Taylor (form Kirk) rst by rq
1802, 7, 2. Cert rec for Joshua & w, Mary, & ch, Charity & Timothy, from Nottingham MM, dtd 1801,11,28, endorsed to Concord MM, N. W. Territory
1803, 12, 30. William dis mou
1804, 11, 30. Ann Winders (form Kirk) dis mcd
1804, 12, 28. Isaiah con mcd
1805, 3, 29. Amos Heston & w, Ann (form Kirk) dis mcd
1807, 7, 31. Esther, w Adam, & dt, Phebe, gct Westland MM
1807, 12, 4. Susanna Bloomfield (form Kirk) dis mou
1810, 11, 2. Rachel Bloomfield (form Kirk) dis mcd
1814, 7, 29. Timothy & w, Edith, rocf York MM, dtd 1814,7,6
1814, 9, 2. Beulah rocf York MM, dtd 1814,7,6
1814, 9, 2. Susan rocf York MM, dtd 1814,7,6
1818, 5, 27. Timothy & w, Edith, gct Plymouth MM, O.
1818, 5, 27. Beulah gct Plymouth MM, O.
1818, 5, 27. Susanna gct Plymouth MM, O.
1818, 9, 23. Allum Creek MM was given permission to rst Benjamin

KNIGHT
1864, 11, 2. William & w, Hannah, & ch, John Fisher, William F. & Mary Hannah, gct Spring Creek MM, Ia.
1864, 11, 2. Henry S. gct Spring Creek MM, Ia.
1864, 11, 2. Ann gct Spring Creek MM, Ia.
1865, 2, 1. Jonathan, s William, gct Spring Creek MM, Ia.

LACKEY
1793, 8, 23. Sarah (form Harlin) dis mou

LAING
1795, 10, 23. David rocf Rahway & Plainfield MM, dtd 1795,6,17
1813, 3, 5. David gct Plainfield MM

LAMB
----, --, --. George & Susannah
    Ch: George   b 1791, 12, 21
        Susannah   " 1793, 10, 6
        Thomas G.   " 1796, 4, 23
        Hannah   " 1798, 3, 23
        James L.   " 1800, 11, 7
1797, 3, 4. John, s George, Kent Co., Md.; m at Providence, Hannah GIBSON, dt Joshua & Lydia, Fayette Co., Pa.
    Ch: Joshua G.   b 1798, 12, 1
        Lydia   " 1800, 5, 19
        Eliza Ann   " 1802, 4, 2

    Ch: Mary Ann   b 1804, 3, 12
        John Gibson " 1806, 8, 10
        Rebecca   " 1808, 2, 13
        Daniel   " 1810, 1, 27

1795, 6, 26. George & w, Susanna, & ch, George & Susannah, rocf Kennet MM, dtd 1794,10,16
1799, 3, 29. Michael rocf Cecil MM, dtd 1798,8,18
1802, 12, 3. George dis
1806, 2, 28. Susanna dis
1811, 10, 4. Michael dis mcd & jas
1816, 10, 23. Baltimore MM for Western District was given permission to rst Michel
1820, 10, 4. Thomas G. rocf Providence MM, dtd 1820,9,19
1821, 5, 2. Susannah & dt, Hannah, rocf Providence MM, dtd 1821,1,23
1822, 7, 3. Thomas G. dis mcd
1822, 10, 2. Sarah (form Pennell) dis mcd
1826, 8, 30. Hannah Mather (form Lamb) dis mcd
1846, 9, 30. Susanna gct Salem MM, Ia.

LAMBERT
1800, 1, 3. Abner & w, Winneford, & ch, Mary, Joseph, Benjamin, Albert, Elizabeth, Abner, Daniel & Anna, rocf Trent MM, N.C., dtd 1799,9,7
1801, 3, 6. Cert rec for Abner some time ago endorsed to Westland MM

LANDIS
1847, 9, 1. Louisa [Landies] rocf Baltimore MM for Eastern & Western Districts, dtd 1847,8,5
1851, 4, 2. Louisa C. gct ND MM, Phila., Pa.

LANE
1836, 3, 30. Hannah & Mary Dix rocf Baltimore MM, dtd 1835,11,5, endorsed by Westland MM, 1836,3,23
1838, 1, 31. Mary D. gct Middleton MM, O.
1838, 5, 30. Hannah Forrester (form Lane) dis mcd

LEA
1801, 3, 6. Cert rec for Elizabeth [Lees] from New Garden MM, Pa., dtd 1800,1,4, endorsed by Hopewell MM, 1800,9,1, endorsed by this mtg back to New Garden MM, Pa.
1813, 7, 30. Thomas G. rocf SD MM. Phila., Pa. dtd 1813,1,27
1817, 11, 26. Elizabeth, dt James, rocf Wilmington MM, dtd 1817,8,1
1818, 7, 22. James & w, Elizabeth, & ch, Susanna & Henry, rocf ND MM, Phila., Pa., dtd 1818,1,27
1822, 7, 31. James & w, Elizabeth, & s, Henry, gct Cincinnati MM, O.
1822, 7, 31. Elizabeth gct Cincinnati MM
1822, 7, 31. Susanna gct Cincinnati MM

LEWIS
1799, 11, 6. John, s Samuel & Cathrine, Wash-
     ington Co., Pa.; m at Redstone, Hannah
     ROBERTS, dt Griffith & Rachel, Fayette
     Co., Pa.
1801, 10, 7. Jacob, s Samuel & Catherine,
     Washington Co., Pa.; m at Redstone, Mary
     BUNDY, dt Joshua & Mourning

1800, 1, 3. Hannah, w John, gct Westland MM
1802, 1, 29. Mary, w Jacob, gct Westland MM

LILLEY
1825, 3, 9. Hannah m John WOOD
1825, 5, 11. Ellis, s Thomas & Ruth, Washing-
     ton Co., Pa.; m at Redstone, Elizabeth
     PHILLIPS, dt Solomon & Martha
1825, 9, 7. Phebe m Ellis PHILLIPS
1825, 10, 3. Robert d ae 30y bur Guernsey, O.

1818, 6, 24. Thomas & w, Ruth, & ch, Jane,
     Ellis, Hannah, Phebe, Ruth & Thomas, rocf
     Westland MM, dtd 1818,5,28
1826, 5, 2. Robert rocf Flushing MM
1829, 9, 2. Jane dis jH
1829, 9, 31. Elizabeth dis jH
1830, 3, 3. Ellis dis jH
1830, 8, 4. Thomas dis disunity
1843, 2, 1. Thomas con mcd (H)
1845, 4, 30. Thomas dis mcd
1848, 8, 2. Ruth Elwood (form Lilley) dis mou
1849, 3, 23. Ellis gct Gunpowder MM, to m
     Honor C. Wheeler (H)
1849, 7, 25. Honor C. rocf Gunpowder MM, dtd
     1849,6,6 (H)
1850, 2, 20. Ruth Elwood (form Lilley) dis
     mcd (H)

LIPSEY
1833, 8, 1. Edmund, s Amasa & Rachel, Jeffer-
     son Co., O.; m at Redstone, Sarah HAINES,
     dt Eli & Ruth, Fayette Co., Pa.

1833, 10, 30. Sarah H. gct Short Creek MM, O.

LLOYD
1845, 4, 3. William, s Isaac & Ruth, Belmont
     Co., O.; m at Redstone, Eliza P. HOUGH, dt
     Washington & Maria, Fayette Co., Pa.

1813, 1, 1. Mary (form Cook) dis mcd
1845, 7, 30. Eliza P. gct Short Creek MM, O.
1851, 1, 1. Eliza P. [Loyd] rocf Short Creek
     MM, O., dtd 1850,8,20
1856, 1, 2. Eliza P. Merrit (form Lloyd) dis
     mcd

LOBB
1808, 4, 1. Cert rec for James from Derby
     MM, dtd 1807,4,2; endorsed to Westland MM

LONG
1819, 3, 24. Sarah (form Miller) dis mcd

LONSDALE
1819, 12, 29. Cert rec for Thomas from MM in
     England, endorsed to Providence MM
1821, 1, 3. Cert rec for John endorsed to
     Providence MM

LYNCH
1836, 8, 3. Lydia (form Worley) dis mcd (H)

McCADDEN
1795, 9, 25. John & Elizabeth [McCaddin] dis
     disunity
1817, 9, 24. Ann dis jas
1820, 10, 4. James [McAaden] dis mcd

McCANN
1801, 7, 3. Cert rec for Tacy from Fairfax
     MM, dtd 1800,11,22, endorsed to Westland
     MM

McCORTNEY
1817, 11, 26. Amy (form Gregg) dis mou

McCOWAN
1824, 6, 30. Jane (form Talbott) dis mou

McCRACKEN
1850, 9, 25. Elizabeth (form Tramer) con mcd
     (H)

McDONNELL
1815, 9, 6. John, Allegheny Co., Pa.; m at
     Redstone, Sabina TOWNSEND, dt Jesse &
     Edith, Fayette Co., Pa.
1822, 9, 4. Wm. P., s John & Sebina M., b
1822, 9, 5. Wm. P. d bur Pittsburgh
1822, 9, 15. John M. d ae 33y bur Pittsburgh

1812, 2, 28. John [McDonald] rocf Dublin MM,
     dtd 1810,8,14, endorsed by Phila. MM,
     1811,6,27
1829, 6, 3. Sabina T. dis jH
1838, 1, 31. Sabina T. gct Green Plains MM,
     O. (H)

McGRAIL
1806, 8, 29. Thomas & w, Rachel, & w, James,
     rocf Monallin MM, dtd 1803,6,23; a dt,
     Mary, b since cert was issued
1809, 6, 2. John & w, Mary, & ch, Moses,
     Elizabeth & Mary, rocf Monallin MM, dtd
     1804,11,21; the following ch b since dte
     of cert also rec: Rebecca, Sarah & Deborah
1815, 6, 2. Thomas & w, Rebecca, & ch, James
     Mary & Ann, gct Plymouth MM
1816, 6, 26. Moses dis mcd
1816, 6, 26. Sarah (form Means) dis mcd

McGREW
----, --, --. James C. & Rachel
     Ch: James W.   b 1796, 1, 10
         Ebeneezer   " 1797, 9, 30
         Rachel   " 1799, 10, 29

McGREW, James C. & Rachel, continued
    Ch: Mary   b 1802, 12, 30
        Dinah   " 1805, 2, 8
        Sinah   " 1807, 7, 15
        Finley   " 1809, 10, 17
1796, 12, 14. Mary m Samuel TALBOTT
1800, 12, 9. Ebenezer d bur Providence
----, --, --. James Jr., s James A. & Jane,
    b 1778,9,29; m Rebeckah -----
    Ch: Mary   b 1802, 12, 18
        Jane   " 1804, 7, 1
        Rosanna   " 1805, 5, 10
1803, 8, 10. Finley, s James A. & Jane, West-
    moreland Co., Pa.; m at Sewickley, Deborah
    BLACKBURN, dt Moses & Mary, Westmoreland
    Co., Pa.
1805, 7, 31. Jane d bur Seweekley

1796, 6, 3. Elizabeth Ong (form McGrew) con
    mou
1796, 9, 30. James rocf Monallin MM, dtd
    1796,7,20
1796, 9, 30. Elizabeth & ch, Nathan, Jane,
    James, Deborah, Joseph, Simeon, Finley &
    Thomas, rocf Monallen MM, dtd 1795,2,9
1798, 3, 2. Deborah (form Blackburn) dis
    mcd
1801, 5, 29. Jacob dis mcd
1801, 5, 29. Jane dis mcd
1802, 5, 28. James Jr., s James A., con mcd
1802, 5, 28. Rebecca (form Ong) con mcd
1802, 7, 2. Nathan con mou
1803, 12, 2. James, s James B., dis mcd
1803, 12, 2. Isabella dis mcd
1805, 2, 1. Deborah con mou
1805, 6, 28. Nathan gct Short Creek MM, O.
1806, 2, 28. Joseph gct Short Creek MM, to
    m Margaret Hammond
1809, 6, 30. Joseph gct Plymouth MM, O.
1810, 3, 2. Thomas dis disunity
1810, 5, 4. Samuel rocf Monallen MM, dtd
    1809,9,20
1810, 6, 1. Rosanna Painter (form McGrew)
    dis mcd
1812, 8, 28. Mary & Martha rocf Monallen MM,
    dtd 1812,4,23
1812, 12, 4. Nathan & w, Martha, & s, Stephen,
    rocf Monallen MM, dtd 1812,3,18
1813, 7, 2. Simon dis mou
1813, 12, 31. Samuel dis disunity
1813, 1, 29. James C. & w, Rachel, & ch,
    James, Rachel, Mary, Dinah, Sinah & Find-
    ley, gct Short Creek MM
1815, 3, 3. James rocf Monallen MM, dtd
    1814,6,20
1815, 6, 30. James, s Nathan, dis disunity
1862, 12, 31. Nathan & Susan dis joining Wil-
    burite Separatists

McGUILKIN (also McQuilkin)
1832, 1, 4. Teresa (late Wiggins) dis mcd

McKAY
1812, 10, 30. Jane (form Underwood) dis mou

McMULLIN
1826, 8, 30. Hannah (form Wiggins) dis mcd

McNUTT
1812, 5, 29. Hannah rocf Notingham MM, dtd
    1811,12,6

McVAY
1796, 2, 26. Asa Cadwalader gct Westland MM,
    to m Jane McVay

MAERKT
1862, 4, 2. Frederick & w, Amelia, & ch,
    Williamina, Hannah G., Jane & Anna, rocf
    Salem MM
1862, 12, 31. Frederick & w, Amelia, & ch,
    Wilhelmina, Hannah C., Jane & Anna, dis
    joining Wilburite Separatists

MARICLE
1798, 3, 2. Rachel (form Blackburn) dis mou

MARSH
1807, 1, 4. Mary Ann, dt James & Edith, b

1806, 5, 2. James & w, Edith, & ch, Zillah,
    Amos & Miriam, rocf Baltimore MM, dtd
    1806,1,9
1808, 4, 29. James & w, Edith, & ch, Zillah,
    Amos, Miriam & Mary Ann, gct Middleton MM
1813, 1, 29. Dinah (form Mains) dis mcd

MARSHALL
1816, 6, 26. William & w, Hannah, & ch, Thom-
    as & Elizabeth, rocf Center MM, Del., dtd
    1816,5,6
1816, 6, 26. Jane [Marshal] rocf Center MM,
    Del., dtd 1816,5,6
1816, 8, 21. Cert rec for William & fam some
    time ago endorsed to Short Creek MM
1816, 8, 21. Cert rec for Jane [Marshal] some
    time ago endorsed to Short Creek MM

MARTIN
1808, 7, 1. Edith, minor, rocf Westland MM,
    dtd 1808,5,28
1812, 10, 30. Edith, minor, gct Westland MM

MASON
1794, 6, 27. Elizabeth (form Garwood) dis
    mou

MATHER
1826, 8, 30. Hannah (form Lamb) dis mcd
1844, 4, 3. Hannah G. rst by rq
1846, 9, 30. Hannah G. gct Salem MM, Ia.

MATHEWS
1807, 12, 9. Miriam m Jacob BURDG

MATHEWS, continued
1807, 10, 2. Miriam rocf Westland MM, dtd
    1807,7,25
1818, 5, 27. Charles rocf Green St. MM,
    Phila., dtd 1818,3,19

MATHIET
----, --, --. George & Ruth [Mathiot]
        Ch: Mary   b 1796, 10, 9
            Joshua   " 1800, 4, 4
            Casandra " 1803, 4, 28
            John   " 1805, 7, 7
            Susan   " 1807, 9, 21
            Ann   " 1810, 2, 13

1797, 9, 29. George & w, Ruth, & ch, Jacob,
    Elizabeth, Catharine & Mary, rocf Indian
    Spring MM, dtd 1797,1,4
1805, 5, 3. George dis disunity
1816, 7, 24. Jacob dis mcd
1816, 10, 23. Elizabeth Davison (form Mathiet)
    dis mou

MAXEN
----, --, --. Stephen & Margaret [Maxson]
        Ch: Jesse   b 1797, 3, 30
            Stephen   " 1801, 10, 17

1794, 7, 25. Jonathan [Maxson] & w, Mary
    Magdalen, & ch, David & Nathan, rocf
    Shrewsbury MM, dtd 1794,5,5
1798, 9, 28. Margaret & ch, Joel & Jesse,
    recrq
1805, 6, 28. Margaret dis disunity
1808, 6, 3. Jonathan [Maxin] & w, Mary Mag-
    dalen, & ch, David, Nathan, John & William,
    gct Plainfield MM
1809, 9, 1. Joel dis mou
1820, 2, 2. Hannah recrq
1824, 11, 3. Hannah [Maxon] gct Plainfield
    MM, O.

MAYLIN
1830, 6, 30. Sarah rocf Phila. MM, dtd 1829,9,
    24
1832, 1, 4. Sarah gct Cincinnati MM, O.

MEANS
----, --, --. James & Rebecca
        Ch: Findley   b 1788, 12, 17
            Elizabeth " 1790, 10, 1
            Dinah   " 1793, 3, 18
            Mary   " 1795, 3, 1
            Sarah   " 1796, 12, 17
            Jane   " 1797, 10, 24
            Rebeckah " 1799, 12, 15
            Margaret " 1801, 6, 15
            James   " 1805, 7, 28
            Deborah   " 1807, 10, 17
            John   " 1809, 7, 9
1797, 11, 15. Jane d bur Seweekley

1795, 9, 25. James & ch, Finley, Elizabeth,

Dinah & Mary, recrq
1796, 6, 3. Rebekah, w James, rocf Monallin
    MM, dtd 1796,3,23
1808, 9, 2. Elizabeth Newlin (form Means)
    dis mou
1811, 11, 29. Finley [Mains] dis mou
1813, 1, 29. Dinah Marsh (form Mains) dis
    mcd
1814, 6, 3. Mary Hendrix (form Mains) dis
    mcd
1816, 6, 26. Sarah McGrail (form Means) dis
    mcd

MECHEM
1836, 3, 2. Joshua [Mechend] rocf Stillwater
    MM, dtd 1835,6,20

MEDHEART
1798, 8, 31. Hannah (form Grave) dis mou

MELTON
1800, 5, 30. William & w, Sarah, & ch, Jona-
    than Bogue, her s by a form m & Fanny &
    Moses Melton, rocf Trent MM, N. C., dtd
    1800,1,12
1802, 12, 31. Cert rec for William & fam some
    time ago endorsed to Concord MM, N. W.
    Territory

MENDENHALL
1832, 2, 5. Jane [Mendinghall] d bur Sandy
    Hill

1794, 5, 23. Jane recrq

MERCER
1799, 8, 30. Rebecca (form Roberts) dis mou
1807, 8, 28. John & w, Hepsibah, & ch, Mathi-
    as, Solomon & Joseph, rocf Kennet MM,
    dtd 1807,4,7
1809, 12, 29. John & w, Hepsibah, & ch, Ma-
    thias, Solomon, Joseph & Daniel, gct West-
    land MM
1816, 4, 24. Stacy Hunt gct Middleton MM, to
    m Rebecca Mercer
1818, 2, 18. Hannah rocf Middleton MM, dtd
    1817,12,15
1822, 5, 1. Hannah gct Providence MM

MERRIT
1856, 1, 2. Eliza P. (form Lloyd) dis mcd

MIFLIN
1797, 6, 30. Eleazer Brown gct Deer Creek MM,
    to m Mary Miflin

MILLER
1806, 10, 10. Anne m Jonathan HOGE
----, --, --. Solomon & Ruth
        Ch: Lydia   b 1807, 4, 8
            Ann   " 1809, 6, 20
            Robert   " 1811, 1, 21
            Thomas N. " 1812, 8, 12

MILLER, Solomon & Ruth, continued
    Ch: Lewis N.   b 1814, 6, 29
1810, 9, 29. Hannah m Amos GIBSON
----, --, --. William & Rebeckah
    Ch: Warrick   b 1811, 12, 5
       Hiram   " 1813, 10, 31
       Sarah   " 1816, 9, 7
       Mary Ann   " 1819, 2, 5
       Cassandrew   " 1821, 3, 3
       Lydia   " 1823, 6, 11
       Jane   " 1825, 6, 30
       Wm. Henry   " 1829, 3, 6
       Oliver   " 1831, 12, 13
1814, 7, 6. Caleb, s Robert & Cassandra,
    Fayette Co., Pa.; m at Redstone, Phebe
    RAY, dt Wm. & Elizabeth
1815, 12, 13. David, s Robert & Cassandra,
    Fayette Co., Pa.; m at Redstone, Eliza-
    beth BENNETT, dt Wm. & Grace, Fayette Co.,
    Pa
    Ch: Maria P.   b 1816, 9, 30
       Hannah G.   " 1817, 12, 17
       Eliza Jane   " 1820, 1, 9
       Sabina   " 1822, 9, 6
       Lydia M.   " 1824, 6, 28
       Rachel Jane " 1826, 5, 6
       Amos   " 1829, 10, 5
       Drusilla   " 1831, 11, 27
       Emmor   " 1835, 4, 20
       Ruthanna   " 1838, 10, 4
1815, 3, 15. Mary m Amos KENWORTHY
1818, 10, 29. Cassandrew d ae 62y bur Redstone
1826, 1, 22. Eliza Jane d
1832, 8, 24. Drusilla d bur Redstone
1833, 11, 14. Rebecca d ae 41y bur Sandy Hill
1840, 12, 9. Mary Ann m Abraham GARWOOD
1842, 5, 5. Hannah m Jonathan STANLEY
1843, 4, 5. Maria P. m Abel CAREY
1847, 1, 7. Joseph H., s Solomon & Ruth,
    Washington Co., Pa.; m at Redstone, Re-
    becca GARWOOD, dt Jesse & Lydia, Fayette
    Co., Pa.
1848, 3, 30. Lydia m William JENKINS
1853, 6, 2. Lydia W. m Emmir FAWCETT
1858, 4, 1. Jane m John KILLE

1803, 4, 29. Robert & w, Cassandra, & ch,
    Hannah, Caleb, Mary, David & Lydia, rocf
    Crooked Run MM, dtd 1803,3,5
1803, 4, 29. Solomon rocf Crooked Run MM,
    dtd 1803,3,5
1803, 4, 29. Sarah rocf Crooked Run MM, dtd
    1803,3,5
1803, 7, 1. William rocf Pipe Creek MM, dtd
    1803,4,16
1803, 9, 30. Solomon gct Crooked Run MM, to
    m Ruth Neal
1804, 6, 1. Ruth, w Solomon, rocf Crooked
    Run MM, dtd 1804,3,3
1808, 1, 1. Joseph dis mou
1810, 5, 4. Hannah, w Reuben, & ch, Martha,
    Sarah, David Willson & Reuben, rocf Abing-
    ton MM, dtd 1809,3,27

1810, 12, 28. Mary Downs (form Miller) dis mou
1810, 12, 28. William con mou
1812, 10, 2. Rebecca recrq
1814, 12, 2. Caleb & w, Phebe, gct Short Creek
    MM
1815, 9, 29. Solomon & w, Ruth, & ch, Lydia,
    Ann, Robert, Thomas & Lewis, gct Miami MM
1817, 6, 25. Phebe rocf Short Creek MM, dtd
    1817,4,22
1817, 12, 24. Phebe gct Cincinnati MM
1818, 9, 23. Warrick, s William, recrq
1819, 3, 24. Martha Elliot (form Miller) dis
    mcd
1819, 3, 24. Sarah Long (form Miller) dis mcd
1820, 11, 29. Lydia Willis (form Miller) dis
    mcd
1821, 4, 4. David & w, Elizabeth, & ch, Ma-
    ria, Hannah & Eliza Jane, gct Miami MM,O.
1823, 4, 2. Robert dis mcd
1826, 11, 29. David & w, Elizabeth, & ch, Ma-
    ria, Hannah G., Sabina, Lydia & Rachel
    Jane, rocf Springborough MM, dtd 1826,10,
    24
1828, 1, 2. David dis mcd
1828, 1, 2. Reuben dis mcd
1835, 6, 3. Sarah Jeffries (form Miller) dis
    mcd
1835, 7, 1. Warwick dis mcd
1835, 7, 1. William dis mcd
1838, 1, 31. Hiram dis mcd
1841, 6, 30. Cassandra Haney (form Miller)
    dis mcd
1846, 9, 30. William rst by rq
1846, 11, 4. Ann recrq
1856, 6, 4. William H. dis mcd & jas
1856, 7, 30. Oliver dis disunity
1857, 4, 1. Rebecca G. gct Westland MM
1861, 7, 3. Lindley M. Rogers gct Springboro
    MM, O., to m Ruth H. Miller
1862, 6, 4. Emmer H. dis jas
1865, 6, 28. Joseph H. & w, Rebecca, & dt,
    Mary H., gct Springborough MM, O.
1865, 11, 29. David & w, Elizabeth, gct Salem
    MM, O.
1865, 11, 29. Sabina gct Salem MM, O.
1865, 11, 29. Rachel Jane gct Salem MM, O.

MILLISON
1814, 9, 14. Elisha, s Wm. & Elizabeth, Wash.
    Co., Pa.; m at Redstone, Hannah CHANDLER,
    dt Enoch & Hannah, Fayette Co., Pa.

1795, 6, 26. James & w, Abigail, & ch, Sarah,
    Mary, Lydia, James, Ann & John, rocf Brad-
    ford MM, dtd 1795,4,17
1795, 6, 26. Caleb rocf Bradford MM, dtd
    1795,4,17
1796, 9, 2. Cert rec for James a short
    time ago endorsed to Westland MM
1796, 9, 2. Caleb [Milleson] dis mou
1814, 12, 30. Hannah gct Westland MM

MILLS
1844, 2, 21. Eli & w, Elizabeth, & ch, Susan
        K., Joseph Jr. & Thomas K., gct Clear
        Creek MM, Ill. (H)

MINIKIN
----, --, --. William & Margaret
        Ch: Sarah
            Simpson   b 1815, 1, 13
            Margaret   " 1819, 3, 7
            William   " 1823, 6, 7
            Gulielma
             Maria Penn " 1826, 9, 2
1824, 7, 14. William d bur Redstone
1827, 5, 14. William d ae 60y bur Redstone
1828, 1, 24. Ann d bur Redstone

1814, 7, 29. William & w, Margaret, & ch,
        Mary, John & Ann, recrq
1815, 6, 2. William & w, Margaret, & ch, Mary,
        John, Ann & Sarah Simpson, gct Westland MM
1818, 3, 25. William [Minikan] & w, Margaret,
        & ch, Mary, Ann, John, Sarah Simpson &
        Hannah, rocf Westland MM, dtd 1818,2,19
1829, 4, 29. Margaret & ch, Sarah Simson, Mar-
        garet & Gulielma Maria Penn, gct Plain-
        field MM, O. (H)
1829, 4, 29. Mary gct Plainfield MM, O. (H)
1829, 7, 1. Margaret & ch, Sarah, Margaret &
        Gulielma, gct Stillwater MM, O.
1829, 7, 29. John dis mcd
1829, 9, 30. John dis mou (H)
1829, 12, 2. John [Miniken] dis jH
1830, 2, 3. Mary [Miniken] dis jH

MITCHEL
1811, 2, 1. Elizabeth (form Campbell) dis mcd

MITCHENER
1802, 1, 6. John, s William & Esther, Fayette
        Co., Pa.; m at Sandy Creek, Neomi WOOD, dt
        Joseph & Abigail, Monongalia Co., Pa.

1801, 12, 4. John rocf Fairfax MM, dtd 1801,
        9,28
1802, 7, 2. Thomas rocf Fairfax MM, dtd
        1802,3,27
1802, 7, 2. Esther & ch, Rachel, Hannah,
        Mordecai & Jonathan, rocf Fairfax MM, dtd
        1802,3,27
1802, 9, 3. Esther Jr. rocf Fairfax MM, dtd
        1802,3,27
1803, 9, 30. Lydia (form Smith) dis mcd
1803, 9, 30. Esther & ch, Hannah, Mordecai &
        Jonathan, gct Westland MM
1803, 10, 28. Esther Jr. dis
1804, 5, 4. Thomas [Michener] gct Westland
        MM
1804, 11, 2. Rachel gct Westland MM
1810, 6, 29. John & w, Naomi, gct Westland MM

MOORE
1805, 1, 3. Mary m Joseph NICHOLSON

1819, 12, 5. Bathsheba d ae 59y bur Redstone
1834, 12, 22. John d ae 80y bur Redstone

1794, 5, 23. Grace recrq
1799, 10, 4. Elizabeth Cock (form Moore) dis
        mou
1800, 7, 4. Mary rocf Trent MM, N. C., dtd
        1800,1,12
1803, 12, 2. David dis mou
1804, 6, 29. Cyrus dis mou

1805, 10, 4. Mordecai dis mou
1808, 7, 29. Joseph dis mou
1810, 6, 29. Joshua dis mou
1817, 8, 27. John Jr. dis mcd
1822, 12, 4. Abner dis mcd
1828, 10, 1. Sarah Gause (form Moore) dis mcd

MORGAN
----, --, --. John & Ann
        Ch: Edith   b 1810, 2, 14
            Edward   " 1815, 1, 17
            Deborah   " 1817, 12, 18
            Ann Eliza " 1820, 2, 8
            Rebecca
             Mathews " 1821, 5, 29
            Charles

1806, 2, 28. John & w, Ann, & ch, Mary, Han-
        nah & Elizabeth, rocf Westland MM, dtd
        1806,1,25
1819, 6, 30. Olover rocf Westland MM, dtd
        1819,5,27
1820, 2, 2. Oliver gct Westland MM
1823, 6, 4. John & w, Ann, & ch, Edith, Ed-
        ward, Deborah, Ann Eliza & Rebecca Ma-
        thews, gct New Garden MM, O.
1823, 6, 4. Hannah gct New Garden MM, O.
1823, 10, 29. Mary gct New Garden MM, O.
1826, 3, 29. Mary & Hannah rocf New Garden
        MM. O., dtd 1825,12,22
1826, 5, 2. John & w, Ann, & ch, Edith, Ed-
        ward, Deborah, Ann Eliza, Rebekah M. &
        Charles, rocf New Garden MM, O., dtd 1826,
        1,26
1827, 1, 31. Mary Green (form Morgan) dis mcd
1832, 1, 4. Ann & dt, Hannah & Edith, dis jH
1832, 2, 29. John dis jH
1839, 12, 4. Edward dis mcd
1845, 1, 1. Rebecca Morris (form Morgan)
        dis joining Separatists
1845, 1, 1. Deborah & Ann Eliza dis joining
        Separatists
1845, 7, 30. Charles dis disunity
1847, 5, 26. Deborah dis jas(H)

MORRIS
1805, 5, 8. Elizabeth m Abraham ROBERTS

1800, 10, 3. Mary (form Bostick) dis mou
1801, 5, 1. Edward & ch, David, Elizabeth,
        Jane, Hannah, Lydia & Edward, rocf Hope-
        well MM, dtd 1801,3,2

MORRIS, continued
1802, 10, 1. David dis
1802, 12, 3. Anthony & w, Hannah, & ch, Barzilla, Esther & Sarah, rocf Burlington MM, N. J., dtd 1802,10,4
1804, 3, 30. Anthony & w, Hannah, & ch, Barzilla, Esther, Sarah & Thomas, gct Middleton MM
1804, 6, 1. Edward & ch, Jane, Hannah, Lydia & Edward, gct Short Creek MM, O.
1804, 6, 29. Cert rec for Richard from Shrewsbury MM, dtd 1802,12,6, endorsed to Westland MM
1826, 10, 4. Susanna (form Jones) dis mcd
1845, 1, 1. Rebecca (form Morgan) dis joining Separatists

MORRISON
1798, 1, 11. Jane m William DIXON

1797, 11, 3. Jane rocf Gunpowder MM, dtd 1797,3,25

MORTON
1807, 7, 9. Mary m Joseph PENROSE
1835, 1, 30. Hannah d ae 63y bur Sandy Creek

1794, 2, 21. Ann Brandon (form Morton) dis mcd
1794, 8, 22. Thomas dis mou
1801, 12, 4. Susanna Neal (form Morten) dis mou
1804, 11, 30. William dis disunity
1811, 3, 29. Edith dis
1811, 3, 29. Phebe dis
1815, 6, 30. Hannah Stroud (form Hannah Morton, Sr.) dis mou
1816, 7, 24. Rebecca gct Short Creek MM

NEAL
1800, 2, 28. Mary (form Atherton) dis mou
1801, 12, 4. Susanna (form Morten) dis mou
1803, 9, 30. Solomon Miller gct Crooked Run MM, to m Ruth Neal
1808, 4, 29. William [Neill] rocf Hopewell MM, dtd 1808,11,2
1811, 3, 1. William [Neil] gct Hopewell MM
1812, 10, 2. Dennings Creek MM was given permission to rst Susanna [Neil]

NEEDLES
1819, 11, 3. James B. rocf Indian Spring MM, dtd 1819,6,18

NEGUS
----, --, --. John & Miriam
    Ch: Sarah   b 1807, 4, 23
        Levinah   " 1809, 2, 19
        Eliza   " 1810, 12, 27
        Israel   " 1812, 8, 13
        Jacob   " 1814, 8, 22
        Lydia   " 1816, 4, 22
1814, 12, 7. Jacob d bur Providence

1830, 1, 6. Joseph, s Shaidlock & Sarah, Fayette Co., Pa.; m at Redstone, Eliza Ann CHALFANT, dt Abel & Hannah, Fayette Co., Pa.
1836, 3, 31. Israel, s John & Miriam, Columbiana Co., O.; m at Redstone, Lydia GARWOOD, dt Jesse & Lydia, Fayette Co., Pa.

1805, 8, 2. Sarah Waites (form Negus) con mou
1806, 5, 2. John gct Westland MM, to m Miriam Burdge
1806, 10, 3. Miriam rocf Westland MM, dtd 1806,8,23
1810, 3, 30. Joshua dis mcd
1813, 5, 28. Joseph dis
1814, 4, 29. Shaidlock gct Westland MM
1836, 6, 1. Lydia G. gct Upper Springfield MM, O.

NEELAN
1833, 8, --. Rachel d bur Providence

NEW
1801, 3, 6. Phebe (form Grist) dis mou

NEWBURN
1837, 8, 15. Tamer d bur Redstone

1800, 1, 3. Sarah Yarnall (form Newburn), w George Jr., dis mou
1800, 2, 28. David rocf Wrightstown MM, dtd 1799,12,3
1800, 11, 28. George rocf Chester MM, dtd 1800,9,29
1808, 4, 1. John con mou
1815, 12, 1. Jacob gct Westland MM
1817, 5, 21. John gct Miami MM, O.
1817, 7, 23. George gct Westland MM
1817, 10, 22. David Jr. gct Miami MM
1825, 2, 2. William dis mcd
1827, 1, 31. Ann gct Westland MM
1830, 8, 4. Rachel dis jH
1835, 7, 29. Mary Vore (form Newburn) dis mou
1846, 2, 18. Rachel gct Clear Creek MM, Ill. (H)

NEWLIN
1801, 7, 3. Ann rocf Warrington MM, dtd 1800,5,10
1808, 9, 2. Elizabeth (form Means) dis mou

NEWPORT
1793, 9, 27. Thomas dis mcd
1793, 9, 27. Mary (form Evans), w Thomas, dis mcd
1795, 4, 24. Elizabeth rocf Abington MM, dtd 1794,10,27
1795, 11, 27. Elizabeth Robins (form Newport) dis mou
1797, 6, 30. Aaron dis disunity
1797, 6, 30. Mary, w Aaron, & ch, Elizabeth, Jesse, Ruth, Joseph, Reece & Nathan, gct

NEWPORT, continued
    Westland MM

NICHOLS
1797, 8, 2. Susanna m Ephraim CRAWFORD

1796, 2, 26. Ellis rocf Kennet MM, dtd 1795,
    8,13
1797, 6, 30. Susanna rocf Kennet MM, dtd
    1796,11,17
1797, 9, 29. Cert rec for Susanna (now Craw-
    ford) some time ago endorsed to Westland MM
1802, 5, 28. Ellis dis disunity

NICHOLSON
1805, 1, 3. Joseph, s George & Elizabeth,
    Belmont Co., O.; m at Sandy Hill, Mary
    MOORE, dt Edward & Marion, Fayette Co.,
    Pa.
1841, 9, 14. Mary d ae 60y bur Sandy Creek

1793, 8, 23. Joseph & ch, James & Elizabeth,
    rocf Westland MM, dtd 1793,7,27
1793, 8, 23. Sarah, w James, rocf Plainfield
    MM, dtd 1793,6,19, endorsed by Westland
    MM, 1793,7,27
1802, 3, 5. Joseph & w, Sarah, & ch, James,
    Elizabeth, George, Hannah & William, gct
    Concord MM, N. W. Territory
1805, 3, 1. Mary gct Concord MM, O.
1821, 10, 3. Isaac, minor s Mary, recrq

NORRIS
1820, 8, 2. Tabitha (form Chandler) dis

NUTT
1811, 11, 29. Cert rec for Hannah from Fair-
    fax MM, dtd 1810,6,29, endorsed by Middle-
    ton MM, 1811,4,13, endorsed to Westland MM

NUZUM
1801, 3, 6. Richard [Newzum] & w, Hannah,
    rocf Chester MM, Pa., dtd 1800;9,29
1806, 1, 3. William rocf Chester MM, dtd
    1801,5,25
1808, 4, 1. George dis mcd
1808, 4, 1. William dis mou

ONG
----, --, --. Rebeckah, dt Jacob & Mary, b

1797, 12, 29. Jesse recrq
1796, 6, 3. Elizabeth (form McGrew) con mou
1802, 5, 28. Rebecca McGrew (form Ong) con
    mcd
1802, 12, 3. Jacob & w, Mary, & ch, Finley,
    Jacob, Isaac, Dinah, Nathan & John, gct
    Concord MM, N. W. Territory
1806, 5, 30. Ann (form Blackburn) con mou
1809, 11, 3. Anne con mou
1809, 12, 1. Anne gct Plymouth MM, O.
1820, 10, 4. Jesse & w, Elizabeth, & ch,
    James & Isabella, gct Providence MM

1820, 11, 1. Jane gct Providence MM
1820, 11, 1. Mary gct Providence MM

OXLEY
1817, 5, 28. Joel, Fayette Co., Pa.; m at
    Redstone, Mary TROTH, dt Henry & Hannah,
    Fayette Co., Pa.
----, --, --. Joel & Sarah
    Ch: Hannah
        Jane   b 1821, 1, 5
        Henry
        Troth   " 1822, 7, 12
        Margaret
        Truman   " 1823, 12, 19
1835, 4, --. Hannah Jane d bur Redstone

1801, 3, 6. Joel recrq
1804, 12, 28. Joel gct Short Creek MM
1816, 2, 21. Joel rocf Hopewell MM, dtd
    1815,9,7
1829, 4, 29. Sarah dis jH
1829, 9, 2. Joel dis jH
1849, 10, 3. Mary dis disunity

PACKER
1801, 1, 30. Moses recrq
1801, 7, 31. Moses gct Westland MM
1831, 9, 28. George rocf Carmel MM, O. (H)

PAINTER
1810, 6, 1. Rosanna (form McGrew) dis mcd

PARISHO
1800, 5, 30. Mary rocf Trent MM, N. C., dtd
    1800,1,12; d shortly after arriving

PARVIANCE (see PURVIANCE)

PATE
1800, 8, 29. Charlotte rocf Trent MM, N. C.,
    dtd 1800,1,12
1801, 10, 2. Cert rec for Richard Jelks & w &
    dt, Charlotte Pate & Priscilla Jelks, some
    time ago endorsed to Westland MM

PATTERSON
1860, 10, 10. Asahel H., s Mahlon & Mary Ann,
    Jefferson Co., O.; m at Redstone, Esther
    P. GRIFFITH, dt Amos & Elizabeth, Fayette
    Co., O.

1841, 3, 31. Ezra Cattell gct Short Creek
    MM, to m Ruthanna Patterson
1849, 10, 3. George Cattell gct Short Creek
    MM, to m Jane H. Patterson
1861, 4, 3. Esther G. gct Short Creek MM, O.

PEARCE
1808, 3, 16. Mary m Samuel GAUSE
1809, 11, 8. Martha m Eli GAUSE

1807, 1, 2. Martha [Peirce] rocf New Garden
    MM, dtd 1806,11,6

PEARCE, continued
1807, 7, 3. Mary [Pierce] rocf New Garden
MM, dtd 1807,1,8

PEARSON
1802, 12, 31. Phebe (form Smith) dis mou
1804, 6, 29. Abraham & w, Ann, & dt, Alice,
rocf Kennet MM, dtd 1804,1,12; dt. Sarah,
b since cert was issued
1809, 2, 3. Abraham [Pierson] dis disunity
1814, 7, 1. Ann & ch, Alice, Susanna, Sarah
& Ann, gct New Garden MM, O.

PECK
1803, 12, 30. John dis disunity

PEDEN
1796, 12, 2. Isaac dis disunity
1799, 8, 30. Hannah Burwell (form Peden) dis
mou
1803, 3, 4. Jacob dis disunity
1815, 3, 3. Thomas [Pedan] rocf Westland MM,
dtd 1814,12,29
1819, 6, 30. Thomas [Peaden] gct Westland MM
1822, 2, 27. Rebecca Canada (form Peden) dis
mcd
1822, 2, 27. Susannah Gillilan (form Peden)
dis mcd
1822, 2, 27. Rachel Harvey (form Peden) dis
mcd
1822, 2, 27. Ruth Hill (form Peden) dis mcd
1822, 7, 31. Isaac gct Middleton MM, O.
1822, 7, 31. Rebecca gct Middleton MM, O.

PENNELL
----, --, --. Jesse & Hannah
Ch: Mary·   b 1794, 4, 13
    Twin dt   " 1795, 6, 5 d 1795, 6, 5
    Maria   " 1796, 10, 22
    Wm. Grubb   " 1798, 5, 10
    Sarah   " 1799, 12, 18
    Robert Dell " 1802, 5, 7
    Wm. Dell   " 1804, 1, 16
    Susannah   " 1805, 10, 12
    Eliza   " 1806, 12, 25
    Esther   " 1808, 10, 24
    Beulah   " 1810, 5, 4
    George W.   " 1812, 2, 17
1795, 8, 18. Mary d bur Redstone
1800, 4, 5. Wm. Grubb d bur Redstone
1811, 9, 17. Beulah d bur Redstone
1818, 6, 3. Maria G. m Washington HOUGH
1819, 2, 5. Jesse d ae 46y bur Redstone
1821, 7, 19. Robert D. d bur Redstone

1795, 8, 21. Jesse [Pennel] & w, Hannah, &
dt, Mary, rocf Crooked Run MM, dtd 1795,4,
4
1815, 3, 31. Maria gct Concord MM, Pa.
1816, 12, 25. Maria rocf Concord MM, Pa., dtd
1816,10,3
1822, 10, 2. Sarah Lamb (form Pennell) dis
mcd

1830, 3, 3. George, minor, gct Short Creek
MM, O.
1830, 3, 31. William gct Stillwater MM, O.
1830, 4, 28. Eliza Binns (form Pennell) dis
mcd
1830, 6, 2. Hannah dis JH
1830, 8, 4. Susanna dis disunity
1830, 9, 29. Esther dis disunity
1834, 7, 2. Susanna & Esther dis jas (H)

PENROSE
1863, 12, 9. Thomas, s John & Ann, Morgan
Co., O.; m at Brownsville, Mary R. GRIF-
FITH, dt Amos & Edith, Fayette Co., Pa.

1803, 6, 3. Jesse & w, Sarah, & ch, Abraham,
Benjamin, Joseph, Phebe, William & Sarah,
rocf Crooked Run MM, dtd 1803,2,28
1804, 3, 2. Abraham dis disunity
1804, 3, 2. Benjamin dis disunity
1810, 9, 28. Phebe Conner (form Penrose) dis
mcd
1810, 12, 28. Joseph & w, Mary, gct Miami MM
1814, 12, 30. Jesse & w, Sarah, gct Plainfield
MM
1815, 3, 3. Sarah Workman (form Penrose) dis
mou
1864, 11, 30. Mary R. gct Chesterfield MM, O.

PETTIT
1835, 11, 4. William Jr. &·w, Jane R., & dt,
Elizabeth H., rocf Upper Springfield MM,
dtd 1835,9,25
1847, 3, 3. William & w, Jane R., & dt,
Elizabeth H., gct WD MM, Phila., Pa.
1865, 6, 28. Oscar J. Griffith gct Short
Creek MM, O., to m Mary Elma Pettit

PHILLIPS
1825, 5, 11. Elizabeth m Ellis LILLEY
1825, 9, 7. Ellis, s Solomon & Martha, Washington Co., Pa.; m at Redstone, Phebe LIL-
LEY, dt Thomas & Ruth
1839, 4, --. Martha d bur Redstone
----, --, --. Jonathan bur Redstone

1813, 12, 31. Samuel [Philips] rocf Westland
MM, dtd 1813,11,23
1814, 3, 4. Solomon & w, Martha, & ch, Solomon, Ruth, Ellis, Elizabeth & Jonathan,
rocf Westland MM, dtd 1813,10,23
1814, 4, 29. James [Philips] rocf Westland
MM, dtd 1813,10,23
1815, 4, 28. Sarah (form Chalfant) dis
1817, 6, 25. James dis mcd
1817, 9, 24. Edith [Philips] (form Dixon) dis
mcd
1828, 10, 1. Sarah (form Wood) dis mcd
1829, 9, 30. Ruth dis jH
1829, 11, 4. Solomon dis jH
1830, 3, 31. Samuel [Philips] dis jH
1830, 3, 31. Solomon [Philips] Jr. dis jH
1831, 6, 29. Elizabeth (form Wood) dis mou &

PHILLIPS, continued
        JH
1832, 2, 1. Ellis dis disunity
1832, 2, 29. Phebe dis disunity
1836, 3, 30. Solomon con mcd (H)

PHIPS
1797, 9, 29. Edith (form Updegraff) dis mou

PICKERING
1806, 7, 4. Cert rec for Mary from Hopewell
    MM, dtd 1806,7,1, endorsed to Concord MM,
    O.

PICKLE
1793, 8, 23. Sarah (form Rees) rpd mcd

PINKHAM
1843, 9, 9. Gilbod Latey [Pinkhan], s Thomas
    & Mary, b

1843, 8, 2. Thomas & w, Mary B., & ch, Mary
    Elizabeth, Thomas Edward, Caroline H.,
    James Parnell & William Penn, rocf Litch-
    field MM, Maine, dtd 1843,5,19, endorsed
    by Providence MM
1845, 4, 2. Thomas & w, Mary B., & ch, Mary
    Elizabeth, Thomas Edward, Caroline H.,
    James Parnell, William Penn & Gilbert
    Latey, gct Salem MM, O.

PITMAN
1802, 12, 3. Cert rec for Elizabeth, w Levi,
    from Burlington MM, dtd 1802,10,4, endors-
    ed to Concord MM, N. W. Territory

PLUMMER
1798, 5, 4. Moses & w, Elizabeth, & ch, Ann,
    Sarah & Ruth, rocf Fairfax MM, dtd 1797,11,
    27

PRAY
1807, 10, 7. Wm., s William & Rachel, Fayette
    Co., Pa.; m at Redstone, Mary AIRY, wd,
    dt John & Betty JONES, Fayette Co., Pa.
    Ch: Joseph   b 1808, 6, 15
        Samuel   " 1809, 10, 19
        Rachel   " 1810, 11, 2
1809, 10, 24. Samuel d bur Redstone
1816, 1, 10. Wm. d bur Redstone

1807, 7, 3. William recrq
1818, 12, 23. Mary & ch, Joseph, Enos & Mary,
    gct White Water MM, Ind.
1819, 6, 30. Rachel, minor, gct White Water
    MM, Ind.

PRICE
1814, 7, 7. Thomas [Priece], s Ezekiel &
    Mercy, Fayette Co., Pa.; m at Providence,
    Mary COPE, dt Isaac & Sarah, Fayette Co.,
    Pa.

1802, 5, 28. William & w recrq
1802, 5, 28. Hannah & h recrq
1814, 4, 29. Thomas recrq
1816, 10, 23. Thomas & w, Mary, & s, Ezekiel,
    gct Marlborough MM, O.
1827, 5, 2. Mary recrq
1827, 5, 30. Mary (form Campbell) dis mcd
1830, 12, 29. Mary dis JH
1836, 5, 4. Rachel (form Smith) dis mou
1838, 10, 31. Westland MM was given permission
    to rst Mary
1847, 12, 29. Mary rst by rq
1862, 12, 31. Israel & w, Margaret, & ch, Jas-
    per & Mary Melissa, dis joining Wilburite
    Separatists

PURVIANCE
1798, 2, 2. David dis mcd
1798, 2, 2. Mary (form Walker), w David, dis
    mcd
1800, 8, 1. David & w, Mary, rst by rq
1800, 8, 1. Sarah, infant dt David & w rec-
    rq
1802, 3, 5. David [Parviance] & w, Mary, &
    ch, Sarah & James, gct Concord MM
1803, 4, 29. James Jr. gct Concord MM, N. W.
    Territory
1805, 10, 4. James Jr. rocf Short Creek MM,
    dtd 1805,7,20
1807, 2, 1. Thomas [Parviance] gct Short
    Creek MM
1812, 10, 2. Joseph [Perviance] gct Plymouth
    MM, O.
1813, 1, 29. James [Parviance] Jr. gct Ply-
    mouth MM, O.
1813, 1, 29. William [Parviance] gct Plymouth
    MM, O.
1814, 6, 3. George [Parviance] gct Plymouth
    MM
1814, 6, 3. Richard [Parviance] gct Plymouth
    MM
1814, 7, 1. Sarah [Perviance], dt Elizabeth,
    gct Plymouth MM, O.
1814, 7, 1. Elizabeth [Perviance] gct Ply-
    mouth MM, O.
1829, 11, 4. John Willets gct Smithfield MM,
    O., to m Elizabeth Purviance

QUAIL
1809, 3, 3. Asenith (form Dennis) dis mou

RAMSEY
1803, 12, 2. Susanna (form Webster) dis mcd

RANDOLPH
1834, 4, 15. Jane [Dixon] d ae 60y

RATCLIFF
1835, 9, 2. Mary (form Smith) dis mou

RAY
1814, 7, 6. Phebe m Caleb MILLER

RAY, continued
1808, 4, 1. Elizabeth (form Dickinson) dis mcd
1814, 4, 29. Phebe rocf Abington MM, dtd 1814, 3,28

REESE
1793, 8, 23. Sarah Pickle (form Rees) rpd mcd
1822, 4, 3. Tamer rocf Goose Creek MM, dtd 1821,11,29
1823, 12, 31. Tamer gct Plainfield MM, O.

RICHARDS
1816, 11, 20. Mary (form Denis) dis mcd

RIDGWAY
1794, 12, 26. Cert rec for Timothy & w, Michal, & ch, Paul, Dinah, Job, Thomas, Lavina & John, endorsed to Westland MM

ROBERTS
1799, 11, 6. Hannah m John LEWIS
1800, 11, 5. Lydia m Jesse GARWOOD
1805, 5, 8. Abraham, s Griffith & Rachel, Fayette Co., Pa.; m at Redstone, Elizabeth MORRIS, dt Edward & Hannah, Fayette Co., Pa.
    Ch: Hannah   b 1806, 1, 13
        Griffith   " 1807, 3, 7
        Morris   " 1808, 11, 8
        Benoni   " 1811, 10, 3
        Rachel   " 1813, 4, 2
        Lydia   " 1815, 4, 19
        Abraham   " 1816, 12, 4
        Elizabeth   " 1820, 1, 10
1819, 5, 19. Abraham d ae 35y
1823, 6, 7. Griffith d ae 73y
1835, 1, 21. Rachel d ae 79y bur Redstone

1799, 3, 1. Griffith & w, Rachel, & s, Abraham, rocf Hopewell MM, dtd 1799,2,4
1799, 3, 1. Lydia rocf Hopewell MM, dtd 1799,2,4
1799, 5, 31. Rebekah rocf Hopewell MM, dtd 1799,2,4
1799, 6, 28. Hannah rocf Bradford MM, dtd 1798,11,6, endorsed by Hopewell MM, 1799, 6,3
1799, 8, 30. Rebecca Mercer (form Roberts) dis mou
1825, 11, 2. Hannah Saladay (form Roberts) dis mcd
1827, 8, 29. Griffith dis mcd
1832, 2, 1. Morris dis mou
1837, 10, 4. Benoni dis mcd
1840, 11, 4. Rachel Hoge (form Roberts) dis mcd
1841, 11, 3. Elizabeth, Lydia & Elizabeth Jr. gct Flushing MM, O.

ROBINS
1795, 11, 27. Elizabeth (form Newport) dis mou

ROBINSON
1819, 6, 30. Charles recrq
1821, 4, 4. Charles gct Short Creek MM, O.

ROGERS
1832, 5, 3. Nathan I., s Philip & Mary, Wash. Co., Pa.; m at Redstone, Atlantic HAINES, dt Eli & Ruth, Fayette Co., Pa.

1798, 8, 3. Joseph recrq
1805, 3, 29. Elizabeth (form Gibson) dis mou
1813 4, 30. Mary recrq
1823, 6, 4. Mary gct Concord MM
1825, 6, 1. Mary rocf Concord MM, O., dtd 1825,5,19
1832, 8, 1. Atlantic gct Westland MM
1840, 9, 2. Nathan & w, Atlantic, & ch, Eli, Jonathan, Lindley & Mary, rocf Westland MM, dtd 1840,7,22
1842, 6, 29. Winston D. rocf Westland MM
1843, 6, 28. Winston D. gct Westland MM
1843, 6, 28. Nathan & w, Atlantic, & ch, Eli, Jonathan, Lindley, Mary, Edith & Elizabeth L., gct Westland MM
1857, 6, 3. Atlantic & ch, Lindly M., Mary & Edith G., rocf Westland MM, dtd 1857,5, 28
1861, 7, 3. Lindley M. gct Springboro MM, O., to m Ruth H. Miller
1861, 7, 31. Mary C. Jones (form Rogers) dis
1862, 6, 4. Lindley M. gct Springborough MM, O.

ROSS
1807, 10, 2. Ruth (form Hough) dis mcd

RUSSELL
1793, 5, 24. Esther rocf Crooked Run MM, Va., dtd 1792,11,3, endorsed by Westland MM, 1793,4,27
1797, 9, 29. Mary (form Vail) dis mou
1804, 11, 30. Esther gct Miami MM
1807, 8, 28. Phebe [Rossel] (form Duly) dis mou

SALADAY
1825, 11, 2. Hannah (form Roberts) dis mcd

SAUNDERS
----, --, --. Paul & Anna
    Ch: Elizabeth b 1794, 11, 23
        Isaac   " 1797, 5, 7
        Joseph   " 1799, 9, 15
        Sarah   " 1802, 8, 25
        Anna   " 1805, 6, 11

1800, 8, 29. Clark & William rocf Duck Creek MM, dtd 1799,12,7
1803, 3, 4. Clark dis disunity
1803, 3, 4. Paul dis disunity
1804, 11, 30. William dis disunity
1807, 10, 2. Ann & ch, Elizabeth, Isaac, Joseph, Sarah & Anna, gct Miami MM

SCHOLFIELD
1804, 6, 29. David rocf Crooked Run MM, dtd
    1804,5,5
1805, 5, 31. David gct Middleton MM

SCHOOLEY
1796, 7, 29. William & w, Ann, gct Fairfax MM
1800, 7, 4. Dorothy rocf Fairfax MM, dtd
    1800,5,24
1805, 3, 29. William dis mcd
1805, 10, 4. Dorothy gct Short Creek MM, O.

SEXTON
1801, 12, 4. Hannah, w Meshack, & dt, Cathe-
    rine, Hannah & Mary, rocf Hopewell MM, dtd
    1801,5,4, endorsed by Westland MM, 1801,8,
    22
1811, 3, 29. Hannah gct Short Creek MM
1811, 3, 29. Mary gct Short Creek MM
1811, 8, 2. Catherine gct Plainfield MM, O.

SHAEFFER
1809, 6, 2. Susanna (form Gibson) dis mcd
1833, 5, 29. Cincinnati MM was given permis-
    sion to rst Susanna [Shaffer]

SHARP
1807, 8, 28. Susanna (form Cook) con mou

SHARPLESS
1801, 5, 13. Benjamin, s Isaac & Elizabeth,
    Fayette Co.; m at Redstone, Amy CADWALADER
    dt Septimus & Sarah, Fayette Co., Pa.

1795, 12, 25. Jonathan & w, Edith, & ch, Sam-
    uel & Elizabeth, rocf Wilmington MM, dtd
    1795,9,16
1804, 3, 30. Benjamin & w, Amy, & s, Isaac,
    gct Middleton MM, O.
1816, 3, 27. Elizabeth Jackson (form Sharp-
    less) con mcd
1833, 7, 3. Hugh Judge & Margaret, ch Samuel
    & Rebecca, rocf Stillwater MM, O., dtd
    1833,1,28
1862, 12, 31. Margaret dis joining Wilburite
    Separatists

SHAW
1802, 10, 29. Ruth (form Crawford) dis mou

SHAY
1821, 5, 2. Phebe (form Sidwell) dis mcd

SHEARON
1844, 10, 2. White Water MM, Ind. was given
    permission to rst Elizabeth

SHEPHERD
1805, 6, 28. Solomon & w, Margaret, rocf
    Westland MM, dtd 1805,4,27
1806, 2, 28. Cert rec for Solomon & w some
    time ago endorsed to Westland MM
1810, 12, 28. Solomon rocf Westland MM, dtd

1810,11,24
1815, 10, 27. Solomon gct Westland MM
1817, 1, 22. Thomas rst by rq
1817, 1, 22. Elizabeth rst by rq
1817, 6, 25. Joseph rst by rq with consent of
    Westland MM
1817, 9, 24. Joseph [Shepperd] gct Providence
    MM

SHOEMAKER
1815, 9, 1. William & Martha rocf Bradford
    MM, dtd 1814,8,3

SHOTWELL
1802, 3, 5. Sarah, dt John, rocf Rahway &
    Plainfield MM, N. J., dtd 1801,10,21
1803, 1, 28. Sarah Hempson (form Shotwell)
    dis mcd
1806, 8, 1. Hope Woodward (form Shotwell)
    con mou
1806, 10, 3. Titus & ch, Marion, Joseph,
    Thomas & Isaac, gct Concord MM, O.
1814, 10, 28. Titus Jr. dis disunity
1819, 5, 26. Edward gct Bridgetown & Plain-
    field MM, East Jersey

SHREVE
1794, 9, 26. Margaret, w Richard, rocf Upper
    Springfield MM, N. J., dtd 1794,2,5
1815, 10, 27. Israel dis mcd
1815, 12, 27. Joseph gct Short Creek MM

SHURN
1820, 3, 1. Elizabeth (form Chalfant) dis
    mou

SIDWELL
1831, 7, --. Hugh d
1832, 7, 11. Mary d
1839, 9, 25. Amy d ae 77y bur Sandy Hill

1796, 12, 30. James & w, Amy, & ch, Margaret
    & Lydia, rocf Hopewell MM, dtd 1796,9,7
1800, 2, 28. Margaret Stevenson (form Sidwell)
    dis mou
1808, 4, 1. Charity Hartley (form Sidwell)
    dis mou

1809, 11, 3. Mary Hartley (form Sidwell) dis
    mou
1812, 10, 30. James dis disunity
1814, 1, 28. Lydia Hackney (form Sidwell)
    dis mcd
1821, 5, 2. Phebe Shay (form Sidwell) dis
    mcd
1821, 5, 2. Rees dis mcd
1821, 5, 2. Jesse dis mcd
1827, 8, 1. Henry dis mcd
1828, 6, 4. Hannah Thomas (form Sidwell) dis
    mcd
1828, 6, 4. Sarah Vandevert (form Sidwell)
    dis mcd
1828, 7, 2. Hugh dis mcd

SILVERTHORN
1796, 9, 2. Thomas dis mou
1798, 5, 4. James dis mou

SIMMS
1802, 3, 5. Sarah (form Weaver) dis mou

SMITH
1799, 5, 10. Ann m Robert BURNETT
1799, 6, 7. David, s Thomas & Deborah, Fayette Co., Pa.; m at Center, Judith KIRK,
dt Joseph & Judith, Fayette Co., Pa.
1803, 3, 10. Richard, s Timothy & Sarah,
Monongaly Co., Pa.; m at Providence,
Elizabeth WALKER, dt Ebeneezer & Mary,
Westmoreland Co., Pa.
----, --, --. Samuel & Catherine
    Ch: Jane
        Harvey   b 1808, 11, 22
        John   " 1810, 11, 3
        Jehu   " 1813, 3, 13
        Sarah   " 1815, 9, 3
        Ann   " 1818, 4, 30
        Elizabeth " 1820, 9, 16
        Amos Har-
        vey   " 1823, 8, 12
        Rebeckah " 1827, 9, 7
        Asa   " 1831, 5, 23
1808, 8, 10. John d ae 66y bur Sandy Creek
1824, 12, 16. Ann m Mahlon BROOMHALL
1830, 10, 26. Saran d ae 81y bur Sandy Creek
1835, 4, 23. Joseph d ae 67y bur Sandy Creek
1845, 2, 6. Asa d ae 13y bur Sandy Creek
1845, 7, 2. Sarah d ae 29y bur Sandy Creek
1847, 3, 11. Samuel d ae 74y bur Sandy Creek
----, --, --. Sarah bur Cincinnati

1793, 12, 27. Randal rocf Wrightstown MM,
Pa., dtd 1792,12,4, endorsed by Westland
MM, 1793,8,24
1795, 7, 24. Cert rec for Anthony & w, Lydia,
from Little Eggharbour MM, dtd 1794,8,14,
endorsed to Westland MM
1795, 8, 21. Cert rec for Samuel from Hopewell
MM, dtd 1794,9,1, endorsed to Westland MM
1795, 9, 25. Jane & s, John, gct Wilmington
MM
1796, 9, 30. Thomas & w, Deborah, & ch, David,
Ann, Lydia, Copathite, John, Margaret &
Elizabeth, rocf Hopewell MM, dtd 1796,3,7,
also Judith & James rec, two ch whose
names did not appear on cert
1797, 4, 24. Aaron gct Fairfax MM
1799, 5, 3. Randolph gct Westland MM
1801, 1, 30. Anthony dis mou
1801, 5, 1. Jonas dis mou
1802, 10, 1. Timothy Jr. dis disunity
1802, 12, 3. Aaron rocf Fairfax MM, dtd 1802,
9,25
1802, 12, 31. Thomas & w, Deborah, & ch, Coperthwite, John, Margaret, Elizabeth, Judith
& James, gct Westland MM
1802, 12, 31. Phebe Pearson (form Smith) dis

mou
1803, 7, 1. Daniel dis mou
1803, 9, 30. Lydia Mitchener (form Smith)
dis mcd
1804, 3, 30. Hannah (form Jacobs) dis mou
1805, 5, 31. Aaron dis mou
1806, 1, 31. David & w, Judith, & ch, Lydia,
William & Thomas, gct Concord MM, O.
1806, 10, 3. Samuel gct Middleton MM, to m
Catharine Harvey
1806, 10, 3. Sarah Garee (form Smith) dis
mou
1807, 5, 29. Catherine, w Samuel, rocf Middleton MM, dtd 1807,1,10
1808, 7, 29. Timothy gct Shrewsbury MM, to m
Hannah Williams
1810, 6, 29. Hannah, w Timothy, rocf Shrewsbury MM, dtd 1810,4,2
1810, 11, 2. James dis mou
1813, 1, 29. Richard dis disunity
1813, 4, 30. Timothy & w, Hannah, gct Westland MM
1824, 4, 28. Sarah Stockwell (form Smith) dis
mcd
1831, 2, 2. Cert rec for Jesse from Sadsbury
MM, endorsed to Providence MM
1835, 4, 1. Cert rec for Micajah & w, Esther, from Providence MM, dtd 1834,2,22,
endorsed back to Providence MM
1835, 4, 1. Cert rec for Hannah from Providence MM, dtd 1834,2,22, endorsed back to
Providence MM
1835, 9, 2. Susanna rocf Providence MM, dtd
1834,2,27
1835, 9, 2. Mary Ratcliff (form Smith) dis
mou
1835, 9, 30. Jane Exline (form Smith) dis mou
1835, 9, 30. Susanna Hollen (form Smith) dis
mou
1835, 11, 4. Timothy dis mou
1836, 3, 30. George dis mou
1836, 3, 30. Ebeneezer dis mou
1836, 5, 4. Rachel Price (form Smith) dis
mou
1836, 11, 2. Jane Jeffries (form Smith) dis
mou
1839, 4, 3. Jehu dis mcd
1842, 2, 2. John dis mcd
1842, 8, 31. Mahala gct Cincinnati MM, O.
1842, 8, 31. Sarah gct Cincinnati MM, O.
1845, 7, 2. Elizabeth Fear (form Smith) dis
mou
1846, 11, 4. Elias gct Cincinnati MM; returned for non-residence
1846, 11, 4. Joseph gct Cincinnati MM; returned for non-residence
1846, 11, 4. John F. dis mou
1849, 11, 28. Rebecca Garner (form Smith) dis
mcd
1849, 11, 28. Anna Guthry (form Smith) dis mcd
1863, 12, 30. Harvey dis mcd & jas

SOPHER
1836, 11, 30. Joseph & w, Sarah, & ch, Hannah
    & Lydia, rocf Westland MM, dtd 1836,11,23
1840, 4, 29. Joseph & w, Sarah, & ch, Hannah
    & Lydia, gct Providence MM

SPARKS
1814, 6, 3. Sarah (form Cook) dis

SPEAKMAN
1821, 1, 3. Esther rocf Phila. MM, dtd 1820,
    3,30
1823, 4, 30. Esther gct ND MM, Phila., Pa.

SPRAGUE
1828, 4, 30. Matilda (form Townsend) dis mou

SPURGEN
1839, 12, 4. Hannah (form Forman) dis mcd

STAATS
1800, 7, 4. Margaret (form Chandler) dis

STANLEY
1838, 1, 10. Abraham, s Jonathan & Mary,
    Fayette Co., Pa.; m at Redstone, Lydia
    HAINES, dt Eli & Ruth
1840, 4, 25. John d bur Salem
1842, 5, 5. Jonathan, s Jonathan & Mary,
    Columbiana Co., O.; m at Redstone, Hannah
    MILLER, dt David & Elizabeth, Fayette
    Co., Pa.
1856, 7, 27. Abraham d ae 52y bur Salem
1860, 5, 23. Lydia m Joseph HAVILAND

1835, 4, 1. Abraham rocf Marlborough MM, O.,
    dtd 1835,3,3
1838, 4, 4. John rocf Salem MM, O., dtd
    1838,2,21
1842, 6, 29. Hannah M. gct Salem MM, O.

STANTON
1800, 5, 30. Benjamin & w, Mary, & ch, Elias,
    Benjamin, Sarah & Dorcas, rocf Trent MM,
    N. C., dtd 1800,1,12
1801, 1, 30. Cert rec for Benjamin & fam
    some time ago endorsed to Westland MM

STERNE
1852, 9, 29. Ann rocf Westland MM, dtd 1852,
    9,22

STEVENSON
1800, 2, 28. Margaret (form Sidwell) dis mou

STICKLE
1814, 7, 29. George & w, Jane, rocf Westland
    MM, dtd 1814,4,23

STOCKDALE
1794, 1, 24. John rocf Gunpowder MM, dtd
    1792,8,31
1800, 10, 3. John dis mou

STOCKWELL
1824, 4, 28. Sarah (form Smith) dis mcd

STONE
1833, 7, 3. Samuel rocf Fairfax MM, dtd
    1833,5,15 (H)
1837, 3, 1. Samuel dis mcd (H)
1842, 11, 2. Joshua Wood gct Fairfax MM, to
    m Eleanor H. Stone (H)

STRATTON
1802, 1, 1. Benjamin & w, Amy, & ch, Rebekah,
    Naomi & Levi, rocf South River MM, Va.,
    dtd 1801,10,10, endorsed by Westland MM,
    1801,12,26
1804, 11, 30. Benjamin [Stratten] & w, Amy,
    & ch, Rebecca, Naomi, Levi & Ephraim, gct
    Middleton MM

STRAUGHN
1800, 10, 3. Thomas [Strawhen] rocf Richland
    MM, dtd 1799,4,20, endorsed by Westland
    MM, 1800,9,27
1800, 11, 28. Job [Strawhan] rocf Richland MM,
    dtd 1798,3,15
1804, 3, 2. Thomas dis disunity
1813, 7, 2. Job [Straughan] dis mou

STREET
1806, 1, 3. Cert rec for Zadock & w, Eunice,
    & dt, Lydia, (the latter d before the
    cert was rec) from Salem MM, N. J., dtd
    1805,10,28, endorsed at next mtg to Salem
    MM, O.
1806, 1, 3. Cert rec for Anna from Salem
    MM, N. J., dtd 1805,10,28, endorsed at
    next mtg to Salem MM, O.
1806, 5, 30. Cert rec for John & w, Ann, from
    Salem MM, N. J., dtd 1805,12,30, endorsed
    to Salem MM, O.

STROUD
1815, 6, 30. Hannah (form Hannah Morton Sr.)
    dis mou

SWAYNE
1798, 11, 2. Joshua rocf London Grove MM, dtd
    1798,8,1
1803, 9, 30. Joshua gct Concord MM, O.

SWINDLER
1818, 8, 26. Elizabeth (form Airy) con mcd
1819, 1, 27. Elizabeth [Swingler] con mou
1819, 6, 30. Elizabeth gct White Water MM,
    Ind.

TALBOTT
1796, 12, 14. Samuel, s John & Mary, Frederick
    Co., Md.; m at Sewickley, Mary M'GREW, dt
    James & Jane, Westmoreland Co., Pa.

1793, 9, 27. Joseph & w, Mary, & ch, Sarah,
    Elizabeth, Allen & William, rocf Pipe

TALBOTT, continued
    Creek MM, dtd 1793,5,18, endorsed by West-
    land MM, 1793,8,24
1796, 10, 28. Samuel [Talbot] rocf Pipe Creek
    MM, dtd 1796,8,13
1802, 4, 2. Joseph & w, Mary, & ch, Sarah,
    Elizabeth, Allen, William, John, Robert,
    Mary & Hannah, gct Concord MM, N. W. Terri-
    tory
1803, 3, 4. Beulah gct Concord MM, O.
1805, 5, 31. Mary gct Short Creek MM
1806, 8, 29. Benjamin & w, Susanna, & ch,
    John, William, Nathan, Margaret, Elizabeth
    & Benjamin, gct Short Creek MM, O.
1821, 1, 31. John [Talbot] rocf Goose Creek
    MM, dtd 1820,6,29
1824, 6, 30. Jane McCowan (form Talbott) dis
    mou
1828, 10, 29. John [Talbot] gct Smithfield
    MM, O.
1830, 8, 4. James [Talbot] dis mcd
1830, 11, 3. Finly gct Smithfield MM, O.
1830, 11, 3. Mary gct Smithfield MM, O.
1841, 9, 29. Findlay M. con mcd (H)
1842, 3, 2. Findlay M. gct Smithfield MM (H)

TATE
1812, 4, 3. Mary (form John) dis mcd
1812, 4, 3. Susannah (form John) dis mcd

TAYLOR
1796, 2, 26. Jesse rocf London Grove MM, dtd
    1796,4,29
1796, 12, 2. Jesse dis mou
1800, 5, 30. Jonathan & w, Ann, & dt, Rebecca,
    rocf Crooked Run MM, Va., dtd 1800,3,1
1801, 1, 30. Cert rec for Jonathan & fam some
    time ago endorsed to Westland MM
1800, 11, 28. Mary (form Kirk) rst by rq
1806, 2, 28. Jesse con mcd

THISTLETHWAITE
1821, 1, 3. Anthony rocf Frankford MM, dtd
    1820,8,25
1822, 1, 30. Anthony gct Frankford MM, Pa.

THOMAS
1800, 11, 28. Patience, minor, rocf Content-
    ney MM, N. C., dtd 1800,3,8
1803, 12, 30. David & s, Able, rocf Westland
    MM, dtd 1803,12,24
1804, 8, 31. Samuel Clark & w, Ruth, & appren-
    tice, Abel Thomas, gct Westland MM
1805, 6, 28. David & w, Mary, gct Middleton
    MM
1807, 12, 4. Samuel Clark & w, Ruth, & appren-
    tice, Abel Thomas, rocf Westland MM, dtd
    1807,7,25
1808, 7, 1. Thomas French & w, Esther, &
    two apprentices, Moses Townsend & Patience
    Thomas, gct Salem MM
1808, 9, 30. Abel, minor, gct Middleton MM
1816, 6, 26. John & w, Elizabeth, & ch,

    Elizabeth, Sarah-ann & Lydia, rocf Center
    MM, Del., dtd 1816,5,6
1816, 6, 26. Alice rocf Center MM, Del., dtd
    1816,5,6
1816, 6, 26. Mary rocf Center MM, Del., dtd
    1816,5,6
1816, 8, 21. Cert rec for John & fam endorsed
    to White Water MM, Ind.
1816, 8, 21. Cert rec for Alice endorsed to
    White Water MM, Ind.
1816, 8, 21. Cert rec for Mary endorsed to
    White Water MM, Ind.
1828, 6, 4. Hannah (form Sidwell) dis mcd

THOMPSON
1816, 1, 24. Mary recrq
1824, 3, 3. Martha recrq
1828, 9, 3. Martha gct Salem MM, O.

THORN
1800, 9, 11. Sarah m Robert VAIL

1802, 12, 31. Isaac & w, Hannah, & ch, Marga-
    ret, William, Elizabeth, Thomas & Mary,
    gct Concord MM, N. W. Territory
1803, 6, 3. Catherine gct Concord MM, O.
1844, 2, 28. Edgar [Thorne] rocf New York
    MM, dtd 1843, directed to Providence MM
    but accepted by this mtg without an en-
    dorsement from Providence MM

TILTON
1816, 5, 22. Enoch & w, Elizabeth, & ch,
    James, Mary, Sarah, Mathias, Enoch, Joseph,
    John & Charles, rocf Westland MM, dtd
    1816,4,25

TOWNSEND
----, --, --. John & Sarah
    Ch: Sarah   b 1792, 8, 23
        Nancy   " 1794, 10, 31
        Hannah   " 1796, 10, 10
        John   " 1800, 4, 3
        Matilda   " 1805, 8, 4
        Wm. Colum-
        bus   " 1808, 7, 13
1815, 9, 6. Sabina m John Mc DONNELL
1837, 8, 24. Sarah d ae 7ly bur Sandy Hill

1794, 4, 25. Edith, w Jesse, gct Westland MM
1796, 4, 22. Hannah, w Joseph, & ch, Eliza-
    beth, Sarah & John Fares, rocf Wilmington
    MM, dtd 1795,12,16, endorsed by Westland
    MM, 1796,3,26
1799, 5, 3. Joseph Jr. rocf Wilmington MM,
    dtd 1799,2,13
1800, 5, 30. Hannah & s, John, gct Westland
    MM
1800, 8, 29. Cert rec for Isaac, s Joseph,
    from Concord MM, dtd 1799,9,4, endorsed to
    Westland MM
1800, 10, 31. Elizabeth gct Westland MM
1803, 4, 1. Joseph Jr. dis mou

TOWNSEND, continued

1803, 7, 1. Moses rocf Westland MM, dtd 1803,6,25

1803, 10, 28. Sarah Evans (form Townsend) dis mcd

1804, 3, 2. Hannah Adams (form Townsend) dis mou

1804, 8, 31. John dis disunity

1805, 11, 1. Jesse & w, Edith, & ch, Sabina, Rees Cadwalader, Ruth & Ann, rocf Westland MM, dtd 1805,10,26

1808, 7, 1. Thomas French & w, Esther, & two apprentices, Moses Townsend & Patience Thomas, gct Salem MM

1809, 7, 28. Amos dis disunity

1809, 7, 28. Moses rocf Salem MM, O., dtd 1809,4,11

1810, 9, 28. Moses dis mou

1812, 2, 28. Robert rocf Baltimore MM for Western District, dtd 1811,8,7

1814, 6, 3. Martha (form Hendrix) dis

1816, 2, 21. Amos Jr. dis mcd

1816, 8, 21. Salem MM, O. was given permission to rst Martha

1816, 9, 25. Robert dis mcd

1818, 2, 18. Thomas gct Marlborough MM, O.

1820, 11, 1. Sarah Hammond (form Townsend) dis mcd

1823, 12, 3. Nancy Hubert (form Townsend) dis mcd (also Hobert)

1825, 9, 28. Ann Hopkins (form Townsend) dis mcd

1827, 7, 4. Reese dis mcd

1827, 10, 31. Hannah gct Salem MM, O.

1828, 4, 30. Matilda Sprague (form Townsend) dis mcd

1829, 4, 29. Edith & Ruth dis JH

1829, 11, 4. Jesse dis JH

1830, 3, 31. John gct Marlboro MM, O.

TRAMER

1850, 9, 25. Elizabeth McCracken (form Tramer) con mcd (H)

TRAYER

1806, 5, 30. Elizabeth rocf Concord MM, O., dtd 1806,1,22

1814, 10, 28. Elizabeth Edwards (form Trayer) dis mcd

TRIMBLE

1802, 4, 2. John [Tremble] & w, Rachel, & ch, Charity, John & William, rocf Southland MM, dtd 1801,12,2

1804, 8, 31. Catherine, minor, rocf Southland MM, dtd 1804,2,1

1806, 5, 30. John & w, Rachel, & ch, William, John & Isaac, gct Miami MM

TROTH

----, --, --. Henry & Hannah
    Ch: Hannah   b 1796, 11, 14
         Elizabeth " 1799, 4, 17 d 1819,5,31

1816, 7, 16. Wm. d ae 31y bur Redstone

1817, 5, 28. Mary m Joel OXLEY

1821, 8, 21. Henry d ae 63y bur Redstone

1823, 10, 2. Hannah S. m Aquila COATS

1828, 3, 11. Hannah d ae 69y bur Redstone

1795, 11, 27. Henry & w, Hannah, & ch, William, Sarah, John, Jane & Margaret, rocf Wilmington MM, dtd 1795,5,13, endorsed by Westland MM, 1795,8,23

1812, 8, 28. John dis

1814, 9, 30. Margaret Truman (form Troth) dis mcd

1826, 11, 29. Jane gct Marlborough MM, O.

TRUMAN

1807, 7, 3. Morris & w, Mary, & s, Morris, rocf Chester MM, dtd 1807,4,27

1807, 8, 28. Joseph rocf Chester MM, dtd 1807,4,27

1807, 8, 28. James rocf Chester MM, dtd 1807,4,27

1814, 7, 29. James dis mcd

1814, 9, 30. Margaret (form Troth) dis mcd

1818, 3, 25. Margaret rst by rq

1829, 4, 29. Mary & Margaret dis JH

1829, 6, 3. Morris dis JH

1834, 2, 26. Joseph dis disunity

1834, 2, 26. Morris dis disunity

TYMANUS (also Temanus)

1806, 7, 4. Margery (form Wiggens) dis mou

TYSON

1818, 10, 21. William R. & Samuel [Tysen], minors, rocf ND MM, Phila., Pa.

1819, 1, 27. Ann, wife Joseph, & ch, Daniel T., Job R., Charles M., Esther F., Joseph Jr. & James Jr. rocf WD MM, Phila., Pa., dtd 1818,12,16

1823, 1, 29. Ann, w Joseph, & ch, Job R., Samuel H., Charles M., Esther F., Joseph & James, gct WD MM, Phila., Pa. (12th St)

UNDERWOOD

1794, 11, 21. Benjamin, minor, rocf Deer Creek MM, dtd 1794,8,28, endorsed by York MM, 1794,10,8

1798, 6, 29. William & w, Sarah, & ch, John, Susannah, Sarah, Benjamin, Willing, Joseph & Betty, rocf Westland MM, dtd 1798,5,26

1800, 5, 2. Willin & w, Sarah, & ch, John, Susannah, Sarah, Benjamin, Joseph, Betty & Willin, gct Westland MM

1801, 1, 2. Benjamin dis disunity

1803, 9, 2. John rocf Westland MM, dtd 1803,7,23

1810, 5, 4. Hannah, w Abraham, & ch, Jane, Elihu & Cyruss, rocf Baltimore MM for the Western District, dtd 1809,1,11

1812, 10, 30. Jane McKay (form Underwood) dis mcd

1813, 1, 29. Elisha dis disunity

UNDERWOOD, continued
1827, 5, 30. Cyrus dis mcd
1847, 3, 31. George W. dis jas
1847, 12, 1. James dis mcd

UPDEGRAFF
1794, 6, 27. James [Updegraft] rocf York MM,
    dtd 1794,2,5
1795, 2, 27. Abner [Updegraft] rocf York MM,
    dtd 1794,7,9
1796, 6, 3. Ann [Updegraft] & ch, Eli, Edith
    & Ann, rocf York MM, dtd 1792,1,4, endors-
    ed by Westland MM, 1795,11,30
1797, 9, 29. Edith Phips (form Updegraff) dis
    mou
1799, 8, 30. James rocf Crooked Run MM, dtd
    1799,6,1
1802, 12, 31. Abner dis mou
1802, 12, 31. James dis disunity
1803, 10, 28. Ann Kerwoo (form Updegraff) dis
    mou (also Kevode & Kervode)
1804, 6, 1. Susanna (form Jackson) dis
1813, 9, 3. Susanna rocf York MM, dtd 1813,
    7,7
1816, 11, 20. Susanna gct Cincinnati MM, O.

VAIL
1800, 9, 11. Robert, s Abraham & Margaret,
    Fayette Co., Pa.; m at Sandy Hill, Sarah
    THORN, dt Isaac & Hannah, Fayette Co., Pa.
----, --, --. Samuel & Agnes
    Ch: Charles   b 1805, 1, 24
        Priscilla " 1806, 8, 29
        Mercy   " 1808, 1, 17
        Hannah   " 1810, 7, 5
        Joel   " 1812, 2, 1
        Jesse   " 1814, 3, 31
1810, 1, 4. Mercy m Jesse BALL

1793, 8, 23. Abraham [Veal] & w, Margaret, &
    ch, Benjamin, Mercy, Robert, Samuel,
    Stephen, Catherine & Taylor, rocf Raway &
    Plainfield MM, dtd 1793,4,17, endorsed by
    Westland MM, 1793,7,27
1797, 9, 29. Mary Russell (form Vail) dis
    mou
1798, 2, 2. Sarah Burge (form Vail) dis mcd
1799, 3, 29. Stephen Jr. dis mou
1800, 1, 3. Shubal dis mou
1802, 4, 30. Benjamin & w, Rebecca, & ch,
    Rachel, Anna & Nathan, gct Concord MM,
    N. W. Territory
1802, 4, 30. Robert & w, Sarah, & s, Isaac,
    gct Concord MM, N. W. Territory
1804, 3, 2. Samuel gct Westland MM, to m
    Agness Griswald
1804, 6, 1. Agnes, w Samuel, rocf Westland
    MM, dtd 1804,5,20
1805, 3, 1. Stephen & w, Mary, & ch, Aaron,
    Randolph, Catherine & Hugh, gct Miami MM;
    rem about 1800
1822, 5, 1. Catharine Davis (form Vail) dis
    mcd

1824, 3, 4. Taylor dis mcd
1824, 6, 2. Eliza (form Ball) dis mcd
1827, 5, 2. Abraham gct Providence MM
1838, 8, 29. Rachel (form Willets) dis mcd
1862, 12, 31. Samuel & w, Elizabeth, & ch, Ed-
    ward, Abraham & Lydia, dis joining Wilbur-
    ite Separatists

VANDEVERT
1828, 6, 4. Sarah (form Sidwell) dis mcd

VERNON
1796, 7, 1. Sarah, w Benjamin, rocf Kennet
    MM, dtd 1796,6,16
1801, 12, 4. Rachel (form Cadwalader) dis mou
1807, 7, 31. Sarah, w Benjamin, gct Westland
    MM
1820, 8, 30. Mary (form Garwood) dis mcd

VIA
1804, 1, 4. Mary m David THOMAS

1803, 7, 1. Mary rocf South River MM, dtd
    1802,9,11, endorsed by Westland MM, 1803,
    5,28

VICKERS
1794, 8, 22. Rebecca rocf Evesham MM, West
    Jersey, dtd 1794,5,9

VORE
1809, 2, 3. Cert rec for Benjamin from Bal-
    timore MM for Western District, dtd 1808,
    9,7, endorsed to Westland MM
1820, 3, 1. Cert rec for Isaac from Balti-
    more MM for Western District, dtd 1820,1,
    7, endorsed to Westland MM
1835, 7, 29. Mary (form Newburn) dis mou

WAINWRIGHT
1834, 6, 4. Thomas B. [Wainright] rocf Phila.
    MM, dtd 1834,1,30
1834, 7, 30. Thomas B. dis mcd

WAITES
1805, 8, 2. Sarah (form Negus) con mou

WALKER
1803, 3, 10. Elizabeth m Richard SMITH
1828, 10, 2. Lewis B., s Abel & Mary, Belmont
    Co., O.; m at Redstone, Tamson HAINES, dt
    Eli & Ruth, Fayette Co., Pa.

1796, 2, 26. George gct Westland MM, to m
    Anna Garrison
1796, 6, 3. Anna rocf Westland MM, dtd 1796,
    4,23
1798, 2, 2. Mary Purviance (form Walker), w
    David, dis mcd
1810, 6, 1. George & w, Anna, & ch, Ebenezar,
    Mary, Isaac & George Bruce, gct Concord
    MM, O.
1814, 9, 30. Isaac, minor, rocf Concord MM,

WALKER, continued
    dtd 1814,7,21
1815, 7, 28. Isaac E., minor, gct Plainfield
    MM, O.
1817, 5, 21. Sina & Leah dis jas
1828, 10, 29. Tamson (form Haines) gct Flush-
    ing MM, O.

WALTER
1800, 2, 28. Thomas rocf Concord MM, dtd
    1799,4,3, endorsed by Westland MM, 1799,
    12,28
1801, 7, 31. Thomas [Walters] dis mou

WALTON
1813, 4, 2. Jesse & w, Ann, & ch, Tacy,
    Uree, Amos, Jehu & Lydia, rocf Fallow-
    field MM, dtd 1812,9,14
1816, 10, 23. Jesse & w, Ann, & ch, Tacy,
    Uree, Amos, Jehu, Lydia, Ann & Benjamin,
    gct Salem MM, O.
1861, 8, 28. Abner Gilbert gct Driftwood MM,
    Ind., to m Anzanette Walton

WANEY
1837, 5, 25. Patience d ae 88y bur Redstone

WARNER
1821, 2, 7. Thomas Ellicott, s Asaph & Ruth,
    Fayette Co., Pa.; m at Redstone, Mary Ann
    WORLEY, dt John & Elizabeth, Fayette Co.,
    Pa.
1823, 12, 12. John, s Thomas & Mary Ann, b

1796, 4, 22. Cert rec for Mary, w Isaac,
    from Kennet MM, dtd 1796,1,14, endorsed
    to Westland MM
1820, 3, 29. Thomas E. rocf Deer Creek MM,
    dtd 1820,3,6
1827, 5, 30. Thomas E. & w, Mary Ann, & s,
    John, gct Deer Creek MM, Md.
1838, 5, 2. Thomas E. & w, Mary Ann, & ch,
    Ruth, Elizabeth & James, rocf Deer Creek
    MM, dtd 1838,3,15 (H)
1843, 12, 27. Thomas E. dis mcd (H)
1845, 1, 22. Thomas E. rst by rq (H)
1845, 9, 24. Mary Ann, dt Thomas E. & Rhoda,
    recrq (H)
1846, 3, 25. Rhoda recrq (H)

WARRINGTON
1839, 3, 6. John R., s Abraham & Keziah,
    Columbiana Co., O.; m at Redstone, Rachel
    GARWOOD, dt Jesse & Lydia, Fayette Co., Pa.

1839, 7, 3. Rachel gct Upper Springfield
    MM, O.

WEAVER
1793, 8, 23. William dis mou
1802, 3, 5. Sarah Simms (form Weaver) dis
    mou
1830, 2, 29. Abraham dis

1830, 2, 29. James dis

WEBB
1798, 8, 3. Hannah (form Kirk) dis mou

WEBSTER
1795, 11, 27. William dis mou
1803, 12, 2. Susannah Ramsey (form Webster)
    dis mou
1805, 3, 1. Hannah, wd Taylor, & s, John,
    gct Miami MM; rem about 1799

WELCH
1806, 8, 29. Jane recrq

WELLS
1800, 5, 2. Levi recrq
1801, 3, 6. John & w, Catherine, & ch,
    Mary, Isaiah, Elizabeth, Susanna, Thomas
    & Sarah, rocf New Garden MM, Pa., dtd [1
    1800,1,4, endorsed by Hopewell MM, 1800,9,
1801, 8, 28. Susannah rocf Hopewell MM, dtd
    1800,6,2
1802, 4, 2. Levi gct Concord MM, N. W. Terri-
    tory
1802, 7, 30. Susannah gct Concord MM, N. W.
    Territory
1802, 10, 1. Mary dis
1803, 4, 29. John & w, Catherine, & ch,
    Isaiah, Elizabeth, Susannah, Thomas & Sa-
    rah, gct Concord MM, O.

WETSEL
1807, 8, 28. Sarah (form Duly) dis mcd

WEYMORE
1817, 1, 22. Margaret (form Johns) dis mcd

WHEELER
1849, 3, 23. Ellis Lilley gct Gunpowder MM,
    to m Honor C. Wheeler (H)

WHITE
1800, 8, 1. Ann (form Brown) con mou
1811, 6, 28. Ann gct Salem MM, O.

WICKERSHAM
1809, 6, 30. Isaac rocf Hopewell MM, dtd
    1808,11,7
1810, 2, 2. Isaac dis disunity
1810, 2, 2. Isaac rocf Wilmington MM, Del.,
    dtd 1809,5,7
1816, 9, 25. Isaac dis mcd
1818, 11, 25. Thomas & w, Susanna, & s, Eli-
    jah, rocf Wilmington MM, dtd 1818,7,31
1819, 2, 24. Sarah, w John, & ch, Sarah
    Evans, Thomas Bartlett, George & David
    Evans, rocf WD MM, Phila., Pa., dtd 1818,
    12,16
1820, 11, 29. Elijah dis mcd
1821, 10, 3. Thomas & w, Sarah, gct Salem MM,
    O.
1823, 4, 30. Sarah, w John, & ch, Sarah

WICKERSHAM, continued
    Evans & William Morrison, gct ND MM,
    Phila., Pa.
1853, 2, 2. Cincinnati MM was given per-
    mission to rst Elijah

WIGGINS
1803, 10, 28. Cuthbert & w, Margaret, & ch,
    Martha & Hannah, rocf Wrightstown MM, dtd
    1802,6,8
1804, 6, 29. Margery rocf Deer Creek MM, dtd
    1804,2,23
1806, 7, 4. Margery Tymanus (form Wiggens)
    dis mou (also Temanus)
1812, 5, 1. Cuthbert dis disunity
1826, 8, 30. Hannah McMullin (form Wiggins)
    dis mcd
1832, 1, 4. Teresa McGuilkin (late Wiggins)
    dis mcd (also McQuilkin)
1835, 9, 2. Eliza Downard (late Wiggins)
    dis mou
1843, 2, 1. Harrison dis mcd
1844, 10, 30. Martha Griffith (form Wiggins)
    dis mou

WILDMAN
1802, 1, 1. John dis disunity
1816, 11, 20. Cinthy gct Clear Creek MM, O.
1816, 11, 20. Rebecca & dt, Zillah, gct Clear
    Creek MM, O.
1816, 12, 25. Townsend gct Clear Creek MM, O.

WILKINS
1804, 5, 4. Cert rec for Amos from Cedar
    Creek MM, Va., dtd 1804,1,14, endorsed to
    Westland MM
1804, 5, 4. Cert rec for Joseph & w, Sarah,
    & ch, Susanna, Rachel, Daniel, Joseph,
    Sarah, Elizabeth, Tamson, William & John,
    from Cedar Creek MM, Va., dtd 1803,11,12,
    endorsed to Middleton MM, O.

WILLETS
----, --, --. Samuel & Elizabeth [Willits]
    Ch: Isaiah   b 1797, 3, 31
        Ellis   " 1798, 10, 16
        John   " 1800, 5, 7
        Eli   " 1801, 8, 25
        Joel   " 1800, 10, 22 (?)
        Taylor   " 1806, 6, 10
        Sarah   " 1809, 11, 13
        Samuel   " 1814, 10, 6
1797, 12, 14. Sarah m Samuel COOPE
1805, 1, 24. Elizabeth m Samuel FORMAN
----, --, --. Jesse & Rebecca [Willits]
    Ch: Israel   b 1809, 11, 24
        Asa   " 1811, 9, 19
        Ruth   " 1813, 5, 29
        Lee   " 1815, 9, 27
        Rachel   " 1818, 4, 4
        Ammi   " 1820, 8, 18
        Ezra C.   " 1824, 6, 5
        Milton   " 1827, 2, 12

    Ch: Mary   b 1830, 11, 29
1809, 6, 8. Jesse, s John & Rachel, Monon-
    galia Co., Pa.; m at Sandy Creek, Rebeccah
    FORMAN, dt Robert & Mary, Monongalia Co.,
    Pa.
1811, 11, 4. Asa d bur Sandy Creek
1826, 7, 11. John d ae 78y bur Sandy Creek
1830, 8, 8. Rachel d ae 83y bur Sandy Creek
1830, 12, 25. Mary d bur Sandy Creek
1830, 10, 24. Mary, dt John & Elizabeth, b
1831, 10, 1. Jesse d ae 47y bur Sandy Creek
1831, 10, 17. Lee d bur Sandy Creek
1845, 12, 21. Milton d bur Sandy Creek

1793, 6, 21. Rachel [Willits], w John, & ch,
    Samuel, Sarah, Ellis, Elizabeth & Jessa,
    rocf Pipe Creek MM, dtd 1793,2,16, endors-
    ed by Westland, 1793,4,27
1801, 7, 3. John rocf Pipe Creek MM, dtd
    1801,2,14
1806, 5, 30. Ellis [Willitts] dis
1810, 11, 2. Jesse & w, Rebeckah, dis
1815, 3, 3. Samuel & w, Elizabeth, & ch,
    Iaaiah, Ellis, John, Eli, Joel, Taylor,
    Sarah & Samuel, gct Short Creek MM
1815, 6, 30. Jesse rst by rq
1815, 6, 30. Rebecca rst by rq
1815, 7, 28. Israel & Ruth, ch Jesse & Re-
    becca, recrq
1821, 5, 2. Smithfield MM was given permis-
    sion to rst Ellis
1823, 6, 4. John M. [Willits] rocf Allum
    Creek MM, O.
1829, 11, 4. John gct Smithfield MM, O., to m
    Elizabeth Purviance
1830, 4, 28. Elizabeth P. rocf Smithfield MM,
    O., dtd 1830,4,19
1831, 11, 2. John & w, Elizabeth, gct Smith-
    field MM, O.
1837, 2, 1. Ruth Frankhouser (form Willets)
    dis mou
1838, 8, 29. Rachel Vail (form Willets) dis
    mcd
1844, 7, 3. Israel [Willits] dis
1844, 12, 4. Ammi [Willetts] gct Smithfield
    MM, O., to m Maria Hammond
1846, 2, 4. Ammi gct Smithfield MM
1853, 3, 2. Ezra gct Alum Creek MM, O.
1853, 6, 1. Rebecca gct Alum Creek MM, O.

WILLIAMS
----, --, --. John & Sarah
    Ch: Benjamin   b 1815, 6, 6
        Hannah   " 1817, 2, 27
        Robert   " 1819, 5, 21
        Ann Shoe-
        bridge   " 1820, 8, 18
        John
        Bouvier   " 1822, 8, 4
        Elizabeth   " 1824, 11, 18

1808, 7, 29. Timothy Smith gct Shrewsbury MM,
    to m Hannah Williams

WILLIAMS, continued

1814, 3, 4. Sarah rocf Stillwater MM, O.,
   dtd 1813,11,30
1814, 4, 29. John rocf Concord MM, dtd 1813,
   10,21
1827, 4, 4. John S. & w, Sarah, & ch, Benjamin, Hannah, Robert, Ann, John & Elizabeth,
   gct Plainfield MM, O.
1846, 12, 2. William Darlington gct Salem MM,
   to m Catherine Williams
1852, 12, 29. Phebe J. gct Sandy Spring MM, O.

WILLIS

----, --, --. Henry & Lydia
   Ch: Joel   b 1821, 5, 20
       Robert   " 1823, 6, 17
       Sarah   " 1825, 4, 25
1832, 11, 1. Lydia m Israel JENKINS

1820, 11, 29. Lydia (form Miller) dis mcd
1822, 1, 2. Lydia M. rst by rq
1822, 1, 30. Henry recrq
1823, 10, 29. Joel, s Henry, recrq
1833, 1, 2. Lydia Jenkins & ch, Joel & Susan Willis, gct Short Creek MM, O.
1840, 9, 30. Joel rocf Short Creek MM
1843, 8, 30. Joel gct Westland MM

WILSON

1794, 1, 24. Martha gct Westland MM
1794, 6, 27. Jeremiah & w, Joanna, rocf Kingwood MM, dtd 1793,5,9, endorsed by Westland MM, dtd 1794,4,26
1797, 11, 3. Mercy & ch, John, Benjamin,
   Isaiah, Robert, Mercy, Caleb, Gabriel &
   Rebekah, rocf Kingwood MM, dtd 1796,9,8
1806, 3, 29. John dis mcd
1806, 1, 31. Benjamin dis mou
1808, 4, 1. Mercy Clelland (form Wilson) dis
   mou
1810, 11, 30. Rebecca gct Miami MM
1810, 11, 30. Jeremiah & w, Joanna, & ch, Gabriel, Elizabeth, Edith, Henry & William,
   gct Miami MM
1810, 11, 30. Gabriel gct Miami MM
1818, 9, 23. Oliver rocf New Garden MM, dtd
   1818,6,4

WINDERS

1796, 2, 26. James [Windor] rocf Kennet MM,
   dtd 1795,10,15
1796, 2, 26. Hannah rocf Kennet MM, dtd
   1795,10,15
1796, 4, 22. Cert rec for John & w, Margaret,
   & ch, Ann, Abner, Mercy & Elizabeth,
   from Kennet MM, dtd 1795,11,12, endorsed
   to Westland MM
1796, 6, 3. Cert rec for Hannah some time
   ago endorsed to Westland MM
1799, 3, 1. James [Winder] gct Westland MM
1804, 11, 30. Ann (form Kirk) dis mou

WOOD

1802, 1, 6. Neomi m John MICHENER
1822, 9, 5. Ann m Job HOLLOWAY
1825, 3, 9. John, s John & Catharine, Fayette Co., Pa.; m at Redstone, Hannah
   LILLEY, dt Thomas & Ruth, Wash. Co., Pa.
1833, 7, 11. Josiah d ae 69y bur Sandy Creek
1842, 8, 30. Catherine d
1845, 2, 9. John d

1795, 7, 24. Jonah rocf Fairfax MM, dtd
   1794,9,27
1800, 3, 28. John & w, Catharine, & ch, Nathan, Rebecca, Sarah & Catherine, rocf
   Hopewell MM, dtd 1799,11,4
1801, 7, 3. Joseph & w, Abigail, & s,
   Jesse, rocf Fairfax MM, dtd 1801,3,28
1801, 10, 2. Naomi rocf Fairfax MM, dtd 1801,
   3,28
1804, 12, 28. Ruth (form Gregg) con mou
1806, 3, 28. Ruth gct Hopewell MM
1809, 3, 31. Joseph & w, Abigail, gct Fairfax
   MM
1809, 4, 28. Jesse gct Fairfax MM
1815, 6, 30. Catherine Johnson (form Wood)
   dis mcd
1816, 2, 21. Joshua rocf Hopewell MM, dtd
   1815,11,9
1818, 12, 23. Jesse rocf Hopewell MM, dtd
   1818,11,3
1824, 3, 31. Jesse gct Hopewell MM, Va.
1828, 10, 1. Sarah Phillips (form Wood) dis
   mcd
1831, 6, 29. Elizabeth Phillips (form Wood)
   dis mou & jH
1831, 8, 31. Hannah dis jH
1833, 9, 4. Joshua dis disunity
1838, 8, 29. Maria Cock (form Wood) dis mcd
1840, 7, 29. John Jr. dis jH
1842, 11, 2. Joshua gct Fairfax MM, to m
   Eleanor H. Stone (H)
1843, 2, 1. John con mcd (H)
1843, 3, 29. Lydia Blackburn (form Wood) dis
   mcd
1843, 10, 25. Eleanor H. rocf Fairfax MM, Va.,
   dtd 1843,8,16 (H)
1846, 11, 4. Amos dis mcd
1850, 5, 22. Joshua gct Fairfax MM, Va. (H)
1850, 5, 22. Eleanor H. gct Fairfax MM (H)
1864, 9, 28. Amos T. Griffith gct Smithfield
   MM, O., to m Mary E. Wood

WOODWARD

1856, 2, 12. Hope d bur Sandy Hill

1806, 8, 1. Hope (form Shotwell) con mou

WORKMAN

1815, 3, 3. Sarah (form Penrose) dis mou

WORLEY   [ER
1821, 2, 7. Mary Ann m Thomas Ellicott WARN-
1821, 2, 14. Ann d ae 8ly bur Redstone

WORLEY
1794, 5, 23. John gct York MM
1797, 3, 3. John rocf York MM, dtd 1796,1,
    6, endorsed by Westland MM, 1796,4,23
1802, 4, 2. John gct York MM
1814, 9, 2. Ann rocf York MM, dtd 1814,6,8
1814, 10, 26. John & w, Elizabeth, & ch, Mary-
    ann, Aron, Jacob, Caleb, Asa & Lydia, rocf
    York MM, dtd 1814,9,7
1829, 7, 29. John dis JH
1830, 2, 3. Elizabeth dis JH
1830, 3, 31. Aaron gct Providence MM
1834, 7, 2. Jacob dis disunity
1834, 7, 2. Lydia dis disunity
1834, 7, 30. Caleb dis disunity
1836, 8, 3. Lydia Lynch (form Worley) dis
    mcd (H)
1840, 6, 3. Asa dis mcd

WORREL
1797, 6, 30. Benjamin [Worrell] rocf Robeson
    MM, dtd 1797,5,24
1801, 7, 31. Cert rec for Eleanor from Robe-
    son MM, dtd 1798,11,27, endorsed to West-
    land MM
1804, 8, 3. Benjamin gct Short Creek MM

WRIGHT
1813, 9, 3. David Cattell gct Hopewell MM,
    to m Margaret Wright

YARNALL
1794, 11, 21. Susanna, George, Mary, Aaron,
    Amos, Eli & Mordecai, ch George, rocf
    Gunpowder MM, dtd 1794,6,28, endorsed by

        *   *   *   *   *   *   *

ANTRAM
1824, 2, 12. Mary m William CAMPBELL

BURNET
1800, 3, 6. Rebecca m Job JEFRIS

CAMPBELL
1796, 12, 15. Mary m Jesse BEESON

COATS
1823, 10, 2. Aquila. s Moses & Mary, Stark
    Co., O.; m at Redstone, Hannah S. TROTH,
    dt Henry & Hannah, Fayette Co., Pa.

COOK
1838, 4, 5. Nathan, s Elisha & Lydia, Colum-
    biana Co., O.; m at Redstone, Ann BINNS,
    dt David & Margaret, Fayette Co., Pa.

GARWOOD
1839, 3, 6. Rachel m John R. WARRINGTON

HUNT
1807, 6, 3. Esther m John COLLINS

Westland MM, 1794,9,27
1796, 9, 2. Susannah Hill (form Yarnall) dis
    mou
1796, 9, 30. Mary [Yarnel] dis jas
1798, 5, 4. George & w, Lydia, rocf Gunpow-
    der MM, dtd 1797,8,26
1800, 1, 3. George Jr. dis mou
1800, 1, 3. Sarah (form Newburn), w George,
    Jr., dis mou
1801, 10, 2. Eli [Yarnell], minor s George,
    gct Abington MM
1806, 5, 2. George & w, Lydia, gct Short
    Creek MM
1812, 12, 4. Mordecai gct Short Creek MM

YEATES
1814, 11, 2. William, s William & Elizabeth,
    Washington, D. C.; m at Redstone, Hannah
    CATTELL, dt Jonas & Elizabeth, Fayette
    Co., Pa.

1814, 12, 30. Hannah [Yeats] gct Indian Spring
    MM, Md.

YEATMAN
1795, 8, 21. John dis disunity

YOUNG
1805, 3, 29. Rachel (form Hayhurst) dis mou
1806, 1, 3. Ann (form Chandler) con mcd
1808, 7, 29. Hercules recrq
1823, 10, 29. Herculus & w, Ann, & ch, Dina,
    Eli, Ann, Morgan, John & Hannah, gct
    Flushing MM, O.

        *   *   *   *   *   *   *

PENROSE
1807, 7, 9. Joseph, s Jesse & Sarah, Monon-
    galia Co., Va.; m at Sandy Creek, Mary
    MORTON, dt Samuel & Hannah, Monongalia
    Co., Va.

SMITH
1815, 9, 14. Joseph, s John & Sarah, Mononga-
    halah Co., Pa.; m at Sandy Hill, Mahala
    FREEMAN, dt Benjamin & Sarah, Fayette Co.,
    Pa.

THOMAS
1804, 1, 4. David, s Jesse & Sarah, Fayette
    Co., Pa.; m at Redstone, Mary VIA, dt Jo-
    seph Stratton & w, Naomi, Fayette Co., Pa.

WILLIAMS
1852, 9, 30. Caspar, s Daniel & Mary, Colum-
    biana Co., O.; m at Redstone, Phebe J.
    ALLEN, dt Joshua & Sybbel Jenkins, Fayette
    Co., Pa.

WOOD
1827, 3, 8. Sabina, dt John & Hanna, b

PROVIDENCE MONTHLY MEETING

Providence Monthly Meeting, located in Fayette County, Pennsylvania, was set up as a Preparative Meeting by Redstone Monthly Meeting in 1789. The Friends met in a one story stone building. The date of the building is unknown but it is believed to have been occupied from the date of organization to 1832. In 1895, Mrs. Mary Binns, a descendant of the early Quakers, rebuilt the meeting house with the materials of the original building.

In January 1832 the Pennsylvania General Assembly approved an act appointing Jesse Coldron and Jesse Negrin as trustees of the Providence Preparative Meeting and further provided that in the case of death or removal of one or both of these trustees, the Providence meeting could appoint new trustees.

Death and removals caused the membership to be so reduced in number that the remaining members were transferred to Redstone meeting at Brownsville between 1832 and 1870. Providence Preparative Meeting was laid down in 1870. The only record we have found concerning a monthly meeting is one in the Redstone Quarterly Meeting records which indicates that Providence Monthly Meeting was established in 1817 and that it was still in existence in 1826.

RECORDS

ALLMON
1868, 9, 24. Thomas Blackburn gct Middleton
     MM, 0., to m Sarah Allmon

ARMSTRONG
1828, 10, 3. Samuel, s James & Ruth, Columbi-
     ana Co., 0.; m in Providence, Elizabeth
     COPE, dt Joshua & Alice, Fayette Co., Pa.

BAILEY
1823, 3, 25. Margaret (form Ghrist) dis mcd

BARRET
1819, 1, 26. Hannah Doyel (form Barret) dis
     mcd

BENEDICT
1841, 10, 9. Charles d bur Providence
1844, 8, 2. Cyrus, s Cyrus & Hannah, Mirrion
     Co., 0.; m in Providence, Hannah COPE, dt
     John & Sarah, Fayette Co., Pa.

1841, 3, 4. Cyrus, minor, rocf Plymouth-
     Smithfield MM, 0., dtd 1841,1,18
1841, 4, 29. Charles, minor, rocf Allum Creek
     MM, 0., dtd 1841,1,28
1845, 10, 2. Cyrus & Hannah gct Allum Creek
     MM, 0.

BLACK
1827, 7, 24. Clayton rocf Upper Springfield
     MM, dtd 1827,4,4
1827, 10, 4. Clayton gct Marlborough MM, 0.

BINNS
1826, 5, 4. James, s John & Sarah, Fayette
     Co., Pa.; m in Providence, Elizabeth HEW-
     ITT, dt Jonathan & Ann, Fayette Co., Pa.
     Ch: Daniel   b 1828, 6, 12
----, --, --. William & Ruth
     Ch: Gibson   b 1830, 12, 10
         Charles   " 1832, 2, 19 d 1838, 5,31
           bur Providence
         Richard   b 1834, 1, 28
         Robert   " 1835, 7, 26 d 1838, 6,21
           bur Providence
         David   b 1837, 2, 18
         Mary   " 1838, 9, 16
         Amos   " 1840, 5, 17
1834, 1, 9. John, s James & Alice, Fayette
     Co., Pa.; m in Providence, Sarah A. HEWITT
     dt Abel & Rachel, Fayette Co., Pa.
1854, 8, 25. Gibson, s William & Ruth, Harri-
     son Co., 0.; m in Providence, Martha V.
     COPE, dt Samuel & Mercy, Fayette Co., Pa.
1865, 9, 24. Jesse C., s Wm. & Sarah Ann, b

1819, 7, 20. James & w, Alice, & ch, Sarah,
     Margaret, William, John, Joseph, Wilson &
     Hannah, rocf Knaresborough MM, Eng., dtd
     1818,8,10, endorsed by Short Creek MM, 0.,

1819,5,18
1820, 8, 20. Jonathan rocf Marsden MM, Eng.,
     dtd 1820,5,4
1821, 2, 20. Margaret Smith (form Binns) dis
     mcd
1821, 6, 19. Jonathan gct Westland MM, Pa.
1829, 1, 1. James dis jH
1829, 12, 3. Wm. dis disunity
1831, 6, 30. Elizabeth dis disunity
1832, 8, 2. Wm. & w, Ruth, & ch, Gibson &
     Charles, rocf Redstone MM, Pa., dtd 1832,
     8,1
1835, 4, 30. James & w, Elizabeth, & ch,
     Wilson, Hannah & Daniel, gct Adrian MM,
     Mich.
1835, 4, 30. John & w, Sarah, & dt, Martha,
     gct Adrian MM, Mich.
1835, 6, 4. Sarah Cockburn (form Binns) dis
     mcd
1835, 8, 27. Joseph gct Adrian MM, Mich.
1841, 6, 3. Wm. & w, Ruth, & ch, Gibson,
     Richard, David, Mary & Amos, gct Redstone
     MM, Pa.

BLACKBURN
1811, 12, 27. Mary d bur Sewickley
1825, 3, 3. Wm., s Wm. & Amy, Washington
     Co., Pa.; m in Providence, Anna HEWITT,
     dt Abel & Rachel, Fayette Co., Pa.
1825, 6, 10. Finley d bur Sewickley
1862, 7, 4. Nathan M., s Wm. & Ann, Wash-
     ington Co., Pa.; m in Providence, Rebecca
     M. COPE, dt Jesse & Elizabeth, Fayette
     Co., Pa.

1822, 6, 25. Moses gct Plymouth-Smithfield
     MM, 0.
1829, 11, 5. Thomas dis disunity
1850, 5, 29. Thomas rst at Allum Creek MM. 0.
     on consent of this mtg
1853, 6, 30. Nathan rocf Westland MM, Pa.,
     dtd 1853,5,25
1868, 4, 2. George gct Salem MM, 0., to m
     Rachel W. Bonsall
1868, 6, 4. Jonathan gct Middleton MM, 0.
1868, 8, 2. George gct Salem MM, 0.
1868, 9, 24. Thos. gct Middleton MM, 0., to
     m Sarah Allmon
1868, 12, 31. Thomas gct Middleton MM, 0.
1869, 12, 2. Wm. & w, Ann, & s, Daniel, gct
     Middleton MM, 0.

BLACKLIDGE
1834, 4, 3. Thomas G. rocf New Garden MM,
     0., dtd 1833,11,21
1835, 2, 5. Thos. G. [Blacklegde] dis mcd

BLANEY
1865, 6, 1. Eliza Ann (form Campbell) dis
     mcd

BONSALL
1868, 4, 2. George Blackburn gct Salem MM,

BONSALL, continued
    O., to m Rachel W. Bonsall

BOTTOMLEY
1856, 9, 13. Hannah d bur Providence

1829, 7, 30. Hannah rocf Redstone MM, Pa.,
    dtd 1829,4,1

BOWMAN
1825, 12, 20. Ruth (form Cook) dis mcd

BOYD
1832, 11, 1. Sarah dis JH
1837, 6, 1. Ruth (form McGrew) dis mcd
1842, 9, 29. Ruth M. rst

BRANSON
1866, 4, 5. Aaron dis
1866, 4, 5. Frances dis
1869, 3, 4. Richard, Susan G., Thomas W. &
    Elma gct Flushing MM, O.
1869, 3, 4. Rebecca Ann gct Flushing MM, O.

BRINTON
1827, 1 29. Wm. P., s John & Sarah, b
1834, 7, 5. Sarah Ann m Dawsey COPE
1839, 7, 12. John d bur Sewickley
1856, 7, 7. Sarah d bur Sewickley

1826, 3, 21. Sarah recrq
1826, 10, 24. John rst (he was dis by Gunpowder
    MM, Md.)
1831, 8, 25. Sarah Ann recrq
1849, 8, 23. Wm. P. dis disunity

BROWN
1818, 4, 21. Elizabeth Parker (form Brown)
    dis mcd
1822, 5, 21. Ann rocf Marlborough MM, O., dtd
    1822,1,27
1825, 10, 25. Eleazer gct Westland MM, Pa., to
    m Elizabeth England
1826, 1, 24. Elizabeth rocf Westland MM, Pa.,
    dtd 1825,12,22
1826, 3, 21. Ann gct Salem MM, O.
1826, 3, 21. Eleazer & w, Elizabeth, gct Marl-
    borough MM, O.
1826, 7, 25. Margaret rocf Marlborough MM, O.,
    dtd 1826,4,25
1829, 2, 5. Margaret dis JH

BUNDY
1856, 5, 3. Wm., s Benjamin & Delitha, Bel-
    mont Co., O.; m in Providence, Sarah Ann
    COPE, dt Jesse & Elizabeth, Fayette Co.,
    Pa.
1865, 10, 20. Elmira d bur Providence

1858, 3, 4. Sarah Ann gct Short Creek MM, O.
1865, 2, 2. Wm. & w, Sarah, & ch, Elizabeth
    D., Effie Ann & Emma Almira rocf Short
    Creek MM, O.

1869, 12, 2. Wm. & w, Sarah Ann, & ch, Eliza-
    beth D., Effie Ann, Jesse & Mary, gct
    Springville MM, Ia.

BURDG
1835, 3, 12. Wm., s Jacob & Miriam, Fayette
    Co., Pa.; m in Providence, Martha COPE,
    dt Joshua & Alice, Fayette Co., Pa.

1829, 7, 30. Jacob & w, Meriam, & ch, Wm.,
    Hannah, Lewis, Oliver & Mary, rocf West-
    land MM, Pa., dtd 1829,6,24
1835, 4, 2. Jacob & w, Miriam, & ch, Lewis,
    Oliver & Mary, gct Upper Springfield MM,
    O.
1835, 4, 2. Hannah gct Upper Springfield MM,
    O.
1835, 4, 30. Wm. & w, Martha, gct Upper
    Springfield MM, O.

BURTON
1839, 5, 2. Tacy (form Hague) dis mcd

CAMPBELL
----, --, --. William & Mary
    Ch: Morgin   b 1825, 1, 18
        Robert   " 1826, 6, 24
        Ruth   " 1828, 10, 28
        Caleb   " 1830, 2, 14
        Reuben   " 1831, 10, 14
        Benjamin   " 1833, 9, 2
        Joseph   " 1836, 4, 15
        Eliza Ann   " 1838, 8, 4
        Samuel   " 1840, 8, 4
        William B.   " 1842, 4, 4
1834, 1, 1. Benjamin d bur Providence
1848, 1, 5. Morgan, s William & Mary, Fay-
    ette Co., Pa.; m in Center, Priscilla H.
    SHARPLESS, dt Jonathan & Margaret, Fay-
    ette Co., Pa.
    Ch: Mary M.   b 1848, 11, 27
        Elizabeth   " 1851, 12, 11
        Ruth Ann   " 1855, 7, 17
1854, 1, 1. Benjamin d bur Providence
1854, 11, 6. Samuel d bur Providence

1829, 7, 30. Wm. & w, Mary, & ch, Morgan,
    Robert & Ruth, rocf Redstone MM, Pa., dtd
    1829,7,29
1855, 5, 3. Reuben Bailey dis mcd
1859, 5, 5. Caleb dis mcd
1863, 7, 30. Morgan dis disunity
1865, 6, 1. Eliza Ann Blaney (form Campbell)
    dis mcd
1865, 8, 31. Robert dis mcd
1867, 5, 9. Joseph dis mcd
1868, 8, 30. Samuel dis mcd

CARREL
1841, 2, 23. Susannah d bur Providence

1821, 12, 25. Susannah rocf Westland MM, Pa.,
    dtd 1821,7,26

CARREL, continued

1827, 11, 29. Susannah [Carrol] gct Upper
    Springfield MM, O.
1837, 8, 24. Susannah [Carrol] rocf New Gar-
    den MM, O., dtd 1837,5,4

CATTELL

1866, 5, 31. Albert, Almira & Esther B., ch
    of Wm. & Mary, gct Upper Springfield MM,
    O.

CHAFFIN

1821, 2, 20. Ananias dis mcd

CHALFANT

1822, 5, 21. Ann gct Salem MM, O.
1829, 12, 3. Joseph Negus gct Redstone MM,
    Pa., to m Eliza Ann Chalfont

COCKBURN

1835, 6, 4. Sarah (form Binns) dis mcd

COLDREN

1856, 10, 22. Jesse d bur Providence

1825, 6, 21. Jesse recrq

COOK

1820, 9, 10. Elizabeth d bur Providence
1841, 6, 5. Uriah d bur Providence
1842, 2, 14. Thomas d bur Providence
1842, 9, 8. Lydia d bur Providence
1844, 10, 6. Anna d bur Providence

1822, 11, 19. Rachel Maxen (form Cook) dis mcd
1822, 12, 24. Thomas con mcd
1825, 12, 20. Ruth Bowman (form Cook) dis mcd
1826, 7, 25. Anna recrq
1827, 3, 20. Nancy Jackson (form Cook) dis mcd
1832, 8, 2. Thomas Jr. dis mcd
1832, 10, 4. Elizabeth Hamer (form Cook) dis
    mcd

COOPER

1847, 9, 30. Amos Cope gct Sandy Spring MM,
    O., to m Rachel Cooper

COPE

----, --, --. Joseph & Elizabeth
    Ch: Ruth   b 1817, 8, 18
        Elihu   " 1819, 1, 21
        Anne   " 1822, 7, 12
        Sarah
          Raily   " 1824, 9, 1
----, --, --. Joshua & Alice
    Ch: Caleb   b 1818, 2, 10
        Joshua   " 1818, 2, 10
        Edith   " 1819, 5, 8
        Benjamin " 1820, 3, 14
1818, 8, 8. Joshua d bur Providence
1818, 8, 12. Caleb d bur Providence
----, --, --. John & Sarah
    Ch: George   b 1820, 6, 11

Ch: Oliver   b 1822, 2, 28
    Isaac
      Perkins   " 1824, 1, 2
    Hannah   " 1826, 4, 14
    John Smith " 1827, 11, 27
    Sarah Ann   " 1829, 8, 10
    Mary Ann   " 1831, 7, 22
    Dawsey   " 1833, 4, 20
    Ruth   " 1835, 6, 24
    Henry   " 1837, 8, 10
    Sarah Jane " 1839, 12, 28
    John Cou-
      sins   " 1842, 5, 3
    Charles   " 1844, 11, 2
1821, 1, 4. Judith m Moses PENNOCK
1821, 5, 24. Sarah m Michael HAGAMAN
1822, 5, 28. Isaac d bur Providence
1823, 11, 26. Sarah m John RALEY
1823, 11, 27. Joseph, s Joseph & Ann, Chester
    Co., Pa.; m in Providence, Rachel W. COPE
    dt Samuel & Sarah, Fayette Co., Pa.
1825, 3, 4. Joseph d bur Providence
1825, 10, 27. Joseph, s John & Grace, Harri-
    son Co., Pa.; m in Providence, Ruth
    GRIFFITH, dt Wm. & Sarah, Fayette Co.,Pa.
1826, 6, 1. Hannah m Geo. D. GILBERT
1827, 8, 22. Ruth m Aaron VANSCOYOC
1828, 10, 3. Elizabeth m Samuel ARMSTRONG
1829, 1, 8. Lydia m Benjamin GILBERT
1829, 9, 2. Samuel Jr., s Samuel & Sarah,
    Fayette Co., Pa.; m in Center, Mercy VAIL,
    dt Samuel & Agnes, Monalen Co., Pa.
    Ch: Joseph   b 1830, 7, 5
        Martha   " 1832, 9, 1
        Lewis   " 1836, 2, 15
        Willets   " 1838, 5, 13
        Elma   " 1840, 12, 25
1830, 5, 31. Sarah Ann d bur Providence
1832, 1, 21. Jasper d bur Providence
1832, 8, 25. John Smith d bur Providence
1833, 12, 6. Jesse, s Isaac & Sarah, Fayette
    Co., Pa.; m in Sewickley, Elizabeth Mc-
    GREW, dt James A. & Rebecca, Westmoreland
    Co., Pa.
    Ch: Rebecca M. b 1834, 11, 3
        Sarah Ann " 1835, 11, 20
        Caroline   " 1837, 4, 30
        Emily   " 1838, 12, 29
        Mary   " 1840, 11, 25
        James A.   " 1842, 10, 14
        Mercy   " 1843, 11, 3
        Albert   " 1846, 10, 26
        Allen   " 1848, 11, 30
        Lydia   " 1850, 12, 27
        Almira   " 1853, 10, 12
1834, 7, 5. Dawsey, s Samuel & Sarah, Fay-
    ette Co., Pa.; m in Sewickley, Sarah Ann
    BRINTON, dt John & Sarah, Allegheny Co.,
    Pa.
    Ch: Rachel   b 1835, 4, 10
        Emmer   " 1836, 8, 24
        Mary   " 1838, 10, 31
        Lydia   " 1841, 5, 29

COPE, Dawsey & Ann, continued
        Ch: Melissa   b 1844, 2, 14
           Lucinda   " 1848, 1, 21
1835, 3, 12. Martha m Wm. BURDGE
1836, 4, 7. Elizabeth m Nathan McGREW
1836, 9, 24. Dawsey d bur Providence
1838, 4, 6. Joseph, s Joseph & Ann, Chester
    Co., Pa., m in Sewickley, Eliza GILBERT,
    dt Abner & Ann, Westmoreland Co., Pa.
1838, 8, 24. Elma m Jesse VAIL
1839, 9, 9. Joshua d bur Providence
1841, 8, 27. Sarah R. m John NAYLOR, Jr.
1843, 4, 25. Samuel d bur Providence
1843, 7, 6. George, s John & Sarah S., Fay-
    ette Co., Pa.; m in Providence, Elmira
    HEWITT, dt Joseph & Ruth, Fayette Co., Pa.
----, --, --. Amos & Edna L.
        Ch: William   b 1835, 7, 13
           Joshua   " 1837, 4, 5
           Thomas
            Clarkson " 1839, 6, 25
           Margaret " 1842, 5, 21
           Hiram   " 1844, 3, 26
1844, 8, 2. Hannah m Cyrus BENEDICT
1845, 5, 19. Hiram d bur Providence
1845, 10, 14. Edeny Emily d bur Providence
----, --, --. Amos & Rachel
        Ch: Mary Ann b 1851, 10, 30
           Calvin   " 1854, 6, 21
1854, 8, 25. Martha V. m Gibson BINNS
1856, 5, 3. Sarah Ann m Wm. BUNDY
1856, 9, 24. Alice d bur Providence
1857, 9, 25. Edward, s Joseph & Rachel, Ches-
    ter Co., Pa.; m in Sewickley, Alice GIL-
    BERT, dt George & Hannah, Westmoreland
    Co., Pa.
        Ch: Charles   b 1858, 8, 7
           Anna   " 1861, 4, 3
1859, 3, 29. Willis d bur Providence
----, --, --. Louis & Hannah
        Ch: Florence N.b 1862, 7, 6
           Edith G. " 1863, 12, 16
           Priscilla " 1865, 6, 5
           Martha V. " 1868, 1, 22
1862, 7, 4. Rebecca m Nathan M. BLACKBURN
1864, 9, 23. William, s Amos & Emily Edna,
    Jefferson Co., Pa.; m in Sewickley, Rachel
    W. COPE, dt Joseph & Eliza, Chester Co.,
    Pa.
        Ch: Francis   b 1865, 10, 28
           Ellen   " 1865, 10, 28
1866, 10, 18. Rachel W. m Daniel J. SCOTT
1867, 11, 16. Robert J., s James A. & Achsia
    H., b
1869, 1, 1. Mary m Simon O. McGREW
1869, 3, 19. Mercy d bur Providence
1869, 6, 8. Sarah d ae 94 (an elder)

1817, 7, 22. Rachel rocf Concord MM, Pa., dtd
    1817,5,1, endorsed by Redstone MM, Pa.,
    1817,6,25
1819, 8, 24. Joseph & w, Elizabeth, & ch,
    Ruth & Elisha, gct Westland MM, Pa.

1819, 8, 24. Joseph & w, Elizabeth, & ch,
    John Negus & Joseph Shreve, gct Westland
    MM, Pa.
1819, 8, 24. John gct Westland MM, Pa., to m
    Sarah Smith
1819, 11, 23. Sarah rocf Westland MM, Pa., dtd
    1819,10,28
1822, 7, 23. Joseph & w, Elizabeth, & ch,
    Ruth, Elihu & Uriah, rocf Westland MM, Pa.
    dtd 1822,6,27
1824, 1, 20. Rachel W. gct Bradford MM, Pa.
1824, 3, 23. Sarah Raley & ch, Ruth & Jesse
    Cope, gct Westland MM, Pa.
1824, 8, 24. Joseph H. gct Concord MM, O.
1825, 12, 20. Ruth gct Short Creek MM, O.
1826, 2, 21. Elihu & Uriah, ch Elizabeth, gct
    Westland MM, Pa.
1826, 8, 22. Isaac gct Marlborough MM, O.
1827, 11, 1. Willets gct Plymouth-Smithfield
    MM, O.
1827, 11, 29. Uriah, minor, rocf Westland MM,
    Pa., dtd 1827,8,23
1832, 10, 4. Elihu, minor, rocf Westland MM,
    Pa., dtd 1832,8,22
1833, 7, 4. John F. gct Middleton MM, O.
1834, 8, 28. Amos dis mcd
1837, 1, 5. Elihu dis disunity
1837, 6, 29. Evan dis disunity
1838, 5, 31. Eliza gct Bradford MM, Pa. (w of
    Joseph)
1839, 5, 2. Hiram gct Upper Springfield MM,
    O.
1839, 7, 4. John F. rocf Carmel MM, O.
1840, 3, 5. Edith gct Upper Springfield MM,
    O.
1840, 7, 2. John F. gct Carmel MM, O.
1840, 7, 30. Ruth Embree (form Cope) con mcd
1843, 8, 24. Geo. & w, Elmira, gct Westland
    MM, Pa.
1843, 11, 30. Amos rst
1844, 1, 4. Edna Emily recrq
1846, 2, 5. Wm., Joshua, Thos. Clarkson &
    Margaret, ch Amos, recrq
1846, 3, 5. John dis disunity
1846, 3, 5. Sarah L. dis
1846, 4, 2. Isaac Perkins gct Westland MM,
    Pa.
1846, 4, 30. Maryann, Dawsey, Ruth, Henry,
    Sarah Jane, John Cousins & Charles Binns,
    ch John & Sarah L., gct Westland MM, Pa.
1846, 4, 30. Benjamin dis mcd
1846, 11, 7. Judgment reversed in case of
    John; retained mbrp
1846, 12, 31. Oliver gct Westland MM, Pa.
1847, 2, 4. Anne dis disunity
1847, 9, 30. Amos gct Sandy Spring MM, O., to
    m Rachel Cooper
1848, 3, 2. Rachel rocf Sandy Spring MM, O.,
    dtd 1848,12,24
1848, 6, 1. John gct Westland MM, Pa.
1858, 9, 23. Edward Y. rocf Birmingham MM,
    Pa., dtd 1858,9,1
1859, 2, 3. Emmor dis mcd

COPE, continued
1859, 3, 31. Elizabeth recrq
1861, 9, 5. Louis gct Middleton MM, O., to m
    Hannah Hollingsworth
1863, 3, 5. Hannah rocf Middleton MM, O.
1864, 6, 30. Rachel W. rocf Birmingham MM,
    Pa., dtd 1864,6,29
1866, 10, 31. John dis disunity
1866, 11, 29. Chas. B. dis disunity
1867, 1, 31. James A. gct Upper Springfield
    MM, O.
1868, 7, 2. Achsah H. rocf Upper Springfield
    MM, O., dtd 1868,5,22
1869, 12, 2. James A. & w, Achsah, gct Middle-
    ton MM, O.

CRAWFORD
1865, 6, 6. Richard I. d bur Redstone
1865, 11, 23. Elizabeth A. d bur Redstone
1869, 3, 4. Priscilla W. d bur Redstone

1822, 3, 26. Mary (form McGrew) dis mcd
1831, 3, 31. Sarah (form Hoge) dis mcd

DARLINGTON
1866, 3, 1. Hannah gct Salem MM, O.
1866, 4, 5. Wm. & w, Catharine, gct Salem
    MM, O.

DENNIS
1818, 10, 20. Martha dis
1819, 2, 23. Aaron rst
1825, 8, 26. Aaron gct Plymouth-Smithfield
    MM, O.
1828, 5, 1. Deborah dis

DEWEES
1844, 12, 11. Isaac, s Wm. & Debby, Washington
    Co., Pa., d 1851,1,7 bur Sewickley; m in
    Sewickley, Rebecca McGREW, dt James & Re-
    becca, Westmoreland Co., Pa.
    Ch: Rebecca   b 1845, 9, 21
        James   " 1848, 9, 13
        Deborah   " 1848, 9, 13
        William   " 1850, 10, 6 d 1851, 8,12
          bur Sewickley
        Mary   b 1850, 10, 6 " 1859,10,15
          bur Sewickley

1845, 6, 5. Isaac rocf Chesterfield MM, O.
1855, 11, 1. Rebecca McGrew (form Dewees)
    dis mcd
1865, 6, 1. Rebecca dis disunity

DEWLY
1817, 8, 26. Maxen gct Plainfield MM
1823, 5, 20. Avis [Duley], w Joshua, gct
    Flushing MM, O.

DINGEE
1869, 12, 2. Adaline gct Middleton MM, O.

DOYEL
1819, 1, 26. Hannah (form Barret) dis mcd

EBERHART
1820, 10, 24. Rachel (form Hutton) dis mcd

EMBREE
1840, 7, 30. Ruth (form Cope) con mcd
1841, 9, 30. Ruth gct Marlborough MM, O.

EMMONS
1869, 2, 4. Ann (form Knight) dis mcd

ENGLAND
1825, 10, 25. Eleazer Brown gct Westland MM,
    Pa., to m Elizabeth England

ENLOWS
1817, 10, 12. Susannah, dt James & Ruth, b

1818, 7, 21. John, minor, rocf Westland MM,
    Pa., dtd 1818,6,25
1818, 7, 21. James & w, Ruth, & ch, John,
    Emily & Susannah, gct Marlboro MM, O.

FARQUHAR
1866, 4, 5. Eli dis mcd

FINCH
1834, 6, 5. Samuel rocf Westland MM, Pa.,
    dtd 1834,5,21

FISHER
----, --, --. Isaac & Elizabeth
    Ch: David   b 1825, 3, 25
        Caleb   " 1830, 6, 14

1824, 11, 23. Isaac & w, Elizabeth, & ch,
    James & John, rocf Dunning Creek MM, dtd
    1824,7,14
1825, 6, 21. Isaac & w, Elizabeth, & ch,
    James, John & David, gct Redstone MM, Pa.
1829, 4, 30. Isaac & w, Elizabeth, & ch,
    James, John & David, rocf Redstone MM,
    Pa., dtd 1829,4,29
1839, 8, 1. Isaac & w, Elizabeth, & ch,
    James, John, David & Caleb, gct West
    Branch MM, O.

FRAZURE
1851, 4, 3. Agnes (form Vail) dis mcd

FURRY
1835, 11, 5. Mary (form Sharpless) dis mcd

GARWOOD
1868, 8, 30. Wm. dis mcd

GIBSON
1852, 3, 24. Hannah J. d

1828, 7, 30. Nathaniel dis disunity
1830, 9, 30. Lydia Powers (form Gibson) dis

126

GIBSON, continued
    mcd

GIDEON
1824, 8, 10. John d bur Providence

GILBERT
1809, 1, 11. Benjamin d bur Sewickley
1821, 12, 10. Jesse d bur Sewickley
1822, 12, 26. Susannah m Archebald B. MEGREW
1826, 6, 1. George D., s Abner & Ann, West-
    moreland Co., Pa.; m in Providence, Hannah
    COPE, dt Joshua & Alice, Fayette Co., Pa.
    Ch: Thomas
        Clarkson b 1827, 8, 12 d 1827,10, 4
        bur Sewickley
        David P. b 1829, 2, 21 " 1829, 4, 9
        bur Sewickley
        Rebecca b 1830, 3, 14
        Ann Eliza " 1832, 8, 17
        Alice   " 1835, 3, 3
        Joshua   " 1837, 11, 18
        Abner   " 1837, 11, 18
        Sarah   " 1840, 1, 20
        Edith   " 1845, 4, 29
        Ellen   " 1851, 3, 31
1829, 1, 8. Benjamin, s Abner & Ann, West-
    moreland Co., Pa.; m in Providence, Lydia
    COPE, dt Samuel & Sarah, Fayette Co., Pa.
    Ch: Sarah Ann b 1829, 10, 27
        Mary   " 1831, 11, 7
        Samuel C. " 1839, 4, 19
        Susan   " 1842, 3, 31
        Eliza C.   " 1834, 9, 23
1831, 5, 31. Abner d ae 67 bur Sewickley (an
    elder)
1831, 5, 31. Margaret d bur Sewickley
1838, 4, 6. Eliza m Joseph COPE
1841, 12, 3. Ann m James W. McGREW
1845, 11, 13. Ann d ae 79 bur Sewickley (an
    elder)
1857, 9, 25. Alice m Edward COPE
1857, 12, 4. Rebecca m Alfred MEGRAIL
1861, 1, 9. Joshua, s George & Hannah, West-
    moreland Co., Pa.; m in Sewickley, Debora
    HUTTON, dt Joel & Ann, Westmoreland Co.,
    Pa.
    Ch: Wilmer H. b 1862, 9, 30
        Edwin D.   " 1864, 8, 23

1863, 3, 5. Abner dis mcd
1863, 7, 2. Edith Newlin (form Gilbert) dis
    mcd

GRABEL
1846, 12, 7. Rachel d

GRAHAM
1845, 5, 1. Philena W. (form McGrew) dis mcd

GRIFFITH
----, --, --. Wm. & Margaret
    Ch: Eli   b 1794, 5, 16

Ch: Samuel   b 1795, 11, 28
    Elizabeth   " 1797, 2, 11
    Abram   " 1798, 12, 13
    Ruth   " 1801, 1, 1
    Sarah   " 1803, 2, 8
    Mary   " 1805, 5, 13
    Wm. Mode   " 1806, 10, 4
    Elisha   " 1808, 8, 21
    Milton   " 1811, 4, 18
    Newlin   " 1811, 4, 18
    Emlin   " 1813, 4, 22
    Elma   " 1816, 3, 4
1805, 6, 18. Mary d bur Providence
1818, 2, 12. Elizabeth d bur Redstone
1825, 4, 20. Sarah m Zachariah B. HAMPTON
1825, 10, 27. Ruth m Joseph COPE

1821, 5, 22. Wm. & w, Sarah, & ch, Wm. Mode,
    Elisha, Milton, Newton, Emlen & Elma, rocf
    Redstone MM, Pa., dtd 1821,4,4
1821, 5, 22. Ruth rocf Redstone MM. Pa., dtd
    1821,2,28
1821, 5, 22. Sarah Jr. rocf Redstone MM, Pa.,
    dtd 1821,2,28
1823, 4, 22. Samuel Vail gct Short Creek MM,
    O., to m Elizabeth Griffith
1823, 6, 24. Samuel dis mcd
1824, 12, 24. Wm. Mode gct Short Creek MM, O.,
    (minor s of Wm.)
1825, 4, 19. Newton, s Wm., gct Short Creek
    MM, O.
1825, 6, 21. Emlin, s Wm., gct Flushing MM,O.
1825, 12, 20. Wm. dis disunity
1825, 12, 20. Sarah dis disunity
1827, 2, 20. Elma, minor, gct Short Creek MM,
    O.
1829, 6, 4. Elisha dis mcd
1834, 8, 28. Milton gct Deerfield MM, O.

GRIST
1794, 8, 17. William d bur Providence
1796, 9, 11. George d bur Providence
1796, 12, 26. Margaret, dt Joseph & Margaret,
    b
1819, 6, 10. Margaret d bur Providence
1829, 3, 31. William d bur Center

1823, 3, 25. Margaret Bailey (form Ghrist)
    dis mcd
1829, 7, 30. Orpha dis JH

GROVE
1843, 6, 1. Elma (form Jackson) dis mcd

HAGAMAN
1821, 5, 24. Michael, s John & Mary, Fayette
    Co., Pa.; m in Providence, Sarah COPE, dt
    Isaac & Sarah, Fayette Co., Pa.
    Ch: Ruth G. b 1822, 6, 10
        Maria   " 1824, 3, 22
        Isaac C.   " 1826, 5, 12
        Anna C.   " 1828, 8, 25
        John C.   " 1831, 3, 9

HAGAMAN, Michael & Sarah, continued
    Ch: Joseph   b 1833, 7, 19
        Sarah Jr. " 1836, 9, 13

1820, 11, 21. Michael recrq
1821, 6, 19. Michael & w, Sarah, gct Westland
    MM, Pa.
1822, 5, 21. Michael & w, Sarah, rocf West-
    land MM, Pa., dtd 1822,4,25
1826, 12, 26. Michael dis
1842, 11, 3. Maria gct Marlborough MM, O.
1845, 2, 27. Ruth Reeder (form Hagaman) dis
    mcd
1845, 2, 27. Sarah & ch, Isaac, Anne, John,
    Joseph, Sarah, Martha & Rachel, gct Marl-
    borough MM, O.

HALLOCK
1825, 6, 21. Thos. rocf Cornwall MM, N. Y.,
    dtd 1824,12,23

HAMER
1832, 10, 4. Elizabeth (form Cook) dis mcd

HAMPTON
1825, 4, 20. Zachariah B., s John & Mary, Bel-
    mont Co., O.; m in Providence, Sarah GRIF-
    FITH, dt Wm. & Sarah, Fayette Co., Pa.

1825, 6, 21. Sarah gct Flushing MM, O.

HANK
1829, 7, 30. Judith rocf Westland MM, Pa.,
    dtd 1829,6,24
1835, 4, 2. Judith gct Upper Springfield MM,
    O.

HANNAH
1848, 2, 3. Rebecca (form Jackson) dis mcd

HARRIS
1843, 10, 5. Emily (form McGrew) con mcd
1843, 11, 2. Emily M. gct Short Creek MM, O.

HARTLEY
1818, 9, 22. Thomas & w, Barbara, & ch, Eliza,
    Leah, Esther, Sarah, Norton & Rachel, gct
    Cincinnati MM, O.

HENDRICKS
1820, 7, 25. Ann gct Salem MM, O.

HEWITT
----, --, --. Abel & Rachel
    Ch: Jesse   b 1818, 10, 2
        David   " 1821, 1, 4
----, --, --. Joseph & Ruth
    Ch: Elmira   b 1818, 8, 1
        Israel   " 1821, 1, 20
        Cynthiann " 1823, 3, 6 d 1826, 6,22
        bur Providence
        Milton   b 1824, 11, 22
        David Por-

    Ch: ter   b 1829, 5, 24
1823, 7, 11. Rebecca d bur Providence
1825, 3, 3. Anna m Wm. BLACKBURN
1826, 5, 4. Elizabeth m James BINNS
1831, 3, 18. Jonathan d bur Providence
1834, 1, 9. Sarah A. m John BINNS
1843, 7, 6. Elmira m Geo. COPE

1817, 11, 25. Rebecca rocf Westland MM, dtd
    1817,9,28
1826, 6, 20. Mary Sparks (form Hewitt) dis
    mcd
1826, 6, 20. Sarah, minor dt Rachel, gct West
    land MM, Pa.
1828, 10, 2. Jonathan Jr. dis disunity
1828, 10, 28. Charles dis mcd
1828, 12, 4. Ann dis JH
1829, 1, 1. John dis disunity
1829, 4, 30. Joseph dis JH
1829, 7, 30. Sarah rocf Westland MM, Pa., dtd
    1829,4,1 (a minor)
1833, 4, 4. Joseph Jr. dis jas
1837, 8, 24. Cyrus dis disunity
1837, 11, 2. Martha gct Adrian MM, Mich.
1840, 4, 30. Amos dis disunity
1843, 5, 4. Jesse dis disunity
1843, 6, 1. Rachel gct Westland MM, Pa.
1844, 4, 4. Joseph Jr. rst at Adrian MM,
    Mich. on consent of this mtg
1845, 7, 3. David dis mcd
1849, 8, 2. Milton dis mcd
1854, 2, 2. Israel dis mcd

HOGE
1829, 2, 21. John d bur Center

1825, 5, 24. Jacob dis disunity
1831, 3, 31. Sarah Crawford (form Hoge) dis
    mcd
1835, 8, 27. Tacy [Hogue] rocf Redstone MM,
    Pa., dtd 1835,7,1
1839, 5, 2. Tacy Burten (form Hogue) dis
    mcd

HUNT
1821, 6, 10. Priscilla, dt Nathan & Ann, b
----, --, --. Stacy & Rebecca
    Ch: Esther   b 1823, 7, 7
        William   " 1825, 10, 8

1820, 8, 20. Nathan & w, Ann, & ch, Ira, Es-
    ther, Enoch, Caleb & Rachel, rocf Marl-
    borough MM, O., dtd 1820,3,25
1822, 6, 25. Stacy & w, Rebecca, & ch,
    George, Dillwyn & Milton, rocf Redstone
    MM, Pa., dtd 1822,5,1
1822, 10, 22. Nathan & w, Ann, & ch, Ira, Es-
    ther, Enoch, Caleb, Rachel & Priscilla,
    gct Salem MM, O.
1830, 6, 3. Stacy & ch, George, Milton, Es-
    ther & Wm., gct Salem MM, O.

HUTTON
----, --, --. Joel d 1862,7,3 bur Sewickley;
    m Ann ----- d 1865,7,7 bur Sewickley
      Ch: James   b 1833, 1, 22 d 1838, 4,30
          bur Sewickley
        Addison   b 1834, 11, 28
        Mary   " 1837, 6, 25
        Finley   " 1839, 12, 11
        Deborah S. " 1841, 11, 17
        Ann   " 1844, 3, 20
        Rebecca   " 1847, 2, 18 d 1849, 2, 4
          bur Center
        Susan   " 1849, 12, 14
        Linnaeus " 18--, 5, 29
        Samuel   " 18--, 8, 19 d 1861,11, 6
          bur Sewickley
1861, 1, 9. Debora m Joshua GILBERT
1861,'11, 18. Joel Jr. d bur Sewickley

1820, 10, 24. Rachel Eberhart (form Hutton)
    dis mcd
1823, 11, 25. James dis
1824, 1, 20. Susannah McGrew (form Hutton)
    dis mcd
1825, 10, 25. Nathan dis disunity
1828, 1, 31. Deborah McGrew (form Hutton) dis
    mcd
1832, 8, 23. Anne (form Mains) con mcd
1834, 5, 1. Joel W. rocf Smithfield MM, O.,
    dtd 1833,10,21
1851, 5, 1. Joel W. & w, Ann, & ch, Adison,
    Mary, Finley, Deborah, Ann, Rebecca & Su-
    san, gct Plymouth MM, O.
1852, 2, 5. Joel W. & w, Ann, & ch, Adison,
    Mary, Finley, Deborah, Ann, Rebecca & Su-
    san, rocf Plymouth MM, O.
1863, 11, 5. Addison gct WDMM, Phila., Pa.

INGRIM
1848, 6, 1. Margaret Ann (form McGrew) dis
    mcd

INNIS
1818, 7, 21. Mary recrq
1821, 12, 25. Mary gct Redstone MM, Pa.

JACKSON
----, --, --. Jesse & Elizabeth
      Ch: Elma   b 1816, 2, 20
        Samuel   " 1819, 3, 20
        Mary   " 1820, 8, 20
        Jonathan
          Sharpless" 1822, 6, 18
        Joseph   " 1825, 1, 5
        Edith
          Nichols " 1827, 1, 24 d 1828, 8,31
          bur Center
        Rebecca   " 1829, 8, 24
1839, 5, 10. Elizabeth d
1839, 9, 8. Jonathan d

1824, 3, 23. Jesse & w, Elizabeth, & ch, Elma,
    Samuel, Mary S. & Jonathan S., gct Red-

stone MM, Pa.
1826, 7, 25. Jesse & w, Elizabeth, & ch, El-
    ma, Samuel, Mary S., Jonathan & Joseph,
    rocf Redstone MM, Pa., dtd 1826,6,28
1827, 3, 20. Nancy (form Cook) dis mcd
1843, 6, 1. Samuel Jr. dis mcd
1843, 6, 1. Elma Grove (form Jackson) dis
1843, 6, 1. Mary Misner (form Jackson) dis
1844, 1, 4. Jesse dis mcd
1848, 2, 3. Rebecca Hannah (form Jackson)
    dis mcd

JOHN
1818, 2, 17. Daniel dis disunity
1818, 6, 23. Samuel dis mcd
1828, 10, 2. Mordecai dis disunity

KINNISON
1869, 1, 7. Sarah (form Vail) rpd mcd

KIRK
1820, 11, 27. Judith d bur Providence

KNIGHT
1866, 5, 31. John F., Wm. & Mary Hannah, ch
    Wm. & Hannah, gct Coal Creek MM, Ia.
1869, 2, 4. Ann Emmons (form Knight) dis mcd

LAMB
1817, 9, 23. James, minor, gct Cincinnati MM,
    O.
1819, 11, 23. Joshua G. gct Cincinnati MM, O.
1820, 8, 20. George dis mcd
1820, 9, 19. Thomas G. gct Redstone MM, Pa.
1820, 12, 26. Susannah & dt, Hannah, gct Red-
    stone MM, Pa.
1820, 12, 26. Sarah Roberts (form Lamb) dis
    mcd
1823, 10, 21. John & w, Hannah, & ch, Mary
    Ann, Rebecca, Daniel S., Phebe G. & John,
    gct Concord MM, O.
1823, 10, 21. Eliza relrq
1824, 2, 24. Eliza dis jas

LEWIS
1917, 8, 26. Hannah rocf SDMM, Phila., Pa.

LONSDALE
1823, 8, 8. Thomas [Lousdale] d bur Centre

1820, 1, 25. Thomas rocf Marsden MM, Eng.,
    dtd 1819,2,4, endorsed by Falls MM, Pa.,
    1819,9,10 & by Redstone MM, Pa., 1819,12,
    29
1821, 2, 20. John rocf Hardshaw MM, Eng., dtd
    1818,12,25, endorsed by Chesterfield MM,
    N. J., 1820,5,2 & by Redstone MM, Pa.,
    1821,1,3
1821, 4, 24. John con mcd
1823, 6, 24. John gct Westland MM, Pa.

McGRAIL
----, --, -. John & Mary [McGraile]

McGRAIL, John & Mary, continued
  Ch: Mary   b 1801, 3, 29
    Sarah " 1806, 6, 30
    Deborah " 1808, 11, 27
    Rachel " 1811, 3, 27
    Isabel " 1813, 10, 19
1814, 4, 5. John d bur Sewickley
1857, 12, 4. Alfred [Megrail], s James & Mary,
  Jefferson Co., O.; m in Sewickley, Rebecca
  GILBERT, dt George & Hannah, Westmoreland
  Co., Pa.

1819, 8, 24. Elizabeth McGrew (form McGrail)
  dis mcd
1822, 12, 24. Rebecca Taylor (form McGreil)
  dis mcd
1823, 1, 21. Sarah gct Plymouth-Smithfield
  MM, O.
1824, 12, 24. Deborah [McGrale], minor, gct
  Plymouth-Smithfield MM, O.
1826, 10, 24. Mary McGrew (form McGrail) dis
  mcd
1832, 5, 21. Mary & ch, Rachel & Isabell, gct
  Plymouth-Smithfield MM, O.
1847, 9, 30. Sarah rst
1855, 5, 31. Mary rocf Plymouth-Smithfield MM,
  O., dtd 1855,4,2
1858, 4, 29. Rebecca gct Short Creek MM, O.
1863, 7, 30. Rebecca & ch, George G. & Amy
  Ann, rocf Short Creek MM, O.

McGREW
----, --, --. James & Rebecca
  Ch: Elizabeth b 1813, 12, 15
    Ruth   " 1815, 2, 8
    Rees   " 1817, 1, 8
    Emly   " 1819, 4, 6
    Rebecca " 1821, 7, 20
    Shepherd " 1823, 10, 7
1812, 4, 9. Finley Sr. d bur Sewickley
1819, 11, 2. Dinah d bur Sewickley
1821, 5, 12. Martha d bur Sewickley
1861, 7, 15. Martha d bur Sewickley
1822, 12, 26. Archebald B., s James B. & Elizabeth, Westmoreland Co., Pa.; m in Sewickley, Susannah GILBERT, dt Abner & Ann,
  Westmoreland Co., Pa.
1823, 2, 10. Elizabeth d bur Sewickley
----, --, --. Archibald d 1843,1,-- bur Sewickley; m Susanna -----
  Ch: Philena
    Wakefield b 1823, 10, 14
    Abner Gil-
    bert   " 1826, 2, 27
    Elizabeth " 1827, 11, 11
    Margaret
    Ann   " 1829, 10, 19
    Mary Jane " 1832, 1, 29
    Benjamin " 1834, 3, 31
    Deborah " 1836, 1, 2
    Isabella " 1837, 3, 29
    Rebecca " 1838, 8, 28
    Phebe

  Ch: Catherine b 1840, 7, 7
    James " 1842, 3, 1
----, --, --. James B. d 1836,10,4 bur Sewickley; m Isabella -----
  Ch: Samuel b 1826, 10, 3
    Lydia " 1828, 8, 30
1828, 11, 10. Nathan d bur Sewickley
1829, 12, 20. Jane d bur Sewickley
1830, 9, 18. Stephen d bur Sewickley
1833, 12, 6. Elizabeth m Jesse COPE
1836, 4, 7. Nathan, s Wm. & Ann, Westmoreland Co., Pa.; m in Providence, Elizabeth
  COPE, dt Isaac & Elizabeth FISHER, Fayette
  Co., Pa.
1841, 3, 10. Elizabeth d bur Providence
1841, 12, 3. James W., s Nathan M. & Elizabeth, Jefferson Co., O.; m in Sewickley,
  Ann GILBERT, dt Asher & Ann, Westmoreland
  Co., Pa.
1842, 12, 31. James d bur Sewickley
1844, 6, 28. James d bur Sewickley
1844, 12, 11. Rebecca m Isaac DEWEES
1847, 6, 27. Rebecca d bur Sewickley
1853, 3, --. Finley d bur Sewickley
1854, 10, 9. Simon B. d bur Sewickley
1855, 8, 16. Deborah d bur Sewickley
1861, 1, 9. James A. d bur Sewickley
1864, 3, 15. Samuel d bur Sewickley
1869, 1, 1. Simon O., s Alexander & Margaret, Muscatine Co., Ia.; m in Providence,
  Mary COPE, dt Jesse & Elizabeth, Fayette
  Co., Pa.

1817, 7, 22. Finley A. & w, Deborah, & ch,
  James, Mary, Moses, Jane, Thomas & Rebecca
  gct Plymouth MM, O.
1817, 9, 23. Thomas gct Plymouth MM, O.
1817, 9, 23. Finley gct Plymouth MM, O.
1818, 10, 20. Jacob con mcd
1819, 8, 24. Elizabeth (form McGrail) dis mcd
1819, 10, 26. John gct Smithfield MM, O.
1821, 5, 22. Elizabeth gct Plymouth MM, O.
1821, 9, 25. Jacob gct Smithfield MM, O.
1822, 3, 26. Mary Crawford (form McGrew) dis
  mcd
1822, 7, 23. Stephen dis mcd
1824, 1, 20. Susannah (form Hutton) dis mcd
1824, 10, 26. James B. rst
1824, 11, 23. Isabella rst
1826, 10, 24. Mary (form McGrail) dis mcd
1827, 6, 19. Dinah dis mcd
1828, 1, 31. Deborah (form Hutton) dis mcd
1831, 9, 27. James A. dis disunity
1833, 2, 28. Nathan recrq
1835, 12, 31. Simon B. rst
1837, 6, 1. Ruth Boyd (form McGrew) dis mcd
1842, 3, 3. Ann G. gct Plymouth-Smithfield
  MM, O.
1842, 9, 29. Margaret (form Vail) con mcd
1843, 2, 2. Samuel recrq
1843, 10, 5. Finley recrq
1843, 10, 5. Emily Harris (form McGrew) con
  mcd

McGREW, continued

1843, 11, 30. Isabella gct Plymouth-Smithfield MM, O.
1845, 1, 2. Simon B. con mcd
1845, 6, 5. Philena W. Graham (form McGrew) dis mcd
1846, 1, 1. Samuel [Megrew] Jr. dis disunity
1846, 10, 1. Abner [Megrew] dis mcd
1848, 6, 1. Margaret Ann Ingrim (form McGrew) dis mcd
1851, 5, 1. Margaret gct Plymouth MM, O.
1852, 2, 5. Mary Jane dis disunity
1852, 7, 1. Elizabeth dis disunity
1855, 11, 1. Rebecca (form Dewees) dis mcd
1858, 7, 1. Benjamin dis mcd
1858, 12, 2. Phebe Catharine Shaner (form McGrew) dis mcd
1860, 7, 5. Rebecca dis disunity
1860, 8, 2. Isabella dis disunity
1860, 8, 2. Deborah dis disunity
1865, 6, 29. Lydia (form Vail) con mcd
1865, 11, 30. Lydia gct Pennsville MM, O.
1868, 9, 3. Simon O. rocf Sewickley MM

MAERKT

1861, 12, 7. Charlotte d bur Sewickley
1861, 12, 17. Louisa d bur Sewickley

1861, 4, 4. Frederick & w, Amelia, & ch, Louisa, Jane J., Ann & Hannah G., rocf New Garden MM, O.
1861, 4, 4. Charlotte D. & Wilhelmina, rocf New Garden MM, O.
1866, 1, 4. Frederick & w, Amelia, & ch, Jane J., Anna & Hannah G., gct Salem MM,O.
1866, 1, 4. Wilhelmina gct Salem MM, O.

MAINS

----, --, --. James & Rebecca
     Ch: John   b 1809, 7, 9
         Ann   " 1812, 1, 31
         Jane   " 1814, 12, 13
         Elma   " 1818, 6, 22
1847, 4, 4. James d bur Sewickley
1852, 11, 10. Rebecca d bur Sewickley

1821, 5, 22. Rebecca Marsh (form Mains) dis mcd
1822, 5, 21. Margaret Price (form Mains) dis mcd
1825, 5, 24. Deborah Shaner (form Mains) dis mcd
1826, 5, 23. James Jr. con mcd
1830, 12, 2. James Jr. dis disunity
1831, 5, 5. John dis mcd
1832, 8, 23. Anne Hutton (form Mains) con mcd
1833, 2, 28. Jane Taylor (form Mains) con mcd
1835, 10, 1. Elma Taylor (form Mains) dis mcd

MARSH

1834, 10, 3. Margaret, dt Wm. & Dinah, b
1840, 3, 10. Rebecca d bur Sewickley
1846, 2, 16. Dinah d bur Sewickley

1847, 7, 25. Martha d bur Sewickley
1853, 4, 30. William d bur Sewickley

1821, 5, 22. Rebecca (form Mains) dis mcd
1832, 11, 29. Dinah rst by rq
1832, 11, 29. Wm. recrq
1834, 10, 13. Rebecca rst by rq
1840, 12, 3. Martha recrq
1854, 11, 2. Margaret dis disunity

MATHIOTT

1821, 11, 20. Mary relrq
1824, 11, 23. Katharine Smith (form Mathiott) dis mcd
1826, 6, 20. Susannah dis jas
1832, 11, 29. Ann Wood (form Methiatt) dis mcd
1836, 8, 4. John [Mathiatt] dis mcd
1836, 8, 4. George [Matthiott] dis mcd
1839, 9, 29. Henry [Matthiott] dis disunity

MAXEN

1818, 11, --. Jesse dis disunity
1822, 10, 22. Stephen Jr. dis mcd
1822, 11, 19. Rachel (form Cook) dis mcd
1826, 6, 20. Stephen [Maxon] dis disunity

MERCER

1822, 7, 23. Hannah rocf Redstone MM, Pa., dtd 1822,5,1
1830, 6, 3. Hannah gct Salem MM, O.

MILLER

1825, 4, 27. Margaret m Jonathan SHARPLESS
1830, 11, 23. Tacy d bur Center
1838, 6, 12. Peter d bur Center
1855, 11, 18. Tacy d bur Center

1819, 12, 21. David dis mcd

MISNER

1843, 6, 1. Mary (form Jackson) dis mcd

NAYLOR

1841, 8, 27. John Jr., s John & Martha, Belmont Co., O.; m in Providence, Sarah R. COPE, dt Joseph & Elizabeth, Fayette Co., Pa.

1841, 9, 30. Sarah R. gct Somerset MM, O.
1848, 5, 4. John & w, Sarah, & ch, David E. & Maria Elizabeth, rocf Marlborough MM, O., dtd 1848,2,29
1853, 6, 2. John & w, Sarah, & ch, David E., Martha Elizabeth, George G. & Uriah C., gct Plymouth MM, O.

NEGUS

----, --, --. John & Miriam
     Ch: Sarah   b 1807, 4, 23
         Levinah " 1809, 12, 19 d 1833, 5, 2
           bur Providence
         Eliza   b 1810, 12, 27
         Israel   " 1812, 8, 13

NEGUS, John & Miriam, continued
    Ch: Jacob   b 1814, 8, 22
        Lydia   " 1816, 4, 22
        Mary Mar-
          tin   " 1818, 5, 31
        John Wayts " 1820, 5, 20
        Isaac   " 1823, 6, 30
        Miriam   " 1824, 11, 17
        Esther   " 1828, 5, 21
1814, 12, 7. Jacob d bur Providence
1821, 10, 13. Sarah d bur Providence
1823, 1, 30. West, s Shaidlock & Sarah, Fay-
    ette Co., Pa.; m in Providence, Mary
    THOMPSON, dt John & Nancy, Allegany Co.,
    Pa.
    Ch: William   b 1823, 12, 20
        Eliza   " 1825, 9, 16
1825, 4, 7. Eliza d bur Providence
----, --, --. Joseph & Eliza
    Ch: Isabel   b 1831, 2, 19 d 1831, 2,23
        bur Providence
        Jonathan B.b 1832, 4, 14 " 1832, 8,14
        bur Providence
        Margaret B.b 1833, 9, 3
        Sarah   " 1835, 9, 14 " 1844, 8,22
        bur Providence
        Hannah La-
          vinah   b 1838, 4, 29 " 1840, 1, 7
        bur Providence
        Albert C. b 1840, 6, 27
        Mary Eliza " 1844, 1, 17
        Lydia S.   " 1846, 7, 22
        Ruthana   " 1847, 3, 24

1820, 1, 25. Joseph rst
1823, 5, 20. Sarah gct Salem MM, O.
1823, 5, 20. John & w, Meriam, & dt, Sarah,
    gct Salem MM, O.
1824, 7, 20. Sarah, minor, rocf Salem MM, O.
1827, 11, 1. West & w, Mary, & ch, Wm. &
    Eliza, gct New Garden MM, O.
1829, 12, 3. Joseph gct Redstone MM, Pa., to
    m Eliza Ann Chalfont
1830, 3, 4. Eliza Ann rocf Redstone MM, Pa.,
    dtd 1830,2,3
1833, 10, 31. John & w, Miriam, & ch, Lydia,
    Mary M., John W., Isaac, Miriam & Esther,
    gct Upper Springfield MM, O.
1833, 10, 31. Israel gct Upper Springfield MM,
    O.
1833, 10, 31. Sarah gct Upper Springfield MM,
    O.
1843, 3, 2. Rebecca gct Upper Springfield.
    MM, O.
1849, 10, 4. Joseph & w, Eliza, & ch, Marga-
    ret B., Albert C., Mary Eliza, Lydia L. &
    Ruthanna, gct Chester MM, Ind.

NEWLIN
1827, 4, 16. Ann [Newlon] d bur Sewickley
1859, 4, 7. Simon [Newlon] d bur Sewickley
1860, 6, 2. Elijah [Newlon] d bur Sewickley

1819, 7, 20. Elizabeth rst
1822, 5, 21. Jane (form Ong) dis mcd
1832, 11, 29. Elijah recrq
1863, 7, 2. Edith (form Gilbert) dis mcd

OMAN
1832, 1, 13. Eli d bur Providence

ONG
1857, 11, 25. Jesse d bur Sewickley

1821, 2, 20. Jesse & w, Elizabeth, & ch,
    James & Isabella, rocf Redstone MM, Pa.,
    dtd 1820,10,4
1821, 2, 20. Mary & Jane rocf Redstone MM,
    Pa., dtd 1820,11,1
1821, 5, 22. Mary Wilson (form Ong) dis mcd
1822, 5, 21. Jane Newlin (form Ong) dis mcd
1832, 1, 3. James dis disunity
1834, 10, 13. Isabel Reed (form Ong) dis mcd
1837, 11, 2. Jesse dis disunity
1841, 4, 29. Jesse rst

OSBURN
1823, 10, 21. Rebecca (form Smith) dis mcd

PARKER
1818, 4, 21. Elizabeth (form Brown) dis mcd

PENNOCK
1821, 1, 4. Moses, s Wm. & Mary, Stark Co.,
    O.; m in Providence, Judith COPE, dt
    Isaac & Sarah, Fayette Co., Pa.

1821, 3, 20. Judith gct Marlborough MM, O.

PIERSOL
1820, 12, 26. Sarah (form Smith) dis mcd
1827, 10, 4. Edith (form Sharpless) dis mcd

PINKHAM
1843, 6, 29. Cert rec for Thomas & w, Mary
    B., & ch, Mary Elizabeth, Thomas Edward,
    Caroline H., James Parnell & Wm. Penn,
    from Litchfield MM, Me., dtd 1843,5,19,
    endorsed to Redstone MM, Pa.

POWERS
1830, 9, 30. Lydia (form Gibson) dis mcd

PRICE
----, --, --. Isaac m Margaret ----- d 1863,9,
    23 bur Sewickley
    Ch: James M.   b 1835, 12, 17 d 1837, 3,28
        bur Sewickley
        Jasper   b 1838, 5, 16
        Mary Me-
          lissa   " 1841, 6, 19

1822, 5, 21. Margaret (form Mains) dis mcd
1825, 8, 23. Hannah Tarr (form Price) dis mcd
1835, 10, 1. Isaac recrq
1835, 10, 1. Margaret rst

PRICE, continued
1841, 9, 30. Mary rocf Westland MM, Pa., dtd
      1841,7,21
1843, 10, 5. Harmon dis mcd
1852, 7, 1. Wm. recrq
1863, 9, 3. Uriah recrq
1863, 9, 3. Wm. & Mary dis joining separa-
      tists in 1854

PYLE
1832, 8, 2. Priscilla (form Vail) dis mcd

RALEY
1823, 11, 26. John, s Robert & Ann, Washing-
      ton Co., Pa.; m in Providence, Sarah COPE,
      dt Joseph & Judith KIRK, Fayette Co., Pa.
1851, 1, 16. Sarah d bur Providence

1824, 3, 23. Sarah & ch, Ruth & Jesse Cope,
      gct Westland MM, Pa.
1826, 7, 25. John & w, Sarah, & her dt, Ruth
      & Jesse Cope, rocf Westland MM, Pa., dtd
      1826,5,25

REED
1834, 10, 13. Isabel (form Ong) dis mcd

REEDER
1845, 2, 27. Ruth (form Hagaman) dis mcd

RICHARDSON
1841, 7, 1. Hannah (form Vail) dis mcd
1850, 10, 3. Hannah D. rst at Pennsville MM,
      O. on consent of this mtg

ROBERTS
1820, 12, 26. Sarah (form Lamb) dis mcd

ROGERS
1869, 2, 24. Jeremiah d bur Westland (an
      elder) (ae 89y)

1869, 12, 2. Ann gct Middleton MM, O.

SCOTT
1866, 10, 18. Daniel J., s Amos & Ann, Chester
      Co., Pa.; m in Providence, Rachel W. COPE,
      dt Dawsy & Sarah Ann, Fayette Co., Pa.

1867, 8, 1. Rachel W. gct Bradfield MM, Pa..

SHANER
1853, 5, 22. Deborah d bur Sewickley

1825, 5, 24. Deborah (form Mains) dis mcd
1834, 10, 13. Deborah rst by rq
1858, 12, 2. Phebe Catharine (form McGrew)
      dis mcd

SHARP
1820, 11, 21. Susannah gct Clear Creek MM, O.

SHARPLESS
----, --, --. Jonathan, s Joseph & Mary, Fay-
      ette Co., Pa., d 1860,1,20; m ----- -----
   Ch: Samuel   b 1793, 2, 25
       Elizabeth   " 1794, 12, 29
       Joseph   " 1796, 12, 17 d 1797,11,
       11 bur Center
       William   b 1798, 2, 5
       Ellis   " 1800, 5, 16 " 1804,11,4
       bur Centre
       Mary   " 1802, 8, 12
       Edith   " 1805, 2, 5 " 1823,5,5
       bur Centre
       Jonathan Jr. b1807, 6, 8 " 1821,9,24
       bur Centre
       Sabina   "1810, 1, 25
   Jonathan m 2nd 1825,4,27 at Center, Marga-
   ret MILLER, dt Peter & Tacy, Fayette Co.,
   Pa.
   Ch: Priscilla
       Hunt   b 1826, 2, 16
       Hannah Pen-
       nell   " 1828, 1, 19 d 1828,10,23
       bur Centre
1848, 1, 5. Priscilla H. m Morgan CAMPBELL

1819, 4, 20. Samuel con mcd
1824, 2, 24. Wm. dis mcd
1826, 7, 25. Samuel gct Carmel MM, O.
1827, 10, 4. Edith Piersol (form Sharpless)
      dis mcd
1833, 5, 30. Samuel rocf Carmel MM, O., dtd
      1832,5,19
1835, 11, 5. Mary Furry (form Sharpless) dis
      mcd
1839, 4, 4. Samuel dis disunity

SHEPHERD
1840, 9, 9. Emily d bur Providence
1844, 7, 9. Joseph Jr. d bur Providence
1852, 5, 6. Elizabeth d bur Providence

1817, 10, 21. Joseph [Shepperd] rocf Redstone
      MM, Pa., dtd 1817,9,24
1817, 10, 21. John, Mary, Solomon, Rachel, Ja-
      cob, Louiza & Willson [Sheperd], ch Joseph
      & Elizabeth, recrq
1823, 6, 24. Joseph & w, Elizabeth, & ch,
      Mary, Solomon, Rachel, Jacob, Louiza, Wil-
      son, Margaret Jane & Emily, gct Westland
      MM, Pa.
1825, 3, 22. John gct Westland MM, Pa.
1827, 10, 4. Thomas dis mcd
1828, 8, 28. Joseph & w, Elizabeth, & ch,
      Solomon, Rachel, Jacob, Lydia, Louiza, Wm.
      Wilson, Margaret Jane, Emily & Joseph,
      rocf Westland MM, Pa., dtd 1828,7,24
1829, 12, 31. Solomon dis disunity
1833, 4, 4. Jacob dis disunity
1837, 6, 1. Rachel dis disunity
1837, 11, 30. Wilson dis disunity
1840, 1, 30. Louisa dis disunity
1841, 8, 26. Margaret dis jas (Cumberland So-

SHEPHERD, continued
   ciety

SHREVE
----, --, --. John m Abigail ----- d 1808,6,4
   bur Providence
   Ch: Joseph   b 1787, 7, 25
      John   " 1789, 11, 15 d 1813, 3,23
        bur Providence
      Mary B.   b 1792, 11, 27
      Israel   " 1795, 3, 22
      George W. " 1798, 1, 28
      Thomas C. " 1800, 9, 8
      Benjamin B." 1802, 11, 18
      Solomon   " 1805, 7, 5
      Eliza   " 1807, 10, 25

1817, 10, 21. Joseph rocf Short Creek MM, O.,
   dtd 1817,8,19
1823, 5, 20. Joseph gct Salem MM, O.
1823, 5, 20. Mary & Eliza gct Salem MM, O.
1823, 6, 24. Geo. W. gct Salem MM, O.
1823, 10, 21. Solomon, minor s John, gct Salem
   MM, O.
1823, 12, 23. Thomas C. gct Salem MM, O.
1824, 5, 25. Benjamin R. gct Salem MM, O.
1826, 8, 22. Benjamin R. rocf Salem MM, O.,
   dtd 1826,6,21
1827, 6, 19. Benj. R. gct Salem MM, O.
1829, 11, 5. John gct Salem MM, O.

SMITH
1842, 11, 22. Hannah, w Timothy, d
1849, 6, 10. Esther d

1819, 8, 24. John Cope gct Westland MM, Pa.,
   to m Sarah Smith
1820, 12, 26. Sarah Piersol (form Smith) dis
   mcd
1820, 12, 26. Wm. dis mcd
1821, 2, 20. Margaret (form Binns) dis mcd
1823, 10, 21. Rebecca Osburn (form Smith) dis
   mcd
1824, 11, 23. Katharine (form Mathiott) dis mcd
1826, 1, 24. Hannah rocf Westland MM, Pa., dtd
   1825,12,22
1830, 3, 4. Joseph rocf Westland MM, Pa.,
   dtd 1830,1,27
1831, 5, 5. Jesse rocf Sadsbury MM, dtd
   1830,12,7, endorsed by Redstone MM, Pa.,
   1831,2,2
1832, 11, 1. Jesse dis mcd
1833, 7, 4. Joseph dis mcd
1834, 2, 27. Micajah & w, Esther, gct Redstone
   MM, Pa.
1834, 2, 27. Hannah gct Redstone MM, Pa.
1834, 2, 27. Susannah gct Redstone MM, Pa.

SOPHER
1829, 8, 6. Joseph, s Joseph & Catharine,
   Washington Co., Pa.; m in Providence, Sarah WAYTS, dt Shaedlock & Sarah NEGUS

1829, 10, 1. Sarah & dt, Susanna Wayts, gct
   Westland MM, Pa.
1840, 6, 4. Joseph & w, Sarah, & ch, Hannah
   & Lydia, rocf Redstone MM, Pa., dtd 1840,
   4,29
1841, 6, 3. Sarah & step-dt, Hannah K. &
   Lydia Soper, gct Spiceland MM, Ind.
1842, 6, 2. Joseph dis

SPARKS
1826, 6, 20. Mary (form Hewitt) dis mcd

STERREN
1838, 4, 5. Anne rocf Denning Creek MM, dtd
   1838,2,22

STICKEL
1829, 7, 11. George d bur Providence
1838, 10, 5. Jane [Sticlle] d bur Providence

TARR
1825, 8, 23. Hannah (form Price) dis mcd

TATE
1828, 1, 31. Sarah (form Tilton) dis mcd

TAYLOR
1822, 12, 24. Rebecca (form McGreil) dis mcd
1828, 7, 30. Jesse dis disunity
1830, 8, 5. Mary gct Marlborough MM, O.
1833, 2, 28. Jane (form Mains) con mcd
1835, 10, 1. Elma (form Mains) dis mcd
1850, 5, 30. Jane dis jas

THOMPSON
1823, 1, 30. Mary m West NEGUS

THORNE
1830, 2, 4. Hallock gct Cornwall MM, N. Y.

TILTON
----, --, --. Enoch & Elizabeth
    Ch: Ann   b 1817, 7, 19
      Morgan   " 1819, 5, 28
      Samuel   " 1821, 4, 6 d 1821, 4,27
        bur Centre
      Elizabeth " 1822, 4, 11 " 1822, 4,30
        bur Centre
      Jobe   " 1823, 7, 16

1825, 12, 20. James dis disunity
1828, 1, 31. Sarah Tate (form Tilton) dis mcd
1828, 4, 2. Mary Whitam (form Tilton) dis
   mcd
1828, 5, 1. Enoch dis disunity
1828, 5, 1. Elizabeth dis disunity
1835, 7, 2. Mathias dis mcd
1835, 10, 1. John dis disunity
1835, 10, 1. Enoch Jr. dis mcd
1835, 11, 5. Joseph dis disunity
1835, 10, 2. Charles dis mcd & jas
1846, 6, 4. Morgan dis mcd & jas
1847, 7, 1. Job dis jas

TILTON, continued
1847, 8, 5. Ann Vancamp (form Tilton) dis
     mcd

VAIL
----, --, --. Samuel d 1865,4,27 bur Centre,
     ae 91; m Agnes ----- d 1821,9,10 bur Cen-
     tre
     Ch: Margaret   b 1818, 3, 21 d 1841, 1,27
         Martha   " 1820, 4, 18 " 1827, 8,7
         Abraham   " 1816, 4, 13
----, --, --. Samuel & Elizabeth
     Ch: Edward   b 1824, 3, 4
         Agnes   " 1826, 10, 12
         Lydia   " 1828, 12, 1
         Abraham   " 1831, 4, 8
1821, 9, 3. Abraham d bur Centre
1829, 9, 2. Mercy m Samuel COPE, Jr.
1838, 8, 24. Jesse, s Samuel & Agnes, Elk-
     hart Co., Ind.; m in Providence, Elma
     COPE, dt Samuel & Sarah, Fayette Co., Pa.
     Ch: Melissa D. b 1839, 8, -- d 1839,11, 9
         Margaret   " 1840, 9, 21
         Samuel C. " 1841, 3, 17
         Louis Wil-
           lets   " 1851, 1, 20
1839, 12, 18. Abraham d bur Centre

1823, 4, 22. Samuel gct Short Creek MM, O.,
     to m Elizabeth Griffith
1823, 9, 23. Elizabeth rocf Short Creek MM,
     O., dtd 1823,7,22
1823, 11, 25. Chas. dis
1827, 5, 22. Abraham rocf Redstone MM, Pa.,
     dtd 1827,5,2
1832, 8, 2. Priscilla Pyle (form Vail) dis
     mcd
1838, 8, 2. Joel dis mcd
1841, 7, 1. Hannah Richardson (form Vail)
     dis mcd
1842, 9, 29. Margaret McGrew (form Vail) con
     mcd
1850, 1, 31. Edward con mcd
1851, 4, 3. Agnes Frazure (form Vail) dis
     mcd
1860, 7, 5. Abram dis mcd
1865, 6, 29. Lydia McGrew (form Vail) con
     mcd
1869, 1, 7. Sarah Kinnison (form Vail) rpd
     mcd

VANCAMP
1847, 8, 5. Ann (form Tilton) dis mcd

VANSCOYOC
1827, 8, 22. Aaron, s Enoch & Lydia, Washing-
     ton Co., Pa.; m in Providence, Ruth COPE,
     dt Isaac & Sarah, Fayette Co., Pa.

1827, 11, 29. Ruth gct Westland MM, Pa.

WALKER
1817, 9, 23. Rutn dis jas (Methodists)

WAYTS
1829, 8, 6. Sarah m Joseph SOPHER
1846, 1, 27. Shaidlock d
1818, 12, 22. Mary, Shaidlock, William & Su-
     sannah, ch Sarah, recrq
1824, 2, 24. Mary, minor dt Sarah, gct West-
     land, Pa.
1829, 7, 2. Wm. gct Sandy Spring MM, O.
     (minor)
1829, 10, 1. Sarah Sopher & dt, Susanna
     Wayts, gct Westland MM, Pa.
1831, 3, 3. Shaidlock gct Westland MM, Pa.
1834, 7, 3. Wm. rocf Haddonfield MM, N. J.,
     dtd 1834,6,9
1834, 8, 28. Wm. dis mcd
1836, 9, 29. Shaidlock N. rocf Westland MM,
     Pa., dtd 1836,7,27

WHITAM
1828, 4, 3. Mary (form Tilton) dis mcd

WILSON
1821, 5, 22. Mary (form Ong) dis mcd
1835, 8, 27. Wm. Jr. recrq
1840, 12, 31. Wm. gct Chesterfield MM, O.
1841, 12, 2. Margaret rst
1851, 6, 5. Margaret gct Plymouth MM, O.

WOOD
1832, 11, 29. Ann (form Methiatt) dis mcd

WORLEY
1830, 8, 5. Aaron rocf Redstone MM, Pa.,
     dtd 1830,3,31
1831, 6, 2. Aaron gct Redstone MM, Pa.
1831, 9, 27. Aaron dis disunity

SEWICKLEY MEETING

Sewickley Meeting was established in 1799 in Westmoreland County, Pennsylvania. It was set up as a Preparative Meeting in 1826 by Redstone Quarterly Meeting. The Meeting was established by pioneer Friends who migrated from Adams, Philadelphia and Washington Counties.

A deed dated December 12, 1832 records the donation of land by James McGrew: "James McGrew willed to the Society of Friends, April 11, 1805, seven acres of land in Sewickley Township for a meeting house and burial ground." From 1799 until 1805 meetings were conducted in members homes. In the latter year, a one room log house was erected. Part of the surrounding seven acres was plotted as a graveyard. By 1893 the meeting declined in membership to the extent that only a few members were left. A deed dated March 16, 1893 says, "The Society of Friends, Sewickley Township, sold to J. M. Guffey of Pittsburgh, Alleghany County, the coal under the seven acres of ground for $628.75." Another deed dated June 6, 1907, states that "the Society of Friends, Sewickley Township, sold to Salem (Ohio) Monthly Meeting the seven acres of ground in their possession."

On authority of the oldest resident of the community, the Meeting held its last session in 1928 and in the same year it was laid down by Salem Quarterly Meeting.

RECORDS

BLACKBURN
1870, 2, 1. Wm. & w, Ann, & s, Daniel, gct
    Middleton MM, O.
1870, 3, 29. Lydia, Martha, Amy & Hannah gct
    Middleton MM, O.
1870, 8, 30. Charles gct Middleton MM, O.
1870, 8, 30. Nathan M. & w, Rebecca M., & ch,
    Annie E., gct Middleton MM, O.
1870, 9, 20. Wm. H. gct Middleton MM, O.

BRANSON
1874, 2, 3. Oliver J. dis mcd

CAMPBELL
1872, 4, 21. Mary d

COPE
1868, 10, 31. Edna, dt Wm. & Rachel W., b
----, --, --. Louis P. & Hannah Y.
    Ch: Samuel W. b 1870, 5, 12
        Louis Jr. " 1873, 6, 22
1870, 5, 26. Eliza d ae 57
1871, 2, 8. Joshua, s Amos & Edna Emily, Co-
    lumbiana Co., O.; m at Sewickley, Eliza
    GILBERT, dt Benjamin & Lydia, Westmoreland
    Co., Pa.
1871, 6, 24. Jesse d

----, --, --. Robert J., minor s James A. &
    Achsah, gct Middleton MM, O.
1870, 11, 29. Amos & w, Rachel, & ch, Mary Ann
    & Calvin, gct Middleton MM, O.
1871, 1, 31. Wm. & w, Rachel W., & ch, Fran-
    cis R. & Edna E., gct Middleton MM, O.
----, --, --. Margaret gct Middleton MM, O.
----, --, --. Thomas C. gct Middleton MM, O.
1871, 11, 28. Edward Y. & w, Alice G., & ch,
    Charles & Anna, gct Newgarden MM, O.
1873, 7, 1. Sarah Ann & ch, Mary M., Melisse
    & Lucinda, gct Salem MM, O.

DEWEES
1869, 6, 1. Deborah Marsh (form Dewees) dis
    mcd & jas
1869, 8, 3. James dis jas

FRITCHMAN
----, --, --. Mary (form Hutton) dis mcd

GIBBONS
1873, 12, 3. Dillon, s James & Elizabeth, Bel-
    mont Co., O.; m at Sewickley, Mary GILBERT
    dt Benjamin & Lydia, Westmoreland Co., Pa.

GILBERT
1869, 1, 1. Elma, dt Joshua & Deborah S., b

1871, 5, 2. George & w, Hannah, & dt, Ellen
    C., gct Newgarden MM, O.
1871, 8, 1. Ann Eliza & Sarah gct New Garden
    MM, O.

1872, 1, 2. Joshua & w, Deborah, & ch, Wil-
    mer H., Edwin D. & Elma, gct New Garden
    MM, O.

HUTTON
1874, 5, 8. Harmon Linnaeus d ae 21 bur Ha-
    verford College

1872, 4, 30. Annie gct New Garden MM, O.
1872, 7, 30. Finley M. gct WDMM, Phila., Pa.
----, --, --. Mary Fritchman (form Hutton) dis
    mcd

KINNISON
----, --, --. Sarah (form Vail) dis mcd

McGRAIL
1867, 12, 28. Mary d ae 91

1871, 1, 30. Sarah gct Plymouth MM, O.
1872, 5, 28. Uriah Price & w, Rebecca, & ch,
    Elizabeth, Edwin G. & Francis Price, &
    George G. & Amy Ann McGrail, gct New Gar-
    den MM, O.

McGREW
1871, 2, 1. Nathan d ae 86
1873, 9, 14. Susannah d ae 69

1867, 1, 29. Simon O. recrq
1868, 7, 28. Simon O. gct Providence MM
1870, 8, 2. Simon O. & Mary gct Hickory
    Grove MM, Ia.

MARSH
1869, 6, 1. Deborah (form Dewees) dis mcd &
    jas

PRICE
1866, 4, 11. Uriah, s Isaac & Margaret, West-
    moreland Co., Pa.; m at Sewickley, Rebecca
    McGRAIL, dt George Gilbert & w, Hannah,
    Westmoreland Co., Pa.
    Ch: Edwin G. b 1868, 9, 25
        Francis " 1872, 1, 25

1866, 7, 3. Jasper Oliver dis mcd
1870, 2, 12. Elizabeth, minor dt Uriah & Re-
    becca, recrq
1872, 5, 28. Uriah & w, Rebecca, & ch, Eliza-
    beth, Edwin G. & Francis Price, & George
    G. & Amy Ann McGrail, gct New Garden MM, O.

SAVERY
1870, 9, 15. Wm., s Wm. & Elizabeth H., Phil-
    adelphia, Pa.; m at Sewickley, Rebecca
    HUTTON, dt Joel W. & w, Ann, Westmoreland
    Co., Pa.

VAIL
1869, 12, 28. Jesse D. dis mcd
1870, 8, 2. Edward G. gct Coal Creek MM, Ia.
----, --, --. Sarah Kinnison (form Vail) dis
    mcd

           *   *   *   *   *   *   *   *   *   *   *   *   *   *

GILBERT   McGRAIL
1871, 2, 8.   Eliza m Joshua COPE   1866, 4, 11.   Rebecca m Uriah PRICE
1873, 12, 3. Mary m Dillon GIBBONS

HUTTON
1870, 9, 15. Rebecca m Wm. SAVERY

CONCORD MONTHLY MEETING

The first established meeting of Friends west of the Alleghany Mountains was at Westland, in southwestern Pennsylvania. This meeting was provided for by action of Hopewell
Monthly Meeting located near Winchester, Virginia, November 11, 1782. Groups of Friends
from Pennsylvania, Maryland and Virginia were augmented by a large movement from the Carolinas and Georgia. Probably the greatest single factor in this movement was the slavery
issue. After the passage of the famous Ordinance of 1787, Friends knew that the territory
north and west of the Ohio River would be forever free from slavery, but there were doubtless other contributing reasons, such as availability of good land at a cheap price, the
lure of the frontier and natural expansion.

The movement into Ohio began in 1796 and an intensified movement began about 1800
when settlements were made west of the Ohio River some miles northwest of Wheeling, Virginia. These were a "meeting-going" population. These people in their migrations had rested
on the First day of the week, and at the accustomed hour had gathered around their campfire
for worship.

There is a tradition that at Concord (Colerain) a group assembled first on the trunk
of a fallen tree, then were invited to the newly erected cabin of Jonathan Taylor, and later moved to a log meeting house. The first Friends moved into eastern Ohio in September
1800. In less than one year, Friends so increased that two preparative meetings were established and on December 19, 1800, Concord Monthly Meeting was opened.

The place of meeting alternated with Short Creek until 3rd Month, 20th, 1804, when a
request was made to Redstone Quarterly Meeting held at Westland that the monthly meeting be
divided - Short Creek Monthly Meeting to be held alternately at Short Creek and Plymouth,
and Concord Monthly Meeting to be held alternately at Concord and Plainfield. This request was granted. In 1804 Concord Monthly Meeting initiated a movement looking forward to
a Quarterly Meeting for the Friends in eastern Ohio.

Among the charter members of Concord Monthly Meeting who were prominent in the begin-
nings of Quakerism in Ohio were Howard Horton, Nathan Updegraff, Jonathan Taylor, Benjamin
Starta, Josiah Bundy, Cadwallader Evans, Bordon Stanton, Jacob Ong, Joseph Hall, Samuel
Lewis, Enoch Harris, Benjamin Vaile, Jonathan Wilson, Malachi Jolly, Mary Jolly, Amara Lip-
sey, Benjamin Steel, David Berry, Joseph Dew, Royal Wade, James Raby, Abner Lambert, Joseph
Arnold, Samuel James, William Kirk, Jesse White, William Satterthwait, Levi Wells, Joshua
Hatcher, Daniel Frazier, Aaron Brown and William Carr.

In the years 1803-1805 the Hopewell meeting of Virginia sent to Concord in Ohio members
of the Lufton, Piggot, Jenkins, Pickering, Miller, Ellis, Steer and Bevan families. Concord Monthly Meeting suffered heavily as a result of the Hicksite Separation in 1828.

Records of Concord Monthly Meeting are preserved by Mable Clark, Custodian, Bridgeport,
Ohio, and in the bank vault at Mount Pleasant. Some records have been lost by fire and as
a result of having been borrowed and never returned.

RECORDS

ALBERTSON
1804, 7, 24. Joseph rocf Contentnea MM, N. C. dtd 1804,2,11

ANSON
1806, 5, 27. Lovesy & Patience rocf Contentnea MM, N. C., dtd 1806,3,9

ARNOLD
1804, 5, 30. Sarah m Samuel WILLIAMS

ASKEW
1807, 4, 30. William, s Parker & Hannah, Belmont Co., O.; m in Plainfield MH, Martha WILSON, dt Isaac & Rebecca, Belmont Co., O.

1806, 11, 18. Wm. rocf SD MM, dtd 1806,9,24

ATHERTON
1804, 7, 24. Richard gct Westland MM

ATKINSON
1807, 6, 23. Thomas & fam rocf Bush River MM, S. C., dtd 1807,1,31, end to Short Creek MM, O. on rq
1818, 8, 19. Daniel & w, Mary, rocf Short Creek MM, dtd 1818,7,21
1821, 5, 23. Daniel & w, Mary, gct Short Creek MM

BAILEY
1807, 10, 28. Suzannah m Jacob CROY

1804, 11, 20. Henry & Jesse rocf Contentnea MM, dtd 1804,9,8
1804, 11, 20. Elizabeth & dt, Mary Ruth & Elizabeth, rocf Contentnea MM, dtd 1804, 9,8
1806, 6, 24. Lucy rocf Black Water MM, dtd 1806,3,19
1807, 7, 21. Micajah & w, Mary, & ch, Marander & Samuel, rocf Black Water MM, Va., dtd 1805,10,24
1807, 7, 21. Mary rocf Black Water MM, Va., dtd 1806,9,24
1808, 6, 23. Stephen rocf Upper MM, Va., dtd 1808,3,19
1809, 5, 22. Zachariah & fam rocf Upper MM, Va., dtd 1809,1,25; cert returned because outward unsettled

BAKER
1830, 6, 23. James Jr. rocf Fallowfield MM, Pa., dtd 1830,2,5 (H)

BALDWIN
1807, 11, 4. Margaret rst on consent of Hopewell MM
1808, 3, 24. Mary, Thomas, David & Rees, ch Margaret Baldwin, rocf Hopewell MM, Va., dtd 1808,2,1, end to Plainfield MM

BALL
1802, 12, 18. Thomas rocf Darby MM, dtd 1802, 9,2
1806, 3, 18. Thomas gct Salem MM

BALLINGER
1808, 1, 19. Daniel rocf Pipe Creek MM, dtd 1807,11,14

BARKER
1840, 9, 23. James dis mcd (H)

BARLEY
1806, 5, 27. Wm. & w, Rebecca, & ch, Susannah, Lucy, Bethany, Rebecca, Wyatt, Barak, Michael, Permilia, Wm., Beuford & Martha, rocf Black Water MM, Va., dtd 1806,3,19

BARNES
1805, 7, 23. John recrq
1805, 9, 24. Henry recrq
1806, 9, 23. David rocf Pipe Creek MM, dtd 1806,6,12
1809, 9, 21. Henry rocf Stillwater MM
1818, 8, 19. Mary con mcd

BATTEN
1803, 12, 17. Richard rocf Wrightsborough MM, dtd 1803,6,4
1828, 12, 24. Ann Jr. rocf New Garden MM, dtd 1828,11,20 (H)
1829, 8, 19. Ann gct New Garden MM (H)

BECK
1825, 8, 24. Lydia dis mcd

BELANGEE
1803, 6, 18. James & w, Grace, & their niece, Mary Engle, rocf Evesham MM, N. J., dtd 1803,4,8

BERRY
1803, 10, 19. Thomas, s David & Hannah, Belmont Co., O.; m in Concord MH, Rachel WHITE, dt Jesse & Mary, Belmont Co., O.
Ch: Mary   b 1807, 2, 3
    David
    Cyrus   " 1809, 4, 5
    Israel
    Jesse W.   " 1812, 9, 26
    Samuel   " 1816, 2, 20
    Reese   " 1817, 10, 6
    Jordan   " 1819, 12, 13
    Asenath   " 1821, 6, 21
    Elizabeth " 1823, 2, 14
1806, 1, 1. Hannah m Samuel DEWEES
1806, 10, 1. Samuel, s David & Hannah, Belmont Co., O.; m in Stillwater MH, Mary HODGIN, dt Wm. & Agness, Belmont Co., O.
----, --, --. Jesse & Esther
Ch: Madison G. b 1837, 3, 28
    Braxton C. " 1840, 4, 14
    Thomas W. " 1843, 1, 7

BERRY, Jesse & Esther, continued
  Ch: Ruth Han-
       nah b 1845, 7, 19
    Edward John
    Culberson " 1851, 5, 20
1839, 2, 27. Reese T., s Thos. & Rachel, Belmont Co., O., b 1817,10,6; m in Concord
  MH, Martha H. VICKERS, dt Thomas & Hannah,
  Belmont Co., O.
  Ch: Theodore b 1839, 12, 11
1839, 5, 29. Mary m Elisha PICKERIN
1878, 5, 23. Laura A. m Theodore CLARK

1804, 9, 18. Thomas & w, Rachel, dis
1805, 4, 23. Thomas & Rachel rst
1810, 8, 23. Samuel & w, Mary, & ch, Hannah,
  rocf Stillwater MM, dtd 1810,10,31
1812, 6, 25. David gct Short Creek MM
1812, 6, 25. Samuel & w, Mary, & ch, Hannah
  & Sarah, gct Stillwater MM
1815, 5, 25. Beulah dis mcd
1817, 8, 20. Samuel & w, Mary, & ch, Hannah,
  Sarah, Ann & William, rocf Stillwater MM,
  dtd 1817,6,28
1822, 2, 20. Samuel & w, Mary, & ch, Hannah,
  Sarah, Ann, Wm., David, Agnes & Samuel,
  gct Stillwater MM
1827, 7, 25. Hannah White (form Berry) dis
  mcd to first cousin
1831, 5, 25. Cyrus con mcd (H)
1833, 5, 22. Cyrus gct Deerfield MM (H)
1837, 2, 22. Jesse dis mcd (H)
1840, 5, 22. Esther Ruth rocf New Garden MM,
  dtd 1839,10,24 (H)
1840, 8, 19. Samuel dis mcd (H)
1850, 4, 24. Julianna rocf Short Creek MM,
  dtd 1850,1,24 (H)
1850, 8, 25. Rees con mcd (H)
1843, 6, 21. Asenath Jobe (form Berry) con
  mcd (H)

BEVAN
1806, 7, 22. Stacy & w, Lydia, & ch, Susanna,
  Eleanor, John & Owen, rocf Hopewell MM,
  Va., dtd 1805,3,4

BISHOP
1815, 7, 20. Joseph gct Stillwater MM

BLACKLEDGE
1814, 6, 23. Cert rec for Rachel from ND MM,
  dtd 1814,2,22, end to Short Creek MM, O.

BLOXSOM
1805, 1, 22. Gideon rocf South River MM, Va.,
  dtd 1804,10,13
1805, 11, 19. Wm. [Bloxom] & w, Mary, & ch,
  James, Ann, Elizabeth & Meriah, rocf South
  River MM, Va., dtd 1805,8,11
1807, 1, 20. Richard [Bloxam] & w, Ann, & ch,
  Ann, Mary, Elizabeth & Charles, & gr ch,
  Unity, Jerusha, Richard, Obediah & Gideon
  Johnson, rocf South River MM, Va., dtd

1806,10,11, end by Miami MM, O., 1806,11,
  13
1808, 6, 23. Richard & w & ch, Ann, Mary &
  Charles, & their gr ch, Jerusha, Unity,
  Richard, Obediah & Gideon Johnson, gct
  Fairfield MM, O.

BOGUE
1803, 1, 15. Jonathan, s Sarah Bogue Melton,
  rocf Trent MM, N. C., dtd 1802,3,12

BOLDEN
1806, 9, 23. Jane (form Mecan) dis mcd

BOLTON
1806, 7, 22. Aquila M. rocf Phila. MM, Pa.,
  dtd 1806,5,30
1807, 6, 23. Joshua rocf ND MM, dtd 1807,4,28
1808, 12, 22. Joshua dis
1810, 2, 22. Aquila M. gct Short Creek MM
1811, 4, 25. Aquila M. rocf Short Creek MM,
  dtd 1811,4,23
1811, 9, 26. Aquila M. dis mcd

BOND
1805, 7, 23. Allen & w, Sarah, & ch, Margaret,
  John, Joseph, Abner, Rebecca & Elizabeth,
  rocf Goose Creek MM, dtd 1805,4,4

BORTON
1806, 1, 21. Benjamin & w, Charity, rocf Evesham MM, N. J., dtd 1805,9,--
1806, 1, 21. Reuben rocf Evesham MM, N. J.,
  dtd 1805,9,--
1806, 9, 23. Keturah Vine (form Borton) dis
  mcd
1808, 1, 19. Martha dis

BOSWELL
1804, 9, 26. Demsey, s Zadoc & Ruth, Belmont
  Co., O.; m in Stillwater MH, Mary MIDDLE-
  TON, dt Joseph & Phebe, Belmont Co., O.

1804, 5, 22. Ruth & ch, Wm. & Penninah, rocf
  Mt. Pleasant MM, Va., dtd 1804,3,25
1804, 6, 19. Dempsey rocf Mt. Pleasant MM,
  Va., dtd 1804,2,25
1804, 6, 19. Thomas & w & s, Jonathan, rocf
  Mt. Pleasant MM, Va., dtd 1804,2,25

BOWMAN
1807, 4, 21. Isaac rocf Salem MM, dtd 1807,
  4,14
1807, 9, 22. Isaac gct Short Creek MM, O.

BRADRICK
1803, 8, 20. Beulah rocf Evesham MM, N. J.,
  dtd 1803,4,8

BRANSON
1826, 11, 16. Eliza, dt Thomas & Anna (Vale),
  b
1805, 9, 24. Jacob & w, Rebecca, & ch, Abi-

BRANSON, continued
    gail, Isaiah, Phebe & Lydia, rocf Crooked
      Run MM, dtd 1805,6,29, end from Short
      Creek MM, 1805,9,21
1807, 2, 24. Elizabeth rocf Crooked Run MM,
    dtd 1806,4,5
1815, 6, 22. Sarah (form Pickering) dis mcd
1818, 2 , 22. Amelia (form Pickering) dis mcd
1818, 5, 20. Isaac rocf Stillwater MM, dtd
    1818,2,28
1819, 5, 19. Isaac gct Westland MM, to m Sa-
    rah Bracken
1824, 12, 22. John Hirst gct Flushing MM, to
    m Elizabeth Branson
1825, 5, 25. Thomas gct Plainfield MM, to m
    Anna Vale
1825, 9, 21. Anna rocf Plainfield MM, dtd
    1825,8,25
1829, 11, 25. Thomas & w, Anna, & dt, Eliza,
    gct Green Plain MM (H)

BRIGGS
1803, 2, 19. Wm. & w, Esther, & ch, Israel
    Shreeve, Samuel Miller, George Green &
    Maria, rocf Westland MM dtd 1802,3,12

BRIGHT
1802, 7, 17. Mary recrq

BROCK
1806, 9, 23. John rocf Westland MM, dtd
    1806,7,26

BROOMHALL
1806, 5, 27. Enos & w, Phebe, & ch, Sarah,
    Isaac, Bartley, James, Jane, Joanna, Su-
    sanna & Martha, rocf Goose Creek MM, Va.,
    dtd 1806,3,4

BROWN
1803, 4, 16. Josiah rocf Richsquare MM, N.C.,
    dtd 1802,8,21
1803, 9, 17. Cert rec for Josiah end back to
    Richsquare MM, N. C., by rq
1805, 6, 18. Josiah rocf Rich Square MM,
    N. C., dtd 1804,3,17
1808, 9, 22. Josiah gct Rich Square MM, N. C.

BUFFKIN
1807, 3, 24. Thomas rocf Western Branch MM,
    dtd 1806,9,27

BUNDY
1807, 12, 2. Lydia m John PEELLE
1812, 9, 30. Susanna m Isaac WELLS
1816, 10, 30. Ruth m John TOWNSEND
1819, 12, 1. Abigail m Joel WHARTON
1832, 8, 23. Ann m George COPE

1802, 1, 16. Josiah & w, Bathia, & ch, Benja-
    min, Moses, Stanton, Susannah, Abigail &
    Ruth, rocf Redstone MM, Pa., dtd 1801,12,
    4, end by Westland MM, 1801,12,26

1805, 9, 24. William & w, Mary, & ch, Moses,
    Lydia & Mary, rocf Mt. Pleasant MM, Va.,
    dtd 1805,4,27
1806, 7, 22. William rocf Contentney MM,
    N. C., dtd 1806,2,8
1806, 7, 22. Sarah & dt, Mary, rocf Content-
    nea MM, N. C., dtd 1806,2,8
1806, 9, 23. Mary rocf Contentnea MM, N. C.,
    dtd 1806,5,10
1807, 12, 27. Joshua rocf Springfield MM, N.C.,
    dtd 1807,7,4
1813, 2, 25. Joshua rocf Short Creek MM, O.
1815, 9, 2. Moses gct Short Creek MM, O., to
    m Ann Townsend
1815, 12, 20. Ann rocf Short Creek MM, O.
1818, 5 , 20. Benjamin gct Stillwater MM, to
    m Mary Bailey
1818, 8, 19. Mary rocf Stillwater MM, dtd
    1818,7,25
1819, 9, 23. Stanton gct Stillwater MM, O.,
    to m Ann Bailey
1820, 1, 19. Stanton gct Stillwater MM, O.
1823, 7, 23. Benjamin gct Stillwater MM, to
    m Delitha Bailey
1824, 1, 21. Delitha rocf Stillwater MM, dtd
    1823,11,22
1827, 10, 24. Moses & w, Ann, & ch, Mary, Jo-
    seph, Townsend, Josiah, Bethia, Lucinda,
    Susanna & Nehemiah Matson, gc
1831, 8, 24. Ann T. recrq (H)
1833, 8, 21. Sarah S. rocf Plainfield MM,
    dtd 1833,6,20 (H)
1834, 12, 24. Josiah recrq (H)

BUTLER
1821, 7, 25. Jared recrq
1822, 6, 19. Jared gct Somerset MM, to m
    Elizabeth Bailey
1823, 3, 19. Jared gct Somerset MM

CADWALADER
1808, 4, 21. Cert rec for Isaac & w, Eliza-
    beth, from Redstone MM, dtd 1807,12,4, end
    to Plainfield MM

CARR
1802, 11, 20. William & w, Sarah, & ch, Jesse,
    Anne, Joshua, Thomas & Susannah, rocf
    Westland MM, dtd 1802,8,28
1802, 12, 18. James & w, Elizabeth, & ch, Ann,
    Samuel, Kinsey, Catharine & Aletta, rocf
    Westland MM, dtd 1802,8,28

CARSON
1806, 6, 24. Cert rec for George & w, Lydia,
    & ch, Phebe, from London Grove MM, end to
    Short Creek MM, O.

CARTER
1819, 2, 24. Richard gct Plainfield MM
1824, 5, 19. Richard rocf Plainfield MM, dtd
    1824,4,22

CARVER
1802, 5, 15. Talitha recrq
1803, 1, 15. John, Rebecca, Henry, Elisabeth
  & James, ch Henry & Talitha, recrq
1805, 11, 19. Henry & w, Talitha, & ch, John,
  Rebecca, Henry, Elizabeth, James, Ann &
  Abner, rocf Short Creek MM, O., dtd 1805,
  5,18

CHAPLINE
1813, 10, 21. Elizabeth (form Fox) dis mcd

CHERINGTON
1806, 10, 29. Anna m Cadwallader FOULKE

1806, 2, 18. Anna [Cherrington] rocf Exeter
  MM, dtd 1805,10,30

CHILDRA
1805, 10, 22. Martha (form Middleton) dis mcd
1816, 11, 20. Martha rst at Stillwater MM, on
  consent of this Mtg

CLARK
1878, 5, 23. Theodore, s Geo. P. & Samaria,
  Jefferson Co., O.; m in home of Reese
  Berry, Laura A. BERRY, dt Reese & Julianna, Belmont Co., O.

COATS
1841, 7, 21. Hannah & Lydia Ann rocf Cherry
  St., Phila. MM, Pa., dtd 1841,4,21 (H)
1842, 3, 23. Hannah & Lydia gct Alum Creek
  MM (H)

COFFEE
1805, 11, 19. John & w, Rachel, & ch, Wm.,
  John, Joseph, Rachel, Mary, Ruth, Mareb,
  Isaac & Charles, rocf Goose Creek MM, Va.,
  dtd 1805,9,5

COLYER
1804, 6, 19. James rocf Great Contentnea MM,
  N. C., dtd 1804,3,10
1806, 7, 22. Joseph rocf Contentnea MM, N.C.,
  dtd 1806,2,8
1807, 7, 21. John [Colyar] & w, Rhody, & ch,
  Benajah & Mary, rocf Contentnea MM, N. C.,
  dtd 1807,2,8
1808, 9, 22. James [Colyar] gct Contentnea
  MM, N. C.

CONARD
1841, 8, 25. Sarah Morris (form Conard) con
  mcd

CONRAD
1810, 6, 21. Thomas & w, Sarah, & ch, William,
  Mary & Hannah, rocf York MM

CONROW
1806, 1, 21. Darling & w, Rachel, & ch, Jacob, Eunice, Thomas & Rebecca, rocf Crook-

ed Run MM, Va., dtd 1805,11,2

COOK
1807, 2, 24. Jeremiah & w, Rachel, & ch,
  Allen, Hannah, Ellis, Sarah & Mary, rocf
  Westland MM, dtd 1806,11,22
1808, 2, 23. Hannah Jolly (form Cook) dis mcd
1809, 5, 22. Allen dis mcd
1810, 4, 26. Jeremiah & w, Rachel, & ch, Sarah & Mary, gct Stillwater MM
1810, 4, 26. Ellis gct Plymouth MM

COOMBS
1807, 11, 24. Benjamin & w, Charity, & ch,
  Mary, Ann, Deborah, John & George, rocf
  Chesterfield MM, N. J., dtd 1807,8,7

COPE
1818, 5, 27. Mary m Thomas WHITE
1819, 4, 28. James, s Geo. & Abigail, Belmont Co., O.; m in Concord MH, Phebe
  PIGGOTT, dt Nathan & Lydia
  Ch: Nathan   b 1820, 6, 21
      Abigail   " 1822, 2, 21
      David   " 1824, 1, 1
      Charles   " 1825, 11, 21
      Elias   " 1827, 11, 9
1820, 4, 26. Joshua, s Geo. & Abigail, Belmont Co., O.; m in Concord MH, Rebecca
  MEDCELF, dt Moses & Susannah, Belmont Co.,
  O.
  Ch: George   b 1821, 1, 26
      Susannah " 1823, 8, 20
      Moses   " 1824, 8, 10
      Alfred   " 1826, 1, 21
      Edward   " 1827, 9, 23
      Caleb   " 1830, 10, 26
1825, 12, 28. Joseph H., s Samuel & Sarah,
  Belmont Co., O.; m in Concord MH, Rebecca
  MILLHOUSE, dt Wm. & Martha, Belmont Co., O.
1832, 8, 23. George, s Geo. & Abigail, Belmont Co., O.; m in Concord MH, Ann BUNDY,
  dt Josiah & Bathiah, Belmont Co., O.
  George m 2nd 1838,5,30 in Concord MH, Juliann TOWNSEND, dt John & Ruth, Monroe
  Co., O.
1864, 9, 15. Julia m John RENNARD

1815, 4, 20. Joshua rocf Short Creek MM, dtd
  1815,3,21
1815, 5, 25. George & w, Abigail, & ch,
  James, George, Abigail, Jane, Sarah, Rachel & Caleb, rocf Short Creek MM, dtd
  1815,4,18
1815, 6, 22. Mary rocf Short Creek MM, dtd
  1815,4,18
1822, 7, 24. Abigail Hoops (form Cope) dis
  mcd
1824, 9, 23. Joseph H. rocf Providence MM,
  dtd 1824,8,24
1826, 5, 24. Joseph H. & w, Rebecca, gct
  Smithfield MM
1835, 7, 22. James gct Short Creek MM, to m

COPE, continued
    Ann E. Lukens (H)
1836, 2, 24. Ann E. rocf Short Creek MM, dtd 1835,11,26 (H)
1837, 4, 19. James & w, Ann E., & ch, Nathan, Abigail, Charles, Elias & Emmaline, gct Deerfield MM (H)
1841, 8, 25. Caleb H. con mcd (H)
1843, 1, 25. Joshua con mcd (H)
1843, 4, 19. Hannah recrq (H)
1843, 11, 22. Abigail & Jane gct Deerfield MM (H)
1846, 10, 21. George Jr. gct Deerfield MM (H)
1851, 7, 23. Caleb dis mcd (H)
1851, 12, 24. Jane rocf Deerfield MM, dtd 1851,10,8 (H)
1854, 1, 25. Emily McCarty (form Cope) con mcd (H)

COPPOCK
1805, 7, 25. Isaac, s Samuel & Ellen, Belmont Co., O.; m in Concord MH, Mary LAMBERT, dt Abner & Winneford, Belmont Co., O.

1802, 5, 15. John & w, Catharine, rocf Nottingham MM, dtd 1801,3,28, end by Redstone MM, Pa., 1802,1,1
1805, 6, 18. Isaac rocf Rich Square MM, N.C., dtd 1804,3,17

COWGILL
1802, 11, 20. Isaac [Cogill] & s, Abraham, recrq
1804, 6, 19. Ralph & Isaac, ch Isaac, recrq
1805, 5, 21. Isaac dis mcd

COX
1806, 3, 18. John [Coxe] & w, Rachel, & ch, Thomas, Levi, Stephen, Anne, Rachel, John & Mary, rocf Wrightsborough MM, Ga., dtd 1805,4,6
1806, 7, 22. Joseph & s, Joel, rocf Contentnea MM, N. C., dtd 1806,2,8
1806, 7, 22. Elizabeth rocf Contentnea MM, N. C., dtd 1806,2,8

CROFT
1807, 6, 23. John, Ridgway, Jesse, Elizabeth, Samuel & Joseph, rocf Little Egg Harbour MM, dtd 1807,2,12

CROSSLEY
1807, 7, 1. Rachel m Housen HARRELL

1803, 11, 19. Tamor & Sarah [Crosley] recrq
1806, 5, 27. John & w, Tamor, & ch, Jonathan, Rachel, Samuel, John, Hannah, Esther, Elizabeth, Moses & Mary, rocf Short Creek MM, dtd 1806,4,19
1806, 5, 27. Sarah [Crosley] rocf Short Creek MM, dtd 1806,4,19

CROY
1807, 10, 28. Jacob, s Richard & Ann, Belmont Co., O.; m in Stillwater MH, Suzannah BAYLY, dt Wm. & Rebecca, Belmont Co., O.

1805, 9, 24. Richard & w & ch, Jacob, John, Margaret, Richard, Mathias, Rebecca & Ann, recrq

CURTIS
1823, 5, 21. Anna (form Fox) dis mcd

DANIELS
1860, 3, 21. Lydia Ann con mcd (H)
1863, 9, 23. Lydiann gct Plainfild MM (H)
1851, 8, 20. Phebe Ann [Daniel] (form Pickering) dis mcd (H)

DAVIS
1803, 7, 16. Harmon & w, Hannah, & ch, Rachel, Joseph & Isaac, rocf Mt. Pleasant MM, Va., dtd 1803,4,30
1805, 7, 23. Moses & w, Ann, & ch, Elizabeth, Charity, Asenath & Jemima, rocf Mt. Pleasant MM, Va., dtd 1805,4,27

DAWSON
1807, 9, 30. Jesse, s Joseph & Patience, Belmont Co., O.; m in Stillwater MH, Elizabeth DOUDNA, dt John & Sarah, Belmont Co., O.
1805, 7, 23. Jesse rocf Contentnea MM, N. C., dtd 1805,3,19

DESELMS
1806, 7, 22. Elizabeth [Diselm] rocf Hopewell MM, Va., dtd 1805,3,4
1807, 3, 24. Jesse [Dezelms] & ch, Hannah, Jacob, Ann, Benjamin, Eleanor, Jonathan, Elizabeth & David, recrq
1817, 6, 25. Jacob & w, Rhoda, & s, Joseph, rocf Plainfield MM, dtd 1817,5,22
1820, 1, 19. Jacob & w, Rhoda, & ch gct Flushing MM

DEVERS
1807, 4, 21. Elizabeth (form Jenkins) dis mcd

DEVULT
1870, 5, 24. Martha (form Wells) con mcd (H)

DEW
1802, 10, 21. Cherry m John HOWARD
1802, 12, 23. Susanna m Joshua JAMES

DEWEES
1806, 1, 1. Samuel, s Owen & Mary, Belmont Co., O.; m in Concord MH, Hannah BERRY, dt David & Hannah, Belmont Co., O.
1815, 12, 27. Mary m Daniel WILSON
1817, 5, 20. Esther m George PARVIANCE

1805, 6, 18. Owen & w, Mary, & ch, Joanna,

DEWEES, continued
Esther, Hannah, Thomas & Mary, rocf Callawissa MM, Pa., dtd 1805,5,25
1805, 6, 18. Margaret rocf Cattawissa MM,
Pa., dtd 1805,5,25
1809, 11, 23. Samuel & w, Hannah, & ch, Owen
& David, rocf Plainfield MM
1813, 2, 25. Samuel & w, Hannah, & ch, Owen,
David, Gulielma & Beulah Emily, rocf
Plainfield MM, dtd 1813,2,27
1816, 4, 24. Samuel & w, Hannah, & ch, Owen,
David, Gulielma, Beulah Emily & Elis, gct
Plainfield MM
1817, 1, 22. Thomas dis mcd
1818, 3, 25. Thomas rst
1818, 10, 21. Mary Jr. & s, Lewis, recrq
1821, 4, 25. Hannah Grimes (form Dewees) con
mcd
1826, 5, 24. James, minor, rocf Stillwater
MM, dtd 1826,3,25
1827, 10, 24. James gct Stillwater MM
1837, 6, 21. Owen, Margaret & Joanna
[Deweese] gct Deerfield MM (H)

DILLON
1808, 1, 19. William dis
1808, 5, 25. Cert rec for Rachel from Goose
Creek MM, Va., dtd 1807,7,27, end to
Plainfield MM

DILWORTH
1824, 11, 24. Rhodes & w, Rebecca, rocf Short
Creek MM, dtd 1824,7,20
1826, 8, 23. Rhodes & w, Rebecca, & ch, Sarah, Jane & Abraham, gct Short Creek MM

DODD
1804, 7, 24. Aaron & w, Rebecca, & ch, Joseph, Daniel, Wm., Nathan, Sarah, Elizabeth, Rebeckah, Ruth, Zilpha, Peninnah &
Piety, rocf Contentnea MM, N. C.
1804, 7, 24. Mary rocf Contentnea MM

DOUDNA
1807, 9, 30. Elizabeth m Jesse DAWSON
1807, 12, 30. Knois, s John & Sarah, Belmont
Co., O.; m in Stillwater MH, Hannah WEB-
STER, dt John & Hannah, Belmont Co., O.
1821, 8, 1. John, s John & Sarah, Belmont
Co., O.; m in Concord MH, Mary STEER, dt
James & Abigail

1804, 6, 19. John rocf Great Contentnea MM,
N. C., dtd 1804,3,10
1804, 6, 19. Knowas & two younger brothers,
Hosea & Joel, rocf Great Contentnea MM,
N. C., dtd 1804,3,10
1804, 7, 24. Sarah & dt, Peninah, Zilpah &
Asenath, rocf Contentnea MM, N. C.
1804, 7, 24. Miriam & dt, Charity, Anna &
Achsah, rocf Contentnea MM, N. C.
1804, 7, 24. Elizabeth & Ann rocf Contentnea
MM, N. C.

1821, 9, 19. Mary gct Somerset MM

DU BOIS
1815, 12, 27. Mary Ann m Israel UPDEGRAFF

1811, 5, 23. Mary Ann, niece of Anna Fox,
rocf Indian Springs MM, dtd 1811,2,15

DUNGAN
1830, 5, 19. Mary rocf Short Creek MM, dtd
1830,4,22 (H)
1834, 5, 21. Sarah S. (form Fox) con mcd (H)
1838, 6, 20. Mary gct Somerset MM (H)   [(H)
1851, 7, 23. Jemima N. (form Vickers) con mcd
1857, 4, 22. Jemima dis disunity (H)

EAVES
1816, 1, 24. Susanna (form Miles) dis mcd
1818, 11, 25. Susanna [Eves] rst at Stillwater
on consent of this MM

EDGERTON
1805, 5, 21. James & w, Sarah, & ch, Richard,
James, John, Jesse, William, Mary, Sarah,
rocf Contentney MM, N. C., dtd 1805,3,9
1806, 8, 19. Samuel & w, Elizabeth, & ch,
Wm., Sarah & Hannah, rocf Haddonfield MM,
N. J.
1808, 2, 23. Richard gct Short Creek MM, O.,
to m

ELLIS
1803, 10, 15. Jonathan & w, Lydia, & ch,
Elizabeth, Rachel & Joshua, rocf Southland MM, Va., dtd 1801,9,30, end from
Westland MM, 1803,9,24
1803, 12, 17. Jonathan Jr. & w, Martha, & ch,
Naomi, Elisha & Elizabeth, rocf Hopewell
MM, Va., dtd 1803,9,5
1805, 7, 23. Theodore & w, Elizabeth, & ch,
Amos & Mary, & gr ch, Elisha Ellis, rocf
Hopewell MM, dtd 1805,4,1
1805, 7, 23. Sarah rocf Hopewell MM, dtd
1805,4,1
1808, 3, 24. Cert rec for Mary, Thomas, David & Rees, ch Margaret Balding, rocf
Hopewell MM, Va., dtd 1808,2,1, end to
Plainfield MM

ELLISON
1810, 6, 21. Thomas rocf ND MM, dtd 1819,12,
26

ELLIOTT
1806, 5, 27. John [Eliot] & w, Rachel, rocf
Pipe Creek MM, Md., dtd 1806,4,19
1831, 12, 21. Isaac Pickering gct Plainfield
MM, to m Elizabeth Elliott (H)

ELY
1820, 11, 22. Elizabeth (form Kenard) dis mcd

EMBRY
1842, 3, 21. Mary Ann (form Pickering) con
     mcd (H)

ENGLAND
1833, 5, 1. Samuel, s Samuel & Tacy, Wash-
     ington Co., Pa.; m in Concord MH, Emma
     GIVEN, dt Moses & Ann, Belmont Co., O.

1833, 7, 24. Emma gct Westland MM (H)
1865, 1, 25. Samuel & w, Emma, rocf Salem MM,
     dtd 1864,10,20 (H)

ENGLE
1805, 10, 3. Ann m John HAINS
1807, 12, 31. Rachel m Nathaniel HAINES

1803, 6, 18. Mary, niece of James & Grace
     Belengee, rocf Evesham MM, N. J., dtd
     1803,4,8
1803, 6, 18. Abraham & w, Patience, & ch, Ra-
     chel & Samuel, & gr s, Abraham Engle, rocf
     Evesham MM, N. J., dtd 1803,4,8
1803, 6, 18. Job & w, Sarah, & dt, Rebeccah,
     rocf Evesham MM, N. J., dtd 1803,4,8
1803, 6, 18. Caleb & w, Mercy, & ch, James,
     Elizabeth, John & Mary, rocf Burlington
     MM, dtd 1803,4,4
1803, 6, 18. Anne & Jane rocf Evesham MM,
     N. J., dtd 1803,4,8
1804, 2, 18. Jacob & fam cert end back to
     Evesham MM
1804, 11, 20. Job & w, Sarah, & dt, Rebecca,
     rocf Evesham MM, dtd 1804,9,7
1805, 8, 20. Cert rec for Mary & ch from Eve-
     sham MM, N. J., dtd 1805,4,5, end to Short
     Creek MM, O.
1808, 2, 23. Jane dis

EVANS
1802, 5, 15. Cadwalader & w, Sarah, & ch,
     Evan, James, John, Asher, Sarah, Benoni
     & Pamelia, rocf Westland MM, Pa., dtd
     1802,3,27
1802, 5, 15. Mary rocf Westland MM, dtd 1802,
     3,27
1811, 9, 26. Joanna rocf Redstone MM, dtd
     1811,8,2
1815, 1, 26. Joanna gct Short Creek MM
1829, 7, 22. Evan & w, Mary, & ch, James
     Cadwalader, Amos Hutton, Sarah, Henrietta,
     Asher Parker & Wm. Jones, rocf Smithfield
     MM, dtd 1829,6,23 (H)
1829, 7, 22. Rebecca rocf Smithfield MM dtd
     1829,6,23 (H)
1831, 11, 23. Evan & w, Mary, & ch, James C.,
     Amos H., Sarah Henrietta, Asher P. & Wm.
     J., gct Deerfield MM (H)
1831, 11, 23. Rebecca gct Deerfield MM (H)
1841, 1, 20. Jonathan recrq (H)

EWERS
1805, 11, 19. Wm. & w, Amy, & ch, Rebecca,

Thomas & Gulielma, rocf Goose Creek MM,
     Va., dtd 1805,9,30

FALKNER
1806, 4, 22. Hannah rocf Crooked Run MM, Va.,
     dtd 1805,8,5

FARIS
1811, 7, 31. Susanna m Abner LAMBERT

1805, 4, 23. John & w, Susannah, rocf Darby
     MM, dtd 1805,3,29

FARQUHAR
1803, 2, 19. Wm. & w, Elizabeth, rocf Red-
     stone MM, dtd 1802,7,2
1806, 6, 24. Wm. rocf Pipe Creek MM, dtd
     1806,5,7
1809, 9, 21. William gct Short Creek MM, to
     m
1810, 2, 22. Sarah rocf Short Creek MM, dtd
     1810,1,23
1811, 12, 26. Sarah gct Concord MM, Pa.

FARRINGTON
1802, 5, 15. Abraham & w, Deborah, & s, Moses,
     rocf Redstone MM, dtd 1801,10,30, end by
     Westland MM, dtd 1802,2,27

FAWCETT
1804, 9, 26. Samuel, s Richard & Mary (Pick-
     ering), Frederick Co., Va.; m in home of
     Jacob Pickering, Belmont Co., O., Rachel
     SMITH, dt Thomas & Martha, Belmont Co., O.
1807, 4, 29. Richard, s Richard & Mary (Pick-
     ering), Belmont Co., O.; m in Flushing MH,
     Sarah GILBERT, dt Joel & Elizabeth, Bel-
     mont Co., O.

1804, 4, 24. Samuel [Fawcitt] roc
1804, 11, 20. Mary & ch, Jonathan, Richard &
     Jacob, rocf Crooked Run MM, dtd 1804,9,29
1804, 11, 20. Hannah rocf Crooked Run MM, dtd
     1804,9,29
1805, 1, 22. Joseph rocf Crooked Run MM, dtd
     1804,9,29
1806, 11, 18. Samuel & w, Rachel, & dt, Eliza-
     beth, gct Short Creek MM, O.
1807, 3, 24. Phebe rocf Crooked Run MM, dtd
     1806,10,4
1808, 3, 24. Hannah dis
1823, 11, 19. Nathan Newport gct Salem MM, to
     m Elizabeth Fawcet
1833, 1, 21. Elisha & w, Rebecca, & ch, Mah-
     lon Taylor, Thos. Wm., Mary Taylor, Frank-
     lin, Joseph Janney & Lydia Ann, rocf Hope-
     well MM, Va., dtd 1832,12,6 (H)

FELL
1803, 8, 20. Aaron rocf Redstone MM, dtd
     1803,8,3
1803, 9, 17. Rachel & ch, Rachel & Joseph,
     rocf Redstone MM, dtd 1803,7,1

FELL, continued
1804, 2, 18. Aaron dis mcd

FERGUSON
1813, 6, 24. Cert rec for Nimrod from South
        River MM, Va., dtd 1805,4,13 & end to
        Miami 1807,10,20 by this mtg has not been
        rec at Miami MM, O.

FISHER
1803, 5, 21. Samuel & w, Ruth, & ch, Rachel,
        Mary, Frances, Joel & Casandra, rocf Red-
        stone MM, dtd 1802,10,1
1805, 7, 23. John & w, Sarah, & ch, Mary,
        Richard, Rachel, Baruch & Joseph, rocf
        Hopewell MM, dtd 1805,1,4

FOULKE
1806, 10, 29. Cadwallader, s Edward & Margaret,
        Ohio Co., Va.; m in Concord MH, Anne CHER-
        INGTON, dt Thomas & Rachel, Belmont Co., O.
1838, 2, 28. Edward, s Evan & Sarah, Wayne
        Co., Ind.; m in Concord MH, Phebe Ann
        VICKERS, dt Thomas & Ann, Belmont Co., O.

1806, 8, 19. Cadwallader rocf ND MM, dtd
        1806,7,22
1807, 8, 18. Sarah rocf Springfield MM, N. J.,
        dtd 1807,5,6
1808, 7, 21. Anna & Sarah gct Short Creek
        MM, O.

1851, 12, 24. Phebe Ann & ch, William H.,
        Amanda Jane, Sarah Ann, Hannah Mary &
        Francis Elwood, gct Short Creek MM (H)

FOX
————, ——, ——. Josiah & Anna
        Ch: Charles   b 1805, 10. 17
            Sarah
            Scantle-
            berry   " 1808, 6, 12
            Francis
            Drake   " 1811, 6, 13
1826, 9, 27. Rebecca Stevens m Elijah PICKER-
        ING
1851, 10, 30. Francis D., s Josiah & Anna,
        Belmont Co., O., b 1811,6,13; m in home of
        Francis D. FOX, Juliana D. UPDEGRAFF, dt
        Israel & Mary Ann, Wheeling

1811, 5, 23. Anna & ch, Elizabeth Miller,
        Anna Applebee, Rebecca Stephen, Charles
        James & Sarah Scantlebury Fox, & minor
        niece, Mary Ann DuBois, rocf Indian Spring
        MM, dtd 1811,2,15
1813, 10, 21. Elizabeth Chapline (form Fox)
        dis mcd
1818, 5, 20. Francis, s Josiah & Anna, recrq
1823, 5, 21. Anna Curtis (form Fox) dis mcd
1834, 5, 21. Sarah S. Dungan (form Fox) con
        mcd (H)
1837, 8, 23. Charles I. con mcd (H)

1850, 10, 23. Francis D. con mcd (H)

FRAZIER
1814, 12, 22. Daniel dis
1815, 4, 20. Nelly & ch, "elly, Daniel & Ann,
        gct Stillwater MM
1815, 4, 20. William gct Stillwater MM

FREEBORN
1814, 11, 24. Samuel rocf Plymouth MM, Md.,
        dtd 1814,9,17
1818, 6, 24. Samuel dis mcd

FRENCH
1807, 6, 23. Emma rocf Pipe Creek MM, dtd
        1806,11,15
1807, 9, 22. Israel rocf Pipe Creek MM, dtd
        1807,6,20
1809, 5, 22. Emma gct Stillwater MM
1814, 1, 20. Joseph Steer gct Stillwater MM,
        O., to m Emma French
1831, 2, 23. Israel & w, Deborah, & dt, Ju-
        lian, rocf Short Creek MM, dtd 1830,12,23
1832, 12, 19. Israel & w, Deborah, gct White
        Water MM, Ind.

FULERTON
1819, 5, 19. Ann (form Lewis) dis mcd

GALBREATH
1803, 5, 21. James & w, Susannah, & ch, Ash-
        er, David & Anne, rocf Deep River MM,
        N. C., dtd 1803,4,4
1839, 10, 23. Thomas Elwood Vickers gct New-
        garden MM, to m Elizabeth [Galbraith]

GAMBLE
1807, 12, 27. Joseph dis disunity
1820, 6, 21. Elizabeth gct Stillwater MM

GARRETSON
1802, 10, 27. Casparus, s Wm. & Mary, Belmont
        Co., O.; m in Plymouth MH, Sarah KIRK,
        dt Wm. & Rachel, Jefferson Co., O.
1803, 5, 25. Mary m Stafford MELTON
1803, 12, 21. Sarah m Caleb KIRK
1804, 4, 26. Joseph, s Wm. & Mary, Belmont
        Co., O.; m in Concord MH, Elizabeth
        WILLIAMS, dt Robert & Anne, Belmont Co., O.

1806, 1, 21. Mary & ch gct Short Creek MM, O.
1809, 10, 26. John & w, Henrietta, & ch, Wm.,
        Joel, Anna, Mary & Hanna, rocf Plymouth
        MM, dtd 1809,10,21
1811, 5, 23. Joseph & w, Elizabeth, & ch,
        Asenath, Asa & Joseph, gct Stillwater MM
1814, 3, 24. Patience rocf Plymouth MM, O.,
        dtd 1814,3,19
1817, 1, 22. Mary & Armelle rocf Plymouth
        MM, dtd 1816,12,23
1823, 11, 19. Wm. gct Warrington MM
1825, 6, 22. Joel gct Plainfield MM

GAUZE
1802, 9, 18. Sarah rocf Redstone MM, dtd
    1802,4,2
1802, 12, 18. Cert for Sarah end to Redstone
    MM

GIBBONS
1805, 10, 22. Joseph & w, Sarah, & ch, Wm.,
    Joseph, Martha, Hannah & Mercy, rocf Uwch-
    lan MM, dtd 1805,8,8
1810, 6, 21. Joseph & w, Sarah, & ch, William,
    Joseph, Martha, Hannah & Mary, gct SD MM
1816, 3, 20. Elizabeth recrq
1823, 8, 20. Jane & Susannah recrq
1823, 12, 24. Elizabeth & Susan gct Somerset
    MM
1824, 10, 20. Jane gct Somerset MM

GILBERT
1806, 12, 31. Abel, s Joel & Elizabeth, Bel-
    mont Co., O.; m in Stillwater MH, Rebecca
    WILLIAMS, dt Daniel & Mary, Belmont Co., O.
1807; 4, 29. Sarah m Richard FAWCETT

1805, 7, 23. Joel & w, Elizabeth, & ch, Abel
    & Sarah, rocf Wrightsborough MM, Ga., dtd
    1805,4,6
1805, 9, 24. John & w, Elizabeth, rocf
    Wrightsborough MM, Ga., dtd 1805,3,23

GILL
1807, 4, 21. Elizabeth dis mcd

GIVEN
----, --, --. Moses & Ann
    Ch: Jane   b 1801, 10, 27
        Joel   " 1803, 6, 10
        Israel   " 1805, 1, 27
        James   " 1808, 2, 16
        Rachel   " 1809, 11, 26
        Amon   " 1812, 1, 30
        Isaac   " 1813, 9, 11
1833, 5, 1. Emma m Samuel ENGLAND

1802, 11, 20. Moses & w, Ann, & ch, Reuben &
    Emma, rocf Pipe Creek MM, Md., dtd 1802,
    8,14
1831, 1, 18. Joel dis mcd (H)
1833, 2, 20. Israel con mcd (H)
1833, 2, 20. Elizabeth (form Leek) con mcd(H)
1861, 9, 25. Ann H. con mcd (H)
1866, 11, 21. Ann H. gct Short Creek MM (H)

GRAHAM
1807, 2, 24. Michael & w, Patience, & ch,
    Elizabeth, Deborah & James, rocf Balti-
    more MM, dtd 1807,1,8
1824, 10, 20. Deborah Tanner (form Graham) dis
    mcd

GRAY
1803, 5, 21. Elijah & w, Mary, & ch, Esther,
    Samuel & David, rocf Redstone MM, dtd 1803,

4,29

GREGG
1804, 2, 23. Ruth m Jonas PICKERING

1802, 6, 19. Samuel & w, Ann, & ch, Mary,
    Abel, Phebe, Ellis, Gulielma & Phinehas,
    rocf Redstone MM, Pa., dtd 1802,4,2
1803, 2, 19. Abner & w, Sarah, & ch, Nathan-
    iel, Ruth, Wm., Stephen, Albina, Mahlon,
    John, Sarah, Rhoda, Mercy & Lydia, rocf
    South River MM, Va., dtd 1802,9,11
1803, 12, 17. Jacob & w, Mary, & ch, Rebecca,
    Esther, James, Anna & Jesse, rocf Goose
    Creek MM, dtd 1803,8,29
1806, 11, 18. Caleb rocf Goose Creek MM, dtd
    1806,5,26
1807, 1, 20. Samuel & w, Guli Elma, & ch,
    Maria, Aquila, Edith & Mary, recrq
1807, 6, 23. Hannah, w Caleb, & ch, Stephen,
    Laban, Abner, Alphard, Elijah Burr &
    Caleb, recrq
1821, 5; 23. Thomas Hirst rqct Plainfield MM,
    to m Anna Gregg
1824, 12, 22. Jesse Medcelf rqct Plainfield MM
    to m Asenath Gregg

GRIFFITH
1804, 7, 24. Cert rec for Ann from Baltimore
    MM, dtd 1804,4,20, end to Short Creek MM
1819, 4, 21. Keturah rocf Short Creek MM, dtd
    1819,4,20
1821, 2, 21. Keturah gct Salem MM
1821, 7, 25. Eli & w, Rachel, & s rocf Plain-
    field MM
1822, 4, 24. Cert rec for Abraham & w, Mary,
    from Plainfield MM, dtd 1821,2,21, end to
    Flushing MM
1823, 6, 25. Eli & w, Rachel, & s, Wm., gct
    Short Creek MM

GRIMES
1821, 4, 25. Hannah (form Dewees) con mcd

HAINS
1805, 10, 3. John, s John & Rachel, Belmont
    Co., O.; m in Plainfield MH, Ann ENGLE,
    dt Abraham & Patience, Belmont Co., O.
1807, 12, 31. Nathaniel, s John & Rachel,
    Belmont Co., O.; m in Plainfield MH, Ra-
    chel ENGLE, dt Abraham & Patience, Bel-
    mont Co., O.

1805, 9, 24. John rocf Middleton MM, O., dtd
    1805,9,14
1807, 7, 21. Nathaniel rocf Mt. Holly MM, dtd
    1806,1,9

HALL
1807, 8, 26. John, s Isaac & Ann, Belmont
    Co., O.; m in Stillwater MH, Phebe WEB-
    STER, dt John & Hannah, Belmont Co., O.
1807, 12, 24. Isaac, s Moses & Elizabeth, Bel-

HALL, Isaac, continued
    mont Co., O.; m in Plainfield MH, Dinah
    PLUMMER, dt Thomas & Phebe, Belmont Co.,O.

1802, 6, 19. Jesse & w, Penninah, & s, Jo-
    seph, rocf Contentney MM, N. C., dtd 1802,
    3,13, end by Westland MM, 1802,5,22
1802, 10, 16. Joseph & w, Christian, & ch,
    Thos., Nathan, Christian & Anne, rocf Great
    Contentnea MM, N. C., dtd 1802,8,14
1802, 11, 20. John, Mary & Sarah rocf Great
    Contentney MM, N. C., dtd 1802,8,14
1804, 6, 19. Isaac & s, Henry, rocf Great
    Contentnea MM, N. C., dtd 1804,3,10
1804, 7, 24. Mary & dt, Zilpah, rocf Content-
    nea MM, N. C.
1805, 7, 23. Isaac & w, Ann, & s, Moses, rocf
    Contentnea MM, N. C., dtd 1805,3,19
1805, 7, 23. Ann rocf Contentnea MM, N. C.,
    dtd 1805,3,19
1805, 8, 20. John rocf Contentnea MM, N. C.,
    dtd 1805,3,9
1806, 5, 27. Levina rocf Short Creek MM, dtd
    1806,4,19
1807, 9, 22. Lavina gct Short Creek MM, O.

HAMMIT
1802, 5, 15. Sarah rocf Salem MM, N. J., dtd
    1801,2,23, end by Redstone MM, Pa., 1802,
    3,5

HAMMOND
1802, 11, 20. George & w, Deborah, & ch, Marga-
    ret, Sarah, James, William, Deborah, Mary,
    Ruth & Benjamin, rocf Monallen MM, dtd
    1802,4,23, end from Redstone MM, 1802,7,30

HANSON
1807, 12, 30. Menoah, s Elijah & Phebe; m in
    Stillwater MH, Rachel STUBS, dt Joseph &
    Zilpha, Belmont Co., O.

HARMOR
1827, 2, 28. Naylor [Harmer], s Amos & Eliza-
    beth, Belmont Co., O.; m in Concord MH,
    Isabella HUNT, dt Geo. & Ann, Belmont Co.,
    O.
1822, 8, 21. George rocf Indian Spring MM,
    Md., dtd 1822,2,15, end by Bradford MM,
    Pa., 1822,5,8, and by Short Creek MM,
    1822,7,23
1822, 8, 21. Elizabeth & ch, Nailor, William,
    Mary Ann, Elwood & Amos Roberts, rocf
    Indian Spring MM, Md., dtd 1822,2,15, end
    by Bradford MM, Pa. 1822,5,8 and by Short
    Creek MM 1822,7,23
1824, 1, 21. Amos rocf Sadsbury MM, Pa., dtd
    1823,8,5
1824, 2, 25. Amos & w, Elizabeth, & ch,
    Nailor, William, Mary Ann, Elwood & Amos
    Roberts, gct Marlborough MM
1824, 2, 25. Geoge gct Marlsborough MM
1825, 6, 22. Amos [Harmer] & w, Elizabeth, &

& ch, Naylor, William, Mary Ann, Elwood &
    Amos R., rocf Marlborough MM, dtd 1825,5,
    18
1825, 6, 22. George [Harmer] rocf Marlborough
    MM, dtd 1825,5,18

HARRELL
1807, 7, 1. Housen, s Samuel & Martha, Bel-
    mont Co., O.; m in Flushing MH, Rachel
    CROSSLEY, dt John & Tamer, Belmont Co., O.

HARRIS
1802, 9, 18. Enoch & w, Lany, & s, David, rocf
    Core Sound MM, N. C., dtd 1802,4,28
1804, 6, 19. Cert rec for Ezekiel & fam from
    Core Sound MM, N. C., dtd 1804,4,11, end
    to Short Creek MM, O.
1804, 6, 19. Cert rec for Uriah from Core
    Sound MM, N. C., dtd 1804,4,11, end to
    Short Creek MM, O.
1804, 6, 19. Cert rec for Thomas from Core
    Sound MM, N. C., dtd 1804,3,31, end to
    Middleton MM by rq
1805, 9, 24. Cert rec for Isaiah from Core
    Sound MM, N. C., dtd 1804,7,27, end to
    Salem MM by rq
1842, 3, 21. Mary Ann (form Ridgeway) con mcd
    (H)

HARTLEY
1810, 2, 22. Cert rec for Elizabeth & s,
    Elias, from Sadsbury MM, dtd 1808,10,4,
    end to Short Creek MM

HASTINGS
1806, 11, 18. Horton Howard gct Wilmington MM,
    Del., to m Hannah Hastings

HATCHER
1804, 4, 24. John dis mcd
1806, 12, 23. Mahlon dis
HERALD
1807, 2, 24. Housin recrq

HERBERT
1802, 10, 16. Ann rocf Westland MM, dtd 1802,
    8,28
1803, 1, 15. William recrq

HESTON
1803, 1, 15. John & w, Elizabeth, & ch, Mar-
    garet, Anne, Tacy, Rebecca, John & Zebulon
    rocf Westland MM, dtd 1802,10,23

HIBBARD
1845, 10, 22. Thomas & w, Margaret, rocf Con-
    cord MM, Pa., dtd 1845,9,25 (H)
1845, 10, 22. Hannah rocf Concord MM, Pa., dtd
    1845,9,25 (H)
1861, 2, 20. Hannah gct Chester MM, Pa. (H)

HICKS
1839, 6, 26. Joseph, s Clement & Mary, Bel-

HICKS, continued
  mont Co., O.; m in Concord MH, Lucinda
  THOMAS, dt Samuel & Sarah SACKET

1808, 7, 21. Cert rec for Mary & ch, Laban,
  James, Asa, Rachel, Joseph & Robert, from
  Black Water MM, Va., dtd 1807,5,23, end
  to Stillwater MM   [1840,1,18 (H)
1840, 2, 19. Joseph rocf Stillwater MM, dtd
HILL
1805, 6, 18. Lydia (form **Perry**) dis mcd

HINES
1804, 12, 18. Patience, w Nathan, & ch, Susanna, Joel, Rachel & Lydia, rocf New Garden MM, N. C., dtd 1803,8,27
1804, 12, 18. Sarah & Isaac rocf New Garden
  MM, N. C., dtd 1803,8,27

HINKSON
1821, 3, 21. Katharine rocf Chester MM, Pa.,
  dtd 1820,11,27

HINSON
1805, 7, 23. Elijah & Borden rocf Contentney
  MM, N. C., dtd 1805,3,19
1805, 7, 23. Manoah rocf Contentnea MM, N.C.,
  dtd 1805,3,19
1805, 9, 24. Susanna & dt, Clerky & Susanna,
  rocf Contentney MM, N. C., dtd 1805,3,9

HIRST
1817, 12, 24. David & w, Ann, & ch, Thomas,
  John, Israel, Asenath, Rachel, Smith &
  Mary, rocf Short Creek MM, O., dtd 1817,
  7,22
1821, 5, 23. Thomas rqct Plainfield MM, to m
  Anna Gregg
1821, 10, 21. Anna rocf Plainfield MM, dtd
  1821,8,23
1822, 2, 20. Thomas gc
1823, 8, 20. Israel gct Flushing MM, to m
  Catharine Branson
1824, 1, 21. Catharine rocf Flushing MM, dtd
  1823,12,26
1824, 12, 22. John gct Flushing MM, to m
  Elizabeth Branson
1825, 5, 25. Elizabeth rocf Flushing MM, dtd
  1825,3,25
1825, 11, 23. Thomas & w, Ann, & ch, Ruthanna
  & Rebecca, gct Plainfield MM
1826, 4, 19. David & w, Ann, & ch, Smith,
  Mary & Hannah, gct Flushing MM
1826, 4, 19. John & w, Elizabeth, & ch, Alpheus, gct Flushing MM
1826, 4, 19. Asenath & Rachel gct Flushing MM
1826, 8, 23. Asa Raley gct Flushing MM, to m
  Asenath Hirst
1827, 4, 25. Israel & w, Catharine, & dt,
  Eliza Jane, gct Flushing MM

HOBSON
1802, 8, 21. Joseph & w, Anne, & ch, Francis,

Mary, Anne, Joseph, Jane, William, Esther Phebe & James, rocf Redstone MM, dtd
  1802,4,30

HODGIN
1806, 10, 1. Mary [Hodgins] m Samuel BERRY

1803, 6, 18. Wm. & w, Agnes, & ch, Mary,
  John, Sarah, Wm., Martha, Laban & Ann,
  rocf Wrightsborough MM, Ga., dtd 1803,3,23
1803, 6, 18. Stephen & w, Elizabeth, & ch,
  Asenath, Eli, Amy & Wm., rocf Wrightsborough MM, Ga., dtd 1803,3,23

HODGSON
1804, 12, 18. Mary rocf New Garden MM, N. C.,
  dtd 1803,8,27
1804, 12, 18. Cert rec for Amos from New Garden MM, N. C., dtd 1804,8,27, end to
  Miami MM, O. by rq

HOGUE
1802, 6, 19. Isaac & w, Elizabeth, & ch,
  James, Absalom, Solomon, Craven, Pleasant,
  Joshua & Asa, rocf Goose Creek MM, Va.,
  dtd 1802,3,29
1804, 5, 22. David & w, Ruth, & ch, Asael,
  Joshua, Ann, Lydia, Rebecca, Sarah, Betsy & Ruth, rocf Goose Creek MM, dtd 1803,
  10,24

HOLLINGSWORTH
1805, 5, 21. Levi & w, Mary, & ch, Thomas,
  David, Sarah, Hannah, Isaac & Susanna,
  rocf Goose Creek MM, dtd 1805,2,25
1806, 6, 24. Christopher & w, Elizabeth, & s,
  John Ferris, rocf Wilmington MM, Del., dtd
  1806,4,10
1806, 6, 24. Samuel rocf Kennet MM, dtd 1806,
  4,8
1808, 5, 25. Samuel dis performing military
  service
1815, 7, 20. Christopher & w, Elizabeth, &
  ch, John Ferris, Samuel, Sarah Ann &
  Charles, gct Plainfield MM

HOLLOWAY
1803, 7, 16. Joseph & w, Eleanor, rocf Southland MM, dtd 1802,12,29
1804, 9, 18. Asa & w, Margaret, & ch, Robert
  & Asa, rocf Southland MM, dtd 1804,5,30
1805, 9, 24. Samuel rocf Crooked Run MM, dtd
  1805,6,1
1807, 3, 24. James recrq
1807, 8, 18. Jacob gct Short Creek MM, O.

HONEYCUTT
1807, 4, 21. Thomas & w, Miriam, & ch, Sarah,
  Deborah, & Thomas, rocf Blackwater MM,
  Va., dtd 1806,7,24

HOOPS
1822, 7, 24. Abigail (form Cope) dis mcd

HORTON

1867, 2, 21. Malin, s Joseph & Agness, Belmont Co., O.; m in house of Wm. Wells, Catherine T. WELLS, dt Wm. & Mary, Belmont Co., O.

1831, 8, 24. Cert rec for Joseph H. & w, Agness, & ch, Elizabeth, Thomas & Joseph, from Cherry St. MM, Phila., Pa., dtd 1830, 6,16, end to Plainfield MM (H)
1845, 8, 20. Joseph & w, Agnes, & ch, Thomas, Joseph & Malin, rocf Plainfield MM, dtd 1843,8,17 (H)
1845, 9, 24. Elizabeth rocf Plainfield MM, dtd 1843,8,17 (H)
1851, 6, 25. Thomas con mcd (H)
1853, 12, 21. Joseph con mcd (H)
1854, 6, 21. Rebecca & ch, Jonathan Street & Joseph Malin, recrq (H)
1868, 6, 24. Thomas con mcd (H)

HOUGH

1802, 11, 20. Benjamin & w, Catharine, & ch, Elizabeth, Rachel & Amos, rocf Westland MM, dtd 1802,3,27

HOWARD

1802, 10, 21. John, s Bartholemew & Ruth, Belmont Co., O.; m in Short Creek MH, Cherry DEW, dt Joseph & Viley, Jefferson Co., O.
           John m 2nd 1813,1,27 in Concord MH, Hannah RALEY, dt James & Rachel, Belmont Co., O.

1802, 8, 21. John rocf New York MM, held at Flushing, dtd 1802,6,3
1802, 10, 16. Orpah recrq
1806, 11, 18. Horton gct Wilmington MM, Del., to m Hannah Hastings
1807, 2, 24. Hannah, w Horton, rocf Wilmington MM, Del., dtd 1807,2,5
1812, 8, 20. Henry dis mcd
1815, 4, 20. Horton & w, Hannah, & ch, Joseph, Rachel, Horton, Sarah, Mary, Ann, Hannah & John, gct Plainfield MM

HOWELL

1807, 4, 30. Deborah m Titus SHOTWELL

1806, 7, 22. Deborah rocf Goose Creek MM, dtd 1805,12,30

HOYLE

1819, 5, 26. Joseph, s John & Sarah, Jefferson Co., O.; m in Concord MH, Ruth NEWPORT, dt Aaron & Mary, Belmont Co., O.
1821, 6, 6. William [Hoyl], s John & Sarah, Jefferson Co., O.; m in Concord MH, Edith NEWPORT, dt Aaron & Mary, Belmont Co., O.

1821, 9, 19. Edith gct Smithfield MM

HUNT

1827, 2, 28. Isabella m Naylor HARMER

1817, 12, 24. Cert rec for Joshua & fam from Short Creek MM, O., end to Plainfield MM
1826, 12, 20. Isabella recrq

HUNTER

1803, 12, 17. Hugh & w, Elizabeth, rocf Goose Creek MM, dtd 1800,10,27, end by Westland MM, 1803,7,23

HURFORD

1803, 11, 19. Sarah.& Rachel recrq
1825, 12, 21. Ruth (form Steele) dis mcd

HUTTON

1804, 1, 21. Joshua & w, Sarah, rocf Westland MM, dtd 1803,10,23
1804, 4, 24. Cert rec for Joseph & w, Sarah, from Westland MM, dtd 1803,10,2, end to Short Creek MM, O.

IMLAY

1812, 3, 26. Richard rocf West Hartford MM, Conn., dtd 1811,1,8
1812, 3, 26. Maria, w Richard, & a minister, rocf Chesterfield MM, N. J., dtd 1811,12,3

JAMES

1802, 12, 23. Joshua, s Samuel & Hannah, Jefferson Co., O.; m in Short Creek MH, Susannah DEW, dt Joseph & Viley, Jefferson Co., O.
1807, 4, 1. Evan, s Samuel & Hannah, Jefferson Co., O.; m in Flushing MH, Rebecca PICKERING, dt Samuel & Phebe, Belmont Co., O.
----, --, --. Isaac & Deborah
      Ch: Josiah   b 1812, 7, 13
          Hervey   " 1816, 4, 3
          Edwin   " 1818, 1, 30
          Chalkley   " 1820, 4, 20
          Rachel   " 1821, 5, 30
          William   " 1824, 5, 24
          Martha   " 1826, 7, 6
          Isaac   " 1828, 11, 20
          Ruth   " 1831, 6, 21
          James   " 1831, 6, 21
          Lydia Ann " 1833, 8, 12
1858, 7, 22. Isaac, s Ezekiel & Keziah, Belmont Co., O.; m in home of Isaac James, Sarah PICKERING, dt Edmond & Mary, Belmont Co., O.

1815, 6, 22. Isaac & w, Deborah, rocf Young Street MM, Upper Canada, dtd 1815,4,13, end by Short Creek MM
1851, 7, 23. Rachel Vickers (form James) rpd mcd (H)
1855, 6, 20. Martha Ward (form James) dis mcd (H)
1865, 8, 23. Lydia Jones (form James) recrq (H)

JELKS
1811, 11, 27. Richard, Jefferson Co., O.; m
    in Concord MH, Lydia STANTON

1812, 1, 23. Lydia gct Plymouth MM

JENKINS
1803, 2, 19. Misael & w, Rachel, & ch, Anne,
    Jacob, Lydia, Betty, Jane, Caty, Pugh &
    John, rocf Hopewell MM, dtd 1802,9,6
1804, 2, 18. Elizabeth & ch, Ruth, Elizabeth,
    James & Evan, rocf Hopewell MM, Va., dtd
    1803,7,11
1805, 4, 23. Mishal Jr. rocf Hopewell MM, dtd
    1804,4,2
1805, 12, 24. Mishael Sr. gct Short Creek MM,
    O., to m
1806, 5, 27. Sarah rocf Short Creek MM, dtd
    1806,4,19
1806, 5, 27. Mishael Jr. dis
1805, 6, 18. Ann Perkins (form Jenkins) dis
    mcd
1807, 4, 21. Elizabeth Devers (form Jenkins)
    dis mcd

JOB
1844, 5, 25. Rachel Ann, dt Samuel & Elizanna,
    b

1841, 2, 24. Samuel, Allen & Daniel rocf
    Short Creek MM, dtd 1840,8,20
1843, 3, 22. Samuel con mcd
1843, 3, 22. Eliza Ann W. con mcd
1843, 6, 21. Allen con mcd
1843, 6, 21. Asenath (form Berry) con mcd
1845, 5, 21. Rebecca & dt, Ann Hannah, rocf
    Short Creek MM, dtd 1845,3,20
1849, 8, 22. Samuel F. & w, Elizanna, & ch,
    Rachel & Hannah Elizabeth, gct Plainfield
    MM
1866, 11, 21. Rebecca gct Short Creek MM
1868, 5, 20. Mary Ann con mcd
1868, 9, 23. Mary Ann gct Plainfield MM

JOHN
1806, 8, 19. Cert rec for Hannah from London
    Grove MM, dtd 1806,5,7, end to Short Creek
    MM, O.
1822, 8, 21. Lydia rocf Short Creek MM

JOHNSON
1807, 1, 20. Unity, Jerusha, Richard, Obediah
    & Gideon, ch Wm. & Sarah Bloxson-Johnson,
    gr ch Richard & Ann Bloxam, rocf South
    River MM, Va., dtd 1806,10,11, end by Mi-
    ami MM, O., 1806,11,13
1808, 6, 23. Jerusha, Unity, Richard, Oba-
    diah & Gideon, gct Fairfield MM, O.

JOLLY
1808, 2, 23. Hannah (form Cook) dis mcd
1810, 11, 22. Hannah rst by Plymouth MM by
    consent of this mtg

JONES
1803, 5, 21. Joseph & w, Mary, & dt, Rachel,
    rocf Wrightsborough MM, Ga., dtd 1803,3,23
1865, 8, 23. Lydia (form James) relrq (H)

JUDKINS
1824, 8, 25. Susanna & ch, Jonathan, Martha,
    Mary & Sarah, rocf Flushing MM, dtd 1824,
    5,--

KELLUM
1803, 5, 21. Nathaniel & w, Elizabeth, & ch,
    John, Elizabeth, Sarah, Nathaniel, Joseph,
    Elijah & Susannah, rocf Wrightsborough MM,
    Ga., dtd 1803,3,23

KENNARD
1817, 3, 19. Levi [Kenard] & w, Ann, & s,
    Levi, rocf Short Creek MM, dtd 1817,1,21
1817, 9, 24. Elizabeth & Mary [Kenard] rocf
    Short Creek MM, dtd 1817,6,24
1820, 11, 22. Elizabeth Ely (form Kenard) dis
    mcd
1823, 5, 21. Levi [Kenard] Jr. con mcd
1832, 9, 19. Jemima & ch, Preston, Delila
    Ann, Elizajane & Hannah Amanda, recrq (H)
1850, 6, 19. Levi dis mcd (H)
1851, 9, 24. Delilah Woodmansee (form Ken-
    nard) dis mcd (H)
1851, 12, 24. Preston dis disunity (H)
1856, 8, 20. Ellen Jane & Amanda dis jas (H)
1865, 11, 22. John & dt, Mary Vilenda, recrq
    (H)

KENNY
1805, 6, 18. Richard & w, Mary, & dt, Jane,
    rocf Uwchlan MM, dtd 1805,4,4

KING
1813, 12, 30. Elizabeth m Josiah UPDEGRAFF

1807, 1, 20. Michael & w, Hannah, & ch, Sam-
    uel, Joseph, Rebeckah, Isaac, Catharine,
    Isabella, Jacob & Mary, rocf Nottingham
    MM, Md., dtd 1806,9,5
1813, 2, 25. John & w, Mary, & ch, Hannah,
    Caroline, Mary, John, Samuel & Elizabeth,
    rocf New York MM, N. Y., dtd 1812,1,8
1813, 4, 22. Jane rocf New York MM, dtd 1812,
    2,12
1815, 5, 25. John & w, Mary, & ch, Hannah,
    Caroline, Mary, John Brown, Samuel, Eliza-
    beth & Catharine Murray, gct Plainfield MM
1815, 1, 22. Jane rocf Plainfield MM
1817, 8, 20. John & w, Mary, & ch, Hannah,
    Caroline, Mary, John Brown, Samuel, Eliza-
    beth, Catharine Murray & Ann, roc dtd
    1817,7,24
1819, 6, 23. John & w, Mary, & ch, Hannah,
    Caroline, Mary, Samuel, Elizabeth, Katha-
    rine & Ann, gct New York MM

KINSEY

1803, 9, 17. Benjamin & Stephen rocf Redstone MM, dtd 1803,3,5
1804, 11, 20. Cert rec for Edmund from London
Grove MM, dtd 1804,5,9, end to Short Creek
MM
1804, 11, 20. Cert rec for James from Bradford
MM, dtd 1804,9,8, end to Short Creek MM
1806, 7, 22. Richard & dt, Jane, gct Uwchlan
MM, Pa.
1812, 6, 25. Edmund rocf Short Creek MM, dtd
1811,12,19
1815, 4, 20. Edmund gct Short Creek MM
1819, 1, 19. John & w, Mary, & ch, Miriam,
Susanna, Hirah & Lydia Ann, recrq

KIRK

1802, 10, 27. Sarah m Casparus GARRETSON
1803, 12, 21. Caleb, s Wm. & Rachel, Jefferson
Co., O.; m in Concord MH, Sarah GARRETSON,
dt Wm. & Mary, Belmont Co., O.

1802, 9, 18. Joshua & w, Mary, & ch, Charity
& Timothy, rocf Nottingham MM, Pa., dtd
1801,11,28, end from Redstone MM, Pa.,
1802,7,2
1802, 12, 18. Caleb rocf Westland MM, dtd
1802,11,27

LACEY

1803, 11, 19. Ephraim rocf Fairfax MM, dtd
1803,9,24

LAMB

1823, 11, 19. John & w, Hannah, & ch, Mary
Ann, Rebecca, Daniel S., Phebe G. & John,
rocf Providence MM, dtd 1823,10,21
1825, 2, 23. Joshua rocf Cincinnati MM, dtd
1824,11,25
1825, 8, 24. Joshua dis disunity
1826, 6, 21. Mary & Rebecca dis disunity

LAMBERT

1805, 7, 25. Mary m Isaac COPPOCK
1811, 7, 31. Abner, Belmont Co., O.; m in
Concord MH, Susanna FARIS

1808, 2, 23. Albert dis mcd
1808, 7, 21. Elizabeth dis
1810, 9, 20. Benjamin dis mcd
1817, 4, 23. Abner Jr. dis mcd

LAY

1804, 5, 22. William rocf Wrightsborough MM,
Ga., dtd 1804,3,3

LEEK

1830, 11, 24. Elizabeth & Maria rocf Indian
Spring MM, Md., dtd 1830,7,7, end by
Flushing MM, 1830,9,25 (H)
1833, 2, 20. Elizabeth Given (form Leek) con
mcd (H)
1833, 4, 24. Maria gct Stillwater MM

LEWIS

1803, 5, 21. Henry & w, Susanna, & ch, Wm.,
Mary, Lewis, Esther, Catharine, Anne,
Samuel & Susannah, rocf Westland MM, dtd
1803,4,23
1803, 5, 21. Jacob & w, Mary, & ch, Hannah,
rocf Westland MM, dtd 1803,4,23
1818, 4, 22. Anna rocf Short Creek MM, dtd
1817,9,23, end by Plainfield MM, 1818,3,25

1819, 5, 19. Ann Fulerton (form Lewis) dis mcd
1839, 6, 19. Evan & w, Rebecca, & ch, Charles,
Martha, Jesse & Elijah, rocf Uwchland MM,
Pa., dtd 1839,4,1 (H)
1841, 4, 21. Evan & w, Rebecca, & ch,
Charles, Martha, Jesse & Elijah, gct Short
Creek MM (H)
1853, 11, 12. Lydia Ann (form Newport) con mcd
(H)

LIGHTFOOT

1827, 3, 7. Joseph, s Samuel & Rachel, Belmont Co., O.; m in Concord MH, Rachel MED-
CELF, dt Moses & Susanna, Belmont Co., O.

1826, 3, 22. Wm. M. rocf Uwchland MM, Pa.,
dtd 1826,1,5
1827, 1, 24. Joseph rocf Goshen MM, Pa., dtd
1826,11,29
1828, 3, 19. Wm. M. gct Springboro MM

LITTLE

1827, 1, 24. Robert rocf Baltimore MM for
West. Dist.
1827, 10, 24. Robert gct Plainfield MM
1840, 7, 22. Isaac P. [Litle] rocf Alexandria MM, D. C. (H)

LUKENS
                              Cope
1835, 7, 22. James/gct Short Creek MM, to m
Anna E. Lukens (H)

LUMAN

1865, 8, 23. Sarah Ann (form Wells) con mcd
(H)

LUNDY

1807, 1, 20. Amos Jr. rocf Mt. Pleasant MM,
Va., dtd 1806,4,26
1810, 1, 25. Benjamin rocf Hardwich & Mend-
ham MM, N. J., dtd 1809,10,5

LUPTON

1803, 9, 22. Solomon, s Wm. & Bathsheba;
m in Short Creek MH, Rachel WOOD, dt Joseph & Rachel, Jefferson Co., O.

1803, 11, 19. Cert rec for William & w, Bathsheba, & ch, Lydia, Grace, Jonathan,
Allen, Mary, Isaac, Wm., Davis & Mahlon,
from Hopewell MM, Va., dtd 1803,10,3, end
to Miami MM, O.
1803, 11, 19. Solomon & w, Rachel, rqct Miami

LUPTON, continued
    MM, O.

McCARTY
1854, 1, 25. Emily (form Cope) con mcd (H)

McKANN
1804, 12, 18. Jane recrq

McMILLEN
1803, 12, 17. Mary rocf Warrington MM, dtd
    1803,7,9

McMULIN
1808, 8, 1. Elizabeth m Thomas SATTERTHWAITE

1810, · 4, 26. Elizabeth [McMullins] recrq

McPHERSON
1803, 6, 18. John rocf Goose Creek MM, Va.,
    dtd 1803,5,7

MACE
1804, 6, 19. Cert rec for William & w, Anna,
    & ch, Katherine, William, Joseph & Anna,
    from Core Sound MM, N. C., dtd 1804,3,31,
    end to Short Creek MM, O.
1804, 8, 21. Hannah rocf Core Sound MM, N. C.
    dtd 1804,3,31
1805, 5, 21. William & fam gct Short Creek
    MM, O.

MARIS
1824, 7, 21. Owen recrq
1825, 9, 21. Owen gct Short Creek MM, to m
    Rachel Jenkins
1826, 4, 19. Owen gct Stillwater MM

MARSH
1832, 5, 23. Susanna N. & Elizabeth rocf
    Smithfield MM, dtd 1832,4,24 (H)
1832, 5, 23. Ann & Mifflin, minors, rocf
    Smithfield MM, dtd 1832,4,24 (H)

MAULE
1831, 11, 23. John rocf Green St. MM, Phila.,
    Pa., dtd 1831,8,18 (H)

MECAN
1806, 9, 23. Jane Bolden (form Mecan) dis mcd

MEDCALF
----, --, --. Abraham & Hannah
    Ch: John   b 1818, 5, 10
        Susanna   " 1820, 8, 14
        Jemima S.   " 1823, 11, 18
        Elizabeth   " 1826, 10, 1
        Lydia Ann   " 1829, 4, 7
        Moses   " 1833, 12, 15
1820, 4, 26. Rebecca m Joshua COPE
1827, 3, 7. Rachel m Joseph LIGHTFOOT

1814, 11, 24. Moses [Medkelf] & w, Susannah,

& ch, Abraham, Mary, Rebecca, Jesse,
Joseph, Rachel, Moses & David, rocf Deer
Creek MM, Md., dtd 1814,8,25, end by Short
Creek MM
1817, 12, 24. Abraham con mcd
1821, 11, 21. Hannah [Midcelf] recrq
1821, 11, 21. John [Midcelf], s Abraham & Han-
    nah, recrq
1824, 12, 22. Jesse [Medcelf] rqct Plainfield
    MM, to m Asenath Gregg
1825, 5, 25. Abraham [Medcelf] & w, Hannah,
    & ch, John, Susanna & Jemima, gct Somer-
    set MM
1825, 7, 20. Asenath [Medcelf] rocf Plain-
    field MM, dtd 1825,6,23
1831, 10, 19. Abram [Medcelf] & w, Hannah, &
    ch, John, Susanna, Jemima S., Elizabeth
    & Lydiann, rocf Plainfield MM, dtd 1831,9,
    22 (H)
1837, 3, 22. Abram [Medcelf] & w, Hannah, &
    ch, John, Susana, Jemima L., Elizabeth,
    Lydiann, Moses & Hannah, gct Deerfield MM
    (H)
1837, 3, 22. Moses [Medcelf] gct Deerfield MM
    (H)

MELTON
1803, 5, 25. Stafford, s Joseph & Tamer, Bel-
    mont Co., O.; m in Concord MH, Mary GARRET-
    SON, dt Wm. & Mary

1803, 2, 19. Wm. & w, Sarah, & ch, Fanny &
    Moses, and Jonathan Bogue, her s by former
    m, rocf Trent MM, N. C., dtd 1800,1,12,
    end from Redstone MM 1802,12,31
1803, 3, 19. Stafford rocf Westland MM, dtd
    1803,2,26
1805, 6, 18. Thomas recrq
1805, 12, 24. Thomas, Henry, Amos & Ann, ch
    Thomas, recrq
1839, 9, 25. Stafford gct Flushing MM (H)

MENDENHALL
1805, 7, 23. Catharine rocf Deep River MM,
    N. C., dtd 1805,4,1

MIDDLETON
1804, 9, 26. Mary m Demsey BOSWELL

1803, 7, 16. Joseph & w, Phebe, & ch, Mary &
    Martha, rocf Mt. Pleasant MM, Va., dtd
    1803,4,30
1803, 7, 16. John & w, Mary, rocf Mt. Pleas-
    ant MM, Va., dtd 1803,4,30
1805, 10, 22. Martha (form Middleton) dis mcd
                    Childra

MILES
1814, 3, 24. Moses, minor, rocf Hopewell MM,
    dtd 1813,10,4, end by Plainfield MM, 1814,
    1,22
1814, 3, 24. Lydia rocf Hopewell MM, dtd
    1813,10,4, end by Plainfield MM, 1814,1,
    22

MILES, continued
1815, 4, 20. Lydia Steele (form Miles) dis
    mcd
1815, 5, 25. Hannah & dt, Susanna, rocf Hope-
    well MM, dtd 1815,3,9
1816, 1, 24. Susanna Eaves (form Miles) dis
    mcd
1820, 12, 20. Moses dis mcd
1820, 12, 20. Hannah gct Stillwater MM

MILIGAN
1836, 8, 24. Sarah L. con mcd (H)

MILLHOUSE
1808, 4, 27. Phebe m David STEER
1825, 12, 28. Rebecca m Joseph H. COPE

1804, 7, 24. Robert & w, Sarah, & s, Daniel,
    rocf Wrightsborough MM, Ga., dtd 1804,3,3
1805, 10, 22. Wm. & w, Hannah, & dt, Jane,
    rocf Uwchlan MM, dtd 1805,8,8
1805, 10, 22. Phebe rocf Uwchlan MM, dtd 1805,
    8,8
1805, 12, 24. William Jr. rocf Uwchlan MM, dtd
    1805,9,5
1813, 11, 25. William & w, Hannah, gct Uwchlan
    MM
1813, 11, 25. Jane gct Uwchlan MM
1825, 8, 24. William & w, Hannah, rocf Exeter
    MM, dtd 1825,6,29

MILLER
1804, 1, 21. John & Margarett rocf Hopewell
    MM, dtd 1803,11,7

MILLS
1806, 1, 21. Nathan & w, Elizabeth, & s,
    Isaac, rocf Deep River MM, N. C., dtd
    1805,10,7
1808, 1, 19. Reuben & w, Sarah, & ch, Mary,
    Gideon & Sally, rocf Deep River MM, N.C.,
    dtd 1807,9,7
1808, 1, 19. Reuben Jr. & w, Clarissa, rocf
    Deep River MM, N. C., dtd 1807,9,7

MILNOR
1806, 9, 23. Dudley & w, Mary, & ch, Anna &
    Caty, rocf South River MM, Va., dtd 1806,
    8,10

MILTON
1803, 11, 19. Mary rocf Hopewell MM, dtd 1803,
    10,3, end by Goose Creek MM, 1803,10,24
1818, 10, 21. Amos dis
1821, 6, 20. Henry dis
1829, 1, 21. Moses con mcd (H)
1832, 3, 21. Thomas, Moses & Thomas Jr. gct
    Deerfield MM

MOORE
----, --, --. William & Lydia
    Ch: Samuel
        John

    Ch: Edward T. b 1822, 1, 9
        Martha   " 1824, 7, 19
        Isabella   " 1827, 3, 15

1806, 9, 23. William rocf Contentnea MM,
    N. C., dtd 1806,5,10
1808, 3, 24. William gct Salem MM
1819, 8, 25. William & w, Lydia, & ch, Sam-
    uel & John, recrq
1829, 3, 25. William & w, Lydia, & ch, Samuel,
    John, Edward, Martha & Isabella, gct Deer-
    field MM (H)

MORGAN
1806, 5, 27. Elizabeth, w Jonathan, & ch,
    Hannah, Jonathan, Isaac & Asa, rocf Piles-
    grove MM, dtd 1806,3,27
1807, 7, 21. D vid rocf Piles Grove MM, dtd
    1807,6,25

MORRIS
1833, 6, 19. Thomas, s Joseph & Abigail,
    Ohio Co., Va.; m in Concord MH, Mary Ann
    UPDEGRAFF, dt Israel & Jane, Ohio Co., Va.

1804, 12, 18. Cert rec for Samuel & s, Aaron,
    from Contentnea MM, N. C., dtd 1804,9,8,
    end to Middleton MM, O.
1804, 12, 18. Cert rec for Benjamin & s,
    Joshua, from Contentnea MM, N. C., dtd
    1804,9,8, end to Middleton MM
1804, 12, 18. Cert rec for William & s, Benja-
    min & Mordecai, from Contentnea MM, N. C.,
    dtd 1804,9,8, end to Middleton MM
1804, 12, 18. Cert rec for Susannah & dt,
    Avice from Contentnea MM, N. C., dtd 1804,
    9,8, end to Middleton MM
1804, 12, 18. Cert rec for Sally & dt, Mary &
    Lydia, from Contentnea MM, N. C., dtd
    1804,9,8, end to Middleton MM
1804, 12, 18. Cert rec for Leah & Lydia from
    Contentnea MM, N. C., dtd 1804,9,8, end to
    Middleton MM
1841, 8, 25. Sarah (form Conard) con mcd (H)

MORTON
1802, 9, 18. Hannah & ch, Ann, Mary, Benja-
    min, John & Hannah, rocf Westland MM, dtd
    1802,7,24

MOTT
1812, 4, 23. William rocf Abington MM, dtd
    1811,12,30, end by Plainfield MM, O.,
    1812,3,28
1812, 8, 20. William gct Short Creek MM, O.

MUSGRAVE
1806, 7, 22. Wm. rocf Contentnea MM, N. C.,
    dtd 1806,2,8

NEAVE
1825, 2, 23. Charles rocf Cincinnati MM, dtd
    1824,11,25

NEAVE, continued
1825, 6, 22. Charles dis disunity

NEWETT
1818, 2, 22. Cert rec for Ruth from Short
    Creek MM, dtd 1817,12,23, end to Plain-
    field MM on rq

NEWPORT
1819, 5, 26. Ruth m Joseph HOYLE
1821, 6, 6. Edith m William HOYL
1821, 11, 28. Abigail m Edward G. POTTS
----, --, --. Nathan & Elizabeth
    Ch: Caroline   b 1824, 9, 14
        Lidia Ann   " 1825, 10, 27
        John Wil-
            liam   " 1828, 3, 22
        Fawcett T. " 1829, 12, 27
        Julia Me-
            riah   " 1828, 3, 22

1805, 12, 24. Mary & ch, Elizabeth, Jesse,
    Ruth, Joseph, Reese, Nathan, Noble, Edith,
    Abigail & Jonah, rocf Westland MM, dtd
    1805,9,28
1807, 9, 22. Edith Sharpless (form Newport)
    dis mcd
1814, 11, 24. Jesse & Rees gct Short Creek MM,
    O.
1815, 7, 20. Joseph gct Cincinnati MM
1823, 11, 19. Nathan gct Salem MM, to m Eliza-
    beth Fawcet
1824, 5, 19. Elizabeth rocf Salem MM, dtd
    1824,4,21
1827, 10, 24. Noble gct Short Creek MM
1829, 1, 21. Jonah gct Goose Creek MM, Va.,
    to m Rachel Smith
1829, 7, 22. Rachel rocf Goose Creek MM, Va.,
    dtd 1829,6,11
1829, 8, 19. Jonah & w, Rachel, gct Spring-
    borough MM
1830, 6, 23. Mary Ann Potts (form Newport)
    con mcd
1839, 10, 23. Mary gct Springboro MM
1853, 11, 12. Julia M. Rice (form Newport) con
    mcd
1853, 11, 12. Lydia Ann Lewis (form Newport)
    con mcd
1857, 4, 22. Elizabeth, Caroline & Narcissa
    dis disunity

NICHOLS
1804, 4, 24. Solomon [Nicholls] & w, Hannah,
    & ch, Thos., James, Elizabeth, John, Dan-
    iel, Hannah, Helen & Amy, rocf Westland
    MM, dtd 1804,4,2
1808, 1, 19. Jean & ch, Eli & Mary, rocf
    Hopewell MM, dtd 1807,10,5
1808, 2, 23. James rpd mcd

NICHOLSON
1802, 4, 17. Joseph & w, Sarah, & ch, James,
    Elizabeth, George, Hannah & Wm., rocf Red-

stone MM, dtd 1802,3,5
1805, 8, 20. Mary rocf Redstone MM, dtd
    1805,3,3

NICKLERS
1808, 4, 21. Martha M. rocf Hopewell MM, dtd
    1808,1,4, end to Plainfield MM

NIXON
1804, 12, 18. Cert rec for Mary from Spring-
    field MM, dtd 1803,10,1, end to Miami MM
    on rq

ONG
1803, 1, 15. Jacob & w, Mary, & ch, Finley,
    Jacob, Isaac, Dinah, Nathan & John, rocf
    Redstone MM, 1802,12,3

OUTLAND
1805, 9, 24. Margaret rocf Contentnea MM,
    N. C., dtd 1805,3,9
1805, 12, 24. William rocf Contentnea MM, N.C.
    dtd 1805,9,14

PACKER
1813, 4, 22. Moses gct Short Creek MM

PANCOAST
1806, 5, 27. Sarah rocf Goose Creek MM, Va.,
    dtd 1806,12,30

PARKER
1817, 7, 23. Joseph & w, Mary, & ch, Abigail,
    Jacob, James, William & Isaac, rocf Short
    Creek MM, dtd 1817,2,18

PARKINS
1806, 3, 18. Jane, w Jonathan, & ch, David,
    Stephen, Nathan, Jane, Elizabeth, Isaac,
    Hannah, Anne & Lydia, rocf Hopewell MM,
    dtd 1805,7,1

PARVIANCE
1817, 5, 20. George, s James & Elizabeth,
    Jefferson Co., O.; m in Concord MH, Esther
    DEWEES, dt Owen & Mary, Belmont Co., O.

PATTERSON
1806, 9, 23. Joseph [Patteson] & w, Mary, &
    ch, Samuel, Esther, Deborah & Laband, rocf
    Short Creek MM, dtd 1806,5,24
1807, 1, 20. Jonathan & w, Ruth, & s, Michael,
    rocf Short Creek MM, O., dtd 1806,9,20
1807, 4, 21. Margaret rocf Short Creek MM,
    dtd 1806,12,20
1807, 5, 19. Catharine rocf Short Creek MM,
    dtd 1806,12,20
1807, 7, 21. Benjamin & ch, Elam & Elijah,
    rocf Short Creek MM, O., dtd 1806,12,20
1808, 5, 25. Cert rec for Wm. Jr. & w,
    Elizabeth, & ch, Silas, Talitha, Jeremiah,
    Axim & Rachel, from Short Creek MM, dtd
    1808,3,22, end to Stillwater MM

PATTERSON, continued
1813, 8, 26. John Williams gct Stillwater MM,
     to m Sarah Patterson

PAXTON
1816, 11, 20. Hannah (form Whitehead) dis mcd
1822, 12, 25. Mary (form Whitehead) dis mcd
1846, 4, 22. Hannah L. W. (form Wells) dis
     mcd (H)

PEARSON
1805, 1, 22. Benjamin & w & ch, William, Anne,
     Jesse & Elizabeth, rocf Cattawissa MM,
     dtd 1804,8,25, end by Short Creek MM, O.,
     1805,1,19

PEELLE
1807, 12, 2. John, s Reuben & Rhoda, N. C.;
     m in Stillwater MH, Lydia BUNDY, dt Wm. &
     Mary, Belmont Co., O.

1807, 6, 23. John rocf Mt. Pleasant MM, Va.,
     dtd 1807,2,28
1808, 3, 24. John & w, Lydia, gct Fairfield
     MM, O.

PENROSE
1828, 11, 19. Isaac & Jesse rocf Plainfield
     MM, dtd 1828,10,23 (H)
1828, 12, 24. Sarah & Rachel rocf Plainfield
     MM, dtd 1828,10,3 (H)
1837, 11, 22. Sarah Ward (form Penrose) con
     mcd (H)
1846, 10, 21. Jesse & Rachel gct Clear Creek
     MM, Ill. (H)

PERDUE
1833, 8, 20. Charles A., s Sarah S. Bundy,
     rocf Plainfield MM, dtd 1833,6,20 (H)

PERRY
1805, 6, 18. Lydia Hill (form Perry) dis mcd

PICKERING
1804, 2, 23. Jonas, s Samuel & Phebe, Belmont
     Co., O.; m in Plainfield MH, Ruth GREGG,
     dt Abner & Sarah, Belmont Co., O.
1805, 10, 2. Sarrah m Jesse WHITE
1806, 3, 26. Rebecca m Job RIDGWAY
1807, 4, 1. Rebecca m Evan JAMES
1813, 3, 10. Ann m Joseph WRIGHT
1813, 10, 27. Leah m David SPENCER
1826, 9, 27. Elijah, s John & Mary, Belmont
     Co., O.; m in Concord MH, Rebecca Stevens
     FOX, dt Josiah & Ann, Belmont Co., O.
     Ch: Anna
          Miller   b 1830, 2, 3
          Sarah Fox " 1832, 3, 24
          Henry Fox " 1827, 12, 19
1832, 3, 28. Lewis, s John & Mary, Belmont
     Co., O.; m in Concord MH, Amanda VICKERS,
     dt Thomas & Ann, Belmont Co., O.
     Ch: Phebe Ann b 1833, 4, 18

     Ch: Thomas V. b 1823, 10, 8
          Caroline   " 1836, 10, 9
          Lydia Ann " 1836, 10, 9
          Lewis   " 1838, 10, 5
1839, 5, 29. Elisha, s John & Mary, Belmont
     Co., O.; m in Concord MH, Mary BERRY, dt
     Thomas & Rachel, Belmont Co., O.
     Ch: Reese   b 1842, 5, 3
1858, 7, 22. Sarah m Isaac JAMES

1803, 4, 16. Samuel & w, Phebe, & ch, Jonas,
     Levi, Samuel, Rebecca, Mary, Phebe &
     Joshua, rocf Crooked Run MM, dtd 1802,10,2
1803, 5, 21. Jacob & w, Hannah, a minister,
     & ch, Jacob, David & Jonathan, rocf South-
     land MM, dtd 1802,12,29
1803, 6, 18. Enos rocf Southland MM, Va., dtd
     1802,12,29
1803, 6, 18. Hannah Jr. rocf Southland MM,Va.
     dtd 1802,9,29
1803, 11, 17. Jacob Jr. & w, Lydia, & ch, Sa-
     rah, Abel, Joseph, Rhoda, Mary & Hannah,
     rocf Hopewell MM, Va., dtd 1803,10,3
1806, 1, 21. Mary & ch, Rebeckah, Ann, John,
     Sarah, Leah, Milla, Samuel, Elijah,
     Elisha & Lewis recrq
1806, 6, 24. Elias & Isaac, ch Jonathan, dec,
     rocf Hopewell MM, dtd 1805,12,2
1807, 2, 24. Mary, dt Jonathan & Sarah, dec,
     rocf Hopewell MM, dtd 1805,7,1, end by
     Redstone MM, 1806,7,4
1807, 12, 27. Jonathan, minor, rocf Hopewell
     MM, dtd 1807,9,7
1808, 2, 23. John recrq
1808, 4, 21. Cert rec for Rachel, Mary &
     Jane, ch Jane, from Hopewell MM, dtd 1807,
     10,5, end to Plainfield MM
1812, 12, 24. John Jr. dis mcd
1815, 6, 22. Sarah Branson (form Pickering)
     dis mcd
                      Branson
1818, 2, 22. Amelia/(form Pickering) dis mcd
1819, 8, 25. John Jr. rst
1820, 2, 23. Elizabeth recrq
1825, 5, 25. Joanna & ch, Sarah Ann, Rebecca,
     Mary Ann, James & Alexander, recrq
1827, 10, 24. Samuel gct Plainfield MM
1830, 1, 20. John & w, Joann, & ch, Sarah
     Ann, Mary Ann, James, Amanda, Thomas &
     Ruthanna, gct Plainfield MM (H)
1830, 4, 21. Samuel & w & dt, Elizabeth, rocf
     Plainfield MM, dtd 1830,3,25 (H)
1831, 12, 21. Isaac gct Plainfield MM, to m
     Elizabeth Elliott (H)
1832, 5, 23. Elizabeth rocf Plainfield MM,
     dtd 1832,4,26 (H)
1839, 11, 20. Elijah & w, Rebecca, & ch,
     Henry, Anna, Sarah, Josiah, John C. &
     Thomas, gct Plainfield MM (H)
1842, 3, 21. Mary Ann Embry (form Pickering)
     con mcd (H)
1845, 2, 19. Isaac & w, Elizabeth, & ch,
     Lamira, Rachel, Eleanor, John & Charles,
     gct Plainfield MM (H)

PICKERING, continued

1851, 5, 21. Elisha & w, Mary, & s, Reese, gct Plainfield MM (H)

1851, 8, 20. Phebe Ann Daniel (form Pickering) dis mcd (H)

1853, 11, 23. Elisha & w, Mary, & s, Reese, rocf Plainfield MM, dtd 1853,10,13 (H)

1869, 10, 20. Elisha & w, Mary S., gct Wapsinonoc MM, Ia. (H)

PIDGEON

1803, 2, 19. Charles [Pigeon] & w, Anne, rocf South River MM, Va., dtd 1802,9,11

1804, 12, 18. Samuel [Pidgion] & ch, Sarah, Elizabeth & Isaac, rocf Springfield MM, dtd 1803,9,3

1806, 6, 24. Wm. & w, Rachel, & dt, Sarah, rocf Goose Creek MM, Va., dtd 1806,5,1

PIGGOTT

1819, 4, 28. Phebe m James COPE

1803, 12, 17. Moses [Pigott] & w, Hannah, & ch, Rachel, Thomas, James, Hannah & Moses, rocf Hopewell MM, dtd 1803,9,5

1805, 2, 19. John & w, Rachel, & ch, Mary & Rebecca, rocf Crooked Run MM, dtd 1805,2, 2

1805, 2, 19. John Jr. rocf Hopewell MM, dtd 1805,2,4

1805, 12, 24. Ruth rocf Hopewell MM, dtd 1805, 10,7

1818, 6, 24. Phebe recrq

1819, 3, 24. Anna recrq

1819, 4, 21. Thomas con mcd

1821, 1, 24. Wm., s Thomas & Rhoda, recrq

1821, 2, 21. Rhoda recrq

1821, 6, 20. Anna Yates (form Piggott) dis mcd

1824, 11, 24. Moses & w, Hannah, & fam gct Stillwater MM

1824, 11, 24. Thomas & fam gct Stillwater MM

1824, 11, 24. James & Hannah Jr. gct Stillwater MM

PITMAN

1803, 2, 19. Elizabeth rocf Burlington MM, dtd 1802,12,3

1806, 11, 18. Levi & ch, John, Uriah, Anthony, Beulah, Ann & Levi, recrq

1827, 5, 23. Anthony & w, Margaret, & ch, Rebecca, Esther & Elias, rocf Plainfield MM, dtd 1827,4,26

1829, 3, 25. Anthony & w, Margaret, & ch, Rebecca, Esther, Elias & Eliza, gct Plainfield MM (H)

PLUMMER

1807, 12, 24. Dinah m Isaac HALL

1803, 11, 19. Robert & w, Rachel, & ch, Elizabeth, John & Abraham, rocf Pipe Creek MM, dtd 1802,11,13

1804, 1, 21. Abraham & John rocf Pipe Creek MM, dtd 1803,10,15

1804, 7, 24. John dis mcd

1805, 8, 20. Ann (form Sidwell) dis mcd

1806, 8, 19. Thomas & w, Phebe, rocf Baltimore MM, dtd 1806,7,10

1806, 9, 23. Eleanor rocf Baltimore MM, dtd 1806,7,10

1807, 1, 20. Dinah rocf Nottingham MM, Md., dtd 1806,9,5

1808, 6, 23. Cert rec for Eli & w, Alice, & ch, James & Sinah, from Sadsbury MM, Pa., dtd 1808,4,5, end to Plainfield MM

1818, 9, 23. Ann rst

1824, 5, 19. Greenberry G. [Plumer] rocf Short Creek MM, dtd 1824,4,20

1825, 3, 23. Greenberry G. gct Exeter MM, to m Jane Milhouse

1825, 8, 24. Jane M. rocf Exeter MM, dtd 1825,6,29

1826, 5, 24. Greenberry G. & w, Jane M., gct Short Creek MM

POOL

1833, 5, 22. Samuel rocf Smithfield MM, dtd 1832,12,18 (H)

POTTS

1821, 11, 28. Edward G., s Samuel & Mary, Belmont Co., O.; m in Concord MH, Abigail NEWPORT, dt Aaron, Belmont Co., O.
Ch: Alfred   b 1822, 9, 12
    Oliver Gold-
              smith" 1824, 12, 21

1805, 4, 23. Samuel & w, Mary, & ch, Ruth Anna, Edward Garrigus, Deborah & Rebecca, rocf Cattawissa MM, dtd 1804,4,21

1806, 11, 18. Samuel & w, Mary, & ch, Ruth Anna, Edward, Deborah, Rebecca & Lindley, gct Centre MM, Pa.

1814, 12, 22. Samuel & w, Mary, & ch, Ruth Anna, Edward, Rebecca, Lindley & John, gct Plainfield MM

1816, 2, 21. Samuel & w, Ruth, & ch, Ruth Anna, Edward, Rebecca, Lindley & John, rocf Plainfield MM, dtd 1815,11,25

1818, 1, 21. Samuel & w, Mary, & ch gct Plainfield MM

1818, 1, 21. Ruth Anna gct Plainfield MM

1818, 4, 22. Samuel & fam & Ruth Anna returned to this mtg; cert returned

1820, 4, 19. Samuel & w, Ruth, & ch, Edward Garagus, Rebecca, Lindley & John, gct White Water MM, Ind.

1820, 4, 19. Ruth Anna gc

1822, 2, 20. Abigail gct Flushing MM

1823, 8, 20. Edward G. & w, Abigail, & s, Alfred, rocf Flushing MM, dtd 1823,3,21, end by Plainfield MM, 1823,7,14

1829, 3, 25. Edward G. & w, Abigail, & ch, Alfred & Oliver, gct Springboro MM (H)[(H)

1830, 6, 23. Mary Ann (form Newport) con mcd

POTTS, continued
1831, 1, 18. Mary Ann gct Springborough MM

PURVIANCE
1802, 4, 17. David & w, Mary, & ch, Sarah &
    James, rocf Redstone MM, dtd 1802,3,5
1803, 5, 21. James rocf Redstone MM, dtd
    1803,4,29

PYLE
1811, 10, 24. Jesse rocf Concord MM, Pa., dtd
    1811,8,9
1814, 7, 21. Jesse dis joining M. E. Church

RALEY
1813, 1, 27. Hannah m John HOWARD

1826, 8, 23. Asa gct Flushing MM, to m
    Asenath Hirst
1827, 4, 25. Asenath rocf Flushing MM, dtd
    1827,2,23

RECKITT
1807, 7, 21. Thomas rocf ND MM, dtd 1807,2,24

REED
1834, 8, 20. Cert rec for John & w, Rebecca,
    & ch, Eliza Jane, Priscilla C. & Joseph
    Durese, from Bradford MM, dtd 1834,5,6,
    end to Westland MM (H)

REEVE
1805, 8, 20. Cert rec for Joshua & w, Amilis-
    cent & ch from Mt. Holly MM, N. J., dtd
    1805,5,9, end to Short Creek MM, O.

RENNARD
1864, 9, 15. John, s Jacob & Vilinda, Belmont
    Co., O.; m in home of Geo. Cope, Julia
    COPE, dt Geo. & Julia Ann, Belmont Co., O.

REYNOLDS
1807, 8, 18. Cert rec for Thomas from Notting-
    ham MM, Pa., dtd 1806,4,11, end to Short
    Creek MM, O., on rq

RICE
1853, 11, 12. Julia M. (form Newport) con mcd
    (H)

RIDGEWAY
1806, 3, 26. Job [Ridgway], s Timothy & Mi-
    chal, Belmont Co., O.; m in Concord MH,
    Rebecca PICKERING, dt John & Sarah, Bel-
    mont Co., O.

1802, 8, 21. Job [Ridgway], apprentice to
    Francis Townsend, rocf Westland MM, dtd
    1802,7,24
1819, 1, 19. Job & w, Rebecca, & ch, Rees,
    David, John, Sarah & Mary Ann, gct Short
    Creek MM
1821, 11, 21. Rebecca [Ridgway] & ch, Rees,

David, John, Sarah, Maryjane & Job, rocf
    Short Creek MM, dtd 1821,11,20
1827, 3, 21. Rebecca dis
1829, 4, 22. Reese [Ridgway] gct Milton MM,
    Ind. (H)
1834, 5, 21. John con mcd (H)
1837, 7, 19. Rebecca recrq (H)
1842, 3, 21. Mary Ann Harris (form Ridgeway)
    con mcd (H)
1857, 4, 22. Job gct Maple Creek MM, Ind.(H)

ROBERTS
1806, 9, 23. Henry & w, Ann, & ch, Wm.,
    Richard, Morris, Isaiah & Rachel, rocf
    Pipe Creek MM, dtd 1806,4,19
1810, 2, 22. Cert rec for Henry from Pipe
    Creek MM, end to Short Creek MM
1822, 1, 23. Joseph rocf Plainfield MM, dtd
    1821,12,20
1827, 12, 19. Joseph con mcd

ROBSON
1807, 6, 23. Sampson rocf Lisburn MM, Ireland,
    dtd 1807,9,18
1807, 9, 22. Sampson Jr. recrq; dis by Antrim
    MM, Ireland, now dissolved
1814, 6, 23. Sampson Sr. gct Plainfield MM, O.

ROGERS
1807, 1, 20. Mary rocf Nottingham MM, Md.,
    dtd 1806,10,10
1807, 1, 20. Josiah & w, Alice, & ch, Jane,
    Evan, John, Josiah, Sarah & Alice, rocf
    Westland MM, dtd 1806,10,25
1823, 6, 25. Mary [Rodgers] rocf Redstone MM,
    dtd 1823,6,4
1824, 5, 19. Mary gct Redstone MM

ROSE
1807, 8, 18. Martha recrq

ROTCH
1812, 1, 23. Thomas & w, Charity, rocf West
    Hartford MM, Conn., dtd 1811,9,11

SACKET
1820, 3, 28. Ann m Geo. SHARPLESS

1812, 10, 22. Ann recrq

SATTERTHWAIT
1808, 8, 1. Thomas [Satterthwaite], s Wm.
    & Meriba, Belmont Co., O.; m in Concord
    MH, Elizabeth McMULIN, dt Richard & Ann

1802, 8, 21. Wm. & ch, Joseph, Thomas & Wm.,
    rocf Chesterfield MM, N. J., dtd 1802,5,4
1809, 1, 20. Richard gct ND MM
1809, 2, 23. Joseph gct Plainfield MM
1809, 5, 22. Ann rocf Plainfield MM, dtd
    1809,--,22
1810, 4, 26. Wm. gct Stillwater MM
1810, 5, 24. Joseph & w, Ann, & ch, Mary,

SATTERTHWAIT, continued
    rocf Plainfield MM
1812, 3, 26. Thomas & w, Elizabeth, & s, Robert Whitehill, gct Stillwater MM

SCOTT
1802, 9, 18. Joshua & w, Elizabeth, & ch, Job, Jesse, Hannah & Anne, rocf Core Sound MM, N. C., dtd 1802,6,9

SHAHL
1806, 9, 23. Isaac & w, Eleanor, & ch, Samuel, Margaret, Stacy, John & Mahlon, rocf Short Creek MM, dtd 1806,7,19

SHARP
1806, 11, 18. Samuel & w, Martha, & ch, Abigail, George, Jeptha, Sarah, Jesse, Lydia, Samuel & Phineas, rocf Crooked Run MM, dtd 1806,10,4

SHARPLESS
1820, 3, 28. George, s Thomas & Martha, Belmont Co., O.; m in Concord MH, Ann SACKET, dt Samuel & Sarah

1806, 6, 24. Samuel rocf Third Haven MM, dtd 1806,2,--
1807, 9, 22. Edith (form Newport) dis mcd
1807, 11, 24. Preston dis mcd
1808, 2, 23. George rocf Wilmington MM
1815, 3, 23. Samuel gct Plainfield MM
1859, 8, 24. Samuel dis jas (H)

SHOTWELL
1807, 4, 30. Titus, s Daniel & Deborah, Belmont Co., O.; m in Plainfield MH, Deborah HOWEL, dt Timothy & Rebecca

1807, 3, 24. Titus & ch, Marion, Joseph, Thomas & Isaac, rocf Redstone MM, dtd 1806,10,3

SIDWELL
1805, 7, 23. Rebecca & ch, Ann, Sarah, John, Nathan, Joseph & Gabrial Baker, rocf Wrightsborough MM, Ga., dtd 1804,7,7
1805, 8, 20. Ann Plummer (form Sidwell) dis mcd
1807, 7, 21. Nathan rocf Bush River MM, S. C. dtd 1806,12,27
1807, 11, 24. Henry & w, Cinah, & ch, Eli, Deborah, Eleanor, Elisha, Thomas, Henry & Cinah, rocf Nottingham MM, Md., dtd 1807,8,7
1822, 7, 24. Rebecca, dt Elizabeth Tomlinson, recrq
1805, 8, 20. Sarah Todd (form Sidwell) dis mcd

SINCLAIR
1805, 9, 24. James & w, Mary, rocf Goose Creek MM, Va., dtd 1804,9,24

SMITH
1804, 9, 26. Rachel m Samuel FAUCETT

1803, 5, 21. Martha & ch, Rachel, John, Sarah, Thomas & Martha, rocf Southland MM, dtd 1802,9,29
1804, 11, 20. Thomas rocf Fairfax MM, dtd 1804,9,22
1806, 3, 18. Mahlon & w, Mary, rocf Crooked Run MM, dtd 1806,11,30
1806, 7, 22. David & w, Judith, & ch, Lydia, Wm. & Thomas, rocf Redstone MM, dtd 1806, 1,31
1806, 11, 18. William & w, Ann, rocf Goose Creek MM, dtd 1806,9,29
1806, 12, 23. George & w, Mary, & ch, William, Samuel, Anna, George, Tamor, Tacy & Benjamin, rocf Westland MM, dtd 1806,11,22
1808, 9, 22. Cert rec for Susannah from Goose Creek MM, dtd 1808,5,30, end to Plainfield MM
1816, 9, 25. Cert rec for Ethan & w, Chloe, from West Hartford MM, Conn., dtd 1816,5, 15, end to Marlborough MM
1818, 2, 22. David & w, Judith, & ch, Lydia, Wm., Joseph, Sarah, Thos. & John, rocf Stillwater MM, dtd 1818,11,27
1821, 5, 23. David & w, Judith, & ch, William, Sarah, Joseph, Thomas & John, gct Stillwater MM
1821, 5, 23. Lydia gct Stillwater MM
1829, 1, 21. Jonah Newport gct Goose Creek MM, Va., to m Rachel Smith (H)

SPEAKMAN
1810, 2, 22. Betty rocf Pipe Creek MM, dtd 1808,4,16

SPENCER
1813, 10, 27. David, s Nathan & Ann, Belmont Co., O.; m in Concord MH, Leah PICKERING, dt John & Mary, Belmont Co., O.
    Ch: Maryan   b 1814, 8, 30
        Samuel   " 1815, 12, 28
        Phebe   " 1817, 11, 30
        Nathan   " 1820, 4, 20
        Eleanor " 1823, 9, 20
        Rebecca " 1825, 4, 25

1806, 4, 22. Nathan & w, Ann, & ch, David, Betcy, Jonathan, Mercy, Abner, Sarah, Phebe & Mary, rocf Goose Creek MM, Va., dtd 1806,3,24
1814, 4, 21. Leah rocf Plainfield MM
1816, 4, 24. David & w, Leah, & ch, Mary Ann & Samuel, rocf Plainfield MM, dtd 1816,3, 20
1839, 8, 21. Mary Ann & Phebe gct Milford MM, Ind. (H)
1839, 9, 25. David & w, Leah, & ch, Nathan, Elenor, Rebecca, Edwin & David P., gct Milford MM, Ind. (H)

STANTON
1811, 11, 27. Lydia m Richard JELKS

1804, 7, 24. Cert rec for Susannah from Core
      Sound MM, N. C., dtd 1804,4,11, end to
      Short Creek MM
1805, 11, 19. Cert rec for James & fam from
      Cane Creek MM, N. C., dtd 1805,4,6, end
      to Salem MM
1808, 9, 22. Borden Jr. dis
1808, 9, 22. Hannah dis
1811, 2, 21. Enoch & Mary dis
1812, 6, 25. Abigail gct Plymouth MM
1812, 8, 20. Hannah rst
1814, 5, 26. Susannah rocf Short Creek MM,
      dtd 1814,3,22
1816, 4, 24. Hannah & ch, Elizabeth & Peninah
      gct Stillwater MM
1817, 6, 25. Borden & w, Charlotte, & ch,
      Hope, Borden, Mary & Lotte, gct Stillwater
      MM
1817, 9, 24. Borden Jr. rst at Stillwater
      MM with consent of this Mtg
1818, 7, 22. Susannah dis
1819, 10, 20. William gct Stillwater MM, O.

STARBUCK
1805, 7, 23. Hezekiah rocf New Garden MM,
      N. C., dtd 1805,2,23
1805, 7, 23. George & w, Elizabeth, & ch,
      John, Rachel, Elisha & Mary, rocf New Gar-
      den MM, N. C., dtd 1805,2,23
1807, 1, 20. Jethro & w, Rebecca, & dt, Sa-
      rah, rocf New Garden MM, N. C., dtd 1806,
      9,27
1807, 3, 24. Hezekiah's cert end to another
      MM on rq
1808, 1, 19. Anna rocf Hopewell MM, dtd 1807,
      10,5

STEELE
1815, 2, 23. Peter dis mcd
1815, 4, 20. Lydia (form Miles) dis mcd
1819, 10, 20. Elijah dis mcd
1825, 12, 21. Ruth Hurford (form Steele) dis
      mcd

STEER
1808, 4, 27. David, s Joseph & Grace, Jeffer-
      son Co., O.; m in Concord MH, Phebe
      MILLHOUSE, dt Wm. & Hannah, Belmont Co.,O.
1821, 8, 1. Mary m John DOUDNA

1804, 5, 22. Joseph & w, Grace, & ch, David,
      Rachel, Samuel & Amos, rocf Hopewell MM,
      dtd 1804,3,5, end to Short Creek MM, O.
1804, 5, 22. Cert rec for Sarah, dt Joseph &
      Grace, from Hopewell MM, dtd 1804,3,5,
      end to Short Creek MM, O.
1808, 6, 23. Phebe gct Short Creek MM, O.
1812, 12, 24. James rocf Hopewell MM, dtd
      1812,5,24, end by Short Creek MM, 1812,11,
      24

1812, 12, 24. Joseph, James Jr., Ruth, Mary &
      Phebe, rocf Hopewell MM, dtd 1812,5,14, end
      by Short Creek MM, 1812,11,24
1814, 1, 20. Joseph gct Stillwater MM, O., to
      m Emma French
1814, 7, 21. Emma rocf Stillwater MM, O., dtd
      1814,4,26
1819, 7, 21. James Jr. gct Flushing MM, O.,
      to m Ruth Wilson
1823, 7, 23. David & w, Phebe, & ch, Hannah,
      Joseph, Wm., Isaac, Benjamin, Jane, Amos
      & Greenberry, rocf Short Creek MM, dtd
      1823,6,24
1823, 7, 23. Emma gct Short Creek MM
1831, 4, 20. Emma rocf Short Creek MM, dtd
      1830,12,23 (H)
1833, 2, 20. Emma gct White Water MM, Ind.
      (H)

STEPHEN
1802, 9, 18. Silas rocf Robeson MM, Pa., dtd
      1802,4,9
1803, 5, 21. Catharine & ch recrq

STRAHL
1806, 1, 21. Ann & ch, Mary, Rebecca, Sarah,
      Elmor & John, rocf Short Creek MM, O., dtd
      1805,12,21

STREET
1826, 10, 25. Isaac & w, Rebecca, & ch, Mary
      Ann & Rachel, rocf Upper Springfield MM,
      dtd 1826,9,23
1828, 10, 22. Isaac & w, Rebecca, & ch, Mary
      Ann, Elizabeth & Belinda, gct Salem MM (H)

STUBS
1807, 12, 30. Rachel m Menoah HANSON

1805, 7, 23. Joseph & w, Zilphah, & ch, Ra-
      chel, Sarah, Jacob, Isaac, Deborah, Abra-
      ham, Elizabeth, Rebecca, Iddo, Eliza &
      Rhoda, rocf Wrightsborough MM, Ga., dtd
      1805,4,6

SWAIN
1804, 1, 21. Joshua rocf Redstone MM, dtd
      1803,11,7

TALBOTT
1802, 6, 19. Joseph & w, Mary, & ch, Sarah,
      Elizabeth, Allen, William, John, Robert,
      Mary & Hannah, rocf Redstone MM, Va., dtd
      1802,4,2

TANNER
1824, 10, 20. Deborah (form Graham) dis mcd

TAYLOR
1806, 1, 21. Ann, dt Joseph, rocf Crooked
      Run MM, Va., dtd 1805,10,5

TEST
1803, 10, 15. Zaccheus & w, Hannah, & ch,
      Isaac, Samuel & Joseph, rocf Woodsbury MM,
      N. J., dtd 1803,8,9

THOMAS
1839, 6, 26. Lucinda m Joseph HICKS

1802, 7, 17. Jesse & w, Avice, & dt, Abigail,
      rocf Core Sound MM, N. C., dtd 1802,4,28
1802, 8, 21. John rocf Core Sound MM, N. C.,
      dtd 1802,4,28
1802, 10, 16. Lovice rocf Core Sound MM, N.C.,
      dtd 1802,4,28
1804, 6, 19. Cert rec for John & w, Hannah,
      from Core Sound MM, N. C., dtd 1804,3,31,
      end to Short Creek MM, O.
1804, 6, 19. Cert rec for Nathaniel & Benja-
      min, from Core Sound MM, N. C., dtd 1804,
      3,31, end to Short Creek MM, O.
1804, 8, 21. Cert rec for Jesse & w, Elizabeth
      & ch from Core Sound MM, N. C., dtd 1804,
      3,31, end to Short Creek MM
1804, 12, 18. Cert rec for Sarah from Core
      Sound MM, N. C., dtd 1804,4,11, end to
      Short Creek MM
1805, 7, 23. Camm & w, Elizabeth, & ch,
      William, Abisha, Asael, Hezekiah, Caty &
      Priscilla, rocf Wrightsborough MM, Ga.,
      dtd 1805,4,6
1805, 7, 23. Rebecca rocf Wrightsborough MM,
      Ga., dtd 1805,4,6
1807, 9, 22. Robert & w, Lucinda, rocf Salem
      MM, dtd 1807,5,12

THOMSON
1803, 6, 18. Bradway, & w, Ann, & ch, Mary,
      John, Couzens, Sarah, Hannah, Samuel &
      Reason, rocf Westland MM, dtd 1803,5,28

THORN
1803, 7, 16. Isaac & w, Hannah, & ch, Wm.,
      Margaret, Elizabeth, Thomas & Mary, rocf
      Redstone MM, dtd 1802,12,31

TIMBERLAKE
1809, 11, 23. Cert rec for Mourning from
      South River MM, dtd 1805,11,9, end to
      Plainfield MM

TODD
1803, 7, 16. Stephen & w, Sibilla, & ch, Re-
      beckah, Mary & Wm., rocf Wrightsborough
      MM, Ga., dtd 1803,3,23
1803, 8, 20. Rebeckah rocf Wrightsborough
      MM, Ga.
1805, 8, 20. Sarah (form Sidwell) dis mcd
1817, 8, 20. Sarah rst by Stillwater MM, on
      consent of this Mtg

TOMLINSON
1819, 11, 24. Elizabeth rocf Little Britain
      MM. Pa., dtd 1819,10,2, end by Short Creek

MM 1819,11,23
1822, 7, 24. Rebecca Sidwell, dt Elizabeth
      Tomlinson, recrq

TOWNSEND
1816, 10, 30. John, s Joseph & Mary, Harrison
      Co., O.; m in Concord MH, Ruth BUNDY, dt
      Josiah & Bathiah, Belmont Co., O.
1838, 5, 30. Juli Ann m George COPE

1802, 8, 21. Francis & w, Marah, & Job Ridg-
      way, his apprentice, rocf Westland MM, dtd
      1802,7,24
1803, 9, 17. Benjamin & w, Jemima, & ch, Mar-
      tha, Aaron, Robert, Edith & Eli, rocf
      Westland MM, dtd 1803,6,25
1805, 11, 19. Cert rec for Judith & ch from
      Greenwich MM, N. J., dtd 1805,5,1, end to
      Salem MM
1806, 1, 21. Francis & w gct Westland MM
1810, 2, 22. Thomas rocf Baltimore MM, dtd
      1808,5,11
1815, 9, 2. Moses Bundy gct Short Creek MM,
      O., to m Ann Townsend
1817, 6, 25. Ruth dis
1818, 5, 20. Ruth rst
1819, 2, 24. Ruth & dt, Guliann, gc

TRAHERN
1820, 6, 21. Asa & w, Elizabeth, & dt, Sina
      rocf Goose Creek MM, Va., dtd 1820,3,30

TRAYER
1805, 3, 17. Elizabeth recrq
1806, 1, 21. Elizabeth gct Westland MM

UPDEGRAFF
1813, 12, 30. Josiah, s Joseph & Mary, Ohio
      Co., Va.; m in Wheeling MH, Elizabeth KING
      dt Thomas & Jane, Ohio Co., Va.
1815, 12, 27. Israel, s Joseph & Mary, Ohio
      Co., Va.; m in Concord MH, Mary Ann Du
      BOIS, dt John Joseph & Juliann
1833, 6, 19. Mary Ann m Thomas MORRIS
1851, 10, 30. Juliana D. m Francis D. FOX

1805, 12, 24. Josiah & w, Hannah, & s, Joseph,
      rocf York MM, Pa., dtd 1805,9,10
1810, 3, 22. Israel rocf York MM, Pa., dtd
      1810,1,10
1817, 1, 22. Elizabeth gct Plainfield MM
1818, 8, 19. Alexander, Mary Ann, Sarah &
      Jane, recrq
1827, 10, 24. Alexander gct Plainfield MM
1846, 1, 21. Edward Jessop gct York MM (H)
1846, 3, 25. Sarah gct Smithfield MM (H)
1850, 12, 25. Josiah dis mcd (H)
1852, 6, 23. Israel con mcd (H)
1853, 8, 24. Sarah rocf Baltimore MM, dtd
      1853,4,7 (H)
1855, 4, 25. Elizabeth Wilson (form Upde-
      graff) con mcd (H)

VAILE
1802, 8, 21. Robert & w, Sarah, & s, Isaac, rocf Redstone MM, dtd 1802,4,30
1802, 8, 21. Benjamin & w, Rebecca, & ch, Rachel, Anne & Nathan, rocf Redstone MM, dtd 1802,4,30

VANLAW
1803, 5, 21. Joseph & w, Mary, & ch, Anne, John, Thomas, George & Samuel, rocf Burlington MM, N. J., dtd 1803,4,4

VANPELT
1808, 2, 23. John & w, Mary, & ch, Jonathan, Nancy, Mary & Catharine, recrq

VERNON
1803, 5, 21. Robert & w, Anne, & dt, Content, rocf Wrightsborough MM, Ga., dtd 1803,3, 23
1803, 6, 18. Amos & Mary & ch, James & Rachel, rocf Wrightsborough MM, Ga., dtd 1803,3,23
1805, 7, 23. James & w, Tamor, & ch, Giana, Thisdate, Wm., Elizabeth & Amos, rocf Mt. Pleasant MM, Va., dtd 1805,4,27

VICKERS
----, --, --. Thomas & Ann G.
    Ch: Amanda M. b 1813, 8, 15
        Thomas
        Elwood   " 1815, 4, 1
        Phebe Ann " 1817, 3, 13
        Thomas m 2nd Hannah P. -----
    Ch: Martha H. b 1820, 7, 12
        Amos H.   " 1821, 6, 26
        Chalkley   " 1822, 9, 16
        Rebecca   " 1824, 1, 27
        John   " 1825, 6, 23
        Jesse   " 1826, 12, 29
        Elijah L. " 1828, 4, 30
----, --, --. Thomas & Hannah
    Ch: Barclay   b 1830, 10, 3
        George   " 1832, 5, 18
        Sanford   " 1834, 2, 24
        Elizabeth " 1836, 1, 8
        Mary Ann " 1837, 8, 31
        Ziba   " 1839, 5, 22
1832, 3, 28. Amanda M. m Lewis PICKERING
1838, 2, 28. Phebe Ann m Edward FOULKE
1839, 2, 27. Martha H. m Reese T. BERRY

1819, 8, 25. Thomas & William rocf Staindrop MM, Durham, England, dtd 1819,3,30
1822, 6, 19. Thomas & w, Hannah, & ch, Amanda M., Thomas Elwood, Phebe Ann, Martha H. & Amos H., rocf Bradford MM, Pa., dtd 1822,5,8, end by Short Creek MM, 1822, 6,18
1824, 12, 22. Thomas gct Lockport MM, N. Y.
1832, 3, 21. Phebe Ann gct Uwchland MM, Pa. (H)
1832, 6, 20. William con mcd (H)

1835, 11, 25. Phebe Ann rocf Uwchland MM, Pa., dtd 1835,9,3 (H)
1836, 1, 20. Jesse H. & w, Margaret, & ch, Samuel, Isaac M., Thomas, Jemima, William & John, rocf Horsham MM, Pa., dtd 1835,7, 29 (H)
1839, 5, 22. Jemima rocf Uwchland MM, Pa., dtd 1839,4,1 (H)
1839, 10, 23. Thomas Elwood gct New Garden MM, to m Elizabeth Galbraith (H)
1839, 12, 25. Thomas Elwood gct Salem MM (H)
1840, 6, 24. Thomas & w, Hannah, & ch, Amos H., Chalkley, Rebecca L., Jesse, Elijah L., Barclay, George, Sanford, Elizabeth H., Mary Ann & Zeba, gct Deerfield MM (H)
1841, 4, 21. Jemima gct Short Creek MM (H)
1842, 7, 20. Samuel P. con mcd (H)
1842, 8, 24. Lucinda B. recrq
1850, 12, 25. Isaac dis mcd
1851, 6, 25. Thomas con mcd
1851, 7, 23. Jemima N. Dungan (form Vickers) con mcd (H)
1851, 7, 23. Rachel (form James) rpd mcd (H)
1851, 9, 24. Rachel dis (H)
1854, 1, 25. William con mcd (H)
1857, 4, 22. Margaret dis disunity (H)

VINE
1806, 9, 23. Keturah (form Borton) dis mcd

VORE
1806, 7, 22. Isaac & w, Eleanor, & ch, William, Isaac, Eleanor & Mordecai, rocf Pipe Creek MM, dtd 1806,2,15
1813, 12, 23. Cert rec for Rebecca from Exeter MM, Pa., dtd 1813,2,24, end to Stillwater MM

WADE
1808, 7, 21. Elizabeth dis
1815, 4, 20. Royal & w, Phebe, & ch, Nathan, Rhoda, Ruth, Hannah, Lydia & Rachel, gct Plainfield MM
1815, 4, 20. Mary and Sarah gct Plainfield MM
1815, 4, 20. Owen gct Plainfield MM

WALKER
1810, 5, 24. George & w, Anna, & ch, Ebenezar, Mary, Isaac & George Bruce, rocf Redstone MM, dtd 1810,6,1
1814, 7, 21. Isaac, minor, gct Redstone MM
1814, 12, 22. Anna dis
1815, 6, 22. George & s, Geo., gct Plainfield MM
1815, 11, 23. Ebenezer gct Short Creek MM
1818, 10, 21. Anna rst at Plainfield on consent of this Mtg

WARD
1837, 11, 22. Sarah (form Penrose) con mcd (H)

WARD, continued
1841, 11, 22. Sarah P. gct Plainfield MM (H)

WARF
1855, 6, 20. Martha (form James) dis mcd (H)

WEBSTER
1807, 8, 26. Phebe m John HALL
1807, 12, 30. Hannah m Knois DOUDNA

1807, 1, 20. John & w, Hannah, & ch, Hannah, John, Nathan, Joshua, Isaac & Eli, rocf Little Britain MM, Pa., dtd 1806,8,9
1807, 1, 20. Thomas rocf Little Britain MM, Pa., dtd 1806,9,8
1807, 3, 24. Wm., Phebe & Ann rocf Little Britain MM, Pa., dtd 1806,8,9

WEEKS
1863, 2, 25. Sarah Jane con mcd

WELLS
1812, 9, 20. Isaac, s Levi & Margaret, Belmont Co., O.; m in Concord MH, Susanna BUNDY, dt Josiah & Bethiah, Belmont Co.,O.
Ch: Josiah   b 1813, 8, 9
    William   " 1815, 8, 6
    Lewis   " 1817, 8, 9
    Moses B.   " 1820, 11, 30
    Jonathan   " 1821, 11, 16
    Elisha M.   " 1824, 4, 25
    Hannah L.   " 1825, 12, 29
    Ann B.   " 1828, 5, 14
    Amos Peas-
         ley   " 1831, 6, 21
    Ruth T.   " 1834, 9, 21
1867, 2, 21. Catherine T. m Malin HORTON

1802, 5, 15. Levi rocf Redstone MM, dtd 1802, 4, 2
1803, 3, 19. Abner & w, Deborah, rocf Nottingham MM, dtd 1802,11,27
1803, 5, 21. John & w, Catharine, & ch, Isaiah, Elizabeth, Susannah, Thomas & Sarah, rocf Redstone MM, dtd 1803,4,29
1804, 12, 18. William recrq
1805, 2, 19. Isaac recrq
1805, 2, 19. Margaret & s, Levi, recrq
1813, 5, 20. William & w, Margaret, & ch, Levi & John, gct Short Creek MM, O.
1814, 12, 22. Isaac & w, Susannah, & s, Josiah, gct Plainfield MM
1822, 7, 24. Isaac & w, Susanna, & ch, Josiah, William, Levi, Moses & Jonathan, rocf Flushing MM, dtd 1822,5,24
1827, 10, 24. Ann M. gct Deersfield MM
1828, 8, 20. Isaac & w, Susanna, & ch, Wm., Levi, Moses, Jonathan, Elisha & Hannah, gct Deerfield MM (H)
1836, 4, 20. Isaac & w, Susanna, & ch, William, Levi, Moses B., Jonathan, Elisha M., Hannah L., Ann B., Amos Peasley & Ruth, rocf Deerfield MM, dtd 1836,3,16

1838, 7, 25. William con mcd (H)
1839, 2, 20. Mary recrq (H)
1842, 3, 23. Isaac & w, Susanna, & ch, Jonathan, Hannah L., Ann, Amos P. & Ruth, gct Plainfield MM (H)
1842, 3, 23. Wm. & w, Mary, & ch, David & Isaac, gct Plainfield MM (H)
1844, 6, 19. Isaac & w, Susanna, & ch, Elisha, Ann B., Amos P. & Ruth, rocf Plainfield MM, dtd 1844,3,14 (H)
1844, 6, 19. Hannah rocf Plainfield MM, dtd 1844,3,14 (H)
1844, 11, 22. Wm. & w, Mary, & ch, David & Sarah Ann, rocf Plainfield MM, dtd 1844, 7,18 (H)
1846, 4, 22. Hannah L. W. Paxton (form Wells) dis mcd (H)
1850, 6, 19. Levi dis mcd (H)
1854, 9, 20. Elisha gct Gwynedd MM, Pa.
1865, 8, 23. Sarah Ann Luman (Looman in women's minutes) (form Wells) con mcd (H)
1865, 8, 23. Slisha rocf Plainfield MM, dtd 1867,3,25 (H)
1870, 5, 24. Martha Devult (form Wells) con mcd (H)   [1867,3,25 (H)]
1867, 9, 25. Elisha rocf Plainfield MM, dtd

WHARTON
1819, 12, 1. Joel, s Ezra & Martha, Harrison Co., O.; m in Concord MH, Abigail BUNDY, dt Josiah & Bathia, Belmont Co., O.

1820, 1, 19. Abijah gct Short Creek MM

WHITACRE
1807, 5, 19. Ann rocf Goose Creek MM, Va., dtd 1806,11,24
1822, 9, 25. Maria rocf Westland MM, dtd 1822,8,22

WHITE
1803, 10, 19. Rachel m Thomas BERRY
1805, 10, 2. Jesse, s Jesse & Mary, Belmont Co., O.; m in "Head of Wheeling", Sarah PICKERING, dt Jacob & Lydia, Jefferson Co., O.
1818, 5, 27. Thomas, s Nathaniel & Phebe, Jefferson Co., O.; m in Concord MH, Mary COPE, dt George & Abigail, Belmont Co., O.
Ch: Eliza   b 1820, 9, 10
    Ann   " 1823, 1, 13
    George   " 1825, 10, 16
    Rachel   " 1828, 12, 21
----, --, --. Isaac & Hannah
Ch: Martha Janeb 1829, 11, 17
    David
      Goucher " 1829, 2, 18
    Rachel Ann " 1831, 4, 5
    Mary Ade-
       line   " 1833, 6, 17
    Thomas
      William " 1834, 10, 24
    Margaret
      Elma   " 1837, 1, 30

WHITE, Isaac & Hannah, continued
    Ch: Asenath
        Anabella   b 1839, 11, 3
        Wm. Hamil-
            ton " 1842, 7, 8

1802, 6, 19. John & w, Jane, & ch, Anne &
    Phebe, rocf Westland MM, dtd 1802,4,24
1802, 6, 19. Jesse & w, Mary, & ch, Rachel,
    Jesse, Israel & Mary, rocf Westland MM,
    dtd 1802,4,24
1807, 1, 20. Isaac & w, Jane, & ch, Sarah,
    Anna, Elizabeth & Aaron, rocf Goose Creek
    MM, dtd 1806,10,27
1818, 4, 23. Jesse & w, Sarah, & ch, Jacob,
    Mary, Lydia, Rhoda, Sarah & Jane, rocf
    Stillwater MM
1818, 8, 19. Mary gct Short Creek MM
1819, 2, 24. Mary returned cert as she will
    reside in limits
1819, 6, 23. Thomas & w, Mary, rocf Short
    Creek MM
1821, 3, 21. Thomas & w, Mary, gct Stillwater
    MM
1823, 9, 24. Mary & ch, Eliza & Ann, gct
    Stillwater MM
1827, 7, 25. Hannah (form Berry) dis mcd to
    first cousin
1829, 2, 25. Isaac rocf New Garden MM, dtd
    1828,12,25 (H)
1833, 3, 20. Hannah recrq (H)
1835, 3, 25. Isaac & w, Hannah, & ch, Mar
    tha Jane, David G. & Mary Adaline, gct
    New Garden MM (H)
1838, 5, 23. Isaac & w, Hannah, & ch, Mar-
    tha Jane, Mary Adaline & Margaret Elma,
    rocf New Garden MM, dtd 1837,10,26 (H)
1854, 9, 20. Martha Jane Hunt (form White)
    con mcd (H)
1860, 6, 20. Isaac & w, Hannah, & s, William,
    gct Salem MM (H)
1860, 6, 20. Margaret Elma & Asenath Ara-
    bella, gct Salem MM (H)

WHITEHEAD
1813, 3, 27. Elisha & w, Ralph, & ch, Samuel,
    Hannah, Jesse, William, Mary, David, rocf
    New York MM, dtd 1812,12,12
1816, 11, 20. Hannah Paxton (form Whitehead)
    dis mcd
1819, 7, 21. Samuel dis
1822, 12, 25. Mary Paxton (form Whitehead)
    dis mcd

WICKERSHAM
1802, 8, 21. Isaac & w, Elizabeth, rocf Hope-
    well MM, dtd 1802,3,1, end from Westland
    MM, 1802,6,26

WILEMAN
1805, 12, 24. Cert rec for Abraham & Latitia
    from South River MM, Va., end to Salem MM

WILEY
1858, 9, 22. Hannah rocf Stillwater MM, dtd
    1858,8,21 (H)
1867, 1, 23. Hannah dis jas (H)

WILLETTS
1805, 12, 24. Elizabeth rocf Deep River MM,
    N. C., dtd 1805,9,2

WILLIAMS
1804, 4, 26. Elizabeth m Joseph GARRETSON
1804, 5, 30. Samuel, s Robert & Anne, Bel-
    mont Co., O.; m in Concord MH, Sarah
    ARNOLD, dt Joseph & Sarah, Belmont Co., O.
    Ch: Joseph
        Anna
        Sally
        Robert
        Mary
        Elizabeth
        Peninah
1806, 12, 31. Rebecca m Abel GILBERT

1802, 8, 21. Richard & Sarah & dt, Elizabeth,
    rocf Core Sound MM, N. C., dtd 1802,6,?
1804, 5, 22. Mary & dt, Rebecca, & Mary, rocf
    Wrightsborough MM, Ga., dtd 1804,3,3
1804, 7, 24. Ruth rocf Wrightsborough MM,
    Ga., dtd 1804,3,3
1805, 5, 21. Richard & fam gct Short Creek
    MM, O.
1805, 7, 23. Henry & w, Zilphah, & ch, Abby,
    Job, Aaron, Isaiah, Elias, Lydia, John &
    Anna, rocf Wrightsborough MM, Ga., dtd
    1805,4,6
1813, 8, 26. John gct Stillwater MM, to m
    Sarah Patterson
1818, 9, 23. Samuel & w, Sarah, & ch, Jo-
    seph, Anna, Sally, Robert, Mary, Eliza-
    beth & Peninah, gct Stillwater MM
1818, 9, 23. Anna gct Stillwater MM

WILSON
1807, 4, 30. Martha m Wm. ASKEW
1815, 12, 27. Daniel, s Skidmore & Sarah,
    Belmont Co., O.; m in Concord MH, Mary
    DEWEES, dt Owen & Mary, Belmont Co., O.

1806, 5, 27. Isaac & w, Rebecca, & ch, Han-
    nah & Stephen, rocf Abington MM, Pa., dtd
    1806,4,28
1806, 5, 27. Hugh rocf Abington MM, Pa., dtd
    1806,4,28
1806, 5, 27. Isaac Jr. rocf Abington MM, Pa.,
    dtd 1806,4,28
1806, 5, 28. Martha rocf Abington MM, Pa.,
    dtd 1806,4,28
1807, 11, 24. Samuel rocf Gwyned MM, Pa., dtd
    1807,9,29
1810, 2, 22. Samuel & fam rocf Pipe Creek
    MM, dtd 1808,4,16
1819, 7, 21. James Steer, Jr. gct Flushing
    MM, O., to m Ruth Wilson

WILSON, continued

1837, 6, 21. Margaret gct Deerfield MM (H)

1841, 6, 23. Susanna rocf Freeport MM, dtd
1841,2,27 (H)

1845, 5, 21. Sarah gct Freeport MM (H)

1855, 4, 25. Elizabeth (form Updegraff) con
mcd (H)

WINTER

1812, 2, 20. Jonathan rocf West Hartford MM,
Conn., dtd 1811,9,11

WITCHEL

1808, 6, 23. John & w, Mary, rocf Abington
MM, Pa., dtd 1808,4,25

1809, 12, 21. John & w, Mary, gct Plainfield
MM

WOOD

1803, 9, 22. Rachel m Solomon LUPTON

1802, 7, 17. Rachel rocf Crooked Run MM, dtd
1801,5,30, end by Westland MM, 1801,12,26

1806, 7, 22. Aaron & w, Elizabeth, & ch,
Moses, Israel, Susanna, Sarah, Catharine,
Zachariah & Wm., rocf Mt. Pleasant MM,
Va., dtd 1805,12,28

1809, 12, 21. Cert rec for Robert & w, Mary,
& ch, Joseph, Sarah, Abigail, Benjamin,
John, Hannah, Jesse & Rachel, from Young
St. MM, Can., dtd 1809,9,14, end to Short
Creek MM

1813, 5, 20. Robert & w, Mary, & ch, Joseph,
Sarah, Abigail, Benjamin, John, Hannah,
Jesse, Rachel, Thomas & Robert. gct Short
Creek MM, O.

WOODMANSEE

1851, 9, 24. Delilah Ann (form Kennard) dis
mcd (H)

WOODROW

1802, 4, 17. Mary rocf Southland MM, Va., dtd
1801,9,30

WORREL

1803, 3, 19. Jonathan & ch, Sarah, Benjamin
& Nathaniel, recrq

1803, 5, 21. Eleanor rocf Robeson MM, dtd
1798,11,27, end by Redstone MM 1801,7,31
& by Westland MM 1803,3,26

*   *   *   *   *   *   *

BRANSON

1822, 7, 24. Abraham D. rocf Hopewell MM, Va.
dtd 1822,1,10

1823, 8, 20. Israel Hirst gct Flushing MM, to
m Catharine Branson

HUNT

1854, 9, 20. Martha Jane (form White) con
mcd (H)

1860, 6, 20. Martha Jane & Mary Adaline gct

WRIGHT

1813, 3, 10. Joseph, s Wm. & Unice, Belmont
Co., O.; m in Concord MH, Ann PICKERING,
dt John & Sarah, Belmont Co., O.

1802, 11, 20. Hannah & ch, Benjamin & Abigail,
rocf Dublin MM, Ireland, dtd 1802,3,16

1803, 6, 18. James & Nehemiah, minors, rocf
Dublin MM, Ireland, dtd 1802,9,15

1803, 6, 18. James rocf Hopewell MM, Va., dtd
1802,9,8, end by Crooked Run MM, 1803,4,2

1803, 6, 18. John rocf Dublin MM, Ireland,
dtd 1802,3,16

1803, 6, 18. Hannah, w James, & dt, Phebe,
rocf Crooked Run MM, dtd 1803,3,5

1803, 6, 18. Joseph Sr. rocf Dublin MM, Ireland, dtd 1802,9,15

1806, 2, 18. Joseph gct Baltimore MM

1807, 1, 20. Sarah rocf Crooked Run MM, dtd
1806,4,5

1807, 1, 20. Wm. & w, Eunice, & ch, John,
William, Elizabeth & Rebecca, rocf Crooked
Run MM, dtd 1806,4,5

1807, 2, 24. Cert rec for Robert & fam from
Fairfax MM, dtd 1806,4,26, end to Short
Creek MM, O.

1807, 8, 18. James gct Baltimore MM

1807, 12, 27. Joseph rocf Hopewell MM, dtd
1807,9,7

1808, 10, 20. Rebecca recrq

1810, 5, 24. Rebecca gct Plainfield MM

1825, 8, 24. Benjamin & w, Hannah, & ch, Wm.
M., Charles, Parvin & Benjamin H., rocf
Exeter MM, dtd 1825,6,29

YARNALL

1802, 11, 20. Phebe rocf Crooked Run MM, Va.,
dtd 1801,1,8, end by Westland MM, 1802,
6,20

YATES

1821, 6, 20. Anna (form Piggott) dis mcd

1826, 9, 20. Anna rst at Plainfield MM on
consent of this mtg

1828, 12, 24. Ann rocf Plainfield MM, dtd
1828,10,3 (H)

*   *   *   *   *   *   *

Salem MM (H)

PATTON

1803, 5, 21. Wm. & w, Rachel, & ch, Grace,
Mahlon, Wm., Rachel, John & Sarah, rocf
Wrightsborough MM, Ga., dtd 1803,3,23

PERKINS

1805, 6, 18. Ann (form Jenkins) dis mcd

SHORT CREEK MONTHLY MEETING

Short Creek Monthly Meeting was established in Jefferson County, Ohio, 3rd Mo. 17th, 1804, by Redstone Quarterly Meeting. It had been a preparative meeting under Concord Monthly Meeting. Short Creek Monthly Meeting was made up of Short Creek and Plymouth Preparative Meetings. Short Creek Monthly Meeting established a meeting for worship called Cross Creek on 6th Mo. 16th, 1804, and this was made a preparative meeting 4th Mo. 20th, 1805 and West Grove Meeting for worship was established 2nd Mo. 20th, 1808. Short Creek Monthly Meeting was divided 2nd Mo. 24th, 1915, Mt. Pleasant and Long Run Preparative Meetings becoming Mt. Pleasant Monthly Meeting and West Grove and Georgetown Preparative Meetings constituting Short Creek Monthly Meeting.

Among the early families who were members of Short Creek Monthly Meeting were Jonathan Taylor, Nathan Updegraph, Israel Wilson, Jacob Holloway, Joseph Wright, Samuel Holloway, John Cadwallader, Isaac Whealdon, William Hoge, Enoch Chandler, Isaac Schooley, Evan Roman, Darwin Conroe, Jacob Cope, Josiah Wood, Jacob Ong, Jacob Lewis, Joseph Talbot, Benjamin Stanton, Henry Lewis, Evans Cadwallader, Jesse Fowke, and a number of others whose names will appear in the genealogical records.

RECORDS

ACKLEY

1805, 3, 16. Hannah recrq

1808, 3, 22. Hannah Gray (form Ackley) dis mou

1822, 5, 21. Mary rocf Sadsbury MM, dtd 1821, 12,4

ADAMS

1870, --, --. Elizabeth d

1881, 1, 8. William d

----, --, --. Ellsworth & Kate (G)
    Ch: Maud   d 1918,--,--
        Anna May   " 1925,10,13

1809, 5, 23. Beulah recrq

1816, 6, 18. Thomas & w, Ann, & dt, Ruth, rocf Falls MM, dtd 1816,4,5

1816, 11, 19. Thomas & fam gct Miami MM

1835, 5, 19. Bulah gct Flushing MM

1862, 11, 19. Rachel dis jW (G)

1865, 8, 23. Rachel gct New Sharon MM, Ia. (G)

1884, 6, 25. Lizzie S. (form Cope) dropped from mbrp (G)

1894, 2, 21. Kate recrq (G)

1895, 9, 25. William & w, Henrietta, recrq (G)

1898, 6, 22. William & Henrietta dropped from mbrp (G)

1902, 2, 19. Mary recrq (G)

1902, 8, 20. William & Henrietta dropped from mbrp (G)

1906, 4, 25. Nellie Lorea recrq (G)

1907, 9, 25. Maud recrq (G)

1911, 4, 19. Edith recrq (G)

1918, 12, 25. Anna May, dt Elsworth & Kate, recrq (G)

1925, 1, 21. Ruth, minor, recrq (G)

ADY

1821, 11, 20. Rachel (form Hall) dis mcd

1824, 3, 23. Levina rst

1824, 6, 22. Betty (form Harris) dis mcd

1831, 10, 18. Cherry [Aidy] (form Howard) dis

AICHER

1892, 10, 19. E. C. recrq (G)

AINSCOUCH

1914, 1, 21. Thomas recrq (G)

AIRN

1898, 5, 25. Ida M. relrq (G)

ALBERTSON

1804, 9, 15. Joseph & w, Elvy, & dt, Penina, rocf Great Contentney MM, N. C., dtd 1804, 2,11, end by Concord MM 1804,7,24

ALEXANDER

1843, 4, 18. Sarah (form Judkins) dis mcd & jas

ALLEN

----, --, --. Reuben d 1875,7,10; m Joanna -----

    d 1869,12,--
    Ch: Isaac   b 1813, 9, 16.
        Rebecca   " 1815, 4, 27
        Esther   " 1816, 9, 23
        Amos   " 1818, 5, 13
        Mary Jane   " 1820, 11, 16 d 1822,10,25 bur Short Creek
        Ruthann   b 1825, 5, 23
        Joanna   " 1827, 8, 2
        James M.   " 1831, 9, 10

----, --, --. Wm. m Mabel Loretta STARBUCK, dt Thos. S. & Abbie S. (Hall), b 1899,5,27

1813, 7, 20. Joanna (form McMillan) dis mcd

1813, 8, 24. Reuben rocf Nottingham MM, dtd 1813,5,7

1819, 10, 19. Joanna rst

1828, 12, 23. Joanna dis jH

1833, 10, 22. Rebecca Packer (form Allen) dis mcd & jH

1834, 3, 18. Isaac dis jH

1835, 1, 20. Esther, Ruthanna, Joanna & James, ch Reuben & Joanna, gct Flushing MM

1835, 4, 23. Reuben & w, Joanna, & ch, Ruth Ann, Joanna & James, gct Flushing MM (H)

1840, 8, 20. Isaac gct Flushing MM (H)

ALLMON

1858, 8, 24. Linton Hall gct Middleton MM, to m Ann W. Allmon

ALLOWAY

1827, 6, 19. Sarah dis

ALSON

1874, 12, 24. Mandales recrq (G)

AMSCOUGH

1895, 3, 20. Jane & Maggie recrq (G)

ANDERSON

1879, 1, 23. John recrq (G)

1898, 2, 23. Nancy R. relrq (G)

1903, 6, 24. John dropped from mbrp (G)

1907, 4, 24. Mathew dropped from mbrp (G)

1929, 7, 24. Charles & Walter dropped from mbrp (G)

ANDREWS

1829, 12, 23. Daniel, s John & Sarah, Columbiana Co., O.; m in Short Creek MH, Mary RATCLIFF, dt Isaac & Margaret, Jefferson Co., O.

1830, 3, 23. Mary gct Upper Springfield MM

1851, 4, 22. John Lloyd gct Upper Springfield MM, to m Margaret Andrew

APPLEGARTH

1907, 4, 24. Martha dropped from mbrp (G)

ARCHER

1892, 10, 19. Evaline recrq (G)

ARMSTRONG
1843, 8, 22. Juliann (form Lewis) rpd mcd

ARNOLD
1862, 11, 19. Caleb & Phebe dis jW
1873, 4, 24. Alfred recrq (G)
1873, 7, 24. Dorotha recrq (G)
1880, 5, 20. Alfred dis disunity (G)
1888, 10, 24. Maggie S. dropped from mbrp (G)
1907, 4, 24. Blanche dropped from mbrp (G)
1914, 4, 22. Rhoda recrq (G)
1915, 2, 24. Orville & Lottie recrq (G)

ARTHERS
1891, 12, 23. Clark recrq (G)

ASHEAD
1857, 8, 18. Hannah (form Hoyle) dis mcd to
first cousin
1866, 8, 21. Hannah rst (W)
1866, 10, 23. Hannah S. gct Upper Evesham MM,
N. Y. (W)

ASHMAN
1914, 1, 21. Charles & Elizabeth recrq (G)

ASHMOND
1907, 4, 24. Dina dropped from mbrp (G)

ASHTON
1874, 9, 23. Richard, s Barak & Jane, Columbiana Co., O.; m in Smithfield, Eliza G.
McGREW, dt James W. & Ann G., Jefferson
Co., O.
1897, 7, 29. Harmon J., s Richard & Eliza,
d bur Harrisville (ae 21)
1901, 10, 23. Rena Jane m Elwood PEACOCK

1875, 5, 18. Eliza G gct Middleton MM (W)
1884, 3, 18. Richard & w, Eliza G., & ch,
Harman J., Rena J., William B. & Albert H.,
rocf Middleton MM, dtd 1884,2,16 (W)
1902, 9, 23. Richard & w, Eliza G., gct Plainfield MM (W)
1908, 2, 18. Albert H. gct Plainfield MM, Ind.
(W)
1908, 2, 18. Wm. B. gct Plainfield MM, Ind.
(W)

ASKEW
1862, 11, 19. Benjamin, Mary, Parker, Rebecca
dis jW

ATKINS
1892, 10, 19. Anne J. recrq (G)

ATKINSON
1812, 4, 30. William, s Thos. & Ann, Jefferson Co., O.; m in Short Creek MH, Nanny
TAYLOR, dt Christopher & Elizabeth, Jefferson Co., O.
   Ch: Keziah   b 1813, 5, 30
       Mary Ann   " 1815, 4, 20

   Ch: Elizabeth
      T.   b 1817, 9, 21 d 1819, 2, 5
      bur Short Creek
      Ruth   b 1820, 5, 13
      Daniel   " 1824, 5, 24
      Thomas   " 1824, 9, 21 (?)
      Rachel   " 1829, 10, 14
1817, 5, 28. Daniel, s Thos. & Ruth, Jefferson Co., O.; m in Mt. Pleasant, Mary HALL,
dt John & Esther
1820, 8, 11. Ruth d
----, --, --. ----- m Catharine WILLIAMS, dt
Wm. C. & Rebecca (Vanlaw), b 1838,12,13
d 1925,4,26 bur Harrisville
1843, 3, 23. Mary d ae 56 bur Short Creek
1844, 8, 28. Daniel, s Thos. & Ruth, Belmont
Co., O.; m in Concord, Rachel BAILY, dt
James & Rachel, Belmont Co., O.
   Ch: Mary   b 1845, 10, 6
      William   " 1847, 8, 20
      Ruth   " 1852, 3, 8
----, --, --. William & Catharine
   Ch: Thomas E. b 1868, 12, 6 d 1889,12,13
      bur Stillwater
      Rachel M. b 1871, 4, 21
      Emma Jane " 1872, 10, 12 " 1878, 5, 8
      Rebecca W." 1874, 11, 3 [bur Harriv.
      Edith   " 1877, 10, 10
      Anna Mary " 1881, 1, 28 " 1898,11,15
      bur Stillwater
1898, 10, 19. Edith m Wm. F. PACKER (W)
1899, 3, 23. Rachel M. m Wilson C. HIRST (W)
1905, 3, 12. William d ae 58 bur Harrisville
1914, 2, 25. Rebecca W. m Edward Y. GAMBLE
(W)

1807, 7, 18. Thomas & w, Ruth, & ch, Rachel,
Ruth, Edy & Daniel, rocf Bush River MM,
S. C., dtd 1807,3,20
1813, 11, 23. Edith Markee (form Atkinson) dis
mcd
1815, 5, 23. Ruth Moore (form Atkinson) dis
mcd
1816, 5, 2. Rachel Oxley (form Atkinson) dis
mcd
1818, 7, 21. Daniel & w, Mary, gct Concord MM
1821, 6, 19. Daniel & w, Mary, rocf Concord
MM, dtd 1821,5,23
1831, 7, 19. Mary dis
1831, 11, 22. Keziah Embree (form Atkinson)
con mcd
1835, 12, 22. William A. & w, Nancy, & ch, Daniel, Thos. & Rachel, gct Stillwater MM
1862, 11, 19. Daniel & w, Rachel, & ch, Mary,
Ruth & Wm., dis jW (G)
1865, 11, 21. Daniel dis jG (W)
1871, 10, 24. William con mcd (W)
1872, 4, 23. Caroline rst on consent of
Flushing MM (W)
1874, 12, 22. Mary Bitler (form Atkinson) dis
mcd & jG (W)
1875, 1, 19. Ruth Packer (form Atkinson) dis
disunity (W)

ATKINSON, continued

1875, 11, 23. Rebecca (form Watson) dis mcd (W)

1876, 2, 22. Thomas E. & Rachel M., ch Wm. & Catharine, recrq (W)

ATWOOD

1904, 3, 23. Clarence C. & w, Lillian, & dt, Hazel, recrq (G)

AULD

1886, 5, 19. Lee recrq (G)

AULT

1840, 8, 20. Amy gct Plainfield MM (H)

1891, 1, 21. Rosa dropped from mbrp (G)

BABB

1892, 2, 24. Lewis A. & Nelie A. recrq (G)

1900, 7, 25. Amelia relrq (G)

BAHL

1902, 10, 7. Martha L. d

1897, 4, 14. Lewis A. d bur Harrisville

BAILEY

1814, 9, 29. Elizabeth Jr. m Chas. LOWNES

1818, 1, 23. Jacob d bur Short Creek

1818, 12, 9. Mary m Wm. DILWORTH

1822, 1, 30. Margaret m Henry CREW

----, --, --. Henry & Mary
  Ch: Jane b 1823, 9, 27
    Sarah " 1825, 3, 1

1833, 9, 25. William, s Stephen & Tabitha, Belmont Co., O.; m in Mt. Pleasant, Sarah FLANNER, dt Wm. & Peninah, Belmont Co., O.

1833, 10, 23. Samuel, s Micajah & Mary, Belmont Co., O.; m in Mt. Pleasant, Harriet EMBRE, dt John & Huldah, Belmont Co., O.

1844, 8, 28. Rachel m Daniel ATKINSON

1846, 10, 28. Jehu, s Edmond & Margaret, Belmont Co., O.; m in Concord, Martha STEER, dt James & Ruth, Belmont Co., O.

1873, 5, 29. Rosella m Jonathan BINNS (W)

1896, 5, 20. Oscar J., s Lindley P. & Elizabeth, Belmont Co., O.; m in Concord, Mary Ann BRACKEN, dt Lindley M. & Anna, Belmont Co., O. (W)
  Ch: Oliver
    Brackin b 1901, 6, 14

1901, 10, 9. Alva C., s Lindley P. & Elizabeth S., Belmont Co., O.; m in Concord, Laura E. STEER, dt Nathan & Mary Jane, Belmont Co., O. (W)

----, --, --. Oliver Brackin, s Oscar J. & Mary Anna (Brackin); m Rebecca STEER, dt Wilson J. & Mary C. (Hall), b 1903,8,10
  Ch: Oscar Wil-
    son b 1925, 7, 23
    Warren
    Oliver " 1927, 8, 28
    Margaret
    Rebecca " 1931, 6, 17

1928, 7, 5. Raymond C., s Alva C. & Laura E., Belmont Co., O.; m in Colerain, Edith M. BRACKIN, dt Ogden J. & Rachel S., Belmont Co., O., b 1906,6,11 (W)

1814, 7, 19. Emmor & w, Elizabeth, & ch, Henry, Mary, Abraham, Jacob, Ezra, Hannah, Phebe, Emmor, Martha & Ann, rocf Baltimore MM for W. Dist., dtd 1814,6,8

1814, 7, 19. Margaret & Elizabeth rocf Baltimore MM for W. Dist., dtd 1814,6,8

1819, 11, 23. Henry gct Plainfield MM, to m Mary Foulke

1820, 4, 18. Henry gct Plainfield MM

1822, 4, 23. Henry & w, Mary, & ch, Elizabeth & Joel, rocf Plainfield MM, dtd 1822, 3,21

1825, 5, 24. Henry & w, Mary, & ch, Elizabeth, Joel, Jane & Sarah, gct Somerset MM

1828, 4, 22. Elizabeth rocf Newgarden MM, dtd 1828,2,26, end to Smithfield

1828, 5, 20. Ezra gct Smithfield MM

1828, 10, 21. Emmor & w, Elizabeth, & ch, Emmor, Martha & Ann, gct Flushing MM

1828, 10, 21. Phebe & Hannah gct Flushing MM

1829, 9, 22. Cert for Emmor & fam lost, new one granted

1829, 11, 26. Hannah gct Flushing MM (H)

1829, 11, 26. Phebe gct Flushing MM (H)

1831, 11, 22. Phebe & Hannah dis jH

1834, 3, 18. Harriett gct Stillwater MM

1836, 1, 19. William rocf Somerset MM, dtd 1835,11,26

1837, 5, 23. William & w, Sarah, & ch, Abigail F. & Elizabeth M., gct Pennsville MM

1847, 3, 23. Martha L. gct Somerset MM

1848, 3, 21. Sally rocf Westland MM, dtd 1848, 2,23

1855, 3, 20. Uriah rocf Stillwater MM, dtd 1855,2,20

1856, 9, 23. Rosella, minor, recrq

1862, 11, 19. Mary dis jW

1862, 11, 19. Adaline dis jW (G)

1862, 11, 19. Allen dis jW (G)

1862, 11, 19. Almedia dis jW (G)

1862, 11, 19. Asenath dis jW (G)

1862, 11, 19. Benjamin dis jW (G)

1862, 11, 19. Caleb dis jW (G)

1862, 11, 19. Charles dis jW (G)

1862, 11, 19. Delitha dis jW (G)

1862, 11, 19. Dempsey dis jW (G)

1862, 11, 19. Edmund dis jW (G)

1862, 11, 19. Edwin H. dis jW (G)

1862, 11, 19. Elizabeth dis jW (G)

1862, 11, 19. Elvira dis jW (G)

1862, 11, 19. Emmor dis jW (G)

1862, 11, 19. Fanny dis jW (G)

1862, 11, 19. Hezekiah dis jW (G)

1862, 11, 19. Isaac dis jW (G)

1862, 11, 19. Isaac Hoover dis jW (G)

1862, 11, 19. Jacob dis jW (G)

1862, 11, 19. James E. dis jW (G)

1862, 11, 19. Jehu dis jW (G)

BAILEY, continued

1862, 11, 19. Jephtha dis jW (G)
1862, 11, 19. Jesse dis jW (G)
1862, 11, 19. Jesse M. dis jW (G)
1862, 11, 19. Joel dis jW (G)
1862, 11, 19. John dis jW (G)
1862, 11, 19. Joseph dis jW (G)
1862, 11, 19. Lindley dis jW (G)
1862, 11, 19. Lucy dis jW (G)
1862, 11, 19. Lydia dis jW (G)
1862, 11, 19. Lydia Jr. dis jW (G)
1862, 11, 19. Lydia J. dis jW (G)
1862, 11, 19. Margaret dis jW (G)
1862, 11, 19. Maria dis jW (G)
1862, 11, 19. Martha dis jW (G)
1862, 11, 19. Martha L. dis jW (G)
1862, 11, 19. Mary dis jW (G)
1862, 11, 19. Mary Ann dis jW (G)
1862, 11, 19. Melvina dis jW (G)
1862, 11, 19. Milicent dis jW (G)
1862, 11, 19. Nancy dis jW (G)
1862, 11, 19. Priscilla dis jW (G)
1862, 11, 19. Prudence dis jW (G)
1862, 11, 19. Rachel dis jW (G)
1862, 11, 19. Robert dis jW (G)
1862, 11, 19. Ruth dis jW (G)
1862, 11, 19. Samuel G. dis jW (G)
1862, 11, 19. Sarah dis jW (G)
1862, 11, 19. Sarah Ann dis jW (G)
1862, 11, 19. Sidney dis jW (G)
1862, 11, 19. Silas dis jW (G)
1862, 11, 19. Sina dis jW (G)
1862, 11, 19. Stephen dis jW (G)
1862, 11, 19. William L. dis jW (G)
1865, 8, 22. Uriah gct Somerset MM (W)
1873, 5, 22. Jane recrq (G)
1882, 5, 23. James Hervey Binns gct Flushing
     MM, to m Ida Bailey (W)
1883, 6, 20. Smith M. recrq (G)
1892, 10, 19. Anna recrq (G)
1894, 7, 25. S. M. dropped from mbrp (G)
1896, 8, 18. Mary Anna gct Stillwater MM (W)
1903, 12, 22. Laura E. gct Stillwater MM (W)
1931, 4, 21. Oliver S. & w, Rebecca S., & ch,
     Oscar Wilson & Warren Oliver, rocf Still-
     water MM, dtd 1931,3,25 (W)

BALDERSON

1820, 4, 21. Mordecai d ae 65 bur Short Creek

1807, 1, 17. Mary [Balderstone] rocf Newgar-
     den MM, dtd 1806,12,4
1809, 10, 24. Deborah Jr. rocf Newgarden MM,
     Pa., dtd 1809,9,7
1809, 10, 24. Mordecai & w, Deborah, & ch,
     Mordecai, Catharine, Joseph, Jonathan &
     Esther, rocf Newgarden MM, Pa., dtd 1809,
     9,14
1811, 6, 18. Mary dis
1811, 6, 18. Deborah Bush (form Balderson)
     dis mcd
1814, 5, 24. Mordecai Jr. dis mcd
1816, 4, 23. Joseph, minor, gct Newgarden MM,

Pa.

1816, 6, 18. Catharine [Balderston] dis
1817, 4, 22. Jonathan dis disunity

BALDWIN

1892, 10, 19. Mary recrq (G)
1911, 3, 22. Mary Shores relrq (G)

BALL

1836, 5, 17. Jane d bur Short Creek

1807, 8, 15. James rocf Fairfax MM, dtd
     1806,11,22
1807, 8, 15. Martha recrq
1809, 8, 22. Henry & w, Jane, rocf Fairfax
     MM, dtd 1808,10,22
1835, 10, 20. James R. gct Smithfield MM, to
     m Mary Ann Talbott
1836, 8, 23. James R. gct Smithfield MM
1837, 11, 21. Sarah (form Pyle) dis mcd
1839, 3, 19. Henry dis mcd
1840, 6, 23. Mary Ann & ch, Henry C. & Mary
     Cassandra, rocf Smithfield MM, dtd 1840,
     6,22
1840, 7, 21. James P. & w, Mary Ann, & ch,
     Henry C. & Cassandra, gct Chesterfield MM
1890, 1, 22. Joseph recrq (G)
1890, 12, 24. Joseph & w & three ch recrq (G)
1897, 9, 22. Joseph & fam relrq (G)
1907, 9, 25. Joseph recrq (G)
1908, 4, 22. David U. recrq (G)
1908, 4, 22. Mary, Martha & Lizzie recrq (G)

BALLARD

1824, 12, 21. Amy recrq
1903, 4, 22. Grant & Lilla recrq (G)
1907, 9, 25. Willard M. recrq (G)
1909, 10, 22. S. G. & Delilah relrq (G)
1913, 5, 21. Ernest dropped from mbrp (G)

BALLINGER

1857, 9, 8. Mary d ae 47
1858, 3, 31. William d ae 99 bur Smithfield

1821, 4, 24. Nathan Updegraff gct Smithfield
     MM, to m Cassandra [Ballenger]
1863, 4, 22. Thos. H. Terrell gct Smithfield
     MM, to m Rebecca Ballinger (W)

BALTEN

----, --, --. Samuel b 1761,11,25; m Sarah
     ----- b 1774,2,29
     Ch: Ruth   b 1796, 3, 11
         Lydia   " 1800, 7, 21
         Jesse   " 1804, 3, 28
         Samuel   " 1807, 12, 30
         Amy   " 1809, 1, 23
         Rhoda   " 1811, 9, 9
         Aaron   " 1813, 8, 8
         Priscilla " 1816, 2, 20
         Ira   " 1818, 4, 30

BANCROFT
1891, 11, 25. Catharine M. recrq (G)
1898, 4, 20. Joseph recrq (G)
1901, 2, 20. Lena Olive recrq (G)

BARBER
----, --, --. Samuel & Ann
    Ch: Sarah   b 1790, 10, 11
        Cornelius " 1793, 3, 21
        Abraham   " 1795, 11, 10
        Doritha   " 1798, 4, 28
        Elizabeth " 1802, 11, 8
        Samuel   " 1805, 8, 30
        Anne   " 1808, 11, 3
        James   " 1811, 12, 15
1808, 12, 28. Sarah m Geo. JAMES
1818, 12, 2. Dorothy m Asa HOLLOWAY
1823, 12, 31. Elizabeth m Moses LUKENS
1835, 1, 28. Ann m Townsend THOMAS
1852, 2, 5. Samuel d ae 84 bur West Grove

1805, 8, 17. Samuel & w, Ann, & ch, Sarah,
    Cornelius, Abram, Dorthy & Elizabeth,
    rocf Redstone MM, dtd 1805,5,3
1815, 9, 4. Cornelius dis mcd
1818, 2, 24. Rachel rocf Plainfield MM, dtd
    1818,1,22
1817, 10, 21. Abram gct Plainfield MM, to m
    Rachel Frame
1819, 12, 21. Abraham & w, Rachel, & dt, Eliza-
    beth, gct Flushing MM
1821, 8, 21. Cornelius rst at Flushing MM on
    consent of this mtg
1822, 11, 19. Rachel, minor, recrq
1823, 9, 23. Rachel & ch, Elizabeth & Ann,
    rocf Flushing MM, dtd 1822,6,21
1823, 9, 25. Abraham & w, Rachel, & ch,
    Elizabeth & Ann, rocf Flushing MM, dtd
    1823,6,21
1827, 5, 22. Elizabeth & ch, Susanna, Naomi &
    Samuel, rocf Flushing MM, dtd 1827,4,27
1829, 12, 22. Cornelius & w, Elizabeth, & ch,
    Susannah, Naomy, Abraham & William, gct
    Flushing MM
1836, 4, 19. James dis mcd
1839, 11, 19. Rachel Erskine (form Barber) dis
    mcd
1843, 5, 23. Samuel & w, Ann, gct Flushing MM
1851, 8, 19. Samuel & w, Ann, rocf Flushing
    MM, dtd 1851,7,24
1874, 6, 25. Rachel (form Crossley) dis mcd &
    jas (G)

BARCROFT
1902, 8, 20. Joseph dropped from mbrp (G)

BARCUS
1881, 2, 26. Leela recrq (G)
1881, 2, 26. Levi recrq (G)

BARKHURST
1888, 10, 24. Lelah dropped from mbrp (G)

BARKER
1894, 7, 25. Mary dropped from mbrp (G)

BARNES
1817, 5, 20. Meriam rocf Stillwater MM, dtd
    1817,2,22
1818, 3, 24. Meriam gct Stillwater MM
1830, 3, 23. Mary dis jH
1849, 1, 23. Sarah Elizabeth (form Hunnicutt)
    dis mcd
1849, 8, 21. Lucy Ann (form Ladd) dis mcd
1876, 5, 25. George E. recrq (G)
1884, 5, 21. Hester A. & Maggie recrq (G)
1884, 6, 25. George A. dropped from mbrp (G)
1886, 5, 19. Rena recrq (G)
1886, 5, 19. William recrq (G)
1886, 5, 19. Mary L. recrq (G)
1889, 2, 20. William dropped from mbrp (G)
1892, 10, 19. Edward recrq (G)

BARNHARD
1814, 7, 19. Alice rocf Newgarden MM, Pa.,
    dtd 1814,4,7
1821, 7, 24. Alice McMillan (form Barnhard)
    dis mcd
1821, 11, 20. Sarah (form Wood) dis mcd
1829, 9, 19. Sarah dis jH
1849, 9, 18. Jane (form Williams) dis mcd

BARNHART
1905, 4, 19. William recrq (G)
1905, 6, 17. Genevra Mary, dt James & Hattie
    (Finley) b (G)
1932, 4, 20. Mary Geneva recrq (G)

BARR
1881, 2, 26. Eliza recrq (G)
1884, 7, 23. Eliza dropped from mbrp (G)

BARRETT
1825, 10, 27. Warden, s Thos. & Margaret, Har-
    rison Co., O.; m in Harrisville, Mary HUR-
    FORD, dt John & Sarah, Jefferson Co., O.
1827, 5, 5. Baldin, s Thomas & Margaret,
    Harrison Co., O.; m in Short Creek MH,
    Mary Ann STREET, dt Griffith & Elizabeth,
    Harrison Co., O.

1810, 8, 20. Sarah, minor, rocf Redstone MM,
    dtd 1810,8,3
1827, 9, 18. Mary Ann gct Flushing MM
1829, 9, 22. Sarah dis jH
1843, 12, 19. Amy Manley (form Barret) con mcd
1850, 2, 11. Mary Ann rocf Flushing MM, dtd
    1849,9,20
1851, 3, 18. Mary Ann dis jH
1861, 9, 22. Mary dis jG
1861, 9, 22. Warden dis jG
1892, 10, 19. Mary recrq (G)

BARTON
1895, 3, 20. John Nelson recrq (G)
1898, 6, 22. John dropped from mbrp (G)

BAST
1892, 10, 19. Jose recrq (G)

BASSETT
1886, 7, 21. Minnie recrq (G)
1892, 10, 19. Minnie gct Cleveland MM (G)
1894, 3, 21. Amanda & Steven recrq (G)
1905, 2, 22. Minnie rocf Carmel MM, Ind. (G)
1912, 8, 14. Minnie rocf Adrian MM, Mich. (G)

BATES
1819, 5, 26. Margaret m Horton BROWN
1820, 10, 22. Sarah Ann, dt Elisha & Sarah J., b
1824, 6, 30. Anna m Ezekiel HARRIS
1825, 3, 30. Mary M. m Horton J. HOWARD
----, --, --. Joseph D. & Mary
    Ch: Thomas W. b 1826, 5, 2
        Joshua   " 1829, 8, 9
        Benjamin   " 1831, 9, 6
        Susanna P. " 1835, 8, 5 d 1856,10,13
          bur Smithfield
        Nathan P. b 1841, 11, 6
1835, 8, 26, Deborah H. m Joseph STEER
1854, 2, 21. Lydia, w Wm., d bur Smithfield
----, --, --. Joshua & Julia Ann   [ae 48
    Ch: Mary Alice b 1858, 7, 15
        Oliver   " 1860, 9, 4
        Catharine
          A.   " 1863, 6, 26
        Emma P.   " 1865, 8, 27 d 1866, 7,10
          Coal Creek, Ia.
        Susan L.   b 1869, 6, 14
        Amos P.   " 1874, 5, 16 " 1875, 8,29
          Coal Creek, Ia.

1817, 6, 24. Elisha & w, Sarah, & ch, Anna,
    Mary M., Lucy H., Rebecca, William J. &
    Deborah, rocf Waynook MM, Va., dtd 1817,5,3
1817, 6, 24. Elizabeth & ch, Matilda Jordan,
    Sarah Jordan, Margaret, Hannah, Benjamin,
    Fleming & Benjamin, rocf Waynook MM, Va.,
    dtd 1817,5,3
1829, 10, 30. Benjamin gct Marlborough MM, to
    m Lydia Johnson
1830, 7, 20. Benjamin gct Marlborough MM
1837, 5, 23. Elisha dis disunity
1838, 1, 23. Martha, Lucy H. & Rebecca dis
    disunity
1838, 1, 23. Wm. J. dis disunity
1838, 3, 20. Ann Scott (form Ricks) dis mcd
1838, 9, 18. Sarah Ann dis jas
1850, 10, 22. Robert B. Lawrence gct Smith-
    field MM, to m Tacy Bates
1856, 6, 24. William S. dis mcd
1856, 6, 24. Thomas dis mcd
1857, 9, 22. Mary Judkins (form Bates) dis mcd
1864, 4, 19. William dis jG

1864, 4, 19. Fleming dis jG
1865, 3, 21. Hannah dis jG (W)
1867, 12, 24. Benjamin L. con mcd (W)
1868, 6, 23. Benjamin L. gct Coal Creek MM,
    Ia. (W)
1877, 9, 18. Joshua con mcd (W)
1877, 9, 18. Julia A. (form Plummer) con mcd
    (W)
1877, 11, 20. Nathan Pusey dis jas & serving
    in Army in Civil War (W)
1878, 5, 21. Joshua & w, Juliann, & ch,
    Oliver L., Catharine A. & Susan L., gct
    Coal Creek MM, Ia. (W)
1878, 5, 21. Mary Alice gct Coal Creek MM, Ia.
    (W)

BATTIN
----, --, --. Samuel & Sarah
    Ch: Ruth   b 1796, 3, 11
        Nathan   " 1798, 2, 24
        Lydia   " 1800, 7, 21 d 1832, 8,31
        Sarah   " 1802, 4, 28
        Jesse   " 1804, 3, 28
        Thomas   " 1806, 1, 2
        Samuel   " 1807, 12, 30
        Amy   " 1810, 1, 23
        Rhoda   " 1811, 9, 9
        Aaron   " 1813, 8, 8
        Priscilla " 1816, 2, 20
        Tace   " 1818, 4, 30
1818, 6, 9. Nathan d bur Short Creek
1824, 12, 1. John, s John & Ann, Columbiana
    Co., O.; m in Mt. Pleasant, Sarah D.
    HOWARD, dt John & Cherry, Jefferson Co.,
    O., b 1804,1,21
1845, 2, 25. Sarah d ae 71
1852, 4, 17. Samuel d ae 90
1858, 5, 19. Ann d ae 88
1909, 8, 17. Emily Tomlinson d

1805, 5, 18. Sarah rocf Westland MM, dtd
    1805,2,23
1805, 11, 16. Samuel recrq
1806, 11, 15. Five minor ch of Samuel recrq
1815, 9, 4. Eli rocf Newgarden MM, dtd 1815,
    8,17
1815, 11, 21. Eli gct Newgarden MM, to m Phebe
    Pennock
1816, 7, 23. Phebe rocf Newgarden MM, dtd
    1816,5,16
1818, 9, 22. Phebe, w Eli, & dt, Jane, gct
    Newgarden MM
1821, 7, 24. Eli gct Sandy Spring MM
1822, 12, 24. John Jr. gct Sandy Spring MM
1823, 10, 21. Sarah Shannon (form Battin) dis
    mcd (1824,2,24 on men's minutes)
1824, 12, 21. Sarah D. gct Sandy Spring MM
1828, 12, 23. Lydia & Amy dis jH
1829, 1, 20. Sarah & Ruth dis jH
1834, 12, 25. Ruth gct Deerfield JM (H)
1835, 9, 22. Priscilla dis jH
1835, 11, 24. Aaron dis mcd
1840, 8, 20. Samuel & w, Sarah, gct Plainfield

BATTIN, continued
   MM (H)
1866, 11, 6. Emily T. gct Salem MM (H)
1874, 7, 21. Ruth Morris (form Battin) rst
   at Plymouth MM on consent of this mtg (W)

BEAL
1892, 10, 19. Samuel, Ida, Mary & Susie
   [Beals] recrq (G)
1903, 4, 22. Frederick D. & Catharine recrq
   (G)
1907, 3, 20. Frederick D. & Catharine dropped
   from mbrp (G)

BEARDSLEY
1892, 5, 24. Martha C. (form Cook) dis mcd
   (W)

BECK
1912, 2, 21. Lawrence recrq (G)

BEESON
1818, 10, 7. Mary m Jonathan FAWCETT
1821, 12, 26. Charity m Jacob P. FLANNER
1824, 12, 1. Rebecca m Isaac BROWN

1816, 7, 23. Charity, Rebecca & Ann rocf
   Middleton MM, dtd 1816,6,10
1816, 7, 23. Henry & w, Mary, & grand-dt,
   Mary, rocf Middleton MM, dtd 1816,6,10
1818, 12, 22. Sarah & ch, Henry, Rachel,
   Charity, Elisha, Jesse, Edward & John,
   rocf Middleton MM, dtd 1818,6,15
1819, 11, 23. Sarah & ch, Henry, Rachel,
   Charity, Elisha, Jesse, Edward & John, gct
   Newgarden MM

BELL
1892, 10, 19. Harriet, Jesse, Charles &
   Arthur recrq (G)

BENEDICT
1812, 12, 22. Aaron & w, Esther, & ch, Sarah,
   Elizabeth & Aaron, rocf Peru MM, dtd 1812,
   9,24
1812, 12, 22. Aaron & w, Elizabeth, rocf Peru
   MM, dtd 1812,9,24
1813, 4, 20. Reuben rocf Peru MM, dtd 1812,9,
   24
1814, 9, 20. William & w, Alice, & ch, Daniel
   & Phebe, rocf Peru MM, N. Y., dtd 1812,12,
   22
1814, 11, 22. Martha recrq
1815, 12, 19. Sarah Kees (form Benedict) rpd
   mcd

BENNETT
1892, 2, 25. James Allen d ae 35
1894, 1, 28. Ruth Allen d

1904, 5, 11. Ruben Grant & s, Lewis G., gct
   New York MM (H)

BENTON
1876, 11, 21. Amy J., w Heber C., dt John &
   Elizabeth (Evans) Scott, b
1913, 12, 23. Amy J. S. con mcd (W)

BERGEN
1907, 4, 24. Grace Updegraff relrq (G)

BERRY
1812, 7, 30. David, Jefferson Co., O., m in
   Short Creek MH, Mary STANTON, Jefferson
   Co., O.

1826, 9, 19. Mary gct Goshen MM, O.
1828, 7, 22. Rachel dis jH
1831, 7, 19. Mary dis jH
1834, 2, 18. Jesse dis jH
1839, 12, 24. Reese dis mcd
1839, 12, 24. Samuel dis mcd
1840, 1, 21. Ascenath & Martha dis jH
1843, 5, 23. Eliza Ann Job (form Berry) dis
   mcd & jH
1850, 1, 24. Julianna gct Concord MM
1884, 5, 21. Ida recrq (G)
1885, 3, 25. Jennie recrq (G)
1886, 5, 19. Thomas recrq (G)
1886, 5, 19. Mary recrq (G)
1889, 3, 20. George recrq (G)
1889, 3, 20. Albert recrq (G)
1893, 6, 21. Eddie N. recrq (G)
1895, 2, 20. Anna E. recrq (G)

BERTRAM
1903, 1, 21. Alice Pennington [Bertrum] relrq
   (G)
1905, 3, 22. William H. & w, Alice, recrq (G)
1906, 9, 19. John Pennington, s Wm. H., recrq
   (G)
1906, 9, 19. Wm. H. & w, Alice, & ch, John P.
   & Louise Marie, gct Milan MM, O. (G)

BESS
1915, 2, 24. Charity recrq (G)

BEVINGTON
1902, 3, 19. Walter B. recrq (G)
1907, 3, 20. Walter dropped from mbrp (G)

BIDDLE
1911, 2, 22. Helen Hawthorn relrq (G)

BIGWELL
1892, 10, 19. Sarah recrq (G)

BINGMAN
1821, 10, 23. Sarah (form Townsend) dis mcd

BINNS
----, --, --. William & Ruth
   Ch: Gibson   b 1830, 12, 10
       Richard   " 1834, 1, 28
       David   " 1837, 2, 18
       Mary   " 1838, 9, 17

BINNS, William & Ruth, continued
 Ch: Amos   b 1840, 5, 16
  John   " 1842, 9, 10 d 1864, 3,11
  Thomas
   Clarkson " 1846, 6, 23
  William
   Henry " 1848, 3, 2
  Hannah " 1850, 5, 31
  Margaret " 1851, 8, 28 " 1866, 2,24
  Oliver H. " 1857, 11, 7
  Thomas C.
1836, 11, 23. Jonathan, s David & Margaret,
 Fayette Co., Pa.; m in Mt. Pleasant, Eliza
 M. HUSSEY, dt Christopher & Lydia, Jeffer-
 son Co., O., d 1863,5,10
1841, 4, 29. David, s David & Margaret, Har-
 rison Co., O., d 1877,5,24 ae 62 bur Har-
 risville; m in Harrisville, Rebecca HALL
 dt Thos. & Mary, Harrison Co., O.
 Ch: Elizabeth b 1844, 5, 21
  Joseph P. " 1847, 2, 18 d 1929, 1, 7
   bur Harrisville
  Margaret
   Ann b 1849, 6, 20
  Jonathan " 1851, 4, 6
  James Har-
   vey " 1853, 3, 3
  David " 1857, 7, 6
  Thomas " 1857, 7, 6
  Addison " 1859, 3, 16
  Mary " 1861, 10, --
1847, 2, 18. Joseph P. b
1849, 4, 25. David Sr. d bur Harrisville
1851, 4, 6. Jonathan b
1851, 4, 27. Caroline H. b
1852, 9, 19. Lizzie A. b
1852, 9, 29. Mary P. m Lewis W. JONES
1858, 11, 3. Margaret Sr. d ae 77
1861, 8, 31. Elizabeth d bur Harrisville
1873, 5, 29. Jonathan, s David & Rebecca,
 Jefferson Co., O.; m in Harrisville, Ro-
 sella BAILEY, dt Stephen & Martha, Bel-
 mont Co., O., d 1905,10,25 ae 55 bur
 Harrisville (W)
 Ch: Oliver b 1874, 7, 13
  Eliza R. " 1877, 3, 25
  Martha " 1879, 3, 30
----, --, --. Joseph & Belinda
 Ch: Edward T. b 1875, 7, 13
  Arthur " 1877, 5, 21
  John A. " 1881, 6, 2
  Mary C. " 1884, 2, 11
1878, 5, 2. Margaret Ann m Lewis HALL (W)
1879, 4, 30. David, s David & Rebecca, Harris-
 ville Co., O., b 1857,7,6; m in Concord,
 Lizzie A. BUNDY, dt Israel & Rachel R.
 SIDWELL, Belmont Co., O., b 1852,9,19 (W)
 Ch: Willis J. b 1880, 1, 29 d 1885,11,19
   bur Concord
  Rachel S. b 1882, 2,18
  Mary Edith " 1883, 1,12
1879, 9, 24. Thos. H., s David & Rebecca,
 Harrison Co., O.; m in Concord, Abza J.

STEER, dt Nathan & Mary J., Belmont Co.,
 Ohio (W)
 Ch: Ida Mary b 1881, 8, 5
  Clara " 1885, 4, 27
  Mira H. " 1889, 7, 21
  Luella " 1891, 6, 9
1880, 5, 19. Mary K. m Walter EDGERTON (W)
----, --, --. Hervey J. b 1853,3,3; m Ida
 ----- b 1854,7,1
 Ch: David M. b 1887, 8, 11
  Rebecca " 1889, 8, 27
  Charles H. " 1893, 6, 25 d 1893, 9,27
   bur Harrisville
  James
   Howard b 1894, 9, 7
1893, 12, 27. Gibson, s Wm. & Ruth, Franklin
 Co., O., d 1897,5,2 ae 66 bur Providence,
 Pa.; m in Colerain, Martha RUSSELL, dt Asa
 & Asenath RALEY, Belmont Co., O. (W)
----, --, --. Oliver, s Jonathan & Rosella,
 b 1874,7,13 d 1933,10,29; m Mariana
 DEWEES, dt Joshua & Martha (Gibbons),
 b 1874,1,18
 Ch: Bertha M. b 1898, 6, 11 d 1917, 2,15
   bur Harrisville
  Gertrude R.b 1903, 4, 14
  Willis J. " 1909, 7, 11
1904, 4, 21. Martha m Walter S. THOMAS (W)
1904, 5, 25. Mary C. m Jesse H. DEWEES (W)
1904, 10, 6. Elza R. m Alfred D. HALL (W)
1907, 8, 7. Martha R., dt Joseph RALEY, d
 bur Colerain
1908, 7, 2. Jonathan, s David & Rebecca H.,
 Jefferson Co., O.; m in Harrisville, Caroline BRANSON, dt Wm. & Mary T. HALL, Jefferson Co., O. (W)
1910, 11, 8. Bertha A., w Willis J., dt Chalkley A. & Luella (Hall) BUNDY, b
1911, 8, 23. Rebecca m Harvey PICKETT (W)
1915, 7, 27. Belinda H., w Joseph P., d bur
 Harrisville
1917, 5, 24. J. Howard, s J. Hervey & Ida,
 Jefferson Co., O., b 1894,9,7; m 1917,5,
 24 in Harrisville, Edith T. STEER, dt
 Louis & S. Louiza, Harrison Co., O.,
 b 1896,1,17 (W)
 Ch: Virginia
   Louise b 1918, 7, 13
  Ruth Mar-
   jorie " 1920, 6, 1
  Gladys Ma-
   rie " 1921, 7, 11
1918, 7, 13. Virginia Louise b
1929, 1, 7. Joseph P. d
1930, 6, 28. Willis J., s Oliver W. & Mariana D., Harrison Co., O., b 1909,7,11; m
 in Harrisville, Bertha A. BUNDY, dt
 Chalkley L. & Luella H. (W)

1819, 5, 18. Cert rec for David & s, John,
 from Otty MM, Yorkshire, Eng., dtd 1818,
 8,10. end to Redstone MM
1819, 5, 18. Cert rec for James & w, Allice,

BINNS, continued
&ch, Sarah, Margaret, Wm., John, Joseph, Wilson & Hannah, from Otty MM, Yorkshire, Eng., dtd 1818,8,10, end to Providence MM
1836, 2, 23. Chas. Kinsey gct Redstone MM, to m Sarah Binns
1837, 4, 18. Eliza gct Redstone MM
1839, 8, 20. David rocf Redstone MM, dtd 1839,7,31
1842, 8, 23. Ruth & ch, Gibson, Richard, David, Mary & Amy, rocf Redstone MM, dtd 1842,6,29 (also William, husband)
1847, 12, 21. Jonathan & w, Eliza, & s, Edward, rocf Redstone MM, dtd 1847,12,1
1849, 4, 24. Mary rocf Redstone MM, dtd 1849, 2,28
1854, 8, 22. Gibson gct Providence MM, Pa., to m Martha V. Cope
1855, 3, 21. Richard gct White Water MM, Ind. (G)
1860, 2, 21. Wm., Ruth & Mary dis jG (W)
1862, 4, 23. Gibson gct Redstone MM (G)
1862, 5, 20. Jonathan dis jG (W)
1862, 10, 21. Amos dis mcd (W)
1862, 10, 22. Amos con mcd (G)
1862, 11, 19. David & w, Rebecca, & ch, Joseph R., Margaret Ann, Jonathan, Hervey, David S., Thomas, Mary H. & Addison, dis jW
1863, 8, 19. Rebecca A. recrq (W)
1865, 3, 21. Gibson dis (W)
1866, 6, 20. Edward dis mcd (G)
1867, 2, 21. David Jr. rpd mcd (G)
1867, 8, 20. David dis jG (W)
1868, 2, 20. Amos G. & w, Rebecca, & dt, Lilla Aurelia, gct White Water MM, Ind.(G)
1872, 4, 23. Hannah G. dis jG (W)
1872, 11, 21. Sarah (form Newlin) con mcd (G)
1874, 2, 24. Joseph P. gct Plymouth MM, to m Belinda Hobson (W)
1874, 9, 22. Belinda H. rocf Plymouth MM, dtd 1874,8,17 (W)
1875, 11, 23. David rstrq (W)
1880, 12, 21. James Hervey gct Flushing MM (W)
1882, 5, 23. James Hervey gct Flushing MM, to m Ida Bailey (W)
1882, 12, 19. James Hervey gct Flushing MM (W)
1886, 3, 23. Addison H. con mcd (W)
1886, 12, 21. James Hervey & w, Ida, & s, William, rocf Flushing MM, dtd 1886,11,25 (W)
1891, 6, 24. Sarah L. relrq (G)
1892, 6, 21. Thomas H. & w, Alza J., & ch, Ida Mary, Clara, Mira H. & Luella, gct Springville MM, Ia. (W)
1893, 6, 20. Gibson rst at Salem MM on consent of this mtg (W)
1894, 6, 19. Addison dis jas (W)
1895, 3, 19. Gibson rocf Salem MM, dtd 1895, 1,23 (W)
1896, 3,24. Edward T. gct Coal Creek MM, Ia., to m Esther L. Brackin (W)
1896, 7, 21. David E. dis disunity (W)
1896, 12, 22. Edward T. gct Coal Creek MM, Ia.

(W)
1897, 5, 18. Oliver gct Somerset MM, to m Mariana Dewees (W)
1897, 8, 24. Arthur H. gct Stillwater MM, to m Tacy M. Bundy (W)
1898, 4, 19. Mariana D. rocf Somerset MM, dtd 1898,3,24 (W)
1902, 6, 24. Arthur H. gct Stillwater MM (W)
1902, 10, 21. John A. gct Salem MM, to m Mary E. Cope (W)
1903, 10, 20. Lizzie S. gct Newgarden MM (W)
1903, 12, 20. Mary E. gct Newgarden MM (W)
1903, 12, 20. Rachel S. gct Newgarden MM (W)
1903, 12, 22. Ogden J. Bracken gct Newgarden MM, O., to m Rachel S. Binns (W)
1905, 6, 20. John A. gct Newgarden MM, O. (W)
1908, 9, 22. John A. & w, Mary E., & dt, Alice Rebecca, rocf Newgarden MM, O., dtd 1908,8,20 (W)
1908, 9, 22. Rachel S. Bracken (form Binns) & dt, Edith Margaret, rocf Newgarden MM, dtd 1908,9,17 (W)
1909, 1, 19. Wm. C. dis mcd (W)
1911, 4, 18. Lizzie A. rocf Newgarden MM (W)
1912, 6, 18. Rebecca Binns Pickett gct Mill Creek MM, Ind.(W)
1922, 5, 23. David M. dis mcd & jas (W)
1928, 1, 22. J. Hervey & w, Ida, gct Plainfield MM, Ind. (W)

BIRD
1835, 4, 29. Matilda m Henry DOUDNA

1834, 10, 21. Matilda recrq

BISCO
1876, 10, 26. Alice (form Johnson) con mcd (G)

BITLER
1874, 12, 22. Mary (form Atkinson) dis mcd & jG (W)

BLACK
1914, 1, 21. John R. & Dinah recrq (G)

BLACKBURN
1892, --, --. Mary d

BLACKLEDGE
----, --, --. William & Elizabeth
  Ch: Robert H. b 1794, 2, 7
      Sarah   " 1795, 6, 20
      Elizabeth " 1798, 9, 5
      Samuel   " 1800, 6, 28
      John   " 1802, 12, 20
      Asa Hart-
      ley   " 1810, 11, 26
1821, 12, 27. Robert H., s William & Elizabeth, Jefferson Co., O.; m in Short Creek MH, Esther THOMPSON, dt Aaron & Sarah, Jefferson Co., O.
  Ch: Ann   b 1823, 7, 12
      Israel   " 1833, 4, 7

BLACKLEDGE, continued
1846, 10, 10. Esther d ae 47 bur Short Creek
1879, 8, 30. Robert d ae 85 bur Harrisville

1809, 7, 18. William & w, Elizabeth, & ch,
     Robert, Sarah, Elizabeth, Samuel & John,
     rocf Westland MM, dtd 1809,6,24
1814, 7, 19. Rachel rocf ND MM dtd 1814,2,22,
     end by Concord MM
1815, 9, 4. David rocf Newgarden MM, dtd
     1815,3,16
1816, 10, 22. Rachel gct ND MM
1821, 12, 18. Samuel dis mcd
1824, 7, 20. John gct Somerset MM
1824, 7, 20. William & w, Elizabeth, & s,
     Asa Hartley, gct Somerset MM
1824, 7, 20. Sarah gct Somerset MM
1825, 12, 20. Robert & w, Esther, & dt, Ann,
     gct Summerset MM
1827, 2, 20. David gct Somerset MM
1828, 12, 23. Esther & ch, Ann & Aaron, rocf
     Somerset MM, dtd 1828,8,25
1844, 12, 24. Ann Hunnicutt (form Blackledge)
     dis mcd
1851, 4, 22. Aaron dis mcd
1862, 11, 19. Sarah dis jW
1901, 2, 20. Ora, Blanch & Blain recrq (G)

BLACKMORE
1908, 7, 22. Ethel recrq (G)

BLAKE
1895, 12, 25. Mary E. recrq (G)
1898, 6, 22. Mary dropped from mbrp (G)
1913, 1, 22. Arthur recrq (G)

BLEAKMORE
1891, 3, 25. Frank recrq (G)

BLOWERS
1862, 11, 19. Andrew J. & w, Rebecca, & ch,
     Ann, Rachel, Jephtha, Rebecca Jr. & Sarah
     Alice, dis jW

BODENHAMER
1892, 5, 2. Harold R. b
1896, 6, 14. John Myron b
1900, 9, 19. Rowan O., s John A. & Miriam O.,
     Hendricks Co., Ind.; m in Colerain, Mary
     STEER, dt Lindley B. & Hanna, Belmont Co.,
     O. (W)

BOLAND
1914, 6, 24. Calvin & Jennie recrq (G)

BOLDKINS
1892, 10, 19. Jack recrq (G)

BOLTON
1823, 3, 27. Levi [Boulton], s James & Hannah,
     Columbiana Co., O.; m in Harrisville, Or-
     pha MENDENHALL, dt Isaac & Lydia, Harrison
     Co., O.

1810, 3, 20. Aquilla M. rocf Concord MM, dtd
     1809,10,22
1811, 4, 23. Aquilla M. gct Concord MM
1819, 9, 21. Jehu rocf Newgarden MM, O., dtd
     1819,7,22
1824, 8, 24. Orpah [Boulton] gct Middleton MM

BOND
1831, 12, 21. Benjamin gct Silver Creek MM,
     Ind.
1846, 7, 21. Elizabeth (form Williams) dis
     mcd
1849, 10, 23. Jane (form Williams) dis mcd

BONE
1879, 4, 24. Pinkney & Sarah Jane recrq (G)
1889, 3, 20. Benjamin & Waller E. recrq (G)
1899, 12, 20. Jennie relrq (G)

BONSALL
1805, 5, 18. Edward [Bonsell] rocf Uchland
     MM, dtd 1805,4,4
1807, 4, 18. Edward gct Salem MM, to m Rachel
     Warrington
1807, 9, 19. Rachel rocf Salem MM, dtd 1807,
     7,4
1808, 6, 21. Martha rocf Hopewell MM, dtd
     1808,3,7
1810, 4, 24. Edward & w, Rachel, & ch, James
     Gibbons, Isaac & Abraham, gct Salem MM
1812, 6, 23. Martha [Bonswel] gct Stillwater
     MM
1843, 3, 21. John C. Hoague gct Salem MM, to
     m Rebecca Bonsall

BOON
1838, 7, 26. Mary gct Deerfield MM (H)

BOOTHE
1814, 11, 22. Elizabeth rocf Westland MM, dtd
     1814,6,2

BORDNER
1900, 10, 10. Jacob d

1886, 7, 2. Jacob recrq (G)

BOSWELL
1862, 11, 19. Anne dis jW
1862, 11, 19. Anne dis jW
1862, 11, 19. Benjamin Sr. dis jW
1862, 11, 19. Benjamin dis jW
1862, 11, 19. James dis jW
1862, 11, 19. James dis jW
1862, 11, 19. Rebecca dis jW
1862, 11, 19. Thomas dis jW
1862, 11, 19. William dis jW

BOWERS
1896, 2, 19. Carrie T. relrq (G)

BOWLS
1882, 7, 19. Lizzie recrq (G)

BOWLS, continued
1893, 6, 21. Susanna [Bowles] recrq (G)

BOWMAN
1807, 11, 26. Isaac, s Richard & Mary, Jefferson Co., O.; m in Cross Creek MH, Ann
HOBSON, dt Joseph & Ann, Jefferson Co., O.
     Ch: Mary   b 1809, 2, 14
         Joseph   " 1810, 10, 25
         Ann   " 1812, 3, 25
1838, 5, 2. Thos., s Isaac & Ann, Stark Co.,
O.; m in Mt. Pleasant, Elizabeth LUPTON,
dt Henry & Achsah, Jefferson Co., O.
1910, 3, 10. Mary d ae 1 yr

1807, 10, 17. Isaac rocf Concord MM, dtd 1807,
9,22
1808, 5, 24. Ann rocf Plymouth MM, dtd 1808,5,
21
1812, 6, 23. Isaac & w, Ann, & ch, Joseph &
Ann, gct Newgarden MM
1839, 4, 23. Elizabeth gct Upper Springfield
MM

BOYLE
1872, 11, 5. Sarah E. gct Clear Creek MM, Ill.
(H)

BRACKIN
1798, 2, 24. Elisha b
----, --, --. Elisha & Phebe [Bracken]
     Ch: Deborah   b 1823, 8, 6 d 1838,3,26
         Rebecca   " 1825, 4, 10
     Elisha m 2nd Esther ----- d 1877,5,20 ae
     75 bur Concord
     Ch: Drusilla   b 1832, 7, 1 d 1832,9,25
            bur Short Creek
         Sarah   b 1833, 8, 28
         Richard F. " 1836, 7, 25
         Martha   " 1838, 11, 26
         Lindley   " 1841, 3, 14
         Lemuel   " 1843, 5, 11
         Phebe   " 1846, 10, 24
1841, 3, 14. Lindley M. b
1844, 10, 21. Rebecca [Bracken] m Israel STEER
1857, 4, 1. Sarah m David J. SCOTT (W)
----, --, --. Lindley m Anna ----- d 1915,11,
1 bur Colerain
     Ch: Esther C. b 1869, 1, 11 d 1869,1,23
            bur Concord
         Edward T. b 1870, 3, 14
         Ogden J.   " 1871, 7, 9
         Martha H. " 1874, 7, 4
         Mary Ann   " 1876, 2, 5
         Sarah J.   " 1878, 5, 30
         Alice M.   " 1880, 7, 15
         Esther   " 1892, 4, 11
1869, 3, 25. Phebe m Asaph WOOD (W)
1874, 7, 6. Caleb d ae 73 bur Concord
1876, 1, 27. Mary d bur Concord
1880, 7, 15. Alice M. [Bracken] b
1881, 4, 11. Elisha d ae 83 bur Concord
1882, 2, 17. Rachel S., w Ogden J., dt David

& Lizzie A. (Sidwell) BINNS, b
1891, 4, 11. Esther b
1895, 10, 23. Martha H. m Frederick C. HOYLE
(W)
1896, 5, 20. Mary Anna m Oscar J. BAILEY (W)
1906, 6, 11. Edith Margaret, dt Ogden J. &
Rachel S., b
1928, 2, 28. Lindley M. d bur Colerain
1928, 7, 5. Edith M. m R. C. BAILEY (W)

1821, 11, 20. Elisha rocf Westland MM, dtd
1821,7,26
1822, 8, 20. Caleb [Braken] rocf Westland MM,
dtd 1822,7,25
1823, 4, 22. Phebe rocf Flushing MM, dtd 1823,
2,21
1824, 9, 21. Caleb gct Smithfield MM
1825, 8, 23. Elisha & w, Phebe, & ch, Deborah
& Rebecca, gct Flushing MM
1827, 2, 20. Phebe & ch, Deborah & Rebecca,
rocf Flushing MM,dtd 1826,12,22
1831, 8, 23. Elisha gct Salem MM, to m Esther
Faucet
1832, 1, 24. Esther rocf Salem MM, dtd 1831,
12,21
1836, 2, 23. Caleb rst at Redstone MM on consent of this mtg
1862, 6, 24. Richard F. dis mcd
1862, 11, 19. Elisha & w, Esther, & ch, Martha, Phebe, Lindley, Lemuel & Richard, dis
jW (G)
1866, 10, 23. Lemuel gct Flushing MM, to m
Mary Hirst (W)
1867, 5, 21. Lemuel gct Coal Creek MM, Ia.
(W)
1867, 10, 22. Lindley M. gct Salem MM, to m
Anna S. French (W)
1868, 11, 19. Anna S. rocf Salem MM, dtd 1868,
10,21 (W)
1883, 2, 20. Martha Janney (form Brackin) dis
mcd (W)
1896, 3, 24. Edward T. Binns gct Coal Creek
MM, Ia., to m Esther L. Brackin (W)
1899, 5, 23. Edward F. gct Goshen MM (W)
1903, 12, 22. Ogden J. gct Newgarden MM, O.,
to m Rachel S. Binns (W)
1908, 8, 18. Martha B. Janney (form Bracken)
rst (W)
1908, 9, 22. Rachel S. (form Binns) & dt,
Edith Margaret, rocf Newgarden MM, dtd
1908,9,17 (W)
1908, 10, 20. Sara J. gct Phila. MM (W)
1919, 9, 23. Sara J. gct Pasadena MM, Calif.
(W)
1924, 7, 22. Esther dis jas (W)
1927, 7, 22. Esther dis jas (W)

BRADY
1914, 12, 23. Lewis & Beulah dropped from
mbrp (G)

BRAINARD
1896, 1, 23. Franklin recrq (G)

BRAINARD, continued
1902, 8, 20. Franklin dropped from mbrp (G)

BRANDON
1840, 11, 24. Eliza rocf Salem MM, dtd 1840,9,
    23

BRANON
1821, 4, 24. Esther (form Watson) dis mcd

BRANSON
----, --, --. Isaac & Sarah
    Ch: Elvira   b 1820, 3, 25
        Elias   " 1821, 11, 23
        Sarah Ann " 1824, 5, 6
        Phebe   " 1826, 3, 30
1831, 6, 2. Abraham, s Rees & Ruth, Belmont
    Co., O.; m in Short Creek MH, Ann WILSON,
    dt Jonathan & Hannah, Jefferson Co., O.
    Ch: Lindley   b 1832, 9, 26 d 1899,12, 8
        Rachel   " 1835, 2, 9
        William   " 1837, 5, 10
        Elizabeth " 1839, 11, 17
        Abraham   " 1846, 12, 9 " 1920, 5,11
        Jonathan   " 1841, 11, 15
        John   " 1844, 3, 16
1833, 8, 28. Mariah m Israel WILSON
1837, 1, 7. Sarah d ae 37 bur Concord
1843, 3, 9. Eliza J. m Caleb B. NEGUS
1844, 5, 1. Sarah A. m Phinehas COWGILL
1846, 4, 30. Asa, s John & Abigail, Jefferson
    Co., O.; m in Harrisville, Rebecca SMART,
    dt Isaac & Rebecca, Salem, N. J.
1855, 5, 2. Rachel m Peter THOMAS
1866, 10, 31. Elizabeth S. m Israel THOMAS
1867, 1, 16. Abraham d
1868, 1, 12. John C. d
1875, 5, 25. Abraham W., s Abraham & Ann W.,
    Harrison Co., O.; m in home of Isaac Thom-
    as, Lucy THOMAS, dt Isaac & Ann L., Harri-
    son Co., O., d 1897,2,15
    Ch: Mary E.   b 1905, 1, 31
        Anne L.   " 1918, 3, 9
1884, 10, 9. Benjamin, s Jacob & Juliann H.,
    Belmont Co., O., d 1886,7,12 ae 37; m in
    Harrisville, Caroline HALL, dt Wm. & Mary
    T., Jefferson Co., O. (W)
1908, 7, 2. Caroline m Jonathan BINNS (W)
1919, 1, 15. Anna M. d

1823, 7, 22. Charles rocf Abington MM, dtd
    1823,5,25
1828, 9, 23. Anna dis jH
1833, 7, 23. Maria rocf Hopewell MM, dtd
    1833,6,5
1833, 11, 19. Eliza Jane rocf Sadsbury MM, dtd
    1833,10,8
1836, 8, 25. Ruth gct Fall Creek MM (H)
1837, 5, 23. William D. rocf Hopewell MM, dtd
    1837,4,5
1840, 6, 23. William D. gct Salem MM, to m
    Eliza Oliphant
1840, 11, 24. Eliza rocf Salem MM, dtd 1840,

9,23
1841, 7, 20. William & w, Eliza, & s, Abner,
    gct Salem MM
1844, 10, 22. Elvira B. Lea (form Branson) con
    mcd
1845, 1, 23. Charles gct Clear Creek MM, Ill.
    (H)
1845, 2, 20. Mary gct Clear Creek MM, Ill.
1845, 8, 19. Asa & s, Joseph, rocf Flushing
    MM, dtd 1845,6,26
1848, 5, 23. Asa & w, Rebecca, & s, Joseph,
    gct Flushing MM
1853, 8, 23. Phebe gct Red Cedar MM, Iowa
1854, 3, 21. Isaac gct Red Cedar MM, Ia.
1857, 4, 21. Nathan Steer gct Flushing MM, to
    m Mary Jane Branson (W)
1861, 2, 19. Abraham dis jG (W)
1861, 8, 20. Lindley dis jG (W)
1863, 3, 25. Wm. W. dis (G)
1867, 10, 22. Elizabeth Thomas (form Branson)
    dis mcd & jG (W)
1870, 12, 20. Abraham W. dis jG (W)
1877, 8, 22. William G. & w, Charlotte S., &
    ch, Hortense S., Russell W., Mary Ann, Ra-
    chel Elma, Loretta M., Lizzie S., John H.
    & Sarah, recrq (G)
1883, 9, 18. Nathan R. Smith gct Flushing MM,
    to m Lizzie M. Branson (W)
1885, 5, 19. Benjamin rocf Flushing MM, dtd
    1885,4,23 (W)

BRANTINGHAM
1871, 5, 23. David Thomas gct New Garden MM,
    to m Lydia Brantingham (W)

BRENNAMAN
1903, 7, 22. Alice H. relrq (G)

BRESSOCK
1903, 3, 25. Joseph Frederick recrq (G)
1907, 3, 20. James F. [Bresock] dropped from
    mbrp (G)

BREWER
1842, 9, 21. Phebe m Joseph K. QUAINTANCE

1808, 10, 18. Mary & ch, Sarah, Rachel, John,
    Richard, Mary, Martha, Ann & Hannah, rocf
    Redstone MM, dtd 1808,7,30
1810, 10, 23. Sarah dis
1812, 12, 22. Rachel gct Plainfield MM
1813, 1, 19. Mary & ch, John, Richard, Mary,
    Martha, Ann & Hannah, gct Plainfield MM
1817, 8, 19. Sarah rst
1819, 11, 23. Sarah gct Flushing MM
1838, 1, 23. Phebe rocf Flushing MM, dtd
    1837,12,21

BRIGGS
---, --, --. William & Esther
    Ch: Israel
        Shreve   b 1792, 4, 24
        Samuel

BRIGGS, William & Esther, continued
    Ch: Miller   b 1796, 10, 30
        George
          Green   " 1798, 10, 9
        Maria   " 1801, 4, 24
        Job   " 1803, 1, 17
        Jonathan T." 1805, 7, 24
        Rebecca
          Moorhead " 1807, 10, 19
        William   " 1810, 3, 7

1811, 3, 19. William & w, Esther, & ch, Israel
    Shreve, Samuel Miller, George Green, Maria,
    Job, Jonathan Taylor, Rebecca Moorehead &
    William, gct Salem MM
1816, 9, 24. George, minor, rocf Salem MM,
    dtd 1816,8,13
1818, 7, 21. George gct Plainfield MM
1849, 1, 23. Sarah T. rocf Flushing MM, dtd
    1848,11,23
1855, 10, 23. Sarah B. gct Stillwater MM (W)
1862, 11, 19. Benjamin dis jW
1862, 11, 19. Elizabeth dis jW
1862, 11, 19. George dis jW
1862, 11, 19. Jonathan dis jW
1862, 11, 19. Josiah dis jW
1862, 11, 19. Mary dis jW
1862, 11, 19. Sarah dis jW
1862, 11, 19. Sarah dis jW
1862, 11, 19. Sarah J. dis jW
1905, 4, 19. James H. & w recrq (G)

BRIGHT
1808, 2, 20. Mary rocf Concord MM, dtd 1807,
    12,22

BRISCO
1876, 10, 26. Alice (form Johnson) con mcd (G)

BROADHURST
1814, 4, 19. Elizabeth (form Townsend) dis
    mcd

BROADRUP
1883, 11, 21. Cornelius recrq (G)
1884, 3, 19. Hannah [Broadrupt] recrq (G)
1885, 10, 21. Hannah G. [Broadruff] dropped
    from mbrp (G)
1894, 7, 25. Cornelius [Broodruff] dropped
    from mbrp (G)

BROCK
1862, 11, 19. Joel dis jW
1862, 11, 19. Martha Ann dis jW
1862, 11, 19. Mary Jane dis jW
1862, 11, 19. Peninah dis jW
1862, 11, 19. Rebecca dis jW
1862, 11, 19. William dis jW

BROOKS
1902, 12, 20. Mary Elizabeth & Esther recrq
    (G)

BROOMHALL
1818, 4, --. Cert rec for John end to Still-
    water MM

BROWN
----, --, --. Aaron & Ann
    Ch: Benjamin   b 1800, 7, 13
        Mary   " 1802, 8, 18
        Zacheus   " 1804, 9, 2
        Ira   " 1806, 12, 27
1810, 2, 23. Aaron, s Isaac & Rebeckah, b
1816, 6, 26. Elizabeth m Wm. CARR
1819, 1, 28. Isaac, s Josiah & Sarah, Jeffer-
    son Co., O.; m in Short Creek MH, Mary
    PATTERSON, dt Wm. & Keziah, Jefferson
    Co., O.
1819, 5, 26. Horton, s Aaron & Mary, Jeffer-
    son Co., O.; m in Mt. Pleasant, Margaret
    BATES, dt Edward & Elizabeth
1823, 8, 1. Rebecca d ae 44 bur Short Creek
1824, 4, 28. Elizabeth m Harmon RHODES
1824, 12, 1. Isaac, s Daniel & Miriam, Jef-
    ferson Co., O.; m in Mt. Pleasant, Rebec-
    ca BEESON, dt Henry & Mary
1871, 2, 1. Edgar Allen, s John & Anna, b
1881, 4, 24. Mary S., w Herbert Raymond, dt
    Lindley B. & Hanna S. (Penrose) STEER, b
1889, 10, 26. Edgar Allen d
1914, 2, 26. Anna Hannah Given d

1805, 12, 21. Naomi rocf Crooked Run MM, dtd
    1805,8,31
1808, 5, 24. Isaac rocf Miami MM, dtd 1808,3,
    10
1809, 4, 18. Isaac & w, Rebecca, & ch, Eliza-
    beth, William & Joseph, rocf Redstone MM,
    dtd 1808,10,28
1810, 3, 20. Daniel & w, Miriam, rocf Hope-
    well MM, dtd 1809,4,20
1810, 12, 18. David roc dtd 1810,6,4
1812, 10, 20. William & w, Grace, rocf Hope-
    well MM, Va., dtd 1812,8,6
1813, 2, 23. Elizabeth rocf Hopewell MM, dtd
    1813,1,1
1815, 6, 20. Benjamin & w, Amy, & dt, Abi-
    gail, rocf Newgarden MM, Pa., dtd 1815,5,
    14
1818, 10, 20. Aaron & w & ch, Benjamin S.,
    Mary, Zacheus, Ira, Asa, Anna, James &
    David, gct Darby Creek MM
1819, 4, 20. Isaac & w, Mary, gct Stillwater
    MM
1819, 8, 24. Horton & w, Margaret, gct Darby
    Creek MM
1826, 7, 18. Benjamin & w, Amy, & ch, Abi-
    gail, Jacob, Joseph, Nathan & Rachel, gct
    Stillwater MM
1828, 5, 20. Susanna (form Updegraff) dis mcd
1837, 11, 21. Samuel gct Clear Creek MM
1837, 11, 21. William & w, Grace, & s, Isaac,
    gct Clear Creek MM
1838, 6, 19. Joseph dis jas
1840, 1, 21. Abrah W. rocf Upper Springfield

BROWN, continued
      MM, dtd 1838,12,22, end by Miami MM, 1839,
      9,25
1840, 7, 21. Abiah W.dis disunity
1842, 11, 22. William gct Salem MM, Iowa.
1843, 1, 24. Abba & ch, Ann, Jane, Hannah,
      Mary & Abijah William, rocf Upper Spring-
      field MM, dtd 1842,12,24
1856, 1, 22. Isaac gct Plymouth MM
1872, 5, 23. Theodore recrq (G)
1873, 4, 24. Elnathan P. recrq (G)
1878, 4, 25. Sarah E. recrq (G)
1881, 2, 26. John J. recrq (G)
1881, 2, 26. Sherman recrq (G)
1881, 11, 24. Theodore relrq (G)
1882, 3, 23. Elnathan P. gct Smithfield MM
      (G)
1888, 3, 21. Sherman H. gct Pleasant View
      MM, Kans. (G)
1888, 10, 24. John J. dropped from mbrp (G)
1890, 7, 23. Elnathan & w, Rachel Ann, & ch,
      Mary Emily & Clarence Elnathan, rocf
      Smithfield MM (G)
1894, 3, 21. Elizabeth N. recrq (G)
1896, 3, 25. E. Garnet recrq (G)
1903, 6, 24. Garnet(Brown)Delmuth relrq (G)
1907, 4, 24. Lizzie dropped from mbrp (G)
1907, 6, 19. John J. dropped from mbrp (G)
1911, 11, 22. Mabel Hawthorn relrq (G)

BRUCE
1907, 9, 25. John recrq (G)

BRYANT
1862, 11, 19. Elizabeth dis jW
1862, 11, 19. Isaac dis jW
1862, 11, 19. James dis jW
1862, 11, 19. Mary dis jW
1862, 11, 19. Tamar J. dis jW
1862, 11, 19. William dis jW

BRYEN
1896, 3, 25. Mary Ellen Griffith (form Bryen)
      rocf Cleveland MM, dtd 1895,9,19 (G)

BUCHANAN
1821, 12, 18. Mary [Buckanan] rocf Goose Creek
      MM, Va., dtd 1821,8,2
1823, 5, 20. Grace [Buckman] (form Fell) dis
      mcd
1874, 8, 20. William recrq (G)
1891, 5, 20. V. W. relrq (G)
1890, 5, 20. William relrq (G)
1902, 12, 24. Charles gct Cleveland MM (G)

BUCKINGHAM
1873, 5, 22. Peter & Mary Ann recrq (G)

BUFKIN
1831, 2, 22. Samuel gct Flushing MM

BULL
1892, 3, 23. Irving F. recrq (G)

BULLOCK
1905, 4, 19. Mona recrq (G)

BUNDY
1815, 9, 28. Moses, s Josiah & Bathiah, Bel-
      mont Co., O., b 1789,12,24; m in Short
      Creek MH, Ann TOWNSEND, dt Joseph & Mary,
      Harrison Co., O., b 1794,5,6
      Ch: Mary   b 1816, 12, 17
          Joseph   " 1818, 3, 25
          Josiah   " 1819, 8, 31
          Bethiah   " 1821, 5, 28
          Lucinda   " 1822, 11, 18
          Susanna   " 1824, 10, 27
          Nehemiah M." 1826, 9, 10
          Ruth Ann   " 182-, 12, 26
----, --, --. Benjamin d 1875,4,26 ae 87 bur
      Concord; m Delitha ----- d 1870,3,24 bur
      Concord
      Ch: William   b 1829, 8, 4
          Sarah   " 1833, 1, 11
          Edmon   " 1834, 11, 25
          Rachel   " 1837, 3, 4
          Ann   " 1839, 3, 3
          David   " 1840, 11, 13
          Jane   " 1842, 3, 11
          Charles   " 1847, 3, 20
1829, 8, 4. Mary Ann d bur Summerset
1835, 3, 14. Martha d bur Concord
1842, 11, 3. Jane d bur Short Creek
1850, 10, 31. Josiah, s Benj. & Delitha, Bel-
      mont Co., O.; m in Harrisville, Asenath
      HALL, dt Thos. & Mary, Jefferson Co.,
      O., d 1907,12,17 bur Concord
      Ch: Wilson   b 1851, 8, 26
          Oliver   " 1852, 10, 20
          Ellen M.   " 1856, 5, 25
          Walter T.   " 1860, 3, 20 d 1880, 7,26
          bur Concord
1854, 8, 23. Sarah m John STARBUCK
----, --, --. William m Sarah Ann ----- d 1909,
      2,17 bur Concord
      Ch. Elizabeth
          D.   b 1858, 1, 15
          Effie Ann   " 1860, 3, 24
          -----   " 1862,11,7   (torn)
          Marylina   " 1869, 7, 26
          Jesse C.   d 1891, 1,16
          bur Concord
----, --, --. Edmund d 1916,7,4 ae 82 bur
      Colerain; m Deborah JONES, dt Joshua & Re-
      becca (Miller), b 1840,2,5 d 1925,11,14
      bur Colerain
      Ch: Elmer J.   b 1864, 1, 14
          Josephine   " 1869, 1, 12
          Laura R.   " 1872, 1, 26 d 1922, 9, 4
          bur Colerain
          Anna Mary   b 1873, 9, 22
          Lyman E.   " 1877, 2, 18
          Rachel E.   " 1882, 1, 2
1864, 1, 14. Elmer J. b
1865, 4, 19. Ann m Robert W. HAMPTON (W)
1869, 7, 26. Marylina b

BUNDY, continued
1872, 1, 26. Laura R. b
----, --, --. Charles & Margaret
    Ch: Frederick b 1873, 9, 30
        Lewis S.   " 1875, 10, 10
        Willis M. " 1877, 9, 30
        Myrtle R. " 1881, 2, 18
        Elden J.   " 1883, 3, 30
        Clarence E." 1885, 5, 27
1873, 9, 24. Wilson, s Josiah & Asenath, Bel-
    mont Co., O., b 1851,8,6 d 1876,11,17 bur
    Concord; m in Concord, Lizzie A. SIDWELL,
    dt Israel & Rachel B., Belmont Co., O. (W)
    Ch: William   b 1874, 7, 6
        Oscar W.   " 1874, 7, 6
        Olive R.   " 1875, 8, 1
1875, 10, 10. Lewis S. b
1879, 4, 30. Lizzie A. m David BINNS (W)
1880, 3, 31. Oliver W., s Josiah & Asenath,
    Belmont Co., O.; m in Concord, Sina H,
    SIDWELL, dt Israel & Rachel B., Belmont
    Co., O. (W)
    Ch: Lawrence G. b 1883, 5, 30
1880, 7, 30. Luella H. b
1880, 9, 22. Ellen M. m Jas. H. LUPTON (W)
1882, 11, 22. Elizabeth D. m Albert H. CAMERON
    (W)
1888, 3, 29. Sarah L. m Louis C. STEER (W)
1892, 9, 7. Josiah d bur Concord
1897, 9, 22. Anna M. m Jos. R. STRATTON
1898, 5, 25. Josephine m Gilbert WARRINGTON
    (W)
1902, 8, 20. Rachel E. m Gilbert E. THOMAS
    (W)
1902, 9, 10. Wallace J., s David & Esther M.,
    Belmont Co., O., b 1874,11,11; m in Con-
    cord, Louisa D. STEER, dt Elisha B. &
    Ellen, Belmont Co., O., b 1875,6,1 (W)
    Ch: Donald
        David   b 1903, 10, 11
        Wallace
        Wayne   " 1906, 5, 2
        Allen E.   " 1908, 11, 25
1903, 10, 22. Chalkley L., s Lindley & Ruanna,
    Belmont Co., O., b 1879,6,30; m in Harris-
    ville, Luella HALL, dt Lewis & Margaret
    Ann, Harrison Co., O. (W)
    Ch: Wilmer L. b 1904, 10, 23
        Clifford M." 1906, 8, 11
        Arthur H. " 1907, 12, 14
        Bertha A. " 1910, 11, 8
        Edna Doro-
        thy   " 1913, 1, 8
        Herbert F. " 1914, 8, 24
        Ruana   " 1917, 4, 15
        Helen   " 1918, 12, 22
1916, 4, 17. William d bur Colerain
1922, 9, 4. Laura R. d
----, --, --. Clifford C., s Chalkley L. &
    Luella (Hall), b 1906,8,11; m Wauneta R.
    DOUDNA, dt Dillwyn W. & Edith R. (Carter)
    b 1908,12,28
    Ch: Bertha

    Ch: Marie   b 1930, 10, 22
1930, 6, 28. Bertha A. m Willis J. BINNS (W)
1932, --, --. Elmer J. d

1813, 4, 20. Joshua rocf Concord MM, dtd
    1813,2,25
1813, 7, 20. Joseph dis disunity
1815, 12, 19. Ann gct Concord MM
1816, 10, 23. John Townsend gct Concord MM,
    to m Ruth Bundy
1819, 11, 23. Joel Watson gct Concord MM, to
    m Abigail Bundy
1828, 4, 22. Ann & ch, Mary, Joseph Townsend,
    Josiah, Bethial, Lucinda, Susanna & Nehe-
    miah Matson Bundy, rocf Concord MM, dtd
    1827,10,24
1829, 11, 24. Ann dis JH
1830, 3, 25. Moses & w, Ann, & ch, Mary, Jo-
    seph T., Josiah, Bethiah, Lucinda, Susan-
    nah, Nehemiah & Ruthanna, gct Deerfield MM
1830, 6, 22. Mary, Joseph, Josiah, Bethiah,
    Lucinda, Nehemiah & Ruthanna, gct Deerfield
    MM
1832, 11, 20. Ann Cope (form Bundy) dis mcd &
    JH
1833, 1, 22. Josiah dis mcd
1841, 4, 20. Pharaby gct Stillwater MM
1847, 10, 19. Josiah gct Flushing MM, to m
    Achsah R. Smith
1848, 5, 23. Achsah R. rocf Flushing MM, dtd
    1848,2,24
1855, 5, 22. Jesse dis mcd
1856, 4, 22. William gct Providence MM, Pa.,
    to m Sarah Ann Cope
1857, 8, 19. Jesse dis mcd
1858, 3, 23. Sarah Ann rocf Providence MM,
    dtd 1858,3,4
1862, 11, 19. Joseph, Asenith, Wilson, Oliver,
    Walter T., Ellen M., Edmund, John D.,
    Stephen Edgar, Nathan, Anna, Joseph, Ma-
    thew, Ezekiel, Sarah, William E., Mary
    Jane, Martha Ann, Anna Maria, John, Han-
    nah, Sarah Alice, Dempsey, Rebecca, Emily,
    Amanda, Jephtha, Jefferson, Chalkley, Sa-
    rah, Lindley, Joel, Nathan, Rachel, Ann,
    William, Lizzie D., Effie Anna, Benjamin,
    Talitha, Charles, David, Mary C., Deborah,
    William, Asenath, Allen, Clarhs, Joel,
    Ellen, Dillwyn, John, Ann, Thomas, Ruth,
    Elizabeth, Jesse, William P., Talitha,
    Lucinda, Rebecca, Emma, Chalkley Jr., El-
    vira, Stanton, Ann, Josiah, Susan, Martha,
    Elizabeth, Mary & Bailey dis jW (G)
1864, 11, 22. Sarah Ann & ch, Elizabeth D.,
    Effie Ann & Emma Almira, gct Providence MM
    (W)
1865, 1, 25. Deborah N. rocf Upper Springfield
    MM (G)
1865, 11, 21. Josiah dis jG (W)
1867, 7, 23. Asenath dis jG (W)
1868, 4, 21. Edmond dis jG (W)
1869, 6, 22. Charles gct Springville MM,
    Iowa (W)

BUNDY, continued

1870, 2, 22. David dis mcd (W)

1872, 5, 20. Parker Hall gct Stillwater MM,
     to m Tabitha D. Bundy (W)

1873, 3, 18. Louisa, dt Tabitha D. Hall, rocf
     Stillwater MM, dtd 1873,1,22 (W)

1873, 8, 19. Deborah M. rocf Upper Spring-
     field MM, dtd 1873,6,27 (W)

1873, 12, 23. Margaret H. rocf Stillwater MM,
     dtd 1873,11,19 (W)

1874, 8, 18. Charles rocf Springville MM,
     Ia. (W)

1875, 10, 19. William & w, Sarah Ann, & ch,
     Elizabeth D., Jesse & Mary Lina, rocf
     Springville MM (W)

1876, 5, 23. Rachel Thomas (form Bundy) dis
     mcd (W)

1878, 3, 21. Deborah M. relrq (W)

1880, 8, 24. Josiah rstrq

1881, 4, 19. Oliver W. dis disunity (W)

1883, 8, 21. Asenath H. rstrq (W)

1887, 11, 22. Sinah H. & ch, Lawrence G. &
     Chester M., gct Newgarden MM (W)

1893, 9, 19. Elmer J. con mcd (W)

1894, 3, 21. Foster recrq (G)

1895, 7, 23. Olive R. Whinery (form Bundy)
     con mcd (W)

1897, 8, 24. Arthur H. Binns gct Stillwater
     MM, to m Tacy M. Bundy (W)

1897, 11, 23. Oscar W. con mcd (W)

1899, 3, 21. Josephine B. Warrington (form
     Bundy) gct Upper Springfield MM (W)

1901, 2, 19. Charles & w, Margaret H., & ch,
     Myrtle K., Eldon J. & Clarence E., gct
     Stillwater MM (W)

1902, 3, 16. Wallace J. recrq (W)

1903, 4, 21. Frederick R. gct Stillwater MM
     (W)

1903, 4, 21. Willis M. gct Stillwater MM (W)

1905, 8, 22. Lyman dis jas (W)

1910, 4, 19. Chalkley L. rocf Stillwater MM,
     dtd 1910,3,23 (W)

1911, 7, 18. Lindley B. Steer gct Stillwater
     MM, to m Ruanna Bundy (W)

1926, 3, 23. Wilmer L. gct West-town MM, Pa.
     (W)

1929, 8, 20. Clifford C. gct Somerset MM, to
     m Wauneta Rosetta Doudna (W)

1930, 3, 18. Wauneta R. rocf Somerset MM,
     dtd 1830,2,20 (W)

BUNKER

1813, 4, 20. Cert rec for Peleg & fam from
     Peru MM, end to Plainfield

1815, 2, 21. Peleg & w, Hannah, & ch, Elihu,
     Lucy, Reuben & Isaac, rocf Plainfield MM,
     dtd 1815,12,24

1816, 1, 23. Isaac rocf Troy MM, dtd 1815,8,9

BUNTING

1892, 10, 19. Solomon & Anna recrq(G)

BURDETT

1882, 7, 19. David, Nancy & Wm. H. recrq (G)

1889, 3, 20. Mary recrq (G)

1891, 1, 21. Nancy, William & David [Bur-
     dette] dropped from mbrp (G)

BURGESS

1847, 3, 24. Clarkson, s John & Margaret,
     Morgan Co., O.; m in Short Creek MH, Susan
     WILLIS, dt Henry & Lydia, Jefferson Co.,
     O.

1847, 5, 18. Susan gct Pennsville MM

BURGY

1914, 3, 25. Harry & Annie recrq (G)

BURK

1881, 3, 24. Albert [Burke] recrq (G)

1888, 10, 24. Albert dropped from mbrp (G)

1895, 3, 20. Cora recrq (G)

1904, 2, 24. Ralph recrq (G)

1913, 1, 22. Charles A. [Burke] recrq (G)

BURKHEART

1912, 2, 21. Natalia recrq (G)

BURNET

1811, 5, 21. Stephen & w, Anibel, rocf Red-
     stone MM, dtd 1811,3,29

1811, 6, 18. Robert [Burnett] & w, Anna, &
     ch, John, David, Rebecca, Rachel & Deborah
     rocf Redstone MM, dtd 1811,3,29

1812, 5, 19. Robert & w, Ann, & ch, John,
     David, Rebecca, Rachel, Deborah & Thomas,
     gct Stillwater MM

1812, 5, 19. Stephen & w, Annable, gct Red-
     stone MM

BURNS

1860, 4, 25. Mary (form Lupton) con mcd

BURR

1808, 2, 7. Ann, dt Wm. & Sarah, b

1823, 10, 2. Ann m John LIPSEY

1824, 10, 28. Jesse, s Wm. & Sarah, Jefferson
     Co., O.; m in Short Creek MH, Martha LIP-
     SEY, dt Amasa & Rachel, Jefferson Co., O.

1807, 12, 19. Joseph & William, minor s Wm.,
     rocf Callawissa MM, dtd 1807,7,25

1809, 1, 24. Vicey (form Thomas) dis mcd

1817, 4, 22. Lavicy rst

1823, 1, 21. Louisa Evans (form Burr) dis mcd

1823, 5, 20. William & w, Sarah, recrq

1823, 6, 24. Merrick & Milton, ch Wm. & Sa-
     rah, recrq

1823, 8, 19. Sarah & Ruthanna, ch Wm. & Sa-
     rah, recrq

1825, 10, 18. Jesse & w, Martha, & ch, Sarah
     Ann, gct Flushing MM

1829, 5, 19. Sarah dis jH

1829, 10, 20. Joseph gct Milford MM

BURR, continued
1829, 10, 30. Wm. Jr. dis JH
1830, 1, 19. Sarah Jr. dis JH
1835, 7, 21. Mary Stedman (form Burr) dis mcd
1836, 11, 24. Sarah Jr. & Ruthanna, gct Plain-
        field MM (H)
1836, 12, 23. William & w, Sarah, & ch, Mer-
        rick S. & Milton J. gct Plainfield MM (H)
1837, 3, 21. Milton & Merrick gct Plainfield
        MM
1841, 9, 21. Ruthanna dis JH

BURRESS
1876, 10, 26. Esther recrq (G)

BURROUGHS
1892, 10, 19. Georgia A. recrq (G)

BURSON
----, --, --. ----- m Hannah ----- b 1770,3,--
        Ch: Thirza   b 1805, 1, 24
            Maria   " 1811, 4, 5
            Ann   " 1812, 9, 12

1820, 12, 19. Hannah rocf Newgarden MM, dtd
        1820,11,23
1822, 8, 20. Thirza, Rachel, Maria & Anna,
        minor ch Hannah, recrq
1824, 12, 21. Rachel Lanning (form Burson) dis
        mcd
1828, 11, 18. Hannah, Maria & Ann dis JH
1828, 12, 23. Thirza dis JH
1846, 4, 26. David & w, Jane, rocf Smithfield
        MM, dtd 1846,4,20
1859, 7, 20. Jane [Berson] gct Smithfield MM

BURT
1811, 5, 21. Daniel recrq
1812, 3, 24. Sarah recrq
1818, 6, 23. Daniel & w, Sarah, gct Plain-
        field MM

BUSH
1811, 6, 18. Deborah (form Balderson) dis mcd

BUTCHER
1871, 12, 21. ·Thomas J. & w, Lodinia, & ch,
        Helen J., David P., Mary E., William B.,
        John E., Lucy D. & Annis S., recrq (G)
1875, 7, 22. Ellen dis disunity (G)

BUTLER
1809, 4, 27. Sarah m Aaron KINSEY
----, --, --. Barak b 1786,8,27; m Hannah ----
        b 1789,10,3
        Ch: Mary   b 18-2, 2, 26
            Jonathan   " 1816, 8, 24
            Deborah   " 1818, 8, 10
            David   " 1820, 10, 20
            Hannah Jane" 1829, 2, 11 (?) d 1833,5,
              ·24
            Mary M.   " 1832, 2, 26 d 1832, 3,19
            Edward Mor-

        Ch: ris   b 1823, 5, 10 (?) d 1833,
            5,21

1808, 4, 19. Sarah recrq
1808, 8, 23. Jane recrq
1815, 10, 24. Hannah (form Morris) dis mcd
1821, 11, 20. Mary rocf New Garden MM, Pa.,
        dtd 1821,4,4
1830, 9, 21. Jane dis JH
1835, 3, 26. Barak & w, Hannah, & ch, Jona-
        than, Deborah & David, gct Alum Creek MM
        (H)
1835, 3, 26. Jane gct Alum Creek MM (H)
1862, 11, 19. Elizabeth, Tabitha, Henry &
        Pharaby dis JW
1870, 10, 20. Isaac Lloyd gct Damascus MM, to
        m Hannah W. Butler (G)

BYE
1812, 12, 3. Susanna m James JUDKINS Jr.
1816, 2, 29. Jonathan Jr., s Jonathan & Mary,
        Jefferson Co., O.; m in Short Creek MH,
        Mary HUNT, dt Joshua & Rachel, Jefferson
        Co., O.

1810, 1, 22. Jonathan & w, Mary, & ch, John,
        Jonathan, Jonas, Sarah & Samuel, rocf
        Indian Spring MM, Md., dtd 1810,11,16
1811, 1, 22. Susanna rocf Indian Spring MM,
        Md., dtd 1810,11,16
1818, 6, 23. Jonathan Jr. & w, Mary, gct
        Plainfield MM
1819, 8, 24. Jonas gct Flushing MM
1820, 3, 21. John gct Flushing MM
1820, 3, 21. Sarah gct Flushing MM
1820, 6, 20. Jonathan & w, Mary, & s, Samuel,
        gct Flushing MM

CADWALADER
----, --, --. Asa & Jane
        Ch: Mary   b 1806, 8, 1
            Susan   " 1808, 7, 15
            Nathan   " 1811, 5,25
            Jacob   " 1813, 11, 21
            Jonah   " 1815, 8, 15
1809, 12, 28. Joseph, s John & Sarah, Tuskara-
        was Co., O.; m in Short Creek MH, Chris-
        tena HALL, dt Joseph & Christena, Jeffer-
        son Co., O.
1812, 2, 27. David, s John & Sarah, Tuskrawas
        Co., O.; m in Short Creek MH, Sarah LYPSEY
        dt Amasa & Penninah, Jefferson Co., O.
1830, 4, 28. Sarah m Wm. F. RATCLIFF
1830, 8, 26. Nathan d bur Short Creek
1830, 9, 14. Harmon d bur Springfield, O.
1833, 2, 27. Eliza m Lewis LEWIS
1836, 3, 23. Edith m Henry CREW
1844, 5, 22. Asa d ae 76 bur Short Creek
1852, 1, 22. Jane d bur Short Creek

1805, 8, 17. Asa & w, Jane, & ch, Abigail,
        William, Rees & Harmon, rocf Redstone MM,
        dtd 1805,5,3

CADWALADER, continued

1806, 6, 21. John Jr. & w, Ruth, & ch, Anne
    & Sarah, rocf Redstone MM, dtd 1806,3,28
1810, 7, 24. Christiana gct Plainfield MM
1812, 5, 19. Sarah gct Plainfield MM
1827, 2, 20. Abby gct Springfield MM
1827, 2, 20. Abby gct Upper Springfield MM
1827, 2, 20. Harmon gct Upper Springfield MM
1827, 2, 20. William gct Upper Springfield MM
1828, 9, 19. Sarah rocf Flushing MM, dtd
    1828,6,27
1828, 12, 23. Eliza rocf Flushing MM, dtd
    1828,8,22
1830, 1, 19. Rees dis jH
1831, 5, 24. Sarah & ch, Elizabeth, Edith,
    Amasa, Sarah & Joseph, rocf Flushing MM,
    dtd 1831,3,24
1841, 3, 23. Sarah & s, Joseph, gct Chester-
    field MM
1841, 3, 23. Sarah Ann gct Chesterfield MM
1842, 4, 19. Amasa dis mcd
1843, 2, 21. Jacob dis mcd
1856, 1, 22. Susan & Mary gct Winnesheik MM,
    Iowa
1856, 10, 22. Jonah gct Wenesheik MM

CALFER

1924, 4, 23. Mrs. Celia E. recrq (G)

CALL

1895, 2, 20. James recrq (G)

CAMERON

1882, 11, 22. Albert H., s Josiah & Hannah,
    Columbiana Co., O.; m in Concord, Eliza-
    beth D. BUNDY, dt Wm. & Sarah, Belmont
    Co., O. (W)

1883, 6, 19. Elizabeth D. gct Salem MM (W)
1907, 3, 19. Barclay S. Hall gct Upper Spring-
    field MM, to m Mary Cameron (W)

CAMPBELL

1823, 6, 24. William gct Redstone MM

CANARY

1813, 11, 23. Sarah (form Hall) dis mcd

CANDLER

1845, 3, 18. Susan J. (form Johnson) con mcd

CANTLEBERRY

1902, 2, 19. Harry recrq (G)
1907, 4, 24. Harry dropped from mbrp (G)

CAROTHERS

1829, 7, 21. Rhoda [Carethers] (form Parker)
    dis mcd
1905, 4, 19. John [Carruthers] recrq (G)
1911, 4, 19. Jay & Esther recrq (G)
1929, 7, 24. Charles, Clark, Jay, John W. &
    Samuel dropped from mbrp (G)

CAREY

1933, 8, 17. Wilford & w, Colleen, recrq (G)

CARMAN

1886, 5, 19. Rosa recrq (G)
1891, 5, 20. Rosa L. Graebe (form Carmon)
    relrq (G)
1893, 6, 21. Edna F. recrq (G)

CARNEY

1892, 10, 19. John W. recrq (G)

CARPENTER

----, --, --. Howard m Esther RODGERS
    Ch: Mary
        Eleanor   b 1908, 8, 30
        Margery
        Rodgers   " 1910, 5, 7
----, --, --. John & Mary H.
    Ch: Howard H. b 1881, 1, 9
        Amy Lee   " 1886, 1, 5

1882, 5, 24. Andrew, Lizzie May & Lyde recrq
    (G)
1888, 10, 24. Andy, Lizzie May & Lida dropped
    from mbrp (G)
1912, 6, 5. John E. & w, Mary H., gct
    Orange Grove MM, Calif. (H)
1912, 6, 5. Howard & ch, Mary Eleanor & Mar-
    gary Rogers, gct Orange Grove MM, Calif.
    (H)

CARR

1816, 6, 23. William, s Aquila & Susanna,
    Jefferson Co., O.; m in West Grove MH,
    Elizabeth BROWN, dt Daniel & Miriam, Har-
    rison Co., O.
1821, 10, 10. Elizabeth, dt Kinsey & Rachel,
    b
1837, 2, 16. James d ae 74 bur Smithfield
1848, 3, 22. Mary H., w Samuel, d bur Smith-
    field
1852, 8, 6. Elizabeth, w James, d bur Smith-
    field
1852, 8, 6. Elizabeth, dt Samuel, d

1805, 4, 20. Priscilla rocf Westland MM, dtd
    1805,1,26
1816, 8, 20. Elizabeth gct Plymouth MM
1817, 1, 21. Thomas, minor, rocf Plymouth MM,
    dtd 1816,12,28
1819, 8, 24. Gideon Lupton gct Smithfield MM,
    to m Susanna Carr
1833, 11, 19. Orpha rocf Smithfield MM, dtd
    1833,9,23
1835, 5, 19. Orpha gct Smithfield MM
1863, 3, 24. Kinsey & Samuel dis jG (W)
1864, 9, 20. Rachel dis jG (W)
1867, 11, 19. Aletta & Ann dis jG (W)
1892, 10, 19. Alice E. & Walter S. recrq (G)
1896, 2, 19. Lizzie G. relrq (G)

CARROLL
1817, 5, 20.   Thomas rocf Newgarden MM, dtd
      1817,4,17
1820, 1, 18.   Thomas gct Whitewater MM, Ind.
1865, 7, 4.   Beulah A. gct Phila. MM, Race
      St. (H)

CARSON
1813, 5, 27.   Phebe m Mordecai YARNEL

1806, 7, 19.   George & w, Lydia, & dt, Phebe,
      rocf London Grove MM, dtd 1806,4,9

CARTER
1832, 1, 24.   Richard gct Sadsbury MM
1833, 12, 24. Richard rocf Fallowfield MM,
      dtd 1833,10,11
1834, 5, 20.   Richard gct Somerset MM
1835, 1, 20.   Susanna dis mcd to first cousin
      & jH
1836, 2, 23.   Mary, minor, rocf Flushing MM,
      dtd 1835,11,26
1836, 12, 20. Richard gct Pennsville MM
1839, 10, 22. Mary gct Chesterfield MM
1862, 11, 19. Sarah, Phebe Eliza, Joel K. &
      Melinda dis jW
1923, 11, 23. Allen E. recrq (G)
1929, 10, 23. Allen E. & w, Nellie, relrq (G)

CARVER
1805, 5, 18.   Henry & fam gct Concord MM
1815, 9, 19.   John C. Thompson gct Concord MM,
      to m Rebecca Carver
1907, 6, 19.   Priscilla J. dropped from mbrp
      (G)

CASE
1876, 5, 25.   Oliver C. & w, Catharine A.,
      recrq (G)
1885, 2, 25.   Joseph & Johnson recrq (G)
1886, 5, 19.   Jacob & Emma recrq (G)
1891, 12, 23. Alice recrq (G)
1894, 5, 23.   Jennie E. recrq (G)
1896, 2, 19.   J. Johnson & w, Alice C., relrq
      (G)
1902, 12, 24. Joseph dropped from mbrp (G)

CASTLE
1892, 10, 19. Julia M. recrq (G)

CASTLEMAN
1886, 5, 19.   Sarah E. recrq (G)

CATTELL
1841, 4, 21.   Ezra, s David & Margaret, Fayette
      Co., Pa.; m in Short Creek MH, Ruthanna
      PATTERSON, dt Mahlon & Maryann, Jefferson
      Co., O.
      Ch: Marianna   b 1842, 9, 5 d 1866, 3,12
          Elma   " 1844, 5, 12
          Edward D. " 1846, 1, 28
          Martha P. " 1848, 5, 16
          Eliza B.   " 1850, 6, 8

      Ch: Lurena P.   b 1852, 7, 18
          Caroline E." 1854, 9, 4
          Lydia H.P. " 1857, 1, 23
          Emeline J. " 1858, 9, 11
          William M. " 1860, 7, 25
          Edith Elma " 1865, 8, 21
1849, 11, 1. Geo. s David & Margaret, Fay-
      ette Co., O., d 1864,3,8 ae 36; m in Short
      Creek MH, Jane H. PATTERSON, dt Mahlon &
      Mary Ann, Jefferson Co., O., d 1858,4,25
      ae 31 bur Short Creek
      Ch: Myra G.   b 1850, 9, 7
          David M. " 1852, 6, 25
          Oliver   " 1855, 5, 4
      Geo. m 2nd Mary -----
      Ch: Harvey G. b 1861, 10, 1
1853, 9, 21. Edith m Samuel LLOYD
1854, 8, 12. Mathew P. d
1865, 2, 10. Elmar d
1865, 3, 10. Eliza B. d
1865, 4, 9. Huldah d
1868, 2, 9. Ezra d ae 51
1874, 5, 28. Mira J. m Robt. W. CHAMBERS (nm)

1841, 10, 19. Ruthanna P. [Cattle] gct Red-
      stone MM
1842, 11, 22. Ezra & w, Ruthanna, rocf Red-
      stone MM, dtd 1842,9,26
1844, 9, 24. Maryanna, minor dt Ezra & Ruth-
      anna, rocf Redstone MM, dtd 1844,9,4
1850, 3, 19. George rocf Redstone MM, dtd
      1850,1,30
1853, 7, 19. Esther rocf Redstone MM, dtd
      1853,6,29
1855, 5, 23. Beulah rocf Redstone MM, Pa.,
      dtd 1855,2,5
1860, 4, 25. Beulah gct Redstone MM
1860, 4, 24. Ezra dis jG
1860, 8, 22. George gct Flushing MM, to m
      Mary B. Ratcliff
1860, 9, 18. George dis jG
1860, 11, 21. Mary B. rocf Flushing MM
1864, 12, 21. Mary B. gct New Sharon MM, Ia.
1864, 12, 21. Mary B. & s, Harvey B., gct New
      Sharon MM, Ia. (G)
1872, 4, 23. Myra J. dis jG (W)
1874, 11, 24. Lurena P. dis jG (W)
1875, 3, 23. Caroline E. dis jG (W)
1875, 4, 20. Edward dis disunity (W)
1877, 10, 25. David M. relrq (G)
1883, 4, 24. William Jr. dis jG (W)
1889, 6, 19. Edward relrq (G)
1893, 10, 25. William M. relrq (G)
1903, 2, 25. Lewis E. recrq (G)
1904, 2, 24. Horace recrq (G)
1904, 3, 23. Edward D., Emma L. & Marjorie
      recrq (G)
1905, 10, 25. Lewis relrq (G)
1906, 4, 25. William M. & w, Edith B., & ch,
      Ezra Brenaman, Stephenson, Cornelia,
      Richard Bartley Channing & William Maurice,
      recrq (G)
1908, 1, 22. Horace M. relrq (G)

CATTELL, continued
1912, 10, 23. Marjorie released (G)

CHAFFIN
1834, 6, 24. James rst

CHALFAN
1834, 10, 2. James, s Aaron & Margaret, Jef-
      ferson Co., O.; m in Short Creek MH, Ruth
      THOMPSON, dt Aaron & Sarah, Jefferson Co.,
      O.
1835, 7, 13. James d ae 29 bur Short Creek
1837, 6, 23. Ruth d ae 26 bur Short Creek

CHAMBERLAIN
1848, 7, 18. Rebecca (form Waterman) dis mcd
1887, 3, 23. Mary F. recrq (G)

CHAMBERS
1874, 5, 28. Robert W. (nm), s David & Nancy,
      Jefferson Co., O.; m in home of Ruthan P.
      Cattell, Mira J. CATTELL, dt Geo. & Jane
      H., Harrison Co., O.
----, --, --. Benjamin, s James & Ann, b 1850,
      12,22 d 1880,6,10 bur West Grove; m Mary
      Jane MADDOX, dt Wilson & Mary, b 1853,4,23
      d 1880,6,10(?) bur West Grove (G)
      Ch: Elizabeth
              H.   b 1886, 2, 18

1809, 1, 24. James & w, Mary, & dt, Ann, rocf
      Lurgan MM, Ireland, dtd 1808,4,18
1809, 10, 24. James & w, Mary, & ch, Ann &
      Jane, gct Newgarden MM
1861, 10, 23. Milton I. Hussey gct Sandy Spring
      MM, to m Mary Jane Chambers
1880, 12, 23. Mary Jane gct Sandy Spring MM
      (G)
1883, 9, 19. Benjamin S. & w, M. J., rocf San-
      dy Spring MM, O., dtd 1883,7,24 (G)
1890, 12, 24. Minnie McGill relrq (G)

CHAMP
1881, 2, 26. John Henry recrq (G)
1888, 10, 24. John H. dropped from mbrp (H)

CHANCE
1825, 1, 18. Vilee (form Stephens) dis mcd

CHANDLER
1876, 5, 25. Judith D. recrq (G)

CHAPMAN
1845, 9, 24. Elwood, s John & Ann, Columbi-
      ana Co., O.; m in Mt. Pleasant, Sarah A.
      WILSON, dt Daniel & Mary, Morgan Co., O.

1816, 5, 2. Ann rocf Kennet MM, dtd 1816,4,2
1817, 12, 23. John recrq
1827, 2, 20. John & w, Ann, & ch, Lydia, El-
      wood & Anna, gct Middleton MM
1846, 2, 24. Sarah Ann gct Middleton MM

CHASE
1877, 2, 20. Mary L. (form Cook) dis mcd &
      jG (W)

CHERRY
1892, 10, 19. Agnes, Sarah & Caroline recrq
      (G)

CHILDERS
1913, 1, 22. Mary A. recrq (G)
1913, 1, 22. Orvy D. recrq (G)

CLARK
1819, 7, 29. Samuel, s John & Mary, Jeffer-
      son Co., O.; m in Short Creek MH, Hannah
      MICHENER, dt John & Martha, Harrison Co.,
      O.
      Ch: Hannah M. b 1820, 8, 4
----, --, --. George & Samaria
      Ch: Charles
          Burley   b 1841, 12, 2 d 1846,10,7
          Wm. Robin-
            son   " 1843, 7, 13 " 1914, 2,7
          Theodore   " 1845, 9, 18
          Francis   " 1848, 9, 14 " 1849, 3,-
          Jane Eliza-
            beth   " 1850, 2, 28 " 1914, 3,30
          Tacy Elthena" 1851, 12, 25
          Mary Alice " 1854, 9, 14
          George   " 1857, 10, 29
          Laurey Sa-
            maria   " 1857, 10, 29
1872, 2, 20. Robert d ae 79
1877, 3, 13. Jane d
1879, 7, 15. Frank W., s Wm. R. & Margaret
      C., b
1881, 10, 24. Ella T. d
1890, 3, 7. George P. d
1893, 8, 23. Laura S. d
1905, 10, 23. Samaria J. d
----, --, --. Frank Ward m Alice JONES
      Ch: Margaret
          Sabina   b 1908, 7, 4
          William
            Elery   " 1910, 1, 14
          Catharine " 1912, 1, 3
          Mildred   " 1913, 10, 16
1912, 3, 8. Margaret Craft d

1819, 2, 23. Samuel rocf Lisburn MM, Ireland,
      dtd 1818,5,14
1826, 9, 19. Solomon gct Somerset MM
1827, 3, 20. Samuel gct Belfastin MM, Ireland
1835, 5, 19. Hannah M. gct Marlborough MM
1881, 2, 26. Emma recrq (G)
1882, 1, 12. Theodore & ch, Horace B. & Anna
      Mabel, gct Concord MM (H)
1888, 10, 24. Emma dropped from mbrp (G)
1895, 1,23. George recrq (G)
1907, 6, 19. George dropped from mbrp (G)

CLAWSON
1873, 12, 23. Charles [Claussen] recrq (G)

CLAWSON, continued
1879, 3, 20. George & w, Josephine, recrq
      (G)
1879, 3, 20. Taylor recrq (G)
1884, 7, 23. Charles dropped from mbrp (G)
1884, 7, 23. George dropped from mbrp (G)
1884, 7, 23. Josephine dropped from mbrp (G)
1888, 10, 24. Mary T. dropped from mbrp (G)
1888, 10, 24. Taylor dropped from mbrp (G)

CLEAVER
1844, 11, 21. Eli gct Westland MM (H)

CLENDENNEN
1862, 11, 19. Hannah [Clendenen] dis jW
1862, 11, 19. Sarah dis jW
1862, 11, 19. Stephen, Elizabeth, Sarah Louiza
      & Matilda Jane dis jW

COBBS
1862, 5, 28. Henry P., s Ansalem & Ann, Mo-
      honan Co.; m in West Grove MH, Anna LADD,
      dt Peter & Catharine, Harrison Co., O.

1863, 5, 20. Annie S. gct Upper Springfield
      MM (G)

COCHRAN
1902, 12, 20. Lucy recrq (G)
1914, 3, 25. John A. & Mary L. recrq (G)

COFFIN
1840, 10, 2. Hannah, w Albert, d bur Cross
      Creek
1843, 1, 2. Charles d bur Cross Creek
1859, 11, 17. Rebecca, w Chas., d ae 79 bur
      Cross Creek

COFFMAN
1880, 4, 22. George recrq (G)
1895, 1, 23. Anna recrq (G)
1896, 9, 23. Charles W. recrq (G)
1897, 5, 19. Lillian May recrq (G)
1900, 4, 25. Edith recrq (G)
1905, 3, 22. Mrs. Earle recrq (G)
1915, 2, 24. Eunice Mary recrq (G)

COFLIN
1869, 6, 24. Elizabeth dis mcd (G)

COKELEY
1875, 10, 21. Jacob recrq (G)

COLEMAN
1881, 2, 26. James recrq (G)
1881, 2, 26. Malvena recrq (G)
1907, 4, 24. Bessie T., Charles A., James,
      Mary C., Mollie T. & Phebe dropped from
      mbrp (G)

COLES
1892, 10, 19. C. H., Anna & Frank recrq (G)

COLLENS
1835, 3, 4. Daniel, s Earnest & Elizabeth, b

COLLINGS
1836, 1, 19. Cert rec for Earnest & w, Eliza-
      beth, & ch from Menden MM, Germany, dtd
      1835,7,5, end to Pennsville MM

COLLINS
1819, 2, 23. Cert rec for Benjamin from
      Farmington MM, N. Y., dtd 1819,2,20, end
      to Alum Creek MM

COMLEY
1858, 4, 13. Sarah d ae 62
1866, 9, 6. David d ae 68 bur Short Creek

1839, 9, 24. David & ch, John, William,
      James, Benjamin & David, recrq
1839, 11, 19. Sarah rst on consent of New-
      garden MM
1839, 12, 24. Eliza Jane [Comly], dt Sarah,
      recrq
1851, 6, 24. John [Comly] dis mcd
1859, 5, 25. Benjamin [Comly] con mcd
1860, 6, 20. David [Comly] Jr. con mcd
1861, 3, 20. Eliza Jane Hoge (form Comley)
      con mcd
1867, 4, 25. William [Comly] con mcd (G)
1879, 10, 23. David B. dis disunity (G)
1882, 8, 22. David B. dis mcd (W)
1882, 8, 22. William dis mcd (W)
1882, 10, 24. James dis jG (W)
1883, 2, 20. Benjamin [Comly] dis mcd (W)
1884, 7, 23. William [Comely] dropped from
      mbrp (G)

CONNARD
1830, 9, 21. William dis jH
1862, 11, 19. Rachel dis jH

CONRAD
1828, 9, 19. Sarah dis jH
1831, 7, 19. Hannah dis jH
1831, 9, 20. Mary dis jH

CONROW
1830, 4, 28. Thomas, s Darling & Rachel,
      Belmont Co., O.; m in Mt. Pleasant, Ruth
      LUPTON, dt John & Rachel, Jefferson Co.,O.
1837, 11, 2. David, s Darling & Rachel, Bel-
      mont Co., O.; m in Harrisville, Anna HALL,
      dt Thos. & Mary, Jefferson Co., O.

1830, 9, 21. Ruth gct Flushing MM
1838, 2, 20. Anna gct Flushing MM
1862, 11, 19. Anne dis jW

COOK
----, --, --. Elisha & Mary Ann
      Ch: Elizabeth
            L.   b 1838, 3, 1
            Benjamin L." 1840, 9, 10

COOK, Elisha & Mary Ann, continued
    Ch: William M. b 1842, 5, 17
      George   " 1845, 2, 27
      James D. " 1847, 6, 6
----, --, --. Nathan & Ann H.
    Ch: Elisha   b 1839, 1, 8
      Margaret B." 1843, 3, 1
      Mary Lou-
        isa   " 1849, 6, 2
      Lydia   " 1852, 12, 12
----, 3, 27. Mary Ann d ae 40 bur Cross Creek

1836, 6, 21. Nathan rocf Deer Creek MM, dtd
    1836,5,5
1837, 10, 24. Nathan gct Upper Springfield MM
1839, 7, 23. Nathan & w, Ann, & s, Elisha,
    rocf Upper Springfield MM, dtd 1839,6,2
1859, 3, 23. Mary Jane (form Pettet) con mcd
1859, 4, 19. Elisha dis mcd
1859, 6, 21. Elizabeth Cunningham (form Cook)
    dis mcd
1859, 7, 20. Mary Jane gct Smithfield MM
1861, 8, 20. Elisha Cook gct Salem MM, to m
    Abbie H. Cook
1862, 5, 20. Abbie H. rocf Salem MM, dtd
    1862,4,23
1862, 5, 20. Mary Jane (form Pettit) dis mcd
    (W)
1862, 11, 19. Nathan & w, Ann, & ch, Margaret
    B., Mary L., Lydia & Elisha, dis jW (G)
1865, 3, 21. William M. dis mcd & military
    service (W)
1876, 11, 21. Margaret B. & Lydia gct Newgar-
    den MM (W)
1877, 2, 20. Mary L. Chase (form Cook) dis
    mcd & jG (W)
1877, 9, 18. Nathan gct Newgarden MM, Pa.(W)
1892, 5, 24. Martha C. Beardsley (form Cook)
    dis mcd (W)

COOPER
1844, 6, 20. Elma gct Fall Creek MM (H)

COPE
----, --, --. ----- m Grace ----- b 1764,3,9
    Ch: Isaac   b 1801, 2, 1
      John   " 1803, 4, 25
----, --, --. Joseph & Rebecca
    Ch: Lindley   b 1826, 10, 16
      William M. " 1829, 10, 22
      Wiletts   " 1833, 5, 20
      Samuel   " 1834, 10, 18
      Benjamin " 1843, 9, 8
      Martha   " 1845, 8, 24
      Sarah   " 1849, 7, 21
----, --, --. Joseph b 1799,1,19; m Ruth -----
    b 1801,1,1
    Ch: Amos   b 1826, 12, 20
      Benjamin " 1828, 5, 15
      Oliver   " 1830, 8, 11
----, --, --. William b 1796,8,1; m Sarah ----
    b 1798,3,12
    Ch: Mary   b 1828, 10, 28

Ch: Grace   b 1830, 1, 4
    John   " 1831, 7, 30
    Charles   " 1834, 7, 15
    Benjamin " 1836, 4, 16
    Isaac   " 1838, 1, 4
    Sarah Ann " 1843, 7, 3
----, --, --. John & Mary
    Ch: Sarah   b 1833, 6, 2
      Lemuel   " 1838, 7, 1 d 1838, 9,23
      Hiram   " 1843, 12, 16
----, --, --. Isaac & Abigail
    Ch: Rachel   b 1841, 4, 28
      Sarah   " 1845, 7, 23
1841, 6, 14. Martha Ann b
1850, 6, 26. Amos L., s Joseph & Ruth, Harri-
    son Co., O.; m in West Grove MH, Elizabeth
    THOMAS, dt Peter & Mary, Harrison Co., O.
    Ch: William
      Albert   b 1851, 3, 8
      Mary Isa-
        bel   " 1853, 4, 7
      Oliver P. " 1855, 4, 2
      Pearson   " 1860, 7, 7
      Rachel E. " 1859, 11, --
1855, 3, 30. Grace d ae 91
----, --, --. Benjamin & Rachel
    Ch: Ruth Ann b 1856, 3, 30
      Lizza S.   " 1859, 6, 19
1855, 10, 4. Ellen P., dt Darlington & Ann, b
1859, 6, --. Rachel E. d
1872, 10, 31. Hiram, s John & Mary, Harrison
    Co., O.; m in home of Isaac Thomas, Martha
    THOMAS, dt Isaac & Anna L., Harrison Co.,
    O., d 1927,5,11
1876, 7, 19. Mary d
1883, 12, 21. Isaac d
1885, 4, 21. Joseph d
1885, 8, 28. Benjamin H., s Darlington & Ann
    D., Belmont Co., O.; m in Concord, Mari-
    etta STARBUCK, dt John & Sarah, Belmont
    Co., O. (W)
    Ch: Amy A.   b 1886, 10, 10
      Hannah M. " 1888, 5, 28
      John S.   " 1889, 8, 28
      Caroline " 1891, 1, 17
      Helena   " 1895, 1, 28 d 1896, 8,24
      bur Concord
      Darlington b 1897, 3, 10
      Byron H. " 1899, 3, 31
      Chalkley B." 1900, 12, 4
1886, 3, 12. Abigail d
1891, 4, 22. John d
1897, 6, 9. Ruth Griffith d
1906, --, --. Rachel d
1908, 10, 19. Sarah T. d
1914, 1, 24. Hanna M. m W. Herbert HAINES (W)

1805, 12, 21. George & w, Abigail, & ch, Mary,
    John, James, George, Abigail & Jane, rocf
    Hopewell MM, dtd 1805,10,7
1807, 7, 18. Jacob & w, Mary, & ch, Opkia,
    rocf Nottingham MM, dtd 1807,4,10
1811, 12, 24. Grace rocf Hopewell MM, dtd

COPE, continued
    1811,10,7
1811, 12, 24. Jacob & w, Mary, & ch, Sophia,
    Rachel, Margaret & Ellis, gct Plainfield
    MM
1815, 3, 21. Joshua gct Concord MM
1815, 4, 18. George & w, Abigail, & ch, James,
    George, Abigail, Jane Sarah, Rachel & Ca-
    leb, gct Concord MM
1815, 4, 18. Mary gct Concord MM
1817, 1, 21. William, Joseph, Isaac, John &
    James, ch John & Grace, recrq
1818, 5, 19. Thomas White gct Concord MM, to
    m Mary Cope
1826, 1, 25. Ruth rocf Providence MM, dtd
    1825,12,20
1828, 7, 22. Abigail, Phebe & Jane dis jH
1829, 4, 21. Grace & Ruth dis jH
1830, 2, 23. Sarah dis jH
1832, 11, 23. Ann (form Bundy) dis jH
1834, 6, 24. Rebecca dis jH
1835, 11, 26. Ann E. gct Concord MM (H)
1840, 11, 24. Sarah Ann (form Gwynn) dis mcd
1845, 3, 20. William & w, Sarah C., & ch,
    Mary, Grace, John, Charles, Benjamin,
    Isaac & Sarah, gct Deerfield MM (H)
1846, 11, 24. Abigail gct Pennville MM
1847, 11, 23. George Jr. dis disunity
1850, 3, 19. Edward dis disunity
1851, 1, 21. Julia Ann (form French) dis mcd
1854, 8, 22. Gibson Binns gct Providence MM,
    Pa., to m Martha V. Cope
1856, 2, 19. Benjamin dis mcd
1856, 3, 18. Rachel (form Lukens) dis mcd
1856, 4, 22. William Bundy gct Providence
    MM, Pa., to m Sarah Ann Cope
1857, 9, 22. Sarah (form Williams) dis mcd
1861, 10, 22. Amos dis disunity
1863, 3, 24. Joseph H. dis jG (W)
1863, 3, 24. Lindley M. dis jG (W)
1864, 9, 20. Rebecca dis jG (W)
1864, 11, 22. Samuel dis jG (W)
1865, 1, 24. Jane dis disunity (W)
1865, 8, 22. Willets dis jH (W)
1865, 9, 19. Martha dis disunity (W)
1869, 4, 20. Benjamin dis disunity (W)
1869, 5, 20. Amos A. & w, Elizabeth L., & ch,
    William Albert, Mary Isabella, Oliver P.
    & Pearson L., gct Springdale MM, Iowa (G)
1870, 11, 22. William M. dis mcd (W)
1876, 5, 25. Benjamin T. & w, Rachel, dis
    disunity (G)
1884, 6, 25. Lizzie S. Adams (form Cope)
    dropped from mbrp (G)
1884, 6, 25. Ruthanna Scott (form Cope)
    dropped from mbrp (G)
1885, 2, 24. Benjamin H. rocf Newgarden MM,
    Pa., dtd 1885,1,7 (W)
1902, 10, 21. John A. Binns gct Salem MM, to
    m Mary E. Cope (W)
1909, 2, 23. Ellen P. rocf Newgarden MM, Pa.,
    dtd 1909,2,3 (W)
1917, 9, 18. Amy gct Paulina MM, Ia. (W)

1917, 9, 18. Benjamin & w, Marietta S., &
    ch, Darlington, Byron & Chalkley B., gct
    Paullina MM, Ia. (W)
1917, 9, 18. Caroline gct Paulina MM, Ia. (W)
1917, 9, 18. Charlotte gct Paulina MM, Ia.
    (W)
1917, 9, 18. John S. gct Paulina MM, Ia. (W)
1922, 6, 20. Ellen P. gct New Garden MM, Pa.
    (W)

COPELAND
1836, 8, 23. Ann & ch, John, James, Bonsel
    & Joseph, roc
1841, 7, 20. Ann & ch, John, James Bonsall
    & Joseph, rocf Somerset MM, dtd 1836,3,27
1841, 8, 24. John dis mcd
1846, 12, 2. James gct Somerset MM
1847, 2, 23. Joseph dis disunity

COPPOCK
1914, 4, 22. Robert E., s Jos. J. & Rebecca
    E., Cedar Co., Ia.; m in Harrisville,
    Mary Emma SMITH, dt Nathan R. & Lizzie
    M., Jefferson Co., O. (W)

1804, 11, 7. Isaac rocf Notingham MM, dtd
    1804,9,7
1805, 6, 15. Isaac gct Concord MM
1806, 4, 19. John & w, Catharine, & ch, Ann,
    Samuel & Timothy, gct Salem MM
1806, 4, 19. Sarah gct Concord MM
1812, 6, 23. Cert rec for Rebecca & Ellin fro
    Little Britain MM, dtd 1812,5,9, end to
    Salem MM
1812, 6, 23. Cert rec for Samuel & ch, Aaron
    & Ruth, from Little Britain MM, dtd 1812,
    5,9, end to Salem MM
1812, 6, 23. Cert rec for Samuel Jr. from
    Little Britain MM, dtd 1812,5,9, end to
    Salem MM
1915, 3, 23. Mary Emma gct Hickory Grove MM,
    Ia. (W)

CORNLIKI
1902, 3, 19. Alice recrq (G)

CORNLIFF
1907, 3, 20. Alice dropped from mbrp (G)

COTANT
1885, 6, 24. Eliza (form Mattox) gct Green-
    wich MM, O. (G)

COUGHLIN
1891, 4, 11. Esther, w Dennis, dt Lindley M.
    & Anna S. (French) Brackin, b

COVEL
1817, 11, 18. Cert rec for Micajah & fam from
    Saratoga MM, N. Y., dtd 1817,6,8, end to
    Alum Creek MM

COWGILL
1844, 5, 1. Phinehas, s Ralph & Betsy, Bel-
    mont Co., O.; m in Concord, Sarah Ann BRAN-
    SON, dt Isaac & Sarah

1843, 8, 22. Pheneas rocf Plainfield MM, dtd
    1843,6,21
1848, 6, 20. Phineas & w, Sarah Ann, & ch,
    Elias B. & R. Henry, gct Plainfield MM
1862, 11, 19. Esther, Isaac, Joseph & Sarah
    dis jW

COX
1819, 3, 4. Sarah m Amasa LIPSEY
1853, 9, 21. Joseph M., s Joseph & Elizabeth,
    Wayne Co., Ind.; m in Mt. Pleasant, Rachel
    M. TERRELL, dt Clark & Mary, Jefferson Co.,
    O.

1819, 1, 19. Sarah rocf Goshen MM, Pa., dtd
    1818,5,29, end by Salem MM
1854, 2, 21. Rachel M. gct Walnut Ridge MM,
    Ind.
1864, 12, 21. Lydia P. rocf Neuse MM, N. C.
    (G)
1872, 1, 25. Lydia M. gct Neuse MM, N. C. (G)
1889, 3, 20. John recrq (G)
1897, 11, 24. Martha Jane recrq (G)
1915, 12, 23. Steuben D. & w, Ruth, & ch,
    Lester, Caspar & Eleanor, rocf Berlin-
    ville MM (G)
1919, 11, 19. Steuben D. & w, Ruth, & ch, Les-
    ter, Casper & Eleanor, relrq (G)

COZENS
1811, 6, 18. John & w, Sarah, rocf Westland
    MM, dtd 1811,5,25

CRAFT
1881, 11, 20. Rachel d

1822, 6, 18. Ann rocf Somerset MM, dtd 1822,
    3,25
1822, 6, 18. Samuel rocf Plainfield MM, dtd
    1822,4,25
1823, 10, 21. Samuel & w, Ann, & s, James,
    gct Somerset MM
1862, 11, 19. Asa, Asa, Ephraim, Evaline,
    Isaac, Joseph, Lindley, Millie & Peninah,
    dis jW (G)
1873, 5, 22. Zipha Eliza recrq (G)

CRAVEN
1831, 1, 18. Hannah (form Walker) dis mcd

CRAWFORD
1906, 9, 19. John B., s Thos. A. & Sarah B.,
    Phila., Pa.; m in Colerain, Alice R.
    STEER, dt Elisha B. & Ellen G., Belmont
    Co., O. (W)
    Ch: Dorothy
        Ellen   b 1908, 1, 13

1908, 12, 22. Alice R. S. & dt, Dorothy Ellen,
    gct Phila. MM (W)
1925, 11, 24. Walter N. Whinery gct Upper
    Springfield MM, to m Deborah Crawford (W)

CREIGHTON
1902, 5, 21. Florence E. (form Jenkins) rel-
    rq (G)

CREW
1822, 1, 30. Henry, s Jacob & Elizabeth,
    Jefferson Co., O.; m in Mt. Pleasant,
    Margaret BAILEY, dt Emmor & Elizabeth,
    Belmont Co., O.
1834, 7, 31. Nancy T. m Nathan PARKER
1836, 3, 23. Henry, s Jacob & Rachel, Bel-
    mont Co., O.; m in Short Creek MH, Edith
    CADWALADER, dt David & Sarah, Jefferson
    Co., O.
1837, 12, 28. Jesse B., s Robert & Nancy,
    Jefferson Co., O., d 1865,7,30; m in
    Short Creek MH, Elizabeth H. JENKINS, dt
    Israel & Elizabeth, Charles City Co., Va.,
    b 1821,11,17 d 1907,4,17
    Ch: Theopilus b 1839, 12, 31
        Ruth Anna " 1841, 8, 13
        Robert Ter-
          rill   " 1846, 8, 12
1841, 5, 3. Theophilus d bur Short Creek
1842, 3, 15. Nancy d ae 67 bur Short Creek
1846, 10, 13. William d
1851, 10, 7. Anna d bur Short Creek
1856, 12, 22. Henry d ae 70 bur Cross Creek
1859, 6, 7. Henry, s Wm. & Deborah, b

1822, 5, 21. Margaret gct Smithfield MM
1832, 4, 23. William, s Nancy, rocf Wayne Oak
    MM, Va., dtd 1832,3,3
1832, 4, 24. Nancy & dt, Nancy T., rocf Wayne
    Oak MM, Va., dtd 1832,3,3
1832, 6, 19. Robert rocf Wayne Oak MM, Va.,
    dtd 1832,5,5 (with Peter Ladd fam)
1833, 4, 23. Jesse B. rocf Wayne Oak MM, Va.,
    dtd 1832,8,4
1836, 8, 23. Edith gct Somerset MM
1840, 2, 18. George Lupton gct Smithfield MM,
    to m Sarah Ann Crew
1842, 4, 19. Edward B. rocf Wayne Oak MM,
    Va., dtd 1839,5,10
1842, 11, 22. Benjamin rocf Cedar Creek MM,
    Va., dtd 1842,10,8
1843, 5, 23. Lemuel & w, Ann, & ch, Margaret
    E., Samuel H., Walter, Tarleton, Deborah
    D., Henrietta & Anna, rocf Ceder Creek
    MM, Va.
1843, 6, 20. Edward B. dis disunity
1849, 4, 24. Micajah rocf Baltimore MM, dtd
    1849,3,8
1849, 9, 18. Henrietta dis
1852, 5, 18. Wqlter dis mcd
1852, 9, 21. Lemuel & dt, Ann, gct Salem MM,
    Iowa
1852, 9, 21. Margaret E. & Deborah D. gct

CREW, continued
    Salem MM, Ia.
1853, 1, 18. Samuel dis jas
1859, 6, 22. Deborah Ann (form Hargrave) con
    mcd
1860, 2, 22. Deborah Ann gct Smithfield MM
1862, 11, 19. John, Asenath, Miriam, Rebecca,
    Abner, Rachel, Josiah, Ann Eliza, Barclay,
    James, Sarah, Aquilla, Rachel, Thomas Jo-
    seph, Chalkley, Farmer, Ann, Oliver, Isaac,
    Tabitha, Drusilla, Elijah, Martha, John,
    Jephtha, Eli, Mary, Ida May, Isaac, Eliza-
    beth, James, John C., Lydia, Sarah, Aquil-
    la & Robert dis jW
1864, 9, 20. Margaret dis jG
1866, 6, 19. William dis jG & mcd (W)
1866, 10, 23. Deborah Ann dis mcd & disunity
    (W)
1866, 10, 23. William dis jG (W)
1869, 2, 25. Robert T. gct Damascus MM, to m
    Anna E. Hole (G)
1869, 10, 19. Elizabeth dis jG (W)
1869, 10, 19. Ruthanna dis jG (W)
1873, 1, 23. Ruthanna Hoge (form Crew) con
    mcd (G)
1902, 10, 20. Robert F. dropped from mbrp (G)

CRON
1892, 10, 19. Ida recrq (G)

CROSSLEY
----, --, --. Moses & Jane
    Ch: Mary Jane b 1843, 4, 17
        Rachel Ann " 1846, 4, 6

1805, 3, 16. Samuel, John, Hannah, Esther,
    Elizabeth, Moses & Mary, ch John, recrq
1805, 3, 16. Jonathan recrq
1805, 3, 16. Rachel recrq
1805, 4, 20. John recrq
1806, 4, 19. John & w, Tamar, & ch, Jonathan,
    Rachel, Samuel, John, Hannah, Esther,
    Elizabeth, Moses, & Mary, gct Concord MM
1812, 9, 22. Samuel rqct Plainfield MM, to
    m Phebe Sinclair
1814, 3, 22. Samuel gct Plainfield MM
1844, 9, 24. Moses & w, Jane, & ch, John,
    Amy, James, Martha, Moses & Rebecca, rocf
    Flushing MM, dtd 1844,7,25
1849, 10, 23. Amy Waterman (form Crossley) con
    mcd
1854, 7, 18. James dis mcd
1860, 4, 25. Moses dis disunity
1863, 9, 23. Mary Jane King (form Crossley)
    con mcd
1863, 9, 23. Rebecca Thornton (form Crossley)
    con mcd
1864, 8, 23. Moses dis jG (W)
1874, 6, 25. Rachel Barber (form Crossley)
    dis mcd & jas (G)
1902, 3, 19. Carl & Elsey A. recrq (G)
1902, 12, 24. Earnest recrq (G)
1910, 2, 23. Earnest & Ora relrq (G)

CROTHERS
----, --, --. William & Adaline
    Ch: Charles H. b 1881, 5, 22
        John W.   " 1883, 9, 4
        Samuel J.   " 1886, 5, 21

1885, 2, 25. George H., Samuel L., Sarah M.,
    Sarah R. & Thomas recrq (G)
1885, 5, 20. Thomas W. & Adeline A. [Crow-
    thers] recrq (G)
1903, 6, 24. George dropped from mbrp (G)

CROZIER
1838, 12, 18. Sarah, minor, gct Stillwater MM
1839, 7, 23. Sarah Webster (form Crozier)
    con mcd
1851, 3, 18. Mary (form Grubb) con mcd

CUNARD
1811, 9, 24. Elizabeth rocf Fairfax MM, dtd
    1810,6,27, end by Stillwater MM

CUNNINGHAM
1910, 1, 19. Viola Belle, w Earnest, dt
    Robert Nicholas & Margaret (Thompson), b
----, --, --. James L. m Hattie FINDLEY, dt
    Jackson & Loretta, b 1868,6,2
    Ch: Finley   b 1912,10,22

1859, 6, 21. Elizabeth (form Cook) dis mcd

CUSICK
1891, 2, 25. James C. & w, Elizabeth, recrq
    (G)
1891, 11, 25. John A. recrq (G)
1891, 11, 25. William H., Sarah M. & Oswell
    H., ch James C. & Elizabeth, recrq (G)
1903, 3, 25. Dora E. recrq (G)
1903, 4, 22. Emily F. recrq (G)
1907, 1, 23. Dora E. relrq (G)
1907, 1, 23. James dropped from mbrp (G)
1913, 11, 19. John & Ona relrq (G)

DANGE
1907, 3, 20. Ida dropped from mbrp (G)

DAUBINS
1892, 10, 19. M. P. & A. F. recrq (G)

DAUDLE
1902, 12, 24. Joseph dropped from mbrp (G)

DAVIS
1804, 5, 19. Edward dis mcd
1805, 4, 20. Phebe gc
1841, 7, 22. Cynthia Horton, minor, gct
    Plainfield MM (H)
1851, 3, 18. John Hall gct Flushing MM, to
    m Deborah S. Davis
1862, 11, 19. Francis, Mary, John F., Jane,
    Smith & Mary dis jW
1896, 3, 25. Mary J. recrq (G)
1901, 7, 24. Margaret recrq (G)

DAVISON
1821, 8, 29. George, s Rees & Ann, Harrison
      Co., O.; m in West Grove MH, Hannah HARRI-
      SON, dt Peter & Sarah, Harrison Co., O.
      Ch: Sarah Ann b 1822, 6, 7
          Emery L.   " 1825, 10, 13
          Parker   " 1827, 11, 18
          Rees   " 1830, 5, 8

1819, 9, 21. George recrq
1837, 9, 19. George [Davidson] & w, Hannah, &
      ch, Sarah Ann, Charlotte, Evry, Parker &
      Reece, gct Alum Creek MM

DAWSON
1862, 11, 19. Annie, Chalkley, Clinton Els-
      worth, Eli, Elmira, Henry, Martha, Mary,
      Mary Matilda, Sarah, Willets, dis jW

DAY
1854, 1, 24. Mary (form Kinsey) dis mcd

DAYORMAN
1881, 3, 24. William C. recrq (G)
1888, 10, 24. William dropped from mbrp (G)

DEAN
1842, 6, 21. Stephen, minor, rocf Smithfield
      MM, dtd 1842,5,23
1844, 2, 20. Stephen gct Smithfield MM

DEFRANCE
1897, 7, 21. Mary (form Richards) relrq (G)

DEGARMA
1914, 3, 25. Maud recrq (G)
1915, 2, 24. Dorothy, Ola & Mildred recrq (G)

DeGARMORE
1882, 5, 24. Iva & Ella recrq (G)
1882, 5, 24. Rachel recrq (G)
1888, 10, 24. Ella dropped from mbrp (G)

DELANEY
1894, 3, 21. Dessie recrq (G)
1902, 8, 20. Bessie dropped from mbrp (G)
1909, 7, 21. Dessie relrq (G)

DELMUTH
1903, 6, 24. Garnet Brown relrq (G)

DEMAINE
1879, 1, 21. Lydia Emily d ae 34

DEMBY
1892, 10, 19. Pauline recrq (G)

DEMING
1825, 5, 24. Margaret (form Masters) con mcd

DEMPSTER
1899, 6, 21. Joseph S. recrq (G)
1900, 1, 24. Ruth H. [Dempter] recrq (G)

1901, 4, 24. Joseph S. dis (G)
1902, 8, 20. Ruth H. dropped from mbrp (G)

DENNING
1831, 1, 18. Margaret dis jas

DENNIS
1845, 4, 23. Mary (form Herrel) dis mcd
1894, 3, 21. Alice J. recrq (G)

DEW
1808, 1, 11. Joseph d ae 60 bur Short Creek
1808, 12, 29. Joseph, s Joseph & Viley, Jef-
      ferson Co., O.; m in Short Creek MH, Fan-
      nah HARRIS, dt Ezekiel & Sarah, Jefferson
      Co., O., d 1843,5,7 bur Short Creek
      Ch: Ezekiel   b 1809, 10, 1
          Sarah   " 1811, 6, 12
          Joseph   " 1813, 12, 29
          Viley   " 1815, 6, 3
          Susanna   " 1818, 9, 15 d 1820, 6,27
          bur Short Creek
          Liverman b 1821, 1, 27 " 1826,12, 9
          bur Short Creek
          Fannah   b 1823, 3, 18
          Elias   " 1825, 8, 11
          Thomas   " 1828, 3, 18
1811, 10, 20. Elias, s Joseph & Viley, Jeffer-
      son Co., O., b 1787,5,2; m in West Grove
      MH, Sarah McMILLAN, dt John & Esther,
      Jefferson Co., O., b 1792,2,28
      Ch: Ruth   b 1812, 8, 15
          John   " 1814, 6, 12
          Mary   " 1816, 4, 21
          Joseph   " 1818, 3, 6
          Esther   " 1820, 8, 11
          Maria   " 1822, 8, 21
          Allen   " 1824, 8, 23
          Albert   " 1827, 7, 27
1812, 12, 3. Abigail m Nehemiah WRIGHT
1830, 2, 15. Joseph d bur Short Creek
1830, 10, 10. Sarah d ae 38
1832, 1, 15. Ezekiel d bur Short Creek
1836, 7, 4. Thomas d bur Short Creek

1815, 10, 24. Elias & w, Sarah, & ch, Ruth &
      John, gct Plainfield MM
1820, 10, 24. Elias & w, Sarah, & ch, Ruth,
      John, Mary & Joseph, rocf Flushing MM, dtd
      1820,6,23
1829, 1, 20. Sarah dis jH
1830, 9, 21. Sarah Humphreville (form Dew)
      rpd mcd
1833, 10, 24. Ruth gct Plainfield MM (H)
1833, 10, 24. Elias & ch, John, Maria, Alen
      & Albert, gct Plainfield MM (H)
1839, 4, 23. Vila Hull (form Dew) dis mcd
1840, 9, 24. Elias & ch, Allen & Albert, gct
      Flushing MM (H)
1842, 1, 20. Allen & Albert, minor ch Elias,
      gct Freeport MM (H)
1845, 2, 18. Joseph dis disunity
1857, 4, 21. Elias dis mcd

DEWALT

1900, 7, 2. Leroy, s Samuel & Anna (Al-
    bright), b (G)

1885, 2, 25. Peter & Lavinia recrq (G)
1886, 5, 19. Maggie May, Anna Lora & Jennie
    recrq (G)
1891, 12, 23. Samuel recrq (G)
1892, 3, 23. Mahlon recrq (G)
1907, 6, 19. Mahlon [Dewault] dropped from
    mbrp (G)
1932, 4, 20. Leroy recrq (G)

DEWEES

----, --, --. Samuel & Hannah
    Ch: Gulielma   b 1810, 5, 1
        Bulyelma   " 1812, 6, 25
        Ellis Lee " 1814, 7, 16
        Thomas Lee " 1817, 5, 11
        Hannah Ma-
        ria   " 1820, 11, 28
        Mary Ann   " 1824, 4, 2
----, --, --. Thomas L. & Mary
    Ch: Charles B. b 1830, 5, 6
        Greenbury
        P.   " 1832, 1, 10
1829, 8, 22. Sarah [Deweese] d
1871, 9, 21. Thomas, s Jesse & Rebecca, Mor-
    gan Co., O.; m in Harrisville, Martha H.
    HALL, dt Wm. & Hannah, Jefferson Co., O.
    (W)
1904, 5, 25. Jesse H., s Thomas & Martha W.,
    Belmont Co., O., b 1873,1,11; m in Harris-
    ville, Mary C. BINNS, dt Jos. P. & Belin-
    da, Harrison Co., O. (W)
    Ch: Florence
        Martha   b 1905, 5, 31
        Clara R. " 1906, 8, 6
        Thomas Ar-
        thur   " 1908, 3, 7
        Mildred Re-
        becca   " 1909, 3, 2
        Margaret H." 1910, 9, 2
        Joseph How-
        ard   " 1912, 1, 24
        James E. " 1914, 8, 26

1821, 2, 20. Samuel & w, Hannah, & ch, Owen,
    David, Gulielma, Bulielma, Ellis & Thomas
    L., rocf Plainfield MM
1821, 11, 20. Sarah rocf Exeter MM, Pa., dtd
    1821,6,27
1829, 8, 18. David B. gct Deerfield MM
1829, 8, 20. Samuel & w, Hannah, & ch, Guliel-
    ma, Bulaelma B., Ellis Lee, Thomas Lee,
    Hannah Maria & Mary Ann, gct Stillwater
    MM (H)
1831, 2, 22. Hannah dis jH
1832, 4, 24. Samuel dis jH
1832, 8, 21. Thomas Jr. rocf Stillwater MM,
    dtd 1832,7,28
1833, 4, 23. Thomas T. & w, Mary, & ch, Lew-
    is W., Jonathan F., Ann M., Isaiah F.,

Mary L., William H., Charles B. & Greenberry P., gct Deerfield MM
1833, 5, 21. Gulielma, Bulielma, Ellis,
    Thomas Lee, Hannah, Mariah & Mary Ann, ch
    Samuel & Hannah, gct Deerfield MM
1833, 6, 18. Gula Elma gct Deerfield MM
1833, 6, 18. Bula Elma gct Deerfield MM
1834, 8, 19. Thomas gct Stillwater MM
1836, 6, 23. James gct Deerfield MM (H)
1837, 6, 20. Mary gct Pennsville MM
1872, 1, 23. Thomas rocf Pennsville MM, dtd
    1871,12,14 (W)
1876, 7, 18. Thomas & w, Martha W., & ch,
    Jesse H. & Ezra, gct Pennsville MM (W)
1897, 5, 18. Oliver W. Binns gct Somerset MM,
    to m Mariana Dewees (W)
1906, 1, 23. Jesse H. rocf Stillwater MM, dtd
    1905,11,22 (W)
1916, 4, 18. Jesse H. & w, Mary, & ch, Flor-
    ence Martha, Clara R., Thos. Arthur, Mil-
    dred Rebecca, Margaret H., Jos. Howard &
    James E. gct Salem MM (W)

DICKERSON

1898, 8, 22. Genevra relrq (G)

DICKEY

----, --, --. Benjamin & L----
    Ch: Phinius   b 1851, 4, 25
        Horace G. " 1859, 2, 26

1850, 5, 21. Leanna (form Waterman) dis mcd
1857, 3, 25. Benjamin & s, Phineas, recrq
1857, 3, 25. Leanah rst
1893, 6, 21. Benjamin H. & Laura M. recrq (G)

DILLINGHAM

1859, 12, 28. Abigail m Joshua JOHNSON

1816, 5, 2. John & w, Mary, & ch, Micajah,
    Sylvanus, Sarah, James, Hiram, Mira & Han-
    nah, rocf Deryter MM, N. Y., dtd 1815,9,27
1857, 9, 23. Jesse Lloyd Jr. gct Goshen MM,
    to m Edith Dillingham
1859, 10, 19. Abigail rocf Goshen MM, dtd
    1859,9,17

DILWORTH

1818, 12, 9. William, s Caleb & Ann, Jeffer-
    son Co., O.; m in Mt. Pleasant, Mary BAIL-
    EY, dt Emmor & Elizabeth, Belmont Co., O.
    Ch: John R.   b 1820, 3, 15
        Elizabeth " 1822, 11, 17
1821, 1, 31. Abraham R., s Caleb & Ann, Jef-
    ferson Co., O.; m in Mt. Pleasant, Martha
    JUDKINS, dt James & Martha, Jefferson Co.,
    O.
----, --, --. Rhodes R. & Rebecca
    Ch: Sarah E.   b 1823, 4, 5
        Jane   " 1824, 11, 16
        Abram   " 1826, 2, 15
        Ann   " 1830, 10, 10
        Charlotte " 1833, 9, 1

DILWORTH, Rhodes R. & Rebecca, continued
    Ch: Lydia   b 1836, 3, 2
       Hannah   " 1838, 3, 11
       Rebecca   " 1841, 6, 28

1814, 9, 5. Caleb & w, Ann, & ch, William,
    Charlotte, Ann, Rhodes, Caleb & Abigail,
    rocf Byberry MM, Pa., dtd 1814,3,29
1817, 8, 19. Abraham R. rocf Byberry MM, Pa.,
    dtd 1817,1,27
1822, 4, 23. Rhodes gct Plainfield MM, to m
    Rebecca Foulke
1823, 7, 22. Rebecca rocf Plainfield MM, dtd
    1823,6,26
1824, 7, 20. Rhodes & w, Rebecca, & dt, Sa-
    rah, gct Concord MM
1825, 5, 24. William & w, Mary, & ch, John
    R. & Elizabeth, gct Flushing MM
1827, 2, 20. Rebecca & ch, Sarah,Jane & Abra-
    ham, rocf Concord MM, dtd 1826,8,23
1829, 1, 20. Rebecca dis jH
1829, 2, 24. Charlotte & Abigail dis jH

1838, 5, 22. Martha Evans (form Dilworth) dis
    mcd
1840, 7, 21. Rankin, Abigail P., Caleb D.,
    Rebecca Ann & Sarah, ch Abraham & Martha,
    gct Cincinnati MM
1844, 2, 20. Jane Russell (form Dilworth) dis
    mcd
1844, 2, 20. Sarah Mashawn (form Dilworth)
    dis mcd
1845, 2, 20. Charlotte gct Clear Creek MM,
    Ill. (H)
1845, 3, 20. Rebecca F. & ch, Abraham, Ann,
    Charlotte, Lydia, Hannah & Rebecca, gct
    Clear Creek MM, Ill. (H)   [mcd
1846, 11, 24. Jane Russell (form Dilworth) dis
1846, 11, 24. Sarah Mashawn (form Dilworth)
    dis mcd
1852, 4, 25. Rhodes gct Plainfield MM, Ill.
    (H)
1898, 3, 23. Charles M. [Dillworth] recrq (G)
1900, 3, 21. Charles M. relrq (G)

DINGEE
1819, 5, 18. John & w, Barshaba, & ch, Ruth
    Martha Nathan & Mary, rocf Westland MM,
    dtd 1819,4,22
1824, 12, 21. John & w, Bathsheba, & ch, Ruth
    Martha, Charles & John, gct Middleton MM

DIXON
1876, 3, 29. Cyrus, s Simon & Elizabeth,
    Harrison Co., O., d 1899,7,13 bur West
    Grove; m in home of Isaac Thomas, Edna
    THOMAS. dt Isaac & Anna L., Harrison Co.,
    O., d 1919,6,8 bur West Grove

1809, 6, 20. William & w, Jane, & ch, Sarah,
    Samuel, Hannah & Susanna, rocf Redstone
    MM, dtd 1809,6,2
1810, 7, 24. William & w, Jane, & ch, Sarah,

    Samuel, Hannah, Susanna & William, gct
    Plainfield MM
1876, 2, 24. Cyrus rocf Salem MM, O. (G)

DODD
----, --, --. Walter, s Felix & Rhoda, b
    1874,3,14; m Lulu CUNNINGHAM, dt James &
    Hattie (Finley), b 1897,5,6
    Ch: Arthur   b 1913, 11, 19
       Howard   " 1915, 4, 29
       Beatrice " 1916, 12, 20

1932, 4, 20. Beatrice recrq (G)

DOAN
1826, 9, 19. Elizabeth (form Wells) dis mcd
1868, 5, 5. David gct Deerfield MM (H)

DOGUE
1903, 4, 22. Ida recrq (G)

DOLL
1914, 3, 25. Charles, Geo. Dewie & Geo. Jr.
    recrq (G)

DOLMEN
1892, 10, 19. John & Joseph recrq (G)

DONARD
1888, 3, 21. William & w, Mary, relrq (G)

DOUDNA
1835, 4, 29. Henry, s Henry & Martha, Belmont
    Co., O.; m in Concord, Matilda BIRD, dt
    Isaac & Mary, Berk Co., Pa.
1860, 2, 14. Thomas d
1929, 12, 25. Alfred M., s Joseph & Nora,
    Belmont Co., O.; m in Harrisville, Alice
    B. STARBUCK, dt Thomas & Abbie H., Belmont
    Co., O.

1835, 12, 22. Henry Jr. rocf Stillwater MM,
    dtd 1835,11,28
1837, 10, 24. Henry & w, Matilda, & ch, Mary,
    gct Pennsville MM
1862, 11, 19. Hosea Jr. & Mary P. dis jW
1862, 11, 19. Joel & Rebecca & ch, Eunice,
    Rebecca Jr. & Joel Jr. dis jW
1862, 11, 19. Asenath, Joseph, Ann, Sarah,
    Jesse, Elisha, Abigail, Hannah, Miriam,
    Thomas, Matilda, Nathan, John, Joseph,
    Belinda, Josiah, Mary, Edwin, Isaac, Mar-
    tha, Benjamin, Suphemia, John, Thomas,
    Flanner, John, Mary Jane, Hannah Ann,
    Samuel C., Martha Ellen, Tabitha C.,
    Joseph, Phebe, John S., Hannah E., Hannah,
    Sina, Jesse, Elisha, Hannah Ann & Mary
    dis jW (G)
1929, 8, 20. Clifford C. Bundy gct Somerset
    MM, to m Wauneta Rosetta Doudna (W)

DOVENER
1893, 2, 21. William N. recrq (W)
1897, 1, 19. William con mcd (W)
1900, 11, 20. William W. dis disunity (W)

DOWDLE
1900, 2, 10. Walter R., s Silas & Amanda
      (Thompson), b (G)

1881, 2, 26. Alice [Dowdell] recrq (G)
1884, 2, 20. William H. & Joseph [Dowdell]
      recrq (G)
1885, 2, 25. Jonas recrq (G)
1885, 2, 25. Silas recrq (G)
1888, 10, 24. Alice [Doudle] dropped from
      mbrp (G)
1903, 6, 24. Sarah dropped from mbrp (G)
1913, 5, 21. Charles relrq (G)
1913, 5, 21. Elmer relrq (G)
1913, 5, 21. George relrq (G)
1932, 4, 20. Walter R. recrq (G)

DOWNARD
1906, 12, 29. W. H. d bur Cadiz, O.

1884, 1, 23. Clara Leona recrq (G)
1885, 2, 25. William & Mary C. recrq (G)
1899, 1, 25. Wm. H. & w, Mary C., recrq (G)

DOWNER
1922, 3, 22. Mary C. relrq (G)

DUCAS
1834, 8, 19. Thomas gct Stillwater MM

DUFF
1827, 3, 20. Ann F. (form Judkins) dis mcd

DUFFIELD
1898, 2, 23. Anna B. (form Grubb) relrq (G)

DULY
1807, 10, 17. Lydia rocf Redstone MM, dtd
      1807,7,21

DUNGAN
1873, 4, 1. Hannah d ae 70

1822, 7, 23. Mary rocf Smithfield MM, dtd
      1822,6,17
1829, 4, 21. Mary dis jH
1830, 4, 22. Mary gct Concord MM (H)

DUNKIN
1814, 11, 22. Elizabeth (form Hatcher) dis mcd

DURBIN
1873, 5, 22. Mary Alice recrq (G)
1874, 6, 25. Sarah recrq (G)
1876, 2, 24. Alice Vernon (form Durban) con
      mcd (G)
1878, 4, 25. Josephine recrq (G)
1879, 4, 24. Edith L. recrq (G)

1881, 2, 26. Annie recrq (G)
1881, 2, 26. William recrq (G)
1881, 3, 24. Lemuel recrq (G)
1901, 2, 20. David E., Walter E., Roy &
      Minnie L. recrq (G)
1904, 2, 24. George recrq (G)
1907, 6, 19. Minnie, Walter E. & Roy dropped
      from mbrp (G)
1912, 3, 20. Maggie & Harry D. recrq (G)
1915, 2, 24. Carnie recrq (G)
1915, 2, 24. George recrq (G)
1915, 2, 24. Lizzie, Harry & Maggie recrq (G)
1929, 7, 24. Alice dropped from mbrp (G)

DUTTON
----, --, --. Robert & Anna
      Ch: Martha Ann b 1834, 12, 22 d 1852, 1,16
          Cynthia   " 1837, 2, 14
          Ezra   " 1839, 1, 7
          Hannah H. " 1840, 12, 15
1836, 10, 13. David d ae 80
1837, 11, 14. Hannah, w David, d ae 76
1845, 4, 2. Robert d

1831, 9, 22. Hannah gct Springborough MM (H)
1839, 7, 25. Sarah & s, John M. Mendenhall,
      gct Newgarden MM (H)
1863, 6, 9. Ezra gct West MM, O. (H)
1879, 7, 24. Robert recrq (G)
1880, 4, 22. Elmer E., Cora Maude, Nettie
      Blanche & Leota, recrq (G)
1888, 10, 24. Robert & Leota dropped from
      mbrp (G)
1888, 10, 24. Annetta dropped from mbrp (G)
1892, 10, 19. Mary recrq (G)
1895, 3, 20. Marvin recrq (G)
1897, 2, 24. Elmer gct Smithfield MM (G)
1898, 3, 23. Murden recrq (G)

DYER
1892, 10, 19. Mary & Emma recrq (G)

EAKIN
1900, 5, 23. Aaron S., s Elias H. & Annie B.,
      Lycoming Co., Pa.; m in Concord, Eva B.
      STARBUCK, dt John & Sarah, Belmont Co., O.
      (W)

EASLEY
1821, 11, 20. Richard rocf Flushing MM, dtd
      1821,9,21

EASTON
1914, 4, 22. Ella recrq (G)

ECHELBERGER
1817, 1, 21. Mary (form Hatcher) dis mcd

ECKLEY
1826, 1, 10. Marry d

ECROYD
1832, 1, 24. Joshua Maule gct Muncy MM, Pa.,

ECROYD, continued
     to m Sarah N. Ecroyd

EDDINGS
1882, 7, 19. Sarah recrq (G)

EDDY
1814, 7, 19. Lavina (form Hall) dis mcd

EDGERTON
1808, 4, 20. Richard, s James & Sarah, Bel-
     mont Co., O.; m in Short Creek MH, Mary
     HALL, dt Joseph & Christian, Jefferson
     Co., O.
1810, 10, 4. James, s James & Sarah, Belmont
     Co., O.; m in Short Creek MH, Anna HALL,
     dt Joseph & Christiana, Jefferson Co., O.
1880, 5, 19. Walter, s Jos. & Anna M., Colum-
     biana Co., O.; m in Harrisville, Mary K.
     BINNS, dt David & Rebecca, Harrison Co.,O.
     Ch: Anna Mabel b 1886, 3, 5   [(W)
         Mildred R.   " 1889, 3, 16
         Wilford D.   " 1891, 10, 16
         Jesse N.   " 1895, 12, 26
         Sarah Mar-
            garet   " 1899, 9, 13
1887, 2, 16. Sarah d ae 27 bur Harrisville
1910, 8, 24. Jesse, s Joseph & Charity, Colum-
     biana Co., O.; m in Colerain, Elizabeth A.
     McGREW, dt James W. & Ann J., Belmont Co.,
     O. (W)

1808, 6, 21. Mary gct Stillwater MM
1810, 12, 18. Ann gct Stillwater MM
1862, 11, 19. David, Esther, Anna, Jane, Rob-
     ert, Charles, Joseph, Anna, Nathan, Jesse,
     Walter, Sarah, Rachel, James, Mary, Wil-
     liam, Rebecca, Joseph & Thomas dis jW
1872, 1, 23. James rocf Concord MM, dtd
     1871,12,29 (W)
1876, 2, 22. James con mcd (W)
1878, 2, 19. James gct Stillwater MM (W)
1880, 12, 21. Mary H. gct Newgarden MM (W)
1884, 5, 20. Walter & w, Mary H., & ch, Hor-
     ace J. & Rebecca Bertha, rocf Coal Creek
     MM, Ia. (W)
1886, 8, 24. Anna M. rocf Newgarden MM, dtd
     1886,7,22 (W)
1886, 8, 24. Sarah rocf Newgarden MM, dtd
     1886,7,22 (W)
1895, 4, 23. Anna M. gct New Garden MM (W)
1901, 8, 21. Walter & w, Mary H., & ch,
     Horace J., Rebecca B., Anna M., Mildred
     R., Wilfred D., Jesse N. & Sara M., gct
     Newgarden MM (W)
1910, 10, 18. Elizabeth A. gct Upper Spring-
EDKIN   [field MM (W)
1911, 4, 18. Eva S. gct Birmingham MM, Pa.(W)

EDMONDSON
1826, 9, 19. Mary rocf Third Haven MM, dtd
     1826,8,17
1827, 11, 20. Mary gct Middleton MM

ELLERMAN
1836, 1, 19. Gottlieb rocf Menden MM, Ger-
     many, dtd 1835,7,5
1836, 9, 20. Gottlieb gct Middleton MM

ELLIOTT
1873, 1, 1. Martha J. (nm) m Oliver THOMAS

ELLIS
1830, 3, 23. Elwood Ratcliff gct Flushing MM,
     to m Mary Ellis

ELLISON
1861, 6, 19. Ezra & w, Beulah C., rocf Red-
     stone MM
1875, 12, 23. Beulah gct Oskaloosa MM, Ia.
     (women's minutes read gct Spring Creek MM,
     Ia.)(G)
1902, 2, 18. Emma S. (form Sidwell) dis jas
     (W)

ELY
1886, 5, 19. Alonzo S. & Amanda R. recrq (G)
1892, 2, 24. R. Amanda relrq (G)

EMBREE
1814, 3, 8. Isaac R., s Samuel & Hannah, b
----, --, --. John & Huldah
     Ch: Abigail   b 1826, 5, 9
         Mordecai M." 1826, 11, 2 (?)
         Sarah   " 1829, 5, 9
----, --, --. James & Keziah
     Ch: William A. b 1834, 5, 24
         John   " 1835, 8, 25
         Lucinda   " 1838, 2, 11
         Sarah   " 1840, 8, 27
         Daniel A.   " 1844, 5, 8
         Mary S.   " 1847, 2, 12
         Dianna T.   " 1850, 9, 30
1833, 10, 23. Harriet m Samuel BAILEY

1812, 5, 19. Samuel & w, Hannah, & ch, Lydia,
     Joseph, Phebe, John, Jesse & Israel, rocf
     Baltimore MM for W. Dist., dtd 1812,1,8
1815, 10, 24. James, minor, rocf Bradford MM,
     dtd 1815,6,7
1816, 2, 20. Lydia gct Stillwater MM
1816, 2, 20. Samuel & w, Hannah, & ch, Jo-
     seph, Phebe, John, James, Jesse, Israel &
     Isaac R., gct Stillwater MM
1827, 4, 24. John & w, Huldah, & ch, James,
     Harriet, Jesse, Elizabeth, Edith, John,
     Abigail & Mordecai [Embra] rocf Flushing
     MM, dtd 1827,1,26
1831, 11, 22. Keziah (form Atkinson) con mcd
1832, 1, 24. James con mcd
1834, 3, 18. Elizabeth gct Stillwater MM
1832, 8, 21. John rst
1834, 5, 20. John & w, Huldah, & ch, Edith,
     John, Abigail, Mordecia & Sarah, gct
     Stillwater MM
1835, 12, 22. James & w, Keziah, & ch, William
     A. & John P., gct Stillwater MM

EMBREE, continued

1840, 2, 18. James & w, Keziah, & ch, Wm. A.,
     John P. & Lucinda, rocf Stillwater MM, dtd
     1839,12,28
1841, 7, 20. Mary Ann (form Pickering) dis
     mcd
1841, 10, 19. Jesse dis mcd
1853, 9, 20. James & w, Keziah, & ch, William
     A., John P., Lucinda, Sarah, Daniel A.,
     Mary L. & Diannah F., gct Red Cedar MM,
     Iowa

EMMONS

1929, 6, 27. Chester W., s Wilson T. & Amy,
     Keokuk Co., Ia.; m in Harrisville, Florence
     HALL, dt Samuel & Anna, Jefferson Co., O.,
     b 1902,11,24

ENFIELD

1885, 2, 25. Henry recrq (G)

ENGLAND

1847, --, --. John d bur Stubenville, O.

1805, 7, 20. John rocf Westland MM, dtd
     1805,3,23
1867, 4, 9. Milton gct Plainfield MM (H)

ENGLE

1901, 2, 20. Harry recrq (G)
1914, 1, 21. Harry recrq (G)

ERNS

1908, 4, 22. Mrs. Erns & ch, Marie & Bartel-
     emy, recrq (G)

EROYD

1859, 8, 23. Sarah M. rocf Plainfield MM, dtd
     1859,7,20

ERSKINE

1839, 11, 19. Rachel (form Barber) dis mcd

ESELICK

1892, 10, 19. Elnorah recrq (G)

EVANS

1833, 5, 24. John [Evens] d ae 38
----, --, --. George & Sarah
     Ch: Elizabeth b 1835, 6, 8
         Julia Ann " 1837, 10, 2
         Evan Grif-
         fith   " 1840, 5, 14
         Sarah El-
         len   " 1842, 2, 27 d 1863, 9,17
         Mary A.   " 1844, 3, 3
         Hannah Jane" 1849, 5, 23
1841, 4, 28. Josiah, s Nathan & Zillah, Bel-
     mont Co., O.; m in Concord, Susan M. THOM-
     AS, dt Samuel & Mary, Montgomery Co., Pa.
1844, 4, 7. Jonathan d ae 65
1846, 4, 18. Sarah d ae 31
----, --, --. Evan Griffith & Rebecca

Ch: Arthur
        William   b 1863, 5, 31
    George
        Austin   " 1865, 4, 10
        Sarah Ella " 1871, 4, 29
    Elery Chan-
        ning   " 1873, 4, 22
        Anna Clare " 1875, 4, 21
        Marietta C." 1879, 12, 1
1864, 10, 11. Anna, w Arthur, dt John & Eliza-
     beth (Evans) SCOTT, b
1876, 9, 20. Mary P. d
1886, 3, 2. George J. d
1895, 12, 26. Delphina S. b
1918, 3, 30. Anna, w Arthur, dt John & Eliza-
     beth (Evans) SCOTT, d bur Hicksite Frs
     Bur Gr., Emerson, O.

1805, 3, 16. Elenor rocf Westland MM, dtd
     1804,11,2'
1807, 8, 15. Elenor Wright (form Evans) dis
     mou
1815, 5, 23. Joanna rocf Concord MM, dtd
     1815,1,26
1819, 5, 18. Joanna, w Benjamin, gct Plain-
     field MM
1823, 1, 21. Louisa (form Burr) dis mcd
1829, 3, 24. Amos, Sarah, Henrietta, Asher,
     Parker & Wm. Jones Evans, minor ch Evan &
     Mary, rocf Smithfield MM, dtd 1829,2,23
1831, 5, 24. Geo. I. rocf Gwynead MM, dtd
     1830,12,30
1835, 2, 24. Amos, Sarah, Henrietta, Asher,
     Parker & Wm., ch Evan & Mary, gct Deer-
     field MM
1835, 3, 24. George dis jH
1835, 3, 24. Sarah dis jH
1838, 5, 22. Martha (form Dilworth) dis mcd
1838, 5, 22. Hannah J., minor, rocf Buckingham
     MM, Pa., dtd 1838,4,2
1840, 4, 21. Josiah rocf Goshen MM, Pa., dtd
     1840,1,30
1840, 10, 20. Martha rst at Cincinnati MM on
     consent of this mtg
1841, 12, 21. Josiah & w, Susannah M., gct
     Frankfort MM, Pa.
1845, 9, 23. Hannah Tomlinson (form Evans)
     dis disunity
1879, 4, 24. Columbus C. & Cassandra recrq (G)
1881, 2, 26. Ella recrq (G)
1894, 3, 20. Anna J. (form Scott) con mcd to
     first cousin (W)
1906, 3, 21. Florence Johnson relrq (G)
1911, 8, 22. Sarah Delphine, dt Anna S.,
     recrq (W)
1924, 3, 18. S. Delphine Vale (form Evans)
     con mcd (W)

EVERETT

1815, 11, 21. John & Sarah rocf Dunnings
     Creek MM
1829, 9, 19. Sarah dis jH
1892, 10, 19. James M. recrq (G)

EVERLY
1869, 11, 25. Adam, Melissa M., William,
    Elizabeth Ann, Thomas E. & Bertha A. (an
    infant) recrq (G)

EYRE
1815, 10, 5. Robert, s Robert & Ann, Harrison
    Co. O.; m in Short Creek MH, Jemima
    GRUBB, dt John & Hannah, Jefferson Co., O.
    Ch: Hannah   b 1816, 8, 21
        Ann   " 1818, 5, 24
1823, 5 20. Robert d ae 88 bur West Grove
1824, 4, 27. Ann d ae 78 bur West Grove
1840, 1, 22. Hannah J. m Elnathan PETTIT
1842, 9, 21. Ann P. m Miller GIBSON
1865, 12, 17. Jemima [Eyeres] d ae 84

1810, 5, 22. Sarah [Eyeres] rocf Hopewell
    MM, dtd 1810,5,3
1811, 5, 21. Robert Sr. & w, Anna, rocf Hope-
    well MM, Va., dtd 1811,1,10
1811, 5, 21. Robert Jr. rocf Hopewell MM, Va.,
    dtd 1811,1,12
1815, 11, 21. Adam rocf Hopewell MM, dtd
    1815,6,8
1822, 6, 18. Martha (form Taylor) dis mcd
1823, 4, 22. Sarah [Ayres] (form Hurford)
    dis mcd
1823, 6, 24. Adam [Eyres] dis mcd
1824, 8, 24. Sarah con mcd

FARMER
1827, 5, 3. William, s John & Mary, Jeffer-
    son Co., O.; m in Short Creek MH, Mary
    PARKER, dt Isaac & Sarah, Jefferson Co.,O.
    Ch: Sarah P. b 1828, 2, 26
        Isaac
        Parker   " 1829, 8, 22

1822, 11, 19. William rocf Sandy Spring MM,
    dtd 1822,3,22
1830, 2, 23. William & Mary & ch, Sarah P.
    & Isaac Parker Farmer, gct Smithfield MM
1843, 7, 18. Wm. & w, Mary, & ch, Sarah,
    Isaac, Parker, Mary Cassandra, John, Mar-
    tha & Abby Ann, rocf Sandy Spring MM, dtd
    1843,6,27
1849, 10, 23. William & w, Mary, & ch, Isaac
    P., Cassander, John, Martha & Abby Ann,
    gct Sandy Spring MM
1850, 6, 18. Sarah Hovey (form Farmer) dis
    mcd

FARQUHAR
1809, 11, 2. William, s Allen & Phebe, Ohio
    Co., Va.; m in Short Creek MH, Sarah
    FOULK, dt Cadwalader & Phebe, Jefferson
    Co., O.
1829, 7, 4. Sarah d bur Richmond (ae 97)
1834, 1, 13. William d ae 79
1834, 8, 13. William [Farquehar] d bur Cross
    Creek
1837, 4, 27. Martha m Joseph HALL

1839, 5, 22. Matilda m Aaron ROBERTS
1844, 1, 21. Benjamin d ae 29 bur Cross Creek

1810, 1, 24. Sarah gct Concord MM
1811, 4, 23. Hannah, w Samuel, & ch, Samuel,
    Caleb, Dinah & Elijah, rocf Pipe Creek
    MM, dtd 1811,3,11
1811, 4, 23. Phebe rocf Pipe Creek MM, dtd
    1811,3,11
1811, 7, 23. Amos rocf Pipe Creek MM, dtd
    1811,3,16
1828, 1, 22. Martha W. & Hannah, minors,
    rocf Flushing MM, dtd 1827,12,21
1828, 2, 19. Matilda, minor, recrq
1855, 7, 26. Hannah Ann gct Westland MM (H)

FARR
1815, 12, 19. James Frame gct Indian Spring
    MM, Md., to m Asenath Farr

FARRINGTON
1805, 1, 19. Abraham & fam gct Redstone MM

FAWCETT
1818, 10, 7. Jonathan, s Richard & Eunice,
    Columbiana Co., O.; m in Mt. Pleasant,
    Mary BEESON, dt Jacob & Lydia, Jefferson
    Co., O.
1862, 10, 29. Jonathan, s Richard & Eunice,
    Belmont Co., O.; m in Short Creek MH,
    Eliza J. NEGUS, dt Reese & Ruth BRANSON,
    Belmont Co., O.
1884, 8, 10. Jonathan d bur Concord
1889, 8, 18. Eliza J. d bur Concord
1907, 9, 25. Clifford, s Jason & Mary E.,
    Morgan Co., O.; m in Concord, Florence H.
    STEER, dt Elisha B. & Ellen G., Belmont
    Co., O. (W)
1908, 8, 19. Clarence Edward, s Jason &
    Mary E., Phila., Pa.; m in Colerain, Mary
    Rebecca NEGUS, dt Oliver S. & Deborah S.,
    Belmont Co., O. (W)

1807, 1, 17. Samuel & w, Rachel, & dt,
    Elizabeth, rocf Concord MM, dtd 1806,1,18
1811, 3, 19. Samuel & w, Rachel, & ch, Eliza-
    beth, Benjamin & Maria, gct Plainfield MM
1818, 12, 22. Mary gct Salem MM
1821, 8, 23. Elisha Bracken gct Salem MM, to
    m Esther [Faucet]
1862, 9, 23. Jonathan rocf Salem MM, dtd
    1862,8,20
1862, 11, 19. Eliza J. dis jW
1908, 12, 22. Florence S. gct Chesterfield
    MM (W)
1909, 1, 19. Mary N. gct Lansdowne MM, Pa.
    (W)

FELL
1846, 3, 12. Marshall, s Joseph & Ann, Bel-
    mont Co., O.; m in Harrisville, Rebecca
    HIRST, dt Thomas & Ann, Jefferson Co., O.

FELL, continued

1811, 3, 19. Rachel Parson (form Fell) dis
    mcd
1814, 3, 22. Joseph dis mcd
1817, 8, 19. Grace & dt, Grace, rocf Bucking-
    ham MM, Pa., dtd 1817,5,5
1823, 5, 20. Grace Buckman (form Fell) dis
    mcd
1824, 10, 19. Rachel gct Mill Creek MM
1830, 6, 22. Grace dis jH
1846, 8, 18. Rebecca gct Goshen MM

FENSTERMAKER

1928, 4, 25. Lottie, minor, recrq (G)

FERRIL

1870, 10, 10. Elma T., w George, dt Elwood D.
    & Asenath (Thomas) Whinery, b
1916, 7, 23. Elma T., w George, dt Elwood D.
    & Asenath (Thomas) Whinery, d bur New
    Athens, Ohio

FIELD

1816, 12, 24. Ann rocf Little Britain MM, dtd
    1816,5,11
1819, 11, 23. Anna gct Flushing MM

FISHER

1816, 5, 2. Elizabeth rocf Dunnings Creek
    MM, dtd 1815,12,13
1820, 12, 19. Elizabeth gct Westland MM
1823, 9, 23. Elizabeth rocf Westland MM, dtd
    1823,6,2
1823, 9, 25. Elizabeth rocf Westland MM, dtd
    1823,11,26
1862, 11, 19. Phebe dis jW

FITCH

1891, 12, 23. Elma recrq (G)
1902, 10, 20. John, Elma & Mary dropped from
    mbrp (G)

FITCHELL

1892, 10, 19. Virginia recrq

FITCHETT

1892, 10, 19. George & Anna recrq

FITZGERALD

1892, 3, 23. Charles H. recrq (G)
1901, 2, 20. Herman H. recrq (G)
1907, 6, 19. Chas. & w dropped from mbrp (G)
1914, 1, 21. Beatrice recrq (G)
1914, 1, 21. Guy A. recrq (G)
1915, 2, 24. Caroline recrq (G)
1915, 2, 24. Herman Jr. recrq (G)

FLAGOR

1905, 5, 24. Albert & w, Margaret; recrq (G)

FLANNER

----, --, --. William & Peninnah
    Ch: Thomas   b 1796, 9, 7

Ch: Abigail   b 1798, 10, 17
    Jacob   " 1801, 2, 15
    William   " 1803, 10, 21
    Peninah   " 1806, 10, 9
    Sarah   " 1811, 6, 30
    Rebecca   " 1814, 3, 6
1821, 12, 26. Jacob P., s Wm. & Peninah, Jef-
    ferson Co., O.; m in Mt. Pleasant, Charity
    BEESON, dt Henry & Mary, Jefferson Co.,O.
Ch: Henry   b 1822, 9, 7
    Mary   " 1826, 9, 22
    William   " 1824, 8, 8
    Edmund   " 1829, 5, 4
    Oliver   " 1831, 3, 21
    Charles   " 1833, 2, 25
    Phebe   " 1835, 1, 12
    Anna   " 1837, 5, 12
1823, 5, 7. Peninah d ae 56 bur Short Creek
1828, 12, 31. William, s Wm. & Peninah, Jef-
    ferson Co., O., b 1803,10,21; m in Mt.
    Pleasant, Mary L. UPDEGRAFF, dt Nathan &
    Ann, Jefferson Co., O.
Ch: Thomas   b 1830, 1, 5
    Ann U.   " 1831, 9, 10
    Peninah   " 1835, 9, 22
1833, 9, 25. Sarah m Wm. BAILEY
1833, 10, 30. Rebecca m Geo. MICHENER
1838, 10, 31. Abigail m Nathan TALBOTT
1842, 10, 11. Edward d bur Short Creek
1843, 10, 4. Phebe d bur Short Creek
1851, 10, 29. Mary m Isaac LUPTON
1858, 5, 27. Oliver, s Jacob B. & Charity B.,
    Jefferson Co., O.; m in Short Creek MH,
    Mary Ann LAWRENCE, dt Thos. & Deborah,
    Jefferson Co., O.
Ch: Luella   b 1859, 7, 14
    Dilwin   " 1861, 11, 23
1858, 9, 26. Wm. d ae 55
1858, 9, --. Wm. Jr. d

1808, 10, 18. William & w, Peninah, & ch,
    Thomas, Abigail, Jacob, William & Peninah
    & Eaton Hays, minor in their care, rocf
    New Garden MM, N. C., dtd 1808,7,30
1816, 6, 18. William & w, Penina, & ch, Abi-
    gail, Jacob, William, Penina, Sarah & Re-
    becca, gct Plymouth MM
1816, 10, 22. Thomas gct Cincinnati MM
1817, 9, 23. William & w, Peninah, & ch, Ja-
    cob, William, Peninah, Sarah & Rebecca,
    rocf Plymouth MM, dtd 1817,9,22
1817, 10, 21. Abigail rocf Plymouth MM, dtd
    1817,9,22
1817, 10, 21. Cert for Thomas granted to
    Cincinnati some time ago now end to Plain-
    field MM
1818, 3, 24. Thomas gct Arch Street MM,
    Phila.
1821, 3, 20. Thomas rocf SD MM, dtd 1821,1,24
1825, 7, 19. Catharine rocf Stillwater MM,
    dtd 1825,4,23
1825, 12, 20. Abigail gct Stillwater MM
1831, 4, 19. William & w, Catharine, gct

FLANNER, continued
    Somerset MM
1831, 10, 18. Abigail rocf Stillwater MM, dtd
    1831,6,25
1836, 10, 18. William & w, Catharine, rocf
    Somerset MM, dtd 1836,9,26
1837, 6, 20. William & w, Catharine, gct
    Somerset MM
1843, 12, 19. Henry dis mcd
1844, 10, 22. Penninah gct Somerset MM
1848, 5, 23. William Jr. dis mcd
1857, 8, 18. Ann U. Townsend (form Flanner)
    dis mcd (W)
1859, 7, 20. Thomas N. dis mcd (G)
1860, 4, 25. Peninah Waite (form Flanner) dis
    mcd (G)
1860, 9, 19. Annie E. dis jas (G)
1861, 1, 22. Charles dis disunity (W)
1861, 4, 24. Peninah Wait (form Flanner) dis
    mcd (G)
1862, 11, 19. Jacob P. & Charity dis jW (G)
1864, 7, 19. Mary Ann dis jG (W)
1864, 8, 23. Oliver dis jG (W)
1883, 5, 22. Luella dis jG (W)

FLEMMING
1839, 6, 18. Nancy (form Gill) dis mcd

FOGG
1877, 9, 28. Isabel C. m Wilson T. SIDWELL
    (W)
1884, 3, 19. Adna S., s Chas. & Esther,
    Cedar Co., Ia.; m in Concord, Mary Ella
    SIDWELL, dt Israel & Rachel B., Belmont
    Co., O. (W)

1876, 3, 21. Esther F. & ch, Adna S. & Emily,
    rocf Hickory Grove MM, dtd 1876,2,5 (W)
1876, 3, 21. Isabella C. rocf Hickory Grove
    MM, dtd 1876,2,5 (W)
1880, 3, 23. Esther F. & ch, Adna S. & Emily
    gct Hickory Grove MM, Ia. (W)

FOOLKS
1892, 10, 19. V. N. recrq (G)

FORD
1881, 2, 26. Charles C. recrq (G)
1881, 2, 26. William T. recrq (G)
1888, 10, 24. William dropped from mbrp (G)

FOREMAN
1895, 3, 20. Ollie Way recrq (G)

FOSTER
1907, 6, 19. Bundy dropped from mbrp (G)

FOULK
1809, 11, 2. Sarah m Wm. FARQUHAR
1810, 8, 30. Anna m Jesse PARKER
1839, 5, 23. Jesse d ae 76 bur Short Creek
----, --, --. Edward & Phebe Ann
    Ch: William

    Ch: Harris   b 1840, 6, 30
        Amanda Jane" 1843, 2, 19
        Sarah Ann   " 1845, 3, 30
        Hannah
        Mary   " 1843, 11, 26
        Francis El-
        wood   " 1850, 9, 5
1840, 3, --. Mary d
----, --, --. Jesse M. & Mary
    Ch: John B.   b 1844, 3, 31
        George   " 1845, 6, 7
        Sarah Ann   " 1846, 11, 20 d 1861, 8,16
        Amasa   " 1849, 8, 29
1895, --, --. Edward [Foulk] d

1808, 8, 23. Ann rocf Concord MM, dtd 1808,
    7,21
1808, 8, 23. Sarah rocf Concord MM, dtd 1808,
    7,21
1819, 11, 23. Henry Bailey gct Plainfield MM,
    to m Mary Foulke
1821, 5, 22. Elizabeth rocf Plainfield MM,
    dtd 1821,3,22
1822, 4, 23. Rhodes Dilworth gct Plainfield
    to m Rebecca Foulke
1822, 4, 23. Elizabeth gct Flushing MM
1822, 6, 18. Thomas Sidwell gct Flushing MM,
    to m Elizabeth Foulke
1830, 11, 23. Jesse dis jH
1832, 2, 21. Silas, minor, rocf Stillwater
    MM, dtd 1831,12,22
1834, 7, 22. Silas gct Stillwater MM
1832, 7, 24. Jesse & w, Sarah, rocf Flushing
    MM, dtd 1832,6,21
1842, 12, 20. Sarah gct Allum Creek MM
1852, 6, 24. Jesse M. & w, Mary, & ch, John
    B., George, Sarah Ann, William & Amasa,
    gct Fall Creek MM, Ill. (H)
1864, 10, 4. Edward & s, Francis E., gct
    Clear Creek MM, Ill. (H)

FOWLER
1823, 12, 23. Sally & Anna M. recrq
1831, 10, 18. Sally & Anna M. gct Westland MM
1847, 11, 23. Joseph Raley gct Westland MM,
    to m Sally Fowler

FOX
----, --, --. Charles & Esther
    Ch: Anna
        Miller   b 1838, 5, 2
        Wm. Spicer " 1839, 9, 22 d 1908, 1,27
        Sarah Coop-
        er   " 1841, 11, 14
        Francis
        Cooper   " 1855, 11, 1 " 1895, 9, 7
----, --, --. William Spicer b 1839,9,22 d
    1908,1,27; m Esther J. -----
    Ch: Mary Moore b 1877, 7, 29
        John Fran-
        cis   " 1878, 12, 4 d 1897, 6, 9
        Erie Esther" 1880, 4, 13
1895, 6, 21. Charles James d

FOX, continued
1896, 2, 1. Esther Cooper d
1913, 5, 24. Esther Moore d

1838, 7, 22. Anna dis jH
1828, 12, 23. Sarah dis jH
1839, 1, 22. Francis dis jH
1854, 8, 22. Juliann (form Updegraff) dis mcd

FRAME
1814, 9, 28. William, s Benj. & Elizabeth,
      Harrison Co., O.; m in West Grove MH, Ru-
      annah THOMAS, dt Isaac & Rachel, Harrison
      Co., O.
      Ch: Aaron   b 1815, 6, 18
          James T.   " 1818, 3, 15
          Peter   " 1820, 4, 15
          William   " 1823, 5, 3
1816, 10, 13. George, s Benj. & Elizabeth,
      Harrison Co., O.; m in West Grove MH, Lyd-
      ia LEWIS, dt Thomas & Mary, Harrison Co.,
      O.
      Ch: Elizabeth
          Ann   b 1818, 8, 13
          Thomas L.   " 1820, 1, 14
1827, 10, 24. Lydia m Nathan P. GRISSELL
1836, 1, 9. Aaron, s Wm. & Ruannah, Belmont
      Co., O.; m in Harrisville, Telitha THOMP-
      SON, dt John C. & Rebecca, Harrison Co.,
      O., d 1860,6,14 ae 43
      Ch: Amasa   b 1839, 6, 26
          Thompson   " 1841, 6, 20
          Mary Ann   " 1843, 3, 2
          Ruanna   " 1845, 3, 30
          Tacy T.   " 1848, 8, 5
          Melissa   " 1848, 8, 5
          John T.   " 1851, 6, 22
          William A.   " 1852, 7, 23
          Oliver C.   " 1854, 5, 24
----, --, --. James T. & Anna
      Ch: Rebecca
          Ann   b 1847, 2, 2
          Joseph W.   " 1848, 10, 14

1813, 6, 22. William rocf Hopewell MM, dtd
      1813,5,6
1813, 7, 20. Benjamin & w, Elizabeth, & ch,
      James & Rachel, rocf Hopewell MM, dtd
      1813,5,6
1813, 7, 20. Jane rocf Hopewell MM, dtd
      1813,5,6
1815, 3, 21. George rocf Hopewell MM, dtd
      1815,2,9
1815, 12, 19. James gct Indian Spring MM, Md.,
      to m Asenath Farr
1816, 8, 20. Asenath rocf Indian Spring MM,
      Md., dtd 1816,5,19
1817, 1, 21. Benjamin & w, Elizabeth, gct
      Plainfield MM
1817, 1, 21. Rachel & Jane gct Plainfield MM
1817, 10, 21. Abram Barber gct Plainfield to
      m Rachel Frame
1818, 6, 23. William & w, Ruannah, & ch,

Aaron & James, gct Plainfield MM
1820, 1, 18. James & w, Asenath, & ch, Mahlon
      & William, gct Indian Spring MM, Md.
1820, 1, 18. William & w, Ruanna, & ch,
      Aaron & James F., rocf Flushing MM, dtd
      1819,8,27
1831, 5, 24. Ruanna & ch, Aaron, James T.,
      Peter & Wm. P., gct Flushing MM
1837, 11, 21. Aaron rocf Flushing MM, dtd
      1837, 8, 24
1838, 10, 23. Ruanna & s, Wm. R., rocf Flush-
      ing MM
1840, 2, 18. James T. rocf Flushing MM, dtd
      1839,6,20
1840, 7, 21. Peter, minor s Ruanna, rocf
      Flushing MM, dtd 1840,6,25
1844, 3, 19. William F. dis mcd
1846, 4, 21. James T. gct Plainfield MM, to
      m Anna Satterthwait
1846, 8, 18. Anna rocf Plainfield MM, dtd
      1846,7,22
1853, 3, 22. James T. & w, Anna, & ch, Re-
      becca Ann & Joseph, gct Salem MM, Iowa
1857, 2, 25. Aaron & w, Tabitha, & ch, Amasa,
      Thompson, Mary Ann, Ruanna, Tacy, William
      A. & Oliver C., gct Red Cedar MM, Iowa
1857, 3, 25. Ruanna gct Cedar MM, Ia.
1863, 1, 20. Aaron & ch, Ruannah T., Tacy T.,
      William A., Oliver & Ira E., gct Hickory
      Grove MM, Ia. (W)
1863, 4, 21. Amasa gct Stillwater MM
1863, 4, 21. Thompson gct Stillwater MM
1863, 9, 22. Mary Ann gct Stillwater MM

FREEMAN
1881, 2, 26. Thomas recrq (G)
1882, 3, 23. Thomas relrq (G)

FRENCH
1813, 5, 21. Juliann, dt Israel & Deborah, b

1813, 4, 20. Israel & w, Deborah, & ch, Ze-
      ruah, rocf Pipe Creek MM, dtd 1812,11,14
1828, 12, 23. Deborah dis jH
1829, 4, 21. Zeruah dis jH
1830, 12, 23. Israel & w, Deborah, & dt, Ju-
      liann, gct Concord MM (H)
1851, 1, 21. Juliann Cope (form French) dis
      mcd
1867, 10, 22. Lindley M. Bracken gct Salem
      MM, to m Anna S. French (W)

FRIEND
1894, 12, 19. Wesley & w, Elizabeth, recrq (G)
1895, 11, 20. Elizabeth & Wesley relrq (G)

FULTON
1882, 5, 24. Maggie recrq (G)
1888, 10, 24. Maggie dropped from mbrp (G)

FURBAY
----, --, --. Lewis b 1851,12,29; m Rebecca
      A. E. WATKINS, dt Eli & Martha J., b 1856,

FURBAY, continued
    7,10
    Ch: Clara   b 1883, 2, 4
        Josephine
        I.   " 1887, 1, 23
        Harriet E. " 1890, 1, 20
1903, 2, 7. Sarah A. d
----, --, --. James R., s W. Leroy & Carrie,
    b 1900,12,31; m Ethel M. WALKER, dt J. E.
    & Cora, b 1900,5,14 (G)
    Ch: Ethel
        Caroline b 1925, 8, 4

1885, ·2, 25. Oliver recrq (G)
1894, 2, 21. Lida recrq (G)
1896, 1, 23. Clara recrq (G)
1896, 1, 23. Josie Irene recrq (G)
1896, 1, 23. Lewis recrq (G)
1896, 1, 23. Rebecca A. E. recrq (G)
1896, 1, 23. Emma recrq (G)
1896, 1, 23. Harriet E. recrq (G)
1900, 5, 23. Eliza dis (G)
1907, 6, 19. Clara dis (G)
1913, 7, 23. Emma relrq (G)
1922, 11, 23. James R. rocf Mt. Gilead MM (G)
1926, 6, 9. Oliver dropped from mbrp (G)
1926, 10, 20. James R. & w, Ethel, & dt, Caro-
    line, gct Goshen MM (G)

FURGASON
1895, 2, 20. William recrq (G)

FURMAN
1869, 11, 25. Elmer & Lydia C. recrq (G)

GALLOWAY
1879, 5, 22. James & Nancy recrq (G)
1901, 2, 20. James L. & May recrq (G)
1912, 3, 20. Mae & Elma recrq (G)
1914, 1, 21. James L. recrq (G)

GAMBLE
1914, 3, 25. Edward Y., s Samuel & Mary Jane,
    Columbiana Co., O.; m in Colerain, Rebec-
    ca W. ATKINSON, dt Wm. & Catherine, Bel-
    mont Co., O. (W)

1915, 4, 20. Rebecca W. gct Salem MM, O. (W)

GARDING
1891, 12, 23. Lemuel recrq (G)
1892, 2, 24. Samuel & Harriett E. recrq (G)

GARRETT
1892, 10, 19. Mary B. recrq (G)
1896, 6, 23. William S. rocf Birmingham MM,
    Pa., dtd 1896,2,26 (W)

GARRETSON
1874, 3, 28. Jazer d ae 86

1806, 2, 15. Mary & dt, Armela & Patience,
    rocf Concord MM, dtd 1806,1,21
1826, 5, 23. Beulah (form Kirk) con mcd
1827, 5, 22. Beulah & dt, Eliza, gct Smith-
    field MM
1832, 4, 24. Anna gct Somerset MM
1832, 4, 24. Hannah gct Somerset MM
1832, 4, 24. John & w, Henrietta, & ch, Re-
    becca, Isaac Parker & Sarah, gct Somerset
    MM
1832, 4, 24. Joseph gct Somerset MM
1833, 1, 22. Patience gct Somerset MM
1841, 10, 19. Armella gct Middleton MM
1862, 11, 19. Asa dis jW
1862, 11, 19. Ruth dis jW
1862, 11, 19. Joseph dis jW
1862, 11, 19. Henrietta dis jW
1863, 6, 9. Jazer gct West MM, O. (H)
1866, 4, 10. Jazer gct West MM, O. (H)

GARRIS
1892, 10, 19. Ida, Katie & Martha recrq (G)

GARWOOD
1809, 11, 21. Jane dis mcd

GASKILL
----, --, --. Rudderrow S. m Phebe S. STEER,
    dt Lindley B. & Hannah (Penrose), b 1882,
    9,14

1915, 5, 18. Phebe Steer con mcd (W)

GAUSE
1821, 4, 24. Jesse & w, Martha, & ch, Har-
    riet Amelia & Hannah, rocf Plainfield MM,
    dtd 1821,6,21
1821, 8, 21. Jesse & w, Martha, & ch, Har-
    riet Amelia & Hannah, gct Kennet MM

GAYNOR
1892, 7, 28. Lucy recrq (G)
1904, 4, 20. Lucy A. relrq (G)

GEISEY
1902, 12, 24. William & Rose relrq (G)

GEORGE
1812, 9, 22. Mary rocf Plainfield MM, dtd
    1812,6,27

GIBBONS
1825, 1, 26. Thomas, s James & Eleanor, Har-
    rison Co., O.; m in West Grove MH, Sarah
    THOMAS, dt Isaac & Susanna, Harrison Co.,
    O.
1838, 5, 8. Thomas d ae 64
1870, 9, 21. Eli W., s Joseph & Penina, Bel-
    mont Co., O.; m in Smithfield, Eliza Jane
    McGREW, dt Finley W. & Rebecca D., Jeffer-

GIBBONS, continued
    son Co., O. (W)
1897, 3, 24. Joseph B., s Joseph & Penina,
    Belmont Co., O.; m in Harrisville, Elma
    THOMAS, dt Bradway & Rachel, Harrison Co.,
    O. (W)

1821, 1, 23. Thomas [Gibons] rocf Concord MM,
    Pa., dtd 1820,11,30
1828, 11, 18. Lydia rocf Farmington MM, N. Y.,
    dtd 1828,9,25
1830, 7, 20. Sarah dis jH
1830, 7, 20. Thomas dis jH
1832, 10, 23. Joseph & w, Lydia H., gct
    Adrien MM, Mich. Territory
1845, 3, 20. Sarah gct Deerfield MM (H)
1861, 7, 24. Amos E., William S., John Edwin,
    Ruthanna & Rebecca W., ch John, rocf Upper
    Springfield MM
1861, 7, 24. Lydia S. & Mary Ann rocf Upper
    Springfield MM
1862, 11, 19. Rachel, Joseph, Penina, Elam,
    Eli, Joseph Jr., Martha, Ann, Elizabeth,
    Lavin, Richard, James, Maria, Dillon, Ma-
    randa, Sarah E., Lucinda, Penninah, John,
    Lydia, William, Tilman, Ruth, John Taylor,
    Lydia Ann, Esther, Lindley, Rachel, Homer,
    Ann, Oliver H. & John Franklin dis jW
1871, 1, 26. Hannah Penrose (form Gibbons)
    con mcd (G)
1871, 7, 18. Eliza Jane gct New Garden MM
    (W)
1875, 7, 22. Isaac Thomas gct Adrian MM,
    Mich., to m Phebe G. Gibbons (G)
1897, 8, 24. Elma T. gct Somerset MM (W)

GIBBS
1892, 10, 19. John W., Sophronia & Rosa recrq
    (G)
1892, 10, 19. John Wilber recrq (G)

GIBSON
1842, 9, 21. Miller, s Amos & Hannah, Fayette
    Co., Pa.; m in Short Creek MH, Ann P.
    EYRE, dt Robert & Jemima, Harrison Co., O.
    Ch: Robert E. b 1843, 12, 9 d 1854, 8,29
        ae 10
        Elizabeth
        M.   " 1846, 9, 7 " 1848, 4,19
        Hannah J. " 1849, 9, 8
        Annie M.   " 1858, 2, 10 " 1864, 1,11
        Albert
1865, 9, 21. Mary d
1881, 7, 1. Rebecca d

1843, 5, 23. Ann T. gct Redstone MM
1844, 9, 24. Miller & w, Ann P., & s, Robert
    E., rocf Redstone MM, dtd 1844,9,4
1848, 5, 23. Mary rocf Redstone MM
1854, 9, 19. Sarah rocf Upper Springfield MM,
    dtd 1854,2,22
1860, 9, 18. Sarah dis jG (W)
1870. 7, 19. Hannah Penrose (form Gibson) dis

    jG & mcd (W)
1870, 7, 19. Miller dis jG (W)
1870, 8, 23. Ann dis jG (W)
1875, 6, 24. Rebecca relrq (G)
1883, 4, 25. Amos G. dis disunity (W)
1892, 10, 19. W. F. recrq (G)
1894, 1, 24. Mabel recrq (G)
1894, 3, 21. William, Harry C., Russell N.,
    Amelia & Oliver E., recrq (G)
1898, 6, 22. William, Amelia, Oliver, Harry
    & Russell dropped from mbrp (G)
1902, 8, 20. Harrie, Russell, Emeline &
    Olive dropped from mbrp (G)
1906, 9, 19. Mabel gct Columbus MM, O. (G)

GIDLEY
1817, 11, 18. Cert rec for William & fam from
    Saratoga MM, N. Y., dtd 1817,6,8, end to
    Alum Creek MM

GIESY
1894, 2, 21. William & Rose recrq (G)

GIFFORD
1865, 12, 19. Lydia dis jG (W)

GILBERT
1850, 4, 4. Abraham, s John & Susan, b
----, --, --. John & Elizabeth
    Ch: Ruth   b 1813, 6, 2
        John   " 1814, 11, 18
1830, 10, 27. Thomas, s John & Elizabeth,
    Belmont Co., O.; m in Mt. Pleasant, Edith
    SMITH, dt Jonathan & Mary
    Ch: Jonathan   b 1832, 7, 9
        Daniel A. " 1834, 10, 21

1815, 5, 23. Elizabeth & ch, Mary, Sarah,
    Thomas, Ruth & John, rocf Stillwater MM,
    dtd 1815,1,31
1818, 7, 21. Elizabeth Vanhorn (form Gilbert)
    dis mcd
1818, 7, 21. Mary, minor, gct Plainfield MM
    with fam of Nehemiah Wright
1825, 4, 19. Sarah, minor in care of Wm.
    Wells, gct Stillwater MM
1828, 5, 22. Thomas & w, Edith, & ch, Jona-
    than, Daniel A. & Mary S., gct Pennsville
    MM
1829, 3, 19. Ruth St. Clair (form Gilbert)
    dis mcd
1849, 6, 19. John gct Flushing MM, to m Su-
    sanna Packer
1850, 1, 22. Susanna P. rocf Flushing MM, dtd
    1849,11,22
1853, 6, 21. John & w, Susannah, & ch, Abram
    & Mary, gct Flushing MM
1857, 11, 24. Alfred McGrail gct Providence
    MM, to m Rebecca Gilbert
1874, 5, 19. Elisha B. Steer gct New Garden
    MM, to m Ellen C. Gilbert (W)

GILBREATH
1804, 5, 19. James gct Middleton MM

GILL
----, --, --. Joseph & Nancy
    Ch: William S. b 1806, 7, 29 d 1869, 3,16
            "somewhere in Illinois"
        John W.   b 1809, 11, 21
        James H.   " 1813, 1, 31
        Nancy   " 1815, 7, 29
1819, 9, 1. Priscilla m Benj. WORRALL
1821, 6, 7. Elizabeth m James HOOPS
1845, 1, 6. Nancy d ae 68 bur Short Creek
1845, 12, 1. Joseph d ae 82 bur Short Creek

1807, 1, 17. Joseph rocf Indian Spring MM,
    dtd 1806,1,17
1808, 12, 20. Ann & s, William, recrq
1810, 10, 23. Susanna recrq
1811, 5, 21. Ann rocf Hopewell MM, dtd 1810,
    12,3
1812, 11, 24. John recrq
1817, 7, 22. Elizabeth recrq
1818, 8, 18. Priscilla recrq
1828, 3, 18. Susanna & ch, John, Susanna &
    Salkel, gct Fairfield MM
1831, 2, 24. John gct Greenplain MM (H)
1836, 5, 24. John W. dis
1837, 5, 23. James dis disunity
1839, 6, 18. Nancy Flemming (form Gill) dis
    mcd
1843, 5, 23. Mary Ann (form Parker) dis mcd
1846, 5, 19. Deborah (form Watkins) dis mcd
1851, 9, 23. Deborah rst
1862, 7, 23. Samuel & ch, Joseph John, Han-
    nah E., Samuel C., James W., Anna L. &
    Mary Ellie, recrq (G)
1874, 4, 23. Mary Ann recrq (G)
1877, 4, 26. Hannah E. relrq (G)
1891, 3, 25. Harry C. recrq (G)
1907, 6, 19. Harry dropped from mbrp (G)
1912, 2, 21. Mary Eva recrq (G)

GILLETT
1912, 11, 20. Elizabeth W. gct Yarba Linda MM,
    Calif. (G)

GIVEN
1828, 12, 23. Ann & Emma dis jH
1830, 1, 19. Israel dis jH
1839, 12, 24. James dis mcd
1840, 4, 21. Amon dis disunity
1841, 3, 23. Isaac dis disunity
1872, 11, 5. Margaret A. & Sarah E. Boyle gct
    Clear Creek MM, Ill. (H)

GLASS
1866, 10, 1. Ruthanna d

1865, 8, 23. Ruth Ann recrq (G)
1865, 12, 20. William recrq (G)
1868, 1, 23. William M. con mcd (G)   [(G)
1868, 3, 26. Mary S. (form Talbott) con mcd

1869, 5, 20. William M. dis disunity (G)
1878, 5, 23. Anne E. gct Gilead MM (G)
1881, 2, 26. Caroline, Wm. K., Wm. M. & Mary
    E. recrq (G)
1907, 11, 20. Mary A. Thornton recrq (G)
1911, 5, 27. Harry recrq (G)

GLENN
1825, 10, 18. Edith (form Thompson) dis mcd

GOFF
1903, 3, 25. Edith recrq (G)

GOMERY
----, --, --. William & Phebe (H)
    Ch: Eli   b 1800, 9, 6
        Swithin   " 1809, 10, 28
        Enoch   " 1814, 8, 27
        William   " 1817, 1, 17
        Hannah   " 1819, 1, 16
        Joshua   " 1821, 1, 2
        Thomas Lew-
          is   " 1823, 1, 16
        Benjamin   " 1825, 2, 21
        Lovina   " 1827, 7, 4

1830, 2, 23. William [Gomere] dis jH
1830, 3, 25. William & w, Phebe, & ch,
    Swithin, Eli, Enoch, William, Hannah,
    Joshua, Thomas, Lewis, Benjamin & Lovina,
    gct Plainfield MM (H)
1830, 4, 22. John Jr. [Gumery] gct Plainfield
    MM (H)
1833, 5, 21. Enoch, William, Hannah, Joshua,
    Benjamin & Lavina [Gumery], ch William,
    gct Stillwater MM
1835, 6, 23. Hannah & Lydia dis jH
1837, 4, 20. Ann [Gummery] gct Plainfield MM
    (H)
1837, 4, 20. Hannah [Gummery] gct Plainfield
    MM (H)
1837, 4, 20. Isaac [Gummery] gct Plainfield
    MM (H)
1837, 4, 20. John [Gummery] & w, Elizabeth,
    & dt, Sarah, gct Plainfield MM (H)
1838, 1, 23. Isaac [Gumery] dis jH
1810, 10, 23. John [Gumery] recrq
1810, 10, 23. Levina [Gumery] & dt, Ann, recrq
1811, 9, 24. Phebe rocf Redstone MM, dtd
    1811,8,2
1813, 1, 19. William recrq
1817, 4, 22. Wm. [Gumere] & w, Phebe, & ch,
    John, Harlen, Ann, Swithen & Eli, recrq
1823, 1, 21. William & w, Phebe, & ch, John,
    Harlem, Ann, Swithen, Eli, Enoch, William,
    Hannah & Joshua, gct Flushing MM
1823, 9, 25. William & w, Phebe, & ch, John,
    Harland, Ann, Swithen, Eli, Enoch, William,
    Hannah, Joshua & Thomas, rocf Flushing MM,
    dtd 1823,8,22
1828, 12, 23. Lavina & Phebe dis jH
1829, 4, 21. Elizabeth dis jH
1833, 5, 21.   Enoch, William, Hannah, Joshua,

GOMERY, continued
    Benjamin & Levina, ch Wm. & Phebe, gct
    Stillwater MM
1829, 10, 30. Harland [Gomere] dis mcd

GOODING
----, --, --. William, s Samuel & Martha P.,
    b 1848,8,20; m Eva Leona RICHARDSON, dt
    Alexander & Catharine R., b 1857,7,4
    d 1924,6,4
        Ch: George A. b 1874, 9, 22
           Mary L.   " 1882, 7, 21
           Danford S. " 1885, 12, 20
           Calvert   " 1889, 6, 24
1930, 11, 26. Harriet E., dt Lemuel & Anna E.,
    d
1894, 2, 21. Emma recrq (G)
1894, 2, 21. Anna E. recrq (G)
1895, 12, 25. William & w, Eva Leona, & ch,
    Mary & Danford Leigh recrq (G)
1896, 1, 23. G. A. recrq (G)
1896, 5, 20. James Calvert, minor, recrq (G)
1897, 9, 22. Lemuel & w, Annie E., relrq (G)
1901, 1, 23. Lillie recrq (G)
1903, 6, 24. Lemuel dropped from mbrp (G)
1903, 6, 24. Monna dropped from mbrp (G)
1903, 6, 24. Anna S. dropped from mbrp (G)
1929, 7, 24. William dropped from mbrp (G)

GOODWIN
1837, 10, 30. Abigail, dt Ezra & Martha Whar-
    ton, d ae 18

1814, 6, 21. Ann rocf Newgarden MM, dtd
    1814,4,7
1832, 2, 21. William recrq
1832, 12, 18. William gct Deerfield MM

GORDING
1898, 12, 21. Samuel released from mbrp (G)

GOVE
1843, 8, 30. Moses D., s Moses & Hannah,
    Essex Co., Mass.; m in Concord, Sally B.
    STROUD, dt Jacob & Ann, Belmont Co., O.

1841, 6, 22. Moses D. rocf Weare MM, N. H.,
    dtd 1841,5,13
1847, 6, 22. Moses D. & w, Sally B., & ch,
    Frederick D. & Anna Ellen, gct Salem MM
1853, 10, 18. Moses D. & w, Sally, & ch, Fred-
    erick D., Anna Ellen & John Howard, rocf
    Salem MM, dtd 1853,9,21

GRACE
----, --, --. Benajah & Grace
    Ch: Isaac   b 1823, 5, 1
        Benajah " 1825, 9, 11
        Rachel   " 1829, 3, 30

GRAEBE
1891, 5, 20. Rosa L. (form Carmon) relrq (G)

GRAFTON
1896, 1, 21. James & w, Mary, & three ch
    rocf Smithfield MM (G)
GRAHAM
1835, 7, 21. Joseph [Greyham] dis disunity
1881, 2, 26. Harry recrq (G)
1886, 7, 21. Harvey relrq (G)
1888, 10, 24. Harvey & Maggie S. dropped
    from mbrp (G)
1895, 12, 25. Clyde recrq (G)
1907, 4, 24. Clyde dropped from mbrp (G)

GRANDON
1914, 1, 21. George recrq (G)

GRANT
1892, 10, 19. George N. recrq (G)

GRAY
----, --, --. Elijah & Mary
    Ch: Esther   b 1797, 7, 30
        Samuel   " 1799, 12, 24
        David   " 1801, 11, 1
        Elijah   " 1804, 8, 2
        Thomas   " 1806, 6, 2
        Elisha   " 1808, 4, 30
1810, 11, 28. Elijah d (a minister)
1817, 6, 4. Esther m Enoch MATSON
1823, 4, 30. Samuel, s Elijah & Mary, Harri-
    son Co., O.; m in West Grove MH, Hannah
    WOOD, dt Robert & Mary, Harrison Co., O.
    Ch: Mary   b 1824, 1, 28
        Elijah   " 1825, 8, 30
        Robert   " 1827, 6, 5
        Rachel   " 1829, 5, 14
        Lemuel   " 1831, 5, 8
        Samuel   " 1833, 2, 12
1827, 5, 30. Thomas, s Elijah & Mary, Harri-
    son Co., O.; m in West Grove MH, Catharine
    LEWIS, dt Thomas & Mary, Harrison Co., O.
    Ch: William S. b 1828, 10, 6
----, --, --. Elisha & Ann
    Ch: Elijah   b 1829, 2, 4
        Peter   " 1832, 1, 11
1830, 7, 22. Robert d
1830, 7, 11. Rachel d
1832, 8, 29. John, s Elijah & Mary, Harrison
    Co., O.; m in West Grove MH, Deborah PYLE,
    dt Wm. & Jane, Tuskrawas Co., O.

1806, 9, 20. Susanna (form Wells) dis mcd
1808, 3, 22. Hannah (form Ackley) dis mou
1819, 8, 24. Hannah rst at Flushing MM on
    consent of this mtg
1828, 7, 22. Thomas & w, Catharine, & s,
    William S., gct Somerset MM
1828, 10, 21. Ann (form Thomas) con mcd
1829, 2, 24. David gct Somerset MM
1829, 7, 21. Elisha dis
1829, 7, 23. Thomas & w, Catharine, & s,
    Wm. S., gct Stillwater MM (H)
1833, 4, 23. Ann rocf Flushing MM, dtd 1833,
    2,21

GRAY, continued

1833, 5, 21. William & Isaac [Grey], ch
    Thos., rocf Flushing MM, dtd 1833,1,24

1833, 8, 22. Thomas & w, Catharine, & ch,
    William, Mary & Atlantic Ocean, gct Still-
    water MM (H)

1833, 11, 19. Elisha [Grey] & w, Ann, & ch,
    Elijah & Peter, gct Somerset MM

1835, 5, 19. Mary gct Somerset MM

1836, 7, 19. John & w, Deborah, & s, John
    White Gray, gct Somerset MM

1837, 4, 18. Hannah & ch, Mary, Elijah, Lem-
    uel, Samuel & Jesse, gct Pennsville MM

1838, 11, 22. Atlantic O. gct Stillwater MM
    (H)

1840, 9, 24. Elijah & w, Charlotte, & ch,
    Emily, Rees, Thos., Mary Ann, Esther,
    Lilburn & Agness, gct Stillwater MM (H)

1852, 2, 24. Rachel, minor, rocf Somerset
    MM, dtd 1851,10,27

1852, 8, 24. Ann Hoops (form Gray) dis mcd

1892, 10, 19. Elizabeth F. recrq (G)

GREEN

1829, 10, 29. Samuel, s Alexander & Eleanor,
    Harrison Co., O.; m in Short Creek MH, Ann
    THOMPSON, dt Aaron & Sarah, Jefferson Co.,
    O.

1862, 10, 29. John H., s John & Mary, Henne-
    pin Co., Minn.; m in Mt. Pleasant, Hannah
    K. TERRELL, dt Clark & Mary, Jefferson
    Co., O.

1867, 6, 10. Ronald M. b

1830, 3, 23. Ann gct Flushing MM

1853, 10, 18. James Steer Jr. gct Stillwater
    MM, to m Mary Green

1856, 11, 18. Joseph Hall gct Stillwater MM,
    to m Rebecca S. Green

1861, 3, 20. Peter L. Thomas gct Flushing MM,
    to m Mary Green

1862, 11, 19. Rachel, John & Lydia dis jW

1864, 11, 23. Hannah L. gct Spring Creek MM,
    Iowa

1866, 4, 25. Marius Edward & Anna Mary Thomas,
    ch Thos. E. & Mary Pinkham, gct Blooming-
    ton MM, Ia. (G)

1873, 5, 22. Mary E. recrq (G)

1886, 5, 19. David H. recrq (G)

1887, 2, 23. Roland M. recrq (G)

1895, 1, 23. Viola recrq (G)

1898, 3, 23. Ronald M. relrq (G)

1898, 11, 24. Anabelle recrq (G)

1907, 3, 20. Alice Patterson & ch, John, Ja-
    cob & Robert E. & Esther Patterson, gct
    Muncie MM, Ind. (G)

1907, 3, 20. Anna Bell dropped from mbrp (G)

GREENHALGH

1897, 3, 24. Sarah A. recrq (G)

GREGG

1814, 9, 29. Eli, s Samuel & Ann, Knox Co.;

m in Owl Creek MH, Knox Co., Martha
    WRIGHT, dt Robert & Rachel, Knox Co., O.

1812, 9, 22. Samuel & w, Ann, & ch, Eli,
    Gulielma, Phineas, William, Isaac, Asa &
    Tacy, rocf Plainfield MM, dtd 1812,6,27

1816, 6, 18. Gulielma Harris (form Gregg) dis
    mcd

1816, 12, 24. Abel & w, Hannah, & ch, David,
    Betty Ann & Jesse, rocf Plainfield MM, dtd
    1816,11,21

1831, 10, 18. Vila (form Howard) dis

1833, 3, 19. Benjamin W., Joseph W., Newton
    & Elmira, minor ch James & Abigail, rocf
    Stillwater MM, dtd 1833,1,26

1862, 11, 19. Hannah dis jW (G)

1862, 11, 19. Mahlon dis jW (G)

1884, 5, 21. Ella recrq (G)

1885, 3, 25. Sylvanus L., Mary L., Josiah P.
    & Oliver T. recrq (G)

1894, 7, 25. Alice dropped from mbrp (G)

GRIFFIN

1847, 11, 23. Joshua V. Millhouse gct Westland
    MM, to m Elizabeth P. Griffin

GRIFFITH

----, --, --. George & Sarah
    Ch: Isaac   b 1816, 2, 29
        Martha   " 1821, 12, 4
        George   " 1826, 5, 2

1819, 10, 28. Charles W., s Evan & Amy, Jeffer-
    son Co., O.; m in Short Creek MH, Hannah
    LEWIS, dt Jacob & Mary, Jefferson Co., O.

----, --, --. Abraham b 1798,12,13; m Mary
    ----- b 1801,2,27
    Ch: Elma   b 1821, 5, 2
        Ann   " 1825, 5, 18
        Reese S.   " 1826, 12, 28
        Charles R. " 1829, 10, 16
        Sarah   " 1831, 12, 24

1820, 7, 19. Amos Lee, s Chas. W. & Hannah, b

1822, 5, 9. Amy m John H. HURFORD

1829, 3, 15. Even Jr. d ae 20

1830, 7, 15. Even Sr. d ae 66

----, --, --. Samuel & Hannah
    Ch: Amy   b 1834, 1, 14
        Evan   " 1836, 11, 16 d 1840, 2,29
        Mercy Jane " 1840, 1, 3

1864, 11, 23. Elenor d ae 79

1865, 7, 26. Oscar J., s Eli L. & Mary Ann,
    Washington Co., Pa.; m in Mt. Pleasant,
    M. Elma PETTIT, dt Joseph & Hannah, Jef-
    ferson Co., O.

1866, 9, 12. Elizabeth d ae 91

1868, 5, 12. Samuel d ae 66

1890, 12, 28. Sarah d

1895, 5, 21. Hannah d

1804, 9, 15. Ann rocf Baltimore MM, dtd

GRIFFITH, continued
     1803,10,20 end by Concord MM 1804,7,24
1806, 7, 19. Ann gct Baltimore MM
1809, 8, 22. Deborah rocf Warrington MM, dtd
     1809,5,18
1813, 11, 23. Deborah gct Warrington MM
1816, 9, 24. Reuben & ch, Ann More, Rebecca,
     Elizabeth, Mary & Keturah, rocf Newgarden
     MM, O., dtd 1816,8,15
1818, 7, 21. Charles rocf Goshen MM, Pa.,
     dtd 1818,4,29 end by Salem MM
1818, 7, 21. Elina rocf Goshen MM, Pa., dtd
     1818,4,29 end by Salem MM
1818, 7, 21. Even & w, Elizabeth, & ch, Amy,
     Samuel, Jane, Evan, Sarah & Elizabeth Ann,
     rocf Goshen MM, Pa., dtd 1818,4,29 end by
     Salem MM
1819, 4, 20. Mary & Kitturah, minor ch Reu-
     ben, gct Concord MM
1819, 6, 22. Elizabeth rocf Redstone MM, dtd
     1819,5,26
1819, 6, 22. Elizabeth gct Flushing MM
1821, 5, 22. George & w, Sarah, & ch, Isaac
     & Juliann, rocf Warrington MM, dtd 1820,
     11,23
1822, 7, 23. Charles & w, Hannah, & s, Amos
     Lee, gct Plainfield MM
1823, 9, 25. Eli & w, Rachel, & ch, William,
     rocf Concord MM, dtd 1823,5,25
1823, 11, 18. Rachel & s, William, rocf Con-
     cord MM, dtd 1823,8,25
1824, 1, 21. Reuben gct WD MM
1824, 8, 24. Abraham & w, Mary, & dt, Vio-
     letta L., rocf Richland MM, dtd 1824,4,30
1825, 3, 22. Abraham & w, Mary W., & dt,
     Violetta L., gct Stillwater MM
1826, 6, 20. Eli & w, Rachel P., & ch, Wm.
     P. & Collins, gct Stillwater MM
1827, 4, 24. Elma, minor, rocf Providence MM,
     Pa., dtd 1827,2,20
1828, 10, 21. Mary & ch, Elma, Ann & Rees,
     rocf Flushing MM, dtd 1828,6,27
1829, 3, 24. Elma, minor, gct Deerfield MM
1829, 4, 21. Newton gct Deerfield MM
1829, 9, 19. Sarah dis jH
1829, 12, 22. Elizabeth & Eleanor dis jH
1829, 12, 22. Samuel dis jH
1830, 1, 19. Jane dis jH
1830, 8, 24. Abraham dis disunity
1830, 9, 21. George dis jH
1834, 6, 24. Mary dis jH
1835, 7, 21. William dis mcd
1836, 10, 18. Charles, minor, gct Pennsville
     MM
1839, 7, 25. Lavinia & ch, Oliver Francis &
     Joel Emlen, gct Westland MM, Pa. (H)
1840, 6, 23. Eliza Ann dis jH
1840, 8, 20. Anna R., Rees L., Charles P. &
     Ruth, ch Abraham, gct Plainfield MM (H)
1843, 5, 25. George & ch, George, John & Sa-
     rah, gct Clear Creek MM, Ill. (H)
1843, 10, 26. Isaac gct Clear Creek MM, Ill (H)
1844, 12, 26. Martha Jane gct New Garden MM(H)

1847, 11, 23. Joshua V. Millhouse gct West-
     land MM, to m Elizabeth P. Griffith
1860, 9, 19. Asahel H. Patterson gct Red-
     stone MM, to m Esther Griffith
1865, 7, 19. Oscar J. rocf Redstone MM, to m
     M. Elma Pettit (G)
1866, 5, 23. Mary Elma gct Minneapolis MM (G)
1872, 7, 25. Elizabeth rocf Salem MM, dtd
     1872,5,23 (G)
1881, 2, 26. James A., Annie & Gracie recrq
1884, 1, 23. Benjamin recrq (G)   [(G)·
1884, 3, 19. Joseph A. recrq (G)
1884, 5, 21. George A. recrq (G)
1884, 7, 23. James A. dropped from mbrp (G)
1886, 2, 24. Laura L. recrq(G)
1886, 5, 19. Grant recrq (G)
1886, 5, 19. William recrq (G)
1888, 10, 24. Anzonetta dropped from mbrp (G)
1888, 10, 24. Grace dropped from mbrp (G)
1889, 2, 20. William dropped from mbrp (W)
1891, 12, 23. Anna R. recrq (G)
1896, 1, 23. James William recrq (G)
1896, 1, 23. Frank recrq (G)
1896, 3, 25. Mary Ellen (form Bryen) rocf
     Cleveland MM, dtd 1895,9,19 (G)
1902, 12, 20. Benjamin gct Guerney MM (G)
1913, 5, 21. Frank dropped from mbrp (G)
1919, 8, 13. Mercy Griffith Hammond gct
     Orange Grove MM, Calif. (H)

GRIMES
1822, 6, 18. Hannah rocf Concord MM, dtd
     1822,4,20
1825, 10, 18. Hannah gct Stillwater MM
1828, 5, 20. Hannah gct Deerfield MM
1904, 2,24. Walker J. & w, Lucy E., & ch,
     Myre E., Carl S., Walker G., Howard W. &
     Harvey J., recrq (G)
1916, 3, 22. Walker, Walter, Myra, Carl L.,
     Howard & Harry J. dropped from mbrp (G)

GRIMSHAW
1878, 12, 20. Joseph gct Smithfield MM (H)

GRISSELL
----, --, --. Thomas & Elizabeth
     Ch: Hannah Ann b 1819, 4, 14
         Edward L.   " 1820, 10, 16
         Elizabeth
           H.   " 1822, 11, 15
         Thomas A.   " 1824, 11, 28
         Simeon   " 1827, 2, 9
         Jesse   " 1829, 3, 9
1823, 5, 22. Elizabeth m Samuel VAIL
1827, 10, 24. Nathan P., s Edward & Hannah,
     Monroe Co., O.; m in West Grove MH,
     Lydia FRAME, dt Thos. & Mary LEWIS, Harri-
     son Co., O.
1883, 3, 9. Rebecca [Grizzell] d

1819, 6, 22. Elizabeth rocf Redstone MM, dtd
     1819,5,26
1824, 9, 21. Thomas & w, Elizabeth, & ch,

GRISSELL, continued
    Hannah Ann, Edward L. & Eliza N., recrq
1825, 11, 22. Hannah recrq
1826, 4, 18. Hannah gct Somerset MM
1828, 6, 24. Lydia gct Somerset MM
1829, 9, 26. Thomas & w, Elizabeth, & ch,
    Hannah Ann, Edward L., Elizabeth H., Thom-
    as & Simeon, gct Stillwater MM (H)
1829, 12, 22. Thomas dis jH
1831, 2, 22. Elizabeth dis jH
1841, 11, 20. Elizabeth & Simon, ch Thos. &
    Eliza, gct Somerset MM
1841, 11, 20. Edward gct Somerset MM
1841, 11, 20. Hannah Ann gct Somerset MM
1852, 5, 20. Rebecca gct Stillwater MM (H)

GRIST
1865, 8, 4. William Elmer d

1856, 10, 21. Ann (form Watson) dis mcd

GROVES
1893, 8, 27. Clifford E., s John & Ida
    (Moore), b

1901, 3, 19. Clifford E., minor, recrq (W)
1924, 9, 23. Clifford E. con mcd (W)

GRUBB
1815, 10, 5. Jemima m Robert EYRE
----, --, --. Curtis & Ann
    Ch: Hannah   b 1826, 2, 1
        Mary   " 1827, 7, 27
        Samuel   " 1829, 4, 25
        Elizabeth " 1831, --, 30
        Lydia
1844, 2, 21. Hannah G. m Milton R. PETTIT
1849, 11, 1. Elizabeth M. m Samuel LLOYD
1851, 12, 28. Mary d ae 75 bur Short Creek

1807, 1, 17. Curtis rocf Indian Spring MM,
    dtd 1806,3,21
1807, 1, 17. Jeremith rocf Wilmington MM,
    dtd 1806,12,4
1807, 1, 17. John rocf Wilmington MM, dtd
    1806,12,4
1807, 1, 17. Mary rocf Wilmington MM, dtd
    1806,12,4
1807, 7, 18. Hannah rocf Wilmington MM, dtd
    1806,12,4
1811, 12, 24. Mary gct Alexandria MM
1818, 4, --. Mary rocf Alexandria MM, dtd
    1817,12,25
1825, 6, 21. Ann & dt, Sarah Crozer, rocf
    Plainfield MM, dtd 1825,5,26
1831, 3, 22. John rst
1851, 3, 18. Mary Crozier (form Grubb) con
    mcd
1867, 12, 24. Samuel S. dis jG (W)
1867, 12, 26. Edith A. rocf Salem MM (G)
1898, 2, 23. Anna B. Duffield (form Grubb)
    relrq (G)
1902, 12, 20. Mary Elizabeth gct Cleveland MM
    (G)

(G)
1912, 3, 20. Edith A. gct East Whittier MM,
    Calif.(G)
1912, 3, 20. Gertrude gct East Whittier MM,
GUMERY   [Calif. (G)
1811, 3, 27. John, s John & Levinah, Jeffer-
    son Co., O., b 1781,11,26; m in West
    Grove MH, Elizabeth THORN dt Isaac &
    Hannah, Jefferson Co., O., b 1788,10,22
    Ch: Isaac   b 1812, 4, 26 d 1871, 6, 9
        Lydia   " 1814, 3, 27
        Hannah   " 1816, 3, 19
        Ann   " 1818, 2, 2
        Sarah   " 1826, 9, 19
1811, 5, 29. Ann m Thos. THORN
1826, 8, 31. Ann m Jesse PARKER
1881, 8, 11. Nancy d

GURYTON
1891, 3, 25. Isaac Oliver recrq (G)

GUTSHALL
1897, 8, 15. Erma, dt Wm. & Belle, b

1910, 3, 23. Clara B. [Gutshaw] relrq (G)
1922, 7, 19. Irma recrq (G)
1926, 6, 9. Irma dropped from mbrp (G)

GUY
1892, 10, 19. Joseph & Isaac recrq (G)

GWINN
----, --, --. Hugh [Guynn] b 1769,3,12 d 1861,
    9,9; m Hannah -- --- b 1787,8,6 d 1830,11,
    16
    Ch: Rachel   b 1814, 3, 5
        Isaac   " 1817, 3, 26 d 1817, 5,22
        Sarah Ann " 1819, 2, 8
        Hannah   " 1822, 5, 13
        Thomas   " 1822, 5, 13
        William   " 1825, 6, 26
1913, 4, 6. Rachel d ae 68
1914, 7, 11. Mary Elizabeth d ae 41

1811, 9, 24. Hannah [Gwynn] (form Thomas) dis
    mcd
1814, 10, 18. Hannah rst
1814, 11, 22. Hugh & ch, Susana & Rachel, recrq
1828, 10, 21. Susanna Maddon (form Gwyn) dis
    mcd
1829, 9, 19. Hannah [Gwyn] dis jH
1835, 6, 23. Rachel dis jH
1840, 11, 24. Sarah Ann Cope (form Gwinn) dis
    mcd
1844, 8, 20. Thomas [Gwyn] dis disunity
1851, 12, 23. Hannah Nealy (form Gwinn) dis mcd
1867, 7, 6. Thomas [Gwynn] gct Plainfield MM
    (H)
1892, 10, 19. Frank [Guynn] recrq (G)
1892, 10, 19. Jequette [Guynn] recrq (G)

HADLEY
----, --, --. Larkin J., s Alva & Ellen,

HADLEY, continued
 b 1889,12,18; m Myrtle ALLEN, dt Ebb. &
 Jennie, b 1888,11,10

1900, 2, 21. Lewis I. rocf Fairfield MM, Ind.
 (G)
1903, 11, 25. Lewis I. gct Portsmouth MM (G)
1927, 1, 5. Larkin & w, Myrtle, rocf Clark
 Ave. MM (G)
1929, 4, 24. Elaine, dt Larkin & Myrtle, recrq (G)
1931, 10, 28. Larkin & w, Myrtle, gct Urbana
 MM. O. (G)

HAGUE
1812, 8, 26. James R., s Francis & Ruth, Tusk-
 rawas Co., O.; m in West Grove MH, Ann
 SANDERS, dt Joseph & Hannah, Jefferson Co.,
 O.
 Ch: Joseph
   Sanders b 1813, 6, 4
   Henry Ball " 1814, 9, 25
   Samuel " 1817, 10, 11 d 1843, 3,26
   Robert " 1820, 11, 6
1835, 5, 28. Joseph S., s James & Nancy, Har-
 rison Co., O.; m in Harrisville, Eliza-
 beth A. RUSSELL, dt James & Sarah, Jeffer-
 son Co., O.
 Ch: James Rus-
   sell b 1838, 1, 7
   John Lup-
   ton " 1840, 4, 17
   William H. " 1842, 8, 8
   Joseph R. " 1846, 12, 16
1837, 4, 6. Henry B., s James R. & Ann,
 Harrison Co., O., d 1847,12,14 bur Short
 Creek; m in Harrisville, Sarah Ann THOMP-
 SON, dt John C. & Rebecca, Harrison Co.,
 O.
 Ch: Ann b 1838, 2, 27
   John T. " 1840, 6, 18 d 1840, 6,21
   bur Short Creek
   Henrietta T." 1847, 4, 2
   Samuel " 1842, 7, 14
----, --, --. ----- & Elizabeth
 Ch: James R. b 1838, --, --
   John " 1840, --, --
   William " 1843, --, --
   Joseph " 1846, --, --
1850, 10, 30. Robert, s James & Ann, Jefferson
 Co., O.; m in Mt. Pleasant, Martha Ann
 JONES dt Samuel & Elizabeth, Jefferson
 Co., O.
 Ch: Elizabeth
   J. b 1851, 7, 28
   Henry W. " 1853, 8, 28
1857, 10, 28. Ann m Samuel J. THOMASSON
1859, 3, 2. Annie, w James, d
1863, 9, 3. Elizabeth A. d ae 50
1863, 9, 5. Elizabeth, dt James Russel, d
 bur Short Creek
1864, 9, 28. Samuel E., s Henry B. & Sarah
 A., Jefferson Co., O.; m in Mt. Pleasant,

Mary HARRISON, dt Richard & Elizabeth,
Jefferson Co., O.
1869, 9, 29. Henrietta L. m Thos. MADDOX

1809, 8, 22. James, gr s of James Rattikane,
 rocf Fairfax MM, dtd 1808,1,22
1809, 8, 22. Sarah rocf Fairfax MM, dtd
 1808,10,22
1811, 5, 21. Sarah Slutts (form Hague) dis
 mcd
1841, 8, 24. Joseph S. dis disunity
1843, 3, 21. John C. gct Salem MM, to m Rebecca Bonsall
1862, 6, 25. James R. Jr. con mcd (G)
1864, 12, 21. Samuel E. & w, Mary H., gct
 Smithfield MM (G)
1865, 7, 19. William H. con mcd (G)
1866, 4, 25. Wm. H. gct Chesterfield MM (G)
1867, 1, 24. Joseph R. gct Spring Creek MM,
 Ia. (G)
1867, 2, 21. James R. Jr. gct Smithfield MM
 (G)
1869, 4, 20. James R. dis jG (W)
1869, 4, 20. Robert S. dis jG (W)
1870, 10, 18. Henrietta T. Maddox (form Hague)
 dis mcd & jG (W)
1875, 1, 21. Samuel E. & w, Mary, & ch, William H., Thos. Wood & Annie W., rocf
 Springdale MM, Ia. (G)

HAINES
1812, 8, 27. Isaac, s Wm. & Martha, Jeffer-
 son Co., O.; m in Short Creek MH, Rachel
 MICHENER, dt John & Martha, Jefferson Co.,
 O.
----, --, --. Timothy & Hannah
 Ch: Elizabeth b 1830, 7, 4
   Joseph " 1833, --, --
   Isaac " 1835, --, --
1877, 5, 24. Clayton, s Zebedee & Elizabeth
 F., Burlington Co., N. J.; m in Smithfield, Lydia B. McGREW, dt James W. & Ann
 G., Jefferson Co., O. (W)
1904, 9, 7. J. Rowland, s Clayton & Lydia
 B., Burlington Co., N. J., b 1878,5,17;
 m in Colerain, Mary MAULE, dt Jacob & Ra-
 chel R., Belmont Co., O., b 1880,11,9 (W)
1901, 12, 27. Thos. Harvey, s Zebedee & Anna
 P., Franklin Co., O.; m in Colerain, Ra-
 chel A. RUSSELL, dt Joseph & Martha, Belmont Co., O., d 1903,9,24 ae 30 bur Colerain (W)
1914, 1, 24. W. Herbert, s Zebedee & Anna P.,
 Chester Co., Pa.; m in Colerain, Hanna M.
 COPE, dt Benj. H. & Marietta, Jefferson
 Co., O., b 1888,5,28 (W)
 Ch: Helen Cope b 1920, 12, 26

1807, 1, 17. Isaac rocf Nottingham MM, dtd
 1805,11,8
1812, 12, 22. William, Ann & Timothy, ch
 Isaac, recrq
1817, 9, 23. Isaac & w, Rachel, & ch, Wil-

HAINES, continued
    liam, Nancy, Timothy, Rebecca & Edwin,
    gct Plainfield MM
1819, 8, 24. Lydia & ch, Smith, Davis, Sam-
    uel, Milton, Hannah, Lydia Ann & Mary,
    rocf Goshen MM, Pa., dtd 1819,4,28
1829, 11, 24. Timothy dis mcd
1830, 10, 19. William dis jH
1833, 7, 23. Edmund Lipsy gct Redstone MM,
    to m Sarah Haines
1838, 11, 22. Timothy & w, Hannah, & ch,
    Elizabeth, Joseph & Isaac, gct Stillwater
    MM (H)
1877, 11, 20. Lydia B. gct Upper Eavesham MM,
    N. J. (W)
1881, 2, 26. David recrq (G)
1914, 1, 19. J. Rowland rocf Upper Evesham
    MM, N. J., dtd 1913,12,12 (W)
1914, 1, 21. John F. [Haynes] recrq (G)
1914, 7, 22. Stella recrq (G)

HALDERMAN
1912, 2, 21. Anna Maddox relrq (G)

HALDY
1910, 10, 19. Herbert rocf Hanover MM (G)
1912, 11, 20. Herbert L. gct Beloit MM, O.(G)
1913, 7, 23. Arthur roc (G)
1913, 12, 24. Elizabeth Mote rocf Tecumseh MM,
    Mich (G)

HALL
1806, 1, 27. Christian d (an elder)
1806, 5, 1. Sarah m Evan HURFORD
1808, 2, 25. John, s Joseph & Christian, Jef-
    ferson Co., O.; m in Short Creek MH, Tacey
    PATTERSON, dt Joseph & Mary
    Ch: Mary   b 1809, 6, 1
        Robert   " 1810, 12, 28
        Christian " 1812, 9, 17
        Joseph   " 1814, 6, 22
        Achsah   " 1816, 8, 5
        Jesse   " 1818, 12, 30
        John   " 1821, 1, 31
        Elizabeth " 1823, 3, 27
        James   " 1829, 3, 28
1808, 4, 20. Mary m Richard EDGERTON
1809, 12, 28. Christena m Joseph CADWALADER
1810, 10, 4. Anna m James EDGERTON
1813, 4, 1. Thomas, s Joseph & Christiana,
    Jefferson Co., O.; m in Short Creek MH,
    Mary PATTERSON, dt Joseph & Mary, Jeffer-
    son Co., O., d 1859,11,16 bur Harrisville
    Ch: David   b 1817, 2, 2
        Rachel   " ----, 12, 27
        Anna   " 1819, 3, 25
        Rebecca " 1821, 3, 10
        Mary   " ----, 1, 27
        Asenath " 1826, 7, 13
        Sarah   " 1828, 7, 23
        Thomas   " 1831, 5, 2
1817, 5, 28. Mary m Daniel ATKINSON
----, --, --. Nathan, s Wm. & Hannah (Wharton)

b 1836,3,23 d 1918,10,23 bur Pasadena,
    Calif; m Hannah -----
    Ch: Maria   b 1824, 8, 20
        William " 1826, 6, 12 d 1885, 4,18
        bur Harrisville
        Elizabeth b 1829, 6, 24
        Hannah   " 1831, 5, 13
Nathan m 2nd Sarah -----
    Ch: Josiah   b 1841, 11, 22 d 1899, 4,12
        bur Harrisville
----, --,--. Nathan P. m Rachel WILSON
    Ch: Israel   b 1825, 10, 4
        Jesse   " 1827, 9, 15
        Isaac   " 1829, 9, 20
        Wilson   " 1832, 1, 25
        Joseph   " 1834, 3, 26
Nathan m 2nd Merab COFFEE
    Ch: Rachel   b 1840, 4, 11
        John C. " 1842, 3, 11
        Charles " 1844, 6, 6
1825, 4, 8. Joseph d ae 75 bur Harrisville
1826, 4, 6. William, s Jesse & Peninah,
    Jefferson Co., O.; m in Harrisville,
    Hannah WHARTON, dt Ezra & Martha, Jeffer-
    son Co., O.
    Ch: Ezra W. b 1827, 1, 25
        Parker   " 1829, 6, 6 d 1838, 8, 8
        bur Harrisville
        Tilman   b 1831, 5, 18
        Linton   " 1833, 8, 22
        Nathan   " 1836, 5, 23
        Peninah " 1839, 12, 16 d 1891, 9,19
        bur Harrisville
        Martha   b 1843, 12, 6
1831, 5, 26. Hannah d ae 30 bur Harrisville
1832, 3, 1. Mary m Josiah RATCLIFF
1832, 6, 18. Hannah d
1835, 2, 21. Sarah T. d bur Short Creek
----, --, --. Thomas & Mary
    Ch: Sarah   b ----, --, --
        Nathan   " 1836, 3, 13
1835, 12, 12. Rachel d ae 30 bur Short Creek
1837, 4, 27. Joseph, s John & Tacy, Jeffer-
    son Co., O.; m in Harrisville, Martha
    FARQUHAR, dt Alan & Edith, Jefferson Co.,
    O.
1837, 11, 1. David, s Thos. & Mary, Jeffer-
    son Co., O.; m in West Grove MH, Sarah
    THOMAS, dt Peter & Mary
1837, 11, 2. Anna m David CONROW
1837, 11, 30. Rachel m Bradaway THOMAS
----, --, --. David & -----
    Ch: Lindley b 1839, 3, 11
        Sarah T. " 1841, 2, 12
        Ellen   " 1852, 6, 11
        Anna M. " 1854, 9, 12
        Martha   " 1863, 3, --
1839, 12, 11. John d ae 59 bur Short Creek
1841, 2, 21. Sarah T. d ae 24 bur Harris-
    ville
1842, 3, 31. Christiana m Elisha KIRK
1841, 4, 29. Rebecca m David BINNS
1841, 12, 2. Mary P. m Pearson SMITH

HALL, continued
1849, 10, 31. Jesse, s Nathan J. & Rachel,
     Jefferson Co., O.; m in West Grove MH,
     Edith THOMAS, dt Peter & Mary, Harrison
     Co., O.
     Ch: Pearson   b 1851, 8, 15
         Henry   " 1854, 4, 22
         Anna Mary   " 1856, 4, 10 d 1921, 7, 4
            bur Harrisville
         Joshua   b 1857, 12, 7 " 1858,12,17
         Rachel M.   " 1859, 11, 15
         Sina W.   " 1863, 4, 10
         Nathan P.   " 1865, 8, 8
184-, 11, 20. Josiah, s Nathan & Deborah, b
----, --, --. William m Mary T. ----- d 1905,
     3,6 ae 73 bur Harrisville
     Ch: Caroline   b 1851, 4, 27
         Maria   " 1853, 2, 2 d 1862, 6, 6
            bur Harrisville
1850, 10, 31. Asenath m Josiah BUNDY
1852, 3, 19. Miriam, dt John & Deborah, b
1854, 6, 29. Elizabeth m Jesse KIRK
----, --, --. Parker m Rebecca ----- d 1866,5,
     16 bur Harrisville
     Ch: Lewis   b 1855, 3, 26
         William   " 1857, 3, 18 d 1921, 1,30
            bur Colerain
         Edwin   b 1860, 4, 24
1855, 3, 26. Louis, s Parker, b
1855, 3, 29. Tilman, s Wm. & Hannah, Harri-
     son Co., O.; m in Harrisville, Mary Eliza
     KINSEY, dt Chas. & Sarah, Harrison Co.,O.
     Ch: Alice Ann   b 1856, 3, 30
         Charles   " 1860, 4, 9
         Ezra   " 1857, 8, 15 d 1858, 9, 7
         Emmer Wm.   " 1861, 10, 26
1856, 4, 10. Anna Mary b
----, --, --. Thomas & Hannah
     Ch: Thomas Aus-
            tin   b 1857, 11, 23
         Paxton   " 1860, 4, 7
         Mary P.   " 1863, 7, 23
----, --, --. Linton & Ann
     Ch: Cyrus   b 1859, 7, -- d 1862, 7,--
            bur Harrisville
         Hiel   b 1861, 9, --
         Hannah Mary" 1863, 3, 25
         Phebe Elma " 1863, 3, 25
         Abner   " 1865, 8, 8
1859, 4, --. Tace d ae 75
----, --, --. William & Mary
     Ch: Elizabeth   b 1863, 8, 14
         Samuel   " 1865, 10, 30
         Joseph   " 1868, 1, 16
----, --, --. Lindley & Millicent
     Ch: Franklin B.b 1864, 4, 5
         Arthur   " 1866, 4, 1
         Mary C.   " 1868, 4, 25
         Emily S.   " 1870, 6, 17
         Margaret   " 1874, 5, 22
         Dilwin E.   " 1876, 8, 23
         Lydia M.   " 1878, 10, 11
         Wilmer L.   " 1881, 2, 15

1864, 10, 27. Anna M. b
----, --, --. Josiah m Deborah ----- d 1911,
     8,18 bur Harrisville
     Ch: Abby   b 1866, 5, 4
         Elma   " 1868, 8, 11
         Alice M.   " 1871, 4, 4
         Walter N.   " 1874, 9, 6
         Miriam C.   " 1880, 7, 20
1865, 10, 30. Samuel b
1866, 11, 20. Jesse, s W. P., d bur Harris-
     ville
1869, 4, 1. Edith m John W. SMITH (W)
1871, 9, 21. Martha H. m Thos. DEWEES (W)
----, --, --. Parker m Tabitha ----- d 1912,
     2,24 bur Harrisville
     Ch: Clara R.   b 1874, 6, 11
         Alfred D.   " 1878, 8, 4
1874, 1, 12. Nathan d ae 72 bur Harrisville
1874, 6, 9. Margaret, infant, d bur Harris-
     ville
1874, 8, 21. Deborah d ae 72 bur Harrisville
1878, 5, 2. Lewis, s Parker & Rebecca,
     Harrison Co., O.; m in Harrisville, Mar-
     garet Ann BINNS, dt David & Rebecca H.,
     Harrison Co., O., b 1849,6,30 d 1921,7,20
     ae 72 bur Harrisville (W)
     Ch: Almeda R.   b 1879, 4, 15
         Luella   " 1880, 7, 30
         Clifton P. " 1883, 2, 26
         Barclay S. " 1884, 10, 4
         Elizabeth B" 1892, 5, 5
1878, 10, 30. Wm. B., s Parker & Rebecca,
     b 1857,3,18 d 1922,1,30; m in Concord,
     Lydia J. SIDWELL, dt Israel & Rachel B.,
     Belmont Co., O., b 1856,9,26 d 1919,12,28
     (W)
     Ch: Oliver W.   b 1879, 6, 14 d 1881,11, 4
            bur Harrisville
         Ogden R.   b 1879, 6, 14 " 1879, 6,14
         Clinton P. " 1880, 11, 4
         Albert E.   " 1882, 5, 24
         George C.   " 1885, 4, 9
         Ellsworth   " 1889, 7, 22
         Francis W. " 1893, 6, 2
         Lura D.   " 1898, 12, 9
         Helen Lou-
            isa   " 1903, 8, 10
1879, 4, 15. Almeda R. b
1880, 5, 18. Thomas Sr. d bur Harrisville
1881, 2, 15. Wilmer L. b
1881, 10, 24. Clifton P., infant s Wm., d bur
     Harrisville
1883, 12, 14. William Sr. d ae 79 bur Harris-
     ville
1884, 10, 9. Caroline m Benj. BRANSON (W)
1886, 4, 29. Eliza m Gilbert McGREW (W)
1887, 1, 25. Joseph d ae 87 bur Harrisville
1889, 7, 22. Elsworth b
1890, 10, 29. Mary C. m Wilson J. STEER (W)
1891, 4, 3. Amy d ae 68 bur Harrisville
----, --, --. Joseph & Olive
     Ch: Emily C.   b 1892, 12, 27
         Albert J.   " 1896, 6, 1

HALL, Joseph & Olive, continued
        Ch: Lindley M. b 1898, 6, 25
1891, 9, 5. Hannah d ae 83 bur Harrisville
1892, 6, 2. Elizabeth m Dillwyn STRATTON (W)
1892, 9, 16. Eliza D. m Edmund S. SMITH (W)
1894, 5, 23. Sina W. m David P. WILLETS (W)
----, --, --. Samuel & Anna
        Ch: Tacy M.   b 1895, 3, 31
            William R.   " 1897, 7, 4
            Sarah M.   " 1900, 5, 15
            Florence   " 1902, 11, 24
            Bertha   " 1908, 5, 9
1895, 4, 24. Edwin, s Parker & Rebecca, Har-
        rison Co., O.; m in Harrisville, Elma E.
        HALL, dt Josiah & Debora, Harrison Co., O.
        (W)
1895, 4, 24. Elma E. m Edwin HALL (W)
1895, 6, 19. Emily S. m Isaac H. SATTERTH-
        WAIT (W)
----, --, --. Samuel, s Wm. Jr. & Mary (Thom-
        as), b 1865,10,30; m Anna M. MOTT, dt
        Richard & Sara (Hampton), b 1864,10,27
        Ch: Wm. R.   b 1897, 7, 4 d 1923, 1,30
                bur Harrisville
            Sarah M.   b 1900, 5, 15
            Bertha   " 1908, 5, 9
1897, 7, 4. William R. b
1898, 6, 2. Abbie S. m Thomas STARBUCK (W)
1898, 12, 9. Lura b
1900, 3, 29. Clara R. m Thos. B. WHINERY (W)
1900, 5, 15. Sarah M. b
1902, 5, 22. Lydia M. m Morris PEACOCK (W)
1902, 11, 24. Florence b
1903, 10, 22. Luella m Chalkley L. BUNDY (W)
1904, 2, 13. Helen, dt Wm. B. & Lydia Jane
        (Sidwell) b
1904, 10, 6. Alfred D., s Parker & Tabitha
        D., b 1878,8,4; m in Harrisville, Elza R.
        BINNS, dt Jonathan & Rosella, Harrison
        Co., O., b 1877,3,25 (W)
        Ch: William R. b 1914, 11, 1 (foster s)
1906, 4, 26. Rachel M. d ae 47 bur Harris-
        ville
1907, 6, 10. Luella Lucretia, dt Clifton &
        Anna, b
1908, 5, 9. Bertha b
1910, 6, 13. Willard, s Barclay S. & Mary C.,
        b
1915, 8, 5. Elizabeth B. m Albert H. SMITH
        (W)
1917, 10, 25. Tacy M. m Chas. D. KIRK (W)
1918, 10, 22. Nathan L. d ae 82 bur Pasadena,
        Calif.
1921, 7, 4. Anna Mary d bur Harrisville
1923, 1, 30. William R. d bur Harrisville
1929, 6, 27. Florence m Chester W. EMMONS (W)

1806, 4, 19. Levinah gct Concord MM
1807, 11, 21. Levina rocf Concord MM, dtd
        1807,8,18
1808, 10, 18. Mary rocf Newgarden MM, N. C.,
        dtd 1808,7,30
1809, 3, 21. Rebecca rocf London Grove MM,

dtd 1808,9,17
1813, 11, 23. Sarah Canary (form Hall) dis mcd
1814, 7, 19. Lavina Eddy (form Hall) dis mcd
1816, 6, 18. Mary gct Plymouth MM
1817, 4, 22. Mary rocf Plymouth MM, dtd
        1817,4,21
1817, 6, 24. Joseph D. gct Westland MM
1818, 2, 24. Rachel gct Westland MM
1819, 12, 21. Rachel rocf Westland MM, dtd
        1819,10,28
1821, 10, 23. Joseph Jr. gct Somerset MM
1821, 11, 20. Rachel Ady (form Hall) dis mcd
1823, 8, 19. Nathan gct Flushing MM, to m
        Hannah Wilson
1823, 12, 23. Hannah rocf Flushing MM, dtd
        1823,11,21
1824, 10, 19. Nathan P. gct Flushing MM, to
        m Rachel Wilson
1829, 7, 21. Lany James (form Hall) dis mcd
1830, 2, 23. Silas rocf Stillwater MM, dtd
        1830,1,23
1831, 8, 23. Silas dis mcd
1836, 2, 23. Robert gct Flushing MM
1836, 5, 24. Nathan gct Stillwater MM, to m
        Sarah Williams
1836, 8, 23. Sarah rocf Stillwater MM
1838, 7, 24. Nathan P. gct Plainfield MM, to
        m Merab Hall
1839, 2, 19. Merab rocf Plainfield MM, dtd
        1838,12,19
1839, 5, 21. Joseph & w, Martha, & dt, El-
        vira, gct Stillwater MM
1845, 12, 23. Hannan Hall (form Hurford) dis
        mcd
1846, 9, 22. Nathan gct Goshen MM, Pa., to
        m Deborah B. Smith
1847, 5, 18. Deborah rocf Goshen MM, Pa.,
        dtd 1846,12,3
1850, 8, 20. David gct Flushing MM, to m
        Amy T. Thomas
1850, 11, 19. William & w, Mary T., gct
        Flushing MM
1851, 1, 21. Amy T. rocf Flushing MM, dtd
        1850,12,26
1851, 1, 21. Jesse gct Upper Springfield MM
1851, 3, 18. John gct Flushing MM, to m
        Deborah S. DAVIS
1851, 10, 21. Deborah S. rocf Flushing MM,
        dtd 1851,9,25
1852, 7, 20. Israel gct Richland MM, Ind.
1852, 7, 20. John & w, Deborah, & dt, Miriam,
        gct Flushing MM
1853, 6, 21. Isaac gct Goshen MM, Pa.
1853, 8, 23. Parker gct Flushing MM, to m
        Rebecca Hobson
1854, 2, 21. Rebecca rocf Flushing MM, dtd
        1853,12,22
1854, 6, 20. William & w, Mary T., & ch,
        Caroline & Maria, rocf Flushing MM, dtd
        1854,4,20
1854, 9, 19. Thomas Jr. dis disunity
1856, 11, 18. Joseph gct Stillwater MM, to m
        Rebecca S. Green

HALL, continued

1857, 5, 19. Wilson gct Salem MM, to m Sina
    Stratton

1857, 12, 22. Sina rocf Salem MM, dtd 1857,10,
    21

1858, 8, 24. Linton gct Middleton MM, to m
    Ann W. Allmon

1858, 10, 20. Silas rst at Sugar River MM on
    consent of this mtg

1858, 12, 21. Ann W. rocf Middleton MM, dtd
    1858,11,20

1859, 4, 19. Joseph gct Stillwater MM

1859, 5, 24. Nathan P. & w, Merab, & ch,
    John C. & Charles P., gct Middleton MM

1859, 5, 24. Rachel gct Middleton MM

1859, 6, 21. Wilson & w, Sina, & s, Edward,
    gct Middleton MM

1859, 12, 20. Achsah gct Upper Springfield MM

1860, 2, 22. Hannah gct Richland MM, Ind.

1860, 2, 21. Sarah dis disunity

1862, 2, 18. Hannah & ch, Thomas Austin &
    Paxton V.,recrq

1862, 2, 18. Thomas Jr. rst

1862, 7, 22. Lindley gct Somerset MM

1863, 4, 7. Sarah gct Stillwater MM (H)

1862, 11, 19. Joseph dis jW

1862, 11, 19. Abner, Alva, Amy, Ann, Ann, Anna,
    Anna Mary, Caroline, Charles, Cyrus, David,
    Deborah, Deborah, Deborah, Deborah, Edith,
    Edwin, Eliza, Eliza, Ellen, Francis, Hall,
    Hannah, Henry, Henry, Henry, Hyall, Jeptha,
    John, John, Joseph, Joseph G., Josiah,
    Lewis, Lewis, Lindley, Lindley, Linton,
    Mansell E., Martha, Martha, Mary, Mary,
    Mary, May, Meriba, Mic(?), Nathan, Nathan
    L., Nathan P., Nathel, Parker, Pearson,
    Penninah, Phebe, Phebe, Rachel, Rachel,
    Rachel Amy, Rebecca, Sarah, Sarah, Sarah,
    Sarah T., Sina, Tacy, Thomas, Thomas,
    Thomas, Thomas, William, William, William
    & Wilson dis jW

1864, 4, 19. Tilman dis jG (W)

1865, 2, 21. Josiah gct Flushing MM, to m
    Deborah Wilson (W)

1865, 9, 19. Deborah W. rocf Flushing MM,
    dtd 1865,7,20 (W)

1866, 7, 24. Mary Eliza dis jG (W)

1866, 12, 18. Wilson & w, Sina, rocf Middle-
    ton MM, dtd 1866,11,17 (W)

1867, 1, 24. Tillman & w, Mary Eliza, & ch,
    Alice Ann, Chas. Henry, Emmer Wm. & Ira
    K., gct Upper Springfield MM (G)

1867, 8, 20. David dis jG (W)

1867, 8, 20. Thomas Jr. dis jG (W)

1867, 8, 20. Amy T. dis jG (W)

1867, 8, 20. Hannah W. dis jG (W)

1869, 2, 23. Linton & w, Ann, & ch, Hial S.,
    Hannah Mary, Phebe Elma, Abner J. & Wil-
    son M., gct Middleton MM (W)

1870, 1, 18. Lindley & w, Millicent, & ch,
    Franklin B., Arthur & Mary C., rocf
    Flushing MM, dtd 1869,12,23 (W)

1870, 11, 22. James E. gct Newgarden MM (W)

1872, 5, 20. Parker gct Stillwater MM, to m
    Tabitha D. Bundy (W)

1873, 3, 18. Tabitha D. & dt, Louisa Bundy,
    rocf Stillwater MM, dtd 1873,1,22 (W)

1873, 5, 20. Pearson gct Middleton MM (W)

1873, 5, 20. Wilson & w, Sina, gct Middleton
    MM (W)

1875, 2, 23. Anna M. Lamhorn (form Hall) dis
    mcd (W)

1875, 5, 18. Ellen Yost (form Hall) dis mcd
    (W)

1876, 5, 23. Sarah T. Williams (form Hall)
    dis mcd (W)

1877, 12, 18. Amy T. rst (W)

1878, 2, 19. Henry gct Frankfort MM, Pa. (W)

1885, 8, 18. Martha B. dis jas (W)

1885, 11, 24. Mary P. dis disunity (W)

1886, 6, 22. Paxton dis disunity (W)

1888, 7, 24. Nathan P. gct Springville MM,
    Ia., to m Elizabeth D. Test (W)

1890, 10, 21. Nathan P. gct Springville MM,
    Ia. (W)

1890, 11, 18. Arthur T. gct Hickory Grove MM,
    Ia. (W)

1891, 3, 24. Joseph gct New Garden MM, to m
    Olive H. Oliphant (W)

1891, 9, 22. Olive H. rocf New Garden MM,
    dtd 1891,8,20 (W)

1892, 4, 19. Samuel gct Springville MM, Ia.,
    to m Anna Mott (W)

1892, 6, 21. Eliza D. rocf Chesterfield MM,
    dtd 1892,6,7 (W)

1892, 11, 22. Elizabeth H. Stratton (form
    Hall) gct New Garden MM (W)

1892, 12, 20. Anna M. rocf Springville MM,
    Ia. (W)

1893, 1, 25. Frank J. & w, Charity, rocf
    Greenwich MM (G)

1896, 4, 21. Franklin B. dis jas (W)

1897, 11, 23. Phebe Elma rocf Middleton MM,
    dtd 1897,10,16 (W)

1898, 3, 22. Edwin & w, Elma E., & dt, Lil-
    lian A., gct Flushing MM (W)

1899, 6, 20. Phebe Elma gct Middleton MM (W)

1903, 4, 21. Walter N. dis mcd (W)

1903, 12, 22. Lindley & w, Millicent, gct
    New Garden MM (W)

1904, 5, 24. Wilmer L. gct Stillwater MM, to
    m Ida J. Stanton (W)

1904, 8, 23. Mariam C. dis disunity (W)

1904, 9, 20. Joseph & w, Olive H., & ch,
    Emily C., Albert J. & Lindley, gct New-
    garden MM (W)

1905, 3, 21. Clifton D. gct Plainfield MM,
    Ind., to m Anna Pickett (W)

1905, 4, 18. Dillwyn E. gct Newgarden MM (W)

1905, 7, 18. Alice M. Meischlan (form Hall)
    dis disunity (W)

1906, 10, 22. Anna rocf Plainfield MM, Ind.,
    dtd 1906,8,29 (W)

1907, 3, 19. Barclay S. gct Upper Spring-
    field MM, to m Mary Cameron (W)

HALL, continued

1907, 9, 24. Mary Cameron rocf Upper Spring-
    field MM, dtd 1809,8,23 (W)
1909, 2, 23. Albert E. dis mcd & jas (W)
1910, 4, 19. George C. dis mcd & jas (W)
1910, 10, 18. Barclay S. & w, Mary Cameron, &
    s, Willard B., gct Newgarden MM, O. (W)
1910, 10, 18. Clifton P. & w, Anna, & ch, Lu-
    ella L., gct Newgarden MM (W)
1914, 6, 23. Francis W. gct Phila. MM, Pa. (W)
1924, 3, 18. Wilmer L. gct Salem MM, O. (W)
1927, 1, 18. William R., minor, recrq (W)
1927, 5, 24. Almeda R. gct Pasadena MM, Calif.
    (W)
1927, 5, 24. Lewis gct Pasadena MM, Calif.
    (W)
1929, 7, 23. R. Leland Thomas gct Newgarden
    MM, to m Luella L. Hall (W)

HAMBLETON

1808, 7, 19. William dis disunity
1808, 8, 23. Joseph, minor, rocf Newgarden
    MM, Pa., dtd 1808,7,4
1816, 8, 20. Benjamin rst at Middleton MM
    on consent of Short Creek MM, O.

HAMILTON

1806, 7, 19. Benjamin & William, minors, rocf
    Little Britton MM, Pa., dtd 1806,3,8
1807, 4, 18. William rocf Baltimore MM, dtd
    1807,2,12
1808, 3, 22. Benjamin dis
1808, 4, 19. Rachel (form Lewis) dis mou
1810, 10, 23. Joseph, minor, gct Baltimore MM
    for Western Dist.
1812, 6, 23. William Jr., minor, gct Plain-
    field MM
1856, 6, 24. Rachel Ann (form Ong) dis mcd
    (W)
1873, 5, 22. James & Eleanor recrq (G)

HAMMER

1901, 11, 20. Martha R. relrq (G)

HAMMOND

1806, 4, 23. Margaret m Joseph McGREW
----, --, --. Benjamin & Margaret
    Ch: Maria   b 1825, 3, 11
        Mary   " 1826, 9, 6
        George   " 1828, 2, 29
        Deborah   " 1829, 12, 20
        Margaret   " 1829, 12, 20
        Hiram   " 1830, 2, 20
        Isaac   " 1834, 1, 19
        James   " 1835, 12, 19
        Anderson   " 1838, 11, 4
        Rachel   " 1840, 11, 8
        William   " 1845, 5, 17
1840, 11, 1. George d ae 79 bur Smithfield
1844, 8, 15. William d ae 56 bur Smithfield
----, --, --. Joseph & Harriet
    Ch: Mary Ann   b 1846, 3, 18
        Amos P.   " 1848, 3, 22

    Ch: Rachel E.   b 1849, 12, 23
        Joseph J.   " 1852, 6, 1
        Oliver B.   " 1857, 6, 14
        Cordelia   " 1860, 2, 21 d 1863, 4, 1
        bur Cross Creek
1853, 2, 9. Sarah d ae 65
1853, 12, 16. Jane N. d ae 17

1806, 12, 20. John rocf Monallen MM, dtd
    1806,5,21
1807, 3, 21. James, Thomas, Robert & Mary,
    ch Rachel, recrq
1833, 11, 19. James C. rocf Smithfield MM,
    dtd 1833,10,21
1837, 2, 21. James C. con mcd
1850, 3, 19. James C. gct Pennsville MM
1856, 10, 21. Margaret Willets (form Hammond)
    dis mcd
1862, 6, 24. Benjamin dis jG (W)
1862, 8, 19. Margaret dis jG (W)
1864, 9, 20. Harriet & Mary dis jG (W)
1864, 9, 20. Joseph & Thomas dis jG (W)
1865, 8, 22. Nathan dis jH (W)
1865, 9, 19. Eliza Jane dis disunity (W)
1866, 11, 20. Ann dis disunity (W)
1877, 6, 19. William dis mcd & jG (W)
1877, 8, 21. John N. dis jG (W)
1877, 8, 21. John A. dis jG (W)
1877, 8, 21. Mary dis jG (W)
1877, 8, 21. Mary Ann dis jG (W)
1877, 8, 21. Rachel dis jG (W)
1877, 11, 20. Amos P. dis jG (W)
1885, 1, 21. Mary E. (form Woodward) gct
    Smithfield MM (G)
1919, 8, 13. Mercy Griffith gct Orange Grove
    MM, Calif. (H)

HAMPTON

1865, 4, 19. Robert W., s John & Mary, Linn
    Co., Ia.; m in Concord, Ann BUNDY, dt
    Benjamin & Delitha, Belmont Co., O.(W)

1816, 5, 2. Charles D. & w, Julia, & dt,
    Emily, rocf Abington MM, dtd 1815,8,28
1819, 1, 19. Charles D. dis disunity
1819, 1, 19. Julia, w Chas., & ch, Emily,
    Oliver & Henry Dennis, gct Cincinnati MM
1825, 12, 20. Emily & ch, Anna W. & Levi,
    rocf Pikecreek MM, dtd 1825,8,15
1828, 1, 22. James & w, Emily, & ch, Amos W.,
    Levi & Mary, gct Plainfield MM
1830, 6, 22. Amos & Mary, minors, rocf Still-
    water MM
1870, 8, 23. Ann B. gct Springville MM, Ia.
    (W)

HANDAL

1898, 10, 19. Mary R. recrq (G)
1899, 3, 22. Daisy M., Clarence B. & Blanche
    B., ch Mary R., recrq (G)

HANNON

1879, 5, 22. William recrq (G)

HANNON
1888, 10, 24. William dropped from mbrp (G)

HANSON
1862, 11, 19. Asa, Lydia, Elijah & Eliza dis
    jW

HANTHON
1894, 3, 21. Mary recrq (G)

HARGRAVE
----, --, --. Charles & Lucy
    Ch: Robert F. b 1826, 4, 7
        Samuel   " 1828, 2, 19
        Anna   " 1830, 6, 14
        Charles E. " 1833, 10, 27
        John   " 1836, 7, 31 d 1923,11,10
        Lydia   " 1836, 7, 31
        Mary   " 1839, 5, 16
----, --, --. Joseph & Deborah
    Ch: Benjamin S.b 1831, 5, 24
        Mariah   " 1834, 4, 17
1837, 4, 10. Mary Louiza, dt Lemuel & Mary
    Ann, b
1837, 4, 21. Mary Ann d ae 33 bur Short Creek
1838, 2, 28. Joseph, s Samuel & Elizabeth,
    Belmont Co., O.; m in Concord, Margaret J.
    LEWIS, dt Elisha & Elizabeth, Southampton
    Co., Va.
    Ch: William   b 1838, 11, 27
        Joseph   " 1838, 11, 27
        Elisha   " 1840, 5, 2
        Sally Ann " 1841, 3, 23
        Martha Jane" 1843, 10, 24
        Mary Catha-
           rine   " 1845, 4, 25
1839, 6, 6. Lucy d bur Short Creek
1843, 11, 1. Elizabeth A. m Benj. HAYCOCK
1844, 10, 2. Lemuel, s Samuel & Elizabeth,
    Jefferson Co., O.; m in West Grove MH,
    Elizabeth O. JOHNSON, dt Jonathan & Jud-
    ith, Harrison Co., O.
1847, 6, 14. Elizabeth D. J. d bur Short
    Creek
1854, 11, 1. Robert F., s Chas. & Lucy, Har-
    rison Co., O.; m in West Grove MH, Ruan-
    nah T. LADD, dt Peter & Mary THOMAS,
    Harrison Co., O.
    Ch: Oliver C. b 1857, 8, 14
        Wm. Henry " 1861, 11, 7
        John H.   " 1866, 8, 19
----, --, --. Robert & Ruanna [Hartgrave]
    Ch: Oliver C. b 1857, 8, 14
        Thomas E. " 1859, 7, 12
        William H. " 1861, 11, 7
1859, 8, 4. Thomas E. d
1863, 12, 15. Mary d
1867, 3, 21. Charles d
1876, 10, 4. Oliver C., s Robert F. & Ro-
    anna, Harrison Co., O.; m in West Grove
    MH, Emily C. WOODARD, dt Isaac & Emily,
    Harrison Co., O.
1898, 8, 7. Rachel, dt Nehemiah Matson, d

1829, 8, 18. Deborah rocf Cedar Creek MM, Va.
    dtd 1829,6,13
1830, 6, 22. Charles & w, Lucy, & ch, Robert
    Fleming & Samuel, rocf Wayne Oak MM, Va.,
    dtd 1830,4,3
1833, 4, 23. Thomas & w, Sarah, & dt, Eliza-
    beth Ann, rocf Wayne Oak MM, Va., dtd
    1833,3,2
1836, 9, 20. Lemuel & w, Mary, & ch, Thomas
    Exum, Sarah Elizabeth & Deborah Ann, rocf
    Wayne Oak MM, Va., dtd 1836,8,6
1836, 9, 20. Samuel & ch, Martha & Jane rocf
    Wayne Oak MM, Va., dtd 1836,8,6
1854, 8, 22. Benjamin dis mcd
1856, 3, 19. Thomas Exum dis mcd
1859, 6, 22. Deborah Ann Crew (form Hargrave)
    con mcd
1360, 11, 21. William dis mcd
1861, 2, 19. Charles dis jG
1861, 5, 22. Ann Harper (form Hargrave) con
    mcd
1861, 5, 21. Joseph dis jG
1861, 6, 15. William dis mcd
1863, 1, 21. Joseph dis (G)
1863, 3, 22. Ruannah dis jG (W)
1866, 7, 25. Lemuel gct Salem MM, Ia. (G)
1866, 7, 25. Sarah Elizabeth gct Salem MM,
    Ia. (G)
1866, 7, 25. Mary Louisa gct Salem MM, Ia.
    (G)
1866, 7, 25. Chas. E.con mcd (G)
1867, 1, 24. Chas. E. gct Spring Creek MM,
    Ia. (G)
1867, 10, 22. Lydia Hussey (form Hargrave)
    dis mcd & jG (W)
1867, 11, 19. Margaret dis jG (W)
1867, 11, 19. Martha dis jG (W)
1867, 11, 19. Jane dis jG (W)
1867, 11, 21. John con mcd (G)
1867, 12, 24. Sally Ann Harrison (form Har-
    grave) dis mcd & jG (W)
1868, 3, 26. Elisha con mcd (G)
1868, 4, 23. Lydia Hussey (form Hargrave)
    con mcd (G)
1869, 4, 22. Mary Catharine Thompson (form
    Hargrave) con mcd (G)
1869, 8, 24. Mary Catharine Thompson (form
    Hargrave) dis mcd (W)
1871, 4, 18. Robert F. dis jG (W)
1874, 12, 24. Sarah E. & ch, Joseph Lewis,
    Martha & James, recrq (G)
1879, 5, 22. Ruthanna T. & s, John Wilson,
    gct Springdale MM, Iowa (G)
1879, 7, 24. Ruanna & s, John W., rocf
    Springdale MM, Iowa, dtd 1879,6,21 (G)
1880, 3, 25. Rachel M. recrq (G)
1880, 9, 23. William R. gct Springdale MM,
    Ia. (G)
1882, 3, 23. Oliver C. & w, Emily C., & ch,
    Rachel, Ann, Charles L. & Tacy B., gct
    Lynn Grove MM, Ia. (G)
1884, 6, 25. Robert F. & Samuel dropped from
    mbrp (G)

HARGRAVE, continued
1896, 3, 25.   Sarah Elizabeth relrq (G)
1901, 2, 20.   Elizabeth recrq (G)
1902, 12, 24.   Lewis dropped from mbrp (G)
1903, 6, 24.   Elisha dropped from mbrp (G)

HARLEN
1819, 11, 23.   Samuel Steer gct Stillwater MM,
      O., to m Harriet Harlen

HARMAN
1820, 12, 19.   Elizabeth (form Stephens) dis
      mcd
1907, 3, 20.   William dropped from mbrp (G)

HARMER
1807, 5, 16.   Elizabeth (form Thomas) dis mcd
1822, 7, 23.   Cert rec for Elizabeth from
      Indian Spring MM, Md., dtd 1822,2,15, end
      by Bradford MM, Pa., end to Concord MM
1822, 7, 23.   Cert rec for George from Indian
      Spring MM, Md., dtd 1822,2,15, end by
      Bradford MM, Pa., end to Concord MM
1822, 7, 23.   Elizabeth & ch, Elwood, Naylor,
      William, Mary Ann & Amos Roberts, rocf
      Indian Spring MM, dtd 1822,2,15, end by
      Bradford MM, Pa., 1822,5,8
1829, 2, 24.   Naylor & w, Isabella, gct Deer-
      field MM
1831, 3, 22.   William gct Deerfield MM
1834, 2, 18.   Amos & w, Elizabeth, & ch, El-
      wood & Amos, gct Deerfield MM
1834, 2, 18.   Mary Ann gct Deerfield MM
1834, 3, 18.   George gct Deerfield MM

HARPER
1861, 5, 22.   Anne (form Hargrave) con mcd

HARRIS
----, --, --.   Enoch d 1845,6,18 ae 73 bur
      Short Creek; m Lany ----- d 1844,12,12 ae
      70 bur Short Creek
      Ch: Ezekiel   b 1803, 10, 20
          Robert   " 1805, 11, 15
          Joseph   " 1808, 8, 27
          Enoch   " 1816, 1, 1
          Sarah   " 1818, 7, 28
1805, 4, 22.   Uriah d ae 24 bur Short Creek
1808, 12, 29.   Fannah m Joseph DEW
1810, 6,   9.   Ezekiel d ae 67 bur Short Creek
----, --, --.   David & Lettice
      Ch: Lany   b 1822, 10, 15
          Rachel Ann " 1824, 2, 19
1824, 6, 30.   Ezekiel, s Enoch & Lany, Jeffer-
      son Co., O., b 1803,10,20; m in Mt. Pleas-
      ant, Anna BATES, dt Elisha & Sarah, Jef-
      ferson Co., O.
1825, 3,   1.   Thomas, s Richard & Beulah, b
1829, 1, 28.   Susanna m Richard KENNY
1832, 3, 28.   Joseph, s Enoch & Lany, Jeffer-
      son Co., O.; m in Mt. Pleasant, Lusinda
      WATKINS, dt John & Elizabeth, Jefferson
      Co., O., d 1833,7,25 bur Short Creek

Ch: John W.   b 1833, 1, 2
Joseph m 2nd 1840,5,27 in West Grove MH,
Christiana HURFORD, dt Evan & Sarah, Har-
rison Co., O.
Ch: William E. b 1841, 3, 23
    Evan H.   " 1844, 7, 18

1804, 8, 18.   Uriah rocf Coursound MM, dtd
      1804,4,11, end by Concord MM, 1804,6,19
1804, 9, 15.   Ezekiel & w, Sarah, & ch, Su-
      sanna, Fanny & Betty, rocf Coursound MM,
      dtd 1804,4,11, end by Concord MM, 1804,7,
      25
1816, 2, 20.   Richard & w, Beulah, & ch, Re-
      becca, Sarah, Mary, Watson & Jonathan,
      recrq
1816, 6, 18.   Gulielma (form Gregg) dis mcd
1818, 12, 22.   Sarah (form Pugh) dis mcd
1821, 6, 19.   Lettis (form Reynolds) con mcd
1821, 7, 24.   David con mcd
1824, 6, 22.   Betty Ady (form Harris) dis mcd
1826, 4, 18.   David & w, Lettice, & ch,
      Lany & Rachel Ann, gct Flushing MM
1829, 10, 20.   Sarah gct Stillwater MM
1830, 4, 20.   Rebecca King (form Harris) dis
      mcd
1832, 2, 21.   Robert gct Newgarden MM, to m
      Sarah Yates
1832, 8, 21.   Robert gct New Garden MM
1832, 11, 20.   Richard & w, Beulah, & ch,
      Jonathan, Sidney, Jordan P., Eli & Thomas,
      gct Deerfield MM
1835, 3, 24.   Watson gct Deerfield MM
1837, 6, 20.   Ezekiel & w, Anna, & ch, Eli-
      sha, Sarah, Mary, Enoch & Caroline, gct
      Plainfield MM
1840, 10, 20.   Elisha, Sarah, Mary, Enoch,
      Caroline & Wm., minor ch Ezekiel & Anna,
      rocf Plainfield MM, dtd 1840,3,20
1843, 2, 21.   Enoch Jr. dis mcd
1844, 1, 23.   Emily rocf Providence MM, dtd
      1843,11,2
1844, 2, 20.   Sarah Ong (form Harris) rpd
      mcd (d before case was finished)
1846, 4, 21.   Elisha dis jas
1860, 1, 25.   John dis mcd
1862, 8, 20.   Emily & ch, James A., Rebecca,
      Enoch, Rees, Sarah, Mary & Ruth Anna, gct
      Salem MM (G)
1864, 9, 20.   Christiana dis jG (W)
1865, 1, 24.   Joseph dis disunity (W)
1865, 6, 20.   Evan dis disunity & military
      service (W)
1865, 7, 18.   William dis jG (W)
1865, 8, 23.   Evan dis disunity (G)
1865, 10, 25.   William dis disunity (G)
1885, 3, 25.   Mattie recrq (G)
1885, 3, 25.   Emma recrq (G)
1891, 1, 21.   Mattie & Emma recrq (G)

HARRISON
1818, 10, 28.   Jordan, s William & Margaret,
      Jefferson Co., O.; m in Mt. Pleasant,

HARRISON, continued
    Susan LOYD,dt John & Mercy, Belmont Co.,
    O.
    Ch: Mercy Ann b 1821, 1, 14
        Mary   " 1822, 8, 6
        Deborah   " 1824, 12, 20
        Margaret J." 1826, 9, 24
        Wm. Jordan " 1828, 4, 20
        Susan Lloyd" 1830, 5, 9
        Samuel J. " 1832, 3, 7
1818, 12, 2. Ruth m Isaac LOYD
1821, 8, 29. Hannah m Geo. DAVISON
1822, 3, 27. Deborah m Elisha KIRK
1825, 4, 25. Sarah d ae 50
1825, 10, 19. Unity m Abel John PELLETT
1825, 11, 24. Margaret m Demcey JOHNSON
1858; 5, 27. Wm. J., s Jordon & Susan, Jef-
    ferson Co., O.; m in Short Creek MH,
    Deborah R. LAWRENCE, dt Thos. & Deborah,
    Jefferson Co., O.
    Ch: Walter L. b 1859, 5, 3
        Ellen Gor-
          dan   " 1861, 6, 13
        Elizabeth
          Fleming " 1864, 3, 26
        Samuel Ir-
          ving   " 1866, 11, 26
1860, 12, 26. Samuel T., s Jordon & Susan,
    d 1864,4,20 bur Short Creek; m in Mt.
    Pleasant, Margaret I. LAWRENCE, dt Thos.
    & Deborah, Jefferson Co., O.
    Ch: Jesse   b 1861, 11, 16
        Anna J.   d 1864,--, 8
      ae 1y
1864, 9, 28. Mary m Samuel E. HAGUE

1813, 5, 18. Sarah rocf Redstone MM, dtd
    1813,1,1
1817, 6, 24. Jordan rocf Waynook MM, Va.,
    dtd 1817,5,3
1817, 6, 24. William & w, Margaret, & ch,
    Margaret, Deborah & Ruth, rocf Waynook
    MM, Va., dtd 1817,5,3
1821, 5, 22. Unity & Hannah recrq
1824, 12, 21. Lydia (form James) dis mcd
1826, 2, 21. Rachel rocf Somerset MM, dtd
    1825,9,26
1837, 8, 22. Jordan dis disunity
1845, 9, 23. Lydia rst
1846, 10, 20. Lydia gct Flushing MM
1861, 3, 20. Mary recrq
1863, 3, 24. Samuel J. dis jG (W)
1865, 3, 21. Mary, Susan L. & Margaret dis
    jG (W)
1867, 7, 23. Deborah & Margaret dis jG (W)
1867, 12, 24. Sally Ann (form Hargrave) dis
    mcd & jG (W)
1867, 12, 24. William J. dis jG (W)
1873, 5, 22. Phebe recrq (G)
1878, 5, 23. Blakey & w, Priscilla J., recrq
    (G)
1907, 6, 19. Margaret J. dropped from mbrp
    (G)

HARTLEY
1908, 8, 19. Arthur J., s Thomas & Rosella,
    Gurnsey Co., O.; m in Harrisville, Mary
    Edith WHINERY, dt Elwood D. & Asenath H.,
    Jefferson Co., O. (W)
    Ch: Lucile   b 1909, 10, 2

1807, 3, 21. Cert rec for Thomas from Buck-
    ingham MM, end to Redstone MM
1810, 3, 20. Elizabeth & s, Elias, rocf Sads-
    bury MM, dtd 1808,10,4, end by Concord MM
    1810,2,22
1862, 11, 19. Mary & Clarkson dis jW
1862, 11, 19. Isaac, Mary, Joseph, Maria,
    Noah, Zimri, Joseph, Sarah, Mahlon, Mary,
    John, Anna, Joel, John, Elizabeth, Henry,
    Mary, Thomas, Martha, Abbie, Noah, Millie,
    Uriah, Samuel, Caleb & Sarah Ellen dis jW
1910, 3, 22. Mary Edith & dt, Lucile, gct
    Somerset MM (W)

HASTINGS
1912, 2, 21. Grace Molmes relrq (G)

HATCH
1881, 2, 26. John E. recrq (G)
1884, 7, 23. John E. dropped from mbrp (G)
1886, 7, 21. Lida recrq (G)

HATCHER
1811, 11, 19. Isaac & w, Rachel, & ch, Mary,
    Elizabeth, Samuel, Isaac, Rachel, Joshua,
    Rebecca & Daniel Hains, rocf Goose Creek
    MM, dtd 1811,10,3
1814, 11, 22. Elizabeth Dunkin (form Hatcher)
    dis mcd
1816, 10, 22. Samuel dis mcd
1817, 1, 21. Mary Echelberger (form Hatcher)
    dis mcd
1818, 3, 24. Isaac & w, Rachel, & ch, Isaac,
    Rachel, Joshua, Rebecca & Daniel, gct
    Darby Creek MM, O.

HATHAWAY
1882, 5, 24. ----- recrq (G)
1884, 7, 23. Mrs. Hathaway dropped from
    mbrp (G)

HAWMIRE
1902, 3, 19. Liewella recrq (G)

HAWTHORN
1894, 4, 25. Ellis Lemoin recrq (G)
1902, 12, 24. Gertrude, Mable & Helen recrq
    (G)
1911, 2, 22. Helen (Hawthorn) Biddle relrq
    (G)
1911, 11, 22. Mabel (Hawthorn) Brown relrq
    (G)

HAYCOCK
1840, 4, 29. Jane m John C. THOMPSON
1843, 11, 1. Benjamin, s Samuel & Esther,

HAYCOCK, Benjamin, continued
    Jefferson Co., O.; m in Mt. Pleasant,
    Elizabeth Abb HARGRAVE, dt Thos. & Sarah,
    Jefferson Co., O.
    Ch: Sarah T.   b 1844, 8, 22
       George Al-
        bert   " 1846, 4, 19
       Anna Maria " 1849, 6, 15
1848. 11, 29. Hannah A. m Joseph RUSSEL

1854, 8, 28. Jane (form Sanders) con mcd
1833, 12, 24. Larkin A. rocf Westland MM, dtd
    1833,10,23
1836, 11, 20. Larkin dis mcd
1840, 4, 21. Parker, Hannah Ann & Lemuel P.,
    ch Jane, recrq
1841, 11, 20. Benjamin [Heacock] rocf Westland
    MM
1842, 2, 22. Meriam rocf Westland MM, dtd
    1841,11,24
1842, 9, 20. Meriam dis jas
1852, 4, 20. Benjamin & w, Elizabeth Ann, &
    ch, Sarah Thomas, George Albert & Anna
    Maria, gct Salem MM, Ia.
1852, 8, 24. Parker & Lemuel gct Goshen MM,O.

HAYS
1808, 10, 18. Eaton, minor in care of Wm.
    Flanner, rocf New Garden MM, N. C., dtd
    1808,7,30
1812, 5, 19. Eaton [Hayse] gct Stillwater MM

HEALD
1824, 9, 2. Abner, s Wm. & Sarah, Columbi-
    ana Co., O.; m in Short Creek MH, Cineh
    SIDWELL, dt Henry & Sinah, Belmont Co.,O.

1824, 10, 19. Sinah gct Middleton MM
1838, 7, 24. Charles rocf Newgarden MM, dtd
    1838,6,21

HEALY
1819, 10, 19. Cert rec for Thomas & w, Sarah,
    & ch, Sarah, William, Lydia, Oliver,
    Thomas, Delila & Charles, from Colemans
    MM, N. Y., end to Stillwater MM

HEATON
1838, 1, 23. Rachel rocf Falls MM, Pa., dtd
    1837,12,7
1881, 2, 26. Cornelius & Martha recrq (G)
1895, 1, 23. Margaretta recrq (G)
1902, 8, 20. Margaret dropped from mbrp (G)
1907, 4, 24. Margaretta dropped from mbrp (G)
1914, 3, 25. Esther & Mayne recrq (G)
1917, 4, 25. Gladys recrq (G)

HEBERLING
1925, 10, 13. Mary J., w Henry G., dt Jona-
    than & Elizabeth Stephens, d (G)

1836, 5, 24. Hannah (form Lewis) dis mcd
1889, 3, 20. George & Matilda recrq (G)

1894, 3, 21. Mary J. & s, George R., recrq
    (G)
1895, 11, 20. G. H. relrq (G)

HELTZ
1899, 5, 24. John relrq (G)

HEMMINGWAY
1898, 8. 22. Emma Ratcliff relrq (G)

HENDEN
1882, 3, 29. Carrolton recrq (G)
1888, 10, 24. Carrollton dropped from mbrp
    (G)

HENDERSHOT
1854, 11, 21. J. A., s Jonathan & Angeline, b
1889, 7, 27. C. O., s John & Elizabeth, b
1893, 4, 17. Icie b
----, --. --. Clyde & Icie
    Ch: Lawrence b 1912, 8, 11
       John   " 1914, 11, 15
       Sarah   " 1918, 1, 14
       Mildred   " 1920, 1, 2
1932, 4, 20. John W. recrq (G)
1932, 4, 20. Lawrence E. recrq (G)

1905, 9, 20. Will Francis & w, Catherine
    Floretta, recrq (G)
1908, 4, 22. Raymond recrq (G)
1909, 5, 19. Katharine relrq (G)
1911, 11, 22. Raymond relrq (G)

HENDRIX
1817, 1, 21. Mary (form Taylor) dis mcd

HENNIS
1885, 2, 25. Thomas recrq (G)
1885, 5, 20. Clara Bell recrq (G)
1886, 5, 19. Nancy recrq (G)

HENRY
1901, 2, 20. Rosco D. recrq (G)
1916, 7, 19. Virgil recrq (G)

HERALD
1824, 12, 20. Housin & w, Rachel, & ch, Amos,
    Rebecca, Tamer & Mary, rocf Flushing MM,
    dtd 1823,10,24
1829, 9, 22. Houseen [Herrel] & w, Rachel, &
    ch, Amos, Mary & Tamer, gct Stillwater MM
1831, 7, 19. Housen & w, Rachel, & ch, Mary
    & Tamer, rocf Stillwater MM, dtd 1831,5,28
1831, 8, 23. Amos [Herrel] rocf Stillwater
    MM, dtd 1831,7,23
1845, 4, 23. Mary Dennis (form Herrel) dis
    mcd
1846, 4, 21. Rachel [Herrold] gct Flushing
    MM
1851, 2, 18. Tamer [Hearld] gct Flushing MM

HESTON
1810, 6, 20. Margaret m Henry SCHOOLEY

HESTON, continued
1813, 4, 20. John & w, Elizabeth, & ch, Anna,
     Tacy, Rebecca, John, Zebulon, Hannah,
     Amos, David & Elizabeth, gct Newgarden
     MM, O.

HETHERINGTON
1856, 5, 21. Pharaby (form Howard) dis mcd
     (W)

HEWLINGS
1855, 6, 25. Lydia S., dt Franklin L. & Ruth
     Anna (Stokes), b

1887, 7, 19. Lydia S. rocf Middleton MM, dtd
     1887,5,21 (W)
1894, 2, 20. Ruth Anna rocf Frankfort MM,
     Pa., dtd 1894,1,25 (W)

HIATT
1831, 4, 28. Jesse, s Jehu & Tamer, Belmont
     Co., O.; m in Short Creek MH, Ruthanna
     VERNON, dt Amos & Mary, Jefferson Co., O.

1831, 12, 20. Ruthanna [Hiat] gct Clear Creek
     MM
1862, 4, 24. Sarah E. recrq

HIBBS
1834, 8, 28. Amos, s Wm. & Mary, Gurnsey Co.,
     O.; m in Short Creek MH, Elizabeth RAT
     CLIFF. dt Sarah, Jefferson Co., O.

1835, 2, 24. Elizabeth gct Flushing MM
1889, 9, 25. Josephine (form Phillips) gct
     Freeport MM, O. (G)

HILERMAN
1837, 7, 18. Rachel (form Updegraff) dis mcd

HILL
1821, 2, 1. John C., s John & Mary, Jeffer-
     son Co., O.; m in Short Creek MH, Rachel
     WILSON, dt Jonathan & Hannah, Jefferson
     Co., O.
     Ch: Mary Ann   b 1822, 1, 6
         Joseph   " 1823, 10, 8
1842, 4, 28. Mary Ann m Lewis TABER
1850, 5, 2. Joseph, s John C. & Rachel,
     Jefferson Co., O.; m in Short Creek MH,
     Deborah PATTERSON dt Mahlon & Mary Ann,
     Jefferson Co., O.
     Ch: John   b 1852, 10, 15
         Horace P.   " 1855, 3, 12
         Mahol P.   " 1857, 1, 27
         Mary Ann   " 1858, 12, 5
         Lewis P.   " 1860, 11, 11
1853, 1, 17. Rachel d ae 54 bur Short Creek
1865, 3, 26. Deborah d

1825, 1, 18. Esther (form Jenkins) dis mcd
1860, 10, 24. John C. gct Smithfield MM, to

     m Hannah Ladd
1861, 2, 20. John C. gct Smithfield MM
1862, 6, 24. Hannah S. dis jG
1862, 8, 19. John C. dis jG
1865, 11, 21. Joseph dis jG (W)
1866, 11, 22. Joseph gct Smithfield MM, to m
     Elizabeth L. Kinsey (G)
1867, 7, 25. Elizabeth L. rocf Smithfield MM
     (G)
1867, 12, 26. J. C. rocf Smithfield MM (G)
1881, 4, 19. Mahlon P. dis disunity (W)
1881, 11, 22. Mary Ann dis jG (W)
1881, 12, 20. John G. dis jG (W)
1887, 9, 21. John G. gct Archer MM, Fla. (G)
1888, 11, 21. Lewis T. gct Pleasant Plain MM,
     Iowa (G)
1889, 6, 19. John & w, Rachel, & dt, Lucy
     Hazel, rocf Archer MM, Fla. (G)
1907, 3, 20. Lillian Coffman dropped from
     mbrp (G)
1911, 3, 22. John G. & fam relrq (G)

HILLIS
1885, 9, 23. Anne U. (form Updegraff) relrq
     (G)

HINKLE
1887, 5, 25. Joseph recrq (G)
1903, 6, 24. Joseph dropped from mbrp (G)
1907, 3, 20. Joseph dropped from mbrp (G)

HIRST
1878, 8, 2. John, s David & Ann, Belmont
     Co., O.; m in Short Creek MH, Maria WIL
     SON, dt Rees & Ruth BRANSON, Jefferson
     Co., O.
1899, 3, 23. John S., s Wilson C. & Mary
     Ann, Cedar Co., Ia.; m in Harrisville,
     Rachel M. ATKINSON, dt Wm. & Catharine,
     Jefferson Co., O., b 1871,4,21 (W)
1846, 3, 12. Rebecca m Marshall FELL
1841, 10, 28. Ruthanna m Thompson WALKER
1829, 5, 27. Thomas, s David & Ann, Belmont
     Co., O.; m in Concord, Ann RALEY, dt
     James & Rachel, Belmont Co., O.
1834, 1, 30. Thomas, s David & Ann, Belmont
     Co., O.; m in Harrisville, Mary SWAYNE,
     dt Benj. & Susanna, Jefferson Co., O.
1897, 5, 27. Wilson C., s John & Maria,
     Cedar Co., Ia.; m in Harrisville, Rachel
     H. TABER, dt Lewis & Mary Ann, Jefferson
     Co., O. (W)

1815, 5, 23. David & w, Ann, & ch, Thomas,
     John, Israel, Asenath, Rachel, Smith &
     Mary, rocf Goose Creek MM, dtd 1815,4,27
1817, 7, 22. David [Hurst] & w, Ann, & ch,
     Thomas, John, Israel, Asenath, Rachel,
     Smith & Mary, gct Concord MM
1829, 9, 22. Ann R. gct Flushing MM
1831, 6, 21. Jonathan Lupton gct Flushing MM,
     to m Rachel Hirst
1834, 5, 20. Thomas & ch, Rebecca, James &

HIRST, continued
      Ann, rocf Flushing MM, dtd 1834,4,24
1835, 8, 18. Ruthanna, minor dt Thomas, rocf
      Flushing MM, dtd 1834,12,25
1838, 11, 20. Maria gct Flushing MM
1849, 11, 20. Thomas gct Chesterfield MM
1852, 1, 20. Ann Jr. gct Plymouth MM
1852, 1, 20. James gct Plymouth MM
1897, 6, 22. Rachel Taber gct Hickory Grove
      MM, Ia. (W)
1901, 3, 19. Rachel M. gct Hickory Grove MM,
      Ia. (W)
1907, 11, 19. Rachel M. rocf Hickory Grove
      MM, Ia. (W)
1928, 7, 28. Rachel M. gct Pasadena MM, Calif.
      (W)

HIXON
1913, 10, 22. Martha B. recrq (G)

HOAR
1881, 2, 26. George B. recrq (G)
1888, 10, 24. George dropped from mbrp (G)
1894, 1, 24. Mabel recrq (G)
1894, 4, 25. Mary recrq (G)
1902, 8, 20. Harry & Margaret dropped from
      mbrp (G)

HOBBS
1839, 12, 24. Barnabas C. rocf Blue River MM,
      Ind., dtd 1839,11,2
1843, 3, 21. Barnabas C. gct Upper Spring-
      field MM, to m Rebecca Tatum
1843, 6, 20. Barnabas gct White Water MM, Ind.
1843, 6, 20. Barnabas C. gct Whitewater MM,
      Ind.

HOBSON
1807, 5, 21. Francis, s Joseph & Ann, Jeffer-
      son Co., O.; m in Short Creek MH, Grace
      MICHENER, dt John & Martha, Jefferson Co.,
      O.
1807, 11, 26. Ann m Isaac BOWMAN
1818, 4, 28. Joseph P., s Wm., d bur Rich-
      mond
1828, 12, 9. Joseph d ae 82 bur Richmond
1835, 9, 22. Esther d ae 20 bur Richmond
1836, 10, 31. Esther M. d ae 20 bur Richmond
1838, 10, 31. Mary Ann d ae 2 bur Smithfield
----, --, --. Thomas & Unity
      Ch: Benjamin J.b 1841, 7, 18
          Mary J.   " 1843, 9, 13
          Sarah A.   " 1844, 10, 15
          Dorothy   " 1847, 5, 14
          John A.   " 1849, 2, 7
          Belinda   " 1851, 8, 9
1842, 6, 6. Mary d ae 27 bur Richmond
1842, 10, 29. Charles d ae 1
1842, 11, 6. Mary T., dt Wm., d bur Richmond
----, --, --. Benjamin & Sarah Ann
      Ch: Edwin T.   b 1851, 4, 5
          Thomas C. " 1853, 1, 24
          Martha Ann " 1854, 11, 28 d 1863,11,19

      Ch: bur Cross Creek
          John A.   b 1859, 11, 6
1851, 12, 19. John d ae 74 bur Cross Creek
1863, 11, 31. Benjamin d ae 40 bur Cross Creek

1804, 5, 19. Belinda & s, Joseph, recrq
1804, 10, 20. John rocf Redstone MM, dtd
      1804,8,29
1815, 9, 19. Jonathan Michener gct Plymouth
      MM, to m Jane Hobson
1853, 8, 23. Parker Hall gct Flushing MM,
      to m Rebecca Hobson
1866, 10, 23. Abraham dis jG (W)
1866, 11, 20. Elizabeth dis disunity (W)
1874, 2, 24. Joseph P. Binns gct Plymouth
      MM, to m Belinda Hobson (W)
1880, 6, 22. Sarah Ann gct Newgarden MM (W)

HOCKADAY
----, --, --. Benjamin & Sarah
      Ch: Robert
          Ladd   b 1828, 3, 21
          Mary Ann   " 1830, 1, 13
          Benjamin B." 1832, 11, 10
          James   " 1836, 11, 25
1833, 2, 5. Mary Ann d bur Short Creek
1842, 4, 9. Sarah d bur Short Creek

1827, 6, 19. Benjamin & w, Sarah, rocf
      Wayne Oak MM, Va., dtd 1827,6,2
1837, 9, 19. Robert dis disunity
1844, 2, 22. Benjamin dis disunity
1855, 8, 21. Robert L. dis disunity
1856, 3, 18. Benjamin Jr. dis disunity

HODGEN
1862, 11, 19. Eli, Eli, Jr., Harriet &
      William dis jW
1914, 10, 21. David G. [Hodgin] & w, Elsie
      F., rocf Columbus MM (G)
1915, 2, 24. Frances Kyne recrq (G)
1915, 2, 24. Jonathan Theodore [Hodgin]
      recrq (G)

HODGES
1892, 10, 19. Lillie recrq (G)
1892, 10, 19. W. G. recrq (G)

HOFFMIRE
1907, 3, 20. Luella M. dropped from mbrp
      (G)

HOGE
----, --, --. Absalom & Rachel [Hogue]
      Ch: Lindley M. b 1826, 6, 29 d 1835, 9,29
          bur Short Creek
          Rachel P. b 1823, 6, 29
1836, 1, 27. Jesse, s Isaac & Elizabeth, Bel-
      mont Co., O.; m in Concord, Susannah
      KINSEY, dt John & Mary, Belmont Co., O.
1838, 5, 3. Mary Ann m Daniel HOLLOWAY
1866, 11, 27. Eliza Jane, dt David & Sarah
      Comley, d ae 34

HOGE, continued
----, --, --. Joseph & Anna M.
    Ch: Mary Elma b 1879, 8, 21 d 1879, 9,14
        bur Concord
        Thomas Wil-
        son   b 1879, 8, 21 " 1879, 8,22
        Charles L. " 1880, 12, 26
1900, 10, 13. Ruthanna, dt Jesse & Elizabeth
    Crew, w Asa Hoge, d bur West Grove (G)

1812, 11, 24. Craver rocf Plainfield MM, dtd
    1812,10,24
1818, 7, 21. Craven [Hogue] gct Plainfield MM
1823, 12, 20. Absolem [Hogue] & w, Rachel, &
    ch, John C., Isaac, Mary Ann, James & Ra-
    chel, rocf Plainfield MM, dtd 1823,11,20
1843, 11, 21. John gct Plainfield MM
1844, 9, 24. Susan gct Plainfield MM
1846, 2, 24. Isaac [Hoage] dis mcd
1847, 3, 23. James gct Upper Springfield MM
1847, 7, 20. Susan [Hogue] & ch, Mary Eliza-
    beth & Laura, rocf Plainfield MM, dtd
    1847,10,21
1850, 1, 22. Absalom [Hogue] & w, Rachel, gct
    Flushing MM
1850, 1, 22. Rachel T. [Hogue] gct Flushing
    MM
1861, 3, 20. Eliza Jane (form Comley) con mcd
1873, 1, 23. Ruthanna (form Crew) con mcd (G)
1876, 2, 24. Sarah Ann [Hogue] rocf Damascus
    MM (G)
1876, 5, 23. Joseph rocf Flushing MM, dtd
    1876,3,23 (W)
1878, 10, 22. Joseph gct Stillwater MM, to m
    Anna M. Steer (W)
1879, 3, 20. Samuel E. & w, Mary H., & ch,
    William H., Thos. W. & Annie W., relrq(G)
1879, 4, 24. Clayton, Kenworthy & Sabina C.
    recrq (G)
1879, 6, 24. Anna M. rocf Stillwater MM, dtd
    1879,5,21 (W)
1881, 2, 26. William [Hogue] recrq (G)
1883, 6, 19. Joseph S. & Anna M. & s, Charles
    L., gct Stillwater MM (W)
1896, 11, 25. Ernest K. & sisters, Lelia &
    Emma, relrq (G)
1898, 3, 23. Margaret B. recrq (G)
1907, 12, 25. Comley K. [Hogue] recrq (G)
1911, 5, 27. Mary B. recrq (G)
1911, 6, 21. Mary Alma, Clara V. & John
    Clayton relrq (G)

HOGGARD
1892, 10, 19. John T. & Anna recrq (G)

HOLE
1869, 2, 25. Robert T. Crew gct Damascus MM,
    to m Anna E. Hole (G)

HOLLAND
1892, 10, 19. Lillie recrq (G)
1892, 10, 19. Maggie & Nina recrq (G)

HOLLIDAY
1895, 3, 20. John & Edith recrq (G)
1901, 2, 20. David K. recrq (G)
1902, 2, 19. Adda May recrq (G)
1902, 3, 20. David dropped from mbrp (G)
1912, 3, 20. David K. recrq (G)
1914, 4, 22. William & Lillian recrq (G)

HOLLOWAY
1813, 4, 29. Jacob, s Asa & Abigail, Belmont
    Co., O.; m in Short Creek MH, Martha
    WARFIELD, dt Jonathan & Mary BYE, Jeffer-
    son Co., O.
1818, 12, 2. Asa, s Asa & Elizabeth, Belmont
    Co., O.; m in West Grove MH, Dorothy ̃
    BARBER, dt Samuel & Ann, Harrison Co., O.
1837, 7, 27. Smith, s Aaron & Rachel, Bel-
    mont Co., O.; m in Short Creek MH, Abi-
    gail PARKER, dt Isaac & Sarah, Jefferson
    Co. O.
1838, 5, 3. Daniel, s Jacob & Martha, Bel-
    mont Co., O.; m in Short Creek MH, Mary
    Ann HOGE, dt Absolam & Rachel, Belmont
    Co., O.

1804, 9, 15. Cert rec for Asa & fam from
    Southland MM, end to Concord MM
1807, 11, 21. Jacob rocf Concord MM, dtd
    1807,8,18
1813, 9, 21. Asa Jr. rocf Plainfield MM,
    dtd 1813,8,28
1813, 12, 21. Jacob & w, Martha, & her ch,
    Maria & John Warfield, gct Plainfield MM
1818, 6, 23. Asa gct Flushing MM
1819, 3, 23. Dorothy gct Flushing MM
1834, 6, 24. Robert S. & w, Abby T., rocf
    Flushing MM, dtd 1834,5,22
1838, 8, 21. Mary Ann gct Flushing MM
1838, 8, 21. Robert S. & w, Abby, gct Flush-
    ing MM
1839, 9, 24. Smith & w, Abigail, & s, Isaac
    Parker, gct Flushing MM
1853, 8, 23. Smith & w, Abigail, & ch,
    Isaac P., Mary E., Samuel S. & Abby P.,
    rocf Plainfield MM, dtd 1853,3,23
1864, 1, 20. Mary E. gct White Lick MM, Ind.
    (G)
1864, 1, 20. Smith & w, Abigail, & s, Samuel
    L., gct White Lick MM, Ind. (G)
1867, 5, 23. Smith & w, Abigail, & s, Samuel
    T., gct Wabash MM, Ind. (G)
1868, 3, 26. Samuel dis (G)
1874, 11, 26. Mary E. gct Spiceland MM, Ind.
    (G)
1877, 11, 20. Branson D. Sidwell gct Flushing
    MM, to m Abbie Holloway (W)

HOLLOWELL
1787, 12, 22. Jane b

1824, 12, 21. Jane recrq
1828, 12, 23. Jane dis jH
1832, 3, 2. Jane gct Deerfield MM (H)

HOLMES

----, --, --. J. Nathan & Grace
    Ch: John Alex-
        ander   b 1914, 1, 19 d 1914, 2,19
        Laura Mary " 1915, 9, 15
        Ella Ge-
        nette   " 1917, 9, 30

1824, 12, 21. Tacy (form Thompson) dis mcd
1893, 1, 25. John W. & Mary J. recrq (G)
1907, 9, 25. Grace recrq (G)
1912, 2, 21. Grace Holmes Hastings relrq (G)
1920, 1, 21. David gct Mt. Pleasant MM, O. (G)
1920, 1, 21. Helen gct Mt. Pleasant MM, O.(G)
1923, 5, 24. Mary gct Mt. Pleasant MM, O. (G)

HOLSTEAD
1892, 10, 19. Benny F. recrq (G)

HOOPER
1914, 3, 25. Clarence, Elmir H., Emma & Eu-
    phemia F. recrq (G)
1915, 2, 24. Clyde, Ella Viola, Mary May &
    Pearl Euphemia recrq (G)

HOOPS
1821, 6, 7. James, s Nathan & Elizabeth,
    Harrison Co., O.; m in York, Elizabeth
    GILL, dt John & Susanna, Harrison Co., O.
    Ch: Sarahann b 1822, 3, 5
        Nathan   " 1824, 3, 10
1819, 3, 3. Sarah [Hoopes] m Nathan WILLIAMS

1805, 3, 16. Elizabeth recrq
1818, 12, 22. Sarah recrq
1819, 7, 20. James recrq
1825, 12, 20. Elizabeth gct Somerset MM
1830, 2, 23. Elizabeth Jr. & ch, Sarah-ann,
    Nathan, John & Elizabeth, gct Deerfield MM
1831, 10, 18. Ann recrq
1840, 1, 21. Ann Scott (form Hoops) dis mcd
1852, 8, 24. Ann (form Grey) dis mcd
1859, 9, 22. Deborah W. gct Beaver Falls MM
    (H)

HORTON
1829, 11, 24. Joseph & w, Agnes, & ch, Eliza-
    beth, Thomas & Joseph, rocf WD MM dtd
    1829,8,19
1830, 5, 18. Agnus dis jH
1830, 5, 18. Joseph H. dis jH
1841, 7, 22. John & w, Rachel, & Cynthia Hor-
    ton Davis, a minor, gct Plainfield MM (H)
1841, 7, 22. Mary Jane gct Plainfield MM (H)
1907, 4, 24. Edith D. [Horten] dropped from
    mbrp (G)

HOSIER
1838, 1, 31. Hannah m Isaac PARKER

1836, 9, 20. Hannah & dt, Hannah, rocf Plain
    field MM, dtd 1836,8,24
1836, 9, 20. Maria rocf Plainfield MM, dtd

1836,8,24
1855, 5, 22. Maria gct Flushing MM (W)

HOUGH
1805, 1, 19. Benjamin dis disunity
1845, 3, 18. Wm. Lloyd gct Redstone MM, to m
    Eliza M. Hough
1873, 9, 25. Zeri & w, Miriam H., rocf New
    Garden MM, Ind. (G)
1875, 6, 24. Zeri & w, Miriam H., gct New
    Garden MM, Ind. (G)

HOUSE
1903, 6, 24. Henry W. dropped from mbrp (G)

HOVEY
1850, 6, 18. Sarah (form Farmer) dis mcd
1850, 10, 22. Sarah [Houey] (form Farmer) dis
    mcd

HOWARD
----, --, --. John & Cherry
    Ch: Sarah   b 1804, 1, 21
        Asa   " 1805, 5, 8
        Ruth   " 1807, 1, 16
        Viley
        Cherry   " 1810, 10, 27
1811, 11, 7. Cherry d ae 32 bur Short Creek
----, --, --. John & Hannah
    Ch: James   b 1814, 3, 22
        Rachel   " 1815, 10, 8
        Abigail   " 1817, 12, 23
        Jane   " 1819, 11, 13
        Pharaby   " 1822, 3, 7
        Isaac   " 1824, 2, 12
        Joseph   " 1826, 3, 13
        John   " 1828, 12, 31
        Charles   " 1830, 12, 25
        Mary   " 1833, 1, 28
        Harvey   " 1835, 1, 8
1821, 8, 2. Joseph, s Horton & Mary, Dela-
    ware Co., O.; m in Short Creek MH, Phara-
    by J. PATTERSON, dt Anselem & Miriam,
    Jefferson Co., O.
1824, 12, 1. Sarah D. m John BATTEN
1825, 3, 30. Horton J., s Horton & Mary,
    Jefferson Co., O.; m in Mt. Pleasant, Mary
    M. BATES, dt Elisha & Sarah, Jefferson
    Co., O.
    Ch: Elisha
        Bates   b 1825, 13, 30
1837, 3, 2. Harvey d bur Harrisville
1839, 5, 2. Jane m John W. TRIBBY
1856, 1, 9. Hannah d ae 66

1813, 1, 19. John gct Concord MM, to m Han-
    nah Railey
1813, 4, 20. Hannah R. rocf Concord MM, dtd
    1813,3,25
1820, 8, 22. Horton Jr. rocf Plainfield MM,
    dtd 1820,7,20
1826, 11, 21. Ruth gct Sandy Spring MM
1827, 3, 20. Horton J. & w, Mary M., & s,

HOWARD, continued
    Elisha B. gct Plainfield MM
1829, 6, 23. John & w, Hannah, & ch, James,
   Rachel, Abigail, Jane, Pharaby, Isaac, Joseph & John, gct Flushing MM
1830, 2, 23. Asa gct New York MM, N. Y.
1831, 7, 19. John & w, Hannah, & ch, James,
   Rachel, Abigail, Jane, Pharaby, Isaac,
   Joseph, John & Charles, rocf Flushing MM,
   dtd 1831,6,23
1831, 10, 18. Cherry Aidy (form Howard) dis
1831, 10, 18. Vila Gregg (form Howard) dis
1837, 4, 18. John relrq
1837, 8, 22. James R. dis disunity
1838, 3, 20. Abigail McCarthy (form Howard)
   dis mcd
1843, 11, 21. Joseph gct Sandy Spring MM
1844, 9, 24. Joseph rocf Sandy Spring MM, dtd
   1844,8,23
1845, 5, 20. Rachel Sumption (form Howard)
   dis mcd
1850, 7, 25. Joseph dis mcd
1850, 8, 20. John dis mcd
1851, 7, 22. Charles dis disunity
1856, 4, 22. Mary Larken (form Howard) dis
   mcd
1856, 5, 21. Pheraba Hetherington (form
   Howard) dis mcd (W)
1898, 3, 23. Effa L. recrq (G)
1904, 10, 19. Effie gct Cleveland MM (G)

HOWES
1888, 4, 25. Henry Wilmer recrq (G)

HOYLE
----, --, --. John & Prudence
    Ch: Joseph   b 1827, 7, 4
       Hannah   " 1824, 4, 14
----, --, --. Benjamin m Juliann ----- d 1891,
   1,2 ae 77 bur Concord
    Ch: Ellis J. b 1835, 9, 13
       Hannah   " 1839, 8, 21
       Rachel   " 1841, 8, 1
       Lydia   " 1843, 3, 12
       Sarah   " 1845, 8, 23 d 1920, 4,13
        bur Colerain
       John Wil-
        lets   b 1848, 2, 5
       Elvira   " 1851, 7, 13
       Mary Eliza " 1853, 12, 10
----, --, --. Joseph & Phebe
    Ch: Annie W.   b 1852, 4, 8
       William   " 1855, 8, 29
       Amos B.   " 1859, 1, 18
1860, 6, 18. Annie d ae 7 bur Smithfield
1843, 12, 11. Prudence, w John, d bur Smithfield
1869, 12, 29. Lydia m Amasa L. NEGUS (W)
1872, 3, 10. John Sr. d ae 84 bur Smithfield
1878, 12, 14. Benjamin d ae 67 bur Concord
1879, 8, 20. Mary Eliza m Jos. WILLIAMS (W)
1895, 10, 23. Frederick C., s Wm. & Hannah,
   Gurnsey Co., O.; m in Colerain, Martha H.

BRACKEN, dt Lindley & Anna S., Belmont
   Co., O. (W)
1902, 3, 20. Howard E., s Lindley & Deborah,
   Jones Co., Ia.; m in Concord, Elma STEER
   dt Nathan & Mary Jane, Belmont Co., O. (W)
1907, 11, 18. Hannah d ae 68 bur Concord
1908, 6, 18. Rachel d ae 67 bur Concord

1842, 6, 21. John Jr. & w, Dorothy, rocf
   Smithfield MM, dtd 1842,5,23
1842, 12, 20. Benjamin & w, Mary, & ch, Hannah & Benjamin, rocf Stillwater MM, dtd
   1842,11,26
1844, 5, 21. John & w, Dorothy, gct Smithfield MM
1845, 12, 23. Benjamin & w, Gulian, & ch, Ellis, Hannah, Rachel, Lydia & Sarah, rocf
   Smithfield MM, dtd 1845,11,19
1847, 3, 23. Benjamin & w, Mary, & ch, Hannah & Benjamin, gct Stillwater MM
1857, 8, 18. Hannah Ashead (form Hoyle) dis
   mcd to first cousin
1862, 11, 19. John G., Elizabeth, Simeon,
   Ezekiel, Benjamin, Mary, Benjamin Jr.,
   William, Thomas, Hannah, Joseph Lindley,
   dis jW
1862, 3, 24. Joseph dis jG (W)
1862, 11, 19. William L. dis jW
1865, 1, 24. Phebe dis disunity (W)
1868, 4, 21. Ellis J. dis mcd (W)
1868, 11, 24. Elvira, dt Benj. Giliann, gct
   Phila. MM (W)
1872, 9, 24. Elvira rocf Phila. MM, dtd
   1872,8,28 (W)
1876, 6, 20. Elvira (form Hoyle) con mcd (W)
1880, 6, 22. John & w, Dorothy, gct New Garden MM (W)
1889, 6, 18. John Willets dis mcd (W)
1896, 8, 18. Martha B. gct Stillwater MM (W)
1904, 4, 19. Elma S. gct Springville MM, Ia.
   (W)

HUBBARD
1870, 11, 30. Wm. G., s John & Abigail,
   Clinton Co., O.; m in Mt. Pleasant,
   Lydia HUSSEY, dt Penrose & Susannah, Jefferson Co., O.

1837, 3, 21. Martha rocf Deep River MM, N.C.,
   dtd 1837,2,2
1837, 9, 19. Jeremiah & w, Martha, gct White
   Water MM, Ind.
1870, 11, 24. William G. rocf Clear Creek
   MM, O., to m Lydia Hussey (G)
1873, 6, 26. Lydia H. & s, Penrose, gct
   Clear Creek MM, O. (G)

HUDGENS
1892, 10, 19. Eliza & John T. recrq (G)

HUDLER
1887, 5, 25. Samuel & Elizabeth recrq (G)

HUEFORD
----, --, --. John & Sarah
 Ch: John
   Rachel

HUFFINGTON
1892, 10, 19. Benny W. recrq (G)

HULFORD
1839, 10, 30. Sarah m Wm. PURVIANCE

HULL
1839, 4, 23. Vila (form Dew) dis mcd

HUMPHREVILLE
1830, 9, 21. Sarah (form Dew) rpd mcd
1842, 8, 23. William recrq
1864, 9, 20. Sarah [Umphreville] dis jG
1865, 1, 24. William [Umphreville] dis disunity (W)
1913, 1, 22. Mildred recrq (G)
1915, 2, 24. Mary & Edra recrq (G)

HUMWELL
1881, 2, 26. Richard K. & Sarah C. recrq (G)
1891, 10, 21. Richard K. relrq (G)

HUNNICUTT
1836, 11, 22. Sarah Elizabeth rocf Smithfield
 MM, dtd 1836,11,21
1844, 12, 24. Ann (form Blackledge) dis mcd
1844, 12, 24. Joseph dis mcd
1847, 1, 19. Thomas dis mcd
1849, 1, 23. Sarah Elizabeth Barnes (form
 Hunnicutt) dis mcd

HUNT
1816, 2, 29. Mary m Jonathan BYE Jr.

1812, 1, 21. Joshua & w, Rachel, & ch, Mary,
 David, Samuel, Joshua & Jonathan, rocf
 Redstone MM, dtd 1811,6,28
1814, 2, 22. Seth rocf Salem MM, dtd 1814,1,
 11
1814, 4, 19. Abigail rocf Salem MM, dtd
 1813,10,12
1817, 7, 22. Joshua & w, Rachel, & ch, David,
 Samuel, Joshua, Jonathan, John & Nathan,
 gct Concord MM
1817, 8, 19. Seth dis disunity
1819, 7, 20. Abigail gct Marlborough MM, O.
1835, 6, 23. Sarah (form Masters) dis mcd

HURFORD
1806, 5, 1. Evan, s John & Sarah, Jefferson
 Co. O.; m in Short Creek MH, Sarah HALL,
 dt Joseph & Christiana, Jefferson Co., O.
 Ch: Aquila   b 1807, 7, 13
1809, 9, 28. Rachel m Jacob PICKERING
1822, 5, 9. John H., s John & Sarah, Jefferson Co., O.; m in Short Creek MH, Amy
 GRIFFITH, dt Evan & Elizabeth, Jefferson
 Co., O.

1824, 12, 30. Ann m Isaac WATERMAN
1825, 10, 27. Mary m Warden BARRETT
1828, 7, 30. Aquilla, s Evan & Sarah, Harri-
 son Co., O.; m in West Grove MH, Rachel
 MATSON, dt Enoch & Sarah, Harrison Co.,
 O.
 Ch: Evan   b 1829, 7, 17 d 1831,11,17
   bur West Grove
  Sarah Ann b 1831, 5, 26
1829, 10, 29. Mary A. m Robt. E. SAUNDERS
1830, 10, 27. Samuel, s John & Sarah, Jeffer-
 son Co., O.; m in West Grove MH, Hannah
 B. RATCLIFF, dt John & Sarah, Harrison
 Co., O.
 Ch: John R.   b 1832, 11, 22
1840, 5, 27. Christiana m Joseph HARRIS
----, --, --. Samuel & K.
 Ch: Anne J.   b 1846, 12, 22
  Alonzo R. " 1848, 5, 14
  Edgar B.   " 1853, 2, 21
1851, 6, 3. John d ae 95
1862, 8, 4. John d ae 67 bur West Grove

1804, 12, 15. Sarah, John, Samuel & Mary, ch
 John, recrq
1805, 1, 19. Evan recrq
1807, 1, 17. John rocf Newgarden MM, dtd
 1806,8,4
1823, 4, 22. Sarah Eyres (form Hurford) dis
 mcd
1835, 7, 21. John con mcd
1842, 6, 21. Samuel con mcd
1845, 7, 22. Aquilla dis disunity
1845, 12, 23. Hannah Hall (form Hurford) dis
 mcd
1845, 11, 18. Joseph dis mcd
1846, 4, 26. Rachel T. dis disunity
1849, 9, 18. Sarah Ann Sharon (form Hurford)
 con mcd
1861, 9, 25. Rachel Moore (form Hurford)
 dis mcd
1862, 1, 21. Samuel dis jG
1864, 8, 24. Keziah & ch, Annie J., Alonzo
 R. & Edgar B. recrq
1872, 6, 20. Anna Jane Phillips (form
 Hurford) con mcd (G)
1876, 8, 22. Keziah gct Oskaloosa MM, Ia.(G)
1877, 4, 26. Edgar J. gct Oskaloosa MM, Ia.
 (G)
1877, 8, 22. Keziah gct Oskaloosa MM, Ia.(G)
1882, 10, 25. Rachel recrq (G)

HURL
1881, 2, 26. John G. recrq (G)
1907, 6, 19. John G. dropped from mbrp (G)

HUSSEY
1820, 3, 30. Mary Ann m Mahlon PATTERSON
1832, 11, 21. Hannah G. m Joseph PETTIT
1834, 4, 23. Jane R. m Wm. PETTIT
1836, 11, 23. Eliza M. m Jonathan BINNS
1847, 8, 25. Lydia d bur Short Creek
1848, 9, 27. Hester G. m Matthew TERRELL

HUSSEY, continued

1851, 12, 23. Christopher d ae 84 bur Short
Creek

1855, 5, 13. Matthew W., s Penrose & Susannah, Jefferson Co., O.; m in Mt. Pleasant
Ann L. TERRELL, dt Clark & Mary, Jefferson Co., O.

1864, 3, 9. Margaret W. m Isaac RATCLIFF

----, --, --. Asahel H. & Martha P.
Ch: Walter J. b 1865, 4, 6
    Anna M.   " 1867, 5, 22
    Helen J.   " 1868, 12, 4

1868, 7, 28. John G. d ae 71

1870, 3, 14. Angeline d ae 28

1870, 11, 30. Lydia m Wm. G. HUBBARD

1872, 12, 23. Penrose, s Christopher & Lydia,
d

1875, 10, 23. Hannah d ae 26

1877, 9, 29. Nathan d

1878, 7, 3. Daniel d

1878, 11, 13. Ruth d

1815, 9, 19. Lydia rocf Miami MM, dtd 1815,
1,25

1816, 9, 24. Mary Ann recrq

1819, 8, 24. John, Penrose, Curtis, Asahel,
Eliza, Hannah, Jane, Hester & Joseph, ch
Christopher & Lydia, recrq

1820, 11, 21. John gct Stillwater MM

1828, 1, 22. Curtis G. gct White Lick MM, Ind.

1830, 10, 19. Penrose gct Smithfield MM, to m
Susannah Wood

1831, 8, 23. Susannah rocf Smithfield MM, dtd
1821,7,18

1836, 2, 23. Penrose & w, Susanna, & ch,
Nathan W., Asahel & Milton, gct Smithfield
MM

1840, 10, 20. Joseph G. gct Sandy Spring MM

1841, 4, 20. John rocf Stillwater MM, dtd
1841,3,27

1842, 2, 22. Christopher rst at Radnor MM on
consent of this mtg

1848, 7, 18. Penrose & w, Susanna, & ch, Nathan W., Asahel, Milton, Lydia & Margaret
W., rocf Smithfield MM, dtd 1848,6,19

1861, 10, 23. Milton L. gct Sandy Spring MM,
to m Mary Jane Chambers

1862, 7, 22. Susan & Margaret dis jG (W)

1862, 10, 22. Asahel H. gct Milford MM, Ind.,
to m Martha P. Newby (G)

1863, 5, 20. Martha P. rocf Milford MM, Ind.
(G)

1863, 9, 23. Milton gct Minneapolis MM, Minn.
(G)

1865, 1, 24. John dis disunity (W)

1867, 10, 22. Lydia (form Hargrave) dis mcd &
jG (W)

1868, 4, 23. Lydia (form Hargrave) con mcd
(G)

1870, 11, 24. Wm. G. Hubbard rocf Clear Creek
MM, O., to m Lydia Hussey (G)

1871, 4, 18. Asahel H. dis mcd & jG (W)

1877, 4, 26. Nathan W. & w, Anna L., & ch,

Charles A. & Elizabeth B., gct Oskaloosa
MM, Ia. (G)

1889, 9, 25. Rebecca U. recrq (G)

1911, 9, 20. A. H. & w gct Whittier MM,
Calif. (G)

HUTCHINS

1850, 8, 20. Amos H. Terrell gct Elk MM, to
m Mary T. Hutchins

HUTCHINSON

1890, 12, 24. Duke & w, Anna, & ch, Hannah
Jane, William, Walter & Mary Ann, recrq
(G)

HUTTON

1847, 12, 26. Joel d ae 79

1873, 3, 20. Finley, s Joel W. & Ann,
Phila., Pa.; m in Smithfield, Eliza
WILLETS, dt Mark & Sarah V., Jefferson
Co., O. (W)

1804, 7, 21. Joseph & w rocf Westland MM,
dtd 1803,10,22, end by Concord MM, 1804,
4,24

1805, 8, 17. Joel & w, Mary, & ch, Elizabeth, Mary, Deborah & James, rocf Redstone MM, dtd 1805,5,31

1807, 2, 21. Amos & w, Beulah, rocf Westland MM, dtd 1807,1,24

1807, 5, 16. Catharine, Joseph, Levina, Sarah & Rebecca, minor ch Amos & Beulah,
recrq

1815, 11, 21. Joseph, minor, rocf Plymouth
MM, dtd 1815,10,21

1824, 2, 24. Joseph dis mcd

1874, 3, 24. Eliza W. gct ND MM (W)

IDDINGS

1887, 5, 25. John recrq (G)

IRVIN

1914, 12, 23. Anna recrq (G)

1915, 2, 24. Jesse recrq (G)

JACKSON

1870, 10, 26. Geo. E., s James & Rebecca,
Morrow Co., O.; m in Mt. Pleasant, Mary
C. PETTIT dt Milton R. & Hannah, Jeffer-
son Co., O.

1872, 1, 25. Mary C. gct Gilead MM (G)

1876, 6, 22. Nancy & ch, George Ross, Robert
H. Emma-Jane & Mary Ella, recrq (G)

1892, 10, 19. George R. relrq (G)

1914, 3, 25. Noah A. & Martha W. recrq (G)

1915, 2, 24. James Wm. recrq (G)

1915, 2, 24. Harry recrq (G)

JAMES

----, --, --. Joshua & Susanna
Ch: Joseph b 1803, 12, 14 d 1822, 3, 9
    bur Short Creek

JAMES Joshua & Susanna, continued
      Ch: Nathan   b 1806, 2, 3 d 1823, 1,17
               bur Short Creek
          Samuel   b 1808, 10, 13
          John   " 1811, 8, 7
          Rachel   " 1814, 6, 15
          Joshua   " 1817, 3, 18 d 1823, 2,12
               bur Short Creek
          Oliver   b 1819, 4, 21
1808, 12, 28. George, s Samuel & Hannah, Jef-
      ferson Co., O.; m in West Grove MH, Sarah
      BARBER, dt Samuel & Ann, Jefferson Co., O.
      Ch: Anna   b 1809, 10, 17
          Hannah   " 1811, 8, 20
          Edith   " 1813, 10, 14
          David   " 1816, 1, 20
          Elizabeth " 1819, 9, 27
1812, 10, 26. Samuel d ae 58 bur Short Creek
----, --, --. Samuel & Lydia
      Ch: Israel   b 1814, 10, 21
          Mary Ann   " 1816, 5, 31
          Sidney   " 1818, 4, 25
          Rebecca   " 1820, 2, 27
          Martha   " 1822, 5, 2
1819, 1, 20. Hannah m Thomas REEDER
1821, 10, 8 . Samuel Jr. d ae 32 bur Short
      Creek
1829, 4, 5. Susanna d bur Short Creek

1807, 3, 21. Evan gct Concord MM, to m Re-
      becca Pickering
1810, 2, 20. Rebecca rocf Plainfield MM, dtd
      1809,8,26
1810, 3, 20. Nancy Smith (form James) dis mcd
1812, 12, 22. Samuel gct Abington MM, Pa.
1813, 5, 18. Evan & w, Rebecca, & ch, Hannah,
      Jonas & Phebe, gct Plainfield MM
1814, 3, 22. Evan & w, Rebecca, & ch, Hannah,
      Phebe & Jonas, rocf Plainfield MM, dtd
      1814,2,26
1814, 3, 22. Margaret Pugh (form James) dis
      mcd
1814, 10, 18. Samuel & w, Lydia, rocf Abing-
      ton MM, Pa., dtd 1814,8,29
1815, 6, 20. Cert rec for Isaac & w, Deborah,
      from Youngstreet MM, Upper Canada, dtd
      1815,4,13, end to Concord MM
1818, 10, 20. Evan & w, Rebecca, & ch, Han-
      nah Pheby, James, Jesse & Joshua P., gct
      Flushing MM
1822, 10, 22. Evan & w, Rebecca, & ch, Han-
      nah, Phebe, Jonas, Jesse, Joshua P. &
      Mary, rocf Flushing MM, dtd 1822,6,21
1823, 6, 24. Evan & w, Rebecca, & ch, Han-
      nah, Phebe, Jonas, Jesse, Joshua & Mary,
      gct White Water MM, Ind.
1824, 4, 20. George & w, Sarah, & ch, Han-
      nah, Edith, David, Elizabeth & Samuel,
      gct Somerset MM
1824, 9, 21. Anna dis
1824, 12, 21. Lydia Harrison (form James) dis
      mcd
1828, 9, 23. Deborah dis jH

1829, 7, 21. Lany (form Hall) dis mcd
1829, 8, 18. Samuel dis mcd
1830, 11, 23. John dis mcd
1834, 4, 22. Rachel gct Upper Springfield MM
1836, 6, 21. Mary Ann Smith (form James) dis
      mcd
1838, 3, 20. Israel dis mcd
1840, 5, 19. Rebecca Sprigs (form James) dis
      mcd
1841, 2, 23. Oliver dis mcd
1844, 7, 23. Rachel Vickers (form James)
      dis mcd
1846, 11, 24. Edwin dis disunity
1846, 11, 24. Martha dis jH
1847, 11, 23. William dis disunity
1868, 8, 20, Samuel E. & w, Lany, rst at
      Damascus MM on consent of this mtg (W)

JANNEY
1913, 3, 3. Martha d bur Colerain

1883, 2, 20. Martha (form Brackin) dis mcd
      (W)
1908, 8, 18. Martha B. (form Bracken) rst
      (W)

JENKINS
----, --, --. Israel & Elizabeth
      Ch: Ruth   b 1803, 1, 8
          Esther   " 1805, 8, 9
          Anna   " 1807, 2, 24
          Jonathan   " 1808, 10, 9
          Mary   " 1811, 4, 23
          Hannah   " 1817, 5, 21
          Elizabeth " 1821, 1, 7
          David   " 1823, 8, 25
          Israel   " 1835, 11, 2
1806, 1, 23. Mishael, s Jacob & Elizabeth,
      Belmont Co., O.; m in Short Creek MH, Sa-
      rah KINSEY, dt George & Mary, Jefferson
      Co., O.
1825, 7, 28. Mary m Clark TERRELL
1825, 10, 27. Rachel m Owen MARIS
1827, 3, 12. Elizabeth d bur Short Creek
1828, 5, 29. Ann m Aaron THOMPSON
1835, 12, 16. Ruth d bur Short Creek
1837, 12, 28. Elizabeth H. m Jesse B. CREW
1841, 9, 30. Geo. R., s Mishael & Sarah,
      Harrison Co., O., d 1879,3,20; m in Short
      Creek MH, Sarah UPDEGRAFF, dt David & Re-
      becca T., Jefferson Co., O.
      Ch: Rebecca
          Ann   b 1842, 7, 5
          Charles
          Henry   " 1846, 6, 5
          David
          Updegraff   " 1851, 7, 25 d 1354, 7,25
          Mary
          Elizabeth   " 1853, 4, 20
          George
          Francis   " 1857, 12, 9 " 1859, 9, 1
1845, 6, 9. Sarah d ae 71 bur Short Creek
1878, 8, 23. George K. d ae 65 (an elder)(G)

JENKINS, continued
1881, 3, 21. Florence Loretta b (G)

1805, 3, 16. Israel rocf Hopewell MM, dtd
    1804,12,3
1810, 2, 20. Elizabeth & ch, Ruth, Esther,
    Ann & Jonathan, recrq
1816, 5, 2. Sarah & ch, John, Rachel, Mary
    & George, rocf Plainfield MM, dtd 1816,3,
    22
1823, 10, 21. John dis
1825, 1, 18. Esther Hill (form Jenkins) dis
    mcd
1832, 10, 23. Israel gct Redstone MM, to m
    Lydia Willis
1833, 1, 22. Lydia & ch, Joel & Susan Willis,
    rocf Redstone MM, dtd 1833,1,2
1835, 3, 24. Jonathan dis mcd
1835, 5, 19. Hannah gct Westland MM
1835, 5, 19. Mary gct Westland MM
1846, 7, 21. David gct Cincinnati MM
1858, 10, 20. Israel W. gct Upper Springfield
    MM, to m Alvina Stanley
1859, 4, 20. Alvina S. rocf Upper Springfield
    MM, dtd 1859,3,26
1861, 10, 23. Israel & w, Alvina L., gct Upper
    Springfield MM
1864, 4, 19. George K. dis jG (W)
1864, 7, 19. Sarah E. dis jG (W)
1864, 11, 22. Lydia dis jG (W)
1865, 2, 22. Lydia N. gct Upper Springfield
    MM (G)
1865, 11, 22. Rebecca A. relrq (G)
1883, 5, 22. Mary Elizabeth dis jG (W)
1885, 2, 25. Lafayette recrq (G)
1885, 5, 20. Rachel recrq (G)
1888, 4, 25. Margaret L. (form Kinsey) gct
    Damascus MM (G)
1891, 12, 23. Florence L. recrq (G)
1895, 2, 20. Dora recrq (G)
1902, 5, 21. Florence E. Creighton (form Jen-
    kins) relrq (G)
1902, 12, 24. Lafayette dropped from mbrp (G)
1903, 6, 24. John dropped from mbrp (G)

JENKINSON
1808, 10, 18. Cert rec for Rebecca & ch, Ann,
    Elizabeth, Mary, John, Sarah & Rebecca,
    end to Plymouth MM

JESSUP
1868, 4, 23. Sarah W. (form Tweedy) dis mcd
    (G)

JINTLE
1915, 2, 24. John recrq (G)
1915, 2, 24. Stephen recrq (G)

JOB
1813, 7, 7. Samuel b
1815, 1, 10. Allen b
1818, 6, 25 Asenith b
1821, 5, 1. Daniel b

1824, 6, 4. Julianna b
1827, 5, 13. Ann Hannah b
1881, 1, 18. Rebecca [Jobe] d

1816, 12, 24. Rebecca & ch, Ruth, Elizabeth,
    Mary, Susanna & Allen, rocf Nottingham
    MM, Md., dtd 1816,7,8
1820, 3, 21. Rebecca & ch, Ruth, Elizabeth,
    Mary, Samuel & Allen, gct Smithfield MM
1823, 2, 23. Rebecca & ch, Ruth, Elizabeth,
    Samuel, Mary & Allen, rocf Smithfield MM,
    dtd 1822,12,23
1828, 12, 23. Mary & Rebecca dis jH
1829, 7, 21. Ruth McMelon (form Job) dis mcd
1836, 3, 22. Elizabeth dis
1838, 4, 24. Samuel & Allen dis disunity
1840, 8, 20. Allen gct Concord MM (H)
1840, 8, 20. Daniel gct Concord MM (H)
1840, 8 20. Samuel gct Concord MM (H)
1843, 4, 18. Eliza Ann (form Berry) dis mcd
    & jH
1845, 3, 20. Rebecca & dt, Ann Hannah, gct
    Concord MM (H)

JOHN
1812, 12, 3. William, s Wm. & Rachel, Jef-
    ferson Co. O.; m in Short Creek MH, Sa-
    rah THOMAS, dt Jesse & Sarah
    Ch: Ann   b 1813, 12, 18
        Hannah   " 1815, 1, 15
        Jesse T.   " 1816, 5, 21
        Susanna   " 1817, 11, 22 d 1820,11, 2
        bur Short Creek
        Rachel   b 1818, 12, 28

1806, 9, 20. Hannah rocf London Grove MM,
    dtd 1806,8,7, end by Concord MM 1806,8,
    19
1809, 3, 21. William [Johns] & ch, George &
    Lydia, recrq
1812, 12, 22. Amasa Lipsey gct Westland MM,
    to m Sarah John
1821, 10, 23. Hannah, minor dt Sarah, gct
    Smithfield MM
1821, 10, 23. Sarah & ch, Ann, Jesse & Rachel,
    gct Somerset MM
1822, 5, 21. Lydia gct Concord MM
1833, 3, 19. Ann rocf Somerset MM, dtd
    1832,12,24
1835, 10, 20. Ann gct Somerset MM
1838, 7, 24. Rachel gct Smithfield MM

JOHNSON
1825, 11, 24. Demcey, s Elijah & Mary, Stark
    Co., O.; m in Mt. Pleasant, Margaret
    HARRISON dt Wm. & Margaret, Jefferson
    Co., O.
1827, 2, 22. Ashley, s Wm. & Elizabeth, Wayne
    Co., Ind.; m in Harrisville, Lydia RHODES,
    dt Joseph & Martha, Harrison Co., O.
1841, 9, 1. Robert, s Jonathan & Judith,
    Harrison Co., O.; m in West Grove MH, Sa-
    rah K. TOWNSEND, dt Thos. & Maria, Harri-

JOHNSON, Robert & Sarah, continued
    son Co., O.
      Ch: Zelinda
          E. D.   b 1842, 7, 2 d 1845, 2, 8
          bur West Grove
         Thomas
          Townsend b 1843, 11, 18
         Jonathan   " 1846, 1, 20
         Juditha
          Douglass " 1848, 7, 14
1844, 10, 2. Elizabeth D. m Lemuel HARGRAVE
1848, 3, 26. Judith d bur West Grove
1849, 5, 2. Achilles D., s Jonathan & Ju-
    dith, Harrison Co., O.; m in West Grove
    MH, Sarah T. LUKENS dt Moses & Elizabeth,
    Harrison Co., O.
      Ch: Elizabeth
         Ann   b 1850, 2, 3
        Judith
         Douglas " 1851, 11, 2
        Achilles
         Douglas " 1854, 3, 20
        Samuel T. " 1857, 12, 17
        Edith   " 1859, 6, 5
        Ellen H.   " 1860, --, --
1849, 5, 2. Deborah m Samuel B. LUKENS
1852, 3, 30. Sarah H. d ae 30 bur West Grove
----, --, --. Wm. C. & Judith (See p. 310)
      Ch: Edith   b 1859, 6, 5
        Ellen H.   " 1861, 1, 2
        Anna M.   " 1863, 11, 11
        William A. " 1867, 4, 24
        Ida   " 1869, 5, 31
        Franklin   " 1877, 1, 26

1823, 2, 23. Sarah (form Judkins) dis mcd
1826, 3, 21. Margaret gct Marlborough MM
1827, 7, 24. Lydia gct White Water MM, Ind.
1829, 10, 30. Benjamin Bates gct Marlborough
    MM, to m Lydia Johnson
1831, 8, 23. Micajah T. & w, Edna, & dt,
    Judith, rocf Wayne Oak MM, Va., dtd 1831,
    7,3
1831, 9, 20. Richard rocf Western Branch
    MM, Va., dtd 1831,7,23
1832, 10, 23. Richard gct Milford MM, Ind.
1838, 6, 19. Robert M. rocf South River MM,
    dtd 1838,4,12
1840, 8, 18. Jonathan [Jonston] & w, Judith,
    & ch, Elizabeth Douglas, Susanna, Achil-
    les Douglas, Mildred Tyree, Deborah Ju-
    dith & Mary Ann, rocf South River MM, Va.,
    dtd 1840,5,27
1845, 3, 18. Susan J. Chandler (form Johnson)
    con mcd
1847, 8, 24. Sarah E. (form Lewis) dis mcd
1855, 2, 20. Micajah T. dis disunity
1856, 3, 18. Judith Wheeler (form Johnson)
    dis mcd
1857, 4, 21. Robert dis disunity
1857, 10, 21. Wm. C. gct Upper Springfield
    to m Judith C. Stanley
1858, 1, 20. Judith C. rocf Upper Springfield

MM, dtd 1857,12,26
1860, 9, 19. Micajah T. dis disunity
1863, 3, 22. Sarah dis jG (W)
1863, 3, 22. Zilinda E. D. dis jG (W)
1864, 6, 21. Mary Ann dis jG (W)
1865, 4, 18. Anne Jane dis jG (W)
1865, 8, 22. Edna dis jG (W)
1867, 1, 21. Sarah McCombs (form Johnson)
    con mcd (G)
1867, 2, 21. Jonathan Jr. gct Gileas MM,
    Mo. (G)
1867, 2, 21. Judith D. gct Gilead MM, Mo.
    (G)
1867, 2, 21. Zelinda E. D. gct Gilead MM, Mo.
    (G)
1867, 11, 19. Elizabeth Ann dis jG (W)
1868, 2, 18. William dis mcd & jG (W)
1868, 4, 21. Jonathan dis jG (W)
1869, 11, 25. Ruel H., Elizabeth Sr., Ammiel,
    Sophia, Isaac Wm., Iva Nellie, Alice E.,
    James A., Ruth, Annas Mat, minor, Milton
    B. & Elizabeth recrq (G)
1869, 11, 25. Samantha Jane, Viola Ann &
    Albert E. recrq (G)
1871, 6, 20. Mary dis jG (W)
1871, 12, 21. Elvira, Margaret V. & Ruel M.
    recrq (G)
1874, 12, 24. Eliza, Margaret R., Olive V. &
    Vernie E. recrq (G)
1875, 11, 25. Elizabeth Ann Scott (form
    Johnson) con mcd (G)
1876, 7, 20. Thomas E. con mcd (G)
1876, 10, 26. Alice Brisco (form Johnson) con
    mcd (G)
1881, 3, 24. Thomas recrq (G)
1882, 5, 24. Anna recrq (G)
1884, 2, 20. Jonah recrq (G)
1888, 10, 24. Anna dropped from mbrp (G)
1889, 3, 20. William recrq (G)
1889, 3, 20. Caroline recrq (G)
1891, 3, 25. Harry recrq (G)
1895, 2, 20. Clarence recrq (G)
1895, 3, 20. Elizabeth rocf Smithfield MM
    (G)
1895, 7, 24. Harvey dropped from mbrp (G)
1905, 4, 19. Lorain D. & Neva recrq (G)
1906, 3, 21. Anna Elva & ch, Mary Lupton &
    Clara Sophia, relrq (G)
1907, 5, 23. Lorain & Neva relrq (G)
1907, 11, 20. Floy Hall rocf Guernsey MM (G)
1914, 11, 25. Alice Kinsey gct Alliance MM(G)
1915, 8, 17. Frank S. relrq (G)
1915, 8, 17. Floy J. relrq (G)
1915, 8, 17. Lida Judith relrq (G)

JOHNSTON
1845, 2, 8. Thomas S. d ae 1 bur West Grove

1804, 8, 18. Sarah [Johnstone] rocf Redstone
    MM, dtd 1804,6,1
1855, 8, 22. Robert dis
1856, 5, 21. Judith J. Wheeler (form John-
    ston) dis mcd

JOLLY
1807, 9, 19. John dis

JONES
1828, 12, 16. Robert B. d ae 7 bur Short Creek
1829, 1, 7. Maria m Thos. THOMASSON
1829, 12, 30. Lemuel, s Samuel & Elizabeth,
    Jefferson Co., O.; m in Mt. Pleasant,
    Mary Ann WALKER dt Lewis & Rachel, Jef-
    ferson Co., O.
    Ch: Lewis W.   b 1831, 3, 9
        Dillwyn P. " 1832, 10, 29
        Albert   " 1840, 5, 7
        Lemuel O.   " 1843, 3, 21 d 1847,11,30
        Francis
          Pendleton " 1845, 11, 30
        Rachel Ann " 1849, 8, 14
        Oliver W.   " 1852, --, --
        Elizabeth   " 1855, --, --
1832, 6, 11. Edward P. d ae 13 bur Mt. Pleas-
    ant
1833, 1, 11. Samuel d ae 54 bur Mt. Pleasant
----, --, --. Joseph & Isabella
    Ch: Samuel P. b 1838, 3, 16 d 1859, 7,30
          bur Smithfield
        Elizabeth
          L.   b 1839, 7, 6
        Mary Ann   " 1841, 5, 7 " 1841, 7,16
        Frances Con-
          ner   b 1842, 4, 7
        Maria W.   " 1844, 4, 2
        Benjamin W." 1847, 2, 20
        Edward W. " 1849, 1, 19
1850, 10, 30. Martha Ann m Robert HAGUE
1852, 9, 29. Lewis W. s Samuel & Mary Ann,
    Jefferson Co., O.; m in Mt. Pleasant,
    Mary P. BINNS, dt Jonathan & Eliza, Jef-
    ferson Co., O.
----, --, --. Benjamin & Amanda
    Ch: Annie S.   b 1861, 8, 29
        Mary Lizzie" 1863, 1, 15
        Alice R.   " 1878, 8, 13
1885, 5, 9. Amanda d
1873, 1, 15. Mary Elizabeth d
1874, 7, 29. Samuel A., s Josiah & Mary,
    Richmond, Va.; m in West Grove MH, Mary
    THOMAS dt Isaac & Anna L., Harrison Co.,
    O.
1804, 7, 21. Joseph & fam gct Middleton MM
1827, 6, 19. Samuel & w & s, Lemuel, & minor
    ch, Maria, Joseph, William, Edward, Robert,
    Mathew & Martha, rocf Western Branch MM,
    Va., dtd 1827,4,28
1837, 4, 18. Joseph gct Smithfield MM, to m
    Isabella Ladd
1837, 9, 19. Isabella L. rocf Smithfield MM,
    dtd 1837,9,18
1842, 11, 22. Joseph & w, Isabella, & ch,
    Samuel Pendleton, Elizabeth Ladd & Fran-
    ces Conner, gct Smithfield MM
1843, 9, 19. Matthew Oliver gct Dover MM
1855, 10, 24. Lemuel dis disunity
1856, 5, 21. Mary Ann & ch, Dillwyn, Albert,

    Francis P., Rachel Ann, Oliver W. &
    Elizabeth P., gct Winnishiek MM, Iowa
1859, 3, 23. Lewis W. & w, Mary, & dt, Anna
    Elizabeth, gct Honey Creek MM, Iowa
1863, 2, 25. Lemuel rst at Winnesheik MM,
    Ia. on consent of this mtg (G)
1863, 3, 24. Joseph dis jG (W)
1865, 9, 19. Isabella L. & Maria W. dis
    disunity (W)
1865, 10, 24. Frances L. dis jG (W)
1874, 10, 22. Mary T. gct Westland MM (G)
1878, 1, 24. Samuel H. & w, Mary T., & ch,
    William Alfred & Isaac Thomas, rocf Colum-
    bus MM, O.
1879, 6, 26. Mary, w Samuel, & ch, William
    A., Isaac Thomas & Cynthia Ann, gct
    Rasin MM, Mich.(G)
1879, 12, 25. Anna E. rocf Roxylvania MM, Ia.
    (G)
1879, 12, 25. Edward, minor, rocf Roxylvania
    MM, Ia. (G)
1880, 2, 26. Samuel H. gct Rasin MM, Mich.
    (G)
1891, 3, 25. Robert recrq (G)
1896, 5, 20. Mildred, minor, recrq (G)
1914, 1, 21. Marie, Pearl Elizabeth &
    Eugene B., recrq (G)
1914, 1, 21. Henry recrq (G)

JUDKINS
----, --, --. James & Abigail
    Ch: Isaac P.   b 1806, 7, 15 d 1811,7,20
          bur Short Creek
        Anna   b 1809, 6, 27
        Robert   " 1812, 9, 4
        Jesse   " 1815, 5, 31
        Isaac   " 1818, 10, 6
        Charles   " 1821, 6, 28
1812, 12, 3. James Jr., s James & Martha,
    Jefferson Co., O.; m in Short Creek MH,
    Susanna BYE, dt Jonathan & Mary, Jeffer-
    son Co., O.
1813, 9, 30. William, s James & Martha, Jef-
    ferson Co., O.; m in Short Creek MH, Ra-
    chel STEER, dt Joseph & Grace, Jefferson
    Co., O.
1821, 1, 31. Martha m Abraham R. DILWORTH
1821, 8, 1. Abigail d bur Short Creek

1813, 11, 23. William & w, Rachel, gct
    Plymouth MM
1815, 6, 20. James Jr. & w, Susanna, & s,
    Jonathan, gct Plymouth MM
1816, 6, 18. James Jr. & w, Susanna, & ch,
    Jonathan & Martha, rocf Plymouth MM, dtd
    1816,6,17
1816, 9, 24. Anderson gct Plymouth MM
1818, 4, --. James Jr. & w, Susanna, & ch,
    Jonathan & Martha, gct Plainfield MM
1819, 11, 23. Stanton gct Smithfield MM
1822, 12, 24. William & w, Rachel, & ch, Sa-
    rah, David & Martha Ann, rocf Smithfield
    MM, dtd 1822,9,23

JUDKINS, continued

1823, 2, 23.   Sarah Johnson (form Judkins) dis
mcd

1827, 3, 20.   Ann F. Duff (form Judkins) dis
mcd

1831, 11, 22.   Susan & ch, Jonathan, Martha,
Mary, Sarah, James & Maria, gct Flushing
MM

1832, 5, 22.   William & w, Rachel, & ch, Sarah, David & Martha Ann, gct Cincinnati MM

1836, 11, 22.   Robert dis disunity

1838, 4, 24.   Jonathan rocf Flushing MM, dtd
1838,3,27

1838, 4, 24.   Martha, Mary & Susanna rocf
Flushing MM

1838, 5, 22.   Jesse gct Cincinnati MM

1839, 11, 19.   Martha gct Stillwater MM

1839, 11, 19.   Mary gct Stillwater MM

1839, 11, 19.   Susa & ch, James & Maria, gct
Stillwater MM

1842, 9, 20.   Jonathan dis mcd

1843, 4, 18.   Sarah Alexander (form Judkins)
dis mcd & jas

1857, 8, 18.   William A. dis mcd

1857, 9, 22.   Mary (form Bates) dis mcd

KANGUESSER

1908, 4, 22.   Jean Joseph recrq (G)

KEES

1815, 12, 19.   Sarah (form Benedict) rpd mcd

KEHBEL

1904, 12, 21.   Ida & ch, Clara, Ella, Elizabeth
& Carl recrq (G)

KEITH

1881, 2, 26.   Mary E. recrq (G)

1888, 10, 24.   Mary dropped from mbrp (G)

1915, 2, 24.   Archibald & Margaret recrq (G)

1915, 2, 24.   Jesse Lemoyne & Dorris Marie
recrq (G)

KELLUM

1807, 5, 16.   John dis disunity

KELLY

1884, 10, 31.   Erma, dt Samuel & Myrtle
(Thompson), b

1884, 2, 20.   John recrq (G)

1885, 2, 25.   William P. recrq (G)

1903, 6, 24.   William dropped from mbrp (G)

KELTZ

1895, 3, 20.   Ellen recrq (G)

1907, 3, 20.   Ellen dropped from mbrp (G)

KEMMERLING

1905, 4, 19.   Mrs. S. B., Grace, Sadie & Mary
recrq (G)

KENESELL

1910, 1, 31.   Henry E. [Kenisell] d (G)

1897, 2, 24.   Henry [Kenisell] & w, Kate P.,
recrq (G)

1898, 2, 23.   Henry recrq (G)

1898, 2, 23.   George Edward recrq (G)

1898, 2, 23.   Lemuel Cornelius recrq (G)

1898, 2, 23.   John Welburn recrq (G)

1903, 6, 24.   H. Slagle [Kennisell] dropped
from mbrp (G)

1915, 1, 20.   Lemuel Cornelius [Kinsell]
dropped from mbrp (G)

1915, 1, 20.   John Milburn [Kinsell] dropped
from mbrp (G)

1926, 7, 29.   George E. [Kenisell] relrq (G)

KENNARD

1813, 12, 30.   Joseph, s Eli, Belmont Co., O.;
m in Short Creek MH, Hannah THOMPSON, dt
Wm.

1815, 11, 2.   Ann [Kenard] m Stephen TOWNSEND

1816, 2, 23.   Eli, s William & Rachel, b

1821, 8, 8.   Thomas d ae 31 bur Short Creek

1823, 5, 29.   Eli d ae 65 bur Short Creek

1811, 11, 19.   Eli & w, Catharine, & ch, Joseph & Betsy Kennard & Hannah & David
Thompson, rocf Wrightstown MM, dtd 1811,
9,--

1811, 11, 19.   Thomas rocf ND MM, dtd 1811,4,
23, end by Wrightstown MM, 1811,8,7

1811, 11, 19.   William rocf Wrightstown MM, dtd
1811,8,7

1812, 5, 19.   William gct Wrightstown MM, Pa.

1814, 9, 20.   Levi & w, Ann, & s, Levi, rocf
Deer Creek MM, dtd 1814,7,28

1814, 9, 20.   Thomas & w, Elizabeth, rocf
Deer Creek MM, dtd 1814,7,28

1814, 10, 18.   Elizabeth & Ann rocf Deer Creek
MM, Md., dtd 1814,7,28

1814, 10, 18.   William & w, Rachel, rocf
Wrightstown MM, dtd 1814,9,7

1814, 12, 20.   Mary rocf Deer Creek MM, dtd
1814,7,28

1815, 5, 23.   Thomas & s, Henry Preston, gct
Plainfield MM

1817, 1, 21.   Levi & w, Ann, & s, Levi, gct
Concord MM

1824, 7, 20.   William & w, Rachel, & s, Eli,
gct Somerset MM

1826, 4, 18.   Joseph & w, Hannah, & ch, Catharine, Esther, Mary, Tacy, William, Eli &
Hannah, gct Stillwater MM

1827, 7, 24.   Catharine & dt, Elizabeth, gct
Deerfield MM

1862, 11, 19.   Eli, Mary, Anne, William, Jesse,
Mary Jr., Abigail, Sarah, Elizabeth & Joseph dis jW

KENNEDY

1892, 4, 20.   Laura L. relrq (G)

KENNY
1829, 1, 28. Richard, s Daniel & Phebe, Mor-
    gan Co., O.; m in Mt. Pleasant, Susanna
    HARRIS, dt Ezekiel & Sarah, Jefferson Co.,
    O.   [1829,7,16
1829, 8, 18. Richard rocf Deerfield MM, dtd
1829, 10, 20. Richard & w, Susanna, gct Still-
1881, 2, 26. Anna Eliza recrq (G) [water MM
1881, 2, 26. Robert H. recrq (G)
1882, 3, 29. William recrq (G)
1884, 7, 23. Ann Eliza dropped from mbrp (G)
1884, 7, 23. Robert dropped from mbrp (G)
1884, 7, 23. William dropped from mbrp (G)

KENT
1905, 11, 22. George Ernest, Nellie G., Arthur
    Thomas & Robert Downard, rocf New Sharon
    MM, Ia. (G)
1909, 9, 22. George E. & fam gct Salem MM (G)

KENWORTHY
1845, 4, 22. Mary M. (form Spencer) con mcd
1845, 10, 21. Mary Ann gct Spiceland MM, Ind.

KEPPORT
1857, 12, 23. Elizabeth (form Kinsey) dis mcd

KERNS
1907, 4, 24. Ida dropped from mbrp (G)

KESTER
1903, 5, 20. Clara D. relrq (G)

KIMBER
1877, 11, 22. Anthony M. & w, Margaret C.
    recrq (G)
1882, 9, 20. Anthony M. & w, Margaret C.,
    gct Rhode Island MM (G)

KIMBERLY
1908, 7, 22. Mrs. Samuel & dt, Mary, relrq
    (G)

KINDER
1903, 4, 22. Ida H., Arthur, Mary, Bertha &
    Margeretta, recrq (G)
1907, 4, 24. Ida H. dropped from mbrp (G)

KING
----, --, --. William G. & Mercy
    Ch: Isaac L.   b 1861, 6, 20
        Edward F. " 1864, 1, 1
        Anna R.   " 1866, 11, 16
        Wm. Irving
----, --, --. Harry & Elizabeth
    Ch: Mary Adel b 1900, 6, 10
        Howard
          Iden   " 1897, 6, 17 d 1916, 7,14

1830, 4, 20. Rebecca (form Harris) dis mcd
1863, 9, 23. Mary Jane (form Crossley) con mcd
1880, 5, 20. Mary Jane dis (G)
1881, 2, 26. Mary recrq (G)

1902, 4, 23. Nathan recrq (G)
1905, 3, 22. Carrie recrq (G)

KINNEY
1805, 5, 18. Cert rec for Richard & fam from
    Uchland MM, Pa., dtd 1805,4,4, end to
    Concord MM

KINSEY
1805, 12, 26. Susana m Joseph UPDEGRAFF
1806, 1, 23. Sarah m Mishael JENKINS
1807, 9, 24. Anna m Daniel MICHENER
1809, 4, 27. Aaron, s Geo. & Mary, Jefferson
    Co., O.; m in Short Creek MH, Sarah BUTLER
    dt John & Jane, Jefferson Co., O.
    Ch: Deborah   b 1810, 3, 2 d 1810, 4,21
        Mary   " 1811, 7, 11
        Charles   " 1813, 10, 7
        Deborah   " 1815, 12, 14 d 1821, 5,31
          bur Short Creek
        Amos G.   b 1818, 9, 14
        Caleb   " 1821, 2, 22
----, --, --. John & Mary
    Ch: Meriman   b 1811, 2, 16
        Susanna   " 1813, 2, 25
        Hiram   " 1815, 6, 22
        Lydia Ann " 1817, 9, 6
        Alfred   " 1819, 10, 10
        Ezra   " 1821, 8, 16
        Oliver J. " 1824, 6, 16
        Mary D.   " 1826, 11, 2
        Elizabeth
          D.   " 1829, 3, 9
        Jephtha   " 1831, 6, 29
        Ruthanna " 1835, 6, 27
1813, 4, 29. James, s Geo. & Mary, Jefferson
    Co., O.; m in Short Creek MH, Ann LOYD,
    dt John & Mercy, Belmont Co., O.
    Ch: Mercy   b 1814, 3, 27
        Jane   " 1815, 8, 21 d 1835,10,12
          bur Short Creek
        John L.   b 1817, 10, 8 " 1836, 1, 4
          bur Short Creek
        Samuel   b 1819, 9, 12
        George   " 1821, 7, 10
        Mary Ann " 1824, 3, 29 " 1825, 6,21
          bur Short Creek
        James G. b 1827, 1, 14
        Isaac   " 1828, 9, 1
        Lemuel   " 1831, 7, 4 " 1833, 6, 8
          bur Short Creek
1815, 6, 1. Charles, s Geo. & Mary, Jefferson
    Co., O.; m in Short Creek MH, Ann WORRAL,
    dt John & Rebecca, Jefferson Co., O.
    Ch: Gulingham b 1832, 1, 24
        Kersey W. " 1823, 11, 2
1821, 4, 12. Sarah d ae 35 bur Short Creek
1825, 10, 1. Mary d ae 71 bur Short Creek
1828, 2, 16. George d ae 76 bur Short Creek
----, --, --. George & Mary
    Ch: Lucinda   b 1829, 9, 30
        William G. " 1832, 5, 18
1832, 5, 30. Miriam m Stephen K. REYNOLDS

KINSEY, continued

1833, 10, 31. Mercy m Jonathan WILSON
1835, 11, 6. Mary d ae 34 bur Short Creek
1835, --, --. Mary Ann d ae 18 bur Smithfield
1836, 1, 27. Susannah m Jesse HOGE
----, --, --. Charles & Sarah
        Ch: Mary Eliza b 1837, 1, 22
            Margaret. " 1837, 12, 17
            George B. " 1849, 8, 6
1839, 12, 17. Margaret b
1845, 8, 6. George B. b
1849, 11, 7. Edmund d ae 71 bur Short Creek
1850, 10, 30. Geo., s James & Ann, Jefferson
        Co., O.; m in Mt. Pleasant, Ann UPDEGRAFF,
        dt Nathan & Casandra, Jefferson Co., O.
        Ch: Cassandra b 1851, 8, 18
            Mary T.   " 1852, 12, 11 d 1853, 8,25
            Nathan J.   " 1854, 11, 27 " 1856, 8,26
            James D.   " 1857, 3, 27
            William   " 1859, 11, 26 " 1860, 2,9
            Susanna   " 1862, 2, 5
            Edith   " 1864, 10, 11 d 1864,12,14
            George Wm. " 1866, 5, 11
1855, 3, 29. Mary Eliza m Tilman HALL
1855, 8, 31. Maria d ae 22 bur Smithfield
----, --, --. James & Elizabeth
        Ch: Anna Lucy b 1856, 9, 4
            Caroline E." 1861, 6, 5
            Evaline   " 1862, 10, 16
1855, 10, 25. Wm. G., s Nathan & Hannah, Hamil-
        ton Co., O.; m in Mt. Pleasant, Mercy
        LLOYD, dt Isaac & Ruth, Belmont Co., O.
1856, 6, 18. James Sr. d ae 75
1856, 8, 2. Ann d ae 61 bur Smithfield
1862, 7, 23. Ann d ae 71
1864, 4, 9. Evaline d ae 1 bur Short Creek
1864, 4, 12. James G. d ae 37 bur Short Creek
1864, 4, 14. Caroline E. d ae 3 bur Short
        Creek
1864, 5, 13. Anna L. d ae 8 bur Short Creek
1864, 5, 26. William Irving d ae 5 bur Short
        Creek
1865, 11, 30. Margaret B. m Jared STANLEY
1867, 9, 4. Charles d

1804, 10, 20. Christopher & w, Mary, & ch, Sa-
        rah, John, Absolom & Nathan, rocf Red-
        stone MM, dtd 1804,8,3
1804, 11, 7. Ann rocf New Garden MM, Pa.,
        dtd 1804,9,6
1804, 11, 7. George & w, Mary, & ch, Aaron,
        John, George & Charles, rocf New Garden
        MM, Pa., dtd 1804,9,6
1804, 11, 7. Sarah rocf New Garden MM, Pa.,
        dtd 1804,9,6
1804, 12, 15. Edmond rocf London Grove MM,
        dtd 1804,9,5, end by Concord MM, 1804,
        11,20
1805, 1, 19. James rocf Bradford MM, Pa., dtd
        1804,11,20, end by Concord MM, 1804,9,5
1805, 3, 16. Susannah rocf Newgarden MM,
        Pa., dtd 1804,9,6
1811, 4, 23. Edmund con mcd

1811, 6, 18. John dis
1812, 5, 19. Edmund gct Concord MM
1814, 12, 20. George Jr. con mcd
1815, 7, 18. Edmund rocf Concord MM, dtd
        1815,4,20
1815, 7, 18. Ruth Anna, minor dt Edmund,
        recrq
1819, 1, 19. John & w, Mary, rst at Concord
        on consent of this MM
1822, 10, 22. George Jr. gct Stillwater MM
1825, 2, 22. Charles & w, Ann, & ch, Gilling-
        ham W. & Kinsey, gct Flushing MM
1828, 5, 20. Mary & dt, Phebe M., Sarah A.,
        Lydia W. & Elizabeth E., recrq
1833, 6, 18. George & w, Mary S., & ch,
        Phebe M., Sarah Ann, Lydia W., Elizabeth
        E., Oliver C. & Lucinda, gct Flushing MM
1836, 2, 23. Chas. gct Redstone MM, to m
        Sarah Binns
1836, 6, 21. Sarah B. rocf Redstone MM, dtd
        1836,6,1
1836, 12, 20. Hirah dis mcd
1837, 11, 21. Lydia Ann Truman (form Kinsey)
        dis mcd
1843, 4, 18. Caleb B. dis mcd
1846, 6, 23. Samuel B. gct Cincinnati MM
1847, 1, 19. Samuel B. con mcd
1847, 8, 24. Amos E. dis mcd
1847, 9, 22. Lydia rocf Flushing MM, dtd
        1847,7,20
1847, 9, 22. Phebe rocf Flushing MM, dtd
        1847,7,20
1847, 9, 22. Sarah Ann rocf Flushing MM, dtd
        1847,7,20
1848, 1, 18. Samuel B. gct Cincinnati MM
1850, 1, 22. Ezra dis mcd
1852, 4, 20. Sarah Ann dis jas
1853, 12, 20. Phebe Martin (form Kinsey) dis
        mcd
1854, 1, 24. Mary Day (form Kinsey) dis mcd
1854, 7, 18. James G. gct Smithfield MM, to
        m Elizabeth L. Wood
1855, 5, 23. Elizabeth rocf Smithfield MM,
        dtd 1855,5,21
1856, 2, 20. Isaac gct Red Cedar MM, Ia.
1856, 5, 21. Mercy L. gct Cincinnati MM
1857, 12, 23. Elizabeth Kepport (form Kinsey)
        dis mcd
1859, 7, 20. Ruth Ann con mcd
1860, 2, 21. Charles dis jG
1860, 3, 20. John dis jG
1860, 9, 18. Sarah & Margaret dis jG (W)
1861, 2, 20. William G. & w, Mercy L., & ch,
        Margaret L. & William Irwin, rocf Cincin-
        nati MM
1861, 8, 20. Ruthanna dis mcd (W)
1863, 2, 24. Ann dis jG (W)
1864, 4, 2. James G., a trustee, d rpd (G)
1865, 6, 21. Elizabeth L. gct Smithfield MM
        (G)
1865, 10, 24. Elizabeth dis jG (W)
1865, 11, 22. Jared Stanley rocf Upper Spring-
        field MM, to m Margaret B. Kinsey (G)

KINSEY, continued

1866, 1, 23. Mercy dis jG (W)

1866, 2, 21. Samuel B. & w, Rachel G., & ch, Hannah Ann, Jane M., Mary, Samuel B., Wm. H. M. & Rachel Ella, rocf Cincinnati MM (G)

1866, 11, 22. Joseph Hill gct Smithfield MM, to m Elizabeth L. Kinsey

1867, 8, 22. Samuel B. & w, Rachel G., & ch, Hannah Ann, Jane, Mary Ann, Samuel, Harrison M. & Rachel Ella, gct Clear Creek MM,O.

1873, 5, 22. George B. gct East Goshen MM (G)

1873, 5, 22. Sarah E. gct East Goshen MM (G)

1875, 9, 23. Cassandra Mansfield (form Kinsey) con mcd (G)

1888, 4, 25. Margaret L. Jenkins (form Kinsey) gct Damascus MM (G)

1893, 3, 22. Isaac L. & w, Edith E. C., relrq (G)

1895, 9, 25. Isaac L. & w, Edith E. C., recrq (G)

1900, 7, 25. William G. & w, Mercy L., & ch, Edward T., Samuel A., Annie R. & Mary E., gct Alliance MM (G)

1901, 10, 23. Isaac L. & w, Edith E., & ch, Alice & Wilma, gct Portsmouth MM, Va. (G)

1903, 8, 19. Isaac L. & w, Edith, & ch, Alice E. & Wilma, rocf Portsmouth MM, Va. (G)

1907, 4, 24. James D. dropped from mbrp

1914, 11, 25. Alice(Kinsey)Johnson gct Alliance MM (G)

KIRBY

1821, 3, 20. Mary rst on consent of Westland MM

KIRK

1805, 11, 27. Wm., s Wm. & Rachel, Jefferson Co., O.; m in Plainfield MH, Martha TOWNSEND, dt Benj. & Jemimah, Jefferson Co., O.

1822, 3, 27. Elisha, s Eli & Edith, Jefferson Co., O.; m in Mt. Pleasant, Deborah HARRISON, dt Wm. & Margaret, Jefferson Co., O.

1824, 1, 29. Susanna m John N. MARSH

----, --, --. Elisha m Rachel ----- d 1840,8, 5 ae 38 bur Short Creek
   Ch: Jesse   b 1828, 1, 17
      Elisha   " 1832, 10, 19 d 1859,10, 6
      Sarah   " 1835, 7, 22
Elisha m 2nd Christiana -----
   Ch: Nathan   b 1844, 2, 16
      Rachel   " 1846, 11, 2

1832, 1, 27. Sarah, dt Wm. & Martha, d ae 9 bur Smithfield

1839, 10, 31. Mary m John WATERMAN

1842, 3, 31. Elisha, s Eli & Edith, Belmont Co. O.; m in Short Creek MH, Christiana HALL, dt John & Tacy, Belmont Co., O.

1847, 9, 12. Martha, w Wm., d ae 63 bur Smithfield

1851, 5, 20. Elisha d ae 59 bur Short Creek

1851, 6, 28. Edith d bur Smithfield

1854, 6, 20. William d ae 72 bur Smithfield

1854, 6, 29. Jesse, s Elisha & Rachel, Belmont Co., O.; m in Short Creek MH, Elizabeth HALL, dt John & Tacy, Belmont Co.,O.

1857, 11, 25. Jesse d ae 30

1862, 5, 6. Susan, dt Wm. & Martha, d ae 45

1870, 1, 2. Erastus d

1914, 6, 24. Elisha T., s Nathan & Mary M., Stark Co., O.; m in Harrisville, Alice Mary STEER, dt Louis C. & S. Louiza, Jefferson Co., O., b 1891,1,4
   Ch: Mary
      Evalyn   b 1915, 7, 22

1917, 10, 25. Chas. D., s Nathan & Mary M., Columbiana Co., O., b 1894,10,9; m in Harrisville, Tacy M. HALL, dt Samuel & Anna, Jefferson Co., O., b 1895,3,31 (W)
   Ch: Walter S. b 1918, 8, 24
      Dorothy
      Mary   " 1921, 5, 14
      Wm. Joshua " 1925, 4, 20
      Oliver
      James   " 1929, 11, 18

1809, 5, 23. Mary & ch, Charity, Timothy, Phebe, Sidwell & Elisha, gct Salem MM

1811, 2, 19. Joshua gct Salem MM

1818, 6, 23. Timothy & w, Edith, rocf Redstone MM, end by Plymouth MM, 1818,5,27

1818, 7, 21. Rachel & Susanna rocf Redstone MM, dtd 1818,5,27, end by Smithfield MM

1819, 9, 21. Elisha rocf York MM, dtd 1819, 5,5

1824, 7, 20. Joseph rocf York MM, dtd 1824, 6,5

1826, 3, 21. Timothy gct Smithfield MM

1826, 5, 23. Beulah Garretson (form Kirk) con mcd

1827, 2, 20. Rachel rocf Flushing MM, dtd 1827,1,26

1839, 9, 24. Mary rocf Salem MM, dtd 1839,7, 24

1847, 2, 23. Timothy rocf Smithfield MM, dtd 1846,12,21

1850, 2, 19. Tijothy gct Baltimore MM

1859, 12, 20. Elizabeth gct Upper Springfield MM

1862, 6, 24. Mary (or Maria) recrq

1862, 11, 19. Christine, Sarah, Nathan & Rachel, dis jW (G)

1864, 4, 19. Christianna & ch, Nathan & Rachel, gct Newgarden MM (W)

1864, 4, 19. Sarah gct Newgarden MM (W)

1880, 3, 23. Joel dis jG (W)

1880, 3, 23. Mary Ann dis jG (W)

1880, 8, 24. Joel rstrq (W)

1881, 5, 24. Maria gct Stillwater MM (W)

1919, 7, 22. Charles D. rocf Middleton MM,O., dtd 1919,6,21 (W)

1922, 1, 24. Charles D. & w, Tacy M., & ch, Walter S. & Dorothy, gct Middleton MM (W)

1924, 11, 18. Alice M. S. & dt, Mary Evaline,

KIRK, continued
    gct Chester MM, Pa. (W)
1928, 3, 20. Charles D., Tacy M. & ch, Wal-
    ter S., Dorothy M. & William J., rocf
    Middleton MM, dtd 1928,2,18 (W)

KIRKPATRICK
1881, 2, 26. Ida recrq (G)

KIRKWOOD
1831, 5, 24. John rocf Sadsbury MM, Pa., dtd
    1831,2,5
1831, 7, 19. John dis mcd

KITHKART
1876, 6, 22. Jennie N. rocf Milford MM, Ind.,
    dtd 1876,4,22 (G)
1885, 12, 23. Jane N. gct Maryville MM, Tenn.
    (G)

KNIGHT
1912, 3, 20. Elizabeth recrq (G)
1913, 7, 23. Elizabeth dropped from mbrp (G)

KNOLL
1906, 10, 24. Zella recrq (G)
1911, 6, 21. Zella relrq (G)

KOLLING
1836, 1, 17. Cert rec for Elizabeth & fam
    from Menden 2 months mtg (German), end to
    Pennsville MM

KUGH
1894, 4, 25. Mary recrq (G)

LACOCK
1815, 9, 4. Naomi gct Plainfield MM

LACY
1805, 5, 18. Amos rocf Gunpowder MM, dtd
    1805,1,26
1816, 8, 20. Ephraim dis disunity

LADD
1832, 4, 12. Elizabeth d ae 45
----, --, --. Peter d 1864,4,6; m Catharine
    ----- d 1866,7,18
    Ch: Deborah   b 1833,11,22
        Martha   " 1839, 7, 19
        Anna   " 1842, 2, 1
        Catharine   " 1848, 6, 26
        Robert
        Sarah
         Ledbetter
1834, 1, 1. Anna m Isaac THOMAS
----, --, --. Benjamin d 1851,5,31 ae 68 bur
    Smithfield; m Hannah -----
    Ch: Elizabeth b 1835, 10, 8
        Lydia   " 1837, 8, 15
        Hannah   " 1839, 9, 28
1836, 11, 30. Mary m Wm. MADDOX
1840, 8, 26. Robert P., s Robert & Mary,

Harrison Co., O.; m in West Grove MH,
Ruanna THOMAS, dt Peter & Mary, Harrison
Co., O.(Robert P. d 1851,7,9 ae 34 bur
    Ch: Sarah Ann b 1842, 11, 2[West Grove
        Mary Eliza-
        beth   " 1846, 2, 28
        Robert P.   " 1851, 7, 19
----, --, --. James D. & Elizabeth
    Ch: Ellen R.   b 1844, 4, 10
        Oliver M.   " 1846, 6, 24
        Mary F.   " 1849, 12, 15
        Virginia   " 1852, 12, --
        Caroline C." 1855, 6, 29
----, --, --. William H. & Caroline E.
    Ch: Ellen C.   b 1849, 8, 8
        Benjamin W." 1851, 9, 8
        Marianna C." 1854, 3, 3
        Charles C. " 1856, 7, 22
        William C. " 1858, 10, 5
1848, 8, 23. Mary E. m Elihu B. STANLEY
1854, 11, 1. Ruannah T. m Robt. T. HARGRAVE
1858, 11, --. Robert d
1858, 12, 1. Sarah L. m Milton R. PETTIT
1862, 5, 28. Anna m Henry P. COBBS
1864, 9, 28. Sarah Ann m David P. STRATTON
1866, 5, 30. Mary E. m Thos. E. THOMPSON

1831, 8, 23. Robert & w, Mary T., & ch, Ann,
    Robert, Pleasant & Mary Ladd, & his step
    dt, Caty Terrell, rocf Wayne Oak MM, Va.,
    dtd 1831,7,2
1832, 6, 19. Peter & w, Catharine, & ch,
    Lucy Ann, Mary, Emily & Robert Crew &
    Sarah LEadbetter, rocf Wayne Oak MM, Va.,
    dtd 1832,5,5
1837, 4, 18. Joseph Jones gct Smithfield MM,
    to m Isabella Ladd
1849, 8, 21. Lucy Ann Barnes (form Ladd) dis
    mcd
1859, 7, 20. Robert d 1858,10,30 ae 85 (an
    elder)
1860, 10, 24. John C. Hill gct Smithfield to
    m Hannah Ladd
1861, 10, 22. Peter dis jG
1863, 3, 22. Darahann dis jG
1864, 7, 19. Catharine dis jG
1864, 7, 19. Deborah dis jG
1864, 9, 21. David P. Stratton rocf Spring-
    dale MM, Ia., to m Sarah Ann Ladd (G)
1865, 1, 24. Elizabeth & Hannah dis disunity
    (W)
1865, 3, 21. Benjamin dis mcd (W)
1865, 6, 20. Thomas dis jG (W)
1866, 8, 22. Mary d 1865,8,15 ae 82 (an
    elder)
1866, 11, 20. Caroline E. dis disunity (W)
1867, 12, 24. Sally Ann Thompson (form Ladd)
    dis mcd & jG (W)
1868, 7, 23. Deborah Thomas (form Ladd) con
    mcd (G)
1873, 7, 24. Robert P. con mcd (G)
1874, 12, 24. Elizabeth & ch, Oliver I. &
    Anna B. recrq (G)

LADD, continued
1877, 5, 22. Robert P. dis mcd & jG (W)
1884, 11, 19. Robert P. & w, Elizabeth, & ch,
     Oliver T., Ella Dora, Virginia & Ida May,
     gct New Sharon MM, Ia. (G)

LAMB
1831, 7, 19. Hannah dis jH
1914, 2, 25. Marie recrq (G)

LAMBERT
1828, 9, 19. Susanna dis jH
1835, 12, 22. Daniel dis disunity

LAMHORN
1875, 2, 23. Anna M. (form Hall) dis mcd (W)

LAMPHREY
1908, 11, 25. Carrie Thompson relrq (G)

LANNING
1824, 12, 21. Rachel (form Burson) dis mcd

LARGE
1818, 6, 23. Sarah & Sarah Jr. rocf Sadsbury
     MM, dtd 1818,4,7

LARKIN
----, --, --. John b 1807,6,18; m Sarah -----
     Ch: Isaac   b 1833, 11, 23
1825, 6, 7. Rees, s Joseph & Rachel, Harri-
     son Co., O., b 1802,2,26; m in Harris-
     ville, Agness ROBERTS, dt Ezekiel & Anna,
     Harrison Co., O., b 1803,3,4
     Ch: Charles   b 1826, 11, 19
         Rachel Ann " 1828, 10, 15
         Joseph   " 1831, 4, 20
         Ezekiel R. " 1833, 5, 27 d 1834, 8,12
         John   " 1834, 5, 12

1817, 10, 21. Joseph & w, Rachel, & ch, Rees,
     John S. & Joseph William, recrq
1828, 11, 18. Rachel dis jH
1829, 6, 23. Agness dis jH
1830, 11, 23. John dis jH
1831, 6, 21. Townsend T. con mcd
1836, 7, 19. Joseph Jr. dis jH
1837, 3, 23. Joseph & w, Rachel, & dt, Ann,
     gct Fall Creek MM (H)
1837, 3, 23. Joseph W. gct Fall Creek MM (H)
1837, 3, 23. Reese & w, Agness, & ch, Charles,
     Rachel Ann, Joseph & John, gct Fall Creek
     MM (H)
1837, 5, 25. John S. & w, Sarah, & ch, Isaac
     & Mary Ann, gct Fall Creek MM (H)
1841, 7, 22. Margaret gct Fall Creek MM (H)
1841, 10, 19. Townsend T. dis mcd
1856, 4, 22. Mary (form Howard) dis mcd

LATHRAM
1869, 11, 25. Frances Ann recrq (G)

LAWRENCE
----, --, --. Thomas & Isabella
     Ch: Robert
          Barclay b 1823, 7, 24
     Thomas m 2nd Deborah -----
     Ch: Thomas   b 1827, 3, 9
         Julia AnnW." 1829, 9, 26
         Deborah
          Ricks   " 1831, 10, 30
         Margaret J." 1834, 8, 30
         Mary Ann   " 1837, 2, 20
         Martha
          Murry   " 1841, 7, 22
1833, 1, 27. Thomas d bur Short Creek
1833, 1, 30. Julia Ann d bur Short Creek
----, --, --. Robert B. & Tacy
     Ch: William Bates
                b 1851, 12, 6
         Thomas   " 1855, 8, 10 d 1858, 8,31
         Edward M. " 1858, 9, 15
         Robert H. " 1861, 5, 1
         Mary Isa-
          bella   " 1863, 7, 3
         Benjamin
          Bates   " 1866, 11, 6
1858, 5, 27. Deborah R. m Wm. J. HARRISON
1858, 5, 27. Mary Ann m Oliver FLANNER
1860, 12, 26. Margaret I. m Samuel HARRISON

1833, 2, 19. Mary & Ann D. rocf Western
     Branch MM, Va., dtd 1832,10,27
1833, 2, 19. Thomas & w, Deborah, & ch,
     Robert Barclay, Thomas, Julian Wilkinson &
     Deborah Ricks Lawrence, rocf Western Branch
     MM, Va., dtd 1832,10,27
1844, 4, 23. Ann D. Test (form Lawrence) con
     mcd
1847, 6, 21. Abigail M. gct Green Plain MM
     (H)
1850, 10, 22. Robert B. gct Smithfield MM, to
     m Tacy Bates
1851, 9, 23. Tacy B. rocf Smithfield MM, dtd
     1851,6,23
1855, 10, 23. Mary gct Salem MM (W)
1863, 2, 24. Tacy dis jG (W)
1867, 5, 21. Deborah & Martha dis jG (W)
1885, 2, 25. Emmet recrq (W)
1886, 2, 24. Robert H. relrq (G)
1903, 6, 24. Emmet dropped from mbrp (G)

LEADBETTER
1832, 6, 19. Sarah rocf Wayne Oak MM, Va.,
     dtd 1832,5,5, with Peter Ladd fam

LEE
1815, 6, 20. Mary rocf Gunpowder MM, dtd
     1813,11,24
1844, 10, 22. Elvira B. [Lea] (form Branson)
     con mcd
1845, 3, 18. Elvira B. gct Smithfield MM
1892, 10, 19. Evelyn recrq (G)

LEESE
1813, 2, 23. Sarah recrq
1816, 10, 22. Sarah Matson (form Lees) dis mcd

LEGGET
1891, 12, 23. Leroy H. recrq (G)
1891, 12, 23. Mary E. recrq (G)
1903, 6, 24. Leander [Leggitt] dropped from
    mbrp (G)

LEMON
1896, 3, 25. George E. recrq (G)
1902, 8, 20. George A. [Lemons] dropped from
    mbrp (G)

LERENBERRY
1891, 3, 25. Charles & Patsy recrq (G)

LESLIE
1813, 8, 24. Cert rec for Margaret & Eliza-
    beth from Nottingham MM, dtd 1813,6,11,
    end to Plymouth MM
1813, 8, 24. Cert rec for Robert & w, Rachel,
    & ch, Thomas, Mary, Sarah, Robert, John-
    son & Levi, from Nottingham MM, dtd 1813,
    6,11, end to Plymouth MM

LEVENBERRY
1895, 8, 21. Patsy relrq (G)

LEVERING
1907, 3, 20. Charles dropped from mbrp (G)
1907, 3, 20. Patsy dropped from mbrp (G)

LEWIS
1759, 8, 10. Henry b
1768, 5, 2. Rebecca b
----, --, --. Henry & Susanna
    Ch: -----   b 1786, 11, 24
        -----   " 1788, 12, 1
        -----   " 1790, 12, 10
        -----   " 1793, 3, 26
        -----   " 1795, 6, 22
        -----   " 1797, 9, 2
        -----   " 1799, 10, 4
        -----   " 1802, 5, 25
        -----   " 1804, 7, 17
        -----   " 1806, 11, 8
-----,--,--.   Thomas & Mary
    Ch: Morgan   b 1789, 7, 25
        Thomas   " 1791, 6, 14
        Mary   " 1795, 4, 5
        Lydia   " 1797, 11, 11
        Enos   " 1799, 10, 9
        Katey   " 1801, 9, 14
        Emrey   " 1803, 6, 11
        Harvey   " 1806, 1, 26
        Ira   " 1807, 6, 8
        Atlantic-
          otion   " 1809, 5, 12
        Sirah   " 1811, 9, 14
        Ensley   " 1814, 8, 13
1795, 4, 5. Mary Jr. b

1797, 10, 9. Enos b
1798, 6, 22. Catharine b
1806, 1, 26. Harvey b
1806, 11, 8. Elijah b
1809, 5, 5. Atlantic 0. b
1809, 9, 17. Mary d ae 21 bur Short Creek
1811, 5, 26. Susanna d ae 47 bur Short Creek
1811, 5, 29. Morgan, s Thos. & Mary, Jeffer-
    son Co., O., b 1789,7,25; m in West Grove
    MH, Mary THORN, dt Isaac & Hannah, Jeffer-
    son Co., O., b 1792,12,17
    Ch: Isaac   b 1812, 11, 19
        Thomas   " 1815, 1, 6
        Hannah   " 1817, 7, 27
        Sarah   " 1820, 1, 21
        Mary Ann " 1822, 8, 28
        William   " 1824, 12, 11
        Parker   " 1827, 3, 4
        Rachel   " 1829, 8, 28
1814, 2, 2. Esther m Benjamin LUNDY
1815, 11, 30. Henry, s Samuel & Katharine,
    Jefferson Co., O.; m in Short Creek MH,
    Rebecca LUPTON, dt Jonathan & Sarah, Jef-
    ferson Co., O.
1816, 10, 13. Lydia m Geo. FRAME
1818, 4, 1. William, s Henry & Susanna, b
    1786,11,24; m in Mt. Pleasant, Lydia
    STANTON, dt Benj. & Abigail, Jefferson
    Co., O., b 1794,10,11
    Ch: Morris   b 1820, 9, 6 d 1823, 9,19
          bur Harrisville
        Maryann   b 1822, 4, 8
        Lucinda   " 1823, 11, 23 " 1829, 6,10
        Susanna   " 1825, 12, 30 " 1829, 5,4
        David Stan-
          ton   " 1827, 10, 17 " 1828, 9,13
        Lucinda Su-
          sanna   " 1830, 10, 15 " 1832, 8, 9
1819, 3, 31. Lewis, s Henry & Susanna, Jef-
    ferson Co., O.; m in Mt. Pleasant, Eliza-
    beth RATCLIFF, dt Wm. & Mary
    Ch: Martha
        Ann   b 1821, 9, 20
        Mary   " 1825, 12, 21
        Susan H.   " 1833, 12, 3
        Wm. Henry " 1835, 2, 3
1819, 10, 28. Hannah m Chas. W. GRIFFITH
1820, 8, 31. David, s Samuel & Sarah, Belmont
    Co., O.; m in Harrisville, Hannah LUKINS,
    dt Moses & Sarah, Belmont Co., O.
1821, 5, 22. Henry Jr. d ae 16 bur Short
    Creek
1826, 3, 2. Thomas, s Thos. & Mary, Harrison
    Co., O.; m in Harrisville, Lydia MORRIS,
    dt Edward & Hannah, Harrison Co., O.
1826, 5, 31. Emry, s Thos. & Mary, Harrison
    Co., O.; m in West Grove MH, Rachel THOMAS
    dt Peter & Mary, Harrison Co., O.
    Ch: Mary Ann   b 1827, 3, 9
        Lorenzo   " 1828, 11, 28
1827, 5, 30. Catharine m Thomas GRAY
1829, 2, 25. Mary d
1830, 1, 21. Elizabeth d bur Short Creek

LEWIS, continued

----, --, --. Harvey b 1806,1,26; m Elma -----
    b 1810,11,7
    Ch: Caroline   b 1832, 6, 4
        Mary Le-
          titia   " 1833, 5, 1
        Lydia G.   " 1835, 10, 21
----, --, --. Isaac & Lydia
    Ch: Henry H.   b 1837, 9, 11 (or 1833)
        John G.   " 1839, 8, 27
        Mary Eliza-
          beth   " 1851, 12, 5
        Louisa   " 1844, 5, 30
        Morgan   " 1847, 1, 9
        Rosetta
          Philothea" 1849, 10, 30
        Isaac Jr.   " 1852, 10, 25
1833, 2, 27. Lewis, s Henry & Susannah, Jef-
    ferson Co., O.; m in ----- Eliza CADWALA-
    DER, dt Isaac & Elizabeth
1836, 4, 21. Catharine d ae 41
1837, 5, 18. Henery d ae 77
1838, 2, 15. Rebecca d
1838, 2, 28. Margaret m Joseph HARGRAVE
1845, 10, 21. Henery, s Isaac & Lydia, d ae 82
1858, 5, 1. Evan d ae 58
1861, 10, --. Morgan d ae 14
1867, 12, 11. Rebecca m John PACKER
1870, 7, 25. Isaac d ae 57
1880, 1, 12. Lydia d

1804, 6, 16. Jehu & w, Susanna, & dt, Metil-
    da, rocf Westland MM, dtd 1804,4,28
1807, 2, 21. Jehu & ch, Matilda Wey & Emly,
    gct Westland MM
1807, 7, 18. Samuel con mcd
1808, 4, 19. Rachel Hamilton (form Lewis) dis
    mou
1808, 10, 18. Mary gct Westland MM
1810, 4, 24. John & w, Hannah, & ch, Rachel,
    John, Adoni, Cynthia & Griffith, rocf
    Westland MM, dtd 1810,3,24
1810, 10, 23. Morgan recrq
1811, 7, 23. Thomas recrq
1811, 12, 24. Beulah gct Westland MM
1812, 1, 21. Mary recrq
1812, 5, 19. Samuel dis disunity
1814, 4, 19. Lydia recrq
1816, 2, 20. Sarah gct Westland MM
1816, 9, 20. Sarah gct Westland MM
1817, 5, 20. Samuel gct Plainfield MM (a min-
    or)
1817, 6, 24. Catharine gct Plainfield MM
1817, 7, 22. Thomas & w, Mary, & ch, Enos,
    Katy, Emery, Hervey, Ira, Atlantic Ocean,
    Sarah & Ensley, recrq
1817, 9, 23. Anna gct Plainfield MM
1821, 6, 19. David & w, Hannah, gct Still-
    water MM
1821, 9, 18. Catharine rocf Plainfield MM,
    dtd 1821,8,23
1822, 3, 19. Jacob & w, Mary, & ch, Rachel,
    Ira, Abel & Rees, gct Plainfield MM

1822, 11, 19. Catharine gct New Hope MM, Tenn.
1823, 3, 18. Susan Timberlake (form Lewis)
    dis mcd
1823, 4, 22. Samuel rocf Plainfield MM
1826, 10, 24. Thomas Jr. & w, Lydia, gct Flush-
    ing MM
1828, 2, 19. Catharine rocf Newhope MM, Tenn.
    dtd 1825,6,18, end by Baltimore MM, W.
    Dist. 1827,8,10
1828, 11, 18. Lydia dis jH
1829, 1, 20. Catharine dis jH
1829, 1, 20. Mary Jr. dis jH
1829, 4, 21. Mary & Atlantic Ocean dis jH
1829, 7, 23. Emory & w, Rachel, & ch, Mary
    Ann & Lorenzo, gct Flushing MM (H)
1829, 12, 22. Rebecca dis jH
1830, 4, 22. Enos gct Newgarden MM (H)
1830, 8, 24. Ira dis jH
1832, 4, 24. Thomas dis disunity
1835, 9, 22. Isaac dis jH
1835, 9, 22. Syra dis jH
1835, 12, 22. Lewis & w, Eliza, & ch, Martha
    Ann, Susan H. & William Henry, gct Penns-
    ville MM
1836, 5, 24. Hannah Heberling (form Lewis)
    dis mcd
1836, 5, 24. Sarah Martin (form Lewis) dis
    mcd
1836, 7, 19. Joseph rocf Western Branch MM,
    Va., dtd 1836,3,--, end by Smithfield
1837, 7, 18. Endsley dis mcd
1837, 7, 18. Thomas dis mcd
1837, 11, 21. Margaret J. rocf Western Branch
    MM, Va., dtd 1837,10,28
1837, 12, 19. Emery dis jH
1838, 1, 23. Rachel dis disunity
1839, 6, 18. Julia & Eliza rocf Stillwater
    MM, dtd 1839,2,23
1840, 8, 20. Mary Jr. gct Stillwater MM (H)
1841, 3, 23. Mary gct Somerset MM
1841, 3, 23. Mary Ann gct Honey Creek MM,
    Ind. (H)
1841, 6, 24. William & w, Lydia, gct Honey
    Creek MM, Ind. (H)
1843, 5, 23. Mary Ann, Lorenzo D. & Tacy T.,
    minor ch Emory & Rachel, gct Stillwater MM
1843, 8, 22. Juliann Armstrong (form Lewis)
    rpd mcd
1843, 10, 26. Emory & w, Rachel, & ch, Mary
    Ann, Lorenzo D., Tacy T. & Lydia E., gct
    Stillwater MM (H)
1845, 7, 23. Mary Ann dis jas
1845, 8, 19. Eliza gct Stillwater MM
1846, 5, 19. William J. dis
1847, 4, 20. Ann L., w Wm. J., & ch, Marga-
    ret Ann, Joseph T. & Lucy J., gct Cincin-
    nati MM
1847, 4, 20. Sarah Elizabeth Johnson (form
    Lewis) dis mcd
1848, 7, 18. Elizabeth (form Watkins) dis
    mcd
1849, 2, 20. Joseph M. gct Lower MM, Va.
1850, 10, 22. William rpd mcd

LEWIS, continued
1851, 3, 18. Parker dis mcd
1851, 10, 21. Ann (form Lukens) dis mcd
1853, 8, 23. Lydia Ann (form Newport) dis
    mcd
1862, 11, 19. Sarah, Abel, Reece & Juliet
    dis jW
1886, 5, 19. David Z. recrq (G)
1887, 11, 25. Benjamin S. recrq (G)
1888, 4, 25. David J. & w, Ella N. J., gct
    Winona MM (G)
1892, 9, 21. Clark E. & w, Emma E. B., & ch,
    Sarah T., Esther B., Jessie E. & Seth B.,
    rocf White Water MM, Ind. (G)
1894, 12, 19. Allen recrq (G)
1896, 1, 23. J. Allen relrq (G)
1898, 11, 24. Clark E. & w, Emma B., & ch,
    Sara T., Esther B., Jesse E. & Seth B.,
    gct Whitewater MM, Ind. (G)
1900, 2, 21. Ella H. rocf Tecumseh MM, Mich.
    (G)
1907, 7, 10. Charles gct Pasadena MM, Calif.
    (H)
1909, 11, 24. Ella H. gct Mt. Hebron MM, N. C.
    (G)
1915, 1, 6. Amy Lee & ch, Evan John & Doro-
    thy Ann, gct Orange Grove MM, Calif. (H)

LIDDLE
1884, 1, 31. George L., s David P. & Matilda
    (Ramsey), b

1933, 7, 19. George recrq (G)

LIGHTFOOT
1841, 5, 8. Samuel d ae 73 bur Concord
1844, 4, 24. Hannah M. m John PENROSE

1829, 1, 20. William gct Springboro MM, O.
1835, 1, 20. Isaac rocf Wrichland MM, end to
    Somerset MM
1835, 5, 19. Joseph & w, Rachel, & ch, Law-
    rence & Foster, gct Deerfield MM
1839, 6, 18. Hannah M. rocf Pennsville MM,
    dtd 1839,5,16
1839, 6, 18. Samuel & w, Rachel, rocf Penns-
    ville MM, dtd 1839,5,16
1842, 5, 24. Hannah M. gct SD MM
1842, 5, 24. Rachel gct SD MM
1843, 9, 19. Hannah M. & Rachel rocf SD MM,
    dtd 1843,6,28
1844, 6, 18. Rachel gct Chesterfield MM
1862, 11, 19. Isaac, Emma, Mary, William, Han-
    nah, Samuel, Sarah & Thomas dis jW (G)
1864, 3, 23. Martha gct Plainfield MM, Ind.
    (G)
1911, 8, 22. Elisha B. Steer gct Salem MM,
    to m Lydia K. Lightfoot

LINDEN
1903, 5, 20. John A. & Emily recrq (G)
1907, 3, 20. John A. & Emily dropped from
    mbrp (G)

LINN
1879, 4, 24. Albert & Mary recrq (G)
1881, 2, 26. Sallie E. recrq (G)
1884, 8, 23. Albert & Mary dropped from mbrp
1888, 10, 24. Sally dropped from mbrp (G)
1903, 9, 23. Chester & Norma, ch Viola, rec-
    rq (G)
1905, 3, 22. Charles [Lynn] recrq (G)

LINTON
1838, 2, 20. Sarah Ann rocf Falls MM, Pa.,
    dtd 1837,12,7

LIPSEY
----, --, --. Amasa & Peninah
    Ch: Sarah   b 1791, 10, 23
        Mary   " 1798, 3, 25
    Amasa m 2nd Rachel -----
    Ch: John   b 1801, 12, 12
        Israel   " 1803, 11, 9
        Martha   " 1805, 5, 28
        Edmond   " 1807, 3, 4
1808, 5, 3. Rachel d bur Short Creek
1814, 10, 27. Mary m Jordan PATTERSON
1817, 9, 7. Sarah d bur Short Creek
1819, 3, 4. Amasa, s Rosco & Tamer, Jeffer-
    son Co., O.; m in Short Creek MH, Sarah
    COX, dt Samuel & Jane WOOLMAN
1823, 10, 2. John, s Amasa & Rachel, Jeffer-
    son Co., O.; m in Short Creek MH, Ann
    BURR, dt Wm. & Sarah, Jefferson Co., O.
    Ch: William B. b 1825, 1, 20
        Elwood   " 1828, 3, 6
        Ruthanna   " 1830, 5, 21
        Mary Jane   " 1832, 7, 1
        Sarah Jo-
          sephine   " 1834, 7, 20
        Chalkley   " 1838, 10, 8
        Albert   " 1842, 9, 21
1824, 10, 28. Martha m Jesse BURR
----, --, --. Edmund & Sarah
    Ch: Lydia H.   b 1834, 7, 19
        Martha
          Jane   " 1835, 8, 31
        Eli H.   " 1837, 2, 1
        Mary Ann   " 1838, 3, 16
        Ruth   " 1839, 5, 5
        Amy   " 1841, 9, 6

1812, 12, 22. Amasa gct Westland MM, to m Sa-
    rah John
1813, 7, 20. Sarah rocf Westland MM, dtd 1813,
    2,22
1824, 3, 23. John & w, Ann, gct Flushing MM
1833, 7, 23. Edmund gct Redstone MM, to m
    Sarah Haines
1833, 11, 19. Sarah H. rocf Redstone MM, dtd
    1833,10,30
1842, 1, 18. Edmund & w, Sarah, & ch, Lydia,
    Martha, Eli, Mary Ann, Ruth & Amy, gct
    New Garden MM
1844, 5, 21. John & w, Ann, & ch, William B.,
    Ellwood, Ruthanna, Mary Jane, Sarah J.,

LIPSEY, continued
  Chalkley T., Lemuel & Albert, gct Middleton MM

LISBY
1882, 5, 24. Anna M. & Jennie recrq (G)
1888, 10, 24. Anna & Jennie [Lisbay] dropped
  drom mbrp (G)

LIVELY
1892, 10, 19. R. J., Acton S. & Orin recrq (G)

LIVESEY
1893, 10, 25. Charles, s Jesse K. & Elizabeth,
  Belmont Co., O.; m in Harrisville, Elizabeth W. SMITH, dt Robert & Rebecca S.,
  Monroe Co., O. (W)

1862, 11, 19. Anna, Charles, Elizabeth, Jesse
  & Joseph dis jW (G)
1894, 2, 20. Elizabeth W. gct Somerset MM

LIVINGSTON
1882, 5, 24. George F. & Lida C. recrq (G)
1888, 10, 24. George & Lida dropped from mbrp
  (G)

LLEWELLYN
1893, 1, 24. Benjamin F. Starbuck gct Pennsville MM, to m Anna Llewellyn (W)

LOCKHARD
1883, 6, 20. Samuel & Martha recrq (G)
1885, 10, 21. Samuel J. dropped from mbrp (G)

LOWNES
1814, 9, 29. Charles, s Joseph & Miriam, Belmont Co., O.; m in Short Creek MH, Elizabeth BAILEY, Jr., dt Emmor & Elizabeth,
  Belmont Co., O.
     Ch: Rebecca   b 1815, 9, 8

1814, 9, 5. Charles rocf Baltimore MM for
  W. Dist., dtd 1814,7,18
1816, 4, 23. Charles & w, Elizabeth, gct
  Plainfield MM

LLOYD
1813, 4, 29. Ann [Loyd] m James KINSEY
1818, 10, 28. Susan [Loyd] m Jordan HARRISON
1818, 12, 2. Isaac [Loyd], s John & Mercy,
  Belmont Co., O.; m in Mt. Pleasant, Ruth
  HARRISON, dt Wm. & Margaret, Jefferson
  Co., O.
     Ch: William   b 1819, 8, 30
         John   " 1821, 1, 12
         Margaret   " 1822, 7, 26
         Joshua   " 1824, 7, 27
         Samuel   " 1826, 6, 5
         Mercy   " 1828, 6, 1
         Isaac   " 1830, 2, 6
         Ruth   " 1831, 10, 9
         Jesse   " 1833, 10, 5

     Ch: Susannah   b 1835, 9, 26
1819, 3, 31. Rachel [Loyd] m Eli NICOLS
1835, 12, 13. Mercy [Loyd] d ae 75 bur Short
  Creek
1838, 3, 15. John [Loyd] d ae 73 bur Short
  Creek
1848, 5, 5. William d bur Short Creek
1849, 11, 1. Samuel, s Isaac & Ruth, Belmont
  Co., O.; m in Short Creek MH, Elizabeth M.
  GRUBB, dt Curtis & Ann, Jefferson Co., O.,
  b 1851,2,26 bur Short Creek
     Ch: William G. b 1850, 8, 18
----, --, --. John & Margaret R.
     Ch: Mary Caro-
         line   b 1852, 3, 18
         Wm. Flem-
           ming   " 1855, 8, 4
1853, 9, 21. Samuel, s Isaac & Ruth, Belmont
  Co., O.; m in Harrisville, Edith CATTELL,
  dt David & Margaret, Fayette Co., Pa.
1855, 10, 25. Mercy m Wm. G. KINSEY
----, --, --. John & Margaret
     Ch: Martha Em-
           ma   b 1858, 2, 19
         Sybil T.   " 1860, 8, 13
         Elizabeth
           T.   " 1863, 4, 10
----, --, --. Jesse & -----
     Ch: Laura   b 1859, 2, --
         Mary Ada   " 1860 11, 20 d 1864, 6,20
           ae 3
         Sarah Elma " 1862, 10, 11 " 1864, 7, 2
           ae 1
         Edward Wm.   " 1867,11,22
1859, 12, 28. Joshua, s Isaac & Ruth, Belmont
  Co., O.; m in Mt. Pleasant, Abigail DIL-
  LINGHAM, dt Micajah & Elizabeth (now Johnson), Belmont Co., O.
     Ch: Charles   b 1861, 4, --
1862, 11, 26. Margaret J. m Nixon MORRIS
1864, 6, 20. Ann Laura d ae 5
1869, 1, 3. Isaac d ae 74

1807, 12, 19. John [Loyd] & w, Mary, & ch,
  Joshua, Ann, Isaac, Jesse, Susanna & Rachel, rocf Callawissa MM, dtd 1807,10,24
1813, 4, 20. Joshua gct Muncy MM, Pa.
1816, 10, 22. Joshua rocf Roaring Creek MM,
  dtd 1816,3,13
1819, 3, 23. Isaac & w, Ruth, gct Stillwater
  MM
1819, 7, 20. Joshua gct Stillwater MM
1821, 9, 18. Isaac & w, Ruth, & ch, William
  & John, rocf Stillwater MM, dtd 1821,7,25
1845, 3, 18. William gct Redstone MM, to m
  Eliza M. Hough
1845, 9, 27. Eliza P. rocf Redstone MM, dtd
  1845,7,30
1850, 8, 20. Eliza P. gct Redstone MM
1851, 4, 22. John gct Upper Springfield MM,
  to m Margaret Andrew
1851, 7, 22. Margaret rocf Springfield MM
1855, 5, 23. Samuel & w, Esther C., & s,

LLOYD, continued
      William G., gct Red Cedar MM, Iowa
1856, 12, 24. Jesse rst
1857, 9, 23. Jesse Jr. gct Goshen MM, to m
      Edith Dillingham
1859, 7, 20. Samuel & s, William G. & Louis
      D., rocf Red Cedar MM, Ia.
1859, 10, 19. Edith rocf Goshen MM, dtd
      1859,9,17
1860, 8, 22. Jesse Jr. & w, Edith, & dt,
      Anne L., gct Upper Springfield MM
1861, 12, 25. Jesse & w, Edith, & ch, Anna
      Laura & Mary Adah, rocf Upper Springfield
      MM
1862, 9, 24. Samuel gct Miami MM, to m Debo-
      rah T. Stanton (G)
1862, 11, 19. Nixon Morris rocf Blue River MM,
      Ind., to m Margaret J. Lloyd (G)
1863, 2, 25. Deborah J. rocf Miami MM (G)
1863, 4, 21. Isaac Sr., Isaac Jr., Jesse,
      John, Joshua & Samuel dis jG (W)
1863, 6, 24. Samuel & w, Deborah J., & ch,
      William G. & Lewis D., gct Blue River MM,
      Ind.
1866, 1, 23. Ruth dis jG (W)
1866, 1, 23. Susan dis jG (W)
1866, 1, 23. Ruth Jr. dis jG (W)
1866, 7, 24. Margaret dis jG (W)
1868, 5, 21. John & w, Margaret A., & ch,
      William F., Elizabeth B. & Ruth H., gct
      Bangor MM, Ia. (G)
1868, 5, 21. Joshua & w, Abigail, & ch,
      Chas. H. & Elwood A., gct Bangor MM, Ia.
      (G)
1870, 10, 20. Isaac gct Damascus MM, to m
      Hannah W. Butler (G)
1872, 6, 20. Hannah W. rocf Damascus MM (G)
1880, 2, 26. Jesse & w, Edith, & ch, Albert
      H., Edward W., Henry B. & Josephine, gct
      Freeport MM, O. (G)
1883, 3, 21. Jesse & w, Edith, & ch, Albert
      H., Edward, Henry B. & Josephine, gct
      Greenwich MM, O. (G)
1886, 6,23.   Jesse & w, Edith, & ch, Albert
      H., Edward W., Henry B. & Josephine, rocf
      Greenwich MM, O., dtd 1886,6,10 (G)

LUKENS
----, --, --. Moses b 1763,1,30; m Sarah -----
      b 1768,10,15
      Ch: William   b 1807, 6, 20
          Rachel   " 1795, 12, 27
          Sarah   " 1805, 8, 25
          Ann   " 1810, 10, 23
          Mary   " 1814, 1, 14
1820, 8, 31. Hannah [Lukins] m David LEWIS
1823, 5, 8. Sarah d bur West Grove
1823, 5, 8. Sarah Jr. d ae 18
1823, 12, 31. Moses, s Moses & Sarah, Harri-
      son Co., O.; m in West Grove MH, Eliza-
      beth BARBER, dt Samuel & Ann, Harrison
      Co., O.
      Ch: Samuel B. b 1825, 3, 9

      Ch: Sarah   b 1828, 11, 6
          Ann B.   " 1831, 11, 2
          Martha   " 1840, 1, 27
          Rachel   " 1834, 7, 6
          Lemuel   " 1837, 2, 9
          Mary C.   " 1843, 4, 17
          Harriet
          Elizabeth " 1846, 3, 2
          William
          Ellis   " 1849, 6, 14
1829, 3, 11. Sarah d ae 61
----, --, --. ----- & Elizabeth
      Ch: Rachel
          Lemuel   b 1837, 2, 9
          Martha S. " 1840, 1, 27
          Mary   " 1843, 4, 17
          Harriet   " 1845, 3, 1
1839, 4, 2. Moses [Lukins] d ae 77
1849, 5, 2. Samuel B., s Moses & Elizabeth,
      Harrison Co., O.; m in West Grove MH,
      Deborah JOHNSON, dt Jonathan & Judith,
      Harrison Co., O.
      Ch: William
          Ellis   b 1849, 6, 14
          Judith J. " 1851, 5, 12
          Charles W. " 1855, 12, 24
          Elizabeth
          D.   " 1860, 12, 7
          Susan J. C." 1862, 12, 22
1849, 5, 2. Sarah T. m Achilles D. Johnson
1866, 5,11.   Phebe d
1882, 2, 17. Rachel d

1816, 4, 23. Phebe [Lukins] rocf Plymouth MM,
      dtd 1816,3,18
1816, 5, 2. Moses & w, Sarah, & ch, Hannah,
      Moses, Mary, Sarah, William & Ann, rocf
      Plymouth MM, dtd 1816,4,22
1817, 7, 22. Benjamin rocf Plymouth MM, dtd
      1816,12,13
1817, 11, 18. Rachel [Lukins] rocf Plymouth
      MM, dtd 1817,7,21
1824, 2, 24. Benjamin [Lukins] dis mcd
1829, 9, 19. Rachel, Mary & Ann dis jH
1831, 4, 19. Moses Jr. dis jH
1835, 9, 27. Elizabeth & ch, Samuel B., Sa-
      rah, Ann B. & Rachel, gct Flushing MM
1840, 2, 18. Elizabeth & ch, Samuel B., Sa-
      rah, Ann B., Rachel & Pennel, rocf Flush-
      ing MM, dtd 1839,8,22
1851, 10, 21. Ann Lewis (form Lukens) dis mcd
1856, 3, 18. Rachel Cope (form Lukens) con
      mcd
1858, 3, 24. Elizabeth & ch, Mary Ellen,
      Harriet Elizabeth & William Ellis, gct
      Raysville MM, Ind.
1858, 3, 24. Martha gct Raysville MM, Ind.
1861, 5, 22. Elizabeth & ch, Mary Ellen,
      Harriet Elizabeth & William E., rocf Rays-
      ville MM, Ind.
1861, 5, 22. Martha S. rocf Raysville MM, Ind.
1863, 3, 22. Samuel B. dis jG (W)
1863, 4, 19. Deborah dis jG (W)

LUKENS, continued

1867, 3, 21. Samuel B. & w, Deborah J., & ch,
    Judith J., Chas. Wm., Elizabeth D., Susan
    J. & Mary Edna, gct Gilead MM (G)
1868, 4, 23. Martha L. Wright (form Lukens)
    con mcd (G)
1869, 11, 25. Mary E. Morgan (form Lukens)
    con mcd (G)
1870, 12, 20. Harriet dis jG (W)
1871, 10, 26. Harriet E. McLaughlin (form
    Lukens) dis mcd (G)
1873, 7, 24. William E. dis mcd (G)
1877, 5, 22. William [Lukins] dis mcd (W)
1893, 7, 19. Anna M. J. relrq (G)

LUNDY

1815, 2, 2. Benjamin, s Joseph & Elizabeth,
    Jefferson Co., O.; m in Short Creek MH,
    Esther LEWIS, dt Henry & Susanna, Jeffer-
    son Co., O.

1812, 10, 20. Benjamin rocf Concord MM, dtd
    1812,9,21
1815, 6, 20. Benjamin & w, Esther, gct Plain-
    field MM
1822, 3, 19. Benjamin & w, Esther, & ch, Su-
    sannah M., Elizabeth S. & Charles T., rocf
    Plainfield MM, dtd 1822,2,21
1823, 10, 21. Esther, w Benjamin, & ch, Su-
    sannah M., Elizabeth S. & Charles L., gct
    New Hope MM, Tenn.
1825, 11, 22. Benjamin gct Baltimore MM

LUPTON

-- -, --, --. Nathan & Margaret
    Ch: Lydia R.   b 1807, 1, 28
        Joshua   " 1811, 4, 21
----, --, --. John & Rachel
    Ch: Ruth   b 1808, 9, 25
        Anna   " 1811, 2, 27
        Rachel   " 1814, 3, 20 d 1814, 5, 3
        bur Short Creek
        Mary   b 1815, 9, 17
1812, 12, 31. Henry, s Nathan & Margaret,
    Jefferson Co., O.; m in Short Creek MH,
    Achsa PATTERSON, dt Joseph & Mary, Jeffer-
    son Co., O.
    Ch: Elizabeth   b 1814, 10, 24
        Nathan   " 1817, 1, 21 d 1864, 4, 9
        Joseph P.   " 1819, 3, 15
        Mary P.   " 1821, 1, 21
        Henry Rees " 1824, 9, 30
        David   " 1830, 11, 24
        Elwood   " 1839, 1, 16
1815, 11, 30. Rebecca m Henry LEWIS
1819, 4, 23. Jonathan d ae 79 bur Short Creek
----, --, --. Martin & Lucina
    Ch: Martha   b 1828, 5, 11
        Emmor   " 1831, 8, 14
1830, 3, 31. Ann m James STEER
1830, 4, 28. Ruth m Thos. CONROW
1832, 5, 24. David, s Jonathan & Rachel, b
1836, 2, 4. Anna d ae 7 bur Short Creek

1838, 5, 2. Elizabeth m Thos. BOWMAN
1839, 8, 21. Nathan, s Henry & Achsah, Jeffer-
    son Co., O.; m in Mt. Pleasant, Deborah
    Ann RICKS, dt Arnold & Mary, S. St. Hamp-
    ton Co., Va.
    Ch: Mary Win-
        ston   b 1840, 5, 18
        Achsah P.   " 1842, 4, 19 d 1848, 3, 9
        bur Short Creek
        Julia Anna b 1846, 4, 6
        Laura   " 1848, 5, 19 " 1864, 2,28
        Deborah Ann" 1853, 12, 17
----, --, --. George & Sarah Ann
    Ch: Charles   b 1841, 11, 25 d 1860,10,26
        Sarah W.   " 1843, 6, 2 " 1855,12,28
        Francis   " 1845, 2, 10
        Benjamin C." 1846, 12, 19
        John S.   " 1849, 3, 3
        Lydia Jane " 1851, 4, 17
        George A.   " 1853, 8, 12
        Albert   " 1856, 3, 13
        Lewis   " 1859, 5, 9
1847, 4, 30. Rachel d ae 74 bur Short Creek
1850, 5, 1. Joseph P., s Henry & Achsah,
    Jefferson Co., O., d 1907,10,11 ae 88
    bur Colerain; m in Concord, Rachel STEER,
    dt James & Ruth, Belmont Co., O., d 1887,
    1,17 bur Concord
    Ch: Martha
        Ann   b 1851, 4, 1 d 1900, 3, 2
        bur Concord
        James H.   b 1852, 11, 1
        Edward   " 1862, 10, 8
        Henry   " 1865, 12, 4
1851, 5, 21. Mary P. m James E. MOTT
1851, 10, 29. Isaac, s Henry & Achsah, Jeffer-
    son Co., O., d 1894,8,1 bur Short Creek;
    m in Mt. Pleasant, Mary FLANNER, dt Jacob
    & Charity, Jefferson Co., O.
1851, --, --. Anna d
1852, 4, 28. David, s Henry & Achsah, Jeffer-
    son Co., O.; m in Mt. Pleasant, Sarah
    STRATTON, dt Joseph & Sarah, Jefferson
    Co., O.
    Ch: Anna   b 1853, 2, 26
1859, 4, 28. Achsah P. m David STEER
1860, 8, 30. Mary W. m Elisha B. STEER
1880, 9, 22. James H., s Jos. & Rachel, Bel-
    mont Co., O., b 1852,11,1 d 1929,4,23; m
    in Concord, Ellen M. BUNDY, dt Josiah &
    Asenath, Belmont Co., O. (W)
    Ch: Myra B.   b 1882, 5, 1
        Walter J.   " 1884, 7, 1 d 1901, 7,17
        bur Concord
        Martha Vi-
        ola   b 1888, 8, 16
1907, 3, 27. Ella B. d ae 51 bur Colerain

1805, 5, 18. Joseph rocf Crooked Run MM, dtd
    1805,3,3
1805, 5, 18. Rebecca rocf Crooked Run MM, Va.,
    dtd 1805,3,30
1806, 1, 18. Jonathan & w, Sarah, rocf

LUPTON, continued
    Crooked Run MM, dtd 1805,11,30
1806, 1, 18. Nathan & w, Margaret, & ch,
    Henry, Ann, Gideon & Martin, rocf Crooked
    Run MM, dtd 1805,11,2
1806, 2, 15. Ruth rocf Crooked Run MM, dtd
    1805,11,30
1809, 2, 21. John & w, Rachel, & ch, David,
    Jonathan, Lydia, Francis & George, rocf
    Hopewell MM, dtd 1808,7,4
1810, 7, 24. Joseph dis mou
1819, 3, 23. David gct Plainfield MM
1819, 8, 24. Gideon gct Smithfield MM, to m
    Susanna Carr
1821, 5, 22. Gideon gct Smithfield MM
1822, 7, 23. Gideon & w, Susanna, & ch, Sa-
    rah & Margaret, rocf Smithfield MM, dtd
    1822,5,20
1823, 6, 24. Gideon & w, Susannah, & ch, Sa-
    rah & Margaret, gct Salem MM
1825, 7, 19. Margaret & ch, Rachel Ann, Levi
    & George, rocf Smithfield MM, dtd 1825,6,
    20
1827, 8, 21. Ann & Lydia R. gct Plainfield MM
1827, 8, 21. Nathan & w, Margaret, & s,
    Joshua, gct Plainfield MM
1827, 10, 23. Lucina rocf Salem MM, dtd 1827,
    9,18
1829, 5, 19. David & w, Margaret, & ch, Ra-
    chel, Ann, Levi, George, Lidia & Jehu,
    gct Somerset MM
1829, 9, 19. Margaret rocf Stillwater MM,
    dtd 1829,6,27
1829, 9, 19. Ann rocf Stillwater MM, dtd
    1829,6,27
1829, 9, 19. Lydia R. rocf Stillwater MM,
    dtd 1829,6,27
1829, 9, 22. Nathan & w, Margaret, rocf
    Stillwater MM, dtd 1829,6,27
1831, 6, 21. Jonathan gct Flushing MM, to m
    Rachel Hirst
1831, 11, 22. Rachel rocf Flushing MM, dtd
    1831,10,20
1832, 10, 23. Jonathan & w, Rachel, & s, David,
    gct Somerset MM
1833, 5, 21. Martin & w, Lucinda, & ch, Mar-
    tha & Emor, gct Upper Springfield MM
1837, 8, 22. Morris rocf Somerset MM, dtd
    1837,6,26
1838, 7, 24. Lydia gct Upper Springfield MM
1838, 7, 24. Nathan & w, Margaret, gct
    Upper Springfield MM
1840, 6, 23. Nathan Jr. & w, Deborah Ann,
    gct Salem MM
1840, 9, 22. Sarah Ann rocf Smithfield MM,
    dtd 1840,8,17
1840, 12, 22. Morris gct Somerset MM
1841, 2, 18. George gct Smithfield MM, to m
    Sarah Ann Crew
1842, 2, 22. Nathan & w, Deborah Ann, & dt,
    Mary Winston, rocf Salem MM, dtd 1842,1,
    19
1851, 6, 24. Henry gct Newgarden MM, to m

    Sarah Stratton
1851, 10, 21. Sarah rocf Newgarden MM, dtd
    1851,8,21
1852, 3, 23. Isaac P. & w, Mary B., gct
    Somerset MM
1856, 11, 18. David & w, Sarah, & ch, Anna V.
    & Mary P., gct Plymouth MM
1859, 4, 19. Henry & w, Sarah, gct New Gar-
    den MM
1860, 4, 25. Mary Burns (form Lupton) con mcd
1860, 5, 22. David & w, Sarah, & ch, Anne,
    Mary B. & Achsah Elizabeth, rocf Plymouth
    MM, dtd 1860,4,23
1861, 3, 20. Nathan Updegraff gct Upper
    Springfield MM, to m Lucina Lupton
1862, 11, 19. Joseph R., Rachel, Martha Ann,
    James H., Edward & John dis jW
1862, 11, 19. Rachel, Josiah, William, Ann,
    Hannah, Thomas, John, Norris, Rebecca,
    Mary, Harvey, David, Margaret, Rachel Ann,
    John, Hannah, Margaret Jr., Ann & Martha
    dis jW
1863, 2, 24. Isaac & w, Mary, rocf Plymouth
    MM, dtd 1863,1,19
1863, 2, 24. Sarah Ann dis jG (W)
1863, 12, 22. David & w, Sarah, & ch, Annie,
    Mary C., Achsah Elizabeth & Drusilla S.,
    gct Newgarden MM
1864, 4, 2. Nathan's d rpd (a trustee) (G)
1865, 7, 18. Deborah Ann dis jG (W)
1866, 7, 25. Julia A. Ratcliff (form Lupton)
    con mcd (G)
1872, 11, 19. Francis, Benjamin C. & Wm. S.
    dis jG (W)
1875, 2, 23. Isaac B. & w, Mary, gct New
    Garden MM (G)
1878, 4, 25. Achsah E. gct Salem MM, O. (G)
1878, 4, 25. Mary P. gct Salem MM, O.
1879, 5, 22. Anna gct Salem MM (G)
1881, 3, 24. Samantha recrq (G)
1881, 8, 23. Anna (form Thomas) dis mcd & jG
    (W)
1882, 6, 20. Isaac B. & w, Mary, rocf New-
    garden MM, dtd 1882,5,25 (W)
1890, 10, 21. Edward F. dis mcd & jas (W)
1890, 10, 21. Henry W. dis mcd (W)
1900, 1, 24. George A. relrq (G)
1904, 5, 24. Myra B. dis jas (W)
1908, 10, 21. George A. recrq (G)
1909, 12, 22. Charles T. gct Washington MM,
    D. C. (G)
1911, 4, 19. A. Russell relrq (G)
1917, 8, 21. Viola Paunoff (form Lupton)
    dis jas (W)

LYNCAN
1819, 8, 24. Ursula (form Taylor) dis mcd

LYON
1882, 7, 19. Charles W. & Martha Jane recrq
    (G)
1890, 10, 22. Charles relrq (G)
1897, 1, 20. John R. recrq (G)

LYON, continued
1900, 5, 23. J. R. relrq (G)
1906, 3, 21. Myrtle recrq (G)
1913, 5, 21. Pearl relrq (G)

LYTLE
1894, 3, 21. William, Minnie & Pearl recrq
    (G)
1902, 8, 20. William & Minnie [Lyttle]
    dropped from mbrp (G)

McALLESTER
1896, 3, 25. William E. recrq (G)
1898, 6, 22. William [McAllister] dropped
    from mbrp (G)
1902, 8, 20. William [McAlister] dropped
    from mbrp (G)

McBRIDE
1848, 7, 18. Ann rocf Salem MM, dtd 1848,5,24
1859, 7, 19. Grace rocf Salem MM, dtd 1859,
    6,22
1861, 1, 22. Grace Packer (form McBride) dis
    mcd

McCAN
1805, 10, 19. Tacy gct Salem MM

McCARTNEY
1881, 3, 24. George & Robert recrq (G)
1881, 7, 21. Alphia & Ella recrq (G)
1888, 10, 24. Ella & George dropped from mbrp
    (G)
1807, 4, 24. Ellen, Ola, Walter T., David &
    Edwin dropped from mbrp (G)
1912, 3, 20. Lota, Hazel & Della recrq (G)
1914, 1, 21. Arnold recrq (G)

McCARTY
1812, 7, 21. Hannah rocf Hopewell MM, dtd
    1812,5,14
1828, 3, 20. Abigail (form Howard) dis mcd
1903, 4, 22. Elmer & Ola recrq (G)
1903, 5, 20. Walter, David T. & Edwin H.
    recrq (G)

McCOMBS
1867, 1, 21. Sarah (form Johnson) con mcd (G)
1868, 2, 20. Sarah & ch, Elizabeth Ann,
    Judith D., Achilles Douglas, Samuel Tiry
    & Martha Ellen Johnson, gct Spring Creek
    MM, Ia.

McCONNELL
1836, 2, 23. Townsend rocf Middleton MM, dtd
    1835,12,21
1841, 9, 21. Townsend dis mcd
1860, 5, 23. Townsend rst at Pleasant Plain
    MM, Ia. on consent of this mtg
1898, 9, 21. Samuel recrq (G)

1907, 6, 19. Samuel dropped from mbrp (G)
1909, 4, 21. Samuel relrq (G)

McCOY
1868, 7, 23. Edmund H. recrq (G)
1868, 7, 23. Edward M. recrq (G)
1879, 4, 24. Halley relrq (G)

McCUE
1903, 3, 25. Lillian M. & Mildred Edna recrq
    (G)
1912, 2, 21. Gertie & Irene recrq (G)
1915, 2, 24. John E. recrq (G)
1915, 2, 24. William, Belle & Hobert recrq
    (G)

McCURRY
1903, 4, 22. Lillie Dale & Mary Elva recrq
    (G)
1916, 3, 23. Lillie, Mary & Pansy dropped
    from mbrp (G)

McGENAISS
1826, 4, 22. Mary, dt James & Mary, b
1827, 1, 1. Mary M. d bur Short Creek

McGHIE
1890, 4, 23. Viola recrq (G)

McGILL
1862, 11, 19. Deborah dis jW (G)
1882, 3, 29. Minnie recrq (G)
1890, 12, 24. Minnie(McGill) Chambers relrq
    (G)

McGREW
1806, 4, 23. Joseph, s James B. & Elizabeth,
    W. Moreland Co., Pa.; m in Plymouth MH,
    Margaret HAMMOND, dt Geo. & Deborah,
    Jefferson Co., O., d 1821,5,6 ae 35
1830, 6, 10. Mary (Ong) [Megrew], w J. B.,
    d ae 37 bur Smithfield
1831, 8, 31. Willets [Megrew], infant, d bur
    Smithfield
1833, 8, 31. Aletta [Megrew], w T. B., d bur
    Smithfield
1837, 5, 17. John B. [Megrew], s Joseph, d
    bur Smithfield
----, --, --. Finley & Rebecca [Megrew]
    Ch: Jacob O.   b 1842, 11, 12
        James   " 1844, 12, 11
        Eliza Jane " 1846, 7, 31
----, --, --. James & Ann C. [Megrew]
    Ch: Elizabeth
        A.   b 1842, 12, 10
        Lydia B.   " 1844, 5, 14
        Gilbert   " 1846, 8, 15
        Susan Jane " 1848, 3, 1
        Eliza G.   " 1851, 11, 4
1844, 11, 3. Elizabeth [Megrew], w Nathan, d
    ae 61 bur Smithfield
1849, 4, 25. Oliver [Megrew] d ae 25 bur
    Smithfield

McGREW, continued
1865, 11, 8. Lindley B. d ae 76
1870, 9, 21. Eliza Jane m Eli W. GIBBONS (W)
1874, 9, 23. Eliza G. m Richard ASHTON (W)
1875, 10, 20. Susan m Robert P. THOMAS (W)
1876, 3, 7. Rebecca D., w Findley, d ae 57
      bur Smithfield
1876, 6, 6. James W. d ae 68 bur Smithfield
1877, 3, 21. Walter, s James C. & Mary, b
1877, 5, 24. Lydia B. m Clayton HAINES (W)
1886, 4, 29. Gilbert, s James M. & Ann G.,
      Harrison Co., O., b 1846,8,15 d 1920,9,29;
      m in Harrisville, Eliza HALL, dt Wm. &
      Mary T., Harrison Co., O., b 1859,2,1 (W)
         Ch: Mary   b 1887, 10, 3 d 1890, 3,22
               bur Harrisville
            Elma   b 1890, 9, 21
            Edith   " 1890, 9, 21
            Anna   " 1893, 3, 19 d 1926,11, 7
            Caroline " 1895, 2, 1
1890, 12, 13. Finley W. d ae 75 bur Ridge
1893, 1, 11. Ann J., w James, bur Harrisville
1910, 8, 24. Elizabeth A. m Jesse EDGERTON
      (W)
1915, 4, 21. Elma m Elmer STARR (W)
1920, 11, 24. Edith m Custis W. SMITH (W)
1924, 6, 5. Caroline m Edmund SMITH (W)
1925, 5, 7. Eliza H. m Wm. G. STEER (W)

1805, 8, 17. Nathan rocf Redstone MM, dtd
      1805,5,3
18-6, 7, 19. Margaret gct Redstone MM
1807, 7, 18. Jane & Elizabeth, minor ch
      Elizabeth, recrq
1807, 8, 15. Elizabeth recrq
1813, 4, 20. Cert for James C. & fam from
      Redstone MM, dtd 1813,1,29, end to Plymouth
      MM
1851, 12, 23. Ann (form Williams) dis mcd
1875, 10, 19. Jacob O. dis mcd (W)
1876, 1, 18. James A. gct Flushing MM, to m
      Mary W. Smith (W)
1876, 12, 19. Mary W. rocf Flushing MM, dtd
      1876,11,23 (W)
1881, 10, 18. James A. & w, Mary W., & ch,
      Walter & Maurice Austin, gct Springville
      MM, Ia. (W)
1898, 6, 22. Althisa recrq (G)
1907, 6, 19. Asa dropped from mbrp (G)
1921, 2, 22. Edith M. Smith (form McGrew) gct
      Bear Creek MM, Ia. (W)
1926, 6, 22. Anna gct Stillwater MM (W)

McHUGH
1882, 3, 29. Dennis & John recrq (G)

McINTIRE
1882, 5, 24. Dora, James R. & Lula recrq (G)
1888, 10, 24. James, Dora & Lulu dropped from
      mbrp (G)

McINTOSH
1902, 3, 19. George W. & Maggie recrq (G)

1914, 1, 21. George W. recrq (G)

McKANE
1885, 9, 23. Armelda (form McManis) relrq (G)

McKIM
1893, 12, 20. Madge Iola recrq (G)

McKOWAN
1908, 4, 22. James H. recrq (G)

McLAIN
1862, 11, 19. Theodate dis jW

McLAUGHLIN
1871, 10, 26. Harriet E. (form Lukens) dis
      mcd (G)
1892, 11, 23. ----- recrq (G)
1896, 1, 23. Sewell & Pearl recrq (G)
1896, 1, 23. Lida recrq (G)
1896, 4,22. Genevra recrq (G)
1900, 5, 23. Ralph Mitchel, s Minnie, recrq
      (G)
1922, 2, 23. Sewell relrq (G)
1933, 11, 28. Paul gct East Richland MM (G)

McLELLAN
1893, 6, 21. Bessie S. recrq (G)
1893, 6, 21. Eliza J. recrq (G)
1903, 5, 20. Harriet A., Ella M. & Paul D.
      recrq (G)
1907, 3, 20. Harriett, Ella M. & Paul D.
      dropped from mbrp (G)

McMANNIS
1893, 2, 23. Cora, w Wilson, dt John & Eliza-
      beth Hendershot, b

1879, 4, 24. James recrq (G)
1881, 1, 20. Charles E. & w, Elizabeth, &
      ch, Clara E. & Martha, recrq (G)
1881, 2, 26. Kate & Imelda [McMammis] recrq
      (G)
1884, 2, 20. Isaiah recrq (G)
1884, 6, 25. Martha E. dropped from mbrp (G)
1885, 9, 23. Armelda McKane (form McManis)
      relrq (G)
1902, 12, 24. Isaiah dropped from mbrp (G)
1907, 10, 23. James F. [McManus] -----(G)
1913, 1, 22. Orville recrq (G)
1913, 1, 22. Grace recrq (G)

1913, 1, 22. Anna recrq (G)

McMASTERS
1897, 5, 19. Ida May recrq (G)

McMILLAN
1788, 11, 28. Jane b
1811, 10, 30. Sarah m Elias DEW
----, --, --. Joseph b 1795,6,9 d 1837,7,--;
      m Elizabeth ------

McMILLAN, continued
    Ch: Joel   b 1822, 4, 14
        Ruthann   " 1827, 9, 8
1837, 10, 28. Sarah Ann, dt Mahlon & Rachel, b
1842, 5, 13. Ira Vale, s Jacob & Sarah, b
1846, 4, 11. Ruth d ae 83
1848, 5, 30. Mahlon d ae 48
1859, 1, 14. Rachel d ae 60
----, --, --. Thomas R. m Julia A. ----- d
    1894,6,28
    Ch: Mary Inez b 1860, 6, 16 d 1900,10,22
        Henry Iden " 1862, 5, 6
        Geo. Addi-
          son   " 1864, 9, 12
        Charles
          Percy   " 1868, 1, 3
        Eleanor R. " 1870, 6, 7
----, --, --. Eli & Adaline
    Ch: Sallie V. b 1866, 10, 30
        Mary Laura " 1868, 12, 20
        Ira S.   " 1871, 1, 14
        Isaac New-
          ton   " 1873, 1, 12
        Albert E. " 1875, 7, 28
        Ina B.   " 1880, 5, 19
        Edith Olga " 1882, 6, 30
        Ethel Ea-
          lora   " 1882, 6, 30
1880, 7, 26. Sarah d
1884, 11, --. Jacob Sr. d
1890, 1, 5. Eli d
1893, 6, 15. ----- d
1896, 5, 3. Jacob d
1899, 5, 14. Thomas d
1902, 8, 13. Alice Eleanor, dt Henry I. &
    Annie, b
1912, 7, 30. Sarah A. d
1914, 1, 1. Ira Vale d
1918, 6, 4. Elizabeth d

1805, 4, 20. Esther rocf Warrington MM, dtd
    1804,12,8
1809, 5, 23. Jane, Joanna & Sarah recrq
1813, 7, 20. Joanna Allen (form McMillan) dis
    mcd
1821, 5, 22. Uriah recrq
1821, 7, 24. Alice (form Barnhard) dis mcd
1822, 5, 21. Uriah gct Flushing MM, to m
    Rachel Ellis
1822, 11, 19. Rachel rocf Flushing MM, dtd
    1822,8,23
1823, 3, 18. James recrq
1823, 9, 23. Elizabeth & s, Joel, rocf
    Warrington MM, dtd 1823,8,20
1823, 9, 25. Jos. & w, Elizabeth, & s, Joe,
    rocf Warrington MM, dtd 1823,8,20
1824, 10, 19. Phebe (form White) dis mcd
1828, 5, 20. Uriah & w, Rachel, gct Smith-
    field MM
1829, 1, 20. Elizabeth dis jH
1829, 7, 21. Ruth (form Job) dis mcd
1829, 9, 19. Mary dis jH
1829, 9, 22. James Jr. dis mcd

1837, 5, 22. James gct Deerfield MM (H)
1838, 7, 26. Alice gct Deerfield MM (H)
1840, 9, 24. Jane gct Flushing MM (H)
1844, 4, 23. Joel dis disunity
1845, 3, 20. Elizabeth gct Salem MM (H)
1845, 8, 19. Ruthanna gct Salem MM
1853, 6, 23. Jane gct Freeport MM (H)
1855, 6, 20. Uriah & w, Rachel, rocf Ver-
    million MM, dtd 1855,5,5
1855, 12, 19. Uriah & w, Rachel, gct Vermillion
    MM, Ill.
1881, 2, 26. Mahlon recrq (G)
1888, 10, 24. Mahlon dropped from mbrp (G)

McNAMEE
1808, 4, 19. Cert rec for Margaret & ch end
    to Plymouth MM

McNICHOLS
1863, 7, 22. Cyrus gct Plainfield MM, Ind.
    (G)
1863, 7, 22. George con mcd (G)
1863, 9, 23. George gct Plainfield MM, Ind.
    (G)
1863, 10, 21. Martha, Mary, Ruth & Hester,
    the last two minors, gct Union MM, Ind.
    (G)

McPHERSON
1884, 2, 20. Hiram recrq (G)
1895, 11, 21. Hiram relrq (G)

MACE
1805, 7, 20. Cert rec for William & fam from
    Concord MM, dtd 1805,5,21, end to Cour-
    sound MM.
1805, 7, 20. Cert rec for Hannah from Con-
    cord MM, dtd 1805,5,21, end to Cour Sound
    MM

MADDOX
1836, 11, 30. William, s Thos. & Jane, Harri-
    son Co., O.; m in West Grove MH, Mary
    LADD, dt Robert & Mary, Harrison Co., O.
    Ch: Eliza   b 1839, 1, 27
        Thomas   " 1841, 6, 22
        Mary Jane " 1853, 4, 23
        Virginia
          Wilson " 1859, 4, 9
1838, 1, 5. Thomas d ae 62 bur West Grove
1858, 12, 30. Jane d ae 85
1859, 4, 29. Wilson d ae 45
1869, 9, 29. Thos., s Wilson & Mary, Harri-
    son Co., O., b 1841,6,22 d 1919,2,27 bur
    West Grove; m in West Grove MH, Henrietta
    L. HAGUE, dt Henry B. & Sarah Ann, Harri-
    son Co., O.
    Ch: Wilson
          Henry   b 1871, 6, 3 d 1931, 4,29
        Anna Mary " 1874, 12, 22
        Caroline
          Eliza   " 1876, 6, 11
1899, 4, 21. Thomas Joseph, s Wilson & Marga-
    ret, b

MADDOX, continued

----, --, --. Wilson H. m Mary L. -----, dt
Joseph & Francina -----, b 1867,10,15 d
1899,4,-- bur Damascus, O.

----, --, --. Wilson H. m Erba LADD, dt Wm. &
Anna, b 1878,7,23

1824, 12, 21. Thomas & w, Jane, & s, Wilson,
rocf Cedar Creek MM, dtd 1824,9,11

1828, 10, 21. Susanna (form Gwyn) dis mcd

1864, 7, 19. Mary & Eliza dis jG (W)

1870, 10, 18. Henrietta T. (form Hague) dis
mcd & jG (W)

1870, 10, 18. Thomas dis mcd (W)

1877, 12, 18. Mary Jane dis jG (W)

1885, 6, 24. Eliza Cotant (form Mattox) gct
Greenwich MM, O. (G)

1895, 2, 20. Margaret L. rocf Damascus MM,
dtd 1895,1,25 (G)

1908, 4, 22. Erba roc (G)

1912, 2, 21. Anna(Maddox) Halderman relrq (G)

1927, 1, 5. Joseph T. relrq (G)

1932, 4, 20. Erba R. gct Damascus MM, O. (G)

MAGINNIS

1826, 10, 24. Cert rec for Mary from Little
Brittain MM, Pa., dtd 1826,9,16, end back
to that mtg

MANLEY

1843, 12, 19. Amy (form Barrett) con mcd

1851, 10, 21. Amy dis disunity

1860, 5, 23. John rst

1863, 9, 23. Amy recrq (G)

1872, 6, 20. John dis disunity (G)

1872, 8, 22. Amy H. relrq (G)

MANSFIELD

1875, 9, 23. Cassandra (form Kinsey) con mcd
(G)

1896, 6, 24. Clara Elizabeth recrq (G)

1907, 6, 19. Cassie dropped from mbrp (G)

MARCHBANK

1914, 3, 25. Howard & Bessie A. recrq (G)

MARIS

1825, 10, 27. Owen, s David & Sarah, Belmont
Co., O.; m in Short Creek MH, Rachel JEN-
KINS, dt Mishael & Sarah, Jefferson Co.,O.
Ch: Sarah J.   b 1826, 8, 21
    Michael   " 1828, 3, 18
    Mary Ann   " 1830, 1, 20
    Phebe B.   " 1831, 12, 1

1836, 10, 18. Owen & w, Rachel, & ch, Sarah
J., Michal, Mary Anna, Phebe B. & George
J., gct Pennsville MM

1885, 8, 18. Rachel rocf Chesterfield MM, dtd
1885,4,18 (W)

MARKEE

1813, 11, 23. Edith (form Atkinson) dis mcd

MARKESOM

1871, 11, 23. Mary Ann (form Pettit) con mcd
(G)

MARKLEY

1911, 2, 22. Mrs. Lena relrq (G)

MARMON

1884, 7, 23. Asa dropped from mbrp (G)

MARSH

1824, 1, 29. John N., s Wm. & Ann, Jefferson
Co., O.; m in York, Susanna KIRK, dt Eli
& Edith

1824, 5, 18. Susanna gct Smithfield MM

1840, 1, 23. Rebecca T. gct Carmel MM (H)

MARSHALL

1817, 1, 21. Jane rocf Centre MM, dtd 1816,5,
6, end by Redstone MM

1817, 4, 22. William & w, Hannah, & ch, Thomas & Elizabeth,rocf Centre MM, Del., dtd
1816,5,6, end by Redstone MM

1817, 4, 22. Jane Sivil (form Marshall) dis
mcd

1818, 3, 24. William & w, Hannah, & ch, Thomas & Elizabeth, gct Stillwater MM

MARTIN

----, --, --. Isaac & Martha
Ch: Rebecca   b 1810, 9, 24
    Thomas   " 1812, 2, 5
    Sarah   " 1813, 7, 17
    Samuel   " 1815, 10, 19
    Amos G.   " 1815, 11, 6 (?)

1810, 6, 19. Sarah (form Michener) dis mcd

1812, 9, 22. Isaac & w, Martha, & ch, Rebecca
& Thomas, rocf Westland MM, dtd 1812,5,23

1824, 2, 24. Isaac & w, Martha, & ch, Rebecca,
Thomas, Sarah, Samuel & Amos G., gct Somerset MM

1836, 4, 19. Sarah (form Lewis) dis mcd

1853, 12, 20. Phebe (form Kinsey) dis mcd

1859, 9, 22. Beulah W. gct Beaver Falls MM(H)

1881, 3, 24. Edward & Nanie recrq (G)

1884, 7, 23. Edward dropped from mbrp (G)

1888, 10, 24. Nannie dropped from mbrp (G)

1901, 7, 24. Benjamin & Margaret recrq (G)

1912, 12, 25. Sadie Martha recrq (G)

MAREMOON

1807, 5, 16. Samuel [Marymoon] & w, Peggy, &
ch, Rachel, Matilda, Martin, Lettes, Marcy & Rebecca, rocf Jack Swamp MM, N. C.,
dtd 1807,3,7

1807, 7, 18. Martin [Marimoon] & w, Susanna,
& ch, James, Watkins, Paley, Anna & Robert
rocf Jack Swamp MM, N. C., dtd 1807,7,3

1807, 7, 18. Obedience [Merimoon] & dt,
Elizabeth, rocf Jack Swamp MM, N. C., dtd
1806,3,7

MAREMOON, continued
1808, 3, 22. Martin & w, Susanna, & ch,
    James, Watkins, Patey, Ann, Robert & Sa-
    rah, gct Miami MM
1808, 3, 22. Samuel & w, Peggy, & ch, Rachel,
    Matilda, Martin, Lettice & Rebecca, gct
    Miami MM
1808, 3, 22. Obedience & dt, Elizabeth, gct
    Miami MM

MASHAWN
1844, 2, 20. Sarah (form Dilworth) dis mcd
1846, 11, 24. Sarah (form Dilworth) dis mcd

MASON
1889, 3, 20. Samuel recrq (G)
1891, 3, 25. Henry & Eleanor recrq (G)
1907, 3, 20. Henry & Elnor dropped from mbrp
    (G)

MASTERS
----, --, --. Isaac & Sarah
    Ch: Sarah   b 1812, 11, 20
        Martha   " 1815, 9, 29
        Mary   " 1818, 9, 8

1813, 6, 22. Isaac & w, Sarah, & ch, Joseph,
    William, Anne, Margaret, David & Sarah,
    rocf Munsey MM, dtd 1813,5,19
1823, 6, 24. Joseph dis mcd
1824, 8, 28. Anna Smith (form Masters) con
    mcd
1825, 5, 24. Margaret Deming (form Masters)
    con mcd
1829, 5, 19. Naomi rocf Smithfield MM, dtd
    1828,10,20
1831, 9, 20. William & w, Naomi, & ch, David
    & James, gct Smithfield MM
1833, 3, 19. David dis mcd
1835, 6, 23. Sarah Hunt (form Masters) dis
    mcd
1838, 2, 20. Mary & Martha dis jas
1881, 2, 26. William K. recrq (G)
1882, 3, 29. David recrq (G)
1888, 10, 24. William dropped from mbrp (G)
1888, 10, 24. David dropped from mbrp (G)

MATHEW
1896, 1, 23. Charles recrq (G)
1896, 4, 22. Elizabeth May recrq (G)

MATSON
1755, 5, 6. Nehemiah b
1812, 5, 27. Enoch, s Nehemiah & Rachel,
    Jefferson Co., O.; m in West Grove MH, Sa-
    rah THOMPSON, dt Bradway & Ann, Jefferson
    Co., O.
1817, 6, 4. Enoch, s Nehemiah & Rachel,
    Harrison Co., O.; m in West Grove MH, Es-
    ther GRAY, dt Elijah & Mary, Harrison Co.,
    O.
----, --, --. William & Sarah
    Ch: William   b 1819, 6, 20

    Ch: David   b ----, 11, 11
        Elijah   " 1817, 7, 11 (?)
1828, 7, 30. Rachel m Aquilla HURFORD
1838, 10, 31. William d bur Harrisville
1838, 11, 7. David d bur Harrisville
1839, 11, 7. Elijah d bur Harrisville
1864, 12, 23. Hanna Mary, dt John & Phebe, b

1812, 1, 21. Enoch recrq
1814, 10, 18. William recrq
1816, 10, 22. Sarah (form Lees) dis mcd
1819, 2, 23. Mary (form Townsend) con mcd
1819, 8, 24. Nehemiah recrq
1831, 2, 22. Sarah recrq
1831, 4, 19. David, Elijah, William, John,
    Morris & Nehemiah, ch Wm. & Sarah, recrq
1845, 4, 22. Morris dis mcd
1888, 5, 22. Hannah Mary recrq (W)
1914, 2, 25. Elnora recrq (G)
1917, 4, 25. Eleanor Douglas relrq (G)
1920, 8, 18. Elnora Douglas recrq (G)

MAULE
----, --, --. Joshua & Sarah
    Ch: James   b 1838, 12, 19
        Jacob   " 1840, 8, 18
        Henry E.   " 1851, 10, 2
1875, 10, 27. Jacob, s Joshua & Sarah N.
    (Echroyd), Belmont Co., O., b 1840,8,18;
    m in Concord, Rachel RALEY, dt Asa & Asen-
    ath, Belmont Co., O., b 1839,1,2 d 1920,
    2,12 bur Colerain (W)
    Ch: Mary   b 1880, 11, 9
1904, 9, 7. Mary m J. Rowland HAINES (W)

1831, 12, 20. Joshua rocf Radnor MM, dtd 1831,
    12,8
1832, 1, 24. Joshua gct Muncy MM, Pa., to m
    Sarah N. ECROYD
1832, 2, 21. Amos Steer gct Radnor MM, to m
    Ann Maule Jr.
1833, 4, 23. Sarah N. rocf Muncey MM, dtd
    1833,2,20
1841, 8, 24. Edward, minor, recrq
1844, 12, 24. Edward, minor, gct Salem MM
1847, 2, 23. Edward, minor, rocf Salem MM,
    dtd 1847,1,20
1852, 11, 23. Edward gct Pennsville MM, to m
    Hannah Penrose
1853, 3, 22. Edward gct Pennsville MM
1862, 11, 19. Joshua, Sarah & Jacob dis jW (G)
1865, 12, 19. Joshua dis jG (W)
1867, 7, 23. Sarah dis jG (W)
1876, 1, 18. James E., minor, recrq (W)
1889, 3, 19. James E. gct Salem MM (W)

MEDCALF
1830, 3, 3. Joseph H., s Moses & Susanna,
    Belmont Co., O.; m in Mt. Pleasant, Matil-
    da PARKER, dt Jesse & Anna, Jefferson
    Co., O.   [Creek
1848, 6, 8. Lydia [Metcalf] d ae 23 bur Short
1814, 11, 22. Moses [Medkeff] & fam rocf Deer

MEDCALF, continued
Creek MM, dtd 1814,8,25, end to Concord MM
1829, 5, 19. Jesse [Metcalf] & w, Asenath, & ch, Oliver, Caroline & Joshua, gct Stillwater MM
1833, 12, 24. David dis mcd
1833, 12, 24. Moses Jr. dis mcd
1836, 11, 22. Mary Wildman (form Medcalf) con mcd
1837, 3, 21. Susanna [Medkiff] gct Pennsville MM
1837, 6, 20. Joseph [Midcaff] & w, Martha, gct Pennsville MM
1847, 7, 20. Lydia S. rocf Baltimore MM for E. & W. Dist., dtd 1847,5,6

MEEK
1892, 3, 23. William Walker recrq (G)
1896, 3, 25. Love recrq (G)
1915, 2, 24. Mary Jane recrq (G)

MEGRAIL
----, --, --. James & Mary
Ch: Alfred   b 1824, 1, 9 d 1862,12,14 bur Cross Creek
    Thomas   b 1825, 6, 19
    Edith   " 1827, 3, 25
    Elmira   " 1829, 1, 16 d 1862,11,17 bur Cross Creek
    William P. b 1831, 2, 7
    George E. " 1833, 8, 16
    John L.   " 1838, 11, 1
    Lindley H. " 1842, 4, 2
1840, 5, 13. Nathan d ae 69 bur Smithfield
1842, 9, 22. Thomas d ae 67 bur Smithfield
1842, 11, 8. Mary d ae 39 bur Smithfield (dt Thomas)
1849, 6, 24. Mary R., dt Alfred & Amy, b
1854, 1, 10. Rebecca, w Thos., d ae 80 bur Smithfield
1854, 7, 4. Amy, w Alfred, d
----, --, --. Alfred & Rebecca
Ch: Mary R.   d 1862,12, 4 ae 14 bur Cross Creek
    George G. b 1859, 6, 27
    Amy Ann   " 1862, 10, 6
1859, 2, 3. William [McGrail] d
1862, 11, 17. Lamira [McGrail] d
1862, 12, 14. Alfred [McGrail], s James, d
1868, 12, 11. Mary [McGrail], w James, d ae 69
1875, 1, 12. James [McGrail] d ae 76 bur Harrisville

1857, 7, 21. George E. dis disunity
1857, 11, 24. Alfred [McGrail] gct Providence MM, to m Rebecca Gilbert
1858, 5, 18. Rebecca rocf Providence MM, dtd 1858,4,29
1861, 1, 22. John L. dis mcd
1863, 5, 19. Rebecca [McGrail] & ch, George G. & Amy Ann, gct Providence MM (W)
1866, 6, 19. Lindley H. dis disunity & military service (W)

MEISCHLAN
1905, 7, 18. Alice M. (form Hall) dis disunity (W)

MELLENGER
1905, 7, 19. Daniel recrq (G)

MELLIGAN
1837, 2, 21. Sarah dis disunity

MELTON
1848, 1, 22. Joseph d bur Short Creek

MENDENHALL
----, --, --. Aaron b 1779,9,2; m Deborah ----- b 1793,10,9
Ch: Elizabeth b 1814, 7, 29
    Isaac B. " 1815, 11, 4
    Joseph   " 1817, 8, 7
    Lydia   " 1819, 8, 9
    Edith   " 1821, 6, 25
    Rachel   " 1823, 2, 14
    Thirza   " 1826, 1, 16
    Naomi   " 1828, 5, 15
----, --, --. ----- & Sarah
Ch: Phebe   b 1814, 12, 31
    Isaac   " 1817, 2, 14
    Hannah   " 1818, 12, 3
    Asenath   " 1821, 2, 11
    Milton   " 1823, 1, 24
    Israel   " 1825, 1, 10
    Pennock   " 1827, 4, 26
1823, 3, 27. Orpha m Levi BOULTON
1835, 9, 30. John, s Aaron & Lydia, Columbiana Co., O.; m in Concord, Hannah MILHOUSE, dt Wm. & Martha, Belmont Co., O.
1844, 8, 1. Milton, s Israel & Sarah, Harrison Co., O.; m in Harrisville, Sarah Jane TRIBBY, dt John & Ann, Harrison Co., O.
Ch: John Tribby b 1845, 7, 23
    Sarah Ann   " 1847, 5, 6
    James   " 1849, 7, 11
    Rachel   " 1851, 9, 12
1848, 4, 27. Cyrus, s Aaron & Rebecca, Columbiana Co., O.; m in Short Creek MH, Anna T. UPDEGRAFF, dt David & Rebecca T., Jefferson Co., O.
1861, 11, 18. Annie T. d ae 41

1815, 6, 20. Israel & w, Sarah, & dt, Phebe, rocf Kennet MM, dtd 1815,4,4
1816, 4, 23. Mary rocf Kennet MM, Pa., dtd 1816,1,2
1817, 6, 24. Aaron & w, Deborah, & ch, Elizabeth & Israel B., rocf Kennet MM, Pa., dtd 1817,4,16
1817, 6, 24. Lydia rocf Kennet MM, Pa., dtd 1817,4,8
1817, 12, 23. Orpha rocf Kennet MM, Pa., dtd 1817,5,6
1821, 10, 23. Mary gct Kennet MM, Pa.
1828, 11, 18. Sarah & Deborah dis jH
1830, 3, 25. Aaron & w, Deborah, & ch, Eliza-

MENDENHALL, continued
    beth, Isaac B., Joseph, Lydia, Edith, Ra-
    chel, Thirza & Naomi, gct Deerfield MM (H)
1830, 3, 25. Sarah & ch, Phebe, Isaac, Han-
    nah, Asenath, Milton, Israel & Peninah,
    gct Middleton MM (H)
1830, 6, 22. Elizabeth, Isaac, Joseph, Lydia,
    Edith, Rachel, Thirza & Naomi, ch Aaron &
    Deborah, gct Deerfield MM
1830, 6, 22. Phebe, Isaac, Hannah, Israel,
    Asceneth, Milton & Penick, gct Middleton
    MM
1835, 12, 22. Hannah gct Middleton MM
1838, 1, 23. Asenath, Milton & Israel, ch
    Israel & Sarah, rocf Middleton MM, dtd
    1837,7,17
1839, 3, 19. Israel, minor, gct Newgarden MM
1839, 7, 25. John M. gct Newgarden MM with
    mother, Sarah Dutton (H)
1855, 10, 24. John & w, Hannah, & ch, William,
    Lydia Ann, Martha & Charles, rocf Allum
    Creek MM, dtd 1855,8,23
1859, 2, 23. William gct White Water MM
1862,10, 21. Milton dis disunity
1862, 11, 19. Cordelia dis jW
1862, 11, 19. Milton & w, Sarah Jane, & ch,
    John T., Sarah Annie, James dis jW
1863, 5, 20. Cyrus gct Cincinnati MM (G)
1863, 5, 20. John & w, Hannah, & s, Charles,
    gct White Water MM, Ind. (G)
1863, 5, 20. Lydia C. gct Whitewater MM, Ind.
    (G)
1865, 6, 21. Phebe recrq (G)
1867, 10, 24. Cyrus & w, Phebe, gct Cincinnati
    MM, O. (G)
1869, 7, 20. Sarah Jane & dt, Cordelia, gct
    Hickory Grove MM, Ia. (W)

MERCER
1912, 6, 1. Belle Pile d

1835, 4, 23. William gct Plainfield MM (H)
1885, 12, 23. Laura E. gct Lawrence MM, Kans.
    (G)
1889, 3, 20. John T. recrq (G)
1911, 4, 19. Nellie recrq (G)
1912, 2, 21. B. C. recrq (G)
1914, 3, 25. Lemoyne recrq (G)

MERRITT
1886, 5, 19. Josiah & Elizabeth recrq (G)

MICHENER
1774, 2, 10. John b
1775, 4, 26. Naomi b
1807, 5, 21. Grace m Francis HOBSON
1807, 9, 24. Daniel, s John & Martha, Jeffer-
    son Co., O.; m in Short Creek MH, Anna
    KINSEY, dt Geo. & Mary, Jefferson Co., O.
    Ch: Mary   b 1808, 7, 20

Ch: Rebecca   b 1810, 8, 1
    George   " 1812, 2, 27
    Charles   " 1813, 11, 17
    Martha   " 1815, 11, 6
    Kinsey   " 1817, 10, 29
    John L.   " 1820, 1, 14
    Joseph L. " 1821, 9, 12
    Rachel   " 1824, 2, 25
1808, 4, 28. Benjamin, s John & Martha, Jef-
    ferson Co., O.; m in Short Creek MH, Abi-
    gail STANTON, dt Benjamin & Abigail, Jef-
    ferson Co., O.
    Ch: Levi   b 1809, 1, 9
    Susanna   " 1810, 5, 16
    John   " 1812, 3, 10
    Lydia   " 1814, 1, 18
    Henry   " 1816, 2, 12
    David   " 1818, 3, 15
    Isaac   " 1820, 7, 10
    Edwin   " 1822, 10, 12
    Martha   " 1825, 3, 14
    Elma   " 1828, 1, 31
1812, 8, 27. Rachel m Isaac HAINES
----, --, --. Jacob b 1791,8,3; m Martha -----
    b 1788,8,30
    Ch: Elizabeth b 1815, 6, 20
    Rebecca W. " 1816, 11, 12
    Sarah   " 1818, 9, 19
    Mary Ann   " 1821, 11, 12
    David   " 1823, 2, 18
    John W.   " 1824, 12, 22
    Seneca   " 1827, 12, 17
    William   " 1831, 6, 2
1816, 8, 29. John, s Mordecai & Sarah, Jef-
    ferson Co., O.; m in Short Creek MH, Re-
    becca WATERMAN, dt James & Mary WOOD,
    Jefferson Co., O.
1816, 10, 19. Joseph, s Jonathan & Jane, b
1819, 7, 29. Hannah m Samuel CLARK
1824, 3, 3. Hannah m Aaron WHINERY
1833, 10, 30. Geo., s Daniel & Anna, Jeffer-
    son Co., O.; m in Mt. Pleasant, Rebecca
    FLANNER, dt Wm. & Peninah, Belmont Co.,O.
    Ch: Elizabeth b 1834, 9, 28
    Mary   " 1838, 5, 13
    William   " 1840, 3, 4
1834, 10, 13. Martha m Benj. B. RATCLIFF
1836, 8, 31. Elizabeth d
1838, 10, 27. Barak d ae 84
1840, 9, 23. Rebecca d ae 70 bur Short Creek
1889, 7, 13. Mary A. d

1805, 11, 16. John [Michiner] & w, Martha, &
    s, Baruch, rocf Newgarden MM, Pa., dtd
    1805,9,5
1806, 10, 18. Three ch of John recrq
1806, 11, 15. Benjamin rocf Phila. MM, dtd
    1806,8,29
1806, 11, 15. Grace & Sarah recrq
1806, 11, 15. Jonathan recrq
1807, 1, 17. Daniel rocf Horsham MM, dtd
    1806,8,27
1807, 11, 21. Esther & ch, Mordecai & Jona-

MICHENER, continued
    than, rocf Westland MM, dtd 1807,7,25
1809, 10, 24. Esther & ch, Mordecai & Jona-
    than, gct Westland MM
1810, 6, 19. Sarah Martin (form Michener) dis
    mcd
1812, 4, 21. John & w, Naomi, rocf Westland
    MM, dtd 1811,6,22
1814, 6, 21. Barak & w, Jane, rocf Newgarden
    MM, Pa., dtd 1814,4,7
1814, 7, 19. Hannah rocf Newgarden MM, Pa.,
    dtd 1814,4,7
1815, 9, 19. Jonathan gct Plymouth MM, to m
    Jane Hobson
1816, 4, 23. Jane rocf Plymouth MM, dtd
    1816,3,18
1817, 5, 20. Jonathan & w, Jane, & s, Joseph,
    gct Marlborough MM
1817, 8, 19. Jacob & w, Martha, & ch, Eliza-
    beth & Rebecca, rocf Buckingham MM, Pa.,
    dtd 1817,5,5
1829, 1, 18. John & w, Rebecca, & her ch,
    Isaac & John Watterman, gct Flushing MM
1824, 2, 24. Baruch Jr. dis mcd
1826, 8, 22. Mary Price (form Michaner) con
    mcd
1828, 12, 23. Martha dis jH
1829, 1, 20. Abigail & Susanna dis jH
1830, 10, 19. John & w, Rebecca, rocf Flushing
    MM, dtd 1830,6,24
1831, 8, 23. Levi dis jH
1832, 4, 24. Baruck rocf Newgarden MM, Pa.,
    dtd 1832,3,8
1832, 4, 24. John [Mitchenor] & w, Mary, &
    ch, Eber, Hannah, Seth, Jesse, Miriam &
    Israel, rocf Newgarden MM, Pa., dtd 1832,
    3,8
1832, 4, 24. Thomas rocf Newgarden MM, Pa.,
    dtd 1832,3,8
1832, 4, 26. Benjamin [Michenor] & w, Abi-
    gail, & ch, John, Henry, David, Isaac, Ed-
    win, Martha & Elma, gct Goshen MM (H)
1832, 10, 23. Barak gct Stillwater MM
1832, 10, 23. John & w, Mary, & ch, Eber, Han-
    nah, Seth, Jesse, Miriam & Israel, gct
    Stillwater MM
1833, 4, 25. Levi gct Goshen MM (H)
1833, 4, 25. Susanna & Lydia gct Goshen MM (H)
1833, 10, 24. John & w, Naomi, gct Deerfield MM
    (H)
1835, 1, 20. John, Lydia, Henry, David, Isaac,
    Edwin, Martha & Elma [Michenor], ch Benj.
    & Abigail, gct Goshen MM
1835, 5, 19. Charles gct Flushing MM
1835, 5, 19. Daniel & w, Ann, & ch, Kinsey,
    John L., Joseph & Rachel, gct Flushing MM
1835, 5, 19. Rebecca gct Flushing MM
1835, 9, 22. Rebecca & Elizabeth dis jH
1836, 2, 25. Jacob & w, Martha, & ch, Mary
    Ann, David, John W., Seneca & William, gct
    Deerfield MM (H)
1836, 3, 24. Elizabeth L. & Rebecca W. gct
    Deerfield MM (H)

1837, 9, 19. Thomas dis mcd
1838, 4, 24. Rebecca rocf Flushing MM, dtd
    1838,3,22
1838, 5, 22. Sarah dis jH
1840, 5, 19. George & w, Rebecca, & ch,
    Mary & William, gct Chesterfield MM
1842, 1, 18. Mary Ann, David, Wilson, Seneca
    & William, ch Jacob & Martha, gct Penns-
    ville MM
1862, 11, 19. Bareck, Lydia, Hannah Emma, Fran-
    cis, John E., Thos. Chalkley, Elizabeth,
    Rebecca & Mary dis jW

MIDDLEMAS
1895, 3, 20. Anna recrq (G)
1907, 4, 24. Robert & Anna dropped from mbrp
    (G)

MIKESELL
1903, 4, 22. Catharine & Adda recrq (G)
1907, 3, 20. Catharine dropped from mbrp (G)

MILHOUSE
1835, 9, 30. Hannah m John MENDENHALL
----, --, --. Joshua V. & Elizabeth P.
    Ch: Franklin   b 1848, 11, 4
        Jesse   " 1851, 5, 11
        Edith J.   " 1853, 11, 1

1808, 4, 19. David Steer gct Concord MM, to
    m Phebe Milhouse
1833, 12, 24. William [Millhouse] Jr. dis mcd
1838, 12, 18. Vickers [Millhouse] dis mcd
1844, 5, 21. Jane Rice (form Millhouse) con
    mcd
1846, 3, 24. Thomas gct Pennsville MM
1847, 11, 23. Joshua V. gct Westland MM, to
    m Elizabeth P. Griffin
1848, 8, 22. Elizabeth P. [Millhouse] rocf
    Westland MM, dtd 1848,5,24
1854, 8, 22. Joshua V. & w, Elizabeth P., &
    ch, Franklin, Jesse G. & Edith, gct Drift-
    wood MM, Ind.
1860, 3, 20. William & Martha dis jG
1879, 7, 22. Benjamin F. Starbuck gct Penns-
    ville MM, to m Sarah Milhouse (W)

MILES
1911, 3, 21. Zoa Caroline recrq (W)
1911, 5, 23. Zoa Caroline gct Upper Spring-
    field MM (W)
1911, 12, 20. Carroll H., Selma P., Inez M.
    A., Iona Hannah & Irene Katy J., gct
    Damascus MM (G)

MILLEGER
1915, 2, 24. Dan & Abbie recrq (G)

MILLER
1816, 3, 29. John d ae 50 bur Short Creek

1810, 12, 18. John & w, Edith, & ch, Lydia,
    Rachel & Wm. John, rocf Baltimore MM E.

MILLER, continued
    Dist., dtd 1810,11,8
1814, 12, 21. Caleb & w, Phebe, rocf Redstone
    MM, dtd 1814,12,2
1817, 4, 22. Phebe gct Redstone MM
1819, 6, 22. Sarah rocf Gwynnedd MM, dtd
    1817,7,31
1819, 9, 21. Cert for Sarah from Gwynnedd end
    to Newgarden MM, O.
1825, 5, 24. Rachel gct Birmingham MM, Pa.
1828, 10, 21. Rachel rocf Birmingham MM, Pa.,
    dtd 1828,6,3
1838, 5, 22. William dis disunity
1841, 8, 24. Margaret D. (form Wilson) dis
    mcd
1862, 11, 19. Lydia & Rachel dis jW (G)
1864, 5, 24. Lydia gct Flushing MM (W)
1864, 5, 24. Rachel gct Flushing MM (W)
1902, 3, 19. Bessie A. recrq (G)

MILHORN
1879, 4, 24. John, Alvina, Anna, Benjamin &
    Sarah recrq (G)
1881, 2, 26. John Jr. recrq (G)
1881, 2, 26. George A. recrq (G)
1881, 3, 24. Sabina recrq (G)
1881, 3, 24. Elizabeth recrq (G)
1884, 7, 23. John [Millhorn]dropped from
    mbrp (G)
1888, 10, 24. William [Millhoan] dropped from
    mbrp (G)
1888, 10, 24. Elizabeth [Millhoan] dropped
    from mbrp (G)
1890, 9, 24. Josephine [Millhorn] relrq (G)
1895, 7, 24. George A. dropped from mbrp
1895, 7, 24. Josephine [Milhone] dropped from
    mbrp (G)
1897, 5, 19. John recrq
MILLIGAN
1901, 2, 20. Maggie B. & Elmira E. recrq (G)
1907, 6, 19. Maggie & Elmira dropped from
    mbrp (G)

MILLS
1862, 11, 19. Reuben & Mary dis jW
1882, 7, 19. Samuel L. & Annis Levenia recrq
    (G)
1883, 6, 20. Elizabeth, John & Georgia A.
    recrq (G)
1885, 3, 25. William Jr. & William Sr. recrq
    (G)
1887, 5, 24. Selma P. (form Taber) dis mcd
    (W)
189-, 7, 23. Carroll H. rocf Winnesheik MM,
    Ia. (G)
1894, 7, 25. Elizabeth, Georgia, John, Sam-
    uel & William dropped from mbrp (G)
1895, 2, 20. Georgia A. recrq (G)
1895, 2, 20. John J. recrq (G)
1908, 4, 22. F. P. & w, Providence, recrq (G)
1908, 4, 22. J. B. recrq (G)
1909, 5, 19. J. Bertram relrq (G)
1909, 6, 23. Fred P. & w, Providence, relrq

    (G)
1914, 3, 25. J. B. & Clara recrq (G)

MILTON
1839, 11, 19. Mary & Mary Jr. gct Flushing MM
1839, 11, 19. Patience gct Flushing MM
1841, 2, 23. Armella gct Flushing MM
1842, 10, 18. John gct Flushing MM

MITCHELL
1891, 6, 10. Mary d ae 81 bur Harrisville

1890, 6, 24. Mary A. rocf Flushing MM, dtd
    1890,5,22 (W)
1892, 10, 19. A. C., Willie & Addie recrq (G)
1892, 10, 19. Cora recrq (G)

MOFFATT
1860, 11, 17. John, s John & Margaret, b (G)

1885, 2, 25. John [Moffit] recrq (G)
1902, 10, 20. John [Moffitt] dropped from mbrp
    (G)

MONTAGUE
1892, 10, 19. Thomas recrq (G)

MOONEY
1814, 7, 19. Elizabeth rocf Hopewell MM, dtd
    1814,5,5

MOORE
1852, 5, 19. Calvin, s Gainer & Mary C.,
    Columbiana Co., O.; m in Harrisville, Sa-
    rah WALTER, dt Thomas & Sidney, Chester
    Co., Pa.
1911, 2, 2. John Enoch, s Charles & Amanda,b
1815, 5, 23. Ruth (form Atkinson) dis mcd
1828, 9, 23. Lydia [More] dis jH
1852, 8, 24. Hannah (form Sanders) dis mcd
1852, 9, 21. Hannah dis
1852, 9, 21. Sarah W. gct Salem MM, O.
1861, 9, 25. Rachel (form Hurford) dis mcd
1892, 10, 19. Anna recrq (G)
1896, 1, 23. G. W. recrq (G)
1912, 3, 20. Viola & Choicey recrq (G)
1914, 12, 23. Grace recrq (G)
1915, 2, 24. John A. recrq (G)
1915, 2, 24. Margaret Virginia recrq (G)
1927, 3, 23. Jennie recrq (G)
1927, 7, 27. John Enoch recrq (G)
1930, 10, 22. George dropped from mbrp (G)

MOORMAN
1814, 6, 21. Rachel rocf Cedar Creek MM,
    Va., dtd 1814,5,14

MORGAN
1869, 11, 25. Mary E. (form Lukens) con mcd (G)
1870, 2, 24. Mary E. gct Ypsilanti MM, Mich.
    (W)
1885, 2, 25. Frederick Y. recrq (G)
1886, 7, 21. B. T. recrq (G)
1896, 1, 23. Charles recrq (G)

MORGAN, continued
1896, 1, 23. Charles recrq (G)
1902, 12,24. Frank dropped from mbrp (G)
1902, 12,24. Charles dropped from mbrp (G)
1914, 1, 21. Rex & Orpha recrq (G)

MORLAND
1892, 10, 19. Emily & Lulu recrq (G)

MORTON
1807, 4, 18. Ann dis
1816, 9, 24. Rebecca rocf Redstone MM, dtd
     1816,7,24
1892, 10, 19. John R. & Lida recrq (G)

MORRIS
1801, 8, 11. Hannah b
1802, 1, 22. Eliza b
1824, 5, 27. Edward, s Edward & Hannah, Har-
     rison Co., O.; m in Harrisville, Hannah
     YOST, dt Michel & Rachel, Harrison Co., O.
     Ch: Michael
            Edward   b 1830, 8, 7
            Rachel   " 1832, 4, 3
            Margaret
              Ann   " 1834, 4, 2
            John Y.   " 1836, 5, 4
            David E. " 1838, 5, 1
            Sarah
              Elizabeth" 1840, 8, 26
            Isaac Thom-
              as   " 1843, 3, 15
            Lydia Fran-
              ces   " 184-, 3, 3
1825, 1, 21. Elias b
1826, 3, 2. Lydia m Thomas LEWIS
1826, 11, 9. Jonathan b
1828, 10, 24. Hannah Jane b
1862, 11, 26. Nixon, s Benoni & Rebecca,
     Washington Co., Ind.; m in Mt. Pleasant,
     Margaret J. LLOYD, dt Isaac & Ruth, Bel-
     mont Co., O.
1863, 10, 15. Elias d ae 33
1880, 4, 22. Edward d
1881, 1, 7. Isaac T. d
1883, 6, 6. Hannah d
1891, 10, 6. Rachel K. d
1892, 7, 23. Hannah J. d
1906, 5, 14. Rachel d bur Colerain
1930, 5, 12. John Wesley, s Everet & Delphia,
     b (G)

1804, 7, 21. Edward & ch, Jane, Hannah,
     Lydia & Edward, rocf Redstone MM, dtd
     1804,6,1
1815, 10, 24. Hannah Butler (form Morris) dis
     mcd
1819, 5, 18. Anna, minor, rocf Salem MM, dtd
     1819,4,21 with fam of Joseph Rhodes
1827, 5, 22. Anne gct Plainfield MM
1828, 12, 23. Eliza dis jH
1829, 11, 24. Hannah dis jH
1833, 2, 19. Thomas Jr. rocf WD MM, dtd
     1832,12,19

1835, 3, 24. Thomas dis mcd
1840, 3, 24. Henry P. rocf WD MM, dtd 1839,
     9,18
1841, 10, 19. Henry P. dis mcd
1847, 3, 23. Elias dis disunity
1852, 7, 20. Jonathan dis disunity
1861, 4, 9. Michael gct Clear Creek MM, Ill.
     (H)
1862, 11, 19. Nixon rocf Blue River MM, Ind.,
     to m Margaret J. Lloyd (G)
1863, 6, 24. Margaret J. gct Blue River MM,
     Ind. (G)
1866, 2, 20. Margaret dis jG (W)
1869, 2, 25. Margaret J. & dt, Edith L., rocf
     Blue River MM, Ind. (G)
1874, 5, 19. Ruth (form Battin) rst at Ply-
     mouth with consent of this mtg (W)
1888, 10, 24. Maud dropped from mbrp (G)
1905, 3, 22. Thomas E. recrq (G)
1905, 3, 22. Winnie recrq (G)
1905, 3, 22. Howard recrq (G)
1907, 6, 19. Thos. E., Minnie & Howard dropped
     from mbrp (G)
1907, 6, 19. Cora dropped from mbrp (G)
1907, 6, 19. Nettie B. dropped from mbrp (G)
1907, 6, 19. Leota dropped from mbrp (G)
1927, 12, 21. Everett & Delphi recrq (G)

MOSHER
1818, 11, 24. Cert rec for Gershom & w, Ruth,
     & ch, Joseph, Samuel, Daniel, David,
     Gulielma & Allen from Derysta MM, N. Y.,
     dtd 1818,1,28, end to Alum Creek MM

MOSTEZ
1907, 3, 20. Mary F. dropped from mbrp (G)

MOTT
1851, 5, 21. James E., s Wm. & Sarah, Athens
     Co., O.; m in Mt. Pleasant, Mary P. LUP-
     TON, dt Henry & Achsah, Jefferwon Co.,
     O.
1926, 9, 8. Wm. A., s Wm. C. & Anna M.,
     Johnson Co., Ia.; m in Harrisville, Doro-
     thy A. STEER, dt Louis C. & S. Louisa,
     Harrison Co., O.

1812, 9, 22. William rocf Concord MM, dtd
     1812,8,20
1814, 7, 19. William gct Marlborough MM, O.
1852, 1, 20. Mary P. gct Plymouth MM
1892, 4, 19. Samuel Hall gct Springville MM,
     Ia., to m Anna Mott (W)
1920, 1, 21. Bernard E. rocf Lupton MM, Mich.
     (G)
1921, 3, 23. Alma S. recrq (G)
1922, 1, 25. Bernard E. & w, Alma, gct Long
     Beach First Friends Church, Calif. (G)
1927, 12, 20. Dorothy A. gct West Branch MM,
     Ia. (W)

MULLIN
1820, 2, 22. Joseph & Samuel rocf Mt. Holly

MULLIN, continued
    MM, N. J., dtd 1819,6,10
1823, 11, 18. Samuel [Mullen] gct Mt. Holly MM,
    N. J.

MUNSAY
1892, 10, 19. Mary E. recrq (G)

MURIE
1805, 12, 21. Ann [Murry] rocf Crooked Run
    MM, dtd 1805,8,31
1901, 2, 20. Peter recrq (G)
1901, 2, 20. Thomas recrq (G)
1901, 2, 20. Jewsie recrq (G)
1906, 10, 24. Effie [Murray] recrq (G)
1912, 3, 20. Jennie, Jesse & Louis recrq (G)
1914, 1, 21. William recrq (G)
1914, 9, 23. John Sr. & Mary recrq (G)
1915, 2, 24. Vernon recrq (G)

NAMETH
1915, 2, 24. Pearl & Helen recrq (G)

NATION
1885, 2, 25. Alonzo O. recrq (G)
1896, 1, 23. Emma recrq (G)
1905, 4, 19. Maggie recrq (G)
1920, 5, 19. Mrs. Alonzo relrq (G)

NAYLOR
----, --, --. John S. m Jane ----- d 1863,4,
    24 ae 60 bur Smithfield; m Jane -----
    d 1863,4,24 ae 60 bur Smithfield
    Ch: Elizabeth b 1824, 4, 1
        Eliza Ann   " 1826, 7, 21
        Rebecca   " 1829, 9, 8
        Nathan M.   " 1832, 8, 10
        Samuel G.   " 1835, 12, 2
        William R.   " 1837, 7, 1
        Oliver
          Price   " 1843, 11, 6
1823, 9, 28. John d ae 81 bur Smithfield
1826, 8, 30. Mary Sr., w John, d bur Smith-
    field

1807, 4, 18. Benjamin Townsend gct Baltimore
    MM, to m Elizabeth Naylor
1862, 11, 19. Lewis, Rachel, Stephen, Benja-
    min, Tabitha, Ezra, Margaret, Mary, Ra-
    chel, Ann Eliza & James dis jW
1866, 6, 19. Oliver P. dis disunity & mili-
    tary service (W)
1867, 7, 23. William B. dis mcd (W)
1867, 9, 24. Nathan M. dis disunity (W)
1867, 9, 24. Samuel dis disunity (W)

NEALY
1851, 12, 23. Hannah (form Gwinn) dis mcd

NEGUS
1843, 3, 9. Caleb B., s Thaidlock & Rachel,
    Columbiana Co., O.; m in Short Creek MM,
    Eliza J. BRANSON, dt Rees & Ruth, Belmont

Co., O.
    Ch: Rachel E. b 1844, 6, 14
        Amasa L.   " 1845, 9, 22
        Oliver S.   " 1847, 10, 30
        Plummer   " 1851, 2, 20
        Anna
          Bracken   " 1854, 1, 22
1849, 5, 3. Sarah S. m Jonathan WILSON
1862, 10, 29. Eliza J. m Jonathan FAWCETT (W)
1869, 12, 29. Amasa L., s Caleb & Eliza J.,
    Belmont Co., O.; m in Concord, Lydia
    HOYLE, dt Benjamin & Gulia Ann, Belmont
    Co., O., d 1911,8,12 ae 68 (W)
    Ch: Benjamin
          Willard b 1872, 7, 1
        Ellis W.   " 1877, 11, 12 (or 11-2)
        Caleb E.   " 1884, 9, --
1876, 11, 1. Oliver S., s Caleb B. & Eliza
    J., Belmont Co., O., b 1847,10,30 d 1918,
    1,22 ae 71 bur Colerain; m in Concord, De-
    borah STEER, dt Israel & Rebecca B., Bel-
    mont Co., O., b 1847,12,17 (W)
    Ch: Anna B.   b 1877, 12, 13 d 1931, 3,20
        Albert J.   " 1880, 3, 7
        Mary R.   " 1882, 9, 28
        Laura E.   " 1885, 10, 14
        Sara D.   " 1888, 1, 5
        Wilson N.   " 1890, 12, 9
----, --, --. Brackin & Eliza
    Ch: Rachel E.   d 1882,12, 3 ae
        40 bur Concord
        Amasa L.   " 1886, 1,26
1895, 1, 16. Jessie Leah C., w Wilson, dt
    Thomas & Sara (Brantingham) Crawford, b
1908, 8, 19. Mary Rebecca m C. E. FAWCETT (W)
1914, 5, 20. Sara D. m Wm. P. TABER (W)
1931, 3, 20. Anna B. d bur Colerain

1842, 3, 22. Caleb B. rocf Upper Springfield
    MM, dtd 1842,2,26
1846, 7, 21. Sarah rocf Upper Springfield MM,
    dtd 1846,6,27
1858, 3, 24. Amasa gct Salem MM, O.; this
    cert was lost & a duplicate sent 1858,5,10
1862, 11, 19. Rachel, Oliver & Ann dis jW
1862, 12, 24. Amos L. rocf Salem MM (G)
1927, 1, 18. Wilson A. gct Newgarden MM, to
    m Jessie C. Steer (W)
1927, 10, 18. Jessie Leah C. rocf Newgarden
    MM (W)

NEVITT
1815, 3, 21. Catharine & Ruth rocf Hopewell
    MM, dtd 1814,12,8
1815, 3, 21. Isaac & w, Rachel, & ch, Isaac,
    Grace, Eliza, Rachel & John, rocf Hope-
    well MM, dtd 1814,1,5
1815, 4, 18. Mary rocf Hopewell MM, dtd 1814,
    12,8
1816, 12, 24. Isaac [Nevit] & w, Rachel, & ch,
    Isaac, John, Grace, Eliza & Rachel, gct
    Plainfield MM
1817, 12, 23. Ruth [Nevit] gct Concord MM

NEVITT, continued
1821, 2, 20. Catharine Wright (form Nevet)
     dis mcd
1823, 7, 22. Mary [Nevet] dis jas
1834, 8, 19. Rachel Jr. rocf Flushing MM, dtd
     1834,2,20

NEWBY
1865, 8, 30. Wm. C., s Thomas & Margaret,
     Henry Co., Ind.; m in Mt. Pleasant, Olive
     P. TERRELL, dt Matthew & Elizabeth D.,
     Jefferson Co., O.

1815, 5, 23. James rocf Stillwater MM, dtd
     1815,4,25
1815, 5, 23. Job rocf Plymouth MM, dtd 1814,9
     17, end by Stillwater MM
1815, 5, 23. Joseph, minor, rocf Stillwater
     MM, dtd 1815,4,25
1816, 11, 19. James, minor, gct Plymouth MM
1817, 1, 21. Job gct Stillwater MM
1862, 10, 22. Asahel H. Hussey gct Milford MM,
     Ind., to m Martha P. Newby (G)
1864, 4, 2. Matthew Terrell gct Milford MM,
     Ind., to m Isabella Newby (G)
1865, 8, 23. Wm. C. rocf Milford MM, Ind., to
     m Olive B. Terrell (G)
1866, 6, 20. Olive B. gct Milford MM, Ind.(G)

NEWLIN
1867, 9, 26. Sarah L. recrq (G)
1872, 11, 21. Sarah Binns (form Newlin) con
     mcd (G)

NEWPORT
1815, 1, 24. Jesse rocf Concord MM, dtd
     1814,11,24
1815, 2, 21. Reese rocf Concord MM, dtd
     1814,11,24
1815, 6, 20. Jesse dis mcd
1817, 3, 18. Rees dis mcd
1829, 1, 20. Mary dis jH
1829, 7, 21. Noble dis
1834, 6, 24. Elizabeth dis jH
1842, 9, 22. Joseph gct Waynsville MM (H)
1853, 8, 23. Lydia Ann Lewis (form Newport)
     dis mcd
1853, 8, 23. Julia Maria Rice (form Newport)
     dis mcd
1854, 6, 20. Caroline dis disunity

NICHOLS
1819, 3, 31. Eli [Nicols], s Eli & Jane, Bel-
     mont Co., O.; m in Mt. Pleasant, Rachel
     LOYD, dt John & Mercy, Belmont Co., O.
1910, --, --. Willard Alvin, s George H. &
     Mary (Rainbow), b (G)

1819, 7, 20. Rachel [Nickles] gct Plainfield
     MM
1886, 5, 19. William recrq (G)
1902, 12, 24. William dropped from mbrp (G)
1903, 6, 24. John dropped from mbrp (G)

1905, 4, 19. James & Nettie recrq (G)

NICHOLSON
1847, 2, 23. Charles & w, Narcissa, & ch,
     William, Benjamin C., Elizabeth Ann,
     George Edwin & John, rocf Smithfield MM,
     dtd 1846,12,21
1847, 3, 23. Narcissa [Nickilson] & ch,
     William, Benjamin C., Elizabeth Ann,
     George Edwin & John, rocf Smithfield MM,
     dtd 1846,12,21
1852, 1, 20. Charles & w, Narcissa, & ch,
     William, Benjamin C., Elizabeth Ann,
     George Edwin, Sarah Allas, John & Eliza
     Jane Crew, gct Flushing MM

NIXON
1836, 4, 20. Martha L. m John STRAUGHAN

1833, 2, 19. Martha rocf Western Branch MM,
     Va., dtd 1832,10,27
1889, 3, 20. George recrq (G)

NOBLE
1873, 5, 22. William recrq (G)
1884, 2, 20. William H. & George L. recrq
     (G)
1885, 2, 25. Joseph & Amanda recrq (G)
1917, 2, 22. Will & w relrq (G)

NOBRAGE
1892, 10, 19. Elizabeth & John G. recrq (G)

NORMAN
1898, 3, 23. George W. recrq   (G)

NORRIS
1912, 3, 20. Floyd recrq (G)
1913, 3, 19. Rose recrq (G)
1914, 1, 21. Harold & Elizabeth G. recrq (G)
1914, 4, 22. Ruby recrq (G)
1915, 2, 24. Elizabeth recrq (G)

NYHART
1913, 3, 19. Hattie recrq (G)

OAKLEY
1913, 1, 22. William recrq (G)
1913, 7, 23. William relrq (G)

OLDS
1878, 3, 21. Orcelius L. & w, Alice M., recrq
     (G)
1881, 9, 22. Orcelius L. & w, Alice M., gct
     Chesterfield MM (G)

OLIPHANT
1840, 6, 23. William D. Branson gct Salem MM,
     to m Eliza Oliphant
1891, 3, 24. Joseph Hall gct New Garden MM,
     to m Olive H. Oliphant (W)

OLIVER
1819, 5, 18. Daniel recrq
1821, 3, 20. Daniel rocf Pool & Ringwood MM,
     Eng., dtd 1820,7,4
1821, 11, 20. Esther recrq
1824, 1, 20. Daniel & w, Esther, gct Flushing
     MM
1824, 1, 20. Esther gct Flushing MM
1872, 7, 25. John recrq (G)

O'NEAL
1832, 8, 21. Ann (form Reynolds) dis mcd

ONG
1828, 9, 26. Nathan d ae 33 bur Smithfield
1829, 1, 8. Mifflin d ae 22 bur Smithfield
1835, 8, 27. Isaac d ae 44 bur Smithfield
----, --, --. Lewis & Elmira
        Ch: Joseph P. b 1840, 7, 17
            Lindley H. " 1841, 9, 3 d 1862, 7, 8
            bur Cross Creek
            Lemuel   b 1844, 9, 20
            Plummer   " 1846, 1, 22
            Ann Eliza " 1849, 2, 22
            Amanda   " 1851, 1, 9
            William P. " 1853, 7, 7
            Lewis   " 1856, 7, 6
            Anderson C." 1858, 4, 12
1843, 3, 1. Jacob d ae 89 bur Smithfield
----, --, --. Miflin m Eliza ----- d 1858,5,1
     ae 37
        Ch: Finley K. b 1848, 1, 7
            William   " 1851, 7, 15
            Martha A. " 1853, 6, 4
            Oliver   " 1855, 2, 28
1852, 6, 7. Mary, w Jacob, d bur Smithfield
1853, 11, 15. Anna d ae 67 bur Smithfield
1860, 5, 30. Catharine d ae 68 bur Smithfield

1806, 6, 21. Findley con mcd
1844, 2, 20. Sarah (form Harris) rpd mcd; d
     before case was finished
1856, 6, 24. Rachel Ann Hamilton (form Ong)
     dis mcd (W)
1864, 1, 20. Mary recrq (G)
1864, 5, 25. Moses H. rst on consent of
     Smithfield MM (G)
1864, 11, 22. Mifflin dis jG (W)
1865, 8, 23. Sarah Jane recrq (G)
1866, 10, 23. Lewis dis jG (W)
1866, 11, 20. Elmira dis disunity (W)
1870, 6, 23. Sarah J. gct Smithfield MM, O.
     (G)
1873, 8, 21. Mary Elizabeth recrq (G)
1874, 6, 25. Emma recrq (G)
1875, 1, 21. Mary Eliza & Emma gct Smith-
     field MM (G)
1875, 1, 21. Moses H. & w, Mary, gct Smith-
     field MM (G)
1886, 4, 21. Osborn rocf Smithfield MM (G)
1903, 9, 23. Osborn B. & w, Mary, & ch,
     Eilene & Ralph, gct Chagrin Valley MM (G)
1911, 6, 21. Iola rocf Pleasant Valley MM(G)

1911, 6, 21. Osborn B. & w, Mary T., & ch,
     Eilene & Ralph O., rocf Pleasant Valley
     MM (G)
1914, 1, 21. Iola C. gct Pasadena MM, Calif.
     (G)
1914, 1, 21. O. B. & w, Mary S. T., & ch, Ei-
OSBORN [lene & Ralph, gct Pasadena MM, Calif (G)
1817, 8, 12. Gideon Swain, s Chas. & Hannah,
     b

1815, 10, 24. David & w, Anna, & ch, Daniel
     Azur, Henry, Dorcas & David, rocf Peru MM,
     dtd 1815,6,22
1817, 4, 22. Charles rocf Lost Creek MM, Tenn.
     dtd 1817,2,22
1817, 4, 22. Hannah, w Chas., & ch, James,
     Josiah, John, Isaiah, Elijah, Lydia, Nar-
     cissa & Cynthia, rocf Lost Creek MM, Tenn.
     dtd 1816,8,31
1818, 10, 20. James gct Newgarden MM, Ind.
1819, 2, 23. Charles & w, Hannah, & ch,
     Isaiah, Lydia, Elijah, Narcissa, Cynthia &
     Gideon Swayne, gct Newgarden MM, Ind.
1819, 12, 21. Josiah & John, minors, gct New-
     garden MM, O.

OSTROSKI
1902, 2, 19. Stana & Mamie recrq (G)
1905, 3, 22. Mary recrq (G)
1912, 3, 20. Agnes [Ostrosci] recrq (G)
1913, 3, 19. Moxie [Ostrosky] recrq (G)
1913, 7, 23. Agnes dropped from mbrp (G)

OXLEY
1805, 1, 19. Joel rocf Redstone MM, dtd
     1804,12,18
1810, 12, 18. Joel gct Hopewell MM
1816, 5, 2. Rachel (form Atkinson) dis mcd
1896, 5, 20. George & Mary, minors, recrq (G)
1902, 3, 19. Charles, Elizabeth May, John W.
     & James E., recrq (G)
1914, 4, 22. Charles recrq (G)
1914, 12, 23. Ada relrq (G)

PACKER
----, --, --. Abraham & Sarah
        Ch: Levi   b 1824, 2, 17
            Eve   " 1826, 10, 17
1828, 1, 19. Ephraim J. b
1829, 11, 22. Elizabeth d
1834, 9, 30. Amos A., s Isaac & Rebecca, b
----, --, --. Elisha m Asenath ----- d 1858,1,
     7 ae 36
        Ch: Milton W. b 1844, 9, 7 d 1859,10,2'
            Aaron   " 1846, 1, 23
            John Thomas" 1848, 12, 12
            Israel   " 1850, 8, 28
            Allen   " 1852, 9, 6
            Eli   " 1854, 6, 19
            Franklin   " 1856, 10, 1
        Elisha m 2nd Grace -----
        Ch: Seth F.   b 1860, 11, 9
            Benjamin   " 1862, 8, 1

PACKER, Elisha & Grace, continued
    Ch: Alice M.   b 1864, 2, 11
1851, 4, 5. Rebecca d ae 66
1867, 12, 11. John, s Eli & Elizabeth, Clark
    Co., O.; m in home of Elisha Packer, Re-
    becca LEWIS, dt Thos. & Jemima VICKERS (H)
----, --, --. Seth T. & S. M.
    Ch: Elva J.   b 1882, 12, 27
        Edith J.   " 1884, 6, 12
        Grace A.   " 1886, 6, 9
1898, 6, 28. Elisha d
1898, 10, 19. Wm. F. s Aaron & Rebecca, Jef-
    ferson Co., O., b 1876,3,11; m in Harris-
    ville, Edith ATKINSON, dt William & Catha-
    rine, Jefferson Co., O., b 1877,10,10 (W)
    Ch: Lillian
        Catharineb 1903, 4, 9 d 1903, 7,24
        bur Harrisville
        Ethel M.   b 1905, 8, 10
        Wm. Atkin-
          son   " 1910, 9, 1
        Fredrick E." 1912, 8, 10
1899, 12, 13. Grace d

1814, 5, 24. Moses rocf Plymouth MM, dtd
    1814,2,19
1824, 7, 20. Sarah & ch, Abigail, Mary & Su-
    sanna, rocf Somerset MM, dtd 1824,4,26
1826, 7, 18. Abraham & w, Sarah, & ch, Abi-
    jah, Mary, Susanna, Levi & Eve, gct Flush-
    ing MM
1826, 7, 18. Elizabeth rocf Muncy MM, dtd
    1826,6,21
1829, 3, 24. Rebecca dis jH
1833, 8, 22. Ann & ch, Philena, George,
    Phebe Ann, Hannah L. & Lydia C., gct Flush-
    ing MM (H)
1833, 8, 22. Louesa gct Flushing MM (H)
1833, 10, 24. Lambern gct Flushing MM (H)
1833, 10, 22. Rebecca (form Allen) dis mcd &
    jH
1833, 12, 24. Isaac dis jH
1835, 12, 22. Sarah dis jH
1837, 6, 20. Thomas dis disunity
1842, 5, 24. Elisha dis disunity
1845, 2, 18. Asenath dis jH
1849, 6, 19. John Gilbert gct Flushing MM, to
    m Susanna Packer
1861, 1, 22. Grace (form McBride) dis mcd
1865, 4, 4. Aaron & w, Ann, gct Green Plain
    MM (H)
1868, 3, 10. Rebecca V. gct Green Plain MM,
    O. (H)
1874, 10, 6. John Thomas gct Marietta MM, Ia.
    (H)
1875, 1, 19. Ruth (form Atkinson) dis disunity
    (W)
1882, 1, 12. Franklin gct Miami MM (H)
1898, 7, 19. Wm. F. recrq (W)
1918, 2, 4. Jesse gct Wakefield MM, Pa. (H)
1918, 2, 4. Sarah gct Wakefield MM, Pa. (H)

PADEN
1825, 9, 20. Lydia & minor sisters, Rachel &
    Margaret, rocf Westland MM, dtd 1825,5,26

PAGE
1904, 12, 21. Louisa relrq (G)

PAINTER
1815, 1, 24. Robert rocf Salem MM, dtd 1814,
    10,11
1841, 9, 21. William rocf Centre MM, dtd
    1841,6,16
1842, 5, 24. William gct Centre MM

PALMER
1818, 12, 22. Abigail [Pelmer] (form Wood) dis
    mcd
1906, 10, 24. Florence G. recrq (G)
1908, 2, 19. Miss Florence relrq (G)

PARKER
----, --, --. Isaac & Sarrah
    Ch: Mary   b 1793, 12, 25
        John   " 1795, 9, 1
        Nathan   " 1798, 3, 28
        Rhoda   " 1800, 12, 13
        Martha   " 1801, 1, 25
        Abigail   " 1806, 3, 18
        Jacob   " 1808, 11, 7
----, --, --. Jacob & Faith
    Ch: Jordan   b 1795, 9, 11
        Caleb   " 1798, 1, 13
        Rhoda   " 1800, 5, 24
        Eliza   " 1802, 10, 10 d 1823, 8,13
        bur Short Creek
        Mary   b 1804, 10, 25
        Peninah   " 1806, 12, 7 " 1824, 5,13
        bur Short Creek
        Sarah   b 1809, 5, 25
        Rebecca   " 1811, 11, 16
        Joel   " 1814, 4, 25
        Edwin   " 1816, 6, 15
----, --, --. Micajah & Julia
    Ch: Lydia   b 1810, 12, 11
        Isaac   " 1812, 12, 7
        Maryann   " 1814, 12, 12
        Sarah   " 1817, 1, 3
        Jane   " 1818, 5, 15
        Rhoda   " 1819, 3, 3
1810, 8, 30. Jesse, s Jacob & Rhoda, Jeffer-
    son Co., O.; m in Short Creek MH, Anna
    FOULKE, dt Thomas & Rachel CHERRINGTON,
    Jefferson Co., O.
    Ch: Matilda   b 1811, 6, 15
        Thomas C. " 1812, 8, 31
        John Cher-
          ington " 1814, 3, 20
        Jacob Her-
          vey   " 1816, 1, 8
        Wm. Darwin " 1817, 7, 2
        Emlen   " 1826, 12, 2 d 1848, 4,20
        bur Short Creek
1816, 4, 6. Rhoda d ae 15 bur Short Creek

PARKER, continued
1821, 4, 29. Faith d ae 47 bur Short Creek
1824, 8, 19. Jacob d ae 53 bur Short Creek
1826, 6, 26. Sarah d ae 54 bur Short Creek
1826, 8, 3. Sarah d ae 53 bur Short Creek
1826, 8, 31. Jesse, s Ephraim & Sarah, Belmont Co., O.; m in Short Creek MH, Ann GUMERY, dt Phebe, Belmont Co., O.
1827, 5, 3. Mary m Wm. FARMER
1829, 3, 24. Oliver, s Joseph & Mary, b
1830, 3, 3. Matilda m Jos. H. MEDKEFF
1833, 7, 17. Jacob d ae 24 bur Short Creek
1833, 11, --. Martha d ae 29 bur Short Creek
1834, 7, 31. Nathan, s Benj. & Grace, Jefferson Co., O.; m in Short Creek MH, Nancy T. CREW, dt Robert & Nancy, Charles City Co., Va.
1835, 9, 23. Emma m Levi T. PENNINGTON
1837, 7, 27. Abigail m Smith HOLLOWAY
1838, 1, 31. Isaac, s Jacob & Rhoda, Jefferson Co., O.; m in Mt. Pleasant, Hannah HOSIER, dt Edward T. & Elizabeth EMMETT, Jefferson Co., O.
1842, 4, 27. John d ae 46 bur Short Creek
1843, 2, 3. Anna d ae 63 bur Short Creek
1845, 10, 29. Jesse, s Jacob & Rhoda, Jefferson Co., O.; m in Mt. Pleasant, Hannah UPDEGRAFF, dt Nathan & Ann, Jefferson Co., O.
1849, 8, 20. Anderson J. d ae 25 bur Short Creek
1858, 9, --. Isaac d
1859, 10, 9. Dr. Isaac d ae 89
1860, 3, 5. Jesse d ae 75

1805, 9, 21. Joseph & w, Mary, & dt, Abigail, rocf Rich Square MM, N. C., dtd 1805,6,15
1807, 5, 16. Benajah rocf Rich Square MM, N. C., dtd 1807,3,21
1807, 7, 18. Faith & ch, Jordon, Caleb, Rhoda, Eliza & Mary, rocf Rich Square MM, N. C., dtd 1806,3,15
1808, 4, 19. Jesse rocf Rich Square MM, N. C., dtd 1807,9,19
1808, 8, 23. Isaac & w, Sarah, & ch, Mary, John, Rhoda, Martha & Abigail, rocf Rich Square MM, N. C., dtd 1808,6,4
1808, 9, 20. George rocf Rich Square MM, N. C., dtd 1808,6,18
1808, 9, 20. Jacob & Rhoda rocf Rich Square MM, N. C., dtd 1808,6,18
1809, 9, 19. Jacob & w, Rhoda, & ch gct Stillwater MM
1809, 10, 24. Benajah & George gct Stillwater MM
1810, 11, 20. Micajah & w, Julia, & dt, Elizabeth, rocf Richsquare MM, N. C., dtd 1810,9,15
1815, 3, 21. Jacob & w, Rhoda, rocf Stillwater MM, dtd 1814,11,29
1817, 2, 18. Joseph & w, Mary, & ch, Abigail, Jacob, James, William & Isaac, gct Concord MM

1819, 1, 19. Micajah dis disunity
1821, 10, 23. Jordan dis mcd
1821, 11, 20. Aaron & w, Rebecca, & ch, Isaac, Thomas L., Sarah & Elizabeth V., rocf Exeter MM, Pa., dtd 1821,7,25, end by Stillwater MM
1822, 12, 24. Julia & ch, Elizabeth, Isaac, Sarah, Jane & Rhoda, gct Rich Square MM, N. C.
1823, 9, 25. Lydia, minor dt of Julia, gct Flushing MM
1824, 2, 24. Abraham & w, Sarah, & ch, Abigail, Mary & Susannah, rocf Somerset MM, dtd 1824,1,26
1824, 8, 24. Jesse rocf Muncy MM, Pa., dtd 1824,4,21
1824, 9, 21. Benajah & w, Grace, & ch, Nathan, Emma, Hannah, Philip Draper, Charity & Isaac, rocf Stillwater MM, dtd 1824,7,28
1828, 7, 22. Abigail Steel (form Parker) dis mcd
1828, 12, 23. Ann dis jH
1829, 7, 21. Rhoda Carethers (form Parker) dis mcd
1830, 4, 22. Ann gct Plainfield MM (H)
1833, 1, 22. James dis mcd
1833, 8, 22. Ann & ch, Philena, George, Phebe Ann, Hannah L. & Lydia C., gct Flushing MM (H)
1834, 4, 22. Lydia rocf Stillwater MM, dtd 1834,3,22
1835, 11, 24. Jacob dis mcd
1836, 6, 21. William J. gct Stillwater MM
1836, 8, 23. Benajah & w, Grace, & ch, Philip Draper, Charity, Isaac, Benajah & Rachel, gct Spiceland MM, Ind.
1836, 8, 23. Hannah Ann gct Spiceland MM, Ind.
1837, 10, 24. Jacob H. dis disunity
1838, 5, 22. Ann rocf Sandy Spring MM, dtd 1838,4,27
1838, 7, 24. Nathan & w, Nancy, & ch, Mary & Martha, gct Spiceland MM, Ind.
1840, 8, 18. William J. rocf Stillwater MM, dtd 1840,5,25
1841, 5, 18. Thomas C. gct Stillwater MM, to m Lydia Jane Thornburgh
1841, 11, 23. Lydia gct Rich Square MM, N. C.
1842, 5, 24. Isaac Jr. gct Somerset MM
1842, 7, 20. Thomas C. gct Stillwater MM
1842, 10, 18. Stanton J. dis mcd
1843, 5, 23. Mary Ann Gill (form Parker) dis mcd
1843, 7, 18. William J. & w, Ann, & ch, Claudius Galin & Joseph John, gct Sandy Spring MM
1844, 6, 18. Isaac Jr. rocf Somerset MM, dtd 1844, 4, 29
1846, 8, 18. Isaac Jr. gct Chesterfield MM
1847, 11, 23. Joseph Jr. gct Chesterfield MM
1857, 8, 19. Hannah d 1854,--,25 ae 80 (an elder)
1861, 2, 19. Oliver dis jG
1863, 2, 24. Hannah dis jG (W)

PARKER, continued
1885, 3, 25. Elizabeth recrq (G)
1885, 3, 25. Mary Bell recrq (G)
1885, 3, 25. William T. recrq (G)
1886, 5, 19. Jno. W. recrq (G)
1888, 1, 25. Isaac & w, Frances C., rocf Fairfield MM (G)

PARKINS
1873, 5, 22. William & Joseph recrq (G)

PARLOTT
1906, 9, 16. Samuel S. d (G)

1894, 2, 21. Emma [Parlet] recrq (G)
1896, 1, 23. Harry recrq (G)
1897, 2, 24. Samuel S. [Parlett] recrq (W)
1929, 7, 24. Harry [Parlett] dropped from mbrp (G)

PARRISH
1816, 7, 23. Rachel rocf Gunpowder MM, dtd 1815,11,22, end by Plymouth MM

PARRY
1835, 9, 23. Thomas Gibbons, s Gibbons & Deborah, b

1836, 8, 25. Deborah B. & s, Thomas Gibbons Parry, gct Stillwater MM (H)
1894, 3, 21. James C. recrq (G)

PARSON
1811, 3, 19. Rachel (form Fell) dis mcd
1825, 10, 18. Mary & ch, George & Hannah, rocf Chester MM, Pa., dtd 1825,7,26
1826, 10, 24. George gct Flushing MM
1826, 10, 24. Israel gct Flushing MM
1826, 10, 24. Mary & dt, Hannah, gct Flushing MM

PARTINGTON
1895, 3, 20. Eliezur recrq (G)
1895, 3, 20. Jennie recrq (G)
1905, 8, 21. Eliezer gct Newberg MM, Wash. (G)
1907, 6, 19. Edna May dropped from mbrp (G)
1910, 2, 23. Margaret recrq (G)

PARVIANCE
1813, 1, 28. Joseph, s James & Elizabeth, Jefferson Co., O.; m in Short Creek MH, Deborah SIDWELL, dt Henry & Sinah, Belmont Co., O.

PATTEN
1826, 8, 31. Sarah m John THOMPSON

1822, 3, 19. Sarah [Patton] rocf Stillwater MM, dtd 1822,2,23

PATTERSON
1806, 10, 22. Ricks, s Anselem & Mariam, b

1808, 2, 25. Tacey m John HALL
1809, 3, 30. Clary m Henry STANTON
1812, 7, 22. William d bur Short Creek
1812, 12, 31. Achsa m Henry LUPTON
1813, 4, 1. Mary m Thomas HALL
1814, 10, 27. Jordan, s Joseph & Mary, Jefferson Co., O.; m in Short Creek MH, Mary LYPSEY, dt Amasa & Peninah, Jefferson Co., O.
Ch: James   b 1816, 5, 27
    Joseph   " 1818, 1, 20
    Sarah   " 1820, 5, 7
    Amasa L. " 1822, 7, 15
    John   " 1824, 8, 21
    Amos   " 1827, 12, 25
    Pharaby " 1830, 10, 8
1815, 2, 8. Mary d ae 45 bur Short Creek
1815, 3, 25. Martha d ae 83 bur Short Creek
1817, 10, 29. Ira, s Jeremiah & Faith (Baldwin), Jefferson Co., O.; m in Mt. Pleasant Mahala TERRELL, dt Mathew & Sally, Jefferson Co., O.
1818, 1, 28. Arnold, s Jeremiah & Faith (Baldwin), Jefferson Co., O.; m in Mt. Pleasant, Rachel TERRELL, dt Mathew & Sally, Jefferson Co., O.
1818, 11, 27. Keziah d bur Short Creek
1819, 1, 28. Mary m Isaac BROWN
1820, 3, 20. Mahlon, s Jeremiah & Faith, Jefferson Co., O.; m in Short Creek MH, Mary Ann HUSSEY, dt Christopher & Lydia, Jefferson Co., O., d 1865,4,1 ae 68 bur Short Creek
Ch: Ruthanna   b 1821, 4, 14
    Lydia   " 1822, 8, 2
    Deborah   " 1824, 12, 14
    Jane H.   " 1826, 9, 27
    Asahel H. " 1829, 11, 2
    Martha   " 1833, 5, 5
1821, 8, 2. Pharaby J. m Joseph HOWARD
1824, 2, 18. John d ae 86 bur Short Creek
1834, 6, 21. Miriam d ae 65 bur Short Creek
1841, 4, 21. Ruthanna m Ezra CATTELL
1847, 9, 12. Martha d ae 15 bur Short Creek
1849, 11, 1. Jane H. m Geo. CATTELL
1850, 5, 2. Deborah m Joseph HILL
1855, 1, 16. Jeremiah d ae 88 bur Short Creek
1856, 9, 25. Lydia H. m Joel WILLIS
1857, 4, 13. Faith d ae 94 bur on home farm
----, --, --. Asael & H----
   Ch: Oscar
      Willis   b 1861, 7, 25
      Alfred F. " 1864, 9, 13

1805, 5, 18. Benjamin & ch, Margaret, Catharine, Elum & Elijah, rocf Jack Swamp MM, N. C., dtd 1805,3,2
1805, 5, 18. Jonathan & w, Ruth, & dt, Michal rocf Jack Swamp MM, N. C., dtd 1805,3,2
1805, 5, 18. Joseph & w, Mary, & ch, Lemuel, Laban, Esther & Deborah, rocf Jack Swamp MM, N. C., dtd 1805,3,2
1805, 11, 16. Enselem & w, Merriam, & dt,

PATTERSON, continued
    Phariba, rocf Jack Swamp MM, N. C., dtd
    1805,9,7
1805, 11, 16. Jeremiah & w, Faith, & ch, Ira,
    Arnal, Mahlon, Edwin & Tilman, rocf Jack
    Swamp MM, N. C., dtd 1805,9,7
1805, 11, 16. Joseph & Mary & ch, Tace, Clarey,
    Mary, Jordan & Achsa, rocf Jack Swamp MM,
    N. C., dtd 1805,9,7
1806, 5, 24. Joseph Jr. & fam gct Salem MM
1806, 9, 20. Jonathan & w, Ruth, & dt, Michal,
    gct Concord MM
1806, 12, 20. Benjamin & ch, Elam & Elijah,
    gct Concord MM
1806, 12, 20. Margaret & Catharine gct Concord
    MM
1807, 1, 17. John & w, Martha, & ch, Marga-
    ret & Mary, rocf Jack Swamp MM, N. C., dtd
    1806,7,5
1807, 5, 16. Joseph & w, Hannah, & ch, Jere-
    miah, Benjamin, John, Elizabeth, Joel, Sa-
    rah, Rebecca & Isaac, rocf Jack Swamp MM,
    N. C., dtd 1807,3,7
1807, 5, 16. William & w, Elizabeth, & ch,
    Tabitha, Silas, Jeremiah, Exum & Rachel,
    rocf Jack Swamp MM, N. C., dtd 1807,2,7
1808, 3, 22. William Jr. & w, Elizabeth, &
    ch, Silas, Delitha, Jeremiah, Axem & Ra-
    chel, gct Concord MM
1808, 6, 21. Joseph & w, Hannah, & ch, Sarah,
    Rebecca & Isaac, gct Stillwater MM
1808, 6, 21. Jemima & Elizabeth gct Still-
    water MM
1808, 7, 19. Cert rec for Jacob from Jack-
    swamp MM, N. C., dtd 1807,12,5, end to
    Miami MM
1808, 10, 18. Benjamin, John & Joel gct Still-
    water MM
1808, 12, 20. Reuben Taylor gct Stillwater MM,
    to m Jemima Patterson
1811, 5, 21. Mary rocf Rich Square MM, N. C.,
    dtd 1810,12,15
1815, 1, 24. Mary gct Stillwater MM
1818, 1, 2. Ira & w, Mahala, gct Stillwater
    MM
1818, 4, --. Arnald & w, Rachel, gct Still-
    water MM
1818, 7, 21. Edwin, minor, gct Plainfield MM
1823, 9, 25. Edwin & w, Gulielma, rocf Plain-
    field MM, dtd 1823,8,2
1823, 9, 23. Gulielma rocf Plainfield MM, dtd
    1823,8,21
1825, 4, 19. Edwin & w, Gulielma, & s, Mil-
    ton, gct Somerset MM
1825, 12, 20. Tremon gct Somerset MM
1827, 2, 20. Rebecca rocf Somerset MM, dtd
    1826,12,25
1829, 2, 24. Tilmon gct Somerset MM
1830, 3, 23. Rebecca gct Somerset MM
1836, 4, 20. Jordon & w, Mary, & ch, James,
    Joseph, Sarah, Amasa, John, Amos, Pharaby
    & Mary, gct Pennsville MM
1840, 3, 24. Rix dis

1849, 12, 18. Elwood rocf Chesterfield MM, dtd
    1849,11,17
1849, 12, 18. Rix rocf Chesterfield MM, dtd
    1849,11,17
1851, 7, 22. Elwood gct Chesterfield MM
1851, 7, 22. Ricks gct Chesterfield MM
1860, 9, 19. Asahel H. gct Redstone MM, to m
    Esther P. Griffith
1861, 4, 26. Esther J. rocf Redstone MM
1862, 11, 19. Mary, Elizabeth, Wilson, Albert
    & Charles dis jW
1862, 11, 19. Lemuel, Hannah, Eli, Talitha,
    Loisa, Lindley, Elwood, Loretta, Eva Lu-
    zene, David, Geo. Wilson, Gulielma, Amy,
    Asa, William, Milton, Bailey, Tilman, Ra-
    chel E., Joseph, Tilman Jr., Rebecca, Sa-
    rah, Rachel & Deborah dis jW
1865, 11, 21. Mahlon dis jG (W)
1865, 11, 21. Asahel dis jG (W)
1888, 1, 25. Lucinda rocf Fairfield MM (G)
1888, 6, 19. Oscar W. dis jG (W)
1902, 3, 19. William A. recrq (G)
1907, 3, 20. William A. dropped from mbrp (G)
1912, 2, 21. William recrq (G)
1915, 2, 24. Gladys recrq (G)

PAUNOFF
1917, 8, 21. Viola (form Lupton) dis jas (W)

PAXTON
1846, 7, 21. Hannah [Paxson] (form Wells) dis
    mcd
1846, 11, 24. Hannah [Pason] (form Wells) dis
    mcd
1881, 2, 26. Edward W. recrq (G)
1888, 10, 24. Edward dropped from mbrp (G)

PAYNE
1879, 1, 23. Leonard & w, Mary L., recrq (G)
1888, 10, 24. Leonard & Lutitia dropped from
    mbrp (G)
1894, 12, 19. William E. & Charles Wesley
    recrq (G)
1896, 3, 25. William Irvin & Chas. Wesley
    relrq (G)
1901, 2, 20. Emily Florence recrq (G)

PEACOCK
1901, 10, 23. Elwood, s Abram & Mary Jane,
    Hendricks Co., Ind.; m in Harrisville,
    Rena Jane ASHTON, dt Richard S. & Eliza
    G., Harrison Co., O. (W)
1902, 5, 22. Morris, s Abram & Mary Jane,
    Hendricks Co., Ind.; m in Concord, Lydia
    M. HALL, dt Lindley & Milicent, Belmont
    Co., O. (W)
1902, 9, 23. Lydia H. gct Plainfield MM, Ind.
    (W)
1902, 10, 21. Rena J. gct Plainfield MM, Ind.
    (W)

PEADEN
1830, 12, 23. Joseph gct Blue River MM, Ind.
    (H)
1830, 12, 23. Alexander [Peadon] gct Blue
    River MM, Ind. (H)

PEARSON
1805, 1, 19. Cert rec for Benjamin & fam from
    Cattawissa MM, end to Concord MM
1824, 9, 21. Phebe rocf Monallen MM, Pa., dtd
    1824,6,24
1845, 3, 20. Ann gct Salem MM (H)

PEELLE
1811, 6, 18. Robert rocf Richsquare MM, N. C.,
    dtd 1811,5,18
1815, 9, 19. Robert [Peale] gct Richsquare MM,
    N. C.
1845, 6, 24. Josiah [Peel] rocf Marlborough
    MM, dtd 1845,5,27
1849, 2, 20. Josiah [Peele] gct Goshen MM, O.

PELLETT
1825, 10, 19. Abel John, s Francis & Mary,
    Columbiana Co., O.; m in West Grove MH,
    Unity HARRISON, dt Peter & Sarah, Harri-
    son Co., O.
1827, 9, 18. Unity [Pellet] gct Carmel MM

PELT
1902, 7, 23. Robert A. rocf Nahanta MM, N.C.
    (G)
1903, 11, 25. Robert A. gct Columbus MM (G)

PENMAN
1907, 4, 24. Thomas H. dropped from mbrp (G)

PENNELL
----, --, --. Jonathan & Rosanna
    Ch: James   b 1804, 5, 4
        Eli   " 1807, 8, 29
        Lewis   " 1812, 2, 9
        Mary Ann   " 1816, 2, 11

1816, 7, 23. Jonathan [Pennel] & w, Rosanna,
    & ch, James M., Ely Y., Lewis & Mary Ann,
    rocf Wilmington MM, dtd 1816,5,3
1825, 5, 24. James M. gct Cincinnati MM
1825, 5, 24. Jonathan & w, Rosanna, & ch,
    Lewis M. & Mary Ann, gct Cincinnati MM
1827, 7, 24. Eli gct Springboro MM
1830, 5, 18. George [Pennel], minor, rocf
    Redstone MM, dtd 1830,3,30

PENNINGTON
1835, 9, 23. Levi T., s Joseph & Deborah,
    Henry Co., Ind.; m in Short Creek MH, Emma
    PARKER, dt Benajah & Grace, Jefferson Co.,
    O.
1835, 12, 22. Emma gct Spiceland MM, Ind.
1894, 8, 21. John & w, Rebecca W., & ch,
    Alice L. & Fred, rocf Stewart MM, Ia. (G)
1895, 7, 24. Eva rocf Stuart MM, Iowa (G)

1895, 12, 25. Deborah rocf Stuart MM, Ia. (G)
1903, 1, 21. Alice Pennington Bertrum relrq
    (G)
1906, 1, 24. Fred W. relrq (G)
1906, 9, 19. John & w, Rebecca, & dt, Deborah,
    gct Ypsilanti MM, Mich. (G)

PENNOCK
1815, 11, 21. Eli Batten gct Newgarden MM, to
    m Phebe Pennock

PENNRAN
1901, 2, 20. Thomas H. recrq (G)

PENROSE
1816, 5, 2. Hannah m Benj. STANTON
1844, 4, 24. John, s Thos. & Sarah, Morgan
    Co., O.; m in Concord, Hannah M. LIGHTFOOT
    dt Samuel & Rachel, Jefferson Co., O.

1813, 3, 23. Thomas & w, Sarah, & ch, Hannah,
    Mahlon, Richard, James, Thomas, John
    Hughes & Jacob Hibbs, rocf Moncey MM,
    Pa., dtd 1812,12,23
1815, 6, 20. Robert & w, Rachel, & ch, Jesse,
    Mark, Isaac, Edwin & Sarah, rocf Young
    Street MM, Upper Canada, dtd 1815,4,13
1818, 9, 22. Robert & w, Rachel, & ch, Jesse,
    Mark, Isaac, Edwin & Sarah, gct Plainfield
    MM
1821, 5, 22. Mahlon dis mcd
1827, 5, 22. Thomas & w, Sarah, & ch, Sarah
    Ann & Joseph, gct Smithfield MM
1827m 5, 22. Thomas Jr. & James gct Smith-
    field MM
1830, 12, 21. John gct Smithfield MM
1833, 6, 18. Richard rst at Deerfield MM on
    consent of this mtg
1839, 6, 18. Lavina, minor, rocf Plainfield
    MM, dtd 1839,3,20
1844, 6, 18. Hannah M. gct Pennville MM
1852, 11, 23. Edward Maule gct Pennville MM,
    to m Hannah Penrose
1868, 10, 20. Lindley B. Steer gct Pennville
    MM, to m Hannah S. Penrose (W)
1870, 7, 19. Hannah (form Gibson) dis mcd &
    jG (W)
1871, 1, 26. Hannah (form Gibbons) con mcd
    (G)
1871, 11, 23. Hannah G. rocf Alliance MM (G)

PERDUE
1841, 1, 19. Charles Atkinson, minor, rocf
    Plainfield MM, dtd 1840,12,23

PERRY
1862, 11, 19. Elizabeth, Ephraim, David, Job,
    Asenath, Asa, Sarah, Rachel, Elizabeth,
    Phebe, Job Jr., Letitia & Rachel dis jW(G)
1893, 1, 25. Samuel recrq (G)
1895, 7, 24. Samuel dropped from mbrp (G)
1901, 7, 24. Mary recrq (G)
1902, 8, 20. James C. dropped from mbrp (G)

PETERSON
1825, 7, 19. Elizabeth (form Taylor) dis mcd
1914, 1, 20. Alice S. dis mcd (W)

PETTIT
1832, 11, 21. Joseph, s Wm. & Mary, Columbiana
      Co., O.; m in Mt. Pleasant, Hannah G.
      HUSSEY, dt Christopher & Lydia, Jefferson
      Co., O., d 1869,11,11 ae 60
1834, 4, 23. William, s Wm. & Mary, Columbus
      Co.; m in Mt. Pleasant, Jane R. HUSSEY,
      dt Christopher & Lydia, Jefferson Co., O.
1840, 1, 22. Elnathan, s Wm. & Mary, Colum-
      biana Co., O.; m in Short Creek MH, Hannah
      J. EYRE, dt Robert & Jemima, Harrison Co.,
      O., d 1861,6,1
      Ch: John Grubb b 1840, 11, 2
          Milton E.   " 1843, 5, 23 d 1862, 4, 5
          Mary Ann   " 1846, 7, 2
1844, 2, 21. Milton R., s Wm. & Mary, Colum-
      biana Co., O.; m in Short Creek MH, Hannah
      G. GRUBB, dt Curtis & Ann, Jefferson Co.,O.
      Ch: Curtice G. b 1844, 12, 31 d 1845, 2, 5
          William   " 1846, 3, 15
          Anna Eliza-
            beth   " 1849, 4, 11
          Mary C.   " 1851, 3k 23
          Frank R.   " 1853, 10, 5
          Hannah G.   " 1856, 9, 30
      Milton R. m 2nd 1858,12,1 in West Grove MH
      Sarah L. LADD, dt Peter & Catharine, Har-
      rison Co., O.
      Ch: Emma C.   b 1859, 9, 17
          Milton E. " 1865, 9, 26 d 1865,10,10
1861, 6, 1. Hannah G. d ae 45
1862, 5, 5. Milton E. Jr. d ae 19
1865, 7, 26. M. Elma m Oscar J. GRIFFITH
1869, 4, 9. Elnathan Jr., s Elnathan & Mar-
      garet, d
1870, 10, 26. Mary C. m Geo. E. JACKSON
1870, 12, 28. Joseph, s Wm. & Mary, Jefferson
      Co., O.; m in Mt. Pleasant, Lydia W. RAN-
      KIN, dt John W. & Elizabeth, Jefferson
      Co., O.

1807, 9, 19. Cert rec for William & w, Mary,
      & ch, Benjamin, Elizabeth & William, from
      Calawissa MM, dtd 1807,5,22, end to Salem
      MM
1833, 5, 21. Hannah gct Sandy Spring MM
1834, 12, 23. Jane R. gct Upper Springfield MM
1840, 7, 21. Hannah G. gct Sandy Spring MM
1841, 8, 24. Elnathan & w, Hannah G., & s,
      John Grubb, rocf Sandy Spring MM, dtd
      1841,6,25
1844, 9, 24. Hannah G. gct Sandy Spring MM
1846, 4, 26. Mary Jane [Pettet] rocf Smith-
      field MM, dtd 1846,4,20
1846, 8, 18. Milton R. [Pettet] & w, Hannah
      G., & s, John G., rocf Sandy Spring MM,
      dtd 1846,6,26
1859, 3, 23. Mary Jane Cook (form Pettet) con
      mcd

1859, 4, 20. Joseph & w, Hannah G., & dt,
      Mary Elma, rocf Sandy Spring MM, dtd
      1859,3,25
1862, 5, 20. Mary Jane Cook (form Pettit) dis
      mcd
1863, 3, 24. Milton R. [Pettitt] dis jG (W)
1863, 3, 24. Elnathan dis jG (W)
1863, 10, 21. Elnathan gct Smithfield MM, to
      m Margaret H. Wood (G)
1864, 8, 24. Margaret H. rocf Smithfield MM
      (G)
1865, 7, 19. Oscar J. Griffith rocf Redstone
      MM, to m M. Elma PETTIT (G)
1867, 1, 22. Sarah L. [Petit] dis jG (W)
1870, 5, 20. Jane P. rocf Burlington MM, N.J.
      (G)
1871, 11, 23. Mary Ann Markeson (form Pettit)
      con mcd (G)
1871, 12, 21. William P. rpd mcd (G)
1872, 3, 21. Franklin R. gct Indianapolis
      MM, Ind. (G)
1872, 5, 23. William B. con misconduct (G)
1872, 7, 25. William B. gct Indianapolis MM,
      Ind. (G)
1874, 11, 26. Jane R. gct Salem MM (G)
1876, 4, 20. Elnathan & w, Margaret H., & s,
      Elnathan, gct Columbus MM, O. (G)
1878, 5, 23. Hannah G. gct Gilead MM (G)
1881, 8, 23. Emma Scott (form Pettit) dis
      mcd (W)

PEW
1831, 12, 20. Achillas gct Cincinnati MM
1835, 10, 20. Hannah gct Cincinnati MM

PHEBUS
1861, 3, 20. Amy (form Waterman) dis mcd

PHELPHOT
1907, 11, 30. Harry, s Lewis & Anna, d (G)

PHILLIPS
1828, 7, 22. Susanna (form Reynolds) rpd mcd
1830, 8, 24. Susanna dis
1872, 5, 20. Anna Jane (form Hurford) con mcd
      (G)
1876, 5, 25. Elmore & ch, Josephine E., Alon-
      zo C., Ida Bell, Jesse E., Smiley E. &
      James Evan, recrq (G)
1885, 7, 22. Ida Williams (form Phillips)
      gct Rush Creek MM (G)
1887, 9, 21. Alonzo C. gct Damascus MM (G)
1889, 9, 25. Josephine Hibbs (form Phillips)
      gct Freeport MM, O. (G)
1915, 12, 23. Smylie S. gct Des Moines MM,
      Ia. (G)

PHILPOT
1881, 2, 26. William recrq (G)
1895, 8, 21. Lewis [Philpott] & w, Anna,
      recrq (G)
1896, 1, 23. Harry recrq (G)
1908, 4, 22. Lewis J. & w, Anna, relrq (G)

PICKERING
1809, 9, 28. Jacob, s Jacob & Hannah, Bel-
     mont Co., O.; m in Short Creek MH, Rachel
     HURFORD, dt John & Sarah, Jefferson Co.,O.

1807, 3, 21. Evan James gct Salem MM, to m
     Rebecca Pickering
1810, 2, 20. Rachel gct Stillwater MM
1813, 6, 22. Jacob Jr. & w, Rachel, & ch,
     John Hurford & Jonathan, rocf Stillwater
     MM, dtd 1813,4,27
1815, 4, 18. Evan, minor, rocf Hopewell MM,
     dtd 1814,8,2
1820, 4, 18. Evan con mcd
1823, 6, 24. Evan gct Flushing MM
1828, 9, 19. Rebecca dis jH
1829, 8, 18. Jacob & w, Rachel, & ch, John
     H., Jonathan E., Sarah Ann, Aquilla, Eli-
     hu & Naomi, gct Duck Creek MM, Ind.
1830, 1, 19. John Sr. dis jH
1831, 2, 22. Mary dis jH
1833, 3, 19. Mary & Elizabeth, minor ch Sam-
     uel & Sarah, rocf Stillwater MM, dtd 1833,
     1,26
1834, 6, 24. Amanda dis jH
1841, 7, 20. Mary Ann Embree (form Pickering)
     dis mcd
1869, 12, 7. Abel gct Clear Creek MM, Ill.
     (H)
1874, 7, 21. Isaac rst at Chesterfield MM on
     consent of this mtg (W)
1875, 6, 24. Josiah F. & w, Rebecca J., recrq
     (G)
1882, 7, 19. Eliza C. & Anna V. recrq (G)
1885, 3, 25. Ellis H. recrq (G)
1893, 6, 21. Rosa May recrq (G)
1895, 2, 20. Clyde Ward recrq (G)

PICKETT
1911, 8, 23. Harvey, s Robert & Irene, Hen-
     dricks Co., Ind.; m in Harrisville, Rebec-
     ca BINNS, dt James Hervey & Ida,Jefferson
     Co., O. (W)
1903, 10, 21. Perley, s Wm. & Rebecca, Belmont
     Co., O.; m in Concord, Sarah E. STEER, dt
     Israel & Rebecca B., Belmont Co., O. (W)

1873, 10, 21. Joseph John H. Taber gct Penns-
     ville MM, to m Mary H. Picket (W)
1904, 4, 19. Perley rocf Stillwater MM (W)
1905, 3, 21. Clifton D. Hall gct Plainfield
     MM, Ind., to m Anna Pickett (W)
1905, 12, 19. Perley & w, Sara E. S., gct
     Stillwater MM (W)
1912, 6, 18. Rebecca Binns gct Mill Creek MM,
     Ind. (W)

PILINGS
1915, 2, 24. Rosa recrq (G)

PINKERTON
1899, 3, 22. Michael L. & w, Helen, & dt,
     Lida B., recrq (G)

1907, 4, 24. Mrs. Mike & fam dropped from
     mbrp (G)

PINKHAM
1864, 5, 18. Mary F., w Thomas, d ae 32

1861, 8, 21. Thos. Edward rocf Salem MM
1861, 11, 20. Mary F. rocf Upper Springfield
     MM
1862, 12, 24. William P. & w, Emma C., & ch,
     Mary Cornelia & Arthur Edwin, rocf Salem
     MM (G)
1865, 3, 22. Wm. P. & w, Emma C., & ch, Mary
     Cornelia & Arthur Edward, gct Honey Creek
     MM, Ia. (G)

PITMAN
1828, 12, 23. Margaret dis jH
1832, 3, 20. Anthony dis jas
1834, 1, 21. Rebecca, Esther, Elias & Eliza,
     ch Anthony & Margaret, gct Allum Creek MM

PLATT
1823, 1, 21. Benjamin rocf Oblong MM, N. Y.,
     dtd 1817,6,16

PLUMMER
1821, 1, 24. Mary, w I. S., d bur Smithfield
1823, 2, 10. Caleb, s Joseph, d bur Richmond
1823, 5, 13. Deborah d bur Richmond
1837, 4, 10. Alice, w John, d bur Richmond
1842, 6, 10. Mary [Plumer], w Joseph, d ae
     41 bur Cross Creek

1823, 3, 18. Greenberry G. recrq
1824, 4, 20. Greenberry G. gct Concord MM
1826, 8, 22. Jane rocf Concord MM, dtd 1826,
     5,24
1862, 9, 24. Greenberry G. & w, Jane M., gct
     Plainfield MM, Indiana (G)
1862, 11, 19. Robert, Jane, Abram, Rachel, Jo-
     seph, Micajah, Hannah, Elizabeth, Lydia
     & John dis jW
1877, 9, 18. Julia A. Bates (form Plummer)
     con mcd (W)

POLLARD
1834, 12, 12. Amy d ae 62 bur Short Creek

1807, 1, 17. Joseph & w, Hannah, & ch, Naomi,
     Benjamin, Elizabeth, Joseph, John, Mariah
     & Emily, rocf Crooked Run MM, dtd 1806,7,3
1816, 12, 24. Benjamin dis mcd
1819, 2, 23   Joseph & w, Hannah, & ch, Mariah,
     Emily, Hannah & Samuel, gct Smithfield MM
1832, 10, 23. Hannah rocf Smithfield MM

PORTER
1884, 7, 23. Lizzie Rankin dropped from mbrp
     (G)
1902, 12, 24. Amy Bell & Susanna recrq (G)
1912, 3, 20. Ida M. recrq (G)
1913, 7, 23. Ida May dropped from mbrp (G)

PORTER, continued
1914, 1, 21. Charles E. & Annie recrq (G)
1914, 1, 21. Harrison recrq (G)
1915, 2, 24. Ida May recrq (G)
1915, 2, 24. Lizzie recrq (G)
1922, 4, 19. Elizabeth recrq (G)

POTTS
1828, 7, 22. Abigail dis jH

POWELL
1892, 10, 19. Roney & Mary recrq (G)

POWERS
1810, 6, 19. Jane (form Welch) dis mcd

PRESTON
1812, 12, 22. Paul & w, Sarah, & s, Joseph,
    rocf Buckingham MM, Pa., dtd 1812,10,5
1819, 2, 23. Paul dis disunity

PRICE
1843, 10, 21. Susanna, w Warrick, d ae 77 bur
    Smithfield
1847, 4, 24. Oliver, s Wm. & Edith, d ae 17
    bur Smithfield
1853, 11, 2. Edith, w Wm., d ae 54 bur Smith-
    field
1856, 7, 2. Wm., s Ivarrick & Susannah, Jef-
    ferson Co., O.; m in Mt. Pleasant, Hannah
    WALKER, dt Lewis & Rachel, Jefferson Co.,O.
1857, 10, 8. Warrick Sr. d ae 88 bur Smith-
    field
1876, 5, 31. Hannah W. m Chas. WRIGHT

1806, 4, 19. Israel & w, Hannah, & ch, Eliza-
    beth, William, Frances & Israel, roc
1816, 6, 18. Samuel rocf Buckingham MM, dtd
    1816,5,6
1819, 8, 24. Samuel gct Miami MM
1826, 8, 22. Mary (form Michanar) con mcd
1829, 11, 24. Mary, dt Joseph, rocf Falls MM,
    Pa., dtd 1829,6,4
1830, 9, 21. Mary gct Flushing MM
1839, 4, 25. Joseph & w, Eliza & ch, Mary,
    Elwood & Eliza Ann, gct Stillwater MM
    (H)
1852, 8, 24. David B. Updegraff gct Smith-
    field MM, to m Rebecca B. Price
·1857, 1, 21. Hannah V. gct Smithfield MM
1862, 1, 22. William & w, Hannah, rocf
    Smithfield MM
1864, 4, 19. William dis jG
1864, 10, 19. Martha J. recrq
1864, 10, 19. Martha Jane recrq (G)
1864, 11, 23. Charles H. & w, Charity D., rocf
    Sandy Spring MM (G)
1865, 7, 18. Hannah dis jG (W)
1914, 6, 24. Maud recrq (G)

PUGH
1807, 7, 18. David, minor, rocf Notingham MM,
    dtd 1807,4,10

1809, 7, 18. Ester & ch, Sarah, Ester,
    Achilles & Rachel, rocf Nottingham MM,
    dtd 1809,5,5
1814, 3, 22. Margaret (form James) dis mcd
1815, 4, 18. David dis mcd
1818, 12, 22. Sarah Harris (form Pugh) dis mcd
1825, 9, 20. Ann recrq·
1826, 8, 22. Rachel White (form Pugh) dis mcd
1830, 6, 22. Anna dis jH
1831, 12, 21. Achilles gct Cincinnati MM
1835, 10, 20. Hannah gct Cincinnati MM
1888, 10, 24. Zilpha dropped from mbrp (G)

PURVIANCE
1816, 10, 19. Sina d ae 2 bur Smithfield
1819, 9, 2. William, s James & Elizabeth,
    Jefferson Co., O.; m in Short Creek MH,
    Eleanor SIDWELL, dt Henry & Sinah
1826, 4, 29. Joseph d ae 45 bur Smithfield
1837, 8, 28. Mary d bur Smithfield
1838, 10, 14. David d bur Smithfield
1839, 10, 30. William, s Joseph & Deborah,
    Jefferson Co., O.; m in West Grove MH, Sa-
    rah HULFORD, dt Evan & Sarah, Harrison
    Co., O.
    Ch: Evan H.   b 1840, 11, 29
        William J. " 1848, 8, 8

1807, 3, 21. Thomas rocf Redstone MM, dtd
    1807,2,1
1808, 2, 20. Thomas dis mcd
1813, 3, 23. Deborah gct Plymouth MM
1815, 4, 6. Eli Sidwell gct Plymouth MM, to
    m Sarah Purviance
1819, 12, 21. Eleanor [Perviance] gct Smith-
    field MM
1840, 5, 19. Sarah gct Smithfield MM
1862, 8, 19. Sarah dis jG
1862, 8, 19. William dis jG
1864, 11, 2. Evan [Perviance] dis jG (W)
1865, 1, 24. Lydia dis disunity (W)

PYLE
1816, 3, 7. Sarah m Israel SCHOOLEY
1824, 7, 31. Jane d bur Grandhutton
1824, 9, 19. William d ae 42 bur Grandhutton
1832, 8, 29. Deborah m John GRAY

1821, 1, 23. William & w, Jane, & ch, Deborah,
    Harland, Isaac, Sarah, George & Caleb,
    recrq
1836, 5, 24. Harland dis mcd
1836, 11, 20. Isaac dis mcd
1837, 7, 18. Sarah Ball (form Pyle) dis mcd
1842, 8, 23. Caleb dis jas
1845, 12, 23. William dis mcd

QUAINTANCE
1842, 9, 21. Joseph K., s Eli & Betty, Dela-
    ware Co., O.; m in Short Creek MH, Phebe
    BREWER, dt Elias & Mary, Jefferson Co.,O.

1807, 11, 21. Joseph & w, Susanna, & ch,

QUAINTANCE, continued
     William, Eli, Ann, Susanna & Fisher, rocf
     Hopewell MM, dtd 1806,8,4
1842, 12, 20. Phebe gct Gilead MM

QUIMBY
1902, 8, 20. Charles & w dropped from mbrp
     (G)

QUINN
1895, 9, 25. Charles C. & w, Ada G., recrq (G)

RALEY
----, --, --. Asa [Railey] m Asenath ----- d
     1890,12,14 ae 85 bur Concord
     Ch: David   b 1827, 5, 5
         Newton   " 1828, 9, 11
         Ann   " 1832, 5, 24
         Mary   " 1834, 9, 15
         Martha   " 1836, 10, 12
         Rachel   " 1839, 1, 2
         Elizabeth " 1842, 5, 12 d 1929, 1,15
         Mellissa
             Ann   " 1844, 11, 18 " 1921, 4,13
             bur Colerain
1829, 5, 27. Ann m Thos. HIRST
1833, 9, --. Ann [Railey] d bur Concord
1835, 1, 15. James [Railéy] d ae 80
1835, 1, 19. James [Railey] d ae 79 bur Con-
     cord
1856, 2, 29. Rachel d ae 91
1861, 12, 13. Ruth d
1871, 12, 27. Mary H. m Edward STRATTON
1872, 10, 30. Martha m Joseph RUSSELL
1873, 3, 24. Asa d ae 76 bur Concord
1875, 1, 19. Joseph d ae 74 bur Concord
1875, 10, 27. Rachel m Jacob MAULE (W)
1882, 3, 31. Mary d ae 81 bur Concord

1813, 1, 19. John Howard gct Concord MM, to
     m Hannah Railey
1815, 1, 24. David rocf Westland MM, dtd
     1814,11,3
1817, 10, 21. Joseph [Raleigh] rocf Newgarden
     MM, O., dtd 1817,8,14
1817, 10, 21. James [Raleigh], minor, rocf
     Newgarden MM, dtd 1817,8,14
1819, 9, 21. Joseph gct Newgarden MM, O.
1822, 6, 18. Thomas rocf Sandy Spring MM,
     dtd 1822,5,24
1822, 7, 23. James gct Sandy Spring MM, O.
1827, 2, 20. Ann [Reighley] rocf Flushing
     MM, dtd 1827,1,26
1831, 2, 26. Eli [Railey] Jr. rocf Westland
     MM, dtd 1831,1,26
1831, 6, 21. Thomas & w, Ann, & ch, Talitha
     Ann, Robert & Sarah Jane, gct Flushing MM
1847, 11, 23. Joseph gct Westland MM, to m
     Sally Fowler
1848, 3, 21. Sally rocf Westland MM, dtd
     1848,2,23
1850, 10, 22. David con mcd
1851, 3, 18. Elizabeth rst on consent of West-

land MM
1854, 2, 21. David gct Red Cedar MM, Ia.
1862, 11, 4. Thomas gct Middleton MM, O. (H)
1862, 11, 19. Elizabeth [Railey] dis jW (G)
1862, 11, 19. Asa & Asenath [Railey] & ch,
     Mary, Martha, Rachel, Elizabeth & Melissa,
     dis jW (G)
1862, 11, 19. Mary [Railey] Sr. dis jW (G)
1862, 11, 19. Joseph & Sally dis jW (G)
1865, 8, 22. Newton dis mcd & military ser-
     vice (W)
1869, 7, 20. Elizabeth gct Hickory Grove
     MM, Ia. (W)
1872, 3, 19. Mary H. gct Middleton MM (W)
1881, 3, 24. James & David [Rail] recrq (G)
1926, 12, 21. Elizabeth T. gct Stillwater MM
     (W)

RANKIN
1870, 12, 28. Lydia W. m Joseph PETTIT

1814, 11, 22. Martha rocf Warrington MM, dtd
     1814,7,21
1815, 5, 23. Martha gct Plainfield MM
1817, 10, 21. John rocf Byberry MM, Pa., dtd
     1817,7,15
1845, 2, 20. Abigail gct Clear Creek MM, Ill.
     (H)
1846, 1, 22. Martha gct Clear Creek MM, Ill.
     (H)
1846, 8, 18. Lydia (form Watkins) dis mcd
1850, 10, 22. Lydia W. rst
1860, 8, 22. Elizabeth & William J. W.,
     minor ch Lydia, recrq
1884, 7, 23. William dropped from mbrp (G)

RATCLIFF
1819, 3, 31. Elizabeth m Lewis LEWIS
1819, 4, 1. Martha m Zebulon WORRALL
1829, 12, 23. Mary m Daniel ANDREWS
1830, 4, 28. Wm. F., s Wm. & Mary, Jefferson
     Co., O.; m in Mt. Pleasant, Sarah CADWALA-
     DER, dt Isaac & Elizabeth, Harrison Co.,O.
     Ch: Isaac C. b 1831, 3, 6
         Mary B.   " 1832, 11, 25
         Elizabeth " 1834, 2, 10
         Martha   " 1836, 6, 19
1830, 10, 27. Hannah B. m Samuel HURFORD
1832, 3, 1. Josiah, s John & Sarah, Harri-
     son Co., O.; m in Harrisville, Mary HALL,
     dt John & Tacy, Jefferson Co., O.
1832, 8, 15. Sally Ann d ae 11 bur Harris-
     ville
1832, 9, 23. Mary d bur Short Creek
1834, 8, 28. Elizabeth m Amos HIBBS
1834, 10, 13. Benj. B., s John & Sarah, Jef-
     ferson Co., O.; m in Short Creek MH, Mar-
     tha MICHENER, dt Daniel & Anna, Jefferson
     Co., O.
1835, 4, 13. Mary d ae 74 bur Short Creek
----, --, --. Ellwood & Martha J.
     Ch: William   b 1838, 7, 21
         Isaac   " 1840, 10, 3

RATCLIFF, continued
1845, 9, 22. Isaac d bur Short Creek
1845, 10, 4. Margaret d bur Short Creek
1864, 3, 9. Isaac, s Elwood & Martha J.,
      Jefferson Co., O.; m in Mt. Pleasant, Mar-
      garet W. HUSSEY, dt Penrose & Susanna,
      Jefferson Co., O.
          Ch: Horace H. b 1867, 10, 6
              Elwood   " 1871, 11, 14
              Anna Lydia " 1875, 10, 27
----, --, --. Wm. R. & Esther W.
          Ch: George M. b 1869, 2, 28 d 1869, 4,27
              Frederick
                 W.   " 1871, 2, 22
1874, 9, 30. Elwood, s Isaac & Margaret, Jef-
      ferson Co., O.; m in Short Creek MH, Re-
      becca B. TERRELL, dt Wm. & Lydia BALLANGER
      Jefferson Co., O.
1878, 8, 23. Rebecca B. d ae 65 (an elder)
      (G)

1811, 5, 21. Isaac & w, Margaret, & ch, Mar-
      tha, Elwood & Mary, rocf Waynoak MM, Va.,
      dtd 1811,4,6
1817, 5, 20. Harrison & w, Mildred, rocf
      Fairfield MM, dtd 1817,3,29
1817, 6, 24. Josiah rocf Waynook MM, Va.,
      dtd 1817,5,3
1817, 6, 24. Mary & ch, Elizabeth, Hannah,
      Fleming & William, rocf Waynook MM, Va.,
      dtd 1817,5,3
1818, 6, 23. Josiah gct Waynoak MM, Va.
1827, 5, 22. Sarah J., Hannah B. & Elizabeth
      rocf Wainoak MM, Va., dtd 1826,10,7
1830, 3, 23. Elwood gct Flushing to m Mary
      Ellis
1830, 8, 24. Mary rocf Flushing MM, dtd 1830,
      7,22
1831, 5, 24. Wm. gct Flushing MM, to m Sarah
      Wood
1831, 10, 18. Harrison & w, Mildred, gct West-
      land MM
1832, 4, 24. William gct Flushing MM
1835, 4, 21. John gct Flushing MM
1835, 5, 19. Benjamin & w, Martha, gct Flush-
      ing MM
1835, 10, 20. Sarah gct Flushing MM
1836, 10, 18. Hannah gct Flushing MM
1837, 8, 22. Elwood gct Springboro MM, to m
      Martha J. Robinson
----, --, --. William F. & w, Sarah, & ch,
      Isaac, Mary, Elizabeth & Martha, gct
      Flushing MM
1837, 9, 19. Robert gct Flushing MM
1837, 10, 24. Martha gct Flushing MM
1837, 10, 24. Robert, minor, gct Flushing MM
1838, 4, 24. Martha J. rocf Springboro MM,
      dtd 1838,2,20
1843, 5, 23. Mary & s, Josiah C., gct Still-
      water MM
1860, 8, 22. George Cattell gct Flushing MM,
      to m Mary B. Ratcliff
1861, 8, 21. Isaac C. & w, Rebecca, & s,

                    Chas. Arthur, rocf Flushing MM
1862, 6, 25. William F. & s, John C. & Wm.
      N., rocf Flushing MM (G)
1862, 5, 20. Elwood dis jG (W)
1862, 6, 25. Hannah Jane rocf Flushing MM (G)
1864, 7, 19. Martha dis jG (W)
1865, 2, 22. Wm. F. & s, John C. & Wm. N.,
      gct New Sharron MM, Ia. (G)
1865, 2, 22. Hannah J. gct New Sharon MM, Ia.
      (G)
1865, 8, 23. William R. rocf Goshen MM, O.,
      to m Sarah Esther WILLIAMS (G)
1865, 9, 20. Isaac C. & w, Rebecca, & ch,
      Charles Augustus & Mary Elizabeth, gct
      Lynn Grove MM, Ia. (G)
1866, 7, 25. Sarah E. rocf Goshen MM (G)
1866, 7, 25. Julia A. (form Lupton) con mcd
      (G)
1867, 8, 20. Isaac & William dis jG (W)
1869, 12, 23. Julia A. gct Spiceland MM, Ind.
      (G)
1901, 6, 19. E. Wood relrq (G)
1907, 4, 24. H. H. & w, Blanche N., & ch,
      Horace Hussey Jr. & Richard Updegraff,
      relrq (G)
1910, 9, 21. Margaret H. relrq (G)

RATHMIER
1894, 7, 25. Ella dropped from mbrp (G)

RATTISKANE
1809, 8, 22. James & w, Susanna, & gr s,
      James Hague, rocf Fairfax MM, dtd 1808,10,
      22

RAWSON
1869, 11, 25. Samuel, Tabitha, Jane, Alice
      Leota & Chas. E. recrq (G)

RAYFIELD
1892, 10, 19. Angeline B. recrq (G)

RAYL
1894, 3, 21. Hannah Jane recrq (G)
1894, 3, 21. Samuel A., Lucy Elizabeth &
      Athelbert recrq (G)
1895, 3, 20. David S. & Athelbert recrq (G)
1902, 8, 20. David P., Lucy, Samuel, Athel-
      bert & Hannah dropped from mbrp (G)

RAYNARD
1894, 3, 21. Charles recrq (G)
1902, 12, 24. Charles dropped from mbrp (G)

REA
1880, 6, 24. Hiram & w, Nancy, recrq (G)
1881, 2, 26. Carrie & Ida recrq (G)
1881, 2, 26. Vena recrq (G)
1884, 7, 23. Ida [Rhea] dropped from mbrp (G)
1888, 10, 24. Vena [Ray] dropped from mbrp
      (G)
1907, 4, 24. Nancy dropped from mbrp (G)

REEDER
1819, 1, 20. Thomas, Columbiana Co., O.; m in
     Short Creek MH, Hannah JAMES, Jefferson
     Co., O.

1819, 3, 23. Hannah gct Newgarden MM, O.
1879, 4, 24. Washington & Martha [Reeder]
     recrq (G)
1895, 7, 24. G. W. & Pearl H. dropped from
     mbrp (G)
1895, 7, 24. Martha C. dropped from mbrp (G)

RECKMAN
1898, 6, 22. Samuel recrq (G)

REDD
1816, 5, 30. Charity m Pusey WOOD

1814, 6, 21. Charity rocf Hopewell MM, dtd
     1814,1,4, end to Plainfield MM
1816, 1, 23. Charity rocf Plainfield MM, dtd
     1815,9,23

REES
1763, 10, 15. Rachel [Reese] b

1813, 6, 22. Rachel recrq
1817, 4, 22. Stephen & Silas, minors, rocf
     Peru MM, N. Y., dtd 1815,8,24
1830, 11, 23. Rachel dis jH
1907, 9, 25. Ruth [Reece] recrq (G)

REEVES
1814, 7, 19. Mary rocf SD MM, dtd 1814,5,25
1819, 10, 19. Mary gct Woodberry MM, N. J.

REICHARD
1909, 7, 21. Lida McLaughlin relrq (G)

REIGEL
1892, 10, 19. Martha recrq (G)

RENSHAW
1920, 6, 23. Frank & w, Elizabeth, & dt, Al-
     berta, recrq (G)
1926, 7, 29. Frank & w, Elizabeth, & dt, Al-
     berta, relrq (G)

REPPERT
1917, 11, 22. Ruth relrq (G)
1922, 10, 25. Julia Stephens relrq (G)
1929, 3, 20. Ellsworth recrq (G)

REVEL
1892, 10, 19. Ocena recrq (G)
1892, 10, 19. Rosa recrq (G)

REYNOLDS
----, --, --. Richard B. & Esther
     Ch: Jeremiah   b 1812, 12, 27
         Matilda   " 1814, 6, 6
         Rachel   " 1815, 11, 21 d 1823, 1,11
           bur Short Creek

     Ch: Susanna   b 1817, 8, 31
         Richard   " 1820, 4, 8
         Oliver   " 1822, 11, 16
         Reuben   " 1824, 9, 3
1832, 5, 30. Stephen K., s Stephen & Hannah
     (now Hannah Wester), Belmont Co., O.; m
     in Concord, Miriam KINSEY, dt John & Mary,
     Belmont Co., O.

1806, 3, 15. Cert for Levi end to Salem MM
1807, 10, 17. Thomas rocf Nottingham, dtd
     1807,4,11, end by Concord MM, 1807,8,18
1808, 1, 16. Thomas dis mou
1809, 5, 23. Cert rec for Micheal from Little
     Britten MM, Pa., dtd 1808,4,9, end to New-
     garden MM, O.
1817, 9, 23. Richard B. & w, Esther, & ch,
     Jeremiah, Mahala & Rachel, rocf Nottingham
     MM, dtd 1817,8,9
1819, 7, 20. Joseph & w, Rachel, & s, Abia,
     rocf Notingham MM, Md., dtd 1819,6,17
1819, 7, 20. Joseph Jr. rocf Notingham MM,
     Md., dtd 1819,6,17
1819, 7, 20. Rebea Susanna Lydia & Lettice
     rocf Notingham MM, Md., dtd 1819,6,17
1819, 8, 24. Cyrus rocf Notingham MM, dtd
     1819,7,9
1820, 9, 19. Joseph & w, Rachel, gct Flush-
     ing MM
1820, 10, 24. Joseph Jr. gct Flushing MM
1821, 4, 24. Lydia Yardley (form Reynolds)
     dis mcd
1821, 5, 22. Rebecca Wells (form Reynolds)
     dis mcd
1821, 6, 19. Lettis Harris (form Reynolds)
     con mcd
1825, 5, 24. Richard B. & w, Esther, & ch,
     Jeremiah, Matilda, Susanna, Richard,
     Oliver & Reuben, gct Flushing MM
1828, 7, 22. Susanna Phillips (form Reynolds)
     rpd mcd
1829, 3, 24. Cyrus [Reanolds] gct Flushing MM
1830, 4, 20. Susanna Phillips (form Reynolds)
     dis mcd
1831, 6, 21. Ann M. rocf Baltimore MM, E. &
     W. Dist., dtd 1831,4,7
1831, 6, 21. Ruthanna & Mary Jane rocf
     Nottingham & Little Britain MM, Md., dtd
     1831,6,10
1831, 6, 21. Stephen K. rocf Baltimore MM
     E. & W. Dist., dtd 1831,4,7
1832, 8, 21. Ann Oneal (form Reynolds) dis
     mcd
1836, 10, 18. Ruthanna & Mary Jane, gct
     Flushing MM
1837, 2, 21. Stephen K. dis jas
1843, 2, 21. Miriam dis jas
1892, 10, 19. Eliza recrq (G)
1892, 10, 19. William recrq (G)

RHODES
1758, 8, 19. Joseph b
1818, 9, 30. Joseph, Columbiana Co., O.; m in

RHODES, Joseph, continued
    Mt. Pleasant, Sally TERRELL
1824, 4, 28. Harmon, s Jos. & Martha, Jeffer-
    son Co., O.; m in Mt. Pleasant, Elizabeth
    BROWN, dt Isaac & Rebecca
1827, 2, 22. Lydia m Ashley JOHNSON
1842, 11, 9. Joseph d ae 84
1866, 3, 14. Mary d ae 87

1819, 5, 18. Joseph & ch, Harmon & Lydia,
    also a minor named Anna Morris, rocf Salem
    MM, dtd 1819,4,21
1822, 11, 19. Lidia, minor dt Joseph, gct
    Clear Creek MM
1827, 1, 23. Lydia rocf Clear Creek MM, dtd
    1826,11,11
1835, 11, 24. Harnan & w, Elizabeth, & ch, Re-
    becca, Martha, William & Isaac, gct Penns-
    ville MM
1843, 5, 23. James Tribby gct Chesterfield
    MM, to m Rebecca Rhodes

RICE
1844, 5, 21. Jane (form Millhouse) con mcd
1853, 8, 23. Julia Maria (form Newport) dis
    mcd
1860, 3, 20. Jane M. dis jG (W)
1861, 9, 25. Jane M. Waters (form Rice) con
    mcd
1864, 11, 23. Charles H. & Charity rocf Sandy
    Spring MM (G)
1869, 4, 22. Chas. H. & w, Charity D., gct
    Alliance MM (G)
1872, 6, 20. Martha Jane Singer (form Rice)
    con mcd (G)

RICHARDS
----, --, --. Samuel & Ann
    Ch: Isaac W.   b 1803, 7, 3 d 1829, 5, 5
        Jacob W.   " 1805, 8, 9
        Beulah W. " 1807, 10, 11
        Mary   " 1809, 12, 3
        Sarah   " 1811, 12, 25
        Samuel   " 1814, 2, 15
        Ann   " 1820, 8, 19
1827, 5, 5. Isaac W. d
1849, 7, 11. Ann d ae 71
1851, 9, 7. Samuel d ae 73
1878, 3, 18. Sarah d

1827, 7, 24. Ann & ch, Beulah, Mary, Sarah,
    Samuel & Ann, rocf Radnor MM, Pa., dtd
    1827,8,18
1828, 12, 23. Ann, Beulah & Sarah dis jH
1829, 2, 24. Mary dis jH
1842, 2. 22. Ann Jr. dis jH (G)
1878, 4, 25. Mary recrq (G)
1879, 5, 22. Martha recrq (G)
1881, 2, 26. Emma recrq (G)
1888, 10, 24. Emma dropped from mbrp (G)
1897, 2, 24. W. S. recrq (G)
1897, 7, 21. Mary Defrance (form Richards)
    relrq (G)

RICHARDSON
1817, 4, 22. Eleanor (form Vore) con mcd
1892, 10, 19. J. C. recrq (G)
1892, 10, 19. Virginia recrq (G)
1895, 3, 20. Buford Seigal & Mary Virginia
    recrq (G)
1905, 5, 24. Desmond recrq (G)

RICHIE
1806, 4, 24. Robert, s Edward & Mary, Jeffer-
    son Co., O.; m in Short Creek MH, Sarah
    STEER, dt Joseph & Grace, Jefferson Co.,O.

1805, 11, 16. Robert recrq
1810, 4, 24. Robert & w, Sarah, & ch, Mary
    Ansley & Joseph Steer Richie, gct SD MM
1814, 5, 24. Robert & w, Sarah, & ch, Mary
    Ansley, Joseph Steer, Edward & Samuel
    Steer Richie, gct Plymouth MM

RIDDLE
1914, 3, 25. Alexander recrq (G)
1914, 3, 25. Eliza recrq (G)

RIDGWAY
1819, 4, 20. Job & w, Rebecca, & ch, Reese,
    David, John, Sarah & Mary Ann, rocf Con-
    cord MM
1821, 11, 20. Rebecca & ch, Rees, David, John,
    Sarah, Mary Ann & Job, gct Concord MM
1831, 3, 22. Rees [Ridgeway] dis jH
1833, 12, 24. John dis mcd
1837, 2, 21. Mary Ann [Ridgeway] dis disunity
1838, 10, 23. David [Ridgeway] dis disunity

RIGG
----, --, --. Jesse b 1778,9,28; m Sarah -----
    b 1777,12,28
    Ch: Nathaniel b 1806, 4, 12
        Hiram   " 1808, 8, 26
        Miriam   " 1810, 8, 20
        Sarah   " 1815, 2, 13
        Anna   " 1817, 7, 29
        Susanna   " 1820, 4, 17
1830, 7, 19. Sarah d ae 52

1816, 6, 18. Jesse & w, Sarah, & ch, Nathaniel,
    Hiram, Miriam & Sarah, rocf Westland MM,
    dtd 1816,2,22
1833, 12, 26. Nathaniel [Rig] gct Stillwater
    MM (H)
1834, 3, 20. Sarah [Rig] gct Stillwater MM
    (H)
1834, 5, 22. Jesse & ch, Anna & Susanna, gct
    Stillwater MM (H)
1836, 10, 22. Sarah & ch, Jesse, Mary Ann &
    David B. M. L., gct Carmel MM (H)
1836, 7, 21. Hiram gct Carmel MM (H)

RIGGLE
1817, 10, 21. Susanna (form Thomas) dis mcd
1829, 9, 19. Susanna dis jH

RIGHTER
1861, 5, 13. Hannah G. d ae 65

RILEY
1901, 8, 18. Thos. Samuel, s Jeremiah & Mary,
    b (G)

1927, 5, 26. Thomas Samuel recrq (G)
1933, 1, 25. Thomas gct Goshen MM (G)

RAINBOW
1881, 2, 26. Jefferson & William recrq (G)
1888, 10, 24. Jefferson & William dropped from
    mbrp (G)
1902, 3, 19. Nettie May recrq (G)
1914, 1, 21. Rosa & Eugene recrq (G)

RING
1910, 5, 25. Beatrice U. relrq (G)

RIPLEY
1889, 3, 20. John recrq (G)
1890, 10, 22. John relrq (G)

ROBB
1840, 8, 20. Ann Eliza gct Goshen MM (H)
1841, 2, 23. Ann Eliza (form Thomas) dis mcd

ROBERTS
----, --, --. Ezekiel b 1775, 12, 19; m -----

        Ch: Charles   b 1808, 1, 19
            John   " 1810, 3, 13
            Nancy   " 1812, 6, 14
            Esther   " 1815, 6, 18
----, --, --. Thomas & Hannah
        Ch: Ann   b 1815, 1, 1
            Abel   " 1816, 7, 27
            Ephraim   " 1818, 4, 8
1825, 6, 7. Agness m Rees LARKIN
1839, 5, 22. Aaron, s Aaron & Elizabeth, Bel-
    mont Co., O.; m in Harrisville, Matilda
    FARQUHAR, dt Wm. & Hannah, Harrison Co.,O.
1849, 8, 22. Israel d ae 42
1860, 9, 17. Richard d ae 79
1867, 4, 3. Eliza Ann d ae 50
----, --, --. Richard Evan, s Ezekiel & Eliza
    Ann, b 1843,3,1; m Mira G. S.------
    Ch: Charles
            Summers b 1874, 5, 24 d 1876, 8,25
1889, --, --. Roland d
1895, 10, 22. Elizabeth d
1897, 2, 12. Mary d
1903, 3, 19. Ezekiel d

1810, 3, 20. Henry & w, Ann, & ch, William,
    Richard, Mercy, Isaiah & Rachel, rocf
    Pipecreek MM, dtd 1806,4,19, end by Con-
    cord MM, 1810,2,22
1814, 1, 18. Thomas & w, Hannah, & ch, Abra-
    ham, John, Judah, Joseph, Lewis & Margaret,
    rocf Fallowfield MM, dtd 1813,9,13
1814, 2, 22. Abel & w, Elenor, & s, Moses,

rocf Plainfield MM, dtd 1814,1,22
1814, 3, 22. Jane rocf Plainfield JM, dtd
    1814,2,26
1814, 6, 21. William dis disunity
1815, 5, 23. Abel & w, Eleanor, & s, Moses,
    gct Plainfield MM
1815, 5, 23. Jane gct Plainfield MM
1817, 8, 19. Ezekiel & w, Ann, & ch, Joseph,
    Mary, Agnes, George, John, Charles, Nancy
    & Esther, rocf Youngstreet MM, Upper Cana-
    da, dtd 1817,5,15
1819, 11, 23. Ezekiel & w, Ann, & ch, Joseph,
    Agnes, George, Charles, John, Ann & Es-
    ther, gct Plainfield MM
1819, 11, 23. Mary gct Plainfield MM
1823, 2, 23. Ezekiel & w, Ann, & ch, George,
    Charles, John, Nancy & Esther, rocf Plain-
    field MM, dtd 1822,12,26
1823, 4, 22. Thomas & w, Hannah, & ch, Abra-
    ham, John, Judah, Joseph, Lewis, Margaret,
    Ann, Able & Ephraim, gct Fall Creek MM
1823, 5, 20. Agnes rocf Plainfield MM, dtd
    1822,12,26
1829, 1, 20. Nancy dis jH
1830, 5, 20. Charles gct Plainfield MM (H)
1830, 5, 20. Ezekiel & ch, John, Nancy & Es-
    ther, gct Plainfield MM (H)
1830, 6, 22. John & Esther, minors, gct
    Stillwater MM
1835, 5, 19. John, minor, s Richard, rocf
    Gwynedd MM, Pa., dtd 1835,4,2
1839, 7, 23. Matilda gct Chesterfield MM
1839, 8, 20. Mary & Phebe rocf Gwynedd MM,
    Pa., dtd 1839,5,30
1839, 11, 19. John gct Gwinedd MM
1845, 5, 20. Mary dis jH
1845, 5, 20. Phebe Waterman (form Roberts)
    dis mcd & jH
1862, 11, 19. Beulah dis jW
1862, 11, 19. Elizabeth dis jW
1862, 11, 19. Jesse dis jW
1901, 2, 20. Frank & Martha J. recrq (G)
1906, 11, 21. Frank relrq (G)

ROBERTSON
1821, 6, 19. Charles rocf Redstone MM, dtd
    1821,6,4
1853, 4, 19. Thomas John rocf Lisbon MM, Ire.

ROBINSON
----, --, --. Thomas & Ann
        Ch: Joseph W. b 1813, 4, 9
            Charles B. " 1815, 5, 31
            Rebecca   " 1817, 10, 28
            Thomas
              Chalkley " 1819, 11, 13
            Emily   " 1824, 12, 17
            William   " 1829, 11, 5
----, --, --. William & Jane
        Ch: Elizabeth b 1814, 2, 7
            Samaria J. " 1818, 11, 25
            Tacy C.   " 1818, 11, 25
1851, 9, 8. Elizabeth d

ROBINSON, continued
1876, 7, 3. Jane d

1816, 1, 23. William & w, Jane, & ch, Hannah
    Jacobs & Elizabeth, rocf Goshen MM, dtd
    1815,11,29
1825, 5, 24. Hannah Jacobs, minor dt Wm.,
    gct Gwynead MM, Pa.
1828, 12, 23. Jane dis jH
1837, 8, 22. Elwood Ratcliff gct Springboro
    to m Martha J. Robinson
1839, 1, 22. Elizabeth, Tacy & Samaria dis jH
1845, 1, 23. Chas. Branson gct Clear Creek MM,
    Ill. (H)
1845, 1, 23. Joseph W. gct Clear Creek MM,
    Ill. (H)
1845, 1, 23. Thomas & w, Anna, & s, William,
    gct Clear Creek MM, Ill. (H)
1845, 1, 23. Thomas Chalkley gct Clear Creek
    MM, Ill. (H)
1845, 2, 20. Rebecca & Emily gct Clear Creek
    MM, Ill. (H)

ROBSON
1816, 2, 20. Sampson Sr. & Sampson Jr. rocf
    Plainfield MM, dtd 1816,1,26
1817, 2, 18. Sampson Jr. dis mcd

ROGERS
1808, 11, 22. Cert for Hannah & Ann from
    Nottingham MM, dtd 1808,9,9, end to Still-
    water MM
1819, 10, 19. Thomas recrq
1828, 5, 20. Thomas & w, Catharine, gct Alum
    Creek MM
1878, 4, 25. Sarah Catharine recrq (G)
1878, 5, 23. James R. & w, Edith M., recrq
    (G)
1879, 4, 24. Addison recrq (G)
1883, 5, 23. James A. relrq (W)
1890, 1, 22. Katharine recrq (G)
1892, 10, 19. Virginia E. recrq (G)
1907, 3, 20. Addison dropped from mbrp (G)

ROOD
1848, 1, 27. Emmor, s Jonathan & Clarissa,
    Augusta, Carroll Co., O.; m in Harris-
    ville, Tacy THOMPSON, dt John C. & Rebec-
    ca, Harrison Co., O.
    Ch: William   b 1849, 1, 12
        Ann Eliza " 1851, 12, 16

1848, 10, 24. Emmor rocf Sandy Spring MM, dtd
    1848,7,--
1852, 8, 24. Emmor & w, Tacy, & ch, William
    & Ann Eliza, gct Salem MM, Iowa

ROSS
1812, 8, 18. Cert rec for Phineas from New-
    garden MM, Pa., dtd 1810,3,8, end to
    Waynesville MM
1812, 8, 18. Cert rec for Thomas from New-
    garden MM, Pa., dtd 1810,3,8, end to

Waynesville MM
1820, 11, 21. Cert rec for Thomas from Hope-
    well MM, dtd 1819,5,6, end to Stillwater
    MM

ROSSELL
1848, --, --. Hannah Ann, dt Joseph, b

ROTTMIER
1895, 2, 20. Margaretta E. recrq (G)
1895, 2, 21. Otto recrq (G)

RUBLE
1905, 11, 22. Rosa & Norah recrq (G)
1912, 3, 20. Earnest recrq (G)

RUCKMAN
1891, 3, 25. Samuel recrq (G)

RUPILL
1849, 9, 24. Hannah Ann, dt J. & H. A., b

RUSH
1904, 1, 20. Nellie B. relrq (G)

RUSSELL
1816, 11, 10. Gulielma, dt James & Sarah, b
1819, 3, 23. Gulielma d bur Short Creek
1835, 5, 28. Elizabeth A. m Joseph S. HAGUE
1848, 11, 29. Joseph, s James & Sarah, Jeffer-
    son Co., O.; m in Mt. Pleasant, Hannah Ann
    HAYCOCK, dt Benj. & Jane, Carroll Co.
1850, 6, 9. James Sr. d ae 90
1858, 9, 8. Sarah A., dt James & Sarah, d
    ae 50
1860, 3, 7. Sarah, w James Sr., d ae 87
1862, 5, 26. John d
1863, 10, 3. Hannah A. d
1871, 11, 2. Hannah Ann m Thos. STANLEY
1872, 10, 30. Joseph, s James & Sarah, Jeffer-
    son Co., O.; m in Concord, Martha RALEY,
    dt Asa & Asenath, Belmont Co., O. (W)
    Ch: Rachel A. b 1873, 7, 27
1889, 3, 31. Joseph d bur Concord
1893, 12, 27. Martha (nee Raley) m Gibson
    BINNS (W)
1901, 12, 27. Rachel A. m Thos. H. HAINES (W)

1816, 2, 20. James & w, Sarah, & ch, John,
    Mary, James, Sarah Ansley, Joseph & Eliza-
    beth Ann, recrq
1844, 2, 20. Jane (form Dilworth) dis mcd
1845, 1, 23. Jane D. gct Clear Creek MM, Ill.
    (H)
1846, 11, 23. Jane (form Dilworth) dis mcd
1847, 12, 21. John con mcd
1862, 1, 21. James & Joseph dis jG (W)
1862, 2, 18. Mary dis jG (W)
1871, 10, 26. Thomas Stanley rocf East Goshen
    MM, dtd 1871,10,21, to m Hannah Ann Rus-
    sel (G)
1872, 7, 22. Joseph rst (W)
1874, 4, 23. Joseph dis jas (G)

RUSSELL, continued
1874, 5, 21. Joseph dis jas (G)
1875, 6, 22. Hannah Ann Stanley (form Russell)
     dis mcd & jG (W)

RUTMIRE
1887, 5, 25. Ella recrq (G)

RICKS
1833, 2, 13. William d bur Short Creek
1833, 8, 21. Mary W. m Thos. H. TERRELL
1839, 8, 21. Deborah Ann m Nathan LUPTON
----, --, --. Nathaniel & Mary L.
     Ch: Nathaniel
             Winston b 1847, 3, 30
         Ann Scott " 1850, 2, 16
         Oswin   " 1852, 11, 19
----, --, --. Nathaniel & Mary W.
     Ch: Edward
             Lynch b 1858, 2, 30
1849, 1, 3. Oswin d bur Short Creek
1861, 11, --. Marcia L. d

1832, 10, 23. Oswin & w, Marcia, & ch, Richard
     L., Nathaniel W. & Ann Scott Ricks, rocf
     Western Branch MM, Va., dtd 1832,8,25
1832, 10, 23. Robert rocf Western Branch MM,
     dtd 1832,8,25
1832, 12, 18. Mary W. & dt, Deborah Ann, rocf
     Wayneoak MM, Va., dtd 1832,10,3
1833, 1, 22. William rocf Western Branch MM,
     Va., dtd 1832,12,22
1833, 2, 19. Millicent rocf Western Branch
     MM, Va., dtd 1832,10,27
1838, 3, 20. Ann Scott Bates (form Ricks) dis
     mcd
1839, 12, 24. Richard dis mcd
1846, 4, 21. Nathaniel con mcd
1848, 8, 22. Mary L. rocf Cedar Creek MM, Va.
     dtd 1847,9,8
1853, 3, 22. Margaret rocf Springborough MM
1861, 12, 25. Richard L. rst
1863, 3, 24. Nathaniel W. dis jG (W)
1867, 1, 22. Mary W. dis jG (W)
1872, 4, 25. Lucy, minor, recrq (G)
1872, 4, 24. Julia recrq (G)
1883, 7, 25. Lucy K. relrq (G)
1887, 4, 20. Richard L. gct Maryville MM,
     Tenn. (G)

SAMPSON
1835, 9, 24. Elizabeth gct Deerfield MM (H)

SANDAL
1895, 7, 24. David recrq (G)

SANDELL
1891, 3, 25. Dama recrq (G)

SANDERS
1812, 8, 26. Ann m James R. HAGUE
1835, 4, 12. Martha, dt Robert & Mary Ann, b
----, --, --. Robert & Mary Ann

Ch: Hannah   b 1830, 10, 29
    Sarah   " 1832, 3, 11
    Martha   " 1835, 4, 12

1810, 4, 24. Joseph & w, Hannah, & ch, Ann,
     Susanna, Mary, Martha, John, Jane & Robert
     rocf Hopewell MM, dtd 1810,1,1
1824, 8, 28. Jane Haycock (form Sanders) rpd
     mcd
1851, 3, 18. Robert dis disunity
1852, 8, 24. Hannah Moore (form Sanders) dis
     mcd
1895, 6, 19. Bessie recrq (G)
1902, 8, 20. Bessie dropped from mbrp (G)
1904, 10, 19. Edgar J. & Elma rocf Legrand
     MM, Ia. (G)

SANDS
1864, 9, 20. John dis mcd & jG

SANTORA
----, --, --. Albert m Lura HALL, dt Wm. B.
     & Lydia Jane (Sidwell), b 1898,12,9

SARBER
1875, 10, 21. Jane recrq (G)

SATTERTHWAIT
1895, 6, 19. Isaac H., s Chas. W. & Adaline
     M., Columbiana Co., O.; m in Concord,
     Emily S. HALL, dt Lindley & Millicent,
     Belmont Co., O. (W)
1932, 7, 9. Wilmer L. [Satterthwaite], s
     Isaac H. & Emily S., Columbiana Co., O.;
     m in Harrisville, Alice R. THOMAS, dt
     Walter S. & Martha B. (W)

1846, 4, 21. James T. Frame gct Plainfield
     MM, to m Anna Satterthwait
1862, 11, 19. Ann dis jW
1862, 11, 19. Edward dis jW
1862, 11, 19. Joseph dis jW
1862, 11, 19. Joseph dis jW
1895, 11, 19. Emily S. gct New Garden MM (W)

SAUNDERS
1829, 10, 28. Robert E., s Joseph & Hannah,
     Harrison Co., O.; m in West Grove MH,
     Mary Ann HURFORD, dt Evan & Sarah

1908, 4, 22. Edgar & w, Elma, gct Legrand
     MM, Ia. (G)

SCHOLFIELD
1848, 11, 1. Jonathan T., s Isachar & Edith,
     Belmont Co., O.; m in Concord, Abigail
     STEER, dt James & Ruth, Belmont Co., O.

1840, 2, 18. Cert rec for Edith from Still-
     water MM, dtd 1840,1,25, end back to that
     mtg
1849, 9, 18. Abigail gct Stillwater MM
1851, 9, 25. Joshua & w, Margaret Ann, & ch,

SCHOLFIELD, continued
    Joseph Clark, Robert Marcus, David, Re-
    becca Jane, William Davis, Samuel Sylves-
    ter & George Clark, gct Salem MM (H)
1862, 11, 19. Jonathan T.. Abigail & Rebecca
    dis jW

SCHOOLEY
1810, 6, 20. Henry, s Wm. & Hannah, Tuskrawas
    Co., O.; m in Short Creek MH, Margaret
    HESTON, dt John & Elizabeth, Tuskrawas
    Co., O.
1816, 3, 7. Israel, s Elisha & Rachel, Colum-
    biana Co., O.; m in Short Creek MH, Sarah
    PYLE, dt James & Lydia

1806, 5, 24. Dorothy rocf Redstone MM, dtd
    1805,10,4
1810, 5, 22. Henry rocf Fairfax MM, dtd 1810,
    2,24
1812, 1, 21. Richard rocf Fairfax MM, dtd
    1810,5,30
1813, 10, 19. Richard con mcd
1813, 11, 23. Henry & w, Margaret, & ch, Han-
    nah & John, gct Newgarden MM
1814, 9, 5. Richard gct Newgarden MM
1816, 5, 2. Sarah gct Salem MM
1879, 4, 24. Clarkson recrq (G)
1884, 4, 23. Clarkson C. dis disunity (G)
1887, 5, 12. Sarah C. gct Somerton MM (H)

SCOTT
1860, 11, 14. Charles F. b
1857, 4, 1. David J., s Amos & Ann, Jeffer-
    son Co., O.; m in Short Creek MH, Sarah
    BRACKIN, dt Elisha & Esther, Jefferson Co.,
    O., d 1859,1,10 (W)
    Ch: David   b 1858, 12, 27
1855, 8, 22. Edith Lukens b
1859, 1, 4. David d
1863, 5, 14. Mary Elizabeth b
1874, 2, 21. Jesse M., s John & Elizabeth, b
1876, 8, 10. John d ae 48 bur Concord
1876, 11, 21. Amy J., dt John & Elizabeth, b
1879, 12, 24. Edith C., dt Geo. & Emma, b
1886, 11, 3. Elizabeth E. d ae 51
1905, 9, 9. Sarah, dt John & Elizabeth, d bur
    Emerson
1926, 9, 13. Charles F. d
1929, 7, --. Edith Lukens d bur Emerson
1930, 7, 27. Mary Elizabeth d

1813, 8, 24. Joshua & w, Elizabeth, & ch,
    Job, Jesse, Anna, Rebecca, Stanton, Enoch
    & Elizabeth, gct Stillwater MM
1818, 8, 18. Mahlon rocf ND MM dtd 1817,8,26,
    end by Indian Spring MM, Md.
1819, 12, 21. Mahlon gct Alexandria MM
1821, 5, 22. Cert for Mahlon S. granted to
    Alexandria some time ago, now returned &
    endorsed to Redstone MM
1840, 1, 21. Ann (form Hoopes) dis mcd
1852, 8, 24. John rocf Radnor MM, Pa., dtd

1852,6,10
1853, 8, 23. John con mcd
1854, 5, 23. David James rocf Bradford MM,
    Pa., dtd 1854,4,5
1860, 4, 24. David J. gct Bradford MM, Pa.
1862, 11, 19. John dis jW (G)
1871, 12, 19. John & w, Elizabeth E., & ch,
    George E., Edith L., Sarah G., Chas. F. W.,
    Mary E., Anna J. & Walter A., recrq (W)
1871, 12, 19. Elizabeth E. recrq (W)
1875, 11, 25. Elizabeth Ann (form Johnson) con
    mcd (G)
1877, 10, 23. Walter, minor, gct Concord MM
    (W)
1881, 3, 22. George dis mcd (W)
1881, 8, 23. Emma (form Pettit) dis mcd (W)
1884, 6, 25. Ruthanna (form Cope) dropped
    from mbrp (G)
1885, 6, 20. George & dt, Edith, recrq (G)
1888, 7, 25. Harrison Newton & Rosa C. recrq
    (G)
1890, 4, 22. Charles F. con mcd (W)
1894, 3, 20. Anna J. Evans (form Scott) con
    mcd to first cousin (W)
1898, 1, 19. Harry N. & w, Rosa B., & ch,
    Clyde Alvin & Earl Hurford, relrq (G)
1911, 1, 24. Jesse dis mcd (W)
1913, 1, 22. Esther Griffith recrq (G)

SEAMAN
1885, 3, 25. Sarah recrq (G)

SEARS
1862, 11, 19. Esther, Mary Ann, Joseph & Wm.
    Henry, dis jW
1862, 11, 19. Peter Jr. & w, Pharaby, & ch,
    Sarah, May & Edwin, dis jW
1862, 11, 19. Peter & Anne dis jW

SEEDS
1892, 10, 19. Alice recrq (G)
1892, 10, 19. Frank recrq (G)

SEIGER
1894, 2, 21. William & Alice recrq (G)

SELMAN
1881, 2, 26. John recrq (G)
1888, 10, 24. John [Sellman] dropped from
    mbrp (G)

SELLS
1886, 5, 19. James & Anna R. recrq (G)
1892, 3, 23. John V. recrq (G)
1895, 7, 24. John C. dropped from mbrp (G)

SHACKLEFORD
1912, 9, 10. Julia Wood d

SHAFFER
1914, 6, 24. James M. & Mary H. recrq (G)

SHALLCROSS
1854, 3, 23. Sarah P. gct Plainfield MM (H)

SHANNON
1823, 10, 21. Sarah (form Battin) dis mcd
1892, 10, 19. J. C. recrq (G)
1915, 2, 24. Wm. Allen & Luella recrq (G)

SHARON
1849, 9, 18. Sarah Ann (form Hurford) con mcd
1850, 1, 22. Sarah Ann gct Smithfield MM
1873, 5, 22. Sarah A. rocf Smithfield MM (G)
1881, 2, 26. Freddie recrq (G)
1884, 7, 23. Freddy dropped from mbrp (G)

SHARP
1859, 10, 19. William Henry & w, Rebecca, & s,
    Samuel T., gct Milford MM, Ind.

SHARPLESS
1830, 2, 23. Ann dis jH

SHAW
1805, 7, 20. John & w, Elizabeth, & ch, Jona-
    than, Benjamin, Sarah, Jane, Joseph &
    John, rocf Newgarden MM, Pa., dtd 1805,5,9
1805, 7, 20. Mary rocf Newgarden MM, Pa., dtd
    1805,5,9
1810, 9, 18. John & w, Elizabeth, & ch, Jo-
    seph & John, gct Miami MM
1810, 9, 18. Sarah gct Miami MM
1891, 9, 22. Russell Z. Taber gct Spring-
    ville MM, Ia., to m Phebe Ellen Shaw (W)

SHEPLER
1886, 5, 19. James Albert recrq (G)
1902, 10, 20. James dropped from mbrp (G)
1907, 3, 20. Amanda D. recrq (G)

SHERMAN
1881, 2, 26. David Romanus recrq (G)
1885, 3, 25. Abram recrq (G)

SHIELDS
1873, 6, 26. Joseph recrq (G)
1873, 6, 26. Maggie C. recrq (G)
1895, 1, 23. Mildred recrq (G)
1895, 1, 23. Sabina Jane recrq (G)
1895, 1, 23. Virginia recrq (G)
1908, 4, 22. Mildred relrq (G)

SHOEMAKER
1838, 8, 29. Alfred, s Thos. & Abi, d ae 3

1813, 11, 23. Mary rocf Plainfield MM, dtd
    1813,10,23
1820, 1, 18. Cert for Mary granted to Chester
    MM, Pa., returned, endorsed back to this
    MM 1821,12,18
1822, 7, 23. Mary Updegraff (form Shoemaker)
    dis mcd
1839, 2, 21. Thomas & w, Abi, & ch, Edwin,
    Isaac B., Ann & Elizabeth T., gct Fall

Creek MM (H)

SHORES
1913, 5, 19. Anna d

1885, 2, 25. William E. recrq (G)
1894, 11, 21. Anna recrq (G)
1896, 1, 23. Philip & Mary recrq (G)
1896, 5, 20. Lonie Martin & Lillie Bell,
    minors, recrq (G)
1911, 3, 22. Mary Shores Baldwin relrq (G)
1914, 1, 21. Lillie Bell & Clara A. relrq (G)
1915, 1, 20. Lewis relrq (G)
1929, 7, 24. Robert dropped from mbrp (G)

SHORKLEY
1892, 10, 19. John R. recrq (G)

SHREEVE
1816, 1, 23. Joseph rocf Redstone MM, dtd
    1815,12,27
1817, 8, 19. Joseph [Shreve] gct Providence
    MM

SICKLES
1912, 3, 20. Simon R. & Oscar recrq (G)
1913, 1, 22. Elsie, Ethel, George W., Isaac,
    Lizzie, Rosie & Sylvia recrq (G)
1913, 1, 22. John & w recrq (G)
1914, 3, 25. William & Izetta Matilda recrq
    (G)
1914, 3, 25. Iva recrq (G)

SIDWELL
1813, 1, 28. Deborah m Joseph Parviance
1819, 9, 2. Eleanor m Wm. PURVIANCE
1822, 8, 29. Elisha, s Henry & Sinah, Belmont
    Co., O.; m in Short Creek MH, Elizabeth
    WILSON, dt Jonathan & Hannah, Jefferson
    Co., O., d 1875,1,19 ae 74 bur Concord
    Ch: Israel   b 1823, 8, 5
        Hannah W.   " 1826, 9, 11
        Oliver   " 1830, 8, 11
        Eliza Ann   " 1832, 10, 20
1824, 9, 2. Cineh m Abner HEALD
1830, 6, --. Sarah d
1834, 4, 20. Eliza Ann d bur Short Creek
1839, 11, 2. Hannah W. d bur Short Creek
----, --, --. Israel & Rachel
    Ch: Branson D. b 1850, 4, 13
        Lizzie Ann " 1852, 9, 19
        Wilson T.   " 1854, 8, 24
        Lydia Jane " 1856, 9, 26
        Sina H.   " 1859, 9, 15
        Ellen   " 1861, 10, 6
        Louisa   " 1864, 5, 15
        Elisha D.   " 1867, 8, 24 d 1878,10, 6
        bur Concord
        Emma   b 1871, 2, 9
1850, 5, 3. Branson D., s Israel & Rachel B.,
    b
1872, 10, 4. Elisha Sr. d ae 73 bur Short
    Creek

SIDWELL, continued

1873, 9, 24. Lizzie A. m Wilson BUNDY (W)

1877, 9, 28. Wilson T., s Israel & Rachel, Belmont Co., O.; m in Concord, Isabell C. FOGG, dt Charles & Esther, Belmont Co., O. (W)

1878, 10, 30. Lydia J. m Wm. B. HALL (W)

1880, 3, 31. Sina H. m O. W. BUNDY (W)

1884, 3, 19. Mary Ella m Adna S. FOGG (W)

1888, 12, 26. Louiza J. m Francis WALTON (W)

1895, 6, 25. Rachel B. d ae 66 bur Concord

1901, 1, 8. Israel d bur Concord

1810, 9, 18. Henry & w, Cinah, & ch, Eli, Deborah, Elenor, Elisha, Thomas, Henry & Cinah, rocf Stillwater MM, dtd 1810,5,29

1815, 4, 6. Eli gct Plymouth MM, to m Sarah Purviance

1815, 10, 24. Eli gct Plymouth MM

1822, 6, 18. Thomas gct Flushing MM, to m Elizabeth Foulke

1822, 11, 19. Thomas gct Stillwater MM

1827, 4, 24. Rebecca White (form Sidwell) dis mcd

1827, 5, 22. Henry & w, Sina, gct Plainfield MM

1848, 11, 21. Israel gct Flushing MM, to m Rachel Branson

1849, 5, 22. Rachel B. rocf Flushing MM, dtd 1849,4,26

1862, 11, 19. Branson D., Lizzie Ann, Wilson T., Lydia Jane, Sina H. & Mary Ellen dis jW

1862, 11, 19. Elisha & Elizabeth dis jW

1862, 11, 19. Israel & Rachel dis jW

1863, 1, 21. Oliver W. con mcd (G)

1865, 4, 18. Oliver dis mcd (W)

1867, 8, 22. Barbary recrq (G)

1874, 4, 23. Laura E. & Frank R., minor ch O. W. & Laura E., recrq (G)

1877, 11, 20. Branson D. gct Flushing MM, to m Abbie Holloway (W)

1880, 7, 20. Branson D. gct Flushing MM (W)

1884, 10, 21. Mary Ella Fogg (form Sidwell) gct Hickory Grove MM (W)

1885, 12, 23. Oliver W. & w, Barbara Ellen, & ch, Frank Russell, Albert E., Walter N., gct Lawrence MM, Kans. (G)

1886, 4, 20. Wilson T. & w, Isabell C., & ch, Clara E., Clarence J. & Luella W., gct Hickory Grove MM, Ia. (W)

1902, 2, 18. Emma S. Ellyson (form Sidwell) dis jas (W)

SILLS

1891, 1, 21. Emma & James dropped from mbrp [G]

SIMMONS

1892, 10, 19. Amelia recrq (G)

1892, 10, 19. William H. recrq (G)

1915, 2, 24. Leonard G. recrq (G)

SIMPSON

1862, 3, 19. Lindley M. Thompson gct Chesterfield MM, to m Rebecca Simpson

1907, 3, 20. Barbary dropped from mbrp (G)

SINCLAIR

1812, 9, 22. Samuel Crossley rqct Plainfield MM, to m Phebe Sinclair

1844, 8, 20. Mary recrq

SINGER

----, --, --. Walter & Mable
  Ch: Dorothea
    Odessa b 1911, 3, 5
    Frances Isa-
     bell b 1915, 4, 20

1872, 6, 20. Martha Jane (form Rice) con mcd (G)

1927, 7, 27. Dorothea Odessa recrq (G)

1927, 7, 27. Frances Isabell recrq (G)

SIVIL

1817, 4, 22. Jane (form Marshall) dis mcd

SLATES

1857, 6, 16. Oscar B. b

1857, 7, 7. Mary E., dt Alexander & Sophia Morgan, b

1909, 8, --. Oscar B. d

1894, 2, 21. Oscar B. & Mary E. [Slater] recrq (G)

SLAY

1873, 5, 22. Elijah & Eleanor recrq (G)

SLUTTS

1811, 5, 21. Sarah (form Hague) dis mcd

SLYTER

1818, 2, 24. Cert rec for Jacob & w, Elizabeth, & ch, Chalkley, Unice & Milla, from Peru MM, N. Y., dtd 1817,9,25, end to Alum Creek MM

SMALLEY

1886, 5, 19. Ezra & Maria recrq (G)

SMALLWOOD

1881, 2, 26. Rosa B. recrq (G)

1884, 7, 23. Rosa B. dropped from mbrp (G)

SMART

1846, 4, 30. Rebecca m Asa BRANSON

1846, 3, 24. Rebecca rocf Salem MM, N. J., dtd 1846,1,28

SMILEY

1881, 2, 26. Ada, Edward, Mary Ann, Melissa, Rezin & Robert recrq (G)

1886, 7, 21. Rezin relrq (G)

SMILEY, continued
1891, 3, 25. Leslie [Smilie] recrq (G)
1914, 4, 22. Melissa E. relrq (G)

SMITH
----, --, --. Jirah & Avice
    Ch: Sarah   b 1802, 1, 19
        Samuel   " 1803, 1, 29
        David   " 1805, 5, 30
        Mary   " 1810, 3, 26
        Job   " 1813, 4, 12
1802, 3, 28. Nathan b
1807, 8, 20. Jonathan, s Jacob & Phebe, Jef-
    ferson Co., O.; m in Short Creek MH, Mary
    SMITH, dt Samuel & Naomi, Jefferson Co.,O.
    Ch: Levi   b 1808, 6, 6
        Anna   " 1810, 5, 12
        Edith   " 1812, 3, 10
        Sarah   " 1814, 7, 21
        Maryann   " 1819, 11, 24
        John   " 1817, 5, 3
        Nathan   " 1823, 6, 19
1807, 8, 20. Mary m Jonathan SMITH
1808, 9, 21. Lydia b
----, --, --. Thomas & Nancy
    Ch: Sarah   b 1810, 10, 22
        James   " 1813, 4, 26
        Hannah   " 1814, 10, 17
        Elizabeth " 1817, 2, 27
        Even   " 1819, 5, 30
1813, 2, 2. Reese b
1815, 2, 5. Jeretta b
1830, 10, 27. Levi, s Jonathan & Mary, Harri-
    son Co., O.; m in West Grove MH, Rebecca
    L. STEPHEN, dt Samuel & Elizabeth, Harri-
    son Co., O.
1830, 10, 27. Edith m Thos. GILBERT
1838, 5, --. Mary d ae 57 bur Short Creek
1841, 12, 2. Pearson, s Amos & Anna, Belmont
    Co., O.; m in Harrisville, Mary P. HALL,
    dt Thos. & Mary, Jefferson Co., O.
    Ch: Lemuel   b 1842, 10, 10
        James   " 1847, 5, 25
        Elwood   " 1849, 6, 20
        Mary Ann   " 1851, 8, 16
----, --, --. John W. m Maria H. ----- d 1867,
    1,9 bur Harrisville
    Ch: Eliza   b 1850, 8, 24
        Walter   " 1855, 6, 17
        Nathan R. " 1858, 4, 9
1850, 8, 24. Eliza, dt John & Maria, b
1859, 1, 14. Lizzie M. b
1869, 4, 1. John W., s Robert H. & Elizabeth
    W., Jefferson Co., O.; m in Harrisville,
    Edith HALL, dt Peter & Mary THOMAS, Harri-
    son Co. O. (W)
1870, 1, 30. Hannah d ae 49
1871, 12, 2. Eliza d ae 22 bur Harrisville
1872, 2, 29. Walter d ae 17 bur Harrisville
1881, 11, 29. Junius L. b
1883, 1, 12. Mary Edith b
----, --, --. Nathan R. d 1908,8,3 ae 50 bur
    Harrisville; m Lizzie -----, dt David &

Sara B. (Holloway) BRANSON, b 1859,1,14
    Ch: Mira B.   b 1884, 12, 6
        Wilmer J. " 1888, 3, 11
        Albert Hen-
        ry   " 1890, 1, 25
        Mary Emma " 1893, 8, 16
        Edith Lil-
        lian   " 1906, 3, 6
----, --, --. Eugene, s Geo. & Sarah, b 1853,
    9,12; m Rebecca ----- (G)
    Ch: Parke E.   b 1892, 3, 7
        William H. " 1892, 3, 7
1892, 9, 16. Edmund S., s Robt. & Rebecca S.,
    Jefferson Co., O.; m in Harrisville,
    Eliza D. HALL, dt John & Deborah, Belmont
    Co., O. (W)
    Ch: Helen
        Rebecca   b 1893, 9, 23
1893, 10, 25. Elizabeth W. m Chas. LIVEZEY (W)
1902, 7, 29. John W. d ae 77 bur Harrisville
1904, 4, 18. Rebecca S., w Robert S., d ae 61
    bur Harrisville
----, --, --. Aaron Thomas, s Stephen & Eliza-
    beth (Roberts), b 1875,8,13; m Rachel
    DEWEES, dt James E. & Anna (Harmer), b
    1877,4,17
    Ch: Irving
        James   b 1907, 2, 27
        Ada Alber-
        ta   " 1909, 12, 2
        Oscar
        Stephen   " 1914, 4, 25
        Clinton
        Lindley   " 1920, 1, 28
----, --, --. Junius L., s Wm. R. & Virginia
    A. (Conner), b 1881,10,29; m Mary Edith
    BINNS, dt David E. & Lizzie A., b 1883,1,
    12
    Ch: Virginia E.b 1909, 6, 12
        Olive L.   " 1910, 11, 19
1909, 6, 12. Virginia E. b
1910, 11, 19. Olive L. b
1911, 4, 19. Wilmer J., s Nathan R. & Lizzie
    M., Jefferson Co. O., b 1888,3,11; m in
    Colerain, Grace Alma STEER, dt Lindley B.
    & Hannah P., Belmont Co., O., b 1889,12,7
    Ch: Donald
        Wilmer   b 1912, 7, 9
        Arthur Na-
        than   " 1914, 7, 24
        Howard
        Penrose   " 1916, 3, 19
        Ralph Lind-
        ley   " 1918, 3, 30
        Raymond W. " 1923, 2, 10
1914, 4, 22. Mary E. m Robt. E. COPPOCK
1915, 8, 5. Albert H., s Nathan R. & Lizzie
    M., Jefferson Co., O., b 1890,1,25; m in
    Harrisville, Elizabeth B. HALL, dt Lewis
    & Margaret A., Harrison Co., O., b 1892,5,5
    Ch: Margaret
        Edith   b 1916, 4, 29
        Lewis Bran-

SMITH, Albert H. & Elizabeth B., continued
   Ch: son   b 1918, 7, 27
         Mabel Ger-
          trude   " 1920, 4, 19
         Albert H.
          Jr.   " 1923, 8, 23
         Carl Nathan" 1930, 10, 12
1916, 4, 29. Margaret Edith b
1917, 7, 13. Edith d ae 9- bur Harrisville
1918, 3, 26. Ralph Lindley b
1920, 4, 19. Mabel Gertrude b
1920, 11, 24. Curtis W., s Marion & Alice M.,
  Warren Co., Ia.; m in Harrisville, Edith
  McGREW, dt Gilbert & Eliza H., Jefferson
  Co., O., b 1890,9,21 (W)
1924, 6, 5. Edmund, s Joshua W. & Eva Irene,
  Linn Co., Ia.; m in Harrisville, Caroline
  McGREW, dt Gilbert & Eliza H., Jefferson
  Co., O. (W)
1927, 3, 26. Marjory A. m Stanley W. STRATTON
  (W)

1806, 3, 15. Naomi & dt, Mary, rocf Westland
  MM, dtd 1806,2,22
1806, 6, 21. Jonathan rocf Westland MM, dtd
  1806,5,21
1809, 10, 24. Cert rec for John from London
  Grove MM, dtd 1809,6,7, end to Plainfield
  MM
1810, 3, 20. Nancy (form James) dis mcd
1814, 7, 19. Cert rec for Thomas & fam from
  Hopewell MM, dtd 1814,6,9, end to Stillwater MM
1815, 2, 21. Jirah & w, Avis, & ch, Sarah,
  Samuel, David & Mary, & one b same dte
  as cert named Job, rocf Peru MM, dtd 1811,
  5,23, end by Pelham MM, Upper Canada
1815, 5, 23. Thomas recrq
1816, 5, 2. Nancy rst
1816, 6, 18. Sarah & Hannah, minor ch Thomas,
  recrq
1817, 11, 18. Cert rec for Samuel & fam from
  Dartmore MM, dtd 1817,6,5, end to Peru MM,
  N. Y.
1821, 8, 21. Thomas & w, Nancy, & ch, Sarah,
  Hannah, Elizabeth & Evan, gct Somerset MM
1822, 2, 19. Hannah & dt, Jureta, recrq
1822, 5, 21. Rebecca, Rachel & Martha, minors
  gct Westland MM
1822, 6, 18. Thomas rst
1822, 6, 18. Peter, Nathan, Tristram, Rees &
  Jurity, ch Thos. & Hannah, recrq
1824, 8, 28. Anna (form Masters) con mcd
1825, 3, 22. Lydia recrq
1826, 6, 20. Jonathan & w, Mary, & ch, Levi,
  Anna, Edith, Sarah, John, Maryann & Nathan,
  gct Somerset MM
1829, 8, 18. Lydia dis jH
1829, 11, 24. Hannah dis jH
1830, 9, 21. Edith rocf Summerset MM, dtd
  1830,6,28
1830, 11, 23. Rees & Tristran dis jH
1832, 9, 18. Nathan dis jH

1835, 4, 21. Mary & ch, Mary Ann & Nathan,
  rocf Stillwater MM, dtd 1834,10,24
1835, 9, 22. Jeretah dis jH
1836, 6, 21. Mary Ann (form James) dis mcd
1837, 6, 20. Cert rec for Sarah from Stillwater MM, end back to Stillwater MM
1839, 2, 21. Nathan gct Fall Creek MM (H)
1839, 5, 21. Levi & w, Rebecca, & ch, Lydia
  Ann, Samuel & Phebe, gct Pennsville MM
1840, 1, 21. Deborah B. rocf ND MM, dtd 1829,
  12,20
1840, 1, 23. Tristram gct Fall Creek MM (H)
1841, 9, 21. Deborah B. gct Goshen MM, Pa.
1841, 10, 19. John Thomas gct Flushing MM, to
  m Miriam B. Smith
1842, 11, 22. Pearson rocf Flushing MM, dtd
  1842,4,21
1844, 5, 21. Nathan dis jas
1847, 10, 29. Josiah Bundy gct Flushing MM, to
  m Achsah R. Smith
1847, 11, 23. Pearson Thomas gct Flushing MM,
  to m Amy T. Smith
1848, 9, 19. Maria H. gct Flushing MM
1849, 3, 20. John P. rocf Upper Springfield
  MM, dtd 1849,2,24
1849, 4, 24. Nathan Jr. rocf Flushing MM, dtd
  1849,1,25
1850, 11, 19. John W. & w, Maria H., rocf
  Flushing MM, dtd 1850,8,22
1851, 1, 21. John P. gct Sadsbury MM, Pa.
1852, 5, 18. Nathan & w, Catharine, rocf
  Flushing MM, dtd 1852,4,22
1852, 5, 18. Catharine B. rocf Flushing MM
1852, 6, 2. Nathan Jr. dis disunity
1853, 10, 8. Nathan dis mcd
1861, 10, 22. Robert H. & w, Elizabeth W., rocf
  Stillwater MM, dtd 1861,9,28
1862, 4, 22. Catharine B. dis disunity
1862, 7, 22. Nathan rst
1862, 11, 19. Barclay, Hannah, Arthur, Benjamin W., Robert, Rebecca & Edmund, dis jW
  (G)
1862, 11, 19. Joel, Deborah & Mary Ellen dis
  jW (G)
1862, 11, 19. John W. & w, Maria, & ch, Eliza,
  Nathan & Walter dis jW (G)
1862, 11, 19. Robert & w, Elizabeth, & dt,
  Rebecca, dis jW (G)
1862, 11, 19. Sinclair, H. M. & Robert Jr. dis
  jW (G)
1865, 4, 18. Robert H. & w, Elizabeth, gct
  Stillwater MM (W)
1871, 4, 18. Robert & w, Rebecca, & ch, Edwin S., Elizabeth W. & Maria H., rocf
  Stillwater MM, dtd 1871,3,22 (W)
1874, 7, 23. John T. recrq (G)
1874, 7, 23. Nancy recrq (G)
1875, 6, 22. Dorothy Ann (form Watson) dis
  mcd (W)
1876, 1, 18. James A. McGrew gct Flushing MM,
  to m Mary W. Smith (W)
1881, 2, 26. William F. & Walker recrq (G)
1882, 9, 19. Catharine S. gct Flushing MM (W)

SMITH, continued
1882, 5, 24. Anna M. recrq (G)
1882, 5, 24. Clinton recrq (G)
1882, 5, 24. Sharron M. recrq (G)
1883, 9, 18. Nathan R. gct Flushing MM, to m
    Lizzie M. Branson (W)
1884, 11, 18. Lizzie M. rocf Flushing MM, dtd
    1884,10,23 (W)
1886, 5, 19. Oliver J. & Evaline recrq (G)
1886, 7, 21. E. Anna recrq (W)
1887, 6, 9. Alice M. gct Salem MM (H)
1888, 10, 24. Anna dropped from mbrp (G)
1888, 10, 24. Clinton dropped from mbrp (G)
1888, 10, 24. Shannon dropped from mbrp (G)
1892, 10, 19. J. R. recrq (G)
1892, 10, 19. Katie M. recrq (G)
1895, 2, 20. Benjamin & w, Abbie, recrq (G)
1895, 3, 20. Eugene & Nettie May recrq (G)
1896, 1, 23. Winnamore recrq (G)
1896, 1, 23. William A. recrq (G)
1896, 1, 23. Rebecca A. recrq (G)
1896, 5, 20. Parks Eugene & Wm. Harvey, min-
    ors, recrq (G)
1902, 2, 18. Edmund S. & w, Eliza D., & dt,
    Helen Rebecca, gct Springville MM, Ia. (W)
1903, 3, 25. Helen recrq (G)
1904, 7, 19. Albert W. Starbuck gct Salem MM,
    to m Ethel C. Smith (W)
1905, 4, 19. William recrq (G)
1907, 3, 20. John T. dropped from mbrp (G)
1907, 6, 19. Rachel E. dropped from mbrp (G)
1907, 6, 19. Emma L. dropped from mbrp (G)
1907, 6, 19. Will T. dropped from mbrp (G)
1910, 1, 18. Maria H. gct Stillwater MM (W)
1910, 1, 18. Robert gct Stillwater MM (W)
1914, 8, 18. Junius L. recrq (W)
1914, 8, 18. Mary E. rst on consent of New
    Garden MM (W)
1914, 8, 18. Virginia E. & Olive L., ch Jun-
    ius & Mary, recrq (W)
1921, 2, 22. Edith M. (form McGrew) gct Bear
    Creek MM, Ia. (W)
1924, 12, 23. Caroline M. gct Springville MM,
    Ia. (W)
1926, 7, 20. Aaron T. & w, Rachel D., & ch,
    Irving James, Ada Alberta, Oscar Stephens,
    Clinton Lindley, rocf Chesterfield MM (W)
1926, 7, 20. Marjorie Anna rocf Chesterfield
    MM (W)
1929, 7, 24. Parks [Smythe] dropped from
    mbrp (G)
1929, 7, 24. Will [Smythe] dropped from
    mbrp (G)
1932, 4, 19. Irving J. gct Coal Creek MM,
    Ia., to m Mary Emmons (W)
1933, 1, 24. Edith Lillian gct West-town MM,
    Pa. (W)

SNODGRASS
1881, 3, 24. Frank recrq (G)

SNYDER
1891, 3, 25. Frank K. recrq (G)

1892, 10, 19. Lizzie recrq (G)
1892, 12, 21. Agnes recrq (G)

SOMERVILLE
1908, 2, 19. Ethel Herbert relrq (G)
1908, 2, 19. James Andrew relrq (G)
1908, 2, 19. Orville William relrq (G)
1908, 2, 19. Ralph Irvin relrq (G)

SPARROW
1858, 6, 16. John C., s Benjamin & Elizabeth,
    b
----, --, --. J. & Elizabeth
    Ch: Clarabelle b 1887, 9, 29
        Sarah E. " 1897, 7, 5
----, --, --. S. Vincent, s Benjamin & Eliza
    B., b 1866,1,21; m Anna Mary CROWN, dt
    Saml. B. & Ruth D., b 1868,5,14
    Ch: Forrest E. b 1898, 11, 8

1894, 2, 21. Samuel Vincent recrq (G)
1894, 2, 21. Anna Mary recrq (G)
1894, 8, 21. John C. & w, Lizzie, recrq (G)
1902, 1, 22. Clara Bell recrq (G)
1905, 11, 22. John C. & w, Lizzie, relrq (G)
1913, 5, 21. Sara E. dropped from mbrp (G)
1914, 6, 24. S. V. relrq (G)
1914, 6, 24. Mollie relrq (G)
1914, 6, 24. Oda relrq (G)
1914, 6, 24. Foust relrq (G)

SPEAKMAN
1810, 3, 20. Betty rocf Pipe Creek MM, dtd
    1808,4,16, end by Concord MM 1810,2,22

SPENCER
1830, 3, 23. Leah dis JH
1845, 4, 22. Mary M. Kenworthy (form Spencer)
    con mcd
1846, 5, 19. Rebecca gct Spiceland MM, Ind.
1897, 5, 19. Iowa May recrq (G)

SPICER
1903, 8, 1. William Jones, s R. Barkley &
    Margaret, b

SPIER
1903, 12, 9. R. Barclay & s, Wm. Jones Spier,
    gct Darby MM, Pa. (H)
1906, 2, 21. Laura [Spies] recrq (G)

SPIRA
1892, 10, 19. Sarah recrq (G)

SPRIGS
1840, 5, 19. Rebecca (form James) dis mcd
1840, 6, 23. Sidney [Sprogs] dis jas (a
    woman)

SPURRIER
1828, 7, 22. Mary (form Worrell) dis mcd

STACKHOUSE
1829, 9, 19. Hannah & dt, Elizabeth, rocf
    ND MM, dtd 1829,6,23
1833, 1, 22. Hannah & dt, Elizabeth, gct
    ND MM

STAFFORD
1892, 10, 19. Genette recrq (G)
1892, 10, 19. Irene recrq (G)
1892, 10, 19. Margaret recrq (G)

STANLEY
1840, 9, 30. Thos. H., s John & Mary, Colum-
    biana Co., O.; m in Concord, Mary WILSON,
    dt Daniel & Mary, Monroe Co., O.
1841, 9, 12. Esther Jane, dt Samuel W. & Mary
    V., b
1848, 8, 23. Elihu B., s John Jr. & Abigail,
    Mahoning Co., O.; m in West Grove MH, Mary
    Emily LADD, dt Peter & Catharine, Harrison
    Co., O.
1860, 8, 29. Daniel H., s Ira & Elizabeth,
    Wayne Co., Ind.; m in Mt. Pleasant, Sarah
    H. TERRELL, dt Matthew & Elizabeth, Jeffer-
    son Co., O.
1865, 11, 30. Jared, s Edmund & Mary, Mahoning
    Co., O.; m in Harrisville, Margaret B.
    KINSEY, dt Chas. & Sarah, Harrison Co., O.
1871, 11, 2. Thos., s Micajah & Unity, Mahon-
    ing Co., O.; m in Harrisville, Hannah Ann
    RUSSELL, dt Joseph & Hannah Ann, Jefferson
    Co., O.

1840, 1, 21. Samuel W. rocf Upper Springfield
    MM, dtd 1839,12,28
1840, 1, 21. Thomas H. rocf Upper Springfield
    MM, dtd 1839,12,28
1840, 9, 22. Samuel W. gct Plainfield MM, to
    m Mary Vail
1840, 12, 22. Mary V. rocf Plainfield MM, dtd
    1840,11,25
1842, 10, 18. Samuel rocf Upper Springfield
    MM, dtd 1842,9,24
1846, 4, 21. Samuel & w, Mary, & ch, Esther
    Jane & Benjamin, gct Plainfield MM
1847, 11, 23. James gct Salem MM, Ia.
1847, 11, 23. Thomas H. & w, Mary W., & s,
    William F., gct Salem MM, Iowa
1849, 2, 20. Mary Emily gct Upper Springfield
    MM
1857, 10, 21. William C. Johnson gct Upper
    Springfield MM, to m Judith C. Stanley
1858, 10, 20. Israel W. Jenkins gct Upper
    Springfield MM, to m Alvina Stanley
1860, 12, 19. Sarah H. gct Milford MM
1865, 11, 22. Jared rocf Upper Springfield
    MM, to m Margaret B. Kinsey (G)
1866, 5, 23. Margaret B. gct Upper Spring-
    field MM (G)
1871, 10, 26. Thomas rocf East Goshen MM, dtd
    1871,10,21, to m Hannah Ann Russel (G)
1872, 6, 20. Hannah gct East Goshen MM (G)
1875, 6, 22. Hannah Ann (form Russell) dis

mcd & jG (W)
1877, 6, 21. Mary Ann rocf Damascus MM, O.
    (G)
1880, 5, 20. Mary Ann gct Damascus MM, O.(G)
1885, 9, 23. Mabel rocf Albion MM, Ia. (G)
1932, 7, 19. Alfred R. Thomas gct Plainfield
    MM, Ind., to m Harriet Stanley (W)

STANTON
----, --, --. Benjamin & Mary
    Ch: Ruth   b 1802, 4, 6
        Martha   " 1804, 5, 8
1804, 6, 11. Martha, an infant, d bur Short
    Creek
1804, 10, --. Ruth d ae 2y bur Short Creek
1807, 5, 14. Benjamin Sr. d ae 51 bur Short
    Creek
1807, 10, 22. Elias, s Benj. & Mary, Jeffer-
    son Co., O.; m in Short Creek MH, Martha
    WILSON, dt Wm. & Elizabeth, Jefferson
    Co., O.
    Ch: Benjamin   b 1809, 6, 4
1808, 4, 28. Abigail m Benjamin MICHENER
1809, 3, 30. Henry, s Benj. Sr. & Abigail,
    Jefferson Co., O.; m Clary PATTERSON, dt
    Joseph & Mary, Jefferson Co., O.
1811, 2, 22. Elias d ae 26 bur Short Creek
1811, 7, 14. Martha d bur Short Creek
1812, 7, 30. Mary m David BERRY
1816, 5, 2. Benjamin, s Benj. & Mary, Jef-
    ferson Co., O.; m in Short Creek MH, Han-
    nah PENROSE, dt Thomas & Sarah, Jefferson
    Co., O.
    Ch: Charles
          Osborn   b 1817, 7, 19
        Mahlon   " 1819, 1, 22
        Ruth   " 1821, 2, 10
        Thomas   " 1823, 2, 25
1818, 4, 1. Lydia m Wm. LEWIS
1825, 6, 5. Abigail d ae 72 bur Harrisville
1831, 11, 24. Daniel, s James & Ann, Warren
    Co., O.; m in Mt. Pleasant, Angelina WAT-
    KINS, dt John W. & Elizabeth, Jefferson
    Co., O.

1804, 9, 15. Susanna rocf Coursound MM, N.C.
    dtd 1804,4,11, end by Concord 1804,7,24
1807, 8, 15. Sarah Taylor (form Stanton) dis
    mou
1812, 5, 19. Henry & w, Clary, & ch, James
    & Joseph, gct Stillwater MM
1814, 3, 22. David dis mcd
1814, 3, 22. Susanna gct Concord MM
1816, 6, 18. Benjamin gct Salem MM
1822, 3, 19. Abigail Jr. rocf Stillwater MM,
    dtd 1821,11,24
1822, 5, 21. Joseph gct Miami MM
1824, 3, 23. Abigail gct Somerset MM
1827, 12, 18. Benjamin gct Smithfield MM
1830, 3, 23. Benjamin & ch, Charles Osborn,
    Mahlon, Ruth, Thomas & Elias, gct Sandy
    Spring MM
1830, 3, 23. Richard, minor s Benjamin, gct

STANTON, continued
    Deerfield MM
1830, 4, 20. Benjamin W. dis mcd
1832, 10, 23. Angelina gct Springborough MM
1862, 9, 24. Samuel Lloyd gct Miami MM, to m
    Deborah I. Stanton (G)
1862, 11, 19. Eli & Mary, Wm. & Sarah B. dis
    jW (G)
1862, 11, 19. Henry Sr. dis jW (G)
1862, 11, 19. Tabitha, Henry Jr., Daniel &
    Benjamin dis jW (G)
1904, 5, 24. Wilmer L. Hall gct Stillwater
    MM, to m Ida J. Stanton (W)

STARBUCK
1854, 8, 23. John, s John & Ann, Belmont Co.,
    O.; m in Concord, Sarah BUNDY, dt Benj. &
    Delitha, Belmont Co., O.
    Ch: B. F.   b 1855, 7, 21
        Addison   " 1857, 2, 11
        Marietta   " 1859, 11, 2
        Anna D.   " 1861, 4, 25
        Eva B.   " 1863, 5, 25
        Thomas   " 1865, 1, 1
        Lorena   " 1866, 2, 28 d 1921,10, 3
            bur Colerain
        Elizabeth   b 1868, 12, 29
        Alice J.   " 1870, 4, 17
        Eunice R.   " 1873, 2, 26 d 1924,11,24
            bur Colerain
1861, 4, 15. Anna D. b
1867, 2, 17. Lorena b
1868, 12, 31. Elizabeth b
1873, 2, 23. Eunice R. b
----, --, --. Benjamin F. & Sarah
    Ch: Edith P.   b 1881, 4, 7 d 1899, 4,22
            bur Concord
        Albert   b 1882, 12, 16
    Benjamin m 2nd Anna -----
    Ch: Lewis C.   b 1885, 3, 5
        Martha   " 1895, 5, 28
        Mary T.   " 1898, 1, 11
        Emily   " 1899, 5, 4
        Jesse   " 1902, 2, 4
1885, 3, 16. Sarah M., w Benj., dt Robert
    Milhouse, d bur Concord
1885, 8, 28. Marietta m Benj. H. COPE (W)
1898, 6, 2. Thomas, s John & Sarah, Belmont
    Co., O., b 1865,1,1 d 1930,9,12 bur Cole-
    rain; m in Harrisville, Abbie S. HALL, dt
    Josiah & Deborah, Jefferson Co., O., b
    1866,5,4 (or 1861,4,15) (W)
    Ch: Mabel   b 1899, 5, 27
        Clinton   " 1906, 6, 26 (or 1906,5,26)
        Alice   " 1910, 2, 18
1899, 5, 27. Mabel Loretta b
1900, 5, 23. Eva B. m Aaron S. EAKIN (W)
1904, 3, 10. John d ae 77 bur Colerain
1908, 3, 30. Sarah d bur Concord
1918, 5, 26. Clinton J. b
1921, 10, 3. Lorena d
1924, 11, 24. Eunice R. d bur Colerain
1929, 12, 25. Alice B. m A. M. DOUDNA

1856, 1, 22. John Jr. rocf Somerset MM, dtd
    1856,11,--
1862, 11, 19. Daniel dis jW
1862, 11, 19. George, Mary, Jesse & Milton
    dis jW
1862, 11, 19. John dis jW
1862, 11, 19. John & w, Sarah, & ch, Benja-
    min F., Addison, Marietta & Anna D., dis
    jW
1862, 11, 19. Ruthanna dis jW
1879, 7, 22. Benjamin F. gct Pennsville MM,
    to m Sarah Millhous (W)
1880, 4, 20. Sarah M. rocf Pennsville MM,
    dtd 1880,2,19 (W)
1893, 1, 24. Benjamin F. gct Pennsville MM,
    to m Anna Llewellyn (W)
1893, 9, 19. Anna L. rocf Pennsville MM (W)
1897, 4, 20. Addison dis mcd & jas (W)
1904, 7, 19. Albert W. gct Salem MM, to m
    Ethel C. Smith (W)
1906, 11, 26. Albert W. gct Salem MM, O. (W)
1917, 7, 24. B. Franklin & w, Anna L., & s,
    Jesse, gct Salem MM, O. (W)
1917, 7, 24. Martha, Mary & Emily gct Salem
    MM, O. (W)
1919, 7, 22. Louis C. dis mcd & jas (W)

STARCHER
1914, 1, 21. Earl E. recrq (G)

STARGLE
1892, 10, 19. S. M. recrq (G)

STARR
1824, 3, 31. Merrick, s Moses & Martha, Jef-
    ferson Co., O.; m in Mt. Pleasant, Ann
    UPDEGRAFF, dt Nathan & Ann, Jefferson Co.,
    O.
    Ch: Nathan   b 1825, 1, 30
        Moses   " 1827, 10, 30
        Hannah   " 1830, 7, 17
1832, 11, 16. Ann d ae 75 bur Short Creek
1915, 4, 21. Elmer, s Mordecai F. & Harriet
    F., York Co., Ontario, Canada; m in Har-
    risville, Elma McGREW, dt Gilbert & Eliza
    H., Jefferson Co., O. (W)

1812, 12, 22. Merrick & w, Ann, rst on con-
    sent of Exeter MM
1818, 11, 24. Merrick rocf Muncy MM, Pa., dtd
    1818,9,23
1832, 4, 24. Moses rocf Muncey MM, Pa., dtd
    1832,2,21
1835, 3, 24. Moses gct Muncey MM, Pa.
1839, 9, 24. Ann dis jas
1839, 10, 22. Merrick dis jas
1840, 7, 21. Nathan W., Hannah & Moses, ch
    Merrick & Ann, gct Alum Creek MM
1917, 4, 24. Elma M. & s, Francis, gct Yonge
    St. MM, Ontario, Canada (W)

ST. CLAIR
1839, 4, 23. Ruth (form Gilbert) dis mcd

ST. CLAIR, continued
1851, 5, 20. Mary gct Mt. Gilead MM
1844, 8, 20. Mary recrq   •

STEDDOM
1856, 9, 25. John F., s Samuel & Susannah,
    Warren Co., O.; m in Mt. Pleasant, Sarah
    J. TERRELL, dt Clark & Mary J., Jefferson
    Co., O.

1854, 1, 24. Thomas Terrell gct Miami MM, to
    m Lydia Steddom
1857, 1, 21. Sarah J. gct Miami MM, O.

STEDMAN
1835, 7, 21. Mary (form Burr) dis mcd

STEEL
1828, 7, 22. Abigail (form Parker) dis mcd

STEER
1806, 4, 24. Sarah m Robert RICHIE
----, --, --. David & Phebe
    Ch: Hannah M. b 1809, 1, 23
        Joseph   " 1811, 1, 27
        William   " 1812, 12, 25
        Isaac   " 1814, 12, 18
        Benjamin   " 1817, 5, 29
        Jane M.   " 1819, 4, 13
        Amos   " 1821, 3, 27
        Greenberry
          P.   " 1822, 8, 14
        Harriet   " 1830, 8, 30
1813, 9, 30. Rachel m Wm. JUDKINS
1819, 11, 13. Grace d ae 61 bur Short Creek
----, --, --. Samuel & Harriet
    Ch: Elizabeth b 1821, 1, 10
        Sarah   " 1822, 3, 19
----, --, --. Amos d 1847,3,26 ae 48 bur Short
    Creek; m Lavina ----- d 1828,11,26 bur
    Short Creek
    Ch: Joshua
          Hood   b 1828, 11, 17
    Amos m 2nd Ann -----
    Ch: Joseph   b 1833, 3, 18
        Anna M.   " 1834, 12, 6
        Deborah Ann " 1837, 7, 22
1830, 3, 31. James, s James & Abigail, Bel-
    mont Co., O.; m in Concord, Ann LUPTON,
    dt Nathan & Margaret, Belmont Co., O.
    Ch: Nathan   b 1830, 12, 20
        Joseph   " 1833, 9, 23
1835, 8, 26. Joseph, s David & Phebe, Lenawee
    Co., Mich. Territory; m in Mt. Pleasant,
    Deborah H. BATES, dt Elisha & Sarah, Jef-
    ferson Co., O.
    Ch: Elisha   b 1836, 5, 31
        David   " 1838, 7, 7
        William   " 1841, 3, 12
1839, 5, 15. Joseph d ae 5 bur Concord
1839, 5, 20. Joseph d bur Concord
1844, 10, 21. Israel, s James & Ruth, Belmont
    Co., O.; m in Short Creek MH, Rebecca

BRACKEN, dt Elisha & Phebe, Jefferson
    Co., O., d 1901,9,3 bur Concord
    Ch: Lindley B. b 1845, 9, 25
        Deborah   " 1847, 12, 27
        Elisha
          Brackin   " 1850, 6, 2
        Phebe Anna " 1852, 12, 6 d 1901, 8,26
          bur Concord
        Sina R.   b 1855, 6, 25
        Wilson J.   " 1859, 10, 31
        Sarah R.   " 1864, 8, 31
1846, 10, 28. Martha m Jehu BAILEY
1848, 11, 1. Abigail m J. T. SCHOLFIELD
1850, 3, 9. Ann M. d ae 51 bur Short Creek
1850, 5, 1. Rachel m Joseph P. LUPTON
1853, 4, 2. Ann d ae 57 bur Short Creek
1854, 10, 24. Anna Mary, dt James & Mary, b
----, --, --. James & Mary
    Ch: William G. b 1856, 5, 15
        Joseph   " 1858, 4, 14
        Rachel G.   " 1860, 4, 16
        Elizabeth   " 1863, 1, 7
----, --, --. Nathan, s Jas. & Ann (Lupton),
    b 1830,12,25 d 1918,6,4 bur Colerain; m
    Mary Jane ----- d 1915,8,1 ae 79 bur
    Colerain
    Ch: Abzie Jane b 1858, 5, 23
        Abbie Lo-
          retta   " 1860, 7, 30
        Louis Clar-
          ence   " 1863, 6, 9
        Lydia Ann   " 1865, 10, 10
        Edwin M.   " 1869, 3, 6
        Elma   " 1873, 1, 27
        Laura E.   " 1877, 11, 1
1859, 4, 28. David, s Joseph & Deborah, Jef-
    ferson Co., O.; m in Short Creek MH, Ach-
    sah P. LUPTON, dt Nathan & Deborah Ann,
    Jefferson Co., O.
    Ch: Ida B.   b 1860, 4, 15
        William E. " 1861, 3, 24
        Charles A. " 1863, 2, 20
1860, 7, 30. Abbie L. b
1860, 8, 30. Elisha B., s Joseph & Deborah,
    Jefferson Co., O.; m in Short Creek MH,
    Mary W. LUPTON, dt Nathan & Deborah, Jef-
    ferson Co., O.
    Ch: E. C.   b 1862, 8, 24
        Clara B.   " 1863, 4, 13
----, --, --. Lindley B., s Israel & Rebecca,
    b 1845,9,25; m Ruanna FRAME, dt Aaron &
    Talitha (Thompson), b 1845,3,30
----, --, --. Lindley B. & Hannah
    Ch: Walter J. b 1873, 4, 30
        Richard
          Arthur   " 1875, 8, 23
        Charles L. " 1877, 10, 11
        Emma R.   " 1879, 7, 16
        Mary   " 1881, 4, 24
        Phebe Elma " 1882, 9, 14
        Horace W.   " 1884, 5, 11
        Jason P.   " 1886, 1, 25
        Clara Ellen " 1887, 9, 3 d 1897, 5,27

STEER, Lindley B. & Hannah, continued
    Ch: bur Concord
       Grace Alma b 1889, 7, 12
1874, 6, 27. James d ae 93 bur Concord
----, --, --. Elisha B. m Ellen G. ----- d
    1909,10,25 bur Concord
    Ch: Louisa D. b 1875, 6, 1
       Alfred G. " 1877, 3, 17
       Wilmer   " 1880, 7, 2
       Alice B.   " 1884, 5, 24
       Florence H." 1886, 7, 18
1875, 6, 1. Louiza D. dt Elisha B., b
1875, 8, 23. Richard Arthur, s Lindley B. &
    Ellen, b
1876, 11, 1. Deborah m Oliver S. NEGUS (W)
1877, 3, 17. Alfred G., s Elisha B. & Ellen,
    b
1879, 9, 24. Alza J. m Thos. H. BINNS (W)
1884, 5, 11. Horace W. b
1886, 1, 25. Jason P. b
1888, 3, 29. Louis C., s Nathan & Mary Jane,
    Belmont Co., O., b 1863,6,9; m in Harris-
    ville, Sarah Louisa BUNDY, dt Wm. P. &
    Tabitha D., Belmont Co., O., b 1865,3,24
    Ch: Alice M. b 1891, 1, 4   [(W)
       Edith   " 1896, 1, 17
       Dorothy
       Allegra " 1906, 2, 12
1890, 10, 29. Wilson J., s Israel & Rebecca
    B., Belmont Co., O.; m in Concord, Mary C.
    HALL, dt Lindley & Millicent, Belmont Co.,
    O. (W)
    Ch: Lindley
       Ellis   b 1891, 1, 31
       Albert   " 1893, 6, 28
       James W.   " 1895, 7, 7
       Margaret R." 1897, 10, 15
       Millicent H! 1900, 1, 24
       Rebecca B. " 1903, 8, 10
1891, 4, 1. Sina R. m James WALTON (W)
1896, 3, 4. Lydia A. m Geo. E. YOUNG (W)
1900, 9, 19. Mary m Rowan O. BODENHAMER (W)
1901, 10, 9. Laura E. m Alva C. BAILEY (W)
1902, 3, 20. Elma m Howard E. HOYLE (W)
1902, 9, 10. Louisa D. m Wallace J. BUNDY (W)
1903, 10, 21. Sarah E. m Perley PICKETT (W)
1905, 6, 7. Israel d bur Colerain
1906, 9, 19. Alice R. m John B. CRAWFORD (W)
1907, 9, 25. Florence H. m Clifford FAWCETT
    (W)
1907, 10, 13. Hannah P. d bur Concord
1911, 4, 19. Grace Alma m W. J. SMITH (W)
1914, 6, 24. Alice Mary m Elisha T. KIRK (W)
1917, 5, 24. Edith T. m J. H. BINNS (W)
1925, 5, 7. Wm. G., s James & Mary G., Bel-
    mont Co., O.; m in Harrisville, Eliza H.
    McGREW, dt Wm. & Mary T. HALL, Harrison
    Co., O. (W)
1926, 9, 8. Dorothy A. m Wm. A. MOTT (W)

1804, 6, 16. Joseph & w, Grace, & ch, David,
    Rachel, Samuel & Amos, rocf Hopewell MM,
    dtd 1804,3,5, end by Concord MM, 1804,5,22

1804, 6, 16. Sarah rocf Hopewell MM, dtd
    1804,3,5, endorsed by Concord MM, 1804,5,
    22
1808, 4, 19. David gct Concord MM, to m
    Phebe Milhouse
1808, 7, 19. Phebe rocf Concord MM, dtd
    1808,6,23
1812, 7, 21. James, Joseph & James Jr., rocf
    Hopewell MM, dtd 1812,5,14
1812, 7, 21. Mary & Phebe rocf Hopewell MM,
    dtd 1812,5,14
1812, 8, 18. Ruth rocf Hopewell MM, dtd
    1812,5,14
1819, 11, 23. Samuel gct Stillwater MM, O.,
    to m Harriet Harlan
1828, 12, 23. Emma dis jH
1820, 7, 18. Harriet A. rocf Stillwater MM,
    dtd 1820,5,27
1823, 6, 24. David & w, Phebe, & ch, Hannah,
    Joseph, William, Isaac, Benjamin, Jane,
    Amos & Greenberry, gct Concord MM
1824, 2, 24. Emma rocf Concord MM, dtd 1823,
    7,23
1828, 3, 18. Lavina rocf Salem MM, dtd 1828,
    2,20
1828, 4, 22. Samuel & w, Harriet A., & ch,
    Elizabeth & Sarah, gct Fallowfield MM,Pa.
1830, 7, 20. Samuel & w, Harriet, & ch,
    Elizabeth & Sarah, rocf Fallowfield MM,
    dtd 1830,5,7
1830, 12, 23. Emma gct Concord MM (H)
1832, 8, 21. Ann M. rocf Radnor MM, dtd
    1832,6,14
1832, 2, 21. Amos gct Radnor MM, to m Ann
    Maule Jr.
1833, 7, 23. Samuel & w, Harriet, & ch,
    Elizabeth & Sarah, gct Cincinnati MM
1833, 11, 19. David & w, Phebe, & ch, William
    M., Isaac, Benjamin W., Jane M., Amos,
    Greenbury P. & Harriet, gct Adrian MM,
    Mich.
1833, 11, 19. Hannah M. gct Adrian MM, Mich.
    Territory
1834, 10, 21. Joseph Jr. gct Adrian MM, Mich.
    Territory
1835, 10, 20. Joseph gct Cincinnati MM, O.
1835, 10, 20. Deborah gct Adrian MM, Mich.
    Territory
1839, 5, 21. Joseph & w, Deborah H., & ch,
    Elisha B. & David Quincy, rocf Adrian
    MM, Mich., dtd 1839,4,11
1840, 5, 19. Deborah H. dis jH
1843, 12, 19. Joseph dis disunity
1848, 6, 20. Joshua, minor, gct Upper Spring-
    field MM
1853, 10, 18. James Jr. gct Stillwater MM, to
    m Mary Green
1854, 5, 23. Joseph gct Red Cedar MM, Ia.
1854, 5, 23. Mary J. rocf Stillwater MM, dtd
    1854,3,25
1855, 1, 23. Anna M. & minor sister, Deborah,
    gct Red Cedar MM, Iowa (G)
1857, 4, 21. Nathan gct Flushing MM, b m

STEER, continued
    Mary Jane Branson (W)
1857, 9, 22. Nathan gct Flushing MM (W)
1860, 11, 21. Joseph & w, Deborah, rst (G)
1862, 5, 20. Nathan & w, Mary Jane, & ch,
    Abzie Ladd & Abbie Loretta, rocf Flushing
    MM, dtd 1862,4,24 (W)
1862, 11, 19. Israel & w, Rebecca, & ch, Wil-
    son, Sina, Deborah, Lindley, Phebe A. &
    Elisha, dis jW (G)
1862, 11, 19. James Sr. & James Jr. dis jW
    (G)
1862, 11, 19. Mary, Anne, William, Joseph, Ra-
    chel & Nathan, dis jW (G)
1865, 1, 24. James Jr. & w, Mary G., & ch,
    Anna M., William J., Joseph, Rachel G. &
    Elizabeth, gct Stillwater MM (W)
1865, 4, 18. William dis mcd (W)
1865, 7, 18. Achsah dis jG (W)
1865, 8, 23. William H. con mcd & jas (G)
1868, 10, 20. Lindley B. gct Pennsville MM, to
    m Hannah S. Penrose (W)
1869, 4, 20. Hannah P. rocf Pennsville MM,
    dtd 1869,3,18 (W)
1869, 5, 18. Lindley B. & w, Hannah P., gct
    Coal Creek MM, Iowa (W)
1869, 11, 25. Sarah Louisa recrq (G)
1874, 5, 19. Elisha B. gct New Garden MM, to
    m Ellen C. Gilbert (W)
1874, 12, 22. Ellen G. rocf Newgarden MM, dtd
    1874,11,26 (W)
1875, 8, 21. Lindley B. & w, Hannah P., & s,
    Walter G., rocf Coal Creek MM (W)
1878, 10, 22. Joseph S. Hoge gct Stillwater
    MM, to m Anna M. Steer (W)
1891, 8, 18. Sina R. Walton (form Steer) gct
    Stillwater MM (W)
1899, 3, 21. Walter J. dis mcd (W)
1902, 11, 18. Edmon M. dis mcd (W)
1902, 5, 21. Elisha B. & w, Mary W., relrq
    (G)
1902, 5, 21. Joseph B. & w, Josie, & ch relrq
    (G)
1905, 1, 24. Alfred G. gct Philadelphia MM
    (W)
1905, 12, 19. Wilson J. & w, Mary C., & ch,
    Lindley Ellis, Albert I., James W., Marga-
    ret R., Millicent H. & Rebecca B., gct
    Newgarden MM (W)
1907, 5, 21. Richard A. dis mcd (W)
1911, 3, 21. Wilmer I. dis mcd (W)
1911, 7, 18. Lindley B. gct Stillwater MM, to
    m Ruanna Bundy (W)
1911, 8, 22. Elisha B. gct Salem MM, to m
    Lydia K. Lightfoot (W)
1912, 2, 20. Ruanna B. rocf Stillwater MM,
    dtd 1912,1,24 (W)
1912, 7, 23. Elisha B. gct Salem MM (W)
1915, 5, 18. Phebe Gaskill (form Steer) con
    mcd (W)
1918, 11, 19. Lindley B. & w, Ruanna, gct
    Stillwater MM (W)
1926, 6, 22. Eliza H. gct Stillwater MM (W)

1927, 1, 18. Wilson A. Negus gct Newgarden
    MM, to m Jessie C. Steer (W)

STEINER
1907, 4, 24. C. Charles dropped from mbrp
    (G)
1907, 6, 19. Jesse [Stiner] dropped from
    mbrp (G)
1932, 5, 26. Violet recrq (G)

STEPHEN
----, --, --. Silas & Catharine
    Ch: Zachariah b 1792, 4, 4
        Mary   " 1795, 9, 9
        Esther   " 1798, 4, 3
        Jonathan   " 1800, 6, 2
        Elizabeth " 1800, 6, 2
        Ann   " 1802, 9, 8
        Viley   " 1805, 8, 16
        Ellenor   " 1811, 6, 5
----, --, --. Zachariah & Elizabeth
    Ch: Samuel   b 1819, 2, 19
        David   " 1821, 1, 26
        Phancinah " 1823, 11, 2
        Catharine " 1825, 1, 15
        Silas   " 1827, 3, 26
        Sarah   " 1829, 12, 8
1830, 10, 27. Rebecca L. m Levi SMITH
1862, 12, 14. Laura b
1879, 1, 16. Jonathan d
1887, 10, 11. Grace M., dt Alexander & Laura,
    b
----, --, --. Lewis, s Jonathan & Elizabeth,
    d 1897,7,3; m Eliza FITZGERALD, dt Nathan
    & Dorcas, d 1906,10,17, bur West Grove
----, --, --. Silas, s Jonathan & Elizabeth,
    d 1929,6,16; m Sarah BARCROFT, dt Jos. &
    Elizabeth, b 1847,12,7 d 1916,1,30
1916, 5, 25. Margaret Anna, dt Harry W., b
    (G)
1918, 12, --. Florence Lukens, w Clarence,
    d bur in Mo.
1927, 7, --. William, s Thos. & Catharine, d

1814, 9, 15. Mary dis mcd
1818, 1, 21. Zachariah recrq
1818, 8, 18. Elizabeth recrq
1820, 12, 19. Elizabeth Harman (form Stephens)
    dis mcd
1825, 1, 18. Vilee Chance (form Stephens) dis
    mcd
1825, 2, 22. Ann Walker (form Stephens) dis
    mcd
1828, 10, 21. Esther dis jas
1829, 8, 18. Elizabeth rocf Robeson MM, Pa.,
    dtd 1829,5,8
1829, 8, 18. Jonathan & w, Esther, & ch, Sam-
    uel, Joseph, Amos L., Elizabeth & Isaac,
    gct Deerfield MM
1829, 8, 18. Cert rec for Rebecca L. from
    Robeson MM, Pa., dtd 1829,5,8, end to
    Deerfield MM
1829, 9, 19. Catharine dis jH

STEPHEN, continued

1829, 9, 22. Cert rec for David & w, Rebecca,
    from Robeson MM, dtd 1829,8,7, end to
    Deerfield MM
1829, 9, 22. William & w, Phebe, & ch, Debo-
    rah, Josiah, Samuel C., Rebecca & Anna D.
    rocf Robeson MM, dtd 1829,5,8, end to
    Deerfield
1831, 2, 22. Cert rec for Wm. & w, Phebe, &
    ch, Deborah, Josiah, Samuel C., Rebecca &
    Ann D., from Rolston MM, dtd 1829,5,8, end
    by this MM to Deerfield 1829,9,22, and by
    that MM to this MM 1831,11,13
1832, 12, 18. Elenor dis jH
1836, 10, 18. Phebe & ch, Deborah, Jonah,
    Samuel C., Rebecca, Anna D. & William M.,
    gct Pennsville MM
1837, 3, 21. William dis jH
1839, 6, 18. Elizabeth & ch, Francina, Catha-
    rine, Silas & Sarah, gct Chesterfield MM
1840, 8, 18. Samuel gct Chesterfield MM
1841, 5, 18. Elizabeth & ch, Catharine, Silas
    & Sarah, rocf Chesterfield MM, dtd 1841,1,1
    16
1843, 7, 18. Catharine gct Flushing MM
1843, 7, 18. David gct Flushing MM
1843, 7, 18. Elizabeth & ch, Silas & Sarah,
    gct Flushing MM
1873, 2, 20. William H. recrq (G)
1874, 12, 24. James & Sarah recrq (G)
1875, 2, 25. Louis recrq (G)
1876, 5, 25. Lemuel recrq (G)
1879, 6, 26. Sarah Elizabeth recrq (G)
1885, 2, 25. Robert recrq (G)
1889, 12, 25. Samuel & w, Elizabeth, relrq
    (G)
1891, 11, 25. Sarah A. recrq (G)
1894, 2, 21. Silas recrq (G)
1902, 1, 22. Grace M. & Texana, recrq (G)
1902, 12, 24. Robert dropped from mbrp (G)
1905, 4, 19. Elsworth, Addie, Sadie recrq
    (G)
1905, 4, 19. William recrq (G)
1906, 2, 21. Mrs. Maggie [Stevens] recrq (G)
1911, 4, 19. Julia recrq (G)
1914, 2, 25. Robert & J. William recrq (G)
1917, 3, 21. Florence E. recrq (G)
1920, 7, 21. Clarence M. recrq (G)
1922, 10, 25. Julia (Stephens) Reppert relrq
    (G)
1927, 7, 27. Margaret Anna recrq (G)
1929, 3, 20. Mrs. Anna recrq (G)
1933, 5, 25. Mahala relrq (G)

STERLING

1881, 2, 26. Caroline recrq (G)
1888, 10, 24. Caroline dropped from mbrp (G)
1893, 12, 20. Dallas M. & Margaret J. recrq
    (G)
1897, 1, 20. Montgomery recrq (G)
1897, 6, 28. William Harry recrq (G)
1904, 10, 19. Margaret & ch recrq (G)
1911, 6, 21. Louisa recrq (G)

1913, 1, 22. Floyd recrq (G)

STEWART

1881, 2, 26. Alfred recrq (G)
1884, 7, 23. Alfred dropped from mbrp (G)
1892, 10, 19. Mary L. recrq (G)
1892, 10, 19. Thomas & Sophia recrq (G)

STILLWAGON

1885, 2, 25. Peter recrq (G)
1885, 2, 25. Sarah Ann recrq (G)
1885, 2, 25. Henry recrq (G)
1885, 2, 25. Hettie recrq (G)
1885, 5, 20. Isaac recrq (G)
1902, 12, 24. Isaac dropped from mbrp (G)
1913, 5, 21. Cretia relrq (G)

STINER

1901, 2, 20. Chris recrq (G)

STOLL

1900, 4, 25. Mary Chamberlain relrq (G)

STOWERS

1892, 10, 19. Margaret G. recrq (G)

STRAHL

----, --, --. Philip & Sarah
    Ch: Daniel   b 1794, 12, 14
        Caspar   " 1796, 5, 10
        Merihab   " 1797, 11, 14
        Phillip   " 1799, 8, 11
        Elizabeth   " 1801, 1, 28
        David
        Rachel   " 1805, 10, 24
        Sarah   " 1807, 4, 12

1804, 9, 15. Ann & ch, Mary, Rebecca, Sarah,
    Elinor & John, rocf Catawisa MM, Pa.,
    dtd 1804,5,26
1804, 11, 7. Philip & w, Sarah, & ch, Daniel,
    Casper, Merihab, Phillip, Elizabeth & Da-
    vid, rocf Cattawisa MM, dtd 1804,8,25
1804, 11, 7. Isaac & w, Ellen, & ch, Samuel,
    Margaret, Stacy, John & Isaac, rocf Catta-
    wisa MM, dtd 1804,8,25
1804, 11, 7. Thomas & w, Martha, & ch, Anna,
    Hannah & Joseph, rocf Cattawisa MM, dtd
    1804,8,25
1806, 7, 19. Isaac & w, Eleanor, & ch, Sam-
    uel, Margaret, Stashey, John, Isaac & Mah-
    lon, gct Concord MM
1810, 5, 22. Philip & w, Sarah, & ch, Daniel,
    Caspar, Merihab, Phillip, Elizabeth, Da-
    vid, Rachel, Sarah & Edmund, gct Still-
    water MM
1814, 2, 22. Daniel rocf Stillwater MM, dtd
    1813,12,18
1815, 12, 19. Thomas & w, Martha, & ch, Anna,
    Hannah, Joseph, Rebecca, William, Jane,
    Jesse & Lovisa, gct Plainfield MM
1817, 6, 24. Daniel gct Stillwater MM

STRATTON
1850, 9, 8. Martha W. d ae 28 bur Salem, O.
1852, 4, 28. Sarah m David LUPTON
1864, 9, 28. David P., s Elisha & Elizabeth,
    Cedar Co., Ia.; m in West Grove MH, Sarah
    Ann LADD dt Robert P. & Ruanna T., Harri-
    son Co., O.
1871, 12, 27. Edward, s Joshua & Rachel, Co-
    lumbiana Co., O.; m in Concord, Mary H.
    RALEY, dt Asa & Asenath, Belmont Co., O.
    (W)
1892, 6, 2. Dillwyn, s Barclay & Hannah H.,
    Columbiana Co., O.; m in Harrisville,
    Elizabeth HALL, dt Wm. & Mary T., Harrison
    Co., O. (W)
1897, 9, 22. Joseph R., s Edward & Mary H.,
    Columbiana Co., O.; m in Colerain, Anna M.
    BUNDY, dt Edmund & Deborah, Belmont Co.,
    O. (W)
1927, 3, 26. Stanley W., s Geo. W. & Melva W.
    Belmont Co., O.; m in Harrisville, Marjor-
    ie Ann SMITH, dt Aaron T. & Rachel D.,
    Harrison Co., O., b 1905,5,16 (W)
1932, 10, 29. Howard, s Geo. W. & Melva W.,
    Belmont Co., O.; m in Harrisville, Mabel
    WHINNERY, dt Thomas B. & Clara H., Jeffer-
    son Co., O. (W)

1848, 8, 22. Martha W. rocf Salem MM, dtd
    1848,7,19
1851, 6, 24. Henry Lupton gct Newgarden MM,
    to m Sarah Stratton
1851, 9, 23. Sarah rocf Newgarden MM, dtd
    1851,8,21
1857, 5, 19. Wilson Hall gct Salem MM, to m
    Sina Stratton
1864, 9, 21. David P. rocf Springdale MM,
    Ia., to m Sarah Ann Ladd (G)
1865, 3, 22. Sarah Ann gct Springdale MM,
    Ia. (G)
1872, 3, 19. Mary H. gct Middleton MM (W)
1873, 7, 22. Barclay & w, Hannah H., & ch,
    Joseph H. & Dilwin, rocf Newgarden MM, dtd
    1873,6,20 (W)
1874, 10, 20. Barclay & w, Hannah, & ch, Jo-
    seph C. & Dillwyn, gct New Garden MM (W)
1892, 11, 22. Elizabeth (form Hall) gct New
    Garden MM (W)
1898, 3, 22. Anna M. gct Salem MM (W)

STRAUGHAN
1836, 4, 20. John, s Daniel & Ann, Columbi-
    ana Co., O.; m Martha L. NIXON, in Short
    Creek MH, dt Robert & Milicent LAWRENCE,
    Jefferson Co., O.

1837, 7, 18. Martha L. [Straughn] gct Salem
    MM

STREET
----, --, --. Griffith b 1755,5,15 d 1840,3,
    17; m Elizabeth----- b 1769,8,31 d 1849,
    10,4 (H)

Ch: Gulielma   b 1797, 1, 22
    Rebecca   " 1803, 10, 25
    Rachel   " 1810, 1, 21
1827, 5, 5. Mary Ann m Baldin BARRETT

1818, 10, 20. Agnes rocf Falls MM, Pa., dtd
    1818,9,11
1819, 6, 22. Griffith & w, Elizabeth, & ch,
    Mary Ann, Rebecca & Rachel, rocf Byberry
    MM, Pa., dtd 1819,4,27
1819, 6, 22. Gulielma rocf Byberry MM, dtd
    1819,4,27
1828, 10, 21. Rebecca dis jH
1828, 12, 23. Elizabeth & Rachel dis jH
1829, 1, 20. Gulielma dis jH
1829, 1, 20. Mary Ann, Rachel & Balinda,
    minor ch Isaac & Rebecca, gct Upper
    Springfield MM
1829, 11, 24. Agnes dis jH
1830, 12, 23. Agness gct Stillwater MM (H)
1852, 3, 23. Hannah (form Wood) dis mcd

STREIGHT
1895, 3, 20. Sarah Catharine recrq (G)

STROUD
----, --, --. Jacob & Ann
    Ch: Mary
        William   b 1842, 1, 20
1843, 8, 30. Sally B. m Moses B. GOVE
1869, 3, 31. Mary B. m Parvin WRIGHT

1842, 1, 18. Sally B. rocf Centre MM, dtd
    1841,11,17
1843, 6, 20. Jacob & w, Ann M., & ch, Mary
    B., Emily H. & William, rocf Centre MM,
    dtd 1843,5,17
1846, 3, 24. Benjamin H. Wright gct Spring-
    boro MM, to m Sally Ann Stroud
1862, 10, 21. Mary B. dis jG (W)
1867, 6, 20. William gct Springfield MM, Kan.
    (G)

SUMPTION
1845, 5, 20. Rachel (form Howard) dis mcd

SUTTON
1914, 1, 21. Clara recrq (G)

SWABDJO
1914, 1, 21. James, Mike & Mary recrq (G)

SWAIN
1832, 8, 21. Joshua d ae 62 bur Harrisville
1834, 1, 30. Mary [Swayne] m Thos. HIRST

1809, 2, 21. Joshua & w, Mary, rocf Plymouth
    MM, dtd 1809,1,18

SWEET
1878, 3, 21. Charles T. recrq (G)
1883, 11, 21. Charles T. gct Cleveland MM (G)

SYKES
1892, 10, 19. Barclay recrq (G)

SYMONS
1899, 9, 20. Robert & w, Gertrude E., rocf
Spiceland MM, Ind. & from Knightstown MM,
Ind. (G)
1905, 11, 22. Robert & w, Gertrude, relrq (G)

TABER
1842, 4, 28. Lewis, s Benj. & Phebe, Jeffer-
son Co., O.; m in Short Creek MH, Mary Ann
HILL, dt John C. & Rachel, Jefferson Co.,
O., d 1910,3,11 bur Harrisville
Ch: Joseph John
                b 1846, 7, 8
    Rachel Han-
       nah   " 1848, 6, 5
    Mary Lewis " 1848, 6, 5 d 1870,11,26
    Selma
       Phebe   " 1859, 10, 6
    Russell
       Zeno   " 1862, 8, 17
----, --, --. Joseph John & Mary P.
    Ch: Anna R.   b 1875, 10, 30
        Louis J. " 1878, 9, 19
        William P. " 1881, 7, 18
        Salma Liz-
           zie   " 1884, 6, 18
1875, 10, 30. Anna R., dt Joseph J. & Mary P.,
b
1887, 12, 7. Lewis d ae 76 bur Harrisville
1893, 8, 23. Melvin Louis [Tabor], s Russell
B. & Phebe Ellen, b
1897, 5, 27. Rachel H. m Wilson C. HIRST (W)
1914, 5, 20. Wm. P., s Joseph John H. & Mary
P. Belmont Co., O.; m in Colerain, Sara
Debora NEGUS, dt Oliver S. & Deborah,
Belmont Co., O., b 1888,1,5 (W)

1841, 3, 23. Lewis rocf Starksborough MM,
Vt., dtd 1841,1,1
1862, 11, 19. Lewis [Tabor] dis jW
1873, 10, 21. Joseph John J. gct Pennville MM,
to m Mary H. Picket (W)
1874, 11, 24. Mary P. rocf Pennsville MM, dtd
1874,10,15 (W)
1884, 7, 23. Joseph John dropped from mbrp
(G)
1884, 7, 23. Mary Ann dropped from mbrp (G)
1884, 7, 23. Rachel dropped from mbrp (G)
1884, 7, 23. Russell dropped from mbrp (G)
1885, 3, 24. Joseph John & w, Mary P., & ch,
Anna R., Louis J., William P. & Selma
Lizzie, gct Stillwater MM (W)
1887, 5, 24. Selma P. Mills (form Taber) dis
mcd (W)
1891, 9, 22. Russell Z. gct Springville MM,
Ia., to m Phebe Ellen Shaw (W)
1892, 4, 19. Phebe Ellen rocf Springville
MM, Ia., dtd 1892,3,19 (W)
1894, 11, 20. Russell Z. & w, Phebe Ellen, &
s, Melvin Louis, gct Springville MM (W)

TALBOTT
1838, 10, 31. Nathan, s Benjamin & Susannah,
Jefferson Co., O.; m in Mt. Pleasant,
Abigail FLANNER, dt Wm. & Peninah, Belmont Co., O.
1842, 6, 11. Deborah d bur Cross Creek
----, --, --. Kinsey d 1853,8,23 ae 75 bur
Cross Creek; m Hannah Y---- d 1851,8,22
ae 70 bur Cross Creek
    Ch: William J.   d 1852, 3.16
          ae 8 bur Cross Creek
        Mary Elizabeth   " 1852, 3,18
          bur Cross Creek
        Eli P.   " 1852, 3,21
          bur Cross Creek
1845, 12, 23. Sarah M. d ae 26 bur Cross Creek
1846, 7, --. Benjamin d ae 88 bur Cross Creek
1847, --, --. Susanna d bur Cross Creek
----, --, --. Kinsey & Caroline
    Ch: Mary S.   b 1849, 9, 4
        Joseph A.   " 1844, 12, 15
        William M. " 1846, 9, 18
        Elizabeth C." 1858, 1, 29
1850, 3, 31. Addison d ae 3 bur Cross Creek
1850, 4, 20. Ann Eliza d bur Cross Creek
1852, 6, 7. Mary d ae 3 bur Cross Creek
1852, 11, 17. Joseph d ae 89 bur Smithfield
1858, 2, 13. Caleb S. d ae 18
1859, 11, 2. Elizabeth d ae 2 bur Cross Creek

1805, 10, 19. Mary [Talbot] rocf Redstone MM,
dtd 1805,5,31
1806, 9, 20. Benjamin [Talbot] & w, Susanna,
& ch, John, William, Nathan, Margaret,
Elizabeth & Benjamin, rocf Redstone MM,
dtd 1806,8,29
1820, 9, 19. Rebecca gct Cincinnati MM
1820, 10, 24. Nathan gct Cincinnati MM
1820, 10, 24. Rachel, w Samuel, & ch, John,
Samuel & David, gct Cincinnati MM
1821, 2, 20. Samuel gct Cincinnati MM
1829, 9, 22. Rebecca dis jH
1835, 10, 20. James R. Ball gct Smithfield
MM, to m Mary Ann Talbot
1839, 6, 18. Abigail F. [Talbot] gct Smithfield MM
1851, 7, 22. Abigail [Talbot] rocf Smithfield MM, dtd 1851,6,23
1865, 1, 24. Caroline dis disunity (W)
1865, 4, 18. Kinsey dis jG (W)
1865, 10, 25. Kinsey M. & w, Caroline E., &
ch, Wm. & Mary Samantha, rocf Smithfield
MM (G)
1867, 12, 26. Jos. A. & w, Esther, & ch,
Delbert R., rocf Gilead MM (G)
1868, 3, 26. Mary S. Glass (form Talbott)
con mcd (G)
1869, 6, 24. William [Talbot] con mcd (G)
1869, 7, 22. Jos. A. [Talbot] & w, Esther,
& s, Robert Delbert, gct Gilead MM (G)
1876, 9, 21. Mary E. & ch, Charles E., Anna
A., Wm. K. & Joseph E., recrq (G)
1885, 1, 21. Emily B. rocf Winona MM (G)

TALBOTT, continued

1889, 12, 25. Joseph & w, Esther, & ch, M.
      Elizabeth & Sarah E., rocf Damascus MM
      (G)
1891, 5, 20. Anna A. gct Scipio MM, N. Y. (G)
1899, 1, 25. Ethel relrq (G)
1902, 2, 19. William [Talbot] gct Damascus MM
      (G)
1906, 9, 19. William & Emily [Talbot] gct
      Damascus MM, O. (G)
1907, 4, 24. Chas. B. & Anna R. dropped from
      mbrp (G)

TATUM

1843, 3, 21. Barnabas C. Hobbs gct Upper
      Springfield MM, to m Rebecca Tatum
1862, 11, 19. George & Hannah dis jW

TAWNER

1901, 7, 24. George, Lurenda, Nellie, Emma,
      Grace, Henry, Henry & Wm. J. B. recrq (G)
1902, 5, 21. George & w, Lurenda, & ch, Emma,
      Nellie, Grace, Henry & William, relrq (G)

TAYLOR

----, --, --. Reuben d 1828,10,21 ae 47 bur
      Short Creek; m Jemima -----
      Ch: Joseph   b 1809, 10, 13 d 1810, 3,25
            bur Short Creek
          Rebecca   b 1812, 2, 28
          Isaac   " 1815, 10, 2
          Eliza   " 1819, 5, 2
          Pharaby P. " 1822, 1, 28
1812, 4, 23. Rebecca m David UPDEGRAFF
1812, 4, 30. Nanny m Wm. ATKINSON
1831, 11, 6. Jonathan d ae 68 bur Short Creek
1862, 11, 13. Ann, w Jonathan, d ae 97
1897, 4, 8. Eliza d bur Concord

1807, 8, 15. Sarah (form Stanton) dis mou
1807, 11, 21. Christopher & w, Elizabeth, &
      ch, Nanne, Keziah, Daniel, Bettie, Ursula,
      Mary, Martha, William & Stace, rocf Jack-
      swamp MM, N. C., dtd 1807,10,3
1808, 8, 23. Reuben rocf Jackswamp MM, N. C.,
      dtd 1808,6,4
1808, 12, 20. Reuben gct Stillwater MM, to m
      Jemima Patterson
1809, 7, 18. Keziah gct Plainfield MM
1809, 8, 22. Jemima rocf Stillwater MM, dtd
      1809,7,25
1811, 5, 21. Simeon & w, Elizabeth, & dt,
      Sally, rocf Jackswamp MM, N. C., dtd 1811,
      3,2
1811, 11, 19. Simeon & fam gct Stillwater MM
1815, 4, 18. Daniel dis enlisting in military
      service
1816, 5, 2. Sarah rst at Darby Creek MM with
      consent of this mtg
1817, 1, 21. Mary Hendrix (form Taylor) dis
      mcd
1818, 1, 2. Ursula gct Stillwater MM
1818, 1, 2. Elizabeth & ch, William & Tacy,

gct Stillwater MM

1818, 6, 23. Cert rec for Joseph from Noting-
      ham MM, dtd 1816,9,6, end to Plymouth MM
1819, 6, 22. Cert for Elizabeth granted to
      Stillwater MM in 1818,1,20 end by that MM
      to this 1819,5,22
1819, 6, 22. Cert for Ursula endorsed back
      to this MM from Stillwater MM
1819, 8, 24. Ursula Lyncan (form Taylor) dis
      mcd
1821, 2, 20. William dis disunity
1821, 11, 20. Martha gct Plainfield MM
1822, 4, 23. Cert for Martha granted in 1821,
      11,20 now returned end by Plainfield MM
1822, 6, 18. Martha Eyre (form Taylor) dis
      mcd
1823, 7, 22. Tacy gct Plainfield MM
1824, 4, 20. Elizabeth gct Plainfield MM
1825, 7, 19. Elizabeth Peterson (form Taylor)
      dis mcd
1847, 6, 22. Isaac dis mcd
1864, 3, 23. Ann d 1862,11,13 ae 97y 34d (G)
1881, 2, 26. John recrq (G)
1881, 2, 26. John W. & Mattie recrq (G)
1881, 2, 26. Noble recrq (G)
1881, 2, 26. Sarah recrq (G)
1883, 6, 20. Lemuel, Dillon & Ola recrq (G)
1885, 10, 21. Dillon dropped from mbrp (G)
1889, 2, 20. Clara dropped from mbrp (G)
1891, 1, 21. Lemuel dropped from mbrp (G)
1894, 3, 21. Maud recrq (G)
1905, 4, 19. Annie recrq (G)
1912, 3, 20. Viola recrq (G)

TEASDALE

1892, 3, 23. John G. recrq (G)
1895, 7, 24. John dropped from mbrp (G)

TERRELL

1817, 10, 29. Mahala m Ira PATTERSON
1818, 1, 28. Rachel m Arnold PATTERSON
1818, 9, 30. Sally m Joseph RHODES
1820, 3, 1. Joanna m Benj. THOMAS
1825, 7, 28. Clark, s Mathew & Sarah, Jeffer-
      son Co., O.; m in Short Creek MH, Mary
      JENKINS, dt Mishael & Sarah, Belmont Co.,
      O.
      Ch: Thomas   b 1826, 7, 14
          Sarah   " 1827, 11, 14
          George   " 1829, 11, 3
          Mathew   " 1829, 11, 3
          Rachel   " 1831, 5, 1
          Ann   " 1832, 12, 17
          Hannah   " 1834, 9, 1
          Mathew   " 1836, 9, 16
          Clark   " 1838, 3, 9
          Mary   " 1840, 5, 17
          Mishael   " 1845, 4, 5
          John   " 1847, 5, 20
          Elizabeth   " 1842, 11, 6
          Rebecca   " 1851, 10, 28
1830, 2, 15. Mathew d bur Short Creek
1833, 8, 21. Thos. H., s Matthew & Sally,

TERRELL, continued
   Jefferson Co., O.; m in Mt. Pleasant, Mary
      W. RICKS, dt Geo. & Judith WINSTON, Rich-
      mond, Va.
----, --, --. Mathew & Elizabeth
      Ch: Lucy Win-
            ston   b 1838, 4, 15
          Sarah   " 1840, 7, 12
          Olive   " 1842, 5, 18
      Mathew m 2nd Hester -----
      Ch: Lydia
            Jane   b 1849, 9, 8
1845, 9, 19. Elizabeth d ae 42 bur Short Creek
1846, 11, 12. Caty d bur West Grove
1848, 9, 27. Matthew, s Matthew & Sarah, Jef-
      ferson Co., O.; m in Mt. Pleasant, Hester
      G. HUSSEY, dt Christopher & Lydia, Jeffer-
      son Co. O.
1852, 8, 25. Elizabeth A. m Timothy WILSON
1853, 9, 21. Rachel M. m Joseph M. COX
1854, 5, 13. Maty W. d ae 59 bur Short Creek
1855, 5, 13. Ann L. m Matthew W. HUSSEY
1856, 9, 25. Sarah J. m John F. STEDDOM
1859, 9, 22. Lucy W. m Franklin WILSON
1860, 8, 29. Sarah H. m Daniel H. STANLEY
1862, 10, 29. Hannah K. m John H. GREEN
1865, 8, 30. Olive B. m Wm. C. NEWBY
1874, 9, 30. Rebecca B. m Elwood RATCLIFF

1814, 3, 22. Sally & ch, Mahlon, Rachel,
      Thomas, Clark, Joana & Mathew, rocf Cedar
      Creek MM, dtd 1813,10,9
1820, 4, 18. Thomas gct Cedar Creek MM, Va.
1834, 4, 22. Mathew & w, Elizabeth, & ch,
      Amos H., Joseph & Elizabeth Ann, rocf
      Upper Springfield MM, dtd 1834,2,22
1850, 8, 20. Amos H. gct Elk MM, to m Mary
      T. Hutchins
1851, 9, 23. Amos H. gct Elk MM, O.
1854, 1, 24. Thomas gct Miami MM, to m Lydia
      Steddom
1856, 5, 21. Thomas gct Miami MM, O.
1862, 7, 22. Thomas H. & Mathew dis jG
1863, 3, 24. Clark Sr. & Clark Jr. dis jG
1863, 4, 22. Clark & w, Mary J., & ch,
      Michael & John, gct Spring Creek MM, Ia
      (G)
1863, 4, 22. Mary F. & Elizabeth C. gct
      Spring Creek MM, Ia. (G)
1863, 4, 22. Thomas H. gct Smithfield MM, to
      m Rebecca Ballinger (G)
1863, 10, 21. Rebecca B. rocf Smithfield MM
      (G)
1864, 4, 2. Matthew gct Milford MM, Ind.,
      to m Isabella Newby (G)
1865, 3, 21. Esther dis jG (W)
1865, 3, 22. Clark Jr. gct Spring Creek MM,
      Ia. (G)
1865, 3, 22. George gct Spring Creek MM, Ia.
      (G)
1865, 3, 22. Matthew Jr. gct Spring Creek MM,
      Ia. (G)
1865, 7, 18. Rebecca dis jG (W)

1865, 8, 23. William C. Newby rocf Milford
      MM, Ind., to m Olive B. Terrell (G)
1871, 4, 20. Matthew & w, Hester G., gct
      Salem MM (G)
1871, 4, 20. Lydia J. gct Salem MM, O. (G)

TEST
1816, 1, 23. Benjamin & w, Mary, & ch, Re-
      becca, Elisha, Rachel, Hannah & Mary,
      rocf Salem MM, dtd 1816,1,16
1816, 2, 20. Rebecca rocf Salem MM, dtd
      1816,1,11
1819, 8, 24. Benjamin & w, Mary, & ch, Re-
      becca, Rachel, Hannah, Mary & Elizabeth,
      gct Stillwater MM
1844, 4, 23. Ann D. (form Lawrence) con mcd
1844, 10, 22. Ann D. gct Salem MM
1888, 7, 24. Nathan P. Hall gct Springville
      MM, Ia., to m Elizabeth D. Test (W)

THOMAS
----, --, --. Jesse & Avis
      Ch: Abigail   b 1798, 6, 23
          William   " 1800, 12, 7
          Nathan   " 1803, 1, 2
          Jonathan   " 1805, 6, 5
          Gulielma   " 1807, 11, 21
          Jesse   " 1810, 9, 29
          David   " 1813, 4, 3
          Annaliza   " 1817, 2, 2
          Joseph   " 1820, 1, 31
1803, 1, 2. Nathan M. b
1808, 6, 29. Peter, s Isaac & Rachel, Jeffer-
      son Co., O.; m in West Grove MH, Mary
      THOMSON, dt Bradway & Ann, Jefferson Co.,
      O., d 1861,8,13 bur West Grove
      Ch: Rachel   b 1809, 4, 27
          Ann   " 1811, 2, 11
          Isaac   " 1813, 6, 1
          Bradway   " 1815, 5, 16
          Sarah   " 1817, 4, 27
          John   " 1819, 6, 4
          Pearson   " 1821, 6, 20
          Ruanna   " 1823, 7, 5
          Mary   " 1826, 1, 8
          Edith   " 1828, 3, 1
          Peter   " 1836, 8, 14
          Elizabeth " 1834, 6, 17
1812, 12, 3. Sarah m Wm. JOHN
1814, 9, 28. Ruannah m Wm. FRAME
1820, 3, 1. Benjamin, s Jonah & Rebecca,
      Belmont Co., O.; m in Mt. Pleasant, Jo-
      anna TERRELL, dt Mathew & Sarah
1824, 12, 24. Isaac d ae 70 bur West Grove
1825, 1, 26. Sarah m Thomas GIBBONS
1825, 12, 24. Isaac d ae 71 bur West Grove
1826, 5, 31. Rachel m Emry LEWIS
1829, 12, 24. Susanna d bur West Grove
1834, 1, 1. Isaac, s Peter & Mary, Harri-
      son Co., O.; m in West Grove MH, Anna
      LADD, dt Robert & Mary, Harrison Co., O.
      Ch: Robert   b 1834, 10, 5
          Joseph   " 1836, 4, 7

THOMAS, continued

Ch: Peter   b 1838, 1, 23
    Israel   " 1839, 7, 16
    Martha Ann " 1841, 6, 14
    Mary   " 1843, 3, 18
    Edna   " 1845, 1, 24
    Oliver   " 1846, 12, 10
    Lucy   " 1848, 9, 25
    Anna   " 1851, 5, 24
    Sarah   " 1854, 1, 1

1835, 1, 28. Townsend, s Townsend & Bula E.,
    Harrison Co., O.; m in West Grove MH, Ann
    BARBER, dt Samuel & Ann, Harrison Co., O.
    Ch: Beulah
        Elma   b 1836, 2, 2
        Chalkley   " 1837, 10, 3
        Samuel E. " 1839, 10, 8
        Mary   " 1843, 12, 17
        Townsend   " 1846, 2, 18
        William Al-
          bert   " 1848, 9, 19
        Clarkson   " 1850, 12, 21
        Rebecca A. " 1853, 9, 16

1837, 11, 1. Sarah m David HALL
1837, 11, 30. Bradaway, s Peter & Mary, Harri-
    son Co., O.; m in Harrisville, Rachel
    HALL, dt Thos. & Mary, Harrison Co., O.
    Ch: David   b 1841, 11, 7
        Asenath H. " 1847, 2, 8
        Mary   " 1851, 11, 6 d 1898. 3,28
          bur Harrisville
        Elma   b 1859, 3, 9

1840, 8, 26. Ruanna m Robert P. LADD
1841, 4, 28. Susan M. m Josiah EVANS
1847, 11, 30. Jesse d
1848, 3, 1. Susan M. b
1848, 6, 18. Pearson d ae 28 bur West Grove
1849, 10, 31. Edith m Jesse HALL
1850, 6, 26. Elizabeth m Amos L. COPE
1855, 5, 2. Peter, s Peter & Mary, Harrison
    Co., O.; m in West Grove MH, Rachel BRAN-
    SON, dt Abraham & Ann, Harrison Co., O.
    Ch: Mary Ann   b 1856, 7, 12
        Sarah Eliza-
          beth   b 1858, 2, 4
        Tacy Eliza-
          beth   b 1859, 6, 23
        Emma B.   " 1861, 5, 30

1856, 10, 29. Beulah E. m Abraham WILSON
1861, 8, 13. Mary d
----, --, --. Peter L. & Mary T.
    Ch: Walter   b 1863, 12, 10
        Marianna " 1867, 9, 17
        Eleanor   " 1870, 4, 12
        Ester   " 1873, 1, 24

1863, 4, 4. Joseph d
1866, 10, 31. Israel, s Isaac & Anna, Harri-
    son Co., O., b 1839,9,16 d 1905,4,14; m
    in West Grove MH, Elizabeth S. BRANSON, dt
    Abraham & Ann, Harrison Co., O., b 1839,
    11,17
    Ch: John B.   b 1868, 1, 19
        Edgar B. " 1870, 2, 15

Ch: Anne R.   b 1877, 11, 12
1869, 12, 22. Harvey, s Samuel & Mary, Dela-
    ware Co., Pa.; m in Smithfield, Lydia S.
    WILLETS, dt Mark & Sarah, Jefferson Co.,
    O. (W)
1872, 5, 9. Anna L. d (an elder) (G)
1872, 10, 31. Martha m Hiram COPE
1873, 1, 1. Oliver, s Isaac & Ann, Harrison
    Co., O.; m in West Grove MH, Martha J.
    ELLIOTT, nm, dt Samuel & Sarah, Harrison
    Co., O.
----, --, --. David & Lydia
    Ch: Mary Eva   b 1874, 7, 4
        Clarkson B." 1877, 3, 14
        Anna L.   " 1880, 8, 25
        Rachel Elma" 1884, 3, 5
1874, 7, 29. Mary m Samuel A. JONES
1875, 5, 25. Lucy m Abraham W. BRANSON
1875, 10, 20. Robert P., s Elwood & Beulah
    A., Beaver Co., Pa., d 1902,4,20 ae 40;
    m in Smithfield, Susan McGREW, dt James W.
    & Ann, Jefferson Co., O., b 1848,3,1 d
    1927,7,12 ae 79 bur Colerain (W)
    Ch: Walter S. b 1878, 5, 1
1876, 3, 29. Edna m Cyrus DIXON
1877, 2, 12. Benjamin J. b
1877, 3, 14. Clarkson B., s David & Lydia, b
1881, 7, 10. Elmira d
1887, 7, 31. Ernest B., s Robert & Susan, b
1895, 2, 5. Elwood d ae 81 bur Harrisville
1897, 3, 24. Elma m Jos. B. GIBBONS (W)
1898, 5, 24. Mary M., dt Elwood & Bulah, d
    bur Harrisville
1900, 5, 4. Beulah, w Elwood, d bur Harris-
    ville
1902, 8, 20. Gilbert E., s Robert P. & Susan
    M., Belmont Co., O., b 1880,3,29; m in
    Concord, Rachel E. BUNDY, dt Edmund &
    Deborah M., Belmont Co., O., b 1882,1,2
    Ch: Mabel S.   b 1904, 11, 30
        Robert L. " 1907, 8, 26
        Byron G.   " 1913, 11, 22
1904, 4, 21. Walter S., s Robert P. & Susan
    M., Belmont Co., O., b 1878,5,1; m in
    Harrisville, Martha BINNS, dt Jonathan &
    Rosella, Harrison Co., O., b 1875,3,20
    (W)
    Ch: J. Howard b 1905, 10, 9 d 1905,10,15
        Alice Ro-
          sella   " 1906, 11, 29
        Alfred R. " 1909, 11, 12
        Margaret
          Elizabeth " 1913, 7, 14
        Bulah Al-
          meda   " 1918, 8, 24
        Leslie
          Binns   " 1920, 9, 11
1920, 9, 11. Leslie B. b
1927, 7, 12. Susan M. d
----, --, --. Robert Leland, s Gilbert E. &
    Rachel (Bundy), b 1907,9,23; m Luella L.
    HALL, dt Clifton P. & Anna (Pickett), b
    1907,6,10

THOMAS, continued
    Ch: Helen
        Phyllis b 1932, 4, 11
1932, 7, 9. Alice R. m W. L. SATTERTHWAIT
    (W)

1804, 8, 18. Benjamin rocf Coursound MM, dtd
    1804,3,31
1804, 9, 15. John & w, Hannah, rocf Coursound
    MM, N. C., dtd 1804,3,31 end by Concord
    MM, 1804,6,10
1804, 9, 15. Nathaniel & w, Dorcas, & s, Abel,
    rocf Coursound MM, N. C., dtd 1804,3,31,
    end by Concord MM, 1804,6,19
1804, 10, 20. Jesse Sr. & w, Elizabeth, & ch,
    Joseph & Scotten, rocf Coursound MM, N.C.,
    dtd 1804,3,31, end by Concord MM, 1804,8,
    21
1805, 1, 19. Sarah rocf Coresound MM, N. C.,
    dtd 1804,4,11, end by Concord MM, 1804,12,
    18
1805, 4, 20. Joseph & John, ch Nathaniel,
    recrq
1806, 7, 19. Nathaniel & fam gct Salem MM
1806, 8, 16. John & fam gct Salem MM
1807, 5, 16. Elizabeth Harmer (form Thomas)
    dis mcd
1807, 10, 17. Isaac & s, Peter, recrq
1807, 10, 17. Susanna & dt, Susanna, Hannah &
    Ruanna, recrq
1809, 1, 24. Vicey Burr (form Thomas) dis mcd
1809, 9, 19. Benjamin gct Coursound MM, N. C.
1811, 9, 24. Hannah Gwynn (form Thomas) dis
    mcd
1814, 7, 19. Sarah recrq
1817, 9, 23. Benjamin con mcd
1817, 10, 21. Susanna Riggle (form Thomas) con
    mcd
1818, 7, 21. Benjamin gct Suttons Creek MM,
    N. C.
1820, 2, 22. Aaron recrq
1820, 2, 22. Joseph rpd mcd
1820, 4, 18. Sarah (form Worrel) con mcd
1820, 9, 19. Cert rec for Eleanor, w Joseph,
    & ch, Jacob & Jesse, from Abington MM,
    dtd 1819,12,27, end to Cincinnati MM
1820, 9, 19. Sarah rocf Abington MM, dtd
    1819,12,27
1821, 3, 20. Joanna gct Plainfield MM
1824, 5, 18. Joseph dis mcd
1826, 12, 19. Jonathan gct Goshen MM
1828, 10, 21. Ann Gray (form Thomas) con mcd
1828, 12, 23. Avis & Abigail dis jH
1829, 6, 23. Lucinda dis jH
1830, 7, 20. Townsend, minor, rocf Concord
    MM, Pa., dtd 1830,6,10
1835, 3, 24. Nathan gct Adrian MM, Mich.
    Territory
1835, 5, 19. Aaron & w, Sarah, & ch, Jonathan,
    Susannah, John, Mary & William, gct Deer-
    field MM
1837, 11, 21. David dis jH
1838, 11, 20. Jesse P. rocf Gwynedd MM, Pa.,

dtd 1838,9,27
1839, 1, 22. Susan M. rocf Abington MM, dtd
    1838,11,26
1841, 2, 23. Ann Eliza Robb (form Thomas)
    dis mcd
1841, 10, 19. John gct Flushing MM, to m Mi-
    riam B. Smith
1842, 5, 24. Miriam B. rocf Flushing MM, dtd
    1842,3,24
1843, 6, 20. John & w, Meriam B., & s, Samuel
    T., gct Flushing MM
1847, 6, 21. Airs gct Green Plain MM (H)
1847, 11, 23. Pearson gct Flushing MM, to m
    Amy T. SMITH
1848, 5, 23. Amy T. rocf Flushing MM, dtd
    1848,2,24
1849, 8, 21. Ann T. gct Flushing MM
1850, 8, 20. David Hall gct Flushing MM, to
    m Amy T. Thomas
1861, 3, 20. Peter L. gct Flushing MM, to m
    Mary Green
1861, 5, 21. Isaac dis jG
1861, 11, 20. Mary T. rocf Flushing MM
1862, 11, 19. Ann dis jW
1862, 11, 19. Brodowa & w, Rachel, & ch, Da-
    vid, Asenath, Mary & Elma, dis jW
1864, 3, 22. Peter Jr. dis jG (W)
1864, 3, 22. Townsend dis jG (W)
1864, 4, 19. Ann dis jG (W)
1864, 4, 19. Rachel B. dis jG (W)
1864, 9, 21. Peter & w, Rachel H., & ch,
    Mary Ann, Sarah Elizabeth, Tacy Edith &
    Emma B., gct Springdale MM, Ia. (G)
1865, 4, 19. Robert gct Springdale MM, Ia.
    (G)
1865, 8, 22. Anna dis jG (W)
1866, 1, 24. Mary P. gct Springdale MM, Ia.
    (G)
1866, 1, 24. Townsend & w, Ann, & ch, Town-
    send, William A., Clarkson & Rebecca Ann,
    gct Springdale MM, Ia. (G)
1867, 10, 22. Elizabeth (form Branson) dis
    mcd & jG (W)
1868, 1, 21. Martha Ann dis jG (W)
1868, 1, 21. Edna, Mary & Lucy dis jG (W)
1868, 7, 23. Deborah (form Ladd) con mcd (G)
1870, 5, 24. Lydia S. gct Concord MM, Pa.
1870, 11, 22. Israel dis jG (W)
1870, 11, 22. Peter L. dis jG (W)
1871, 5, 23. David gct New Garden MM, to m
    Lydia Brantingham (W)
1871, 11, 21. Lydia B. rocf Newgarden MM, dtd
    1871,10,26 (W)
1874, 12, 24. Martha J. recrq (G)
1875, 7, 22. Isaac gct Adrian MM, Mich., to
    m Phebe G. Gibbons (G)
1875, 11, 25. Phebe G. rocf Adrian MM, Mich.
    (G)
1875, 9, 21. Rachel dis disunity (W)
1875, 12, 21. Bradway dis disunity (W)
1876, 5, 23. Rachel (form Bundy) dis mcd
    (W)
1876, 8, 22. Ann dis disunity (W)

SHORT CREEK MONTHLY MEETING

THOMAS, continued

1876, 8, 22. Susan M. gct Middleton MM (W)

1876, 10, 24. Asenath Whinery (form Thomas) con mcd (W)

1877, 5, 22. Oliver dis mcd & jG (W)

1877, 11, 20. Sarah Woodward (form Thomas) dis mcd & jG (W)

1881, 1, 26. Edith J. relrq (G)

1881, 8, 23. Anna Lupton (form Thomas) dis mcd & jG (W)

1884, 5, 21. Peter L. & w, Mary T., & ch, Walter, Mary-Ann, Elenor G. & Esther H., gct Oskaloosa MM, Ia. (G)

1884, 6, 25. Chalkley dropped from mbrp (G)

1885, 12, 22. Robert P. & w, Susan M., & ch, Benjamin J., Walter S. & Gilbert E., rocf Middleton MM, dtd 1885,11,21 (W)

1887, 5, 24. Elwood & w, Beulah A., rocf Middleton MM, dtd 1887,4,16 (W)

1887, 7, 19. Mary M. rocf Middleton MM, dtd 1887,5,21 (W)

1890, 12, 23. David & w, Lydia B., & ch, Mary Eva, Clarkson B., Anna L. & Rachel Emma, gct Plainfield MM (W)

1899, 6, 21. Adella B. recrq (G)

1902, 2, 19. Edgar B. relrq (G)

1903, 2, 25. Olive Myra recrq (G)

1908, 3, 25. Martha J. relrq (G)

1908, 4, 22. Howard recrq (G)

1909, 5, 19. Anderson E. & w, Adella B., & ch, Howard & Halford, relrq (G)

1912, 10, 23. Anna R. relrq (G)

1914, 9, 22. Earnest B. con mcd (W)

1926, 9, 21. Benjamin J. gct Uwchlan MM, Pa. (W)

1926, 9, 21. Ernest B. gct Uwchlan MM, Pa. (W)

1929, 7, 23. R. Leland gct Newgarden MM, O., to m Luella L. Hall (W)

1931, 7, 21. Luella L. rocf Newgarden MM, dtd 1931,6,25 (W)

1932, 7, 19. Alfred R. gct Plainfield MM, Ind., to m Harriet Stanley (W)

1933, 2, 21. Harriet S. rocf Plainfield MM, Ind., dtd 1933,2,1 (W)

THOMASSON

1829, 1, 7. Thomas, s Thos. & Sarah, Belmont Co., O.; m in Mt. Pleasant, Maria JONES, dt Samuel & Elizabeth, Jefferson Co., O.
    Ch: Samuel
        Jones   b 1829, 8, 28

1843, 11, 29. Mariah m Wm. WATSON

1851, 5, 28. Samuel J., s Thos. & Maria, Jefferson Co., O.; m in Mt. Pleasant, Mary B. UPDEGRAFF, dt Nathan & Cassander, Jefferson Co., O.

1853, 9, 9. Mary d ae 24

1857, 10, 28. Samuel J., s Thos. & Maria, Jefferson Co., O.; m in Mt. Pleasant, Ann HAGUE, dt Henry B. & Sarah Ann, Jefferson Co., O.

Ch: Anna M.   b 1860, 7, 7
    Mary S.   " 1861, 12, 1
Samuel J. m 2nd Mary W. -----
Ch: Thomas W. b 1868, 5, 30 d 1868, 8, 6

1860, 12, 7. Ann [Thomason] d

1861, 12, 8. Annie d ae 23

1830, 2, 23. Thomas [Thomason] rocf Stillwater MM, dtd 1830,1,23

1837, 11, 21. Thomas Jr. & w, Mariah, & s, Samuel, gct Plainfield MM

1841, 1, 19. Maria & s, Samuel J., rocf Plainfield MM, dtd 1840,12,23

1844, 5, 21. Samuel J., minor, gct Smithfield MM

1862, 11, 19. John, Eunice, Abigail, Sarah, Joseph, Thomas, Mary, John Jr. & Nathan, dis jW

1863, 2, 24. Maria [Thomason] dis jG (W)

1866, 10, 25. Samuel J. gct Smithfield MM, to m Mary Wood (G)

1868, 3, 26. Mary W. rocf Smithfield MM, dtd 1868,1,-- (G)

1904, 2, 24. Virginia & Myra recrq (G)

1910, 2, 23. Will & w & ch relrq (G)

THOMPSON

----, --, --. Bradway & Ann
    Ch: Mary   b 1792, 3, 8
        John Cozens" 1794, 12, 19
        Sarah   " 1796, 2, 8
        Benoni   " 1798, 4, 13
        Hannah   " 1799, 8, 4
        Samuel   " 1799, 8, 4
        Reasin   " 1801, 7, 17
        Ezra   " 1803, 10, 16
        Tacy   " 1806, 3, 10
        Edith   " 1808, 10, 20
        Israel   " 1812, 9, 26
----, --, --. Aaron & Sarah
    Ch: Esther   b 1798, 11, 19
        William   " 1801, 1, 3
        John   " 1803, 6, 28
        Aaron   " 1805, 9, 13
        Ann   " 1808, 6, 13
        Ruth   " 1810, 4, 10
        Lewis   " 1813, 11, 21
        Israel   " 1818, 1, 4

1808, 6, 29. Mary [Thomson] m Peter THOMAS

1812, 5, 27. Sarah m Enoch MATSON

1813, 12, 30. Hannah m Joseph KENNARD

----, --, --. John C. m Rebecca ----- d 1837, 3,27 ae 43 bur Harrisville
    Ch: Talitha   b 1816, 9, 8
        Sarah Ann   " 1818, 2, 22
        Mary   " 1819, 7, 11
        Bradway   " 1820, 9, 14
        Eliza   " 1822, 11, 26
        Carver   " 1824, 7, 16
        Tacy   " 1826, 8, 25
        Ezra   " 1829, 1, 14
        John H.   " 1831, 2, 11
        Rozen   " 1834, 8, 26

THOMPSON, continued
1817, 7, 30. Hannah m Ebeneezer WALKER
1821, 12, 27. Esther m Robert H. BLACKLEDGE
1825, 4, 28. William, s Aaron & Sarah, Jeffer-
son Co., O.; m in Short Creek MH, Rachel
VERNON, dt Amos & Mary, Belmont Co., O.
1826, 8, 31. John, s Aaron & Sarah, Jefferson
Co., O.; m in Short Creek MH, Sarah PATTEN
dt Wm. & Rachel, Belmont Co., O.
 Ch: Eliza Ann b 1827, 9, 30
   Elisha " 1829, 7, --
   Lewis " 1832, 6, 13
----, --, --. William & Rachel
 Ch: Amos V. b 1827, 8, 30
   Isaac " 1829, 2, 28
   Israel " 1831, 1, 31
   Eli   " 1833, 3, 11
   Ruth-anna " 1835, 4, 28 d 1851, 7, 3
   William " 1837, 7, 9
   Aaron " 1840, 6, 30
1828, 5, 29. Aaron, s Aaron & Sarah, Jeffer-
son Co., O.; m in Short Creek MH, Ann
JENKINS, dt Israel & Elizabeth
 Ch: Stephen b 1829, 10, 27 d 1837, 7, 2
   bur Short Creek
   Elizabeth b 1832, 8, 26 " 1837, 6,21
   bur Short Creek
   Sarah b 1832, 8, 26
   Martha " 1835, 5, 24 " 1846,10,18
   bur Short Creek
   Linley
   Murray b 1838, 7, 11
   Elwood " 1841, 4, 9
   Thomas El-
   wood " 1841, 4, 9
   Israel
   Jenkins " 1844, 9, 14
1829, 10, 29. Ann m Samuel GREEN
1834, 10, 2. Ruth m James CHALFAN
----, --, --. ----- & Ann
 Ch: Lindley M. b 1837, --, --
   Thomas El-
   wood " 1841, --, --
   Israel Jen-
   kins " 1844, --, --
1836, 9, 1. Telitha m Aaron FRAME
1837, 1, 14. Mary d ae 17 bur Harrisville
1837, 2, 3. Bradway d ae 16 bur Harrisville
1837, 4, 6. Sarah Ann m Henry B. HAGUE
1838, 6, 23. Aaron Sr. d bur Short Creek
1838, 11, 21. Ann, dt Bradbury & Rachel, b
1840, 4, 29. John C., s Bradway & Ann, Harrison Co., O.; m in West Grove MH, Jane
HAYCOCK, dt Joseph & Hannah LOUDERS,
Carrel Co., O.
1846, 8, 2. Aaron Jr. d ae 40 bur Short
Creek
1846, 9, 26. Sarah d ae 68 bur Short Creek
1848, 1, 27. Tacy m Emmor ROOD
----, --, --. Lindley & Julia
 Ch: George H. b 1866, 4, 10
   Annie L. " 1867, 8, 12
   Charles D. " 1869, 8, 21

 Ch: John S. b 1872, 2, 26
1866, 5, 30. Thos. E., s Aaron & Ann, Harri-
son Co., O.; m in West Grove MH, Mary E.
LADD, dt Robert P. & Ruannah T., Harrison
Co., O.
 Ch: Viola b 1867, 2, 4
   Willard L. " 1868, 9, 15
----, --, --. Alvin E. & Minnie
 Ch: Pearl b 1885, 8, 29
   Edward " 1889, 3, 4
   Lester " 1891, 7, 3
   Clarence " 1895, 10, 10
1912, 10, 7. Anna Craft d

1805, 8, 17. Esther, William & John, ch
Aaron, recrq
1805, 9, 21. Aaron recrq
1810, 1, 24. Joshua recrq
1811, 11, 19. Hannah & David & parents Eli
& Catharine Kennard, rocf Wrightstown MM,
dtd 1811,9,--
1812, 3, 24. Sarah recrq
1812, 6, 23. William & Joseph, minor ch
Joshua, recrq
1814, 2, 22. John rocf London Grove MM, dtd
1813,11,3
1814, 6, 21. Levi rocf Newgarden MM, dtd
1813,9,12
1815, 6, 20. Ann rocf Newgarden MM, Pa., dtd
1815,5,4
1815, 9, 19. John C. gct Plainfield MM, to m
Rebecca Carver
1816, 7, 23. John dis mcd
1816, 7, 23. Levi dis mcd to first cousin
1816, 12, 24. Rebecca rocf Plainfield MM, dtd
1816,12,22
1817, 10, 21. Ann Wirstel (form Thompson) con
mcd
1820, 2, 22. Joshua dis mcd
1824, 4, 20. Joseph rocf New Garden MM, dtd
1824,2,5
1824, 6, 22. Samuel dis mcd
1824, 10, 19. Ezra dis mcd
1824, 12, 21. Tacy Holmes (form Thompson) dis
mcd
1825, 10, 18. Edith Glenn (form Thompson) dis
mcd
1826, 11, 21. Mary recrq
1828, 1, 22. Joseph M., Esther & Joshua,
minors, gct Deerfield MM
1828, 6, 24. David gct Deerfield MM
1830, 11, 23. Samuel & w, Mary, gct Deerfield
MM
1831, 6, 21. William & s, Joshua, dis mcd
1832, 1, 24. Rezin dis jas
1832, 10, 23. Ann gct Deerfield MM
1833, 6, 18. Joshua rocf Deerfield MM, dtd
1833,5,16
1833, 11, 19. Ann rocf Deerfield MM, dtd
1833,10,7
1837, 10, 24. Lewis dis mcd
1840, 2, 18. Joshua dis mcd
1841, 8, 24. Eliza dis jas

THOMPSON, continued

1842, 4, 19. Samuel & w, Mary, rocf Flushing MM, dtd 1842,2,24

1843, 7, 18. Jane dis disunity

1843, 8, 22. Israel dis mcd

1843, 8, 22. John C. dis

1846, 6, 23. Mary dis disunity

1846, 9, 22. Carver dis mcd

1846, 9, 22. Samuel dis disunity

1850, 9, 24. Ezra dis mcd

1853, 1, 18. John H. dis disunity

1856, 10, 22. Reazin gct Red Cedar MM, Iowa

1857, 3, 24. Elisha dis mcd

1857, 3, 25. Ann gct Cedar MM, Ia.

1858, 3, 23. William dis disunity

1860, 5, 23. Israel dis mcd

1860, 6, 19. Sarah dis jG

1860, 7, 24. John dis jG

1862, 3, 19. Lindley M. gct Chesterfield MM, to m Rebecca Simpson

1862, 8, 13. Rebecca M. rocf Chesterfield MM

1863, 1, 21. Aaron con mcd (G)

1864, 9, 20. Aaron dis jG (W)

1864, 9, 20. William Jr. dis jG & mcd (W)

1864, 10, 19. John C. denied consent to be rst at Springdale MM, Ia. (G)

1864, 11, 22. William Sr. dis jG (W)

1864, 12, 20. Israel dis mcd (W)

1865, 1, 25. William Jr. dis mcd (G)

1865, 6, 21. Lindley con mcd (G)

1866, 4, 24. Ann dis jG (W)

1867, 12, 24. Mary Elizabeth (form Ladd) dis mcd & jG (W)

1869, 4, 22. Mary Catharine (form Hargrave) con mcd (G)

1869, 5, 20. Israel Jenkins con mcd (G)

1869, 6, 22. Israel Jenkins dis mcd & jG (W)

1869, 8, 24. Mary Catharine (form Hargrave) dis mcd (W)

1870, 2, 24. Wm. Sr. con mcd (G)

1871, 6, 22. Julia & ch, George, Anna Lewis & Charles, recrq (G)

1871, 7, 20. Israel & w, Abi, & ch, Franklin S., Mary Tacy, James Eli & Wm. Albert, recrq (G)

1872, 6, 20. Mary B. recrq (G)

1873, 5, 22. John & Jane recrq (G)

1873, 5, 22. Sarah Elizabeth recrq (G)

1873, 6, 26. William recrq (G)

1881, 2, 26. Rhoda, Kersey, Lydia J., Austin B., Oscar, Charlie, Walter F. & Effie recrq (G)

1883, 10, 24. Thomas E. & w, Mary E., & ch, Viola R., Robert B., Harvey & Elwood, gct Chicago MM (G)

1884, 2, 20. John W. & Amanda Bell recrq (G)

1885, 2, 25. Arminda recrq (G)

1885, 2, 25. Berney, Edwin Stanton & George recrq (G)

1887, 3, 23. Anna relrq (G)

1891, 12, 23. Boyd recrq (G)

1896, 1, 23. Ida recrq (G)

1896, 1, 23. Laura recrq (G)

1903, 6, 24. Edwin S. dropped from mbrp (G)

1910, 9, 21. Emma J. relrq (G)

1912, 3, 20. Paul & Allen recrq (G)

1913, 1, 22. Mrs. Allen recrq (G)

1913, 5, 21. Carrie relrq (G)

1914, 3, 25. Effie, Lorene & Paul recrq (G)

1914, 6, 24. Effie recrq (G)

1914, 11, 25. Margaret relrq (G)

1915, 2, 24. Etta, Mildred & Naomi recrq (G)

1926, 6, 9. Lester dropped from mbrp (G)

1926, 6, 9. Clarence dropped from mbrp (G)

1929, 7, 24. Adeline Enfield dropped from mbrp (G)

1929, 7, 24. Alvin E., Edward & John W. dropped from mbrp (G)

1929, 10, 23. Birney & Laura relrq (G)

THORN

1805, 7, 2. Isaac d bur Short Creek

1811, 3, 27. Elizabeth m John GUMERY

1811, 5, 29. Mary m Morgan LEWIS

1811, 5, 29. Thomas, s Isaac & Hannah, Jefferson Co., O.; m in West Grove MH, Ann GUMERY, dt John & Levinah, Jefferson Co., O.

   Ch: John   b 1814, 8, 27
       William   " 1816, 10, 4
       Hannah   " 1821, 1, 30
       Isaac   " 1823, 5, 14
       Sarah   " 1825, 9, 20
       Elizabeth   " 1828, 4, 30

1807, 12, 19. Catharine gct Miami MM

1807, 12, 19. William gct Miami MM

1826, 9, 19. Rachel (form White) dis mcd

1828, 12, 23. Ann dis jH

1834, 2, 20. Thomas & ch, John, William, Hannah, Isaac, Sarah & Elizabeth, gct Plainfield MM (H)

1835, 8, 18. Isaac rocf Green Plain MM, dtd 1835,5,30

1837, 2, 21. Isaac gct Green Plain MM

1841, 5, 18. Hannah gct Cesars Creek MM

1841, 5, 18. Isaac, Sarah & Elizabeth, ch Thomas, gct Greenplain MM

THORNBURGH

1841, 5, 18. Thomas C. Parker gct Stillwater MM, to m Lydia Jane Thornburgh

THORNTON

1863, 9, 23. Rebecca (form Crossley) con mcd

1874, 11, 26. Rebecca gct Smithfield MM (G)

TIMBERLAKE

1823, 3, 18. Susan (form Lewis) dis mcd

TIPTON

1823, 6, 24. Luke & w, Priscilla, & ch, David, Mary, Esther, Rachel, Abigail, Elihu, John & Hannah, rocf Deer Creek MM, end by Smithfield MM, 1823,1,16

TIPTON, continued
1824, 3, 23. Luke & w, Priscilla, & ch, Da-
     vid, Mary, Esther, Rachel, Abijahk Elihu,
     John, Hannah & Susannah, gct Somerset MM
1862, 11, 19. Tacy Ann, Luke, Priscilla,
     Phebe Ann, Joseph, Elisha, Sarah, Ann
     Elizabeth, Rachel, Levi, Susan, Phebe,
     Hannah & William dis jW

TOLBERT
1817, 10, 21. Samuel & w, Rachel, & ch, Na-
     than, Rebecca, John, Samuel & David, rocf
     Westland MM, dtd 1817,8,28
1851, 7, 22. Abigail rocf Smithfield MM

TOMLINSON
----, --, --. Isaac & Mary
     Ch: Samuel   b 1810, 1, 15
         Aaron   " 1811, 11, 22
         Rebecca   " 1814, 2, 26
         Carvar   " 1816, 6, 13
         Susanna   " 1818, 8, 30
         Thomas   " 1821, 5, 22
         Comley   " 1823, 12, 29
         Sarah   " 1826, 6, 10
         Chalkley " 1830, 6, 25
1831, 3, 15. Caroline d ae 23
----, --, --. Samuel b 1810,1,15; m Rachel
     ----- b 1810,1,21 d 1880,11,2
     Ch: Griffith S.b 1832, 12, 23 d 1872, 8,16
         Emily   " 1835, 1, 5
         Isaac   " 1837, 11, 6
         Mary Eliza-
           beth   " 1840, 3, 23
         Rebecca   " 1842, 9, 19
         Edwin   " 1845, 5, 9
         Wm. Francis" 1849, 5, 26
----, --, --. Thomas b 1812,9,15; m Allette
     ----- b 1815,9,14
     Ch: Allazanna b 1835, 12, 28
----, --, --. Thomas & Hannah
     Ch: Laura B.   b 1844, 5, 20
         Menerva   " 1847, 11, --
         Elizabeth
           E.   " 1850, 7, 11
1854, 10, 25. Aaron P. d ae 42
1860, 1, 13. Isaac d ae 76
1872, 4, 8. Mary d ae 82
1899, 12, 17. Samuel S. d
1913, 12, 3. Mary Elizabeth d

1819, 8, 24. Isaac & w, Mary, & ch, Samuel,
     Aaron, Rebecca, Carven & Elizabeth, rocf
     Byberrey MM, Pa., dtd 1819,7,27
1819, 11, 23. Cert rec for Elizabeth from
     Little Britain MM, Pa., dtd 1819,10,22,
     end to Concord MM
1824, 2, 24. Joseph rocf Byberry MM, dtd
     1823,11,25
1826, 2, 21. Elizabeth & dt, Caroline & Han-
     nah, recrq
1827, 1, 23. Elizabeth & dt, Rebecca Sidwell,
     rocf Concord MM, dtd 1826,12,20

1828, 12, 23. Mary, Elizabeth, Hannah & Caro-
     line, dis jH
1830, 6, 22. Elizabeth gct Somerset MM
1832, 6, 19. Samuel dis jH
1834, 7, 22. Aaron dis jH
1835, 3, 24. Rebecca dis jH
1836, 10, 20. Joseph & w, Elizabeth, gct
     Stillwater MM (H)
1840, 1, 23. Thomas & w, Aletta, & ch, Ala-
     zanna, John N. & Joseph, gct Smithfield
     MM (H)
1844, 4, 23. Thomas dis disunity
1844, 10, 22. Carter dis disunity
1845, 9, 23. Hannah (form Evans) dis disunity
1847, 10, 19. Comley dis disunity
1863, 7, 22. Martha N. rocf Newgarden MM (G)
1870, 1, 20. Martha recrq (G)
1883, 10, 11. Comly gct Salem MM (H)
1898, 3, 23. Walter M. recrq (G)
1902, 10, 20. Orlando C. & w, Emeline J., &
     ch, Sibyl, Mira & Wymond, rocf Portsmouth
     MM, Va. (G)
1904, 12, 21. Orlando & w, Emily, & ch,
     Sibyl, Mira & Weymond, gct Damascus MM
     (G)

TOWNSEND
1805, 11, 27. Martha m Wm. KIRK
1810, 1, 14. Seneca b
1815, 9, 28. Ann m Moses BUNDY
1815, 11, 2. Stephen, s Joseph & Mary, Har-
     rison Co., O.; m in Short Creek MH, Ann
     KENARD, dt Levi & Ann, Belmont Co., O.
1841, 9, 1. Sarah K. m Robert JOHNSON
1869, 10, 25. Anna d ae 69

1806, 11, 15. Edith, minor dt Benj., gct Salem
     MM
1807, 4, 18. Benjamin gct Baltimore MM, to m
     Elizabeth Naylor
1807, 12, 19. Elizabeth rocf Baltimore MM,
     dtd 1807,10,13
1810, 3, 20. Thomas rocf Baltimore MM, dtd
     1808,5,11, end by Concord MM, 1810,2,22
1810, 6, 19. Thomas con mcd
1810, 9, 18. Elizabeth con mcd
1814, 1, 18. David dis mcd
1814, 1, 18. David, Joseph Jr. & Elizabeth
     rocf Buckingham MM, Pa., dtd 1813,9,6
1814, 1, 18. Joseph & w, Mary, & ch, Ste-
     phen, John, Levi, Amos, Sarah, Samuel &
     Seneca, rocf Buckingham MM, Pa., dtd
     1813,9,6
1814, 4, 19. Elizabeth Broadhurst (form
     Townsend) dis mcd
1816, 9, 24. Joseph dis mcd
1816, 10, 22. John gct Concord MM, to m
     Ruth Bundy
1817, 8, 19. John dis
1819, 2, 23. Mary Matson (form Townsend)
     con mcd
1820, 8, 22. Levi gct Plainfield MM, to m
     Mary Watson

TOWNSEND, continued
1820, 11, 21. Amos dis mcd
1821, 3, 20. Levi gct Flushing MM
1821, 10, 23. Sarah Bingman (form Townsend)
    dis mcd
1823, 5, 20. Eli rocf Plainfield MM, dtd
    1823,4,26
1827, 4, 24. Stephen & w, Ann, & ch, Maryann,
    Sarah, Levi & Eliza, gct Somerset MM
1840, 8, 20. Eli gct Stillwater MM (H)
1841, 6, 22. Sarah H. recrq
1857, 8, 18. Ann (form Flanner) dis mcd (W)
1862, 11, 19. Hannah, Hannah Jr. & Stephen
    dis jW

TRAHERN
1840, 9, 22. Asa & w, Elizabeth, gct Miami MM
1840, 9, 22. Sinah gct Miami MM

TRIBBY
1817, 1, 29. John, s John & Martha, Harrison
    Co., O.; m in West Grove MH, Ann WHITE, dt
    John & Jane, Harrison Co., O.
    Ch: John W.   b 1818, 8, 20
        James   " 1820, 5, 19 d 1843,11,12
          bur Harrisville
        Samuel   b 1822, 12, 6
        Sarah Jane " 1825, 5, 27
        Isaac B.   " 1829, 6, 7
        Lewis L.   " 1838, 11, 18
        Martha Ann " 1844, 8, 11
1839, 5, 2. John W., s John & Ann, Harrison
    Co., O.; m in Harrisville, Jane HOWARD,
    dt John & Hannah, Harrison Co., O.
    Ch: Martha Ann b 1842, 8, 11
        Juliet   " 1846, 7, 29
        Samuel   " 1848, 7, 7
        Hannah Mary" 1850, 10, 19
        Ella J.   " 1853, 2, 7
        Charles H. " 1855, 2, 18
1844, 8, 1. Sarah J. m Milton MENDENHALL
1845, 3, 10. Samuel d ae 22 bur Harrisville
1850, 9, 2. Samuel d

1816, 11, 19. John recrq
1842, 9, 20. John W. & w, Jane, & s, Lindley,
    gct Sandy Spring MM
1843, 5, 23. James gct Chesterfield MM, to m
    Rebecca Rhodes
1844, 9, 24. John W. & w, Jane, & ch, Lind-
    ley, rocf Sandy Spring MM, dtd 1844,8,23
1852, 5, 18. Isaac B. dis disunity
1861, 3, 19. Lewis L. dis disunity
1862, 11, 19. John W., Jane & ch, Martha Ann,
    Juliett, Hannah May, Ella, Charles, Ma-
    lissa & Lois S., dis jW
1862, 11, 19. John & Ann dis jW (G)
1869, 7, 20. John & w, Ann, gct Hickory Grove
    MM, Ia. (W)
1869, 7, 20. John W. & w, Jane H., & ch,
    Ella T., Chas. H. & Melissa B., gct Hick-
    ory Grove MM, Ia. (W)

TRUMAN
1837, 11, 21. Lydia Ann (form Kinsey) dis mcd

TUCKER
1892, 10, 19. Nora recrq

TURNER
1873, 5, 22. James & Jane recrq (G)
1877, 10, 25. James & w, Jane, & ch, Mary,
    gct Smithfield MM (G)

TWEEDY
1864, 8, 24. Sarah (form Wood) con mcd (G)
1865, 6, 20. Sally W. [Twedy] (form Wood)
    dis mcd (W)
1868, 4, 23. Sarah W. Jessup (form Tweedy)
    dis mcd (G)
1879, 4, 24. George & Hannah G. recrq (G)
1896, 4, 22. Wilmer J. & w, Alice, & s, Wini-
    fred, recrq (G)
1909, 12, 22. Winford relrq (G)
1913, 3, 19. Wilmer dis disunity (G)
1914, 11, 25. Alice relrq (G)

UMBORS
1881, 2, 26. Leonora recrq (G)

UMPHREVILLE
----, --, --. William & Sarah
    Ch: Fanny   b 1843, 9, 4
        Henry Lew-
          is   " 1848, 1, 7

UNDERHILL
1846, 9, 22. Jonathan T. Updegraff gct Fair-
    field MM, Ind., to m Phebe W. Underhill

UPDEGRAFF
----, --, --. Nathan & Ann
    Ch: Ann   b 1801, 4, 8
        Mary   " 1804, 1, 2
        Thomas   " 1806, 6, 15
        Josiah   " 1810, 12, 14
1805, 12, 26. Joseph, s Nathan & Ann, Jeffer-
    son Co., O.; m in Short Creek MH, Susana
    KINSEY, dt Geo. & Mary, Jefferson Co., O.
    Ch: Mary   b 1806, 8, 19
        Sarah   " 1809, 6, 10
        Susanna   " 1811, 9, 14
        James   " 1813, 10, 16
        Rachel   " 1816, 4, 11
        Eliza   " 1818, 9, 17
        Ruthana   " 1821, 6, 29
1810, 9, 27. Rachel m Lewis WALKER
1812, 4, 23. David, s Nathan & Ann, Jeffer-
    son Co., O.; m in Short Creek MH, Rebecca
    TAYLOR, dt Jonathan & Ann, Jefferson Co.,
    O.
    Ch: Mary Ann b 1813, 3, 5 d 1822, 5,15
          bur Short Creek
        Eliza   b 1816, 5, 9 " 1817, 3, 3
          bur Short Creek
        Sarah E. b 1818, 2, 18

UPDEGRAFF, continued
    Ch: Ann T.   b 1820, 6, 10
        Jonathan T." 1822, 5, 13 d 1882,11,30
        David B.   " 1830, 8, 23 " 1894, 5,23
        Rebecca A. " 1824, 9, 15 " 1848, 5, 9
        Elizabeth   " 1827, 4, 5
----, --, --. Nathan m Cassandra ----- d 1832,4,
    8 bur Short Creek
    Ch: William   b 1822, 4, 4
        David   " 1824, 1, 21
        Ann   " 1825, 12, 20
        Mary   " 1829, 11, 2
        Lewis W.   " 1832, 4, 3
1824, 3, 31. Ann m Merrick STARR
1827, 2, 3. Nathan d ae 68 bur Short Creek
1828, 12, 31. Mary L. m Wm. FLANNER
1833, 12, 25. Ann d ae 67 bur Short Creek
1840, 4, 7. Elizabeth d ae 12 bur Short
    Creek
1840, 4, 8. Elizabeth P. d ae 13 bur Short
    Creek
1840, 5, 16. Joseph d
1841, 9, 30. Sarah m Geo. R. JENKINS
1843, 1, 21. Susannah d
1845, 10, 29. Hannah m Jesse PARKER
1847, 11, 23. Robert D., s Jonathan & Phebe, b
1848, 4, 27. Anna T. m Cyrus MENDENHALL
1848, --, --. Robert W., s Jonathan T., b
1850, 2, 6. Phebe W. d ae 24 bur Short Creek
1850, 10, 30. Ann m Geo. KINSEY
1851, 5, 28. Mary B. m Samuel J. THOMASSON.
----, --, --. David & Rebecca
    Ch: Oliver
        Price   b 1857, 12, 20
        William
        Ross   " 1860, 12, 5
        Russell
        Taylor   " 1862, 11, 28
        Anna E.   " 1854, 8, --
1864, 12, 20. David d
1865, 8, 11. Rebecca B., w D. B., d ae 35
1867, 6, 2. Rebecca T. d

1819, 4, 20. Sarah rocf Monallen MM, Pa.,
    dtd 1819,1,20
1821, 4, 24. Nathan gct Smithfield MM, to m
    Cassandra Ballenger
1821, 9, 18. Cassandra rocf Smithfield MM,
    dtd 1821,8,20
1822, 7, 23. Mary (form Shoemaker) dis mcd
1828, 5, 20. Susanna Brown (form Updegraff)
    dis mcd
1828, 9, 19. Mary Ann dis jH
1828, 12, 23. Susanna, Mary & Sarah dis jH
1829, 11, 24. Joseph dis jH
1831, 9, 20. Mary Ann Jr. & Jane dis jH
1837, 2, 21. Josiah dis mcd
1837, 7, 18. Rachel Hilerman (form Updegraff)
    dis mcd
1837, 11, 21. James dis jH
1846, 9, 22. Jonathan T. gct Fairfield MM,
    Ind., to m Phebe W. Underhill
1848, 7, 18. David Jr. con mcd

1848, 11, 21. Phebe W. rocf Fairfield MM, dtd
    1848,8,17
1849, 6, 19. David Jr. gct Smithfield MM
1852, 8, 24. David B. gct Smithfield MM, to m
    Rebecca B. Price
1853, 7, 19. Rebecca B. rocf Smithfield MM,
    dtd 1853,5,23
1854, 8, 22. Juliann Fox (form Updegraff)
    dis mcd
1854, 9, 19. Sarah dis jH
1855, 8, 22. Elizabeth Wilson (form Updegraff)
    dis disunity
1856, 7, 22. Jonathan T. dis mcd
1860, 11, 21. William B. con mcd
1861, 3, 20. Nathan gct Upper Springfield MM,
    to m Lucina Lupton
1861, 3, 20. William D. gct Winnesheik MM,
    Ia.
1861, 6, 19. Lucina rocf Springfield MM
1861, 12, 24. Israel dis mcd
1861, 12, 24. Josiah dis mcd
1862, 7, 22. Rebecca dis jG
1865, 1, 24. Nathan dis disunity (W)
1865, 3, 21. Rebecca Jr. dis jG (W)
1865, 5, 24. Lewis W. gct Winnesheik MM, Ia.
    (G)
1865, 7, 18. David B. dis jG (W)
1867, 1, 24. David B. con mcd (G)
1871, 8, 24. Lucina gct Springdale MM, Ia.
    (G)
1881, 2, 26. R. Blanche, Eliza Jane & Mary
    Ada recrq (G)
1882, 9, 20. Laura recrq (G)
1882, 10, 25. Jonathan T. & w, Elizabeth W.,
    & ch, Frederick Clark & Charles Taylor,
    recrq (G)
1885, 9, 23. Anna U. Hillis (form Updegraff)
    relrq (G)
1888, 10, 24. Robert D. dropped from mbrp (G)
1889, 3, 20. Alice M. & David Benjamin recrq
    (G)
1891, 2, 25. Eliza J. recrq (G)
1892, 4, 20. William R. & Laura A. relrq (G)
1906, 3, 21. David B. relrq (G)
1912, 5, 22. Charles Taylor relrq (G)

URNSHAW
1822, 9, 2. Hannah d bur Richmond

VAIL
----, --, --. Olton m Delphine EVANS, dt
    Arthur & Anna D. (Steer), b 1895,12,26
1823, 5, 26. Samuel, s Abraham & Margaret,
    Fayette Co., Pa.; m in West Grove MH,
    Elizabeth GRISSELL, dt Edward & Hannah,
    Harrison Co., O.

1823, 7, 22. Elizabeth gct Providence MM
1832, 7, 24. John gct Smithfield MM
1833, 11, 19. John & w, Esthér, rocf Smith-
    field MM, dtd 1833,9,23
1835, 6, 23. John & w, Esther, & dt, Phebe,
    gct Upper Springfield MM

VAIL, continued
1840, 9, 22. Samuel W. Stanley gct Plainfield
    MM, to m Mary Vail
1862, 11, 19. Semira dis jW (G)
1862, 11, 19. Mary dis jW (G)
1862, 11, 19. Isaac dis jW (G)
1862, 11, 19. Jesse dis jW (G)
1862, 11, 19. John dis jW (G)
1862, 11, 19. Abigail dis jW (G)
1862, 11, 19. Benjamin dis jW (G)
1862, 11, 19. Harvey dis jW (G)
1862, 11, 19. Anna dis jW (G)
1862, 11, 19. David dis jW (G)
1862, 11, 19. John Jr. dis jW (G)
1862, 11, 19. Abigail Jr. dis jW (G)
1862, 11, 19. Joseph S. dis jW (G)
1924, 3, 18. S. Delphine [Vale] (form Evans)
    con mcd (W)

VANHORN
1818, 7, 21. Elizabeth (form Gilbert) dis mcd
1829, 1, 20. Elizabeth rocf Flushing MM, dtd
    1828, 10,24
1839, 5, 21. Elizabeth gct Pennsville MM
1882, 7, 19. George McClelland recrq (G)

VANLAW
1822, 3, 19. Elizabeth rst at Smithfield MM
    on consent of this MM

VANNERSON
1892, 10, 19. Betty recrq (G)

VARNEY
1817, 6, 24. Abel & w, Hannah, & ch, Anna,
    Mary, William & Isaac, rocf Ferrisboro
    MM, dtd 1817,4,2
1820, 5, 23. Mary dis
1822, 5, 21. Anna gct Salem MM
1822, 5, 21. Hannah & ch, William, Isaac &
    Able gct Salem MM

VERMELION
1913, 8, 13. Flora Watkins dropped from mbrp
    (G)

VERNON
1825, 4, 28. Rachel m Wm. THOMPSON
1831, 4, 28. Ruthanna m Jesse HIATT
1848, 4, 6. Abigail b
1851, 7, 14. Charles D. b
1877, 11, 27. Estella, dt Chas. D. & Abigail
    (Thomasson), b
1922, 3, 23. Abigail d
1923, 11, --. Estella, dt Chas. D. & Abigail
    (Thomasson), d

1818, 11, 24. Theodate rocf Stillwater MM,
    dtd 1818,10,24
1821, 1, 23. Theodate gct Stillwater MM
1822, 5, 21. Ruthanna, minor, rocf Stillwater
    MM, dtd 1822,2,23, end by Concord MM
1825, 8, 23. Theodate rocf Stillwater MM

1827, 2, 20. Theodate gct Flushing MM
1873, 7, 24. Dempsey recrq (G)
1876, 2, 24. Alice (form Durban) con mcd (G)
1876, 2, 24. Dempsey con mcd (G)
1884, 7, 23. Dempsey & w, Alice, & ch, Emma
    Olive & Charles Edgar, dropped from mbrp
    (G)
1901, 9, 24. Charles D. & w, Abigail, rocf
    Somerset MM, dtd 1901,8,22 (W)
1901, 9, 24. Estella rocf Somerset MM, dtd
    1901,8,22 (W)
1912, 3, 20. Wallace W. & Mary recrq (G)
1913, 7, 23. Wallace W. & Mary dropped from
    mbrp (G)

VICKERS
1841, 12, 9. Eugene, s Joseph & Elizabeth, b

1822, 6, 18. Cert rec for Thomas & w, Hannah,
    & ch, Amanda M., Thomas Elwood, Phebe
    Ann, Martha H. & Amos H., from Bradford
    MM, Pa., dtd 1822,5,8, end to Concord MM
1830, 3, 23. Hannah dis jH
1832, 8, 21. William dis mcd
1838, 3, 20. Phebe Ann dis jH
1839, 12, 24. Thos. Elwood dis jH
1842, 9, 20. Chalkley, Rebecca L., Jesse
    Elijah & Barclay L., ch Thos. & Hannah,
    gct Chesterfield MM
1843, 6, 20. Amos dis mcd
1844, 7, 23. Rachel (form James) dis mcd
1845, 12, 25. Jemima gct Uchland MM, Pa. (H)
1854, 2, 23. Joseph & w, Elizabeth, & ch,
    Jonathan, Joseph, Eugene & Lydia Anna,
    gct Fallowfield MM, Pa. (H)

VORE
1812, 9, 22. Isaac & w, Eleanor, & ch, Wil-
    liam, Isaac, Eleanor & Mordecai, rocf
    Plainfield MM, dtd 1812,6,27
1815, 11, 21. William dis mcd
1817, 4, 22. Eleanor Richardson (form Vore)
    con mcd

WAITE
1860, 4, 24. Peninah (form Flanner) dis mcd
1861, 4, 24. Peninah [Wait] (form Flanner)
    dis mcd

WALDRESSE
1907, 3, 20. Harrison R. dropped from mbrp
    (G)

WALDRON
1880, 5, 20. Angie recrq (G)
1880, 5, 20. Harrison Riley & w, Nancy Jane,
    recrq (G)
1880, 5, 20. Robert recrq (G)
1884, 7, 23. Harrison R. dropped from mbrp
    (G)
1888, 10, 24. Robert dropped from mbrp (G)
1913, 1, 22. Ella recrq (G)
1913, 1, 22. Hane recrq (G)

WALDRON, continued
1913, 1, 22. Mable recrq (G)
1913, 1, 22. Velma recrq (G)
1913, 1, 22. Winfield recrq (G)

WALKER
1810, 9, 27. Lewis, s Abel & Mary, Jefferson
    Co., O.; m in Short Creek MH, Rachel UP-
    DEGRAFF, dt Nathan & Rachel, Jefferson
    Co., O.
    Ch: Mary Ann b 1812, 6, 16
        Hannah U. " 1815, 2, 25
        Elizabeth " 1818, 2, 10
        Nathan U. " 1823, 5, 28
        Lewis
        James   " 1825, 10, 21
1817, 7, 30. Ebeneezer, s Geo. & Anna, Gurn-
    sey Co., O.; m in West Grove MH, Hannah
    THOMPSON, dt Bradway & Ann, Harrison Co.,
    O.
    Ch: Thomson   b 1819, 9, 3
        Tacy   " 1823, 6, 27
1829, 12, 30. Mary A. m Lemuel JONES
1841, 10, 28. Thompson, s Ebeneezer & Hannah,
    Harrison Co., O.; m in Harrisville, Ruth-
    anna HIRST, dt Thos. & Anna, Harrison Co.,
    O.
1849, 1, 19. Lewis Sr. d ae 73 bur Short
    Creek
----, --, --. Jeremiah C. d 1904,5,7; m Ruth-
annah -----
    Ch: Mahlon M. b 1852, 2, 2 d 1916,11, 6
        Thomas El-
        wood   " 1855, 5, 13
        Watson A. " 1857, 3, 20
        Lewis J.   " 1863, 7, 18
        Wallace   " 1871, 9, 8
1851, 8, 28. Rachel d
----, --, --. Abel M. d 1908,3,6; m Amy G.

    Ch: Mary H.   b 1857, 1, 31
        Samuel G. " 1861, 1, 24 d 1896, 6, 5
        Anna Bath-
        sheba   " 1866, 2, 21
1856, 7, 2. Hannah m Wm. PRICE
1875, 2, 17. Mary d ae 77
1877, 10, 22. Joel d
----, --, --. Thomas Elwood & Alice M.
    Ch: Ernest   b 1883, 3, 8
        Irene Sa-
        maria   " 1888, 5, 12
1898, 10, 9. J. Wallace d
----, --, --. George & Elenor R.
    Ch: Mary
        Inez   b 1902, 8, 23
        Channing
1902, 4, 5. Ruth Hannah d
1906, 11, 3. Elias Hicks d (H)
----, --, --. Ernest & Effie M.
    Ch: James Mur-
        ry   b 1908, 5, 2
        Helen
        Irene   " 1910, 3, 1

    Ch: Donald
        Ernest   b 1914, 10, 24
1909, 8, 16. Joel A. d
1912, 6, 2. Anna Bashabe d

1810, 8, 20. Lewis rocf Hopewell MM, dtd
    1810,7,28
1816, 1, 23. Ebeneezer rocf Concord MM, dtd
    1815,11,23
1818, 3, 24. Ebeneezer & w, Hannah, gct
    Plainfield MM
1824, 11, 23. Ebeneazar & w, Hannah, & ch,
    Thompson & Tacy, rocf Flushing MM, dtd
    1824, 7, 23
1825, 2, 22. Ann (form Stephens) dis mcd
1831, 1, 19. Hannah Craven (form Craven) dis
    mcd
1831, 7, 21. Jesse gct Flushing MM (H)
1831, 9, 20. Thompson & Tacy, minor ch Han-
    nah Craven, gct Deerfield MM
1831, 10, 18. Samuel & Mary, minors, gct
    Flushing MM
1839, 10, 22. Thompson rocf Pennsville MM,
    dtd 1839,8,15
1840, 1, 21. Hannah U. gct Middleton MM
1840, 1, 21. Elizabeth gct Middleton MM
1840, 2, 18. Lewis & w, Rachel, & ch, Nathan
    U. & Lewis, gct Middleton MM
1842, 10, 18. Thompson & w, Ruth Anna, & ch,
    Amanda, gct Chesterfield MM
1843, 5, 23. Lewis & w, Rachel, & ch, Nathan
    M., Lewis & James, rocf Middleton MM, dtd
    1843,5,11
1843, 5, 23. Hannah M. rocf Middleton MM,
    dtd 1843,5,11
1845, 10, 21. Samuel T. rocf Flushing MM, dtd
    1845,9,25
1848, 8, 22. Samuel dis mcd
1849, 2, 20. Nathan dis mcd
1900, 4, 25. Loyal recrq (G)
1912, 5, 22. Anna gct Yorba Linda MM, Calif.
    (G)
1912, 6, 5. Watson A. gct Orange Grove MM,
    Calif. (H)
1913, 5, 21. Amey G. gct Orange Grove MM,
    Calif. (H)
1916, 10, 8. Elwood T., Alice & Irene S.
    gct Orange Grove MM, Calif. (H)
1916, 10, 8. Ernest R. & ch, James Murray,
    Helen Irene & Donald Everet, gct Orange
    Grove MM, Calif. (H)

WALLACE
1861, 10, 23. William A. recrq
1868, 1, 23. William A. con mcd (G)
1873, 2, 20. William A. relrq (G)

WALLER
1883, 6, 20. James recrq (G)
1894, 3, 21. Effie recrq (G)

WALLIN
1894, 4, 25. Huldah S. recrq (G)

WALTER

1852, 5, 19. Sarah m Calvin MOORE

1848, 8, 22. Sarah rocf Kennet MM, Pa., dtd
        1848,4,4
1861, 9, 25. Jame M. (form Rice) con mcd
1862, 4, 22. Jane M. gct West Branch MM, O.
1863, 4, 22. Cert sent to West Branch MM
        some time ago for Jane [Waters] returned
        unused & accepted (G)
1881, 3, 24. Mary E. recrq (G)
1882, 7, 19. Luetta recrq (G)

WALTON

1830, 8, 26. Sarah d
1839, 3, 29. Elizabeth d ae 75
1888, 12, 26. S. Francis, s Samuel & Sarah J.,
        Belmont Co., O.; m in Colerain, Louiza J.
        SIDWELL, dt Israel & Rachel B., Belmont
        Co., O. (W)
1891, 4, 1. James, s Samuel & Sarah J., Bel-
        mont Co., O.; m in Colerain, Sina R. STEER,
        dt Israel & Rebecca B., Belmont Co., O.
        (W)
1897, 7, 23. Priscilla S. d

1812, 11, 24. Joseph rocf Buckingham MM, Pa.,
        dtd 1812,10,5
1817, 12, 23. Joseph gct Buckingham MM, Pa.
1821, 10, 23. Margaret & Elizabeth rocf Buck-
        ingham MM, Pa., dtd 1821,9,3
1821, 10, 25. Joseph rocf Buckingham MM, Pa.,
        dtd 1821,9,3
1821, 11, 30. Sarah rocf Buckingham MM, Pa.,
        dtd 1821,9,3
1828, 12, 23. Elizabeth dis jH
1842, 3, 22. Rebecca rocf Philadelphia MM,
        dtd 1842,2,24
1843, 8, 22. Rebecca gct Radnor MM
1862, 11, 19. Joseph dis jW
1862, 11, 19. Samuel & Sarah, Joseph, James,
        Ann & Walter, dis jW
1889, 6, 18. Louisa S. gct Stillwater MM (W)
1891, 8, 18. Sina R. (form Steer) gct Still-
        water MM (W)

WARE

1898, 8, 22. Alfred F. & w, Lillie H., & s,
        Alfred Raymond, rocf Marshalltown MM, Ia.
        (G)
1900, 3, 21. Alfred T. & w & ch, Alfred Ray-
        mond & Wm. Hadley, gct Lewiston MM, Me.
        (G)

WARFIELD

1813, 4, 29. Martha m Jacob HOLLOWAY

1813, 2, 23. Martha rst on consent of Indian
        Spring MM
1813, 2, 23. Mariah & John Warfield recrq of
        mother, Martha

WARNER

1858, 5, 18. Yardley & w, Hannah, & ch,
        Charles A., Anne, Rebecca, William G. &
        George Malin, rocf Goshen MM, Pa., dtd
        1858,4,29
1861, 4, 23. Yardley & w, Hannah, & ch,
        Charles A., Anne, Rebecca, William Y. &
        George Mahlon, gct SD MM

WARREN

1909, 1, 20. Iven recrq (G)
1910, 5, 25. Iven relrq (G)

WARRINGTON

----, --, --. Linneas & Sina
        Ch: Mary Ellen b 1884, 4, 10
            Sarahetta " 1888, 1, 11
1898, 5, 25. Gilbert, s Thomas & Lydia, Colum-
        biana Co., O.; m in Concord, Josephine
        BUNDY, dt Edmund & Debora M., Belmont
        Co., O. (W)

1807, 4, 18. Edward Bonsall gct Salem MM, to
        m Rachel Warrington
1883, 11, 20. Linneus & w, Sina, & ch, Leora,
        Cyrus J. & Phebe Ellen, rocf Hickory
        Grove MM (W)
1889, 4, 23. Linneus & w, Sina, & ch, Anna
        Leora, Cyrus J., Phebe Elma, Mary Ellen &
        Saretta, gct Stillwater MM (W)
1899, 3, 21. Josephine B. (form Bundy) gct
        Upper Springfield MM

WATERMAN

----, --, --. Charles & Rebecca
        Ch: William   b 1816, 11, 29
            Mary   " 1817, 10, 6
            Hannah   " 1820, 2, 5
            Charles   " 1823, 7, 6
            Joseph   " 1827, 1, 29
            Rebecca Ann" 1829, 7, 4
1816, 8, 29. Rebecca m John MICHENER
1824, 12, 30. Isaac, s Phineas & Rebecca, Jef-
        ferson Co., O.; m in Harrisville, Ann
        HURFORD, dt John & Sarah, Jefferson Co.,O.
1839, 10, 31. John, s Phineas & Rebecca, Jef-
        ferson Co., O.; m in Harrisville, Mary
        KIRK, dt Caleb & Sarah, Jefferson Co., O.
1842, 7, 7. Mary d ae 24
1849, 2, 22. Rebecca d ae 59
1855, 11, 25. Ann T. d
1862, 12, 5. Charles d

1814, 10, 18. Rebecca & ch, Isaac & John,
        rocf Abington MM, Pa., dtd 1814,8,29
1820, 1, 18. Isaac & John, ch Rebecca Michen-
        er, gct Flushing MM
1825, 2, 22. Rebecca & ch, William, Mary &
        Charles Johnson, rocf Fallowfield MM, Pa.
1825, 3, 22. Ann gct Flushing MM
1826, 2, 21. Hannah, minor dt Chas. & Rebec-
        ca, rocf Fallowfield MM, Pa., dtd 1825,10,
        7

WATERMAN, continued
1828, 9, 19. Ann & ch, Leannah & Rebecca,
       rocf Flushing MM, dtd 1828,6,27
1829, 1, 18. Isaac & John rocf Flushing MM
       with mother, Rebecca Michener
1829, 4, 21. Rebecca dis jH
1838, 4, 24. John rocf Flushing MM, dtd
       1838,3,27
1840, 6, 23. Mary & Hannah dis jH
1841, 1, 19. John & w, Mary, gct Gillead MM
1845, 2, 18. William dis mcd
1845, 5, 20. Phebe (form Roberts) dis mcd &
       jH
1848, 7, 18. Rebecca Chamberlain (form Water-
       man) dis mcd
1850, 5, 21. Leanna Dickey (form Waterman)
       dis mcd
1849, 10, 23. Amy (form Crossley) con mcd
1849, 10, 23. Charles Johnson con mcd
1850, 5, 21. Leanna Dickey (form Waterman)
       dis mcd
1852, 4, 20. Joseph con mcd
1855, 6, 19. Isaac dis disunity
1861, 3, 20. Amy Phebus (form Waterman) dis
       mcd

WATKINS
1831, 11, 24. Angelina m Daniel STANTON
1832, 3, 28. Lusinda m Joseph HARRIS
1851, 8, 5. Elizabeth d ae 67

1830, 6, 22. John W. & w, Elizabeth, & ch,
       Angelina, Lucinda, Robert, William, Su-
       sanna, Elizabeth, Deborah, Lydia & John,
       rocf Upper MM, Va., dtd 1830,4,17
1837, 1, 24. Robert J. gct Goshen MM
1840, 2, 18. William gct Goshen MM
1846, 5, 19. Deborah Gill (form Watkins)
       dis mcd
1846, 8, 18. Lydia Rankin (form Watkins) dis
       mcd
1848, 7, 18. Elizabeth Lewis (form Watkins)
       dis mcd
1894, 3, 21. Flora recrq (G)
1896, 1, 23. Harry recrq (G)
1896, 1, 23. Creighton recrq (G)
1913, 8, 12. Flora(Watkins) Vermelion dropped
       from mbrp (G)
1926, 6, 9. Creighton dropped from mbrp (G)
1926, 6, 9. Harry dropped from mbrp (G)

WATSON
1840, 11, 24. Anne M., w Mathew, d ae 31 bur
       Cross Creek
1842, 8, 1. Phebe, dt Wm., d ae 47
1843, 9, 18. John d ae 88 bur Cross Creek
1843, 11, 29. William, s John & Ann, Jefferson
       Co., O.; m in Mt. Pleasant, Mariah THOMAS-
       SON, dt Samuel & Elizabeth JONES, Jeffer-
       son Co., O.
----, --, --. Mathew & Eliza
       Ch: James H.   b 1846, 6, 16
           William   " 1847, 9, 6

       Ch: Mary H.   b 1848, 10, 25
           Barclay S. " 1850, 2, 8
           Flounders   " 1852, 2, 25
           Benezett   " 1854, 10, 1
1850, 1, --. Benjamin d ae 4 bur Cross Creek
----, --, --. Nathan & Eliza
       Ch: Flounders   d 1853, 5,21
           ae 1
           Benezet   " 1856, 9,14
1861, 7, 5. Mathew d ae 58 bur Cross Creek
1862, 1, 4. Joseph d ae 74
1862, 1, 9. Mathew, infant s John & Eliza, d
       bur Cross Creek
1862, 1, 14. Joseph d
1886, 3, 21. William d bur Mt. Pleasant
1896, 3, 21. Marcia, w Wm., d

1810, 5, 22. Rachel rocf Hopewell MM, dtd
       1810,4,2
1819, 11, 23. Joel gct Concord MM, to m Abi-
       gail Bundy
1819, 11, 23. Michal, minor, rocf Smithfield
       MM, dtd 1819,10,18
1821, 4, 24. Esther Branon (form Watson) dis
       mcd
1824, 4, 20. Michael, minor, gct Smithfield
1844, 4, 23. Maria gct Smithfield MM
1846, 7, 21. Wm. & w, Maria, & s, Samuel
       Thomason, rocf Smithfield MM, dtd 1846,6,
       22
1856, 10, 21. Ann Grist (form Watson) dis mcd
1864, 9, 20. John dis jG
1875, 6, 22. Dorothy Ann Smith (form Watson)
       dis mcd (W)
1875, 11, 23. Rebecca Atkinson (form Watson)
       dis mcd (W)
1876, 10, 24. John dis mcd (W)
1878, 2, 19. Anna Mary & Phebe Eva dis jG (W)
1878, 5, 21. Hannah dis disunity (W)
1882, 5, 24. Iva D. recrq (G)
1882, 5, 24. Amy recrq (G)
1886, 5, 19. William recrq (G)
1888, 10, 24. Eva & Amy dropped from mbrp (G)
1894, 2, 21. Lindley recrq (G)

WATTERS
1879, 7, 24. Martha M. recrq (G)

WATTERSON
1858, 8, 20. Martha T. d

WEATHERSON
1913, 1, 22. Myrtle M. recrq (G)
1914, 3, 25. Margaret recrq (G)

WEAVER
1833, 11, 19. Edwin A., minor, rocf ND MM,
       dtd 1833,8,27

WEBB
1892, 10, 19. Maria recrq (G)
1892, 10, 19. Pauline recrq (G)

WEBSTER
----, --, --. Nailor & Jemima
    Ch: John V.   b 1839, 1, 15
        Mary V.   " 1841, 2, 17
        Lydia Ma-
          ria   " 1843, 2, 26
        George J. " 1845, 9, 8
        Isabel   " 1847, 5, 14
        William R. " 1849, 5, 16
1839, 7, 23. Sarah (form Crozier) con mcd
1840, 5, 19. Sarah gct Stillwater MM
1862, 11, 19. John dis jW
1862, 11, 19. Eliza Jane dis jW
1862, 11, 19. Mary M. dis jW
1862, 11, 19. Henry dis jW
1862, 11, 19. Samuel dis jW
1862, 11, 19. John dis jW
1862, 11, 19. Charles dis jW
1862, 11, 19. Mary dis jW
1862, 11, 19. Sarah Jane dis jW
1862, 11, 19. Jephtha dis jW
1862, 11, 19. Hannah dis jW
1862, 11, 19. Joseph G. dis jW
1862, 11, 19. Nathan dis jW
1862, 11, 19. Thomas dis jW
1862, 11, 19. Ann P. dis jW
1862, 11, 19. Ruth Ann dis jW
1862, 11, 19. Thomas P. dis jW
1862, 11, 19. Lydia dis jW
1862, 11, 19. Sarah dis jW
1862, 11, 19. James dis jW
1862, 11, 19. Lydia dis jW
1862, 11, 19. Abner dis jW
1862, 11, 19. Elizabeth dis jW
1862, 11, 19. Charles dis jW

WEIR
1898, 2, 23. Charles Lorell, Eva Rose &
    Gretta Elizabeth recrq (G)
1903, 6, 24. Gretta E. & Chas. S. dropped
    from mbrp (G)

WELCH
1810, 6, 19. Jane Powers (form Welch) dis mcd
1810, 6, 19. Mary dis mcd
1901, 7, 24. Alice recrq (G)
1901, 7, 24. Harvey R. recrq (G)
1901, 7, 24. Rayton H. recrq (G)
1902, 5, 21. Abner & w, Rachel, & ch, Harvey
    B., Payton H., Lucy E. & Alice, gct Colum-
    bus MM, O. (G)

WELDON
1856, 8, 16. Rachel d ae 45

WELLAN
1862, 11, 19. Mary dis jW

WELLS
1757, 8, 25. Catharine b
1826, 4, 7. John d ae 69 bur Harrisville

1806, 9, 20. Susanna Gray (form Wells) dis

mcd
1807, 8, 15. Israel dis disunity
1813, 7, 20. William & w, Margaret, & ch,
    Levi & John, rocf Concord MM, dtd 1813,
    5,20
1821, 5, 22. Rebecca (form Reynolds) dis mcd
1825, 4, 19. Levi gct Stillwater MM
1825, 4, 19. William & w, Margaret, & s, John
    & Sarah Gilbert, a minor in their care,
    gct Stillwater MM
1826, 9, 19. Elizabeth Done (form Wells) dis
    mcd
1827, 4, 24. Abner & w, Deborah, gct Plain-
    field MM
1828, 9, 23. Susanna dis jH
1829, 5, 19. William, Levi, Moses, Jonathan,
    Elisha & Hannah, minor ch Isaac & Susanna,
    gct Deerfield MM
1836, 11, 20. Moses, Jonathan, Elisha & Han-
    nah, ch Isaac & Susanna, rocf Pennsville
    MM, dtd 1836,8,18
1841, 10, 19. Moses D. dis mcd
1843, 1, 24. Hannah, dt Isaac & Susannah,
    gct Plainfield MM
1843, 1, 24. Jonathan gct Plainfield MM
1844, 10, 22. Hannah rocf Plainfield MM
1846, 11, 24. Hannah Paxon (form Wells) dis
    mcd
1853, 12, 22. Rebecca gct Deerfield MM (H)
1856, 8, 19. Elisha dis jH

WEST
1870, 9, 22. Anna (form Wood) con mcd

WETZEL
1896, 1, 23. J. E. recrq (G)

WHARTON
----, --, --. Ezra b 1778,8,26; m Martha
    ----- b 1778,5,19
    Ch: Anna   b 1800, 7, 17
        Amos   " 1803, 2, 28
        Linton   " 1805, 9, 27
----, --, --. Eli & Martha
    Ch: Daniel   b 1811, 1, 7
        James   " 1813, 8, 1
        Silas   " 1817, 1, 16
        Abigail   " 1819, 3, 19
        Levi   " 1821, 8, 13
        Ezra   " 1824, 7, 3 d 1832, 8,18
1826, 4, 6. Hannah m Wm. HALL
1842, 5, 3. Silas d ae 27
1847, 5, 16. Ezra d ae 68
1866, 12, 9. Martha d ae 88

1818, 10, 20. Ezra & w, Martha, & ch, Joel,
    Anna, Amos, Linton, Hannah, Daniel,
    James & Silas, rocf Wrightstown MM, Pa.,
    dtd 1818,8,5
1820, 2, 22. Abigail rocf Concord MM, dtd
    1820,1,19
1828, 1, 22. Abigail & ch, Martha, Rachel &
    Josiah, gct Flushing MM

WHARTON, continued
1828, 12, 23. Martha & Anna dis jH
1832, 6, 19. Linton & Daniel dis disunity
1836, 5, 26. Daniel gct Flushing MM (H)
1836, 12, 20. James dis jH
1838, 5, 22. Silas dis jH
1839, 2, 19. Bethiah, minor, gct Flushing MM
1847, 5, 20. Levi gct Salem MM (H)
1849, 12, 18. Talitha Ann rocf Flushing MM,
     dtd 1849,10,25
1867, 2, 19. Talitha Ann gct Flushing MM (W)

WHEALDON
----, --, --. Nathan m Ruth ----- d 1821,10,7
     ae 34 bur Short Creek
     Ch: Rebecca   b 1808, 9, 28
         Rachel
         Isaac   " 1815, 7, 30
         Martha   " 1818, 4, 15
         Alphred   " 1820, 10, 10
     Nathan m 2nd Ruth -----
     Ch: Meriha   b 1826, 4, 20

1815, 7, 18. Nathan recrq
1815, 11, 21. Ruth rst on consent of Westland
     MM & ch, Rebecca, Ruth & Isaac, minors,
     recrq
1822, 5, 21. Rebecca, Rachel & Martha Smith,
     minors, gct Westland MM
1824, 7, 20. Rachel, minor, rocf Westland
     MM, dtd 1824,5,27
1825, 11, 22. Ann [Wealdon] rocf Westland MM,
     dtd 1825,7,28
1826, 9, 19. Nathan [Wealdon] & w, Ann, & ch,
     Rachel, Isaac, Alfred & Meriba, gct
     Flushing MM
1840, 4, 21. Martha [Wheldon] rocf Westland
     MM, dtd 1840,2,19
1843, 10, 24. Martha [Weldon] gct Westland MM

WHEELER
----, --, --. Wm. m Judith J. D. JOHNSON, dt
     Micajah & Edna L., b 1831,5,23 d 1905,6,
     17 (G)

1817, 10, 21. Gould rocf Simons Creek MM,
     N. C., dtd 1817,9,20
1819, 7, 20. Gould gct Westland MM
1856, 3, 18. Judith J. (form Johnston) dis mcd
1873, 5, 22. Judith J. D. recrq (G)
1892, 11, 23. Sarah R. & Florence M. recrq (G)

WHINERY
1824, 3, 3. Aaron, s George & Mary, Jeffer-
     son Co., O.; m in West Grove MH, Hannah
     MICHENER, dt Barak & Jane, Harrison Co.,O.
1845, 2, 1. Elwood D., s Mahlon & Hanna
     (Dean), b
----, --, --. Elwood & Asenath
     Ch: Elma T.   b 1870, 10, 10
         Hervey M. " 1872, 8, 16 d 1887, 1, 9
           bur Harrisville
         Thomas B. b 1875, 1, 6

     Ch: Chester E. b 1880, 6, 16
         Mary
         Edith   " 1887, 2, 3
1897, 9, 30. Asenath H. d ae 50 bur Harris-
     ville
1900, 3, 29. Thomas B., s Elwood D. & Asen-
     ath, Harrison Co., O., b 1875,1,6; m in
     Harrisville, Clara R. HALL, dt Parker &
     Tabitha D., Harrison Co., O., b 1874,6,11
     (W)
     Ch: Walter N. b 1901, 5, 23
         Wilson J. " 1902, 12, 4 d 1902, 12,8
         Alfred L. " 1904, 7, 1 " 1926, 3, 8
         Mabel   " 1906, 6, 6
         Melva Ra-
         chel   " 1907, 11, 20
         Louisa M. " 1910, 2, 15
         Francis   " 1911, 6, 25
1908, 8, 19. Mary Edith m Arthur J. HARTLEY
     (W)
----, --, --. Walter, s Thos. B. & Clara R.
     (Hall), b 1902,5,23; m Debora -----, dt
     Thos. A. & Sara CRAWFORD, b 1904,3,15
     Ch: Lewis Al-
         fred   b 1926, 8, 27
         Walter Jr. " 1928, 8, 3
         Patricia
         Ann   " 1930, 1, 9
1932, 10, 20. Mabel m Howard STRATTON

1822, 6, 18. Abigail rocf Newgarden MM, dtd
     1822,4,25
1824, 4, 20. Abigail gct New Garden MM
1876, 10, 24. Asenath (form Thomas) con mcd
     (W)
1877, 2, 20. Elwood D. rocf Newgarden MM, dtd
     1877,1,25 (W)
1895, 7, 23. Olive R. (form Bundy) con mcd
     (W)
1901, 6, 18. Olive R. B. dis jas (W)
1913, 1, 21. Chester dis mcd (W)
1925, 11, 24. Walter N. gct Upper Springfield
     MM, to m Deborah Crawford (W)
1926, 5, 18. Deborah Crawford rocf Upper
     Springfield MM, O., dtd 1896,4,23 (W)

WHITACRE
1830, 11, 23. Maria gct Westland MM

WHITE
----, --, --. John & Jane
     Ch: Ann   b 1799, 8, 8
         Phebe   " 1801, 9, 1
         James   " 1803, 11, 27
         Rachel   " 1806, 12, 18
1817, 1, 29. Ann m John TRIBBY
1840, 4, 6. John d ae 83 bur West Grove

1818, 2, 24. Thomas rst with consent of
     Fairfax MM
1818, 5, 19. Thomas gct Concord MM, to m
     Mary Cope
1818, 12, 22. Cert rec for Mary from Concord

WHITE, continued
    Concord MM, dtd 1818,8,19, end back to
    that mtg
1819, 3, 23. Thomas gct Concord MM
1824, 10, 19. Phebe McMillen (form White) dis
    mcd
1826, 8, 22. Rachel (form Pugh) dis mcd
1826, 9, 19. Rachel Thorn (form White) dis mcd
1827, 4, 24. Rebecca (form Sidwell) dis mcd
1828, 9, 19. Mary dis jH
1837, 4, 18. James dis mcd
1856, 7, 22. George dis mcd
1876, 5, 25. Arthur B. & w, Belinda, & ch,
    Elnora & Sylvanus, recrq (G)
1879, 5, 22. Arthur relrq (G)
1882, 3, 29. Belinda & ch, Elma & Sylvanus,
    relrq (G)
1892, 10, 19. Lillie recrq (G)
1906, 1, 24. Julia W. relrq (G)

WHITEHEAD
1830, 9, 21. David dis jH

WHITTEN
1906, 1, 24. Orwell recrq (G)
1908, 4, 22. William & w, Lucy, & ch, For-
    rest & Glenn, recrq (G)

WIER
1881, 2, 26. George M. recrq (G)
1881, 3, 24. Sadie recrq (G)
1884, 7, 23. Eliza dropped from mbrp (G)
1907, 3, 20. Sadie dropped from mbrp (G)

WILDMAN
1829, 9, 22. Joshua, Mary, Martha & Solomon
    [Wileman] rocf Falls MM, Pa., dtd 1829,6,4
    (minor ch of Jos. & Elizabeth)
1829, 9, 22. William [Wileman] rocf Falls MM,
    Pa., dtd 1829,6,4
1829, 11, 24. Mary, Joshua, Martha & Solomon,
    minor ch Joseph & Elizabeth, rocf Falls
    MM, Pa., dtd 1829,6,4
1835, 6, 23. Joshua [Wileman] dis mcd
1836, 11, 22. Mary (form Medcalf) con mcd
1837, 1, 24. William dis mcd
1837, 5, 23. Mary [Wileman] gct Pennsville MM
1838, 4, 24. Martha gct Stillwater MM
1838, 5, 22. Mary [Wileman] dis jH
1838, 5, 24. Joseph & w, Elizabeth, & s, Solo-
    mon, gct Stillwater MM (H)
1838, 5, 24. Mary gct Stillwater MM (H)
1838, 11, 20. Solomon, minor, gct Stillwater
    MM
1840, 10, 22. Walter B. & w, Lydia, & ch,
    Hannah Jane, Thomas Smith & David Baker
    gct Clear Creek MM (H)

WILEY
1833, 5, 23. Gulielma gct Smithfield MM (H)

WILKINS
1892, 10, 19. Sarah J. recrq (G)

WILLETS
----, --, --. Ellis & Hannah
    Ch: Lydia   d 1827, 3,22
        ae 14 bur Smithfield
        Rachel   " 1836, 5,23
        ae 27 bur Smithfield
1830, 2, 6. Eliza d ae 19 bur Smithfield
----, --, --. Mark & Sarah (Sarah bur at Smith-
    field)
    Ch: Hannah b 1845, 6, 20 d 1845, 7,15
        Lydia S. " 1846, 6, 9
        Eliza   " 1848, 2, 28
        Hannah R. " 1849, 8, 24
        Sarah Ann " 1851, 12, 15
        David   " 1853, 12, 8
        Mary   " 1855, 12, 8
        Ellis
        Campbell
1844, 10, 21. Hannah d bur Smithfield
1854, 12, 4. Ellis d bur Smithfield
1869, 12, 22. Lydia S. m Harvey THOMAS (W)
1873, 3, 20. Eliza m Finley HUTTON (W)
1874, 8, 18. Mark d ae 69 bur Smithfield
1894, 5, 23. David P., s Mark & Sarah V.,
    Lynn Co., Ia.; m in Harrisville, Sina W.
    HALL, dt Jesse & Edith, Jefferson Co., O.
    (W)

1815, 9, 4. Samuel & w, Elizabeth, & ch,
    Isaiah, Ellis, John, Eli, Joel, Taylor,
    Sarah & Samuel, rocf Redstone MM, dtd
    1815,2,3
1840, 8, 18. Joel gct Redstone MM
1856, 10, 21. Margaret (form Hammond) dis mcd
1865, 3, 21. John rpd mcd (W)
1882, 9, 19. Ellis C. gct Springville MM,
    Ia. (W)
1882, 9, 19. Mary S. gct Springville MM, Ia.
    (W)
1882, 9, 19. Sarah V. gct Springville MM,
    Ia. (W)
1885, 2, 24. David gct Springville MM, Ia.
    (W)
1885, 2, 24. Hannah gct Springville MM, Ia.
    (W)
1894, 12, 18. Sina W. gct Springville MM, Ia.
    (W)

WILLIAMS
----, --, --. Richard & Sarah
    Ch: Elizabeth b 1799, 9, 9
        Abigail " 1802, 9, 18
        Dearmon " 1804, 10, 12
        Deborah " 1806, 11, 30
        Benjamin " 1808, 12, 27
1819, 3, 3. Nathan, s Abraham & Margaret,
    Fayette Co., Pa.; m in West Grove MH, Sa-
    rah HOOPES, dt Nathan & Elizabeth, Harri-
    son Co., O.
    Ch: Elizabeth b 1820, 10, 12

WILLIAMS, continued
    Ch: Ann   b 1822, 11, 26
        Mary   " 1824, 8, 27
        William " 1827, 1, 30
        Thomas   " 1828, 11, 29
        Jane   " 1830, 11, 2
        John   " 1832, 9, 29
        Nathan   " 1834, 11, 1
        Sarah   " 1837, 2, 4
        Joseph   " 1839, 5, 27
1826, 7, 20. Mary d bur West Grove
1841, 7, 30. Nathan d ae 60 bur West Grove
1850, 9, 23. William d ae 24
1879, 8, 20. Joseph, s Daniel & Martha S.,
    Belmont Co., O.; m in Concord, Mary Eliza
    HOYLE, dt Benjamin & Guli Ann, Belmont Co.,
    O.

1805, 7, 20. Richard & w, Sarah, & ch, Eliza-
    beth, Abigail & Dearman, rocf Concord MM,
    dtd 1805,5,21
1812, 7, 21. Richard & w, Sarah, & ch, Eliza-
    beth, Abigail, Dearman, Deborah, Asa &
    Mary, gct Newberry MM, O.
1817, 5, 20. Nathan rocf Dunnings Creek MM,
    dtd 1817,4,6
1836, 5, 24. Nathan Hall gct Stillwater MM,
    to m Sarah Williams
1837, 6, 20. Daniel & w, Elizabeth, & ch,
    Hannah & Joseph, rocf Salem MM, dtd 1837,
    5,24
1839, 3, 19. Daniel & w, Elizabeth, & ch,
    Hannah, Joseph & Lindley M., gct Salem MM
1846, 7, 21. Elizabeth Bond (form Williams)
    dis mcd
1848, 6, 20. Joseph & w, Lydia M., rocf Flush-
    ing MM, dtd 1848,5,25
1849, 9, 18. Jane Barnard (form Williams) dis
    mcd
1849, 10, 23. Jane Bond (form Williams) dis
    mcd
1851, 12, 23. Ann McGrew (form Williams) dis
    mcd
1854, 5, 23. Joseph & w, Lydia M., gct
    Spiceland MM
1856, 10, 22. Abner & w, Mary Ann, & ch,
    William Talbott & Ann Eliza, gct Honey
    Creek MM, Ind.
1856, 10, 22. Albert & w, Mary Ann, gct
    Honey Creek MM, Ind.
1856, 10, 22. Henry gct Honey Creek MM, Ind.
1856, 10, 22. Job & w, Elizabeth, & ch, Benja-
    min, James & Job, gct Honey Creek MM, Ind.
1857, 9, 22. Sarah W. Cope (form Williams)
    dis mcd
1862, 2, 19. John dis mcd
1862, 2, 19. Nathan dis mcd
1862, 2, 19. Thomas dis mcd
1862, 11, 19. Ephraim, Anna & Sarah dis jW
    (G)
1865, 8, 23. Wm. R. Ratcliff gct Goshen MM,
    O., to m Sarah Esther Williams (G)
1874, 4, 23. Jesse recrq (G)

1876, 5, 23. Sarah T. (form Hall) dis mcd
    (W)
1879, 5, 22. Annie M. recrq (G)
1880, 1, 20. Mary Eliza gct Flushing MM (W)
1881, 2, 26. Mary recrq (G)
1882, 3, 29. Wm. K. & Sally C. K. recrq (G)
1884, 6, 25. Joseph dropped from mbrp (G)
1884, 6, 25. Thomas dropped from mbrp (G)
1884, 6, 25. John dropped from mbrp (G)
1885, 7, 22. Ida (form Phillips) gct Rush
    Creek MM (G)
1887, 4, 20. Sarah E. & Charles K. recrq (G)
1892, 3, 23. Duncan recrq (G)
1892, 10, 19. John H. & Stephen recrq (G)
1894, 12, 19. Charles recrq (G)
1895, 2, 20. Charles recrq (G)
1901, 7, 24. Chas. & Eliza recrq (G)

WILLIAMSON
1885, 3, 25. Frank recrq (G)
1886, 5, 19. Henry recrq (G)
1886, 5, 19. Edmund recrq (G)
1886, 5, 19. Ines recrq (G)
1886, 5, 19. Peter S. recrq (G)
1886, 5, 19. Mary recrq (G)
1886, 5, 19. Jennie recrq (G)
1886, 5, 19. John A. recrq (G)
1886, 5, 19. Abraham recrq (G)
1893, 6, 21. Minerva S., Joseph C. & Lillie
    May recrq (G)

WILLIS
1847, 3, 24. Susan m Clarkson BURGESS
1856, 9, 25. Joel, s Henry & Lydia, Hardin
    Co., Ia.; m in Short Creek MH, Lydia H.
    PATTERSON, dt Mahlon & Mary Ann, Jefferson
    Co., O.
1856, 11, 18. Lydia H. d ae 35 bur Rocksylvan-
    ia, Hardin Co., Iowa

1832, 10, 23. Israel Jenkins gct Redstone MM,
    to m Lydia Willis
1833, 1, 22. Joel & Susan rocf Redstone MM
    with mother, Lydia Jenkins, dtd 1833,1,2
1840, 8, 18. Joel gct Redstone MM

WILSON
----, --, --. Jonathan & Hannah
    Ch: Rachel   b 1799, 9, 22
        Elizabeth " 1801, 4, 25
        Ann   " 1805, 3, 14
        Israel   " 1807, 2, 16
        Jonathan " 1813, 7, 5
1807, 10, 22. Martha m Elias STANTON
----, --, --. Thomas & Hannah (H)
    Ch: Yarnall   b 1815, 3, 3
        Phebe   " 1817, 3, 30
        Jane   " 1819, 4, 9
        Cyrus   " 1821, 8, 10
        Thomas Jr. " 1828, 12, 10
1821, 2, 1. Rachel m John C. HILL
1822, 8, 29. Elizabeth m Elisha SIDWELL
1831, 4, 24. Jonathan d ae 60 bur Short Creek

WILSON, continued

1831, 6, 2. Ann m Abraham BRANSON

1833, 8, 28. Israel, s Jonathan & Hannah, Jefferson Co., O.; m in Concord, Mariah BRANSON, dt Rees & Ruth, Belmont Co., O.
Ch: Abraham   b 1834, 9, 8
    Israel   " 1836, 9, 4

1833, 10, 31. Jonathan, s Jonathan & Hannah, Jefferson Co., O.; m in Short Creek MH, Mercy KINSEY, dt James & Ann, Jefferson Co., O., d 1848,2,27 bur Short Creek
Ch: James K.   b 1835, 5, 17
    Israel   " 1837, 4, 12
    Jane   " 1839, 2, 10 d 1851, 4, 5
    Mary Ann   " 1841, 12, 16 " 1849,11,25
    John   " 1843, 1, 31
    Lemuel   " 1845, 5, 24
Jonathan m 2nd 1849,5,3 in Short Creek MH, Sarah S. NEGUS, dt Shedloc & Rachel, Jefferson Co., O.

1836, 4, 16. Israel d bur Short Creek

1838, 4, 16. Israel Jr. d bur Short Creek

1838, 8, 2. Maria (nee Branson) m John HIRST

1840, 9, 30. Mary m Thos. H. STANLEY

1843, 9, 2. Hannah d ae 71 bur Short Creek

1845, 9, 24. Sarah A. m Elwood CHAPMAN

1848, 10, 10. Mary d ae 57 bur Short Creek

1852, 8, 25. Timothy, s John W. & Margaret, Wayne Co., Ind.; m in Mt. Pleasant, Elizabeth Ann TERRELL, dt Matthew & Elizabeth D., Jefferson Co., O.

1856, 10, 29. Abraham, s Israel & Maria, Jefferson Co., O.; m in West Grove MH, Beulah E. THOMAS, dt Townsend & Ann, Harrison Co., O.

1859, 9, 22. Franklin, s John W. & Margaret W., Wayne Co., Ind.; m in Mt. Pleasant, Lucy W. TERRELL, dt Matthew & Elizabeth D., Jefferson Co., O.

1894, 5, 8. Eliza d ae 81 bur Harrisville

1807, 6, 20. Martha rocf Westland MM, dtd 1807,4,25

1810, 3, 20. Samuel & w, Hannah, & s, Joseph, rocf Pipecreek MM, dtd 1808,4,16, end by Concord MM, 1810,2,22

1816, 11, 19. Asa rocf Buckingham MM, Pa., dtd 1816,9,2

1817, 11, 18. Hannah, w Thomas, & ch, Yarnal & Phebe, recrq

1819, 3, 23. Asa gct Cincinnati MM

1823, 8, 19. Nathan Hall gct Flushing MM, to m Hannah Wilson

1823, 10, 21. Mary recrq

1823, 10, 21. Thomas recrq on consent of Byberry MM, Pa.

1824, 4, 20. Elizabeth rocf Falls MM, Pa., dtd 1824,2,7

1824, 5, 18. Cyrus & Jane, ch Thos. & Hannah recrq

1824, 5, 18. Jane, dt Hannah, recrq

1824, 10, 19. Nathan P. Hall gct Flushing

MM, to m Rachel Wilson

1829, 9, 19. .Ann, w Geo., rocf Falls MM, Pa., dtd 1829,6,4

1829, 11, 24. Elizabeth dis JH

1830, 2, 23. Hannah dis JH

1830, 11, 25. Elizabeth gct Stillwater MM (H)

1831, 7, 19. Mary & ch, Margaret, Sarah, Mary, Rachel, Daniel, Ruth, William & Owen, rocf Deerfield MM, dtd 1831,5,19

1833, 4, 25. Thos. & w, Hannah, & ch, Yarnal, Phebe, Jane, Cyrus & Thomas, gct Plainfield MM (H)

1833, 5, 21. Yarnal, Phebe Jane, Cyrus & Thomas, ch Thos., gct Stillwater MM

1834, 7, 24. Elizabeth gct Deerfield MM (H)

1838, 4, 24. Ann gct Stillwater MM

1841, 4, 20. Mary & ch, Rachel, Daniel, Ruth, William, Owen, Thomas & Catharine, gct Somerset MM

1841, 8, 24. Margaret D. Miller (form Wilson) dis mcd

1852, 11, 23. Sarah, w Jonathan, & ch, James K., Israel & Lemuel, gct Salem MM, Ia.

1852, 12, 21. Elizabeth Ann gct Honey Creek MM, Ind.

1854, 1, 24. Jonathan dis

1855, 8, 22. Elizabeth (form Updegraff) dis disunity

1859, 2, 23. Jonathan rst at Red Cedar MM, Ia. on consent of this mtg

1859, 7, 20. John L., minor, s Jonathan, gct Red Cedar MM, Ia.

1859, 12, 21. Lucy T. gct Milford MM

1862, 11, 19. Edwin & Deborah dis JW

1862, 11, 19. Israel dis JW

1862, 11, 19. Catharine dis JW

1862, 11, 19. Ann Eliza dis JW

1862, 11, 19. Rachel dis JW

1862, 11, 19. Israel Jr. dis JW

1862, 11, 19. Joseph dis JW

1862, 11, 19. William C. dis JW

1862, 11, 19. Esther dis JW

1862, 11, 19. Charles dis JW

1862, 11, 19. Francis dis JW

1862, 11, 19. Levi dis JW

1862, 11, 19. Ann dis JW

1862, 11, 19. Elizabeth dis JW

1863, 8, 19. Abraham & w, Beulah E., & ch, Anna Maria, Israel T. & Townsend, gct Red Cedar MM, Ia. (G)

1865, 2, 21. Josiah Hall gct Flushing MM, to m Deborah Wilson (W)

1873, 4, 24. Robert recrq (G)

1880, 5, 20. Caroline C. recrq (G)

1889, 2, 19. Eliza rocf Flushing MM, dtd 1889,1,24 (W)

1892, 10, 19. James & Lizzie recrq (G)

1902, 6, 25. Annie recrq (G)

1902, 7, 22. Joseph G. dis mcd & military surgeon in the army (W)

1905, 2, 22. Anna relrq (G)

WINN
1892, 10, 19. Daisy recrq (G)
1892, 10, 19. William A. recrq (G)

WINSTON
1855, 8, 19. Nathaniel d ae 59

1848, 9, 19. Nathaniel rocf South River MM,
     Va., dtd 1846,4,9, end by Cincinnati MM
1849, 6, 19. Zalinda rocf Cedar Creek MM,
     Va., dtd 1849,4,11

WIRSTEL
1817, 10, 21. Ann (form Thompson) con mcd

WOLLER
1881, 2, 26. Oliver recrq (G)

WOOD
----, --, --. Robert & Mary
     Ch: Keester   b 1814, 10, 15
         Josiah   " 1817, 3, 7
         Mary Ann   " 1819, 9, 26
1816, 5, 30. Pusey, s Thos. & Susanna, Jef-
     ferson Co., O.; m in Short Creek MH, Char-
     ity REDD, dt Geo. & Rachel, Jefferson Co.,
     O., d 1833,12,10 ae 29 bur Smithfield
1823, 4, 30. Hannah m Samuel GRAY
----, --, --. Samuel & Lucy
     Ch: Ann Maria b 1828, 2, 21
         Nathan L. " 1830, 4, 10
         Elizabeth
           L.   " 1832, 10, 5
         Margaret
           H.   " 1835, 5, 18
         Jane   " 1838, 1, 24
         Mary E.   " 1845, 1, 9
1827, 7, 25. Mary, w Wm., d ae 66 bur Smith-
     field
1829, 9, 20. Isaac, infant, d bur Smithfield
----, --, --. Thomas & Elizabeth
     Ch: Mary   b 1834, 7, 28
         Martha   " 1837, 5, 19
         Anna   " 1839, 2, 1
         Lydia B.   " 1841, 2, 14
         William   " 1844, 6, 18
         Henry C.   " 1849, 7, 8
         Elizabeth
           C.   " 1852, 12, 15
         Cornelia
           J.   " 1855, 12, 27
1844, 6, 4. William d ae 87 bur Smithfield
----, --, --. Joseph & Mary
     Ch: James   b 1837, 10, 5
         Sarah   " 1840, 3, 6
         Mary Ann   " 1845, 5, 6
         Elizabeth " 1849, 7, 6
1838, 10, 5. John d bur Short Creek
----, --, --. Joel & Elizabeth
     Ch: George R. b 1839, 5, 16
         Mary Caro-
           line   " 1844, 6, 2
         William

     Ch: Henry   b 1847, 8, 16
         Oliver R. " 1855, 12, 1
         Lucy J.   " 1860, 9, 9
1851, 10, 5. Margaret, w Nathan, d ae 76
1859, 4, 2. Charles W., s Nathan & Mary, b
1869, 3, 25. Asaph, s Elisha M. & Martha,
     Morgan Co., O.; m in Concord, Phebe
     BRACKIN, dt Elisha & Esther, Belmont Co.,
     O.

1807, 12, 19. William & w, Mary, & ch, Joshua,
     Richard, Wm., Thomas, Mary & Lydia, rocf
     Pipe Creek MM, dtd 1807,10,7
1808, 2, 20. Elizabeth rocf Pipe Creek MM,
     dtd 1807,11,14
1809, 11, 21. Robert & w, Mary, & ch, Joseph,
     Sarah, Abigail, Benjamin, John, Hannah,
     Jesse & Rachel, rocf Youngstreet MM, Upper
     Canada, dtd 1809,9,14
1813, 7, 20. Robert & w, Mary, & ch, Joseph,
     Sarah, Abigail, Benjamin, John, Hannah,
     Jesse, Rachel, Thomas & Robert, rocf Con-
     cord MM, dtd 1813,5,20
1815, 10, 24. Daniel & w, Phebe, & ch, Anna
     & Levi, rocf Peru MM, dtd 1815,6,22
1816, 8, 20. Charity gct Plymouth MM
1818, 2, 24. Cert rec for Jonathan & w, Ra-
     chel, & ch, Israel, Lydia, Jonathan, Reu-
     bin, Rachel & Matilda, from Peru MM, N.Y.,
     dtd 1817,9,25, end to Alum Creek MM
1818, 12, 22. Abigail Pelmer (form Wood) dis
     mcd
1820, 11, 21. John, minor s Robert, gct Fair-
     fax MM
1821, 10, 23. Joseph gct Flushing MM
1821, 11, 20. Sarah Barnard (form Wood) dis
     mcd
1821, 12, 18. Benjamin dis mcd
1822, 11, 19. John rocf Fairfax MM, dtd 1822,
     10,16
1825, 7, 19. John gct Somerset MM
1828, 10, 25. Mary, w Robert, & ch, Thomas,
     Robert, Kester, Josiah & Mary Ann, gct
     Deerfield MM
1828, 11, 20. Robert gct Deerfield MM (H)
1830, 2, 25. Rachel gct Deerfield MM (H)
1830, 6, 22. Rachel gct Deerfield MM
1830, 10, 19. Penrose Hussey gct Smithfield
     MM, to m Susannah Wood
1830, 10, 21. Zeruah gct Smithfield MM (H)
1831, 5, 24. William Ratcliff gct Flushing
     MM, to m Sarah Wood
1832, 2, 21. Charles Wright gct Smithfield
     MM, to m Mary Wood
1832, 9, 18. Jesse dis disunity
1836, 10, 18. Joseph recrq
1836, 11, 22. Mary & dt, Hannah, recrq
1837, 2, 21. Benjamin, John & Jonathan, ch
     Joseph, recrq
1838, 2, 20. Joel & w, Elizabeth, rocf Smith-
     field MM, dtd 1838,2,19
1839, 3, 19. Lewis rocf Smithfield MM, dtd
     1839,2,18

WOOD, continued
1841, 3, 23. Lewis dis mcd
1843, 10, 21. Rosina recrq
1851, 7, 22. Benjamin dis disunity
1852, 3, 23. Hannah Street (form Wood) dis
    mcd
1854, 7, 18. James G. Kinsey gct Smithfield
    MM, to m Elizabeth Wood
1857, 2, 24. Joseph dis disunity
1859, 4, 20. Jonathan rpd mcd
1860, 8, 21. Elizabeth dis jG (W)
1860, 8, 21. Joel dis jG (W)
1861, 2, 19. Rosina dis jG (W)
1861, 2, 20. James dis jas (G)
1862, 8, 19. Lucy dis jG (W)
1862, 11, 19. John W. dis jW (G)
1862, 11, 19. Almeda dis jW (G)
1862, 11, 19. Elam dis jW (G)
1862, 11, 19. Allen dis jW (G)
1863, 3, 24. Thomas dis jG (W)
1863, 10, 21. Elnathan Pettit gct Smithfield
    MM, to m Margaret H. Wood (G)
1864, 6, 24. Samuel dis jG (W)
1864, 7, 19. James dis disunity (W)
1864, 8, 24. Sarah Tweedy (form Wood) con mcd
1864, 9, 20. Mary dis jG (W)
1865, 1, 24. Mary & Elizabeth dis disunity
    (W)
1865, 6, 20. Sally W. Twedy (form Wood) dis
    mcd (W)
1865, 8, 22. Nathan L. dis jH (W)
1865, 11, 22. Lewis rst (G)
1866, 7, 25. Rosina dis jas (G)
1866, 10, 25. Samuel J. Thomasson gct Smith-
    field MM, to m Mary Wood (G)
1867, 10, 24. Sarah B. & Anna U. recrq (G)
1867, 12, 24. Pusey dis mcd (W)
1867, 12, 26. Rosina recrq (G)
1869, 9, 23. Elizabeth dis jas (G)
1870, 8, 23. Phebe B. & s, Clarence E., gct
    Coal Creek MM, Ioaa (W)
1870, 9, 22. Anna West (form Wood) con mcd
    (G)
1871, 12, 21. William con mcd (G)
1872, 1, 25. William Allen recrq (G)
1872, 4, 23. Henry dis mcd & jG (W)
1872, 4, 23. William dis mcd & jG (W)
1877, 8, 21. Elizabeth C. dis jG (W)
1877, 9, 18. Cornelia J. dis jG (W)
1880, 9, 23. Allen dis disunity (W)
1883, 11, 21. Lucy rocf Smithfield MM (G)
1889, 12, 25. Joseph U. recrq (G)
1890, 5, 21. Rose relrq (G)
1895, 1, 23. Rose recrq (G)
1902, 4, 23. Rose relrq (G)
1909, 7, 21. Lizzie C. rocf Smithfield MM,
    dtd 1909,6,23 (G)
1912, 10, 23. Elizabeth C. relrq (G)

WOODWARD
1845, 3, 26. Sarah d ae 28
----, --, --. Isaac & Sarah Ann
    Ch: Mary E.   b 1857, 3, 13

    Ch: John S.   b 1855, 1, 28
1876, 10, 4. Emily C. [Woodard] m Oliver C.
    HARGRAVE
1910, 6, 22. Sarah Ann [Woodard] d bur West
    Grove (G)

1853, 11, 22. Sarah Ann con mcd
1862, 2, 18. Sarah Ann [Woodard] dis jG
1864, 8, 24. Isaac & ch, Charles Eli, Emily
    C., John T. & Mary E., recrq (G)
1876, 7, 20. Charles E. [Woodard] dis mcd
    (G)
1877, 11, 20. Sarah (form Thomas) dis mcd &
    jG (W)
1885, 1, 21. Mary E. Hammond (form Woodward)
    gct Smithfield MM (G)
1891, 3, 25. John L. & w, Sarah T., & ch,
    Clara E. & Walter J., relrq (G)

WOOSTER
1892, 10, 19. Addie recrq (G)
1892, 10, 19. J. F. recrq (G)

WORRELL
----, --, --. Jonathan & Eleanor
    Ch: Sarah   b 1795, 12, 13
        Benjamin   " 1798, 2, 7
        John   " 1800, 4, 18
        Nathaniel " 1802, 7, 24
        George   " 1804, 9, 19
        Joseph   " 1807, 1, 20
        Elizabeth " 1809, 7, 10
        Rebecca   " 1811, 12, 18
        Mordecai   " 1815, 2, 2
        Isaac   " 1817, 3, 31
1815, 6, 1. Ann [Worrel] m Chas. KINSEY
1819, 4, 1. Zebulon [Worrall], s John &
    Rebecca, Delaware Co., Pa.; m in Short
    Creek MH, Martha RATCLIFF, dt Isaac &
    Margaret, Jefferson Co., O.
    Ch: Isaac   b 1820, 2, 22
        John   " 1822, 1, 2
        Rebecca   " 1824, 2, 10
        Margaret   " 1824, 2, 10
1819, 9, 1. Benjamin [Worrall], s Jonathan
    & Eleanor, Harrison Co., O.; m in West
    Grove MH, Priscilla GILL, dt John &
    Sunna, Harrison Co., O.
1824, 6, 16. Thomas d ae 38 bur West Grove
1868, 8, 31. William P. d ae 83
1868, 9, 14. Daniel d ae 83

1804, 9, 15. Benjamin [Worrel] rocf Red-
    stone MM, dtd 1804,8,3
1806, 10, 18. Isaiah & w, Sarah, & ch, Daniel
    & Eliza Ann, rocf Philadelphia MM, dtd
    1806, 8, 26
1807, 2, 21. Jacob [Worrel] rocf Abington
    MM, dtd 1806,11,24
1807, 3, 21. Jonathan [Worrel] & w, Eleanor,
    & ch, Sarah, Benjamin, John, Nathaniel,
    George & Joseph, gct Salem MM
1807, 4, 18. Jacob [Worrel] gct Abington MM

WORRELL, continued

1811, 5, 21. Jonathan & w, Eleanor, & ch,
Sarah, Benjamin, Nathaniel, George, Joseph & Elizabeth, rocf Salem MM, dtd
1810,12,11

1812, 12, 22. Thomas & w, Eleanor, & ch, Mary,
Burgess & Hannah, recrq

1814, 10, 18. Ann [Worrall] rocf Abington MM,
Pa., dtd 1814,8,29

1820, 4, 18. Sarah Thomas (form Worrel) con
mcd

1828, 5, 20. Jonathan [Worrall] & w, Eleanor,
& ch, Rebecca, Mordecai & Isaac, gct
Deerfield MM

1828, 7, 22. Mary Spurrier (form Worrell)
dis mcd

1828, 8, 19. Elizabeth gct Deerfield MM

1828, 11, 18. Benjamin [Worral] Sr. gct Deerfield MM

1829, 4, 21. Esther & ch, Hannah, Ruth,
Lydia, Elizabeth, Amos & Miriam, gct Deerfield MM

1830, 7, 20. Benjamin Jr. & w, Priscilla, &
ch, Eleanor, Ann, Sarah & Elizabeth, gct
Deerfield MM

1837, 7, 18. Zebulon & w, Martha, & ch, John,
Rebecca, Margaret, Mary, Zebulon, Elwood,
Elizabeth & Martha, gct Pennsville MM

1832, 4, 24. Burgess dis disunity

1845, 1, 21. Isaac R. [Worrel] gct Westland
MM

1884, 5, 20. Nathaniel rst at Hickory Grove
MM on consent of this mtg (W)

WORSTELL

1797, 1, 19. Ann [Worstel] b

1830, 6, 22. Ann dis JH

1855, 6, 21. Ann [Worstel] gct Deerfield MM
(H)

1874, 4, 23. Sarah C. rocf Chesterfield MM
(G)

1885, 12, 23. Sarah E. [Wirstell] relrq (G)

1894, 3, 21. John recrq (G)

1896, 1, 23. Ruth Ann recrq (G)

1896, 1, 23. Clarence recrq

1929, 7, 24. Clarence dropped from mbrp (G)

1929, 10, 23. Ruth relrq (G)

WORTHINGTON

1879, 5, 22. Sarah recrq (G)

WORTHY

1873, 5, 22. John & w, Margaret, & ch, Elizabeth, Edward, Franklin & Edith, recrq (G)

1875, 6, 24. John & w, Margaret, & ch, Edith,
gct Smithfield MM (G)

WRIGHT

1812, 12, 3. Nehemiah, s Joseph & Mary, Jefferson Co., O.; m in Short Creek MH, Abigail DEW, dt Joseph & Vilee, Jefferson Co.,
O.

Ch: Joseph D.   b 1813, 8, 17
    Martha   " 1815, 12, 28
    John D.   " 1818, 2, 16

1814, 9, 29. Martha m Eli GREGG

----, --, --. Charles & Mary
Ch: William M. b 1832, 12, 6
    Elizabeth   " 1834, 10, 19
    Francis   " 1837, 7, 1
    Benjamin   " 1843, 12, 11
    Edward Bon-
      sall   " 1847, 3, 2

1838, 2, 21. Benjamin d ae 64 bur Short Creek

----, --, --. Parvin m Ellen S. ----- d 1861,5
--
Ch: Henry C.   b 1844, 4, 10
    Morris P.   " 1849, 4, 9
    Walter   " 1851, 7, 18

----, --, 0-. Benjamin H. & Sally Ann
Ch: Susan S.   b 1847, 3, 1
    Charles
      Stroud   " 1849, 5, 6
    Hannah M.   " 1851, 5, 5
    Mary E.   " 1853, 7, 25
    George P.   " 1855, 3, 15
    Jane P.   " 1858, 1, 31

1869, 3, 31. Parvin, s Benj. & Hannah, Belmont Co., O.; m in Mt. Pleasant, Mary B.
STROUD, dt Jacob & Ann

1876, 5, 31. Charles, s Benj. & Hannah, Belmont Co., O.; m in Mt. Pleasant, Hannah
W. PRICE, dt Lewis & Rachel WALKER, Harrison Co., O.

1807, 3, 21. Robert & w, Rachel, & ch, William, Martha, John, Mary, Paxson & Susan,
rocf Fairfax MM, Va., dtd 1806,4,26, end
by Concord MM 1807,--,--

1807, 8, 15. Elenor (form Evans) dis mou

1808, 12, 20. Nehemiah rocf Plainfield MM, dtd
1808,11,26

1817, 3, 18. Sarah rocf Plainfield MM

1818, 7, 21. Nehemiah & w, Abigail, & ch,
Joseph, Martha & John, gct Plainfield MM,
also Mary Gilbert, minor, gct Plainfield
MM

1821, 2, 20. Catharine (form Nevet) dis mcd

1829, 9, 19. Mary A. rocf ND MM, dtd 1829,6,
23

1832, 2, 21. Chas. gct Smithfield to m Mary
Wood

1832, 8, 21. Mary A. gct ND MM

1832, 9, 18. Mary rocf Smithfield MM, dtd
1832,9,17

1833, 5, 21. Ann B. rst at Flushing MM on
consent of this mtg

1838, 3, 20. Samuel & w, Lydia, rocf Philadelphia MM, dtd 1838,1,25

1838, 4, 24. Beulah R. & Jane A. rocf Philadelphia MM, dtd 1838,1,25

1839, 10, 22. Parvin gct Centre MM, to m Ellen Stroud

1840, 2, 18. Ellen S. rocf Center MM, dtd
1840,1,15

WRIGHT, continued

1840, 5, 19. Mary Ann rocf Exeter MM, dtd
    1840,3,25
1841, 11, 23. Beulah dis disunity
1841, 11, 23. Jane dis disunity
1846, 3, 24. Benjamin H. gct Springboro to
    m Sally Ann Stroud
1846, 11, 24. Sally Ann rocf Springfield MM,
    dtd 1846,7,21
1850, 2, 19. Mary Ann gct ND MM
1850, 4, 23. Lydia gct Cincinnati MM
1858, 4, 21. Charles & w, Mary, & ch, Fran-
    cis, Benjamin & Elwood B., gct Gilead MM,
    O.
1858, 4, 21. Elizabeth gct Gilead MM
1859, 1, 19. Benjamin H. & w, Sally Ann, &
    ch, Susan S., Chas. Stroud, Hannah M.,
    Mary E., Geo. P. & Jane D., gct Blue
    River MM, Ind.
1859, 1, 19. Hannah & s, Benjamin H., gct
    Blue River MM, Ind.
1859, 7, 20. William W. rpd mcd; dropped from
    mbrp
1860, 5, 23. William M. gct Blue River MM,
    Ind.
1860, 6, 19. Ellen S. dis jG (W)
1860, 6, 19. Parvin dis jG (W)
1861, 7, 23. William dis mcd & jG (W)
1863, 1, 20. Benjamin dis jG (W)
1863, 2, 24. Charles dis jG (W)
1868, 4, 23. Henry C. rpd mcd (G)
1868, 4, 23. Martha L. (form Lukens) con mcd
    (G)
1868, 9, 24. Henry C. gct White Water MM,
    Ind. (G)
1868, 11, 28. Marillia L. gct Ypsilanti (G)
1870, 3, 24. Parvin & w, Mary B. L., & ch,
    Morris P. & Walter B., gct White Water MM,
    Ind. (G)
1870, 4, 21. Charles & w, May, & ch, Eliza-
    beth, Benjamin & Edward B., rocf Indianapo-
    lis MM, Ind. (G)
1879, 4, 24. Anna Bell recrq (G)
1881, 5, 26. Elizabeth gct Indianapolis MM,
    Ind. (G)
1881, 6, 23. Martha rocf Ypsilanti MM, Mich.
    (G)
1883, 1, 23. Benjamin Jr. dis mcd & jG (W)
1883, 4, 24. Henry C. dis mcd (W)
1883, 4, 24. Morris P. dis mcd (W)
1884, 4, 22. Francis D. dis mcd (W)
1884, 4, 22. Walter B. dis mcd & jas (W)
1886, 2, 23. Elizabeth M. dis jG (W)
1887, 9, 21. Elizabeth rocf Indianapolis MM,
    Ind. (G)
1898, 3, 23. Edward relrq (G)
1898, 4, 20. Benjamin F. & w, Anna Bell, &
    dt, Anna Mary, gct Indianapolis MM, Ind.
    (G)
1898, 4, 20. Charles dropped from mbrp (G)
1902, 12, 20. Benjamin F., Annie B. & Charles
    recrq (G)
1911, 3, 22. Paul Howard & w, Orpha, & dt,

Dorothy Evelyn, rocf Miami MM (G)
1913, 1, 22. Carolyn recrq (G)
1913, 1, 22. Morris English recrq (G)
1913, 1, 22. Dorothy recrq (G)
1913, 1, 22. Virginia recrq (G)
1914, 1, 21. Ch of Alice relrq (G)

WRITER
1851, 6, 24. Hannah C. rocf Gwyned MM, Pa.,
    dtd 1851,5,1

WYANT
1910, 9, 21. Isaac & w, Nettie, recrq (G)

WYMAN
1895, 3, 20. Nerva recrq (G)

WYTCHERLY
1895, 9, 25. Edward recrq (G)
1896, 3, 25. Edward relrq (G)
1902, 8, 20. Edward [Wicherly] dropped from
                                [mbrp (G)

YADER
1915, 2, 24. George recrq (G)

YARBY
1901, 7, 24. Isabella & Morrison recrq (G)

YARDLEY
1821, 4, 24. Lydia (form Reynolds) dis mcd

YARNAL
1813, 5, 27. Mordecai, s Geo. & Lydia, Jef-
    ferson Co., O.; m in Short Creek MH,
    Phebe CARSON, dt Geo. & Lydia, Jefferson
    Co., O.

1806, 5, 24. George & w, Lydia, rocf Red-
    stone MM, dtd 1806,5,2
1813, 1, 19. Mordecai rocf Redstone MM, dtd
    1812,12,4
1817, 6, 24. Mordecai [Yarnall] & w, Phebe,
    & ch, Hannah & Susanna, gct Stillwater MM

YATER
1912, 3, 20. Lillie recrq (G)
1913, 7, 23. Lillie dropped from mbrp (G)

YOCUM
----, --, --. Samuel & Rebecca
    Ch: Hannah   b 1796, 5, 10
        Thomas   " 1797, 8, 25
        Jacob   " 1801, 12, 12
        Samuel   " 1803, 12, 7
        Mark   " 1806, 4, 27
        John   " 1808, 8, 13

1805, 11, 16. Rebecca [Yocum] rocf Catawesa
    MM, Pa., dtd 1805,9,21
1808, 3, 22. Samuel recrq
1808, 4, 19. Hannah, Thomas, Jacob, Samuel &
    Mark, ch Samuel, recrq
1811, 5, 21. Samuel & fam gct Stillwater MM

YORE
1892, 10, 19. Lovie recrq (G)

YOST
1769, 3, 28. Rachel b
1812, 10, 9. Sarah b
1815, 10, 1. Margaret b
1824, 5, 27. Hannah m Edward MORRIS
1842, 8, 18. Rachel d ae 73
1863, 11, 13. Mary d
18--, 9, 9. Mary b

1822, 6, 18. Hannah [Yhost] & Mary, elder dt
    Rachel, recrq
1822, 6, 18. Rachel [Yhost] & minor dt, Sa-
    rah & Margaret, recrq
1828, 12, 23. Rachel & Mary [Youst] dis JH
1831, 10, 18. Sarah dis JH
1835, 9, 22. Margaret dis JH
1858, 8, 25. Martha rst (he was dis by Con-
    cord MM before the separation, but MM not
    asked for consent)
1875, 5, 18. Ellen (form Hall) dis mcd (W)

YOUNG
1896, 3, 4. Geo. E., s Job & Mary B., Linn
    Co., Ia.; m in Concord, Lydia A. STEER,
    dt Nathan & Mary J., Belmont Co., O. (W)
    Ch: Lawrence   b 1897, 7, 23

1896, 11, 24. Lydia A. gct Springville MM (W)
1907, 6, 19. Mrs. C. N. dropped from mbrp (G)
1912, 3, 20. Lila recrq (G)
1913, 3, 19. C. A. recrq (G)
1914, 1, 21. Maude & Don C. recrq (G)
1914, 8, 18. Lawrence N. rocf Springville MM,
    Ia. (W)
1931, 1, 20. Lawrence N. dis mcd (W)

ZIMMERMAN
1902, 1, 22. J. Grace recrq (G)
1905, 7, 19. Grace relrq (G)

ZOOK
----, --, --. Paul L., s Jacob & Sadie E.,
    b 1907,6,6; m Esther LINDLEY, dt Paul &
    Mary, b 1907,7,9 (G)
    Ch: Paul
        Lindley   b 1926, 7, 25

1931, 9, 22. Paul & w, Esther, & s, Paul,
    recrq (G)

    *   *   *   *   *   *   *

FITCH
1896, 1, 23. John recrq (G)

FRAME
1863, 1, 20. Ruanna gct Hickory Grove MM, Ia.
    (W)

JOHNSON
----, --, --. Jonathan & Edna (W)

Ch: Mary Ann
    Judith   b 1831, 5, 23
    William C. " 1833, 5, 24
    Jonathan   " 1835, 5, 23
    Robert L.   " 1838, 1, 18
    Mary T.   " 1842, 9, 18
    Elizabeth
      Ann   " 1845, 12, 7
    Thomas El-
      wood   " 1848, 3, 27
[Mother's & ch's names are same on two cards;
father's name is Jonathan on one card & Micajah
on the other. Micajah appears to be right
name of father. Micajah T. Johnson m Edna
Ladd, 1830, at Wayne Oak MM, Va. & removed to
Short Creek MM with dt, Judith, in 1831]
----, --, --. Wm. C., s Macajah T. & Edna L.,
    b 1833,5,24 d 1901,6,24; married Judith
    C. STANLEY, dt John Jr. & Abigail, b 1835,
    12,22 d 1904,12,9

KENN
1818, 9, 22. Cert rec for Joseph from Peru
    MM, N. Y., dtd 1815,3,22, endorsed to
    Alum Creek MM

LIPSEY
1812, 2, 27. Sarah [Lypsey] m David CADWALA-
    DER

PACKER
----, --, --. Aaron & Rebecca
    Ch: Isaac   b 1812, 2, 29
        Thomas   " 1814, 2, 16
        Sarah   " 1816, 10, 22
        Elisha   " 1821, 10, 30
        Benjamin " 1824, 8, 27
1848, 7, 3. Benjamin d ae 20y

STANTON
1862, 11, 19. William Sr. & Elizabeth dis JW
    (G)

WORRELL
1818, 12, 22. Zebulon rocf Abington MM, Pa.,
    dtd 1818,9,28

RECORDS

AIRES
1832, 10, 25. Ann recrq

ALLEN
1835, 7, 23. Rebecca Packer (form Allen) dis
    mcd
1840, 9, 24. Ester McCormick (form Allen) dis
    (Flushing MM had been rq to treat with her
    on behalf of this mtg)

AULT
1838, 11, 22. Amy (form Battin) con mou

BABB
1850, 11, 21. Martha (form Lewis) dis mcd

BANE
1844, 5, 23. Ann (form Richards) con mcd

BARRETT
1829, 11, 26. Sarah rmt Hiram Pegg

BATTIN
1838, 11, 22. Amy Ault (form Battin) con mou
1839, 8, 22. Rhoda Bishop (form Battin) dis
    mcd
1839, 8, 22. Tacy Ducker (rorm Battin) dis
    mcd
1840, 4, 23. Priscilla [Batton] dis
1855, 2, 22. Ann rocf Deer Creek MM, dtd 1854,
    11,25

BECK
1839, 8, 22. Rachel (form Dutton) con mou

BERRY
1848, 8, 24. July Anna con misconduct

BISHOP
1839, 8, 22. Rhoda (form Battin) dis mcd

BOON
1828, 12, 25. Mary rocf Roaring Creek MM, dtd
    1828,2,13

BRANSON
1834, 9, 25. Mary, minor under care of Martha
    Rankin, recrq
1835, 12, 21. Ruth rocf Sadsbury MM, Pa., dtd
    1835,9,3

BURSON
1830, 2, 25. Maria Morris (form Burson) dis
    mcd

BUTLER
1830, 11, 25. Jonathan, Deborah, David, Ed-
    ward Morris & Hannah Jane, ch Hannah,
    recrq

CADWALADER
1830, 5, 20. Rees rmt Mary Updegraff

CARTER
1835, 4, 23. Susannah (form Tomlinson) dis
    mcd

CLARK
1840, 11, 26. George P. rmt Samaria I. Robin-
    son

COOPER
1844, 5, 23. John rmt Elma Griffith

COPE
1832, 5, 24. Sarah & h & ch, Mary, Grace &
    John, recrq
1832, 8, 23. John rmt Mary Lukens
1835, 9, 24. James rmt Ann E. Lukens
1833, 8, 22. Abigail recrq
1839, 5, 23. Abigail con mou
1840, 4, 23. Sarah Ann (form Gwynn) dis mcd

DAVIS
1840, 6, 25. John Horton & w, Rachel, & a
    minor under their care, Cynthia Horton
    Davis, rocf Marlborough MM, dtd 1840,4,25

DEW
1833, 10, 24. Ruth, dt Elias, gct Plainfield
    MM
1838, 8, 26. Ruth rocf Plainfield MM, dtd
    1838,3,15
1842, 10, 20. Ester Maxwell (form Dew) dis
    mcd (committee to write to Deerfield MM,
    to treat with her on behalf of this mtg)

DILWORTH
1832, 5, 24. Abigail R. Rankin (form Dil-
    worth) con mcd
1844, 12, 26. Jane D. Russell (form Dilworth)
    con mou

DUCKER
1839, 8, 22. Tacy (form Battin) dis mcd

DUTTON
1830, 4, 22. Hannah rocf Baltimore MM for
    Western Dist., dtd 1829,11,12
1831, 5, 21. David & w, Susannah, rocf Hope-
    well MM, dtd 1831,1,6
1833, 4, 26. Rachel recrq
1833, 10, 24. Robert rmt Anna Wharton
1839, 5, 23. Joseph rmt Sarah Mendenhall
1839, 8, 22. Rachel Beck (form Dutton) con
    mou
1849, 11, 22. Anna rmt Levi Townsend

EVANS
1834, 8, 21. George I. rmt Sarah Griffith
1838, 12, 20. Hannah I. rocf Buckingham MM,
    Pa., dtd 1838,8,6
1844, 4, 25. Hannah I. rmt Thomas D. Tomlin-
    son

EVANS, continued
1848, 7, 20. George P. rmt Mary P. Richards
1852, 2, 24. Elizabeth rmt John Scott

FARQUHAR
1854, 11, 23. Hannah Ann (form Walker) rpd
    mcd (residing within limits of Westland
    MM; committee to ask them to treat with
    her on behalf of this mtg)
1855, 5, 24. Hannah Ann con mcd

FOULKE
1831, 4, 21. Jesse M. rmt Mary Yost
1843, 10, 26. Mary [Foulk] rocf Fall Creek MM
1853, 6, 23. Phebe Ann & minor ch, William
    H., Amanda Jane, Sarah Ann, Hannah Mary &
    Francis Elwood, rocf Concord MM, dtd
    1851,12,24

FRENCH
1830, 4, 22. Zemah rmt Joel Wood

GARRETSON
1835, 2, 26. Lavinia rocf Monallen MM, Pa.,
    dtd 1834,2,18

GARRISON
1835, 7, 23. Levina Griffeth (form Garrison)
    con mou

GILBERT
1831, 5, 26. Sarah rocf Deerfield MM, dtd
    1830,11,21. "The mtg is informed that
    she has gone with the Orthadox party".

GOODWIN
1846, 10, 22. Ruth rocf Deerfield MM, dtd
    1846,7,6

GRAY
1832, 7, 27. Thomas & w, Catharine, & ch,
    William, Mary & Atlantic Ocean, rocf
    Stillwater MM, dtd 1832,4,21
1837, 9, 21. Atlantic O. (form Lewis) rpd mcd
1838, 9, 20. Atlantic O. con mcd

GREGG
1829, 1, 22. Nathaniel & fam rocf Somerset MM,
    dtd 1828,5,26, endorsed by Duck Creek MM,
    1828,9,25 & now endorsed to Westland MM
    on rq

GRIFFITH
1833, 6, 20. Hannah rocf Plainfield MM, dtd
    1823,5,23
1834, 8, 21. Sarah rmt George I. Evans
1835, 1, 22. Jane Wilson (form Griffith) con
    mcd
1835, 7, 23. Levina [Griffeth] (form Garri-
    son) con mou
1840, 8, 20. Anna R., Rees L., Charles R. &
    Ruth, minor ch Abraham, dec, & Mary, gct
    Plainfield MM

1841, 4, 22. Elizabeth Ann rmt Ezekiel
    Roberts
1844, 5, 23. Elma rmt John Cooper
1844, 12, 26. Martha Jane gct New Garden MM
1853, 3, 24. Amos L. rmt Sarah D. Tomlinson
1854, 11, 23. Amy rmt Abel M. Walker

GRISELL
1852, 4, 22. Nathan P. rmt Rebecca Street

GUMERY
1830, 3, 25. William [Gummery] & w, Phebe, &
    minor ch, Swithen, Eli Enoch William Han-
    nah Joshua Thomas L. Benjamin & Lavina,
    gct Plainfield MM (9ch)
1837, 4, 20. Ann gct Plainfield MM
1837, 4, 20. Elizabeth & h & dt, Sarah, gct
    Plainfield MM
1837, 4, 20. Hannah gct Plainfield MM
1838, 6, 21. Lydia (form Gumery) con mou
    (Lydia Lewis)
1846, 2, 26. Nancy rocf Plainfield MM, dtd
    1845,12,18
1846, 2, 26. Sarah rocf Plainfield MM, dtd
    1846,1,15

GWYNN
1840, 4, 23. Sarah Ann Cope (form Gwynn) dis
    mcd

HAINES
1830, 5, 20. Hannah (form Tomlinson) con mcd

HEBERLING
1836, 5, 19. Hannah (form Lewis) dis mcd (H)

HOGE
1829, 7, 23. Abigail M. (form Thomas) con
    mcd
1847, 8, 26. Abigail M. rmt Joseph Lawrence

HORTON
1840, 6, 25. John & w, Rachel, & a minor un-
    der their care, Cynthia Horton Davis, rocf
    Marlborough MM, dtd 1840,4,25
1840, 6, 25. Mary J. rocf Marlborough MM, dtd
    1840,4,25

JOB
1830, 5, 20. Ruth M'Millan (form Job) con mcd

JOHN
1845, 9, 25. Mary Ann Tomlinson (form John)
    rpd mcd (a mbr of Westland MM & they rq
    this mtg to treat with her; this mtg rpd
    to them 10-23-1845 that she did not de-
    sire to retain mbrp

KINSEY
1844, 10, 24. Sarah M. (form Medcalf) con mcd

LARKIN
1832, 12, 20. John rmt Sarah Yost

LARKIN, continued
1840, 11, 26. Joseph W. rmt Margaret Yost

LAWRENCE
1847, 8, 26. Joseph rmt Abigail M. Hoge

LEWIS
1830, 5, 20. Lydia rocf Flushing MM, dtd
    1830,3,27
1832, 4, 26. Elma recrq
1836, 5, 19. Hannah Heberling (form Lewis)
    dis mcd (H)
1836, 6, 23. Sarah Martin (form Lewis) dis
    mcd
1837, 9, 21. Atlantic O. Gray (form Lewis)
    rpd mcd
1838, 6, 21. Lydia (form Gumery) con mou
1840, 8, 20. Mary, Jr. gct Stillwater MM
1841, 4, 22. Evan, Rebecca & ch, Charles
    Martha Jesse Elijah, rocf Concord MM, dtd
    1841,4,21
1850, 11, 21. Martha Babb (form Lewis) dis mcd

LUKENS
1832, 8, 23. Mary [Lukkens] rmt John Cope
1835, 9, 24. Ann E. rmt James Cope

McCORMICK
1840, 9, 24. Ester (form Allen) dis mcd
    (Flushing MM had been rq to treat with
    her on behalf of this mtg)

McMILLAN   (form Job)
1830, 5, 20. Ruth [M'Millan]/con mcd
1830, 7, 22. Alice, form dis mcd; now ack-
    nowledgment accepted
1836, 7, 21. Ruth rocf Warrington MM, Pa.,
    dtd 1836,5,19   & w, Rachel,
1836, 12, 22. Mahlon [McMillin]/& minor ch,
    William, Ruth, Hannah & Thomas, rocf
    Little Britain MM, dtd 1836,8,13
1838, 2, 22. Ruth & h gct Deerfield MM
1842, 5, 26. Jane [McMillain] gct Freeport MM,
    dtd 1840,9,24; now returned she having re-
    turned within limits of this mtg
1842, 10, 20. Jacob [McMillen] & w, Sarah, &
    minor ch, Eli, Sarah Ann, Ruth Elizabeth &
    Jacob, rocf Warrington MM, Pa., dtd 1842,
    7,21
1846, 1, 22. Ruth Ann relrq
1851, 1, 23. Ruth Hanna rmt Jeremiah C. Walk-
    er

MARSH
1839, 11, 21. Amos rmt Rebecca Tomlinson

MARTIN
1836, 6, 23. Sarah (form Lewis) dis mcd

MAXWELL
1842, 10, 20. Ester (form Dew) dis mcd (Deer-
    field MM had been rq to treat with her on
    behalf of this mtg)

MEDCALF
1839, 12, 26. Sarah M. rocf Baltimore MM for
    Western Dist., dtd 1839,8,11
1844, 10, 24. Sarah M. Kinsey (form Medcalf)
    con mcd

MENDENHALL
1839, 5, 23. Sarah rmt Joseph Dutton
1843, 10, 26. Asenath rmt Elisha Packer

MICHENER
1832, 4, 26. Lydia gct Goshen MM
1832, 4, 26. Susanna gct Goshen MM
1834, 11, 20. Mary recrq
1843, 11, 23. Sarah Woodward (form Michener)
    con mcd

MORRIS
1830, 2, 25. Maria (form Burson) dis mcd
1833, 9, 26. Eliza Wilson (form Morris) rpd
    mcd (committee appointed to write to
    Deerfield MM within whose limits she now
    resides to rq them to treat with her on
    behalf of this mtg)

NEWPORT
1834, 6, 26. Sarah (form Updegraff) dis mcd;
    now living within limits of Springborough
    MM

PACKER
1831, 9, 22. Ann & ch, Wilson, Lewess & Cal-
    vin H., rocf Centre MM, Pa., dtd 1831,2,
    10
1831, 11, 24. Philena, George, Phebe Ann, Han-
    nah L. & Lydia C., ch Wm. L. & Ann, recrq
1835, 7, 23. Rebecca (form Allen) dis mcd
1838, 7, 26. Sarah P. Shalcross (form Packer)
    con mou
1843, 10, 26. Elisha rmt Asenath Mendenhall
1846, 11, 26. Margaret rocf Westland MM, dtd
    1846,10,22
1852, 12, 23. Ann rocf Deer Creek MM, dtd
    1852,11,27

PARKER
1830, 4, 22. Ann & s, Ephraim I., gct Plain-
    field MM

PARRY
1833, 4, 26. Gibbons & w, Deborah, rocf
    Chester MM, Pa., dtd 1833,2,25

PEARSON
1830, 2, 25. Ann rocf Monallen MM, dtd 1829,
    12,25

PEGG
1829, 11, 26. Hiram rmt Sarah Barrett

PRICE
1829, 12, 24. Joseph & w, Eliza, & dt, Mary,
    rocf Falls MM, Pa., dtd 1829,11,7

PRICE, continued
1839, 4, 25. Eliza & h & ch, Mary, Ellwood &
    Eliza Ann, gct Stillwater MM

RANKIN
1830, 1, 21. Martha rocf Plainfield MM, dtd
    1829,10,22
1832, 5, 24. Abigail R. (form Dilworth) con
    mcd
1834, 9, 25. Mary Branson, minor under care of
RHODES   Martha Rankin, recrq
1834, 12, 25. Mary rocf Plainfield MM, dtd
    1834,8,14

RICHARDS   Bane
1844, 5, 23. Ann/(form Richards) con mcd
1848, 7, 20. Mary P. rmt George P. Evans

ROBB
1840, 6, 25. Ann Eliza (form Thomas) con mou

ROBERTS
1838, 8, 26. Phebe rocf Guynedd MM, Pa., dtd
    1838,8,2
1840, 12, 24. Mary rocf Guynedd MM, Pa., dtd
    1840,12,3
1841, 4, 22. Ezekiel rmt Elizabeth Ann
    Griffith
1845, 8, 21. Phebe/(form Roberts) dis mcd
                Waterman
ROBINSON
1829, 2, 26. Thomas & w, Anna, & ch, Joseph
    Walker, Charles Branson, Rebecca, Thomas
    Chalkley & Emily, rocf Radnor MM, dtd 1828,
    12,11
1839, 6, 20. Elizabeth rocf Gwynedd MM, Pa.,
    dtd 1839,5,30
1840, 11, 26. Samaria I. rmt George P. Clark
1844, 1, 25. Elizabeth relrq

RUSSELL
1844, 12, 26. Jane D. (form Dilworth) con mou

SCHOLFIELD
1845, 6, 26. Margaret Ann [Schofield] & h &
    ch, Joseph, Clark, Robert Marcus, David
    & Rebecca Jane, rocf Salem MM, dtd 1845,2,
    19
1847, 6, 24. Margaret Ann & h & ch rqct Salem
    MM

SCHOOLEY
1853, 9, 22. Sarah, dt Jemima Webster, con
    mcd

SCOTT
1852, 2, 24. John rmt Elizabeth Evans

SHALCROSS
1838, 7, 26. Sarah P. (form Packer) con mou

SHOEMAKER
1838, 7, 26. Thomas & w, Abi, & minor ch, Ed-

win, Alfred, Isaac B., Ann & Elizabeth
    T., rocf Little Britain MM, held at Dru-
    more, dtd 1838,6,16

SMITH
1831, 7, 21. Lydia (form Smith) con mcd
    (Lydia Wildman)
1837, 9, 21. Jeretha dis
1845, 11, 20. David G.rmt Hannah W. Waterman

STEPHENS
1853, 6, 23. Rebecca rmt Thomas M. Wells

STREET
1831, 12, 22. Rachel rmt Samuel Tomlinson
1833, 2, 21. Elma ltm Abel Wiley
1835, 4, 26. Agness rocf Stillwater MM, dtd
    1833,1,15
1852, 4, 22. Rebecca rmt Nathan P. Grisell

THOMAS
1829, 7, 23. Abigail M. Hoge (form Thomas)
    con mcd
1835, 8, 20. Elizabeth [Tomas] gct Dear-
    field MM
1840, 6, 25. Ann Eliza (form Thomas) con mou
    (Ann Eliza Robb)
1849, 6, 21. Avis gct Green Plain MM

THOMPSON
1832, 6, 21. Elizabeth rocf Deerfield MM,
    dtd 1832,5,16

TOMLINSON   Haines
1830, 5, 20. Hannah/(form Tomlinson) con mcd
1831, 12, 22. Samuel rmt Rachel Street
1835, 4, 23. Susannah/(form Tomlinson) dis
    mcd   Carter
1835, 12, 21. Aletta rocf Smithfield MM, dtd
    1835,12,22 (?)
1839, 11, 21. Rebecca rmt Amos Marsh
1844, 4, 25. Thomas D. rmt Hannah I. Evans
1845, 9, 25. Mary Ann (form John) rpd mcd
    (a mbr of Westland MM & they rq this mtg
    to treat with her; this mtg rpd to them
    1845,10,23 that she did not desire to re-
    tain her mbrp)
1847, 7, 22. Deborah W. recrq
1853, 3, 24. Sarah D. rmt Amos L. Griffith

TOWNSEND
1849, 11, 22. Levi rmt Anna Dutton

UPDEGRAFF
1830, 5, 20. Mary rmt Rees Cadwalader
1834, 6, 26. Sarah Newport (form Updegraff)
    dis mcd (now living within limits of
    Springborough MM

VANHORN
1834, 4, 24. Charles & w, Sarah, & ch,
    George W., James M., Robert & Mary, rocf
    Makefield MM

VICKERS
1841, 3, 25. Joseph & w, Elizabeth P., & minor ch, Jonathan & Joseph P., rocf Uwchlan MM, Pa., dtd 1840,6,7
1841, 4, 22. Jemima rocf Concord MM, dtd 1841,4,21

WALDON
1853, 10, 20. Rachel rocf Freaport MM, dtd 1853,7,23

WALKER
1840, 8, 20. Joel & w, Mary, & ch, Lewis M., Isaac John, Elias H., Abel, Jeremiah C., Hannah Ann, Rachel M. & Joel Aaron, rocf Smithfield MM, dtd 1840,6,23
1851, 1, 23. Jeremiah C. rmt Ruth Hannah McMillan
1854, 11, 23. Abel M. rmt Amy Griffith
1854, 11, 23. Hannah Ann Farquhar (form Walker) rpd mcd (residing within limits of Westland MM; committee to ask them to treat with her on behalf of this mtg

WATERMAN
1845, 8, 21. Phebe (form Roberts) dis mcd
1845, 11, 20. Hannah W. rmt David G. Smith

WEBSTER
1837, 4, 20. Naylor & w, Jemima M., & ch, Abigail P., Sarah C. & Hannah, rocf Sadsbury MM, dtd 1837,2,8
1853, 9, 22. Sarah Schooley, dt Jemima Webster, con mcd
1854, 2, 3. Jemima dis allowing her dt, Sarah, to be m by a Justice of the Peace & joining the Progressive Friends

WELLS
1853, 6, 23. Thomas M. rmt Rebecca Stephens

WHARTON
1833, 10, 24. Anna rmt Robert Dutton

WHEELER
1846, 2, 26. Hannah rocf Plainfield MM, dtd 1845,12,18

WILDMAN
1829, 9, 24. Joseph & w, Elizabeth, & ch, Walter B., Mary, Joshua, Martha & Solomon, rocf Falls MM, dtd 1829,8,8
1831, 7, 21. Lydia (form Smith) con mcd
1840, 10, 22. Walter B. & w, Lydia, & ch, Joseph, Hannah Jane, Thomas Smith & David Baker, gct Fall Creek MM

WILEY
1833, 2, 21. Abel ltm Gulia Elma Street

WILSON
1833, 2, 21. Mary recrq
1833, 9, 26. Eliza (form Morris) rpd mcd (Committee appointed to write to Deerfield MM within whose limits she now resides, to rq them to treat with her on behalf of this mtg
1835, 1, 22. Jane (form Griffith) con mcd
1837, 3, 23. Rachel (form Guyin) dis mcd

WOOD
1830, 4, 22. Joel rmt Zemah French

WOODWARD
1843, 11, 23. Sarah (form Michener) con mcd

YOST
1831, 4, 21. Mary rmt Jesse M. Foulke
1832, 12, 20. Sarah rmt John Larkin
1840, 11, 26. Margaret rmt Joseph W. Larkin

PLAINFIELD MONTHLY MEETING

Plainfield Monthly Meeting, Belmont County, Ohio, was set off from Concord Monthly Meeting, 3rd Mo. 26th, 1828, by Short Creek Quarterly Meeting and was composed of Plainfield and Flushing Preparative Meetings.

This meeting was later divided in such a way by separations that the records are found among Hicksite, Orthodox and Conservative records.

RECORDS

ADAMS
1809, 2, 25. Lydia rocf Hopewell MM, dtd 1808,10,7

AGNEW
1820, 5, 25. Hannah (form Tuder) dis mcd

AIRY
1838, 5, 17. Phebe & s, Robert Cook, rocf Green St. MM, Phila., Pa., dtd 1838,3,22 (H)

ALEXANDER
1845, 2, 13. James rocf New Garden MM, dtd 1844,11,21 (H)

ALLEN
1822, 3, 27. Moses, s Benjamin & Hannah, Belmont Co., O.; m in St. Clairsville, Jane FOULKE, dt Isachar & Jane, Belmont Co., O.
1834, 10, 22. Elizabeth m Joseph BOND (H)

1811, 12, 28. Benjamin & w, Hannah, & ch, Moses, Unice, Daniel, Mary, Jehu, Hannah & Benjamin, rocf Hopewell MM, dtd 1811,10, 7
1812, 1, 25. Elizabeth rocf Hopewell MM, dtd 1811,10,7
1826, 4, 20. Moses & w, Jane, & ch, William & Walton, gct Somerset MM
1827, 5, 24. Daniel H. gct Flushing MM
1830, 6, 24. Daniel A. & w, Eliza, & ch, Amos G. & Benjamin, rocf Flushing MM, dtd 1830,5,22 (H)
1835, 3, 19. Jehu gct Flushing MM, to m Mary Ann Garretson (H)
1836, 1, 14. Mary Ann rocf Flushing MM, dtd 1835,9,26 (H)
1837, 11, 15. Hannah Carter (form Allen) dis mcd (H)
1839, 8, 15. Daniel H. & w, Eliza, & ch, Amos G., Benjamin, Lindley, Mary Ann, Narcissa & Louisa, gct Milford MM, Ind. (H)
1839, 8, 15. Jehu & w, Mary Ann, & ch, Mary & Rebecca, gct Milford MM, Ind. (H)
1847, 1, 14. Benjamin dis mcd (H)
1850, 4, 18. Mary Lewis (form Allen) con mcd (H)
1878, 3, 14. Eunice recrq (H)
1885, 3, --. Eunice Cash (form Allen) con mcd (H)

ASKEW
1817, 11, 26. Parker, s Parker & Hannah, Belmont Co., O.; m in St. Clairsville, Hannah WILSON, dt Isaac & Rebeckah, Belmont Co., O.
1836, 9, 29. Parker, s Parker & Hannah, Belmont Co., O.; m in Plainfield MH, Rebecca VAIL, dt Benj. & Rebecca, Belmont Co., O.
Ch: Benjamin b 1837, 7, 30

Ch: Mary b 1841, 4, 19
1840, 6, 3. Hannah m John D. WRIGHT
1847, 10, 21. Rebecca W. m Cornelius DEWEES
1860, 10, 3. Martha d bur Plainfield

1817, 11, 20. Parker Jr. rocf Wilmington MM, Del., dtd 1817,10,3
1837, 8, 23. Sarah Grove (form Askew) dis mcd
1839, 8, 21. Joseph dis disunity
1843, 7, 19. Rebecca Heaton (form Askew) dis mcd
1845, 5, 21. Elizabeth Neiswanger (form Askew) dis mcd
1847, 3, 24. Martha Tidball (form Askew) dis mcd
1848, 5, 24. William dis disunity
1850, 6, 19. Samuel dis mcd
1852, 12, 22. Isaac dis disunity
1853, 3, 23. Clarissa Neiswanger (form Askew) dis mcd
1853, 4, 20. Margaret dis disunity
1853, 5, 27. Ann & Hannah dis disunity

ATHERTON
1814, 9, 1. Boaz & w, Mary, rocf Westland MM, Pa., dtd 1814,4,23

BABB
1824, 4, 22. Ann (form Rodgers) dis mcd

BAILEY
1819, 12, 1. Henry, s Emmor & Elizabeth, Belmont Co., O.; m in St. Clairsville, Mary FOULKE, dt Isachar & Jane, Belmont Co., O.
1857, 12, 24. Tabitha m Eli PATTERSON

1815, 2, 25. Elizabeth (form Craft) dis mcd & jas
1820, 4, 20. Henry rocf Short Creek MM, O., dtd 1820,4,18
1822, 3, 21. Henry & w, Mary, & ch, Elizabeth & Joel, gct Short Creek MM, O.
1829, 7, 23. Emmor & w, Elizabeth, & ch, Emmor, Martha & Ann, rocf Short Creek MM, O., dtd 1828,10,21, end by Flushing MM (H)
1830, 3, 25. Emmer & w, Elizabeth, & ch, Emmor, Martha & Ann, gct Springborough MM(H)
1850, 5, 16. Lot Gregg gct Salem MM, to m Hannah Bailey (H)
1854, 6, 13. Maria A. (form Frazier) con mcd (H)
1857, 11, 25. Tabitha rocf Chesterfield MM, dtd 1857,10,17
1857, 11, 25. Elwood rocf Chesterfield MM, dtd 1857,10,17
1857, 11, 25. Robert & Mary Ann, minors, rocf Chesterfield MM, dtd 1857,10,17
1891, 3, 19. Maria E. gct Lincoln, Neb. Executive Mtg (H)

BAKER
1823, 10, 23. Cert rec for Amos & w, Sarah, & ch, George H., John T., Mary, Joseph,

BAKER, continued
    Elizabeth & Lydia from Chester MM, Pa.,
    dtd 1823,8,25, end to Fall Creek MM

BALDWIN
1808, 5, 28. Mary, Thomas, David & Rees
    Ellis, ch Margaret, rocf Hopewell MM, end
    by Concord MM, 1808,2,1
1809, 9, 23. Margaret & ch, Thomas, Davis &
    Rees Ellis, gct Fairfield MM
1872, 10, 17. Priscilla (form White) con mcd
    (H)

BALES
1821, 5, 24. Thomas recrq

BALLANGER.
1818, 6, 25. James & w, Rebecca, & s, John,
    rocf Little Egg Harbor MM, dtd 1818,4,9

BARBER
1817, 10, 29. Abraham, s Samuel & Ann, Harri-
    son Co., O.; m in Flushing MH, Rachel
    FRAME, dt Benjamin & Elizabeth, Belmont
    Co., O.

1818, 1, 22. Rachel gct Short Creek MM, O.

BARNES
1813, 10, 23. James recrq
1814, 1, 22. James gct Stillwater MM
1822, 1, 24. David gct Stillwater MM

BARRETT
1813, 2, 27. Thomas & w, Mary, & dt, Esther,
    Amy, Ann, Melinda & Elizabeth, recrq
1813, 2, 27. Thomas & w, Margaret, & ch,
    Warden, Esther, Amy, Baldwin, Ann, Arthur,
    Belinda & Rachel, recrq
1818, 7, 23. David & w, Winnefred, & ch,
    William, Thomas, Elizabeth, Uriah, Albert
    & Sarah, recrq
1883, 5, 17. Rosa B. (form White) con mcd (H)

BATTEY
1856, 1, 11. Rachel E. (form Pickering) con
    mcd (H)
1856, 2, 14. Rachel E. [Batty] (form Picker-
    ing) gct Maple Grove MM, Pa. (H)

BATTON
1840, 9, 17. Samuel & w, Sarah, rocf Short
    Creek MM, O., dtd 1840,8,20 (H)
1840, 10, 15. Cert rec for Samuel & w, Sarah,
    returned to Short Creek MM (H)

BEAN
1818, 7, 23. Levi rocf Middleton MM, dtd
    1818,3,16
1828, 4, 24. Levi [Beans] dis disunity

BEARD
1844, 1, 18. Rebecca relrq (H)

1844, 2, 15. Rebecca dis jas (H)

BECK
1818, 8, 20. Jesse & w, Elizabeth, rocf
    Stillwater MM, dtd 1818,6,27
1821, 12, 20. Samuel Craft gct Somerset MM,
    to m Ann Beck
1822, 9, 26. Samuel Craft gct Sommerset MM,
    to m Lydia Beck

BEESON
1817, 10, 29. Anna m Amos SMITH

BELANGEE
1837, 9, 20. Mary dis jH
1845, 1, 16. John gct Clear Creek MM, Ill.(H)
1845, 2, 13. James, Rebecca & Aaron gct Clear
    Creek MM, Ill. (H)
1882, 5, 18. Jane Wilson P. [Bellangee] (form
    Pennington) con mcd (H)
1883, 6, 14. Jane Penington gct Clear Creek
    MM, Ill. (H)

BELL
1864, 6, 16. Mary C. P. (form Pickering) con
    mcd (H)

BERT
1818, 7, 23. Daniel & w, Sarah, rocf Short
    Creek MM, O., dtd 1818,6,23

BEVAN
1818, 2, 4. Stacy, s Samuel & Naomi, Bel-
    mont Co., O.; m in Sinclairsville, Eunice
    FAWCETT, dt Thomas & Martha, Belmont Co.,
    O.

1817, 6, 26. Stacy Jr. recrq

BILLINGSBY
1815, 9, 27. William [Billingsly], s James &
    Margaret, Belmont Co., O.; m in Flushing
    MH, Sarah JONES, dt James & Grace

1813, 11, 27. William recrq
1814, 4, 23. Ruth recrq

BLACKLEDGE
1828, 7, 2. Sarah m Samuel PICKERING (H)

1816, 1, 26. Mary rocf Goshen MM, dtd 1815,
    8,2, end by Westland MM
1817, 6, 20. Mary gct Salem MM
1818, 12, 24. Thomas [Blacklidge] rocf Rich-
    land MM, Pa., dtd 1818,9,4
1824, 8, 26. Sarah [Blacklidge] & Phebe rec-
    rq

BLOCKSOME
1809, 8, 26. William & w, Mary, & ch, James,
    Ann, Elizabeth, Maria, Priscilla & Sarah,
    gct Stillwater MM

BOGUE
1812, 1, 2. Jonathan, s Mark & Sarah, Tus-
    caraways Co., O.; m in Big Stillwater, Sa-
    rah EASLEY, dt Daniel & Edith, Tuscaraways
    Co., O.
1813, 2, 4. Huldah m Wm. SMITH
1813, 4, 9. Job, s Robert & Miriam, Harrison
    Co., O.; m in Notingham, Mary Ann EASLEY,
    dt Daniel & Edith, Harrison Co., O.

1809, 5, 27. Job gct Plymouth MM
1809, 12, 23. Jonathan rocf Plymouth MM, dtd
    1809,9,16
1812, 4, 25. Job rocf Plymouth MM, dtd 1812, [5,16
1812, 6, 27. Huldah rocf Plymouth MM, dtd
    1812,5,16
1816, 3, 22. Jonathan & w, Sarah, & ch, Mary
    Ann & Ruth, gct Stillwater MM

BOND
1820, 3, 29. Joseph, s Allen & Sarah, Belmont
    Co., O.; m in Goshen MH, Ester GREGG, dt
    Jacob & Mary, Belmont Co., O.
    Joseph m 2nd 1834,10,22 in Goshen MH,
    Elizabeth ALLEN, dt Benjamin & Hannah, Bel-
    mont Co., O.
1826, 3, 8. Rebecca m James BROOMHALL

1821, 3, 22. Abner dis disunity
1824, 7, 22. John dis
1829, 11, 26. Elizabeth Smith (form Bond) con
    mcd (H)
1837, 4, 13. Allen Jr. dis mcd (H)
1844, 7, 24. Jonathan dis disunity
1848, 5, 18. Alcinda Burr (form Bond) dis
    mcd (H)

BONSEL
1847, 3, 18. Mary Jane (form Horner) dis mcd
    (H)

BOSWELL
1812, 10, 24. Martha rocf Short Creek MM, dtd
    1812,6,23

BOWLES
1822, 3, 27. Thomas [Bowls], s Thos. & Eliza-
    beth, Belmont Co., O.; m in Goshen MH,
    Amy NICHOLS, dt Solomon & Hannah, Belmont
    Co., O.

1828, 4, 24. Thomas dis mcd
1828, 7, 24. Hannah (form Strahl) dis mcd(H)
1845, 3, 13. John con mcd (H)
1845, 8, 20. John dis mcd

BOYD
1841, 6, 23. Elizabeth (form Price) dis mcd

BRADRICK
1812, 8, 22. Beulah gct Miami MM

BRANSON
1818, 8, 26. Smith, s Isaac & Jane, Belmont

Co., O.; m Jane FRAME, dt Benjamin &
    Elizabeth, Belmont Co., O.
----, --, --. David & Lydia
    Ch: Amy   b 1820,12,29
        Smith   " 1822, 10, 12
        Lydia Jane " 1826, 8, 27
        Elizabeth " 1831, 12, 6
1825, 6, 9. Thomas, s Abraham & Sarah, Bel-
    mont Co., O.; m in Plainfield MH, Anna
    VAIL, dt Benjamin & Rebecca, Belmont Co.,
    O.
1838, 9, 27. Lydia m John VANLAW
1840, 2, 19. Elizabeth d ae 8 bur Plainfield
1840, 12, 31. Amy m Thos. VANLAW

1813, 6, 26. Rees & w, Ruth, & ch, Abraham &
    Maria, rocf Hopewell MM, dtd 1813,5,6, al-
    so a dt, Elizabeth, b since cert granted
1815, 2, 25. John & w, Abigail, & ch, Mariam,
    Nancy, Asa, & Eliza, rocf Hopewell MM, Va.,
    dtd 1814,8,12
1816, 4, 26. Ruth & ch, Eliza & William, gct
    Sadsbury MM
1816, 7, 26. Mary (form Pickering) dis mcd
1817, 11, 20. Abraham & Mariah, minors, gct
    Hopewell MM
1818, 5, 21. Smith recrq
1825, 8, 25. Anna gct Concord MM
1841, 9, 22. Smith & Lydia Jane, ch Lydia
    Vanlaw, gct Chesterfield MM
1862, 11, 13. Hannah Priscilla (form Gregg)
    con mcd (H)
1870, 7, 14. Isaac Elsworth & Josephine, ch
    Pickering, recrq (H)
1876, 9, --. Hannah Priscilla Hutchison (form
    Branson) con mcd (H)

BREWER
1813, 2, 29. Rachel rocf Short Creek MM, dtd
    1812,12,22
1813, 6, 26. Mary & ch, John, Richard, Mary,
    Martha, Ann & Hannah, rocf Short Creek MM,
    O., dtd 1813,2,23
1815, 3, 25. Mary dis disunity

BRIGGS
1818, 5, 21. William & w, Esther, & ch, Ma-
    riah, Job, Jonathan, Rebecca M., William &
    Henry, rocf Smithfield MM, dtd 1818,4,20
1818, 5, 21. Samuel rocf Smithfield MM, dtd
    1818,4,20
1818, 6, 25. Israel & w, Mary, & ch, Esther
    & Ann, rocf Stillwater MM, dtd 1818,4,25
1818, 7, 23. George Green rocf Short Creek
    MM, O., dtd 1818,7,21
1857, 4, 22. Jonathan & w, Elizabeth, & ch,
    William, Sarah M., Benjamin, Josiah &
    Robert, rocf Flushing MM, dtd 1857,3,26
1857, 4, 22. George rocf Flushing MM, dtd
    1857,3,26
1857, 4, 22. Mary rocf Flushing MM, dtd
    1857,3,26
1858, 4, 21. Robert M. dis mcd

BRIGGS, continued
1864, 8, 24. Jonathan & w, Elizabeth, & ch,
     Benjamin & Josiah, gct Stillwater MM
1864, 8, 24. George gct Stillwater MM
1864, 8, 24. Mary & Sarah M. gct Stillwater
     MM

BROCK
1816, 8, 20. Catherine m Wm. PEARSON

1812, 2, 22. Stephen rst on consent of Hope-
     well MM
1814, 4, 23. Mary, Catharine, Ann, John,
     David, Jane & Sarah, ch Stephen, recrq
1814, 4, 23. Ann recrq
1818, 8, 20. Elizabeth rocf Stillwater MM,
     dtd 1818,6,27

BROOMHALL
1818, 4, 1. Barclay, s Enos & Phebe, Belmont
     Co., O.; m in Goshen MH, Rebeckah EWERS,
     dt Wm. & Amy, Belmont Co., O.
1826, 3, 8. James, s Enos & Phebe, Belmont
     Co., O.; m in Goshen MH, Rebecca BOND, dt
     Allen & Sarah, Belmont Co., O.

1811, 7, 27. Isaac dis disunity
1820, 2, 24. Orpha rocf Kennet MM, Pa., dtd
     1820,1,4
1823, 7, 24. Martha Hoover (form Broomhall)
     dis mcd
1824, 5, 20. Jane Wright (form Broomhall)
     dis mcd
1824, 6, 24. Joanna McKisson (form Broomhall)
     dis mcd
1824, 7, 22. Joanna W. Kizser (form Broom-
     hall) dis mcd
1826, 8, 24. Susanna Moore (form Broomhall)
     dis mcd
1828, 10, 23. Barkley & w, Rebecca, & ch,
     William E., Enos J., Arminda & Amy J., gct
     Stillwater MM (H)
1832, 12, 20. Orpha gct Stillwater MM (H)
1849, 6, 14. Elihu dis (H)
1849, 6, 14. Elizabeth Gregg (form Broomhall)
     dis mcd (H)
1859, 10, 13. Olinda Palmer (form Broomhall)
     con mcd (H)

BROWN
1837, 3, 30. John C., s Jos. & Phebe; m in
     Plainfield MH, Abigail WALTER, dt Wm. &
     Phebe, Belmont Co., O.

1808, 4, 23. Elizabeth (form Pickering) dis
     mcd
1813, 6, 26. Lydia (form Hoge) dis mcd
1820, 5, 25. Pleasant (form Hough) dis mcd
1837, 1, 25. John C. rocf Newgarden MM, Pa.,
     dtd 1836,11,9
1838, 1, 24. John C. & w, Abigail, gct Ches-
     terfield MM
1848, 3, 16. Sarah Hoge Jr. gct Stillwater

MM, to m Agnes Ann Brown (H)
1860, 6, 14. Catharine gct Miami MM, O.;
     cert returned 1861,8,15 "she was united
     with those called Spiritualists" (H)
1882, 1, 19. Catharine gct Miami MM, O. (H)

BUFKINS
1809, 7, 26. Thomas, s Samuel & Bathsheba,
     Belmont Co., O.; m in Flushing MH, Ruth
     DAWSON, dt John & Sarah CADWALLADER,
     Tushar Co.

BUNDY
1811, 1, 26. Susanna rocf Concord MM, dtd
     1810,11,22
1812, 2, 22. Susanna gct Concord MM
1833, 5, 23. Sarah con mcd (H)
1833, 6, 20. Sarah & s, Charles, gct Concord
     MM (H)

BUNKER
1813, 5, 22. Peleg & w, Hannah, & ch, Elihu,
     Lucy & Reuben, rocf Peru MM, dtd 1812,9,24
     end by Short Creek MM, 1813,4,20
1814, 12, 24. Peleg & w, Hannah, & ch, Elihu,
     Lucy, Reuben & Isaac, gct Short Creek MM,
     O.

BURK
1811, 10, 26. Rachel con mcd

BURR
1853, 2, 24. Sarah m Wm. STANTON (H)

1837, 1, 19. Sarah Jr. rocf Short Creek MM,
     dtd 1836,11,21 (H)
1837, 2, 16. William & w, Sarah, & ch, Mer-
     riah & Milton, rocf Short Creek MM, O.,
     dtd 1836,12,22 (H)
1837, 3, 16. Ruthann rocf Short Creek MM,
     dtd 1836,11,24 (H)
1847, 8, 19. Milton J. dis disunity (H)
1848, 5, 18. Alcinda (form Bond) dis mcd (H)
1855, 4, 19. Merrick B. con mcd (H)

BURT
1818, 8, 20. Sarah rocf Short Creek MM, O.,
     dtd 1818,6,23

BYE
1818, 7, 23. Jonathan & w, Mary, & ch,
     Joshua, rocf Short Creek MM, O., dtd
     1818,6,23

CADWALADER
1808, 4, 23. Elizabeth rocf Redstone MM, dtd
     1807,12,14
1808, 6, 25. Isaac & w, Elizabeth, rocf Red-
     stone MM, end by Concord MM, 1807,4,12
1808, 8, 27. John & w, Ruth, & ch, Ann, Sa-
     rah & Isaac, rocf Plymouth MM, dtd 1808,
     8,20
1808, 8, 26. Ruth rocf Plymouth MM, dtd

CADWALADER, continued
1808,8,20
1809, 2, 25. Jno. & w, Sarah, rocf Redstone
   MM, dtd 1809,2,3
1809, 6, 24. Joseph rocf Redstone MM, dtd
   1809,6,2
1809, 11, 25. Joseph gct Short Creek MM, O.,
   to m Christian Hall
1810, 4, 28. David rocf Redstone MM, dtd
   1809,9,29
1810, 10, 27. Christina rocf Short Creek MM,
   O., dtd 1810,7,24
1812, 1, 25. David gct Short Creek MM, O.,
   to m Sarah Lipsey
1812, 6, 27. Sarah rocf Short Creek MM, O.,
   dtd 1812,5,19
1813, 12, 25. Rees & w, Hannah, & ch, Dillon
   & Alfred, rocf Redstone MM, dtd 1813,10,1

CARLETON
1824, 4, 28. Mary m Nathan CRAWFORD
1826, 8, 29. Hannah m Wm. GREGG

1819, 3, 25. Abner [Carlton] recrq
1820, 1, 20. Mark [Carlton] & w, Bulah, rocf
   Kennet MM, Pa., dtd 1819,12,7
1824, 1, 22. Hannah & Mary [Carlton] recrq
1825, 7, 21. Abner dis mcd

CARPENTER
1812, 2, 22. Atlantic (form Fawcett) dis jas
   & mcd
1816, 7, 26. Susannah (form Fawcett) dis mcd

CARROLL
1824, 9, 23. Thomas & w, Ann L., & s, Foster
   W., rocf New Garden MM, dtd 1824,7,22
1843, 4, 19. Foster W. & Robert W., minor ch
   Thomas & Ann, gct Cincinnati MM
1839, 8, 15. Cert rec for Joseph & w, Elizabeth, & ch (10 not named) from New Garden
   MM, dtd 1839,10,25, end to Fall Creek MM(H)
1841, 10, 14. Thomas [Carrol] & w, Ann, &
   ch, William Foster, Robert & Laura A.,
   gct Cincinnati MM (H)

CARSON
1818, 1, 22. Andrew & w, Isabel, & ch, Robert,
   Catharine, John, Rachel, Andrew, Isabel &
   Jeremiah, rocf Plymouth MM, dtd 1817,9,22
1818, 5, 21. Amy rocf Plymouth MM, dtd 1817,9,
CARTER   [22
1819, 3, 31. Richard, s Daniel & Margery,
   Belmont Co., O.; m in St. Clairsville,
   Mary FAWCETT, dt Thos. & Martha, Belmont
   Co., O.

1819, 3, 25. Richard rocf Concord MM, dtd
   1819,2,24
1824, 4, 22. Richard gct Concord MM
1837, 11, 15. Hannah (form Allen) dis mcd (H)

CARVER
1815, 9, 28. Rebekah m John C. Thompson

1816, 3, 22. John gct Westland MM, Pa., to
   m Abigail Millison
1816, 6, 21. Abigail rocf Westland MM, dtd
   1816,5,22
1818, 7, 23. Elizabeth Covington (Coffington
   on women's record) (form Carver) dis mcd

CASH
1885, 3, --. Eunice (form Allen) con mcd (H)

CHALFANT
1818, 9, 24. Robert & w, Elizabeth, & s,
   Millera, rocf Kennet MM, Pa., dtd 1818,6,
   2
1820, 11, 23. Lydia rocf Fallowfield MM, Pa.,
   dtd 1820,9,8
1821, 1, 25. Cert rec for Jesse & w, Rachel
   from Fallowfield MM, Pa., dtd 1820,9,8,
   end to Stillwater MM
1821, 1, 25. Cert rec for Ezekiel & Joel from
   Fallowfield MM, Pa., dtd 1820,9,8, end to
   Stillwater MM
1821, 4, 26. Cert rec for Jesse from Fallowfield MM, Pa., dtd 1820,9,3, end to Stillwater MM
1821, 5, 24. Lydia gct Stillwater MM
1843, 8, 23. Phebe Satterthwait (form Chalfant) dis mcd
1843, 9, 20. Rachel & Mary dis jH
1843, 9, 20. Miller dis mcd
1843, 10, 25. Milton dis disunity
1845, 3, 13. Abel & Hannah rocf Redstone MM,
   dtd 1844,12,25 (H)
1845, 4, 17. Milton dis mcd (H)
1847, 9, 16. Miller dis mcd (H)
1848, 12, 14. Mary dis (H)
1852, 5, 13. Ephraim dis jas (H)
1852, 5, 19. Rachel N. Smith (form Chalfant)
   con mcd (H)
1852, 6, 19. Rachel Smith (form Chalfant)
   con mcd (H)
1853, 11, 17. Lydia Malory (form Chalfant)
   dis mcd (H)
1864, 4, 16. Abel & w, Hannah, gct Green
   Plain MM, O.

CHAMBERLAIN
1841, 5, 28. Elizabeth d ae 60 bur St. Clairsville

1818, 11, 26. Elizabeth & ch, John, William,
   Hannah, Ann & James, rocf Sadsbury MM,
   dtd 1818,7,8
1836, 7. 20. William dis disunity
1836, 11, 23. John dis disunity [lain) dis mcd
1837, 4, 24. Hannah Greenlief (form Chamber
1837, 6, 21. Ann dis disunity
1842, 1, 19. Mary Wilson (form Chamberlain)
   dis disunity

CHAMBERS

1823, 10, 2. John, s Samuel & Deborah, Belmont Co., O.; m in Plainfield MH, Ann
COMBS, dt Benj. & Charity, Belmont Co., O.

----, --, --. Samuel & Tamer
    Ch: Deborah   b 1831, 11, 19
        William   " 1833, 10, 8
        Thomas   " 1836, 3, 18
1840, 5, 9. Deborah d ae 70
1843, 5, 30. Mary m Wm. LLEWELLYN
1845, 3, 20. Margaret m David COULSON
1846, 11, 8. Samuel d ae 35 bur Knox Co.

1815, 1, 28. Samuel & w, Deborah, & ch, John,
Robert, Deborah, Samuel, Margaret, Mary &
James, rocf Butternut MM, N. Y., dtd 1814,
5,4, end by New Garden MM, 1814,10,13
1817, 9, 25. James & w, Mary, & ch, Ann,
Thomas, Ellen, Elizabeth & James, rocf
New Garden MM, dtd 1817,4,17
1818, 10, 22. Thomas rocf Butternut MM, dtd
1818,3,12
1819, 4, 22. James & w, Mary, & ch gct New
Garden MM
1820, 2, 24. John gct Creek MM, N. Y.
1821, 12, 20. Robert dis mcd
1822, 10, 24. John rocf Creek MM, N. Y., dtd
1822,8,16
1823, 12, 25. John & w, Mary Ann, gct Allum
Creek MM
1826, 7, 20. Samuel gct Sandy Spring MM, to
m Tamer Winder
1827, 3, 22. Tamer rocf Sandy Spring MM, dtd
1827,1,26
1836, 10, 19. Samuel dis disunity
1847, 7, 21. Tamar & ch, Margaret, Ann, Deborah, William, Thomas, Levi, Benjamin,
Samuel & Mary, gct Flushing MM

CHANDLER

1812, 8, 22. Eli rocf Redstone MM, dtd 1812,
7,3
1816, 10, 24. Enoch & w, Hannah, rocf Redstone MM, dtd 1816,4,26
1816, 12, 26. Mary rocf Redstone MM, dtd 1816,
6,26
1816, 12, 26. Hannah rocf Redstone MM, dtd
1816,4,24
1817, 6, 26. Enoch Jr. rocf Westland MM, dtd
1817,4,24
1819, 7, 22. Eli dis mcd
1823, 1, 23. Eli rst at Flushing MM on consent
of this mtg
1841, 8, 19. Sarah Jane (form Hogue) con mcd
(H)

CHAPLINE

1852, 9, 16. Margaret S. (form Thomas) con
mcd (H)

CHICKEN

1815, 10, 28. Daniel & w, Elenor, & ch, John,
Daniel, David & Mary, rocf Duck Creek MM,

dtd 1815,7,8

CHRISTY

1852, 7, 15. Sarah Jane (form Pickering) con
mcd (H)

CLARK

1839, 3, 15. Margaret Ann m Joshua SCHOFIELD
(H)
1843, 6, 22. Hugh P., s Robert & Jane, Belmont Co., O.; m in home of John Piggott,
Lydia Ann FITZSIMMONS, dt Stephen & Hannah, Morgan Co., O. (H)
1843, 10, 26. Isaac N., s Robert & Jane, Belmont Co., O.; m in home of Mary Hustler,
Elizabeth HUSTLER, dt John & Mary, Belmont
Co., O. (H)

1830, 10, 21. Jane recrq (H)
1831, 10, 20. Robert recrq (H)
1831, 10, 20. Margaret & Elizabeth, ch Jane,
recrq (H)
1835, 10, 15. George, minor, gct Stillwater
MM (H)
1844, 2, 21. Elizabeth (form Hustler) dis mcd
1844, 7, 18. Lydia Ann recrq (H)
1859, 6, 16. Elizabeth W. rocf Green St. MM,
Phila., Pa., dtd 1859,5,19 (H)
1859, 9, 15. Robert & w, Jane, gct Short
Creek MM, O. (H)
1866, 9, 13. Elizabeth W. gct Phila. MM, Pa.
(H)

CLOSE

1835, 5, 14. Mary (form Smith) dis mcd (H)

COBBS

1827, 9, 20. Eliza rocf Marlborough MM, dtd
1827,7,31

COBLE

1829, 4, 23. Eliza McClarey (form Coble) dis
mcd (H)

COFFEE

1811, 10, 30. Rachel [Coffey] m Absalom HOGE
1814, 9, 26. John, s John & Rachel, Belmont
Co., O.; m in Plainfield MH, Alice SPEN-
CER, dt John & Lydia, Belmont Co., O.
1827, 8, 13. Isaac, s John & Rachel, Belmont
Co., O.;.m in Goshen MH, Betsey SPENCER,
dt John & Lydia, Belmont Co., O.
1835, 6, 4. Lydia S. m Samuel GREGG
1836, 1, 8. John d ae 49 bur Wrightstown
1838, 8, 2. Merab m Nathan P. HALL
1851, 5, 27. Alice d ae 63 bur Wrightstown

1810, 11, 24. William gct South River MM, Va.
1812, 5, 23. Joseph dis mcd
1812, 7, 25. William rocf South River MM,
Va., dtd 1811,9,11
1813, 4, 27. Mary Spencer (form Coffee) dis
mou

COFFEE, continued
1815, 5, 27. Ann rocf Hopewell MM, Va., dtd
     1815,3,9
1819, 6, 24. William dis
1837, 11, 22. Isaac & w, Betty, & ch, Rachel
     Ann & Charles W., gct Miami MM, O.
1839, 4, 24. John S. gct Stillwater MM
1839, 5, 22. Jonathan gct Salem MM
1837, 2, 24. Thomas Elwood dis disunity
1848, 8, 23. Mary Ann & Eliza dis disunity

COMBS
1823, 10, 2. Mary Ann m John CHAMBERS

1827, 4, 26. Deborah Eaton (form Combs) dis
     mcd
1827, 11, 22. Benjamin & w, Charity, & ch,
     Benjamin, Rebecca & Samuel, gct Allum
     Creek MM
1827, 11, 22. George gct Allum Creek MM

COOK
1862, 4, 17. Henry F. Pickering gct West MM,
     O., to m Hannah F. Cook (H)

COOPER
1839, 8, 15. Nicholas rocf Flushing MM, dtd
     1839,6,22 (H)

COPE
1812, 4, 25. Jacob & w, Mary, & ch, Sophia,
     Rachel, Margaret & Ellis, rocf Short Creek
     MM, O., dtd 1811,12,24

COULSON
1845, 3, 20. David, s Jehu & Jane, Columbi-
     ana Co., O.; m in Plainfield MH, Margaret
     CHAMBERS, dt Samuel & Deborah, Belmont
     Co., O.

1845, 5, 21. Margaret gct Sandy Spring MM

COVINGTON
1818, 7, 23. Elizabeth (form Carver) dis mcd
     (Coffington on women's minutes)

COWGILL
1816, 10, 31. Ralph [Cogal], s Isaac & Sarah,
     Belmont Co., O.; m in Plainfield MH, Bet-
     sey SPENSER, dt Nathan & Ann, Belmont Co.,
1817, 11, 26. Sarah m Jonathan SPENCER   [O.
1824, 9, 2. Isaac, s Isaac & Sarah, Belmont
     Co., O.; m in Plainfield MH, Jane FOULKE,
     dt Judah & Sarah, Monroe Co., O.
     Ch: Jane   b 1836, 2, 22 d 1837, 5, 1
          bur in fam lot on farm of Isaac Cow-
          gill
        Isaac Jr. b 1840, 5, 13
     Isaac m 2nd 1847,12,2 in Plainfield MH,
     Esther ROBERTS, dt Aaron & Elizabeth, Bel-
     mont Co., O.
1834, 9, 29. Isaac d ae 5 bur in fam bur gr
     near St. Clairesville

1842, 9, 29. Jonathan, s Ralph & Betsey, Bel-
     mont Co., O.; m in Plainfield MH, Rebecca
     SATTERTHWAIT, dt Joseph & Ann, Belmont Co.,
     O.
1843, 4, 28. Jane d ae 44
1844, 4, 22. Rebecca d bur in fam bur gr near
     St. Clairsville
1851, 1, 21. Betsy d ae 58 bur in fam plot
1851, 4, 21. Ralph d ae 57
1852, 12, 1. Ann S. m Nathan SATTERTHWAIT
1853, 3, 31. Abraham, s Isaac & Jane, Belmont
     Co., O.; m in Plainfield MH, Lydia Ann
     SPENCER, dt Abner & Harriet, Belmont Co.,
     O.
     Ch: Adaline   b 1854, 4, 26
         Elma   " 1857, 8, 4
1861, 1, 18. Isaac d ae 65 bur in fam ground
     near St. Clairesville

1816, 11, 21. Sarah recrq
1843, 6, 21. Phinehas gct Short Creek MM, O.
1847, 11, 24. Jephthah gct Stillwater MM
1848, 8, 23. Phinehas & w, Sarah Ann, & ch,
     Elias B. & Henry, rocf Short Creek MM, dtd
     1848,6,20
1851, 3, 19. Ralph, an elder, d 1851,4,12 ae
     58
1853, 2, 23. Phineas & w, Sarah Ann, & ch,
     Elias B. & Henry, gct Salem MM, Iowa
1853, 8, 24. Sarah gct Red Cedar MM, Iowa
1854, 3, 22. Jonathan & s, Samuel, gct Red
     Cedar MM, Ia.
1855, 6, 20. William dis mcd

COX
1810, 11, 24. Sarah gct Stillwater MM

COZINS
1817, 11, 20. Benjamin rocf Dublin MM, dtd
     1817,6,10
1819, 6, 24. Benjamin [Cousins] gct SD MM

CRAFT
1834, 6, 25. Wm., s John & Margaret, Belmont
     Co., O.; m in St. Clairsville, Rachel
     SPENCER, dt Nathan & Ann, Belmont Co., O.
1834, 8, 27. Margaret d ae 66 bur St. Clairs-
     ville

1810, 1, 27. Margaret, w John, & ch, William
     & Stacey, rocf Baltimore MM for E. Dist.,
     dtd 1809,8,10
1815, 2, 25. John dis mcd
1815, 2, 25. Elizabeth Bailey (form Craft)
     dis mcd & jas
1815, 3, 25. Ridgeway dis military service
1817, 1, 23. Stacy dis mcd
1817, 4, 24. William dis mcd
1821, 1, 25. William rst
1821, 10, 25. Samuel Jr. rocf Chesterfield
     MM, N. J., dtd 1821,7,3
1821, 12, 20. Samuel gct Somerset MM, to m
     Ann Beck

CRAFT, continued
1822, 4, 25. Samuel gct Short Creek MM, O.
1822, 9, 26. Samuel gct Sommerset MM, to m
     Lydia Beck
1822, 12, 26. Lydia rocf Somerset MM, dtd
     1822,11,25
1844, 5, 22. Mary dis disunity
1861, 8, 15. Rachel & dt, Ann, Margaret & Re-
     becca, gct Short Creek MM, O. (H)

CRAWFORD
1824, 4, 28. Nathan, s Seaborn & Frances,
     Washington Co., Pa; m in Goshen MH, Mary
     CARLETON, dt Mark & Beulah, Belmont Co.,
     O.

1824, 7, 22. Mary gct Westland MM, Pa.

CROSSLEY
1811, 10, 30. Sarah m John PIGGOTT
1812, 10, 29. Samuel, s John & Tamer, Jeffer-
     son Co., O.; m in Plainfield MH, Phebe
     SINCLAIR, dt George & Jane, Belmont Co.,O.

1812, 2, 22. Samuel gct Short Creek MM
1812, 3, 28. Jonathan dis mcd
1814, 6, 25. Samuel rocf Short Creek MM, O.,
     dtd 1814,3,22

CROZIER
1812, 10, 28. James [Crozer], s John & Elener,
     Belmont Co., O.; m in Flushing MH, Mary
     PICKERING, dt Samuel & Phebe, "of Flush-
     ing"
     James m 2nd 1817,8,27 in Flushing MH, Ra-
     chel WOOD, dt Joshua & Hannah, Belmont
     Co., O.
     James m 3rd 1820,4,27 in Plainfield MH,
     Ann FOULKE, dt Judah & Sarah, Belmont Co.,
     O.
1825, 2, 25. Ann [Crosier] m Curtis GRUBB

1808, 5, 28. Levi Pickering gct Middleton MM,
     to m Susannah Crozier
1812, 7, 25. James recrq
1817, 12, 25. Thomas recrq
1820, 6, 22. Ann [Crozer] gct Flushing MM
1824, 6, 24. Ann & dt, Sarah, rocf Flushing
     MM, dtd 1824,5,21
1825, 5, 26. Sarah, dt Ann Grubb, gct Short
     Creek MM, O.

DANIELS
1864, 4, 14. Lydia Ann rocf Concord MM, dtd
     1863,9,25 (H)

DAVID
1816, 2, 1. Sarah m Richard KINSEY

1815, 2, 25. Ruth (form Easley) con mcd

DAVIS
1809, 11, 25. Keziah (form Taylor)dis mou

1813, 12, 25. Margaret, Nehemiah, Sarah &
     Mary, ch John, rocf Duck Creek MM, Del.,
     dtd 1813,6,12
1814, 6, 25. Sarah rocf Duck Creek MM, Del.,
     dtd 1814,2,12
1825, 5, 26. Cert rec for Miles & s, Hiram E.
     from Westland MM, dtd 1825,4,25, end to
     Stillwater MM
1841, 9, 16. Cynthia Horton, minor with John
     & Rachel Horton, rocf Short Creek MM, dtd
     1841,7,22 (H)
1846, 10, 15. Gideon rocf New Garden MM, dtd
     1846,9,24 (H)
1848, 8, 17. Cynthia Horton, minor with John
     & Rachel Horton, gct Westland MM (H)

DAWSON
1809, 7, 26. Ruth m Thomas BUFKINS

1809, 2, 25. Ruth & ch, Lydia, Isaac, Susan
     & Sina, rocf Redstone MM, dtd 1808,10,28
1817, 12, 25. Lydia Dooly (form Dawson) con
     mcd

DESELMS
1811, 2, 27. Hannah m Abel GREGG
1815, 12, 27. Jacob, s Jesse & Elizabeth, Bel-
     mont Co., O.; m in Flushing MH, Rhoda
     PICKERING, dt Jacob & Lydia, Belmont Co.,
     O.
1817, 5, 22. Jacob & w, Rhoda, & s, Joseph,
     gct Concord MM

DEW
1815, 10, 28. Elias & w, Sarah, & ch, Ruth &
     John, rocf Short Creek MM, O., dtd 1815,
     10,24
1834, 1, 23. Elias & ch, John, Maria, Allen
     & Albert, rocf Short Creek MM, O., dtd
     1833,10,24 (H)
1834, 2, 20. Ruth rocf Short Creek MM, O.,
     dtd 1833,10,24 (H)
1838, 3, 15. Elias & ch, Maria, Allen & Al-
     bert, gct Short Creek MM (H)
1838, 3, 15. Ruth gct Short Creek MM (H)

DEWEESE
1847, 10, 21. Cornelius [Dewees], s Wm. &
     Debby, Wash. Co.; m in St. Clairsville,
     Rebecca W. ASKEW, dt Wm. & Martha, Bel-
     mont Co., O.

1810, 1, 27. Samuel & w, Hannah, & ch, David
     & Owen, rocf Concord MM, dtd 1809,11,23
1813, 2, 27. Samuel & w, Hannah, & ch, Owen,
     David, Gulielma & Buly Emly, gct Concord
     MM
1816, 7, 26. Samuel [Dewees] & w, Hannah, &
     ch, Owen, David, Gulielma, Bulielma &
     Ellis, rocf Concord MM, dtd 1816,4,24
1820, 11, 23. Samuel & w, Hannah, & ch, Owen,
     David, Gulielma, Bulielma, Ellis & Thomas
     L., gct Short Creek MM, O.

DEWEESE, continued
1848, 2, 23. Rebecca W. gct Chesterfield MM

DICKS
1818, 9, 24. John & w, Sarah, & ch, Joseph,
    Peter, James & Harland, recrq

DILLON
1836, 1, 26. Mary d ae 81 bur Plainfield
1854, 6, 26. Rhoda d ae 60 bur Wrightstown

1808, 7, 23. Rachel [Dillen] rocf Goose Creek
    MM, Va., dtd 1807,7,27; end by Concord MM
    1808,6,26
1810, 1, 27. Sarah rocf Hopewell MM, dtd
    1809,9,4
1813, 12, 25. Isaac rocf Baltimore MM for W.
    Dist., dtd 1813,8,11, end by Stillwater
    MM, 1813,11,30
1814, 2, 26. Moses & w, Hannah, rocf Gun-
    powder MM, end by Stillwater MM, 1813,12,
    28
1814, 2, 26. Edith & ch, Lloyd, Keziah, Moses,
    Hannah & Margaret, recrq
1817, 5, 22. Rhoda (form Gregg) con mcd
1817, 11, 20. Elizabeth recrq
1818, 11, 26. Rebecca (form Hoge) dis mcd

DILWORTH
1822, 5, 1. Rhoads R., s Caleb & Ann, Jeffer-
    son Co., O.; m in St. Clairsville, Re-
    becca FOULKE, dt Isachar & Jane, Belmont
    Co., O.

1823, 6, 26. Rebecca gct Short Creek MM, O.

DIXON
1810, 10, 27. William & w, Jane, & ch, Sarah,
    Samuel, Hannah, Susannah & William, rocf
    Short Creek MM, O., dtd 1810,7,24

DOBBINS
1826, 2, 23. Edith (form Gregg) dis mcd
1830, 12, 23. Susanna (form Gregg) dis mcd (H)
1837, 7, 13. Mary (form Gregg) dis mcd (H)

DODD
1811, 12, 28. Isaac Wilson Jr. gct Stillwater
    MM, to m Elizabeth Dodd

DOOLY
1817, 9, 25. Maxin rocf Providence MM, dtd
    1817,8,26
1817, 12, 25. Lydia (form Dawson) con mcd
1817, 12, 25. Maxon [Duly] con mcd

DOWNS
1816, 12, 26. Jeremiah & w, Anna, rocf Red-
    stone MM, dtd 1816,10,23
1817, 6, 26. Elizabeth, Sarah, William &
    Thomas, ch Jeremiah & Anna, recrq

DRAPER
1827, 10, 25. Cert rec for Elizabeth Sr. &
    Elizabeth Jr. from Western Branch MM, Va.,
    dtd 1827,9,22, end to Marlborough MM

DRUMMOND
1849, 6, 14. Sarah (form Vanlaw) con mcd (H)

DUNGAN
1815, 7, 22. Mary rocf Muncy MM, dtd 1814,
    11,23 end to Plymouth MM, 1815,8,31

DUNN
1883, 10, 18. Precilla recrq (H)

EASLEY
1812, 1, 2. Sarah m Jonathan BOGUE
1813, 4, 9. Mary Ann m Job BOGUE

1809, 6, 24. Daniel & w, Edith, & ch, Sarah,
    Mary Ann, Ruth, John, Daniel, Richard,
    Isaac & Stephen, rocf South River MM, dtd
    1809,4,8
1815, 2, 25. Ruth David (form Easley) con
    mcd

EATON
1827, 4, 26. Deborah (form Combs) dis mcd
1847, 4, 15. Lydia (form Elliott) con mcd
    (H)

ECKROYD
1859, 10, 4. Martha [Ecroyd] d ae 24 bur
    Plainfield

1853, 6, 22. John H. & w, Sarah W., & ch,
    Elizabeth W., Martha, Henry, Rachel W.,
    Sarah, John Hayworth & Louisa, rocf Mun-
    cey MM, dtd 1853,5,18
1853, 6, 22. Hannah rocf Muncey MM, dtd
    1853,5,18
1853, 12, 21. Hannah [Ecroyd] dis jas
1859, 7, 20. Sarah M. gct Short Creek MM, O.
1863, 6, 24. Henry [Echroyd] rpd mcd

EDGERTON
1822, 10, 30. William, s James & Sarah, Bel-
    mont Co., O.; m in St. Clairsville, Sarah
    FOULKE, dt Issachar & Jane, Belmont Co.,O.
1852, 9, 30. James, s Joseph & Charity, Bel-
    mont Co., O.; m in Plainfield MH, Mary
    Ann WILLIAMS, dt Wm. C. & Rebecca, Bel-
    mont Co., O.

1822, 12, 26. Sarah gct Stillwater MM
1845, 12, 24. Ann, Bathsheba & Jane dis dis-
    unity
1852, 12, 22. Mary Ann gct Somerset MM
1837, 6, 15. Sarah & ch, Jane, Bathsheba &
    Ann, rocf Stillwater MM, dtd 1836,11,19
    (H)
1837, 8, 23. John Vail gct Somerset MM, to
    m Abigail Edgerton

EDGERTON, continued
1847, 2, 24. John Thomasson gct Somerset MM,
    to m Eunice Edgerton

ELLIOTT
1831, 12, 1. Lamira m Eli WILLITS (H)
1831, 12, 29. Elizabeth m Isaac PICKERING (H)
----, --, --. Jesse H., s John & Rachel, Bel-
    mont Co., O.; m Rachel HAINES, dt Nathan-
    iel & Rachel, Belmont Co., O. (H)

1832, 4, 26. Elijah gct Deerfield MM (H)
1835, 2, 19. Rhesa gct Deerfield MM; returned
    for mcd (H)
1835, 4, 16. Rhese con mcd (H)
1835, 10, 15. Rhesa gct Deerfield MM (H)
1836, 1, 14. Joel dis (H)
1836, 2, 18. Cert for Rhesa to Deerfield MM,
    returned as he resides here (H)
1836, 7, 14. Lucinda (form Vanlaw) con mcd
    (H)
1836, 10, 13. Matilda recrq (H)
1836, 12, 21. Jesse dis jH
1837, 1, 25. Rachel (form Haines) dis jH
1838, 10, 18. Rheas & w, Matilda, gct Deer-
    field MM (H)
1840, 8, 13. Jesse H. & w, Rachel, & ch,
    Phebe Ann & Elizabeth, gct Deerfield MM
    (H)
1843, 12, 20. Lydia dis disunity
1847, 4, 15. Lydia Eaton (form Elliott) con
    mcd

ELLIS
1808, 5, 28. Mary rocf Hopewell MM, end by
    Concord MM 1808,2,1
1809, 9, 23. Mary gct Fairfield MM
1810, 5, 27. Sarah Vanpelt (form Ellis) dis
    mcd
1811, 5, 25. Amos dis disunity

ELY
1854, 4, 20. James S., s Jacob & Sarah, Bel-
    mont Co., O.; m in Plainfield MH, Emily E.
    HOGUE, dt Samuel & Mary, Belmont Co., O.
    (H)

1833, 8, 22. Sarah B. & s, William Brown
    Waters & Edward Waters, rocf Baltimore MM
    for W. Dist., dtd 1833,5,10
1857, 7, 16. Emily E. gct Stillwater MM (H)

EMBREE
1817, 10, 23. John & w, Huldah, & ch, Mary,
    James, Harriet, Elizabeth & Jesse, rocf
    New Garden MM, dtd 1817,8,14

ENGLAND
1867, 1, 17. Margaret recrq (H)
1867, 5, 16. Milton V. rocf Short Creek MM,
    dtd 1867,4,9 (H)
1875, 12, 16. Margaret gct Salem (H)

ENGLE
1813, 12, 1. Abraham, Belmont Co., O.; m in
    Flushing MH, Phebe PICKERING, wd Samuel,
    Belmont Co., O.

1809, 5, 27. Job & w, Sarah, & ch, Rebecca &
    Hannah, gct Evesham MM, N. Y.
1810, 4, 28. Samuel dis disunity
1812, 9, 26. Abraham, minor, gct Miami MM, O.
1816, 2, 23. Caleb gct Stillwater MM, to m
    Rachel Plummer
1816, 4, 26. Caleb & ch, Mary, Rebecca, Anna
    Mercy, Caleb & Maria, gct Stillwater MM
1816, 5, 24. Elizabeth gct Stillwater MM
1819, 3, 25. Mary dis
1820, 4, 20. John, minor, gct Stillwater MM

EVANS
1815, 3, 25. Evan & w, Mary, & ch, Rebecca,
    James, Cadwalader & Amos Hutton, rocf
    Plymouth MM, dtd 1814,9,17
1815, 9, 23. Asher [Evins] rocf Plymouth MM,
    dtd 1815,5,20
1815, 11, 25. Benoni rocf Plymouth MM, dtd
    1815,9,16
1816, 6, 21. Jacob Smith gct Goose Creek MM,
    Va., to m Martha Evans
1819, 8, 26. Joanna rocf Short Creek MM, O.,
    dtd 1819,5,18
1832, 11, 22. Sally (form Paxon) dis mcd (H)

EWERS
1818, 4, 1. Rebeckah m Barclay BROOMHALL
1823, 3, 26. Gulielma m Edwin PATTERSON

1818, 2, 26. Thomas dis jas
1831, 6, 23. Gladney dis mcd (H)
1831, 8, 25. Elizabeth (form Hogue) dis mcd
    (H)
1835, 10, 15. Jesse dis mcd (H)   [(H)
1838, 2, 15. Lydia Hoge (form Ewers) con mcd
1839, 1, 17. William gct Stillwater MM (H)

FARQUHAR
1817, 11, 27. Alan, s Thos. & Hannah, Jeffer-
    son Co., O.; m in Notingham, Edith WILSON,
    dt Israel & Martha, Harrison Co., O.

1818, 1, 22. Edith gct Smithfield MM

FAWCETT
1812, 1, 1. William, s Thos. & Sarah; m in
    Plainfield MH, Abigail SHARP, dt Samuel &
    Martha, Belmont Co., O.
1813, --, --. Robert, s John & Mary, Belmont
    Co., O.; m Mary PICKERING, dt John & Jane,
    Belmont Co., O.
1815, 11, 2. Thomas, s Thos. & Martha, Bel-
    mont Co., O.; m in Plainfield MH, Rachel
    VAIL, dt Benjamin & Rebekah, Belmont Co.,
    O.

1818, 2, 4. Eunice m Stacy BEVAN
1818, 3, 4. Rachel m Wm. McNICHOLS

FAWCETT, continued

1819, 3, 31. Mary m Richard CARTER
1828, 3, 26. Benjamin, s Samuel & Rachel,
    Belmont Co., O.; m in St. Clairsville,
    Lydia Ann HORNER, dt John & Lydia, Belmont
    Co., O.
----, --, --. Elijah & Sarah
    Ch: Reece L.   b 1834, 2, 23 d 1840, 2,14
        bur Plainfield
        Linley M. b 1835, 8, 17
        Samuel G. " 1837, 6, 21
1836, 10, 24. Phebe d bur Wrightstown
1836, 10, 30. David d ae 59 bur Wrightstown
1843, 8, 24. Mary T. m Thos. R. HOGE (H)
1855, 1, 24. Rebecca J. m Joseph W. HOLMES
    (H)

1809, 10, 28. William rocf Hopewell MM, dtd
    1808,12,5
1809, 10, 28. Mary & ch, Robert, Atlantic,
    Joshua, Susannah, John, Mahlon, Darcus,
    Nancy & Washington, rocf Hopewell MM, dtd
    1809,10,2
1811, 5, 25. Richard & dt, Elizabeth, gct
    Stillwater MM
1811, 11, 23. Samuel & w, Rachel, & ch, Eliza-
    beth, Benjamin & Mariah, rocf Short Creek
    MM, O., dtd 1811,3,19
1812, 2, 22. William & w, Abigail, gct Salem
    MM
1812, 2, 22. Atlantic Carpenter (form Faw-
    cett) dis mcd & jas
1812, 12, 26. Jonathan gct Stillwater MM, to
    m Rebecca Strall
1813, 5, 22. Jonathan gct Stillwater MM
1813, 10, 23. Robert rmt Mary Pickering
1814, 6, 25. Jonathan & w, Rebecca, & s,
    Jesse, rocf Stillwater MM, dtd 1814,3,29
1814, 7, 23. Robert dis military service
1814, 12, 24. Mary rocf Hopewell MM, dtd
    1814,10,3
1814, 12, 24. Thomas & w, Martha, & s, Thomas,
    rocf Hopewell MM, dtd 1814,10,3
1815, 1, 28. Eunice rocf Hopewell MM, dtd
    1814,10,3
1815, 4, 22. Jonathan & w, Rebecca, & s,
    Jesse, gct Stillwater MM
1816, 7, 26. Susannah Carpenter (form Faw-
    cett) dis mcd
1816, 9, 26. Joshua dis military service
1817, 4, 24. Jacob dis mcd
1818, 5, 21. Jane (form Pickering) dis mcd
1818, 10, 22. John dis disunity
1820, 6, 22. David rst in mbrp, was dis at
    Crooked Run MM, now laid down
1823, 2, 20. Amos recrq
1831, 11, 24. Rachel (form Miller) dis mcd (H)
1833, 7, 25. Elisha & w, Rachel, & ch, Mah-
    lon Taylor, Thomas Williams, Mary Taylor,
    Franklin, Joseph, Janny & Lydia Ann, rocf
    Hopewell MM, dtd 1832,12,6, end by Concord
    MM
1837, 2, 22. Elijah & w, Sarah, & ch, Rease

& Lindley, rocf Flushing MM, dtd 1836,10,
    20
1837, 6, 21. Rebecca dis JH
1837, 8, 23. Joel dis JH
1838, 12, 13. Joel dis disunity (H)
1839, 10, 17. Elisha gct New Garden MM, to m
    (H)
1840, 9, 17. Herphilia rocf New Garden MM,
    dtd 1840,5,21 (H)
1841, 8, 25. Simeon dis disunity
1841, 12, 22. Elijah & w, Sarah, & ch, Lind-
    ley & Samuel, gct Chesterfield MM
1842, 6, 22. Benjamin & w, Lydia Ann, & ch,
    Samuel, Rachel, Drusilla, Ann Eliza &
    Lydia Jane, rocf Somerset MM
1843, 10, 19. Mahlon T. con mcd (H)
1844, 2, 15. Thomas W. con mcd (H)
1844, 7, 24. Benjamin & w, Lydia Ann, & ch,
    Samuel, Rachel, Drusilla, Ann Eliza &
    Lydia Jane, gct Somerset MM
1844, 9, 25. Levi dis disunity
1845, 10, 16. Simeon dis disunity (H)
1848, 5, 18. Franklin dis mcd (H)
1848, 6, 21. Nathan dis disunity
1848, 8, 23. Amos dis mcd
1848, 12, 14. Levi & w, Sarah A., con mcd (H)
1849, 5, 17. Amos con mcd (H)
1852, 7, 15. Sina (form Gregg) dis mcd (H)
1852, 8, 19. Thomas dis mcd (H)
1855, 2, 15. Levi & w, Sarah Anne, & ch,
    Thomas & John, gct Clear Creek MM, Ill.
    (H)
1856, 1, 11. Mary Wells (form Fawcett) con
    mcd (H)
1860, 7, 18. Sarah Ann & ch, Thomas, John &
    Rachel Ann, gct Prairie Grove MM, Ia. (H)
1866, 11, 15. Thomas Jr. con mcd (H)
1860, 6, 14. Amos relrq (H)

FENLEY
1813, 5, 5. Hannah m Benj. VAIL

1812, 6, 27. Hannah & dt, Eunice, rocf Hope-
    well MM, dtd 1812,4,19

FESLER
1843, 12, 20. Asenath (form Gregg) dis mcd

FIELDS
1830, 8, 26. Sarah rocf Flushing MM, dtd
    1830,6,26 (H)

FISHER
1815, 4, 22. Mary Linton (form Fisher) dis
    mcd
1816, 10, 24. Richard dis disunity
1817, 7, 24. Rebeckah gct Stillwater MM
1817, 11, 20. Joseph, minor, gct Stillwater MM

FITZSIMMONS
1843, 6, 22. Lydia Ann m Hugh P. CLARK (H)

FLANNER
1817, 9, 25. Cert rec for Thomas from Short
    Creek MM, O., end back to that mtg

FORD
1816, 2, 23. Ann rocf Duck Creek MM, dtd
    1815,8,12

FOREMAN
1823, 6, 26. Rachel (form Lewis) dis mcd

FOULKE
1819, 12, 1. Mary m Henry BAILEY
1819, 12, 2. Thomas, s Judah & Sarah, Bel-
    mont Co., O.; m in Plainfield MH, Sarah
    SPENCER, dt Nathan & Ann, Belmont Co., O.
1820, 4, 27. Ann m James CROZER
1822, 1, 31. Amelia m John WILSON
1822, 3, 27. Jane m Moses ALLEN
1822, 5, 1. Rebecca m Rhoads R. DILWORTH
1822, 10, 30. Sarah m. Wm. EDGERTON
1824, 9, 2. Jane m Isaac COWGILL
1829, 10, 28. Barton, s Issachar & Jane, Bel-
    mont Co., O.; m in St. Clairsville, Mary
    MINNIKAN, dt William & Margaret, Belmont
    Co., O. (H)
1833, 3, 27. Hannah m Samuel GRIFFITH (H)
1852, 9, 23. Aaron, s Isaachar & Jane, Bel-
    mont Co., O.; m in home of Eli SIDWELL,
    Phebe SIDWELL, dt Eli & Sarah, Belmont
    Co., O.

1810, 6, 23. Issachar & w, Jane, & ch, Pris-
    cilla, Bathsheba, Mary, Sarah, Rebecca,
    Jane, Aaron & Barton, roof Richland MM,
    dtd 1810,4,12
1812, 6, 27. Jesse & w, Sarah, & ch, Ellen,
    Hannah, Rachel, William & Jesse, rocf
    Muncy MM, dtd 1812,4,22
1819, 5, 20. Thomas rocf Richland MM, Pa.,
    dtd 1818,10,2, end by Miani MM, O., 1819,
    2,24
1819, 5, 20. Judah & w, Sarah, & ch, Amelia,
    Cadwalader, Jesse, Mercy, Grace, Sylvas
    & John, rocf Richland MM, Pa., dtd 1818,10,
    2m end by Miami MM, O., 1819,2,24
1819, 6, 24. Jane rocf Chester MM, dtd 1819,
    2,4
1819, 7, 22. Ann rocf Richland MM, dtd 1818,
    10,21, end by Miami MM; original cert
    lost "she having resided in this mtg since
    leaving Richland, is accepted"
1819, 11, 25. Elizabeth rocf Abington MM, dtd
    1819,9,28, end by Miami MM, O., 1819,10,27
1821, 3, 22. Elizabeth gct Short Creek MM, O.
1822, 2, 21. Cadwalader, minor, gct Richland
    MM, Pa.
1824, 9, 23. Judah & w, Sarah, & ch, Jesse,
    Mercy, Grace, Silas & John, gct Somerset
    MM
1826, 8, 24. Thomas & w, Sarah, & ch, Joshua
    & Milton, gct Stillwater MM
1827, 2, 22. Cert rec for Cadwalader from

Gwyned MM, Pa., dtd 1826,11,30, end to
    Somerset MM
1829, 4, 23. Anthony & w, Eleanor, & ch, Sa-
    rah P., Phebe & William W., rocf Alexan-
    dria MM, dtd 1829,1,22 (H)
1830, 5, 30. Anthony & w, Eleanor, & ch, gct
    Flushing MM (H)
1838, 7, 19. Isechar [Folk] d 1838,8,5 ae 79
    (elder) (H)
1858, 5, 13. Priscilla White (form Foulk) con
    mcd (H)
1863, 2, 19. Sarah McDowell (form Foulk)
    relrq (H)
1870, 12, 15. Rosa Bell White, dt Priscilla,
    (form Foulke) recrq (H)
1871, 6, 15. Barton con mcd (H)

FRAME
1817, 10, 29. Rachel m Abraham BARBER
1818, 8, 26. Jane m Smith BRANSON
1846, 4, 30. James T., s Wm. & Ruanna, Harri-
    son Co., O.; m in Plainfield MH, Anna SAT-
    TERTHWAITE, dt Joseph W. & Ann, Belmont
    Co., O.

1817, 2, 20. Jane rocf Short Creek MM, O.,
    dtd 1817,1,21
1817, 2, 20. Benjamin & w, Elizabeth, rocf
    Short Creek MM, O., dtd 1817,1,21
1817, 4, 24. Rachel rocf Short Creek MM, O.,
    dtd 1817,1,21
1818, 7, 23. William & w, Ruanna, & ch,
    Aaron & James, rocf Short Creek MM, O.,
    dtd 1818,6,23
1846, 7, 22. Anna gct Short Creek MM, O.

FRAVEL
1893, 1, 25. Rebecca S. m J. Clement MERRITT
    (H)

1876, 4, 13. Rebecca S. & s, William J., rocf
    Miami MM, O., dtd 1876,2,23 (H)
1886, 9, 16. Rebecca S. & ch, Wm. J. & Maria
    S., gct Race St. MM, Phila., Pa. (H)
1892, 8, 18. Rebecca S. & Myra J. rocf Phila.
    MM, Pa., dtd 1892,7,20 (H)

FRAZIER
1817, 10, 2. William, s Daniel & Elener, Bel-
    mont Co., O.; m Anna ROSS, dt Reuben &
    Elizabeth, Harrison Co., O.

1818, 1, 22. Ann gct Stillwater MM
1830, 2, 25. Elinor (form Pickering) con mcd
    (H)
1836, 8, 16. James Whalen [Frasier] recrq (H)
1836, 8, 16. Maria Ann & Thomas Smith [Fras-
    er], ch James Whalen & Eleanor, recrq (H)
1854, 6, 13. Maria A. Bailey (form Frazier)
    con mcd (H)
1867, 4, 18. Sarah Piper (form Frazier) con
    mcd (H)

FRED
1846, 9, 17. Viley W. (form Wright) con mcd
    (H)

GARRETSON
1814, 2, 26. Amos & w, Mary, & ch, Nancy,
    Elisha, Mary Ann & Talbot, rocf Plymouth
    MM, dtd 1813,12,18
1825, 7, 21. Joel rocf Concord MM
1826, 11, 23. Joel gct Stillwater MM
1835, 3, 19. Jehu Allen gct Flushing MM, to
    m Mary Ann Garretson
1838, 12, 13. Amos & w, Hannah, & dt, Martha,
    rocf Flushing MM, dtd 1838,11,24 (H)
1844, 7, 18. Martha gct Fall Creek MM, Ind.
    (H)
1847, 11, 24. Martha Lucetta, minor dt Sarah
    Michener, rocf Flushing MM, dtd 1847,5,20
1846, 8, 19. John Michener gct Flushing MM,
    to m Sarah Garretson
1856, 10, 22. Martha Lucetta dis jas
1857, 5, 14. Amos & w, Hannah F., gct Fall
    Creek MM, Ind. (H)

GATCHEL
1818, 2, 26. Elizabeth rocf Nottingham MM,
    dtd 1817,11,7
1818, 6, 25. Hannah [Getchel] (form Rodgers)
    dis mcd
1829, 8, 20. Jeremiah [Gitchell] & w, Deborah,
    & ch, Maria, Gainer, Nathan, Robert B.,
    Elizabeth, Hannah E., Deborah & Ann, rocf
    Nottingham MM, dtd 1829,2,13, end by Still-
    water MM (H)
1831, 6, 23. Jeremiah [Gitchell] dis disunity
    (H)
1832, 12, 20. Deborah [Gatchell] & ch, Maria,
    Garner, Nathan, Robert, Elizabeth, Hannah,
    Deborah Ann & John, gct Stillwater MM (H)

GAUSE
1816, 7, 26. Jesse & w, Martha, rocf ND MM,
    dtd 1816,4,23
1821, 5, 24. Jesse & w, Martha, & ch, Harriet
    Amelia & Hannah, gct Short Creek MM, O.
1821, 6, 2-. Martha gct Short Creek MM, O.

GAY
1820, 7, 20. Asa & w, Nancy, & ch, Sarah,
    Charles, Ephraim, Mary, William, David,
    Asa, Hyram, Cyrus, Eliphilet, Jesse, Rob-
    ert & Elvin, rocf Vasselborough MM, Maine,
    dtd 1816,3,20, end by Stillwater MM 1820,
    5,27

GEORGE
1810, 4, 28. Mary (form Gregg) dis mcd
1811, 11, 23. Mary rst
1812, 6, 27. Mary gct Short Creek MM
1832, 3, 22. Edith R. (form White) con mcd
    (H)
1839, 9, 19. Harriett recrq (H)
1841, 6, 17. Edith dis joining Baptist Socie-

ty (H)

GIFFORD
1818, 11, 26. Cert rec for Marven from mtg
    held at Harlem, dtd 1818,9,16, end to
    Stillwater

GILBERT
1810, 9, 22. Joel & w, Elizabeth, gct Still-
    water MM
1810, 9, 22. Abel, s Joel & Elizabeth, & w,
    Rebecca, & ch, Ruth & Achsah, gct Still-
    water MM
1811, 9, 28. John & w, Elizabeth, & ch, Mary,
    Thomas & Sarah, gct Stillwater MM
1818, 7, 23. Mary, minor with fam of Nehemiah
    Wright, rocf Short Creek MM, O., dtd 1818,
    7,21
1825, 3, 24. Mary dis

GIVENS
1881, 6, 16. Mary Ann gct Clear Creek MM, Ill.
    (H)

GORE
1813, 12, 30. Anne m Thomas WEBSTER
1812, 10, 29. Sarah m Jephthah SHARP

1811, 7, 24. Ann recrq
1812, 3, 28. Sarah recrq

GREEN
1808, 11, 26. Alexander & w, Mary, & ch, Thom-
    as, John, Abigail, Samuel, James & Isaac,
    rocf Lurgan MM, Ireland, dtd 1808,4,16,
    "directed to N.Y. MM but not presented
    there"
1825, 4, 21. John gct Sandy Spring MM, to m
    Mary Hole
1826, 6, 22. Mary Wright (form Green) dis
    mcd
1826, 9, 21. John gct Flushing MM
1827, 7, 26. Isaac dis mcd
1828, 2, 21. Samuel gct Flushing MM
1835, 11, 25. Ellen dis
1836, 7, 20. Samson dis mcd
1847, 7, 21. Maria Lewis (form Green) dis mcd

GREENLIEF
1837, 4, 24. Hannah (form Chamberlain) dis
    mcd

GREGG
1811, 2, 27. Abel, s Samuel & Ann, Belmont
    Co., O.; m in Flushing MH, Hannah DESELMS,
    dt Jesse & Elizabeth, Belmont Co., O.
1811, 2, 27. Phebe m James HOLLOWAY
1813, 1, 28. Albina m John WEBSTER
1813, 10, 27. Stephen, s Abner & Sarah, Bel-
    mont Co., O.; m in Flushing MH, Hannah
    PICKERING, dt Jacob & Hannah, Belmont Co.,
    O.
1814, 4, 28. Samuel, s Abraham & Mary, Bel-
    [mont

GREGG, Samuel, continued
    Co., O.; m in Plainfield MH, Jane NICHOLS,
    dt Geo. & Mary FALLIS
1816, 5, 2. Sarah m Samuel WILSON
1816, 10, 31. John, s Abner & Sarah, Belmont
    Co., O.; m in Plainfield MH, Mary HATCHER,
    dt Joshua & Jane, Belmont Co., O.
1820, 3, 29. Ester m Joseph BOND
1821, 5, 30. James, s Jacob & Mary, Belmont
    Co., O.; m in Belmont Co., Abigail WRIGHT,
    dt Joseph & Hannah, Belmont Co., O.
1821, 6, 27. Anna m Thomas HIRST
1821, 12, 26. Harriet m Abner SPENCER
1822, 5, 4. Mariah m Joel JUDKINS
1823, 9, 24. Elijah, s Caleb & Hannah, Bel-
    mont Co., O.; m in Plainfield MH, Phebe
    SPENCER, dt Nathan & Ann, Belmont Co., O.
1824, 12, 29. Asenath m Jesse MEDCELF
1825, 2, 25. Lydia m Jesse WILEMAN
1825, 10, 26. Malinda m Tilman PATTERSON
1826, 8, 29. William, s Samuel & Ann, Belmont
    Co., O.; m in Goshen MH, Hannah CARLETON,
    dt Mark & Beulah, Belmont Co., O.
1834, 5, 13. Mary m Joseph RHODES (H)
1835, 4, 2. Lucinda m Abel LEWIS
1835, 6, 4. Samuel, s Stephen & Asenath,
    Belmont Co., O.; m in Plainfield MH, Lydia
    S. COFFEE, dt John & Alice, Belmont Co., O.
    Ch: Lydia Ann b 1836, 5, 20
1835, 8, 10. Lydia d bur Wrightstown
1836, 11, --. Phebe m Washington HOGE (H)
1840, 2, 14. Lydia Ann m Chas. LEWIS (H)
1841, 5, 26. Margaret S. m Isaac HAINS (H)
1842, 10, 6. Elias d ae 21 bur Wrightstown
1842, 11, 20. Ruth d ae 25 bur Wrightstown
1842, 11, 26. Abner d ae 85 bur Wrightstown
1843, 8, 9. Mahlon d ae 53 bur Wrightstown
1844, 12, 9. Stephen d ae 76 bur Plainfield
1850, 4, 24. Ann m Thomas E. HOGE (H)
1855, 11, 19. Phebe P. d ae 28 bur Wrights-
    town
1873, 3, 27. Eliza m Samuel P. VICKERS (H)

1810, 4, 28. Mary George (form Gregg) dis mcd
1810, 9, 22. Nathaniel gct Westland MM, to m
    Elizabeth Mills
1811, 5, 25. Elizabeth rocf Westland MM, dtd
    1811,1,26
1811, 6, 22. Stephen Jr. gct Goose Creek
    MM, Va.
1812, 6, 27. Samuel & w, Ann, & ch, Eli, Gu-
    lielma, Phinehas, William, Israel, Asa &
    Tacy, gct Short Creek MM, O.
1812, 9, 26. Stephen & w, Asenath rst on con-
    sent of Goose Creek MM, Va. (Ch; Harriett,
    Asenath, Lucinda, Elizabeth & Sarah, rec-
    rq)
1813, 3, 27. William dis mcd
1813, 6, 26. Nathaniel & w, Elizabeth, & ch,
    Henry, gct Westland MM
1813, 8, 23. Stephen Jr. rocf Goose Creek
    MM, Va., dtd 1813,6,3
1815, 3, 25. Nathaniel & w, Elizabeth, & s,

    Henry, rocf Westland MM, dtd 1815,3,2
1816, 11, 21. Hannah & ch, David, Betsyann &
    Jesse, gct Short Creek MM, O.
1816, 12, 26. Mahlon gct Stillwater MM, O., to
    m Hannah Miles
1817, 5, 22. Rhoda Dillon (form Gregg) con mcd
1817, 5, 22. Hannah rocf Stillwater MM, O.,
    dtd 1817,4,26
1818, 1, 22. Joshua Jr. rocf Goose Creek MM,
    Va., dtd 1817,8,28
1818, 2, 26. Laban dis
1819, 4, 22. Susannah & ch, Sarah Ann & Han-
    son, recrq
1820, 7, 20. Susannah & ch, Sarah Ann & Han-
    son, gct Flushing MM
1821, 4, 26. Stephen Jr. dis mcd
1823, 3, 20. Jane dis disunity
1823, 6, 26. Mary Phillips (form Gregg) dis
    mcd
1823, 10, 23. Susannah & ch, Sarah Ann & Han-
    son, rocf Flushing MM, dtd 1823,5,23
1825, 1, 20. Joshua gct Goose Creek MM, Va.
1825, 6, 23. William rocf Alum Creek MM, dtd
    1825,1,27
1825, 9, 22. Nathaniel & w, Elizabeth, & ch,
    Ruth Ann, Jonas & Martin, gct Somerset MM
1825, 9, 22. Abner Sr. gct Goose Creek MM,
    Va., to m Mary Hatcher
1826, 2, 23. Edith Dobbins (form Gregg) dis
    mcd
1826, 7, 20. Mary rocf Goose Creek MM, Va.,
    dtd 1826,3,26
1826, 10, 26. William & w, Hannah, gct Flush-
    ing MM
1827, 7, 26. Jesse dis mcd
1828, 7, 24. Mary rocf Centre MM, Del., dtd
    1828,5,5 (H)
1829, 10, 22. Abner dis (H)
1830, 7, 22. Nathaniel & w, Elizabeth, & ch,
    Ruthanna, Jonas, Martin, Nathan, Pusey &
    Nimrod, rocf Westland MM, Pa., dtd 1830,5,
    27 (H)
1830, 12, 23. Susanna Dobbins (form Gregg) dis
    mcd (H)
1831, 4, 21. Nathaniel & w, Elizabeth, & ch,
    Jonas, Martin, Nathan Pusey & Nimrod, gct
    Stillwater MM (H)
1831, 4, 21. Burr dis mcd (H)
1832, 9, 20. James dis disunity (H)
1833, 5, 23. Amy Heald (form Gregg) con mcd(H)
1835, 6, 18. Alfred dis mcd (H)
1835, 11, 19. Ruth Anna gct Stillwater MM (H)
1836, 2, 18. Laban recrq (H)
1836, 7, 20. Sarah Jane dis jH
1837, 2, 16. Lot gct Stillwater MM (H)
1837, 5, 18. Sarah Jane Lewis (form Gregg)
    dis mcd (H)
1837, 7, 13. Mary Dobbins (form Gregg) dis
    mcd (H)
1838, 6, 20. Lydia Ann dis disunity
1838, 7, 25. Hanson dis jH
1839, 6, 13. Lot & w, Ruth, & s, Bennett,
    rocf Stillwater MM, dtd 1839,5,18 (H)

GREGG, continued

1841, 8, 25. Sarah Ann (form Wright) dis mcd
1841, 9, 22. Margaret Haines (form Gregg) dis mcd & jas
1842, 5, 19. Hanson dis mcd (H)
1842, 10, 13. Amos, Nicholas, Hannah, Ann & Hamelton, ch Laban, recrq (H)
1843, 8, 17. John dis (H)
1843, 8, 17. Stephen C. recrq (H)
1843, 11, 22. Mary gct Pennsville MM
1843, 12, 20. Asenath Fesler (form Gregg) dis mcd
1845, 10, 22. Lydia Way (form Gregg) dis mcd
1845, 11, 13. Nathan gct Stillwater MM, to m Mary Ann Price (H)
1847, 1, 14. Mary Ann rocf Stillwater MM, dtd 1846,8,15
1847, 8, 25. Elias & Nathan dis disunity
1847, 10, 20. Stephen dis disunity
1847, 12, 22. William dis disunity
1848, 2, 17. Elias dis mcd (H)
1849, 5, 23. Mary Ann Rogers (form Gregg) dis mcd
1849, 6, 14. Elizabeth (form Broomhall) dis mcd (H)
1850, 5, 16. Lot gct Salem MM, to m Hannah Bailey
1850, 12, 25. Abner dis disunity
1851, 3, 13. Hannah B. rocf Salem MM, dtd 1850,12,25 (H)
1852, 5, 13. Sina Fawcett (form Gregg) dis mcd (H)
1852, 8, 19. Abner dis mcd (H)
1853, 8, 18. Nathan con mcd (H)
1854, 4, 13. Elijah & w, Phebe, & ch, Jonathan, Albert, Mariam & Sylvanes, gct Stillwater MM (H)
1854, 4, 13. Nathan & s, Spencer, gct Stillwater MM (H)
1856, 11, 12. Mary Eliza Wright (form Gregg) dis mcd (H)
1860, 11, 15. Susanna gct Prairie Grove MM, Ia. (H)
1862, 11, 13. Hannah Priscilla Branson (form Gregg) con mcd (H)
1863, 11, 19. Hannah McKisson (form Gregg) con mcd (H)
1870, 5, 19. Hannah B. & s, Kenworthy, gct West MM, Mahoning Co., O. (H)
1881, 6, 16. Joshua C. gct Race St. MM, Philadelphia, Pa. (H)
1881, 11, 17. Lot gct Stillwater MM (H)

GREWELL

1817, 4, 24. Mary & dt, Sarah Ann & Rachel, recrq

GRIFFITH

1821, 5, 2. Abram, s Wm. & Sarah, Belmont Co., O.; m in St. Clairsville, Mary ROBERTS, dt Ezekiel & Ann, Belmont Co., O.
1833, 3, 27. Samuel, s Evan & Elizabeth, Jefferson Co., O.; m in St. Clairsville,

Hannah FOULK, dt Issachar & Jane, Belmont Co., O.

1819, 9, 23. Eli & Rachel & s, William, rocf Stillwater MM, dtd 1819,8,28
1820, 4, 20. Abraham rocf Redstone MM, dtd 1820,3,1
1821, 5, 24. Eli & w, Rachel, & s, William, gct Concord MM
1822, 2, 21. Abraham & w, Mary, gct Concord MM
1822, 9, 26. Charles W. & w, Hannah, & s, Amos L., rocf Short Creek MM, O., dtd 1822,7,23
1833, 5, 23. Hannah gct Short Creek MM, O.(H)
1840, 9, 17. Anna R. & Rees L., Charles P. & Ruth, minor ch Abraham, dec, rocf Short Creek MM, O., dtd 1840,8,20 (H)
1844, 7, 24. Amos Lee & Jacob Lewis dis disunity
1852, 2, 19. Jacob Lewis con mcd (H)
1853, 2, 17. Amos L. gct Short Creek MM, O., to m Sarah Tomlinson (H)
1853, 3, 17. Charles W. & w, Hannah, & ch, Abel L., Samuel, Charles Lee & Mary Ellen, gct Clear Creek MM, Ill. (H)
1855, 8, 16. Amos gct Clear Creek MM, Ill.(H)

GRISSELL

1865, 7, 13. Nathan P. & w, Rebecca, rocf Stillwater MM, dtd 1865,6,17 (H)
1870, 8, 18. Rebecca gct Short Creek MM, O. (H)
1870, 7, 14. Rebecca gct Short Creek MM, O. (H)

GROVE

1837, 8, 23. Sarah (form Askew) dis mcd

GRUBB

1825, 2, 25. Curtis, s John & Hannah, Jefferson Co., O.; m in Goshen MH, Ann CROSIER, dt Judah & Sarah FOULKE, Monroe Co., O.

1825, 5, 26. Ann & dt, Sarah Crozier, gct Short Creek MM, O.

GUMERY

1830, 5, 30. John Jr. rocf Short Creek MM, O., dtd 1830,4,22 (H)
1830, 6, 24. William & w, Phebe, & ch, Swithen, Eli, Enoch, William, Hannah, Thomas, Lewis, Benjamin & Lavina, rocf Short Creek MM, O., dtd 1830,3,25 (H)
1832, 7, 26. Eli [Gumeree] con mcd (H)
1835, 5, 14. Enoch con mcd (H)
1835, 9, 17. William & w, Phebe, & ch, William, Hannah, Joshua, Benjamin, Lavina & gr s, Ephraim J. Parker, gct Green Plain MM (H)
1836, 8, 16. Swithen gct Green Plain MM (H)
1837, 7, 13. Hannah & Ann rocf Short Creek MM, O., dtd 1837,4,20 (H)

GUMERY, continued
1837, 12, 14. Eli [Gumere] dis disunity (H)
1844, 5, 16. Hannah Wheeler (form Gumery) con
    mcd (H)
1845, 12, 18. John [Gomery], Nancy & Isaac
    gct Short Creek MM, O. (H)
1846, 1, 15. Sarah [Gomery] gct Short Creek
    MM, O. (H)

GURNSEY
1837, 7, 13. John & w, Elizabeth, & dt, Sa-
    rah, rocf Short Creek MM, dtd 1837,4,20
    (H)
1837, 7, 13. Isaac rocf Short Creek MM, dtd
    1837,4,20 (H)
1837, 7, 13. Hannah & Ann rocf Short Creek
    MM, dtd 1837,4,20 (H)

GUYNN
1840, 8, 13. Mary Ann [Gwin] rocf Purchase
    MM, dtd 1838,10,10 (H)
1853, 8, 18. Mary Ann [Guian] gct Stillwater
    MM (H)
1869, 8, 19. Thomas rocf Short Creek MM, O.,
    dtd 1869,6,7 (H)
1870, 2, 17. Albert recrq (H)
1870, 2, 17. Mary & ch, John, Sarah, Amanda,
    Hugh Oliver, Thomas F., Elizabeth A.,
    Mary L. & William S., recrq (H)
1872, 5, 16. Albert L. con mcd (H)
1872, 7, 18. Rachel recrq (H)
1881, 6, 16. Mary Ann gct Clear Creek MM, Ill.
    (H)
1883, 5, 18. Albert [Gwynn] & w, Rachel, &
    ch, Mary Elizabeth & Minnie Wanita, gct
    Short Creek MM, O. (H)
1889, 6, 13. Sarah Amanda McKnight (form
    Guinn) con mcd (H)

HAINES
1832, 12, 26. Mary [Hains] m Stephen PANCOAST
    (H)
1833, 1, 2. Sarah [Hains] m Taylor SMITH
    (H)
1836, 3, 2. Wm., s John & Ann, Belmont Co.,
    O.; m in St. Clairsville, Eunice HORNER,
    dt John & Lydia, Belmont Co., O. (H)
1836, 3, 24. Rachel m Jesse H. ELLIOTT (H)
1841, 5, 26. Isaac [Hains], s Nathan & Rachel,
    Belmont Co., O.; m in Goshen MH, Margaret
    S. GREGG, dt John & Mary, Belmont Co., O.
    (H)

1810, 1, 27. Nathaniel dis
1817, 12, 25. Isaac & Rachel [Hains] & ch,
    William, Nancy, Timothy, Rebeckah & Edwin,
    rocf Short Creek MM, O., dtd 1817,9,23
1822, 6, 22. James rocf Burlington MM, N. J.,
    dtd 1821,12,6
1826, 3, 23. Rachel Parrish (form Haines)
    con mcd
1831, 8, 25. Joseph con mcd (H)
1832, 2, 23. Mary recrq (H)

1832, 11, 22. Joseph & w, Mary, & dt, Esther
    Ann, gct Salem MM (H)
1835, 1, 15. Phebe Lemon (form Haines) dis
    mcd (H)
1836, 12, 21. William dis JH
1837, 1, 25. Rachel (form Elliott) dis mcd &
    jas
1837, 5, 18. Charles con mcd (H)
1838, 3, 15. Charles gct Stillwater MM (H)
1839, 2, 14. John A. con mcd (H)
1841, 9, 22. Margaret (form Gregg) dis mcd
    & JH
1841, 11, 22. Isaac dis mcd & JH
1841, 12, 22. Eliza dis JH
1844, 12, 25. Elisha dis mcd
1845, 1, 16. Elisha con mcd
1845, 1, 16. Lydia Jane (form White) con mcd
    (H)
1845, 1, 22. Mary Vanlaw (form Haines) dis
    mcd
1845, 2, 13. Mary Vanlaw (form Haines) con
    mcd (H)
1848, 3, 16. Eliza Hoge (form Haines) con mcd
    (H)
1858, 12, 16. Elisha dis joining M. E. Church
    (H)
1859, 1, 13. Joseph & w, Mary, & ch, Mary R.,
    Simpson G., Maria E., Seldon T., Dempsy
    T. & Valinda J., rocf Stillwater MM, dtd
    1858,10,16 (H)
1861, 7, 18. William & w, Eunice, & ch, Os-
    car, Mary Emily, Anna & John Willis, gct
    Prairie Grove MM, Ia. (H)
1871, 10, 19. Mary Emily (form Mead) con mcd
    (H)
1882, 1, 19. Margaret d 1881,1,25 ae 60, w
    Isaac (H)
1882, 8, 17. ----- con mcd (H)
1892, 11, 17. Elizabeth Mitchner recrq (H)

HALL
1838, 8, 2. Nathan P., s Jesse & Peninah,
    Jefferson Co., O.; m in Plainfield MH,
    Merab COFFEE, dt John & Rachel, Belmont
    Co., O.
1845, 5, 22. Isaac W., s John & Phebe,
    Gurnsey Co., O.; m in Plainfield MH, Eliza-
    beth VAIL, dt Robert & Sarah, Belmont Co.,
    O. (H)

1809, 11, 25. Joseph Cadwalader gct Short
    Creek MM, O., to m Christian Hall
1838, 12, 19. Merab gct Short Creek MM, O.
1849, 3, 21. Robert & ch, Tacy & Hervey,
    rocf Flushing MM, dtd 1849,2,22
1849, 3, 21. Mary rocf Chesterfield MM, dtd
    1849,2,17
1850, 4, 24. Robert & w, Mary, & ch, Tacy,
    Hervey & Martha, gct Somerset MM
1846, 2, 19. Elizabeth gct Stillwater MM (H)

HAMBLETON
1812, 8, 22. William rocf Short Creek MM,

HAMBLETON, continued
    dtd 1812,6,23

HAMPTON
1828, 2, 21. James & w, Emily, & ch, Amos W.,
    Levi & Mary, rocf Short Creek MM, O., dtd
    1828,1,22
1831, 2, 24. Emily & ch, Amos, Levi, Mary &
    Hiram, gct Stillwater MM (H)

HARRIS
1837, 10, 22. Ezekiel & w, Anna, & ch, Elisha,
    Sarah, Mary, Enoch & Caroline, rocf Short
    Creek MM, O., dtd 1837,6,20
1838, 1, 24. Ezekiel & w, Anna, dis disunity
1839, 3, 20. Elisha, Sarah, Mary, Enoch,
    Caroline & William, minor ch Ezekiel &
    Anna, gct Short Creek MM, O.

HARRISON
1836, 9, 21. Thomas dis jas

HARTLEY
1823, 3, 20. Aaron & w, Phebe, & dt, Ann
    Lundy, rocf Muncy MM, dtd 1822,11,20
1828, 7, 24. Aaron & w, Phebe, & ch, Anna
    Lundy, William Watson, Mary Ann & Joseph,
    gct Muncy MM, Pa. (H)
1830, 10, 21. Cert rec for Aaron & fam from
    Muncy MM, Pa., dtd 1828,7,24, returned to
    that mtg since they returned to reside in
    limits of that mtg (H)
1836, 1, 14. Aaron & ch, Anna Lundy, Wm. Wil-
    son, Maryann, Joseph, Hannah Jane & Eliza-
    beth, gct Goshen MM (H)

HARVEY
1833, 10, 24. Margaret (form Minikin) con mcd
    (H)
1836, 1, 14. Margaret & dt, Julia Elna Maria
    Miniken, gct Westland MM (H)

HATCHER
1811, 10, 31. Sarah m Asahel HOGE
1816, 10, 31. Mary m John GREGG

1813, 2, 27. William dis
1821, 3, 22. Elijah dis disunity
1825, 9, 22. Abner Gregg, Sr. gct Goose Creek
    MM, Va., to m Mary Hatcher
1854, 2, 16. Rachel rocf Goose Creek MM,
    Va., dtd 1854,1,12 (H)
1855, 4, 19. Mary (form Kennard) con mcd (H)

HAWLEY
1818, 12, 3. Richard, s Caleb & Hannah, Colum-
    biana Co., O.; m in Plainfield MH, Rachel
    PAXSON, dt Benjamin & Ruth, Belmont Co., O.

1820, 3, 23. Richard & w, Rachel, & dt, Ann,
    gct West Grove MM, Ind.

HEAD
1819, 5, 20. Elizabeth (form White) dis mcd

HEALD
1833, 5, 23. Amy (form Gregg) con mcd (H)

HEATON
1843, 7, 19. Rebecca (form Askew) dis mcd

HESTER
1827, 11, 22. Cert rec for Ruth from Muncey
    MM, dtd 1827,4,18, end to Stillwater MM

HESTON
1835, 6, 24. Mahlon rocf New Garden MM, Pa.,
    dtd 1834,12,3
1837, 11, 22. Mahlon gct Flushing MM

HIBERT
1846, 7, 16. Thomas rocf Concord MM, Pa., dtd
    1845,9,25 (H)

HILL
1817, 6, 26. Elizabeth (form Tuder) dis mcd
    (Hull on women's minutes)

HILLIS
1844, 12, 19. Nathan & w, Sarah, & ch, Skip-
    with C., Wm., Robert, Rachel Ann, Samuel
    & John P., rocf Middleton MM, dtd 1844,
    1,12, end by Stillwater MM (H)
1850, 1, 17. Scipwith C. [Hilles] con mcd
    (H)
1859, 11, 17. Skipwith C. con mcd (H)
1867, 2, 14. Samuel con mcd (H)

HILTON
1830, 7, 22. Ann (form Pittman) con mcd (H)

HIRST
1821, 6, 27. Thomas, s David & Ann, Belmont
    Co., O.; m in Goshen MH, Anna GREGG, dt
    Jacob & Mary, Belmont Co., O.

1821, 8, 23. Anna gct Concord MM
1826, 4, 20. Thomas & w, Anna, & ch, Ruth
    Anna & Rebecca, rocf Corcord MM, dtd 1825,
    11,23
1826, 5, 25. Thomas & w, Anna, & ch, Ruth
    Anne, Rebecca & Amanda, gct Flushing MM
1852, 3, 18. Phebe (form Wilson) dis mcd (H)
1863, 8, 20. Able Lewis gct Flushing MM, to
    m Hannah [Hurst]

HOBSON
1818, 7, 23. Francis & w, Grace, & ch, Ann,
    John, Martha & Esther, rocf Smithfield MM,
    dtd 1818,6,22

HOFF
1886, 8, 19. Mary E. rocf Short Creek MM, O.,
    dtd 1886,7,8 (H)

HOGE

1808, 4, 27. William, s John & Mary, Belmont
    Co., O.; m in Flushing MH, Sarah WRIGHT,
    dt Wm. & Eunice, Belmont Co., O.
1811, 10, 30. Absalom, s Isaac & Elizabeth,
    Belmont Co., O.; m in Goshen MH, Rachel
    COFFEY, dt John & Rachel, Belmont Co., O.
1811, 10, 31. Asahel, s David & Ruth, Belmont
    Co., O.; m in Plainfield MH, Sarah HATCHER,
    dt Joshua & Jane, Belmont Co., O.
1836, 11, --. Washington, s Samuel & Elizabeth,
    Belmont Co., O.; m in Goshen MH, Phebe
    GREGG, dt Jacob & Mary, Belmont Co., O.
    (H)
----, --, --. John C. & Rebecca B.
    Ch: Lindley M. b 1844, 6, 18
        Hannah E. " 1848, 7, 12
        Edward   " 1853, 10, 2
1843, 8, 24. Thomas R., s Abner & Sarah, Bel-
    mont Co., O.; m in Plainfield MH, Mary T.
    FAWCETT, dt Elisha & Lydia, Belmont Co.,O.
1850, 4, 24. Thomas E., s Samuel & Mary, Bel-
    mont Co., O.; m in Goshen MH, Ann GREGG,
    dt Elijah & Phebe, Belmont Co., O.
1854, 4, 20. Emily E. [Hogue] m James S. ELY
    (H)

1810, 7, 28. Ann Tompkins (form Hoge) dis mcd
1812, 10, 24. Craven gct Short Creek MM, O.
1813, 5, 22. James con mcd
1813, 6, 26. Lydia Brown (form Hoge) dis mcd
1813, 12, 25. James gct Goose Creek MM, Va.
1814, 1, 22. Solomon dis mcd
1817, 10, 23. Pleasant Norris (form Hoge) dis
    mcd
1818, 7, 23. Craven rocf Short Creek MM, O.,
    dtd 1818,7,21
1823, 11, 20. Absalom & w, Rebecca, & ch,
    John, Isaac, Maryann, James & Rachel, gct
    Short Creek MM
1825, 4, 21. Ruth Palmer (form Hogue) dis mcd
1827, 7, 26. Asa [Hogue] dis mcd
1829, 6, 25. Samuel & w, Mary, & ch, Susan,
    Washington, William, Samuel, Solomon &
    Thomas Elwood, rocf Goose Creek MM, Va.,
    dtd 1829,4,16 (H)
1830, 7, 22. Jonathan [Hogue] con mcd (H)
1830, 7, 22. Susan (form Hoge) con mcd (H)
1831, 8, 25. Elizabeth Ewers (form Hogue) dis
    mcd (H)
1832, 7, 26. Bushrod [Hogue] con mcd (H)
1835, 12, 23. Jesse gct Short Creek MM, O., to
    m Susannah Kinsey
1836, 6, 22. Jane dis jH
1836, 10, 19. Jesse dis jH
1838, 2, 15. Lydia (form Ewers) con mcd (H)
1838, 3, 15. Jonathan con mcd (H)
1838, 4, 19. Mary Palmer (form Hoge) con mcd
    (H)
1838, 8, 22. Nimrod dis jH (H)
1838, 10, 18. Amy con mcd (H)
1839, 2, 14. Jonathan & w, Lydia, & ch,
    William H., Theodoric & Susanna, gct

Stillwater MM (H)
1839, 4, 13. Nimrod con mcd & rst (H)
1839, 11, 14. David E. con mcd (H)
1840, 2, 13. William dis mcd (H)
1840, 3, 19. David E. gct Stillwater MM (H)
1841, 8, 19. Sarah Jane Chandler (form Hogue)
    con mcd (H)
1843, 12, 20. John C. rocf Short Creek MM, O.,
    dtd 1843,11,21
1843, 12, 20. Rebecca B. rocf Salem MM, dtd
    1843,10,25
1844, 11, 20. Susan rocf Short Creek MM, O.,
    dtd 1844,9,24
1845, 4, 17. Joshua H. dis mcd (H)
1845, 7, 23. Hannah (form Wilson) dis mcd
1846, 10, 21. Susanna & ch, Mary Elizabeth &
    Laura, gct Short Creek MM, O.
1846, 12, 17. Hannah (form Wilson) con mcd
    (H)
1847, 6, 23. Joshua dis mcd
1848, 3, 16. Samuel Jr. gct Stillwater MM,
    to m Agnes Ann Brown (H)
1848, 3, 16. Eliza (form Haines) con mcd
    (H)
1848, 5, 18. Solomon, Samuel Jr. & Nimrod
    gct Stillwater MM (H)
1851, 4, 17. Hannah B. gct Clear Creek MM,
    Ill. (H)
1851, 4, 17. Elijah gct Stillwater MM (H)
1852, 4, 15. Thomas Elwood & w, Ann, & dt,
    Mary Emily, gct Stillwater MM (H)
1857, 7, 16. Mary gct Stillwater MM (H)
1858, 1,14. Abner E. con mcd (H)
1858, 7, 21. John C. [Hogue] & w, Rebecca,
    ch, Lindley, Hannah Elma & Edward, gct
    Flushing MM
1858, 12, 16. Ruthanna Plumley (form Hoge)
    con mcd (H)
1867, 8, 15. Lundy B. [Hogue] con military
    service (H)
1870, 7, 14. Lundy B. [Hogue] con mcd (H)
1886, 7, 15. Eliza [Hogue] relrq (H)

HOLE
1825, 4, 21. John Green gct Sandy Spring MM,
    to m Mary Hole

HOLLIDAY
1817, 8, 21. Fanny (form Melton) dis mcd

HOLLINGSWORTH
1814, 4, 27. David, s Levi & Mary, Belmont
    Co., O.; m in Flushing MH, Hannah JONES,
    dt James & Grace

1815, 4, 22. Sarah Packer (form Hollings-
    worth) con mcd
1815, 9, 23. Christopher & w, Elizabeth, &
    ch, John Ferris, Samuel, Sarah Ann &
    Charles, rocf Concord MM, dtd 1815,7,20
1821, 3, 22. Christopher & w, Elizabeth, &
    ch, John, Faris, Samuel, Sarah Ann, Chris-
    ropher & Edward, gct Salem MM

HOLLOWAY

1811, 2, 27. James, s James & Mary, Belmont
Co., O.; m in Goshen MH, Phebe GREGG, dt
Samuel & Ann, Belmont Co., O.
1812, 1, 2. Ann m Thomas VANLAW
1813, 5, 26. Robert, s Asa & Abigail, Belmont Co., O.; m in Flushing MH, Rebecca
PICKERING, dt John & Jane
1816, 10, 30. Samuel, s Asa & Abigail, Belmont
Co., O.; m in Plainfield MH, Amy TRAHERN,
dt James & Dinah, Belmont Co., O.
1840, 12, 31. Elisha J., s James & Phebe, Belmont Co., O.; m in Plainfield MH, Lydia S.
VANLAW, dt John & Sarah, Belmont Co., O.

1811, 9, 28. Ann recrq
1813, 8, 23. Asa Jr. gct Short Creek MM, O.
1814, 3, 26. Jacob & w, Martha, & ch, Mariah
& John Warfield, rocf Short Creek MM, O.,
dtd 1813,12,21
1818, 7, 23. Asa rocf Short Creek MM, O., dtd
1818,6,23
1818, 10, 22. Asa gct Short Creek MM, O., to
m
1820, 4, 20. Margaret rocf Flushing MM, dtd
1820,3,24
1825, 4, 21. James & w, Phebe, & ch, Samuel,
Asa & Elisha, gct Flushing MM
1841, 2, 24. Lydia S. gct Flushing MM
1841, 8, 25. Smith & w, Abigail, & ch, Isaac
Parker & Elvira, rocf Flushing MM
1853, 3, 23. Smith & w, Abigail, & ch, Isaac
P., Mary E., Samuel & Abby P., gct Short
Creek MM, O.

HOLMES

1848, 12, 15. Jesse, s Joseph & Elizabeth,
Columbiana Co., O.; m in Plainfield MH,
Marcy LLOYD, dt Joshua & Mary, Belmont Co.,
O. (H)
1855, 1, 24. Joseph W., s William & Eliza
T., Louden Co., Va.; m in house of Elisha
FAWCETT, Rebecca J. FAWCETT, dt Elisha &
Rebecca, Belmont Co., O. (H)

1842, 8, 18. Jesse & Rebecca & ch, Elizabeth
Hannah & Orlando Wm., rocf New Garden MM,
dtd 1842,7,21 (H)
1843, 10, 19. Jesse & w, Rebecca, & ch,
Elizabeth & Kerry Orlando, gct New Garden
MM (H)
1849, 5, 17. Mercy L. gct Salem MM (H)
1857, 4, 16. Rebecca gct Goose Creek MM, Va.
(H)

HOOVER

1823, 7, 24. Martha (form Broomhall) dis mcd
1860, 10, 18. Lewis Henry, s Amelia Pickering,
recrq (H)

HORNER

1828, 3, 21. Thomas F., s John & Lydia, Belmont Co., O.; m in St. Clairsville, Mary-

ann PARKER, dt Thos. & Rachel, Belmont
Co., O.
1828, 3, 26. Lydia Ann m Benj. FAWCETT
1836, 3, 2. Eunice m Wm. HAINES (H)

1815, 11, 25. Thomas F. rocf Alexander MM,
Va., dtd 1815,4,20
1820, 2, 24. Martha B., minor, rocf Alexandria MM, dtd 1819,12,23
1821, 3, 22. Lydia & ch, Elizabeth, Lydia
Ann, Isaac & John, rocf Alexandria MM,
dtd 1820,12,21
1828, 5, 22. Thomas F. & w, Mary Ann, gct
Salem MM
1831, 4, 21. Amos, s Lydia, recrq (H)
1831, 5, 26. Eunice, Sarah, Mary Jane, Phebe
Ellen & Druzilla, ch Lydia, recrq (H)
1841, 9, 22. Isaac dis disunity
1841, 12, 16. Phebe Ellen Thompson (form
Horner) dis mcd (H)
1843, 2, 22. John Jr. dis disunity

1847, 3, 18. Mary Jane Bonsel (form Horner)
dis mcd (H)
1847, 10, 14. Amos dis military service (H)
1859, 1, 13. Druzilla Williams (form Horner)
dis mcd

HORSMAN

1818, 8, 20. Mary recrq

HORTON

1831, 9, 22. Joseph H. [Horten] & w, Agnes,
& ch, Elizabeth, Thomas & Joseph, rocf
Cherry St. MM, Phila., Pa., dtd 1830,6,16,
end by Concord MM (H)
1841, 9, 16. Mary J. rocf Short Creek MM, dtd
1841,7,22 (H)
1841, 9, 16. John & w, Rachel, & Cynthia Horton Davis, minor, rocf Short Creek MM, dtd
1841,7,22 (H)
1842, 1, 13. Mary H. Sriver (form Horton)
con mcd (H)
1843, 3, 16. Joseph H. & w, Agnes, & ch,
Thos., Joseph & Mahlon, gct Concord MM (H)
1843, 8, 17. Elizabeth gct Concord MM (H)
1848, 8, 17. John & w, Rebecca, & Cynthia
Horton Davis, minor, gct Westland MM (H)

HOSIER

1835, 12, 23. Hannah & dt, Maria, rocf Baltimore MM for E. & W. Dist., dtd 1835,10,12
1836, 8, 24. Hannah & Maria gct Short Creek
MM, O.

HOUGH

1842, 4, 28. Thomas, s John & Elizabeth,
Jefferson Co., O.; m in Plainfield MH,
Hannah VAIL, dt Benj. & Hannah, Belmont
Co., O.

1812, 5, 23. Jonah & w, Pleasant, & ch, Is-

HOUGH, Jonah, continued
      rael J. & James, rocf Goose Creek MM, Va.,
      dtd 1812,2,--
1812, 7, 25. Pleasant rocf Goose Creek MM,
      Va., dtd 1812,4,2
1830, 5, 25. Pleasant Brown (form Hough) dis
      mcd

HOWARD
1815, 4, 22. Horton & w, Hannah, & ch, Joseph,
      Rachel, Horton, Sarah, Mary, Ann, Hannah &
      John, rocf Concord MM, dtd 1815,4,20
1820, 7, 20. Horton & w, Hannah, & ch, Sarah,
      Mary, Ann, Hannah & John, gct Alum Creek
      MM
1820, 7, 20. Howard Horton Jr. & Rachel gct
      Allum Creek MM
1827, 5, 24. Horton & w, Mary, & s, Elisha
      B., rocf Short Creek MM, O., dtd 1827,3,20
1836, 3, 23. Horton J. & w, Mary, dis disunity

HOYLE
----, --, --. Thomas & Hannah
      Ch: William C. b 1845, 2, 25

1842, 8, 24. Hannah V. gct Smithfield MM
1843, 6, 21. Thomas & w, Hannah V., & s, Jo-
      seph Lindley, rocf Smithfield MM, dtd
      1843,5,22
185-, 12, 25. Thomas & w, Hannah, & ch, Jo-
      seph Lindley & William G., gct Newgarden
      MM
1857, 5, 20. Thomas & w, Hannah V., & ch, Jo-
      seph Lindley & William G., rocf Newgarden
      MM, dtd 1857,3,26

HUNT
1818, 1, 22. Joshua & w, Rachel, & ch, David,
      Samuel, Joshua, Jonathan, John & Nathan,
      rocf Short Creek MM, dtd 1817,7,22, end by
      Concord MM 1817,12,24

HURFORD
1809, 8, 26. Jacob Pickering Jr. gct Short
      Creek MM, O., to m Rachel Hurford

HUSTLER
1843, 10, 26. Elizabeth m Isaac N. CLARK (H)

1838, 2, 21. Anna & Elizabeth rocf Phila. MM
      for N. Dist., dtd 1838,1,23
1838, 5, 17. Mary & dt, Ann & Elizabeth, rocf
      Green St. MM, Phila., Pa., dtd 1838,3,22
      (H)
1844, 2, 21. Elizabeth Clark (form Hustler)
      dis mcd
1849, 12, 19. Ann Meek (form Hustler) dis mcd

HUTCHISON
1876, 9, --. Hannah Priscilla (form Branson)
      con mcd (H)

INNIS
1818, 10, 22. Cert rec for Robert & w, Isa-
      bella, & dt, Emla, from Concord MM, dtd
      1818,7,30, end to Flushing MM

JAMES
1809, 8, 20. Rebeckah gct Short Creek MM
1813, 6, 26. Evan & w, Rebecca, & ch, Han-
      nah, Phebe & Jonas, rocf Short Creek MM,
      O., dtd 1813,5,18
1814, 2, 26. Evan & w, Rebecca, & ch, Hannah,
      Phebe & Jonas, gct Short Creek MM, O.
1838, 10, 24. Rachel rocf Upper Springfield
      MM, dtd 1838,7,28

JANNEY
1809, 12, 23. Amos rocf New Garden MM, dtd
      1809,10,19
1810, 1, 27. Amos dis mcd

JEFFERS
1820, 8, 24. Caleb & w, Phebe, & ch, Emmer &
      Rhoda, rocf Westland MM, dtd 1820,7,27
1829, 9, 24. Rhoda dis (H)
1831, 4, 21. Caleb & w, Phebe, & s, Emmor,
      gct Owl Creek MM (H)

JENKINS
1812, 12, 30. Lydia m David PERKINS
1815, 12, 27. Elizabeth m Thos. KENNARD

1808, 4, 23. Ruth Willes (form Jenkins) dis
      mcd
1816, 3, 22. Sarah & ch, John, Rachel Mary &
      George, gct Short Creek MM, O.
1816, 8, 23. Evan dis military service
1816, 9, 26. James dis disunity
1816, 12, 26. Catharine Morgan (form Jenkins)
      dis mcd
1823, 4, 24. Thomas Pugh dis mcd

JOB
1849, 11, 15. Samuel & w, Eliza Ann, & ch, Ra-
      chel Ann & Hannah Elizabeth, rocf Concord
      MM, dtd 1849,8,22 (H)
1868, 12, 14. Mary Ann [Jobe] roc (H)

JOHNSON
1812, 9, 26. Rachel rst on consent of Goose
      Creek MM, Va.
1813, 6, 26. Hannah & Lucretia recrq
1818, 12, 24. Martha (form Tudor) con mcd
1819, 10, 21. Martha (form Tuder) con mcd
1820, 3, 23. Sarah (form Hoge) dis mcd
1820, 5, 25. William rocf Stillwater MM, dtd
      1820,4,22
1821, 12, 20. Martha [Jonson] dis joining
      M. E. Church

JONES
1814, 4, 27. Hannah m David HOLLINGSWORTH
1815, 9, 27. Sarah m Wm. BILLINGSLY
1818, 3, 2. Hannah m Micajah J. WILLIAMS

JONES, continued

1812, 10, 24. Sarah & Hannah recrq

1818, 1, 26. Hannah rocf Cincinnati MM, dtd
1817,12,18, end by Stillwater MM 1818,1,24

1853, 5, 19. Emily (form Kenard) con mcd (H)

1856, 11, 13. Yearsly rocf Stillwater MM, dtd
1856,10,18 (H)

1862, 2, 13. Yearsly relrq (H)

JOSLIN

1821, 11, 22. Mary (form Piatt) dis mcd

JUDGE

1815, 6, 24. Cert rec for Hugh & w, Susannah
from Indian Spring MM, Md., dtd 1815,4,21
end to Stillwater MM 1815,8,31

1815, 6, 24. Cert rec for Phebe & Rebecca
from Indian Spring MM, Md., dtd 1815,4,21,
end to Stillwater MM, 1815,8,31

1834, 8, 14. Hugh rocf Stillwater MM, O., dtd
1834,6,21 (H)

JUDKINS

1822, 5, 4. Joel, s Nicholas & Mary, Belmont
Co., O.; m in Plainfield MH, Mariah GREGG,
dt Samuel & Gulielma, Belmont Co., O.

1817, 1, 23. Catharine Morgan (form Judkins)
dis mcd

1818, 5, 21. James Jr. & w, Susanna, & ch,
Jonathan & Martha, rocf Short Creek MM,
O., dtd 1818,4,21

1822, 7, 25. Maria gct Stillwater MM

1829, 6, 25. Maria & s, Hiram, rocf Stillwater MM, dtd 1829,4,18 (H)

KEITH

1864, 1, 21. Mary Ann m Thomas WILSON (H)

KELSE

1847, 1, 20. Mary (form McNichols) dis mcd

KENNARD

1815, 12, 27. Thomas, s Levi & Ann, Belmont
Co., O.; m in St. Clairsville, Elizabeth
JENKINS, dt Mishael & Rachel, Belmont Co.,
O.

1842, 11, 24. Wm., s Eli & Elizabeth, Monroe
Co., O.; m in Plainfield MH, Sarah ROBERTS
dt Aaron & Elizabeth, Belmont Co., O.

1815, 6, 24. Thomas & s, Henry Preston, rocf
Short Creek MM, O., dtd 1815,5,23

1830, 6, 24. Thomas & w, Elizabeth, & ch,
Henry P., Rachel, Levi, John, Jacob, Jenkins & Thomas, gct Flushing MM (H)

1831, 12, 22. Henry P., minor, rocf Flushing
MM, dtd 1831,11,26 (H)

1832, 7, 26. Anthony & w, Elizabeth, & ch,
Sarah, Levi, Emily & Mary, recrq (H)

1843, 2, 22. Sarah gct Somerset MM

1848, 5, 18. Sarah White (form Kenard) dis

mcd (H)

1853, 5, 19. Emily Jones (form Kenard) con
mcd (H)

1855, 4, 19. Mary Hatcher (form Kennard)
con mcd (H)

KENNY

1821, 5, 24. Margaret rocf Lurgan MM, Ireland
dtd 1818,2,14

1822, 10, 24. Jane, of Stillwater, ltm Thos.
Smith Jr.

1825, 2, 24. Alice (form Pearson) dis mcd

KESTER

1835, 1, 21. David, s John & Martha, Gurnsey
Co., O.; m in Goshen MH, Ann PARKER, dt
Wm. & Phebe GUMMERE, Belmont Co., O. (H)

1826, 12, 21. John & w, Martha, & ch, Jonathan, Hartley, Benjamin, David, Jesse,
Lavina, John B., Aaron, James Kitely,
Martha, Robert & Sarah E., rocf Muncy MM,
dtd 1826,10,18

1826, 12, 21. Cert rec for William & w, Mary,
& dt, Elizabeth, from Muncy MM, dtd 1826,
10,18, end to Stillwater MM

1827, 11, 22. Ruth rocf Muncy MM, Pa., dtd
1827,4,18

1835, 9, 17. Ann gct Stillwater MM (H)

KING

1815, 5, 27. John & w, Mary, & ch, Hannah,
Caroline, Mary, John Bowne, Samuel, Elizabeth & Catharine Murry, rocf Concord MM,
dtd 1815,5,25

1817, 4, 24. Jane rocf Concord MM, dtd 1817,
1,22

1817, 7, 24. John & w, Mary, & ch, Hannah,
Caroline, Mary, John Brown, Samuel, Eliza-
beth, Catharine Murry & Ann, gct Concord
MM

KINSEY

1814, 3, 1. Sarah m David MAXSON

1816, 2, 1. Richard, s Absalom & Ridley,
Harrison Co., O.; m in Notingham, Sarah
DAVID, dt Daniel & Ann

1809, 4, 22. Richard & w, Rhoda, & ch, Jesse,
Nancy & John, rocf Plymouth MM, dtd 1809,
3,18

1812, 8, 22. Christopher & w, Mary, & ch, Sarah, John, Absalam, Nathan, Ruth, Edmond,
Susannah & Rachel, rocf Plymouth MM, dtd
1812,3,21

1835, 12, 23. Jesse Hoge gct Short Creek MM,
O., to m Susannah Kinsey

1849, 11, 15. Oliver rocf New Garden MM, dtd
1849,9,6 (H)

1889, 4, 18. Oliver gct Argonia MM, Kans. (H)

KIRK

1813, 9, 29. Nathan, s Eli & Edith, Belmont

KIRK, continued
    Co., O.; m in St. Clairsville, Amelia
TOWNSEND, dt Thos. & Elizabeth, Belmont
Co., O.

1810, 10, 27. Esther & dt, Phebe, rocf West-
    land MM, dtd 1809,12,23
1811, 6, 22. Rachel (form Pickering) con mcd
1812, 5, 23. Phebe Pickering (form Kirk) dis
    mcd
1812, 9, 26. Nathan rocf York MM, Pa., dtd
    1812,4,8
1824, 3, 23. Nathan & w, Amelia, & ch, Louisa,
    Almira, Mary & Elizabeth, gct Driftwood
    MM, Ind.

KIZSER
1824, 7, 22. Johanna W. (form Broomhall) dis
    mcd

KNIGHT
1839, 6, 13. Mary Ann (form Vanlaw) con mcd
    (H)

LACOCK
1815, 11, 25. Naomi rocf Short Creek MM, dtd
    1815,9,4

LAING
1813, 7, 24. David rocf Redstone MM, Pa., dtd
    1813,3,5

LEMON
1835, 1, 15. Phebe (form Haines) dis mcd (H)

LESLIE
1819, 5, 26. Margaret m David LUPTON

1819, 3, 25. Robert & w, Rachel, & ch, Thom-
    as, Mary, Robert, Johnson, Sarah & Levi,
    rocf Smithfield MM, dtd 1819,2,22
1819, 3, 25. Margaret & Elizabeth rocf Smith-
    field MM, dtd 1819,2,22
1820, 6, 22. Robert & w, Rachel, & ch, Robert
    Johnson, Sarah & Levi L., gct Stillwater
    MM
1820, 6, 22. Elizabeth & Mary gct Stillwater
    MM

LEWIS
1835, 4, 2. Abel, s Jacob & Mary, Belmont
    Co., O.; m in Plainfield MH, Lucinda
    GREGG, dt Stephen & Asenath, Belmont Co.,
    O., d 1861,12,22 ae 54 bur Plainfield
    Ch: Wilson   b 1836, 1, 4
        Reese   " 1838, 5, 2
        Stephen A. " 1844, 1, 1 d 1861,12,19
            bur Plainfield
        Juliet C. b 1848, 6, 22
1840, 2, 14. Charles, s Isaac & Mary, Wash.
    Co.; m in Goshen MH, Lydia Ann GREGG, dt
    John & Mary, Belmont Co., O. (H)

1859, 1, 7. Mary d ae 81 bur Plainfield

1817, 9, 25. Catharine rocf Short Creek MM,
    O., dtd 1817,6,24
1817, 11, 20. Samuel rocf Short Creek MM, O.,
    dtd 1817,5,20
1818, 3, 26. Ann rocf Short Creek MM, O.,
    dtd 1817,9,23, end by Concord MM
1821, 8, 23. Catharine gct Short Creek MM, O.
1822, 4, 25. Jacob & w, Mary, & ch, Rachel,
    Ira, Able & Reese, rocf Short Creek MM,
    O., dtd 1822,3,19
1823, 3, 20. Samuel gct Short Creek MM, O.
1823, 6, 26. Rachel Foreman (form Lewis) dis
    mcd
1836, 12, 21. Reece dis mcd
1837, 5, 18. Sarah Jane (form Gregg) dis mcd
    (H)
1847, 7, 21. Maria (form Green) dis mcd
1859, 3, 23. John Milton dis disunity
1863, 8, 20. Able gct Flushing MM, to m Han-
    nah Hurst
1864, 1, 20. Hannah rocf Flushing MM, dtd
    1863,11,26
1850, 4, 18. Mary (form Allen) con mcd (H)
1852, 5, 13. Mary rocf Westland MM, dtd 1851,
    9,25 (H)
1855, 9, 13. Thomas recrq (H)
1856, 1, 17. Charles & w, Lydia, & ch, Isaac,
    John Ira & Wm. Harvey, rocf Westland MM,
    dtd 1855,10,25 (H)
1881, 6, 16. Wm. H. gct Race St. MM, Phila.,
    Pa. (H)

LIGHTFOOT
1819, 9, 23. William rocf Chester MM, Pa.,
    dtd 1818,8,31, end by Cincinnati MM, 1819,
    8,19
1821, 12, 20. William gct New Garden MM
1855, 2, 21. Abner Spencer gct Pennsville MM,
    to m Rachel Lightfoot

LILLY
1818, 4, 23. Robert rocf Westland MM, dtd
    1818,3,26

LINTON
1815, 4, 22. Mary (form Fisher) dis mcd

LIPSEY
1812, 1, 25. David Cadwalader gct Short Creek
    MM, O., to m Sarah Lipsey

LLEWELLYN
1843, 5, 30. William, s Wm. & Mary, Morgan
    Co., O.; m in Plainfield MH, Mary CHAM-
    BERS, dt Samuel & Deborah, Belmont Co., O.

1843, 11, 22. Mary gct Pennsville MM

LLOYD
1820, 8, 30. Joshua [Loyd], s John & Mercy,
    Belmont Co., O.; m in St. Clairville, Mary

LLOYD, Joshua, continued
    & Mercy, Belmont Co., O.; m in St. Clair-
    ville, Mary NICHOLS, dt Eli & Jane, Bel-
    mont Co., O.
1843, 5, 6. Mary d ae 41 bur Plainfield
1848, 12, 15. Mercy m Jesse HOLMES (H)

1819, 1, 27. Eli Nickols gct Short Creek MM,
    O., to m Rachel LLoyd
1822, 7, 25. Joshua [Loyd] rocf Stillwater
    MM, dtd 1822,6,22
1826, 7, 20. Joshua [Loyd] dis disunity
1847, 6, 23. Mercy & Jane dis disunity
1848, 4, 19. Edward dis disunity
1853, 10, 17. Susan dis disunity

LOWNS
1816, 5, 24. Charles & w, Elizabeth, & dt,
    Rebecca H., rocf Short Creek MM, O., dtd
    1816,4,23
1832, 5, 24. Charles & w, Elizabeth, & ch,
    Rebecca, Joseph, Emmor & Elizabeth, gct
    Stillwater MM (H)

LUKENS
1815, 1, 28. Cert rec for Moses & w, Sarah,
    & 8 ch from Muncy MM, end to Plymouth MM
1815, 1, 28. Cert rec for Rachel & Lydia from
    Muncy MM, dtd 1814,10,19, end to Plymouth
    MM

LUNDY
1815, 7, 22. Benjamin & w, Esther, rocf Short
    Creek MM, dtd 1815,6,20
1822, 2, 21. Benjamin & w, Esther, & ch, Su-
    sannah M., Elizabeth S. & Charles T., gct
    Short Creek MM, O.

LUPTON
1819, 5, 26. David, s John & Lydia, Jeffer-
    son Co., O.; m in Goshen MH, Margaret
    LESLIE, dt Robert & Rachel, Belmont Co.,
    O.

1821, 4, 26. David & w, Margaret, & ch, Ra-
    chel Ann, gct Smithfield MM
1827, 10, 25. Nathan & w, Margaret, & s, Josh-
    ua, rocf Short Creek MM, O., dtd 1827,8,21
1827, 10, 25. Ann & Lydia rocf Short Creek MM,
    O., dtd 1827,8,21
1856, 12, 18. Joshua B. rocf Hopewell MM, Va.,
    dtd 1856,6,5 (H)
1857, 7, 16. Lydia Ann con mcd (H)

LUTTON
1837, 6, 15. Margaret (form Miniken) con mcd
    (H)

McCLAREY
1829, 4, 23. Eliza (form Coble) dis mcd

McDOWELL
1863, 2, 19. Sarah (form Foulk) relrq (H)

McGIRR
1823, 9, 25. Arthur & w, Elizabeth, & ch,
    Frances, Nancy & Sarah, rocf Westland MM
    Pa., dtd 1823,4,23

McGREW
1818, 6, 25. Rachel Jr. rocf Smithfield MM,
    dtd 1818,2,23
1818, 6, 25. Rachel & ch, Mary, Dinah, Sinah,
    Finley & Elizabeth, rocf Smithfield MM,,
    dtd 1818,2,23

McKAY
1809, 11, 25. Jacob & w, Rebeccah, rocf Hope-
    well MM, dtd 1809,9,4

McKISSON
1824, 6, 24. Joanna (form Broomhall) dis mcd
1844, 12, 19. Joanna recrq (H)
1863, 11, 19. Hannah (form Gregg) con mcd (H)

McKNIGHT
1889, 6, 13. Sarah Amanda (form Gwinn) con
    mcd (H)

McMELLON
1811, 8, 24. Hannah gct Center MM

McMILLAN
1811, 5, 29. Jonathan, s Wm. & Deborah, Clin-
    ton Co., O.; m in St. Clairsville, Hannah
    SEXTON, dt Meshack & Hannah, Belmont Co.,
    O.

1830, 11, 25. Susannah (form Smith) dis mcd
    (H)

McNAMEE
1814, 6, 25. Margaret & ch, William, Reuben,
    Cyrus, Helena, Cynthia, Ann & Israel, rocf
    Hopewell MM, dtd 1813,10,4, end by Short
    Creek MM, O., 1814,6,21
1817, 8, 21. Mashach rocf Plymouth MM, dtd
    1817,3,17
1818, 4, 23. Isaac rst on consent of Westland
    MM

McNICHOLS
1808, 4, 23. Martha rocf Hopewell MM, end by
    Concordia MM 1808,1,4
1813, 7, 24. William recrq
1818, 9, 24. William & w, Rachel, & ch, Eliza-
    beth, Benjamin, Maria & John Fawcett, gct
    Stillwater MM
1824, 1, 22. Joseph, Mary & Rachel, ch Mar-
    tha, recrq
1835, 4, 22. Rachel Shamlin (form McNichols)
    dis mcd
1847, 1, 20. Mary Kelse (form McNichols) dis
    mcd

MALORY
1853, 11, 17. Lydia (form Chalfant) dis mcd(H)

MARTIN
1813, 5, 22. Jane (form Rogers) dis mcd
1816, 11, 21. Agnes rst on consent of Goose
    Creek MM, Va.
1834, 4, 24. Martha (form Smith) con mcd (H)
1849, 8, 16. Martha gct Plainfield MM, Ill.

MATHER
1854, 2, 16. Rachel rocf Goose Creek MM, Va.
    (H)

MAXON
1814, 3, 1. David [Maxson], s Jonathan &
    Mary M., Harrison Co., O.; m in Notingham,
    Sarah KINSEY

1808, 10, 22. Jonathan [Maxin] & w, Mary Mag-
    dalin, & ch, David, Nathan, John & William
    rocf Redstone MM, dtd 1808,6,3
1816, 3, 22. Nathan dis
1818, 9, 24. Susannah & ch, Sarah & Mary,
    recrq
1819, 5, 20. Nathan rst at Flushing on con-
    sent of this mtg
1825, 5, 26. Hannah rocf Redstone MM, dtd
    1824,11,3
1826, 7, 20. Hannah gct Stillwater MM

MEAD
1871, 10, 25. M. Cornelia m Leander VICKERS
    (H)

1829, 6, 25. Joseph Philo, Benjamin & John,
    rocf Goose Creek MM, dtd 1829,4,16 (H)
1839, 8, 15. Joseph gct Goose Creek MM, Va.
    (H)
1840, 1, 16. Joseph con mcd (H)
1840, 2, 13. Philo con mcd (H)
1840, 7, 16. Phebe G. rocf Goose Creek MM,
    Va., dtd 1840,5,14 (H)
1842, 1, 13. Joseph, Phebe G. & Philo gct
    Stillwater MM (H)
1848, 5, 18. Benjamin con mcd (H)
1848, 5, 18. Ann Eliza [Meed] (form White)
    con mcd (H)
1851, 7, 17. Sarah E., John H., Alonzo,
    Joseph M. & Joshua G., ch Philo & Mariah,
    recrq (H)
1851, 7, 17. Mariah recrq (H)
1855, 6, 14. Joseph & w, Phebe, & ch, Thomas,
    William, Joseph James, Charles Elwood,
    Mary Emily, Francis Julian & Phebe Alice,
    rocf Freeport MM, dtd 1855,5,26 (H)
1867, 4, 18. Joseph P. con military service
    (H)
1868, 2, 13. Philco & w, Maria, & ch, Joseph
    W., Joshua R., Guela Elma, Mary M. & Elma
    E., gct Wapsonoboc MM, Ia. (H)
1868, 2, 13. John & Alonzo gct Wapsanonoc MM,
    Ia. (H)
1869, 9, 16. Benjamin & Ann Eliza & ch,
    Aaron W., John S., Philo D. & Nathan Or-
    ville, gct Wapsanonoc MM, Ia. (H)

1871, 10, 19. Mary Emily Haines (form Mead)
    con mcd (H)
1882, 1, 19. Phebe G., minister, elder & over-
    seer, w Joseph, d 1881,8,24 (H)

MEDCALF
1824, 12, 29. Jesse [Medcelf], s Moses & Su-
    sannah, Belmont Co., O.; m in Goshen MH,
    Asenath GREGG, dt Stephen & Asenath, Bel-
    mont Co., O.

1825, 6, 23. Asenath gct Concord MM
1829, 10, 22. Abraham [Medcalph] & w, Hannah,
    & ch, John, Susannah, Jeremiah S., Eliza-
    beth & Lidea Ann, rocf Stillwater MM, dtd
    1829,9,19 (H)
1831, 9, 22. Abraham [Medkalf] & w, Hannah,
    & ch, John, Susannah, Jeremiah S., Eliza-
    beth & Lydia Ann, gct Concord MM (H)
1836, 5, 25. Jesse & w, Asenath, & ch, Oliver,
    Caroline, Joshua, Stephen, Adaline, William
    & Asenath, gct Pennsville MM

MEEK
1849, 12, 19. Ann (form Hustler) dis mcd

MERCER
1813, 5, 22. Elizabeth (form Perkins) dis mcd
1835, 6, 18. William rocf Short Creek MM, O.,
    dtd 1835,4,23 (H)

MERRIT
1893, 1, 25. J. Clement [Merritt], s John &
    Sarah, Belmont Co., O.; m in Plainfield
    MH, Rebecca S. FRAVEL, dt Jacob & Jane
    Downing (H)

1814, 12, 24. Isaac rocf Mt. Holly MM, N. J.,
    dtd 1814,10,6
1815, 1, 28. Isaac dis mcd
1815, 11, 25. Mary [Merritt] recrq
1818, 8, 20. Hannah (form Perkins) dis mcd
1822, 10, 24. Hannah [Merrett] rst at Still-
    water on consent of this MM
1855, 2, 15. Margaret M. gct Clear Creek MM,
    Ill. (H)

MICHENER
----, --, --. Barak & Lydia
    Ch: Elizabeth b 1834, 1, 16
        Charles   " 1835, 9, 30
        Robert Lin-
            ley " 1837, 9, 4 d 1854, 3,19
         bur Plainfield
        Hannah Emma b 1853, 2, 25
1843, 4, 7. Mary d ae 59 bur Plainfield
1863, 8, 23. Thomas Chalkley d ae 16 bur
    Plainfield

1839, 4, 24. Barak & w, Lydia, & ch, Eliza-
    beth, Charles & Robert Lindley, gct Still-
    water MM
1846, 8, 19. John gct Flushing MM, to m Sa-

MICHENER, John, continued
rah Garretson
1847, 2, 24. Jesse dis disunity
1847, 11, 24. Sarah & dt, Martha Lucette
Garretson, rocf Flushing MM, dtd 1847,5,20
1850, 9, 25. Seth dis mcd
1851, 3, 19. Miriam dis disunity
1852, 6, 23. Barak & w, Lydia, & ch, Charles,
Robert Lindley, John, Rebecca, Mary, Thomas Chalkley & Francis, rocf Somerset MM,
dtd 1852,4,26
1852, 6, 23. Elizabeth rocf Somerset MM, dtd
1852,4,25
1856, 12, 24. Sarah dis disunity
1863, 7, 22. John Sr. dis jG

MILES
1814, 1, 22. Cert rec for Hannah from Hopewell MM, dtd 1813,10,--, end to Stillwater
MM, 1814,7,23
1814, 1, 22. Cert rec for Lydia & Moses from
Hopewell MM, Va., dtd 1813,10,4, end to
Concord MM
1814, 1, 22. Hannah Jr. rocf Hopewell MM
1816, 12, 26. Mahlon Gregg gct Stillwater MM,
O., to m Hannah Miles

MILLER
1808, 10, 22. John & w, Margaret, & ch, Joshua
& Elizabeth, gct Fairfield MM
1810, 6, 23. Hannah W. gct Center MM
1815, 3, 25. Daniel & w, Sarah, & ch, Milton,
Susannah, Reuben, Lydia, Warrick, Rachel
& Mary Ann, rocf Sadsbury MM, Pa., dtd
1815,2,7
1815, 5, 27. Robert rocf Sadsbury MM, Pa., dtd
1815,2,7
1815, 6, 24. Mason & w, Ruth, & ch, Asa, Eli,
Stephen, Nathan, Sarah, Mary, Richard &
William, rocf Plymouth MM, dtd 1815,4,15
1815, 11, 25. Robert gct Stillwater MM
1817, 5, 22. Levi rocf Sadsbury MM, Pa., dtd
1816,8,10
1821, 5, 24. Milton dis mcd
1821, 8, 23. Sina (form Plummer) dis mcd
1821, 9, 20. Lydia & ch, Jesse & Newton, rocf
Stillwater MM, dtd 1821,8,25
1822, 5, 23. Levi dis disunity
1822, 12, 26. Lydia & ch, Jesse & Newton, gct
Stillwater MM
1827, 1, 25. Reuben dis disunity
1831, 11, 24. Rachel Fawcett (form Miller) dis
mcd (H)
1865, 11, 16. Anna Pickering (form Miller)
con mcd (H)

MILLISON
1816, 3, 22. John Carver gct Westland MM,
Pa., to m Abigail Millison
1817, 6, 26. Elisha & w, Hannah, rocf Westland MM, dtd 1817,4,24
1817, 8, 21. James Jr. & w, Dorothy, & ch,
Jonathan & Ann, rocf Westland MM, dtd

1817,6,26
1817, 11, 20. William [Milison] & w, Elizabeth, rocf Westland MM, Pa., dtd 1817,6,
26
1829, 7, 23. Elizabeth [Milison] (form Sinclair) con mcd (H)

MILLS
1839, 9, 20. Henry, s Joseph & Sarah, Wash.
Co., O.; m in St. Clairsville, Esther
RHODES, dt Moses & Susannah, Belmont Co.,
O.

1810, 9, 22. Nathaniel Gregg gct Westland
MM, to m Elizabeth Mills
1841, 4, 15. Esther gct Honey Creek MM, Ind.
(H)

MILNER
1808, 9, 24. Dudley & w, Mary, & ch gct Fairfield MM
1846, 2, 13. Athanissa [Miliner] (form Pancoast) con mcd (H)

MILTON
1808, 8, 27. William & w, Sarah, & ch, Fanny
& Moses, rocf Plymouth MM, dtd 1808,8,20
1817, 8, 21. Fanny Holliday (form Melton)
dis mcd

MINIKIN
1829, 10, 28. Mary [Minnikan] m Barton FOULKE
(H)

1829, 5, 21. Margaret & ch, Sarah Samson,
Margaret & Gulielma Maria Penn, rocf Redstone MM, dtd 1829,4,29
1829, 5, 21. Mary rocf Redstone MM, dtd 1829,
4,29
1833, 7, 25. Sarah [Miniken] dis mcd
1833, 10, 24. Margaret Harvey (form Minikin)
con mcd (H)
1837, 6, 15. Margaret Lutton (form Miniken)
con mcd (H)

MITCHELL
1842, 5, 19. Lydia E. con mcd (H)
1885, 5, 20. David [Mitchel] recrq (H)

MONDAY
1855, 7, 19. Susanna [Munday] (form Pickering) con mcd (H)
1864, 11, 17. Barclay recrq (H)
1865, 12, 15. Barclay & w, Susan, gct Wapsa-
nonock MM, Ia. (H)

MOORE
1817, 5, 22. Jane & dt, Sarah, rocf Sadsbury
MM, Pa., dtd 1816,10,8
1817, 5, 22. Anna rocf Sadsbury MM, dtd
1816,10,8
1826, 8, 24. Susan (form Broomhall) dis mcd

MORGAN
1808, 4, 23. David gct Fairfield MM
1808, 4, 23. Elizabeth & ch, Hannah, Jona-
    than, Isaac & Asa, gct Fairfield MM
1817, 1, 23. Catharine (form Judkins) dis mcd

MORRIS
1828, 3, 5. Anna m Amos WILSON

1809, 11, 25. Esther rocf London Grove MM,
    dtd 1809,10,4
1812, 10, 24. Esther gct Fallowfield MM, Pa.
1821, 11, 22. Cert rec for John & Abraham from
    Burlington MM, N. J., dtd 1821,9,3, end
    to Salem MM
1821, 11, 22. Cert rec for Joseph & w, Rachel,
    & ch, Joseph, Rachel, Esther, Caleb, Eliza-
    beth & Beulah, from Burlington MM, N. J.,
    dtd 1821,9,3, end to Salem MM
1821, 11, 22. Cert rec for Sarah & Rebecca
    from Burlington MM, N. J., dtd 1821,9,3,
    end to Salem MM
1827, 7, 26. Anna rocf Short Creek MM, O.,
    dtd 1827,5,22

MOTT
1812, 3, 28. William rocf Abington MM, dtd
    1811,12,30

MUSGROVE
1819, 1, 21. Mary rocf Goose Creek MM, Va.,
    dtd 1818,10,29

NEFF
1840, 12, 17. Rebecca con mcd (H)
1861, 7, 18. Rebecca gct Prairie Grove MM,
    Ia. (H)

NEISWANGER
1845, 5, 21. Elizabeth (form Askew) dis mcd
1853, 3, 23. Clarissa (form Askew) dis mcd

NEVIT
1818, 4, 30. Ruth m John RIDGWAY

1817, 4, 24. Isaac [Nevitt] & w, Rachel, &
    ch, Isaac, Grace, Eliza, & Rachel, rocf
    Short Creek MM, O., dtd 1816,12,24
1818, 3, 26. Ruth rocf Short Creek MM, O.,
    dtd 1817,12,23, end by Concord MM

NEWPORT
1831, 6, 23. Jonah & w, Rachel, & ch, Anna
    Maria, rocf Springborough MM, dtd 1831,
    2,22 (H)
1846, 7, 16. Jonah & w, Rachel, & ch, Anna
    Mariah, Elvira, David Noble, Bernard,
    Taylor, Jesse R. & Ruthanna, gct Clear
    Creek MM, Ill. (H)
1871, 8, 17. Cert for Jonah & fam returned
    by Clear Creek MM, Ill. (H)

NICHOLS
1820, 8, 30. Mary m Joshua LOYD
1822, 3, 27. Amy m Thomas BOWLS
1891, 12, 30. Flora M. m Chas. H. WILLIS (H)

1808, 4, 23. Martha rocf Hopewell MM, dtd
    1808,1,4
1811, 5, 25. Hannah dis
1813, 8, 23. David dis disunity
1814, 4, 23. Thomas dis mcd
1815, 6, 24. Hannah rst
1819, 1, 27. Eli [Nickols] gct Short Creek
    MM, O., to m Rachel Lloyd
1819, 8, 26. Rachel rocf Short Creek MM, O.,
    dtd 1819,7,20
1828, 3, 20. Sarah rocf Goose Creek MM, Va.,
    dtd 1828,2,13
1831, 9, 22. Elizabeth (form Hogue) con mcd
    (H)
1835, 11, 19. Sarah rocf Goose Creek MM, Va.,
    dtd 1835,8,13 (H)
1838, 6, 14. Emmor & w, Maria P., & ch, Na-
    than B., William, Albert, Mary, Lydia,
    Ann, Eli & Martha B., rocf Goose Creek
    MM, Va., dtd 1838,4,12 (H)
1839, 5, 22. Rachel dis disunity
1844, 1, 24. Jesse dis disunity
1844, 12, 25. Jane dis disunity
1846, 2, 25. Charles dis disunity
1846, 10, 21. Eliza, Lloyd, Eugene, Susan &
    Hortentia, ch Eli & Rachel, gct Alum
    Creek MM
1846, 12, 23. Mary dis
1855, 4, 19. Nathan B. con mcd (H)
1855, 7, 18. William con mcd (H)
1857, 5, 20. Mercy Ann dis disunity
1860, 4, 19. Thomas T. recrq (H)
1860, 10, 18. Lydia Ann Taylor (form Nichols)
    con mcd (H)
1867, 8, 15. William con "military service"
1871, 9, 14. Sarah Elenor & ch, William, Ed-
    gar, John Wilbur, Clayton Amor, Mary
    Emma, Flora Mariah & Nathan Clifford,
    recrq (H)
1882, 1, 19. Maria, w Amor, d 1882,2,14 bur
    Plainfield (an elder) (H)

NICHOLSON
1811, 3, 23. Joseph dis
1812, 1, 25. George, Hannah & William, ch
    Joseph, gct Stillwater MM
1812, 1, 25. Elizabeth gct Stillwater MM
1815, 2, 25. John con mcd

NICKERSON
1814, 11, 26. Jonathan & w, Polly, rocf
    Butternut MM, N. Y., dtd 1814,5,4, end by
    New Garden MM, 1814,9,15
1817, 6, 26. Polly Thompson (form Nickerson)
    dis mcd

NORRIS
1817, 10, 23. Pleasant (form Hoge) dis mcd

NORRIS, continued
1830, 12, 23. Ann (form Smith) con mcd (H)

O'NEAL
1819, 1, 21. Cert rec for Hannah from Hope-
    well MM, Va., dtd 1818,10,5, end back/that
    mtg   to

ORISON
1818, 12, 24. Helen con mcd

OSBURN
1825, 5, 26. John rocf Springfield MM, Ind.,
    dtd 1824,11,17

PACKER
1815, 4, 22. Sarah (form Hollingsworth) con
    mcd
1815, 8, 31. Sarah rst
1818, 8, 20. Abraham recrq

PAINTER
1814, 12, 24. Eunice rocf Hopewell MM, dtd
    1814,10,3

PALMER
1817, 6, 26. Levick & w, Elizabeth, & ch,
    John, Mary, Samuel Fisher Palmer, Hannah
    Fisher Palmer & Sarah Cowgill Palmer, rocf
    Duck Creek MM, Del., dtd 1817,2,8
1825, 4, 21. Matilda (form White) dis mcd
1825, 4, 21. Ruth (form Hogue) dis mcd
1836, 8, 18. George recrq (H)
1838, 4, 19. Mary (form Hoge) con mcd (H)
1859, 4, 14. Daniel recrq (H)
1859, 10, 13. Olinda (form Broomhall) con mcd
    (H)
1860, 3, 15. Sarah Ann recrq (H)
1860, 6, 14. Abigail recrq (H)
1875, 8, 19. Daniel gct Clear Creek MM, Ill.
    (H)

PANCOAST
1821, 8, 30. Lydia m Samuel VANLAW
1832, 12, 26. Stephen, s Joseph & Mary, Bel-
    mont Co., O.; m in St. Clairsville, Mary
    HAINS, dt John & Ann, Belmont Co., O. (H)

1813, 9, 25. Joseph & ch, Mercy, Elizabeth,
    John, Lydia, Samuel & Stephen, recrq
1815, 3, 25. Mercy dis
1819, 10, 21. Elizabeth Pittman (form Pan-
    coast) dis mcd
1824, 6, 24. John dis mcd
1832, 4, 26. Samuel con mcd (H)
1843, 8, 17. Arthanissa recrq (H)
1846, 2, 13. Athanissa Miliner (form Pancoast)
    con mcd (H)

PARKER
1828, 3, 21. Maryann m Thos. F. HORNER
1835, 1, 21. Ann m David KESTER (H)

1826, 8, 24. Mary Ann recrq
1830, 5, 30. Ann & s, Ephraim J., rocf Short
    Creek MM, O., dtd 1830,4,22 (H)
1835, 9, 17. Ephraim J. gct Green Plain MM
    with his gr parents, Wm. & Phebe Gumery (H)

PARRISH
1826, 3, 23. Rachel (form Haines) con mcd

PATTERSON
1823, 3, 26. Edwin, s Jeremiah & Faith, Bel-
    mont Co., O.; m in Goshen MH, Gulielma
    EWERS, dt Wm. & Amy, Belmont Co., O.
1825, 10, 26. Tilman, s Jeremiah & Faith,
    Jefferson Co., O.; m in Goshen MH, Malin-
    da GREGG, dt Jacob & Mary, Belmont Co., O.
1857, 12, 24. Eli, s Isaac & Rebecca, Belmont
    Co., O.; m in St. Clairsville, Tabitha
    Bailey, dt Uriah & Susannah, Belmont Co.,
    O.
1818, 7, 23. Edwin rocf Short Creek MM, O.,
    dtd 1818,7,21
1823, 8, 21. Edwin & w, Gulielma, gct Short
    Creek MM, O.
1825, 12, 22. Malinda gct Somerset MM
1859, 2, 23. Tabitha gct Somerset MM

PAXON
1818, 12, 3. Rachel [Paxson] m Richard HAW-
    LEY

1817, 12, 25. Benjamin [Paxton] & w, Mary, &
    ch, John, Rachel, Samuel, Isaac, Charles,
    Sally & Ruth, rocf Middleton MM, dtd 1817,
    10,13
1821, 12, 20. John con mcd
1822, 11, 21. John gct West Grove MM, Ind.
1832, 11, 22. Sally Evans (form Paxon) dis
    mcd (H)
1833, 6, 20. Isaac con mcd (H)
1833, 9, 26. Samuel con mcd (H)
1833, 10, 24. Benjamin [Paxton] & w, Mary, &
    ch, Ruth, Aaron, Lydia & Webster, gct Mil-
    ford MM

PEARSON
1816, 8, 20. William S., s Benj. & Jane,
    Belmont Co., O.; m in Flushing MH, Cathe-
    rine BROCK, dt Stephen & Ann, Belmont Co.,O.
1824, 3, 11. Jesse, s Benj. & Jane, Belmont
    Co., O.; m in Plainfield MH, Cynthia SIN-
    CLAIR, dt George & Jane, Belmont Co., O.

1818, 1, 26. Anna & ch, Alice, Susanna, Sa-
    rah, Anna & Isaac, rocf New Garden MM,
    dtd 1817,12,18, end by Stillwater MM
1824, 5, 20. Cynthia gct Flushing MM
1825, 1, 20. Alice Kinney (form Pearson) dis
    mcd
1839, 12, 25. Ann [Pierson] Jr. & Jane dis
    jas
1843, 9, 20. Isaac [Pierson] dis disunity

PENNELL
1819, 6, 24. Rhoda (form Wade) dis mcd

PENNINGTON
1840, 9, 17. Margaret (form Wilson) con mcd
     (H)
1840, 9, 23. Margaret (form Smith) dis mcd &
     jH
1847, 9, 16. Margaret gct Green Plain MM (H)

PENROSE
1828, 3, 5. Edwin, s Robert & Rachel, Bel-
     mont Co., O.; m in St. Clairsville, Mary
     SPENCER, dt Nathan & Ann, Belmont Co., O.
1836, 3, 7. Jesse d bur near St. Claires-
     ville
1840, 11, 25. Sarah d ae 80 bur near St.
     Clairesville

1815, 5, 27. Jesse & w, Sarah, rocf Redstone
     MM, Pa., dtd 1815,3,2
1818, 11, 26. Albert & w, Rachel, & ch, Jesse,
     Mark, Isaac, Edwin & Sarah, rocf Short
     Creek MM, O., dtd 1818,9,22
1828, 10, 23. Rachel, Sarah, Jesse & Isaac gct
     Concord MM (H)
1839, 3, 20. Lavina gct Short Creek MM, O.
1841, 9, 16. Edwin & w, Mary, & ch, Lavina,
     Eliza, Ann, Rachel & Nathan, gct Allum
     Creek MM (H)
1847, 1, 14. Mark con mcd (H)
1847, 2, 18. Mark gct Clear Creek MM, Ill.
     (H)

PERDUE
1831, 12, 22. Sarah & s, Charles A., rocf
     Birmingham MM, Pa., dtd 1831,11,26 (H)
1840, 12, 23. Charles Atkinson [Perdew],
     minor, gct Short Creek MM, O.

PERKINS
1812, 12, 30. David, s Jonathan & Rachel, Bel-
     mont Co., O.; m in Flushing MH, Lydia
     JENKINS, dt Mishael & Rachel, Belmont Co.,
     O.
1810, 1, 27. Nathan dis mcd
1810, 10, 27. Jonathan rocf New Garden MM, dtd
     1809,11,16
1811, 10, 26. Stephen dis mcd
1813, 5, 22. Elizabeth Mercer (form Perkins)
     dis mcd
1818, 8, 20. Hannah Merrit (form Perkins)
     dis mcd

PERRY
1818, 1, 22. John & w, Rachel, & ch, Ruanna,
     Hannah, Deborah, Thomas & Job, recrq
1837, 8, 23. Lydia (form Pool) dis mcd

PHILIPS
1838, 12, 26. Mery d ae 42

1823, 6, 26. Mary [Phillips] (form Gregg)

dis mcd

PICKERING
1812, 10, 28. Mary m James CROZER
1813, 5, 26. Rebecca m Robert HOLLOWAY
1813, --, --. Mary m Robert FAWCETT
1813, 10, 27. Hannah m Stephen GREGG
1813, 12, 1. Phebe m Abraham ENGLE
1815, 6, 28. Phebe m Jacob WOOD
1815, 12, 27. Rhoda m Jacob DESELMS
1828, 7, 2. Samuel, s John & Mary, Belmont
     Co., O.; m in St. Clairsville, Sarah
     BLACKLEDGE, dt Thomas & Sarah, Belmont
     Co., O.
1831, 12, 29. Isaac, s John & Mary, Belmont
     Co., O.; m in Plainfield MH, Elizabeth
     ELLIOTT, dt John & Rachel, Belmont Co., O.

1808, 4, 23. Elizabeth Brown (form Pickering)
     dis mcd
1808, 5, 28. Levi gct Middleton MM, to m
     Susannah CROZIER
1808, 7, 23. Jane & dt, Rachel, Mary & Jane,
     rocf Hopewell MM, dtd 1807,5,10, end by
     Concord MM
1808, 11, 26. Susanna rocf Middleton MM, dtd
     1808,8,13
1809, 8, 26. Jacob Jr. gct Short Creek MM,
     O., to m Rachel Hurford
1809, 10, 28. Enos dis mcd
1810, 4, 28. Jacob Jr. gct Stillwater MM
1810, 12, 22. Rebecca rocf Hopewell MM, dtd
     1810,2,5
1811, 10, 26. Rebecca gct Hopewell MM
1812, 3, 28. Samuel dis
1812, 5, 22. Phebe (form Kirk) dis mcd
1813, 1, 23. Joseph Wright gct Concord MM, to
     m Ann Pickering
1813, 3, 27. Rebecca rocf Hopewell MM, dtd
     1812,5,18
1813, 4, 24. Abel dis
1813, 9, 25. David Spencer gct Concord MM,
     to m Leah Pickering
1813, 10, 23. Mary rmt Robert Fawcett
1815, 5, 27. Samuel & w, Phebe, rst
1815, 8, 31. Rebecca, James & Hiram, ch Sam-
     uel, recrq
1815, 8, 31. Joseph dis mcd
1815, 10, 28. David dis mcd
1816, 2, 23. Jonathan dis
1816, 7, 26. Mary Branson (form Pickering)
     dis mcd
1817, 5, 22. Elias dis mcd
1818, 4, 23. Jane Fawcett (form Pickering)
     dis mcd
1818, 6, 25. Isaac, minor, rocf Hopewell MM,
     dtd 1816,11,7, end by Fairfield MM, 1817,
     10,25
1828, 4, 24. Samuel rocf Concord MM, 1827,
     10,24
1830, 1, 21. John & w, Joanna, & ch, Sarah
     Ann, Mary Ann, James, Amanda, Thomas &
     Ruthanna, rocf Concord MM, dtd 1830,1,20(H)

PICKERING, continued

1830, 2, 25. Elinor Frazier (form Pickering) con mcd (H)

1830, 3, 25. Samuel & w, Sarah, & dt, Elizabeth, gct Concord MM (H)

1832, 4, 26. Elizabeth gct Concord MM (H)

1837, 11, 22. Levi Jr. dis mcd & jH

1838, 7, 19. Samuel dis disunity (H)

1840, 3, 19. Elijah & w, Rebecca Stevens, & ch, Henry Fox, Anna Miller, Sarah Fox, Josiah Fox, John Charles & Francis Drake Pickering, rocf Concord MM, dtd 1839,11,20

1840, 3, 25. Simeon dis jH

1840, 3, 25. Elias rst at Chesterfield MM on consent of this mtg

1841, 4, 21. Sarah Ann (form Smith) dis mcd

1841, 12, 22. Susanna Jr. dis jH

1843, 7, 13. Sarah Ann (form Smith) dis mcd (H)

1843, 10, 19. John con mcd (H)

1843, 10, 25. John dis mcd (H)

1844, 1, 18. Simeon dis mcd (H)

1845, 3, 15. Isaac & w, Elizabeth, & ch, Lamira, Rachel, Elenor, John E. & Chas. Lewis, rocf Concord MM (H)

1847, 2, 18. Levi Jr. & John gct Stillwater MM (H)

1847, 9, 16. Isaac & w, Elizabeth, & ch, Rachel, Ellen, John E., Lemira & Chas. Lewis, gct Fall Creek MM (H)

1847, 10, 20. Elizabeth dis disunity

1851, 6, 16. Elisha & w, Mary, & s, Rees, rocf Concord MM, dtd 1851,5,21 (H)

1851, 6, 16. John L. & ch, John & Jane W., gct Clear Creek MM, Ill. (H)

1851, 6, 16. James, Thomas & Ruthanna gct Clear Creek MM, Ill. (H)

1851, 12, 18. John rocf Stillwater MM, dtd 1851,9,17 (H)

1852, 7, 15. Sarah Jane Christy (form Pickering) con mcd (H)

1852, 12, 16. Isaac & w, Elizabeth, & ch, Lamira, Rachel, Eleanor, John Elliott & Chas. Lewis, rocf Fall Creek MM, Ind., dtd 1852,11,11 (H)

1853, 10, 13. Elisha & w, Mary S., & s, Rees, gct Concord MM (H)

1853, 12, 15. William con mcd (H)

1854, 1, 19. Sarah F. Seamans (form Pickering) con mcd (H)

1854, 10, 19. Margaret J. (form Foulke) dis mcd (H)

1855, 7, 19. Susanna Munday (form Pickering) con mcd (H)

1856, 1, 11. Rachel E. Battey (form Pickering) con mcd (H)

1856, 2, 14. Rachel E. Batty (form Pickering) gct Maple Grove MM, Ia. (or Ind.) (H)

1856, 2, 14. Samira John Eliot, Chas Lewis & Ellen, ch Isaac, gct Maple Grove MM, Ind. (H)

1856, 2, 14. Isaac con mcd (H)

1860, 1, 19. John E. & Chas. L., ch Isaac,

rocf Maple Grove MM, Ind., dtd 1859,11,12 (H)

1860, 10, 18. Amelia, w Isaac, & ch, Lewis Henry Hoover & Mary Elizabeth, recrq (H)

1862, 4, 17. Henry F. gct West MM, O., to m Hannah K. Cook (H)

1863, 1, 15. Hannah K. rocf West MM, Mahoning Co., O., dtd 1862,10,24 (H)

1864, 6, 16. Mary C. P. Bell (form Pickering) con mcd (H)

1864, 11, 17. John C. gct Wapsenonock MM, Ia. (H)

1865, 11, 16. Anna (form Miller) con mcd (H)

1867, 4, 18. William T. con mcd (H)

1867, 5, 16. Isaac & w, Amelia, & s, Lewis Henry Hoover, gct Deerfield MM (H)

1871, 8, 17. Wm. Thomas gct Prairie Grove MM, Ia. (H)

1871, 10, 19. Sarah E. (form Mead) con mcd (H)

1871, 12, 14. Sarah E. gct Wapsinonoc MM, Ia. (H)

1872, 8, 15. John Chas. con mcd (H)

1880, 8, 19. Hannah K, w Henry F., d 1880,1, 25 (an elder & overseer) (H)

1882, 8, 17. Henry F. gct Green Plain MM, O., to m Ann F. Thorp (H)

1883, 7, 19. Ann F. rocf Green Plain MM, O. (H)

PICKET

1840, 11, 25. Eli dis disunity

PIDGEON

1816, 2, 28. Sarah m Robert WRIGHT

1847, 2, 15. Charles [Pigeon] d ae 74 bur Plainfield

1856, 6, 24. PIDGEON, Ann d ae 75 bur Plainfield

PIGGOTT

1808, 10, 27. John, s Henry & Hannah, Belmont Co., O.; m in Plainfield MH, Elenor PLUMMER, dt Thomas & Phebe, Belmont Co., O.

1811, 10, 30. John, s John & Phebe, Belmont Co., O.; m in Flushing MH, Sarah CROSSLEY, dt John & Tamar, Belmont Co., O.

1833, 2, 22. Phebe E. [Piggot] m Asa SPENCER (H)

1815, 5, 27. Amos & w, Susannah, & ch, Ann, Mary, Elizabeth, Lucinda, John & Harriet, recrq

1846, 7, 16. Eli con mcd (H)

1860, 6, 14. Eli L. relrq (H)

PIOTT

1821, 11, 22. Mary Joslin (form Piatt) dis mcd

1821, 12, 20. Susanna dis joining M. E. Church

PIPER

1867, 4, 18. Sarah (form Frazier) con mcd (H)

PITMAN

1821, 6, 28. Anthony, s Levi & Elizabeth, Bel-
    mont Co., O.; m Margaret VAIL, dt Benjamin
    & Rebecca, Belmont Co., O.
1822, 8, 1. Elizabeth m Geo. SINCLAIR

1819, 10, 21. John dis mcd
1819, 10, 21. Elizabeth [Pittman] (form Pan-
    coast) dis mcd
1822, 7, 25. Uriah dis mcd
1823, 2, 20. Levi [Pittman] gct Stillwater MM
1827, 4, 26. Anthony & w, Margaret, & ch, Re-
    becca, Esther & Elias, gct Concord MM
1829, 3, 26. Anthony & w, Margaret, & ch, Re-
    becca, Esther, Elias & Eliza, rocf Concord
    MM
1829, 8, 20. Aaron dis (H)
1830, 7, 22. Ann Hilton (form Pittman) con
    mcd (H)
1832, 10, 25. Anthony & w, Margaret, & ch,
    Rebecca, Esther, Elias & Eliza, gct Alum
    Creek MM (H)
1833, 7, 25. Bulah gct Allum Creek MM (H)

PLUMLEY
1858, 12, 16. Ruthanna (form Hoge) con mcd (H)

PLUMMER
1808, 10, 27. Elenor m John PIGGOTT
1854, 6, 9. Alice [Plumer] d ae 88 bur St.
    Clairesville

1816, 2, 23. Caleb Engle gct Stillwater MM,
    to m Rachel Plummer

POOL
1837, 2, 12. Susannah d ae 52 bur Plainfield

1824, 6, 24. Susanna rst on consent of Goose
    Creek MM, Va.
1825, 5, 26. Lydia, Samuel & Timothy, ch Su-
    sannah, recrq
1837, 8, 23. Lydia Perry (form Pool) dis mcd
1844, 5, 22. Samuel dis mcd

POTTS
1826, 4, 26. Rebecca m Jesse WOOD

1814, 12, 24. Samuel & w, Mary, & ch, Ruth
    Anna, Edward, Rebecca, Lindley & John,
    rocf Concord MM, dtd 1814,12,22
1815, 11, 25. Samuel & w, Mary, & ch, Ruth
    Anna, Edward, Rebecca, Lindley & John, gct
    Concord MM
1822, 4, 25. Samuel & w, Mary, & ch, Rebecca,
    Lindley & John, rocf Flushing MM, dtd
    1822,3,22
1823, 7, 24. Edward G. & w, Abigail, & s, Al-
    fred, rocf Flushing MM, dtd 1823,3,21
1823, 10, 23. Samuel & w, Mary, & ch, Rebecca,
    Lindley & John, gct Miami MM, O.
1824, 3, 23. Cert rec for Samuel & fam re-
    turned, end from Miami MM, O.

1827, 5, 24. Samuel & w, Mary, & ch, Lindley
    & John, gct Miami MM, O.

PRICE
1818, 10, 22. John H. rocf Baltimore MM for
    W. Dist., dtd 1818,3,6, end by Smithfield
    MM, 1818,8,17
1825, 4, 21. Uriah, Edith, Ruthann, Eliza-
    beth & George, ch John & w, recrq
1825, 6, 23. Rachel recrq
1829, 11, 26. John H. & w, Rachel, & ch, Uriah,
    Edith, Ruthann, Elizabeth, George J., Mary-
    ann & Rachel, gct Stillwater MM
1839, 2, 20. Uriah dis jH
1840, 1, 28. Ruthanna dis iH
1841, 6, ·23. Elizabeth Boyd (form Price) dis
    mcd
1845, 11, 13. Nathan Gregg gct Stillwater MM,
    to m Mary Ann Price
1855, 2, 15. John H. & w, Rachel, rocf Still-
    water MM, dtd 1855,7,15 (H)

PUSEY
1815, 5, 27. Nathan & w, Martha, rocf West-
    land MM, dtd 1815,3,2
1816, 5, 24. Nathan [Pewsey] & w, Martha, &
    s, Joseph, gct Westland MM

RANKIN
1815, 6, 24. Martha rocf Short Creek MM, O.,
    dtd 1815,5,23   [1824,8,27
1825, 1, 20. Martha rocf Flushing MM, dtd
1829, 10, 22. Martha [Rankins] gct Short
    Creek MM, O. (H)

READ
1819, 6, 24. Isaiah, minor, rocf Smithfield
    MM, dtd 1819,5,17

REASE
1824, 10, 21. Tamer [Riese] rocf Redstone
    MM, dtd 1823,12,31
1845, 6, 25. Tamor dis disunity

REAVES
1817, 9, 25. John & w, Bathsheba, & s, Math-
    ew, recrq

1822, 5, 23. Cert rec for Samuel [Reeve] from
    Salem MM, dtd 1821,11,21, end to Still-
    water MM

REDD
1814, 6, 25. Charity rocf Hopewell MM, dtd
    1813,10,4, end by Short Creek MM, O.,
    1814,6,21
1815, 9, 23. Charity gct Short Creek MM, O.
1822, 2, 21. Isaiah [Red] gct Smithfield MM
1825, 2, 24. Mary rocf Smithfield MM, dtd
    1824,12,20

REMINGTON
1842; 5, 19. Jane W. con mcd (H)

REYNOLDS
1843, 1, 25. Oliver, minor, rocf Flushing MM,
    dtd 1842,9,22
1841, 6, 17. Joseph [Renolds] rocf Flushing
    MM, dtd 1841,5,22 (H)

RHODES
1834, 5, 23. Joseph, s Moses & Mary, Harrison
    Co., O.; m in Plainfield MH, Mary GREGG
    dt Abraham & Mary, Belmont Co., O. (H)
1839, 9, 20. Esther m Henry MILLS (H)

1834, 8, 14. Mary gct Short Creek MM, O. (H)

RICKET
1809, 11, 25. Thomas gct Miami MM

RIDGEWAY
1816, 10, 3. Thomas [Ridgway], s Timothy &
    Michal, Harrison Co., O.; m in Flushing
    MH, Elizabeth WRIGHT, dt Schooley & La-
    vina, of Flushing
1818, 4, 30. John [Ridgway], s Timothy &
    Michel, Harrison Co., O.; m in Notingham,
    Ruth NEVIT, dt Isaac & Rachel, Harrison
    Co., O.

1812, 4, 25. Timothy & w, Michal, & ch,
    John, Richard & Keziah, rocf Westland MM,
    dtd 1812,3,28
1812, 4, 25. Thomas rocf Westland MM, dtd
    1812,3,28
1816, 8, 23. Levina rst on consent of West-
    land MM

ROBERTS
1821, 5, 2. Mary m Abram GRIFFITH
1839, 8, 22. Anna m Silas TABER
1840, 5, 12. Mary d ae 27 bur Plainfield
1842, 11, 24. Sarah m Wm. KENNARD
1847, 12, 2. Esther m Isaac COWGILL
1854, 10, 22. Aaron d ae 78 bur Plainfield
1857, 2, 26. Rebecca m Wm. H. SHARP
1812, 6, 27. Abel & w, Eleanor, & s, Moses,
    rocf Muncy MM, dtd 1812,4,22
1812, 7, 25. Jane rocf Muncy MM, dtd 1812,4,
    22
1814, 1, 22. Abel & w, Eleanor, & s, Moses,
    gct Short Creek MM, O.
1814, 2, 26. Jane gct Short Creek MM, O.
1815, 6, 24. Abel & w, Elenor, & s, Moses,
    rocf Short Creek MM, dtd 1815,5,23
1815, 6, 24. Jane rocf Short Creek MM, O.,
    dtd 1815,5,23
1820, 3, 25. Ezekiel & w, Ann, & ch, Joseph,
    Agnes, George, Charles, Ann, John & Es-
    ther, rocf Short Creek MM, O., dtd 1819,
    7,29
1820, 3, 25. Mary rocf Short Creek MM, O.,
    dtd 1819,11,23
1821, 12, 20. Joseph gct Concord MM
1822, 12, 26. Ezekiel & w, Amy, & ch, George,
    Charles, John, Nancy & Esther, gct Short

Creek MM, O.
1822, 12, 26. Agnes & Anna gct Short Creek
    MM
1830, 6, 24. Ezekiel & ch, John, Nancy & Es-
    ther, rocf Short Creek MM, O., dtd 1830,5,
    20 (H)
1830, 6, 24. Charles rocf Short Creek MM, O.,
    dtd 1830,5,20 (H)
1830, 12, 23. Charles dis mcd (H)
1833, 2, 21. Nancy Taggert (form Roberts) dis
    mcd (H)
1837, 9, 14. John dis mcd (H)
1838, 6, 20. Aaron & w, Elizabeth, & ch, Beu-
    lah, Joseph & Lydia, rocf Flushing MM, dtd
    1838,5,28
1838, 6, 20. Jesse,& minor dt, Rebecca, rocf
    Flushing MM, dtd 1838,5,28
1838, 6, 20. Esther, Sarah, Anna & Elizabeth
    rocf Flushing MM, dtd 1838,6,20
1839, 9, 25. Mary rocf Flushing MM, dtd 1839,
    4,25
1840, 6, 18. Ezekiel gct Fall Creek MM (H)
1842, 5, 25. Elizabeth Jr. gct Gilead MM
1844, 3, 20. Joseph gct Gilead MM
1846, 11, 25. Lydia Thomasson (form Roberts)
    dis mcd

ROBSON
1815, 2, 25. Sampson Sr. rocf Concord MM, dtd
    1815,6,23
1816, 1, 26. Sampson Sr. & Sampson Jr. gct
    Short Creek MM

ROGERS
1811, 3, 22. Evan dis disunity
1812, 6, 27. John, Josiah, Sarah, Alice &
    Mary, ch Josiah & Alice, gct Stillwater MM
1812, 8, 22. Josiah & Alice dis jas
1813, 5, 22. Jane Martin (form Rogers) dis
    mcd
1816, 7, 26. Hannah & Anna, minors, rocf
    Stillwater MM, dtd 1816,2,24
1818, 6, 25. Hannah Getchel (form Rodgers)
    dis mcd
1849, 5, 23. Mary Ann Rogers (form Gregg)
    dis mcd
1824, 4, 22. Ann Babb (form Rodgers) dis mcd

ROMANS
1818, 12, 24. Moses & ch, Mary Ann, Robert,
    Lydia, Elisha, Hannah & Moses, rocf Brad-
    ford MM, dtd 1818,10,17
1818, 12, 24. Evan & w, Mary, & ch, Jane &
    Mary, rocf Bradford MM, dtd 1818,10,17
1818, 12, 24. Cert rec for Hannah from Brad-
    ford MM, dtd 1818,10,17, end to Flushing
    MM

ROSS
1817, 10, 2. Anna m Wm. FRAZIER

1815, 4, 22. Reuben & w, Elizabeth, & ch,
    Anna, Elizabeth & Phebe, rocf Westland

ROSS, Reuben, continued
    MM, dtd 1815,3,30

SAMUELS
1832, 6, 21. Mary & Jane rocf Richland MM,
    Pa., dtd 1832,1,6
1852, 3, 18. Jane [Samuel] rocf White Water
    MM, Ind., dtd 1852,2,19 (H)

SATTERTHWAIT
1809, 3, 2. Joseph W. [Satterthwaite], s
    Wm. & Maraha, Belmont Co., O.; m in Plain-
    field MH, Ann VANLAW, dt Jos. & Mary, Bel-
    mont Co., O.
1842, 9, 29. Rebecca m Jonathan COWGILL
1852, 12, 1. Nathan, s Jos. W. & Ann, Belmont
    Co., O.; m in St. Clairsville, Ann S. COW-
    GILL, dt Ralph & Betsy, Belmont Co., O.
1863, 8, 15. ----- d bur Plainfield

1809, 7, 22. Ann gct Concord MM
1810, 7, 28. Joseph & w, Ann, & dt, Mary,
    rocf Concord MM, dtd 1810,5,24
1815, 9, 23. Cert rec for Mary from Chester-
    field MM, N. J., dtd 1815,7,4, end to
    Stillwater MM
1835, 2, 23. William dis mcd
1836, 10, 19. Mary Sharp (form Satterthwaite)
    dis mcd
1843, 8, 23. Joshua dis mcd
1843, 8, 23. Phebe (form Chalfant) dis mcd
    & jH
1843, 10, 19. Phebe [Saterthwait] (form Chal-
    fant) dis mcd (H)
1853, 7, 20. Nathan [Satterthwaite] & w,
    Ann S., gct Red Cedar MM, Iowa
1861, 8, 21. Samuel dis mcd

SCHOFIELD
1839, 3, 15. Joshua, s David & Rebecca,
    Columbiana Co., O.; m in St. Clairsville,
    Margaret Ann CLARK, dt Robert & Jane, Bel-
    mont Co., O. (H)

1839, 6, 13. Margaret Ann gct Salem MM (H)

SCHOOLEY
1816, 1, 26. Isaac & w, Sarah, & ch, Phineas,
    Samuel, Nancy & Sarah, rocf Goose Creek MM,
    dtd 1815,11,2
1816, 1, 26. William rocf Goose Creek MM,
    dtd 1815,11,2
1818, 7, 23. William dis mcd
1821, 9, 20. William rst
1821, 9, 20. Agnes recrq
1826, 5, 25. William & w, Agnes, & ch, Clark-
    son & Lindley (nothing more on manuscript,
    McM.)

SCOT
1836, 7, 20. Robert dis disunity

SEAMANS
1854, 1, 19. Sarah F. (form Pickering) con
    mcd (H)

SEXTON
1811, 5, 29. Hannah m Jonathan McMILLAN

1811, 4, 27. Hannah rocf Redstone MM, dtd
    1811,3,29, end by Short Creek MM, O., dtd
    1811,4,23
1811, 5, 25. Mary rocf Redstone MM, dtd
    1811,3,29, end by Short Creek MM, O.,
    1811,4,23
1811, 9, 28. Catharine rocf Redstone MM, dtd
    1811,1,2
1813, 9, 25. Catharine & Mary gct Centre MM

SHALLCROSS
1854, 6, 15. Sarah P. rocf Short Creek MM,
    O., dtd 1854,3,23 (H)

SHAMBLAIN
1835, 4, 22. Rachel (form McNichols) dis mcd
    (Shamlin on women's minutes)

SHARP
1812, 4, 29. Sarah m John VANLAW
1812, 10, 29. Jephthah, s Samuel & Martha, Bel-
    mont Co., O.; m in Plainfield MH, Sarah
    GORE, dt Thomas & Mercy, Belmont Co., O.
1857, 2, 26. William H., s Samuel T. & Mary
    V., Cedar Co.; m in Plainfield MH, Rebecca
    ROBERTS, dt Jesse & Lydia, Belmont Co., O.
    Ch: Samuel T. b 1857, 12, 30
        Jesse R.   " 1860, 10, 27

1814, 11, 26. Samuel & w, Martha, & ch,
    George, Lydia & Phineas, gct Goose Creek
    MM, Va.
1823, 2, 20. Jesse gct Hopewell MM, Va.
1826, 5, 25. Samuel rocf Hopewell MM, Va.,
    dtd 1825,12,8
1835, 8, 19. Mary dis mcd
1836, 10, 19. Mary (form Satterthwaite) dis
    mcd

SHARPLESS
1815, 8, 31. Cert rec for Samuel from Con-
    cord MM, dtd 1815,3,23, end to Stillwater
    MM
1817, 11, 20. Samuel & w, Rebecca G., rocf
    Stillwater MM, dtd 1817,5,24

SHOEMAKER
1812, 1, 25. Mary rocf SD MM, dtd 1811,12,25
1813, 10, 23. Mary gct Short Creek MM, O.

SHOTWELL
1810, 6, 23. Deborah & ch, Priscilla, Bath-
    sheba, Mary, Sarah, Rebecca & Jane, rocf
    Richland MM, Pa., dtd 1810,4,12
1810, 6, --. Titus & w, Deborah, & ch, Marion,
    Thomas, Isaac, Rebecca & Mahlon, gct

SHOTWELL, Titus, continued
    Stillwater MM

SHRIVER
1842, 1, 13. Mary H. [Sriver] (form Horton)
    con mcd (H)
1848, 7, 13. William Henry, s Mary, recrq (H)
1848, 8, 17. Mary & s, Wm. Henry, gct West-
    land MM (H)

SIDWELL
1852, 9, 23. Phebe m Aaron FOULKE (H)

1824, 3, 23. Thomas & w, Elizabeth, & s,
    James C., rocf Stillwater MM, dtd 1824,2,
    28
1827, 6, 26. Henry & w, Sina, rocf Short
    Creek MM, O., dtd 1827,5,22
1842, 6, 16. Eli & ch, Elma & Henry, rocf
    Smithfield MM, dtd 1842,5,24 (H)
1842, 8, 18. Mary M. rocf White Water MM,
    Ind., dtd 1842,6,22 (H)
1843, 1, 19. Thomas & w, Elizabeth, & ch,
    James, John, Elwood, Sina, Robert E. &
    Lindley, gct Honey Creek MM, Ind. (H)
1844, 6, 13. Isabella recrq (H)
1845, 6, 19. Mary gct Clear Creek MM, Ill.
    (H)
1851, 9, 18. Phebe rocf Smithfield MM, dtd
    1851,7,22 (H)
1886, 6, --. Plummer, form mbr at Smithfield,
    now laid down, recrq (H)

SINCLAIR
1812, 10, 29. Phebe m Samuel CROSSLEY
1822, 8, 1. George, Belmont Co., O.; m in
    Plainfield MH, Elizabeth PITMAN, Belmont
    Co., O.
1824, 3, 11. Cynthia m Jesse PEARSON

1809, 6, 24. Elizabeth, Phebe, Albinah, Eden,
    Cinthia, Mary & James, ch George, recrq
1819, 10, 21. Albinah gct Allum Creek MM
1823, 9, 25. Albina rocf Allum Creek MM
1823, 11, 20. George dis disunity
1825, 2, 24. Mary dis joining M. E.
1829, 3, 26. James dis military service (H)
1829, 7, 23. Elizabeth Milison (form Sinclair)
    con mcd (H)
1835, 6, 18. Elizabeth gct Allum Creek MM (H)
1835, 7, 16. Abbina gct Stillwater MM (H)

SMITH
1813, 2, 4. William, s Geo. & Mary, Gurnsey
    Co., O.; m in Big Stillwater, Huldah
    BOGUE, dt Josiah & Mary, Tuskaraways Co.,
    O.
1817, 4, 30. Samuel, s Geo. & Mary, Gurnsey
    Co., O.; m in Flushing MH, Elizabeth
    WRIGHT, dt William & Eunice, Belmont Co.,
    O.
1817, 10, 29. Amos, s Geo. & Mary, Gurnsey Co.,
    O.; m in Flushing MH, Anna BEESON, dt

Benjamin & Jane, Belmont Co., O.
1825, 4, 27. Eliza m Thos. SWAYNE
1833, 1, 2. Taylor, s Mahlon & Sarah, Bel-
    mont Co., O.; m in St. Clairsville, Sarah
    HAINS, dt John & Ann, Belmont Co., O.
1845, 5, 17. Margaret m Levi WARNER (H)
1860, 10, 25. John M., s Nathan & Catherine,
    Gurnsey Co., O.; m in Plainfield MH,
    Lydia VAIL, dt Benj. & Hannah, Belmont
    Co., O.

1808, 9, 24. Susanna rocf Goose Creek MM,
    dtd 1808,5,30, end by Concord MM
1809, 5, 27. Susanna gct Goose Creek MM, Va.
1809, 10, 28. John rocf London Grove MM, end
    by Short Creek MM, O., 1809,6,7
1811, 5, 25. John dis mcd
1814, 7, 23. John W. & w, Alice, rocf New
    Garden MM, dtd 1814,6,9
1815, 6, 24. Catharine rocf Plymouth MM, dtd
    1815,4,15
1815, 11, 25. Mary rocf Goose Creek MM, Va.,
    dtd 1815,8,3
1816, 4, 26. Jacob & ch, Anna, Nathan, Le-
    titia, Gulielma, Mary, Ezra & Sarah, rocf
    Goose Creek MM, Va., dtd 1816,2,1
1816, 6, 21. Jacob gct Goose Creek MM, Va.,
    to m Martha Evans
1816, 9, 26. Martha rocf Goose Creek MM, Va.,
    dtd 1816,8,29
1817, 2, 20. Mary gct Goose Creek MM, Va.
1820, 8, 24. Margaret & Eliza rocf London
    Grove MM, Pa., dtd 1820,7,5
1821, 3, 22. Mahlon gct New Garden MM, Pa.,
    to m Margaret Wilson
1821, 8, 23. Margaret rocf New Garden MM,
    Pa., dtd 1821,8,9
1821, 11, 22. Aaron rst on consent of Goose
    Creek MM, Va.
1821, 11, 22. Ann recrq
1822, 10, 24. Thomas Jr. gct Stillwater MM, to
    m Jane Kenny
1822, 10, 24. Thos. Smith Jr. ltm Jane Kenny,
    of Stillwater
1823, 7, 24. Thomas Jr. gct Stillwater MM
1824, 9, 23. Thomas Jr. & w, Jane, & dt,
    Mary, rocf Stillwater MM, dtd 1824,6,28
1825, 11, 24. Margaret gct London Grove MM,
    Pa.
1827, 10, 25. Thomas Jr. & w, Jane, & ch,
    Mary & Martha, gct Stillwater MM
1828, 8, 21. Rebecca (form Strahl) dis mcd
    (H)
1829, 9, 24. Susannah recrq (H)
1829, 11, 26. Elizabeth (form Bond) con mcd
    (H)
1830, 11, 25. Susannah McMillan (form Smith)
    dis mcd (H)
1830, 12, 23. Ann Morris (form Smith) con mcd
    (H)
1831, 6, 23. Rebecca (form Nichols) dis mcd
    (H)
1832, 11, 22. Taylor recrq (H)

SMITH, continued
1834, 4, 24. Martha Martin (form Smith) con
             mcd (H)
1835, 5, 14. Mary Close (form Smith) dis mcd
             (H)
1837, 5, 18. Alice & ch, Sarah Ann & Thomas
             Wilkinson, rocf Flushing MM, dtd 1837,2,
             25 (H)
1837, 12, 14. Esther (form Roberts) dis mcd
             (H)
1838, 6, 20. Wilkinson & Sarah Ann, minor ch
             Alice, rocf Flushing MM, dtd 1838,2,--
1838, 11, 21. Thomas Wilkinson, minor, gct
             Milford MM
1840, 9, 23. Margaret Pennington (form Smith)
             dis mcd & jas
1841, 4, 21. Sarah Ann Pickering (form Smith)
             dis mcd & jas
1843, 7, 13. Sarah Ann Pickering (form Smith)
             dis mcd (H)
1844, 12, 25. Mahlon dis disunity
1852, 5, 19. Rachel N. (form Chalfant) con
             mcd (H)
1861, 1, 23. Lydia gct Flushing MM

SMITHFIELD
1827, 8, 23. Mary gct Smithfield MM

SPENCER
1814, 9, 26. Alice m John COFFEE
1816, 10, 31. Betsy m Ralph COWGILL
1817, 5, 1. George, s John & Lydia, Belmont
             Co., O.; m in Plainfield MH, Eunice FERN-
             LEY, dt Wm. & Hannah
1817, 11, 26. Jonathan, s Nathan & Ann, Bel-
             mont Co., O.; m in St. Clairsville, Sarah
             COWGILL, dt Isaac & Sarah, Belmont Co., O.
1819, 12, 2. Sarah m Thomas FOULKE
1821, 12, 26. Abner, s Nathan & Ann, Belmont
             Co., O.; m in Goshen MH, Harriet GREGG,
             dt Stephen & Asenath, Belmont Co., O.
1823, 9, 4. Phebe m Elijah GREGG
1827, 8, 13. Betsey m Isaac COFFEE
1828, 3, 5. Mary m Edwin PENROSE
1833, 2, 22. Asa, s Nathan & Ann, Belmont
             Co., O.; m in St. Clairsville, Phebe E.
             PIGGOT, dt John & Elinor, Belmont Co., O.
             (H)
1834, 6, 25. Rachel m Wm. CRAFT (H)
1839, 3, 7. Amy m Jephthah S. VANLAW
1840, 2, 21. Joseph d ae 18 bur Plainfield
1840, 10, 1. Samuel, s John & Mary,Jefferson
             Co., O.; m in Plainfield MH, Mary VAIL, dt
             Benj. & Hannah, Belmont Co., O.
             Ch: Thomas E. b 1847, 4, 16
                 Morris   " 1849, 8, 5
                 Hannah   " 1855, 10, 5
1848, 2, 12. Harriet d ae 46 bur Plainfield
1853, 3, 31. Lydia Ann m Abraham COWGILL

1810, 4, 28. Sarah (form White) dis mcd
1813, 4, 27. Mary (form Coffee) dis mou
1813, 9, 25. David gct Concord MM, to m Leah

Pickering
1814, 4, 23. Alice recrq
1814, 11, 26. Leah rocf Concord MM, dtd 1814,
             4,21
1815, 5, 27. Joseph & ch, Wm. & Elisha,
             recrq
1815, 6, 24. Sarah rst
1816, 3, 22. David & w, Leah, & ch, Maryann
             & Samuel, gct Concord MM
1816, 12, 26. George recrq
1818, 3, 26. Mercy Windham (form Spencer) con
             mcd
1818, 9, 24. Mary rocf Middleton MM, dtd 1818,
             4,18
1823, 7, 24. Jonathan & w, Sarah, gct Still-
             water MM
1826, 6, 22. Betsy recrq
1833, 3, 21. George & w, Eunice, & ch, Lou-
             isa, Athamissa, William F., Lydia, John,
             Elwood, Eunice & Hannah Jane, gct Allum
             Creek MM (H)
1834, 4, 24. Asa & w, Phebe, gct Stillwater
             MM (H)
1835, 10, 21. Jonas dis jH (H)
1836, 3, 23. Abner & w, Harriett, & ch,
             Lydia Ann & Asenath, gct Pennsville MM
1838, 7, 25. George dis mcd
1839, 6, 19. Abner & w, Harriett, & ch,
             Lydia, Asenath & Ira, rocf Pennsville MM,
             dtd 1839,5,16
1855, 2, 21. Abner gct Pennsville MM, to m
             Rachel Lightfoot
1855, 6, 20. Abner & s, Ira, gct Pennsville
             MM
1855, 6, 20. Asenath gct Pennsville MM

STAATS
1815, 10, 28. Margaret rocf Westland MM, Pa.,
             dtd 1815,8,3

STANLEY
1840, 11, 25. Mary V. gct Short Creek MM, O.
1846, 6, 24. Samuel W. & w, Mary, & ch, Es-
             ther Jane & Benjamin V., rocf Short Creek
             MM, O.

STANTON
1823, 4, 13. Joseph, s Benj. & Abigail,
             Wash. Co., O.; m in St. Clairsville, Mary
             TOWNSEND, dt Thomas & Elizabeth, Belmont
             Co., O.
1853, 2, 24. William, s Enoch & Mary, Bel-
             mont Co., O.; m in house of Wm. BURR, Sa-
             rah BURR, dt William & Sarah, Belmont Co.,
             O. (H)

1823, 6, 26. Mary gct Miami MM, O.
1855, 2, 15. Sarah Burr gct Stillwater MM (H)

STEWART
1820, 3, 23. Elizabeth D. rocf Wilmington MM,
             dtd 1818,12,4, end by Stillwater MM,
             1819,6,26

STRAHL

1812, 12, 26. Jonathan Fawcett gct Stillwater
MM, to m Rebecca Strahl
1816, 6, 21. Thomas & w, Martha, & ch, Anna,
Hannah, Joseph, Rebecca, William, Jane,
Jesse & Levina, rocf Short Creek MM, O.,
dtd 1815,12,19
1825, 6, 23. Thomas & w, Martha, & ch, Hannah, Joseph, Rebecca, William, Jane,
Jesse & Lavina, rocf Flushing MM
1827, 3, 22. Thomas dis disunity
1828, 7, 24. Hannah Bowles (form Strahl) dis
mcd (H)
1828, 8, 21. Rebecca Smith (form Strahl) dis
mcd (H)
1829, 6, 25. Joseph dis mcd (H)
1830, 7, 22. Martha & ch, Jane, Jesse & Lavisa, gct Stillwater MM (H)
1830, 7, 22. William gct Stillwater MM

SWAYNE

1825, 4, 27. Thomas, s Joshua & Rebecca, Belmont Co., O.; m in Goshen MH, Eliza SMITH,
dt James & Mary

1826, 12, 21. Eliza & dt, Mary Ann, gct Flushing MM

SYLVESTER

1819, 5, 20. Ann (form Pyott) dis mcd

TABER

1839, 8, 22. Silas, s Benj. & Phebe, Marion
Co., O.; m in Plainfield MH, Anna ROBERTS,
dt Aaron & Elizabeth, Belmont Co., O.

1839, 10, 23. Anna gct Gilead MM

TAGGART

1833, 2, 21. Nancy (form Roberts) dis mcd

TALBOTT

1819, 6, 24. John & w, Rachel, & ch, Susanna & Mary, rocf Smithfield MM, dtd
1819,5,17
1821, 5, 24. Isaac [Talbert] & w, Rachel, &
ch, Susanna, Mary & David, gct Flushing
MM

TAYLOR

1808, 12, 25. Mary recrq
1809, 8, 20. Keziah rocf Short Creek MM, dtd
1809,7,12
1809, 11, 25. Keziah Davis (form Taylor) dis
mou
1810, 6, 23. Anna gct Stillwater MM
1811, 7, 24. Cert rec for Mary from Exeter
MM, Pa., dtd 1811,5,20, end to Stillwater
MM
1814, 9, 1. Rouse & w, Mary, & ch, Peter &
James, rocf Plymouth MM, dtd 1814,7,16
1818, 7, 23. Joshua rocf Nottingham MM, Md.,
dtd 1816,9,6, end by Short Creek MM, O.,

1818,6,23
1821, 11, 22. Martha rocf Short Creek MM, O.,
dtd 1821,11,20
1823, 10, 23. Tacy rocf Short Creek MM, O.,
dtd 1823,7,22
1824, 6, 24. Elizabeth rocf Short Creek MM,
O., dtd 1824,4,20
1825, 6, 23. Joseph gct Flushing MM
1827, 1, 25. Tacie dis jas
1860, 10, 18. Lydia Ann (form Nichols) con mcd
(H)
1867, 4, 18. Lydia A. gct Wapsanonoc MM, Ia.
(H)

TEARL

1820, 1, 20. Benjamin Thomas gct Short Creek
MM, to m Joanna Tearl

THOMAS

1846, 1, 12. Sarah C. m Chas. H. WILLIAMS
(H)

1813, 1, 23. Alisha, minor, rocf Stillwater
MM
1814, 4, 23. Abisha gct Stillwater MM
1819, 1, 21. Benjamin rocf Baltimore MM, E.
Dist., dtd 1818,8,6
1820, 1, 20. Benjamin gct Short Creek MM, to
m Joanna Tearl
1821, 7, 26. Joanna rocf Short Creek MM, O.,
dtd 1821,3,20
1835, 10, 15. Asahel & w, Phebe, & ch, Christopher H., Susannah, Hugh Judge & William,
rocf Stillwater MM, dtd 1835,4,18 (H)
1837, 6, 15. Ashel relrq (H)
1839, 12, 25. Edith (form Price) dis mcd & jH
1841, 10, 20. Sarah C. dis jH
1843, 6, 21. Susann, Hugh J. & William, minor,
rocf Stillwater MM, dtd 1843,5,27
1846, 11, 25. Terrell dis disunity
1846, 2, 19. Phebe & dt, Susanna, gct Cincinnati MM (H)
1852, 9, 16. Margaret S. Chapline (form
Thomas) con mcd (H)

THOMASSON

1839, 12, 11. Thomas Jr. d ae 36 bur St.
Clairsville
1841, 5, 23. Thomas d ae 68 bur St. Clairsville
----, --, --. John & Eunice
Ch: Abigail   b 1848, 4, 6
    Joseph   " 1849, 8, 17
    Sarah   " 1850, 12, 7
    Thomas   " 1852, 7, 18
1848, 5, 18. Sarah d ae 71 bur St. Clairsville

1824, 12, 23. Thomas & w, Sarah, & s, John,
rocf Greenstreet MM, Phila., Pa.
1837, 12, 20. Thomas Jr. & w, Maria, & s,
Samuel J., rocf Short Creek MM, O., dtd
1837,11,21

THOMASSON, continued
1840, 12, 23. Maria & s, Samuel, gct Short
      Creek MM, O.
1846, 11, 25. Lydia [Tummelson] (form Roberts)
      dis mcd
1847, 2, 24. John gct Somerset MM, to m
      Eunice Edgerton
1847, 6, 23. Eunice [Thomason] rocf Somerset
      MM, dtd 1847,5,24
1854, 1, 25. John & w, Eunice, & ch, Abigail,
      Joseph, Sarah & Thomas, gct Somerset MM

THOMPSON
1815, 9, 28. John C., s Bradway & Ann, Harri-
      son Co., O.; m in Notingham, Rebekah CAR-
      VER, dt Henry & Talitha, Harrison Co., O.

1815, 11, 25. Rebecca gct Short Creek MM;
      another cert sent 1816,10,24 as the other
      was mislaid
1817, 6, 26. Polly (form Nickerson) dis mcd
1841, 12, 16. Phebe (form Horner) dis mcd (H)

THORP
1823, 9, 25. Thomas & w, Mary, & ch, Samuel,
      James, Eleanor, Jabez, Hannah & Elizabeth,
      rocf Frankford MM, Pa., dtd 1823,5,23
1834, 10, 16. Cert rec for Thomas & w, Marga-
      ret, & ch, James, Eleanor, Jabez, Hannah,
      Elizabeth, Jesse, Mary, Thomas & Ann, from
      Deerfield MM, dtd 1834,2,20, end to Green
      Plain MM, O.(H)
1835, 6, 18. Samuel gct Deerfield MM (H)
1839, 3, 20. James & Jabez gct Chesterfield
      MM
1839, 3, 20. Thomas, minor, gct Chesterfield
      MM
1882, 8, 17. Henry F. Pickering gct Green
      Plain MM, O., to m Ann F. Thorp (H)

TIDBALL
1847, 3, 24. Martha (form Askew) dis mcd

TIMBERLAKE
1810, 1, 27. Mourning rocf South River MM,
      Campbell Co., Va., dtd 1805,11,9

TOMPKINS
1810, 7, 28. Ann [Tomkin] (form Hoge) dis mou

TOMLINSON
1853, 2, 17. Amos L. Griffith gct Short
      Creek MM, O., to m Sarah Tomlinson

TOWNSEND
1813, 9, 29. Amelia m Nathan KIRK
1820, 8, 21. Levi, s Joseph & Mary, Harrison
      Co., O.; m in Plainfield MH, Mary WATSON,
      dt Abner & Elizabeth, Belmont Co., O.
1823, 4, 13. Mary m Joseph STANTON

1813, 7, 24. Thomas & w, Eliza, & ch, Amelia,

Mary, Morris & Harriet, rocf Westland MM,
      dtd 1813,3,27
1816, 9, 26. Eli, minor, rocf Plymouth MM
1819, 11, 25. Eli rocf Smithfield MM, dtd
      1819,9,20
1821, 3, 22. Mary gct Flushing MM
1821, 7, 26. Morris dis disunity
1823, 4, 24. Eli gct Short Creek MM, O.
1824, 3, 23. Thomas & w, Elizabeth, gct Miami
      MM, O.
1824, 4, 22. Harriett gct Miami MM, O.
1830, 8, 26. Eli gct Short Creek MM, O. (H)

TRAHERN
1816, 10, 30. Amy m Samuel HOLOWAY
1810, 7, 28. Amy rocf Goose Creek MM, Va.,
      dtd 1810,6,20
1828, 4, 24. Israel rocf Goose Creek MM, Va.,
      dtd 1828,1,17 (H)
1829, 2, 26. Israel [Trahorn] dis mcd (H)

TUDER
1815, 8, 31. Elizabeth [Tuider] rocf Gun-
      powder MM, Md., dtd 1815,4,5
1816, 4, 26. Isaac [Tuider] & w, Martha, &
      ch, William, Abraham, Martha & Hannah,
      rocf Goose Creek MM, Va., dtd 1816,2,1
1817, 6, 26. Elizabeth Hill (form Tuder) dis
      mcd
1818, 12, 24. Martha Johnson (form Tudor) con
      mcd
1819, 6, 24. Isaac [Tueder] gct Monallen MM,
      Pa.
1819, 10, 21. Martha Johnson (form Tudor) con
      mcd
1820, 5, 25. Hannah Agnew (form Tuder) dis mcd

TURK
1817, 4, 24. Sarah (form Smith) dis mcd

TWYFORD
1812, 9, 26. Elizabeth (form Nichols) dis mcd

UNDERWOOD
1827, 1, 25. Mordecai T. rocf Baltimore MM,
      W. Dist., dtd 1826,9,8, end by Somerset MM
1827, 2, 22. Mordecai P. dis mcd

UPDEGRAFF
1817, 3, 20. Elizabeth rocf Concord MM, dtd
      1817,1,22

VAIL
1813, 5, 5. Benjamin, s Abraham & Margrat,
      Belmont Co., O.; m in Flushing MH, Hannah
      FENLY, dt Thomas & Martha FAWCETT, Bel-
      mont Co., O.
1815, 11, 2. Rachel m Thos. FAWCETT
1821, 6, 28. Margaret m Anthony PITMAN
1825, 6, 9. Anna m Thos. BRANSON
1827, 8, 24. Esther m John T. WELLS
1836, 9, 29. Rebecca m Parker Askew

VAIL, continued
----, --, --. John & Abigail
    Ch: Semira L. b 1838, 9, 3
        Isaac   " 1840, 1, 30
        Mary   " 1842, 4, 6
        Benjamin " 1844, 1, 10
        Hervey " 1845, 11, 22
        John   " 1847, 12, 25 d 1848, 9, 16
          bur Plainfield
        Eunice b 1849, 8, 3 " 1849, 8, 7
          bur Plainfield
        David   b 1851, 4, 21
        Anna   " 1853, 2, 14
        John Jr. " 1857, 4, 11
        Abigail E." 1858, 12, 5
        Joseph S. " 1861, 4, 12
        Walter E. " 1863, 2, 11
1837, 9, 21. Hannah m George VANLAW (H)
1840, 10, 1. Mary m Samuel STANLEY
1842, 4, 28. Hannah m Thos. HOUGH
1844, 8, 22. Sarah m Mark WILLETS
1845, 5, 22. Elizabeth m Isaac W. HALL (H)
1847, 4, 16. Benjamin d ae 80 bur Plainfield
1860, 9, 28. Hannah, w Benjamin, d ae 82 bur
    Plainfield
1860, 10, 25. Lydia m John M. SMITH

1831, 4, 21. Nathan dis mcd (H)
1833, 6, 20. Isaac gct Short Creek MM, O. (H)
1842, 7, 14. Sarah Jane, gr dt Sarah, recrq
    (H)
1837, 8, 23. John gct Somerset MM, to m Abi-
    gail Edgerton
1838, 4, 25. Abigail rocf Somerset MM, dtd
    1838,3,26
1839, 5, 22. Robert Jr. dis jH
1841, 8, 25. Elisha dis disunity
1848, 12, 20. Jesse con mcd
1850, 12, 25. Jesse gct Chesterfield MM
1857, 8, 19. Jesse rocf Plymouth MM, dtd
    1857,7,20
1864, 8, 24. John & w, Abigail, & ch, Harvey,
    David, Anna, John, Abigail, Joseph S. &
    Walter E., gct Coal Creek MM, Ia.
1864, 8, 24. Lemira S. & Mary gct Coal Creek
    MM, Iowa
1864, 10, 19. Isaac N. gct Stillwater MM, to
    m Rachel D. Wilson

VANLAW
1809, 3, 2. Ann m Jos. W. SATTERTHWAIT
1812, 1, 2. Thomas, s Joseph & Mary, Belmont
    Co., O.; m in Plainfield MH, Ann HOLLOWAY
1815, 6, 1. George, s Joseph & Mary, Belmont
    Co., O.; m in Plainfield MH, Anne WHITE,
    dt Isaac & Jane, Belmont Co., O.
    George m 2nd 1837,9,21 in Plainfield MH,
    Hannah VAIL, dt Robert & Sarah, Belmont
    Co., O.(H)
1821, 8, 30. Samuel, s Joseph & Mary, Bel-
    mont Co., O.; m in Plainfield MH, Lydia
    PANCOAST, dt Joseph & Sarah, Belmont Co.,
    O.

1812, 4, 29. John, s Joseph, Belmont Co.,
    O.; m in Goshen MH, Sarah SHARP, dt Samuel
    & Martha, Belmont Co., O.
1837, 4, 19. Sarah d ae 43 bur Plainfield
1838, 9, 27. John, s Jos. & Mary, Belmont Co.,
    O.; m in Plainfield MH, Lydia BRANSON, dt
    John & Lydia SPENCER, Belmont Co., O.
    Ch: Ann   b 1840, 8, 23
1839, 3, 7. Jephthah S., s John & Sarah,
    Belmont Co., O.; m in Plainfield MH, Amy
    SPENCER, dt Joseph & Sarah, Belmont Co.,
    O.
1840, 12, 31. Lydia S. m Elisha J. HOLLOWAY
1840, 12, 31. Thomas, s Thos. & Ann, Belmont
    Co., O.; m in Plainfield MH, Amy BRANSON,
    dt David & Lydia, Belmont Co., O.

1825, 4, 21. Ann & ch, Joseph, Rebecca &
    Thomas Elwood, gct Flushing MM
1833, 5, 23. Samuel & w, Lydia, & ch, Joseph
    P., Sarah P., Pearson L. & William, gct
    Owl Creek MM (H)
1835, 7, 22. Lucinda dis jH
1836, 7, 14. Lucinda Elliott (form Vanlaw)
    con mcd (H)
1838, 7, 25. Mary Ann & Sarah dis disunity
1838, 7, 25. Elisha gct Pennsville MM, to m
    Anna Worthington
1838, 10, 24. Elisha gct Chesterfield MM
1839, 4, 24. Jephthah S. & w, Amy, gct Ches-
    terfield MM
1841, 2, 24. Amy B. gct Chesterfield MM
1841, 9, 22. John & w, Lydia, & ch, Smith
    & Lydia Jane Branson & Eliza, John, Sam-
    uel C., Jesse, Thomas & Ann S. Vanlaw,
    gct Chesterfield MM
1841, 9, 22. Louisa M. & Lucinda gct Ches-
    terfield MM
1842, 4, 21. Joseph, Sarah & Reason, minor
    ch Samuel, rocf Alum Creek MM, dtd 1842,
    1,27
1844, 1, 24. Isaac dis disunity
1844, 12, 25. Joseph dis mcd
1845, 1, 22. Mary (form Haines) dis mcd
1845, 2, 19. Sarah dis disunity
1839, 6, 13. Joseph A., Sarah P., Resin L.,
    William & George, ch Samuel & Lydia, dec,
    rocf Alum Creek MM, dtd 1839,2,21 (H)
1839, 6, 13. Mary Ann Knight (form Vanlaw)
    con mcd (H)
1845, 1, 16. Joseph con mcd (H)
1846, 3, 19. Isaac dis mcd (H)
1849, 6, 14. Sarah Drummand (form Vanlaw)
    con mcd (H)
1855, 2, 15. George Jr. dis mcd (H)

VANPELT
1810, 5, 27. Sarah (form Ellis) dis mcd
1814, 11, 26. John & w, Mary, & ch, Hannah,
    Jonathan, Ann, Mary, Katy, Elisha, Mahlon
    & Phebe, gct Fall Creek MM
1816, 9, 26. Sarah rst

VICKERS
1871, 10, 25.   Leander, s Isaac & Rachel, Bel-
     mont Co., O.; m in house of Jos. MEAD,
     M. Cornelia MEAD, dt Joseph & Phebe, Bel-
     mont Co., O. (H)
1873, 3, 27.   Samuel P., s Jesse K. & Marga-
     retta, Belmont Co., O.; m in Plainfield
     MH, Eliza GREGG, dt Lott & Ruth, Belmont
     Co., O. (H)

1871, 5, 18.   Samuel P. & w, Lucinda, & ch,
     Clara, John, Morris & Mary, rocf Concord
     MM, dtd 1871,4,19 (H)
1892, 7, 14.   Morris gct Concord MM (H)

VORE
1812, 6, 27.   Isaac & w, Eleanor, & ch, Wil-
     liam, Isaac, Eleanor & Mordecai, gct
     Short Creek MM

WADE
1815, 5, 27.   Royal & w, Phebe, & ch, Nathan,
     Rhoda, Ruth, Hannah, Lydia & Rachel, rocf
     Concord MM, dtd 1815,4,20
1815, 5, 27.   Owen rocf Concord MM, dtd 1815,
     5,25
1815, 5, 27.   Mary & Sarah rocf Concord MM,
     dtd 1815,4,20
1819, 3, 25.   Nathan dis disunity
1819, 4, 22.   Rhoda Pennel (form Wade) dis mcd
1819, 7, 22.   Royal & w, Phebe,& Ruth, Hannah,
     Lydia & Rachel, gct Stillwater MM
1819, 7, 22.   Owen gct Stillwater MM
1819, 7, 22.   Mary gct Stillwater MM
1823, 1, 23.   Sarah gct Somerset MM
1827, 1, 25.   Sarah rocf Somerset MM, dtd
     1826,10,30
1827, 4, 26.   Sarah rocf Somerset MM, dtd
     1826,10,30

WALKER
1811, 6, 22.   Mary & ch, Martha, Joseph,
     Lewis, Eliza & Isaac, rocf Middleton MM,
     dtd 1811,5,9
1815, 7, 22.   George & s, George, rocf Con-
     cord MM, dtd 1815,6,22
1815, 8, 31.   Isaac E., minor, rocf Redstone
     MM, dtd 1815,7,28
1816, 2, 23.   Mary D. rocf Concord MM, dtd
     1816,2,20
1818, 5, 21.   Ebenezer & w, Hannah, rocf Short
     Creek MM, O., dtd 1818,3,24
1818, 10, 22.   Anna recrq on consent of Con-
     cord MM

WALTER
1837, 3, 30.   Abigail m John C. BROWN

1826, 12, 21.   Abigail recrq
1837, 1, 25.   Hannah (form Michner) dis mcd
1839, 7, 24.   Phebe gct Pennsville MM
1875, 9, 16.   Bennett G. [Walters] & w, Emily,
     recrq (H)

1875, 9, 16.   Branson Hollowell [Walters]
     recrq (H)

WARD
1842, 2, 17.   Sarah P. rocf Concord MM, dtd
     1841,11,24 (H)   [(H)
1847, 2, 18.   Sarah gct Clear Creek MM, Ill.

WARNER
1845, 5, 17.   Levi, s John & Lydia, Ross Co.,
     O.; m in St. Clairsville, Margaret SMITH,
     dt David & Margaret WILSON, Belmont Co.,
     O. (H)

1845, 7, 17.   Margaret gct Greenplain MM (H)

WATERS
1844, 1, 18.   Edward dis mcd (H)

WATSON
1820, 8, 21.   Mary m Levi TOWNSEND

1817, 1, 23.   Abner & w, Elizabeth, & ch,
     William, Deborah, Phebe, Ann & Mark, rocf
     Middleton MM, dtd 1816,12,16
1817, 2, 20.   Hannah rocf Middleton MM, dtd
     1816,12,16
1817, 9, 25.   Mary rocf Middleton MM, dtd
     1817,7,14
1821, 5, 24.   Abner & w, Elizabeth, & ch,
     William, Phebe, Ann & Mark, gct Stillwater
     MM
1821, 10, 25.   Hannah & Deborah gct Stillwater
     MM
1824, 3, 23.   Cert rec for Joseph from Muncie
     MM, Pa., end to Marlborough MM, O.
1840, 8, 13.   Sarah con mcd (H)   [(H)
1842, 3, 17.   Sarah dis joining Meth. Society

WAY
1823, 6, 26.   Robert, minor, rocf Somerset
     MM, dtd 1823,5,26
1824, 9, 23.   Robert gct Sommerset MM
1845, 10, 22.   Lydia (form Gregg) dis mcd

WEBSTER
1813, 1, 28.   John, s John & Hannah, Gurnsey
     Co., O.; m in Plainfield MH, Albina GREGG,
     dt Abner & Sarah, Gurnsey Co., O.
1813, 12, 30.   Thomas, s John & Hannah, Gurnsey
     Co., O.; m in Plainfield MH, Anne GORE,
     dt Thomas & Mercy, Belmont Co., O.

1813, 4, 27.   Albina gct Stillwater MM
1814, 4, 23.   Ann gct Stillwater MM
1814, 11, 26.   John & w, Abbina, rocf Stillwater
     MM, dtd 1814,10,25
1816, 2, 23.   John & w, Albina, & s, Charles,
     gct Stillwater MM

WELDON
1815, 9, 23.   Isaac & w, Elizabeth, & ch,
     Ann, John, Isaac, Nathan & Joseph, recrq

WELLS

1827, 8, 24. John T., s Wm. & Margaret, Morgan Co., O.; m in Plainfield MH, Esther VAIL, dt Benj. & Rebecca, Belmont Co., O.

1814, 12, 24. Isaac & w, Susannah, & s, Josiah, rocf Concord MM, dtd 1814,12,22

1827, 12, 20. Esther gct Deerfield MM

1828, 7, 24. Abner & w, Deborah, rocf Short Creek MM, dtd 1828,4,24 (H)

1842, 4, 14. Isaac & w, Susanna, & ch, Jonathan, Hannah L., Elisha, Ann B., Amos P. & Ruth, rocf Concord MM, dtd 1842,3,23 (H)

1842, 4, 14. William & w, Mary, & ch, David & Isaac, rocf Concord MM, dtd 1842,3,23 (H)

1843, 5, 24. Jonathan rocf Short Creek MM, O., dtd 1843,1,24

1843, 5, 24. Hannah, minor, rocf Short Creek MM, O., dtd 1843,1,24

1844, 7, 18. Mary & ch, David S. & Sarah Ann, gct Concord MM (H)

1844, 3, 14. Hannah L. gct Concord MM (H)

1844, 4, 18. Isaac & w, Susannah, & ch, Elisha, Anna B., Amos P. & Ruth, gct Concord MM (H)

1844, 7, 18. William & w, Mary, & ch, David T. & Sarah Ann, gct Concord MM (H)

1844, 7, 24. Hannah gct Short Creek MM, O.

1856, 1, 11. Martha (form Fawcett) con mcd (H)

1856, 5, 15. Martha gct Deerfield MM, O. (H)

1863, 11, 19. Elisha rocf Gwynedd MM, Pa., dtd 1863,7,30 (H)

1867, 8, 15. Elisha gct Concord MM (H)

WHEELER

1845, 12, 18. Hannah gct Short Creek MM, O. (H)

1844, 5, 16. Hannah (form Gumery) con mcd (H)

WHINERY

1838, 12, 13. Edward rocf New Garden MM, dtd 1838,5,24 (H)

WHITE

1815, 6, 1. Anne m Geo. VANLAW

1810, 4, 28. Sarah Spencer (form White) dis mcd

1816, 7, 26. Benjamin rocf Butternut MM, N.Y., dtd 1816,4,5, end by New Garden MM

1819, 5, 20. Elizabeth Head (form White) dis mcd

1819, 7, 22. Benjamin gct Allum Creek MM

1821, 5, 24. Aaron dis mcd

1824, 1, 22. Thomas dis mcd

1825, 4, 21. Matilda Palmer (form White) dis mcd

1831, 8, 25. Jane Williams (form White) con mcd (H)

1832, 3, 22. Edith R. George (form White)

con mcd (H)

1833, 8, 22. Aaron & w, Amy, & ch, William, Analiza S. & Lydia Jane, recrq (H)

1844, 9, 19. Sarah recrq (H)

1845, 1, 16. Lydia Jane Haines (form White) con mcd (H)

1848, 5, 18. Ann Eliza Meed (form White) con mcd (H)

1848, 5, 18. Sarah (form Kenard) dis mcd (H)

1848, 6, 15. William dis mcd (H)

1858, 5, 13. Priscilla (form Foulk) con mcd (H)

1858, 12, 16. David con mcd (H)

1870, 8, 18. Rose B. recrq (H)

1870, 12, 15. Rosa Bell, dt Priscilla White (form Foulke) recrq (H)

1872, 10, 17. Priscilla Baldwin (form White) con mcd (H)

1883, 5, 17. Rosa B. Barrett (form White) con mcd (H)

WILEMAN

1825, 2, 25. Jesse, s Abraham & Letitia, Stark Co., O.; m in Goshen MH, Lydia GREGG, dt Abner & Sarah, Belmont Co., O.

1825, 5, 26. Lydia gct Marlborough MM

WILKINSON

1816, 1, 26. James rocf New Garden MM, Pa., dtd 1815,12,7

WILLIAMS

1818, 3, 2. Micajah J., s Jesse & Sarah, Harrison Co., O.; m in Banesville, Hannah JONES, dt Aquilla & Elizabeth

1846, 1, 12. Charles H., s Micajah T. & Hannah, Lucas Co., O.; m in home of Benjamin Thomas, Sarah C. THOMAS, dt Benjamin & Joanna, St. Clairsville, O. (H)

1851, 11, 12. Thomas E. d ae 2 bur Plainfield

1852, 9, 30. Mary Ann m Jas. EDGERTON

----, --, --. William C. & Rebecca Ch: Lydia M.   b 1854, 10, 15

1854, 3, 24. Elizabeth d ae 16, bur Plainfield

1818, 5, 21. Hannah gct Cincinnati MM

1823, 6, 26. William & w, Lydia, & dt, Hannah, rocf Somerset MM, dtd 1823,5,26

1825, 7, 21. William & w, Lydia, & ch, Hannah C. & Mary, gct Somerset MM

1827, 5, 24. Cert rec for John S. & w, Sarah, & ch, Benjamin, Hannah, Robert, Ann, John & Elizabeth, from Redstone MM, dtd 1827,4,4, end to Stillwater MM

1828, 12, 26. Sarah & ch, Benjamin, Hannah, Anne, John, Robert, Elizabeth & Joseph, rocf Stillwater MM, dtd 1828,8,23 (H)

1831, 8, 25. Jane (form White) con mcd (H)

1845, 5, 15. Jane gct Stillwater MM (H)

1849, 12, 19. Wm. C. & w, Rebecca, & ch, Mary Ann, Phebe H., Elizabeth, Caroline, Ra-

WILLIAMS, Wm. C., continued
    chel, Amy B., Joseph John & Thomas G.,
    rocf Flushing MM, dtd 1849,11,22
1857, 4, 22. Phebe H. & Catharine gct Flush-
    ing MM
1857, 5, 20. Wm. C. & w, Rebecca, & ch, Ra-
    chel, Amy B., Joseph John & Lydia M., gct
    Flushing MM
1859, 1, 13. Druzilla (form Horner) dis mcd

WILLIS
1891, 12, 30. Charles H., s Peter & Martha,
    Carolina Co., Md.; m in house of N. B.
    Nichols, Flora M. NICHOLS, dt Nathan B. &
    Sarah E., Belmont Co., O. (H)

1808, 4, 23. Ruth [Willes] (form Jenkins) dis
    mcd

WILLITS
1831, 12, 1. Eli, s Samuel & Elizabeth,
    Knox Co., O.; m in Plainfield MH, Lamira
    ELLIOTT, dt John & Rachel, Belmont Co., O.
1844, 8, 22. Mark [Willets], s Ellis & Han-
    nah, Jefferson Co., O.; m in Plainfield
    MH, Sarah VAIL, dt Benj. & Hannah, Belmont
    Co., O.

1817, 1, 23. Joseph rocf Deep River MM, N.C.,
    dtd 1816,11,11
1817, 4, 24. Joseph gct Fairfield MM
1832, 8, 23. Lemira [Willets] gct Allum Creek
    MM (H)
1844, 11, 20. Sarah V. gct Smithfield MM

WILSON
1816, 5, 2. Samuel, s Isaac & Rebeckah, Bel-
    mont Co., O.; m in Plainfield MH, Sarah
    GREGG, dt Abner & Sarah, Belmont Co., O.
1817, 11, 26. Hannah m Parker ASKEW
1817, 11, 27. Edith m Alan FARQUHAR
1822, 1, 31. John, s Israel & Martha, Harri-
    son Co., O.; m in Plainfield MH, Amelia
    FOULKS, dt Judah & Sarah, Belmont Co., O.
1828, 3, 5. Amos, s David & Margaret, Bel-
    mont Co., O.; m in St. Clairsville, Anna
    MORRIS, dt Samuel & Salley, Belmont Co.,O.
1846, 1, 21. Thomas, s Amos & Hannah, Belmont
    Co., O.; m in St. Clairsville, Mary Ann
    KEITH, dt Lloyd & Anna, Belmont Co., O.(H)

1810, 12, 22. Israel & w, Martha, & ch, Ruth,
    William, Edith, John, Hannah, David, Ra-
    chel, Israel & Jonathan, rocf Westland MM,
    dtd 1812,10,27
1811, 3, 23. Hugh con mcd
1811, 6, 22. Hugh gct Stillwater MM
1811, 12, 28. Edward rocf Buckingham MM, Pa.,
    dtd 1810,4,2
1811, 12, 28. Isaac Jr. gct Stillwater MM, to
    m Elizabeth Dodd
1812, 2, 22. Edward dis mcd & taking part in
    military exercise

1812, 7, 25. Elizabeth rocf Stillwater MM,
    dtd 1812,6,30
1818, 10, 22. Cert rec for Sarah from Sadbury
    MM, Pa., dtd 1818,9,3, end to Flushing MM
1819, 9, 23. Isaac gct Baltimore MM, W. Dist.
1820, 6, 22. Henry rocf Westland MM, dtd
    1820,3,23
1820, 6, 22. Isaac & w, Elizabeth, & ch, Sam-
    uel, Rebecca, Aaron, Sarah & Stephen, gct
    Stillwater MM
1821, 3, 22. Mahlon Smith gct New Garden
    MM, Pa., to m Margaret Wilson
1822, 3, 21. Amelia gct Flushing MM
1825, 5, 26. Stephen dis mcd
1825, 11, 24. Ruth rocf New Garden MM, Pa.,
    dtd 1825,10,6
1826, 12, 21. Amos & w, Hannah, & ch, Joshua
    B., Margaret, David, Thomas & Hannah B.,
    rocf Center MM, Del., dtd 1826,10,2
1829, 1, 22. Henry dis jas (H)
1833, 5, 23. Thomas & w, Hannah, & ch, Yar-
    nal, Phebe, Jane, Cyrus & Thomas, rocf
    Short Creek MM, O., dtd 1833,4,25 (H)
1833, 11, 21. Elizabeth gct Stillwater MM (H)
1837, 6, 21. Phebe dis jH
1839, 3, 20. Yarnal dis jH
1840, 9, 17. Margaret Pennington (form Wil-
    son) con mcd (H)
1840, 10, 20. Jane dis jH
1841, 6, 17. Joshua B. con mcd (H)
1841, 6, 23. Joshua dis disunity
1841, 12, 22. Margaret dis jH
1842, 1, 19. Mary (form Chamberlain) dis mcd
1842, 11, 22. Cyrus con mcd
1843, 12, 14. Cyrus con mcd (H)
1846, 8, 19. David dis mcd
1846, 10, 21. Thomas dis disunity
1846, 12, 17. Hannah Hoge (form Wilson) con
    mcd (H)
1847, 5, 13. Thomas dis (H)
1851, 4, 17. Amos & w, Anne, & ch, Rebecca,
    Sarah P., Elizabeth, Morris A., Laura C.,
    Mary, Amos & Oliver, gct Clear Creek MM,
    Ill. (H)
1864, 10, 19. Isaac N. Vail gct Stillwater
    MM, to m Rachel D. Wilson
1871, 4, 13. Joshua B. gct Clear Creek MM,
    Ill. (H)
1847, 4, 15. Daniel con mcd (H)
1847, 5, 13. Thomas dis (H)
1852, 1, 15. Phebe Hurst (form Wilson) dis
    mcd (H)
1855, 7, 19. David gct Clear Creek MM, Ill.
    (H)
1871, 4, 13. Joshua B. gct Clear Creek MM,
    Ill. (H)

WINDER
1826, 7, 20. Samuel Chambers gct Sandy
    Spring MM, to m Tamer Winder

WINDHAM
1818, 3, 26. Mercy (form Spencer) con mcd

WINDHAM, continued
1833, 1, 24.   Mercy gct Allum Creek MM (H)

WINTER
1812, 3, 28.   Jonathan rocf Westheartford MM,
    Conn., dtd 1811,9,11, end by Concord MM,
    1812,2,20
1815, 4, 22.   Jonathan gct Marlborough MM

WITCHEL
1814, 6, 2.   John [Witchell], s John & Mary,
    Belmont Co., O.; m in Plainfield MH, Bath-
    sheba FOULKE, dt Isachar & Jane, Belmont
    Co., O.

1809, 12, 23.   John & w, Mary, rocf Concord MM,
    dtd 1809,12,21
1814, 2, 26.   John Jr. rocf Abington MM, dtd
    1814,1,31
1815, 7, 22.   John & w, Mary, gct Richland MM,
    Pa.
1815, 7, 22.   John Jr. & w, Bathsheba, gct
    Richland MM, Pa.
1817, 1, 23.   John Jr. & w, Bethsheba, & dt,
    Jane, rocf Stroudsburgh MM, dtd 1816,11,28
1819, 4, 22.   John & w, Bethsheba, & ch, Jane,
    Mary & Isaac, gct Flushing MM

WOOD
1815, 6, 28.   Jacob, s Joshua & Hannah, Bel-
    mont Co., O.; m in Flushing MH, Phebe [O.
    PICKERING, dt Samuel & Phebe, Belmont Co.,
    O.
1817, 8, 27.   Rachel m James CROZER

1809, 12,23.   Joshua & w, Hannah, & ch, Jacob,
    Rachel, Jesse, Sarah & Asenith, rocf
    Hopewell MM, dtd 1809,11,6
1820, 6, 22.   William rocf Smithfield MM, dtd
    1820,6,19
1821, 2, 22.   William dis disunity
1826, 6, 22.   Rebecca gct Milford MM, Ind.

WORTHINGTON
1838, 7, 25.   Elisha Vanlaw gct Pennsville
    MM, to m Anna Worthington

WRIGHT
1808, 4, 27.   Sarah m Wm. HOGE
1816, 2, 28.   Robert, s Anthony & Martha,
    Knox Co., O.; m in Goshen MH, Sarah PIDGEON
    dt Wm. & Rachel, Belmont Co., O.
1816, 10, 3.   Elizabeth m Thomas RIDGWAY
1817, 4, 30.   Elizabeth m Samuel SMITH
1821, 5, 30.   Abigail m James GREGG
1840, 6, 3.   John D., s Nehemiah & Abigail,
    Belmont Co., O.; m in St. Clairsville, Han-
    nah ASKEW, dt Wm. & Martha, Belmont Co., O.
    Ch: Isaac A.   b 1841, 3, 27
        Mary I.   " 1843, 11, 8

1808, 11, 26.   Nehemiah gct Short Creek MM
1809, 10, 28.   Schooley & w, Lavina, & ch, Mary,

Elizabeth, Hannah, Amos, Sarah, Aaron, Re-
    becca, William & Fanny, rocf Westland MM,
    dtd 1809,7,22
1810, 6, 23.   Rebecca rocf Concord MM, dtd
    1810,5,24
1813, 1, 23.   Joseph gct Concord MM, to m
    Ann Pickering
1813, 5, 22.   John gct Baltimore MM
1813, 9, 25.   James dis mcd
1813, 10, 23.   Ann rocf Concord MM, dtd 1813,
    10,21
1815, 11, 25.   Rebecca gct Fairfield MM
1816, 8, 23.   Sarah gct Short Creek MM, O.
1817, 1, 23.   Hannah recrq
1817, 8, 21.   James rst
1818, 7, 23.   Nehemiah & w, Abigail, & ch,
    Joseph Dew, Martha & John D., also a min-
    or, Mary Gilbert, rocf Short Creek MM, O.,
    dtd 1818,7,21
1820, 8, 24.   Paxton, minor, rocf Allum Creek
    MM, dtd 1820,6,1
1824, 4, 22.   Benjamin G. dis mcd
1824, 5, 20.   Jane (form Broomhall) dis mcd
1826, 6, 22.   Mary (form Green) dis mcd
1836, 8, 24.   Martha dis jH
1839, 10, 23.   Sarah Ann rocf Alum Creek MM,
    dtd 1839,6,20
1840, 9, 17.   Joseph Dew dis mcd (H)
1841, 8, 25.   Sarah Ann Gregg (form Wright)
    dis mcd
1842, 8, 24.   James D. dis disunity
1842, 11, 22.   Viley dis jH
1843, 3, 16.   Sarah rocf Allum Creek MM, dtd
    1842,10,20 (H)
1845, 5, 21.   John D. & w, Hannah, & ch,
    Isaac A. & Mary J., gct Chesterfield MM
1846, 9, 17.   Viley W. Fred (form Wright) con
    mcd (H)
1848, 6, 15.   James D. con mcd (H)
1849, 8, 22.   Jenkinson dis mcd
1850, 11, 14.   Jenkinson dis mcd (H)
1856, 11, 12.   Mary Eliza (form Gregg) dis mcd
    (H)
1856, 12, 18.   Emmett dis mcd
1875, 8, 19.   Louisa G. (form Gregg) gct Clear
    Creek MM, Ill.
1875, 7, 15.   Mary J. gct Clear Creek MM, Ill.
1898, 1, 13.   Myra F. gct Race St. MM, Phila.,
    Pa. (H)

YATES
1826, 10, 26.   Anna rst on consent of Concord
    MM

YOCUM
1866, 11, 15.   Joseph rocf Stillwater MM, dtd
    1866,9,15 (H)
1866, 3, 15.   Samuel & w, Jane, & ch, Lindly
    & Mary J., rocf Stillwater MM, dtd 1866,
    1,20 (H)
1866, 6, 14.   John D. [Yokum] & w, Hannah T.,
    & s, Nathan G., rocf Stillwater MM (H)
1869, 9, 16.   Samuel con mcd (H)

YOCUM, continued
1869, 12, 16. Samuel Sr. gct Deerfield MM (H)

*   *   *   *   *   *   *   *

PLUMMER
1808, 9, 24. Eli & w, Alice, & ch, James &
        Sina, rocf Saddsbury MM, end by Concord
        MM, 1808,4,5
1821, 8, 23. Sina Miller (form Plummer) dis
        mcd
1822, 3, 21. James dis disunity
1828, 12, 26. Eli dis disunity (H)

1871, 8, 17. Aaron D. rocf Stillwater MM,
        dtd 1871,1,21 (H)

*   *   ..   *   *   *   *   *

WOOD
1826, 4, 26. Jesse, s Joshua & Hannah, Bel-
        mont Co., O.; m in St. Clairsville, Rebec-
        ca POTTS, dt Samuel & Mary, "of the town
        of St. Clairsville"

STILLWATER MONTHLY MEETING

Stillwater Monthly Meeting, Belmont Co., Ohio, was established by Short Creek Quarterly Meeting, 3rd Mo. 29th, 1808, being set off from Concord Monthly Meeting. This meeting was divided by the Hicksite Separation in 1829 and became the center of the Wilbur group later.

RECORDS

ADAMS

1844, 11, 28. Edward G., s Thomas & Lydia, Monroe Co., O.; m in home of Wm. Thomas, Harriet THOMAS, dt Wm. & Rebecca, Belmont Co., O. (H)

1873, 1, 18. Elnora (form Hogue) con mcd (H)
1880, 7, 17. Rebecca Ann Smith (form Adams) con mcd (H)

AGUR

1819, 7, 24. Rebecca (form Croy) dis mcd

ALBERTSON

1816, 1, 11. Penninah m Joel PATTERSON

1813, 3, 2. Joseph & w, Elvira, & dt, Peninah, rocf Plymouth MM, dtd 1812,11,21

ALLEN

1823, 7, 25. John Milten d ae 18y 5m 24d

1817, 12, 27. Philip & w, Elizabeth, & ch, John Milton, Jacob H. & Samuel, rocf Oswego MM, end by Smithfield MM, 1817,12,22
1829, 1, 24. Benjamin dis JH
1829, 1, 24. Benjamin Jr. dis JH
1829, 1, 24. Eunice dis JH
1829, 1, 24. Hannah dis JH
1829, 1, 24. Hannah Jr. dis JH
1829, 1, 24. Jehu dis JH
1829, 1, 24. Mary dis JH
1829, 9, 26. Philip dis JH
1829, 10, 24. Elizabeth dis JH
1829, 10, 24. Elizabeth Jr. dis JH
1830, 1, 23. Jacob dis JH
1830, 4, 17. Phillip & w, Elizabeth, & ch, Jacob & Samuel, gct Westfield MM, O. (H)
1830, 5, 22. Samuel gct Silver Creek MM
1834, 2, 22. Betsy (form Horner) dis mcd
1839, 8, 17. Moses & w, Jane, & ch, William, Walton, Aaron, Sarah, Hannah, Unice & Isaac, gct Whitewater MM, Ind.

ALWINE

1883, 3, 11. Ida May, w Homer P., dt Jeptha W. & Abi (Hartley) HALL, b

1907, 5, 22. Ida M. (form Hall) con mcd

AMOS

1831, 3, 28. Susannah m Wm. WOOD

1826, 9, 23. Moses Dillon gct Little Falls MM, Md., to m Martha Amos
1831, 2, 26. Susannah [Amoss] rocf Gunpowder MM, Md., dtd 1831,3,1

ANDERSON

1924, 10, 22. Dorothy (form Bailey) dis mcd & jas

ANDREWS

1815, 8, 28. Richard & ch, Arrena & Lucy, recrq
1815, 8, 29. Polly, w Richard, rst; dis by Seacock MM, Va., now laid down

ARNET

1811, 3, 26. Anderson & Thomas rocf Springfield MM, N. C., dtd 1809,2,4, end by Miami MM 1811,1,30

ARNOLD

1819, 7, 29. Thomas, s Asa & Susanna, Belmont Co., O.; m in Ridge, Elizabeth BAILEY, dt Henry & Elizabeth, Guernsey Co., O.
    Ch: William   b 1824, 6, 29
        Henry   " 1829, 7, 24
        James   " 1831, 11, 10
        Caleb   " 1834, 11, 4
1834, 1, 30. Thomas, s Asa & Susanna, Guernsey Co., O.; m in Richland, Elizabeth HALL, dt Caleb & Silva (Patterson), Guernsey Co., O.
    Ch: Nathan   b 1836, 12, 13
        Maria   " 1836, 12, 13
        Joseph   " 1839, 12, 31 d 1842,11,28
        bur Richland
        Amanda
        Jane   b 1843, 5, 3
1846, 8, 5. Thomas d bur Richland
1854, 12, 21. Elizabeth, w Thomas, d bur Richland
1859, 10, 27. Caleb, s Thomas & Elizabeth, Guernsey Co., O.; m in Richland, Phebe HARTLEY, dt Noah & Milicent, Guernsey Co., O.
    Ch: Milly Rose-
        lee   b 1862, 5, 7
        Rhoda   " 1866, 8, 29
        Cora Ellen
        May   " 1868, 5, 10
        Phebe De-
        lora Da-
        zelln   " 1870, 9, 6
        Noah P.
        Hartley   " 1873, 4, 16
1867, 2, 20. Rhoda d ae 5m 22d bur Richland

1811, 3, 26. Susannah & dt, Hannah, rocf Springfield MM, dtd 1809,2,4, end by Miami MM, 1811,1,30
1833, 5, 25. William & James Hadly, minors in care of Nathan & Ruth Dodd, gct Somerset MM
1846, 5, 23. William dis disunity
1859, 3, 26. Maria A. gct Somerset MM
1876, 9, 20. Amanda Dyer (form Arnold) dis jas & mcd
1888, 9, 19. Ellen May Dotson (form Arnold) dis mcd
1905, 7, 19. Phebe E. Wilcox (form Arnold) dis mcd

ARNOLD, continued
1909, 6, 23. Milicent Rosaline Hill (form
    Arnold) dis mcd

ASHEAD
1894, 6, 21. J. Morris, s Amos & Hannah (Hoyle)
    Burlington Co., N. J.; m in Stillwater MH,
    Elizabeth T. HALL, dt John & Deborah (Davis)
    Belmont Co., O.

1895, 3, 20. Elizabeth T. (form Hall) gct
    Salem MM, O.

ASKEW
----, --, --. William & Martha
    Ch: Isaac   b 1810, 10, 17
        Hannah   " 1813, 1, 27
        Rebecca W. " 1815, 6, 12
        Joseph   " 1817, 7, 22
        -----   " 1819, 8, 28
        Martha   " 1822, 6, 10
        William   " 1824, 11, 18
        Margaret   " 1827, 12, 3
        Clarissa R." 1831, 6, 18
----, --, --. Parker & Hannah
    Ch: Sarah   b 1818, 12, 26
        Rebecca   " 1821, 4, 7
        Elizabeth S" 1823, 6, 18
        Samuel   " 1825, 11, 24
        Peter Hat-
        ton   " 1828, 3, 3
        Isaac
        Blackfan   " 1830, 10, 9

1829, 10, 24. William dis jH
1831, 2, 26. Parker W. dis disunity
1833, 12, 28. Isaac dis disunity
1866, 1, 27. Parker & w, Rebecca, gct Spring-
    field MM, Iowa
1866, 1, 27. Mary gct Springfield MM, Iowa
1866, 7, 28. Benjamin gct Springville MM,
    Iowa

ATHERTON
1849, 5, 21. Richard, s Boah & Mary, Morgan
    Co., Ohio; m Marahda BAILEY, dt Barak &
    Elizabeth, Belmont Co., O. (H)

1838, 4, 28. David, Ann, Reuben, Ross,
    Richard & Elizabeth, minors, rocf Flush-
    ing MM, dtd 1837,10,25
1849, 6, 16. Reuben R. gct Plainfield MM (H)

ATKINSON
1850, 3, 27. Daniel, s William & Anne, Bel-
    mont Co., O.; m in Stillwater MH, Sabilla
    BUTLER, dt William & Rebecca SMITH, Bel-
    mont Co., O.

1836, 2, 27. William & w, Nanny, & ch, Daniel,
    Thomas & Rachel, rocf Short Creek MM, dtd
    1835,12,22
1849, 6, 23. Thomas dis mcd

1849, 8, 25. Rachel Williams (form Atkinson)
    con mcd
1852, 11, 27. Daniel & w, Sabilla, gct Three
    Rivers MM, Ia.
1854, 10, 28. William & w, Nancy, gct Walnut
    Ridge MM, Ind.
1914, 2, 25. Edward Y. Gamble gct Short Creek
    MM, to m Rebecca W. Atkinson

BACKES
1928, 6, 25. Margaret B. (form Bundy) gct
    Falls MM, Pa.

BAILEY
----, --, --. Jesse & Pharaba
    Ch: Edmund   b 1795, 10, 2
        Abigail   " 1798, 3, 28
        Uriah   " 1800, 12, 27
        Delitha   " 1803, 4, 9
        Matilda   " 1807, 3, 28
        Mary   " 1810, 2, 28
        David   " 1813, 1, 28 d 1832,11, 9
        bur Stillwater
        Jesse Jr. b 1815, 1, 11
----, --, --. Zachariah m Mary ----- d 1859,
    2,14 bur Stillwater
    Ch: Ira W.   b 1798, 8, 14 d 1803,12,21
        Eliza S.   " 1799, 8, 20
        Wiley S.   " 1801, 10, 27
        Mahala R.   " 1806, 7, 19
        Ira W.   " 1812, 5, 19
        Diza Ann   " 1814, 6, 7
        Robert C.   " 1819, 10, 8
----, --, --. Micajah & Mary
    Ch: Maranda   b 1804, 2, 28
        Samuel   " 1806, 2, 11
        Maria   " 1808, 11, 28
        Jesse   " 1811, 3, 8
        Joshua   " 1813, 7, 13
        Matthews   " 1815, 12, 23
        Jane   " 1817, 1, 27
        Joseph   " 1819, 5, 23
        Hezekiah   " 1821, 10, 23
1808, 9, 14. Stephen, s Edmond & Elizabeth,
    Belmont Co., O.; m in Stillwater MH, Ti-
    litha PATTERSON, dt Wm. & Elizabeth, Bel-
    mont Co., O.
    Ch: Elizabeth b 1809, 6, 17
        William   " 1810, 11, 24
        Benjamin   " 1812, 11, 18
        Exum   " 1815, 1, 18
1809, 5, 3. Jesse, s Henry & Elizabeth,
    Belmont Co., O.; m in Stillwater MH, Mary
    BUNDY, dt Wm. & Mary, Belmont Co., O.
    Ch: Lydia   b 1812, 8, 8
        Rachel   " 1814, 8, 21 d 1834, 5,29
        Mary   " 1817, 5, 9 [bur Rich.
        Ruth   " 1819, 4, 7
        Elizabeth   " 1821, 8, 10 d 1835,12,27
        Achsah   " 1824, 7, 11 [bur Rich.
        Jesse W.   " 1827, 10, 5 " 1898, 5,14
----, --, --. Jesse & Hannah
    Ch: Rachel   b 1813, 7, 10

BAILEY, Jesse & Hannah, continued
    Ch: Even   b 1814, 12, 31
1812, 11, 5. Bethany m James HICKS
1814, 11, 2. Ruth m Nathan DODD
1815, --, --. Matther d bur Stillwater
1816, 2, 28. Mahlon, s John & Rebecca, Belmont Co., O.; m in Stillwater MH, Charity DAVIS, dt Moses & Ann, Belmont Co., O.
1816, 10, 2. Edmund, s Jesse & Pheraba, Belmont Co., O.; m in Stillwater MH, Margaret DOUDNA, dt Henry & Martha, Belmont Co., O.
    Ch: Martha   d 1898, 2, 8
        Sarah M. b 1833, 7, 3 " 1924, 6,13
----, --, --. Jesse & Mary
    Ch: David   b 1817, 10, 7
        Susann   " 1819, 6, 11
        Jehu   " 1821, 8, 13
1818, 5, 27. Mary m Benjamin BUNDY
1819, 1, 28. Lucy m John PATTERSON
1819, 4, 1. Barak, s Wm. & Rebecca, Belmont Co., O.; m in Ridge, Elizabeth VERNON, dt James & Tamer, Belmont Co., O.
1819, 7, 29. Elizabeth m Thomas ARNOLD
1819, 9, 27. Ann m Stanton BUNDY
1819, 12, 2. Michel m Joseph DAVIS
1820, 7, 17. Phareba d ae 49 bur Stillwater
1822, 7, 15. Jesse d bur Meigs Creek
1823, 7, 30. Abigail m Marvin GIFFORD
1823, 7, 30. Delitha m Benjamin BUNDY
1823, 12, 3. Jesse, Belmont Co., O.; m in Stillwater MH, Sarah MILLHOUSE, Belmont Co., O.
1824, 1, 28. Susan Ann d bur Meigs Creek, ae 4y 7m 7d
1824, 4, 28. Maranda m Borden STANTON
1826, 11, 30. Matilda m Wm. PIERPOINT
1827, 5, 3. Mary m Caleb BUTLER
1829, 12, 10. Lydia m Wm. DOUDNA
----, --, --. Uriah & Susannah
    Ch: Tabitha   b 1831, 10, 3
        David   " 1833, 5, 16
1831, 3, 30. Mary m William CREW
1834, 12, 3. Jesse, s Micajah & Mary, Belmont Co., O.; m Nancy HODGIN, dt John & Prudence, Belmont Co., O.
    Ch: Laban   b 1836, 10, 28 d 1852,10,13
        bur Stillwater
        Edwin   b 1839, 9, 28
        Maria   " 1841, 10, 27
        Mary Ann   " 1843, 7, 28
        Lindley   " 1846, 3, 26
        Lydia Jane " 1847, 12, 27
        Robert H. " 1850, 3, 1
        Prudence   " 1852, 10, 21
        Sarah H.   " 1854, 12, 3
        Fanny   " 1857, 4, 14
1834, 12, 19. Henry d
1835, 3, 12. Mary m Isaac HALL
1835, 6, 4. Joshua, s Micajah & Mary, Belmont Co., O.; m in Captina, Elizabeth EMBREE
1836, 9, 28. Jane m Robert PLUMMER
1837, 3, 29. Jesse, s Jesse & Pharaby, Bel-

mont Co., O.; m in Stillwater MH, Asenath PATTERSON, dt Silas & Rachel, Belmont Co., O., d 1905,11,29 bur Stillwater
    Ch: Silas   b 1839, 7, 14
        Sarah
         Elizabeth " 1841, 5, 13 d 1863, 6, 6
         bur Stillwater
        John   b 1845, 10, 5
        Lindley P. " 1850, 3, 8 " 1928, 1,10
         bur Stillwater
        Rachel   b 1855, 11, 15 " 1862,11,30
         bur Stillwater
        Allen   b 1858, 6, 11
        Mary Jane " 1863, 6, 16 " 1864, 7,26
         bur Stillwater
1837, 9, 25. Sarah, w Jesse, d bur Concord
1838, 2, 28. Ann m Joel STRAHL (H)
1839, 3, 25. Rachel W., w Elihu, dt Matthew Wood, d
1844, 7, 20. Sarah, wd Joseph, d bur Stillwater
1844, 8, 28. Maria m Joseph A. HARTLEY
1845, 12, 21. Hezekiah, s Micajah & Mary, Belmont Co., O.; m in Stillwater MH, Elizabeth BUNDY, dt William & Sarah, Belmont Co., O.
    Ch: Sarah   b 1846, 10, 14
        Mary   " 1848, 11, 16
        Demsey   " 1851, 2, 5
        Melvina   " 1854, 5, 6
        Almeda   " 1856, 3, 8
        Adaline   " 1858, 8, 26
        Lucinda   " 1864, 9, 1
1846, 2, 28. Jeptha, s Joseph & Achsah, b
1847, 8, 29. Elizabeth, wd Henry, d bur Richland
1847, 8, 31. Mary, w Jesse, d bur Richland
1849, 5, 21. Maranda m Richard ATHERTON (H)
1849, 10, 31. Milton, s Edmund & Margaret, Belmont Co., O.; m in Stillwater MH, Sarah Ann BUTLER, dt Jared & Elizabeth, Belmont Co., O.
1851, 11, 17. Sarah Ann, w Milten, d bur Stillwater
1859, 8, 26. Margaret d bur Stillwater
----, --, --. Joel & Lydia H.
    Ch: Charles   b 1860, 3, 3
        Albert H. " 1862, 11, 20
1871, 3, 8. Mary m Henry STANTON
1871, 7, 26. Lindley P., s Jesse & Asenath, Belmont Co., O., b 1850,3,8 d 1928,1,10 bur Stillwater; m in Stillwater MH, Elizabeth STANTON, dt Joseph & Mary (Hodgin), b 1846,2,24
    Ch: Edwin M. b 1872, 7, 18
        Oscar J.   " 1874, 12, 5
        Annie   " 1876, 8, 16
        Clara   " 1878, 6, 25
        Alva C.   " 1880, 4, 26
        Jesse S.   " 1884, 4, 15
1871, 11, 1. Priscilla m John E. STRATTON
1873, 3, 5. Melvina m Joseph GARRETSON
1874, 6, 22. Lillian, w Edwin M., dt Josiah

BAILEY, continued
& Ruth (Bundy) Doudna, b
1876, 11, 19. Mary, w Micajah, d bur Stillwater
1880, 3, 31. Allen, s Jesse & Asenath (Patterson), Belmont Co., O., b 1858,6,11; m
Eva L. PATTERSON, dt David & Eunice (Starbuck), b 1860,11,25
Ch: Clifford   b 1883, 6, 6
    Wilson   " 1894, 12, 15
    Dorothy M. " 1897, 11, 17
1883, 11, 1. Adaline m Robert H. SMITH
1893, 6, 28. Edwin M., s Lindley P. & Eliza-
beth S., Belmont Co., O.; m in Stillwater
MH, Lillian M. DOUDNA, dt Josiah W. &
Ruth B., Belmont Co., O.
Ch: Herbert J. b 1896, 6, 8
----, --, --. Oscar J. m Mary Anna BRACKEN
Ch: Alfred L. b 1897, 3, 16
    Oliver
     Bracken   " 1901, 6, 14
    Joseph Os-
     car   " 1903, 7, 5
    Edward
     French   " 1907, 1, 30
    Lindley P.
     Jr.   " 1911, 8, 9
Oscar J. m 2nd Sarah Lavada STOCKDALE, dt
Wm. & Elizabeth (Bond), b 1886,12,23
Ch: Sarah
    Josephine b 1924, 9, 3
1896, 6, 8. Herbert, s Edward & Lillian
(Doudna), b
----, --, --. Alva C., s Lindley P. & Eliza-
beth (Stanton), b 1880,4,26; m Laura
STEER, dt Nathan & Mary Jane (Branson), b
1877,11,1
Ch: Harmon Eu-
     gene   b 1902, 7, 14
    Mary Eliza-
     beth   " 1904, 9, 20; m Vernon
    WARD
    Raymond C. " 1907, 6, 28
    Roland A. " 1909, 6, 28
    David Bran-
     son   " 1913, 1, 29
    Nathan   " 1914, 6, 17
    Ralph W.   " 1921, 2, 21
1901, 6, 14. Alfred Bracken, s Oscar J. &
Mary Anna (Brackin), b
1902, 5, 24. Anna m Clarence R. PATTEN
1903, 9, 9. Anna E. m J. Clarkson EDGERTON
1903, 10, 28. Clara m Frederick R. BUNDY
1904, 9, 22. Ethel E. m Lewis N. ELLYSON
1909, 10, 27. Edna A. m Louis J. TABOR
----, --, --. Jesse S., s Lindley P. & Elizabeth, b 1884,4,15; m Lydia M. HOGE, dt
Wm. & Rachel (Huff), b 1883,9,13 d 1925,
5,28 bur Stillwater
Ch: Elizabeth
     S. Jr.   b 1911, 5, 16
    Florence
     Eleanor   " 1913, 6, 27

Ch: Lester Wm. b 1915, 11, 22
    Charles
     Lloyd   " 1918, 3, 20
    Jesse S. Jr" 1925, 3, 23
1914, 10, 22. Mary Alma m Arthur E. STANTON
----, --, --. Alfred L., s Oscar J. & Mary
Anna (Bracken), b 1897,3,16; m Anna
BUNDY
----, --, --. Joseph Oscar, s Oscar J. & Mary
Anna (Brackin), b 1903,7,5; m Frances
DOUDNA
----, --, --. Oliver m Rebecca S. STEER, dt
Wilson J. & Mary S. (Hall), b 1903,8,10
Ch: Oscar Wil-
     son   b 1925, 7, 23
    Warren
     Oliver   " 1927, 9, --
----, --, --. Raymond C., s Alva C. & Laura
(Steer), b 1907,6,28; m Edith BRACKIN
Ch: Helen
     Margaret b 1930, 1, 5
    Martha
     Louise   " 1931, 4, 6

1808, 7, 28. Stephen rocf Gravelly Run MM,
Va., dtd 1808,3,19, end by Concord MM,
1808,6,23
1811, 10, 1. Jesse & w, Phariba, & ch, Edmund, Abigail, Uriah, Talitha, Matilda &
Mary, rocf Upper MM, Va., dtd 1811,3,16,
end by Salem MM 1811,8,13
1811, 10, 29. Rebecca & ch, Mahlon, Hiram,
Abidon, Joseph, Mary, John & Rebeckah,
recrq
1811, 10, 29. Elizabeth rocf Gravely Run MM,
Va., dtd 1811,6,13
1811, 11, 26. Sarah & ch, Betsy, Michal &
Nancy, rocf Gravely Run MM, Va., dtd
1811,9,21
1812, 3, 31. Sarah (form Hunnicutt) dis mcd
1812, 4, 28. Peninah (form Boswell) dis mcd
1812, 9, 29. Mary & ch, Eliza, Wiley & Mahala, rocf Upper MM, Va., dtd 1812,7,18
1812, 12, 29. Mary Hall (form Bailey) con mcd
1813, 8, 31. Margaret rocf Upper MM, dtd
1813,2,20
1813, 9, 28. Zachariah rocf Upper MM, Va.,
dtd 1813,5,23
1813, 10, 26. Margaret Young (form Bailey)
dis mcd
1814, 7, 26. Mary & Ann recrq
1814, 10, 25. Rebecca Wooton (form Bailey)
dis mcd
1815, 2, 28. Peninah rst at White Water MM,
Ind., on consent of this mtg
1815, 2, 28. Rebeckah & ch, Hiram, Sarah,
Abidon, Joseph, Mary, John & Rebeckah,
gct Center MM, O.
1815, 8, 29. Betsy Hawkins (form Bailey) dis
mcd
1816, 5, 25. Wyat dis mcd
1816, 7, 22. Hiram rocf Center MM, O., dtd
1816,4,20

BAILEY, continued
1817, 2, 22. Hiram gct Center MM, O.
1819, 1, 23. Sarah recrq
1819, 3, 27. James recrq
1819, 3, 27. Sarah & ch, Elizabeth, Henry, Sarah, Susanna, Anna & Martha, recrq
1819, 11, 27. Jesse & w, Mary, & ch, Rachel, Evan & David, rocf London Grove MM, dtd 1819,3,3
1821, 12, 21. Elizabeth gct Center MM
1822, 6, 22. Michel Ghant (form Bailey) dis mcd
1823, 7, 26. Eliza D. Gammon (form Bailey) dis mcd
1825, 2, 26. Ann Johnson (form Bailey) dis mcd
1827, 2, 24. Elizabeth (form Judkins) dis mcd
1830, 2, 27. Wiley dis mcd
1830, 6, 26. Mahala dis
1830, 9, 25. Uriah gct Flushing MM, to m Susannah Farmer
1831, 6, 25. Susannah rocf Flushing MM, dtd 1831,4,21
1833, 9, 28. Samuel gct Short Creek MM, to m Harriet Embree
1833, 11, 23. Zachariah dis disunity
1834, 4, 26. Harriet rocf Short Creek MM, dtd 1834,3,18
1834, 4, 26. Rachel Prouty (form Bailey) rpd mcd
1835, 11, 28. Mary, w Zachariah, & s, Robert, gct Goshen MM
1836, 3, 26. George Starbuck gct Somerset MM, to m Lydia Bailey
1836, 8, 27. Elizabeth dis
1836, 8, 27. Evan dis disunity
1836, 8, 27. Joshua dis
1836, 10, 22. Ira dis mcd
1837, 10, 22. Samuel & w, Harriet, & ch, Burden, gct Pennsville MM
1838, 5, 26. Jesse & w, Nancy, & s, Laban, gct Chesterfield MM
1838, 8, 25. Sarah d 1837,9,25 ae 65 (an elder)
1838, 11, 24. Rachel (form Wood) con mcd
1839, 1, 26. Uriah & w, Susannah, & ch, Tabitha, David, Elwood & Robert, gct Pennsville MM
1841, 4, 24. Ruth Parry (form Bailey) dis mcd
1844, 11, 23. Joseph gct Somerset MM, to m Achsah Edgerton
1845, 7, 26. Uriah rocf Chesterfield MM, dtd 1845,5,17
1845, 7, 26. Achsah rocf Somerset MM, dtd 1845,5,26
1845, 11, 22. Mary rocf New Garden MM, dtd 1841,11,20
1845, 11, 22. Robert rocf New Garden MM, dtd 1841,11,20
1846, 4, 25. Robert dis jas
1847, 11, 27. Achsah & fam gct Somerset MM
1848, 6, 24. Jesse & w, Nancy, & ch, Laban, Edwin, Maria, Mary Ann, Lindley & Lydia

Jane, rocf Chesterfield MM, dtd 1848,3,18
1848, 10, 28. Jesse W. dis jas
1848, 12, 25. Amy rocf Birmingham MM, Pa., dtd 1848,11,29
1849, 6, 23. Achsah Bowlin (form Bailey) dis mcd
1849, 7, 28. Joseph & w, Achsah, & ch, Jeptha & Joseph E., rocf Somerset MM, dtd 1849,6,25
1850, 9, 28. Milton rocf Somerset MM, dtd 1850,6,24
1851, 8, 23. Jesse dis mcd
1853, 11, 26. Mary Jane gct Chesterfield MM
1854, 7, 22. Joseph & w, Achsah, & ch, Jeptha & Joseph, gct Somerset MM
1855, 1, 27. Milton dis mcd
1855, 2, 24. Uriah gct Short Creek MM
1856, 9, 27. James & w, Rhoda, & s, John Henry, rocf Pennsville MM, dtd 1856,8,14
1857, 2, 28. Sarah F. & ch, Thomas F., George M. & William, rocf Somerset MM, dtd 1856,12,29
1858, 6, 26. James & w, Rachel, & ch, John Henry & Rebecca Alice, gct Chesterfield MM
1858, 8, 28. Joel rocf Somerset MM, dtd 1858,7,26
1859, 4, 23. Joel gct Flushing MM, to m Lydia Holloway
1859, 9, 24. Sarah F. dis disunity
1859, 12, 26. Lydia H. rocf Flushing MM, dtd 1859,11,24
1861, 8, 24. Ephraim Parry gct Somerset MM, to m Elizabeth Bailey
1862, 3, 22. Sidney, Priscilla, Isaac, Jacob & Lydia, ch Joel, rocf Somerset MM, dtd 1862,2,24
1863, 3, 28. Jesse & w, Nancy, & ch, Lindley, Lydia Jane, Robert H., Prudence, Sarah & Fanny, gct Hickory Grove MM, Ia.
1863, 3, 28. Maria & Mary Ann gct Hickory Grove MM, Ia.
1863, 4, 25. Silas dis mcd
1866, 2, 24. John dis mcd & military service
1866, 6, 23. Mary Ann Hartley (form Bailey) con mcd
1867, 10, 24. Phebe (form Parry) dis mcd & jas
1868, 1, 25. Edwin dis mcd & military service
1868, 2, 22. Asa Parry gc to m Sarah Ann Bailey
1873, 4, 23. Dempsey dis mcd
1875, 5, --. Isaac dis mcd
1875, 7, 21. Sarah Wilcox (form Bailey) dis mcd
1876, 4, 19. Martha rocf Somerset MM, dtd 1876,3,23
1880, 10, 20. Almedia Garretson (form Bailey) dis mcd
1887, 10, 19. Samuel C. Smith gct Flushing MM, to m Sarah Elma Bailey
1889, 4, 24. Charles gct Damorris MM, Kans.
1896, 4, 22. Oscar J. gct Short Creek MM, to m Mary Anna Brakin
1896, 9, 23. Mary Anna rocf Short Creek MM,

BAILEY, continued
     dtd 1896,8,18
1901, 8, 21. Alva C. gct Short Creek MM, to
     m Laura E. Steer
1903, 4, 23. Anna recrq
1904, 2, 24. Laura E. rocf Short Creek MM,
     dtd 1903,12,22
1906, 10, 24. Daniel rst; dis by Somerset
1911, 2, 22. Lydia M. recrq
1911, 3, 22. Jesse S. con mcd
1915, 7, 20. Ernest dis mcd
1917, 1, 24. Oscar J. dis mcd
1917, 5, 23. Sarah Lavada recrq
1917, 11, 21. Edwin M. dis disunity
1919, 2, 25. Alfred S. con mcd
1922, 11, 22. Oliver B. gct New Garden MM, to
     m Rebecca Steer
1923, 2, 21. G. Wilson dis mcd
1924, 6, 25. Rebecca Steer rocf New Garden MM,
     dtd 1924,5,22
1924, 8, 20. Sarah M. d 1924,6,13 ae 91 (an
     elder)
1924, 10, 22. Dorothy Anderson (form Bailey)
     dis mcd & jas
1928, 4, 25. Raymon C. gct Short Creek MM, to
     m Edith M. Bracken
1931, 2, 25. Herbert dis mcd & jas
1931, 3, 25. Oliver B. & w, Rebecca S., & ch,
     Warren Oliver & Oscar Wilson, gct Short
     Creek MM, O.

BAIN
1814, 3, 1. Rhoda & ch, Mary, Sarah, Lavina,
     Almedia & John, recrq

BALDERSON
1857, 4, 25. Deborah rocf Pennsville MM, dtd
     1857,3,19

BALLENGER
1810, 5, 29. Henry [Balanger] rocf Pipe Creek
     MM, dtd 1810,4,14
1810, 6, 26. Daniel gct Pipe Creek MM

BARBER
1859, 4, 27. Mary m Jason DOUDNA
1860, 5, 1. Samuel, s Jacob & Mary Ann,
     Columbiana Co., O.; m in Stillwater MH,
     Elizabeth HALL, dt Joseph & Martha, Bel-
     mont Co., O.

1859, 3, 26. Mary rocf Flushing MM, dtd
     1859,3,24
1860, 10, 27. Elizabeth gct New Garden MM

BARNES
1833, 9, 30. David d bur Stillwater
1843, 3, 8. James d

1809, 9, 26. Henry [Barns] rocf Concord MM,
     dtd 1809,9,21
1811, 2, 26. Marion (form Shotwell) con mcd
1814, 3, 1. James rocf Plainfield MM, dtd

     1814,1,23
1817, 1, 25. Henry dis mcd
1817, 2, 22. Marion (Merion) gct Short Creek
     MM
1818, 5, 23. Marion rocf Short Creek MM, dtd
     1818,3,24
1822, 3, 23. David rocf Plainfield MM, dtd
     1822,1,24
1824, 7, 24. Merian rocf Somerset MM, dtd
     1824,5,24
1832, 11, 24. Merian dis
1844, 4, 27. Sarah Ann (form Wilson) dis mcd
1860, 9, 15. Mary (form Barnes) rel (H)
1863, 9, 19. Rachel Blackledge (form Barnes)
     dis mcd & jas (H)

BARTON
1897, 10, 20. Altie (form Hall) con mcd

BATES
1866, 1, 27. Martha gct Coal Creek MM, Iowa

BAY
1894, 12, 19. Florence W. (form Webster) dis
     mcd

BEARDMORE
1868, 5, 16. Rebecca (form Frame) rel (H)

BEATY
1852, 1, 24. Susannah (form Smith) dis mcd
1917, 3, 21. Herman J. [Battey] & w, Isa-
     bella H., & ch, Lois Margaret, Richard
     Chester & Ralph D., rocf Paulina MM, dtd
     1917,2,10
1918, 3, 20. Irene [Beatty] (form Edmundson)
     con mcd
1919, 4, 23. Herman J. [Batty] & w, Isabelle
     H., & ch, Richard Chester, Lois Margaret &
     Ralph D., transferred to Fairhope MM, Ala.
1919, 4, 23. M. Irene & Samuel Franklin trans-
     ferred to Fairhope MM, Ala.

BECK
----, --, --. John & Rachel
     Ch: Jesse   b 1793, 3, 14
         Lydia   " 1797, 2, 13
         Ann   " 1800, 7, 1
         Phebe   " 1802, 3, 1
         Sally   " 1804, 3, 26
         Jemima   " 1806, 4, 11
         Martha   " 1808, 11, 13
         John Jr. " 1810, 1, 23
1818, 4, 29. Jesse, s John & Rachel, Belmont
     Co., O.; m in Stillwater MH, Elizabeth
     ENGLE, dt Caleb & Mercy, Belmont Co., O.
     Ch: Rachel E. b 1819, 3, 24
         Mary P.   " 1820, 12, 21 d 1821, 4,26
         bur Stillwater
         Grace C.   b 1822, 8, 8

1808, 12, 27. John & w, Rachel, & ch, Jesse,
     Lydia Ann, Phebia Sally Jemima & Martha,

BECK, continued
  rocf Mt. Pleasant MM, Va., dtd 1808,10,29
1818, 6, 27. Jesse & w, Elizabeth, gct Plainfield MM
1820, 5, 27. Jesse & w, Elizabeth, & dt, Rachel, rocf Flushing MM, dtd 1820,4,21
1823, 4, 26. Jesse & w, Elizabeth, & fam gct
  Somerset MM
1859, 11, 26. Jesse rocf Chesterfield MM, dtd
  1859,10,15

BEDELL
1861, 12, 28. William P. & ch, Samuel, Mahlon,
  Sarah Etta, Cynthia, Amelia & Elwood, recrq (residing in Lynn Co., Iowa)
1868, 11, 28. Tilman Patterson Jr. gct Springville MM, Ia., to m Sarah E. Bedell

BEERS
1919, 12, 24. Laura A. (form Doudna) dis mcd &
  jas

BEESON
1861, 12, 28. Richard H. & w, Rebecca H., &
  ch, Ephraim L., Ruthanna W., Phebe S.,
  John S., Rachel Armatta & Erwin, recrq
  (residing in Linn Co., Ia.)

BEGGS
1932, 5, 25. Anna Plummer rpd mcd & jas

BELANGEE
----, --, --. James & Rebecca
  Ch: John   b 1813, 4, 29
      Aaron   " 1823, 9, 26
1832, 3, 7. James d ae 87y 8m bur Plainfield

1829, 1, 24. Rebecca [Balgee] dis jH
1829, 2, 28. James [Bellange] dis jH
1830, 6, 26. Grace dis jH

BENNETT
1828, 8, 28. Daniel R., s Titus & Rachel B.,
  Phila., Pa.; m in Stillwater, Maria A.
  TAYLOR, dt Israel & Susan, Belmont Co., O.
  (H)

1875, 8, 25. Rachel [Bennet] (form Naylor)
  dis mcd

BENSON
1844, 4, 23. Julia m James CARTER (H)

1857, 10, 17. Mary D. (form Hall) dis mcd (H)
1862, 7, 19. Rachel L. Doudna (form Benson)
  con mcd (H)
1883, 7, 25. Tabitha C. (form Doudna) con mcd
1900, 8, 18. Levi L. relrq (H)

BERRY
----, --, --. Samuel & Mary
  Ch: William
      David

Ch: Agnes
    Samuel
    Thomas
    Mary

1809, 10, 31. Samuel & fam gct Concord MM
1812, 7, 28. Samuel & w, Mary, & ch, Hannah
  & Sarah, rocf Concord MM, dtd 1812,6,25
1817, 6, 28. Samuel & fam gct Concord MM, O.
1822, 8, 24. Samuel & w, Mary, & ch, Hannah,
  Sarah, Ann, William, David, Agnes & Samuel, rocf Concord MM, dtd 1822,3,20
1826, 9, 23. Anna White (form Berry) dis mcd
1829, 2, 28. Ann dis jH
1829, 2, 28. Mary dis jH
1829, 2, 28. Samuel dis jH
1829, 2, 28. Sarah dis jH
1838, 3, 24. William dis disunity
1839, 7, 27. Agnes dis jH
1840, 7, 25. David dis disunity
1846, 8, 22. Samuel Jr. dis disunity
1849, 6, 23. Thomas dis mcd
1866, 7, 28. Elizabeth Anna (form Parker)
  dis mcd
1869, 3, 27. Elizabeth Ann (form Parker) dis
  mcd

BEVAN
1844, 8, 28. Joseph, s Stacy & Eunice, Belmont Co., O.; m in Richland, Maria HALL,
  dt Stephen & Mary, Guernsey Co., O.

1831, 10, 22. Stacy & w, Eunice, & ch, Joseph,
  Martha, Susannah, Naomi, Lydia Ann &
  Elizabeth, gct Flushing MM
1846, 6, 27. Maria [Biven] gct Flushing MM

BINFORD
1826, 8, 26. Hannah rocf Rich Square MM,
  N. C., dtd 1826,3,18, end by Somerset MM
1827, 6, 23. Hannah gct Duck Creek MM, Ind.

BINNS
1897, 6, 26. Arthur H., s Joseph P. & Belinda (Hobson), Harrison Co., O.; m in
  Stillwater MH, Tacie M. BUNDY, dt Lindley & Ruanna (Frame), Belmont Co., O.
  Ch: Francis S. b 1899, 6, 6
      Mildred M. " 1901, 4, 14
      Dorothy A. " 1903, 1, 22
      John Edward" 1908, 3, 31
      J. Alfred " 1910, 2, 12

1902, 7, 23. Arthur H. rocf Short Creek MM,
  dtd 1902,6,24
1904, 4, 20. Jesse H. Dewees gct Short Creek
  MM, O., to m Mary C. Binns
1905, 11, 22. Arthur H. & w, Tacy M., & ch,
  Francis S., Mildred M. & Dorothy A., gct
  Flushing MM

BIRCH
1834, 11, 22. Sarah (form Hall) dis mcd

BIRD
1835, 3, 28. Henry Doudna gct Short Creek MM,
    to m Matilda Bird

BISHOP
1815, 10, 5. Joseph, s Joseph & Elizabeth,
    Belmont Co., O.; m in Capteanna Creek,
    Mary WHITE, dt Jesse & Mary

1815, 8, 29. Joseph rocf Concord MM, dtd
    1815,7,20
1866, 5, 19. Louisa relrq (H)

BLACKBURN
1909, 2, 24. Samuel Carter gct Middleton MM,
    O., to m Mary Elma Blackburn

BLACKLEDGE
1836, 12, 1. Asa, s William & Elizabeth,
    Monroe Co., O.; m in Sunberry, Sarah RIGG,
    dt Jesse & Sarah, Monroe Co., O.
1859, 11, 29. Elizabeth m Elijah GRAY

1829, 10, 24. Thomas dis jH
1830, 2, 27. Phebe dis jH
1839, 3, 23. Rachel rocf Phila. MM, Pa., dtd
    1839,1,24, end to Somerset
1854, 10, 21. John relrq (H)
1863, 9, 19. Rachel (form Barnes) dis mcd &
    jas (H)
1877, 9, 21. Susanna Thomas (form Blackledge)
    con mcd (H)

BLOCKSOM
1809, 9, 26. William & w, Mary, & ch, James,
    Ann, Elizabeth, Maria, Priscilla & Sarah,
    rocf Plainfield MM, dtd 1809,8,26
1811, 4, 30. William [Bloxom] & w, Mary, &
    ch, Ann, Elizabeth, Maria, Priscilla, Sa-
    rah & Mary, gct Fairfield MM

BLOVELT
1814, 5, 31. Sarah (form Strahl) dis mcd

BLOWERS
----, --, --. Andrew J. & Rebecca D.
    Ch: Mary   b 1841, 6, 6
        Ann D.   " 1846, 1, 27
        Rachel   " 1850, 10, 26
        Lucinda   " 1853, 8, 16
        Jeptha D.   " 1855, 8, 10
        Rebecca   " 1859, 6, 25
        Salah Alice" 1861, 7, 17
        Hosetta   " 1863, 3, 16
----, --, --. Jeptha m Eliza Blanche CREW
    Ch: Mary Ethel b 1884, 12, 26
        Ida R.   " 1893, 6, 7
1888, 3, 28. Sarah A. m Elwood HARTLEY

1840, 5, 23. Rebecca (form Doudna) dis mcd
1849, 4, 28. Rebecca rst
1850, 3, 23. Mary & Ann, ch Andrew & Rebecca,
    recrq

1866, 5, 26. Ann Hall (form Blowers) dis mcd
1882, 3, 22. Jeptha D. gct Pennsville MM, to
    m Eliza B. Crew
1882, 8, 23. Rebecca S. Bufkin (form Blowers)
    con mcd
1889, 11, 20. Andrew J. dis mcd
1893, 4, 19. Rachel Darby (form Blowers) dis
    mcd
1909, 7, 21. Hosetta B. Sinton (form Blowers)
    con mcd
1911, 7, 19. Blanche & dt, Ida R., rocf Ches-
    terfield MM, dtd 1911,6,17
1914, 10, 21. Ida Gibbons (form Blowers) dis
    mcd
1915, 7, 20. Jeptha & Eliza B. gct Pasadena
    MM, Calif.

BOGUE
1816, 4, 27. Jonathan & w, Sarah, & ch, Mary
    Ann & Ruth, rocf Plainfield MM, dtd 1816,
    3,22
1821, 5, 26. Sarah & ch, Ruth, Mary Ann, Mark
    & John, gct Flushing MM

BOLES
1823, 1, 27. John, s Thomas & Amy, b
1824, 4, 25. Amy, w Thomas, d

BOND
----, --, --. Joseph & Esther
    Ch: Jonathan   b 1821, 2, 18
        Abner   " 1823, 4, 21 d 1822, 5, 4
        Alinda   " 1824, 7, 31
        Eliza   " 1826, 10, 4

1826, 4, 22. Benjamin & Eli, minors, rocf
    Deer Creek MM, dtd 1825,9,15
1827, 4, 28. Benjamin gct Short Creek MM
1829, 1, 24. Allen dis jH
1829, 1, 24. Joseph dis jH
1829, 1, 24. Sarah dis jH
1829, 2, 28. Abner, Jr. dis jH
1829, 11, 28. Esther dis jH
1833, 11, 23. Silas Jr. gct Milford MM, Ind.

BONE
1829, 1, 24. Sarah dis jH

BORTON
----, --, --. Orville G. m Altie T. HALL, dt
    Joseph W. & Sarah (Webster), b 1866,9,10
    Ch: Elsie B.   b 1902, 12, 4
        Joseph Or-
        ville   " 1896, 6, 5
        Jennie Ger-
        trude   " 1898, 10, 15 d 1900, 8, 8
        bur Richland
        Walter Eu-
        gene   b 1900, 9, 28
        Elsie Bell " 1902, 12, 14
        Sarah Ellen" 1905, 8, 19 d 1905, 8,22
        bur Richland
        Wilford A. b 1907, 2, 17

BORTON, continued

1809, 7, 25. Reuben con mcd
1812, 9, 29. Rachel Marsh (form Borton) dis mcd
1812, 12, 29. Benjamin Jr. dis
1813, 9, 28. Vashti Dillon (form Borton) dis mcd
1817, 2, 22. Mary Tidrick (form Borton) dis mcd
1822, 5, 25. James dis mcd
1824, 4, 22. Reuben dis disunity
1831, 4, 23. Benjamin dis jH
1902, 11, 19. Orville A. & ch, Joseph O. & Walter E., recrq
1929, 7, 24. Elsie B. Vorhies (form Borton) con mcd
1930, 7, 23. Joseph con mcd
1930, 12, 24. Walter con mcd

BOSWELL

----, --, --. Demsey & Mary
        Ch: Anna   b 1805, 9, 11
            Lydia   " 1807, 4, 12
            Jesse   " 1808, 12, 3
            John   " 1811, 4, 26
1815, 10, 4. William, s Zadok & Ruth, Belmont Co., O.; m in Stillwater MH, Rachel DAVIS, dt Harmon & Hannah, Belmont Co., O.
        Ch: Ruth   b 1816, 8, 22
            Zadok   " 1818, 11, 9 d 1818,12,20
            Elizabeth   " 1820, 4, 13
            Asenath   " 1823, 1, 28
            Rebeckah   " 1824, 12, 28
1817, 3, 22. Zadock d ae 65 y 7 d
1817, 5, 28. Benjamin, s Wm. & Sarah, Belmont Co., O.; m in Stillwater MH, Asenath DOUDNA, dt John & Sarah, Belmont Co., O.
        Ch: William   b 1819, 4, 16
            Sarah   " 1822, 2, 27
            Mary   " 1824, 7, 25

1812, 4, 28. Peninah Bailey (form Boswell) dis mcd
1814, 4, 26. Zodak rocf Symons Creek MM, N. C., dtd 1814,1,15
1815, 7, 25. Benjamin recrq
1824, 12, 25. Demsey & w, Mary, & ch gct Somerset MM
1824, 12, 25. Anna gct Somerset MM
1825, 12, 24. Benjamin & w, Asenath, & fam gct Somerset MM
1827, 4, 28. William & w, Rachel, & ch, Ruth, Elizabeth, Asenath, Rebecca & Isaac, gct Somerset MM
1827, 5, 26. Demsey & w, Mary, & ch, Jesse, John & Phebe, rocf Somerset MM, dtd 1827, 4,3
1827, 10, 27. Ruth gct Somerset MM
1828, 5, 24. Ruth rocf Somerset MM, dtd 1828, 4,28
1829, 3, 28. Demsey & w, Mary, & ch, Jesse, John & Phebe, gct White Water MM, Ind.
1829, 5, 23. Ruth, a minister, gct White

Water MM, Ind.

BOWLIN

1840, 6, 21. Mary (form Smith) dis mcd
1849, 6, 23. Achsah (form Bailey) dis mcd

BOWLS

1830, 9, 25. Hannah (form Strahl) dis mcd

BOYD

1817, 8, 23. Mary recrq
1822, 1, 26. Mary Lingo (form Boyd) dis mcd
1931, 6, 24. Martha (form Carter) con mcd

BRACKEN

1895, 9, 25. Frederick C. Hoyle gct Short Creek MM, to m Martha H. Brakin
1896, 4, 22. Oscar J. Bailey gct Short Creek MM, to m Mary Anna Brakin
1928, 4, 25. Raymon C. Bailey gct Short Creek MM, to m Edith M. Bracken

BRAIDLEY

1839, 4, 27. Angelina (form Strahl) dis mcd

BRANSON

1828, 8, 25. Isaiah, s Jacob & Rebecca, Belmont Co., O.; m in Stillwater MH, Sarah G. LAWTON, dt James & Susanna, Washington Co., O.

1816, 12, 22. Isaac rocf Indian Spring MM, Va., dtd 1816,8,16
1829, 1, 24. Sarah G. gct Flushing MM
1834, 6, 28. Smith, s Lydia, recrq
1834, 6, 28. Lydia & ch, Amy, Lydia & Elizabeth, recrq
1837, 8, 26. Asa & w, Mary, & ch, Abigail & Joseph, rocf Flushing MM, dtd 1837,8,24
1838, 4, 28. Asa & w, Mary, & ch, Abigail & Joseph, gct Flushing MM
1873, 9, 24. Chalkley Dawson gct Flushing MM, to m Rebecca Anna Branson
1886, 7, 21. James Walton gct Flushing MM, to m Anna L. Branson

BRIGGS

1831, 9, 28. Jonathan, s Wm. & Esther, Belmont Co., O.; m in Stillwater MH, Elizabeth MILLHOUSE, dt Robert & Sarah, Belmont Co., O.
1866, 10, 31. Sarah S. m Benjamin WINDER

1816, 8, 24. Israel & w, Mary, & ch, Esther & Ann, rocf Salem MM, dtd 1816,7,16
1818, 4, 25. Israel & fam gct Plainfield MM
1831, 12, 24. Elizabeth gct Flushing MM
1849, 10, 27. Benjamin Sears gct Flushing MM, to m Esther Briggs
1855, 11, 24. Sarah S. rocf Short Creek MM, dtd 1855,10,23
1864, 9, 24. Jonathan & w, Elizabeth, & ch, Benjamin & Josiah, rocf Plainfield MM,

BRIGGS, continued
    dtd 1864,8,24
1864, 9, 24. George rocf Plainfield MM, dtd
    1864,8,24
1864, 9, 24. Mary & Sarah M. rocf Plainfield
    MM, dtd 1864,8,24
1865, 4, 22. Sarah W. rocf Flushing MM, dtd
    1865,2,23
1865, 6, 24. Jonathan & w, Elizabeth, & ch,
    Benjamin & Josiah, gct Coal Creek MM, Ia.
1865, 6, 24. George gct Coal Creek MM, Ia.
1865, 6, 24. William gct Coal Creek MM, Ia.
1865, 6, 24. Mary & Sarah M. gct Coal Creek
    MM, Ia. •
1872, 1, 24. Sarah Sears (form Briggs) con
    mcd

BROCK
----, --, --. James & Martha
    Ch: Robert   b 1810, 4, 13
        James Jr.   " 1811, 12, 25
        Sarah   " 1813, 12, 7
1831, 3, 9. Robert, s James & Martha, Bel-
    mont Co., O.; m in Stillwater MH, Peninah
    DAWSON, dt Jesse & Elizabeth, Belmont Co.,
    O.

1809, 8, 29. James & w, Martha, rocf Gravelly
    Run MM, Va., dtd 1809,5,27
1831, 5, 28. Nathan Dawson gct Somerset MM,
    to m Sarah Brock
1831, 9, 24. Peninah gct Somerset MM

BROOKS
----, --, --. William & Mary
    Ch: Esther   b 1819, 5, 1
        Martha   " 1820, 6, 18
        Teacy   " 1821, 3, 25
        Mary J.   " 1823, 6, 7
        Joel E.   " 1825, 4, 6
        Eadith   " 1827, 1, 1
        Ruth
1822, 7, 27. William & w, Mary, & ch, Esther,
    Martha & Tacy, rocf Westland MM, Pa., dtd
    1822,4,25
1830, 8, 28. William dis disunity·
1830, 8, 28. Mary dis disunity

BROOMHALL
----, --, --. Barkley & Rebecca
    Ch: William E. b 1819, 8, 1
        Enos J.   " 1821, 11, 30
        Arminda   " 1824, 6, 19
        Amy   " 1827, 2, 10
1856, 10, 23. Lydia J. m Jesse L. SMITH (H)

1818, 8, 22. John rocf Fallowfield MM, dtd
    1817,9,8, end by Short Creek MM, 1818,4,
    21
1819, 6, 26. Phebe, w John Jr., & ch,
    William, Orphah, Minerva, Hannah, John &
    Webb, rocf Kennet MM, dtd 1819,3,3

1827, 4, 28. Minerva Price (form Broomall)
    dis mcd
1829, 1, 24. Orpha [Broomall] dis JH
1829, 5, 23. Orpha Wood (form Broomhall) dis
    mcd
1829, 10, 24. Rebecca dis JH
1829, 12, 26. Hannah dis JH
1830, 1, 23. William dis disunity
1830, 8, 28. James dis JH
1830, 9, 25. John dis JH
1832, 12, 23. Barclay dis JH
1832, 12, 23. Rebecca dis JH
1833, 1, 26. William, Enos, Arminda, Amy,
    Phebe & Townsend, ch Berkley & Rebecca,
    gct Somerset MM
1860, 9, 15. Thomas relrq (H)

BROWN
1847, 1, 20. John, s Stephen & Axey, Monroe
    Co., O.; m in house of Emery Lewis, Mary
    Ann LEWIS, dt Emery & Rachel, Monroe Co.,
    O.
1848, 3, 22. Agnes Ann m Samuel HOGUE (H)

1819, 6, 26. Isaac & w, Mary, rocf Short
    Creek MM, dtd 1819,4,30
1826, 8, 26. Benj. & w, Amy, & ch, Abigail,
    Jacob, Joseph, Nathan & Rachel, rocf
    Short Creek MM, dtd 1826,3,18
1849, 10, 27. Mary Ann (form Lewis) dis mcd
1853, 1, 15. Silas & w, Mary Ann, gct White
    Water MM, Ind.
1853, 12, 17. Tacy (form Lewis) dis mcd (H)
1854, 10, 21. John & Mary Ann relrq (H)

BRYANT
1830, 12, 8. Jane Vernon m Jesse DAWSON
----, --, --. John & Mary
    Ch: Lucinda   b 1859, 11, 16 d 1866, 9,19
            bur Stillwater
        Alice   b 1861, 12, 13 " 1866, 9,23
            bur Stillwater
        Jane D.   b 1863, 11, 21
        Mary Lou-
        isa   " 1865, 8, 13
        Harriet Em-
        ma   " 1867, 5, 1 d 1870, 4,25
        Charles
        Wesley   " 1869, 10, 25
        John L.   " 1873, 8, 12
1862, 1, 8. Rachel m Lindley H. GIBBONS
1866, 12, 22. Jesse D., s John & Mary, d bur
    Stillwater
1870, 1, 27. William, s John & Mary, Belmont
    Co., O.; m in Richland, Rachel PARRY, dt
    Job & Asenath, Guernsey Co., O.
    Ch: Lillie   b 1871, 11, 12
        Roseine   " 1872, 11, 4
        John Thomas" 1874, 6, 26

1815, 3, 28. Jenny (form Vernon) dis mcd
1827, 11, 24. Jane rst
1850, 3, 23. John rocf Somerset MM, dtd

BRYANT, continued
    1850,2,25
1854, 5, 27. John gct Red Cedar MM, Ia.
1859, 4, 23. Mary recrq
1859, 6, 25. Rachel, Elizabeth, James,
    William, Tamar Jane, Esther & Joel, ch
    John & Mary, recrq
1871, 2, 22. John dis paying bounty money
1873, 8, 20. James dis mcd
1873, 12, 24. Elizabeth Norris (form Bryant)
    dis mcd & jas
1875, 8, 21. Tamar Jane Hogue (form Bryant)
    con mcd (H)
1876, 7, 19. Esther dis disunity
1878, 2, 20. William dis disunity

BUFFKIN
1882, 8, 23. Rebecca S. (form Blowers) con
  mcd

BUNDY
----, --, --. Thomas & Milisent
    Ch: Jonathan b 1803, 9, 17
        Exum   " 1806, 10, 1
        William   " 1808, 3, 27
        Elias   " 1809, 12, 12
        Benjamin " 1811, 8, 18
        David   " 1813, 7, 24
        Thomas Jr. " 1815, 3, 13
        Pennina   " 1817, 2, 7
        Ruth   " 1818, 9, 23
----, --, --. William & Sarah
    Ch: Mary   b 1805, 2, 25
        Ezekiel   " 1807, 7, 26 d 1866,11, 2
        Eli   " 1809, 3, 31
        Charity   " 1811, 2, 3
        John   " 1813, 2, 17
        Nathan   " 1814, 10, 16
        Sarah   " 1817, 1, 29
        William   " 1819, 10, 10 d 1905, 5,10
        bur Stillwater
1809, 5, 3. Mary m Jesse BAILEY
1818, 5, 27. Benjamin, s Josiah & Bethiah,
    Belmont Co., O.; m in Stillwater MH, Mary
    BAILEY, dt Matthew & Susanna, Belmont Co.,
    O.
1819, 9, 27. Stanton, s Josiah & Bathiah,
    Belmont Co., O., d 1873,10,18; m in Still-
    water MH, Ann BAILEY, dt Matthew & Susan-
    nah, Belmont Co., O.
    Ch: Susannah b 1820, 7, 14
        Bailey   " 1823, 1, 8
        Matthew   " 1826, 3, 24
        Josiah   " 1829, 4, 11
        Mary   " 1833, 9, 1
        Elizabeth " 1836, 8, 30
----, --, --. Wilson & Sarah
    Ch: Demsey   b 1821, 8, 8
        Chalkley   " 1823, 2, 24
        Elizabeth " 1826, 5, 28
1823, 7, 30. Benjamin, s Josiah & Bethiah,
    Belmont Co., O.; m in Stillwater MH, De-
    litha BAILEY, dt Jesse & Phariba, Belmont

Co., O.
1824, 12, 8. Mary m Wm. FRENCH
1828, 6, 21. William d ae 48y 5m 20d bur
    Deerfield
1829, 10, 28. William, s Thomas & Milisent,
    Belmont Co., O.; m in Stillwater MH, Mary
    PEEBLES, dt Mordecai & Abigail
1830, 10, 27. Ezekiel, s Wm. & Sarah, Belmont
    Co., O.; m in Stillwater MH, Mariah ENGLE,
    dt Caleb & Mercy, Belmont Co., O.
    Ch: Sarah   b 1831, 8, 6 d 1833, 6,24
        bur Stillwater
        Elizabeth b 1834, 8, 11
        Nathan   " 1837, 8, 22
        Caleb   " 1839, 7, 23 d 1859,12,15
        bur Stillwater
        Rachel   b 1841, 10, 2 " 1841,10, 2
        bur Stillwater
        William E. b 1843, 3, 11
        Mary Jane " 1845, 5, 20
        Martha Ann " 1848, 1, 10
        Anne Maria " 1850, 1, 25
1831, 3, 9. Eli, s Wm. & Sarah, Belmont
    Co., O.; m in Stillwater MH, Sarah VERNON,
    dt Amos & Mary, Belmont Co., O.
    Ch: William C. b 1832, 3, 15
        Mary   " 1834, 3, 21
        Ruth Anna " 1836, 5, 5
1833, 10, 30. John, s Wm. & Sarah, Belmont
    Co., O.; m in Stillwater MH, Ruth PATTEN,
    dt Wm. & Sally, Belmont Co., O., d 1841,2,
    17 bur Stillwater
    Ch: William   b 1835, 2, 15
        Sarah   " 1835, 2, 15
        Martha   " 1836, 9, 16 d 1842,11,20
        bur Stillwater
        Mary P.   b 1837, 12, 18
        Charity   " 1839, 4, 17 " 1841, 4,10
        Thomas   " 1844, 12, 6
        Ephraim   " 1845, 5, 13 " 1845, 6,19
        bur Stillwater
        Ruth   b 1849, 1, 7
        Rebecca   " 1851, 2, 10
        Jesse E. " 1852, 9, 23
        Wilson H. " 1855, 7, 22
        Elizabeth " 1858, 10, 4
    (John had to m again to have ch from
    Thos. on. McM)
1835, 4, 29. Sarah m Joel DAWSON
1836, 12, 7. Nathan, s Wm. & Sarah, Belmont
    Co., O.; m in Stillwater MH, Sarah DOUDNA
    dt Henry & Martha, Belmont Co., O.
1842, 12, 7. William, s Wm. & Sarah, Belmont
    Co., O.; m in Stillwater MH, Prudence
    WOOD, dt John & Esther, Belmont Co., O.,
    d 1844,5,2 bur Stillwater
    Ch: Allen   1844, --, 23 d 1867, 7, 3
        bur Stillwater
1843, 4, 26. Demsey, s Wm. & Sarah, Belmont
    Co., O.; m in Stillwater MH, Ann WOOD,
    dt John & Esther, Belmont Co., O., d 1847,
    3,9 bur Stillwater
    Ch: Emila   b 1844, 2, 4

BUNDY, Demsey & Ann, continued
  Ch: Amanda b 1846, 5, 25
  Demsey m 2nd in Stillwater MH, 1848,11,1
  Ann CREW, dt Jacob & Rachel, Belmont Co.,
  O.
  Ch: Jeptha b 1850, 4, 13
   Melvina " 1852, 7, 7 d 1857, 2, 2
    bur Stillwater
   Jefferson b 1854, 5, 24
1843, 6, 28. Charity m James STANTON
1844, 3, 27. Chalkley, s William & Sarah, Bel-
  mont Co., O., d 1866,12,1 bur Stillwater;
  m in Stillwater MH, Sarah DOUDNA, dt Joel
  & Rebecca, d 1862,8,1 bur Stillwater
  Ch: Lindley b 1845, 1, 28
   Joel D. " 1846, 10, 22
   Nathan " 1848, 6, 11
   Lucinda " 1850, 9, 11
   Rebecca D. " 1853, 12, 11
   Emma " 1856, 12, 8 d 1863, 8,25
    bur Stillwater
   Mary Eliza-
   beth b 1860, 5, 23
   Chalkley " 1862, 6, 5 " 1862, 9,28
    bur Stillwater
1845, 6, 16. Sidney, w John, d bur Stillwater
1845, 12, 21. Elizabeth m Hezekiah BAILEY
1847, 6, 30. William, s William & Sarah, Bel-
  mont Co., O.; m in Stillwater MH, Asenath
  DOUDNA, dt Joel & Rebecca, Belmont Co., O.
  Ch: Prudence b 1849, 4, 3 d 1850, 9, 8
    bur Stillwater
   Clarkson b 1850, 12, 18
   Joel H. " 1852, 10, 28
   Almeda " 1854, 10, 28 d 1857, 9,14
    bur Stillwater
   Evaline b 1858, 1, 17 d 1860,12,24
    bur Stillwater
   Charles b 1859, 1, 17 d 1860,12,31
    bur Stillwater
   Dillwyn C. b 1861, 3, 30
   Rebecca H. " 1863, 1, 3
1850, 10, 30. Elizabeth m John G. HOYLE
1851, 1, 1. Pheriba m Peter SEARS
1851, 1, 11. Maria, w Ezekiel, d bur Still-
  water
1852, 9, 29. Ezekiel, s William & Sarah, Bel-
  mont Co., O.; m in Stillwater MH, Sarah
  STANTON, dt Benjamin & Tabitha HOYLE, Bel-
  mont Co., O.
  Ch: John H. b 1853, 7, 25
   Hannah H. " 1855, 10, 22 d 1870, 3,13
    bur Stillwater
   Ezekiel b 1857, 8, 31 " 1861, 1,16
    bur Stillwater
   Chalkley
   Clinton b 1859, 6, 27 " 1861, 1,18
    bur Stillwater
   Sarah
   Alice b 1861, 6, 5
1853, 1, 5. William, s Eli & Sarah, Belmont
  Co., O.; m in Stillwater MH, Edith STAN-
  TON, dt James & Rachel, Belmont Co., O.

  Ch: Henry b 1853, 12, 22
   Ellen   d 1865,10,27
1853, 3, 9. Mary m John DOUDNA
1853, 5, 8. Sarah, wd Wm., d bur Stillwater
1854, 5, 4. Wilson H., s John & Anne, d bur
  Stillwater
1854, 10, 7. Ann, w Dempsey, d bur Stillwater
1855, 11, 7. Esther m Robert H. DOUDNA
1856, 12, 6. Rebecca, dt John & Anne, d bur
  Stillwater
----, --, --. Dempsey m Rebecca W. SMITH, dt
  Samuel & Elizabeth (Wright), b 1832,1,9
  d 1923,5,14 bur Stillwater
1856, 3, 26. Sarah m Asher MOTT
1856, 10, 1. Ruthanna m Gersham MOTT
1857, 12, 9. Mary P. m Eli STANTON
1858, 12, 29. William P., s John & Ruth, Belmont Co., O., d 1870,6,17; m in Stillwater
  MH, Tabitha DOUDNA, dt Joel & Rebecca
  (Hodgin), Belmont Co., O.
  Ch: John D. b 1859, 2,12 d 1864, 7,24
    bur Stillwater
   Stephen
   Edgar b 1861, 11, 18 d 1869, 6,21
    bur Stillwater
   Sarah Lou-
   isa b 1865, 3, 24
   Wilson C. " 1867, 2, 17 d 1868, 9,10
    bur Stillwater
   Harvey W. b 1869, 2, 26 " 1870, 2,11
    bur Stillwater
1859, 3, 30. Caleb, s Ezekiel & Maria, Bel-
  mont Co., O.; m in Stillwater MH, Deborah
  HANSON, dt Elijah & Eliza, Belmont Co., O.
  Ch: Mary Caleb b 1860, 2, 3
1859, 3, 30. Nathan, s Ezekiel & Mariah, Bel-
  mont Co., O.; m in Stillwater MH, Anna
  STANTON, dt Joseph & Mary, Belmont Co., O.
  Ch: Joseph S. b 1860, 1, 19
   Caleb L. " 1862, 12, 12
   Mary Maria " 1864, 7, 7
   Clara Elma " 1871, 11, 7
1862, 10, 1. Mary Jane m Jesse STARBUCK
1864, 4, 27. William, s Ezekiel & Maria, Bel-
  mont Co., O.; m in Stillwater MH, Rebecca
  DOUDNA, dt Joel & Rebecca, Belmont Co., O.
----, --, --. William m Rebecca DOUDNA
  Ch: Elmer Els-
   worth b 1865, 2, 11
   Agnes May " 1872, 10, 11
   Bertram H. " 1876, 5, 27
1864, 9, 7. Emily m Thompson FRAME
1864, 12, 7. Chalkley, s William & Sarah, Bel-
  mont Co., O.; m in Stillwater MH, Deborah
  H. HANSON, dt Elijah & Eliza, Belmont Co.,
  O.
1867, 12, 4. Martha Ann m Joseph PLUMMER
1869, 10, 6. Nathan H., s Chalkley & Sarah,
  Belmont Co., O.; m in Stillwater MH, Anna
  S. DAWSON, dt Joel & Mary, Belmont Co., O.
  Ch: Aurora E. b 1870, 7, 10
   Russel C. " 1871, 8, 22
----. --, --. Charles, s Benj. & Delitha

BUNDY, Charles, continued
    (Bailey), b 1847,3,2 d 1919,3,17; m Marga-
    ret NAYLOR, dt Louis & Rachel (Bailey),
    b 1849,12,26 d 1919,10,7 bur Stillwater
1870, 3, 9. Lucinda m Benjamin H. HANSON
1870, 12, 7. Lindley, s Chalkley & Sarah
    (Doudna), Belmont Co., O.; m in Stillwater
    MH, Ruanna FRAME, dt Aaron & Tabitha, Bel-
    mont Co., O.
    Ch: Sara C.   b 1872, 12, 16
       Carver T. " 1874, 8, 9
       Tacy M.   " 1876, 10, 28
       Chalkley L." 1879, 6, 9
       Bertha R. " 1882, 9, 24
1871, 10, 7. Emma L., dt Joel D. & Mary Ellen,
    b
----, --, --. Josiah W. m Ruth DOUDNA
    Ch: Albert H. b 1872, 8, 12
       Lillian   " 1874, 6, 22
       Ernest J. " 1886, 4, 9
       Mary Alice " 1888, 8, 22
1872, 3, 27. Jeptha, s Demsey & Ann (Crew),
    Belmont Co., O., b 1850,4,13 d 1920,3,9;
    m in Stillwater MH, Myra DAWSON, dt Joel
    & Mary, Belmont Co., O., d 1922,2,28
    Ch: Alvin J. b 1873, 4, 5
       Clara Le-
         anna   " 1874, 7, 18
       Randall   " 1883, 9, 5
1872, 5, 23. Tabitha D. m Parker HALL
1872, 10, 9. Rebecca D. m Daniel STANTON
1873, 3, 26. John H., s Ezekiel & Sarah
    (Hoyle), Belmont Co., O.; m in Stillwater
    MH, Mary D. DOUDNA, dt Thomas & Rachel,
    Belmont Co., O., d 1908,7,29 bur Salem, O.
    Ch: Clinton T. b 1874, 1, 5
       Sarah A. " 1881, 1, 14
1873, 7, 30. Deborah (nee HANSON) m Eli STAN-
    TON
1874, 7, 18. Clara L., dt Jeptha & Myra (Daw-
    son), b; m Harry REED
1878, 10, 30. Thomas Clarkson, s Wm. & Asen-
    ath (Doudna), Belmont Co., O.; m in Still-
    water MH, Rachel CREW, dt John & Asenath,
    Belmont Co., O.
    Ch: Howard C. b 1879, 9, 7
       William J. " 1881, 4, 23
       Mary A.   " 1883, 10, 11
       Edith M. " 1885, 11, 3
       Elva   " 1889, 3, 4
       Melva   " 1889, 3, 4
1879, 9, 25. Mary E. m Jason FAWCETT
----, --, --. Allen m Eva L. PATTERSON
    Ch: Ethel E. b 1881, 2, 18
       Clifford J." 1883, 6, 6
       Ernest D. " 1885, 10, 10
       Edna A.   " 1888, 2, 29
       Mary Alma " 1892, 9, 14
       George Wil-
         son   " 1894, 12, 15
       Dortha M. " 1897, 11, 17
1885, 5, 27. Clarence, s Charles & Margaret
    (Naylor), b

1886, 9, 9. Dillwyn C., s William & Asenath
    (Doudna), Belmont Co., O.; m in Stillwater
    MH, Elizabeth STEER, dt James & Mary G.,
    Belmont Co., O.
    Ch: Ellis   b 1888, 5, 22
       Annie   " 1893, 11, 7
       Walter A. " 1894, 12, 15 d 1902, 8,15
       bur Stillwater
       Mary E.   b 1898, 11, 5
       Margaret " 1902, 1, 18
       Anna Rebec-
         ca   " 1903, 12, 5
1892, 10, 6. Elizabeth m Ira S. FRAME
1893, 1, 26. Aurora E. m Louis W. EMMONS
1893, 9, 21. Sarah C. m Charles HOLLOWAY
1897, 8, 26. Tacie M. m Arthur H. BINNS
1898, 9, 18. John, s William, d bur Still-
    water
1901, 3, 6. Carver T., s Lindley & Ruanna,
    Belmont Co., O.; m in Barnsville MH, Eva-
    lyn C. PLUMMER, dt Abram & Miriam (Crew),
    Belmont Co., O., b 1877,3,7 d 1927,9,20
    bur Stillwater
    Ch: Edith M. b 1906, 10, 9
       Ralph A. " 1908, 2, 14
1903, 10, 28. Frederick R., s Charles & Mar-
    garet H. (Naylor), Belmont Co., O., b
    1873,9,30; m in Stillwater MH, Clara
    BAILEY, dt Lindley P. & Elizabeth(Stanton)
    Belmont Co., O., b 1878,6,25
    Ch: Willard L. b 1906, 4, 2
       Joseph
         Stanton " 1911, 1, 28
----, --, --. Chalkley m Luella HALL
    Ch: Wilmer L. b 1904, 10, 23
       Clifford
         Carver " 1906, 8, 11
       Arthur H. " 1907, 12, 13
       Bertha A. " 1910, 11, 8
1904, 5, 26. Anna, w John, d bur Stillwater
1905, 9, 21. Bertha m Lindley C. LARSON
1911, 7, 20. Ruanna (Frame) m Lindley B.
    STEER
1914, 4, 23. Rebecca H. m John J. CADWALADER

1808, 8, 30. Mary Sinclair (form Bundy) dis
    mcd
1818, 7, 25. Mary gct Concord MM
1820, 4, 23. Stanton rocf Plainfield MM, dtd
    1820,1,19
1823, 11, 22. Delitha gct Concord MM
1830, 1, 23. Mary gct Somerset MM
1832, 2, 25. Elias rocf Somerset MM, dtd
    1833,1,30
1834, 6, 28. Elias con mcd
1835, 10, 24. Elizabeth & dt, Maria, recrq
1836, 1, 23. Elias & w, Elizabeth R., & dt,
    Mariah, gct Pennsville MM
1836, 12, 24. Eli dis
1837, 2, 25. Nathan & w, Sarah, gct Penns-
    ville MM
1837, 8, 26. Eli rst
1838, 9, 22. Eli & w, Sarah, & ch, William,

BUNDY, continued

Mary & Ruthanna, gct Chesterfield MM

1841, 5, 22. Pharaby rocf Short Creek MM, dtd 1841,4,20

1842, 3, 26. Eli Hodgin gct Chesterfield MM, to m Sarah Bundy

1842, 6, 25. William, Mary, Ruthanna & Esther, ch Sarah Hodgin, rocf Chesterfield MM, dtd 1842,6,18

1843, 1, 28. John gct Somerset MM, to m Sidney Tipton

1843, 7, 22. Sidney rocf Somerset MM, dtd 1843,3,27

1849, 1, 27. John gct Somerset MM, to m Anna Edgerton

1849, 6, 23. Anna rocf Somerset MM, dtd 1849, 5,28

1857, 3, 28. Demsey gct Flushing MM, to m Rebecca W. Smith

1857, 9, 26. Rebecca W. rocf Flushing MM, dtd 1857,8,20

1858, 2, 27. Wm. C. & w, Edith, & ch, Henry & Ellen, gct Chesterfield MM

1861, 12, 28. Achsah recrq (residing in Linn Co., Ia.)

1862, 9, 27. Josiah dis mcd

1864, 5, 28. Ellen, minor, rocf Chesterfield MM, dtd 1864,4,16

1864, 7, 23. Susannah Wood (form Bundy) dis mcd

1866, 4, 28. Thomas dis enlisting in army

1866, 6, 23. Amanda French (form Bundy) dis mcd

1866, 7, 28. Bailey dis paying bounty money

1866, 11, 24. Mathew dis mcd

1867, 10, 24. Nathan dis jas & paying bounty money

1869, 5, 22. Anna Maria Watt (form Bundy) dis mcd

1871, 8, 23. Joel dis mcd

1873, 1, 22. Sarah Louisa & mother Tabitha D. Hall, gct Short Creek MM

1873, 5, 21. Margaret (form Naylor) con mcd

1873, 11, 19. Margaret H. gct Short Creek MM

1879, 1, --. Jefferson dis mcd

1882, 6, 21. Nathan W. dis mcd

1886, 12, 22. Emma, niece of Lindley & Ruanna, recrq

1888, 8, 22. Elmer E. dis mcd

1889, 4, 24. William E. & w, Rebecca, & ch, Agnes M. & Bertram H., gct Springville MM, Ia.

1889, 8, 21. Mary Colpitt (form Bundy) dis mcd

1891, 3, 25. Jesse dis mcd

1889, 9, 25. Mary C. Smith (form Bundy) dis mcd

1891, 5, 20. Henry dis mcd

1901, 3, 20. Charles & w, Margaret H., & ch, Myrtle R., Eldon J. & Clarence E., rocf Short Creek MM, dtd 1901,2,19

1903, 6, 24. Frederick R. rocf Short Creek MM, dtd 1903,4,2

1903, 6, 24. Willis M. rocf Short Creek MM, dtd 1903,4,2

1903, 9, 23. Chalkley L. gct Short Creek MM, to m Luella Hall

1905, 2, 22. Clinton T. dis mcd & military service in Spanish American War

1906, 8, 22. Alice D. Martin (form Bundy) dis mcd

1906, 12, 19. Russel C. dis mcd

1907, 6, 19. Myrtle Naylor (form Bundy) dis mcd

1908, 1, 22. Willis M. dis mcd

1910, 3, 23. Chalkley L. gct Short Creek MM, O.

1910, 3, 23. Ruanna gct Salem MM

1911, 1, 25. Thomas Clarkson dis jas

1911, 1, 25. Rachel dis jas

1911, 3, 22. Ruanna rocf Salem MM, O., dtd 1911,2,22

1913, 7, 23. Eldon dis mcd

1914, 2, 25. Eldon C. dis

1914, 8, 19. William E. rocf Springville MM; returned as he does not reside in our limits

1915, 2, 24. C. Ellis dis mcd & jas

1917, 8, 22. Amy B. Pierce (form Bundy) dis mcd

1925, 2, 23. Clarence E. gct Pasadena MM, Calif.

1928, 6, 25. Margaret B. Backes (form Bundy) gct Falls MM, Pa.

BURDG

1868, 11, 28. Henry, minor, rocf Chesterfield MM, dtd 1868,8,15

BURNET

----, --, --. Robert & Anna

Ch:		
John	b 1800,	3, 25
David	" 1803,	2, 4
Rebecca	" 1805,	1, 23
Rachel	" 1807,	2, 21
Deborah	" 1810,	12, 21
Thomas	" 1811,	1, 4
Lydia	" 1813,	10, 22
Stephen	" 1815,	10, 22
William	" 1817,	10, 23

1812, 6, 30. Robert & w, Ann, & ch, John, David, Rebeckah, Rachel, Deborah & Thomas, rocf Short Creek MM, dtd 1812,5,19

1812, 6, 30. Ann & dt, Rebecca, Rachel & Deborah rocf Short Creek MM, dtd 1812,5, 19

1813, 8, 31. Stephen rocf Redstone MM, dtd 1813,1,29

1816, 8, 24. John [Burnett] gct Miami MM

1820, 11, 25. Robert & fam gct Flushing MM

1823, 12, 27. Rebecca rocf Pipe Creek MM, dtd 1823,10,24

1826, 12, 23. Rebecca gct Miami MM

BUTLER

----, --, --. Jared d 1860,2,2 bur Stillwater;

BUTLER, Jared, continued
  m Elizabeth ----- d 1867,12,16 bur Stillwater
  Ch: William b 1823, 5, 17 d 1846, 7,23
    bur Stillwater
    Aseph   b 1825, 7, 1 " 1846, 6,27
    bur Stillwater
    James   b 1827, 6, 5
    Sarah Ann " 1829, 3, 16
    Tabitha " 1831, 12, 12
    Martha " 1835, 8, 14 d 1851,11, 3
    bur Stillwater
    Henry   b 1837, 9, 12 " 1870,10,29
    bur Stillwater
    Pheriba b 1839, 5, 8
    Robert " 1840, 10, 29 " 1853, 1, 1
    bur Stillwater
    Jared   b 1845, 7, 10 " 1846, 3,19
    bur Stillwater
1827, 5, 3. Caleb, s John & Jane, Muskingdon
  Co., O.; m in Blue Rock, Muskingdon Co.,
  O., Mary BAILEY, dt Joel & Martha, Muskingdon Co., O.
1845, 12, 10. William, s Jared & Elizabeth,
  Belmont Co., O.; m in Stillwater MH, Sabilla SMITH, dt Wm. & Rebecca, Belmont
  Co., O.
1849, 10, 31. Sarah Ann m Milton BAILEY
1850, 3, 27. Sabilla Smith m Daniel ATKINSON

1824, 7, 24. Jared & w, Elisabeth, & s,
  William, rocf Somerset MM, dtd 1824,5,24
1825, 4, 23. Mary (form Starbuck) dis mcd
1825, 8, 27. Caleb recrq
1857, 4, 25. James dis mcd
1864, 8, 27. Tabitha dis
1873, 8, 20. Phariba Patterson (form Butler)
  dis mcd

BYE
----, --, --. Jonathan & Mary
  Ch: Joshua b 1816, 12, 3
    Catharine " 1823, 3, 24
    Mariah " 1826, 3, 22
    Jonathan " 1828, 3, 15
    Rachel " 1830, 2, 25
    Susanna " 1833, 2, 15

1822, 5, 25. Jonathan & w, Mary, & ch, Joshua,
  Phebe & Mary, rocf Flushing MM, dtd 1822,
  4,26
1834, 1, 25. Jonathan & Mary dis JH
1842, 5, 28. Joshua dis mcd
1842, 9, 24. Mary (form Judkins) dis mcd

CADWALADER
----, --, --. Rees m Hannah D. ----- d 1829,1,
  23 bur Zanesville
  Ch: Moses
    Dillon b 1810, 8, 14
    Alfred " 1812, 8, 9
    Edith   " 1814, 11, 4
    Edwin   " 1816, 8, 26

  Ch: Howard b 1818, 4, 22
    Rees   " 1821, 10, 3 d 1822, 8,22
    bur Zanesville
    Loyd   b 1823, 10, 5
    Isaac D. " 1825, 8, 7
1828, 8, 30. Mary P., dt Rees, d bur Zanesville
1914, 4, 23. John J., s Mifflin & Sarah J.,
  Columbiana Co., O.; m in Stillwater MH,
  Rebecca H. BUNDY, dt William & Asenath,
  Belmont Co., O.

1819, 9, 25. Rebecca [Cadwiler] (form Dodd)
  dis mcd
1830, 4, 24. Emlin rocf Redstone MM, dtd
  1830,3,3
1834, 11, 22. Reece gct New Garden MM, to m
  Sarah Johnson
1835, 2, 28. Alfred dis disunity
1835, 6, 27. Sarah rocf New Garden MM, dtd
  1835,3,26
1836, 8, 27. Reese & w, Sarah, & ch, Edith,
  Loyd D. & Isaac D., gct Pennsville MM
1840, 6, 27. Howard, s Rees, gct Upper
  Springfield MM
1842, 1, 22. Moses D. dis jas
1915, 3, 24. Rebecca H. gct Middleton MM

CALHOUN
1824, 10, 27. John [Calhoon], s Wm. & Mary,
  Belmont Co., O.; m in Stillwater MH,
  Elizabeth MIDDLETON, dt Jehu & Mary, Bel-
  mont Co., O.
  Ch: William b 1825, 7, 17

1824, 1, 24. John recrq
1828, 2, 23. Elizabeth, w John, & ch, William
  & Mary, gct Miami MM
1828, 10, 25. John dis disunity

CAMPBELL
1836, 8, 27. Eleanor (form Hicks) dis mcd

CARLISLE
1825, 2, 26. Leah recrq

CARLTON
1829, 10, 24. Buley dis jH
1830, 3, 29. Mark dis disunity

CARROLL
1829, 1, 24. Thomas dis jH
1829, 1, 24. Ann dis jH

CARTER
1844, 4, 23. James, s Joel & Margaret,
  Guernsey Co., O.; m in house of Levi BEN-
  SON, Julia BENSON, dt Levi & Rachel,
  Guernsey Co., O. (H)
1853, 9, 29. Mary Jane m John DOUDNA
----, --, --. Samuel m Sarah DOUDNA
  Ch: Phebe
    Eliza   b 1856, 2, 22

CARTER, Samuel & Sarah, continued
    Ch: Joel D.   b 1858, 2, 8
----, --, --. Beulah R., dt Joseph & Rachel
    (Kirk) ROBERTS, b 1849,7,6 d 1922,5,9
----, --, --. Ellis Tucker, s Levi & Beulah
    (Roberts); m Mary Alice HALL, dt Mansel E.
    & Martha (Hartley) b 1881,1,20
        Ch: Mansel
           Levi   b 1902, 5, 12
           Wilma Al-
             berta   " 1904, 2, 2
           Martha
             Beulah   " 1906, 6, 4
           Russel
             Stephen " 1908, 4, 9
           Harold
             Robert   " 1912, 8, 3
           Alice Edna " 1919, 1, 26

1818, 8, 22. Benjamin rocf Piles Grove MM,
    N. J., dtd 1818,6,25
1829, 2, 28. Benjamin dis jH
1831, 10, 22. Mary, minor, in care Stacy Bevan,
    gct Flushing MM
1843, 10, 28. Sarah (form Doudna) dis mcd
1853, 5, 28. Mary Jane rocf Baltimore MM, E.
    Dist., dtd 1853,4,7
1853, 6, 25. Sarah rst
1855, 2, 17. Elizabeth (form Outland) dis mcd
    (H)
1855, 7, 20. Mary J. Doudna (form Carter) dis
    mcd (H)
1857, 6, 20. James & w, Julia, & ch, Joel B.,
    Joseph H., Elton C., Levi S. & John S.,
    gct Alum Creek MM (H)
1861, 8, 24. Malinda (form Hartley) dis mcd
1868, 3, 28. Philip recrq
1873, 7, 23. Philip dis mcd
1876, 6, 21. Hannah Ann recrq
1886, 7, 21. Sarah Ellen recrq
1894, 2, 21. Hannah Ann Hall (form Carter)
    con mcd
1900, 5, 23. Sarah Ellen Galloway (form
    Carter) con mcd
1900, 12, 19. Hannah R. recrq
1902, 4, 23. Ellis T. recrq
1904, 7, 20. Samuel recrq
1905, 6, 21. Phebe E. Hartley (form Carter)
    con mcd
1909, 1, 20. Beulah recrq
1909, 2, 24. Samuel gct Middleton MM, O., to
    m Mary Elma Blackburn
1909, 8, 25. Samuel gct Middleton MM, O.
1912, 3, 20. Hannah R. gct Somerset MM
1915, 1, 20. Elma L. (form Hall) dis mcd &
    jas
1931, 6, 24. Martha Boyd (form Carter) con
    mcd

CECILLE
1845, 12, 27. Mary (form Romans) con mcd
1847, 6, 26. Mary gct Flushing MM

CHALFANT
1822, 6, 5. Lydia m Abner WILLIAMS
1822, 6, 26. Jesse, s Robert & Elizabeth,
    Guernsey Co., O.; m in Stillwater MH, Ann
    WEBSTER, dt John & Hannah, Guernsey Co.,O.

1821, 3, 24. Jesse & w, Rachel, rocf Fallow-
    field MM, Pa., dtd 1820,9,8, end by
    Plainfield MM, 1821,1,25
1821, 3, 24. Joel rocf Fallowfield MM, Pa.,
    dtd 1820,9,8, end by Plainfield MM, 1821,
    1,25
1821, 3, 24. Ezekiel rocf Fallowfield MM,
    Pa., dtd 1820,9,8, end by Plainfield MM,
    1821,1,25
1821, 4, 28. Jesse rocf Fallowfield MM, Pa.,
    dtd 1820,9,8, end by Plainfield MM, 1821,
    4,26
1821, 7, 28. Lydia rocf Plainfield MM, dtd
    1821,5,24
1825, 6, 25. Joel gct Fallowfield MM, Pa.
1829, 9, 26. Jesse [Chalfin] dis jH
1829, 9, 26. Ann [Chalfin] dis jH
1829, 10, 24. Robert dis jH
1829, 10, 24. Elizabeth dis jH

CHAMBERS
----, --, --. Samuel & Tamer
    Ch: Margaret   b 1827, 10, 3
        Ann   " 1829, 8, 8
1832, 6, 7. Abigail m Benjamin WAY
1833, 8, 1. Deborah m John WEBSTER
----, --, --. Chas. Theodore & Edith
    Ch: Jennie Ida
        Emma   b 1910, 2, 10
        Elma Cailet-
         ta   b 1911, 6, 16

1829, 10, 24. Samuel Jr. & w, Tamer, & ch,
    Margaret & Ann, gct Alum Creek MM
1832, 9, 22. Samuel & w, Tamer, & ch, Marga-
    ret, Ann & Deborah, rocf Alum Creek MM,
    dtd 1832,3,29
1834, 2, 22. Mary T. rocf Somerset MM, dtd
    1834,1,27
1834, 3, 22. James & w, Mary, & s, Samuel,
    gct Alum Creek MM

CHILDRE
1816, 12, 28. Martha rst on consent of Con-
    cord MM
1822, 11, 23. Phebe & Sarah recrq
1827, 6, 23. Martha, Phebe & Sally [Childra]
    gct White Water MM, Ind.

CINARD
1810, 9, 25. Elizabeth rocf Fairfax MM, dtd
    1810,6,27

CLARK
1835, 6, 20. Solomon & w & ch, Joseph, De-
    borah & Curtis, gct Goshen MM (H)
1840, 1, 18. Hannah gct Deerfield MM (H)

CLARK, continued

1853, 2, 19. Solomon & w, Ann, & ch, Mary,
     Elizabeth & Jesse, gct White Water MM, Ind.
     (H)
1923, 12, 19. Jennie Ida Emma & Elma Carlotta,
     rocf Somerset MM, dtd 1923,11,22

CLENDENON

----, --, --. Isaac & Hannah
     Ch: Elizabeth b 1793, 10, 19
         Benjamin   " 1795, 11, 7
         Rebeckah   " 1798, 5, 14
         Esther   " 1800, 12, 4
         Lydia   " 1803, 8, 2
         Isaac   " 1806, 5, 2
         Maria   " 1808, 10, 21
         Hannah   " 1812, 6, 8 d 1819, 8,28
1815, 8, 2. Elizabeth [Clendenning] m Job M.
     WILLIAMS
1821, 9, 26. Benjamin, s Isaac & Hannah, Bel-
     mont Co., O.; m in Stillwater MH, Amy HOD-
     GIN, dt Stephen & Elizabeth, Belmont Co.,
     O.
     Ch: Sarah   b 1826, 4, 24
         Lydia   " 1828, 12, 18
         Stephen   " 1835, 5, 28
         Hannah   " 1836, 8, 7
1821, 10, 31. Lydia m Wm. WILLIAMS
1822, 10, 30. Esther m Daniel MILLHOUSE
1823, 3, 26. Rebecca m Joseph EMBREE
1848, 12, 27. Lydia m Elisha SMITH
1854, 2, 1. Stephen, s Benjamin & Amy, Bel-
     mont Co., O.; m in Stillwater MH, Matilda
     DAWSON, dt Joel & Sarah, Belmont Co., O.,
     d 1857,1,5 bur Stillwater
1855, 5, 10. Sarah Louisa, dt Wm. & Joanna,
     b
1859, 8, 16. Benjamin, s Stephen & Elizabeth,
     d bur Stillwater
----, --, --. Stephen & Elizabeth
     Ch: Matilda
         Jane   b 1860, 3, 30
         Benjamin E." 1862, 2, 21
         Isaac Wil-
         son   " 1863, 6, 12
1863, 3, 17. Benjamin E. d bur Stillwater

1808, 5, 31. Hannah recrq
1808, 10, 25. Isaac rocf Robeson MM, dtd 1808,
     8,5
1808, 11, 29. Elizabeth, Benjamin, Rebecca,
     Esther, Lydia & Isaac, ch Isaac & Hannah,
     recrq
1827, 4, 28. Maria gct Deerfield MM
1827, 5, 26. Isaac & w, Hannah, gct Deerfield
     MM
1829, 6, 27. Isaac Jr. gct Deerfield MM
1859, 2, 26. Stephen gct Flushing MM, to m
     Elizabeth Branson
1860, 4, 28. Elizabeth rocf Flushing MM, dtd
     1860,3,22
1864, 12, 24. Amy & Hannah [Clendennon] gct
     Coal Creek MM, Ia.

1866, 4, 28. Stephen & fam gct Coal Creek
     MM, Iowa

CLIFF

1863, 6, 20. Sarah (form James) dis mcd &
     jas

COBBS

1830, 2, 27. Agatha, minor, rocf Upper
     Springfield MM, dtd 1829,12,26
1830, 7, 24. Agathy Winters (form Cobb) dis
     mcd

COCKAYNE

1835, 9, 26. Elizabeth rocf Wilmington MM,
     Del., dtd 1835,9,5
1839, 12, 28. Elizabeth gct White Water MM,
     Ind.; this cert was lost & another granted
     1841,7,24

COFFEE

----, --, --. John & Alice
     Ch: John S.   b 1815, 7, 22
         Lydia S.   " 1815, 7, 22
         William   " 1817, 7, 7
         Thomas El-
         wood   " 1823, 1, 14
         Mary Ann   " 1823, 1, 14
         Eliza   " 1827, 5, 11
1828, 7, 2. Rachel A., dt Isaac & Betsy, b
1833, 3, 28. Ruth m David SATTERTHWAIT

1839, 5, 25. John S. rocf Plainfield MM, dtd
     1839,4,24

COFFMAN

1917, 5, 2. Minerva E. m Jesse N. EDGERTON

1912, 1, 24. Minerva E. recrq

COLBURN

1898, 7, 20. Emily E. (form Hall) dis mcd &
     jas

COLES

----, --, --. Charles & Elizabeth
     Ch: Mary Par-
         wina   b 1808, 12, 26
         Debora   " 1810, 11, 18
         Lydia Ann   " 1813, 3, 3
         Chas. Cy-
         renius   " 1815, 1, 23
         Elizabeth   " 1817, 3, 23
         Sarah M.   " 1821, 2, 26
         Ann Margaret 1824, 6, 27

1815, 8, 29. Charles & w, Elizabeth, & ch,
     Mary, Deborah, Lydia Ann & Charles Cy-
     renius, recrq
1827, 4, 28. Mary (form Starbuck) dis mcd
1829, 4, 25. Charles dis jH
1829, 5, 16. Charles [Coals] gct Westfield
     MM (H)

COLES, continued
1829, 6, 27. Mary & Deborah gct Elk MM
1829, 6, 27. Elizabeth & ch, Lydia Ann,
     Charles Cyrenus, Elizabeth, Sarah M., Ann
     Margret & Paerson, gct Elk MM
1830, 1, 23. Eliza McClary (form Coles) dis
COLLINS   [mcd
1819, 12, 25. Peninah (form Dodd) dis mcd

COLPITT
1889, 8, 21. Mary (form Bundy) dis mcd

COLLYER
1811, 10, 29. John & fam gct Miami MM
1811, 10, 29. Rhoda [Colyer] & dt, Mary &
     Elizabeth, gct Miami MM

CONNARD
1861, 3, 16. John H. dis (H)

CONROW
1876, 8, 25. Anna, w Darling, d bur Stillwater

1862, 3, 22. Anna rocf Somerset MM, dtd 1862,
     2,24

COOK
1812, 12, 16. Jeremiah, s Stephen & Hannah,
     Belmont Co., O.; m in Capteene, Lovice
     HANSON, dt Elijah & Susanna, d 1839,3,26

1810, 7, 31. Jeremiah & w, Rachel, & ch, Sa-
     rah & Mary, rocf Concord MM, dtd 1810,4,26
1812, 6, 30. Sarah Williams (form Cook) dis
     mcd
1813, 4, 27. Mary gct Plymouth MM
1816, 10, 26. Mary recrq
1819, 8, 28. Jeremiah & w, Lovise, gct Darby
     Creek MM
1832, 12, 22. Barak Michenor gct New Garden MM
     to m Lydia R. Cook
1837, 9, 23. Lovisa rocf Goshen MM, dtd 1837,
     8,19

COOPER
1857, 7, 25. Evan & w, Mary, & ch, Albert,
     Ann & Sarah, rocf Sandy Spring MM, dtd
     1857,5,23
1857, 7, 25. Hinchman rocf Sandy Spring MM,
     dtd 1857,5,23
1857, 8, 22. Martha rocf Sandy Spring MM,
     dtd 1857,6,27
1861, 11, 23. Evan & w, Mary, & ch, Albert,
     Ann & Sarah, gct Pennsville MM

COPE
1880, 4, --. Isaac N. Vail gct Salem MM, to
     m Mary M. Cope
1902, 12, 24. Thomas C. & w, Mary J., & ch,
     Mary Ella, rocf Flushing MM
1914, 7, 22. J. Wetherill Hutton gct New Gar-
     den MM, to m Ellen S. Cope
1916, 7, 19. Wm. Macy Stanton gct Woodbury

MM, N. J., to m Edith Mary Cope
1917, 2, 21. Mary Jane gct Dartmouth MM, Mass.
1917, 2, 21. Mary Ellen gct Dartmouth MM,
     Mass.

COPELAND
1820, 1, 22. David & Ann & ch, Mary & Sarah
     Ann, recrq

COPPOCK
1810, 7, 31. Mary dis
1810, 11, 27. Mary rst
1812, 2, 25. Mary dis
1830, 6, 26. Isaac dis JH
1830, 6, 26. Mary gct Somerset MM

COUGHLIN
1850, 9, 28. Eliza (form Harrison) dis mcd

COVENTRY
1888, 11, 21. Asenath P. (form Webster) dis
     mcd

COWDEN
1856, 5, 24. Penninah (form Heartley) dis
     mcd

COWGILL
----, --, --. Ralph & Betsy
     Ch: Phinneas   b 1817, 9, 29
         Jonathan   " 1818, 10, 27
         Jeptha   " 1820, 8, 9
         Ann   " 1822, 10, 29
         Sarah   " 1826, 1, 29
         Isaac   " 1829, 2, 28
         William   " 1832, 3, 25
----, --, --. Isaac & Jane
     Ch: Joseph   b 1828, 11, 18 d 1898, 4,11
         bur Stillwater
         Abraham   b 1830, 7, 6
         Sarah   " 1832, 12, 1
1867, 1, 30. Joseph, s Isaac & Jane, Belmont
     Co., O.; m in Stillwater MH, Rebecca
     SMITH, dt Robert H. & Elizabeth W., Bel-
     mont Co., O.
1871, 5, 27. Esther, dt Aaron & Elizabeth
     Roberts , d
1876, 8, 1. Isaac d bur Plainfield

1898, 3, 6. Rebecca, w Joseph, d bur Still-
     water

1847, 12, 25. Jeptha rocf Plainfield MM, dtd
     1847,11,24
1848, 8, 25. Jeptha dis mcd
1855, 7, 20. Ellen P. (form Spencer) con mcd
     (H)
1875, 11, 24. Sarah F. Wallace (form Cowgill)
     con mcd

COWPERTHWAIT
1898, 10, 20. William C., s Levi R. & Ella,
     Camden Co., N. J.; m in Stillwater MH,

COWPERTHWAIT, continued
    Mary M. SMITH, dt Sinclair & Tacy (Hall),
    Belmont Co., O.

1899, 7, 19. Mary M. gct Haddonfield MM, N.J.

COX
----, --, --. John & Rachel
    Ch: Thomas   b 1786, 7, 25
        Levi   " 1789, 10, 21
        Stephen   " 1791, 5, 7
        Anna   " 1796, 5, 27
        Rachel   " 1799, 10, 12
        John   " 1802, 3, 14
        Mary   " 1803, 12, 12
        Deborah   " 1806, 7, 27
----, --, --. Joseph & Elizabeth
    Ch: Joel M.   b 1805, 6, 2
        Rebecca   " 1807, 2, 23
        Elizabeth " 1808, 10, 16 d 1809, 9,21
          bur Stillwater
        Priscilla b 1810, 5, 5
        Marmaduke " 1812, 1, 3 " 1812, 2,28
          bur Stillwater
        Elizabeth b 1813, 5, 22
        Drusilla " 1815, 5, 23
        Bennet   " 1817, 1, 25
        Seth   " 1819, 4, 19
        William   " 1821, 5, 28
        Moriah   " 1822, 9, 15
1815, 3, 15. Anna m Asa HICKS
1819, 3, 30. Rachel m Borden HANSON
1827, 6, 27. Deborah m John WILLIAMS

1810, 12, 25. Sarah rocf Plainfield MM, dtd
    1810,11,24
1813, 4, 27. Elizabeth (form Stubbs) dis mcd
1813, 5, 25. Stephen dis mcd
1823, 7, 26. Elizabeth & dt, Rebecca, Pris-
    cilla, Elizabeth, Drucilla & Mariah, gct
    Somerset MM
1824, 8, 28. John Jr. dis mcd
1825, 12, 24. Mary Murphy (form Cox) dis mcd
1826, 10, 28. Walter Edgerton gct Somerset
    MM, to m Rebecca Cox
1827, 5, 26. Stephen & Elizabeth rst at Som-
    erset MM, on consent of this mtg
1828, 10, 25. Levi con mcd
1831, 7, 28. Rachel gct Springfield MM, Ind.
1831, 7, 28. Thomas gct Springfield MM, Ind.
1831, 7, 28. Levi gct Springfield MM, Ind.

CRAFT
----, --, --. William & Lydia
    Ch: Mary   b 1823, 8, 4
        William   " 1825, 5, 22
        John   " 1827, 5, 4
1846, 4, 30. Asa, s James & Mary, Belmont
    Co., O.; m in Richland, Peninah HALL, dt
    Isaac & Mary, Guernsey Co., O., d 1891,8,7
    bur Richland
    Ch: Ephraim b 1847, 3, 3 d 1869, 8,20
          bur Richland

    Ch: Lindley   b 1848, 4, 19
        Millisent " 1850, 4, 24
        Asa   " 1853, 4, 4
        Evaline   " 1855, 4, 12
        Isaac   " 1857, 8, 4
        Joseph   " 1859, 4, 19
1848, 11, 1. Ann m Demsey BUNDY
1873, 4, 10. Asa d

1823, 7, 26. Jesse dis mcd
1829, 1, 24. Lydia dis JH
1829, 5, 23. William dis JH
1837, 5, 27. Asa rocf Somerset MM, dtd 1837,
    4,24
1840, 4, 25. Asa gct Somerset MM
1845, 7, 26. Asa rocf Somerset MM, dtd 1845,
    6,30
1849, 6, 23. Rebecca (form Hanson) dis mcd
1881, 11, 23. Lindley dis jas
1890, 11, 19. Joseph L. dis mcd
1897, 1, 20. Millie Duvall (form Craft) dis
    mcd
1905, 10, 25. Eveline Hall (form Craft) con
    mcd

CRAMBLETT
1833, 3, 23. Elizabeth (form Hall) dis mcd
1835, 8, 22. William [Cramblet] recrq
1836, 11, 26. Elizabeth [Cramlet] rst
1848, 9, 23. Eliabeth dis disunity

CREW
----, --, --. Jacob & Rachel
    Ch: Henry   b 1811, 7, 16
        Priscilla " 1813, 9, 26
        Aquilla   " 1815, 11, 10
        John   " 1817, 9, 15
        Joseph   " 1819, 10, 19
1813, 9, 23. Eli, s Isaac & Judith, b
1820, 9, 28. Rebecca m Isaac PATTERSON
1831, 3, 30. William, s Jacob & Rachel, Bel-
    mont Co., O.; m in Stillwater MH, Mary
    BAILEY, dt Jesse & Phariba, Belmont Co.,O.
1839, 10, 30. Aquilla, s Jacob & Rachel, Bel-
    mont Co., O.; m in Stillwater MH, Rachel
    FARMER, dt Thomas & Ann, Belmont Co., O.
1843, 4, 26. John, s Jacob & Rachel, Athens
    Co., O.; m in Stillwater MH, Ann DOUDNA,
    dt Hosea & Mary, Belmont Co., O.
----, --, --. John & Asenath
    Ch: Rachel   b 1855, 8, 25
        Josiah   " 1857, 1, 11
        Ann Eliza " 1858, 12, 25
        Barclay   " 1861, 9, 1
        Mary A.   " 1863, 6, 26
1865, 3, 29. Mariam m Abram PLUMMER
1868, 3, 6. John d bur Stillwater
1878, 1, 15. Asenath, w John, d bur Still-
    water
1878, 10, 30. Rachel m Thos. Clarkson BUNDY

1811, 5, 28. Jacob & w, Rachel, & ch, Re-
    becca, James, William & Edwin, rocf Jack

CREW, continued
      Swamp MM, N. C., dtd 1811,3,2
1811, 6, 25. Judith & Anna rocf Jackswamp MM,
      N. C., dtd 1811,3,2
1831, 6, 25. Mary gct Somerset MM
1840, 3, 28. Rachel F. gct Somerset MM
1843, 7, 22. Ann gct Chesterfield MM
1843, 9, 23. Henry D. Williams gct Somerset
      MM, to m Rachel Crew
1847, 7, 24. Ann rocf Somerset MM, dtd 1847,
      5,24
1848, 10, 28. John W. Wood gct Somerset MM,
      to m Almedia Crew
1850, 2, 23. Rachel rocf Somerset MM, dtd
      1850,1,28
1850, 2, 23. Priscilla rocf Somerset MM, dtd
      1850,1,28
1855, 5, 26. John & ch, Miriam, Rebecca &
      Abner, rocf Somerset MM, dtd 1855,4,30
1855, 5, 26. Asenath rocf Flushing MM, dtd
      1855,4,26
1861, 10, 26. Martha (form Hodgin) dis mcd
1870, 8, 24. Rebecca W. gct Springville MM,
      Iowa
1874, 7, 22. Abner F. gct Springville MM, Ia.
1882, 3, 22. Jeptha D. Blowers gct Penns-
      ville MM, to m Eliza B. Crew
1884, 7, 23. Barclay dis mcd
1884, 11, 26. Ann Eliza Price (form Crew) dis
      mcd
1889, 4, 24. Mary A. gct Coal Creek MM, Ia.

CROSSLEY
1829, 7, 25. Moses & w, Jane, & ch, Leana,
      Jonathan, Caroline & John, rocf Flushing
      MM, dtd 1829,7,23

CROY
1811, 1, 29. Margaret dis joining M. E.
1811, 3, 26. John dis disunity
1811, 4, 30. Richard & s, Richard, dis join-
      ing M. E.
1811, 4, 30. Ann dis joining M. E.
1819, 7, 24. Rebecca Agur (form Croy) dis
      mcd
1821, 5, 26. Ann Vore (form Croy) dis mcd
1823, 8, 23. Mathias dis disunity

CROZER
1832, 5, 26. Samuel rocf Flushing MM, dtd
      1832,5,24
1861, 12, 28. Sarah [Crozier] recrq (residing
      in Linn Co., Ia.)

DARBY
1893, 4, 19. Rachel (form Blowers) dis mcd

DAVIS
---- --, --. Harmon & Hannah
      Ch: Joseph   b 1800, 3, 28
          Isaac   " 1802, 4, 24
          Anne   " 1804, 10, 21
          Thomas   " 1806, 11, 30

      Ch: Sarah   b 1812, 2, 11
          Jehu   " 1814, 6, 11
          Hannah   " 1816, 12, 28
          Eunice   " 1819, 6, 30
1810, 1, 3. Amos, s Abiather & Lydia, Bel-
      mont Co., O.; m in Stillwater MH, Sarah
      HODGIN, dt Wm. & Agnes, Belmont Co., O.
1815, 10, 4. Rachel m Wm. BOSWELL
1816, 2, 28. Charity m Mahlon BAILEY
1817, 3, 26. Elizabeth m Laben HICKS
1819, 12, 2. Joseph, s Harmon & Hannah, Bel-
      mont Co., O.; m in Ridge, Michel BAILEY,
      dt Wm. & Rebecca, Belmont Co., O.
1822, 5, 1. Ann m Isaac KING
----→ --, --. Francis, s John & Ann, b 1819,
      7,9 d 1889,8,20 bur Stillwater; m Mary
      ----- d 1910,3,30
      Ch: Josiah   d 1861,10,11
          Lindley   " 1861, 9,25
          Smith   " 1863,10, 8
          John F.   " 1899,12,12
          bur Elizabeth City, N. C.
1864, 1, 27. Jane m William STANTON
1864, 3, 30. John F., s Francis & Mary, Bel-
      mont Co., O.; m in Stillwater MH, Tabitha
      STANTON, dt Edmund & Sarah (Hoyle), Bel-
      mont Co., O., b 1845,3,13 d 1920,2,13 bur
      Stillwater
      Ch: Melvina   b 1865, 2, 4 d 1867,--,--
          Francis
           Edgar   " 1871, 12, 12 d 1889, 6,27
           bur Phila.
          Henry Clin-
           ton   " 1884, 8, 26 " 1885, 5,26
1866, 1, 10. Sarah Eleanor, dt Archibald &
      Susanna (Hanlon) Giffin, b
1868, 2, 20. William C., s Francis & Mary, b

1810, 1, 30. Sarah [Davies] gct W. Branch MM
1818, 9, 26. John & w, Annie, rocf Enis-
      corthy MM, Ireland, dtd 1817,12,9
1819, 12, 25. William rocf Eniscorthy MM, Wex-
      ford Co., Ireland, dtd 1819,5,4
1820, 8, 26. Joshua rocf Westland MM, dtd
      1820,7,27
1820, 10, 28. Hannah rocf Amesbury MM, dtd
      1820,5,4
1821, 11, 24. William dis mcd
1823, 11, 22. John F. & w, Ann, & fam gct
      Flushing MM
1825, 9, 24. Miles & s, Hiram E., rocf West-
      land MM, dtd 1825,4,21, end by Plainfield
      MM, 1825,5,26; returned to that mtg as
      not within limits of this MM
1825, 10, 24. Miles & s, Hiram, rocf Westland
      MM
1825, 11, 26. Hiram E., s Miles, gct Alum
      Creek MM
1826, 2, 25. Hqrmon & w, Hannah, & fam gct
      Milford MM, Ind.
1826, 5, 27. Miles dis
1827, 10, 27. Isaac gct Milford MM
1828, 1, 26. Joseph & w, Michale, gct Somer-

DAVIS, continued
    set MM
1841, 6, 26. Elva (form Wood) dis mcd
1843, 8, 26. Matilda Ann (form Reeves) dis mcd
1845, 4, 26. Elmy Ann (form Reeves) dis mcd
1852, 7, 24. Martha (form Smith) dis mcd
1860, 6, 23. Francis & w, Mary, & ch, John F.,
    Jane S., Josiah, Lindley & Smith rocf
    Flushing MM, dtd 1860,5,24
1889, 4, 24. John F. & w, Tabitha, & s, Fran-
    cis Edgar, gct ND MM
1913, 7, 23. William C. con mcd
1914, 4, 22. Sarah E. G. recrq

DAWSON
----, --, --. Jesse m Elizabeth DOUDNA
    Ch: Nathan   b 1809, 1, 9
        Joseph   " 1810, 8, 6
        Peninah   " 1812, 3, 8
        Joel   " 1814, 2, 21 d 1859,10, 2
          bur Stillwater
        Sarah   b 1816, 4, 19 " 1833, 8,12
          bur Stillwater
        Patience b 1818, 4, 11
        Martha   " 1820, 5, 26
        Mary   " 1820, 5, 26 " 1836, 3,28
          bur Stillwater
        Elizabeth b 1832, 1, 11
        Tamer J. "" 1835, 6, 5
1825, 5, 13. Elizabeth d ae 40 bur Captina
1830, 12, 8. Jesse, s Joseph & Patience, Bel-
    mont Co., O.; m in Stillwater MH, Jane
    BRIANT, dt James & Tamer VERNON, Belmont
    Co.. O.
    Ch: Elizabeth   d 1833, 7,29
          bur Stillwater
1831, 3, 9. Peninah m Robert BROCK
1835, 4, 29. Joel, s Jesse & Elizabeth
    (Doudna), Belmont Co., O., d 1859,10,2
    bur Stillwater; m in Stillwater MH, Sarah
    BUNDY, dt William & Sarah, Belmont Co., O.,
    d 1842,4,22 bur Stillwater
    Ch: Chalkley b 1836, 2, 1
        Malinda   " 1837, 8, 30
        Eli   " 1839, 12, 17
        Jesse   " 1841, 8, 23
    Joel m 2nd 1843,9,27 in Stillwater MH,
    Mary P. STANTON, dt Henry & Clary, Belmont
    Co., O., d 1901,3,23 bur Stillwater
    Ch: Sarah   b 1844, 12, 18
        Henry   " 1847, 3, 19
        Clary   " 1849, 8, 4 d 1851,10,30
          bur Stillwater
        Anna   b 1852, 6, 26
        Mira   " 1854, 8, 29
        Elvira   " 1857, 11, 30 d 1861, 2,17
          bur Stillwater
        Joel   b 1860, 1, 24 " 1861, 2,20
          bur Stillwater
1854, 2, 1. Matilda m Stephen CLENDENON
1856, 10, 1. Tamor m Daniel HODGIN
1859, 9, 28. Chalkley, s Joel & Sarah, Bel-
    mont Co., O., m in Stillwater MH, Martha

GARRETSON, dt Asa & Ruth, Belmont Co.,
O.
    Ch: Mary Ma-
       tilda   b 1860, 8, 5 d 1874, 5,27
       bur Stillwater
       Willis   b 1861, 9, 28 " 1863, 8,28
       bur Stillwater
       Melvina   b 1863, 3, 31
       Sina   "1889, 5,18
       bur Richland
1861, 11, 6. Clinton Elsworth, s Eli & Es-
    ther, b
1865, 1, 13. Jesse Jr. d bur Stillwater
1869, 10, 6. Anna S. m Nathan H. BUNDY
1872, 3, 27. Myra m Jeptha BUNDY
1875, 5, 2. Martha S., dt Chalkley & Rebecca
    b
1877, 7, 20. Rebecca Ann, w Chalkley, d bur
    Stillwater
1885, 10, 22. Melvina m Elisha GAMBLE

1831, 5, 28. Nathan gct Somerset MM, to m
    Sarah Brock
1831, 12, 24. Sarah rocf Somerset MM, dtd
    1831,8,29
1832, 5, 26. Joseph dis disunity
1832, 12, 22. Nathan & w, Sarah, gct Somerset
    MM
1838, 9, 22. Joel & w, Sarah, & ch, Chalkley
    & Matilda, gct Chesterfield MM
1839, 4, 24. Martha Parker (form Dawson) dis
    mcd
1839, 10, 26. Joel & w, Sarah, & ch, Chalkley
    & Matilda, rocf Chesterfield MM, dtd 1839,
    10,19
1843, 8, 26. Patience Shriner (form Dawson)
    dis mcd
1860, 11, 24. Eli gct Somerset MM, to m Es-
    ther Tipton
1862, 4, 26. Esther & s, Clinton Ellsworth
    Dawson, rocf Somerset MM, dtd 1861,3,24
1864, 10, 22. Chalkley & w, Martha, & ch,
    Mary M., Melvina & Caleb, gct Coal Creek
    MM, Iowa
1864, 12, 24. Esther W. & ch gct Hickory
    Grove MM, Ia.
1866, 10, 27. Sarah French (form Dawson) dis
    mcd
1868, 11, 28. Eli dis military service
1872, 3, 20. Chalkley & ch, Mary Matilda,
    Melvina, Caleb & Sina, rocf Coal Creek
    MM, Ia., dtd 1872,2,9
1872, 12, 25. Jesse dis mcd
1873, 9, 24. Chalkley gct Flushing MM, to
    m Rebecca Anna Branson
1876, 1, 19. Rebecca Ann rocf Flushing MM,
    dtd 1875,12,28
1883, 8, 22. Chalkley dis mcd

DAY
1867, 5, 25. Sarah (form Parry) dis mcd
1895, 10, 23. Annie L. (form Webster) con mcd

DENNIS
1823, 12, 31. Increase m Hezekiah THOMAS

1823, 6, 28. Increase W. recrq

DEPUE
1812, 6, 30. Margaret (form Williams) dis mcd

DEWEESE
----, --, --. William & Deborah
     Ch: Mary   b 1811, 1, 11
         James   " 1813, 9, 10 d 1826, 8, 5
           bur Captina
         Sarah   b 1815, 9, 25
         Ellis   " 1817, 8, 28 " 1826, 8, 21
           bur Captina
         Isaac   b 1819, 11, 10
         Cornelius " 1821, 10, 23
         William   " 1825, 9, 13
----, --, --. Thomas & Jane [Dewees]
     Ch: Jesse   b 1821, 4, 20 d 1907, 5, 10
           bur Stillwater
         Joseph   b 1823, 7, 3
         Hannah   " 1826, 1, 2
         Ellis   " 1828, 5, 16
         Thomas   " 1812, 3, 18 (sic)
         John   " 1814, 11, 4
         Rebecca   " 1817, 6, 15
         Aaron   " 1819, 4, 11
1826, 12, 28. Sarah m Thomas YOCOM
1830, 5, 11. James [Dewees], s Wm. Jr. & Sa-
     rah, b
1841, 12, 9. Aaron, s Thomas & Jane, Belmont
     Co., O.; m in Captina, Mary WOOD, dt
     Matthew & Margaret, Belmont Co., O.
     Ch: Matthew W. b 1843, 4, 20
         Watson   " 1845, 7, 30
         Margaret
          Jane   " 1847, 9, 2
         Almedia   " 1849, 10, 1
1883, 3, 22. Jesse [Dewees], s Thomas & Sarah,
     Morgan Co., O.; m in Stillwater MH, Mariam
     P. HALL, dt John & Deborah (Davis), Bel-
     mont Co., O.
1899, 11, 2. William [Dewees], s William &
     Sarah, Belmont Co., O., b 1840,11,12 d
     1926,7,20; m in Barnsville MH, Anna EDGER-
     TON, dt David & Esther (Ellyson), Belmont
     Co., O.
1815, 11, 28. Daniel Wilson gct Concord MM, to
     m Mary [Dewees]
1817, 6, 28. William [Dewees] & w, Debby, & ch,
     Mary, James & Sarah, rocf Exeter MM, dtd
     1817,4,30
1821, 2, 24. Thomas recrq
1821, 2, 24. Jane recrq
1821, 9, 22. Sarah rocf Exeter MM, Pa., dtd
     1821,6,21, end to Short Creek MM
1822, 7, 27. Sarah, James, William, Jane,
     Thomas, John, Rebecca & Aaron, ch Thomas
     & Jane, recrq
1826, 3, 25. James gct Concord MM (a minor)
1828, 3, 22. James rocf Concord MM, dtd

1827,10,24
1828, 12, 27. William Jr. gct Somerset MM
1829, 6, 27. James dis jH
1830, 2, 27. William & w, Sarah, rocf Somer-
     set MM, dtd 1830,1,25
1830, 4, 24. Jane Jr. dis jH
1830, 7, 17. Gulielma gct Deerfield MM (H)
1830, 7, 17. Samuel & w, Hannah, & ch, Buly
     Elma, Ellis Lee, Thomas Lee, Hannah Ma-
     riah & Mary Ann, gct Deerfield MM
1831, 4, 23. William Jr. & w, Sarah, & ch,
     James, gct Somerset MM
1832, 7, 28. Thomas Jr. gct Short Creek MM
1832, 7, 21. James gct Short Creek MM (H)
1833, 11, 23. John, minor, gct Flushing MM
1834, 3, 22. Thomas & w, Jane, & ch, Rebecca,
     Aaron, Jesse, Joseph, Hannah & Ellis, gct
     Deerfield MM
1834, 12, 27. Thomas Jr. rocf Short Creek MM
1834, 12, 27. Thomas Jr. dis mcd
1836, 3, 26. William & w, Deborah, & ch,
     Isaac, Cornelius, William, Deborah &
     Griffith, gct Pennsville MM
1836, 3, 26. Mary gct Pennsville MM
1836, 3, 26. Sarah gct Pennsville MM
1837, 2, 25. James Doudna gct Pennsville MM,
     to m Sarah Deweese
1842, 2, 26. Aaron rocf Somerset MM, dtd
     1842,1,24
1851, 10, 25. Aaron & w, Mary, & ch, Matthew
     W., Watson, Margaret Jane & Almeda, gct
     Pennsville MM
1861, 12, 28. Maria recrq (residing in Linn
     Co., Ia.)
1875, 11, 24. James E. & w, Anna, & dt, Mary
     Emma, rocf Pennsville MM, dtd 1875,10,14
1878, 2, 20. James [Dewees] & w, Anna, & ch,
     Mary E. & Rachel, gct Pennsville MM
1883, 7, 25. Miriam P. [Dewees] gct Penns-
     ville MM
1892, 8, 24. Lewis W. Plummer gct Spring-
     ville MM, Ia., to m Mary R. Deweese
1900, 6, 20. Thomas [Dewees] & w, Martha W.,
     rocf Pennsville MM, dtd 1900,6,14
1900, 6, 20. Jesse H. rocf Pennsville MM,
     dtd 1900,6,14
1902, 7, 23. William [Dewees] rocf Somerset
     MM, dtd 1902,6,26
1904, 4, 20. Jesse H. [Dewees] gct Short
     Creek MM, O., to m Mary C. Binns
1905, 11, 22. Jesse H. gct Short Creek MM
1906, 12, 19. Jesse [Dewees] & w, Mariam P.,
     rocf Chesterfield MM, dtd 1906,11,17
1907, 8, 21. Jesse d 1907,5,18 ae 86 (an
     elder)
1917, 8, 22. Thomas [Dewees] & w, Martha W.,
     gct Salem MM
1927, 6, 22. Miriam P. gct Pasadena MM, Calif.

DILLON
1794, 10, 4. Isaac, s Moses & Hannah, b
----, --, --. John & Edith
     Ch: Loyd   b 1803, 2, 2

DILLON, John & Edith, continued
```
Ch: Keziah    b 1805,  4,  8
    Moses     " 1808, 12,  4
    Hannah    " 1810,  8, 10
    Margaret  " 1812, 12, 26
    John      " 1815, 10, 27
    Elizabeth " 1817, 10, 19
    Asahel    " 1819, 11,  5
    Isaac     " 1823, 10, 22
```

1813, 9, 28. Vashti (form Borton) dis mcd
1813, 11, 30. Isaac, minor, rocf Baltimore MM, W. Dist., end to Plainfield MM
1813, 12, 28. Moses & w, Hannah, rocf Gunpowder MM, dtd 1813,10,27 (women's minutes say end to Plainfield)
1813, 12, 28. John dis entering military service
1816, 5, 25. Elizabeth Wilson (form Dillon) dis mcd
1821, 8, 25. Rachel Schogin (form Dillon) dis mcd
1822, 5, 25. Noah dis mcd
1823, 7, 26. Keziah Flanner (form Dillon) con mcd
1823, 12, 27. Ann Marsh (form Dillon) dis mcd
1824, 2, 28. Edith dis jas
1826, 9, 23. Moses gct Little Falls MM, Md., to m Martha Amos
1827, 8, 25. Martha rocf Littlefalls MM, Md., dtd 1827,1,2
1828, 7, 26. Isaac dis mcd
1829, 1, 24. Elizabeth dis jH
1830, 5, 22. Sarah dis jH
1830, 9, 25. Rachel dis disunity
1830, 9, 25. Hannah Morehead (form Dillon) dis joining M. E. Church
1832, 5, 26. Lloyd dis mcd
1841, 10, 23. Martha gct Smithfield MM
1931, 8, 19. Bertha (form Hall) dis mcd

DOAN
1827, 11, 24. William recrq
1827, 11, 24. Deborah & Mary recrq

DODD
1808, 9, 14. Joseph, s Aaron & Rebecca, Belmont Co., O.; m in Stillwater MH, Anna HALL, dt Isaac & Ann, Belmont Co., O.
```
Ch: Aaron   b 1809,  8, 13
    Orpah   " 1811, 10, 18
    Celah   " 1813,  9, 14
    Rachel  " 1815,  9, 25
```
1812, 1, 8. Elizabeth m Isaac WILSON
1814, 11, 2. Nathan, s Aaron & Rebecca, Belmont Co., O.; m in Stillwater MH, Ruth BAILEY, dt Henry & Elizabeth, Belmont Co., O.
1811, 2, 26. Mary dis
1812, 6, 30. Sarah Webster (form Dodd) dis mcd
1817, 10, 25. Ruth Hudson (form Dodd) dis mcd
1819, 9, 25. Rebecca Ford (form Dodd) dis mcd

1819, 9, 25. Rebecca Cadwiler (form Dodd) dis mcd
1819, 12, 25. Peninah Collins (form Dodd) dis mcd
1819, 12, 25. Piety dis
1828, 4, 26. Nathan & w, Ruth, gct Somerset MM
1832, 8, 25. Nathan & w, Ruth, rocf Somerset MM, dtd 1832,6,25
1833, 5, 25. Nathan & w, Ruth, & William & James Hadly Arnold, minors in their care, gct Somerset MM

DOTSON
1888, 9, 19. Ellen May (form Arnold) dis mcd

DOUDNA
----, --, --. Henry m Martha DANIELD
```
Ch: Elizabeth  b 1793, 10,  9
    Sally      " 1797,  4,  4 d 1815, 2,29 bur Stillwater
    Margaret   b 1799,  8, 26
    Temperance " 1802,  5, 17
    Mary       " 1804,  1,  1
    Joseph     " 1806,  7,  2
    Milesent   " 1809,  8,  3
    Henry      " 1812,  8, 25
    Martha     " 1814,  7, 18
    James      " 1816, 11, 20
    Sarah      " 1819,  7, 19
```
1810, 3, 14. Anna m Peter SEARS
1813, 4, 7. Peninnah m James LISLE
----, --, --. Knowes m Hannah WEBSTER
```
Ch: Cynah  b 1812,  9,  8 d 1895, 6,28 bur Richland
    David  b 1814,  6,  3
    Sarah  " 1816, 11, 18
    Joseph " 1819, 11,  8
    Hannah " 1822,  4, 12 d 1865,10,21 bur Richland
    Mary   b 1824,  3, 15 " 1895, 2,16 bur Richland
    Elisha b 1826,  6, 19
    John   " 1828,  6,  6 " 1887, 1,28 bur Richland
    Jesse           " 1880,11,30 bur Richland
```
1816, 10, 2. Margaret m Edmund BAILEY
1816, 10, 13. Zilpah m John EDGERTON
1817, 1, 29. Sarah Knowles m Joseph MIDDLETON
1817, 5, 28. Asenath m Benjamin BOSWELL
1818, 4, 2. Charity m Joseph EDGERTON
1818, 10, 29. Anne m Exum PATTERSON
1818, 12, 2. Temperance m Daniel WILLIAMS
1819, 5, 30. Elisha, s John & Miriam (Hall) b
1819, 6, 22. Miriam, w John, d ae 39y 10m 21d bur Ridge Bur. Grounds
1820, 3, 29. Hosea, s John & Sarah (Knowles), Belmont Co., O.; m in Stillwater MH, Mary FARMER, dt Thomas & Ann, Columbiana Co., O., d 1842,4,9 bur Stillwater
```
Ch: Rebeckah  b 1821,  3,  4
```

DOUDNA, Hosea & Mary, continued
 Ch: Ann b 1823, 1, 10
  John " 1826, 9, 27 d 1828, 1, 6
   bur Stillwater
  Thomas b 1828, 1, 1 " 1860, 2,14
   bur Kansas
  Joseph b 1824, 12, 18
  Willoughby " 1830, 11, 8
  Robert " 1833, 12, 1 d 1852, 5,27
   bur Stillwater
  Jason b 1835, 5, 25
  Hosea " 1837, 3, 9 " 1878, 7,25
   bur Stillwater
  Ephraim b 1840, 4, 12
1823, 10, 29. Joel, s John & Sarah, Belmont
 Co., O.; m in Stillwater MH, Rebecca
 HODGINS, dt Wm. & Agnes, Belmont Co., O.,
 d 1877,4,1 bur Stillwater
 Ch: Sarah b 1824, 9, 16
  William " 1826, 10, 17
  Asenath " 1828, 9, 20
  Stephen " 1830, 9, 13 d 1854,12,17
   bur Stillwater
  John b 1832, 12, 17
  Robert " 1835, 3, 11
  Tabitha " 1837, 4, 14
  Eunice " 1840, 3, 7 d 1868, 8,22
   bur Stillwater
  Henry b 1842, 5, 4
  Rebecca " 1844, 2, 4
  Agnes H. " 1846, 8, 31 " 1867, 1,19
   bur Stillwater
  Joel b 1849, 12, 5 " 1864, 2,10
   bur Stillwater
1826, 4, 26. Mary m Thomas PICKET
1828, 1, 6. Henry, s Joel & Rebecca, d bur
 Stillwater
1828, 10, 29. Milisent m Caleb GREGG
1829, 12, 10. William, s John & Miriam, Bel-
 mont Co., O.; m in Richland, Lydia BAILEY,
 dt Jesse & Mary, Guernsey Co., O.
 Ch: Joseph b 1830, 12, 2
  Mary " 1833, 4, 2
  George " 1835, 4, 9
  Ann " 1837, 4, 22
  Hetty " 1839, 6, 3
  Elisha " 1841, 5, 30
  Benjamin " 1843, 1, 15
  Lydia Jane " 1846, 11, 2
1830, 10, 7. Joseph, s Henry & Martha, Bel-
 mont Co., O.; m in Plainfield, Mary VANLAW,
 dt John & Sarah, Belmont Co., O.
 Ch: Jeptha b 1831, 7, 16
  Samuel " 1833, 6, 3
1833, 5, 1. Isaac, s John & Miriam (Hall),
 Belmont Co., O.; m in Stillwater MH, Mar-
 tha PEEBLES, dt Mordecai & Deborah, Bel-
 mont Co., O.
1836, 12, 7. Sarah m Nathan BUNDY
1843, 3, 9. Joseph, s Knowles & Hannah,
 Guernsey Co., O.; m in Richland, Phebe
 SMITH, dt John S. & Elizabeth, Guernsey
 Co., O.

 Ch: John b 1844, 1, 17
  Hannah " 1846, 10, 10
1843, 4, 26. Ann m John CREW
----, --, --. Elisha m Mary PICKETT d 1860,
 2,4 bur Stillwater
 Ch: Abigail b 1844, 5, 17
  Hannah " 1846, 4, 24
  James " 1848, 7, 6 d 1852, 1, 7
   bur Stillwater
  Miriam b 1851, 3, 12
  Thomas P. b 1853, 3, 5
  Matilda " 1854, 10, 12
  Nathan M. " 1856, 12, 16
----, --, --. John & Asenath (Garretson)
 Ch: Jesse I. b 1844, 6, 8 d 1928, 5,30
1844, 3, 27. Sarah m Chalkley BUNDY
1847, 6, 30. Asenath m William BUNDY
1852, 9, 7. Louisa, w Jesse I., dt Eli &
 Pharabi (Bailey) Patterson, b
1853, 3, 9. John, s Joel & Rebecca, Belmont
 Co., O.; m in Stillwater MH, Mary BUNDY,
 dt Eli & Sarah, Belmont Co., O.
1853, 9, 29. John, s Knowles & Hannah, Guern-
 sey Co., O.; m in Richland, Mary Jane
 CARTER, dt Samuel & Susanna, Guernsey Co.,
 O., d 1895,9,21 bur Richland
 Ch: Hannah
  Anne b 1854, 12, 21
  Samuel C. " 1857, 3, 3
  Martha
  Ellen " 1859, 8, 11
  Tabitha C. " 1861, 11, 27
  John El-
  wood " 1864, 2, 28
  Mary Jane " 1865, 11, 10
  Willis E. " 1874, 5, 23 d 1887,10,10
   bur Richland
  Eddie b 1876, 11, 28
----, --, --. Thomas m Rachel ----- d 1907,6,
 13 bur Salem, O.
 Ch: Mary b 1855, 3, 24
  Ann " 1857, 1, 9
1855, 11, 7. Robert H., s Joel & Rebecca
 (Hodgin), Belmont Co., O.; m in Still-
 water MH, Esther BUNDY, dt Eli & Sarah,
 Belmont Co., O.
1858, 11, 3. Knowes, s John & Sarah (Knowles)
 d bur Richland
1858, 12, 29. Tabitha m Wm. P. BUNDY
1859, 4, 27. Jason, s Hosea & Mary, Guernsey
 Co., O.; m in Stillwater MH, Mary BARBER,
 dt Abraham & Rachel, Guernsey Co., O.
 Ch: Charles b 1860, 3, 17
  Rachel " 1861, 10, 31
  Elwood " 1863, 8, 17
1860, 5, 30. Alonzo b
1861, 3, 6. Hosea, s Hosea & Mary, Belmont
 Co., O.; m in Stillwater MH, Mary PLUMMER,
 dt Robert & Jane, Belmont Co., O., b 1837,
 12,11 d 1928,2,28 bur Stillwater
1864, 4, 27. Rebecca m William BUNDY
1867, 1, 31. Joel, s John & Sarah (Knowles),
 d bur Stillwater

DOUDNA, continued

1871, 11, 1. Mary H. m Simeon S. HOYLE
1871, 12, 15. Josiah W., s Joseph & Belinda, Belmont Co., O.; m in Stillwater MH, Ruth BUNDY, dt John & Anna, Belmont Co., O.
1873, 3, 26. Mary D. m John H. BUNDY
1875, 4, 29. Joseph, s John & Asenath (Garretson), Belmont Co., O.; m in Richland, Rosetta HALL, dt Joseph W. & Sarah (Webster), Guernsey Co., O.
1878, 3, 27. Anna m George K. SMITH
----, --, --. John m Anna B. DOUDNA
        Ch: Laura A.   b 1886, 10, 29
            Erma L.   " 1889, 3, 23
1885, 12, 21. Martha E. m Lindley HALL
1893, 6, 28. Lillian M. m Edwin M. Bailey
1893, 12, 6. Albert H., s Josiah W. & Ruth B., Belmont Co., O.; m in Stillwater MH, Blanche D. HALL, dt Thomas P. & Rebecca W., Belmont Co., O.
        Ch: Waneta M. b 1894, 12, 13
            Frances P. " 1903, 9, 20
1896, 5, 7. Belinda, w Joseph T., dt Joseph & Ruth Hobson, d
1898, 12, 7. Joseph F., s Hosea & Mary, Belmont Co., O.; m in Stillwater MH, Ann Eliza WILSON, dt Israel & Catharine, Belmont Co., O.
1899, 1, 22. Rachel Ann (Lupton), w Elisha, d bur Richland
1905, 6, 22. Joseph H., s Joseph W. & Rosetta H., Belmont Co., O.; m in Richland, Norah E. HARTLEY, dt Thomas & Rosella, Guernsey Co., O.
1909, 5, 20. Erma L. m Elmer I. HALL
1926, 6, 16. Chester E., s Joseph H. & Nora E., Belmont Co., O.; m in Richland, Marion Ethlyn HALL, dt Louis L. & Anna M., Guernsey Co., O.

1813, 9, 28. Patty (later given Martha) & ch, Sally, Margaret, Temperance, Mary, Joseph, Milicent & Henry, recrq
1818, 1, 24. Henry recrq
1830, 5, 22. William rocf Somerset MM, dtd 1830,4,26
1833, 7, 27. Martha gct Somerset MM
1835, 3, 28. Henry gct Short Creek MM, to m Matilda Bird
1835, 11, 28. Henry Jr. gct Short Creek MM
1836, 4, 23. Joseph & w, Mary, & ch, Jeptha, Samuel & Joshua, gct Pennsville MM
1837, 2, 25. James gct Pennsville MM, to m Sarah Deweese
1837, 4, 22. Henry & w, Martha, gct Pennsville MM
1837, 4, 22. James gct Pennsville MM
1837, 4, 22. Martha Jr. gct Pennsville MM
1840, 5, 23. Rebecca Blowers (form Doudna) dis mcd
1840, 11, 28. Lydia dis disunity
1841, 12, 25. Mary P. rocf Pennsville MM, dtd 1841,12,16

1842, 8, 27. Elisha rocf Somerset MM, dtd 1842,4,25
1843, 10, 28. Sarah Carter (form Doudna) dis mcd
1847, 10, 23. Joseph gct Flushing MM, to m Belinda Hobson
1847, 12, 25. William dis mcd
1848, 3, 25. Mary Grubs (form Doudna) dis mcd
1848, 7, 22. Joseph gct Flushing MM
1849, 8, 25. Knowis dis mcd
1853, 4, 23. John & w, Mary B., gct Chesterfield MM
1854, 1, 28. Thomas gct Flushing MM, to m Rachel Wood
1854, 6, 21. Rachel W. rocf Pennsville MM, dtd 1854,1,19
1855, 7, 20. Mary J. (form Carter) dis mcd (H)
1855, 7, 28. David dis mcd
1856, 9, 27. Robert H. & w, Esther, gct Chesterfield MM
1860, 6, 23. Willoughby dis mcd
1862, 7, 19. Rachel L. (form Benson) con mcd (H)
1862, 9, 27. Elisha & fam gct Somerset MM
1862, 9, 27. Abigail gct Somerset MM
1862, 10, 25. Jesse con mcd
1863, 1, 24. Rachel Ann rocf Somerset MM, dtd 1862,12,29
1863, 6, 27. Hosea dis jG
1864, 2, 29. Joseph & w, Belinda, & ch, Josiah, Mary, Edwin & Ruth, rocf Somerset MM, dtd 1864,1,25
1865, 3, 25. William dis disunity
1865, 3, 25. Ephraim dis volunteering his services at war
1865, 11, 25. Jason & w, Mary, & ch, Charles, Rachel, Elwood & Ann B., gct Flushing MM
1869, 9, 22. Ann Eliza (form Hanson) dis mcd
1873, 3, 19. John S. gct Somerset MM, to m Sarah Thomason
1873, 5, 21. Joseph & w, Phebe, gct Somerset MM
1873, 5, 21. Hannah gct Somerset MM
1873, 12, 24. John S. gct Somerset MM
1875, 3, 24. Eli B., Clarissa & Walter, ch John, rocf Chesterfield MM, dtd 1874,12,19
1876, 8, --. Eli dis mcd
1877, 4, 28. Rosetta gct Somerset MM
1877, 11, 24. Rosa, Claud & Maud, ch in care of Elisha & Rachel Ann Doudna, recrq; no surname given for the children
1881, 7, 20. Hannah Ann Hall (form Doudna) con mcd
1882, 10, 25. Ruth S. Hibbs (form Doudna) dis mcd
1883, 7, 25. Tabitha C. Benson (form Doudna) con mcd
1883, 6, 20. Edwin dis mcd
1885, 9, 23. John E. gct Flushing MM, to m Anna B. Doudna

DOUDNA, continued

1886, 10, 20. Samuel C. dis mcd
1889, 4, 24. Clarissa gct Hickory Grove MM, Ia.
1897, 2, 24. John E. con mcd
1899, 5, 24. Edward B. dis mcd
1899, 6, 21. Mary Jane (form Doudna) dis mcd
1901, 8, 21. Jesse I. & w, Louisa, & ch, William, Wallace & Mary Ethel, rocf Somerset MM, dtd 1901,7,25
1903, 9, 23. Ruth S. dis jas
1903, 10, 21. Josiah W. dis jas
1903, 12, 23. Joseph F. & Ann Eliza W. gct Pasadena MM, Calif.
1904, 1, 20. Albert H. dis jas
1904, 1, 20. Blanche dis jas
1906, 7, 25. Nora E. gct Somerset MM
1908, 4, 22. Russel J., minor, gct Somerset MM
1908, 4, 22. Wallace dis mcd
1910, 9, 21. Alva B. Hartley gct Somerset MM, to m Elizabeth C. Doudna
1910, 10, 19. Alice dis jas
1912, 9, 25. Ernest J. dis jas
1919, 12, 24. Laura A. Beers (form Doudna) dis mcd & jas.
1926, 9, 22. Ethelyn (form Hall) gct Somerset MM

DUVALL

1897, 1, 20. Millie (form Craft) dis mcd

DWIGGINS

1910, 9, 21. Mabel H. (form Hoyle) dis mcd

DYER

1820, 5, 27. Bracket rocf Harlem MM, Dist. of Me., dtd 1816,6,18, end to Alum Creek MM
1876, 9, 20. Amanda (form Arnold) dis mcd & jas

EARSH

1820, 4, 23. John rocf Plainfield MM, dtd 1820,4,20

ECROYD

1866, 5, 26. John & w, Sarah, & ch, John H. & Louisa, gct Coal Creek MM, Iowa
1866, 6, 23. Henry gct Coal Creek MM, Iowa

EDGERTON

----, --, --. James & Sarah
  Ch: William   d 1827,12, 6
          ae 28y 7m 8d bur Captina
      Mary   d 1828, 1, 8
          ae 23y 8m 27d bur Captina
      Walter   b 1806, 8, 6
      Aquilla   " 1810, 9, 10 d 1827,12, 8
          ae 17y 2m 18d bur Captina
----, --, --. Richard m Mary HALL
  Ch: Christiana b 1809, 1, 13
      Nathan   " 1810, 11, 19

Ch: Anna   b 1811, 5, 14
    Jesse   " 1817, 7, 30
1811, 7, 7. Rachel, dt James & Anna, b
1813, 2, 17. Ruth, dt Richard & Mary, b
1813, 4, 19. Nathan d
1813, 9, 16. Reuben, s Joseph & Martha, Belmont Co., O.; m in Captene, Patience HANSON, dt Elijah & Susannah, Belmont Co., O.
  Ch: Avice   b 1814, 6, 13
      Louisa   " 1816, 11, 13 d 1817, 2,15
      Benajah   " 1816, 11, 13
      Elizabeth " 1818, 10, 22
1815, 11, 25. Nathan, s James & Anna (Hall), b
1816, 10, 13. John, s James & Sarah, Belmont Co., O.; m in Stillwater MH, Zilpah DOUDNA dt John & Sarah (Knowles), Belmont Co., O.
  Ch: Abijah   b 1817, 8, 26
      Elizabeth " 1819, 5, 7
      James   " 1823, 7, 26
      Asenath   " 1825, 2, 9
      Richard   " 1827, 4, 7
      John   " 1829, 5, 19
      Sarah   " 1833, 6, 8
1821, 8, 2. Sarah m Wm. MOTT
1817, 7, 31. William, s Joseph & Martha, Belmont Co., O.; m in Capteen, Nelly FRAZIER, dt Daniel & Nelly, Belmont Co., O.
1818, 4, 2. Joseph, s James & Sarah, Belmont Co., O.; m in Ridge, Charity DOUDNY, dt John & Miriam
----, --, --. William & Sarah
  Ch: Jane   b 1823, 10, 19
      Bathsheba " 1825, 6, 28
      Ann   " 1827, 2, 26
1825, 1, 21. James d ae 60 bur Captina
1828, 1, 18. Sarah d ae 58y 4m 23d
1837, 11, 28. Abijah, s John & Zilpha, Athens Co., O.; m in Captina, Rhoda VERNON, dt Robert & Deborah, Belmont Co., O.
----, --, --. David, s James, d 1904,6,1 bur Stillwater; m Esther ELLYSON, d 1907,9,14 bur Stillwater
  Ch: Robert   b 1850, 12, 19 d 1931, 5, 3
      Sarah S. " 1853, 1, 3
1857, 4, 29. John, s Joseph & Charity, Belmont Co., O.; m in Stillwater MH, Asenath HODGIN, dt Eli & Mary, Belmont Co., O.
----, --, --. James & Amy
  Ch: John
      Clarkson b 1878, 11, 16
      Carleton " 1881, 6, 8
      Esther   " 1883, 3, 6
----, --, --. Wm. D., s James & Mary Ann (Williams), b 1854,9,3; m Louisa GIBBONS, dt Wm. & Caroline (Tomlinson), b 1858,2, 26 d 1923,5,4 bur Stillwater
  Ch: Mary Emma b 1884, 8, 22
1892, 9, 23. Ellen B. m Thomas E. PARKER
1898, 9, 7. Walter J., s James & Mary Ann, Belmont Co., O., b 1871,1,11 d 1928,9,24; m in Stillwater MH, Anna R. TABER, dt Joseph John & Mary, Belmont Co., O.

EDGERTON, Walter J. & Anna R., continued
  Ch: Elizabeth
      M.   b 1908, 6, 10
      Mabel S.   " 1912, 5, 1
      Louis J.   " 1914, 1, 28
      Florence   " 1918, 10, 27
1899, 11, 2. Anna m William DEWEES
1903, 4, 18. Dessie Terrell b
1903, 8, 20. Esther m Wm. P. JOHNSON
1903, 9, 9. J. Clarkson, s James & Amy L.,
    Belmont Co., O., b 1878,11,16; m in Still-
    water MH, Anna E. BAILEY, dt Dempsey &
    Sarah E., Belmont Co., O., b 1877,9,17
    Ch: Gilbert D. b 1904, 9, 7
        Willard B. " 1907, 9, 10
1917, 5, 2. Jesse N., s Walter & Mary, Colum-
    biana Co., O.; m in Stillwater MH, Minerva
    E. COFFMAN, dt (foster) Elmer & Elizabeth
    HOGE, Belmont Co., O., b 1893,1,23
1930, 6, 6. Elizabeth m Glenn R. ROCKWELL

1808, 6, 28. Mary rocf Short Creek MM, dtd
    1808,6,21
1810, 8, 28. James Jr. gct Short Creek MM,
    to m Anna Hall
1810, 12, 25. Ann rocf Short Creek MM, dtd
    1810,12,18
1812, 12, 29. Reuben rocf Deer Creek MM, dtd
    1812,9,5
1815, 11, 28. Samuel & w, Elizabeth, & ch,
    William, Sarah, Hannah, Prudence, Rachel
    & Tabitha, gct Miami MM
1815, 11, 28. Joseph & w, Martha, & ch,
    William, Joseph, Samuel, Martha & Daniel,
    rocf Deep Creek MM, N. C., dtd 1815,8,5
1819, 2, 27. Reuben & w, Patience, & fam gct
    Darby Creek MM
1819, 6, 26. Thomas & w, Mary, recrq
1819, 7, 24. Thomas & w, Mary, gct Darby
    Creek MM
1821, 3, 24. Joseph & w, Martha, & ch, Sam-
    uel, Martha & Daniel, gct Derby Creek MM
1822, 9, 28. William gct Plainfield MM, to
    m Sarah Foulke
1823, 1, 25. Sarah Jr. rocf Plainfield MM,
    dtd 1822,12,26
1826, 10, 28. Walter gct Somerset MM, to m
    Rebecca Cox
1830, 8, 28. Sarah dis JH
1835, 4, 25. John & w, Zilpha, & ch, Abijah,
    Elizabeth, James, Asenath, Richard, John
    & Sarah, gct Deerfield MM
1836, 11, 19. Sarah & ch, Jane, Bathsheba &
    Ann, gct Plainfield MM (H)
1838, 1, 27. Rhoda gct Chesterfield MM
1849, 1, 27. John Bundy gct Somerset MM, to
    m Anna Edgerton
1857, 7, 25. Asenath gct Somerset MM
1877, 7, 25. David & w, Esther, & ch,
    Charles & Ellen, rocf Somerset MM, dtd
    1877,5,24
1878, 2, 20. James Jr. rocf Short Creek MM
1884, 7, 23. Charles gct Evesham MM, N. J.

1887, 3, 23. James gct New Garden MM, Pa.
1889, 3, 20. Wm. D. & w, Louisa, & ch, Alice
    Caroline & Mary Emma, rocf Somerset MM,
    dtd 1889,2,21
1890, 11, 19. John Clarkson, Carelton & Es-
    ther, ch James, recrq
1901, 6, 19. Jesse & w, Susan G., rocf
    Middleton MM, dtd 1901,6,15
1904, 4, 20. Walter J. rocf Somerset MM, dtd
    1904,3,24
1906, 5, 23. Jesse & w, Susan G., gct
    Springfield MM
1907, 6, 19. Alice McMillan (form Edgerton)
    dis mcd & jas
1911, 3, 22. Dessie T., foster dt Wm. D. &
    Louisa, recrq
1911, 10, 25. Henry Alden Hall gct New Garden
    MM, O., to m Anna Mabel Edgerton
1918, 12, 25. Minerva E. gct New Garden MM, O.
1930, 1, 22. J. Clarkson & w, Anna B., gct
    Salem MM, O.

EDMUNDSON
1838, 7, 28. William rocf Wilmington MM,
    Del., dtd 1837,6,3
1910, 6, 22. Franklin rst on consent of Coal
    Creek MM, Ia.
1910, 6, 22. Mary Irene, dt Franklin & Alice
    H., recrq
1910, 7, 20. Alice H. rst on consent of
    Cottonwood MM, Kans.
1918, 3, 20. Irene Beatty (form Edmundson)
    con mcd
1919, 4, 23. Franklin & Alice transferred to
    Fairhope MM, Ala.

ELKINTON
1885, 9, 24. Alfred C., s Joseph S. & Malin-
    da (Patterson), Phila., Pa.; m in Barns-
    ville MH, Abby WALTON, dt Samuel & Sarah
    (Edgerton), Belmont Co., O.

1886, 3, 24. Abby W. gct Phila. MM, Pa.

ELLIOTT
1829, 5, 23. Elizabeth dis JH
1829, 5, 23. John dis JH
1829, 5, 23. Lamira dis JH
1829, 5, 23. Rachel dis JH
1829, 10, 24. Elijah dis JH
1829, 12, 26. Resea dis JH
1832, 4, 28. Joel dis JH
1844, 6, 22. Samira Willets (form Elliott)
    rst at Alum Creek MM on consent of this
    mtg

ELLYSON
1844, 6, 26. Robert, s Zachariah & Mary,
    Columbiana Co., O.; m in Stillwater MH,
    Mary RATCLIFF, dt Jaon & Tacy HALL, Bel-
    mont Co., O.
1904, 9, 22. Lewis N., s Benjamin & Elma
    C., Cedar Co., Iowa; m in Stillwater MH,

ELLYSON, Lewis, continued
    Ethel E. BAILEY, dt Allen & Eva L., Bel-
    mont Co., O., b 1881,2,18

1844, 9, 28. Mary & s, Josiah C. Ratcliff,
    gct Upper Springfield MM
1932, 4, 20. Ethel Bailey gct West Branch MM,
    Ia.

ELY
1857, 8, 15. Emily rocf Plainfield MM, dtd
    1857,7,16 (H)

EMBREE
1816, 5, 15. Samuel Jr., s Samuel & Hannah, b
1817, 1, 1. Phebe m Wm. PATTON
1817, 9, 3. Lydia m Robert MILLER
1823, 3, 26. Joseph, s Samuel & Hannah, Bel-
    mont Co., O.; m in Stillwater MH, Rebecca
    CLENDENNON, dt Isaac & Hannah, Belmont
    Co., O.
      Ch: Eliza   b 1823, 12, 26 d 1824, 2, 6
          bur Stillwater
        Maria   b 1825, 1, 20
1833, 12, 12. Israel, s Samuel & Hannah, Mor-
    gan Co., O.; m in Captina, Mary Ann VERNON,
    dt Robert & Deborah, Belmont Co., O.
----, --, --. James & Keziah
    Ch: William A. b 1834, 5, 25
        John P.   " 1835, 8, 25
----, --, --. John & Huldah
    Ch: Jonah   b 1834, 7, 8 d 1836, 9, 6
1835, 6, 4. Elizabeth m Joshua BAILEY
1840, 2, 26. John d

1816, 3, 23. Lydia rocf Short Creek MM, dtd
    1816,2,20
1816, 3, 23. Samuel & w, Hannah, & ch, Jo-
    seph, Phebe, John, James, Jesse, Israel
    & Isaac, rocf Short Creek MM, dtd 1816,2,
    20
1833, 5, 25. Israel rocf Deerfield MM, dtd
    1833,5,16
1833, 9, 28. Samuel Bailey gct Short Creek
    MM, to m Harriet Embree
1834, 1, 25. Israel & w, Maryann, gct Deer-
    field MM
1834, 4, 26. Elizabeth rocf Short Creek MM,
    dtd 1834,3,18
1834, 7, 26. John & w, Huldah, & ch, Edith,
    John, Abigail, Mordecai & Sarah, rocf
    Short Creek MM, dtd 1834,5,20
1836, 2, 27. James & w, Kesiah, & ch, William
    & John P., rocf Short Creek MM, dtd 1835,
    12,22
1839, 12, 28. James & w, Keziah, & ch, William
    A., John P. & Lucinda, gct Short Creek MM
1842, 4, 23. Edith Hiatt (form Embree) dis
    mcd
1844, 3, 23. John dis disunity
1846, 2, 28. Abigail dis disunity
1846, 8, 22. Sarah McCane (form Embree) dis
    mcd

1851, 8, 23. Mordecai dis mcd
1861, 12, 28. Achsah recrq (residing in Linn
    Co., Ia.)

EMMONS
1893, 1, 26. Louis W., s Abner & Rachel
    (Crew), Keokuk Co., Ia.; m in Stillwater
    MH, Aurora E. BUNDY, dt Nathan W. & Anna
    D., Belmont Co., O.

1896, 3, 25. Aurora E. gct Coal Creek MM, Ia.
1896, 10, 21. Randall, infant s Louis W. &
    Aurora E., gct Coal Creek MM, Ia.

ENDICOTT
1842, 11, 26. Susannah (form Hanson) con mcd
1864, 8, 27. Susannah dis disunity

ENGLAND
1822, 12, 22. Esther rocf Westland MM, dtd
    1822,9,26

ENGLE
----, --, --. Caleb & Mercy
    Ch: Elizabeth b 1796, 8, 12
        John   " 1800, 9, 13
        Mary   " 1802, 8, 11
        Rebecca   " 1804, 5, 6
        Anna M.   " 1806, 5, 20
        Caleb   " 1808, 6, 12
        Mariah   " 1813, 3, 17
1816, 2, 28. Caleb, s Abraham & Patience,
    Belmont Co., O.; m in Stillwater MH, Ra-
    chel PLUMMER, dt John & Mary, Belmont Co.,
    O.
1818, 4, 29. Elizabeth m Jesse BECK
1822, 3, 27. John, s Caleb & Mercy, Belmont
    Co., O.; m in Stillwater MH, Deborah
    WATSON, dt Abner & Elizabeth, Belmont Co.,
    O., d 1836,9,10
      Ch: Maria   b 1823, 7, 3
        Jesse B.   " 1825, 10, 11 d 1825,12,3
        bur Stillwater
        Sarah B.   b 1828, 1, 6
        Mary   " 1830, 9, 18
1822, 10, 2. Mary m Eli HODGINS
1824, 6, 2. Anna M. m John MARSHALL
1829, 4, 29. Caleb, s Caleb & Mercy, Belmont
    Co., O.; m in Stillwater MH, Sarah FAW-
    CETT, dt Richard & Mary, Belmont Co., O.
      Ch: Mary   b 1830, 4, 13 d 1830, 6,26
        bur Stillwater
        Richard   b 1831, 11, 9
1830, 10, 27. Mariah m Ezekiel BUNDY
1839, 6, 19. Joshua, s Joshua & Hannah, Green
    Co., O.; m in Richland, Sarah A. SWAYNE,
    dt Samuel & Margaret, Guernsey Co., O.
1847, 4, 12. Caleb d bur Stillwater
1851, 1, 2. Mary m Isaac HARTLEY
1856, 4, 22. Rachel, w Caleb, d bur Still-
    water

1816, 5, 25. Caleb & ch, Mary, Rebecca, Anna

ENGLE, continued
    Mercy, Caleb & Maria, rocf Plainfield MM,
    dtd 1816,4,26
1816, 5, 25. Elizabeth rocf Plainfield MM,
    dtd 1816,5,24
1822, 6, 22. Rebecca Smith (form Engle) dis
    mcd
1830, 4, 24. Elizabeth (form Willits) rst at
    Short Creek MM, on consent of this mtg
1830, 5, 22. Elizabeth gct Clear Creek MM
1834, 1, 25. Caleb Jr. & w, Sarah, & ch,
    Richard & John, gct Deerfield MM
1837, 1, 28. John & ch, Mariah, Sarah &
    Ephraim gct Pennsville MM
1839, 8, 17. Sarah A. gct Greenplain MM (H)
1853, 8, 27. Ephraim W., minor, rocf Plymouth
    MM, dtd 1853,6,20

EVES
1818, 10, 24. Hannah, dt James & Susannah,
    recrq
1818, 11, 28. Susannah rst on consent of Con-
    cord MM
1821, 2, 24. James recrq
1836, 5, 21. James & w, Susanna, & ch, Lydia,
    Ruthan, John, Susan, Ellen, Mary & Agnes
    S., gct Deerfield MM (H)

EWERS
-----, --, --. William & Amy
    Ch: Amy   b 1815, 1, 18
        Lydia
        Jesse
1839, 6, 19. William, s John & Sarah, Belmont
    Co., O.; m in Somerset, Abigail STANTON,
    dt William & Lydia, Belmont Co., O.

1829, 2, 28. Gladney dis JH
1829, 2, 28. William dis JH
1829, 3, 28. Amy dis JH
1829, 3, 28. Lydia dis JH
1832, 10, 27. Amy dis JH
1833, 1, 26. Jesse dis JH
1834, 6, 28. Martha (form Wood) dis mcd
1857, 12, 26. Zilpha W. (form Hanson) dis mcd

FARMER
1816, 11, 27. William, s Wm. & Catharine,
    Montgomery Co., O.; m in Stillwater MH,
    Ruth WILLIAMS, dt Daniel & Mary, Montgom-
    ery Co., O.
1820, 3, 29. Mary m Hosea DOUDNA
1833, 4, 4. Elijah, s Joseph & Amelia, Bel-
    mont Co., O.; m in Plainfield, Sarah
    GREGG, dt Stephen & Cenith, Belmont Co.,
    O.
----, --, --. Taylor & Mary Ann
    Ch: Joseph   b 1835, 10, 10
        Adaline   " 1837, 6, 21
1839, 10, 30. Rachel m Aquilla CREW

1817, 2, 22. Ruth gct West Branch MM
1820, 2, 26. Mary rocf New Garden MM, O., dtd

1820,11,25
1820, 7, 22. Susannah rocf New Garden MM,
    O., dtd 1820,3,23
1820, 12, 23. Ann, a minister, & ch, Tabitha,
    Joseph, Taylor, Jesse, Rachel & Thomas,
    rocf New Garden MM, dtd 1820,11,23
1821, 7, 28. Taylor, a minor in care of Jo-
    seph Jones & w gct Flushing MM
1821, 12, 21. Ann & ch, Susannah, Tabitha,
    Joseph, Rachel & Thomas, gct Flushing MM
1830, 9, 25. Uriah Bailey gct Flushing MM,
    to m Susannah Farmer
1831, 5, 28. Jesse gct Upper Springfield MM
    (dt Ann Langstaff)
1833, 4, 27. Jesse rocf Upper Springfield MM;
    returned not in limits of this MM
1835, 1, 24. Taylor & w, Maryann, rocf Flush-
    ing MM, dtd 1834,12,20
1836, 5, 28. Rachel rocf Upper Springfield
    MM, dtd 1836,4,23
1837, 10, 22. William J. Parker gct Sandy
    Spring MM, to m Ann Farmer
1839, 9, 28. Taylor & w, Mary Ann, & ch, Jo-
    seph & Adaline, gct Flushing MM

FARO
1828, 1, 26. Rachel recrq
1830, 9, 25. Rachel [Farrow] dis JH

FARQUHAR
1842, 10, 22. David rocf Short Creek MM, dtd
    1842,8,25
1846, 3, 25. David gct Milford MM, Ind.

FARRA
1838, 2, 28. Levina m Uriah PRICE (H)

FAWCETT
----, --, --. Samuel & Rachel
    Ch: Elizabeth b 1806, 3, 1
        Benjamin   " 1807, 11, 18
        Mariah   " 1810, 1, 16
        John Smith " 1814, 9, 30
1808, 4, 27. Elizabeth, dt Richard & Sarah,
    b
1811, 9, 11. Richard, s Richard & Mary, Bel-
    mont Co., O.; m in Stillwater MH, Mary
    WILLIAMS, dt Daniel & Mary, Belmont Co.,O.
    Ch: Sarah   b 1812, 5, 30
        Philip   " 1814, 2, 19
        Mary   " 1815, 2, 26
        Samuel   " 1817, 4, 10
        Sibilla   " 1819, 4, 15
        Rachel   " 1820, 12, 26 d 1838,10,
        14 bur Stillwater
        Ruth   b 1822, 1, 22
        Lydia   " 1826, 7, 15
        Joel   " 1810, 4, -- (sic)
1813, 1, 6. Jonathan, s Richard & Mary,
    Belmont Co., O.; m in Stillwater MH, Re-
    becca STRAHL, dt John & Ann, Belmont Co.,
    O.
    Ch: Jesse   b 1813, 11, 5

FAWCETT, Jonathan & Rebecca, continued
  Ch: Mary Ann b 1815, 12, 14 d 1823, 9, 1
    bur Stillwater
    Eli   b 1818, 4, 27
    Martha W. " 1820, 7, 13
    Armela " 1822, 12, 4
    Sarah   " 1825, 4, 8
1826, 7, 17. Mary d ae 36y 6m 25d bur Stillwater
1827, 3, 7. Elizabeth m Joel GARRETSON
1828, 4, 30. Richard, s Richard & Mary, Belmont Co., O.; m in Stillwater MH, Deborah
 PEEBLES, dt Anderson & Huldah SIMMONS,
 Belmont Co., O.
  Ch: Eli   b 1829, 2, 4
    Jane   " 1831, 6, 11
    Deborah " 1835, 4, 5
1829, 4, 29. Sarah m Caleb ENGLE
1835, 12, 9. Mary m Joseph SMITH
1838, 12, 26. Sibilla m Austen SIMPSON
1839, 8, 1. Rachel, dt Samuel & Mary Ann, b
1840, 9, 14. Richard d bur Stillwater
1848, 11, 29. Jeptha, s William & Abigail,
 Mahoney Co., O.; m in Stillwater MH, Rachel WILLIAMS, dt Daniel & Temperance,
 Belmont Co., O.
1879, 9, 25. Jason, s Abner & Martha (Doudna)
 Morgan Co., O.; m in Stillwater MH, Mary
 E. BUNDY, dt Charles & Sarah

1811, 8, 27. Richard & dt, Elizabeth, rocf
 Plainfield MM, dtd 1811,5,25
1813, 6, 29. Jonathan [Faucet] rocf Plainfield
 MM, dtd 1813,6,22
1814, 3, 29. Jonathan & w, Rebecca, & ch,
 Jesse, gct Plainfield MM
1815, 5, 30. Jonathan & w, Rebecca, & s, Jesse,
 rocf Plainfield MM, dtd 1815,4,22
1818, 10, 24. Elizabeth, Benjamin, Maria &
 John [Faucet], ch Rachel McNichols, rocf
 Plainfield MM, dtd 1818,9,24
1825, 8, 27. Jonathan & w, Rebecca, & ch,
 Jesse, Eli, Martha, Amelia & Sarah, gct
 Flushing MM
1828, 1, 26. Maria McNichols (form Fawcett)
 dis mcd
1828, 2, 23. Benjamin gct Plainfield MM, to
 m Lydia Horner
1828, 6, 28. Elizabeth gct Somerset MM
1829, 1, 24. Rachel dis jH
1829, 2, 28. Thomas dis jH
1829, 7, 25. Amos gct Salem MM
1830, 8, 28. Lydia (form Miller) dis mcd
1832, 10, 27. Benjamin & w, Lydiann, & ch,
 Samuel & Rachel, gct Somerset MM
1833, 5, 25. Sarah gct Flushing MM
1833, 10, 26. John S. rocf Somerset MM, dtd
 1833,8,26
1835, 8, 22. John gct Somerset MM
1839, 3, 23. Mary Ann rocf Pennsville MM,
 dtd 1839,2,14
1840, 11, 28. Samuel & w, Mary, & dt, Rachel,
 gct Chesterfield MM

1841, 10. 23. Deborah & ch, Lydia & Eli,
 Jane & Deborah, gct Chesterfield MM
1841, 10, 23. Ruth gct Chesterfield MM
1849, 6, 23. Rachel gct Upper Springfield MM
1880, 6, 23. Mary E. gct Chesterfield MM

FINLEY
1886, 10, 20. Melissa (form Hartley) dis mcd
1893, 7, 19. Minnie (form Hartley) dis mcd
1917, 8, 22. Elsie (form Hall) dis mcd

FISHER
----, --, --. John & Sarah
  Ch: Joseph b 1804, 5, 29
    John   " 1811, 11, 15
1825, 4, 27. Joseph, s John & Sarah, Belmont
 Co., O.; m in Stillwater MH, Hannah HARRY,
 dt Absolam & Rebecca, Washington Co., O.
  Ch: William b 1826, 6, 13
    Sarah " 1828, 9, 7

1817, 11, 22. Rebecca, minor, rocf Plainfield
 MM, dtd 1817,9,24
1818, 1, 24. Joseph, minor, rocf Plainfield
 MM, dtd 1817,11,20
1820, 6, 24. Rebeckah, minor in care of
 Elizabeth Pickering, gct Flushing MM
1821, 8, 25. John, minor, rocf Flushing MM,
 dtd 1821,7,27
1828, 3, 22. John gct Flushing MM
1829, 12, 26. John, minor, rocf Flushing MM,
 dtd 1829,9,24
1832, 1, 28. Joseph dis mcd
1833, 10, 26. John dis disunity
1841, 6, 26. William & Hannah, ch Joseph,
 gct Chesterfield MM

FLANNER
----, --, --. Thomas m Keziah ---- d 1825,11,
 29 ae 20y 7m 21d
  Ch: Casper
    Wister b 1823, 10, 22

1825, 3, 3. William, s Thomas & Trinity,
 Jefferson Co., O.; m in Capitina, Catha-
 rine VERNON, dt Benjamin & Esther PATTER-
 SON, Belmont Co., O.

1869, 6, 12. Peninnah, dt Wm. & Peninnah, d
 bur Stillwater
1823, 1, 25. Thomas rocf Short Creek MM,
 dtd 1822,12,24
1823, 7, 26. Thomas dis mcd
1823, 7, 26. Keziah (form Dillon) con mcd
1825, 4, 23. Catharine gct Short Creek MM
1826, 3, 25. Abigail rocf Short Creek MM,
 dtd 1825,12,20
1831, 6, 25. Abigail gct Short Creek MM
1845, 5, 24. Thomas W. dis mcd
1845, 11, 22. Keziah Hazelett (form Flanner)
 dis mcd
1861, 1, 26. Peninah rocf Somerset MM, dtd
 1860,10,29

FORD
1819, 9, 25. Rebecca (form Dodd) dis mcd

FOSTER
1924, 9, 5. Henry Cope, s Horace B. & Mary C., Kent Co., R. I.; m in Stillwater MH, Thyra Jane MEYERS, dt Joseph E. & Mary W., Belmont Co., O.
1930, 11, 29. Marianna m W. Mifflin HALL

1925, 11, 25. Thyra Jane gct Nantucket MM, R. I.
1930, 9, 24. Mariana rocf Scipio MM, N. Y., dtd 1930,8,20

FOULKE
1817, 2, 19. John b
----,--,--. Thomas & -----
    Ch: Joshua   b 1823, 5, 30
        Milten   " 1826, 1, 23
        Phebe   " 1827, 10, 21
----,--,--. Juda d 1847,11,30 bur Richland; m Sarah ----- d 1843,10,30

1822, 9, 28. William Edgerton gct Plainfield MM, to m Sarah Foulke
1826, 12, 23. Thomas & w, Sarah, & ch, Joshua & Milton, rocf Plainfield MM, dtd 1826,8, 4.
1828, 12, 27. Thomas dis jH
1829, 1, 24. Aaron dis jH
1829, 1, 24. Barton dis jH
1829, 1, 24. Hannah dis jH
1829, 1, 24. Issachar dis jH
1829, 1, 24. Jane dis jH
1829, 1, 24. Priscilla dis jH
1829, 3, 28. Sarah dis jH
1829, 5, 23. Judah & w, Sarah, & ch, Silas & John, rocf Somerset MM, dtd 1829,4,27
1831, 10, 22. Silas gct Short Creek MM (a minor)
1834, 7, 26. Silas rocf Short Creek MM, dtd 1834,7,22
1835, 8, 22. Silas dis mcd
1835, 11, 28. Hannah (form Webster) dis mcd
1839, 8, 17. Sarah & ch, Joshua, Milton, Phebe, Mary, Nathan & Miles, gct Deer- field MM
1840, 11, 28. John con mcd
1841, 9, 25. Joshua, Milton, Phebe & Mary, ch Thomas & Sarah, gct Pennsville MM

FRAME
1844, 11, 28. Thomas L., s George & Lydia, Monroe Co., O.; m in house of Wm. Thomas, Elizabeth THOMAS, dt William & Rebecca, Belmont Co., O. (H)
1846, 10, 2. Elizabeth m James SAWYER (H)
1852, 7, 23. William A., s Aaron, b
1855, 10, 8. Florence, w Wm., dt Joseph & Phebe D. (Thomas) Outland, b
1863, 10, 28. Mary Ann m Wm. H. HOLLAWAY
1864, 9, 7. Thompson, s Aaron & Tabitha,

Belmont Co., O.; m in Stillwater MH, Emily BUNDY, dt Demsey & Ann, Belmont Co., O., d 1878,5,26 bur Stillwater
    Ch: Mary T.   b 1867, 11, 21
1864, 9, 28. Amasa, s Aaron & Tabitha, Bel- mont Co., O., d 1896,2,10 bur Stillwater; m in Stillwater MH, Elizabeth R. KENNARD, dt William & Sarah, d 1865,6,4 bur Still- water
1868, 12, 30. Tacy m Milton STARBUCK
1869, 10, 27. Amasa, s Aaron & Tabitha, Bel- mont Co., O.; m in Stillwater MH, Rachel E. PLUMMER. dt Robert & Jane, Belmont Co., O.
    Ch: Elizabeth
        K.   b 1871, 11, 22
        Clara E.   " 1875, 1, 13
1870, 12, 7. Ruanna m Lindley BUNDY
1875, 10, 2. Achsah, w Aaron, (form Smith) d bur Stillwater
-----, --, --. William A. m Laura OUTLAND
    Ch: Lura L.   b 1878, 9, 16
        Emily D.   " 1880, 4, 10
        Joseph A.   " 1891, 4, 9
        Mary Elma   " 1893, 6, 7
1878, 10, 3. Margaret H. m Daniel C. MARTIN (H)
1881, 4, 17. Ruanna (Thompson), mother of Aaron, d bur Stillwater
1892, 10, 6. Ira S., s Aaron & Tabitha, San Diago, Calif.; m in Barnsville MH, Elizabeth BUNDY, dt John & Anna, Belmont Co., O.
1896, 5, 21. Aaron, s Wm. & Ruana, d bur Stillwater
1902, 8, 21. Clara E. m Edward F. STRATTON
1907, 4, 25. Emily Dennis m Charles B.

LLEWELLYN
1863, 5, 23. Amas & Thompson rocf Short Creek MM, dtd 1863,4,21
1863, 9, 26. Mary Ann rocf Short Creek MM, dtd 1863,9,22
1864, 6, 25. Aaron & ch, Tacy T., William A., Oliver C. & Ira S., rocf Hickory Grove MM, Ia., dtd 1864,4,20
1864, 6, 25. Achsah rocf Flushing MM, dtd 1864,5,26
1865, 3, 25. Ruanna T. rocf Hickory Grove MM, Ia., dtd 1865,2,22
1868, 5, 16. Rebecca Beardmore (form Frame) released from mbrp (H)
1868, 9, 19. Ruanna rocf Hickory Grove MM, Ia., dtd 1868,8,19
1872, 7, 20. Mary Selby (form Frame) con mcd (H)
1875, 1, 16. Lyda G. Spencer (form Frame) con mcd (H)
1875, 11, 24. Thompson gct Kennet MM, Pa.
1877, 11, --. William A. con mcd
1881, 7, 18. Thomas L. & w, Elizabeth, & dt, Georgia Anna, gct Miami MM (H)
1881, 7, 18. Phebe Alice gct Miami MM (H)

FRAME, continued
1884, 10, 22. Aaron gct Flushing MM. to m La-
    vinia H. Wright
1885, 2, 25. Mary F., dt Thompson, gct Kennet
    MM, Pa.
1885, 4, 22. Lavina H. rocf Flushing MM, dtd
    1885,3,26
1886, 12, 22. Oliver C. dis mcd
1891, 11, 25. Laura L., Emily D. & Joseph A.,
    ch William A. & Florence M., recrq
1895, 1, 23. Oliver C. rst
1900, 1, 24. Lavina H. gct Hickory Grove MM,
    Ia.
1901, 9, 25. Ira S. & w, Elizabeth B., gct
    Phila. MM, Pa.
1903, 7, 22. Mary E., dt Wm. A. & Florence
    M., recrq
1903, 10, 21. Florence M. recrq
1904, 7, 20. Elizabeth R. Hogue (form Frame)
    dis mcd & jas
1910, 5, 25. Rachel E. gct Salem MM, O.
1915, 2, 24. Lura L. gct Pasadena MM, Calif.
1919, 7, 23. Mary F. Tinder (form Frame) dis
    mcd & jas
1925, 5, 20. Joseph E. dis mcd
1930, 2, 19. William A. & Florence M. gct
    Pasadena MM, Calif.
1931, 10, 21. Oliver C. gct Pasadena MM, Calif.

FRAZIER
1815, 5, 30. Nelly & ch, Nelly, Daniel &
    Ann, rocf Concord MM, dtd 1815,4,20
1815, 5, 30. William rocf Concord MM, dtd
    1815,4,20
1817, 8, 23. William gct Plainfield MM, to m
    Anne Ross
1818, 3, 28. Anna rocf Plainfield MM, dtd
    1818,1,22

FRENCH
1814, 2, 2. Emma m Joseph STEER
1817, 7, 31. Nelly m Wm. EDGERTON
1820, 8, 16. Israel d ae 73y 11m bur Still-
    water
1824, 12, 8. William, s Otho & Elizabeth,
    Belmont Co., O.; m in Stillwater MH, Mary
    BUNDY, dt Wm. & Sarah, Belmont Co., O.
1826, 2, 1. Rhoda Ann m Philip STRAHL

1809, 7, 25. Emma rocf Concord MM, dtd 1809,
    6,22
1822, 10, 26. William recrq
1822, 10, 26. Elizabeth & Rhoda Ann recrq
1827, 4, 28. William dis jas
1827, 4, 28. Mary & s, Eliel, gct Deerfield
    MM
1827, 4, 28. Elizabeth dis jas
1866, 6, 23. Amanda (form Bundy) dis mcd
1866, 10, 27. Sarah (form Dawson) dis mcd
1884, 7, 23. Joseph G. Steer gct Salem MM, to
    m Elmira T. French

GALLOWAY
1850, 9, 25. Sarah Ellen, w Caleb, dt Samuel
    & Sarah (Doudna) Carter, b
1900, 5, 23. Sarah Ellen (form Carter) con
    mcd

GAMBLE
1885, 10, 22. Elisha, s Harrison & Phebe,
    Columbiana Co., O.; m in Barnsville MH,
    Melvina DAWSON, dt Chalkley & Martha, Bel-
    mont Co., O., d 1886,4,13 bur Salem, O.

1820, 7, 22. Elizabeth rocf Concord MM, dtd
    1820,6,21
1913, 7, 23. Edwin Y. rocf Paulina MM, Ia.,
    dtd 1913,8,9
1914, 2, 25. Edward Y. gct Short Creek MM,
    to m Rebecca W. Atkinson

GAMMON
1823, 7, 26. Eliza D. (form Bailey) dis mcd

GARRET
1826, 6, 24. William rocf White Water MM,
    dtd 1826,5,20
1827, 6, 23. William gct White Water MM

GARRETSON
----, --, --. Joseph m Elizabeth WILLIAMS
    Ch: Asenith   b 1805, 1, 25
        Asa   " 1807, 6, 5
        Joseph   " 1811, 8, 3
        Elizabeth " 1815, 9, 21
1827, 3, 7. Joel, s John & Henrietta, Bel-
    mont Co., O.; m in Stillwater MH, Eliza-
    beth FAWCETT, dt Richard & Sarah, Belmont
    Co., O.
1859, 9, 28. Martha m Chalkley DAWSON
1873, 3, 5. Joseph, s Asa & Ruth, Belmont
    Co., O.; m in Stillwater MH, Melvina
    BAILEY, dt Hezekiah & Elizabeth, Belmont
    Co., O., d 1875,10,15
    Ch: Mary
        Leora   b 1874, 2, 14
----, --, --. Asa d 1890,10,27 bur Stillwater;
    m Ruth EDGERTON, dt Richard & Mary, d
    1877,6,24 bur Stillwater

1811, 10, 29. Joseph & w, Elizabeth, & ch,
    Asenath, Asa & Joseph, rocf Concord MM,
    dtd 1811,8,22
1826, 12, 23. Joel rocf Plainfield MM, dtd
    1826,11,23
1830, 4, 24. Joel & w, Elizabeth, & s, Wil-
    liam, gct Deerfield MM
1832, 5, 26. Anna rocf Short Creek MM, dtd
    1832,4,24
1836, 3, 26. Anna gct Pennsville MM
1858, 6, 26. Asa & w, Ruth, & s, Joseph,
    rocf Somerset MM, dtd 1858,5,29
1858, 7, 24. Martha rocf Somerset MM, dtd
    1858,6,28

GARRETSON, continued

1859, 11, 26. Joel & w, Elizabeth, & ch, Hannah & Emily Sophia, rocf Plymouth MM, dtd 1859,10,17
1880, 9, --. Joseph dis mcd
1880, 10, 20. Almedia (form Bailey) dis mcd
1897, 2, 24. Ora dis jas

GATCHEL

1834, 1, 22. Gainer m Jesse YOCUM (H)

GAY

1823, 7, 26. Sarah Massey (form Gay) dis mcd
1830, 2, 27. Asa dis mcd

GENNIT

1835, 7, 25. Ellsberg L. rocf Contentna MM, N. C., dtd 1835,5,20
1836, 3, 26. Ellsbury J. [Gennet] con mcd
1836, 10, 22. Elsbury L. gct Bloomfield MM

GHANT

1822, 6, 22. Michel (form Bailey) dis mcd

GIBBONS

1862, 1, 8. Lindley H., s John & Mary, Belmont Co., O.; m in Stillwater MH, Rachel BRYANT, dt John & Mary, Belmont Co., O.

1862, 10, 25. Rachel B. rocf Somerset MM
1914, 10, 21. Ida (form Blowers) dis mcd

GIFFORD

1823, 7, 30. Marvin, s Abraham & Patience, Morgan Co., O.; m in Stillwater MH, Abigail BAILEY, dt Jesse & Phariba, Belmont Co., O.
       Ch: Phariba   b 1824, 8, 16
           Levi   " 1826, 7, 31

1818, 11, 28. Marven rocf Harlem MM, Maine Dist., dtd 1817,9,16, end by Plainfield MM, 1818,11,26
1823, 6, 28. Isabell (form King) dis mcd
1825, 11, 26. Alexander M. recrq
1825, 11, 26. Isabella recrq
1826, 8, 26. Abel & Michael King, ch Alexander & Sarah, recrq
1827, 2, 24. Owen recrq

GILBERT

----, --, --. Abel & Rebecca
       Ch: Ruth   b 1807, 10, 21
           Achsah   " 1809, 6, 26
           Rachel   " 1811, 12, 23
           Mary   " 1814, 5, 27
           Joel   " 1816, 10, 7
           Daniel W. " 1819, 8, 16
           Eli   " 1822, 10, 17

1810, 10, 30. Joel & w, Elizabeth, rocf Plainfield MM, dtd 1810,9,22
1810, 10, 30. Abel & w, Rebeckah, & ch, Ruth

& Achsah, rocf Plainfield MM, dtd 1810,9, 22
1811, 11, 26. John & w, Elizabeth, & ch, Mary, Thomas & Sarah, rocf Plainfield MM, dtd 1811,9,28
1815, 1, 31. Elizabeth & ch, Mary, Thomas, Sarah, Ruth & John, gct Short Creek MM
1825, 4, 23. Sarah, minor in care of Margaret Wells, rocf Short Creek MM, dtd 1825,4,19

GILLILAND

1867, 11, 23. Harriet (form Hodgin) dis mcd

GOMERY

1833, 7, 27. Enoch, William, Hannah, Joshua, Benjamin & Lovina, ch Wm. & Phebe, rocf Short Creek MM, dtd 1833,5,21
1834, 5, 24. Enoch dis mcd

GORE

1813, 11, 30. Thomas Webster gct Plainfield MM, to m Anna Gore

GRATIGNY

1876, 12, 20. Hannah H. (form Parry) dis mcd

GRAY

1859, 11, 29. Elijah, s Elijah & Mary, Monroe Co., O.; m in house of Sarah Blackledge, Elizabeth BLACKLEDGE, dt Wm. & Elizabeth, Monroe Co., O. (H)
1820, 5, 27. Cert rec for Asa [Grey] & w, Nancy, & ch from Vasselborough MM, Mass., Dist. of Me., dtd 1816,3,20, end to Plainfield MM
1832, 4, 21. Thomas & w, Catharine, & ch, William, Mary & Atlantic Ocean, gct Short Creek MM (H)
1851, 4, 19. Catharine & ch, William & Mary (of ae) & Atlantic, Sarah, Thomas L. & Morgan (minors), gct Richmond MM, Ind.(H)
1852, 4, 17. Catharine & ch, Atlantic, Sarah, Thomas L. & Morgan, gct White Water MM Ind. (H)
1854, 10, 21. Atlantic relrq (H)
1855, 5, 19. Mary Ann Walters (form Gray) dis mcd (H)

GREEN

----, --, --. Alexander & Mary
       Ch: Sarah   b 1810, 10, 20
           Sampson   " 1813, 3, 19
           Ellen   " 1813, 3, 19
           Mary Ann " 1815, 10, 15
           William   " 1817, 9, 22
           Maria   " 1819, 11, 12
           Ruth   " 1822, 1, 17
----, --, --. William, s Wm. & Mary, d 1862,2, 26; m Rachel -----, dt John & Sarah HOYLE, d 1882,1,18 bur Stillwater
       Ch: Mary   b 1828, 2, 28
           Rachel   " 1830, 2, 20 d 1831,12,19 bur Stillwater

GREEN, William & Rachel, continued
    Ch: William   b 1832, 3, 24 d 1843, 9,18
          bur Stillwater
      John S.   b 1834, 4, 26 " 1873,11,14
          bur fam burying ground, Putnam Co.,
          Ill.
      Rebecca   b 1836, 4, 7
      Lydia   " 1838, 8, 6
      Benjamin " 1841, 5, 8 d 1841, 9, 2
          bur Stillwater
      Josiah   b 1844, 4, 5 " 1844, 8,16
          bur Stillwater
1844, 6, 5. Hannah m George TATUM Jr.
1853, 10, 26. Mary m James STEER Jr.
1856, 12, 3. Rebecca m Joseph HALL
1864, 3, 9. Lydia m Joseph PATTERSON

1826, 11, 25. William & w, Rachel, & ch, Han-
    nah, Joseph & Sarah, rocf Smithfield MM,
    dtd 1826,10,23
1830, 4, 24. James dis mcd
1830, 4, 24. Alexander dis mcd
1832, 5, 26. Mary Ann & William, minors, gct
    Flushing MM
1832, 5, 26. Sarah gct Flushing MM
1848, 4, 22. Sarah Parker (form Green) dis
    mcd
1850, 10, 26. Joseph dis mcd
1873, 1, 22. John dis mcd
1882, 7, 19. Rachel d 1882,1,18 ae 83 (an
    elder)

GREGG
----, --, --. Stephen m Asenath ----- d 1818,
    4,5 ae 41y 17d bur Plainfield
    Ch: Harriett b 1801, 2, 28
      Asenath   " 1805, 7, 26
      Lucinda   " 1807, 5, 17
      Elizabeth " 1809, 7, 2
      Sarah   " 1811, 8, 6
      Stephen   " 1813, 8, 21
      Samuel   " 1813, 8, 21
      Joshua   " 1815, 10, 2
1817, 1, 1. Mahlon, s Abner & Sarah, Bel-
    mont Co., O.; m in Stillwater MH, Hannah
    MILES, dt George & Hannah, Belmont Co., O.
    Ch: Ruth   b 1817, 10, 10
      Asenath   " 1819, 7, 3
      Elias   " 1821, 7, 27
      Mahlon Jr. " 1823, 6, 8
      Mary Ann " 1825, 11, 6
      Phebe   " 1827, 5, 17
      Lydia   " 1833, 7, 26
----, --, --. James & Abigail
    Ch: Benjamin
      W.   b 1822, 4, 4
      Joseph
      Wright   " 1824, 7, 30
      Newton   " 1825, 8, 29
      Elmira   "
1828, 10, 29. Caleb, s Caleb & Hannah, Belmont
    Co., O.; m in Stillwater MH, Milicent
    DOUDNA, dt Henry & Martha, Belmont Co., O.

    Ch: Henry   b 1829, 8, 25
      Martha   " 1830, 9, 15
      Elizabeth
      W.   " 1831, 12, 17
1833, 4, 4. Sarah m Elijah FAWCETT
1837, 4, 20. Lot, s Caleb & Hannah, Belmont
    Co., O.; m in Stillwater, Ruth THOMAS, dt
    Camm & Elizabeth, Belmont Co., O. (H)
1845, 11, 26. Nathan, s Elijah & Phebe, Bel-
    mont Co., O.; m in Centre, Mary Ann PRICE,
    dt John & Rachel, Belmont Co., O. (H)

1812, 12, 29. John Webster gct Plainfield MM,
    to m Albinah Gregg
1817, 4, 26. Hannah gct Plainfield MM
1822, 3, 23. Joel Judkins gct Plainfield MM,
    to m Maria Gregg
1829, 2, 24. Abner dis
1829, 2, 24. Amy dis JH
1829, 2, 24. Aquilla dis JH
1829, 2, 24. Hannah dis JH
1829, 2, 24. Hannah Sr. dis JH
1829, 2, 24. John dis JH
1829, 2, 24. Mary, w John, dis JH
1829, 2, 24. Mary Jr. dis JH
1829, 2, 24. Samuel dis JH
1829, 2, 28. Eliza dis JH
1829, 2, 28. Jacob dis JH
1829, 2, 28. Mary dis JH
1829, 2, 28. Rebecca dis JH
1829, 6, 27. John Jr. dis disunity
1829, 8, 22. Elizabeth Lewis (form Gregg)
    dis mcd
1829, 10, 24. Abigail dis JH
1829, 10, 24. Burr dis JH
1829, 10, 24. Elijah dis JH
1829, 10, 24. James dis JH
1829, 10, 24. Phebe dis JH
1829, 10, 24. Susannah dis JH
1830, 3, 29. Alfred dis JH
1831, 1, 22. Lot dis JH
1831, 1, 22. Thomas dis JH
1831, 3, 26. Caleb & w, Milicent, & ch,
    Henry & Martha, gct Somerset MM
1832, 1, 28. Caleb & w, Milicent, & ch, Hen-
    ry & Martha, rocf Somerset MM, dtd 1831,
    11,28
1832, 10, 27. Cinah dis JH
1832, 10, 27. Hiram dis JH
1832, 10, 27. Phebe dis JH
1832, 10, 27. Sarah Ann dis JH
1833, 1, 26. Benjamin W., Joseph W., Newton
    & Elmira gct Short Creek MM (ch of Abi-
    gail & James)
1834, 1, 25. Caleb & w, Milisent, & ch, Hen-
    ry, Martha & Elijah W., gct Deerfield MM
1839, 5, 16. Lot & w, Ruth, & s, Bennet, gct
    Plainfield MM (H)
1846, 8, 15. Mary Ann gct Plainfield MM (H)
1854, 6, 19. Deborah (form Hartley) con mcd
    (H)
1854, 6, 19. Elijah & w, Phebe, & ch, Jona-
    than, Albert, Mariam & Sylvanus, rocf

GREGG, continued
    Plainfield MM (H)
1854, 7, 15. Deborah gct White Water MM, Ind.
    (H)
1865, 1, 21. Elijah & w, Phebe, & s, Sylvanus,
    gct Wapsanonoc MM, Iowa (H)
1870, 8, 24. Mahlon dis mcd & paying bounty
    money

GRIFFIN
1873, 9, 24. Elizabeth (form Parry) dis mcd
    & jas
1887, 7, 20. Melissa (form Webster) dis mcd

GRIFFITH
1818, 7, 1. Eli, s Wm. & Sarah, Belmont Co.,
    O.; m in Stillwater MH, Rachel PATTON, dt
    Wm. & Rachel, Belmont Co., O.

1818, 6, 27. Eli rocf Redstone MM, dtd 1818,
    5,27
1819, 8, 28. Eli & w, Rachel, gct Plainfield
    MM
1825, 10, 24. Emlen, minor, rocf Flushing MM,
    dtd 1825,10,21
1826, 2, 25. Abraham & w, Mary, & dt, Vio-
    letta L., rocf Short Creek MM, dtd 1825,
    3,22
1826, 6, 24. Eli & w, Rachel P., & ch, Wm. P.
    & Collins, rocf Short Creek MM, dtd 1826,
    6,20
1829, 2, 28. Charles dis JH
1829, 3, 28. Hannah dis JH

GRIMES
1825, 12, 24. Hannah rocf Short Creek MM, dtd
    1825,10,18
1828, 3, 22. Hannah gct Deerfield MM

GRIMSHAW
1861, 7, 20. Hannah d

1836, 7, 23. John Sears gct Smithfield MM,
    to m Phebe Grimshaw
1837, 5, 27. Hannah rocf Smithfield MM, dtd
    1837,5,22
1851, 10, 25. Hannah gct Chesterfield MM

GRISSELL
1857, 6, 24. Hannah T. m John D. YOCUM (H)

1856, 9, 20. Emily relrq (H)
1865, 6, 17. Nathan P. & w, Rebecca, gct
    Plainfield MM (H)
1877, 9, 21. Sarah Ann (form Tomlinson) dis
    mcd (H)

GRUBS
1848, 3, 25. Mary (form Doudna) dis mcd

GUINDON
----, --, --. Joseph W., s Francis T. & Su-
    sanna H. (Batley); m Zoa Caroline MILES,

dt Carroll H. & Selma P. (Taber), b 1887,
9,10
Ch: Carroll
    Taber   b 1913, 1, 27
    George Al-
    bert   " 1914, 8, 31
    Frances
    Ruth   " 1919, 8, 11
    Dorothy
    Inez   " 1924, 1, 21
1918, 9, 26. Albert W., s Francis T. & Su-
    sanna H., Addison Co., Vt., b 1893,5,7;
    m in Barnsville MH, Bertha R. HALL, dt
    Wilford T. & Sarah B., Belmont Co., O.,
    b 1892,12,16
Ch: William
    Raymond   b 1921, 4, 14
    Clifford
    Joseph   " 1923, 10, 8
    Mary Eva   " 1926, 2, 8
    Wilford
    Francis   " 1930, 8, 17

1921, 9, 21. Albert W. rocf Nantucket MM,
    dtd 1921,8,25
1930, 6, 25. Joseph N. & w, Zoa C., & ch,
    Carrol Taber, George Albert, Frances
    Ruth & Dorothy Inez, rocf Fairhope MM,
    Ala.

HAINES
----, --, --. Isaac & Lydia
    Ch: Smith   b 1805, 4, 12
        Davis   " 1806, 8, 11
        Samuel   " 1808, 2, 20
        Milton   " 1810, 5, 22
        Hannah   " 1811, 10, 8
        Lydia Ann   " 1813, 7, 8
        Mary   " 1815, 2, 6
----, --, --. Nathaniel & Rachel [Hains]
    Ch: Joseph   b 1808, 12, 1
        Charles   " 1810, 8, 3
        John A.   " 1812, 8, 28
        Phebe   " 1814, 10, 3
        Rebecca   " 1816, 4, 27
        Rachel   " 1818, 4, 17
        Isaac   " 1819, 10, 11
        Elisha   " 1822, 6, 3
        Ann   " 1824, 3, 12
1848, 12, 19. Elizabeth T. m Lorenzo D. LEWIS
    (H)

1819, 12, 25. Isaac & w, Lydia, & ch, Smith,
    Davis, Samuel, Milton, Hannah, Lydia Ann
    & Mary, rocf Goshen MM, Pa., dtd 1819,4,
    28, end by Short Creek MM 1819,8,24
1825, 3, 26. David gct Birmingham MM, Pa.
    (a minor)
1829, 5, 23. Ann dis JH
1829, 10, 24. John dis JH
1829, 10, 24. Rachel dis JH
1830, 6, 26. Mary dis JH
1830, 6, 26. Sarah dis JH

HAINES, continued
1830, 6, 25. Sarah gct Deerfield MM
1831, 4, 23. Joseph dis jH
1831, 4, 23. Charles dis jH
1832, 5, 26. James gct Flushing MM
1832, 9, 22. Phebe dis jH
1832, 9, 22. Rebecca dis jH
1834, 7, 26. John Jr. dis jH
1854, 10, 21. Timothy relrq (H)
1854, 10, 21. Hannah relrq (H)
1858, 10, 16. Joseph & w, Mary, & ch, Mary R.,
     Simpson G., Maria E., Seldon T., Dempsy S.
     & Vilinda J., gct Plainfield MM
1884, 4, 23. Elizabeth (form Michener) dis mcd

HALL
----, --, --. John & Miriam
     Ch: Charity   b 1797, 7, 16
         Anna   " 1801, 3, 6
         Achsah   " 1803, 5, 28
         Lydia   " 1812, 10, 5
         William   " 1806, 5, 6
         John   " 1808, 5, 30
         Isaac   " 1810, 8, 31
----, --, --. Isaac m Mary DOUDNA d 1878,1,26
     bur Richland
     Ch: Zilpah   b 1801, 8, 12
         Henry   " 1803, 2, 6 d 1895, 4,22
           bur Richland
         William   b 1804, 11, 20 " 1821, 8,25
           bur Stillwater
         John   b 1806, 10, 13
         Millicent " 1808, 1, 4
         Sarah   " 1809, 9, 22
         Isaac   " 1811, 6, 28 " 1876, 9, 7
           bur Richland
         Mary   b 1813, 5, 9
         Peninah   b 1815, 3, 23
         Anna   " 1818, 7, 3 " 1820, 9, 1
           bur Stillwater
1806, 3, 23. Ann d ae 53y 9m 13d
----, --, --. John m Phebe WEBSTER
     Ch: Cyrus   b 1808, 5, 31
         Isaac   " 1810, 7, 15
         Thomas   " 1812, 2, 14
         John   " 1813, 8, 26
         Hannah A. " 1817, 8, 3
         Eli   " 1819, 6, 7
         Jesse   " 1821, 8, 31
         Eliza   " 1824, 9, 22
1808, 9, 14. Anna m Joseph DODD
1808, 12, 14. Moses, s Isaac & Ann (White),
     Belmont Co., O.; m in Stillwater MH,
     Elizabeth PATTERSON, dt Joseph & Hannah,
     Belmont Co., O.
----, --, --. Caleb m Sylvia PATTERSON
     Ch: Nathan   b 1809, 12, 18
         Exum   " 1812, 3, 4
         Elizabeth " 1813, 7, 16
         Sarah   " 1814, 12, 19
         William   " 1816, 10, 8
         Piety   " 1819, 4, 26
         Asenath   " 1820, 4, 15

     Ch: Caleb   b 1822, 12, 18
         Silvia   " 1824, 12, 24
----, --, --. Stephen & Mary
     Ch: Jesse   b 1814, 1, 19
         Elizabeth " 1816, 7, 1
         Priscilla " 1820, 2, 25
         Mary   " 1824, 3, 15
         Maria   " 1827, 10, 25
         Ruth   " 1834, 10, 11
----, --, --. Benjamin m Sarah ----- d 1849,8,
     18 bur Richland
     Ch: James   b 1823, 6, 22
         Sarah   " 1825, 8, 26
         Zilpah   " 1829, 1, 25
1824, 4, 28. Henry, s Isaac & Mary, Guernsey
     Co., O., d 1895,4,22 bur Richland; m in
     Stillwater MH, Phebe WATSON, dt Abner &
     Elizabeth, Belmont Co., O., d 1874,9,8
     Ch: Joseph W. b 1825, 2, 13 d 1910, 3,11
           bur Richland
         Abner   b 1827, 2, 21
         Lindley H. " 1836, 4, 17 " 1865, 4,12
           bur Richland
         Emily   b 1840, 7, 30 " 1859, 3, 1
           bur Richland
1826, 2, 2. Zilpah m John HARTLEY
1827, 1, 31. Caleb, s Benjamin & Sarah,
     Guernsey Co., O., d 1840,1,27; m in Still-
     water MH, Mary HICKS, dt Joseph & Mary
     BAILEY, Belmont Co., O., d 1839,4,14 bur
     Stillwater
1827, 9, 27. Milicent m Noah HARTLEY
1828, 3, 26. John, s Isaac Jr. & Mary, Guern-
     sey Co., O.; m in Stillwater MH, Anna
     SCOTT, dt Joshua & Elizabeth, Belmont Co.,
     O.
1828, 10, 2. Sarah m Joseph HARTLEY
1831, 9, 28. Jesse, s Stephen & Mary, Guern-
     sey Co., O.; m in Stillwater MH, Eliza-
     beth HARTLEY, dt Mahlon & Charity, Bel-
     mont Co., O.
     Ch: Noah   b 1832, 12, 20
         Charity   " 1834, 7, 3
         Stephen   " 1835, 12, 31
         Joseph
           Hartley " 1838, 3, 1
         Mary   " 1840, 3, 31
1832, 3, 21. Cyrus, s John & Phebe, Belmont
     Co., O.; m in Somerset, Ellen STRAHL,
     dt Isaac & Ellen, Belmont Co., O.
1832, 3, 29. Nathan, s Caleb & Silvia,
     Guernsey Co., O., d 1880,2,8; m in Rich-
     land, Deborah PERRY, dt John & Rachel,
     Guernsey Co., O., d 1844,2,1 bur Richland
     Ch: Hannah Ann b 1833, 11, 29
         Amos   " 1837, 3, 30 d 1882, 3,15
           bur Richland
         Thomas   b 1840, 11, 22
1834, 1, 30. Elizabeth m Thomas ARNOLD
1834, 7, 17. Isaac d bur Stillwater
1835, 3, 12. Isaac, s Isaac & Mary, d 1876,
     9,7 bur Richland; m in Richland, Mary
     BAILEY, dt Jesse & Mary, Guernsey Co., O.

HALL, Isaac & Mary, continued
    Ch: Rachel   b 1837, 8, 2 d 1856, 9,28
        bur Richland
       Phebe   b 1839, 7, 22 " 1904, 3,24
        bur Richland
       Ruthann   b 1843, 7, 4
       Jesse B. " 1846, 7, 11 " 1894, 8,28
        bur Richland
1836, 6, 8. Nathan, s Joseph & Christiana,
Jefferson Co., O.; m in Stillwater MH, Sarah WILLIAMS, dt Daniel & Jane, Belmont
Co., O.
1836, 12, 8. Mary m William HALL
1836, 12, 8. William, s Caleb & Silvy, Guernsey Co., O.; m in Richland, Mary HALL, dt
Isaac & Mary, Guernsey Co., O., d 1856,4,
14 bur Richland
    Ch: Deborah   b 1837, 9, 21
       Asenath   " 1838, 11, 15 d 1854,12, 5
        bur Richland
       Jesse D. b 1840, 9, 13 " 1903, 9, 1
        bur Richland
       Asa   b 1842, 2, 25
       Caleb   " 1850, 9, 14 " 1854,10, 3
        bur Richland
       William   " 1854,10,27
        bur Richland
----, --, --. Joseph & Martha
    Ch: Elvira   b 1838, 5, 20
       Hannah   " 1840, 4, 26
       Elizabeth " 1842, 7, 19
       John   " 1844, 11, 14 d 1845, 6, 3
        bur Stillwater
       Mary   b 1846, 5, 21
       Joseph   " 1849, 1, 7
1839, 8, 1. Asenath m Job PARRY
1841, 3, 24. Isaac W., s John & Phebe, Guernsey Co., O.; m in Somerset, Margaret
THOMAS, dt William & Rebecca, Belmont Co.,
O.
1844, 8, 28. Maria m Joseph A. BEVAN
1846, 4, 30. Nathan, s Caleb & Sylvia (Patterson), Guernsey Co., O.; m in Stillwater MH, Phebe SEARS, dt John & Margaret
GRIMSHAW, Jefferson Co., O., d 1849,3,30
bur Richland
1846, 4, 30. Peninah m Asa CRAFT
1847, 12, 30. Joseph W., s Henry & Phebe
(Watson), Guernsey Co., O.; m in Richland,
Sarah WEBSTER, dt Thomas & Anna, Guernsey
Co., O., d 1891,3,14 bur Richland
    Ch: Thomas
       Henry   b 1849, 1, 16 d 1851, 7,22
        bur Richland
       Rosetta   b 1850, 10, 5
       Joseph Gore" 1852, 8, 1
       Louis Webster
               b 1854, 9, 21 d 1859, 7,11
        bur Richland
       Mansel Eu-
        gene   b 1856, 4, 3
       Jeptha   " 1858, 11, 22
       Cassius C. " 1860, 12, 23

    Ch: Elmer Els-
       worth   b 1862, 10, 17 d 1928, 3,19
        bur Quaker City, O.
       Alvin E.   b 1864, 12, 8
       Altie Isa-
        bella   " 1866, 9, 10
       Tilman L. " 1870, 7, 25
1848, 4, 2. George d
1848, 6, 30. Joseph d bur Stillwater
1851, 5, 1. Benjamin, s John & Sarah, Guernsey Co., O.; m in Richland, Deborah WEB-
STER, dt Samuel & Deborah CHAMBERS, Belmont Co., O.
1851, 11, 27. Abner, s Henry & Phebe (Watson),
Guernsey Co., O.; m in Richland, Phebe
WEBSTER, dt Thomas & Anne, Guernsey Co.,
O., d 1885,7,31 bur Richland
    Ch: Ann   b 1855, 9, 6
       Lindley   " 1859, 7, 31
       Thomas Hen-
        ry   " 1857, 9, 28
       Wilmer   " 1861, 8, 9
       Milton   " 1863, 11, 2
       Emily E.   " 1865, 12, 11
1853, 2, 14. Letitia, w George, d
1853, 10, 27. Hannah Ann m Jeptha L. WEBSTER
1856, 12, 3. Joseph, s Nathan P. & Rachel
(Wilson), Jefferson Co., O.; m in Still-
water MH, Rebecca GREEN, dt William & Rachel (Hoyle), Belmont Co., O.
    Ch: George
       Dillwyn   b 1857, 12, 17
       William G. " 1859, 10, 11
----, --, --. John m Deborah DAVIS, dt John
F. & Ann, d 1886,7,12 bur Stillwater
    Ch: Tacy   b 1854, 10, 13 d 1929,11,27
        bur Pasadena, Calif; m Ralph ATWOOD
       Rachel G. b 1858, 3, 30
       Francis D. " 1860, 3, 26
       Elizabeth " 1862, 9, 10
1857, 9, 24. Eli, s John & Phebe, Guernsey
Co., O.; m in house of Wm. THOMAS, Priscilla THOMAS, dt Wm. & Rebecca, Belmont
Co., O.
1858, 6, 3. Amos, s Nathan & Deborah (Parry)
Guernsey Co., O.; m in Richland, Deborah
WEBSTER, dt Thomas & Ann, Guernsey Co., O.
d 1889,1,24 bur Richland
    Ch: Alva   b 1859, 8, 8
       Clarence   " 1859, 1, 28
       Clayton   " 1866, 10, 22
1860, 5, 1. Elizabeth m Samuel BARBER
1860, 10, 31. Martha (nee FARQUHAR) m Saml.
HOLLINGSWORTH
1861, 11, 23. Sarah B., w Wilford T., dt
Eli & Mary P. (Bundy) Stanton, b
1866, 7, 27. Deborah d bur Richland
----, --, --. Thomas P. m Rebecca W. RICHARD-
SON, dt Samuel & Hannah Dingy (Vail),
b 1846,4,3 d 1926,3,30 bur Stillwater
    Ch: Milford T. b 1869, 8, 29
       Blanche D. " 1874, 5, 22
       Everette G." 1878, 6, 11

HALL, Thomas & Rebecca, continued
        Ch: Elma C.   b 1878, 6, 11
            Elsie H.   " 1880, 5, 22
1872, 5, 23. Parker, s William & Hannah,
    Harrison Co., O.; m in Stillwater MH, Tabi-
    tha D. BUNDY, dt Joel & Rebecca (Hodgin),
    Belmont Co., O.
1874, 9, 3. Joseph G., s Joseph W. & Sarah
    (Webster), Guernsey Co., O.; m in Rich-
    land, Sarah HARTLEY, dt Joseph & Marion
    (Bailey), Guernsey Co., O., b 1854,2,28
        Ch: Albert   b 1876, 3, 9
            Elwood   " 1877, 8, 2
            Walter   " 1879, 7, 21
            Homer   " 1882, 2, 3
1875, 4, 29. Rosetta m Joseph DOUDNA
1875, 5, 15. John, s John & Tacy (Patterson),
    d bur Stillwater
1877, 9, 27. Ann m Ezekiel B. HOYLE
1878, 10, 31. Mansel E., s Joseph W. & Sarah,
    Guernsey Co., O., b 1856,4,3; m in Rich-
    land, Martha HARTLEY, dt Henry & Mary,
    Guernsey Co., O., b 1858,3,7 d 1927,4,3
    bur Richland, O.
        Ch: Lewis   b 1879, 8, 16
            Mary Alice " 1881, 1, 20
            Sarah Anise" 1883, 7, 21 d 1884, 7,13
              bur Richmond
            Elmer   b 1887, 3, 18
            Melissa H. " 1889, 3, 12
            Annie M.   " 1885, 5, 8
            Charles A. " 1892, 10, 17
            Edith J.   " 1894, 12, 31 d 1896, 2, 8
              bur Richland
            Harriet E. b 1897, 2, 3
            Wilmer Es-
              ther   " 1901, 10, 6
            Irene   " 1903, 9, 8
1882, 4, 27. Jeptha W., s Joseph W. & Sarah
    W., Guernsey Co., O., b 1858,11,21 d 1925,
    5,11 bur Quaker City, O.; m in Richland,
    Abi HARTLEY, dt Henry & Mary (Webster),
    b 1860,10,18 d 1928,11,25 bur Quaker City,
    O.
        Ch: Ida May   b 1883, 3, 11
            Elma L.   " 1886, 9, 27
            Charles
              Arthur   " 1885, 7, 18 d 1885, 5, 9
              bur Richland
            Freda
              Blanche   b 1899, 9, 11 " 1918,10,19
              bur Quaker City, O.
1882, 9, 21. Sina A. m John W. MOTT
1883, 3, 22. Mariam P. m Jesse DEWEESE
1885, 10, 29. Cassius, s Joseph W. & Sarah
    (Webster), Guernsey Co., O.; m in Richland,
    Deborah E. HARTLEY, dt Henry & Mary (Web-
    ster), Guernsey Co., O.
        Ch: Henry
              Alden   b 1887, 1, 23
            Alvin
              Ernest   " 1891, 5, 28
            Verna

        Ch: Idella   b 1893, 2, 24 d 1894, 5, 8
              bur Richland
            William T. b 1897, 7, 14
            Thomas C. " 1901, 7, 1
1885, 12, 21. Lindley, s Abner & Phebe (Web-
    ster), Guernsey Co., O.; m in Richland,
    Martha E. DOUDNA, dt John & Mary Jane,
    Guernsey Co., O., d 1897,9,28 bur Richland
        Ch: Elsie May b 1893, 8, 24
----, --, --. Elmer E. m Mary Bell HARTLEY, dt
    Isaac & Nancy (Whitcraft) HARTLEY
        Ch: Arthur
              Hartley b 1889, 3, 30
            Golda Bell " 1894, 3, 26
            Carl Whit-
              craft   " 1896, 6, 21
            Chester
              Blane   " 1899, 12, 27
            Homer
              Cecil   " 1903, 8, 13
1891, 9, 25. Mary Eva b
1892, 12, 16. Bertha R. b
1893, 12, 6. Blanche D. m Albert H. DOUDNA
----, --, --. Hannah Ann C., dt Samuel & Sarah
    (Doudna) CARTER, b 1843,12,19 d 1925,2,28
    bur Stillwater
1894, 6, 21. Elizabeth T. m J. Morris ASHEAD
----, --, --. Tilman L. m Mary Belle DOUGLAS
    d 1901,9,2 bur Richland
        Ch: William T. b 1895, 11, 20 d 1897, 7,12
              bur Richland
            Sarah   b 1898, 12, 23
            Sarah
              Myrtie   " 1899, 12, 23 (sic)
            Joseph J.   " 1901, 3, 8
1896, 9, 11. Hannah A., w Alonzo, dt Jno. &
    M. J. Doudna, d bur Richland
1898, 9, 8. Elwood, s Joseph G. & Sarah
    (Hartley), Guernsey Co., O., b 1877,8,2;
    m in Richland, Cora E. HALL, dt Jesse D.
    & Jane (Whitcraft) b 1878,12,1
        Ch: Jesse   b 1900, 5, 9 d 1900, 5,29
              bur Richland
            Willis
              Herbert b 1902, 7, 7
            Perley J. " 1905, 1, 19
            Sarah   " 1911, 6, 13
1898, 9, 8. Cora E. m Elwood HALL
1899, 6, 30. Helen E., dt Wilford & Sarah B.
    (Stanton), b
----, --, --. Elmer E. m Mary B. HARTLEY
        Ch: Chester B. b 1900, 12, 27
            Homer C.   " 1903, 8, 13
            Bertha
              Mary   " 1909, 4, 10
----, --, --. Tillman L., s Joseph W. & Sarah
    (Webster), b 1870,7,25; m Evaline CRAFT,
    dt Asa & Penina (Hall), b 1856,4,12
----, --, --. Alvin Edgar m Elma Maria -----,
    dt Henry & Mary (Webster) HARTLEY, b 1868,
    10,6
        Ch: Mary W.   b 1902, 6, 4
            Joseph W. " 1905, 5, 12

HALL, continued

1904, 5, 26. Wilmer L., s Lindley & Millicent Belmont Co., O.; m in Stillwater MH, Ida J. STANTON, dt Benjamin & Elizabeth, Belmont Co., O.
Ch: Dorothy
Lucile   b 1906, 2, 2
Howard
Stanton   " 1908, 8, 26

----, --, --. Louis L., s Mansel E. & Martha (Hartley), b 1879,8,16; m Annie M. GALLO-WAY, dt Caleb & Emaline (Low), b 1880,8,7
Ch: Olive
Winifred b 1906, 4, 26
Dean
Robert   " 1916, 8, 13
Lester G. " 1918, 5, 13

----, --, --. Wilson Mifflin, s Linton & Ann W. (Allmon), b 1868,1,4; m Mary Anna ED-GERTON, dt Jesse & Samira (Stratton) b 1866,8,15
Ch: Edward
Stratton b 1907, 12, 6

1909, 4, 10. Bertha Mary, dt Elmer E. & Mary B. (Hartley), b

1909, 5, 20. Elmer I., s Manuel E. & Martha H., Guernsey Co., O.; m in Richland, Erma L. DOUDNA, dt John E. & Anna B., Guernsey Co., O., b 1889,3,23

1911, 7, 24. Marian Helen b

----, --, --. Henry Alden, s Cassius C. & Deborah C. (Hartley), b 1887,1,23; m Anna Mable EDGERTON, dt Walter & Mary (Binns), b 1886,3,5
Ch: Herbert
Walter   b 1913, 9, 1
Clara
Luella   " 1917, 8, 5
Clarence
James   " 1919, 6, 8
Irving
Cassius   " 1923, 6, 17

1914, 6, 25. Mary Eva m Guy WOODWARD

----, --, --. Howard Theophilus, s Abner & Anna (Morlan), b 1891,6,1; m Anna Florence COPE, dt Albert & Phebe (Ashton), b 1893, 1,6
Ch: David Ab-
ner   b 1917, 5, 18
Richard
Albert   " 1919, 12, 19
Phebe Jane " 1923, 12, 10

1918, 9, 26. Bertha R. m Albert W. GUINDON

----, --, --. Wilford Linton, s Mifflin & Mary Ann (Edgerton); m Ethel PICKETT, dt Phineas & Harriett (Kerr), b 1895,8,3
Ch: Delbert
Lester   b 1923, 5, 7
Wilford
Leland   " 1925, 3, 2
Donald
Linton   " 1928, 1, 2
Harold La-

Ch: verne   b 1829, 8, 26
Narville
Lloyd   " 1932, 3, 15

1926, 6, 16. Marion Ethlyn m Chester E. DOUDNA

1929, 10, 5. Josephine m Harry W. PEACOCK

1930, 11, 29. W. Mifflin, s Linton & Ann W., Columbiana Co., O.; m in Stillwater MH, Mariana FOSTER, dt Edward & Emma, Belmont Co., O.

1809, 8, 29. George & w, Letitia, & dt, Nancy, recrq

1809, 10, 31. Sarah (form Stubbs) dis mcd

1810, 8, 28. James Edgerton Jr. gct Short Creek MM, to m Anne Hall

1812, 12, 1. Stephen rocf Contentney MM, N. C., dtd 1811,9,14

1812, 12, 1. Stephen con mcd

1812, 12, 29. Mary (form Bailey) con mcd

1821, 11, 24. Sarah rst

1822, 3, 23. Benjamin recrq

1826, 5, 27. Caleb & ch, Silas, Nathan, Exum, William, Caleb, Elizabeth, Sarah, Piety, Asenath & Sylvia Jane, rocf Contentnea MM, N. C., dtd 1836,3,11

1828, 7, 26. John Jr. dis JH

1828, 7, 26. Anna dis JH

1829, 9, 26. John dis JH

1829, 9, 26. Phebe dis JH

1829, 10, 24. Isaac Sr. dis JH

1830, 1, 23. Silas gct Short Creek MM

1831, 7, 28. Cyrus dis JH

1831, 7, 28. Isaac Jr. dis JH

1833, 2, 23. Hannah recrq

1833, 3, 23. Elizabeth Cramblett (form Hall) dis mcd

1834, 11, 22. Sarah Birch (form Hall) dis mcd

1836, 5, 28. Betsy Hays (form Hall) dis mcd

1836, 7, 23. Piety Hays (form Hall) dis mcd

1836, 7, 23. Sarah gct Short Creek MM

1839, 5, 25. Joseph & w, Martha, & dt, Elvira, rocf Short Creek MM, dtd 1839,1,21

1839, 5, 25. Thomas dis JH

1839, 5, 25. John Jr. dis JH

1842, 6, 25. Sylvia Jane Smith (form Hall) dis mcd

1843, 2,.25. Jesse & w, Elizabeth, & ch, Noah, Charity, Stephen, Joseph H., Mary & George S., gct Flushing MM

1844, 6, 22. Priscilla Hayes (form Hall) dis mcd

1844, 8, 24. Sarah Kuntz (form Hall) dis mcd

1844, 8, 24. James dis mcd

1844, 8, 24. Jesse dis mcd

1844, 10, 26. Eli dis disunity

1845, 7, 26. Stephen & w, Mary, & dt, Ruth, gct Flushing MM

1845, 11, 22. Mary L. gct Flushing MM

1846, 5, 23. Caleb dis mcd

1848, 3, 25. John W. Smith rocf Short Creek MM, to m Maria Hall

1854, 7, 22. Zilpha King (form Hall) dis mcd

HALL, continued
1857, 2, 28. Benjamin dis disunity
1857, 4, 25. John & w, Deborah, & ch, Mariam
    P., Eliza D., Tacy Ellen & Sina Ann, rocf
    Flushing MM, dtd 1857,3,26
1857, 8, 22. Deborah Hayes (form Hall) dis
    mcd
1857, 10, 17. Mary D. Benson (form Hall) con
    mcd (H)
1859, 4, 23. Joseph rocf Short Creek MM, dtd
    1859,3,19
1860, 4, 28. Sinclair Smith gct Somerset MM,
    to m Tacy M. Hall
1861, 1, 19. Ann H. Hilton (form Hall) con
    mcd (H)
1861, 1, 26. Mary & Joseph, ch Martha Hollings-
    worth, gct Middleton MM
1861, 2, 23. Elvira gct Middleton MM
1861, 5, 18. Phebe Kenan (form Hall) con mcd
    (H)
1861, 7, 27. Asa dis mcd
1862, 4, 26. Lindley H. rpd mcd
1863, 4, 25. Zilpha King (form Hall) dis mcd
1863, 5, 18. Sarah rocf Short Creek MM, dtd
    1863,4,7 (H)
1866, 1, 27. Isaac con mcd
1866, 1, 27. David dis mcd
1866, 4, 28. Rachel (form Hanson) con mcd
1866, 5, 26. Ann (form Blowers) dis mcd
1873, 1, 22. Tabitha D. & dt, Sarah Louisa
    Bundy, gct Short Creek MM
1874, 7, 22. Jesse B. con mcd
1876, 4, 15. Phebe H. recrq (H)
1877, 2, 17. Mary Alice rocf Goose Creek MM
    (H)
1883, 2, 21. Alva B. con mcd
1881, 7, 20. Hannah Ann (form Doudna) con mcd
1884, 9, 24. Francis D. gct Springville MM,
    Ia.
1884, 9, 24. Eliza D. gct Chesterfield MM,
    N. J.
1885, 4, 22. Wilmer dis mcd
1885, 8, 19. Clarence W. dis mcd
1886, 11, 24. Milton dis mcd
1887, 11, 30. Elmer E. con mcd
1889, 9, 25. Alva B. dis jas
1890, 5, 21. Thomas Henry dis mcd
1890, 12, 24. Clayton F. dis mcd
1892, 2, 24. Sarah (form Stanton) con mcd
1894, 1, 24. Abner con mcd
1894, 2, 21. Hannah Ann (form Carter) con mcd
1895, 3, 20. Elizabeth T. Ashead (form Hall)
    gct Salem MM
1895, 5, 22. Tillman L. con mcd
1895, 5, 22. Lewis W. dis mcd & jas
1895, 8, 21. Mary B. recrq
1895, 8, 21. Cora E., dt Jesse D. & Jane,
    recrq
1897, 6, 23. Mary B. & ch, Arthur H., Goldie
    B. & Carl W., recrq
1897, 10, 20. Altie Barton (form Hall) con
    mcd
1898, 7, 20. Emily E. Colburn (form Hall) dis

mcd & jas
1898, 12, 21. Rachel G. gct Phila. MM, Pa.
1899, 5, 24. Mary Eva & Bertha R., ch Wil-
    ford & Sarah B., recrq
1902, 3, 19. Alvin E. con mcd
1902, 3, 19. Albert dis mcd
1902, 4, 23. Elma M. (form Hartley) con mcd
1902, 11, 19. Walter con mcd
1903, 6, 20. Sarah M. recrq (H)
1903, 6, 24. Lindley con mcd
1903, 9, 23. Chalkley L. Bundy gct Short
    Creek MM, to m Luella Hall
1905, 4, 15. Franz K. recrq (H)
1905, 10, 25. Eveline (form Craft) con mcd
1905, 10, 25. Tilman L. con mcd
1906, 12, 19. Lewis L. con mcd
1907, 5, 22. Ida M. Alwine (form Hall) con
    mcd
1907, 11, 20. Silas Hartley gct Somerset MM,
    to m Elizabeth J. Hall
1908, 4, 22. Homer con mcd
1910, 4, 20. Everett dis mcd
1911, 10, 25. Henry Alden gct New Garden MM,
    O., to m Anna Mabel Edgerton
1912, 5, 22. Anna Mabel rocf New Garden MM,
    dtd 1912,4,25
1912, 9, 25. Joseph D. Henderson gct Middle-
    ton MM, to m Vesta M. Hall
1914, 7, 22. Arthur H. con mcd
1915, 1, 20. Elma L. Carter (form Hall) dis
    mcd & jas
1915, 6, 23. Charles E. dis mcd
1916, 6, 21. Charles E. dis mcd
1916, 9, 20. Anna T. rocf Salem MM, dtd
    1916,6,21
1917, 1, 24. Anna M. & ch, Marian E., Olive
    W., Lois J. & Dean R., recrq
1917, 5, 24. Anna M. Stillion (form Hall)
    con mcd
1917, 8, 22. Elsie Finley (form Hall) dis
    mcd
1917, 11, 21. Everett G. rst
1920, 7, 21. Malissa Kutz (form Hall) dis
    mcd
1922, 1, 25. Wilson Mifflin & w, Mary Anna
    E., & s, Edward S., also Marion Ellen
    Hall, a minor in their care, rocf Upper
    Springfield MM, dtd 1921,12,23
1923, 5, 23. Erma L. dis jas
1923, 5, 23. Elmer I. dis jas
1923, 5, 23. Erma L. dis jas
1924, 3, 19. Ida Stanton & ch, Dorothy L.,
    Howard S. & Gertrude M., gct Salem MM, O.
1924, 2, 20. John A. & Ronald J., ch Dora
    M., recrq
1924, 8, 20. Edna H. Jones (form Hall) dis
    mcd & jas
1924, 12, 24. Hallie Olive recrq
1925, 3, 25. Walter & w, Dora Myrtle, & ch,
    Ronald Joseph & John A., gct Somerset MM
1925, 3, 25. Hallie Olive gct Somerset MM
1925, 10, 21. Myrtle D. Peters (form Hall)
    dis mcd

HALL, continued

1926, 6, 23. Chester B. con mcd
1926, 6, 23. Carl W. con mcd
1926, 8, 25. Wilson Mifflin & w, Mari-anna
E., & ch, Edward & Marian H., gct Upper
Springfield MM
1926, 9, 22. Ethelyn Doudna (form Hall) gct
Somerset MM
1927, 5, 25. Golda B. H. Yourex (form Hall)
con mcd
1927, 7, 20. Harold recrq
1927, 8, 24. Lizzie Ball recrq
1928, 2, 22. Wilford L. & ch, Delbert Lester,
Wilford Leland & Donald Linton, rocf Upper
Springfield MM
1928, 3, 21. Ethel Pickett rocf Plainfield
MM, dtd 1928,2,1
1928, 7, 25. Homer C. con mcd
1928, 7, 25. Joseph J. dis mcd
1929, 7, 24. Olive W. Nimmo (form Hall) con
mcd
1930, 6, 25. Perley dis mcd
1931, 7, 22. Mariana Foster gct Upper Springfield MM, O.
1931, 8, 19. Bertha Dillon (form Hall) dis
mcd

HAMBLETON

1827, 10, 27. Rachel rocf Little Britain MM,
Pa., dtd 1827,2,27, end to Deerfield MM

HAMILTON

1909, 4, 25. Rebecca (form Thomas) dis mcd

HAMPTON

----, --, --. Thomas & Hannah [Hamton]
Ch: Cary   b 1813, 10, 11
    Eunice   " 1819, 2, 6
    Jason   " 1822, 1, 14
    Amos   " 1826, 6, 6

1821, 2, 24. Thomas & w, Hannah, & ch,
Charles & Eunice, rocf Fallowfield MM,
Pa., dtd 1820,9,8
1825, 6, 25. Asa C. rocf Pipe Creek MM, dtd
1825,4,16
1825, 6, 25. Bethula rocf Pipe Creek MM, dtd
1825,4,16
1825, 6, 25. Asenath rocf Pipe Creek MM, dtd
1825,4,16
1825, 10, 24. Sarah & fam rocf Flushing MM,
dtd 1825,10,21
1826, 1, 28. Mary & ch, John, Samuel, Mary
Ann & Cary, rocf Pipe Creek MM, dtd 1825,
12,17
1826, 9, 23. John rst (dis by Pipe Creek MM)
1827, 9, 22. Asa C. gct Deerfield MM, to m
Esther Patterson
1829, 1, 24. James dis jH
1829, 2, 28. Emily dis jH
1830, 5, 22. Amos & Mary gct Short Creek MM
1834, 12, 27. Amos W., Levi, Mary & James
Hiram, gct Somerset MM

1846, 3, 28. Amos & w, Mary, rocf Somerset
MM, dtd 1846,3,2
1850, 9, 28. Amos W. & w, Mary, gct Salem
MM, Ia.
1853, 12, 17. Elizabeth recrq (H)
1857, 8, 15. Ruth Anna Williams (form Hampton) con mcd (H)

HANSON

----, --, --. Manoah d 1858,11,21 bur Stillwater; m Rachel ----- d 1847,4,17
Ch: Deborah   b 1808, 10, 16
    Isaac   " 1809, 12, 22
    Jesse   " 1811, 4, 29
    Ida   " 1813, 1, 8
    Eliza   " 1814, 4, 17
    Elijah   " 1815, 10, 29 d 1876, 2, 7
    bur Stillwater
    Elizabeth b 1817, 4, 18
    Manoah   b 1819, 12, 8 d 1858,12,39
    bur Stillwater
1813, 9, 16. Patience m Reuben EDGERTON
1813, 12, 16. Lovice m Jeremiah COOK
1814, 4, 7. Clarkey m Isaac WOOD
1818, 8, 26. Elijah, s Elijah & Susannah,
Belmont Co., O.; m in Stillwater MH, Eliza
STUBBS, dt Joseph & Zilpah, Belmont Co.,
O., d 1877,3,21 bur Richland
Ch: William   b 1819, 6, 18
    Joseph   " 1821, 1, 21
    Deborah   " 1839, 1, 26
    Lydia   " 1842, 2, 16
    Isaac   " 1845, 2, 17 d 1845,11,30
    Benjamin   " 1849, 7, 11 " 1886,11,10
    bur Stillwater
1819, 3, 30. Borden, s Elijah & Susannah,
Belmont Co., O.; m in Stillwater MH, Rachel COX, dt John & Rachel, Belmont Co.,O.
Ch: John   b 1820, 7, 10
1821, 12, 27. Jesse d ae 10y 7m bur Captina
1826, 5, 15. Susanna d ae 66y 2m 22d bur
Captina "on her own place"
1828, 10, 2. Deborah m Wm. VERNON
1835, 10, 20. Eliza m Eli VERNON
1839, 12, 5. William, s Elijah & Eliza, Belmont Co., O.; m in Captina, Joanna HICKS,
dt James & Bethany, Belmont Co., O.
Ch: Westley H. b 1840, 9, 19 d 1842, 4,22

    James   " 1842, 5, 28
1840, 12, 10. Joseph, s Elijah & Eliza, Belmont Co., O.; m in Captina, Lydia HICKS,
dt James & Bethany, Belmont Co., O., d
1841,8,6
----, --, --. Manoah & Millicent
Ch: Lovise   b 1844, 8, 10
    Phoebe   " 1846, 4, 21
    Demsey   " 1848, 7, 17
    David   " 1850, 4, 6 d 1851, 8,21
    bur Stillwater
    John Milton b 1852, 6, 9
1844, 5, 28. Rachel m Edwin MORRIS
1845, 10, 29. Robert, s Elijah & Eliza, Bel-

HANSON, Robert, continued
    mont Co., O.; m in Stillwater MH, Prudence
    McNICHOLS, dt George & Martha, Belmont
    Co., O.
1859, 3, 30. Deborah m Caleb BUNDY
1864, 12, 7. Deborah H. m Chalkley BUNDY
1870, 3, 9. Benjamin H., s Elijah & Eliza,
    Belmont Co., O., d 1886,11,10 bur Still-
    water; m in Stillwater MH, Lucinda BUNDY,
    dt Chalkley & Sarah (Doudna), Belmont Co.,
    O., b 1850,9,11
    Ch: Cora Sa-
        rah   b 1870, 3, 27
        Eliza Al-
        vin   " 1873, 6, 10 d 1874,10, 1
        bur Stillwater
        Maud Ella b 1875, 6, 23
        Mary E.   " 1877, 9, 2
        Caleb L. " 1880, 1, 15
        Benjamin
        Herman   " 1883, 5, 4

1817, 7, 26. Isaac dis mcd
1822, 9, 28. Elijah & Eliza & fam gct Somer-
    set MM
1823, 7, 26. Rachel & dt, Ann, gct Somerset
    MM
1830, 11, 27. Isaac Jr. dis mcd
1836, 2, 27. Elizabeth White (form Hanson)
    dis mcd
1836, 5, 28. Iddo dis mcd
1837, 7, 22. Elijah & w, Elizabeth, & ch,
    William, Joseph, Susannah, Robert, Elijah,
    Zilpha, Eliza, John, Asa & Edo, rocf Somer-
    set MM, dtd 1837,5,29
1839, 2, 23. Elijah Jr. dis mcd
1841, 4, 24. Mary (form Lisle) dis mcd
1842, 11, 26. Susannah Endicott (form Hanson)
    con mcd
1843, 7, 22. Manoah Jr. gct Chesterfield MM
1843, 7, 22. Joseph gct Chesterfield MM
1843, 9, 23. Lavisa Williams (form Hanson)
    con mcd
1845, 2, 22. William & w, Joannah, & ch,
    James & Elijah, gct Pennsville MM
1846, 5, 23. Robert & w, Prudence, gct Somer-
    set MM
1848, 9, 23. Manoah Jr. & w, Milicent, & ch,
    Levisa & Phebe, rocf Chesterfield MM, dtd
    1848,6,17
1849, 6, 23. Rebecca Craft (form Hanson) dis
    mcd
1850, 2, 23. Elijah Jr. dis disunity
1850, 9, 28. Eliza Coughlin (form Hanson) dis
    mcd
1851, 7, 26. Joseph dis mcd
1851, 11, 22. Clarkey dis disunity
1855, 8, 25. Rachel & ch, John, Clarkson,
    Ann Eliza, William Lindley, Henry, Martha
    & Mary, rocf Plymouth MM, dtd 1855,7,23
1857, 12, 26. Zilpha W. Ewers (form Hanson)
    dis mcd
1858, 6, 26. Iddo dis mcd

1858, 9, 25. John dis disunity
1859, 4, 23. Joanna & ch, James, Elijah,
    Malinda, Isaac, Cidney & William, rocf
    Pennsville MM, dtd 1859,3,17
1859, 5, 28. Milicent & ch, Lovisa W.,
    Phebe J., Demsey B., John M., George F.
    & Mary E., gct Plymouth MM
1866, 4, 28. Rachel Hall (form Hanson) con
    mcd
1869, 1, 23. Asa dis mcd
1869, 9, 22. Ann Eliza Doudna (form Hanson)
    dis mcd
1875, 6, 23. Martha Mills (form Hanson) dis
    mcd & jas
1875, 6, 23. Mary Hartley (form Hanson) dis
    mcd
1891, 4, 22. Cora Van Hostein (form Hanson)
    dis mcd
1905, 4, 19. Maud dis jas
1905, 6, 21. Caleb L. dis military service

HARDON
1825, 10, 24. Zachariah B. & w, Sarah, rocf
    Flushing MM, dtd 1825,10,21

HARLAN
----, --, --. Enoch & Hannah
    Ch: William   b 1797, 3, 1
        John   " 1802, 10, 26 d 1821, 3,11
        bur Meigs Creek
        George   b 1804, 7, 6
        Humphrey " 1806, 5, 19
        Gibbons " 1808, 2, 16
        Samuel   " 1810, 7, 7
        Rebecca " 1812, 1, 12
1819, 12, 27. Harriet A. m Samuel STEER

1816, 12, 22. Enoch & w, Hannah, & ch,
    William, John, George, Humphrey, Gibbons,
    Samuel & Rebecca, rocf Fallowfield MM,
    Pa., dtd 1816,9,9
----, --, --. Harriet rocf Fallowfield MM,
    Pa., dtd 1816,9,9
1857, 5, 16. Caleb & w, Pamelia, & ch, Ed-
    ward, Mary Jane, Lewis, Oliver, Phebe Ann,
    Henry & John W., gct Alum Creek MM, O.(H)

HARRINGTON
1889, 5, 22. Lineus & w, Sina B., & ch,
    Anna Leora, Cyrus J., Phebe Elma, Mary
    Ellen & Sara Etta, rocf Short Creek MM,
    dtd 1889,4,23

HARRIS
1829, 11, 28. Sarah rocf Short Creek MM
1830, 6, 26. Sarah gct Deerfield MM
1833, 3, 23. David & w, Lettuce, & ch,
    Eleanor, Rachel Ann, Susan & Sarah, rocf
    Flushing MM, dtd 1833,1,24
1835, 6, 27. David dis mcd
1847, 10, 23. Elana Eliza McCartney (form
    Harris) dis mcd
1851, 7, 26. Rachel Holton (form Harris) dis

HARRIS, continued
    mcd

HARRISON
1832, 8, 25. Thomason rocf Phila. MM, dtd
    1832,7,26

HARROLD
1820, 2, 15. Dotty, dt Jacob & Mary, b

1820, 7, 22. Jacob & w, Mary, & ch, Joseph,
    Charity & Amasa, rocf Union MM, N. C.,
    dtd 1819,7,28, end by Fairfield MM, 1812,
    5,27
1829, 11, 28. Housen [Harrel] & w, Rachel, &
    ch, Amos, Mary & Tamer, rocf Short Creek
    MM, dtd 1829,9,22
1831, 5, 28. Howsen [Herril] & w, Rachel, &
    ch, Mary & Tamer, gct Short Creek MM
1831, 7, 28. Amos [Herrol] gct Short Creek MM

HARRY
----, --, --. William & Hannah
    Ch: John   b 1813, 6, 3
        Rebecca   " 1816, 4, 2
        Absalom   " 1819, 3, 4
1825, 4, 27. Hannah m Joseph FISHER

1817, 8, 23. William rocf Kennet MM, dtd 1817,
    5,6
1818, 10, 24. Hannah & ch, John & Rebecca, rec-
    rq
1820, 6, 24. Hannah rocf Kennet MM, Pa., dtd
    1820,4,4
1827, 5, 26. William & w, Hannah, & ch, John,
    Rebecca, Absalom & Mary, gct Deerfield MM

HARTLEY
1826, 2, 2. John, s Mahlon & Charity, Bel-
    mont Co., O.; m in Richland, Zilpah HALL,
    dt Isaac & Mary (Doudna), Guernsey Co., O.,
    d 1841,7,26 bur Richland
    Ch: Charity   b 1827, 11, 2
        James   " 1829, 1, 3 d 1875, 7, 2
        David   " 1830, 9, 12
        Isaac   " 1832, 3, 7
        Benjamin   " 1834, 1, 22
        Peninah   " 1836, 1, 18
        Joel   " 1837, 12, 24
        Mary D.   " 1840, 3, 13
1827, 9, 27. Noah, s Mahlon & Charity, Bel-
    mont Co., O., d 1889,11,2 bur Richland;
    m in Richland, Milicent HALL, dt Isaac &
    Mary, Guernsey Co., O., d 1866,8,5 bur
    Richland
    Ch: Maryann   b 1828, 6, 28
        Mahlon   " 1829, 10, 28 d 1868, 9, 2
          bur Richland
        Phebe   b 1831, 7, 18
        John   " 1833, 5, 18 " 1834, 9,27
        William   " 1835, 5, 3
        Joseph   " 1837, 1, 20 " 1854,12,14
          bur Richland

    Ch: Malinda   b 1838, 10, 25
        Uriah   " 1841, 4, 2
        Cyrus   " 1843, 5, 14 d 1845, 5,16
          bur Richland
        Caleb   b 1845, 6, 18
        Samuel S.   " 1847, 5, 28
        Sarah
         Eleanor   " 1849, 12, 20
        Noah P.   " 1852, 4, 9
1828, 10, 2. Joseph, s Mahlon & Charity,
    Belmont Co., O., d 1890,8,2 bur Richland;
    m in Richland, Sarah HALL, dt Isaac Jr. &
    Mary, Guernsey Co., O., d 1844,1,20 bur
    Richland
    Ch: Isaac   b 1829, 8, 30
        Henry   " 1831, 1, 25
        Eli   " 1833, 1, 16 d 1833, 2,21
        Noah   " 1834, 2, 20
        Jesse   " 1836, 1, 4
        Martha   " 1837, 6, 6
        Zimri   " 1841, 7, 4
1829, 12, 24. Malinda m Benjamin KESTER (H)
1831, 9, 28. Elizabeth m Jesse HALL
1843, 3, 29. John, s Mahlon & Charity,
    Guernsey Co., O.; m in Stillwater MH, Sa-
    rah SEARS, dt Peter & Ann (Doudna), Bel-
    mont Co., O., d 1845,2,24 bur Stillwater
1844, 2, 21. Elizabeth, dt John & Sarah, b
1844, 8, 28. Joseph A., s Mahlon & Charity,
    Guernsey Co., O.; m in Stillwater MH, Ma-
    ria BAILEY, dt Micajah & Mary, Belmont
    Co., O.
    Ch: Joseph B. b 1848, 6, 4
        Mary   " 1850, 4, 15 d 1858, 3,16
          bur Richland
        Sarah   b 1854, 2, 28
1846, 6, 3. John, s Mahlon & Charity, Guern-
    sey Co., O., d 1885,9,20 bur near Mc-
    Arthur, O.; m in Stillwater MH, Anna
    WILLIAMS, dt Henry & Zilpha, Belmont Co.,
    O., d 1887,6,1 bur Stillwater
    Ch: Rebecca   b 1847, 12, 24 d 1849, 3, 3
          bur Richland
        John   b 1849, 3 , 19
1851, 1, 2. Isaac, s Joseph & Sarah (Hall),
    Guernsey Co., O.; m in Richland, Mary
    ENGLE, dt John & Deborah (Watson), b 1830,
    9,18 d 1925,4,15 bur Green Lawn Cemetery,
    Quaker City, O.
    Ch: Lewis   b 1852, 12, 5 d 1859, 7,22
          bur Richland
        Abner W.   b 1856, 2, 24 " 1859, 7,30
          bur Richland
        Alva   b 1862, 10, 25 " 1888, 1,26
          bur Richland
1855, 3, 8. Martha m Josiah SMITH
1855, 12, 27. Henry, s Joseph & Sarah (Hall)
    Guernsey Co., O.; m in Richland, Mary WEB-
    STER, dt John & Deborah, Guernsey Co., O.,
    d 1900,3,27 bur Richland
    Ch: Thomas   b 1856, 10, 13
        Martha   " 1858, 3, 7
        Abi   " 1860, 10, 18

HARTLEY, Henry & Mary, continued
    Ch: Elwood   b 1863, 11, 30
        Debora   " 1866, 2, 25
        Maria Elma " 1868, 10, 6
1856, 2, 22. Phebe, w Noah E., dt Samuel &
    Sarah (Doudna) Carter, b
1856, 9, 14. Charity, w Mahlon, d bur Richland
1859, 10, 27. Phebe m Caleb ARNOLD
----, --, --. Mahlon & Mary
    Ch: Clarkson   b 1861, 8, 27 d 1873, 4,20
                 bur Richland
        Melissa   b 1862, 9, 18
        Phebe   " 1864, 9, 27 " 1884, 4,29
        Minnie   " 1866, 7, 3
----, --, --. Uriah & Mary Ann
    Ch: Rosa R.   b 1867, 10, 10
        Harriet B. " 1876, 3, 4
        Fred M.   " 1882, 2, 9
1874, 9, 3. Sarah m Joseph G. HALL
1878, 10, 31. Martha m Mansel E. HALL
----, --, --. Thomas, s Henry & Mary (Webster)
    b 1856,10,13; m Rosella MARSHALL, dt Jesse
    & Rebecca (Tope), b 1856,12,5
    Ch: Silas H.   b 1881, 3, 19
        Arthur J.   " 1886, 5, 25
        Alva B.   " 1889, 7, 23
        Nora Elmer " 1884, 10, 17
        Homer T.   " 1893, 5, 21
        Elmer C.   " 1897, 12, 8
1882, 4, 27. Abi m Jeptha W. HALL
1885, 10, 29. Deborah C. m Cassius C. HALL
1888, 3, 28. Elwood, s Henry & Mary, Guernsey
    Co., O.; m in Stillwater MH, Sarah A.
    BLOWERS, dt Andrew J. & Rebecca, Belmont
    Co., O.
    Ch: Charles An-
        drew   b 1889, 2, 25
        Mary Etta   " 1892, 10, 20
        Eva Rebec-
        ca   " 1894, 7, 14
        Viola R.   " 1897, 3, 2
        Alfred J.   " 1899, 9, 1
1903, 7, 13. Mary, w Joseph, d bur Richland
1905, 6, 22. Nora E. m Joseph H. DOUDNA
1908, 5, 21. Roanice m William PATTEN
----, --, --. Silas H. m Elizabeth HALL
    Ch: Mary R.   b 1909, 7, 20
        Harry John " 1911, 7, 15
        Anna Mabel " 1913, 8, 21
----, --, --. Arthur J., s Thos. & Rosella
    (Marshall), b 1886,5,25; m Mary Edith
    WHINERY b 1887,2,3
    Ch: Lucile   b 1909, 10, 2
        Laura E.   " 1911, 11, 28
        Willard
        Everett   " 1913, 12, 27
        Clifford B." 1916, 1, 4
        Sarah Alice" 1917, 11, 24
1918, 8, 23. Homer J., s Thomas & Rosella J.
    (Marshall), Guernsey Co., O., b 1896,5,21;
    m in Richland, Martha Eliza LOUHOFF, dt
    Frederic Charles & Julia (or Judith)
    (Kaiser), b 1891,3,31

    Ch: Naomi
        Louise   b 1920, 5, 9
        Chester
        Earl   " 1925, 9, 20
        Shirley   " 1929, 2, 25
----, --, --. Alfred J., s Elwood & Sarah
    Alice (Blowers), b 1899,9,1; m Ethel
    STANLEY, dt Wm. & Edith A. (Wiles),
    b 1898,9,11
    Ch: Dorothy
        Lucile   b 1928, 9, 8

1818, 3, 28. Mahlon & w, Charity, & ch,
    John, Noah, Sarah, Joseph, Melinda,
    Elizabeth, Mary & Abia, rocf Smithfield
    MM, dtd 1818,2,23
1830, 10, 23. Mahlon dis disunity
1830, 10, 23. Malinda Kester (form Hartley)
    dis mcd
1831, 1, 22. Aaron dis jH
1831, 1, 22. Phebe dis jH
1835, 6, 27. Mary Hollinshead (form Hartley)
    dis mcd
1836, 2, 27. Abi Vore (form Hartley) dis mcd
1839, 6, 22. Phebe James (form Hartley) con
    mcd
1847, 11, 27. Charity dis jas
1849, 12, 22. Mary Ann Kester (form Hartley)
    dis mcd
1852, 4, 24. David con mcd
1853, 9, 24. Isaac W. [Heartley] dis mcd
1854, 6, 19. Deborah Gregg (form Hartley)
    con mcd (H)
1855, 2, 17. Aby gct Honey Creek MM, Ind.
    (H)
1856, 5, 24. Penninah Cowder (form Heartley)
    dis mcd
1857, 2, 28. William dis mcd
1858, 8, 28. David dis jas
1858, 12, 25. Mary Starbuck (form Hartley)
    dis mcd
1861, 8, 24. Malinda Carter (form Hartley)
    dis mcd
1864, 8, 27. Noah Jr. dis mcd
1865, 6, 27. Zimri dis mcd
1866, 1, 27. Uriah con mcd
1866, 6, 23. Mary Ann (form Bailey) con mcd
1867, 6, 22. Elizabeth dis jas
1869, 6, 26. Joseph Jr. dis mcd
1873, 3, 19. John Jr. dis mcd
1874, 7, 22. Samuel dis mcd
1874, 9, 23. Sarah Ellen Smith (form Hartly)
    dis mcd
1874, 10, 21. Mary Jones (form Hartly) dis
    mcd
1875, 6, 23. Mary (form Hanson) dis mcd
1879, 1, --. Caleb dis mcd
1880, 7, 21. Thomas con mcd
1880, 7, 21. Rosella recrq
1881, 10, 19. Uriah dis paying bounty money
1884, 1, 23. Alva B. con mcd
1886, 10, 20. Melissa Finley (form Hartley)
    dis mcd

HARTLEY, continued
1893, 7, 19. Minnie Finley (form Hartley)
     dis mcd
1903, 4, 23. Elma M. Hall (form Hartley) con
     mcd
1904, 8, 24. Henry gct Pasadena MM, Calif.,
     to m Margaret C. Williams
1905, 6, 21. Phœbe E. (form Carter) con mcd
1907, 11, 20. Silas gct Somerset MM, to m
     Elizabeth J. Hall
1908, 2, 19. Elizabeth J. rocf Somerset MM,
     dtd 1908,1,23
1908, 7, 22. Arthur J. gct Short Creek MM,
     O., to m Mary Edith Whinnery
1910, 6, 22. Arthur J. gct Somerset MM
1910, 9, 21. Alva B. gct Somerset MM, to m
     Elizabeth C. Doudna
1911, 11, 22. Alva B. gct Somerset MM
1914, 10, 21. Silas H. & w, Elizabeth J., &
     ch, Mary R., Harry J. & Anna M., gct
     Somerset MM
1915, 1, 20. Arthur J. & w, Mary Edith, &
     ch, Laura E., Lucile & Willard Everett,
     rocf Somerset MM
1919, 5, 21. Arthur J. & w, Mary Edith, &
     ch, Lucile, Laura E., W. Everett, Clifford
     B. & Sarah Alice, gct Somerset MM, Ohio
1923, 6, 23. Alfred J. gct Springville MM,
     Ia., to m Ethel A. Stanley
1925, 10, 21. Ethel A. rocf Springville MM,
     Ia., dtd 1925,5,16
1931, 10, 21. Alfred J. & ch, Dorothy Lucile
     & Wm. Elwood, gct New Garden MM
1932, 2, 24. Ethel A. gct New Garden MM

HATCHER
1829, 1, 24. Joshua dis JH
1829, 11, 28. Jane dis JH

HATTON
1814, 6, 28. Edward rocf Centre MM, Pa.,
     dtd 1814,3,19
1814, 10, 25. Edward gct Center MM, O.

HAVILAND
1817, 12, 28. Harriet & dt, Rebecca, rocf
     Fallowfield MM, Pa., dtd 1816,9,9

HAWKINS
1815, 8, 29. Betcy (form Bailey) dis mcd

HAYES
1812, 6, 30. Eaton rocf Short Creek MM, dtd
     1812,5,19
1813, 7, 27. Eaton dis enlisting as a mili-
     tary soldier
1819, 3, 27. Mary [Hays] rst
1829, 6, 27. Mary [Hays] dis JH
1836, 5, 28. Betzy [Hays] (form Hall) dis mcd
1836, 7, 23. Piety [Hays] (form Hall) dis mcd
1844, 6, 22. Priscilla (form Hall) dis mcd
1857, 8, 22. Deborah (form Hall) dis mcd

HAZELETT
1845, 11, 22. Keziah (form Flanner) dis mcd

HEADLEY
1883, 4, 25. Robert Barclay [Headly], s
     Samuel H. & Jane, recrq
1900, 1, 24. Robert B. con mcd
1900, 8, 22. Samuel H. recrq

HEALD
1861, 12, 28. Eliza Ann recrq (residing in
     Linn Co., Ia.)

HEALY
1824, 4, 28. Sarah m Laban B. PATTERSON

1819, 12, 25. Thomas & w, Sarah, & ch, Sarah,
     William P., Hannah, Lydia, Alice, Thomas,
     Delia & Charles, rocf Coyemans MM, N. Y.,
     dtd 1819,7,21, end by Short Creek MM,
     1819,10,19
1824, 8, 88. Thomas dis disunity
1824, 10, 23. Sarah dis disunity; rst by QM
                                1825,1,6
HEATH
1818, 7, 25. Ralph & w, Elizabeth, & ch,
     William Philpot, Robert, Eleanor, Joshua,
     Joanna, Isaac & John, recrq

HENDERSON
1887, 10, 20. James, s Joseph & Isabella,
     Oxford Co., Ontario, Can.; m in Stillwater
     MH, Eunice H. SMITH, dt Israel & Margaret
     Ch: Joseph
             (Dempsey) b 1888, 9, 11
          Lloyd Israel 1896, 1, 28
          Edith
             Jeanette b 1897, 7, 2
----, --, --. Joseph D., s James & Eunice H.
     (Smith), b 1888,9,11; m Vestal M. HALL,
     dt Abner & Anna (Morlan), b 1892,7,23
     Ch: James
             Chalmers b 1913, 11, 13
          Winifred
             Ann   " 1915, 9, 7
          Virginia
             Eunice   " 1923, 4, 3
          Beatrice
             Eva   " 1926, 7, 11

1875, 6, 19. Lucinda (form Thomas) con mcd
     (H)
1888, 8, 22. Eunice H. gct Norwich MM, On-
     tario, Can.
1894, 6, 20. James & w, Eunice H., & s, Jo-
     seph D., rocf Phila. MM, Pa.
1912, 9, 25. James D. gct Middleton MM, to
     m Vesta M. Hall
1913, 1, 22. Vesta M. rocf Middleton MM, dtd
     1913,1,18
1926, 5, 19. Edith J. Skinner (form Hender-
     son) dis mcd
1926, 7, 21. Lloyd I. con mcd

HENDERSON, continued
1929, 6, 19. Edith J. Skinner (form Hender-
     son) dis mcd & jas

HESTER
1836, 5, 21. David & w, Ann, & dt, Phebe, gct
     Green Plain MM

HESTON
1835, 5, 23. Mahlon rocf New Garden MM, Pa.,
     dtd 1834,12,3, end to Plainfield MM

HIATT
1816, 10, 2. Jehu [Hiat], Belmont Co., O.; m
     in Stillwater MH, Tamer VERNON, Belmont
     Co., O.
----, --, --. Elijah & Anne
     Ch: Demsey   b 1826, 11, 12
         Jehu   " 1828, 12, 2

1814, 11, 29. Jehu [Highet] recrq
1815, 2, 28. Elijah, Jonathan, Amos, Jesse,
     Sussana, Ann & Jehu [Highet], ch Jehu,
     recrq
1826, 4, 22. Lydia (form Hodgin) dis mcd
1827, 7, 28. Elisha & w, Anna, & s, Demsey,
     rocf Somerset MM, dtd 1827,5,28
1829, 3, 28. Elisha & w, Anna, & ch, Demsey
     & Jehu, gct White Water MM, Ind.
1842, 4, 23. Edith [Hiat] (form Embree) dis
     mcd

HIBBERT
1830, 8, 28. Caleb rocf Flushing MM, dtd
     1830,7,22
1830, 12, 25. Caleb dis jH
1833, 10, 19. Caleb gct Flushing MM (H)

HIBBS
1882, 10, 25. Ruth S. (form Doudna) dis mcd

HICKS
1812, 11, 5. James, s Clemens & Mary, Belmont
     Co., O.; m in Stillwater MH, Bethany
     BAILEY, dt Wm. & Rebekah, Belmont Co., O.
     Ch: Mary   d 1841,11,15
1815, 3, 15. Asa, s Clemmon & Mary, Belmont
     Co., O.; m in Stillwater MH, Anna COX, dt
     John & Rachel, Belmont Co., O.
     Ch: Israel   b 1816, 7, 15
         Ellen   " 1818, 3, 26
         Asenith   " 1820, 3, 8
         Eli   " 1822, 4, 5
         Milten   " 1824, 7, 5
         Asa   " 1826, 11, 5
         Anna   " 1829, 2, 5
         Harrison   " 1831, 3, 4
         Elwood   " 1833, 1, 3
         Emaline   " 1834, 12, 8
1817, 3, 26. Laben, s Clemons & Mary, Belmont
     Co., O.; m in Stillwater MH, Elizabeth
     DAVIS, dt Moses & Ann, Belmont Co., O.
1827, 1, 31. Mary Bailey m Caleb HALL

1839, 12, 5. Joanna m William HANSON
1840, 12, 10. Lydia m Joseph HANSON
1843, 11, 30. James, s James & Bethany, Bel-
     mont Co., O.; m in Captina, Zilpha VERNON
     dt Robert & Deborah, Belmont Co., O.
     Ch: Mary Jane b 1845, 2, 2
         Lucina   " 1846, 8, 18
         Lydia Ann " 1848, 4, 11
         Malinda   " 1849, 12, 26
1845, 11, 27. Martha m Joseph VERNON

1808, 7, 28. Mary & ch, Laban, James, Rachel,
     Joseph Robert & Asa, rocf Blackwater MM,
     Va., dtd 1808,5,23, end by Concord MM,
     1808,7,21
1816, 5, 25. Laban dis serving in army
1816, 12, 22. Laban [Hix] rst
1817, 1, 25. Rachel Parsons (form Hicks) dis
     mcd
1820, 8, 26. Joseph dis
1833, 7, 27. Robert dis mcd
1835, 1, 24. Asa dis disunity
1836, 8, 27. Eleanor Campbell (form Hicks)
     dis mcd
1838, 7, 28. Joanna rocf Somerset MM, dtd
     1838,6,25
1838, 7, 28. Lydia rocf Somerset MM, dtd
     1838,6,25
1838, 10, 27. James & w, Bethany, & ch, Mary,
     James, Martha, Bethany & Robert, rocf
     Somerset MM, dtd 1838,9,7
1838, 10, 27. William rocf Somerset MM, dtd
     1838,9,7
1840, 1, 18. Joseph gct Concord MM (H)
1840, 3, 28. William dis mcd
1847, 2, 27. Bethena Wilson (form Hicks) dis
     mcd
1849, 1, 27. Israel dis mcd
1849, 6, 23. Asenath Scott (form Hicks) dis
     mcd
1852, 8, 28. Asa dis mcd
1852, 8, 28. Milton dis mcd
1852, 11, 27. James Jr. & w, Zilpah, & ch,
     Mary Jane, Lucinda & Malinda, gct Spring
     Creek MM, Ia.
1853, 2, 26. Robert dis mcd

HILL
1909, 6, 23. Milicent Rosaline (form Arnold)
     dis mcd

HILTON
1861, 1, 19. Ann H. (form Hall) con mcd (H)

HINSHAW
1894, 12, 26. John E., s Andrew & Sarah A.,
     Lyon Co., Kans.; m in Stillwater MH,
     Elizabeth B. SMITH, dt Barclay & Hannah
     H., Belmont Co., O.

1897, 1, 20. Elizabeth & s, Howard B., gct
     Cottonwood MM, Kans.

HIRST

----, --, --. Wilson C., s John & Maria
    (Branson), b 1846,10,27; m Rachel TABER,
    dt Louis & Mary Ann (Hill); b 1848,6,5

1907, 11, 20. Wilson C. & w, Rachel Taber,
    rocf Hickory Grove MM, Ia., dtd 1907,2,11
1926, 6, 23. Wilson C. con mcd

HOBSON
1847, 10, 23. Joseph Doudna gct Flushing MM,
    to m Belinda Hobson

HODGIN

----, --, --. William m Agnes ----- d 1841,9,9
    bur Stillwater
    Ch: Mary   b 1788, 11, 13
        John   " 1791, 2, 19
        Sarah   " 1793, 3, 22
        William " 1795, 6, 6
        Martha   " 1798, 2, 19
        Laban   " 1800, 9, 15 d 1816, 5,21
            bur Stillwater
        Ann   b 1802, 10, -- " 1803, 6,--
        Robert   " 1805, 3, 3
        Rebecca " 1807, 4, 21
        Stephen " 1809, 11, 23
----, --, --. Stephen m Elizabeth ----- d 1841,
    10,8 bur Stillwater
    Ch: Asenath b 1796, 10, 20
        Eli   " 1798, 10, 28
        Amy   " 1800, 6, 10
        William " 1802, 7, 15
        Lydia   " 1806, 11, 22
        Mary   " 1810, 4, 10
1810, 1, 3. Sarah m Amos DAVIS
----, --, --. John & Prudence
    Ch: Nancy   b 1816, 4, 4
        William " 1817, 10, 21
        Leah   " 1819, 8, 1
        Elias   " 1821, 4, 23
        Agnes   " 1822, 1, 3 d 1826, 4,26
            bur Deerfield
        Frances b 1824, 12, 9
        Edwin   " 1827, 4, 11
1819, 9, 1. William, s Wm. & Agnes, Belmont
    Co., O.; m in Stillwater MH, Mary WILLIAMS
    dt Daniel & Mary, Belmont Co., O.
1820, 11, 15. William d ae 54y 8m 11d bur New
    Garden, N. C.
1821, 9, 26. Amy m Benjamin CLENDENON
1822, 10, 2. Eli, s Stephen & Elizabeth, Bel-
    mont Co., O.; m in Stillwater MH, Mary
    ENGLE, dt Caleb & Mercy, Belmont Co., O.,
    Ch: Asenath b 1823, 7, 21[d 1840,10,19
        Caleb   " 1825, 5, 3 d 1825, 5,15
            bur Stillwater
        Stephen b 1826, 6, 25
        John E. " 1830, 11, 12
        Daniel W. " 1833, 10, 27
        Ezekiel " 1836, 8, 7 d 1840,10, 7
            bur Stillwater
        William b 1839, 11, 1

1823, 10, 29. Rebecca m Joel DOUDNA
1832, 9, 26. Mary m Joseph STANTON
1834, 12, 3. Nancy m Jesse BAILEY
----, --, --. Eli & Sarah
    Ch: Eli   b 1843, 1, 5
        Amos   " 1848, 5, 11
        Jesse   " 1852, 1, 30 d 1852, 2,12
            bur Stillwater
1847, 6, 2. Stephen, Belmont Co., O.; m in
    Stillwater MH, Abba WILLIAMS, dt Henry &
    Zilpha, Belmont Co., O., d 1873,5,5
1852, 5, 20. Barclay, s Wm. & Mary, Belmont
    Co., O.; m in house of Wm. Schooley, Mary
    E. SCHOOLEY, dt Wm. & Agness, Belmont Co.,
    O.
1853, 3, 23. Clarkson, s Stephen & Mary, b
1853, 6, 21. Stephen d bur Stillwater
1856, 10, 1. Daniel, s Eli & Mary, Belmont
    Co., O.; m in Stillwater MH, Tamar DAW-
    SON, dt Jesse & Jane, Belmont Co., O.
1857, 4, 29. Asenath m John EDGERTON

1815, 9, 26. John dis mcd
1815, 12, 23. Asenath Starbuck (form Hodgin)
    dis mcd
1817, 4, 26. Robert & w, Ann, & ch, John,
    Lydie, Mary Ann, Elizabeth, William, Rob-
    ert & Stephen, rocf Mill Creek MM, dtd
    1816, 10,26
1817, 8, 23. Prudence recrq
1818, 3, 28. John recrq
1820, 2, 26. Martha Steele (form Hodgin) dis
    mcd
1820, 8, 26. Mary (form Williams) dis mcd
1820, 9, 23. William Jr. dis
1822, 5, 25. William dis mcd
1824, 2, 28. John & w, Prudence, & ch, Nancy,
    Leah & Agnes, rocf Somerset MM, dtd 1823,
    12,29
1826, 4, 22. Lydia Hiatt (form Hodgin) dis
    mcd
1829, 1, 3. Robert dis mcd
1829, 1, 24. Eunice (form Strahl) dis mcd
1829, 6, 27. Prudence & ch, Nancy, William,
    Leah, Elias, Frances & Edwin E., rocf
    Deerfield MM, dtd 1829,3,19
1832, 5, 26. Stephen dis mcd
1837, 1, 28. Leah dis
1839, 11, 23. Elias gct Chesterfield MM
1840, 1, 25. Prudence & ch, Francis & Edwin,
    gct Chesterfield MM
1840, 7, 25. William gct Chesterfield MM
1842, 3, 26. Eli gct Chesterfield MM, to m
    Sarah Bundy
1842, 6, 25. Sarah & ch, William, Mary,
    Ruthanna & Esther Bundy, rocf Chesterfield
    MM, dtd 1842,6,18
1848, 9, 23. William & w, Martha, & ch, Mar-
    garet, rocf Chesterfield MM, dtd 1848,6,17
1852, 2, 28. Stephen Jr. gct Pennsville MM,
    to m Sarah Millhouse
1852, 9, 25. Sarah M. rocf Pennsville MM,
    dtd 1852,8,19

HODGIN, continued

1853, 8, 27. Stephen & w, Sarah M., & s,
    Clarkson, gct Pennsville MM
1853, 10, 22. William dis mcd
1855, 4, 28. John gct Plymouth MM
1857, 10, 24. Daniel & w, Tamor, gct Chester-
    field MM
1861, 10, 26. Martha Crew (form Hodgin) dis
    mcd
1863, 1, 24. Prudence rocf Chesterfield MM,
    dtd 1862,12,20
1864, 11, 26. Eli Jr. dis military service
1866, 2, 24. William dis military service
1867, 3, 23. Eli & w, Sarah, gct Springville
    MM, Iowa
1867, 11, 23. Harriet Gilliland (form Hodgin)
    dis mcd
1874, 12, 23. Amos dis mcd
1906, 8, 22. Edmund C. Stanton gct Spring-
    ville MM, Ia., to m Sina M. Hodgin

HODGSON

1901, 5, 22. Robert & w, Emma, rocf Frankfort
    MM, Phila., Pa., dtd 1901,4,25
1909, 2, 24. Robert & Emma relrq "to become
    mbr at Marsden MM, England"

HOGUE

1848, 3, 22. Samuel, s Samuel & Elizabeth,
    Belmont Co., O.; m in house of Stephen
    BROWN, Agnes Ann BROWN, dt Stephen &
    Asenath, Monroe Co., O. (H)
1878, 10, 24. Joseph S., s Levi & Mary (Hirst)
    Belmont Co., O., b 1852,10,18; m in Still-
    water MH, Anna M. STEER, dt James & Mary,
    Belmont Co., O., b 1852,10,24
    Ch: Chas. Levi d 1891, 10, 17

1829, 1, 24. David dis JH
1829, 1, 24. Elizabeth dis JH
1829, 1, 24. Elizabeth dis JH
1829, 1, 24. Ruth dis JH
1829, 2, 28. Elizabeth, dt David, dis JH
1829, 2, 28. Joshua dis JH
1829, 9, 26. Bushrod dis JH
1829, 9, 26. Isaac dis JH
1829, 10, 24. David Jr. dis JH
1829, 10, 24. Jonathan dis JH
1830, 1, 23. Haseal [Hoge] dis JH
1830, 6, 26. Mary [Hoge] dis JH
1830, 6, 26. Sarah [Hoge] dis JH
1851, 3, 15. Jonathan L. & w, Lydia, & ch,
    William Homes, Theodoric, Susannah, Philo
    Mead, Amy & Romona, gct Deerfield MM
1853, 8, 27. Asa Benjamin rocf Hopewell MM,
    dtd 1853,5,5
1857, 8, 15. Mary rocf Plainfield MM, dtd
    1857,7,16 (H)
1858, 3, 20. Elizabeth recrq (H)
1864, 5, 21. Thomas E. & w, Ann, & ch, Mary
    Emily, Sylvanus G., Orilla C. & Orison,
    gct Prairie Grove MM, Ia. (H)
1873, 1, 18. Elnora Adams (form Hogue) con

mcd (H)
1875, 8, 21. Isaac N. con mcd (H)
1875, 8, 21. Tamar Jane (form Bryant) con
    mcd (w of Isaac) (H)
1879, 5, 21. Anna M. gct Short Creek MM
1883, 8, 25. Joseph G. & w, Anna M., & s,
    Charles L., rocf Short Creek MM
1904, 7, 20. Elizabeth (form Frame) dis mcd
    & jas

HOLLAND

1846, 1, 24. Sarah (form Kester) dis mcd

HOLLINGSHEAD

1835, 6, 27. Mary (form Hartley) dis mcd

HOLLINGSWORTH

1860, 10, 31. Samuel, s Er & Phebe, Columbi-
    ana Co., O.; m in Stillwater MH, Martha
    HALL, dt Allen & Edith FARQUHAR, Harrison
    Co., O.

1857, 4, 25. William rocf Pennsville MM,
    dtd 1857,3,19
1861, 1, 26. Martha & ch, Mary Hall & Joseph
    Hall, gct Middleton MM
1865, 6, 24. William gct Coal Creek MM, Iowa

HOLLOWAY

1830, 4, 1. Samuel, s Asa & Abigail, Bel-
    mont Co., O.; m in Plainfield, Sarah
    SHARP, dt Thomas & Mercy, Belmont Co., O.
----, --, --. David & Rachel (Pidgeon)
    Ch: David   b 1838, 6, 12 d 1928, 9,10
        bur Stillwater
1863, 10, 28. William H., s Samuel & Mary,
    Belmont Co., O.; m in Stillwater MH, Mary
    Ann FRAME, dt Aaron & Talitha, Ia.
----, --, --. David & Ann (Cooper)
    Ch: Charles   b 1868, 11, 29
        John   " 1875, 11, 10
----, --, --. David m Eliza M. WILLIAMS, dt
    Francis H. & Mary (Owen), b 1851,1,4 d
    1926,1,4 bur Stillwater
1893, 9, 21. Charles, s David & Ann, Keokuk
    Co., Ia.; m in Stillwater MH, Sarah C.
    BUNDY, dt Lindley & Ruanna, Belmont Co.,O.
    Ch: Mabel Anna b 1894, 7, 31 d 1919, 1,18
        bur Stillwater
        Harrold L. b 1895, 12, 28
        Mary Ru-
        anna   " 1901, 11, 15
        Charles
        Francis   " 1908, 7, 29
----, --, --. Walter m Alice VAIL
    Ch: Rola Vail b 1898, 7, 27
        Walter M. " 1899, 10, 25
----, --, --. Willis & Louisa (Penrose)
    Ch: Francis
        Iral   b 1902, 7, 1
        John LeRoy " 1900, 4, 25
        Theodore R." 1903, 8, 25
        Leslie Da-

HOLLOWAY, continued
　　Ch: vid　b 1906,12,19
----, --, --. Charles m Sarah C. BUNDY, dt
　　Lindley & Ruanna (Frame), b 1872,12,16
　　Ch: Mary R.　　b 1901, 11, 15
　　　　Charles
　　　　　Francis　"　1908, 7, 29
----, --, --. Harold, s Charles & Sarah C.
　　(Bundy); m Helen E. HALL, dt Wilford & Sa-
　　rah B. (Stanton) b 1899,6,30
　　Ch: Paul W.　　b 1919, 12, 21
　　　　Dorothy
　　　　　Louella　"　1923,　6, 24
　　　　Harold Jr.　"　1928,　8, 12

1830, 7, 24.　Sarah & dt, Ann Sharp, gct
　　Flushing MM
1843, 4, 22.　Paul Sears gct Flushing MM, to
　　m Abigail Holloway
1859, 4, 23.　Joel Bailey gct Flushing MM, to
　　m Lydia Holloway
1869, 1, 23.　Mary Ann F. gct Flushing MM
1888, 1, 25.　William H. & s, Emerson W., rocf
　　Flushing MM, dtd 1887,11,24
1890, 5, 21.　Walter E. Vail gct Flushing MM,
　　to m Deborah Holloway
1896, 8, 19.　Sarah C. & ch, Mabel Anna &
　　Harold Lindley, gct Flushing MM
1903, 5, 20.　Charles & w, Sarah, & ch, Mable
　　Anna, Harold L. & Mary Ruanna, rocf Flush-
　　ing MM, dtd 1903,4,23
1903, 11, 25.　Alice (form Vail) dis mcd
1905, 7, 19.　John B. rocf Coal Creek MM, Ia.,
　　dtd 1905,7,8
1908, 7, 22.　Willis L. & w, Louisa S., & ch,
　　Leroy, Iral, Ernest & Leslie, rocf Hickory
　　Grove MM, Ia., dtd 1908,7,4
1908, 10, 21.　David & w, Eliza M., rocf Coal
　　Creek MM, Ia., dtd 1908,10,10
1910, 2, 23.　John B. con mcd
1912, 9, 25.　Willis L. dis disunity
1912, 9, 25.　Louisa dis disunity
1920, 11, 24.　Charles E. dis disunity
1923, 6, 23.　Harold L. con mcd
1926, 8, 25.　Eliza M. d 1926,4,7 ae 74 (an
　　elder)
1926, 12, 22.　Sarah C. & s, Charles Francis,
　　gct Pasadena MM, Calif.
1926, 12, 22.　Mary R. gct Pasadena MM, Calif.
1929, 9, 25.　David d 1928,9,10 ae 91 (a
　　minister)

HOLLOWELL
1845, 3, 20.　Lydia m Samuel YOCUM (H)

1843, 1, 21.　Thomas C. gct Rochester MM, N.Y.
　　(H)

HOLTON
1851, 7, 26.　Rachel (form Harris) dis mcd

HOOPES
1819, 3, 4.　Sidney [Hoops] m Lewis MARIS

1817, 6, 28.　Sidney rocf Bradford MM, dtd
　　1817,5,7
1819, 8, 28.　Sidney Maris (form Hoopes) dis
　　mcd

HORNER
1828, 2, 23.　Benjamin Fawcett gct Plainfield
　　MM, to m Lydia Horner
1830, 5, 22.　Lydia dis disunity
1830, 7, 24.　Martha dis JH
1834, 2, 22.　Betsy Allen (form Horner) dis
　　mcd

HOUGH
1833, 11, 23.　Sarah Jane Morton (form Hough)
　　dis mcd
1834, 2, 22.　Israel dis JH

HOYLE
----, --, --. Benjamin, s John & Sarah, Bel-
　　mont Co., O., d 1875,2,3 bur Stillwater;
　　m Tabitha ----- d 1828,4,2 ae 30y bur
　　Stillwater
　　Ch: Sarah　　b 1821, 1, 11
　　　　Josiah　"　1822, 10, 29 d 1825, 2,20
　　　　　bur Stillwater
　　　　John G.　b 1827, 4, 10
Benjamin m 2nd 1830,3,10 in Stillwater MH
　　Mary MILLHOUSE, dt Robert & Sarah, Belmont
　　Co., O., d 1895,5,4 bur Stillwater
　　Ch: Tabitha　　b 1831, 6, 8 d 1837, 4, 2
　　　　　bur Stillwater
　　　　Hannah　　b 1834, 6, 2
　　　　Benjamin Jr"　1837, 8, 5 "　1905,10,25
　　　　　bur Stillwater
　　　　Elizabeth b 1841, 5, 26 "　1841, 5,28
　　　　　bur Stillwater
　　　　William　b 1847, 7, 17
1840, 7, 1.　Sarah m Edmund STANTON
1850, 10, 30.　John G., s Benjamin & Tabitha,
　　Belmont Co., O.; m in Stillwater MH,
　　Elizabeth BUNDY, dt Ezekiel & Maria, Bel-
　　mont Co., O.
　　Ch: Simeon　　b 1851, 10, 31
　　　　Ezekiel B.　"　1855, 12, 16
　　　　Nathan B.　"　1854, 8, 5 d 1855, 2, 5
　　　　　bur Stillwater
1856, 10, 29.　Hannah m Barclay SMITH
1869, 3, 31.　William, s Benjamin & Mary, Bel-
　　mont Co., O., b 1847,7,17 d 1928,5,23 bur
　　Stillwater; m in Stillwater MH, Hannah W.
　　PLUMMER, dt Robert & Jane, Belmont Co.,
　　O., b 1848,7,13 d 1928,4,4 bur Stillwater
　　Ch: Frederick
　　　　　C.　　b 1870, 12, 26
　　　　Albertus　"　1872, 6, 27
　　　　Laura Jo-
　　　　　sephine　"　1876, 3, 13
　　　　Mabel Jane "　1881, 3, 27
1871, 11, 1.　Simeon S., s John G. & Eliza-
　　beth, Belmont Co., O.; m in Stillwater
　　MH, Mary H. DOUDNA, dt Joseph F. & Bel-
　　linda (Hobson), Belmont Co., O.

HOYLE, Simeon S. & Mary, continued
    Ch: Alice Cary b 1874, 1, 11
1877, 9, 27. Ezekiel B., s John G. & Elizabeth
    (Bundy), Belmont Co., O.; m in Richland,
    Ann HALL, dt Abner & Phebe (Webster),
    Guernsey Co., O.
    Ch: Emory D.   b 1878, 6, 11
        Nathan A. " 1880, 2, 23
        Elmer R.   " 1882, 5, 1
        Webster B. " 1887, 3, 8
        Clara P.   " 1888, 8, 24
----, --, --. Frederick C., s Wm. & Hannah
    (Plummer), b 1870,12,26; m Martha BRACKEN,
    dt Lindley & Anna S. (French), b 1874,7,4
    Ch: Mildred   b 1897, 1, 26
        Helen   " 1899, 3, 21
        Robert
         Bracken " 1903, 2, 11

1827, 2, 24. Benjamin & w, Tabitha, & dt,
    Sarah, rocf Smithfield MM, dtd 1827,2,19
1842, 11, 26. Benjamin & w, Mary, & ch, Hannah
    & Benjamin, gct Short Creek MM
1847, 3, 27. Benjamin & w, Mary, & ch, Hannah
    & Benjamin, rocf Short Creek MM, dtd 1847,
    3,23
1865, 7, 22. Thomas & w, Hannah, & s, William
    G., gct Hickory Grove MM, Ia.
1865, 7, 22. Joseph Lindley gct Hickory Grove
    MM, Ia.
1875, 8, 25. Benjamin d 1875,2,3 ae 78 (a
    minister)
1884, 3, 19. Simeon & w, Mary H., & dt, Alice
    Cary, gct Cottonwood MM, Kans.
1884, 4, 23. John G. & w, Elizabeth, gct
    Cottonwood MM, Kans.
1889, 5, 22. Ezekiel & w, Anna, & ch, Emery
    D., Nathan H., Elmer R., Webster B. &
    Clarence P., gct Damorris MM, Kans.
1895, 3, 20. Albertus C. gct Flushing MM, to
    m Mabel B. Wilson
1895, 9, 25. Fredrick C. gct Short Creek MM,
    to m Martha H. Brakin
1895, 10, 23. Albertus L. gct Phila. MM, Pa.
1896, 9, 23. Martha B. rocf Short Creek MM,
    dtd 1896,8,18
1910, 9, 21. Mabel H. Dwiggins (form Hoyle)
    dis mcd
1922, 8, 23. Mildred & Helen dis jas

HUDSON
1817, 10, 25. Ruth (form Dodd) dis mcd

HUGHES
1832, 3, 24. Ellis, Edwin & Moses rocf New
    Garden MM, dtd 1831,10,20

HULL
1819, 12, 25. Ann rocf Baltimore MM, W. Dist.,
    dtd 1819,6,11
1820, 8, 26. Ann rocf Baltimore MM, W. Dist.,
    dtd 1819,6,11, end to Smithfield MM

HUNNICUTT
1812, 3, 31. Sarah Bailey (form Hunnicutt)
    dis mcd
1816, 4, 27. Deborah Wilson (form Hunnicutt)
    dis mcd
1819, 4, 24. Thomas dis mcd
1828, 10, 25. William P. & w, Edna, & s, Mor-
    decai P., rocf Upper MM, Va., dtd 1829,1,
    19
1829, 9, 26. Wm. P. & w, Edna, & ch, Morde-
    cai P. & Burwell, gct Springborough MM

HUNT
1831, 6, 30. Samuel P., s Joshua & Rachel,
    Belmont Co., O.; m in Stillwater, Eliza-
    beth THOMAS, dt Camm & Elizabeth, Belmont
    Co., O. (H)

1820, 5, 27. Joshua & w, Rachel, & ch, Sam-
    uel, Joshua, Jonathan, John, Nathan &
    Charles, rocf Flushing MM, dtd 1820,4,21
1823, 12, 27. David rocf Flushing MM, dtd
    1823,10,24
1829, 1, 3. William dis jH
1830, 6, 26. Rachel dis jH
1830, 9, 25. Jonathan dis jH
1832, 3, 24. Moses rocf New Garden MM, dtd
    1831,10,20
1832, 3, 24. Joshua dis jH
1844, 3, 16. Samuel P. & w, Elizabeth, & ch,
    Thomas, John Eberly, Elizabeth & Martha,
    gct Miami MM (H)

HUSSEY
1821, 1, 27. John rocf Short Creek MM, dtd
    1821,11,21
1841, 3, 21. John gct Short Creek MM

HUSTLER
1831, 5, 28. Sarah recrq
1832, 11, 24. Jeremiah Jr. recrq
1836, 11, 26. Hannah recrq
1839, 3, 23. Jeremiah Jr. gct Knesborough
    MM, England
1839, 3, 23. Hannah & dt, Sarah, gct Knes-
    borough MM, Eng.

HUTCHINSON
1832, 7, 28. Becca (form Williams) dis mcd

HUTTON
----, --, --. J. Wetherill, s Richard &
    Elizabeth (Thompson), b 1866,4,28; m
    Ellen C. COPE, dt Charles & Rachel (Edger-
    ton), b 1887,6,1
    Ch: Elizabeth
          R.   b 1915, 6, 16
        Chas.
         Wetherill " 1917, 1, 9

1912, 11, 20. J. Wetherill rocf Kennet MM,
    Pa., dtd 1912,11,5
1914, 7, 22. J. Wetherill gct New Garden MM,

HUTTON, continued
    to m Ellen S. Cope
1914, 12, 23. Ellen rocf New Garden MM, dtd
    1914,11,26

INGRAM
----, --, --. Robert & Hannah
    Ch: Harlan   b 1821, 1, 30
        Mary   " 1822, 12, 28

1822, 6, 22. Robert & w, Hannah, & s, Harlen,
    rocf Bradford MM, dtd 1822,1,9

JACKSON
1885, 8, 19. Stephen & w, Frances, & ch,
    Israel Ernest & Mari-Frances, recrq (form
    mbr Orthodox Frs)
1887, 6, 22. Stephen & w, Frances, & ch gct
    Springville MM, Ia.

JAMES
----, --, --. Caleb & Elizabeth
    Ch: Mary Ann b 1816, 8, 31
        Lorenzo   " 1814, 3, 13
        Curtis
         Hoops   " 1818, 8, 16
        Elizabeth " 1822, 3, 6
        Caleb   " 1826, 9, 25
        Isaac   " 1830, 4, 12

1820, 6, 24. Caleb & w, Elizabeth, & ch, Lo-
    renzo, Mary Ann & Curtis, rocf Goshen MM,
    Pa., dtd 1819,6,30
1828, 12, 27. Caleb dis disunity
1833, 10, 26. Elizabeth dis disunity
1839, 6, 22. Phebe (form Hartley) con mcd
1845, 2, 22. Lorenzo dis mcd
1845, 2, 22. Curtis dis mcd
1845, 12, 27. Mary Ann Jewett (form James) dis
    mcd
1846, 6, 27. Elizabeth dis disunity
1852, 3, 27. Phebe gct South River MM, Ia.;
    returned 7-24 & then gct Spring Creek MM,
    Ia.
1860, 6, 23. Jesse rocf Middleton MM, dtd
    1860,6,16
1860, 6, 23. Mary Catharine rocf Middleton
    MM, dtd 1860,6,16
1863, 6, 20. Sarah Cliff (form James) dis
    mcd & jas (H)
1914, 12, 23. William Carson & w, Amy R., &
    ch, Walter S. & Eva Rachel, rocf Spring
    River MM, Kans.
1919, 4, 23. Wm. Carson & w, Amy R., & ch,
    Walter S. & Eva Rachel, transferred to
    Fairhope MM, Ala.

JEFFRIES
1829, 2, 28. Phebe dis jH
1829, 6, 27. Rhoda dis

JEWELL
1845, 12, 27. Mary Ann (form James) dis mcd

JOHNSON
1821, 2, 3. William d
1903, 8, 20. William P., s Ashley & Eliza-
    beth H., Morgan Co., O.; m in Barnsville
    MH, Esther EDGERTON, dt James & Amy L.,
    Belmont Co., O.
----, --, --. Roy Lamont, s Albert & Frances
    A.; m Emma L. McGREW, dt Eli W. & Eliza
    J., b 1884,3,31 (Roy Lamont b 1884,12,27)
----, --, --. Roy m Emma GIBBONS
    Ch: Edith
        Rebecca b 1924, 1, 11
        Allen Nel-
         son   " 1926, 11, 4
        Myron Roy " 1928, 5, 28

1818, 6, 27. William rocf Nottingham MM, dtd
    1818,7,11
1818, 9, 26. William con mcd
1820, 4, 23. William gct Plainfield MM
1825, 2, 26. Ann (form Bailey) dis mcd
1829, 1, 24. Rachel dis jH
1905, 2, 22. Esther E. gct West Union MM,
    Ind.
1923, 12, 19. Emma L. rocf Somerset MM, dtd
    1923,11,22

JOLLEY
1812, 8, 26. Malachi m in Stillwater MH, Su-
    sannah NEWBY

1813, 3, 2. Susannah gct Plymouth MM
1817, 9, 27. Susannah & dt, Elizabeth, rocf
    Plymouth MM, dtd 1817,6,23
1818, 10, 24. Susannah dis
1826, 9, 23. Elizabeth, minor, gct Elk MM

JONES
----, --, --. Joseph d 1837,11,26 bur Still-
    water; m Mary ----- d 1835,12,22 bur
    Stillwater
1846, 12, 24. Aquilla, s Yearsley & Susannah,
    Belmont Co., O.; m in house of Samuel
    Wells, Sarah WELLS, dt Samuel & Hannah,
    Belmont Co., O.

1814, 1, 25. George Parker gct New Garden
    MM, O., to m Rachel Jones
1816, 4, 27. Joseph & w, Mary, & Aaron
    Morris, a minor in their care, rocf New
    Garden MM, O., dtd 1816,2,15
1818, 1, 24. Hannah rocf Cincinnati MM, dtd
    1817,12,18
1821, 7, 28. Joseph & w, Mary, gct Flushing
    MM
1828, 10, 25. Thomas Thomason gct Short Creek
    MM, to m Mariah Jones
1832, 5, 26. Joseph & w, Mary, rocf Flushing
    MM, dtd 1832,4,24
1834, 3, 15. Abner & w, Maria, & dt, Rebecca,
    gct White Water MM (H)
1835, 8, 22. Joseph rocf Concord MM, Pa., dtd
    1835,4,3

JONES, continued

1849, 5, 26. Sarah (form Wells) dis mcd
1849, 5, 26. Susannah (form Wood) dis mcd
1856, 10, 18. Yearsley gct Plainfield MM (H)
1866, 9, 15. Susanna J. Price (form Jones)
    con mcd (H)
1874, 10, 21. Mary (form Hartly) dis mcd
1924, 8, 20. Edna H. (form Hall) dis mcd &
    jas

JORDAN
1819, 2, 27. Rebecca (form Starbuck) dis mcd

JUDGE
1816, 4, 3. Rebecca Y. m Samuel Sharpless
1818, 8, 26. Phebe m Asahel THOMAS
1827, 9, --. Susannah, w Hugh, d bur Still-
    water

1815, 9, 26. Hugh & w, Susannah, rocf Indian
    Spring MM, dtd 1815,4,21, end by Plain-
    field MM, 1815,8,31
----, --, --. Phebe rocf Indian Spring MM,
    dtd 1815,4,21, end by Plainfield MM,
    1815,8,31
----, --, --. Rebeckah Y. rocf Indian Spring
    MM, dtd 1815,4,21, end by Plainfield MM,
    1815,8,31
1828, 8, 23. Susannah d 1827,9,29 ae 74 (an
    elder)
1829, 6, 27. Hugh dis jH
1834, 6, 21. Hugh gct Plainfield MM (H)

JUDKINS
1812, 6, 10. Elizabeth m Edward THORNBROUGH
1818, 5, 8. Lucy d bur Stillwater

1811, 5, 28. Joel & w, Lucy, & dt, Elizabeth,
    rocf New Garden MM, N. C., dtd 1811,3,30
1811, 5, 28. Carolius & w, Charity, & ch,
    Thomas, Jesse, Joel, Anderson, Elizabeth
    & James, rocf New Garden MM, N. C., dtd
    1811,3,30
1820, 1, 22. Thomas dis mcd
1822, 3, 23. Joel gct Plainfield MM, to m
    Maria Gregg
1823, 5, 24. Maria rocf Plainfield MM, dtd
    1821,7,25
1827, 2, 24. Elizabeth Bailey (form Judkins)
    dis mcd
1827, 3, 24. Joel dis disunity
1829, 1, 3-. Anderson relrq
1829, 4, 18. Maria & s, Hiram, gct Plainfield
    MM (H)
1829, 9, 26. Carolus dis jH
1829, 9, 26. Jesse dis jH
1829, 10, 24. Mariah dis jH
1829, 12, 26. Charity dis jH
1831, 4, 23. Nicholas dis disunity
1832, 9, 22. Joel dis paying a muster fine
1833, 5, 25. James dis jH
1833, 9, 28. Rachel dis jH
1840, 2, 22. Susannah & ch, James & Maria,

rocf Short Creek MM, dtd 1839,11,19
1840, 2, 22. Martha rocf Short Creek MM, dtd
    1839,11,19
1840, 2, 22. Mary rocf Short Creek MM, dtd
    1839,11,19
1841, 9, 25. Martha Shriver (form Judkins)
    dis mcd
1842, 9, 24. Mary Bye (form Judkins) dis mcd
1846, 3, 25. Susannah & dt, Mariah, gct
    White Water MM, Ind.
1848, 5, 27. James dis mcd

KENAN
1861, 5, 18. Phebe (form Hall) con mcd (H)

KENNARD
----, --, --. Thomas & Elizabeth
    Ch: Henry
        Preston   b 1814, 10, 26
        Rachel   " 1816, 12, 6
        Levi   " 1819, 2, 7
        John   " 1820, 11, 20
        Joseph   " 1822, 12, 12
        Jacob   " 1825, 2, 3
        Jenkins   " 1826, 12, 4
----, --, --. Eli & Mary (Edgerton)
    Ch: Abby W.   b 1860, 8, 27
        Alferd E. " 1865, 4, 26
----, --, --. Eli m Mary EDGERTON d 1902,1,29
    bur Stillwater
    Ch: Mary E.   b 1857, 11, 8
        Abby W.   " 1860, 8, 27
        Sarah J.   " 1862, 9, 5
        Lizzie   d 1904,12,20
1862, 8, 13. William d bur Stillwater
1864, 9, 28. Elizabeth R. m Amasa FRAME
1885, 8, 18. Eli, s William, d bur Stillwater
1892, 10, 11. Sarah, w William, dt Aaron &
    Elizabeth ROBERTS, d bur Stillwater
----, --, --. Anna D., dt John B. & Mary
    Eleanor Bulger, b 1870,2,1 d 1933,7,14
1909, 12, 15. Mary Elizabeth, dt Alferd E. &
    Anna (Bulger), b

1826, 6, 24. Eli & w, Hannah, & ch, Catha-
    rine, Esther, Mary, Tacy, Wm., Eli & Han-
    nah, rocf Short Creek MM, dtd 1826,4,18
1829, 10, 24. Elizabeth dis jH
1829, 12, 26. Thomas dis jH
1856, 5, 24. Eli & w, Mary, & ch, Anna,
    William & Jesse, rocf Somerset MM, dtd
    1856,4,28
1860, 1, 28. William & w, Sarah, & ch,
    Elizabeth R. & Joseph, rocf Somerset MM,
    dtd 1860,12,26
1864, 7, 23. Eli & w, Mary, & ch, William,
    Jesse, Mary E., Abby & Sarah J., gct
    Hickory Grove MM, Iowa
1865, 1, 28. Annie C. gct Hickory Grove MM,
    Ia.
1868, 9, 19. Eli & w, Mary, & ch, William,
    Jesse, Mary E., Abby W., Sarah J., Al-
    fred E. & Elizabeth, rocf Springville

KENNARD, continued
    MM, Ia., dtd 1868,8,19
1869, 1, 23. Annie rocf Springville MM, Ia.,
    dtd 1868,12,19
1874, 7, 22. Jesse dis mcd
1873, 10, --. William gct Frankford MM, Pa.
1889, 9, 25. Sarah J. & Elizabeth gct Phila.
    MM, Pa.
1890, 7, 23. Alfred E. dis mcd
1896, 2, 19. Joseph dis mcd
1921, 2, 23. Mary E. gct Phila. MM, Pa.
1924, 6, 25. Alfred E. rst
1924, 6, 25. Annie D. & dt, Mary Elizabeth,
    recrq (w & dt of Alfred)

KENNY
1822, 10, 31. Jane m Thomas SMITH

1808, 8, 30. Richard rocf Uwchland MM, Pa.,
    dtd 1808,8,4
1809, 6, 26. Richard gct Baltimore MM, W.
    Dist.
1821, 8, 25. Richard rocf Uwchlan MM, dtd
    1821,7,5
1821, 8, 25. Jane rocf Uwchlan MM, dtd 1821,
    7,5
1829, 11, 28. Richard & w, Susannah, rocf
    Short Creek MM, dtd 1829,10,29
1830, 6, 26. Richard & w, Susannah, gct
    Deerfield MM
1839, 10, 26. Richards & w, Susanna, rocf
    Pennsville MM, dtd 1839,10,17
1840, 5, 23. Richard & w, Susannah, gct
    Pennsville MM

KESTER
1829, 12, 24. Benjamin, s John & Martha,
    Guernsey Co., O.; m in Stillwater, Malinda
    HARTLEY, dt Mahlon & Charity, Belmont Co.,
    O.

1826, 12, 23. John & w, Martha, & ch, Jona-
    than Hartley, Benjamin, David, Jesse, La-
    vinia, John B., Aaron, James Kitely, Mar-
    tha, Robert & Sarah E., rocf Muncy MM,
    dtd 1826,10,18, end by Plainfield MM,
    1826,12,21
1826, 12, 23. William & w, Mary, & dt, Eliza-
    beth, rocf Muncy MM, dtd 1826,10,18, end
    by Plainfield MM, 1826,12,21
1827, 12, 22. Ruth rocf Muncy MM, dtd 1827,4,
    18, end by Plainfield MM, 1827,11,22
1829, 6, 27. Hannah dis jH
1829, 6, 27. John dis jH
1829, 6, 27. Martha dis jH
1829, 6, 27. Mary dis jH
1829, 6, 27. Ruth dis jH
1829, 6, 27. William dis jH
1829, 10, 24. David dis jH
1830, 2, 27. Benjamin dis jH
1830, 5, 22. Jonathan H. dis disunity
1830, 10, 23. Malinda (form Hartley) dis mcd
1834, 5, 24. Jesse dis mcd

1839, 2, 23. Elizabeth, dt Wm. & Mary, gct
    Chesterfield MM
1839, 5, 25. John Jr. dis jH
1839, 6, 22. Lovina dis jH
1840, 1, 18. Benjamin & w, Malinda, & ch,
    Mary, Mahlon, Abi & Ephraim Williams, gct
    Deerfield MM (H)
1840, 1, 18. William & w, Mary, & ch, Eliza-
    beth, Ruth Anna, Sarah, Aaron & Mary Jane,
    gct Deerfield MM (H)
1841, 8, 28. Aaron dis disunity
1846, 1, 24. James dis mcd
1846, 1, 24. Sarah Holland (form Kester)
    dis mcd
1846, 4, 25. Robert dis disunity
1846, 4, 25. Robert dis disunity
1849, 12, 22. Mary Ann (form Hartley) dis mcd
1850, 3, 22. Ann (form Webster) dis mcd
1854, 2, 18. Benjamin & w, Melinda, & ch,
    Ephraim W., Melissa, Phebe Ann & Charity,
    gct Honey Creek MM, Ind. (H)
1854, 10, 21. Mahlon gct Honey Creek MM, Ind.
    (H)

KING
----, --, --. Michael & Hannah
    Ch: Abel   b 1809, 1, 12
        Deborah " 1814, 12, 14
1813, 10, 7. Samuel, s Michael & Hannah,
    Guernsey Co., O.; m in Leatherwood, Phebe
    WILLIAMS, dt Joseph & Sarah, Guernsey
    Co., O.
1816, 10, 31. Rebekah m Nimrod WILLIAMS
1818, 10, 28. Joseph, s Michael & Hannah,
    Guernsey Co., O.; m in Stillwater MH,
    Mary MORRIS, dt Samuel & Sally, Columbi-
    ana Co., O.
    Ch: Michael b 1819, 9, 10
        Samuel   " 1821, 3, 29
        William " 1823, 3, 9
1820, 4, 14. Phebe d ae 25y 11m 17d bur
    Deerfield
1821, 7, 30. Samuel, s Michael & Hannah,
    Morgan Co., O.; m in Stillwater MH, Con-
    tent VERNON, dt Robert & Ann, Morgan Co.,
    O.
    Ch: Ann   b 1822, 8, 12
        Obed   " 1824, 12, 1
1822, 5, 1. Isaac, s Michael & Hannah, Mor-
    gan Co., O.; m in Stillwater MH, Ann
    DAVIS, dt Harmon & Hannah, Belmont Co.,O..

1823, 6, 28. Isabell Gifford (form King) dis
    mcd
1825, 9, 24. James & w, Rebecca, & ch, Jo-
    seph, James, Sarah, Rebecca, Phebe &
    Mercy, rocf Little Britain MM, dtd 1825,
    5,14
1826, 9, 23. Isaac & w, Ann, & ch, Harmon,
    Hannah & Phebe, gct Milford MM, Ind.
1854, 7, 22. Zilpha (form Hall) dis mcd
1857, 4, 25. Jacob & w, Sarah, & ch, Martha
    & Jeptha, rocf Pennsville MM, dtd 1857,3,

KING, continued

1857, 4, 25. Phebe rocf Pennsville MM, dtd
    1857,3,19
1863, 4, 25. Zilpha (form Hall) dis mcd

KINSEY
1823, 1, 25. George Jr. rocf Short Creek MM,
    dtd 1822,9,11
1827, 6, 23. Benjamin & ch, Aaron & Abi, rocf
    Little Britain MM, dtd 1827,3,17
1827, 6, 23. Tacy rocf Goshen MM, dtd 1827,5,
    2, end to Deersfield MM
1827, 6, 23. Cert for Martha from Goshen MM,
    1827,5,2, end to Deerfield MM
1827, 7, 28. George gct Short Creek MM

KIRK
1843, 8, 19. Augustus S. & w, Eliza Anna, gct
    Deerfield MM (H)
1843, 8, 19. Henry C. & w, Margaretta, & ch,
    Alvertas, William, Henry, Ann, Lydia, Eli,
    Oliver & Elmor, gct Smithfield MM (H)
1856, 4, 19. Erastus W. & w, Mary Ann, & dt,
    Ann, gct Short Creek MM (H)
1856, 4, 19. Philena & Emily gct Short Creek
    MM (H)
1881, 6, 22. Mariah rocf Short Creek MM, dtd
    1881,5,24
1889, 12, 20. Maria gct Chesterfield MM
1920, 7, 21. Albert J. Livezey gct Middle-
    ton MM, O., to m Rachel Kirk

KITE
1867, 5, 8. James R., s James & Lydia,
    Phila., Pa.; m in Stillwater MH, Ruth
    MILLHOUSE, dt Robert & Martha, Morgan Co.,
    O.

1868, 1, 25. Ruth gct Pennsville MM

KUNTZ
1844, 8, 24. Sarah (form Hall) dis mcd

KUTZ
1920, 7, 21. Malissa (form Hall) dis mcd

LADD
1824, 10, 27. Ann m William SMITH

LAMBERT
1817, 4, 26. Elizabeth (form Stanton) dis mcd
1819, 9, 25. Elizabeth recrq

LANE
1829, 10, 24. Theodate M. rocf Somerset MM,
    dtd 1829,7,27

LANGSTAFF
1839, 9, 10. Ann, w Thomas, dt Mary Jones,
    d bur Stillwater

1836, 5, 28. Thomas & w, Ann, rocf Upper
    Springfield MM, dtd 1836,4,23
1841, 8, 28. Thomas D. & w, Hannah, & ch,
    Rhoda, Elnathan & William, rocf Chester-
    field MM, dtd 1841,3,20
1843, 4, 22. Thomas D. & w, Hannah, & ch,
    Rhoda, Elnathan, Wm. & Enoch, gct Ches-
    terfield MM

LARSON
1905, 9, 21. Lindley C., s Nicholas & Lydia,
    Cedar Co., Ia.; m in Stillwater MH, Ber-
    tha BUNDY, dt Lindley & Ruanna, Belmont
    Co., O.

1906, 5, 23. Bertha R. (form Bundy) gct West
Branch MM

LAUGHLIN
1833, 7, 27. Rhoda (form Starbuck) dis mcd

LAWTON
1828, 8, 25. Sarah G. m Isaiah BRANSON

1828, 6, 28. Sarah G. recrq

LAY
1813, 2, 2. William d ae 73

LEACH
1860, 4, 28. Thomas & w, Elizabeth, & ch,
    John, Deborah, Jane, Charles, Lewis &
    Ross, rocf Middleton MM, dtd 1860,3,17

LEE
1820, 11, 25. Ruth (form Wade) dis mcd
1823, 6, 28. Lydia rocf Roaring Creek MM,
    Pa., dtd 1823,5,14, end to Somerset MM
1823, 6, 28. Cert rec for Margaret & dt, Mar-
    garet, from Roaring Creek MM, Pa., dtd
    1823,5,14, end to Somerset MM
1856, 8, 16. John E. & w, Elizabeth B., &
    ch, Levi B., Rachel N., Sabella R., Mar-
    tha E., Eliza Jane & Phebe E., gct Alum
    Creek MM, O. (H)
1856, 8, 16. Harriet Ann gct Alum Creek MM,
    O. (H)
1864, 4, 16. John E. & w, Elizabeth, & ch,
    Sabella A., Martha E., Eliza J., Phebe
    E. & Sarah P., rocf Alum Creek MM, dtd
    1864,2,25 (H)
1864, 7, 16. Rachel N. rocf Alum Creek MM,
    dtd 1864,3,25 (H)
1869, 5, 22. Ellis P. rocf Exeter MM, Pa.,
    dtd 1869,4,28

LEE, continued
1870, 9, 21. Ellis P. dis disunity
1876, 7, 15. Eliza Jane Thomas (form Lee) con
     mcd

LEEDS
----, --, --. Henry Brown, s Charles & Susanna
     R., b 1864,6,18; m Eliza FOSTER, dt Edward
     H. & Emma Jane (Walmsley) b 1879,6,14
     Ch: Mariana
          Priscilla b 1917, 9, 15

1928, 6, 25. Eliza T. & dt, Marianna Pris-
     cilla, rocf Scipio MM, N. Y., dtd 1928,4,
     25
1928, 6, 25. Henry B. rocf Burlington MM,
     N. J., dtd 1928,5,17

LEEKE
1831, 6, 2. Samuel, s Joseph & Ann, Harrison
     Co., O.; m in Stillwater, Martha WILLIAMS,
     dt Joshua & Lydia MENDENHALL, Belmont Co.,
     O. (H)
1833, 6, 20. Maria m Thomas SCHOFIELD (H)

LENT
1825, 12, 24. Elizabeth (form Sidwell) dis mcd

LESLIE
1820, 6, 24. Robert & w, Rachel, & ch, Sarah,
     Johnson & Levi L., rocf Plainfield MM, dtd
     1820,6,22
1820, 6, 24. Thomas rocf Plainfield MM, dtd
     1820,6,22
1820, 6, 24. Elizabeth rocf Plainfield MM,
     dtd 1820,6,22
1820, 6, 24. Mary rocf Plainfield MM, dtd
     1820,6,22

LEWIS
----, --, --. Jacob & Mary
     Ch: Abel   b 1810, 6, 2
         Reece   " 1813, 8, 24
1847, 1, 20. Mary Ann m John BROWN (H)
1849, 12, 19. Lorenzo D., s Emery & Rachel,
     Monroe Co., O.; m in house of Timothy
     HAINES, Elizabeth T. HAINES, dt Timothy
     & Hannah, Monroe Co., O.
1886, 10, 21. Hannah, w Able, d bur Colerain
1886, 12, 21. Able d bur Barnesville

1821, 5, 26. David & w, Hannah, rocf Short
     Creek MM, dtd 1821,5,19
1828, 3, 22. David dis disunity
1829, 2, 28. Ira dis mcd
1829, 6, 27. Hannah dis jH
1829, 8, 22. Elizabeth (form Gregg) dis mcd
1829, 10, 24. Elizabeth dis jH
1839, 2, 23. Julia & Eliza, ch Hannah McCune,
     gct Short Creek MM
1840, 1, 25. Sarah Shankland (form Lewis)
     dis mcd
1843, 8, 26. Mary Ann, Lorenzo & Tacy F., ch

Emery & Rachel, rocf Short Creek MM, dtd
     1843,5,23
1845, 9, 27. Eliza rocf Short Creek MM, dtd
     1845,8,19
1849, 1, 25. Eliza Smith (form Lewis) dis mcd
1849, 6, 23. Lorenzo D. & Tacy T., ch Emor &
     Rachel, gct Somerset MM
1849, 10, 27. Mary Ann Brown (form Lewis) dis
     mcd
1853, 12, 17. Tacy Brown (form Lewis) dis mcd
     (H)
1854, 10, 21. Elizabeth relrq (H)
1854, 10, 21. Emery relrq (H)
1854, 10, 21. Lorenzo D. relrq (H)
1854, 10, 21. Rachel relrq (H)
1866, 2, 24. Reece dis military service
1867, 7, 27. Julia dis jas

LINGO
1822, 1, 26. Mary (form Boyd) dis mcd

LISLE
1813, 4, 7. James, s Henry & Lettice, Bel-
     mont Co., O.; m in Stillwater MH, Peninnah
     DOUDNA, dt John & Sarah (Knowles)
     Ch: George   b 1814, 2, 20
         John   " 1815, 12, 10
         Joseph   " 1818, 3, 15
         Henry   " 1820, 8, 3
         Mary   " 1822, 6, 1
         James Jr. " 1824, 7, 21
1824, 9, 9. James d ae 34y 8m bur Captina

1809, 8, 29. James [Lile] recrq
1833, 11, 23. George dis mcd
1834, 1, 25. Phebe (form Wood) dis mcd
1839, 7, 27. Joseph dis mcd
1840, 7, 25. John dis mcd
1841, 4, 24. Mary Hanson (form Lisle) dis mcd
1842, 1, 22. Peninnah [Liles] dis disunity
1850, 1, 26. Henry dis mcd
1851, 2, 22. James dis mcd

LIVEZEY
----, --, --. Charles, s Jesse K. & Elizabeth
     (Patterson), b 1861,3,7 d 1927,8,20 bur
     Stillwater; m Elizabeth W. SMITH, dt
     Robert & Rebecca (Stanton), b 1863,1,7
     Ch: Robert S. b 1894, 11, 27 d 1895, 3, 7
           bur Somerset
         Walter   b 1899, 1, 24
         Albert J.   " 1897, 3, 6 (sic)
         Jesse R. Jr." 1901, 1, 31
         William E. " 1903, 8, 11
----, --, --. Albert J., s Charles & Eliza-
     beth W., b 1897,3,6; m Rachel KIRK, dt
     Nathan & Mary (Morlan), b 1896,12,19
     Ch: Ruth
         Elizabeth b 1923, 7, 16
         Dorothy Mary" 1924, 5, 12
         Mildred
         Anna   " 1926, 6, 11
         Helen Edith " 1927, 11, 4

LIVEZEY, Albert & Rachel, continued
    Ch: Paul
        Albert   b 1919, 9, 26
        Bertha M. " 1931; 3, 6

1827, 4, 28. John H. & w, Sarah, rocf Fallow-
    field MM, Pa., dtd 1827,3,9
1927, 5, 26. Oliver, Hannah Ann, Jesse K. &
    Jeremiah, ch John H. & Sarah, recrq
1901, 9, 25. Charles & w, Elizabeth, & ch,
    Albert J., Walter C. & Jesse K., rocf
    Somerset MM, dtd 1901,8,22
1920, 7, 21. Albert J. gct Middleton MM, O.,
    to m Rachel Kirk
1921, 1, 19. Rachel K. rocf Middleton MM, O.,
    dtd 1921,1,15
1921, 4, 20. Walter C. gct New Garden MM, to
    m Emma L. Gamble
1922, 5, 24. Walter C. gct New Garden MM, O.
1925, 12, 23. Jesse K. gct New Garden MM, O.

LLEWELLYN
----, --, --. William & Sarah
    Ch: Thomas   b 1822, 5, 24
        Joseph   " 1825, 1, 5
        Ezra   " 1827, 3, 22
1907, 4, 25. Charles B., s Elisha & Abigail
    S., Phila., Pa.; m in Stillwater MH, Emily
    Dennis FRAME, dt William A. & Florence,
    Belmont Co., O.

1825, 3, 26. William [Llewelyn] & w, Sarah,
    & s, Thomas, rocf Goshen MM, Pa., dtd
    1824,9,1
1829, 1, 24. William [Llewelyn] & fam gct
    Deerfield MM
1829, 1, 24. Sarah [Llewelyn] & fam gct Deer-
    field MM
1909, 2, 24. Emily D. gct Phila. MM, Pa.

LLOYD
----, --, --. Joshua & Mary
    Ch: Jane   b 1822, 7, 28
        Mercy   " 1824, 5, 19
        Edward   " 1826, 8, 2
        Charles   " 1829, 9, 18
1819, 5, 22. Isaac & w, Ruth, rocf Short
    Creek MM, dtd 1819,3,23
1819, 7, 24. Joshua rocf Short Creek MM, dtd
    1819,7,20
1820, 7, 22. Joshua gct Plainfield MM, to m
    Mary Nichols
1821, 8, 25. Isaac & w, Ruth, & fam gct Short
    Creek MM
1822, 6, 22. Joshua gct Plainfield MM

LONG
1870, 3, 5. Maud, w G. M., dt Ervin & Eliza-
    beth Roosa, b

1918, 11, 20. Maud dis jas

LOUHOFF
1918, 8, 23. M. Elizabeth m Homer J. HARTLEY

1918, 7, 24. M. Elizabeth rocf Phila. MM,
    Pa., dtd 1918,6,27

LOWNS
----, --, --. Charles & -----
    Ch: Joseph   b 1818, 10, 23
        Emmor B. " 1822, 6, 19
        Esther   " 1824, 10, 11
1834, 7, 26. Rebecca, dt Chas. & Elizabeth,
    d bur Springborough, O.

1829, 10, 24. Charles dis jH
1829, 10, 24. Eliza dis jH
1839, 4, 20. Charles [Lownes] & w, Eliza-
    beth, & ch, Joseph, Emmor & Elmira, gct
    Springborough MM, O.
1840, 4, 25. Emor [Lownds] gct Springborough
    MM
1840, 4, 25. Joseph [Lownds] gct Spring-
    borough MM
1840, 8, 22. Emmor [Lounds] gct Springborough
    MM, dtd 1840,4,25; returned to this mtg,
    he does not reside in their limits

LUNDY
1812, 1, 28. Amos con mcd
1812, 10, 27. Amos gct Fairfield MM

LUPTON
1829, 6, 27. Nathan & w, Margaret, gct Short
    Creek MM
1829, 6, 27. Ann gct Short Creek MM
1829, 6, 27. Ann gct Short Creek MM

McBROOME
1877, 9, 21. Mary Catharine (form Tomlinson)
    dis mcd (H)

McCANE
1846, 8, 22. Sarah (form Embree) dis mcd

McCARTNEY
1847, 10, 23. Elana Eliza (form Harris) dis
    mcd

McLANE
1881, 3, 19. Theodate [McClain], w William,
    d bur Stillwater

1821, 11, 24. Theodate (form Vernon) dis mcd
1823, 11, 22. Theodate rst
1824, 10, 23. Theodate gct Somerset MM

McCLARY
1830, 1, 23. Eliza (form Coles) dis mcd

McCOY
1893, 7, 19. Martha (form Webster) dis mcd

McGIRR

1824, 1, 24. Arthur & w, Elizabeth, & ch, Frances, Nancy & Sarah, rocf Westland MM, dtd 1823,4,24, end by Plainfield MM, 1823, 9,25

1826, 5, 27. Arthur & w, Elisabeth, & ch, Francis J., Nancy H., Sarah C. & Alexander C., gct Somerset MM

1839, 3, 16. Arthur & w, Elizabeth, & ch, Sarah C., Alexander C., Eliza Ann, Mary C., Rebecca & William P., gct Deerfield MM (H)

1839, 4, 20. Nancy H. gct Deerfield MM (H)

McGREW

----, --, --. Gilbert & Eliza (Hall)
    Ch: Anna   b 1893, 3, 19 d 1926, 11,7

1925, 3, 25. William G. Steer gct Short Creek MM, to m Eliza C. McGrew

1926, 6, 23. Anna rocf Short Creek MM, dtd 1926,6,22

McKINLEY

1860, 7, 28. Jane (form Smith) dis mcd

McMILLAN

1907, 6, 19. Alice (form Edgerton) dis mcd & jas

McMINN

1817, 3, 22. Prudence rocf Mill Creek MM, O., dtd 1817,10,26

McMULLEN

1837, 11, 25. Wilma (form Satterthwait) dis mcd

McNICHOLS

1819, 3, 1. Nathaniel, s William & Rachel, b
----, --, --. George & Martha
    Ch: Prudence   b 1825, 12, 23
        John   " 1827, 11, 23
        Thomas   " 1827, 11, 19
        Jane   " 1833, 4, 18
        George   " 1836, 4, 11
        Cyrus   " 1838, 4, 25
        Martha   " 1840, 3, 26
        Mary   " 1842, 5, 8
        Ruth   " 1846, 10, 10
        Esther   " 1849, 10, 23
1845, 10, 29. Prudence m Robert HANSON

1818, 10, 24. William & w, Rachel, & her ch by a form h, Elizabeth, Benjamin, Maria & John Faucett, rocf Plainfield MM, dtd 1818,9,24

1825, 3, 26. Martha (form Williams) dis mcd

1828, 1, 26. Maria (form Fawcett) dis mcd

1828, 4, 26. William & Rachel & ch, Nathaniel, Mary, Smith, William & John, gct Somerset MM

1831, 10, 22. Joseph dis disunity

1833, 9, 28. Charity (form Newsome) dis mcd

1838, 12, 22. Martha rst at Somerset MM on consent of this mtg

1839, 12, 28. George & w, Martha, & ch, Prudence, John, Thomas, Jane, George & Cyrus, rocf Somerset MM, dtd 1839,10,28

1840, 5, 23. Mary (form Nicelson) dis mcd

1851, 2, 22. George dis disunity

1852, 9, 25. Martha dis disunity

1853, 5, 28. John dis mcd

1853, 8, 27. Jane dis disunity

1853, 9, 24. Thomas dis disunity

1879, 7, --. George con mcd

1880, 6, 23. George gct Coal Creek MM, Ia.

McVEY

1848, 4, 22. Phebe (form Williams) dis mcd

MARIS

1819, 3, 4. Lewis, s David & Sarah, Belmont Co., O.; m in Captina, Sidney HOOPS, dt Isaac & Mary, Belmont Co., O.

1818, 7, 25. Lewis recrq

1819, 8, 28. Lewis dis

1819, 8, 28. Sidney (form Hoopes) dis mcd

1822, 6, 22. Sidney rst

1835, 6, 27. Rachel & Phebe, dt Sidney, recrq

1844, 6, 22. Sidney & dt, Rachel & Phebe, gct Somerset MM

MARSH

1812, 9, 29. Rachel (form Borton) dis mcd

1823, 12, 27. Ann (form Dillon) dis mcd

MARSHALL

----, --, --. William & Hannah
    Ch: Thomas   b 1813, 6, 15
        Elizabeth   " 1815, 9, 5
        Hannah P.   " 1818, 6, 11
        James   " 1822, 4, 18
        Martha   " 1825, 5, 17
        William P. " 1828, 7, 17
1824, 6, 2. John, s Samuel & Elizabeth, Guernsey Co., O.; m in Stillwater MH, Anna Mercy ENGLE, dt Caleb & Mercy, Belmont Co., O.
    Ch: James E.   b 1825, 5, 15
        Caleb   " 1826, 11, 1
        Elizabeth V. 1829, 3, 23 d 1833, 7,14

        Jesse B.   b 1834, 6, 3

1818, 8, 22. William & w, Hannah, & ch, Thomas & Elizabeth, rocf Short Creek MM, dtd 1818,3,24

1824, 1, 24. John recrq

1829, 6, 27. Hannah dis jH

1829, 6, 27. William dis jH

1837, 11, 25. Anna Mercy & fam gc

1839, 5, 25. Thomas dis mcd

1841, 4, 17. Hannah & ch, James, Martha, [(H)
    William P. & John, gct Whitewater MM, Ind.

MARSHALL, continued
   (H)
1841, 4, 17. Thomas gct Whitewater MM, Ind.
   (H)

MARTIN
1878, 10, 3. Daniel C., s Samuel & Drucilla,
   Belmont Co., O.; m in house of Thos. L.
   Frame, Margaret H. FRAME, dt Thos. L. &
   Elizabeth, Belmont Co., O. (H)

1830, 10, 23. Agnes dis jH
1853, 8, 20. Mary Patton (form Martin) con
   mcd (H)
1906, 8, 22. Alice D. (form Bundy) dis mcd

MASON
1826, 8, 26. Hannah [Maxon] rocf Plainfield
   MM, dtd 1826,7,20
1836, 7, 23. Martha (form Satterthwait) dis
   mcd

MASSEY
1817, 2, 22. William [Massy] rocf Goshen MM,
   Pa., dtd 1817,1,29
1819, 3, 27. William dis mcd
1823, 7, 26. Sarah (form Gay) dis mcd
1859, 8, 27. William rst at Pennsville MM, on
   consent of this mtg

MASTERS
----, --, --. David & Priscilla (Worthington)
   Ch: William   b 1858, 7, 12 d 1931,12,14
      bur Stillwater

1909, 2, 24. William rocf Chesterfield MM,
   dtd 1909,2,20

MAYES
1878, 2, 21. Jacob, s Wm. & Mary, Belmont
   Co., O.; m in house of Joshua Swayne, Rebecca B. SWAYNE, dt Samuel & Margaret,
   Guernsey Co., O. (H)

MEAD
1848, 6, 17. Joseph & w, Phebe, & ch, Thomas
   William Joseph Charles Elwood & Mary (5)
   gct Freeport MM, O. (H)
1856, 2, 16. Ruth Annah (form Stanton) con
   mcd (H)

MEECHUM
1835, 4, 18. John & w, Lydia, & ch, Elisha
   J. & Jonathan E., gct Goshen MM, O. (H)
1835, 6, 20. Joshua, minor s John, gct Redstone MM (H)

MENDENHALL
1907, 12, --. J. Lindley gct Miami MM (H)

MERRILL
----, --, --. Richard & Hannah
   Ch: Jonathan   b 1818, 12, 19

Ch: Margaret   b 1821, 10, 10
   Joseph   " 1823, 12, 12
   Jesse   " 1825, 3, 15 (or 1826)
   Stephen   " 1828, 5, 10
   Richard   " 1830, 11, 21 d 1831, 7, 7
      bur Captina

1822, 6, 22. Richard recrq
1822, 11, 23. Hannah rst on consent of Plainfield MM
1823, 4, 26. Jonathan & Margaret, ch Richard
   & Hannah, recrq
1831, 8, 27. Richard [Merril] dis
1835, 8, 22. Hannah [Merril] & ch, Jonathan,
   Margaret, Joseph, Jesse, Stephen, Isaac &
   Hannah, gct Somerset MM

METCALF
----, --, --. Jesse & Asenath
   Ch: Oliver J. b 1825, 11, 6
      Caroline   " 1827, 6, --
      Joshua   " 1828, 9, 19
      Stephen   " 1830, 4, 12
      Adaline   " 1831, 12, 3
1884, 1, 9. Hannah, w Jesse, d bur Stillwater

1829, 5, 23. Jesse & w, Acenath, & ch,
   Oliver, Caroline & Joshua, rocf Short
   Creek MM, dtd 1829,5,19
1829, 9, 19. Abraham [Medkeff] & w, Hannah,
   & ch, John, Susannah, Jemimah S., Elizabeth & Lydia Ann, gct Plainfield MM (H)
1881, 5, 24. Matilda rst on consent of Pennsville MM
1881, 8, 24. Hannah D. rst on consent of
   Pennsville MM

MEYERS
1894, 12, 20. Joseph D., s William D. & Mary
   R. (Warner), Cedar Co., Ia., b 1858,12,
   21; m in Barnsville MH, Mary J. WORTHING-
   TON, dt Jacob & Lydia, Morgan Co., O.,
   b 1862,4,24 d 1925,3,6 bur Stillwater
   Ch: Charles
      Lionel   b 1900, 8, 5
      Ambrose
      Worthing-
      ton   " 1904, 1, 5
      Thyra Jane " 1898, 3, 12
      Bernice
      Lydia   " 1896, 5, 20
1924, 9, 5. Thyra Jane [Myers] m Henry Cope
   FOSTER

1831, 10, 22. Sarah [Miers] (form Pearson)
   dis mcd
1896, 1, 22. Mary W. gct Hickory Grove MM,
   Ia.
1908, 8, 19. Joseph E. [Myers] & w, Mary
   W., & ch, Bernice L., Thyra Jane, Charles
   Lionel & Ambrose Worthington, gct Hickory
   Grove MM, Ia.

MEYERS, continued
1931, 8, 19. Bernice L. gct Chester MM, Pa.
1931, 10, 21. Joseph E. gct Nantucket MM, R.I.

MICHENER
----, --, --. Barak & Lydia R.
    Ch: John   b 1840, 6, 5
        Rebecca   " 1842, 5, 14
        Emma   " 1853, 2, 25
        Mary L.   d 1883, 2, 1

1832, 10, 27. John & w, Mary, & ch, Eber, Han-
    nah, Seth, Jesse, Miriam & Israel, rocf
    Short Creek MM, dtd 1832,10,23
1832, 10, 27. Barak rocf Short Creek MM, dtd
    1832,10,23
1832, 12, 22. Barak gct New Garden MM, to m
    Lydia R. Cook
1833, ·2, 23. Wilson [Michenor], minor, rocf
    New Garden MM, Pa., dtd 1832,11,17
1833, 5, 25. Lydia B. [Mitchener], w Barak,
    rocf New Garden MM, Pa., dtd 1833,4,3
1839, 5, 25. Barak [Michaner] & w, Lydia, &
    ch, Elizabeth, Charles & Robert Lindley,
    rocf Plainfield MM, dtd 1839,4,24
1843, .3, 23. Borak & w, Lydia, & ch, Eliza-
    beth, Charles, Robert-Lindley, John & Re-
    becca, gct Somerset MM
1850, 6, 22. George & w, Rebecca, & ch, Mary,
    William, Anna, Joseph, Sarah, Penninah &
    Amy, rocf Chesterfield MM, dtd 1850,6,15
1850, 10, 26. George & w, Rebecca, & ch, Mary,
    William, Anna, Joseph, Sarah, Peninah &
    Amy, gct Chesterfield MM
1861, 12, 28. Charles & w, Lydia, & ch, Anne &
    Charles K., recrq (residing in Linn Co.,
    Ia.)
1865, 10, 28. John E. [Michiner] rpd mcd &
    military service
1866, 3, 24. John E. gct Middleton MM
1868, 10, 24. Lydia Ann (form Webster) dis mcd
1874, 2, 25. Barach & Lydia dis disunity
1884, 4, 23. Elizabeth Haines (form Michiner)
    dis mcd

MIDDLETON
----, --, --. Jehu & Mary
    Ch: Joseph   b 1805, 11, 3
        Elizabeth " 1808, 4, 25
        Phebe   " 1810, 7, 5
        Hannah   " 1815, 7, 25
        Richard   " 1817, 10, 24
        Rachel   " 1820, 4, 8
1815, 12, 19. Phebe d ae 73y 7m 24d bur Still-
    water
1817, 1, 29. Joseph, Belmont Co., O.; m in
    Stillwater MH, Sarah (Knowles) DOUDNA,
    d 1843,6,4 bur Stillwater
1824, 10, 27. Elizabeth m John CALHOON
1828, 10, 13. Joseph d ae 73 y 7m 21d

1827, 11, 24. Jehu dis disunity
1827, 11, 24. Mary, w Jehu, & ch, Phebe, Han-

nah, Richard & Rachel, gct White Water
    MM, Ind.
1829, 3, 21. Joseph gct Miami MM (H)
1829, 8, 22. Joseph d 1828,10,13 ae 74 (an
    elder)
1830, 1, 23. Sarah gct Somerset MM
1831, 1, 22. Sarah rocf Somerset MM, dtd
    1830,12,27
1835, 11, 28. Joseph dis jH

MILES
1817, 1, 1. Hannah m Mahlon GREGG

1814, 7, 26. Hannah Jr. rocf Hopewell MM,
    Va., dtd 1813,10,4 end by Plainfield MM,
    1814,7,23
1821, 2, 24. Hannah rocf Concord MM, dtd 1820
    12,20, end to Somerset MM

MILLER
1817, 9, 3. Robert, s David & Sarah, Bel-
    mont Co., O.; m in Stillwater MH, Lydia
    EMBREE, dt Samuel & Hannah, Belmont Co.,
    O.
1815, 11, 28. Robert rocf Plainfield MM, dtd
    1815,11,25
1821, 3, 24. Robert dis disunity
1821, 8, 25. Lydia & s, Jesse, gct Plain-
    field MM
1823, 1, 25. Lydia & ch, Jesse & Newton,
    rocf Plainfield MM, dtd 1822,12,26
1829, 1, 24. David dis jH
1829, 1, 24. Rachel dis jH
1829, 1, 24. Sarah dis jH
1830, 4, 24. Warrick dis jH
1830, 8, 28. Lydia Fawcett (form Miller) dis
    mcd
1842, 3, 26. Sarah Ann (form Parry) dis mcd
1842, 11, 26. Jerusha (form Satterthwait) dis
    mcd

MILLHOUSE
----, --, --. Robert & Sarah
    Ch: Daniel   b 1800, 3, 13
        Samuel   " 1802, 8, 6 d 1803, 9,17
        bur Stillwater
        Elizabeth b 1804, 10, 2
        Mary   " 1806, 12, 26
        Robert   " 1811, 4, 15
1810, 11, 22. Robert d
1822, 10, 30. Daniel, s Robert & Sarah, Bel-
    mont Co., O.; m in Stillwater MH, Esther
    CLENDENON, dt Isaac & Hannah, Belmont
    Co., O.
    Ch: William   b 1823, 8, 27
1823, 12, 3. Sarah m Jesse BAILEY
1830, 3, 10. Mary m Benjamin HOYLE
1831, 9, 28. Elizabeth m Jonathan BRIGGS
1836, 3, 9. Robert, s Robert & Sarah, Mor-
    gan Co., O.; m in Stillwater MH, Martha
    SEARS, dt Peter & Anna (Doudna), Belmont
    Co., O.
1867, 5, 8. Ruth m James R. KITE

MILLHOUSE, continued
1834, 5, 24. Robert gct Deerfield MM
1836, 5, 28. Martha gct Pennsville MM
1852, 2, 28. Stephen Hodgin Jr. gct Penns-
      ville MM, to m Sarah Millhouse
1862, 12, 27. Ruth gct Pennsville MM, dtd
      1862,11,13

MILLISON
1829, 1, 24. Elizabeth (form Sinclair) dis
      mcd

MILLS
----, --, --. Gideon & Edith
      Ch: Eli   b 1809, 5, 30
          Elisha   " 1810, 11, 10
          Esther   " 1812, 9, 5
          Lewis   " 1814, 7, 28
          Isaac   " 1817, 2, 20
          Hugh J.   " 1818, 10, 28
          Reuben   " 1820, 11, 19
          Thomas   " 1822, 12, 31
1843, 11, 29. Reuben, s Reuben & Sarah, Bel-
      mont Co., O., d 1873,3,13 bur Stillwater;
      m in Stillwater MH, Mary REDD, dt Geo. &
      Rachel, Belmont Co., O., d 1868,3,26 bur
      Stillwater

1809, 2, 28. Gideon dis mcd
1810, 1, 30. Elizabeth dis
1810, 8, 28. Mary dis
1811, 2, 26. Nathan dis disunity
1814, 7, 26. Hannah rocf Hopewell MM, dtd
      1813,10,4, end by Plainfield MM, 1814,7,
      23
1815, 9, 26. Sally Wilson (form Mills) dis
      mcd
1816, 11, 23. Gideon rst
1817, 1, 25. Edith & dt, Esther, recrq
1817, 4, 26. Eli, Elisha & Lewis, ch Gideon,
      recrq
1875, 6, 23. Martha (form Hanson) dis mcd &
      jas

MINICAN
1829, 9, 26. Margaret & dt, Sarah, Margaret
      & Gulielma, rocf Redstone MM, dtd 1829,7,1
1830, 2, 27. Margaret dis jH
1830, 2, 27. Sarah dis jH

MONTGOMERY
----, --, --. Thomas & Sarah Ann
      Ch: Ruthanna b 1835, ·5, 13
          William H. " 1836, 12, 25
          Henry C. " 1839, 3, 2
          Jane   " 1841, 2, 23
          Mary   " 1843, 3, 9
          Sarah   " 1845, 1, 4 d 1846,12,14
            bur Stillwater
          Joel   b 1847, 3, 18

1838, 11, 24. Thomas recrq
1840, 11, 28. Sarah Ann recrq

1843, 12, 23. Ruth Ann, William H. & Henry C.,
      ch Thomas & Sarah Ann, recrq
1848, 12, 25. Thomas & w, Sarah Ann, & ch,
      Ruthanna, William H., Henry C., Jane,
      Mary & Joel, gct Chesterfield MM

MOREHEAD
1830, 9, 25. Hannah (form Dillon) dis join-
      ing M. E.

MOORE
1829, 10, 24. Jane dis jH
1831, 11, 26. Sarah dis disunity

MORRIS
1813, 6, 2. Sally m William PATTON
----, --, --. Joshua & Rachel
      Ch: Ellen   b 1817, 2, 1
          Samuel   " 1818, 8, 22 d 1819, 7, 5
          Benjamin " 1819, 1, 14
1818, 9, 22. Ruth, dt William & Susannah, b
1818, 10, 28. Mary m Joseph KING
1833, 11, 14. Samuel, s Nathan & Tacy, b
1834, 7, 22. Lydia, dt Aaron & Phebe, b
1844, 5, 28. Edwin, s Mordecai & Alice, Wash-
      ington Co., O.; m in Captina, Rachel HAN-
      SON, dt Manoah & Rachel, Belmont Co., O.
1846, 7, 30. Mary E., w Samuel, dt Robert &
      Eunice (Hampton) Todd, b

1813, 5, 25. Sally rocf Salem MM, dtd 1813,
      4,13
1814, 12, 27. William & w, Susannah, & ch,
      Benjamin, Ava, Mordecai, Jesse, Jonathan,
      Sarah, William, Susannah & Lydia, rocf
      Salem MM, dtd 1814,11,15
1816, 4, 27. Aaron, minor in care of Joseph
      Jones, rocf New Garden MM, O., dtd 1816,
      2,15
1817, 10, 25. Mary rocf Salem MM, dtd 1817,9,
      16
1817, 10, 25. Nathan rocf Salem MM, dtd 1817,
      9,16 (a minor)
1818, 11, 28. Joshua & w, Rachel, & ch, Ellen
      & Samuel, rocf Salem MM, dtd 1818,10,21
1819, 1, 23. Lydia rocf Salem MM, dtd 1818,
      10,21
1822, 12, 22. Sarah (form Starbuck) dis mcd
1829, 11, 28. Lydia rocf Westland MM, dtd
      1829,9,23
1830, 7, 24. Susannah (form Pierson) dis mcd
1832, 2, 25. Aaron rocf Flushing MM, dtd 1831,
      12,22
1832, 5, 19. Joshua & w, Rachel, & ch, Ellen,
      Benjamin, Rebecca, Rachel, Joshua & Ma-
      tilda, gct Deerfield MM (H)
1832, 6, 16. Rebecca gct Miami MM (H)
1833, 1, 26. Nathan gct Flushing MM, to m
      Tacy Perkins
1833, 5, 25. Tacy rocf Flushing MM, dtd
      1833,4,25
1833, 7, 27. Aaron gct Flushing MM, to m
      Phebe Perkins

MORRIS, continued
1833, 11, 23. Phebe rocf Flushing MM, dtd
     1833,10,24
1835, 4, 25. Lydia gct Miami MM
1835, 4, 25. Nathan & w, Tacy, & s, Samuel,
     gct Somerset MM
1835, 11, 28. Aaron & w, Phebe, & dt, Lydia,
     gct Pennsville MM
1845, 2, 22. Rachel gct Chesterfield MM
1915, 10, 20. Mary E. rocf Springville MM,
     Ia., dtd 1915,8,21

MORTON
1833, 11, 23. Sarah Jane (form Hough) dis mcd

MOSSBURGH
1827, 9, 22. Susannah recrq
1831, 3, 26. Susannah gct Smithfield MM

MOTT
1821, 8, 2. William, s John & Eleanor, Bel-
     mont Co., O.; m in Stillwater MH, Sarah
     EDGERTON, dt James & Sarah, Belmont Co.,
     O.
     Ch: Daniel
          Milhouse b 1822, 9, 19
1856, 3, 26. Asher, s Wm. & Sarah (Edgerton),
     Athens Co., O.; m in Stillwater MH, Sarah
     BUNDY, dt John & Ruth, Belmont Co., O.,
     d 1857,2,14 bur Southland
1856, 10, 1. Gersham, s William & Sarah,
     Athens Co., O.; m in Stillwater MH, Ruth-
     anna BUNDY, dt Eli & Sarah, Morgan Co., O.
1882, 9, 21. John W., s Richard & Sarah W.
     (Hampton), Limo Co., Iowa; m in Stillwater
     MH, Sina A. HALL, dt John & Deborah S.
     (Davis), Belmont Co., O.

1817, 2, 22. William rocf Marlborough MM,
     dtd 1816,10,16
1823, 6, 28. William & w, Sarah, & s gct
     Somerset MM
1857, 1, 24. Ruth Anna gct Plymouth MM
1883, 1, 24. Sina A. gct Springville MM, Ia.
1883, 5, 23. Richard & w, Sarah, rocf Spring-
     ville MM, Ia., dtd 1883,5,19
1886, 2, 24. Richard & w, Sarah gct Spring-
     ville MM, Ia.

MURPHY
1825, 12, 24. Mary (form Cox) dis mcd

NAYLOR
----, --, --. ----- m Rachel BAILEY, dt Stephen
     & Tabitha (Patterson), b 1821,1,13 d 1918,
     1,10 bur Stillwater
1878, 3, 27. Mary K. m Wm. Henry SEARS
1880, 10, 24. Maria W., dt Lewis & Rachel
     (Bailey) d bur Stillwater
1892, 12, 30. Ross, s Ezra & Rachel E., d
     bur Stillwater
1884, 12, 27. James, s Ezra & Rachel (Stephens)
     b

1906, 8, 9. Louis, s James & Rachel, d bur
     Stillwater

1870, 5, 25. Lewis & w, Rachel, & ch, Mary
     K., Rachel F. & Maria, rocf Somerset MM,
     dtd 1870,3,24
1870, 5, 25. Margaret H. rocf Somerset MM,
     dtd 1870,3,24
1870, 5, 25. Ezra rocf Somerset MM, dtd
     1870,3,24
1873, 5, 21. Margaret Bundy (form Naylor)
     con mcd
1875, 8, 25. Rachel Bennet (form Naylor) dis
     mcd
1880, 1, 21. Ezra gct Flushing MM
1889, 8, 21. Ezra & w, Rachel, & ch, Mary E.,
     Charles B., James & Ross D., rocf Flushing
     MM, dtd 1889,7,25
1907, 6, 19. Myrtle (form Bundy) dis mcd
1911, 10, 25. Ezra W. dis disunity
1911, 10, 25. Rachel E. dis disunity
1912, 7, 24. Charles B. dis jas
1913, 10, 22. Mary E. Seaman (form Naylor)
     dis mcd

NEGUS
1914, 4, 22. Wm. P. Taber gct Short Creek
     MM, to m Sarah D. Negus

NEWBY
1812, 8, 26. Susannah m Malachi JOLLEY

1813, 11, 30. Job gct Plymouth MM
1815, 3, 28. Job rocf Plymouth MM, dtd 1814,
     9,27, end to Short Creek MM
1815, 4, 25. James & Joseph gct Short Creek
     MM
1817, 2, 22. Job rocf Short Creek MM, dtd
     1817,1,21
1817, 12, 27. James rocf Short Creek MM, end
     by Plymouth MM, 1817,5,19
1820, 9, 23. Job gct Driftwood MM
1822, 9, 28. Jesse dis disunity
1826, 10, 28. Henry gct Elk MM

NEWLIN
1927, 7, 20. Robert H. Smith gct Plainfield
     MM, Ind., to m Alice Newlin

NEWSOM   [5,29 bur Stillwater
----, --, --. Jordan m Elizabeth ----- d 1839,
     Ch: Susannah b 1815, 1, 30
          Mary   " 1818, 2, 14 d 1835, 5,10
          bur Stillwater
          Joseph   b 1812, 9, 22
          Elizabeth " 1820, 4, 16 " 1835, 5,12
          bur Stillwater
          Rachel   b 1822, 8, 24
          Martha
          Chiles   " 1826, 2, 20 " 1826,10,17
          bur Stillwater

1813, 9, 28. Elizabeth & ch, William, Edwin,

NEWSOM, continued
    Charity & Joseph Jourdan, recrq
1817, 3, 22. Jordan rocf Contentney MM, N.C.,
    dtd 1816,12,24
1818, 10, 24. Charles recrq
1822, 12, 22. Jordon dis disunity
1830, 1, 23. Edwin [Newsome] dis disunity
1833, 2, 23. Joseph dis disunity
1833, 9, 28. Charity McNichols (form Newsome)
    dis mcd
1835, 1, 24. William [Newsome] gct Deerfield
    MM
1841, 7, 24. Susan & Rachel gct Pennsville
    MM

NIBLOCK
1902, 6, 25. Mary (form Sears) dis mcd

NICHOLS
----, --, --. Eli & Rachel
    Ch: Rebecca b 1820, 5, 3
        Jesse " 1821, 10, 1
        Charles " 1822, 12, 26
        Jane " 1824, 2, 22
        Mercy Ann " 1825, 10, 8
        Mary " 1827, 2, 23
        Loyd " 1829, 2, 21
        Paxton " 1830, 6, 9
        Eliza " 1831, 8, 7

1820, 7, 22. Joshua Lloyd gct Plainfield MM,
    to m Mary Nichols
1829, 1, 24. Hannah dis jH
1829, 10, 24. Eli dis jH
1830, 1, 23. Rebecca dis jH
1832, 5, 26. Sarah dis disunity
1873, 5, 17. Lydia J. (form Adams) con mcd
1874, 4, 18. Lydia gct Salem MM, O.

NICHOLSON
----, --, --. Jacob & Mary
    Ch: Daniel S. b 1806, 11, 28
        George " 1815, 9, 28
        Job Scott " 1819, 3, 15
        Rebecca " 1808, 10, 10
        Hannah " 1810, 12, 2
        Elizabeth " 1813, 2, 15
        Mary " 1823, 3, 5
1812, 2, 6. Elizabeth m Israel WOOD

1812, 1, 28. Joseph & ch, George, Hannah &
    William, rocf Plainfield MM, dtd 1812,1,25
1812, 1, 28. Elizabeth rocf Plainfield MM,
    dtd 1812,1,25
1812, 1, 28. Hannah rocf Plainfield MM, dtd
    1812,1,25
1814, 9, 27. Hannah Perkins (form Nicholson)
    dis mcd
1817, 2, 22. Mary recrq
1817, 2, 22. Jacob recrq
1817, 5, 24. William dis mcd
1817, 9, 27. Jacob & w, Mary, & ch, Rebecca,
    Hannah & Elizabeth, recrq

1828, 8, 23. Jacob dis jH
1828, 8, 23. Rebecca dis jH
1828, 8, 23. Hannah dis jH
1828, 9, 27. Daniel dis jH
1828, 9, 27. Elizabeth dis jH
1828, 9, 27. Mary dis jH
1839, 9, 28. George dis jH
1840, 5, 23. Mary McNicles (form Nicelson)
    dis mcd
1845, 8, 25. Job S. dis disunity

NIMMO
1929, 7, 24. Olive W. (form Hall) con mcd

NORRIS
1873, 12, 24. Elizabeth (form Bryant) dis mcd

OLIVER
1850, 12, 28. Daniel & w, Esther, rocf Flush-
    ing MM, dtd 1850,10,24

ORN
1836, 7, 23. Ann (form Satterthwait) dis mcd

OSBORN
----, --, --. Thomas & Rebecca
    Ch: Owen b 1812, 6, 19
        Mary " 1814, 4, 9
        Nellie " 1817, 4, 17
        Martha " 1819, 1, 22

1815, 8, 29. Thomas & w, Rebeckah, & s, Owen,
    rocf Deep Creek MM, N. C., dtd 1813,1,2
1819, 8, 28. Thomas & Rebecca [Osborne] gct
    Darby Creek MM
1829, 10, 24. John dis jH

OUTLAND
1815, 10, 12. Rebecca m Wm. THOMAS
1821, 1, 4. Elizabeth m John S. SMITH

1809, 10, 31. Rebecca, Elizabeth & Josiah, ch
    Margaret, recrq
1850, 9, 28. Phebe (form Thomas) dis mcd
1855, 2, 17. Phebe (form Thomas) dis mcd (H)
1855, 2, 17. Elizabeth Carter (form Outland)
    dis mcd (H)
1855, 3, 24. Martha (form Starbuck) dis mcd
1863, 3, 28. Ann P. (form Webster) con mcd
1865, 6, 27. Ann P. gct Somerset MM

ORRISON
1850, 8, 1. Rebecca m Aquilla THOMAS (H)

PACKER
1819, 6, 26. Abraham & w, Sarah, & ch, Mary
    & Abijah, rocf Flushing MM, dtd 1819,6,21
1821, 9, 22. Cert rec for Aaron & fam from
    Exeter MM, Pa., dtd 1821,6,27, end to
    Short Creek MM

PALMER
1908, 6, 25. Charles W., s Lewis & Mary C.,

PALMER, continued
    Chester Co., Pa.; m in Stillwater MH, Anna
    C. STANTON, dt William & Jane, Belmont Co.,
    O.

1909, 7, 21. Anna Stanton gct Chester MM, Pa.

PANCOAST
1823, 12, 27. Mary [Panecast] rocf Pipe Creek
    MM, dtd 1823,3,12
1829, 10, 24. Samuel dis jH
1829, 10, 24. Stephen dis jH
1830, 3, 29. Alfred dis disunity
1830, 3, 29. Sarah dis jH

PARISH
1830, 11, 27. Rachel dis jH

PARKER
1810, 2, 7. Benajah, s Jacob & Rhoda, Bel-
    mont Co., O.; m in Stillwater MH, Grace
    PATTEN, dt Wm. & Rachel, Belmont Co., O.
    Ch: Nathan   b 1810, 11, 30
        Emma   " 1812, 12, 15
        Hannah Ann " 1815, 12, 3
        Philip
          Draper   " 1818, 4, 21
        Charity   " 1821, 5, 10
----, --, --. George & Rachel
    Ch: Joseph J. b 1815, 6, 10
        Jacob B. " 1818, 1, 14
        Lindley " 1820, 4, 13
        Mary   " 1821, 12, 28
        Ezra   " 1824, 1, 4
        Rhoda   " 1825, 2, 15
        Elisha   " 1829, 7, 30
        Isaac   " 1831, 9, 9
        Rachel A. " 1833, 8, 24
        Martha   " 1836, 9, 17
        John   " 1838, 1, 11
1831, 10, 5. John, s George & Rachel, d bur
    Stillwater
1841, 6, 30. Thomas C., s Jesse & Anna,
    Ohio Co., Va.; m in Stillwater MH, Lydia
    Jane THORNBURGH, dt Edward & Elizabeth,
    Belmont Co., O., d 1845,9,9 bur Stillwater
    Ch: Elizabeth
          Ann   b 1842, 4, 19
        Edward
          Thornburgh" 1843, 9, 4
        Joel Judkins
             b 1844, 6, 24
1892, 9, 23. Thomas E., s Isaac & Jane H.,
    Northampton Co., N. C., b 1860,3,21; m
    in Stillwater MH, Ellen B. EDGERTON, dt
    David & Esther, Belmont Co., O., b 1865,
    12,18
    Ch: David
          Howard   b 1893, 9, 14
        Beulah
          Roads   " 1897, 9, 1

1809, 10, 31. Jacob & w, Rhoda, rocf Short

Creek MM, dtd 1809,9,19
1809, 11, 28. Benajah rocf Short Creek MM,
    dtd 1809,10,25
1809, 11, 28. George rocf Short Creek MM,
    dtd 1809,10,25
1814, 1, 25. George gct New Garden MM, O.,
    to m Rachel Jones
1814, 11, 29. Jacob & Rhoda gct Short Creek
    MM
1815, 4, 25. George gct New Garden MM, O.
1816, 4, 27. George & w, Rachel, & s, Joseph,
    rocf New Garden MM, O., dtd 1815,11,18
1821, 5, 26. George & w, Rachel, & ch, Jo-
    seph Jones, Jacob Bolman & Timothy, gct
    Flushing MM
1822, 3, 23. Grace & fam gct Short Creek MM
1824, 8, 28. Benajah & w, Grace, & fam gct
    Short Creek MM
1832, 5, 26. Geo. & w, Rachel, & ch, Joseph
    J., Jacob B., Lindley, Mary G., Ezra,
    Rhoda D., Elisha & Isaac, rocf Flushing
    MM, dtd 1832,4,24
1832, 5, 26. Lydia rocf Flushing MM, dtd
    1832,4,24
1834, 3, 22. Lydia gct Short Creek MM
1836, 11, 26. William rocf Short Creek MM,
    dtd 1836,6,21
1837, 10, 22. William J. gct Sandy Spring MM,
    to m Ann Farmer
1839, 7, 27. Joseph dis mcd
1839, 4, 24. Martha (form Dawson) dis mcd
1840, 4, 25. William J. rocf Short Creek MM
1840, 9, 26. Mary I. gct Chesterfield MM
1841, 4, 24. George & w, Rachel, & ch, Ezra,
    Rhoda, Elisha, Isaac, Rachel Ann & Martha,
    gct Chesterfield MM
1841, 5, 22. Lindley gct Chesterfield MM
1841, 5, 22. Jacob gct Chesterfield MM
1842, 10, 22. Thomas C. rocf Short Creek MM,
    dtd 1842,7,19
1844, 6, 22. Thomas C. dis disunity
1848, 4, 22. Sarah (form Green) dis mcd
1866, 7, 28. Elizabeth Anna Berry (form
    Parker) dis mcd
1867, 9, 21. Joel dis jas & joining military
    organization
1868, 3, 28. Edward dis disunity
1869, 3, 27. Elizabeth Ann Berry (form Park-
    er) dis mcd
1901, 11, 20. Isaac T. E. rocf Rich Square MM,
    N. C., dtd 1901,2,16
1904, 3, 23. Anna B. gct Springville MM, Ia.
1921, 12, 21. Thomas E. & w, Ellen E., gct
    Birmingham MM, Pa.
1921, 12, 21. D. Howard gct Birmingham MM, Pa.
1921, 12, 21. Beulah R. gct Birmingham MM, Pa.

PARRY
----, --, --. John d 1850,5,13 bur Richland;
    m Rachel ----- d 1859,5,3 bur Richland
    Ch: Ruannah   b 1809, 9, 16 d 1829, 7, 2
        bur Stillwater
        Hannah   b 1812, 8, 27 " 1829, 5,15

PARRY, John & Rachel, continued
    Ch: bur Stillwater
        Deborah   b 1814, 1, 7
        Thomas   " 1816, 11, 16
        Job   " 1818, 8, 1
        David   " 1819, 7, 9
        Sarahann " 1821, 6, 16
        John   " 1822, 11, 22 d 1861, 1,10
        Rachel   " 1825, 7, 31
        Elizabeth " 1831, 8, 13
1839, 8, 1. Job, s John & Rachel, Guernsey
    Co., O.; m in Richland, Asenath HALL, dt
    Caleb & Silvia, Guernsey Co., O., d 1882,
    11,14 bur Stillwater
    Ch: Eliza Jane b 1840, 5, 15
        Ephraim   " 1841, 9, 6
        Asa   " 1842, 11, 19
        Sarah   " 1844, 3, 20
        Phebe   " 1847, 1, 1
        Rachel   " 1848, 12, 4
        Elizabeth " 1850, 2, 29
        Job Jr.   " 1855, 11, 28 d 1875,12, 8
        bur Stillwater
        Letitia   b 1858, 4, 15
1858, 10, 28. Eliza Jane m John WEBSTER
1870, 1, 27. Rachel m William BRYANT

1830, 10, 23. John & w, Rachel, & ch, Deborah,
    Thomas, Job, David, Sarah, John & Rachel,
    rocf Flushing MM, dtd 1830,9,23
1841, 2, 27. Thomas dis mcd
1841, 4, 24. Ruth (form Bailey) dis mcd
1842, 3, 26. Sarah Ann Miller (form Parry)
    dis mcd
1854, 4, 22. Elizabeth Perkins (form Parry)
    dis mcd
1861, 8, 24. Ephraim gct Somerset MM, to m
    Elizabeth Bailey
1863, 3, 28. Ephraim gct Somerset MM
1867, 5, 25. Sarah Day (form Parry) dis mcd
1867, 10, 24. Phebe Bailey (form Parry) dis
    mcd & jas
1868, 2, 22. Asa gc to m Sarah Ann Bailey
1873, 9, 24. Elizabeth Griffin (form Parry)
    dis mcd & jas
1874, 8, 19. Job dis disunity
1876, 12, 20. Hannah H. Gratigny (form Parry)
    dis mcd
1881, 4, 20. Sarah Ann & ch rocf Somerset
    MM, dtd 1881,3,24
1886, 2, 24. Asa & w, Sarah Ann, & ch, Ro-
    sella, Eli & Alice, gct Hickory Grove MM,
    Ia.

PARSONS
1817, 1, 25. Rachel (form Hicks) dis mcd
1826, 4, 22. Benjamin recrq
1830, 11, 27. Benjamin L. dis disunity

PATTERSON
----, --, --. Jonathan & Ruth
    Ch: Edwin   b 1808, 10, 2
        Benjamin " 1810, 6, 18

1808, 9, 14. Tilitha m Stephen BAILEY
1808, 12, 14. Elizabeth m Moses HALL
1808, 12, 28. Jemima m Ruben TAYLOR
1812, 12, 16. Jeremiah, s Wm. & Elizabeth,
    Belmont Co., O.; m in Stillwater MH,
    Elizabeth PLUMMER, dt Robert & Rachel,
    Belmont Co., O.
    Ch: Eliza Jane b 1813, 10, 29
        Rachel P. " 1815, 8, 25
        Sarah B.   " 1817, 9, 23
        William L. " 1819, 9, 20
1813, 9, 16. Sarah m John WILLIAMS
1813, 11, 4. Margaret m Matthew WOOD
----, --, --. Thomas & Achsah
    Ch: Jonathan b 1815, 1, 20
        Isaac   " 1817, 7, 4
        Sarah   " 1814, 1, 20
1814, 5, 4. Silas, s Wm. & Elizabeth (Ladd)
    Belmont Co., O.; m in Stillwater MH, Ra-
    chel STARBUCK, dt George & Elizabeth,
    Belmont Co., O.
    Ch: Elizabeth b 1815, 10, 26 d 1901, 1, 4
        bur Stillwater
        Mary   b 1818, 2, 17 " 1843, 8,27
        bur Stillwater
        Asenath   b 1820, 7, 4
        George S. " 1822, 12, 19
        Nathan   " 1826, 4, 28
1815, 10, 5. Catharine m Amos VERNON
1816, 1, 11. Joel, s Joseph & Hannah, Belmont
    Co., O.; m in Stillwater MH, Penninah
    ALBERTSON, dt Joseph & Elvy, Belmont Co.,
    O.
1816, 8, 1. Elam, s Benjamin & Patience,
    Monroe Co., O.; m in Captina Creek, Ann
    WOOD, dt Matthew & Mary, Monroe Co., O.
1817, 3, 27. Rachel m John PLUMMER
1818, 10, 29. Exum, s Wm. & Elizabeth, Bel-
    mont Co., O.; m in Ridge, Anne DOUDNA, dt
    John & Miriam
1819, 1, 27. Mary d ae 49y bur Ridge
1819, 1, 28. John, s Joseph & Hannah, Bel-
    mont Co., O.; m in Stillwater MH, Lucy
    BAILEY, dt Wm. & Rebecca, Belmont Co., O.
1820, 9, 28. Isaac, s Joseph & Hannah, Bel-
    mont Co., O.; m in Ridge, Rebecca CREW,
    dt Jacob & Rachel, Belmont Co., O.
1820, 12, 26. Mary m John PERVIS
1824, 4, 28. Laban, s Joseph & Mary, Belmont
    Co., O.; m in Stillwater MH, Sarah HEALY,
    dt Thomas & Sarah, Morgan Co., O.
1826, 3, 22. Amos, s Jared & Angeline, b
1828, 4, 9. Silas d ae 39y bur Stillwater
1833, 3, 6. Amasa, s Jared & Angelina, Bel-
    mont Co., O.; m in Stillwater MH, Lydia
    STARBUCK, dt George & Elizabeth, Belmont
    Co., O.
    Ch: James   b 1834, 2, 4
        Eliza Ann " 1837, 7, 14
        Rachel   " 1840, 1, 18
1836, 10, 26. James B., s Jared & Angelina,
    Belmont Co., O.; m in Stillwater MH,
    Elizabeth STARBUCK, dt George & Elizabeth,

PATTERSON, James B. & Elizabeth, continued
    Belmont Co., O.
1837, 3, 29. Asenath m Jesse BAILEY
1842, 12, 28. Rachel m John PARTEN
1850, 3, 27. Nathan, s Silas & Rachel (Star-
    buck), Belmont Co., O.; m in Stillwater
    MH, Mary WILSON, dt Edwin & Deborah, Bel-
    mont Co., O.
      Ch: Wilson   b 1851, 4, 16
          Albert   " 1854, 5, 27
          Lewis   " 1858, 1, 6
          Charles   " 1860, 10, 1
          Anna   " 1864, 4, 17
1853, 9, 18. Mary Elizabeth, dt George &
    Artemisa (Burns), b
1856, 3, 26. David, s Isaac & Rebecca (Crew)
    Belmont Co., O.; m in Stillwater MH,
    Eunice STARBUCK, dt George & Lydia (Bail-
    ey), Belmont Co., O.
1861, 11, 1. Louis d bur Stillwater
1864, 3, 9. Joseph, s Tillman & Rachel
    (Edgerton), Belmont Co., O.; m in Still-
    water MH, Lydia GREEN, dt William & Rachel
    (Hoyle), Belmont Co., O.
1880, 3, 31. Eva L. m Allen BAILEY

1808, 5, 31. William & w, Elizabeth (Ladd),
    & ch, Silas, Talitha, Jeremiah, Axum &
    Rachel, rocf Short Creek MM, dtd 1808,3,
    22, end by Concord MM, 1808,5,26
1808, 6, 28. Joseph Sr. & w, Hannah, & ch,
    Sarah, Rebecca & Isaac, rocf Short Creek
    MM, dtd 1808,6,21
1808, 6, 28. Elizabeth & Jemima rocf Short
    Creek MM, dtd 1808,6,21
1808, 10, 25. Benjamin Jr. rocf Short Creek
    MM, dtd 1808,10,18
1808, 10, 25. Joel rocf Short Creek MM, dtd
    1808,10,18
1808, 11, 29. John rocf Short Creek MM, dtd
    1808,10,18
1812, 10, 27. David & w, Rhoda, & ch, Obedi-
    ence, Milicent Jones & Rhoda, rocf Jack-
    swamp MM, N. C., dtd 1812,6,6
1812, 12, 1. Thomas rocf Jack Swamp MM, N. C.
    dtd 1812,7,4
1813, 10, 26. Achsah rocf Rich Square MM,
    N. C., dtd 1812,9,19
1814, 3, 1. Jacob rocf Darby Creek MM, dtd
    1813,11,20
1815, 5, 30. Mary rocf Short Creek MM, dtd
    1815,1,24
1817, 4, 26. David & w, Rhoda, & ch, Mili-
    cent & Rhoda, gct Darby Creek MM
1817, 4, 26. Obedience gct Derby Creek MM
1817, 4, 26. Jacob gct Derby Creek MM
1818, 4, 25. Ira and w, Mahala, rocf Short
    Creek MM, dtd 1818,1,20
1818, 4, 25. Elijah rpd mcd
1818, 6, 27. Arnold & w, Rachel, rocf Short
    Creek MM, dtd 1818,4,21
1819, 7, 24. Elijah dis
1824, 7, 24. Sarah gct Somerset MM

1825, 11, 26. Jared & w, Angelina, & ch,
    Amasa, James, Elihu, Asenath, Eliza &
    Mary, rocf Somerset MM, dtd 1825,10,24
1826, 9, 23. Laban B. & w, Sarah, rocf Somer-
    set MM, dtd 1826,8,29
1827, 9, 22. Asa C. Hampton gct Deerfield MM,
    to m Esther Patterson
1830, 6, 26. Edwin & w, Ann, & ch, Unice &
    Sarah Ann, rocf Somerset MM, dtd 1830,5,24
1831, 11, 26. Edwin & w, Anna, & ch, Eunice,
    Sarah Ann & Nathan, gct Somerset MM
1833, 5, 25. Rachel rocf Somerset MM, dtd
    1833,1,28
1836, 3, 26. Jared & w, Angelina, & ch,
    Elihu, Asenath, Eliza, Mary & Amos, gct
    Walnut Ridge MM, Ind.
1837, 7, 22. James B. & w, Elizabeth, gct
    Somerset MM
1837, 9, 23. Rachel gct Walnut Ridge MM, Ind.
1841, 3, 21. Amacy & w, Lydia, & ch, Tamer,
    Eliza & Rachel, gct Walnut Ridge MM, Ind.
1846, 9, 26. Elizabeth gct Pennsville MM
1851, 10, 25. George dis disunity
1854, 1, 28. Nathan dis disunity
1854, 6, 21. Elizabeth rocf Pennsville MM,
    dtd 1854,1,19
1858, 7, 24. Eunice & s, George Wilson Pat-
    terson, gct Somerset MM
1863, 4, 25. Tilman & w, Rachel E., & ch,
    Tilman, Rebecca, Sarah, Rachel & Deborah,
    rocf Somerset MM, dtd 1863,3,30
1863, 4, 25. Joseph rocf Somerset MM, dtd
    1863,3,30
1865, 1, 28. Joseph & w, Lydia, gct Hickory
    Grove MM, Ia.
1867, 12, 28. Sarah J. gct Springville MM, Ia.
1868, 11, 28. Tilman Jr. gct Springville MM,
    Ia., to m Sarah E. Bedell
1868, 12, 26. Tillman & w, Rachel E., & dt,
    Deborah, gct Springville MM, Ia.
1870, 2, 23. Rebecca gct Phila. MM. S. Dist.
1873, 3, 19. Tillman Jr. gct Springville
    MM, Ia.
1873, 4, 23. Mary dis jas
1873, 8, 20. Phariba (form Butler) dis mcd
1880, 1, 21. Eva L. rocf Somerset MM, dtd
    1879,12,25
1882, 12, 20. Benjamin S. Sears gct Somerset
    MM, to m Ellen Patterson
1887, 7, 20. Mary E. recrq

PATTEN
----, --, --. William & Rachel [Patton]
    Ch: Williams Jr.
                b 1790, 5, 28
       Rachel   " 1793, 6, 23
       John   " 1796, 2, 27
       Sarah   " 1799, 4, 18
1810, 2, 7. Grace m Benajah PARKER
1811, 9, 28. Rachel [Patton] d bur Still-
    water
1813, 6, 2. William [Patton], Belmont Co.,
    O.; m in Stillwater MH, Sally MORRIS,

PATTEN, William & Sally, continued
        d 1849,11,30 but Stillwater
        Ch: Ruth   b 1814, 3, 11
1814, 7, 26. Ezekiel, s Mahlon & Ephraim, b
1816, 11, 27. John [Patton], s Wm. & Rachel,
        Belmont Co., O.; m in Stillwater MH, Re-
        becca STUBBS, dt Joseph & Zilpah, Belmont
        Co., O.
        Ch: Rhoda   b 1822, 3, 16
            Joseph   " 1823, 7, 10
1817, 1, 1. William, s Wm. & Rachel, Belmont
        Co., O.; m in Stillwater MH, Phebe EMBREE,
        dt Samuel & Hannah, Belmont Co., O.
        Ch: Elihu H.   b 1818, 1, 18
            Hannah Ann " 1820, 5, 22
            Rachel   " 1822, 8, 17
            Mary   " 1824, 4, 1
1818, 7, 1. Rachel [Patton] m Eli GRIFFITH
1833, 10, 30. Ruth m John BUNDY
1840, 10, 15. William [Patton] d bur Still-
        water
1842, 12, 28. John, s Wm. & Rachel, Morgan
        Co., O.; m in Stillwater MH, Rachel
        PATTERSON, dt Geo. & Elizabeth STARBUCK,
        Belmont Co., O.
1902, 5, 24. Clarence R., s Richard & Lydia
        (Pierpoint), Lynn Co., Ia., b 1881,6,7;
        m in Stillwater MH, Anna BAILEY, dt Lind-
        ley P. & Elizabeth (Stanton), Belmont Co.,
        O., b 1876,8,16
        Ch: Bertha E. b 1903, 6, 1 d 1933, 4,11
            Beulah
             Lydia   " 1907, 2, 23
            Oscar
             Marion   " 1909, 3, 20
1908, 5, 21. William, s Richard & Lydia, Linn
        Co., Ia.; m in Stillwater MH, Roanice
        HARTLEY, dt Uriah & Mary Ann, Belmont Co.,
        O.
1809, 2, 28. Mahlon dis mcd
1822, 2, 23. Sarah gct Short Creek MM
1824, 2, 28. Euphemia [Patton] recrq
1824, 6, 26. Mahlon & ch, Smith & Ezekiel,
        recrq
1828, 7, 26. Rachel (form Strahl) dis mcd
1831, 1, 22. Smith [Patton] dis disunity
1838, 4, 28. Mahlon & w, Euphamy, gct Ches-
        terfield MM
1843, 2, 25. Rachel gct Pennsville MM
1844, 2, 24. David Sears gct Pennsville MM,
        to m Rachel B. Patton
1853, 8, 20. Mary [Patton] (form Martin) con
        mcd (H)
1904, 2, 24. Mary H. Rouse (form Patten) con
        mcd
1904, 3, 23. Anna B. gct Springville MM, Ia.
1909, 4, 21. Clarence R. & w, Anna B., & ch,
        Bertha Elizabeth & Beulah Lydia, rocf
        Springville MM, Ia., dtd 1909,2,20
1915, 12, 22. Roanice gct Springville MM, Ia.

PAXTON
1829, 1, 24. Isaac dis JH

1829, 1, 24. Benjamin dis JH
1829, 1, 24. Mary dis JH
1831, 7, 28. Sally dis JH
1832, 5, 26. Charles dis JH
1833, 1, 26. Ruth, Lydia, Aaron & Webster
        gct Milford MM, Ind.

PEACOCK
1929, 10, 5. Harry Wetherill, s Elwood &
        Rena, Hendricks Co., Ind.; m in Richland,
        Lois Josephine HALL, dt Lois L. & Anna M.,
        Guernsey Co., O.

1930, 7, 23. Lois J. gct Plainfield MM, Ind.

PEARSON
1830, 7, 24. Susannah Morris (form Pierson)
        dis mcd
1831, 10, 22. Sarah Miers (form Pearson) dis
        mcd
1832, 9, 22. Ann dis disunity

PECKHAM
1917, 3, 21. Daniel J. & w, Nancy J., & dt,
        Marian E., rocf Paulina MM, dtd 1917,2,10
1918, 12, 25. Marian E. gct Paulina MM, Ia.
1919, 4, 23. Daniel J. & Nancy J. trans-
        ferred to Fairhope MM, Ala.

PEEBLES
1828, 4, 30. Deborah Simmons m Richard
        FAWCETT
1829, 10, 28. Mary m William BUNDY
1831, 4, 27. Burwell, s Mordecai & Abigail,
        Belmont Co., O.; m in Stillwater MH,
        Asenath TODD, dt Stephen & Sibilla, Bel-
        mont Co., O.
1833, 5, 1. Martha m Isaac DOUDNA
1837, 11, 1. William, s Mordecai & Deborah,
        Morgan Co., O.; m in Stillwater MH, Ra-
        chel PLUMMER, dt John & Rachel, Belmont
        Co., O.

1828, 1, 26. Deborah & ch, William Simmons,
        Martha & Susannah Ladd, rocf Upper MM,
        Va., dtd 1825,9,15, end by Springborough
        MM, O., 1827,11,17
1828, 7, 26. Burwell rocf Upper MM, Va., dtd
        1828,6,21
1829, 2, 28. Mary Jr. rocf Upper MM, Va., dtd
        1828,9,20
1833, 9, 28. Susan gct Deerfield MM
1834, 10, 25. Burwell & w, Asenath, & ch,
        Chalkley & Daniel, gct Deerfield MM
1834, 12, 27. William gct Deerfield MM
1838, 4, 28. Rachel T. gct Pennsville MM

PEELLE
1839, 10, 2. Anna [Peel] m Isaiah WILLIAMS

1815, 9, 26. Ann rocf Contentnea MM, N. C.,
        dtd 1815,7,8
1828, 10, 25. Anna [Peal] gct Somerset MM

PEELLE, continued
1837, 4, 22. Ann [Peal] rocf Somerset MM, dtd
     1837,2,27

PEEPER
1853, 8, 20. Rachel dis (H)

PENNEL
1830, 4, 24. William rocf Redstone MM, dtd
     1830,3,31

PENNINGTON
----, --, --. Josiah & Deborah
     Ch: Leroy
          Talbott   b 1812, 4, 30
          Mary   " 1813, 10, 9
          Susannah " 1815, 7, 18 (sic)
          John   " 1815, 3, 11 (sic)
          Eliza   " 1818, 11, 30
          Rachel   " 1821, 3, 8

1812, 2, 25. Deborah rocf Pipe Creek MM, dtd
     1811,11,16
1812, 6, 30. Josiah rocf Center MM, Pa., dtd
     1812,3,14
1822, 3, 23. Josiah & w, Deborah, & ch, Levi,
     Talbert, Mary, Susannah, John, Elizabeth
     & Rachel, gct Miami MM
1822, 3, 23. Elizabeth (form Thompson) dis
     mcd
1828, 11, 22. Charity (form Williams) dis mcd

PENROSE
----, --, --. Barclay, s Richard & Ann Eliza-
     beth (Swickard), b 1841,5,8 d 1923,4,20
     bur Pennsville; m Mary GILBERT, dt Joel &
     Elizabeth (Smith) b 1843,1,1 d 1929,1,11
     bur Pennsville
     Ch: Oliver J. b 1862, 6, 14

1829, 10, 24. Isaac dis jH
1829, 10, 24. Rachel dis jH
1829, 10, 24. Sarah dis jH
1829, 11, 28. Mary dis jH
1829, 12, 26. Edwin dis jH
1829, 12, 26. Jesse dis jH
1907, 12, 25. Barclay & w, Mary P., rocf
     Somerset MM, dtd 1907,11,21
1913, 10, 22. Barclay & Mary P. gct Somerset
     MM
1917, 7, 25. Barclay & w, Mary B., rocf Somer-
     set MM, dtd 1917,5,24
1917, 12, 19. Oliver J. rst

PERDUE
1831, 7, 28. Sarah & s, Charles, rocf Bir-
     mingham MM, Pa., dtd 1831,4,25
1831, 11, 26. Sarah dis disunity

PERKINS
1814, 9, 27. Hannah (form Nicholson) dis mcd
1833, 1, 26. Nathan Morris gct Flushing MM, to
     m Tacy Perkins

1833, 7, 27. Aaron Morris gct Flushing MM,
     to m Phebe Perkins
1854, 4, 22. Elizabeth (form Parry) dis mcd

PERRY
1832, 3, 29. Deborah m Nathan HALL

PERVIS
1820, 12, 28. John, s John & Winifred, Bel-
     mont Co., O.; m in Captina, Mary PATTER-
     SON, dt Jonathan & Temperance, Belmont
     Co., O.
     Ch: Jonathan b 1821, 10, 19

1809, 3, 28. John [Pervies] rocf Contentney
     MM, N. C., dtd 1808,10,8
1857, 4, 25. Levi rocf Pennsville MM, dtd
     1857,3,19
1857, 4, 25. Ann rocf Pennsville MM, dtd
     1857,3,19

PERYGO
1827, 8, 25. Sarah (form Hartley) dis mcd

PETERS
1848, 2, 28. Robert d bur Stillwater

1817, 1, 25. Robert recrq
1925, 10, 21. Myrtle D. (form Hall) dis mcd

PHILLIPS
1833, 7, 27. Mercy [Philips] recrq "was
     mbr at Plainfield MM at time it was dis-
     continued"
1879, 7, --. Albert recrq
1884, 12, 24. Albert S. gct Cottonwood MM,
     Kans.

PIAT
1827, 12, 22. Elizabeth Smith (form Piat) dis
     mcd
1828, 9, 27. Lucinda dis jas
1828, 9, 27. Elizabeth Smith (form Piet) dis
     mcd

PICKERING
1810, 7, 31. Jacob rocf Plainfield MM, dtd
     1810,4,28
1810, 8, 28. Rachel rocf Short Creek MM, dtd
     1810,2,20
1813, 4, 27. Jacob & w, Rebecca, & ch gct
     Short Creek MM
1820, 2, 26. Elizabeth rst on consent of
     Concord MM
1820, 6, 24. Elizabeth & Rebecca Fisher, a
     minor in her care, gct Flushing MM
1829, 1, 24. Levi dis jH
1829, 1, 24. Susannah dis jH
1829, 1, 24. Eleanor dis jH
1832, 10, 27. Samuel dis jH
1833, 1, 26. Mary & Elizabeth, ch Samuel &
     Sarah, gct Short Creek MM
1833, 2, 23. Sarah dis jH

PICKERING, continued
1834, 1, 25. Lydia dis JH
1834, 3, 22. Samuel dis JH
1851, 7, 19. John gct Plainfield MM

PICKETT
1826, 4, 26. Thomas [Picket], s Moses & Han-
        nah, Morgan Co., O.; m in Stillwater MH,
        Mary DOUDNA, dt Henry & Martha, Belmont
        Co., O.
----, --, --. Wm. & Rebecca (Worthington)
        Ch: Elizabeth b 1848, 7, 12 d 1926, 6,24
----, --, --. Wm. m Rebecca ----- d 1904,11,20
        Ch: Edward   d 1899, 1,10
1873, 4, 24. Perley [Picket], s William & Re-
        becca, Morgan Co., O., b 1851,2,8 d 1931,
        2,12 bur Stillwater; m in Stillwater MH,
        Rebecca M. SCHOLFIELD, dt Jonathan & Abi-
        gail, Belmont Co., O., d 1901,7,29 bur
        Stillwater
----, --, --. Perley m Sarah E. STEER, dt
        Israel & Rebecca (Brackin), b 1864,8,30
        Ch: Edith R. b 1906, 11, 22
1909, 10, 28. William, s Thos. & Rhoda, d bur
        Stillwater
1930, 8, 23. Edith R. m Arthur John STRATTON

1830, 8, 28. Phebe [Picket] dis JH
1846, 1, 24. Hannah (form Thorp) dis mcd
1874, 10, 21. Perley [Picket] rocf Pennsville
        MM, dtd 1874,10,10
1879, 3, --. Wm. G. Steer gct Pennsville MM,
        to m Louisa Pickett
1883, 11, 21. William [Picket] & w, Rebecca,
        & s, Edward, rocf Pennsville MM, dtd
        1883,11,15
1883, 11, 21. Elizabeth [Picket] rocf Penns-
        ville MM, dtd 1883,11,15
1903, 9, 23. Perley gct Short Creek MM, to m
        Sarah E. Steer
1904, 3, 23. Perley gct Short Creek MM
1904, 4, 20. Sarah M. rocf Pennsville MM, dtd
        1904,4,14
1905, 8, 23. Rebecca d 1904,11,20 ae 84 (an
        elder)
1906, 1, 24. Perley & w, Sarah E., rocf
        Short Creek MM, O., dtd 1905,12,19
1910, 8, 24. William d 1909,10,28 ae 90 (an
        elder)
1915, 1, 20. Sarah M. rocf Phila. MM, Pa.

PIERCE
1917, 8, 22. Amy B. (form Bundy) dis mcd

PIERPOINT
1826, 11, 30. William, s Jonathan & Ann, Mor-
        gan Co., O.; m in Stillwater MH, Matilda
        BAILEY, dt Jesse & Phariba, Belmont Co.,O.

1826, 6, 24. Jonathan & w, Ann, & ch, Benja-
        min, Elizabeth, John, Mary & Eli, rocf
        New Garden MM, dtd 1826,3,23
1826, 6, 24. William rocf New Garden MM, dtd

1826,3,23
1826, 6, 24. Obed rocf New Garden MM, dtd
        1826,3,23

PIGGOTT
1824, 12, 25. Moses & w, Hannah, & dt, Mary,
        rocf Concord MM, dtd 1824,11,24
1824, 12, 25. Thomas & ch, William & Mary,
        rocf Concord MM, dtd 1824,11,24
1824, 12, 25. Hannah Jr. rocf Concord MM, dtd
        1824,11,24, end to Flushing MM
1825, 10, 24. Moses rocf Concord MM, dtd
        1825,5,25
1829, 1, 24. John dis JH
1829, 1, 24. Eleanor dis JH

PITMAN
----, --, --. Anthony & Margaret
        Ch: Rebecca   b 1822, 4, 18
            Esther   " 1824, 1, 15
            Elias   " 1825, 12, 27

1823, 4, 26. Levi rocf Plainfield MM, dtd
        1823,2,20
1829, 1, 24. Aaron [Pittman] dis
1829, 2, 28. Bula [Pittman] dis JH
1829, 5, 23. Ann [Pittman] dis JH
1830, 2, 27. Levi dis mcd

PLUMLEY
1839, 5, 16. Jonathan S. & w, Rebecca, &
        ch, Jacob N., William D., Mary Ann,
        Clarkson & Peasley, gct Deerfield MM (H)
1875, 7, 17. Anna Whitacre (form Plumley)
        con mcd (H)

PLUMMER
1809, 2, 1. Mary T., dt Robert & Rachel, b
1812, 12, 16. Elizabeth m Jeremiah PATTERSON
1814, 7, 25. Robert d ae 42y 11m 10d
1816, 2, 28. Rachel m Caleb ENGLE
1817, 3, 27. John, s Robert & Rachel, Bel-
        mont Co., O.; m in Stillwater MH, Rachel
        PATTERSON, dt Wm. & Elizabeth (Ladd), Bel-
        mont Co., O.
        Ch: Elizabeth
            P.   b 1818, 7, 2 d 1836, 7,10
            bur Stillwater
            Rachel T. b 1819, 12, 23
            Deborah
            Talitha   b 1822, 1, 28
            Robert   " 1823, 10, 8
            Mary B.   " 1825, 2, 28
            William   " 1827, 2, 28
            Exum   " 1829, 4, 24
            Talitha   " 1831, 2, 21
            Anjaline " 1835, 12, 10
            John   " 1838, 2, 4
1821, 8, 29. Abram, s Robert & Rachel, Bel-
        mont Co., O.; m in Stillwater MH, Eliza-
        beth STRAHL, dt Philip & Sarah, Belmont
        Co., O.
        Ch: Sarah S.   b 1822, 8, 2

PLUMMER, Abram & Elizabeth, continued
        Ch: Talbert   b 1824, 4, 23
            Casper   " 1825, 12, 26
            Rachel   " 1827, 7, 31
            Elizabeth " 1829, 9, 16
            Ruth Ann   " 1831, 4, 10
1828, 7, 30. Mary m Elisha STARBUCK
1836, 9, 28. Robert, s Robert & Rachel, Bel-
    mont Co., O., b 1813,2,25 d 1894,9,2 bur
    Stillwater; m in Stillwater MH, Jane BAIL-
    EY, dt Micajah & Mary, Belmont Co., O.
        Ch: Mary   b 1837, 12, 11
            Abram   " 1839, 10, 20 d 1910, 3,26
                bur Stillwater
            Rachel   b 1842, 1, 11
            Joseph   " 1844, 2, 16 " 1918, 1,21
                bur Stillwater
            Micajah   b 1846, 5, 18
            Hannah   " 1848, 7, 13
            Elizabeth " 1850, 9, 17
            Lydia   " 1853, 4, 17 d 1863, 5,30
                bur Stillwater
            John   b 1856, 4, 24
1837, 11, 1. Rachel m William PEEBLES
1861, 3, 6. Mary m Hosea DOUDNA
1865, 3, 29. Abram, s Robert & Jane (Bailey)
    Belmont Co., O.; m in Stillwater MH, Ma-
    riam CREW, dt John & Anna (Doudna), Bel-
    mont Co., O.
        Ch: Louis W.   b 1866, 2, 15 d 1930, 2,18
            Clarence O." 1867, 11, 14 " 1868, 1,29
                bur Stillwater
            Herbert E. b 1870, 4, 16
1867, 12, 4. Joseph, s Robert & Jane, Belmont
    Co., O.; m in Stillwater MH, Martha Ann
    BUNDY, dt Ezekiel & Maria, Belmont Co., O.
1869, 3, 31. Hannah W. m Wm. HOYLE
1869, 10, 27. Rachel E. m Amasa FRAME
1870, 4, 16. Herbert W., s Abram & Miriam
    (Crew), b
1870, 10, 26. Elizabeth m Benjamin STANTON
----, --, --. Micajah, s Robert & Jane (Bail-
    ey), b 1846,5,18/bur Stillwater; m Ida
    WRIGHT   d 1923,9,1
        Ch: Ralph H.   b 1888, 7, 9
            Raymond   " 1896, 8, 11
----, --, --. Louis W. m Mary DEWEESE, dt Wm.
    & Maria (Embree), b 1867,4,20
        Ch: Edward D. b 1893, 11, 23
            Alfred A. " 1895, 3, 27
            William
              Everett " 1898, 11, 14 d 1899, 3, 3
                bur Flushing
            Robert
              Allen   b 1903, 8, 28
            Anna D.   " 1906, 8, 7
1901, 3, 6. Evalyn C. m Carver T. BUNDY

1814, 8, 30. Susannah & ch, Joseph, Caleb,
    Mary, John, Thomas & Deborah, rocf Pipe
    Creek MM, dtd 1814,7,16
1818, 9, 26. Ann rst on consent of Concord MM

1819, 5, 22. Susannah & six ch gct Smith-
    field MM
1830, 1, 23. Eli [Plumer] dis disunity
1832, 3, 24. John & w, Rachel, & ch, Eliza-
    beth, Deborah, Robert, Mary, William,
    Exum & Tabitha, rocf Somerset MM
1834, 4, 26. Abraham & w, Elizabeth, & ch,
    Sarah, Talbert, Casper, Rachel, Eliza-
    beth, Ruthann & Thomas, gct Deerfield MM
1835, 5, 23. John & w, Rachel, & ch, Eliza-
    beth, Deborah, Robert, Mary B., William,
    Exum, Talitha & Rebecca, rocf Somerset MM,
    dtd 1834,4,27
1839, 3, 23. John & w, Rachel, & ch, Deborah,
    Robert, Mary B., William, Exam, Tabitha,
    Rebecca, Angelina & John, gct Chesterfield
    MM
1871, 3, 22. Abram & w, Miriam, & ch gct
    Springville MM, Ia.
1878, 7, --. Micajah con mcd
1879, 3, --. Micajah gct Springville MM, Ia.
1883, 5, 23. Abraham & ch, Lewis W., Herbert
    E. & Evaline C., rocf Springville MM, Ia.,
    dtd 1883,4,21
1884, 3, 19. Joseph W. & w, Martha Ann, gct
    Cottonwood MM, Kans.
1889, 2, 20. John D. con mcd
1892, 8, 24. Lewis W. gct Springville MM,
    Ia., to m Mary R. Deweese
1895, 1, 23. Mary R. rocf Springville MM,
    Ia., dtd 1894,12,15
1896, 1, 22. John D. dis mcd & jas
1898, 12, 21. Joseph W. rocf Damorris MM, Kan.
1903, 12, 23. Herbert E. con mcd
1910, 6, 22. Raymond I., s Micajah C. &
    Ida B., recrq
1917, 9, 19. Ralph N. recrq

POOL
----, --, --. Timothy & Susannah
        Ch: Lydia   b 1818, 8, 3
            Samuel   " 1830, 6, 29
            Timothy   " 1823, 4, 29 d 1831,11, 7

PORTER
1835, 1, 24. Rebecca (form Wilson) dis mcd

POWELL
1830, 6, --. John d bur St. Clairsville

1829, 7, 25. John rocf Chester MM, Pa., dtd
    1829,7,3

PRICE
1838, 2, 28. Uriah, s John H. & Rachel, Bel-
    mont Co., O.; m in Center, Levina FARRA,
    dt Rees & Rachel, Belmont Co., O. (H)
1839, 5, 29. Edith m James THOMAS (H)
1845, 11, 26. Mary Ann m Nathan GREGG (H)

1827, 4, 28. Minerva (form Broomhall) dis
    mcd
1829, 3, 28. John H. dis jH

PRICE, continued
1829, 3, 28. Rachel dis JH
1854, 7, 15. John H. & w, Rachel, gct Plain-
     field MM (H)
1866, 9, 15. Susanna J. (form Jones) con mcd
     (H)
1884, 11, 26. Ann Eliza (form Crew) dis mcd

PROUTY
1834, 4, 26. Rachel (form Bailey) rpd mcd

RALEY
----, --, --. Asa & Asenath (Hirst)
     Ch: Elizabeth b 1842, 5, 12 d 1929, 1,15
          T.

1926, 12, 22. Elizabeth T. rocf Short Creek
     MM, dtd 1926,12,21

RANDALL
1819, 11, 27. Mary recrq

RATCLIFF
1844, 6, 26. Mary m Robert ELLYSON

1843, 7, 22. Robert F. rocf Flushing MM, dtd
     1844,6,22
1843, 8, 26. Mary & s, Josiah, rocf Short
     Creek MM, dtd 1843,5,23
1844, 9, 28. Josiah C., s Mary Ellyson, gct
     Upper Springfield MM

REDD
1825, 6, 8. Isaiah, s George & Rachel,
     Jefferson Co., O.; m in Stillwater MH, Ann
     St. CLEAR, dt James & Catharine, Belmont
     Co., O.
     Ch: Catharine b 1826, 4, 23
          Rachel
1845, 10, 29. Israel d
1843, 11, 29. Mary m Reuben MILLS

1825, 11, 26. Isaiah rocf Smithfield MM, dtd
     1825,8,22
1828, 5, 24. Isaiah dis JH
1828, 7, 26. Ann dis JH
1841, 12, 25. Mary rocf Chesterfield MM, dtd
     1841,12,18
1843, 3, 23. Israel rocf Smithfield MM, dtd
     1843,12,19

REEVES
1844, 2, 19. Anne d

1822, 5, 25. Samuel [Reeve] rocf Salem MM,
     dtd 1822,4,21, end by Plainfield MM, dtd
     1822,5,23
1824, 2, 28. Samuel C. gct Salem MM
1838, 12, 22. Anne & Matilda Ann rocf Somer-
     set MM, dtd 1838,11,26
1838, 12, 22. Elma-anna rocf Somerset MM, dtd
     1838,11,26
1839, 4, 27. Joseph [Reeve] rocf Somerset MM,

dtd 1839,3,25
1841, 12, 25. Joseph con mcd
1843, 8, 26. Matilda Ann Davis (form Reeves)
     dis mcd
1845, 4, 26. Elmy Ann Davis (form Reeves)
     dis mcd
1846, 7, 25. Joseph gct Somerset MM

RICHARDSON
----, --, --. Samuel W. & Hannah Dingy (Vail)
     Ch: Margaret V. b 1843, 7, 25 d 1928, 5,18

1860, 3, 24. Thomas Webster gct Pennsville
     MM, to m Lydia P. Richardson
1911, 12, 20. Margaret V. rocf Chesterfield
     MM, dtd 1911,12,16

RIGG
1836, 12, 1. Sarah m Asa BLACKLEDGE (H)

RING
1820, 8, 26. Rachel rocf Little Britain MM,
     Pa., dtd 1820,2,5

ROBERTS
----, --, --. Aaron m Elizabeth ----- d 1870,
     2,27
     Ch: Jesse   d 1886,3, 13
          bur Stillwater
          Beula   " 1896, 2,20
          bur Stillwater

1830, 8, 28. John & Esther, minors, rocf
     Short Creek MM, dtd 1830,6,22
1880, 4, 17. Melissa (form Spencer) relrq
     (H)

ROCKWELL
1930, 6, 6. Glenn R., s Edwin C. & Louella
     W., Belmont Co., O., b 1908,5,19; m in
     Stillwater MH, Elizabeth EDGERTON, dt
     Walter J. & Anna T., Belmont Co., O.
1914, 10, 21. Franklin & w, Maria A., & s,
     Reuben L. rocf Cottonwood MM, Kans., dtd
     1914,10,10
1917, 3, 21. Roy W. & w, Oletia A., & ch,
     Hubert Joshua, Eleanor M., Howard Fran-
     cis, Owen Lorenzo & Heston Ellis, rocf
     Paulina MM, dtd 1917,2,10
1917, 4, 25. Edwin C. & w, Luella W., & ch,
     Glenn Rudolph, Helen Luella, Margaret
     Georgiana & Carl Franklin, rocf Pasadena
     MM, Calif.
1917, 5, 23. Arthur R. & w, Clara D., & ch,
     Dorothy, Francis Hall, Chester Arthur,
     Harvey Whiting & Cecil Floyd, rocf Spring-
     ville MM, Ia., dtd 1917,4,21
     (all of the above Rockwell fam were trans-
     ferred to Fairhope MM, Ala. on the es-
     tablishment of a MM there)
1930, 4, 23. Glenn R. rocf New Garden MM, O.,
     dtd 1930,3,20

ROGERS

1809, 1, 31. Ann rocf Nottingham MM, Md., dtd
    1808,9,9, end by Short Creek MM, dtd 1808,
    11,22
1809, 1, 31. Hannah & Ann, dt Joseph, rocf
    Nottingham MM, dtd 1808,9,9, end by Short
    Creek MM, 1808,11,27
1812, 7, 28. John, Josiah, Sarah Alice & Mary,
    ch Josiah & Alice, rocf Plainfield MM, dtd
    1812,6,27
1816, 2, 24. Hannah & Ann gct Plainfield MM
1816, 5, 25. Josiah dis joining M. E.
1816, 6, 22. John dis joining M. E.
1817, 11, 22. Sarah & Alice dis jas
1829, 10, 24. Mary dis jH
1930, 7, 23. Dessie dis mcd & jas

ROMAN

----, --, --. Isaac & Mary
    Ch: Ephraim   b 1814, 8, 1
        Ezra   " 1816, 4, 21
        Sarah Ann   " 1818, 4, 19
        Amos   " 1820, 8, 23
        Hamton   " 1823, 3, 27
1844, 2, 1. Thomas J., s Even & Mary, Guerns-
    ey Co., O.; m in Richland, Susan WEBSTER,
    dt John & Elizabeth, Guernsey Co., O.

1816, 9, 28. Hannah [Romine] rocf Hopewell
    MM, dtd 1816,4,4
1820, 9, 23. Isaac & w, Mary, & ch, Ephraim,
    Ezra & Sarah Ann, rocf Fallowfield MM,
    Pa., dtd 1820,7,7
1842, 5, 28. Thomas I. rocf Flushing MM, dtd
    1842,4,21
1844, 9, 28. Thomas C. & w, Susan, gct Flush-
    ing MM
1845, 8, 25. Mary rocf Flushing MM, dtd 1845,
    7,24
1845, 9, 27. Thomas L. rocf Flushing MM, dtd
    1845,5,24
1845, 12, 27. Mary Cecille (form Romans) con
    mcd
1846, 11, 28. Thomas I. dis mcd

ROOSA

1870, 3, 5. Claud, s Ervin & Elizabeth, b

1893, 4, 19. Claud con mcd

ROSS

1817, 8, 23. William Frazier gct Plainfield
    MM, to m Anne Ross
1820, 11, 25. Thomas rocf Hopewell MM, Va.,
    dtd 1819,5,6, end by Short Creek MM,
    1820,11,21
1826, 8, 26. Thomas dis

ROUSE

----, --, --. Albert m Mary E. HANSON, dt Ben-
    jamin & Lucinda, b 1877,9,2
    Ch: Miles   b 1903, 7, 12
        AlbertaMay " 1905, 9, 26

    Ch: Julia Maud b 1911, 7, 28
        Jane Hanson" 1913, 8, 25
        William
        Henry   " 1916, 5, 15
1925, 7, 23. Helen R. m Loran A. STANLEY
----, --, --. Miles m Agnes McELROY, dt Robert
    J. F. & Agnes A. (Holahan), b 1904,8,1
    Ch: Robert
        Miles   " 1930, 5, 5
        James Wil-
        ford   " 1932, 1, 28

1904, 2, 24. Mary H. (form Patten) con mcd
1917, 9, 19. Helen Ruth, Miles Fay, Alberta
    May, Julia Maude, Jane Hanson & Wm. Henry,
    ch Albert & Mary Hanson Rouse, recrq
1929, 4, 24. Miles F. con mcd
1929, 6, 19. Agnes recrq

ROWND

1804, 2, 20. James S. recrq (H)

RUTLIDGE

1848, 8, 26. Elizabeth (form Strahl) dis mcd
1852, 6, 28. Elizabeth [Rudledge] (form
    Strahl) dis mcd

SATTERTHWAIT

----, --, --. Joseph & Ann
    Ch: Mary   b b 1809, 11, 29
        William   " 1811, 10, 5
        Joshua   " 1813, 3, 8
        Rebeckah   " 1815, 12, 5
        Anne   " 1818, 2, 23
        Samuel   " 1820, 1, 6
        Nathan   " 1821, 9, 21
        Joseph   " 1824, 12, 2
        Edward   " 1827, 2, 14
----, --, --. Thomas & Elizabeth
    Ch: Robert W. b 1811, 5, 24 d 1814, 5,24
        bur Seneca
        Merribah b 1813, 3, 23
        Martha   " 1815, 7, 20
        Ann   " 1817, 11, 27
        Richard   " 1820, 1, 15
        Jerusha   " 1823, 1, 18
----, --, --. William W. & Mary
    Ch: Sarah Ann b 1816, 1, 30 d 1816, 2, 1
        Judge Ma-
        son   " 1817, 6, 28 " 1817, 9,18
        Wilma   " 1819, 3, 7
----, --, --. David & Sarah
    Ch: Hutchin   b 1821, 4, 29
        Lydia-ann   " 1818, 4, 17
        Joshua W.   " 1823, 7, 9
1833, 3, 28. David, s Joshua & Ann, Guernsey
    Co., O.; m in Plainfield, Ruth COFFEE, dt
    John & Rachel, Belmont Co., O.
1896, 4, 29. Nathan, s Joseph W. & Ann,
    Ceder Co., Ia.; m in Stillwater MH,
    Elizabeth J. SPALDING, dt William & Ann,
    Belmont Co., O.

SATTERTHWAIT, continued
1810, 7, 31. William rocf Concord MM, dtd
     1801,4,26
1812, 9, 29. William dis disunity
1812, 12, 1. Thomas & w, Elizabeth, & s,
     Robert W., rocf Concord MM, dtd 1812,3,26
1815, 9, 26. Mary rocf Chesterfield MM, N.J.,
     dtd 1815,7,4, end by Plainfield MM, 1815,
     8,23
1818, 9, 26. David rocf Chesterfield MM, dtd
     1818,6,2
1818, 9, 26. Sarah, w David, rocf Upper
     Springfield MM, dtd 1818,5,6
1827, 2, 24. Elizabeth dis jas
1827, 3, 24. David dis mcd
1828, 5, 24. William dis jH
1828, 5, 24. Thomas dis jH
1828, 5, 24. Mary dis jH
1828, 9, 27. Maribah dis jas
1831, 5, 28. David rst
1835, 4, 25. David & w, Ruth, & ch, Huchin,
     Lydia Ann & Charles W., gct Salem
1836, 7, 23. Martha Mason (form Satterthwait)
     dis mcd
1836, 7, 23. Ann Orn (form Satterthwait) dis
     mcd
1837, 11, 25. Wilma McMullen (form Satterth-
     wait) dis mcd
1842, 8, 27. Richard dis mcd
1842, 11, 26. Jerusha Miller (form Satterth-
     wait) dis mcd
1865, 7, 22. Joseph W. gct Hickory Grove MM,
     Ia.
1865, 7, 22. Joseph Jr. gct Hickory Grove MM,
     Ia.
1866, 6, 23. Edward con mcd
1867, 2, 23. Edward gct Hickory Grove MM, Ia.
1883, 3, 21. Arthur H. Smith gct Hickory
     Grove MM, Ia., to m Ida Satterthwait
1883, 12, 19. Benjamin H. Smith gct Hickory
     Grove MM, Ia., to m Sarah Ann Satterthwait

SAWYER
1846, 10, 21. James, s Archibald & Mary, Mon-
     roe Co., O.; m in house of Nathan P.
     Grissell, Elizabeth FRAME, dt George &
     Lydia, Monroe Co., O.

1851, 4, 19. James & w, Elizabeth Ann, & ch,
     George F. & Thomas A., gct Richmond MM,
     Ind.

SCHOGIN
1821, 8, 25. Rachel (form Dillon) dis mcd

SCHOLFIELD
----, --, --. Issachar d 1834,1,10 bur Still-
     water; m Edith -----
     Ch: Thomas
           Marshall b 1803, 5, 1
         Andrew   " 1805, 5, 23
         William
           Grubb   " 1807, 8, 18

Ch: Mary   b 1809, 6, 25 d 1812,12,28
    Rachel   " 1811, 8, 4
    Cidney   " 1814, 8, 18
    Martha   " 1817, 6, 10
    Jonathan   " 1820, 2, 6 " 1903, 2,15
1830, 3, 31. Rachel m James STANTON
1833, 6, 20. Thomas, s Isaachar & Edith,
     Belmont Co., O.; m in Stillwater, Mariah
     LEEKE, dt Samuel & Ann, Belmont Co., O.
     (H)
1838, 8, 1. Martha m Daniel WILLIAMS
----, --, --. Jonathan T., s Isaachar & Edith,
     d 1903,2,15; m Abigail STEER, dt James &
     Ruth, d 1896,4,27 bur Stillwater
     Ch: Joseph
           Jessup   b 1850, 6, 3 d 1861,11,15
           bur Stillwater
         Rebecca
           Marshall b 1852, 12, 28
         James
           Steer   " 1854, 8, 28 d 1861,10, 2
           bur Stillwater
         Frederick b 1857, 10, 28 " 1861,10, 9
           bur Stillwater
         Franklin   b 1863, 8, 22 " 1864, 5,28
           bur Stillwater
1873, 4, 24. Rebecca M. m Perley PICKET

1816, 5, 25. Isaachar & w, Edith, & ch,
     Thomas Marshall, William Grubb, Rachel &
     Sidney, rocf Indian Spring MM, Md., dtd
     1815,12,15
1816, 6, 22. Andrew rocf Indian Spring MM,
     dtd 1816,5,2
1823, 2, 23. Thomas M., minor, gct Concord MM
1826, 5, 27. Rachel G. rocf Smithfield MM,
     dtd 1826,3,20
1832, 2, 25. Andrew & w, Rachel, & ch, Thom-
     as, John & Margaret, gct Alum Creek MM
1833, 10, 26. William G. gct Baltimore MM
1840, 1, 25. Edith gct Short Creek MM
1840, 3, 28. Edith gct Short Creek MM; re-
     turned to this mtg by her rq, end by that
     mtg 1840,2,18
1845, 6, 28. Jonathan rocf Baltimore MM, W.
     Dist., dtd 1845,5,8
1848, 9, 23. Jonathan T. gct Short Creek MM,
     to m Abigail Steer
1849, 10, 27. Abigail rocf Short Creek MM,
     dtd 1849,9,18
1867, 9, 21. Anna (form Smith) dis mcd & jas

SCHOOLEY
1852, 5, 20. Mary E. m Barclay HODGIN (H)

SCOTT
----, --, --. Joshua & Elizabeth
     Ch: Job   b 1795, 3, 1
         Jesse   " 1793, 7, 23 (sic)
         Hannah   " 1799, 11, 19 d 1807, 8,14
           bur Short Creek
         Anna   b 1802, 4, 19
         Rebecca " 1804, 11, 1

SCOTT, Joshua & Elizabeth, continued
    Ch: Stanton   b 1807, 6, 26
        Enoch M. " 1810, 2, 27
        Elizabeth " 1812, 7, 29
        Joshua   " 1815, 7, 14
        Benjamin S." 1821, 1, 14
1817, 10, 1. Job, s Joshua & Elizabeth, Bel-
    mont Co., O.; m in Stillwater MH, Maribah
    STRAHL, dt Philip & Sarah, Belmont Co., O.
    Ch: Lydia Lee b 1818, 8, 28
        Martha
          Williams " 1820, 2, 29
        David   " 1822, 4, 17
        Evaline " 1825, 6, 28
1822, 10, 20. Jesse, s Joshua & Elizabeth,
    Belmont Co., O.; m in Stillwater MH, Han-
    nah WATSON, dt Abner & Elizabeth, Belmont
    Co., O.
    Ch: Pennington b 1823, 10, 31
        Watson   " 1825, 8, 4
1828, 3, 26. Anna m John HALL

1813, 8, 31. Joshua & w, Elizabeth, & ch, Job,
    Jesse, Anne, Rebecca, Stanton, Enoch &
    Elizabeth, rocf Short Creek MM, dtd 1813,
    8,24
1824, 3, 27. Deborah & ch, Sarah Ann, Robert,
    Cyrus, Mary Ann, Samuel & Thomas, rocf
    Falls MM, Pa.
1825, 10, 24. Jesse & w, Hannah, & fam gct
    Somerset MM
1827, 8, 25. Jesse & w, Hannah, & ch, Penning-
    ton & Watson, rocf Somerset MM, dtd 1827,
    7,30
1828, 7, 26. Joshua, Job & Enoch dis jH
1828, 7, 26. Stanton & Elizabeth & Rebecca
    dis jH
1828, 12, 27. Elizabeth Jr. dis jH
1829, 3, 28. Jesse dis jH
1829, 6, 27. Hannah dis jH
1829, 12, 26. Meriby dis jH
1830, 3, 20. Joshua & w, Elizabeth, & ch,
    Enoch M., Elizabeth W., Joshua & Benjamin,
    gct Goshen MM (H)
1830, 3, 20. Stanton gct Goshen MM (H)
1830, 3, 20. Rebecca gct Goshen MM (H)
1830, 5, 22. Joshua & Benjamin gct Darby Creek
    MM
1831, 4, 16. Job & w, Meribah, & ch, Lydia
    Lee, Martha Williams, David, Evaline,
    Jason & Elizabeth, gct Goshen MM (H)
1832, 8, 25. Robert rocf Deerfield MM, dtd
    1832,7,19
1833, 6, 22. Lydia, Martha, David, Avelina,
    Jason & Elizabeth, gct Miami MM
1849, 6, 23. Asenath (form Hicks) dis mcd
1904, 8, 20. Mary D. gct Camden MM, Ind. (H)

SEAMAN
1913, 10, 22. Mary E. (form Naylor) dis mcd

SEARS
1810, 3, 14. Peter, s John & Sarah, Belmont

Co., O., d 1863,7,12 bur Stillwater; m in
    Stillwater MH, Anna DOUDNA, dt John &
    Sarah (Knowles), Belmont Co., O., d 1878,
    11,5 bur Stillwater
    Ch: Sarah   b 1810, 12, 14
        Martha   " 1812, 1, 9
        Zillah   " 1813, 7, 30 d 1839, 3, 8
        bur Stillwater
        John   b 1814, 11, 10 " 1844, 9,20
        bur Stillwater
        Peter   b 1816, 5, 20 " 1898, 4,22
        bur Stillwater
        Paul   b 1818, 2, 1
        David   " 1819, 9, 14
        Huldah   " 1821, 9, 3 " 1846, 3,24
        bur Stillwater
        Ann   b 1823, 8, 30 " 1844,10,27
        bur Stillwater
        Benjamin b 1825, 6, 23 " 1857, 8,30
        bur Stillwater
        Joseph   b 1827, 5, 10 " 1833, 7, 8
        bur Stillwater
        Elizabeth b 1830, 3, 29 " 1832, 8, 3
        bur Stillwater
1836, 3, 9. Martha m Robert MILLHOUSE
----, --, --. John & Phebe
    Ch: Jane   b 1837, 10, 31
        Margaret " 1842, 11, 16 d 1859,8,11
        bur Chesterfield
        John   b 1844, 1, 15
1843, 3, 29. Sarah m John HARTLEY
1846, 4, 30. Phebe (nee Grimshaw) m Nathan
    HALL
----, --, --. Benjamin & Esther
    Ch: Mary Ann b 1851, 3, 23 d 1862,10,26
        bur Stillwater
        Joseph J. b 1853, 2, 24
        William
        Henry   " 1856, 3, 31
1851, 1, 1. Peter, s Peter & Anna, Belmont
    Co., O.; m in Stillwater MH, Pheriba
    BUNDY, dt Benjamin & Mary, Belmont Co.,O.,
    d 1879,1,16 bur Stillwater
    Ch: Mary B.   b 1852, 10, 11
        Sarah D. " 1854, 8, 11 d 1905, 2, 5
        bur Stillwater
        Benjamin
        Stanton b 1857, 1, 22
        Edwin W. " 1858, 11, 29 " 1925, 6,30
        bur Stillwater
1878, 3, 27. William Henry, s Benjamin & Es-
    ther (Briggs), Belmont Co., O., b 1856,
    3,31; m in Stillwater MH, Mary H. NAYLOR,
    dt Lewis & Rachel (Bailey), Belmont Co.,
    O., b 1854,2,24
    Ch: Frederick
        L.   b 1879, 8, 19
        Walter B. " 1881, 4, 3
        Alice E. " 1886, 10, 27
        Ethel R. " 1891, 5, 28 d 1891, 1,30
        bur Stillwater
        Edna M.   b 1891, 5, 28 " 1921, 4, 3
        bur Stillwater

SEARS, continued

1905, 1, 22. Esther (Briggs), w Benjamin, d
bur Stillwater

1809, 11, 28. Peter rocf Upper MM, Va., dtd
1809,9,16
1828, 1, 26. Paul & ch, Maria, Lydia Ladd &
John, rocf Upper MM, Va., dtd 1827,9,15,
end by Springborough MM, O., 1827,11,17
1828, 4, 26. Paul & s, John G., gct Springborough MM
1828, 4, 26. Lydia Ladd & Mariah gct Springborough MM
1829, 10, 24. Huldah rocf Upper MM, dtd 1829,8,
15, end to Somerset MM
1836, 7, 23. John gct Smithfield MM, to m
Phebe Grimshaw
1836, 8, 27. John gct Smithfield MM
1837, 5, 27. John & w, Phebe, rocf Smithfield
MM, dtd 1837,5,22
1843, 4, 22. Paul gct Flushing MM, to m
Abigail Holloway
1843, 12, 23. Abigail rocf Flushing MM, dtd
1843,9,21
1844, 2, 24. David gct Pennsville MM, to m
Rachel B. Patton
1844, 6, 22. Rachel B. rocf Pennsville MM,
dtd 1844,6,13
1844, 12, 28. David & w, Rachel B., gct Goshen
MM
1845, 7, 26. Paul & w, Abigail, & dt, Rebecca,
gct Flushing MM
1849, 10, 27. Benjamin gct Flushing MM, to m
Esther Briggs
1850, 3, 22. Esther rocf Flushing MM, dtd
1850,2,21
1862, 6, 28. Peter Jr. & w, Pheribah, & ch,
Mary B., Sarah D., Benjamin S. & Edwin W.,
gct Pennsville MM
1868, 4, 25. Peter & w, Phariba, & ch, Mary,
Sarah, Benjamin & Edward, rocf Coal Creek
MM, Iowa, dtd 1868,4,11
1872, 1, 24. Sarah (form Briggs) con mcd
1873, 1, 22. Sarah W. rst at Coal Creek MM,
Ia. on consent of this mtg
1873, 8, 20. John dis mcd
1876, 8, --. Joseph dis mcd
1879, 12, 24. Jane H. gct Chesterfield MM
1882, 12, 20. Benjamin S. gct Somerset MM, to
m Ellen Patterson
1883, 7, 25. Benjamin S. gct Springville MM,
Ia.
1902, 6, 25. Mary Niblock (form Sears) dis
mcd
1905, 1, 25. Frederic L. dis mcd
1908, 11, 25. Walter B. dis mcd

SELBY

1855, 9, 15. Sarah relrq (H)
1872, 7, 20. Mary (form Frame) con mcd (H)
1880, 5, 15. Mary relrq (H)

SHANKLAND

1840, 1, 25. Sarah (form Lewis) dis mcd

SHARP

----, --, --. Jeptha & Sarah
Ch: Samuel   b 1813, 9, 15
    Martha   " 1815, 11, 3
    Ann   " 1818, 7, 24
1818, 9, 3. Jeptha d
1824, 2, 24. Jesse d
1830, 4, 1. Sarah m Samuel HOLLOWAY

1831, 12, 24. Samuel gct Flushing MM
1839, 2, 23. Ephraim Williams gct Flushing
MM, to m Ann Sharp

SHARPLESS

1816, 4, 3. Samuel, s Thomas & Martha,
Belmont Co., O.; m in Stillwater MH, Rebecca Y. JUDGE, dt Hugh & Susannah, Belmont Co., O.

1815, 9, 26. Samuel rocf Concord MM, dtd
1815,3,23
1817, 5, 24. Samuel & w, Rebecca, gct
Plainfield MM
1829, 1, 24. Rebecca dis jH
1829, 2, 28. Samuel dis jH
1833, 1, 26. Hugh Judge & Margaret, ch Samuel & Rebecca, gct Redstone MM, Pa.

SHARRACK

1810, 10, 30. Constant (form Williams) dis mcd

SHEWARD

1822, 8, 24. John recrq
1819, 6, 26. Cert rec for Elizabeth D.
[Sherwood] from Wilmington MM, Del., dtd
1819,4,2, end to Plainfield MM
1830, 9, 25. Elizabeth D. dis jH

SHIPLEY

1860, 7, 21. Ann (form Spencer) con mcd (H)

SHOTWELL

----, --, --. Titus & Deborah
Ch: Rebeckah b 1808, 5, 8 d 1828, 4,--
    bur Stillwater
    Mahlon   b 1810, 4, 2
    Nathan   " 1812, 5, 28
1821, 12, 5. Isaac, s Titus & Deborah, Belmont Co., O.; m in Stillwater MH, Hope
STANTON, dt Borden & Charlotta, Belmont
Co., O.
1828, 3, 25. Titus d ae 69y 7m 12d bur
Stillwater
1895, 9, 5. Nathan d bur Stillwater

1810, 6, 26. Titus & w, Deborah, & ch, Merion, Thomas, Isaac, Rebeckah & Mahlon,
rocf Plainfield MM, dtd 1810,6,23
1811, 2, 26. Merion Barnes (form Shotwell)
con mcd

SHOTWELL, continued
1818, 3, 28. Thomas dis mcd
1826, 6, 24. Isaac & w, Hope, & ch, Mary,
    Ruth & Titus, gct Somerset MM
1832, 5, 26. Mahlon dis jH & mustering in a
    military Parade
1839, 4, 20. Isaac & w, Hope, & ch, Mary,
    Ruth, Titus, Jonathan, Elias, Charlotte,
    Emily & Thomas, gct Deerfield MM (H)
1851, 8, 23. Nathan rocf Somerset MM, dtd
    185-,6,30

SHRINER
1843, 8, 26. Patience (form Dawson) dis mcd

SHRIVER
1841, 9, 25. Martha (form Judkins) dis mcd

SIDWELL
1810, 5, 29. Henry & w, Cineh, & ch, Deborah,
    Eleanor & Cinah, gct Short Creek MM
1814, 5, 31. John dis mcd
1822, 8, 24. Elizabeth rocf Flushing MM, dtd
    1822,8,23
1823, 1, 25. Thomas rocf Short Creek MM, dtd
    1822,9,11
1823, 11, 22. Nathan Jr. dis disunity
1824, 2, 28. Thomas & w, Elizabeth, & s, James,
    gct Plainfield MM
1824, 6, 26. Gabriel B. dis disunity
1825, 3, 26. Jesse dis disunity
1825, 12, 24. Elizabeth Lent (form Sidwell)
    dis mcd
1829, 1, 24. Henry dis jH
1829, 1, 24. Cinah dis jH
1830, 1, 23. Thomas dis jH
1830, 5, 22. Elizabeth dis jH
1888, 11, 21. S. Francis Walton gct Short
    Creek MM, to m Lovisa Sidwell

SIMPSON
1838, 12, 26. Austen, s John & Sarah, Morgan
    Co., O.; m in Stillwater MH, Sibilla FAW-
    CETT, dt Richard & Mary, Belmont Co., O.

1839, 2, 23. Sabilla F. gct Pennsville MM

SINCLAIR
1808, 8, 30. Mary (form Bundy) dis mcd
1824, 2, 28. Ann & Phebe recrq
1829, 1, 24. Elizabeth Millison (form Sin-
    clair) dis mcd
1829, 2, 28. Elizabeth dis jH
1829, 5, 23. Albina dis jH
1830, 8, 28. James B. dis military service
1830, 8, 28. Phebe dis jH

SINTON
1909, 7, 21. Hosetta B. (form Blowers) con
    mcd

SKINNER
1926, 5, 19. Edith J. (form Henderson) dis

mcd
1929, 6, 19. Edith J. (form Henderson) dis
    mcd & jas

SMITH
----, --, --. David & Judith
    Ch: Lydia   b 1800, 2, 12
        William   " 1801, 11, 1
        Thomas   " 1805, 10, 25 d 1809, 7,24
                   bur Stillwater
        Joseph   b 1808, 5, 23
        Sally   " 1811, 2, 1
        Thomas 2nd" 1813, 4, 12
        John   " 1815, 12, 6 d 1841,10, 2
                   bur Stillwater
1821, 1, 4. John S., s Thomas & Phebe, Bel-
    mont Co., O.; m in Ridge, Elizabeth OUT-
    LAND, dt Wm. & Margaret, Belmont Co., O.
    Ch: Phebe   b 1822, 1, 26
        William   " 1824, 3, 19 d 1828, 3,13
        James L.   " 1829, 4, 20
        Josiah   " 1829, 8, 27
        Robert   " 1832, 7, 19 d 1837, 8,26
        Margaret   " 1835, 3, 7
        Jonah   " 1837, 7, 3 " 1837, 7,11
        Rebeckah   " 1837, 7, 3
        John S.   " 1839, 12, 31
1821, 12, 26. William, s Thomas & Phebe, Bel-
    mont Co., O.; m in Stillwater MH, Rebecca
    TODD, dt Stephen & Sibilla, Belmont Co.,O.
    Ch: Thomas   b 1822, 12, 12
        Sibilla   " 1824, 8, 30
        Elisha   " 1826, 5, 14
        Mary Ann   " 1828, 4, 15
        Asenath   " 1830, 3, 29
        Elwood   " 1832, 4, 27
        Hannah   " 1834, 6, 1
        William   " 1836, 7, 3
1822, 10, 31. Thomas, s Thomas & Martha, Bel-
    mont Co., O.; m in Capteana, Jane KENNY,
    dt Richard & Mary, Belmont Co., O.
    Ch: Mary   b 1824, 1, 16
        Martha   " 1826, 9, 19
        Richard   " 1829, 2, 6
        Susanna   " 1832, 4, 30
        Thomas   " 1836, 4, 4 d 1853,12, 6
                   bur Stillwater
        Jane   b 1834, 5, 28
        John   " 1842, 2, 13 d 1846, 8,20
        Ann   " 1847, 6, 19
1822, 12, 4. Robert, s Thomas & Phebe, Bel-
    mont Co., O., d 1878,10,7; m in Still-
    water MH, Elizabeth WILLIAMS, dt Daniel &
    Jane, Belmont Co., O.
    Ch: Daniel W. b 1823, 9, 1 d 1824, 7,21
                   bur Stillwater
        John W.   b 1825, 1, 1
        Rebecca   " 1826, 12, 16
        Barclay   " 1829, 1, 25
        Sinclair   " 1831, 5, 19 d 1879, 9,15
                   bur Stillwater
        Ephraim   b 1833, 9, 26
        Joel   " 1836, 4, 11

SMITH, Robert & Elizabeth, continued
    Ch: Robert   b 1838, 3, 11 d 1930, 6, 4
       Jane   " 1840, 3, 18 " 1841, 3, 3
        bur Stillwater
       William b 1842, 4, 5
1824, 10, 27. William, s David & Judith, Belmont Co., O.; m in Stillwater MH, Ann LADD, dt Stephen & Sibilla, Belmont Co., O.
    Ch: Mary T.   b 1825, 8, 26
       David   " 1827, 8, 29
       Humphrey " 1829, 9, 4
       Stephen   " 1831, 9, 4
       Elihu   " 1833, 4, 28
1827, 6, 6. Sally m Elisha TODD
1832, 5, 31. Stephen d ae 8m 27d bur Stillwater
1834, 10, 1. Thomas, s David & Judith, Belmont Co., O.; m in Stillwater MH, Elizabeth STARBUCK, dt Samuel & Asenath, Logan Co., O.
1835, 12, 9. Joseph, s David & Judith, Belmont Co., O.; m in Stillwater MH, Mary FAWCETT, dt Richard & Mary, Belmont Co.,O.
1836, 5, 1. Rebecca E., w Jonah, dt Caleb Engle, d
1843, 3, 9. Phebe m Joseph DOUDNA
1845, 12, 10. Sabilla m William BUTLER
1848, 12, 27. Elisha, s William & Rebecca, Morgan Co., O.; m in Stillwater MH, Lydia CLENDENON, dt Benjamin & Amy, Belmont Co., O.
    Ch: Amy   b 1849, 9, 16
       Rebecca T. " 1851, 9, 16
1855, 3, 8. Josiah, s John S. & Elizabeth, Guernsey Co., O.; m in Richland, Martha HARTLEY, dt Josiah & Sarah (Hall), Guernsey Co., O.
1856, 10, 23. Jesse L., s Thomas W. & Mary, Belmont Co., O.; m in house of Barkley Broomhall, Lydia J. BROOMHALL, dt Barclay & Rebecca, Belmont Co., O.
1856, 10, 29. Barclay, s Richard H. & Elizabeth (Williams), Belmont Co., O.; m in Stillwater MH, Hannah HOYLE, dt Benj. & Mary (Milhouse), Belmont Co., O.
    Ch: Arthur   b 1857, 8, 25
       Benjamin " 1859, 10, 25
       Anna Mary " 1864, 12, 16
       Elizabeth
        B.   " 1869, 11, 11
1858, 9, 16. Thomas d
1860, 2, 3. Mary Caleb, w Thompson, dt Caleb & Deborah (Hanson) Bundy, b
----, --, --. Sinclair m Tacy HALL d 1869,10, 25 bur Stillwater
    Ch: Robert K. b 1861, 2, 16
       Samuel C. " 1863, 8, 1
       Mary M.   " 1867, 8, 15
1860, 9, 26. Robert, s Robert & Elizabeth (Williams) Belmont Co., O., b 1838,3,11; m in Stillwater MH, Rebecca STANTON, dt Edmund & Sarah, Belmont Co., O.
    Ch: Edmund   b 1861, 9, 18 d 1924, 2,16

    Ch: bur Pasadena
       Elizabeth
       W.   b 1863, 1, 7
       Maria H.   " 1868, 1, 9
1860, 11, 7. Joel, s Robert H. & Elizabeth (Williams), Belmont Co., O.; m in Stillwater MH, Deborah Ann STRATTON, dt Ross & Mary P., Columbiana Co., O.
    Ch: Mary Ellen b 1862, 1, 19
       Emma J.   " 1864, 12, 8
       William C. " 1867, 5, 7
       Dillwyn R. " 1870, 6, 30
1867, 1, 30. Rebecca m Joseph COWGILL
----, --, --. Joshua P., s Evan & Mary (Burgess), b 1850,10,20 d 1930; m Mary M. WILLIAMS, dt Francis & Mary (Hadwin), b 1853,12,24
1877, 3, 5. Samuel d bur Stillwater
1878, 3, 27. George K., s Samuel & Catharine, Guernsey Co., O.; m in Stillwater MH, Anna DOUDNA, dt Thomas & Rachel (Wood), Belmont Co., O.
    Ch: Elbert J. b 1879, 3, 28
       Edgar T.   " 1880, 3, 29 d 1882,12,10
        bur Stillwater
1878, 10, 7. Robert H. d bur Stillwater
1883, 11, 1. Robert H., s Sinclair & Tacy (Hall), Belmont Co., O., b 1861,2,16; m in Barnesville, O., Adaline BAILEY, dt Hezekiah & Elizabeth (Bundy), Belmont Co., O.
    Ch: Lucinda M. b 1896, 7, 15 d 1896, 7,15
       Tacy E.   " 1899, 4, 30
1884, 10, 18. Elizabeth, w Samuel, d bur Stillwater
----, --, --. Edmund S., s Robert & Rebecca (Stanton), b 1861,9,18 d 1924,2,16 bur Pasadena, Calif.; m Eliza D. HALL, dt John & Delora (Davis), b 1853,4,23
1887, 9, 22. Anna W. m William T. SPENCER
1887, 10, 20. Eunice H. m James HENDERSON
1894, 12, 26. Elizabeth B. m John E. HINSHAW
1898, 10, 20. Mary M. m Wm. C. COWPERTHWAIT
----, --, --. Samuel C. & Elma (Bailey)
    Ch: William
       Joseph   b 1905, 7, 15 d 1906, 2,14
----, --, --. Robert H., s Sinclair & Tacy (Hall), b 1861,2,16; m Alice NEWLIN, dt Eli & Mary (Picket), b 1898,7,24

1814, 8, 30. Thomas & w, Phebe, & ch, John S., Jonah, William & Robert H., rocf Hopewell MM, dtd 1814,6,9, end by Short Creek MM, 1814,7,19
1814, 12, 27. Susannah (form Wood) con mcd
1815, 6, 27. Sarah (form Wood) dis mcd
1817, 12, 27. David & fam gct Concord MM
1821, 5, 26. David & w, Judith, & ch, William, Sarah, Joseph, Thomas & John, rocf Concord MM, dtd 1821,4,23
1821, 5, 26. Lydia rocf Concord MM, dtd 1821, 4,23
1822, 5, 25. Jonah dis mcd

SMITH, continued

1822, 6, 22. Rebecca (form Engle) dis mcd
1822, 12, 22. Lydia Williams (form Smith) dis mcd
1823, 8, 23. Thomas Jr. rocf Plainfield MM, dtd 1823,7,24
1824, 8, 28. Jane & dt, Mary, gct Plainfield MM
1827, 12, 22. Thomas & w, Jane, & ch, Mary & Martha, rocf Plainfield MM, dtd 1827,10,25
1827, 12, 22. Elizabeth (form Piat) dis mcd
1828, 9, 27. Elizabeth (form Piet) dis mcd
1829, 1, 24. Mahlon dis jH
1829, 1, 24. Mary dis jH
1829, 1, 24. Ann dis jH
1829, 1, 24. Martha dis jH
1829, 1, 24. Margaret dis jH
1829, 1, 24. Martha Jr. dis jH
1829, 2, 28. Thomas dis jH
1829, 8, 22. Phebe dis jH
1829, 9, 26. Thomas dis jH
1829, 10, 24. Ann dis jH
1830, 2, 27. Susannah dis jH
1830, 10, 23. John L. dis disunity
1831, 6, 25. Rebecca (form Strahl) dis mcd
1831, 7, 28. Mary & ch, Sarah, John, Mary Ann & Nathan, rocf Somerset MM, dtd 1831, 4,25
1831, 7, 28. Rebecca dis
1835, 1, 24. Mary & ch, Maryann & Nathan, gct Short Creek MM
1835, 2, 28. Rebecca rst
1836, 3, 26. Joseph & w, Mary, gct Pennsville MM
1836, 7, 23. Sarah gct Short Creek MM
1836, 11, 26. William & w, Ann, & ch, Mary T., David, Humphrey, Elihu & Lydia, gct Pennsville MM
1837, 2, 18. Jonathan gct Short Creek MM (H)
1837, 4, 22. Thomas & w, Elizabeth, & s, William, gct Pennsville MM
1837, 5, 27. John C. dis mcd
1837, 11, 25. Sarah Jr. gct Short Creek MM, 1836,7,23, now returned to this mtg end 1837,6,20
1839, 10, 26. Sarah dis
1840, 5, 23. William & w, Rebecca, & ch, Thomas, Sibilla, Mary Ann, Asenath, Elwood, Hannah, William & Stephen, gct Chesterfield MM
1840, 6, 27. Mary Bowlin (form Smith) dis mcd
1841, 11, 27. David & w, Judith, gct Chesterfield MM
1842, 6, 25. Sylvia Jane (form Hall) dis mcd
1842, 8, 27. Rebecca & ch, Thomas, Sabilla, Elisha, Mary Ann, Asenath, Elwood, Hannah, Stephen & Phebe, rocf Chesterfield MM, dtd 1841,7,16
1845, 3, 22. Thomas con mcd
1847, 4, 24. James dis disunity
1847, 4, 24. Mary Ann Spencer (form Smith) dis mcd
1848, 3, 25. John W. rocf Short Creek MM, to

m Maria Hall

1848, 7, 22. John W. gct Flushing MM
1848, 9, 23. Rebecca & ch, Hannah, Stephen & Phebe, gct Chesterfield MM
1849, 1, 25. Eliza (form Lewis) dis mcd
1849, 12, 22. Thomas gct Chesterfield MM
1851, 7, 26. Richard dis mcd
1851, 11, 22. Asenath gct Spring Creek MM, Ia.
1852, 1, 24. Susannah Beaty (form Smith) dis mcd
1852, 7, 24. Martha Davis (form Smith) dis mcd
1854, 7, 22. Elisha & w, Lydia, & ch, Amy & Rebecca, gct Three Rivers MM, Ia.
1855, 1, 20. Sarah W. (form Webster) con mcd (H)
1857, 3, 28. Demsey Bundy gct Flushing MM, to m Rebecca W. Smith
1857, 7, 25. Ephraim gct Birmingham MM, Pa.
1858, 4, 17. Louisa recrq (H)
1858, 9, 25. Janedis disunity
1860, 4, 28. Sinclair gct Somerset MM, to m Tacy M. Hall
1861, 2, 23. Tacy rocf Somerset MM, dtd 1860,10,29
1861, 9, 28. Robert H. & w, Elizabeth, gct Short Creek MM
1861, 12, 28. Barak & w, Mary, recrq (residing in Linn Co., Ia.
1864, 8, 27. Samuel & w, Elizabeth, rocf Flushing MM, dtd 1864,7,25
1865, 4, 22. William W. gct Salem MM, to m Hannah Street
1865, 6, 27. Robert H. & w, Elizabeth, rocf Short Creek MM, dtd 1865,5,18
1865, 6, 27. Elizabeth gct Coal Creek MM, Ia.
1866, 6, 23. Hannah S. rocf Salem MM, dtd 1866,5,23
1867, 9, 21. Anna Scholfield (form Smith) dis mcd & jas
1869, 9, 22. Eunice H., gr dt Samuel & Elizabeth, recrq
1871, 3, 22. Robert Jr. & w, Rebecca S., & ch, Edwin S., Elizabeth W. & Maria H., gct Short Creek MM
1874, 9, 23. Sarah Ellen (form Hartly) dis mcd
1880, 7, 17. Rebecca Ann (form Adams) con mcd (H)
1882, 5, 24. George K. & w, Anna D., & ch, Elbert J. & Edgar T., gct Flushing MM
1882, 7, 19. Elizabeth W. d 1881,10,16 ae 80 (a minister)
1882, 10, 25. Mary Ellen gct Hickory Grove MM, Ia.
1883, 3, 21. Arthur H. gct Hickory Grove MM, Ia., to m Ida Satterthwait
1883, 12, 19. Benjamin H. gct Hickory Grove MM, Ia., to m Sarah Ann Satterthwait
1885, 8, 19. Elizabeth d 1884,10,18 ae 92 (an elder)
1887, 10, 19. Samuel C. gct Flushing MM, to m Sarah Elma Bailey

SMITH, continued

1887, 11, 30. William D. dis mcd

1888, 3, 21. Benjamin H. gct Hickory Grove
MM, Ia.

1888, 3, 21. Sarah Elma rocf Flushing MM, dtd
1888,2,23

1889, 2, 20. Wm. C. gct Hickory Grove MM, Ia.

1889, 7, 24. Emma J. gct Hickory Grove MM, Ia.

1889, 9, 25. Mary C. (form Bundy) dis mcd

1892, 4, 20. Joel J. & w, Deborah Ann, gct
West Branch MM, Ia.

1895, 8, 21. Mary C. rst

1895, 10, 23. Mary Acice & William S., ch
Thompson & Mary C., recrq

1902, 2, 19. Barclay & Hannah H. gct Springville MM, Ia.

1910, 2, 23. Robert rocf Short Creek MM, dtd
1910,1,18

1910, 2, 23. Maria H. rocf Short Creek MM, dtd
1910,1,18

1914, 8, 19. Edmund S. & Eliza rocf Springville MM, dtd 1914,7,18

1914, 10, 21. Marion & w, Alice M., & ch, Curtis W. & Josephine A., rocf Cottonwood MM,
Kans.

1915, 6, 23. Mary Avice Webster (form Smith)
con mcd

1919, 4, 23. Marion & w, Alice M., & ch, Curtis W., Josephine A., Samuel C. & Sarah
Elma, transferred to Fairhope MM, Ala. on
the establishment of a mtg there

1922, 11, 22. Edmund J. & w, Eliza D., gct
Pasadena MM, Calif.

1927, 3, 23. Joshua P. & w, Mary M., rocf
Fairhope MM, Ala., dtd 1927,1,12

1927, 7, 20. Robert H. gct Plainfield MM,
Ind., to m Alice Newlin

1928, 4, 25. Alice Newlin rocf Plainfield MM,
Ind., dtd 1929,5,2

1929, 7, 24. Lucinda Weaver (form Smith) con
mcd

1930, 8, 20. Joshua P. d 1930,6,15 ae 80 (a
minister)

SPALDING

1895, 8, 21. Elizabeth J. recrq

1896, 4, 29. Elizabeth J. m Nathan SATTERTH-
WAIT

SPENCER

----, --, --. Joseph & Sarah
Ch: John   b 1811, 1, 10 d 1811, 4 9
    William   " 1812, 3, 20 " 1832, 8,20
    Elisha   " 1814, 6, 3 " 1818, 3,--
    George   " 1816, 6, 12
    Amy   " 1819, 1, 10
    Joseph   " 1821, 5, 23

1821, 2, 15. Joseph d ae 34y 3m 3d

1830, 9, 30. Sarah m John VANLAW

1831, 2, 22. Lydia Ann, dt Abner & Harriet, b

1861, 7, 18. Sarah d bur Captina

1887, 9, 22. William T., s Elwood & Anna,

Mohaska Co., Ia.; m in Stillwater MH,
Anna W. SMITH, dt Barclay & Hannah H.,
Belmont Co., O.

1823, 8, 23. Jonathan & w, Sarah, rocf
Plainfield MM, dtd 1823,7,24

1829, 1, 24. Ann dis jH

1829, 1, 24. Asa dis jH

1829, 1, 24. Nathan dis jH

1829, 1, 24. Rachel dis jH

1829, 4, 25. Unice relrq

1829, 5, 23. George dis jH

1829, 10, 24. Mariah dis jH

1829, 11, 28. Jonathan dis jH

1831, 12, 24. George gct Flushing MM

1833, 9, 28. Louiza, Athanesa, William,
Lydia, John, Elwood & Eunice, ch Geo. &
Eunice, gct Alum Creek MM

1834, 2, 22. George rocf Flushing MM, dtd
1833,12,26

1847, 4, 24. Mary Ann (form Smith) dis mcd

1855, 7, 20. Ellen P. Cowgill (form Spencer)
con mcd

1860, 7, 21. Ann Shipley (form Spencer) con
mcd (H)

1875, 1, 16. Lyda G. (form Frame) con mcd
(H)

1880, 4, 17. Melissa Roberts (form Spencer)
relrq (H)

1888, 6, 20. Anna M. gct Coal Creek MM, Ia.

1904, 7, 16. Rachel N. relrq (H)

1906, 7, 21. Rachel N. rst rq (H)

STANLEY

1925, 7, 23. Loran A., s Wm. B. & Edith A.
(Wiles), Baldwin Co., Ala., b 1901,8,17;
m in Stillwater MH, Helen R. ROUSE, dt
Albert M. & Mary N., Montgomery Co., Md.,
b 1901,12,10
Ch: Arthur
    Loren   b 1926, 10, 31
    Clarence
    Wilbur   " 1928, 7, 5
    Verna Marie " 1932, 6, 14

1818, 2, 28. James C. & w, Mary, & ch,
Jesse, Littleberry, Lemuel, Jonathan &
Rhoda, rocf Salem MM, dtd 1818,1,13

1818, 6, 27. James & w, Rachel, & ch, Israel
& Jesse, rocf Salem MM, dtd 1818,5,12

1819, 1, 23. James Jr. & w, Rachel, gct
Salem MM, O.

1917, 8, 22. William B. & w, Edith A., & ch,
Loren Alverda, Clayton Robert & Ralph
Ernest, rocf Hickory Grove MM, Ia., dtd
1917,8,4

1919, 4, 23. Wm. B. & w, Edith A., & ch,
Loran Alverdo, Clayton Robert, Ralph
Ernest, Louisa May & Lillian transferred
to Fairhope MM, Ala.

1923, 6, 23. Alfred J. Hartley gct Springville MM, Ia., to m Ethel A. Stanley

1925, 5, 20. Loran A. rocf Fairhope MM, Ala.

STANTON
----, --, --. Henry & Clarey
    Ch: Anna   b 1814, 4, 21
        Edmund   " 1816, 10, 14 d 1850,12,14
          bur Stillwater
        Jordon   " 1818, 11, 25 " 1839,12,16
          bur Stillwater
        Mary P.   b 1821, 5, 8
        Henry   " 1824, 10, 20 " 1844,10,16
          bur Stillwater
        Daniel   b 1827, 6, 12 " 1844,11,16
          bur Stillwater
1821, 12, 5. Hope m Isaac SHOTWELL
1824, 4, 28. Borden, s Borden & Charlotte,
    Belmont Co., O.; m in Stillwater MH, Maran-
    da BAILEY, dt Micajah & Mary, Belmont Co.,
    O.
    Ch: Jane   b 1825, 1, 29
        Charlotte   " 1826, 11, 29
1830, 3, 31. James, s Henry & Clara, Belmont
    Co., O.; m in Stillwater MH, Rachel SCHOL-
    FIELD, dt Issachar & Edith, Belmont Co.,
    O., d 1836,9,1 bur Stillwater
    Ch: David   b 1831, 2, 4
        Lindley   " 1832, 11, 5
        Edith   " 1834, 5, 25
        Lydia   " 1836, 2, 7
1832, 9, 26. Joseph, s Henry & Clary, Bel-
    mont Co., O.; m in Stillwater MH, Mary
    HODGIN, dt Stephen & Elizabeth, Belmont
    Co., O., d 1857,9,27 bur Stillwater
    Ch: Eli   b 1835, 2, 12
        Anna   " 1837, 8, 8
        William   " 1839, 9, 15 d 1918, 5, 5
          bur Stillwater
        Eunice   b 1843, 10, 19 " 1849, 9, 6
          bur Stillwater
        Elizabeth   b 1846, 12, 24
1836, 12, 2. Anna, dt Thomas, d bur Stillwater
1837, 1, 26. William, s Enoch & Mary, Bel-
    mont Co., O.; m in Stillwater, Catharine
    THOMAS, dt William & Rebecca, Belmont Co.,
    O.
1839, 6, 19. Abigail m William EWERS (H)
1840, 7, 1. Edmund, s Henry & Clara, Belmont
    Co., O.; m in Stillwater MH, Sarah HOYLE,
    dt Benjamin & Tabitha, Belmont Co., O.
    Ch: Rebecca   b 1842, 7, 5
        Tabitha   " 1845, 3, 13
        Henry   " 1847, 6, 25
        Benjamin H.   " 1849, 4, 22
        Daniel E.   " 1850, 8, 28 d 1919, 4,25
          bur Stillwater
1843, 6, 28. James, s Henry & Clara, Belmont
    Co., O.; m in Stillwater MH, Charity
    BUNDY, dt Wm. & Sarah, Belmont Co., O., d
    1852,3,20 bur Stillwater
1843, 9, 27. Mary P. m Joel DAWSON
1851, 1, 20. James, s Henry & Clara, d bur
    Stillwater
1852, 9, 29. Sarah m Ezekiel BUNDY
1853, 1, 5. Edith m Wm. C. BUNDY
1857, 12, 9. Eli, s Joseph & Mary, Belmont

Co., O.; m in Stillwater MH, Mary P.
    BUNDY, dt John & Ruth, Belmont Co., O.,
    d 1871,12,6 bur Stillwater
    Ch: William
        Henry   b 1860, 8, 2
        Sarah B.   " 1861, 11, 23
        Emma C.   " 1864, 10, 5
1859, 3, 30. Anna m Nathan BUNDY
1860, 9, 26. Rebecca m Robert SMITH
1863, 6, 6. Henry d bur Stillwater
1864, 1, 27. William, s Joseph & Mary (Hod-
    gin), Belmont Co., O.; m in Stillwater
    MH, Jane DAVIS, dt Francis & Mary (Smith),
    Belmont Co., O., d 1910,3,8 bur Still-
    water
    Ch: Eva T.   b 1868, 8, 20
        Mary D.   " 1870, 4, 24 d 1884,10, 4
          bur Stillwater
        Joseph E.   b 1872, 8, 26
        Francis W.   " 1875, 4, 5 " 1886, 8, 8
          bur Stillwater
        John
        Lindley   b 1877, 4, 17 " 1897, 3,20
          bur Stillwater
        Elwood Dean   b 1880, 8, 20
        Anna Clara   " 1883, 4, 9
        Edna M.   " 1886, 4, 26
        Ellen D.   " 1886, 4, 26
        William
        Macy   " 1888, 9, 15
1864, 3, 30. Tabitha m John F. DAVIS
1870, 10, 26. Benjamin, s Edmund & Sarah,
    Belmont Co., O., d 1898,8,6 bur Still-
    water; m in Stillwater MH, Elizabeth
    PLUMMER, dt Robert & Jane (Bailey), Bel-
    mont Co., O., b 1850,9,17
    Ch: Mildred
        Leroy   b 1872, 12, 10
        Howard A.   " 1876, 2, 24 d 1898,11, 1
          bur Stillwater
        Ida Jane   b 1881, 7, 22
        Arthur E.   " 1891, 9, 6
1871, 3, 8. Henry, s Edmond & Sarah
    (Hoyle), Belmont Co., O.; m in Stillwater
    MH, Mary BAILEY, dt Hezekiah & Elizabeth
    (Bundy), Belmont Co., O., b 1848,11,16
    d 1925,11,5 bur Stillwater
1871, 7, 26. Elizabeth m Lindley P. BAILEY
1872, 10, 9. Daniel, s Edmund & Sarah, Bel-
    mont Co., O.; m in Stillwater MH, Rebecca
    D. BUNDY, dt Chalkley & Sarah (Doudna),
    Belmont Co., O., b 1853,12,11 d 1926,5,9
    bur Stillwater
    Ch: Sarah El-
        ma   b 1873, 8, 4
        Edmund C.   " 1877, 9, 17
1873, 7, 30. Eli, s Joseph & Mary, Belmont
    Co., O.; m in Stillwater MH, Deborah
    BUNDY, dt Elijah & Eliza (Stubbs) HANSON,
    Belmont Co., O., b 1839,1,26 d 1926,4,25
    bur Stillwater
    Ch: Nathan   b 1875, 1, 26
1875, 1, 26. Nathan E., s Nathan & Annie

STANTON, continued
     (Hanson), b
1888, 8, 23. Emma A. m Willis V. WEBSTER
1904, 5, 26. Ida J. m Wilmer L. HALL
1907, 6, 20. Sarah E. m Nathan E. STANTON
1907, 6, 20. Nathan E., s Eli & Deborah
     (Hanson), Emmet Co., Ia.; m in Stillwater
     MH, Sarah E. STANTON, dt Daniel E. & Re-
     becca D. (Bundy), Belmont Co., O.
     Ch: Edith Re-
          becca   b 1908, 4, 15
        Merion Dan-
          iel   " 1910, 2, 13
        William
          Hanson   " 1914, 1, 8
1908, 6, 25. Anna C. m Charles W. PALMER
----, --, --. Edmund, s Daniel E. & Rebecca
     (Bundy), b 1877,9,17; m Sina M. HODGIN,
     dt Clarkson & Elizabeth (Wood), b 1872,3,
     11
     Ch: Henry Ed-
          mund   b 1910, 7, 22
        Alfred
          Hodgin   " 1912, 10, 15
1914, 10, 22. Arthur E., s Benjamin & Eliza-
     beth (Plummer), Belmont Co., O.; m in
     Stillwater MH, Mary Alma BAILEY, dt Allen
     & Eva L. (Patterson), b 1892,9,14 (Arthur
     E. b 1891,9,6)
     Ch: Pauline B. b 1917, 12, 23
        Howard Ar-
          den   " 1926, 6, 23

1812, 6, 30. Henry & w, Clary, & ch, James &
     Joseph, rocf Short Creek MM, dtd 1812,5,19
1816, 7, 27. Hannah & ch, Elizabeth &
     Peninah, rocf Concord MM, dtd 1816,4,24
1817, 4, 26. Elizabeth Lambert (form Stanton)
     dis mcd
1817, 6, 24. Ann recrq
1817, 7, 26. Bordon & w, Charity, & ch, Hope,
     Borden, Mary & Lotte, rocf Concord MM, dtd
     1817,6,25
1817, 10, 25. Borden Jr. rst
1818, 10, 24. Abigail rocf Smithfield MM, dtd
     1818,8,17
1818, 10, 24. William & ch, Enoch & Mary, rec-
     rq
1819, 3, 27. Lydia, Mary & Sarah, ch Borden
     Jr. & Ann, recrq
1820, 4, 23. William rocf Plainfield MM, dtd
     1819,10,20
1821, 11, 24. Abigail Jr. gct Short Creek MM
1826, 5, 27. Mary Williams (form Stanton)
     dis mcd
1828, 2, 23. Borden dis disunity
1828, 6, 28. Charlotte & Lotte dis jH
1828, 8, 23. Borden Jr. dis jH
1829, 6, 27. Maranda dis jH
1840, 6, 20. Maranda & ch, James, Charlotte,
     Edmund, Micajah & David, gct Deerfield MM
     (H)
1840, 10, 24. Edmund & w, Sarah, gct Chester-

field MM
1842, 5, 21. Borden gct Deerfield MM (H)
1845, 2, 22. Edmund & w, Sarah, & dt, Re-
     becca, rocf Chesterfield MM
1850, 8, 17. William & w, Mary, & ch,
     Schooley, Lydia, Mary Jane & Sarah, gct
     Deerfield MM (H)
1852, 4, 24. David gct Flushing MM, to m
     Martha Wilson
1853, 6, 25. David gct Flushing MM
1855, 4, 21. Sarah Burr rocf Plainfield MM,
     dtd 1855,2,15 (H)
1856, 2, 16. Ruth Annah Mead (form Stanton)
     con mcd (H)
1858, 8, 28. Mary d 1857,9,27 ae 48 (an
     elder)
1859, 7, 23. Joseph gct Flushing MM, to m
     Achsah Smith
1859, 8, 27. Joseph d 1859,7,26 ae 48 (an
     elder)
1860, 6, 23. Lindley dis mcd
1881, 4, 20. Wm. Henry gct Phila. MM, Pa.
1881, 9, 21. Henry & w, Mary, gct Flushing MM
1892, 2, 24. Sarah Hall (form Stanton) con
     mcd
1893, 4, 19. Everette G., Elma C. & Elsie H.,
     ch Rebecca W., recrq
1893, 5, 24. Rebecca W. dis by Pennsville MM
1893, 5, 24. Blanch D. recrq
1893, 5, 24. Wilford T. recrq
1904, 1, 20. Henry E. & w, Mary, rocf Flush-
     ing MM, dtd 1903,12,24
1904, 8, 24. Eva T. gct Phila. MM, Pa.
1906, 8, 22. Edmund C. gct Springville MM,
     Ia., to m Sina M. Hodgin
1907, 2, 20. Elwood Dean gct Phila. MM, Pa.
1907, 11, 20. Sina M. rocf Springville MM,
     Ia., dtd 1907,2,16
1911, 8, 23. Ellen D. & Edna M. gct Lans-
     down MM, Pa.
1916, 7, 19. Wm. Macy gct Woodbury MM, N. J.,
     to m Edith Mary Cope
1919, 5, 21. W. Macy gct Lawnsdowne MM, Pa.
1922, 3, 22. Joseph E. gct West-town MM, Pa.
1925, 12, 23. Edmund C. & w, Sina M., & ch,
     Henry Edmund & Alfred Hodgin, gct West-
     town MM, Pa.

STARBUCK
----, --, --. Jethro & Rebecca
     Ch: Sarah   b 1806, 5, 23
        Mary   " 1808, 1, 29
        Elizabeth " 1810, 1, 18
        Rhoda   " 1812, 1, 27
        Hilda   " 1814, 2, 7
----, --, --. George & Elizabeth
     Ch: Lydia   b 1807, 2, 12
        Eunice   " 1809, 8, 24 (sic)
        Elizabeth " 1809, 5, 31 (sic)
        George   " 1814, 3, 8
----, --, --. Hezekiah & Anne
     Ch: Nathan
        Hussey   b 1807, 8, 16

STARBUCK, Hezekiah & Anne, continued
    Ch: Alfred   b 1809, 12, 19 d 1810, 1,24
        Joseph   " 1811, 2, 8
        Irena   " 1813, 4, 19
        Sidney   " 1815, 5, 5
        Lydia   " 1817, 10, 7
1814, 5, 4. Rachel m Silas PATTERSON
----, --, --. Samuel & Asenath
    Ch: Elizabeth b 1816, 8, 20
        Sibilla   " 1819, 12, 10 d 1824, 2, 1
        bur Stillwater
1815, 12, 19. Jethro d ae 30y 7m 4d bur Still-
    water
----, --, --. John & Ann
    Ch: George   b 1821, 7, 8
        Samuel   " 1823, 5, 12
        Hezekiah   " 1825, 8, 19
1825, 12, 12. George d ae 40y 8m 4d bur Still-
    water
1828, 7, 30. Elisha, s George & Elizabeth,
    Belmont Co., O.; m in Stillwater MH, Mary
    PLUMMER, dt Robert & Rachel, Belmont Co.,O.
    Ch: Robert   b 1829, 6, 26
        George   " 1830, 11, 12
        Abram   " 1832, 7, 4
        Rachel   " 1834, 9, 6
        Elizabeth " 1836, 8, 1
        Sarah   " 1833, 6, 24
        Elisha   " 1840, 9, 9
        John   " 1842, 3, 11
        Mary Jane " 1844, 3, 4
        Hezekiah   " 1846, 7, 11
1833, 3, 6. Lydia m Amasa PATTERSON
1834, 10, 1. Elizabeth m Thomas SMITH
----, --, --. George m Lydia BAILEY d 1851,
    11,3 bur Stillwater
    Ch: Martha   b 1837, 1, 18
        Eunice   " 1838, 10, 3
        Jesse   " 1841, 4, 23
        Milton   " 1843, 5, 27
        Edmund   " 1845, 4, 10 d 1848, 2, 8
        bur Stillwater
        Joseph   b 1847, 6, 19 " 1861,10,24
        bur Stillwater
        Margaret   " 1849, 8, 17 " 1862, 5,13
        bur Stillwater
1836, 10, 26. Elizabeth m James B. PATTERSON
1845, 4, 5. Elizabeth d bur Stillwater
1856, 3, 26. Eunice m David PATTERSON
----, --, --. George & Mary (Painter)
    Ch: Lydia Ellen b 1858, 7, 23 d 1862, 1,12
1862, 10, 1. Jesse, s George & Lydia (Bailey)
    Belmont Co., O.; m in Stillwater MH, Mary
    Jane BUNDY, dt Ezekiel & Maria (Engle),
    Belmont Co., O.
    Ch: Caleb L. b 1863, 12, 4
        Joseph
          Clinton " 1865, 10, 17
        Clyde L.   " 1868, 3, 17
        Clara L.   " 1875, 4, 27 d 1886,11,17
        Adelbert W." 1877, 5, 14
        Edith M.   " 1882, 9, 12
1868, 12, 30. Milton, s George & Lydia (Bailey)

Belmont Co., O.; m in Stillwater MH,
Tacy FRAME, dt Aaron & Tabitha (Thompson), Belmont Co., O.
    Ch: Melissa T. b 1872, 4, 7
        Mabel D.   " 1876, 10, 28
        Viola C.   " 1880, 7, 28
        Joseph
          Earle   " 1887, 11, 16

1809, 6, 26. Hezekiah rocf New Garden MM,
    N. C., dtd 1809,4,29
1811, 4, 30. Anna Williams (form Starbuck)
    dis mcd
1811, 10, 1. Nathan Hussey & Joseph, ch
    Hezekiah, recrq
1811, 11, 26. Ann recrq
1815, 12, 23. Asenath (form Hodgin) dis mcd
1816, 11, 23. Asenath rst
1817, 3, 22. Asenath gct Darby Creek MM, O.
1819, 2, 27. Rebecca Jordan (form Starbuck)
    dis mcd
1819, 3, 27. Hezekiah & w, Ann, & fam gct
    Darby Creek MM, O.
1820, 10, 28. John dis mcd
1821, 7, 28. Elizabeth & Sabilla, minors,
    rocf Darby Creek MM, dtd 1821,5,19
1822, 12, 22. Sarah Morris (form Starbuck)
    dis mcd
1823, 10, 28. Ann recrq
1824, 1, 24. George & Samuel, ch John &
    Ann, recrq
1825, 4, 23. Mary Butler (form Starbuck) dis
    mcd
1827, 4, 28. Mary Coles (form Starbuck) dis
    mcd
1828, 9, 27. Elizabeth, dt Jethro, dis jas
1829, 5, 23. John & w, Ann, & ch, George,
    Samuel, Hezekiah, John & Robert, gct
    Somerset MM
1833, 7, 27. Rhoda Laughlir (form Starbuck)
    dis mcd
1834, 9, 27. Huldah dis jas
1836, 3, 26. George gct Somerset MM, to m
    Lydia Bailey
1854, 10, 28. Robert dis mcd
1855, 3, 24. Rachel dis disunity
1855, 9, 22. George gct Salem MM, to m
    Mary P. Stratton
1855, 3, 24. Martha Outland (form Starbuck)
    dis mcd
1856, 4, 26. Mary P. & dt, Deborah Ann
    Stratton, rocf Salem MM, dtd 1856,3,19
1858, 12, 25. Mary (form Hartley) dis mcd
1859, 1, 22. Abraham dis mcd
1863, 11, 28. George dis disunity
1863, 11, 28. Mary P. dis disunity
1864, 5, 28. Mary dis disunity
1867, 11, 23. Elisha Jr. dis mcd & enlisting
    in Army
1882, 2, 22. Jesse dis paying bounty money
1884, 6, 25. Joseph Clinton gct Phila. MM,
    Pa.
1884, 8, 20. Milton dis disunity

STARBUCK, continued
1890, 7, 23. Caleb B. dis mcd
1911, 1, 25. Mary Jane dis jas

ST. CLEAR
1825, 6, 8. Ann m Isaiah REDD

STEELE
1820, 2, 26. Martha (form Hodgin) dis mcd

STEER
1814, 2, 2. Joseph, s James & Abigail, Bel-
     mont Co., O.; m in Stillwater MH, Emma
     FRENCH, dt Israel & Margaret, Belmont Co.,
     O.
1819, 12, 27. Samuel, s Joseph & Grace, Jeffer-
     son Co., O.; m in Stillwater MH, Harriet
     A. HARLAN, dt Enoch & Hannah, Muskingdon Co
     Co., O.
1853, 10, 26. James Jr., s James & Ruth (Wil-
     son), Belmont Co., O.; m in Stillwater MH,
     Mary GREEN, dt William & Rachel (Hoyle),
     Belmont Co., O., d 1903,2,7 bur Stillwater
     Ch: Anna Mary b 1854, 10, 24
         William G. " 1856, 5, 13
         Joseph   " 1858, 4, 14 d 1904,11,26
           bur Stillwater
         Rachel G. b 1860, 4, 16
         Elizabeth " 1863, 1, 7
         Charles • " 1865, 2, 4 " 1884,11,15
           bur Stillwater
         Rebecca   b 1867, 11, 23 " 1868, 7,19
           bur Stillwater
         Abby   b 1871, 1, 12 " 1872, 8,25
1878, 10, 24. Anna M. m Joseph S. HOGE
----, --, --. Joseph m Elmira FRENCH
     Ch: Bertha M. b 1885, 8, 12
         Edith   " 1887, 7, 16 d 1888, 1,29
           bur Stillwater
         John Ogden b 1888, 12, 15
         Anna   " 1890, 9, 27
         Harold
         James   " 1896, 4, 18
1886, 9, 9. Elizabeth m Dillwyn C. BUNDY
----, --, --. Wm. G. m Louisa D. PICKETT, dt
     Wm. & Rebecca (Worthington), b 1856,1,28
     d 1923,9,9
----, --, --. Wm. G., s James & Mary (Green),
     b 1856,5,13; m Eliza Hall, dt Wm. Jr. &
     Mary (Thomas), b 1859,2,1 (she m Gilbert
     McGREW 1886,4,29 and later m Wm. G. Steer)
1911, 7, 20. Lindley B., s Israel & Rebecca
     (Bracken), Belmont Co., O., b 1845,9,25;
     m in Stillwater MH, Ruanna BUNDY, dt
     Aaron & Tabitha (Thompson) FRAME, Belmont
     Co., O.
1911, 9, 12. Alfred Gilbert, s Elisha B. &
     Ellen G., Delaware Co., Pa.; m in Still-
     water MH, Selma L. TABER, dt Joseph John &
     Mary P., Belmont Co., O.

1814, 4, 20. Emma gct Concord MM
1820, 5, 27. Harriet A. gct Short Creek MM

1848, 9, 23. Jonathan T. Schofield gct Short
     Creek MM, to m Abigail Steer
1854, 3, 25. Mary G. gct Short Creek MM
1865, 2, 25. James & w, Mary G., & ch, Anna
     M., William G., Joseph, Rachel G. & Eliza-
     beth, rocf Short Creek MM, dtd 1865,1,24
1879, 3, --. William G. gct Pennsville MM, to
     m Louisa Pickett
1879, 12, 24. Louisa D. rocf Pennsville MM,
     dtd 1879,12,18
1884, 7, 23. Joseph G. gct Salem MM, to m
     Elmira T. French
1885, 10, 21. Elmira T. rocf Salem MM, dtd
     1885,8,19
1901, 8, 21. Alva C. Bailey gct Short Creek
     MM, to m Laura E. Steer
1903, 9, 23. Perley Pickett gct Short Creek
     MM, to m Sarah E. Steer
1912, 1, 24. Ruanna Bundy gct Short Creek MM
1912, 6, 19. Selina Taber gct Lansdowne MM,
     Pa.
1916, 9, 20. Ella T. & Anna B. gct Salem MM
1917, 1, 24. Bertha M. dis jas
1918, 12, 25. Lindley B. & w, Ruanna B., rocf
     Short Creek MM, O., dtd 1918,11,19
1922, 11, 22. Oliver B. Bailey gct New Garden
     MM, to m Rebecca Steer
1925, 3, 25. William G. gct Short Creek MM,
     to m Eliza C. McGrew
1926, 4, 21. Lindley B. & w, Ruanna B., gct
     Pasadena MM, Calif.
1926, 6, 23. Eliza H. rocf Short Creek MM,
     dtd 1926,6,22

STEPHEN
----, --, --. David & Eliza
     Ch: William   b 1847, 3, 11
         Abigail   " 1848, 11, 28
         Barclay   " 1852, 3, 12
         Mary Jane " 1854, 6, 17

1855, 7, 28. David & w, Eliza, & ch, Wilson,
     Abigail, Barclay & Mary Jane, rocf Flush-
     ing MM, dtd 1855,5,24
1861, 6, 22. David & fam gct Flushing MM
1892, 10, 19. David rocf Flushing MM, dtd
     1892,9,22

STILLION
1885, 5, 8. Annie M., w George C., dt Man-
     sel E. & Martha (Hartley) Hall, b

1917, 5, 24. Anna M. (form Hall) con mcd

STRAHL
----, --, --. Philip & Sarah
     Ch: Edmund   b 1809, 8, 26
         Thomas   " 1811, 2, 13
         Ann   " 1813, 5, 2
         Eli   " 1815, 4, 20
         Amos G.   " 1818, 10, 18
1813, 1, 6. Rebecca m Jonathan FAWCETT
1817, 10, 1. Maribah m Job SCOTT

STRAHL, continued

1818, 9, 29. Margaret m Owen WADE

1817, 10, 29. Casper, s Philip & Sarah, Bel-
mont Co., O.; m in Stillwater MH, Mary
TODD, dt Stephen & Sibbella, Belmont Co.,O.
Ch: Osborn   b 1818, 7, 29
    Angelina   " 1821, 1, 18
    Stephen   " 1824, 8, 3
    Philip   " 1826, 10, 25
    Rebecca
     Ann   " 1830, 9, 12
    Mary Jane   " 1834, 8, 5
    Sibbila   " 1838, 2, 9

1820, 8, 30. Samuel, s Isaac & Ellen, Belmont Co., O.; m in Somerset, Hannah WADE,
dt Royal & Phebe, Belmont Co., O.

1821, 8, 29. Elizabeth m Abram PLUMMER

1825, 9, 28. Sarah m David WILLIAMS

1826, 2, 1. Philip, s Philip & Sarah, Bel-
mont Co., O.; m in Stillwater MH, Rhoda
Ann FRENCH, dt Otho & Elizabeth, Belmont
Co., O.

1832, 3, 21. Ellen m Cyrus HALL (H)

1838, 2, 28. Joel, s Isaac & Ellen, Belmont
Co., O.; m in Sumerton, Ann BAILEY, dt
Mahlon & Charity, Belmont Co., O. (H)

1810, 6, 26. Philip & w, Sarah, & ch, Daniel
Caspar, Meriba, Philip, David, Rachel, Sarah & Edmund, rocf Short Creek MM, dtd
1810,5,22

1811, 3, 26. Mary gct Salem MM

1813, 12, 28. Daniel, minor, gct Short Creek
MM

1814, 5, 31. Sarah Blovelt. (form Strahl) dis
mcd

1817, 9, 27. Daniel rocf Short Creek MM, dtd
1817,6,24

1819, 9, 25. Daniel dis mcd

1820, 2, 26. Casper dis disunity

1825, 3, 26. David dis disunity

1827, 4, 28. Philip Jr. dis jas

1827, 4, 28. Rhoda Ann dis jas

1828, 7, 26. Rachel Patten (form Strahl) dis
mcd

1828, 10, 25. Mary & ch, Osborn, Angelina,
Stephen & Philip, rocf Deerfield MM, dtd
1823,9,18

1828, 10, 25. Philip dis jH

1828, 11, 22. Sarah dis jH

1829, 1, 24. Eunice Hodgin (form Strahl) dis
mcd

1829, 6, 27. Joseph dis mcd

1829, 10, 24. Joseph dis jH

1830, 8, 28. Jane dis jH

1830, 8, 28. Lovisa dis jH

1830, 8, 28. Martha dis jH

1830, 9, 25. Hannah Bowls (form Strahl) dis
mcd

1831, 6, 25. Rebecca Smith (form Strahl) dis
mcd

1832, 2, 25. Ann dis jH

1832, 7, 28. Edmond dis jH

1832, 11, 24. Thomas dis jH

1832, 7, 21. Ann W. gct Miami MM (H)

1832, 7, 21. Philip & w, Sarah, & ch, Eli &
Amos G., gct Miami MM (H)

1833, 1, 26. Eli & Amos gct Miami MM

1833, 3, 23. William dis disunity

1833, 3, 23. Jesse dis jH

1839, 4, 27. Angelina Braidley (form Strahl)
dis mcd

1839, 4, 27. Mary & ch, Osborn, Philip,
Stephen, Rebecca, Mary Jane & Rebecca, gct
Pennsville MM

1848, 8, 26. Elizabeth Rutlidge (form Strahl)
dis mcd

1852, 6, 26. Elizabeth Rudledge (form Strahl)
dis mcd

STRATTON

1860, 11, 7. Deborah Ann m Joel SMITH

1871, 11, 1. John E., s Ross & Mary (Painter)
Belmont Co., O.; m in Stillwater MH,
Priscilla BAILEY, dt Joel & Ruth Anna
(Patterson), Belmont Co., O.
Ch: Ruthanna   b 1872, 11, 25
    Ross J.   " 1878, 9, 15
    Charles   " 1879, 11, 9

1902, 8, 21. Edward F., s Edward & Mary H.,
Columbiana Co., O.; m in Stillwater MH,
Clara E. FRAME, dt Amasa & Rachel E.,
Belmont Co., O.

1930, 8, 23. Arthur John, s Geo. W. & Melva
W., Belmont Co., O.; m in Stillwater MH,
Edith R. PICKETT, dt Perley & Sarah E.,
Belmont Co., O.

1855, 9, 22. George Starbuck gct Salem MM,
to m Mary P. Stratton

1856, 4, 26. Deborah Ann, dt Mary P. Starbuck, rocf Salem MM, dtd 1856,3,19

1861, 12, 28. Elizabeth B. recrq (residing in
Linn Co., Ia.)

1863, 6, 27. John E. rocf Salem MM, dtd
1863,5,20

1876, 3, 22. Barclay & w, Hannah, & ch, Joseph C. & Dillwyn, rocf New Garden MM,
dtd 1876,2,24

1881, 5, 24. Barclay & w, Hannah, & s, Dillwyn, gct New Garden MM

1881, 5, 24. Joseph gct New Garden MM

1881, 7, 20. John & w, Priscilla, & ch
gct Coal Creek MM, Ia.

1886, 3, 24. Barclay & w, Hannah, rocf New
Garden MM, dtd 1886,2,25

1890, 5, 21. Barclay & w, Hannah H., gct
New Garden MM

1902, 12, 24. Clara F. gct Salem MM, O.

1911, 5, 24. Joseph C. & w, Elizabeth B.,
rocf New Garden MM, dtd 1911,4,20

1914, 7, 22. Joseph C. & Elizabeth B. gct
New Garden MM, O.

STREET

1832, 9, 15. Agnes gct Short Creek MM (H)

STREET, continued
1865, 4, 22. Wm. W. Smith gct Salem MM, to m
   Hannah Street

STUBBS
----, --, --. Joseph &·Zilpah
     Ch: Mary   b 1784, 6, 4
         Rachel   " 1785, 11, 21
         Sarah   " 1787, 1, 3
         Jacob   " 1789, 11, 17
         Isaac   " 1790, 3, 4
         Deborah   " 1792, 3, 2
         Abraham   " 1793, 5, 28 d 1815,10,25
         Elizabeth " 1795, 3, 2
         Rebecca   " 1796, 5, 10
         Idda   " 1798, 1, 3
         Zilpha   " 1800, 12, 3
         Eliza   " 1802, 3, 18
         Rhoda   " 1803, 12, 3
         Joseph   " 1805, 11, 2
1811, 11, 6. Deborah m Robert VERNON
1816, 5, 1. Joseph d ae 53 bur Stillwater
1816, 11, 27. Rebecca m John PATTON
1818, 8, 26. Eliza m Elijah HANSON
1823, 6, 4. Rhoda m James VERNON
----, --, --. Isaac m Elizabeth DOUDNA
     Ch: Isaac   b 1825, 9, 24
         Henry   " 1829, 8, 22
         Margaret " 1831, 8, 26

1809, 10, 31. Sarah Hall (form Stubbs) dis mcd
1810, 1, 30. Jacob dis disunity
1810, 6, 26. Isaac dis disunity
1813, 4, 27. Elizabeth Cox (form Stubbs) dis
   mcd
1819, 9, 25. Iddo dis
1824, 12, 25. Elizabeth recrq
1825, 2, 26. Isaac recrq
1830, 7, 24. Sarah recrq
1830, 8, 28. Joseph dis mcd
1832, 3, 24. Isaac & w, Elizabeth, & ch,
   Isaac, Henry & Margaret, gct Deerfield MM
1832, 3, 24. Sarah gct Deerfield MM
1832, 9, 22. Isaac Vernon gct Deerfield MM,
   to m Sarah Stubbs

SWAYNE
1839, 6, 19. Sarah A. m Joshua ENGLE (H)
1878, 2, 21. Rachel B. m Jacob MAYES (H)

1824, 12, 25. Rebecca rocf Fairfax MM, dtd
   1824,9,15, end to Flushing MM
1826, 5, 27. Samuel & w, Margaret, & ch,
   Isaac, Sarah Ann, Mary, Joshua, Rachel,
   Samuel, John Thomas & Noah, gct Hopewell
   MM, Va., dtd 1826,4,6
1827, 11, 24. Samuel & w, Margaret, & ch,
   Isaac, Sarah, Mary, Joshua, Rachel, Samuel, John, Thomas, Noah & Margaret, gct
   Somerset MM
1832, 5, 19. Isaac B. gct Hopewell MM, Va.
   (H)
1839, 4, 20. Samuel F. gct Green Plane MM(H)

1858, 1, 16. Mary B. Wilson (form Swain) con
   mcd (H)
1861, 5, 18. Elias M. gct Whitewater MM, Ind.
   (H)

TABER
1898, 9, 7. Anna R. m Walter J. EDGERTON
1909, 10, 27. Louis J. [Tabor], s Joseph J. &
   Mary P., Belmont Co., O.; m in Stillwater
   MH, Edna A. BAILEY, dt Allen & Eva L.
   (Patterson), Belmont Co., O., b 1888,2,29
     Ch: Joseph
         Paul   b 1911, 3, 22
         Francis
         Bailey   " 1915, 5, 25
1911, 9, 12. Selma L. m Alfred Gilbert
   STEER
----, --, --. Joseph John H. [Tabor], s Lewis
   & Mary Ann, d 1893,2,1 bur Stillwater; m
   Mary P. PICKETT, d 1906,3,2 bur Still-
   water
----, --, --. William P., s Joseph John &
   Mary (Pickett), b 1881,7,18; m Sarah
   NEGUS
     Ch: Mary A.   b 1916, 8, 11
         Helen   " 1918, 5, 1
         Joseph J. " 1920, 2, 6
         William P.
         Jr.   " 1927, 10, 29

1885, 5, 20. Joseph John H. & w, Mary P., &
   ch, Anna R., Louis J., William P. & Selma
   Lizzie, rocf Short Creek MM, dtd 1885,3,24
1914, 4, 22. William P. gct Short Creek MM,·
   to m Sarah D. Negus

TALBOTT
1894, 8, 22. Emma M. recrq
1914, 3, 25. Emma M. gct Nantucket MM, Mass.

TANNER
1826, 1, 28. Lydia recrq

TATUM
1844, 6, 5. George Jr., s George & Beulah,
   Columbiana Co., O.; m in Stillwater MH,
   Hannah GREEN, dt Wm. & Rachel, Belmont
   Co., O.
1886, 9, 6. George d bur Stillwater
1902, 9, 7. Hannah, w George, d bur Stillwater

1844, 9, 28. Hannah gct Upper Springfield MM
1846, 4, 25. George & w, Hannah, rocf Upper
   Springfield MM, dtd 1846,2,28, end by
   Somerset MM, 1846,3,20
1904, 8, 24. Hannah d 1902,9,7 ae 81 (an
   elder)

TAYLOR
1808, 12, 28. Ruben, s Christopher & Elizabeth, Jefferson Co., O.; m in Stillwater
   MH, Jemima PATTERSON, dt Joseph & Hannah,

TAYLOR, Ruben & Jemima, continued
    Belmont Co., O.
---, --, --. Simeon & Elizabeth
    Ch: Lucy Mason b 1812, 4, 8
        Elbina
          Smith   " 1813, 11, 25
        Angelina P." 1815, 9, 24
        John Mos-
          by   " 1819, 7, 4
1820, 7, 13. Mary d ae 68y 7m 10d bur Still-
    water
1828, 8, 28. Maria A. m Daniel R. BENNETT (H)
1848, 5, 29. Mary, w Rouse, d bur Stillwater

1809, 7, 25. Jamima gct Short Creek MM
1810, 6, 26. Ann rocf Plainfield MM, dtd
    1810,6,23
1811, 3, 26. Ann Wilson (form Taylor) con
    mcd
1811, 6, 25. Mary rocf Exeter MM, dtd 1811,5,
    29 end by Plainfield MM, 1811,5,27
1812, 1, 28. Simeon & w, Elizabeth, & dt,
    Sally, rocf Short Creek MM, dtd 1811,11,19
1822, 8, 24. Joseph rocf Chesterfield MM,
    N. J., dtd 1822,8,6
1826, 12, 23. Israel & w, Susan, & ch, Mariah
    Ann, George R., Charles M., Israel W.,
    Lydia S. & Edith S., rocf Chesterfield
    MM, N. J., dtd 1826,12,5
1828, 6, 28. Maria Ann dis JH
1828, 7, 26. Joseph relrq
1829, 4, 18. Israel & w, Susan, & ch, George
    R., Charles M., Israel W., Lydia S.,
    Edith S. & Jane, gct Cincinnati MM (H)
1829, 6, 27. Susannah dis jH
1830, 2, 27. Peter dis mcd
1830, 5, 22. George R., Charles M., Israel W.,
    Lydia S., Edith S. & Jane, gct Cincinnati
    MM
1833, 2, 23. James dis disunity

TEST
1819, 10, 23. Benjamin & w, Mary, & ch, Re-
    becca, Rachel, Hannah, Mary & Elizabeth,
    rocf Short Creek MM, dtd 1819,7,22
1823, 5, 24. Benjamin & w, Mary, & fam gct
    Salem MM

THOMAS
----, --, --. Camm & Elizabeth
    Ch: William   b 1791, 8, 28
        Abishai   " 1793, 5, 25 d 1814,10, 9
        Asahel   " 1795, 9, 5
        Hezekiah   " 1798, 2, 17
        Caty   " 1800, 4, 9 d 1814, 4,29
        Henry Camm " 1802, 8, 11 " 1803, 1,17
        Priscilla " 1803, 12, 7
        Asa   " 1806, 5, 31
        Elizabeth " 1808, 5, 17
        Camm Jr.   " 1810, 8, 5
        Rebecca   " 1812, 6, 17
        Ruth   " 1815, 10, 10
----. --, --. Jesse & Rebecca

    Ch: Elizabeth b 1810, 1, 1
        Sarah   " 1811, 4, 17
        Mary Ann " 1813, 3, 7
        Joseph   " 1814, 12, 5
        Deborah   " 1817, 3, 21
        Philena   " 1819, 10, 9
        Joanna   " 1822, 1, 21
        Jonathan H." 1824, 3, 25 d 1825, 6,30
          bur Blue Rock
        Eli   b 1826, 5, 19
1815, 10, 12. William, s Camm & Elizabeth,
    Belmont Co., O.; m in Stillwater MH, Re-
    becca OUTLAND, dt Wm. & Margaret, Belmont
    Co., O.
    Ch: Catharine b 1817, 2, 13
        Margaret " 1819, 3, 16
1818, 8, 26. Asahel, s Camm & Elizabeth, Bel-
    mont Co., O.; m in Stillwater MH, Phebe
    JUDGE, dt Hugh & Susannah, Belmont Co., O.
1823, 12, 31. Hezekiah, s Camm & Elizabeth,
    Belmont Co., O.; m in Stillwater MH, In-
    crease DENNIS, dt John & Phebe, Burlington
    Co., N. J.
1827, 3, 28. Precilla m Moses M. WHITACRE
1831, 6, 30. Elizabeth m Samuel P. HUNT (H)
1837, 1, 26. Catharine m William STANTON (H)
1837, 4, 20. Ruth m Lot GREGG (H)
1839, 5, 29. James, s Isaac & Rebecca, Monroe
    Co., O.; m in Center, Edith PRICE, dt
    John H, & Rachel, Belmont Co., O. (H)
1841, 3, 24. Margaret m Isaac HALL (H)
1844, 11, 28. Elizabeth m Thomas L. FRAME (H)
1844, 11, 28. Harriet m Edward G. ADAMS (H)
1850, 8, 1. Aquilla, s William & Rebecca,
    Belmont Co., O.; m in house of Amos ORRI-
    SON, Rebecca ORRISON, dt Amos & Helen,
    Belmont Co., O.(H)
1851, 4, 23. Robert P., s Wm. & Rebecca, Bel-
    mont Co., O.; m in Richland, Phebe WEB-
    STER, dt Eli & Mercy, Guernsey Co., O.(H)
1857, 9, 24. Priscilla m Eli HALL (H)

1809, 4, 25. Rebecca Hamilton (form Thomas)
    dis mcd
1812, 12, 1. Abisha gct Plainfield MM
1814, 5, 21. Abisha rocf Plainfield MM, dtd
    1814,4,23
1820, 9, 23. Jesse & w, Rebecca, & ch,
    Elizabeth, Sarah, Mary Ann, Joseph, Debo-
    rah & Philena, rocf Fallowfield MM, dtd
    1820,5,5
1822, 2, 23. Camm & w, Elisabeth, & ch, Heze-
    kiah, Priscilla, Asa, Camm, Elisabeth,
    Rebecca, Ruth & Sidney, rocf Somerset MM,
    dtd 1822,1,28
1828, 5, 24. Asahel dis JH
1828, 5, 24. Camm dis JH
1828, 5, 24. Elizabeth dis JH
1828, 5, 24. Elizabeth Jr. dis JH
1828, 5, 24. Rebecca dis JH
1828, 5, 24. Phebe dis JH
1828, 6, 28. Hezekiah dis JH
1828, 11, 22. Increase dis JH

THOMAS, continued
1828, 12, 27. Camm Jr. dis disunity
1829, 1, 24. Joanna dis JH
1829, 2, 28. Benjamin dis JH
1835, 3, 28. Cidney dis JH
1835, 4, 18. Azael & w, Phebe, & ch, Christo-
    pher H., Susanna, Hugh Judge & William, gct
    Plainfield MM (H)
1835, 4, 25. Ruth dis JH
1843, 5, 27. Susannah, Hugh & William gct
    Plainfield MM; returned 1843,6,24 with in-
    formation they were not within their lim-
    its
1849, 3, 24. Philip Mason dis disunity
1850, 9, 28. Phebe Outland (form Thomas) dis
    mcd
1851, 6, 28. Phebe (form Webster) dis disunity
1855, 2, 17. Phebe Outland (form Thomas) dis
    mcd (H)
1855, 5, 26. Sarah rocf Plymouth MM, dtd
    1855,4,23
1858, 3, 20. Jonah & w, Phebe, & ch, Martha
    A., Lewis B. & Levi L., recrq (H)
1859, 6, 18. Isaac relrq (H)
1860, 8, 18. William & w, Mary B., con mcd
    (H)
1861, 12, 28. Miriam B. recrq (residing in
    Linn Co., Ia.)
1862, 1, 25. Samuel S., Rebecca, William,
    Pearson, Elizabeth S., Mary & Peter, ch
    John & Miriam B., recrq
1866, 1, 27. Eliza dis disunity
1870, 5, 21. Elmira gct Short Creek MM (H)
1875, 6, 19. Lucinda Henderson (form Thomas)
    con mcd (H)
1876, 7, 15. Eliza Jane (form Lee) con mcd
    (H)
1877, 9, 21. Susanna (form Blackledge) con
    mcd (H)
1881, 8, 20. Pluma Ellen & ch, Arloff, Alvin,
    Ross & Frederick, recrq (H)

THOMASON
1828, 10, 25. Thomas Jr. gct Short Creek MM,
    to m Mariah Jones
1830, 1, 23. Thomas Jr. gct Short Creek MM
1873, 3, 19. John S. Doudna gct Somerset MM,
    to m Sarah Thomason

THOMPSON
1818, 3, 28. Elizabeth rocf Center MM, Pa.,
    dtd 1818,2,14
1822, 3, 23. Elizabeth Pennington (form
    Thompson) dis mcd

THORNBURGH
1812, 6, 10. Edward [Thornbrough], s Joseph
    & Rachel, Belmont Co., O.; m in Still-
    water MH, Elizabeth JUDKINS, dt Joel &
    Lucy, Belmont Co., O.
    Ch: Joel Jud-
        kins   b 1815, 3, 30 d 1815, 6,21
    Joseph

    Ch: Brown   b 1815, 3, 30 d 1815, 9,14
        Edna   " 1817, 3, 8 " 1824, 5,--
        bur Stillwater
        Lydia Jane b 1820, 1, 15
        Lucy Stan-
        ton   " 1822, 6, 5 " 1823,10, 3
        bur Stillwater
1828, 11, 24. Elizabeth d ae 33y 7m bur Still-
    water
1841, 6, 30. Lydia Jane m Thos. C. PARKER

1811, 5, 28. Edward [Thornborough] rocf New
    Garden MM, N. C., dtd 1811,3,30

THORP
----, --, --. Thomas & Mary
    Ch: Samuel   b 1811, 10, 25
        James   " 1813, 10, 24
        Elenor   " 1815, 9, 2
        Jabesh   " 1817, 3, 22
        Hannah   " 1819, 4, 18
        Elizabeth " 1822, 3, 13
        Thomas
        Jesse   " 1825, 1, 24
        Mary   " 1827, 5, 5

1829, 2, 28. Thomas dis JH
1829, 12, 26. Mary dis JH
1834, 6, 28. Eleanor dis JH
1834, 7, 26. Samuel dis JH
1846, 1, 24. Hannah Pickett (form Thorp) dis
    mcd

TIDRICK
1816, 12, 28. Mary (form Borton) dis mcd
1817, 2, 22. Mary (form Borton) dis mcd

TINDER
1919, 7, 23. Mary F. (form Frame) dis mcd &
    jas

TIPTON
1839, 1, 31. Abijah, s Luke & Priscilla,
    Monroe Co., O.; m in Captina, Sidney
    WOOD, dt John & Esther, Belmont Co., O.

1839, 4, 24. Sidney gct Somerset MM
1843, 1, 28. John Bundy gct Somerset MM, to
    m Sidney Tipton

TODD
----, --, --. Stephen & Sibilla
    Ch: Rebecca   b 1800, 6, 9
        Mary   " 1800, 6, 9
        William   " 1802, 12, 1
        Daniel   " 1804, 9, 1 d 1814, 4,24
        Elisha   " 1806, 6, 6
        Ann   " 1808, 4, 20
        John   " 1810, 1, 16 " 1814, 4,28
        Humphrey   " 1810, 1, 16 " 1814, 4,29
        Robert   " 1812, 4, 15
        Asenath   " 1814,/ 4, 6
        Elihu   " 1817, 6, 28

TODD, continued

----, --, --. Robert & Sarah
    Ch: James   b 1811, 11, 25
        Ann   " 1814, 1, 12
        Theodate   " 1815, 10, 28
        Rebeckah   " 1818, 6, 11
        Robert   " 1820, 8, 9
        Maranda   " 1822, 3, 28
1817, 10, 29. Mary m Casper STRAHL
1821, 12, 26. Rebecca m Wm. SMITH
1827, 6, 6. Elisha, s Stephen & Sibilla,
    Belmont Co., O.; m in Stillwater MH, Sally
    SMITH, dt David & Judith, Belmont Co., O.
    Ch: Emily   b 1829, 10, 17
        Shannon   " 1832, 6, 14
        Lydia   " 1832, 6, 14
        John   " 1834, 11, 4
        Lindley   " 1837, 4, 28
        Sibbilla   " 1840, 4, 26
1831, 4, 27. Asenath m Burwell PEEBLES

1808, 6, 28. Robert recrq
1817,· 9, 27. Sarah rst at Concord MM on con-
    sent of this mtg
1818, 1, 24. James, Ann & Theodate, ch Robert
    & Sarah, recrq
1826, 1, 28. William dis mcd
1838, 4, 28. Stephen & w, Sibilla, & s, Eli-
    hu, gct Chesterfield MM
1838, 4, 28. Robert gct Chesterfield MM
1839, 10, 26. Robert rocf Chesterfield MM, dtd
    1839,10,19
1842, 1, 22. Robert gct Chesterfield MM
1842, 3, 26. Elisha & w, Sally, & ch, Nancy,
    Emily, Lydia & Sabilla, gct Chesterfield
    MM

TOMLINSON
1860, 10, 20. Mariam con mcd (H)
1869, 5, 22. Mariam relrq (H)
1877, 9, 21. Alesanna Williams (form Tomlin-
    son) dis mcd (H)
1877, 9, 21. Mary Catharine McBroome (form
    Tomlinson) dis mcd (H)
1877, 9, 21. Sarah Ann Grissell (form Tom-
    linson) dis mcd (H)

TOWNSEND
1819, 5, 22. Ruth & dt, Juli Ann, rocf Con-
    cord MM, dtd 1819,2,24
1821, 8, 25. Ruth & dt, Juliann, gct Flushing
    MM
1823, 2, 23. Ruth & dt, Juliann, rocf Flush-·
    ing MM, dtd 1822,12,29
1830, 5, 22. Eli dis jH
1831, 3, 26. Ruth & dt, Juliann, gct Deer-
    field MM
1835, 3, 21. Levi & w, Mary, & ch, Elizabeth,
    Eli, William W., Joseph & Abner W., gct
    Goshen MM, O. (H)
1850, 7, 20. Abigail gct Deerfield MM (H)

TRIMBLE

----, --, --. John & Lydia
    Ch: Elisha   b 1815, 2, 6
        James   " 1817, 2, 20
        Caleb Har-
          lan   " 1819, 10, 5
        Mary   " 1822, 2, 24

1819, 2, 27. John & w, Lydia, & ch, Elisha I.
    & James, rocf Birmingham MM, Pa., dtd
    1818,12,10

TUDOR
1823, 8, 29. Martha d bur Zanesville

TURNER
1832, 11, 24. Rebecca (form Vernon) dis mcd

UMSTEAD
1827, 3, 24. Nancy (form Hall) dis mcd

VAIL
1804, 12, 29. Rebecca, dt Benjamin & Rebeckah,
    b
----, --, --. Benjamin & Hannah
    Ch: John   b 1814, 6, 6
        Hannah   " 1816, 4, 28
        Mary   " 1818, 7, 25
        Sarah   " 1820, 6, 13
        Lydia   " 1822, 9, 15
        Jesse   " 1825, 8, 24
1864, 10, 26. Isaac W., s John & Abigail,
    Belmont Co., O.; m in Stillwater MH, Ra-
    chel D. WILSON, dt Israel & Catharine,
    Belmont Co., O., d 1877,2,21 bur Still-
    water
    Ch: Alice Jane b 1868, 7, 1
        Lydia C.   " 1870, 8, 27

1829, 1, 24. Robert dis jH
1829, 1, 24. Isaac dis jH
1829, 1, 24. Sarah dis jH
1829, 1, 24. Hannah Jr. dis jH
1829, 1, 24. Mercy dis jH
1829, 1, 24. Elizabeth dis jH
1829, 1, 24. Randal dis jH
1829, 10, 24. Nathan dis jH
1870, 1, 19. Benjamin gct Coal Creek MM, Ia.
1873, 8, 20. Isaac N. & w, Rachel, & ch gct
    Goshen MM
1875, 11, 24. Isaac & w, Rachel D., & ch,
    Alice J. & Lydia C., rocf Goshen MM, Pa.,
    dtd 1875,11,28(?)
1880, 4, --. Isaac N. gct Salem MM, to m
    Mary M. Cope
1880, 12, 22. Mary C. rocf Salem MM
1885, 10, 21. Walter C. rocf Coal Creek MM,
    Ia., dtd 1885,10,10
1890, 5, 21. Walter E. gct Flushing MM, to m
    Deborah Holloway
1895, 3, 20. Isaac N. & w, Mary C., gct
    Pasadena MM, Calif.
1901, 10, 23. Lydia C. gct Chester MM, Media,

VAIL, continued
    Pa.
1903, 11, 25. Alice Holloway (form Vail) dis
    mcd

VAN HOSTEIN
1891, 4, 22. Cora (form Hanson) dis mcd

VANLAW
----, --, --. John m Sarah ----- d 1829,8,3
    Ch: Mary   b 1813, 5, 7
        Jeptha
         Sharp   " 1814, 11, 7
        Elisha   " 1816, 7, 24
        Louisa M. " 1818, 4, 22
        Lydia
         Sharp   " 1820, 5, 1
        Lucinda " 1822, 1, 30
        Eliza   " 1824, 2, 11
        John   " 1826, 2, 27
        Samuel   " 1828, 1, 3
    John m 2nd Sarah SPENCER
    Ch: Jesse   b 1831, 9, 5
        Thomas   " 1834, 5, 25
----, --, --. George & Ann
    Ch: Lucinda b 1816, 8, 2
        Mary Ann " 1818, 4, 14
        Sarah   " 1820, 4, 19
        Isaac W. " 1822, 2, 18
1830, 9, 20. John, s Joseph & Mary, Belmont
    Co., O.; m in Plainfield, Sarah SPENCER,
    dt Isaac & Jane, Belmont Co., O.
1830, 10, 7. Mary m Joseph DOUDNA

1829, 5, 23. George dis jH
1829, 5, 23. Anna dis jH
1829, 10, 24. Lydia dis jH
1829, 12, 26. Samuel dis jH
1833, 9, 28. Joseph, Sarah & Reasin, ch Sam-
    uel & Lydia, gct Alum Creek MM

VERNON
----, --, --. James & Tamer
    Ch: Janney   b 1797, 4, 21
        Theodate " 1799, 4, 22
        William   " 1801, 2, 16
        Elizabeth " 1802, 12, 16
        Amos   " 1804, 10, 26
        Asa   " 1806, 12, 25
        James   " 1809, 3, 15
        Jesse   " 1811, 4, 6
        Eli   " 1813, 4, 15
----, --, --. Amos & Mary
    Ch: James   b 1800, 4, 18
        Rachel   " 1802, 2, 16
        Theodate " 1804, 7, 11
        Ruthanna " 1806, 1, 2
        Isaac   " 1809, 8, 20
        Sarah   " 1811, 10, 12
1810, 6, --. Anne d bur Stillwater
1811, 11, 6. Robert, s James & Content, Bel-
    mont Co., O.; m in Stillwater MH, Deborah
    STUBBS, dt Joseph & Zilpah, Belmont Co.,O.

Ch: Mary Ann b 1812, 11, 10
    Rebecca   " 1814, 6, 4
    Rhoda   " 1816, 2, 1
    Robert   " 1818, 2, 12
    Joseph   " 1820, 2, 29
    Zilpah   " 1822, 6, 4
    Elijah   " 1828, 3, 1
    Thomas   " 1830, 4, 24
    James   " 1832, 4, 27
1813, 8, 26. Mary d bur Stillwater
1815, 10, 5. Amos, s James & Content, Bel-
    mont Co., O.; m in Stillwater MH, Catha-
    rine PATTERSON, dt Benjamin & Esther,
    Belmont Co., O.
1816, 10, 2. Tamer m Jehu HIAT
1819, 4, 1. Elizabeth m Barak BAILEY
1821, 7, 30. Content m Samuel KING
1823, 6, 4. James, s Amos & Mary, Belmont
    Co., O.; m in Stillwater MH, Rhoda STUBBS,
    dt Joseph & Zilpah, Belmont Co., O.
    Ch: Mary   b 1824, 3, 26
        Isaac   " 1826, 7, 6
        Benjamin " 1828, 2, 22
        Joseph   " 1830, 5, 22
        Amos   " 1833, 5, 20
        James   " 1835, 9, 19
        Abner   " 1837, 1, 19
1825, 3, 3. Catharine Patterson m Wm.
    FLANNER
1828, 10, 2. William, s Robert & Ann, Bel-
    mont Co., O.; m in Captina, Deborah HAN-
    SON, dt Manoah & Rachel, Belmont Co., O.
1831, 3, 9. Sarah m Eli BUNDY
----, --, --. Amos & Jane
    Ch: Ann   b 1832, 7, 23 d 1832,12,27
        bur Stillwater
        Robert   b 1823, 9, 25 (sic)
1833, 1, 12. Mary Ann m Israel EMBREE
1835, 10, 20. Eli, s James & Thamer, Belmont
    Co., O.; m in Captina, Eliza HANSON, dt
    Manoah & Rachel, Belmont Co., O.
    Ch: Tamer   b 1836, 8, 6
        Rachel   " 1838, 4, 27
        Deborah H. " 1840, 8, 5
1835, 11, 7. James d
1837, 11, 28. Rhoda m Abijah EDGERTON
1843, 11, 30. Zilpha m James HICKS
1845, 11, 27. Joseph, s Robert & Deborah, Bel-
    mont Co., O.; m in Captina, Martha HICKS,
    dt James & Bethany, Belmont Co., O.
    Ch: John T. b 1846, 10, 19

1815, 3, 28. Jenny Bryant (form Vernon) dis
    mcd
1818, 10, 24. Theodate gct Short Creek MM
1821, 2, 24. Theodate rocf Short Creek MM,
    dtd 1821,1,23
1821, 11, 24. Theodate McLane (form Vernon)
    dis mcd
1822, 1, 26. Catharine rocf Somerset MM, dtd
    1822,12,24
1822, 2, 23. Ruthanna gct Concord MM
1825, 3, 26. Rachel gct Short Creek MM

VERNON, continued

1825, 5, 28. Theodate gct Short Creek MM
1826, 4, 22. James, minor, gct Somerset MM
1831, 9, 24. Amos gct Somerset to m Jane WAY
1832, 1, 28. Jane rocf Somerset MM, dtd
    1831,12,26
1832, 9, 22. Isaac gct Deerfield MM, to m
    Sarah Stubbs
1832, 11, 24. Jesse gct Clear Creek MM
1832, 11, 24. Rebecca Turner (form Vernon)
    dis mcd
1835, 7, 25. Amos & w, Jane, & s, Robert, gct
    Somerset MM
1836, 8, 27. Jesse rocf Clear Creek MM, dtd
    1836,3,22
1837, 7, 22. Jesse gct Alum Creek MM
1838, 3, 24. James & w, Rhoda, & ch, Mary,
    Joseph, Isaac, Benjamin, Amos & Abner, gct
    Pennsville MM
1842, 8, 27. Eli & w, Eliza, & ch, Tamer,
    Rachel & Deborah, gct Chesterfield MM
1843, 1, 28. Robert Jr. con mcd
1850, 3, 23. Joseph & w, Martha, gct Somerset
    MM
1852, 9, 25. Martha Ann recrq
1853, 2, 26. Elijah dis mcd
1853, 5, 28. Thomas dis mcd
1854, 5, 27. Robert & w, Deborah, gct Red
    Cedar MM, Ia.
1854, 5, 27. James gct Red Cedar MM, Ia.
1860, 3, 24. Deborah gct Plymouth MM
1861, 12, 28. Sarah recrq (residing in Linn
    Co., Ia.)

VINCENT

1815, 9, 26. Elizabeth recrq (dis by Jack
    Swamp MM, N. C. now laid down)
1817, 4, 26. Elizabeth gct Darby Creek MM

VORE

1813, 12, 28. Rebecca rocf Exeter MM, dtd 1813,
    2,24, end by Concord MM 1813,12,23
1821, 5, 26. Ann (form Croy) dis mcd
1829, 3, 28. Rebecca gct Deerfield MM
1836, 2, 27. Abi (form Hartley) dis mcd

VORHIES

1929, 7, 24. Elsie B. (form Borton) con mcd

WADE

1819, 9, 29. Owen, s Royal & Phebe, Belmont
    Co., O.; m in Somerset, Margaret STRAHL,
    dt Isaac & Elen, Belmont Co., O.
1820, 8, 30. Hannah m Samuel STRAHL

1819, 7, 24. Royal & w, Phebe, & ch, Ruth,
    Hannah, Lydia & Rachel, rocf Plainfield
    MM, dtd 1819,7,22
1819, 7, 24. Owen rocf Plainfield MM, dtd
    1819,7,22
1819, 10, 23. Mary rocf Plainfield MM, dtd
    1819,7,22
1820, 11, 25. Ruth Lee (form Wade) dis mcd

WALLACE

1875, 11, 24. Sarah F. (form Cowgill) con mcd
1876, 4, 19. Sarah F. gct Hickory Grove MM,
    Ia.

WALTERS

1834, 4, 26. Phebe rocf New Garden MM, Pa.,
    dtd 1834,3,5
1855, 5, 19. Mary Ann (form Gray) dis mcd
    (H)

WALTON

----, --, --. Samuel m Sarah EDGERTON
    Ch: James   b 1857, 10, 20
        Anna   " 1859, 5, 6
        Samuel Fran-
        cis   " 1861, 8, 28
        Abby   " 1864, 5, 20
1885, 9, 24. Abby m Alfred C. ELKINTON
1888, 4, 27. Annie L., w James, d bur Still-
    water
----, --, --. James, s Samuel & Sarah (Edger-
    ton); m Sina R. STEER, dt Israel & Rebec-
    ca (Bracken), b 1855,6,25
    Ch: Rebecca   b 1894, 7, 29
        Joseph J. " 1896, 7, 13 d 1918,10,11
        bur Stillwater
        William   b 1898, 7, 1 " 1899, 4,30
        bur Stillwater
1899, 3, 22. Samuel, s Joseph & Abi, d bur
    Stillwater

1857, 11, 28. Samuel & w, Sarah J., & s, Jo-
    seph, rocf Phila. MM, S. Dist., dtd 1857,
    9,23
1878, 8, --. Joseph J. gct Chesterfield MM,
    N. J.
1882, 10, 25. Anna gct Phila. MM, Pa.
1886, 7, 21. James gct Flushing MM, to m
    Anna L. Branson
1887, 5, 25. Anna rocf Flushing MM, dtd
    1887,4,21
1888, 11, 21. S. Francis gct Short Creek MM
    to m Lovisa Sidwell
1889, 7, 24. Louisa S. rocf Short Creek MM,
    dtd 1889,6,18
1891, 9, 23. Sina R. rocf Short Creek MM,
    dtd 1891,8,18
1901, 9, 25. S. Francis & w, Louisa S., gct
    Phila. MM, Pa.
1903, 1, 21. Sarah J. gct Phila. MM, Pa.

WARRINGTON

1888, 1, 11. Saraetta, dt Linneaus & Sina
    (Brantingham), b

1891, 7, 22. Linneus & w, Sina B., & ch,
    Cyrus J., Phebe Ellen, Mary Elma, Saraetta
    & Melva L., gct New Garden MM

WATKINS

----, --, --. Reuben & Anna
    Ch: James   b 1812, 12, 23

WATKINS, Reuben & Anna, continued
       Ch: Susannah   b 1814, 10, 2
           Joel   " 1816, 3, 30
           Unity   " 1817, 12, 31

1809, 11, 28. Benjamin rocf Upper MM, Va.,
    dtd 1809,9,16
1811, 11, 26. Reuben & w, Anna, & ch, Lemuel,
    Edwin, Iry, Bennet & William, rocf
    Gravely Run MM, Va., dtd 1811,9,21
1812, 5, 26. Benjamin gct Darby Creek MM

WATSON
1822, 3, 27. Deborah m John ENGLE
1822, 10, 30. Hannah m Jesse SCOTT
1824, 4, 28. Phebe m Henry HALL
1824, 12, 2. Abner d ae 57y 2m bur Stillwater

1821, 5, 26. Abner & w, Elizabeth, & ch,
    William, Phebe, Ann & Mark, rocf Plainfield
    MM, dtd 18--,5,24
1821, 10, 27. Deborah rocf Plainfield MM, dtd
    1821,10,25
1821, 11, 24. Hannah rocf Plainfield MM, dtd
    1821,10,25
1825, 4, 23. Elisabeth & s, Mark, gct Somer-
    set MM
1825, 4, 23. William gct Somerset MM
1825, 4, 23. Ann gct Somerset MM

WATT
1869, 5, 22. Anna Maria (form Bundy) dis mcd

WAY
1832, 6, 7. Benjamin, s David & Anne, Bel-
    mont Co., O.; m in Plainfield, Abigail
    CHAMBERS, dt Samuel & Deborah, Belmont
    Co., O.

1820, 7, 22. David & w, Ann, & ch, Benjamin,
    Robert, Alice, Hannah, Sarah, Jane, Mary,
    Elizabeth & Jacob, rocf Smithfield MM, O.,
    dtd 1820,6,21
1827, 6, 23. Robert & w, Lydia, & dt, Mili-
    cent, rocf Somerset MM, dtd 1827,4,30
1828, 11, 22. Benjamin & w, Jane, & s, John,
    rocf Somerset MM, dtd 1828,10,27
1829, 3, 28. Robert & w, Lydia, & ch, Mili-
    cent & Mary Ann, gct White Water MM, Ind.
1829, 6, 27. Benjamin & w, Jane, & s, John,
    gct Somerset MM
1831, 9, 24. Amos Vernon gct Somerset MM,
    to m Jane Way
1832, 3, 24. Benjamin rocf Smithfield MM,
    dtd 1832,3,19
1833, 3, 23. Benjamin & w, Abigail, gct
    Somerset MM
1834, 6, 28. Robert & w, Lydia, & ch, Milli-
    cent, Maryann, David L. & Sarah, rocf
    Milford MM, Ind., dtd 1834,5,24
1835, 8, 22. Robert & w, Lydia, & ch, Mili-
    cent, Maryann, David & Sarah, gct Somer-
    set MM

WEAVER
1852, 9, 25. Deborah (form Williams) dis mcd
1929, 7, 24. Lucinda (form Smith) con mcd

WEBSTER
1808, 3, 22. John d ae 56y 2m 26d bur
    Leatherwood
----, --, --. Thomas m Anna GORE, d 1854,7,8
    bur Richland
    Ch: John   b 1814, 11, 21 d 1822,12,12
        bur Richland
        Hannah   b 1817, 4, 11
        Joseph G. " 1819, 7, 28
        Jeptha   " 1821, 11, 16
        Ann   " 1824, 2, 10
        Sarah   " 1827, 3, 1
        Phebe   " 1830, 9, 25
----, --, --. John m Albina GREGG d 1820,6,25
    ae 31y 5d bur Leatherwood
    Ch: Charles P. b 1815, 4, 17
        Abner   " 1816, 12, 3
        Lydia   " 1818, 12, 6 " 1820, 3,23
        bur Leatherwood
        Albina   b 1820, 5, 22 " 1820, 6,25
        bur Leatherwood
    John m 2nd Elizabeth ----- d 1831,7,25
    Ch: Ann   b 1823, 5, 24 d 1823, 7,23
        Susan   " 1824, 11, 10
        Warner   " 1826, 11, 28
        Elizabeth " 1831, 5, 28 " 1831, 9, 7
1820, 6, 25. Joshua d ae 31y 5d bur Leather-
    wood
1822, 6, 26. Ann m Jesse CHALFANT
1823, 11, 5. Nathan d bur Leatherwood
----, --, --. Eli & Mercy
    Ch: Ann   b 1826, 5, 18
        Phebe   " 1827, 8, 26
1833, 8, 1. John, s John & Hannah, Guernsey
    Co., O.; m in Plainfield, Deborah CHAM-
    BERS, dt Samuel & Deborah, Belmont Co.,O.
    Ch: Mary   b 1835, 8, 16
        John   " 1839, 11, 29
        Samuel   " 1839, 4, 6
----, --, --. Charles P. & Sarah
    Ch: Albina   b 1841, 1, 20 d 1853, 8,13
        bur Richland
        James C.   b 1842, 9, 14
        Lydia Ann " 1844, 9, 15
        Abner   " 1847, 3, 3
        Elizabeth " 1849, 4, 17
        Lindley   " 1851, 5, 4 d 1851, 8, 4
        bur Richland
        John   b 1852, 4, 30
        Charles   " 1854, 5, 29
        Sarah Jane " 1857, 3, 26
        Mary   " 1859, 12, 7
1844, 2, 1. Susan m Thos. J. ROMANS
1847, 3, 15. John d
1847, 12, 30. Sarah m Joseph W. HALL
1851, 4, 23. Phebe m Robert P. THOMAS (H)
1851, 5, 1. Deborah Chambers m Benjamin HALL
1851, 11, 27. Phebe m Abner HALL
1853, 10, 27. Jeptha L., s Thomas & Anne,

WEBSTER, Jeptha L., continued
    Guernsey Co., O.; m in Richland, Hannah
    Ann HALL, dt Nathan & Deborah (Parry),
    Guernsey Co., O.
      Ch: Joseph G. b 1854, 10, 13
          Nathan
           Thomas   " 1858, 1, 6
          Florence " 1862, 9, 28
          Louis Alton" 1865, 7, 8
          Edson C. " 1868, 9, 3
          Horner J. " 1871, 2, 1
1855, 12, 27. Mary m Henry HARTLEY
1858, 6, 3. Deborah m Amos HALL
1858, 10, 28. John, s John & Deborah, Guernsey
    Co., O.; m in Richland, Guernsey Co., O.;
    Eliza Jane PARRY, dt Job & Asenath (Hall),
    Guernsey Co., O.
      Ch: Mary
          Melissa   b 1859, 8, 9
          Henry   " 1861, 7, 1
          Martha   " 1865, 1, 19
          Asenath P. " 1866, 6, 28
          Warner   " 1867, 8, 12
          Deborah Ann" 1874, 5, 23
----, --, --. Thomas m Lydia P. RICHARDSON,
    dt Samuel & Hannah Dingee (Vail), b 1841,
    8,25 d 18--,4,21
      Ch: Willis V. b 1861, 2, 15
          Annie
           Laura   " 1863, 8, 27 d 1928, 3,21
           bur Quaker City, O.
          Harriet G. b 1865, 10, 23
          Franklin T." 1868, 1, 3
          Walter Alva" 1873, 2, 20
          Albert D.R." 1871, 7, 18 d 1872, 4,24
           bur Richland
1874, 5, 23. Debora Ann, dt John & Eliza Jane
    (Perry), b
1888, 8, 23. Willis V., s Thomas & Lydia
    (Richardson), Guernsey Co., O., b 1861,3,
    1; m in Stillwater MH, Emma A. STANTON,
    dt Eli & Mary P. (Bundy), Belmont Co., O.,
    b 1864,10,5
      Ch: Harlan
           Stanton b 1889, 9, 6
          Raymond
           Nathan   " 1893, 7, 27
          Thomas Jr. " 1897, 6, 25
          Mary Lydia " 1904, 6, 11
          Deborah
           Harriet   " 1901, 7, 6 (sic)
----, --, --. Harlan Stanton, s Willis V. &
    Emma C. (Stanton); m Mary Avice SMITH, dt
    Thompson & Mary Caleb (Bundy), b 1891,11,
    12
      Ch: Willis
          William b 1914, 7, 8

1808, 10, 25. Thomas gct Little Briton MM, Pa.
1810, 3, 27. William dis attending muster
1811, 6, 25. Thomas rocf Little Britain MM,
    dtd 1811,4,6
1812, 6, 30. Sarah (form Dodd) dis mcd

1812, 12, 29. John gct Plainfield MM, to m
    Albina Gregg
1813, 4, 27. Albina rocf Plainfield MM, dtd
    1813,4,24
1813, 6, 29. William rocf Plainfield MM, dtd
    1813,4,24
1813, 11, 30. Thomas gct Plainfield MM, to m
    Anna Gore
1814, 8, 30. Anna rocf Plainfield MM, dtd
    1814,5,28
1814, 10, 25. John & Albina gct Plainfield MM
1816, 3, 23. John & w, Albina, & s, Charles,
    rocf Plainfield MM, dtd 1816,2,23
1822, 7, 27. John dis mcd
1824, 2, 28. Elizabeth recrq
1825, 5, 28. Mercy rocf Somerset MM, dtd
    1825,2,26
1829, 6, 27. Isaac dis jH
1829, 6, 27. Eli dis jH
1829, 6, 27. Mercy dis jH
1829, 6, 27. Hannah dis jH
1835, 11, 28. Hannah Foulke (form Webster)
    dis mcd
1839, 3, 23. Charles P. con mcd
1840, 7, 25. Sarah rocf Short Creek MM, dtd
    1840,5,19
1841, 5, 22. Abner dis mcd
1850, 3, 22. Ann Kester (form Webster) dis
    mcd
1851, 6, 28. Phebe Thomas (form Webster) dis
    disunity
1854, 7, 22. Joseph G. dis mcd
1855, 1, 20. Sarah W. Smith (form Webster)
    con mcd (H)
1855, 2, 17. Mary gct Honey Creek MM, Ind.
    (H)
1860, 3, 24. Thomas gct Pennsville MM, to m
    Lydia P. Richardson
1861, 6, 22. Lydia P. rocf Pennsville MM,
    dtd 1861,6,13
1861, 7, 27. Samuel dis mcd
1863, 3, 28. Ann P. Outland (form Webster)
    con mcd
1866, 1, 27. Sarah C., w Chas., & ch, Abner,
    Elizabeth, John, Charles & Sarah Jane,
    gct Hickory Grove MM, Iowa. (women's
    minutes also add ch, Mary & Lewis after
    Sarah Jane
1868, 10, 24. Lydia Ann Michener (form Web-
    ster) dis mcd
1882, 1, 25. Joseph G. dis mcd
1886, 10, 20. Henry H. dis mcd
1886, 11, 24. Nathan T. dis mcd
1887, 7, 20. Melissa Griffin (form Webster)
    dis mcd
1888, 11, 21. Asenath P. Coventry (form Web-
    ster) dis mcd
1892, 7, 20. John dis disunity
1893, 7, 19. Martha E. McCoy (form Webster)
    dis mcd
1894, 8, 22. Marner L. dis mcd
1894, 12, 19. Florence W. Bay (form Webster)
    dis mcd

WEBSTER, continued
1895, 10, 23. Annie L. Day (form Webster) con
     mcd
1898, 2, 23. Franklin P. con mcd
1899, 2, 22. Edson C. dis mcd
1899, 6, 21. Walter A. dis mcd
1913, 7, 23. Harlan S. con mcd
1915, 6, 23. Mary Avice (form Smith) con mcd
1933, 10, 25. Thomas Jr. & Frederick Stuckey,
     ch Thomas, recrq

WELLONS
1869, 1, 23. Mary dis jas

WELLS
----, --, --. Samuel & Hannah
     Ch: Thomas   b 1824, 8, 2 d 1826,10, 5
          ae 2y 2m 3d
1846, 12,24. Sarah m Aquilla JONES (H)

1821, 5, 26. Hannah (form Yocum) dis mcd
1824, 3, 27. Hannah rst
1825, 4, 23. William & w, Margaret, & ch,
     John T. & Sarah G., rocf Short Creek MM,
     dtd 1825,4,19
1825, 4, 23. Levi rocf Short Creek MM, dtd
     1825,4,19
1828, 8, 23. Hannah dis jH
1829, 6, 27. Abner & w, Deborah, rocf Short
     Creek MM, dtd 1827,4,24 (it was addressed
     to Plainfield MM but not presented there
     before that MM was laid down)
1829, 6, 27. Samuel dis jH
1830, 1, 23. Abner dis disunity
1830, 4, 24. Deborah dis jH
1849, 5, 26. Sarah Jones (form Wells) dis jas

WHINNERY
1908, 7, 22. Arthur J. Hartley gct Short Creek
     MM, O., to m Mary Edith Whinnery

WHITACRE
1827, 3, 28. Moses M., s Robert & Patience,
     Warren Co., O.; m in Stillwater MH, Pre-
     cilla THOMAS, dt Camm & Elizabeth, Belmont
     Co., O.

1827, 5, 26. Priscilla gct Miami MM
1830, 8, 28. Ann dis jH
1875, 7, 17. Anna (form Plumley) con mcd

WHITE
1815, 10, 5. Mary m Joseph BISHOP
1817, 5, 1. Israel, s Jesse & Mary, Belmont
     Co., O.; m in Captina Creek, Catharine
     WOOD, dt Aaron & Elizabeth, Belmont Co.,O.
1820, 9, 10. Eliza, dt Thos. & Mary, b

1818, 6, 27. Jesse Jr. & w, Sarah, & ch, Ja-
     cob, Mary, Lydia, Rhoda, Sarah & Jane,
     rocf Concord MM, O., dtd 1818,4,22
1821, 5, 26. Thomas & w, Mary, & dt, Eliza,
     rocf Concord MM, dtd 1821,3,21

1823, 1, 25. Thomas dis
1823, 7, 26. Mary & ch, Eliza & Ann, gct
     Concord MM
1824, 10, 23. Israel dis disunity
1825, 7, 23. Catharine & ch, Aaron, Mary &
     Elizabeth, gct Somerset MM
1826, 9, 23. Anna (form Berry) dis mcd
1826, 10, 28. Hannah (form Berry) dis mcd
1828, 5, 24. Jesse dis jH
1828, 8, 23. Mary dis jH
1829, 5, 23. Isaac dis jH
1829, 5, 23. Jane Jr. dis jH
1829, 10, 24. Edith dis jH
1830, 7, 24. James dis jH
1836, 2, 27. Elizabeth (form Hanson) dis mcd
1856, 9, 20. Hannah Wiley (form White) con
     mcd (H)

WILCOX
1875, 7, 21. Sarah (form Bailey) dis mcd
1905, 7, 19. Phebe E. (form Arnold) dis mcd

WILDMAN
1838, 5, 26. Martha [Wileman] rocf Short
     Creek MM, dtd 1838,4,24
1839, 1, 26. Solomin, minor, rocf Short
     Creek MM, dtd 1838,11,2
1839, 3, 23. Mary rocf Pennsville MM, dtd
     1829,2,14
1841, 1, 23. Mary gct Chesterfield MM
1841, 11, 27. Solomon [Wileman] dis mcd
1864, 6, 25. Martha dis disunity

WILLETS
1810, 7, 31. Elizabeth dis
1820, 9, 23. Henry rocf Lees Creek MM, dtd
     1820,7,15
1820, 10, 28. Charity rocf Lees Creek MM, dtd
     1820,7,15
1821, 5, 26. Joseph rocf Fairfield MM, dtd
     1820,7,30, end to Somerset MM
1830, 4, 24. Elizabeth Engle (form Willits)
     rst at Short Creek MM, on consent of this
     mtg
1844, 6, 22. Samira (form Elliott) rst at
     Alum Creek MM with consent of this mtg

WILLIAMS
----, --, --. Henry m Zilpah ----- d 1855,11,
     23 bur Sunsbury
     Ch: Abbie   b 1791, 3, 30
         Job M.   " 1792, 12, 29
         Aaron   " 1795, 5, 21
         Isaiah   " 1797, 2, 25
         Elias   " 1798, 12, 18
         Lydia   " 1800, 12, 1
         John   " 1802, 11, 9
         Anna   " 1804, 11, 23
         Charity " 1807, 2, 28
         Rhoda   " 1810, 4, 6
         Bekah   " 1812, 2, 10
1811, 9, 11. Mary m Richard FAWCETT
1813, 9, 16. John, s Robert & Anna, Belmont

WILLIAMS, John, continued
    Co., O.; m in Stillwater MH, Sarah PATTER-
SON, dt Joseph & Hannah, Belmont Co., O.
1813, 10, 7. Phebe m Samuel KING
1814, 5, 5. Mary d ae 66y 10m 24d
1815, 8, 2. Job, s Henry & Zilpha, Belmont
    Co., O.; m in Stillwater MH, Elizabeth
    CLENDENNON, dt Isaac & Hannah, Belmont
    Co., O.
    Ch: Seth   b 1816, 8, 4
        Jesse   " 1819, 1, 19
1816, 10, 31. Nimrod, s Joseph & Sarah, Guern-
    sey Co., O.; m in Leatherwood, Rebekah
    KING, dt Michael & Hannah, Guernsey Co.,O.
1816, 11, 27. Ruth m Wm. FARMER
1818, 12, 2. Daniel, s Thos. & Prudence; m
    in Stillwater MH, Temperance DOUDNA, dt
    Henry & Martha
    Ch: Henry D.   b 1819, 10, 7
        Rachel P. " 1821, 5, 12
        Isachar   " 1823, 3, 1
        Martha   " 1825, 4, 18 d 1847, 5,24
            bur Stillwater
        Joseph   b 1827, 3, 9 " 1850,12, 7
            bur Stillwater
        Joel   b 1829, 2, 14 " 1844, 4, 3
            bur Stillwater
        Sarah   b 1823, 2, 18
        Prudence   " 1833, 2, 7
        Mary   " 1835, 2, 25
        Esther   " 1838, 8, 7
        Temperance " 1840, 7, 6 d 1843, 9,17
            bur Stillwater
        Eliza F.   b 1842, 9, 12
        Margaret   " 1845, 5, 15 " 1845, 9,14
            bur Stillwater
1819, 4, 29. Esther m John WOOD
1819, 9, 1. Mary m Wm. HODGIN
----, --, --. Manoah & Rachel
    Ch: Rachel   b 1821, 11, 28
        Joseph   " 1823, 8, 31
        Lovice   " 1825, 4, 5
        Clarkay   " 1827, 12, 17
        Rebeckah " 1829, 7, 28
        Elizabeth " 1817, 4, 18
        Manoah   " 1819, 12, 8
1821, 10, 31. William, s Daniel & Mary, Bel-
    mont Co., O.; m in Stillwater MH, Lydia
    CLENDENON, dt Isaac & Hannah, Belmont Co.,
    O.
1822, 6, 5. Abner, s Joseph & Sarah, Guern-
    sey Co., O.; m in Stillwater MH, Lydia
    CHALFANT, dt Jesse & Rachel, Guernsey Co.,
    O.
1822, 12, 4. Elizabeth m Robert SMITH
1825, 9, 28. David, s Daniel & Jane, Belmont
    Co., O.; m in Stillwater MH, Sarah STRAHL,
    dt Philip & Sarah, Belmont Co., O.
1825, 10, 23. Daniel d ae 68y 7m 10d bur Still-
    water
1827, 6, 22. Joseph, s John S. & Sarah, b
1827, 6, 27. John, s Henry & Zilpah, Belmont
    Co., O.; m in Stillwater MH, Deborah COX,

    dt John & Rachel, Belmont Co., O.
1831, 6, 2. Martha m Samuel LEEKE (H)
1834, 8, 15. Henry d bur Stillwater
1836, 6, 8. Sarah m Nathan HALL
1838, 8, 1. Daniel, s Joseph & Mary, Bel-
    mont Co., O.; m in Stillwater MH, Martha
    SCHOLFIELD, dt Issachar & Edith, Belmont
    Co., O.
----, --, --. Ephraim m Ann ----- d 1893,10,
28 bur Stillwater
    Ch: Sarah   b 1840, 5, 19 d 1927, 2, 1
        Samuel   " 1844, 3, 25 " 1851, 5,20
            bur Stillwater
        Daniel   b 1849, 9, 5 " 1849, 9,17
            bur Stillwater
1839, 10, 2. Isaiah, s Henry & Zilpha, Bel-
    mont Co., O.; m in Stillwater MH, Anna
    PEEL, dt John & Anna, Nash Co., N. C.
    Ch: John P.   b 1840, 8, 5
        David W. " 1842, 2, 5
        Nathan   " 1844, 11, 29
----, --, --. Henry D. & Rachel
    Ch: Francis R. b 1845, 10, 14
        Ann   " 1846, 3, 27
        Mary   " 1846, 3, 27
        Martha   " 1848, 3, 3
        Thomas   " 1849, 8, 29
        Velina A. " 1857, 4, 13
        Rebecca P. " 1859, 4, 24
1846, 6, 3. Anna m John HARTLEY
1847, 6, 2. Abba m Stephen HODGIN
1848, 11, 29. Rachel m Jeptha FAWCETT
1850, 3, 20. John d bur Stillwater
1887, 4, 15. Ephraim d bur Stillwater

1809, 9, 26. Prudence & dt, Esther & Martha,
    recrq
1810, 3, 27. Sarah, w Joseph, & ch, Anthony,
    Constance, Margaret, Nimrod, Phebe, Abner,
    Joseph & Jacob, rocf Pipe Creek MM, dtd.
    1809,3,18
1810, 10, 30. Constant Sharrack (form Williams)
    dis mcd
1811, 4, 30. Anna Williams (form Starbuck)
    dis mcd
1812, 5, 26. Anthony dis mcd
1812, 6, 30. Sarah (form Cook) dis mcd
1812, 6, 30. Margaret Depue (form Williams)
    dis mcd
1817, 11, 22. Thomas recrq
1818, 10, 24. Joseph & fam rocf Uwchland MM,
    Pa., end to Flushing MM
1818, 9, 26. Daniel & w, Martha, & ch,
    Elizabeth, David J., Sarah & Ephraim,
    rocf Bradford MM, dtd 1818,8,5
1818, 10, 24. John rocf Bradford MM, dtd 1818,
    8,5
1818, 10, 24. William rocf Bradford MM, dtd
    1818,8,5
1818, 10, 24. Mary rocf Bradford MM, dtd
    1818,8,5
1818, 10, 24. Anne rocf Concord MM, O., dtd
    1818,9,23

WILLIAMS, continued

1818, 10, 24. Samuel & w, Sarah, & ch, Joseph,
    Anne, Sally, Robert, Mary, Elizabeth &
    Peninah, rocf Concord MM, O., dtd 1818,9,
    23
1820, 8, 26. Mary Godgin (form Williams) dis
    mcd
1822, 3, 23. George dis mcd
1822, 6, 22. William & w, Lydia, gct Somerset
    MM
1822, 10, 26. Elias dis mcd
1822, 12, 22. Lydia (form Smith) dis mcd
1824, 11, 24. Jacob & Joseph dis disunity
1825, 3, 26. Martha McNichols (form Williams)
    dis mcd
1826, 1, 28. Nimrod dis disunity
1826, 5, 27. Isaiah gct Abington MM, Pa.
1826, 5, 27. Mary (form Stanton) dis mcd
1827, 5, 26. John S. & w, Sarah, & ch, Ben-
    jamin, Hannah, Robert, Ann, John & Eliza-
    beth, rocf Redstone MM, dtd 1827,4,4, end
    by Plainfield MM, 1827,5,24
1827, 5, 26. David & w, Sarah, & dt, Rachel,
    gct Somerset MM
1827, 7, 28. John S. relrq
1827, 12, 22. Aaron dis mcd
1828, 8, 23. Martha dis jH
1828, 11, 22. Charity Pennington (form
    Williams) dis mcd
1829, 5, 23. Rebecca & ch, Miriam, Lavina,
    Phebe & Deborah, rocf Somerset MM, dtd
    1829,4,16
1830, 4, 24. Thomas dis jH
1830, 5, 22. John & w, Deborah, rocf Somerset
    MM
1831, 2, 26. Rhoda dis mcd
1831, 3, 26. Isaiah rocf Frankfort MM, Pa.,
    dtd 1831,3,1
1831, 8, 27. Ephraim gct Salem MM
1831, 8, 27. Abner dis mcd
1832, 7, 28. Becca Hitchinson (form Williams)
    dis mcd
1834, 2, 22. Isaiah gct Somerset MM
1834, 9, 20. David J. & w, Sarah, & ch, Ra-
    chel S., Jane, Philip Strahl & Casper, gct
    Deerfield MM (H)
1835, 1, 24. Sarah & ch, Benjamin, Hannah,
    Robert, Ann, John, Eliza, Joseph, Sarah-
    jane, Marylouisa & Martha Bell, gct Cin-
    cinnati MM
1835, 3, 28. Ephraim rocf Salem MM, dtd 1834,
    12,21
1838, 1, 27. Isaiah & s, Elias, rocf Ches-
    terfield MM, dtd 1837,11,18
1838, 12, 22. Martha gct Flushing MM
1839, 1, 26. Rachel & Jane rocf Chesterfield
    MM, dtd 1838,12,15
1839, 2, 23. Ephraim gct Flushing MM, to m
    Ann Sharp
1839, 4, 24. Ann rocf Flushing MM, dtd 1839,
    7,25
1841, 3, 21. Rebecca & ch, Marian, Levy,
    Phebe, Deborah, Joseph, Willit, Ezra,

Peninnah, Preston & Isaac, gct Chester-
    field MM
1843, 9, 23. Lavisa (form Hanson) con mcd
1843, 9, 23. Henry D. gct Somerset MM, to
    m Rachel Crew
1844, 3, 23. Rachel rocf Somerset MM, dtd
    1844,1,29
1844, 3, 22. Rachel rocf Somerset MM, dtd
    1844,1,29
1845, 6, 28. Sarah & ch, Jane T., Ephraim &
    Otho F., gct Somerset MM
1845, 9, 27. Rachel L. gct Somerset MM
1846, 3, 28. Isaiah & w, Anna, & ch, Elias,
    John P. & Nathan, gct Chesterfield MM
1846, 8, 22. Rebecca & ch, Deborah, Jeptha,
    Willet, Ezra, Penninah, Preston & Isaac,
    rocf Chesterfield MM, dtd 1846,7,18
1846, 8, 22. Phebe rocf Chesterfield MM, dtd
    1846,7,18
1848, 4, 22. Phebe McVey (form Williams) dis
    mcd
1848, 5, 27. William & w, Lydia, & ch,
    Lindley, Elwood & Elizabeth, rocf Penns-
    ville MM, dtd 1848,4,13
1849, 8, 25. Rachel (form Atkinson) con mcd
1850, 1, 26. Rachel gct Springfield MM, Ind.
1850, 4, 27. William & w, Lydia, & ch,
    Lindley, Elwood & Elizabeth, gct Somerset
    MM
1851, 2, 22. Isaachar dis mcd
1852, 6, 26. Willet dis mcd
1852, 9, 25. Deborah Weaver (form Williams)
    dis mcd
1852, 10, 23. Daniel & w, Temperance, & ch,
    Mary, Esther & Eliza F., gct Vermillion
    MM, Ill.
1852, 10, 23. Sarah M. gct Vermillion MM, Ill.
1852, 10, 23. Prudence gct Vermillion MM, Ill.
1857, 8, 15. Ruth Ann (form Hampton) con mcd
    (H)
1877, 9, 21. Alesanna (form Tomlinson) dis
    mcd (H)
1904, 8, 24. Henry Hartley gct Pasadena
    MM, Calif., to m Margaret C. Williams

WILLIS

1840, 3, 28. Joseph, minor, rocf Cherry
    Grove MM, dtd 1840,1,15
1844, 8, 24. Joseph gct Cherry Grove MM, Ind.

WILSON

1812, 1, 8. Isaac, s Isaac & Rebecca, Bel-
    mont Co., O.; m in Stillwater MH, Eliza-
    beth DODD, dt Aaron & Rebeckah, Belmont
    Co., O.
    Ch: Samuel   b 1813, 8, 1
        Rebecca   " 1814, 9, 11
        Aaron   " 1816, 1, 23
        Sarah   " 1818, 3, 23
        Stephen   " 1820, 5, 1
        Joseph   " 1822, 4, 12
        Martha   " 1824, 6, 11
        Elizabeth   " 1826, 6, 27

WILSON, continued
----, --, --. Daniel & Mary
    Ch: Margaret D.b 1817, 4, 22
        William   " 1818, 9, 28
        Sarah Ann " 1819, 10, 8
        Mary   " 1821, 10, 6
        Rachel   " 1823, 7, 29
        Daniel   " 1825, 3, 7
----, --, --. Edwin m Deborah ----- d 1878,10,
  27 bur Stillwater
    Ch: Thomas H. b 1818, 7, 24
        Sarah Ann " 1820, 7, 28
        Demsey   " 1823, 2, 2
        Mary   " 1826, 1, 16
        Hannah   " 1828, 1, 21 d 1846,12,28
          bur Stillwater
1850, 3, 27. Mary m Nathan PATTERSON
----, --, --. William C. m Esther ----- d 1886,
  4,22 bur Stillwater
    Ch: Edwin   b 1862, 8, 12
        Mary   " 1865, 9, 27 d 1889, 3,18
          bur Stillwater
1864, 10, 26. Rachel D. m Isaac W. VAIL
----, --, --. Israel m Catharine ----- d 1878,
  7,21
    Ch: Israel J.   d 1863,11,26
        Joseph D.   " 1865,10,22
        William C.   " 1866, 2, 8
1865, 4, 16. Israel d bur Stillwater
1865, 12, 27. Edwin d bur Stillwater
1898, 12, 7. Ann Eliza m Joseph F. DOUDNA

1811, 3, 26. Ann (form Taylor) con mcd
1811, 6, 25. Hugh rocf Plainfield MM, dtd
  1811,6,22
1812, 6, 30. Elizabeth gct Plainfield MM
1815, 9, 26. Sally (form Mills) dis mcd
1815, 10, 31. Daniel rocf Concord MM, Pa., dtd
  1815,9,8
1815, 11, 28. Daniel gct Concord MM, to m Mary
  Dewees
1816, 4, 27. Deborah (form Hunnicutt) dis mcd
1816, 5, 25. Elizabeth (form Dillon) dis mcd
1816, 7, 27. Mary rocf Concord MM, dtd 1816,
  4,24
1820, 6, 24. Isaac Jr. & w, Elizabeth, & ch,
  Samuel, Rebecca, Aaron, Sarah & Stephen,
  rocf Plainfield MM, dtd 1820,6,22
1822, 5, 28. Isaac & w, Elizabeth, & ch,
  Samuel, Rebecca, Aaron, Sarah, Stephen &
  Joseph, rocf Somerset MM, dtd 1822,4,29
1822, 8, 24. Edwin & Deborah recrq
1822, 12, 22. Thomas H. & Sarah Ann, ch Edwin
  & Deborah, recrq
1824, 11, 24. Daniel dis disunity
1828, 3, 22. Mary & ch, Margaret, Sarah,
  Mary, Rachel, Daniel & Ruth, gct Deerfield
  MM
1828, 5, 24. Hugh dis jH
1828, 7, 26. Ann dis jH
1828, 8, 23. Joseph dis jH
1829, 4, 18. Hugh & w, Ann, & ch, Joseph
  Taylor, Isaac B., Rebecca, James, Stephen,

Mary Jane, Sarah & Ann, gct Cincinnati MM
1829, 10, 24. Ruth dis jH   [(H)
1830, 5, 22. Isaac, James, Stephen, Rebecca,
  Mary Jane, Sarah & Ann, gct Cincinnati MM
1830, 8, 28. Isaac dis jH
1833, 7, 27. Yarnal, Phebe, Jane, Cyrus &
  Thomas, ch Thomas & Hannah, rocf Short
  Creek MM, dtd 1833,5,21
1835, 1, 24. Rebecca Porter (form Wilson)dis
  mcd
1835, 7, 25. Aaron dis disunity
1835, 7, 25. Sarah dis disunity
1836, 7, 23. Samuel dis mcd
1838, 5, 26. Ann rocf Short Creek MM, dtd
  1838,4,24
1838, 7, 28. Elizabeth dis jas
1838, 7, 28. Martha dis jas
1840, 9, 26. Joseph, Isaac, Hannah, Nathan &
  Ann Elizabeth, ch Isaac & Elizabeth, gct
  Chesterfield MM
1841, 3, 21. Stephen dis disunity
1841, 12, 25. Ann gct Gilead MM
1844, 4, 27. Sarah Ann Barnes (form Wilson)
  dis mcd
1845, 3, 22. Thomas H. dis mcd
1847, 2, 27. Bethena (form Hicks) dis mcd
1852, 1, 24. Dempsy dis mcd
1858, 1, 16. Mary B. (form Swain) con mcd (H)
1861, 6, 22. Israel & w, Catharine, & ch,
  Israel I. & Joseph D., rocf Flushing MM,
  dtd 1861,5,23
1861, 6, 22. Ann Eliza & Rachel D. rocf Flushing MM, dtd 1861,5,23
1862, 4, 26. Wm. C. & w, Esther, & ch,
  Charles, Francis & Levi F., rocf Flushing
  MM, dtd 1861,11,21
1878, 1, --. Charles dis mcd
1884, 5, 21. Francis dis mcd
1885, 11, 25. Edwin dis mcd
1888, 7, 25. Levi dis mcd
1895, 3, 20. Albertus C. Hoyle gct Flushing
  MM, to m Mabel B. Wilson

WINDER
1866, 10, 31. Benjamin, s William & Ada, Columbiana Co., O.; m in Stillwater MH, Sarah
  S. BRIGGS, dt William & Esther, Belmont
  Co., O.
1889, 11, 28. Joseph, s Lenard & Ruth Anna
  (Coppock), b

1917, 7, 25. Joseph C. rocf New Garden MM,
  O., dtd 1917,6,21
1922, 3, 22. Joseph C. gct Chester MM, Pa.

WINDHAM
1829, 5, 25. Mercy dis jH

WING
1818, 8, 22. Sarah & dt, Lydia, rocf Butternut MM, dtd 1816,10,30, end by Nine Partners MM, N. Y., 1818,2,19 & Smithfield MM
  1818,6,22

WING, continued
1819, 6, 26. Phebe, dt Sarah, recrq
1823, 12, 27. Sarah & dt, Phebe, gct Alum
    Creek MM

WINTERS
1830, 7, 24. Agathy (form Cobb) dis mcd

WOOD
1802, 8, 23. William, s Matthew & Mary, b
----, --, --. Abraham & Jane
    Ch: Lewis   b 1811, 9, 12
        James   " 1813, 1, 19
        Phebe   " 1814, 12, 11
        Martha   " 1816, 11, 15
        Mary Ann   " 1820, 12, 2
        Abraham   " 1823, 2, 6
        John   " 1825, 5, 22
        Nathan   " 1827, 2, 9
        Amos   " 1829, 7, 1
1812, 2, 6. Israel, s Aaron & Elizabeth,
    Belmont Co., O.; m in Capteanna Creek MH,
    Elizabeth NICHOLSON, dt Joseph & Sarah,
    Belmont Co., O.
1813, 11, 4. Matthew, s James & Mary; m in
    Stillwater MH, Margaret PATTERSON, dt
    Benjamin & Esther
    Ch: Elam   b 1815, 1, 13 d 1836,11,29
        Mary   " 1816, 5, 17
        Rachel " 1817, 10, 18
        Matthew " 1819, 4, 10 d 1839, 3,17
1814, 4, 7. Isaac, s Matthew & Mary, Belmont
    Co., O.; m in Stillwater MH, Clarkey HAN-
    SON, dt Elijah & Susanna, Belmont Co., O.
    Ch: Seth   b 1815, 1, 24
        Hanson " 1816, 11, 20
        Elvy   " 1819, 6, 13
        Isaac   " 1821, 6, 19
        Elijah " 1823, 10, 7
        William " 1826, 1, 28
        Susanna
1816, 8, 1. Ann m Elam PATTERSON
1817, 5, 1. Catharine m Israel WHITE
1819, 4, 29. John, s Matthew & Mary, Belmont
    Co., O.; m in Captina, Esther WILLIAMS,
    dt Thomas & Prudence, Belmont Co., O.
    Ch: Sidney   b 1820, 3, 13
        Jane   " 1821, 12, 10
        Prudence " 1824, 2, 5
        Ann   " 1826, 4, 24
        John
        Worthing-
        ton
        Thomas
1831, 3, 28. William, s Wm. & Margaret, Jef-
    ferson Co., O.; m in Stillwater MH, Susan-
    nah AMOS, dt Wm. & Susannah, Hartford Co.,
    Md.
1839, 1, 31. Sidney m Abijah TIPTON
1841, 12, 9. Mary m Aaron DEWEESE
1842, 12, 7. Prudence m William BUNDY
1843, 4, 26. Ann m Densey BUNDY
1850, 3, 4. Matthew d bur Stillwater

1810, 7, 31. Moses dis mcd
1812, 5, 26. Mathew & ch, Ann, John &
    William, rocf Goshen MM, dtd 1812,3,6
1812, 5, 26. Isaac rocf Goshen MM, dtd 1812,
    3,6
1812, 5, 26. Abraham rocf Goshen MM, dtd
    1812,3,6
1814, 7, 26. Jane recrq
1814, 12, 27. Susannah Smith (form Wood) con
    mcd
1815, 6, 27. Sarah Smith (form Wood) dis mcd
1818, 5, 23. Lewis & James, ch Abram & Jane,
    recrq
1826, 2, 25. William, s Mathew, dis mcd
1826, 5, 27. Israel & w, Elizabeth, & ch, Jo-
    seph, Wilson, Ann, John & Sarah, rocf
    Somerset MM, dtd 1826,4,24
1826, 11, 25. William dis disunity
1827, 2, 24. Ann dis disunity
1827, 12, 22. Samuel rocf Pipe Creek MM, dtd
    1827,6,16
1828, 1, 26. Zachariah dis mcd
1829, 3, 28. Samuel dis JH
1829, 5, 23. Orpha (form Broomhall) dis mcd
1829, 11, 28. Aaron dis JH
1829, 11, 28. Elizabeth dis JH
1829, 11, 28. Mary dis JH
1830, 2, 27. Isaac dis JH
1830, 7, 24. James dis jas
1830, 9, 25. Clarry dis JH
1831, 1, 22. John dis disunity
1831, 6, 25. Susannah gct Smithfield MM
1831, 6, 25. Lewis dis mcd
1832, 8, 25. Esther dis disunity
1834, 1, 25. Phebe Lisle (form Wood) dis mcd
1834, 6, 28. Martha Ewers (form Wood) dis mcd
1835, 1, 24. Abraham & w, Jane, & ch, Mary-
    ann, Abraham, John, Nathan & Emmor, gct
    Deerfield MM
1835, 5, 23. Cidney, Jane, Prudence, Ann,
    John W., Thomas & Mary, gct Somerset MM
1836, 5, 28. Seth dis mcd
1838, 5, 26. Cidney, Prudence, Ann, John W.,
    & Thomas M., minor ch John & Esther, rocf
    Somerset MM, dtd 1838,3,26
1838, 6, 23. Ann, minor, gct Flushing MM
1838, 11, 24. Rachel Bailey (form Wood) con
    mcd
1841, 6, 26. Elva Davis (form Wood) dis mcd
1841, 9, 25. Ann rocf Flushing MM, dtd 1841,
    8,26
1846, 9, 26. Eliajh dis disunity
1848, 10, 28. John W. gct Somerset MM, to m
    Almedia Crew
1849, 5, 26. Susannah Jones (form Wood) dis
    mcd
1849, 9, 22. William dis disunity
1851, 10, 25. Margaret gct Pennsville MM
1854, 1, 28. Thomas Doudna gct Flushing MM,
    to m Rachel Wood
1865, 8, 25. John W. gct Somerset MM
1864, 7, 23. Susannah (form Bundy) dis mcd

WOODWARD
1914, 6, 25. Guy, s Miles & Louisa J., Madi-
     son Co., Ind.; m in Stillwater MH, Mary
     Eva HALL, dt Wilford & Sarah B., Belmont
     Co., O., b 1891,9,26 d 1919,2,26 bur
     Stillwater

WOOTON
1814, 10, 25. Rebecca (Bailey) dis mcd
1817, 8, 23. Rebecca rst

WORTHINGTON
1894, 12, 20. Mary J. m Joseph E. MEYERS

1893, 8, 23. Mary J. rocf Somerset MM, dtd
     1893,7,20
1894, 10, 24. Amy Leanna recrq
1910, 9, 21. Leanna gct Plainfield MM, Ind.

WRIGHT
----, --, --. Nehemiah & Abigail
     Ch: Joseph Dew b 1813, 8, 17
         Martha   " 1815, 12, 28
         John D.   " 1818, 2, 16
         James D.   " 1820, 11, 30
         Viley   " 1823, 4, 7
         Jenkinson " 1827, 5, 28
1888, 8, 20. William d bur Stillwater

1829, 5, 23. Nehemiah dis jH
1829, 12, 26. William dis jH
1832, 10, 27. Abigail dis jH
1833, 3, 23. Joseph D. dis jH
1884, 10, 22. Aaron Frame gct Flushing MM, to
     m Lavina H. Wright
1886, 1, 20. William recrq

WYLIE
----, --, --. Joseph m M. Ethel DOUDNA, dt
     Jesse I. & Louisa (Patterson), b 1885,7,24
     Ch: Grace Mar-
             tha   b 1912, 2, 11
         Myrtle
         Ellen   " 1917, 5, 16
         Jessie Al-
         berta   " 1919, 9, 27

1818, 4, 25. David & w, Elizabeth, & ch, Sa-
     rah & Joseph, rocf Salem MM, dtd 1818,3,17
1856, 9, 20. Hannah (form White) con mcd (H)
1858, 8, 21. Hannah gct Concord MM (H)
1925, 6, 24. Grace M., Myrtle E. & J. Alberta
     ch Joseph W. & Ethel, recrq

YARNALL
1817, 9, 27. Mordecai & w, Phebe, & ch, Han-
     nah & Susannah, rocf Short Creek MM, dtd
     1817,6,24

YEARSLEY
1818, 6, 27. Abigail rocf Wilmington MM, dtd
     1818,4,3

YEATES
1833, 2, 23. Ann dis jH

YOCUM
----, --, --. Samuel & Rebecca
     Ch: Rebecca   b 1813, 7, 11
         Mary   " 1817, 9, 8
1826, 12, 28. Thomas, s Samuel & Rebecca,
     Belmont Co., O.; m in Capitena, Sarah DE-
     WEESE, dt Thomas & Jane, Belmont Co., O.
     Ch: Samuel   b 1828, 8, 13
1834, 1, 22. Jesse, s Samuel & Rebecca, Bel-
     mont Co., O.; m in Centre, Gainer GATCHEL,
     dt Jeremiah & Deborah, Belmont Co., O.
     (H)
1845, 3, 20. Samuel, s Jacob & Maria, Bel-
     mont Co., O.; m in Sunbury, Lydia HOLOWELL,
     dt John & Lydia EDWARDS, Monroe Co., O.
     (H)
1857, 6, 24. John D., s Samuel & Jane, Bel-
     mont Co., O.; m in Somerset, Hannah T.
     GRISSELL, dt Nathan P. & Lydia, Belmont
     Co., O. (H)

1811, 10, 1. Samuel & w, Rebeckah, & ch,
     Hannah, Thomas, Jacob, Samuel, Mark,
     John & Jesse, rocf Short Creek MM, dtd
     1811,5,21
1821, 5, 26. Hannah Wells (form Yocom) dis
     mcd
1823, 6, 28. Jacob gct Somerset MM
1827, 6, 23. David & w, Lydia, & ch, Phebe &
     Samuel, rocf Somerset MM, dtd 1827,5,28
1828, 5, 24. Jacob dis disunity
1828, 8, 23. Samuel dis jH
1828, 8, 23. Mark & Rebecca dis jH
1828, 9, 27. Lydia & Rebecca Jr. dis jH
1829, 6, 27. Thomas dis jH
1829, 6, 27. Samuel Jr. dis jH
1829, 6, 27. John dis jH
1829, 6, 27. Sarah dis jH
1830, 2, 27. Jesse dis jH
1839, 7, 27. Mary dis jH
1866, 1, 20. Samuel & w, Jane, & ch, Lindley
     & Mary, gct Plainfield MM (H)
1866, 1, 20. Hannah & s, Nathan G., gct
     Plainfield MM (H)
1866, 4, 21. John D. gct Plainfield MM (H)
1866, 9, 15. Joseph gct Plainfield MM (H)
1866, 9, 15. Isaac gct Plainfield MM (H)

YOUNG
1813, 10, 26. Margaret (form Bailey) dis mcd

YOUREX
----, --, --. Moses & Golda (Hall)
     Ch: Mary Ar-
             line   b 1930, 3, 28
         Paul Hall   " 1931, 9, 21
1927, 5, 25. Golda B. H. (form Hall) con mcd
1929, 9, 25. Moses R. recrq

*   *   *   * | *   *   *   *

WILSON
1829, 4, 25. Ann rocf Smithfield MM, dtd
     1829,1,19

1829, 5, 23. Amos dis JH
1829, 5, 23. Ann dis JH

PLYMOUTH-SMITHFIELD MONTHLY MEETING

Plymouth-Smithfield Monthly Meeting, located in Jefferson County, Ohio, was organized as early as 1802. The first meetings were held in the private residences of members until about 1804 when a log building was erected. This was used until 1813 when a substantial brick building took its place.

The meeting was originally called Plymouth Monthly Meeting, but in 1818 the name was changed to Smithfield.

The first marriage in this meeting was that of Evan Evans and Mary Bright, 4th Mo. 20, 1808.

RECORDS

ABRAMS

1926, 10, 2. Ethel May, dt William & May, b

1931, 1, 21. Rev. Will & w, May, & ch, Rod-
ney & Ethel May, rocf Highland Avenue MM,
Columbus, O.

ALBERTSON

1812, 11, 20. Joseph & w, Elva, & dt, Peninah,
gct Stillwater MM

ALLEN

1817, 10, 20. Cert rec for Phillip & w, Elizabeth, & ch, John Milton, Jacob H. & Samuel
from Oswego MM, N. Y., dtd 1817,8,20, end
to Stillwater MM 1817,12,22

ALLMAN

1842, 6, 21. John [Allmon], s Wm. & Lydia,
Stark Co., O.; m in Cross Creek MH, Eliza-
beth FARQUHAR, dt Jos. & Beulah FARQUHAR,
Jefferson Co., O.
  Ch: Lydia   b 1844, 11, 8
      Beulah E. " 1846, 2, 22
1843, 8, 31. Joseph, s Wm. & Lydia, Stark
Co., O.; m in Cross Creek MH, Hannah Maria
FARQUHAR, dt Wm. & Hannah, Jefferson Co.,
O.

1842, 8, 22. Elizabeth [Almon] gct Marlborough
MM
1843, 10, 23. Hannah Maria gct Marlborough MM
1844, 6, 17. John & w, Elizabeth, & dt, Mary
F., rocf Marlborough MM, dtd 1844,4,30
1846, 7, 20. Joseph [Allmon] & w, Hannah,
rocf Marlborough MM
1849, 3, 19. Joseph & w, Hannah, gct Salem MM,
Iowa
1854, 5, 22. John & w, Elizabeth, & ch, Mary
F., Lydia & Bulah Elma, gct Spring Creek
MM, Ia.

AMOS

1831, 3, 21. William Wood gct Stillwater MM,
to m Susanna Amos

ARMS

1904, 3, 23. Lizzie recrq

ARMSTRONG

1904, 2, 24. B. J. C. recrq

ARNOLD

1850, 10, 21. Rebecca (form McGrew) dis mcd

ASHBA

1906, 10, 24. Frank D., minister, rocf New
London MM, Ind.
1908, 3, 25. Rev. Frank D. gct Salem MM

ATKINSON

1862, 8, 18. Rebecca (form Watson) dis mcd

BABCOCK

1902, 9, 22. Maria C. recrq
1906, 1, 24. Maria C. relrq

BAILEY

----, --, --. Ezra & Elizabeth
  Ch: Elmira   b 1829, 1, 12
      Hezekiah B." 1830, 11, 9
1840, 5, 25. Elizabeth [Baley] m James BOWMAN

1822, 1, 21. Henry Crew gct Short Creek MM,
to m Margaret Bailey
1828, 6, 23. Elizabeth rocf New Garden MM,
O., dtd 1828,2,26, end by Short Creek MM,
O.
1828, 8, 18. Ezra rocf Short Creek MM, O.,
dtd 1828,5,20
1831, 4, 18. Ezra & w, Elizabeth, & ch, Elmira S. & Hezekiah B., gct Cincinnati MM,
O.
1840, 9, 21. Elizabeth rocf Somerset MM, dtd
1840,8,31

BALES

1824, 6, 21. Joseph D. rocf Waynoak MM, dtd
1824,3,5

BAKE

1837, 11, 11. Gilbert, s Gilbert & Margaret, b

1865, 4, 17. Gilbert H. recrq
1890, 6, 23. Gilbert relrq

BALL

1810, 8, 20. Martha m John NAYLOR
1812, 12, 2. Elizabeth m Wm. HAMMOND
1814, 3, 24. Rachel m John TALBOTT
1821, 6, 10. Ruth Ball, dt Jas., d bur Richmond
1824, 1, 24. Ruth m Joseph HOBSON
1825, 9, 29. David, s Jas. & Ruth, Jefferson
Co., O.; m in Cross Creek MH, Juliann PAR-
SONS, dt Amos & Gaynor, Jefferson Co., O.
  Ch: Gaynor   b 1826, 8, 9
      Ruth   " 1828, 4, 22
      Mary   " 1830, 1, 25 d 1833, 5,16
       bur Cross Creek
      Alice Ann b 1833, 3, 18
      Abigail   " 1835, 6, 6
1827, 10, 23. Naomi m Wm. MASTERS
1835, 11, 26. James R., s Henry & Jane, Carroll Co., O.; m in Cross Creek MH, Mary
Ann TALBOTT, dt John & Cassandra, Jefferson Co., O.
1837, 3, 1. Rebecca m Pusey WOOD

1810, 9, 15. Ruth & ch, Rebecah, David, Abigail, Naomi, Ruth & Susannah, recrq
1810, 9, 15. Rachel recrq
1812, 6, 20. Elizabeth recrq

BALL, continued

1824, 8, 23. Abigail Naylor (form Ball) con
               mcd
1836, 2, 22. David & w, Juliann, & ch, Gay-
               nor, Ruth, Alice Ann & Abigail, gct
               Pennsville MM
1836, 9, 19. James R. rocf Short Creek MM, O.
1840, 6, 22. Mary Ann & ch, Henry & Mary Cas-
               sandra, gct Short Creek MM, O.

BALLINGER

1821, 5, 30. Cassandra m Nathan UPDEGRAFF
1825, 4, 27. Edith m Wm. PRICE
1836, 3, 8. Lydia, w Wm., d bur Smithfield
1858, 3, 31. William d bur Smithfield
1859, 9, 8. Mary d bur Smithfield
1863, 5, 27. Rebecca m Thos. H. TERRIL

1819, 11, 22. William & w, Lydia, & ch, Sam-
               uel, Mary & Rebecca, rocf Pipe Creek MM,
               Md., dtd 1819,10,16
1819, 11, 22. Edith & Casander rocf Pipe Creek
               MM, Md., dtd 1819,10,16
1858, 7, 19. Samuel dis mcd
1864, 8, 22. Mary C. [Balenger] rst
1875, 4, 19. Samuel [Balenger] recrq

BARBER
1881, 2, 21. Charles recrq

BARCRAFT
1817, 12, 22. Lydia rocf Baltimore MM, dtd
               1817,6,5
1819, 9, 20. Rebecca recrq
1825, 9, 19. Rebecca Paxon (form Barcroft)
               dis mcd

BARCUS
1881, 2, 21. John & Emma L. recrq
1891, 7, 20. Emma & ch relrq

BARKHURST
1905, 8, 21. Mary E. relrq

BATES
1825, 6, 29. Joseph Denson, s James & Ann,
               Jefferson Co., O., d 1872,11,17 bur Smith-
               field; m in Smithfield MH, Mary P. WOOD,
               dt Thomas & Susanna
               Ch: Thomas W. b 1826, 5, 2
                   Joshua   " 1829, 8, 9
                   Benjamin L." 1831, 9, 6
                   Susanna P. " 1835, 8, 5 d 1856,10,13
                    bur Smithfield
                   Nathan
                   Pusey   b 1841, 11, 6
1829, 4, 1. Wm. Savory, s Benj. & Tace,
               Jefferson Co., O.; m in Smithfield MH,
               Lydia WOOD, dt Wm. & Mary, Jefferson Co.,
               O., d 1854,2,20 bur Smithfield
               Ch: Tace   b 1830, 3, 15
                   Mary Wood " 1832, 5, 25
                   Benjamin   " 1837, 3, 16

----, --, --. Thomas W., s Jos. & Mary P.,
               b 1826,5,2 d 1898,10,--; m Sarah C. GILL,
               dt John & Elizabeth, b 1831,2,16
1850, 11, 21. Tacy m Robt. B. LAWRENCE
----, --, --. Thomas W. & Sarah C.
               Ch: Idamay   b 1863, 5, 25
                   Mary E.   " 1867, 12, 15
                   William   " 1870, 5, 7

1828, 8, 18. William Savery rocf Ceder Creek
               MM, Va., dtd 1828,7,12
1828, 10, 20. Joseph Hargrave gct Cedar Creek
               MM, Va., to m Deborah Bates
1856, 1, 21. William S. dis mcd
1856, 9, 22. Thomas dis mcd
1857, 10, 19. Mary W. Judkins (form Bates)
               dis mcd
1858, 11, 22. Benjamin dis mcd
1858, 11, 22. Joshua con mcd
1859, 7, 18. Joshua gct Spring Creek MM, Ia.
1867, 10, 21. Nathan Pusey dis military ser-
               vice
1873, 11, 17. Thomas W. & w, Sarah Catherine,
               & ch, Ida-May, Mary Elizabeth & William,
               recrq
1906, 7, 25. Elizabeth H. relrq

BELL
1887, 1, 17. Moses B. recrq
1893, 7, 17. Moses dropped from mbrp

BENEDAL
1836, 1, 18. Henry, minor, rocf Alum Creek MM
               dtd 1835,11,20

BENEDICT
1837, 10, 23. Cyrus, minor, rocf Alum Creek
               MM, dtd 1837,6,22
1841, 1, 18. Cyrus, minor, gct Providence MM,
               Pa.
1843, 8, 21. Henry gct Upper Springfield MM,
               to m Eliza T. Stanley
1844, 1, 22. Henry gct Gilead MM, O.

BERGETT
1906, 10, 24. William recrq

BINFORD
1850, 12, 23. Josiah rocf Lower MM, Va., dtd
               1850,11,23
1854, 10, 23. Josiah gct Walnut Ridge MM, Ind.

BLACKBURN
1828, 7, 14. Moses d bur Richmond
----, --, --. Charles, s Thomas & Margaret;
               m Mary E. NAYLOR, dt Samuel & Mariah,
               b 1850,7,4 (Charles b 1845,8,12)
               Ch: Maud   b 1882, 10, 24 d 1888, 6, 5
                   S. Denzil b 1889, 8, 9

BLACKBURN, continued
1886, 6, 21. Keziah relrq

BLACKISON
1814, 1, 15. Ann rst on consent of Gunpowder
     MM
1830, 12, 20. Ann [Blackiston] dis jH

BLAKEMORE
1842, 6, 20. Juliann (form McGrew) dis mcd

BOGUE
1809, 8, 17. Job rocf Plainfield MM, dtd
     1809,3,27
1809, 9, 16. Jonathan gct Plainfield MM
1810, 5, 19. Meriam Rheubel (form Bogue) dis
     mcd
1811, 5, 18. Catharine Smith (form Bogue) dis
     mcd
1812, 4, 18. Job gct Plainfield MM
1812, 5, 16. Huldah gct Plainfield MM

BOWMAN
1833, 6, 27. Joseph, s Isaac & Anne, Jeffer-
     son Co., O.; m in Cross Creek MH, Eliza-
     beth SPENCER, dt Miller & Sidney, Jeffer-
     son Co., O.
1840, 5, 25. James, s Isaac & Anna, Stark
     Co., O.; m in Cross Creek MH, Elizabeth
     BALEY, dt Henry & Mary, Belmont Co., O.

1808, 5, 21. Ann [Boman] gc
1827, 9, 17. James rocf Marlborough MM, dtd
     1827,6,26
1830, 10, 18. Richard, minor, gct Marlborough
     MM
1834, 4, 21. Joseph & w, Elizabeth, gct
     Marlborough MM
1842, 7, 15. James & w, Elizabeth, gct Marl-
     borough MM

BRESARD
1840, 10, 19. Elizabeth (form McGrew) dis mcd

BRIGGS
1849, 12, 19. William, s Wm. & Esther, Belmont
     Co., O.; m in Smithfield MH, Hannah CREW,
     dt Benjamin & Sarah, Jefferson Co., O.
     William m 2nd 1856,9,24 in Smithfield MH,
     Rachel KIRK, dt Wm. & Martha, Jefferson
     Co., O.

1817, 8, 18. William & w, Esther, & ch, Sam-
     uel M., Mariah, Job, Jonathan T., Rebecca
     M., William & Henry, rocf Salem MM, dtd
     1817,5,13
1818, 4, 20. William & w, Esther, & ch, Ma-
     riah, Job, Jonathan T., Rebecca M., Wil-
     liam & Henry, gct Plainfield MM
1818, 4, 20. Samuel M. gct Plainfield MM
1850, 4, 22. Hannah C. gct Flushing MM
1857, 2, 23. Rachel gct Flushing MM, O.
1862, 10, 20. Mifflin Ong gct Flushing MM, O.,

to m Mary R. Briggs

BRITE
1808, 4, 20. Mary m Evan EVANS

BROWN
1810, 10, 20. Miriam & ch, Sarah, Jane, Mary,
     Elizabeth, Ruth & Aaron, gct Miami MM, O.
1832, 9, 17. Elizabeth Updegraff & Jane,
     minor dt Henry & Jane, rocf Sandy Spring
     MM, dtd 1832,8,24
1833, 1, 21. Eliza Updegraff rocf Sandy
     Spring MM, dtd 1832,8,24
1833, 1, 21. Abigail rocf Sandy Spring MM,
     dtd 1832,8,24
1882, 4, 17. Elnathan P. rocf Short Creek
     MM, O.
1890, 6, 23. Nathan & fam gct Short Creek
     MM, O.
1915, 9, 22. Lewis rocf Murry MM
1916, 8, 16. Lewis relrq

BRUCE
1889, 7, 22. George O. & w, Emeline, recrq
1899, 1, 23. George dropped from mbrp

BRYANT
1827, 6, 18. Thomas French gct Upper Spring-
     field MM, to m Martha Bryant

BUCHANAN
1889, 2, 18. Stephen & Victoria recrq
1900, 9, 17. Stephen & Victoria dropped from
     mbrp

BURGESS
1815, 2, 22. John, s Jos. & Ann, Jefferson
     Co., O.; m in Plymouth MH, Margaret
     PLUMMER, dt Thos. & Susanna WOOD, Jeffer-
     son Co., O.
     Ch: Ann   b 1815,12 22 d 1820, 4,28
          bur Smithfield
        Clarkson   b 1817, 3, 18
        Elwood   " 1818, 7, 11
        Mary
        Ann   " 1821, 5, 19
        Elizabeth "
        Sarah   " 1824, 8, 26
1831, 12, 24. Ann, w Joseph, d bur Smithfield

1812, 6, 20. Joseph [Burges] & w, Ann, rocf
     Deer Creek MM, dtd 1811,5,23, end by Bal-
     timore MM, E. Dist. 1811,9,12
1812, 6, 20. John [Burges] rocf Deer Creek
     MM, dtd 1811,5,23, end by Baltimore MM,
     E. Dist., 1811,9,12
1836, 5, 23. John & w, Margaret, & ch, Clark-
     son, Elwood, Mary, Anne, Elizabeth & Sa-
     rah, gct Pennsville MM
1838, 7, 23. Joseph gct Pennsville MM

BURGETT
1908, 5, 20. William relrq

BURNET

----, --, --. John, s Elias & Ann, b 1798,3,
     13; m Eliza GARRETSON, dt Isaac & Beulah,
     b 1827,2,19
1864, 11, 21. Eliza [Bernett] rocf Chesterfield
1874, 10, 19. John recrq   [MM

BURRES

1839, 12, 23. Mary (form Wood) dis mcd

BURWON

1867, 12, 12. Jane, w David, d bur Smithfield

1819, 2, 22. David & w, Jane, rocf Westland
     MM, dtd 1818,9,24
1846, 4, 20. Daniel & w, Jane, gct Short
     Creek MM, O.
1859, 8, 22. Jane rocf Short Creek MM, O.,
     dtd 1859,8,20

CADWALLADER

1808, 8, 20. John & w, Ruth, & ch, Ann, Sa-
     rah & Isaac, gct Plainfield MM
1844, 3, 18. Israel D. rocf Salem MM, dtd
     1844,2,21
1848, 2, 21. Isaac D. gct Cincinnati MM, O.;
     returned with same cert 1848,6,19

CANE

1814, 3, 19. Ann dis mcd

CAREY

----, --, --. Lewis & Rachel
     Ch: Susan   b 1808, 3, 4
         Abel   " 1809, 10, 2
         William   " 1811, 8, 9
         Aaron   " 1813, 8, 17
         Edmund   " 1815, 10, 27
         Isabella   " 1817, 9, 14
         Sarah   " 1819, 9, 4

1816, 4, 22. Lewis rst
1816, 4, 22. Susannah, Abel, William, Aaron &
     Edmond, ch Lewis & Rachel, recrq
1822, 10, 21. Lewis & w, Rachel, & ch, Susan,
     Abel, William, Aaron, Edmond, Isabella,
     Sarah & George, gct Alum Creek MM, O.
1827, 7, 23. Isabelle recrq
1831, 11, 21. Isabella Sidwell (form Cary) dis
     mcd

CARPENTER

1864, 9, 14. Charles G., s Walter T. & Susan
     M., Wayne Co., Ind.; m in Smithfield MH,
     Elizabeth A. NEWLIN, dt Jas. & Matilda,
     Jefferson Co., O.

1864, 3, 20. Elizabeth A. gct White Water MM,
     Ind.

CARR

----, --, --. William & Sarah
     Ch: Jesse   b 1792, 5, 10

     Ch: Nancy
         (alias Ann) b 1794, 9, 26
         Joshua   " 1797, 2, 13
         Thomas   " 1798, 10, 10
         Susanna   " 1801, 10, 16
         James   " 1804, 7, 27
         Prisilla   " 1807, 7, 11
1806, 7, 31. Ann d bur Smithfield
1809, 9, 20. Ann m Daniel WORRELL
1809, 12, 31. Jesse d bur Smithfield
1815, 1, 24. Sarah d bur Smithfield
1816, 10, 30. Samuel, s James & Elizabeth,
     Jefferson Co., O.; m in Plymouth MH, Mary
     HUTTON, dt Joel & Mary, d 1848,3,22,
     Jefferson Co., O.
     Ch: James   b 1818, 3, 18 d 1853, 3,13
         bur Smithfield
         Mary   b 1819, 9, 27
         Elizabeth " 1823, 8, 27 " 1852, 8, 6
         bur Smithfield
         Joel   b 1825, 11, 29
         Ann   " 1828, 10, 3
1817, 5, 28. Catharine m Anderson JUDKINS
1818, 1, 21. Aletta m Finley B. McGREW
1819, 9, 29. Susanna m Gideon LUPTON
1820, 11, 29. Kinsey, s Jas. & Elizabeth,
     Jefferson Co., O.; m in Smithfield MH, Ra-
     chel SCOTT, dt Amos & Rachel, Jefferson
     Co., O.
     Ch: Elizabeth b 1821, 10, 10
1824, 6, 30. James, s Wm. & Sarah, Jefferson
     Co., O.; m in Smithfield MH, Mary GRIFFITH,
     dt Reuben & Elizabeth, Jefferson Co., O.
     Ch: Sarah   b 1826, 5, 8
         Elizabeth " 1829, 9, 15
         Mary G.   " 1835, 11, 26
1828, 12, 24. Priscilla m Fleming STANLEY
1830, 10, 27. Aquilla, s Jas. & Elizabeth,
     Jefferson Co., O., d 1867,1,28 bur Smith-
     field; m in Smithfield MH, Mary B. ONG,
     dt Finley & Anna, Jefferson Co., O.
     Ch: Aletta   b 1833, 7, 11
         Ann   " 1836, 3, 16
         Addison   "
1833, 2, 27. Esther m John VAIL
1833, 11, 1. Elizabeth, w William, d bur
     Smithfield
1837, 2, 16. James d bur Smithfield
1847, 4, 3. Elizabeth, w James, d bur Smith-
     field
1865, 9, 17. Kinsey d bur Smithfield

1813, 9, 18. Orpha con mcd
1816, 6, 17. William gct Short Creek MM, O.,
     to m
1816, 9, 23. Elizabeth rocf Short Creek MM,
     O., dtd 1816,8,20
1816, 12, 23. Thomas gct Short Creek MM, O.
1817, 8, 18. Joshua dis mcd
1821, 7, 23. Esther, minor dt Orpha, recrq
1833, 9, 23. Orphia gct Short Creek MM, O.
1835, 8, 17. Orpha rocf Short Creek MM, O.,
     dtd 1835,5,19

CARR, continued

1837, 4, 17. James & ch, Sarah, Elizabeth &
     Mary G., gct Adrian MM, Mich.
1837, 9, 18. William gct Upper Springfield
     MM, to m Lydia Pool
1837, 12, 18. Lydia rocf Upper Springfield
     MM, dtd 1837,11,25
1840, 3, 23. William gct Adrian MM, Mich.
1841, 12, 20. Lydia gct Adrian MM, Mich.
1841, 12, 20. Mary Carter (form Carr) dis mcd
1843, 6, 19. Elizabeth Mather (form Carr) dis
     mcd
1844, 8, 19. Mary, w Aquilla, dis jas
1844, 9, 23. Aquilla dis jas
1853, 7, 18. Joel H. dis mcd
1859, 8, 22. Anna gct Salem MM
1864, 6, 20. Aletta gct Salem MM
1864, 10, 17. Aquilla rst

CARREL

1810, 5, 19. Sarah rocf Westland MM, dtd
     1810,3,24

CARSON

1811, 3, 16. Andrew & w, Isabel, & ch, Wil-
     liam, Amy, Robert, Catherine, John, Ra-
     chel & Andrew, recrq
1817, 9, 22. Andrew & w, Isabel, & ch, Robert,
     Catharine, John, Rachel, Andrew, Isabella
     & Jeremiah, gct Plainfield MM
1817, 9, 22. Amy gct Plainfield MM
1819, 3, 22. William dis mcd

CARTER

1816, 4, 22. Sarah (form Evans) dis mcd
1816, 6, 17. Pamelia (form Evans) dis mcd
1841, 12, 20. Mary (form Carr) dis mcd
1843, 2, 20. Ruth Ann (form Kinsey) dis mcd

CASE

1881, 2, 21. Charles G. recrq
1881, 4, 18. Charles G. gct Oak Ridge MM, Ind.

CATTELL

1919, 12, 24. Lydia H. P. roc
1931, 11, 25. Lydia H. P. gct Damascus MM, O.

CELLEM

1810, 5, 19. Elizabeth dis

CHADWELL

1852, 1, 19. Emily (form Ong) dis mcd
1874, 10, 19. Emily recrq

CHAPMAN

1823, 4, 22. Aaron, s Aaron & Mary, Stark
     Co., O.; m in Cross Creek MH, Mary HOBSON,
     dt Joseph & Ann, Jefferson Co., O., d
     1824,9,18 bur Richmond

1813, 5, 15. Aaron recrq
1815, 4, 15. Aaron gct Marlborough MM, O.
1823, 7, 21. Mary gct Marlborough MM

CLAPP

1819, 4, 20. Deborah m Richard PURVIANCE

1817, 9, 22. James rocf Hudson MM, N. Y., dtd
     1817,7,22
1818, 10, 19. Catharine recrq
1819, 2, 22. Deborah recrq
1827, 4, 23. Eliza (form McGrew) dis mcd
1828, 9, 22. James dis jH
1829, 2, 23. Catharine dis jH

COFFIN

1835, 12, 22. Albert M., s Chas. & Mary,
     Stark Co., O.; m in Cross Creek MH, Hannah
     FARQUHAR, dt Joseph & Beulah, Jefferson
     Co., O., d 1840,10,2 bur Cross Creek
     Ch: Joseph   b 1836, 11, 27
1837, 3, 21. Charles, s Obed & Deborah,
     Jefferson Co., O.; m in Cross Creek MH,
     Rebecca HOBSON, dt John & Mary TALBOTT,
     d 1859,11,17 bur Cross Creek
1843, 1, 2. Charles d bur Cross Creek
1838, 3, 1. Elizabeth m Wm. FARQUHAR

1836, 2, 22. Hannah gct Marlborough MM
1837, 3, 20. Charles & ch, Elizabeth &
     Charles B., rocf Marlborough MM
1840, 5, 18. Albert & w, Hannah, & s, Joseph,
     rocf Marlborough MM, dtd 1840,4,28
1843, 2, 20. Rachel (form Johns) dis mcd
1845, 7, 21. Albert M. gct Middleton MM, to
     m Elmira Townsend
1846, 4, 20. Elmira T. rocf Middleton MM, dtd
     1846,5,12
1850, 1, 21. Charles B. dis mcd
1854, 4, 17. Albert M. & w, Elmira T., & s,
     Joseph, gct Pleasant Plain MM, Ia.

COLE

1860, 9, 5. Rolen, s John & Margaret, b
----, --, --. William, s Joseph & Sarah, b
     1822,8,18; m Achsah -----, dt Elijah & M.,
     b 1822,8,18 d 1889,8,31
     Ch: Viola   b 1863, 7, 2

1808, 8, 20. Sarah dis mcd
1815, 11, 16. Sarah recrq
1832, 4, 23. Mahala (form Talbott) dis mcd
1885, 5, 22. William, Achsa R., Viola T. &
     Mary Ella V., recrq
1891, 3, 23. William relrq
1898, 2, 21. Roland recrq
1913, 2, 19. Raymond recrq
1933, 9, 20. Rolland & Viola gct Salem MM

COLLINS

1863, 3, 5. Sampson Thorton m Rebecca
     Collins, dt Moses & Jane CROSSLEY,
     b 1840,4,20
1923, 11, 30. Rebecca d

1878, 3, 18. Rebecca relrq
1880, 10, 18. Rebecca recrq

COOK

1837, 5, 31. Elisha, s Elisha & Lydia, Jefferson Co., O.; m in Smithfield MH, Mary Ann
LADD, dt Benj. & Elizabeth, d ----,3,27
bur Cross Creek
    Ch: Elizabeth b 1838, 3, 1
       Benjamin L." 1840, 3, 16
       William
          Mode   " 1842, 5, 17
       George   " 1845, 2, 27
       James D. " 1847, 6, 6
----, --, --. Elisha & Mary Jane
    Ch: Edward B. b 1860, 12, 5
       Mary Eva   " 1862, 3, 12
       Oliver M. " 1863, 7, 31
       Florence P." 1865, 5, 11

1810, 5, 19. Elias rocf Concord MM, dtd 1810,
    4,26
1813, 6, 19. Mary rocf Stillwater MM, dtd
    1813,4,27
1813, 10, 16. Elis dis mcd
1827, 4, 23. Eleanor, minor, recrq
1836, 10, 17. Elisha Jr. rocf Baltimore MM,
    E. & W. Dist., dtd 1836,9,8
1840, 2, 17. Eleanor gct Middleton MM
1858, 8, 25. Elizabeth L. Cunningham (form
    Cook) dis mcd
1859, 1, 17. Elisha Jr. con mcd
1859, 8, 22. Mary Jane rocf Short Creek MM,
    O., dtd 1859,8,20
1866, 7, 23. William M. dis violating testi-
    mony against war & mcd
1869, 2, 22. Elisha Jr. & w, Mary Jane, &
    ch, Edward B., Mary Eva, Oliver M.,
    Florence P. & Abbie Louesa, gct Spring
    Creek MM, Ia.
1880, 12, 20. Benjamin, George & James gct
    Salem MM, O.

COPE

----, --, --. Joseph H. & Rebecca M.
    Ch: Lindley   b 1826, 10, 16
       William M. " 1829, 10, 22
       Willett   " 1833, 5, 21
       Samuel   " 1834, 10, 18
1833, 8, 21. Willets, s Samuel, d
1843, 3, 8. Benjamin b
----, --, --. Joseph m Rebecca MILLHOUSE, dt
    Wm. & Martha, b 1808,3,29
    Ch: Mattie M. b 1845, 8, 24
       Sarah   " 1849, 7, 21
1845, 8, 24. Martha M. b
1849, 7, 21. Sarah b
1861, 3, 27. Samuel, s Jos. H. & Rebecca M.,
    Jefferson Co., O., b 1835,10,18; m in
    Smithfield MH, Jane L. WOOD, dt Samuel &
    Lucy, Jefferson Co., O., b 1838,1,24
    Ch: Ernest F. b 1843, 3, 31
       Francis M. " 1865, 1, 21
       Lucy B.   " 1873, 9, 17
1861, 3, 27. Willits, s Jos. H. & Rebecca M.,
    Jefferson Co., O.; m in Smithfield MH,

Martha WOOD, dt Thos. & Elizabeth, Jefferson Co., O.
    Ch: Mary E.   b 1863, 9, 14
       Thomas W. " 1865, 7, 26
       Frederick
          J.   " 1867, 6, 20
       Martha W. " 1873, 9, 11
----, --, --. William M., s J. H. & R. M.,
    b 1829,10,22; m M. A. JOHNSON, dt John &
    N., b 1843,11,19
    Ch: Ida M.   b 1868, 5, 6
       Charles C. " 1870, 5, 4
1868, 2, 24. Lindley d bur Smithfield
----, --, --. Benjamin & Amelia
    Ch: Walter T. b 1870, 3, 30
       Florence S." 1872, 3, 9
       Burton H. " 1876, 3, 18
       Alice M.   " 1882, 10, 5
       June   " 1885, 6, 4
       Harold   " 1890, 5, 3
----, --, --. Willets, s Joseph & Rebecca, b
    1833,5,20; m Martha J. -----, dt Thos. &
    Elizabeth A., b 1837,5,19
    Ch: Howard b 1881, 3, 26
----, --, --. Wood, s Willets & Mattie, b
    1866,7,26; m Elizabeth UPDEGRAFF, dt Ed-
    win & Mollie, b 1869,3,21
    Ch: Cornelius b 1895, 2, 13

1826, 7, 17. Joseph H. & w, Rebecca, rocf
    Concord MM, dtd 1826,5,24
1827, 11, 19. Willets rocf Providence MM,
    Pa., dtd 1827,11,1
1852, 1, 19. Lindley con mcd
1865, 7, 17. Elizabeth H. recrq
1869, 1, 18. William M. con mcd
1870, 4, 18. Benjamin W. con mcd
1874, 11, 23. Mary Ann recrq
1875, 4, 19. Amelia & ch, Walter T. & Flor-
    ence S., recrq
1880, 12, 20. Elizabeth gct Salem MM, O.
1881, 2, 21. Ida M., Charles & Louis T.,
    recrq
1887, 3, 21. Samuel & w, Jennie L., & ch,
    Lulu, relrq
1887, 12, 19. Frederic J. & Mary Etta V.,
    gct Freeport MM, O.
1888, 1, 23. E. I. gct Cleveland MM, O.
1888, 1, 23. Franklin M. gct Lawrence MM,
    Kans.
1889, 11, 18. F. J. & w, Etta V., & ch, Inez
    A., rocf Freeport MM, O.
1893, 4, 17. F. J. & w, Etta V., & ch, Inez
    A., gct Winona MM
1895, 4, 22. Lewis J. relrq
1895, 12, 23. Elizabeth W. rocf Fairfield MM,
    Ind.
1895, 12, 23. Cornelius Crew, s Elizabeth,
    rocf Fairfield MM, Ind.
1896, 10, 19. Arthur L. relrq
1899, 10, 23. Charles C. relrq
1900, 11, 19. T. W. & w, Elizabeth W., & s,
    Cornelius C., gct Goshen MM, O.

COPE, continued
1906, 9, 19. Howard gct First Friends Ch.,
    Alliance, O.
1909, 3, 24. Mary A. dropped from mbrp
1910, 7, 20. Frederick J. & w, Marietta
    (Etta) V., & ch, Inez & Lois, rocf Adrian
    MM, Mich.
1932, 8, 21. June relrq

COPELAND
1850, 10, 7. Mary, dt Nathan & Eliza, b

1911, 2, 22. John M. recrq

COPPOCK
1840, 12, 30. Joshua, s John & Catharine,
    Columbiana Co., O.; m in Smithfield MH,
    Jane HOYLE, dt John & Elizabeth, Jefferson
    Co., O.

1841, 5, 17. Jane H. gct Newgarden MM

COWGILL
1869, 10, 22. John, s Thos. & Sarah, Cham-
    paign Co., O.; m in Smithfield MH, Eleanor
    H. CREW, dt Jacob & Mary H., Belmont Co.,
    O.

1869, 12, 20. Eleanor H. gct Goshen MM

COX,
----, --, --. William m Elvirah -----, dt
    Joseph & Jane, b 1850,5,2
    Ch: John   b 1872, 1, 8
        James W.   " 1874, 6, 6
        Lena   " 1884, 8, 23

1889, 2, 19. Walter, John & James recrq
1891, 12, 21. Alvira E. recrq
1893, 3, 20. Lena May recrq
1899, 5, 22. Alvira & dt, Lena, relrq
1900, 9, 17. Walter dropped from mbrp

CREW
----, --, --. Henry d 1856,12,22 bur Cross
    Creek; m Margaret ----- d 1873,4,7 bur
    Cross Creek
    Ch: Elizabeth b 1823, 4, 14 d 1833, 2,25
            bur Richmond
        James   b 1826, 1, 21
        William
          Henry   " 1829, 6, 10 d ----, --,--
            bur Cross Creek
        Benjamin L.b 1831, 4, 10
1830, 4, 28. Anna m John PENROSE
1833, 5, 2. Elizabeth Ann m Thos. WOOD
1833, 11, 27. Narcissa m Chas. NICHOLSON
1834, 2, 26. Jacob, s Jacob & Elizabeth,
    Jefferson Co., O.; m in Smithfield MH,
    Mary HARVEY, dt Job & Eleanor, Washington
    Co., Pa.
1840, 4, 1. Sarah Ann m Geo. LUPTON
1849, 12, 19. Hannah m Wm. BRIGGS

----, --, --. William H. & Deborah
    Ch: Henry   b 1859, 6, 7
        Charles H. " 1861, 3, 16
        Caroline L." 1864, 12, 4
        Winona B. " 1867, 1, 20
1869, 10, 22. Eleanor H. m John COWGILL
1881, 4, 10. Benjamin, s Henry & Margaret, b

1817, 2, 17. Henry rocf Wayn Oak MM, Va., dtd
    1816,12,7
1822, 1, 21. Henry gct Short Creek MM, to m
    Margaret Bailey
1822, 7, 22. Margaret rocf Short Creek MM, O.,
    dtd 1822,5,21
1826, 5, 22. Anna rocf Waine Oak MM, Va., dtd
    1826,3,4
1828, 9, 22. Jacob rocf Wayn Oke MM, Va., dtd
    1828,8,2
1828, 9, 22. Elizabeth & dt, Elizabeth A.,
    rocf Wayn Oke MM, Va., dtd 1828,8,2
1832, 7, 23. Sarah & dt, Narcissa, Sarah Ann,
    Hannah & Eliza Jane, rocf Wayne Oak MM,
    Va., dtd 1832,6,2
1836, 5, 23. Jacob & w, Mary, & dt, Eliza-
    beth, gct Flushing MM
1845, 7, 21. James gct WD MM
1847, 4, 19. James rocf SD MM, dtd 1847,3,24
1850, 5, 20. James con mcd
1858, 1, 19. James gct Cincinnati MM, O.
1859, 1, 17. William H. con mcd
1860, 3, 19. Deborah A. rocf Short Creek MM,
    O.
1863, 5, 16. Benjamin L. con mcd
1867, 3, 18. Mary & Eleanor rocf Flushing
    MM, O., dtd 1867,2,23
1871, 9, 18. Mary H. gct Goshen MM, O.
1873, 4, 21. Deborah A. & ch, Henry, Caro-
    line L. & Winona B., gct Wilmington MM
1900, 12, 17. Benjamin L. relrq

CRIPPEN
----, --, --. William [Crippin], s Henry & Sa-
    rah, b 1847,9,28; m Catharine STUBBINS,
    dt Thomas & Elizabeth, b 1851,5,5
    Ch: Ora   b 1880, 3, 18
        Robert   " 1882, 8, 5

1879, 11, 17. William recrq
1881, 6, 20. Catharine recrq
1898, 2, 21. Ora recrq
1912, 4, 24. Catharine relrq

CROSS
1883, 10, 22. Elizabeth gct Kansas City MM,
    Mo.

CROSSLEY
1925, 11, 25. Plummer & w, Jessie, recrq

CUMLEY
1814, 10, 15. Priscilla con mcd
1815, 6, 17. John rst on consent of Gun-
    powder MM, Md.

CUNNINGHAM
1858, 8, 25. Elizabeth L. (form Cook) dis mcd

CURL
1887, 1, 17. John G. recrq

DAUGHERTY
1840, 9, 21. Sarah (form Watson) dis mcd

DAVIDSON
1881, 2, 21. James & Luella recrq
1888, 5, 21. James dropped from mbrp

DAVIS
1809, 2, 23. Ellis, s Abram & Hannah, Jeffer-
        son Co., O.; m in Cross Creek MH, Ann
        QUAINTANCE, dt Joseph & Susanna, Jeffer-
        son Co., O.

1809, 6, 17. Ellis & w, Ann, gct New Garden
        MM

DAWSON
1884, 4, 21. Susan C. recrq
1885, 5, 22. William E. dropped from mbrp
1885, 6, 22. Ella C. dropped from mbrp

DEAN
1840, 4, 20. Stephen [Deen], minor, rocf
        Newgarden MM, dtd 1840,2,20
1842, 5, 23. Stephen gct Short Creek MM, O.
1844, 4, 22. Stephen rocf Short Creek MM, O.,
        dtd 1844,2,20
1845, 6, 23. Milton, minor, rocf New Garden
        MM, dtd 1845,5,22
1847, 8, 23. Stephen gct Salem MM
1848, 4, 17. Milton gct New Garden MM

DEGARMO
1933, 12, 20. Ola May recrq

DENNIS
1825, 12, 19. Aaron rocf Providence MM, dtd
        1825,8,26
1826, 5, 22. Aaron gct Flushing MM

DEWEES
1828, 8, 28. David B., s Samuel & Hannah,
        Jefferson Co., O.; m in Cross Creek MH,
        Rachel KIRBY, dt Thomas & Rebecca, Jeffer-
        son Co., O.

1829, 7, 20. Rachel gct Deerfield MM

DIFFORD
1906, 6, 20. William B. & Mary A. rocf First
        Friends Ch., Cleveland, O.

DILLON
1842, 2, 21. Martha rocf Stillwater MM, dtd
        1841,10,23
1850, 8, 19. Martha gct Baltimore MM

DULA
1813, 7, 17. Lydia dis

DULING
1827, 9, 17. Elizabeth (form Hammond) dis mcd

DUNGAN
1815, 10, 21. Mary [Dungen] rocf Muncey MM,
        dtd 1814,11,23, end by Plainfield MM,
        1815,8,31
1822, 6, 17. Mary gct Short Creek MM, O.
1884, 12, 22. William O. recrq
1893, 7, 17. Oliver dropped from mbrp

EARNSHAW
1823, 1, 2. Mary m James MEGRAIEL
1824, 12, 2. George Jr., s Geo. & Ann, Jef-
        ferson Co., O.; m in Cross Creek MH, Sa-
        rah PLUMMER, dt Joseph & Mary, Jefferson
        Co., O.

1821, 3, 19. George [Ernshaw] & w, Ann, rocf
        Pontifract MM, Eng., dtd 1820,7,17
1821, 3, 19. Hannah [Ernshaw] rocf Ponti-
        fract MM, Eng., dtd 1820,7,17
1821, 7, 23. Mary rocf Brig House MM, Eng.,
        dtd 1820,8,18
1821, 8, 20. George Jr. rocf Hollowfield MM,
        Pa., dtd 1821,2,9
1829, 4, 20. George Sr. gct Alum Creek MM
1829, 4, 20. George Jr. & w, Sarah, gct
        Alum Creek MM

EASLEY
1822, 3, 18. Isaac, minor, rocf Flushing MM,
        O., dtd 1822,1,25
1831, 10, 17. Isaac dis mcd

ELLIOTT
1900, 2, 19. Cora Hammond relrq

EMBREE
1852, 11, 19. Samuel gct Pennsville MM, O.

ENGLAND
1839, 9, 23. Elizabeth (form McGrew) dis mcd

ERVINE
1881, 10, 17. Mary Virginia recrq

EVANS
1808, 4, 20. Evan, s Cadwallader & Sarah,
        Jefferson Co., O.; m in Plymouth MH, Mary
        BRITE, dt Wm. Jones & Rebecca, Jefferson
        Co., O.

1814, 9, 17. Evan & w, Mary, & ch, Rebeckah,
        James Cadwallader & Amos Hutton, gct
        Plainfield MM
1814, 11, 19. James dis mcd
1815, 5, 20. Asher gct Plainfield MM
1815, 9, 16. Benjamin gct Plainfield MM
1816, 4, 22. Sarah Carter (form Evans) dis

EVANS, continued
mcd
1816, 6, 17.   Pamelia Carter (form Evans) dis
mcd
1823, 10, 20.   John dis jas
1825, 1, 17.   Evan & w, Mary, & ch, Rebecca,
James, Cadwalader, Amos Hutton, Sarah,
Henrietta & Asher, rocf Flushing MM, dtd
1824,6,25
1828, 11, 17.   Evan, James, Mary & Rebecca dis
jH
1829, 2, 23.   Amos, Sarah, Henrietta, Asher
Park & Wm. Jones, ch Evan, gct Short Creek
MM, O.
1840, 7, 20.   Amanda (form McGrew) dis mcd

FARMER
1830, 6, 21.   William & w, Mary, & ch, Sarah
& Isaac Parker, rocf Short Creek MM, O.,
dtd 1830,2,23
1836, 4, 18.   William & w, Mary, & ch, Sarah
P., Isaac Parker, Mary Cassander, John &
Jacob, gct Sandy Spring MM
1856, 5, 19.   Warrick Price gct Sandy Spring
MM, to m Beulah R. Farmer
1859, 5, 23.   William B. Price gct Sandy
Spring MM, to m Ellen A. Farmer

FARQUHAR
1810, 4, 26.   Joseph, s Thos. & Hannah, Washington Co., Pa.; m in Cross Creek MH, Beulah TALBOTT, dt Benjamin & Susannah, Jefferson Co., O.
Ch: Hannah   b 1811, 2, 22
    Elizabeth " 1812, 10, 23
    Benjamin   " 1814, 9, 21 d 1844,11,21
      bur Cross Creek
    William   b 1816, 4, 5
    Mary S.   " 1818, 5, 13
1829, 7, 4.   Sarah d bur Richmond
1834, 1, 13.   William d
1834, 8, 13.   William d bur Cross Creek
1835, 12, 3.   John, s Thos. & Hannah, Jefferson Co., O.; m in Cross Creek MH, Mary T.
TALBOTT, dt Kinsey & Deborah, Jefferson
Co., O.
1835, 12, 22.   Hannah m Albert M. COFFIN
1838, 3, 1.   William, s Jos. & Beulah, Jefferson Co., O.; m in Cross Creek MH,
Elizabeth COFFIN, dt Chas. & Mary, Jefferson Co., O.
Ch: Beulah T. b 1840, 9, 3
    Mary C.   " 1843, 6, 4
    Charles C. " 1845, 1, 18
    Hannah   " 1847, 7, 25
    Benjamin   " 1849, 1, 11
1842, 6, 21.   Elizabeth m John ALLMON
1843, 8, 31.   Hannah Maria m Jos. ALLMAN
1847, 12, 30.   Mary S. m Jos. PLUMMER

1810, 3, 17.   Joseph rocf Westland MM, dtd
1810,2,24
1810, 7, 21.   Allen rocf Westland MM, dtd

1810,6,23
1812, 5, 16.   Allen gct Westland MM
1813, 6, 19.   Sarah rocf Redstone MM, dtd
1813,5,28
1816, 2, 19.   Allen rocf London Grove MM,
Pa., dtd 1815,12,6
1816, 7, 22.   William rocf Westland MM, dtd
1816,6,27
1817, 10, 20.   Allen gct Plainfield MM, to m
1818, 2, 23.   Edith rocf Plainfield MM, dtd
1818,1,22
1818, 7, 21.   William dis mcd to first cousin
1818, 7, 21.   Hannah (form Talbott) dis mcd
to first cousin
1822, 4, 22.   Alan & w, Edith, & ch, Martha &
Hannah, gct Flushing MM, O.
1835, 3, 23.   John rocf Westland MM, dtd 1835,
2,18
1836, 10, 17.   Hannah Maria, minor, recrq
1840, 2, 17.   Elizabeth Sr. gct Middleton MM
1854, 4, 17.   Joseph & w, Beulah, gct Spring
Creek MM, Ia.
1854, 4, 17.   William & w, Elizabeth, & ch,
Bula T., Mary C., Charles C., Hannah,
Benjamin & Rebecca, gct Spring Creek MM,
Ia.

FARRINGTON
1825, 12, 19.   Judith rocf Sandy Spring MM,
dtd 1825,11,25
1826, 3, 20.   Jesse rocf Sandy Spring MM, dtd
1826,2,24
1828, 10, 20.   Judith gct Sandy Spring MM
1844, 10, 21.   Jesse K. [Ferrington] dis disunity

FISHER
----, --, --.   Francis & Susanna
Ch: Joshua   b 1823, 10, 14
    Susanna   " 1825, 2, 9
    Samuel D. " 1826, 12, 13
    John   " 1828, 10, 10

1809, 7, 15.   Samuel dis
1810, 5, 19.   Rachel Pickering (form Fisher)
dis mcd
1819, 4, 19.   Cassander Morton (form Fisher)
dis mcd
1819, 5, 17.   Ann dis
1821, 3, 19.   Joel dis mcd
1821, 3, 19.   Francis con mcd
1822, 10, 21.   Susanna recrq
1828, 9, 22.   Ruth dis jas
1831, 9, 18.   Francis dis jas
1831, 10, 17.   Susanna dis jas
1844, 4, 22.   Joshua dis mcd
1844, 6, 17.   Susanna James (form Fisher) dis
mcd
1887, 1, 17.   Mary recrq
1887, 1, 17.   Joshua, Maude J., Henry A.,
Susan M. & Sarah V., recrq
1893, 7, 17.   Henry dropped from mbrp

FLANNER
1816, 7, 22. William & w, Peninah, & ch, Abigail, Jacob, William, Peninah, Sarah & Rebecca, rocf Short Creek MM, dtd 1816,6,18
1817, 9, 22. William & w, Peninah, & ch, Jacob, William, Peninah, Sarah & Rebecca, gct Short Creek MM, O.
1817, 9, 22. Abigail gct Short Creek MM, O.
1817, 9, 22. William & w, Peninah, & ch, Jacob, William, Peninah, Sarah & Rebecca, gct Short Creek MM, O.
1838, 10, 22. Nathan Talbott gct Short Creek MM, O., to m Abigail Flanner

FOLGER
1842, 7, 15. James Ladd gct Marlborough MM, to m Elizabeth Folger
1844, 5, 20. Mary rocf Marlborough MM, dtd 1844,3,26

FORD
1885, 1, 19. Jacob recrq
1887, 1, 17. Joseph recrq
1887, 5, 23. Joshua recrq
1893, 7, 17. Joshua & Joseph dropped from mbrp

FOREMAN
1813, 7, 17. Rachel rocf Redstone MM, dtd 1813,2,7
1818, 4, 20. Rachel Naylor (form Foreman) dis mcd with first cousin
1822, 9, 23. John rocf Redstone MM, Pa., dtd 1822,7,3
1826, 9, 18. Jane gct Redstone MM, Pa.

FORNER
1884, 12, 22. David H. recrq
1889, 2, 18. H. D. relrq

FRANCIS
1892, 5, --. Ida M. relrq

FREEBORN
1811, 7, 20. Samuel rocf Rhode Island MM, dtd 1811,4,25
1814, 9, 17. Samuel gct Concord MM

FRENCH
1817, 7, 3. Thomas, s James & Sarah, Jefferson Co.; m in Cross Creek MH, Elizabeth TALBOTT, dt Jos. & Mary, Jefferson Co., O., d 1824,2,15 bur Richmond
     Ch: Allen T.   b 1818, 4, 2
         Joseph T.   " 1819, 8, 21
         James F.   " 1821, 6, 10
         William F. " 1823, 3, 30
         Thomas m 2nd 1827,--,--, Martha BRYANT, in Upper Springfield MM
     Ch: Hannah   b 1828, 3, 15

1817, 3, 17. Thomas recrq
1827, 6, 18. Thomas gct Upper Springfield

MM, to m Martha Bryant
1828, 6, 23. Martha rocf Upper Springfield MM, dtd 1827,12,22
1833, 6, 17. Thomas & w, Martha, & ch, Allen, Joseph T., James, William F., Karon, Elizabeth & Newton, gct Upper Springfield MM

FRY
1884, 12, 22. George recrq

FULTON
1841, 4, 5. Hannah d

1824, 5, 17. Hannah rst on consent of Fairfax MM, Va.

GARRETSON
----, --, --. Casparis d 1866,5,31 bur Smithfield; m Sarah ----- d 1863,9,20 bur Smithfield
     Ch: Rachel   b 1806, 9, 10
         Isaac   " 1808, 1, 28
         Nathan   " 1809, 4, 20
         Joseph   " 1810, 12, 15
         Hannah   " 1812, 7, 3
         Mary Ann " 1814, 8, 23

1809, 10, 22. John & w, Henrietta, & ch, William, Joel, Anna, Mary & Hannah, gct Concord MM
1813, 5, 15. Amos & w, Mary, & ch, Eliza, Mary Ann & Talbott, rocf Pipe Creek MM, dtd 1812,12,19
1813, 12, 18. Amos & fam gct Plainfield MM
1814, 3, 19. Patience gct Concord MM
1816, 12, 23. Mary & Armella gct Concord MM
1826, 7, 17. Isaac dis mcd
1826, 9, 18. Mary, minor, rocf Pipe Creek MM, dtd 1826,8,19
1827, 1, 22. Elizabeth rocf Indian Spring MM, dtd 1826,7,5
1827, 10, 22. Bulah & dt, Eliza, rocf Short Creek MM, O., dtd 1827,5,22
1828, 1, 21. Jazar rocf Pipe Creek MM, dtd 1827,11,17
1825, 11, 21. Rachel Kirk (form Garretson) dis mcd
1828, 9, 22. Jazar dis jH
1828, 11, 17. Elizabeth dis jH
1829, 2, 23. Nathan dis jH
1832, 1, 23. Hannah Wiley (form Garretson) dis mcd
1835, 5, 18. Beulah & ch, Eliza, Emily, David & Eli, gct Deerfield MM
1835, 7, 26. Mary dis jH
1837, 4, 17. Joseph dis mcd
1846, 8, 17. Mary Ann Hussey (form Garretson) con mcd

GARDNER
1888, 3, 19. John B. W. recrq

GASAWAY
1881, 2, 21. Carrie recrq

GEARY
1881, 2, 21. Laura recrq
1883, 12, 17. Laura [Garey] dis

GEORGE
1816, 3, 18. Sarah (form Purviance) dis mcd
1826, 1, 23. Sarah rst at Flushing MM on con-
    sent of this mtg
1832, 4, 23. Mary (form Purviance) dis mcd

GIFFORD
1863, 9, 30. William, s Isaac R. & Phebe R.,
    Bristol Co., Mass.; m in Smithfield MH,
    Lydia LADD, dt Benj. W. & Hannah T., Jef-
    ferson Co., O.

1854, 7, 18. Thomas gct Dartmouth MM, Mass.,
    to m Hannah P. Gifford
1874, 12, 21. Lydia & ch, Robert Austin &
    Isaac Reynard, gct Chicago MM, Ill.

GILBERT
1841, 11, 22. James W. McGrew gct Providence
    MM, Pa., to m Anne Gilbert

GOODWIN
1875, 4, 19. Jesse & w, Alice Ann, & ch,
    Mary Ida, Ella & Anna Lillie, recrq
1881, 4, 18. Jesse & w, Alice A., & ch, Mary
    Ida & Ellen, gct Oak Ridge MM, Ind.

GRAFTON
----, --, --. George W., s Israel & Jane,
    b 1841,5,21; m Lucinda MORROW
    Ch: Hettie   b 1868, 3, 23
        Sadie   " 1879, 8, 17
        Victor   " 1884, 8, 12
        Florence

1886, 3, 22. Hettie, James W. & Emerson F.
    recrq
1889, 3, 18. George W. & w, Lucinda, recrq
1896, 1, 20. James & w, Mary, & ch gct Short
    Creek MM, O.
1898, 2, 21. Sarah recrq
1925, 6, --. G. W. d 1925,6,11 ae 84

GREEN
1821, 5, 30. William, s Wm. & Mary, Jeffer-
    son Co., O.; m in Smithfield MH, Rachel
    HOYLE, dt John & Sarah, Montgomery Co.,
    Pa.
    Ch: Hannah   b 1822, 2, 19
        Joseph   " 1823, 12, 21
        Sarah   " 1826, 2, 17

1818, 11, 23. William rocf Allendale MM, Eng.,
    dtd 1818,5,20
1826, 10, 23. William & w, Rachel, & ch, Han-
    nah, Joseph & Sarah, gct Stillwater MM

GRIFFITH
1824, 6, 30. Mary m James CARR
1864, 10, 26. Amos, s Amos & Edith, Fayette
    Co., Pa.; m in Smithfield MH, Mary E.
    WOOD, dt Samuel & Lucy, Jefferson Co., O.

1819, 8, 23. Mary, minor, rocf Short Creek
    MM, O., dtd 1819,4,20
1823, 6, 23. Elizabeth rocf Flushing MM, dtd
    1823,4,25
1837, 4, 17. Elizabeth gct Adrian MM, Mich.
1865, 9, 18. Mary E. gct Redstone MM, Pa.
1868, 3, 23. Amos T. & w, Mary E., & dt,
    Lucy Amelia, rocf Salem MM, dtd 1868,2,20
1870, 5, 23. Amos T. & w, Mary E., & dt,
    Lucy Amelia, gct Alliance MM

GRIMSHAW
----, --, --. John m Margaret ----- d 1835,10,
    16 bur Carmel, O.
    Ch: Rachel   b 1804, 10, 20
        Margaret " 1812, 9, 21
1820, 3, 1. Tabitha m Benj. HOYLE
1825, 10, 19. Rachel m Andrew SCHOLFIELD
1826, 11, 1. Sarah m David WORRELL
1827, 2, 21. Jane m Chas. HAMBLETON
1836, 6, 1. Margaret m Jos. F. TALBOTT
1836, 8, 24. Phebe m John SEARS

1817, 10, 20. John & w, Margaret, & dt, Sarah,
    Hannah, Tabitha, Jane, Margaret, Rachel &
    Phebe, rocf Nine Partners MM, N. Y., dtd
    1817,9,18
1825, 3, 21. Jane gct New Garden MM
1826, 11, 20. Jean rocf New Garden MM, dtd
    1826,10,26
1837, 5, 22. Hannah gct Stillwater MM

GRIST
1867, 6, 22. Ann W. rst
1868, 8, 26. Ann W. m Abraham J. HOBSON

GRUMMEN
1888, 3, 19. Victor W. recrq
1891, 2, 23. V. W. [Grummans] dropped from
    mbrp

HAGUE
1865, 1, 23. Samuel E. & w, Mary H., rocf
    Short Creek MM, O.
1867, 5, 20. James R. rocf Short Creek MM,
    O., dtd 1867,2,21
1870, 12, 19. Samuel & w, Mary, & ch, William
    H., Thos. W. & Anna N., gct Springdale
    MM, Iowa
1872, 12, 23. James R. dis jas

HAINES
1828, 5, 19. Atlantic rocf Redstone MM, Pa.,
    dtd 1828,2,27
1829, 10, 19. Atlantic gct Redstone MM
1849, 11, 19. Mary (form Nailor) dis mcd
1853, 8, 18. Elizabeth [Haynes] (form Nay-

HAINES, continued
    lor) dis mcd
1886, 12, 20. Lizzie [Haynes] (form Ong) relrq

HALL
1816, 8, 19. Mary rocf Short Creek MM, O.,
    dtd 1816,6,18
1885, 1, 19. George W. recrq
1888, 3, 19. George recrq
1893, 7, 17. George dropped from mbrp

HAMBLETON
1827, 2, 21. Charles, s Wm. & Mary, Columbiana
    Co., O.; m in Smithfield MH, Jane GRIMSHAW,
    dt John & Margaret, Jefferson Co., O.

1827, 4, 23. Jane gct Carmel MM
1858, 4, 19. Nathan L. Wood gct Driftwood MM,
    Ind., to m Mary Hambleton

HAMILTON
1856, 9, 22. Rachel Ann (form Ong) dis mcd

HAMMOND
----, --, --. John m Rachel ----- d 1827,2,23
    bur Richmond
    Ch: James   b 1799, 4, 1
        John   " 1800, 9, 27 d 1801,12,--
        bur Richmond
        Thomas   b 1802, 4, 10
        Robert   " 1804, 3, 11 " 1825, 4,21
        bur Richmond
        Mary   b 1806, 1, 10
        Elizabeth " 1807, 12, 29
        John   " 1809, 12, 5
        George   " 1812, 3, 31
        Samuel   " 1814, 5, 31 d 1815,10,--
        bur Richmond
        Mahala   b 1816, 6, 6 d 1836,10,13
        bur Richmond
        Joseph   b 1818, 5, 13
        Amy   " 1820, 6, 16
1812, 12, 2. William, s Geo. & Deborah, Jef-
    ferson Co., O., d 1844,8,15; m in Smith-
    field MH, Elizabeth BALL, dt James & Mary,
    Brook Co., Va.
    Ch: Rachel   b 1815, 7, 31
        Joseph   " 1817, 12, 30
        Nathan   " 1822, 4, 28
1815, 10, 25. Ruth m Abraham NAYLOR
1822, 4, --. Nathan, s Wm. & Elizabeth, b
1824, 4, 28. Benjamin, s Geo. & Deborah,
    Jefferson Co., O.; m in Smithfield MH,
    Margaret NAYLOR, dt James & Margaret, Jef-
    ferson Co., O.
    Ch: Maria   b 1825, 3, 11
        Mary   " 1826, 9, 11
        George   " 1828, 2, 29
        Deborah   " 1829, 12, 20
        Margaret   " 1829, 12, 20
        Hiram   " 1830, 2, 20
        Isaac   " 1834, 1, 17
        James   " 1835, 12, 13 d 1853,12,16

    Ch: Anderson   b 1838, 11, 4
        Rachel   " 1840, 11, 8
        William   " 1845, 5, 17
1826, 7, 21. Eliza Ann, dt John T. & Jane
    NAYLOR, b
1826, 8, 16. Deborah, w George, d bur Smith-
    field
1828, 5, 1. John, s James & Mary, Jefferson
    Co., O.; m in Cross Creek MH, Mary PLUM-
    MER, dt Joseph & Mary, Jefferson Co., O.
1840, 11, 1. George d bur Smithfield
1844, 12, 25. Maria m Ammi WILLITS
----, --, --. Joseph & Harriet
    Ch: Mary Ann   b 1846, 3, 18
        Amor P.   " 1848, 3, 23
        Rachel E. " 1849, 12, 23
        Joseph I. " 1852, 6, 1
        Oliver B. " 1857, 6, 14
        Cordelia   " 1860, 3, 21
1845, 11, 16. John d
1846, 12, 30. Thomas, s John & Rachel, Jeffer-
    son Co., O.; m in Smithfield MH, Ann ME-
    GRAIL, dt Thos. & Rebecca, Jefferson Co.,
    O.
----, --, --. Joseph m Harriet PIDGEON, dt
    Amos & Ann, b 1819,11,20
    Ch: Amos P.   b 1848, 3, 23
        Oliver B. " 1857, 6, 14
1847, 9, 2. Amy m Alfred MEGRAIL
----, --, --. Nathan & Eliza Ann
    Ch: Mary   b 1850, 10, 7
        William   " 1853, 5, 2
        John N.   " 1856, 2, 16
        Henry N.   " 1859, 12, 13
1850, 7, 18. Hannah M., dt James, b
1857, 3, 13. Mary E., dt J. & S. A., b
1860, 12, 26. Mary m Joel WILLITTS
1863, 10, 4. Hannah, w Thomas, d bur Smith-
    field
----, --, --. Hugh, s Bezaleel & Louisa,
    b 1845,10,20; m Elizabeth C. CARTER, dt
    J. W. & Mary, b 1844,2,25
1865, 1, 4. Cordelia, dt James & Harriett, d
1867, 3, 2. Mary d bur Cross Creek
1868, 5, 16. Thomas d bur Smithfield
1871, 10, 29. Thomas d
1871, 1, 27. Amanda d bur Smithfield
1874, 2, 22. Joseph d
----, --, --. William, s Nathan & E. A., b
    1853,5,2; m Ida E. ONG, dt M. & C. A.,
    b 1855,4,6
    Ch: Mary C.   b 1875, 10, 20
        Annie C.   " 1876, 10, 16
        Frank N.   " 1878, 2, 14
        Frederick M. 1878, 2, 14
----, --, --. Oliver B., s Joseph & Harriet,
    b 1857,6,14; m Jessie F. WHITE, dt Thos.
    & Maggie, b 1861,8,17
    Ch: J. Edgar   b 1886, 11, 9
1886, 2, 13. Clarence, s Wm. & Mary, b
----, --, --. George N., s Nathan & Anna,
    b 1861,6,11; m Ora HILL, dt J. E., b 1861,
    1,6

HAMMOND, George N. & Ora, continued
     Ch: Edwin   b 1888, 4, 18
          Mary   " 1891, 4, 18
1932, --, --. Amos d

1811, 5, 18. Deborah McGrew (form Hammond)
     dis mcd
1813, 12, 18. Elizabeth recrq
1815, 12, 18. Mary dis
1816, 2, 19. James dis mcd
1819, 11, 22. James gct Monallen MM, Pa.
1825, 12, 19. James recrq
1827, 9, 17. Elizabeth Duling (form Hammond)
     dis mcd
1833, 10, 21. James C. gct Short Creek MM, O.
1835, 12, 21. Thomas con mcd
1839, 6, 17. Joseph dis mcd
1840, 7, 20. John Jr. dis mcd
1841, 10, --. George con mcd
1843, 10, 23. Joseph gct Pennsville MM, to m
     Harriet Pigeon
1844, 6, 17. Harriet rocf Pennsville MM, O.,
     dtd 1844,5,16
1845, 1, 20. Elizabeth dis disunity
1849, 4, 23. Deborah McGrew (form Hammond)
     con mcd
1850, 6, 17. Nathan con mcd
1850, 6, 17. Eliza Ann con mcd
1855, 8, 20. George & Hiram gct Western Plain
     MM, Ia.
1855, 9, 17. Margaret Willets (form Hammond)
     con mcd
1859, 9, 19. Hannah rst
1859, 11, 21. Hannah gct Salem MM, O.
1861, 1, 17. Hannah & Amanda rocf Salem MM
1861, 6, 17. Laura E., minor in care of Jo-
     seph & Isabella L. Jones, recrq
1861, 10, 21. Hannah M., minor in care of Jo-
     seph & Phebe Hoyle, recrq
1863, 2, 23. Catharine recrq
1864, 1, 18. Benjamin & w, Margaret, & s,
     William, gct LeGrand MM, Ia.
1864, 1, 18. Isaac N., Anderson & Rachel gct
     LeGrand MM, Ia.
1864, 12, 19. Thomas recrq
1869, 7, 19. Bezaleel recrq
1871, 10, 23. Laura E., minor, gct Chicago
     MM, Ill.
1871, 11, 20. Catharine gct Salem MM
1873, 3, 17. Hugh & Elizabeth recrq
1875, 4, 19. Ida recrq
1884, 12, 22. Kittie S. & Jesse recrq
1884, 12, 22. Olive Lena, dt Henry & Kittie,
     recrq
1885, 2. 23. Mary E. rocf Short Creek MM, O.,
     dtd 1885,1,21
1886, 12, 20. Orah W. recrq
1888, 9, 17. Hugh & w relrq
1900, 6, 18. George N. & fam relrq
1903, 10, 21. Frank relrq
1904, 3, 23. Anna dropped from mbrp
1913, 4, 23. Oliver B. & w, Jessie, relrq

HARGRAVE
1827, 12, 17. Joseph rocf Wayne Oak MM, Va.,
     dtd 1827,11,3
1828, 10, 20. Joseph gct Cedar Creek MM, Va.,
     to m Deborah Bates
1829, 4, 20. Joseph gct Short Creek MM, O.

HARTLEY
1815, 3, 18. Mahlon & w, Charity, & ch, John,
     Noah, Sarah, Joseph, Melinda & Elizabeth,
     rocf Nottingham MM, Md., dtd 1813,3,13
1818, 2, 23. Mahlon & w, Charity, & ch, John,
     Noah, Sarah, Joseph, Malinda, Elizabeth,
     Mary & Ebi, gct Stillwater MM

HARVEY
1834, 2, 26. Mary m Jacob CREW

1821, 11, 19. Amos rocf Westland MM, Pa., dtd
     1821,10,29
1821, 11, 19. Mary rocf Westland MM, Pa., dtd
     1821,10,29
1833, 4, 22. Amos dis mcd

HASHMAN
1915, 9, 22. Charles recrq

HAWORTH
1912, 12, 25. Arthur J. & w, Daisy S., & ch,
     Francis Murray & Ruth Esther, gct Ceiling
     MM, Okla.
1916, 12, 20. Arthur J. & w, Daisy S., & ch,
     Francis Murry & Ruth Esther, gc

HEALD
1845, 7, 21. Matthew Watson gct Sandy Spring
     MM, to m Eliza Heald

HEATON
----, --, --. John P., s Amos & Sarah, b 1844,
     5,24; m Cassie KANE
     Ch: Comly T.   b 1869, 10, 25
          Rutherford " 1876, 11, 9
               B.
          John C.   " 1878, 12, 26
          Evan P.   " 1881, 1, 23

1874, 12, 21. Cassie & ch, Comley T. & Mary
     Edna, recrq
1875, 3, 22. James P. recrq
1875, 10, 18. Amos recrq
1900, 4, 28. John P. relrq
1904, 9, 21. John C. gct West Elkton MM, O.
1910, 6, 22. John C. rocf West Elkton MM, O.

HEMSLEY
1874, 7, 14. Mary E., w Wm., dt E. W. & W. E.
     Phipps, b

1904, 3, 23. William R. & Howard recrq

HENDERSON
1892, 12, 19. Ida M. relrq

HENRY
1932, 8, 21. Mrs. Katheryn recrq

HEXTON
1824, 5, 17. Maria (form Pool) dis mcd

HICKS
----, --, --. John & Martha
       Ch: Frank   b 1870, 10, 13
           Daniel   " 1876, 10, 10
----, --, --. Charles, s Daniel & Sarah,
      b 1864,11,1; m Emma -----, dt Sampson &
      Rebecca, b 1869,5,3

1898, 2, 21. Frank & Daniel recrq
1898, 3, 21. Charlie recrq
1900, 8, 20. Frank relrq
1906, 12, 19. Emma relrq
1907, 9, 25. Charles relrq
1907, 12, 25. George M. & w, Jennie, (minister)
      rocf Cleveland MM, O.
1908, 4, 22. George Lawrence, s Geo. M. &
      Jennie M., rocf Cleveland MM, O.
1910, 10, 17. George & w, Jennie, & s, Geo.
      Lawrence, gct Raisin Center MM

HILER
1819, 4, 19. Catharine recrq

HILL
1860, 11, 28. John C., s John & Mary, Jeffer-
      son Co., O.; m in Smithfield MH, Hannah
      S. LADD, dt John & Lydia WOOD, Jefferson
      Co., O.
1866, 12, 26. Joseph, s John C. & Rachel,
      Jefferson Co., O.; m in Smithfield MH,
      Elizabeth L. KINSEY, dt Samuel & Lucy
      WOOD, Jefferson Co., O.
1867, 4, 17. Hannah S., w John C., d bur
      Smithfield

1810, 2, 17. Mary dis mcd
1861, 4, 22. John C. rocf Short Creek MM, O.
1867, 7, 22. Hannah S. d 1867,4,19 ae 66 (an
      elder)
1867, 7, 17. Elizabeth L. gct Short Creek MM,
      O.
1867, 11, 18. John C. gct Short Creek MM, O.

HOBSON
----, --, --. John d 1851,12,19 bur Cross
      Creek; m Belinda ----- d 1837,11,27 bur
      Richmond
      Ch: Joseph   b 1802, 12, 10 d 1827,12, 9
            bur Richmond
          William   b 1804, 11, 10 " 1807,10,24
            bur Cross Creek
          Stephen   b 1806, 11, 2
          John   " 1808, 8, 24
          Ann   " 1810, 7, 20 " 1842,12, 1
            bur Richmond
          Thomas   b 1812, 7, 13
          Mary   " 1815, 3, 13 " 1842, 6, 6

      bur Richmond
      Ch: Phebe   b 1817, 4, 14
          Belinda   " 1820, 9, 5
----, --, --. Francis m Grace ----- d 1832,7,
23 bur Richmond
      Ch: Anne H.   b 1808, 11, 28
          John   " 1811, 6, 4
          Martha   " 1814, 2, 21
          Esther   " 1817, 5, 17 d 1836,10,31
            bur Richmond
          Rebecca   b 1820, 3, 1
1815, 10, 26. Jane m Jonathan MICHENER
1817, 5, 29. William, s Jos. & Ann, Jeffer-
      son Co., O.; m in Cross Creek MH, Mahale
      PLUMMER, dt Jos. & Mary, Jefferson Co., O.
----, --, --. Wm. & M.
      Ch: Joseph P.   d 1818, 4,28
            bur Richmond
          Mary T.   " 1819,11, 6
            bur Richmond
----, --, --. Joseph & Rebecca
      Ch: Elizabeth
            F. b 1820, 8, 25
          Abraham   " 1824, 12, 18
1822, 9, 3. William, s Joseph, d bur Rich-
      mond
1822, 12, 18. Anna W., w Abram, dt Jos. & M.
      Watson, b
1823, 4, 22. Mary m Aaron CHAPMAN
1823, 9, 25. Phebe m Wm. WATSON
1824, 1, 24. Joseph, s John & Belinda, Jef-
      ferson Co., O.; m in Cross Creek MH, Ruth
      BALL, dt James & Ruth, Jefferson Co., O.
      Ch: Belinda   b 1825, 4, 30
          Hannah   " 1826, 1, 12
          Rebecca   " 1828, 2, 17
          Stephen   " 1830, 4, 17
1828, 12, 9. Joseph Sr. d bur Richmond
1832, 5, 2. John Jr., s John & Belinda,
      Jefferson Co., O.; m in Smithfield MH,
      Rebecca P. NAYLOR, dt Samuel & Rebecca,
      Jefferson Co., O.
      Ch: Samuel   b 1833, 4, 5
          Belinda   " 1834, 10, 9
          Mary Ann " 1836, 10, 23 d 1838,10,31
            bur Smithfield
          Phebe   b 1838, 9, 13
          Charles   " 1841, 2, 22 " 1842,10,29
            bur Smithfield
          Thomas   b 1843, 7, 26
----, --, --. Stephen & Lydia
      Ch: Jane   b 1832, 8, 15
          Belinda   " 1834, 3, 20
          John   " 1835, 12, 7
          James   " 1838, 10, 11
          William   " 1842, 6, 24
1835, 9, 22. Esther d bur Richmond
1837, 3, 21. Rebecca (nee Talbott) m Chas.
      COFFIN
1837, 11, 2. Mary Ann m John WATSON
1838, 10, 31. Maryann, dt J. & R., d bur
      Smithfield
----, --, --. Thomas & Unity

HOBSON, Thomas & Unity, continued
    Ch: Benjamin
                G.   b 1841, 7, 18
        Mary   " 1843, 3, 13
        Sarah Ann " 1844, 10, 15
        Dorothy " 1847, 5, 14
        John M. " 1849, 2, 7

1845, 1, 1. John, s Jos. & Ann, Jefferson
    Co., O.; m in Smithfield MH, Isabella Mc-
    GREW, dt Jas. & Jane, Westmoreland Co.,
    Pa.
----, --, --. Benjamin d 1863,11,31 bur Cross
    Creek; m Sarah Ann -----
    Ch: Edwin F. b 1851, 4, 5
        Thomas C. " 1853, 1, 24
        Martha Ann " 1854, 11, 28 d 1863,11,19
        bur Cross Creek
        John A. b 1859, 11, 6
1863, 11, 31. Benjamin d bur Cross Creek.
1868, 8, 26. Abraham J., s Jos. & Rebecca,
    Jefferson Co., O.; m in Smithfield MH, Ann
    W. GRIST, dt Jos. & Mary WATSON, Jefferson
    Co., O.

1813, 1, 20. Joseph Jr. gct Pipe Creek MM,
    Md., to m Rebekah Talbott
1813, 10, 16. Rebecca rocf Pipe Creek MM, dtd
    1813,5,15
1816, 3, 18. Joseph Jr. & w, Rebecca, & ch,
    William & Mary Ann, gct Marlborough MM, O.
1818, 6, 22. Francis & w, Grace, & ch, Ann,
    John, Martha & Esther, gct Plainfield MM
1822, 3, 18. James dis mcd
1822, 5, 22. Grace & ch, Ann, John, Martha,
    Esther & Rebecca, rocf Flushing MM, dtd
    1822,3,22
1826, 5, 22. Ann M. Watson (form Hobson) dis
1828, 3, 17. Mahala Skelly (form Hobson) dis
    mcd
1829, 5, 18. Rebecca & ch, William, Mary,
    Ann, John, Joseph, Elizabeth Farquhar,
    Benjamin & Abraham Johns, rocf Marlbor-
    ough MM, dtd 1829,4,28
1831, 8, 22. Joseph & w, Ruth, & ch, Belinda,
    Hannah, Rebecca & Stephen, gct Flushing MM
1832, 2, 20. Stephen dis mcd
1836, 6, 20. John M. dis mcd
1837, 6, 19. Stephen rst
1837, 7, 17. Lydia recrq
1839, 3, 18. John, s Joseph, gct Flushing MM
1839, 11, 11. Thomas gct Newgarden MM, to m
    Unity Johnson
1840, 3, 23. Joseph gct Salem MM
1840, 6, 22. Unity rocf Newgarden MM, dtd
    1840,4,23
1842, 4, 18. Caleb P. dis jas
1842, 4, 18. Rebecca Scott (form Hobson) dis
    mcd
1844, 12, 23. John rocf Chesterfield MM
1845, 5, 19. Mary E. recrq
1847, 6, 21. William dis mcd
1847, 10, 18. Stephen & w, Lydia, & ch, Jane,

Belinda, John, James, William & Mary Ann,
    gct Chesterfield MM
1848, 1, 17. John T. & w, Mary E., & s, Ben-
    jamin, gct Gilead MM
1850, 4, 22. Benjamin gct New Garden MM, to
    m Sarah Ann Johnson
1850, 9, 23. Sarah Ann rocf New Garden MM
1852, 4, 19. Thomas & w, Unity, & ch, Benja-
    min J., Mary, Dorothy, John A. & Belinda,
    gct Plymouth MM, O.
1852, 6, 21. Ann, Phebe & Belinda gct Ches-
    terfield MM
1852, 7, 19. John d 1851,12,19 ae 74 (an
    elder)
1852, 7, 19. John & w, Rebecca, & ch, Samuel
    N., Belinda H., Phebe N., Thomas C. & Re-
    becca Jane, gct Plymouth MM, O.
1864, 6, 20. Sarah Ann & ch, Edwin L., Thom-
    as Chalkley & John A., gct Upper Spring-
    field MM
1901, 7, 22. Ann d 1900,10,9 ae 78 (an elder)

HODGIN
1903, 7, 20. T. C. & w recrq
1910, 11, 23. Thomas C. & w, Ida M., & ch,
    Lenna, gct Piney Wood MM, N. C.

HOGE
1850, 9, 23. Samuel C. McGrew gct Flushing
    MM, O., to m Rachel P. Hoge

HOOD
1881, 3, 29. Charles Wesley & w recrq

HOOPER
1884, 12, 22. Minnie, John E. & Euphemia recrq
1885, 1, 19. Kate & Olive recrq
1885, 2, 23. Minnie relrq
1887, 1, 17. John B. & Sarah recrq
1888, 11, 19. Sarah relrq
1893, 3, 20. Lillie May recrq
1900, 8, 20. John relrq
1900, 9, 17. Lilly May dropped from mbrp

HOWARD
1817, 4, 21. Joshua recrq
1837, 11, 20. Joshua dis disunity

HOYLE
1817, 7, 9. Hannah m John SHARP
----, --, --. Joseph & Ruth
    Ch: Edward   b 1820, 3, 5 d 1821, 4,18
        bur Smithfield
        Sabina   b 1821, 11, 28
        William   " 1825, 2, 7
        Mary Ann " 1828, 2, 12
1820, 3, 1. Benjamin, s John & Sarah, Jef-
    ferson Co., O.; m in Smithfield MH, Tabi-
    tha GRIMSHAW, dt John & Margaret, Jeffer-
    son Co., O.
    Ch: Sarah   b 1821, 1, 11
        Josiah   " 1822, 10, 29 d 1825, 2,20
        bur Smithfield

HOYLE, continued
1820, 4, 26. Mary m Joseph WATSON
1821, 5, 30. Rachel m William GREEN
----, --, --. William & Edith
      Ch: Elma C.   b 1823, 6, 27
          Lindley   " 1826, 6, 15
1825, 3, 4. William d bur Smithfield
1825, 11, 11. Ann, w John, d bur Smithfield
1826, 3, 12. John d bur Smithfield
1834, 3, 26. Benjamin, s John & Elizabeth,
      Jefferson Co., O.; m in Smithfield MH,
      Guliann WILLETS, dt Ellis & Hannah, Jef-
      ferson Co., O.
          Ch: Ellis   b 1835, 9, 3
              Elizabeth   " 1837, 3, 29
1840, 12, 30. Jane m Joshua COPPOCK
1843, 12, 11. Prudence, w John, d bur Smith
      field
----, --, --. Joseph, s John & Prudence, b
      1829,7,4; m Phebe WATSON, dt Matthew &
      Anna M., b 1832,6,27
          Ch: Annie W.   b 1853, 4, 8
              William   " 1855, 8, 29
              Amos B.   " 1859, 1, 18
              John   " 1863, 10, 24 d 1865,--,--
              Matthew W. " 1865, 7, 3
              Elizabeth
                    P.   " 1868, 12, 24
              Lucy   " 1872, 8, 7
              Morris J   " 1875, 8, 30
1860, 6, 18. Amie d bur Smithfield
1864, 11, 26. John d

1816, 2, 19. John & w, Ann, & ch, Mary, Jo-
      seph, William, Benjamin & Rachel, rocf
      Pontefract MM, York Co., Eng., dtd 1815,5,
      15, end by New York MM, 1816,1,3
1816, 4, 22. Hannah rocf Hardshaw MM, Warring-
      ton Co., Eng., dtd 1815,11,16
1817, 11, 17. Ann Shiletto, gr dt John & Ann
      Hoyle, recrq
1819, 5, 17. Joseph gct Concord MM
1819, 12, 20. Ruth rocf Concord MM, dtd 1819,
      8,25
1821, 1, 22. John & w, Ann, & gr dt, Ann
      Shellita, gct Gwynead MM, Pa.
1821, 5, 21. William gct Concord MM, to m
      Edith Newport
1821, 11, 19. Edith rocf Concord MM, O., dtd
      1821,9,19
1823, 6, 23. John Sr. & w, Ann, rocf Gwynedd
      MM, Pa., dtd 1823,5,1
1823, 9, 22. John Jr. & w, Prudence, & his
      ch, Benjamin, John, Jane & Thomas, & her
      dt, Elizabeth Morris, rocf Gwynedd MM,
      Pa., dtd 1823,7,3
1827, 2, 17. Benj. & w, Tabitha, & dt, Sa-
      rah, gct Stillwater MM
1828, 10, 20. William dis jH
1828, 11, 17. Joseph dis jH
1828, 12, 22. Edith dis jH
1829, 3, 23. Ruth dis jH
1837, 9, 18. John Jr. gct Newgarden MM, to m

Dorothy Johnson
1838, 4, 23. Dorothy rocf Newgarden MM, dtd
      1838,1,25
1842, 4, 18. Thomas gc
1842, 5, 23. John Jr. & w, Dorothy, gct Short
      Creek MM, O.
1842, 10, 17. Hannah V. rocf Plainfield MM,
      dtd 1842,8,24
1843, 5, 22. Thomas & w, Hannah, & s, Joseph
      Lindley, gct Plainfield MM
1844, 8, 19. John Jr. & w, Dorothy, rocf
      Short Creek MM, O., dtd 1844,5,21
1845, 11, 17. Benjamin & w, Julian, & ch, El-
      lis, Hannah, Rachel, Lydia & Sarah, gct
      Short Creek MM, O.
1846, 3, 23. Elmira Wilson (form Hoyle) dis
      mcd
1846, 3, 23. Sabina Merrite (form Hoyle) dis
      mcd
1846, 4, 20. John gct Upper Evesham MM, N.J.
1847, 2, 22. Sarah rocf Upper Evesham MM,
      N. J., dtd 1847,2,6
1861, 10, 21. Hannah M. Hammond, minor in
      care of Joseph & Phebe Hoyle, recrq
1862, 12, 22. John, John Jr. & Dorothy dis
      jW
1885, 1, 19. Louisa recrq
1894, 1, 22. Matthew Watson gct Plymouth
      Ch., White Oaks, New Mexico

HULL
1821, 8, 20. Ann rocf Baltimore MM, W. Dist.,
      dtd 1819,6,11, end by Stillwater MM, 1821,
      4,--
1821, 11, 19. Ann Ridgley (form Hull) dis mcd

HUNNICUTT
1832, 6, 18. Rachel & ch, Benjamin Thomas,
      Joseph & Sarah Elizabeth, rocf Wayne Oak
      MM, Va., dtd 1832,5,5
1836, 11, 21. Sarah Elizabeth, minor, gct
      Short Creek MM, O.
1836, 11, 21. Benjamin T. & Joseph, minors,
      gct Short Creek MM, O.

HUNT
1824, 8, 23. Diana recrq
1829, 4, 20. Diana dis jH

HURFORD
1839, 10, 21. William Purviance gct Short
      Creek MM, O., to m Sarah Hurford

HURL
1893, 7, 17. John dropped from mbrp

HUSSEY
1830, 12, 1. Penrose, s Christopher & Lydia,
      Jefferson Co., O.; m in Smithfield MH, Su-
      sanna WOOD, dt Nathan & Margaret, Jeffer-
      son Co., O.
          Ch: Nathan W. b 1831, 11, 18
              Asael   " 1833, 11, 23

HUSSEY, Penrose & Susanna, continued
  Ch: Milton b 1835, 5, 22
    Lydia " 1839, 3, 6
    Margaret " 1843, 9, 18

1836, 4, 18. Penrose & w, Susannah, & ch, Nathan W., Asahel & Milton, rocf Short Creek MM, O., dtd 1836,2,23
1846, 8, 17. Mary Ann (form Garretson) con mcd
1848, 6, 19. Penrose & w, Susanna, & ch, Nathan, Asahel, Milton, Lydia & Margaret, gct Short Creek MM, O.
1851, 6, 23. Mary Ann gct Salem MM, Iowa

HUTTON
----, --, --. Joel d 1847,12,26 bur Smithfield m Mary -----
  Ch: Elizabeth b 1794, 11, 17
    Samuel " 1796, 9, 22
    Mary " 1798, 3, 9
    Deborah " 1801, 12, 3 d 1819, 9,21
     bur Smithfield
    James b 1804, 5, 25
    Samuel " 1806, 8, 22
    John Mc-
     Grew " 1809, 2, 20
    Joel W. " 1811, 6, 7
    Ann   " 1813, 11, 3
    Rebecca " 1817, 7, 11
    Nathan " 1820, 5, 3 d 1822, 8,21
     bur Smithfield
1816, 10, 30. Mary m Samuel CARR
1831, 3, 2. Ann W. m Moses McGrew

1815, 2, 18. Levina, minor, gct Westland MM
1815, 10, 21. Joseph gct Short Creek MM, O.
1817, 1, 20. Elizabeth Judkins (form Hutton) dis mcd
1818, 5, 18. Lavina rocf Westland MM, dtd 1817,10,23
1820, 11, 20. Levinah dis
1822, 12, 23. Sarah gct Fairfield MM
1825, 4, 18. Rebecca McHatten (form Hutton) dis mcd
1829, 8, 17. William gct Westland MM
1831, 2, 21. James dis disunity
1831, 5, 23. Ann (form Wiley) dis mcd
1832, 5, 21. Joel Jr. con mcd
1832, 9, 17. Samuel dis mcd
1833, 10, 21. Joel Jr. gct Providence MM
1834, 2, 17. John M. dis mcd
1836, 7, 18. Rebecca Talbott (form Hutton) dis mcd
1836, 8, 22. Joel & w, Mary, gct Flushing MM
1836, 8, 22. Matilda (form Wiley) dis mcd
1841, 12, 20. Joel & w, Mary, rocf Flushing MM, dtd 1841,10,21; she dec since cert was issued

HYLER
1824, 4, 19. Catherine Longten (form Hyler)

dis mcd

ILER
1887, 5, 23. William recrq

JAMES
1844, 6, 17. Susanna (form Fisher) dis mcd
1880, 12, 20. Benjamin gc

JEFFERS
1927, 1, 5. Guy & w, Myriam, recrq
1933, 12, 20. Miriam rocf Mt. Pleasant MM, O.

JELKS
1811, 10, 19. Richard gct Concord MM, to m Lydia Stanton
1812, 2, 15. Lydia rocf Concord MM, dtd 1812, 1,23
1812, 7, 18. Priscilla Marchant (form Jelks) dis mcd

JENKINSON
1809, 9, 16. Rebecca & ch, Ann, Elizabeth, Mary, John, Sarah & Rebeckah, rocf Redstone MM, Pa., dtd 1807,10,2, end by Short Creek MM, 1808,10,18
1816, 12, 23. John dis jas
1819, 4, 16. Sarah Spencer (form Jinkenson) dis mcd
1838, 11, 19. Isaac rst on consent of Westland
1828, 8, 18. Rebecca Tracy (form Jenkinson) dis mcd
1840, 9, 21. Ann dis jas
1840, 9, 21. M. dis jas

JEWELL
1902, 4, 21. S. V., minister, & w, Lucretia A., rocf Friendswood MM, Texas

JOB
1820, 5, 22. Rebecca & ch, Ruth, Elizabeth, Mary, Samuel & Allen, rocf Short Creek MM, O., dtd 1820,3,21
1822, 12, 23. Rebecca & ch, Ruth, Elizabeth, Mary, Samuel & Allen, gct Short Creek MM, O.

JOHN
1839, 3, 21. Hannah T. m Kinsey TALBOTT

1822, 1, 21. Hannah rocf Short Creek MM, O., dtd 1821,10,23
1841, 1, 18. Rachel rocf Somerset MM, dtd 1840,10,26
1843, 2, 20. Rachel Coffin (form Johns) dis mcd

JOHNSON
----, --, --. Isaac m Annie J. -----, dt Matthew W., b 1835,1,12
1861, 10, 9. Isaac W., s Jas. & Sarah V., Columbiana Co., O.; m in Smithfield MH,

JOHNSON, Isaac W., continued
     Jane WATSON, dt Matthew & Annie M., Jef-
     ferson Co., O.

1837, 9, 18. John Hoyle Jr. gct New Garden
     MM, to m Dorothy Johnson
1839, 11, 11. Thomas Hobson gct Newgarden MM,
     to m Unity Johnson
1850, 4, 22. Benjamin Hobson gct New Garden
     MM, to m Sarah Ann Johnson
1862, 3, 17. Anna Jane [Johnston] gct New
     Garden MM
1895, 6, 17. Elizabeth gct Short Creek MM, O.
1895, 12, 20. Annie Jane rocf Oskaloosa MM,
     Ia.

JOLLY
1810, 12, 15. Hannah rst on consent of Concord
     MM
1812, 8, 15. Malachi gct Stillwater MM, to m
     Susannah Newby
1813, 3, 20. Susanna rocf Stillwater MM
1817, 6, 23. Susanna & dt, Elizabeth, gct
     Stillwater MM
1818, 5, 18. Hannah gct Darby MM, O.
1820, 3, 20. Malachi dis mcd
1821, 8, 20. Philip gct Salem MM, Ind.
1825, 7, 18. Eunice Watlin (form Jolly) rpd
     mcd

JONES
1837, 5, 31. Joseph, s Samuel & Elizabeth,
     Belmont Co., O.; m in Smithfield MH, Isa-
     bella LADD, dt Benj. & Elizabeth
     Ch: Samuel
           Pendleton b 1838, 3, 16 d 1859, 7,30
             bur Smithfield
           Elizabeth
               Ladd   b 1839, 7, 6
           Frances
             Conner   " 1842, 7, 4
           Maria W.   " 1844, 4, 2
           Benjamin W." 1847, 2, 20
           Edward W.   " 1849, 1, 19
----, --, --. Reason, s John & Elizabeth, b
     1817,10,19; m Rebecca ONG, dt Finley &
     Anna,
     Ch: Anna   b 1854, 12, 5
1862, 9, 3. Elizabeth L. m Geo. M. TATUM
1865, 4, 30. John Sr. d

1810, 5, 19. Amy rocf Redstone MM, dtd 1809,
     11,3
1810, 5, 19. Mary rocf Westland MM, dtd 1809,
     10,28
1817, 5, 19. Isaac recrq
1817, 7, 21. Ester (form Linton) dis mcd
1817, 12, 22. Eli, Abigail, James & Jonathan,
     ch Isaac & Mary, recrq
1821, 8, 20. Isaac & w, Mary, & ch, Eli,
     Abigail, James, Jonathan & Mary, gct
     Flushing MM
1830, 10, 18. Amy gct Flushing MM

1831, 7, 18. Margaret (form Marsh) dis mcd
1837, 9, 18. Isabella L. gct Short Creek
     MM, O.
1840, 11, 28. Rebecca (form Ong) dis mcd
1843, 2, 20. Joseph & w, Isabella, & ch,
     Samuel Pendleton, Elizabeth Ladd & Fran-
     cis Conner, rocf Short Creek MM, O., dtd
     1842,11,21
1861, 6, 17. Laura E. Hammond, minor in care
     of Joseph & Isabella L. Jones, recrq
1867, 7, 22. Rebecca rst
1867, 10, 21. Joseph & w, Isabella, & ch,
     Benjamin L. & Edward W., gct Chicago MM,
     Ill.
1867, 10, 21. Francis & w, Maria W., gct
     Chicago MM, Ill.
1875, 4, 9. John Sr. recrq
1875, 4, 19. Rezin recrq
1875, 8, 23. Anna recrq
1875, 8, 23. Louisa & ch, Mary Vanetta &
     Walter, recrq
1875, 9, --. Louisa recrq
1880, 3, 22. John N. recrq
1884, 9, 22. John dis
1886, 3, 22. Louisa relrq
1904, 3, 23. David recrq

JORDAN
1832, 10, 22. Rebecca & ch, Edward Thomas,
     Benjamin Harris, William Foster, Sarah
     Isabella & Deborah Ann, rocf Cedar Creek
     MM, Va.
1838, 9, 17. Joseph dis disunity
1849, 8, 20. William Foster dis jas
1851, 12, 22. Deborah Ann Stroud (form Jordan)
     dis mcd & jas
1851, 12, 22. Sarah Isabella dis jas

JUDKINS
----, --, --. William & Rachel
     Ch: Sarah   b 1814, 6, 11
         David   " 1817, 7, 17
1817, 5, 28. Anderson, s Jas. & Martha, Jef-
     ferson Co., O.; m in Plymouth MH, Catha-
     rine CARR, dt Jas. & Elizabeth, Jefferson
     Co., O.
1843, 8, 24. David, s Wm. & Rachel, Hamilton
     Co., O.; m in Smithfield MH, Susan P. Mc-
     GREW, dt Thos. B. & Ann, Jefferson Co., O.

1813, 12, 18. William & w, Rachel, rocf Short
     Creek MM, O., dtd 1813,11,23
1815, 7, 15. James Jr. & w, Susannah, & s,
     Jonathan, rocf Short Creek MM, O., dtd
     1815,6,20
1816, 6, 17. James Jr. & w, Susanna, & ch,
     Jonathan & Martha, gct Short Creek MM, O.
1816, 12, 23. Anderson rocf Short Creek MM,
     O., dtd 1816,9,24
1817, 1, 20. Elizabeth (form Hutton) dis mcd
1818, 5, 18. Anderson & Catherine dis
1820, 2, 21. Stanton rocf Short Creek MM, O.,
     dtd 1819,11,23

JUDKINS, continued
1821, 9, 17. Anderson & Catherine rst
1821, 9, 17. Elizabeth & Martha, ch Anderson & Catherine, recrq
1822, 7, 22. Stanton dis mcd
1822, 9, 23. Wm. & w, Rachel, & ch, Sarah, David & Martha Ann, gct Short Creek MM, O.
1833, 10, 21. Anderson dis disunity
1836, 9, 19. Elizabeth dis jas
1838, 6, 18. Martha dis jas
1844, 4, 22. Susan P. gct Cincinnati MM
1847, 11, 22. Ann Mason (form Judkins) dis mcd
1852, 9, 20. Maria Louisa dis jas
1857, 10, 19. William A. dis mcd
1857, 10, 19. Mary W. (form Bates) dis mcd

KAMINSKI
1883, 4, 23. Anna recrq
1895, 7, 22. Annie gct White Water MM, Ind.

KEIM
1913, 10, 22. Maud relrq

KELLUM
1810, 3, 17. Nathaniel [Kilham] & w, Elizabeth, & ch, Nathaniel, Joseph, Elijah & Susanna, gct Miami MM, O.
1810, 3, 17. Sarah [Kilham] gct Miami MM, O.
1830, 3, 22. Sarah [Kellem] (form Hutton) dis mcd

KEYS
1835, 6, 22. Rachel (form Willits) dis mcd
1906, 1, 24. Thomas recrq

KIMBERLING
1887, 4, 18. Louisa recrq
1888, 5, 21. Louisa [Kimberly] dropped from mbrp

KING
1889, 2, 18. Fred recrq
1893, 7, 17. Fred dropped from mbrp

KINNY
1895, 7, 22. Sadie R. relrq

KINSEY
1813, 11, 25. Stephen, s Absalom & Ridley, Jefferson Co., O.; m in Cross Creek MH, Anna ONG, dt Jacob & Mary, Jefferson Co., O.
    Ch: Mary Ann b 1817, 2, -- d 1835,--,-- bur Smithfield
        Lewis   b
        Jacob   " 1818, 12, 8
        Absolom   " 1821, 2, 20
        Ruthann   " 1823, 12, 10
        Rebecca   " 1826, 8, 18
        Elizabeth " 1831, 8, 9
        Maria   " 1833, 3, 28 d 1855, 8,31 bur Smithfield
1852, 3, 18. Mary Elizabeth d

1854, 8, 30. James G., s Jas. & Ann, Jefferson Co., O.; m in Smithfield MH, Elizabeth L. WOOD, dt Samuel & Lewcy, Jefferson Co., O.
1866, 12, 26. Elizabeth L. m Jos. HILL

1809, 3, 18. Richard & w, Rhoda, & ch, Jesse, Nancy & John, gct Plainfield MM
1810, 6, 16. Benjamin dis disunity
1812, 3, 21. Christopher & w, Mary, & ch, Sarah, John, Absolom, Nathan, Ruth, Edmond, Susanna & Rachel, gct Plainfield MM
1830, 12, 20. Stephen dis disunity
1837, 1, 23. Lewis dis mcd
1840, 11, 28. Jacob dis mcd
1843, 2, 20. Ruth Ann Carter (form Kinsey) dis mcd
1848, 4, 17. Absolom dis mcd
1850, 4, 22. Rebecca Matthews (form Kinsey) dis mcd
1855, 5, 21. Elizabeth L. gct Short Creek MM, O.
1855, 5, 21. Elizabeth Wheeler (form Kinsey) dks mcd
1865, 7, 17. Elizabeth L. rocf Short Creek MM, O.

KIRBY
1828, 8, 28. Rachel m David B. DEWEES

1827, 4, 23. Rebecca, Rachel & Isaac [Kerby] recrq
1829, 7, 20. Thomas & w, Rebecca, & ch, Eleanor, Elizabeth-Farquhar, Ann, Hannah & Kiturah, gct Deerfield MM
1829, 7, 20. Isaac gct Deerfield MM
1912, 4, 24. Alice M. gct Highland Avenue Ch. Cleveland, Ohio

KIRK
----, --, --. William d 1854,6,20 bur Smithfield; m Martha ----- d 1847,9,12 bur Smithfield
    Ch: Mahlon   b 1807, 2, 1
        Joseph   " 1809, 3, 18
        Rachel   " 1810, 11, 16
        Joel   " 1812, 6, 29
        Edith   " 1815, 5, 3 d 1851, 6,28
        Susanna " 1817, 7, 21 " 1862, 5, 6
        Elizabeth " 1820, 9, 6
        Sarah   " 1823, 4, 10 " 1832, 1,27
1810, 11, 21. Betta m Eli QUAINTAINCE
1811, 1, 24. Timothy, s Wm. & Rachel, Jefferson Co., O.; m in Cross Creek MH, Susanna QUAINTANCE, dt Jos. & Susanna, Jefferson Co., O.
    Ch: William   b 1812, 2, 13
        Sarah Ann " 1815, 4, 11
        Joseph   " 1813, 9, 13
        Rachel   " 1817, 4, 18
        Mary   " 1819, 9, 20
1826, 5, 21. Henry C., s Caleb & Lydia,.Jefferson Co., O.; m in Smithfield MH, Marga-

KIRK, Henry C., continued
    ret MARSH, dt Wm. & Ann, Jefferson Co., O.
      Ch: Albertus T.b 1827, 3, 19
         William H. " 1828, 2, 19
----, --, --. Joel & Mary Ann
      Ch: Catherna   b 1837, 3, 31
         Lindley W. " 1839, 9, 20
         Amy T.   " 1841, 10, 15
         Zadock P. " 1844, 1, 3
         Martha   " 1846, 4, 17
         Chalkley   " 1848, 11, 20
1839, 10, 30. Edith m John M. SMITH
1847, 3, 31. Elizabeth m Mifflin ONG
1855, 10, 23. Catharine S. m Samuel R. SMITH
1856, 9, 24. Rachel m Wm. BRIGGS

1814, 9, 17. Caleb & w, Sarah, & ch, Isaac,
    Mary, Armelle, John & Joseph, gct New Gar-
    den MM
1815, 1, 21. Susanna Sherron (form Kirk) dis
    mcd
1816, 1, 22. Caleb & ch, Isaac, Mary, Armella,
    John & Joseph, rocf Newgarden MM, dtd
    1815,10,19
1816, 8, 19. Caleb gct Newgarden MM
1818, 6, 22. Cert rec for Timothy & w, Edith,
    from Redstone MM, Pa., dtd 1818,5,27, end
    to Short Creek MM, O.
1818, 6, 22. Cert rec for Beulah & Susannah
    from Redstone MM, Pa., dtd 1818,5,27, end
    to Short Creek MM, O.
1823, 9, 22. Timothy & w, Susannah, & ch,
    William, Joseph, Sarah Ann, Rachel, Mary
    & Rebecca, gct Alum Creek MM, O.
1824, 1, 19. John N. Marsh gct Short Creek
    MM, to m Susanna Kirk
1825, 11, 21. Rachel (form Garretson) dis mcd
1826, 2, 20. Caleb & w, Lydia, rocf Marl-
    borough MM, dtd 1826,1,31
1826, 2, 20. Henry C. rocf Marlborough MM,
    dtd 1826,1,31
1826, 5, 22. Aquilla N. & w, Sarah, & ch,
    Elmira, Lydia Ann, Elizabeth N. & Catha-
    rine, rocf Marlborough MM, dtd 1826,4,25
1826, 7, 17. Timothy rocf Short Creek MM, O.,
    dtd 1826,3,21
1827, 10, 22. Mary rocf Newgarden MM, dtd 1827,
    6,21
1828, 5, 19. Rachel G. rst
1828, 9, 22. Caleb dis jH
1828, 12, 22. Henry dis jH
1829, 2, 23. Sarah & Lydia dis jH
1829, 2, 23. Aquilla dis jH
1829, 8, 17. Margaret dis jH
1829, 10, 19. Mahlon dis mcd
1830, 1, 18. Mary (form Naylor) dis mcd
1832, 3, 19. William, minor, rocf Alum Creek
    MM, dtd 1831,7,29
1832, 3, 19. Mary G. gct Sandy Spring MM
1832, 7, 23. Joseph dis mcd
1836, 4, 16. Joel gct Flushing MM, to m Mary
    Ann Smich
1836, 6, 20. Joseph rst at Flushing MM on

consent of this mtg
1836, 7, 18. Mary Ann rocf Flushing MM, dtd
    1836,5,23
1838, 2, 19. Elmina Worrell (form Kirk) dis
    mcd & jH
1841, 2, 22. Lydia Ann & Elizabeth dis jH
1846, 12, 21. Timothy gct Short Creek MM, O.
1850, 10, 21. Sarah Ann & Catharine dis jH
1853, 4, 18. Rachel G. dis disunity
1858, 5, 17. Joel & w, Mary, & ch, Lindley
    M., Amy T., Zadok, Chalkley H., Martha,
    Anna, Mary & Rachel, gct Upper Spring-
    field MM
1862, 7, 21. Joel rocf Flushing MM, O., dtd
    1862,5,24
1865, 2, 20. Joel T. gct Flushing MM

KLEIN
1903, 11, 25. Mrs. H. E. recrq

KLIEVES
1882, 2, 20. Dr. Frank A. recrq
1883, 10, 22. Dr. F. A. dis

LADD
1814, 4, 20. Benjamin W., s James & Isabella,
    Charles City Co., O., d 1851,5,31; m in
    Plymouth MH, Elizabeth WOOD, dt Wm. &
    Mary, Jefferson Co., O., d 1832,12,4
      Ch: Isabella   b 1815, 3, 22
         Mary Ann   " 1816, 9, 17
         Lydia   " 1818, 11, 23 d 1819, 6, 5
         bur Smithfield
         James   b 1820, 7, 16
         William   " 1823, 3, 12
         Rebecca   " 1825, 2, 24
         Benjamin   " 1830, 8, 24
         Thomas W. " 1832, 12, 4
    Benjamin W. m 2nd 1834,--,-- Hannah S.
    WOOD in Birmingham MM, Pa.
      Ch: Elizabeth b 1835, 10, 8
         Lydia   " 1837, 8, 15
         Hannah   " 1839, 9, 28
1837, 5, 21. Isabella m Joseph JONES
1837, 5, 31. Mary Ann m Elisha COOK
----, --, --. James & Elizabeth
      Ch: Ellen R.   b 1844, 1, 11
         Oliver M. " 1846, 6, 24
         Mary Fol-
           ger   " 1849, 12, 15
         Virginia   " 1852, 12, --
         Caroline C." 1855, 6, 29
1845, 8, 16. Eleanor d bur Richmond
1848, 8, 24. William H., s Benj. & Elizabeth,
    b 1823,3,13; m Caroline -----
      Ch: Ellen C.   b 1849, 8, 8
         Benjamin W." 1851, 9, 8
         Mariana C. " 1854, 3, 31
         Charles C. " 1856, 7, 22
         William C. " 1858, 10, 5
1860, 11, 28. Hannah S. m John C. HILL
1863, 9, 30. Lydia m Wm. GIFFORD

LADD, continued
1814, 5, 21. Elizabeth gct Weynoke MM, Va.
1815, 9, 16. Benjamin W. & w, Elizabeth, & dt, Isabella, rocf Waynoak MM, Va., dtd 1815,7,1
1816, 9, 23. Oliver & Mariah, minors, rocf Wayn Oak MM, Va., dtd 1816,8,3
1819, 5, 17. Anna Maria gct Birmingham MM, Pa.
1820, 1, 17. Oliver gct Wynoke MM, Va.
1828, 11, 17. Anna Maria Minge (form Ladd) dis mcd
1823, 12, 22. Anna Maria rocf Burmingham MM, dtd 1823,9,4
1834, 7, 21. Benjamin W. gct Birmingham MM, Pa., to m Hannah S. Wood
1834, 11, 17. Hannah S. rocf Birmingham MM, Pa., dtd 1834,10,1
1842, 7, 15. James gct Marlborough MM, to m Elizabeth Folger
1843, 3, 20. Elizabeth F. rocf Marlborough MM, dtd 1843,1,3
1848, 7, 17. William H. gct White Water MM, Ind., to m
1848, 11, 20. Caroline E. (Coffin) rocf White Water MM, Ind., dtd 1848,10,25
1851, 7, 21. Benjamin W. d 1851,5,31 ae abt 68 (an elder)
1854, 7, 18. Thomas gct Dartmouth MM, Mass., to m Hannah P. Gifford
1855, 2, 19. Hannah P. rocf Dartmouth MM, Mass.
1857, 11, 23. Thomas W. & w, Hannah P., gct Cincinnati MM, O.
1859, 1, 17. Benjamin con mcd
1865, 4, 17. Benjamin gct Spring Creek MM, Iowa
1867, 4, 22. William H. & w, Caroline E., & ch, Ellen C., Benjamin W., Marianna C., Charles F. C. & William C., gct New York MM, N. Y.
1867, 7, 17. James D. & w, Elizabeth, & ch, Oliver M., May F., Caroline C. & Warren F., gct Spring Creek MM, Ia.
1871, 9, 18. Elizabeth & Hannah gct Spring Creek MM, Ia.

LANGSTAFF
1830, 2, 22. James rocf Salem MM, dtd 1829, 11,25
1832, 4, 23. James Jr. gct Cincinnati MM, O.

LAPPAN
1825, 11, 21. Sarah (form McGrail) dis mcd

LARK
1826, 4, 26. Lucy L. m Samuel WOOD

1817, 11, 17. Lucy, minor, recrq

LARKIN
1816, 2, 19. Lydia Smith (form Larkin) dis

LAWRENCE
1850, 11, 21. Robert B., s Thos. & Isabella, Jefferson Co., O.; m in Smithfield MH, Tacy BATES, dt Wm. S. & Lydia, Jefferson Co., O.

1851, 6, 23. Tace B. gct Short Creek MM, O.

LEE
1845, 4, 21. Elvira B. rocf Short Creek MM, O., dtd 1845,3,18
1853, 12, 19. Elvira B. gct Red Cedar MM, Ia.

LEMASTER
1875, 4, 19. Belvia recrq
1884, 2, 16. Belle dropped from mbrp

LEMON
1911, 2, 22. George G. recrq
1917, 11, 21. Margaret recrq

LESLIE
1813, 12, 18. Robert & w, Rachel, & ch, Thomas, Mary, Sarah, Robert, Johnson & Levi, rocf Nottingham MM, Pa., dtd 1813,6,11, end by Short Creek MM, 1813,8,24
1819, 2, 22. Margaret & Elizabeth gct Plainfield MM
1819, 2, 22. Robert & w, Rachel, & ch, Thomas, Mary, Robert, Johnson, Sarah & Levi L., gct Plainfield MM

LEWIS
1826, 3, 17. Eliza, w Isaac, dt Finley ONG, b

1834, 5, 19. Wm. G. & w, Ann, & dt, Sarah E., rocf Cedar Creek MM, Va.
1836, 7, 18. Cert rec for Joseph from Western Branch MM, Va., dtd ----, --, --, end to Short Creek MM, O.
1836, 12, 19. Wm. J. & w, Anne, & ch, Sarah Elizabeth & Margaret Anne, rocf China MM, Me., dtd 1836,1,19
1850, 3, 18. Elizana (form Ong) dis mcd
1876, 5, 22. Eliza Ann recrq
1885, 10, 19. Kate recrq

LINTON
1809, 12, 16. Hannah & ch, Elizabeth, Esther, William & Samuel, rocf Baltimore MM for W. Dist., dtd 1809,3,8
1817, 7, 21. Ester Jones (form Linton) dis mcd
1818, 11, 23. David, Albert, Thomas, Harriett, John, Sarah & Isaiah, ch Wm. & Hannah, recrq
1819, 3, 22. William & w, Hannah, & ch, William, Samuel, David, Albert, Thomas, Harriet, John, Sarah, Isaiah & Hannah, gct Center MM, O.
1819, 3, 22. Elizabeth gct Center MM, O.
1919, 1, 22. H. Lawrence & w, Effie A., & ch,

LINTON, continued
     Lois, roc

LIVTIR
1817, 2, 17. William rocf Wrightstown MM, Pa.,
     dtd 1817,1,8

LOGAN
1890, 5, 19. Mary W. relrq

LONGTEN
1824, 4, 19. Catherine (form Hyler) dis mcd

LORD .
1896, 11, 23. Edwin Jay, a minister, & w, Jo-
     sephine, rocf Portsmouth MM, R. I.
1897, 10, 18. E. Jay, a minister, & w relrq

LUKENS
1812, 10, 17. Jacob & w, Tace, & ch, John, Re-
     becca, Merrican, Ruth & Alice, rocf Gun-
     powder MM, dtd 1812,6,24
1815, 3, 18. Moses & w, Sarah, & ch, Benja-
     min, Phebe, Hannah, Moses, Mary, Sarah,
     William & Anna, rocf Muncy MM, dtd 1814,
     10,19, end by Plainfield MM, 1815,1,28
1815, 4, 15. Rachel rocf Muncy MM, dtd 1814,
     10,19
1815, 4, 15. Lydia rocf Muncey MM, dtd 1814,
     10,19, end by Plainfield MM, 1815,1,28
1816, 3, 18. Phebe gct Short Creek MM, O.
1816, 4, 22. Moses & w, Sarah, & ch, Hannah,
     Moses, Mary, Sarah, William & Anna, gct
     Short Creek MM, O.
1816, 12, 23. Benjamin gct Short Creek MM, O.
1817, 7, 21. Rachel gct Short Creek MM, O.
1823, 12, 22. Rebecca Snee (form Lukins) dis
     mcd
1825, 2, 21. Ruth dis jas
1825, 12, 19. Merican gct Center MM
1828, 1, 21. Alice dis jas

LUPTON
1819, 9, 29. Gideon, s Nathan & Margaret,
     Jefferson Co., O.; m in Smithfield MH,
     Susanna CARR, dt Wm. & Sarah, Jefferson
     Co., O.
1840, 4, 1. George, s John & Sarah, Jeffer-
     son Co., O.; m in Smithfield MH, Sarah Ann
     CREW

1821, 5, 21. David & w, Margaret, & dt, Ra-
     chel Ann, rocf Plainfield MM, dtd 1821,4,
     26
1821, 9, 17. Gideon rocf Short Creek MM, O.,
     dtd 1821,6,19
1822, 5, 22. Gideon & w, Susannah, & ch, Sa-
     rah & Margaret, gct Short Creek MM, O.
1825, 6, 20. David & w, Margaret, & ch, Ra-
     chel Ann, Levi & George, gct Short Creek
     MM, O.
1829, 1, 19. Gideon & w, Susanna, & ch, Sarah,
     Margaret & William, rocf Salem MM, dtd

     1828,12,24
1835, 11, 23. Gideon & w, Susanna, & ch, Sa-
     rah C., Margaret & William, gct Adrien MM,
     Mich. Territory
1840, 8, 17. Sarah Ann gct Short Creek MM, O.

McADAMS
1913, 2, 19. Samuel G. recrq

McBRIDE
1828, 10, 20. Benjamin Stanton gct Sandy
     Spring MM, to m Betsy McBride

McCLAIN
----, --, --. William B., s John & Rebecca,
     b 1852,2,5; m Isabella WEBSTER, dt Naylor
     & Jamima, b 1855,11,7

1884, 12, 22. William B. [McLAIN] recrq
1889, 1, 21. Isabel recrq
1897, 6, 21. Noah C. [McLean] & w, Cora E.,
     rocf Marshall MM, Ind.
1899, 3, 20. Isabel relrq
1909, 12, 22. Noah C. & w gct Cleveland MM, O.

McCONNELL
1918, 1, 23. Beryl Whitten relrq

McGRAIL
1842, 9, 22. Thomas d bur Smithfield
1842, 11, 8. Mary, dt Thomas, d bur Smith-
     field
1849, 6, 24. Mary, dt Alfred & Amey, b
1854, 1, 10. Rebecca, w Thomas, d
1854, 4, 7. Amy, w Alfred, d bur Richmond

1815, 9, 16. Thomas & w, Rebecca, & ch,
     James, Mary & Ann, rocf Redstone MM, dtd
     1815,6,2
1823, 8, 18. Sarah rocf Providence MM, Pa.,
     dtd 1823,1,21
1825, 2, 21. Deborah, minor, rocf Providence
     MM, Pa., dtd 1824,12,21
1825, 11, 21. Sarah Lappan (form McGrail) dis
     mcd
1832, 7, 23. Mary & dt, Rachel & Isabella,
     rocf Providence MM, dtd 1832,5,30
1860, 9, 17. John dis mcd
1862, 12, 22. Ann dis jW
1862, 12, 22. Edith dis jW
1862, 12, 22. Eliza dis jW
1862, 12, 22. Elizabeth A. dis jW
1862, 12, 22. Finley dis jW
1862, 12, 22. Gilbert dis jW
1862, 12, 22. James dis jW
1862, 12, 22. James W. dis jW
1862, 12, 22. Lydia M. dis jW
1862, 12, 22. Mary dis jW
1862, 12, 22. Susan dis jW

McGREW
----, --, --. Nathan d 1849,5,19 bur Smith-
     field; m Elizabeth ----- d 1844,11,3 bur

McGREW, Nathan & Elizabeth, continued
   Smithfield
     Ch: Jane   b 1803, 10, 9
        Eliza   " 1805, 12, 1
        James W. " 1808, 6, 17
        David   " 1810, 10, 15
        Thomas   " 1813, 4, 26
        Finley   " 1815, 12, 17
        Deborah   " 1818, 6, 8 d 1819, 8, 8
          bur Smithfield
        Samuel   b 1822, 2, 8
        Mary Rebec-
               ca " 1823, 12, 17
1803, 8, 10. Finley A. & Deborah
     Ch: James   b 1804, 3, 8
        Mary   " 1805, 8, 26
        Moses   " 1807, 4, 25
        Jane   " 1810, 10, 17
        Thomas   " 1813, 10, 31
        Rebecca   " 1815, 8, 8 d 1828, 9,10
          bur Smithfield
        William L. b 1817, 11, 18
        Eli   " 1820, 5, 7 " 1820, 5,20
          bur Smithfield
        Elizabeth b 1820, 5, 7
        Oliver   " 1827, 8, 2
----, --, --. Joseph m Margaret HAMMOND, d
   1821,5,6 bur Smithfield
     Ch: James   b 1808, 4, 2
        Deborah   " 1810, 6, 15
        John   " 1812, 9, 1
        George   " 1814, 8, 29
        Jacob   " 1816, 7, 23
        Elizabeth " 1818, 8, 30
        May   " 1820, 11, 29
1818, 1, 21. Finley B., s Jas. B. & Elizabeth,
   Jefferson Co., O.; m in Smithfield MH,
   Aletta CARR, dt Jas. & Elizabeth, Jefferson Co., O., d 1833,8,21 bur Smithfield
     Ch: Elizabeth b 1819, 4, 20
        James   " 1824, 6, 20
        Anderson J." 1823, 12, 31
        William   " 1826, 12, 21
        Ann   " 1830, 5, 17
        Finley Jr. " 1833, 8, 8
1819, 5, 26. Thomas B., s James B. & Elizabeth, Jefferson Co., O.; m in Smithfield
   MH, Ann PRICE, dt Warrick & Susanna, Jef-
   ferson Co., O.
     Ch: Susanna b 1820, 9, 4
        Samuel   " 1822, 3, 3
        Oliver   " 1823, 11, 12 d 1849, 4,25
        Addison   " 1827, 9, 6
        Willett   " 1830, 10, 14 " 1831, 8,31
        Thomas   " 1833, 4, 24
1820, 6, 28. John B., s Jas. & Elizabeth,
   Jefferson Co., Pa.; m in Smithfield MH,
   Mary ONG, dt Jacob & Mary, Jefferson Co.,
   O.
     Ch: Amanda   b 1821, 5, 9
        Julian   " 1823, 12, 23
        Mary Jane " 1827, 3, 4 d 1830, 6,10
          bur Smithfield

1823, 2, 26. Jane m John NAYLOR
----, --, --. Jacob & Martha
     Ch: Finley   b 1832, 4, 8
        Dorsey   " 1834, 10, 31
        James B.   " 1837, 9, 9
        Elizabeth
            M. " 1839, 12, 29
1831, 3, 2. Moses, s Finley A. & Deborah,
   Jefferson Co., O.; m in Smithfield MH,
   Ann W. HUTTON, dt Joel & Mary, Jefferson
   Co., O.
     Ch: Rebecca   b 1832, 9, 15
        Thomas P. " 1835, 7, 10
        Mary H.   " 1838, 2, 5
        James Addi-
            son " 1840, 3, 8
        Joel H.   " 1842, 8, 8
1837, 8, 30. Elizabeth m Joel WOOD
1837, 5, 17. John B., s Joseph, d bur Smithfield
----, --, --. Finley & Rebecca
     Ch: Jacob A. b 1842, 11, 13
        James   " 1844, 12, 11
        Eliza Jane " 1846, 7, 31
----, --, --. James & Ann G.
     Ch: Elizabeth
          Ann b 1842, 12, 10
        Lydia B.   " 1844, 5, 14
        Gilbert   " 1846, 8, 15
        Susan Jane " 1848, 1, 3
1843, 8, 24. Susan P. m David JUDKINS
1845, 1, 1. Isabella m John HOBSON
----, --, --. Simeon, s Elijah, b 1822,12,21;
   m Mary Ann ----- b 1821,3,5
     Ch: Eliza Jane b 1856, 3, 30
        Ross   " 1858, 6, 24
        Mary Emily " 1862, 6, 15
----, --, --. Ross, s Simeon & Mary Ann, b
   1858,6,24; m Sarah BOOP, dt Joseph &
   Julia, b 1860,3,4
     Ch: Jesse   b 1887, 10, 29
        Ida   " 1894, 10, 13

1809, 12, 16. Joseph rocf Redstone MM, Pa.,
   dtd 1809,6,30
1811, 5, 18. Deborah (form Hammond) dis mcd
1813, 5, 15. James C. & w, Rachel, & ch,
   James W., Rachel, Mary, Dinah, Sinah &
   Finley, rocf Redstone MM, dtd 1813,1,29,
   end by Short Creek MM, 1813,4,20
1816, 1, 22. James Jr. dis mcd
1817, 9, 22. James C. dis disunity
1817, 10, 20. Finley A. & w, Deborah, & ch,
   James, Mary, Moses, Jane, Thomas & Rebeckah, rocf Providence MM, Pa., dtd 1817,7,
   22
1817, 12, 22. Finley rocf Providence MM, dtd
   1817,9,23
1818, 1, 19. Thomas rocf Providence MM, Pa.,
   dtd 1817,9,23
1818, 2, 23. Rachel & ch, Mary, Dinah, Sinah,
   Finley & Elizabeth, gct Plainfield MM
1818, 2, 23. Rachel Jr. gct Plainfield MM

McGREW, continued
1819, 6, 21. Eleanor rst on consent of War-
     rington MM, Pa.
1819, 12, 20. John rocf Providence MM, Pa.,
     dtd 1819,10,26
1821, 9, 17. Elizabeth rocf Providence MM,
     dtd 1821,5,22
1822, 5, 22. Jacob rocf Providence MM, dtd
     1821,9,25
1823, 9, 22. Joseph dis mcd
1827, 1, 22. James dis mcd
1827, 4, 23. Eliza Clapp (form McGrew) dis
     mcd
1829, 10, 19. Jane Talbott (form McGrew) dis
     mcd to first cousin
1830, 1, 18. Finley A. dis jH
1830, 3, 22. Martha recrq
1831, 11, 21. Finley B. dis jH
1833, 1, 21. John B. dis
1833, 4, 22. David dis mcd
1833, 7, 22. James H. dis mcd
1839, 1, 21. George dis mcd
1839, 9, 23. Elizabeth England (form McGrew)
     dis mcd
1839, 9, 23. Mary Price (form McGrew) dis mcd
1840, 5, 18. Thomas dis mcd
1840, 7, 20. Amanda Evans (form McGrew) dis
     mcd
1840, 8, 17. Mary Weldy (form McGrew) dis mcd
1840, 10, 19. William Leslie dis mcd
1841, 2, 22. Finley W. con mcd
1841, 11, 22. James W. gct Providence MM, Pa.,
     to m Anne Gilbert
1842, 3, 21. Anne C rocf Providence MM, Pa.,
     dtd 1842,3,3
1842, 6, 20. Juliann Blakemore (form McGrew)
     dis mcd
1843, 5, 22. Rebecca recrq
1844, 1, 22. Jacob A. & s, Finley W., & Re-
     becca, recrq
1844, 1, 22. Isabella rocf Providence MM,
     Pa., dtd 1843,11,30
1844, 10, 21. James C. dis mcd
1846, 1, 19. Jacob dis
1848, 4, 17. Jacob B. & w, Martha, & ch, Fin-
     ley, Dorsey, James B. & Benjamin H., gct
     Alum Creek MM, O.
1849, 4, 23. Deborah (form Hammond) con mcd
1849, 5, 21. Deborah gct Alum Creek MM, O.
1850, 2, 18. Ann P. & s, Thomas O., gct
     Cincinnati MM, O.
1850, 9, 23. Samuel C. gct Flushing MM, O.,
     to m Rachel P. Hoge
1850, 10, 21. Rebecca Arnold (form McGrew) dis
     mcd
1851, 4, 21. Rachel P. rocf Flushing MM, O.,
     dtd 1851,3,20
1852, 9, 20. Samuel P. con mcd
1853, 2, 21. Samuel C. & w, Rachel P., gct
     Flushing MM
1853, 9, 18. Samuel P. gct Cincinnati MM
1853, 9, 19. Ann E. Wallace (form McGrew) dis
     mcd

1853, 9, 19. Joseph A. gct Cincinnati MM
1857, 1, 19. Thomas B. gct Cincinnati MM, O.
1862, 12, 22. Findley, Rebecca, Jacob, James
     & Eliza J. dis jW
1864, 9, 19. Jemima recrq
1864, 11, 21. Annaletta, Josephine K., Wil-
     liam B., Mary-Tabitha, Elizabeth W. & Mar-
     tha J., ch James C. & Jemima, recrq
1871, 11, 20. Finley C. dis
1874, 7, 20. Jemima & ch, Elizabeth W. & Mar-
     tha, gct Columbus MM, O.
1874, 10, 19. William B. gct Columbus MM, O.
1874, 10, 19. Anna L., Josephine K. & Mary T.
     gct Columbus MM, O.
1881, 2, 21. Simon B., Mary A., Rachel A.,
     Jennie & Mary Emily, recrq
1885, 1, 19. Mary recrq
1886, 3, 22. Ross H. & Sarah recrq
1903, 9, 23. Ross & fam dropped from mbrp

McHATTEN
1825, 4, 18. Rebecca (form Hutton) dis mcd

McNAMEE
1808, 5, 21. Margaret & ch, Barnabas, Mary,
     Sarah, Meshack, Elias, Ruben, William,
     Cyrus & Helana, rocf Westland MM, Pa.,
     dtd 1807,9,26, end by Short Creek MM, O.,
     dtd 1808,4,19
1810, 10, 20. Mary Naylor (form McNamee) dis
     mcd
1812, 2, 15. Barnabas dis mcd
1812, 2, 15. Sarah Snider (form McNamee) dis
     mcd
1813, 12, 18. Margaret & ch, Reuben, William,
     Cyrus, Helena, Cynthia Ann & Isaac, gct
     Plainfield MM
1817, 3, 17. Meshack gct Plainfield MM, O.
1818, 11, 23. Elias gct Flushing MM
1826, 8, 21. William Marsh Jr. gct Flushing
     MM, to m Cynthiann McNamee

McNICHOLS
1818, 3, 4. William, s Nathaniel & Martha,
     Belmont Co., O.; m in St. Clairsville, Ra-
     chel FAWCETT, dt Thomas & Martha SMITH,
     Belmont Co., O.
1848, 5, 31. Martha d ae 74 bur Plainfield

MARCHANT
1812, 7, 18. Priscilla (form Jelks) dis mcd
1825, 2, 21. Priscilla rst
1826, 6, 19. Priscilla gct Flushing MM
1830, 8, 23. Priscilla rocf Flushing MM, dtd
     1830,6,24

MARIS
1861, 5, 2. Caleb, s Jonathan & Thomason,
     Mahoning Co., O.; m in Cross Creek MH,
     Deborah WATSON, dt Matthew & Annie M.,
     Jefferson Co., O.

1845, 11, 17. Mary (form Purviance) con mcd

MARIS, continued
1845, 12, 22. Mary gct Somerset MM
1861, 9, 23. Deborah gct Upper Springfield MM

MARSH
----, --, --. William m Ann ----- d 1829,1,19
    bur Smithfield
    Ch: John
        Margaret
        William Jr.b 1806, 3, 5
        Susanna
        Isaac
        Elizabeth
        Ann
        Mifflin   " 1816, --, --
----, --, --. Jonathan & Lavina
    Ch: Margaret b 1807, 3, 16
        Mary   " 1808, 8, 1
        John   " 1810, 11, 10
        Hugh   " 1813, 2, 13
        Elizabeth " 1816, 2, 6
        Jonathan " 1818, 7, 13
        Abraham   " 1820, 4, 25
        Sarah   " 1823, 5, 10
        Dillon   " 1827, 6, 14
1826, 5, 21. Margaret m Henry C. KIRK

1810, 5, 19. Wm. & w, Ann, & ch, John, Marga-
    ret, William & Susannah, rocf Gunpowder
    MM, dtd 1810,4,25
1811, 3, 16. Jonathan & w, Lavina, & ch, Mar-
    garet & Mary, rocf Baltimore MM for W.
    Dist., dtd 1810,8,8
1813, 9, 18. William dis disunity
1824, 1, 19. John N. gct Short Creek MM, to
    m Susanna Kirk
1824, 7, 19. Susanna rocf Short Creek MM, O.,
    dtd 1824,5,18
1826, 8, 21. Mary Orr (form Marsh) dis mcd
1826, 8, 21. William Jr. gct Flushing MM, to
    m Cynthiann McNamee
1828, 9, 22. Wm. Jr. dis disunity
1828, 12, 22. John dis JH
1829, 1, 19. Isaac dis JH
1829, 12, 21. Susannah Sr., w John, dis JH
1829, 12, 21. Susanna Jr., dt Wm., dis JH
1831, 7, 18. Margaret Jones (form Marsh) dis
    mcd
1832, 10, 22. Jonathan & w, Lavina, & ch,
    Hugh, Elizabeth, Jonathan, Abraham, Sarah
    & Dillon, gct Flushing MM
1832, 10, 22. John gct Flushing MM
1833, 7, 22. Elizabeth dis disunity
1833, 7, 22. Ann dis JH
1835, 12, 21. Cynthia Ann & ch, Mary Ann,
    Thaddeus & Edgar, rocf Flushing MM, dtd
    1835,9,24

MARSHALL
1849, 10, 22. Anna Maria (form Wood) dis mcd

MARTIN
1812, 1, 18. Benjamin dis disunity

1931, 11, 25. James S. recrq
1932, 4, 20. James relrq

MASON
1847, 11, 22. Ann (form Judkins) dis mcd

MASTERS
1827, 10, 23. William, s Isaac & Sarah, Jef-
    ferson Co., O.; m in Cross Creek MH, Na-
    omi BALL, dt James & Ruth, Jefferson Co.,
    O.
1828, 10, 20. Naomi gct Short Creek MM, O.
1832, 2, 20. William & w, Naomi, & ch, David
    & James, rocf Short Creek MM, O., dtd
    1831,9,2
1833, 4, 22. William & w, Naomi, & ch, David,
    James & Ruthanna, gct Deerfield MM

MATHER
1843, 6, 19. Elizabeth (form Carr) dis mcd

MATHEWS   [1809,5,25
1809, 12, 16. Mary rocf Gunpowder MM, dtd
1850, 4, 22. Rebecca [Matthews] (form Kinsey)
    dis mcd

MEGRAIL
1823, 1, 2. James, s Thos. & Rebecca, Jef-
    ferson Co., O.; m in Cross Creek MH, Mary
    EARNSHAW, dt Geo. & Ann, Jefferson Co., O.
    Ch: Alfred   b 1824, 1, 9
        Thomas   " 1825, 6, 19
        Edith   " 1827, 3, 25
        Elmira   " 1829, 1, 1
        William P. " 1831, 2, 7
        George E. " 1833, 8, 16
        John L.   " 1838, 11, 1
        Lindley H. " 1842, 4, 2
1837, 5, 31. Isabella m John C. TALBOTT
1846, 12, 20. Ann m Thos. HAMMOND
1847, 9, 2. Alfred, s James & Mary, Jeffer-
    son Co., O., b 1824,1,9; m in Cross Creek
    MH, Amy HAMMOND, dt John & Rachel, Jeffer-
    son Co., O.

1855, 10, 22. Thomas dis mcd
1857, 5, 18. George dis disunity

MEHOLIN
1887, 12, 19. John W. recrq
1903, 9, 23. John dropped from mbrp

MELTON
1808, 8, 20. William & w, Sarah, & ch, Fanny
    & Moses, gct Plainfield MM

MERRYMAN
1867, 11, 6. Anna, w Wm., dt Matthias &
    Celia Ong, b

1899, 6, 19. Anna [Merriman] relrq
1903, 2, 23. Rosa & Anna recrq

MERRITE
1846, 3, 23. Sabina (form Hoyle) dis mcd

MITCHEL
1824, --, --. Nelson, s Wm. & Mary, b

MICHENER
1815, 10, 26. Jonathan, s John & Martha, Jef-
     ferson Co., O.; m in Cross Creek MH, Jane
     HOBSON, dt Joseph & Ann, Jefferson Co., O.

1816, 3, 18. Jane [Mitchner] gct Short Creek
     MM, O.

MILLER
1815, 4, 15. Mason & w, Ruth, & ch, Asa, Eli,
     Stephen, Nathen, Sarah, Mary, Richard &
     William, gct Plainfield MM
1887, 1, 17. James W. recrq
1902, 10, 21. William J. & w & six ch recrq
1903, 2, 23. Charles E. recrq
1925, 12, 30. Mib(?) recrq

MILLIGAN
1831, 4, 18. Joseph rocf Upper Springfield
     MM, dtd 1831,3,25
1833, 10, 21. Joseph gct Marlborough MM; re-
     turned unaccepted
1834, 5, 19. Joseph dis mcd

MILLS
1893, 11, '20. Julia relrq

MINGE
1828, 11, 17. Anna Maria (form Ladd) dis mcd

MOONEY
1879, 10, 1. Eva P., w F. H., dt Wm. & Mary
     E. -----, b
1879, 10, 1. Eva P., w J. H., dt N. O. & H. E.
     Phipps, b

1904, 3, 23. J. H. recrq
1911, 2, 22. Malcolm recrq
1913, 2, 19. Edward & Marie recrq

MORGAN
1825, 11, 21. Ann rocf Westland MM, dtd 1825,
     1,27
1833, 11, 18. Ann dis jas

MORRIS
1823, 9, 22. Elizabeth, dt Prudence Hoyle,
     rocf Gwynedd MM, Pa., dtd 1823,7,3
1850, 10, 21. Elizabeth gct Salem MM
1889, 8, 19. Frederick & Carrie recrq
1889, 11, 18. Frederick & Carrie relrq

MORTON
1808, 6, 18. Mary dis
1818, 6, 22. John dis disunity
1819, 4, 19. Cassander (form Fisher) dis mcd
1824, 10, 18. Cassander rst

1831, 10, 17. Cassandra & Hannah gct Flushing
     MM

MOSSBURGH
1831, 4, 18. Susanna rocf Stillwater MM, dtd
     1831,3,26
1833, 3, 18. Susanna dis

NAYLOR
----, --, --. Samuel & Rebecca
     Ch: John L.   b 1800, 3, 19
         Joseph P.   " 1802, 10, 3
         Charles P.   " 1804, 9, 12
         Mary   " 1806, 10, 10
         Rebecca   " 1808, 11, 13
         Samuel   " 1812, 5, 21 d 1814, 9,15
           bur Smithfield
         Abraham P. b 1814, 3, 15
         Samuel   " 1816, 2, 26
1810, 8, 20. John, s John & Mary, Jefferson
     Co., O.; m in Cross Creek MH, Martha BALL,
     dt James & Ruth, Jefferson Co., O.
     Ch: Matilda   b 1812, 12, 7
         Ruth   " 1814, 11, 3
         John N.   " 1816, 4, 24
         Joseph   " 1817, 12, 25
         Narsissa   " 1819, 2, 25
         Naomi   " 1821, 8, 7
         Farlin   " 1823, 11, 20
         David   " 1825, 10, 5
1815, 10, 25. Abraham, s John & Mary, Jeffer-
     son Co., O.; m in Plymouth MH, Ruth HAM-
     MOND, dt Geo. & Deborah, Jefferson Co.,
     O., d 1844,--,-- bur Smithfield
     Ch: William   b 1816, 8, 30
         David   " 1818, 5, 28
         Sarah   " 1820, 3, 17
         Deborah   " 1822, 8, 9
         George   " 1824, 9, 22
         Mary G.   " 1827, 6, 21
         Caroline   " 1830, 2, 2
         Elizabeth   " 1833, 6, 7
         Presley I.   " 1836, 9, 6
1823, 2, 26. John L., s Samuel & Rebecca,
     Jefferson Co., O.; m in Smithfield MH,
     Jane McGREW, dt Nathan & Elizabeth, Jef-
     ferson Co., O., d 1863,4,24
     Ch: Elizabeth b 1824, 1, 4 d 1826, 2, 9
         Eliza Ann   " 1826, 7, 21
         Rebecca   " 1829, 8, 9 " 1835, 2,14
         Nathan M.   " 1832, 10, 8
         Samuel G.   " 1835, 2, 13
         William
           Bates   " 1837, 1, 7
         Oliver
           Price   " 1843, 6, 11
1823, 9, 28. John d bur Smithfield
1824, 4, 28. Margaret m Benj. HAMMOND
1826, 8, 30. Mary Sr., w John, d
1832, 5, 2. Rebecca P. m John HOBSON, Jr.
1835, 4, 1. Abraham, s Samuel & Rebecca,
     Jefferson Co., O.; m in Smithfield MH,
     Rachel Ann WOOD, dt Joshua & Esther, Jef-

NAYLOR, Abraham & Rachel Ann, continued
ferson Co., O.
1844, --, --. Ruth, w Abraham, d bur Smithfield
1845, 4, 18. Ruth, w Abraham G., d bur Smithfield
1845, 11, 7. William Henry, s Samuel & Sarah,
b
----, --, --. William B. m Eliza J. ----- b
1838,10,15
    Ch: Harry C. b 1868, 6, 16
        Charles W. " 1869, 12, 4
        Oliver G. " 1871, 10, 20
        Bartley G. " 1874, 5, 11 (or 1874,5,6)
        Lulu   " 1876, 5, 18
        Mary   " 1880, 8, 21
----, --, --. Oliver P. & Margaret Jane
    Ch: Etta Jane b 1868, 10, 3
        John Oscar " 1870, 4, 3
        Howard
        Elliott   " 1873, 12, 6
1929, 10, 2. Oliver d
1930, 6, 28. J. Oscar d

1810, 1, 20. John rocf Gunpowder MM, dtd
1809,11,22
1810, 10, 20. Samuel & w, Rebecca, & ch, Ann,
John, Joseph, Charles, Mary & Rebeckah,
rocf Gunpowder MM, dtd 1810,8,22
1810, 10, 20. Mary (form McNamee) dis mcd
1812, 5, 16. John & w, Mary, & ch, Abraham,
rocf Gunpowder MM, dtd 1812,3,25
1813, 9, 18. Margaret, minor, rocf Baltimore
MM, E. Dist., dtd 1813,5,13
1818, 4, 20. Rachel (form Foreman) dis mcd
with first cousin
1824, 8, 23. Abigail (form Ball) con mcd
1825, 3, 21. Rachel rst
1825, 10, 17. Mary Wolf (form Naylor) dis mcd
1826, 5, 22. Mary, minor, recrq
1827, 3, 19. Joseph dis mcd
1829, 9, 21. Abigail gct Deerfield MM
1829, 10, 19. Charles dis mcd
1830, 1, 18. Mary Kirk (form Naylor) dis mcd
1833, 11, 18. Matilda dis jas
1834, 8, 18. James rst on consent of Baltimore MM
1834, 11, 17. Lewis, minor s James & Rachel,
recrq
1837, 5, 22. James & w, Rachel, & s, Lewis,
gct Somerset MM, O.
1837, 8, 21. John & ch, Farland & David, gct
Somerset MM, O.
1837, 10, 23. William dis mcd
1838, 5, 21. Ruth & Naomi dis jas
1838, 6, 18. Joseph dis mcd
1838, 7, 23. John Jr. gct Somerset MM
1837, 11, 19. Narcissa gct Somerset MM
1839, 7, 22. Absalom P. & w, Rachel Ann, &
ch, Albert & Mary Jane, gct Pennsville
MM, O.
1844, 1, 22. Samuel Jr. con mcd
1844, 11, 18. Sarah, w Samuel Jr., recrq

1845, 1, 20. Sarah Purviance (form Naylor)
dis mcd
1846, 1, 19. Abraham dis mcd
1847, 4, 19. David dis
1847, 10, 18. Deborah Porter (form Naylor)
dis mcd
1849, 11, 19. Mary Haines (form Nailor) dis
mcd
1851, 6, 23. George dis mcd
1853, 8, 18. Elizabeth Haynes (form Naylor)
dis mcd
1855, 6, 18. Samuel & w, Sarah, & s, William
Henry, gct Western Plain MM, Ia.
1864, 1, 18. Caroline gct LeGrand MM, Ia.
1865, 2, 20. Caroline dis jas; LeGrand MM rpd
she had jas before cert was issued
1867, 7, 17. Maria recrq
1868, 10, 19. William B. con mcd
1869, 2, 22. Oliver con mcd
1869, 7, 19. Margaret recrq
1869, 10, 18. Etta Jane, dt Oliver & Margaret,
recrq
1870, 3, 20. Nathan M. con mcd
1872, 9, 18. Eliza Jane & ch, Harry, Charles
& Oliver, recrq
1876, 6, 19. Abram & Mary H. recrq
1879, 2, 17. Nathan M. dis disunity
1880, 6, 21. Samuel G. relrq
1898, 1, 17. Oscar relrq
1902, 9, 22. Charles relrq
1908, 4, 22. Nathan O. recrq
1917, 11, 21. Virginia recrq
1920, 4, 21. Jessie Belle & Annie E. recrq
1924, 9, 24. Eliza J. d 1924,8,30
1928, 8, 15. Oscar I. recrq

NEAL
1860, 1, 23. Margaret, w Archibald, dt John &
Mariah Smith, b
                                   [rq
1881, 2, 21. Archibald & Margaret [Neil] rec-

NEGUS
1854, 10, 23. John Watson gct New Garden MM,
to m Eliza Negus

NEUBEN
1932, 1, 20. Nicholas recrq

NEWBY
1812, 8, 15. Malachi Jolly gct Stillwater
MM, to m Susannah Newby
1814, 1, 15. Job rocf Stillwater MM, dtd
1813,11,30
1814, 9, 17. Job gct Stillwater MM
1817, 2, 17. James, minor, rocf Short Creek
MM, O., dtd 1816,11,19
1817, 5, 19. Cert rec for James, minor, end
to Stillwater MM

NEWLIN
1864, 9, 14. Elizabeth A. m Chas. G. CARPEN-
TER

NEWLIN, continued
1834, 5, 19. Matilda (form Ong) dis mcd
1860, 3, 19. James recrq   [recrq
1861, 1, 21. Elizabeth, dt James & Matilda,
1881, 2, 21. Annie recrq
1886, 10, 18. Anna relrq

NEWPORT
1821, 5, 21. William Hoyle gct Concord MM, to
    m Edith Newport

NICHOLSON
----, --, --. John & Alice
    Ch: William L. b 1805, 1, 26
        Eliza   " 1808, 7, 4
        Charles   " 1813, 2, 5
        Aletta   " 1815, 7, 14
        John   " 1819, 4, 13
1833, 11, 27. Charles, s John & Alice, Jeffer-
    son Co., O., b 1813,2,5; m in Smithfield
    MH, Narcissa CREW, dt Benj. & Sarah, Jef-
    ferson Co., O.
    Ch: William   b 1836, 4, 8
        Benjamin C." 1838, 9, 20

1814, 9, 17. John & w, Alice, & ch, William
    L., Eliza & Charles L., rocf Baltimore MM,
    W. Dist., dtd 1814,8,10
1828, 9, 22. Eliza Shaddock (form Nicholson)
    dis mcd
1829, 5, 18. John & Alice dis jH
1835, 8, 17. Aletta Tumbleson (form Nichol-
    son) dis jH & mcd
1844, 11, 18. Alice rst
1846, 12, 21. Charles & w, Narcissa, & ch,
    William, Benjamin C., Elizabeth Ann,
    George Edwin & John, gct Short Creek MM,
    O.
1847, 3, 22. John dis mcd
1853, 10, 17. Alice gct Somerset MM
1904, 3, 23. Mrs. Bell [Nichison] recrq

NOBLE
1887, 1, 17. Eliza Jane & Lyman A. recrq
1903, 2, 23. Rose recrq
1911, 6, 21. Ross gct Mt. Pleasant MM, O.

ONG
----, --, --. Finley d 1874,3,10; m Anna
    ----- d 1853,11,15 bur Smithfield
    Ch: Jacob   b 1806, 10, 26
        Mary   " 1808, 9, 10
        Harlem   " 1810, 12, 15
        Matilda " 1813, 4, 21
        Lewis   " 1815, 3, 18
        Rebecca " 1817, 4, 15
        Mifflin " 1819, 6, 7
        Elizanna " 1821, 3, 14
        Enly   " 1824, 8, 15
        Rachel Ann " 1834, 4, 15
1813, 11, 25. Anna m Stephen KINSEY
1820, 6, 28. Mary m John B. McGREW
----, --, --. J. & M.

Ch: Nathan   d 1828, 9,26
    bur Smithfield
    Mifflin J.   " 1829, 1, 8
    bur Smithfield
1830, 10, 27. Mary B. m Aquilla CARR
1839, 10, 2. Lewis, s Finley & Anna, Jeffer-
    son Co., O.; m in Smithfield MH, Elmira
    PURVIANCE, dt Jos. & Deborah, Jefferson
    Co., O.
    Ch: Joseph P. b 1840, 7, 17
        Lindley H. " 1841, 9, 3 d 1862, 7, 8
        Lemuel   " 1844, 3, 30
        Plummer   " 1846, 1, 22
        Ann Eliza " 1849, 3, 22
        Amanda   " 1851, 3, 1
        William P. " 1853, 7, 7
        Lewis   " 1856, 7, 6
        Anderson C." 1858, 4, 12
        Delbert B. " 1861, 4, 24
1847, 3, 31. Mifflin, s Finley & Ann, Jeffer-
    son Co., O., d 1869,4,4; m in Smithfield
    MH, Elizabeth KIRK, dt Wm. & Martha, Jef-
    ferson Co., O., d 1858,5,1 bur at Smith-
    field
    Ch: Finley K. b 1848, 1, 7
        William   " 1851, 7, 15
        Martha Ann " 1853, 6, 4
        Oliver   " 1855, 2, 28
1849, 9, 1. Jacob d
1853, 11, 15. Anna d bur Smithfield
----, --, --. Moses & Mary
    Ch: Zola   b 1856, 11, 20
        A. R.   " 1846, 10, 9
----, --, --. Miffen, s Harlen & Mary, b 1836,
    2,8; m Sarah J. HUSSEY, dt Nathan & Ruth,
    b 1839,6,9
1860, 5, 30. Catharine d bur Smithfield
1875, 10, 19. Mary C., w Moses, d bur Smith-
    field
----, --, --. Matthias F., s J. F. & M. J.,
    b 1831,1,1; m Celia A. WHITE, dt Wm. &
    Sarah, b 1835,12,20
    Ch: Mabel C.   b 1876, 11, 20
        Jessie L. " 1879, 1, 27
        Fred   " 1873, 12, 20
        Clarence   " 1864, 12, 25 (sic)
1882, 2, 19. Howard, s Wm. & Rachel E., b

1810, 4, 21. Anna rocf Redstone MM, dtd
    1809,12,1
1810, 7, 21. Isaac dis mcd
1813, 1, 16. Jacob Jr. dis disunity
1815, 6, 17. Nathan dis
1819, 8, 23. John dis mcd
1820, 8, 21. Isaac rst
1820, 11, 20. Hannah recrq
1821, 9, 17. Isaac gct Flushing MM
1823, 12, 22. Catharine recrq
1830, 3, 22. Jacob, s Finley, dis mcd
1833, 12, 23. Moses H. dis mcd
1834, 5, 19. Matilda Newlin (form Ong) dis
    mcd
1840, 11, 28. Rebecca Jones (form Ong) dis

ONG, continued
mcd
1849, 7, 23.   Jacob d 1849,1,1 ae 90 (a minister & mbr of this mtg)
1850, 3, 18.   Elizana Lewis (form Ong) dis mcd
1852, 1, 19.   Emily Chadwell (form Ong) dis mcd
1852, 7, 19.   Mary d 1852,6,7 ae 89 (an elder)
1856, 9, 22.   Rachel Ann Hamilton (form Ong) dis mcd
1862, 10, 20. Mifflin gct Flushing MM, O., to m Mary R. Briggs
1863, 5, 16.   Mary rocf Flushing MM, O.
1864, 5, 23.   Moses H. rst at Short Creek MM, O., on consent of this mtg
1867, 8, 19.   Joseph P. gct Damascus MM, to m Rhoda Stratton
1868, 6, 22.   Lewis & w, Elmira, & ch, Amanda, William P., Lewis B., Anderson C. & Delbert, gct Damascus MM, O.
1868, 6, 22.   Lemuel M. dis mcd
1868, 10, 19. Joseph gct Damascus MM, O.
1870, 7, 18.   Sarah J. rocf Short Creek MM, O.
1870, 7, 18.   Mary H. & s, Lewis H., gct New Sharon MM, Ia.
1872, 10, 21. Lewis & w, Elmira, & ch, Lewis B., Anderson C. & Delbert L., rocf Damascus MM
1873, 4, 21.   Anna Simpson (form Ong) dis mcd
1874, 5, 18.   Matthas T. recrq
1874, 7, 20.   Lewis & w, Elmira, & ch, Lewis B., Anderson C. & Delbert T., gct Columbus MM, O.
1874, 10, 19. Celia recrq
1875, 2, 22.   Moses H. & w, Mary, rocf Short Creek MM, O.
1875, 2, 22.   Emma & Mary Elizabeth rocf Short Creek MM, O.
1877, 4, 23.   Osborn & Iola recrq
1879, 11, 17. Albert R. recrq
1880, 12, 20. Oliver, William, Finley & Martha, gc
1880, 12, 20. William P. gc
1881, 2, 21.   Shepherd, Rebecca & Elva L. recrq
1881, 2, 21.   Ross & Annie L. recrq
1886, 3, 22.   Osborn gct Short Creek MM, O.
1886, 3, 22.   Harlin & Naomi recrq
1886, 10, 18. Finley, Oliver & Mattie relrq
1886, 12, 20. Lizzie Haynes (form Ong) relrq
1888, 3, 19.   Clarence W. & Ella P. recrq
1888, 5, 21.   Emma L. Smith (form Ong) relrq
1890, 6, 23.   Shepherd dropped from mbrp
1890, 7, 21.   Rebecca & ch, Elva, Harlin & Nancy gct Newberg MM, Oregon
1891, 8, 17.   Shepherd rst by QM
1891, 11, 22. Shepherd gct Newberg MM, Oregon
1898, 3, 21.   Howard recrq
1899, 11, 20. A. R. relrq
1903, 8, 17.   Clarence & Rosa relrq
1903, 8, 17.   Iola C. gct Chagrin MM
1911, 5, 24.   Howard relrq

ORR
1826, 8, 21.   Mary (form Marsh) dis mcd

OXLEY
1903, 2, 23.   William recrq

PACKER
1813, 5, 15.   Moses rocf Concord MM, dtd 1813,4,22
1814, 2, 19.   Moses gct Short Creek MM, O.

PANCOAST
1824, 2, 23.   Mary rocf Pipe Creek MM, dtd 1823,3,15 end by Stillwater MM, 1823,12,27
1825, 12, 19. Mary gct Salem MM

PARISH
1816, 2, 19.   Cert rec for Rachel from Gunpowder MM, Md., dtd 1815,11,22, end to Short Creek MM, O.

PARKS
1871, 10, 23. Mariah A., w Wm., dt Chas. & Mary E. Blackburn, b

1911, 2, 22.   Pauline May & John Wm. recrq
1913, 2, 19.   William W. & William G. recrq
1915, 4, 21.   Marguerite Ford recrq
1921, 4, 20.   Mary Margaret recrq
1930, 2, 19.   Henry Isaac recrq
1931, 3, 25.   Phillis Jane relrq
1931, 11, 25. John W. relrq

PARSHALL
1931, 11, 25. Alphaus recrq
1932, 9, 21.   Alpheus relrq

PARSON
1799, 10, 14. Mary, w Chas., dt J. & Mary Talbert, b
1825, 9, 29.   Juliann m David BALL
1830, 4, 1.   Mary m Joseph PLUMMER
1832, 5, 31.   Alice m John PLUMMER

1814, 1, 15.   Susanna rocf Gunpowder MM, dtd 1813,10,27
1817, 4, 21.   Susanna dis
1819, 12, 20. Ganah rocf Deer Creek MM, Md., dtd 1819,4,5
1825, 2, 21.   Juliann & Mary recrq
1826, 12, 18. William, minor s of Ganor, recrq
1832, 2, 23.   Alice recrq
1836, 2, 22.   William dis mcd
1841, 10, --. Mary (form Talbott) dis mcd
1851, 4, 21.   Gainor gct Pennsville MM
1860, 3, 19.   Mary (Talbott) con mcd

PARVIANCE
1815, 4, 19.   Sarah m Eli SIDWELL

PAXON
1825, 9, 19.   Rebecca (form Barcroft) dis mcd

PAYNE
1885, 1, 19. Adda recrq
1885, 6, 22. Ada dropped from mbrp

PELT
1907, 4, 24. Anna W. gct Beloit MM

PENN
1916, 4, 19. Golda relrq

PENROSE
1830, 4, 28. John, s Thos. & Sarah, Jefferson
    Co., O.; m in Cross Creek MH, Anna CREW,
    dt Jacob & Elizabeth, Jefferson Co., O.

1827, 9, 17. Thomas & w, Sarah, & ch, Sarah
    Ann & Joseph, rocf Short Creek MM, O., dtd
    1827,5,22
1827, 9, 17. Thomas Jr. rocf Short Creek MM,
    O., dtd 1827,5,22
1827, 9, 17. James rocf Short Creek MM, O.,
    dtd 1827,5,22
1829, 10, 19. Thomas Jr. gct Deerfield MM
1830, 3, 22. Thomas & w, Sarah, & ch, Sarah
    Ann & Joseph, gct Deerfield MM
1831, 4, 18. John rocf Short Creek MM, dtd
    1830,12,21
1831, 7, 18. John & w, Anna, gct Deerfield MM
1832, 7, 23. James gct Deerfield MM

PERRINE
1913, 2, 19. Altha recrq

PETTIT
1863, 12, 2. Elnathan [Pettet], s Wm. P. &
    Mary, Jefferson Co., O.; m in Smithfield
    MH, Margaret H. WOOD, dt Samuel & Lewcy,
    Jefferson Co., O.

1833, 1, 21. Mary Jane, minor, rocf New Gar-
    den MM, dtd 1832,10,25
1846, 4, 20. Mary Jane gct Short Creek MM, O.
1864, 8, 22. Margaret H. [Pettitt] gct Short
    Creek MM, O.

PHIPPS
1850, 2, 8. William, s Wm. & Mary, b
----, --, --. E. W. & W. E.
    Ch: Earla   b 1880, 3, 10
        Charles   " 1887, 8, 27

1813, 8, 21. Susanna recrq
1820, 7, 17. Susanna dis
1882, 4, 17. Emma W. recrq
1885, 9, 21. Emma relrq
1888, 3, 19. Eva recrq
1888, 3, 19. Elisha W., Emma W., Mary E. &
    Earla E. recrq
1903, 2, 23. Marie recrq

PICKERING
1810, 5, 19. Rachel (form Fisher) dis mcd

PIDGEON
1819, 1, 28. Amos, s John & Susanna, Jeffer-
    son Co., O.; m in Cross Creek MH, Ann
    PLUMMER, dt Jos. & Mary, Jefferson Co., O.
    Ch: Harriet   b 1819, 11, 20
        Joseph W. " 1824, 9, 21

1816, 4, 22. Amos rocf Pipe Creek MM, dtd
    1816,3,16
1832, 11, 19. Amos & w, Ann, & ch, Harriet,
    Joseph & John, gct Deerfield MM
1843, 10, 23. Joseph Hammond gct Pennsville
    MM, to m Harriet Pigeon

PLUMMER
1815, 2, 22. Margaret (nee Wood) m John
    BURGESS
1817, 5, 29. Mahale m Wm. HOBSON
1819, 1, 28. Ann m Amos PIDGEON
1821, 1, 24. Mary, w J. L., d bur Richmond
1823, 5. 13. Deborah, dt S., d bur Richmond
1823, 10, 2. Caleb, s Joseph, d bur Richmond
1824, 12, 2. Sarah m Geo. EARNSHAW
1828, 5, 1. Mary m John HAMMOND
1828, 7, 28. Lydia W., dt Samuel, d bur
    Smithfield
1830, 4, 1. Joseph, s Thos. & Susanna, Jef-
    ferson Co., O.; m in Cross Creek MH, Mary
    PARSONS, dt Amos & Gaynor, d 1842,6,10 bur
    Cross Creek
    Ch: Thomas   b 1831, 1, 6
        Amos P.   " 1832, 9, 12
        Mary   " 1834, 12, 12
        Benjamin L." 1837, 8, 12
    Joseph m 2nd 1847,12,30 in Cross Creek MH,
    Mary S. FALQUHAR, dt Joseph & Beulah, Jef-
    ferson Co., O.
1832, 5, 31. John, s Thos. & Susanna, Jeffer-
    son Co., O.; m in Cross Creek MH, Alice
    PARSONS, dt Amos & Gaynor, Jefferson Co.,
    O., d 1837,4,10 bur Richmond
    Ch: Juliann   b 1834, 2, 24

1813, 4, 17. Samuel & w, Margaret, & ch,
    Richard, Lydia, William, Rebecca, Joshua,
    Thomas & Susanna, rocf Pipe Creek MM, Md.,
    dtd 1813,3,13
1814, 9, 17. Mary, Sarah, Ann & Mahala rocf
    Pipe Creek MM, dtd 1814,7,16
1815, 8, 20. Caleb rocf Pipe Creek MM, dtd
    1815,4,15
1815, 9, 16. Mary rocf Pipe Creek MM, dtd
    1815,5,13
1818, 5, 18. Rebecca, minor, gct Westland MM,
    Pa.
1819, 9, 20. Susannah & ch, Joseph, Mary,
    John, Caleb, Thomas & Deborah, rocf Still-
    water MM, dtd 1819,5,22
1821, 12, 17. Rebecca rocf Westland MM, Pa.,
    dtd 1821,5,24
1823, 10, 20. Mary Teeple (form Plummer) con
    mcd
1831, 9, 18. Caleb dis mcd

PLUMMER, continued
1832, 1, 23. Thomas gct Alum Creek MM
1833, 8, 19. Cert for Thomas granted some
     time ago to Alum Creek, now returned un-
     used
1836, 6, 20. Rebecca gct Pennsville MM
1836, 7, 18. Joshua gct Pennsville MM
1836, 10, 17. Richard & Thomas gct Penns-
     ville MM
1836, 10, 17. Susannah W. gct Pennsville MM
1841, 2, 22. John dis disunity
1842, 2, 21. Thomas rpd mcd
1843, 5, 22. Thomas dis mcd a yr ago
1855, 3, 19. Joseph & w, Mary, & ch, Benjamin
     L., Elizabeth, William, Susanna T. & Han-
     nah Maria, gct Western Plain MM, Ia.
1855, 3, 14. Susanna Mary T. & Juli Ann gct
     Western Plain MM, Ia.
1862, 6, 23. Thomas rst at LeGrand MM, Ia.,
     on consent of this mtg

POOL
1819, 6, 21. Joseph & w, Hannah, & ch, Maria,
     Emily, Samuel & Hannah, rocf Short Creek
     MM, O., dtd 1819,2,23
1824, 5, 17. Maria Hexton (form Pool) dis mcd
1832, 9, 17. Hannah & Elizabeth gct Short
     Creek MM, O.
1837, 9, 18. William Carr gct Upper Spring-
     field MM, to m Lydia Pool

PORTER
1847, 10, 18. Deborah (form Naylor) dis mcd
1931, 5, 20. Mary relrq

POWELL
1927, 10, 19. Chas., Essie, Walter & Thomas
     recrq

PRICE
1819, 5, 26. Ann m Thos. B. MEGREW
1825, 4, 27. William, s Warrick & Susanna,
     Jefferson Co., O.; m in Smithfield MH,
     Edith BALLINGER, dt Wm. & Lydia, Jefferson
     Co., O., d 1853,11,2 bur Smithfield
     Ch: Lydia   b 1826, 4, 30 d 1830, 5,24
          bur Richmond
        Oliver   b 1828, 1, 20 " 1847, 1,24
        Warick   " 1829, 4, 12
        Rebecca   " 1831, 3, 19
        Wm. Ballin-
             ger " 1836, 2, 27
        Ann   " 1839, 3, 21 " 1839, 8,31
          bur Richmond
1828, 3, 26. Susanna m John WOOD
1833, 4, 1. Isaac, s Warrick, d bur Smith-
     field
1843, 10, 21. Susannah, w Warrick, d bur
     Smithfield
1852, 9, 23. Rebecca B. m David B. UPDEGRAFF
1857, 10, 8. Warrick Sr. d bur Smithfield

1808, 11, 19. Israel & ch, Elizabeth, William,

Frances & Israel, gct Baltimore MM, E.
Dist.
1811, 11, 16. Warrick & w, Susannah, & ch,
     William, Ann, Isaac & Susannah, rocf Bal-
     timore MM, E. Dist., dtd 1811,10,10
1818, 8, 17. Cert rec for John W. from Bal-
     timore MM, W. Dist., dtd 1818,3,6, end to
     Plainfield MM
1826, 11, 20. Daniel Williams gct Gunpowder
     MM, Md., to m Elizabeth Price
1839, 9, 23. Mary (form McGrew) dis mcd
1851, 12, 22. Warrick gct Alum Creek MM, O.
1856, 5, 19. Warrick gct Sandy Spring MM, to
     m Beulah R. Farmer
1856, 6, 23. William gct Short Creek MM, O.,
     to m Hannah W. Walker
1857, 2, 23. Hannah W. rocf Short Creek MM,
     O., dtd 1857,2,21
1857, 4, 20. Warrick rocf Alum Creek MM, O.,
     dtd 1857,1,22
1859, 5, 23. William B. gct Sandy Spring MM,
     to m Ellen A. Farmer
1861, 12, 23. William & w, Hannah W., gct
     Short Creek MM, O.
1863, 12, 21. Warrick & William B. gct Sandy
     Spring MM

PUGH
1825, 5, 23. John rst on consent of Notting-
     ham MM, Pa.
1826, 5, 22. John gct Somerset MM

PURVIANCE
----, --, --. David d 1838,10,14; m Mary -----
     d 1837,8,28
     Ch: James   b 1800, 12, 28
        David   " 1804, 4, 8
        Mary   " 1806, 3, 11
        Elizabeth " 1810, 2, 10 d 1816,10,10
          bur Smithfield
        Amos   b 1812, 2, 19 " 1822, 7.17
          bur Smithfield
----, --, --. Joseph d 1826,4,29 bur Smithfield
     m Deborah -----
     Ch: William   b 1816, --, --
        Henry   " 1818, --, --
        Elmira   " 1821, --, --
        Israel   " 1823, --, --
        Elwood   " 1826, --, --
1816, 10, 19. Sinah d bur Smithfield
----, --, --. George & Esther
     Ch: Samuel   b 1818, 6, --
        Isaac   " 1820, --, --
        Mary   " 1821, --, --
        Martha   " 1823, --, --
        Richard B. " 1823, 3, 25 d 1850, 7,25
          bur Smithfield
        George   b 1824, 11, 1
        Owen   " 1827, 2, 5
        Elizabeth " 1828, 11, 4 " 1850, 7, 7
          bur Smithfield
        Esther   b 1830, 2, 26
        Nathan   " 1834, 3, 23

PURVIANCE, continued

1819, 4, 20. Richard, s Jas. & Elizabeth, Jefferson Co., O.; m in Smithfield MH, Deborah CLAPP, dt Jas. & Catharine, Jefferson Co., O.
   Ch: Nathaniel b 1820, 1, 22
       Alfred G. " 1820, 10, --
       Elisha   " 1823, 4, --
       Joseph R. " 1827, 12, --

1820, --, --. Plummer, s Wm. & Ellen, b

1827, 3, 28. David, s David & Mary, Jefferson Co., O.; m in Smithfield MH, Sarah WILLITS dt Ellis & Hannah, Jefferson Co., O.
   Ch: Elis   b 1828, 4, 6

1829, 11, 25. Elizabeth m John WILLITS

1837, 8, 28. Mary d

1838, 10, 14. David d

1839, 10, 2. Elmira m Lewis ONG

----, --, --. William, s Jos. & D., b 1816,11, 19 d 1899,5,7; m Sarah -----, dt Evan & Sarah HEIFERD, b 1817,10,7
   Ch: Evan   b 1840, 12, 30

----, --, --. William & Sarah
   Ch: Evan H.   b 1840, 11, 29
       William I. " 1848, 8, 8

1862, 10, 1. Evan H., s Wm. & Sarah, Jefferson Co., O.; m in Smithfield MH, Lydia B. WOOD, dt Thos. & Elizabeth A., Jefferson Co., O.
   Ch: Thomas W. b 1863, 12, 7
       Willie   " 1870, 8, 4 d 1871, 1, 7
       Charles L. " 1872, 3, 10
       Samuel   " 1873, 6, 21

----, --, --. Evan, s Wm. & Sarah, b 1840,12, 30; m Lydia B. WOOD, dt Thomas & Elizabeth, b 1841,2,14
   Ch: Thomas W. b 1863, 12, 7
       William H. " 1870, 8, 4
       Charles T. " 1872, 3, 10
       Samutl T. " 1874, 6, 21
       Annie W. " 1876, 3, 8

1866, 11, 15. Nellie, w Thomas W., dt Wm. & Rebecca Judkins, b

1873, 6, 21. Samuel b

----, --, --. William S., s Wm. & S., b 1848, 8,7; m Elizabeth JONES, dt Joshua & R., b 1846,8,12
   Ch: Mary S.   b 1879, 8, 3
       Samuel   "

----, --, --. Chas. A. m Alice M. KELLERS, dt Wm. & Margaret, b 1871,3,24
   Ch: Hannah
       May   b 1895, 10, 7
       Thomas Wm. " 1897, 10, 5

1810, 11, 17. Thomas rst

1812, 10, 17. Joseph rocf Redstone MM, dtd 1812,10,2

1813, 1, 16. Joseph gct Short Creek MM, to m Deborah Sidwell

1813, 4, 17. James Jr. rocf Redstone MM, dtd 1813,1,29

1813, 7, 17. Deborah [Perviance] rocf Short

Creek MM, dtd 1813,3,23

1813, 7, 17. William rocf Redstone MM, dtd 1813,2,27

1814, 6, 18. George rocf Redstone MM, dtd 1814,5,3

1814, 7, 16. Richard rocf Redstone MM, dtd 1814,6,3

1814, 9, 17. Elizabeth & Sarah rocf Redstone MM, dtd 1814,7,1

1816, 5, 20. David & w, Mary, & ch, James, David, Mary, Elizabeth & Amos, gct Plainfield MM; returned unused 1816,8,19

1817, 5, 19. George gct Concord MM, to m

1818, 1, 19. Esther rocf Concord MM, dtd 1817,8,20

1816, 3, 18. Sarah George (form Purviance) dis mcd

1819, 8, 23. William gct Short Creek MM, O., to m

1820, 2, 21. Elenor rocf Short Creek MM, O., dtd 1819,12,21

1820, 3, 20. James con mcd

1822, 11, 18. James Jr. dis mcd

1829, 2, 23. Thomas dis jH

1829, 4, 20. Deborah, w Richard, dis jH

1829, 5, 18. Richard dis jH

1829, 5, 18. Deborah Sr., wd Joseph, dis jH

1829, 7, 20. James dis jH

1829, 7, 20. George dis jH

1830, 11, 22. William dis disunity

1831, 4, 18. David Jr. & w, Sarah, & ch, Ellis & Martin Ezra, gct Flushing MM

1832, 4, 23. Mary George (form Purviance) dis mcd

1834, 5, 19. David & w, Mary, gct Flushing MM

1836, 6, 20. David & w, Mary, rocf Flushing MM, dtd 1836,5,25

1839, 10, 21. William gct Short Creek MM, O., to m Sarah Hurford

1840, 2, 17. Martha Scott (form Purviance) dis mcd

1840, 5, 18. Samuel dis mcd

1840, 8, 17. Henry dis mcd

1842, 11, 21. Sarah rocf Short Creek MM, O., dtd 1840,8,19

1843, 5, 22. Isaac dis disunity

1844, 11, 18. Alfred dis mcd

1844, 12, 23. Israel dis mcd

1845, 1, 20. Sarah (form Naylor) dis mcd

1845, 6, 23. Plummer W. dis disunity

1845, 11, 17. Mary Maris (form Purviance) con mcd

1847, 12, 20. George Jr. con mcd

1850, 1, 21. Elwood dis mcd

1850, 11, 18. Henry S. rst at Alum Creek MM, on consent of this mtg

1851, 5, 19. George dis jas

1852, 12, 20. Esther Walters (form Purviance) dis mcd

1858, 12, 20. Nathan dis mcd

1862, 6, 23. Owen dis mcd

1866, 12, 17. William & w, Sarah H., & ch,

PURVIANCE, continued
    William, gct Damascus MM, O.
1877, 4, 23. Samuel recrq
1878, 5, 20. William & Sarah rocf Damascus MM
1878, 6, 17. William S. & Elizabeth L. rocf
    Damascus MM
1895, 1, 21. Alice M. recrq
1896, 1, 20. Nellie recrq
1897, 1, 18. Hannah M. relrq
1899, 2, 20. Nellie relrq
1899, 7, 17. William d 1899,5,7 ae 83 (an
    elder)
1902, 7, 21. Sarah d 1901,9,11 ae 84y 8m 4d
    (a minister)
1902, 9, 22. Elizabeth M. rocf Fairfield MM,
    Ind.
1905, 5, 24. Anna H. recrq
1907, 9, 25. Samuel T. dis disunity; his w.
    Bessie, & ch, Evan Hurford & Ethel May
    dropped from mbrp
1907, 9, 25. William S., Annie Hurford &
    Lydia B. dropped from membership
1909, 2, 24. Samuel T. rst by QM
1909, 3, 24. Samuel T. joined M. E. Church;
    dropped from mbrp

QUAINTANCE
1809, 2, 23. Ann m Ellis DAVIS
1810, 11, 21. Eli, s Jos. & Susanna, Jefferson
    Co., O.; m in Plymouth MH, Betty KIRK,
    dt Wm. & Rachel, Jefferson Co., O.
    Ch: Joseph   b 1812, 4, 25
        Lewis C. " 1814, 1, 12
        Susanna " 1816, 9, 2
        Rachel   " 1818, 7, 26
        William " 1820, 6, 19
1811, 1, 24. Susanna m Timothy KIRK
----, --, --. Fisher & Sarah
    Ch: Ann   b 1817, 2, 26
        Eli   " 1818, 8, 16
        Hannah " 1819, 2, 20 d 1821, 9,17
          bur Smithfield
        Irey   b 1822, 4, 7
        Susanna " 1824, 1, 11
        Dawson   " 1826, 6, 22
        Joseph W. " 1828, 8, 31
1819, 8, 20. Rachel d

1808, 7, 16. Wm. con mcd
1815, 4, 15. Eli & w, Betty, & ch, Joseph &
    Lewis Carey, gct New Garden MM
1815, 12, 27. Fisher gct Newgarden MM, to m
1816, 9, 23. Sarah rocf Newgarden MM, dtd
    1816,3,14
1818, 9, 21. Eli & w, Betsy, & ch, Joseph,
    Lewis & Susannah, rocf Newgarden MM, dtd
    1818,7,16
1819, 9, 20. Esther recrq
1825, 9, 19. Eli & w, Betty, & ch, Joseph,
    Lewis Cary, Susannah, William, Edward
    Courtney & Ann, gct Alum Creek MM
1829, 4, 20. Joseph & w, Susanna, gct Alum
    Creek MM

1830, 12, 20. Fisher & w, Sarah, & ch. Ann,
    Eli P., Irey, Susannah, Dawson & Joseph
    W., gct Alum Creek MM
1830, 12, 20. William & w, Esther, & ch, Re-
    becca, Charlotte, Joseph & Wm., gct Alum
    Creek MM

RABB
1904, 7, 20. Jennie relrq
1923, 1, 24. Jennie [Robb] recrq

RAMSEY
1886, 1, 18. Annis W. (form Whitten) rpd
    mcd; released from mbrp

REDD
1824, 5, 26. Lydia m Caleb WOOD

1817, 8, 18. Mary rocf Hopewell MM, dtd
    1817,5,--
1817, 9, 22. Israel rocf Hopewell MM, Va.,
    dtd 1817,3,8
1817, 9, 22. Isaiah & Lydia rocf Hopewell
    MM, Va., dtd 1817,3,8
1819, 5, 17. Isaiah, minor, gct Plainfield MM
1822, 8, 19. Isaiah rocf Plainfield MM, dtd
    1822,2,21
1824, 12, 20. Mary gct Plainfkeld MM
1825, 5, 23. Isaiah gct Stillwater MM, to m
    Ann St Clair
1825, 8, 22. Isaiah gct Stillwater MM
1827, 10, 22. Mary rocf Plainfield MM, dtd
    1827,8,23
1837, 8, 21. Mary gct Flushing MM
1842, 12, 19. Israel gct Stillwater MM

REED
1844, 11, 18. Elizabeth (form Watson) con mcd

REESE
----, --, --. Seth C., s Zachery, b 1854,8,6;
    m Huldah A. ----- b 1855,10,15 bur Cherry
    Grove, Ind.
    Ch: Byrum G. b 1877, 9, 30
        Loring   " 1882, 3, 23

1884, 5, 19. Seth & w, Huldah, & ch, Byron
    J. & Loring W., rocf Raysville MM, Ind.,
    dtd 1884,4,26
1889, 4, 22. Seth S. & w, Huldah A., & ch
    gct Adrian MM, Mich.
1890, 3, 17. Seth C. & w, Huldah A., & ch,
    Byron & Loring, rocf Adrian MM, Mich.,
    dtd 1890,2,22
1898, 7, 18. Memorial for Hulda Ann, w Seth,
    dt Nathan W. & Malinda Johnson, b 1855,10,
    15 d 1898,6,-- (a minister)
1900, 2, 19. Mrs. Frida M. [Rees] recrq
1902, 9, 22. Edith C. recrq
1911, 1, 25. Seth C. & fam relrq

RHEUBEL
1810, 5, 19. Meriam (form Bogue) dis mcd

RICHARDS
1827, 9, 17. Joseph rocf Marlborough MM, dtd
    1827,6,26

RICHIE
----, --, --. Robert & Sarah
    Ch: Mary Annes-
              ley b 1807, 2, 21
        Joseph
          Steer   " 1809, 12, 17
        Edward   " 1812, 3, 27
        Samuel
          Steer   " 1814, 5, 8
        Hannah   " 1816, 9, 29
        Sarah   " 1818, 10, 18

1814, 6, 18. Robert [Richee] & w, Sarah, &
    ch, Mary, Ansley, Joseph Steer, Edward &
    Samuel Steer, rocf Short Creek MM, dtd
    1814,5,24
1822, 3, 18. Robert & w, Sarah, & ch, Mary,
    Joseph, Edward, Samuel, Hannah & Sarah,
    gct WD MM

RIDGLEY
1821, 11, 19. Ann (form Hull) dis mcd

ROBERTS
1877, 6, 18. Nathan recrq
1877, 10, 22. Amanda recrq
1881, 2, 21. Clarence M., Alena V. & Ella M.
    recrq '
1886, 10, 18. Nathan & fam relrq

ROBINSON
1821, 11, 19. Charles rocf Redstone MM, Pa.,
    dtd 1821,4,4, end by Short Creek MM, O.
1827, 4, 23. Charles gct Marlborough MM

RODGERS
1927, 12, 21. Allison & w, Inez, gct Portland
    MM, Oregon

ROSS
1881, 2, 21. Hunter & Sherman recrq
1885, 1, 19. Jessie & Mina recrq
1888, 3, 19. Luella relrq
1888, 3, 19. William & Bates, Bessie & Edna
    recrq
1891, 12, 21. Belle recrq
1893, 7, 17. Bates, Edna, Sherman & Bessie
    dropped from mbrp
1905, 7, 19. Clara Bell recrq

ST. CLAIR
1825, 5, 23. Isaiah Redd gct Stillwater MM,
    to m Ann St. Clair

SANDS
1850, 5, 2. Ann, w John, d bur Smithfield

1828, 5, 19. John recrq
1828, 11, 17. Ann recrq

1864, 7, 18. John con mcd
1866, 9, 17. Margaret recrq

SATTERTHWAITE
1846, 4, 30. Anna m Jas. T. FRAME

SCHELL
1892, 8, 22. Lettie relrq

SCHOLFIELD
1825, 10, 19. Andrew, s Issachar & Edith,
    Belmont Co., O.; m in Smithfield MH, Ra-
    chel GRIMSHAW, dt John & Margaret, Jeffer-
    son Co., O.

1826, 3, 20. Rachel J. gct Stillwater MM

SCOTT
1814, 11, 23. Esther m Joshua WOOD
1820, 11, 29. Rachel m Kinsey CARR

1814, 7, 16. William & w, Rachel, rocf Gun-
    powder MM, dtd 1814,4,27
1814, 7, 16. Easter rocf Gunpowder MM, dtd
    1814,4,27
1820, 6, 19. William dis mcd
1839, 5, 20. Sarah Ann (form Talbott) dis mcd
1840, 2, 17. Martha (form Purviance) dis mcd
1842, 4, 18. Rebecca (form Hobson) dis mcd
1848, 8, 21. Rebecca dis jas

SCUDDER
1847, 8, 23. Elizabeth (form Talbott) dis mcd

SEARS
1836, 8, 24. John, s Peter & Anna, Belmont
    Co., O.; m in Smithfield MH, Phebe GRIM-
    SHAW, dt John & Margaret, Jefferson Co.,O.

1836, 11, 21. John rocf Stillwater MM, dtd
    1836,9,24
1837, 5, 22. John & w, Phebe, gct Stillwater
    MM

SELMON
1903, 9, 23. Alice recrq

SHADDOCK
1828, 9, 22. Eliza (form Nicholson) dis mcd

SHAFER
1887, 1, 17. Philip, Ada R., Edith M. & Eva
    E., recrq
1893, 7, 17. Philip, Ada, Edith, Eva dropped
    from mbrp

SHANE
1869, 10, 11. Mary Eva, w James, dt Chas. &
    Mary E. Blackburn, b

SHANON
1867, 1, 21. Esther recrq

SHARON
1815, 1, 21. Susanna [Sherron] (form Kirk)
     dis mcd
1825, 6, 20. Susan [Sharron] rst
1850, 2, 18. Sarah Ann rocf Short Creek MM,
     O., dtd 1850,1,22
1873, 5, 19. Sarah Ann gct Short Creek MM, O.

SHARP
1817, 7, 9. John, s John & Hannah, Phila.,
     Pa.; m in Smithfield MH, Hannah HOYLE,
     dt John & Sarah, Jefferson Co., O.

1817, 8, 18 Hannah gct Phila. MM, Pa.

SHILETTO
1817, 11, 17. Ann Jr., gr dt John & Ann Hoyle,
     recrq
1821, 1, 22. Ann [Shellita] & gr parents,
     John & Ann Hoyle, gct Gwynead MM, Pa.

SIDWELL
1815, 4, 19. Eli, s Henry & Sinah, Belmont
     Co., O.; m in Plymouth MH, Sarah PAR-
     VIANCE, dt James & Elizabeth, Jefferson
     Co., O.
     Ch: Nathan P. b 1816, 3, --
         Plummer   " 1818, --, --
         Phebe   " 1820, 1, --
         Sina W.   " 1822, 4, --
         Elma   " 1824, 8, --
         Eli   " 1829, 1, 24
1830, 6, --. Sarah d

1813, 1, 16. Joseph Purviance gct Short Creek
     MM, to m Deborah Sidwell
1816, 4, 22. Eli rocf Short Creek MM, O.,
     dtd 1815,10,24
1829, 1, 19. Eli dis jH
1831, 11, 21. Isabella (form Cary) dis mcd
1844, 11, 18. Sina gct Middleton MM
1847, 10, 18. Phebe & Elma dis jH

SIMPSON
1873, 4, 21. Anna (form Ong) dis mcd

SINSMITH
1885, 1, 19. Maggie & Julia recrq
SKELLY
1828, 3, 17. Mahala (form Hobson) dis mcd

SLEIN
1911, 2, 22. Clyde recrq

SMICH
1836, 4, 16. Joel Kirk gct Flushing MM, to m
     Mary Ann Smich

SMITH
1839, 10, 30. John M., s Nathan & Catharine,
     Guernsey Co., O.; m in Smithfield MH,
     Edith KIRK, dt Wm. & Martha, Jefferson
     Co., O.

1845, 11, 18. Samuel B., s Nathan & Catharine,
     Guernsey Co., O.; m in Smithfield MH,
     Lydia Ann WOOD, dt John & Lydia, Chester
     Co., Pa.
1855, 10, 23. Samuel R., s Geo. & Elizabeth
     G., Guernsey Co., O.; m in Smithfield MH,
     Catharine S. KIRK, dt Joel & Mary Ann,
     Jefferson Co., O.

1811, 5, 18. Catharine (form Bogue) dis mcd
1814, 10, 15. Catharine rst
1815, 4, 15. Catharine gct Plainfield MM
1816, 2, 19. Lydia (form Larkin) dis mcd
1819, 7, 19. Richard recrq
1820, 9, 18. Richard gct Staffordshire MM,
     Eng.
1839, 12, 23. Edith K. gct Flushing MM
1843, 4, 17. Samuel B. gct Flushing MM
1846, 2, 23. Lydia Ann gct Flushing MM
1848, 8, 21. John M. & w, Edith R., & ch,
     Deborah T., William R., Catharine & El-
     wood, rocf Flushing MM, O., dtd 1848,6,22
1852, 4, 19. John M. & ch, Deborah F., Wil-
     liam K., Catharine L., Elwood Thomas &
     Samuel K., gct Flushing MM, O.
1856, 4, 21. Catharine S. gct Flushing MM, O.
1880, 12, 20. Dorothy A. gc
1888, 5, 21. Emma L. (form Ong) relrq

SNEE
1823, 12, 22. Rebecca (form Lukins) dis mcd

SNIDER
1812, 2, 15. Sarah (form McNamee) dis mcd

SPEARS
1915, 4, 21. Fannie recrq

SPENCER
1833, 6, 27. Elizabeth m Joseph BOWMAN

1819, 4, 19. Sarah (form Jinkenson) dis mcd
1827, 3, 19. Elizabeth recrq

SPERRY
1918, 2, 20. Charles Herbert, Harriett Vir-
     ginia & Clency C. recrq

STANLEY
1828, 12, 24. Fleming, s Jonathan & Mary,
     Columbiana Co., O.; m in Smithfield MH,
     Priscilla CARR, dt Wm. & Sarah, Jefferson
     Co., O.
1833, 6, 26. Priscilla (nee Carr) m Benj. T.
     TALBOTT

1829, 2, 23. Priscilla gct Salem MM
1829, 10, 19. Priscilla gct Salem MM
1843, 8, 21. Henry Benedict gct Upper Spring-
     field MM, to m Eliza T. Stanley

STANTON
1811, 10, 19. Richard Jelks gct Concord MM,

STANTON, continued
    to m Lydia Stanton
1812, 10, 17. Abigail rocf Concord MM, dtd
    1812,7,23
1818, 8, 17. Abigail gct Stillwater MM
1828, 1, 21. Benjamin rocf Short Creek MM,
    O., dtd 1827,11,17
1828, 10, 20. Benjamin gct Sandy Spring MM,
    to m Betsy McBride
1830, 3, 22. Benjamin rocf Sandy Spring MM

STARR
1881, 2, 21. George & Mary A. recrq
1888, 8, 24. George [Star] dropped from mbrp

STINARD
1933, 12, 20. Lucy Velma recrq
STRATTON
1867, 8, 19. Joseph P. Ong gct Damascus MM,
    to m Rhoda Stratton

STROUD
1851, 12, 22. Deborah Ann (form Jordan) dis
    mcd & jas

STUBBS
1903   4, 20. Bertha recrq

SUMMERS
1884, 2, 16. Deborah dropped from mbrp

SWANE
1808, 11, 24. Joshua, s Francis & Betty, Jef-
    ferson Co., O.; m in Cross Creek MH, Mary
    TALBOTT, dt Benjamin & Susan, Jefferson
    Co., O.

1809, 2, 18. Joshua [Swayne] & w, Mary, gct
    Short Creek MM

TALBOTT
----, --, --. Benjamin d 1846,7,-- bur Cross
    Creek; m Susannah ----- d 1847,--,-- bur
    Cross Creek
    Ch: Mary   b 1786, 6, 24
        Beulah   " 1788, 4, 28
        John   "" 1790, 8, 31
        William   " 1793, 6, 3
        Nathan   " 1796, 2, 21
        Margaret   " 1798, 5, 21
        Joseph   " 1801, 8, 9 d 1802, 5,13
          bur Richmond
        Elizabeth b 1803, 3, 18 " 1822, 2,11
          bur Richmond
        Benjamin I.b 1806, 1, 31
        George C. " 1809, 3, 9 " 1829, 3,19
          bur Richmond
----, --, --. Kinsey d 1853,8,23 bur Cross
    Creek; m Deborah ----- d 1863,9,20 bur
    Cross Creek
    Ch: Elijah   b 1800, 11, 3
        Elisha   " 1802, 8, 1
        Joseph   " 1804, 10, 28

    Ch: Mary   b 1806, 2, 11
        John   " 1808, 2, 28
        Mahala   " 1810, 10, 22
        Sarah A.   " 1812, 3, 25
        Kinsey   " 1815, 8, 5
        Caleb   " 1817, 3, 10
        Deborah   " 1819, 11, 24 d 1842, 6,11
          bur Cross Creek
        Rachel A. b 1824, 11, 10
1808, 11, 24. Mary m Joshua SWANE
1810, 4, 26. Beulah m Joseph FARQUHAR
1814, 3, 24. John, s Benj. & Susanna, Jeffer-
    son Co., O.; m in Cross Creek MH, Rachel
    BALL, dt James & Ruth, Jefferson Co., O.
1815, 6, 28. Cassandra, w John, d bur Rich-
    mond
1817, 7, 3. Elizabeth m Thomas FRENCH
----, --, --. Allen & Mary
    Ch: Rebecca L. b 1820, 9, 20
        Mary F.   " 1823, 9, 16
----, --, --. Robert & Matilda
    Ch: Sarah   b 1820, 11, 10 d 1825,12,23
          bur Cross Creek
        Joseph   b 1822, 6, 30
        Elizabeth " 1825, 4, 15
----, --, --. Robert, s Joseph & Mary, b 1799,
    3,21 d 1881,1,28; m Matilda MORGAN, dt
    Thomas & Esther, d 1881,1,28
1833, 6, 26. Benjamin T., s Benj. & Susanna,
    Jefferson Co., O.; m in Smithfield MH,
    Priscilla STANLEY, dt Wm. & Sarah CARR,
    Jefferson Co., O.
1835, 11, 26. Mary Ann m James R. BALL
1835, 12, 3. Mary T. m John FARQUHAR
1836, 6, 1. Joseph F., s Jos. & Mary, Jef-
    ferson Co., O.; m in Smithfield MH, Mar-
    garet GRIMSHAW, dt John & Margaret, Jef-
    ferson Co., O.
1837, 5, 31. John C., s Kinsey & Deborah,
    Jefferson Co., O.; m in Smithfield MH,
    Isabella MEGRAIL, dt John & Mary, West-
    moreland Co., Pa.
    Ch: Thomas C. b 1838, --, --
        Mary   " 1840, 11, 23
        Deborah Ann" 1845, 8, 14
        Addison M. " 1847, 7, 14 d 1850, 3,31
          bur Cross Creek
        Kinsey P. b 1850, 11, 5
        M. Kelley " 1853, 1, 24
1839, 3, 21. Kinsey Jr., s Kinsey & Deborah,
    b 1815,8,5; m in Cross Creek MH, Hannah T.
    JOHN, dt Wm. & Sarah
    Ch: Caleb   b 1840, 2, 12 d 1858, 2,13
        Ann Eliza " 1842, 1, 13 " 1850, 4,20
        William J. " 1845, 2, 1 " 1852, 3,16
        Eli P.   " 1847, 7, 10 " 1852, 3,21
        Mary Eliza-
          beth   " 1851, 4, 15 " 1852, 3,18
        Sarah E.   " 1853, 10, 16
        Deborah P. " 1856, 5, 21
1843, 6, 1. Mary d
----, --, --. Kinsey & Caroline
    Ch: Joseph A. b 1844, 12, 15

TALBOTT, Kinsey & Caroline, continued
    Ch: William M. b 1846, 9, 18
        Mary   " 1849, 4, 9
        Elizabeth C" 1858, 1, 29 d 1859,11, 2
        bur Cross Creek
1851, 8, 22. Hannah, w Kinsey Jr., d bur
    Cross Creek
1852, 11, 17. Joseph d bur Richmond
1872, 9, 5. Mary d bur Cross Creek

1813, 1, 20. Joseph Hobson Jr. gct Pipe Creek
    MM, Md., to m Rebekah Talbott
1814, 9, 17. Kinsey & w, Deborah, & ch, Eli-
    jah, Elisha, Mary, John, Mahala & Sarah-
    ann, rocf Pipe Creek MM, Md., dtd 1814,7,
    16
1816, 6, 17. John dis mcd
1817, 12, 22. William A. dis mcd
1818, 2, 23. Casander recrq
1818, 3, 23. John recrq
1818, 7, 21. Hannah Farquhar (form Talbott)
    dis mcd to first cousin
1819, 5, 17. John & w, Rachel, gct Plain-
    field MM
1819, 8, 23. Mary Ann, infant dt John, recrq
1819, 9, 20. Ann recrq
1819, 9, 20. Robert gct Newgarden MM, to m
1819, 10, 18. Alen gct Pipe Creek MM, Md., to
    m
1820, 2, 21. Matilda M. rocf Newgarden MM,
    dtd 1819,12,23
1820, 5, 22. Mary rocf Pipe Creek MM, Md.,
    1820,1,15
1821, 2, 19. William A. rst
1821, 11, 19. John dis mcd
1821, 12, 17. Joseph & Eliza Jane, ch Wm. A.,
    recrq
1826, 6, 19. Elisha dis disunity
1826, 7, 17. Elijah dis mcd
1826, 10, 23. Mary Jr. dis
1828, 11, 17. John rocf Redstone MM, dtd
    1828,10,29
1828, 11, 17. Benjamin I. gct Middleton MM;
    end back to this mtg 1829,7,20
1829, 8, 17. John dis mcd with first cousin
1829, 10, 19. Jane (form McGrew) dis mcd with
    first cousin
1829, 10, 19. Allen & w, Mary, & ch, Rebecca,
    Mary & John R., gct Alum Creek MM
1830, 11, 22. Finley rocf Redstone MM, dtd
    1830,11,3
1831, 1, 17. Mary rocf Redstone MM, dtd 1830,
    11,3
1832, 4, 23. Mahala Cole (form Talbott) dis
    mcd
1832, 7, 23. William A. & w, Ann, & ch, Jo-
    seph, Eliza Jane, John, Kinsey, Allen &
    William, gct Deerfield MM
1833, 6, 17. Mary J. rst
1835, 4, 20. Benjamin I. & w, Priscilla, gct
    Adrian MM, Mich.
1835, 8, 17. Thomas dis mcd
1836, 7, 18. Rebecca (form Hutton) dis mcd

1836, 7, 18. Joseph & w, Margret, gct Penns-
    ville MM
1836, 7, 18. Finley M. dis mcd
1837, 11, 20. William gct Middleton MM, to m
    Adaline Townsend
1838, 10, 22. Nathan gct Short Creek MM, O.,
    to m Abigail Flanner
1839, 5, 20. Sarah Ann Scott (form Talbott)
    dis mcd
1840, 11, 28. Nathan dis disunity
1841, 2, 22. Caleb dis
1841, 2, 22. William dis disunity
1841, 10, --. Mary Parsons (form Talbott) dis
    mcd
1844, 8, 19. Kinsey M. con mcd
1845, 9, 22. Joseph W. dis disunity
1847, 8, 23. Elizabeth Scudder (form Talbott)
    dis mcd
1847, 8, 23. Thomas M. dis jas
1848, 6, 19. Caroline E. recrq
1848, 6, 19. William rst at Middleton MM with
    consent of this meeting
1851, 6, 23. Joseph M. & William, ch Kinsey
    M. & Caroline, recrq
1851, 6, 23. Wm. rst at Middleton MM on con-
    sent of this mtg
1851, 6, 23. Abigail gct Short Creek MM, O.
1853, 9, 19. Rachel Ann dis
1854, 4, 17. Margaret gct Spring Creek MM, Ia.
1855, 12, 17. Esther Matilda dis jas
1858, 11, 22. Thomas M. rst
1860, 2, 20. Kinsey con mcd
1860, 2, 20. Thomas C. dis mcd
1860, 3, 19. Mary Parsons (form Talbott) con
    mcd
1863, 11, 23. John C. dis disunity
1864, 12, 19. Joseph A. gct Gilead MM, O.
1865, 9, 18. Kinsey M. & w, Caroline E., &
    ch, William M. & Mary S., gct Short Creek
    MM, O.
1866, 5, 21. Deborah A. dis disunity
1871, 12, 18. Thomas M. gct Baltimore MM, Md.
1874, 6, 22. Kinsey P. dis mcd
1879, 2, 17. Kelly dis disunity
1880, 12, 20. Robert & Matilda gc
1934, 3, 21. Almon & w, Mary Jane, & ch, Mar-
    tha & Erving, recrq

TANKIMAN
1843, --, --. Isaac d bur Cross Creek

TANNER
1914, 2, 25. William recrq

TATNALL
1902, 7, 21. Ashton R. recrq
1907, 4, 24. Ashton R. relrq

TATUM
1862, 9, 3. Geo. M., s Wm. R. & Sarah M.,
    Gloucester Co., N. J.; m in Smithfield
    MH, Elizabeth L. JONES, dt Jos. & Isa-
    bella, Jefferson Co., O.

TATUM, continued
1869, 12, 20. Elizabeth L. & ch, Joseph Fran-
     cis & William, gct Woodbury MM, N. J.

TAYLOR
1814, 7, 16. Rouse & w, Mary, & ch, Peter &
     James, gct Plainfield MM
1811, 7, 20. Rowse & w, Mary, & ch, Peter &
     James, rocf Rhode Island MM, dtd 1811,4,25

TEAS
1909, 1, 20. Thomas C. gct Bloomfield MM (a
     minister)

TEPLES
1838, 8, 30. Sarah Ann T., dt Henry & Mary, b

1823, 10, 20. Mary (form Plummer) con mcd
1837, 3, 20. Henry [Teeples] recrq
1842, 10, 17. Thomas, s Henry & Mary, recrq
1847, 2, 22. Henry & w, Mary, & ch, Thomas &
     Sarah Ann, gct Gilead MM

TERRIL
1863, 5, 27. Thomas H., s Matthew & Sarah,
     Jefferson Co., O.; m in Smithfield MH, Re-
     becca BALLINGER, dt Wm. & Lydia BALLANGER,
     Jefferson Co., O.

1863, 9, 21. Rebecca B. [Terrell] gct Short
     Creek MM, O.

THOMAS
1829, 4, 20. Scatten dis mcd

THOMASSON
1866, 11, 28. Samuel J., s Thos. & Maria, Jef-
     ferson Co., O.; m in Smithfield MH, Mary
     WOOD, dt Thos. & Elizabeth Ann, Jefferson
     Co., O.

1843, 11, 25. William Watson gct Short Creek
     MM, O., to m Maria Thomasson
1844, 12, 23. Samuel G., minor, rocf Short
     Creek MM, O.
1846, 6, 22. William Watson & w, Maria, & s,
     Samuel Thomasson, gct Short Creek MM, O.
1867, 12, 21. Mary W. gct Short Creek MM, O.

THOMPSON
1911, 2, 22. Louise recrq

THORN
1830, 12, 20. Catharine recrq

THORNBERRY
1880, 4, 19. William J. & w, Mary, & ch,
     Risher W. & Rhoda, rocf Walnut Ridge MM,
     Ind.
1883, 3, 19. William J. & fam gct Freeport
     MM, O.

THORNTON
1865, 3, 20. Alwilda, dt Sampson & Rebecca,
     b
1874, 12, 21. Rebecca rocf Short Creek MM, O.
1885, 3, 23. Alwilda & Emma A. recrq

THWAITE
1842, 10, 17. James [Thwait] & w, Mary Ann, &
     ch, Edward, Mary Ann, Sophia, Maria &
     Amelia, rocf Brighouse MM, Eng., dtd
     1842,7,15
1843, 7, 17. James & w, Mary Ann, & ch, Ed-
     ward, Mary Ann, Sophia, Maria & Amelia,
     gct Flushing MM
1851, 1, 20. Cert rec for Richard from Pres-
     ton MM, Eng., dtd 1850,7,11, end to Cin-
     cinnati MM

TIPTON
1823, 5, 19. Cert rec for Luke & w, Pris-
     cilla, & 8 ch, from Deer Creek MM, dtd
     1823,1,10, end to Short Creek MM, O.

TOLERTON
1812, 1, 18. James gct Salem MM
1811, 4, 20. James recrq
1812, 1, 18. James [Towlerton] gct Salem MM

TOMLINSON
----, --, --. Orlando C., s Allen & Martha,
     b 1860,9,8; m Jennie E. -----, dt Joel
     & Eliza CLAMPITT, b 1863,9,10
     Ch: Syble E.   b 1887, 10, 23
         Myra M.   " 1889, 5, --
         Wymond J.   " 1891, 8, 8

1897, 7, 19. Orlando C. & w, Jennie E., & ch,
     Sibyl E., Mira M. & Wymond J., rocf West-
     field MM
1900, 2, 19. O. C. & fam gct Greenville,
     Clay Co., Ia.

TOWNSEND
1808, 8, 28. Robert, minor, s Benj., gct
     Baltimore MM for W. Dist.
1809, 8, 19. Aaron gct Westland MM, Pa.
1809, 9, 16. Benj. & w, Elizabeth, gct New-
     Garden MM
1811, 3, 16. Francis & w, Marrah, rocf West-
     land MM, dtd 1810,10,27
1813, 9, 18. Aaron rocf Westland MM, dtd
     1813,2,27
1815, 9, 16. Aaron dis mcd
1816, 8, 19. Eli gct Plainfield MM
1819, 9, 20. Eli, minor, gct Plainfield MM
1837, 11, 20. William Talbott gct Middleton
     MM, to m Adaline [Towsend]
1845, 7, 21. Albert M. Coffin gct Middleton
     MM, to m Elmira Townsend

TRACY
1828, 8, 18. Rebecca (form Jenkinson) dis
     mcd

TUMBLESON
1835, 8, 17. Aletta (form Nicholson) dis jH
    & mcd

TURNER
----, --, --. James b 1843,--,--; m Jane
    -----. dt John & Margaret WORTHY, b 1851

1877, 11, 19. James & w, Jane, & dt, Mary,
    rocf Short Creek MM, O.
1883, 3, 19. James & fam gct Oskaloosa MM,
    Ia.

TURNEY
1881, 12, 19. William B. & w, Vashti E., recrq
1885, 10, 19. William & Vashti E. relrq

TURPIN
1875, 3, 22. Elizabeth recrq
1880, 12, 20. Elizabeth gc

UPDEGRAFF
1821, 5, 30. Nathan, s Nathan & Ann, Jeffer-
    son Co., O.; m in Smithfield MH, Cassan-
    dra BALLINGER, dt Wm. & Lydia, Jefferson
    Co., O.
1852, 9, 23. David B., s David & Rebecca T.,
    Jefferson Co., O.; m in Smithfield MH,
    Rebecca B. PRICE, dt Wm. & Edith, Jeffer-
    son Co., O.

1821, 8, 20. Cassander gct Short Creek MM, O.
1836, 11, 21. Eliza Jane (form Wood) dis mcd
1849, 7, 23. David Jr. rocf Short Creek MM,
    O., dtd 1849,6,19
1853, 5, 23. Rebecca B. gct Short Creek MM,
    O.
1913, 2, 19. Lance recrq
1914, 2, 25. Anna recrq

VAIL
1833, 2, 27. John, s Samuel & Lydia, Jeffer-
    son Co., O.; m in Smithfield MH, Esther
    CARR, dt Thos. & Orpah, Jefferson Co., O.,
    b 1816,6,17

1833, 1, 21. John rocf Short Creek MM, O.,
    dtd 1832,7,24
1833, 9, 23. John & w, Esther, gct Short
    Creek MM, O.
1844, 8, 19. Mark Willets gct Plainfield MM,
    to m Sarah Vail
1845, 11, 17. Jacob G. rocf Deer Creek MM,
    Md., dtd 1845,10,9
1847, 9, 20. Jacob G. dis mcd

VANHORN
1822, 5, 22. Elizabeth rst on consent of
    Short Creek MM, O.
1826, 10, 23. Elizabeth gct Flushing MM

VICKERS
1829, 7, 20. Thomas rocf Hartland MM, N. Y.,

dtd 1829,3,31
1906, 2, 21. Lena, Mamie & Nettie recrq

VORE
----, --, --. Jesse & Ann
    Ch: Susannah   b 1819, 9, 2
        Maria   " 1820, 9, 13
        Joseph   " 1822, 8, 13
        Sarah   " 1823, 11, 12
        Blackburn " 1825, 12, 1
        Ann   " 1828, 9, 25

1828, 8, 18. Jesse & w, Anne, & ch, Susanna,
    Maria, Joseph, Sarah & Blackburn, rocf
    Dunnings Creek MM, dtd 1828,5,14
1831, 8, 22. Jesse & w, Ann, & ch, Susannah,
    Maria, Joseph, Sarah & Blackburn, gct
    Alum Creek MM

WALKER
1833, 2, 7. Martha, dt Joseph & Maria, b
1872, 6, --. Gertrude D., w Clinton, dt
    Thomas & Maggie -----, b

1832, 8, 20. Joseph & w, Maria, rocf Flush-
    ing MM, dtd 1832,6,21
1837, 5, 22. Joseph & w, Maria, & ch, Martha
    & Daniel, gct Flushing MM
1856, 6, 23. William Price gct Short Creek
    MM, O., to m Hannah W. Walker
1899, 1, 23. Gertrude recrq
1903, 8, 17. Gertie relrq

WALLACE
1831, 3, 21. Deborah dis mcd
1853, 9, 19. Ann E. (form McGrew) dis mcd

WALTERS
1852, 12, 20. Esther (form Purviance) dis mcd

WATKINS
1849, 11, 22. Benjamin, s Jas. & Anna, Logan
    Co., O.; m Susanna A. WOOD, dt Wm. & Su-
    sanna AMOS

1849, 2, 19. Susanna A. gct Goshen MM, O.

WATLIN
1825, 7, 18. Eunice (form Jolly) rpd mcd

WATSON
1820, 4, 26. Joseph, s John & Elizabeth,
    Jefferson Co., O.; m in Smithfield MH,
    Mary HOYLE, dt John & Mary, Jefferson Co.,
    O.
    Ch: Sarah   b 1821, 1, 28
        Ann   " 1822, 12, 9
        Joseph   " 1825, 12, 13 d 1850, 1,--
        bur Cross Creek
1823, 9, 25. William, s John & Ann, Jefferson
    Co., O.; m in Cross Creek MH, Phebe HOB-
    SON, dt Joseph & Ann, Jefferson Co., O.,
    d 1842,8,1 bur Richmond

WATSON, continued

----, --, --. Matthew d 1861,7,5 bur Cross
  Creek; m Ann M. HOBSON d 1840,11,24 bur
  Cross Creek
    Ch: Grace   d 1835, 5,25
            bur Cross Creek
        Ann Jane   " 1830, 7,30
            bur Cross Creek
        John   b 1829, 12, 30 " 1843, 9,18
            bur Cross Creek
        Phebe   b 1832, 6, 27
        Ann Jane " 1835, 1, 12
        Esther Han-
              nah " 1836, 10, 31
        Deborah " 1839, 4, 24
    Matthew m 2nd 1845,--,-- in Sandy Spring
    MM, Eliza HEALD
    Ch: James H. b 1846, 6, 16
        William   " 1847, 6, 9
        Mary H.   " 1848, 10, 25
        Barclay S." 1850, 8, 2
        Flounder " 1852, 2, 25 d 1853, 5,21
            bur Richmond
        Benezett b 1854, 10, 1 " 1856, 9,14
            bur Richmond
1837, 11, 2. John, s Jos. & Dorothy, Jeffer-
    son Co., O.; m in Cross Creek MH, Mary Ann
    HOBSON, dt Joseph & Rebecca, Jefferson
    Co., O., d 1860,3,3 bur Athens Co., O.
    Ch: Rebecca   b 1838, 8, 3
        Joseph W. " 1840, 6, 3
        Dorothy Ann" 1842, 5, 3
        Benjamin P.   d 1850, 1,-
            bur Cross Creek
        Charles C. b 1847, 1, 24
        Elizabeth " 1849, 1, 18
        Emma Jane " 1854, 3, 26
        Sarah A.   " 1857, 6, 10
        Oliver J. " 1859, 6, 7
1852, 5, 27. Pheby m Jos. HOYLE
----, --, --. John & Eliza
    Ch: Phebe E. b 1855, 7, 28
        Anna Mary " 1856, 6, 28
1861, 5, 2. Deborah m Caleb MARIS
1861, 10, 9. Jane m Isaac W. JOHNSON
1862, 1, 9. Matthew, s John & Eliza, d bur
    Cross Creek

1818, 10, 19. Joseph rst on consent of New
    Castle MM, Eng.
1819, 2, 22. Michael, Elizabeth & John, ch
    Joseph, recrq
1819, 9, 20. John & w, Ann, & ch, William &
    Martha, rocf Newcastle MM, Eng., dtd
    1819,5,11
1819, 10, 18. Michael gct Short Creek MM, O.
1824, 9, 20. Michael, minor, rocf Short Creek
    MM, O., dtd 1824,4,20
1826, 5, 22. Mathew dis
1826, 5, 22. Ann M. (form Hobson) dis
1828, 9, 22. Anne M. rst
1828, 9, 22. Matthew rst
1828, 10, 20. Joseph dis jH

1829, 2, 23. Michael dis jH
1829, 8, 17. Mary dis jH
1830, 1, 18. Grace & Ann Jane, ch Mathew &
    Ann, recrq
1830, 5, 17. Mathew & w, Ann, & ch, Grace,
    Ann Jane & John, gct Flushing MM
1833, 7, 22. Mathew & w, Anna, & ch, Grace,
    John & Phebe, rocf Flushing MM
1839, 5, 20. John Jr. & w & ch gct Chester-
    field MM
1842, 6, 20. Mary Ann & ch, Rebecca & Joseph,
    rocf Chesterfield MM, dtd 1842,5,21
1840, 9, 21. Sarah Daugherty (form Watson)
    dis mcd
1843, 7, 17. Phebe d 1842,8,1 ae 47 (an
    elder)
1843, 11, 25. William gct Short Creek MM, O.,
    to m Maria Thomasson
1844, 5, 20. Maria rocf Short Creek MM, O.,
    dtd 1844,4,23
1844, 11, 18. Elizabeth Reed (form Watson) con
    mcd
1845, 7, 21. Matthew gct Sandy Spring MM, to
    m Eliza Heald
1845, 10, 20. Eliza rocf Sandy Spring MM, dtd
    1845,9,20
1846, 6, 22. William & w, Maria, & s, Samuel
    Thomasson, gct Short Creek MM, O.
1851, 1, 20. John rocf Chesterfield MM, dtd
    1850,12,21
1854, 10, 23. John gct New Garden MM, to m
    Eliza Negus
1855, 3, 19. Eliza T., w John, rocf New Gar-
    den MM
1855, 11, 19. Ann dis jH
1862, 8, 18. Eliza & ch, James W., William,
    Mary H. & Barclay, gct Upper Springfield
    MM
1862, 8, 18. Rebecca Atkinson (form Watson)
    dis mcd
1865, 4, 17. John S. dis mcd
1866, 10, 22. John & w, Eliza J., & ch, Phebe
    Eva & Anna Mary, gct New Garden MM
1871, 9, 18. John rst at Spring Grove MM,
    Ia., on consent of this mtg
1880, 12, 20. Sarah A. & Hannah gc
1884, 2, 16. Oliver, Elizabeth & Sarah
    dropped from mbrp

WATTS
1914, 2, 25. Lucia & ch, Mary & Margaret,
    recrq

WAY
1816, 11, 18. David recrq
1817, 6, 23. Ann rst on consent of Deer Creek
    MM, Md.
1818, 3, 23. Benjamin, Robert, Alice, Hannah,
    Sarah, Jane, Mary & Elizabeth, ch David
    & Ann, recrq
1820, 7, 17. David & w, Ann, & ch, Benjamin,
    Robert, Alice Hannah, Sarah, Jane, Mary,
    Elizabeth & Jacob, gct Stillwater MM

WAY, continued
1831, 6, 20. Benjamin rocf Somerset MM, dtd
    1831,5,25
1832, 3, 19. Benjamin gct Stillwater MM

WEIR
1890, 6, 23. George, minister, & w, Martha,
    rocf Alum Creek MM, O., dtd 1890,6,19
1894, 12, 17. George & w, Martha, & ch, Den-
    zlon & Jessie, gct Greenwich MM

WELDY
1840, 8, 17. Mary (form McGrew) dis mcd

WEST
1884, 12, 22. James P. recrq
1885, 5, 22. James dropped from mbrp

WHEELER
1855, 5, 21. Elizabeth (form Kinsey) dis mcd
1881, 2, 21. Ellen recrq

WHICHER
1884, 1, 21. Mary recrq

WHITE
1817, 9, 22. Ann rocf Salem MM, dtd 1817,5,13
1818, 5, 18. Robert L. recrq
1819, 7, 19. Nathan recrq
1819, 7, 19. Sarah, Lewis, Jesse, Israel,
    Paul & Ann, ch Robert L. & Ann, recrq
1824, 4, 19. Robert L. & w, Ann, & ch, Lewis,
    Jesse, Israel, Paul & Anna, gct Marlbor-
    ough MM
1824, 4, 19. Sarah gct Marlborough MM
1824, 12, 20. Nathan gct Marlborough MM
1881, 2, 21. Thomas, Margaret, Frank L. &
    Gertrude recrq
1885, 1, 19. Frederica recrq
1888, 9, 17. Thomas & w & ch, Frank, Gertie
    & Freddie, gct Freeport MM, O.; cert lost
1892, 1, 18. Thomas & fam gct Freeport MM, O.

WHITTEN
----, --, --. William m Mary LIPTON, dt S. &
    R., b 1860,7,7
    Ch: Glennie   b 1880, 12, 28
        Frank   " 1882, 10, 16
----, --, --. Wm. T. m Elizabeth JONES, dt
    J. C. & Sarah, b 1838,10,4
    Ch: Lemuel   b 1880, 3, 28

1884, 12, 22. Elizabeth recrq
1885, 1, 19. William, Mary V., John J. & Sa-
    rah J., recrq
1885, 1, 19. Mary J. recrq
1885, 4, 20. Lizzie recrq
1885, 5, 22. Anna recrq
1885, 12, 21. Sadie R. recrq
1886, 1, 18. Annis W. Ramsey (form Whitten)
    rpd mcd; released from mbrp
1893, 7, 17. John dropped from mbrp
1898, 2, 21. Frank recrq

1903, 2, 23. Wm. Jr., Bery C., Alwilda &
    Golda recrq
1911, 2, 22. Margaret Elizabeth & Florence
    recrq
1913, 2, 19. Walter recrq

WICKERSHAM
1841, 12, 28. Elizabeth d bur Smithfield

WILBER
1889, 8, 19. William & Hannah recrq
1891, 3, 22. William & w, Hannah K., gct
    Rochester MM, N. Y.

WILCOXEN
1917, 11, 21. Nancy E. recrq
1919, 1, 22. Thomas O. & w, Edith, & dt,
    Eloise, gct Rush Creek MM

WILEY
----, --, --. Abel & Rebecca
    Ch: John   b 1808, 9, 23
        Ann   " 1810, 8, 2
        Mary   " 1812, 10, 14
        Matilda   " 1814, 7, 4
        William F. " 1816, 6, 22
        Richard S. " 1818, 6, 21 d 1826, 6,21
          bur Smithfield
        Benjamin   b 1821, 3, 25
        Richard   " 1822, 9, 8

1816, 8, 19. Abel recrq
1816, 10, 21. Rebecca recrq
1817, 4, 21. John, Ann, Mary & William T.,
    ch Abel & Rachel, recrq
1830, 5, 17. Abel dis jH
1831, 5, 23. Ann Hutton (form Wiley) dis mcd
1831, 9, 18. John dis mcd
1832, 1, 23. Hannah (form Garretson) dis mcd
1833, 5, 20. Hannah rst
1833, 8, 19. Hannah gct Deerfield MM
1834, 1, 20. Mary dis jas
1836, 8, 22. Matilda Hutton (form Wiley) dis
    mcd
1836, 12, 19. Wm. F. dis disunity
1895, 12, 20. Frank recrq
1901, 3, 18. Frank relrq
1907, 7, 24. Ora relrq

WILLITS
----, --, --. Ellis d 1854,12,4 bur Smithfield
    m Hannah ----- d 1844,10,21 bur Smithfield
    Ch: Mark   b 1805, 10, 17
        Sarah   " 1807, 4, 8
        Rachel   " 1809, 9, 9 d 1836, 5,23
        Guli Ann   " 1813, 11, 22
        Eliza   " 1816, 5, 18 " 1830, 2, 6
        Lydia   " 1822, 1, 25 " 1827, 3,22
        John   " 1823, 11, 10
1827, 3, 28. Sarah m David PURVIANCE
1829, 11, 25. John, s Samuel & Elizabeth,
    Preston Co., Va.; m in Smithfield MH,
    Elizabeth PURVIANCE, dt David & Mary,

WILLITS, continued
    Jefferson Co., O.
1834, 3, 26. Guliann m Benj. HOYLE
----, --, --. Mark & Sarah
    Ch: Hannah   b 1845, 6, 20 d 1845, 7,15
            bur Smithfield
        Lydia S.   b 1846, 6, 9
        Eliza   " 1848, 2, 28
        Hannah R. " 1849, 8, 24
        Sarah Ann " 1851, 2, 15
        David   " 1853, 12, 8
        Mary   " 1855, 12, 8
1844, 12, 25. Ammi, s Jesse & Rebecca, Pres-
    ton Co., Va.; m in Smithfield MH, Maria
    HAMMOND, dt Benj. & Margaret, Jefferson
    Co., O.
    Ch: Milton   b 1847, 7, 31
        Mary H.   " 1850, 8, 26
1860, 12, 26. Joel, s Ellis & Rachel, Marshall
    Co., Ia.; m in Smithfield MH, Mary HAMMOND
    dt Benj. & Margaret, Jefferson Co., O.

1820, 10, 23. Hannah [Willets] recrq
1821, 6, 18. Ellis rst on consent of Redstone
    MM, Pa.
1822, 11, 18. Mark, Sarah, Rachel, Juleann &
    Elizabeth [Willets], ch Elis & Hannah,
    recrq .
1830, 4, 19. Elizabeth P. [Willets] gct Red-
    stone MM
1831, 11, 21. John [Willets] & w, Elizabeth,
    rocf Redstone MM, dtd 1831,11,2
1832, 3, 19. John [Willets] & w, Elizabeth,
    gct Alum Creek MM
1835, 6, 22. Rachel Keys (form Willits) dis
    mcd
1844, 8, 19. Mark [Willets] gct Plainfield
    MM, to m Sarah Vail
1844, 12, 23. Sarah [Willets] rocf Plainfield
    MM
1846, 2, 23. Annie [Willets] rocf Redstone
    MM, Pa., dtd 1846,2,4
1852, 3, 23. Ammi & w, Maria, & ch, Milton &
    Mary H., gct Alum Creek MM, O.
1855, 9, 17. Margaret [Willets] (form Ham-
    mond) con mcd
1855, 10, 22. Margaret [Willets] gct Allum
    Creek MM, O.
1861, 7, 22. Mary gct LeGrand MM, Ia.
1862, 12, 22. Mark, Sarah, Lydia, Eliza &
    Hannah, dis jas (Wilburites)
1862, 12, 22. David, Mary & Ellis dis jW
1863, 2, 23. John rpd mcd

WILLIAMS
1821, 7, 23. Daniel rocf Uwchland MM, Pa.,
    dtd 1821,6,7
1826, 11, 20. Daniel gct Gunpowder MM, Md.,
    to m Elizabeth Price
1827, 7, 23. Elizabeth rocf Gunpowder MM,
    dtd 1827,4,4
1829, 5, 18. Daniel & w, Elizabeth, & dt,
    Hannah, gct Salem MM

WILSON
1823, 3, 17. Anna rocf Hardwick MM, N. J.,
    dtd 1819,6,3, end by Cincinnati MM, O.
1829, 1, 19. Ann gct Stillwater MM
1846, 3, 23. Elmira (form Hoyle) dis mcd

WING
1818, 6, 22. Cert rec for Sarah & dt, Lydia
    from Butternut MM, N. Y., dtd 1816,10,30,
    end by Nine Partners MM, N. Y., end to
    Stillwater MM

WOLF
1825, 10, 17. Mary (form Naylor) dis mcd
1876, 2, 21. Mary recrq
1893, 2, 20. Eli recrq

WOOD
----, --, --. Nathan d 1863,3,23 bur Smith-
    field; m Margaret ----- d 1851,10,5 bur
    Smithfield
    Ch: Samuel   b 1802, 2, 19
        Susannah   " 1805, 1, 5
        Joel   " 1807, 5, 16
        Sarah   " 1810, 9, 22
        Thomas   " 1814, 8, 22
1814, 4, 20. Elizabeth m Benjamin W. LADD
1814, 11, 23. Joshua, s Wm. & Mary, Jefferson
    Co., O.; m in Plymouth MH, Esther SCOTT,
    dt Amos & Rachel, Jefferson Co., O.
----, --, --. Pusy m Charity ----- d 1833,12,
    10
    Ch: Grandvil   b 1817, 3, 27
        Nathan R. " 1818, 5, 13
        Greenbury " 1820, 6, 19
        Ann   " 1822, 1, 7
        Isaiah   " 1823, 5, 8
        Rachel   " 1825, 1, 16
        Pusey   " 1826, 12, 18
        Charity   " 1828, 11, 11
        Mary R.   " 1831, 4, 8
1824, 5, 26. Caleb, s Thos. & Susanna, Jef-
    ferson Co., O.; m in Smithfield MH, Lydia
    REDD, dt George & Rachel, Jefferson Co.,
    O.
    Ch: Milton   b 1826, 11, 9
        Alfred   " 1828, 11, 8
        Mary M.   " 1830, 11, 17
        William C. " 1833, 8, 24
1825, 6, 29. Mary P. m Jos. D. BATES
1826, 4, 26. Samuel, s Nathan & Margaret,
    Jefferson Co., O.; m in Smithfield MH,
    Lucy L. LARK, dt Tenison & Lucy, York Co.,
    Va.
    Ch: Ann Maria b 1828, 2, 21
        Nathan L. " 1830, 4, 10
        Elizabeth L. 1832, 10, 5
        Margaret H." 1835, 5, 18
        Jane   " 1838, 1, 25
        Mary E.   " 1845, 9, 1
1827, 7, 25. Mary, w Wm., d bur Smithfield
1828, 3, 26. John, s Joel & Elizabeth, Jef-
    ferson Co., O.; m in Smithfield MH, Su-

WOOD, John, continued
    sanna PRICE, dt Warrick & Susanna, Jeffer-
    son Co., O.
    Ch: Isaac   b 1829, 5, 4 d 1829, 9,20
        bur Smithfield
        Elizabeth b 1830, 10, 11
1829, 4, 1. Lydia m Wm. S. BATES
1830, 12, 1. Susanna m Penrose HUSSEY
----, --, --. Thomas m Elizabeth A. CREW, dt
    Jacob & Elizabeth, b 1810,10,25 d 1898,5,5
1832, 3, 22. Mary m Chas. WRIGHT
1833, 5, 2. Thomas, s Wm. & Mary, Jefferson
    Co., O.; m in Cross Creek MH, Elizabeth
    Ann CREW, dt Jacob & Elizabeth
    Ch: Mary   b 1834, 7, 28
        Martha   " 1837, 5, 19
        Anna   " 1839, 2, 1
        Lydia B. " 1841, 2, 14
        William   " 1844, 6, 18
        Henry C. " 1849, 7, 8
        Elizabeth C. 1852, 12, 15
        Cornelia I." 1855, 12, 27
1833, 12, 10. Charity d
1835, 4, 1. Rachel Ann m Abraham NAYLOR
1837, 3, 1. Pusey, s Thos. & Susanna, Jef-
    ferson Co., O.; m in Smithfield MH, Re-
    becca BALL, dt James & Ruth, Jefferson
    Co., O.
1837, 8, 30. Joel, s Joel & Elizabeth, Bel-
    mont Co., O.; m in Smithfield MH, Eliza-
    beth McGREW, dt Finley B. & Aletta McGREW,
    Jefferson Co., O.
----, --, --. Thomas & Elizabeth
    Ch: William T. b 1844, 6, 18
        Henry C.   " 1849, 7, 8
        Elizabeth C. 1854, 12, 15
        Cornelia J. 1857, 12, 27
1844, 6, 4. William d bur Smithfield
1845, 11, 18. Lydia Ann m Saml B. SMITH
1848, 11, 22. Susanna A. m Benj. WATKINS
1854, 8, 30. Elizabeth L. m James G. KINSEY
----, --, --. Nathan L., s Samuel & Lucy, b
    1830,4,10; m Mary H. ----- b 1830,5,23
    Ch: Charles D. b 1859, 4, 2
        Frederick S. 1861, 6, 23
        Herbert   " 1865, 11, 10
        Maida   " 1869, 2, 12
1861, 3, 27. Jane L. m Samuel COPE
1861, 3, 27. Martha m Willits COPE
1862, 10, 1. Lydia B. m Evan H. PURVIANCE
1864, 10, 26. Mary E. m Amos GRIFFITH
1866, 11, 28. Mary m Samuel J. THOMASSON
1863, 12, 2. Margaret H. m Elnathan PETTIT
1871, 8, --. Thomas Jr., s William & Emma, b
1871, 11, 4. Annie P. d bur Smithfield
1871, 12, 18. Thomas d bur Smithfield

1810, 5, 19. William & s, Richard, gct Pipe
    Creek MM, Md.
1813, 6, 19. Joel & w, Elizabeth, & ch, John,
    Mary, Lewis & Susanna, rocf Pipe Creek
    MM, dtd 1813,4,17
1813, 9, 18. Richard rocf Pipe Creek MM, dtd

1813, 7. 17
1813, 12, 18. Caleb rocf Pipe Creek MM, dtd
    1813,11,13
1814, 11, 19. Nathen & w, Margaret, & ch,
    Samuel, Susannah & Joel, rocf Pipe Creek
    MM, dtd 1814,8,13; also Thomas b since
    issuance of cert
1815, 4, 15. Richard gct Fairfax MM, Va., to
    m
1815, 11, 16. Pusey rocf Pipe Creek MM, dtd
    1815,6,17
1816, 2, 19. Richard gct Fairfax MM, Va.
1816, 5, 20. Pusey gct Short Creek MM, O.,
    to m
1816, 9, 23. Charity rocf Short Creek MM, O.,
    dtd 1816,8,20
1818, 1, 19. Mary rocf Pipe Creek MM, Md.,
    dtd 1817,11,15
1818, 7, 21. William Jr. gct Baltimore MM,
    W. Dist.
1819, 8, 23. William Jr. rocf Baltimore MM,
    W. Dist., dtd 1819,7,9
1820, 6, 19. William Jr. gct Plainfield MM
1826, 9, 18. Joshua & w, Esther, & ch, Ra-
    chel Ann, Eliza Jane, Mary, Lydia, Adison
    & William, gct Flushing MM
1829, 12, 21. Joel dis jH
1830, 6, 21. Joshua & w, Esther, & ch, Ra-
    chel Ann, Eliza Jane, Mary, Lydia, Addi-
    son, William & Gerard Hopkins Wood, rocf
    Flushing MM, dtd 1830,3,25
1831, 3, 21. William gct Stillwater MM, to m
    Susanna Amos
1831, 8, 22. Susanna A. rocf Stillwater MM,
    dtd 1831,6,25
1834, 7, 21. Benjamin W. Ladd gct Birmingham
    MM, Pa., to m Hannah S. Wood
1835, 12, 21. Caleb & w, Lydia, & ch, Newton,
    Alfred, Mary Ann & William, gct Penns-
    ville MM
1836, 11, 21. Eliza Jane Updegraff (form
    Wood) dis mcd
1837, 6, 19. Lydia Ann rocf Birmingham MM,
    dtd 1837,4,26
1838, 2, 19. Joel & w, Elizabeth, gct Short
    Creek MM, O.
1839, 2, 18. Lewis gct Short Creek MM, O.
1839, 7, 27. Joshua & w, Esther, & ch,
    Lydia, Addison, William, Gerard Hopkins,
    Thomas, Esther Maria & Susan Amos Wood,
    gct Pennsville MM
1840, 3, 23. John P. & w, Susanna, & ch,
    Elizabeth, gct Pennsville MM
1841, 6, 21. Sarah, minor, gct Salem MM
1841, 6, 21. Isaiah gct Salem MM
1843, 5, 22. Greenberry P. gct Springfield
    MM
1843, 7, 17. Thomas Jr. dis mcd
1843, 10, 23. Lydia Ann gct Pennsville MM
1844, 7, 22. Elizabeth d 1844,2,9 ae 62 (an
    elder)
1844, 7, 22. William d 1844,6,4 ae 87 (a
    minister & mbr of this mtg)

WOOD, continued

1845, 10, 20. Lydia rocf Pennsville MM, dtd
    1845,10,16
1848, 4, 17. Nathan R. dis mcd
1848, 5, 22. Ann gct Flushing MM
1849, 10, 22. Anna Maria Marshall (form Wood)
    dis mcd
1853, 4, 18. Pusey & w, Rebecca, gct Flushing
    MM, O.
1853, 4, 18. Granville rpd mcd
1853, 4, 18. Charity & Mary R. gct Flushing
    MM, O.
1854, 1, 23. Rachel gct Flushing MM, O.
1858, 4, 19. Nathan L. gct Driftwood MM, Ind.,
    to m Mary Hambleton
1859, 1, 17. Mary H. rocf Driftwood MM, Ind.
1864, 11, 21. Granville dis mcd
1870, 5, 23. William T. con mcd
1873, 3, 17. Henry C. con mcd
1881, 2, 21. Jessie E. recrq
1881, 7, 18. Emma M. recrq
1882, 7, 17. Nathan L. & w, Mary H., & ch,
    Thomas Herbert & Mary, gct Lawrence MM,
    Kans.
1883, 11, 19. Lucy L. gct Short Creek MM, O.
1884, 1, 21. Emma gc
1885, 1, 19. Cora recrq
1885, 5, 22. Jessie E. relrq
1889, 2, 18. Thomas recrq
1893, 3, 20. Cora C. relrq
1894, 4, 23. Mary V. relrq
1899, 2, 20. Mary H. & dt, Mary, rocf Law-
    rence MM, Kans.
1901, 10, 21. Anna recrq
1901, 11, 18. William T. gct White Water MM,
    Ind.
1909, 3, 24. Thomas & Anna dropped from mbrp
1909, 6, 23. Lizzie C. gct Short Creek MM, O.
1909, 7, 21. Cornelia J. d 1908,12,10 (an
    elder)
1919, 10, 1. Mary rec in mbrp at Whittier MM,
    Calif.

WOLLAM

1902, 3, 17. Hiram [Woolam] & w, Emma, & ch,
    Arthur J., Roy H. & Ruby Frances, rocf
    Elk MM, West Elkton, O.
1905, 2, 22. Hiram S. & w, Rubie, gct Hope-
    well MM, Ind.
1905, 2, 22. Roy gct Hopewell MM, Ind.
1905, 8, 21. Arthur gct Stillwater MM, Ind.

WORRELL

1809, 9, 20. Daniel, s Isaiah & Sarah, Jef-

*   *   *   *   *   *   *

BLACKBURN

1811, 2, 16. James rst on consent of Westland
    MM
1813, 1, 16. Deborah rocf Redstone MM, dtd
    1812,9,3
1819, 12, 21. Sarah recrq
1819, 3, 17. John [Blackbourn] rst on consent
    of Monallen MM, Pa.

ferson Co., O.; m in Plymouth MH, Ann
CARR, dt James & Elizabeth, Jefferson Co.,
O.
    Ch: Elizabeth b 1812, 6, 1
        Susanna   " 1810, 7, 10
        Isaiah   " 1815, 1, 25
        Sarah   " 1817, 4, 20
        James C.   " 1819, 10, 8
        Warrick   " 1822, 8, 9
1826, 11, 1. David, s Isaiah & Sarah, Jeffer-
    son Co., O.; m in Smithfield MH, Sarah
    GRIMSHAW, dt John & Margaret, Jefferson
    Co., O.
1829, 1, 5.   Daniel, s Daniel & Sarah, b

1828, 12, 22. Elizanne dis jH
1829, 2, 23. Isaiah dis jH
1829, 3, 23. Sarah Sr. dis jH
1830, 3, 22. Daniel dis disunity
1832, 12, 17. Elizabeth dis jH
1836, 9, 19. Susannah dis jH
1837, 5, 22. Isaiah Jr. dis jH
1838, 2, 19. Elmina (form Kirk) dis mcd & jH
1838, 3, 19. Sarah Jr. dis jH
1851, 8, 18. Sarah G. gct Chesterfield MM

WORTHY

----, --, --. John b 1820,--,--; m Margaret
    ----- b 1826,--,--

1875, 7, 19. John, a minister, & w, Margaret,
    & ch, Edward, Franklin & Edith, rocf
    Short Creek MM, O.
1880, 12, 20. John & w, Margaret, & ch, Ed-
    ward, Franklin & Edith, gc

WRIGHT

1832, 3, 22. Charles, s Benj. & Hannah, Bel-
    mont Co., O.; m in Smithfield MH, Mary
    WOOD, dt Joel & Elizabeth, Jefferson Co.,
    O.

1832, 9, 17. Mary gct Short Creek MM, O.

WYLIE

1872, 7, 28. Frank, s Wm. & Jane, b

ZINK

----, --, --. John, s Wm. & Mary, b 1826,10,
    20; m Susie -----, dt Moses & Mary, b
    1856,7,14
    Ch: Agnes   b 1891, 11, 14

1880, 3, 22. John recrq

*   *   *   *   *   *   *

1822, 8, 19. Moses [Blackbourn] rocf Provi-
    dence MM, Pa., dtd 1822,6,25
1872, 9, 18. Charles M. & w, Mary E., & ch,
    Mary E. & Maria A., recrq
1881, 2, 21. Iazer & Keziah recrq
1882, 1, 23. Susanna B. recrq

FLUSHING MONTHLY MEETING

Flushing Monthly Meeting, Belmont County, Ohio, was set up 10th Mo. 23rd, 1818, by Plainfield Monthly Meeting. It was composed of Flushing, Nottingham, Bushy Fork, Westchester, Lower Flushing and Guernsey Preparative Meetings. In 1817, Nottingham Preparative Meeting built a large, brick house, planned for a quarterly meeting house and the name was changed from Nottingham to Freeport. Among early ministers at Flushing were Jacob Branson and Abigail Branson; other ministers in the limits of the monthly meeting were Joseph Cadwallader and Israel Wilson. Henry Carver, Jr. and Ann Strahl were the first to marry in Flushing Monthly Meeting, 12th Mo. 25th, 1818.

In 3rd Mo. 24th, 1820, the monthly meetings of Flushing, Plainfield and Stillwater united in asking for a new quarterly meeting to be known as Stillwater. In 1828 it was decided to hold the Flushing Monthly Meeting at Guernsey and Flushing all the time. Bushy Fork meeting belonged to this monthly meeting. It was laid down 1st Mo. 24, 1823; then set up again 2nd Mo. 27th 1824. It was again laid down 5th Mo. 24th 1832.

A library was placed in the Flushing and Freeport local meetings in 1822. From the establishment of Flushing Monthly Meeting until the close of 1854, there was no interruption in the work of the meeting, but on 11th Mo. 23rd 1854, the meeting was divided as a result of the Conservative separation. In 1875, the large, brick house on the hill near Freeport was torn down and rebuilt in the town with the date inscribed over the doorway, "Rebuilt in 1875", leaving the original date of 1817 in the gable.

RECORDS

ABEL
1839, 10, 24. Abigail (form Millison) dis mcd

ADAMS
1835, 6, 25. Beulah rocf Short Creek MM, O.,
    dtd 1835,5,19

AIKENS
1822, 10, 25. Hannah (form Dawson) dis mcd

ALFRED
1846, 11, 26. Anna G. (form Melton) dis mcd

ALLEN
1827, 4, 27. Daniel rmt Eliza Garretson
1828, 12, 26. Daniel H. dis JH
1829, 7, 23. Eliza dis jH
1835, 2, 26. Esther, Ruthanna, Joanna & James,
    minor ch Reuben & Joanna, rocf Short Creek
    MM, O., dtd 1835,1,20
1841, 11, 25. Sarah (form Barrett) dis mcd

ASHTON
1876, 5, 31. Wm. L., s Barak & Jane, Columbi-
    ana Co., O., b 1848,8,3 d 1924,12,7; m in
    Flushing MH, Eliza F. HOLLOWAY, dt Jacob
    & Sarah F., Belmont Co., O., b 1854,8,20
    d 1889,3,29 bur Flushing
----, --, --. William L. m Dorothy HOBSON, dt
    Thos. & Unity (Johnson), b 1847,5,14
    d 1934,3,31 bur Flushing

1877, 10, 25. William L. rocf Middleton MM, dtd
    1877,9,15
1891, 12, 24. Wm. L. gct New Garden MM
1892, 5, 26. Dorothy S. & s, George W. Strat-
    ton, rocf New Garden MM, dtd 1892,4,21

ATHERTON
----, --, --. Boaz & Mary
    Ch: Ann   b 1821, 11, 9
        Reuben R. " 1823,12, 15
        Richard   " 1825, 12, 10
        David   " 1818, 2, 9

1828, 12, 26. Boaz dis jH
1829, 1, 23. Mary dis jH
1838, 1, 25. David, Ann, Reuben Ross, Richard
    & Elizabeth, gct Stillwater MM

ATKINSON
1872, 3, 21. Catharine rst at Short Creek
    MM, O., on consent of this mtg

BAILEY
----, --, --. Jesse & Lydia
    Ch: Rachel   b 1828, 1, 21
        Joseph
        Lydenham   " 1830, 2, 10
        Rebecca   " 1831, 11, 26
        Elizabeth " 1833, 7, 26 d 1834, 8,24

    bur Flushing
    Ch: Lydia Pa-
        melia   b 1835, 3, 29 d 1842, 2,12
        bur Flushing
        Hannah L. b 1837, 4, 6
        Thomas
        Clarkson   " 1839, 10, 12
        John   " 1842, 7, 23
        Dillwyn G. " 1845, 10, 28
1859, 6, 2. Joel, s Edmund & Margaret, Bel-
    mont Co., O.; m in Guernsey MH, Lydia HOL-
    LOWAY, dt Robert & Rebecca, Guernsey Co.,O.
1861, 11, 22. Joseph, s Micajah & Mary, Bel-
    mont Co., O.; m in Flushing MH, Elvira
    PURVIANCE, dt David & Sarah, Belmont Co.,
    O., d 1895,10,23 bur Flushing (Joseph
    b 1819,5,23 d 1911,11,25)
    Ch: Irving E. b 1862, 12, 4; m Elma
        DOUDNA   [bur Flushing
        Mary R.   " 1866, 11, 1; d 1911,8,25
1882, 5, 31. Ida m James Hervey BINNS
1887, 10, 26. Sarah Elma m Samuel C. SMITH
----, --, --. Sydenham m Phebe W. HOGE, dt
    Elisha & Lydia (Vanpelt), b 1840,11,2

1826, 1, 27. Jesse rocf Salem MM, dtd 1826,11,
    23
1826, 6, 23. Jesse gct Middleton MM, O., to
    m Lydia Townsend
1827, 2, 23. Asenath gct Concord MM
1827, 8, 24. Lydia rocf Middleton MM, dtd
    1827,8,9
1829, 12, 24. Emmor & w, Elizabeth, & ch,
    Emmor, Martha & Ann, rocf Short Creek MM,
    dtd 1828,10,21
1830, 3, 25. Elizabeth & ch, Emmor, Martha
    & Ann, rocf Short Creek MM, O., dtd 1828,
    10,21
1830, 11, 25. Uriah rmt Susannah Farmer
1831, 4, 21. Susanna gct Stillwater MM, O.
1831, 6, 23. Ann & Martha rqct Springborough
    MM; returned from Springborough, Ind.,
    1831,11,24 because of their disunity be-
    fore cert was granted
1831, 12, 22. Elizabeth dis JH
1832, 5, 24. Martha & Ann dis jH
1832, 8, 23. Emmor & Emmor Jr. dis jH
1838, 1, 25. Jesse & w, Lydia, & ch, Rachel,
    Joseph S., Rebecca, Amelia & Hannah, gct
    Salem MM
1839, 7, 25. Jesse & w, Lydia, & ch, Rachel,
    Joseph, Sidenham, Rebecca, Lydia Pamelia
    & Hannah L., rocf Salem MM, dtd 1839,6,19
1857, 8, 20. Stephen Hobson gct Somerset MM,
    to m Margaret Bailey
1858, 5, 20. Jesse dis disunity
1858, 6, 24. Lydia dis jG
1860, 3, 22. Hannah Lavina & Rebecca T. dis
    jG
1860, 4, 26. Ida, minor, in care of Isaac &
    Mary Mitchel, recrq
1860, 5, 22. Rachel dis jG
1860, 11, 22. Joseph Sydenham dis jG

BAILEY, continued
1861, 1, 24. Jesse dis jG
1861, 1, 24. Phebe W. (form Hoge) dis mcd &
    jG
1862, 2, 20. Elvira P. gct Somerset MM
1864, 12, 22. Thomas C. & John Quincey dis jG
1865, 4, 20. Joseph & w, Elvira, & ch, Jep-
    tha, Joseph E., Elizabeth, Irving & Sarah
    Elma, rocf Somerset MM
1874, 9, 24. Joseph E. dis mcd
1919, 7, 24. Irving E. gct Somerset MM, to m
    Asenath Elma Doudna
1921, 7, 21. Irving E. gct Somerset MM
1841, 5, 20. Ann (form Young) dis mcd

BARBER
----, --, --. Abraham m Rachel ----- d 1879,
    2,22 bur Guernsey
    Ch: Elizabeth b 1819, 2, 2
        Ann   " 1820, 12, 22
        Jane   " 1823, 7, 11
        Asenith " 1826, 6, 19
        Asa   " 1828, 8, 13 d 1844, 9,14
            bur Guernsey
        Benjamin b 1830, 10, 2
        Samuel   " 1833, 12, 14
        Mary   " 1836, 10, 18
----, --, --. Cornelius & Elizabeth
    Ch: Susannah b 1822, 2, 10 d 1845, 7, 3
            bur Flushing
        Naomi   b 1823, 7, 23
        Samuel   " 1825, 5, 26 d 1829,11,27
            bur Guernsey
        Abraham b 1827, 8, 17 " 1831,11,13
            bur Guernsey
        William b 1829, 8, 23
        Anne   " 1832, 5, 10
1839, 5, 1. Ann m Jason A. HIBBS
1854, 11, 1. Asenath m John CREW
1860, 9, 28. Samuel Jr. d bur Guernsey

1820, 2, 25. Abraham & w, Rachel, & dt,
    Elizabeth, rocf Short Creek MM, O., dtd
    1819,12,21
1821, 7, 27. Elizabeth recrq
1821, 8, 24. Cornelius rst on consent of
    Short Creek MM, O.
1822, 4, 26. Abraham & w, Rachel, & ch,
    Elizabeth & Ann, gct Short Creek MM, O.
1823, 11, 21. Abraham & fam gct Short Creek
    MM, O., 1823,6, returned end by Short
    Creek MM, O.
1827, 4, 27. Cornelius & w, Elizabeth, & ch,
    Susannah, Naomi & Samuel, gct Short Creek
    MM, O.
1830, 1, 21. Cornelius & w, Elizabeth, & ch,
    Susanna, Naomi, Abraham & William, rocf
    Short Creek MM, O., dtd 1829,12,22
1843, 8, 24. Samuel & w, Ann, rocf Short
    Creek MM, O., dtd 1843,5,23
1844, 10, 24. Naomi Brock (form Barber) dis
    mcd
1851, 4, 24. Jane Hoge (form Barber) dis mcd

1851, 7, 24. Samuel & w, Ann, gct Short Creek
    MM, O.
1853, 1, 20. Ann gct Vermillion MM, Ill.
1853, 2, 24. Cert for Wm. to Vermillion MM,
    Ill., returned 1853,8,25 with information
    he was not living in limits
1859, 3, 24. Mary gct Stillwater MM
1867, 6, 20. Benjamin rst at Chesterfield
    MM on consent of this mtg

BARRETT
----, --, --. Thomas m Margaret ----- d 1838,
    5,14 bur Flushing
    Ch: Warden   b 1799, 10, 10
        Esther   " 1801, 2, 12
        Amy   " 1802, 7, 12
        Baldwin " 1804, 6, 24
        Ann   " 1805, 12, 27
        Arthur   " 1807, 9, 16
        Belinda " 1809, 6, 22
        Rachel   " 1812, 5, 15
        Thomas   " 1813, 12, 8
----, --, --. David & Winifred
    Ch: William b 1808, 1, 7
        Thomas   " 1809, 12, 11
        Elizabeth " 1811, 8, 27
        Uriah   " 1813, 11, 4
        Albert   " 1815, 7, 18
        Sarah   " 1817, 5, 29
        Ruth   " 1819, 8, 27
        David   " 1821, 8, 26
        Winifred " 1823, 6, 11
        Joseph   " 1825, 4, 18
1829, 1, 14. Immer, s Baldwin & Mary Ann, b
1844, 11, 27. David d bur Flushing

1825, 9, 23. Warden gct Short Creek MM, O.,
    to m Mary Hurford
1826, 11, 24. Esther rmt David Wilson
1827, 3, 23. Baldwin gct Short Creek MM, O.,
    to m Mary Ann Street
1828, 4, 25. Warden gct Short Creek MM, O.
1828, 5, 23. Mary Ann rocf Short Creek MM,
    O., dtd 1827,9,18
1830, 1, 21. William dis mcd
1830, 4, 22. Belinda rmt John Cadwalader
1832, 4, 26. Ann dis
1832, 6, 21. Amy Spurrier (form Barrett) dis
    mcd
1833, 5, 23. Rachel dis disunity
1835, 2, 26. Elizabeth Hughes (form Barrett)
    dis mcd
1836, 2, 23. Arthur dis mcd
1836, 4, 21. Thomas dis mcd
1841, 2, 25. Thos. Jr. dis military training
1841, 11, 25. Sarah Allen (form Barrett) dis
    mcd
1842, 4, 21. Baldwin dis disunity
1844, 2, 22. Albert dis mcd
1844, 2, 22. Winifred Walker (form Barrett)
    dis mcd
1846, 4, 23. Thomas dis mcd
1849, 5, 24. David dis

BARRETT, continued
1849, 9, 20. Mary Ann gct Short Creek MM, O.
1849, 12, 20. Emmer dis disunity
1852, 7, 22. Uriah dis mcd

BARTHELOW
1838, 5, 24. Mary (form Miller) dis mcd

BARTON
1825, 9, 23. Susannah (form Dixon) dis mcd

BECK
1820, 4, 21. Jesse & w, Elizabeth, & ch, Ra-
    chel, gct Stillwater MM

BELL
1916, 5, 25. James F. Walker gct Haddonfield
    MM, N. J., to m Alice M. Bell

BENNETT
1830, 1, 27. Ann & ch, Thomas, Lydia, William
    & Smith, gc

BERRY
1829, 2, 27. Martha dis mcd

BETHEL
1863, 11, 26. Mary (form Hall) dis mcd

BEVAN
----, --, --. Stacy & Lydia
    Ch: Mary   b 1793, 5, 18
        Susanna   " 1795, 12, 16
        Eleanor   " 1798, 4, 19
        John   " 1800, 12, 25
        Owen   " 1813, 1, 1
        Samuel   " 1807, 1, 6
        Abel   " 1810, 2, 18
        Elizabeth
        Phamyann   d 18--, 2,12
----, --, --. Stacy & Eunice
    Ch: Joseph A. b 1819, 2, 27
        Martha   " 1820, 12, 19
        Susanna   " 1822, 9, 22
        Naomi   " 1824, 8, 23
        Lewis   " 1826, 3, 13
        Lydia Ann   " 1827, 2, 22
        Elizabeth   " 1830, 4, 1
        Stacy Ewing " 1834, 1, 19
        Mary E.   " 1835, 6, 9
        Samuel   " 1838, 9, 16
1826, 4, 17. Lewis d bur Flushing
1844, 12, 23. David b

1821, 12, 21. Eleanor rmt John Kinsey
1823, 2, 21. Naomi recrq
1824, 6, 25. Stacy & w, Lydia, & ch, John,
    Owen, Samuel, Abel & Elizabeth, gct Fall
    Creek MM
1827, 1, 26. Nancy (form Fawcett) dis mcd
1831, 11, 24. Stacy & w, Eunice, & ch, Joseph,
    Martha, Susanna, Naomi, Lydia Ann & Eliza-
    beth, rocf Stillwater MM, dtd 1831,10,22

1833, 5, 23. Stacy rmt Jane Roberts
1844, 8, 22. Joseph A. gct Stillwater MM, to
    m Maria Hall
1846, 7, 23. Stacy & w, Jane, & ch, Stacy
    Ewing, Mary Elizabeth, Gulielma, Aaron &
    David C., gct Goshen MM
1846, 7, 23. Mariah rocf Stillwater MM, dtd
    1846,6,27
1847, 2, 25. Naomi McCall (form Bevan) dis
    mcd
1850, 5, 23. Martha Ramsey (form Bevan) dis
    mcd
1861, 3, 21. Elizabeth Scott (form Bevans)
    dis mcd

BILLINGSLY
----, --, --. William m Sarah ----- d 1865,12,
    14
    Ch: James   b 1816, 7, 24
        Elijah   " 1818, 1, 21
        Samuel K.   " 1819, 10, 29
        Margaret   " 1822, 5, 17
        Rachel   " 1824, 8, 17
        William P. " 1828, 10, 8
1832, 4, 8. Ruth d bur Flushing

1838, 4, 26. James dis mcd
1840, 4, 23. Samuel K. & Elijah dis jas
1847, 7, 22. William P. dis jas
1848, 7, 20. Rachel Meldrom (form Billingsly)
    dis mcd

BINNS
1882, 5, 31. James Hervey, s David & Rebecca
    H., Harrison Co., O.; m in Flushing MH,
    Ida BAILEY, dt Stephen & Martha, Belmont
    Co., O.
    Ch: Wm.   b 1884, 4, 29

1882, 12, 21. James Hervey rocf Short Creek
    MM, O., dtd 1882,12,19
1886, 11, 25. James Hervey & w, Ida, & s,
    William C., gct Short Creek MM, O.
1906, 1, 25. Arthur H. & w, Tacy M., & ch,
    Frances S., Mildred M. & Dorothy A., rocf
    Stillwater MM, O.
1908, 2, 20. Arthur H. & w, Tacie M., & ch,
    Frances S., Mildred M. & Dorothy A., gct
    Salem MM, O.

BISHOP
1883, 5, 25. Wm., s John & Rebecca F., Burl-
    ington Co., N. J.; m in Flushing MH, Mar-
    tha M. HOLLOWAY, dt Jacob Jr. & Sarah, b
    1856,10,10

1883, 11, 22. Martha H. gct ND MM

BOGUE
----, --, --. Jonathan & Sarah
    Ch: Maryann   b 1813, 2, 21
        Ruth   " 1814, 10, 16
        Mark   " 1816, 10, 26

BOGUE, Jonathan & Sarah, continued
    Ch: John   b 1819, 1, 21
1820, 4, 8. Jonathan [Boge] Jr. d bur Free-
    port
----, --, --. Job & Mary Ann
    Ch: Joel H.   b 1824, 8, 23
        Jonathan " 1822, 7, 10
        Sarah   " 1815, 3, 24
        Elizabeth " 1816, 10, 1
        Daniel E. " 1818, 7, 5
        Edith A. " 1820, 6, 17

1821, 12, 21. Sarah & ch, Mary Ann, Ruth,
    Mark & John, rocf Stillwater MM, dtd
    1821,5,26
1839, 1, 24. Job & w, Mary Ann, & ch, Sarah
    Elizabeth, Daniel, Edith, Jonathan, Joel,
    Robert & Phebe, gct Vermillion MM, Ill.
1839, 1, 24. Sarah & ch, Mary Ann, Ruth &
    John, gct Vermillion MM, Ill.

BOSWELL
1847, 5, 26. William, s Benjamin & Asenath,
    Belmont Co., O.; m in Guernsey MH, Hannah
    BRIGGS, dt Samuel & Phebe, Belmont Co., O.

1847, 7, 22. Hannah gct Somerset MM

BRACKEN
1866, 10, 26. Lemual [Brackin], s Elisha & Es-
    ther, Belmont Co., O.; m in Flushing MH,
    Mary HIRST, dt Israel & Catharine, Bel-
    mont Co., O.

1822, 11, 22. Elisha rmt Phebe Branson
1823, 2, 21. Phebe gct Short Creek MM, O.
1825, 8, 26. Elisha & w, Phebe, & ch, Deborah
    & Rebecca, rocf Short Creek MM, O., dtd
    1825,8,23
1826, 12, 22. Elisha & w, Phebe, & ch, Deborah
    & Rebecca, gct Short Creek MM, O.
1842, 3, 24. Caleb & w, Mary, rocf Redstone
    MM, Pa., dtd 1842,2,2
1860, 7, 26. Caleb & w, Mary, gct Short Creek
    MM, O.
1868, 1, 23. Mary H. gct Coal Creek MM, Ia.

BRANSON
----, --, --. John m Abigail ----- d 1826,7,
    16 bur Flushing
    Ch: Miriam   b 1802, 10, 1
        Nancy   " 1804, 2, 26
        Gulielmah " 1806, 6, 3
        Samuel   " 1809, 3, 19
        Asa   " 1810, 7, 8 d 1909, 5,
        29 bur Flushing
        Eliza   b 1813, 5, 26
        John W.   " 1815, 10, 15
1808, 12, 22. Ann, dt Jacob Sr. & Rebecca
    (Holloway), b
----, --, --. Smith m Jane ----- d 1853,6,17
    bur Flushing
    Ch: Benjamin b 1819, 7, 7 d 1822, 7,10

bur Flushing
    Ch: Elisha S. b 1820, 12, 25 d 1822, 6,
      25 bur Flushing
      Lydia   b 1823, 2, 20
      William   " 1824, 12, 3 d 1840,11,13
      bur Flushing
      David   b 1827, 2, 23
      Rachel   " 1829, 8, 25
      Asa   " 1832, 4, 26
      Elizabeth " 1834, 3, 26
      Mary Jane " 1836, 7, 17
      Smith Jr. " 1838, 11, 19
1822, 8, 25. Deborah, dt Jacob & Rebecca, d
    bur Flushing
----, --, --. Aquilla & Lydia E.
    Ch: Lydia Jane b 1826, 9, 16
      Jonathan E." 1828, 3, 14
      Isaac L.   " 1829, 9, 23
      William E. " 1831, 5, 9
      Mary R.   " 1832, 10, 10 d 1833,8,29
      Levi   " 1834, 3, 18
      Israel   " 1835, 9, 17
      Elizabeth " 1837, 4, 5
      Rachel   " 1838, 11, 10
----, --, --. Josiah & Sarah
    Ch: Elizabeth b 1829, 7, 27
      James Law-
          ton   " 1831, 4, 3
      Rebecca   " 1833, 5, 7
      Susannah " 1835, 6, 24
      Jesse   " 1837, 6, 16
      Martha   " 1839, 8, 21
      Phebe   " 1841, 9, 21
      Jacob   " 1844, 5, 4
----, --, --. Asa, s John & Abigail (Holloway)
    b 1810,7,8 d 1909,5,29 bur Flushing; m
    Mary BYE d 1844,1,13
    Ch: Abigail   b 1834, 10, 29 d 1842, 6,12
      Joseph   " 1837, 1, 1 " 1880, 4,16
    Asa m 2nd Rebecca SMART d 1896,6,28 bur
    Flushing
1834, 10, --. Rebecca, w Jacob, d bur Flush-
    ing
1843, 11, 1. Lydia m John HOGE
----, --, --. Jacob, s Jacob & Rebecca (Hollo-
    way), b 1816,7,19 d 1868,2,16 bur Flush-
    ing; m Julian H. JOHNSON, dt John & Hanna
    (Pennock), b 1816,2,12 d 1892,6,23 bur
    South Western Grounds, Phila., Pa.
    Ch: Levi   b 1844, 11, 2 d 1905, 6, 3
      Angelica, N. Y.
      Joseph H. b 1846, 11, 29 " 1890, 6,26
      bur S. W. Grounds, Phila., Pa.
      Benjamin b 1848, 12, 15 d 1886, 7,12
      bur Harrisville
      Deborah b 1851, 2, 10 d 1891, 3, 2
      bur Flushing
      John J.   b 1853, 9, 20 " 1855, 9,11
      bur Flushing
      Mary Eliza-
        beth b 1856, 9, 5 " 1892, 5,16
      bur Springfield, Pa.
      Anne L.   b 1859, 2, 6

BRANSON, continued
1845, 6, 27. Jacob d bur Flushing
1848, 11, 29. Rachel m Israel SIDWELL
1857, 4, 29. Mary Jane m Nathan STEER
1861, 5, 8. Smith d bur Flushing
----, --, --. Samuel & Sarah
      Ch: Daniel H. b 1849, 1, 17
          Francis W. " 1850, 11, 25
          Albert
          Laurence   " 1858, 1, 11
1849, 5, 14. Elizabeth d bur Flushing
1850, 10, 30. David, s Smith & Jane, Belmont
    Co., O., d 1903,12,18 bur Flushing; m in
    Flushing MH, Sarah B. HOLLOWAY, dt Jacob
    & Martha, Belmont Co., O., b 1827,4,10
    d 1894,3,15 bur Flushing
      Ch: Martha H. b 1851, 8, 24
          Ann Eliza " 1854, 1, 23
          Mary Ellen " 1856, 8, 14
          Lizzie   " 1859, 1, 14
          Emma Jane " 1862, 11, 21; m James
            Hervey DEWEES
          Mira D.   b 1869, 3, 8; m Albert
            HAYES
1859, 3, 25. Elizabeth m Stephen CLENDENAN
----, --, --. Joseph H. m Ruthanna STRATTON,
    dt Benjamin & Ellen (Stanley), b 1849,4,7
    d 1912,12,31 bur South Western Grounds,
    Phila., Pa.
      Ch: Elma   b 1870, 9, 28; m (1) 1892,
            9,7, Robert Wood MARIS; m (2) Edwin
            F. HOLLOWAY
          Walter J. b 1871, 10, 29
          Albert D. " 1873, 7, 26 d 1885, 1,27
            bur Flushing
          Anne Mary b 1875, 11, 27; m (1) James
            Arthur HOLLOWAY; m (2) Wm. D. OLI-
            PHANT; d 19--, 2, -- bur Winona
          Jula Ellen b 1889, 10, 7
          Howard
1873, 6, 27. Martha H. m John A. HOBSON
1873, 10, 8. Rebecca Anna m Chalkley DAWSON
1874, 5, 27. Susan G. m Eulyssus A. McGREW
1882, 10, 4. Ann Eliza m Henry HALL
1883, 9, 26. Lizzie M. m Nathan R. SMITH
1886, 7, 28. Annie L. m James WALTON
1891, 4, 11. Ann d bur Flushing
1891, 8, 21. Myra D. m Albert HAYES
1892, 9, 23. Emma J. m Jas. Henry DEWEES

1820, 5, 26. Sarah rst on consent of Concord
    MM
1820, 12, 22. Elizabeth recrq
1821, 12, 21. Miriam rmt Joshua Ellis
1822, 11, 22. Phebe rmt Elisha Bracken
1823, 2, 21. Catharine recrq
1823, 9, 25. Catharine rmt Israel Hirst
1824, 3, 26. Aquilla recrq
1824, 11, 26. Aquila rmt Lydia Ellis Jr.
1825, 1, 21. Elizabeth rmt John Hirst
1826, 11, 24. Nancy rmt Samuel Fawcett
1828, 8, 22. Isaiah gct Stillwater MM, to m
    Sarah G. Laughton

1833, 11, 21. Lydia rmt Jesse Roberts
1833, 12, 26. Asa rmt Mary Bye
1834, 3, 20. Sarah dis jH
1836, 4, 21. Aaron gct Redstone MM, Pa.
1837, 5, 25. Eliza rmt Joseph Wilson
1837, 8, 24. Asa & w, Mary, & ch, Abigail &
    Joseph, gct Stillwater MM
1838, 6, 21. Asa & w, Mary, & ch, Abigail &
    Joseph, rocf Stillwater MM, dtd 1838,4,28
1838, 11, 22. Samuel gct Redstone MM, Pa.
1839, 1, 24. John gct Spiceland MM, Ind.
1841, 8, 26. Aquilla & w, Lydia, & ch, Lydia
    Jane, Jonathan Ellis, Isaac L., Wm. E.,
    Levi, Israel, Elizabeth & David, gct Ver-
    million MM, Ill.
1841, 12, 23. Samuel rocf Redstone MM, Pa.,
    dtd 1841,11,3
1842, 5, 26. Jacob Jr. gct Salem MM
1845, 6, 26. Asa & s, Joseph, gct Short Creek
    MM, O.
1846, 7, 23. Jacob & w, Julian H., & s, Levi,
    rocf Salem MM, dtd 1846,5,20
1848, 3, 23. Samuel gct Fall Creek MM, O., to
    m Sarah A. Huff
1848, 6, 22. Asa & w, Rebecca, & s, Joseph,
    rocf Short Creek MM, O., dtd 1848,5,23
1852, 1, 22. Sarah A. rocf Fairfield MM, dtd
    1851,11,15
1852, 4, 22. Elizabeth R. & Rebecca G. gct
    Chester MM, Ind.
1852, 4, 22. Isaiah J. & w, Sarah G., & ch,
    Susannah, Jesse, Martha, Phebe & Jacob,
    gct Chester MM, Ind.
1862, 2, 20. Asa Jr. dis
1862, 6, 26. Smith dis disunity
1869, 3, 25. Rebecca Ann rocf Providence MM,
    Pa., dtd 1869,3,4
1869, 3, 25. Richard, Susan G., Thomas W. &
    Elenor P., rocf Providence MM, Pa., dtd
    1869,3,4
1869, 8, 26. Joseph H. gct New Garden MM, to
    m Ruthanna Stratton
1870, 3, 24. Ruth Anna rocf New Garden MM,
    dtd 1870,2,24
1872, 12, 26. Joseph H. & w, Ruthanna, & ch,
    Elma & Walter J., gct Salem MM
1873, 7, 24. Joseph H. & w, Ruthanna, & ch,
    Elma & Walter J., rocf Salem MM, dtd 1873,
    6,25
1873, 12, 25. Thomas H. dis mcd
1876, 12, 21. Daniel H. dis mcd
1878, 1, 24. Francis W. dis jas
1880, 7, 22. Joseph d 1880,4,16 ae 44 (an
    elder)
1882, 3, 23. Elma P. January (form Branson)
    dis mcd
1884, 8, 21. Benjamin gct Short Creek MM, O.,
    to m Caroline Hall
1885, 4, 23. Benjamin gct Short Creek MM, O.
1888, 5, 24. Samuel rst
1888, 12, 20. Levi dis mcd
1890, 6, 26. Joseph H. & w, Ruthanna, & ch,
    Elma, Walter J., Anna Mary & Julia E., gct

BRANSON, continued
    Chester MM, Pa.
1891, 1, 22. Sarah A. dis jas
1892, 5, 26. Juliann H. gct Chester MM, Pa.
1899, 6, 22. Richard dis disunity
1917, 2, 22. Mary Ellen gct Salem MM, O.

BREWER
1819, 11, 26. Martha Buffington (form Brewer)
    dis mcd
1820, 4, 21. Sarah rocf Short Creek MM, O.,
    dtd 1819,11,23
1821, 4, 27. John dis mcd
1823, 7, 25. Ann Keech (form Brewer) dis mcd
1825, 1, 21. Richard dis disunity
1825, 10, 21. John rst
1828, 3, 21. Mary Jr. dis
1829, 10, 22. Hannah gct Blue River MM, Ind.
1833, 2, 21. John con mcd
1834, 2, 20. Phebe recrq
1834, 6, 26. John gct Blue River MM, Ind.
1837, 12, 21. Phebe gct Short Creek MM, O.

BRIGGS
1818, 8, 27. Sarah S., dt Wm. & Esther, b
----, --, --. Israel & Mary
    Ch: George G. b 1822, 6, 17
        Benjamin   " 1823, 9, 3
        Job   " 1826, 5, 30
        William   " 1828, 11, 2
1822, 7, 13. George d bur Guernsey
----, --, --. Samuel M. m Phebe ----- d 1830,
    9,1 bur Guernsey
    Ch: Hannah   b 1823, 8, 4
        Esther S. " 1825, 2, 21
        Sarah   " 1826, 7, 19
        Eliza   " 1828, 8, 18
    Samuel m 2nd Elizabeth H. ----- d 1841,7,
    25 bur Guernsey
    Ch: Mary Ann   b 1833, 3, 13
        William   " 1835, 2, 1
        Phebe S.   " 1837, 7, 7
1829, 3, 27. William d bur Guernsey
1830, 7, 12. Mary d bur Guernsey
----, --, --. Job & Ann
    Ch: Thomas   b 1831, 5, 31 d 1831,12,26
            bur Guernsey
        Hannah   b 1832, 10, 30
        Lydia   " 1834, 3, 13
        Maria   " 1835, 11, 15
        Jesse   " 1839, 2, 14
        Amos   " 1839, 5, 1
        Liza Ann   " 1840, 11, 8 d 1853, 1,10
            bur Guernsey   .
        Cynthia   b 1842, 8, 9 " 1853, 1, 9
            bur Guernsey
        Keziah   b 1844, 2, 12 " 1853, 1, 7
            bur Guernsey
        Harriett   b 1849, 3, 15
----, --, --. Jonathan & Elizabeth
    Ch: Mary   b 1832, 7, 2
        George   " 1834, 3, 12
        Robert M. " 1836, 3, 25

    Ch: Sarah M.   b 1840, 12, 24
        William   " 1838, 3, 16
        Benjamin   " 1844, 2, 25
        Josiah   " 1846, 8, 12
----, --, --. William m Jane ----- d 1845,2,7
    bur Guernsey
    Ch: Mary R.   b 1834, 10, 16
        Thomas   " 1837, 2, 4
        Evan   " 1839, 9, 29
        Jordan   " 1843, 1, 15 d 1844,10,29
            bur Guernsey
1837, 8, 8. Esther, w Wm., d bur Guernsey
1842, 10, 26. Henry, s Wm. & Esther, Guernsey
    Co., O.; m in Guernsey MH, Betsy HOLLOWAY,
    dt Robert & Rebecca, Guernsey Co., O.,
    d 1865,11,27 bur Guernsey
    Ch: Rebecca   b 1843, 11, 1
        Martha   " 1845, 3, 21
        Luceta   " 1847, 4, 3 d 1866, 1, 3
            bur Guernsey
        Joseph   b 1850, 10, 31 " 1852,12, 7
            bur Guernsey
        Jonathan   b 1852, 11, 13
        Mariah   " 1855, 6, 25
    Henry m 2nd 1867,5,2 in Guernsey MH, Ta-
    litha Ann WHARTON, dt Joel & Abigail,
    Harrison Co., O.
    Ch: Abigail   b 1869, 6, 4
1843, 6, 28. Maria m Robert HOLLOWAY
1845, 4, 30. Samuel, s Wm. & Esther, Belmont
    Co., O.; m in Guernsey MH, Elizabeth
    STEVEN, dt Jesse & Francina SCHOOLEY,
    Guernsey Co., O., d 1881,4,16 bur Guernsey
1845, 10, 1. Eliza m David STEPHEN
1847, 5, 26. Hannah m Wm. BOSWELL
1849, 11, 28. Esther m Benjamin SEARS
1860, 8, 30. Mary Ann m Nathan MICHENER
1878, 9, 27. Martha m Thomas E. MOTT
1884, 9, 26. Rebecca m Samuel B. SMITH
1885, 2, 27. Maria m Wilson HODGIN

1822, 11, 22. Samuel M. rmt Phebe Wright
1830, 7, 22. Job rmt Ann Romans
1831, 9, 22. Jonathan gct Stillwater MM, to
    m Stephen Millhouse (?)
1831, 12, --. Samuel M. rmt Elizabeth Hibbs
1832, 2, 23. Elizabeth rocf Stillwater MM,
    dtd 1831,12,24
1832, 4, 26. Israel & w, Mary, & ch, Esther,
    Ann, John S., Benjamin, Job & William, gct
    Deerfield MM
1833, 5, 23. William rmt Jane Romans
1838, 5, 24. Rebecca Parkins (form Briggs)
    dis mcd
1848, 3, 23. William gct New Garden MM, to m
    Mary Johnston
1848, 11, 23. Sarah S. gct Short Creek MM, O.
1849, 11, 22. William gct Smithfield MM, to m
    Hannah Crew
1850, 6, 20. Hannah C. rocf Smithfield MM,
    dtd 1850,4,22
1854, 8, 24. Hannah, Lydia & Maria gct Spring
    Creek MM, Ia.

BRIGGS, continued
1854, 8, 24. Job & w, Anna, & ch, Jesse,
    Amos & Harriet gct Spring Creek MM, Ia.
1855, 7, 26. Wm. Jr. dis jas
1857, 3, 26. George & Mary gct Plainfield MM
1857, 3, 26. Jonathan & w, Elizabeth, & ch,
    William, Sarah M., Benjamin, Josiah &
    Robert M., gct Plainfield MM
1858, 3, 25. Phebe L. dis jas
1861, 5, 23. Wm. dis jG
1862, 5, 22. Martha (form Ratcliff) dis mcd
1863, 7, 23. Evan dis military service
1864, 12, 22. Thomas dis jG

1865, 2, 23. Sarah W. gct Stillwater MM
1876, 4, 20. Elwood R. dis disunity
1879, 12, 25. Jonathan dis mcd
1908, 9, 24. Abigail gct Salem MM, O.

BRINTON
1911, 5, 25. John French Wilson gct Birming-
    ham MM, Pa., to m Anna Hoopes Brinton

BROCK
----, --, --. Stephen & Anne
    Ch: Mary   b 1796, 4, 10
        Catharine " 1798, 9, 13
        Anne   " 1801, 5, 2
        John   " 1803, 5, 14
        David   " 1806, 7, 2
        Jane   " 1808, 10, 13
        Sarah   " 1812, 1, 28
        Stephen   " 1815, 8, 12
        Abigail   " 1817, 12, 15
1822, 7, 10. Sarah d bur Flushing
1822, 7, 11. Abigail d bur Flushing

1829, 4, 24. David dis jH
1830, 3, 25. Jane Day (form Brock) dis mcd
1831, 8, 25. Ann Wilson (form Brock) dis mcd
1831, 9, 22. Stephen & w, Ann, & ch, Mary,
    John & Stephen, gct Somerset MM
1844, 10, 24. Naomi (form Barber) dis mcd

BROKAW
1845, 8, 21. Elizabeth (form Fell) dis mcd

BROOMHALL
1821, 10, 26. Sarah Fields (form Broomhall)
    dis mcd

BROWN
1820, 11, 24. Mary (form Pickering) dis mcd
1824, 4, 23. Sinah (form Dawson) dis mcd

BUCK
1828, 4, 25. Eleanor (form Chicken) dis mcd

BUFFINGTON
1819, 11, 26. Martha (form Brewer) dis mcd

BUFKIN
----, --, --. Thomas & Ruth

    Ch: Samuel   b 1810, 5, 31
        John   " 1811, 9, 12
        Bathsheba " 1813, 1, 19
        Warner   " 1814, 5, 20
        Gulyelma   " 1815, 8, 30
        Sarah   " 1817, 4, 4
        Ruth   " 1820, 3, 25

1829, 4, 24. Samuel gct Short Creek MM, O.
1830, 11, 21. Thomas [Buffkin] & w, Ruth, &
    ch, John, Bathsheba, Warner, Julia Elma,
    Sarah & Ruth, gct Springborough MM
1831, 3, 24. Samuel rocf Short Creek MM, O.,
    dtd 1831,2,22
1832, 6, 21. Samuel dis mcd
1840, 11, 26. Samuel rst at Spiceland MM, Ind.
    on consent of this mtg

BUNDY
1847, 12, 1. -----, s Benjamin & Delitha,
    Belmont Co., O.; m in Guernsey MH, Achsah
    R. SMITH, dt Nathan & Catharine, Guernsey
    Co., O., b 1825,3,18
1857, 4, 30. Demsey, s Wm. & Sarah, Belmont
    Co., O.; m in Guernsey MH, Rebecca W.
    SMITH, dt Samuel & Elizabeth, Guernsey Co.,
    O.

1848, 2, 24. Achsah R. gct Short Creek MM, O.
1857, 8, 20. Rebecca W. gct Stillwater MM

BURKE
1836, 8, 25. Rachel gct Duck Creek MM, Ind.

BURKHEAD
1831, 5, 26. Susanna dis mcd

BURNETT
----, --, --. Robert & Ann [Burnet]
    Ch: John   b 1800, 3, 25
        David   " 1804, 2, 4
        Rebecca   " 1805, 1, 23
        Rachel   " 1807, 2, 21
        Deborah   " 1810, 12, 21
        Thomas   " 1811, 10, 4
        Lydia   " 1813, 10, 22
        William   " 1817, 10, 23
        Smith   " 1820, 3, 2

1823, 10, 24. Rebecca gct Stillwater MM
1827, 7, 27. David gct Miami MM, O.
1828, 3, 21. Rachel gct Miami MM, O.
1830, 1, 21. Robert & w, Ann, & ch, Thomas,
    Lydia, William & Smith, gct Miami MM, O.

BURR
----, --, --. Jesse & Martha
    Ch: Sarah Ann b 1825, 8, 20
        Amy H.   " 1826, 12, 15
        Rachel L. " 1828, 12, 21
        Amanda   " 1830, 5, 6
        Rebecca S. " 1832, 3, 24

BURR, continued
1825, 12, 23. Jesse & w, Martha, & dt, Sarah
Ann, rocf Short Creek MM, O., dtd 1825,
10,18
1830, 2, 24. Jesse dis disunity

BURT
1832, 5, 27. Daniel d bur Flushing

BYE
----, --, --. Jonathan m Mary ----- d 1846,10,
23 bur Flushing
Ch: Martha   b 1786, 12, 11
    Susanna   " 1788, 8, 14
    John   " 1790, 2, 12
    Jonathan   " 1793, 3, 25
    Jonas   " 1794, 9, 7
    Samuel   " 1795, 10, 10
----, --,---. Jonas & Martha
Ch: Abel W.   b 1821, 6, 8
    Edward   " 1822, 9, 14
    Samuel   " 1824, 10, 30
    Elisha
    Elizabeth
    Lewis   " 1832, 4, 27
1846, 4, 7. Jonathan d bur Flushing
1858, 10, 22. Lewis, s Jonas & Martha, Morgan
Co., b 1832,4,27; m in Flushing MH, Phebe
H. WILLIAMS, dt Wm. C. & Rebecca, Belmont
Co., O.
----, --, --. William S. m Mary R. H. HOLLOWAY
dt Lindley M. & Martha (Walker), b 1855,
2,2

1819, 9, 24. Jonas rocf Short Creek MM, O.,
dtd 1819,8,24
1820, 4, 21. John & Sarah rocf Short Creek
MM, O., dtd 1820,3,21
1820, 8, 25. Jonathan & w, Mary, & s, Samuel,
rocf Short Creek MM, O., dtd 1820,6,20
1820, 11, 24. Jonas rmt Martha Walker
1821, 12, 21. Sarah Crozer (form Bye) dis mcd
1824, 8, 27. Mary recrq
1833, 12, 26. Mary rmt Asa Branson
1839, 10, 24. Jonas & w, Martha, & ch, Abel
W., Edward, Samuel, Elisha, Elizabeth,
Lewis & William, gct Chesterfield MM
1841, 12, 23. Martha (form Cope) dis mcd
1859, 2, 24. Phebe H. gct Chesterfield MM
1894, 1, 25. Mary R. (form Holloway) dis mcd

CADWALADER
----, --, --. John & Ruth
Ch: Ann   b 1801, 12, 19
    Sarah   " 1804, 4, 17
    Isaac   " 1806, 8, 25
    Ruth   " 1809, 3, 1
    John   " 1812, 2, 29
    Sabina   " 1814, 4, 10
    Rees   " 1816, 9, 16
    Mary   " 1818, 11, 22
    Jesse K.   " 1824, 7, 28
----, --, --. Joseph & Christiana

Ch: Martha   b 1812, 1, 25
    David   " 1813, 11, 13
    Ruth   " 1815, 11, 9
    Joseph   " 1817, 7, 13
    Achsar   " 1821, 4, 28
    Nathan   " 1824, 4, 25
----, --, --. David & Sarah [Cadwallader]
Ch: Elizabeth   b 1813, 3, 29
    Edith   " 1814, 10, 26
    Isaac   " 1816, 12, 16
    Amasa   " 1819, 3, 19
    Sarah   " 1821, 2, 28
    Joseph   " 1824, 1, 26
1812, 11, 29. Elizabeth d bur Freeport
1813, 1, 26. Isaac d bur Freeport
1825, 10, 16. Christopher d bur Freeport
1825, 12, 19. Isaac d bur Freeport
1832, 4, 16. Rachel Ann, dt John & Belinda,
b
1821, 12, 21. David dis disunity
1825, 9, 23. Anna Howard (form Cadwalader)
dis mcd
1827, 1, 26. Isaac dis
1827, 5, 25. Joseph gct Lick Creek MM, Ind.
1828, 5, 23. Martha, David, Ruth, Joseph &
Rebecca, ch Joseph, gct Blue River MM,
Ind.
1828, 8, 22. Eliza & Sarah gct Short Creek
MM, O.
1830, 4, 22. John rmt Belinda Barrett
1831, 3, 24. Sarah & ch, Elizabeth, Edith,
Amasa, Sarah & Joseph, gct Short Creek
MM, O.
1839, 1, 24. John & w, Ruth, & ch, Ruth,
John, Sabina, Mary (Margaret) & Jesse Kersey Cadwalader, gct Vermillion MM, Ill.
1842, 10, 20. Caroline (form Crossley) dis
mcd
1878, 9, 26. Edwin F. Holloway gct Middleton MM, to m Mary Cadwalader

CARSON
----, --, --. Andrew & Isabel
Ch: William   b 1795, 8, 7
    Naomi   " 1797, 5, 12
    Robert   " 1798, 10, 29
    Catharine   " 1800, 4, 19
    John   " 1801, 12, 4
    Rachel   " 1805, 7, 13
    Andrew   " 1807, 5, 8
    Isabel   " 1811, 10, 19
    Jeremiah   " 1816, 5, 4
1820, 6, 29. Jeremiah d bur Freeport
1821, 4, 13. Robert d bur Freeport
1826, 5, 3. Catharine d bur Freeport

1819, 8, 27. Mary (form McGrew) dis mcd
1820, 2, 25. Andrew dis disunity
1824, 12, 24. John dis mcd
1826, 11, 24. Naomi Meach (form Carson) dis
mcd
1831, 10, 20. Rachel dis mcd
1842, 3, 24. Rachel recrq

CARSON, continued
1858, 3, 25. Rachel James (form Carson) dis
    mcd

CARTER
1831, 11, 24. Mary, minor in care of Eunice
    Bevan, rocf Stillwater MM, dtd 1831,10,22
1835, 11, 26. Mary, minor, gct Short Creek MM,
    O.

CARVER
----, --, --. Henry m Talitha ----- d 1845,3,
    31 bur Freeport
    Ch: John   b 1791, 7, 6
        Rebecca   " 1793, 7, 15
        Henry   " 1795, 4, 4 d 1836,11,16
          bur Flushing
        Elizabeth b 1797, 4, 15
        James   " 1799, 9, 21
        Anne   " 1802, 10, 7
        Abner   " 1805, 1, 23
        Mary   " 1807, 2, 27
        Elijah   " 1810, 7, 17
1818, 12, --. Henry, s Henry & Talitha, b 1795,
    4,4; m in Flushing MH, Anna STRAHL, dt
    Thomas & Martha, Belmont Co., O., b 1799,9,
    16
    Ch: Thomas   d 1820, 5,25
          bur Freeport
        John   b 1822, 4, 28
        William T. " 1824, 4, 21
        James   " 1826, 5, 17
        Ruth   " 1828, 10, 4
        Dimsdill " 1831, 2, 9
        Alexander " 1833, 12, 15 d 1834, 1,4
          bur Freeport
        Henry M. b 1835, 4, 1
1820, 11, 24. John d bur Freeport
1856, 1, 23. Anna d bur Freeport

1820, 12, 22. James rqct Fairfield MM, to m
    Mary Ferguson
1821, 3, 23. Abigail & ch, Betsy Ann, Henry
    & James Millison Carver, gct Westland MM,
    Pa.
1821, 9, 21. Mary rocf Fairfield MM
1822, 11, 22. James & w, Mary, gct Fairfield MM
1826, 11, 24. Mary dis
1826, 11, 24. Ann rmt Thomas Raley
1828, 1, 25. James & w, Mary, rocf Fairfield
    MM, dtd 1827,8,25
1828, 7, 25. Henry dis disunity
1830, 10, 21. Abner dis mcd
1833, 12, 26. Elijah dis jH
1833, 12, 26. James & w, Mary, gct Sugar River
    MM, Ind.
1847, 7, 22. James dis disunity
1847, 10, 21. William dis disunity
1853, 5, 26. John dis mcd
1855, 8, 23. Henry M. dis disunity

CECILLE
1847, 7, 22. Mary rocf Stillwater MM, dtd
    1847,6,26

CHAMBERS
1847, 8, 28. Tamer & ch, Margaret, Ann, Debo-
    rah, Wm., Thomas, Levi, Benjamin, Samuel
    & Mary, rocf Plainfield MM, dtd 1847,7,21

CHANDLER
----, --, --. Eli & Mary
    Ch: Enoch   b 1819, 3, 14
        Hannah   " 1822, 1, 2
        Catharine " 1824, 1, 19
        John   " 1827, 12, 25
        Mary   " 1831, 12, 19
        Elisha   " 1834, 4, 28
        Maria   " 1837, 1, 7
        Elizabeth
          Ann   " 1839, 7, 28
        Matilda B. " 1841, 12, 7
----, --, --. Enoch Jr. & Rachel
    Ch: Anne   b 1821, 4, 22
        Isaac   " 1823, 8, 23
----, --, --. Swithen m Mary P. PACKER, dt
    Abram & Sarah (Hollingsworth), b 1817,10,
    3 d 1889,5,19 bur Flushing, O.
1874, 3, 4. Sarah m Thos. E. FARMER

1819, 3, 26. Mary Wood (form Chandler) dis
    mcd
1820, 8, 25. Martha & ch, Esther, Rachel,
    Jane, Mary & Jason, rocf Redstone MM, Pa.,
    dtd 1820,6,28
1821, 7, 27. Jane rmt Moses Crossley
1823, 2, 21. Eli rst on consent of Plainfield
1823, 10, 24. Swithen rocf Redstone MM, Pa.,
    dtd 1823,7,2
1826, 2, 24. Rachel Moore (form Chandler)
    dis mcd
1827, 9, 21. Mary dis jas
1828, 12, 26. Enoch dis jH
1829, 1, 23. Martha dis jH
1830, 4, 22. Jason dis mcd
1830, 8, 26. Enoch Jr. dis mcd
1832, 2, 23. Mary recrq
1835, 6, 25. Enoch, Hannah, Catharine & John,
    ch Eli & Mary, recrq
1839, 1, 24. Ann & Isaac, ch Enoch, gct Ver-
    million MM, Ill.
1844, 11, 21. Eli & w, Mary, & ch, John C.,
    Mary, Elisha M., Maria F., Elizabeth Ann,
    Matilda B. & Bennett, gct Fairfield MM,
    O.
1844, 11, 21. Enoch, Hannah & Catharine gct
    Fairfield MM, O.
1849, 2, 22. Mary Chandler (form Parker) con
    mcd
1863, 4, 23. Sarah Ann & Rebeckah W., ch
    Mary, recrq
1892, 12, 22. Rebecca W. Doudna (form Chand-
    ler) dis mcd

CHARNOCK
1862, 9, 25. Elizabeth Ann (form Nicholson)
    dis mcd

CHICKEN
----, --, --. Daniel & Eleanor
    Ch: John   b 1806, 1, 16
       Daniel Da-
           vid " 1809, 2, 16
       Anne   " 1809, 2, 16
       Mary   " 1811, 1, 6
       Henry Far-
           son " 1815, 9, 16
1824, 2, 23. Daniel d bur Freeport

1828, 4, 25. Eleanor Buck (form Chicken) dis
    mcd
1830, 3, 25. John dis disunity
1831, 5, 26. Daniel dis jH
1831, 7, 21. Mary Green (form Chicken) dis
    jH
1847, 6, 24. Mary (form Hall) dis mcd

CLARK
1820, 8, 4. Hannah M., dt Samuel & Hannah, b

CLAY
1843, 2, 22. Catharine (form Stephens) dis mcd

CLENDENAN
1859, 3, 25. Stephen, s Benjamin & Amy, Bel-
    mont Co., O.; m in Flushing MH, Elizabeth
    BRANSON, dt Smith & Jane, Belmont Co., O.

1860, 3, 22. Elizabeth gct Stillwater MM

COLE
1831, 10, 20. Mary (form Pearson) dis mcd

CONARD
1831, 10, 20. Sinai (form McGrew) dis mcd
1842, 3, 24. Sinah [Connard] rst

CONROW
----, --, --. Thomas m Ruth ----- d 1872,3,20
    bur Flushing
    Ch: Francis   b 1831, 1, 30
       Josiah   " 1833, 8, 11 d 1857, 1,10
       bur Flushing
       David J. b 1835, 12, 13 " 1857, 2,20
       bur Flushing
       Lewis   b 1837, 12, 8 " 1838, 6, 2
       bur Flushing
       Albert   b 1839, 11, 3
       Darling   " 1842, 6, 16 " 1857, 1,24
       bur Flushing
----, --, --. Darling m Rachel ----- d 1834,2;
    24 bur Flushing
    Ch: Lydia   d 1834, 2,14
       bur Flushing
       Mary   d 1835, 5,
       21 bur Flushing
       Rachel   " 1835, 5,25
       bur Flushing
       Darling Jr.   " 1836, 7,26
       bur Flushing
       Martha   " 1837,12, 7

    bur Flushing
    Ch: Thomas   d 1846, 4, 28
       bur Flushing
       Rebecca   " 1857, 1, 10
1838, 3, 4. Aquilla d bur Flushing
----, --, --. David & Anne
    Ch: Joseph   b 1841, 9, 16
       Thomas H. " 1843, 7, 23
----, --, --. Thomas H., s David & Annie
    (Hall), b 1843,7,23 d 1910,7,6 bur Flush-
    ing; m Mary J. ----- b 1843,3,13 d 1921,7,
    18 bur Flushing
    Ch: Charles D. b 1867, 7, 11
       Edward H.   " 1873, 5, 14
       Edith A.   " 1873, 5, 14
1871, 10, --. Joseph d bur Flushing
----, --, --. Chas. D., s Thos. & Mary J. (Hob-
    son), b 1867,7,11; m Deborah HAYES, dt
    Chas. T. & Deborah (Fawcett)
    Ch: Carlton H. b 1896, 1, 7
       T. Rollin   " 1900, 9, 12
----, --, --. Edward H., s Thos. H. & Mary J.
    (Hobson); m Martha ROCKWELL
    Ch: Edith M.   b 1897, 3, 14
       Mary Moore " 1899, 3, 26; m Willard
         BLACKBURN
       Gertrude
         Ellen   " 1901, 6, 17
       Harvey Rock
         well" 1905, 11, 15
       Alfred Ed-
         ward " 1907, 5. 3
       Elizabeth
         Ruth   " 1917, 4, 27
1898, 5, 27. Edith Anna m Jas. W. EDGERTON

1821, 4, 27. Jacob dis disunity
1830, 3, 25. Thomas gct Short Creek MM, O.,
    to m Ruth Lupton
1830, 10, 21. Ruth rocf Short Creek MM, O.,
    dtd 1830,9,21
1837, 9, 21. David gct Short Creek MM, O., to
    m Anna Hall
1838, 1, 25. Darling gct Somerset MM, to m
    Anna Edgerton
1838, 4, 26. Anne rocf Short Creek MM, O.,
    dtd 1838,2,20
1853, 6, 23. Francis dis mcd
1863, 12, 24. Albert dis mcd
1866, 6, 21. Anna dis
1866, 6, 21. David dis jG
1868, 3, 26. Thomas dis mcd & jG
1874, 3, 26. Thomas H. rst
1875, 2, 25. Thomas H. & w, Mary J., & ch,
    Chas. D., Edward H. & Edith A., recrq
1893, 9, 21. Chas. D. gct Salem MM, to m
    Deborah F. Hayes
1894, 8, 23. Deborah Hayes rocf Salem MM
1895, 11, 24. Edmund H. gct Paulina MM, Ia.,
    to m Martha M. Rockwell
1897, 7, 22. Martha M. rocf Paulina MM, Ia.
1910, 6, 23. Edward H. & w, Martha R., & ch,
    Edith A., Mary Moore, Gertrude Ellen,

CONROW, continued
      Harvey Rockwell & Alfred Edward, gct
      Paulina MM, Ia.
1914, 2, 26. Edward H. & w, Martha R., & ch,
      Edith A., Mary M., Gertrude E., Harvey R.,
      Alfred E. & Elizabeth, rocf Paulina MM,
      Ia., dtd 1914,2,14

COOK
1836, 4, 21. Thomas recrq
1836, 12, 22. Thomas gct Duck Creek MM, Ind.
1851, 8, 21. Mary Ann (form Hirst) dis mcd
1854, 8, 24. Daniel Williams gct New Garden
      MM, Pa., to m Hannah Francena Cook
1854, 10, 26. Mary Ann rst at Spiceland MM,
      Ind. on consent of this mtg
1863, 9, 24. Elizabeth (form Hirst) dis mcd
1868, 5, 20. Elizabeth H. rst at Hickory
      Grove MM, Ia. with consent of this mtg

COOPER
1837, 6, 28. Sarah Jr. m Joseph GARRETSON

1821, 6, 22. Elizabeth (form Downes) dis mcd
1822, 9, 27. Susan (form Dawson) dis mcd
1824, 12, 24. William recrq
1828, 12, 26. William dis jH
1829, 3, 27. Samuel rocf Uwchlan MM, Pa., dtd
      1829,1,8
1831, 9, 22. Sarah & ch, Gulielma, Nicholas,
      Eli B., Esther, Martha, Ann, Margaret &
      Priscilla, rocf Gunpowder MM, dtd 1831,8,3
1831, 9, 22. Martha Esther Ann Margaret &
      Priscilla rocf Gunpowder MM, Md., dtd
      1831,8,3
1832, 9, 20. Sarah rocf Baltimore MM E & W
      Dist., dtd 1832,7,9
1833, 4, 28. Ann McConnal (form Cooper) rpd
      mcd
1834, 5, 22. Nicholas dis disunity
1835, 8, 20. Sarah Sr. dis disunity
1836, 5, 26. Margaret Lukins (form Cooper)
      dis mcd
1836, 7, 21. Guli Elma dis disunity
1836, 8, 25. Priscilla Dunn (form Cooper) dis
      mcd
1836, 11, 24. Eli B. dis disunity
1837, 12, 21. Esther Fox (form Cooper) dis mcd
1838, 4, 26. Esther Fox (form Cooper) dis mcd
1842, 1, 20. Martha Bye (form Cooper) dis mcd
1850, 10, 24. Samuel gct Short Creek MM, O.

COPE
----, --, --. Jacob & Mary
      Ch: Sophia   b 1806, 6, 2
          Rachel   " 1807, 10, 11
          Margaret   " 1809, 5, 4
          Ellis   " 1811, 9, 4
          Hannah   " 1813, 9, 11
          Nathan   " 1815, 7, 15
          Elizabeth   " 1817, 6, 22
          Martha   " 1821, 2, 15
          Mary   " 1823, 4, 7

      Ch: John P.   b 1824, 8, 15
1823, 6, 22. Mary d bur Brushy Fork
1876, 9, 22. Thomas C., s Amos & Edna E.,
      Columbiana Co., O.; m in Guernsey MH,
      Maria WILSON, d 1886,2,22 bur "near
      Guernsey MH"
      Ch: Walter C. b 1878, 5, 22
      Thomas m 2nd 1889,8,29 in Guernsey MH,
      Mary J. STEPHENS, dt David & Eliza,
      Guernsey Co., O.
      Ch: Mary Ella b 1891, 12, 14

1826, 3, 23. Sophia rmt George Parsons
1826, 12, 22. Rachel rmt Israel Parsons
1828, 12, 26. Jacob dis jH
1829, 9, 24. Mary dis jH
1830, 1, 21. Margaret dis jH
1834, 2, 20. Hannah Parsons (form Cope) dis
      jas
1835, 3, 26. Ellis dis jH
1841, 4, 22. Elizabeth Hastings (form Cope)
      dis mcd
1841, 6, 24. Martha dis jH
1841, 7, 22. Nathan dis jH
1878, 3, 21. Thomas C. rocf Middleton MM, dtd
      1878,1,19
1902, 11, 20. Thomas C. & w, Mary J., & dt,
      Mary Ella, gct Stillwater MM

COVENTRY
1872, 9, 26. Susanna (form Wharton) dis mcd

COVINGTON
1820, 4, 21. Elizabeth rst
1831, 1, 20. Elizabeth dis jH

COX
1828, 8, 22. Sarah rocf Little Britain MM,
      Pa., dtd 1828,4,19
1830, 4, 22. Sarah dis jH

CREW
----, --, --. Jacob & Mary H.
      Ch: Eleanor   b 1838, 8, 26
          Elizabeth " 1851, 5, 28
1854, 11, 1. John, s Jacob & Rachel, Belmont
      Co., O.; m in Guernsey MH, Asenath BARBER,
      dt Abraham & Rachel, Guernsey Co., O.

1836, 5, 26. Jacob & w, Mary H., & ch, Eliza-
      beth, rocf Smithfield MM, dtd 1836,5,23
1849, 11, 22. Wm. Briggs gct Smithfield MM,
      to m Hannah Crew
1855, 4, 26. Asenath gct Stillwater MM
1859, 1, 20. Mary H. dis jG
1860, 6, 21. Jacob dis jG

CROSSLEY
----, --, --. John & Thamar [Crosley]
      Ch: Sarah   b 1786, 5, 12
          Rachel   " 1789, 4, 1
          Samuel   " 1792, 9, 29
          John   " 1794, 5, 19 d 1868,3,6

CROSSLEY, John & Thamar, continued
          bur Flushing
     Ch: Hannah   b 1796, 8, 19
         Hester   " 1798, 7, 29
         Elizabeth " 1800, 5, 2
         Moses   " 1802, 1, 8
         Mary   " 1804, 11, 2 d 1885,12, 4
          bur Flushing
----, --, --. Samuel C. & Phebe [Crossly]
     Ch: George   b 1813, 8, 10
         Rebecca   " 1816, 12, 27
         Martha   " 1819, 8, 1
         Lydia   " 1822, 5, 1
         Simeon   " 1824, 10, 6
1820, 7, 10. John d bur Flushing
----, --, --. Moses & Jane [Crossly]
     Ch: Leannah   b 1822, 6, 2
         Jonathan   " 1823, 6, 20
         Caroline   " 1825, 1, 1
         John   " 1827, 10, 5
         Amy   " 1829, 12, 25
         James   " 1832, 7, 7
         Martha   " 1834, 12, 16
         Moses   " 1837, 7, 27
         Rebecca   " 1840, 4, 21
1843, 2, 1. Elizabeth m David HOLLINGSWORTH
----, --, --. Hannah, dt Jos. & Eliza Wilson,
     d bur Flushing

1821, 7, 21. Moses rmt Jane Chandler
1829, 7, 23. Moses & w, Jane, & ch gct Still-
     water MM
1829, 12, 24. Esther dis
1831, 8, 25. Moses & w, Jane, & ch, Leana,
     Jonathan, Caroline, John & Amy, rocf Still-
     water MM, dtd 1831,7,23
1840, 5, 21. Jordon, minor in care of John,
     recrq
1842, 10, 20. Caroline Cadwalader (form Cross-
     ly) dis mcd
1844, 1, 25. George dis mcd & jas
1844, 1, 25. Samuel dis mcd
1844, 2, 22. Rebecca Watson (form Crosley)
     dis mcd
1844, 2, 22. Martha Sargent (form Crosley)
     dis mcd
1844, 2, 22. Simeon, minor, gct Cincinnati
     MM
1844, 3, 21. Lydia gct New York MM, N. Y.;
     returned 1845,7,24 she could not be found
1844, 3, 21. Mary, minor, gct Cincinnati MM
1844, 4, 25. Moses & w, Jane, & ch, John,
     Amy, James, Martha, Joseph & Rebecca, gct
     Short Creek MM, O.
1844, 7, 25. Jonathan gct Cincinnati MM
1862, 9, 25. Jordon dis mcd

CROZER
1814, 4, 30. Samuel, s James & Mary, b
1818, 5, 18. Joshua W., s James & Rachel, b
1818, 6, 24. Rachel, w James, d bur Flushing
1821, 1, 16. Sarah, dt James & Anne, b
1821, 9, 2. James d bur Flushing

1820, 3, 24. James gct Plainfield MM, to m
     Ann Foulke
1820, 5, 26. Thomas dis
1820, 6, 23. Ann rocf Plainfield MM, dtd
     1820,6,22
1821, 12, 21. Sarah (form Bye) dis mcd
1822, 12, 27. Thomas rst
1823, 1, 24. James, s Thos. & Sarah, recrq
1823, 1, 24. Sarah rst
1823, 6, 27. Thomas & w, Sarah, & s, James,
     gct Sandy Spring MM
1824, 5, 21. Ann & dt, Sarah, gct Plainfield
     MM
1831, 7, 21. Samuel, minor, gct Middleton MM
1832, 5, 24. Samuel, minor, gct Stillwater MM
1842, 6, 23. Joshua W. gct Fall Creek MM

DARNALD
1853, 8, 25. Susannah (form Wright) dis mcd

DAVID
1831, 7, 21. Ruth dis jH

DAVIS
1823, 7, 10. Deborah, dt John F. & Anne, b
1840, 4, 1. Francis, s John F. & Ann, Bel-
     mont Co., O.; m in Guernsey MH, Mary
     SMITH, dt Amos & Anne, Guernsey Co., O.
     Ch: John F.   b 1842, 1, 13
         Wilson   " 1843, 11, 27 d 1843,12,31
          bur Flushing
         Jane S.   b 1846, 7, 15
         Josiah   " 1849, 11, 13
         Lindley   " 1852, 9, 25
         Anna   " 1856, 4, 22
1843, 4, 27. Eliza, dt Jno & Anne, d bur
     Flushing
1851, 4, 2. Deborah m John HALL

1824, 1, 23. John F. & w, Ann, & ch, Francis,
     Ann Eliza & Deborah, rocf Stillwater MM,
     dtd 1823,11,--
1827, 3, 23. Catharine recrq
1827, 12, 21. Catharine rmt Israel Wilson
1830, 4, 22. Ann rmt Israel Wilson
1860, 5, 26. Frances & w, Mary S., & ch,
     John F., James S., Josiah, Lindley & Smith,
     gct Stillwater MM

DAWSON
1873, 10, 8. Chalkley, s Joel & Sarah, Bel-
     mont Co., O.; m in Flushing MH, Rebecca
     Anna BRANSON, dt Aaron & Frances, Belmont
     Co., O.

1822, 9, 27. Susan Cooper (form Dawson) dis
     mcd
1822, 10, 25. Hannah Aikens (form Dawson) dis
     mcd
1824, 3, 26. Sinah Brown (form Dawson) dis
     mcd
1830, 9, 23. Isaac gct Springborough MM
1875, 12, 23. Rebecca Ann gct Stillwater MM

DAY
1830, 3, 25. Jane (form Brock) dis mcd
1878, 11, 21. Mary Jane (form Smith) dis mcd

DENNIS
1828, 2, 22. Aaron rocf Smithfield MM, dtd
    1826,5,22

DERRY
1840, 6, 21. Bethia (form Wharton) dis mcd

DEW
1820, 5, 26. Susanna Mason (form Dew) dis
    mcd
1820, 6, 29. Elias & w, Sarah, & ch, Ruth,
    John, Mary & Joseph, gct Short Creek MM,
    O.

DEWEES
1892, 9, 23. James Henry, s Wm. P. & Maria,
    Chester Co., Pa.; m in Flushing MH, Emma
    J. BRANSON, dt David & Sarah H., Belmont
    Co., O.

1834, 1, 23. John, minor, rocf Stillwater
    MM, dtd 1833,5,25
1837, 1, 26. John dis mcd
1848, 7, 21. Robert Hall gct Chesterfield
    MM, to m Mary Dewees
1893, 2, 23. Emma J. gct Goshen MM, Pa.

DICKS
1835, 3, 60. John d bur Freeport

1824, 3, 26. Evan dis jas
1826, 5, 26. Peter dis disunity
1832, 4, 26. James [Dix] dis mcd

DILWORTH
----, --, --. William & Mary
    Ch: James   b 1825, 10, 29
        Eleanor   " 1828, 2, 24

1825, 7, 22. William & w, Mary, & ch, John
    & Elizabeth, rocf Short Creek MM, O., dtd
    1825,5,24
1829, 10, 22. Mary dis
1833, 6, 20. William dis jH

DISSELMES
----, --, --. Jesse & Elizabeth
    Ch: Jacob
        Hannah   b 1792, 10, 13
        Benjamin   " 1799, 3, 30
        Eleanor   " 1801, 1, 21
        Elizabeth   " 1805, 9, 26
        David   " 1806, 12, 19
        Polly   " 1809, 5, 4
        Phebe   " 1811, 8, 15
        Jonas   " 1814, 12, 21
        Jesse   " 1816, 9, 15
        Ruthanna   " 1819, 4, 13
        Jonathan   " 1803, 3, 28 (sic)
1835, 8, 10. Phebe [Deselmes], dt Jesse & C.,

d bur Flushing
----, --, --. Jacob & Rhoda [Deselms]
    Ch: Joseph   b 1816, 10, 29
        Elizabeth   " 1818, 10, 28
        Lydia   " 1820, 12, 28
1819, 5, 7. Joseph [Diselms] d bur Flushing

1820, 4, 21. Jacob [Desselms] & w, Rhoda, &
    dt, Elizabeth, rocf Concord MM, dtd 1820,
    1,19
1820, 5, 26. Eleanor [Desselms] dis
1823, 3, 21. Benjamin [Deselms] dis mcd
1827, 10, 26. Jacob [Deselms] dis mcd
1832, 5, 24. Jonathan [Deselms] dis mcd
1834, 7, 24. David [Deselms] dis mcd
1836, 5, 26. Ruthanna Kennard (form Deselms)
    dis mcd & jas
1837, 2, 23. Jonas [Deselms] gct Duck Creek
    MM
1837, 5, 25. Mary gct Duck Creek MM, Ind.

DIXON
1821, 2, 23. Samuel dis
1822, 6, 21. William dis disunity
1823, 2, 21. Sarah gct Redstone MM, Pa.
1825, 9, 23. Susannah Barton (form Dixon) dis
    mcd
1827, 1, 26. Jane & ch, Wm. & Joseph, gct
    Redstone MM, Pa.
1828, 12, 26. Sarah dis mcd
1829, 2, 27. Sarah dis jH
1840, 3, 26. Elizabeth (form McGrew) dis mcd

DOUDNA
1847, 12, 1. Joseph, s Hosea & Mary, Belmont
    Co., O.; m in Flushing MH, Belinda A. HOB-
    SON, dt Joseph & Ruth, Belmont Co., O.
    Ch: Josiah   b 1849, 9, 26
        Mary H.   " 1853, 3, 26
1854, 3, 1. Thomas, s Hosea & Mary, Belmont
    Co., O.; m in Flushing MH, Rachel WOOD,
    dt Pusey & Charity, Belmont Co., O.
----, --, --. Jason & Mary
    Ch: Hosea   b 1867, 1, 21
        Asenath El-
        ma   " 1873, 11, 22
        Joel J.   " 1879, 3, 31
1885, 9, 25. John E., s John & Mary, Belmont
    Co., O.; m in Guernsey MH, Anna B. DOUDNA,
    dt Jason & Mary, Harrison Co., O.
1885, 9, 25. Anna B. m John E. DOUDNA

1848, 7, 21. Joseph rocf Stillwater MM, dtd
    1848, 7,22
1853, 5, 26. Joseph & w, Belinda, & ch, Jo-
    siah & Mary H., gct Somerset MM
1854, 5, 25. Rachel W. gct Stillwater MM
1865, 12, 21. Jasin & w, Mary, & ch, Charles,
    Rachel, Elwood & Ann R., rocf Stillwater
    MM
1886, 10, 21. Elwood T. dis mcd
1886, 12, 23. Hosea B. dis disunity
1889, 2, 21. Charles A. dis disunity

DOUDNA, continued
1892, 12, 22. Rebecca W. (form Chandler) dis
    mcd
1919, 7, 24. Irving E. Bailey gct Somerset
    MM, to m Asenath Elma Doudna

DOWNS
----, --, --. Jeremiah & Anna
    Ch: Elizabeth b 1803, 3,   4
        Sarah   " 1806, 4,   6
        William   " 1810, 12,   3
        Thomas   " 1813, 9, 18

1821, 6, 22. Elizabeth Cooper (form Downes)
    dis mcd
1827, 4, 27. Jeremiah & w, Anna, & ch, Wm.
    & Thomas, gct Marlborough MM
1827, 4, 27. Sarah gct Marlborough MM

DUNN
1836, 8, 25. Priscilla (form Cooper) dis mcd

DULEY
----, --, --. Maxon & Lydia [Douled]
    Ch: Ruthanna   b 1818, 10,. 4
        William D. " 1820, 8, 10
        Susanna   " 1822, 11, 25
        Sinai Jane " 1825, 3, 9

1823, 10, 24. Avis, w Joshua, rocf Providence
    MM, Pa., dtd 1823,5,20
1830, 11, 25. Maxon [Dewley] & w, Lydia, & ch,
    Ruthanne, William, Dawson, Susanna, Sinah
    Jane, Eliza Annah & Thomas Elwood, gct
    Marlborough MM

EASLY
1808, 8, 8. Stephen [Easely], s Daniel &
    Edith, b
1820, 3, 6. Edith d bur Freeport
1820, 3, 21. Daniel d bur Freeport
1820, 4, 17. Rachel d bur Freeport
----, --, --. John & Nancy
    Ch: Edith   b 1823, 6, 24
        Jane D. " 1825, 5, 1
1825, 8, 5. Daniel Jr. d bur Freeport

1820, 12, 22. John rmt Nancy Kinsey
1821, 9, 21. Richard gct Short Creek MM, O.
1822, 1, 25. Isaac, minor, gct Smithfield
    MM
1825, 8, 26. Stephen, minor, gct Short Creek
    MM, O.
1828, 8, 22. John dis disunity
1829, 4, 24. Nancy dis jH
1831, 6, 23. Phebe Knock (form Easly) dis mcd
1831, 11, 24. Isaac rpd mcd
1839, 2, 21. Rhoda, Jane B., Rachel & Sarah
    Ann, ch John, gct Vermillion MM, Ill.

EDGERTON
1853, 4, 27. Joseph, s Joseph & Charity, Bel-
    mont Co., O.; m in Flushing MH, Lydia P.

MITCHELL, dt Isaac & Lydia, Belmont Co.,
    O.
    Ch: William   b 1854, 5, 1
        Mary Eliza   " 1857, 12, 26
        Edward   " 1861, 9, 14
        Sarah Eliza-
            beth b 1863, 11, 11
1898, 5, 27. James Warder, s James & Mary
    Ann, Delaware Co., Pa.; m in Flushing MH,
    Edith Anna CONROW, dt Thomas H. & Mary J.,
    Belmont Co., O., b 1873,5,14
    James Warder m 2nd 1905,12,22 in Flushing
    MH, Bertha Mary WALKER, dt Abel & Hannah
    L., Belmont Co., O., b 1878,10,12

1838, 1, 25. Darling Conrow gct Somerset MM,
    to m Anna Edgerton
1854, 6, 22. Joseph Jr. rocf Somerset MM, dtd
    1854,4,24
1864, 12, 22. Joseph & w, Lydia S., & ch, Wil-
    liam, Mary Eliza, Edward & Sarah Eliza-
    beth, gct Coal Creek MM, Ia.
1898, 12, 22. Edith Conrow gct Chester MM, Pa.
1907, 4, 25. Bertha W. gct Chesterfield MM,
    N. J.

EDWARDS
1823, 7, 25. Jane (form Parkins) dis mcd

ELLIS
----, --, --. Jonathan & Martha
    Ch: Theodore   b 1813, 3, 26
        Peter Marsh " 1814, 8, 21
        Martha   " 1816, 9, 4
        Solomon
            Jehu   " 1818, 8, 21
        Catharine   " 1820, 7, 11
----, --, --. Joshua & Mariam
    Ch: Abigail B. b 1822, 8, 18
        Lydia   " 1824, 9, 30
        Rachel M. " 1827, 6, 16
        Asa   " 1830, 3, 25
        Jonathan   " 1832, 11, 17
        John   " 1835, 1, 30 d 1838, 4,13
            bur Guernsey
        William   b 1837, 4, 2
        Mary   " 1840, 9, 4 " 1844, 8,19
            bur Guernsey
        Martha   b 1843, 6, 14
        Miriam Jr. " 1846, 11, 19
1825, 9, 11. Theodore d bur Flushing
----, --, --. Elisha & Hannah
    Ch: Levi   b 1828, 2, 14
        Mary Jane " 1829, 4, 2
        Mary Anne " 1831, 7, 1
        Hannah   d 1841, 2,11
            bur Freeport
        Elisha   b 1842, 6, 9 " 1848,12,27
            bur Freeport
        Sarah Eliza-
            beth   b 1845, 10, 5
----, --, --. Jonathan & Susannah
    Ch: Susanna   b 1835, 5, 6

ELLIS, Jonathan & Susannah, continued
    Ch: Jonathan M.b 1837, 8, 15
        Hannah   " 1841, 1, 27
1835, 3, 16. Elizabeth, w Theodore, d bur
    Flushing
1840, 2, 6. William d

1819, 7, 23. Mary Garrett (form Ellis) dis
    mcd
1821, 12, 21. Joshua rmt Miriam Branson
1821, 12, 21. Naomi rmt Jesse Kinsey
1822, 4, 26. Elizabeth rmt Jonah Hole
1822, 6, 21. Rachel rmt Uriah McMillan
1824, 11, 26. Lydia Jr. rmt Aquila Branson
1825, 1, 21. Sarah recrq
1826, 5, 26. Elisha dis mcd
1826, 5, 26. John dis mcd
1827, 3, 23. Elizabeth rmt Eli Hollingsworth
1827, 5, 25. Elisha rmt Hannah Hollingsworth
1829, 4, 24. Jonathan M. dis jH
1829, 5, 22. Elisha dis jH
1829, 6, 25. Bevan dis jH
1829, 7, 23. Sarah dis jH
1830, 4, 22. Mary rmt Elwood Ratcliff
1833, 3, 21. Fannie dis jH
1833, 4, 25. Jonathan Jr. gct Clear Creek MM
1834, 3, 20. Sarah gct Fall Creek MM
1834, 7, 24. Martha & ch, Peter, Martha,
    Solomon & Catharine, gct Fall Creek MM
1836, 11, 24. Jonathan & w, Lydia, gct Ver-
    million MM, Ill.
1836, 11, 24. Rebecca, William & Lewis gct
    Vermillion MM, Ill.
1847, 10, 21. Mary Jane Smith (form Ellis)
    dis mcd
1847, 10, 21. Levi dis disunity
1852, 7, 22. Asa gct Duck Creek MM
1853, 10, 20. Abigail gct Duck Creek MM, Ind.
1853, 10, 20. Jonathan gct Duck Creek MM,
    Ind. (s Joshua)
1853, 10, 20. Joshua & ch, Martha & Miriam,
    gct Duck Creek MM, Ind.
1853, 10, 20. Lydia gct Duck Creek MM, Ind.
1854, 5, 25. Sarah (form Stephens) dis mcd
1855, 7, 26. Martha Ann & Susanna A. dis jas
1867, 6, 20. Rachel M. Gause (form Ellis) dis
    mcd
1869, 1, 21. Sarah Elizabeth dis joining
    M. E. Society

EMBRY
1824, 5, 9. Abigail, dt John & Huldah, b

1826, 8, 25. Mary Hammer (form Embree) dis
    mcd
1827, 1, 26. John & w, Huldah, & ch, James,
    Harriett, Jesse, Elizabeth, Edith, John,
    Abigail & Mordecai, gct Short Creek MM, O.

ENGLE
1823, 9, 26. Phebe gct White Water MM, Ind.
1843, 3, 23. Elizabeth (form Marsh) dis mcd

ETHERTON
1822, 5, 24. Eliza (form Nevitt) dis mcd

EVANS
1819, 11, 26. Benoni dis mcd
1821, 2, 23. Asher dis
1824, 5, 21. Evan & w, Mary, & ch, Rebecca,
    James, Cadwalader, Amos Hutton, Sarah
    Henrietta & Asher Parker, gct Smithfield
    MM

FARMER
----, --, --. Taylor d 1899,3,27 bur Flushing;
    m Maryann ----- d 1873,1,22 bur Flushing
    Ch: Armila C. b 1840, 7, 4
        Rhoda   " 1843, 8, 1
        John T.   " 1847, 10, 3 d 1848, 1,24
        bur Flushing
        Thomas   b 1849, 5, 29
        Jesse   " 1854, 9, 13
1874, 3, 4. Thomas E., s Taylor & Mary Ann,
    Belmont Co., O.; m in Flushing MH, Sarah
    CHANDLER, dt Swithen & Mary, Belmont Co.,
    O.
    Ch: Lynden T. b 1875, 8, 20
        Emmet S.   " 1878, 11, 20
        Loray G.   " 1880, 7, 31
        Oakley J. " 1883, 11, 3

1821, 8, 24. Taylor, minor, rocf Stillwater
    MM, dtd 1821,7,28
1822, 1, 25. Ketura rocf New Garden MM
1822, 2, 22. Ann & ch, Susanna, Talitha, Jo-
    seph, Rachel & Thomas, rocf Stillwater MM
1824, 10, 22. Ann rmt Thomas Langstaff
1828, 7, 25. Susanna rocf Upper Springfield
    MM, dtd 1828,6,28
1830, 11, 25. Susannah rmt Uriah Bailey
1832, 4, 26. Keturah gct Sandy Spring MM
1833, 4, 25. Taylor rocf Upper Springfield
    MM, dtd 1833,3,23
1834, 10, 23. Taylor rmt Mary Ann Fawcett
1834, 12, 25. Taylor & w, Mary Ann, gct Still-
    water MM
1839, 10, 24. Taylor & w, Mary Ann, & ch, Jo-
    seph & Adaline, rocf Stillwater MM, dtd
    1839,9,28
1855, 9, 20. Adeline Piggott (form Farmer)·
    dis mcd
1858, 7, 22. Taylor & w, Mary Ann, & ch,
    Amelia, Rhoda & Thomas, gct Somerset MM
1861, 4, 25. Joseph dis joining M. E. Society
1863, 9, 24. Taylor & w, Mary Ann, & s, Thom-
    as, rocf Somerset MM, dtd 1863,7,27
1870, 12, 22. Rhoda dis joining M. E. Society
1890, 1, 23. Thomas & Sarah P. dis jas

FARQUHAR
----, --, --. Allen & Edith
    Ch: Martha W. b 1818, 9, 19
        Hannah   " 1820, 7, 22
        David   " 1822, 10, 1
1823, 8, 14. Edith d bur Freeport

FARQUHAR, continued
1822, 7, 26. Allen & w, Edith, & ch, Martha
     & Hannah, rocf Smithfield MM
1827, 12, 21. Martha W. & Hannah, minors, gct
     Short Creek MM, O.
1833, 6, 20. David, minor, gct Duck Creek MM,
     Ind.
1839, 4, 25. Aaron Roberts gct Short Creek
     MM, O., to m Matilda Farquhar
1842, 8, 25. David, minor, gct Stillwater MM

FAWCETT
----, --, --. Joseph m Amelia ----- d 1854,--,
     -- bur Flushing
     Ch: Samuel   b 1802, 7, 14
         Elijah   " 1804, 3, 28
         Jonathan " 1806, 6, 14
         Nancy   " 1808, 7, 12
         Joseph   " 1810, 11, 2
         George   " 1813, 1, 18
         Mary Ann " 1815, 3, 30
         Jonas   " 1817, 12, 7
         Armelia   " 1820, 12, 17
1826, 2, 12. Washington d bur Flushing
----, --, --. Samuel & Nancy
     Ch: Allen B.   b 1828, 4, 29 d 1829, 1, 5
         Abigail H." 1829, 11, 23
         Eliza Jane" 1832, 2, 2
         Joseph Jr." 1834, 5, 19
         Alpheus   " 1837, 9, 15
         Semilda   " 1841, 1, 11
         John Wm.   " 1842, 11, 24
         Benjamin
               F. " 1845, 1, 28
1843, 8, 14. Joseph d bur Flushing
1845, 7, 23. Phebe d bur Freeport
1854, 3, 29. Jehu, s Thos. & Sarah, Columbi-
     anna Co., O.; m in Flushing MH, Deborah S.
     HOLLOWAY, dt Isaac & Rebecca SMART, Bel-
     mont Co., O.
1883, 10, 20. Jeptha Anna, dt Jeptha & Lydia
     Anne, d bur Flushing

1822, 6, 21. Dorcas Howel (form Fawcett) dis
     mcd
1823, 6, 27. Mahlon gct Sandy Spring MM
1825, 9, 23. Jonathan & w, Rebecca, & ch,
     Jesse, Eli, Martha, Amelia & Sarah, rocf
     Stillwater MM, dtd 1825,8,27
1826, 11, 24. Samuel rmt Nancy Branson
1827, 1, 26. Nancy Bevan (form Fawcett) dis.
     mcd
1832, 4, 26. Mary & Lucinda gct Centre MM
1832, 9, 20. Robert recrq
1833, 1, 24. Robert & w, Mary, & ch, Char-
     lotte, Jane, Maryann, Milton, Sarah B.,
     Jonathan P. & Elizabeth, gct Centre MM
1833, 3, 21. Elijah gct Stillwater MM, to m
     Sarah Gregg
1833, 8, 22. Nancy rmt John Trigg
1833, 9, 26. Thomas dis mcd
1834, 1, 23. Sarah rocf Stillwater MM, dtd
     1833,5,23

1834, 2, 20. Thomas dis jH
1834, 10, 23. Mary Ann rmt Taylor Farmer
1834, 12, 25. Jonathan & w, Rebecca, & ch,
     Eli, Martha W., Amelia, Sarah, Susannah &
     Maria, gct Deerfield MM
1835, 10, 22. Jesse gct Pennsville MM
1836, 10, 20. Elijah & w, Sarah, & ch, Reese &
     Lindly, gct Plainfield MM
1838, 1, 25. George dis
1838, 4, 26. Jonas dis mcd
1839, 6, 20. Jonathan con mcd
1840, 3, 26. Samuel dis disunity
1846, 12, 24. Amelia Hoover (form Fawcett) dis
     mcd
1848, 8, 24. Jacob Holloway Jr. gct Salem MM,
     to m Sarah Fawcett
1850, 7, 25. Abigail dis jas
1852, 8, 26. Eliza Jane gct Duck Creek MM, Ind.
1852, 9, 23. Wm. C. Wilson gct Salem MM, to m
     Esther Fawcett
1853, 12, 22. Nancy & ch, Joseph, Alpheus, Se-
     milda, John Wm., & Benjamin T., gct Duck
     Creek MM, Ind.
1854, 5, 25. Deborah S. gct Salem MM
1854, 11, 23. Joseph dis mcd
1868, 1, 23. Jonathan [Faucett] gct Hickory
     Grove MM, Ia.
1871, 7, 20. Daniel Williams gct Chester-
     field MM, to m Lydia Ann Fawcett
1871, 12, 21. Jeptha Ann, dt Lydia Ann Wil-
     liams, rocf Chesterfield MM, dtd 1871,11,
     18

FELL
----, --, --. Joseph & Ann
     Ch: Samuel K. b 1832, 9, 14 d 1833, 5,18
         bur Flushing
         Lydia Ann b 1834, 7, 16
         Joseph J. " 1838, 9, 30 d 1840, 6,11
         bur Flushing
         Lewis   " 1841, 4,20
         bur Flushing
1839, 12, 4. Thomas, s Jos. & Ann, Belmont
     Co., O.; m in Flushing MH, Phebe L. WRIGHT
     dt Joseph & Ann, Belmont Co., O.
     Ch: Joseph
         Townsend b 1840, 8, 29 d 1845,12,12
         bur Flushing
         William W.b 1842, 11, 14
         Lewis L. " 1845, 5, 9
         John W.   " 1848, 3, 2
         Marshal   " 1850, 7, 30
         Howard
         Wilson   " 1852, 10, 11

1832, 9, 20. Joseph & w, Ann, & ch, Thomas,
     Marshall, Elizabeth, Esther H., Emily &
     Lewis, rocf New Garden MM, Pa., dtd 1832,
     9,5
1845, 8, 21. Elizabeth Brokaw (form Fell)
     dis mcd
1846, 1, 22. Marshall gct Short Creek MM, O.,
     to m Rebecca Hirst

FELL, continued
1846, 8, 20. Marshall gct Goshen MM
1846, 9, 24. Joseph & w, Ann, & ch, Emily &
        Lydia Ann, gct Goshen MM
1846, 9, 24. Esther gct Goshen MM
1847, 10, 21. Alpheus Hirst gct Goshen MM, O.,
        to m Esther H. Fell
1857, 6, 25. Thomas dis disunity
1861, 11, 21. Marshal Jr. & Martha gct Brad-
        ford MM, Pa.

FERGUSON
1820, 12, 22. James Carver rqct Fairfield MM,
        to m Mary Ferguson

FIELDS
1820, 5, 26. Anna [Field] rocf Short Creek
        MM, O., dtd 1819,11,23
1821, 10, 26. Sarah (form Broomhall) dis mcd
1825, 5, 27. Sarah rst
1831, 10, 20. Sarah dis jH

FISHER
1873, 1, 17. Eve, w Samuel, dt A. Packer, d
        bur Flushing

1821, 7, 27. John gct Stillwater MM
1823, 3, 21. Barak dis mcd
1826, 11, 24. Rebecca dis jas
1828, 6, 27. John, minor, rocf Stillwater MM,
        dtd 1828,3,22
1829, 9, 24. John gct Stillwater MM
1847, 5, 20. Eve (form Parker) dis mcd
1851, 1, 23. Eve rst

FORD
1820, 12, 31. Ann d bur Freeport

FOULKE
----, --, --. Jesse & Sarah
    Ch: Ellen   b 1798, 9, 29
        Hannah   " 1800, 7, 16
        Rachel   " 1802, 9, 16
        William   " 1805, 5, 6
        Jesse R.   " 1811, 8, 24
        Sarah Ann   " 1814, 11, 28 d 1832, 3, 2
            bur Flushing

1820, 3, 24. James Crozer gct Plainfield MM,
        to m Ann Foulke
1822, 5, 24. Elizabeth rocf Short Creek MM,
        O., dtd 1822,4,23
1822, 7, 26. Elizabeth rmt Thomas Sidwell
1826, 11, 24. Rachel rmt Elisha Kirk
1829, 9, 24. Wm. rmt Eliza Walker
1829, 10, 22. William & w, Eliza, gct Deer-
        field MM
1829, 10, 26. Hannah rmt Jehu Lewis
1832, 6, 21. Jesse & w, Sarah, gct Short
        Creek MM, O.
1832, 6, 21. Jesse Jr. gct Deerfield MM

FOWLER
1826, 3, 24. Rachel (form Pickering) dis mcd

FOX
1837, 12, 21. Esther (form Cooper) dis mcd
1838, 4, 26. Esther (form Cooper) dis mcd

FRAME
1832, 7, 1. Benjamin d bur Guernsey
1863, 9, 29. Aaron, s Wm. & Ruanna, Cedar
        Co., Iowa; m in Guernsey MH, Achsah SMITH,
        dt Samuel & Elizabeth, Guernsey Co., O.
        Aaron m 2nd 1884,10,24 in Guernsey MH, La-
        vina H. WRIGHT, dt Wm. & Anne, Washtenaw
        Co., Mich.

1820, 8, 27. Wm. & w, Ruanna, & ch, Aaron &
        James, gct Short Creek MM, O.
1831, 6, 23. Ruanna & ch, Aaron, James,
        Peter & Wm. P., rocf Short Creek MM, O.,
        dtd 1831,5,25
1836, 7, 21. Aaron gct Short Creek MM, O., to
        m Tabitha Thompson
1837, 8, 24. Aaron gct Short Creek MM, O.
1838, 6, 21. Ruanna & s, Wm. P., gct Short
        Creek MM, O.
1839, 6, 20. James T. gct Short Creek MM, O.
1840, 6, 25. Peter gct Short Creek MM, O.
1840, 6, 25. Rhuanna & s, Peter, gct Short
        Creek MM, O.
1863, 5, 26. Achsah gct Stillwater MM
1863, 10, 22. Wm. H. Holloway gct Stillwater
        MM, to m Mary Ann Frame
1864, 5, 26. Achsah gct Stillwater MM
1885, 3, 26. Lavina H. gct Stillwater MM

FREET
1849, 9, 20. Rachel (form Nevit) dis mcd

FRENCH
----, --, --. Samuel m Mary J. PARRY, dt Da-
        vid & Hannah (Jones), b 1817,10,7 d 1912,
        3,11 bur Flushing
1846, 9, 2. Zadok, s Robert & Anna, Columbi-
        ana Co., O.; m in Guernsey MH, Miriam
        HOLLOWAY, dt Robert & Rebecca, Guernsey
        Co., O.

1846, 11, 26. Miriam gct Salem MM
1873, 8, 21. Benjamin Wilson gct Salem MM,
        to m Mary A. French
1876, 10, 26. Abel Walker gct Salem MM, to m
        Hannah L. French
1879, 10, 23. Mary J. rocf Salem MM, dtd 1879,
        9,24

GARRETSON
----, --, --. Amos & Mary
    Ch: Angalina   b 1803, 1, 8 d 1807, 9,27
        Eliza   " 1806, 1, 1
        Mary Anne   " 1808, 9, 5
        Talboth   " 1810, 9, 6
        Peggy   " 1814, 1, 22

GARRETSON, Amos & Mary, continued
    Ch: Angelina b 1816, 2, 5
        Joel   " 1818, 2, 6
        Martha   " 1821, 2, 22
1837, 6, 28. Joseph, s John & Henrietta, Mon-
    roe Co., O.; m in Flushing MH, Sarah Coop-
    er, dt Nicholas & Sarah, Belmont Co., O.
1846, 8, 26. Sarah m John MICHENER

1827, 4, 27. Eliza rmt Daniel Allen
1828, 7, 25. Amos dis disunity
1829, 6, 25. Talbott, Mary & Mary Ann dis jH
1833, 5, 23. Peggy dis jH
1834, 9, 25. Angelina dis jH
1837, 11, 23. Sarah gct Somerset MM
1842, 9, 22. Sarah C. & dt, Martha Luceta,
    rocf Somerset MM, dtd 1842,2,28
1843, 9, 21. Joel gct Duck Creek MM
1847, 5, 20. Luceta, dt Sarah Mitchener, gct
    Plainfield MM

GARRETT
1819, 7, 23. Mary (form Ellis) dis mcd
1821, 5, 25. Mary rst
1839, 2, 21. Mary gct Cherry Grove MM, Ind.

GATCHEL
1822, 1, 24. Elizabeth d

GAUSE
1867, 6, 20. Rachel M. (form Ellis) dis mcd

GEORGE
1826, 2, 24. Sarah rst on consent of Smith-
    field
1839, 12, 26. Sarah dis jas

GIBBONS
1892, 8, 26. James E., s James & Lydia, Bel-
    mont Co., O.; m in Guernsey MH, Eliza M.
    STEPHEN, dt David & Anna, Guernsey Co.,
    O., d 1926,1,10 bur Pasadena, Calif.
    Ch: Wilbert
        Carlton   b 1893, 6, 20
        Ronald D. " 1898, 4, 25
1839, 4, 25. Susan (form Gruell) dis mcd

GILBERT
1849, 6, 27. John, s John & Elizabeth, Harri-
    son Co., O.; m in Flushing MH, Susannah
    PACKER, dt Abraham & Sarah, Belmont Co.,
    O.
    Ch: Abraham b 1850, 4, 4
        Mary   " 1852, 8, 9 d 1857, 8,12
        Daniel   " 1854, 2, 18
        Sarah   " 1858, 8, 27
        Abijah   " 1861, 9, 11
1870, 4, 21. John d bur Flushing

1849, 11, 22. Susan P. gct Short Creek MM, O.
1853, 11, 24. John & w, Susanna, & ch, Abraham
    & Mary, rocf Short Creek MM, O., dtd 1853,
    6,21

1872, 7, 25. Abraham con mcd
1878, 3, 20. Daniel dis joining M. E. Society
1879, 6, 26. Sarah dis joining M. E. Society
1884, 5, 22. Abijah dis joining M. E. Society
1890, 7, 24. Abraham dis disunity

GRAY
----, --, --. Thomas & Hannah
    Ch: Ebenezer
        Atherton b 1808, 11, 3
        Anna   " 1810, 7, 25
        Thomas   " 1812, 6, 29
        James   " 1814, 10, 25
        John   " 1814, 10, 25
        William   " 1817, 9, 24
        Isaac   " 1820, 8, 20
1825, 5, 2. Hannah d bur Freeport

1819, 7, 23. Thomas & ch recrq
1819, 9, 24. Hannah, w Thomas, recrq on con-
    sent of Short Creek MM, O.
1826, 3, 24. Lydia (form Parkins) dis mcd
1827, 3, 23. Thomas dis mcd
1832, 10, 25. Ebenezer dis mcd
1832, 12, 20. James gct Cincinnati MM
1832, 12, 20. Thomas, John & James, ch Thomas,
    gct Cincinnati MM
1832, 12, 20. Wm. & Isaac, minors, s Thomas,
    gct Short Creek MM, O.
1833, 2, 1. Anne gct Short Creek MM, O.
1839, 1, 24. Ann (form Millison) dis mcd
1905, 12, 21. Elma (form Doudna) dis mcd

GREAVES
1821, 12, 21. George & w, Sarah, & ch, Alfred
    & Charles, rocf Balby MM, York Co., Great
    Britain, end by Radnor MM, Pa.

GREEN
----, --, --. John & Mary
    Ch: Thomas   b 1826, 5, 12
        Sophia   " 1827, 10, 23
        Rachel   " 1830, 5, 15
        John   " 1832, 6, 16
        Mary   " 1834, 5, 27
        Jacob   " 1836, 9, 24
        James   " 1838, 11, 6 d 1839, 3,14
        bur Freeport
        Abigail   b 1840, 1, 30
        Rebecca   " 1844, 5, 4
----, --, --. Samuel & Ann
    Ch: William   b 1830, 10, 29
        James   " 1833, 9, 16
        Aaron   " 1836, 5, 6
        Sarah   " 1838, 10, 31 d 1838,10,31
        bur Freeport
        Samuel   b 1840, 12, 5
        Ruth T.   " 1843, 6, 18
        Israel   " 1845, 11, 11
1838, 3, 29. Sarah m Valentine HIBBS

1825, 10, 21. Mary rocf Sandy Spring MM, dtd
    1825,6,24

GREEN, continued

1826, 10, 27. John rocf Plainfield MM, dtd
    1826,9,21
1828, 3, 21. Samuel rocf Plainfield MM, dtd
    1828,2,21
1830, 4, 22. Ann rocf Short Creek MM, O., dtd
    1830,3,23
1831, 7, 21. Mary (form Chicken) dis jH
1832, 6, 21. Mary Ann & William, minors, rocf
    Stillwater MM, dtd 1832,5,26
1832, 8, 23. Sarah rocf Stillwater MM, dtd
    1832,6,23
1841, 1, 21. William dis mcd
1846, 7, 23. Eliza Jane (form Hirst) dis mcd
1862, 7, 24. John, Samuel & Ann & Mary dis jG
1863, 6, 25. Sophia Hopkins (form Green) dis
    mcd
1863, 6, 25. Thomas dis mcd
1868, 8, 10. Ruth L. dis jG
1868, 10, 22. Jacob A. dis mcd & jG
1869, 10, 21. Israel & Aaron dis jG
1869, 10, 21. Rachel Wherry (form Green) dis
    mcd & jG
1869, 11, 25. Mary Ann dis jG
1872, 6, 20. William dis mcd & jG
1872, 9, 26. James dis jG

GREENFIELD
1843, 8, 24. Mary (form Hibbs) dis mcd

GREGG
----, --, --. Stephen & Hannah
    Ch: Anne   b 1814, 10, 9
        Hannah   " 1817, 1, 10
        Sarah   " 1819, 6, 12
        Asahel   " 1818, 2, 28
        Eula   " 1821, 4, 14
----, --, --. William & Hannah
    Ch: Carleton b 1827, 6, 3
        Samuel   " 1828, 9, 25
        Mark C.   " 1830, 7, 9
        Beulahann " 1833, 1, 13
        Lydia L. " 1835, 11, 7
        Phebe H. " 1838, 1, 29
        James
        William

1822, 6, 21. David, Betsy Ann, Jesse, Phebe
    & Nancy, ch Abel & Hannah, rocf Alum Creek
    MM
1823, 5, 23. Susanna & ch, Sarahann & Hanson,
    gct Plainfield MM
1823, 9, 26. Hannah rocf Alum Creek MM
1826, 11, 24. William & w, Hannah, rocf Plain-
    field MM, dtd 1826,10,26
1828, 2, 22. Stephen dis disunity
1829, 3, 27. Hannah & ch, Ann, Hannah, Asahel,
    Sarah, Lydia, Eliza & Mary, gct Duck Creek
    MM, Ind.
1830, 10, 21. William dis disunity
1833, 3, 21. Elijah Fawcett gct Stillwater
    MM, to m Sarah Gregg
1845, 8, 21. Hannah & ch, Carleton, Samuel,

Mark, Beula Ann, Lydia, Phebe H., James
    & William, gct Somerset MM
1877, 1, 23. Lucy (form Thwaite) dis mcd

GREWELL
1820, 1, 1. Mary d bur Freeport

1821, 3, 23. John dis mcd
1821, 5, 25. Sarah dis mcd
1822, 11, 22. Ruth, w Thos., & ch, Thomas,
    Ezekiel, Isaac, Susan & Mary Ann, recrq
1830, 10, 21. Sarah Niblack (form Grewell) dis
    mcd
1831, 5, 26. Ruth dis jH
1832, 2, 23. Thomas dis jH
1832, 4, 26. Mary Ann Weldon (form Grewell)
    dis mcd
1835, 6, 25. Daniel dis disunity
1835, 7, 23. Ezekiel & Isaac dis disunity
1838, 6, 21. Rachel Shamel (form Gruell) dis
    mcd
1839, 4, 25. Susan Gibbons (form Gruell) dis
    mcd
1841, 6, 24. Thomas D. [Gruell] dis mcd
1845, 12, 25. John rst at Chesterfield MM on
    consent of this mtg

GRIFFITH
1819, 7, 23. Elizabeth rocf Short Creek MM,
    O., dtd 1819,6,22
1822, 5, 24. Abraham & w, Mary, rocf Plain-
    field MM, dtd 1822,2,22, end by Concord
    MM
1823, 4, 25. Elizabeth gct Smithfield MM
1825, 7, 22. Emlen, minor, rocf Providence
    MM, Pa., dtd 1825,6,21
1825, 10, 21. Emlen, minor, in care of Zacha-
    riah B. & Sarah Hampton, gct Stillwater MM
1828, 6, 27. Abraham & w, Mary, & ch, Elma,
    Ann & Reese, gct Short Creek MM, O.

GUMERE
1823, 1, 24. William & w, Phebe, & ch, John,
    Harlan, Ann, Swithen, Eli, Enoch, William,
    Hannah & Joshua, roc
1823, 8, 22. William & w, Phebe, & ch, John,
    Harlan, Ann, Swithen, Eli, Enoch, William,
    Hannah, Joshua & Thomas, gct Short Creek
    MM, O.

HAINES
----, --, --. Isaac & Rachel
    Ch: William   b 1804, 7, 16
        Nancy   " 1805, 12, 27
        Timothy   " 1807, 7, 30
        Rebecca   " 1813, 7, 2
        Edwin   " 1815, 7, 29
        John   " 1820, 4, 10 d 1821, 9,15
          bur Brushy Fork
        Ruth   b 1821, 12, 13
        John M.   " 1824, 7, 6
        Jacob M. " 1824, 7, 6
        Daniel Long-

HAINES, Isaac & Rachel, continued
            streath b 1825,11, 16
1824, 7, 10. Jacob d
1824, 7, 22. John d

1827, 3, 23. Timothy gct Short Creek MM, O.
1830, 2, 24. William dis jH
1831, 6, 23. Rachel dis jH
1832, 6, 21. James, minor, rocf Stillwater
    MM, dtd 1832,5,26
1832, 8, 23. Isaac dis jH
1833, 5, 23. Rebecca Stewart (form Haines)
    dis mcd
1837, 6, 22. James dis disunity

HALL
----, --, --. Jesse & Elizabeth
    Ch: Noah   b 1832, 12, 20
        Charity   " 1834, 7, 3
        Stephen   " 1835, 12, 3
        Joseph
        Hartley   " 1838, 3, 1
        Mary   " 1840, 3, 1
        George S. " 1842, 2, 2
        Sarah   " 1844, 3, 7
        John Green " 1846, 7, 29
        Mahlon   " 1848, 10, 10
        Phebe   " 1850, 8, 15
        Ephraim   " 1852, 9, 29
        Jesse
        Franklin   " 1855, 6, 16
----, --, --. Robert m Martha ----- d 1841,5,
    26 bur Flushing
    Ch: Hervy   b 1837, 3, 20
        Tacy   " 1838, 12, 27
1850, 8, 28. David, s Thomas & Mary, Jeffer-
    son Co., O.; m in Guernsey MH, Amy T.
    THOMAS, dt Nathan & Catharine, Guernsey
    Co., O.
----, --, --. William & Mary T.
    Ch: Caroline   b 1851, 4, 27
        Maria   " 1853, 2, 2
1851, 4, 2. John, s John & Tacy, Belmont
    Co., O.; m in Flushing MH, Deborah DAVIS,
    dt John F. & Ann, Harrison Co., O., b
    1823,7,10
1853, 8, 31. Parker, s Wm. & Hannah, Jeffer-
    son Co., O.; m in Flushing MH, Rebecca
    HOBSON, dt Joseph & Ruth, Belmont Co., O.
1865, 2, 24. Josiah, s Nathan & Sarah, Jeffer-
    son Co., O.; m in Guernsey MH, Deborah
    WILSON, dt Joseph & Eliza, Guernsey Co.,O.
1882, 10, 4. Henry, s Jesse & Edith, Chester
    Co., Pa.; m in Flushing MH, Ann Eliza
    BRANSON, dt David & Sarah, Belmont Co., O.,
    b 1854,1,23

1823, 9, 26. Nathan rmt Hannah Wilson
1823, 11, 21. Hannah gct Short Creek MM, O.
1824, 11, 26. Nathan P. rmt Rachel Wilson
1825, 3, 25. Rachel W. gct Short Creek MM, O.
1836, 2, 25. Robert rocf Short Creek MM, O.,
    dtd 1836,2,23

1836, 4, 21. Robert rmt Martha Wilson
1837, 9, 21. David Conrow gct Short Creek
    MM, O., to m Anna Hall
1838, 7, 26. Lydia (form Pearson) dis mcd
1843, 3, 23. Jesse & w, Elizabeth, & ch,
    Noah, Charity, Stephen, Joseph H., Mary &
    George S., rocf Stillwater MM, dtd 1843,2,
    25
1844, 8, 22. Joseph A. Bevan gct Stillwater
    MM, to m Maria Hall
1845, 8, 21. Stephen & w, Mary, & dt, Ruth,
    rocf Stillwater MM, dtd 1845,7,26
1845, 12, 25. Mary L. rocf Stillwater MM, dtd
    1845,11,22
1847, 6, 24. Mary Chicken (form Hall) dis
    mcd
1848, 7, 21. Robert gct Chesterfield MM, to
    m Mary Dewees
1849, 2, 23. Robert & ch, Henry & Tacy, gct
    Plainfield MM
1850, 11, 21. Wm. & w, Mary T., rocf Short
    Creek MM, O., dtd 1850,11,19
1850, 12, 26. Amy T. gct Short Creek MM, O.
1851, 9, 25. Deborah S. gct Short Creek MM, O.
1852, 8, 26. John & w, Deborah S., & dt, Ma-
    rian, rocf Short Creek MM, O., dtd 1852,7,
    20
1853, 12, 22. Rebecca gct Short Creek MM, O.
1854, 4, 20. William & w, Mary T., & ch,
    Caroline & Maria, gct Short Creek MM, O.
1855, 6, 21. Noah dis mcd
1857, 3, 26. John & w, Deborah S., & ch, Wm.
    P., Eliza D., Tacy Ellen & Sina Ann, gct
    Stillwater MM
1861, 2, 21. Elizabeth dis jG
1861, 3, 21. Jesse dis jG
1863, 1, 22. Joseph Heartly dis mcd
1863, 11, 26. Mary Bethel (form Hall) dis mcd
1864, 7, 21. Stephen dis jG
1864, 8, 25. George S. dis jG
1864, 11, 24. Charity dis jG
1865, 5, 25. Sarah dis jG
1865, 7, 20. Deborah gct Short Creek MM, O.
1866, 1, 23. Lindley & w, Milicent, & s,
    Franklin B., rocf Somerset MM, dtd 1865,
    10,31
1866, 9, 20. John G. dis military service
1869, 7, 22. Phebe dis jG
1869, 12, 23. Lindley & w, Milicent, & ch,
    Franklin B., Arthur & Mary C., gct Short
    Creek MM, O.
1871, 7, 20. Mahlon dis disunity
1877, 5, 24. Jesse Franklin dis jG
1878, 1, 24. Ephraim dis jG
1883, 4, 26. Ann Eliza rocf Goshen MM, Pa.
1898, 4, 21. Edwin & w, Elma E., & dt,
    Lillian A., rocf Short Creek MM, O.

HAMBLETON
1820, 7, 21. William Jr. gct Carmel MM

HAMMER
1826, 8, 25. Mary (form Embree) dis mcd

HAMMOND
1870, 4, 21. Caroline B. (form Hirst) dis mcd

HAMPTON·
1853, 6, 24. William, s Zachariah & Sarah,
    Linn Co., Ia.; m in Flushing MH, Charity
    WOOD, dt Pusey & Charity, Belmont Co., O.

1825, 3, 25. Zachariah B. rocf Goose Creek
    MM, Va., dtd 1825,1,13
1825, 3, 25. Zachariah B. gct Providence MM,
    Pa., to m Sarah Griffith
1825, 7, 22. Sarah rocf Providence MM, Pa.,
    dtd 1825,6,21
1825, 10, 21. Zachariah B. & w, Sarah, & Em-
    len Griffith, a minor, gct Stillwater MM
1853, 8, 25. Charity gct Red Cedar MM, Ia.

HANKISON
1819, 12, 24. Edward Y. recrq
1821, 9, 21. Edward Y. gct White Water MM,
    Ind.

HARRIS
1826, 6, 23. David & w, Lettice, & ch, Lany
    & Rachel, rocf Short Creek MM, O., dtd
    1825,7,18
1833, 1, 24. David & w, Lettuce, & ch, Elana,
    Rachel Ann, Susan & Sarah Eliza, gct
    Stillwater MM
1836, 8, 25. Hannah (form Millison) dis mcd
1917, 12, 20. Martha H. (form Holloway) con
    mcd

HARRISON
1846, 11, 26. Lydia rocf Short Creek MM, O.,
    dtd 1846,10,20

HASTINGS
1841, 4, 22. Elizabeth (form Cope) dis mcd

HAYES
1891, 8, 21. Albert, s Chas. & Deborah F.,
    Columbiana Co., O.; m in Flushing MH,
    Myra D. BRANSON, dt David & Sarah H.,
    Belmont Co., O.

1891, 12, 24. Myra D. gct Salem MM
1893, 9, 21. Chas. D. Conrow gct Salem MM, to
    m Deborah F. Hayes

HERALD
1875, 1, 30. Tamar d bur Flushing

1823, 10, 24. Housen & w, Rachel, & ch, Amos,
    Rebecca, Tamar & Mary, gct Short Creek
    MM, O.
1846, 5, 21. Rachel rocf Short Creek MM, O.,
    dtd 1846,4,21
1852, 2, 26. Tamar rocf Short Creek MM, O.,
    dtd 1851,2,18

HESTON
1838, 6, 21. Mahlon rocf Plainfield MM, dtd
    1837,11,22

HIBBARD
1821, 8, 24. Caleb rocf Goshen MM, Pa.
1830, 7, 22. Caleb [Hibberd] gct Stillwater
    MM

HIBBS
----, --, --. William d 1844,8,28 bur Guern-
    sey; m Mary ----- d 1832,2,12 bur Guernsey
    Ch: Elizabeth b 1804,10,24
        Valentine " 1807, 1, --
        Amos   " 1809, 5, 4
        William   " 1814, 5, 8
        Anne   " 1811, 12, 13
        Jason   " 1816, 7, 17
        George   " 1819, 11, 22 d 1828, 3, 3
        bur Guernsey
        Mary   b 1822, 7, 30
        Elijah   " 1824, 8, 21
1828, 3, 31. George d
1824, 8, 28. Elijah d
----, --, --. Amos m Elizabeth R. - --- d 1875,
    3,9 bur Guernsey
    Ch: John R.   b 1835, 7, 18
        William G. " 1838, 7, 31
        Amos E.   " 1841, 5, 13
        Barclay   " 1846, 10, 27
1838, 3, 29. Valentine, s Wm. & Mary, Guern-
    sey Co., O.; m in Freeport MH, Sarah GREEN
    dt Alexander & Mary, Belmont Co., O.
    Ch: Mary   b 1839, 2, 13
        John G.   " 1840, 7, 23
        William B. " 1842, 1, 4
        Maria   " 1843, 10, 25
        Elizabeth " 1845, 10, 2
        Sarah G.   " 1847, 8, 10
        George S. " 1849, 5, 9
        Phebe Ann " 1852, 5, 17
1838, 5, 2. William, s Wm. & Mary, Harrison
    Co., O.; m in Guernsey MH, Martha RATCLIFF
    dt Josiah & Rachel
    Ch: Rachel R. b 1839, 1, 21
        Mary C.   " 1841, 7, 24
        Robert F.R." 1844, 3, 12 d 1844, 4,11
        Benjamin
        Franklin   " 1846, 8, 25
1839, 5, 1. Jason A., s Wm. & Mary, Guernsey
    Co., O.; m in Guernsey MH, Ann BARBER, dt
    Abraham & Rachel, Guernsey Co., O.
    Ch: Abraham   b 1840, 4, 4
        George   " 1842, 3, 5 d 1844, 8, 8
        William   " 1845, 1, 28
        Amasa   " 1847, 5, 13

1819, 6, 25. Wm. & w, Mary, & ch, Wm., Valen-
    tine, Jason, Elizabeth & Nancy, recrq
1823, 7, 25. Margaret recrq
1827, 4, 27. Mary (form Hibbs) dis mcd
1831, 12, --. Elizabeth rmt Samuel Briggs
1834, 7, 24. Amos gct Short Creek MM, O.,

HIBBS, continued
      to m Elizabeth Ratcliff
1835, 3, 26. Elizabeth rocf Short Creek MM,
    O., dtd 1835,2,24
1843, 8, 24. Mary Greenfield (form Hibbs)
    dis mcd
1849, 8, 23. Lydia (form Smith) dis mcd
1851, 5, 22. William dis disunity
1851, 7, 24. Sarah recrq
1852, 6, 24. Jason A. & w, Anne, & ch, Abra-
    ham, William, Amasa & Rachel Ann, gct Duck
    Creek MM, Ind.
1853, 6, 23. Valentine & w, Sarah, & ch, Mary,
    John G., Wm. B., Maria, Elizabeth, Sarah
    G., Geo. S. & Phebe Ann, gct Pleasant Plain
    MM, Ia.
1853, 8, 25. Martha & ch, Rachel R., Mary C.
    & Josiah R., gct Spring Creek MM
1858, 4, 22. John R. dis mcd
1859, 4, 21. Lydia (form Smith) dis mcd
1860, 2, 23. Amos Jr. dis mcd
1864, 2, 25. Wm. G. dis mcd
1873, 1, 23. Barclay dis mcd

HIRST
----, --, --. Thomas m Anna ----- d 1827,6,22
    bur Flushing
    Ch: Ruthanna   b 1822, 5, 4
        Rebecca   " 1823, 11, 30
        Amanda   " 1825, 11, 20
----, --, --. Israel & Catharine
    Ch: Eliza Jane b 1824, 10, 28
        Oliver W. " 1827, 8, 1
        Joseph Addi-
             son 1830, 5, 20
        David
        Rebecca   " 1837, 2, 4
        Mary   " 1839, 10, 9
        Caroline   " 1842, 3, 17
----, --, --. John m Elizabeth BRANSON, d
    1837 bur Flushing
    Ch: Alpheus   b 1825, 1, 25
        Mary Ann   " 1828, 1, 5
        Lindley Mur-
            ray b 1836, 8, 9
----, --, --. Thomas m Ann Raley d 1832,6,10
    bur Flushing
    Ch: James   b 1830, 3, 22
        Ann   " 1832, 6, 5
1838, 11, 28. Mary m Levi HOGE
----, --, --. John m Maria WILSON
    Ch: Elizabeth b 1840, 3, 20
        Israel Wil-
            son " 1846, 10, 21
1839, 4, 4. David d bur Flushing
1847, 9, 24. Amanda m Allen T. LEE
1848, 11, 19. Ann Maria, dt Alpheus & Esther
    F., b
1863, 8, 26. Hannah m Abel LEWIS
1866, 10, 26. Mary m Lemuel BRACKIN

1823, 9, 26. Israel rmt Catharine Branson
1823, 12, 26. Catharine gct Concord MM

1825, 1, 25. John rmt Elizabeth Branson
1825, 3, 25. Elizabeth gct Concord MM
1826, 5, 26. Asenath & Rachel rocf Concord
    MM, O., dtd 1826,4,19
1826, 5, 26. David & w, Ann, & ch, Smith,
    Mary & Hannah, rocf Concord MM, dtd 1826,
    4,19
1826, 5, 26. John & w, Elizabeth, & s, Al-
    pheus, rocf Concord MM, O., dtd 1826,4,19
1826, 5, 26. Thomas & w, Anna, & ch, Ruth-
    anna, Rebecca & Amanda, rocf Plainfield
    MM, dtd 1826,5,25
1826, 9, 22. Asenath rmt Asa Raley
1827, 7, 27. Israel & w, Catharine, & dt,
    Elizajane, rocf Concord MM, O., dtd 1827,
    4,25
1829, 4, 24. Thos. gct Short Creek MM, O., to
    m Ann Raley
1829, 12, 24. Ann rocf Short Creek MM, O., dtd
    1829,9,21
1833, 12, 26. Thomas gct Short Creek MM, O.,
    to m Mary Swayne
1834, 4, 24. Thomas & ch, Rebecca, James &
    Ann, gct Short Creek MM, O.
1834, 12, 25. Ruthanna gct Short Creek MM, O.
1838, 6, 21. John gct Short Creek MM, O., to
    m Maria Wilson
1839, 1, 24. Maria rocf Short Creek MM, O.,
    dtd 1838,11,20
1839, 9, 26. Israel T. dis disunity
1846, 1, 22. Marshall Fell gct Short Creek
    MM, O., to m Rebecca Hirst
1846, 7, 23. Eliza Jane Green (form Hirst)
    dis mcd
1847, 10, 21. Alpheus gct Goshen MM, O., to m
    Esther H. Fell
1848, 3, 23. Esther H. [Hurst] rocf Goshen
    MM, O., dtd 1848,1,15
1850, 2, 21. Alpheus & w, Esther, & dt, Ann
    Maria, gct Goshen MM
1851, 3, 20. Smith dis mcd
1851, 8, 21. Mary Ann Cook (form Hirst) dis
    mcd
1852, 3, 25. David dis disunity
1857, 6, 25. Lydia (form Hoge) dis mcd
1863, 9, 24. Elizabeth Cook (form Hirst) dis
    mcd
1863, 11, 26. John [Hurst] & w, Miriah, & s,
    Israel Wilson, gct Hickory Grove MM, Ia.
1870, 4, 21. Caroline B. Hammond (form
    Hirst) dis mcd

HOBBS
1827, 9, 21. Juliann (form Leeke) dis mcd
1844, 3, 21. Wilson rocf Walnut Ridge MM,
    dtd 1844,2,17, end to White Water MM, Ind.

HOBSON
----, --, --. Francis & Grace
    Ch: Anne   b 1808, 11, 28
        John M.   " 1811, 6, 4
        Martha   " 1814, 2, 21
        Esther   " 1817, 5, 17

HOBSON, Francis & Grace, continued
    Ch: Rebecca   b 1820, 3, 21
1821, 8, 21. Francis d bur Brushy Fork
1847, 12, 1. Belinda A. m Joseph DOUDNA
1853, 5, 27. Hannah m Barclay STRATTON
1853, 8, 31. Rebecca m Parker HALL
----, --, --. Stephen, s Joseph & Ruth (Ball),
    d 1887,7,17; m Margaret BAILEY
    Ch: Rebecca   b 1858, 9, 11 d 1889, 5, 9
           bur Flushing
        Edward L. b 1860, 3, 27 " 1918,--,--
           bur Cleveland, O.
        Joseph F. b 1861, 8, 30 " ----,--,--
           bur Cleveland, O.
        Alice   b 1864, 2, 13 " 1886, 7,12
           bur Flushing
        Mary S. b 1870, 9, 16
        Clarence C." 1882, 3, 30
1871, 3, 7. Joseph d bur Flushing
1873, 6, 27. John A., s Thos. & Unity, Wash-
    ington Co., O., d 1913,2,21 bur Flushing;
    m in Flushing MH, Martha H. BRANSON, dt
    David & Sarah H., Belmont Co., O., b 1851,
    8,24 d 1910,11,15 bur Flushing
    Ch: Mary Bertha b 1874, 4, 20 d 1877, 2,25
           bur Flushing
        Emma Ger-
           trude b 1876, 8, 10; m Ray D.
           JUDKINS
        Anna S.   " 1879,11, 4; m Dr. Van
           NOrton MARSH
        James David b 1884,11, 17
        Alfred   " 1892,--, --
1876, 3, 23. Ruth, w Joseph, d bur Flushing
1887, 7, 17. Stephen, s Jos. & Ruth, d bur
Flushing

1822, 3, 22. Grace & ch, Ann, John, Martha,
    Esther & Rebecca, gct Smithfield MM
1831, 11, 24. Joseph & w, Ruth, & ch, Belinda,
    Hannah, Rebecca & Stephen, rocf Smithfield
    MM, dtd 1831,8,22
1840, 5, 21. John rocf Smithfield MM, dtd
    1839,3,18
1840, 6, 25. John con mcd
1840, 11, 26. John gct Chesterfield MM
1857, 8, 20. Stephen gct Somerset MM, to m
Margaret Bailey
1858, 6, 24. Margaret rocf Somerset MM, dtd
    1858,3,29
1874, 5, 21. John A. rocf Plymouth MM, dtd
    1874,4,20
1887, 5, 26. Joseph T. dis disunity
1899, 1, 26. Emma Gertrude & Anna dis jas

HODGINS
1885, 2, 27. Wilson [Hodgin], s Stephen & Sa-
    rah, Linn Co., O.; m in Guernsey MH, Maria
    BRIGGS, dt Henry & Betsy, Harrison Co., O.

1886, 4, 22. Maria gct Damorris MM, Kans.
1890, 4, 24. Wilson & w, Maria B., & ch, Sa-
    rah P., rocf Damoeris MM, Kans., dtd 1890,

4,4
1891, 4, 23. Wilson & w, Maria, & ch, Sarah
    B. & Henry S., gct Springville MM, Ia.

HOGE
----, --, --. William, s John & Mary (Jen-
    kins), b 1779 d 1845,4,22 bur Flushing;
    m Sarah ----- d 1866,3,25 bur Flushing
    Ch: Levi   b 1809, 3, 11
        Mary   " 1811, 9, 9
        Elisha   " 1814, 2, 6 d 1847,10, 4
           bur Flushing
        Ellazan   b 1816, 3, 14 " 1818, 9,17
           bur Flushing
        Eunice   b 1818, 1, 31
        John   " 1820, 3, 22
----, --, --. Absalom, s Isaac & Elizabeth
    (Nichols), d 1865,9,17 bur Flushing; m
    Rachel COFFEE, d 1862,11,9 bur Flushing
    Ch: John C.   b 1813, 7, 2 d 1893,8,25
        James M.D.
        Mary Ann   " 1895, 2, 5
           ae 78; m ----- HOLLOWAY
        Isaac
        Rachel P.   " 1854, 7,15
           ae 32; m ----- McGREW
1838, 5, 2. Mary m Samuel G. HOLLOWAY
1838, 11, 28. Levi, s Wm. & Sarah, Belmont Co.
    O., b 1809,3,11 d 1857,4,5 bur Flushing;
    m in Flushing MH, Mary HIRST, dt David &
    Ann, Belmont Co., O., d 1855,4,27
    Ch: David   b 1839, 10, 10
        Asa   " 1842, 2, 23 d 1923, 3, 1
           bur West Grove, O.
        Thomas   b 1845, 2, 25
        Rebecca W. " 1847, 10, 22; m Joshua
           GILBERT
        John Bar-
           clay " 1850, 1, 9 d 1922,12, 9
           bur St. Clairsville, O.
        Joseph   b 1852, 10, 18
1840, 11, 2. Phebe W., dt Elisha & Lydia, b
1840, 12, 4. David d bur Flushing
1841, 10, 27. Eunice W. m Asa HOLLOWAY
----, --, --. John C., s Absolam & Rachel
    (Coffee), b 1813,7,2 d 1893,8,25 bur Flush-
    ing; m Rebecca BONSALL, dt Edward & Ra-
    chel (Warrington), b 1818,7,5 d 1879,7,22
    bur Flushing
    Ch: Lindley M. b 1844, 6, 18 d 1897,12,26
           bur Chester Co., Pa.
        Hannah El-
           ma b 1848, 1, 12
        Edward B. " 1853, 2, 10
    John C. m 2nd 1882,6,29 in Guernsey MH,
    Ann B. WOOD, dt Pusey & Charity (Redd),
    Guernsey Co., O., d 1910,12,24 bur Flush-
    ing
1843, 11, 1. John, s Wm. & Sarah (Wright),
    Belmont Co., O.; m in Flushing MH, Lydia
    BRANSON, dt William & Sarah, Belmont Co.,
    O.
    Ch: William   b 1844, 9, 22

HOGE, John & Lydia, continued
    Ch: Eliza   b 1846, 4, 1; m Nathan
      HEALD
      Elisha   " 1848, 2, 19
      Rachel B. " 1850, 3, 15
      Smith B. " 1852, 5, 19
      James Ed-
          win " 1854, 9, 17
      Mary Jane " 1857, 5, 13
      David J. " 1860, 12, 4 d·1865, 4, 4
        bur Coal Creek, Ia.
      Samuel G. b 1863, 2, 8
1850, 10, 2. Rachel P. m Samuel McGREW
1868, 10, 28. Hannah Elma m Asa G. HOLLOWAY
1886, 11, 7. Florence, dt Lindley & Martha,
    d bur Flushing (or 1886,7,11)

1823, 9, 26. Craven dis mcd
1835, 9, 24. Anna & s, Peter Miller Hoge,
    rocf Redstone MM, Pa., dtd 1835,6,3
1838, 3, 22. Daniel Holloway gct Short Creek
    MM, O., to m Mary Ann Hoge
1839, 9, 26. Elisha gct Fall Creek MM, to m
    Lydia Vanpelt
1839, 12, 26. Anna dis jH
1840, 3, 26. Lydia rocf Fall Creek MM, dtd
    1840,2,19
1850, 1, 24. Absalom & w, Rachel, rocf Short
    Creek MM, O., dtd 1850,1,22
1850, 3, 21. Rachel P. rocf Short Creek MM,
    O., dtd 1850,1,22
1851, 4, 24. Jane (form Barber) dis mcd
1857, 6, 25. Lydia Hirst (form Hoge) dis mcd
1858, 8, 26. John C. & w, Rebecca, & ch,
    Lindley, Hannah Elma & Edward B., rocf
    Plainfield MM, dtd 1858,7,21
1861, 1, 24. Phebe W. Bailey (form Hoge) dis
    mcd & jG
1865, 9, 21. Eliza gct Coal Creek MM, Ia.
1865, 9, 21. John & w, Lydia, & ch, William,
    Rachel B., Elisha, Smith B., James Edwin,
    David & Samuel G., gct Coal Creek MM, Ia.
1869, 9, 23. Thomas C. gct Kennet MM, Pa.
1869, 11, 25. Lindley M. gct Concord MM, Pa.,
    to m Martha C. Smith
1872, 9, 26. Asa dis mcd
1876, 3, 23. Joseph L. gct Short Creek MM, O.
1877, 5, 24. John Barclay dis mcd
1885, 9, 24. Martha C. & ch, Mary, Estella,
    Florence, James S., Ulyssus & Samuel T.,
    rocf Concord MM, Pa.,
1885, 12, 24. Edward B. dis mcd
1886, 11, 25. Mary Estella, minor dt Lindley
    M. & Martha C., gct Phila. MM, Pa.
1888, 10, 25. James S., Eulyssus, Samuel &
    Grace, ch Lindley & Martha, gct WD MM
1889, 5, 23. Martha S. dis disunity
1891, 11, 26. Rebecca W. gct Hickory Grove MM,
    Ia.
HOLE
----, --, --. Jonah & Elizabeth
    Ch: Lydia Ann b 1823, 1, 14
      Mary   " 1824, 1, 28

    Ch: Jonathan   b 182-,12,13
      Elizabeth " 1828, 8, 8
      Jonah   " 1831, 4, 6

1821, 12, 21. Jonah rocf New Garden MM, dtd
    1821,8,23
1822, 4, 26. Jonah rmt Elizabeth Ellis
1840, 5, 21. Jonah & w, Elizabeth, & ch,
    Lydia Ann, Mary, Jonathan, Elizabeth &
    Jonah, gct Goshen MM

HOLLINGSWORTH
----, --, --. Levi & Mary
    Ch: Thomas   b 1790, 6, 11
      David   " 1791, 12, 11
      Rachel   " 1793, 11, 17
      Sarah   " 1796, 1, 29
      Hannah   " 1798, 11, 18
      Isaac   " 1801, 3, 2
      Susannah " 1803, 3, 3
      Levi   " 1805, 3, 26
      Eli   " 1807, 4, 12
      John   " 1809, 5, 29
      Mary   " 1811, 3, 19
      Elihu   " 1813, 1, 12
1790, 4, 24. Thomas d bur Flushing
1795, 3, 9. Rachel d
1811, 3, 25. Mary d bur Flushing
----, --, --. David m Hannah ----- d 1838,9,5
    bur Flushing
    Ch: Grace   b 1815, 3, 13
      Eliza   " 1818, 4, 2
      Mary   " 1821, 8, 29
      Hannah   " 1824, 6, 11 d 1834, 3,20
      Elwood   " 1827, 1, 22
      Levi   " 1829, 4, 3
      Sarah   " 1835, 9, 7
----, --, --. Eli & Elizabeth
    Ch: Jonathan M. b 1827, 12, 14
      Isaac   " 1830, 2, 29
      Mary Anne " 1831, 12, 30
1829, 6, 11. Levi d bur Flushing
1834, 2, 1. David, s Levi & Mary, Belmont
    Co., O.; m in Flushing MH, Elizabeth CROSS-
    LEY, dt John & Tamar, Belmont Co., O.
1852, 7, 13. Mary d
1885, --, --. Elizabeth d bur Flushing

1824, 3, 26. Susanna Scholes (form Hollings-
    worth) dis mcd
1827, 3, 23. Eli rmt Elizabeth Ellis
1827, 5, 25. Hannah rmt Elisha Ellis
1829, 8, 20. Isaac dis jH
1831, 5, 26. Levi dis mcd
1831, 11, 24. Grace Williams (form Hollings-
    worth) dis mcd
1834, 12, 25. John dis disunity
1835, 1, 22. Elihu dis disunity
1835, 8, 20. Eliza rmt John Holloway
1837, 8, 24. Eli & w, Elizabeth, & ch, Jona-
    than M. E., Isaac & Mary Ann, gct Old
    Chester MM, Ind.
1840, 12, 24. Mary J. dis jas

HOLLINGSWORTH, continued
1845, 11, 23. Elwood dis jas
1851, 4, 24. Levi dis mcd
1854, 5, 25. Sarah Wherry (form Hollingsworth)
    dis mcd

HOLLOWAY
----, --, --. James Sr. & Mary
    Ch: James b 1786,--,-- d 1836, 4,15
----, --, --. Daniel & Mary
    Ch: Jonas   b 1802, 9, 13
        James   " 1804, 3, 6 d 1830, 3,19
        bur Freeport
        Mahala   b 1806, 10, 25
        Nancy   " 1808, 10, 17
        Catharine " 1810, 9, 4
        John   " 1812, 2, 23
        Mary   " 1824, 9, 24
----, --, --. Joseph & Eleanor
    Ch: Asa   b 1803, 11, 19 d 1829, 7,27
        bur Flushing
        David   b 1805, 9, 19
        Hannah   " 1808, 3, 19
        Betsy Ann " 1810, 8, 18 " 1831, 2,10
        bur Flushing
        Margaret   b 1813, 4, 17
        Nancy   " 1821, 4, 27
----, --, --. Jacob m Martha ----- d 1866,12,
    4 bur Flushing
    Ch: Daniel B. b 1814, 3, 4
        Eliza   " 1816, 5, 5 d 1842, 8,20
        .bur Flushing
        William   b 1818, 11, 23
        Martha   " 1820, 12, 11 (or 1820,11,
        23)
        Jacob   " 1823, 3, 6 d 1893, 7,24
        bur Flushing
        Sarah   b 1827, 4, 10
----, --, --. Robert m Rebecca ----- d 1836,6,
    30 bur Guernsey
    Ch: Betsy   b 1814, 11, 25
        Joseph   " 1816, 12, 29
        Aaron   " 1818, 9, --
        Miriam   " 1820, 10, 11
        Abigail   " 1824, 9, 1
        Jane   " 1822, 10, 1
        Lydia   " 1827, 1, 27
----, --, --. Samuel m Amy ----- d 1821,12,1
    bur Flushing
    Ch: Chalkley T.b 1817, 9, 27
    Samuel m 2nd Sarah ----- d 1835,6,11 bur
    Flushing
    Ch: Lindley
        Murray   b 1831, 2, 5 d 1859, 2, 7
        bur Flushing
        Rebecca B.
1820, 7, 16. Martha d bur Flushing
----, --, --. Asa & Dorothy
    Ch: Elisha   b 1823, 4, 11
        Cornelius
            B.   " 1825, 12, 22
        Anne B.   " 1828, 7, 10
        Samuel Bar-

                    ber   b 1831, 4, 5
    Ch: Asa   b 1833, 5, 17 d 1836, 7,18
        bur Guernsey
        Abraham B. b 1835, 10, 29 " 1835,12,18
        bur Guernsey
        Elizabeth b 1837, 8, 24
        Jacob M.   " 1840, 1, 28
        Sarah Jane " 1842, 9, 6
1824, 9, 20. Mahala d bur Freeport
1828, 8, 24. William, s Asa & Maria, b
1829, 3, 20. Nancy d bur Freeport
----, --, --. Aaron & Rachel
    Ch: Asa C.   d 1831,11,30
        bur Flushing
        Abigail   " 1831,11,26
        bur Flushing
1831, 2, 5. Rebecca b
----, --, --. Robert S., s Aaron & Rachel,
    Belmont Co., O., d 1851,6,22 bur Guernsey;
    m Abby T. TABER, dt Francis & Lydia, d
    1844,11,24 bur Guernsey
    Ch: Lydia T.   b 1834, 7, 13 d 1836, 2,13
        bur Short Creek
        Rachel   b 1839, 1, 26
        Mary   " 1841, 2, 19 d 1841, 2,19
        bur Guernsey
        Francis
        Taber   b 1842, 4, 29 " 1842, 7,27
        bur Guernsey
    Robert S. m 2nd 1849,5,2 in Flushing
    MH, Deborah SMART, dt Isaac & Rebecca,
    Salem Co., O.
1836, 5, --. Rachel, dt A. & Rachel, d bur
    Flushing
1836, 6, 30. Robert b
1836, 11, 3. Daniel d bur Freeport
----, --, --. Daniel m Mary Ann HOGE, dt Ab-
    solam & Rachel (Coffee), d 1894,2,5 bur
    Flushing
    Ch: Jacob   b 1839, 2, 14
        Lindley Hoge" 1840, 11, 10
        Wm. Coffee " 1844, 1, 3
        Eliza B.   " 1848, 6, 12 d 1851,7,20
        James D.   " 1852, 11, 28 " 1860,8,22
        Rachel M. " 1858, 10, 19 " 1859,8,16
        Daniel   " 1860, 12, 31
1838, 5, 2. Samuel G., s James & Phebe, Bel-
    mont Co., O., b 1813,9,23 d 1852,7,23 bur
    Chester Hill, O.; m in Flushing MH, Mary
    HOGE, dt William & Sarah (Wright), Belmont
    Co., O., b 1811,9,11 d 1877,8,22 bur Flush-
    ing
    Ch: James   b 1839, 3, 13 d 1852,8,16
        bur Chester Hill, O.
        William   b 1841, 2, 20
        Asa   " 1843, 3, 7
        Ephraim   " 1845, 4, 7 " 1887, 5,4
        bur Flushing
----, --, --. Elisha m Lydia S. VANLAW
    Ch: Phebe
        Louisa   b 1841, 11, 13; m Samuel
        KIRBY
        Mary Lucy " 1847, 6, 13; m Wm.STEEL

HOLLOWAY, Elisha & Lydia, continued
    Ch: Lucinda b 1849, 5, 10
1840, 6, 20. Rachel, w Aaron, d bur Flushing
1841, 3, 31. Samuel, s Asa & Abigail, Bel-
    mont Co., O.; m in Guernsey MH, Sarah I.
    HOLLOWAY, dt John & Sarah, Belmont Co., O.
1841, 3, 31. Sarah I. m Samuel HOLLOWAY
1841, 10, 27. Asa, s James & Phebe, Belmont
    Co., O., d 1861,8,3 bur Flushing; m in
    Flushing MH, Eunice W. HOGE, dt William &
    Sarah (Wright), Belmont Co., O., b 1818,1,
    31
    Ch: Rebecca
            Ann   b 1842, 9, 5; m Lindley
        Hoge HOLLOWAY
      Jeptha V. b 1845, 4, 21 d 1917,11, 9
      bur Middleton, O.
1842, 10, 26. Betsy m Henry BRIGGS
1843, 6, 7. Abigail m Paul SEARS
1843, 6, 28. Robert, s Asa & Abigail, Guernsey
    Co., O.; m in Guernsey MH, Maria BRIGGS,
    dt William & Esther, Belmont Co., O., d
    1844,9,6 bur Guernsey
1843, 8, 30. James B., s John & Eliza, b
1845, 1, 4. Aaron Sr. d bur Flushing
1845, 12, 16. Phebe, w James Jr., dt Samuel &
    Ann (Sinclair) GREGG, d bur Flushing
1846, 9, 2. Miriam m Zadok FRENCH
----, --, --. Jacob m Sarah FAWCETT, dt Jehu
    & Abigail (Williams), d 1906,10,24 bur
    Flushing
    Ch: Abigail   b 1850, 4, 7
        Edwin F.   " 1852, 10, 31 d 1930, 5,11
        bur Flushing
        Eliza T.   b 1854, 8, 20
        Anna   " 1856, 8, 8
        Martha   " 1858, 10, 10
        Emma   "" 1860, 10, 18
        Deborah   " 1862, 9, 18
1850, 10, 30. Sarah B. m David BRANSON
1851, 4, 9. Samuel d bur Flushing
1851, 4, 10. Jacob Sr. d bur Flushing ae 68y
    6m 18d
1853, 12, 28. Lindley M., s Samuel & Sarah,
    Belmont Co., O., b 1831,2,5 d 1859,2,7
    bur Flushing; m in Flushing MH, Martha H.
    WALKER, dt Joseph & Maria, Belmont Co., O.,
    b 1833,2,7 bur in Iowa
    Ch: Mary Rebec-
            ca b 1855, 2, 1
        Chalkley
        Clinton   " 1857, 7, 14 d 1918,12,16
        bur Columbus
1854, 3, 29. Deborah S. m Jehu FAWCETT
1857, 3, 15. Robert d bur Guernsey
1858, 3, 26. Rebecca B. m David WICKERSHAM
1859, 6, 2. Lydia m Joel BAILEY
1860, 3, 16. James d bur Woodford Co., Ill.
1861, 8, 3. Asa, s James & Phebe, d bur
    Flushing
----, --, --. Wm. H., s Samuel G. & Mary
    (Hoge), b 1841,2,20 d 1904,5,14 bur
    Flushing; m Mary Ann FRAME, dt Aaron &

Talitha (Thompson), d 1880,3,20 bur Flush-
    ing
    Ch: Louisa
        Tabitha   b 1865, 2, 13
        Murray S.   " 1868, 5, 11
        Emerson W. " 1874, 3, 22
        Emma F.   " 1874, 3, 22
----, --, --. William C., s Daniel B. & Mary
    Ann (Hoge), b 1844,1,3 d 1912,3,29; m Re-
    becca S. SCATTERGOOD, dt Samuel & Mary,
    d 1933,8,6 bur Cadiz, O.
    Ch: Walter S. b 1868, 6, 17 d 1914, 1,13
        Ellen
        Leeds   " 1871, 2, 19
        Mary Scat-
        tergood   " 1877, 11, 18
        Henry
        Earle   " 1879, 3, 30
        Margaret W." 1883, 5, 12
1868, 10, 28. Asa G., s Samuel G. & Mary, Bel-
    mont Co., O., b 1843,7,3 d 1916,12,22 bur
    Flushing; m in Flushing MH, Hannah Elma
    HOGE, dt John C. & Rebecca (Bonsell), Bel-
    mont Co., O., b 1848,1,12
    Ch: Ellazan R. b 1871, 5, 31
        Howard
        John   " 1875, 4, 21
        Martha Mary" 1878, 10, 16; m Lemoyne
        Albert HARRIS
        Ephraim Asa b 1894, 7, 14 d 1919, 4,17
        bur Flushing
1870, 6, 1. Ephraim, s Samuel G. & Mary
    (Hoge), Belmont Co., O., b 1845,4,7 d 1887,
    5,4 bur Flushing; m in Flushing MH, Semira
    Clementine PURVIANCE, dt David & Sarah
    (Willits), b 1847,9,21
    Ch: Melva
        Willets   b 1872, 11, 13
        James Ar-
        thur   " 1874, 11, 4
1876, 5, 31. Eliza F. m Wm. L. ASHTON
1877, 11, 28. Abbie m Branson D. SIDWELL
1883, 5, 25. Martha M. m Wm. BISHOP
----, --, --. Edwin F. & Mary C.
    Ch: J. Edwin b 1885, 1, 17 d 1885, 1,17
1890, 6, 23. Deborah m Walter E. VAIL
1895, --, --. Ellazan R. m Wm. D. OLIPHANT
1900, 5, 2. Minerva W. m Geo. W. STRATTON
----, --, --. James Arthur, s Ephraim W. &
    Semira Clementine (Purviance), b 1874,11,
    4 d 19--,4,15 bur Flushing; m Anna Mary
    BRANSON
    Ch: Clement
        Purviance b 1907, 1, 17
        Joseph
        Branson   " 1911, 6, 22

1819, 6, 25. Dorothy rocf Short Creek MM, O.,
    dtd 1819,3,25
1820, 3, 24. Margaret gct Plainfield MM
1820, 8, 25. Daniel & w & ch, Jonas, James,
    Mahala, Ann, Catharine & John, recrq
1825, 2, 25. Aaron & w, Rachel, & ch, Robert,

HOLLOWAY, continued
    Smith, Asa, Elvira, Rachel, Abigail, Sam-
    uel & James, rocf Goose Creek MM, Va., dtd
    1824,11,11
1825, 5, 27. James & w, Phebe, & ch, Samuel,
    Asa & Elisha, rocf Plainfield MM, dtd
    1825,4,21
1826, 11, 24. Jonas con mcd
1826, 12, 22. David & w, Mary, & ch, Joseph &
    Asa, gct Duck Creek MM, Ind.
1827, 12, 21. Asa rmt Mary Warfield
1829, 10, 26. Abigail rmt Jason Williams
1830,   3, 25. Samuel gct Stillwater MM, to m
    Sarah Sharp
1830,   9, 23. Sarah & dt, Ann Sharp, rocf
    Stillwater MM, dtd 1830,7,24
1830, 11, 25. Catharine rmt John Nevitt
1832,   4, 26. Maria rmt Joseph Walker
1833,   8, 22. Robert S. gct New Bedford MM,
    Mass., to m Abby Taber
1833, 11, 21. David rmt Mary S. Williams
1834,   2, 20. Abby rocf New Bedford MM, Mass.,
    dtd 1834,1,23
1834,   5, 22. Robert S. & w, Abby T., gct
    Short Creek MM, O.
1835,   8, 20. John rmt Eliza Hollingsworth
1836,   9, 22. Joseph & w, Eleanor, & ch, Han-
    nah, Margaret & Nancy, gct Duck Creek MM,
    Ind.
1836,   9, 22. William, minor grandson of Jos.
    & Eleanor, gct Duck Creek MM, Ind.
1826, 12, 22. David & w, Mary, & ch, Joseph
    & Asa, gct Duck Creek MM, Ind.
1837,   6, 22. Smith gct Short Creek MM, O., to
    m Abigail Parker
1837,   9, 21. Smith gct Short Creek MM, O.
1838,   3, 22. Daniel gct Short Creek MM, O.,
    to m Mary Ann Hoge
1838,   9, 20. Robert S. & w, Abby, rocf Short
    Creek MM, O., dtd 1838,8,21
1838, 11, 22. Jonas dis mcd
1838, 11, 22. Mary Ann rocf Short Creek MM,
    O., dtd 1838,9,18
1839, 10, 24. Asa dis disunity
1839, 10, 24. Smith & w, Abigail, & s, Isaac
    Parker, rocf Short Creek MM, O., dtd 1839,
    9,24
1840, 11, 26. Elisha J. gct Plainfield MM, to
    m Lydia Vanlaw
1841,   3, 26. Lydia S. rocf Plainfield MM,
    dtd 1841,2,24
1841,   4, 22. Smith & w, Abigail, & ch, Isaac
    Parker & Elvira, gct Plainfield MM
1841,   6, 24. Joseph con mcd
1843,   9, 21. Aaron Jr. dis mcd
1843,   9, 21. Elizabeth (form Barber) dis mcd
1843, 12, 21. Dorothy & ch, Elisha, Cornelius
    B., Ann B., Samuel B., Elizabeth, Jacob &
    Sarah Jane, gct Chesterfield MM
1844,   7, 25. Elisha J. & w, Lydia, & ch,
    Phebe Louisa, gct Chesterfield MM
1845,   5, 22. Mary Randall (form Holloway) dis
    mcd

1846,   5, 21. Chalkley T. dis mcd
1846,   9, 24. Wm. W. dis mcd
1847,   1, 27. Elisha J. & w, Lydia S., & ch,
    Phebe Louisa, rocf Chesterfield MM, dtd
    1846,11,21
1847,   2, 25. Samuel S. dis mcd
1848,   8, 24. Jacob Jr. gct Salem MM, to m
    Sarah Fawcett
1849,   2, 23. Sarah F. rocf Salem MM, dtd
    1849,1,24
1849, 10, 25. Elisha & w, Lydia, & ch, Phebe
    Louisa, Mary S. & Lucinda, gct Chester-
    field MM
1852,   6, 25. Samuel G. & w, Mary, & ch,
    James, Wm., Asa & Ephraim, gct Chester-
    field MM
1853,   1, 20. James gct Vermillion MM, Ill.;
    returned 1853,8,25, not living in limits
1853,   3, 24. Mary & ch, Wm., Asa & Ephraim
    rocf Chesterfield MM, dtd 1853,2,19
1858, 11, 25. Rachel A. gct Phila. MM, Pa.
1859, 11, 24. Rebecca Lewis (form Holloway)
    dis mcd
1860,   2, 23. Sarah J. dis jG
1861,   5, 23. Robert A. dis joining M. E.
    Society
1863,   4, 23. Lindley dis
1863,   6, 25. Rebecca Ann dis mcd
1863, 10, 22. Wm. H. gct Stillwater MM, to m
    Mary Ann Frame
1863, 11, 26. Jacob A. dis military service
1864,   5, 26. Daniel dis disunity
1866,   7, 26. William C. gct Muncy MM, Pa.,
    to m Rebecca Scattergood
1867,   8, 22. Rebecca S. rocf Muncy MM, Pa.,
    dtd 1867,6,19
1868,   2, 20. Elvira gct Phila. MM, Pa.; re-
    turned 8-10 as she was leaving their
    limits
1869,   5, 20. Mary Ann F. rocf Stillwater MM,
    dtd 1869,2,27
1873,   3, 20. Rebecca Ann rst
1873,   6, 24. Eunice W. gct Hickory Grove MM,
    Ia.
1873,   9, 25. Rebecca Ann gct Hickory Grove
    MM, Ia.
1878,   9, 26. Edwin F. gct Middleton MM, to m
    Mary Cadwalader
1879,   6, 26. Mary E. rocf Middleton MM
1885, 10, 22. Chalkley C. dis disunity
1885, 11, 26. Daniel W. dis disunity
1887, 11, 24. Wm. H. & s, Emerson, gct Still-
    water MM
1888, 12, 20. Jeptha con mcd
1890,   1, 23. Jeptha gct Hickory Grove MM, Ia.
1890,   2, 20. Louisa T. dis
1893,   3, 23. Ella H. Otis (form Holloway) con
    mcd
1894,   1, 25. Mary R. Bye (form Holloway) dis
    mcd
1896,   6, 25. Charles rocf Coal Creek MM, Ia.
1896,   9, 24. Sarah C. & ch, Mabel Ann &
    Harold Lindley, rocf Stillwater MM

HOLLOWAY, continued
1898, 12, 22. Mary H. Judkins (form Holloway)
     dis mcd
1899, 6, 22. Murray S. dis mcd & enlisting in
     the Navy
1900, 7, 26. Walter dis mcd
1903, 4, 23. Charles & w, Sarah C., & ch,
     Mabel Ann, Harold Lindley & Mary Ruanna,
     gct Stillwater MM
1905, 7, 20. James Arthur gct Phila. MM, Pa.,
     to m Anna M. Branson
1910, 1, 20. Margaret W. dis disunity
1915, 4, 22. Anna M. B. & s, Clement Purvi-
     ance, rocf Phila. MM, Pa., dtd 1915,3,25
1917, 12, 20. Martha H. Harris (form Holloway)
     con mcd
1918, 6, 20. Mary C. d 1918,2,26 ae 69 (an
     elder)
1920, 1, 22. Edwin F. gct Lansdowne MM, Pa.,
     to m Elma B. Maris
1920, 8, 26. Elma B. M. rocf Lansdowne MM,
     Pa., dtd 1920,7,29
1924, 9, 25. Anna M. B. & ch, Clement P. &
     Jpseph B., gct Westown MM, Pa.
1925, 2, 26. Edwin F. & Elma B. M. gct Lans-
     downe MM, Pa.

HOOVER
1846, 12, 24. Amelia (form Fawcett) dis mcd

HOPKINS
1863, 6, 25. Sophia (form Green) dis mcd

HOSIER
1855, 6, 21. Mariah rocf Short Creek MM, O.,
     dtd 1855,5,22

HOWARD
1830, 12, 25. Charles, s John & Hannah, b

1825, 9, 23. Anna (form Cadwalader) dis mcd
1829, 6, 25. John & w, Hannah, & ch, James,
     Rachel, Abigail, Jane, Pharoby, Isaac, Jo-
     seph & John, rocf Short Creek MM, O., dtd
     1829,6,23
1831, 6, 23. John & w, Hannah, & ch, James,
     Rachel, Abigail, Jane, Pharaby, Isaac, Jo-
     seph, John & Charles, gct Short Creek MM,
     O.
HOWEL
1822, 6, 21. Dorcas (form Fawcett) dis mcd
1856, 8, 21. Mary (form Sissle) dis mcd &
     jas

HOYLE
1895, 4, 26. Alburtus L., s Wm. & Hannah,
     Phila., Pa.; m in Flushing MH, Mabel B.
     WILSON, dt Benjamin & Mary A., Belmont
     Co., O.
1867, 8, 10. Joseph L., s Thomas & ·Hannah,
     Linn Co., Ia.; m in Guernsey MH, Deborah
     T. SMITH, dt John N. & Edith H., Guernsey
     Co., O.

1868, 3, 26. Deborah T. gct Springville MM,
     Ia.
1879, 7, 26. Joseph Williams gct Short Creek
     MM, O., to m Mary E. Hoyle
1895, 10, 24. Mabel B. gct Phila. MM, Pa.

HOZIER
1862, 5, 19. Maria d

HUFF
1848, 3, 23. Samuel Branson gct Fall Creek
     MM, O., to m Sarah A. Huff

HUGHES
1835, 2, 26. Elizabeth (form Barrett) dis
     mcd

HUNT
1820, 4, 21. Joshua & w, Rachel, & ch, Sam-
     uel, Joshua, Jonathan, John, Nathan &
     Charles, gct Stillwater MM
1822, 10, 25. David con mcd
1823, 10, 24. David gct Stillwater MM
1879, 11, 20. Martha T. (form Romans) dis mcd
     & jas
1880, 9, 20. Eliza Jane Crew Hunt (form
     Nicholson) dis mcd

HURFORD
1825, 9, 23. Warden Barrett gct Short Creek
     MM, O., to m Mary Hurford

HUTTON
1837, 2, 23. Joel & w, Mary, rocf Smithfield
     MM, dtd 1836,8,--
1841, 10, 21. Joel & w, Mary, gct Smithfield
     MM

INNIS
1841, 12, 19. Isabella d bur Flushing
1841, 12, 19. Robert d bur Flushing

1818, 10, 23. Robert & w, Isabella, & dt, Im-
     lah, rocf Concord MM, Pa., dtd 1818,7,30
     end by Plainfield MM
1842, 2, 24. Emily Swallow (form Innis) dis
     mcd

JAMES
----, --, --. George & Sarah
     Ch: Edith   d 1837,11,13
         Rebecca   b 1831, 3, 31

1818, 11, 27. Evan & w, Rebecca, & ch, Hannah,
     Phebe, Jonas, Jesse & Joshua P., rocf
     Short Creek MM, O., dtd 1818,10,20
1822, 6, 21. Evan & w, Rebecca, & ch, Hannah,
     Phebe, Jonas, Jesse, Joshua P. & Mary, gct
     Short Creek MM, O.
1830, 3, 25. Sarah & ch, Hannah, Edith, Da-
     vid, Elizabeth, Samuel B. & Rachel, rocf
     Somerset MM, dtd 1829,11,30
1835, 6, 25. Hannah Martin (form James) dis

JAMES, continued
mcd
1839, 6, 20. David dis mcd
1843, 5, 25. Elizabeth gct Chesterfield MM
1843, 5, 25. Sarah & ch, Samuel B., Rachel &
Rebecca D., gct Chesterfield MM
1859, 3, 25. Rachel (form Carson) dis mcd
1874, 4, 23. David & Rachel C. rst at Coal
Creek MM, Ia., on consent of this mtg

JANUARY
1882, 3, 23. Elma P. (form Branson) dis mcd

JENKINS
1829, 6, 25. Elizabeth dis JH

JOHNSTON
1848, 3, 23. Wm. Briggs gct New Garden MM, to
m Mary Johnston

JONES
----, --, --. Isaac & Mary
Ch: Eli   b 1808, 1, 16
    Abigail   " 1810, 3, 31
    James   " 1812, 4, 1
    Jonathan   " 1815, 2, 12
    Mary   " 1817, 6, 10
    Hiram   " 1820, 1, 20
    Isaac   " 1823, 4, 21
    Joel   " 1826, 6, 15
    Asa   " 1832, 7, 23
1821, 3, 28. Hiram d bur Freeport
1838, 3, 24. Maryann, dt Eli & Sarah, b
1907, 6, 26. Lloyd Balderston, s S. Morris &
Jane C. B., Chester Co., Pa.; m in Flush-
ing MH, Luella Letitia WALKER, dt Abel &
Hannah L., Belmont Co., O.
Ch: Charles
    Walker   b 1909, 6, 29
    Helen H. " 1910, 10, 22 d 1929, 1,23
    Margaret M." 1914, 10, 18

1821, 8, 24. Joseph & w, Mary, rocf Stillwater MM, dtd 1821,7,28
1821, 9, 21. Isaac & w, Mary, & ch, Eli, Abigail, James, Jonathan & Mary, rocf Smithfield MM
1824, 12, 24. William recrq
1831, 1, 20. Amy rocf Smithfield MM, dtd
1830,10,18
1831, 11, 24. Eli rmt Sarah Miller
1832, 4, 26. Joseph & w, Mary, gct Stillwater
MM
1834, 7, 24. Eli dis disunity
1836, 2, 25. James dis mcd
1836, 6, 26. Jonathan & Mary Jr. dis disunity
1840, 2, 20. Abigail gct Salem MM, Ia.
1840, 2, 20. Isaac & w, Mary, & ch, Isaac
M. & Joel, gct Salem MM, Iowa
1840, 3, 26. Sarah & ch, Asa, Hirah & Mary
Ann, gct Salem MM, Ia.
1842, 11, 24. Hannah (form Knight) dis mcd
1919, 4, 24. Luella Walker dis jas

JUDKINS
----, --, --. James & Susanna
Ch: Jonathan b 1813, 10, 25
    Martha   " 1816, 4, 1
    Mary   " 1818, 12, 23
    Sarah   " 1821, 4, 24
    James Jr. " 1825, 3, 24
    Mariah   " 1829, 7, 27
1822, 6, 21. James dis disunity
1824, 5, 21. Susannah & ch, Jonathan, Martha,
Mary & Sarah, gct Concord MM
1831, 11, 24. Susannah & ch, Jonathan, Martha,
Mary, Sarah, James & Maria, rocf Short
Creek MM, O., dtd 1831,11,22
1838, 3, 22. Martha, Mary & Jonathan gct
Short Creek MM, O.
1838, 3, 22. Susanna & ch, Sarah, James & Maria, gct Short Creek MM, O.
1899, 1, 26. Mary H. (form Holloway) dis mcd

KEECH
1823, 7, 25. Ann (form Brewer) dis mcd

KENNARD
1836, 5, 26. Ruthanna (form Deselms) dis mcd
& jas

KING
1820, 10, 14. Jane d bur Flushing

KINSEY
----, --, --. Christopher & Mary
Ch: Sarah   b 1795, 9, 9
    John   " 1798, 8, 23
    Absolam   " 1801, 1, 21
    Nathan   " 1803, 3, 16
    Ruth   " 1805, 2, 7
    Edmund   " 1807, 3, 10
    Susannah " 1809, 3, 21
    Rachel   " 1811, 10, 8
    Mary Anne " 1814, 5, 4
    Christopher" 1817, 2, 9
    Fanny   " 1819, 12, 18
----, --, --. Richard & Sarah
Ch: Daniel D. b 1817, 1, 6
    Rees   " 1819, 1, 27
    Stephen   " 1821, 3, 1
----, --, --. John & Eleanor
Ch: Jonathan B.b 1822, 12, 14
    Samuel B. " 1824, 9, 19
----, --, --. Jesse & Naomi
Ch: Martha E. b 1823, 1, 13
    Julia E. " 1824, 5, 21
1835, 4, 4. Simeon, s Geo. & Mary, b
1844, 2, 29. George d bur Salem, O.

1820, 12, 22. Nancy rmt John Easly
1821, 12, 21. Jesse rmt Naomi Ellis
1821, 12, 21. John rmt Eleanor Bevan
1825, 1, 21. Absalom dis mcd
1825, 4, 22. Charles & w, Ann, & ch, Gillingham W. & Kinsey, rocf Short Creek MM, O.,

KINSEY, continued
    dtd 1825,2,22
1826, 3, 24. John & w, Eleanor, & ch, John
    B. & Samuel B., gct Centre MM, O.
1827, 4, 27. Ruth gct Center MM
1827, 6, 22. Christopher & w, Mary, & ch,
    Edmund, Susanna, Rachel, Mary Ann, Chris-
    topher & Fanny, gct Centre MM
1827, 12, 21. Charles dis mcd
1828, 6, 27. John dis disunity
1829, 1, 23. Sarah dis jH
1829, 6, 25. Naomi dis jH
1829, 10, 22. Richard dis disunity
1830, 10, 21. Jesse dis jH
1833, 9, 24. George & w, Mary S., & ch,
    Phebe M., Sarah Ann, Lydia W., Elizabeth
    E., Oliver C. & Lucinda, rocf Short Creek
    MM, O., dtd 1833,6,18
1834, 6, 26. Daniel dis jas
1839, 4, 25. Martha Eliza, Claudius, Richard
    & Rhoda Emeline, ch Jesse & Naomi, gct
    White Water MM, Ind.
1843, 7, 20. Rease dis mcd
1846, 1, 22. Elizabeth Maholin (form Kinsey)
    dis mcd
1846, 7, 23. Eliza (form Ridgway) dis mcd
1846, 12, 24. Mary dis disunity
1847, 5, 20. Oliver dis disunity
1847, 7, 22. Phebe, Sarah Ann & Lydia gct
    Short Creek MM, O.
1851, 11, 20. Lucinda dis

KIRK
----, --, --. Joseph & Mary
    Ch: Elizabeth b 1833, 6, 7
        James B.   " 1834, 12, 9
        Joel T.   " 1836, 4, 17
        William   " 1840, 7, 12
1840, 7, 18. Martha d bur Guernsey
1842, 3, 20. Joseph, s Wm. & Martha, Guernsey
    Co., O.; m in Guernsey MH, Phebe SMITH, dt
    George & Mary, Jefferson Co., O.

1820, 10, 27. William recrq on consent of
    Kennet MM, Pa.
1822, 7, 26. Phebe recrq
1826, 11, 24. Elisha rmt Rachel Foulke
1827, 1, 26. Rachel gct Short Creek MM, O.
1831, 1, 20. Phebe dis jH
1836, 5, 26. Joel rmt Mary Ann Smith
1836, 6, 23. Mary Ann gct Smithfield MM
1839, 6, 20. Mary recrq
1839, 6, 20. Mary & ch, Elizabeth, James B.
    & Joel T., recrq
1839, 9, 26. John Smith gct Smithfield MM, to
    m Edith Kirk
1858, 12, 23. Joel dis mcd & jas
1862, 6, 26. Elizabeth Romans (form Kirk) dis
    mcd & jG
1862, 6, 26. Joseph dis jG
1863, 12, 24. James B. dis mcd & jG
1864, 1, 21. Elvira R. (form Ridgeway) dis
    mcd

1865, 9, 21. William dis serving as a soldier
1883, 12, 20. Joseph T. dis jG

KNIGHT
----, --, --. John & Katharine
    Ch: William   b 1801, 6, 19 d 1822, 8,16
        bur Brushy Fork
        Hiram   b 1806, 7, 12
        Lydia   " 1808, 11, 26
        John B.   " 1810, 11, 3
        Catharine " 1812, 3, 3
        Joseph   " 1813, 12, 31
        Emmor   " 1815, 11, 21
        Abijah   " 1818, 5, 30
        Needham   " 1820, 2, 16
        Elizabeth " 1822, 12, 16
        Hannah   " 1824, 10, 25

1819, 8, 27. John & w & ch, Hiram, Lydia,
    John Brown, Catharine, Joseph, Immer &
    Abijah, recrq
1819, 8, 27. William recrq
1827, 1, 26. Hiram dis mcd
1828, 12, 26. John dis jH
1829, 9, 24. Catharine dis jH
1831, 6, 23. Catharine Jr. dis jH
1841, 6, 24. Elizabeth Romans (form Knight)
    dis mcd
1841, 7, 22. Joseph dis jas
1842, 11, 24. Hannah Jones (form Knight) dis
    mcd

KNOX
1848, 7, 20. Hannah (form Romans) dis mcd

KOREY
1850, 8, 22. Francina (form Stephen) dis

LANGSTAFF
1824, 10, 22. Thomas rmt Ann Farmer
1825, 2, 25. Ann & ch, Susanna, Tabitha, Jo-
    seph, Rachel & Thomas, gct Salem MM

LAUGHTON
1828, 8, 22. Isaiah Branson gct Stillwater
    MM, to m Sarah G. Laughton

LAWTON
1837, 9, 21. James & w, Susannah, rocf Penns-
    ville MM, dtd 1837,7,15
1838, 6, 21. James & w, Susannah, gct Penns-
    ville MM

LEE
1847, 9, 24. Allen T., s Samuel & Cynthia,
    Monroe Co., O.; m in Flushing MH, Amanda
    HIRST, dt Thomas & Anne, Harrison Co., O.

1848, 2, 24. Amanda T. gct Chesterfield MM

LEEKE
1827, 7, 14. Hannah Ann, dt Philip W. &
    Elizabeth, b

LEEKE, continued
1826, 5, 26. Philip W. & w, Elizabeth, rocf
    Indian Spring MM, Md., dtd 1826,4,5
1834, 11, 20. Philip W. & w, Elizabeth, & dt,
    Hanna-Ann, gct Deerfield MM

LENFESTY
1851, 5, 22. Sarah Ann (form Piggott) dis mcd

LEWIS
----, --, --. Emery & Rachel
    Ch: Mary Ann   b 1827, 3, 9
        Lorenzo   " 1828, 10, 28
        Atlantic O." 1831, 3, 6
----, --, --. Thomas & Lydia
    Ch: Hannah M. b 1828, 5, 3
        Thomas   " 1830, 6, 26
        Edward M. " 1833, 5, 19
1856, 7, 12. Anna d bur Flushing
1863, 8, 26. Abel, s Jacob & Mary, Belmont
    Co., O.; m in Flushing MH, Hannah HIRST,
    dt David & Ann, Belmont Co., O.

1821, 10, 26. Adoni, minor, rocf Alum Creek
    MM
1821, 11, 23. John rmt Jane Roberts
1822, 2, 22. Jane gct Alum Creek MM
1826, 10, 27. Thomas Jr. & w, Lydia, rocf
    Short Creek MM, O., dtd 1826,10,24
1828, 6, 27. Adoni rmt Rebeckah Wright
1828, 8, 22. Aaron & w, Rebecca H., gct
    Allum Creek MM
1829, 10, 26. Jehu rmt Hannah Foulke
1830, 2, 24. Hannah gct Allum Creek MM
1859, 11, 24. Rebecca (form Holloway) dis mcd
1863, 11, 26. Hannah gct Plainfield MM

LIGHTFOOT
1831, 11, 24. William rocf Sandy Spring MM,
    dtd 1831,10,21
1832, 6, 21. William gct Sandy Spring MM

LILLY
1826, 2, 24. Robert gct Redstone MM, Pa.

LIPSEY
1825, 1, 20. William D., s John & Ann, b
1824, 5, 21. John [Lipsy] & w, Ann, rocf
    Short Creek MM, O., dtd 1824,3,23

LUKENS
1835, 11, 26. Elizabeth & ch, Samuel B., Sa-
    rah, Ann B. & Rachel, rocf Short Creek MM,
    dtd 1835,9,22
1836, 5, 26. Margaret [Lukins] (form Cooper)
    dis mcd
1839, 8, 22. Elizabeth & ch, Samuel B., Sa-
    rah, Ann B., Rachel & Lemuel, gct Short
    Creek MM, O.

LUPTON
1830, 3, 25. Thomas Conrow gct Short Creek
    MM, O., to m Ruth Lupton

1831, 7, 21. Jonathan rmt Sarah Wood
1831, 10, 20. Rachel gct Short Creek MM, O.

McCALL
1847, 2, 25. Naomi (form Bevan) dis mcd

McCLURE
1841, 2, 25. Abel T. rocf Middleton MM, O.,
    dtd 1841,2,11

McCONNELL
1833, 4, 28. Ann [McConnal] (form Cooper)
    dis mcd
1836, 12, 22. Ann rst
1837, 2, 23. Anna gct Gunpowder MM, Va.

McGREW
1850, 10, 2. Samuel, s Nathan & Elizabeth,
    Jefferson Co., O.; m in Flushing MH, Ra-
    chel P. HOGE, dt Absalom & Rachel, Bel-
    mont Co., O., d 1854,7,16 bur Flushing
    (Samuel d 1862,7,23 bur Flushing)
1866, 1, 30. Anna, dt Geo. & Anne, d bur
    Flushing
1874, 5, 27. Eulyssus A., s Samuel C. & Ra-
    chel P., Belmont Co., O., b 1853,4,7; m
    in Flushing MH, Susan G. BRANSON, dt
    Aaron & Frances, Belmont Co., O.
1876, 3, 2. James A., s Finley W. & Rebecca,
    Jefferson Co., O.; m in Guernsey MH, Mary
    W. SMITH, dt Samuel B. & Lydia Ann,
    Guernsey Co., O.

1818, 10, 23. Rachel Williams (form McGrew)
    dis mcd
1819, 8, 27. Mary Carson (form McGrew) dis
    mcd
1825, 9, 23. Dinah Williams (form Magrew)
    dis mcd
1831, 10, 20. Sinai Conard (form McGrew) dis
    mcd
1832, 4, 26. Finley dis mcd
1840, 3, 26. Elizabeth Dixon (form McGrew)
    dis mcd
1851, 2, 20. Rachel P. gct Smithfield MM
1853, 2, 24. Samuel C. & w, Rachel P., rocf
    Smithfield MM, dtd 1853,2,21
1864, 7, 21. Elenor dis jG
1876, 11, 23. Mary W. gct Short Creek MM, O.
1884, 9, 25. Eulyssus A. dis mcd

McGUIRE
1867, 4, 25. George W., minor, recrq
1880, 5, 20. George W. dis disunity

McMILLAN
1822, 6, 21. Uriah rmt Rachel Ellis
1822, 8, 28. Rachel gct Short Creek MM, O.
1828, 7, 25. Uriah & w, Rachel, rocf Short
    Creek MM, O., dtd 1828,5,20
1836, 11, 24. Uriah & w, Rachel, gct Ver-
    million MM, Ill.

McNAMEE

----, --, --. Isaac & Margaret
 Ch: William J. b 1802, 2, 1
   Cyrus K. " 1803, 11, 10
   Hellen A. " 1806, 1, 10
   Cynthiann " 1808, 3, 4
   Isaac P. " 1813, 7, 27
   Rachel
    Cairy " 1814, 12, 20

1820, 2, 25. Mashac dis mcd
1820, 4, 21. Elias B. dis disunity
1821, 6, 22. Reuben dis disunity
1822, 8, 28. William dis disunity
1825, 2, 25. Isaac dis disunity
1826, 9, 22. Cynthia Ann rmt Wm. Marsh
1828, 9, 26. Helena rmt Hiram Pickering
1829, 1, 23. Elizabeth & Margaret dis JH
1829, 3, 27. Cyrus dis JH
1836, 11, 24. Isaac dis disunity

MAHOLIN

1846, 1, 22. Elizabeth (form Kinsey) dis mcd

MARIS

1920, 1, 22. Edwin F. Holloway gct Lansdowne
 MM, Pa., to m Elma B. Maris

MARSH

1826, 9, 22. Willaim rmt Cynthia Ann McNamee
1833, 11, 21. John rocf Smithfield MM, dtd
 1833,10,22
1833, 11, 21. Jonathan & w, Lavina, & ch,
 Hugh, Elizabeth, Jonathan, Abraham, Sarah-
 Dillin, rocf Smithfield MM, dtd 1833,10,22
1835, 9, 24. Cynthia Ann & ch, Myra Ann,
 Thaddeus & Edgar, gct Smithfield MM
1843, 3, 23. Elizabeth Engle (form Marsh) dis
 mcd
1843, 5, 25. Hugh dis jas
1843, 8, 24. Abraham dis jas
1853, 6, 23. Lavina gct Pennsville MM

MARTIN

1835, 6, 25. Hannah (form James) dis mcd
1842, 2, 24. Hannah J. rst
1850, 2, 21. Hannah dis

MAXON

----, --, --. David & Sarah
 Ch: Nathan b 1815, 4, 8
   Ira " 1816, 9, 26
   Ruth " 1818, 8, 12
   Jonathan " 1820, 6, 11
----, --, --. Nathan & Susanna
 Ch: Sarah b 1819, 12, 9
   Priscilla " 1820, 10, 27
   Lydia " 1821, 10, 28
   Alfred " 1824, 10, 16
1825, 6, 6. Jonathan d bur Freeport

1819, 5, 21. Nathan rst on consent of Plainfield MM, O.

1820, 1, 21. John dis mcd
1820, 5, 26. Susanna [Mason] (form Dew) dis
 mcd
1827, 5, 25. William dis disunity
1828, 1, 25. Sarah [Maxson] & ch, Nathan,
 Ira, Ruth, Jonathan, Stephen & Mary Hannah, gct Centre MM
1831, 6, 23. Susannah [Maxson] dis JH
1831, 7, 21. Mary dis JH
1831, 8, 25. Nathan dis JH

MEACH

1826, 11, 24. Naomi (form Carson) dis mcd

MELDROM

1848, 7, 20. Rachel (form Billingly) dis mcd

MELTON

1821, 7, --. Sarah d bur Freeport

1823, 10, 24. Moses dis jas
1841, 3, 25. Armella rocf Short Creek MM, O.,
 dtd 1841,2,23
1842, 11, 24. John rocf Short Creek MM, O.,
 dtd 1842,10,18
1846, 11, 26. Anna G. Alfred (form Melton)
 dis mcd
1848, 6, 22. John dis mcd
1852, 3, 25. Armella dis disunity
1857, 7, 23. Patience & Mary G. dis disunity

MERCHANT

1826, 9, 22. Priscilla rocf Smithfield MM,
 dtd 1826,5,19
1830, 6, 24. Priscilla gct Smithfield MM

MICHENER

1837, 2, 4. John d
1837, 11, 1. Charles, s Daniel & Ann, Guern-
 sey Co., O.; m in Guernsey MH, Lydia
 PICKERING, dt Jacob & Lydia, Harrison
 Co., O., b 1811,6,13
 Ch: Lindley H. b 1838, 11, 22
   Harriet " 1839, 12, 13
   Ezra " 1841, 10, 12 d 1842, 7,18
   bur Flushing
   Anne b 1845, 3, 12
   Charles K. " 1849, 5, 9
1837, 12, 27. Kinsey, s Daniel & Ann, Guernsey
 Co., O.; m in Guernsey MH, Rachel SMITH,
 dt Nathan & Catharine, Guernsey Co., O.
 Ch: Nathan S. b 1839, 8, 14
   Catharine S. 1842, 6, 15 d 1844, 7,18
   bur Guernsey
   Wm. Galon b 1844, 7, 15
   Lydia Ann " 1846, 12, 17
   Amy T. " 1850, 8, 14 d 1863, 9,26
   bur -----
   Elmir " 1852, 5, 7
   David H. " 1854, 5, 30
   Mary Cor-
    nelia " 1856, 9, 23
1844, 8, 16. Anne, w Daniel, d bur Guernsey

MICHENER, continued

1846, 8, 26. John, s Barak & Jane, Belmont
    Co., O.; m in Flushing MH, Sarah GARRET-
    SON, dt Nicholas & Sarah COOPER
1847, 11, --. Rebecca [Michiner] m Amos SMITH
1854, 6, --. Daniel d bur Guernsey
1860, 8, 30. Nathan, s Kinsey & Rachel,
    Guernsey Co., O.; m in Guernsey MH, Mary
    Ann BRIGGS, dt Samuel & Elizabeth, Belmont
    Co., O.
    Ch: Chas.
        Ellsworth b 1861, 6, 1 d 1862, 3, 7
          bur Guernsey
        Mary E.   b 1863, 2, 23
        Sarah Alice" 1865, 5, 14
        William   " 1867, 2, 18

1820, 4, 21. John [Mitchener] & w, Rebekah,
    & ch, Isaac & John Waterman, rocf Short
    Creek MM, O., dtd 1820,1,18
1830, 6, 24. John [Mitchner] & w, Rebeckah,
    gct Short Creek MM, O.
1835, 6, 25. Charles & Rebecca rocf Short
    Creek MM, O., dtd 1835,5,19
1835, 6, 25. Daniel & w, Ann, & ch, Kinsey,
    John L., Joseph & Rachel, rocf Short
    Creek MM, O., dtd 1835,5,19
1838, 3, 22. Rebecca gct Short Creek MM, O.
1840, 4, 23. John L. gct White River MM, Ind.
1847, 5, 20. Sarah [Mitchner] & dt, Luceta
    Garretson, gct Plainfield MM
1854, 10, 26. Charles & w, Lydia, & ch, Lind-
    ley H., Harriet, Anna & Chas. R., gct
    Red Cedar MM, Ia.
1865, 9, 21. Wm. dis serving as a soldier
1866, 8, 23. Kinsey [Mitchener] & w, Rachel,
    & ch, Elmor, David H. & Mary C., gct
    Hickory Grove MM, Ia.
1867, 7, 25. Lydia Ann [Mitchener] gct Hick-
    ory Grove MM, Ia.
1868, 10, 22. Nathan S. [Mitchener] & w, Mary
    Ann, & ch, Mary Evaline, Sarah Alice & Wm.
    Arthur, gct Hickory Grove MM, Ia.

MILHOUSE

1831, 9, 22. Jonathan Briggs gct Stillwater
    MM, to m Stephen(?) Millhouse
1871, 4, 20. David Stephen gct Pennsville
    MM, to m Anna Milhouse

MILLER

----, --, --. Mason & Ruth
    Ch: Asa   b 1800, 10, 24
        Eli   " 1802, 4, 7
        Stephen   " 1804, 5, 16
        Nathan   " 1806, 2, 15
        Sarah   " 1808, 2, 14
        Mary   " 1809, 8, 1
        Rachel   " 1811, 8, 18
        William   " 1814, 10, 23
        Thomas   " 1816, 11, 11
        Edith   " 1819, 12, 13
        Elijah   " 1822, 8, 12 d 1823, 8, 3

       bur Freeport
----, --, --. Stephen & Phebe
    Ch: Elijah   b 1828, 2, 6
        Amos   " 1833, 2, --
1852, 9, 27. Ruth d bur Freeport
1871, --, --. Rachel d
1882, 7, 28. Lydia d bur Flushing

1827, 5, 25. Stephen rmt Phebe Ross
1831, 11, 24. Sarah rmt Eli Jones
1832, 2, 23. Nathan dis mcd
1832, 3, 22. Stephen dis jH
1832, 9, 20. William dis disunity
1833, 1, 24. Richard dis mcd
1836, 9, 22. Asa & Eli dis disunity
1838, 5, 24. Mary Barthelow (form Miller) dis
    mcd
1851, 2, 20. Matilda (form Wharton) dis mcd
1864, 6, 23. Lydia & Rachel rocf Short Creek
    MM, O., dtd 1864,5,24

MILLISON

----, --, --. James & Dorothy
    Ch: Jonathan b 1815, 7, 24
        Anne   " 1816, 10, 16
        Rachel   " 1818, 1, 29
        Abigail   " 1819, 3, 14
        Abel   " 1820, 11, 4
        James   " 1823, 3, 21
        Rebecca   " 1825, 1, 23
1822, 7, 30. Rachel d bur Guernsey

1828, 8, 22. James dis disunity
1829, 7, 23. Dorothy dis jH
1836, 8, 25. Hannah Harris (form Millison)
    dis mcd
1837, 12, 21. Jonathan dis mcd
1839, 1, 24. Ann Gray (form Millison) dis mcd
1839, 10, 24. Abigail Abel (form Millison) dis
    mcd
1841, 4, 22. Abel, James, Noah & Leah, ch
    James & Dorothy, gct Salem MM, Ia.

MILTON

1840, 2, 20. Mary & dt, Anna, rocf Short
    Creek MM, O., dtd 1839,11,19
1840, 2, 20. Mary Jr. & Patience, rocf Short
    Creek MM, O., dtd 1839,11,19

MITCHELL

1840, 1, 14. Laban, s Isaac, b
1853, 4, 27. Lydia P. m Joseph EDGERTON
1862, 1, 6. Laban, s Isaac, d
1879, 4, 24. Isaac d ae 75 yr (an elder)

MOORE

1826, 2, 24. Rachel (form Chandler) dis mcd

MORRIS

1831, 12, 22. Aaron gct Stillwater MM
1833, 3, 21. Nathan rmt Tacie Parkins
1833, 4, 25. Tacy gct Stillwater MM
1833, 9, 26. Aaron rmt Phebe Parkins

MORRIS, continued
1833, 10, 24. Phebe gct Stillwater MM
1846, 3, 26. Joseph Williams gct Salem MM, to
    m Lydia Morris

MORTON
1831, 11, 24. Cassandra rocf Smithfield MM,
    dtd 1831,10,17
1832, 2, 23. Hannah rocf Smithfield MM, dtd
    1831,10,17
1834, 2, 20. Cassandra dis jH

MOTT
1878, 9, 27: Thomas E., s Richard & Sarah,
    Linn Co., Ia.; m in Guernsey MH, Martha
    BRIGGS, dt Henry & Betsy, Guernsey Co., O.

1879, 1, 23. Martha B. gct Springville MM,
    Ia.

MURRY
1867, 4, 25. Mary R. (form Woods) dis mcd

NAIL
1860, 9, 20. John M. Smith gct Plainfield
    MM, to m Lydia Nail

NAYLOR
1879, 2, 21. Ezra W., s Lewis & Rachel, Bel-
    mont Co., O.; m in Guernsey MH, Rachel E.
    STEPHEN, dt David & Eliza, Guernsey Co., O.
    Ch: Mary E.   b 1880, 4, 27

1880, 2, 26. Ezra W. rocf Stillwater MM, dtd
    1880,1,21
1889, 7, 25. Ezra W. & w, Rachel, & ch, Mary
    B., Charles B., James & Ross D., gct
    Stillwater MM

NEVITT
----, --, --. Isaac & Rachel [Nevit]
    Ch: John   b 1798, 9, 29
        Rachel   " 1806, 4, 22
        Joseph   " 1797, 7, 24
        Isaac   " 1796, 8, 28
1825, 3, 26. Isaac [Nevit] d bur Freeport
1825, 5, 7. Joseph [Nevit] d bur Freeport
1831, 5, 3. Katharine, w Jno., d bur Free-
    port
1839, 1, 13. Isaac d bur Freeport

1819, 12, 24. Isaac [Nevit] dis mcd
1820, 9, 22. Thomas & Joseph rocf Hopewell
    MM, dtd 1820,6,8
1821, 4, 27. Grace rmt Richard Ridgeway
1821, 10, 26. Thomas rmt Keziah Ridgeway
1822, 5, 24. Eliza Etherton (form Nevitt)
    dis mcd
1825, 6, 24. Isaac Jr. rst
1830, 11, 25. John rmt Catharine Holloway
1834, 2, 20. Rachel [Nevit] Jr. gct Short
    Creek MM, O.
1835, 12, 24. Thomas [Nevit] & w, Keziah, &

ch gct Spiceland MM, Ind.
1836, 12, 24. Thomas & w, Keziah, & ch, Lu-
    vina, Isaac, David, Maryann & Thomas J.,
    gct Spiceland MM, Ind.
1837, 7, 20. John [Nevit] dis mcd
1849, 9, 20. Rachel Freet (form Nevit) dis
    mcd

NIBLACK
1830, 10, 21. Sarah (form Grewell) dis mcd

NICHOLS
1837, 2, 23. John gct Duck Creek MM, Ind.
1862, 2, 20. Lydia [Nicholas] (form Romans)
    dis mcd & jG

NICHOLSON
1852, 2, 26. Charles & w, Narcissa, & ch,
    William, Benjamin C., Elizabeth, Ann Jane,
    George Edwin, Sarah Alice, John & Eliza,
    rocf Short Creek MM, O., dtd 1852,1,20
1859, 6, 23. Benjamin C. dis mcd & jG
1860, 8, 23. Charles & Narcissa dis jG
1861, 8, 22. William dis jG
1862, 9, 25. Elizabeth Ann Charnock (form
    Nicholson) dis mcd
1864, 12, 22. George Edwin dis mcd
1880, 9, 20. Eliza Jane Crew Hunt (form
    Nicholson) dis mcd
1880, 11, 25. Phebe Ann Greenfield Winrod
    (form Nicholson) dis mcd

NOCK
1826, 6, 23. Rachel & ch, Daniel C., Ezekiel
    & Rachel, rocf Duck Creek MM, Del., dtd
    1826,6,--
1826, 6, 23. William & Jane rocf Duck Creek
    MM, Del., dated 1826,6,--
1826, 8, 25. Sarah rocf Duck Creek MM, dtd
    1826,5,6
1829, 1, 23. Sarah & Rachel dis jH
1829, 7, 23. William & Daniel dis jH
1831, 6, 23. Jane dis jH
1831, 6, 23. Phebe [Knock] (form Easly) dis
    mcd
1831, 7, 21. Rachel [Knock] dis jH

NORRIS
1837, 9, 21. Jane R. rocf Guynnedd MM, Pz.,
    dtd 1837,8,3
1849, 2, 22. Jane gct Plainfield MM

OLIPHANT
1895, --, --. Wm. D., s John & Hannah P.,
    Columbiana Co., O.; m in Flushing MH,
    Ellazan R. HOLLOWAY, dt Asa G. & Hannah
    Elma, Belmont Co., O., b 1871,5,31 d 1896,
    3,26 bur Winona, O.
    Ch: Howard John b 1897, 2, 19
        Arthur G.   " 1899, 3, 26
        Beulah H.   " 1906, 7, 17
1896, 3, 26. Ellazan [Olliphant] gct New Gar-

OLIPHANT, continued
    den MM, O.

OLIVER
1824, 2, 27. Daniel & w, Esther, rocf Short
    Creek MM, O., dtd 1824,1,20
1850, 10, 24. Daniel & w, Esther, gct Still-
    water MM
1852, 3, 25. Sarah (form Wright) dis mcd
1853, 2, 24. Sarah (form Wright) dis mcd

ORR
1819, 3, 26. Ann (form Parkins) dis mcd
1837, 11, 23. Ruthanna [Ore] (form Reynolds)
    dis mcd
1852, 11, 20. Anna (form Schooley) dis mcd

OTIS
1893, 3, 23. Ella H. (form Holloway) con mcd
1897, 2, 25. Ella H. Vance (form Otis) dis
    mcd

PACKER
----, --, --. Abraham m Sarah ----- d 1867,7,
    30 bur Flushing
    Ch: Jordan   b 1832, 3, 15 d 1844, 8,21
            bur Flushing
        David   b 1835, 8, 15 " 1835, 1, 4
            bur Flushing
        Isaac   b 1838, 4, 23
        Levi   " 1845, 8, 7
1849, 6, 27. Susanna m John GILBERT
1857, 5, 23. Abraham d bur Flushing
1857, 12, 30. Isaac d

1818, 11, 27. Abijah & Mary, ch Abraham, recrq
1819, 5, 21. Abraham & w, Sarah, & ch, Abijah
    & Mary, gct Stillwater MM
1827, 6, 22. Abraham & w, Sarah, & ch, Abi-
    jah, Mary, Susanna, Levi & Eve, rocf Short
    Creek MM, O., dtd 1827,6,19
1838, 4, 26. Abijah dis mcd

PALMER
1821, 3, 23. Levick & w, Elizabeth, & ch,
    John, Mary, Samuel, Hannah, Sarah & Daniel,
    gct Duck Creek MM, Del.
1838, 11, 22. Elizabeth rst; dis by Sandy
    Spring MM, now inexistent

PARKER
----, --, --. George & Rachel
    Ch: Joseph J. b 1815, 6, 10
        Jacob Bel-
                man " 1818, 1, 14
        Lindley   " 1820, 4, 13
        Mary G.   " 1821, 12, 28
        Ezra   " 1824, 1, 4
        Rhoda D.   " 1825, 2, 15

1821, 7, 27. George & w, Rachel, & ch, Jo-
    seph Jones, Jacob Belman & Lindley, rocf
    Stillwater MM, dtd 1821,6,25

1824, 3, 26. Lydia, minor, rocf Short Creek
    MM, O., dtd 1823,9,23
1832, 4, 26. George & w, Rachel, & ch, Jo-
    seph S., Jacob B., Lindley, Mary G., Eva,
    Rhoda D., Elisha & Isaac, gct Stillwater
    MM
1832, 4, 26. Lydia gct Stillwater MM
1837, 6, 22. Smith Holloway gct Short Creek
    MM, O., to m Abigail Parker
1847, 5, 20. Eva Fisher (form Parker) dis
    mcd
1849, 2, 22. Mary Chandler (form Parker) con
    mcd

PARKINS
----, --, --. David & Lydia
    Ch: Lucinda   b 1813, 9, 28
        Mishael   " 1815, 10, 2
        Rachel   " 1817, 6, 29
        Jacob   " 1819, 6, 30
        Levi   " 1821, 6, 20
        Eliza   " 1823, 5, 23 d 1825, 3, 6
        bur Flushing
        John   b 1825, 4, 9
        Mary   " 1827, 7, 9
        Sarah J.   " 1831, 6, 20
        David   " 1833, 4, 14
----, --, --. Isaac & Nancy
    Ch: Sarah   b 1822, 8, 9
        Jesse   " 1824, 4, 30
        Jane   " 1825, 2, 11
        Louisa   " 1828, 10, 30
1878, 12, 26. Stephen d

1819, 3, 26. Ann Orr (form Parkins) dis mcd
1820, 11, 24. Isaac rmt Nancy Schooley
1823, 7, 25. Jane Edwards (form Parkins) dis
    mcd
1823, 8, 22. Stephen recrq
1824, 11, 26. Jacob dis mcd
1825, 12, 23. Tacy recrq
1826, 3, 24. Lydia Gray (form Parkins) dis
    mcd
1829, 4, 24. Isaac dis jH
1829, 6, 25. Nancy dis jH
1830, 5, 20. Phebe recrq
1833, 3, 21. Tacie rmt Nathan Morris
1833, 9, 26. Phebe rmt Aaron Morris
1838, 1, 25. David & w, Lydia, & ch, Jacob,
    Levi, John, Mary, Sarah J. & David, gct
    Chesterfield MM
1838, 1, 25. Lucinda & Rachel gct Chester-
    field MM
1838, 1, 25. Rachel gct Chesterfield MM
1838, 1, 25. Sarah, Jesse, James & Louisa,
    ch Isaac & Nancy, gct Allum Creek MM
1838, 5, 24. Rebecca (form Briggs) dis mcd
1873, 9, 25. Jonathan [Perkins] gct Chester-
    field MM

PARRY
----, --, --. John & Rachel
    Ch: Rhevanna   b 1809, 9, 16

PARRY, John & Rachel, continued
    Ch: Hannah   b 1812, 8, 27
        Thomas   " 1816, 11, 16
        Deborah   " 1814, 1, 7
        Job G.   " 1818, 8, 1
        David   " 1819, 7, 9
        Sarah Ann " 1821, 6, 18
        John   " 1825, 7, 13

1830, 9, 23. John & w, Rachel, & ch, Deborah,
    Thomas, Job, David, Sarah, John & Rachel,
    gct Stillwater MM

PARSONS
1826, 3, 23. George rmt Sophia Cope
1826, 10, 27. George & Isaac rocf Short Creek
    MM, O., dtd 1826,10,24
1826, 11, 24. Mary & dt, Hannah, rocf Short
    Creek MM, O., dtd 1826,10,24
1826, 12, 22. Israel rmt Rachel Cope
1828, 12, 26. George dis disunity
1830, 1, 21. Sophia & Rachel dis jH
1830, 4, 22. Mary dis jH
1834, 2, 20. Hannah (form Cope) dis jas
1834, 8, 21. Israel dis jH

PEARSON
1821, 8, 27. John d bur Flushing
1829, 10, 17. David, s William & Catharine, b
1830, 4, 27. Benjamin, s Thos. & Elizabeth,
    d bur Flushing

1824, 1, 23. Jesse gct Plainfield MM, to m
    Cynthia Sinclair
1824, 8, 27. Cynthia rocf Plainfield MM, dtd
    1824,5,20
1825, 2, 25. Elizabeth rmt Benjamin Smith
1831, 2, 25. William & Catharine, & ch, Ben-
    jamin, Enoch, Maryann & David, gct Deer-
    field MM
1831, 3, 24. Jesse & w, Cynthia, & ch, Thom-
    as, George & Mary Jane, gct Deerfield MM
1831, 10, 20. Mary Cole (form Pearson) dis
    mcd
1838, 7, 26. Lydia Hall (form Pearson) dis
    mcd
1851, 1, 23. Jane gct Chesterfield MM

PICKERING
----, --, --. Jacob d 1832,2,28 bur Flushing;
    m Lydia ----- d 1833,2,24 bur Flushing
    Ch: William b 1778, 12, 28
        Sarah   " 1790, 3, 30
        Abel   " 1792, 6, 10
        Joseph   " 1795, 5, 1
        Rhoda   " 1798, 3, 30
        Hannah   " 1800, 7, 5
        Mary   " 1803, 5, 19
        Rachel   " 1806, 2, 14
        Hiram   " 1809, 1, 16
        Lydia   " 1811, 6, 13
        Jacob   " 1815, 9, 3
----, --, --. Jonas & Ruth

    Ch: Abner   b 1805, 3, 9
        Abigail   " 1806, 8, 25
        Samuel   " 1807, 11, 30
        Sarah   " 1809, 4, 7
        Phebe   " 1811, 6, 30
        Jonas   " 1812, 9, 8
        Mahlon   " 1814, 6, 15
        Ruthanna " 1816, 2, 25
        Joseph   " 1818, 1, 27
        Jordan   " 1820, 5, 31
1833, 6, 11. Jonathan d bur Flushing
1837, 11, 1. Lydia m Chas. MICHENER
1840, 3, 16. Jacob d bur Gurnsey

1819, 7, 23. Joshua dis mcd
1820, 11, 24. Mary Brown (form Pickering) dis
    mcd
1822, 2, 22. Samuel & w, Phebe, & ch, Rebecca,
    James, Hiram, Esther, Susanna & Samuel,
    gct White Water MM, Ind.
1823, 6, 27. Jonas & w, Ruth, & ch, Abner,
    Abigail, Samuel, Sarah, Phebe, Jonas, Mah-
    lon, Ruthanna, Joseph & Jordan, gct White
    Water MM, Ind.
1823, 9, 26. Evan rocf Short Creek MM, O.
1824, 4, 23. Elizabeth gct Somerset MM
1826, 3, 24. Rachel Fowler (form Pickering)
    dis mcd
1828, 5, 23. Sarah rst on consent of Hope-
    well MM
1828, 9, 26. Hiram rmt Helena McNamee
1829, 7, 23. Hiram dis jH
1829, 8, 20. Helena dis jH
1832, 8, 23. Jonathan recrq
1836, 8, 25. Sarah gct Duck Creek MM, Ind.
1837, 1, 26. Elizabeth (form Whealdon) dis
    jH
1837, 5, 25. Jacob Jr. dis mcd
1877, 2, 22. Armelia rst at Chesterfield MM,
    with consent of this mtg

PICKETT
1930, 7, 24. Arthur J. Stratton gct Still-
    water MM, O., to m Edith R. Pickett

PIGGOTT
----, --, --. John & Rachel
    Ch: Mary   b 1799, 12, 29
        Rebecca   " 1801, 6, 24
        Samuel   " 1805, 1, 16
        Isaac   " 1809, 5, 29
----, --, --. John & Sarah
    Ch: John Cros-
        ley   b 1813, 3, 29
        David   " 1814, 7, 15
        Israel   " 1816, 9, 3
        Joshua   " 1818, 2, 5
        Jordan   " 1821, 1, 2
        Sarahann " 1823, 1, 1
        William   " 1824, 10, 12
1819, 3, --. Rebecca d bur Flushing

1822, 3, 22. Mary Wilkinson (form Piggot)

PIGGOTT, continued
    dis mcd
1825, 6, 24. Samuel gct Goose Creek MM, Va.
1837, 10, 28. Israel dis mcd
1846, 7, 23. Joshua dis disunity
1851, 5, 22. Sarah Ann Lenfesty (form Piggott)
    dis mcd
1855, 9, 20. Adeline (form Farmer) dis mcd

POTTS
1821, 8, 24. Samuel & w, Mary, & ch, Rebecca,
    Lindley & John, rocf White Water MM, Ind.,
    dtd 1821,7,28
1821, 10, 26. Edward gct Concord MM, to m
    Abigail Newport
1822, 3, 22. Samuel & w, Mary, & ch, Rebecca,
    Lindley & John, gct Plainfield MM
1822, 4, 26. Abigail rocf Concord MM, dtd
    1822,2,20
1823, 3, 21. Edward G. & w, Abigail, & s, Al-
    fred, gct Plainfield MM

PRICE
1830, 10, 21. Mary rocf Short Creek MM, O.,
    dtd 1830,9,21

PURVIANCE
----, --, --. David, s David & Mary (Walker),
    b 1804,4,8 d 1853,9,14 bur Flushing; m
    Sarah WILLITS, dt Ellis & Hannah (Coldren)
    b 1807,4,8 d 1889,9,5 bur Flushing
    Ch: Ellis   b 1828, 4, 6 d 1881, 8,15
        bur Flushing
        Marten Ez-
          ra b 1830, 8, 14 " 1833, 5,17
        Elvira   " 1833, 7, 1 " 1895,10,23
          bur Flushing
        Eliza   b 1835, 12, 4 " 1837, 1, 2
          bur Flushing
        Ketura H. b 1840, 4, 6 " 1907, 8,30
        Mark W.   " 1842, 5, 18 " 1844, 6, 7
        Guliann   " 1845, 7, 13
        Semira
        Clementine " 1847, 9, 21
1861, 11, 22. Elvira m Joseph BAILEY
1870, 6, 1. Semira Clementine m Ephraim
    HOLLOWAY
1874, 4, 29. Guli Ann m Joseph WILLIAMS

1831, 5, 26. David Jr. & w, Sarah, & ch, El-
    lis & Martin Ezra, rocf Smithfield MM, dtd
    1831,4,18
1834, 9, 25. David & w, Mary, rocf Smithfield
    MM, dtd 1834,5,19
1836, 5, 26. David & w, Mary, gct Smithfield
    MM

RALEY
----, --, --. Thomas & Ann
    Ch: Talitha
          Ann b 1827, 7, 28
        Robert   " 1828, 10, 3
        Sarah Jane " 1830, 11, 7

    Ch: Abner   b 1832, 11, 10
        Phebe   " 1834, 9, 1
1836, 9, 24. Thomas [Railey] d bur Freeport
1852, 4, 29. Talitha Ann m Jonathan RIDGWAY

1826, 9, 22. Asa rmt Asenath Hirst
1826, 11, 24. Thomas rmt Ann Carver
1827, 1, 26. Ann gct Short Creek MM, O.
1831, 7, 21. Thomas [Raleigh] & w, Ann, &
    ch, Tabitha, Ann, Robert & Sarah Jane,
    rocf Short Creek MM, O., dtd 1831,6,31
1854, 10, 26. Ann [Railey] & dt, Sarah Jane &
    Phebe, gct Red Cedar MM, Ia.
1854, 10, 26. Robert [Railey], minor, & Ab-
    ner, gct Red Cedar MM, Ia.

RAMSEY
1850, 5, 23. Martha (form Bevan) dis mcd

RANDALL
1845, 5, 22. Mary (form Holloway) dis mcd

RANKINS
1824, 8, 27. Martha gct Plainfield MM

RATCLIFF
----, --, --. William & Sarah
    Ch: Jesse   b 1832, 2, 29
        Elisha B. " 1833, 9, 18
        Joshua   " 1835, 11, 13 d 1838, 1,12
          bur Flushing
        Edward   b 1837, 10, 21
        Hannah   " 1840, 2, 24
        Lewis   " 1841, 12, 14
        Fleming   " 1846, 10, 17
        Mary   " 1843, 7, 1 d 1845, 2,21
          bur Flushing
----, --, --. Benjamin B. & Martha M.
    Ch: Lemuel   b 1835, 10, 23
        Sarah Ann " 1837, 10, 25
        Charles   " 1839, 9, 3
        Eliza W. " 1841, 8, 21
----, --, --. William F. m Sarah ----- d 1851,
    4,7 bur Guernsey
    Ch: Hannah
        Jane   b 1839, 1, 23
        Jacob F. " 1841, 12, 20 d 1847, 9, 7
          bur Guernsey
        John   b 1844, 3, 12
        William N. " 1846, 6, 11
        Benjamin S." 1849, 2, 28
        Sarah   "   d 1851, 4, 2
          bur Guernsey
        Lewis   " 1841,12,14
1838, 5, 2. Martha m Wm. HIBBS
1842, 4, 1. John d bur Guernsey

1830, 4, 22. Elwood rmt Mary Ellis
1830, 7, 22. Mary gct Short Creek MM, O.
1831, 6, 23. William rmt Sarah Wood
1832, 5, 24. William rocf Short Creek MM, O.,
    dtd 1832,4,--.
1834, 7, 24. Amos Hibbs gct Short Creek MM,

RATCLIFF, continued
   O., to m Elizabeth Ratcliff
1835, 6, 25. Benjamin & w, Martha, rocf Short
   Creek MM, O., dtd 1835,5,19
1835, 6, 25. John rocf Short Creek MM, O.,
   dtd 1835,4,21
1835, 11, 26. Sarah rocf Short Creek MM, O.,
   dtd 1835,10,20
1836, 11, 24. Wm. F. & w, Sarah, & ch, Isaac,
   Mary, Elizabeth & Martha, rocf Short Creek
   MM, O., dtd 1836,10,18
1837, 8, 24. Hannah rocf Short Creek MM, O.,
   dtd 1836,10,18
1837, 11, 23. Robert, minor, rocf Short Creek
   MM, O., dtd 1837,9,19
1837, 11, 23. Martha, minor, rocf Short Creek
   MM, O., dtd 1837,10,21
1843, 5, 25. Robert F., minor, gct Stillwater
   MM
1844, 11, 21. Benjamin R. & w, Martha, & ch,
   Lemuel, Sarah Ann, Chas., Eliza & John,
   gct Pennsville MM
1857, 2, 26. William dis jG
1859, 6, 23. Isaac dis jG
1859, 9, 22. Jesse dis jG
1860, 4, 26. Rebecca (form Hirst) dis mcd &
   jG
1860, 5, 26. Sarah dis jG
1860, 9, 20. Elizabeth dis jG
1861, 2, 21. Wm. F. dis jG
1861, 11, 21. Hannah dis jG
1862, 5, 22. Martha Briggs (form Ratcliff)
   dis mcd
1865, 10, 26. Elisha & Edward [Ratliff] dis mcd
   & jG

RED
1837, 11, 23. Mary rocf Smithfield MM, dtd
   1837,8,21
1839, 8, 22. Mary gct Chesterfield MM

REEVES
1829, 11, 26. John dis mcd
1842, 4, 21. Matthew [Reeve] dis disunity

REYNOLDS
1825, 7, 22. Richard B. & w, Esther, & ch,
   Jeremiah, Matilda, Susanna, Richard,
   Oliver & Reuben, rocf Short Creek MM, O.,
   dtd 1825,5,24
1829, 4, 24. Joseph Jr. dis jH
1829, 5, 22. Cyrus rocf Short Creek MM, O.,
   dtd 1829,3,24
1830, 4, 22. Siras dis disunity
1830, 6, 24. Rachel dis jH
1830, 8, 26. Joseph Jr. dis jH
1831, 6, 23. Esther dis jH
1834, 12, 25. Matilda Shepherd (form Reynolds)
   fis mcd
1835, 5, 21. Susanna dis jH
1835, 10, 22. Jeremiah dis disunity
1836, 11, 24. Mary Jane & Ruthanna rocf Short
   Creek MM, O., dtd 1836,10,18

1837, 11, 23. Ruthanna Ore (form Reynolds) dis
   mcd
1838, 5, 24. Mary Jane gct Pennsville MM
1842, 8, 25. Richard dis mcd
1842, 9, 22. Oliver, minor, gct Plainfield MM
1843, 5, 25. Esther Ann dis jas
1849, 4, 26. Reuben dis mcd & jas

RIDGEWAY
----, --, --. Thomas & Elizabeth
   Ch: Jonathan   b 1817, 8, 13
       Elizann   " 1818, 9, 23
       Aaron   " 1820, 7, 13 d 1826,12,26
       bur Freeport
       Hannah   b 1822, 6, 25
       Mary   " 1825, 2, 15
       Phebe   " 1827, 4, 3
       Anna   " 1829, 6, 13
       Elvira   " 1831, 7, 5
       Thomas El-
       wood   " 1833, 7, 15
----, --, --. John & Ruth
   Ch: Abijah J. b 1819, 3, 8
       Lydia   " 1820, 12, 10
       Daniel   " 1822, 11, 26
       Jane   " 1825, 2, 23
       Catharine " 1827, 2, 4 d 1832, 8, 9
       bur Freeport
       Richard   b 1829, 6, 10
       Ruthanna " 1831, 8, 21
       John   " 1838, 6, 28
----, --, --. Richard & Grace
   Ch: Rachel   b 1823, 7, 1
       Keziah   " 1825, 12, 31
       Joseph   " 1828, 3, 9
       John J.   " 1830, 5, 3
       Mary   " 1832, 5, 13
       Isaac   " 1834, 6, 16
1833, 6, 26. Mary d bur Freeport
1834, 12, 31. Michal [Ridgway], w Timothy, d
   bur Freeport
1835, 12, 24. Timothy d bur Freeport
1848, 6, 29. Phebe [Ridgway]m Geo. SMITH
1852, 4, 29. Jonathan [Ridgway], s Thos. &
   Elizabeth, Harrison Co., O.; m in Freeport MH, Talitha Ann RALEY, dt Thomas &
   Ann, Harrison Co., O.
1854, 4, 21. Anna [Ridgway] m Elwood SPENCER

1821, 4, 27. Richard rmt Grace Nevitt
1821, 10, 26. Keziah rmt Thomas Nevitt
1822, 9, 27. Lavina dis disunity
1834, 5, 22. John [Ridgway] & w, Ruth, & ch,
   Abijah, Lydia, Daniel, Jane, Richard,
   Ruth Anna & John, gct Milford MM, Ind.
1838, 8, 23. Richard [Ridgway] & w, Grace, &
   ch, Rachel, Kezia, Joseph, John, Johnson,
   Isaac & Michal, gct Westfield MM
1844, 7, 25. Jonathan [Ridgway] dis mcd
1846, 7, 23. Eliza Kinsey (form Ridgway) dis
   mcd
1850, 2, 21. Mary [Ridgway] gct Alum Creek MM
1854, 10, 26. Jonathan & w, Tabitha Ann, & ch,

RIDGEWAY, continued
    Elizabeth Ann, gct Red Cedar MM, Ia.
1862, 11, 20. Thomas & Elizabeth dis jG
1864, 1, 21. Elvira R. Kirk (form Ridgeway)
    dis mcd
1868, 7, 23. Thomas Elwood dis jG

ROBERTS
----, --, --. Aaron & Elizabeth
    Ch: Jesse   b 1801, 11, 21
        Esther   " 1803, 2, 6
        Sarah   " 1804, 11, 13
        Reuben   " 1806, 7, 1
        Jane   " 1808, 8, 11
        Aaron   " 1810, 9, 14
        Mary   " 1812, 10, 17
        Anna   " 1814, 8, 11
        Amos   " 1816, 5, 13 d 1830, 5,13
            bur Flushing
        Elizabeth b 1818, 6, 2
        Beulah   b 1820, 5, 4
        Joseph   " 1822, 12, 27
        Lydia   " 1825, 1, 26
----, --, --. Lydia, dt Jacob BRANSON, w
    Jesse, d bur Flushing

1821, 11, 23. Jane rmt John Lewis
1822, 7, 26. Ann recrq
1824, 3, 26. Aaron & w, Elizabeth, & ch,
    Jesse, Esther, Sarah, Reuben Lundy, Jane,
    Aaron, Mary, Anna, Amos, Elizabeth, Beulah
    & Joseph, rocf Muncy MM, dtd 1824,1,21
1829, 5, 22. Ann dis jH
1833, 4, 25. Reuben L. gct Allum Creek MM
1833, 5, 23. Jane rmt Stacy Bevans
1833, 11, 21. Jesse rmt Lydia Branson
1838, 5, 24. Jesse & dt, Rebecca, gct Plain-
    field MM
1838, 5, 24. Aaron & w, Elizabeth, & ch, Beu-
    lah, Joseph & Lydia, gct Plainfield MM
1838, 5, 24. Sarah, Esther, Elizabeth Jr. &
    Anna, gct Plainfield MM
1839, 4, 25. Aaron gct Short Creek MM, O., to
    m Matilda Farquhar
1839, 4, 25. Mary gct Plainfield MM
1839, 10, 24. Aaron Jr. gct Chesterfield MM
1841, 12, 23. Elizabeth, Lydia & Elizabeth
    Jr. rocf Redstone MM, Pa., dtd 1841,11,3

ROCKWELL
----, --, --. Edward & Martha
    Ch: Edith M. b 1897, 3, 14
        Mary Moore" 1899, 3, 26
        Gertrude
            Ellen " 1901, 6, 17
        Harvey
        Rockwell " 1905, 11, 15
        Alfred Ed-
            ward " 1907, 5, 3
        Elizabeth " 1913, --, --
        Ruth   " 1919, 4, 27

1895, 11, 24. Edmund H. Conrow gct Paulina

MM, Ia., to m Martha M. Rockwell

ROGERS
----, --, --. Joseph m Pamela ----- d 1822,4,
    13
    Ch: Joseph   b 1806, 1, 19
        Susannah " 1808, 1, 1
        Lydia   " 1811, 9, 30
        Elijah   " 1813, 7, 12
        Maryann   " 1816, 3, 27
----, --, --. Samuel & Sarah
    Ch: Lewis   b 1814, 5, 16
        Rachel   " 1816, 4, 26
        Susannah B" 1818, 4, 28
        Thomas   " 1820, 6, 21
        Thomas 2nd" 1822, 12, 18
        Rowland   " 1825, 5, 2
1822, 4, 13. Thomas d

1818, 11, 27. Mary rocf Hopewell MM, dtd
    1818,1,8
1820, 3, 24. Joseph & w, Pamela, & ch, Joshua,
    Susanna, Lydia, Elijah & Mary Ann, recrq
1820, 6, 23. Samuel & w, Sarah, & ch, Lewis,
    Rachel, Thos. & Susanna, recrq
1828, 12, 26. Joseph dis jH
1829, 10, 22. Joseph Jr. dis mcd
1831, 6, 23. Sarah & Lydia dis jH
1832, 8, 23. Samuel dis jH
1834, 1, 23. Elijah & Lewis dis jas
1834, 2, 20. Rachel & Susanna dis jH

ROMANS
----, --, --. Evan & Mary
    Ch: Thomas   b 1819, 1, 15
        Hannah   " 1821. 8, 26
1821, 9, 3. Hannah d
1822, 7, 24. Mary d bur Guernsey
----, --, --. Evan m Tacy SMITH
    Ch: George   b 1824, 12, 18 d 1828,10, 7
            bur Guernsey
        Tamar   b 1827, 3, 9 " 1835,11,24
            bur Guernsey
        Jordan   b 1828, 12, 29 " 1845, 1, 14
            bur Guernsey
        Phebe   b 1831, 8, 4
        Evan D.   " 1834, 2, 10
        Lydia   " 1836, 5, 27
----, --, --. Jacob & Mary
    Ch: Hannah H. b 1827, 12, 12
        William   " 1833, 2, 20
        Valentine " 1834, 9, 15
        Joseph   " 1836, 1, 21
1841, 5, 19. Hannah d bur Guernsey
1845, 1, 26. Susan W., w Thomas, d bur
    Leatherwood
1860, 10, 6. Hannah d bur Guernsey

1818, 12, 25. Evan & w, Mary, & ch, Jane &
    Mary, rocf Bradford MM, Pa., dtd 1818,10,
    7 end by Plainfield MM
1818, 12, 25. Hannah rocf Bradford MM, Pa.,
    dtd 1818,10,7 end by Plainfield MM

ROMANS, continued
1818, 12, 25. Moses & ch, Mary Ann, Robert,
     Lydia, Elisha, Hannah & Moses, rocf Brad-
     ford MM, Pa., dtd 1818,10,7 end by Plain-
     field MM
1822, 1, 25. Hannah recrq
1824, 3, 27. Evan rmt Tacy Smith
1828, 12, 26. Moses dis jH
1829, 5, 22. Lydia & Mary Ann dis jH
1830, 2, 24. Ann recrq
1830, 7, 22. Ann rmt Job Briggs
1832, 12, 20. Jacob & w, Mary, & dt, Hannah,
     recrq (Mary rst)
1833, 5, 23. Jane rmt Wm. Briggs
1834, 3, 20. Robert dis jH
1836, 9, 22. Elisha & Moses dis jH
1841, 6, 24. Elizabeth (form Knight) dis mcd
1842, 4, 21. Thomas J. gct Stillwater MM
1843, 1, 26. Jacob dis disunity
1844, 12, 26. Thomas J. & w, Susan H., rocf
     Stillwater MM, dtd 1844,9,28
1845, 5, 22. Thomas J. gct Stillwater MM
1845, 7, 24. Mary gct Stillwater MM
1848, 7, 20. Hannah Knox (form Romans) dis
     mcd
1850, 10, 24. Wm. dis jas
1859, 1, 20. Evan & Tacy dis jG
1862, 3, 20. Evan D. dis mcd & jG
1862, 3, 20. Mary dis jas
1862, 6, 26. Elizabeth (form Kirk) dis mcd &
     jG
1863, 6, 26. Phebe S. dis jG
1863, 6, 25. Joseph dis mcd & military ser-
     vice
1879, 11, 20. Mary P. dis jas
1879, 11, 20. Martha T. Hunt (form Romans)
     dis mcd & jas

ROSS
1822, 10, 25. Elizabeth Seward (form Ross) dis
     mcd
1827, 5, 25. Phebe rmt Stephen Miller
1829, 1, 23. Elizabeth dis jH

RUSSELL
1878, 7, 12. Samuel d bur Flushing

1854, 9, 21. Samuel recrq

SARGENT
1844, 2, 22. Martha (form Crosley) dis mcd

SCHOLES
1824, 3, 26. Susanna (form Hollingsworth) dis
     mcd

SCHOLFIELD
1833, 8, 22. Rachel rocf Hopewell MM, Va.,
     dtd 1833,6,5
1838, 7, 26. Daniel Williams gct Stillwater
     MM, to m Martha Scholfield
1850, 7, 25. John [Schofield] rocf Vermillion
     MM, dtd 1850,6,1

1858, 7, 22. John G. gct Chesterfield MM

SCHOOLEY
----, --, --. Phineas & Mary
     Ch: Mahlon   b 1820, 11, 3
         Samuel   " 1822, 5, 14
         Isaac Ever-
              ett   " 1823, 5, 11
         Asenath   " 1825, 4, 2 d 1848, 3,16
           bur Guernsey
         Addison   b 1827, 4, 4
         Leah   " 1829, 1, 17
         Sarah   " 1830, 11, 13
         Ann   " 1833, 10, 9
         George W.   " 1836, 4, 6
         William   " 1838, 6, 16
         Ebenezer W." 1840, 11, 28
         Susan   " 1844, 1, 22
1820, 11, 16. Mahala d bur Guernsey
1822, 6, 20. Samuel d bur Guernsey
1845, 3, 8. Mary D., dt Geo. & Anne Walker,
     d bur Guernsey

1819, 12, 24. Phinehas rmt Mary D. Walker
1820, 11, 24. Nancy rmt Isaac Parkins
1823, 9, 26. Samuel dis mcd
1828, 5, 23. Isaac dis disunity
1828, 12, 26. Sarah dis jH
1829, 2, 27. Phineas & Sarah Jr. dis jH
1848, 8, 24. Addison dis disunity
1848, 11, 23. Isaac E. gct Gilead MM
1848, 11, 23. Sarah dis disunity
1849, 2, 23. Leah dis disunity
1852, 11, 20. Anna Orr (form Schooley) dis mcd

SCOTT
1861, 3, 21. Elizabeth (form Bevans) dis mcd

SEARS
1843, 6, 7. Paul, s Peter & Ann, Belmont Co.,
     O.; m 1843,6,7 in Guernsey MH, Abigail
     HOLLOWAY, dt Robert & Rebecca, Guernsey
     Co., O., d 1912,7,6 bur Flushing
     Ch: Rebecca   b 1845, 1, 1
           bur Friends Cemetery, Pasadena, Cal.
         Anne   b 1846, 9, 9
           bur Flushing
         Robert S.   b 1851, 3, 15 d 1930,10,29
           bur Fr. Cem., Pasadena, Cal.
         Rachel T.   b 1851, 3, 15
1849, 11, 28. Benjamin, s Peter & Anna, Bel-
     mont Co., O.; m in Guernsey MH, Esther
     BRIGGS, dt Samuel & Phebe, Belmont Co., O.

1843, 9, 21. Abigail gct Stillwater MM
1845, 8, 21. Paul & w, Abigail, & dt, Rebec-
     ca, rocf Stillwater MM, dtd 1845,7,26
1850, 2, 21. Esther S. gct Stillwater MM
1902, 4, 24. Rebecca gct ND MM
1906, 8, 23. Rebecca rocf ND MM
1912, 7, 25. Abigail d 1912,7,6 ae 88 (an
     elder)
1930, 7, 24. Rebecca d 1930,1,25 ae 85 (an

SEARS, continued
          elder)

SEWARD
1822, 10, 25. Elizabeth (form Ross) dis mcd

SHAMEL
1838, 6, 21. Rachel (form Gruell) dis mcd

SHARP
1830, 5, 19. Martha, dt Sarah, d bur Flushing
1839, 3, 27. Ann m Ephraim WILLIAMS

1830, 9, 23. Ann, dt Sarah Holloway, rocf
        Stillwater MM
1832, 1, 26. Samuel F. rocf Stillwater MM,
        dtd 1831,12,24
1835, 2, 26. Samuel T. dis mcd

SHEPHERD
1834, 12, 25. Matilda (form Reynolds) dis mcd

SIDWELL
1848, 11, 29. Israel, s Elisha & Elizabeth,
        Belmont Co., O.; m in Flushing MH, Rachel
        BRANSON, dt Smith & Jane, Belmont Co., O.
1877, 11, 28. Branson, s Israel & Rachel B.,
        Belmont Co., O.; m in Flushing MH, Abbie
        HOLLOWAY, dt Jacob & Sarah F., Belmont
        Co., O., b 1850,4,7
        Ch: Edwin H.   b 1878, 9, 15
            Dallas J.   " 1880, 5, 23
            William T. " 1882, 4, 23
            Mary   " 1883, 3, 23
            Wilson   " 1884, 11, 5
            Edith   " 1887, 1, 16
            Albert   " 1889, 3, 11
            Anna E.   " 1892, 5, 1
            Florence   " 1893, 12, 22

1822, 7, 26. Thomas rmt Elizabeth Foulke
1822, 8, 28. Elizabeth rocf Stillwater MM
1849, 4, 26. Rachel gct Short Creek MM, O.
1880, 9, 23. Branson D. rocf Short Creek
        MM, O., dtd 1880,7,20
1898, 1, 20. Branson D. & Abbie H. & ch, Ed-
        win H., Dallis J., Mary, Wilson, Edith
        Albert B., Anna E. & Florence, gct Spring-
        ville MM, Ia.

SINCLAIR
1821, 4, 27. Eden dis

SISSLE
1856, 8, 21. Mary Howel (form Sissle) dis mcd
        & jas

SMART
1849, 5, 2. Deborah m Robert S. HOLLOWAY

1849, 3, 23. Deborah rocf Salem MM, N. J.,
        dtd 1849,2,28
1852, 8, 26. Ruth rocf Salem MM, N. J., dtd

1852,7,28
1855, 8, 23. Ruth gct Salem MM

SMITH
----, --, --. Nathan & Catharine
        Ch: Samuel B. b 1811, 9, 5
            Mary Ann   " 1813, 6, 5
            John M.   " 1815, 4, 6
            Rachel   " 1817, 9, 3
            Lydia   " 1820, 2, 13
            Amy T.   " 1822, 8, 16
            Achasah R. " 1825, 3, 18
            Nathan   " 1827, 11, 17
            Catharine B." 1830, 3, 23
----, --, --. John W. & Alice
        Ch: Allen   b 1812, 2, 22
            Elizabeth " 1814, 9, 24
            Mary   " 1817, 8, 28
            Eleanor   " 1820, 2, 11
            Sarah Ann " 1821, 8, 3
            Thomas Wil-
              kinson   " 1823, 10, 11
----, --, --. William & Huldah
        Ch: George B. b 1813, 12, 19
            Josiah   " 1816, 3, 7
            Amos   " 1819, 9, 29
----, --, --. Samuel & Elizabeth
        Ch: Mariam B. b 1818, 4, 11
            John W.   " 1820, 2, 15 d 1821, 8,22
              bur Guernsey
            Achsah   b 1822, 2, 22
            William   " 1823, 10, 4 d 1827, 8,22
              bur Guernsey
            Israel   b 1825, 9, 1
            Elisha   " 1827, 7, 22
            Joshua   " 1829, 5, 18
            Rebecca   " 1832, 1, 9
            Samuel   " 1834, 3, 12
----, --, --. Amos m Anne ----- d 1845,2,13
        bur Guernsey
        Ch: Pearson   b 1818, 8, 8
            William   " 1819, 10, 29 d 1819,11,18
              bur Guernsey
            Mary   b 1820, 9, 25
            Jane   " 1822, 6, 29
            George   " 1823, 10, 7
            Jesse P.   " 1825, 2, 25
            Phebe   " 1826, 12, 16
            Isaac   " 1828, 8, 1
            Lewis   " 1829, 7, 12
            Hannah J. " 1831, 8, 5
            Lydia P.   " 1835, 7, 16
            Rachel   " 1837, 6, 3
1818, 8, 30. D---- d bur Guernsey
1820, 2, 12. Eleanor d bur Flushing
1820, 5, 7. William d bur Guernsey
1820, 9, 28. Lydia d bur Guernsey
1821, 8, 19. Isaiah d bur Guernsey
1822, 8, 11. George d bur Guernsey
----, --, --. Benjamin & Elizabeth
        Ch: Lydia   b 1825, 12, 6
            Martha   " 1829, 10, 6
            Tacy   " 1827, 8, 26

SMITH, Benjamin & Elizabeth, continued
    Ch: Abraham   b 1831, 8, 28
        Mary Jane " 1834, 2, 8
        Candace   " 1836, 10, 28
        Anne   " 1839, 8, 13 d 1845,10,24
            bur Guernsey
        William P.b 1846, 8, 12
----, --, --. George & Elizabeth G.
    Ch: William G.b 1831, 4, 4
        Samuel R. " 1833, 3, 19
        Mary Ann   " 1836, 8, 14 d 1846,11,13
            bur Guernsey
1837, 12, 27. Rachel m Kinsey MICHENER
----, --, --. John M. d 1876,6,28 bur Guern-
    sey; m Edith R. -----
    Ch: Deborah T. b 1840, 8, 19
        William K. " 1843, 3, 28
        Catharine L." 1845, 3, 21
        Elwood Thom-
            as " 1846, 11, 17
        Lemuel   " 1851, 4, 29
1840, 4, 1. Mary m Francis DAVIS
1841, 10, 27. Miriam B. m John THOMAS
1842, 3, 20. Phebe m Joseph KIRK
1842, 8, 20. Jane d bur Guernsey
----, --, --. Samuel B. & Lydiann
    Ch: Louisa P. b 1847, 9, 18
        Amy T.   " 1849, 6, 19
        Morris C.   " 1850, 9, 8
        Mary W.   " 1853, 6, 14
        Joshua Wal-
            ter " 1858, 1, 14
1847, 11, --. Amos, s George & Mary, Guernsey
    Co., O.; m in Guernsey MH, Rebecca MICHEN-
    ER, dt Daniel & Anna, Guernsey Co., O.
1847, 12, 1. Achsah R. m ----- BUNDY
1847, 12, 1. Amy T. m Pearson THOMAS
1848, 6, 29. George, s Amos & Anna, Guernsey
    Co., O.; m in Freeport MH, Phebe RIDG-
    WAY, dt Thomas & Elizabeth, Harrison Co.,
    O.
    Ch: Francis D. b 1849, 9, 20
1850, 4, 2. Mary, dt Wm. & Ruth Hibbs, d bur
    Guernsey
1854, 4, 26. Hannah J. m David STANTON
1854, 6, 28. Wm. G., s Geo. & Elizabeth G.,
    Guernsey Co., O.; m in Guernsey MH, Mary
    Ann THWAITE, dt James & Mary Ann, Guernsey
    Co., O.
    Ch: Mary Jane b 1855, 4, 20
1857, 4, 30. Rebecca W. m Demsey BUNDY
1863, 9, 29. Achsah m Aaron FRAME
1867, 8, 10. Deborah T. m Joseph L. HOYLE
1872, 9, 27. Catharine L. m Morris STANLEY
1875, 1, 22. Amy T. m Thos. E. STANLEY
1876, 3, 2. Mary W. m Jas. A. McGREW
----, --, --. George K. & Anna
    Ch: Elbert J. b 1879, 3, 2
        Edgar T.   " 1880, 3, 29 d 1882,12,10
            bur Guernsey
        Ethel C.   b 1884, 3, 10
        Eva M.   " 1889, 2, 10 " 1890, 2,18
            bur Guernsey

        Ch: Mary R.   b 1890, 6, 1
            Iva D.   " 1900, 3, 22
1883, 9, 26. Nathan R., s John W. & Maria,
    Jefferson Co., O.; m in Flushing MH,
    Lizzie M. BRANSON, dt David & Sarah H.,
    Belmont Co., O., b 1862,1,14
1884, 9, 26. Samuel B., s Nathan & Catharine,
    Guernsey Co., O.; m in Guernsey MH, Rebec-
    ca BRIGGS, dt Henry & Betsy, Guernsey Co.,
    O.
1887, 10, 26. Samuel C., s Sinclair & Tacy,
    Belmont Co., O.; m in Flushing MH, Sarah
    Elma BAILEY, dt Joseph & Elvira P., Bel-
    mont Co., O., b 1865,1,27
1892, 8, 31. Catharine, w Samuel B., d bur
    Guernsey

1819, 6, 25. Geo. Jr. dis mcd
1820, 8, 25. Nathan & ch, Samuel, Mary Ann,
    John, Rachel & Lydia, recrq
1821, 8, 24. Jacob & w, Martha, & ch, Anna,
    Letitia, Nathan, Gulielma, Mary, Ezra,
    Samuel & James, gct White Water MM, Ind.
1823, 11, 21. George rst
1824, 3, 27. Tacy rmt Evan Romans
1824, 7, 23. Huldah dis
1825, 2, 25. Benjamin rmt Elizabeth Pearson
1825, 8, 26. Elizabeth G. recrq
1828, 12, 26. John W. dis jH
1829, 1, 23. Alice dis jH
1832, 6, 21. George B. dis disunity
1832, 12, 20. Elizabeth dis jH
1835, 1, 22. Mary (form Smith) dis mcd
1836, 5, 26. Mary Ann rmt Joel Kirk
1838, 1, 25. Wilkinson & Sarah Ann, ch Alice,
    gct Plainfield MM
1838, 8, 23. Samuel B. gct Smithfield MM
1839, 9, 26. John M. gct Smithfield MM, to
    m Edith Kirk
1839, 12, 26. Amos Jr. dis mcd
1840, 1, 23. Edith K. rocf Smithfield MM, dtd
    1839,12,23
1841, 10, 21. Pearson gct Short Creek MM, O.,
    to m Mary P. Hall
1842, 4, 21. Pearson gct Short Creek MM, O.
1843, 5, 25. Samuel B. rocf Smithfield MM,
    dtd 1843,4,17
1845, 10, 23. Samuel B. gct Smithfield MM, to
    m Lydia B. Wood
1846, 4, 23. Lydiann rocf Smithfield MM, dtd
    1846,2,23
1847, 8, 28. Mary Jane (form Ellis) dis mcd
1848, 6, 22. John M. & w, Edith R., & ch,
    Deborah T., Wm. R., Catharine & Elwood,
    gct Smithfield MM
1848, 7, 21. John W. rocf Stillwater MM, dtd
    1848,7,22
1848, 10, 26. Maria H. rocf Short Creek MM,
    O., dtd 1848,9,19
1849, 1, 25. Nathan Jr. gct Short Creek MM,
    O.
1849, 6, 21. Jesse P. dis mcd
1849, 8, 23. Lydia Hibbs (form Smith) dis mcd

SMITH, continued

1850, 8, 22. John W. & w, Maria H., gct Short Creek MM, O.

1851, 1, 23. Benjamin & w, Elizabeth P., & ch, Abraham, Mary Jane, Candace & Wm. P., gct Pleasant Plain MM, Iowa

1851, 1, 23. Tacy & Martha gct Pleasant Plain MM, Ia.

1852, 4, 22. Nathan & w, Catharine, gct Short Creek MM, O.

1852, 4, 22. Catharine B. gct Short Creek MM, O.

1852, 5, 20. John M. & ch, Deborah T., Wm. K., Catharine L., Elwood Thomas & Lemual K., rocf Smithfield MM

1852, 6, 24. Elisha gct Spring Creek MM, Iowa

1852, 9, 23. Sarah (form Wright) dis mcd

1853, 7 21. Israel gct Three Rivers MM, Iowa

1854, 1, 26. Joshua gct Red Cedar MM, Ia.

1854, 2, 23. George Jr., Phebe R. & ch, Francis D. & Amos, gct Three Rivers MM, Ia.

1854, 5, 25. Isaac gct Three Rivers MM, Ia.

1854, 11, 23. Lewis rpd mcd

1859, 3, 24. George dis jG

1859, 4, 21. Lydia Hibbs (form Smith) dis mcd

1860, 6, 21. Amos, Elizabeth G. & Rebecca M. dis jG

1860, 9, 20. John M. gct Plainfield MM, to m Lydia Nail

1861, 2, 21. Lydia rocf Plainfield MM, dtd 1861,1,23

1861, 7, 25. Thamor dis jG

1861, 12, 26. Samuel R. dis mcd & jG

1862, 3, 20. Mary Ann dis jG

1862, 3, 20. Samuel B. dis jG

1864, 8, 25. Samuel & w, Elizabeth, gct Stillwater MM

1866, 7, 26. William R. dis jG

1869, 3, 25. Louisa P. Spaulding (form Smith) dis mcd

1869, 11, 25. Lindley M. Hoge gct Concord MM, Pa., to m Martha C. Smith

1872, 6, 20. Elwood gct Springville MM, Ia.

1876, 2, 24. Lemuel gct Springville MM, Ia.

1878, 2, 21. George K. gct Stillwater MM, to m Anna Doudna

1878, 5, 23. George K. gct Stillwater MM

1878, 11, 21. Mary Jane Day (form Smith) dis mcd

1879, 2, 20. Lydia gct Springville MM, Ia.

1882, 1, 26. Morris C. gct Springville MM, Ia.

1882, 3, 23. Joel K. dis mcd

1882, 6, 22. George K. & w, Ann, & ch, Elbert J. & Edgar, rocf Stillwater MM, dtd 1882,5,24

1882, 9, 21. Catharine S. rocf Short Creek MM, O., dtd 1882,9,19

1884, 1, 24. Joshua W. gct Plymouth MM, to m Eva Irene Fowler

1884, 10, 23. Lizzie M. gct Short Creek MM, O.

1885, 12, 24. Joshua W. gct Springville MM, Ia.

1887, 6, 23. Rebecca gct Salem MM

1887, 11, 24. Samuel dis disunity

1888, 2, 23. Sara Elma gct Stillwater MM

1888, 6, 21. Harvey W. dis mcd

1891, 7, 23. Murray L. dis jas

1897, 4, 22. Mark con mcd

1901, 1, 24. Walter dis mcd & jas

1902, 6, 26. Ethel C. gct Salem MM, O.

1904, 1, 21. George K. dis disunity

1904, 2, 25. Anna D. & ch, Mary R., Ella T. & Eva D., gct Salem MM, O.

1927, 2, 24. Stanley W. Stratton gct Short Creek MM, O., to m Marjorie A. Smith

SPAULDING

1869, 3, 25. Louisa P. (form Smith) dis mcd

SPENCER

1854, 4, 21. Elwood, s Geo. & Eunice, Mahaska Co., Ia.; m in Freeport MH, Anna RIDGWAY, dt Thomas & Elizabeth, Harrison Co., O.

1832, 1, 26. George, minor, rocf Stillwater MM, dtd 1831,12,24

1833, 12, 26. George gct Stillwater MM

1837, 5, 25. Elizabeth gct Duck Creek MM, Ind.

1854, 7, 20. Anna gct Spring Creek MM, Ia.

SPURRIER

1832, 6, 21. Ann (form Barrett) dis mcd

STANLEY

1872, 9, 27. Morris, s Samuel & Mary, Linn Co., Ia.; m in Guernsey MH, Catharine L. SMITH, dt John M. & Edith, Guernsey Co.,O.

1875, 1, 22. Thomas E., s Samuel W. & Mary, Linn Co., Ia.; m in Guernsey MH, Amy T. SMITH, dt Samuel B. & Lydia, Guernsey Co., O.

1875, 6, 24. Amy F. gct Springville MM, Ia.

STANTON

1852, 6, 3. David, s James & Rachel, Belmont Co., O.; m in Freeport MH, Martha WILSON, dt Israel & Catharine, Harrison Co., O., d 1852,12,27 bur Stillwater David m 2nd 1854,4,26 in Guernsey MH, Hannah J. SMITH, dt Amos & Anna, Guernsey Co., O.

1853, 7, 21. Daniel rocf Stillwater MM, dtd 1853,6,25

1882, 1, 26. Henry & Mary rocf Stillwater MM, dtd 1881,12,24

19-3, 12, 24. Henry & w, Mary, gct Stillwater MM, O.

STEER

1857, 4, 29. Nathan, s James & Ann, Belmont

STEER , Nathan, continued
    Co., O.; m in Flushing MH, Mary Jane BRAN-
    SON, dt Smith & Jane, Belmont Co., O.
    Ch: Alzie Jane b 1858, 5, 23
        Abby Loret-
                ta " 1860, 7, 31

1819, 8, 27. James rmt Ruth Wilson
1857, 10, 22. Nathan rocf Short Creek MM, O.
1862, 4, 24. Nathan & w, Mary Jane & ch, Al-
    zie Jane & Abbie Loretta, gct Short Creek
    MM, O.

STEPHEN
1845, 4, 30. Elizabeth [Steven] (nee Schooley)
    m Samuel BRIGGS
1845, 10, 1. David, s Zachariah & Elizabeth,
    Harrison Co., O.; m in Guernsey MH, Eliza
    BRIGGS, dt Samuel M. & Phebe, Harrison
    Co., O., d 1866,10,1 bur Guernsey
    Ch: Wilson   b 1847, 2, 11
        Abigail   " 1848, 11, 28
        Barclay   " 1852, 3, 12
        Mary Jane   " 1854, 6, 19
        Rachel Es-
            ther   " 1860, 1, 18
1872, 5, 3. Eliza M., dt David & Anna, b
1879, 2, 21. Rachel E. m Ezra W. NAYLOR
1880, 7, 25. Anna M., w David, d bur "near
    Guernsey MH"
1889, 8, 29. Mary J. m Thomas C. COPE
1892, 8, 26. Eliza M. m James E. GIBBONS

1843, 8, 24. David [Stephens] rocf Short
    Creek MM, O., dtd 1843,7,18
1843, 8, 24. Elizabeth [Stephens] & ch,
    Silas & Sarah, rocf Short Creek MM, O.,
    dtd 1843,7,18
1843, 8, 24. Catharine [Stephens] rocf Short
    Creek MM, O., dtd 1843,7,18
1844, 2, 22. Catharine Clay (form Stephens)
    dis mcd
1844, 7, 25. Francina [Stephens] rocf Ches-
    terfield MM, dtd 1844,6,15
1849, 12, 20. Sylas dis mcd
1850, 8, 22. Francina Korey (form Stephen)
    dis
1854, 5, 25. Sarah Ellis (form Stephens) dis
    mcd
1854, 7, 20. Samuel [Stephens] gct Red Cedar
    MM, Ia.
1855, 5, 24. David [Stephens] & w, Elizabeth,
    & ch, Wilson, Abigail, Barclay & Mary Jane,
    gct Stillwater MM
1861, 7, 25. David & w, Elizabeth, & ch,
    Wilson, Abigail, Barclay, Mary Jane, Ra-
    chel & Esther, rocf Stillwater MM
1867, 7, 25. Wilson dis joining M. E. Society
1868, 3, 26. Abigail dis jas
1871, 4, 20. David gct Pennsville MM, to m
    Anna Milhouse
1872, 1, 25. Anna M. [Stevens] rocf Penns-
    ville MM, dtd 1871,12,14

1872, 11, 21. Mary Jane [Stephens] dis jas
1876, 3, 23. Mary Jane [Stephens] rst
1883, 10, 25. David gct Chesterfield MM, to m
    Sarah Todd
1884, 3, 20. Sarah T. [Stephens] rocf Ches-
    terfield MM, dtd 1884,2,16
1892, 9, 22. David gct Stillwater MM

STEWART
1833, 5, 23. Rebecca (form Haines) dis mcd

STOTZ
1829, 12, 24. Margaret dis jH

STRAHL
----, --, --. Thomas & Martha
    Ch: Anne   b 1799, 9, 16
        Hannah   " 1801, 7, 18
        Joseph   " 1803, 6, 15
        Rebecca   " 1805, 12, 2
        William   " 1808, 12, 1
        Jane   " 1811, 1, 25
        Jesse   " 1813, 11, 8
        Lavisa   " 1815, 9, 16
1818, 12, --. Anna m Henry CARVER

1825, 4, 22. Thomas & w, Martha, & ch, Han-
    nah, Joseph, Rebecca, William, Jane,
    Jesse & Lavisa, gct Plainfield MM
1831, 6, 23. Elmer rocf Somerset MM, dtd
    1831,4,25
1835, 10, 22. Elmer gct Pennsville MM

STRATTON
1847, 1, --. Michael Jr., s Daniel & Abigail,
    Mahoning Co., O.; m in Flushing MH, Mar-
    tha WILLIAMS, dt Joseph & Mary, Belmont
    Co., O.
1853, 5, 27. Barclay, s Daniel & Abigail,
    Columbiana Co., O.; m in Flushing MH, Han-
    nah HOBSON, dt Joseph & Ruth, Belmont Co.,
    O.
----, --, --. Charles, s Benj. & Ellen (Stan-
    ley), b 1854,2,5; m Mary F. FRENCH, dt
    David & Eliza (Hole), b 1858,3,12
    Ch: Benjamin
        Laurance b 1891, 2, 12 (or 1891,3,
        12)
        Albert C.
1900, 5, 2. George W., s John F. & Dorothy
    (Hobson), Belmont Co., O., b 1876,9,12;
    m in Flushing MH, Minerva W. HOLLOWAY,
    dt Ephraim W. & Semira Clementine (Pur-
    viance), b 1872,11,13
    Ch: Arthur
        John   b 1901, 2, 3
        William
        Ashton   " 1902, 12, 12
        Stanley
        Willitts   " 1904, 10, 29
        Howard
        Ephraim   " 1907, 1, 18
        Charles

STRATTON, George W. & Minerva W., continued
       Abram   b 1909, 4, 29
----, --, --. Stanley Willits, s George W. &
    Melva W. (Holloway; m Marjorie Anna SMITH,
    dt Thos. & Rachel (Dewees), b 1905,5,--
    (Stanley b 1904,10,29)
      Ch: James Edward b 1930, 12, 26
         Eleanor Lou-
              ise " 1933, 5, 22
1932, 6, 4. Wilmer Joseph, s Arthur J. &
    Edith (Pickett), b

1830, 12, 23. Sina, minor, rocf Salem MM, dtd
    1830,10,20

1838, 4, 26. Sina gct Salem MM
1847, 2, 25. Martha W. gct Salem MM
1853, 8, 25. Hannah H. gct Salem MM
1869, 8, 26. Joseph H. Branson gct New Gar-
    den MM, to m Ruthanna Stratton
1880, 11, 25. Charles rocf New Garden MM,
    dtd 1880,10,21
1889, 7, 25. Charles gct Stillwater MM
1890, 5, 22. Mary F. rocf Salem MM
1892, 5, 26. George W., s Dorothy S. Ashton,
    rocf New Garden MM
1912, 2, 22. Charles & w, Mary, & ch, Benja-
    min Laurance & Albert Clifton, gct Bir-
    mingham MM, Pa.
1927, 2, 24 Stanley W. gct Short Creek MM,
    O., to m Marjorie A. Smith
1927, 6, 23. Marjorie A. rocf Short Creek
    MM, O., dtd 1927,6,21
1930, 7, 24. Arthur J. gct Stillwater MM, O.,
    to m Edith R. Pickett
1932, 9, 22. Howard E. gct Short Creek MM, O.,
    to m Mabel Whinery

STREET
1827, 3, 23. Baldwin Barrett gct Short Creek
    MM, O., to m Mary Ann Street

SWALLOW
1842, 2, 24. Emily (form Innis) dis mcd

SWAYNE
1825, 1, 21. Rebecca rocf Fairfax MM, Va.,
    dtd 1824,9,15
1826, 8, 25. Joshua rocf Fairfax MM, Va.,
    dtd 1826,7,12
1827, 1, 26. Eliza & dt, Mary Ann, rocf
    Plainfield MM, O., dtd 1826,12;21
1829, 1, 23. Joshua dis disunity
1829, 9, 24. Eliza dis jH
1830, 5, 20. Rebeckah dis jH
1833, 12, 26. Thomas Hirst gct Short Creek MM,
    O., to m Mary Swayne

TABER
1833, 8, 22. Robert S. Holloway gct New Bed-
    ford MM, Mass., to m Abby Taber

TALBOTT
----, --, --. John & Rachel
    Ch: Susannah C.b 1815, 3, 27
       Mary   '" 1817, 2, 7
       David B. " 1820, 8, 8

1821, 5, 25. John & w, Rachel, & ch, Su-
    sanna, Mary & David, rocf Plainfield MM,
    dtd 1821,5,24
1835, 6, 25. John [Talbot] & w, Rachel, &
    ch, David B., gct Adrian MM, Mich.
1835, 6, 25. Susanna C. & Mary S. gct Adrian
    MM, Mich.

TAYLOR
1825, 9, 23. Joseph rocf Plainfield MM, dtd
    1825,6,23

THOMAS
1841, 10, 27. John, s Peter & Mary, Harrison
    Co., O.; m in Guernsey MH, Miriam B.
    SMITH, dt Samuel & Elizabeth, Guernsey
    Co., O.
    Ch: Samuel S. b 1842, 8, 15
       Rebecca " 1844, 2, 6
       William " 1845, 4, 6
       Lydia H. " 1847, 1, 25 d 1847, 6,12
         bur Freeport
       Pearson b 1848, 4, 3
1847, 12, 1. Pearson, s Peter & Mary, Harri-
    son Co., O.; m in Guernsey MH, Amy T.
    SMITH, dt Nathan & Catharine, Guernsey
    Co., O.
1850, 8, 28. Amy T. m David HALL

1832, 12, 20. John gct Cincinnati MM
1842, 3, 24. Miriam B. gct Short Creek MM, O.
1843, 8, 24. John & w, Miriam B., & ch, Sam-
    uel T., rocf Short Creek MM, O., dtd
    1843,6,20
1848, 2, 24. Amy T. gct Short Creek MM, O.
1849, 11, 22. Amy T. rocf Short Creek MM, O.,
    dtd 1849,8,21
1853, 3, 23. John & w, Mariam B., & ch, Sam-
    uel T. S., William, Pearson, Elizabeth &
    Mary, gct Red Cedar MM, Ia.

THOMSON
1836, 7, 21. Aaron Frame gct Short Creek MM,
    O., to m Tabitha [Thompson]
1839, 6, 20. Mary rocf Chesterfield MM, dtd
    1839,5,18
1841, 5, 20. Samuel B. rocf Chesterfield MM,
    dtd 1841,4,17
1841, 6, 24. Samuel B. & w, Mary, gct Short
    Creek MM, O.
1842, 2, 24. Samuel B. & w, Mary, gct Short
    Creek MM, O.

THWAITE
----, --, --. James & Mary Ann
    Ch: Isabel   b 1844, 2, 14
       James T. " 1846, 9, 17

THWAITE, James & Mary Ann, continued
    Ch: Lucy   b 1849, 9, 10
        Jane   " 1851, 8, 2
        John   " 1853, 9, 17
1854, 6, 28. Mary Ann m Wm. G. SMITH

1843, 7, 20. James & w, Mary Ann, & ch, Ed-
    ward, Mary Ann, Sopia, Maria & Amelia, rocf
    Smithfield MM, dtd 1843,7,17
1851, 12, 25. Richard rocf Preston MM, Eng-
    land, dtd 1850,11,7, end by Cincinnati
    MM, O., 1851,8,21
1853, 12, 22. Richard gct Preston MM, Lanca-
    shire, Eng.
1856, 4, 24. Edward [Thwait] dis mcd
1861, 8, 22. James [Thwait] dis jG
1864, 7, 21. Isabella dis
1876, 3, 23. James dis mcd
1877, 1, 23. Lucy Gregg (form Thwaite) dis
    mcd
1878, 1, 24. Jane dis disunity

TODD
1883, 10, 25. David Stephen gct Chesterfield
    MM, to m Sarah Todd

TOMLINSON
1847, 7, 22. Elizabeth rocf Somerset MM, dtd
    1847,4,26

TOWNSEND
1821, 3, 23. Levi rocf Short Creek MM, O.,
    dtd 1821,3,20
1821, 10, 26. Ruth & dt, Guli Ann, rocf Alum
    Creek MM
1822, 12, 27. Ruth & dt, Julia Ann, gct Still-
    water MM
1824, 2, 27. Levi & w, Mary, & ch, Elizabeth
    & Eli, gct Somerset MM
1826, 6, 23. Jesse Bailey gct Middleton MM,
    O., to m Lydia Townsend

TRIGG
1831, 3, 24. John recrq
1833, 8, 22. John rmt Mary Fawcett
1834, 9, 25. John & Nancy dis
1857, 1, 22. Nancy rst
1869, 2, 25. Nancy dis

UPDEGRAFF
1820, 10, 14. Eliza, niece of Jane King, d
    bur Flushing

VAIL
1890, 6, 23. Walter E., s John & Abigail,
    Belmont Co., O.; m in Flushing MH, Debo-
    rah HOLLOWAY, dt Jacob & Sarah F., Bel-
    mont Co., O.

1890, 9, 20. Deborah H. gct Chester MM, N. J.

VANCE
1897, 2, 25. Ella H. (form Otis) dis mcd

VANHORN
1827, 2, 23. Elizabeth rocf Smithfield MM,
    dtd 1826,10,23
1828, 10, 24. Elizabeth gct Short Creek MM, O.

VANLAW
1832, 3, 25. Ann d bur Flushing
1833, 8, 6. Joseph H., s Thos. & Anne, d

1825, 5, 27. Ann & ch, Rebecca, Joseph &
    Thomas Elwood, rocf Plainfield MM, dtd
    1825,4,21
1832, 12, 20. Rebecca rmt Wm. C. Williams
1840, 11, 26. Elisha J. Holloway gct Plain-
    field MM, to m Lydia Vanlaw
1840, 11, 26. Thomas E. gct Plainfield MM, to
    m Amy Branson
1841, 3, 25. Thomas E. gct Chesterfield MM

VANPELT
1831, 5, 26. Sarah gct Fall Creek MM
1839, 9, 26. Elisha Hoge gct Fall Creek MM,
    to m Lydia Vanpelt

VERNON
1827, 3, 23. Theodate rocf Short Creek MM,
    O., dtd 1827,2,20
1828, 7, 25. Theodate gct Deerfield MM

WALKER
1815, 12, 21. Anna, dt George & Anna, b
1817, 11, 13. George d bur Guernsey
1822, 8, 5. Isaac E. d bur Guernsey
----, --, --. Joseph, s Abel & Mary (Branson)
    b 1803,2,21 d 1877,11,7 bur Flushing; m
    Maria HOLLOWAY, dt Wm. & Martha (Bye)
    WARFIELD; Maria m 1st 1827,11,18 Asa
    Holloway; Maria b 1807,10,7 d 1898,5,28
    bur Flushing
    Ch: Daniel   b 1835, 8, 28 d 1911,12,27
               bur Flushing
        Rebecca   b 1837, 6, 10 d 1848, 3,22
               bur Flushing
        Deborah   b 1839, 2, 17 " 1921, 8,10
               bur Flushing
        Eliza H.   b 1843, 1, 3 " 1844, 8,14
               bur Flushing
        Lewis T.   b 1844, 8, 16 d 1908, 4, 8
               bur Flushing
        Abel   b 1849, 6, 7
----, --, --. Isaac & Lydia
    Ch: William b 1841, 4, 21
        Miriam   " 1843, 1, 25
        Israel   " 1844, 4, 15
1843, 9, 20. Mary d bur Flushing
1844, 6, 19. Anna d bur Guernsey
1853, 12, 28. Martha H. m Lindley M. HOLLOWAY
----, --, --. Abel, s Jos. & Maria, b 1849,6,7;
    m Hannah L. FRENCH, dt Samuel & Mary J.,
    b 1851,9,15
    Ch: Bertha M. b 1878, 10, 12; m James W.
        EDGERTON
        Luella L. " 1880, 5, 3; m Lloyd B.

WALKER, Abel & Hannah, continued
    JONES
        Ch: Joseph S. b 1887, 4, 3 d 1887, 9,30
            bur Flushing
            Julia M. b 1887, 4, 3 " 1887, 8, 1
            bur Flushing
            James
            French b 1889, 11, 1
1905, 12, 22. Bertha Mary m Jas. W. EDGERTON
1907, 6, 26. Luella Letitia m L. B. JONES

1819, 12, 24. Mary D. rmt Phinehas Schooley
1820, 9, 22. Jesse, minor, rocf Westland MM,
    Pa., dtd 1820,7,27
1820, 11, 24. Martha rmt Jonas Bye
1824, 7, 23. Ebenezer & w, Hannah, & ch,
    Thomas & Tacy, gct Short Creek MM, O.
1825, 7, 22. Aaron rq to be mbr Westland MM,
    Pa.; consent given but Aaron dec mean-
    while
1828, 9, 26. Lewis B. gct Redstone MM, Pa.,
    to m Tamson Haines
1828, 11, 21. Tamson rocf Redstone MM, Pa.,
    dtd 1828,10,29
1829, 3, 27. Jesse gct Short Creek MM, O.
1829, 9, 24. Eliza rmt William Foulke
1830, 5, 20. Lewis B. & w, Tamson, & s, Eli,
    gct New Garden MM
1832, 1, 26. Stacy & Samuel, minors, rocf
    Short Creek MM, O., dtd 1831,10,18
1832, 4, 26. Joseph rmt Maria Holloway
1832, 6, 21. Joseph & Maria gct Smithfield
    MM
1837, 2, 23. Isaac gct New Garden MM
1837, 5, 25. Joseph & w, Maria, & ch, Martha
    & Daniel, rocf Smithfield MM, dtd 1837,5,
    22
1841, 11, 25. Isaac & w, Lydia N., & s, Wil-
    liam, rocf Upper Springfield MM, dtd 1841,
    10,23
1843, 5, 25. Tacy gct Chesterfield MM
1844, 2, 22. Winifred (form Barrett) dis mcd
1845, 9, 25. Samuel T., minor, gct Short
    Creek MM, O.
1846, 12, 24. Isaac & w, Lydia, & ch, William,
    Miriam, Israel & Eliza Ann, gct Chester-
    field MM
1856, 11, 20. Anne M. Gwoir (form Walker) con
    mcd
1869, 4, 23. Lewis dis mcd
1876, 10, 26. Abel gct Salem MM, to m Hannah
    L. French
1878, 6, 20. Hannah rocf Salem MM, dtd 1878,
    5,22
1878, 6, 20. Joseph d 1877,11,7 (an elder)
1882, 12, 21. Daniel dis mcd
1916, 5, 25. James F. gct Haddonfield MM,
    N. J., to m Alice M. Bell
1917, 5, 24. James F. gct Haddonfield MM, N.J.
1924, 2, 21. Abel & Hannah L. gct Birmingham
    MM, Pa.

WALTON
1886, 7, 28. James, s Samuel & Sarah J.,
    Belmont Co., O.; m in Flushing MH, Annie
    L. BRANSON, dt Jacob & Juliann H., Bel-
    mont Co., O., b 1859,2,6 d 1888,4,15 bur
    Stillwater
1888, 4, 11. Anna S. d bur Stillwater

1887, 4, 21. Annie L. gct Stillwater MM

WARFIELD
1806, 11, 7. Mary Bye d

1827, 12, 21. Mary rmt Asa Holloway
1835, 8, 20. John dis mcd

WATERMAN
1825, 11, 14. Leannah, dt Isaac & Ann, b

1824, 11, 26. Isaac gct Short Creek MM, O.,
    to m Ann Hurford
1825, 4, 22. Ann rocf Short Creek MM, O.,
    dtd 1825,3,22
1828, 6, 27. Isaac & w, Ann, & ch, Hannah &
    Rebeckah, gct Short Creek MM, O.
1838, 3, 22. John gct Short Creek MM, O.

WATSON
1830, 7, 22. Matthew & w, Ann M., & ch,
    Grace, Ann Jane & John, rocf Smithfield
    MM, dtd 1830,5,17
1833, 5, 23. Matthew & w, Ann, & ch, Grace,
    John & Phebe, gct Smithfield MM
1844, 2, 22. Rebecca (form Crosley) dis mcd

WEBSTER
1837, 5, 25. Hannah & ch, Jesse, Isaac, Sa-
    rah, rocf Little Britain & Nottingham MM,
    dtd 1837,3,10
1838, 5, 24. Hannah & ch, Jesse, Isaac & Sa-
    rah, gct Pennsville MM

WELDON
1832, 4, 26. Mary Ann (form Grewell) dis mcd
1842, 6, 23. Tabitha [Wheldon] dis disunity

WELLS
1822, 5, 24. Isaac & w, Susanna, & ch, Jo-
    siah, William, Levi, Moses & Jonathan,
    gct Concord MM

WHARTON
----, --, --. Joel & Abigail
    Ch: Martha b 1820, 10, 3
        Rachel " 1823, 10, 31
        Josiah Bun-
            dy " 1825, 9, 4
        Delitha Ann" 1828, 2, 3
        Matilda " 1830, 5, 1
        Ezra " 1833, 6, 21
        Abigail B. " 1835, 7, 1 d 1836,10, 8
        bur Freeport

WHARTON, Joel & Abigail, continued
    Ch: Susanna   b 1838, 10, 8
1872, 3, 11. Abigail d bur Guernsey
1867, 5, 2. Talitha Ann m Henry BRIGGS

1828, 2, 22. Abigail & ch, Martha, Rachel,
    Josiah, rocf Short Creek MM, O., dtd 1828,
    1,22
1839, 7, 25. Bethia rocf Short Creek MM, O.,
    dtd 1839,2,19
1840, 6, 21. Bethia Derry (form Wharton) dis
    mcd
1848, 2, 24. Josiah dis mcd
1849, 10, 25. Tabitha Ann gct Short Creek MM,
    O.
1851, 2, 20. Matilda Miller (form Wharton)
    dis mcd
1867, 3, 21. Talitha Ann rocf Short Creek MM,
    O., dtd 1867,2,19
1872, 6, 20. Ezra dis mcd
1872, 9, 26. Susanna Coventry (form Wharton)
    dis mcd

WHEALDON
----, --, --. Isaac & Elizabeth
    Ch: Ann   b 1806, 1, 4
        John   " 1808, 12, 20
        Isaac   " 1809, 10, 5
        Nathan   " 1811, 5, 6
        Joseph   " 1813, 8, 2
        Elizabeth " 1815, 12, 16
        Ruth   " 1818, 1, 16
        Tabitha " 1820, 3, 7

1826, 9, 22. Nathan & w, Ann, & ch, Rachel,
    Alfred, Isaac & Meriba, rocf Short Creek
    MM, O., dtd 1826,9,19
1828, 12, 26. Isaac dis jH
1829, 1, 23. Elizabeth dis jH
1829, 3, 27. Nathan dis jH
1829, 4, 24. John dis mcd
1829, 9, 24. Ann dis jH
1831, 7, 21. Nathan & Isaac Jr. dis disunity
1832, 4, 26. Rachel & Ann dis jH
1832, 5, 24. Mary Ann (form Grewell) dis mcd
1836, 2, 25. Joseph dis disunity
1836, 12, 22. Elizabeth & Ruth dis jH
1837, 1, 26. Elizabeth Pickering (form Wheal-
    don) dis jH
1837, 2, 23. Isaac dis jH

WHERRY
1854, 5, 25. Sarah (form Hollingsworth) dis
    mcd
1869, 10, 21. Rachel (form Green) dis mcd &
    jG

WHINERY
1832, 9, 22. Howard E. Stratton gct Short
    Creek MM, O., to m Mabel Whinery

WICKERSHAM
1858, 3, 26. David, s Thomas & Ann, Columbi-

ana Co., O.; m in Guernsey MH, Rebecca B.
HOLLOWAY, dt Robert & Rebecca, Guernsey
Co., O.

1858, 8, 26. Rebecca gct Middleton MM

WILKINSON
1822, 3, 22. Mary (form Piggot) dis mcd
1833, 7, 25. Mary rocf Hopewell MM, Va., dtd
    1833,6,5
1840, 6, 25. George R., minor, rocf New Gar-
    den MM, Pa., dtd 1840,5,6
1845, 7, 24. George R. dis mcd
1852, 6, 24. Mary gct Spring Creek MM, Iowa

WILLIAMS
----, --, --. Joseph m Mary ----- d 1844,2,4
    bur Flushing
    Ch: Jasen   b 1808, 7, 5
        William C. " 1810, 3, 16
        Mary T.   " 1812, 1, 23
        Daniel   " 1813, 7, 13
        Hannah C. " 1817, 11, 29
        Eliza   " 1820, 10, 26 d 1844,11,11
          bur Flushing
        Martha   b 1822, 12, 21
----, --, --. Jason & Abigail
    Ch: Sarah   b 1830, 8, 17
        Hannah   " 1832, 6, 23
        Joseph H. " 1834, 8, 19
        Mary Ellen " 1836, 6, --
1832, 5, 6. Hannah, dt Jas. & Mary, d
----, --, --. Wm. C. m Rebecca ----- d 1874,4,
    1, bur Flushing
    Ch: Mary Ann b 1833, 9, 3
        Phebe H. " 1835, 4, 30
        Elizabeth " 1837, 4, 15
        Catharine " 1838, 12, 13
        Rachel G. " 1841, 9, 17
        Amy B.   " 1843, 12, 22 d 1860, 1,21
          bur Flushing
        Joseph Johnb 1847, 1, 10
        Thomas E. " 1848, 11, 19
        Lydia M. " 1854, 10, 15
----, --, --. Daniel, s Joseph & Mary, b 1813,
    7,13 d 1896,6,1; m Martha S. ----- d 1853,
    4,12 bur Flushing
    Ch: Mary   b 1839, 8, 12 d 1877, 2,19
          bur Flushing
        Edith S. b 1841, 8, 13 " 1883, 8, 9
          bur Flushing
        Cidney
        Eliza   b 1843, 11, 9 " 1871,12,14
          bur Flushing
        Joseph   b 1845, 10, 16
        Jonathan " 1848, 9, 22 " 1864, 1,13
          bur Flushing
        Jason   b 1852, 9, 24 " 1853, 4, 7
          bur Flushing
        Daniel   " 1877, 2,19
          bur Flushing
Daniel m 2nd Hannah COOK, dt T. & H., b
1827,6,5 d 1868,2,22 bur Flushing

WILLIAMS, continued

1839, 3, 27. Ephraim, s Daniel & Jane, Belmont Co., O.; m in Flushing MH, Ann SHARP,
dt Jeptha & Sarah, Belmont Co., O.

1847, 1, --. Martha m Michael STRATTON, Jr.

1858, 10, 22. Phebe H. m Lewis W. BYE

1874, 4, 29. Joseph, s Daniel & Martha S.,
Belmont Co., O.; m in Flushing MH, Guli
Ann PURVIANCE, dt David & Sarah W., Bel-
mont Co., O., b 1845,7,13 d 1877,4,11 bur
Flushing

1877, 4, 11. Clement P., s Joseph & Gulie A.,
b

1877, 4, 11. Clement P. d bur Flushing

1882, 5, 23. Sidwell, s Branson D. & Abbie, d
bur Flushing

----, --, --. Joseph m Mary E. HOYLE
Ch: Ernest Dan-
iel b 1883, 9, 7 d 1922, 3,25
bur Flushing
Myrtle El-
vira b 1886, 8, 16

1818, 10, 23. Rachel (form McGrew) dis mcd

1818, 11, 27. Joseph & w, Mary, & ch, Jason,
Wm. C., Mary S., Daniel & Hannah, rocf
Uwchlan MM, Pa., end by Stillwater MM

1825, 9, 23. Dinah (form Magrew) dis mcd

1829, 10, 26. Jason rmt Abigail Holloway

1831, 11, 24. Grace (form Hollingsworth) dis
mcd

1832, 12, 20. Wm. C. rmt Rebecca Vanlaw

1833, 11, 21. Sarah S. rmt David Holloway

1836, 9, 22. Jason & w, Abigail, & ch, Sarah, Hannah, Joseph & Mary Ellen, gct
Duck Creek MM, Ind.

1838, 7, 26. Daniel gct Stillwater MM, to m
Martha Scholfield

1839, 1, 24. Martha rocf Stillwater MM, dtd
1838,12,22

1839, 7, 25. Ann gct Stillwater MM

1846, 3, 26. Joseph gct Salem MM, to m Lydia
Morris

1846, 12, 24. Lydia M. rocf Salem MM, dtd
1846,11,25

1848, 5, 25. Joseph & w, Lydia M., gct Short
Creek MM, O.

1849, 11, 22. Wm. C. & w, Rebecca, & ch, Mary
Ann, Phebe H., Elizabeth, Catharine, Rachel, Amy B., Joseph John & Thomas Elwood,
gct Plainfield MM

1854, 8, 24. Daniel gct New Garden MM, Pa.,
to m Hannah Francena Cook

1855, 1, 25. Hannah Francena rocf New Garden
MM, Pa., dtd 1854,12,6

1857, 6, 25. Phebe H. & Catharine rocf Plainfield MM, dtd 1857,4,22

1857, 6, 25. Wm. C. & w, Rebecca, & ch, Rachel, Amy, Joseph, John & Lydia M., rocf
Plainfield MM, dtd 1857,5,20

1863, 2, 26. Rachel dis

1866, 5, 24. Wm. C. dis jG

1866, 6, 21. Rebecca dis jG

1867, 9, 26. Catharine dis jG

1871, 7, 20. Daniel gct Chesterfield MM, to
m Lydia Ann Fawcett

1871, 12, 21. Lydia Ann & dt, Jeptha Anna
Fawcett rocf Chesterfield MM, dtd 1871,11,
18

1873, 9, 25. Wm. C. & Rebecca rst

1875, 2, 25. Wm. C. & Lydia H. gct Chesterfield MM

1879, 7, 26. Joseph gct Short Creek MM, O.,
to m Mary E. Hoyle

1880, 2, 26. Mary Eliza rocf Short Creek MM,
O., dtd 1880,1,20

WILSON

----, --, --. Israel m Martha ----- d 1825,3,
6 bur Freeport
Ch: Ruth b 1794, 10, 20
William " 1895, 11, 22 (sic) (?)
Edith " 1897, 3, 7 (") (?)
John " 1799, 1, 5
Hannah " 1800, 12, 2
David " 1802, 12, 3
Rachel " 1805, 3, 29
Israel " 1807, 6, 9
Jonathan " 1809, 8, 12
Susan " 1811, 6, 26 d 1840,--,--
bur Flushing
Martha b 1813, 4, 9
Joseph " 1815, 3, 24 " 1871, 6,17
bur Guernsey

----, --, --. John & Amelia
Ch: Edith b 1823, 10, 13
Mary " 1825, 2, 5

----, --, --. Israel Jr. & Catharine
Ch: William b 1828, 10, 28
Martha " 1830, 6, 23
Elisha " 1832, 7, 19 d 1857,10, 1
bur Freeport
Jane b 1834, 8, 16 " 1858,12,11
bur
Ann Eliza " 1836, 10, 6
Mary H. " 1838, 9, 19 " 1858, 4, 9
bur
Rachel D. " 1841, 6, 28
Israel J. " 1843, 8, 12
Joseph D. " 1845, 8, 7

----, --, --. Joseph, s Israel & Martha,
b 1815,2,3 d 1871,6,17; m Eliza BRANSON,
dt John & Abigail (Holloway), b 1813,5,26
Ch: Abigail B. b 1838, 10, 18 d 1860, 1,21
bur Guernsey
Lindley b 1840, 9, 10
Martha Ann " 1842, 2, 16 d 1886,10,21
bur Flushing
Deborah b 1843, 12, 3 " 1911, 8,18
bur Harrisville; m Josiah HALL
Maria b 1846, 1, 31 " 1886, 2,22
bur Smyrna, O.; m Thomas COPE
Benjamin b 1849, 10, 11
Miriam " 1851, 9, 8 d 1879, 4,21

1841, 3, 13. Lindley, s Jas. & Eliza, d bur
Guernsey

WILSON, continued
1852, 6, 3. Martha m David STANTON
1852, 11, 12. Israel d bur Flushing
----, --, --. William & Esther
    Ch: Charles   b 1853, 11, 29
       Francis   " 1855, 11, 14
       Levi Faw-
         cett   " 1858, 1, 29
1856, 12, 23. Anne, w Israel, d bur Flushing
1865, 2, 24. Deborah m Josiah HALL
----, --, --. Benjamin, s Joseph & Eliza (Branson), b 1849,10,11 d 1910,6,23 bur Flushing; m Mary Ann FRENCH, dt John & Martha
   (Ogden), b 1853,9,14 d 1911,11,5
    Ch: Joseph   b 1874, 6, 22
       Mabel B.   " 1876, 2, 27; m Albertus
        HOYLE
       George J.   " 1878, 12, 11
       John French " 1886, 4, 15
1876, 9, 22. Maria m Thos. C. COPE
1886, 10, 21. Martha A. d bur Flushing
1895, 4, 26. Mabel B. m Alburtus L. HOYLE

1818, 10, 23. Sarah rocf Sadsbury MM, Pa., dtd
   1818,9,8 end by Plainfield MM
1819, 8, 27. Ruth rmt James Steer
1821, 12, 21. John gct Plainfield MM, to m
   Amelia Foulke
1822, 4, 26. Amelia rocf Plainfield MM, dtd
   1822,3,21
1823, 9, 26. Hannah rmt Nathan Hall
1824, 11, 26. Rachel rmt Nathan P. Hall
1826, 11, 24. David rmt Esther Barrett
1827, 12, 21. Israel Jr. rmt Catharine Davis
1827, 12, 21. John C. & w, Amelia, & ch,
   Edith, Mary & Ann, gct Milford MM, Ind.
1829, 1, 23. Sarah dis JH
1830, 4, 22. Israel rmt Ann Davis
1831, 8, 25. Ann (form Brock) dis mcd
1833, 2, 21. David & w, Esther, & ch, Margaret, Isaac & Amy, gct Duck Creek MM, Ind.
1833, 6, 20. Jonathan gct Duck Creek MM, Ind.
1835, 7, 23. Ann (form Brock) rst at Somerset on consent of this mtg
1836, 4, 21. Martha rmt Robert Hall
1837, 5, 25. Joseph rmt Eliza Branson
1838, 6, 21. John Hirst gct Short Creek MM,
   O., to m Maria Wilson
1852, 9, 23. Wm. C. gct Salem MM, to m Esther Fawcett
1853, 5, 26. Esther rocf Salem MM, dtd 1853,
   4,20
1861, 5, 23. Israel & w, Catharine, & ch, Israel & Joseph D., gct Stillwater MM
1861, 5, 23. Rachel D. & Ann Eliza gct Stillwater MM
1861, 11, 21. William C. & w, Esther, & ch,
   Charles, Frances & Levi F., gct Stillwater MM
1873, 8, 21. Benjamin gct Salem MM, to m
   Mary A. French
1875, 11, 25. Mary A. rocf Salem MM, dtd
   1875,10,20

1889, 1, 24. Eliza gct Short Creek MM, O.
1900, 3, 22. George J. gct Birmingham MM,
   Pa., to m Sarah Edna Hoffman
1902, 6, 26. Joseph G. dis mcd & serving as
   a surgeon in the Army
1911, 5, 25. John French gct Birmingham MM,
   Pa., to m Anna Hoopes Brinton
1911, 5, 25. John French & Mary A. gct Salem
   MM, O.

WINROD
1880, 11, 25. Phebe Ann Greenfield (form
   Nicholson) dis mcd

WITCHELL
----, --, --. John & Bathsheba [Witchel]
    Ch: Jane   b 1815, 8, 31
       Mary   " 1818, 6, 21
       Isaac   " 1818, 6, 21

1819, 5, 21. John & w, Bathsheba, & ch, Jane,
   Mary & Isaac, rocf Plainfield MM, O., dtd
   1819,4,22
1828, 10, 24. John dis disunity
1828, 10, 24. Bathsheba dis disunity
1834, 10, 23. Jane [Witchel] dis JH
1836, 2, 25. Isaac & Mary [Witchel], ch John
   & Bathsheba, gct White Water MM, Ind.
1844, 12, 26. Isaac & w, Mary A., & ch, Lydia
   S., Hannah & Laban, rocf Nantucket MM,
   Mass., dtd 1844,10,31

WOOD
----, --, --. Joshua & Hannah
    Ch: Jacob   b 1793, 4, 2
       Rachel   " 1795, 10, 30
       Jesse M. " 1798, 4, 20
       Arbina   " 1800, 12, 23
       Sarah   " 1803, 6, 17
       Asenath " 1805, 10, 27
       Lewis   " 1810, 9, 3
1844, 5, 7. Hannah d
1848, 4, 7. Joshua d bur Flushing
1854, 3, 1. Rachel m Thomas Doudna
1875, 9, 17. Pusey d bur Flushing
1882, 6, 29. Ann B. m John C. HOGE

1819, 3, 26. Mary (form Chandler) dis mcd
1821, 12, 21. Joseph rocf Short Creek MM, O.,
   dtd 1821,10,23
1822, 2, 22. Jacob & w, Phebe, & ch, Hannah
   & Simeon, rocf New Garden MM
1826, 3, 24. Jesse M. gct Plainfield MM, to
   m Rebecca P. Potts
1826, 6, 23. Jesse M. gct Milford MM, Ind.
1827, 1, 26. Joshua & w, Esther, & ch, Rachel Ann, Elizabeth , Mary, Lydia, Adde-
   son & William, rocf Smithfield MM, O.,
   dtd 1826,9,18
1828, 1, 25. Joseph gct Deerfield MM
1830, 3, 25. Joshua & w, Esther, & ch, Rachel Ann, Eliza-Jane, Mary, Lydia, Addison, William & Gerard Hopkins, gct Smith-

WOOD, continued
    field MM
1831, 6, 23. Sarah rmt Wm. Ratcliff
1831, 7, 21. Sarah rmt Jonathan Lupton
1836, 9, 22. Lewis con mcd
1838, 7, 26. Ann, minor, rocf Stillwater MM,
    dtd 1838,7,23
1840, 5, 21. William recrq
1841, 8, 26. Ann gct Stillwater MM
1841, 9, 23. Mary rst at Chesterfield MM on
    consent of this mtg
1844, 7, 25. William gct Pennsville MM
1845, 10, 23. Samuel B. Smith gct Smithfield
    MM, to m Lydia B. Wood
1846, 1, 22. Lewis dis mcd
1848, 7, 20. Ann B. rocf Smithfield MM, dtd
    1848,5,22
1853, 4, 21. Charity & Mary R. rocf Smith-
    field MM, dtd 1853,4,18
1853, 5, 26. Pusey & w, Rebecca, rocf Smith-
    field MM, dtd 1853,4,18
1854, 1, 26. Rachel rocf Smithfield MM, dtd
    1854,1,23
1861, 1, 24. Ascenath dis jG
1866, 9, 20. Rebecca dis jG
1866, 10, 25. Pusey dis jH
1867, 4, 25. Mary R. Murry (form Wood) dis
    mcd
1869, 5, 20. Arthur P. dis jG
1871, 9, 20. Pusey rst

WRIGHT
----, --, --. James & Hannah
    Ch: Phebe   b 1801, 12, 8
        Mary   " 1804, 2, 15
        Sarah   " 1807, 11, 17
1805, 9, 5. Mary d bur Flushing
----, --, --. Joseph & Anne
    Ch: William B. b 1815, 3, 12
        Susannah   " 1816, 12, 14
        Phebe   " 1819, 4, 2
        Samuel   " 1821, 4, 13
        Sarah   " 1823, 3, 17
        John   " 1825, 3, 19
        Elisha   " 1827, 6, 28
        Joseph   " 1830, 8, 26
1822, 9, 10. Rhoda [Right] d bur Flushing
1822, 9, 10. Sarah d bur Flushing
1825, 7, 20. William d bur Flushing
----, --, --. Amos & Ann
    Ch: Sarah   b 1832, 3, 25
        Schooley   " 1834, 4, 20
        Lindley H. " 1836, 6, 10
        John   " 1839, 1, 6
1839, 12, 4. Phebe L. m Thos. FELL
1843, 5, 20. Ann d

    *   *   *   *   *   *   *
HOGE
1873, 5, 22. John Barclay dis disunity
1874, 2, 26. John B. rst by QM

1843, 6, 27. Sarah d bur Flushing
1843, 6, 30. Mary, dt Schooley, d bur Flush-
    ing
1862, 10, 9. Joseph d
1863, 5, 25. John d bur Flushing
1868, 12, 17. William d bur Flushing
1872, 11, 16. Rebecca d bur Flushing
1884, 10, 24. Lavina H. m Aaron FRAME

1822, 6, 21. Hannah gct Springfield MM, N. J.
1822, 11, 22. Phebe rmt Samuel M. Briggs
1827, 5, 25. Aaron gct White Water MM, Ind.
1828, 6, 27. Rebeckah rmt Adoni Lewis
1829, 9, 24. James & Hannah dis jH
1830, 3, 25. William dis disunity
1831, 1, 20. Aaron rocf White Water MM, Ind.,
    dtd 1830,11,24
1831, 3, 24. Amos dis mcd
1833, 8, 22. Ann B. rst on consent of Short
    Creek MM, O.
1835, 8, 20. Amos recrq
1835, 11, 26. Rachel gct Alum Creek MM
1836, 8, 25. Sarah & Schooley, ch Amos & Ann,
    recrq
1840, 6, 21. Ann recrq
1845, 7, 24. Samuel dis mcd
1846, 3, 26. John Jr. dis disunity
1849, 4, 26. Aaron gct Allum Creek MM
1852, 9, 23. Sarah Smith (form Wright) dis
    mcd
1852, 11, 20. Joseph Jr. dis disunity
1853, 8, 25. Susannah Darnald (form Wright)
    dis mcd
1853, 10, 20. Elisha dis disunity
1854, 6, 22. Ann gct Allum Creek MM
1878, 3, 21. Lavina recrq

YOUNG
----, --, --. Herculus & Ann
    Ch: Dinah   b 1811, 10, 9
        Eli   " 1813, 1, 20
        Ann   " 1814, 12, 4
        Morgan   " 1816, 10, 9
        John   " 1819, 2, 1
        Hannah   " 1820, 8, 25
        Elizabeth " 1824, 7, 21

1824, 2, 27. Hercules & w, Ann, & ch, Dinah,
    Eli, Ann, Morgan, John & Hannah, rocf Red-
    stone MM, Pa., dtd 1823,10,29
1825, 6, 24. Hercules dis disunity
1833, 8, 22. Ann dis disunity
1834, 9, 25. Dinah dis jH
1841, 5, 20. Ann Baker (form Young) dis mcd
1842, 12, 22. Hannah & Elizabeth dis disunity

RECORDS

ADAMS
1838, 7, 28. William recrq
1853, 2, 26. Elizabeth & Eliza Jane recrq

ATHERTON
1837, 10, 28. Boaz & w, Mary, & ch, David, Ann, Reuben, Ross, Richard & Elizabeth, gct Deerfield MM

ALLEN
1830, 5, 22. Daniel H. & w, Eliza, & ch, Amos G. & Benjamin, gct Plainfield MM
1835, 4, 25. Jehu rmt Mary Ann Garretson
1835, 5, 23. Reuben & w, Joanna, & ch, Ruthann, Joanna & James M., rocf Short Creek MM, O., dtd 1835,4,23
1835, 9, 26. Mary Ann gct Plainfield MM
1840, 9, 28. Isaac rocf Short Creek MM, O.
1844, 7, 27. Isaac rpd mcd
1856, 5, 24. Ruthann Benet (form Allen) con mcd

BAILEY
1829, 2, 28. Cert rec for Emmor & w, Elizabeth, & ch, Emmor, Martha & Ann, from Short Creek MM, O., dtd 1828,10,21, endorsed to Plainfield
1829, 12, 26. Hannah & Phebe rocf Short Creek MM, O., dtd 1829,11,26
1830, 3, 27. Hannah & Phebe gct Springborough MM

BENET
1856, 5, 24. Ruthann (form Allen) con mcd

BIRKHEAD
1831, 10, 22. Susanna (form Rogers) dis mcd

BRANSON
1835, 9, 26. Sarah Ann gct Milford MM, Ind.

BROWN
1840, 1, 23. Mary H. rocf Little Falls MM, Md.

CARTER
1833, 5, 25. John rocf Little Falls MM, Md., dtd 1832,11,6

CHANDLER
1830, 8, 28. Sarah (form Knock) dis mcd

CHICKEN
1831, 6, 25. Mary Green (form Chicken) con mcd

CLARK
1853, 3, 26. Runame recrq

COPE
1834, 8, 23. Hannah Parsons (form Cope) dis

mcd
1838, 4, 28. Ellis dis mcd
1838, 10, 27. Jacob dis
1831, 6, 25. Margaret Tomlinson (form Cope) con mcd

COOPER
1829, 9, 26. Nicholas & w, Sarah, & ch, Ely, Margaret & Gulielma, rocf Little Falls MM, Md., dtd 1829,8,4
1830, 6, 26. Cert for Nicholas from Little Falls MM, Md., returned because of non-attendance
1831, 11, 26. Nicholas rocf Little Falls MM, Md., dtd 1831,5,7
1837, 3, 25. Eli dis disunity
1839, 6, 22. Nicholas gct Plainfield MM

DEW
1840, 11, 28. Cert for Elias & fam from Short Creek MM, O., not accepted; dis disunity
1842, 2, 26. Allen & Albert, minor s Elias, rocf Short Creek MM, O., dtd 1842,1,22

DILWORTH
1845, 4, 26. William & w, Mary, & ch gct MM in Illinois

ELLIS
1831, 3, 26. Sarah Lister (form Ellis) dis mcd
1831, 5, 28. Bevan dis mcd
1834, 3, 22. Jonathan M. & w, Martha, & ch, Theodore, Peter M., Martha, Solomon Jehu & Catherine, gct Fall Creek MM, O.
1834, 3, 22. Jonathan Jr. & Phamy gct Fall Creek MM, O.
1835, 4, 25. Cert granted Phamy 1834,3,22, now returned; unaccepted because of a complaint against her
1835, 4, 25. Phamy dis

FOULKE
1830, 7, 24. Anthony & w, Eleanor, & ch, Sarah P., Phebe & William W., rocf Plainfield MM, dtd 1830,5,20
1832, 4, 28. Anthony & w, Eleanor, & ch, Sarah P., Phebe & William W. gct White Water MM, Ind.

FIELDS
1830, 6, 27. Sarah gct Plainfield MM

GARRETSON
1835, 4, 25. Mary Ann rmt Jehu Allen
1837, 1, 28. Hannah T. rocf Bradford MM, Pa.
1837, 3, 25. Talbert dis mcd
1838, 6, 23. Amos & w, Hannah L., & dt, Martha, gct Short Creek MM, O.
1839, 7, 27. Peggy & Angeline gct Milton MM, Ind.
1843, 10, 28. Joel gct Fall Creek MM, Ind.

GREEN
1831, 6, 25. Mary (form Chicken) con mcd

GRIEST
1859, 10, 21. William Elmer & w, Ann, rocf
    Smithfield MM, dtd 1859,10,3

HAINES
1829, 12, 26. William con mcd
1830, 12, 25. William gct Centre MM, O.
1833, 1, 26. Rebecca Stewart (form Haines)
    dis mcd
1838, 1, 27. Edwin con mcd
1838, 7, 28. Isaac & w, Rachel, & five ch gct
    Whitewater MM, Ind.
1838, 7, 28. Edwin gct Whitewater MM, Ind.

HAMILTON
1836, 2, 27. William recrq

HARMER
1830, 4, 24. John & w, Parthenia, & ch, Han-
    nah & Isaiah C., rocf Deer Creek MM, Md.,
    dtd 1830,2,11

HIBBARD
1830, 10, 23. Caleb gct Stillwater MM
1834, 5, 24. Caleb rocf Stillwater MM, dtd
    1833,10,19

HUNT
1833, 5, 25. Diana rocf Smithfield MM, dtd
    1833,3,19

HOLLET
1858, 12, 22. Joseph gct Deerfield MM, to m
    Mary P. Colsen
1859, 5, 28. Mary P. rocf Deerfield MM. dtd
    1859,5,4
1860, 7, 14. Hannah Elizabeth, dt Mary P.,
    recrq

HOLLINGSWORTH
1831, 4, 23. Isaac rmt Phebe Kirk
1854, 4, 22. Phebe recrq
1857, 5, 23. Lydia dis jas
1860, 8, 11. Phebe dis jas

KENNARD
1830, 6, 26. Thomas & w, Elizabeth, & ch,
    Henry P., Rachel, Levi, John, Jacob, Jen-
    kins & Thomas, rocf Plainfield MM, dtd
    1830,6,24
1831, 11, 26. Henry P. gct Plainfield MM
1834, 8, 23. Thomas & w, Elizabeth, & ch, Ra-
    chel, Levi, John, Jacob, Jenkins, Thomas,
    Joseph & Mishael, gct Milford MM, Ind.

KINSEY
1838, 5, 26. Jesse H. & w, Naomi, & ch gct
    Whitewater MM, Ind.

KIRK
1831, 4, 23. Phebe rmt Isaac Hollingsworth

KNIGHT
1830, 2, 27. Lydia rmt Ira Lewis
1834, 4, 26. John B. dis mcd
1838, 4, 28. Immor dis mcd
1843, 6, 24. Joseph dis mcd
1843, 10, 28. Neadham dis mcd
1851, 1, 26. Amos Peasley dis mcd & jas

KNOCK
1830, 8, 28. Sarah Chandler (form Knock) dis
    mcd
1831, 8, 27. Daniel C. dis mcd
1832, 3, 24. William dis disunity
1832, 9, 22. Jane Merrill (form Knock) dis
    mcd
1833, 1, 26. Ezekiel dis disunity
1833, 7, 27. Rachel dis jas

LEEKE
1830, 9, 25. Samuel & ch, Samuel & Rebecca,
    rocf Indian Spring MM, Md., dtd 1830,7,7
1830, 9, 25. Cert rec for Elizabeth from
    Indian Spring MM, Md., dtd 1830,7,7, en-
    dorsed to Concord MM
1831, 4, 23. Samuel gct Stillwater MM, to m
    Martha Williams
1831, 7, 23. Samuel & ch, Samuel & Rebecca,
    gct Stillwater MM

LEWIS
1830, 2, 27. Ira rmt Lydia Knight
1830, 3, 27. Lydia gct Short Creek MM, O.

LISTER
1831, 3, 26. Sarah (form Ellis) dis mcd

McMATH
1846, 5, 23. Hannah dis

McNAMEE
1839, 10, 26. Cyrus dis disunity
1843, 10, 28. Isaac dis disunity

MARSH
1833, 8, 24. Cynthia Ann & ch, Myraan &
    Thaddeus Constantine, rocf Smithfield MM

MEAD
1848, 7, 22. Joseph & w, Phebe, & ch, Thom-
    as, William, Joseph James, Charles El-
    wood & Mary Emily, rocf Stillwater MM,
    dtd 1848,6,17
1855, 5, 26. Joseph & w, Phebe, & seven ch
    gct Plainfield MM

MELTON
1840, 6, 27. Stafford rocf Concord MM, dtd
    1839,9,25

MERRILL
1832, 9, 22. Jane (form Knock) dis mcd

PACKER
1834, 1, 25. Ann & ch, Philena, George,
     Phebe Ann, Hannah L. & Lydia C., rocf
     Short Creek MM, O., dtd 1833,8,22
1834, 1, 25. Lewessa rocf Short Creek MM, O.,
     dtd 1834,8,22
1834, 5, 24. Lamborn rocf Short Creek MM, O.,
     dtd 1833,10,24
1836, 4, 23. Lamborn dis disunity

PARKINS
1835, 8, 22. Isaac & w, Nancy, & ch, Sarah,
     Jesse, Jane, Luis & Hannah, gct Allum
     Creek MM

PARSONS
1834, 4, 26. Israel dis mcd
1834, 8, 23. Hannah (form Cope) dis mcd
1835, 8, 22. George dis jas
1836, 6, 25. Sophia & ch, Mahlon H., Joseph
     H., Jacob, Israel & Martha, rqct Deer-
     field MM

PICKERING
1837, 1, 28. Able recrq
1842, 8, 26. Jesse B. recrq
1849, 6, 23. Jesse B. & w, Elizabeth, gc
1854, 10, 28. Jacob recrq

REYNOLDS
1841, 5, 22. Joseph gct Plainfield MM

ROBERTS
1830, 4, 27. Ann gct Deerfield MM

ROGERS
1831, 10, 22. Susanna Birkhead (form Rogers)
     dis mcd
1835, 5, 23. Mary Ann dis jas
1833, 5, 25. Elijah dis jas
ROMANS
1830, 2, 27. Sally (form Schooley) dis mcd
1833, 7, 27. Robert gct New Garden MM
1842, 6, 25. Elisha con mcd
1844, 7, 27. Moses Jr. dis mcd

SCHOOLEY
1830, 2, 27. Sally Romans (form Schooley) dis
     mcd
1835, 2, 28. Isaac & w, Sarah gct Allum Creek
     MM
1850, 1, 26. Phinehas dis mcd

SMITH
1836, 6, 25. Elizabeth relrq
1837, 2, 25. Alice & ch, Thomas Wilkerson &
     Sarah Ann, gct Plainfield MM
1835, 3, 25. Mary con mcd

STAATS
1838, 7, 28. Margaret dis

STEWART
1833, 1, 26. Rebecca (form Haines) dis mcd

SWAYNE
1834, 7, 26. Thomas recrq
1839, 3, 23. Thomas & w, Eliza, & ch, Joshua,
     Mary Ann, Rebecca, Eliza & Thomas Jr., gct
     Green Plain MM

TERRELL
1835, 7, 25. Lydia con mcd

TOMLINSON
1831, 6, 25. Margaret (form Cope) con mcd

TOWNSEND
1834, 8, 23. Joseph & w, Elizabeth, & ch,
     Anthony, Mary Ann, Ross & James recrq
1839, 2, 23. Joseph & w, Elizabeth, & ch,
     Anthony, Mary Ann, Rose & James, gct
     Deerfield MM

WALKER
1829, 3, 28. Jesse gct Short Creek MM, O.

WHEALDON
1829, 2, 28. John dis mcd
1840, 6, 27. Nathan & w, Ann, & ch, Alfred,
     Marybe, Elizabeth, Ann, Abel & Jonathan,
     gct Stillwater MM
1841, 1, 23. Isaac con mcd
1849, 6, 23. Elizabeth & Ann gc

WILLIAMS
1831, 4, 23. Samuel Leeke gct Stillwater MM,
     to m Martha Williams
1832, 6, 23. Cert rec for Wisper & w, Han-
     nah & ch, Thomas, Charles & Mary, from
     Exeter MM, dtd 1832,2,29, endorsed to Sa-
     lem MM

WILLIS
1840, 6, 27. Amos recrq
1845, 10, 25. Amos dis disunity

WITCHELL
1834, 10, 25. John & w, Bathsheba, & ch,
     Jane, Mary, Isaac & Barton, gct White-
     water MM, Ind.

WRIGHT
1832, 3, 24. James dis disunity

SOMERSET MONTHLY MEETING

Somerset Monthly Meeting, located in Belmont County, Ohio, was established by Stillwater Quarterly Meeting 12th Mo. 25th 1820, and consisted of Somerset and Ridge Preparative
Meetings.

RECORDS

ADAMS

1826, 8, 31. Hannah m John BLACKLEDGE
1828, 3, 17. Mary A., dt Thomas & Lydia, b
1838, 5, 10. John T., s Thomas & Lydia, Monroe Co., Ohio, m in Sunbury, Patience GARRETSON, dt John & Henrietta, Monroe Co., Ohio
     Ch: William G. b 1839, 2, 10
         Edward   " 1840, 4, 8
         Henrietta   " 1841, 12, 4
         John T.   " 1843, 5, 23

1826, 1, 30. Thomas & w, Lydia, & ch, Hannah, Elizabeth, John, Nathan C., Edward G., Ira L. & Margaret, recrq
1829, 7, 27. Lydia & Elizabeth dis jH
1830, 5, 24. Thomas dis jH
1834, 6, 30. Nathan dis jH
1834, 9, 29. John dis disunity
1838, 2, 26. John T. rst
1838, 4, 30. Rachel (form Tipton) con mcd
1840, 11, 30. Ira dis mcd
1843, 11, 27. John & w, Patience, & ch, Wm. G., Edward, Henrietta & John T., gct Chesterfield MM
1845, 1, 27. Harriett dis jH
1847, 3, 29. Rachel gct Chesterfield MM
1854, 12, 25. Rachel rocf Plymouth MM, dtd 1854,10,20

ALLEN

----, --, --. Moses & Jane
     Ch: William b 1824, 3, 29
         Walton   " 1825, 12, 13
         Aaron   " 1828, 6, 7

1826, 5, 29. Moses & w, Jane, & ch, William & Walton, rocf Plainfield MM, dtd 1826,4, 20
1828, 4, 28. Moses dis jH
1829, 7, 27. Jane dis jH
1842, 3, 28. William, Walker & Aaron, ch Moses & Jane, gct White River MM, Ind.

ANDREWS

1822, 10, 28. Richard dis mcd
1828, 3, 24. Irena Varner (form Andrews) dis mcd
1832, 3, 26. Lucy Varner (form Andrews) dis mcd
1832, 4, 30. Lucy Warner (form Andrew) dis mcd
1836, 9, 26. Malinda Varner (form Andrews) dis mcd

ARNOLD

1824, 2, 5. Hannah m Lemuel PATTERSON
1843, 12, 15. Susanna d ae 92 bur Ridge
1846, 8, 14. Joseph d ae 93 bur Ridge
1850, 3, 7. Anderson, s Asa & Susannah, Belmont Co., Ohio; m in Ridge MH, Bethula

ARNOLD, dt John & Mary HAMPTON
1855, 12, 4. Bethula d ae 63 bur Ridge
1859, 4, 18. Mary d bur Ridge
1859, 7, 6. Maria A. m Emmor BAILEY
1862, 2, 7. Anderson d ae 77 bur Ridge

1829, 11, 30. Joseph gct Deerfield MM, to m Bethula Hampton
1830, 8, 30. Bethula rocf Deerfield MM, dtd 1830,7,15
1833, 5, 27. Wm. & James, minors in care of Nathan & Ruth Dodd, rocf Stillwater MM, Ohio, dtd 1833,5,25
1859, 3, 28. Maria A. rocf Stillwater MM, Ohio, dtd 1839,3,26

BAILEY

----, --, --. Edmund & Margaret
     Ch: Lydia   b 1817, 8, 27
         Sidney   " 1819, 4, 20
         Jehu   " 1821, 3, 3
         Joel   " 1822, 10, 11
         Milton   " 1825, 8, 22
         Martha   " 1827, 6, 9
         Daniel   " 1829, 1, 18
         Pharaby " 1831, 2, 28
         Sarah   " 1833, 7, 3
         Margaret " 1835, 9, 18
         Caleb   " 1841, 12, 7
----, --, --. Stephen & Talitha
     Ch: Rachel   b 1821, 1, 13
         Stephen " 1825, 7, 28
----, --, --. James & Sarah
     Ch: George   b 1821, 5, 29
         James   " 1829, 3, 21
1820, 5, 4. Sidney d bur Stillwater
1820, 11, 17. Elizabeth d bur Ridge
1822, 6, 27. Elizabeth m Jared BUTLER
----, --, --. Henry & Mary
     Ch: Hannah   b 1826, 9, 26 d 1895, 4,11 bur Somerset
         Margaret   b 1828, 3, 28
         Elizabeth " 1820, 12, 1
         Joel   " 1822, 1, 1
         Jane   " 1823, 9, 2
         Issachar   " 1829,12, 14 d 1835, 3,16 bur Sunsbury
         Rebecca   b 1833, 10, 27 d 1835, 6,21 bur Sunsbury
         Emmor   b 1836, 6, 16
         Ann   " 1838, 6, 26
         Martha   " 1840, 5, 29
         Rachel   " 1832, 3, 13
1825, 10, 31. Sarah d bur Sunsbury
1825, 12, 5. William d ae 73 bur Ridge
1836, 4, 7. Lydia m George STARBUCK
1834, 4, 9. Rebecca d ae 71 bur Ridge
1834, 8, 7. Benjamin, s Stephen & Tabitha (Patterson), Belmont Co., Ohio, d 1888,5, 5, ae 75, bur Ridge; m in Ridge MH, Lucy CREW, dt Isaac & Judith, Belmont Co., O., d 1892,1,14 ae 75 bur Ridge
     Ch: Talitha   b 1835, 6, 29

BAILEY, Benjamin & Lucy, continued
    Ch: Eli C.   b 1839, 3, 11
        Phebe   " 1838, 8, 13
        Elizabeth " 1842, 1, 6
        William L. " 1844, 1, 17
        Sarah Ann " 1848, 7, 18
        John   " 1850, 11, 27
        Lewis   " 1853, 3, 4
        Stephen   " 1855, 6, 2
        George W. " 1858, 12, 25
        Isaac H.   " 1861, 6, 2
1840, 5, 7. Rachel m Lewis NAYLOR
1843, 11, 30. Martha m Elisha M. WOOD
1844, 4, 4. Joel, s Edmond & Margaret, Bel-
    mont Co., Ohio: m in Ridge MH, Ruth Anna
    PATTERSON
    Ch: Sidney   b 1845, 7, 2
        Priscilla " 1847, 3, 8
        Isaac   " 1848, 10, 21
        Jacob   " 1850, 9, 11
        Lydia   " 1852, 7, 14
1844, 12, 5. Joseph, s Micajah & Mary, Bel-
    mont Co., Ohio; m in Ridge MH, Achsah ED-
    GERTON, dt Joseph & Charity (Doudna), Bel-
    mont Co., Ohio
    Ch: Joseph E. b 1848, 4, 20
        Elizabeth " 1855, 2, 12
        Jeptha   " 1846, 2, 28
        Miriam   " 1850, 1, 31 d 1852, 1, 9
          bur Ridge
----, --, --. Jehu & Martha S.
    Ch: Ruth   b 1847, 12, 16
        Nathan   " 1851, 4, 4
        James E.   " 1855, 4, 19
        Sina   " 1860, 5, 29
        Melissa   " 1863, 11, 11
----, --, --. William & Sarah
    Ch: William   b 1850, 11, 16
1850, 5, 9. Pharaba m Eli PATTERSON
1852, 3, 11. Abigail F. m Jacob CREW
1853, 6, 26. Lewis d bur Ridge
1853, 9, 19. Nathan d ae 2 bur Ridge
1854, 1, 9. Henery d ae 58 bur Sunsbury
1856, 11, 29. Ruthanna d ae 29 bur Ridge
1857, 1, 26. Rachel m James McGIRR (dte is
    that on which report of m was made to MM.
    Exact dte of m is not recorded)
1857, 9, 3. Margaret m Stephen HOBSON
1859, 6, 4. Achsah d ae 35 bur Ridge
1859, 7, 6. Emmor, s Henry & Mary, Belmont
    Co., Ohio, b 1836,6,16 d 1898,7,22; m in
    Somerset MH, Maria A. ARNOLD, dt Thomas &
    Elizabeth, Belmont Co., Ohio
    Ch: Samuel G. b 1861, 4, 29
1860, 9, 26. Benjamin F. d ae 2 bur Ridge
1861, 4, 26. Stephen d ae 83 bur Ridge
1861, 9, 5. Elizabeth m Ephraim PARRY
----, --, --. Joseph m Elvira PURVIANCE
    Ch: Irving C. b 1862, 12, 4 d 1932, 7,11
          bur Ridge
1862, 1, 16. Mary d ae 64 bur Sunsbury
1862, 12, 4. Millicent m Lindley HALL
1864, 4, 25. Sarah d ae 77

1865, 11, 6. Talitha d ae 78 bur Ridge
1866, 1, 29. Melissa d ae 2 bur Ridge
1867, 3, 12. Caleb d ae 25 bur Ridge
1868, 3, 5. Sarah Ann m Asa PARRY
1873, 4, 8. Edmund d ae 78 bur Ridge
1873, 5, 18. Margaret d ae 73 bur Ridge
1875, 2, 25. With(?) d ae 74 bur Ridge
1887, 11, 25. Sina m George JOHN
1889, 9, 5. Maria d ae 53
1919, 9, 4. Irving E., s Joseph & Elvira
    P., Belmont Co., Ohio; m in Ridge MH,
    Asenath Elma DOUDNA, dt Joseph W. & Ro-
    setta (Hall), Belmont Co., Ohio, b 1877,9,
    21

1824, 6, 28. Permelia Butler (form Bailey)
    dis mcd
1825, 6, 27. Henry & w, Mary, & ch, Elizabeth,
    Joel, Jane & Sarah, rocf Short Creek MM,
    Ohio, dtd 1825,5,24
1827, 1, 29. William dis mcd
1827, 2, 26. Martha Wooten (form Bailey) dis
    mcd
1828, 5, 26. Sarah dis jH
1828, 6, 30. Mahlon dis jH
1828, 6, 30. Charity dis jH
1828, 9, 29. Elizabeth dis jH
1829, 10, 26. Wm. Doudna gct Stillwater MM,
    Ohio, to m Lydia Bailey
1831, 2, 28. Wm. Crew gct Stillwater MM, Ohio
    to m Mary Bailey
1831, 5, 30. Henry dis mcd
1833, 8, 26. Wm. gct Short Creek MM, Ohio, to
    m Sarah Flanner
1835, 1, 26. James dis disunity
1835, 7, 27. Susanna Hall (form Bailey) dis
    mcd
1835, 11, 30. Wm. gct Short Creek MM, Ohio
1838, 12, 24. Ann Strahl (form Bailey) dis jH
1840, 6, 29. John dis mcd
1840, 8, 31. Elizabeth gct Smithfield MM
1841, 3, 1. Matilda dis jH
1842, 8, 29. Exum dis mcd
1842, 10, 24. Mary (form Brock) dis mcd
1844, 6, 24. Joel gct Chesterfield MM
1844, 8, 26. Elisha dis mcd
1845, 5, 26. Achsah gct Stillwater MM, Ohio
1846, 6, 29. Henry rst at Pennsville MM on
    consent of this mtg
1846, 9, 28. John gct Short Creek MM, Ohio,
    to m Jehu(?) Bailey
1847, 4, 26. Martha rocf Short Creek MM,
    Ohio, dtd 1847,3,23
1847, 7, 26. Joseph dis disunity
1848, 2, 28. Joseph & w, Achsah, & s, Jeph-
    thah, rocf Stillwater MM, Ohio, dtd 1847,
    11,27
1849, 6, 25. Joseph & w, Achsah, gct Still-
    water MM, Ohio
1849, 9, 24. Milton gct Stillwater MM, Ohio
1849, 10, 29. Margaret gct Chesterfield MM
1850, 6, 24. Sarah & ch, Abigail, Elizabeth,
    Thomas F. & George M., rocf Chesterfield

BAILEY, Sarah, continued
    MM, dtd 1850,5,18
1850, 5, 27. Milton gct Stillwater MM, Ohio
1850, 12, 30. Stephen dis mcd
1851, 2, 24. George dis mcd
1851, 2, 24. Martha (form Edgerton) dis mcd
1853, 7, 25. Daniel dis mcd
1854, 3, 27. James gct Pennsville MM, to m
    Rhoda Patton
1854, 9, 25. Joseph & w, Achsah, & ch, Jep-
    thah & Joseph, rocf Stillwater MM, Ohio,
    dtd 1854,7,22
1855, 3, 26. Mariam (form Doudna) dis mcd
1855, 6, 26. Telitha Fisher (form Bailey) dis
    mcd
1855, 10, 29. Mary West (form Bailey) dis mcd
1856, 12, 29. Sarah F. & ch, Thomas F., George
    M. & William, gct Stillwater MM, Ohio
1857, 1, 26. Elizabeth Parsons (form Bailey)
    dis mcd
1857, 11, 30. Eli Patterson gct Plainfield MM,
    to m Tabitha Bailey
1858, 5, 24. Phebe Fisher (form Bailey) dis
    mcd
1858, 7, 26. Joel gct Stillwater MM, Ohio
1859, 7, 25. Eli rpd mcd; he d before testi-
    mony was produced
1861, 10, 28. Joseph gct Flushing MM, Ohio, to
    m Elvira Purviance
1862, 2, 24. Five minor ch of Joel gct Still-
    water MM, Ohio
1862, 2, 24. Elvira P. rocf Flushing MM, dtd
    1862,2,20
1860, 11, 26. Jane Warfield (form Bailey) con
    mcd
1865, 3, 27. Joseph & w, Elvira, & ch, Jep-
    tha, Joseph E., Elizabeth, Irving & Sarah,
    gct Flushing MM, Ohio
1865, 10, 30. Uriah rocf Short Creek MM, Ohio,
    dtd 1865,8,22
1866, 3, 26. Ann gct Plymouth MM
1866, 4, 30. Edmund Jr. dis military service
1868, 4, 27. Wm. L. dis mcd
1874, 12, 24. John dis mcd
1876, 3, 23. Martha gct Stillwater MM, Ohio
1876, 3, 23. Sarah M. gct Stillwater MM, Ohio
1876, 3, 23. Martha Ring (form Bailey) dis
    mcd
1876, 8, 24. Almedia (form Starbuck) dis mcd
1877, 1, 25. Stephen dis mcd
1879, 9, 25. James E. gct New Garden MM, to
    m Sarah Coppock
1880, 11, 25. James E. gct New Garden MM
1880, 11, 25. George W. dis mcd
1885, 7, 23. Isaac H. dis mcd
1888, 7, 26. Samuel G. dis
1895, 5, 23. Ruth gct New Garden MM, Ohio
1898, 5, 26. Jehu gct New Garden MM, Ohio
1906, 10, 25. Daniel rst at Stillwater MM, on
    consent of this mtg
1921, 8, 25. Irving E. rocf Flushing MM

BANE
1823, 1, 14. Rhoda d bur Ridge
1826, 5, 4. Sarah [Bain] m James CREW

1824, 3, 1. Elijah recrq
1824, 11, 29. Anna & Martha, minor ch Elijah,
    recrq
1825, 11, 28. Mary Cato (form Bane) dis mcd
1828, 3, 24. Lavina Cadle (form Bane) dis mcd
1828, 6, 30. Elijah & s, John, gct Deerfield
    MM, Ohio
1829, 10, 26. Almedia [Bain] dis disunity
1831, 7, 25. Anna & Martha [Bain], dt Elijah,
    gct Deerfield MM, Ohio

BARBER
1854, 9, 25. John Crew gct Flushing MM, Ohio,
    to m Acenath Barber

BARNES
1824, 5, 24. Miriam gct Stillwater MM, Ohio
    (Baines in one record)

BAXTER
1872, 6, 20. Sarah (form Lightfoot) dis mcd

BECK
1822, 1, 9. Ann m Samuel CRAFT
1822, 10, 9. Lydia m Wm. CRAFT
1823, 7, 15. Phebe d bur Stillwater
----, --, --. Jesse & Eliza
    Ch: L. Sarah b 1826, 2, 3

1823, 4, 28. Jesse & w, Elizabeth, & ch, Ra-
    chel E. & Grace E., rocf Plainfield MM,
    dtd 1823,4,26
1826, 12, 25. Jemimah Glover (form Beck) dis
    mcd
1827, 8, 27. Sarah Lundy (form Beck) dis mcd
1835, 3, 20. Martha Nicholson (form Beck)
    dis mcd
1835, 3, 30. Jesse & w, Elizabeth, & ch, Ra-
    chel, Grace & Sarah, gct Deerfield MM, O.
1835, 6, 29. John Jr. dis disunity
1838, 11, 26. John & w, Rachel, gct Chester-
    field MM, Ohio

BERRY
1842, 6, 27. Sarah Ann (form Couplin) dis
    mcd

BINFORD
1826, 7, 24. Hannah rocf Rich Square MM,
    N. C., dtd 1826,3,18, end by Stillwater
    MM, O.

BINNS
1897, 5, 21. Oliver W., s Jonathan & Rosella
    (Bailey), Harrison County, O.; m in Ridge
    MH, Mariana DEWEES, dt Joshua & Martha
    (Gibbons), Belmont Co., O.

1898, 3, 24. Mary Anna D. gct Harrisville MM

BISHOP
----, --, --. Joseph & Mary
    Ch: James   b 1816, 8, 31
        Elizabeth " 1818, 8, 1
        Jesse
        Mary   " 1823, 2, 15
1824, 7, 31. Elizabeth d bur Somerset

1825, 8, 29. Joseph dis mcd
1839, 8, 26. Mary Palmer (form Bishop) dis
    mcd
1842, 10, 24. James dis disunity
1842, 10, 24. Jesse dis disunity

BLACKLEDGE
1826, 8, 31. John, s Wm. & Elizabeth, Monroe
    Co., O.; m in Sunbury, Hannah ADAMS, dt
    Thomas & Lydia
    Ch: Lydia   b 1827, 7, 29
----, --, --. Robert & Esther
    Ch: Aaron   b 1827, 8, 24
1853, 5, 9. Rachel d ae 75 bur Sunsbury
1864, 1, 7. Sarah d ae 68 bur Sunbury

1824, 7, 26. William [Blacklidge] & w, Eliza-
    beth, & s, Asa Hartley, rocf Short Creek
    MM, O., dtd 1824,7,20
1824, 7, 26. John [Blacklidge] rocf Short
    Creek MM, O., dtd 1824,7,20
1824, 7, 26. Sarah [Blacklidge] rocf Short
    Creek MM, O., dtd 1824,7,20
1824, 7, 26. Elizabeth [Blacklidge] rocf
    Short Creek MM, O., dtd 1824,7,20
1825, 12, 26. Robert H. & w, Esther, & dt, Ann,
    rocf Short Creek MM, O., dtd 1825,12,20
1827, 2, 26. David rocf Short Creek MM, O.,
    dtd 1827,2,20
1828, 8, 25. Robert H. & w, Esther, & ch,
    Ann & Aaron, gct Short Creek MM, O.
1829, 10, 26. John dis JH
1829, 12, 28. Wm. dis JH
1830, 5, 24. Elizabeth dis JH
1830, 5, 24. Elizabeth Jr. dis JH
1830, 8, 30. David dis JH
1831, 4, 25. Hannah dis JH
1834, 6, 30. Asa dis JH
1839, 3, 25. Rachel rocf Philadelphia MM,
    Pa., dtd 1839,12,24, end by Stillwater
    MM, O., 1839,3,23

BOSWELL
1825, 8, 4. Lydia m Robert WAY
1825, 11, 3. Anne m Elijah HIETT
----, --, --. William & Rachel
    Ch: Isaac   b 1827, 2, 18
        Joseph   " 1828, 9, 13
----, --, --. Benjamin & Asenath
    Ch: Benjamin   b 1831, 1, 25
        James   " 1833, 4, 5
        Rebecca
          Anna   " 1838, 7, 20
          Anne   " 1842, 7, 15
1833, 2, 7. Jesse, s Dempsey & Mary, Belmont

Co., O.; m in Ridge MH, Eliza PATTERSON,
dt Jeremiah & Elizabeth
1844, 1, 4. William, s Benjamin & Asenath
    (Doudna), Belmont Co., O.; m in Ridge MH,
    Susannah L. PEEBLES, dt Mordecai & Deborah
    Ch: Joel D.   b 1844, 10, 19 d 1846, 5,28
        bur Ridge
1845, 7, 7. Susannah d ae 28 bur Ridge
----, --, --. William & Hannah
    Ch: Samuel   b 1849, 1, 16 (or 1848)
        Benjamin   " 1850, 5, 13
        William   " 1852, 4, 2
        John H.   " 1854, 12, 6
        Susannah   " 1861, 6, 6
        Nathan M. " 1864, 6, 9
1854, 2, 24. William d ae 1 bur Ridge
1865, 4, 13. Benjamin d ae 76
1891, 12, 10. William d ae 72 bur Ridge
1893, 5, 27. Hannah d ae 69 bur Ridge

1824, 12, 27. Densey & w, Mary, & ch, Lydia,
    Jesse, John & Phebe, rocf Stillwater MM,
    O., dtd 1824,12,25
1824, 12, 27. Anne rocf Stillwater MM, O.,
    dtd 1824,12,25
1826, 1, 30. Benjamin & w, Asenath, & ch,
    William, Sarah & Mary, rocf Stillwater MM,
    O., dtd 1825,12,24
1827, 4, 30. Dempsey & w, Mary, & ch, Jesse,
    John & Phebe, gct Stillwater MM, O.
1827, 5, 28. William & w, Rachel, & ch, Ruth,
    Elizabeth, Asenath, Rebecca & Isaac, rocf
    Stillwater MM, O., dtd 1827,4,28
1827, 10, 29. Ruth rocf Stillwater MM, O., dtd
    1827,10,27
1829, 3, 2. William & w, Rachel, & ch, Ruth,
    Asenath, Elizabeth, Rebecca, Isaac & Jo-
    seph, gct White Water MM, Ind.
1833, 4, 29. Eliza gct Deerfield MM, O.
1842, 7, 25. Sarah Dew (form Boswell) dis mcd
1842, 7, 25. Mary Turner (form Boswell) dis
    mcd
1847, 4, 26. Wm. gct Flushing MM, to m Hannah
    Briggs
1847, 9, 29. Hannah rocf Flushing MM, dtd
    1847,7,22
1851, 5, 26. Benjamin Jr. dis mcd
1856, 3, 24. Rebecca dis jas
1876, 3, 23. Samuel dis mcd
1876, 7, 20. Benjamin dis mcd
1876, 11, 23. John H. dis mcd
1892, 4, 21. Susanna McGill (form Boswell)
    dis mcd
1895, 1, 24. Nathan M. dis disunity

BRANTINGHAM
1857, 3, 30. Joseph Edgerton gct New Garden
    MM, to m Anna M. Brantingham
1857, 7, 27. Lydia & Sina rocf New Garden
    MM with mother, Anna M. Edgerton
1865, 3, 27. Lydia & Sina gct Coal Creek MM,
    Ia.

BRIGGS
1847, 4, 26. Wm. Boswell gct Flushing MM, to
m Hannah Briggs

BROCK
----, --, --. Robert & Peninah
Ch: Jesse   b 1832, 2, 9 d 1836, 4, 4
                 bur Ridge
    James   b 1833, 12, 2 " 1836, 4, 8
                 bur Ridge
    Sarah   b 1836, 3, 10 " 1855,10,12
                 bur Ridge
    William   b 1840, 5, 11
    Martha Ann " 1843, 5, 13 " 1862,10,17
                 bur Ridge
    Elizabeth b 1845, 2, 20 " 1846, 5,28
                 bur Ridge
    Mary   b 1849, 3, 22
    Lydia Jane " 1851, 3, 4 " 1865, 4,13
                 bur Ridge
    Joel   b 1838, 2, 25
    Rebecca   " 1853, 6, 18
1831, 6, 9. Sarah m Nathan DAWSON
1833, 4, 5. John d ae 3 bur Ridge
1833, 8, 26. Jane d ae 21 bur Ridge
1835, 2, 16. Stephen d ae 20 bur Ridge
1841, 7, 8. Stephen d ae 74 bur Ridge
1855, 10, 5. Robert d ae 45 bur Ridge
1857, 4, 26. Martha d ae 75 bur Ridge

1831, 1, 24. Robert gct Stillwater MM, O.,
   to m Peninah Davison
1831, 10, 24. Stephen & w, Ann, & ch, Mary,
   John & Stephen, rocf Flushing MM, O., dtd
   1831,9,22
1831, 11, 28. Peninah rocf Stillwater MM, O.,
   dtd 1831,9,24
1842, 10, 24. Mary Bailey (form Brock) dis mcd
1861, 10, 28. Joel dis mcd & jas
1863, 9, 28. Wm. dis mcd
1866, 9, 24. Mary Warrick (form Brock) dis
   mcd
1870, 6, 23. Penninah Hogue (form Brock) dis
   mcd
1870, 9, 22. Rebecca dis jas

BROOMHALL
1833, 4, 29. Wm., Enos, Arminda, Amy, Phebe
   & Townsend, minor ch Berkley & Rebecca,
   rocf Stillwater MM, O., dtd 1833,1,28
1848, 9, 25. Amy Patterson (form Broomhall)
   dis mcd
1850, 3, 25. Wm. dis mcd

BROWN
1835, 4, 27. Isaac & w, Mary, gct Deerfield
   MM, O.
1840, 8, 31. Esther (form Tipton) dis mcd
1853, 11, 28. Tacy (form Lewis) dis mcd

BRUCE
1831, 4, 25. Susanna (form Gibbons) dis mcd
1831, 5, 30. Susanna dis JH

BRYANT
1849, 3, 26. John recrq
1850, 2, 28. John gct Stillwater MM, O.
1861, 11, 25. Lindley Gibbons gct Stillwater
   MM, O., to m Rachel Bryant

BUNDY
1808, 12, 14. William d ae 52
----, --, --. Thomas & Milisent
Ch: Lydia   b 1820, 8, 4
    Zadock   " 1824, 9, 6
1824, 5, 6. Jonathan, s Thomas & Milisent,
   Belmont Co., O.; m in Ridge MH, Achsah
   DOUDNA, dt John & Miriam, Belmont Co., O.
Ch: John   b 1826, 9, 5
    Mary   " 1825, 6, 3
    Sarah   " 1830, 6, 4
1828, 7, 9. Exum, s Thomas & Milisent, Bel-
   mont Co., O.; m in Somerset MH, Sally
   WILLIAMS, dt Samuel & Sarah, Belmont Co.,
   O.
Ch: Joseph   b 1829, 9, 24
    Josiah   " 1831, 6, 15
    Elizabeth " 1833, 3, 6
1828, 11, 3. Mary d ae 81
----, --, --. William & Mary
Ch: Abigail b 1830, 8, 16
1842, 1, 28. John d ae 15 bur Ridge
1843, 2, 9. John, s Wm. & Sarah, Belmont
   Co., O.; m in Ridge MH, Sidney TIPTON,
   dt John & Sarah WOOD, Belmont Co., O.
1844, 2, 8. Mary m Amos W. HAMPTON
1840, 2, 8. John, s Wm. & Sarah, Belmont
   Co., O.; m in Ridge MH, Anne EDGERTON,
   dt Richard & Mary (Hall), Belmont Co., O.
1865, 12, 7. Thomas W., s John & Sidney,
   Belmont Co., O.; m in Ridge MH, Abbie
   DOUDNA, dt Elisha & Mary, Belmont Co., O.
Ch: Clinton b 1866, 11, 25 d 1871, 8, 3
    Frank Wood-
         ward " 1869, 4, 16 " 1870,10,10
    Mary E.   " 1870, 8, 28
1929, 8, 24. Clifford C., s Chalkley L. &
   Luella, Jefferson Co., O.; m in Ridge MH,
   Wauneta Rosetta DOUDNA, dt Dillwyn W. &
   Edith R., Belmont Co., O.

1821, 4, 30. Thomas named overseer
1829, 9, 28. Wm. gct Stillwater MM, O., to m
   Mary Peebles
1830, 1, 25. Mary rocf Stillwater MM, O., dtd
   1830,1,23
1830, 10, 25. Jonathan & w, Achsah, & ch, Mary,
   John & Sarah, gct Deerfield MM
1830, 10, 25. Wm. & w, Mary, & ch, Abigail,
   gct Deerfield MM
1832, 1, 30. Elias gct Stillwater MM, O.
1833, 4, 29. Thomas & w, Millicent, & ch,
   David, Thomas, Peninah, Ruth, Lydia &
   Zadock, gct Deerfield MM
1833, 6, 24. Benjamin gct Deerfield MM, O.
1834, 4, 28. Exum & w, Sally, & ch, Joseph,
   Josiah & Elizabeth, gct Deerfield MM, O.

BUNDY, continued

1834, 4, 28. Moses gct Deerfield MM, O.
1841, 3, 1. Jonathan & w, Achsah, & ch, John,
        Mary, Sarah, Lydia, Peninah & Thomas, rocf
        Chesterfield MM, dtd 1840,12,19
1843, 3, 27. Cidney gct Stillwater MM, O.
1849, 5, 29. Anna gct Stillwater MM, O.
1851, 8, 25. Jonathan & w, Achsah, & ch,
        Peninah & Thomas, gct Pennsville MM
1851, 8, 25. Sarah M. gct Pennsville MM
1851, 8, 25. Lydia gct Pennsville MM
1854, 7, 24. John Starbuck Jr. gct Short Creek
        MM, O., to m Sarah T. Bundy
1930, 2, 30. Wauneta R. gct Short Creek MM, O.

BURKHART

1895, 8, 22. Ella (form Parry) dis mcd

BUTLER

1822, 6, 27. Jared, s Asaph & Lucy, Belmont
        Co., O.; m in Ridge, Elizabeth BAILEY, dt
        James & Sarah, Belmont Co., O.

1824, 5, 24. Jared & w, Elizabeth, & s, Wm.,
        gct Stillwater MM, O.
1824, 6, 28. Permelia (form Bailey) dis mcd

CADLE

1828, 3, 24. Lavina (form Bane) dis mcd

CADWALLADER

1836, 2, 29. Henry Crew gct Short Creek MM,
        O., to m Edith Cadwallader

CARR

1837, 6, 26. Orpah rocf Upper Springfield
        MM, O., dtd 1837,5,27
1838, 5, 28. Orpha gct Pennsville MM, O.

CARTER

----, --, --. Phillip m Hannah R. REYNOLDS,
        dt Josiah & Mary (Swigart), b 1841,3,2
        d 1929,11,4
1906, 5, 3. Edith m Dillwun DOUDNA

1834, 7, 28. Richard rocf Short Creek MM,
        O., dtd 1834,5,20
1836, 4, 25. Richard gct Short Creek MM, O.
1906, 3, 22. Edith R. recrq
1912, 3, 21. Hanna R. rocf Stillwater MM,
        O., dtd 1912,3,20

CATO

1825, 11, 28. Mary (form Bane) dis mcd

CHAMBERS

1833, 4, 4. James, s Samuel & Deborah, Bel-
        mont Co., O.; m in Sunbury, Mary TIPTON,
        dt Luke & Priscilla, Monroe County, O.

1834, 1, 27. Mary gct Stillwater MM, O.

CLARK

1826, 11, 8. Solomon, s Abraham & Mary, Bel-
        mont Co., O.; m in Somerset MH, Ann WAT-
        SON, dt Abner & Elizabeth, Belmont Co.,
        O.
        Ch: Joseph   b 1827, 8, 16
----, --, --. Chas. T. m Edith GIBBONS, dt
        Eli W. & Eliza Jane (McGrew), b 1875,10,
        19)
        Ch: Jennie Ida
               Emma b 1910, 2, 10
            Elma Char-
               lotta b 1911, 6, 16

1826, 9, 25. Solomon rocf Short Creek MM, O.,
        dtd 1826,9,19
1828, 5, 26. Ann dis jH
1828, 6, 30. Solomon dis jH
1835, 6, 29. Joseph, s Solomon & Ann, gct
        Goshen MM, O.
1868, 1, 27. Amy (form Patterson) dis mcd
1910, 2, 24. Edith G. (form Gibbons) con mcd
1910, 8, 22. Jennie Ida Emma, infant dt
        Edith, recrq
1918, 8, 22. Elma Carlotta, infant dt Edith,
        recrq
1923, 9, 20. Edith G. dis disunity
1923, 11, 22. Jennie Ida Emma & Elma Carlotta,
        minors, gct Stillwater MM, O.

CONARD

1863, 2, 8. Rachel d ae 27 bur Sunsbury

1862, 5, 27. Rachel K. [Connard] (form Light-
        foot) con mcd

CONROW

1838, 2, 7. Darling, s Jacob & Eunice, Bel-
        mont Co., O.; m in Somerset MH, Anna EDGER-
        TON, dt Joseph & Christiana HALL, Belmont
        Co., O.
        Ch: Lydia   b 1838, 11, 20 d 1850, 2,22
               bur Somerset
1847, 2, 18. Darling d bur Somerset

1838, 7, 30. Darling rocf Flushing MM, O.,
        dtd 1838,6,21
1862, 2, 24. Anna gct Stillwater MM, O.
1898, 4, 21. James W. Edgerton gct Flushing
        MM, O., to m Edith Conrow

COOK

1925, 7, 30. Alva G., s Wm. & Florence J.
        (Vansyoc), Belmont Co., O., b 1904,3,31;
        m in Ridge MH, Hallie Olive HALL, dt J.
        Walter & Dora Myrtle, Belmont Co., O.
        Ch: Bertha
            Myrtle   b 1926, 9, 8 d 1928, 2, 7
               bur Ridge
            Carl Alva b 1927, 12, 23
            Donald Ce-
               cil   " 1930, 7, 10

COOK, continued
1920, 8, 26. Alva G. recrq

COOPER
1837, 5, 29. Joseph F. Garretson gct Flushing
    MM, O., to m Sarah Cooper

COPE
1839, 7, 27. Julia Ann (form Townsend) dis
    mcd
1841, 7, 26. John Naylor gct Providence MM,
    to m Sarah R. Cope

COPELAND
----, --, --. David & Ann
    Ch: Mary   b 1815, 12, 1
        Sarah A.   " 1817, 10, 26
        John   " 1819, 12, 18
        James B.   " 1822, 3, 6
        Joseph   " 1825, 9, 2
1833, 5, --. David [Couplin] d
1843, 3, --. Ann [Couplin] d bur Concord

1821, 6, 25. Mary, Sarah, Ann & John, minor
    ch of David & Ann, recrq
1836, 6, 27. Ann [Couplin] & ch, James, John
    Bonsel & Joseph, gct Short Creek MM, O.
1837, 4, 24. Mary Hiatt (form Couplin) dis
    mcd
1842, 6, 27. Sarah Ann Berry (form Couplin)
    dis mcd
1847, 3, 29. James [Couplin] rocf Short Creek
    MM, O., dtd 1846,12,22
1849, 4, 30. James [Couplin] dis disunity
1850, 9, 30. Lydia [Couplin] (form Lupton)
    dis mcd

COPPOCK
1830, 6, 28. Mary rocf Stillwater MM, dtd
    1830,6,26
1837, 5, 29. Mary gct Pennsville MM, O.
1879, 9, 25. James E. Bailey gct New Garden
    MM, to m Sarah Coppock

COVENTRY
1873, 8, 21. Sarah (form Doudna) dis mcd

COX
----, --, --. Joseph & Elizabeth
    Ch: Rachel   b 1825, 3, 27
        Joseph   " 1827, 4, 2
1826, 11, 9. Rebecca m Walter EDGERTON
1827, 12, 3. Elizabeth d bur Ridge

1823, 7, 23. Joseph & w, Elizabeth, & ch,
    Joel, Rebecca, Priscilla, Elizabeth, Dru-
    silla, Bennet, Seth, William & Mariah,
    rocf Stillwater MM, O., dtd 1823,6,28
1825, 12, 26. Joel gct White Water MM, Ind.
1827, 5, 28. Stephen & Elizabeth rst on con-
    sent of Stillwater MM, O.
1829, 8, 24. Joseph & w, Elizabeth, & dt,
    Priscilla, & minor ch, Drucilla, Bennett,

Seth, William, Maria, Rachel & Joseph, gct
Milford MM, Ind.
1831, 7, 25. Stephen & w, Elizabeth, & s,
Stephen & Jared, gct Springfield MM, Ind.

CRAFT
1821, 1, 9. Samuel, s James & Mary, Belmont
    Co., O.; m in Somerset MH, Ann BECK, dt
    John & Rachel, Belmont Co., O.
    Ch: John W.   b 18--, 11, 12
        James L.   " 1822, 10, 26
        Rachel B.   " 1827, 6, 28
        Jesse   " 1832, 5, 7
        William   " 1830, 7, 26
        Martha   " 1830, 7, 26
1822, 10, 9. William, s John & Margaret, Bel-
    mont Co., O.; m in Somerset MH, Lydia BECK,
    dt John & Rachel, Belmont Co., O.
1832, 3, 2. Martha d bur Somerset
1889, 3, 24. Sarah d ae 78 bur Ridge

1822, 3, 25. Ann gct Short Creek MM, O.
1822, 11, 25. Lydia gct Plainfield MM
1823, 12, 29. Samuel & w, Ann, rocf Short
    Creek MM, O., dtd 1823,10,21
1825, 2, 28. Asa rocf Chesterfield MM, N. J.,
    dtd 1824,11,2
1825, 8, 29. Asa dis mcd
1828, 8, 25. Asa rst
1837, 4, 24. Asa gct Stillwater MM, O.
1838, 11, 26. Samuel & w, Ann, & ch, James,
    John, Rachel B., Wm. & Jesse, gct Chester-
    field MM, O.
1840, 7, 27. Asa rocf Stillwater MM, O.,
    dtd 1840,4,25
1845, 6, 30. Asa gct Stillwater MM, O.
1885, 3, 26. Sarah rocf Pennsville MM, dtd
    1885,3,19

CREW
----, --, --. Isaac & Judith
    Ch: Lucy   b 1815, 4, 12
        Mary   " 1817, 3, 13
        Edna   " 1818,10, 30
        Rebecca   " 1822,10, 12
1823, 11, 1. Isaac d ae 41 bur Ridge
1826, 5, 4. James, s Jacob & Rachel, Bel-
    mont Co., O.; m in Ridge MH, Sarah BAIN,
    dt Elijah & Rhoda, Belmont Co., O.
    Ch: Isaac   b 1827, 3, 14
        Jacob   " 1828, 9, 22
        Almedia   " 1830, 8, 3
        Edwin   " 1832, 7, 24
        George   " 1833, 12, 9
        Robert   " 1836, 3, 15
        Rebecca   " 1837, 12, 17
        Elijah   " 1839, 9, 24
        John   " 1841, 9, 12
        Jepthah   " 1843, 9, 16
        Eli   " 1846, 3, 11
        Mary   " 1848, 6, 11
        Hosea   " 1851, 2, 16
1829, 9, 15. Edwin d ae 21 bur Ridge

CREW, continued
1830, 11, 4. Judith (nee Bailey) m Robert
     RICKS
----, --, --. William & Mary
     Ch: Delitha   b 1832, 6, 11
         Phariba   " 1833, 12, 1
         Elias   " 1836, 1, 2
1834, 8, 7. Lucy m Benjamin BAILEY
1834, 12, 30. Ann d ae 82 bur Ridge
1835, 4, 17. Eli d ae 21 bur Ridge
----, --, --. Aquilla & Rachel
     Ch: Thomas   b 1840, 12, 25
         Emily   " 1842, 2, 18
         Joseph   " 1843, 9, 30
         Chalkley   " 1845, 4, 24
         Farmer   " 1846, 12, 28
         Ann   " 1849, 6, 29
         Oliver   " 1852, 2, 10
         Isaac   " 1854, 3, 11
         Tabitha   " 1856, 5, 2
         Drucilla   " 1859, 7, 14
         Milton   " 1862, 7, 19
1843, 5, 10. Rachel m Henry D. WILLIAMS
1845, 7, 24. Jacob d ae 66 bur Ridge
----, --, --. Joseph & Esther
     Ch: Joseph Le-
          ander   b 1847, 3, 11
1847, 5, 17. Joseph d ae 28 bur Ridge
1848, 11, 16. Almedia m John W. Wood
1851, 5, 7. Isaac, s James & Sarah (Baine),
     Belmont Co., O.; m Elizabeth GIBBONS, dt
     John & Lydia, Belmont Co., O.
     Ch: James   b 1852, 7, 22
         Lydia   " 1854, 8, 21
         John C.   " 1857, 7, 6
         Sarah D.   " 1859, 9, 6
         Aquila   " 1862, 5, 3
1851, 5, 23. Ann d ae 30 bur Stillwater
1852, 3, 11. Jacob, s James & Sarah, Belmont
     Co., O.; m in Ridge MH, Abigail F. BAILEY,
     dt Wm. & Sarah (Flanner), Belmont Co., O.
     Ch: Esther El-
            len b 1853, 2, 16
         Charlie   " 1857, 11, 28
         Sarah Lizzy" 1860, 3, 28
         Kate   " 1862, 5, 4
1852, 4, 20. Osborn d ae 3 bur Ridge
1853, 9, 29. Hosea d bur Ridge
1856, 8, 7. Rebecca m Wm. STARBUCK
1859, 1, 18. Emily, dt John & Ann, d ae 16,
     bur Ridge
1864, 4, 30. Isaac d ae 37 bur Coal Creek, Ia.
1864, 8, 27. James d ae 60 bur Coal Creek, Ia.

1821, 4, 30. Jacob named overseer
1826, 2, 27. Ann rocf Rich Square MM, N. C.,
     dtd 1825,10,15
1831, 2, 28. William gct Stillwater MM, O.,
     to m Mary Bailey
1831, 6, 27. Mary rocf Stillwater MM, O., dtd
     1831,6,25
1835, 1, 26. Anna Day (form Crew) dis mcd
1836, 2, 29. Henry gct Short Creek MM, O., to

m Edith Cadwalader
1836, 4, 25. Mary Day (form Crew) dis mcd
1836, 9, 26. Edna dis disunity
1836, 9, 26. Edith rocf Short Creek MM, O.,
     dtd 1836,8,23
1836, 10, 24. Wm. & w, Mary, & ch, Delitha,
     Phariba & Elias, gct Pennsville MM, O.
1838, 4, 30. John gct Chesterfield MM
1838, 7, 30. Rebecca Day (form Crew) dis mcd
1839, 7, 27. Henry & w, Edith, & s, Elwood,
     gct Chesterfield MM, O.
1839, 9, 30. Aquilla gct Stillwater MM, O.,
     to m Rachel Farmer
1840, 3, 30. Rachel F. rocf Stillwater MM,
     O., dtd 1840,3,23
1846, 1, 26. Joseph gct Upper Springfield
     MM, to m Esther Crew
1847, 1, 25. Esther rocf Upper Springfield
     MM, dtd 1847,10,24
1848, 5, 29. Esther & s gct Upper Spring-
     field MM
1850, 1, 28. Rachel gct Stillwater MM, O.
1850, 1, 28. Priscilla gct Stillwater MM, O.
1850, 6, 24. John & w, Ann, & ch, Mariam,
     Rebecca, Abner & Osborn. rocf Chesterfield
     MM, dtd 1850,6,15
1854, 9, 25. John gct Flushing MM, O., to m
     Acenath Barber
1854, 10, 30. Jacob & w, Abigail, & dt, Es-
     ther, gct Chesterfield MM
1855, 4, 30. John & ch, Mariam, Rebecca &
     Abner, gct Stillwater MM, O.
1856, 2, 25. Edwin gct Pennsville MM, to m
     Mary B. Doudna
1856, 3, 24. George dis mcd
1858, 11, 27. Edwin gct Pennsville MM
1858, 11, 27. Robert gct Chesterfield MM
1862, 2, 24. Elijah dis mcd
1864, 11, 28. Aquilla & w, Rachel, & ch, Jo-
     seph, Chalkley, Farmer, Ann, Oliver,
     Isaac, Tabitha, Drucilla & Milton, gct
     Hickory Grove MM, Ia.
1864, 11, 28. Sarah & ch, Eli & Mary, & gr dt,
     Sarah Starbuck, gct Hickory Grove MM, Ia.
1865, 2, 27. Elizabeth & ch, James, Lydia,
     John Calvin, Sarah D. & Aquilla I., gct
     Hickory Grove MM, Ia.
1865, 6, 26. Thomas gct Hickory Grove MM, Ia.
1866, 7, 30. John dis mcd

CROY
1828, 9, 29. Judith relrq
1830, 3, 29. Binford dis disunity
1832, 5, 28. Rebecca Parsons (form Croy) dis
     mcd
1832, 9, 24. Susannah dis disunity
1834, 1, 27. Elizabeth Parsons (form Croy)
     dis mcd
1844, 4, 29. William dis disunity

CUMMINS
1834, 6, 30. Lana (form Hall) dis mcd

DAVIS

1825, 7, 6.   Jemima m Jonathan HIETT

1828, 3, 24. Joseph & w, Michael, rocf Still-
     water MM, O., dtd 1828,1,26
1828, 3, 24. Asenath Wellins (form Davis) dis
     mcd
1828, 6, 30. Moses dis jH
1829, 3, 2.   Joseph gct White Water MM, Ind.
1829, 6, 29. Sarah dis jH
1829, 10, 26. Hannah dis jH
1829, 11, 30. Edith dis jH
1831, 5, 30. Ann & Phariba dis jH
1862, 9, 29. Mary (form Tipton) dis mcd

DAVISON

1831, 1, 24. Robert Brock gct Stillwater MM,
     O., to m Penina Davison

DAWSON

1831, 6, 9.   Nathan, s Jesse & Elizabeth,
     Belmont Co., O.; m in Ridge MH, Sarah
     BROCK, dt James & Martha, Belmont Co., O.
     Ch: Martha   b 1832, 11, 12 d 1857, 4, 5
         bur Ridge
1836, 4, 12. Nathan d ae 27 bur Ridge
1860, 12, 6. Eli B., s Joel & Sarah, Belmont
     Co., O.; m in Ridge MH, Esther W. TIPTON,
     dt Abijah & Sidney, Monroe County, O.

1831, 8, 29. Sarah gct Stillwater MM, O.
1833, 1, 20. Nathan & w, Sarah, & dt, Martha,
     rocf Stillwater MM, O., dtd 1832,12,22
1840, 5, 25. Sarah Vandyke (form Dawson) dis
     mcd
1862, 3, 24. Esther & s, Clinton Elsworth,
     gct Stillwater MM, O.

DAY

1835, 1, 26. Anna (form Crew) dis mcd
1836, 4, 25. Mary (form Crew) dis mcd
1838, 7, 30. Rebecca (form Crew) dis mcd

DEW

1842, 7, 25. Sarah (form Boswell) dis mcd

DEWEES

1829, 4, 15. William, s Thomas & Jane, Bel-
     Mont Co., O.; m in Somerset MH, Sarah
     SMITH, dt Thomas & Nancy, Belmont Co., O.
1847, 10, 27. Jesse [Deweese], s Thomas &
     Jane, Monroe Co., O.; m in Somerset MH,
     Rebecca EDGERTON, dt James & Anna (Hall)
     Belmont Co., O.
     Ch: Thomas   b 1848, 10, 12
         James   " 1850, 9, 7
1866, 4, 5.   Aaron, s Wm. & Sarah (Smith),
     Belmont Co., O., b 1844,10,6 d 1926,3,6
     bur Ridge; m in Ridge MH, Maranda GIBBONS,
     dt James & Elizabeth, Belmont Co., O., d
     1891,7,28 ae 45 bur Ridge
1870, 3, 31. Joshua, s Wm. & Sarah (Smith),
     Belmont Co., O.; m in Ridge MH, Martha

GIBBONS, dt Joseph & Peninah (Williams),
     d 1901,1,1 ae 48 bur Ridge
     Ch: Elwood   b 1871, 3, 13
         Mary A.   " 1875, 1, 18
         Joseph   " 1875, 9, 13
         William N. " 1879, 5, 9 d 1880, 9,20
           bur Ridge
         Clifton E. " 1887, 9, 4 " 1888, 2,27
           bur Ridge
1897, 5, 21. Mariana m Oliver W. BINNS
1900, 6, 26. Aaron, s Wm. & Sarah (Smith),
     Belmont Co., O., d 1926,3,6 ae 81 bur
     Ridge; m in Ridge MH, Penina E. GIBBONS,
     dt James & Elizabeth (Williams), b 1854,
     7,17 d 1927,3,12 ae 72 bur Ridge
1927, 3, 12. Penina E. G. d ae 73 (an elder)
1828, 12, 29. William rocf Stillwater MM, O.,
     dtd 1828,12,27
1830, 1, 25. Wm. Jr. & w, Sarah, gct Still-
     water MM, O.
1831, 4, 25. Wm. & w, Sarah, & s, James, rocf
     Stillwater MM, O., dtd 1831,4,23
1834, 1, 27. Wm. & w, Sarah, & ch, James &
     Thomas, gct Deerfield MM, O.
1838, 1, 29. Aaron rocf Pennsville MM, O.,
     dtd 1837,12,14
1840, 5, 25. Rebecca rocf Pennsville MM, O.,
     dtd 1840,4,16
1841, 10, 25. Aaron [Deweese] gct Stillwater
     MM, O., to m Mary Wood
1842, 1, 21. Aaron gct Stillwater MM, O.
1848, 4, 26. Jesse [Deweese] & minor nephew,
     Joshua Deweese, roc dtd 1848,3,16
1848, 4, 26. Joshua [Deweese], minor with
     uncle Jesse Deweese, roc dtd 1848,3,16
1850, 1, 28. Rebecca dis disunity
1851, 10, 27. Jesse & w, Rebecca, & ch, Thom-
     as & James, & nephew, Joshua Dewees, gct
     Pennsville MM
1851, 10, 27. Joshua gct Pennsville MM with
     uncle, Jesse, & fam
1866, 2, 26. Aaron rocf Pennsville MM, dtd
     1866, 2, 15
1869, 9, 23. Joshua rocf Pennsville MM, O.,
     dtd 1869,9,16
1871, 3, 23. Aaron & w, Miranda, gct Penns-
     ville MM
1872, 3, 21. Aaron & w, Miranda, rocf Penns-
     ville MM, O., dtd 1872,2,15
1876, 10, 26. Aaron & w, Miranda, gct Penns-
     ville MM
1882, 3, 23. Joshua dis "obtaining a pension
     for military service"
1890, 6, 26. Aaron & w, Miranda G., rocf
     Pennsville MM, dtd 1890,5,15
1899, 7, 20. Wm. rst on consent of Chester-
     field MM
1899, 9, 21. Wm. gct Stillwater MM, O., to
     m Anna Edgerton
1899, 11, 23. Elwood dis mcd
1902, 6, 26. Wm. gct Stillwater MM, O.
1903, 3, 26. Joseph dis mcd

DODD

1837, 6, 8. Nathan, s Aaron & Rebecca, Bel-
mont Co., O.; m in Ridge MH, Anne Williams
PATTERSON, dt Samuel & Sarah WILLIAMS,
Belmont Co., O.

1828, 6, 30. Nathan & w, Ruth, rocf Stillwater
MM, O., dtd 1828,4,26
1831, 8, 29. Orpha dis jas
1832, 1, 30. Rachel Snyder (form Dodd) dis mcd
1832, 6, 25. Nathan & w, Ruth, gct Stillwater
MM, O.
1833, 5, 27. Nathan & w, Ruth, & Wm. & James
Arnold, minors in their care, rocf Stillwater MM, O., dtd 1833,5,25
1835, 7, 27. Celia Statler (form Dodd) dis
mcd
1842, 2, 28. Nathan & w, Ann, & ch, Eunice,
Ruth & Joseph Patterson, gct Chesterfield
MM
1844, 4, 29. Aaron dis
1845, 12, 29. Joseph & w, Anna, gct Fall Creek
MM

DOUDNA

----, --, --. John & Miriam
    Ch: John   d 1848, 4, 3
            bur Ridge (ae 39)
        Miriam   " 1842, 9,25
            bur Ridge (ae 29)
1824, 5, 6. Achsah m Jonathan BUNDY
----, --, --. Isaac m Martha ----- d 1885,9,28
    ae 70
    Ch: Deborah   b 1834, 10, 29
        Miriam   " 1836, 1, 29
        Benjamin   " 1840, 12, 14 d 1862, 7,12
        John   " 1843, 9, 4
        Thomas   " 1847, 3, 21
        Martha E. " 1849, 11, 7
        Isaac H.   " 1852, 2, 4
        William F. " 1854, 2, 21
        Frank E.   " 1856, 7, 6
        Barnwell P.
        or Burwell
            P.   " 1859, 8, 21 d 1862,12,18
        Edgar S.   " 1862, 5, 7
1840, 10, 8. John Jr., s John & Miriam (Hall)
Belmont Co., O.; m in Ridge MH, Asenath
GARRETSON, dt Joseph & Elizabeth (Williams)
Belmont Co., O., d 1892,2,10 ae 87 bur
Ridge
    Ch: Joseph W. b 1841, 12, 26 d 1933, 1,21
            bur Ridge
        Ann   " 1843, 2, 10
        Jesse   " 1844, 6, 8
        Sarah   " 1846, 7, 5
----, --, --. Joseph & Balinda
    Ch: Edwin   b 1857, 6, 6
        Ruth   " 1862, 8, 3
1860, 10, 8. Mary d ae 86 (w John) bur Ridge
1862, 8, 7. Elisha, s Nowis & Hannah, Guern-
sey Co., O.; m in Sunsbury, Rachel Ann
LUPTON, dt David & Margaret, Monroe Co.,

O.
1863, 11, 29. John, s John & Sarah, d ae 90
bur Ridge
1865, 12, 7. Abbie m Thos. W. BUNDY
1873, 3, 27. John S., s Joseph & Phebe
(Smith), Belmont Co., O., b 1844,1,17
d 1918,2,20 bur Ridge; m in Ridge MH,
Sara THOMASSON, dt John & Eunice (Edgerton)
    Ch: Eunice   b 1874, 10, 26 d 1882,11,25
            bur Ridge
        Smith   " 1877, 2, 24
        Joseph Ell-
            mer   " 1879, 9, 30
        Phebe Anna " 1885, 3, 28
----, --, --. Joseph, s John & Asenath (Garretson), b 1841,12,26 d 1933,1,21 bur
Ridge; m Rosetta H. HALL, dt Joseph & Sarah (Webster), b 1850,10,5
    Ch: Mary   b 1876, 2, 15
        Sarah   " 1876, 2, 15 d 1926, 5,27
        Asenath E. " 1877, 9, 21
        Dilwyn   " 1879, 2, 4
        Elizabeth " 1881, 7, 27
        Joseph H. " 1883, 6, 11
        John A.   " 1887, 2, 2
        Rosetta   " 1889, 4, 25
1880, 1, 1. Jesse, s John & Asenath (Garretson), Belmont Co., O., b 1844,6,8; m
in Ridge MH, Louisa PATTERSON, dt Eli &
Pheriba (Bailey), Belmont Co., O.
    Ch: William W. b 1880, 10, 10
        Martha W.M." 1891, 7, 14 d 1892, 4, 7
            bur Ridge
1894, 2, 3. Phebe, w Joseph, d ae 72 bur
Ridge
1897, 8, 7. Joseph, s Knowis & Hannah (Webster) d ae 77 bur Ridge
----, --, --. Joseph H., s Joseph H. & Rosetta (Hall), b 1883,3,11; m Nora Elma
HARTLEY, dt Thomas & Rosella J. (Marshall),
b 1884,10,17
    Ch: Russell J. b 1906, 3, 14
        Chester E. " 1907, 9, 3
        Alfred M. " 1909, 4, 21
        Delbert H. " 1911, 9, 13
1906, 5, 3. Dillwyn W., s Joseph H. & Rosetta (Hall), Belmont Co., O., b 1879,2,4;
m in Ridge MH, Edith R. CARTER, dt Philip
& Hannah, Guernsey Co., O., b 1879,6,30
    Ch: Margery H. b 1907, 7, 9; m Wm. How-
            ard PEACOCK
        Wauneta R. b 1908, 12, 28; m Clifford
            C. BUNDY
        Joseph Syl-
            vester " 1912, 8, 6
        Ruth Vir-
            ginia " 1918, 9, 13
        Elma May   " 1920, 5, 18
----, --, --. John A., s Joseph W. & Rosetta
(Hall), b 1887,2,2; m Mary Etta CARTER,
dt Levi & Beulah (Roberts), b 1887,9,28
    Ch: Beulah M. b 1910, 3, 13

DOUDNA, John A. & Mary Etta, continued
    Ch: Stanley J. b 1912, 1, 9
        Kenneth L. " 1914, 1, 4
1910, 9, 23. Elizabeth C. m Alva B. HARTLEY
1918, 2, 20. John S., s Joseph & Phebe, d ae
    74 bur Ridge
1919, 9, 4. Asenath Elma m Irving G. BAILEY
1922, 9, 6. Rosetta B. m Frank Allen LOUHOFF
----, --, --. Chester, s Joseph H. & Nora El-
    ma (Hartley), b 1907,9,3; m Marian Ethlyn
    HALL, dt Lewis & Anna (Galloway), b 1904,
    4,5
    Ch: Robert Gene b 1928, 7, 14 d 1928, 7,14
        bur Ridge
1928, 4, 5. Russell J., s Joseph H. & Nora
    E., Belmont Co., O.; m in Ridge MH, Bertha
    L. GALLOWAY, dt Charles A. & Aby L.,Guern-
    sey Co., O., b 1904,3,5
----, --, --. Alfred M., s Joseph H. & Nora
    E., b 1909,4,21; m Alice Bertha STARBUCK,
    dt Thomas & Abbie S. (Hall), b 1910,8,12
    Ch: Richard
        Gene   b 1930, 6, 16
        Harold Ed-
        mund " 1932, 5, 27
1929, 8, 24. Wauneta m Clifford C. BUNDY
1930, 8, 23. Margery H. m Howard PEACOCK

1821, 6, 25. John gct Concord MM, to m Mary
    Steer
1821, 11, 26. Mary rocf Concord MM, dtd 1821,
    9,19
1829, 10, 26. Wm. gct Stillwater MM, O., to
    m Lydia Bailey
1833, 3, 25. Isaac gct Stillwater MM, O., to
    m Martha Peebles
1833, 7, 29. Martha rocf Stillwater MM, O.,
    dtd 1833,7,27
1836, 11, 28. Isaac & w, Martha, & ch, Debo-
    rah & Miriam, gct Pennsville MM, O.
1837, 10, 30. Isaac & w, Martha, & ch, Debo-
    rah & Miriam, rocf Pennsville MM, O., dtd
    1837,10,19
1841, 9, 27. Elisha gct Pennsville MM, to m
    Mary Picket
1842, 4, 25. Elisha gct Stillwater MM, O.
1853, 5, 30. Joseph & w, Belinda, & ch, Jo-
    siah & Mariah (Mary H. on women's minutes)
    rocf Flushing MM, dtd 1853,5,26
1854, 8, 28. Joshua, minor, rocf Chesterfield
    MM, dtd 1854,7,15
1855, 3, 26. Mariam Bailey (form Doudna) dis
    mcd
1855, 10, 29. Deborah dis disunity
1856, 2, 25. Edwin Crew gct Pennsville MM, to
    m Mary B. Doudna
1857, 8, 24. Joshua dis mcd
1860, 5, 28. Deborah E. McGill (form Doudna)
    rpd mcd
1862, 12, 29. Rachel Ann gct Stillwater MM, O.
1862, 12, 29. Elisha & ch, Hannah, Miriam,
    Thomas, Matilda & Nathan, rocf Stillwater
    MM, O., dtd 1862,9,27

1862, 12, 29. Abigail rocf Stillwater MM, O.,
    dtd 1862,9,27
1864, 1, 25. Joseph & w, Belinda, & ch, Jo-
    siah, Mary, Edwin & Ruth, gct Stillwater
    MM, O.
1864, 9, 26. Deborah McGill (form Doudna)
    dis mcd
1865, 2, 27. Elisha dis mcd
1868, 10, 26. Hannah Lightfoot (form Doudna)
    dis mcd
1872, 12, 26. Ann Myers (form Doudna) dis mcd
1873, 5, 22. Joseph & w, Phebe, rocf Still-
    water MM, O., dtd 1873,5,21
1873, 5, 22. Hannah E. rocf Stillwater MM,
    O., dtd 1873,5,21
1873, 8, 21. Sarah Coventry (form Doudna) dis
    mcd
1873,12, 25. John S. rocf Stillwater MM, O.,
    dtd 1873,12,24
1874, 11, 26. Matilda Hodgin (form Doudna)
    dis mcd
1875, 3, 25. Joseph W. gct Stillwater MM, O.,
    to m Rosetta Hall
1877, 5, 24. Rosetta rocf Stillwater MM, O.,
    dtd 1877,4,25
1878, 12, 26. John M. dis mcd & military ser-
    vice
1878, 12, 26. Isaac Jr. dis mcd
1881, 6, 23. Jesse & w, Louisa, & ch, Wm. W.,
    gct Pennsville MM
1883, 5, 24. Miriam dis disunity
1883, 7, 26. Wm. D. rst
1884, 3, 20. Nathan W. dis disunity
1887, 11, 24. Isaac dis disunity
1888, 3, 22. Jesse I. & v, Louiza P., & ch,
    Wm. W. & Mary E., rocf Pennsville MM, O.,
    dtd 1887,3,17
1889, 11, 21. Sarah F. dis
1892, 11, 24. Hannah White (form Doudna) con
    mcd
1901, 7, 25. Jesse & w, Louiza, & ch, Wm.
    Wallace, & Mary Ethel, gct Stillwater MM,
    O.
1901, 12, 26. Smith dis disunity
1905, 5, 25. Joseph H. gct Stillwater MM, O.,
    to m Nora Hartley
1902, 3, 20. Phebe Anna Vandyne (form Doudna)
    dis mcd
1906, 8, 23. Nora E. rocf Stillwater MM, O.,
    dtd 1906,7,25
1907, 8, 22. Joseph Elmer dis mcd & jas
1908, 7, 13. Russel J. rocf Stillwater MM,
    O., dtd 1908,4,22
1910, 10, 20. John A. [Dowdna] con mcd
1911, 4, 20. Mary Etta [Dowdna] & dt, Bula
    M., recrq
1926, 4, 22. Chester E. gct Stillwater MM,
    O., to m Marian Ethelyn Hall
1926, 10, 21. Marian Ethelyn rocf Stillwater
    MM, O., dtd 1926,9,22
1929, 11, 21. Alfred M. gct Short Creek MM,
    O., to m Alice B. Starbuck
1930, 10, 23. Alice B. rocf Short Creek MM,

DOUDNA, continued
    O., dtd 1930,9,23

EATON
1839, 10, 16. Rachel d bur Sunsbury

1839, 3, 25. Rachel rocf Deer Creek MM, dtd
    1839,1,10

EDGERTON
----, --, --. James m Anna HALL
    Ch: Rachel   b 1811, 7, 7
        Joseph   " 1813, 3, 25 d 1828, 3, 7
          bur Somerset
        Nathan   b 1815, 11, 25 " 1828, 3, 1
          bur Somerset
        David   b 1817, 12, 10
        Abigail   " 1820, 9, 29
        Rebecca   " 1822, 9, 10
        Mary   " 1824, 10, 12
        Sarah J.   " 1826, 12, 19
----, --, --. Richard, s James & Sarah (Cox),
    d 1827,10,28 ae 41 bur Ridge; m Mary HALL,
    dt John & Christiana, d 1844,4,6 ae 60 bur
    Ridge
    Ch: Jesse   d 1844, 8, 5
          ae 27 bur Ridge
        Thomas   " 1847, 9, 1
          ae 25 bur Ridge
----, --, --. Joseph & Charity
    Ch: Miriam   b 1819, 10, 4 d 1821, 8,20
          bur Ridge
        Eunice   b 1821, 11, 18
        Achsah   " 1823, 11, 10
        Lydia   " 1825, 8, 26 " 1842,12,10
          bur Ridge
        James   " 1828, 12, 26 " 1907, 9,30
          bur Ridge
         Joseph   " 1830, 11, 18
        William   " 1832, 11, 2 " 1835,12,19
          bur Ridge
        Mary   " 1834, 6, 30
        John   " 1836, 2, 6
        Nathaniel " 1838, 8, 24
        Isaac   " 1842, 5, 29 d 1847, 4,16
        Jesse   " 1845, 7, 12
        Martha   " 1827, 3, 2 sic
1826, 11, 9. Walter, s James & Sarah, Belmont
    Co., O.; m in Ridge MH, Rebecca COX, dt
    Joseph & Elizabeth, Belmont Co., O.
    Ch: William   b 1827, 11, 4
1828, 2, 28. James, s James & Sarah (Cox) d
    ae 40 bur Somerset
1828, 11, 6. Christianna m David GRAY
1829, 4, 8. Rachel m Tilman PATTERSON
1830, 11, 11. Ruth m Asa GARRETSON
1837, 8, 31. Abigail m John VAIL
1838, 2, 7. Anna (nee HALL) m Darling CONROW
1842, 6, 4. Sarah m Isaac HUESTIS
1844, 4, 3. Mary m Eli KENNARD
1844, 12, 5. Achsah m Joseph BAILEY
1847, 3, 11. Eunice m John THOMASSON
1847, 10, 27. Rebecca m Jesse DEWEESE

1849, 2, 8. Anne m John BUNDY
----, --, --. David & Esther
    Ch: Sarah   b 1853, 1, 7
        Lydia   " 1855, 7, 12 d 1858, 3,12
          bur Somerset
        Charles   b 1858, 1, --
        Ellen   " 1865, 12, 18
----, --, --. James & Mary Ann
    Ch: William D. b 1854, 9, 3
        Rebecca   " 1856, 7, 23
        Joseph S.   " 1858, 6, 24
        Thomas D.   " 1861, 12, 22 d 1885, 7,18
        Caroline   " 1864, 5, 14
        Mary   " 1865, 12, 11
        Sarah T.   " 1868, 2, 2
        Walter J.   " 1871, 1, 11
        James W.   " 1872, 11, 9
        Annie E.   " 1875, 3, 8
1854, 7, 26. Sarah J. m Samuel WALTON
1855, 12, 2. Charity, w Joseph, dt John &
    Miriam DOUDNA, d ae 56 bur Ridge
1857, 3, 31. Mary m Allen T. LEE
----, --, --. Joseph & Anna M.
    Ch: Walter   b 1858, 9, 21
        Sarah   " 1860, 8, 13
        Rachel   " 1862, 2, 5
----, --, --. John & Asenath
    Ch: Annie   b 1859, 5, 14
1876, 9, 7. Rebecca m Joseph B. GIBBONS
----, --, --. William D. & Louiza
    Ch: Mary Emma b 1884, 8, 22
1883, 11, 1. Joseph S., s James & Mary Ann
    (Williams); m in Ridge MH, Loretta F.
    PATTERSON, dt Eli & Talitha (Bailey) Bel-
    mont Co., O.
    Ch: Lloyd B.   b 1886, 6, 6
1892, 10, 21. Sarah T. m Allen MAXWELL
1907, 9, 30. James, s Joseph & Charity, d
    ae 78 bur Ridge
1911, 1, 10. Mary Ann, w James, dt Wm. WIL-
    LIAMS, d ae 77 bur Ridge

1823, 11, 24. William & w, Nellie, & ch, Eli
    & Owen, gct Darby Creek MM
1827, 8, 27. Walter rocf Stillwater MM, O.,
    dtd 1827,6,23
1829, 8, 24. Walter & w, Rebecca, & s, Wm.,
    gct Milford MM, Ind.
1837, 3, 27. Albert Lambert gct Pennsville
    MM, O., to m Elizabeth Edgerton
1842, 10, 24. David gct Pennsville MM
1844, 8, 26. Mary d 1844,4,6 ae 61 (an elder)
1851, 2, 24. Martha Bailey (form Edgerton)
    dis mcd
1851, 10, 27. David & w, Esther, & ch, Anna,
    James & Robert, rocf Chesterfield MM, dtd
    1851,9,20
1852, 8, 30. James gct Plainfield MM, to m
    Mary Ann Williams
1853, 1, 24. Mary Ann rocf Plainfield MM,
    dtd 1852,12,22
1853, 3, 28. Joseph Jr. gct Flushing MM, O.,
    to m Lydia S. Mitchel

EDGERTON, continued
1856, 8, 25. Charity d 1855,12,2 ae 57
1875, 3, 30. Joseph gct New Garden MM, to m Anna M. Brantingham
1857, 3, 30. John gct Stillwater MM, O., to m Asenath Hodgin
1857, 7, 27. Sarah T. & ch, Lydia & Sina Brantingham, rocf New Garden MM, dtd 1857, 6,25
1857, 8, 24. Asenath rocf Stillwater MM, O., dtd 1857,7,25
1862, 6, 30. Nathan H. gct Goshen MM, Pa.
1864, 10, 24. John & w, Acenith, & dt, Anna Mary, gct Coal Creek MM, Ia.
1865, 3, 27. Joseph & w, Anna, & ch, Jesse Edgerton, Lydia & Sina Brantingham & Walter, Sarah & Rachel Edgerton, gct Coal Creek MM, Ia.
1868, 7, 27. James Jr. gct Concord MM, Pa.
1877, 4, 26. Robert gct Stillwater MM, O.
1877, 5, 24. Anna gct Stillwater MM, O.
1877, 5, 24. Sarah S. gct Stillwater MM, O.
1877, 7, 27. David & w, Esther, & ch, Charles & Ellen, gct Stillwater MM, O.
1882, 1, 26. Wm. D. dis mcd
1883, 8, 23. Louisa & dt, Alice Caroline, recrq
1884, 12, 25. Caroline gct Chester MM, Pa.
1884, 12, 25. Mary A. gct Chester MM, Pa.
1889, 2, 21. Wm. D. & w, Louesa, & ch, Alice Caroline & Mary Emma, gct Stillwater MM, O.
1894, 3, 22. Joseph E. dis
1898, 4, 21. James W. gct Flushing MM, O., to m Edith Conrow
1898, 7, 21. Walter J. gct Stillwater MM, O., to m Anna R. Taber
1898, 12, 22. James W. gct Chester MM, Pa.
1899, 9, 21. Wm. Dewees gct Stillwater MM, O , to m Anna Edgerton
1904, 3, 24. Walter J. gct Stillwater MM, O.
1913, 8, 21. Annie E. dis
1914, 1, 22. Lloyd B. con mcd
1918, 6, 20. Jesse Wilmer Hall gct New Garden MM, to m Mildred Rachel Edgerton
1926, 2, 25. Loretta F. gct West Branch MM, Ia.

ELKINGTON
1856, 9, 3. Joseph S., s Joseph & Mary, Phila., Pa.; m Malinda PATTERSON, dt Tilman & Rachel (Edgerton), Belmont Co., O.

1856, 12, 29. Malinda gct SD MM

ELLIS
1848, 9, 25. Mary (form Hampton) dis mcd

EMBREE
1829, 5, 28. John, s Samuel & Hannah, Morgan Co., O.; m in Sunsbury Ava MORRIS, dt Wm. & Susannah, Monroe Co., O.

1829, 7, 27. Ava gct Deerfield MM

EVANS
1856, 7, 28. Rebecca (form Tipton) dis mcd

EVES
----, --, --. James & Susanna
    Ch: Ruthann   b 1822, 6, 3
        John   " 1824, 11, 4
        Hannah
        Lydia
        Susanna

1822, 6, 24. Lydia, minor dt Susanna, recrq
1828, 6, 30. James & Susanna dis JH
1835, 11, 30. Hannah Plumley (form Eves) dis mcd
1837, 1, 30. Ruthanna, Susanna & John, minor ch James & Susanna, gct Pennsville MM, O.
1838, 3, 26. Lydia Wells (form Eves) dis mcd

FARMER
1860, 11, 8. Amelia m Able GILBERT

1839, 9, 30. Aquilla Crew gct Stillwater MM, O., to m Rachel Farmer
1858, 7, 26. Taylor & w, Mary Ann, & ch, Armelia, Rhoda & Thomas, rocf Flushing MM, O., dtd 1858,7,22
1863, 7, 27. Taylor & w, Mary Ann, & s, Thomas, gct Flushing MM, O.
1863, 7, 27. Rhoda gct Flushing MM, O.

FAWCETT
----, --, --. Benjamin & Lydia Ann
    Ch: Samuel   b 1828, 12, 13
        Rachel   " 1831, 10, 1
        Drusilla   " 1834, 11, 27

1828, 6, 30. John rocf Stillwater MM, O., with fam of Wm. McNichols, dtd 1828,4,26
1828, 7, 28. Elizabeth rocf Stillwater MM, O., dtd 1828,6,28
1829, 8, 24. Elizabeth Mason (form Fawcett) dis mcd
1832, 10, 29. Benjamin & w, Lydia Ann, & ch, Samuel & Rachel, rocf Stillwater MM, O., dtd 1832,10,27
1833, 8, 26. John gct Stillwater MM, O.
1835, 8, 24. John rocf Stillwater MM, O., dtd 1835,7,25
1837, 1, 30. Mary (form Gibbons) con mcd
1837, 1, 30. John con mcd
1841, 3, 29. John & w, Mary, gct Chesterfield MM
1842, 1, 24. Benjamin & w, Lydia Ann, & ch, Samuel, Rachel, Drucilla, Anna Eliza & Lydia Jane, gct Plainfield MM, O.
1843, 5, 29. Elizabeth [Faucett] (form Gibbons) dis mcd
1845, 9, 29. Benjamin & w, Lydia Ann, & ch, Samuel, Rachel, Drusilla, Ann Eliza & Lydia Jane, rocf Plainfield MM, dtd 1845,

FAWCETT, Benjamin, continued
    7,24

FINCH
1834, 2, 24. Sarah (form Stanton) dis mcd

FISHER
1855, 6, 26. Telitha (form Bailey) dis mcd
1858, 5, 24. Phebe (form Bailey) dis mcd

FLANNER
1837, 12, 31. William d ae 72 bur Ridge
1872, 1, 8. Catharine d ae 87 bur Ridge

1831, 5, 30. Wm. & w, Catharine, rocf Short
    Creek MM, O., dtd 1831,4,19
1833, 8, 26. Wm. Bailey gct Short Creek MM,
    O., to m Sarah Flanner
1836, 9, 26. Wm. & w, Catharine, gct Short
    Creek MM, O.
1837, 10, 30. Wm. & w, Catharine, rocf Short
    Creek MM, O., dtd 1837,6,20
1844, 11, 25. Peninah gct Short Creek MM, O.
    (women's minutes read rocf Short Creek MM,
    dtd 1844,10,22)
1860, 10, 29. Peninah gct Stillwater MM, O.

FOULKE
1825, 1, 6. Mery m Eli WEBSTER
1826, 9, 14. Grace m Ellis HOOPS Jr.

1824, 9, 27. Judah & w, Sarah, & ch, Jesse,
    Mercy, Grace, Silas & John, rocf Plainfield
    MM, dtd 1824,9,23
1827, 2, 26. Cadwallader Jr. rocf Guynned MM,
    Pa., dtd 1826,1,30, end by Plainfield MM
1827, 7, 30. Jesse M. gct Short Creek MM, O.
1829, 4, 27. Judah & w, Sarah, & ch, Silas
    & John, gct Stillwater MM, O.
1829, 4, 27. Judah & w, Sarah, & ch, Silas
    & John, gct Stillwater MM, O.
1830, 3, 1. Cadwallader dis mcd

FRAME
1827, 9, 24. Nathan P. Grissell gct Short
    Creek MM, O., to m Lydia Frame
1844, 3, 25. Elizabeth Ann dis jas
1845, 1, 27. Elizabeth (form Thomas) dis jH

FRAZIER
----, --, --. William & Anne
    Ch: Elizabeth b 1818, 7, 8
        Mary   " 1820, 4, 5
        David   " 1821, 9, 21
        Nelly   " 1823, 7, 29
        Daniel   " 1825, 11, 8

1823, 5, 26. Charity (form Willets) dis mcd
1823, 11, 24. Anna gct Derby Creek MM
1823, 12, 29. Daniel gct Derby Creek MM
1828, 7, 28. Anna dis jH
1828, 8, 25. William dis jH

GALLOWAY
1928, 4, 5. Bertha L. m Russell J. DOUDNA

1928, 2, 23. Bertha L. recrq

GARRETSON
1830, 11, 11. Asa, s Joseph & Elizabeth, Bel-
    mont Co., O.; m in Ridge MH, Ruth EDGER-
    TON, dt Richard & Mary (Hall), Belmont Co.,
    O.
    Ch: Ann   b 1832, 1, 24
        Martha   " 1839,12, 17
        Mary   " 1847, 8, 28 d 1851, 10, 3
        bur Ridge
        Joseph   " 1852, 3, 17
----, --, --. Joseph F. d 1840,10,19 ae 29 bur
    Fremont, Ill; m Sarah -----
    Ch: Martha Lu-
        cetta   b 1838, 4, 19
1838, 5, 10. Patience m John T. ADAMS
1840, 6, 18. Joseph, s Joseph & Elizabeth
    (Williams) d ae 28
1840, 10, 8. Asenath m John DOUDNA Jr.
1841, 5, 6. Rebecca m Norris LUPTON
1848, 11, 16. Hannah m Stephen TOWNSEND
----, --, --. Joseph & Penina
    Ch: Anna   b 1852, 6, 26
        Martha   " 1852, 6, 26
        Elizabeth " 1854, 9, 11
1855, 4, 13. Joseph, s Wm. & Mary, d ae 72
    bur Ridge
1856, 4, 2. Ann m Homer GIBBONS
1858, 2, 26. Elizabeth (Williams), w Joseph,
    d ae 79 bur Ridge
1864, 1, 9. Henrietta d ae 83

1832, 6, 25. John & w, Henrietta, & ch, Re-
    becca, Isaac Parker & Sarah, rocf Short
    Creek MM, O., dtd 1842,4,24
1832, 6, 25. Joseph rocf Short Creek MM, O.,
    dtd 1832,4,24
1832, 4, 24. Hannah rocf Short Creek MM, O.,
    dtd 1832,4,24
1834, 1, 27. Patience rocf Short Creek MM,
    O., dtd 1834,1,22
1837, 5, 29. Joseph F. gct Flushing MM, O.,
    to m Sarah Cooper
1837, 12, 25. Sarah C. rocf Flushing MM, O.,
    dtd 1837,11,23
1842, 2, 28. Sarah C. & dt, Martha Lucetta,
    gct Flushing MM, O.
1842, 6, 27. Isaac P. con mcd
1847, 12, 27. Sarah Oblinger (form Garretson)
    dis mcd
1857, 5, 20. Elizabeth Wilson (form Garret-
    son) con mcd
1848, 10, 30. Isaac dis mcd
1858, 5, 24. Asa & w, Ruth, & ch, Joseph, gct
    Stillwater MM, O.
1858, 6, 28. Martha gct Stillwater MM, O.

GIBBONS
1825, 5, 4. Jane m Benjamin WAY

GIBBONS, continued
----, --, --. John & Lydia
  Ch: Elizabeth b 1831, 4, 26
    Homer " 1832, 12, 29
    Lindley H. " 1836, 6, 20
    Margaret W." 1838, 4, 8 d 1840, 9,25
     bur Somerset
    William b 1840, 8, 4
    Tilman " 1841, 10, 19
    Ruth   " 1844, 3, 21
    John Taylor" 1846, 7, 5
    Lydia Ann " 1848, 12, 3
    Esther " 1851, 3, 31
----, --, --. Joseph & Penina (Williams)
  Ch: Elam b 1838, 10, 23 d 1923, 2, 3
    bur Ridge
1840, 9, --. Elizabeth d bur Somerset
----, --, --. Joseph & Peninah
  Ch: Mary b 1847, 3, 19 d 1848, 5, 7
    bur Somerset
    James b 1847, 3, 19
    Joseph C. " 1850, 2, 6 d 1911,11,28
     bur Ridge
    Lavina H. " 1860, 8, 25 " 1923, 4,30
    Edward W. " 1862, 4, 15
1848, 3, 28. James d bur Sunsbury
1851, 5, 7. Elizabeth m Isaac CREW
1851, 8, 27. James W., infant s James & Elizabeth, d bur Ridge
1856, 1, 22. Edmund d ae 13 bur Somerset
1856, 3, 11. Elizabeth d ae 40 bur Somerset
1856, 4, 2. Homer, s John & Lydia, Belmont
 Co., O.; m in Somerset MH, Ann GARRETSON,
 dt Asa & Ruth (Edgerton), Belmont Co., O.
  Ch: Oliver H. b 1857, 8, 11
    John F. " 1859, 1, 6
    Elvira W. " 1862, 11, 14
1860, 8, 25. Lavina H. d ae 62 bur Ridge
----, --, --. Lindley & Rachel
  Ch: Almeda
    Ellen b 1862, 11, 4
1864, 2, 1. John d ae 58
1864, 4, 8. Sarah E. d bur Ridge
1864, 5, 23. Maria d ae 21 bur Ridge
1866, 4, 5. Maranda m Aaron DEWEES
1870, 3, 31. Martha m Joshua DEWEES
----, --, --. Eli W., s Joseph & Penina (Williams), b 184-,6,27 d 1922,6,27; m Eliza
 Jane McGREW, dt Finley & Rebecca D. (Ong),
 b 1846,7,31 d 1918,4,29 bur Ridge
  Ch: Frederick R. b 1871, 9,22 d 1881, 6,21
    bur Ridge
    Edith El-
     mira " 1875,10, 19
    Albert Wil-
     lard " 1879, 10, 8 d 1883,4,8
     bur Ridge
    Emma Laura " 1884, 3,31
    Edwin D. " 1886, 10,28 " 1887,7,26
     bur Ridge
    Ernest M. " 1886, 10,28 " 1888,3,11
     bur Ridge
----, --, --. James m Lydia HOLLINGSWORTH

Ch: James E. b 1877, 6, 7
1876, 9, 7. Joseph C., s Joseph & Peninah
 (Williams), Belmont Co., O.; m in Ridge
 MH, Rebecca EDGERTON, dt Jas. & Mary Ann
 (Williams), Belmont Co., O. (Joseph C. b
  Ch: Nathan   [1850,2,6
    Allen b 1877, 7, 21
1877, 7, 21. Nathan Allen, s Joseph B. & Rebecca (Edgerton), b
1886, 9, 24. Elizabeth m David WINDER
1888, 1, 16. Penina d ae 70 bur Ridge
1888, 1, 31. Lucinda, dt James & Elizabeth,
 d ae 35 bur Ridge
----, --, --. Joseph B. m Elma THOMAS, dt
 Bradway & Rachel (Hall), b 1859,3,9
  Ch: Clara Bun-
    dy b 1889, 4, 25 d 1900, 5, 9
    bur Ridge
1891, 10, 23. Rebecca E., w Joseph B., dt Samuel & Sarah WILLIAMS, d ae 35
----, --, --. James E. & Lida M.
  Ch: Wilbur Carlton b 1893, 6, 20
    Ronald D. " 1898, 4, 25
1894, 2, 17. Lydia d ae 60 bur Ridge
1896, 9, 25. Anna m George T. SPENCER
1897, 10, 19. James d ae 78 bur Ridge
1898, 4, 28. Edward V., s Joseph & Penina
 (Williams), Belmont Co., O., b 1862,4,15;
 m in Ridge MH, Olive R. PATTERSON, dt Eli
 & Talitha (Bailey), Belmont Co., O.,
 b 1869,10,11 d 1930,2,8, ae 60 bur Ridge
  Ch: Leland S. b 1900, 9, 12
    Mortimer
    Claude " 1909, 3, 2
1900, 6, 26. Penina E. m Aaron DEWEES
1906, 8, 28. Joseph d ae 94 bur Ridge
1911, 11, 28. Joseph B. d ae 61 bur Ridge
1920, 9, 21. Emma Laura m Lamont JOHNSON

1824, 4, 26. Susan rocf Concord MM, dtd 1823,
 12,24
1824, 4, 26. Elizabeth rocf Concord MM, dtd
 1823,12,24
1825, 2, 28. Jane rocf Concord MM, dtd 1824,
 10,20
1827, 10, 29. Elizabeth & Rachel, dt Elizabeth, recrq
1829, 7, 27. Lydia (form Stanton) dis mcd
1830, 1, 25. Mary recrq
1831, 4, 25. Susanna Bruce (form Gibbons) dis
 mcd
1832, 6, 25. Mary (form Stanton) dis mcd
1833, 5, 27. Lydia (form Reeves) dis mcd
1837, 1, 30. Mary Fawcett (form Gibbons) con
 mcd
1837, 5, 29. Peninah (form Williams) con mcd
1838, 11, 26. Lydia rst
1838, 12, 26. John recrq
1840, 6, 29. Elizabeth, Homer, Lindley H. &
 Margaret W., minor ch John & Lydia, recrq
1842, 2, 28. Rachel Williams (form Gibbons)
 dis mcd
1842, 4, 25. Elizabeth Gibbons (form Williams)

GIBBONS, Elizabeth, continued
      dis mcd
1843, 5, 29. Elizabeth Faucett (form Gibbons)
      dis mcd
1846, 10, 26. Joseph recrq
1847, 10, 25. Lydia Ann rst
1851, 6, 30. Lydia Ann gct Bloomfield MM, Ind.
1853, 9, 26. Elam, Eli & Edmund, minor ch
      Joseph & Peninah, recrq
1854, 6, 26. Elizabeth rst
1854, 7, 24. James recrq
1855, 2, 26. Maria, Dillon, Maranda, Sarah
      Elizabeth, Lucinda & Penina, minor ch
      James & Elizabeth, recrq
1861, 11, 25. Lindley H. gct Stillwater MM, O.,
      to m Rachel Bryant
1862, 10, 27. Maria dis
1862, 12, 29. Rachel B. rocf Stillwater MM,
      O., dtd 1862,10,25
1864, 10, 24. Homer & w, Ann, & ch, Oliver
      H., John Franklin & Elvira, gct Coal Creek
      MM, Ia.
1864, 12, 26. Lindley H. & w, Rachel, & dt,
      Amanda Ellen, gct Hickory Grove MM, Ia.
1865, 1, 30. Lydia & ch, John Taylor, Lydia
      Ann & Esther, gct Coal Creek MM, Ia.
1865, 1, 30. Ruth gct Coal Creek MM, Ia.
1866, 4, 30. Wm. dis mcd
1869, 9, 23. James gct Pennsville MM, O., to
      m Lydia Worthington
1870, 8, 25. Eli W. gct Short Creek MM, O.,
      to m Eliza Jane McGrew
1871, 6, 22. Lydia & ch, Zinas Ruben Sarah
      Ann & Mary J. Worthington, rocf Pennsville
      MM, dtd 1871,6,15
1871, 8, 24. Eliza Jane rocf Short Creek MM,
      O., dtd 1871,7,18
1873, 11, 20. Dillon gct Sewickley MM, Pa., to
      m Mary Gilbert
1875, 12, 25. Charles E., minor s James, rec-
      rq
1878, 8, 22. Dillon gct Salem MM
1892, 7, 21. James E. gct Flushing MM, O., to
      m Eliza M. Stephen
1895, 6, 20. Charles E. con mcd
1897, 2, 25. Joseph B. gct Short Creek MM,
      O., to m Elma Thomas
1897, 9, 23. Elma F. rocf Short Creek MM, O.,
      dtd 1897,8,24
1910, 1, 20. N. Allen con mcd
1910, 2, 24. Edith G. Clark (form Gibbons)
      con mcd
1918, 3, 21. Charles E. gct Salem MM, O.
1919, 4, 24. James E. dis disunity
1914, 1, 24. Edward V. dis disunity
1927, 11, 24. Nathan Allen dis jas

GILBERT
1852, 2, 23. Anna d ae 47 bur Sunsbury
1852, 5, 3. Rebecca d bur Sunsbury
1860, 11, 8. Able, s Able & Anna, Belmont
      Co., O.; m in Ridge MH, Amelia Farmer,
      dt Taylor & Mary Ann, Belmont Co., O.

1848, 10, 30. Anna & ch, Rebecca & Abel, rocf
      Chesterfield MM, dtd 1848,9,16
1857, 12, 28. Abel, minor, gct Pennsville MM
1861, 6, 24. Armelia C. gct Plymouth MM
1873, 11, 20. Dillon gct Sewickley MM, Pa.,
      to m Mary Gilbert

GLOVER
1823, 6, 30. Mary (form Wade) dis mcd
1826, 12, 25. Jemimah (form Beck) dis mcd

GOODWIN
1865, 10, 30. Mary (form Lupton) dis mcd

GRAY
----, --, --. Elisha & Ann
      Ch: Elijah   b 1829, 2, 4
          Peter   " 1832, 1, 11
          Rachel   " 1834, 3, 24
1828, 11, 6. David, s Elijah & Mary, Harri-
      son Co., O.; m in Ridge MH, Christianna
      EDGERTON, dt Richard & Mary, Belmont Co.,
      O.
      Ch: Richard E. b 1829, 8, 31
          Elijah   " 1831, 3, 11
          Joseph   " 1833, 6, 18
          Elisha   " 1835, 8, 2
          Mary   " 1837, 7, 10
          Nathan   " 1839, 7, 30
          Sarah   " 1841, 4, 25
          Ann   " 1843, 9, 30
          Jesse   " 1846, 7, 23 d 1846, 8,10
          bur Ridge
----, --, --. Joseph & Deborah
      Ch: John White b 1835, 3, 29
          Lewis C.   " 1837, 8, 13 d 1844, 7,--
          bur Chesterfield
1835, 5, --. Ann d bur W. Grove, Monroe Co.,
      O.
----, --, --. John & Deborah
      Ch: Mary   b 1841, 5, 3
1848, 3, 28. David d bur Sunsbury
1852, 4, 10. Mary d ae 81 bur Somerset
1853. 4, 26. Christianna m George SMITH

1828, 8, 25. Thomas & fam rocf Short Creek
      MM, O.; returned for jH
1829, 3, 2. David rocf Short Creek MM, O.,
      dtd 1829.2.24
1834, 1, 27. Elisha & w, Ann, & ch, Elijah &
      Peter, rocf Short Creek MM, O., dtd 1833,
      11,19   [dtd 1835,5,19
1835, 6, 29. Mary rocf Short Creek MM, O.,
1836, 11, 28. John & w, Deborah, & s, John
      Whittier, rocf Short Creek MM, O., dtd
      1836,7,19
1837, 1, 30. Elisha dis mcd
1844, 7, 29. Deborah dis disunity
1844, 8, 26. John dis disunity
1851, 3, 24. Elijah dis jas
1851, 10, 27. Rachel gct Short Creek MM, O.
1855, 1, 29. Richard E. dis mcd

GREEN
1887, 7, 21. Rhoda dis disunity

GREGG
1875, 7, 9. Hannah d ae 73

1825, 11, 28. Nathaniel & w, Elizabeth, & ch,
      Ruthanna, Jonas & Martha, rocf Plainfield
      MM, dtd 1825,9,22
1828, 5, 26. Nathaniel & w, Elizabeth, & ch,
      Ruthanna, Joseph, Martin & Nathan, gct
      Duck Creek MM, Ind.
1831, 3, 28. Caleb & w, Millisent, & ch,
      Henry & Martha, rocf Stillwater MM, O.,
      dtd 1831,3,26
1831, 11, 28. Caleb & w, Millisent, & ch,
      Henry & Martha, gct Stillwater MM, O.
1845, 9, 29. Hannah & ch, Carlton, Samuel,
      Mark, Bula Ann, Lydia, Phebe H., James &
      William, rocf Flushing MM, O., dtd 1845,
      8,21
1849, 11, 26. Mark dis disunity
1851, 3, 24. Carlton dis mcd
1875, 11, 25. Phebe McAbe (form Gregg) dis mcd
1876, 10, 26. Lydia Harras (form Gregg) dis
      mcd
1877, 2, 22. Wm. dis mcd & military service
1877, 5, 24. James dis mcd & jas

GRISSELL
1826, 6, 26. Hannah [Grizzell] rocf Short
      Creek MM, O., dtd 1826,4,16
1826, 9, 25. Nathan recrq
1827, 9, 24. Nathan P. gct Short Creek MM,
      O., to m Lydia Frame
1828, 4, 28. Nathan P. dis jH
1828, 7, 28. Lydia & dt, Elizabeth Ann Frame,
      rocf Short Creek MM, O., dtd 1828,6,24
1829, 1, 26. Lydia [Grissle] dis jH
1841, 12, 27. Elizabeth & Simeon [Grissel],
      minor ch Thomas, rocf Short Creek MM, O.,
      dtd 1841,11,23
1842, 8, 29. Hannah Ann Tipton (form Grissel)
      dis mcd
1844, 3, 25. Elizabeth [Grissel] dis jH
1844, 9, 30. Edward [Grissel] dis mcd

HALL
----, --, --. Moses & Elizabeth
      Ch: Rachel   b 1810, 5, 28
          Lanah   " 1812, 1, 25
          Sarah   " 1813, 9, 24
          Joseph   " 1816, 2, 24
          Benjamin   " 1816, 2, 24
          Elihu   " 1817, 12, 25
          Elizabeth " 1821, 12, 28
----, --, --. Robert & Mary
      Ch: Sarah   b 1851, 4, 4
          Deborah D. " 1852, 9, 24
1855, 9, 11. Robert d ae 44 bur Short Creek
1860, 5, 10. Tacy M. m Sinclair SMITH
1861, 4, 24. Henry d ae 24 bur Ridge
1862, 12, 4. Lindley, s David & Sarah S.,

Belmont Co., O.; m in Ridge MH, Millicent
BAILEY, dt Edmund & Margaret, Belmont Co.,
O.
1867, 11, 28. Mary m Robert MILLER
1883, 12, 21. John G., s John & Hannah (Graham)
      Columbiana Co., O., b 1834,12,23 d 1918,
      3,6 ae 74 bur Ridge; m in Ridge MH, Anna
      LIVEZEY, dt Jesse & Elizabeth (Patterson),
      Belmont Co., O., b 1851,6,29
      Ch: Elizabeth
               G. b 1884, 10, 21
          Jesse Wil-
               mer " 1886, 2, 8
1906, 12, 15. Nellie Ruth, dt Edwin P. &
      Minnie Catharine (Lehman), b
1907, 11, 22. Elizabeth m Silas HARTLEY
----, --, --. Walter, s Joseph G. & Sara
      (Hartley), b 1879,7,21; m Dora M. LAY, dt
      Adam & Harriet Ann (Cline), b 1880,9,6
      Ch: John A.   b 1911, 3, 11
          Ronald J. " 1915, 5, 17·
----, --, --. J. Wilmer, s John G. & Anna,
      b 1886,2,8; m Mildred EDGERTON, dt Walter
      & Mary H. (Binns), b 1889,3,16
      Ch: Lillian
             Mary   b 1921, 8, 28
          John Ed-
             ward   " 1923, 3, 7
          Elenor Sa-
             ra   " 1924, 10, 30
          Melva Anna " 1927, 2, 27
1925, 7, 30. Hallie Olive m Alva J. COOK
1928, 9, 27. John A., s Walter & Dora M.,
      Belmont Co., O.; m in Ridge MH, Mary Re-
      becca HARTLEY, dt Silas & Elizabeth J.
      (Hall), Belmont Co., O.
      Ch: Olive Mar-
             garet   b 1931, 9, 17
          John Robert" 1933, 10, 25

1928, 10, 4. Verna C. m Wm. L. JOHNS
----, --, --. Ronald J., s Walter & Dora,
      b 1915,5,17; m Anna Mabel HARTLEY, dt
      Silas H. & Elizabeth J. (Hall), b 1913,8,
      21

1821, 11, 26. Joseph rocf Short Creek MM, dtd
      1821,10,23
1831, 6, 27. Sarah Lowry (form Hall) dis mcd
1831, 6, ·27. Moses dis mcd
1833, 7, 29. Rachel dis
1834, 6, 30. Lana Cummins (form Hall) dis mcd
1835, 7, 27. Susanna (form Bailey) dis mcd
1838, 3, 26. Joseph & Elihu gct Pennsville
      MM, O.
1838, 8, 24. Benjamin dis jas
1844, 5, 27. Elizabeth dis
1850, 5, 27. Robert & w, Mary, & ch, Hervey,
      Tacy & Martha, rocf Plainfield MM, dtd
      1850,4,24
1862, 9, 29. Lindley rocf Short Creek MM, O.,
      dtd 1862,7,22
1865, 10, 30. Lindley & w, Milicent, & s,

HALL, Lindley, continued
      Franklin, gct Flushing MM, O.
1868, 12, 28. Martha, Sarah R. & Deborah D.,
      with their mother, Mary H. Miller, gct
      Sandy Spring MM
1884, 2, 21. John G. rocf Middleton MM, dtd
      1884,2,16
1918, 6, 20. Jesse Wilmer gct New Garden MM,
      to m Mildred Rachel Edgerton
1919, 1, 23. Mildred R. rocf New Garden MM
1925, 4, 23. Hallie Olive rocf Stillwater
      MM, dtd 1925,3,25
1926, 4, 22. Chester E. Doudna gct Stillwater
      MM, O., to m Marian Ethelyn Hall
1928, 7, 26. Verna Cecelia, gr dt Sarah Hall,
      recrq
1933, 7, 20. Nellie R. rocf Holly Spring MM,
      N. C.

HAMPTON
1830, 5, 5. John, s John & Mary (Betts),
      Belmont Co., O.; m in Somerset MH, Mary
      WILLIAMS, dt Samuel & Sarah, Belmont Co.,
      O.
      Ch: Anna   b 1840, 4, 3
          Elizabeth " 1844, 4, 5
          Lavina   " 1846, 6, 27
          John W.   " 1849, 5, 8 d 1850, 5, 1
            bur Ridge
          Edward   " 1851, 6, 2 [bur Ridge
          Samuel   " 1851, 6. 2 d 1851, 8,26
1838, 12, 6. Mary Ann m Elihu ROBINS
1844, 2, 8. Amos W., s James & Emily, Bel-
      mont Co., O.; m in Ridge MH, Mary BUNDY,
      dt Jonathan & Achsah (Doudna)
1849, 1, 4. Levi, s James & Emily, Belmont
      Co., O.; m in Ridge MH, Lydia Ann PATTER-
      SON, dt Laben B. & Sarah, Washington Co.,
      O.
1850, 5, 2. Lydia Ann, infant, d Salem,
      Iowa
1852, 4, 8. Sarah W. m Richard MOTT

1829, 4, 27. Asa & w, Esther, & dt, Martha,
      rocf Deerfield MM, dtd 1829,4,16
1829, 11, 30. Joseph Arnold gct Deerfield MM,
      to m Bethula Hampton
1829, 12, 28. John rocf Deerfield MM, dtd
      1829,12,17
1830, 11, 29. John & w, Mary, & s, Carey, rocf
      Deerfield MM, dtd 1830,10,14
1833, 1, 28. Asa C. & w, Esther, & ch, Mar-
      tha, Joseph & Benjamin, gct Deerfield MM,
      O.
1834, 3, 24. Cary gct Deerfield MM, O.
1834, 4, 28. John Jr. & w, Mary, & ch,
      Oliver & Sarah, gct Deerfield MM, O.
1834, 12, 29. Emily & ch, Amos, Levi, Mary &
      James Hiram, rocf Stillwater MM, O., dtd
      1834,12,27
1835, 7, 27. John & w, Mary, & Levi Hampton,
      a minor in their care, gct Pennsville MM,
      O.

1835, 7, 27. Levi, minor in care of John &
      Mary, gct Pennsville MM, O.
1835, 7, 27. Mary Anna gct Pennsville MM, O.
1838, 5, 28. John rocf Pennsville MM, O., dtd
      1838,4,19
1838, 5, 28. Mary Ann rocf Pennsville MM, O.,
      dtd 1838,4,19
1838, 6, 25. Levi, minor rocf Pennsville
      MM, O.
1839, 10, 28. John & w, Mary, & ch, Oliver,
      Sarah, Robert & Lucinda, rocf Chester-
      field MM, dtd 1839,10,19
1840, 11, 30. John gct Pennsville MM
1846, 3, 2. Amos & w, Mary, gct Stillwater
      MM, O.
1848, 9, 25. Mary Ellis (form Hampton) dis
      mcd
1849, 10, 29. James H. gct Pennsville MM
1852, 1, 26. Levi gct Salem MM, Ia.
1854, 3, 27. John & w, Mary, & ch, Robert,
      Lucinda, Anna, Lavina, Elizabeth & Edward,
      gct Vermillion MM, Ill.
1854, 3, 27. Oliver gct Vermillion MM, Ill.

HANSON
----, --, --. Elijah & Eliza
      Ch: William   b 1819, 6, 18
          Joseph S. " 1821, 1, 21
          Susanna   " 1823, 2, 17
          Robert   " 1825, 2, 18
          Elijah   " 1827, 1, 20
          Zilpha   " 1829, 5, 28
          Eliza   " 1831, 4, 21
          John   " 1833, 3, 6
          Asa   " 1835, 4, 15
          ------   " 1837, 3, 17
----, --, --. Borden & Rachel
      Ch: Levi   b 1824, 6, 18
          Edwin   " 1826, 10, 8
          Thomas   " 1828, 11, 16
----, --, --. Robert & Prudence
      Ch: Eliza   b 1846, 8, 19 d 1848, 6,18
          Martha   " 1849, 4, 5

1822, 10, 28. Elijah & w, Eliza, & ch, Wil-
      liam & Joseph, rocf Stillwater MM, O., dtd
      1822,9,28
1823, 8, 25. Borden & w, Rachel, & ch, John &
      Ann, rocf Stillwater MM, O., dtd 1823,7,
      26
1825, 9, 26. Rachel gct Short Creek MM, O.
1831, 7, 21. Borden & w, Rachel, & ch, John,
      Ann, Levi, Edwin, Thomas & Elisha, gct
      Springfield MM, Ind.
1837, 5, 29. Elijah & w, Eliza, & ch, Wil-
      liam, Joseph, Susanna, Robert, Elijah,
      Zilpha, Eliza, John, Asa & J----, gct
      Stillwater MM, O.
1846, 6, 29. Robert & w, Prudence, rocf Still-
      water MM, O., dtd 1846,5,23
1852, 11, 25. Robert & w, Prudence, & ch,
      Thomas Osburn, gct Plymouth MM, O.

HAROLD
1823, 8, 25. Jacob dis disunity
1829, 3, 2. Charity dis
1835, 5, 25. Joseph dis disunity
1840, 2, 24. Amasa dis disunity
1841, 8, 30. Caty [Harrold] dis disunity
1853, 11, 28. Mary gct Chesterfield MM

HARPER
1825, 7, 25. Lydia (form White) dis mcd
1828, 7, 28. Rhoda (form White) dis mcd
1828, 8, 25. Rhoda dis jH

HARRAS
1876, 10, 26. Lydia (form Gregg) dis mcd

HARRISON
1823, 8, 25. Rachel rocf Alum Creek MM, dtd
    1823,5,1
1825, 9, 26. Rachel gct Short Creek MM, O.

HARTLEY
1860, 5, 2. Mahlon, s Noah & Milicent,
    Guernsey Co., O.; m in Ridge MH, Mary
    PATTERSON, dt Lemuel & Hannah (Arnold),
    Belmont Co., O.
1907, 11, 22. Silas, s Thomas & Rosella (Mar-
    shall), Guernsey Co., O., b 1881,3,19;
    m in Ridge MH, Elizabeth J. HALL, dt John
    G. & Anna (Livezey), b 1884,10,21
    Ch: Harry John b 1911, 7, 15
        Walter G. " 1919, 10, 30
        Ellen Gra-
            ham   " 1926, 7, 18
----, --, --. Arthur J., s Thomas & Rosella J.
    (Marshall), b 1886,5,25 d 1927,7,26 bur
    Ridge; m Mary Edith WHINERY, dt Elwood D.
    & Asenath (Thomas), b 1887,2,3
    Ch: Lucile   b 1909, 10, 2; m Kelsall
        Laura E.   " 1911, 11, 28
        Willard
        Everett " 1913, 12, 27
        Clifford B." 1915, 1, 4
        Sara Alice " 1915, 1, 4
        Robert E. " 1920, 11, 18
        Albert T. " 1922, 9, 8
        Flora Sina " 1925, 7, 10
1910, 9, 23. Alva B., s Thomas & Rosella
    (Marshall), Guernsey Co., O., b 1889,7,23;
    m in Ridge MH, Elizabeth C. DOUDNA, dt
    Joseph W. & Rosetta (Hall), Belmont Co.,
    O., b 1881,7,27
    Ch: Cecil   b 1913, 5, 15 d 1913, 5,15
            bur Ridge
        Luella   " 1914, 7, 27 " 1914, 7,27
            bur Ridge

1862, 6, 30. Mary & s, Clarkson, gct Still-
    water MM, O.
1905, 5, 25. Joseph H. Doudna gct Stillwater
    MM, O., to m Nora Hartley
1908, 1, 23. Elizabeth J. gct Stillwater MM,
    O.

1910, 3, 24. Mary Edith & dt, Lucila, rocf
    Short Creek MM, O, dtd 1910,3,22
1910, 8, 22. Arthur J. rocf Stillwater MM,
    O., dtd 1910,6,22
1911, 12, 21. Alva B. rocf Stillwater MM, O.,
    dtd 1911,11,22
1914, 11, 26. Silas & w, Elizabeth J., & ch,
    Mary R., Harry J. & Anna M., rocf Still-
    water MM, O., dtd 1914,10,21
1914, 12, 24. Arthur J. & w, Mary Edith, &
    ch, Lucile, Laura E. & Willard Everet,
    gct Stillwater MM, O.
1919, 6, 26. Arthur J. & w, Mary Edith, &
    ch, Lucile, Laura E., W. Everett Clifford
    B. & Sarah Alice, rocf Stillwater MM, O.,
    dtd 1919,5,21
1926, 7, 22. Arthur J. & w, Mary Edith, &
    ch, Lucile, Laura E., Willard Everett,
    Clifford B., Sara A., Robert Elmer &
    Flora S., gct Plainfield MM, Ind.
1927, 7, 21. Arthur J. & w, Mary Edith, &
    ch, Lucile, Laura E., W. Everett, Clifford
    B., Sara A., Robert E., Albert T. & Flora
    S., rocf Plainfield MM, Ind., dtd 1927,7,
    29
1931, 3, 26. Lucile Kelsel (form Hartley)
    con mcd
1931, 10, 22. Mary Edith Holloway (form Hart-
    ley) con mcd

HEALY
1824, 3, 1. Laban B. Patterson gct Still-
    water MM, O., to m Sarah Healy

HERALD
1848, 10, 30. Mary Jr. dis disunity

HIATT
1825, 7, 6. Jonathan [Hiett], s Jehu &
    Tamar, Belmont Co., O.; m in Somerset MH,
    Jemima DAVIS, dt Moses & Ann, Belmont
    Co., O.
    Ch: Elisha   b 1826, 4, 4
        Lewis   " 1827, 11, 30
1825, 11, 3. Elijah [Hiett], s Jehu & Tamar,
    Belmont Co., O.; m in Somerset MH, Anne
    BOSWELL, dt Dempsey & Mary, Belmont Co., O.

1827, 5, 28. Elijah & w, Anna, & s, Dempsey,
    gct Stillwater MM, O.
1829, 7, 27. Susanna rocf Stillwater MM, O.,
    dtd 1829,7,25
1831, 3, 28. Jesse gct Short Creek MM, O.,
    to m Ruthanna Vernon
1831, 12, 26. Jehu & w, Thamer, gct Clear
    Creek MM
1831, 12, 26. Jonathan & w, Jemima, & ch,
    Elisha, Lewis & Wilson, gct Clear Creek
    MM, O.
1831, 12, 26. Amos gct Clear Creek MM, O.
1831, 12, 26. Jesse gct Clear Creek MM, O.
1831, 12, 26. Susanna gct Clear Creek MM, O.
1831, 12, 26. Ann gct Clear Creek MM, O.

HIATT, continued
1835, 6, 29. Jehu dis disunity
1837, 4, 24. Mary (form Couplin) dis mcd

HICKS
----, --, --. James & Bethany
    Ch: Loiza   b 1813, 8, 5
        Joanna   " 1814, 11, 27
        William   " 1816, 3, 18
        Lydia   " 1818, 12, 28
        Elias   " 1820, 9, 4 d 1822, 5,10
          bur Somerset
        Mary   b 1822, 1, 12
        James   " 1823, 10, 17
        Martha   " 1825, 11, 10
        Bethany   " 1827, 8, 18
        Robert   " 1829, 11, 7

1825, 3, 28. Laban [Hix] dis
1833, 6, 24. Louisa Wilson (form Hix) dis mcd
1838, 6, 25. Joanna gct Stillwater MM, O.
1838, 6, 25. Lydia gct Stillwater MM, O.
1838, 6, 25. James & w, Bethany, & ch, Mary,
    James, Martha, Bethany & Robert, gct
    Stillwater MM, O.
1838, 7, 30. Wm. gct Stillwater MM, O.

HOBBS
1842, 8, 29. Rachel Ann (form Stanton) dis
    mcd

HOBSON
1857, 9, 3. Stephen, s Joseph & Ruth (Ball)
    Belmont Co., O.; m in Ridge MH, Margaret
    BAILEY, dt Edmund & Margaret (Doudna),
    Belmont Co., O.

1858, 3, 29. Margaret gct Flushing MM, O.

HODGIN
1821, 7, 30. Ann (Nancy) & Wm., minor ch
    John & Prudence, recrq
1822, 4, 29. Lydia Willits (form Hodgin) dis
    mcd
1823, 12, 29. John & w, Prudence, & ch, Wil-
    liam, Leake Elias & Agness, gct Still-
    water MM, O.
1824, 5, 24. Ann Willits (form Hodgin) dis
    mcd
1827, 5, 28. Mary Mann (form Hodgin) dis mcd
1831, 5, 30. Robert dis jH
1831, 6, 27. Ann, w Robert, & ch, Elizabeth,
    John, William, Robert, Stephen, Joseph &
    Benjamin, gct Sugar River MM, Ind.
1857, 3, 30. John Edgerton gct Stillwater MM,
    O., to m Asenath Hodgin
1874, 11, 26. Matilda (form Doudna) dis mcd
1885, 8, 20. Thomas Thomasson gct Springville
    MM, Ia., to m Mary E. Hodgin

HOGUE
1870, 6, 23. Penninah (form Brock) dis mcd

HOLLOWAY
1931, 10, 22. Mary Edith (form Hartley) con
    mcd

HOOPS
1826, 9, 14. Ellis Jr., s Ellis & Elizabeth,
    Belmont Co., O.; m in Somerset, Grace
    FOULKE, dt Judah & Sarah, Monroe Co., O.
    Ch: Margaret   b 1828, 4, 30
1850, 3, 20. Elizabeth d ae 68 bur Sunsbury

1826, 1, 30. Ellis recrq
1831, 10, 24. Grace [Hoopes] dis
1832, 1, 30. Ellis & ch, Margaret, Elizabeth
    & Sarah, gct Milford MM, Ind.

HUESTIS
1842, 6, 4. Isaac, s Aaron & Esther, Athens
    Co., O.; m in Ridge MH, Sarah EDGERTON,
    dt Richard & Mary (Hall), Belmont Co., O.

1842, 7, 25. Sarah gct Chesterfield MM

JAMES
----, --, --. George & Sarah
    Ch: Rachel   b 1827, 3, 1

1824, 5, 24. George & w, Sarah, & ch, Hannah,
    Edith, David, Samuel & Elizabeth, rocf
    Short Creek MM, O., dtd 1824,4,20
1829, 7, 27. George dis
1829, 11, 30. Sarah & ch, Edith, David, Eliza-
    beth, Samuel & Rachel, gct Flushing MM
1829, 11, 30. Hannah gct Flushing MM, O.

JARRET
1867, 8, 27. Hannah (form Lightfoot) dis mcd

JOHN
1887, 11, 15. George, s Jesse & Amy (Dean),
    Morgan Co., O.; m in Ridge MH, Sinah
    BALEY, dt Jehu & Martha (Steer), Belmont
    Co., O.
1928, 10, 4. Wm. Leroy, foster s Alva B. &
    Elizabeth C. HARTLEY, Belmont Co., O.,
    b 1910,12,13; m in Ridge MH, Verna C. HALL
    dt Albert & Lillie M., Belmont Co., O.,
    b 1912,2,23
    Ch: Dorothy Mae b 1929, 9, 29
        Kenneth Wm. " 1932, 10, 17

1821, 11, 26. Sarah & ch, Ann, Jesse & Rachel,
    rocf Short Creek MM, dtd 1821,10,23
1824, 7, 26. Sara gct Salem MM
1832, 12, 24. Ann gct Short Creek MM, O.
1835, 12, 28. Ann rocf Short Creek MM, O., dtd
    1835,10,20
1836, 10, 24. Ann gct Pennsville MM, O.
1838, 10, 29. Jesse gct Chesterfield MM
1840, 10, 26. Rachel gct Smithfield MM
1888, 6, 21. Sina gct Chesterfield MM, O.
1920, 10, 21. Wm. Leroy [Johns], foster s Al-
    va B. & Lizzie C. Hartley, recrq

JOHNSON
1920, 9, 21. Roy Lamont, s Chester N. & Fran-
    ces A., Winsor Co., Vt.; m in Ridge MH,
    Emma Laura GIBBONS, dt Eli W. & Eliza
    Jane (McGrew), b 1884,3,31 (Roy Lamont
    b 1884,12,27)
    Ch: Jennie
        Frances   b 1922, 5, 1 d 1922, 5, 1

1920, 7, 22. Roy L. recrq
1923, 11, 22. Roy L. & w, Emma L., gct Still-
    water MM, O.

JONES
1840, 6, 29. Jane (form Wood) dis mcd

KELSEL
1931, 3, 26. Lucile (form Hartley) con mcd
1931, 5, 21. Lucile Hartley gct Chester MM,
    Pa.

KENNARD
1836, 3, 10. Mary m David TIPTON
1840, 10, 11. Rachel d ae 58 bur Sunsbury
----, --, --. William & Sarah
    Ch: Elizabeth b 1843, 12, 15
        Joseph   " 1845, 9, 8
1844, 4, 3. Eli, s Wm. & Rachel, Monroe Co.,
    O.; m in Somerset MH, Mary EDGERTON, dt
    James & Ann, Belmont Co., O.
    Ch: Anna   b 1846, 5, 20
        William   " 1848, 11, 5
        Jesse   " 1851, 8, 23
        Rachel   " 1853, 9, 19 d 1855, 2,21
            bur Somerset

1824, 7, 26. William & w, Rachel, & s, Eli,
    rocf Short Creek MM, O., dtd 1824,7,20
1830, 8, 30. Mary, minor, rocf Deerfield MM,
    dtd 1830,7,15
1832, 8, 27. Eli Jr. rocf Deerfield MM, dtd
    1832,6,14
1842, 5, 30. Eli Jr. gct Pennsville MM
1842, 10, 24. Wm. gct Plainfield MM, to m Sa-
    rah Roberts
1843, 5, 29. Sarah rocf Plainfield MM, dtd
    1843,2,22
1856, 4, 28. Eli & w, Mary, & ch, Anna, Wil-
    liam & Jesse, gct Stillwater MM, O.
1859, 12, 26. William & w, Sarah, & ch, Eliza-
    beth R. & Joseph, gct Stillwater MM, O.

KING
1848, 4, 26. Joseph, s Michael & Hannah, Mor-
    gan Co., O.; m in Ridge MH, Anna PATTERSON
    dt John & Miriam (Hall) DOUDNA, Belmont
    Co., O., d 1883,1,24 ae 81 bur Ridge

1848, 6, 26. Anna gct Pennsville MM

KOONTZ
1852, 10, 25. Elizabeth (form Williams) dis
    mcd

LAMBERT
----, --, --. Albert & Elizabeth
    Ch: Rachel   b 1838, 3, 25
        John   " 1839, 9, 6

1827, 1, 29. Sarah recrq
1835, 11, 30. Sarah, minor dt Sarah, recrq
1835, 12, 28. Albert recrq
1836, 4, 25. Elizabeth gct Pennsville MM, O.
1837, 3, 27. Albert gct Pennsville MM, O., to
    m Elizabeth Edgerton
1838, 1, 29. Elizabeth rocf Chesterfield MM,
    dtd 1837,12,16
1840, 3, 30. Albert & w, Elizabeth, & ch, Ra-
    chel & John, gct Chesterfield MM
1844, 5, 27. Sarah Neptune (form Lambert) con
    mcd
1852, 8, 30. Sarah gct Goshen MM

LEE
1857, 3, 31. Allen T., s Samuel & Cynthia,
    Morgan Co., O.; m in Ridge MH, Mary EDGER-
    TON, dt Joseph & Charity, Belmont Co., O.

1823, 7, 23. Margaret & dt, Margaret, rocf
    Roaring Creek MM, Pa., dtd 1823,5,14, end
    by Stillwater MM 1823,6,28
1823, 7, 23. Lydia rocf Roaring Creek MM,
    Pa., dtd 1823,5,14, end by Stillwater MM,
    O., 1823,6,28
1827, 4, 30. Jonathan rocf Roaring Creek MM,
    dtd 1825,9,14
1828, 6, 30. Lydia dis jH
1828, 9, 29. Jonathan dis jH
1857, 7, 27. Mary E. gct Chesterfield MM

LESLIE
1821, 10, 3. Elizabeth m Benjamin MORRIS
1821, 10, 3. Mary m Wm. STANTON
1826, 4, 6. Sarah m John WOOD

1823, 12, 29. Thomas dis jas
1826, 7, 24. Johnson dis mcd
1828, 4, 28. Robert dis jH
1828, 5, 26. Rachel dis jH
1829, 10, 26. Levi dis jH
1836, 1, 25. Sarah (form Thomas) dis mcd

LEWIS
----, --, --. Henry & Sarah
    Ch: Anna D.   b 1865, 3, 25
        Hiram P. " 1867, 6, 12
        Frank   " 1868, 11, 11
1868, --, --. Frank d ae 80 bur Ridge
1873, 2, 1. Henry C. d ae 41 bur Ridge
1899, 11, 22. Sarah M., dt Exum & Anna (Doud-
    na) PATTERSON, d

1841, 4, 26. Mary rocf Short Creek MM, O.,
    dtd 1841,3,23
1850, 1, 28. Lorenzo D. & w, Tacy T., rocf
    Stillwater MM, O., dtd 1849,7,28
1852, 4, 26. Lorenzo dis mcd

LEWIS, continued

1853, 11, 28. Tacy Brown (form Lewis) dis mcd
1860, 6, 25. Sarah Lewis (form Patterson) dis mcd
1863, 7, 27. Sarah M. rst
1866, 1, 29. Henry C. & s, Samuel E., recrq
1893, 8, 24. Samuel E. dis mcd
1893, 9, 21. Anna D. dis jas
1895, 2, 21. Hiram H. dis jas

LIGHTFOOT

1835, 3, 12. Isaac, s Samuel & Rachel, Monroe Co., O.; m in Sunsbury, Emma SCHOOLEY, dt Mahlon & Honor, d 1893,9,12 ae 82 bur Ridge
 Ch: Rachel K. b 1835, 12, 20
   Mary   " 1837, 5, 12
   William K. " 1840, 8, 17
   Hannah " 1842, 1, 28
   Elizabeth " 1844, 4, 3 d 1845, 5,24
    bur Sunsbury
   Samuel b 1846, 10, 11
   Thomas " 1855, 12, 12
1881, 5, 6. Isaac d ae 75 bur Ridge

1835, 1, 26. Isaac rocf Uwchlan MM, Pa., dtd 1835,1,20
1861, 5, 27. Rachel K. Connard (form Lightfoot) con mcd
1866, 3, 26. Wm. dis military service
1866, 3, 26. Samuel dis military service
1867, 8, 27. Hannah Jarret (form Lightfoot) dis mcd
1868, 10, 26. Hannah (form Doudna) dis mcd
1872, 6, 20. Sarah Baxter (form Lightfoot) dis mcd
1873, 11, 20. Mary dis
1879, 9, 25. Thomas dis mcd & military service

LIVEZEY

1849, 12, 27. Jesse K., s John H. & Sarah (Romans), Morgan Co., O., d 1913,12,12 ae 90; m in Ridge MH, Elizabeth PATTERSON, dt Exum & Anna, Belmont Co., O., d 1897,10,17 ae 76 bur Ridge
 Ch: Anna   b 1851, 6, 29
   John P. " 1854, 1, 27 d 1861, 8, 2
   Oliver " 1855, 12, 22 " 1858, 6,20
    bur Ridge
   Joseph Ex-
    um " 1858, 6, 8 " 1872, 8, 7
    bur Ridge
   Charles " 1861, 3, 7
   Albert H. " 1864, 8, 24 " 1865, 2,20
    bur Ridge
1883, 12, 21. Anna m John G. HALL
----, --, --. Charles & Elizabeth W.
 Ch: Robert S. b 1894, 11, 27 d 1895, 3, 4
    bur Ridge
   Albert J. " 1897, 3, 6
   Walter E. " 1899, 1, 24
   Jesse K. " 1901, 1, 31

1850, 5, 27. Jesse K. rocf Chesterfield MM, dtd 1850,4,20
1893, 9, 21. Charles gct Short Creek MM, O., to m Elizabeth W. Smith
1894, 4, 26. Elizabeth W. rocf Short Creek MM, O., dtd 1894,2,20
1901, 8, 22. Charles & w, Elizabeth W., & ch, Albert J., Walter C. & Jesse K., gct Stillwater MM, O.

LOUHOFF

1859, 11, 27. Frederick Charles, s Frederick & Mary (Miller), b
1922, 9, 6. Frank Allen, s Frederick C. & Julia Kaiser, Belmont Co., O., b 1895,7, 24; m in Ridge MH, Rosetta B. DOUDNA, dt Joseph W. & Rosetta (Hall), Belmont Co., O., b 1889,4.25

1919, 4, 24. Frederick C. recrq
1919, 5, 22. Frank A. recrq
1924, 3, 20. Frederick C. dis disunity

LOVE
1900, 6, 21. Sarah Ann dis jas

LOWRY
1831, 6, 27. Sarah (form Hall) dis mcd

LUNDY
1827, 8, 27. Sarah (form Beck) dis mcd

LUPTON
----, --, --. David & Margaret
 Ch: Rachel Ann b 1820, 4, 4
   Martin " 1821, 8, 19 d 1821,10,26
    bur Sunsbury
   Levi b 1823, 2, 11
   George " 1824, 9, 23
   Lydia " 1826, 8, 6
   Jehu " 1828, 7, 17
   Oliver " 1830, 8, 20 d 1836, 3,12
    bur Sunsbury
   Sarah b 1832, 10, 2 " 1836, 3, 2
    bur Sunsbury
   Lewis b 1835, 4, 20 " 1860, 4,30
    bur Sunsbury
----, --, --. Jonathan & Rachel
 Ch: David b 1832, 5, 24 d 1833, 7,14
    bur Sunsbury
   Smith b 1833, 12, 25 " 1834, 8, 4
    bur Sunsbury
   Asenath b 1835, 4, 18 " 1840, 1,30
    bur Sunsbury
   Josiah b 1837, 3, 18 " 1863, 4,26
    "d in Army"
   William b 1839, 6, 16
   Ann   " 1842, 1, 19
   Hannah " 1844, 9, 22
   Thomas " 1846, 8, 19
   Jonathan " 1849, 3, 10
1841, 5, 6. Norris, s Joseph & Mary, Monroe Co., O., d 1865,6,7 ae 49 bur Sunsbury; m

LUPTON, Norris, continued
    in "mtg held near Malaga, Monroe Co., O.",
    Rebecca GARRETSON, dt John & Henrietta,
    Monroe Co., O.
      Ch: Joseph   b 1842, 6, 8 d 1859, 2,25
          bur Sunsbury
          Mary   b 1844, 1, 16
          John G. " 1857, 9, 13 " 1861, 1,23
1857, 11, 20. Jonathan d ae 59 bur Ridge
1862, 8, 7. Rachel Ann m Elisha DOUDNA
1863, 3, 17. Margaret d ae 69 bur Sunsbury
1873, 10, 3. Lewis d ae 35 bur Ridge

1852, 4, 26. Isaac B. & w, Mary B., rocf
    Short Creek MM, O., dtd 1852,3,23
1856, 4, 28. Isaac D. & w, Mary B., gct Ply-
    mouth MM
1863, 5, 25. Jehu dis mcd
1864, 1, 25. Hannah dis jas
1864, 4, 25. Rachel & ch, Thomas & Jonathan,
    gct Hickory Grove MM, Iowa
1864, 4, 25. Ann gct Hickory Grove MM, Ia.
1865, 3, 27. David gct Coal Creek MM, Ia.
1865, 10, 30. Rebecca gct Coal Creek MM, Ia.
1865, 10, 30. Mary Goodwin (form Lupton) dis
    mcd
1866, 4, 30. Harvey con mcd
1866, 9, 24. Harvey gct Coal Creek MM, Ia.
1829, 6, 29. David & w, Margaret, & ch, Ra-
    chel Ann, Levi, George, Lydia & Jehu, rocf
    Short Creek MM, O., dtd 1829,3,19
1833, 1, 20. Jonathan & w, Rachel, & s, Da-
    vid, rocf Short Creek MM, O., dtd 1833,1,
    23 (?)
1834, 1, 27. Norris recrq
1837, 6, 26. Norris gct Short Creek MM, O.
1841, 3, 29. Norris rocf Short Creek MM, O.,
    dtd 1840,12,28
1844, 6, 24. Norris & w, Rebecca, & ch, Jo-
    seph & Mary, gct Chesterfield MM
1846, 7, 27. Levi dis disunity
1849, 1, 29. Norris & w, Rachel, & ch, Jo-
    seph, Mary & Harvey, rocf Chesterfield MM,
    dtd 1848,12,16
1849, 9, 24. George dis mcd
1850, 9, 30. Lydia Couplin (form Lupton) dis
    mcd

LYMIN
1829, 3, 2. Lucy Mason (form Taylor) dis mcd

LYNUM
1830, 2, 28. Sarah (form Taylor) dis mcd

McABE
1875, 11, 25. Phebe (form Gregg) dis mcd

McGILL
1860, 5, 28. Deborah E. (form Doudna) rpd mcd
1864, 9, 26. Deborah E. (form Doudna) dis mcd
1892, 4, 21. Susanna (form Boswell) dis mcd

McGIRR
1857, 1, 26. James, s James & Sarah, Wash-
    ington Co., O.; m in Sunbury, Rachel
    BAILEY, dt Henry & Mary, Belmont Co., O.
    (dte is that on which report of m was made
    to MM. Exact dte of m is not recorded)

1826, 7, 24. Arthur [McGur] & w, Elizabeth,
    & ch, Francis J., Nancy H., Sarah C. &
    Alexander C., rocf Stillwater MM, O., dtd
    1826,5,27
1828, 6, 30. Elizabeth dis jH
1842, 4, 25. Frances, Nancy H., Sarah C. &
    Alexander C., ch Arthur & Elizabeth, gct
    Chesterfield MM
1857, 6, 29. Rachel gct Plymouth MM, O.

McGREW
1870, 8, 25. Eli W. Gibbons gct Short Creek
    MM, O., to m Eliza Jane McGrew

McLEAN
1824, 11, 29. Theodate rocf Stillwater MM, O.,
    dtd 1824,10,23
1829, 7, 27. Theodate [McClane] gct Still-
    water MM, O.

McNICHOLS
1832, 3, 8. Rachel (nee SMITH) m David WAY
1839, 4, 10. Rachel d bur Sunsbury

1828, 6, 30. Wm. & w, Rachel, & ch, Smith,
    Nathaniel, Mary & Wm., also John Fawcett,
    rocf Stillwater MM, O., dtd 1828,4,26
1838, 11, 26. George recrq
1838, 11, 26. Ch of George & Rachel recrq
1838, 12, 26. ----- rst on consent of Still-
    water MM, O.
1839, 10, 28. George & w, Martha, & ch, Pru-
    dence, John, Thomas, Jane, George & Cyrus,
    gct Stillwater MM, O.
1839, 12, 30. Nathaniel dis mcd
1840, 11, 30. Mary Nicholson (form McNichols)
    dis mcd
1844, 4, 29. Smith dis mcd
1846, 6, 29. Wm. dis mcd

MANN
1827, 5, 28. Mary (form Hodgins) dis mcd
1839, 12, 30. Phebe (form Strahl) dis mcd

MARIS
1844, 7, 29. Sidney rocf Stillwater MM, O.,
    dtd 1844,6,22
1844, 7, 29. Rachel rocf Stillwater MM, O.,
    dtd 1844,6,22
1844, 7, 29. Phebe rocf Stillwater MM, O.,
    dtd 1844,6,22
1846, 3, 2. Mary rocf Smitnfield MM, dtd
    1845,12,22, end to Pennsville MM
1848, 2, 28. Cidney, Rachel & Phebe gct
    Pennsville MM

MARTIN
1828, 6, 30. Martha dis JH
1829, 3, 30. Rebecca dis JH
1831, 11, 28. Thomas dis JH
1840, 2, 24. Samuel dis JH
1843, 12, 25. Amos dis JH

MASON
1829, 8, 24. Elizabeth (form Fawcett) dis mcd

MATCHET
1846, 12, 26. Eliza (form Townsend) dis mcd

MAXWELL
1892, 10, 21. Allen, s Albert & Maria, Harri-
     son Co., O.; m in Ridge MH, Sarah T. ED-
     gerton, dt James & Mary Ann (Williams),
     Belmont Co., O.

1893, 11, 23. Sarah T. gct Plainfield MM, Ind.

MERRIL
1835, 8, 24. Hannah & ch, Jonathan, Margaret,
     Joseph, Jesse, Stephen, Isaac & Hannah,
     rocf Stillwater MM, O., dtd 1835,7,25
1839, 12, 30. Jonathan dis mcd
1844, 1, 29. Joseph dis disunity

METCALF
1825, 7, 25. Abraham & w, Hannah, & ch, John,
     Susanna & Jemima Stephenson, rocf Concord
     MM, dtd 1825,5,25
1829, 3, 30. Abraham [Medkeff] dis JH
1841, 3, 29. Abraham rst at Pennsville MM on
     consent of this mtg
1841, 9, 27. Jemima S., Elizabeth E. & Lydia
     Ann [Medkeff], minor ch Abraham & Hannah,
     gct Pennsville MM
1841, 9, 27. John B. gct Pennsville MM
1842, 1, 21. Susanna Pennel (form Metcalf)
     dis mcd

MICHENER
----, --, --. Barak & Lydia P.
     Ch: Mary   b 1844, 12, 10
         Chalkley
           Thomas   " 1847, 1, 25
         Francis   " 1850, 2, 25

1843, 4, 24. Barak & w, Lydia, & ch, Eliza-
     beth, Charles, Robert-Lindley, John & Re-
     becca, rocf Stillwater MM, O., dtd 1843,
     3,25
1852, 4, 26. Barak & w, Lydia, & ch, Charles,
     Lindley, John, Rebecca, Mary, Thomas,
     Chalkley & Francis, gct Plainfield MM, O.
1852, 4, 26. Elizabeth gct Plainfield MM, O.

MIDDLETON
1830, 3, 1. Sarah rocf Stillwater MM, O.,
     dtd 1830,1,23
1830, 12, 27. Sarah gct Stillwater MM, O.

MILES
1821, 2, 26. Hannah (or Mills) rocf Concord
     MM, dtd 1820,11,20, end by Stillwater
     1821,2,24
1821, 12, 24. George recrq
1828, 6, 30. Geo. & Hannah dis JH

MILLER
1867, 11, 28. Robert, s Levi & Deborah, Colum-
     biana Co., O.; m in Ridge MH, Mary HALL,
     dt Wm. & Debby (Hoopes), Washington Co.,
     O.

1868, 12, 28. Mary H. & ch, Martha, Sarah R.
     & Deborah D. Hall, gct Sandy Spring MM
1877, 9, 20. Rebecca L. recrq
1882, 10, 26. Rebecca Lillian Price (form
     Miller) dis mcd

MITCHEL
1853, 3, 28. Joseph Edgerton Jr. gct Flush-
     ing MM, O., to m Lydia S. Mitchel

MORRIS
----, --, --. William & Susannah
     Ch: Mary   b 1821, 1, 13 d 1821, 9, 9
         bur Ridge
         Rachel   " 1824, 1, 15
1821, 10, 3. Benjamin, s Wm. & Susannah, Bel-
     mont Co., O.; m in Somerset MH, Elizabeth
     LESLIE, dt Robert & Rachel, Monroe Co., O.
     Ch: Robert L. b 1822, 8, 25
1823, 4, 2. Mordecai, s Wm. & Susanna, Bel-
     mont Co., O.; m in Somerset MH, Alice WEY,
     dt David & Ann, Monore Co., O.
     Ch: Edwin   b 1824, 1, 1
         David   " 1825, 10, 1
         Tamson   " 1827, 1, 9 d 1835, 4, 1
         bur Sunsbury
         Martin   b 1828, 11, 7
         Robert   " 1831, 11, 18 " 1835, 3,27
         bur Sunsbury
         Ann   b 1833, 11, 23 " 1834, 8,19
         bur Sunsbury
         Susannah   b 1835, 8, 3
1829, 5, 28. Ava m John EMBREE
----, --, --. Nathan & Tacy
     Ch: Samuel   b 1833, 11, 14
         Jonathan   " 1835, 4, 23
----, --, --. Joshua & Rachel
     Ch: Ellen
         Benjamin
         Rebecca
         Joshua
         Rachel

1827, 1, 29. Jesse dis mcd
1828, 6, 30. Rachel dis JH
1828, 8, 25. Elizabeth dis JH
1829, 10, 26. Sarah gct Deerfield MM
1829, 12, 28. Wm. Jr. dis disunity
1830, 3, 1. Jonathan gct Deerfield MM
1830, 4, 26. William & w, Susanna, & ch,

MORRIS, William & Susanna, continued
    Susanna, Lydia, Ruth & Rachel, gct Deer-
    field MM
1830, 5, 24. Benjamin dis
1834, 4, 28. William rst at Milford MM, Ind.,
    on consent of this mtg
1835, 5, 25. Nathan & w, Tacy, & ch, Samuel
    & Jonathan, rocf Stillwater MM, O., dtd
    1835,4,25
1836, 4, 25. Mordecai & w, Alice, & ch, Ed-
    win, David, Martin & Susanna, gct Penns-
    ville MM, O.
1836, 10, 24. Benjamin, Rebecca, Rachel &
    Joshua, ch Joseph & Rachel, gct Pennsville
    MM, O.
1836, 10, 24. Eleanor gct Pennsville MM, O.
1837, 2, 27. Nathan & w, Tacy, & ch, Samuel &
    Jonathan, gct Pennsville MM, O.
1844, 6, 24. Robert L. dis jas
1845, 11, 24. Susan Jane (form Thomas) dis mcd

MOTT
----, --, --. William & Sarah
    Ch: Mary   b 1825, 2, 17
        James E.   " 1826, 12, 15
        Richard   " 1828, 11, 8
        Gershon   " 1830, 11, 28
        Asher   " 1832, 10, 19
        George W.   " 1834, 6, 21
        Sarah   " 1836, 4, 20 d 1837, 3,13
        Eleanor   " 1838, 7, 9
1852, 4, 8. Richard, s William & Sarah (Ed-
    gerton), Belmont Co., O.; m in Ridge MH,
    Sarah W. HAMPTON, dt John & Mary (Wil-
    liams), Belmont Co., O.

1823, 7, 23. William & w, Sarah, & s, Daniel
    Millhouse, rocf Stillwater MM, O., dtd
    1823,6,28
1839, 4, 29. Wm. & w, Sarah, & ch, Daniel M.,
    Mary, James E., Richard, Gershom, Asher,
    George Wm. & Elenor, gct Chesterfield MM,O.
1847, 4, 26. Richard, minor, rocf Chester-
    field MM, dtd 1847,4,17
1854, 3, 27. Cert for Richard & w, Sarah, &
    s, John, granted to Vermillion MM, Ill;
    later end to Red Cedar MM, Ia., but never
    used because of a split in the mtg; became
    mbr of SMM again on rq 1862,3,24
1862, 7, 28. Richard & w, Sarah, & s, John W.,
    gct Hickory Grove MM, Ia.

MYERS
1872, 12, 26. Ann (form Doudna) dis mcd

NAYLOR
1838, 8, 21. Rachel d ae 71 bur Somerset Twp.
1840, 5, 7. Lewis, s James & Rachel, Bel-
    mont Co., O.; m in Ridge MH, Rachel BAILEY
    dt Stephen & Talitha (Patterson), Belmont
    Co., O.
    Ch: Stephen B. b 1841, 7, 1
        Benjamin   " 1842, 11, 15 d 1865, 9,18

    bur Ridge
    Ch: Tabitha
        Jane   b 1844, 11, 18
        Ezra W.   " 1847, 7, 30
        Margaret   " 1849, 12, 26
        Mary K.   " 1854, 2, 24
        Rachel F.   " 1856, 6, 12
        James N.   " 1858, 4, 11 d 1860,11, 5
        bur Malaga Twp.
        Maria W.   b 1860, 9, 30
----, --, --. John & Sarah R.
    Ch: Nathan   b 1842, 9, 30 d 1843, 1, 2
        bur Somerset Twp.
        David E.   b 1844, 2, 18
1857, 12, 31. John Sr. d ae 82 bur Wayne Twp.
1864, 3, 7. James Sr. d ae 86

1837, 5, 29. James & w, Rachel, & s, Lewis,
    rocf Smithfield MM, dtd 1837,5,22
1837, 12, 25. John & ch, Farlend & David, rocf
    Smithfield MM, O., dtd 1837,8,21
1839, 1, 28. John rocf Smithfield MM, dtd
    1838,7,23
1839, 5, 27. Narcissa rocf Smithfield MM, O.,
    dtd 1838,11,19
1839, 9, 30. Narcissa dis jas
1841, 7, 26. John gct Providence MM, to m
    Sarah R. Cope
1841, 11, 29. Sarah R. rocf Providence MM, Pa.,
    dtd 1841,11,14
1845, 2, 24. John & w, Sarah R., & s, David,
    gct Marlborough MM, O.
1846, 4, 27. Farlin dis mcd
1846, 4, 27. Jane (form Williams) dis mcd
1853, 9, 26. David dis jas
1864, 2, 29. Talitha Steward (form Naylor)
    dis mcd
1868, 8, 24. Stephen B. dis mcd
1870, 3, 24. Lewis & w, Rachel, & ch, Mary
    K., Rachel F. & Maria W., gct Stillwater
    MM, O.
1870, 3, 24. Margaret H. gct Stillwater MM,
    O.
1870, 3, 24. Ezra gct Stillwater MM, O.

NEPTUNE
1844, 5, 27. Sarah (form Lambert) con mcd
1849, 9, 24. Sarah Werniecke (form Neptune)
    dis mcd

NICHOLSON
1856, 5, 24. Allice d ae 78 bur Wayne Twp

1835, 3, 20. Martha (form Beck) dis mcd
1840, 11, 30. Mary (form McNichols) dis mcd
1854, 2, 27. Alice rocf Smithfield MM, dtd
    1853,10,17

OBLINGER
1847, 12, 27. Sarah (form Garretson) dis mcd
1857, 7, 27. Sarah T. [Oplinger] recrq of
    aunt, Hannah G. Townsend

OUTLAND
----, --, --. William & Margaret
    Ch: William   b 1805, 12, 2
1823, 11, 29. Margaret d ae 50 bur Ridge
1874, 7, 4. Ann d bur Richland

1824, 6, 28. Josiah dis mcd
1826, 4, 24. William con mcd
1865, 6, 26. Ann rocf Stillwater MM, O., dtd
    1865,5,27

PACKER
1824, 1, 26. Abraham & w, Sarah, & ch, Abi-
    jah, Mary & Susanna, gct Short Creek MM,O.

PALMER
1839, 8, 26. Mary (form Bishop) dis mcd
1889, 8, 22. Lucy (form Parry) dis mcd

PARKER
1842, 6, 27. Isaac Jr. rocf Short Creek MM,
    O., dtd 1842,5,24
1844, 4, 29. Isaac gct Short Creek MM, O.

PARRY
1861, 9, 5. Ephraim, s Job & Asenath, Guern-
    sey Co., O.; m in Ridge MH, Elizabeth
    BAILEY, dt Benjamin & Lucy, Belmont Co., O.
    Ch: Anna Lu-
        titia   b 1863, 9, 9
      Benjamin F." 1863, 9, 16 (sic)
      Lucy B.   " 1867, 11, 4
      Ella Viola " 1876, 6, 2
1868, 3, 5. Asa, s Job & Asenath (Hall)
    Guernsey Co., O.; m in Ridge MH, Sarah Ann
    BAILEY, dt Benjamin & Lucy (Crew) Belmont
    Co., O.
    Ch: Clara L. b 1874, 1, 24 d 1880,1,23
        bur Stillwater
      Rosella b 1876, 5, 27
      Eli   " 1878, 6, 19
      Alice   " 1880, 5, 1
1876, 4, 30. Mary Esther d ae 13 bur Ridge
1891, 11, --. Ephraim d
1892, 8, 5. Benjamin d ae 28 bur Filmore Co.,
    Nebraska

1863, 3, 30. Ephraim rocf Stillwater MM, O.,
    dtd 1863,3,28
1881, 5, 26. Elizabeth dis
1889, 8, 22. Lucy Palmer (form Parry) dis mcd
1895, 8, 22. Ella Burkhart (form Parry) dis
    mcd

PARSONS
1832, 5, 28. Rebecca (form Croy) dis mcd
1834, 1, 27. Elizabeth (form Croy) dis mcd
1857, 1, 26. Elizabeth (form Bailey) dis mcd

PATTERSON
----, --, --. Arnold & Rachel
    Ch: Sarah   b 1819, 3, 2
        Joanna   " 1822, 2, 8 d 1826, 6,18

    bur Somerset
    Ch: Rebecca b 1825, 4, 3
        Clark   " 1828, 3, 10
        Rachel   " 1834, 11, 21
----, --, --. Ira m Mahala TERRIL
    Ch: Edna T. b 1819, 12, 23
        Mathew T. " 1821, 12, 31
        Jane   " 1823, 5, 4 d 1825,10,20
        bur Somerset
      Harriot   b 1825, 3, 6 " 1825,11, 5
        bur Somerset
      Emily   b 1826, 9, 23
      Elwood   " 1828, 4, 20
      Pharaby   " 1830, 6, 21
      Bicks   " 1832, 1, 10
      Thomas J. " 1836, 9, 4
----, --, --. Exum m Anne DOUDNA
    Ch: Phebe   b 1820, 2, 3 d 1836, 8,13
        bur Ridge
      Elizabeth b 1821, 9, 24
      Mary   " 1823, 12, 31 " 1836, 8, 7
      bur Ridge   ⌊bur Ridge
      John   " 1826, 6, 4 " 1827, 5,12
      Sarah   " 1828, 5, 12
----, --, --. Isaac d 1835,4,14 ae 40 bur
    Ridge; m Rebecca CREW
    Ch: Lydia   b 1821, 6, 10 d 1822, 7, 7
        bur Ridge
      Rachel   " 1822, 9, 9 " 1836, 8,13
      bur Ridge
      Eli   " 1823, 12, 4
      Elisha   " 1825, 9, 8 " 1826, 3, 1
      bur Ridge
      Ruthanna " 1826, 12, 8
      Martha   " 1828, 9, 1 " 1836, 8,17
      bur Ridge
      Isaac   " 1830, 2, 8 " 1836, 8, 6
      bur Ridge
      David   " 1832, 12, 21
      Sidna   " 1832, 11, 10 " 1836, 8,18
      bur Ridge
----, --, --. Jeremiah & Elizabeth
    Ch: Caleb   b 1821, 11, 1
        Jared   " 1824, 1, 31
        Robert   " 1826, 3, 28
        Silas   " 1828, 5, 5
1822, 9, 28. Joseph d ae 47 bur Ridge
----, --, --. Edwin m Guly Elma EWERS d 1864,
    7,27 ae 62 bur Ridge
    Ch: Milton   b 1824, 8, 1
        William " 1826, 10, 12
        Bailey   " 1832, 4, 7
        Jeremiah " 1836, 11, 20
        Asa   " 1840, 3, 1
        Gladney " 1842, 5, 29
        Amy   " 1844, 12, 24
1824, 2, 5. Lemuel, s Joseph & Mary, Bel-
    mont Co., O., d 1868,3,6 ae 67 bur Ridge;
    m in Ridge MH, Hannah ARNOLD, dt Asa &
    Susanna
    Ch: Joshua   b 1825, 2, 12
        Samuel   " 1827, 9, 12
        Elisha   " 1831, 9, 28

PATTERSON, Lemuel & Hannah, continued
    Ch: Mary   b 1833, 6, 5
1825, 8, 13. Joseph, s Laban & Sarah, b
----, --, --. Tilmon & Malinda
    Ch: Jesse   b 1826, 12, 27
1826, 8, 15. Joseph d ae 1 bur Deerfield
1826, 11, 8. Edwin, s Jonathan & Ruth, Bel-
    mont Co., O.; m in Somerset MH, Ann WIL-
    LIAMS, dt Samuel & Sarah, Belmont Co., O.
    Ch: Sarah A.   b 1828, 11, 28 d 1841, 5,13
            bur Ridge
        Eunice   " 1827, 10, 1 (sic)
        Nathan   " 1830, 9, 13
        Ruth   " 1832, 11, 24
        Joseph   " 1834, 8, 24
1827, 3, 18. Malinda d ae 21 bur Goshen
1828, 11, 30. Exum d ae 33 bur Ridge
1829, 4, 8. Tilman, s Jeremiah & Faith
    (Bailey), Belmont Co., O.; m in Somerset
    MH, Rachel EDGERTON, dt James & Anna, Bel-
    mont Co., O.
    Ch: James   b 1833, 1, 27 d 1847, 2,23
            bur Somerset
        Malinda   b 1836, 4, 27
        Joseph   " 1838, 1, 17
        Mary   " 1840, 1, 14 d 1857, 4,28
            bur Somerset
        Anna   b 1842, 1, 28 " 1847, 2,13
            bur Somerset
        Tilman   b 1844, 5, 28
        Rebecca   " 1846, 5, 27
        Sarah J.   " 1848, 11, 28
        Rachel   " 1850, 9, 26
        Deborah H. " 1853, 3, 10
1833, 2, 7. Eliza m Jesse BOSWELL
1833, 12, 20. William d ae 71 bur Ridge
1837, 6, 8. Anne W. (nee WILLIAMS) m Nathan
    DODD
1837, 10, 16. Edwin d ae 27 bur Ridge
1838, 5, 19. Benjamin d ae 87 bur Ridge
1844, 4, 4. Ruthanna m Joel BAILEY
1848, 4, 26. Anna (nee DOUDNA) m Joseph KING
1849, 1, 4. Lydia Ann m Levi HAMPTON
1849, 12, 27. Elizabeth m Jesse K. LIVEZEY
1850, 5, 9. Eli, s Isaac & Rebecca (Crew),
    Belmont Co., O.; m in Ridge MH, Phariba
    BAILEY, dt Edmund & Margaret (Doudna),
    Belmont Co., O.
    Ch: Lewis   b 1851, 2, 9 d 1852, 2,14
            bur Ridge
        Louiza   " 1852, 9, 7
        Lindley   " 1856, 12, 16
1854, 10, 16. Pharaby d ae 23
1855, 3, 9. Jonathan d ae 75
1856, 9, 3. Malinda m Joseph ELKINGTON
1857, 6, --. John d ae 76 bur Ridge
----, --, --. Eli m Tabitha BAILEY d 1904,12,
    20 ae 73 bur Ridge
    Ch: Ellen   b 1858, 10, 31
        Loretta   " 1861, 3, 25
        Lucetta C. " 1867, 11, 11
        Ohio R.   " 1869, 10, 11
1857, 12, 2. Lucy d ae 71 bur Ridge

1858, 8, 17. Rebecca d ae 56 bur Ridge
----, --, --. David & Eunice
    Ch: Eva Luzena b 1860, 11, 25
1860, 5, 2. Mary m Mahlon HARTLEY
1862, 3, 19. Ruth d ae 95 bur Ridge
1875, 1, 27. Hannah d ae 81 bur Ridge
1880, 1, 1. Louisa m Jesse DOUDNA
1882, 11, 1. Loretta F. m Joseph S. EDGERTON
1882, 12, 28. Ellen m Benj. S. SEARS
1898, 4, 28. Olive R. m Edward V. GIBBONS
1904, 12, 20. Tabitha, dt Uriah & Susannah
    (Farmer) Bailey, d ae 73

1821, 4, 30. Ira named overseer
1821, 5, 21. Elim dis disunity
1824, 3, 1. Laban B. gct Stillwater MM, O.,
    to m Sarah Healy
1824, 8, 30. Sarah rocf Stillwater MM, dtd
    1824,7,24
1825, 4, 25. Jared & w, Angelina, & ch,
    Amasa, James, Elihu, Asenath, Eliza &
    Mary, rocf Rich Square MM, N. C., dtd
    1825,2,19 & 1825,3,19 (sic)
1825, 4, 25. Edwin & w, Guli Elma, & s, Mil-
    ton, rocf Short Creek MM, O., dtd 1825,4,
    19
1825, 10, 24. Jared & w, Angelina, & ch,
    Amasa, James, Elihu, Asenath, Eliza &
    Mary, gct Stillwater MM, O.
1826, 12, 26. Tilman rocf Short Creek MM, O.,
    dtd 1825,12,20
1826, 4, 24. Malinda rocf Plainfield MM, dtd
    1825,12,22
1826, 8, 28. Laban B. & w, Sarah, gct Still-
    water MM, O.
1826, 12, 25. Rebecca gct Short Creek MM, O.
1827, 5, 28. Tilman & s, Jesse, gct Short-
    Creek MM, O.
1827, 7, 30. Esther gct Plainfield MM
1828, 6, 30. Edwin dis jH
1828, 12, 29. Thomas dis jH
1829, 3, 2. Tilman rocf Short Creek MM, O.,
    dtd 1829,2,24
1829, 9, 28. Rachel rocf Richsquare MM, N.C.,
    dtd 1829,6,20
1830, 4, 26. Joel dis jH
1830, 4, 26. Penina dis jH
1830, 5, 24. Edwin & w, Anna, & ch, Eunice &
    Sarah, gct Stillwater MM, O.
1830, 6, 28. Rebecca rocf Short Creek MM, O.,
    dtd 1830,3,23
1831, 5, 30. Wm. & w, Elizabeth, gct Milford
    MM, Ind.
1831, 12, 26. Edwin & w, Anna, & ch, Eunice,
    Sarahann & Nathan, rocf Stillwater MM, O.,
    dtd 1831,11,26
1832, 8, 27. William & w, Elizabeth, rocf
    Milford MM, Ind., dtd 1832,7,28
1832, 1, 20. Rebecca gct Goshen MM
1833, 1, 20. Rachel gct Stillwater MM, O.
1833, 9, 30. Jeremiah dis; he appealed to QM
1833, 11, 25. Elizabeth, w Jeremiah, & ch, Ra-
    chel, Sarah, Wm., Caleb, Jared, Robert,

PATTERSON, Elizabeth, continued
    Silas, Isaac B. & Mary, gct Deerfield MM,
    O.
1835, 3, 20. Jeremiah gct Deerfield MM, O.
1836, 2, 29. Elizabeth gct Walnut Ridge MM,
    Ind.
1836, 10, 24. Arnold & w, Rachel, & ch, Sarah
    Rebecca Clark & Rachel, gct Pennsville
    MM, O.
1837, 8, 24. James B. & w, Elizabeth, rocf
    Stillwater MM, O., dtd 1837,7,22
1837, 10, 30. Anna dis jas
1837, 10, 30. Elvy dis jas
1838, 7, 30. Benjamin dis mcd
1839, 3, 25. Achsah & ch, Frances E., Marma-
    duke, Priscilla, Thomas P. & John G., gct
    Chesterfield MM
1839, 3, 25. Sarah gct Chesterfield MM
1840, 2, 24. Ira & w, Mahala, & ch, Mathew
    T., Emily, Elwood, Pharaby, Rix & Thomas
    T., gct Chesterfield MM, O.
184-, 2, 24. Edna T. gct Chesterfield MM, O.
1841, 4, 26. James & w, Elizabeth, & s, Jared
    gct Walnut Ridge MM, Ind.
1845, 5, 26. Jesse dis mcd
1845, 7, 28. Joel dis jas
1845, 7, 28. Hannah & Peninah dis jas
1847, 8, 30. Jesse dis jas & mcd
1848, 6, 26. Joshua dis mcd
1848, 9, 25. Amy (form Broomhall) dis mcd
1848, 11, 27. Lydia Ann rocf Pennsville MM,
    dtd 1848,8,17
1854, 3, 27. Bailey dis mcd
1854, 11, 27. Elisha dis mcd
1855, 6, 26. Nathan dis mcd
1855, 12, 24. Samuel dis mcd
1856, 2, 25. David gct Stillwater MM, O., to
    m Eunice Starbuck
1857, 11, 30. Eli gct Plainfield MM, to m
    Tabitha Bailey
1858, 11, 27. Eunice & s, George Wilson, rocf
    Stillwater MM, O., dtd 1848,7,24
1859, 3, 28. Tabitha rocf Plainfield MM, dtd
    1859,2,23
1860, 6, 25. Sarah Lewis (form Patterson) dis
    mcd
1861, 7, 29. Asa dis mcd
1863, 3, 30. Tilman & w, Rachel, & ch, Til-
    man, Rebecca, Sarah, Rachel & Deborah,
    gct Stillwater MM, O.
1863, 3, 30. Joseph gct Stillwater MM, O.
1864, 2, 29. David dis mcd & mustering with
    militia
1864, 4, 25. Eli dis mustering with militia
1868, 1, 27. Amy Clark (form Patterson) dis
    mcd
1877, 12, 25. Eva L. gct Stillwater MM, O.
    (On men's minutes this dte is 1879,12,25)
1878, 1, 24. Lindley dis mcd
1887, 5, 26. George W. dis mcd
1894, 4, 26. Claudia gct West Branch MM, Ia.

PEACOCK
1930, 8, 23. Wm. Howard, s Morris & Lydia
    H., Hendricks Co., Ind.; m in Ridge MH,
    Margery H. DOUDNA, dt Dillwyn & Edith R.,
    Belmont Co., O.
1931, 7, 23. Marjarie H. gct Plainfield MM,
    Ind.

PEEBLES
1844, 1, 4. Susannah L. m Wm. BOSWELL
1829, 9, 28. Wm. Bundy gct Stillwater MM, O.,
    to m Mary Peebles
1833, 3, 25. Isaac Doudna gct Stillwater MM,
    O., to m Martha Peebles
1837, 10, 30. Susanna rocf Pennsville MM, O.,
    dtd 1837,10,19

PEELE
1828, 11, 24. Anna rocf Stillwater MM, O., dtd
    1828,10,25
1837, 2, 27. Anna gct Stillwater MM, O.

PENNEL
1842, 1, 21. Susanna (form Metcalf) dis mcd

PENROSE
1901, 3, 21. Barclay & w, Mary P., rocf
    Pennsville MM, dtd 1901,3,14
1907, 11, 21. Barclay & w, Mary P., gct Still-
    water MM, O.
1913, 10, 23. Barclay & w, Mary P., rocf
    Stillwater MM, O., dtd 1913,10,22
1917, 5, 24. Barclay & w, Mary P., gct Still-
    water MM, O.

PICKERING
1824, 7, 26. Elizabeth rocf Flushing MM, dtd
    1824,4,23
1835, 11, 30. Elizabeth gct Pennsville MM, O.

PICKET
1841, 9, 27. Elisha Doudna gct Pennsville
    MM, to m Mary Picket

PLUMLEY
1835, 11, 30. Hannah (form Eves) dis mcd

PLUMMER
----, --, --. John m Rachel PATTERSON
    Ch: Rebecca   b 1834, 10, 2

1832, 3, 26. John & w, Rachel, & ch, Eliza-
    beth, Deborah, Robert, Mary B., William,
    Exum & Talitha, rocf Stillwater MM, O.,
    dtd 1832,3,24
1835, 4, 27. John [Plunner] & w, Rachel, &
    ch, Elizabeth, Deborah, Robert, Mary B.,
    William, Exum, Telitha & Rebecca, gct
    Stillwater MM, O.

PRICE
1882, 10, 26. Rebecca Lillian (form Miller)
    dis mcd

PUGH
1826, 5, 29. John rocf Smithfield MM, dtd
    1826,5,22
1829, 10, 26. John gct Cincinnati MM

PURVIANCE
1861, 10, 28. Joseph Bailey gct Flushing MM,
    O., to m Elvira Purviance

REEVE
1824, 5, 24. Benjamin L. rocf WD MM, dtd
    1824,1,21
1824, 5, 24. Abraham, minor, rocf Piles
    Grove MM, dtd 1824,1,27
1824, 6, 28. Anna, w Joseph, & ch, Joseph,
    Lydia Ann, Elma Ann & Matilda Ann, rocf
    Green St. MM, Phila., Pa., dtd 1824,1,22
1826, 6, 26. Abraham [Reeves] dis mcd
1833, 5, 27. Lydia Gibbon (form Reeves) dis
    mcd
1838, 11, 26. Elma Anna gct Stillwater MM, O.
1838, 11, 26. Anna & dt, Matilda Ann, gct
    Stillwater MM, O.
1839, 4, 29. Joseph gct Chesterfield MM, O.
1842, 4, 25. Benjamin [Reeves] dis mcd
1846, 8, 26. Joseph rocf Stillwater MM, O.,
    dtd 1846,7,26
1847, 4, 26. Joseph dis mcd

RICKS
1830, 11, 4. Robert, s Thomas & Elizabeth,
    Belmont Co., O.; m in Ridge MH, Judith
    CREW, dt Wm. & Rebecca BAILEY, Belmont
    Co., O., d 1835,4,29 ae 50 bur Ridge

1830, 6, 28. Robert & s, James, rocf Western
    Branch MM, Va., dtd 1830,4,24
1830, 6, 28. John rocf Western Branch MM,
    Va., dtd 1830,4,24
1832, 9, 24. John W. [Rix] gct Goshen MM
1833, 5, 27. James T., minor s Robert, gct
    Goshen MM
1835, 9, 28. Robert gct Goshen MM, O.

RING
1876, 3, 23. Martha (form Bailey) dis mcd

ROBERTS
1842, 10, 24. William Kennard gct Plainfield
    MM, to m Sarah Roberts

ROBBINS
1838, 12, 6. Elihu [Robins], s Thomas &
    Miriam, Belmont Co., O.; m in Ridge MH,
    Mary Ann HAMPTON, dt John & Mary, Belmont
    Co., O.

1838, 8, 27. Elihu recrq
1840, 4, 27. Elihu & w, Mary Ann, & s, Zach-

eriah H., gct Pennsville MM, O.

ROSE
1848, 9, 12. Martha d ae 85 bur Ridge

ROSS
1832, 5, 28. Margaret recrq
1840, 4, 27. Margaret gct Chesterfield MM, O.

SCHOLFIELD
1833, 9, 30. Rachel rocf Hopewell MM, Va.,
    dtd 1833,6,5, end by Flushing MM, O.,
    1833,8,22
1836, 6, 27. Rachel N. gct Hopewell MM, Va.

SCHOOLEY
1835, 3, 12. Emma m Isaac LIGHTFOOT
----, --, --. William & Agnes
        Ch: Clarkson
            Lindley
            Addison

1826, 6, 26. William & w, Agnes, & ch, Clark-
    son & Lindley, rocf Plainfield MM, dtd
    1826,5,25
1828, 4, 28. William dis jH
1828, 6, 30. Agness dis jH
1832, 6, 25. Emma recrq
1844, 4, 29. Clarkson dis mcd
1848, 9, 25. Lindley dis disunity
1852, 12, 27. Addison dis mcd

SCOTT
1825, 10, 24. Jesse & w, Hannah, & ch, Pen-
    nington & Watson, rocf Stillwater MM, O.,
    dtd 1825,10,22
1827, 7, 30. Jesse & w, Hannah, & Pennington
    & Watson, gct Stillwater MM, O.

SEARS
1882, 12, 28. Benjamin S., s Peter & Phariba
    (Bundy), Lynn Co., Ia.; m in Ridge MH,
    Ellen PATTERSON, dt Eli & Tabitha (Bailey)
    Belmont Co., O.

1829, 10, 26. Huldah rocf Upper MM, Va., dtd
    1829,8,15, end by Stillwater MM, O., 1829,
    10,24
1836, 8, 29. Huldah gct Springfield MM, O.
1883, 7, 26. Ellen P. gct Springville MM, Ia.

SHOTWELL
1826, 7, 24. Isaac & w, Hope, & ch, Mary,
    Ruth & Titus, rocf Stillwater MM, O., dtd
    1826,6,22
1828, 8, 25. Isaac & Hope dis jH
1842, 4, 25. Mary, Ruth & Titus, ch Isaac &
    Hope, gct Chesterfield MM
1850, 5, 27. Nathan rocf Stillwater MM, O.,
    dtd 1850,4,27
1851, 6, 30. Nathan gct Stillwater MM, O.
1881, 3, 24. Ruth Ella (form Starbuck) dis
    mcd

SMITH
----, --, --. Thomas & Nancy
    Ch: Sarah   b 1810, 10, 22
        Hannah   " 1814, 10, 17
        Elizabeth " 1817, 2, 27
        Evan   " 1819, 5, 30
        Samuel   " 1821, 11, 11
        Rachel   " 1823, 12, 6
        James   " 1826, 3, 16
        Margaret " 1828, 3, 31 d 1830, 8,17
          bur Somerset
        Mary   b 1830, 5, 15 " 1830, 8,27
          bur Somerset
1853, 4, 26. George, s Abraham & Sarah, Wash-
    ington Co., Pa.; m in Sunbury, Christianna
    GRAY, dt Richard & Mary EDGERTON, Monroe
    Co., O.
1829, 4, 15. Sarah m William DEWEES
1860, 5, 10. Sinclair, s Robert H. & Eliza-
    beth (Williams), Belmont Co., O.; m in
    Ridge MH, Tacy M. HALL, dt Robert & Mar-
    tha (Wilson), Belmont Co., O.

1821, 8, 27. Thomas & w, Nancy, & ch, Sarah,
    Hannah, Elizabeth & Evan, rocf Short Creek
    MM, dtd 1821,8,21
1826, 7, 24. Jonathan & w, Mary, & ch, Levi,
    Anna, Edith, Sarah, John, Mary Annis & Na-
    than, rocf Short Creek MM, O., dtd 1826,6,
    20
1827, 12, 24. Levi gct Short Creek MM, O.
1828, 7, 28. Jonathan dis jH
1829, 4, 27. Anna dis jH
1830, 6, 28. Edith gct Short Creek MM, O.
1831, 4, 25. Mary & ch, Sarah, John, Mary
    Ann & Nathan, gct Stillwater MM, O.
1834, 3, 24. Hannah gct Upper Springfield MM,
    O.
1834, 3, 24. Thomas & w, Nancy, & ch, Eliza-
    beth, Even, Samuel, Rachel, James & Thom-
    as, gct Upper Springfield MM, O.
1853, 6, 27. Christiana & ch, Mary, Sarah,
    Nathan & Ann Gray, gct Westland MM, Pa.
1860, 5, 28. Tacy gct Stillwater MM, O.
1893, 9, 21. Charles Livesey gct Short Creek
    MM, O., to m Elizabeth W. SMITH

SNYDER
1832, 1, 30. Rachel (form Dodd) dis mcd

SPENCER
1896, 9, 25. George T., s John & Mary R.,
    Keokuk Co., Ia.; m in Ridge MH, Anna GIB-
    BONS, dt Joseph & Peninah (Williams), Bel-
    mont Co., O.

1897, 3, 25. Anna G. gct Coal Creek MM, Ia.

STANLEY
1821, 2, 26. Jesse dis mcd
1821, 3, 26. James C. & w, Mary, & ch, Little-
    berry, Lemuel, Jonathan & Rhoda, gct New
    Garden MM

STANTON
----, --, --. Enoch & Mary
    Ch: William   b 1816, 2, 24
        Sarah S. " 1819, 5, 24 d 1822, 7,9
          bur Somerset
        Nathan   b 1822, 5, 3
1821, 10, 3. William, s William & Lydia, Bel-
    mont Co., O.; m in Somerset MH, Mary LES-
    LIE, dt Robert & Rachel, Monroe Co., O.
    Ch: Rachel Ann b 1822, 7, 23
        Isaac   " 1824, 5, 20 d 1826, 2, 3
        Abigail
        Thomas
1822, 12, 4. Peninah m William VERNON
1833, 12, 18. Hannah d ae 60
----, --, --. Bordon & Nancy
    Ch: Mary
        Sarah
        David
        Margaret
        Jonathan
        John
        Hannah

1824, 6, 28. Abigail rocf Short Creek MM, O.,
    dtd 1824,3,23
1828, 4, 28. Borden dis jH
1828, 4, 28. William dis jH
1828, 6, 30. Ann dis jH
1829, 1, 26. Mary J. dis jH
1829, 4, 27. Abigail dis jH
1829, 6, 29. Enoch dis jH
1829, 7, 27. Lydia Gibbons (form Stanton) dis
    mcd
1831, 5, 30. Mary dis jH
1832, 6, 25. Mary Gibbons (form Stanton) dis
    mcd
1834, 2, 24. Sarah Finch (form Stanton) dis
    mcd
1837, 12, 25. William dis jH
1838, 3, 26. Catharine (form Thomas) dis jH
1842, 8, 29. Rachel Ann Hobbs (form Stanton)
    dis mcd
1844, 2, 26. Jonathan dis mcd
1844, 3, 25. Martha (form Williams) dis mcd
1846, 3, 2. Abigail Townsend (form Stanton)
    dis mcd
1847, 6, 28. John dis jas
1852, 12, 27. Thomas dis mcd

STARBUCK
----, --, --. John d 1864,3,13 ae 66 bur
    Ridge; m Ann ----- d 1850,11,2 ae 55 bur
    Ridge
    Ch: -----   b 1821, 7, 8
        Samuel   " 1823, 5, 12
        Hezekiah " 1825, 8, 19
        John   " 1827, 4, 10
        Robert   " 1829, 5, 3 d 1841, 6,22
          bur Ridge
        William   " 1831, 2, 8
        Elizabeth " 1833, 4, 14 " 1853,10,13
          bur Ridge

STARBUCK, John & Ann, continued
        Ch: Daniel   b 1835, 9, 25
            Ruthanna   " 1837, 12, 22
            Elisha   " 1839, 5, 24 d 1840, 3,21
              bur Ridge
            Thomas   " 1843, 3, 8 " 1864, 5,--
              "Anderson Prison in Civil War"
1836, 4, 7. George, s George & Elizabeth,
    Belmont Co., O.; m in Ridge MH, Lydia
    BAILEY, dt Edmund & Margaret (Doudna), Bel-
    mont Co., O.
1840, 10, 20. George d ae 19 bur Ridge
1856, 8, 7. William, s John & Ann, Belmont
    Co., O.; m in Ridge MH, Rebecca CREW, dt
    James & Sarah, Belmont Co., O.
        Ch: Almeda   b 1857, 1, 29
            Sarah   " 1858, 10, 20
            Ruth Ellen " 1860, 3, 23
1860, 10, 1. Rebecca d ae 22 bur Clayton, Ill.

1829, 5, 25. John & w, Ann, & ch, George,
    Samuel, Hezekiah, John & Robert, rocf
    Stillwater MM, O., dtd 1829,5,23
1836, 7, 25. Lydia gct Stillwater MM, O.
1851, 5, 26. Samuel dis mcd
1854, 7, 24. John Jr. gct Short Creek MM, O.,
    to m Sarah T. Bundy
1855, 11, 26. John Jr. gct Short Creek MM, O.
1856, 2, 25. David Patterson gct Stillwater
    MM, O., to m Eunice Starbuck
1857, 4, 27. Wm. dis
1861, 2, 25. Daniel dis
1864, 11, 28. Sarah, gr dt Sarah Crew, gct
    Hickory Grove MM, Ia.
1867, 7, 29. Ruth Ann dis disunity
1876, 7, '24. Almedia Bailey (form Starbuck)
    dis mcd
1881, 3, 24. Ruth Ella Shotwell (form Star-
    buck) dis mcd

STATLER
1835, 7, 27. Celia (form Dodd) dis mcd

STEER
1821, 6, 25. John Doudna gct Concord MM, to
    m Mary Steer

STEPHEN
1892, 7, 21. James E. Gibbons,gct Flushing
    MM, O., to m Eliza M. Stephen

STEWARD
1864, 2, 29. Talitha (form Naylor) dis mcd

STRAHL
----, --, --. Isaac & Ellen
        Ch: Samuel   b 1796, 9, 11
            Margaret   " 1798, 10, 25
            Stacy   " 1800, 12, 2
            John   " 1803, 2, 7
            Isaac   " 1803, 2, 7
            Mahlon   " 1805, 3, 10
            Abdon(?)   " 1807, 10, 10 d 1807,10,23

        Ch: Ellen   b 1808, 10, 3
            Daniel   " 1811, 4, 5
            Jason   " 1813, 10, 30
            Joel   " 1816, 3, 4
            Ira   " 1820, 8, 28
1827, 7, 4. Mahlon, s Isaac & Ellen, Bel-
    mont Co., O.; m in Somerset MH, Mary WHITE
    dt Jesse & Sarah, Belmont Co., O.
----, --, --. Samuel & Hannah
        Ch: Phebe
            Lydia
            Marinda
            Alfred

1821, 4, 30. Isaac named overseer
1823, 2, 24. Stacy dis mcd
1827, 5, 28. John Jr. dis disunity
1828, 6, 30. Isaac & Hannah dis jH
1828, 6, 30. Isaac Jr. dis jH
1828, 7, 28. Ellen dis jH
1828, 8, 25. Mahlon dis jH
1828, 8, 25. Samuel dis jH
1828, 8, 25. Ellen Jr. dis jH
1828, 9, 29. John dis jH
1829, 3, 2. Mary dis jH
1831, 4, 25. Elmor gct Flushing MM
1831, 12, 26. Daniel dis jH
1837, 11, 27. Jason dis jH
1837, 12, 25. Joel dis jH
1838, 12, 24. Ann (form Bailey) dis jH
1839, 12, 30. Phebe Mann (form Strahl) dis mcd
1840, 6, 29. Lydia Truax (form Strahl) dis
    mcd
1843, 12, 25. Ira dis jH

STUBBS
1872, 9, 26. Rhoda recrq

SWAYNE
----, --, --. Elias, s Samuel & Margaret

1827, 11, 28. Samuel & w, Margaret, & ch,
    Isaac, Sarah, Mary, Joshua, Rachel, Samuel
    John, Noah & Margaret, rocf Stillwater MM,
    O., dtd 1827,11,24
1828, 8, 25. Margaret dis jH
1829, 3, 2. Sarah Ann dis jH
1833, 10, 28. Isaac B. dis jH

TABER
1898, 7, 21. Walter J. Edgerton gct Still-
    water MM, O., to m Anna R. Taber

TATUM
1846, 3, 30. George & w, Hannah, rocf Upper
    Springfield MM, dtd 1846,2,28

TAYLOR
----, --, --. Simeon & Elizabeth
        Ch: Sally B.   b 1809, 9, 23
            Lucy M.   " 1812, 4, 8
            Elbina S.   " 1813, 11, 25
            Angelina P." 1815, 9, 24

TAYLOR, Simeon & Elizabeth, continued
    Ch: John M.   b 1819, 7, 4
        Daniel G.   " 1822, 1, 24
        Allen D.   " 1825, 10, 29

1829, 3, 2. Lucy Mason Lymin (form Taylor)
    dis mcd
1830, 11, 29. Simeon & w, Elizabeth, & ch, El-
    bina L., Angelina P., John M., Daniel G.
    & Allen D., gct Duck Creek MM, Ind.
1831, 2, 28. Sarah Lynum (form Taylor) dis
    mcd

THOMAS
----, --, --. William & Rebecca
    Ch: Catharine b 1817, 2, 13
        Margaret   " 1819, 3, 16
        Elizabéth   " 1821, 5, 27
        Harriet   " 1824, 4, 1
        Robert P.   " 1826, 8, 30

1831, 8, 29. Jehu & w, Susannah, & ch, Han-
    nah, Rachel, Aquilla, Sarah, Samuel, John,
    Susan, Jane, Mary, Ann & Elizabeth Ann,
    rocf Deer Creek MM, dtd 1831,6,10
1832, 2, 27. Jehu dis jH
1832, 3, 26. Susanna dis jH
1832, 5, 28. Rachel dis jH
1832, 5, 28. Hannah dis jH
1836, 1, 25. Sarah Leslie (form Thomas) dis
    mcd
1838, 3, 26. Catharine Stanton (form Thomas)
    dis jH
1845, 1, 27. Elizabeth Frame (form Thomas)
    dis jH
1845, 11, 24. Susan Jane Morris (form Thomas)
    dis mcd
1897, 2, 25. Joseph B. Gibbons gct Short
    Creek MM, O., to m Elma Thomas
1821, 7, 30. Nathaniel & w, Dorcas, & ch,
    William, Ruth, Enos & Nathan, rocf New-
    garden MM, O., dtd 1821,6,21
1821, 11, 26. Joseph & w, Temperance, rocf
    Newgarden MM, O.
1822, 1, 28. Camm & w, Elizabeth, & ch, Heze-
    kiah, Priscilla, Asa, Elizabeth, Camm, Re-
    becca, Ruth & Sidna, gct Sillwater MM, O.
1822, 1, 28. Temperance & dt, Sarah, rocf New
    Garden MM, O., dtd 1821,9,20
1822, 9, 30. Abel, minor, rocf New Garden MM,
    O., dtd 1822,8,22
1824, 6, 28. Abel dis jas
1824, 11, 29. Nathaniel & w, Dorcas, & ch,
    William, Ruth, Enos & Nathan, gct Goshen
    MM
1824, 11, 29. Joseph & w, Temperance, & ch,
    Margaret & Mary, gct Goshen MM
1828, 2, 24. William dis disunity
1828, 8, 25. Rebecca dis jH

THOMASSON
1847, 3, 11. John, s Thomas & Sarah, Belmont
    Co., O., d 1884,4,21 ae 74 bur Ridge; m in

Ridge MH, Eunice EDGERTON, dt Joseph &
    Charity (Doudna), Belmont Co., O.
    Ch: Mary   b 1854, 2, 22
        John   " 1856, 3, 19
        Samuel   " 1858, 8, 10 d 1860, 2, 6
        bur Ridge
        Nathan   " 1861, 4, 15
        James   " 1864, 6, 30 " 1865, 9,25
        bur Ridge
1873, 3, 27. Sara m John S. DOUDNA
1876, 12, 28. Abigail m Chas. D. VERNON
1882, 2, 10. John J. d
----, --, --. Nathan & Mary A.
    Ch: Arthur E. b 1888, 9, 21
        Joseph
        Earl   " 1889, 10, 5
----, --, --. Thomas & Mary E.
    Ch: Jesse J.   b 1889, 4, 16

1847, 5, 24. Eunice gct Plainfield MM
1854, 2, 27. John & w, Eunice, & ch, Abigail,
    Joseph, Sarah & Thomas, rocf Plainfield MM
1872, 5, 22. Joseph gct Coal Creek MM, Ia.
1878, 3, 21. John J. dis
1882, 7, 20. Joseph rocf Coal Creek MM, Ia.,
    dtd 1882,7,8
1884, 4, 24. Joseph dis mcd
1885, 8, 20. Thomas gct Springville MM, Ia.,
    to m Mary E. Hodgin
1886, 4, 22. Mary E. rocf Springville MM,
    Ia., dtd 1886,4,17
1887, 10, 20. Nathan gct Plymouth MM, O.
1888, 4, 26. Mary A. rocf Plymouth MM, dtd
    1888,3,19
1889, 7, 25. Thos. & w, Mary E., gct Spring-
    ville MM, Ia.
1889, 12, 26. Nathan & w, Mary A., & ch,
    Arthur Everett & Joseph Earl, gct Plymouth
    MM
1896, 1, 23. Eunice gct Pasadena MM, Calif.
1896, 1, 23. Mary gct Pasadena MM, Calif.
1901, 1, 24. Joseph rst
1901, 6, 20. Joseph gct Phila. MM, Pa.

TIPTON
----, --, --. Luke d 1854,4,5 ae 65 bur Suns-
    bury; m Priscilla -----
    Ch: Samuel   b 1823, 9, 7 d 1900, 2,5
        Rebecca   " 1825, 10, 5
        Susanna   " 1827, 1, 20
        Sarah   " 1828, 9, 7 " 1835, 3,10
        bur Sunsbury
        Phebe   b 1830, 3, 27
        Abigail   " 1831, 9, 6 d 1835, 3,15
        bur Sunsbury
1833, 4, 4. Mary m James CHAMBERS
1836, 3, 10. David, s Luke & Priscilla, Mon-
    roe Co., O., d 1853,10,20 ae 41 bur Suns-
    bury; m in Sunbury, Mary KENNARD, dt Jo-
    seph & Hannah
    Ch: William   b 1836, 1, 2
        Tacy Ann   " 1838, 1, 9
        Luke   " 1840, 4, 30

TIPTON, David & Mary, continued
    Ch: Priscilla b 1845, 2, 24
----, --, --. Abijah d 1840,9,6 bur Sunsbury;
    m Sidney ----- Ch: Hester b 1839,11,13
----, --, --. John & Mary Ann
    Ch: Stephen   b 1840, 7, 1 d 1870, 10,
    5 bur Sunsbury
1841, 1, 1. Mary Ann d ae 24 bur Sunsbury
1839, 12, 5. Elihu, s Luke & Priscilla, Mon-
    roe Co., O., d 1867,11,26 ae 49 bur Suns-
    bury; m in Sunbury, Sarah TOWNSEND, dt
    Stephen & Ann, d 1877, --,5 ae 58 bur Suns-
    bury
    Ch: Ann Eliza-
            beth b 1841, 4, 15
        Rachel   " 1843, 2, 24
        Levi K.   " 1845, 11, 10
        William B. " 1848, 9, 21 d 1849, 2,13
            bur Sunsbury
1843, 2, 9. Sidney m John BUNDY (nee WOOD)
1854, 10, 31. Joseph d ae 26
1860, 12, 6. Esther W. m Eli B. DAWSON

1824, 6, 28. Luke & w, Priscilla, & ch, Da-
    vid, Mary, Esther, Rachel, Abijah, Elihu,
    John, Hannah & Samuel, rocf Short Creek
    MM, O., dtd 1824,3,23
1838, 4, 30. Rachel Adams (form Tipton) con
    mcd
1838, 12, 26. Abijah gct Stillwater MM, O., to
    m Sidney Wood
1839, 9, 30. Cisney rocf Stillwater MM, O.,
    dtd 1839,8,24
1840, 7, 27. Mary Ann (form Townsend) con
    mcd
1840, 7, 27. John dis mcd
1840, 8, 31. Esther Brown (form Tipton) dis
    mcd
1842, 8, 29. Hannah Ann (form Grissel) dis
    mcd
1847, 5, 24. David & w, Mary, & ch, Wm.,
    Tacy-Ann, Luke & Priscilla, gct Alum Creek
    MM, O.
1851, 3, 24. David & w, Mary, & ch, Wm. K.,
    Tacy, Ann, Luke, Priscilla, Phebe, Jane
    & Joseph, rocf Alum Creek MM, dtd 1850,10,
    24
1856, 7, 28. Rebecca Evans (form Tipton) dis
    mcd
1859, 8, 29. Samuel con mcd
1860, 1, 30. Hannah dis jas
1861, 3, 25. William dis jas
1862, 4, 28. Phebe dis disunity
1862, 9, 29. Mary Davis (form Tipton) dis
    mcd
1865, 1, 30. Tacy Ann dis jas
1869, 3, 1. Levi dis mcd
1870, 12, 22. Samuel gct Hickory Grove MM,
    Ia.
1876, 7, 20. Luke dis mcd & jas
1899, 3, 23. Samuel rocf Hickory Grove MM,
    Ia., dtd 1899,3,4

TOMLINSON
1830, 6, 28. Elizabeth rocf Short Creek MM,
    O., dtd 1830,6,26
1835, 1, 26. Daniel recrq
1846, 4, 27. Daniel dis mcd
1847, 4, 26. Elizabeth gct Flushing MM

TOWNSEND
----, --, --. Stephen d 1850,5,3 ae 55 bur
    Sunsbury; m Ann ----- d 1835,3,12 ae 43
    bur Sunsbury
    Ch: Mary G. b 1816, 8, 9
        Sarah   " 1817, 8, 7
        Levi   " 1821, 12, 4
        Eliza   " 1825, 4,30
        Joseph   " 1828, 3,17
        William   " 1830, 11,30 d 1851, 4,10
        bur Sunsbury
        Emily   b 1833, 6,12 " 1852, 5,10
        bur Sunsbury
1839, 12, 5. Sarah m Elihu TIPTON
1840, 11, 24. Ruth d bur Sunsbury
1847, 8, 20. Frances Ann d ae 54 bur Sunsbury
1848, 11, 16. Stephen, s Joseph & Mary, Bel-
    mont Co., O.; m in Sunbury, Hannah GARRET-
    SON, dt John & Henrietta, Monroe Co., O.
    Ch: Stephen b 1850, 2, 23
        Hannah G. " 1850, 2, 23
----, --, --. Levi & Mary
    Ch: Elizabeth
        Eli
        William
        Joseph

1824, 4, 26. Levi & w, Mary, & ch, Elizabeth
    & Eli, rocf Flushing MM, dtd 1824,2,27
1827, 4, 30. Stephen & w, Ann, & ch, Mary
    Ann, Sarah, Levi & Eliza, rocf Short Creek
    MM, O., dtd 1827,4,24
1828, 6, 30. Mary dis jH
1835, 5, 25. Elizabeth, Eli, William & Jo-
    seph, minor ch Levi & Mary, gct Goshen MM,
    O.
1837, 3, 27. Stephen con mcd
1837, 5, 29. Ruth rocf Pennsville MM, O., dtd
    1837,5,18
1837, 5, 29. Julia Ann rocf Pennsville MM, O.,
    dtd 1837,5,18
1838, 6, 25. Frances Ann recrq
1839, 7, 27. Julia Ann Cope (form Townsend)
    dis mcd
1840, 7, 27. Mary Ann Tipton (form Townsend)
    con mcd
1845, 9, 29. Levi con mcd
1846, 3, 2. Abigail (form Stanton) dis mcd
1846, 12, 26. Eliza Matchett (form Townsend)
    dis mcd
1850, 12, 30. Levi gct Plymouth MM
1850, 12, 30. Joseph gct Plymouth MM

TRUAX
1840, 6, 29. Lydia (form Strahl) dis mcd

TURNER
1842, 7, 25. Mary (form Boswell) dis mcd

UNDERWOOD
----, --, --. Mordecai P. rocf Baltimore MM,
      W. Dist., dtd 1826,9,3

VAIL
1837, 8, 31. John, s Benjamin & Hannah, Bel-
      mont Co., O.; m in Somerset MH, Abigail
      EDGERTON, dt James & Anne, Belmont Co., O.

1837, 6, 26. John & w, Esther, & ch, Phebe
      & Orpah, rocf Upper Springfield MM, O.,
      dtd 1837,5,27
1838, 3, 26. Abigail gct Plainfield MM, O.
1838, 5, 28. John & w, Esther C., & ch,
      Phebe & Orpah, gct Pennsville MM, O.

VANDYKE
1840, 5, 25. Sarah (form Dawson) dis mcd

VANDYNE
1902, 3, 20. Phebe Anna (form Doudna) dis mcd

VARNER
1828, 3, 24. Irene (form Andrews) dis mcd
1832, 3, 26. Lucy (form Andrews) dis mcd
1836, 9, 26. Malinda (form Andrews) dis mcd

VERNON
1816, 10, 1. Elijah, s Amos & Catharine, b
1821, 8, 10. Elijah d ae 3 bur Ridge
1822, 12, 4. William, s James & Tamar, Bel-
      mont Co., O.; m in Ridge MH, Peninah STAN-
      TON, dt Joseph & Hannah
      Ch: Elijah   b 1823, 9, 25
          Elisha   " 1826, 8, 9
          Joseph   " 1829, 9, 30
          Tamer   " 1832, 5, 11
1831, 10, 6. Amos, s James & Tamar, Belmont
      Co., O.; m in Sunbury, Jane WAY, dt David
      & Ann, Monroe Co., O.
----, --, --. Joseph & Martha
      Ch: George W. b 1849,12,26
          Robert N.   " 1852, 3,13
1876, 12, 28. Charles D., s James & Lydia,
      Lynn Co., Ia.; m in Ridge MH, Abigail
      THOMASSON, dt John & Eunice (Edgerton),
      Belmont Co., O.

1821, 12, 24. Catharine gct Stillwater MM, O.
1826, 4, 24. James, minor, rocf Stillwater
      MM, O., dtd 1825,12,22
1831, 3, 28. Jesse Hiatt gct Short Creek MM,
      O., to m Ruthanna Vernon
1831, 12, 26. Jane gct Clear Creek MM, O.
1835, 8, 24. Amos & w, Jane, & s, Robert,
      rocf Stillwater MM, O., dtd 1835,7,25
1835, 9, 28. James gct Alum Creek MM, O., to
      m Rachel Wood
1837, 2, 27. James gct Alum Creek MM, O.
1837, 6, 26. Amos & w, Jane, & ch, Robert,

David & Mary, gct Pennsville MM, O.
1838, 3, 26. William & w, Peninah, & ch,
      Elisha, Joseph, Tamar & Elizabeth, gct
      Chesterfield MM, O.
1850, 4, 29. Joseph & w, Martha, & ch, John
      T., Wm. & George W., rocf Stillwater MM,
      O., dtd 1850,3,23
1877, 8, 23. Abigail T. gct Springville MM
1889, 8, 22. Charles D. & w, Abigail, & dt,
      Estella, rocf Springville MM, Ia., dtd
      1889,7,20
1901, 8, 22. Charles D. & w, Abigail, gct
      Short Creek MM, O.
1901, 8, 22. Estella gct Short Creek MM, O.

WADE
1823, 9, 3. Lydia m Jacob YOCOM
----, --, --. Owen & Margaret
      Ch: Ellen
          Rebecca
          Mary
          Lindley   d 1850, 9,21

1823, 2, 24. Sarah rocf Plainfield MM, dtd
      1823,11,23
1823, 6, 30. Mary Glover (form Wade) dis mcd
1826, 10, 20. Sarah gct Plainfield MM, O.
1828, 6, 30. Phebe dis JH
1828, 7, 28. Rachel dis JH
1828, 8, 25. Owen dis JH
1829, 1, 26. Margaret dis JH
1844, 1, 29. Rebecca dis JH
1844, 4, 29. Ellen Wilson (form Wade) dis
      mcd

WALTON
1854, 7, 26. Samuel, s Joseph & Abi, Phila.,
      Pa.; m in Somerset MH, Sarah J. EDGERTON,
      dt James & Anna, Belmont Co., O.

1854, 9, 25. Sarah J. gct Philadelphia MM,
      Pa. (w of Samuel)

WARFIELD
1860, 11, 26. Jane (form Bailey) con mcd

WARNER
1832, 4, 30. Lucy (form Andrew) dis mcd

WARRICK
1866, 9, 24. Mary (form Brock) dis mcd

WATKINS
1827, 2, 26. Lemuel gct Goshen MM
1832, 3, 26. Ira gct Goshen MM, O.
1832, 3, 26. Ira gct Goshen MM
1832, 3, 26. Bennett gct Goshen MM
1832, 9, 24. Reuben & w, Anna, & ch, James,
      Susanna, Joel, Unity & Lucinda, gct Goshen
      MM, O.
1832, 9, 24. William gct Goshen MM, O.

WATSON

1826, 11, 8. Ann m Solomon CLARK

1825, 6, 27. William rocf Stillwater MM, O., dtd 1825,4,24
1825, 6, 27. Elizabeth & s, Mark, rocf Stillwater MM, O., dtd 1825,4,24
1825, 6, 27. Ann rocf Stillwater MM, O., dtd 1825,4,24
1828, 8, 25. William dis jH
1829, 7, 29. Elizabeth dis jH
1831, 11, 28. Mark dis jH

WAY

----, --, --. David d 1852,1,28 ae 73 bur Sunsbury; m Ann ----- d 1829,11,17 ae 49 bur Sunsbury
 Ch: Benjamin b 1802, 10, 3
     Robert   " 1804, 6, 29
     Alice   " 1806, 2, 23
     Hannah   " 1809, 9, 27
     Sarah   " 1811, 8, 27
     Jane   " 1814, 5, 28
     Mary   " 1814, 5, 28 d 1835,3,29 bur Sunsbury
     Elizabeth b 1816, 10, 30
     Jacob   " 1818, 11, 13
1823, 4, 2. Alice [Wey] m Mordecai MORRIS
1825, 5, 4. Benjamin, s David & Ann, Monroe Co., O., b 1802,10,3; m in Somerset MH, Jane GIBBONS, dt John & Elizabeth, Belmont Co., O.
 Ch: John b 1827, 5, 22
     Jane " 1830, 12, 10
1825, 8, 4. Robert, s David & Ann, Monroe Co., O.; m in Ridge MH, Lydia BOSWELL, dt Dempsey & Mary, Belmont Co., O.
 Ch: Milicent b 1827, 2, 19
     Mary Ann " 1828, 5, 25
     David L. " 1830, 12, 15
     Sarah   " 1833, 10, 22
1830, 12, 23. Jane d bur Somerset
1831, 10, 6. Jane m Amos VERNON
1832, 3, 8. David, s Robert & Hannah, Monroe Co., O.; m in Sunbury, Rachel McNICHOLS, dt Thomas & Martha SMITH, Belmont Co., O.
----, --, --. Benjamin & Abigail
 Ch: Deborah b 1834, 7, 31
1834, 4, 3. Hannah m Isaiah WILLIAMS
1835, 4, 4. Jane d ae 4 bur Sunsbury
1859, 2, 11. Rachel d bur Sunsbury

1823, 5, 26. Robert, minor, gct Plainfield MM
1824, 9, 27. Robert rocf Plainfield MM, dtd 1824,9,23
1827, 4, 30. Robert & w, Lydia, & dt, Milicent, gct Stillwater MM, O.
1829, 10, 27. Benjamin & w, Jane, & s, John, gct Stillwater MM, O.
1829, 6, 29. Benjamin & w, Jane, & s, John, rocf Stillwater MM, O., dtd 1829,6,27
1831, 4, 25. Benjamin gct Smithfield MM
1833, 3, 25. Benjamin & w, Abigail, rocf

Stillwater MM, O., dtd 1833,3,23
1835, 8, 24. Robert & w, Lydia, & ch, Millicent, Mary Ann, David & Sarah, rocf Stillwater MM, O., dtd 1835,7,25
1835, 9, 28. Benjamin & Abigail & ch, John & Deborah, gct Pennsville MM, O.
1836, 3, 28. Robert & w, Lydia, & ch, Millicent, Mary Ann, David & Rachel, gct Pennsville MM, O.
1836, 11, 28. Sarah gct Pennsville MM, O.
1837, 11, 27. Elizabeth gct Chesterfield MM
1839, 11, 25. Jacob dis mcd

WEBSTER

1825, 1, 6. Eli, s John & Hannah, Guernsey Co., O.; m in Sunbury, Mercy FOULKE, dt Judah & Sarah, Monroe Co., O.

1825, 2, 28. Mercy gct Stillwater MM, O.

WELLINS

1828, 3, 24. Asenath (form Davis) dis mcd

WELLS

1838, 3, 26. Lydia (form Eves) dis mcd

WERNIECKE

1849, 9, 24. Sarah (form Neptune) dis mcd

WEST

1855, 10, 29. Mary (form Bailey) dis mcd

WHITE

1827, 7, 4. Mary m Mahlon STRAHL
----, --, --. Jesse & Sarah
 Ch: Jesse
     Matilda

1825, 7, 25. Lydia Harper (form White) dis mcd
1825, 9, 26. Catharine & ch, Aaron, Elizabeth & Mary, rocf Stillwater MM, O., dtd 1825, 7,23
1828, 6, 30. Jesse dis jH
1828, 7, 28. Rhoda Harper (form White) dis mcd
1829, 3, 30. Jacob dis mcd
1829, 10, 26. Sarah dis jH
1839, 10, 28. Sarah dis jH
1892, 11, 24. Hannah (form Doudna) con mcd
1896, 8, 20. Hannah E. dis disunity

WILEY

1821, 3, 26. David & w, Elizabeth, & ch, Sarah, Joseph & Mary, gct Salem MM, O.

WILLIAMS

----, --, --. Job & Elizabeth
 Ch: Ezra   b 1821, 8, 31
     Isaac C. " 1823, 11, 23
     Abner   " 1826, 8, 30
     Jesse   " 1829, 6, 22 d 1831, 8,21
     Henry   " 1831, 11, 25

WILLIAMS, Job & Elizabeth, continued
  Ch: Benjamin b 1834, 4, 20
   James " 1836, 10, 5
   Job   " 1839, 9, 20
----, --, --. Samuel & Sarah
  Ch: Martha b 1822, 4, 7
   Richard " 1824, 5, 6 d 1843, 8, 6
   bur Somerset
   Samuel b 1827, 3, 27
1826, 11, 8. Anne m Edwin PATTERSON
1828, 7, 9. Sally m Exum BUNDY
1830, 5, 5. Mary m John HAMPTON
1834, 4, 3. Isaiah, s Henry & Zilpha, Monroe Co., O.; m in Sunbury, Hannah WAY,
  dt David & Ann, Belmont Co., O.
  Ch: Elias b 1835, 1, 26
1843, 5, 10. Henry, s Daniel & Temperance,
  Belmont Co., O.; m in Ridge MH, Rachel
  CREW, dt Jacob & Rachel, Belmont Co., O.
1845, 6, 9. Ann d ae 96 bur Somerset
1853, 4, 3. William T., s Abner & Mary Ann,
  b
1856, 5, 26. Sarah, w Samuel, dt Joseph & Sarah ARNOLD, d bur Ridge

1822, 9, 30. William & w, Lydia, rocf Stillwater MM, O., dtd 1822,6,22
1823, 5, 26. Wm. & w, Lydia, & dt, Hannah,
  gct Plainfield MM
1825, 10, 24. Wm. & w, Lydia, & ch, Hannah C.
  & Mary, rocf Plainfield MM, dtd 1825,7,21
1827, 4, 30. Wm. & w, Lydia, & ch, Hannah
  Clendenon & Daniel Melton, gct Deerfield
  MM
1827, 6, 25. David & w, Sarah, & dt, Rachel
  S., rocf Stillwater MM, O., dtd 1827,5,26
1828, 6, 30. Samuel dis jH
1828, 11, 24. David dis jH
1829, 7, 27. Sarah Jr. dis jH
1830, 5, 24. John & w, Deborah, rocf Stillwater MM, O., dtd 1830,5,22
1831, 7, 25. John & Deborah gct Stillwater
  MM, O.
1833, 4, 29. Robert dis disunity
1824, 2, 24. Isaiah rocf Stillwater MM, O.,
  dtd 1834,2,22
1835, 5, 25. Rachel & Jane, minor ch David &
  Sarah, gct Deerfield MM, O.
1836, 9, 29. Isaiah & w, Hannah, & s, Elias,
  gct Pennsville MM, O.
1837, 5, 29. Peninah Gibbons (form Williams)
  con mcd
1840, 6, 29. Sarah rst at Stillwater MM, O.,
  on consent of this mtg
1841, 4, 26. Seth gct Chesterfield MM
1842, 2, 28. Rachel (form Gibbons) dis mcd
1842, 4, 25. Elizabeth Gibbons (form Williams)
  dis mcd
1844, 1, 29. Rachel gct Stillwater MM, O.
1844, 3, 25. Martha Stanton (form Williams)
  dis mcd
1844, 11, 25. Ezra dis mcd
1845, 6, 30. Sarah & ch, Jane J., Ephraim &

  Otho F., rocf Stillwater MM, O.
1845, 11, 24. Rachel S. rocf Stillwater MM,
  O., dtd 1845,9,27
1846, 4, 27. Jane Naylor (form Williams) dis
  mcd
1850, 3, 25. Isaac con mcd
1850, 5, 27. Wm. & w, Lydia, & ch, Lindley,
  Elwood & Elizabeth, rocf Stillwater MM, O.,
  dtd 1850,4,27
1850, 9, 30. Isaac C. gct Springfield MM,
  Ind.
1851, 1, 27. Samuel dis mcd
1851, 9, 29. Lindley dis disunity
1851, 10, 27. Abner gct Pennsville MM
1852, 8, 30. James Edgerton gct Plainfield MM,
  to m Mary Ann Williams
1852, 10, 25. Abner & w, Mary Ann, rocf Pennsville MM, dtd 1852,10,14
1852, 10, 25. Elizabeth Koontz (form Williams)
  dis mcd
1853, 7, 25. Elwood dis mcd
1853, 9, 26. Sarah & Rachel dis jas
1854, 1, 30. Jesse dis mcd
1854, 2, 27. Wm. dis disunity
1854, 2, 27. Lydia gct Pleasant Plain MM, Ia.
1855, 2, 26. Abner & w, Mary Ann, & s, Wm.
  Talbat, gct White Lick MM, Ind.
1856, 11, 24. Job M. dis disunity
1889, 4, 25. Job dis mcd

WILLITS
1821, 5, 21. Joseph rocf Fairfield MM, O.,
  dtd 1820,9,30, end by Stillwater MM, O.,
  1821,5,20
1822, 2, 25. Henry dis mcd
1822, 4, 29. Lydia (form Hodgin) dis mcd
1823, 5, 26. Charity Frazier (form Willets)
  dis mcd
1823, 6, 30. Joseph dis mcd
1824, 5, 24. Ann (form Hodgin) dis mcd

WILSON
1833, 9, 4. Mary Ann, dt Charles & Ann, b
1837, 3, 9. Isaac d ae 67 bur Ridge
1844, 12, 22. Mary Ann d ae 11 bur Ridge
1867, 1, 9. Ann, dt Joseph & Penina GIBBONS,
  d ae 65 bur Ridge
1892, 9, 3. Elizabeth, dt Joseph & Elizabeth
  GARRETSON, d ae 79

1822, 4, 29. Isaac & w, Elizabeth, & ch, Rebecca & Sarah, gct Stillwater MM, O.
1833, 5, 24. Louisa (form Hix) dis mcd
1835, 7, 27. Ann rst on consent of Flushing
  MM
1835, 11, 30. Isaac recrq
1835, 11, 30. Mary Ann, infant dt Ann, recrq
1841, 4, 26. Mary & ch, Rachel, Daniel, Ruth,
  William, Owen, Thomas & Catharine, rocf
  Short Creek MM, O., dtd 1841,4,20
1843, 2, 27. Mary & minor ch gct Pennsville
  MM
1844, 3, 25. Rachel gct Pennsville MM

WILSON, continued
1844, 4, 29. Ellen (form Wade) dis mcd
1857, 5, 20. Elizabeth (form Garretson) con
    mcd

WINDER
1886, 9, 24. David, s Joseph & Lydia, Keokuk
    Co., Ia.; m in Ridge MH, Elizabeth GIBBONS
    dt Joseph & Penina (Williams), Belmont Co.,
    O.
1887, 10, 10. Elizabeth G. d ae 33 bur Ridge

WOOD
----, --, --. Israel & Elizabeth
    Ch: Joseph   b 1813, 4, 30
        Aaron   " 1815, 9, 18
        Wilson   " 1818, 3, 25
        Ann   " 1820, 9, 24
        John   " 1822, 12, 11
1826, 4, 6. John, s Robert & Mary, Monroe
    Co., O.; m in Sunbury, Sarah LESLIE, dt
    Robert & Rachel, Monroe Co., O.
1843, 11, 30. Elisha M., s Joseph & Mary,
    Washington Co., O.; m in Ridge MH, Martha
    BAILEY, dt James & Sarah, Belmont Co., O.
1848, 11, 16. John W., s John & Esther, Bel-
    mont Co., O.; m in Ridge MH, Almedia CREW,
    dt James & Sarah, Belmont Co., O.
    Ch: Elam   b 1855, 8, 21
        George C.   " 1858, 1, 14 d 1861, 6,24
            bur Ridge
        Allen D.   " 1860, 4, 27
        Mary R.   " 1862, 9, 29

1825, 9, 26. John rocf Short Creek MM, O.,
    dtd 1825,7,29
1826, 4, 24. Israel & w, Elizabeth, & ch, Jo-
    seph, Wilson, Ann, John & Sarah, gct
    Stillwater MM, O.
1828, 6, 30. John dis jH
1829, 1, 26. Sarah dis jH
1835, 5, 25. Sidney, Jane, Prudence, Ann,
    John W., Thomas & Mary, minors, rocf
    Stillwater MM, O., dtd 1835,5,23

        *   *   *   *   *   *   *
ADAMS
1844, 3, 25. Margaret dis jas
1844, 6, 24. Edward dis jH

        *   *   *   *   *   *   *
HARTLEY
1928, 9, 27. Mary Rebecca m John. A. HALL

1835, 9, 28. James Vernon gct Alum Creek
    MM, O., to m Rachel Wood
1838, 3, 26. Cidney, Prudence, Ann, John W.
    & Thomas, minor ch John & Esther, gct
    Chesterfield MM
1838, 12, 26. Abijah Tipton gct Stillwater
    MM, O., to m Sidney Wood
1840, 6, 29. Jane Jones (form Wood) dis mcd
1841, 10, 25. Aaron Dewees gct Stillwater MM,
    O., to m Mary Wood
1844, 1, 29. Martha gct Chesterfield MM
1855, 8, 27. John rocf Stillwater MM, O.,
    dtd 1855,8,25
1865, 2, 27. John & w, Almeda, & ch, Elma D.
    & Mary R., gct Hickory Grove MM, Ia.

WOOTEN
1827, 2, 26. Martha (form Bailey) dis mcd
1840, 2, 24. Rebecca gct Chesterfield MM, O.

WORTHINGTON
1869, 9, 23. James Gibbons gct Pennsville
    MM, O., to m Lydia Worthington
1871, 6, 22. Zinas Ruben Sarah Ann & Mary J.
    & their mother, Lydia Gibbons, rocf Penns-
    ville MM, dtd 1871,6,15
1875, 11, 25. Zenas dis mcd
1890, 8, 21. Reuben dis mcd
1893, 7, 20. Mary J. gct Stillwater MM, O.

YARNALL
1822, 10, 28. Mordecai & ch, Hannah, Susanna
    & George, gct Flushing MM, O.
1823, 11, 24. Mordecai dis jas

YOCOM
1823, 9, 3. Jacob, s Samuel & Rebecca, Bel-
    mont Co., O.; m in Somerset MH, Lydia WADE
    dt Royal & Phebe, Belmont Co., O.

1823, 7, 23. Jacob rocf Stillwater MM, O.,
    dtd 1823,6,28
1827, 5, 28. Jacob & w, Lydia, & ch, Phebe &
    Samuel, gct Stillwater MM, O.

        *   *   *   *   *   *   *
ARNOLD
1850, 3, 7. Bethula (nee HAMPTON) m Anderson
    ARNOLD

MIDDLETON MONTHLY MEETING

Middleton Monthly Meeting, Columbiana County, Ohio, was established by Redstone Quarterly Meeting 9th Mo. 5, 1803. On the discontinuance of Carmel Monthly Meeting on 1st Mo. 11th 1855, the members were joined to Middletown Monthly Meeting and on 8th Mo. 16th 1855, members of Carmel Monthly Meeting and Carmel Preparative Meeting were attached to this meeting.

Among the charter members of the meeting were the Bingham, Cadwallader, Dixon, Hanna, Heald, Holloway, Pettit, Schooley, Test, and Wright families.

RECORDS

ADAMS
1863, 8, 15. Ruth (form Neil) dis mcd

ADAMSON
1814, 9, 15. Ruth m Thomas HATCHER
1816, 11, 21. Thos., s James & Hannah, Columbiana Co., O.; m at Middleton, Elizabeth WOODS, dt John & Rebecca, Columbiana Co., O.
   Ch: Rebecca b 1817, 9, 13
      Hannah " 1818, 10, 28
      John W. " 1820, 5, 23
      James " 1822, 2, 24
      Samuel " 1822, 11, 30
      Nathan " 1825, 7, 5
      Lydia " 1826, 11, 19
      Thomas " 1828, 9, 26
      Joseph " 1831, 5, 3
1816, 1, 18. Rebecca m John HATCHER
1818, 10, 22. Esther m Samuel WOODS
1827, 3, 14. John, s James & Hannah, Columbiana Co., O.; m at Fairfield, Sarah ERWIN, dt Samuel & Sarah, Columbiana Co., O.
   Ch: Elizabeth b 1827, 12, 15
      Ruth " 1830, 4, 2
      Mary " 1832, 1, 14
      Wm. " 1834, 7, 7
      Susannah " 1836, 12, 12
      James H. " 1839, 7, 21
      Samuel E. " 1842, 1, 8
      Sarah Ann " 1843, 9, 22
      Erwin " 1848, 5, 18
1833, 1, 23. Mary d bur Middleton
1833, 1, 23. Ruth d bur Middleton
1837, 5, 13. James d
1842, 10, 12. Samuel, s John & Sarah, d bur Middleton

1806, 7, 12. Hannah rocf Westland MM, dtd 1806,1,6
1811, 8, 8. John, s James & Hannah, recrq of mother
1811, 8, 8. Thomas recrq
1811, 8, 8. Ruth recrq
1811, 8, 8. Rebecca & Esther, ch Hannah, recrq of mother
1811, 11, 7. James recrq
1823, 2, 17. Thomas & w, Elizabeth, & ch, Rebecca, Hannah, John W. & James, gct Sandy Spring MM
1829, 4, 9. Thomas & w, Elizabeth, & ch, Rebecca, Hannah, John, James, Samuel, Nathan, Lydia & Thos., rocf Sandy Spring MM, dtd 1829,2,27
1835, 8, 17. Thomas & w, Elizabeth, & ch, Rebecca, Hannah, John W., James, Samuel, Nathan, Lydia, Thomas, Joseph & Ellis, gct Upper Springfield MM
1846, 6, 11. Elizabeth James (form Adamson) dis mcd
1850, 11, 7. Sarah dis disunity

1850, 12, 12. John dis disunity
1872, 4, 20. William dis mcd
1872, 12, 21. James dis mcd
1874, 4, 18. Susannah Richardson (form Adamson) dis mcd (first rpd 1872,7,20)

ALFORD
1812, 12, 10. John rocf Kennett MM, dtd 1812,10,6

ALLEN
----, --, --. James & Orpha
   Ch: Thos. b 1799, 11, 11
      Hannah " 1802, 7, 14
      David M. " 1805, 2, 14
      Jesse " 1807, 9, 12
      Nathan " 1810, 3, 26
      Ann " 1813, 1, 1
      Sarah " 1816, 3, 14
----, --, --. Isaac & Sarah
   Ch: Benj. b 1801, 2, 15
      John " 1803, 6, 27
      Lydia " 1805, 12, 23
      Sally Ann " 1808, 7, 26
      Isaac " 1811, 12, 18
      Martha " 1813, 8, 1
1807, 11, 26. Jesse, s Benj. & Hannah, Columbiana Co., O.; m at Middleton, Ann MERCER, dt David & Sarah, Columbiana Co.,O.
1815, 12, 17. Isaac d bur Middleton
1819, 4, 29. Sarah m John McCLUN
1820, 12, 6. David, s Isaac & Sarah, Columbiana Co., O.; m Cynthia McCLUN, dt John & Elizabeth, Columbiana Co., O.
   Ch: Jonathan b 1821, 9, 10
      John Mercer " 1824, 6, 6
1824, 9, 9. Cynthia d
1827, 8, 25. Cynthia Ann, dt David & Sarah K., b
1828, 8, 14. Lydia m Israel HEALD
1838, 9, 20. Jesse M., s James & Orpha, Columbiana Co., O.; m at Columbiana, Mary NICHOLS, dt Wm. & Mary, Columbiana Co., O. (H)
1839, 11, 9. Martha, dt John & Phebe, b
1923, 8, 30. Howard A., s Joseph & Orpha, Hendricks Co., Ind.; m at Middleton, Dorothy EDGERTON, dt J. Howard & Lavina, Columbiana Co., O.

1807, 9, 12. Jesse rocf Chester MM, dtd 1807,7,27
1817, 6, 16. Benjamin, minor, gct Marlborough MM
1822, 2, 18. Hannah gct Marlborough MM
1822, 2, 18. Thomas gct Marlborough MM
1822, 2, 18. James & w, Orpah, & ch, David, Nathan, Ann & Sarah, gct Marlborough MM
1823, 9, 22. Benjamin rocf New Garden MM, Pa., dtd 1823,7,10
1824, 7, 19. Benjamin dis mou
1824, 8, 23. Hannah (form McClun) dis mou

ALLEN, continued
1826, 8, 21. David gct Upper Springfield MM,
   to m Sarah K. Isenhour
1827, 2, 8. Sarah K. rocf Upper Springfield
   MM, dtd 1827,1,27
1829, 1, 8. Ann dis JH
1829, 1, 8. Jesse dis joining Separatists
1829, 2, 12. John gct Marlborough MM
1829, 3, 12. Sarah K. dis JH
1829, 3, 12. David & John, Jr. dis JH
1829, 3, 12. Sally Ann dis JH
1829, 3, 12. Cert granted John to Carmel MM
   returned; com for JH
1829, 7, 9. John dis JH
1830, 3, 11. Martha dis JH
1831, 6, 9. Jesse, Jr. dis JH
1831, 7, 7. Isaac dis disunity
1831, 7, 7. David dis mcd (H)
1831, 7, 7. Jesse dis mcd (H)
1831, 10, 6. Sally Ann Firestone (form Allen)
   dis mcd (H)
1833, 3, 7. Deborah (form Taylor) dis mou &
   JH
1833, 8, 8. Deborah (form Taylor) dis mcd
   (H)
1835, 6, 11. Martha Mendenhall (form Allen)
   con mcd (H)
1837, 5, 11. John con mcd (H)
1837, 5, 11. Phebe con mcd (H)
1837, 7, 17. Jonathan, John Mercer & Cynthia
   Ann, ch David, gct Pennsville MM

1843, 9, 14. Cinthy Ann, minor, rocf Chesterfield MM, dtd 1843,8,18
1843, 11, 9. Martha (form Ladner) dis mou
1847, 2, 11. Cynthia Swigert (form Allen)
   dis mou
1848, 10, 12. Mary Ann (form Armstrong) dis
   mcd
1924, 6, 21. Dorothy E. gct Plainfield MM,
   Ind.

ALLMON
----, --, --. Jno. & Hannah [Almon]
   Ch: Wm.   b 1785, 8, 4
      Ebenezer " 1786, 12, 22
      Thos.   " 1788, 10, 6
      John   " 1796, 5, 26
      Jesse   " 1798, 10, 16
      Hannah   " 1801, 2, 24
      Jehu   " 1804, 10, 11
1809, 11, 16. Ebenezer, s Jno. & Hannah, Co-
   lumbiana Co., O., b 1786,12,22; m at
   Middleton, Rebeccah OLIPHANT, dt Samuel
   & Elizabeth, Columbiana Co., O., b 1788,
   4,24
   Ch: Hannah   b 1810, 8, 18
      Elizabeth " 1812, 10, 10
      Ann   " 1814, 11, 13
      Israel   " 1816, 9, 28
      Rachel   " 1818, 12, 21

   Ch: Thos.   b 1821, 4, 2
      Samuel   " 1824, 4, 5
      George   " 1826, 7, 16
      Margaret " 1828, 6, 13
      Aaron   " 1830, 4, 8
      Eli   " 1832, 8, 9
      Ephraim " 1835, 1, 5
1809, 10, 18. William, s John & Hannah, Columbiana Co., O.; m at Elkrun, Lydia
   WALKER, dt James & Elizabeth, Columbiana
   Co., O.
----, --, --. John, s Jno. & Hannah, b 1785,
   8,4; m Lydia WALKER, dt James & Elizabeth,
   b 1790, 5,18
   Ch: Isaac   b 1810, 7, 27
      John   " 1811, 10, 5
      James   " 1813, 5, 9
      Joseph   " 1817, 7, --
1811, 9, 16. John d bur Middleton
1819, 12, 2. Thomas, s John & Hannah, Columbiana Co., O., b 1788,10,6 d 1858,9,17;
   m at Middleton, Abigail BOULTON, dt James
   & Hannah, Columbiana Co., O., b 1800,1,
   21 d 1871,10,20
   Ch: Silas   b 1820, 8, 24
      Sarah   " 1823, 11, 23
      Mary   " 1826, 12, 23
      Meader   " 1830, 7, 5
      Phebe   " 1834, 12, 27
1822, 4, 8. Jesse, s Wm. & Lydia, b
1832, 2, 26. Jehu, s John & Hannah, Columbiana Co., O., b 1804,10,11 d 1875,11,30;
   m at Middleton, Hannah WICKERSHAM, dt
   Thos. & Ann, Columbiana Co., O., b 1817,
   3,28 d 1875,7,19
   Ch: Phebe Ann b 1833, 5, 26 d 1833, 6,17
      Esther   " 1834, 11, 27
      Lydia   " 1836, 7, 28
      Ann   " 1838, 7, 12
      Abner   " 1843, 5, 17
      Sarah   " 1846, 7, 25
1832, 9, 14. Elizabeth m William MILLIGAN
1833, 2, 9. George d bur Middleton
1833, 6, 17. Phebe Ann, dt J. & H., d bur
   Middleton
1841, 6, 8. Hannah, w John, d bur Middleton
----, --, --. Silas & Phebe
   Ch: Lucy Ann
      Levi
      James B.
1851, 11, 13. Meader, s Thomas & Abigail, Columbiana Co., O., b 1830,7,5; m at
   Middleton, Susannah H. COPE, dt Israel &
   Elizabeth, Columbiana Co., O., b 1829,7,14
   Ch: Webster
      Allison b 1853, 4, 25
      Morris
      Cope   " 1856, 4, 13 d 1857,10,25
      Luanna C. " 1859, 6, 9
      Wilmer
      Joseph   " 1868, 3, 16
1853, 10, 13. Esther m Isaac S. CADWALADER
1858, 9, 23. Ann W. m Linton HALL

ALLMON, continued

1868, 10, 22. Sarah m Thomas BLACKBURN

1869, 10, 21. Abner, s Jehu & Hannah W., Columbiana Co., O., b 1843,5,17 d 1899,7,15;
m at Middleton, Lucinda Ann HARRISON, dt
Benj. & Mary (Dixon), b 1848,12,24 d
1922,6,18 bur Middleton
Ch: Chas.
        Franklin b 1872, 4, 11
        Hannah Mary" 1874, 6, 3 d 1882,10,26
        Albert J. " 1877, 2, 4 " 1882, 6,11
        Alfred
          Clarence " 1892, 8, 30

1872, 3, 21. Webster, s Meader & Susanna,
Columbiana Co., O., b 1853,4,25; m Tacy
M. ELLYSON, dt Robert & Mary, Columbiana
Co., O., b 1851,3,2
Ch: Emmit   b 1873, 2, 25
    Mary L.   " 1875, 5, 5
    Albert
      Robert " 1877, 12, 31

1885, 12, 23. Hannah, dt John, d

1805, 6, 19. Hannah & ch, William, Ebenezer,
Thomas, John, Jesse & Hannah, rocf Westland MM, dtd 1804,4,28

1825, 5, 23. William & w, Lydia, & ch, Isaac,
John, James, Joseph & Jesse, gct Marlborough MM

1827, 10, 11. Jesse gct Marlborough MM

1829, 10, 8. Isaac, minor, rocf Marlborough
MM, dtd 1829,7,28

1833, 10, 10. Israel gct Salem MM

1833, 11, 7. Isaac gct Marlborough MM

1836, 9, 19. Israel rocf Marlborough MM, dtd
1836,5,31

1837, 5, 11. Israel dis disunity

1837, 6, 19. Ann Woods (form Allmon) dis mcd

1839, 6, 6. Hannah Carey (form Allman) con
mou

1839, 10, 10. Ebenezer & w, Rebecca, & ch,
Thomas, Samuel, Margaret, Aaron, Eli &
Ephraim, gct Goshen MM, O.

1839, 10, 10. Rachel gct Goshen MM, O.

1840, 6, 11. Silas gct Carmel MM, to m Phebe
Elma Heald

1840, 10, 8. Phebe Elma rocf Carmel MM, dtd
1840,9,19

1842, 10, 6. John gct Goshen MM

1846, 12, 10. Silas & w, Phebe Elma, & ch,
Lucy Ann, Levi & James B., gct Gillead MM

1847, 5, 6. Ruth (form Garwood) dis mcd

1848, 11, 9. Sarah Murvin (form Allmon) dis
mou

1851, 12, 11. Mary Richey (form Allmon) con
mou

1857, 7, 9. Lydia Heston (form Allmon) con
mcd

1858, 4, 17. Meader [Allman] & w, Susannah,
& ch, Webster Alison, gct Upper Springfield MM

1860, 5, 19. Phebe Detzell (form Allmon) dis
mcd

1860, 7, 21. Meader & w, Susanna, & ch,
Webster Allison & Luanna C., rocf Upper
Springfield MM, dtd 1860,5,25

1881, 11, 19. Tacy M. dis joining separatists

1882, 7, 15. Meader & w, Susannah, & ch, Wilmer J., gct Hickory Grove MM, Ia.

1882, 7, 15. Luanna C. [Almon] gct Hickory
Grove MM, Ia.

1882, 10, 21. Emmet M., Mary L. & Albert R.,
ch Webster A. & Tacy M., gct Hickory
Grove MM, Ia.

1894, 10, 20. Charles F. dis jas

1917, 8, 18. Alfred C. dis mcd

1921, 8, 20. Alfred C. dis mcd

ANDERSON

1815, 9, 7. Elizabeth (form Boyce) dis mou

ANTRIM

1817, 1, 13. Ann rocf Chesterfield MM, N.J.,
dtd 1816,10,8

1817, 5, 12. James P., Daniel & Elizabeth,
ch Levi & w recrq

ARMSTRONG

1807, 11, 19. John W., s James & Ruth, Colum-
biana Co., O.; m at Middleton, Sarah
BEAL, dt Joseph & Hannah. Columbiana Co.,
O.

1808, 12, 22. Phebe m Jonathan MARSH

1811, 1, 3. James, s James & Ruth, Columbiana Co., O.; m at Middleton, Mary HEALD,
dt John & Phebe, Columbiana Co., O.

1814, 4, 14. Bennet, s James & Ruth, Colum-
biana Co., O.; m at Middleton, Elizabeth
CRAIG, dt Wm. & Deborah, Columbiana Co.,
O.
Ch: James C. b 1814, 12, 14
    Deborah
      Elma   " 1816, 10, 12
    Wm.   " 1818, 8, 21
    Bennett   " 1820, 3, 17
    Jane Emily " 1822, 3, 7

1818, 10, 29. Sarah m Nathan HOLE

1821, 11, 29. Samuel, s James & Ruth, Columbiana Co., O.; m at Middleton, Anna WAL-
TON, dt Abraham & Mary, Columbiana Co.,O.

1822, 12, 6. Mary, dt Samuel & Anna, d

----, --, --. John & Sarah
Ch: John C.   b 1825, 1, 7
    Rachel Ann " 1827, 9, 8

1841, 8, 10. Lucinda C. b

----, --, --. Samuel & Elizabeth
Ch: Martha   b 1830, 8, 8
    Thomas   " 1832, 2, 2

1853, 4, 14. Joseph, s Nathan H. & Rebecca,
Columbiana Co., O.; m at Middleton, Sarah
OLIPHANT, dt Samuel & Rachel, Mahoning Co.
O.

1855, 10, 18. Dawsey, s Nathan H. & Rebecca,
Columbiana Co., O.; m at Middleton, Sarah
Emily BAKER, dt Jesse & Eliza, Columbiana
Co., O.

ARMSTRONG, continued

1856, 11, 13. Israel, s Nathan H. & Rebecca,
      Columbiana Co., O.; m at Middleton, Sina
      OLIPHANT, dt Samuel & Rachel, Mahoning
      Co., O.
1865, 9, 21. Elma C. m Benjamin ELLYSON
1867, 9, 25. Samuel, s Nathan H. & Rebecca,
      Columbiana Co., O.; m at Carmel, Emeline
      COPE, dt Isaac & Rachel, Columbiana Co.,O.

1806, 10, 11. James & w, Ruth, & ch, Sarah,
      Bennett, Ruth, Samuel & Nathan, rocf Ken-
      net MM, dtd 1806,8,5
1806, 10, 11. Emmely rocf Kennet MM, dtd
      1806,8,5
1806, 10, 11. Phebe rocf Kennet MM, dtd 1806,
      8,5
1807, 9, 12. Emily Morlin (form Armstrong)
      con mcd
1808, 2, 13. John W. & w, Sarah, gct Salem MM
1811, 10, 10. James & w, Mary, gct New Garden
      MM
1812, 8, 6. James gct New Garden MM, to m
      Deborah Craig
1813, 2, 11. Deborah Armstrong & dt, Lydia
      Craig, rocf New Garden MM, dtd 1812,11,
      19
1817, 8, 11. John W. & w, Sarah, & ch, Phebe,
      Milton, Elizabeth & Samuel, rocf New Gar-
      den MM, dtd 1817,6,19
1823, 6, 23. Nathan gct Carmel MM
1826, 3, 20. Bennet & w, Elizabeth, & ch,
      James C., William, Bennet, Jane Emily &
      Maryann, gct Sandy Spring MM
1826, 3, 20. Deborah gct Sandy Spring MM
1828, 9, 11. Samuel gct Providence MM, Pa.
1828, 10, 9. John W. dis joining Separatists
1829, 2, 12. Sarah dis joining Separatists
1829, 3, 12. Elizabeth rocf Providence MM,
      dtd 1829,2,5
1829, 6, 11. Phebe dis jH
1830, 8, 12. Phebe Garwood (late Armstrong)
      con mou (H)
1833, 12, 12. Milton dis jH
1834, 1, 9. Samuel & w, Elizabeth, & ch,
      Mary Ann, Martha, Thomas & Joshua, gct
      Carmel MM
1835, 11, 10. Elizabeth dis jH
1837, 11, 9. Milton dis mcd (H)
1839, 6, 6. Samuel dis performing military
      service (H)
1840, 10, 8. Samuel, s John, dis mcd & jas
1842, 5, 12. Hannah Elliott (form Armstrong)
      con mcd (H)
1844, 9, 12. Nathan, minor s Bennett, dec,
      rocf Carmel MM, dtd 1844,7,20
1844, 12, 12. Mary Ann rocf Carmel MM, dtd
      1844,10,19
1848, 10, 12. Mary Ann Allen (form Armstrong)
      dis mcd
1852, 8, 12. Nathan gct Carmel MM
1854, 5, 11. Joseph rocf Carmel MM, dtd 1854,
      4,15

1855, 1, 11. Nathan H., Jr., mbr Carmel MM,
      dis mou
1858, 1, 8. Sarah Josephine (form Lipsey)
      dis mcd
1858, 2, 11. Thomas dis mcd
1862, 8, 16. Joseph & w, Sarah, gct Hickory
      Grove MM, Ia.
1863, 3, 21. Martha A. More (form Armstrong)
      dis mcd
1863, 7, 18. Nathan & Joshua dis joining
      Separatists
1864, 2, 20. Dawsy dis mcd
1864, 11, 14. Israel & w, Sina, & ch, Ann
      Eliza & Martha, gct Hickory Grove MM,Ia.
1865, 5, 20. Elizabeth dis joining Separa-
      tists
1869, 2, 20. Ruth A. Stanley (form Armstrong)
      rpd mcd (d before case was settled)
1875, 1, 16. Lucinda C. rst by rq
1879, 4, 19. Alice Anna gct Hickory Grove
      MM, Ia.
1879, 4, 19. Rebecca gct Hickory Grove MM,
      Ia.
1888, 8, 18. Samuel & s, Nathan Edgar, gct
      Hickory Grove MM, Ia.

ARNOLD
1833, 9, 12. Lydia Ann, minor, rocf Sandy
      Spring MM, dtd 1833,7,26
1837, 12, 18. Lydia Ann gct Sandy Spring MM

ASHTON
----, --, --. Barak b 1824,7,26 d 1890,5,7;
      m Jane LEECH, dt Wm. & Jane, b 1821,3,1
      d 1888,4,18
      Ch: Martha   b 1846, 5, 18
          Wm. L.   " 1848, 8, 3
          Richard S.   " 1850, 9, 15 (or 9-13-
              1850)
          Phebe Y.   " 1853, 5, 16
          Eliza M.   " 1856, 1, 8
          Thomas L.   " 1867, 1, 11 d 1911, 6, 7
1865, 10, 25. Martha m Seth SHAW
1867, 1, 13. Martha d ae 84y (an elder)
1873, 2, 20. Phebe Y. m Albert M. COPE
----, --, --. Richard S. b 1850,9,13; m
      Eliza G. McGREW, dt James & Ann, b 1851,
      11,4
      Ch: Harmon J. b 1876, 11, 11
          Reno Jane   " 1878, 11, 28
1884, 12, 25. Eliza M. m David F. MORLAN
1898, 3, 24. Thomas L., s Barak & Jane, Co-
      lumbiana Co., O.; m at Middleton, Ida
      BLACKBURN, dt Jonathan K. & Emily, Colum-
      biana Co., O.

1825, 8, 22. Jacob, minor, rocf Carmel MM,
      dtd 1825,8,20
1834, 7, 10. Jacob F. dis mcd
1874, 9, 19. Richard gct Short Creek MM, to
      m Eliza McGrew
1875, 6, 19. Eliza G. rocf Short Creek MM,
      O., dtd 1875,5,18 .

ASHTON, continued

1876, 5, 20. William L. gct Flushing MM, O., to m Eliza F. Holloway
1877, 9, 15. William L. gct Flushing MM, O.
1880, 12, 18. Thomas L., minor under care of Barak & Jane, recrq
1880, 12, 18. Catharine Longshore, minor under care of Barak & Jane Ashton, recrq
1884, 2, 16. Richard & w, Eliza G., & ch, Harmon J., Rena J., William B. & Albert H., gct Short Creek MM
1913, 8, 16. Ida B. gct Upper Springfield MM

ATKINSON

1838, 4, 23. Theophilos Ellerman gct ND MM, Phila., Pa., to m Sarah Atkinson

BADER

1833, 3, 7. John Valentine recrq (H)
1833, 5, 9. John Valentine gct New Garden MM (H)

BAILEY

1826, 11, 20. Jesse [Baily], s Joseph & Elizabeth, Belmont Co., O.; m at Beaver Falls, Lydia TOWNSEND, dt Joseph & Sinah, Columbiana Co., O.

1805, 10, 12. Cert rec for Joseph & w, Elisabeth, & ch, Jesse, Yarnall, Hoops & Pennock, from Goshen MM, Pa., dtd 1805,6,7, endorsed to Salem MM
1825, 6, 20. Rachel, minor, rocf New Garden MM, dtd 1825,4,21
1827, 8, 9. Lydia gct Flushing MM
1829, 2, 12. Randal [Baily] gct New Garden MM (H)
1829, 10, 8. Randal dis JH

BAKER

----, --, --. Jesse C. b 1800,2,20; m Eliza ----- b 1805,1,29
    Ch: Elizabeth b 1823, 3, 30 d 1859, 5, 5
        Hannah   " 1824, 11, 2
        Isaac R.   " 1831, 7, 4
        Sarah Emily" 1834, 8, 14 d 1859,10, 1
        Lewis W.R. " 1836, 10, 19
        Benezet   " 1839, 4, 15
        Jesse   " 1840, 10, 10
        Wm. N.   " 1844, 11, 17
1846, 8, 13. Hannah m James M. HOLE
1855, 10, 18. Sarah Emily m Dawsey ARMSTRONG

1844, 3, 7. Jesse & ch, Isaac, Sarah Emily, Lewis, Benezet & Jesse, recrq
1844, 3, 7. Eliza, w Jesse, recrq
1844, 3, 7. Elizabeth & Hannah recrq
1858, 6, 19. Jesse & w, Eliza, & ch, Benezett, Jesse & William, gct Salem MM
1858, 6, 19. Elizabeth gct Salem MM
1859, 10, 15. Isaac dis mou
1863, 6, 20. Jesse & w, Eliza, & s, William, rocf Salem MM, dtd 1863,5,20

1864, 11, 19. Jesse dis disunity
1866, 5, 19. Eliza gct Upper Springfield MM

BALDWIN

1806, 10, 11. Mary (form Newport) dis mou

BARBER

1805, 8, 10. Rebecca rocf Piles Grove MM, N. J., dtd 1805,3,21, endorsed by Redstone MM, 1805,8,2
1805, 9, 14. Isaac & w, Mary, & ch, Abraham, Isaac, Jacob, Mary Ann & Jane, rocf Piles Grove MM, N. J., dtd 1805,3,21, endorsed by Redstone MM, dtd 1805,8,2

BARKER

1864, 8, 17. Rebecca (form Hoops) attached to this mtg when Beaver Falls MM, Pa., was laid down (H)

BARTLEY

1843, 4, 6. Francis [Bartly] recrq
1845, 3, 6. Francis dis joining Methodist Society
1847, 4, 8. Francis rst by rq

BASSETT

1838, 11, 8. Charles rocf Sandwich MM, New Hampshire
1844, 5, 9. Charles D. [Basset] gct Salem MM, to m Ann W. Hunt
1844, 10, 10. Charles D. gct Salem MM
1848, 12, 7. Charles D. & w, Ann W., & s, Nathan H., rocf Salem MM, dtd 1848,11,22
1852, 7, 8. Charles D. & w, Ann W., & ch, Nathan H. & James Alvin, gct Salem MM

BATTEY

----, --, --. Thomas C. b 1828,2,19 d 1897,8, 28; m 2nd Lucinda -----
    Ch: Mary B.   b 1866, 12, 15
        Lavina H. " 1871, 10, 5
        Malinda   " 1875, 9, 14
Thomas C. m 3rd 1891,4,2 at Middleton, O., Deborah CADWALLADER, dt Mifflin & Sarah, Columbiana Co., O.
1893, 8, 24. Lavina H. m J. Howard EDGERTON
1898, 4, 19. Malinda E. m Elbert L. COPE

1891, 6, 20. Thomas C. & dt, Melinda E., rocf Springville MM, Ia., dtd 1891,5,16
1891, 6, 20. Lavina H. rocf Springville MM, Iowa, dtd 1891,5,16
1893, 12, 16. Mary R. [Batty] rocf Springville MM, Ia., dtd 1893,11,18
1898, 12, 17. Mary R. [Batty] gct Paulina MM, Ia.
1918, 6, 15. Deborah C. gct Salem MM

BATTIN

1805, 8, 10. Catharine & ch, John, Catharine & Jonathan, rocf Wrightsborough MM, Ga., dtd 1805,3,23

BATTIN, continued
1806, 12, 13. Sarah rocf Fairfax MM, dtd
     1806,10,26
1808, 6, 11. Abigail dis disunity
1819, 2, 22. Phebe, w Eli, & ch, Jane, rocf
     Short Creek MM, dtd 1818,8,18, endorsed
     by New Garden MM, 1818,11,26
1821, 5, 21. Phebe & dt, Jane W., gct Sandy
     Spring MM
1829, 1, 8. Abigail recrq (H)

BEAL
1806, 12, 18. Hannah m John DIXON
1807, 11, 19. Sarah m John W. ARMSTRONG
1809, 8, 17. Rachel m David HAWLY

1805, 1, 12. Hannah rocf Fairfax MM, Va., dtd
     1804,10,27
1805, 1, 12. Ann & dt, Pamelia Maria, rocf
     Fairfax MM, Va., dtd 1804,10,27
1806, 12, 13. Sarah rocf Fairfax MM, dtd
     1806,10,26
1817, 9, 15. Pamelia Maria, gr dt Hannah,
     gct Salem MM
1821, 12, 17. Mariah Mildred rocf Salem MM,
     dtd 1821,8,22
1823, 6, 23. Pemela Maria Stuck (form Beal)
     dis mou
1829, 3, 12. Hannah dis JH

BEANS
1811, 4, 13. Levi rocf Goose Creek MM, dtd
     1811,1,3
1816, 4, 15. Mary (form Burns) con mou
1818, 3, 16. Levi gct Plainfield MM
1828, 5, 8. Mary (form Garwood) dis mou
1830, 3, 11. Mary [Beens] dis JH

BEESON
1804, 7, 18. John, s Henry & Mary, Columbi-
     ana Co., O.; m at Salem, Sarah SCHOOLEY,
     dt Elisha & Rachel, Columbiana Co., O.
1804, 9, 13. Richard, s Henry & Mary, Colum-
     biana Co., O.; m at Middleton, Ann OLI-
     PHANT, dt Samuel & Elizabeth, Columbiana
     Co., O.
     Ch: Elizabeth b 1805, 8, 27
         Mary   " 1807, 2, 5
         Rebecca   " 1808, 5, 18
         Henry M.   " 1809, 6, 6
         Ann   " 1811, 3, 14
         Rachel   " 1814, 5, 13
         Samuel   " 1815, 11, 9
         Richard   " 1817, 9, 21
         Jacob   " 1819, 8, 1
         Ephraim   " 1822, 4, 17
         John Oli-
          phant   " 1826, 7, 3
         Mahlon   " 1830, 1, 9

1807, 5, 14. Pheby m John SCHOOLEY
1820, 8, 15. Jacob, s Richard, d bur Middle-
     ton
1833, 9, 19. Ann m Zimri ENGLE
1839, 10, 17. Rebecca m Joseph LYNCH
----, --, --. Richard H. b 1817,9,21; m Re-
     becca HEALD
     Ch: Smith   b 1840, 10, 5
         Ephraim
          Lycurgas   " 1843, 7, 2
         Ruth Anna   " 1844, 12, 23
         Phebe   " 1847, 5, 15
1843, 10, 2. Ephraim, s Richard, d bur Salem,
     Ia.
1856, 5, 9. Richard d bur Middleton
1877, 3, 9. Mary, dt Richard & Ann, d
1878, 4, 26. Ann, w Richard, d

1807, 1, 10. Mary & dt, Charrity, recrq
1807, 1, 10. Ann, Rebecca & Phebe, dt Mary,
     recrq
1807, 9, 12. Henry recrq
1808, 10, 8. Mary, gr dt of Mary, recrq
1810, 2, 10. John dis
1816, 6, 10. Henry & w, Mary, & gr dt, Mary,
     gct Short Creek MM
1816, 6, 10. Ann, Rebecca & Charity gct
     Short Creek MM
1818, 6, 15. Sarah [Beason] & ch, Henry,
     Rachel, Charity, Elisha, Jesse, Edward &
     John, gct Short Creek MM
1824, 1, 19. Elizabeth Thompson (form Beeson)
     dis mou
1831, 6, 9. Henry dis mcd
1831, 7, 7. Ruth (form Cope) dis mcd
1834, 6, 12. Rachel Smith (form Beeson) dis
     mou
1837, 7, 17. Samuel dis mou
1840, 5, 7. Rebecca H. rocf Carmel MM, dtd
     1840,4,18
1850, 10, 10. Richard H. & w, Rebecca H., &
     ch, Smith H., Ephraim Lycurgas, Ruth Anna
     & Phebe S., gct Salem MM, Ia.
1858, 4, 17. Mahlon dis mou
1869, 1, 16. John [Beason] dis mou
1897, 11, 13. John O. rst by rq
1900, 2, 17. John O. gct Salem MM, O.

BELL
1872, 5, 30. Martha d bur Elkrun

1809, 4, 8. Martha rocf Maurice River MM,
     N. J., dtd 1808,6,3

BENNETT
1807, 8, 8. John rocf Concord MM, Pa., dtd
     1807,4,8
1811, 1, 12. Phebe rocf Kennett MM, dtd 1810,
     10,2 (Uwchland MM in women's minutes)
1811, 9, 12. Phebe gct Uwchlan MM, Pa.

BISHOP
1821, 12, 27. David, s Nicholas & Hannah, Co-

BISHOP, continued
    lumbiana Co., O.; m at Fairfield, Mary
    HAWLEY, dt Caleb & Hannah, Columbiana
    Co., O.

1806, 4, 12. Hannah rocf Kennet MM, dtd 1805,
    9,3
1815, 12, 7. William, David, Thomas, Sarah &
    Martha, ch Hannah, recrq
1827, 10, 11. David & w, Mary, & ch, Ann,
    Eliza, Amos & Hannah, gct Marlborough MM
1827, 11, 8. William gct Upper Springfield
    MM, to m Lydia Mather
1828, 5, 8. Lydia rocf Upper Springfield
    MM, dtd 1828,4,26
1828, 11, 6. Thomas dis mou
1829, 3, 12. Hannah, Lydia, Sarah dis JH
1829, 3, 12. William dis JH
1830, 3, 11. Martha dis JH
1833, 10, 10. Susan (form Ladner) dis mou
1838, 4, 12. William & w, Lydia, & ch, Thom-
    as, Sarah & Lydia, gct Marlborough MM (H)

BLACKBURN
----, --, --. Wm., s Wm. & Amy, b 1803,11,8
    d 1876,3,29; m Ann HEWITT, dt Abel & Ra-
    chel, b 1804,10,16 d 1877,8,24
    Ch: Joseph   b 1825, 12, 30 d 1826, 5,11
        Abel Hew-
          itt   " 1827, 3, 24
        David   " 1828, 9, 11
        Lydia   " 1830, 2, 3 d 1892, 2, 5
        Rachel H. " 1831, 9, 23
        Martha   " 1833, 3, 23 " 1888, 8, 5
        Nathan   " 1834, 10, 24 " 1910,11, 8
        Amy   " 1836, 5, 21 " 1894,12,29
        Hannah   " 1837, 10, 18
        Wm. H.   " 1839, 11, 30 (or 1839,
        12 ,30) d 1888,9,8
        George   b 1841, 7, 18
        Jonathan " 1841, 7, 18
        Chas.   " 1844, 3, 17 d 1912,10,19
        Thomas   " 1846, 12, 29
        Daniel   " 1849, 4, 21 d 1927, 2,22
        bur Middleton
----, --, --. Abel H. b 1827,3,24; m Caroline
    HOAGLAND, dt James & Sarah, b 1834,12,31
    Ch: Wm. J.   b 1862, 3, 24
        Abby J.   " 1865, 1, 28
        Mary   " 1869, 1, 28
        Edward   " 1871, 9, 24 d 1883, 7,28
        bur Carmel
        Henry   " 1872, 12, 24
1868, 10, 22. Thomas, s Wm. & Ann, Washington
    Co., Pa., b 1846,12,29; m at Middleton,
    Sarah ALLMON, dt Jehu & Hannah, b 1846,
    7,25
    Dt: Elizabeth b 1869, 10, 25
1868, 10, 21. Wm. H., s Wm. & Ann, Washington
    Co., Pa., b 1839,12,30 d 1888,9,8; m
    at Carmel, Sarah H. GAMBLE, dt Harrison
    & Phebe, b 1848,3,15
    Ch: Phebe   b 1869, 11, 28 d 1870, 7,29

Ch: John   b 1870, 12, 11 d 1894, 6, 5
    Elisha B. " 1873, 2, 13
    Dora   " 1875, 7, 18
    Edith   " 1877, 1, 29
    Howard   " 1878, 8, 5
    Olive   " 1881, 7, 13 d 1881, 7,15
----, --, --. Nathan M. b 1834,10,24 d 1910,11,
    8; m Rebecca COPE, dt Elizabeth M., b
    1834,11,3 d 1917,7,13
    Ch: Annie E. b 1870, 1, 25
        Myra J.   " 1872, 6, 14
1870, 6, 22. Jonathan, s William & Anna, Co-
    lumbiana Co., O., b 1841,7,18; m at Car-
    mell, Emily HOLLOWAY, dt David & Rachel,
    b 1840,2,25
    Ch: Arthur   b 1871, 3, 20
        George R. " 1873, 7, 14
        Ida   " 1876, 6, 15
        Infant   " 1878, 11, 7 d 1878,11, 7
1873, 5, 22. Daniel, s Wm. & Anna, Columbi-
    ana Co., O., b 1849,4,21; m at Middleton,
    Matilda Ellen HARRISON, Columbiana Co.,
    O., b 1852,5,21 d 1911,9,10
    Ch: Henrietta F.
               b 1876, 7, 1
        Mary Alice " 1881, 10, 29
----, --, --. Chas. b 1844,3,17 d 1912,10,19;
    m Sarah C. HOLLINGSWORTH, dt Edwin & Bet-
    sy (Heald), b 1852,2,19 d 1920,10,26
    Ch: Eliza W.
        (Lida)   b 1876, 4, 20
        Anna P.   " 1878, 12, 13
        Hannah J. " 1880, 5, 9
        Mary Elma " 1886, 11, 9
        Rolland   " 1895, 12, 9
        Willard C. " 1898, 2, 23
1879, 10, 30. Martha m Barzillai FRENCH
1881, 2, 14. Inetta P., dt Warren Stookes-
    berry, b
1898, 3, 24. Ida m Thomas L. ASHTON
1905, 3, 23. Anna P. m Walter M. COOPER
1906, 3, 22. Jessie H. m Howard T. JONES
1909, 3, 25. Mary Elma m Samuel CARTER

1868, 6, 20. Jonathan rocf Providence MM, dtd
    1868,6,4
1869, 2, 20. Thomas rocf Providence MM, Pa.,
    dtd 1868,12,31
1870, 2, 19. William & w, Anne, & s, Daniel,
    rocf Sewickley MM, Pa., dtd 1870,2,1
1870, 4, 16. Lydia, Martha, Amy & Hannah rocf
    Sewickly MM, Pa., dtd 1870,3,29
1870, 9, 17. Charles rocf Sewickly MM, Pa.,
    dtd 1870,8,30
1870, 10, 15. Nathan M. & w, Rebecca M., & ch,
    Anna E., rocf Sewickly MM, Pa., dtd 1870,
    9,30
1874, 8, 15. Charles gct Plymouth MM, O., to
    m Sarah Hollingsworth
1875, 3, 20. Sarah C. rocf Plymouth MM, O.,
    dtd 1874,12,21
1878, 1, 19. Thomas & w, Sarah, & dt, Eliza-
    beth, gct Coal Creek MM, Ia.

BLACKBURN, continued

1882, 4, 15. Jonathan & w, Emily H., & ch,
Arthur, George R. & Ida E., gct Salem MM

1886, 2, 20. Abel H. & w, Caroline, & ch,
Mary & Henry, gct Mill Creek MM, Ind.

1886, 7, 17. William J. gct Chester MM, N.J.,
to m M. Elizabeth Cóleman

1887, 1, 15. William J. gct Mill Creek MM,
Ind.

1887, 1, 15. Abbie T. gct Mill Creek MM, Ind.

1890, 8, 16. Jonathan K. & w, Emily H., &
ch, Arthur, George R. & Ida, rocf Salem
MM, O., dtd 1890,7,23

1896, 12, 19. Sarah H. dis joining Separatists

1899, 1, 21. Elisha dis jas

1899, 7, 15. Edith dis joining Separatists

1905, 6, 17. George R. dis mcd

1911, 4, 15. Myra J. & Anna E. gct Salem MM,
O.

1912, 4, 20. Jonathan K. & w, Emily H., & s,
Arthur, gct Upper Springfield MM

1915, 5, 15. Alice B. Meiser (form Blackburn)
dis mcd & jas

1924, 8, 16. Rolland gct Upper Springfield MM,
to m Julietta Pemberton

1926, 12, 18. Rolland gct Upper Springfield MM

BLACKLEDGE

1808, 2, 13. Joseph [Blacklidge] gct Salem MM

1808, 7, 9. Rachel rocf Salem MM, dtd 1808,
5,17

1809, 5, 13. Joseph & w, Rachel, & s, Thomas
G., gct New Garden MM

BONSALL

1881, 5, 26. Isaac E., s Isaac & Hannah
(Evans), Mahoning Co., O., b 1852,7,2;
m at Middleton, Annie CADWALADER, dt
Isaac S. & Esther (Allmon), Columbiana
Co., O., b 1857,9,18

1882, 1, 21. Anna C. gct Salem MM

1826, 12, 18. Isaac E. & w, Annie C., rocf
Salem MM

BOULTON

----, --, --. James & Hannah
Ch: Levi   b 1796, 10, 30
    Abigail   " 1800, 1, 21
    Daniel   " 1803, 11, 30
    Rebecca   " 1808, 2, 13
    Sarah   " 1810, 3, 25
    Wm.   " 1812, 6, 5

1815, 11, 15. Levi, s James & Hannah, Columbiana Co., O.; m at Elkrun, Ann HEALD,
dt Nathan & Rachel, Columbiana Co., O.
Ch: Rachel   b 1816, 6, 27
    Reuben   " 1818, 3, 3
    Phebe   " 1820, 1, 30

1816, 10, 27. Rachel, dt Levi & Ann, d bur
Middleton

1819, 12, 2. Abigail m Thomas ALLMON

1820, 12, 17. Anne, dt Levi & Ann, d bur

Middleton

1821, 2, 5. Sarah, dt James & Hannah, d bur
Middleton

1837, 8, 2. James d bur Middleton

1838, 4, 20. Reuben, s Levi, d

1840, 9, 24. Phebe m Joseph PRICHETT

1865, 7, 16. Rebecca, dt James, d bur Middleton

1865, 7, 29. Hannah, w James, d ae 86y bur
Middleton

1872, 1, 18. Orpah, w Levi, d bur Middleton

1882, 4, 18. Levi d bur Middleton

1806, 11, 8. James & w, Hannah, & ch, Levi,
Abigail & Dinah, rocf Upper Evesham MM,
N. J., dtd 1806,6,9

1823, 2, 17. Levi gct Short Creek MM, to m
Orpah Mendenhall

1824, 9, 20. Orpah rocf Short Creek MM, dtd
1824,8,24

1827, 11, 8. Daniel gct Upper Springfield MM,
to m Esther Morris

1828, 8, 7. Daniel gct Salem MM

1830, 4, 8. William, minor, gct Salem MM

1847, 1, 7. William & w, Mary, & ch, Elisabeth, James & Charles, rocf Salem MM, dtd
1846,11,25

1854, 1, 12. William & w, Mary, & ch, James
& Charles, gct Gilead MM

1854, 1, 12. Elizabeth gct Gilead MM

BOYCE

1804, 9, 8. Sarah, w Robert, & ch, Richard,
Susannah, Timothy, Elisabeth, Robert,
Deborah, Jane, Sarah, John, Joshua & Isaac
rocf Lisburn MM, Ire., dtd 1801,3,12 (s,
Samuel & Joseph b since cert was granted)

1807, 11, 14. Richard [Boys] dis disunity

1807, 11, 14. Timothy [Boys] dis disunity

1812, 11, 12. Susannah Phelps (form Boyce)
dis mou

1815, 9, 7. Elizabeth Anderson (form Boyce)
dis mou

1838, 11, 8. Mary [Boice] (form Cope) dis mou

BOYD

1813, 4, 8. Sarah (form Hoops) con mou

1813, 11, 11. Sarah gct Redstone MM

1814, 4, 7. Sarah rocf Centre MM, Pa., dtd
1813,7,7

BRADFIELD

1842, 5, 12. Amy (form Harrison) dis mcd

BRADWAY

1837, 10, 12. Mark D. rocf Green St. MM,
Phila., dtd 1837,8,17 (H)

1840, 6, 11. Emeline (form McConnel) dis mou

BRIGGS

1834, 5, 8. Isaac rocf Bridgewater MM, N.Y.,
dtd 1833,8,2

1839, 6, 6. Mary (form Ladnor) dis mou

BRIGGS, continued
1842, 10, 6. Isaac dis disunity
1908, 12, 19. Hiel S. Hall gct Salem MM, O.,
   to m Abigal Briggs

BROOKS
1844, 10, 10. Adaline, w Isaac, recrq (H)

BROOMALL
1834, 9, 11. Sarah T. rocf New Garden MM, dtd
   1834,7,24
1835, 5, 7. Sarah T. rocf New Garden MM, dtd
   1835,3,26 (H)
1837, 2, 9. Sarah Townsend (form Bramwell)
   con mcd (H)
1838, 4, 23. Sarah B. Townsend (form Broomhall
   hall) dis mou

BROWN
1806, 12, 18. Nathan, s Eleazar & Sarah,
   Fayette Co., Pa.; m at Middleton, Amy
   STRATON, dt Daniel & Mary, Columbiana
   Co., O.
1823, 2, 1. Jeremiah, s Jeremiah & Phebe,
   Columbiana Co., O.; m at Middleton, Debo-
   rah SHARP, dt Enoch & Sarah, Columbiana
   Co., O.
   Ch: Sarah Ann b 1823, 10, 21
      Abner   " 1825, 9, 11
1824, 1, 1. Prophet, s Jeremiah & Phebe,
   Columbiana Co., O.; m at Middleton, Rachel
   SAMMS, dt John & Sarah, Columbiana Co.,O.
   Ch: John S.   b 1825, 1, 14
      Jeremiah   " 1826, 7, 19

1808, 6, 11. Amy gct Salem MM
1820, 5, 22. Phebe rocf Carmel MM, dtd 1820,
   5,20
1820, 6, 19. Prophet rocf Carmel MM, dtd
   1820,6,17
1821, 6, 18. Asa & Jeremiah, Jr. recrq
1821, 6, 18. Phebe & Hannah recrq
1827, 5, 10. Jeremiah, Jr. & w, Deborah, &
   ch, Sarah Ann & Abner, gct New Garden MM
1828, 2, 7. Prophet & w, Rachel, & ch,
   John S. & Jeremiah, gct New Garden MM
1828, 5, 8. Phebe & dt, Phebe & Hannah, gct
   New Garden MM
1828, 5, 8. Asa gct New Garden MM
1830, 9, 9. Prophet & w, Sarah, & ch, John
   S., Jeremiah & Sarah, rocf New Garden MM,
   dtd 1830,5,20 (H)
1836, 12, 8. Prophet & w, Rachel, & ch, John
   S., Jeremiah, Sarah, William, Phebe Ann &
   Lydia, gct New Garden MM (H)
1839, 1, 10. Jesse Nichols gct Goose Creek
   MM, Va., to m Mary E. Brown (H)

BUNDY
1914, 4, 18. John J. Cadwalader gct Stillwater MM, to m Rebecca H. Bundy

BURNS
1810, 5, 17. Rachel [Byrnes] m Jesse M.
   McCONNAL

1816, 4, 15. Mary Beans (form Burns) con mou
1828, 9, 11. Mary (form Underwood) dis mou

BURSON
1805, 8, 10. Abigail & ch, Susannah Mary Sarah Catharine & Anne, rocf Goose Creek MM,
   Va., dtd 1805,6,24
1827, 4, 12. Harriet (form Reeves) dis mou

BUTLER
1845, 5, 15. Moses V., s Lawrence W. & Sarah,
   Columbiana Co., O.; m at Middleton, Emily
   SCHOOLY, dt Israel & Sarah, Columbiana
   Co., O.

1845, 8, 7. Emily S. gct Upper Springfield
   MM

BYE
1814, 4, 7. Sarah rocf Centre MM, Pa., dtd
   1813,7,17
1816, 4, 15. Sarah gct New Garden MM

CADWALADER
1806, 12, 25. Eliza m Talbot TOWNSEND
----, --, --. Eli & Catharine
   Ch: John   b 1826, 1, 11
      James D.   " 1828, 4, 13
      Wm.   " 1830, 9, 11
1829, 10, 9. Mifflin, s Jonah & Ann, Mercer
   Co., Pa., b 1803,7,17 d 1886,1,4; m at
   Middleton, Ellen T. SHARPLESS, dt Benja-
   min & Amy, Mercer Co., Pa., b 1806,10,16
   d 1836,3,10 bur Mahoning, Mercer Co.,
   Pa. (H)
   Ch: Isaac S.   b 1831, 2, 2 d 1872, 9, 8
      Jonah   " 1833, 2, 11 " 1855,11, 7
      Ellen   " 1835, 9, 14
   Mifflin, 2nd 1837,4,27, Sarah WICKERSHAM,
   dt Thos. & Ann, b 1815,8,24 d 1846,7,18
   bur Middleton
   Ch: Levi   b 1838, 12, 9
      Ann   " 1840, 8, 17
      Deborah   " 1842, 12, 5
   Mifflin m 3rd Sarah J. JAMES, dt John &
   Martha, b 1812,7,28 d 1903,10,21
   Ch: Mary   b 1849, 9, 20
      James   " 1851, 6, 13 d 1853, 9, 3
      John J.   " 1853, 7, 6
1829, 9, 11. Lydia m William B. IRISH (H)
1841, 3, 18. Eli, s Septimus & Sarah, Mercer
   Co., Pa.; m at Falling Springs, Elizabeth
   HAWLEY, dt David & Rachel, Mercer Co.,Pa.
1853, 10, 13. Isaac, s Mifflin & Ellen, Colum-
   biana Co., O., b 1831,2,2 d 1872,9,8;; m
   at Middleton, Esther ALLMON, dt John &
   Hannah, Columbiana Co., O., b 1834,11,27
   d 1878,5,17
   Ch: Thomas

CADWALADER, Isaac & Esther, continued
    Ch: Mifflin b 1856, 3, 18
        Anna Hannah
                b 1857, 9, 19
        Elma D.   " 1860, 5, 25
        Allan Jonah
                b 1868, 8, 14
        Isaac Dal-
           las   " 1872, 4, 10
1862, 4, --. Rebecca b
1877, 2, 22. John J., s Mifflin & Sarah J.,
    Columbiana Co., O.; m at Middleton, Mary
    Ann COPE, dt Amos & Rachel, Columbiana
    Co., O.
----, --, --. James J., s Mifflin & Sarah
    (James), b 1853,7,6; m˜Rebecca H. BUNDY,
    dt William & Asenath (Doudna), b 1863,1,3
    James J. m 2nd Mary Ann COPE, dt Amos &
    Rachel, b 1851,10,31
    Ch: Celesta M. b 1879, 7, 2
        Edgar M.   " 1889, 1, 30
1891, 4, 2. Deborah [Cadwallader] m Thomas
    C. BATTEY
----, --, --. Elizabeth, wd Rees, bur Middle-
    ton

1805, 7, 13. Sarah & ch, Samuel, Septamus,
    Joseph, Eli & Lydia, rocf Redstone MM,
    dtd 1805,5,3
1805, 7, 13. Mary, Elisa & Sarah, ch Sarah,
    rocf Redstone MM, dtd 1805,5,3
1814, 11, 10. Joseph [Cadwallader] dis
1816, 7, 15. Septamus dis mou
1819, 7, 19. Eli con mcd
1823, 12, 22. Mary Robbins (form Cadwallader)
    con mou
1827, 7, 12. Catharine recrq
1829, 9, 10. Mifflin [Cadwallader] rocf Red-
    stone MM, dtd 1829,7,29 (H)
1829, 9, 10. Lydia dis jH
1829, 9, 24. Eli dis jH
1830, 7, 8. Eleanor (form Sharpless) dis
    mcd & joining Separatists
1830, 10, 7. Elen dis
1831, 5, 12. Catharine dis jH
1834, 12, 11. Mifflin rst by rq
1834, 12, 11. Ellin T. rst by rq
1837, 7, 17. Mifflin & w, Sarah, gct Salem MM
1842, 3, 10. Mifflin & w, Sarah, & ch, Isaac
    S. & Jonah, rocf Salem MM, dtd 1842,2,23
1848, 8, 17. Eli & w, Elizabeth, & dt, Exi-
    mina, gct Clear Creek MM, Ill. (H)
1848, 10, 12. Mifflin gct Salem MM, to m Sa-
    rah James
1849, 1, 11. Sarah rocf Salem MM, dtd 1848,12,
    20
1862, 11, 15. Ellen C. Hoops (form Cadwalader)
    con mcd
1876, 11, 18. Deborah gct Salem MM, O.
1879, 7, 19. Thomas M. dis jas
1883, 8, 18. Allen J. & Dallas P., minors
    under care of Ellen C. Ogden, gct ND MM,
    Phila.. Pa.

1885, 11, 21. Deborah rocf Salem MM, dtd
    1885,10,21
1889, 3, 16. Elma D. Cummings (form Cadwala-
    der) dis mcd
1903, 10, 17. John J. dis disunity
1903, 10, 17. Mary Ann dis disunity
1904, 4, 16. Celesta M. Williamson (form
    Cadwalader) dis mcd
1913, 12, 20. John J. rst by rq
1914, 4, 18. John J. gct Stillwater MM, to
    m Rebecca H. Bundy
1915, 6, 19. Rebecca H. rocf Stillwater MM,
    dtd 1915,3,24
1918, 6, 15. John J. & w, Rebecca H., gct
    Salem MM
1921, 10, 15. Edgar M. dis mcd

CALDWELL
1836, 5, 12. Sarah (form McConnell) con mou
    (H)
1837, 8, 21. Sarah (form McConnell) dis mcd
    & jH
1838, 8, 9. Sarah relrq (H)
1847, 1, 14. Elizabeth (form Garwood) con
    mcd (H)

CAMPBELL
1808, 4, 9. Rebeckah gct Salem MM

CAMERON
1836, 9, 1. Josiah, s Alexander & Jane,
    Columbiana Co., O.; m at Middleton, Hannah
    MENDENHALL, dt Israel & Sarah, Beaver Co.,
    Pa.

1836, 11, 21. Hannah gct New Garden MM

CAREY
1839, 6, 6. Hannah (form Allman) con mou
1839, 10, 10. Hannah gct Goshen MM, O.
1894, 3, 17. Edna E. (form Cope) con mcd
1922, 1, 21. Edna E. dis jas

CARROLL
1817, 12, 18. Edward, s Edward & Elizabeth,
    Columbiana Co., O.; m at Carmel, Rachel
    HAMBLETON, dt William & Mary, Columbiana
    Co., O.

1809, 1, 14. Edward [Carrol] & w, Elizabeth,
    & ch gct New Garden MM
1809, 1, 14. Joseph & Edward [Carrol], Jr.
    gct New Garden MM
1809, 1, 14. Sally & Margery, dt Edward, gc

CARTER
1909, 3, 25. Samuel C., s Philip & Hannah R.,
    (Reynolds), Guernsey Co., O., b 1874,10,
    27 d 1931,8,19 bur Middleton; m at Middle-
    ton, Mary Elma BLACKBURN, dt Chas. & Sa-
    rah (Hollingsworth) Columbiana Co., O.,
    b 1886,11,9
    Ch: Chas. S.   b 1916, 2. 15

CARTER, Samuel C. & Mary Elma, continued
    Ch: Alfred R. b 1919, 4, 6

1909, 10, 16. Samuel rocf Stillwater MM, O.,
    dtd 1909,8,25
1922, 7, 15. Elma B. dis
1925, 9, 19. Maria S. con mcd
1926, 1, 16. Levi recrq

CEMERY
1913, 11, 15. Miriam W. (form Wickersham) dis
    mou

CHAIN
1830, 4, 8. Anna (form Hatcher) dis mou

CHAMBERLAIN
1828, 4, 10. Eliza (form Harrison) dis mou
1838, 2, 8. Mary (late Hoops) con mou (H)
1864, 8, 17. Mary attached to this mtg when
    Beaver Falls MM, Pa. was laid down (H)

CHAPMAN
----, --, --. John & Ann
    Ch: Orpha   b 1816, 11, 11 d 1823,12, 8
        bur Harrisville
        Lydia   b 1818, 11, 1
        Elwood   " 1822, 5, 10
        Anna   " 1825, 10, 8 d 1827, 8, 3
        bur Beaver Falls
        Sally Ann b 1827, 9, 21
----, --, --. Elwood b 1822,5,10; m Sarah Ann
----- b 1819,10,8
    Ch: Jane
        Phemer   b 1846, 7, 20
        Mary W.   " 1850, 6, 10

1827, 6, 7. John & w, Ann, & ch, Lydia, El-
    wood & Anna, rocf Short Creek MM, dtd 1827,
    3,20
1828, 12, 11. John dis joining Separatists
1828, 12, 11. Ann dis jH
1845, 9, 11. Ellwood gct Short Creek MM, to
    m Sarah Ann Wilson
1846, 3, 12. Sarah Ann rocf Short Creek MM,
    dtd 1846,2,26
1851, 10, 9. Elwood & w, Sarah Ann, & ch,
    Jane P. & Mary W., gct Gilead MM
1853, 12, 8. Seely Ann dis jH

CHINEWITH
1817, 11, 10. Rebecca (form Reynolds) dis mou

COALE
1841, 6, 20. Benjamin T., s Joseph B. & Sarah
    P., b

1829, 12, 10. David Townsend gct Sadsbury MM,
    to m Mary B. [Cowl] (H)
1830, 6, 10. Mary B. Townsend & ch, Joseph
    B., Charles & Susanna Coale, rocf Sadsbury
    MM, Pa.,.dtd 1830,3,2
1831, 6, 9. Joseph B., Charles & Susannah

[Coal], ch Mary Townsend, rocf Sadsbury
    MM, dtd 1830,8,2
1835, 10, 8. Sarah W. [Coles] rocf Radnor
    MM, dtd 1835,4,9 (H)
1836, 2, 11. Sarah [Cole] gct Honey Creek
    MM, Ind. (H)
1841, 1, 7. Joseph [Coal] con mcd (H)
1841, 3, 11. Joseph B. dis mou
1841, 6, 10. Sarah B. [Cole] recrq (H)
1864, 8, 17. Benjamin S., W. L. Garrison &
    Joseph B. attached to this mtg when Bea-
    ver Falls MM, Pa. was laid down (H)
1864, 8, 17. Charles & w, Mary Anna, attach-
    ed to this mtg when Beaver Falls MM, Pa.
    was laid down (H)
1864, 8, 17. Sarah, wd Joseph, attached to
    this mtg when Beaver Falls MM, Pa. was
    laid down (H)

COFFIN
1845, 8, 11. Albert M., s Charles & Mary,
    Jefferson Co., O.; m at Middleton, Elmina
    TOWNSEND, dt David & Mary, Beaver Co.,Pa.

1846, 3, 12. Elmina T. gct Smithfield MM

COLEMAN
1886, 7, 17. William J. Blackburn gct Chester
    MM, N. J., to m M. Elizabeth Coleman

CONRAD
1913, 2, 20. Emerson, s Ellwood B. & Phebe
    W., Columbiana Co., O.; m at Middleton,
    Eva M. NEILL, dt Dillwin B. & Ella C.,
    Columbiana Co., O.

1914, 3, 21. Eva N. gct Upper Springfield MM

COOK
1841, 8, 18. Elenor m Enos H. NEAL

1838, 10, 11. Isaac H. rocf Salem MM, dtd
    1838,8,22
1840, 9, 10. Eleanor rocf Smithfield MM, dtd
    1840,2,17
1841, 2, 11. Isaac dis

COOPER
----, --, --. Cyrus, s Samuel & Sarah (Pen-
    nock), b 1860,11,24; m Bertha A. ATWATER,
    dt Levi H. & Mary M. (Crane), b 1862,5,8
    Ch: Samuel   b 1904, 12, 30
1905, 3, 23. Walter M., s Samuel & Sarah
    (Pennock), Chester Co., Pa., b 1870,12,20;
    m Anna B. BLACKBURN, dt Chas. & Sarah C.
    (Hollingsworth), Columbiana Co., O., b
    1878,12,13
    Ch: Sarah
        Elizabeth b 1907, 8, 14
        James R. " 1909, 7, 27
        Thos.
        Charles   " 1911, 1, 15
        Joseph

COOPER, Walter M. & Anna B., continued
    Ch: Barclay b 1915, 11, 9 d 1916, 2, 8
        Wilmer A. " 1920, 4, 20

1811, 12, 12. Cert rec for Anne from Sadsbury
    MM, dtd 1811,9,3, endorsed to New Garden
    MM
1907, 6, 15. Walter M. rocf New Garden MM,
    Pa., dtd 1907,5,8
1910, 1, 15. Cyrus & w, Bertha A., & ch,
    Samuel, rocf Salem MM, O., dtd 1909,12,22

COPE
----, --, --. John, s John & Mary, b 1768,7,
    15; m Ruth DIXON, dt Henry & Elizabeth, b
    1776,3,17
    Ch: Elizabeth b 1794, 10, 17
        Caleb   " 1796, 3, 23
        Simon   " 1798, 11, 18
        Mary   " 1801, 12, 17
        Edith   " 1809, 5, 22
----, --, --. Jesse & Margaret
    Ch: Elizabeth b 1802, 8, 11
        Mary   " 1805, 10, 3
        Hannah   " 1809, 1, 3
        Ellis   " 1812, 1, 19
        Samuel   " 1815, 5, 5
        Ann   " 1818, 5, 10
        Hiram   " 1821, 12, 11
1806, 12, 16. Israel, s John & Mary, Columbi-
    ana Co., O.; m at Middleton, Elizabeth
    DIXSON, dt Henry & Elizabeth, Columbiana
    Co., O.
    Ch: Mary   b 1807, 11, 1
        Rebecca   " 1809, 7, 26
        Lydia   " 1811, 5, 4
        Ruth   " 1813, 5, 6
        Eliza   " 1815, 4, 13
        Ann   " 1817, 12, 23
        Joseph   " 1820, 6, 3
        Elizabeth
         Dixon   " 1822, 11, 14
        Israel   " 1825, 11, 16
        Susannah H." 1829, 7, 14
----, --, --. Joseph & Elizabeth
    Ch: John   b 1806, 2, 8
        Ellis   " 1808, 1, 24
        Samuel   " 1810, 3, 18
        John Dixon " 1812, 7, 21
        Joseph   " 1815, 5, 9
        Nathan   " 1817, 11, 19
        Mary N.   " 1819, 7, 25
        Ruth   " 1824, 8, 28
        Allen   " 1827, 8, 4
----, --, --. Sarah Ann b 1808,11,22 d 1888,6,
    6
1810, 12, 28. Ellis, s Joseph & Elizabeth, d
    bur Middleton
1811, 1, 3. John D., s Joseph & Elizabeth,
    d bur Middleton
1811, 8, 1. Ruth, w John, d bur Middleton
1814, 12, 14. John, s John & Mary, Columbia
    Co., O.; m at Elkrun, Ann STRATTON, dt

Daniel & Susannah Antrim, Stafford Co.,
    Va.
1815, 10, 1. Ruth, dt John & Ann, d
1817, 11, 13. Caleb, s John & Ruth, Columbi-
    ana Co., O.; m at Fairfield, Rebecca
    STRATTON, dt Benjamin & Amy, Columbiana
    Co., O.
1818, 4, 2. Joseph, s John & Ann, b
----, --, --. Elizabeth Dixon b 1822,11,14
    d 1890,1,16
1822, 10, 3. Elizabeth m Mahlon ERWIN
1827, 2, 14. Mary m Joseph TAYLOR
1827, 12, 12. Isaac, s Isaac & Sarah, Stark
    Co., O.; m at Fairfield, Rachel EMBREE,
    dt Moses & Abigail, Columbiana Co., O.
1833, 7, 5. Joseph, Jr. d bur Middleton
----, --, --. Ellis & Amy
    Ch: Reason   b 1834, 4, 25
        Wm.   " 1836, 8, 23
        John   " 1839, 11, 17
----, --, --. Amos b 1811,1,23 d 1873,11,1;
    m Rachel H. ----- b 1813,8,3 d 1898,1,16
----, --, --. Joseph b 1820,6,3 d 1879,6,11;
    m Phebe HOLE, dt Nathan & Sarah, b 1819,
    8,23 d 1894,7,2
    Ch: Lycurgas b 1841, 11, 26
        Lucina   " 1843, 10, 1 d 1905, 7,15
        James   " 1845, 8, 11
        Oliver   " 1847, 6, 7
        Mary   " 1849, 3, 10
        Eliphus   " 1851, 6, 9
        Edith   " 1853, 6, 9 d 1903, 4, 3
        Emor   " 1855, 3, 25
        Sarah Emily" 1857, 10, 3 " 1858, 8,28
----, --, --. Nathan b 1817,11,19 d 1877,1,24;
    m Jane HOLE, dt Nathan & Sarah, b 1825,3,
    31
    Ch: James Byron
                   b 1842, 10, 27
        Melinda   " 1844, 12, 17
        Louiza   " 1847, 8, 3
        Joseph
         Warren   " 1849, 4, 20
        John Dixon " 1851, 3, 7
        Allen Ben
         nett   " 1852, 4, 5
        Franklin
         Samuel   " 1855, 1, 20
        Chas. L.   " 1856, 12, 3 d 1885,12,11
        Sarah Emma " 1858, 10, 13
        Mary
         Elizabeth " 1862, 3, 9
1842, 3, 17. Mary N. m Ethan Allen HOLE
1845, 9, 18. Elizabeth d bur Middleton
1845, 6, 30. Joseph d bur Middleton
1848, 1, 21. Lucinda b
1851, 11, 13. Susannah m Meader ALLMON
----, --, --. Israel b 1825,11,16 d 1899,2,17;
    m Sarah ----- b 1826,9,3
    Ch: Harvey
         Cleaver   b 1853, 11, 6 d 1855,12, 7
        Harvey D. " 1856, 10, 12
        Maria Elma " 1858, 4, 20

COPE, Israel & Sarah, continued
Ch: Ella La-
vina   b 1862, 3, 13 d 1890, 2,15
----, --, --. Wm. b 1835,7,13 d 1871,6,23; m
Rachel COPE, dt Joseph & Eliza, b 1839,3,
23 d 1874,10,18
Ch: Francis R. b 1865, 10, 28
Ellen P.   " 1865, 10, 28 d 1866, 8, 8
Edna E.   " 1868, 10, 31
----, --, --. James A. b 1842,10,14; m Achsah
ELLYSON, dt Robert & Mary, b 1847,8,3
Ch: Robert J. b 1867, 11, 16
Ellen B.   " 1870, 9, 22
Elizabeth M.
b 1874, 3, 1
1867, 9, 25. Emeline m Samuel ARMSTRONG

1873, 2, 20. Albert M., s Benjamin & Eliza-
beth (McGrew), Columbiana Co., O., b
1847,1,19 d 1923,1,6, bur Middleton; m at
Middleton, Phebe Y. ASHTON
Ch: Wm. Logan b 1889, 7, 29
1877, 2, 22. Mary Ann m John J. CADWALADER
1898, 4, 19. Elbert L., s Albert M. & Phebe
Y. (Ashton), Westmoreland Co., Pa., b
1874,4,19; m at Middleton, Malinda E.
BATTEY, dt Thomas C. & Lucinda (Hampton)
(Gregg), b 1875,9,14
Ch: Howard
Herman   b 1899, 5, 29
Chester
Albert   " 1901, 9, 9
Arthur
Morris   " 1906, 9, 27
Wm. David " 1908, 5, 19 d 1913, 3,22
Ernest
Luther   " 1912, 9, 2
Helen
Phebe   " 1914, 3, 26
----, --, --. Wm. L. m Rachel Tacy MOTT, dt
John W. & Sina (Hall), b 1889,12,26 d
1926,2,14
Ch: Alfred
Louis   b 1917, 9, 6
Wm. Loren " 1919, 5, 31
Elmer Dean " 1926, 2, 8
Wm. L. m 2nd Celia PIKE, dt Alpheus &
Jane (Haworth), b 1895,1,10
1933, 9, 20. Helen P. m Frances E. PRICE

1804, 5, 12. Ruth & ch, Caleb, Susan & Mary,
rocf Redstone MM, dtd 1804,3,2
1805, 11, 9. Joseph & w, Elizabeth, rocf Redstone MM, dtd 1805,8,30
1817, 7, 14. Simon, minor, gct Salem MM
1819, 5, 17. Caleb & w, Rebecca, & dt, Ruth,
gct West Grove MM, Ind.
1819, 12, 20. John Cope & w, Ann, & ch, John,
Sarah, Rebecca & Owen Stratton, & Mary,
Edith, Ruth & Joseph Cope, gct Darby Creek
MM
1820, 2, 21. Simon rocf Salem MM, dtd 1819,

12,22
1821, 2, 19. Henry dis disunity
1822, 8, 19. Elizabeth, w Israel, & ch, Mary,
Rebecca, Lydia, Ruth, Eliza, Ann & Joseph,
gct Carmel MM
1824, 2, 23. Simon dis mou
1828, 5, 8. Rachel gct Marlborough MM
1829, 12, 10. Elisabeth, w Israel, & ch, Ruth,
Eliza, Ann, Joseph, Elizabeth & Israel,
rocf Carmel MM, dtd 1829,8,15
1830, 1, 7. Hannah dis jH
1830, 7, 8. Ellis dis joining Separatists
1830, 9, 9. Margaret dis jH
1831, 7, 7. Ruth Beeson (form Cope) dis mcd
1831, 7, 7. Jesse dis jH
1831, 7, 7. Samuel dis mou
1831, 9, 8. Eliza Edmundson (form Cope) dis
mou
1831, 9, 8. Eli dis disunity
1831, 9, 8. John, s Caleb, dis disunity
1831, 9, 8. Samuel, s Caleb, dis disunity
1832, 1, 12. Caleb, Jr. dis disunity
1833, 8, 8. John F. rocf Providence MM, Pa.,
dtd 1833,7,4
1833, 12, 12. Ellis con mcd (H)
1833, 12, 12. Amy con mcd (H)
1834, 1, 9. John F. con mou
1834, 2, 6. Elizabeth, w Israel, & ch, Ann,
Joseph, Elizabeth, Israel, Susannah & Samuel, gct Carmel MM
1834, 6, 12. Israel dis disunity
1834, 6, 12. John D. dis mou
1834, 9, 11. John F. gct Carmel MM
1837, 9, 18. Samuel D. dis disunity
1838, 11, 8. Mary Boice (form Cope) dis mou
1841, 8, 12. Nathan gct Carmel MM, to m
1842, 2, 10. Jane H. rocf Carmel MM, dtd
1841,12,18
1844, 10, 10. Elisabeth Cope, w Israel, & ch,
Elisabeth, Israel & Susannah, & gr dt,
Mary Marsh, rocf Carmel MM, dtd 1844,7,20
1846, 11, 12. Elizabeth Cope, w Israel, & ch,
Elizabeth & Susannah, & gr dt, Mary Marsh,
gct Carmel MM
1846, 12, 10. Israel, Jr. gct Carmel MM
1848, 11, 9. Allen dis disunity
1848, 12, 7. Ruth dis disunity
1849, 10, 11. Rachel (form Prichett) dis mou
1850, 8, 8. Elizabeth & dt, Elizabeth D.,
rocf Carmel MM, dtd 1850,7,20
1850, 8, 8. Susannah Cope & Mary H. Marsh
rocf Carmel MM, dtd 1850,7,20
1862, 9, 20. Lycurgas con mcd
1863, 9, 19. James Byron dis mou
1864, 8, 20. Israel rst by rq
1865, 3, 18. Malinda A. dis jas
1866, 3, 17. Emeline rocf Upper Springfield
MM, dtd 1866,2,23
1868, 5, 16. Louisa L. Grey (form Cope) dis
mcd
1869, 12, 18. James A. & w, Achsah, rocf
Providence MM, Pa., dtd 1869,12,2
1870, 4, 16. Robert, s James A., rocf Sewick-

COPE, continued
ly MM, Pa., dtd 1870,3,29
1871, 1, 21. Amos & w, Rachel, & ch, Mary
Ann & Calvin, rocf Sewickly MM, Pa., dtd
1870,11,29
1871, 2, 18. William & w, Rachel W., & ch,
Francis R. & Edna E., rocf Sewickly MM,
Pa., dtd 1871,1,31
1871, 2, 18. Thomas C. rocf Sewickly MM, Pa.,
dtd 1871,1,31
1871, 2, 18. Margaret rocf Sewickley MM, Pa.,
dtd 1871,1,31
1871, 8, 19. James con mou
1872, 1, 20. John D. dis mcd
1873, 6, 21. Lycurgas dis joining Separatists
1873, 7, 19. Phebe gct New Garden MM
1874, 3, 21. Joseph W. dis mou
1874, 4, 18. Oliver con mou
1875, 3, 20. James A. & w, Achsah, & ch, Robert J., Ellen B. & Elizabeth M., gct Upper
Springfield MM
1876, 1, 15. Oliver gct New Garden MM, O.
1876, 2, 19. Samuel Franklin dis mou
1876, 5, 20. Allen B. dis mou
1876, 9, 16. Eliphus con mou
1876, 9, 16. Thomas C. gct Flushing MM, to
m Maria Wilson
1877, 4, 21. Mary C. Rogers (form Cope) dis
mcd (first rpd 1874,8,15)
1878, 1, 19. Thomas C. gct Flushing MM, O.
1878, 11, 16. Calvin C. dis mcd
1880, 4, 17. Maria Elma Stooksberry (form
Cope) con mcd
1880, 5, 15. Charles P. Hall gct Salem MM, to
m Melissa Cope
1881, 1, 15. Mary Elizabeth (form Philips) dis
disunity
1881, 8, 20. Sarah Emma dis jas
1883, 1, 20. Emmor con mcd
1883, 3, 17. Jane dis disunity
1884, 11, 15. Harvey D. dis mcd
1886, 9, 18. Ella L. May (form Cope) con mou
1887, 6, 18. Lucinda rocf Salem MM, dtd
1887,5,25
1887, 6, 18. Sarah Ann rocf Salem MM, dtd
1887,5,25
1890, 2, 15. Joseph W. rocf Upper Springfield
MM, dtd 1889,12,27
1894, 3, 17. Edna E. Carey (form Cope) con mcd
1895, 2, 16. Emmor dis jas
1896, 1, 18. Lucinda gct Pasadena MM, Calif.
1896, 9, 19. Francis dis mcd
1897, 3, 20. James dis disunity
1897, 3, 20. Eliphus dis disunity
1898, 9, 17. Malinda E. gct Salem MM, O.
1903, 8, 15. Elbert L. & w, Malinda E., & ch,
Howard H. & Chester A., rocf Salem MM, O.,
dtd 1903,6,24
1913, 4, 19. Lewis J. Kirk gct Salem MM, to
m Elizabeth Alice Cope
1920, 8, 21. William L. & w, Rachel Tacy, &
ch, Alfred Louis & William Lorin, rocf
Salem MM, dtd 1920,7,21

1921, 3, 19. Albert M. rocf Salem MM, dtd
1921,2,23
1928, 8, 18. William L. gct Plainfield MM,
Ind., to m Celia Pike
1929, 8, 17. Celia Pike rocf Plainfield MM,
Ind., dtd 1929,5,29

COPELAND
1814, 6, 9. Rebecca (form Dixon) con mou
1829, 5, 7. Rebecca dis disunity

COPPOCK
----, --, --. Rebecca b 1821,4,12 d 1899,1,21
1871, 11, 20. Jeremiah, s John & Catharine,
Columbiana Co., O.; m at Middleton, Rebecca SHAW, dt Thomas & Rachel, Columbiana Co., O.

1872, 4, 20. Rebecca gct New Garden MM
1887, 7, 16. Rebecca rocf New Garden MM, dtd
1887,6,23

CORNTHWAIT
1837, 4, 6. Alisanna rocf Baltimore MM for
Western Dist., dtd 1836,12,9 (H)
1841, 7, 8. William Peck [Cornthwate] rocf
Baltimore MM, dtd 1841,4,8
1842, 4, 7. Robert recrq (H)
1846, 4, 9. C. W. rocf Baltimore MM, dtd
1846,3,5 (H)

COULSON
----, --, --. Jehu & Jane
  Ch: Uriah   b 1790, 2, 19
      Jehue   " 1792, 4, 20
      David   " 1794, 10, 7
      Jabez   " 1797, 1, 17
      Rachel   " 1800, 7, 2
      Jesse   " 1803, 2, 4
1761, 9, 24. Jehu b
1759, 12, 1. Jane b

1805, 6, 19. Jane & ch, Amos, Catharine,
Harvey, Uriah, Jehu, David, Jabez, Rachel
& Jesse, rocf Redstone MM, dtd 1804,6,1
1811, 9, 12. Jehu & w, Jane, & ch, Jehu, David, Jabez, Rachel & Jesse, gct New Garden MM
1815, 4, 6. Uriah gct New Garden MM
1856, 3, 6. Ann & s, Seth, gct Sandy Spring
MM

COURTNEY
1866, 8, 23. Eva D. b
1906, 6, 28. Eva D. m Lewis T. MORLAN

1881, 9, 17. Eva D., minor under care of Morton & Ann Neill, recrq

COWGILL
----, --, --. Thos. & Sarah
  Ch: Ann   b 1800, 11, 27
      Henry   " 1802, 10, 30

COWGILL, Thos. & Sarah, continued
    Ch: Susannah b 1804, 11, 1
        Daniel   " 1806, 10, 9
        Sarah   " 1809, 9, 3
        Thos.   " 1812, 6, 19
        Joseph   " 1814, 12, 15
----, --, --. James & Charlotte
    Ch: Lemuel
        Crew   b 1805, 12, 1
        Margaret " 1808, 2, 29
        Israel   " 1810, 5, 23
1806, 2, 20. Caleb, s Henry & Ruth, Columbi-
    ana Co., O., b 1783,4,2; m at Middleton,
    Rachel OLIPHANT, dt Samuel & Elizabeth,
    b 1781,11,22
    Ch: Samuel   b 1808, 4, 18 d 1810, 3,19
        bur Elkrun
        Ruth   b 1809, 8, 9 " 1810, 4,26
        bur Elkrun
        Henry   b 1811, 4, 18
1815, 1, 18. Rachel m James STANLEY
1815, 12, 16. Henry d bur Elkrun

1804, 7, 14. Sarah rocf Crooked Run MM, dtd
    1804,3,3
1805, 1, 12. Charlottee & ch, Rachel, Abigail,
    John, James, Simpson & Joel, rocf Cedar
    Creek MM, Va., dtd 1804,10,13
1805, 2, 9. Anna & Henry, ch Thomas & Sa-
    rah, recrq
1805, 6, 19. Ruth rocf Southland MM, dtd
    1804,2,28
1817, 11, 10. Thomas & w, Sarah, & ch, Ann,
    Henry, Susanna, Daniel, Sarah, Thomas, Jo-
    seph & Levi, gct Derby MM
1863, 6, 20. Lydia (form McClure) dis mcd

COX
1837, 7, 6. Benjamin D. rocf Third Haven
    MM, dtd 1837,4,13 (H)
1837, 7, 6. Isaac P. Jr. rocf Third Haven
    MM, dtd 1837,4,13 (H)
1837, 7, 6. Noel P. rocf Third Haven MM, dtd
    1837,4,13 (H)
1837, 8, 21. Nowel, Benjamin & Powel rocf
    Wilmington MM, Del., dtd 1837,6,3
1839, 5, 9. Isaac Powel dis disunity

CRAIG
1814, 4, 14. Elizabeth m Bennett ARMSTRONG

1812, 8, 6. James Armstrong gct New Garden
    MM, to m Deborah Craig
1813, 2, 11. Deborah Armstrong & dt, Lydia
    Craig, rocf New Garden MM, dtd 1812,11,9
1813, 9, 9. Elizabeth rocf New Garden MM,
    dtd 1813,7,15
1819, 5, 17. Lydia Davis (form Craig) con mou
1824, 7, 19. Eleanor rocf New Garden MM, dtd
    1824,5,20
1824, 11, 22. Elenor dis jas

CROZER
1808, 6, 13. Susannah m Levi PICKERING
----, --, --. Thos. b 1794,2,17; m Sarah -----
    b 1796,11,10
    Ch: James   b 1822, 7, 8
        Mary   " 1824, 3, 6
        Jonathan   " 1826, 4, 1
        Elisabeth " 1828, 6, 3
        Reasin   " 1830, 8, 2
        Susannah   " 1832, 8, 15
        Martha   " 1836, 2, 17
        Charles   " 1837, 11, 28 d 1839,9, 8
        ae 1y 9m 10d

1807, 9, 12. Susannah recrq
1824, 12, 20. Thomas & w, Sarah, & ch, James
    & Mary, rocf Sandy Spring MM, dtd 1824,11,
    26
1831, 11, 10. Samuel, minor, rocf Flushing MM,
    dtd 1831,7,27
1841, 6, 10. Thomas & w, Sarah, & ch, James,
    Mary, Jonathan, Elizabeth, Reason, Susan-
    nah & Martha, gct Carmel MM

CUMMINGS
1892, 5, 2. Ethel M. b

1889, 3, 16. Elma D. (form Cadwalader) dis
    mcd
1907, 4, 20. Ethel Margaret recrq
1911, 6, 17. Ethel M. Dunlap (form Cummings)
    dis mcd

CURL
1815, 10, 12. Samuel Jr. rocf Darby Creek MM,
    dtd 1815,9,16
1817, 12, 15. Samuel gct Clear Creek MM

DAMSON
1885, 10, 17. Elisha Gamble gct Stillwater MM.
    O., to m Melvina Damson

DANIEL
1805, 5, 16. Rebecca m Thomas SHINN

1808, 10, 8. Jesper dis mou
1809, 12, 9. William dis disunity
1814, 8, 11. Mary gct Salem MM
1816, 12, 16. Hannah Stockhouse (form Daniel)
    con mou
1817, 6, 16. Mary rocf Salem MM, O., dtd
    1817,2,14
1819, 2, 22. John [Daniels] dis mou
1819, 11, 22. Mary Morell (form Daniel) dis
    mou
1826, 6, 19. Tace Galaway (form Daniel) dis
    mou
1829, 5, 7. James dis disunity

DAVIS
1804, 5, 12. Mary & ch, Mary, William, Rachel,
    Elizabeth & Joshua, rocf Redstone MM, dtd
    1804,3,2

DAVIS, continued
1804, 5, 12. Rebekah rocf Redstone MM, dtd
     1804,3,2
1805, 9, 14. Phebe rocf Short Creek MM, dtd
     1805,4,20
1805, 12, 14. Cert rec for Abraham & w, Han-
     nah, & ch, from Short Creek MM, dtd 1805,
     7,20, endorsed to Salem MM
1815, 2, 9. Edith (form Richards) con mou
1815, 7, 6. Edith gct New Garden MM
1817, 11, 10. Joshua rocf Westland MM, dtd
     1817,7,24
1819, 5, 17. Lydia (form Craig) con mou
1819, 8, 23. Lydia gct New Garden MM
1825, 11, 21. Benjamin rocf Marlborough MM,
     dtd 1825,4,21
1829, 10, 8. Benj. dis JH
1829, 12, 10. Benjamin gct Marlborough MM (H)

DENNING
1864, 8, 17. John attached to this mtg when
     Beaver Falls MM, Pa., was laid down (H)

DENNY
1814, 5, 12. Sarah (form Richardson) dis mou

DETZELL
1860, 5, 19. Phebe (form Allmon) dis mcd

DILLON
1816, 11, 21. James, s Thomas & Rebecca, Colum-
     biana Co., O.; m at Carmel, Elizabeth
     UNDERWOOD, dt Willin & Sarah, Columbiana
     Co., O.

1816, 4, 15. James recrq
1824, 12, 20. James & w, Elisabeth, rocf Car-
     mel MM, dtd 1824,12,18
1829, 1, 8. James dis joining Separatists
1829, 6, 11. Elizabeth dis joining Hicksites
1835, 7, 9. James [Dillen] & w, Elizabeth,
     gct Marlborough MM (H)

DINGEE
----, --, --. Elizabeth, w Jacob, dt Martin &
     Magdaline (Andrews) Ressler, b 1855,10,16
     d 1925,10,11 bur Middleton
1883, 3, 31. Rebecca b
1912, 2, 22. Rebecca m Henry Salonis HARVEY

1825, 2, 21. John & w, Bethsheba, & ch, Ruth,
     Martha, Charles & John, rocf Short Creek
     MM, dtd 1825,1,18
1828, 10, 9. John dis joining Separatists
1828, 10, 9. Bathsheba dis JH
1831, 12, 8. John & w, Bathsheba, & ch,
     Charles & John, gct Centre MM, O. (H)
1831, 12, 8. Ruth & Martha gct Center MM, O.
     (H)
1833, 6, 6. Charles & John, ch John & Bath-
     sheba, gct Center MM, O.
1834, 5, 8. Ruth & Martha dis JH
1869, 12, 18. Adaline rocf Providence MM, Pa.,

     dtd 1869,12,2
1909, 4, 17. Rebecca recrq
1921, 12, 17. Elizabeth B. recrq

DIXON
----, --, --. Joshua [Dixson] b 1750,10,20;
     m ----- -----
     Ch: Hannah   b 1774, 9, 29
         Emanuel   " 1776, 9, 28
     Joshua m 2nd Dinah ----- b 1760,2,28
     Ch: John   b 1783, 12, 28
         Rachel   " 1785, 7, 19
         Elizabeth " 1788, 11, 22
         Rebecca   " 1790, 12, 22
         Joshua   " 1792, 12, 7
         Nathan   " 1794, 8, 25
         Thomas   " 1797, 10, 3
         Dinah   " 1799, 8, 27 d 1804,10, 7
         Lydia   " 1801, 10, 24
         Levi   " 1803, 8, 25 " 1804, 8,25
1803, 12, 15. Rachel [Dixson] m Benjamin HANNA
1806, 12, 16. Elizabeth [Dixson] m Israel COPE
1806, 12, 18. Simon [Dixson], s Henry & Eliza-
     beth, Columbiana Co., O.; m at Middleton,
     Elizabeth JAMES, dt Isaac & Sarah, Colum-
     biana Co., O.
----, --, --. John & Hannah [Dixson]
     Ch: Lydiann   b 1807, 11, 14
         Lucena   " 1809, 10, 2
         Newton   " 1812, 3, 9
         Lot   " 1814, 2, 11
         Emanuel   " 1816, 5, 26
         Eliza   " 1816, 5, 26
         Rebecca   " 1818, 6, 8
         Samuel B. " 1820, 10, 30
1808, 12, 15. Elizabeth [Dixson] m Isaac TOWN-
     SEND
1810, 3, 15. Mary [Dixson] m William HARRISON
1811, 2, 26. Lucena [Dixson], dt John & Han-
     nah, d
1816, 3, 7. Elizabeth [Dixson], w Simon, d
     bur Elkrun
1823, 10, 22. Isaac, s John & Mary, Fayette
     Co., Pa.; m at Middleton, Jane HICKLEN, dt
     Samuel & Lydia, Columbiana Co., O.
1827, 5, 31. Henry [Dixson] d
----, --, --. Newton & Eliza Ann
     Ch: Hannah   b 1839, 5, 9
         Joshua   " 1841, 10, 9
1841, 1, 14. Eliza m Lot HOLMES (H)
1843, 11, 16. Mary m Nathan WARRINGTON
1846, 6, 18. Sarah Ann m Mahlon OLIPHANT
1846, 12, 24. Rebecca A. m George N. HAPGOOD
     (H)

1804, 6, 19. Elizabeth [Dixson] & ch, Simon,
     Elisabeth & Mary, rocf Westland MM, dtd
     1804,5,26
1809, 1, 14. Henry [Dixson], Jr. dis mcd
1809, 7, 8. Elizabeth Townsend (form Dixon)
     dis
1814, 6, 9. Nathan [Dixson] con mou
1814. 6, 9. Lucretia (form Pettit) con mcd

DIXON, continued

1814, 6, 9. Rebecca Copeland (form Dixon) con mou

1818, 2, 16. Nathan [Dixson] & fam gct New Garden MM

1818, 7, 13. Cert granted 1818,2,16, to Nathan & w, Lucretia, & ch, Mary Ann, Martha & John, to New Garden MM, forwarded to Carmel MM

1820, 2, 21. Simon [Dixson] gct Salem MM, to m Elizabeth Pidgeon

1820, 5, 22. Thomas [Dixson] dis disunity

1820, 5, 22. Hannah gct Redstone MM

1820, 8, 21. Elizabeth rocf Salem MM, dtd 1820,6,21

1820, 9, 18. Nathan & w, Lucretia, & ch, Mary Ann, Martha, John & Joshua, rocf Carmel MM, dtd 1820,9,16

1821, 8, 20. Samuel & w, Hannah, & s, John N., rocf Redstone MM, dtd 1821,6,30

1822, 5, 20. Abner Heald gct Redstone MM, to m Ruth Dixson

1822, 11, 18. Lydia Steward (form Dixson) dis mou

1824, 3, 22. Jane gct Redstone MM

1824, 10, 18. Joshua [Dixson], Jr. dis mou

1825, 6, 20. Nathan [Dixson] dis jas

1825, 6, 20. Lucretia dis jas

1826, 3, 20. Simon & w, Elizabeth, & ch, John, Ruth, Sarah, Matilda & Mary, gct Marlborough MM

1828, 8, 7. John dis disunity

1829, 1, 8. Hannah, w John, dis joining Separatists

1829, 3, 12. Joshua dis jH

1829, 3, 12. Lydia Ann & Dinah dis jH

1830, 8, 12. Lydia Ann Holloway (form Dixon) con mou (H)

1832, 10, 11. John Pettit, Joshua, Lydia & Charity, ch Nathan & Lucretia, gct Salem MM

1834, 7, 10. Martha & Mary Ann dis jH

1836, 9, 19. John, Jr. rocf Red Stone MM, dtd 1836,8,3

1838, 5, 10. Newton gct Marlborough MM, to m Eliza Ann Scott (H)

1839, 2, 7. Eliza Ann S. rocf Marlborough MM, dtd 1838,11,24 (H)

1840, 6, 11. Newton dis mou

1840, 8, 6. Eliza & Rebecca dis jH

1843, 12, 7. John N. dis jH

1857, 6, 11. Samuel & w, Hannah, gct Upper Springfield MM

1872, 1, 20. Cyrus dis joining Separatists

DOWNING

1817, 2, 10. William & w, Beulah, & ch, Daniel & Rebecca, rocf Center MM, Del., dtd 1816,9,16

1822, 11, 18. William & w, Beulah, & ch, Daniel, Rebecca & John, gct Carmel MM

DUKEHART

1832, 4, 12. John Peck, Margaret Ann & Sarah Jane, ch John & Ann, rocf Baltimore MM for Eastern & Western Dist., dtd 1832,3,8

1833, 4, 11. John, Jr. & w, Ann, & ch, John Peck, Margaret Ann & Sarah Jane, rocf Baltimore MM for Western Dist., dtd 1832,11,9

1836, 2, 11. John & w, Ann P., & ch, John Peck & Sarah Jane, gct Baltimore MM (H)

1841, 7, 8. John, Jr. & w, Ann, & dt, Sarah Jane, rocf Baltimore MM for Western Dist., dtd 1841,6,11 (H)

1844, 6, 6. Ann & dt, Sarah Jane, gct Baltimore MM (H)

1846, 8, 13. Margaret Ann relrq (H)

DUNLAP

1911, 6, 17. Ethel M. (form Cummings) dis mcd

EASTMAN

1840, 8, 6. Lovisa rst by rq

1844, 5, 9. Lavisa & s, Benjamin Franklin, gct Salem MM

EDGERTON

1865, 9, 21. Jesse, s Joseph & Charity, Keokuk Co., Ia., b 1845,7,12; m at Carmel, O., Semira STRATTON, dt Edward & Mary, Columbiana Co., O., b 1844,5,5 d 1878,9,11
Ch: Mary Anna b 1866, 8, 15
    Edward F. " 1867, 4, 13 d 1867,11,22
    J. Howard " 1869, 3, 13
    Arthur
    Howell   " 1871, 6, 6
    Wilson   " 1873, 6, 24 d 1903, 9, 3
    Semira
    Ellen   " 1875, 9, 30
Jesse m 2nd Susan GILBERT, dt Benjamin & Lydia, b 1842,3,31

1891, 5, 21. Mary Anna m Wilson M. HALL

1893, 8, 24. J. Howard, s Jesse & Semira (Stratton), b 1869,3,13; m at Middleton, Lavina H. BATTEY, dt Thomas C. & Lucinda (Hampton) (Gregg), b 1871,10,5
Ch: Alice
    Semira   b 1894, 6, 6
    Chester J. " 1895, 7, 13
    Ruth   " 1897, 9, 4
    Joseph B. " 1900, 9, 2
    Dorothy   " 1902, 4, 23
    Lucinda   " 1903, 6, 7
    Mary Ellen " 1905, 10, 17
    Laura Susan" 1909, 3, 10
    J. Howard
    Jr.   " 1917, 2, 21

1899, 7, 20. Semira Ellen m Charles P. MORLAN

1923, 8, 30. Dorothy m Howard A. ALLEN

----, --, --. Joseph B. m Elsie MAXWELL, dt Arthur B. & Arsinoe (Peacock), b 1902,5,30
Ch: Stephen
    Arthur   b 1928, 5, 8
    Anthony J. " 1931, 5, 17

EDGERTON, continued
1866, 6, 16. Jesse rocf Coal Creek MM, Ia.,
    dtd 1866,5,12
1875, 1, 16. Jesse & w, Semira, & ch, Mari-
    anna, Joshua Howard & Arthur H., gct New
    Garden MM
1884, 2, 16. Jesse & ch, Mary Anna, J. Howard,
    Arthur H. & Semira Ellen, rocf New Garden
    MM, dtd 1884,1,24
1884, 2, 16. Susan G. rocf Salem MM, dtd
    1884,1,23
1894, 11, 17. Arthur H. dis mcd
1901, 6, 15. Jesse & w, Susanna G., gct
    Stillwater MM
1906, 9, 15. Walter G. gct Upper Springfield
    MM
1925, 5, 16. Joseph B. gct Plainfield MM,
    Ind., to m Elsie Maxwell
1928, 8, 18. Elsie Maxwell rocf Plainfield
    MM, Ind., dtd 1928,8,1
1932, 3, 19. Chester J. con mcd

EDMUNDSON
1820, 11, 2. Eli, s John & Ann, Columbiana
    Co., O.; m at Middleton, Ruth HEALD, dt
    John & Phebe, Columbiana Co., O.
    Ch: Phebe   b 1821, 6, 29
        John   " 1822, 11, 11
        Jonathan   " 1824, 8, 23
        Abner   " 1826, 5, 13
        Ann   " 1828, 3, 15
        Sarah   " 1831, 3, 27
        Jane   " 1832, 5, 7
        Thos.   " 1835, 11, 25 d 1857,11,21
        William   " 1840, 1, 8
1848, 7, 13. John, s Eli & Ruth, b 1822,11,11;
    m at Middleton, Ruth HEALD, Columbiana
    Co., O., dt Abner & Sina, b 1831,1,5
    Ch: Mary   b 1849, 4, 22
        Abner   " 1851, 5, 31
        Sina Ann   " 1855, 7, 6
1848, 8, 17. Jonathan, s Eli & Ruth, Columbi-
    ana Co., O., b 1824,8,23; m at Middleton,
    Phebe Ann HOLLINGSWORTH, Columbiana Co.,
    O., dt Samuel & Margaret, b 1827,9,25
    Ch: Samuel L. b 1849, 6, 26
        Hannah   " 1851, 10, 11
        Ellen   " 1853, 8, 27
        Isaac New-
        ton   " 1855, 9, 19
1858, 3, 10. Ruth d bur Middleton
1852, 4, 15. Ann m Joel WICKERSHAM
1857, 11, 21. Thos. d bur Iowa
1866, 2, 18. Eli d bur Middleton

1807, 1, 10. John [Edmonson] & w, Ann, & ch,
    Jonathan, Eli, Sarah & John, rocf Waring-
    ton MM, dtd 1806,9,13
1820, 11, 20. Thomas Taylor gct Carmel MM, to
    m Sarah Edmundson
1820, 12, 18. Ruth gct Carmel MM
1822, 4, 22. Eli & w, Ruth, & dt, Phebe,
    rocf Carmel MM, dtd 1822,4,20

1822, 4, 22. John, Jr., minor, rocf Carmel
    MM, dtd 1822,4,20
1823, 5, 19. John, Jr. gct Carmel MM
1825, 2, 21. Eli & w, Ruth, & ch, Phebe,
    John & Jonathan, gct Carmel MM
1828, 4, 10. Mary rocf Short Creek MM, dtd
    1827,11,20
1830, 6, 10. Eli & w, Ruth, & ch, Phebe,
    John, Jonathan, Abner, Ann & Sarah, rocf
    Carmel MM, dtd 1830,5,15
1831, 9, 8. Eliza (form Cope) dis mou
1831, 12, 8. Mary gct SD MM, Phila., Pa.
1837, 5, 11. Gulielma (form Icenhour) dis mou
1838, 12, 6. Hiram rocf Carmel MM, dtd 1838,
    11,7
1843, 8, 10. Ann (form Icenhour) dis mcd
    (first rpd 1838,4,23)
1850, 2, 7. Hiram con mou
1854, 6, 8. Abner dis
1856, 1, 10. Phebe McBride (form Edmundson)
    dis mou
1857, 12, 10. Hyram dis mcd
1860, 7, 21. Jane dis joining Methodost Soci-
    ety
1860, 7, 21. Sarah dis joining Methodist Soci-
    ety
1866; 5, 19. William dis mou

ELLERMAN
1836, 11, 21. Theophilus rocf Short Creek
    MM, dtd 1836,9,20
1838, 4, 23. Theophilos gct ND MM, Phila.,
    Pa., to m Sarah Atkinson
1838, 10, 11. Sarah rocf ND MM, Phila., Pa.,
    dtd 1838,7,24
1839, 6, 6. Theopholis & w, Sarah, gct Upper
    Springfield MM

ELLIOT
1816, 6, 10. Elizabeth rocf Warrington MM,
    dtd 1816,3,21
1817, 5, 12. Elizabeth gct New Garden MM
1842, 5, 12. Hannah [Elliott] (form Arm-
    strong) con mcd (H)

ELLIS
1806, 2, 8. Enos & w, Mary, & ch gct Salem
    MM
1833, 9, 12. Mary (form Hill) dis mou

ELLYSON
1865, 5, 25. Robert, s Zachariah & Mary, Ma-
    honing Co., O.; m at Middleton, Phebe
    WICKERSHAM, dt Thomas & Ann, Columbiana
    Co., O.
1865, 9, 21. Benjamin, s Robert & Hannah,
    Cedar Co., Ia.; m at Carmel, O., Elma C.
    ARMSTRONG, dt Nathan H. & Rebecca, Colum-
    biana Co., O.
1871, 5, 25. David, s Robert & Mary, Columbi-
    ana Co., O.; m at Middleton, Margaret
    COPE, dt Amos & Emily Edna, Columbiana
    Co., O.

ELLYSON, continued
1872, 3, 21. Tacy M. m Webster A. ALLMON
1917, 11, 24. Phebe d ae 94y (an elder)

1865, 9, 16. Phebe gct Upper Springfield MM
1865, 12, 16. Elma C. gct Hickory Grove MM, Ia.
1867, 6, 15. Robert & w, Phebe, & ch, Tacy M., rocf Upper Springfield MM, dtd 1867, 5,24
1871, 9, 16. Margaret gct Upper Springfield MM
1876, 1, 15. Pearson Hall gct Hickory Grove MM, Ia., to m Miriam Ellyson
1876, 11, 18. Phebe gct Salem MM, O.
1885, 12, 19. Phebe rocf Upper Springfield MM, dtd 1885,9,22

EMBREE
----, --, --. Moses & Abigail
  Ch: Stephen   b 1805, 8, 28
      Rachel   " 1808, 2, 18
      Mary   " 1810, 4, 6
      Charity   " 1813, 1, 7
      Wm.   " 1816, 3, 4
      Moses R.   " 1820, 9, 11
1827, 12, 12. Rachel m Isaac COPE
1831, 2, 26. Wm. d bur Fairfield
1842, 3, 17. Moses, Columbiana Co., O.; m at Columbiana, Ann MARIS, Columbiana Co., O. (H)

1805, 12, 14. Moses & w, Abigail, rocf Goose Creek MM, Va., dtd 1805,5,2 (s, Stephen, b since cert was granted)
1806, 7, 12. Cert rec for John & w, Huldah, from Goose Creek MM, dtd 1806,5,1, endorsed to Salem MM
1830, 4, 24. Mary & Charity dis jH
1830, 6, 10. Moses dis disunity
1830, 11, 11. Abigail dis jH
1831, 7, 7. Mary Underwood (form Embree) con mcd (H)
1836, 4, 18. Stephen dis mou
1844, 4, 11. Moses, Jr. dis mcd
1844, 7, 11. Charity rocf Marlborough MM, dtd 1844,5,28
1845, 12, 11. Charity gct Marlborough MM

ENGLE
----, --, --. Josiah & Mary
  Ch: Nathaniel b 1800, 1, 2
      Chas.   " 1801, 12, 23
      Joann   " 1803, 9, 8
      Josiah   " 1808, 3, 2
      Zimri   " 1811, 7, 9
      Nathan   " 1814, 6, 13
1833, 9, 19. Zimri, s Josiah & Mary, Columbiana Co., O.; m at Middleton, Ann BEESON, dt Richard & Ann, Columbiana Co., O.
----, --, --. Nathan b 1814,6,13; m Catharine HOLE, dt Chas. & Esther, b 1815,1,24
  Ch: Lemuel   b 1841, 10, 20

  Ch: Esther   b 1844, 2, 4
      Robert   " 1845, 12, 5
      Charles   " 1849, 3, 20

1805, 10, 12. Mary & ch, Nathaniel, Charles & Joann, rocf Evesham MM, N. J., dtd 1805,4, 5, endorsed by Concord MM, 1805,8,20
1827, 8, 9. Charles gct Upper Springfield MM, to m Jane Malsberry
1829, 3, 12. Charles gct Upper Springfield MM
1830, 1, 7. Josiah, Jr. dis mou
1834, 1, 9. Zimri & w, Ann B., gct Upper Springfield MM
1840, 11, 12. Joana Wall (form Engle) dis mou
1841, 4, 8. Catharine rocf Carmel MM, dtd 1841,3,20
1863, 2, 21. Catharine dis joining Separatists
1865, 5, 8. Nathaniel dis jas

ERWIN
----, --, --. Samuel & Sarah
  Ch: Wm.   b 1794, 1, 17
      James   " 1795, 6, 9
      Mary   " 1797, 3, 5
      John   " 1798, 11, 20
      Mahlon   " 1800, 6, 18
      Elisha   " 1802, 6, 7
      Elizabeth " 1804, 5, 5
      Sarah   " 1806, 5, 5
      Susannah   " 1810, 8, 7
      Samuel   " 1814, 3, 12
1819, 12, 30. Mary m Richard MORLAN
----, --, --. Mahlon & Elizabeth
  Ch: Reuben   b 1823, 11, 2
      Samuel   " 1825, 8, 9
      Lydia Ann " 1827, 8, 22
      Jesse   " 1829, 9, 12
      Margaret   " 1835, 1, 12
      Sarah   " 1837, 8, 9
1823, 1, 2. Elizabeth m Isaiah GARWOOD
1827, 3, 14. Sarah m John ADAMSON
----, --, --. James & Hannah Ann
  Ch: Elma   b 1831, 3, 31
      Mary Ann   " 1833, 9, 29
      Celicia   " 1836, 3, 4
      Sarah H.   " 1838, 5, 18
1826, 6, 12. Elisha dis mou
1828, 11, 6. Samuel, Mahlon & James dis joining Separatists
1828, 11, 6. Sarah dis jH
1829, 3, 12. Susannah, Jr. dis jH
1829, 10, 8. Susannah dis jH
1830, 1, 7. Elizabeth dis jH
1832, 10, 11. James con mcd (H)
1833, 1, 10. Hannah & dt, Elma, recrq (H)
1837, 6, 19. Samuel, Jr. dis mou
1837, 11, 9. Samuel, Jr. con mcd (H)
1841, 2, 11. William dis disunity
1848, 7, 6. Lydia Ann Rogers (form Erwin) dis mou
1848, 8, 10. Samuel, s Mahlon, dis mou
1864, 8, 17. James & w, Hannah Ann, & ch,

ERWIN, continued
    Elma, Mary, Celicia, Sarah H., Aclice Ann
    & Caroline E. attached to this mtg when
    Beaver Falls MM, Pa. was laid down

EVANS
1805, 6, 8. Elizabeth rocf Derby MM, Pa.,
    dtd 1804,3,29
1816, 3, 11. Eli rocf Uwchlan MM, Pa., dtd
    1815,5,8
1829, 2, 12. Eli dis joining Separatists

FARMER
1805, 8, 10. Mary & ch, William James & Re-
    becca, rocf Wrightsborough MM, dtd 1805,
    3,23
1805, 8, 10. Ann & ch, Mary & Susannah, rocf
    Wrightsborough MM, dtd 1805,3,23

FARQUHAR
1840, 9, 10. Elizabeth, Sr. rocf Smithfield
    MM, dtd 1840,2,17

FAWCETT
1837, 3, 2. Josiah, s Richard & Eunice,
    Columbiana Co., O.; m at Middleton, Sarah
    OLIPHANT, dt Ephraim & Elizabeth, Columbi-
    ana Co., O.

1837, 7, 17. Sarah gct Salem MM

FERRALL
1806, 6, 14. Nancy [Ferral] rocf Smith River
    MM, dtd 1806,4,12
1811, 5, 9. Nancy Jones (form Ferrall) con
    mou
1814, 9, 8. Martha, Benjamin, Edmond, Lucy
    Ann & Judith, ch Mary, recrq
1820, 3, 26. James dis mcd
1823, 6, 23. Mary & dt, Martha, Lucy Ann &
    Judith, dis jas
1824, 6, 21. Benjamin [Ferral] dis mou
1828, 4, 10. Edmund dis mou

FIRESTONE
1831, 10, 6. Sally Ann (form Allen) dis mcd
    (H)

FISH
----, --, --. Joseph & Deborah
    Ch: Celia   b 1804, 7, 1
        Amon   " 1806, 3, 14
        Emma Jane " 1808, 3, 15
        Albert   " 1810, 4, 12
        Lemuel   " 1812, 8, 18
        Mary   " 1815, 1, 18
        Anna   " 1817, 9, 2
        Harry   " 1823, 5, 26
----, --, --. Stephen & Hannah
    Ch: John   b 1804, 12, 2
        Selim   " 1807, 8, 26
        Phebe   " 1814, 4, 18
        Solomon   " 1816, 1, 23

    Ch: Lydia   b 1818, 2, 8
        Gardner   " 1820, 8, 27
1825, 3, 17. Celia m Isaac PADEN

1818, 3, 16. Stephen & w, Hannah, & ch, John,
    Selem, Phebe & Solomon, rocf Rensselaer-
    ville MM, dtd 1817,9,25
1818, 10, 19. Joseph & w, Deborah, & ch, Celia,
    Amon, Emma Jean, Albert, Samuel, Mary,
    Scott & Anne, rocf Bridgewater MM, N. Y.,
    dtd 1818,4,3
1828, 5, 8. Amon dis mcd
1829, 11, 12. Hannah dis jH
1829, 11, 12. John dis jH
1829, 11, 12. Selim dis jH
1829, 11, 12. Stephen dis jH
1830, 2, 11. Joseph dis jH
1831, 1, 6. Deborah dis disunity
1831, 1, 6. Emma Jane dis disunity
1833, 7, 11. Albert dis mou
1837, 10, 12. Sarah recrq (H)
1855, 8, 16. Stephen gct Salem MM, to m
    Hannah K. Hanna (H)

FISHER
----, --, --. Joseph, Jr. b 1766,2,20; m Han-
    nah ----- b 1774,11,30
    Ch: Silvanus b 1797, 10, 8
        Rachel   " 1799, 5, 14
        Wm.   " 1800, 11, 24
        Isaac   " 1802, 5, 18
        Amasa   " 1803, 10, 12
        Anna
        Knight   " 1806, 4, 8
        Joseph
        Scars-
        borough   " 1806, 4, 8
        Elias   " 1808, 1, 10
        Ruth   " 1811, 6, 29

1805, 12, 14. Jonathan & w, Rachel, & ch,
    Robert & Joseph, rocf South River MM, dtd
    1805,8,10
1807, 8, 8. Joseph & w, Hannah, & ch, Syl-
    vanus, Rachel, William, Isaac, Amasa &
    Anna Knight, rocf South River MM, Va., dtd
    1807,5,9, endorsed by Salem MM, 1807,7,14
1815, 2, 9. Joseph & w, Ann, rocf Marl-
    borough MM, dtd 1814,11,16
1817, 11, 10. John & w, Rachel, & ch, Robert,
    Joseph, Elizabeth, Thomas & Marietta, gct
    White Water MM
1824, 10, 18. Elias, minor, rocf Carmel MM,
    dtd 1824,10,16
1825, 12, 19. Elias, minor, gct Carmel MM

FITSPATRICK
1840, 12, 10. Eliza (form Woods) dis jas

FITZ RANDOLPH
1814, 8, 11. Edward [Fitts Randolph] rocf
    Westland MM, dtd 1812,7,25
1814, 10, 6. Edward con mou
1814, 12, 8. Richard rocf Westland MM, dtd

FITZ RANDOLPH, continued
    1812,7,25
1815, 4, 6. Richard [Fitts Randolph] dis
    disunity
1822, 6, 17. Edward gct Carmel MM

FOULK
1840, 1, 9. Charles, minor, rocf Derby MM,
    Pa., dtd 1839,6,25 (H)
1840, 11, 12. Charles gct Spruce St. MM,
    Phila. (H)

FOWLER
1817, 10, 13. Caleb rocf Pipe Creek MM, Md.,
    dtd 1817,5,17
1817, 11, 10. Lydia rocf Pipe Creek MM, dtd
    1817,5,17
1817, 11, 10. Rebecca rocf Pipe Creek MM, dtd
    1817,5,17
1818, 8, 10. Cert rec for Mary & s, Samuel,
    from Pipe Creek MM, dtd 1818,2,14, endors-
    ed to Carmel MM

FRENCH
1879, 10, 30. Barzillai, s Barzillai & Mary,
    Columbiana Co., O.; m at Middleton, Mar-
    tha BLACKBURN, dt Wm. & Ann, Columbiana
    Co., O.

1841, 6, 10. Thomas Y. rocf Upper Spring-
    field MM, dtd 1841,5,22
1842, 8, 11. Thomas Y. gct Salem MM
1865, 1, 21. Thomas Y. & w, Rachel H., & s,
    Clarkson, rocf Salem MM, dtd 1864,11,23
1871, 6, 17. Thomas Y. & w, Rachel H., & s,
    Clarkson, gct Salem MM
1880, 3, 20. Martha B. gct Salem MM

GALBREATH
1804, 9, 8. Susannah & ch, Ashur, David,
    Ann & Sarah, rocf Short Creek MM, dtd
    1804,5,19
1805, 8, 10. Rhoda [Gallbreath] rocf Bush
    River MM, S. C., dtd 1805,4,27
1805, 9, 14. William & w, Hannah, & ch,
    William, rocf Bush River MM, S. C., dtd
    1805,4,27

GALAWAY
1826, 6, 19. Tace (form Daniel) dis mou

GAMBLE
1844, 3, 1. Samuel, s Harrison & Phebe, b
----, --, --. Elisha b 1854,11,28 d 1895,3,
    10; m Melvina ----- d 1886,4,13
----, --, --. Elisha b 1882,7,8; m Mable B.
    ----- b 1881,8,7
    Ch: Robert S. b 1909, 12, 5
        J. Howard " 1911, 11, 10
        Mary Ger-
            trude   " 1916, 10, 25

1844, 1, 11. Phebe rocf Pennsville MM, dtd

    1843,11,16
1844, 4, 11. Harrison P. rocf Salem MM, dtd
    1844,3,20
1845, 6, 12. Harrison P. & w, Phebe, & s,
    Samuel, gct Upper Springfield MM
1858, 3, 9. Eliza [Gammel] (form Townsend)
    dis mou (first rpd 1843,5,11)
1858, 5, 15. Harrison & w, Phebe, & ch, Sam-
    uel, Charles, Sarah, William, Martha Jane,
    Elisha & Ruth Ellen, rocf New Garden MM,
    dtd 1858,4,22
1864, 8, 17. Eliza [Gammel] (form Townsend)
    attached to this mtg when Beaver Falls MM,
    Pa. was laid down (H)
1866, 7, 21. Samuel gct Salem MM
1867, 11, 9. Harrison dis mou
1869, 6, 19. Charles gct Hickory Grove MM,Ia.
1875, 12, 18. William dis mou
1885, 10, 17. Elisha gct Stillwater MM, O., to
    m Melvina Damson
1913, 7, 19. Alvin H. rocf New Garden MM, dtd
    1913,6,26
1914, 9, 19. Mabel B. recrq
1916, 9, 15. Robert S. & J. Howard, ch Alvin
    H. & Mabel B., recrq
1917, 7, 21. Alvin H. & w, Mabel B., & ch,
    Robert S., J. Howard & Mary Gertrude, gct
    Salem MM

GANTZ
1856, 3, 6. Celicia L. (form Townsend) dis
    mou

GARRETSON
----, --, --. Armele b 1788,10,2 d 1874,11,24

1842, 3, 10. Armella rocf Short Creek MM,
    dtd 1841,10,19

GARWOOD
1807, 3, 19. Daniel, s Isaiah & Mary, Colum-
    biana Co., O.; m at home of James Erwin,
    Mary HOLLOWAY, dt Asa & Mary, Columbiana
    Co., O.
    Ch: Isaiah   b 1811, 2, 1
        Isaac   " 1812, 9, 11
        Daniel   " 1816, 1, 19
1807, 3, 26. Mary m David STRATTON
1807, 10, 15. Esther m John STRATTON
1809, 3, 16. Thos., s Isaiah & Mary, Colum-
    biana Co., O.; m at Middleton, Mary
    STRATTON, dt Daniel & Shady, Columbiana
    Co., O.
    Ch: Elias   b 1810, 10, 22
        John   " 1812, 5, 19
        Daniel   " 1816, 3, 24
        Levi   " 1820, 3, 28
        Thos.   " 1823, 1, 11
        Hope   " 1826, 4, 18
        Sidney   " 1828, 12, 10
----, --, --. Isaac & Alice
    Ch: Isaiah   b 1812, 1, 2
        Lucy   " 1813, 10, 19

GARWOOD, Isaac & Alice, continued
    Ch: Sarah   b 1816, 1, 19
        Levi   " 1818, 5, 30
        Isaac   " 1820, 7, 24
        John   " 1823, 12, 14
        Sidney   " 1825, 9, 2
1815, 8, 17. Hope m Isaac HOLLOWAY
1816, 8, 15. Sarah m Aaron HOLLOWAY
1823, 1, 2. Isaiah, s Isaiah & Mary, Colum-
    biana Co., O.; m at Fairfield, Elizabeth
    ERWIN, dt Samuel & Sarah, Columbiana Co.,
    O.
    Ch: Hannah   b 1824, 3, 7
        Sarah   " 1825, 10, 5
        Mary   " 1827, 11, 12
1823, 3, 26. Daniel, s Isaiah & Mary, Colum-
    biana Co., O.; m at Fairfield, Ann WALKER,
    dt James & Elizabeth, Columbiana Co., O.
    Ch: Elizabeth b 1824, 10, 2
        Ruth   " 1826, 2, 4
        John   " 1827, 7, 8
        David   " 1829, 4, 4
        Joseph   " 1831, 5, 12
        Levi   " 1832, 9, 7
        George   " 1836, 5, 16
1825, 12, 28. Hannah m Abel JAMES
1827, 10, 6. Hope, s Thos. & Margaret, d bur
    Fairfield
1850, 6, 13. John, s Daniel & Ann, Columbiana
    Co., O., b 1827,7,8; m at Middleton,
    Asenath POOL, dt Jonas & Ann, Columbiana
    Co., O., b 1825,6,5
    Ch: Sylvanus P.
               b 1851, 9, 24
        Ann Eliza " 1853, 6, 20
        Elizabeth
         Jane   " 1854, 9, 22
        Lewis   " 1856, 9, 9 d 1881,10,--
        Tilman " 1860, 3, 19 " 1860, 4,11
        Anna
         Priscilla " 1861, 6, 18

1803, 12, 10. Mary & ch, Thomas, Mary, Es-
    ther, Sarah, Hope, Hannah & Josiah, rocf
    Southland MM, dtd 1803,9,28, endorsed by
    Westland MM, dtd 1803,11,26
1818, 12, 21. Isaac & w, Alice, & ch, Isaiah,
    Lucy Ann, Sarah & Levi, rocf Upper Eve-
    sham MM, N. J., dtd 1818,7,11
1820, 9, 18. Samuel recrq
1822, 9, 23. Mary, Sr. rocf Redstone MM, dtd
    1822,7,31
1824, 2, 23. Jesse recrq
1824, 2, 23. Anna recrq
1827, 10, 11. Alice dis disunity
1828, 5, 8. Mary Beans (form Garwood) dis
    mou
1829, 1, 8. Isaac dis disunity
1829, 4, 9. Asa dis disunity
1829, 11, 12. Anne dis jas
1830, 1, 7. Thomas dis disunity
1830, 1, 7. Elizabeth dis jH
1830, 6, 10. Elias dis disunity

1830, 8, 12. Phebe (late Armstrong) con mou
    (H)
1830, 9, 9. Isaiah, s Isaac, dis disunity
1830, 9, 9. Samuel dis jH
1831, 8, 11. Isaiah, s Daniel, dis disunity
1831, 8, 11. Mary dis disunity
1832, 9, 13. John dis disunity
1833, 6, 6. Isaiah dis jH
1834, 7, 10. Daniel, Jr. gct Salem MM
1834, 12, 11. Lucy Ann Holloway (form Gar-
    wood) dis mou
1836, 9, 19. Sarah, minor, gct Salem MM
1837, 5, 11. Daniel, s Thomas, dis mou
1839, 5, 9. Sarah dis joining Methodist
    Society
1844, 5, 9. Mary Nigh (form Garwood) dis
    mcd
1844, 7, 11. Sidney dis jas
1845, 5, 8. John dis joining Baptist Socie-
    ty
1845, 5, 8. Sidney, dt Thomas, dis jas
1847, 1, 14. Elizabeth Caldwell (form Gar-
    wood) con mcd (H)
1847, 5, 6. Ruth Allmon (form Garwood) dis
    mcd
1847, 5, 6. Thomas dis mou
1847, 6, 10. Elizabeth dis disunity
1848, 5, 11. Levi dis mou
1848, 8, 10. David, minor, gct Goshen MM
1851, 2, 6. Isaac dis mou
1857, 12, 10. Levi dis mcd
1858, 6, 19. Daniel & w, Ann, gct Salem MM
1859, 3, 19. Joseph dis mou
1864, 8, 20. John W. & w, Asenath H., & ch,
    Sylvanus P., Ann Eliza, Elizabeth J.,
    Lewis J. & Anna Pricilla, gct New Garden
    MM
1882, 7, 15. John W. & w, Asenath, & ch,
    Joseph & Rachel, rocf Springfield MM, dtd
    1882,6,23
1888, 11, 17. John W. & Asenath H. gct North
    Branch MM, Ia.
1888, 11, 17. Joseph gct North Branch MM, Ia.
1888, 11, 17. Rachel gct North Branch MM, Ia.

GEORGE
1817, 11, 10. Henry & w, Tamer, & ch, Caleb
    & Mary, rocf Hopewell MM, dtd 1817,9,4

GIBBONS
1834, 7, 10. Edward, minor, rocf Upper
    Springfield MM, dtd 1834,6,28
1846, 3, 12. Edward gc (H)
1864, 8, 17. Edward S. & Mary Ann attached
    to this mtg when Beaver Falls MM, Pa.
    was laid down (H)
1864, 8, 17. Francis attached to this mtg
    when Beaver Falls MM, Pa., was laid down
    (H)

GILBERT
1884, 6, 4. Walter b
1903, 10, 22. Rachel C. m Elisha LLEWELLYN

GILBERT, continued
1910, 8, --. Sarah W. d

1873, 5, 17. Sarah W. recrq
1899, 5, 20. Rachel C. (form Wickersham) dis
    mcd
1902, 12, 20. Rachel C. rst by rq

GODERT
1856, 6, 12. Frances (form Morlan) dis mou

GRAHAM
1834, 10, 9. Maria (form Hoops) con mou (H)
1844, 10, 10. Maria dis jas (H)

GREEN
1804, 7, 14. Lydia rocf Westland MM, dtd
    1804,4,28
1817, 12, 15. Lydia gct New Garden MM

GREWELL
1831, 4, 7. Moses, minor, rocf Marlborough
    MM, dtd 1831,1,25
1832, 6, 7. Moses [Grewel] gct Marlborough
    MM

GREY
1868, 5, 16. Louisa L. (form Cope) dis mcd

GRIFFITH
1856, 5, 15. Emmor H., s Israel & Letitia,
    Washington Co., Pa.; m at Middleton, Cyn-
    thea HEALD, dt Thomas & Mariam, Columbiana
    Co., O.

1818, 3, 16. William rocf Warrington MM, dtd
    1817,11,20
1819, 3, 22. William gct New Garden MM
1862, 5, 17. Cynthia gct Westland MM

GRISELL
1804, 3, 10. Martha & ch, Joseph, Rachel,
    Ann, Samuel, Thomas, Martha, Charles,
    Margaret & Hannah, rocf Westland MM, dtd
    1803,12,24

GROSSCUP
1855, 1, 11. Amanda (form Morlan) dis mou &
    jas

HAINES
1805, 1, 17. Hannah m Joseph REEDER
1806, 5, 13. Mahlon, s Levi & Elizabeth, Co-
    lumbiana Co., O.; m at Middleton, Rachel
    HATCHER, dt William & Mary, Columbiana
    Co., O.
1811, 10, 24. Levi, s Levi & Elizabeth, Co-
    lumbiana Co., O.; m at Middleton, Sarah
    HATCHER, dt William & Mary, Columbiana
    Co., O.

1804, 7, 14. Elizabeth & s, Levi, rocf South-
    land MM, Va., dtd 1804,5,2

1804, 7, 14. Hannah rocf Southland MM, dtd
    1804,5,2
1809, 5, 13. Mahlon [Hains] & w, Rachel, gct
    New Garden MM
1814, 7, 7. Rachel & ch, Enos, William, Mary,
    Anna & Elizabeth, rocf New Garden MM, dtd
    1814,6,16
1823, 11, 17. Enos, minor, gct New Garden MM
1830, 6, 10. Mary dis mcd
1864, 8, 17. Pauline attached to this mtg
    when Beaver Falls MM, Pa. was laid down
    (H)

HALL
----, --, --. Nathan P. b 1802,6,-- d 1867,
    5,19; m Rachel WILSON, dt Israel & Martha,
    b 1805,3,29 d 1835,12,12
    Ch: Israel   b 1825, 4, 10
        Jesse   " 1827, 9, 15 d 1866,11,30
        Isaac   " 1829, 9, 20
        Wilson   " 1832, 1, 25 d 1890, 4, 2
        Joseph   " 1834, 3, 26
    Nathan P. m 2nd Mareb COFFEE, dt John &
    Rachel, b 1800,9,16 d 1877,9,9
    Ch: Rachel   b 1840, 4, 11 d 1867, 6,26
        John C.   " 1842, 3, 12
        Chas. P.   " 1844, 6, 6
1858, 9, 23. Linton, s William & Hannah,
    Jefferson Co., O., b 1833,8,22 d 1910,2,
    28; m at Middleton, Ann W. ALLMON, dt
    Jehu & Hannah, Columbiana Co., O., b 1838,
    7,12 d 1916,4,15
    Ch: Cyrus   b 1859, 7, 15 d 1862, 7,31
        Hiel   " 1861, 9, 18
        Hannah Mary" 1863, 3, 25
        Phebe Elma " 1863, 3, 25
        Abner J.   " 1865, 8, 8 d 1917, 3,24
        Wilson M.   " 1868, 1, 4
        Chas. W.   " 1871, 5, 5
        Martha P.   " 1873, 4, 28
        Sarah L.   " 1876, 6, 1
        Edwin P.   " 1879, 11, 19
----, --, --. Wilson b 1832,1,25 d 1890,4,2;
    m Sina STRATTON, dt Joshua & Rachel, b
    1820,5,27 d 1896,3,20
    Ch: Edward   b 1858, 11, 22 d 1861,11,27
----, --, --. Joseph b 1834,3,26; m Rebecca S.
    ----- b 1836,4,7
    Ch: Wm. G.   b 1859, 10, 11
        Rachel W.   " 1862, 1, 22
1863, 6, 25. Elvira m Abner WOOLMAN
----, --, --. Pearson b 1851,8,15; m Miriam
    ELLYSON, dt Benjamin & Abigail, b 1850,3,
    17
    Ch: Edith E.   b 1870, 6, 8
        Bertha D.   " 1880, 4, 5
1877, 9, 9. Mary d ae 77y
----, --, --. Chas. P. b 1844,6,6; m Melissa
    ARMSTRONG, dt Dawsey & Sarah Ann, b 1844,
    2,14 d 1895,10,3
    Ch: Lillian B. b 1883, 3, 7
        Willis D.   " 1885, 1, 2
1886, 12, 23. Abner P., s Linton & Ann W.,

HALL, Abner P., continued
 Columbiana Co., O., b 1865,8,8 d 1917,3,
 24; m at Middleton, Anna M. MORLAN, dt
 Theophilus & Sarah P., b 1865,2,21
 Ch: Sarah
  Mabel b 1888, 4, 18
  Harlon L. " 1889, 10, 20 d 1890, 7,12
  Howard T. " 1891, 6, 1
  Vesta M. " 1892, 7, 23
  Bertha A. " 1895, 8, 4 d 1895,10,15
  Herbert D. " 1896, 8, 16
  Allen J. " 1902, 4, 8
----, --, --. Hiel S., s Linton & Ann W.
 (Allmon), b 1861,9,18 d 1928,5,27 bur
 Middleton; m Abigail BRIGGS, dt Henry &
 Talitha Ann (Wharton), b 1869,6,4
1897, 8, 26. Hannah Mary m Daniel S. MASTERS
1891, 5, 21. Wilson M., s Linton S. & Ann,
 Columbiana Co., O.; m at Middleton, Mary
 Anna EDGERTON, dt Jesse & Semira, Colum-
 biana Co., O., b 1866,8,15
 Ch: Jessie M. b 1894, 6, 23
  Foster A. " 1896, 10, 17
  Wilford F. " 1902, 2, 20
----, --, --. Charles W. b 1871,5,5; m Nettie
 M. BURT b 1874,3,26
 Ch: Velma M. b 1904, 1, 4
  Mildred " 1909, 8, 8
----, --, --. Edwin P. b 1879,11,19; m Minnie
 ----- b 1883,12,8
 Ch: Nellie Ruth
    b 1906, 12, 15
  Henry Lee " 1908, 11, 2
  Walter Lin-
  ton " 1910, 8, 3
  Ezra Ben-
  jamin " 1911, 12, 2
  Oscar
  Charles " 1913, 8, 20
  Harry Ed-
  win " 1916, 3, 31
1911, 11, 23. Sarah Mable m Thomas C. WARRING-
 TON
1912, 10, 22. Vestal M. m Joseph D. HENDERSON
----, --, --. Allen J. m Martha Frances MOORE,
 adopted dt of Harry & Frances (Cooper), b
 1902,9,9
 Ch: Margaret
  Louise b 1924, 6, 3
  Mabel Lu-
  cile " 1926, 3, 8
  Ralph
  Harlan " 1928, 8, 26
  Harry Er-
  vin " 1930, 5, 25 d 1933, 4, 9
  bur Middleton
----, --, --. Herbert David, s Abner G. &
 Anna (Morlan), b 1896,8,16; m Martha S.
 STARBUCK, dt Benjamin F. & Anna M. (Llew-
 ellyn), b 1895,5,28
 Ch: Kenneth
  Franklin b 1926, 12, 13

1858, 11, 20. Ann W. gct Short Creek MM
1859, 6, 18. Nathan P. & w, Mareh, & ch,
 John C. & Charles P., rocf Short Creek
 MM, dtd 1859,5,24
1859, 6, 18. Rachel rocf Short Creek MM, dtd
 1859,5,24
1859, 8, 20. Wilson & w, Sinah, & s, Edward,
 rocf Short Creek MM, dtd 1859,6,21
1860, 10, 20. Samuel Hollingsworth gct Still
 water MM, to m Martha Hall
1861, 2, 16. Martha Hollingsworth & ch, Mary
 Hall & Joseph Hall, rocf Stillwater MM,
 dtd 1861,1,26
1861, 4, 20. Elvira rocf Stillwater MM, dtd
 1861,2,23
1865, 11, 18. Martha Hollingsworth & s, Joseph
 Hall, gct New Garden MM
1865, 11, 18. Mary gct New Garden MM
1866, 11, 17. Wilson & w, Sina, gct Short
 Creek MM
1869, 3, 20. Linton & w, Ann, & ch, Hiel
 S., Hannah Mary, Phebe Elma, Abner J. &
 Wilson M., rocf Short Creek MM, dtd 1869,
 2,23
1872, 8, 17. John C. gct Frankford MM, Pa.
1873, 6, 21. William & w, Sinà, rocf Short
 Creek MM, dtd 1873,5,20
1873, 6, 21. Pearson rocf Short Creek MM,
 dtd 1873,5,20
1876, 1, 15. Pearson gct Hickory Grove MM,
 Ia., to m Miriam Ellyson
1877, 7, 21. Miriam rocf Hickory Grove MM,
 Ia., dtd 1877,6,2
1880, 5, 15. Charles P. gct Salem MM, to m
 Melissa Cope
1880, 12, 18. Melissa C. rocf Salem MM, dtd
 1880,11,24
1882, 3, 18. Pearson & w, Miriam, & ch,
 Edith E. & Bertha D., gct Hickory Grove
 MM, Ia.
1882, 12, 16. Joseph & w, Rebecca S., rocf
 Hickory Grove MM, Ia., dtd 1882,12,2
1883, 6, 16. John G. recrq (form mbr of Poplar Ridge MM, N. Y.)
1883, 12, 15. John G. gct Somerset MM, to m
 Anna Livezey
1884, 2, 16. John G. gct Somerset MM
1885, 5, 16. William G. rocf Hickory Grove
 MM, Ia.
1885, 5, 16. Rachel W. rocf Hickory Grove MM,
 Ia., dtd 1885,5,2
1887, 6, 18. William G. gct Hickory Grove MM,
 Ia.
1888, 5, 19. Joseph & w, Rebecca S., gct
 Goshen MM, Pa.
1889, 8, 17. Rachel W. gct Goshen MM, Pa.
1896, 4, 18. Charles P. & ch, Lillian B. &
 Willis D., gct Pasadena MM, Calif.
1897, 10, 16. Phebe Elma gct Short Creek MM,
 O.
1898, 1, 15. Hiel S. dis jas
1899, 1, 21. Charles W. con mcd
1899, 7, 15. Phebe Elma rocf Short Creek MM,

HALL, continued
dtd 1899,6,20
1899, 8, 19. Martha P. Smith (form Hall) con mcd
1901, 2, 16. Sarah L. Howard (form Hall) dis mcd
1907, 1, 18. Edwin P. dis mcd & jas
1907, 3, 16. Wilson M. & w, Maryanna, & ch, Jessie M., Foster A. & Wilford Linton, gct Upper Springfield MM
1908, 8, 15. Hiel S. rst by rq
1908, 12, 19. Hiel S. gct Salem MM, O., to m Abigail Briggs
1909, 4, 17. Abigail B. rocf Salem MM, O.
1913, 9, 20. Phebe E. Heston (form Hall) con mou
1915, 7, 17. Edwin P. rst in mbrp
1915, 9, 18. Minnie C. recrq
1915, 10, 16. Nellie Ruth, Henry Lee, Walter Linton, Ezra Benjamin & Oscar Charles, ch Edwin P. & Minnie C., recrq
1916, 3, 18. Howard T. gct Salem MM, to m
1916, 9, 15. Howard T. gct Stillwater MM
1917, 10, 20. Charles D. Kirk gct Short Creek MM, to m Tacy M. Hall
1918, 1, 19. Nettie M. & dt, Velina M. & Mildred, recrq
1918, 2, 16. Edwin P. & w, Minnie Catharine, & ch, Nellie Ruth, Henry Lee, Walter Linton, Ezra Benjamin, Oscar Charles & Harry Edwin, gct Upper Springfield MM
1919, 6, 21. Herbert D. gct Salem MM, to m Martha Starbuck
1920, 10, 16. Martha S. rocf Salem MM, O., dtd 1920,9,22
1923, 6, 16. Allen J. gct Salem MM, to m Martha F. Moore
1927, 4, 16. Martha Frances rocf Salem MM, dtd 1927,3,23
1928, 4, 21. Charles W. & w, Nettie M., & dt, Mildred, gct Upper Springfield MM

HAMBLETON
1815, 12, 14. Benjamin, s John & Rachel, Columbiana Co., O.; m at Carmel, Ann HANNA, dt Robert & Catherine, Columbiana Co., O.
1817, 12, 18. Rachel m Edward CARROLL
1814, 3, 10. Charles & Benjamin [Hamilton] rocf Baltimore MM, dtd 1814,1,12
1815, 3, 9. James & w, Martha, & ch, Mary & Edward, rocf Baltimore MM, dtd 1814,1,11
1815, 3, 9. Martha & dt, Mary, rocf Baltimore MM, dtd 1815,1,11
1815, 12, 7. Rachel rocf London Grove MM, Pa., dtd 1815,9,6
1816, 9, 16. Benjamin recrq (form dis by Short Creek MM)
1817, 12, 18. Mary [Hamilton] (form Hatcher) dis mou
1826, 7, 17. Mary rocf Carmel MM, dtd 1826, 7,15
1827, 6, 7. Mary Townsend (form Hambleton) dis mou

HAMLIN
1816, 9, 19. William, s Charles & Martha, Stark Co., O.; m at Fairfield, Hannah HOLLOWAY, dt Asa & Mary, Columbiana Co.,O.

1816, 11, 11. Hannah gct Marlborough MM

HANNA
----, --, --. Robert & Catharine
        Ch: Thos.   b 1777, 5, 2
            Benj.   " 1779, 6, 14
            Esther   " 1781, 7, 6
            David   " 1784, 1, 9
            Caleb   " 1786, 8, 4
            Robert   " 1789, 5, 28
            Esther   " 1792, 4, 10; m Chas.
             Hole
            Catharine " 1794, 11, 25
            Ann   " 1797, 7, 30
            Joshua   " 1802, 2, 16
1790, 7, 15. Caleb d
1791, 10, 24. David d
1791, 11, 5. Esther d bur South River Mtg
1803, 12, 15. Benj., s Robert & Catharine, Columbiana Co., O., b 1779,6,14; m at Middleton, Rachel DIXSON, dt Joshua & Dinah, Columbiana Co., O., b 1785,7,19
        Ch: Joshua   b 1804, 11, 8
            Leonard   " 1806, 3, 4
            Levi   " 1808, 2, 7
            Zalinda   " 1810, 2, 23
            Robert   " 1812, 8, 15
1804, 9, 11. Joshua d bur Middleton
1811, 5, 16. Esther m Charles HOLE
1815, 12, 14. Ann m Benj. HAMBLETON
1835, 2, 19. Anne m Thomas MERCER (H)

1808, 7, 9. Thomas gct Salem MM
1809, 5, 13. Thomas & w, Anne, rocf Salem MM, dtd 1809,1,17
1809, 6, 10. Thomas [Hannah] & w, Anna, rocf Salem MM, dtd 1809,1,17
1811, 3, 9. Robert, Jr. dis joining Methodist Society
1814, 12, 8. Rachel & fam gct Salem MM
1815, 1, 12. Benjamin & w, Rachel, & ch, Joshua, Leonard, Levi, Zalinda, Robert, Tryphena & Tryphosa, gct Salem MM
1833, 8, 8. Samuel Nichols gct Newgarden MM, to m Triphena Hanna (H)
1835, 1, 8. Anne rocf New Garden MM, dtd 1834,11,20 (H)
1855, 8, 16. Stephen Fish gct Salem MM, to m Hannah K. Hanna (H)

HAPGOOD
1846, 12, 24. George N., s George & Adeline, Columbiana Co., O.; m at Columbiana, Rebecca A. DIXON, dt John & Hannah, Columbiana Co., O. (H)

1848, 3, 16. Rebecca A. gct Salem MM (H)

HARDY
1830, 8, 12. Benjamin F. rocf Sandwich MM,
    New Hampshire, dtd 1830,7,15
1834, 5, 8. Benjamin gct Radnor MM, Pa.

HARRIS
----, --, --. Wm. & Elizabeth
    Ch: Mary   b 1772, 7, 29
        Hannah   " 1775, 9, 25
        Levi   " 1777, 9, 27
        Jonas   " 1779, 1, 30

1819, 8, 23. Jonas & w, Hannah, & ch, Mary,
    William, Charity, Henry, Jesse, Jonas,
    Jacob & Lydia, gct Blue River MM
1830, 6, 10. Ann Elizabeth, minor, rocf Sads-
    bury MM, dtd 1830,3,2 (H)
1845, 11, 6. Ann Elizabeth gct Cherry St.
    MM, Phila. (H)

HARRISON
----, --, --. Latham b 1785,2,25 d 1877,10,31
1809, 4, 12. Latham, s Benjamin & Miriam,
    Columbiana Co., O.; m at Elkrun, Mary
    JAMES, dt Isaac & Sarah, Columbiana Co.,
    O.
1810, 3, 15. William, s Benjamin & Mirriam,
    Columbiana Co., O.; m at Fairfield, Mary
    DIXON, dt Henry & Elizabeth, Columbiana
    Co., O.
1812, 9, 16. Ann m Joseph JAMES
----, --, --. Benjamin b 1822,1,11; m Mary
    ----- b 1821,2,3 d 1900,1,9
    Ch: Mary
        Elizabeth b 1844, 7, 1
        Lucinda
        Ann   " 1848, 12, 24
        Matilda
        Ellen   " 1852, 5, 22 d 1911, 9,10
        John Frank-
        lin   " 1856, 9, 10
        Sabina Jane " 1859, 9, 6
1869, 10, 21. Lucinda Ann m Abner ALLMON
1873, 5, 22. Matilda E. m Daniel BLACKBURN
1806, 4, 12. Benjamin & w, Mariam, & ch,
    Latham, William, Ann & Thomas, rocf Pipe
    Creek MM, dtd 1805,12,14
1806, 9, 13. Elizabeth & Rachel [Harison]
    rocf Redstone MM, dtd 1806,5,30
1811, 5, 9. Rachel & Elizabeth gct New Gar-
    den MM
1813, 6, 10. Rachel rocf New Garden MM, dtd
    1813,5,13
1828, 4, 10. Eliza Chamberlain (form Harri-
    son) dis mou
1829, 5, 7. William dis disunity
1829, 5, 7. Mary dis disunity
1833, 9, 12. Ann dis disunity
1842, 5, 12. Amy Bradfield (form Harrison)
    dis mcd
1851, 2, 6. William, Jr. dis mou
1858, 2, 11. Edward H. dis mou
1878, 11, 16. John Franklin dis mcd

1880, 4, 17. Sabina Jane dis disunity
1892, 2, 20. Benjamin dis disunity
1911, 8, 19. Mary Elizabeth gct Salem MM, O.

HARVEY
1806, 10, 13. Catharine m Samuel SMITH
1912, 2, 22. Henry Salonis, s Henry S. &
    Andromeda, Los Angeles Co., Calif., b
    1888,7,5; m Rebecca DINGEE, dt Jacob &
    Rebecca A., Columbiana Co., O., b 1883,3,
    31
    Ch: Elizabeth
        Meda   b 1913, 3, 30
        Jacob Mar-
        vin   " 1915, 8, 9
        Jesse Hen-
        ry   " 1918, 9, 14
        Anna Mary   " 1922, 4, 18 d 1923, 4,21
        bur Frds Cemetery, Pasadena, Calif.

1912, 6, 15. Henry Salonis rocf Pasadena MM,
    Calif., dtd 1912,5,15
1923, 6, 16. Henry Salonis & w, Rebecca D.,
    & ch, Elizabeth Meda, Jacob Marvin, Jesse
    Henry & Lydia Beulah, gct Pasadena MM,
    Calif.

HATCHER
----, --, --. Wm. b 1765,5,27; m Mary -----
    b 1771,1,7
    Ch: Rachel   b 1790, 2, 7
        John   " 1791, 5, 10
        Sarah   " 1792, 4, 3
        Thos.   " 1793, 11, 3
        John   " 1795, 12, 9
        Hannah   " 1797, 12, 20
        Jesse   " 1799, 10, 7
        Wm.   " 1803, 4, 10
        Mary   " 1805, 1, 28
        Samuel   " 1807, 7, 9
        Joshua   " 1809, 5, 12
        Ann   " 1812, 3, 29
1806, 5, 13. Rachel m Mahlon HAINES
1811, 10, 24. Sarah m Levi HAINES
1814, 9, 15. Thomas, s William & Mary, Colum-
    biana Co., O.; m at Middleton, Ruth ADAM-
    SON, dt James & Hannah, Columbiana Co., O.
1816, 1, 18. John, s William & Mary, Columbi-
    ana Co., O.; m at Middleton, Rebecca ADAM-
    SON, dt James & Hannah, Columbiana Co., O.
    Ch: Rachel   b 1817, 1, 2
        Nathan   " 1818, 11, 30
        Ruth   " 1820, 2, 18
        Mary Ann   " 1822, 1, 12
1819, 5, 6. Nathan, s John, d bur Middleton
1820, 3, 30. Hannah m Samuel DIXON
1836, 3, 24. Rachel m John P. MERCER (H)

1817, 5, 12. Thomas & w, Ruth, & ch, Hannah
    & James, gct New Garden MM
1818, 12, 21. Jesse dis disunity
1819, 5, 17. Thomas & w, Ruth, & ch, Hannah
    & James, rocf New Garden MM, dtd 1819,3,25

HATCHER, continued
1822, 1, 29. William, Jr. dis disunity
1823, 1, 20. Thomas dis mou
1824, 9, 20. Mary Hamilton (form Hatcher) dis
    mou
1829, 1, 8. John dis joining Separatists
1829, 10, 8. Rebecca dis jH
1830, 4, 8. Anna Chain (form Hatcher) .dis
    mou
1830, 6, 10. Joshua dis disunity
1831, 1, 6. Samuel dis disunity
1833, 2, 5. Hannah & James, ch Thomas, gct
    Marlborough MM
1833, 12, 12. Lydia rocf Goose Creek MM, Va.,
    dtd 1833,10,17 (H)
1836, 7, 18. Rachel Mercer (form Hatcher) dis
    mou & jH
1846, 8, 13. Lydia gct Stillwater MM, O. (H)
1847, 2, 11. Lydia Ann Woods (form Hatcher)
    dis mou
1847, 12, 9. Eliza Ann dis disunity

HATFIELD
1815, 10, 12. James recrq
1820, 5, 22. James gct Marlborough MM

HAWLEY
1809, 8, 17. David, s Caleb & Hannah, Colum-
    biana Co., O.; m at Fairfield, Rachel
    BEAL, dt Joseph & Hannah, Columbiana Co.,
    O.
1817, 10, 15. Caleb, s Caleb & Hannah, Colum-
    biana Co., O.; m at Elkrun, Catharine
    JAMES, dt Isaac & Sarah, Columbiana Co.,O.
1821, 12, 27. Mary m David BISHOP
1841, 3, 18. Elizabeth m Eli CADWALADER (H)

1810, 12, 8. Amos dis disunity
1818, 11, 23. Richard gct Plainfield MM, to
    m Rachel Paxton
1819, 5, 17. Caleb & w, Catharine, & s, Jo-
    seph, gct New Garden MM
1819, 9, 20. Richard gct Plainfield MM
1823, 4, 21. Elisha & Jesse gct Salem MM
1823, 4, 21. Hannah, Sr. & Hannah, Jr. gct
    Salem MM
1823, 5, 19. Benjamin gct Salem MM
1829, 1, 8. Rachel dis jH
1831, 7, 7. Amanda & Elizabeth dis jH
1848, 8, 17. Rachel & Amanda gct Clear Creek
    MM, Ill. (H)

HAYCOCK
1808, 4, 9. Jonathan [Heacock] rocf Derby
    Creek MM, Pa., dtd 1807,12,3
1809, 1, 14. Sarah (form Underwood) con mcd
1809, 1, 14. Jonathan dis mou
1809, 3, 11. Susanna con mcd
1817, 3, 10. Jacob [Heacock] rocf Darby MM,
    Pa., dtd 1816,11,26
1817, 4, 14. Ann Sarah & Elizabeth, ch Su-
    sannah, recrq

HEALD
1768, 4, 18. Elisabeth b
1879, 10, 11. Abi, minister, d ae 60y
----, --, --. John b 1763,9,5; m Phebe -----
    b 1763,6,18
    Ch: Rebecca   b 1787, 6, 21
        Mary   " 1789, 2, 10
        Joseph   " 1791, 2, 14
        Martha   " 1793, 6, 7
        Ruth   " 1795, 6, 5
        Thos.   " 1797, 5, 25
        Nathan   " 1799, 12, 26
        Jane   " 1802, 11, 15
----, --, --. Wm. b 1766,1,10 d 1867,4,6; m
    Sarah ----- b 1767,11,29
    Ch: Rachel   b 1793, 7, 16
        Joseph   " 1795, 1, 7 d 1802, 5,15
        Elizabeth " 1796, 10, 3
        Wm. W.   " 1798, 4, 27
        Abner   " 1799, 11, 20 d 1847, 8,13
        Sarah   " 1802, 1, 31
        John   " 1804, 2, 3
        Israel   " 1807, 1, 11
        Lydia   " 1810, 8, 22
----, --, --. Nathan Jr. b 1777,11,10; m Ra-
    chel ----- b 1781,10,3
    Ch: Anne   b 1799, 2, 4
        Jesse   " 1801, 1, 3
        Hannah   " 1802, 10, 22
        Sarah   " 1805, 2, 10
        Ruth   " 1806, 5, 19
        Wm.   " 1808, 9, 13
        Rachel
        Smith   " 1810, 6, 30
        Lizzy
        Stokes   " 1812, 7, 22
        Smith   " 1814, 6, 22
        Nathan   " 1817, 1, 22
1808, 1, 14. James, s Nathan & Rebecca, Co-
    lumbiana Co., O.; m at Middleton, Mary
    WILSON, dt Wm. & Elizabeth, Washington
    Co., Pa.
    Ch: Levi   b 1808, 11, 27
        Wm. W.   " 1810, 6, 13
        Hannah   " 1812, 2, 14
        Chas.   " 1814, 2, 24
1810, 9, 20. Rachel m Thomas SHAW
1811, 1, 3. Mary m James ARMSTRONG
1814, 11, 7. Hannah, dt James, d
1814, 11, 17. Rachel m Samuel OLIPHANT
1816, 1, 18. Elizabeth m Ephraim OLIPHANT
1816, 11, 14. Joseph, s John & Phebe, Colum-
    biana Co., O.; m at Carmel, Ury Betsy
    HOLE, dt Jonah & Betsy, Bedford Co., Va.
1818, 10, 29. William W., s William & Sarah,
    Columbiana Co., O.; m at Middleton, Su-
    sanna HUTTON, dt John & Jane, Washington
    Co., Pa.
    Ch: Jane   b 1819, 7, 31
        Sarah   " 1821, 9, 18
        Joseph   " 1823, 10, 12
        Amy   " 1825, 3, 29
        Hannah   " 1826, 12, 16

HEALD, William W. & Susanna, continued
        Ch: Rachel   b 1828, 11, 4
            Joel   " 1830, 8, 2
            Celina   " 1832, 4, 30
            Ann   " 1834, 2, 4
            Elizabeth   " 1835, 11, 2
1820, 3, 2. Sarah m Elisha HOLLINGSWORTH
1820, 11, 20. Rebecca, w Nathan, d
1820, 11, 2. Ruth m Eli EDMUNDSON
1822, 1, 3. Rebecca m Aden MORLAN
----, --, --. Abner b 1799,11,20 d 1847,8,13
     bur Middleton; m Ruth DIXON, dt John,
     d 1822,9,1
        Ch: Sidwell   b 1825, 8, 3
            Jonathan   " 1827, 11, 3 d 1847, 8,19
              (or 1847,8,13) bur Middleton
            Ruth   b 1831, 1, 5
            Henry   " 1839, 7, 14
            Sinah
            Sllen   " 1844, 7, 21
            Wm.   " 1846, 9, 11
1826, 12, 14. Nathan d bur Middleton
1828, 8, 14. Israel, s William & Sarah, Co-
     lumbiana Co., O.; m at Middleton, Lydia
     ALLEN, dt Isaac & Sarah, Columbiana Co.,O.
----, --, --. Israel b 1807,1,11; m Lydia
     ALLEN, dt Isaac & Sarah, b 1805,12,23 d
     1837,9,11 bur Middleton
        Ch: Allen   b 1829, 7, 1
            Isaac   " 1831, 7, 9
     Israel m 2nd Rebecca HOLE, dt Chas. & Es-
     ther, b 1813,11,13
        Ch: Ezra   b 1843, 8, 24
            Lydia A.   " 1845, 2, 2 d 1859,10, 8
            Mary Ann   " 1846, 9, 12
            Lindley   " 1848, 3, 25
            Esther   " 1850, 3, 31 d 1852, 9,21
            Cynthia   " 1852, 3, 3
            Charles   " 1854, 4, 25 d 1855, 4, 2
----, --, --. Nathan & Elizabeth
        Ch: David   b 1832, 12, 25
            Louis   " 1835, 1, 22
            Mahlon   " 1837, 1, 21
            John   " 1839, 9, 6
            Abner   " 1841, 5, 24
1834, 3, 13. Ann, dt W. W., d bur Middleton
1836, 3, 31. Lydia m Albert T. SHARPLIS
1840, 8, 29. Sarah, w W., d bur Middleton
1840, 4, 16. Jane m Daniel WALKER
1841, 5, 26. John d bur Middleton
1842, 11, 17. Edith m Austin McCONNELL
1845, 8, 14. Phebe m William SHAW
1846, 3, 19. Sidwell, s Abner & Sina, Colum-
     biana Co., O.; m at Middleton, Mary HICK-
     LEN, dt Samuel & Susannah, Columbiana Co.,
     O.
1847, 5, 18. Phebe, w John, d bur Middleton
1848, 7, 13. Ruth m John EDMUNDSON
1848, 10, 19. Maria m John OLIPHANT
1856, 5, 15. Cynthia m Emmor H. GRIFFITH
1858, 8, 5. Martha, dt John & Phebe, d bur
     Middleton
----, --, --. Matthew b 1850,6,22; m Sarah

     Ellen ------ b 1854,10,16
        Ch: Sarah
            Ellen   b 1876, 1, 19
            David M.   " 1879, 7, 5
            Eva A.   " 1882, 6, 10
            Edwin C.   " 1884, 12, 11
1879, 10, 23. Joseph, s James & Abi, Linn
     Co., Ia.; m at Middleton, Adaline STAPLE-
     TON, dt David & Martha, Johnson Co., Ia.

1805, 10, 12. Rachel rocf Westland MM, dtd
     1805,9,28
1816, 2, 12. James & w, Mary, & ch, Levi,
     William W. & Charles, gct New Garden MM
1818, 6, 15. Joseph & w, Ury, & s, Hiel, gct
     Carmel MM
1821, 6, 18. Tacy recrq
1821, 10, 22. Thomas gct Carmel MM, to m
     Miriam Marsh
1822, 2, 18. Miriam rocf Carmel MM, dtd
     1822,2,16
1822, 5, 20. Abner gct Redstone MM, to m
     Ruth Dixson
1822, 10, 21. Tacy gct New Garden MM
1824, 7, 19. Abner gct Short Creek MM, to m
     Cinah Sidwell
1824, 11, 22. Cinah rocf Short Creek MM, dtd
     1824,9,19
1826, 6, 12. William, minor, rocf Carmel MM,
     dtd 1826,2,16
1827, 8, 9. John, Jr. dis mou
1828, 7, 10. Jane dis
1829, 3, 12. William W. dis JH
1830, 3, 11. William, Jr. gct Carmel MM
1830, 9, 9. Nathan, Jr. gct Sandy Spring
     MM, to m Elizabeth Heston
1831, 5, 12. Nathan, Jr. gct Sandy Spring MM
1832, 8, 9. Nathan & w, Elizabeth, rocf
     Sandy Spring MM, dtd 1832,6,22
1832, 11, 8. Jane rst in mbrp
1838, 8, 9. Samuel Shaw gct Carmel MM, to
     m Peninah Heald
1840, 6, 11. Silas Allmon gct Carmel MM, to
     m Phebe Elma Heald
1842, 7, 7. Israel gct Carmel MM, to m Re-
     becca Hole
1842, 10, 6. Rebecca rocf Carmel MM, dtd
     1842,9,17
1844, 12, 12. William W. & w, Susannah, & ch,
     Joseph, Hannah, Rachel, Joel, Celina &
     Elizabeth, gct Gilead MM
1844, 12, 12. Sarah gct Gilead MM
1845, 5, 8. Amy gct Gilead MM
1845, 9, 11. Elizabeth, w Nathan, & ch, Da-
     vid, Lewis, Mahlon, John & Abner, gct San-
     dy Spring MM
1848, 7, 6. Nathan gct Sandy Spring MM
1849, 10, 11. Allen gct Carmel MM, to m Re-
     becca Neal
1850, 7, 11. Rebecca rocf Carmel MM, dtd
     1850,6,15
1851, 4, 10. Sidwell con mou
1851, 7, 10. William Shaw gct Gilead MM, to

HEALD, continued
to m Hannah Heald

1852, 1, 8. Sidwell gct Allum Creek MM
1858, 4, 17. James & w, Abi, & ch, Joseph S.,
Mathew, Edwin, Francis & Charles, rocf
New Garden MM, dtd 1858,3,25
1858, 7, 17. Ury B. & s, Abner, gct Plymouth
MM
1858, 7, 17. Martha Jane gct Plymouth MM
1862, 1, 18. Sina L. & ch, Sina Ellen &
William, gct Pennsville MM
1862, 1, 18. Henry gct Pennsville MM
1864, 3, 19. Jane gct Salem MM
1864, 5, 21. Isaac con mou
1865, 2, 18. Lucena H. Michener (form Heald)
con mcd
1866, 3, 17. Isaac gct Hickory Grove MM, Ia.
1866, 12, 15. Israel & w, Rebecca, & ch, Lindley & Cynthia, gct Hickory Grove MM, Ia.
1866, 12, 15. Ezra gct Hickory Grove MM, Ia.
1866, 12, 15. Mary Ann gct Hickory Grove MM,
Ia.
1867, 10, 19. Sarah gct Hickory Grove MM, Ia.
1869, 6, 19. Thomas & w, Miriam, gct Hickory
Grove MM, Ia.
1869, 6, 19. Cyrus gct Hickory Grove MM, Ia.
1870, 7, 16. John dis mcd
1870, 9, 17. Joseph S. gct Springville MM,
Ia.
1870, 10, 15. Allen & w, Rebecca, & ch, Alice,
William F. & Clarence, gct Coal Creek MM,
Ia.
1875, 6, 19. Matthew W. con mou
1876, 1, 15. Sarah Ellen recrq
1876, 5, 20. Matthew W. & w, Sarah Ellen, &
dt, Sarah Elnora, gct Springville MM, Ia.
1876, 5, 20. Edwin T. gct Springville MM, Ia.
1880, 3, 20. Adeline S. gct Springville MM,
Ia.
1881, 4, 16. Lewis J. con mou
1882, 3, 18. James & Lewis J. gct Hickory
Grove MM, Ia.
1886, 8, 21. Sarah & ch, Sarah Elnora, David
M., Eva A. & Edwin C., rocf Springville
MM, Ia., dtd 1886,7,17
1887, 3, 19. Matthew rocf Springville MM,
Ia., dtd 1887,2,19
1905, 6, 17. Eva A. Huntley (form Heald) dis
mou & jas
1905, 6, 17. Elnora S. Stewart (form Heald)
dis mcd
1906, 9, 15. David M. dis mcd & jas
1906, 9, 15. Edwin C. dis mcd & jas

HENDERSON

1912, 10, 22. Joseph D., s James & Eunice
H., Belmont Co., O.; m at Middleton, Vesta
M. HALL, dt Abner I. & Anna M., Columbiana
Co., O.

1913, 1, 18. Vesta M. gct Stillwater MM

HENRY

1819, 6, 21. Susannah (form Lewis) con mou
1829, 7, 9. Susannah dis disunity

HEPBOURN

1812, 6, 11. Thomas recrq

HESTON

----, --, --. Lydia, w Cyrus, b 1836,7,28
d 1909,11,19
1863, 3, 25. Phebe Elma, w Cyrus, dt Linton
& Ann W. (Allmon) Hall, b

1830, 9, 9. Nathan Heald, Jr. gct Sandy
Spring MM, to m Elizabeth Heston
1857, 7, 9. Lydia (form Allmon) con mcd
1813, 9, 20. Phebe E. (form Hall) con mou

HEWLING

1867, 7, 20. Lydia S. [Hewlings], minor,
recrq
1887, 5, 21. Lydia S. gct Short Creek MM

HICKLEN

----, --, --. Samuel b 1777,3,25 d 1867,11,14;
m Susannah DIXON, dt John, b 1786,4,13
d 1856,10,--
Ch: Ruth D.   b 1821, 3, 19 d 1893, 5, 1
John   " 1823, 10, 25 " 1847,11, 8
Mary   " 1827, 1, 12 " 1848,11,15
1823, 10, 22. Jane m Isaac DIXON
1846, 3, 19. Mary m Sidwell HEALD
1846, 9, 24. John, s Samuel & Susannah, Columbiana Co., O., b 1823,10,25 d 1847,11,
8 bur Middleton; m at Middleton, Mary Ann
OLOPHANT, dt Ephraim & Elizabeth, Columbiana Co., O., b 1827,3,30
Ch: Sarah Ann b 1847, 10, 15

1820, 5, 22. Samuel & w, Susannah, & ch,
Jane & Susanna, rocf Marlborough MM, dtd
1820,4,20
1832, 7, 12. Susannah, Jr. dis jH
1862, 3, 15. Mary Ann Jackson (form Hicklen)
dis mcd
1805, 11, 9. Lydia rocf Kennet MM, dtd 1805,
10,8
1830, 3, 11. Lydia dis jH
1841, 5, 6. Lydia gct Marlborough MM (H)
1847, 1, 7. Martha (form Mercer) dis mou

HILL

1822, 12, 9. Phebe, dt Wm., b
1825, 7, 21. Amos Line, s Wm. & Ruth, b

1822, 5, 20. William recrq
1822, 9, 23. Ruth rocf Redstone MM, dtd
1822,7,31
1826, 4, 17. Mary, William, Elihu & Ruth, ch
William & Ruth, recrq
1833, 9, 12. Mary Ellis (form Hill) dis mou
1839, 5, 9. Elihu dis mou
1841, 1, 7. William, Jr. dis mou

HILL, continued
1841, 6, 10. Ruth Matthews (form Hill) dis
    mcd
1845, 1, 9. Phebe Miller (form Hill) dis
    mcd

HILLIS
1840, 8, 6. Nathan & w, Sarah, & ch, Skip-
    with C., William, Robert, Samuel & Rachel
    Ann, rocf Salem MM, dtd 1840,7,22 (H)
1844, 9, 12. Nathan & w, Sarah, & ch, Skip-
    with C., William, Robert, Samuel, Rachel
    Ann & John P., gct Plainfield MM, O.

HIRST
----, --, --. Mary b 1810,10,21 d 1891,4,30

1873, 8, 16. Mary Ann rocf Plymouth MM, O.,
    dtd 1873,7,21

HOAG
1838, 1, 6. Nathan Lindley, s Joseph D. &
    Dorcas, b

1837, 10, 23. Joseph D. & w, Dorcas, & s, Jo-
    seph Jonathan, rocf Berwick MM, Maine,
    dtd 1837,8,17
1843, 3, 9. Joseph D. & w, Dorcas T., & ch,
    Joseph Jonathan & Nathan Lindley, gct
    Salem MM, Ia.

HOBSON
1855, 2, 8. Ann M. gct Plymouth MM

HODGE
1832, 4, 12. Mary (form Taylor) dis mcd & JH

HOLE
1811, 5, 16. Chas., s Jacob & Mary, Columbi-
    ana Co., O., b 1783,6,27; m at Middleton,
    Esther HANNA, dt Robt.& Catharine, b
    1792,4,10
    Ch: Thos.   b 1812, 1, 2
        Rebecca   " 1813, 11, 13
        Catharine " 1816, 1, 24
1816, 9, 19. Tacy m Daniel MERCER
1816, 11, 14. Ury Betsy m Joseph HEALD
1818, 10, 29. Nathan, s Jacob & Mary, Columbi-
    ana Co., O.; m at Middleton, Sarah ARM-
    STRONG, dt James & Ruth, Columbiana Co.,O.
1842, 3, 17. Ethan Allen, s Nathan & Sarah,
    Columbiana Co., O., d 1878,11,23; m Mary
    N. COPE, dt Joseph & Elizabeth, Columbiana
    Co., O.
    Ch: Mary Nichols b 1842,11, 13
    Ethan Allen m 2nd Hannah WOODS, dt Samuel
    & Esther, b 1824,4,7 d 1890,3,3
    Ch: Samuel T.   b 1847, 7, 6
        Sarah Ann   " 1851, 6. 18 (or 1851,6,25)
        John Frank
        lin   " 1853, 8, 29
1842, 11, 19. Mary Nichols, w E. A., d bur
    Middleton

1846, 7, 16. Ethan Allen, s Nathan & Sarah,
    Columbiana Co., O.; m at Middleton, Hannah
    WOODS, dt Samuel & Esther, Columbiana Co.,
    O.
1846, 8, 13. James M., s Nathan & Sarah, Co-
    lumbiana Co., O.; m at Middleton, Hannah
    BAKER, dt Jesse & Eliza, Columbiana Co.,O.
1849, 10, 18. Samuel, s Nathan & Sarah, Co-
    lumbiana Co., O.; m at Middleton, Rebecca
    WOODS, dt Samuel & Esther, Columbiana
    Co., O., b 1827,5,6
    Ch: Mary
        Louisa   b 1850, 6, 30
        Emerson
        Bennett   " 1853, 4, 22
        Ruth Anna " 1855, 8, 10

1808, 8, 13. Ann, Tacy & Elizabeth recrq
1809, 7, 8. Charles recrq
1812, 8, 6. Charles & Esther recrq
1814, 12, 8. Ury Betsy recrq
1815, 9, 7. David & w, Anne, & ch, Elen,
    Catharine, Tacy, Jesse, Tirzah & Mary,
    recrq
1817, 10, 13. John recrq
1818, 12, 21. Sarah gct New Garden MM
1842, 7, 7. Israel Heald gct Carmel MM, to
    m Rebecca Hole
1843, 11, 9. Ethan Allen rocf Carmel MM, dtd
    1843,7,15
1847, 3, 11. Hannah B. gct Salem MM
1850, 7, 11. Samuel rocf Carmel MM, dtd
    1850,6,15
1852, 1, 8. Nathan & w, Sarah, rocf Carmel
    MM, dtd 1851,12,20
1852, 1, 8. Sarah Jr. rocf Carmel MM, dtd
    1851,12,20
1853, 12, 8. Nathan & w, Sarah, gct Salem MM
1854, 2, 9. Sarah Roller (form Hole) dis mou
1860, 10, 20. Mary Teegarden (form Hole) dis
    mou
1863, 7, 18. Benjamin & Jacob dis joining
    Separatists
1864, 11, 19. Hannah dis joining Separatists
1873, 1, 18. Samuel J. dis mcd
1873, 4, 19. Mary Louisa Young (form Hole)
    dis mcd
1873, 11, 15. Samuel T. dis mcd
1873, 12, 20. Mary N. dis jas
1878, 6, 15. Franklin dis mcd
1882, 4, 15. Emerson B. dis mcd & jas

HOLLAND
1811, 8, 8. Sarah & ch, William W., Susannah
    John B. & Catharine, recrq
1814, 12, 8. Samuel H. & w, Sarah, & ch,
    William, Susannah, John, Catharine, Sarah
    & Hannah, gct New Garden MM

HOLLINGSWORTH
1818, 12, 29. Sarah, dt E., d bur Middleton
1819, 7, 16. E. d bur Middleton
1820, 3, 2. Elisha, s Er & Phebe, Columbi-

HOLLINGSWORTH, Elisha, continued
    ana Co., O., b 1798,12,16 d 1869,8,22
    bur Middleton; m Sarah HEALD, dt Wm. & Sa-
    rah, b 1802,1,31 d 1839,10,21
    Ch: Edwin   b 1821, 6, 29
        Ruth   " 1823, 7, 7
        Phebe   " 1825, 2, 17
        Er   " 1827, 5, 3
        Martha   " 1829, 6, 11
        Wm.   " 1831, 8, 15
        Lydia   " 1833, 5, 31
        Ezra   " 1836, 1, 22
1823, 10, 13. Phebe m William LEECH
----, --, --. Samuel b 1796,8,2 d 1864,5,18;
    m Margaret LEECH, dt Wm., b 1804,12,8
    d 1856,4,1
    Ch: Jane   b 1825, 4, 13 d 1838, 5, 6
         bur Middleton
        Phebe Ann b 1827, 9, 25
        Louis   " 1831, 3, 5
        Sarah   " 1833, 8, 12
        Thomas   " 1835, 11, 1
        Hannah   " 1838, 1, 4
        Mary L.   " 1840, 4, 20 d 1840, 7,29
         bur Middleton
        Wm.   b 1842, 2, 12 " 1854, 9,30
        Margaret " 1844, 6, 7
        Samuel A. " 1847, 8, 26 " 1854, 9,28
        James Er " 1850, 7, 30 " 1854, 9,17
----, --, --. Edwin b 1821,6,29 d 1905,7,3;
    m Betsy H. ----- b 1823,5,12 d 1900,10,27
1848, 8, 17. Phebe Ann m Jonathan EDMUNDSON
1861, 9, 24. Hannah Y. m Louis COPE
1863, 9, 24. Margaret m Joseph S. VAN LAW

1817, 6, 16. Er & w, Phebe, & ch, Samuel,
    Elisha, Sarah Jane, Ann & Mahlon, rocf
    Centre MM, Del., dtd 1817,5,5
1824, 1, 19. Phebe Leech & ch, Ann & Mahlon
    Hollingsworth, gct Carmel MM
1824, 4, 19. Samuel gct Carmel MM, to m Mar-
    garet Leech
1824, 10, 18. Margaret rocf Carmel MM, dtd
    1824,8,21
1828, 7, 10. Jane Kimble (form Hollingsworth)
    dis mou
1831, 5, 12. Mahlon, minor, rocf Carmel MM,
    dtd 1831,4,16
1837, 5, 11. Elisha & w, Sarah, & ch, Edwin,
    Ruth, Phebe, Er, Martha, William, Lydia &
    Ezra, gct Pennsville MM, O.
1838, 10, 11. Mahlon dis disunity
1839, 7, 11. Louisa rocf WD MM, Phila., Pa.,
    dtd 1839,4,24
1849, 5, 10. Lewis gct Salem MM
1860, 10, 20. Samuel gct Stillwater MM, to m
    Martha Hall
1861, 2, 16. Martha Hollingsworth & ch, Mary
    Hall & Joseph Hall, rocf Stillwater MM,
    dtd 1861,1,26
1862, 3, 15. Thomas dis mou
1865, 11, 18. Martha Hollingsworth & s, Jo-
    seph Hall, gct New Garden MM

1874, 8, 15. Charles Blackburn gct Plymouth
    MM, O., to m Sarah Hollingsworth
1894, 4, 21. Edwin & w, Betsy H., rocf Ply-
    mouth MM, dtd 1894,3,19

HOLLOWAY
1807, 3, 19. Mary m Daniel GARWOOD
1808, 10, 13. Sarah m Israel SCOTT
1812, 10, 14. Aaron, s Jesse & Sarah, Colum-
    biana Co., O.; m at Middleton, Olive
    MERCER, dt Daniel & Alice, Columbiana Co.,
    O.
1815, 8, 17. Isaac, s Asa & Mary, Columbiana
    Co., O.; m at Fairfield, Hope GARWOOD, dt
    Isaiah & Mary, Columbiana Co., O.
    Ch: Chas.   b 1816, 9, 10
        Samuel   " 1818, 2, 25 d 1827,11,25
        Mary   " 1819, 10, 11 " 1827,11,19
         bur Fairfield
        Eli   b 1823, 6, 29
        George   " 1827, 1, 21
        Isaiah   " 1829, 8, 11
1816, 8, 15. Aaron, s Amos & Hephzibah,
    Stark Co., O.; m at Fairfield, Sarah GAR-
    WOOD, dt Isaiah & Mary, Columbiana Co.,O.
1816, 9, 19. Hannah m William HAMLIN
1870, 6, 22. Emily m Jonathan BLACKBURN
1878, 10, 24. Edwin F., s Jacob & Sarah F.,
    Belmont Co., O.; m at Middleton, Mary
    CADWALLADER, dt Mifflin & Sarah J., Colum-
    biana Co., O.
----, --, --. Jeptha b 1845,5,21 d 1917,11,8;
    m Luanna C. ALLMON, dt Meader & Susannah
    H., b 1859,6,9
    Ch: Howard S. b 1890, 9, 21
----, --, --. Cyrus D., s Wm. E. & Lydia
    (Davis), b 1859,5,16; m Esther E. -----
    b 1862,8,19
    Ch: Wilid F. b 1903, 11, 20
        Jesse O.   " 1891, 6, 27
1916, 4, 20. Alfred Howard, s Cyrus D. & Es-
    ther E., Mahoning Co., O.; m at Middleton,
    Edith Lydia KIRK, dt Nathan & Mary, Co-
    lumbiana Co., O.

1806, 2, 8. Cert rec for Amos & w, Hephzi-
    bah, & ch from South River MM, Va., dtd
    1805,8,10, endorsed to Salem MM
1806, 6, 14. Jesse & Sarah & ch rocf Crook-
    ed Run MM, dtd 1806,5,4
1806, 6, 14. Hannah rocf Crooked Run MM, dtd
    1806,5,4
1806, 6, 14. Susannah rocf Crooked Run MM,
    dtd 1806,5,4
1812, 12, 10. Olive gct Salem MM
1816, 11, 11. Sarah gct Marlborough MM
1824, 12, 20. James dis mou
1825, 3, 21. Eli dis mou
1825, 5, 23. Mary recrq
1826, 9, 17. Elias dis disunity
1829, 5, 7. Asa dis disunity
1830, 1, 7. Asa, Jr. dis disunity
1830, 1, 7. Isaac dis disunity

HOLLOWAY, continued

1830, 8, 12. Lydia Ann (form Dixon) con mou (H)
1830, 9, 9. Mary, Jr. dis disunity
1830, 10, 7. Hope dis disunity
1830, 10, 7. Mary dis JH
1834, 6, 12. Amos, Jr., minor, rocf Marlborough MM, dtd 1834,4,29
1834, 12, 11. Lucy Ann (form Garwood) dis mou
1839, 2, 7. Charles dis joining Methodist Society
1852, 3, 11. Hannah (form Taylor) con mcd
1852, 8, 12. Isiah dis mou
1858, 3, 11. David Wickersham gct Flushing MM, to m Rebecca R. Holloway
1870, 1, 15. Emily rocf Salem MM, dtd 1869, 12,22
1876, 5, 20. William L. Ashton gct Flushing MM, O., to m Eliza F. Holloway
1879, 5, 17. Mary C. gct Flushing MM, O.
1882, 9, 16. Hannah dis disunity
1910, 6, 18. Jephtha & w, Luanna C., & s, Howard, prcf Hickory Grove MM, Ia.
1917, 2, 17. Edith Lydia K. gct Salem MM, O.
1921, 6, 18. A. Howard & w, Edith L., & ch, Carol Thelma, Lois Marjorie & Mabel Lydia, rocf Salem MM, dtd 1921,4,20
1921, 7, 16. J. Howard con mcd
1923, 10, 20. A. Howard & w, Edith, & ch, Carol T., Lois M., Mabel L., Edgar B. & Warren O., gct New Garden MM
1923, 10, 20. Cyrus D. & s, Willid, recrq
1923, 10, 20. Esther E. recrq
1924, 4, 19. Rachel Anna recrq
1924, 6, 21. Jesse O. recrq
1928, 9, 15. Rachel Llewellyn (form Holloway) dis mcd
1929, 3, 16. Jesse O., Cyrus D. & Willid dis disunity

HOLMES

----, --, --. Lot & Eliza
    Ch: Mary   b 1820, 1, 28
        Elizabeth " 1832, 6, 13
        Joseph   " 1836, 4, 4
1852, 5, 20. Mary m George WHEALON (H)

1833, 2, 7. Lot & w, Sarah, & ch, Mary & Elizabeth, rocf Goose Creek MM, dtd 1832, 9,13 (H)
1833, 2, 7. Jesse rocf Goose Creek MM, dtd 1832,9,13 (H)
1837, 4, 6. Jesse gct New Garden MM (H)

HOOPS

----, --, --. David & Elizabeth
    Ch: Joshua   b 1820, 6, 7 d 1820, 8, 6 bur Beaver Falls
        Cynthia T. b 1821, 8, 17
        Caroline   " 1823, 11, 27
        Rebecca   " 1826, 2, 8
        Franklin   " 1829, 4, 29(1828,4,29 in
        Thomas   " 1831, 2, 8   [H]

        Ch: Lewis   b 1833, 6, 24
            Evan   " 1836, 1, 9
            Sarah Elma " 1838, 8, 21
----, --, --. Edward & Cynthia
    Ch: Wm. P.   b 1826, 9, 24
        Robert E. " 1829, 7, 14
        Henry   " 1831, 12, 18
        Ellen   " 1834, 10, 13
        Pamelia   " 1837, 8, 29
1826, 4, 19. Rebecca m Benjamin MARSHALL
1829, 3, 19. Susanna m Levi McCONNELL (H)
----, --, --. John R. & Lydia G.
    Ch: Rachel   b 1834, 6, 27
        Samuel G. " 1835, 11, 1
        Elizabeth " 1837, 10, 1
1882, 10, 24. Ellen C. [Hoopes] m Richard T. OGDEN

1804, 7, 14. Sarah & ch, Esther, John Wilson & Isaac, rocf New Garden MM, dtd 1803,8,6, endorsed by Westland MM, 1804,3,24
1805, 4, 13. Jane & ch, Esther David Sarah Rebekah Susannah & John R., rocf New Garden MM, Pa., dtd 1804,8,9
1805, 6, 8. Esther rocf New Garden MM, Pa., dtd 1804,5,5
1805, 8, 10. Lydia rocf New Garden MM, Pa., dtd 1805,5,5
1810, 6, 9. Jesse dis disunity
1811, 5, 9. Esther Taylor (form Hoops) con mou
1813, 4, 8. Sarah Boyd (form Hoops) con mou
1814, 9, 8. John Wilson & Isaac, ch Jesse, gct Baltimore MM
1816, 7, 15. Eleanor & ch, Edward, Francis, Mary, Charles & Hambleton, recrq
1820, 6, 19. Elizabeth recrq
1826, 3, 20. Edward [Hoopes] con mou
1826, 8, 21. Cynthia [Hoopes] recrq
1828, 10, 9. David dis joining Separatists
1828, 10, 9. Thomas & Edward dis joining Separatists
1828, 10, 9. Eleanor dis JH
1829, 4, 9. Cynthia & Mary dis JH
1829, 4, 9. Francis [Hoopes] dis joining Separatists
1829, 6, 11. John dis JH
1829, 6, 11. John Wilson rocf Baltimore MM, dtd 1829,2,-- (H)
1829, 7, 9. Elizabeth dis JH
1829, 7, 9. Esther dis JH
1829, 8, 6. Mariah dis JH
1829, 9, 24. Susannah McConnell (form Hoops) dis mcd & JH
1829, 11, 12. Mary, Sr. dis JH
1830, 2, 11. Ann L. dis JH
1831, 4, 7. John Wilson [Hoopes] rocf Baltimore MM, dtd 1831,1,6
1831, 7, 7. John Wilson [Hoopes] dis JH
1833, 10, 10. John R. con mcd (H)
1834, 2, 6. Lydia G. rocf Salem MM, dtd 1833,12,25 (H)
1834, 10, 9. Maria Graham (form Hoops) con

HOOPS, continued
mou (H)
1835, 4, 9. Wilson con mcd (H)
1836, 8, 11. Ann McIlwain (form Hoops) con
mou (H)
1838, 2, 8. Mary Chamberlain (late Hoops)
con mou (H)
1841, 7, 8. Isaac N. [Hoopes] rocf Baltimore
MM, dtd 1841,4,8
1844, 8, 8. Jesse, s Ann, recrq
1845, 11, 6. Samuel McClure & w, Cynthia T.
(form Hoops), con mcd (H)
1854, 2, 9. Jesse dis mou & joining Methodist Society
1854, 6, 8. Ann gct Marlborough MM
1862m 11, 15. Ellen C. (form Cadwalader) con
mcd
1864, 8, 17. Charles & Francis attached to
this mtg when Beaver Falls MM, Pa. was
laid down (H)
1864, 8, 17. Edward & w, Cynthia, & ch, R.
Emmett, Henry Ellen & Pamela, attached to
this mtg when Beaver Falls MM, Pa. was
laid down (H)
1864, 8, 17. John R. & w, Deborah W. attached to this mtg when Beaver Falls MM, Pa.
was laid down (H)
1864, 8, 17. Joseph & David attached to this
mtg when Beaver Falls MM, Pa., was laid
down (H)
1864, 8, 17. Sarah, Elma, Franklin, Thomas,
Lewis, Evan, David, Jr. & Esther attached
to this mtg when Beaver Falls MM, Pa. was
laid down (H)
1864, 8, 17. Rebecca Barker (form Hoops) attached to this mtg when Beaver Falls MM,Pa.
was laid down (H)
1864, 8, 17. Caroline Shipman (form Hoops)
attached to this mtg when Beaver Falls MM,
Pa. was laid down (H)
1864, 8, 17. Elizabeth Wade (form Hoops) attached to this mtg when Beaver Falls MM,
Pa. was laid down (H)

HOWARD
1901, 2, 16. Sarah L. (form Hall) dis mcd

HUESTIS
1873, 11, 20. Job [Hustis], s Aaron & Esther,
Columbiana Co., O., b 1819,10,13 d 1900,
9,11; m at Middleton, Rachel COPE, dt
Joseph & Eliza, Chester Co., Pa., b 1839,
3,23 d 1874,10,18
Ch: Edward C. b 1874, 9, 30
----, --, --. Rebecca b 1812,9,22 d 1894,6,11

1808, 6, 11. Aaron [Heustis] & w, Esther, &
dt, Elizabeth, rocf Mountholly MM, N. J.,
dtd 1808,5,5
1900, 2, 17. Edward C. dis mcd

HUGHS
1807, 8, 13. Elizabeth m Enos WOOD

1807, 3, 14. Elizabeth recrq
1807, 6, 13. Rebecca [Hewes] rocf Gunpowder
MM, Md., dtd 1807,3,25
1811, 7, 11. Gideon [Hewes] & ch, Edith &
Ellis, gct New Garden MM

HUMPHREY
1813, 1, 6. James, s John & Martha, d

HUNT
1816, 5, 23. Stacy, s Joshua & Esther, Fayette Co., Pa.; m at Middleton, Rebecca
MERCER, dt Daniel & Alice, Columbiana Co.,
O.

1804, 7, 14. Abigail & ch, John & Seth, rocf
Redstone MM, dtd 1804,3,30
1805, 6, 19. Phebe & s, Robert, rocf Redstone MM, dtd 1804,3,2
1816, 8, 12. Rebecca gct Redstone MM
1844, 5, 9. Charles D. Basset gct Salem MM,
to m Ann W. Hunt

HUNTLEY
1905, 6, 17. Eva A. (form Heald) dis mou &
jas

HUSEY
1807, 11, 14. George dis disunity

HUTTON
----, --, --. John & Mercy
Ch: Wm.   b 1789, 11, 2
    Gulielma   " 1791, 12, 11
    James   " 1795, 12, 30
    Hannah   " 1797, 9, 20
    Mary   " 1800, 3, 6
    Sarah   " 1802, 9, 20
    John   " 1805, 2, 1
    Benjamin   " 1807, 6, 4
1818, 10, 29. Susannah m William W. HEALD
1839, 4, 22. Mary, dt J. & R., b
1840, 3, 23. Mary, dt J., d bur New Britain
1840, 12, 4. Rachel, w John, d bur New
Britain
1841, 2, 28. John, Sr. d bur Middleton

1804, 8, 11. John & ch, William, Gulielma,
James, Hannah, Polly & Sarah, rocf Cane
Creek MM, N. C., dtd 1803,12,24
1809, 2, 11. John & ch gct Salem MM
1817, 2, 10. John, Jr. rocf Westland MM, dtd
1817,1,21
1818, 9, 21. Susannah rocf Westland MM, dtd
1818,8,27
1819, 4, 19. John rocf Westland MM, dtd
1819,3,25
1824, 11, 22. John gct Carmel MM
1830, 8, 12. John rocf Carmel MM, dtd 1830,
7,17
1830, 12, 9. John gct West Grove MM, Ind.
1832, 10, 11. John & w, Rachel, & ch, Samuel
W. & Margaret Jane, rocf Salem MM,

HUTTON, continued
    dtd 1832,7,25
1833, 12, 12. John rocf West Grove MM, Ind.,
    dtd 1833,9,14
1834, 6, 12. John, Jr. & w, Rachel, & ch,
    Samuel W., Margaret Jane & William, gct
    Upper Springfield MM
1834, 7, 10. John gct Salem MM
1838, 10, 11. John & w, Rachel, & ch, Samuel
    W., Margaret Jane & William H., rocf Upper
    Springfield MM, dtd 1838,8,25
1841, 11, 11. John & ch, Samuel W., Margaret
    Jane & William H., gct White Water MM,Ind.

ICENHOUR
1836, 10, 2. Mary d bur Middleton

1804, 6, 19. Mary [Isenhour] rocf Westland
    MM, dtd 1804,4,28
1826, 8, 21. David Allen gct Upper Springfield
    MM, to m Sarah K. Isenhour
1832, 9, 13. Mary [Isenhour] & ch, Gulielma,
    Ann & John, rocf Upper Springfield MM,
    dtd 1832,8,25
1832, 9, 13. Mary, Jr. rocf Upper Spring-
    field MM, dtd 1832,8,25
1837, 5, 11. Gulielma Edmundson (form Icen-
    hour) dis mou
1839, 4, 11. Mary Ward (form Icenhour) dis
    mou
1842, 12, 8. John E. dis mou
1843, 8, 10. Ann Edmundson (form Icenhour)
    dis mcd (first rpd 1838,4,23)

IDEN
1838, 1, 11. Thomas J. rocf Scipio MM,
    N. Y., dtd 1837,9,14 (H)
1842, 2, 10. Thomas G. con mcd (H)
1842, 7, 7. Thomas G. gct Buckingham (or
    Solsbury) MM, Pa. (H)

INGLEDUE
1819, 5, 27. Ann m Hosea MORLAN
1820, 8, 31. Mary m Elias STRATTON

1812, 6, 11. Magdalene recrq
1818, 10, 19. Ann, Mary & Rachel recrq

1830, 2, 11. Rachel dis joining Separatists
1836, 7, 7. Rachel gct Marlborough MM (H)
1857, 3, 12. Triphenia (form Woods) dis mcd

IRISH
1829, 9, 11. William B., city of Pittsburgh;
    m at Columbiana, Lydia CADWALADER (H)

1832, 10, 11. William B. & s, Nathaniel W. &
    Franklin, rocf Redstone MM, dtd 1832,2,29
1832, 11, 8. William B. & w, Lydia, & ch,
    Franklin, Elias H. & Dallas C., gct New
    Garden MM (H)

JACKSON
1861, 11, 13. Phebe con mcd (H)
1862, 3, 15. Mary Ann (form Hicklen) dis mcd

JAMES
----, --, --. Isaac, s Thos. & Sarah, b 1763,
    8,31; m Sarah BARKER, dt Thos. & Catha-
    rine, b 1768,3,7
    Ch: John   b 1787, 9, 30
        Elizabeth   " 1789, 4, 18
        Joseph   " 1791, 3, 30
        Mary   " 1793, 2, 29
        Catharine   " 1795, 3, 5
        Rachel   " 1796, 12, 25
        Sarah   " 1798, 12, 1
        Isaac   " 1801, 4, 3
        David   " 1803, 5, 11
        Jesse   " 1805, 4, 30
----, --, --. John & Martha
    Ch: Elizabeth b 1801, 4, 16
        Abel   " 1802, 12, 19
        Tacy   " 1805, 3, 16
        Humphrey   " 1807, 8, 27
        Thomas   " 1809, 12, 3
        Sarah   " 1812, 7, 28
        Mary   " 1815, 1, 1
        Rachel   " 1817, 8, 22 (or 1819)
        Lucy   " 1820, 3, 4
        John   " 1821, 6, 18
1806, 12, 18. Elizabeth m Simon DIXSON
1809, 4, 12. Mary m Latham HARRISON
1809, 6, 14. James, John, s Isaac & Sarah,
    Columbiana Co., O.; m at Elkrun, Esther
    RICHARDS, dt Abijah & Esther, Columbiana
    Co., O.
1812, 9, 16. Joseph, s Isaac & Sarah, Colum-
    biana Co., O.; m at Elkrun, Ann HARRISON,
    dt Benjamin & Meriam, Columbiana Co., O.
    Ch: Benj.   b 1813, 6, 16
        Miriam   " 1814, 12, 23
1817, 8, 13. Sarah Jr. m Atticus SIDDALL
1817, 10, 15. Catharine m Caleb HAWLEY
----, --, --. Rachel b 1819,8,22 (or 1817) d
    1888,5,2
1825, 12, 28. Abel, s John & Martha, Columbi-
    ana Co., O.; m at Fairfield, Hannah GAR-
    WOOD, dt Isaiah & Mary, Columbiana Co.,O.
    Ch: Emeline   b 1826, 6, 10
        Phebe   " 1830, 9, 7
        Lydia Ann   " 1832, 11, 29

1806, 1, 11. John & w, Martha, & ch gct Sa-
    lem MM
1806, 9, 13. Isaac, Hannah, Sarah & Phebe,
    ch Thomas & Hannah, recrq
1810, 6, 9. Thomas & w, Hannah, & ch,
    Isaac, Hannah, Thomas, Sarah & Phebe,
    gct Miami MM
1813, 6, 10. John & w, Martha, & ch, Eliza-
    beth, Abel, Tacy, Umphrey, Thomas & Sa-
    rah, rocf New Garden MM, dtd 1813,5,13
1829, 11, 12. Thomas dis disunity
1830, 9, 9. Elizabeth dis

JAMES, continued
1832, 11, 8. John & w, Martha, & ch, Mary,
        Rachel & John, gct Upper Springfield MM
1832, 11, 8. Tacy gct Upper Springfield MM
1833, 4, 11. Abel & w, Hannah, & ch, Ema-
        line, Phebe & Lydia Ann, gct Upper Spring-
        field MM
1841, 1, 7. Sarah gct Sandy Spring MM
1843, 9, 14. Phebe (form Wickersham) dis mou
1846, 6, 11. Elizabeth (form Adamson) dis
        mcd
1848, 10, 12. Mifflin Cadwalader gct Salem MM,
        to m Sarah James
1860, 6, 16. Mary Catharine & Jesse James,
        ch Elizabeth Leech, gct Stillwater MM
1870, 9, 17. Rachel rocf Hickory Grove MM,
        Ia., dtd 1870,8,6

JAMIESON
1856, 5, 8. Mary Jane (form Lipsey) dis mou

JEWEL
1807, 2, 14. Patience rocf Redstone MM, dtd
        1806,7,4

JOHN
1808, 10, 8. Aden Morelan gct Salem MM, to m
        Amy John
1813, 5, 6. Nathan [Johns] & w, Rachel, &
        ch, Elizabeth, John, Richard, Samuel &
        Sarah, rocf Westland MM, dtd 1813,1,23
1862, 9, 17. Phebe gct Westland MM (H)

JOHNSON
1815, 12, 7. Sarah (form Middleton) dis mou

JONES
1906, 3, 22. Howard T., s William P. & Eliza-
        beth Leeds, Atlantic Co., N. J.; m at
        Middleton, Jessie H. BLACKBURN dt Charles
        & Sarah C., New Waterford

1804, 9, 8. Mary & dt, Rachel, rocf Cane
        Creek MM, dtd 1804,7,21
1811, 5, 9. Nancy (form Ferrell) con mou
1814, 8, 11. Nancy gct Salem MM
1837, 4, 6. Samuel D. rocf Darby MM, dtd
        1837,2,28 (H)
1837, 4, 6. Susanna D. rocf Darby MM, dtd
        1837,2,22 (H)
1840, 7, 9. Mary Anna L., Deborah F. &
        Oliver H., ch Susan, recrq (H)
1849, 8, 16. Mary Ann Longstreth, Debby Ann
        & Oliver H., ch Paul M., gct Cherry St.
        MM, Phila. (H)
1903, 2, 21. Margaret M. (form Shimbron) dis
        mou
1907, 5, 18. Jessie B. gct Haddonfield MM,
        N. J.

JUNKINS
1864, 8, 17. Alice Ann (form Townsend) at-
        tached to this mtg when Beaver Falls MM,

Pa. was laid down (H)

JUSTICE
1820, 11, 20. Mariah (form Reynolds) dis mou

KEELY
----, --, --. George A., s Geo. & Louisa
        Jane (Adams), b 1869,9,22; m Beulah E.
        SHARPLESS, dt Townsend T. & Addie (Wal-
        ton), b 1875,3,13 d 1925,11,9 bur Kimbles
        Gr. Yd.
        Ch: Esther   b 1901, 3, 23
            Mary E.   " 1902, 9, 21 d 1927, 3,20
            bur at Clarkson
            George S. b 1913, 1, 12

1912, 6, 15. George A. & w, Beulah E., & ch,
        Esther S. & Mary E., rocf Wilmington MM,
        dtd 1912,6,6

KERNS
1813, 4, 8. William rocf New Garden MM,
        Pa., dtd 1812,10,5
1815, 5, 11. William dis mou

KILBREATH
1901, 2, 16. Katharine L. (form Longshore)
        dis mcd

KIMBLE
1812, 5, 7. Ruth [Kimbal] rocf Morris River
        MM, dtd 1812,1,3
1812, 9, 10. Ruth [Kemble] gct Maurice River
        MM, N. J.
1828, 7, 10. Jane (form Hollingsworth) dis
        mou

KINSEY
1812, 8, 6. Sarah (form Smith) con mou
1822, 6, 17. Sarah rocf Carmel MM, dtd
        1822,5,18
1823, 10, 20. Sarah gct Carmel MM

KIRK
1886, 12, 23. Nathan, s Elisha & Christiana,
        Columbiana Co., O., b 1844,2,16 d 1910,4,4
        m at Middleton, Mary MORLAN, dt Theophi-
        lus & Lydia F., Columbiana Co., O., b
        1857,8,14
        Ch: Elisha T. b 1887, 11, 24
            Louis J.   " 1889, 9, 9
            Edith L.   " 1892, 2, 28
            Chas. D.   " 1894, 10, 9
            Rachel S. " 1896, 12, 19
            Anna C.   " 1900, 11, 20
----, --, --. Louis J., s Nathan & Mary M.,
        b 1889,9,9; m Alice C. COPE, dt Albert
        N. & Phebe Y. (Ashton), b 1886,4,20
        Ch: Florence J.b 1914, 2, 19
            Robert
              Louis   " 1917, 4, 6
            Edward N. " 1920, 7, 7
            Morris

KIRK, Louis J. & Alice C., continued
    Ch: Lindley   b 1922, 2, 1
1916, 4, 20. Edith Lydia m Howard HOLLOWAY
----, --, --. Wilford N., s Chas. D. & Tacy
    M. (Hall), b 1923,10,2 d 1923,10,20
    bur Middleton

1887, 8, 20. Nathan rocf New Garden MM, dtd
    1887,6,23
1913, 4, 19. Lewis J. gct Salem MM, to m
    Elizabeth Alice Cope
1914, 1, 17. Alice C. rocf Salem MM, dtd
    1913,12,24
1914, 6, 20. Elisha T. gct Short Creek MM,
    to m Alice Mary Steer
1917, 2, 17. Mary M. gct New Garden MM
1917, 10, 20. Charles D. gct Short Creek MM,
    to m Tacy M. Hall
1919, 6, 21. Charles D. gct Short Creek MM
1922, 2, 18. Charles D. & w, Tacy M., & ch,
    Walter S. & Dorothy M., rocf Short Creek
    MM, O.
1924, 11, 10. Elisha T. gct Media MM, Pa.
1928, 2, 18. Charles D. & w, Tacy M., & ch,
    Walter S., Dorothy M. & William J., gct
    Short Creek MM

KOLL
----, --, --. Daniel & Julie
    Ch: Benj.   b 1836, 5, 26
        Lydia   " 1839, 8, 25
        Esther   " 1841, 12, 11
        Joseph   " 1844, 2, 24

1836, 7, 17. Daniel & w, Julia (form Seebohm)
    rocf Pyrmont & Minden MM, Prusia, dtd
    1836,3,6, endorsed by Baltimore MM for
    East or West Dist., 1836,6,9
1844, 5, 9. Daniel & w, Julia, & ch, Benja-
    min, Lydia, Esther & Joseph, gct Salem MM

KOLLING
1839, 7, 11. Louiza [Kollings] rocf WD MM,
    Phila., Pa., dtd 1839,4,24
1842, 8, 11. Louisa Miller (form Kolling) con
    mou
1846, 7, 9. Elizabeth Jr. rocf Chesterfield
    MM, dtd 1846,5,16
1850, 12, 12. Elizabeth gct Salem MM, Ia.

KRUGER
1842, 9, 15. Cert rec for Christian from Min-
    den (2 months) Mtg, Germany, dtd 1841,9,5,
    endorsed to Carmel MM
1859, 1, 15. Christian dis disunity

LADNER
1825, 1, 17. David recrq
1827, 3, 8. John V., Susan W., James Vail,
    Mary, Martha & Elizabeth, ch David, recrq
1833, 10, 10. Susan Bishop (form Ladner) dis
    mou
1833, 9, 12. John dis mou

1839, 6, 6. Mary Briggs (form Ladnor) dis
    mou
1843, 11, 9. Martha Allen (form Ladner) dis
    mou

LANE
1838, 3, 19. Mary D. rocf Redstone MM, dtd
    1838,1,31

LAWRENCE
1825, 8, 9. Isaac T., s Obed & Clariss, b

1824, 2, 23. Clarissa recrq
1825, 1, 17. Obed recrq
1825, 6, 20. Alfred & Derimon, ch Obed &
    Clarissa, recrq
1829, 11, 12. Clarissa dis joining Separatists
1830, 2, 11. Obed dis JH

LAWSON
1825, 1, 17. Cornelius recrq
1825, 1, 17. Caroline recrq
1825, 6, 20. Patty Ann, Harvey, William & Al-
    fred, ch Cornelius & Caroline, recrq
1830, 2, 11. Cornelius dis JH
1830, 6, 10. Caroline dis JH

LEECH
1823, 10, 13. William, s Thomas & Phebe, Co-
    lumbiana Co., O.; m at Middleton, Phebe
    HOLLINGSWORTH, dt David & Sarah Mercer,
    Columbiana Co., O.
1865, 1, 1. Wm. d (an elder)

1816, 6, 10. William & w, Jane, & ch, Re-
    becca, Phebe, Margaret, Cornelius, Han-
    nah, Sarah, Mariah & Thomas, rocf War-
    rington MM, dtd 1816,3,21
1824, 1, 19. Phebe Leech & ch, Ann & Mahlon
    Hollingsworth, gct Carmel MM
1824, 4, 19. Samuel Hollingsworth gct Car-
    mel MM, to m Margaret Leech
1860, 3, 17. Thomas & w, Elisabeth, & ch,
    John, Deborah, Jane, Charles & Ross, gct
    Stillwater MM
1860, 6, 16. Mary Catharine & Jesse James,
    ch Elizabeth Leech, gct Stillwater MM
1878, 2, 16. Cornelius dis mou

LENHART
1852, 2, 12. Lenora M. (form Morlan) dis
    mou & joining Methodist Society

LEWIS
1821, 8, 30. Rebecca m Barzilla MORLAN
1834, 2, 24. Jane d bur Fairfield

1814, 5, 12. Jason con mou
1819, 6, 21. Susannah Henry (form Lewis) con
    mou
1820, 9, 18. Jason dis joining Baptist So-
    ciety
1827, 11, 8. Amos rocf Carmel MM, dtd 1827,9,

LEWIS, continued
15
1842, 4, 7. Jesse gct Bloomfield MM, Ind.

LINE
1821, 10, 22. Amos & w, Phebe, & ch, Joseph,
    Isaac, Smith, James, Mary & Rachel, rocf
    Rahway & Plainfield MM, N. J., dtd 1821,
    2,21
1828, 5, 8. Isaac gct Rahway & Plainfield
    MM, N. J., to m Bathsheba Shotwell
1829, 8, 6. Isaac dis mcd
1829, 11, 12. Phebe dis jH
1829, 11, 12. Amos dis jH
1829, 11, 12. Joseph dis jH
1833, 7, 11. Smith dis mcd
1839, 6, 6. Mary Slocum (form Line) dis mou
1859, 12, 14. Isaac, s Amos, gct Plainfield
    MM, N. J. (H)

LIPSEY
----, --, --. John b 1801,12,12 d 1889,9,13;
    m Ann BUR, dt Wm. & Sarah, b 1806,2,7
    Ch: Wm. B.   b 1825, 1, 20
        Ellwood   " 1828, 3, 26 d 1853, 1,21
        Ruth Anna " 1830, 5, 21
        Mary Jane " 1832, 7, 1
        Sarah   " 1834, 7, 20
        Chalkley   " 1838, 10, 8
        Lemuel   " 1840, 8, 7
        Albert   " 1842, 9, 2 d 1851,10,18
        Eliza Ann " 1844, 5, 10
        John Alonzo" 1849, 1, 3 " 1849,10,29
        Elvira   " 1850, 4, 15 " 1850, 9,10
1834, 2, 24. Jane d bur Fairfield

1844, 10, 10. John & w, Ann, & ch, William B.,
    Elwood, Ruth Anna, Mary Jane, Sarah J.,
    Chalkley T., Lemuel & Albert, rocf Short
    Creek MM, dtd 1844,5,21 (dt, Eliza Ann, b
    since cert was issued)
1848, 8, 10. William B. gct Gilead MM, O.
1856, 5, 8. Mary Jane Jamieson (form Lipsey)
    dis mou
1858, 1, 8. Sarah Josephine Armstrong (form
    Lipsey) dis mcd
1863, 10, 17. Lemuel J. dis mou
1868, 7, 18. Ann Eliza Trueblood (form Lip-
    sey) dis mcd
1873, 11, 15. John & w, Ann, gct Coal Creek
    MM, Ia.
1886, 11, 20. John rocf Coal Creek MM, Ia.,
    dtd 1886,10,9

LIVEZEY
1896, 12, 19. Rachel S., w Albert J., dt Na-
    than & Mary M. (Morlan) Kirk, b
1920, 8, 24. Albert J., s Charles & Eliza-
    beth W., Belmont Co., O.; m at Middleton,
    Rachel S. KIRK, dt Nathaniel & Mary M.,
    Columbiana Co., O.
----, --, --. Jesse K. [Livezy], s Chas. &
    Elizabeth (Smith), b 1901,1,31; m Alice

Rebecca BINNS, dt John A. & Mary E.
    (Cope), b 1906,1,16
    Ch: Donald Wm. b 1927, 1, 17
        Ralph Ar-
        thur   " 1928, 8, 13

1883, 12, 15. John G. Hall gct Somerset MM,
    to m Anna Livesey
1921, 1, 15. Rachel K. gct Stillwater MM
1929, 8, 17. Jesse K. [Livzey] & w, Alice,
    & ch, Donald William & Ralph Arthur, rocf
    New Garden MM, O., dtd 1929,7,25

LLEWELLYN
1856, 2, 23. Rachel A., w Ezra, dt Wm. E. &
    Lydia (Davis) Holloway, b
1903, 10, 22. Elisha, s Thos. & Martha (Hol-
    lingsworth), Columbiana Co., O., b 1856,
    9,6 d 1920,5,13 bur Winona; m at Middle-
    ton, Rachel E. WICKERSHAM, dt David & Re-
    becca (Holloway), Columbiana Co., O.,
    b 1863,4,3

1904, 3, 19. Rachel C. gct New Garden MM
1915, 1, 16. Elisha & w, Rachel C., rocf
    Chesterfield MM, O., dtd 1914,12,17
1920, 11, 13. Rachel C. gct Salem MM
1928, 9, 15. Rachel (form Holloway) dis mcd

LOGUE
1817, 2, 10. Cert rec for Stephen, Jr. from
    Centre MM, Del., dtd 1816,11,4, endorsed
    to Marlborough MM

LONGSHORE
1871, 2, 5. Catharine J. b

1858, 8, 21. Sarah (form Woods) dis mcd
1862, 2, 12. Mary (form Raley) con mcd (H)
1880, 12, 18. Catharine Longshore, minor un-
    der care of Barak & Jane Ashton, recrq
1901, 2, 16. Katharine L. Kilbreath (form
    Longshore) dis mcd

LYNCH
1839, 10, 17. Joseph, s Joshua & Rachel, Co-
    lumbiana Co., O., b 1813,11,25; m Rebecca
    BEESON, dt Richard & Ann, Columbiana Co.,
    O., b 1808,5,18
    Ch: Rachel   b 1842, 1, 23
        Asenath E. " 1848, 5, 28
1840, 1, 9. Rebecca gct Upper Springfield MM
1847, 6, 10. Joseph & w, Rebecca, & dt,
    Rachel, rocf Upper Springfield MM, dtd
    1847,4,24
1851, 5, 8. Joseph & w, Rebecca, & ch,
    Rachel & Ascenith, gct Upper Springfield
    MM

McBRIDE
----, --, --. James, Sr. b 1786,10,31 d 1870,
    4,23; m Elizabeth BATTEN, dt John & Ann,
    b 1796,12,1 d 1877,1,29
    Ch: James Jr. b 1830, 9, 8 d 1846,10,30

McBRIDE, continued

1846, 12, 10. Elizabeth & ch, Elihu, Grace,
     Benjamin, Lydia, Rachel & Abisha, rocf
     Carmel MM, dtd 1846,10,17
1847, 3, 11. Hannah rocf Salem MM, dtd
     1847,1,20
1850, 1, 10. Elizabeth, w James, & ch, Benja-
     min, Lydia, Rachel & Abisha, gct Salem MM
1850, 1, 10. Grace gct Salem MM
1850, 11, 7. Elihu dis disunity
1851, 6, 12. Hannah Smathers (form McBride)
     dis mcd
1855, 8, 9. James & w, Elizabeth, & s,
     Abishai, rocf Salem MM, dtd 1855,7,25
1856, 1, 10. Phebe (form Edmundson) dis mou
1858, 2, 11. Benjamin dis mou
1869, 5, 15. Coal Creek MM, Ia. was granted
     permission to rst Phebe
1871, 1, 21. Abishai dis mcd & jas

McCLUNN

----, --, --. John [McClun] d 1826,5,5 bur
     Columbiana; m Elizabeth ----- d 1813,8,18
     bur Columbiana
     Ch: Isaac   b 1810, 12, 13
1819, 4, 29. John [McClun], s Thomas & Han-
     nah, Columbiana Co., O.; m at Middleton,
     Sarah ALLEN, dt David & Sarah Mercer, Co-
     lumbiana Co., O.
1820, 12, 6. Cynthia [McClun] m David ALLEN
1825, 12, 29. Rachel [McClun] m Willen UNDER-
     WOOD

1806, 5, 10. John & w, Elizabeth, & ch, Jo-
     seph Beal, Cinthia, Hannah & Rachel, rocf
     Goose Creek MM, dtd 1805,11,28
1824, 8, 23. Hannah Allen (form McClunn) dis
     mou
1826, 3, 20. Joseph B. dis mou
1829, 3, 12. Sarah dis jH
1833, 7, 11. Isaac dis mou

McCLURE

1844, 11, 11. Louisa m Matthew PATTERSON

1810, 9, 8. Mary (form Townsend) dis mou
1812, 7, 9. Mary recrq
1824, 6, 21. Hannah Allen (form McClure) dis
     mou
1837, 8, 21. Mary & ch, Abel T., Sinah-Ann,
     Lydia, Seth, Jr., Endley & Mira S., rocf
     Carmel MM, dtd 1837,8,19
1837, 8, 21. Joseph rocf Carmel MM, dtd
     1837,8,19
1837, 8, 21. Louisa rocf Carmel MM, dtd
     1837,8,19
1841, 2, 11. Abel T. gct Flushing MM
1842, 9, 15. Joseph gct Cincinnati MM
1845, 11, 6. Samuel & w, Cynthia T. (form
     Hoops), con their mcd (H)
1863, 6, 20. Lydia Cowgill (form McClure) dis
     mcd

McCONNELL

1810, 5, 17. Jesse M. [McConnal], s James &
     Rachel, Columbiana Co., O.; m at Fairfield
     Rachel BYRNES, dt James & Mary, Columbiana
     Co., O.
1812, 6, 17. Edward [McConnel], s James & Ra-
     chel, Columbiana Co., O.; m at Elkrun,
     Lydia TOWNSEND, dt David & Mary, Beaver
     Co., Pa.
     Ch: Albert   b 1829, 8, 20
         Jonathan   " 1832, 1, 2
         Ruth   " 1834, 4, 18
1813, 3, 18. Levi, s James & Rachel, Beaver
     Co., Pa.; m at Big Beaver, Ruth TOWNSEND,
     dt David & Mary, Beaver Co., Pa.
     Ch: Emeline   b 1814, 2, 27
         Sarah   " 1815, 12, 21
         David   " 1818, 3, 1
         Joseph   " 1820, 3, 18
         Austin   " 1822, 4, 22
     Levi m 2nd 1829,3,19 at Beaver Falls, Su-
     sanna HOOPS, dt Thomas & Mary, Beaver
     Co., Pa.
     Ch: Minerva   b 1830, 3, 29
         Wm.   " 1831, 12, 11
         Thomas   " 1833, 10, 11
         Edwin   " 1835, 12, 11
         Ruth Ann   " 1838, 4, 2
         Henry H.   " 1840, 5, 24
1826, 12, 29. Ruth [McConnel] d bur Beaver
     Falls
1828, 7, 19. Amos [McConnel], s Edward &
     Lydia, d bur Beaver Falls
1842, 11, 17. Austin, s Levi & Ruth, Columbi-
     ana Co., O., b 1822,4,22 d 1866,10,7;
     m at Middleton, Edith HEALD, dt T. & M.,
     (dt Thomas & Mariam), Columbiana Co., O.,
     b 1823,9,27
     Ch: Mary Ann   b 1843, 8, 4
         Emeline   " 1846, 3, 22
         Chas.   " 1851, 3, 24
         Emmet   " 1848, 2, 26
         Thomas   " 1850, 2, 10 d 1850, 5, 1
         Hadley   " 1854, 9, 10 " 1855, 8, 4
         Annabel   " 1858, 9, 13
         Laura   " 1861, 5, 3 " 1866, 9,10

1828, 7, 10. Edward [McConnel] & w, Lydia, &
     ch, Townsend, Talbot, Orpah, James, Ada-
     line, Nathan & Amos, rocf Carmel MM, dtd
     1828,5,17
1828, 10, 9. Levi [McConnel] dis joining
     Separatists
1829, 2, 12. Jesse [McConnel] dis jH
1829, 3, 12. Rachel, w Jesse, & ch, Eliza
     Ann, Mary, Harriet, Rachel, Susan-Jane,
     Nelson & Melissa, gct Carmel MM
1829, 9, 24. Susannah (form Hoops) dis mcd &
     jH
1835, 6, 22. Edward [McConnel] & w, Lydia,
     & ch, Talbot, Orpah, James, Adaline, Na-
     than, Albert, Jonathan & Ruth, gct Upper
     Springfield MM

McCONNELL, continued
1835, 12, 21. Townsend [McConnel] gct Short
     Creek MM
1836, 5, 12. Sarah Caldwell (form McConnell)
     con mou (H)
1837, 10, 23. Sarah Chaldwell (form McConnell)
     dis mcd
1840, 6, 11. Emeline Bradway (form McConnel)
     dis mou
1841, 1, 7. David [McConnel] con mcd (H)
1843, 6, 8. David dis mou
1844, 9, 12. Joseph dis mou
1849, 7, 12. Austin [McConnel] dis disunity
1850, 10, 10. Mary gct Pleasant Plain MM, Ia.
1864, 8, 17. Levi & w, Susan, & ch, Mary,
     Minerva, William C., Thomas, Edwin, Ruth
     Ann, Henry & Amelia, attached to this mtg
     when Beaver Falls MM, Pa. was laid down (H)
1864, 8, 17. Joseph & w, Edith M., attached
     to this mtg when Beaver Falls MM, Pa. was
     laid down (H)
1864, 8, 17. David attached to this mtg when
     Beaver Falls MM, Pa. was laid down (H)
1864, 8, 17. John & Lewis attached to this
     mtg when Beaver Falls MM, Pa. was laid
     down (H)
1869, 6, 19. Emmit gct Hickory Grove MM, Ia.
1869, 6, 19. Edith & ch, Charles & Annabelle,
     gct Hickory Grove MM, Ia.
1869, 6, 19. Mary Ann gct Hickory Grove MM,
     Ia.
1871, 8, 19. Emaline gct Hickory Grove MM,
     Ia.

McGREW
1874, 9, 19. Richard Ashton gct Short Creek
     MM, to m Eliza McGrew
1875, 10, 16. Robert P. Thomas gct Short
     Creek MM, O., to m Susan McGrew

McILWAIN
1836, 8, 11. Ann (form Hoops) con mou (H)

McINTIRE
1806, 4, 12. Rachel dis

McMILLEN
1812, 5, 7. Thomas & w, Jane, & ch, Taylor
     & Jane, rocf Westland MM, dtd 1811,11,23
1867, 6, 15. Elizabeth J. (form Tulliss) dis
     mcd

McNEELY
1827, 7, 12. Abigail rocf Sandy Spring MM,
     dtd 1827,4,27
1832, 6, 7. Abigail [McNealy] gct Salem MM

MALSBERRY
1827, 8, 9. Charles Engle gct Upper Spring-
     field MM, to m Jane Malsberry

MANKIN
1817, 6, 16. Elizabeth (form Morlan) dis mou

MANN
1840, 9, 10. Charity (form Morlan) dis mou

MARIS
1842, 3, 17. Ann m Moses EMBREE (H)

1825, 3, 21. Ann (form Marsh) dis mou
1842, 2, 10. Ann rst by rq (H)

MARSH
1808, 12, 22. Jonathan, s Jonathan & Ann, Co-
     lumbiana Co., O.; m at Middleton, Phebe
     ARMSTRONG, dt James & Ruth, Columbiana Co.,
     O.
1820, 8, 31. Jonathan, s Jonathan & Ann, Co-
     lumbiana Co., O.; m at Middleton, Ann
     WICKERSHAM, dt Sampson & Elizabeth, Colum-
     biana Co., O.

1808, 7, 9. James & w, Edith, & ch, Zillah,
     Amos, Miriam & Mary Ann, rocf Redstone
     MM, dtd 1808,4,29
1808, 11, 12. Jonathan, Jr. rocf Warrington
     MM, dtd 1808,7,21
1817, 8, 11. Joseph Scott gct New Garden MM,
     to m Jane Marsh
1821, 10, 22. Thomas Heald gct Carmel MM, to
     m Miriam Marsh
1822, 2, 18. James & Ruth, ch Jonathan, rocf
     Carmel MM, dtd 1822,1,28
1825, 3, 21. Ann Maris (form Marsh) dis mou
1829, 1, 8. James, Jr. gct Carmel MM
1829, 2, 12. Ruth gct Carmel MM
1844, 10, 10. Elisabeth Cope, w Israel, & ch,
     Elisabeth, Israel & Susannah, & gr dt,
     Mary Marsh, rocf Carmel MM, dtd 1844,7,20
1846, 11, 12. Elizabeth Cope, w Israel, & ch,
     Elizabeth & Susannah, & gr dt, Mary Marsh,
     gct Carmel MM
1850, 8, 8. Mary H. rocf Carmel MM, dtd
     1850,7,20
1850, 8, 8. Susannah Cope & Mary H. Marsh
     rocf Carmel MM, dtd 1850,7,20
1863, 12, 19. Mary H. Stanley (form Marsh) dis
     mcd

MARSHALL
1826, 4, 19. Benjamin, s William & Mary,
     Portage Co., O.; m at Beaver Falls, Re-
     becca HOOPS, dt Thomas & Mary, Beaver
     Co., Pa.

1804, 9, 8. Mary & ch, Joseph & Sarah, rocf
     Cane Creek MM, S. C., dtd 1803,12,24
1808, 4, 9. Joseph gct Salem MM
1808, 4, 9. Sarah gct Salem MM
1808, 4, 9. Mary gct Salem MM
1826, 6, 19. Rebecca gct Marlborough MM
1839, 3, 7. Susanna con mcd (H)
1841, 1, 7. James C. rocf Upper Springfield
     MM, dtd 1840,11,28
1842, 7, 7. James C. con mou
1842, 9, 15. James C. gct Salem MM

MARTIN
----, --, --. Joseph R. & Sarah
    Ch: Biard   b 1831, 2, 23
        Elizabeth " 1833, 8, 15
1842, 11, 17. Joseph R., widower, Beaver Co.,
    Pa.; m at Beaver Falls, Elizabeth WILSON,
    wd, Beaver Co., Pa. (H)

1831, 5, 12. Rebecca, John A., Thomas &
    James, ch Joseph R. & Sarah, rocf Carmel
    MM, dtd 1831,3,19
1839, 8, 8. John, Thomas & James, ch Joseph
    R., gct Carmel MM
1839, 8, 8. Rebecca gct Carmel MM
1841, 2, 11. John, Thomas & James, ch Joseph
    R., rocf Carmel MM, dtd 1841,1,16
1841, 2, 11. Rebecca rocf Carmel MM, dtd
    1841,1,16
1843, 7, 6. Rebecca dis jas
1849, 12, 6. Thomas gct Gilead MM
1864, 8, 7. Beulah M., wd Joseph R., attach-
    ed to this mtg when Beaver Falls MM, Pa.
    was laid down (H)

MARVIN
1848, 10, 12. Sarah (form Almon) dis mou

MASTERS
1897, 8, 26. Daniel S., s Joseph & Esther,
    Columbiana Co., O.; m at Middleton, Hannah
    Mary HALL, dt Linton & Ann W., Columbiana
    Co., O.

1897, 11, 20. Hannah Mary gct New Garden MM,O.

MATHER
1827, 11, 8. William Bishop gct Upper Spring-
    field MM, to m Lydia Mather

MATTHEWS
1841, 6, 10. Ruth (form Hill) dis mcd

MAXWELL
1925, 5, 16. Joseph B. Edgerton gct Plain-
    field MM, Ind., to m Elsie Maxwell

MAY
1886, 9, 18. Ella L. (form Cope) con mou

MEISER
1915, 5, 15. Alice B. (form Blackburn) dis
    mcd & jas

MENDENHALL
1805, 11, 21. Aaron, s Moses & Sarah, Beaver
    Co., Pa.; m at Middleton, Lydia RICHARD-
    SON, dt John & Lydia, Columbiana Co., O.
    Ch: John   b 1806, 8, 19
       Moses   " 1808, 7, 15
       Cyrus   " 1810, 11, 3
       George   " 1814, 5, 5
1805, 1, 17. Jonathan, s Moses & Sarah, Beaver
    Co., Pa.; m at Beaver Falls, Lydia TOWN-

SEND, dt Benjamin & Edith, Beaver Co.,Pa.
----, --, --. Jonathan & Lydia
    Ch: Jesse   b 1809, 12, 5
       Harrison " 1812, 5, 3
----, --, --. Israel & Sarah
    Ch: Phebe   b 1814, 12, 31
       Isaac   " 1817, 2, 14
       Hannah   " 1818, 12, 3
       Asenath   " 1821, 2, 11
       Milton   " 1823, 1, 24
       Israel   " 1825, 1, 10
       Pennock   " 1827, 4, 26
1828, 9, 26. Aaron d bur Middleton
1832, 4, 1. Pennock d
1836, 10, 17. Esther d
1836, 10, 12. Wm., s John & Hannah, b
1836, 9, 1. Hannah m Josiah CAMERON
1836, 9, 26. Cyrus, s Aaron & Lydia, Cuyahoga
    Co., O.; m at Middleton, Esther RUNDAL,
    dt Isaac & Rebecca, Henry Co., O.

1807, 8, 8. James & w, Sarah, & ch, Marga-
    ret, Susan & Stephen, rocf Concord MM,
    Del.,Co., dtd 1807,4,8
1813, 2, 11. James dis disunity
1813, 3, 11. Sarah, w James, & ch, Margaret,
    Susan P., Stephen D., Sarahann & Pennell,
    gct Uwchlan MM, Pa.
1823, 2, 17. Levi Boulton gct Short Creek
    MM, to m Orpah Mendenhall
1829, 4, 9. Lydia dis jH
1830, 2, 11. Jesse dis jH
1830, 8, 12. Phebe, Isaac, Hannah, Asenath,
    Milton, Israel & Pennock, ch Israel & Sa-
    rah, rocf Short Creek MM, dtd 1830,6,22
1830, 9, 9. Lydia dis jH
1831, 1, 6. Sarah & ch, Phebe, Isaac, Han-
    nah, Ascenath, Milton, Israel & Pennock,
    rocf Short Creek MM, dtd 1830,3,25 (H)
1831, 6, 9. George, minor, gct Salem MM
1833, 6, 6. Phebe Young (form Mendenhall)
    dis mcd (H)
1834, 6, 12. Cyrus gct Radnor MM, Pa.
1834, 7, 10. Moses dis mou
1834, 7, 10. Phebe Young (form Mendenhall)
    dis mou
1834, 9, 11. Cert to Radnor MM, Pa. for Cy-
    rus returned
1835, 6, 11. Martha (form Allen) con mcd (H)
1835, 8, 17. John gct Short Creek MM, to m
    Hannah Millhouse
1836, 2, 22. Hannah rocf Short Creek MM, dtd
    1835,12,22
1837, 2, 9. Sarah & ch, Asenath, Milton &
    Israel, gct Short Creek MM (H) (& John M.)
1837, 7, 17. Asenath, Milton & Israel, ch
    Israel & Sarah, gct Short Creek MM
1837, 7, 17. Isaac gct Pennsville MM
1838, 5, 21. John & w, Hannah, & s, William,
    gct Pennsville MM
1839, 5, 9. Israel, minor, rocf Short Creek
    MM, dtd 1839,3,19
1841, 1, 7. Harrison con mcd (H)

MENDENHALL, continued
1843, 2, 9. Harrison dis mou
1847, 5, 6. Israel gct Sandy Spring MM, to m Ann Reader
1847, 9, 9. Ann rocf Sandy Spring MM, dtd 1847,8,27
1848, 4, 6. Cyrus gct Short Creek MM, to m Anna T. Updegraff
1848, 10, 12. Israel & w, Ann, gct Gilead MM
1848, 10, 12. Cyrus gct Short Creek MM
1864, 8, 17. Lydia & Harrison attached to this mtg when Beaver Falls MM, Pa. was laid down (H)

MERCER
1807, 11, 26. Ann m Jesse ALLEN
1808, 3, 17. Thos., s David & Sarah, Columbiana Co., O.; m at Middleton, Hannah RICHARDSON, dt John & Lydia, Columbiana Co., O.
  Ch: Sarah   b 1809, 7, 5
      Lydia   " 1811, 4, 20
      John K.   " 1813, 4, 22
      Phebe   " 1816, 6, 23
      Faithful   " 1819, 10, 16
      Cyrus   " 1821, 1, 3
      Thomas   " 1824, 11, 30
1812, 10, 14. Olive m Aaron HOLLOWAY
1816, 5, 23. Rebecca m Stacy HUNT
1816, 9, 19. Daniel, s Solomon & Olive, Columbiana Co., O.; m at Carmel, Tacy HOLE, dt Charles & Mary, Columbiana Co., O.
1830, 6, 11. Sarah m Nathan TOWNSEND (H)

1832, 2, 25. Sarah d
1832, 10, 10. David d bur Columbiana
1835, 2, 19. Thomas m Anne HANNA (H)
1836, 3, 24. John P., s Thomas & Hannah, Columbiana Co., Co.; m at Columbiana, Rachel HATCHER, dt John & Rebecca, Columbiana Co., O. (H)
1837, 9, 14. Faithful m Stacy NICHOLS (H)

1806, 7, 12. Ann rocf Kennet MM. dtd 1806,5, 6
1806, 7, 12. David & w, Sarah, rocf Kennet MM, dtd 1806,1,6
1806, 7, 12. Martha rocf Kennet MM, dtd 1806,5,6
1807, 8, 8. Thomas rocf Kennet MM, dtd 1807, 7,7
1810, 3, 10. William & w, Charity, & ch, Martha, Mary Ann, George, William, John & Daniel, rocf Sadsbury MM, dtd 1809,11, 7, endorsed by New Garden MM, 1810,2,15
1811, 9, 12. Daniel & w, Alice, & ch, Rebecca, Mary, Hannah, Rachel, Solomon & Phebe, rocf Kennett MM, dtd 1811,5,7, endorsed by Salem MM, 1811,8,13
1812, 9, 10. Olive rocf New Garden MM, dtd 1812,8,13
1817, 4, 14. Martha Pettit (form Mercer) dis mcd

1817, 12, 15. Hannah gct Redstone MM
1819, 3, 22. Rachel gct Salem MM
1821, 2, 19. Solomon, minor, gct New Garden MM
1821, 7, 23. Mary gct New Garden MM
1827, 12, 6. Solomon rocf New Garden MM, dtd 1827,11,22
1829, 11, 12. Thomas dis jH
1830, 3, 11. Hannah, Sarah, Jr. & Lydia dis jH
1830, 11, 11. Solomon dis mou
1831, 7, 7. Daniel gct Salem MM, to m Sarah Schooley
1831, 11, 10. Lydia Wilson (form Mercer) con mou (H)
1832, 3, 8. Sarah Mercer & ch, Rachel & Emley Schooly, rocf Salem MM, dtd 1831,9,21
1832, 11, 8. Ruth, dt Daniel, gct Sandy Spring MM
1833, 5, 9. Phebe gct Salem MM
1833, 6, 6. John dis disunity
1834, 4, 10. Rachel Schooly, minor dt Sarah Mercer, gct Sandy Spring MM
1835, 10, 8. John R. recrq (H)
1836, 7, 18. Rachel (form Hatcher) dis mou & jH
1838, 3, 19. Faithful Nichols (form Mercer) dis mcd
1838, 6, 7. Phebe dis jH
1847, 1, 7. Martha Hickman (form Mercer) dis mou
1849, 10, 11. Cyrus dis mou
1853, 3, 10. Daniel & w, Sarah, gct Salem MM, Ia.
1856, 10, 16. Anne gct Salem MM (H)

METZGER
1839, 12, 12. Margery (form Nichols) dis mou (H)

MICHENER
1843, 5, 1. Lucina [Michenor] b
1866, 3, 27. Chas. C. [Michenor] b

1865, 2, 18. Lucena H. (form Heald) con mcd
1866, 4, 24. John E. rocf Stillwater MM, dtd 1866,3,24
1869, 2, 20. John E. & w, Lucena H., & ch, Charles C. & Eva H., gct Hickory Grove MM, Ia.

MIDDLETON
1804, 7, 14. Deborah & ch, Nathaniel, Sarah, Levi, Hudson & Hannah, rocf Southland MM, dtd 1804,5,30
1815, 12, 7. Sarah Johnson (form Middleton) dis mou
1816, 7, 15. Nathaniel con mou
1817, 7, 14. Hudson, Jr., minor, gct Salem MM
1817, 7, 14. Dorothy & dt, Sarah, recrq
1818, 8, 10. Nathaniel & w, Dorothy, & ch, Sarah & Ira, gct New Garden MM
1819, 7, 19. Deborah & ch, Hannah, Mary,

MIDDLETON, continued
    Lydia & Deborah, gct New Garden MM
1821, 4, 23. Levi gct Lees Creek MM

MILBOURN
1806, 9, 13. Betty, dt Sarah, recrq
1806, 10, 11. Sarah & ch gct Salem MM

MILLER
1807, 9, 12. Susannah (form Wilkins) con mou
1808, 4, 9. Susannah gct Westland MM
1823, 7, 31. Susannah (form Reeves) dis mou
1842, 8, 11. Louisa (form Kolling) con mou
1845, 1, 9. Phebe (form Hill) dis mcd

MILLHOUSE
1835, 8, 17. John Mendenhall gct Short Creek
    MM, to m Hannah Millhouse

MILLIGAN
1832, 9, 14. William, s John & Abigail,
    Stark Co., O.; m at Middleton, Elizabeth
    ALLMON, dt Ebenezer & Rebecca, Columbiana
    Co., O.
1837, 6, 1. Jesse, s John & Abigail, Colum-
    biana Co., O.; m at Middleton, Ruth WOODS,
    dt Samuel & Esther, Columbiana Co., O.
    Ch: Rebecca
          Ann   b 1839, 7, 14
          Esther   " 1843, 7, 8
          Samuel L. " 1845, 6, 1

1833, 1, 10. Elizabeth gct Marlborough MM
1836, 9, 19. William & w, Elizabeth, & ch,
    Lindley H., rocf Marlborough MM, dtd
    1836,5,31
1837, 1, 23. Jesse, minor, rocf Marlborough
    MM, dtd 1836,12,27
1839, 10, 10. William & w, Elizabeth, & dt,
    Hannah Ruth, gct Goshen MM, O.
1847, 5, 6. Jesse & w, Ruth, & ch, Rebecca
    Ann, Esther & Samuel L., gct Goshen MM,O.

MINARD
1884, 12, 9. Sarah b bur Carmel

1884, 5, 17. Sarah rocf Muncy MM, Pa., dtd
    1884,3,19

MINER
1832, 4, 18. Caroline (form Pugh) con mcd
    (H)
1832, 6, 7. Caroline P. (form Pugh) con
    mcd (H)

MOORE
1863, 3, 21. Martha A. [More] (form Arm-
    strong) dis mcd
1923, 6, 16. Allen J. Hall gct Salem MM, to
    m Martha F. Moore

MORELL
1819, 11, 22. Mary (form Daniel) dis mou

MORGAN
1816, 12, 19. Eliza m Elis. WICKERSHAM
----, --, --. Lewis & Elizabeth
    Ch: Thomas   b 1823, 1, 28
        John C.   " 1824, 10, 6
        Joshua W. " 1826, 9, 24
        Eliza   " 1828, 11, 21
        James   " 1832, 8, 7
        Susanna   " 1834, 10, 11

1814, 11, 10. Sarah [Morgen] rocf New Garden
    MM, dtd 1814,8,18
1816, 1, 15. Elizabeth & ch, Eliza & Thomas,
    recrq (Elizabeth had been dis by Westland
    MM)
1817, 6, 16. Sarah, minor, gct New Garden MM
1829, 10, 8. Elizabeth dis jH
1834, 5, 8. Lewis & w, Elizabeth, & ch,
    Thomas, John C., Joshua W., Eliza & James,
    recrq (H)
1845, 8, 7. Joel dis disunity
1847, 8, 19. Lewis & w, Elizabeth, & ch,
    Joshua, James & Susan, gct Marleborough
    MM (H)

MORLAN
----, --, --. Jason & Martha
    Ch: Elisabeth b 1798, 8, 5
    Jason m 2nd Mary -----
    Ch: Mary   b 1800, 9, 25
        Chas.   " 1803, 2, 24
        Ann   " 1805, 1, 10
----, --, --. Isaac & Martha
    Ch: Albert   b 1814, 10, 23
        Charity " 1816, 9, 12
        Joel   " 1819, 7, 7
        Joseph   " 1822, 7, 14
        Harriet " 1824, 4, 11
        Isaac   " 1826, 9, 28
        Mary   " 1829, 9, 14
        Martha   " 1831, 2, 26
1819, 5, 27. Rosea, s Stephen & Mary, Colum-
    biana Co., O.; m at Fairfield, Ann INGLE-
    DUE, dt William & Magdalene, Columbiana
    Co., O.
    Ch: Wm.   b 1820, 4, 15
        Amos   " 1823, 4, 19
        Abner   " 1824, 8, 29
        Rachel   " 1828, 4, 25
        Sally Ann " 1829, 9, 18
1819, 12, 30. Richard, s Stephen & Mary, Co-
    lumbiana Co., O.; m at Fairfield, Mary
    ERWIN, dt Samuel & Sarah, Columbiana Co.,
    O.
    Ch: Samuel E. b 1821, 11, 8
        Stephen R. " 1823, 9, 14
        James H. " 1825, 11, 14
        Wm. S.   " 1828, 4, 19
        Charles L. " 1830, 9, 11
        Erwin C. " 1835, 8, 7
1821, 8, 30. Barzilla, s Stephen & Mary, Co-
    lumbiana Co., O.; m at Fairfield, Rebecca
    LEWIS, dt Jesse & Jane, Columbiana Co., O.

MORLAN, continued

----, --, --. Mordecai & Eliza Ann
    Ch: Edwin D.   b 1822, 4, 18
       Lenora   " 1823, 10, 22
       Theophelus " 1826, 6, 16
       Roxana   " 1828, 1, 30
       Caroline   " 1831, 8, 18
       Micajah   " 1833, 7, 29
       Newberry   " 1835, 6, 3
       Elmira   " 1837, 3, 11
       Amelia   " 1839, 9, 20
1822, 1, 3. Aden, s Stephen & Mary, Columbi-
    ana Co., O.; m at Middleton, Rebecca
    HEALD, dt John & Phebe, Columbiana Co., O.
1827, 12, 10. Wm. d bur Fairfield
1827, 12, 29. Abner d bur Fairfield
1830, 1, 9. Mary d bur Fairfield
1837, 11, 2. Mary d bur Fairfield
----, --, --. Theopholus b 1826,6,26 d 1902,1,
    16; m Lydia FRENCH, dt B. & M., b 1827,12,
    2 d 1859,4,26
    Ch: Mary M.   b 1857, 8, 14
    Theopholus m 3rd Sarah P. HOLLOWAY, dt
    D. & R., b 1830,8,23 d 1908,1,7
    Ch: David H.   b 1862, 4, 8
       Anna   " 1865, 2, 21
       Wilson C.   " 1867, 2, 20 d 1867,10,11
       Mordecai   " 1869, 1, 22 " 1871, 3,21
       Charles P. " 1871, 8, 16
       Lewis T.   " 1874, 8, 11 " 1909, 2,21
1884, 12, 25. David H., s Theophilus & Sarah
    P. (Holloway), Columbiana Co., O., b
    1862,4,8; m at Middleton, Eliza A. ASHTON,
    dt Barak & Jane (Leech), b 1856,1,8
1886, 12, 23. Anna m Abner S. HALL
1886, 12, 23. Mary F. m Nathan KIRK
1899, 7, 20. Chas. P., s Theophilus & Sarah
    P., Columbiana Co., O., b 1871,8,16; m at
    Middleton, Semira Ellen EDGERTON, dt Jesse
    & Semira, Columbiana Co., O., b 1875,9,30
    Ch: Laurence L.
             b 1902, 11, 12
       Melva S.   " 1906, 5, 31 d 1909, 1,10
       Anna Mary   " 1908, 1, 31
1906, 6, 28. Louis T., s Theophilus & Sarah
    P., Columbiana Co., O., b 1874,8,11 d
    1909,2,21; m at Middleton, Eva D. COURT-
    NEY, dt Joseph Addison & Jennie B., Co-
    lumbiana Co., O., b 1866,8,23

1803, 12, 10. Mary [Morland] & dt, Elisabeth,
    rocf Goose Creek MM, dtd 1802,9,4, en-
    dorsed by Westland MM
1803, 12, 10. Jonah [Moreland] & w, Mary, rocf
    Goose Creek MM, dtd 1802,9,4, endorsed by
    Westland MM, 1803,11,26
1807, 9, 12. Emily [Morlin] (form Armstrong)
    con mcd
1808, 8, 13. Jonah [Morelan] recrq
1808, 10, 8. Aden [Morelan] gct Salem MM, to
    m Amy John
1809, 1, 14. Amy [Moreland] rocf New Garden
    MM, dtd 1809,12,15

1810, 3, 10. Ruth Anna [Morelan], dt Jonah &
    Emela, recrq
1811, 4, 13. Jason & w, Ann, recrq
1813, 12, 9. Mary & ch, Mordecai, Hosea &
    Barsilla, rocf Goose Creek MM, Va., dtd
    1813,9,2
1813, 12, 9. Isaac rocf Goose Creek MM, Va.,
    dtd 1813,9,2
1813, 12, 9. Richard rocf Goose Creek MM,
    Va., dtd 1813,9,2
1814, 1, 6. Isaac gct Salem MM, to m Martha
    Wright
1814, 7, 7. Martha rocf Salem MM, dtd 1814,
    5,17
1817, 6, 16. Elizabeth Mankin (form Morlan)
    dis mou
1818, 4, 13. Barzilla [Morelan], minor s Mary
    gct Salem MM
1821, 4, 23. Barzillan rocf Salem MM, dtd
    1821,3,21
1822, 2, 18. Rebecca gct Carmel MM
1822, 10, 21. Barzilla dis jas
1823, 1, 20. Mordecai & w, Eliza Ann, & ch,
    Edwin D., rocf Sandy Spring MM, dtd
    1822,9,27
1823, 11, 17. Huldah rocf New Garden MM, dtd
    1823,8,2
1826, 6, 19. Huldah Smith (form Morlan) dis
    mou
1827, 1, 11. Stephen, minor, rocf New Garden
    MM, dtd 1826,12,21
1828, 12, 11. Mary dis jH
1829, 7, 9. Rebecca [Morlin] dis jH
1830, 10, 7. Ann dis jH
1830, 11, 11. Hosea dis joining Separatists
1831, 7, 7. Mordecai & w, Eliza Ann, & ch,
    Edwin, Lanora, Theopholis & Rosina, gct
    Salem MM
1834, 12, 11. Matilda & Jesse Lewis, ch Bar-
    zillai, gct Marlborough MM
1836, 6, 9. Ann & ch, Amos, Rachel, Sally
    Ann, Lucy Ann & Huldah A., gct Marl-
    borough MM (H)
1836, 9, 19. Amos, Rachel & Sally Ann, ch
    Hosea & Ann, gct Marlborough MM
1838, 4, 23. Albert gct Chesterfield MM
1839, 12, 12. Mordecai & w, Eliza Ann, & ch,
    Edwin D., Lanora, Theopholis, Roxana,
    Caroline, Micajah, Newberry, Elmira &
    Amelia, rocf Sandy Spring MM, dtd 1839,
    11,22
1840, 9, 10. Charity Mann (form Morlan) dis
    mou
1844, 1, 11. Harriet Shaw (form Morlan) dis
    mcd
1844, 3, 7. Edwin D. dis disunity
1844, 4, 11. Harriet Shaw (form Morlan) dis
    mou
1845, 4, 10. Lydia Ann (form Townsend) dis
    mcd
1846, 4, 9. Lydia Ann [Morland] (form Town)
    send) con mcd (H)
1847, 5, 6. Joseph dis mou

MORLAN, continued

1851, 2, 6. Martha Williams (form Morlan) dis mou

1851, 9, 18. Theophilis gct Salem MM

1851, 9, 18. Caroline dis joining Methodist Society

1851, 10, 9. Roxana Wilson (form Morlan) dis joining Methodist Society

1852, 2, 12. Lenora M. Lenhart (form Morlan) dis mou & joining Methodist Society

1852, 6, 10. Mordicai & w, Eliza Ann, & ch, Micajah, Newberry, Amelia, Elmira & Albert, gct Salem MM, Ia.

1855, 1, 11. Amanda Grosscup (form Morlan) dis mou & jas

1856, 6, 12. Frances Godert (form Morlan) dis mou

1860, 6, 16. Mary Shafer (form Moreland) dis mou & joining Methodist

1861, 5, 18. John dis mou

1863, 5, 16. Theophilus & w, Sarah P., & ch, Mary M. & David H., rocf Salem MM, dtd 1863,4,22

1863, 7, 18. Martha Rhodes (form Morland) dis mcd

1864, 8, 17. Richard & w, Caroline O., & ch, Samuel E., Stephen R., James H., Charles L., Edwin C., William S., Albert & Mary, attached to this mtg when Beaver Falls MM, Pa. was laid down (H)

1864, 8, 17. Lydia Ann (form Townsend) attached to this mtg when Beaver Falls MM, Pa. was laid down (H)

1871, 2, 18. Harvey dis mcd & jas

1872, 11, 16. Theophilus & w, Sarah P., & ch, Mary M., David H., Anna & Charles P., gct Salem MM, O.

1873, 5, 17. Amy Jane gct Salem MM, O.

1880, 6, 19. Isaac dis mcd

1883, 6, 16. David H. rocf Salem MM

1883, 10, 20. Theophilus & w, Sarah P., & ch, Charles P. & Lewis T., rocf Salem MM, dtd 1883,9,19

1883, 10, 20. Mary F. & Anna rocf Salem MM, dtd 1883,9,19

1909, 6, 19. Charles P. & w, S. Ellen, & ch, Lawrence L. & Anna Mary, gct Salem MM, O.

1918, 7, 20. Eva D. gct Salem MM

MORRIS

1804, 7, 14. Hannah & ch, Barzilla, Esther, Sarah & Thomas, rocf Redstone MM, dtd 1804,5,4

1805, 8, 10. Sally & ch, Mary & Lydia, rocf Contentney MM, N. C., dtd 1804,9,8, endorsed by Concord MM, 1804,12,18

1805, 8, 10. Susannah & dt, Amy, rocf Contentney MM, N. C., dtd 1804,9,8, endorsed by Concord MM, 1804,12,18

1805, 8, 10. Lydia rocf Contentney MM, N. C., dtd 1804,9,8, endorsed by Concord MM, 1804,12,18

1811, 11, 7. Isaiah & w, Mary, & ch, Joseph,

Lydia & John, recrq

1827, 11, 8. Daniel Boulton gct Upper Springfield MM, to m Esther Morris

1862, 9, 20. Amasa dis mou

1873, 4, 19. Martha A. (form Tullos) dis mcd

MORSE

1898, 4, 7. Kenneth, s Wm. H. Perry & Emma Jane (Lobb), b

1930, 7, 19. Kenneth rocf Salem MM, dtd 1930,6,25

MOSS

1859, 8, 20. Margaret (form Neal) dis mou (first rpd 1856,6,12)

MURPHY

1846, 12, 10. Sarah (form Prichett) dis mou

MYERS

1805, 5, 11. Alice & ch, William & Elizabeth, rocf Westland MM, dtd 1805,3,23

1864, 8, 17. Mary T. (form Townsend), w Wm., attached to this mtg when Beaver Falls MM, Pa. was laid down (H)

NEILL

----, --, --. Morton b 1811,9,4 d 1887,12,4; m Ann ------ b 1817,12,23 d 1884,12,29
    Ch: Guli Elma b 1839, 7, 9
        Edith C.   " 1844, 11, 13

1841, 8, 18. Enos [Neal], s Elijah & Comfort, Beaver Co., Pa.; m at New Brighton, Belmont Co., O., Eleanor COOK, dt Ellis & Elizabeth
    Ch: Hannah W. b 1842, 5, 22
        Elizabeth
        C.   " 1843, 11, 9

1892, 3, 12. Eva M. b

1913, 2, 20. Eva M. m Emerson CONRAD

1837, 7, 17. Enos H. [Neal] rocf North Berwick MM, Maine, dtd 1837,6,27

1849, 10, 11. Allen Heald gct Carmel MM, to m Rebecca Neal

1850, 7, 11. Enos H. [Neal] & w, Eleanor C., & ch, Hannah W., Elizabeth C. & Mary Agnes, gct Pleasant Plain MM, Iowa

1859, 8, 20. Margaret Moss (form Neal) dis mou (first rpd 1856,6,12)

1863, 7, 18. John [Neil] dis disunity

1863, 8, 15. Martha Watson (form Neil) dis mcd

1863, 8, 15. Ruth Adams (form Neil) dis mcd

1869, 11, 20. Edith E. Stanley (form Neill) rpd mcd (d before case was settled)

1881, 9, 17. Eva D. Courtney, minor under care of Morton & Ann Neill, recrq

1908, 3, 21. Eva M. recrq

NEWPORT

1806, 10, 11. Mary Baldwin (form Newport) dis

NEWPORT, continued
    mou

NICHOLS
----, --, --. Samuel & Tryphena
    Ch: Benjamin   b 1836, 9, 23
        Wm.   " 1838, 10, 30
1837, 9, 14. Stacy, s William & Mary, Colum-
    biana Co., O.; m at Columbiana, Faithful
    MERCER, dt Thomas & Hannah, Columbiana
    Co., O. (H)
    Ch: Martha Ann b 1839, 3, 24
        Thomas   " 1841, 4, 4
1838, 9, 20. Mary m Jesse M. ALLEN (H)
----, --, --. Wm., s Wm. & Mary (Mathers), b
    1879,1,1; m Minnie LINHOSS, dt Adam & Eva
    (Wenger), b 1875,3,28
    Ch: Wm.
        Linhoss   b 1903, 5, 4
        Mary Vir-
         ginia   " 1904, 9, 17 d 1929,--,--
        Elwood
         Keagy   " 1907, 3, 22
        David Al-
         pheus   " 1912, 4, 5
        Paul Adam " 1916, 7, 12
1929, 12, 28. Richard Elwood, s Elwood K. &
    Julia (Patten), b 1929,12,28
----, --, --. Alpheus, s Jesse & Mary E.

1833, 2, 7. Samuel rocf Goose Creek MM, dtd
    1832,9,13 (H)
1833, 8, 8. Samuel gct Newgarden MM, to m
    Triphena Hanna (H)
1835, 1, 8. Tryphena rocf New Garden MM, dtd
    1834,10,23 (H)
1835, 1, 8. Zilpha rocf New Garden MM, dtd
    1834,10,23 (H)
1835, 11, 12. Stacy & w, Martha Ann, rocf
    Goose Creek MM, dtd 1835,10,15 (H)
1836, 6, 9. William & w, Cassandra, & ch,
    Margery, William & Mahlon, rocf Goose
    Creek MM, dtd 1836,4,14 (H)
1836, 6, 9. Jesse rocf Goose Creek MM, dtd
    1836,4,14 (H)
1836, 6, 9. Mary rocf Goose Creek MM, dtd
    1836,4,14 (H)
1838, 3, 19. Faithful (form Mercer) dis mcd
1839, 1, 10. Jesse gct Goose Creek MM, Va.,
    to m Mary E. Brown (H)
1839, 12, 12. Mary E. rocf Goose Creek MM,
    Va., dtd 1839,9,12 (H)
1839, 12, 12. Margery Metzger (form Nichols)
    dis mou (H)
1847, 9, 16. Mahlon gct Goose Creek MM, Va.,
    to m Ruth Hannah Pancoast (H)
1848, 7, 13. Ruth Hannah rocf Goose Creek MM,
    Va., dtd 1848,4,13 (H)
1920, 10, 16. William recrq
1921, 1, 15. Minnie L. recrq
1921, 7, 16. Ch of William & Minnie recrq
1928, 6, 16. Elwood K. gct New Garden MM, to
    m Julia Patten

NIGH
1844, 5, 9. Mary (form Garwood) dis mcd

NORTH
1839, 2, 14. Jesse, s John & Margaret, Colum-
    biana Co., O.; m at Middleton, Elizabeth
    PRICHETT, dt Joab & Mary, Columbiana Co.,
    O.
    Ch: Sarah   b 1839, 10, 30
        Mary Jane " 1841, 11, 8

1838, 12, 6. Jesse rocf Upper Evesham MM,
    N. J., dtd 1838,11,10
1839, 10, 10. Abel rocf Frankford MM, Pa., dtd
    1839,7,30
1841, 5, 6. Abel dis mcd
1845, 6, 12. Jesse & w, Elizabeth, & ch, Sa-
    rah, Mary Jane & John, gct Upper Spring-
    field MM

NUTT
1807, 1, 10. Jonathan [Nut] & w, Elizabeth,
    rocf Fairfax MM, dtd 1806,7,27
1811, 5, 9. Cert rec for Hannah from Fair-
    fax MM, endorsed to Westland MM

OAKLEY
1808, 11, 12. Alicean [Okeley] (form Wilson)
    dis mou
1813, 7, 8. Baltimore MM granted permission
    to rst Elisana
1820, 5, 22. Alisana rocf Indian Spring MM,
    Md., dtd 1820,3,17
1829, 7, 9. Alice Ann dis jH

OGDEN
1882, 10, 24. Richard T., s John & Hannah W.,
    Phila., Pa.; m at Middleton, Ellen C.
    HOOPES, dt Mifflin & Ellen Cadwallader,
    Columbiana Co. O.

1806, 3, 8. Stephen & w, Hannah, rocf Darby
    MM, dtd 1805,1,16
1883, 8, 18. Ellen C. H. Ogden & Allen J. &
    Dallas P. Cadwalader, minors under her
    care, gct ND MM, Phila., Pa.

OGLESBY
1811, 4, 13. Margaret (form Stratton) dis mou

OLIPHANT
----, --, --. Samuel & Elizabeth
    Ch: Rachel   b 1781, 11, 22
        Wm.   " 1783, 5, 5
        Ann   " 1785, 10, 11
        Rebecca   " 1888, 4, 24
        Samuel   " 1790, 1, 22
        Ephraim   " 1792, 1, 28
1787, 8, 11. Wm. d bur Beaver Falls
1804, 9, 13. Ann m Richard BEESON
1806, 2, 20. Rachel m Caleb COWGILL
1809, 11, 16. Rebecca m Ebenezer ALLMON
1814, 11, 17. Samuel, s Samuel & Elizabeth,

OLIPHANT, Samuel, continued
Columbiana Co., O.; m at Middleton, Rachel
HEALD, dt Wm. & Sarah, Columbiana Co., O.
Ch: Wm.   b 1816, 5, 14
    Elizabeth " 1817, 10, 8
    Ann   " 1820, 5, 7
    John   " 1822, 5, 20
    Rachel   " 1824, 4, 15
    Sarah   " 1826, 4, 19
    Israel   " 1828, 8, 20
1816, 1, 18. Ephraim, s Samuel & Elizabeth,
Columbiana Co., O., b 1792,1,28; m at
Middleton, Elizabeth HEALD, dt Wm. & Sa-
rah, Columbiana Co., O., b 1796,10,3
d 1847,12,17
Ch: Sarah   b 1817, 3, 23
    Abner   " 1819, 9, 10
    Mahlon   " 1824, 11, 15
    Mary Ann   " 1827, 3, 30
    Israel   " 1836, 12, 16
    Jonathan   " 1839, 6, 11
1837, 3, 2. Sarah m Josiah FAWCETT
1845, 5, 15. William H., s Samuel & Rachel,
Columbiana Co., O.; m at Middleton, Sina
W. SIDWELL, dt Eli & Sarah, Belmont Co.,
O.
1846, 6, 18. Mahlon, s Ephraim & Elizabeth,
Columbiana Co., O.; m at Middleton, Sarah
Ann DIXON, dt Samuel & Hannah, Columbiana
Co., O.
1846, 9, 24. Mary Ann [Olophant] m John HICK-
LEN
1847, 8, 8. Sarah Ann, dt Samuel Dixson, d
bur Middleton
1848, 10, 19. John, s Samuel & Rachel, Mahoning Co., O.; m at Middleton, Maria HEALD,
dt Thomas & Miriam, Columbiana Co., O.
1853, 4, 14. Sarah m Joseph ARMSTRONG
1856, 11, 13. Sina m Israel ARMSTRONG
1820, 1, 17. Ephraim & w, Elizabeth, & ch,
Sarah H. & Abner, rocf Carmel MM, dtd
1820,1,15
1829, 10, 8. Ephraim & w, Elisabeth, & ch,
Sarah, Abner, Mahlon, Mary Ann & Lydia,
gct Salem MM
1830, 1, 7. Samuel, Jr. & w, Rachel, & ch,
William H., Eliza Ann, John, Sarah, Rachel & Israel, gct Salem MM
1836, 8, 22. Ephraim & w, Elizabeth, & ch,
Abner, Mahlon, Mary Ann & Ruth, rocf Salem MM, dtd 1836,6,22
1836, 8, 22. Sarah rocf Salem MM, dtd 1836,
6,22
1845, 12, 11. Sina W. gct Salem MM
1849, 2, 8. Maria gct Salem MM
1849, 7, 12. Abner [Olliphent] gct Gilead MM
1850, 3, 7. Ephraim gct Upper Springfield
MM, to m Sarah Smith
1850, 7, 11. Rachel & ch, Samuel, Sina &
Lydia, rocf Salem MM, dtd 1850,6,19
1850, 7, 11. Sarah rocf Salem MM, dtd 1850,6,
19
1850, 11, 7. Sarah rocf Upper Springfield MM,

dtd 1850,9,28
1850, 12, 12. Ann rocf Salem MM, dtd 1850,11,
20
1850, 12, 12. Rachel rocf Salem MM, dtd 1850,
11,20
1852, 5, 6. Mahlon gct Salem MM, Ia.
1852, 7, 8. Ephraim & w, Sarah, & ch, Israel & Jonathan, gct Salem MM
1852, 10. 7. Ruth gct Salem MM
1862, 7, 19. Samuel gct Hickry Grove MM
1862, 7, 19. Ann gct Hickory Grove MM. Ia.
1864, 9, 17. Lydia gct Hickery Grove MM, Ia.
(d before cert was sent)

PACKER
1814, 5, 12. George rocf Warrington MM, dtd
1813,12,2

PADEN
1825, 3, 17. Isaac, s Isaac & Rebecca, Crawford Co., Pa.; m at Conniautt, Celia
FISH, dt Joseph & Deborah, Crawford Co.,
O.

1822, 9, 23. Isaac rocf Redstone MM, dtd
1822,7,31
1822, 9, 23. Rebecca rocf Redstone MM, dtd
1822,7,31
1830, 2, 11. Isaac dis disunity
1830, 6, 10. Celia dis jH

PAINTER
1804, 1, 4. Jacob & w, Mary, & ch, David,
Samuel, Robert, Abigail & Joseph, rocf
Crooked Run MM, dtd 1802,10,2, endorsed
by Westland MM, dtd 1803,10,22
1823, 2, 17. Hannah (form Reynolds) dis mou

PANCOAST
1847, 9, 16. Mahlon Nichols gct Goose Creek
MM, Va., to m Ruth Hannah Pancoast (H)

PARKER
1845, 7, 12. Melanethon, ch Wm. & Ann, b

1844, 3, 7. William & w, Ann, & ch,
Claudius Galin & Joseph John, rocf Short
Creek MM, dtd 1843,7,18, endorsed by
Sandy Spring MM, 1844,2,23
1849, 5, 10. William J. dis disunity
1873, 3, 15. Melancthan dis mcd
1873, 5, 17. Joseph dis mcd
1873, 11, 15. Ann F. dis joining Separatists

PATTEN
1928, 6, 16. Elwood K. Nichols gct New Garden
MM, to m Julia Patten

PATTERSON
1844, 11, 11. Matthew, s Ira & Mahala, Athens
Co., O.; m at Middleton, Louisa McCLURE,
dt Seth & Mary, Beaver Co., Pa.

PATTERSON, continued
1845, 2, 6. Louisa gct Chesterfield MM

PAUL
1836, 6, 9. William & w, Mary Ann, & ch,
Abigail W., Hannah T. & Sarah, rocf Morris
River MM, dtd 1836,4,14 (H)
1838, 4, 12. William M. & w, Mary Ann, & ch,
Abigail K., Hannah T., Sarah & Michal,
gct Springborough MM (H)

PAXSON
1811, 9, 18. Benjamin, s Jacob & Mary, Columbiana Co., O.; m at Elkrun, Mary WALKER,
dt James & Elizabeth, Columbiana Co., O.

1803, 10, 8. Ruth & ch, William, Mary, John,
Rachel & Sarah, rocf Goose Creek MM, dtd
1802,10,16, endorsed by Westland MM, dtd
1803,9,24
1805, 10, 12. Sarah [Paxon] rocf Fairfax MM,
dtd 1805,6,22
1816, 8, 12. Mary Spencer (form Paxton) con
mcd
1817, 10, 13. Benjamin & w, Mary, & ch, John,
Rachel, Samuel, Isaac, Charles, Sally &
Ruth, gct Plainfield MM
1818, 11, 23. Richard Hawley gct Plainfield
MM, to m Rachel Paxton
1820, 8, 21. William [Paxton] dis mou

PEARSON
1817, 11, 10. Sarah (form Reynolds) dis mou

PECK
1829, 5, 14. Ann m John PUGH (H)

1829, 4, 9. Ann rocf Baltimore MM, dtd 1829,
2,6
1829, 8, 6. Ann Pugh (form Peck), mbr Baltimore MM, dis mcd & jH

PELLETT
1807, 9, 12. Francis & w, Mary, & ch, Eleanor,
Abel, John, Mary & Elizabeth, rocf Westland MM, dtd 1807,7,27

PEMBERTON
1924, 8, 16. Rolland Blackburn gct Upper
Springfield MM, to m Julietta Pemberton

PENNOCK
1800, 6, 30. Hannah d
1811, 1, 16. John, s William & Mary, Columbiana Co., O.; m at Elkrun, Sarah WALKER,
dt James & Elizabeth, Columbiana Co., O.

1811, 3, 9. Sarah gct Salem MM

PETTIT
1810, 7, 14. Daniel [Pettet] & w, Martha, &
dt, Rebecca, rocf Sadsbury MM, dtd 1810,6,
5

1810, 7, 14. Lucretia [Pettet] rocf Sadsbury
MM, dtd 1810,6,5
1811, 1, 12. Cert rec for Charles [Pettet]
from Sadsbury MM, some time ago, endorsed
to New Garden MM
1814, 6, 9. Lucretia Dixon (form Pettit) con
mcd
1817, 4, 14. Martha (form Mercer) dis mcd
1824, 5, 17. Sarah, minor, rocf Sandy Spring
MM, dtd 1824,3,26
1825, 6, 20. Rebecca dis jas
1826, 4, 17. Mary, minor, rocf Carmel MM,
dtd 1826,3,18
1829, 2, 12. Sarah & Mary, minors, gct Carmel MM

PHAGON
1814, 5, 12. Harmin [Phagin] & w, Lydia, rocf
Centre MM, Pa., dtd 1813,10,16
1814, 5, 12. Ephemia [Phagen] rocf Centre
MM, Pa., dtd 1813,10,16
1817, 11, 10. Harmon & w, Lydia, gct New
Garden MM
1817, 12, 15. Uphemia gct New Garden MM

PHARO
1812, 2, 6. Elizabeth rocf Chesterfield
MM, N. J., dtd 1811,11,5

PHELPS
1812, 11, 12. Susannah (form Boyce) dis mou
1814, 7, 7. Sarah con mou

PHILIPS
1881, 1, 15. Mary Elizabeth Philips (form
Cope) dis disunity

PICKERING
1808, 6, 13. Levi, s Samuel & Phebe, Belmont
Co., O.; m at Middleton, Susannah CROZER,
dt John & Elenor, Columbiana Co., O.

1808, 8, 13. Susannah gct Plainfield MM

PIDGEON
1820, 2, 21. Simon Dixson gct Salem MM, to
m Elizabeth Pidgeon

PIERCE
1811, 12, 12. Cert rec for Jane from Sadsbury MM, dtd 1811,9,3, endorsed to New
Garden MM
1822, 7, 22. James rocf Warrington MM, dtd
1822,4,17
1825, 5, 23. James gct Salem MM

PIKE
1928, 8, 18. William L. Cope gct Plainfield
MM, to m Celia Pike

PIM
----, --, --. I(aac) & C(aroline)
Ch: Sarah   b 1841, 5, 28
    Eliza   " 1843, 3, 8

PIM, continued

1824, 1, 19. Garrett [Pimm], minor, rocf
        Sandy Spring MM, dtd 1823,12,26
1826, 12, 7. Garret gct Sandy Spring MM
1841, 8, 12. Isaac [Pimm] & w, Caroline S.,
        & ch, Harvey, Hannah & Sarah, rocf Sandy
        Spring MM, dtd 1841,6,25
1848, 4, 6. Isaac & w, Caroline S., & ch,
        Harvey, Hannah, Sarah, Eliza, Lydia &
        Mary, gct Sandy Spring MM

POOL

----, --, --. Priscilla b 1827,2,16 d 1908,10,
        18

1845, 7, 10. Jonas & w, Ann, & dt, Sarah
        Jane, rocf Carmel MM, dtd 1845,6,21
1845, 7, 10. Asenath H. & Priscilla H.
        [Poole] rocf Carmel MM, dtd 1845,6,21
1885, 4, 18. Sarah Jane dis disunity

POTTS

1834, 9, 11. Ann rocf Radner MM, dtd 1834,8,14
        (H)
1836, 2, 11. Ann gct Honey Creek MM, Ind. (H)

PRICE

1933, 9, 20. Frances E., s Edwin G. & Irene,
        Columbiana Co., O.; m at Middleton, Helen
        P. COPE, dt Elbert Loren & Malinda P., Co-
        lumbiana Co., O.

1864, 8, 17. John T. & w, Rebecca W., & ch,
        Ferris W., Charles C. & Hannah B., attach-
        ed to this mtg when Beaver Falls MM, Pa.
        was laid down (H)
1934, 1, 20. Helen C. gct New Garden MM

PRICHETT

----, --, --. Joab & Mary
        Ch: Isaac   b 1806, 8, 4
            Rachel   " 1808, 8, 3
            Sarah   " 1810, 9, 6
            Elizabeth   " 1813, 4, 12
            Hannah   " 1815, 9, 2
            Wm.   " 1818, 11, 7
            Joseph   " 1821, 8, 8
----, --, --. Phebe b 1820,1,30 d 1904,1,10
1821, 9, 30. Wm., s Joab & Mary, d bur Middle-
        ton
1829, 5, 14. John S., Beaver Co., Pa.; m at
        Beaver Falls, Ann PECK, Baltimore, Md. (H)
1839, 2, 14. Elizabeth m Jesse NORTH
----, --, --. J. & P.
        Ch: Mary Ann   b 1841, 9, 15
            Wm. Henry   " 1846, 7, 2
            Rheuben
              Emmett   " 1850, 12, 7
1851, 5, 3. Joel d
1858, 1, 4. Hannah d

1817, 7, 14. Joab [Prichet] & ch, John,
        Isaac, Rachel, Sarah, Elizabeth & Hannah,

recrq

1817, 11, 10. Mary rocf Greenwich MM, dtd
        1817,8,27
1829, 2, 12. John gct White Water MM
1833, 12, 12. Isaac dis disunity
1845, 6, 2. Joseph dis disunity
1846, 12, 10. Sarah Murphy (form Prichett)
        dis mou
1849, 10, 11. Rachel Cope (form Prichett) dis
        mou
1874, 3, 21. Reuben dis mcd
1885, 1, 17. Mary Ann dis disunity

PUGH

----, --, --. John & Sarah
        Ch: Jonathan   b 1805, 5, 8
            Mary Ann   " 1807, 4, 24
            Joseph   " 1909, 5, 6
            Caroline   " 1812, 3, 3
1806, 9, 16. Jonathan, s John & Sarah, d
1826, 7, 16. Sarah, w John, d bur Beaver
        Falls

1804, 8, 11. Lydia rocf Uwickland MM, dtd
        1804,4,5
1804, 9, 8. Sarah rocf Ewchland MM, dtd
        1804,5,10
1828, 7, 10. Mary Ann Sealy (form Pugh) dis
        mou
1828, 10, 9. Evan dis joining Separatists
1828, 10, 9. John dis joining Separatists
1828, 12, 11. Lydia dis JH
1829, 7, 9. Joseph T. dis JH
1829, 7, 9. Caroline dis JH
1829, 8, 6. Ann (form Peck), mbr Baltimore
        MM, dis mcd & JH
1832, 4, 18. Caroline Miner (form Pugh) con
        mcd (H)
1832, 6, 7. Caroline P. Miner (form Pugh)
        con mcd (H)
1834, 1, 9. Joseph T. con mcd (H)
1864, 8, 17. Joseph T. attached to this mtg
        when Beaver Falls MM, Pa. was laid down
        (H)

PYLE

1857, 3, 24. Henry, s Benjamin & Elizabeth,
        Columbiana Co., O.; m at home of Benjamin
        Taylor, Rebecca TAYLOR, dt Joshua &
        Elizabeth (H)

1830, 7, 8. Joseph & w, Abigail, & ch, Jo-
        seph & Gardner, rocf Chester MM, Pa., dtd
        1830,4,30
1830, 7, 8. William rocf Chester MM, Pa.,
        dtd 1830,4,30
1830, 10, 7. Naomi, Martha & Sarah, rocf
        Chester MM, Pa., dtd 1830,4,30
1831, 7, 7. Joseph dis disunity
1831, 7, 7. Abigail, Naomi, Martha & Sarah
        dis JH
1831, 8, 11. William dis JH
1852, 6, 17. Aaron rocf Carmel MM, dtd 1852,

PYLE, continued
3,20 (H)

RALEIGH
1858, 11, 17. Thomas gct Short Creek MM (H)

RALEY
1807, 3, 14. Robert & fam gct Salem MM
1862, 2, 12. Mary Longshore (form Raley) con
mcd (H)
1865, 5, 20. John [Railey] dis mou
1871, 12, 16. Edward Stratton gct Short Creek
MM, to m Mary H. Raley

RANDLE
1816, 7, 15. William, Jr. & w, Esther, rocf
Warrington MM, Pa., dtd 1816,4,17

RANDOLPH
1822, 6, 17. Edward F. gct Carmel MM

RAWLINGS
1890, 6, 21. Abbie T. (form Wickersham) dis
mcd

REED
1854, 1, 12. White Water MM, Ind. was granted
permission to rec Mary B. in mbrp

REEDER
1805, 1, 17. Joseph, s Thomas & Priscilla,
Columbiana Co., O.; m at Middleton, Hannah
HAINS, dt Levi & Elisabeth, Columbiana
Co., O.

1806, 1, 11. Cert rec for Thomas [Reader]
& w, Priscilla, & ch from South River MM,
Va., dtd 1805,10,9, endorsed to Salem MM
1844, 6, 6. Ann [Reader] recrq
1845, 1, 9. Achsah rocf Carmel MM, dtd
1844,12,21
1846, 7, 9. Ann gct Sandy Spring MM
1847, 5, 6. Israel Mendenhall gct Sandy
Spring MM, to m Ann Reader
1876, 2, 19. Achsah [Reader] gct Upper
Springfield MM, O.

REEVES
1805, 9, 14. Joshua [Rieve] & w, Mellicent,
& ch, Hannah, Samuel Carr & Ellen, rocf
Mt. Holly MM, dtd 1805,9,5
1807, 5, 9. Mary recrq
1808, 6, 11. Mary gct Salem MM
1814, 6, 9. Benjamin [Reaves] & w, Ann, &
ch, Ann, Matilda, Susannah & Harriett,
recrq
1823, 7, 31. Susannah Miller (form Reeves)
dis mou
1824, 8, 23. Ann Robinson (form Reeves) dis
mou
1827, 4, 12. Harriet Burson (form Reeves)
dis mou

1829, 7, 9. Benjamin dis disunity
1829, 10, 8. Ann dis disunity
1830, 3, 11. Matilda dis disunity
1830, 3, 11. Benjamin & w, Ann, gct Carmel
MM (H)

REYNOLDS
----, --, --. James & Hannah
Ch: Rebecca   b 1791, 1, 29
Elizabeth   " 1793, 7, 29
John   " 1795, 6, 27
Nancy   " 1797, 10, 3
Maria   " 1800, 10, 4

1805, 1, 12. Hannah & ch, Henry, Sarah, Rebekah, Elisabeth, John, Ann, Moriah &
Hannah, rocf Westland MM, dtd 1804,10,27
1811, 12, 12. Henry dis mou
1817, 11, 10. Rebecca Chinewith (form Reynolds) dis mou
1817, 11, 10. Sarah Pearson (form Reynolds)
dis mou
1818, 2, 16. Elizabeth dis joining Methodist Society
1820, 11, 20. Mariah Justice (form Reynolds)
dis mou
1823, 2, 17. Hannah Painter (form Reynolds)
dis mou
1823, 3, 17. John dis mou
1856, 2, 7. John dis mou
1859, 5, 21. Isaac dis mou & joining Methodist Society

RHODES
1846, 8, 6. Caroline (form Townsend) dis
mou
1863, 7, 18. Martha (form Morland) dis mcd
1864, 8, 17. Caroline (form Townsend) attached to this mtg when Beaver Falls MM, Pa.
was laid down (H)

RICHARDS
----, --, --. Abijah, s Rowland & Mary, b
1753,5,23; m Esther DANIEL, dt Wm. & Es-
ther, b 1766,12,9
Ch: Samuel   b 1789, 4, 4
Esther   " 1792, 6, 18
Edith   " 1794, 3, 16
Abijah   " 1796, 6, 30
Mary   " 1800, 6, 11
Rowland   " 1806, 6, 3
Eli   " 1807, 6, 9
1809, 6, 14. Esther m John JAMES
----, --, --. Elizabeth b 1824,1,22 d 1911,2,4
1855, 5, 22. Esther d ae 89y (an elder)

1815, 2, 9. Edith Davis (form Richards) con
mou
1816, 7, 15. Abijah, Jr. con mou
1860, 1, 21. Elizabeth Young (form Richards)
con mou

RICHARDSON
1805, 11, 21. Lydia m Aaron MENDENHALL
1808, 3, 17. Hannah m Thomas MERCER

1804, 6, 19. Lydia rocf Westland MM, dtd
     1804,4,28
1804, 6, 19. Mary rocf Westland MM, dtd
     1804,4,28
1814, 5, 12. John, Jr. con mou
1814, 5, 12. Sarah Denny (form Richardson)
     dis mou
1874, 4, 18. Susannah (form Adamson) dis mcd
     (first rpd 1872,7,20)

RICHEY
1851, 12, 11. Mary (form Allmon) con mou
1864, 7, 16. Mary dis jas

RIGG
----, --, --. Hiram & Sarah
     Ch: Jesse   b 1833, 1, 20
         David   " 1834, 4, 15
         Thomas   " 1836, 6, 3
         Joseph   " 1838, 4, 28
         Hannah   " 1840, 3, 23

1847, 3, 9. Hiram & w, Sarah, & ch, Jesse,
     Mary Ann, David B. M. L. & Thomas W.,
     rocf Carmel MM, dtd 1836,10,15

ROBBERMAN
----, --, --. Henry & Caroline [Roberman]
     Ch: Helena   b 1837, 4, 29
         Mary   " 1839, 6, 30
         Lewis N.   " 1842, 1, 11

1837, 10, 23. Henry rocf two months mtg at
     Menden, Prussia
1837, 10, 23. Henry, Jr. rocf two months mtg
     at Menden, Prussia
1837, 12, 18. Caroline recrq
1838, 1, 22. Charlotte, Henry & Hallena, ch
     Henry, Jr. & Caroline, recrq
1841, 5, 6. Charlotte gct Chesterfield MM
1841, 6, 10. Henry, Sr. gct Chesterfield MM
1841, 6, 10. Henry D. [Roberman], minor, gct
     Chesterfield MM
1842, 10, 6. Henry [Raberman], Jr. & w, Caro-
     line, & ch, Hellena, Mary & Lewis W., gct
     Chesterfield MM

ROBBINS
1823, 12, 22. Mary (form Cadwallader) con mou
1825, 2, 21. Mary gct Salem MM

ROBINSON
1824, 8, 23. Ann (form Reeves) dis mou

ROGERS
----, --, --. Ann b 1792,10,9 d 1876,12,29

1848, 7, 6. Lydia Ann (form Erwin) dis mou
1869, 12, 18. Ann rocf Providence MM, dtd

1869,12,2
1877, 4, 21. Mary C. (form Cope) dis mcd
     (first rpd 1874,8,15)

ROLLER
1854, 2, 9. Sarah (form Hole) dis mou

ROTHCHILD
1826, 6, 19. Alice Edgerton dis

RUDIBOUGH
1841, 12, 9. Isabel (form Woods) dis mcd

RUNDEL
1836, 9, 26. Esther [Rundal] m Cyrus MENDEN-
     HALL

1835, 8, 17. Esther recrq

SAMMS
----, --, --. John b 1758,4,23 d 1842,5,17;
     m Sarah ----- b 1762,--,--
     Ch: Ann   b 1786, 5, 17
         John   " 1789, 5, 11
         Benj.   " 1790, 9, 3
         Jesse   " 1793, 2, 10
         Rachel   " 1796, 7, 5
         Isaac   " 1804, 3, 3 d 1804,10,12
1803, 11, 17. Sarah m Samuel SHAW
1804, 10, 12. Isaac d bur Middleton
1813, 9, 16. Ann m Thomas WICKERSHAM
1819, 11, 14. Sarah, w John, d bur Middleton
1824, 1, 1. Rebecca m Prophet BROWN
1842, 2, 8. John, Jr. d bur Middleton

1821, 6, 18. Jesse con mou
1823, 4, 21. John gct Carmel MM
1825, 6, 20. John, Jr. rocf Carmel MM, dtd
     1825,6,18
1828, 11, 6. John dis joining Separatists
1829, 3, 12. Benjamin dis jH
1830, 8, 12. Jesse dis jH
1836, 9, 19. John, Jr. gct Salem MM
1839, 1, 10. John rst by rq (form dis jH)
1840, 5, 7. John, Jr. rocf Salem MM, dtd
     1840,4,22

SANDERS
1804, 8, 11. Ann & ch, Sarah, Charity, Abi-
     shai, Benjamin, Rebeckah, Levi & Jesse,
     rocf Wrightsborough MM, Ga., dtd 1804,4,7

SCHOOLEY
1805, 6, 12. Mary m Benjamin TEST
1845, 5, 15. Emily [Schooly] m Moses V. BUT-
     LER
----, --, --. James & Rebeccah [Schooly]
     Ch: Israel   b 1846, 8, 1
         Sarah Jane " 1848, 3, 9
1807, 10, 10. Phebe gct Salem MM
1831, 7, 7. Daniel Mercer gct Salem MM, to
     m Sarah Schooley
1832, 3, 8. Sarah Mercer & ch, Rachel &

SCHOOLEY, continued
    Emley Schooly, rocf Salem MM, dtd 1831,9,
    21
1834, 4, 10. Rachel [Schooly], minor dt Sa-
    rah Mercer, gct Sandy Spring MM
1836, 4, 18. Elisha [Schooly], minor, rocf
    Salem MM, dtd 1836,3,23
1842, 9, 15. Elisha [Schooly] dis jas
1847, 6, 10. James & w, Rebecca, & s, Israel,
    rocf Upper Springfield MM, dtd 1847,4,24
1849, 12, 6. James & w, Rebecca, & ch, Is-
    rael M. & Sarah Jane, gct Salem MM, Ia.

SCOTT
1808, 10, 13. Israel, s Benjamin & Sarah, Co-
    lumbiana Co., O.; m at Middleton, Sarah
    HOLLOWAY, dt Asa & Mary, Columbiana Co.,
    O.

1807, 12, 12. Benjamin & w, Sarah, & ch, Is-
    rael, Ann, Elizabeth, Joseph, William,
    Benjamin, Sarah & Jacob, rocf Goose Creek
    MM, Va., dtd 1807,9,28
1812, 1, 9. Israel & w, Sarah, & ch, Mary &
    Phebe, gct Salem MM
1816, 12, 16. Israel & w, Sarah, & ch, Mary,
    Phebe, Eli, Eliza Ann & Job, rocf Salem
    MM, dtd 1816,11,12
1817, 4, 14. Israel & w, Sarah, & ch, Mary,
    Phebe, Eli, Eliza Ann & Job, gct Marlboro
    MM
1817, 8, 11. Joseph gct New Garden MM, to m
    Jane Marsh
1838, 5, 10. Newton Dixon gct Marlborough MM,
    to m Eliza Ann Scott (H)

SEALY
1828, 7, 10. Mary Ann (form Pugh) dis mou

SEEBOHM
1836, 7, 17. Daniel Koll & w, Julia (form
    Seebohm) rocf Pyrmont & Minden MM, Prussia,
    dtd 1836,3,6, endorsed by Baltimore MM
    for East or West Dist., 1836,6,9

SHAFER
1860, 6, 16. Mary (form Moreland) dis mou &
    joining Methodist

SHANE
1832, 8, 9. Samuel, minor, rocf Sandy Spring
    NM, dtd 1832,6,22

SHARP
1823, 2, 1. Deborah m Jeremiah BROWN

1816, 6, 10. Sarah & ch, Deborah, Isaac, Sa-
    rah & Mary, recrq
1818, 8, 10. Enoch recrq
1819, 2, 22. Enoch rocf Evesham MM, N. J.,
    dtd 1818,12,11
1820, 4, 17. Deborah dis
1822, 10, 21. Deborah rst in mbrp

1827, 5, 10. Isaac gct Sandy Spring MM
1828, 5, 8. Enoch & w, Sarah, & dt, Mary,
    gct Upper Springfield MM
1828, 5, 8. Sarah, Jr. gct Upper Springfield
    MM

SHARPLESS
----, --, --. Benjamin b 1777,4,16; m Amy
    CADWALADER, dt S. & S., b 1779,12,16
    Ch: Isaac   b 1802, 4, 15
        Septimus C." 1804, 6, 21
        Ellen T.   " 1806, 10, 16 d 1836, 3,10
        Edwin A.   " 1809, 4, 26
        Albert F. " 1811, 5, 1
1829, 10, 9. Ellen T. m Mifflin CADWALLADER
    (H)
----, --, --. Septimus C. b 1804,6,21 d 1865,
    6,24 bur Falling Springs; m Sarah NEGUS,
    dt John & Mariam, b 1807,4,23 d 1824,8,
    18 bur Falling Springs
    Ch: Isaac   b 1836, 5, 2
        John   " 1837, 4, 2
        Nathan   " 1838, 4, 11
        Lavina   " 1839, 7, 21
        Amy   " 1840, 11, 26
        Miriam   " 1841, 11, 29
        Evi   " 1844, 6, 3
        Israel   " 1847, 12, 7
        Lydia   " 1848, 6, 25
1836, 3, 31. Albert [Sharplis], s Benjamin &
    Amy, Mercer Co., Pa.; m at Middleton,
    Lydia HEALD, dt Wm. & Sarah, Mercer Co.,
    Pa.
    Ch: Benj.   b 1837, 2, 2
        Ellen   " 1839, 8, 22
        Sarah   " 1842, 1, 23

1804, 4, 14. Amy & s, Isaac, rocf Redstone
    MM, dtd 1804,3,30
1830, 7, 8. Eleanor Cadwalader (form Sharp-
    less) dis mcd & joining Separatists
1830, 8, 12. Edwin dis joining Separatists
1831, 9, 8. Amy dis disunity
1834, 6, 12. Septimus C. gct Salem MM
1836, 5, 12. Edwin con mou (H)
1843, 1, 12. Septimus C. & w, Sarah, & ch,
    Isaac, Nathan, Lavina, Amy & Miriam, rocf
    Upper Springfield MM, dtd 1842,12,24
1845, 5, 8. Albert & fam gct Gilead MM
1851, 12, 11. Septamus C. [Sharples] & w, Sa-
    rah, & ch, Isaac, Nathan, Lavina, Amy,
    Miriam, Evi & Lydia, gct Salem MM, Ia.

SHAW
1803, 11, 17. Samuel, s Samuel & Mary, Wash-
    ington Co., Pa.; m at Middleton, Sarah
    SAMMS, dt Thomas & Mary Carrington, Co-
    lumbiana Co., O.
1810, 9, 20. Thomas, s Samuel & Susannah,
    Columbiana Co., O.; m at Middleton, Rachel
    HEALD, dt Nathan & Rebecca, Columbiana
    Co., O.
----, --, --. Samuel b 1813,12,25 d 1879,9,

SHAW, continued
    25; m Penina HEALD, dt Joseph & Ury, b
    1819, 3,1 d 1900,10,20
      Ch: Hiel   b 1839, 8, 3 d 1864,10,29
          Seth   " 1843, 4, 17
----, --, --. Nathan & Miriam
      Ch: Thos. E.   b 1840, 8, 11
          Ezra   " 1842, 7, 31
          Eliza Ann   " 1844, 4, 10
          Susannah   " 1845, 10, 29
1840, 3, 14. Joseph L., s N. & M., d bur Elk-
    run
1845, 8, 14. William, s Thomas & Rachel, Co-
    lumbiana Co., O.; m at Middleton, Phebe
    HEALD, dt Thomas & Miriam, Columbiana Co.,
    O.
1847, 1, 9. Phebe, w Wm., d bur Middleton
----, --, --. Wm. b 1824,12,29; m Hannah -----
    b 1826,12,16
      Ch: Lindley   b 1852, 5, 26 d 1888,11,10
          Milton   " 1854, 9, 8
          Wm. Wilson " 1856, 10, 9
          Phebe Ellen" 1860, 2, 24
          Thos. H.   " 1862, 5, 29 d 1862, 7,24
          Charles   " 1864, 6, 4
          Susanna   " 1866, 9, 8
1865, 10, 25. Seth, s Samuel & Penina (Heald),
    Columbiana Co., O., b 1843,4,17 d 1930,7,
    28 bur Middleton; m at Elk Run, Martha S.
    ASHTON, dt Barak & Jane (Leech), Columbi-
    ana Co., O., b 1846,5,18
1871, 11,'20. Rebecca m Jeremiah COPPOCK

1805, 3, 16. Sarah dis disunity
1811, 2, 9. Rachel gct New Garden MM
1838, 8, 9. Samuel gct Carmel MM, to m
    Peninah Heald
1839, 1, 10. Peninah rocf Carmel MM, dtd
    1828,12,15
1840, 2, 6. Nathan & w, Miriam, & ch, Jo-
    seph L., Rachel H. & Sarah Ann, rocf Car-
    mel MM, dtd 1840,1,18
1842, 11, 10. William, minor, rocf Sandy
    Spring MM, dtd 1842,9,23
1844, 1, 11. Harriet (form Morlan) dis mcd
1844, 4, 11. Harriet (form Morlan) dis mou
1847, 4, 8. Nathan & w, Mariam, & ch, Ra-
    chel H., Sarah Ann, Thomas E., Ezra,
    Eliza Ann & Susannah, gct Goshen MM, O.
1847, 12, 9. Thomas rocf Sandy Spring MM,
    dtd 1847,9,24
1848, 8, 10. Thomas gct Sandy Spring MM
1851, 7, 10. William gct Gilead MM, to m
    Hannah Heald
1851, 10, 9. Thomas rocf Sandy Spring MM,
    dtd 1851,5,23
1851, 11, 6. Hannah rocf Gilead MM, dtd 1851,
    9,20
1852, 1, 8. Rebecca rocf Sandy Spring MM,
    dtd 1851,11,21
1862, 8, 10. Hiel gct Salem MM
1867, 11, 9. William dis joining Separatists
1868, 1, 18. Hannah dis joining Separatists

1872, 9, 21. Lindley, Milton, William Wil-
    son, Phebe Ellen, Charles & Susannah,
    ch William & Hannah, gct New Garden MM,O.
1873, 6, 21. Hannah rst by rq
1873, 10, 18. William rst by rq
1881, 3, 19. Margaret Maria Shinbron, minor
    under care of Seth & Martha Shaw, recrq
1922, 7, 15. Seth dis
1925, 8, 15. Seth rst by rq

SHINBRON
1872, 3, 28. Margaret M. b

1881, 3, 19. Margaret Maria, minor under
    care of Seth & Martha Shaw, recrq
1903, 2, 21. Margaret M. Jones (form Shim-
    bron) dis mou

SHINN
1805, 5, 16. Thomas, s Caleb & Mary, Columbi-
    ana Co., O.; m at Middleton, Rebecca
    DANIEL, dt James & Hannah, Columbiana Co.,
    O.

1803, 10, 8. Thomas & w, Abigail, & ch, Mary
    & Joshua, rocf Mountholly MM, N. J., dtd
    1803,7,7, endorsed by Westland MM, 1803,9,
    24
1803, 11, 12. Mary rocf Upper Springfield MM,
    N. J., dtd 1803,8,3, endorsed by Westland
    MM, 1803,9,24

SHIPMAN
1864, 8, 17. Caroline (form Hoops) attached
    to this mtg when Beaver Falls MM, Pa. was
    laid down

SHOEMAKER
1843, 5, 11. Samuel rocf Goose Creek MM, dtd
    1843,3,16 (H)
1845, 11, 6. Samuel gct Goose Creek MM, Va.

SHORE
1804, 7, 14. James & ch, Rebekah, Alice &
    Rachel, rocf Westland MM, dtd 1804,4,28
1804, 7, 14. Sarah rocf Goose Creek MM, dtd
    1803,12,2, endorsed by Westland 1804,3,24

SHOTWELL
1828, 5, 8. Isaac Line gct Rahway & Plain-
    field MM, N. J., to m Bathsheba Shotwell

SIDDALL
1817, 8, 13. Atticus, s Sarah Burke, Columbi-
    ana Co., O.; m at Elkrun, Sarah JAMES, dt
    Isaac & Sarah, Columbiana Co., O.

1805, 11, 9. William [Siddle] & w, Sarah, &
    dt, Hannah, rocf Fairfax MM, Va., dtd
    1805,6,22
1817, 5, 12. Atticus recrq

SIDWELL
1845, 5, 15. Sina W. m William H. OLIPHANT

1804, 2, 11. Isaac & w, Rebecca, rocf Fair-
    fax MM, dtd 1803,12,24
1824, 7, 19. Abner Heald gct Short Creek MM,
    to m Cinah Sidwell
1845, 3, 6. Sina W. rocf Smithfield MM, dtd
    1844,11,18

SIMMS
1812, 4, 9. Jane recrq
1829, 7, 9. Jane dis jH

SLOCUM
1839, 6, 6. Mary (form Line) dis mou

SMATHERS
1851, 6, 12. Hannah (form McBride) dis mcd

SMITH
1806, 10, 13. Samuel, s John & Sarah, Mononga-
    hela Co., Pa.; m at Middleton, Catharine
    HARVEY, dt Jacob & Jane, Beaver Co., Pa.

1804, 12, 8. Rachel & ch, Samuel, Thomas,
    Phebe & Sarah, rocf Westland MM, dtd 1804,
    11,24
1805, 5, 11. Elisabeth (form Townsend) dis
    mou
1807, 1, 10. Catharine gct Redstone MM
1808, 8, 13. Thomas, Jr. dis disunity
1808, 12, 10. Phebe Webb (form Smith) dis mou
1810, 10, 13. Samuel con mou
1812, 8, 6. Sarah Kinsey (form Smith) con
    mou
1817, 3, 10. Joanna recrq
1826, 6, 19. Huldah (form Morlan) dis mou
1834, 6, 12. Rachel (form Beeson) dis mou
1836, 11, 10. Phebe rocf New Garden MM, dtd
    1836,2,25 (H)
1844, 11, 7. Dover MM, Ind. was given per-
    mission to rec Huldah in mbrp
1850, 3, 7. Ephraim Oliphant gct Upper
    Springfield MM, to m Sarah Smith
1899, 8, 19. Martha P. (form Hall) con rcd
1917, 4, 21. Martha P. dis jas

SPENCER
1816, 8, 12. Mary (form Paxton) con mcd
1817, 12, 15. Mary gct Plainfield MM

STACKHOUSE
1816, 12, 15. Hannah (form Daniel) con mou
1818, 12, 21. Hannah gct New Garden MM

STANLEY
1815, 1, 18. James, s James Crew & Mary, Co-
    lumbiana Co., O.; m at Elkrun, Rachel COW-
    GILL, dt James & Charlotte, Columbiana
    Co., O.

1805, 12, 14. Thomas & w, Unity, & ch rocf

rocf Cedar Creek MM, Va., dtd 1805,10,12
1806, 6, 14. Jonathan & w, Mary, & ch rocf
    Cedar Creek MM, dtd 1805,11,9
1815, 11, 9. Rachel gct Salem MM
1863, 12, 19. Mary H. (form Marsh) dis mcd
1869, 2, 20. Ruth A. (form Armstrong) rpd
    mcd (d before case was settled)
1869, 11, 20. Edith E. (form Neill) rpd mcd (d
    before case was settled)
1923, 9, 15. Sina E. recrq
1924, 7, 19. Sina E. gct Salem MM, O.

STANTON
1864, 8, 17. David attached to this mtg when
    Beaver Falls MM, Pa. was laid down (H)

STAPLETON
1879, 10, 23. Adaline m Joseph HEALD

1814, 8, 11. Susannah rocf Westland MM, dtd
    1814,4,23
1815, 6, 8. Joshua rocf Westland MM, dtd
    1814,9,1
1816, 10, 14. Samuel rocf Westland MM, dtd
    1816,5,23
1879, 5, 17. Adaline recrq

STARBUCK
1919, 6, 21. Herbert D. Hall gct Salem MM, to
    m Martha Starbuck

STARR
1815, 12, 7. Rebecca rocf Gwynedd MM, Pa.,
    dtd 1815,4,27
1816, 12, 16. Rebecca Stokes (form Starr) dis
    mou
1824, 3, 22. George L. rocf Green St. MM,
    Phila., Pa., dtd 1823,11,20
1826, 6, 12. George dis mcd

STEER
1914, 6, 20. Elisha T. Kirk gct Short Creek
    MM, to m Alice May Steer

STEWARD
1822, 11, 18. Lydia (form Dixson) dis mou
1826, 5, 22. Aaron & w, Mercy, & ch, Eliza,
    Samuel, Joseph, John & William, recrq
1828, 11, 6. Aaron & w, Massey, & ch, Eliza,
    Samuel, Joseph, John & William, gct Upper
    Springfield MM
1905, 6, 17. Elnora S. [Stewart] (form Heald)
    dis mou & jas

STOCK
----, --, --. Eliza b 1810,1,16 d 1896,8,28

STOKES
1840, 5, 13. Beulah Ann m Elwood THOMAS

1816, 12, 16. Rebecca (form Starr) dis mou
1837, 7, 17. Rachel V. recrq
1837, 8, 21. John S. rocf ND MM, Phila., Pa.,

STOKES, continued
  dtd 1837,6,27
1838, 1, 22. Malvina F. & Alice R., ch John
 & Rachel, recrq
1838, 7, 12. Caleb & w, Ruth, & dt, Ruthanna,
 rocf Phila. MM, Pa., dtd 1838,5,24
1838, 7, 12. Beulah Ann rocf Phila. MM, dtd
 1838,5,24
1841, 10, 7. Caleb & w, Ruth, gct 12th St.
 MM, for Western Dist., Phila., Pa.
1841, 10, 7. Ruth Anna gct 12th St. MM for
 Western Dis., Phila., Pa.
1842, 6, 9. John S. & w, Rachel V., & ch,
 Melvina F. & Alice R., gct Burlington MM,
 N. J.

STOKESBERRY
1881, 2, 14. Inetta P. b

1807, 3, 14. Sarah rocf Crooked Run MM, dtd
 1807,5,31
1816, 4, 15. Ruth, Susannah, Rachel, Isaac,
 William, Henry & John, ch Sarah, recrq
1856,. 6, 12. John, Jr. dis mou
1880, 4, 17. Maria Elma [Stooksberry] (form
 Cope) con mcd
1887, 10, 15. Inetta Pearl [Stookesberry] recrq
1903, 5, 16. Emma M. [Stokesbery] dis disunity

STRATTON
----, --, --. Joseph & Ann
 Ch: Daniel b 1800, 9, 25
  John   " 1803, 2, 29
  Sarah " 1805, 5, 7
  Rebecca " 1807, 4, 21
  Owen " 1809, 11, 11
----, --, --. Jacob & Rebeccah
 Ch: Joel b 1801, 10, 13
  Hannah " 1803, 9, 29
  Ann   " 1805, 11, 19
  Mark " 1807, 11, 21
  Sarah " 1810, 1, 5
1807, 10, 15. John [Stratan], s Daniel & Mary,
 Columbiana Co., O.; m at Middleton, Hes-
 ter (Esther) GARWOOD, dt Isaiah & Mary,
 Columbiana Co., O.
 Ch: Amy b 1809, 12, 4
  Ruth " 1812, 4, 21
  Sabina " 1814, 6, 16 d 1827,11,26
   bur Fairfield
  David b 1816, 6, 28
  Levi " 1819, 9, 10 d 1827,11,24
   bur Fairfield
  Isaiah b 1822, 3, 14 " 1827,12, 1
   bur Fairfield
  John b 1824, 11, 6 " 1827,11,24
   bur Fairfield
  Mary b 1827, 8, 26
1807, 3, 26. David, s Daniel & Mary, Columbi-
 ana Co., O.; m at home of James Erwin, Mary
 GARWOOD, dt Isaiah & Mary, Columbiana Co.,
 O.

1809, 3, 16. Mary m Thomas GARWOOD
1814, 12, 14. Ann m John COPE
1817, 11, 13. Rebecca m Caleb COPE
1819, 3, 4. Joshua, s Michal & Rhoda, Colum-
 biana Co., O.; m at Beaver Falls, Rachel
 TOWNSEND, dt Joseph & Sarah, Beaver Co.,
 Pa.
1820, 8, 31. Elias, s Daniel & Shady, Colum-
 biana Co., O.; m at Fairfield, Mary INGLE-
 DUE, dt William & Magdalene, Columbiana
 Co., O.
----, --, --. Edward b 1822,5,20; m Mary
 ----- b 1815,1,1 d 1869,12,23
 Ch: Lemira b 1844, 5, 5
  Joshua " 1847, 3, 2
 Edward m 2nd Mary H. RALEY, dt Asa &
 Asenath, b 1834,9,15
 Ch: Alfred b 1872, 12, 23
1865, 9, 21. Semira m Jesse EDGERTON

1804, 1, 4. Joseph & w, Naomi, & ch, Hannah,
 & Joel, rocf South River MM, Va., dtd
 1802,11,9, endorsed by Westland MM, 1803,
 12,24
1804, 3, 10. Rebekah [Straton], w Jacob, &
 dt, Hannah, rocf South River MM, dtd
 1802,9,11, endorsed by Westland MM, 1803,
 12,24
1804, 7, 14. Ann rocf Crooked Run MM, dtd
 1804,3,3
1805, 3, 9. Amy recrq
1805, 4, 13. Amy & ch, Rebekah, Naomi, Levi
 & Ephraim, rocf Redstone MM, dtd 1804,11,
 30
1807, 10, 10. Joseph, Jr. rocf Upper Evesham
 MM, dtd 1807,8,8
1810, 5, 12. Jacob & w, Rebecca, & ch, Hannah
 & Sarah, gct Miami MM
1810, 5, 12. Joseph & w, Naomi, gct Miami MM
1810, 5, 12. Hannah, dt Joseph & Naomi, gct
 Miami MM
1810, 5, 12. Joel gct Miami MM, O.
1810, 7, 14. Margaret gct Salem MM, O.
1810, 11, 10. Cert granted to Salem MM for
 Margaret returned with information that
 she had mou
1811, 4, 13. Margaret Oglesby (form Stratton)
 dis mou
1811, 8, 8. Daniel, John & Sarah, ch Ann,
 recrq
1816, 7, 15. David & w, Mary, & ch, Isaac,
 Mary, John & Hope, gct Salem MM
1817, 7, 14. Daniel, minor, gct Salem MM
1819, 4, 19. Benjamin & w, Amy, & ch, Levi,
 Ephraim, Benjamin, Jerusha, Martha, Mary,
 Joseph & Samuel, gct West Grove MM
1819, 4, 19. Naomi gct West Grove MM, Ind.
1819, 4, 19. Rachel gct Salem MM
1819, 12, 20. John Cope & w, Ann, & ch, John,
 Sarah, Rebecca & Owen Stratton, & Mary,
 Ruth, Edith & Joseph Cope, gct Darby Creek
 MM
1820, 2, 21. Daniel dis mou

STRATTON, continued

1822, 1, 29. Elias dis disunity
1823, 2, 17. Daniel gct Darby Creek MM, O.
1823, 7, 31. Mary dis jas
1825, 6, 20. Sarah dis
1827, 10, 11. Evi rocf Salem MM, dtd 1827,6,20
1829, 2, 12. Shady & Almira, ch Elias & Mary, gct Darby Creek MM, O.
1830, 1, 7. Ruth dis disunity
1830, 2, 11. Amy dis jH
1831, 7, 7. Esther dis disunity
1835, 11, 23. Evi gct Upper Springfield MM
1837, 8, 21. David dis disunity
1859, 4, 16. Edward & w, Mary, & ch, Semira & Joshua, rocf Salem MM, dtd 1859,3,23
1867, 11, 9. William W., adopted s Edward & Mary, recrq
1871, 12, 16. Edward gct Short Creek MM, to m Mary H. Raley
1872, 4, 20. Mary H. rocf Short Creek MM, dtd 1872,3,19
1874, 1, 17. Edward & w, Mary H., & s, Alfred, & William W. Stratton, a minor under their care, gct Salem MM
1885, 8, 15. Joshua dis mcd

STUART

----, --, --. Aaron & Mercy
     Ch: Elisa   b 1813, 9, 10
         Samuel   " 1817, 9, 15
         Joseph   " 1820, 4, 1
         John   " 1822, 11, 18
         Wm.   " 1825, 9, 28

STUCK

1823, 6, 23. Pemela Maria (form Beal) dis mou

SWEENEY

1923, 10, 20. Maria S. rocf Scipio MM, N. Y., dtd 1923,8,15

SWIGERT

1847, 2, 11. Cynthia (form Allen) dis mou

TALBOTT

1838, 1, 31. William, s Benjamin & Susannah, Jefferson Co., O.; m at New Brighton, Pa., Adaline TOWNSEND, dt David & Mary, Beaver Co., Pa.

1829, 6, 11. Cert rec for Benjamin I. [Talbot] from Smithfield MM, dtd 1828,11,17, returned to that mtg
1851, 8, 9. William rst by rq (form dis by Smithfield MM)
1852, 6, 10. William & w, Adeline, gct Pleasant Plain MM, Ia.

TAYLOR

----, --, --. Thomas b 1798,12,18 d 1867,9,30; m Sarah EDMUNDSON, dt John, b 1802,12,13 d 1875,6,14
1827, 2, 14. Joseph, s Joseph & Sarah, Colum-

biana Co., O.; m at Fairfield, Mary COPE, dt Jesse & Margaret, Columbiana Co., O., d 1882,9,13
     Ch: Lavina   b 1828, 4, 27
         Amos   " 1829, 12, 23
         Hannah   " 1832, 5, 17
         Cinthy Ann " 1835, 5, 17 d 1838,11,24 bur Middleton
         Oliver   b 1840, 9, 14
         Mary Louisa " 1844, 5, 12 " 1848, 8,19 bur Middleton
1840, 12, 15. Steven d bur Middleton
1846, 8, 26. Sarah, w Joseph, Sr., d
1854, 9, 21. Amos, s Joseph & Mary, Columbiana Co., O., b 1829,12,23; m at Middleton, Ruth Anna LIPSEY, dt John & Ann, Columbiana Co., O., b 1830,5,21
     Ch: Wilmer L.   b 1855, 6, 22
1857, 3, 24. Rebecca m Henry PYLE
1882, 12, 26. Joseph d bur Middleton
1882, 5, 8. Sarah d bur Middleton

1811, 5, 9. Esther (form Hoops) con mou
1812, 8, 6. Joseph & w, Sarah, & ch, Thomas, Joseph, John, Amos, Sarah & Jacob, recrq
1820, 11, 20. Thomas gct Carmel MM, to m Sarah Edmundson
1821, 3, 19. Sarah, w Thomas, rocf Carmel MM, dtd 1821,3,17
1825, 2, 21. John dis mou
1828, 12, 11. Esther dis jH
1830, 1, 7. Sarah, w Thomas, dis jH
1831, 12, 8. Joseph, Sr. dis disunity
1832, 4, 12. Mary Hodge (form Taylor) dis mcd & jH
1832, 7, 12. Jacob dis disunity
1833, 3, 7. Deborah Allen (form Taylor) dis mou & jH
1833, 8, 8. Deborah Allen (form Taylor) dis mcd (H)
1833, 4, 11. Sarah, Jr. dis jH
1839, 2, 7. Sarah E. rst by rq
1841, 4, 8. Stephen con mou
1848, 1, 6. Lavina dis disunity
1852, 3, 11. Hannah Holloway (form Taylor) con mcd
1856, 10, 18. Amos dis disunity
1859, 6, 18. Ruth Anna dis disunity
1860, 3, 17. Olover dis mou

TEEGARDEN

1860, 10, 20. Mary (form Hole) dis mou

TEST

1805, 6, 12. Benjamin, s Zaccheus, Columbiana Co., O.; m at Salem, Mary SCHOOLEY, dt Elisha & Rachel, Columbiana Co., O.

1803, 11, 12. Hannah & ch, Isaac, Samuel & Joseph, rocf Woodburgh MM, dtd 1803,8,9, endorsed by Concord MM, dtd 1803,10,15

THOMAS

1840, 5, 13. Elwood, s Samuel & Mary, Beaver
    Co., Pa., b 1814,5,15; m at New Brighton,
    Pa., Beulah A. STOKES, dt Caleb & Ruth,
    Beaver Co., Pa., b 1810,7,18
        Ch: Mary M.   b 1841, 3, 1
            Levi
            Stokes   " 1843, 12, 13
            Samuel C.   " 1846, 12, 12
            Robert P.   " 1851, 5, 1
            Lydia K.   " 1855, 6, 25
----, --, --. Robert P. b 1851,5,1; m Susan
    McGREW
        Ch: Benjamin J.b 1877, 2, 12
            Walter T.   " 1878, 5, 1
            Gilbert E. " 1880, 3, 29

1805, 12, 14. David & w, Mary, rocf Redstone
    MM, dtd 1805,6,28
1809, 1, 14. Abel rocf Redstone MM, dtd 1808,
    9,30
1810, 5, 12. David & w, Mary, & s, Abel, gct
    Miami MM
1836, 4, 7. Lydia & ch, John H., Elijah,
    Evan, Mary Jane, Oliver F. & Reese D.,
    rocf Gwyned MM, Pa., dtd 1836,3,3 (H)
1837, 12, 18. Harvey rocf ND MM, Phila., Pa.,
    dtd 1837,11,21
1838, 1, 22. Ellwood rocf Abington MM, Pa.,
    dtd 1837,11,27
1839, 1, 10. Samuel rocf Abington MM, Pa.,
    dtd 1838,11,26
1840, 5, 7. John H. gct Radnor MM, Pa. (H)
1840, 7, 9. Lydia & ch, Mary Jane, Evan D.,
    Oliver & Reese D., gct Radnor MM (H)
1840, 7, 9. Elizabeth H. gct Radnor MM (H)
1841, 10, 7. Elijah gct Horseham MM (H)
1843, 6, 8. Harvey gct Upper Springfield MM
1850, 8, 8. Elwood & w, Beulah Ann, & ch,
    Mary M., Levi Stokes & Samuel Caleb, gct
    Frankford MM, Pa.
1852, 6, 10. Cert granted to Frankford MM,
    Pa., 1850,8,8 for Elwood & fam returned;
    now living within limits of this mtg
1864, 7, 16. Rachel gct Plymouth MM
1870, 7, 16. Elwood & Samuel dis joining
    Separatists
1871, 8, 19. Levi gct Kennet MM, Pa.
1874, 1, 17. Samuel C. rst in mbrp
1875, 10, 16. Levi & s, Arthur H., gct Goshen
    MM, Pa.
1875, 10, 16. Robert P. gct Short Creek MM,
    O., to m Susan McGrew
1876, 9, 16. Sarah M. rocf Short Creek MM,
    dtd 1876,8,22
1881, 12, 17. Elmer H., Bertha A., Beulah May
    & Carrie E., ch Samuel C. & Josephine,
    recrq
1882, 2, 18. Elwood rst by rq
1885, 11, 21. Robert P. & w, Susan M., & ch,
    Benjamin J., Walter S. & Gilbert E., gct
    Short Creek MM
1887, 4, 16. Elwood & w, Beulah A., gct Short

Creek MM, O.
1887, 5, 21. Mary M. gct Short Creek MM
1891, 10, 17. Samuel C. dis disunity
1897, 3, 20. Bertha A., Beulah M. & Carrie
    E. dis disunity
1897, 4, 17. Elmer H. dis disunity

THOMPSON
1811, 10, 10. Rachel recrq
1813, 9, 9. Joseph recrq
1824, 12, 24. Elizabeth (form Beeson) dis mou

THORN
1826, 8, 21. Peter M. recrq
1829, 11, 12. Peter M. dis JH

TOWNSEND
1805, 1, 17. Lydia m Jonathan MENDENHALL
1806, 12, 25. Talbot, s Francis & Rachel, Bea-
    ver Co., Pa.; m at Middleton, Eliza CAD-
    WALADER, dt Septimus & Sarah, Mercer Co.,
    Pa.
1808, 12, 15. Isaac, s Francis & Rachel, Bea-
    ver Co., Pa.; m at Middleton, Elizabeth
    DIXSON, dt Joshua & Dinah, Columbiana Co.,
    O.
1812, 6, 17. Lydia m Edward McCONNALL
1813, 3, 18. Ruth m Levi McCONNEL
1817, 4, 24. Abel, s Joseph & Sinah, Beaver
    Co., Pa.; m at Beaver Falls, Rebecca WAY,
    dt John & Mary, Alegany Co., Pa.
        Ch: Mary Way   b 1818, 9, 9
            John   " 1819, 4, 24
            Joseph Tal-
            bott   " 1820, 10, 2
            Mira   " 1822, 6, 4
            Celicia   " 1824, 11, 29
            Lydia   " 1826, 7, 7 d 1827, 7,25
            bur Beaver Falls
            Lazetta   b 1828, 1, 11
----, --, --. Tolbert & Edith
        Ch: Elizabeth b 1818, 3, 15
            Milton   " 1820, 11, 3
            Lydia   " 1824, 11, 6
            Caroline   " 1826, 2, 20
            Alfred   " 1827, 8, 20
            Alizan   " 1830, 4, 10
1819, 3, 4. Rachel m Joshua STRATTON
1825, 7, 26. Mary d bur Beaver Falls
1826, 11, 20. Lydia m Jesse BAILY
1830, 6, 11. Nathan, s David & Mary, Beaver
    Co., Pa.; m at Columbiana, Sarah MERCER,
    dt Thomas & Hannah, Columbiana Co., O.
----, --, --. David & Mary
        Ch: David   b 1833, 7, 29
            Mary   " 1836, 8, 19
1833, 8, 25. Arvine, s Francis & Ann, b
1838, 1, 31. Adaline m William TALBOTT
1841, 10, 13. Milo A., s Talbot & Edith,
    Beaver Co., Pa.; m at New Brighton, Pa.,
    Elizabeth WALKER, dt Lewis & Rachel, Bea-
    ver Co., Pa.
1842, 7, 22. Lemuel J. G., s Milo A. & Eliza-

TOWNSEND, continued
beth N., b
1845, 8, 11. Elmina m Albert M. COFFIN

1804, 9, 8. Lydia rocf New Garden MM, dtd
1804,5,5
1805, 5, 11. Elisabeth Smith (form Townsend)
dis mou
1808, 8, 13. Abel gct Westland MM
1808, 8, 13. Hannah, dt Sarah, gct Westland
MM
1808, 11, 12. Sinah & ch, Rachel, Martha &
Francis, gct Westland MM
1809, 1, 14. Lewis, minor, gct Hopewell MM
1809, 7, 8. Elizabeth (form Dixon) dis
1809, 9, 9. Isaac dis
1810, 9, 8. Mary McClure (form Townsend) dis
mou
1813, 1, 7. Abel rocf Westland MM, dtd
1812,7,25
1813, 1, 7. Francis, minor, rocf Westland
MM, dtd 1812,7,25
1814, 6, 9. John dis mou
1815, 9, 7. Talbert gct Salem MM, to m Edith
Ware
1816, 2, 12. Edith rocf Salem MM, dtd 1815,
12,12
1816, 5, 13. Rachel rocf Hopewell MM, Va.,
dtd 1816,2,8
1817, 3, 10. Sina rocf Hopewell MM, Va.,
dtd 1816,6,6
1817, 7, 14. Sina gct Salem MM, O.
1817, 11, 10. Hannah rocf Westland MM, dtd
1817,10,23
1821, 6, 18. Hannah gct Salem MM
1822, 11, 18. New Garden MM was given permission to rst Isaac & Elizabeth
1826, 3, 20. Francis gct Salem MM
1827, 6, 7. Mary (form Hambleton) dis mou
1828, 10, 9. David dis joining Separatists
1829, 2, 12. Talbot dis joining Separatists
1829, 5, 7. Benjamin recrq (H)
1829, 5, 7. Pamela recrq (H)
1829, 6, 11. Nathan dis jH
1829, 8, 6. Isaac & w, Elizabeth, & ch, Samuel, John Dixon, Mary, Caroline, Rachel,
Elizabeth, Lydia & Rebecca, rocf New Garden MM, dtd 1829,6,25 (H)
1829, 8, 6. Maria rocf New Garden MM, dtd
1829,6,25 (H)
1829, 12, 10. David gct Sadsbury MM, to m Mary
B. Cowl (H)
1830, 2, 11. James Dallas dis jH
1830, 6, 10. Mary B. Townsend & ch, Joseph
B., Charles & Susanna Coale, rocf Sadsbury
MM, Pa., dtd 1830,3,2 (H)
1831, 3, 10. James D. con mou (H)
1831, 6, 9. Joseph B., Charles & Susannah
Coal, ch Mary Townsend, rocf Sadsbury MM,
dtd 1831,2,8
1831, 7, 7. Isaac & w, Elizabeth, & ch, Samuel, Mary, Caroline, Rebecca, Elizabeth,
Lydia, Rachel & Isaac, gct New Garden MM

1831, 7, 7. Edith dis jH
1832, 6, 7. Ann & ch, Emmor, Lewis & Joseph,
rocf Carmel MM, dtd 1832,5,19
1834, 2, 6. Ann, w Francis, & ch, Emmor,
Lewis, Joseph & Ervine, gct Upper Springfield MM
1835, 3, 12. Nathan & w, Sarah, & ch, Lydia
Ann & Thomas M., gct Marlborough MM   (H)
1837, 2, 9. Sarah (form Bramwell) con mcd
(H)
1837, 7, 17. Rachel B. dis mou
1837, 11, 9. Nathan & w, Sarah, & ch, Lydia
Ann, Thomas M. & David W., rocf Marlborough MM, dtd 1837,5,27 (H)
1838, 4, 23. Sarah B. (form Broomhall) dis
mou
1843, 8, 10. Joseph T. gct Adrien MM, Mich.
1843, 12, 7. Milo N. dis disunity
1844, 1, 11. Milton dis disunity
1844, 6, 6. Abel W. dis disunity
1845, 4, 10. Lydia Ann Morlan (form Townsend) dis mcd
1846, 4, 9. Lydia Ann Morland (form Townsend) con mcd (H)
1846, 8, 6. Caroline Rhodes (form Townsend)
dis mou
1848, 3, 9. Eliza Gammel (form Townsend)
dis mou (forst rpd 1843,5,11)
1848, 7, 6. Pleasant Plain MM, Ia., was
granted permission to rst Sarah
1854, 10, 12. Mira H. dis
1856, 3, 6. Celicia L. Gantz (form Townsend)
dis mou
1862, 1, 18. Sina & ch, Sina Ellen & William,
gct Pennsville MM
1862, 5, 17. Tazetta Walton (form Townsend)
dis mcd
1863, 2, 21. Rebecca W. dis joining Separatists
1864, 8, 17. Mary B. attached to this mtg
when Beaver Falls MM, Pa., was laid down
(H)
1864, 8, 17. Milton attached to this mtg
when Beaver Falls MM, Pa. was laid down
(H)
1864, 8, 17. Talbot B. & w, Edith W., attached to this mtg when Beaver Falls MM, Pa.
was laid down (H)
1864, 8, 17. Eliza Gammel (form Townsend)
attached to this mtg when Beaver Falls
MM, Pa. was laid down (H)
1864, 8, 17. Alice Ann Junkins (form Townsend) attached to this mtg when Beaver
Falls MM, Pa. was laid down (H)
1864, 8, 17. Lydia Ann Morlan (form Townsend)
attached to this mtg when Beaver Falls MM,
Pa. was laid down (H)
1864, 8, 17. Mary T. Myers (form Townsend),
w William, attached to this mtg when Beaver Falls MM, Pa., was laid down (H)
1864, 8, 17. Caroline Rhodes (form Townsend)
attached to this mtg when Beaver Falls MM,
Pa. was laid down (H)

TOWNSEND, continued
1871, 9, 16. Elizabeth W. dis joining Separa-
      tists
1872, 3, 16. Lemuel dis mcd
1872, 5, 18. Charles W. dis disunity

TRUEBLOOD
1868, 7, 18. Ann Eliza (form Lipsey) dis mcd

TULLIS
----, --, --. John [Tulloss] b 1762,9,26; m
      Sarah ------ b 1766,9,12
      Ch: Rebecca   b 1791, 4, 28
          Richard   " 1794, 2, 2
          Jane   " 1797, 8, 27
          Nancy   " 1801, 1, 11
          Rhoda   " 1803, 5, 8
----, --, --. Richard & Ann
      Ch: Wm.   b 1796, 12, 15
          Jason   " 1798, 6, 1
          Ann   " 1800, 5, 1
          Jane   " 1802, 12, 5
          Sarah   " 1805, 5, 18
          Joseph   " 1807, 8, --
          Elizabeth " 1810, 1, --
          Catharine " 1812, 4, --
----, --, --. Jason & Hannah [Tulloss]
      Ch: Jonathan   b 1821, 11, 6
          Eliza   " 1822, 12, 13
          Sarah Ann " 1824, 7, 17
          Nathan   " 1826, 3, 24
          Lewis   " 1828, 2, 3 d 1831, 3, 4
            bur Elkrun
          Rachel   " 1830, 3, 24 " 1831, 3, 9
            bur Elkrun

1804, 3, 10. Sarah & ch, Rebekah, Richard,
      Jane & Naomi, rocf South River MM, dtd
      1802,11,9, endorsed by Westland MM, 1803,
      11,26
1804, 9, 8. Ann & ch, William, Jason, Ann &
      Jane, rocf Goose Creek MM, dtd 1802,2,6,
      endorsed by Westland MM, 1804,7,28
1813, 10, 7. Rebecca dis
1816, 12, 16. Richard [Tulloss], Jr. dis dis-
      unity
1832, 7, 12. Jason [Tulloss] & w, Hannah, &
      ch, Jonathan, Eliza Ann, Sarah Ann & Na-
      than, rocf Carmel MM, dtd 1832,6,16
1833, 7, 11. Jason [Tulloss] & w, Hannah, &
      ch, Jonathan, Eliza Ann, Sarah Ann & Na-
      than, gct Carmel MM
1854, 10, 12. Jane rocf Carmel MM, dtd 1854,
      9,16
1857, 10, 8. Richard dis mou
1861, 5, 18. Smith [Tulliss] com mou (d be-
      fore settlement of case)
1865, 8, 19. Err dis disunity
1867, 6, 15. Elizabeth J. McMillen (form
      Tullis) dis mcd
1873, 4, 19. Martha A. Morris (form Tullos)
      dis mcd

UNDERWOOD
1816, 11, 21. Elizabeth m James DILLON
1825, 12, 29. Willen, s Willen & Sarah, Colum-
      biana Co., O.; m at Middleton, Rachel Mc-
      CLUN, dt John & Elizabeth, Columbiana Co.,
      O.
----, --, --. Amos & Mary
      Ch: Stephen   b 1833, 6, 7
          Sarah   " 1835, 12, 20
          Rachel   " 1837, 7, 13
1838, 8, 23. Wm. M., s Leonard, d bur New
      Britain
1844, 1, 23. Elizabeth M., dt Leonard & Anna
      H., b

1806, 8, 9. Sarah rocf Westland MM, dtd
      1806,4,26
1807, 6, 13. Susannah rocf Westland MM, dtd
      1807,4,25
1807, 12, 12. Willin & w, Sarah, & ch, Sarah,
      Benjamin, Joseph, Betty, Willin & Amos,
      rocf Westland MM, dtd 1807,11,28
1809, 1, 14. Sarah Haycock (form Underwood)
      con mcd
1809, 5, 13. John dis mou
1811, 7, 11. Deborah rocf Westland MM, dtd
      1811,5,25
1814, 1, 6. Benjamin gct Westland MM
1814, 2, 10. Joseph, minor, gct New Garden
      MM
1814, 12, 8. Joseph & w, Fanny, rocf New Gar-
      den MM, dtd 1814,8,18
1817, 6, 16. Joseph & w, Fanny, gct New Gar-
      den MM
1817, 6, 16. Hannah recrq
1818, 3, 16. Cert rec for Isaac from Centre
      MM, Pa., endorsed to Carmel MM
1818, 3, 16. Cert rec for Rebecca & Mary from
      Center MM, dtd 1818,1,17, endorsed to Car-
      mel MM
1825, 2, 21. Willin rocf Carmel MM, dtd 1825,
      2,19
1825, 8, 22. Fanny & ch, Elias, Susannah &
      Amos, rocf Carmel MM, dtd 1825,8,20
1828, 1, 10. Amos rocf Salem MM, dtd 1827,
      12,19
1828, 1, 10. Mary rocf Salem MM, dtd 1827,11,
      21
1828, 1, 10. Sarah & dt, Rachel, rocf Salem
      MM, dtd 1827,11,21
1828, 9, 11. Mary Burns (form Underwood) dis
      mou
1828, 10, 9. Rachel & Sarah dis jH
1829, 1, 8. Amos dis joining Separatists
1829, 1, 8. Willin dis joining Separatists
1829, 1, 8. Rachel dis jH
1829, 11, 12. Fanny dis disunity
1831, 7, 7. Amos con mcd (H)
1831, 7, 7. Mary (form Embree) con mcd (H)
1833, 3, 7. Willin & w, Rachel, & ch, Cyn-
      thia & Mary, gct Marlborough MM (H)
1834, 11, 6. Cynthia, dt Willin & Rachel,
      gct Marlborough MM

UNDERWOOD, continued
1835, 3, 12. Sarah gct Marlborough MM (H)
1837, 8, 10. Mary & ch, Stephen & Sarah, gct
    Zanesfield MM (H)
1838, 8, 9. Leonard & w, Ann, & s, William
    M., rocf Salem MM, Mass., dtd 1838,6,6 (H)
1841, 7, 8. Anna H. dis disunity
1842, 7, 7. Leonard dis disunity
1849, 3, 8. Leonard & dt, Elisabeth M., gct
    Swansey MM, Mass.

UPDEGRAFF
1848, 4, 6. Cyrus Mendenhall gct Short Creek
    MM, to m Anna T. Updegraff

VALE
1814, 6, 9. John & w, Deborah, & ch, Deborah,
    John, Jacob & Caroline, rocf Warrington
    MM, dtd 1814,5,19
1815, 5, 11. Phebe rocf Warrington MM, dtd
    1815,1,19
1816, 4, 15. Eli & w, Ann, rocf Warrington
    MM, Pa., dtd 1815,12,20
1860, 10, 11. Lewis W. & w, Sarah W., & s,
    Wilmer P., gct Prairie Grove MM, Ia. (H)

VAN LAW
1863, 9, 24. Joseph S., s Thomas E. & Amy
    B., Morgan Co., O.; m at Middleton, Marga-
    ret HOLLINGSWORTH, dt Samuel & Margaret,
    Columbiana Co., O.

1863, 11, 21. Margaret H. gct Chesterfield MM

VOTAW
1805, 8, 10. Phebe & s, Benjamin, rocf West-
    land MM, dtd 1804,12,27 (& s, Isaac, b
    since cert was granted)
1805, 8, 10. Rebecca & ch, Ann, Mary, James,
    Lydia, Leah & Rachel, rocf Westland MM,
    dtd 1805,3,23
1805, 9, 14. Isaac & w, Ann, rocf Westland
    MM, dtd 1805,8,24
1805, 9, 14. Moses & w, Mary, & ch, Elisa-
    beth, Isaac, Sarah, Ann, Joseph, Mary &
    Daniel, rocf Westland MM, dtd 1805,6,22
1849, 7, 12. Mississiniwa MM, Ind. was given
    permission to rec Rachel in mbrp

WADE
1864, 8, 17. Elizabeth (form Hoops) attached
    to this mtg when Beaver Falls MM, Pa.,
    was laid down

WALL
1840, 11, 12. Joana (form Engle) dis mou

WALKER
1809, 10, 18. Lydia m William ALLMON
1811, 1, 16. Sarah m John PENNOCK
1811, 9, 18. Mary m Benjamin PAXSON
1823, 3, 26. Ann m Daniel GARWOOD
1840, 4, 16. Daniel, s Thomas & Charlotte,

Columbiana Co., O.; m at Middleton, Jane
    HEALD, dt William W. & Susannah, Columbi-
    ana Co., O.
1841, 10, 13. Elizabeth m Milo. A. TOWNSEND

1806, 3, 8. Abel & w, Mary, & ch, Martha,
    Joseph & Lewis, rocf Hopewell MM, dtd
    1805,11,4
1807, 10, 10. Elizabeth recrq
1807, 10, 10. Mary recrq
1809, 6, 10. Lydia recrq
1811, 5, 9. Mary & ch, Martha, Joseph,
    Lewis, Eliza & Isaac, gct Plainfield MM
1816, 10, 14. Rachel recrq
1820, 8, 21. Tacy & Ann recrq
1820, 12, 18. Tacy gct Salem MM
1822, 4, 22. Tacy rocf Salem MM, dtd 1822,3,
    20
1824, 12, 20. Tacy gct Carmel MM
1839, 12, 12. Daniel recrq
1840, 3, 12. Lewis & w, Rachel, & ch, Nathan
    U. & Lewis J., rocf Short Creek MM, dtd
    1840,2,18
1840, 3, 12. Elizabeth rocf Short Creek MM,
    dtd 1840,1,21
1840, 3, 12. Hannah U. rocf Short Creek MM,
    dtd 1840,1,21
1843, 5, 11. Lewis & w, Rachel, & ch, Nathan
    U. & Lewis James, gct Short Creek MM
1843, 5, 11. Daniel & w, Jane H., gct Ches-
    terfield MM, O.
1843, 5, 11. Hannah U. gct Short Creek MM

WALTON
1821, 11, 29. Anna m Samuel ARMSTRONG

1810, 1, 13. Martha rocf New Garden MM, dtd
    1809,11,10
1810, 12, 8. Martha gct New Garden MM
1812, 1, 9. Hannah, Ruth, Anne, Eber Ach-
    sah, Rachel, Abram & Amos, ch Abram &
    Mary, gct Wilmington MM, Del.
1815, 4, 6. Abraham dis mcd
1817, 6, 16. New Garden MM was given per-
    mission to rst John
1818, 12, 21. Abram con mcd
1821, 8, 20. Anna rocf Richland MM, Pa., dtd
    1821,6,1
1821, 8, 20. Ruth, Eber, Rachel & Abraham,
    ch Abram, rocf Richland MM, Pa., dtd
    1821,6,1
1823, 5, 19. Eber gct Richland MM
1824, 11, 22. Phebe rocf Richland MM, dtd
    1824,7,30
1825, 2, 21. Achsah rocf Wilmington MM, dtd
    1824,7,30
1826, 10, 23. Ruth dis
1828, 10, 9. Abraham dis joining Separatists
1829, 8, 6. Phebe dis jH
1831, 1, 6. Rachel dis jH
1831, 2, 10. Abraham gct Salem MM, O.
1831, 6, 9. Achsah gct Salem MM
1837, 7, 6. Abraham con mou (H)

WALTON, continued
1862, 5, 17. Tazetta (form Townsend) dis mcd
1864, 8, 17. Edward H., William & Edward, Jr. attached to this mtg when Beaver Falls MM, Pa. was laid down
1864, 8, 17. Thornton & w, Rachel B., & s, Wilmer, attached to this mtg when Beaver Falls MM, Pa. was laid down (H)
1866, 7, 18. James Edward gct Race St. MM, Phila. (H)
1866, 7, 18. William gct Race St. MM, Phila. (H)
1866, 7, 18. Edward U. con mcd (H)
1866, 9, 12. Edward U. gct Phila. MM (H)

WARD
1839, 4, 11. Mary (form Icenhour) dis mou

WARE
1815, 9, 7. Talbert Townsend gct Salem MM, to m Edith Ware

WARRINGTON
1843, 11, 16. Nathan, s Abraham & Keziah, Columbiana Co., O.; m at Middleton, Mary DIXON, dt Samuel & Hannah, b 1822,5,15
    Ch: Samuel D. b 1844, 9, 24 d 1849, 5, 8
        Linnaeas   " 1847, 6, 22
        Henry   " 1849, 7, 31
        Sarah Ann " 1852, 12, 4
        Hannah   " 1855, 4, 1
1911, 11, '23. Thomas C., s Edgar & Hannah C., Columbiana Co., O.; m at Middleton, Sarah Mable HALL, dt Abner I. & Anna M., Columbiana Co., O.

1805, 11, 9. Cert rec for Abraham & w, Rachel, & ch from Burlington MM, N. J., dtd 1805, 9,10, endorsed to Salem MM
1844, 7, 11. Nathan rocf Upper Springfield MM, dtd 1844,4,27
1857, 6, 11. Nathan & w, Mary, & ch, Lineas, Henry, Sarah Ann & Hannah, gct Upper Springfield MM
1912, 9, 21. Sarah Mabel gct Upper Springfield MM

WATSON
1816, 6, 10. Abner & w, Elizabeth, & ch, William, Deborah, Phebe, Ann & Mark, rocf Goshen MM, Pa., dtd 1816,5,1
1816, 6, 10. Mary & Hannah rocf Goshen MM, dtd 1816,5,1
1816, 12, 16. Abner & w, Elizabeth, & ch, William, Deborah, Phebe Ann & Mark, gct Plainfield MM
1816, 12, 15. Hannah gct Plainfield MM
1817, 7, 14. Mary gct Plainfield MM
1863, 8, 15. Martha (form Neil) dis mcd

WAY
1817, 4, 24. Rebecca m Abel W. TOWNSEND

1808, 12, 10. Phebe (form Smith) dis mou

WEST
----, --, --. George b 1755,6,17; m Elizabeth ----- b 1772,2,9
    Ch: Mary   b 1792, 11, 1
        Priscilla " 1796, 1, 10
        Hannah   " 1798, 5, 23
        Stephen   " 1800, 3, 8
        Rachel   " 1803, 3, 2
        Samuel   " 1806, 1, 10

1803, 11, 12. May, dt George, recrq

WHEALON
1852, 5, 20. George, s Frederick & Jane, Columbiana Co., O.; m at Columbiana, Mary HOLMES, dt Lot & Sarah, Columbiana Co., O. (H)

WHINERY
1805, 2, 9. Phebe & ch, Abigail & Phebe, rocf Westland MM, dtd 1804,8,25 (dt, Lydia, b since cert was granted)

WHITACRE
1805, 4, 13. Martha [Whitecor] & ch, Mahlon, John, Isaac, Martha, Edward, Kezia, Phebe & Asael, rocf Westland MM, dtd 1805,1,26
1805, 4, 13. Ann [Whitecor] rocf Fairfax MM, Va., dtd 1804,11,24
1805, 4, 13. Phebe [Whitecor] rocf Westland MM, dtd 1804,12,22
1809, 6, 10. Mary [Whiteacre] rocf New Garden MM, dtd 1809,4,13
1816, 9, 16. Samuel recrq
1816, 9, 16. John, Rebecca, William, Elizabeth Rachel Levi Samuel, Joseph & Jonathan, ch Mary, recrq

WHITE
1840, 10, 11. Adrian C., s Timothy B. & Olive B., b

1838, 1, 11. Timothy B. & w, Olive B., & s, Adrian A., rocf Scipio MM, N. Y., dtd 1837,9,14 (H)
1864, 8, 7. Timothy B. & w, Olive, & Adrian, Adeline, Lucretia, Samuel & Timothy, Jr. attached to this mtg when Beaver Falls MM, Pa. was laid down (H)
1864, 8, 17. Sarah attached to this mtg when Beaver Falls MM, Pa., was laid down (H)

WHITEZELL
1866, 12, 15. Elizabeth gct Cole Creek MM, Ia.

WICKERSHAM
1813, 9, 16. Thomas, s Sampson & Elizabeth, Columbiana Co., O., b 1777,3,4 d 1868,8, 16; m at Middleton, Ann SAMMS, dt John & Sarah, Columbiana Co., O., b 1786,5,13

WICKERSHAM, Thomas & Ann, continued
    d 1856,5,21
    Ch: Nathan
        Hunt   b 1814, 7, 4 d 1814,12,22
         bur Middleton
        Sarah   b 1815, 8, 24 " 1846, 7,18
        Hannah   " 1817, 3, 28 " 1875, 7,19
        John   " 1820, 5, 18 " 1822, 9,25
         bur Middleton
        Phebe   b 1824, 8, 12 " 1917,11,24
        Joel   " 1826, 4, 12 " 1863, 3,15
        David   " 1828, 8, 19 " 1901, 5,27
1816, 12, 19. Elis, s Abner & Mary, Columbiana
    Co., O.; m at Middleton, Eliza MORGAN, dt
    William & Elizabeth, Columbiana Co., O.
----, --, --. Joseph & Margaret
    Ch: Eliza Ann b 1817, 1, 19
        Job   " 1818, 12, 3
        Phebe   " 1820, 11, 3
        Thomas   " 1823, 5, 11
        Mary   " 1826, 2, 11
        Ellis   " 1828, 2, 11
        Cyrus   " 1830, 9, 11
1820, 8, 31. Ann m Jonathan MARSH
1832, 2, 26. Hannah m John ALLMON
1852, 4, 15. Joel, s Thomas & Ann, Columbiana
    Co., O., b 1826,4,12 d 1863,3,15; m at
    Middleton, Ann EDMUNDSON, dt Eli & Ruth,
    b 1828,3,15
    Ch: Ruth Anna b 1853, 1, 22
        Sarah   " 1854, 8, 9 d 1857,11,17
        Hannah   " 1856, 1, 14 " 1856, 1,28
        Thomas E. " 1857, 4, 27
        Mariah   " 1859, 4, 16
        Phebe
         Flovilla " 1861, 2, 27 d 1865, 2,--
----, --, --. David b 1828,8,19 d 1901,5,27;
    m Rebecca ----- b 1831,2,5 d 1891,10,10
    Ch: Abby T.   b 1861, 5, 26
        Rachel C. " 1863, 4, 3
        Levi B.   " 1867, 11, 7 d 1887, 7,20
        Marium   " 1869, 8, 20
        Joseph P. " 1873, 1, 17
1865, 5, 25. Phebe m Robert ELLYSON

1811, 7, 11. Thomas rocf Centre MM, dtd 1811,
    6,3
1816, 5, 13. Ellis rocf Kennett MM, Pa., dtd
    1816,3,5
1816, 9, 16. Joseph rocf Kennett MM, Pa.,
    dtd 1816,8,6
1819, 7, 19. Ann rocf New Garden MM, Pa.,
    dtd 1819,6,10
1826, 4, 17. Joseph & w, Margaret, & ch,
    Eliza Ann, Job, Phebe, Thomas & Mary, rocf
    Carmel MM, dtd 1826,4,15
1826, 6, 19. Thomas dis disunity
1828, 11, 6. Thomas recrq (H)
1843, 1, 12. Joseph & w, Margaret, & ch,
    Thomas, Mary, Elis, Cyrus, Hannah & Pearce,
    gct Upper Springfield MM
1843, 1, 12. Eliza Ann gct Upper Springfield
    MM

1843, 9, 14. Phebe James (form Wickersham)
    dis mou
1844, 7, 11. Job, s Joseph, dis mcd
1858, 3, 11. David gct Flushing MM, to m
    Rebecca R. Holloway
1858, 11, 20. Rebecca B. rocf Flushing MM,
    dtd 1858,8,26
1865, 2, 18. Thomas rst in mbrp
1873, 6, 21. Ann & ch, Thomas E. & Maria,
    gct Coal Creek MM, Ia.
1873, 6, 21. Ruth Anna gct Coal Creek MM,Ia.
1890, 6, 21. Abbie T. Rawlings (form Wicker-
    sham) dis mcd
1894, 12, 15. Joseph P. dis jas
1899, 5, 20. Rachel C. Gilbert (form Wicker-
    sham) dis mcd
1913, 11, 15. Miriam W. Cemery (form Wicker-
    sham) dis mou

WILEY
1809, 2, 11. David recrq
1810, 3, 10. David gct Salem MM
1811, 12, 12. William recrq

WILKINS
1804, 7, 14. Sarah & ch, Susannah, Rachel,
    Daniel, Joseph, Sarah, Elisabeth, Tam-
    zon, William & John, rocf Cedar Creek MM,
    Va., dtd 1803,11,12, endorsed by Redstone
    MM, 1804,5,4
1806, 10, 11. Joseph & fam gct Salem MM
1807, 9, 12. Susannah Miller (form Wilkins)
    con mou

WILLIAMS
----, --, --. Isaiah b 1761,8,14; m Dinah
    ----- b 1764,10,10
    Ch: Benjamin b 1785, 8, 26
        Mary   " 1787, 4, 8
        Tasa   " 1790, 4, 4
        Martha   " 1792, 2, 14
        Abraham " 1793, 6, 28
        Wm.   " 1793, 6, 28 d 1793, 7,19
        Susanna " 1795, 8, 14
        Ann   " 1797, 4, 14
        Hannah   " 1799, 1, 24
        John   " 1801, 4, 30
        Elizabeth " 1803, 10, 28

1804, 12, 8. Dinah & ch, Mary, Tace, Martha,
    Abraham, Susanna, Ann, Hannah, John &
    Elizabeth, rocf Westland MM, dtd 1804,10,
    27
1807, 3, 14. Dinah & fam gct Salem MM
1807, 10, 10. Benjamin gct Salem MM
1851, 2, 6. Martha (form Morlan) dis mou

WILLIAMSON
1904, 4, 16. Celesta M. (form Cadwalader) dis
    mcd

WILSON
1808, 1, 14. Mary m James HEALD

WILSON, continued

1805, 4, 13. Susannah & ch, Mireanna, David &
      John Webster, rocf Baltimore MM, dtd 1805,
      1,10

1808, 11, 12. Alicean Okeley (form Wilson) dis
      mou

1809, 5, 13. Elizabeth rocf Phila. MM, dtd
      1808,12,29

1813, 3, 11. David, minor s Isaac, gct Balti-
      more MM

1817, 10, 13. David rocf Indian Spring MM,
      Md., dtd 1817,4,18

1828, 10, 9. Isaac dis joining Separatists

1828, 10, 9. Susannah & Elizabeth dis jH

1829, 5, 7. David H. dis jH

1830, 1, 7. John Webster dis jH

1831, 11, 10. Lydia (form Mercer) con mou (H)

1834, 9, 11. Elizabeth gct Spruce St. MM,
      Phila. (H)

1842, 4, 7. Elizabeth rocf Spruce St. MM,
      Phila., dtd 1842,2,24 (H)

1842, 11, 17. Elwood Chapman gct Short Creek
      MM, to m Sarah Ann Wilson

1851, 10, 9. Roxana (form Morlan) dis joining
      Methodist Society

1864, 8, 17. David H., John Webster & Lydia,
      w James, attached to this mtg when Beaver
      Falls MM, Pa. was laid down (H)

1876, 9, 16. Thomas C. Cope gct Flushing MM,
      to m Maria Wilson

WISE

1845, 9, 11. Ruth rocf Sandy Spring MM, dtd
      1845,5,23

WOODS

----, --, --. John & Rebecca
      Ch: Elizabeth   b 1796, 9, 7
          Samuel   " 1798, 7, 16
          Lydia   " 1814, 4, 10
----, --, --. Joshua & Elizabeth
      Ch: Albert   b 1806, 1, 12
          David   " 1810, 9, 7
          Hannah   " 1811, 12, 30
          Anne   " 1813, 12, 29
          Enos Lewis " 1815, 2, 25
          Joshua   " 1816, 8, 15
          Wm.   " 1818, 3, 25
          Sarah   " 1819, 9, 10
          Eliza   " 1821, 4, 9

1807, 8, 13. Enos, s Jacob & Isabel, Colum-.
      biana Co., O.; m at Middleton, Elizabeth
      HUGHS, dt James & Isabel, Green Co., Pa.
      Ch: James   b 1811, 11, 16
          Joseph   " 1813, 3, 9
          Jacob   " 1815, 9, 3
          Isabel   " 1818, 5, 8
          Lydia   " 1821, 9, 5
          John   " 1824, 2, 7
          Elizabeth   " 1827, 1, 31
          Kezia   " 1829, 7, 10

1816, 11, 21. Elizabeth m Thomas ADAMSON

1818, 10, 22. Samuel, s John & Rebecca, Colum-

biana Co., O.; m at Middleton, Esther
ADAMSON, dt James & Hannah, Columbiana
Co., O.
      Ch: Ruth   b 1819, 7, 31
          Elizabeth   " 1821, 7, 17
          Hannah   " 1824, 4, 7
          Rebeccah   " 1827, 5, 6
          Mary Ann   " 1829, 8, 28
          Tryphena   " 1832, 5, 2
          John L.   " 1838, 1, 27
          Sylvanus   " 1840, 11, 23

1824, 2, 7. John d bur Middleton

1836, 3, 19. Rebecca d bur Middleton

1837, 6, 1. Ruth m Jesse MILLAGAN

1846, 7, 16. Hannah m Ethan Allen HOLE

1849, 10, 18. Rebecca m Samuel HOLE

1816, 2, 12. Elizabeth & ch, Albert, David,
      Hannah, Ann & Enos Lewis, recrq

1816, 7, 15. Joshua [Wood] recrq

1828, 3, 6. Enos & w, Elizabeth, & ch,
      James, Joseph, Jacob, Isabel, Lydia, John
      & Elizabeth, rocf Sandy Spring MM, dtd
      1828,11,23

1829, 4, 9. Albert G. dis disunity

1831, 4, 7. Joshua dis jH

1831, 4, 7. Elizabeth, w Joshua, dis jH

1831, 5, 12. Hannah dis jH

1832, 3, 8. Ann dis jH

1833, 1, 10. David dis disunity

1833, 7, 11. James dis mcd

1834, 6, 12. Enos L. dis disunity

1834, 7, 10. Hannah dis mou (H)

1837, 2, 20. Jacob [Wood] dis disunity

1837, 6, 19. Ann (form Allmon) dis mcd

1839, 9, 12. Joshua dis disunity

1839, 10, 10. William dis joining Methodist
      Society

1840, 12, 10. Eliza Fitspatrick (form Woods)
      dis jas

1840, 8, 6. Sarah dis jas

1841, 5, 6. Enos & w, Elizabeth, & ch,
      Elizabeth & Kesiah, gct Goshen MM, O.

1841, 5, 6. Joweph gct Goshen MM

1841, 5, 6. Lydia gct Goshen MM, O.

1841, 12, 9. Isabella Rudibough (form Woods)
      dis mcd

1847, 2, 11. Lydia Ann (form Hatcher) dis
      mou

1848, 8, 10. Lewis dis mcd

1848, 10, 12. Elizabeth (form Woods) dis mcd

1853, 2, 10. Lydia gct Upper Springfield MM

1857, 1, 8. Mary Ann (form Woods) dis mcd

1857, 3, 12. Triphenia Ingledue (form Woods)
      dis mcd

1858, 8, 21. Sarah Longshore (form Woods) dis
      mcd

1863, 1, 17. John [Wood] dis mou

1863, 1, 17. Sylvanus [Wood] dis mou

1866, 1, 20. Samuel dis jas

1873, 12, 20. Esther dis joining Separatists

WOOLMAN
1863, 6, 25. Abner, s Aaron & Mary W., Columbiana Co., O.; m at Middleton, Elvira HALL,
dt Joseph & Martha, Belmont Co., O.

1805, 11, 9. Cert rec for Samuel & w, Rebecca,
from Burlington MM, dtd 1805,10,7, endorsed
to Salem MM
1863, 9, 19. Elvira H. gct Upper Springfield
MM

WRIGHT
1803, 11, 12. Elisabeth & ch, John, Benjamin,
Martha, Charity & Judith, rocf Goose Creek
MM, Va., dtd 1802,8,7, endorsed by Westland MM, 1803,9,24
1806, 5, 10. Latitia recrq
1814, 1, 6. Isaac Morlan gct Salem MM, to m
Martha Wright
1817, 4, 14. Letitia gct Clear Creek MM, O.

YOUNG
1813, 9, 9. Joseph & Ann recrq

*   *   *   *   *   *   *

COPE
1861, 9, 24. Louis, s Samuel & Mercy, Fayette
Co., Pa.; m at Middleton, Hannah Y. HOL-
LINGSWORTH, dt Samuel & Margaret, Columbiana Co., O.

GAMBLE
1868, 10, 21. Sarah H. m William H. BLACKBURN

HUGHS
1807, 3, 14. Elizabeth recrq

McCONNELL
1824, 8, 14. Mary, dt Levi & Ruth, b
1838, 8, 16. Emeline m Mark D. BRADWAY

BRADWAY
1838, 8, 16. Mark D., s Ezra & Mary, Salem
Co., N. J.; m at Beaver Falls, Emeline
McCONNELL, dt Levi & Ruth, Beaver Co., Pa.

DIXON
1806, 12, 18. John [Dixson], s Joshua & Dinah,
Columbiana Co., O.; m at Middleton, Hannah
BEAL, dt Joseph & Hannah, Columbiana Co.,O.

CADWALADER
1881, 5, 26. Annie H. [Cadwallader] m Isaac
E. BONSALL

1816, 10, 14. Thomas, Joseph, William, Jane,
Daniel & Sarah, ch Joseph & Ann, recrq
1829, 8, 6. Joseph & w, Ann, & ch, Daniel &
Sarah, rocf Carmel MM, dtd 1829,7,18
1829, 8, 6. Jane rocf Carmel MM, dtd 1829,6,
20
1829, 11, 12. Joseph, Jr. rocf Carmel MM, dtd
1829,10,17
1832, 3, 8. Joseph, Jr. gct Upper Springfield MM
1832, 6, 7. Joseph & w, Ann, gct Upper
Springfield MM
1832, 6, 7. Daniel gct Upper Springfield MM
1832, 6, 7. Sarah & Jane gct Upper Springfield MM
1833, 6, 6. Phebe (form Mendenhall) dis mcd
(H)
1834, 7, 10. Phebe (form Mendenhall) dis mou
1860, 1, 21. Elizabeth (form Richards) con
mou
1873, 4, 19. Mary Louisa (form Hole) dis
mcd

*   *   *   *   *   *   *

PRICHETT
1840, 9, 24. Joseph, s Joab & Mary, Columbiana Co., O.; m at Middleton, Phebe BOUL-
TON, dt Levi & Anna, Columbiana Co., O.

SCHOOLEY
1804, 7, 18. Sarah m John BEESON
1807, 5, 14. John, s Elisha & Rachel, Columbiana Co., O.; m at home of James Erwin,
Phebe BEESON, dt Henry & Mary, Columbiana Co., O.

STRATTON
1806, 12, 18. Amy [Straton] m Nathan BROWN

WICKERSHAM
1837, 4, 27. Sarah m Mifflin CADWALADER

WILSON
1842, 11, 17. Elizabeth, wd, Beaver Co., Pa.;
m Joseph R. MARTIN (H)

SALEM MONTHLY MEETING

In 10th Mo. 1804, Salem Preparative Meeting was set up by Redstone Quarterly Meeting of Baltimore Yearly Meeting and in the following year the monthly meeting was established in Columbiana Co., Ohio. The early Friends at Salem came from Pennsylvania. They cut the first roads through the forest, built the first log hut, and laid the foundations of the community which was named Salem or the City of Peace. Many of the settlers were prominent business men and merchants. Salem's first schools were under the supervision of Friends. In 1806 a school was started under the care of Jacob Branson.

In the period preceding the Civil War and during the war, Salem was conspicuous for its stand against slavery. The records of this period are full of dealings with Friends for entering the army and otherwise aiding the war. Edwin Coppick, who was connected with John Brown in his raid on Harpers Ferry, lived in this vicinity and was the son of Quaker parents. He was captured and hanged in Virginia, but his body was later brought back and buried at Salem.

The land originally owned by the meeting occupied the site of the present business center of Salem. In 1828 the followers of Elias Hicks took the northern part of the property and erected a meeting house. After the conservative separation, the two branches held the property jointly until 1871. The Wilburs held their meetings in the forenoon and the Gurneys in the afternoon. The pastoral system was introduced into the Gurney meeting about 1890. Elisha and Virginia Blackburn went as missionaries to British East Africa from this meeting.

RECORDS

ADAMS

1885, 8, 25. Cora Mullett, dt George & Della Gardner, b (G)

1932, 6, 29. Cora Mullett dropped from mbrp

AIKEN

1882, 5. 30. Homer L., s Elmer & Lydia, b (G)

1911, 12, 20. Lee rec in mbrp
1925, 3, 25. Homer L. recrq
1925, 3, 25. Mabel recrq
1932, 6, 29. Homer & Mabel dropped from mbrp

ALDRICH

1884, 3, 20. Joseph & Jennie recrq

ALFORD

1910, 2, 23. R. recrq

ALLEN

1808, 5, 5. Joseph A. b (W)
1829, 9, 25. Christopher, Jr. b (W)
1853, 12, 28. Christopher, s Richard & Martha, Columbiana Co., O.; m at Salem, Abigail ROOD, dt Michael & Rhoda STRATTON, Columbiana Co., O. (G)
----, --, --. L. Ebbert, s Ebenezer & Sarah J., b 1881,12,8; m Carrie OYSTER, dt Samuel & Sarah J., b 1882,4,26 (G)

1827, 5, 23. Adnah B. Silvin & w, Lydia, & dt, Sarah, & Joseph P. Allen, an apprentice, rocf Piles Grove MM, N.J., dtd 1827,3,27
1831, 12, 21. Joseph P. gct Greenwich MM, N.J.
1849, 11, 22. Elizabeth (form Waterworth) con mcd (H)
1849, 12, 19. Christopher, Jr. recrq
1852, 3, 24. Christopher, Jr. gct Sandy Spring MM
1852, 9, 22. Casper Williams gct Redstone MM, to m Phebe J. Allen
1854, 3, 22. Abigail gct New Garden MM (W)
1911, 12, 20. L. E. & Carry rec in mbrp
1911, 12, 20. Verna rec in mbrp
1912, 5, 22. Myrtle gct Goshen MM, O.
1913, 1, 31. Ebanezer recrq
1913, 10, 22. Verna gct Beloit MM
1915, 11, 24. Roy recrq
1915, 12, 22. Myrtle O. rocf Lupton MM
1917, 8, 15. Donald Wade recrq
1917, 8, 15. Earl dis disunity
1917, 8, 15. Maud dis disunity
1918, 5, 22. Lowell & Leroy relrq
1918, 11, 20. Myrtle O. gct Cleveland MM, O.
1924, 8, 10. A. Ward rocf Goshen MM
1924, 10, 22. Mary W. recrq
1924, 11, 19. Dorothea Elizabeth & Gordon Elthan, ch Ward & Mary, recrq

ALLISON

----, --, --. ----- m Rebecca ----- b 1770,3, 12 d 1838,6,21 (W)
Ch: Martha   b 1798, 4, 7 d 1863, 6,19
    Sarah L.   " 1811, 4, 4
1833, 10, 30. Sarah L., s George & Rebecca, Columbiana Co., O.; m at Salem, Sarah BALL, dt Thos. & Elizabeth, Columbiana Co., O. (H)

1855, 5, 30. Sarah m James STANLEY (W)

1832, 10, 24. George & w, Rebecca, & s, George, rocf Exeter MM, Pa., dtd 1832,9,26
1832, 10, 24. Mahlon rocf Exeter MM, Pa., dtd 1832,9,26
1832, 10, 24. Samuel L. rocf Exeter MM, Pa., dtd 1832,9,26
1832, 10, 24. Martha & Sarah L. rocf Exeter MM, Pa., dtd 1832,9,26
1833, 9, 25. Samuel L. rocf Exeter MM, Pa., dtd 1833,7,31 (H)
1833, 11, 20. George dis disunity
1833, 11, 20. Samuel dis jH
1836, 4, 20. George W. dis disunity
1836, 7, 20. Mary (form Chrisman) dis mcd
1836, 7, 20. Mahlon dis mcd
1862, 12, 25. Martha [Alison] dis joining separatists (W) of 1854

ALLMAN

1817, 7, 1. Joseph b (G)
1823, 6, 28. Hannah Maria, dt Thomas & Hannah Hammond, b (G)

1833, 10, 23. Israil [Allmon], minor, rocf Middleton MM, dtd 1833,10,10
1834, 4, 23. Joseph, minor, rocf Marlborough MM, dtd 1834,2,25
1838, 8, 22. Joseph gct Marlborough MM
1859, 11, 24. Joseph & w, Hannah Mariah, rocf Westland MM, Ia.
1862, 12, 25. Jehu, Hannah, Esther C., Lydia, Ann W., Abner & Sarah [Almon] dis joining separatists (W) of 1854
1862, 12, 25. Abigail dis joining separatists (W) of 1854
1875, 8, 11. Joseph & w, Hannah Mariah, gct San Jose MM, Calif.
1880, 2, 26. Webster & w, Tacy M., recrq
1880, 3, 25. Emmet M., Mary S. & Albert R. recrq
1880, 12, 11. David [Allmon] & w, Hannah M., rocf LeGrand MM, Ia.
1881, 2, 9. Joseph & Hannah M. rocf Legrand MM, Ia., dtd 1880,12,11
1882, 5, 25. Webster A. [Alman] & w, Tacy, & ch, Emmet M., Mary S. & Albert R., gct Springdale MM, Ia.
1886, 3, 25. Joseph & Hannah Mariah gct Archer MM, Florida

ALTHER

1885, 2, 6. Louisa M. recrq

ANDERSON
1891, 4, 28. Roy Andrew, s Andrew & Nettie,
     b
1928, 4, 30. Phebe Jane, dt Roy & Jennie, b

1923, 12, 19. Roy Andrew recrq
1923, 12, 19. Mrs. Jessie Crawford recrq
1924, 1, 23. Mary Annetta & Joseph Gerald
     recrq

ANTRAM
----, --, --. Frances b 1771,5,5 d 1855,8,24
     (W)
----, --, --. Hannah D., 2nd w John, b 1775,6,
     26 Chester Co., Pa. d 1857,3,3 bur Sandy
     Spring (W)
----, --, --. Benjamin [Antrim] b 1801,9,25 d
     1876,5,14; m Elizabeth D. ----- b 1806,5,6
     The following ch entrusted to their care
          Taylor F. Langstaff b 1829, 11, 26
          Drusilla Langstaff " 1831, 1, 24
----, --, --. Aaron [Antrim] m Elizabeth H.
     ----- b 1814,2,12 d 1842,7,17 (W)

1806, 6, 17. John [Antrem] rocf Burlington
     MM, dtd 1806,5,5
1810, 12, 11. Francis rocf Egg Harbour MM,
     N. J., dtd 1810,5,4
1818, 7, 14. John gct New Garden MM, to m
1818, 12, 23. Hannah rocf New Garden MM, dtd
     1818,11,26
1834, 7, 23. Benjamin & w, Elizabeth, rocf
     Upper Springfield MM, dtd 1834,6,28
1837, 4, 19. Elizabeth (form Halderman) con
     mou
1854, 4, 19. Benjamin & w, Elizabeth, gct Red
     Cedar MM, Ia. (W)
1855, 7, 25. Hannah gct Sandy Spring MM (W)
1857, 6, 25. Benjamin & w, Elizabeth, rocf
     Bloomington MM, Ia., dtd 1857,2,7
1858, 2, 24. Benjamin recrq (W)
1862, 12, 25. Benjamin & Elizabeth dis joining
     separatists (W) of 1854
1871, 2, 22. Elizabeth D. recrq (belonged to
     a mtg in Ia., but owing to a separation
     in Ia. Mtg could not get cert) (W)

ARMITAGE
1794, 4, 12. Sarah b (H)
----, --, --. Charles b 1794,2,14 d 1835,2,14;
     m Jane ----- b 1796,10,7 (H)
     Ch: Rachel   b 1823, 1, 25
         Oliver   " 1825, 1, 9 d 1836, 7,14
         Phebe   " 1827, 5, 20
         Dearborn " 1830, 1, 28
         Zebidee   " 1835, 2, 14 d 1835, 5,14

1829, 6, 24. Charles & w, Jane, & ch, Rachel,
     Oliver & Phebe, rocf Solebury MM, Pa., dtd
     1829,3,3 (H)
1830, 1, 20. Cert rec for Rachel, Oliver &
     Phebe, ch Charles, from Buckingham MM, dtd
     1829,12,7, endorsed to Upper Spring MM

1838, 2, 21. Charles gct Buckingham MM, Pa.,
     to m Sarah Beans (H)
1838, 8, 22. Sarah rocf Buckingham MM, Pa.,
     dtd 1838,8,6 (H)

ARMSTRONG
----, --, --. Robert b 1764,3,3; m Anne -----
     b 1779,6,16 (W)
     Ch: Wm.   b 1800, 7, 23
         James   " 1802, 11, 11
         John   " 1805, 9, 27
         Joel   " 1808, 8, 9
         Mary Ann " 1811, 11, 12
         Lydia   " 1812, 11, 17
         Rebecca   " 1815, 7, 31
         Robert   " 1817, 12, 8
         Sarah P. " 1820, 7, 31
----, --, --. James & Mary
     Ch: Phebe   b 1812, 4, 5 d 1836, 7, 3
         Ruth   " 1814, 2, 19
         Titus   " 1816, 4, 5
         Martha   " 1818, 4, 26 d 1844, 8, 3
         Hannah   " 1820, 6, 28 " 1862,11,17
         John   " 1822, 10, 23 " 1824, 8,13
         Rachel   " 1825, 4, 2 " 1860, 4, 6
         Joseph   " 1828, 1, 15 " 1828, 4,14
         Sarah   " 1829, 10, 5

1808, 7, 12. John W. & w, Sarah, rocf Middle-
     ton MM, dtd 1808,2,13
1813, 1, 12. Robert & w, Ann, & ch, Wm.,
     James, John, Joel, Mary Ann & Lydia, recrq
1855, 6, 21. Elizabeth & ch, Nathan, Dorcas,
     Phebe B., Ruth Anna, Edith & Sarah Emily,
     gct Driftwood MM, Ind.
1855, 6, 21. Alice gct Driftwood MM, Ind.
1855, 6, 21. Joshua gct Driftwood MM, Ind.
1855, 6, 21. Martha gct Driftwood MM, Ind.
1855, 6, 21. Thomas gct Driftwood MM, Ind.
1859, 7, 21. Sarah J. (form Lipsey) con mcd
1859, 8, 25. Sarah J. gct Driftwood MM, Ind.
1862, 12, 25. Isral, Sinia, Wm., Ann Eliza &
     Nathan dis joining separatists (W) of 1854
1862, 12, 25. Nathan, Rebecca, Elma, Samuel,
     Ruth, Dasey, Eliza Ann & Oscar Allen dis
     joining separatists (W) of 1854

ARNOLD
1790, 2, 21. Rachel b (W)
1818, 3, 29. John Wright b (H)
1819, 10, 27. Samuel b (H)
1824, 10, 16. Lydia Ann b (W)
----, --, --. John, s Edward & Sarah, b 1872,8,
     16; m Pauline McCALLUM, dt Duncan & An-
     thrina, b 1890,2,9 (G)

1831, 6, 22. Levi & w, Hannah, & ch, John W.
     & Samuel, rocf Green St. MM, Phila., Pa.,
     dtd 1831,4,21 (H)
1831, 8, 24. Hannah, w Levi, & s, John W. &
     Samuel, rocf ND MM, Phila., Pa., dtd 1831,
     5,24
1832, 3, 21. Hannah dis JH

ARNOLD, continued

1835, 9, 23. Edwin A. rocf Phila. MM held at
    Cherry St., dtd 1835,5,20 (H)
1836, 3, 23. Levi dis administering oaths (H)
1840, 6, 24. Edwin A. dis mou (H)
1844, 7, 24. John con mcd (H)
1850, 5, 22. Rachel rocf Sandy Spring MM, dtd
    1850,4,26
1850, 7, 24. Lydia Ann rocf Sandy Spring MM,
    dtd 1850,5,24
1862, 12, 25. Lydia Ann & Rachel dis joining
    separatists (W) of 1854
1865, 9, 20. Lydia Ann gct New Garden MM (W)
1872, 3, 20. Rachel gct Plymouth MM, O. (W)
1932, 12, 29. John recrq

ASHBA

1910, 3, 23. Frank D. gct Georgetown MM, Ill.

ASHEAD

----, --, --. J. Morris, s Amos & Hannah (Hoyle)
    b 1866,10,21; m Elizabeth T. HALL, dt John
    & Deborah S. (Davis), b 1862,9,10 d 1931,4,
    13 (W)
    Dt: Mary R.   b 1895, 6, 6
1908, 10, 22. Oliver P., s Benjamin S. & Ava-
    linda (Dudley), b 1882,2,21; m Sarah Edith
    ZELLEY, dt J. Howard & Edith (Fawcett),
    b 1887,4,5 (W)
    Ch: Dudley
            Fawcett   b 1909, 11, 12
        Joseph
        Howard   " 1913, 8, 13

1895, 4, 24. J. Moris rocf Chester MM, N. J.,
    dtd 1895,3,20 (W)
1895, 4, 25. Elizabeth T. rocf Stillwater MM,
    dtd 1895,3,20 (W)
1911, 2, 22. Oliver P. rocf Haddonfield MM,
    N. J., dtd 1911,2,8 (W)
1927, 11, 23. J. Morris & Elizabeth T. gct
    Pasadena MM, Calif. (W)
1927, 11, 23. Mary R. gct Pasadena MM, Calif.
    (W)

ASHTON

1862, 12, 25. Barok, Jane, Martha, Mariam,
    Richard, Phebe & Eliza Margaret dis join-
    ing separatists (W) of 1854
1862, 12, 25. Martha dis joining separatists
    of 1854 (W)

ATKINSON

1824, 4, 28. Warner, s Samuel & Hannah, Colum-
    biana Co. O.; m at Salem, Maria STANLEY,
    dt Joshua & Rachel, Columbiana Co., O.

1823, 6, 25. Warner rocf Burlington MM, N. J.,
    dtd 1823,5,5
1826, 6, 21. Robert gct Burlington MM, N. J.
1850, 3, 20. David Coulson gct Upper Spring-
    field MM, to m Rachel Atkinson
1852, 4, 21. Theophilus Morlan gct Upper

Springfield MM, to m Sarah Atkinson

BAILEY

1818, 12, 22. Isaac b (H)
----, --, --. Hoopes [Baily] b 1801,7,18; m
    Anne B. ----- b 1810,1,25 (H)
    Ch: Mary Emily b 1833, 11, 27 (or 1833,11,
            26)
        Howard H.   " 1836, 9, 8
        Edward P.   " 1839, 2, 17
        Wm. Penn   " 1841, 1, 10
1850, 5, 23. Hannah m Lot GREGG (H)
1868, 9, 29. Harding [Baily], s George & Ann,
    Mahoning Co., O.; m at home of Eli Garret-
    son, Lucretia M. GARRETSON, dt Eli & Sarah,
    Mahoning Co., O. (H)
----, --, --. Rev. Charles, s George, b 1889,4,
    25; m Ethel SHREVE, dt Calvin & Anna, b
    1891,12,15 (G)
    Ch: Walter   b 1914, 5, 17
        Lois   " 1917, 6, 17
        Paul   " 1918, 11, 3
        Eldene   " 1926, 2, 8

1805, 10, 15. Joseph & w, Elizabeth, & ch,
    Jesse, Yarnall, Hoops & Penock, rocf Goshen
    MM, Pa., dtd 1805,6,7, endorsed by Middle-
    ton MM, 1805,10,12
1807, 5, 12. Robert & w, Sarah, & ch, Joseph,
    Ruth, John, James, Amos & Thomas, rocf
    Middleton MM, dtd 1807,4,11
1816, 5, 14. Yarnall, minor, rocf New Garden
    MM, dtd 1816,4,18
1811, 6, 11. Jesse & w, Pheriba, & ch, Ed-
    mund, Abigail, Uriah, Delisha, Matilda &
    Mary, rocf Gravelly Run MM (Upper MM) Va.,
    dtd 1811,3,16
1811, 6, 11. Cert rec for Elizabeth from Upper
    MM, Va., dtd 1811,3,16, endorsed to Still-
    water MM
1820, 10, 25. Yarnall gct New Garden MM
1825, 11, 23. Jesse gct Flushing MM
1831, 10, 19. Hannah (form Garretson) dis mou
    (H)
1837, 8, 23. Joseph [Baily] & w, Elizabeth,
    rocf New Garden MM, dtd 1837,6,22 (H)
1837, 8, 23. Elizabeth [Baily], Jr. rocf New
    Garden MM, dtd 1837,6,22 (H)
1837, 8, 23. Hannah [Baily] rocf New Garden
    MM, dtd 1837,6,22 (H)
1837, 8, 23. Rachel [Baily] rocf New Garden
    MM, dtd 1837,6,22 (H)
1837, 11, 22. Hoopes & w, Anne, & ch, Mary
    Emily & Howard H., rocf New Garden MM, dtd
    1837,8,24 (H)
1838, 2, 21. Jesse & w, Lydia, & ch, Rachel,
    Joseph Sidingham, Rebecca, Lydia-Pamelia &
    Hannah, rocf Flushing MM, dtd 1838,1,25
1839, 6, 19. Jesse & w, Lydia, & ch, Rachel,
    Joseph Sydenham, Rebecca, Lydia Pamelia &
    Hannah, gct Flushing MM
1842, 4, 20. Isaac recrq (H)
1842, 11, 23. Mary Ann [Baily] rocf New Garden

BAILEY, continued
MM
1846, 12, 23. Eliza [Baley] gct Sandy Spring
MM
1852, 5, 20. Rachel Vernon (form Bailey) dis
    mcd (H)
1918, 5, 22. Anna dropped from mbrp
1928, 9, 19. Charles & fam rocf Adrian MM

BAKER
----, --, --. Bertha, dt Moses & Elizabeth /b DICKEY
----, --, --. Jesse C. b 1800,2,20; m Eliza
    R. ----- b 1805,1,29 (W)
    Ch: Elizabeth
        W.   b 1823, 3, 30
        Benezet   " 1839, 4, 15 d 1859, 5, 6
        Jesse P.   " 1840, 10, 10
        Wm. N.   " 1844, 11, 17
----, --, --. Eliza b 1805,1,29 d 1884,8,25

1839, 2, 20. Nehemiah Colvin & w, Lydia, &
    adopted ch, Caroline S. Colvin & Thos. S.
    Baker, rocf Adrian MM, dtd 1838,7,12
1840, 5, 20. Nehemiah Colvin & w, Lydia, & ch,
    (adopted) Caroline C. Colvin & Thomas L.
    Baker, gct Adrian MM, Mich.
1858, 7, 21. Jesse & w, Eliza, & ch, Benezett,
    Jesse & Wm., rocf Middleton MM, dtd 1858,6,
    19 (W)
1858, 7, 21. Elizabeth rocf Middleton MM, dtd
    1858,6,19 (W)
1862, 12, 25. Jesse, Eliza, Isaac, Lewis, Bene-
    zet & Wm. dis joining separatists (W) of
    1854
1863, 5, 20. Jesse & w, Eliza, & s, Wm., gct
    Middleton MM (W)
1872, 12, 25. Benezet dis jas (W)
1876, 8, 23. Eliza rocf Upper Springfield MM,
    dtd 1876,6,23 (W)
1931, 5, 20. Bertha recrq

BALL
----, --, --. Nathan b 1762,7,8 d 1842,4,26 (H)
----, --, --. Nathan b 1762,7,8; m Atlantic
    ----- b 1775,9,24 d 1857,3,21 (W)
    Ch: Hannah   b 1798, 5, 2
        John   " 1799, 5, 25 d 1799, 7,20
        bur Philadelphia
        Joseph   b 1802, 6, 9
        Benjamin   " 1803, 2, 10
----, --, --. Thomas b 1766,5,8; m Elizabeth
    ----- b 1782,4,4 (W)
    Ch: John Manning b 1803, 11, 9
        Samuel Sack-
          ett   " 1805, 8, 15
        Sarah Alli-
          son   " 1807, 5, 20
        David   " 1811, 3, 29
        Lydia Mont-
          gomery   " 1814, 3, 17
        Thomas L. " 1816, 5, 30
        Joseph R. " 1819, 10, 5
        Elizabeth " 1822, 6, 18

1815, 5, 24. Hannah m David FAWCETT
----, --, --. Joseph, s Nathan, b 1802,6,9; m
    Hannah ----- b 1805,9,23 d 1839,2,28 (H)
    Ch: Jane   b 1827, 9, 6
        John   " 1829, 5, 3
        Martha   " 1830, 7, 20 d 1833, 1,15
        James   " 1831, 12, 24
        Elizabeth
         B.   " 1834, 1, 28
        David F.   " 1835, 10, 10
        Benjamin
         Franklin " 1837, 12, 24
----, --, --. Benjamin b 1808,2,10; m Hannah
    ----- b 1811,10,17 (W)
    Ch: Nathan   b 1831, 8, 18
        Rachel   " 1833, 4, 17
        Martha   " 1835, 7, 3
        Charles   " 1837, 8, 15
        Joshua L. " 1839, 4, 18
        Ann   " 1841, 2, 3
        Joseph Al-
         len   " 1843, 7, 16
        Samuel C. " 1846, 5, 9
        Sarah H.   " 1848, 6, 20
1833, 10, 30. Sarah m Samuel L. ALLISON (H)
1838, 11, 28. David, s Thomas & Elizabeth, Co-
    lumbiana Co., O.; m at Salem, Rachel SCHOL-
    FIELD, dt David & Rebecca, Columbiana Co.,
    O. (H)

1806, 5, 13. Thomas rocf Concord MM, dtd
    1806,2,18
1806, 9, 16. Nathan & w, Atlantic, & ch, Han-
    nah & Joseph, rocf Phila. MM, dtd 1806,6,
    27
1806, 12, 16. Elizabeth Ball, sister of Lucin-
    da Sackett, & ch, John Manning & Samuel
    Sackett Ball, recrq
1812, 6, 16. Thomas & w, Elizabeth, & ch,
    John-Manning, Samuel Sackett, Sarah & Da-
    vid Thomas, gct Darby MM, Pa.
1813, 11, 16. Thos. & w, Elizabeth, & ch, Sam-
    uel Sacket, Sarah & David, rocf Darby MM,
    Pa., dtd 1813,8,31
1815, 2, 14. John Manning, minor, rocf Darby
    MM, dtd 1814,9,27
1827, 1, 24. Hannah P. rocf Upper Springfield
    MM, dtd 1827,12,16
1828, 12, 24. Nathan & Joseph dis JH
1829, 1, 21. John dis JH
1829, 1, 21. Thomas dis JH
1829, 1, 21. Elizabeth & Sarah dis JH
1829, 12, 23. Hannah dis JH
1830, 8, 25. Samuel dis disunity
1830, 5, 19. John con mou (H)
1830, 10, 20. Benjamin gct Upper Springfield
    MM, to m Hannah Lynch
1831, 1, 19. Hannah L. rocf Upper Springfield
    MM, dtd 1830,12,25
1831, 10, 19. Hannah & dt, Sarah Ann, rocf Car-
    mel MM, dtd 1831,7,16 (H)
1833, 8, 21. David dis JH
1833, 8, 21. Lydia dis JH

BALL, continued

1837, 12, 20. Thomas dis JH

1839, 3, 20. Lydia Montgomery (form Ball) con mou (H)

1840, 12, 23. Joseph gct New Garden MM, to m Elizabeth Lamburn (H)

1841, 5, 19. Joseph P. dis JH

1841, 7, 21. Elizabeth L. rocf New Garden MM, dtd 1841,6,22 (H)

1841, 11, 24. Elizabeth Bean (form Ball) dis mcd

1842, 10, 19. Elizabeth Beens (form Ball) con mcd (H)

1847, 9, 22. Jane dis JH

1850, 8, 21. Benjamin & w, Hannah, & ch, Nathan, Rachel, Martha, Charles, Joshua L., Ann, Joseph Allen, Samuel C. & Sarah H., gct Salem MM, Ia.

1861, 8, 22. Elizabeth L. gct Prairie Grove MM, Ia. (H)

1873, 9, 25. John gct Wappsenonoc MM, Ia. (H)

1876, 6, 22. Sarah Ann gct Marrietta MM, Ia. (H)

BARBER

----, --, --. Isaac b 1756,4,5 d 1825,4,18; m Mary LIPPINCOTT, dt Samuel & Elizabeth, b 1762,10,-- (W)
    Ch: Rebecca   b 1787, 1, 19
        Abram   " 1889, 10, 29
        Isaac   " 1792, 7, 27
        Mary   " 1798, 6, 29
        Jane   " 1800, 10, 8

---, --, --. Jacob b 1796,2,19 d 1877,6,8 (W)

----, --, --. Mary S. b 1805,9,23 d 1874,10,27 (W)

1810, 2, 21. Abraham, s Isaac & Mary, Columbiana Co., O., b 1789,10,29 d 1863,11,10 bur Salem; m at Salem, Drusilla GAUS, dt Enoch & Sarah, Columbiana Co., O., b 1792,12,9 d 1868,3,4 bur Salem (W)
    Ch: Israel   b 1811, 3, 31
        Ruth   " 1813, 3, 11 d 1831, 2, 9 bur Salem
        Ezekiel   " 1815, 3, 26
        Sarah   " 1817, 4, 23
        Mary   " 1819, 4, 12
        Isaac   " 1821, 6, 31
        Ann   " 1823, 12, 3
        Hannah G. " 1825, 12, 22
        Emmaline   " 1828, 7, 10
        Benj. W.   " 1830, 7, 17
        Elizabeth " 1833, 5, 31

----, --, --. Israel b 1811,3,31 d 1890,12,31 (W)

----, --, --. Isaac b 1792,7,27; m Alice ----- b 1794,3,5 (H)
    Ch: Hannah   b 1815, 10, 23
        Joseph   " 1817, 5, 27
        Rebecca   " 1818, 11, 27
        Rachel   " 1820, 10, 29
        Mary Ann   " 1822, 7, 9
        Sarah   " 1824, 5, 14
        Isaac, Jr. " 1826, 6, 21

    Ch: Edith   b 1828, 3, 15 (3-14-1828 in W)
        Barclay   " 1830, 3, 15
        Levi A.   " 1831, 12, 2
        James   " 1834, 4, 4 d 1834, 5, 5
        Emmor   " 1836, 1, 3 " 1836, 2,17
        Elmy   " 1837, 8, 14

1815, 8, 13. Mary Ann m Samuel TEST

----, --, --. Ann L. b 1828,7,4 d 1859,1,8 (W)

1837, 4, 26. Sarah m Josiah ENGLAND

1839, 11, 14. Rachel m Barton HAYCOCK (H)

----, --, --. Israel b 1811,3,31; m Lydia ----- b 1817,11,8 d 1889,2,9 bur Salem (W)
    Ch: Mary A.   b 1841, 2, 8
        Jacob   " 1842, 3, 30
        Benjamin " 1844, 7, 8 d 1863, 5,29
        Anna   " 1848, 8, 3

1840, 5, 27. Jacob, s Isaac & Mary, Columbiana Co., O.; m at Salem, Mary STRATTON, dt Michael & Rhoda, Columbiana Co., O.

1843, 3, 2. Sarah m Uriah HEACOCK (H)

1843, 6, 28. Ann m Thomas YOUNG

1852, 10, 27. Hannah m Isaac B. VOTAW

1808, 6, 14. Rebecca Straughan (form Barber) dis mcd

1814, 12, 13. Isaac, Jr. gct New Garden MM, to m

1815, 4, 11. Alice rocf New Garden MM, dtd 1815,2,16

1819, 1, 17. Jacob dis

1821, 3, 21. Jane Venabal (form Barber) dis mcd

1821, 11, 21. Jacob rst by rq

1823, 9, 24. Jacob dis

1828, 7, 30. Isaac rocf New Garden MM, dtd 1828,7.24 (H)

1828, 8, 20. Isaac dis JH

1835, 5, 20. Alice & ch, Joseph, Rebecca, Rachel, Mary Ann, Sarah, Isaac, Edith, Barclay & Levi Arnold, gct Upper Springfield MM

1837, 8, 23. Hannah Haycock (form Barber) dis mcd (H)

1838, 11, 5. Jacob rst by rq

1839, 8, 21. Israel [Barba] gct Upper Springfield MM, to m Lydia Newburn

1839, 12, 25. Rebecca Mathers (form Barber) con mcd (H)

1840, 1, 22. Israel [Barba] gct Upper Springfield MM

1842, 7, 20. Ezekiel dis mcd

1842, 10, 19. Ann (form Mather) dis mcd (H)

1843, 5, 24. Mary Ann Harlon (form Barber) dis mcd (H)

1846, 10, 21. Israel & w, Lydia, & ch, Mary N., Jacob & Benjamin, rocf Upper Springfield MM, dtd 1846,9,26

1846, 10, 21. Isaac, Jr. dis mcd

1850, 8, 21. Ann L. rocf New Garden MM, dtd 1850,6,20

1853, 4, 20. Mary Whinery (form Barber) con mcd

BARBER, continued

1853, 10, 19. Benjamin W. dis mcd

1861, 7, 24. Mary N. Roose (form Barber) dis
mcd (W)

1862, 12, 25. Abraham, Drusilla, Elizabeth,
Emaline, Jacob, Mary S., Israel, Lydia,
Benjamin & Anna, dis joining for joining
separatists (W) of 1854

1862, 12, 25. Jacob dis joining separatists
(W) of 1854

1863, 3, 25. Jacob dis disunity (W)

1867, 11, 20. Emaline Fisher (form Barber) dis
mcd (W)

1869, 6, 23. Benjamin dis mcd (W)

1870, 10, 19. Annie Hoopes (form Barber) dis
mcd (W)

BARD

----, --, --. George, s Emery & Elizabeth, b
1931,3,25; m Catherine RANCH, dt Jacob &
Barbara, b 1855,11,1 (G)

1849, 3, 21. Mary (form Heald) dis mcd

1931, 3, 25. George recrq

BARKER

----, --, --. M. Luther, s Ezra & Mary Ellen
(Stalker), b 1871,10,5; m Emma LAMBORN (W)
Ch: Lawrence
La Rue   b 1896, 2, 14

1917, 6, 20. M. Luther rocf New Garden MM, O.,
dtd 1917,5,24 (W)

1917, 6, 20. La Rue rocf New Garden MM, O.,
dtd 1917,5,24 (W)

1920, 4, 21. Harvey & fam recrq

1923, 7, 25. La Rue con mcd (W)

1929, 6, 19. Harvey & w, Ella, & ch, William
& Genieve, relrq

1933, 8, 23. Lawrence La Rue dis disunity (W)

BARKHOUSE

1882, 12, 21. Frederick recrq

BARLEY

----, --, --. Benjamin m Rebecca SIFERD, dt
A. J. & Mary, b 1860,11,2 d 1929,12,2 (G)
Ch: James A.   b 1896, 8, 18
Mary   " 1900, 8, 31

1910, 12, 21. Charles gct Damascus MM, O.

1911, 12, 20. James A. rec in mbrp

1913, 1, 31. Mary recrq

1915, 11, 24. Mary recrq

1932, 6, 29. James dropped from mbrp

BARNABE

----, --, --. James b 1781,--,--; m Ann -----
b 1784,--,-- (H)
Ch: Lea   b 1813, 11, 25
James   " 1819, 2, 9
Ann   " 1821, 9, 15
Rachel   " 1824, 3, 15

Ch: Clarkson   b 1826, 10, 12

----, --, --. Stephen b 1808,12,7; m Cathe-
rine ----- b 1809,5,12 (H)
Ch: Howard   b 1833, 3, 14
Louiza   " 1835, 6, 2
Samuel P.   " 1838, 4, 18
Leander   " 1840, 7, 10

1843, 7, 26. James [Barnaby] Jr., s James &
Ann, Stark Co., O.; m at Salem, Laura
STANTON, dt Benjamin & Martha, Columbiana
Co., O. (H)

1837, 1, 25. Stephen [Barneba] & w, Catharine,
& ch, Howard & Louiza, rocf Sadsberry MM,
dtd 1839,11,9 (H)

1837, 7, 19. James [Barneba] & w, Ann, & ch,
James, Ann, Rachel & Clarkson, rocf Sadsbury MM, Pa., dtd 1837,4,5 (H)

1837, 8, 23. Lea [Barnabe] rocf Sadsbury MM,
Pa., dtd 1837,4,5 (H)

1837, 10, 25. Cert rec for James, Ann, Rachel
& Clarkson [Barnaba], ch James & Ann, from
Sadsberry MM, dtd 1837,8,8, endorsed to
Marlborough MM

1839, 9, 25. Joseph [Barnabee] rocf Sadsbery
MM, Pa., dtd 1839,8,7 (H)

1843, 6, 21. Lee [Barnaby] con mcd (H)

1843, 7, 19. Ann Reeves (form Barnaby) con
mcd (H)

BARNARD

1921, 5, 25. Doris L. recrq

1922, 10, 25. Ralph recrq

1932, 6, 29. Ralph dropped from mbrp

BARNES

1871, 4, 24. Alice, dt Felix & Mary Otlip, b
(G)

----, --, --. Charles, s James & Alice, b
1888,8,31; m Ida MORRIS (G)
Ch: Olive   b 1891, 5, 28
Donna Rose " 1930, 5, 28

1929, 4, 24. Olive & Mary A. recrq

1932, 6, 29. Goldie Blackburn dropped from
mbrp

BARR

1858, 11, 24. Elizabeth rocf Goshen MM, Pa.,
dtd 1858,7,1 (W)

1863, 7, 22. Elizabeth E. Steer (form Barr)
dis mcd (W)

BARTON

1885, 1, 11. Loretta, dt James & Mary, b (G)

BASSETT

1844, 5, 29. Chas. D., s John & Ruth, Henry
Co., Ia., b 1816,5,13; m at Salem, Ann W.
HUNT, dt Nathan & Ann, Columbiana Co.,O.,
b 1824,1,5 (G)
Ch: Nathan H. b 1845, 4, 22
James Alvin" 1851,10, 24 d 1909, 1,1

BASSETT, continued
1844, 11, 20. Charles D. [Basset] rocf Middle-
    ton MM, dtd 1844,10,10
1848, 10, 25. Charles D. & w, Ann W., & ch,
    Nathan H., gct Middleton MM
1852, 8, 25. Charles D. & w, Ann W., & ch,
    Nathan H. & James Alvin, rocf Middleton MM,
    dtd 1852,7,8
1864, 6, 22. Charles D. dis joining separatists
    of 1854 (W)
1864, 9, 21. Ann W. dis joining separatists
    of 1854 (W)
1868, 7, 23. Charles D. & w, Ann W., & s,
    James, gct Ypsilanti MM, Mich.

BATES
1932, 6, 29. Mary Elizabeth Gardner dropped
    from mbrp

BATTEY
----, --, --. Deborah C., dt Mifflin & Sarah
    (Wickersham), b 1842,12,5 d 1933,2,15 (W)

1898, 3, 23. Elbert L. Cope gct Middleton MM,
    to m Malinda E. Battey (W)
1910, 1, 19. Walter recrq
1914, 1, 21. Walter [Battie] & w dropped from
    mbrp
1918, 6, 19. Deborah C. rocf Middleton MM, O.,
    dtd 1918,6,15 (W)

BATTIN
1807, 2, 19. Catherine m Benj. WILLIAMS
----, --, --. Robert b 1795,7,12; m Abigail
    ----- b 1797,7,3 (H)
    Ch: Benjamin b 1822, 9, 4
        Hannah C. " 1824, 5, 3
        Thomas   " 1829, 5, 20
        Ann   " 1832, 10, 2
        David   " 1838, 8, 24
        Rachel G. " 1841, 1, 6
----, --, --. John b 1800,2,2; m Sarah D. -----
    b 1804,1,21 (G)
    Ch: Mary   b 1834, 6, 14
        Lucinda M. " 1838, 12, 27
        Ruthanna   " 1840, 10, 14
----, --, --. Samuel R. & Emily T. (H)
    Ch: Orlando T. b 1867, 5, 19
        Kersey R. " 1869, 5, 23
        Martha Alma" 1872, 7, 4
1875, 9, 16. John d ae 76y (an elder)
1875, 12, 3. Sarah D. d ae 72y (an elder)

1806, 10, 14. Richard, Jr. gct Bush River MM,
    S. C.
1811, 7, 16. John [Batten] & w, Ann, & ch,
    Eli, Robert, Elizabeth, Lydia, John, Fan-
    ney, David, Ann, Joshua & Ezra, rocf West-
    land MM, dtd 1811,5,25
1814, 5, 17. John & w, Ann, & ch, Eli, Robert,
    Elizabeth, Lydia, John, Fanny, David, Ann,
    Joshua & Ezra, gct New Garden MM
1840, 7, 22. Robert & w, Abigail, & ch. Benja-

min, Hannah, Thomas, Ann & David C.,
    rocf New Garden MM, dtd 1840,4,23 (H)
1843, 4, 19. Benjamin gct Marlborough MM, to
    m Hannah G. Hoag (H)
1843, 10, 25. Hannah G. rocf Marlborough MM,
    dtd 1843,7,22 (H)
1858, 8, 26. John & w, Sarah D., & ch, Ruth
    Anna, rocf Sandy Spring MM, dtd 1858,7,22
1858, 8, 26. Lucinda M. rocf Sandy Spring MM,
    dtd 1858,6,25
1858, 8, 26. Mary rocf Sandy Spring MM, dtd
    1858,6,25
1861, 1, 24. Robert & w, Abigail, rocf West
    MM, dtd 1860,12,21 (H)
1861, 1, 24. Hannah C. & Ann [Batten] rocf
    West MM, dtd 1860,12,21 (H)
1861, 7, 25. Ann B. Edkin (form Battin) con
    mcd (H)
1861, 11, 21. Hannah C. Cobbs (form Battin)
    con mcd (H)
1863, 12, 24. Mary & Lucinda M. dis jas
1866, 12, 20. Emily T. rocf Short Creek MM,
    dtd 1866,11,6 (H)
1874, 6, 25. Samuel R. & w, Emily T., & ch,
    Orlando T., Kersey R. & Martha Elma, gct
    Green Plain MM, O. (H)

BAUM
1860, 1, 25. Mary Jane (form Hewit) dis mcd
    (W)
1860, 2, 23. Mary Jane (form Hewit) dis mcd

BAYARD
1915, 9, 22. Bell C. gct Alliance MM, O.

BEACH
----, --, --. Harry, s Erskine & Mary, b 1874,
    2,4; m Iva Catherine WALTER, dt James &
    Christy, b 1885,8,27 (G)

1931, 11, 18. Harry [Beech] recrq

BEAL
1817, 11, 11. Pamelia Mariah, minor, rocf
    Middleton MM, dtd 1817,9,15
1821, 8, 22. Maria Mildred gct Middleton MM

BEAN
1838, 2, 21. Charles Armitage gct Buckingham
    MM, Pa., to m Sarah Beans (H)
1841, 11, 24. Elizabeth (form Ball) dis mcd
1842, 10, 19. Elizabeth (form Ball) con mcd (H)

BECK
1807, 1, 13. Edward & w, Ruth, & ch, Jemima &
    Sarah, rocf Westland MM, dtd 1806,11,22
1807, 3, 17. Preston & w, Sarah, & ch, Paul,
    Rachel, Mary, Preston, Richard, John & Sa-
    rah, rocf Westland MM, dtd 1806,10,23

BEDELL
1924, 4, 23. Jesse R. Starbuck gct Springville
    MM, Ia., to m Clara Esther Bedell (W)

BEEDEE
1823, 6, 25. Abram recrq

BEESON
----, --, --. John O. b 1826,7,31 d 1911,2,19
    bur Grandview Cemetery, Salem, O.

1807, 4, 14. John Schooley gct Middleton MM,
    to m Phebe Beason
1862, 12, 25. Anna, John & Malon [Beason] dis
    joining separatists (W) of 1854
1872, 8, 22. John O. rst by rq
1888, 2, 23. John O. relrq
1900, 2, 10. John O. rocf Middleton MM, O.,
    dtd 1900,2,17 (W)

BELL
1862, 12, 25. Martha dis joining separatists
    (W) of 1854
1915, 8, 18. Edna Donnelly gct Valley MM
1932, 6, 29. Elizabeth Kirk dropped from
    mbrp
1932, 6, 29. Ida Ritchie [Belle] dropped from
    mbrp

BENEDICT
1866, 11, 23. Jonathan Stanley gct Alum Creek
    MM, to m Amelia F. Benedict
1877, 12, 20. Edward A. & w, Susan H., & ch,
    Carlos Christy & Mary, rocf Alum Creek MM,
    dtd 1877,11,15
1884, 10, 31. Ella M. rocf Gilead MM, O.

BENFIELD
----, --, --. Cora, dt Joel & Abby Stratton,
    b 1858,3,28 d 1930,3,29 (G)

BENSON
----, --, --. Robert, s Josiah & Ruth (Osborn),
    b 1870,1,18; m Martha KERN, dt Seth & Lu-
    cinda (Anthony), b 1869,10,25 (G)
    Ch: Catharine b 1892, 6, 10
        Wm.   " 1896, 11, 23

BENTLEY
1846, 10, 21. Ruth (form McMillan) dis mcd

BENNETT
1862, 12, 25. Allen [Bennet] dis joining sepa-
    ratists (W) of 1854
1910, 2, 23. George E. & w recrq

BERGEN
1891, 8, 20. Walter B. rocf Central Executive
    Mtg, Chicago, Ill. (H)

BERRY
1811, 8, 13. David recrq
1813, 5, 11. David gct White Water MM, Ind.

BETTS
1837, 11, 22. Elizabeth rocf Buckingham MM,
    Pa., dtd 1837,6,5 (H)

1879, 7, 24. Sallie [Betz] con mcd

BINFORD
1930, 3, 1. Lucy d (G)

1916, 2, 23. Lucie A. rocf Damascus MM
1916, 2, 23. Pearl rocf Damascus MM

BINNS
1804, 8, 23. Jonathan b (W)
----, --, --. Gibson b 1830,10,12; m Martha V.
    ----- b 1832,9,1 d 1892,1,-- (W)
----, --, --. Arthur H. b 1877,5,21, s Joseph
    P. & Belinda (Hobson); m Tacie M. BUNDY,
    dt Lindley & Ruanna, b 1876,10,28 (W)
    Ch: Frances S. b 1899, 6, 6
        Mildred M. " 1901, 4, 14
        Dorothy A. " 1903, 1, 22
        John Edward" 1908, 3, 31
        Jonathan
          Alfred   " 1910, 2, 13
        Martha D. " 1912, 1, 10
----, --, --. John A., s Joseph P. & Belinda
    (Hobson), b 1881,6,2 d 1927,1,20 bur
    Friends Burying Ground, Winona, O.; m at
    Sewickley, Pa., Mary E. COPE, dt Albert
    M. & Phebe Y. (Ashton), b 1881,12,19 d
    1905,2,22 bur Friends Burying Ground, Wi-
    nona, O. (W)
    Ch: Alice Re-
          becca   b 1906, 1, 16
        Esther Mary" 1913, 3, 24
        Albert John" 1916, 6, 29
1920, 8, 26. Frances S. m Francis E. MOTT (W)

1829, 10, 21. Jonathan gct Redstone MM
1829, 12, 23. Jonathan's cert returned by Red-
    stone MM
1829, 12, 23. Jonathan con mcd
1830, 8, 25. Jonathan gct Redstone MM
1880, 8, 25. Elma (form Cope) dis mcd (W)
1888, 4, 26. William rocf Columbus MM, O.,
    dtd 1888,2,1
1893, 7, 19. Gibson rst by rq (form dis by
    Short Creek MM (W)
1893, 11, 22. Gibson gct Short Creek MM, to m
    Martha Russell (W)
1895, 1, 23. Gibson gct Short Creek MM (W)
1905, 6, 21. Mary E. gct New Garden MM, O. (W)
1908, 3, 25. Arthur H. & w, Tacie M., & ch,
    Francis S., Mildred M. & Dorothy A., rocf
    Flushing MM, dtd 1908,2,20 (W)
1911, 8, 23. John A. & w, Mary E., & dt,
    Alice Rebecca, rocf Short Creek MM, O.,
    dtd 1911,7,18 (W)
1921, 7, 20. John A. & w, Mary E., & ch,
    Alice Rebecca, Esther Mary & Albert John,
    gct New Garden MM, O. (W)

BISHOP
----, --, --. Jacob b 1808,8,28 d 1885,5,6; m
    Fanny ----- b 1814,3,3 d 1889,1,21 (W)
    Ch: Henry H. b 1833, 12, 27 d 1840, 1, 7

BISHOP, Jacob & Fanny, continued

Ch: Abram T.   b 1835, 2, 21
    Mary E.   " 1836, 3, 19 d 1837,10,20
    Phebe J.   " 1837, 4, 15 " 1837, 4,29
    Mary E.   " 1839, 3, 10 " 1885, 7, 4
    Victoria   " 1841, 1, 3 " 1903,11,23
    Phebe J.   " 1842, 11, 10
    Isaac T.   " 1844, 6, 4
    Joseph F. " 1845, 11, 20
    Anna L.   " 1847, 8, 20
    Fanny J.   " 1849, 9, 3
    Jacob R.   " 1851, 5, 10 d 1880, 1, 3
    John C.   " 1853, 10, 18 " 1861, 9,22
    Delila E. " 1855, 7, 19
    Harriet E. " 1858, 1, 30

1838, 2, 21. Jacob rocf Danby MM, dtd 1836,11,
   10
1839, 6, 19. Fanny recrq
1886, 9, 23. William & w recrq
1890, 6, 26. William & w dropped from mbrp

BLACK
----, --, --. Geo. Edward m Laura Marguerite
   DRYDEN (W)
   Ch: Doris   b 1919, 9, 10
       Eleanor
       Marguerite" 1917, 2, 20

1930, 6, 25. Eleanor, dt George Edward &
   Laura Dryden, recrq (W)
1933, 12, 20. Doris, dt George Edward & Laura
   Dryden, recrq (W)

BLACKBURN
1812, 10, 14. Sarah m Abram STANLEY
1818, 10, 28. Barbee, s David & Margaret, Co-
   lumbiana Co., O.; m at Goshen, Elizabeth
   HINCHMAN, dt Henry & Ruth, Columbiana Co.,
   O.
----, --, --. Barbe b 1796,1,11; m Elizabeth
   ----- b 1797,1,1 (W)
   Ch: Hannah   b 1819, 7, 25
       Sarah Ann " 1821, 7, 2
       Mary   " 1823, 5, 4
1823, 10, 13. Margaret m John STANLEY
----, --, --. Abel H. m Caroline HOAGLAND (W)
   Ch: Abbie T.   b 1865, 1, 28
       Mary   " 1869, 1, 28
----, --, --. Thomas, s Wm. & Anne (Hewitt),
   b 1846,12,29; m Louisa S. SMITH, dt Evan
   & Mary (Burgess), b 1846,2,20 d 1929,11,30
   bur Salem, O. (W)
1868, 4, 27. George, s Wm. & Anna (Hewitt),
   Washington Co., Pa., b 1841,7,18 d 1924,1,
   25; m at Salem, Rachel W. BONSALL, dt
   Isaac & Hannah, Mahoning Co., O., b 1836,
   7,13 d 1908,6,8 (W)   [(W)
1869, 10, 25. Elizabeth, dt Thomas & Sarah, b
----, --, --. Jonathan K. b 1841,7,18; m Emily
   H. ----- b 1840,2,25 (W)
   Ch: Arthur   b 1871, 3, 20
       George R. " 1873, 7, 14

Ch: Ida   b 1876, 6, 15
----, --, --. Nathan M. m Rebecca COPE (W)
   Ch: Annie E.   b 1870, 1, 25
       Myra J.   " 1872, 6, 14
1877, 6, 4. Mary Elizabeth, dt John & Kathe-
   rine Bare, b (G)
----, --, --. Dr. Wm. J., s Abel H. & Caroline
   (Hoagland), b 1862,3,24; m Elizabeth COLE-
   MAN, dt Samuel & Sarah (Uncles), b 1860,9,
   19 (W)
   Ch: Harold C. b 1887, 10, 26 d 1916,10,26
       bur Byberry, Pa.
       Caroline H.b 1889, 7, 25
       Wm., Jr.   " 1891, 10, 18
       Alice M.   " 1895, 1, 9
1905, 10, 31. Mabel M., foster dt Abbie T. &
   Mary, b (W)
1909, 9, 23. Elizabeth m Jesse R. TUCKER
1914, 5, 21. Caroline Hoagland m Robert P.
   LOVETT (W)
1922, 10, 26. Alice Marie m John Howard OLI-
   PHANT (W)
1930, 5, 28. Elizabeth C. d ae 70y (an elder
   (H)
----, --, --. Wm. J., Jr. m Lorena YOUNG (W)
   Ch: Wm. J. 3rd b 1931, 1, 2
       Thos.
       Mott   " 1932, 1, 24

1812, 9, 15. David & w, Margaret, & ch, Nancy, Sarah, Polly, Barbee, Margaret, Temperance, Thomas & James Crew, rocf Cedar
   Creek MM, Va., dtd 1812,7,11
1813, 8, 17. Elisabeth rocf Cedar Creek MM,
   Va., dtd 1813,1,9
1815, 6, 13. Nancy dis mcd with first cousin
1819, 12, 22. Polly Maria Vaughan (form Blackburn) dis mcd
1824, 7, 21. Thomas [Blackbourn] dis disunity
1827, 6, 20. Ann (form Teetars) dis mcd
1862, 3, 19. Thomas Y. French gct Westland
   MM, to m Rachel H. Blackburn (W)
1868, 8, 19. Abel H. & w, Caroline, & ch,
   William J. & Abbie T., rocf Muncy MM, Pa.,
   dtd 1868,6,17 (W)
1868, 12, 23. Abel H. & w, Caroline, & ch,
   William J. & Abbie T., gct Middleton MM
   (W)
1879, 9, 24. Barzillai French gct Middleton
   MM, to m Martha Blackburn (W)
1882, 5, 24. Jonathan & w, Emily H., & ch,
   Arthur, George R. & Ida, rocf Middleton
   MM, dtd 1882,4,15 (W)
1884. 3, 20. Cert rec for Joseph from Damascus MM, returned because of obstruction
1890, 7, 23. Jonathan & w, Emily H., & ch,
   Arthur, George R. & Ida, gct Middleton MM
   (W)
1893, 2, 22. William J. & w, Elizabeth E., &
   ch, Harold E., Caroline H. & William J.,
   rocf Chester MM, N. J., dtd 1893,2,7 (W)
1908, 12, 23. Elizabeth rocf Coal Creek MM,
   Ia., dtd 1908,12,12 (W)

BLACKBURN, continued

1911, 5, 24. Annie E. & Myra J. rocf Middle-
    ton MM, dtd 1911,5,20 (W)
1911, 11, 22. Harold C. gct WD MM, Phila., Pa.
    (W)
1913, 1, 31. Andrew & w, Mary, recrq
1913, 2, 19. Sarah & Howard dropped from mbrp
1914, 9, 25. Emma recrq
1915, 11, 24. Edward recrq
1917, 8, 15. Harriet Goldie recrq
1917, 8, 15. James recrq
1921, 2, 23. Elisha & w, Virginia, & ch,
    Dosia Esther, Margaret L. & John Hollings-
    worth, gct Cleveland MM, O.
1921, 10, 19. Sarah J. recrq
1928, 8, 15. Mr. & Mrs. relrq
1928, 12, 19. Thomas & w, Louisa, rocf Mill
    Creek MM, Ind., dtd 1928,11,22 (W)
1928, 12, 19. Abbie T., Mary & Mabel M. rocf
    Mill Creek MM, Ind., dtd 1928,11,22 (W)
1929, 12, 18. William J., Jr. gct Springville
    MM, Ia., to m Anna Lorena Young (W)
1931, 6, 24. Mary recrq

BLACKLEDGE
1808, 3, 17. Joseph, s Robert & Joanna, Colum-
    biana Co., O.; m at New Garden, Rachel
    GRISSELL, dt Thomas & Martha, Columbiana
    Co., O.

1807, 1, 13. Robert dis mou
1808, 5, 17. Rachel gct Middleton MM
1817, 10, 14. Mary rocf Plainfield MM, dtd
    1817,6,26
1818, 11, 25. Mary gct ND MM, Phila., Pa.
1830, 7, 21. Mary rocf New Garden MM, dtd
    1830,6,24

BOE
1879, 6, 26. Mary recrq
1887, 1, 20. Mary dropped from mbrp

BOLGER
1878, 2, 20. Alice Carey (now Bolger) dis
    jas (W)

BONHAM
1823, 9, 24. Ephraim rocf Hamburgh MM, New
    York, dtd 1823,5,28
1824, 12, 22. Ephraim dis disunity

BONNER
1921, 4, 20. Thelma recrq
1929, 4, 24. Charles recrq

BONSALL
----, --, --. Edward b 1775,9,2 d 1862,8,29;
    m 2nd Rachel ----- b 1787,10,30 d 1864,9,
    29 (W)
    Ch: James G.   b 1800, 5, 17
        Daniel   " 1802, 11, 13
        Isaac   " 1808, 5, 30
        Abraham   " 1809, 7, 3

Ch: Mark   b 1812, 4, 13
    Edward   " 1814, 4, 26
    Thomas   " 1816, 6, 10 (or 1816,6,
      11) d 1832,9,26
    Rebecca   b 1818, 7, 5
    Hannah   " 1821, 2, 6
    Evan   " 1823, 2, 7
    Rachel   " 1825, 3, 12
    Joshua   " 1827, 3, 2
    John   " 1830, 3, 16 d 1832, 2, 1
    Richard   " 1832, 9, 30 " 1832,11,22
1807, 5, 14. Edward, s Edward & Hannah, Jeffer
    son Co., O.; m at Salem, Rachel WARRINGTON,
    dt Abraham & Rachel, Columbiana Co., O.
1825, 8, 31. Daniel, s Edward & Rebecca, Co-
    lumbiana Co., O., b 1802,11,13; m at Salem,
    Martha W. SHARP, dt Joel & Rebecca, Colum-
    biana Co., O., b 1805,6,3 d 1841,8,8 (H)
    Ch: Joel S.   b 1826, 8, 13
        Rebecca H. " 1829, 1, 12
        Deborah G. " 1831, 9, 4
        Thomas   " 1835, 5, 1 d 1838,11,15
        Sarah   " 1837, 1, 6
        Charles   " 1839, 11, 19
----, --, --. Isaac d 1831,10,3 ae 65y 11m 5d
    (a minister)
1832, 5, 2. Isaac, s Edward & Rachel, Colum-
    biana Co., O., b 1808,5,30 d 1869,3,10; m
    at Salem, Hannah EVINS, dt Jonathan &
    Elizabeth, Columbiana Co., O., b 1811,6,5
    d 1880,10,14 (W)
    Ch: Jonathan   b 1833, 3, 22
        Elizabeth   " 1834, 8, 16 d 1910, 9,22
        Rachel W.   " 1836, 7, 13
        Priscilla   " 1838, 6, 22
        Henry   " 1842, 8, 26
        Isaac E.Jr." 1852, 7, 2
1834, 4, 30. Abraham, s Edward & Rachel, Co-
    lumbiana Co., O., b 1809,7,3; m at Salem,
    Deborah MIDDLETON, dt Hudson & Deborah,
    Columbiana Co., O., b 1812,10,22 (W)
    Ch: Priscilla   b 1835, 3, 8 d 1835, 5, 2
        Joseph   " 1836, 2, 25
        Thomas   " 1838, 12, 24 " 1839,10,19
        Levi   " 1837, 6, 25
        Edwin   " 1842, 4, 2 " 1842, 7,18
        Emmor   " 1840, 10, 9
        Amos   " 1843, 5, 21
        Charles   " 1844, 9, 10 " 1845, 3,--
        Anna   " 1851, 8, 22
        -----   " 1854, 3, 30 " 1854, 8, 1
1837, 11, 1. Mark, s Edward,& Rachel, Colum-
    biana Co., O., b 1812,4,13 d 1888,10,18; m
    at Salem Hannah JOHNSON, dt Wm. & Sarah, b
    1815,9,11 d 1894,5,29 (W)
    Ch: Sarah   b 1838, 8, 8 d 1920, 4,15
        bur Highland Cemetery, near Salem, O.
        Martha   b 1841, 10, 22
        Wm.   " 1846, 9, 2
1839, 11, 27. Edward, s Edward & Rachel, Colum-
    biana Co., O., b 1814,4,26 d 1901,12,13; m
    at Salem, Hannah F. JONES, dt Joseph &
    Elizabeth, Phila. Co., Pa., b 1808,11,14

BONSALL, Edward & Hannah F., continued
    d 1893,12,27
    Ch: Joseph
        Jones   b 1840, 9, 16 d 1841,10,26
        Sidney Ann " 1843, 6, 23
        Robert   " 1846, 5, 25
        Joseph Ed-
        ward   " 1848, 6, 22
        Elizabeth
        J.   " 1851, 5, 6 d 1932, 2, 6
1840, 12, 2. Edward S., s Thos. & Elizabeth, Columbiana Co., O., b 1818,3,19; m Sarah EVANS, dt Jonathan & Elizabeth, Columbiana Co., O., b 1816,11,20 (m at Salem)
1843, 1, 4. Daniel, s Edward & Rebecca, Columbiana Co., O.; m at Salem, Ann HOOPES, Jr., dt Wm. & Ann, Columbiana Co., O. (H)
1843, 4, 26. Rebecca m John C. HOGE
1846, 5, 27. Hannah m Edward HEADLY
----, --, --. Joshua b 1827,3,2 d 1864,3,3; m Elazan ----- b 1824,8,19 (W)
    Ch: James R.   b 1853, 4, 2 d 1853, 7,13
        Elizabeth
        R.   " 1856, 4, 2
        Edward Wm. " 1861, 10, 18
        Elazan   " 1864, 2, 28
1853, 4, 27. Evan, s Edward & Rachel, Mahoning Co., O., b 1823,2,7; m at Salem, Caroline W. SATTERTHWAIT, dt Richard & Rebecca, Columbiana Co., O., b 1820,10,16 (W)
    Ch: Wm. T.   b 1854, 3, 29
        Richard S. " 1856, 4, 17
        Lewis   " 1859, 3, 4
        Rebecca Eva" 1860, 6, 15
1853, 5, 4. Rachel W. m John STRATTON
1856, 8, 14. Mary Ellen, dt David & Sarah (Holloway), b (W)
1864, 3, 30. Sidney Ann m Thomas F. FAWCETT
1867, 5, 29. Wm., s Mark & Hannah J., Columbiana Co., O., b 1846,9,2; m at Salem, Eliza STANLEY, dt Jonathan & Hannah M., Columbiana Co., O., b 1848,7,6 (W)
    Ch: Hannah
        Emma   b 1869, 8, 17 d 1870, 2, 9
        Isabella " 1871, 5, 12
1868, 4, 27. Rachel W. m George BLACKBURN (W)
----, --, --. Jonathan b 1833,3,22; m Rebecca W. ----- b 1834,1,10 d 1881,5,4 (W)
    Ch: Anna S.   b 1870, 3, 22
        Laura R.   " 1873, 1, 17
----, --, --. Isaac E. b 1852,7,2; m Anna CADWALLADER dt Isaac S. & Esther (Allmon), b 1857,9,18 (W) (Isaac, s Isaac & Hannah (Evans)
    Ch: Alice   b 1882, 5, 9 d 1887,11,11

1807, 7, 14. Rachel gct Short Creek MM
1810, 6, 12. Edward & w, Rachel, & ch, James Gibbons, Isaac & Abraham. rocf Short Creek MM, dtd 1810,4,24
1813, 9, 14. James Gibbons, minor s Edward, gct Sadsbury MM, Pa.
1816, 5, 14. James G., minor, rocf Sadbury MM,

dtd 1816,1,31
1819, 3, 24. James G. gct Sadsbury MM, Pa.
1824, 9, 22. Daniel rocf Sadsbury MM, Pa., dtd 1824,8,3
1828, 10, 22. Daniel dis jH
1828, 10, 22. Martha dis jH
1831, 6, 22. Isaac rocf Phila. MM for Western District, dtd 1831,5,18
1838, 8, 22. Edward S., minor, rocf Phila. MM, dtd 1838,7,25
1841, 6, 23. Joseph Scarrett rocf SD MM, Phila., Pa., dtd 1841,4,28
1842, 6, 22. Eliza, w Thomas, rocf Chesterfield MM, N. J., dtd 1842,6,7
1843, 11, 22. Eliza gct Chesterfield MM, N. J.
1845, 4, 23. Francis B. Rich recrq (a minor under care of Edward & Rachel Bonsall)
1845, 8, 20. Edward S. & fam gct Marlborough MM
1846, 10, 21. Joseph Scarrett, minor, gct SD MM, Phila., Pa.
1852, 5, 19. Joshua W. gct Sandy Spring MM, to m Elazan Raleigh
1852, 11, 24. Elazan rocf Sandy Spring MM, dtd 1852,9,24
1856, 4, 23. Joel S. dis mcd (W)
1858, 9, 23. Abraham & w, Deborah, & ch, Emmor, Amos & Anna, gct Spring Creek MM, Ia.
1858, 9, 23. Evan & w, Caroline W., & ch, William & Richard, gct Spring Creek MM, Ia.
1858, 9, 23. Joseph gct Spring Creek MM, Ia.
1858, 9, 23. Levi gct Spring Creek MM, Ia.
1862, 12, 25. Ed & w, Hannah F., & ch, Sidney Ann, Robert, Joseph Elwood & Elizabeth, dis for joining separatists (W) of 1854
1862, 12, 25. Isaac & w, Hannah E., & ch, Elizabeth, Jonathan, Rachel, Priscilla, Henry & Isaac, Jr. dis joining separatists (W) of 1854
1862, 12, 25. Hannah J., Mark, Sarah, Martha & William J. dis joining separatists (W) of 1854
1862, 12, 25. Rachel W., Joshua W., Elizabeth R. & Edward William dis joining separatists of 1854
1863, 6, 24. Joshua W. dis disunity (W)
1863, 7, 22. Evan & w, Caroline W., & ch, William T., Richard S., Lewis H. & Rebecca Eva, gct Pennsville MM (W)
1864, 9, 21. Joshua W. [Bonsal] dis disunity (W)
1866, 5, 23. Emmor dis disunity (W)
1868, 2, 19. Henry dis mcd (W)
1868, 7, 22. Martha D. (form Stratton) dis mcd (W)
1868, 9, 23. Priscilla Grennell (form Bonsall) dis mcd (W)
1869, 1, 20. Rebecca W. rocf Upper Evesham MM, dtd 1868,12,12 (W)
1869, 3, 24. Laura (form Stanley) dis mcd (W)
1869, 7, 21. Jonathan con mcd (W)
1870, 7, 20. Elizabeth R. & Edward William, ch Joshua W., gct Coal Creek MM, Ia. (W)

BONSALL, continued

1871, 4, 19. Joseph E. dis mcd (W)

1875, 3, 21. Robert dis mcd (W)

1876, 9, 21. William rst by rq

1878, 7, 24. William J. dis joining separatists of 1854 (W)

1878, 7, 24. Eliza dis joining separatists of
1854 (W)

1881, 4, 20. Isaac E. gct Middleton MM, to m
Annie H. Cadwallader (H)

1882, 2, 22. Anna C. rocf Middleton MM, dtd
1882,1,21 (W)

1885, 2, 6. Bella recrq

1886, 4, 21. Jonathan dis mcd (W)

1891, 11, 25. Anna S. & Laura R. gct Upper
Evesham MM, N. J. (W)

1893, 4, 19. Isabella dis jas (W)

1918, 6, 19. Rebecca Eva rocf West Branch
MM, Ia., dtd 1918,6,8 (W)

1926, 9, 22. Isaac E. & w, Annie E., gct
Middleton MM (W)

BOOK

1883, 8, 16. Oliver & Enna recrq

BOONE

----, --, --. James [Boon] m Rebecca THOMAS,
dt Jacob & Mary, b 1786,9,27 d 1860,4,12
(W)
    Ch: Jacob
         Thomas   b 1815, 10, 31
        Joshua
         James   " 1820, 2, 10
        Jesse
         Thomas   " 1822, 6, 28

----, --, --. Jesse T. b 1822,6,28 d 1891,3,26
(W)

1828, 7, 30. Isaac & w, Esther, & ch, Thomas
Chalkley, James & Phebe Jane, rocf New Garden MM, dtd 1828,7,24 (H)

1834, 4, 23. Rebecca [Boon] & ch, Jacob Thomas, Joshua James & Jesse Thomas, rocf Exeter MM, Pa., dtd 1834,2,26

1845, 4, 23. Jacob T. dis disunity

1845, 4, 23. Joshua J. dis disunity

1847, 7, 21. Maria L. [Boon] (form Thomas)
con mcd (H)

1851, 2, 19. Mary (form Lee) dis mcd (with
first cousin)

1857, 10, 21. Hannah (form Lee) dis mcd (wtih
first cousin) (W)

1858, 6, 24. Hannah (form Lee) con mcd

BOOTH

1920, 8, 18. Pauline Broomal gct Stella MM,
Okla.

BORTON

----, --, --. ----- & Jane (H)
    Ch: Emmaline   b 1833, 3, 10
        Angeline   " 1835, 5, 11
        Jane D.   " 1837, 1, 12

1832, 5, 3. Ezra, s Samuel & Mercy, Stark
Co., O.; m at West MH, Jane D. HEACOCK,
dt Nathan & Dinah, Columbiana Co., O. (H)

1832, 6, 20. Jane D. gct Marlborough MM (H)

1846, 5, 20. Jane D. rocf Marlborough MM, dtd
1846,2,28 (H)

BOULTON

----, --, --. Sarah b 1778,6,19 d 1864,--,14
(W)

----, --, --. Joseph b 1769,2,25 d 1828,9,17;
m Azubah ----- b 1769,7,4 d 1823,5,5 bur
Salem (W)
    Ch: Margaret   b 1796, 11, 9
        John   " 1798, 9, 29
        James   " 1803, 5, 30
        Joseph Jr. " 1807, 1, 23

----, --, --. Daniel b 1803,11,30 d 1880,4,6;
m Esther ----- b 1799,8,12 d 1880,9,16 (W)

----, --, --. Wm. b 1812,6,5; m Mary -----
b 1811,8,12 (W)
    Ch: Elizabeth b 1833, 9, 9
        Sarah   " 1836, 6, 5 d 1842, 7, 3
        James   " 1838, 12, --
        Charles   " 1841, 5, 10

1810, 12, 11. Joseph & w, Azubah, & ch, Margaret, John, James & Joseph, rocf Great Egg
Harbour MM, N. J., dtd 1810,9,3

1824, 9, 22. Sarah rocf Marlborough MM, dtd
1824,8,20

1824, 11, 24. Sarah gct New Garden MM

1828, 9, 24. Daniel rocf Middleton MM, dtd
1828,8,7

1828, 11, 19. Esther rocf Upper Springfield MM,
dtd 1828,9,27

1830, 5, 6. William, minor, rocf Middleton
MM, dtd 1830,4,8

1830, 8, 25. John dis disunity

1830, 11, 24. Margaret Brown (form Boulton)
dis mcd

1831, 2, 23. Joseph dis mcd

1832, 10, 24. William gct Upper Springfield
MM, to m Mary Morris

1833, 7, 24. Mary rocf Upper Springfield MM,
dtd 1833,4,27

1838, 6, 20. Sarah rocf Upper Springfield MM,
dtd 1838,5,24

1839, 9, 25. Evan [Bolton] & w, Mary Ann, &
dt, Sarah, rocf Little Britton MM, dtd
1839,8,17 (H)

1842, 2, 23. Evan [Bolton] & w, Mary Ann, &
dt, Sarah, gct New Garden MM (H)

1842, 11, 23. New Garden MM was given permission to rec Joseph in mbrp

1846, 11, 25. William & w, Mary, & ch, Elizabeth, James & Charles, gct Middleton MM

1862, 12, 25. Daniel & Esther dis joining
separatists (W) of 1854

1862, 12, 25. Rebecca, Levi & Orphah dis
joining separatists (W) of 1854

1862, 12, 25. Hannah dis joining separatists

BOULTON, continued
    (W) of 1854
1862, 12, 25. Sarah dis joining separatists
    (W) of 1854

BOWMAN
1807, 4, 14. Isaac gct Concord MM
1828, 12, 24. Ann gct Marlborough MM
1883, 8, 16. C. W. recrq
1886, 1, 21. Walter gct Winona MM

BOYD
1890, 8, 29. Ruth M. d (W)

1867, 5, 22. Wilhelmina [Boyed] (form Maerkt)
    con mcd (W)
1905, 2, 22. Wilhelmina dis jas (W)

BRACKIN
1831, 9, 22. Elisha, s Caleb & Rebecca, Jef-
    ferson Co., O.; m at Salem, Esther FAWCETT
    dt Richard & Eunice, Columbiana Co., O.
1867, 10, 24. Lindley M., s Elisha & Esther,
    Belmont Co., O.; m at Salem, Anna FRENCH,
    dt John & Martha H., Columbiana Co., O. (W)

1808, 8, 16. Caleb Whitacre gct Westland MM,
    to m Rebecca Bracken
1831, 12, 21. Esther gct Short Creek MM
1868, 10, 21. Anna S. gct Short Creek MM (W)

BRADSHAW
1833, 11, 20. Sarah & ch, Townsend, Maryann,
    James, Rebecca & William, rocf Buckingham
    MM, Pa., dtd 1833,9,2
1840, 1, 22. Mary Ann Brown (form Bradshaw)
    con mou (H)
1842, 6, 22. Rebecca T. Hinchman (form Brad-
    shaw) con mou (H)
1844, 4, 24. Sarah F. (form Fogg) con mcd (H)
1844, 12, 25. James dis mcd (H)

BRADWAY
1863, 5, 1. James L. W. b (W)

1883, 4, 25. Samuel Gamble & w, Mary Jane,
    & ch, Charles W., Phebe Jane, Edward Y.,
    Mary R., Irene H. & Alvin H. & their s,
    James L. W. Bradway, gct New Garden MM

BRANIN
----, --, --. Ezra b 1788,10,9; m Rachel -----
    b 1789,10,9 (H)
    Ch: Abigail   b 1812, 7, 23
        Hannah   " 1814, 7, 10
        Elijah   " 1816, 8, 23 d 1819,12,21
        Susannah   " 1818, 10, 10
        Mahlon   " 1820, 8, 10
        Nathaniel " 1825, 4, 18
        Rachel   " 1827, 2, 19

1824, 6, 23. Ezra & w, Rachel, & ch, Abigail,
    Hannah, Susannah & Mahlon, rocf Abington

MM, Pa., dtd 1824,3,29
1828, 7, 23. Ezra [Brannin] dis JH
1828, 7, 30. Ezra & w, Rachel, & ch, Abigail,
    Hannah, Susannah, Mahlon, Nathaniel & Ra-
    chel, rocf New Garden MM, dtd 1828,7,24
1828, 8, 20. Rachel dis JH
1833, 3, 20. Susanna, Mahlon, Nathaniel & Ra-
    chel [Brannin], ch Ezra & Rachel, gct
    Upper Springfield MM
1833, 10, 23. Abigail & Hannah [Brannon] dis
    JH
1835, 7, 22. Abigail Shaw (form Branin) con
    mcd (H)
1841, 10, 20. Susannah Snode (form Branin) con
    mou (H)

BRANSON
1840, 6, 25. Wm., s Rees & Ruth, Harrison Co.,
    O., b 1814,4,26; m at Salem, Eliza OLI-
    PHANT, dt Samuel & Rachel, Columbiana Co.,
    O., b 1817,8,10 (W)
    Ch: Abner   b 1841, 4, 28
        Rees   " 1842, 8, 20
        Milton   " 1844, 9, 1 d 1846, 9,16
        Sinah Ann " 1847, 2, 2
        Samuel   " 1849, 6, 2
        Rachel El-
          len   " 1852, 3, 26
1842, 11, 30. Jacob, s Jacob & Rebecca, Colum-
    biana Co., O.; m at Salem, Julian H. JOHN-
    SON, dt John H. & Hannah, Columbiana Co.,
    O.

1840, 9, 23. Eliza gct Short Creek MM
1841, 9, 22. William D. & w, Eliza, & s, Ab-
    ner, rocf Short Creek MM, dtd 1841,7,20
1842, 6, 22. Jacob rocf Flushing MM, dtd
    1842,5,26
1846, 5, 20. Jacob & w, Juliann, & ch, Levi,
    gct Flushing MM
1853, 7, 20. William D. & w, Eliza, & ch, Ab-
    ner, Reese, Sina Ann & Samuel, gct Red
    Cedar MM, Ia.
1873, 2, 19. Joseph H. & w, Ruthanna, & ch,
    Elma & Walter J., rocf Flushing MM, dtd
    1872,12,26 (W)
1873, 6, 25. Joseph H. & fam gct Flushing MM
    (W)
1891, 7, 22. Albert Hays gct Flushing MM, to
    m Myra D. Branson (W)
1917, 3, 21. Mary Ellen rocf Flushing MM, O.,
    dtd 1917,2,22 (W)

BRANTINGHAM
1790, 1, 3. Martin b (W)
----, --, --. George b 1770,11,7 d 1845,10,29
    (an elder); m Phebe ----- b 1773,6,7 d
    1853,3,11 (W)
    Ch: Hannah   b 1809, 3, 1
1821, 9, 26. Martin, s Hugh & Mary, Stark
    Co., O.; m at Salem, Margaret HOLLOWAY,
    dt Jesse & Sarah, Columbiana Co., O.
----, --, --. Elisha K. m Mary A. MASTERS, dt

BRANTINGHAM, Elisha K. & Mary A., continued
    Joseph & Esther (Stratton), b 1870,8,25 (W)
      Ch: C. Wilmer b 1894, 11, 28
         E. Anetta " 1893, 8, 16

1818, 9, 23. Martin rocf New Castle MM, dtd
    1818,5,13
1822, 1, 31. Martin & w, Margaret, gct Marl-
    borough MM
1824, 8, 25. George & w, Phebe, & ch, Joseph,
    Hannah, George & Sarah Hopper, rocf Marl-
    borough MM, dtd 1824,6,26
1824, 11, 24. George & w, Phebe, & ch, Joseph,
    Hannah, George & Sarah Hopper, gct New
    Garden MM
1838, 6, 20. George & w, Phebe, rocf Upper
    Springfield MM, dtd 1838,5,26
1838, 6, 20. Hannah C. rocf Upper Spring-
    field MM, dtd 1838,5,26
1862, 12, 25. Hannah C. dis joining separa-
    tists (W) of 1854
1867, 1, 23. Hannah C. dis disunity (W)
1911, 9, 20. Mary A. & ch, E. Anetta & C. Wil-
    mer, rocf New Garden MM, O., dtd 1911,8,24
    (W)
1916, 12, 20. Mary A. gct Phila. MM, Pa. (W)
1920, 1, 21. C. Wilmer gct Phila. MM, Pa. (W)

BRAYTON
1870, 8, 25. Isaac recrq

BRIDENSTINE
1881, 5, 26. Samuel recrq
1884, 5, 25. Samuel [Bridenstein] gct Colum-
    bus MM, O.

BRIGGS
1813, 6, 30. Israel Shreeve, s Wm. & Esther,
    Columbiana Co., O.; m at Salem, Mary
    STRAHL, dt John & Ann, Belmont Co., O.
1908, 12, 13. Abigail, m Heil S. HALL (W)

1807, 3, 17. Rebecca recrq
1811, 4, 16. William & w, Esther, & ch, Is-
    rael Shreve, Samuel Miller, George Green,
    Mariah, Job, Jonathan Taylor, Rebecca More-
    head & William, rocf Short Creek MM, dtd
    1811,3,19
1816, 7, 16. Israel S. & w, Mary, & ch, Es-
    ther & Ann, gct Stillwater MM
1816, 8, 13. George G., minor, gct Short Creek
    MM
1817, 5, 13. William & w, Esther, & ch, Sam-
    uel M., Maria, Job, Jonathan T., Rebecca
    M., William & Henry, gct Plymouth MM
1819, 5, 19. John & w, Rebecca, & ch, John,
    Jr. & Rebecca Ann, gct New Garden MM
1908, 10, 21. Abigal rocf Flushing MM, O., dtd
    1908,9,24 (W)
1911, 12, 20. Blanch rec in mbrp

BROOKE
----, --, --. James d 1839,11,15; m Esther

----- (W)
  Ch: Isaiah
      Boone   b 1800, 12, 30
      Basil   " 1803, 2, 6
      Hannah
      Pancoast   " 1805, 9, 23
      Gerard   " 1808, 3, 16
      James   " 1810, 8, 6
      Ann Eliza
      Pleasant   " 1813, 4, 5
      Pollina
      Snowden   " 1816, 7, 30
      Jane Grey   " 1819, 2, 10
1824, 6, 30. Isaiah B. [Brook], s James & Es-
    ther, Columbiana Co., O.; m at Goshen,
    Deborah CATTELL, dt James & Deborah, Co-
    lumbiana Co., O.

1817, 1, 14. James [Brook] & w, Hester, & ch,
    Isaiah Boone, Bazil, Hannah Pancoast, Ge-
    rard, James & Ann Eliza Pleasant, rocf
    Farmington MM, dtd 1816,8,22
1829, 6, 24. James & w, Hester, & minor ch,
    James, Ann, Elisa P., Paulina S. & Jane
    Gray Brooke, mbrp transferred from Upper
    Springfield by rq
1834, 7, 23. Paulina S. Hughs (form Brook)
    con mcd (H)
1866, 11, 23. Ruth Anna [Brooks] (form Miller)
    dis mcd

BROOMALL
1911, 2, 22. S. J. & w, Lida, & ch, Pauline,
    Raymond & Vernon, rocf Winona MM, O., dtd
    1911,1,25
1919, 11, 26. Effie (White) [Broomal] recrq
1923, 1, 24. S. J., Lida, Vernon & Glenn rel-
    rq
1923, 10, 24. R. W. & w, Effie (White), & ch,
    relrq

BROSIUS
1797, 10, 11. Phebe [Brosins] b (H)
----, --, --. Harper b 1799,6,15; m Phebe G.
    ----- b 1807,3,22 (H)
  Ch: Edward
      Hicks   b 1827, 10, 29
      Samuel
      Gatchel   " 1829, 8, 30
      Amos Pres-
      ton   " 1831, 12, 12
      Joseph   " 1834, 2, 13
      Wm.   " 1835, 8, 21 d 1837, 3,21
      Enos   " 1837, 2, 26
      Harper   " 1839, 2, 27
      Chalkley   " 1840, 11, 13
----, --, --. Charles b 1811,1,18; m Mary L.
    ----- b 1810,5,1 (H)
  Ch: Robert
      Hillis   b 1834, 4, 11
      David L.   " 1836, 9, 28
      Wm. Henry   " 1839, 1, 21
----, --, --. Amos b 1814,2,3; m Esther C.

BROSIUS, Amos, continued
----- b 1813,11,5 (H)
Dt: Adaline   b 1840, 6, 11

1830, 1, 20. Harper & w, Phebe, & s, Edward
     Hicks, rocf Fallowfield MM, Pa., dtd 1829,
     5,6 (H)
1835, 12, 23. Charles & w, Mary L., & s, Robert
     Hillis, rocf Fallowfield MM, Pa., dtd 1835,
     11,7
1838, 12, 19. Amos rocf Fallowfield MM, Pa.,
     dtd 1838,11,10
1839, 9, 25. Phebe rocf Sadsbury MM, Pa., dtd
     1839,6,5 (H)
1840, 7, 22. Amos con mou
1840, 9, 23. Esther C. & dt, Adaline, recrq
     (H)
1841, 2, 24. Amos & w, Esther C., & dt, Ada-
     line, gct White Water MM, Ind. (H)
1841, 9, 22. Cert for Amos & fam granted
     1841,2,24, returned, since they were again
     within limits of the mtg (H)
1846, 6, 24. Phebe gct West MM (H)
1857, 8, 20. Charles & w, Mary, & ch, David
     L., William H., Amos Preston, Dalton
     Arvine & Laura Jane, gct West MM (H)
1857, 8, 20. Robert Hilles con mou

BROWN
----, --, --. Nathan b 1780,5,12 d 1849,6,28;
     m Amy ----- b 1778,6,6 d 1846,2,6 (W)
     Ch: Mary   b 1808, 12, 27
         Atlantic   " 1809, 7, 9
         David   " 1811, 1, 29
         Sarah   " 1813, 9, 9
         Almira   " 1817, 11, 4 d 1847, 4, 6
----, --, --. David b 1811,11,29 d 1889,12,28;
     m Ann ----- b 1819,3,30 d 1897,11,29 (W)
     Ch: Hiram W.   b 1847, 2, 9
1851, 2, 20. Huldah m Thomas MATHER (H)

1806, 6, 17. Nathan rocf Redstone MM, dtd
     1806,3,28
1808, 10, 11. Amy rocf Middleton MM, dtd 1808,
     6,11
1808, 10, 11. Mary rocf Middleton MM, dtd
     1808,6,11
1809, 1, 17. Joseph & w, Sarah, & ch, Ann,
     Ruth, Alice & Margaret, rocf Redstone MM,
     dtd 1808,9,2
1818, 5, 12. Joseph & w, Sarah, & ch, Ann,
     Ruth, Alice, Margaret, Eliza, Amy & Bath-
     sheba, gct Marlborough MM
1822, 7, 24. Hervey rocf Sandy Spring MM, dtd
     1822,6,21
1823, 4, 23. Jane recrq
1825, 1, 19. Ruth rocf Marlborough MM, dtd
     1824,12,25
1825, 12, 21. Ruth gct Marlborough MM
1826, 3, 22. Eliza Updegraff, minor dt Hervey
     & Jane, recrq
1826, 4, 19. Ann rocf Providence MM, Pa., dtd
     1826,3,21

1826, 9, 20. Hervey & w, Jane, & ch, Eliza
     Updegraff & Abigail, gct Sandy Spring MM
1826, 11, 22. Ann gct Marlborough MM
1830, 7, 21. Phebe rocf New Garden MM, dtd
     1830,5,20 (H)
1830, 11, 24. Margaret (form Boulton) dis mcd
1831, 5, 25. Cert rec for William, minor,
     from Burlington MM, N. J., dtd 1831,5,2,
     endorsed to Upper Springfield MM
1832, 9, 19. Phebe gct New Garden MM (H)
1833, 5, 22. Mary, Atlantic & Sarah gct Upper
     Springfield MM
1833, 6, 19. David gct Upper Springfield MM
1833, 6, 19. Nathan & w, Amy, & dt, Almira,
     gct Upper Springfield MM
1836, 11, 23. Nathan & w, Amy, rocf Upper
     Springfield MM, dtd 1836,10,22
1836, 11, 23. David rocf Upper Springfield MM,
     dtd 1836,10,22
1837, 1, 25. Mary, Atlantic & Almira rocf
     Upper Springfield MM, dtd 1836,10,22
1840, 1, 22. Mary Ann (form Bradshaw) con
     mou (H)
1840, 8, 19. Eliza T. Nickum (form Brown) con
     mcd (H)
1846, 2, 25. David gct New Garden MM, to m
     Ann Whinery
1846, 6, 24. Ann rocf New Garden MM, dtd
     1846,5,26
1848, 2, 23. Huldah rocf Friendsville MM, dtd
     1847,2,12 (H)
1853, 1, 20. Stephen & w, Hannah L., & s,
     Isaac L., rocf Scipio MM, N. Y., dtd 1852,
     11,18 (H)
1862, 12, 25. David, Ann, Hiram, Mary & Atlan-
     tic dis joining separatists (W) of 1854
1868, 5, 20. Mary & Atlantic dis disunity (W)
1875, 3, 21. Hiram W. dis mcd (W)
1881, 8, 24. Jonathan recrq (form mbr but
     joined separatists at time of split in
     mtg) (W)
1883, 2, 7. Hugh Edward, Phebe Ann, Florence
     E., William H., Carrie & Emma J. recrq
1883, 2, 22. Margaret rocf Pickering MM, Cana-
     da
1884, 6, 25. Jonathan gct New Garden MM (W)

BRUCK
1825, 3, 23. Cert rec for William A. & w,
     Catharine, & ch from Phila. MM, dtd 1825,
     1,27, endorsed to New Garden MM

BRUFF
1821, 3, 1. James B., s Christopher & Mary,
     Columbiana Co., O., b 1797,9,28; m at
     Springfield, Sarah MORRIS, dt Anthony &
     Hannah, Columbiana Co., O., b 1802,5,31
     (W)
     Ch: Lydia B.   b 1822, 1, 26
         Hannah   " 1823, 8, 27
         Charles   " 1825, 2, 24
1848, 11, 1. Joseph, s James B. & Sarah, Ma-

BRUFF, continued
      honing Co., O.; m at Salem, Anna M. OGDEN,
      dt John & Ann, Salem Co., N. J.

1819, 12, 22. James B. rocf ND MM, Phila., Pa.,
      dtd 1819,11,23
1849, 2, 21. Anna M. gct Upper Springfield MM
1851, 3, 19. William H. Oliphant gct Upper
      Springfield MM, to m Lydia B. Bruff

BUCEY
1912, 3, 10. Lewis & Rhoda [Bucy] recrq
1915, 9, 22. Lewis & fam released from mbrp
      for joining Church of Nazarine

BUCK
1823, 10, 2. John, s Henry & Rachel, Columbi-
      ana Co., O.; m at Springfield, Miriam
      LAMBORN, dt Parmenas & Hannah, Columbiana
      Co., O.

1823, 11, 19. Miriam gct New Garden MM
1847, 5, 19. Phebe rocf Redstone MM endorsed
      by New Garden MM, dtd 1847,4,22 (H)

BUFKIN
1807, 3, 17. Thomas rocf Western Branch MM,
      Va., dtd 1806,9,27

BULL
1839, 4, 24. Mary Ann (form Garretson) con
      mcd (H)
1844, 7, 24. Mary Ann dis jas (H)

BUMBAUGH
1879, 6, 26. Etta recrq
1881, 5, 26. Drusilla recrq
1881, 11, 23. Drusilla S. (form Lupton) dis
      mcd & joining separatists of 1854 (W)
1882, 2, 8. George recrq
1882, 2, 8. Charles Claud, s George, recrq
1885, 2, 6. George H. recrq
1890, 6, 26. Drusilla dropped from mbrp

BUNDY
----, --, --. Lindley m Ruanna FRAME, dt Aaron
      & Tabitha (Thompson), b 1845,3,30 (W)

1897, 8, 25. Joseph R. Stratton gct Short
      Creek MM, to m Anna M. Bundy (W)
1810, 4, 20. Ruanna rocf Stillwater MM, dtd
      1910,3,23 (W)
1911, 2, 22. Ruanna gct Stillwater MM, O. (W)
1932, 3, 23. Ethel recrq

BURDEN
----, --, --. Job b 1763,9,8; m Mary -----
      b 1770,7,9 (W)
      Ch: Sarah   b 1788, 5, 19
          Reuben   " 1792, 2, 26
          Hannah   " 1794, 2, 14
          Job   " 1796, 1, 10
          Joel   " 1798, 6, 2
          Mary   " 1800, 8, 23

      Ch: Lydia   b 1803, 4, 30
          David   " 1805, 8, 16
          Anna   " 1807, 10, 31
          Rachel   " 1810, 8, 3
1811, 7, 24. Sarah m Garland STANLEY
1813, 4, 28. Hannah m Wm. HUTTON
1812, 1, 1. Levi, s Job & Mary, Fayette Co.,
      Pa.; m at Lexington, Rhoda HOLLOWAY, dt
      Amos & Hephzibah, Fayette Co., Pa.

1808, 8, 16. Job & w, Mary, & ch, Reuben,
      Hannah, Job, Joel, Mary, Lydia & Ann, rocf
      Westland MM, dtd 1808,4,23
1809, 10, 17. Sarah rocf Westland MM, dtd
      1809,7,22
1812, 2, 11. Rhody gct Redstone MM, Pa.
1815, 3, 14. Reuben dis mcd

BURNS
1832, 5, 23. Hope (form Stratton) dis mcd
1836, 11, 23. Lydia (form Stratton) dis mcd

BURRELL
1914, 9, 25. Mary [Burrill] recrq
1915, 6, 23. George & Margaret recrq
1822, 2, 22. George & Margaret [Birrell] rel-
      rq

BURRIER
----, --, --. Oscar E., s George & Nettie
      (Boyd), b 1903,4,17; m Bertha YOCUS, dt
      Nicholas & Etta (Hutson), b 1903,10,23
      Dt: Virginia   b 1930, 1, 10
BURSON
1807, 12, 15. Elizabeth (form Myers) dis mcd
1808, 1, 12. John rocf Goose Creek MM, Va.,
      dtd 1807,5,25

BURTON
1808, 9, 13. Elizabeth recrq

BUSH
1880, 2, 26. James recrq
1880, 3, 25. Harvey, George M. & Annie recrq

BUTLER
----, --, --. Benjamin b 1762,8,21; m Hannah
      ----- b 1771,8,7 (W)
      Ch: Lawrence W.b 1797, 9, 15
          Eleanor   " 1799, 2, 1
          Hannah   " 1802, 1, 2
          John   " 1803, 6, 14
          Meribah   " 1805, 7, 14
          Ann   " 1807, 9, 22
          Sarah   " 1809, 6, 20
          Lydia   " 1811, 10, 7
          Wm.   " 1814, 10, 5
1818, 9, 30. Hannah m Robert ELYSON
1825, 8, 31. John, s Benjamin & Hannah, Colum-
      biana Co., O.; m at Salem, Drusilla FAW-
      CETT, dt Richard & Eunice, Columbiana Co.,O
1834, 1, 29. Ann m Clark FRESCOTT

BUTLER, continued

1812, 7, 14. Hannah, w Benjamin, & ch, Law-
    rence, Ellener, Hannah, John, Meribah,
    Ann & Sarah, rocf Radnor MM, Pa., dtd
    1811,12,12
1813, 7, 13. Benjamin rocf Radnor MM, Pa.,
    dtd 1812,11,12
1820, 3, 22. Lawrence gct New Garden MM, to m
1820, 7, 19. Sarah rocf New Garden MM, dtd
    1820,5,25
1822, 4, 24. Lawrence W. & w, Sarah, gct San-
    dy Spring MM
1833, 8, 21. Ann rocf Upper Springfield MM,
    dtd 1833,7,27
1835, 10, 21. Samuel Stout gct Upper Spring-
    field MM, to m Sarah Butler
1837, 8, 23. Ellen gct Upper Springfield MM

CADWALADER

----, --, --. Rees b 1785,9,4; m Sarah -----
    b 1799,10,27 (W)
    Ch: Isaac D.   b 1825, 8. 7
        Mary P.   " 1828, 7, 24
----, --, --. Mifflin b 1803,7,17; m -----
    ----- (W)
    Ch: Isaac L.   b 1831, 2, 2
        Jonah   " 1833, 2, 11
    Mifflin m 2nd Sarah -----
    Ch: Levi   b 1838, 12, 9 d 1839, 8,30
        Ann   " 1840, 8, 17 " 1841, 8,12
1834, 8, 21. Edith m Asa WILLIAMS
1842, 12, 5. Deborah b
----, --, --. Howard b 1811,4,22; m Margaret
    ----- b 1820,6,13 (W)
    Ch: Rees J.   b 1843, 6, 27
        Edwin   " 1844, 2, 13
        John H.   " 1846, 1, 18
1848, 11, 1. Mifflin [Cadwallader], s Jonah
    & Ann, Columbiana Co., O.; m at Salem,
    Sarah JAMES, dt John & Martha, Carroll
    Co., O.
----, --, --. John J., s Mifflin & Sarah
    (James), b 1853,7,6 d 1920,11,2 bur Damas-
    cus, O.; m Rebecca H. BUNDY, dt Wm. &
    Asenath (Doudna), b 1863,1,3 (W)

1820, 12, 20. Edith, minor, rocf Redstone MM,
    dtd 1819,5,26
1827, 5, 23. Elma rocf Redstone MM, dtd 1827,
    4,4
1830, 8, 25. Elma Howel (form Cadwalader) dis
    mcd
1837, 12, 20. Mifflin & w, Sarah, rocf Middle-
    ton MM, dtd 1837,7,17
1839, 4, 24. Isaac S. & Jonah, ch Mifflin &
    Sarah, recrq
1842, 1, 19. Margaret rocf New Garden MM,
    dtd 1841,12,23
1842, 2, 23. Mifflin & w, Sarah, & ch, Isaac
    & Jonah, gct Middleton MM
1842, 2, 23. Howard rocf Upper Springfield
    MM, dtd 1842,1,22
1842, 6, 22. Reece & w, Sarah, & ch, Lloyd D.

& Isaac D., rocf Chesterfield MM, O., dtd
    1842,5,21
1846, 6, 24. Loyd dis disunity
1848, 12, 20. Sarah J. gct Middleton MM
1850, 12, 25. Reese & w, Sarah, gct White
    Water MM, Ind.
1851, 1, 22. Howard & w, Margaret, & ch,
    Reese D., Edwin C. & John H., gct White
    Water MM, Ind.
1862, 12, 25. Mifflin, Sarah, Mary, John, Debo-
    rah, Isaac, Esther, Thomas, Anna & Elma,
    dis joining separatists (W) of 1854
1876, 12, 20. Deborah rocf Middleton MM, dtd
    1876,11,18 (W)
1881, 4, 20. Isaac E. Bonsall gct Middleton
    MM, to m Annie H. Cadwallader (W)
1885, 10, 21. Deborah gct Middleton MM (W)
1918, 6, 19. John J. & w, Rebecca H., rocf
    Middleton MM, O., dtd 1918,6,15 (W)

CALENDER

1851, 1, 22. Mary W. (form Hollingsworth)
    dis mcd

CAMPF

1931, 3, 26. Carl recrq .

CAMERON

----, --, --. Albert, s Josiah & Hannah (Men-
    denhall), b 1840,12,20 d 1915,3,18 bur
    Grandview Burying Grounds, Salem, O.; m
    Elizabeth BUNDY, dt Wm. M. & Sarah Ann
    (Cope) b 1858,1,15 (W)
    Ch: Effie
        Alice   b 1885, 5, 22
        Clara B.   " 1887, 9, 20
        Holland W. " 1895, 7, 5

1883, 7, 25. Elizabeth D. rocf Short Creek
    MM, dtd 1883,6,19 (W)
1883, 12, 19. Albert [Camron] rocf New Garden
    MM, dtd 1883,9,-- (W)
1913, 7, 23. William D. Satterthwait gct Up-
    per Springfield MM, to m Mabel H. Cameron
    (W)

CAMPBELL

----, --, --. Wm. d 1875,12,19; m Mary -----
    d 1872,4,22 (W)
    Ch: Ruth   b 1828, 10, 28
        Clark   " 1842, 4, 4
        Priscilla
        Elizabeth " 1851, 12, 11
        Mary M.   " 1848, 11, 27
        Ruthanna   " 1855, 7, 17
----, --, --. Morgan m Pricella SHARPLESS, dt
    Jonathan (W)

1808, 7, 12. Rebecca rocf Middleton MM, dtd
    1808,4,9
1864, 6, 23. Lucy Ann (form Taber) con mcd
1880, 1, 21. Clark dis mcd (W)
1886, 8, 25. Elizabeth Cummings (form Camp-

688

CAMPBELL, continued
     bell) dis mcd (W)
1887, 1, 20. Lucy dropped from mbrp
1889, 7, 24. Ruth C. Henderson (form Camp-
     bell) dis mcd (W)
1902, 1, 22. Mary & Ruth dis jas (W)

CAPEL
1928, 11, 30. George b 1854,5,16 d 1928,11,30
     (G)

1919, 9, 24. Margaret recrq
1920, 6, 23. Kate recrq
1923, 12, 19. George recrq

CAREY
----, --, --. Abel b 1810,9,10 d 1872,1,9; m
     Mariah ----- b 1816,9,30 d 1885,6,29 (W)
     Ch: Isabella b 1844, 6, 20 d 1845,8,15
        Ashbel   " 1846, 1, 6
        Barclay   " 1847, 3, 20 d 1848, 8,28
        David   " 1849, 7, 6
        James R.   " 1851, 4, 17
        Chas. M.   " 1853, 5, 14
        Lewis   " 1855, 5, 14 d 1857, 1, 8
        Alice   " 1857, 9, 17
        William B. " 1860, 12, 9

1831, 6, 22. Abel rocf Allum Creek MM, dtd
     1831,3,3
1832, 9, 19. Edmund [Cary], minor, rocf Al-
     lum Creek MM, dtd 1832,6,21
1833, 4, 24. Abel [Cary] gct Sandy Spring MM
1838, 1, 24. Edmund [Cary] gct Upper Spring-
     field MM
1843, 10, 25. Maria P. [Cary] rocf Redstone
     MM dtd 1843,6,28
1844, 4, 24. Abel [Cary] rocf Sandy Spring
     MM, dtd 1844,2,3
1862, 12, 25. Abel, Maria, Abel, David, James
     R., Charles, Alice & William B. [Carry]
     dis joining separatists (W) of 1854
1873, 6, 25. David dis mcd (W)
1875, 3, 21. James R. dis jas (W)
1876, 11, 22. Charles M. dis disunity (W)
1878, 2, 20. Alice (now Bolger) dis jas (W)
1879, 1, 29. Ashbel dis mcd (W)

CARLE
1857, 9, 13. Sidney, s Daniel & Catharine, b
     (G)

CARMAN
1845, 10, 22. Lydia P. (or Garman) gct Battle
     Creek MM (H)

CARPENTER
----, --, --. Edmund M. b 1831,5,24; m Anna
     H. ----- b 1832,7,17 (H)
     Ch: Edith H. b 1862, 8, 4
        Mary Emma " 1864, 7, 15

1881, 8, 25. Edmund M. & w, Anna H., & ch,

Edith H. & Mary Emma, rocf Rochester MM,
     dtd 1881,6,24 (H)
1886, 1, 21. Mary Emma Wray (form Carpenter).
     con mcd (H)
1886, 5, 20. Edmund M. & w, Anna H., gct
     Rochester MM, N. Y. (H)
1886, 5, 20. Edith H. Keintz (form Carpenter)
     gct Rochester MM, N. Y. (H)
1886, 5, 20. Emma Wray (form Carpenter) gct
     Rochester MM, N. Y. (H)

CARR
1797, 2, 3. Patience b
1836, 3, 16. Annie, dt Aquilla & Mary, b

1815, 3, 14. Patience (form Thomas) con mcd
1825, 6, 22. Isaac & w, Ann, & ch, Samuel,
     George & Isaac Ridgeway, rocf Mt. Holly
     MM, N. J., dtd 1825,4,7
1826, 6, 21. Isaac & w, Ann, & ch, Samuel,
     George & Isaac Ridgeway, gct Upper Spring-
     field MM
1828, 11, 19. Stanley Fleming gct Smithfield
     MM, to m Priscilla Carr
1844, 5, 22. Henry R. rocf Mt. Holley MM, en-
     dorsed by Marlborough MM, 1843,6,8
1859, 11, 24. Anna rocf Smithfield MM, dtd
     1859,8,22
1886, 6, 24. Kittie B. recrq
1911, 12, 20. Elizabeth rec in mbrp

CARROLL
1826, 7, 4. Mary Ann, dt Edward, b

1838, 11, 21. Mary Ann, minor, rocf New Garden
     MM, dtd 1838,8,23
1849, 10, 24. Mary Ann gct Cincinnati MM

CARSON
----, --, --. John b 1789,6,25; m Jemima
     ----- b 1787,7,27 (W)
     Ch: Wm.   b 1811, 1, 7
        Phebe   " 1813, 6, 22
        Benjamin
         Yates   " 1815, 3, 9
        Sarah   " 1818, 4, 25
        Alfred   " 1820, 12, 13 d 1822, 7,27
        John T.   " 1824, 9, 7

1811, 8, 13. Jemima rocf New Garden MM, dtd
     1811,7,18
1821, 5, 23. John, h of Jemima, & ch, Wil-
     liam, Phebe, Benjamin Yates, Sarah & Al-
     fred, recrq

CARVER
1885, 2, 6. Alonzo T. & w, Agnes, recrq

CASE
----, --, --. Margaret Price, dt Isaiah &
     Ureann (Price), b 1859,3,26 d 1920,2,9
     bur Sewickley, Pa.(W)

CASE, continued
1906, 3, 21. Margaret P. recrq (W)

CATHON
1824, 10, 20. Cert rec for Josiah West from
Western Branch MM, Va., dtd 1824,8,28,
endorsed to Marlborough MM

CATTELL
----, --, --. James b 1771,6,4; m Deborah -----
b 1774,1,13 (W)
Ch: Ann   b 1793, 9, 6
Hannah   " 1795, 11, 16 d 1819, 8,14
bur Salem
Elizabeth " 1797, 9, 17
Sarah   " 1799, 9, 19 " 1819,--,--
bur Springfield
Deborah b 1801, 11, 30
Mary   " 1804, 6, 11
Isaac   " 1807, 1, 4 d 1807, 2, 2
bur -----
Joseph   " 1808, 3, 19
Ezra   " 1810, 6, 20
Esther   " 1813, 5, 27
James   " 1815, 8, 18
Martha   " 1818, 2, 25 d 1818, 3,10
bur Springfield
Lydia   b 1819, 5, 7
----, --, --. Allen b 1804,11,1 d 1829,--,--
(W)
----, --, --. Enoch b 1782,11,4 d 1815,5,22
bur Salem; m Martha DINGEE, dt Charles &
Martha, b 1788,3,13 d 1815,5,27 (W)
Ch: Jonas D. b 1813, 6, 17
Martha   " 1815, 5, 18 d 1815, 8,16
1813, 4, 22. Ann m Benjamin MARSHALL
1815, 5, 25. Elizabeth m Isaac ELLISON
1818, 12, 3. Sarah m Samuel STANLEY
1819, 2, 4. Hannah m Matthew SEBRELL
1824, 6, 30. Deborah m Isaiah B. BROOK

1807, 12, 15. Hope rocf Evesham MM, dtd 1807,
10,9
1810, 12, 11. James & w, Deborah, & ch, Ann,
Hannah, Elizabeth, Sarah, Deborah, Mary &
Joseph, rocf London Grove MM, Pa., dtd
1810,7,4
1813, 8, 17. Enoch & w, Martha, rocf Redstone
MM, dtd 1813,4,2
1819, 4, 21. Allen recrq
1837, 8, 23. Jones D. dis mcd
1844, 8, 21. James & dt, Juliann, rocf Upper
Springfield MM, dtd 1844,6,22
1844, 8, 21. Ann D., w James, rocf Redstone
MM, dtd 1844,7,31
1848, 12, 20. James & w, Ann D., & ch, Julia-
Ann & Orlando, gct Salem MM, Ia.

CHALFANT
1822, 10, 23. Ann rocf Providence MM, dtd
1822,5,21
1840, 3, 25. Gauis rocf London Grove MM, Pa.,
dtd 1839,7,3

CHAMBERS
1848, 4, 15. Eliza b (W)
1850, 12, 22. Benjamin b (W)
1855, 3, 27. James N. b (W)
1856, 10, 20. Valentine b (W)

CHAMPION
1885, 2, 6. Edgar R. recrq

CHAPMAN
1832, 5, 24. Aaron, s Aaron & Mary, Stark
Co., O.; m at Salem, Mary INNIS, dt Robert
& Mary

1832, 7, 25. Mary gct Marlborough MM

CHELLIS
1911, 12, 20. Freida rec in mbrp
1914, 9, 25. Freda dropped from mbrp

CHERINGTON
1840, 1, 20. Abigail & dt, Emily, rocf Fallowfield MM, dtd 1839,4,6 (H)
1866, 4, 26. Abigail gct Pennsgrove MM, Pa.
(H)

CHESSINGTON
1841, 1, 20. Abigail & dt, Emly, rocf Fallowfield MM, Pa., dtd 1839,4,6

CHRISTIAN
1914, 9, 25. Alma recrq
1917, 10, 24. David & fam dropped from mbrp

CLARK
----, --, --. Henry b 1816,2,3 d 1878,12,16
(W)
----, --, --. Jane b 1820,4,4 d 1885,3,4 (W)
----, --, --. Robert, s Wm. & Maria, b 1865,11,
11; m Clara WHINNERY, dt Wm. & Mary, b
1874,9,10 (G)
Ch: Francis E. b 1896, 11, 22
Joseph W. " 1899, 12, 30
Estella A. " 1914, 8, 28

1839, 2, 20. Joshua Schofield gct Plainfield
MM, to m Margaret Ann Clark (H)
1911, 12, 20. Francis rec in mbrp
1921, 2, 23. Leona relrq

CLAY
1809, 4, 11. Mary (form Pennock) con mou

CLAYTON
1859, 2, 26. Lydia B. (form Lamborn) dis mcd
(W)

CLEMSON
----, --, --. James b 1791,8,15 d 1867,5,24; m
Ann ----- b 1797,9,25 d 1873,6,24 (W)
Ch: Hannah   b 1816, 10, 5 d 1894,10,22
Reuben   " 1818, 5, 22
Wm. Penn " 1820, 7, 5

CLEMSON, James & Ann, continued
    Ch: James Lee b 1823, 11, 22 d 1857, 7,13
        John   " 1826, 1, 9
        Isaac   " 1828, 7, 13 " 1896, 3,11
        Joseph   " 1828, 7, 13 " 1864, 8,28
        Pusy   " 1828, 7, 13
        Mary Ann " 1831, 5, 7
        Lydia
        Starr   " 1834, 11, 6

1837, 11, 22. Bradford MM, Pa. rq this mtg to
    treat with Rubin for mou; he settled here
1837, 12, 20. Reuben wished to retain mbrp;
    Bradford MM, Pa. informed
1840, 4, 22. Reuben rocf Bradford MM, Pa., dtd
    1839,9,3, endorsed to New Garden MM by rq

CLOSSEN
1885, 2, 6. Dominicus [Classon] recrq
1886, 10, 21. Dominicus dropped from mbrp

COATES
1883, 10, 24. Sarah B. (form Thomas) con mcd
    (W)

COBBS
----, --, --. Pleasant b 1760,11,5; m Amy
    ----- b 1766,11,8 (W)
    Ch: Thos.
        Terrell   b 1786, 4, 21 d 1814, 4, 5
        bur Springfield
        Rebecca   b 1787, 10, 20
        Mary   " 1789, 3, 18
        Rhoda   " 1790, 9, 30
        Abigail   " 1792, 3, 28
        Elizabeth " 1793, 11, 19
        Pleasant " 1795, 12, 13
        Joseph   " 1797, 6, 21
        Anselm   " 1799, 4, 16
        Amy   " 1800, 12, 23
        Joanna   " 1803, 6, 17
        Robert
        Venenor   " 1806. 2, 26
1809, 10, 24. Eliza b (W)
1811, 10, 13. Lucinda b (W)
1811, 12, 26. Rhoda m James STANLEY
1812, 7, 2. Abigail m Joseph STANLEY
1813, 6, 24. Elizabeth m Benjamin STANLEY
1813, 9, 2. Agatha b
1813, 6, 24. Mary m Solomon STANLEY
1813, 10, 21. Rebecca m Samuel COPPOCK
1815, 7, 13. Thomas T. b
1818, 12, 3. Amy m Aaron COPPOCK
1819, 12, 2. Pleasant, s Pleasant & Amy, Co-
    lumbiana Co., O.; m at Springfield, Eliza-
    beth ISENHOUR, dt John & Mary, Columbiana
    Co., O.
----, --, --. Pleasant b 1795,12,13; m Elizabeth
    ----- b 1801,3,29 (W)
    Ch: John   b 1820, 10, 8
        Mary Ann   " 1822, 5, 6
1820, 11, 2. Joseph, s Pleasant & Amy, Colum-
    biana Co., O., b 1797,6,21; m at Spring-

field, Tacy WALTON, dt Jesse & Ann, Colum-
    biana Co., O., b 1803,1,22 (W)
    Ch: Jesse   b 1821, 10, 13 d 1822,12,22
        Ura   " 1823, 10, 8
1826, 1, 5. Lindsey, s Waddy & Margaret,
    Columbiana Co., O.; m at Springfield,
    Ann WOOLMAN, dt Abner & Martha, Columbiana
    Co., O.

1810, 8, 14. Pleasant & w, Amy, & ch, Re-
    becca, Mary, Rhoda, Abigail, Elizabeth,
    Pleasant, Joseph, Anselm, Amy, Joanna &
    Robert, rocf Cedar Creek MM, Va., dtd
    1810,4,14
1810, 8, 14. Thomas Terrell & w, Martha, &
    dt, Eliza rocf Cedar Creek MM, Va., dtd
    1810,4,14
1818, 1, 13. Martha dis
1823, 3, 19. Ansalem dis mcd
1824, 8, 25. Linsey recrq
1824, 10, 20. Ansalem rst by rq
1861, 11, 21. Hannah C. (form Battin) con mcd
    (H)
1813, 11, 19. William & Rose [Cobb] dropped
    from mbrp
1923, 3, 21. Albert rocf Damascus MM
1927, 3, 23. A. J. & fam gct Beloit MM
1930, 9, 24. Mabel [Cobb] recrq

COBOURN
----, --, --. John, s Benjamin & Abigail, b
    1795,7,18; m Sarah JOHN, dt Griffith &
    Sarah, b 1795,7,11 (G)
    Ch: Nathan   b 1826, 8, 4
----, --, --. Ezra & Thirza
    Ch: John A.   b 1852, 11   6
        Joseph L. " 1857, 4, 2
----, --, --. Nathan m Harriet J. CARLE, dt
    Geo. & Elizabeth, b 1839,9,18 (G)
    Ch: Sarah L.   b 1861, 10, 14
        John G.   " 1863, 7, 20
        Wm. F.   " 1867, 11, 18
        Curtis L. " 1871, 1, 15
        Mary E.   " 1875, 10, 18
1874, 11, 11. John d (G)
1877, 7, 21. Sarah d (G)

1865, 5, 25. John & w, Sarah, & gr ch, John
    Alexander & Joseph Lawrence, rocf Sandy
    Spring MM, dtd 1865,3,21
1866, 1, 25. Nathan [Couborn] rocf Sandy
    Spring MM
1874, 8, 5. Harriet J., w Nathan, & ch, Sa-
    rah Lenora, John George, William Franklin
    & Kurtis S., recrq
1883, 8, 16. Annie R. recrq
1885, 8, 20. Sabina [Coborn] recrq
1891, 8, 20. Joseph & Annie R. relrq
1891, 8, 20. Ella Ida recrq

COFFEE
----, --, --. Isaac b 1802,10,18; m Betsy ----
    b 1805,10,24 (W)

COFFEE, Isaac & Betsy, continued
     Ch: Rachel Ann b 1828, 7, 2
        Charles W. " 1832, 7, 2
1842, 8, 1. Jonathan W., s John & Rachel,
   Columbiana Co., O., b 1809,7,19 d 1871,6,21
   m at Salem, Priscilla HUNT, dt Nathan &
   Ann, Columbiana Co., O., b 1821,6,10 d
   1874,8,9 (W)

1840, 11, 25. Jonathan rocf Plainfield MM, dtd
   1840,5,22
1848, 8, 23. Isaac & w, Betsy, & s, Charles
   W., rocf Miami MM, dtd 1848,6,21
1848, 8, 23. Rachel Ann rocf Miami MM, dtd
   1848,6,21
1857, 2, 25. Rachel Ann dis disunity (W)
1858, 9, 23. Isaac & w, Betsy, gct Red Cedar
   MM, Ia.
1858, 9, 23. Charles gct Red Cedar MM, Ia.
1859, 4, 21. Rachel Ann gct Red Cedar MM, Ia.
1862, 12, 25. Jonathan W. dis joining separatists (W) of 1854
1862, 12, 25. Priscilla dis joining separatists (W) of 1854
1864, 8, 24. Isaac & w, Betsy, gct Hickory
   Grove MM, Ia. (W)

COFFIN
1809, 8, 20. Albert b (W)

1831, 7, 20. Albert M. gct Marlborough MM
1838, 11, 21. William, minor, rocf Marlborough
   MM, dtd 1838,10,30
1842, 7, 20. William dis mcd
1923, 1, 24. Merrill M. & w, Anna, & ch,
   Thomas Eugene, Louis Haldy & Katharine
   Ellouise, rocf Alliance MM, O.
1923, 10, 24. Merrill M. & fam gct Alliance
   MM, O.

COHNS
1933, 1, 1. Joel & Mary recrq

COLVIN
----. --, --. Nehemiah b 1776,4,11; m Lydia
   ----- b 1778,5,19 (W)
   Ch: (adopted)
     Caroline
      M. C.   b 1826, 9, 30
     Thomas L.
      Baker   " 1827, 4, 6

1839, 2, 20. Nehemiah & w, Lydia, & adopted
   ch, Caroline S. Colvin & Thomas S. Baker,
   rocf Adrian MM, Mich., dtd 1838,7,12
1840, 5, 20. Nehemiah & w, Lydia, & adopted
   ch, Caroline C. Colvin & Thomas L. Baker,
   gct Adrian MM, Mich.
1845, 6, 25. Nehemiah rocf Raisin MM, dtd
   1845,3,12, endorsed by Marlborough MM,
   1845,5,27

CONARD
1860, 10, 24. George S. Satterthwait gct New
   Garden MM, Pa., to m Sarah C. Conard (W)

CONN
----, --, --. Esther b 1771,12,25 d 1833,6,30
   (H)

1808, 7, 12. Esther rocf Burlington MM, N.J.,
   dtd 1808,5,7
1815, 4, 11. Patience [Con] con mcd
1828, 10, 22. Esther dis jH
1868, 8, 20. Dinah Ann (form White) con mcd
   & jas
1871, 2, 22. Dinah Ann (form White) dis mcd
   (W)

CONRAD
----, --, --. Elwood B., s Lewis & Rebecca
   Adamson (Bailey), b 1850,1,25; m Phebe
   DEAN, dt Jonathan & Elizabeth (Branting-
   ham), b 1855,12,14 (W)
   Ch: Samuel   b 1884, 7, 6
     Emmerson "" 1890, 11, 29
     Mary E.   " 1894, 3, 28
1905, 9, 21. Joseph L., s Elwood B. & Phebe
   W., Columbiana Co., O.; m Elma G. HUTTON,
   dt Finley & Eliza, Columbiana Co., O., b
   1875,5,18 (W)
   Ch: Joseph
     Lewis   b 1907, 3, 25 d 1907, 3,27
     bur Friends Burying Ground, German-
     town, Phila., Pa.
     Frederick
     Conrad   b 1908, 8, 27

1903, 6, 24. Elwood B. & w, Phebe W., & ch,
   Samuel, Emmerson & Mary, rocf Upper
   Springfield MM, dtd 1903,5,22
1911, 10, 25. Samuel E. dis mcd (W)
1913, 1, 22. Emerson gct Middleton MM, to m
   Eva M. Neill (W)
1914, 3, 25. Emerson gct Upper Springfield
   MM (W)
1933, 7, 19. Elwood B. & w, Phebe B., rocf
   Pasadena MM, Calif., dtd 1933,7,12 (W)

CONROW
1893, 10, 26. Chas. D., s Thos. H. & Mary J.,
   Belmont Co., O.; m at Salem, Deborah F.
   HAYES, dt Chas. I. & Deborah F., Columbiana Co., O.

1894, 7, 25. Deborah Hayes gct Flushing MM,O.
   (W)

COOK
----, --, --. Stacy [Cooke] b 1790,2,5 d 1876,
   3,13 (W)
----, --, --. Martha [Cooke] b 1794,11,9 d
   1874,9,27 (an elder) (W)
----, --, --. Stacy & Martha
   Ch: Isaac H.   b 1814, 10, 31

COOK, Stacy & Martha, continued
    Ch: James   b 1816, 7, 28
        Stacy Jr. " 1818, 5, 26
        Charles L. " 1821, 3, 16
        Martha Jr. " 1822, 11, 30
        Alexander
          W.   " 1827, 1, 16
        Wm.   " 1828, 10, 2
        Sarah   " 1837, 1, 15
        Abigail H. " 1839, 6, 16
----, --, --. Caleb b 1788,10,15; m Hannah
   ----- b 1791,9,19 (H)
    Ch: Enos   b 1821, 5, 13
        Sarah   " 1823, 7, 4
        Elizabeth " 1827, 3, 23
        Fransena " 1829, 9, 22
        Hannah   " 1833, 4, 11
1840, 10, 28. Stacy [Cooke], s Stacy & Martha,
   Columbiana Co., O., b 1818,5,26 d 1884,3,
   4; m at Salem, Martha JOHNSON, dt Wm. &
   Sarah, Columbiana Co., O., b 1818,11,28
   d 1910,9,27 bur Grandview Cemetery, Salem,
   O. (W)
    Ch: Wm. Henry b 1843, 5, 8
        Edwin   " 1848, 7, 22 d 1924, 5,26
        bur Grandview Cemetery, Salem, O.
1842, 1, 27. Sarah I. m Eli GARRETSON (H)
1843, 3, 29. Charles L., s Stacy & Martha,
   Columbiana Co., O.; m at Salem, Lydia
   FAWCETT, dt Jonathan & Mary, Columbiana
   Co., O.
1844, 1, 31. Martha, Jr. m John STREET, Jr.
1844, 4, 25. Enos, s Caleb & Hannah, Columbiana Co., O.; m at house of James Michener,
   Ann E. MICHENER, dt James & Eliza, Columbiana Co., O. (H)
1861, --, --. Della Haven, dt Wm. & Mary Jane
   McDevitt, b (G)
1880, 6, 2. Edwin [Cooke], s Stacy, Jr. &
   Martha (Johnson), b 1848,7,22 d 1924,5,26
   bur Grandview Cemetery, Salem, O.; m Mary
   H. HAYES, dt Chas. I. & Deborah (Fawcett),
   b 1858,5,30 d 1898,5,30 bur Friends Burying Ground, Salem, O. (W)
1914, 8, 26. Ella Lillian [Cooke] m Dillwyn
   STRATTON (W)

1836, 1, 20. Caleb rocf New Garden MM, Pa.,
   dtd 1835,12,10
1836, 4, 20. Stacy & w, Martha, & ch, James,
   Stacy, Charles L., Martha, Alexander W.
   & William, rocf Frankford MM, Pa., dtd
   1836,3,29
1837, 3, 22. Isaac H. rocf Frankford MM, Pa.,
   dtd 1837,1,30
1837, 5, 24. Hannah & ch, Enos, Sarah, Elizabeth, Francena & Hannah, recrq (H)
1838, 8, 22. Isaac H. gct Middleton MM
1843, 1, 25. James H. dis disunity
1843, 10, 25. Mary Ann rocf New Garden MM, Pa.,
   dtd 1843,4,6 (H)
1849, 6, 20. Alexander W. dis mcd
1851, 11, 19. William dis mcd

1852, 8, 28. Edith Ann recrq
1853, 7, 23. Charles L. dis disunity
1862, 3, 19. Edith Ann dis jas (W)
1862, 4, 23. Abbie H. gct Short Creek MM (W)
1862, 12, 24. Drusilla (form Young) dis mcd
   (W)
1862, 12, 25. Abigail dis joining separatists
   (W) of 1854
1862, 12, 25. Stacy, Martha, Stacy Jr.,
   William Henry & Edwin dis joining separatists (W) of 1854
1863, 2, 25. Sarah C. Fawcett (form Cook)
   dis mou (W)
1873, 6, 26. Edith Ann relrq
1914, 5, 20. Ella Lillian [Cooke] recrq (W)
1914, 12, 23. Ella Lilian Stratton (form
   Cooke) gct New Garden MM, O. (W)
1918, 5, 22. William H. [Cooke] dis disunity
   (W)

COOPER
1806, 10, 27. M. H. b (W)
----, --, --. Elizabeth C., dt Cyrus & Asenath A., b 1837,--,-- d 1916,10,9 bur Damascus, O. (W)
1858, 2, 8. Lydia A. b (W)
----, --, --. Samuel m Sarah PENNOCK, dt Caleb & Mary (Dinge), b 1834,5,8 d 1918,1,
   18 bur Damascus, O. (W)
    Ch: Mary E.   b 1859, 3, 22
        Alice   " 1869, 4, 2
        Harry E. " 1866, 10, 28
1863, 12, 10. Edith G., dt Louis & Hannah Y.
   (Hollingsworth) Cope, b (W)
----, --, --. Cyrus b 1860,11,21; m Bertha
   ----- b 1862,5,8 (W)
    Ch: Samuel   b 1903, 12, 30
----, --, --. Harry E. m Ruth C. SATTERTHWAIT,
   dt Chas. W. & Adaline M. (Bye), b 1871,4,
   11 (W)
    Ch: Chas. H. b 1906, 7, 22
1908, 5, 27. Lydia A. m Lewis A. WOOLMAN (W)

1852, 2, 25. Mary H. rocf Evesham MM, N. J.,
   dtd 1852,1,8
1857, 3, 25. Mary H. gct Woodbury MM, N. J.
   (W)
1869, 5, 20. Ella (form Trescott) dis mcd
1871, 2, 23. Sarah M. & ch, Harry J., Charles
   E. & Mary E., rocf Greenfield MM, Ind.,
   dtd 1871,2,18
1871, 11, 8. Sarah Stevens (form Cooper) con
   mcd
1876, 11, 8. Moses C. Stevens & w, Sarah M.,
   & ch, Harry, Charley & Mary E. Cooper &
   Martha D. Stevens, gct Damascus MM
1902, 6, 25. Cyrus & w, Bertha A., rocf New
   Garden MM, Pa., dtd 1902,6,4 (W)
1907, 3, 20. Lydia A. rocf New Garden MM,
   Pa., dtd 1907,3,6 (W)
1907, 4, 24. Mary E. rocf New Garden MM, Pa.,
   dtd 1907,4,3 (W)
1909, 12, 22. Cyrus & w, Bertha A., & s, Sam-

COOPER, continued
    uel, gct Middleton MM (W)
1916, 3, 22. Elizabeth C. rocf New Garden MM,
    Pa., dtd 1916,3,8 (W)
1916, 7, 19. Sarah P. & Alice rocf New Garden
    MM, Pa., dtd 1916,6,7 (W)
1916, 8, 23. Harry E. & w, Ruth C., & s,
    Charles H., rocf New Garden MM, Pa., dtd
    1916,8,9 (W)
1926, 1, 20. Mary E. gct Upper Springfield
    MM (W)

COPE
----, --, --. George b 1820,6,11 d 1889,6,19;
    m Elmira ----- b 1818,8,1 d 1913,3,14 bur
    New Albany, Ind. (W)
1828, 7, 12. Hannah b (H)
----, --, --. Jesse m Elizabeth ----- b 1813,
    12,15 d 1876,2,3 (W)
    Ch: Caroline b 1837, 4, 30
        Emily   " 1838, 12, 29
        Mercey   " 1844, 11, 3
        Albert   " 1846, 10, 26 d 1907, 1, 4
        Allen   " 1848, 11, 30
        Lydia   " 1850, 12, 27
        Almira   " 1853, 10, 12
----, --, --. ----- m Sarah Ann ----- b 1808,11,
    22 (W)
    Ch: Mary M.   b 1838, 10, 31
        Melissa   " 1844, 2, 14
        Lucinda   " 1848, 1, 21
        Amy Jane " 1825, 12, 11 d 1911,12,17
        bur Friends Grave Yard, Middleton, O.
1840, 12, 25. Elma b (W)
1852, 8, 27. Hannah R. m Benjamin HANNA (H)
1852, 11, 27. Oliver, s Ezra & Hannah, Colum-
    biana Co., O.; m at house of Thos. Gal-
    breath, Hannah GALBREATH, dt Thomas & Ann,
    Columbiana Co., O. (H)
1856, 4, 2. Oliver E. b (H)
----, --, --. Louis, s Samuel, Jr. & Mercy
    (Vail), b 1836,2,15 d 1923,6,9, bur Provi-
    dence Burying Ground, Pa.; m Hannah Y.
    HOLLINGSWORTH, dt Samuel & Margaret (Leech)
    b 1838,1,4 d 1900,8,1 bur Providence Bury-
    ing Ground, Pa. (W)
----, --, --. Joshua b 1837,4,5; m Eliza GIL-
    BERT, dt Benjamin & Lydia (Cope), b 1834,
    9,23 d 1906,3,12 bur Friends Burying Ground,
    Sewickly, Pa. (W)
----, --, --. Louis b 1836,2,15; m Hannah Y.
    ----- b 1838,1,4 d 1900,8,1(W)
    Ch: Florence N.b 1862, 7, 6
        Edith G. " 1863, 12, 16
        Priscilla " 1865, 6, 5
        Martha   " 1868, 1, 22
        Samuel W. " 1870, 5, 12 d 1896, 2,28
        bur Providence Burying Ground, Pa.
        Louis   b 1873, 6, 7
        Elma   " 1877, 11, 22
        Jasper   " 1881, 8, 13
1862, 9, 26. Wm. B. b (H)
----, --, --. Albert M., s Benjamin & Elizabeth

(McGrew), b 1847,1,19 d 1923,1,6 bur
Friends Burying Ground, near Middleton,O.;
m Phebe Y. ASHTON, dt Barak & Jane (Leech),
b 1853,5,16 d 1920,11,24 bur Friends Burying Ground, Middleton O. (W)
Ch: Elbert
    Lorain   b 1874, 4, 19
    Barak A.   " 1879, 12, 9
    Mary Ellen " 1881, 12, 19
    Jane L.   " 1884, 7, 14
    Elizabeth
    Alice   " 1886, 4, 26
    Wm. Logan " 1889, 7, 29
    Anna Flo-
    rence   " 1893, 1, 6
1880, 5, 26. Mary M. m Isaac N. VAIL (W)
1880, 5, 26. Melissa m Chas. P. HALL (W)
1883, 5, 24. Elizabeth W. d (W)
----, --, --. Elbert Lorain b 1874,4,19; m
    Malinda E. ----- b 1875,9,14 (W)
    Ch: Howard
        Herman   b 1899, 5, 29
        Chester
        Albert   " 1901, 9, 9
1902, 10, 23. Mary E. m John A. BINNS (W)
1913, 4, 30. Elizabeth Alice m Louis J. KIRK
    (W)
1916, 3, 23. Anna Florence m Howard Theophi-
    lus HALL (W)
----, --, --. Wm. Logan, s Albert M. & Phebe
    Y., b 1889,7,29; m Rachel Tacy MOTT, dt
    John W. & Sana A. (Hall), b 1889,12,26
    (W)
    Ch: Alfred
        Louis   b 1917, 9, 6
        Wm. Logan
        Jr.   " 1919, 5, 31

1817, 7, 13. Simon, minor, rocf Middleton MM,
    dtd 1817,6,14
1819, 12, 22. Simon gct Middleton MM
1850, 6, 19. Hannah K. & Sarah rocf Birming-
    ham MM,   Pa., dtd 1850,4,27
1850, 6, 19. Mary Ann rocf West MM, dtd
    1850,5,24 (H)
1862, 12, 25. Israel, Sarah, Henry & Mariah El-
    ma dis joining separatists (W) of 1854
1862, 12, 25. Joseph, Phebe, Laycurgas, Lucin-
    da, James, Oliver, Mary, Elipha, Edith &
    Emma, dis joining separatists (W) of 1854
1862, 12, 25. Nathan, Jane, James Byron & Ma-
    tilda Ann dis joining separatists (W) of
    1854
1862, 12, 25. Hannah Y. dis joining separatists
    (W) of 1854
1873, 7, 23. Sarah Ann & dt, Mary M., Melissa
    & Lucinda, rocf Sewickley MM, Pa., dtd
    1873,7,1 (W)
1877, 7, 25. Allen dis (W)
1877, 9, 19. Caroline, Emily, Mercy, Lydia &
    Almira gct Upper Springfield MM (W)
1878, 11, 20. Albert & w, Phebe Y., & ch, El-
    bert Lorain, rocf New Garden MM, dtd 1878,

COPE, continued
10,24 (W)

1879, 2, 6. Lycurgus & w, Eliza Ann, & ch, Sherman B., Susanah D., William G. & Edith E., rocf Mt. Gilead MM, dtd 1879,1,14

1880, 2, 26. Eliphas & w, Emma, recrq

1880, 2, 26. James & w, Mary, recrq

1880, 3, 25. Albertha & Bernard recrq

1880, 3, 25. Price & Paul S. recrq

1880, 8, 25. Elma Binns (form Cope) dis mcd (W)

1881, 3, 24. Elizabeth rocf Smithfield MM, dtd 1880,12,20

1886, 10, 21. Licurgus & Eliza Ann dropped from mbrp

1887, 5, 25. Sarah Ann & Lucinda gct Middleton MM (W)

1888, 7, 25. Florence N. Lackey (form Cope) dis mcd (W)

1891, 7, 22. Edith G. dis jas (W)

1893, 8, 23. Priscilla C. Goslin (form Cope) dis mcd (W)

1893, 11, 22. Albert B. dis mou & jas (W)

1898, 3, 23. Elbert L. gct Middleton MM, to m Malinda E. Battey (W)

1898, 9, 21. Malinda E. rocf Middleton MM, O., dtd 1898,9,17 (W)

1898, 10, 19. Martha C. Forsythe (form Cope) dis mcd (W)

1903, 6, 24. Elbert L. & w, Malinda E., & ch, Howard H. & Chester A., gct Middleton MM (W)

1909, 3, 24. Elma Forsythe (form Cope) dis mcd & jas (W)

1915, 7, 21. William L. gct Springville MM, Ia., to m Rachel Tacy Mott (W)

1916, 3, 22. Howard T. Hall prcf Middleton MM, dtd 1916,3,18, to m Anna F. Cope (W)

1917, 6, 20. Rachel Tacy rocf Springville MM, Ia. (W)

1918, 3, 20. Jasper dis mou (W)

1920, 7, 21. William L. & w, Rachel Tacy, & ch, Alfred Lewis & William Loren, gct Middleton MM (W)

1921, 2, 23. Albert M. gct Middleton MM (W)

1921, 8, 24. Barak A. dis mcd & jas (W)

COPEHART
1910, 2, 23. Ira recrq

COPPOCK
1748, 11, 3. Samuel b (W)

1784, 12, 23. Rebecca b (W)

1786, 3, 24. Ellen b (W)

1804, 7, 25. Ann b (W)

1813, 10, 21. Samuel, s Samuel & Eleanor, Columbiana Co., O., b 1787,8,12; m at Springfield, Rebecca COBBS, dt Pleasant & Amy, Columbiana Co., O., b 1787,10,20 (W)
Ch: Pleasant b 1815, 8, 14
    Samuel
      Robert   " 1821, 5, 28 d 1823,11, 9
    Rhoda   " 1822, 9, 16

Ch: Isaac   b 1825, 3, 23

1814, 1, 20. Jehu, s Samuel & Ellen, Columbiana Co., O., b 1791,2,10; m at Springfield Judith STANLEY, dt Thos. & Unity, Columbiana Co., O., b 1793,9,28 (W)
Ch: Ellen   b 1816, 2, 26
    Unity   " 1818, 10, 26
    Abigail   " 1821, 7, 9

1814, 6, 20. Rachel m Joshua MORRIS

1818, 12, 3. Aaron, s Samuel & Elen, Columbiana Co., O., b 1797,1,24; m at Springfield, Amy COBB, dt Pleasant & Amy, Columbiana Co., O., b 1800,12,23 (W)
Ch: Thomas   b 1819, 10, 1
    James   " 1821, 4, 25

1819, 1, 28. Ruth m Andrew STANLEY

1823, 4, 3. Rebecca m Clayton KILLE

1839, 1, 4. Barclay b (W)

1857, 10, 29. Mehetable J. m Abraham MORRIS

----, --, --. Wm. G. b 1842,2,19; m Abigail D. ----- b 1841,11,13 (W)
Ch: Barton D. b 1863, 4, 31
    Elizabeth
    Jane   " 1868, 3, 24
    Harlen   " 1870, 1, 22

----, --, --. Benj. H. b 1843,10,15; m Esther W. ----- b 1844,1,25 (W)
Ch: Elmer B. b 1866, 11, 20

1806, 7, 15. John & w, Catharine, & ch, Ann Samuel & Timothy, rocf Short Creek MM, dtd 1806,4,19

1812, 7, 14. Samuel, Jr. rocf Little Britain MM, Pa., dtd 1812,5,9, endorsed by Short Creek MM, 1812,6,23

1812, 7, 14. Ellen [Coppeck] rocf Little Britain MM, Pa., dtd 1812,5,9, endorsed by Short Creek MM, 1812,6,23

1812, 8, 11. Samuel & ch, Aaron & Ruth, rocf Little Britain MM, Pa., dtd 1812,5,9, endorsed by Short Creek MM, 1812,6,23

1812, 9, 15. Rebecca rocf Little Britain MM, Pa., dtd 1812,5,9, endorsed by Short Creek MM, 1812,6,23

1813, 5, 11. Jehu [Coppeck] rocf Little Britain MM, Pa., dtd 1813,2,6

1814, 3, 15. Rachel rst by rq with permission of Little Britain MM, Pa.

1819, 1, 20. Aaron & w, Amy, gct Marlborough MM

1820, 4, 19. Aaron & w, Amy, & ch, Thomas, rocf Marlborough MM, dtd 1820,3,23

1823, 8, 20. Samuel, Sr. dis disunity

1833, 2, 20. Ellen rocf Upper Springfield MM, dtd 1833,1,31

1843, 8, 23. Barclay, minor, rocf Upper Springfield MM, dtd 1843,7,22

1845, 6, 25. Maria, dt Ann, rocf Upper Springfield MM, dtd 1845,4,26

1846, 6, 24. Ann rocf Upper Springfield MM, dtd 1846,4,25

1850, 3, 20. Levi, minor, rocf Gilead MM, dtd 1850,2,19

COPPOCK, continued

1850, 8, 21. Ann L. & ch, Levi & Maria B., gct Salem MM, Ia.

1853, 9, 21. Barclay, minor, gct Red Cedar MM, Ia.

1856, 3, 20. Mahitable J. rocf New Garden MM, O., dtd 1856,3,19

1862, 5, 21. Ezra & w, Ann, & dt, Hannah Lavina, rocf New Garden MM, dtd 1862,4,24 (W)

1863, 5, 20. Ezra dis disunity (W)

1866, 9, 19. Esther W. rocf Sandy Spring MM, dtd 1866,8,25 (W)

1866, 11, 21. Benjamin H. rocf New Garden MM, dtd 1866,10,25 (W)

1867, 6, 19. Benjamin H. & w, Esther W., & ch, Elmer B., gct New Garden MM (W)

CORDRAY

1910, 2, 23. Emma recrq

1910, 2, 23. Ethel S. recrq

CORNELL

1882, 5, 25. George T. & w, Margaret, rocf Rhode Island MM, R. I.

1884, 5, 25. George T. & w gct Providence MM, R. I.

COULSON

----, --, --. David b 1794,10,7 d 1863,11,24; m Elizabeth ----- b 1786,5,2 d 1841,4,26 (W)

Ch: Allen   b 1830, 7, 30 d 1839, 8,13

David m 2nd Lydia ----- b 1809,8,21

David m 3rd Margaret ----- b 1805,12,22

----, --, --. John & Della (G)

Ch: Frank H.   b 1887, 1, 10

Laura   " 1896, 9, 17

----, --, --. Frank m Edith GARDNER, dt Frank H. & Rosetta, b 1895,1,7 (G)

Ch: Dorothy

Jane   b 1921, 6, 5

Martha Rose" 1924, 7, 25

Ruth May " ----, --, --

1846, 9, 23. David, minor, rocf Upper Springfield MM, dtd 1846,8,22

1850, 3, 20. David gct Upper Springfield MM, to m Rachel Atkinson

1850, 12, 25. David gct Salem MM, Ia.

1911, 12, 20. Laura rec in mbrp

1912, 4, 24. Frank H. rocf Sandy Spring MM, dtd 1912,4,6

1912, 4, 24. Elizabeth A. rocf Sandy Spring MM, dtd 1912,4,6

1920, 9, 22. Laura V. rocf Sandy Spring MM

1924, 9, 24. John & w, Della, rocf Alliance MM

COURTNEY

1823, 5, 7. Edward, s Dozier & Ann, Columbiana Co., O., b 1794,10,11; m at Goshen, PHEBE G. VOTAW, dt Isaac & Sarah, Columbi-

ana Co., O., b 1799,11,22 (H)

Ch: Sarah   b 1824, 2, 7

John   " 1825, 3, 7

Ann   " 1826, 7, 8

Isaac   " 1827, 12, 2

Mary V.   " 1830, 12, 19

Emaline   " 1834, 1, 22

Nathan   " 1835, 2, 17

Judith   " 1837, 1, 29

Alonzo   " 1838, 11, 24

Phebe C. " 1840, 10, 6

1838, 5, 3. Israel, s Dozier & Anne, Columbiana Co., O.; m at West MH, Susan HAYHURST dt Wm. & Jane, Columbiana Co., O., b 1817,4,4 (H)

Ch: Wm. H.   b 1840, 3, 29

Thomas M. " 1842, 1, 3

----, --, --. Wm., s J. M. & Rebecca Emily, b 1864,5,29; m Nettie BETZ, dt Henry & Mary Ann, b 1866,8,27 (G)

1807, 8, 11. Dozier & w, Ann, & ch, Edward, John, Mary-Ann, Hannah, James, Martha & Moses, recrq

1823, 11, 19. Edward rocf New Garden MM, dtd 1823,9,25

1829, 4, 22. Edward & w, Phebe, & ch, Sarah, John, Ann & Isaac, mbrp transferred from Upper Springfield MM by rq (H)

1838, 4, 25. Israel [Cortney] prcf New Garden MM, dtd -----,3,22, to m Susan Hayhurst (H)

1910, 5, 25. William M. & w, Nettie, rocf East Goshen MM, dtd 1910,5,21

1910, 5, 25. James M. rocf East Goshen MM, dtd 1910,5,21

1911, 12, 20. Orlan rec in mbrp

COWGILL

1801, 11, 28. Sarah b (W)

1820, 10, 12. Charlotte b (W)

1822, 4, 24. Joseph b (W)

1823, 1, 9. James Simpson, s James & Charlotte, Columbiana Co., O., b 1801,5,23; m at Springfield, Lucy STANLEY, dt Woddy & Rebecca, Columbiana Co., O., b 1801,4,9

1814, 12, 13. James Stanley, Jr. gct Middleton MM, to m Rachel Cowgill

1822, 6, 19. James Simpson rocf Carmel MM, dtd 1822,5,18

1823, 4, 23. Joel & w, Rebecca, rocf Carmel MM, dtd 1823,3,15

1823, 6, 25. Sarah & ch, Charlotte & Joseph, rocf Carmel MM, dtd 1823,5,17

1824, 4, 21. Joel & w, Rebecca, & s, Joseph, gct Sandy Spring MM

1827, 5, 23. Sarah [Cowgil] & ch, Charlotte, Joseph, Ann & Lucinda, gct Fairfield MM, Ind.

1859, 10, 20. Lydia (form McCluer) con mcd

1859, 11, 24. Lydia gct Red Cedar MM, Ia.

COX
1779, 11, 10. Thomas b (W)

1818, 8, 11. Sarah rocf Goshen MM, Pa., dtd
1818,5,27
1819, 6, 23. Thomas rocf Farmington MM, N.Y.,
dtd 1818,9,24

COY
1911, 12, 20. Mable A. rec in mbrp

CRAFT
1832, 2, 22. Susan R. rocf ND MM, Phila., Pa.,
dtd 1831,12,27
1834, 2, 19. Susan R. Pippett (form Craft)
dis mcd

CRAIG
1808, 10, 19. James, s Wm. & Deborah, Columbiana Co., O.; m at Sandy Spring, Mary
RHODES, Jr., dt Wm. & Mary, Columbiana
Co., O.

1806, 10, 14. James rocf Goose Creek MM, Va.,
dtd 1806,8,25
1806, 10, 14. Deborah rocf Goose Creek MM,
Va., dtd 1806,8,25

CRAWFORD
1880, 5, 20. Charles H. recrq

CREW
----, --, --. Judith b 1739,6,19 d 1824,3,15
(W)
----, --, --. James m Mary STANLEY (W)
Ch: Garland   b 1790, 2, 12
    James   " 1792, 9, 15
    Nathaniel
     Jarrett   " 1795, 3, 4
    Elizabeth " 1799, 12, 15
    Jesse   " 1800, 5, 27
    Littlebery " 1803, 6, 17
    Lemuel   " 1805, 10, 4
    Sarah   " 1808, 6, 19
    Jonathan   " 1811, 1, 24
----, --, --. Obadiah b 1767,3,31; m Mary -----
b 1776,1,11
    Ch: John   b 1800, 8, 31
    Sarah   " 1802, 4, 4
    Judith   " 1804, 1, 1
    Eliza Ann " 1805, 12, 18
    Unity   " 1807, 9, 7
    Rebecca   " 1809, 8, 11
    Mary   " 1811, 1, 13
    Clotilda   " 1812, 9, 20
    Rachel   " 1814, 6, 20
    Esther   " 1816, 3, 21
    Isabella   " 1819, 7, 19
1812, 10, 15. Joshua, s Benjamin & Margaret,
Columbiana Co., O., b 1782,2,8; m at
Springfield, Milly STANLEY, dt Thos. &
Edith, Columbiana Co., O., b 1791,9,7 (W)
    Ch: Caroline b 1813, 8, 19

Ch: Nancy   b 1815, 2, 5
    Thomas   " 1816, 9, 8
    Fleming   " 1818, 7, 20
1822, 11, 27. John, s Obediah & Mary, Columbiana Co., O.; m at Goshen, Margery ELLY-
SON, dt Zacheriah & Mary, Columbiana Co.,
O.
1823, 1, 2. Sarah m Barzillai MORRIS
1824, 4, 29. Judith m Wm. B. FRENCH
1825, 10, 27. Eliza Ann m Asa WARE, Jr.

1807, 6, 11. Obadiah & w, Mary, & ch, John,
Sarah, Judith & Elisa Ann, rocf Cedar
Creek MM, Va., dtd 1807,4,11
1808, 1, 12. Littleberry & w, Huldah, & ch,
James, Benjamin, Mildred, Judith & Sarah,
rocf Cedar Creek MM, Va., dtd 1807,11,14
1808, 1, 12. Judith rocf Cedar Creek MM, Va.,
dtd 1807,12,12
1812, 9, 15. Joshua rocf Wayneoak MM, Va.,
dtd 1812,8,1
1837, 5, 24. Isaiah Stanley gct Upper Springfield MM, to m Nancy Crew
1870, 3, 20. Phebe Jane (form Trescott) dis
mcd (W)
1879, 12, 25. Henry rocf Damascus MM, dtd
1879,11,22

CRISMAN
1834, 4, 23. Mary H. rocf Exeter MM, Pa.,
dtd 1834,2,26
1836, 7, 20. Mary Allison (form Chrisman)
dis mcd

CRISPIN
1831, 5, 25. Hannah rocf Upper Springfield
MM, dtd 1831,3,26
1833, 5, 22. Hannah gct Upper Springfield MM

CROOKS
1927, 9, 21. Laura B. rocf First Friends
Church, Cleveland, O.

CROSSLEY
1911, 12, 20. Flora [Crosley] rec in mbrp
1916, 8, 16. Emma recrq
1920, 4, 21. Emily recrq

CULLENBERGER
1891, 6, 21. Hazel R., dt Mr. & Mrs. Geo.
Capel, b

1923, 12, 19. Hazel Ruby recrq

CULLER
----, --, --. Byron m Haidee TALBOT, dt Harry
& Mary, b 1883,3,28 (G)
    Ch: Kenneth b 1910, 10, 16

1924, 1, 23. Kenneth recrq
1932, 6, 29. Hadie & Kenneth dropped from
mbrp

CUMMINGS
1886, 1, 20. Elizabeth (form Campbell) dis
	mcd (W)

CURL
1807, 3, 4. Susannah [Curle] m Elijah FRENCH

1806, 2, 11. Caleb Stratton, Naomi, Joseph,
	Elias, James & John, ch Joseph, recrq
1806, 7, 15. Joseph [Curle] rocf South River
	MM, dtd 1806,2,8
1809, 9, 12. Joseph & w, Sarah, & ch, Caleb
	Stratton, Naomi, Joseph, Elias, James,
	John, Joel & Benjamin gct Miami MM
1809, 11, 14. Samuel dis mcd
1815, 9, 12. Darby Creek MM was given per-
	mission to rec Samuel in mbrp

CURRY
1860, 9, 27. Emma C. m Wm. P. PINKHAM

1860, 2, 23. Emma C. recrq

DANIEL
1842, 10, 26. Wm., s Wm. & Rachel, Columbiana
	Co., O., b 1821,1,17 (or 1821,1,21) d
	1902,2,12; m at Salem, Martha STRATTON, dt
	Chas. & Hannah, b 1821,12,1 (G)

1814, 11, 15. Mary rocf Middleton MM, dtd
	1814,8,11
1817, 2, 11. Mary gct Middleton MM
1838, 11, 21. William [Daniels], minor, rocf
	Sadsbury MM, Pa., dtd 1838,10,2
1864, 6, 22. William dis joining separatists
	of 1854 (W)
1864, 7, 20. Martha dis joining separatists
	of 1854 (W)

DARLINGTON
----, --, --. Hannah b 1808,3,2 d 1884,11,9
	(W) (an elder)
1829, 8, 26. Brinton, s Stephen & Rachel, Co-
	lumbiana Co., O., b 1804,12,3; m at Salem,
	Martha THOMPSON, dt John & Ann, Columbiana
	Co., O., b 1801,12,25 (W)
	Ch: Rachel	b 1830, 8, 27
	    Ann	" 1832, 5, 16
	    Esther	" 1833, 12, 29
	    Wm. T.	" 1835, 9, 30
	    Mary	" 1838, 10, 23
	    Martha	" 1838, 10, 23
	    Elma C.	" 1841, 7, 28
1836, 8, 31. Thomas, s Stephen & Rachel, Lu-
	cas Co., O.; m at Salem, Esther HUNT, dt
	Nathan, Cuyahoga Co., O.
1846, 12, 30. Wm., s Stephen & Rachel, Fayette
	Co., Pa., b 1815,3,9 d 1872,5,16; m at
	Salem, Catharine WILLIAMS, dt Daniel &
	Jane, Columbiana Co., O., b 1807,3,13 d
	1896,9,-- (W)
1872, 11, 4. Wm. Sanford, s John & Mary
	(Stitt), b (G)

1836, 7, 20. Thomas rocf Redstone MM, dtd
	1836,6,29
1842, 4, 20. Brinton & w, Martha, & ch, Ra-
	chel, Ann, Esther, William, Mary & Elma
	C., gct Salem MM, Ia.
1842, 11, 23. Thomas gct Salem MM, Ia.
1847, 10, 20. Jane Catharine W. gct Redstone
	MM
1866, 4, 25. William & w, Catharine W., rocf
	Providence MM, Pa., dtd 1866,4,5 (W)
1866, 4, 25. Hannah rocf Providence MM, dtd
	1866,4,5 (W)

DAVENPORT
1856, 7, 24. Almira Jane (form Thomas) dis
	mcd (H)

DAVIDSON
1928, 4, 25. Betty Manley relrq

DAVIS
----, --, --. Samuel b 1762,12,3 d 1836,4,15
	bur Salem; m Mary ----- b 1758,6,14 d
	1842,4,27 bur Salem (W)
	Ch: Rebecca	b 1784, 5, 25
	    Samuel	" 1789, 1, 9
	    Mary	" 1791, 8, 10
	    Wm.	" 1794, 6, 17
	    Elizabeth	" 1797, 2, 4
	    Rachel	" 1799, 8, 17
	    Joshua	" 1802, 3, 17
1805, 11, 20. Rebecca m David SCHOLFIELD
1813, 11, 24. Wm., s Samuel & Mary, Columbi-
	ana Co., O.; m at Salem, Anna FAWCETT,
	dt Richard & Eunice, Columbiana Co., O.
1818, 2, 25. Rachel m Lewis TOWNSEND
1819, 9, 13. Esther b (H)
1824, 5, 26. Joshua, s Samuel & Mary, Colum-
	biana Co., O., b 1802,3,17; m at Salem,
	Rachel MERCER, dt Daniel & Alice, Columbi-
	ana Co., O., b 1801,10,11 (H)
	Ch: Mary M.	b 1826, 7, 2
	    Alice	" 1828, 9, 14 (or 1828,9,7)
	    Joseph	" 1830, 9, 28
	    Rebecca	" 1833, 5, 21
1825, 2, 2. Mary m Benj. HAWLEY
1830, 12, 1. Elisabeth m Wm. WATERWORTH (H)
1836, 4, 15. Samuel's d rpd ae 74y (an elder)
----, --, --. Benjamin B. b 1811,1,21; m Mary
	B. ----- b 1816,1,22 (H)
	Ch: Lucinda	b 1834, 8, 29
	    Rebecca T.	" 1836, 3, 13
	    Susan T.	" 1840, 4, 3
	    Maria L.	" 1842, 2, 12
1843, 3, 29. Louiza [Davees] m James STRATTON
1846, 10, 28. Martha [Davies] m Jeremiah STAN-
	LEY
----, --, --. ----- m Anna ----- b 1797,10,23
	Ch: David
	    Mary	b 1858, 3, 12
	    Elma	" 1860, 4, 21
	    Sophia	" 1862, 7, 4
	    Elisha L.	" 1866, 3, 3

DAVIS, continued

1806, 2, 11. Abraham & w, Hannah, & ch, Ellis & Rachel, rocf Short Creek MM, dtd
1805,7,20, endorsed by Middleton MM, 1805,
12,14

1807, 12, 15. Isaac & w, Hannah, rocf Hopewell
MM, dtd 1807,9,7

1812, 4, 14. Hannah recrq (form dis by a mtg
not now in existence)

1813, 3, 16. Mary, Eli, Joseph & Benjamin,
ch Hannah, recrq

1819, 10, 20. Joseph, minor, rocf Marlborough
MM, dtd 1819,8,28

1828, 7, 30. Joshua & w, Rachel, & dt, Mary,
rocf New Garden MM, dtd 1828,7,24 (H)

1828, 7, 30. Samuel & w, Mary, rocf New Garden MM, dtd 1828,7,24 (H)

1828, 7, 30. Elizabeth rocf New Garden MM,
dtd 1828,7,24 (H)

1828, 8, 20. Elizabeth dis jH

1828, 8, 20. Mary dis jH

1828, 8, 20. Samuel dis jH

1828, 9, 24. Joshua dis jH

1828, 11, 19. Rachel dis jH

1830, 11, 24. William Watterworth prcf Carmel
MM, dtd 1830,11,20, to m Elizabeth Davis
(H)

1831, 5, 25. Anna & ch, Martha, Samuel, Esther, Louiza, Eunice & Lydia, rocf Upper
Springfield MM, dtd 1831,2,26

1831, 6, 22. Joseph dis jH

1838, 6, 20. Benjamin B. & w, Mary, & ch, Lucinda & Rebecca T., rocf New Garden MM,0.,
dtd 1838,5,24 (H)

1838, 11, 21. Samuel gct Upper Springfield MM

1838, 11, 21. Anna & ch, Eunice & Lydia, gct
Upper Springfield MM

1839, 8, 21. Esther dis jH

1843, 7, 19. Sarah (form Silvers) dis mcd (H)

1843, 7, 19. Anna & dt, Eunice & Lydia, rocf
Upper Springfield MM, dtd 1843,5,27 (H)

1843, 9, 22. Esther Ingling (form Davis) con
mcd (H)

1848, 2, 23. Mary dis disunity

1848, 2, 23. Alice dis disunity

1849, 9, 19. Mary B. dis (H)

1852, 2, 25. Eunice Whinery (form Davis) dis
mcd

1853, 2, 23. Lydia Holloway (form Davis) dis
mcd

1862, 12, 25. Anna dis joining separatists
(W) of 1854

1872, 5, 23. Caleb recrq

1879, 12, 25. Huldah Elizabeth relrq (H)

1880, 5, 5. Caleb relrq

DEAN

----, --, --. Barton, s Jonathan R. & Hannah,
Carroll Co., O., b 1803,8,26 d 1887,4,21;
m Hannah ----- b 1808,11,21 d 1838,12,3 (W)
Ch: Ephraim   b 1827, 2, 13
    David   " 1828, 8, 28
    Jonathan   " 1830, 8, 20

Ch: Isaac   b 1832, 6, 10
    Ann   " 1833, 9, 24
    Amos   " 1836, 2, 25 d 1836, 2,26
Barton m 2nd at Salem, 1840,12,2, Eliza-
beth STRATTON, dt Michael & Rhoda, Columbi-
ana Co., O., b 1800,1,10 d 1866,6,7 (W)
Ch: Abigail   b 1841, 11, 13
    Joshua S. " 1843, 10, 2
Barton m 3rd Ann ----- b 1820,5,7

1842, 5, 4. Edith m John H. PAINTER

1847, 9, 29. Stephen, s James Hervey &
Eleanor, Columbiana Co., O.; m at Salem,
Phebe E. PAINTER, dt David & Ann, Columbi-
ana Co., O.

1841, 2, 24. Elizabeth gct Sandy Spring MM

1842, 3, 23. Edith rocf New Garden MM, dtd
1842,2,24

1847, 8, 25. Stephen rocf Smithfield MM, dtd
1847,8,23

1847, 12, 22. Stephen & w, Phebe E., gct Salem MM, Ia.

DEFENBAUGH

1910, 2, 23. Ray G. & w recrq

DELZELL

1862, 12, 25. Phebe dis joining separatists
(W) of 1854

DENNIS

----, --, --. Charles b 1792,5,14; m Jane
----- b 1788,6,17 (H)
Ch: Esther
      Speakman b 1822, 8, 23

1817, 2, 11. Charles rocf Monsey MM, Pa., dtd
1816,5,22

1819, 12, 22. Charles dis mcd

1820, 3, 22. Jane (form Heacock) dis mcd (with
first cousin)

1821, 6, 20. Charles rst by rq

1821, 6, 20. Jane rst by rq

1828, 10, 22. Charles dis jH

1828, 11, 19. Jane dis jH

1847, 5, 19. Esther dis jH

DERR

----, --, --. Edgar, s James & Lydia Ann, b
1878,7,24; m Lillian DAVIS, dt J. K. &
Elizabeth, b 1882,3,3 (G)
Ch: Lamoine   b 1908, 4, 29

1916, 3, 22. Edgar, Lillian, Naomi & Isabella recrq

1916, 9, 20. Lemoine, s Edgar & Lillian, rocf
Winona MM, O., dtd 1916,6,21

DEW

1922, 8, 20. Walter Arthur, s Clyde Allen &
Clara May (Beeson), b 1900,6,4; m at Sa-
lem, Mary Eleanor STRATTON, dt Joseph R.
& Anna Mary (Bundy), b 1900,6,27 (W)

DEW, Walter Arthur & Mary Eleanor, continued
 Ch: Thomas
   Roderick b 1929, 6, 6

1922, 6, 21. Walter A. recrq (W)
1932, 2, 24. Walter A. & w, M. Eleanor, & s, Thomas Roderick, gct Wilmington MM, Del. (W)

DEWEES
----, --, --. Thomas, s Jesse & Rebecca (Edgerton), b 1848,10,12 d 1929,3,30 bur Friends Burying Ground, Barnesville, O.; m Martha -----
 Ch: Jesse H. b 1873, 1, 11 d 1918, 1,23 bur Friends Burying Ground, Salem, O.
1891, 12, 15. Deborah d (W)
1904, 5, 25. Jesse H., s Thomas & Martha (Hall), b 1873,1,11 d 1918,1,23 bur Friends Burying Ground, Salem, O.; m Mary C. BINNS dt Joseph P. & Belinda (Hobson), b 1884,2, 11 (W)
 Ch: Florence
   Martha b 1905, 5, 31
   Clara R. " 1906, 8, 6
   Thomas
   Arthur " 1908, 3, 7
   Mildred
   Rebecca " 1909, 3, 2
   Margaret H." 1909, 3, 2
   Joseph
   Howard " 1912, 1, 24
   James E. " 1914, 8, 26
   Jesse H. " 1918, 2, 14
----, --, --. Chas. W. [Deweese], s Griffith & Ruth Anna (Masters), b 1865,4,28; m Mary GAMBLE, dt Samuel & Mary Jane, b 1876,7,12 (W)
 Ch: Isaac
   Edwin b 1905, 3, 30
1919, 3, 20. Mary C. m Edward J. WOOLMAN (W)

1878, 5, 22. Deborah rocf Chesterfield MM, dtd 1878,4,20 (W)
1916, 5, 24. Jesse H. & w, Mary C., & ch, Florence Martha, Thomas Arthur, Margaret H., James E., Clara R., Mildred Rebecca & Joseph Howard, rocf Short Creek MM, O. (W)
1917, 9, 19. Thomas & w, Martha W., rocf Stillwater MM, O., dtd 1917,8,22 (W)
1920, 9, 22. Mary C. Woolman (form Dewees) & ch, Florence Martha, Margaret Hannah, Joseph Howard, James Ezra & Jesse Hall Dewees, gct New Garden MM (W)
1929, 11, 24. Clara Rosella, Thomas Arthur & Mildred Rebecca Dewees, ch Mary Dewees Woolman, gct Birmingham MM, Pa. (W)
1933, 7, 19. Charles W. & w, Mary G., & s, Isaac E., rocf Upper Springfield MM, O., dtd 1933,6,23 (W)

DICKEY
1880, 10, 11. James & Rebecca recrq

DIXON
1820, 3, 1. Simon, s Henry, Columbiana Co., O.; m at Salem, Elizabeth PIGEON, dt Wm. & Alice, Columbiana Co., O.
----, --, --. Isaac b 1801,3,29; m Jane ----- b 1809,3,10 (W)
 Ch: Rebecca b 1830, 8, 10
   Mary Jane " 1831, 7, 9 d 1841, 9,25
   Eliza " 1835, 10, 15
   Samuel " 1837, 7, 31
   Nathan " 1842, 1, 22
   Isabella " 1844, 9, 22
   Ruth " 1847, 4, 11
1854, 8, 7. Jane b (W)

1820, 6, 21. Elizabeth gct Middleton MM
1825, 7, 20. Jane recrq
1832, 10, 24. John Petit, Joshua, Lydia & Charity, ch Nathan & Lucretia, rocf Middleton MM, dtd 1832,10,11
1847, 2, 24. Jane, w Isaac, & ch, Lydia, Rebecca, Samuel, Eliza, Nathan & Isabella, rocf Redstone MM, dtd 1847,1,12
1847, 6, 25. Lydia McDonal (form Dixon) dis mcd
1853, 7, 23. Joshua dis mcd
1853, 9, 21. Lydia Washburn (form Dixon) dis mcd & jas
1853, 10, 19. John P. dis jas
1853, 10, 19. Charity dis jas
1854, 1, 25. Rebecca Estell (form Dixon) dis mcd
1862, 1, 23. Samuel & w, Hannah, gct Upper Springfield MM, O.
1862, 12, 25. John [Dickson] dis joining separatists (W) of 1854
1874, 5, 6. James S. recrq
1876, 2, 9. Cyrus gct Short Creek MM
1879, 11, 5. James relrq

DOLE
1804, 3, 26. Sarah b (W)
----, --, --. Elizabeth b 1806,1,2 d 1821,2,27 (W)
1808, 7, 19. Michael b (W)
1817, 12, 12. Mark d bur Salem (W)

1812, 12, 15. James Langstaff & w, Elisabeth, & Elizabeth Dole, minor, rocf Maurices River MM, N. J., dtd 1812,10,2
1816, 12, 17. Michael, minor, rocf Maurice MM, N. J., dtd 1816,11,1
1817, 11, 11. Mark rocf Maurice River MM, N. J., dtd 1817,8,1
1818, 11, 25. Sarah rocf Maurice River MM, N. J., dtd 1817,11,3
1819, 8, 25. Daniel rocf Maurice River MM, N. J., dtd 1819,6,4
1819, 12, 22. Daniel dis mcd
1824, 3, 24. Sarah Owen (form Dole) dis

DOLE, continued
1831, 7, 20. Michael dis JH
1846, 5, 20. Ann (form Strech) dis mou (H)
1885, 2, 6. Byron & w, Julia A., recrq
1885, 2, 6. Rebecca G. recrq
1886, 10, 21. Byron dropped from mbrp
1886, 10, 21. Julia & ch dropped from mbrp

DONELLY
1911, 12, 20. Edna rec in mbrp

DROUGHT
----, --, --. Wallace, s Mansfield & Margaret
     Megrin, b 1856,--,-- d 1933,2,24 (G)

1924, 1, 23. Mary B. & Wallace R. recrq
1926, 4, 21. Mr. & Mrs. relrq
1927, 9, 21. Mr. & Mrs. W. R.recrq

DUGDALE
1827, 6, 20. Sarah & ch, Joseph, Wm., Mary,
     Thomas, Charles & Sarah, rocf Solesbury
     MM, dtd 1827,4,3 (Solesbury MM, Pa.)
1828, 7, 23. John dis disunity
1828, 7, 23. Sarah dis disunity
1828, 8, 20. Joseph dis JH
1833, 3, 20. Wm., Mary, Thomas, Charles, Sa-
     rah & Rachel, ch John & Sarah B., gct New
     Garden MM

DUNLAP
1885, 2, 6. John H. recrq
1886, 10, 21. John dropped from mbrp

DURBIN
1910, 2, 23. Ida recrq
1910, 2, 23. Joseph S. & w recrq
1910, 2, 23. Margaret recrq
1910, 2, 23. Pearl recrq
1910, 2, 23. Thomas E. & w recrq

DURHAM
1835, 11, 25. Hannah (form Schooley) dis mcd
     & jas

DYSON
1872, 8, 7. Mason & w, Eleanor, & dt, Agnes
     Ann & Sarah Wilhelmina, rocf White Water
     MM, Ind., dtd 1872,6,26
1872, 12, 26. Eleanor & dt, Agnes Ann & Sarah
     Wilhelmina, gct Kendal MM, England
1873, 2, 5. William rocf White Water MM,
     Ind., dtd 1872,12,25
1878, 2, 21. Mason gct Brighouse MM, England

EAGHTIN (or Eagletin)
1911, 12, 20. Clarence C. rec in mbrp

EARL
1871, 9, 17. Hannah M. & ch, Elma Jessie,
     Mary Hannah & Susan Emily, rocf Winne-
     shiek MM
1874, 8, 20. Elma J. gct Greenwich MM, R. I.

1924, 4, 23. Sidney V. & Lillie [Earle] recrq

EARLY
1904, 4, 8. Blanche, dt Charles & Grace
     O'Connell, b (G)

1932, 6, 29. Blanche dropped from mbrp

EASTMAN
----, --, --. Richard b 1781,4,18; m Lovica
     ----- b 1802,12,30 (W)
     Ch: Pascal   b 1829, 5, 17
         Mary   " 1830, 11, 3
         Julea   " 1832, 2, 18
         Henrietta   " 1835, 7, 19
         Chas. Ed-
           win   " 1837, 10, 5
         Benj. F.   " 1842, 1, 17

1844, 6, 19. Lovisa & s, Benjamin Franklin,
     rocf Middleton MM, dtd 1844,5,9
1844, 11, 20. Richard rocf North Berwich MM,
     Maine, dtd 1844,7,25
1845, 5, 21. Pascal Morel, Mary, Julia Fran-
     cis, Harriett & Charles Edwin, ch Richard
     & Lovisa, recrq
1845, 7, 23. Julia Frances, dt Richard &
     Lovis, gct Sandy Spring MM
1848, 10, 25. Pascal Morrell, minor, gct
     Frankford MM, Pa.
1849, 8, 22. Richard & w, Lovisa, & ch, Hen-
     rietta, Charles Edwin & Benjamin Franklin,
     gct Sandy Spring MM
1849, 9, 19. Mary gct Sandy Spring MM

ECKSTEIN
1917, 7, 25. R. C. recrq

EDDY
1872, 8, 7. Allen W. (Eddie) rocf Greenwich
     MM, dtd 1872,6,13
1874, 12, 24. Allen W. gct Alum Creek MM

EDGERTON
1882, 3, 29. Jesse, s Joseph & Charity, Co-
     lumbiana Co., O.; m at Se-
     wickley, Pa., Susan GILBERT, dt Benjamin &
     Lydia, Westmoreland Co. (W)
----, --, --. J. Clarkson, s James & Amy L.
     (Hammond), b 1878,11,16; m Anna BAILEY,
     dt Dempsey & Sarah E., b 1877,9,19 (W)

1884, 1, 23. Susan G. gct Middleton MM (W)
1930, 2, 19. J. Clarkson & w, Anna B., rocf
     Stillwater MM (W)

EDKIN
1860, 1, 26. Joanna rocf Richland MM, Pa.,
     dtd 1859,12,30 (H)
1861, 7, 25. Ann B. (form Battin) con mcd
     (H)
1863, 11, 26. Joanna gct Fishing Creek MM,
     Pa. (H)

EDMUNDSON
1858, 9, 23. Jonathan [Edmunson] & w, Phebe,
   & ch, Samuel L., Hannah, Ellen, Oscar &
   Isaac N., gct Spring Creek MM, Ia.
1858, 9, 23. John & w, Ruth, & ch, Mary, Abner & Sina, gct Spring Creek MM, Ia.
1862, 12, 25. Jane dis joining separatists
   (W) of 1854

EDSAL
1885, 1, 22. Ruth A. [Edsil] con mcd (H)
1885, 2, 26. Ruth A. gct Marietta MM, Ia. (H)

EDWARDS
1840, 10, 21. Mary rocf Fallowfield MM, dtd
   1840,5,9 (H)
1843, 10, 25. Mary dis jas (H)
1882, 8, 9. Irene & Alexander recrq
1887, 3, 20. Maggie dropped from mbrp

ELDER
----, --, --. Flora C., dt Jordan & Emily
   Crossley, b 1867,--,-- d 1929,1,29 (G)

ELDRIDGE
1836, 8, 24. Rachel (form Hunt) dis mcd

ELIAS
----, --, --. Andrew Curtis m Myra S. JESSUP,
   dt James H. & Martha D. (Stratton), b
   1890,12,10 d 1927,2,22 bur Hope Cemetery,
   Salem, O. (W)

ELLIOTT
1810, 8, 14. Joseph & w, Elizabeth, & ch,
   Mary, Isaac & John, rocf Westland MM, dtd
   1810,3,24

ELLIS
1806, 4, 15. Enos & w, Mary, & ch, Gainer,
   Elizabeth, Enos & Mary More, rocf Middleton MM, dtd 1806,2,8
1808, 1, 12. Enos dis disunity
1811, 8, 13. Enos gct New Garden MM
1913, 2, 19. Lizzie dropped from mbrp

ELLYSON
----, --, --. Zachariah b 1762,10,6; m Mary
   ----- b 1768,10,12 (W)
   Ch: Isaac   b 1789, 8, 28
      Gideon   " 1791, 11, 21
      Zachariah " 1794, 4, 2
      Robert   " 1796, 4, 11
      Wm.   " 1798, 10, 9
      Margery   " 1800, 10, 20
      Anna   " 1803, 6, 3
      John   " 1806, 2, 6
      Joseph   " 1807, 12, 21 d 1813,11,23
      Mary   " 1812, 9, 17
1815, 5, 25. Isaac, s Zachariah & Mary, Columbiana Co., O., b 1789,8,28; m at Springfield, Elizabeth CATTELL, dt James & Deborah, Columbiana Co., O., b 1797,9,17 (W)
   Ch: Deborah b 1816, 5, 5

   Ch: Mary   b 1818, 9, 13
      Ann   " 1820, 7, 12
      Enoch   " 1822, 7, 26 d 1823, 3,20
      Joseph   " 1824, 1, 30
1818, 9, 30. Robert, s Zachariah & Mary, Columbiana Co., O., b 1796,4,11; m at Salem,
   Hannah BUTLER, dt Benjamin & Hannah, Columbiana Co., O., b 1802,1,2 (W)
   Ch: Esther   b 1820, 3, 27
      Miriam   " 1821, 12, 7
      Benjamin " 1824, 1, 29
1822, 11, 27. Margery m John CREW
1824, 8, 12. Phebe b (W)
1830, 5, 26. John, s Zachariah & Mary, Columbiana Co., O.; m at Salem, Lydia STREET,
   dt Aaron & Mary, Columbiana Co., O. (W)
1861, 10, 2. Robert [Ellison], Jr., s Robert
   & Hannah, Mahoning Co., O.; m at Salem,
   Eunice FAWCETT, dt Josiah & Sarah, Columbiana Co., O. (W)
----, --, --. Homer, s Walter & Sadie, b
   1901,11,1; m Mary JACKSON, dt Sylvester &
   Edith, b 1905,10,30 (G)
   Ch: Betty   b 1923, 11, 1
      Bobby   " 1927, 3, 27

1811, 11, 12. Isaac [Ellison] rocf Westland
   MM, dtd 1811,8,24
1816, 10, 15. Zachariah [Elleson] & w, Mary,
   & ch, Robert, Wm., Margery, Anna, John &
   Mary, rocf Westland MM, dtd 1816,9,26
1821, 12, 19. William con mou
1830, 11, 24. Lydia gct Upper Springfield MM
1842, 10, 19. Jeremiah Stanley gct Upper
   Springfield MM, to m Ann Elyson
1862, 6, 25. Eunice gct Upper Springfield
   MM (W)
1862, 12, 25. Eunice dis joining separatists
   (W) of 1854
1876, 11, 22. Phebe rocf Middleton MM, dtd
   1876,11,18 (W)
1883, 8, 22. Phebe gct Upper Springfield MM
   (W)
1829, 12, 26. Homer & w, Mary, & ch rocf Damascus MM

ELTON
----, --, --. Grant J., s Richard & Emily, b
   1873,12,24; m Rose M. OTLIP, dt Felix &
   Mary, b 1879,9,3 (G)

EMBREE
1806, 7, 15. John & w, Huldah, rocf Goose
   Creek MM, Va., dtd 1806,5,1, endorsed by
   Middleton MM, 1806,7,12

EMERY
1923, 12, 19. Minnie Lewis gct Alliance MM

EMMONS
1808, 1, 12. Thomas & w, Mary, & ch, David,
   Rebecca & Cassandra, recrq
1831, 3, 23. Cert rec for Jacob, minor, from

EMMONS, continued
    Sandy Spring MM, dtd 1830,8,22, endorsed
    back to Sandy Spring MM as he had returned
    there to reside

ENGLAND
1799, 2, 11. Matilda b (W)
----, --, --. Joseph b 1769,3,8 d 1866,1,27 bur
    Salem; m Hannah ----- b 1791,10,2 d 1853,4,
    27 bur Salem (W)
    Ch: Sarah   b 1813, 7, 19 d 1894, 5, 1
        Josiah   " 1815, 4, 7
        Mary   " 1818, 5, 11 " 1858, 1,17
        Gideon   " 1820, 2, 22 " 1830, 5,25
        Tacy Jr.   " 1823, 5, 28 " 1872, 8,28
        James R.   " 1825, 3, 8
        George   " 1827, 5, 1
        Ann   " 1829, 5, 25
----, --, --. ----- b 1896,4,29; m Edith ELTON
    dt Grant & Rose, b 1901,12,14
    Ch: Betty   b 1922, 6, 22
        Don James   " 1931, 7, 24

1819, 6, 23. Joseph, Jr. & w, Hannah, & ch,
    Sarah & Mary, rocf Westland MM, dtd 1819,
    4,22
1819, 9, 22. Matilda recrq
1821, 12, 19. Tacy rocf Westland MM, dtd 1821,
    11,22
1826, 4, 19. Tacy gct Westland MM
1829, 4, 24. Harold & Betty recrq
1830, 12, 22. Jane rocf Westland MM, dtd 1830,
    10,27
1838, 8, 22. Josiah & w, Sarah, gct Marl-
    borough MM
1850, 7, 24. James dis mcd
1860, 3, 21. Ann Shreeve (form England) dis
    mcd (W)
1862, 12, 25. Joseph, Sarah & Tacy dis joining
    separatists (W) of 1854
1864, 10, 20. Samuel & w, Emma, gct Concord
    MM (H)
1864, 12, 21. George dis mcd (W)

ENGLE
1856, 1, 24. Nathan & w, Catharine, & ch,
    Lemuel, Esther, Robert, Charles H. & Mary
    Elma, gct Driftwood MM, Ind.

ERWIN
1884, 8, 10. Mahlon b 1800,6,18 d 1884,8,10
    (H)

ESTABROOK
1873, 11, 19. Jane (form Young) dis mcd (W)

ESTELL
1854, 1, 25. Rebecca (form Dixon) dis mcd

EVANS
----, --, --. Jonathan b 1774,3,7 d 1849,8,27
    bur Salem; m Elizabeth ----- b 1778,12,7
    d 1840,8,21 (W)

    Ch: Philip   b 1804, 7, 16
        Lydia   " 1808, 3, 3
        Hannah   " 1811, 6, 5
        Joshua   " 1813, 5, 14
        Susannah   " 1814, 6, 16
        Sarah   " 1816, 11, 20
        Rachel   " 1824, 5, 16 d 1840, 9,22
        bur Salem
1827, 3, 28. Lydia m Samuel MATHER
1832, 5, 2. Hannah m Isaac BONSALL
1834, 5, 17. Susannah [Evins] m George
    STRATTON
1840, 12, 2. Sarah m Edward BONSALL
----, --, --. Philip b 1804,7,16; m Esther
    ----- b 1809,3,10 d 1847,4,26 (Philip,
    s of Jonathan) (W)
    Ch: Rachel   b 1843, 9, 24 d 1847, 8, 5
        Jonathan   " 1847, 4, 24
1880, 8, 8. Philip d (G)
1930, 2, 3. Nettie d (G)
1931, 9, 16. James d (G)

1841, 4, 21. Philip gct Upper Springfield
    MM, to m Esther Morris
1841, 7, 21. Esther rocf Upper Springfield
    MM, dtd 1841,6,26
1852, 8, 25. Philip dis mcd
1857, 2, 26. Philip rst by rq
1873, 6, 25. Jonathan M. dis mcd (W)
1910, 2, 23. Mrs. Jennie recrq
1920, 6, 23. Nellie recrq
1921, 10, 19. James E. & Nettie recrq
1927, 6, 22. Lillie dropped from mbrp

EVERSTINE
----, --, --. George Henry, s Charles & Au-
    gusta; m Lorna Pauline OTT, dt John &
    Mary, b 1895,1,12 (G)
    Ch: Charles   b 1920, 7, 30
        Maxine   " 1924, 8, 10
        Geraldine   " 1924, 8, 10
        Genevieve   " 1926, 1, 19

1930, 2, 19. George Henry & w, Lorna Pauline,
    [Everstein] & ch recrq
1931, 3, 25. George Henry & w, Lorna Pauline,
    & ch, Charles, Genevieve, Geraldine &
    Maxine, relrq

FANLEY
1809, 2, 14. Thomas & w, Martha, rocf Hope-
    well MM, dtd 1808,9,5

FARLAND
1817, 1, 14. Joseph & w, Hannah, rocf Kennet
    MM, Pa., dtd 1816,12,3

FARMER
1824, 8, 25. Thomas Langstaff gct Flushing
    MM, to m Ann Farmer
1865, 6, 22. Elizabeth rocf Sandy Spring MM,
    dtd 1865,5,23
1865, 6, 22. James & w, Maribah, rocf Sandy

FARMER, continued
    Spring MM, dtd 1865,5,23

FARQUHAR
1834, 8, 20. Elizabeth & dt, Sarah, rocf Car-
    mel MM, dtd 1834,6,21
1834, 11, 19. Sarah rocf Carmel MM, dtd 1834,
    9,20
1838, 12, 19. Elizabeth & dt, Sarah W., gct
    Middle Town MM, Pa. (H)
1839, 12, 25. Carmel MM rq this mtg to treat
    with Edward for misconduct; rpd 1840,1,22,
    that he did not wish to retain mbrp; Car-
    mel MM to be notified (H)
1840, 5, 20. Carmel MM rq this mtg to serve
    Edward their testimony of disownment (H)

FARR
1883, 2, 7. Edwin H. & w, Abbie E., & ch,
    Mabel E., Wm. E. & Edwin Wilson rocf Scipio
    MM

FARRINGTON
1834, 10, 23. Abraham, s Joseph & Phebe, Co-
    lumbiana Co., O.; m at Salem, Sarah JOHN,
    dt Jesse & Sarah Thomas, Columbiana Co.,O.
    (H)

1815, 9, 12. Abraham & w, Deborah, & ch,
    Moses, Judith, Jesse Kirk, Phebe, Billion
    & John, rocf Redstone MM, dtd 1815,6,2
1816, 4, 16. Abraham & w, Deborah, & ch,
    Moses, Judith, Jesse Kirk, Phebe, Billion,
    John & Deborah, gct New Garden MM
1834, 10, 22. Abraham prcf New Garden MM, dtd
    1834,9,25, to m Sarah John (H)
1834, 12, 24. Sarah gct New Garden MM (H)
1836, 6, 22. Abraham [Farington] & w, Sarah,
    rocf New Garden MM, dtd 1836,4,21 (H)
1838, 7, 25. Abraham & w, Sarah, gct New Gar-
    den MM (H)

FAULKNER
1817, 11, 11. Abigail (form Painter) dis mcd

FAWCETT
----, --, --. Richard b 1771,9,22 d 1845,8,6;
    m Eunice ----- b 1776,11,26 d 1839,9,9 (W)
    Ch: David   b 1793, 11, 11
        Jonathan   " 1796, 4, 14
        Anna   " 1797, 10, 23
        Wm. F.   " 1799, 1, 27
        Esther   " 1801, 8, 13
        Drusilla   " 1805, 6, 26
        Martha   " 1808, 9, 19
        Richard B. " 1811, 11, 17
        Jonah   " 1815, 4, 5
----, --, --. Simeon b 1801,4,1 d 1817,6,28 (W)
1801, 4, 1. Levi b (W)
1803, 7, 10. Jehu b (W)
----, --, --. Deborah S. b 1807,2,12 d 1876,8,
    20 (W)
----, --, --. Wm. b 1784,10,18; m Abigail

----- b 1787,8,8
Ch: Samuel
    Sharp   b 1812, 10, 21
    Abner   " 1814, 9, 1
    Lucinda   " 1816, 2, 25
    Simeon   " 1817, 10, 19
    Jephthah   " 1821, 7, 23
    Jason   " 1825, 8, 16
1813, 11, 24. Anna m Wm. DAVIS
1815, 5, 24. David, s Richard & Eunice, Co-
    lumbiana Co., O., b 1793,11,11 d 1862,2,5;
    m at Salem, Hannah BALL, dt Nathan & At-
    lantic, Columbiana Co., O., b 1798,5,2 d
    1846,12,29 (W)
    Ch: Ann   b 1816, 4, 4
        Eli   " 1818, 1, 22
        Nathan B.   " 1819, 12, 30 d 1870, 2, 9
        Lydia   " 1822, 11, 3
        Joseph   " 1825, 8, 31
        Sarah T.   " 1828, 5, 19
        Eunice   " 1837, 5, 9
1815, 9, 11. Eli d
----, --, --. Jonathan [Fawcet] b 1796,4,14;
    m Mary ----- b 1797,9,9 (W)
    Ch: Lydia   b 1819, 6, 24 d 1851, 6,17
        Henry B.   " 1820, 12, 9
        Elvira   " 1822, 12, 8
        Edward W. " 1825, 10, 30
        Jacob   " 1828, 7, 21
        Martha   " 1830, 5, 11
        Richard   " 1832, 5, 10
        Lewis   " 1835, 1, 14
        Isaac   " 1837, 5, 14
        Elwood   " 1839, 12, 16
1824, 5, 6. Lydia M., dt David & Elizabeth
    Miller, b (G)
1824, 1, 1. Elizabeth m Nathan NEWPORT
1825, 4, 27. Wm. F., s Richard & Eunice, Co-
    lumbiana Co., O., b 1799,10,27 d 1857,7,5;
    m at Salem, Elizabeth R. TEST, dt Zacheus
    & Hannah, Columbiana Co., O., b 1805,8,17
    d 1873,5,12 (W)
    Ch: Emmor   b 1826, 10, 27
        Isaac   " 1828, 2, 14 d 1848, 5,17
        Zaccheus   " 1830, 2, 13
        Elmina   " 1832, 4, 8 d 1834, 5,31
        Hannah C. " 1834, 11, 10
        Thomas F. " 1837, 5, 5
        Esther   " 1840, 10, 4 (or 1840,4,
        10)
        Jonathan   " 1842, 10, 5
        Samuel T. " 1845, 10, 22
        Martha   " 1848, 8, 9
1825, 6, 29. Martha m George W. SHREVE
1825, 8, 31. Drusilla m John BUTLER
----, --, --. Jehu, s Thomas & Sarah, Columbi-
    ana Co., O., b 1803,7,10 d 1867,2,8 bur
    Salem; m Abigail ----- b 1802,9,19 d 1835,
    10,10 bur Salem, O. (W)
    Ch: Sarah   b 1826, 10, 11
        Edwin   " 1828, 7, 6 d 1849, 1,24
        bur Salem
        Elisha   " 1832, 4, 20 " 1852, 6, 7

FAWCETT   Jehu & Abigail, continued
        bur Salem
      Ch: Deborah   b 1834, 10, 26
    Jehu m 2nd 1837,5,31, Mary THOMAS, dt Ja-
      cob & Mary, b 1796,7,27 d 1850,4,30 bur
      Salem   [bur Salem
      Ch: Thomas   b 1840, 2, 21 d 1840,11,14
    Jehu m 3rd Deborah ----- b 1807,2,12
1826, 12, 29. Wm. T. b (W)
----, --, --. Levi [Fawcet] b 1801,4,1 d 1841,
      8,17; m Mary ----- b 1810,1,10 (W)
      Ch: Hannah   b 1830, 11, 20 d 1831, 3,31
          Esther   " 1832, 4, 11
          Elma   " 1835, 7, 23
          Abigail   " 1838, 3, 18
          Sina   " 1841, 4, 27 d 1841, 9,13
1831, 9, 22. Esther m Elisha BRACKIN
1832, 8, 8. Amos, s David & Phebe, Columbi-
      ana Co., O., b 1800,4,8; m at Salem, Han-
      nah MIDDLETON, dt Hudson & Deborah, Bel-
      mont Co., O., b 1802,3,7 d 1867,5,20 (W)
      Ch: Deborah   b 1833, 6, 21 d 1833,10,29
          Phebe   " 1835, 1, 2
          Phineas   " 1836, 4, 27 d 1836, 7,28
          Lemuel   " 1837, 4, 7 " 1837, 7,25
          Albert   " 1839, 3, 12 " 1862, 4,24
          Mary   " 1840, 6, 7 " 1840,11,29
          Levi   " 1842, 1, 27 " 1863, 8,25
1834, 8, 27. Richard B., s Richard & Eunice,
      Columbiana Co., O., b 1811,11,17 d 1888,10,
      8 (an elder); m at Salem, Edith TEST, dt
      Zacheus & Hannah, Columbiana Co., O., b
      1815,7,19 d 1852,1,23 (W)
      Ch: Ezra   b 1835, 7, 7
          Benjamin " 1840, 3, 23
          Edith   " 1852, 1, 14
    Richard B. m 2nd Rebecca B. ----- b 1815,
      3,4
----, --, --. Josiah b 1815,4,5 d 1888,9,24;
      m Sarah OLIPHANT, dt Ephraim & Elizabeth,
      b 1817,3,23 d 1867,3,28 (W)
      Ch: Lemuel   b 1838, 12, 23
          Eunice   " 1840, 5, 29
          Ruth   " 1842, 4, 4
          John   " 1848, 8, 3
    Josiah m 2nd 1868,10,28, Catharine STANLEY
      dt Moses & Susannah, Columbiana Co., O.
      (W) b 1817,6,21 d 1903,5,4

1848, 5, 31. Edward, s Jonathan & Mary, Co-
      lumbiana Co., O. b 1825,10,30; m at Sa-
      lem, Esther NEGUS, dt John & Miriam, Co-
      lumbiana Co., O. b 1828,5,21 (W)
      Ch: Martha M. b 1849, 7, 16
          Willis G. " 1852, 4 12
          Mary Emma " 1856, 5, 1
          Flora   " 1858, 3, 29
1848, 9, 21. Sarah m Jacob HOLLOWAY
1848, 12, 27. Elvira m Elisha NEGUS
1852, 10, 21. Esther m Wm. C. WILSON
1855, 5, 2. Deborah m Charles G. HAYS (W)
1859, 2, 25. Sarah L. m Louis STREET

1859, 9, 28. Hannah C. m Louis HOLLINGSWORTH
      (W)
1859, 9, 29. Eunice m David STREET
1861, 10, 2. Eunice m Robert ELLISON (W)
----, --, --. Joseph b 1825,8,31 d 1899,2,13;
      m Mary FISHER, b 1830,4,24 d 1908,3,23 (W)
      Ch: Alice S. b 1863, 8, 3
          Hannah R. " 1866, 2, 16
1864, 3, 30. Thomas F., s William & Elizabeth
      (Test) b 1837,5,5 d 1911,3,16 bur Grand-
      view Cemetery, Salem, O.; m Sidney Ann BON-
      SALL, dt Edward & Hannah (Jones), b 1843,
      6,23 d 1928,6,12 bur Grandview Cemetery,
      Salem, O., (W)
      Ch: Wm. Elmer b 1865, 5, 22
          Emma L.   " 1867, 2, 3 d 1928,11,11
          Edward
            Cloudsley " 1871, 10, 23
          Howard   " 1877, 4, 12
          Ralph F. " 1880, 2, 9
          Esther S. " 1882, 9, 23
          Luther T. " 1885, 1, 6
1870, 10, 5. Elma m Charles T. HAYES (W)
1876, 12, 25. Mary G. m Andrew SHIELL (H)
1877, 3, 28. Phebe m Reuben PAINTER (W)
1884, 3, 26. Edith m J. Howard ZELLEY (W)
1889, 6, 26. Hannah R. m James E. MAULE (W)
1902, 8, 27. Edward C., s Thomas F. & Sidney,
      Columbiana Co., O., b 1871,10,23; m at Sa-
      lem, Sarah HAYES, dt Chas. I. & Deborah,
      Columbiana Co., O., b 1865,6,13 (W)
      Ch: James E. b 1904, 8, 25 d 1904, 8,28
          Thos. Hayes" 1905, 10, 7
          Elma   " 1908, 8, 6
          Margaret " 1910, 8, 22
          Edward C.
            Jr.   " 1912, 2, 25
1909, 7, 28. Esther Sidney m Elwood Dean
      STANTON (W)
1912, 9, 25. George W. d (an elder)
1928, 11, 11. Sidney A. d (W)

1807, 12, 15. Richard & w, Eunice, & ch, Da-
      vid, Anna, Jonathan, William, Esther &
      Drusilla, rocf Hopewell MM, dtd 1807,10,5
1812, 4, 14. William & w, Abigail, rocf
      Plainfield MM, dtd 1812,2,22
1814, 6, 14. John gct Hopewell MM, Va.
1814, 8, 16. Eli [Fawcet] rocf Hopewell MM,
      dtd 1814,5,5
1817, 5, 13. Simeon & Levi [Fawcet], minors,
      rocf Hopewell MM, dtd 1817,3,6
1818, 8, 11. Jonathan [Fawcet] gct Short
      Creek MM, to m
1819, 1, 17. Mary [Fawcet] rocf Short Creek
      MM, dtd 1818,12,20
1820, 4, 19. Jehu, minor, rocf Hopewell MM,
      dtd 1819,12,9
1823, 6, 25. Elizabeth rocf Hopewell MM, Va.,
      dtd 1823,4,10
1823, 11, 19. Jehu gct Flushing MM
1824, 3, 24. Jehu returned cert granted to
      Flushing MM; now residing within limits

FAWCETT, continued
of this mtg
1829, 8, 19. Amos rocf Stillwater MM, dtd 1829,7,25
1829, 9, 23. Mahlon dis mcd
1829, 12, 23. Levi gct Marlboro MM, to m Mary Johnson
1830, 5, 19. Mary G. rocf Marlborough MM, dtd 1830,5,4
1837, 1, 25. Josiah gct Middleton MM, to m Sarah Oliphant
1837, 8, 23. Cert rec for Sarah from Middleton MM, dtd 1837,7,19, endorsed to Upper Springfield MM
1843, 6, 21. Jonathan dis
1846, 4, 22. Mary & ch, Edward, Jacob, Martha, Richard, Lewis, Isaac & Elwood, gct Salem MM, Ia.
1846, 4, 22. Elvira gct Salem MM, Ia.
1846, 6, 24. Eli dis mcd
1848, 4, 19. Cert granted to Salem MM, Ia., 1846,4,-- for Mary & ch, Edward, Jacob, Martha, Richard, Lewis, Isaac & Elwood, endorsed back to this mtg (Martha had d)
1848, 4, 19. Cert granted to Salem MM, Ia., 1846,4,-- for Elvira, endorsed back to this mtg
1848, 5, 24. Henry dis mcd
1850, 6, 19. William T. rocf Hopewell MM, Va., dtd 1850,5,2
1853, 4, 20. Mary & ch, Richard, Lewis, Isaac & Elwood, gct Blue River MM, Ind.
1853, 5, 25. Emmor gct Redstone MM, to m Lydia W. Miller
1853, 12, 21. Cert granted to Blue River MM, Ind. for Mary & ch returned (she d before cert was rec)
1854, 2, 22. Jehu gct Flushing MM, to m Deborah S. Holloway (W)
1854, 4, 19. Lydia M. rocf Redstone MM, dtd 1854,5,3 (W)
1854, 5, 24. Lydia M. rocf Redstone MM, Pa., dtd 1854,5,3 (W)
1854, 6, 21. Deborah S. rocf Flushing MM, dtd 1854,5,25 (W)
1854, 11, 22. Zaccheus dis disunity (W)
1855, 2, 21. Richard B. gct ND MM, Phila., Pa., to m Rebecca B. Mattock (W)
1855, 5, 24. William T. gct Allum Creek MM
1855, 11, 21. Rebecca B. rocf ND MM, Phila., Pa., dtd 1855,10,23 (W)
1857, 0, 23. Jacob dis mou (W)
1857, 9, 23. Jonathan rst by rq (W)
1858, 3, 24. Ezra dis mou (W)
1859, 1, 20. Edward W. dis disunity
1859, 1, 20. Isaac gct Blue River MM, Ind.
1860, 7, 26. Esther dis jas
1862, 4, 23. Joseph gct Woodbury MM, N. J., to m Mary R. Fisher (W)
1862, 8, 20. Jonathan gct Short Creek MM (W)
1862, 11, 19. Julius Rasche gct Upper Springfield MM, to m Elizabeth G. Fawcett (W)
1862, 12, 25. Elizabeth, Thomas, Esther, Jona-

than, Samuel & Martha dis joining separatists (W) of 1854
1862, 12, 25. Hannah, Phebe & Lewis dis joining separatists (W) of 1854
1862, 12, 25. Joseph & Nathan dis joining separatists (W) of 1854
1862, 12, 25. Josiah, Sarah, Lemuel, Ruth & John dis joining separatists (W) of 1854
1862, 12, 25. Mary J., Elma, Jehu & Deborah dis joining separatists (W) of 1854
1862, 12, 25. Richard B., Rebecca & Edith dis joining separatists (W) of 1854
1862, 12, 25. Sarah dis joining separatists (W) of 1854
1863, 2, 25. Sarah C. (form Cook) dis mou
1863, 3, 25. Mary R. rocf Woodbury MM, N. J., dtd 1863,2,24 (W)
1863, 8, 19. Edward dis joining Methodist Society (W)
1863, 8, 19. Esther N. dis jas (W)
1864, 4, 20. Amos dis joining separatists of 1854 (W)
1865, 7, 19. Sina F. Pennock (form Fawcett) dis mcd (W)
1866, 3, 21. Sarah T. Street (form Fawcett) dis joining separatists of 1854 (W)
1868, 1, 22. Esther dis jas (W)
1868, 7, 22. Jonathan W., Jr. dis serving as a volunteer in the army & mcd (W)
1868, 8, 19. Mary J. Koll (form Fawcett) dis attending mtg set up contrary to discipline & mcd (W)
1869, 12, 22. Emmor dis disunity (W)
1870, 5, 25. Richard dis mcd (W)
1871, 5, 24. John dis mcd (W)
1871, 5, 24. Samuel dis mcd (W)
1872, 4, 24. Elwood dis jas (W)
1872, 9, 25. Isaac dis participating in the late war (W)
1873, 1, 22. Ruth dis jas (W)
1875, 7, 21. Martha M. Tatum (form Fawcett) dis mcd & jas (W)
1875, 8, 26. Mary Emma dis jas (W)
1876, 8, 24. Mary G. recrq (H)
1879, 7, 23. Martha dis jas (W)
1880, 6, 23. Lemuel dis mcd (W)
1880, 7, 21. Anna (form Johnson) dis mcd (W)
1881, 1, 19. Flora B. dis jas (W)
1881, 5, 25. Willis G. dis mcd (W)
1884, 5, 25. Emmer & w gct Baltimore MM, Md.
1889, 9, 25. Rebecca B. gct ND MM, Phila., Pa. (W)
1892, 7, 20. William E. dis mou (W)
1903, 12, 23. Ralph F. dis mcd (W)
1909, 8, 25. Howard gct Stavanger MM, Ia. (W)
1910, 11, 12. Alice S. gct Woodbury MM, N. J. (W)
1912, 12, 25. Luther T. dis jas (W)
1917, 8, 15. Clara gct First Friends Church, Cleveland, O.
1925, 6, 24. Alice S. rocf Woodbury MM, N.J. (W)
1927, 11, 23. Howard S. gct Pasadena MM, Calif.

FAWCETT, continued
(W)
1927, 12, 21. Thomas Hayes gct Westtown MM,
    Pa. (W)

FEANLEY
----, --, --. Martha b 1739,3,1 d 1815,12,12
    bur Salem (W)
----, --, --. Thos. b 1744,9,20 d 1829,1,25
    (W)
1815, 12, 22. Martin d (W)

FEICHT
----, --, --. Vera Smith, dt Edgar & Minnie
    Smith, b (G)
1928, 6, 28. Harry Morell, s Ellsworth & Ver-
    die, b (G)

1932, 6, 29. Vera Smith dropped from mbrp
1932, 12, 29. Harry M. & Vera recrq

FELTS
1813, 2, 18. Cherry recrq

FENTON
1847, 11, 24. James, s Jacob, gct Alexandria
    MM (H)

FIELD
1776, 11, 16. Elizabeth b (W)

1811, 8, 13. Mary, William & Ambrose, ch
    John, rocf Mt. Holly MM, N. J., dtd 1811,
    7,4
1811, 8, 13. Hannah rocf Mt. Holly MM, N.J.,
    dtd 1811,7,4
1813, 2, 18. Elizabeth (form Pine) con mcd
1815, 3, 14. Mary, minor dt John, gct ND MM,
    Phila., Pa.
1821, 12, 19. Ambrose, minor, gct Mt. Holly
    MM, N. J.
1822, 4, 24. William dis disunity
1827, 4, 25. Elizabeth gct Upper Springfield
    MM

FINNERAN
1913, 2, 19. William & w dropped from mbrp

FINNEY
1885, 2, 6. Clara A. recrq
1887, 8, 25. Clara relrq

FISH
1855, 9, 21. Stephen, s Silas & Susannah,
    Crawford Co., Pa.; m at Salem, Hannah K.
    HANNA, dt Jesse & Elizabeth Kersey, Colum-
    biana Co., O. (H)

FISHER
1729, 9, 29. Joseph b (W)
1741, 10, 20. Ann b (W)

1808, 7, 14. Anne m Thomas HANNA
----, --, --. Joseph d 1848,4,3 bur Salem; m
    Hannah -----
    Ch: Asahel   b 1820, 4, 5
    Joseph m 2nd at Salem, 1826,4,26, Marga-
    ret RAWLINGS, dt Joseph & Ann, Bucks Co.,
    Pa., d 1843,6,15 bur Salem
    Ch: Thomas R. b 1829, 8, 16

1832, 8, 29. William, s Joseph & Hannah, Co-
    lumbiana Co., O., b 1800,11,24 d 1889,2,8;
    m at Salem, Priscilla WARRINGTON, dt Abra-
    ham & Rachel, Columbiana Co., O., b 1795,
    8,15 d 1855,9,7 bur Salem (W)
    Wm. m 2nd at Salem, 1857,3,4, Ruth SMART,
    dt Isaac & Rebecca, Salem Co., N. J.
    b 1819,1,7 d 1885,6,3 (W)
1807, 7, 14. Joseph & w, Hannah, & ch, Sil-
    vanus, Rachel, William, Isaac, Amasa &
    Anna Knight, rocf South River MM, Va., dtd
    1807,5,9
1808, 5, 17. Hannah & Anna rocf South River
    MM, Va., dtd 1808,4,9
1808, 11, 15. Joseph & w, Ann, rocf South
    River MM, Va., dtd 1808,6,11
1826, 6, 21. Margaret gct Carmel MM
1831, 6, 22. Joseph & w, Margaret, & ch,
    Asahel Exchange & Thomas Rawlings, rocf
    Carmel MM, dtd 1831,5,21
1832, 2, 22. William rocf Carmel MM, dtd
    1831,11,19
1838, 11, 5. Isaac & w, Eunice, & ch, Cyrus
    W. & Lydia Ann, rocf Miami MM, dtd 1838,8,
    22
1839, 4, 23. Isaac & w, Eunice, & ch, Cyrus
    W. & Lydia Ann, gct Miami MM
1849, 4, 25. Asahel E. gct Springfield MM, O.
1853, 10, 19. Thomas R. gct Miami MM
1862, 4, 23. Joseph Fawcett gct Woodbury MM,
    N. J., to m Mary R. Fisher (W)
1862, 12, 25. William & Ruth dis joining
    separatists (W) of 1854
1867, 11, 20. Emaline (form Barber) dis mcd
    (W)
1875, 3, 21. Asahel rec in mbrp again (cert
    sent to mtg in Ind. but never rec) (W)

FLEMING
1828, 11, 19. Stanley gct Smithfield MM, to m
    Priscilla Carr

FLESHLEY
1913, 12, 29. Clara Kaiser dropped from mbrp

FLETCHER
1920, 6, 23. Minnie & Henry recrq

FOGG
----, --, --. Elisha b 1786,1,12; m Tacy -----
    b 1794,9,20 (W)
    Ch: Aaron   b 1815, 9, 28
        Hannah   " 1817, 12, 20
        Josiah   " 1820, 9, 28

FOGG, Elisha & Tacy, continued
    Ch: Sarah   b 1824, **5, 6**

1827, 5, 23. Elisha & w, Tacy, & ch, Aron,
    Hannah, Josiah & Sarah, rocf Greenwich MM,
    N. J., dtd 1827,3,29
1829, 1, 29. Elisha dis jH
1829, 1, 29. Tacy dis jH
1829, 10, 21. Ebenezer & w, Mary, & ch, Ed-
    mund, Edwin, Charles & Adna, rocf Piles
    Grove MM, N. J., dtd 1829,5,26 (H)
1833, 5, 22. Hannah, Aaron, Josiah & Sarah,
    ch Elisha & Tacy, gct Upper Springfield
    MM
1836, 6, 22. Ebenezer dis not attending mtg
    (H)
1841, 5, 19. Aaron dis training with the mili-
    tia (H)
1844, 4, 24. Sarah F. Bradshaw (form Fogg)
    con mcd (H)
1873, 8, 21. Sarah & Rebecca M. recrq
1874, 2, 26. Hannah Ann recrq
1912, 12, 26. Sarah [Fog] gct Reamon Ave.
    Friends Church, Pasadina, Calif.

FORSYTHE
----, --, --. Frank W. m Martha COPE, dt
    Louis & Hannah Y. (Hollingsworth), b 1868,
    1,22 (W)
----, --, --. Wm. m Elma COPE, dt Louis &
    Hannah Y. (Hollingsworth), b 1877,11,22
    (W)

1898, 10, 19. Martha C. (form Cope) dis mcd
    (W)
1909, 3, 24. Elma C. (form Cope) dis mcd &
    jas (W)

FOUGHTY
1825, 6, 22. Anna (form Stanley) dis mcd

FOWLER
1821, 11, 21. Joseph rocf Carmel MM, dtd 1821,
    10,20
1823, 4, 23. Joseph rocf Sandy Spring MM, dtd
    1823,3,19
1835, 10, 21. Samuel & w, Phebe, & ch, Mary
    Ann, Joseph, James & Elihu, rocf New Gar-
    den MM, dtd 1835,7,23 (H)
1844, 3, 20. Samuel & w, Phebe, & ch, Maryann,
    Joseph, James, Elisha, Deborah, Sarah &
    Levi, gct Marlborough MM (H)
1882, 12, 21. Charles E. & Elizabeth recrq
1929, 6, 17. Elisha B. Steer gct New Garden
    MM, O., to m Hannah C. Fowler (W)

FRAME
----, --, --. Amasa m Rachel E. PLUMMER, dt
    Robert & Jane (Bailey), b 1842,1,11 d
    1930,9,12 bur Stillwater, Barnesville, O.

1902, 7, 23. Edward F. Stratton gct Still-
    water MM, to m Clara E. Frame (H)

1910, 6, 22. Rachel E. rocf Stillwater MM,
    O., dtd 1910,5,25 (H)

FRAMPTON
1910, 2, 23. C. A. & w recrq
1910, 2, 23. Dessie recrq

FRANKLIN
1862, 12, 25. Lemuel dis joining separatists
    (W) of 1854

FRAZEE
1793, 3, 28. Rachel b (W)

1842, 5, 25. Rachel rocf Farmington MM, N.Y.,
    dtd 1841,7,22

FRENCH
----, --, --. Thos. b 1773,3,13 d 1852,1,23;
    m Esther ----- b 1780,3,28 d 1856,7,27 (W)
----, --, --. James b 1773,3,13; m Mary -----
    b 1780,1,29 (W)
    Ch: Wm. R.   " 1802, 6, 13
        Ann   " 1808, 12, 10
        James   " 1814, 5, 24
        Charles " 1816, 9, 3 d 1821, 9,13
        Richard " 1818, 10, 13
1807, 2, 25. Robert, s Thos. & Mercy, Colum-
    biana Co., O., b 1779,4,24 d 1862,2,13; m
    at Salem, Anna STREET, dt Zadok & Eunice,
    b 1784,8,17 d 1842,3,26 (W)
    Ch: Zadok   b 1808, 1, 7
        Joseph   " 1810, 5, 19 d 1813, 3,25
        Ann   " 1816, 4, 12
        Lydia   " 1819, 5, 11 " 1840, 6,28
        John   " 1822, 9, 20
        Samuel   " 1822, 9, 20
1807, 3, 4. Elijah, s Thomas & Mary, Columbi-
    ana Co., O., b 1784,5,4 d 1815,4,8; m at
    Salem, Susannah CURLE, dt Joseph & Rebecca,
    Columbiana Co., O., b 1787,8,7 (W)
    Ch: Thomas   b 1808, 1, 5
        Rebecca " 1808, 1, 5
        Eliza Ann " 1809, 10, 13
        Joseph C. " 1810, 12, 26
        Maria   " 1812, 9, 20 d 1813, 8, 5
        Elijah   " 1814, 10, 2
----, --, --. Barzillai b 1781,7,22; m Mary
    ----- b 1785,3,17 (W)
    Ch: Elizabeth b 1811, 10, 30
        Albert   " 1815, 7, 9
        Thos. Yates" 1816, 7, 21
        Robert   " 1817, 8, 2
        Ezra   " 1820, 11, 22
        Martha   " 1822, 6, 9 d 1822, 8, 4
        David   " 1823, 11, 3
        Barzillai " 1826, 2, 14
        Lydia   " 1827, 12, 2
----, --, --. Robert, Jr., s Barzilla & Mary,
    b 1817,8,2 d 1836,10,19 (W)
1824, 4, 29. Wm. B., s James & Mary, Columbia-
    Co., O.; m at Springfield, Judith
    CREW, dt Obediah & Mary, Columbiana Co.,O.

FRENCH, continued

----, --, --. Rachel b 1838,7,21 d 1893,3,20 (W)

----, --, --. Albert, s Barzilla, b 1815,7,9; m Elizabeth M. ----- b 1807,3,25 (G)
Ch: Wm. Henry b 1840, 10, 25
  Anna " 1842, 5, 10
  Rebecca " 1845, 9, 17
  Albert E. " 1850, 10, 12

1844, 10, 30. Ann m John W. JOHNSON

1845, 3, 26. John, s Robert & Anna, Columbiana Co., O. b 1822,9,20 d 1889,5,22; m at Salem, Martha HOGDEN, dt John & Ann (Howey), b 1826,1,1 d 1911,9,7 bur Grand View Cemetery (W)
Ch: Anna S. b 1846, 10, 7
  Joseph " 1850, 5, 28
  Mary Ann " 1853, 9, 14
  Sarah J. " 1856, 6, 5
  Elmira T. " 1858, 5, 15
  George " 1861, 1, 23
  Edward " 1863, 12, 27
  Charles Og-
  den   " 1869, 8, 1

1847, 3, 31. Samuel, s Robert & Anne, Columbiana Co., O., b 1822,9,20 d 1871,10,1; m at Salem, Mary J. PERRY, dt David & Hannah, Bucks Co., Pa., b 1817,10,6 d 1912,3,11 (W)
Ch: Sarah b 1849, 7, 1 d 1869,10,15
  Hannah " 1851, 9, 15
  Lewis " 1853, 7, 7
  Charles " 1855, 10, 17 d 1856,10,22

----, --, --. Zadok S. b 1808,1,7; m Mariam ----- b 1820,11,10 d 1904,8,12 (W)
Ch: Robert b 1848, 1, 23
  Lydia " 1850, 5, 28
  Amy " 1856, 8, 6 d 1881, 1,18

----, --, --. Barzillai b 1826,2,14 d 1902,8, 31; m Deborah M. ----- b 1828,9,16 d 1872, 11,9 (W)
Ch: Edgar b 1853, 8, 13
  Mary " 1854, 8, 8 d 1858, 4,--
  bur Salem
  Henrietta " 1859, 9, 13
  Barzillai M.
    b 1865, 8, 13
Barzillai m 2nd Martha B.----- b 1833,3,23 d 1888,8,5

----, --, --. David b 1823,11,3; m Eliza M. ----- b 1833,4,19 (W)
Ch: Mary b 1858, 3, 12
  Elma " 1860, 4, 21
  Sophia " 1862, 7, 4
  Elisha L. " 1866, 3, 3

----, --, --. Henrietta, dt Barzillai & Deborah (Miller), b 1859,9,13 d 1915,10,20, bur Damascus, O. (W)

----, --, --. Thomas Y. b 1816,7,21 d 1895,4, 13; m Rachel H. ----- b 1831,9,23 d 1904, 12,2 (W) (both elders)
Ch: Clarkson b 1863, 8, 26

1865, 9, 6. Wm. H. d (G)

----, --, --. Elisha S., s David & Eliza (Miller), b 1866,3,3 d 1928,3,4 bur West Chester, Pa. (W)

1867, 10, 24. Anna m Lindley M. BRACKEN (W)

1873, 9, 25. Mary A. m Benjamin WILSON (W)

1876, 11, 23. Hannah L. m Abel WALKER

----, --, --. Edgar b 1853,8,15; m Ruth ----- b 1858,9,5 (W)
Ch: Holland M. b 1879, 7, 13 d 1897, 6,--
  Hubert " 1882, 10, 24

1888, 3, 28. Clarkson S., s Thomas Y. & Rachel H. (Blackburn), Columbiana Co., O., b 1863,8,26; m Annie B. YOUNG, dt Thos. & Ann (Barber), b 1854,11,2 (W)

1889, 8, 22. Mary French m Charles STRATTON (W)

----, --, --. Eli m Lorinda GREENAMYER, dt George & Eva, b 1855,2,25 d 1931,7,1 (G)
Ch: Paul C. b 1891, 9, 16

1910, 10, 6. Eli d ae 57y

1805, 11, 12. Robert rocf Abington MM, dtd 1805,8,26

1807, 1, 13. Elijah rocf Haddonfield MM, dtd 1806,11,10

1807, 7, 14. Barzillai rocf Abington MM, Pa., dtd 1807,4,27

1808, 8, 16. Thomas French & w, Esther, & their apprentices, Moses Townsend & Patience Thomas, rocf Redstone MM, dtd 1808,7,1

1810, 10, 16. Barzillai gct New Garden MM, to m Mary Yates

1811, 2, 12. Mary rocf New Garden MM, dtd 1811,1,17

1817, 5, 13. Susannah & s, Elijah, gct Derby Creek MM, O.

1820, 5, 24. James & w, Mary, & ch, William R., Ann, James, Charles & Richard, rocf Chester MM, N. J., dtd 1820,4,5

1825, 12, 21. Eliza Ann gct Darby Creek MM

1826, 11, 22. Rebecca gct Goshen MM

1828, 12, 24. Thomas dis disunity

1830, 10, 20. Robert, minor, rocf Upper Springfield MM, dtd 1830,9,25

1833, 6, 19. Joseph C. gct Frankford MM, Pa.

1835, 10, 21. Thomas rocf Upper Springfield MM, dtd 1835,8,22

1837, 10, 25. Thomas gct Upper Springfield MM

1841, 7, 21. Samuel H. rocf Woodberry MM, N. J., dtd 1841,5,31 (H)

1842, 9, 21. Thomas Y. rocf Middleton MM, dtd 1842,8,11

1843, 9, 20. Samuel con mou (H)

1843, 11, 22. Uriah rocf Woodbury MM, N. J., dtd 1843,6,26 (H)

1845, 1, 22. Zadok dis

1845, 8, 20. Zadok rst in mbrp by QM

1846, 7, 22. Zadok gct Flushing MM, to m Meriam Holloway

1847, 1, 20. Meriam rocf Flushing MM, dtd

FRENCH, continued
  dtd 1846,11,26
1856, 3, 19. Theophilus Morlan gct Upper
  Springfield MM, to m Lydia French (W)
1856, 7, 24. Albert & w, Elizabeth, & ch,
  William Henry, Anna, Rebecca C. & Albert
  E. rocf Upper Springfield MM, dtd 1856,6,
  28
1857, 7, 22. Barzillia, Jr. & w, Deborah M.,
  & ch, Edgar & Mary, rocf Upper Springfield
  MM, dtd 1857,3,27 (W)
1857, 8, 19. Eliza M. rocf Sandy Spring MM,
  dtd 1857,6,27 (W)
1857, 9, 23. David rocf Upper Springfield MM,
  dtd 1857,6,26 (W)
1862, 3, 19. Thomas Y. gct Westland MM, to
  m Rachel H. Blackburn (W)
1862, 7, 23. Rachel H. rocf Westland MM, dtd
  1862,6,25 (W)
1862, 12, 25. Anna, Mary Jane, Joseph, Sarah,
  Elmira & George dis joining separatists
  (W) of 1854
1862, 12, 25. Samuel, Mary J., Sarah, Hannah,
  Lewis, John & Martha dis joining separatists (W) of 1854
1862, 12, 25. Thomas Y. & Rachel dis joining
  separatists (W) of 1854
1862, 12, 25. Zadok, Meriam, Robert, Lydia &
  Amy dis joining separatists (W) of 1854
1864, 12, 21. Thomas Y. & w, Rachel H., & s,
  Clarkson, gct Middleton MM (W)
1865, 8, 23. David dis disunity (W)
1866, 1, 24. Rachel S. (form Satterthwait)
  con mcd (W)
1867, 2, 20. Zadok S. dis disunity
1868, 11, 25. Eliza M. dis disunity (W)
1869, 8, 26. Rebecca C. relrq
1870, 8, 25. Hannah rocf Sandy Spring MM,
  dtd 1870,8,23
1871, 6, 21. Thomas Y. & w, Rachel H., & s,
  Clarkson, rocf Middleton MM, dtd 1871,6,17
  (W)
1873, 3, 20. Albert E. relrq
1876, 5, 24. Joseph dis mcd (W)
1877, 8, 22. Edgar con mcd (W)
1878, 7, 22. Deborah D. (form Hall) dis mcd
  (W)
1878, 9, 25. Lewis B. dis mcd (W)
1879, 1, 29. Emma rocf Upper Springfield MM,
  dtd 1878,11,22 (W)
1879, 9, 24. Barzillai gct Middleton MM, to
  m Martha Blackburn (W)
1879, 9, 24. Mary J. gct Flushing MM (W)
1880, 3, 24. Robert dis disunity (W)
1880, 3, 24. Lydia dis (W)
1880, 3, 24. Martha B. rocf Middleton MM,
  dtd 1880,3,20 (W)
1880, 6, 23. Miriam dis (W)
1882, 12, 21. Lewis G. & w, Ella B., & dt,
  Rosa Ermina, rocf East Goshen MM, O.
1884, 9, 24. Miriam rst by rq (W)
1887, 3, 20. Louis & w, Ella, dropped from
  mbrp

1890, 12, 24. Edgar dis jas (W)
1891, 1, 21. Emma dis jas (W)
1893, 11, 22. Elma F. Olover (form French)
  dis mcd & joining separatists of 1854 (W)
1897, 2, 24. Barzillai Moris dis disunity &
  mou (W)
1897, 10, 20. Edward O. con mou (W)
1907, 12, 25. Hubert C. dis mcd (W)
1911, 12, 20. Paul C. rec in mbrp
1926, 12, 22. Mary Lucile rocf Beloit MM, O.

FRESCOTT
1834, 1, 29. Clark, s Samuel & Sophia, Columbiana Co., O.; m at Salem, Ann BUTLER, dt
  Benjamin & Hannah, Columbiana Co., O.

FRITCHMAN
----, --, --. Emerson B., s Joseph & Mary
  (Hutton), b 1868,3,7 d 1930,11,17 bur
  Hartzell Farm, near North Benton, O.;
  m Lucy HARTZELL (W)
  Ch: Mary
      Louise   b 1899, 10, 16

1915, 7, 21. Emerson B. rst by rq (form dis
  by New Garden MM (W)
1915, 7, 21. Mary Louise, dt Emerson B. &
  Lucy H., recrq (W)

FRYE
1914, 5, 10. Merlin M. recrq
1927, 6, 22. Merlin [Fry] dropped from mbrp

FULLAM
1928, 1, 25. Mrs. Esther recrq
1932, 6, 29. Esther dropped from mbrp

FULLER
----, --, --. Abigail b 1788,4,28 d 1822,8,2
  (W)

1820, 8, 23. Abigail rocf Farmington MM,
  N. Y., dtd 1820,5,25
1861, 4, 25. Thomas Edward Pinkham gct
  Upper Springfield MM, to m Mary Fuller

GALBREATH
1852, 11, 27. Hannah m Oliver COPE (H)

1852, 10, 21. Hannah recrq (form mbr of New
  Garden MM which had been laid down (H)
1855, 5, 24. Thomas recrq (form mbr of Grove
  MM which had been laid down) (H)
1884, 8, 21. Francis C. & w, Deborah G., &
  ch Cornelia & William F., gct Wapsinonoc
  MM, Ia. (H)

GAMBLE
----, --, --. Harrison b 1815,5,--; m Phebe

GAMBLE, Harrison & Phebe, continued
----- b 1825,2,17
    Ch: Samuel   b 1842, 1, 3
        Charles   " 1846, 3, 10
        Sarah   " 1848, 3, 15
        Wm.   " 1850, 3, 4
        Martha   " 1852, 7, 20
----, --, --. Samuel b 1844,3,1; m Mary Jane
----- b 1838,4,7 (W)
    Ch: Chas. W. b 1868, 10, 31
        Phebe Jane " 1870, 9, 3
        Edward Y. " 1874, 10, 12
        Mary R.   " 1876, 7, 12
        Irene H.   " 1879, 8, 1
        Alvin H.   " 1882, 7, 8
        Homer
1876, 5, 31. Chas., s Harrison & Phebe, Co-
lumbiana Co., O., b 1846,3,10; m at Salem,
Martha HALL, dt Robert & Mary (Dewees), b
1849,9,1 d 1928,3,1 bur Winona, O. (W)
----, --, --. Edward Y., s Samuel & Mary Jane
(Fogg), b 1874,10,12; m Rebecca A. ATKIN-
SON, dt Wm. & Catharine, b 1874,11,3 (W)
----, --, --. Alvin H., s Samuel & Mary Jane
(Fogg), b 1882,7,8; m Mabel BEESON, dt
John O. & Rosaltha V. (Heacock), b 1881,8,
7 (W)
    Ch: Robert S. b 1909, 12, 5
        J. Howard " 1911, 11, 10
        Mary Ger-
          trude   " 1916, 10, 25

1841, 6, 23. Harrison P. [Gambell] rocf
Marlborough MM, dtd 1841,5,25
1842, 9, 21. Harrison P. gct Pennsville MM,
to m Phebe Hollingsworth
1844, 3, 20. Harrison P. gct Middleton MM
1846, 6, 24. Harrison P. & w, Phebe, & ch,
Samuel & Charles, rocf Upper Springfield
MM, dtd 1846,5,23
1853, 5, 25. Harrison & w, Phebe, & ch, Samuel, Charles, Sarah, William & Martha
Jane, gct New Garden MM
1866, 7, 25. Samuel [Gambell] rocf Middleton
MM, dtd 1866,7,21 (W)
1869, 1, 20. Samuel con mcd (W)
1875, 5, 19. Charles rocf Hickory Grove MM,
dtd 1875,4,3 (W)
1876, 2, 24. Jannette recrq
1881, 2, 23. Mary Jane recrq (W)
1881, 2, 23. Charles W., Phebe Jane, Edward
Y., Mary R. & Irena H., ch Samuel & Mary
Jane, recrq (W)
1883, 4, 25. Samuel Gamble & w, Mary Jane, &
ch, Charles W., Phebe Jane, Edward Y.,
Mary R., Irene H. & Alvin H. & their s,
James L. W. Bradway, gct New Garden MM
(W)
1897, 5, 19. Charles & w, Martha H., gct New
Garden MM (W)
1915, 1, 20. Adelbert & w, Mary, & ch dropped
from mbrp
1915, 5, 19. Edward Y. rocf Stillwater MM,

O., dtd 1915,4,21 (W)
1915, 5, 19. Rebecca W. rocf Short Creek
MM; O., dtd 1915,4,20 (W)
1915, 8, 25. Martha H. rocf New Garden MM,
O., dtd 1915,7,22 (W)
1917, 7, 25. Alvin H. & w, Mabel B., & ch,
Robert S., J. Howard & Mary Gertrude,
rocf Middleton MM, O., dtd 1917,7,21 (W)

GANTZ
1855, 11, 22. Celicia (form Townsend) con mcd

GARDNER
1867, 8, 28. Rosetta, dt Wm. & Maria Clark, b
(G)
1888, 2, 21. Viola A., dt Philip A. & Mary
E. Butler, b (G)

1911, 12, 20. Viola A. & Edythe rec in mbrp
1917, 8, 15. Elizabeth recrq

GARMAN
1845, 10, 22. Lydia P. (or Carman) gct Battle
Creek MM (H)

GARRETSON
----, --, --. Joseph b 1789,3,23 d 1837,1,28;
m Mariah ----- b 1798,4,13 (H)
    Ch: Mary Ann   b 1817, 9, 11
        Rebecca W. " 1823, 4, 8
        Maria M.   " 1827, 4, 27
        Ruth Ann   " 1830, 4, 18
----, --, --. Peirce b 1808,8,14 d 1876,6,13;
m Sarah H. ----- b 1814,8,17 (H)
    Ch: Franklin   b 1836, 2, 27
        Samantha M." 1837, 12, 15 d 1838, 4,21
        Barclay   " 1839, 5, 10
1842, 1, 27. Eli, s John & Anna, Columbiana
Co., O.; m at West MH, Sarah I. COOK, dt
Caleb & Hannah, Knox Co., O. (H)
1844, 4, 25. Maria m Isaac Newton PEIRCE (H)
1868, 9, 29. Lucretia M. m Harding BAILY (H)

1830, 8, 25. John & w, Ann, & ch, Eli, Mariah, Sidney & Ann, rocf Warrington MM,
dtd 1830,5,20, endorsed by New Garden MM,
1830,7,22 (H)
1830, 8, 25. Price [Garetson] rocf Warrington
MM, dtd 1830,5,20, endorsed by New Garden
MM, 1830,7,22 (H)
1830, 8, 25. Rebecca & Hannah rocf Warrington
MM, dtd 1830,5,20, endorsed by New Garden
MM, 1830,7,22
1831, 10, 19. Hannah Bailey (form Garretson)
dis mou (H)
1835, 3, 25. Pierce gct New Garden MM, to m
Sarah H. Myers (H)
1835, 10, 21. Sarah H. rocf New Garden MM, dtd
1835,8,20 (H)
1836, 10, 19. Joseph & w, Maria, & ch, Mary
Ann, Rebecca Maria & Ruth Ann, rocf Warrington MM, dtd 1836,8,17 (H)
1838, 8, 22. Jesse rocf New Garden MM, dtd
1838,4,26 (H)

GARRETSON, continued
  1835, 8, 20 (H)
1839, 4, 24. Mary Ann Bull (form Garretson)
  con mcd (H)
1842, 1, 19. Rebecca W. Pettit (form Garretson) con mou (H)

1843, 3, 22. Jesse gct New Garden MM (H)
1846, 8, 19. John & w, Ann, gct West MM (H)
1846, 8, 19. Ann P. gct West MM (H)
1846, 8, 19. Rebecca gct West MM (H)
1850, 9, 25. Mariah Lamb (form Garetson) dis
  mcd (H)
1852, 3, 25. John W. Satterthwait gct West
  MM, to m Rebecca Garretson (H)
1854, 7, 20. Ruth Ann Lee (form Garretson)
  dis mcd (H)
1864, 12, 22. Eli & w, Sarah, & ch, Rebecca &
  Lucretia M., rocf West MM, dtd 1864,10,21
  (H)
1876, 8, 24. Margaret A. rocf Rochester MM,
  N. Y., dtd 1876,7,28 (H)
1884, 2, 21. Anna M. Grove (form Garretson)
  con mcd (H)

GARRIGUES
----, --, --. Wm. Henry, s William & Margaret,
  b 1823,8,6; m Gulielma W. ----- b 1820,9,
  16 (W)
  Ch: Anna H. b 1849, 3, 10
    Alfred
    Linden " 1853, 5, 27 d 1858, 2, 8

1839, 4, 24. Richard H. [Garigus] rocf Marlborough MM, dtd 1839,2,26
1840, 3, 25. Richard H. [Garriguis] dis mcd
1840, 5, 20. Edward, minor, rocf Marlborough
  MM, dtd 1840,4,28
1843, 4, 19. Edward H. [Garrigus] dis joining Baptist Society
1852, 10, 20. William Henry & w, Guli Elma,
  & dt, Ann H., rocf Marlborough MM, dtd
  1852,9,28
1864, 11, 11. William H. dis joining separatists of 1854 (W)
1865, 6, 21. Gulielma dis joining separatists
  of 1854 (W)
1870, 8, 24. Anna H. gct ND MM, Phila., Pa.
  (W)

GARWOOD
1794, 10, 3. Ann b (W)
----, --, --. Daniel b 1779,2,15 d 1867,8,16
  (W)
----, --, --. John W. b 1827,7,8; m Asenith
  ----- b 1825,5,6 (W)
  Ch: Sylvanus P.b 1851, 9, 24
    Elizabeth
     Jane " 1854, 9, 22 d 1875, 5,13
    Lewis J. " 1856, 9, 9
    Anna
     Priscilla " 1861, 6, 18
    Joseph D. " 1865, 7, 6

  Ch: Rachel H. b 1867, 8, 12
1858, 9, 10. Lydia Margaret b (W)

1834, 7, 23. Daniel rocf Middleton MM, dtd
  1834,7,10
1836, 10, 19. Sarah, minor, rocf Middleton
  MM, dtd 1836,9,19
1836, 10, 19. Sarah, minor, rocf Middleton MM,
  dtd 1836,9,19
1837, 6, 21. Daniel dis joining Methodist
  Society
1844, 4, 24. Sarah Levan (form Garwood) dis
  mcd
1858, 7, 21. Daniel & w, Ann, rocf Middleton
  MM, dtd 1858,6,19 (W)
1862, 12, 25. David, Ann & David dis joining
  separatists (W) of 1854
1862, 12, 25. John, Asenath, Sylvanus, Ann
  Eliza, Elizabeth Jane, Adam & Priscilla
  dis joining separatists (W) of 1854
1866, 7, 26. Jesse R. & w, Mira C., & ch,
  Benjamin & Margaret, gct Spring Creek MM,
  Ia.
1866, 7, 26. David C. gct Spring Creek MM,
  Ia.
1871, 2, 22. John W. & w, Asenath, & ch,
  Sylvanus P., Elizabeth Jane, Lewis J.,
  Anna Priscilla, Joseph D. & Rachel H.,
  rocf New Garden MM, dtd 1871,1,26 (W)
1876, 9, 20. John W. & w, Asenath H., & ch,
  Lewis J., Anna P., Joseph D. & Rachel H.,
  gct New Garden MM (W)
1878, 10, 23. Lydia Margaret gct Coal Creek
  MM, Ia. (W)
1907, 3, 20. Sylvanus P. dis jas (W)

GASKILL
----, --, --. Israel b 1772,7,22 d 1836,8,24;
  m Rebecca ----- b 1777,4,17 d 1828,4,2 (W)
  Ch: Nathan
    Roberts b 1817, 9, 1
  Israel m 2nd Elizabeth ----- b 1771,2,8
  (H)

1829, 5, 27. Israel, s Daniel & Huldah, Colum-
  biana Co., O.; m at Salem, Elizabeth
  SHREVE, dt Joshua & Anna, Columbiana Co.,
  O. (H)

1810, 9, 11. Hannah con mcd (dis by Mount
  Holly MM, N. J.)
1810, 10, 18. Hannah recrq
1811, 5, 14. Hannah rocf Mt. Holly MM, N.J.,
  dtd 1811,4,4
1816, 9, 17. Israel recrq
1817, 7, 15. Rebecca (form Reed) dis
1817, 8, 12. Israel dis
1820, 2, 23. Elizabeth (form Pennock) dis mcd
1820; 3, 22. Cert rec for Edward from Upper
  Springfield MM, N. J., dtd 1819,5,5, endorsed to Waynesville MM (Miami MM)
1821, 5, 23. Israel rst in mbrp
1821, 6, 20. Rebecca rst by rq
1824, 7, 21. Nathan, s Israel, recrq

GASKILL, continued

1828, 4, 23. Avaline (form Reed) dis mcd

1828, 7, 30. Israel & s, Nathan R., rocf New Garden MM, dtd 1828,7,24 (H)

1828, 11, 19. Israel dis jH

1829, 11, 25. Elizabeth (form Shreve) dis mcd & jH

1838, 6, 20. Nathan R. dis joining Methodist Society

1840, 6, 24. Nathan dis mcd (H)

1883, 2, 9. Huldah rocf Van Wert MM, O.

GAUSE

----, --, --. Sarah b 1754,9,18 d 1826,9,9 (W)

1810, 2, 21. Drusilla [Gaus] m Abraham Barber

1806, 6, 17. Sarah, w Enoch, rocf Redstone MM, dtd 1806,5,2

1807, 3, 17. Drusilla [Gaus], dt Sarah, recrq

1812, 11, 27. Ann Rebecca rocf New Garden MM, dtd 1812,7,16

1830, 8, 25. Rebecca Ann dis disunity

GHOLD

1885, 2, 6. John C. recrq

GIBBONS

----, --, --. Wm. [Gibbins] b 1799,4,6 d 1843, 8,26; m Mary Ann ----- b 1804,4,12 (W)
    Ch: Isaiah H. b 1831, 5, 6
        Benjamin F." 1833, 2, 12
        David   " 1834, 6, 8
        Thomas   " 1836, 4, 1
        Samuel W. " 1841, 8, 11

----, --, --. Charles E., s Wm. & Maria, b 1862,7,10; m Mary GILBERT, dt Benjamin & Lydia (Cope), b 1831,11,7 d 1908,1,2 bur Friends Bur. Ground, Sewickley, Pa. (W)

----, --, --. Dillon b 1844,1,22; m Mary G. ----- b 1831,11,7 d 1908,1,2 (W)

1818, 12, 2. Edward J. b (H)

1819, 6, 18. Mary Ann b (H)

1860, 1, 23. Ellen b (H)

1829, 1, 21. Mary Ann rocf Uwchland MM, dtd 1828,10,9

1830, 8, 25. Samuel [Gibbens] rocf Sadsbury MM, dtd 1830,6,8 (an approved minister) (H)

1830, 11, 24. Hugh, Edward, Isaac & Samuel, ch Samuel, rocf Sadsbury MM, dtd 1830,11, 2 (H)

1831, 3, 23. Lydia rocf Sadsbury MM, dtd 1831, 1,4 (H)

1831, 5, 25. Cert rec for HughJudge, Edward, Isaac & Samuel, ch Samuel, from Sadsbury MM, dtd 1831,2,1, endorsed to Upper Springfield MM

1833, 7, 24. Lydia Hoopes (form Gibbons) con mcd (H)

1834, 7, 23. Hugh-Judge, Isaac & Samuel, ch Samuel, rocf Upper Springfield MM, dtd 1834,6,28

1841, 5, 19. Hugh dis jas (H)

1843, 6, 21. Isaac H. dis disunity

1843, 6, 21. Samuel, Jr. dis joining Baptist Society

1845, 12, 24. Edward gct Middleton MM (H)

1848, 3, 22. Mary Ann Hardman (form Gibbons) dis mcd

1856, 1, 23. Isaiah K. dis mcd (W)

1861, 9, 25. Benjamin F. dis disunity (W)

1863, 2, 25. David dis disunity (W)

1872, 1, 24. Thomas D. dis mcd (W)

1872, 2, 21. Samuel dis serving as a volunteer in army (W)

1878, 9, 25. Dillon rocf Somerset MM, dtd 1878,8,22 (W)

1911, 12, 20. Dillon dis (W)

1918, 5, 22. Charles E. rocf Somerset MM, O., dtd 1918,3,21 (W)

1927, 6, 22. Edith Glass dropped from mbrp

GIBBS

1915, 3, 1. Florence May [Gibb], dt Oscar & Lucy, b (G)

1932, 12, 29. Florence May recrq

GIBSON

----, --, --. Sarah b 1755,--,-- d 1840,6,8 (W)

1840, 4, 1. Prudence H. m Nathan WHITE

1814, 8, 16. Catharine recrq

1820, 6, 21. Aaron rocf Evesham MM, N. J., dtd 1819,5,7

1824, 5, 19. Asa & w, Mary, & ch, Sarah H. & Lettitia, rocf Evesham MM, N. J., dtd 1824,3,5

1824, 6, 23. Sarah rocf Chester MM, N. J., dtd 1824,3,4

1827, 10, 24. Sarah gct Chester MM, Ind.

1830, 5, 6. Aaron gct Upper Springfield MM

1833, 4, 24. Sarah rocf Chester MM, Ind., dtd 1832,11,21

1838, 10, 24. Ruth R. recrq (H)

1839, 9, 25. Prudence recrq

1841, 5, 19. Martha rocf New Garden MM, Ind., dtd 1841,3,25

1843, 9, 20. Martha gct Marlborough MM

1844, 10, 23. Ruth R. dis disunity (H)

1911, 12, 20. Kenneth rec in mbrp

1915, 11, 24. Keith recrq

1918, 5, 22. Ethel dropped from mbrp

1920, 3, 24. Myrtle & Kenneth gct Cleveland MM

GILBERT

----, --, --. Benjamin, s Abner & Ann (Cooper) b 1800,12,13 d 1887,4,7 bur Sewickley Bur. Gr., Pa.; m Lydia COPE, dt Samuel & Sarah (Willets), b 1808,3,12 d 1882,8,26 (or 1882,8,27 bur Friends Bur. Gr., Sewickley, Pa. (W)
    Ch: Sarah Ann b 1829, 10, 27 d 1913, 6,20

GILBERT, continued
      bur Friends Bur. Gr., Sewickley, Pa.
      Ch: Samuel C. b 1839, 4, 19 d 1908, 9,26
          (or 1908,9,25) bur Friends Bur. Gr.,
          Sewickley, Pa.
        Susan   b 1842, 3, 31
1882, 3, 29. Susan m Jesse EDGERTON (W)
----, --, --. James m Rachel C. WICKERSHAM, dt
   David & Rebecca B. (Holloway), b 1863,4,3
   d 1899,7,-- bur East Springfield, Pa. (W)
1903, 10, 22. Rachel C. m Elisha LLEWELLYN
----, --, --. Howard Kent, s Wilmer & Adda,
   b 1888,11,22; m Mary C. INGRAM, dt Jesse
   & Matilda, b 1890,3,27 (W)
   Ch: Jane
       Audrey   b 1921, 2, 6
      John
       Lowell   " 1931, 8, 5

1808, 4, 12. Ann rocf Goose Creek MM, Va., dtd
   1807,11,26
1873, 3, 20. Abner & w, Anzonetta, & ch,
   Mary, Dillwin & Gertie, rocf Grove MM,
   Ind., dtd 1873,4,12
1876, 5, 25. Abner & w, Anzonetta, & ch,
   Mary, Dilwin, Gurtie & Edith, gct Grove
   MM, Ind.
1927, 5, 25. Kent & Jane recrq

GILLAM
1922, 2, 22. Mary relrq

GLASS
1915, 11, 24. Edith recrq

GLOVER
1824, 6, 23. Mary recrq

GOLD
1858, 12, 2. John C. b (G)

GOLDY
----, --, --. Edward S., s J. S. & D. C., b
   1876,1,2 d 1930,3,1; m Jennie B. FINERAN,
   dt Martin, b 1875,7,2 (G)

GONGWER
1881, 5, 26. Catharine & Rosa recrq

GOODMAN
1890, 2, 20. Ella gct Gilead MM, O.

GORDON
1911, 10, 25. Carrie relrq

GOSLIN
----, --, --. Wm. m Priscilla COPE, dt Louis &
   Hannah Y. (Hollingsworth), b 1865,6,6

1893, 8, 23. Priscilla C. (form Cope) dis
   mcd (W)

GOVE
----, --, --. Moses D. b 1816,5,28; m Sally
   B. ------ b 1823,9,18 (W)
   Ch: Frederic
      Dennis   " 1844, 9, 3
      Anna Ellen " 1846, 11, 9
      John
      Howard   " 1849, 10, 7

1847, 9, 22. Moses D. & w, Sallie B., & ch,
   Frederick D. & Anna Ellen, rocf Short
   Creek MM, dtd 1847,6,22
1853, 9, 21. Moses D. & w, Sally B., & ch,
   Frederick D., Anna Ellen & John Howard,
   gct Short Creek MM

GRATE
1880, 10, 11. George W. & w, Lydia M., recrq

GREEN
1849, 11, 28. Daniel, s John & Mary, Columbiana Co., O., b 1804,2,26; m at Salem, Esther STANLEY, dt Moses & Susanna, Columbiana Co., O., b 1811,7,23 (W)
   Ch: Mary S.   b 1852, 5, 12

1816, 7, 16. Thomas [Greene] rocf New Garden
   MM, dtd 1816,5,16
1841, 12, 22. Daniel rocf SD MM, Phila., Pa.,
   dtd 1841,11,24
1846, 7, 22. Daniel gct Cincinnati MM
1849, 8, 22. Daniel rocf Cincinnati MM, dtd
   1849,6,14
1865, 9, 20. Daniel & w, Esther, & ch, Mary
   S., gct Hickory Grove MM, Ia. (W)
1911, 12, 20. Jesse May rec in mbrp

GREENFIELD
1920, 3, 24. Mary & Verlin rec in mbrp

GREGG
1850, 5, 23. Lot, s Caleb & Hannah, Belmont
   Co., O.; m at house of Joseph Bailey, Hannah BAILEY, dt Joseph & Elizabeth, Columbiana Co., O. (H)

1850, 12, 25. Hannah gct Plainfield MM (H)

GREINER
1847, 3, 24. Rebecca Ann (form Thomas) dis
   mcd

GRENNELL
1868, 9, 23. Priscilla (form Bonsall) dis mcd
   (W)

GREWELL
1880, 8, 26. John P., s Timothy & Alice, Mahaska Co., Ia.; m at Salem, Phebe F.
   PAINTER, dt Amos & Hannah F. Fawcett, Columbiana Co., O. (W)

1807, 9, 15. Timothy & w, Alice, & ch, Sa-

GREWELL, continued
    rah, Mary & Elizabeth Clemens, rocf South
    River MM, Va., dtd 1807,5,9
1836, 10, 19. Thomas P. Stanley gct Marl-
    borough MM, to m Hannah Grewell
1880, 6, 23. John P. [Gruwell] rocf Upper
    Springfield MM, dtd 1880,5,21 (W)
1884, 6, 25. John P. [Gruwell] & w, Phebe
    F., gct Upper Springfield MM (W)
1905, 5, 24. Phebe F. rocf Upper Springfield
    MM, O., dtd 1905,4,21 (W)
1908, 10, 21. Phebe F. [Gruell] gct Coal
    Creek MM, Ia. (W)

GRIES
1873, 4, 24. Nathan & w, Mary Ann, rocf Cen-
    tre MM, Pa., dtd 1873,2,6 (H)

GRIFFITH
1803, 7, 15. Mary b (H)
1822, 10, 22. Eliza Jane b (H)
----, --, --. Reuben b 1774,2,3; m Hannah
    ----- b 1781,7,5 (H)
    Ch: Sarah
        Emaline   b 1824, 12, 13
        Rachel   " 1826, 12, 10
1844, 1, 28. Keturah P. d (W)
1871, 9, 10. Amos d (G)

1808, 5, 17. Reuben & w, Elizabeth, & ch,
    Ann Moore, Rebecca, Elizabeth Mary & Ka-
    turah, rocf Gunpowder MM, dtd 1808,2,24
1818, 7, 14. Cert rec for Evan & fam from
    Goshen MM, Pa., dtd 1818,4,29, endorsed
    to Short Creek MM
1818, 7, 14. Cert rec for Eleanor from
    Goshen MM, Pa., dtd 1818,4,29, endorsed
    to Short Creek MM
1820, 10, 25. Cert rec for Charles William from
    .Goshen MM, Pa., dtd 1818,4,29, endorsed to
    Short Creek MM
1820, 10, 25. Rebecca rocf Short Creek MM, dtd
    1820,5,23, endorsed by New Garden MM,
    1820,8,24
1821, 2, 21. Rebecca Painter (form Griffith)
    dis mcd
1821, 7, 25. Keturah, minor, rocf Concord MM,
    dtd 1821,2,21
1839, 12, 25. Reuben & w, Hannah, & ch, Sarah
    Emaline & Rachel, rocf Radnor MM, Pa., dtd
    1839,10,10 (H)
1841, 4, 21. Emeline & Rachel, ch Reuben &
    Hannah, rocf WD MM, Phila., Pa., dtd 1841,
    1,20
1846, 12, 23. Sarah Emeline dis jH
1846, 12, 23. Rachel dis jH
1854, 6, 22. Sarah Emeline gct Wilmington
    MM, Del. (H)   [(H)
1854, 6, 22. Rachel H. gct Wilmington MM, Del.
1866, 9, 20. Oscar J. gct Minneapolis MM,
    Minn.
1868, 2, 20. Amos T. & w, Mary E., & dt, Lucy
    Amelia, gct Smithfield MM

1872, 5, 23. Edith gct Short Creek MM
1876, 7, 20. Israel gct Marietta MM, Ia. (H)
1878, 4, 24. Cynthia dis jas (W)
1878, 4, 24. Emmor dis jas (W)
1879, 10, 23. Samuella relrq (H)
1882, 2, 8. William H. & Nettie recrq
1884, 3, 20. John recrq
1887, 2, 24. William dropped from mbrp
1890, 6, 26. Nettie & s, Harry, dropped from
    mbrp

GRIMMESY
1845, 8, 20. Lucinda [Grimacy] (form Painter)
    dis mcd
1845, 9, 23. Lucinda (form Painter) dis mou
    (H)
1877, 8, 8. Lydia Ann [Grimmisy] recrq

GRISSELL
1808, 3, 17. Rachel m Joseph BLACKLEDGE
1847, 4, 27. Thomas E. [Grisell], s Joseph &
    Letitia, Columbiana Co., O.; m at house of
    Oliver Griffith, Mary A. Wierman, dt Alex-
    ander & Mary, Adams Co., Pa. (H)

GRIST
1807, 4, 14. John rocf Redstone MM, dtd 1807,
    4,3
1815, 1, 17. John [Ghrist] dis mcd

GRONER
1904, 6, 16. Naomi Derr, dt Edgar & Lillian,
    b (G)

GROVES
1908, 12, 18. Chalmer W., s Edward & Ada, b
    (G)

1884, 2, 21. Anna M. [Grove] (form Garretson)
    con mcd (H)
1925, 3, 25. Chalmer W. recrq
1932, 6, 29. Chalmers dropped from mbrp

GRUBB
1867, 10, 24. Edith P. gct Short Creek MM

GUINDON
1896, 9, 7. Lydia M., dt Francis T. & Susan-
    nah H. (Battey), b (W)

1922, 1, 25. Lydia M. rocf Nantucket MM, R.I.
    (W)
1925, 2, 25. Lydia M. gct Fairhope MM, Ala.
    (W)

HAGGERTY
1883, 11, 7. John recrq
1886, 10, 21. John & ch dropped from mbrp

HAINES
1853, 6, 22. Elizabeth, dt John & Fannie
    Saynor, b (G)
1869, 4, 14. Eli d (G)

HAINES, continued

----, --, --. Alfred S. m Edith HAYES, dt
Chas. I. & Elma (Fawcett), b 1876,9,3 (W)

1827, 4, 25. Angelina [Hains] (form Reed) dis
mcd
1833, 10, 20. Joseph [Hanes] & w, Mary, & ch,
Esther Ann, rocf Plainfield MM, dtd 1833,
11,22 (H)
1836, 10, 19. Joseph & w, Mary, & ch, Esther
Ann & Rachel, gct Stillwater MM (H)
1867, 10, 23. Sarah (form Painter) dis mcd (W)
1909, 6, 23. Edith Hayes gct New Garden MM,
Pa. (W)

HALDERMAN

1832, 4, 25. David & w, Ann, & ch, Jacob,
Elizabeth, Ann, Martha, David, Susannah,
Tamar, Joseph & Mary, rocf Sandy Spring MM,
dtd 1832,3,23
1833, 3, 20. Benjamin rocf Sandy Spring MM,
dtd 1833,12,21
1834, 4, 23. David & w, Ann, & ch, Ann, Martha, David, Susannah, Tamer, Joseph & Mary,
gct Sandy Spring MM
1834, 6, 25. Benjamin [Holderman] dis mcd
1837, 4, 19. Elizabeth Antrim (form Halder-
nan) con mou
1838, 4, 25. David & w, Ann, & ch, David, Susannah, Tamor, Joseph & Mary, rocf Sandy
Spring MM, dtd 1838,3,23
1838, 4, 25. Martha rocf Sandy Spring MM, dtd
1838,3,23
1840, 4, 22. David [Holderman] & w, Ann, &
ch, David, Susannah, Joseph, James & Mary,
gct Sandy Spring MM
1840, 4, 22. Martha gct Sandy Spring MM
1842, 8, 24. Jacob & w, Margery, rocf Sandy
Spring MM, dtd 1842,7,22
1842, 8, 24. David, Jr. rocf Sandy Spring
MM, dtd 1842,7,22
1844, 1, 24. David [Holdaman], Jr. gct Sandy
Spring MM
1845, 5, 21. Jacob [Haldeman] & fam gct Sandy
Spring MM

HALL

----, --, --. ----- m Mary ----- b 1812,1,11
d 1897,8,13 (W) (Mary later w of Robert
Miller)
Ch: Martha   b 1849, 9, 1
    Sarah R.   " 1851, 4, 4
    Deborah D. " 1852, 9, 24
1857, 7, 1. Wilson, s Nathan P. & Rachel,
Jefferson Co., O.; m at Salem, Sina STRAT-
TON, dt Joshua & Rachel, Columbiana Co.,
O. (W)
1876, 5, 31. Martha m Charles GAMBLE (W)
1880, 5, 26. Chas. P., s Nathan R. & Merel,
Columbiana Co., O.; m at Salem, Melissa
COPE, dt Dawsey & Sarah, Columbiana Co.,
O. (W)
1903, 9, 9. Martha F. (Moore), b (W)

----, --, --. Wilmer L., s Lindley & Millicent (Bailey), b 1881,2,15; m Ida STANTON,
dt Benjamin & Elizabeth (Plummer), b 1881,
7,22 (W)
Ch: Dorothy
    Lucile   b 1906, 2, 2
    Howard
    Stanton   " 1908, 8, 26
    Gertrude M." 1912, 2, 22
1908, 12, 13. Heil S., s Linton & Ann W., Columbiana Co., O.; m at Salem, Abigail
BRIGGS, dt Henry & Talitha, Columbiana
Co., O. (W)
1916, 3, 23. Howard T., s Abner T. & Anna
M., Columbiana Co., O.; m at Salem, Anna
Florence COPE, dt Albert M. & Phebe (Ashton), b 1893,1,6 (W)
1919, 6, 26. Herbert W., s Abner T. & Anna
M., Columbiana Co., O.; m at Salem, Mar-
tha STARBUCK, dt Benj. F. & Anna M.
(Llewellyn), Columbiana Co., O., b 1895,
5,28 (W)
1923, 6, 27. Allan, s Abner J. & Anna M.,
Columbiana Co., O.; m at Salem, Martha
Frances MOORE, dt Chas. & Alma Blanche
(West) FISH, b 1903,9,9 (W)
Dt: Margaret
    Louise   b 1924, 6, 3

1857, 10, 21. Sina gct Short Creek MM (W)
1874, 4, 22. Martha, Sarah R. & Deborah D.
rocf New Garden MM, dtd 1874,3,26 (W)
1878, 7, 22. Deborah D. French (form Hall)
dis mcd (W)
1880, 11, 24. Melissa C. gct Middleton MM (W)
1881, 10, 19. Sarah R. Sawyer (form Hall) dis
mcd (W)
1909, 3, 24. Abigail B. gct Middleton MM, O.
(W)
1916, 3, 22. Howard T. prcf Middleton MM, dtd
1916,3,18, to m Anna F. Cope (W)
1916, 6, 21. Anna F. gct Stillwater MM, O.(W)
1920, 9, 22. Martha S. gct Middleton MM (W)
1924, 4, 23. Wilmer L. rocf Short Creek MM,
O., dtd 1923,3,18 (W)
1924, 4, 23. Ida Stanton & ch, Dorothy L.,
Howard E. & Gertrude M., rocf Stillwater
MM, O., dtd 1924,3,19 (W)
1927, 3, 23. Martha Frances gct Middleton MM
(W)

HAMILTON
1856, 8, 21. Oliver dis mcd
1869, 7, 22. James [Hambleton] gct Green
Plain MM (H)

HAMLIN
----, --, --. John b 1863,3,8; m Elizabeth -
----- b 1775,5,24 (W)
Ch: Sally   b 1795, 10, 28
    Phariba   " 1797, 9, 30
    Lydia   " 1800, 8, 5
    Martha   " 1804, 7, 11

HAMLIN, continued
        Ch: Mary   b 1807, 2, 9
            John   " 1810, 2, 5

1807, 6, 11. John & w, Elizabeth, & ch, Sally,
    Pharaby, Lydia, Martha & Mary, rocf Black-
    water MM, dtd 1807,3,25
1808, 6, 14. William rocf Black Water MM,
    Va., dtd 1807,5,23
1810, 8, 14. Elizabeth recrq
1810, 10, 16. William, Mary & Joshua, ch
    Charles, dec, rocf Upper MM, Va., dtd
    1810,12,16
1811, 2, 12. Susannah, Charles, William &
    Stephen, ch William & Elizabeth, recrq

HAMMET
1823, 8, 20. Sarah recrq
1828, 3, 19. Sarah gct Salem MM, N. J.

HAMMOND
1772, 2, 2. Ruth b (H)

1828, 7, 23. Ruth rocf Monallen MM, dtd 1827,
    11,21 (H)
1860, 1, 26. Hannah rocf Smithfield MM, dtd
    1859,11,21
1860, 3, 22. Amanda recrq
1860, 4, 26. Jane L. (form Leach) con mcd
1860, 8, 22. Jane L. gct Westland MM, Ia.
1861, 4, 25. Hannah gct Smithfield MM
1861, 4, 25. Amanda gct Smithfield MM
1871, 11, 20. Catharine rocf Smithfield MM
1872, 2, 7. Catharine rocf Smithfield MM,
    dtd 1871,11,20
1872, 6, 20. Anna recrq
1880, 5, 5. Catharine & Anna B. gct Rose
    Hill MM, Ia.

HAMPTON
1920, 4, 28. Russell B., s Clinton E. & Sarah,
    Columbiana Co., O.; m Mary Ellen SATTERTH-
    WAIT, dt Wm. D. & Ida A. (Newlin), b 1898,
    8,23 (W)

1920, 6, 23. Mary E. gct New Garden MM (W)

HANCOCK
1875, 5, 2. Hannah b (W)
1876, 11, 28. Wm. d bur Westland, Pa.
1897, 12, 31. Sabina d bur Westland, Pa. (w of
    Wm.)

1884, 4, 23. Jesse dis mcd (W)
1884, 12, 24. Mary Millikin (form Hancock) dis
    mcd (W)
1889, 4, 24. George dis mcd (W)

HANLY
1823, 8, 1. Benjamin rocf Middleton MM, dtd
    1823,5,19

HANEY
1917, 10, 24. Sarah dropped from mbrp

HANNA
1808, 7, 14. Thomas, s Robert & Catharine,
    Columbiana Co., O.; m at Lexington, Anne
    FISHER, dt Joseph & Ann, Stark Co., O.
1852, 8, 27. Benjamin, s Robert & Catharine,
    Columbiana Co., O.; m at house of Hannah
    R. Cope, Hannah R. COPE, dt Jesse & Eliza-
    beth Kersey, Columbiana Co., O. (H)
1855, 9, 21. Hannah K. m Stephen FISH (H)

1808, 7, 12. Thomas [Hannah] rocf Middleton
    MM, dtd 1808,7,9
1809, 1, 17. Thomas & w, Anne, gct Middleton
    MM
1815, 2, 14. Benjamin & w, Rachel, & ch,
    Joshua, Leonard, Lewis, Zalinda, Robert,
    Tryphena & Tryphosea, rocf Middleton MM,
    dtd 1815,1,12
1819, 5, 19. Benjamin & w, Rachel, & ch,
    Joshua, Leonard, Levi, Zalinda, Robert,
    Triphenia, Rebecca & Thomas, gct New Gar-
    den MM

HAPGOOD
1848, 4, 19. Rebecca A. rocf Middleton MM,
    dtd 1848,3,16 (H)

HARDMAN
1848, 3, 22. Mary Ann (form Gibbons) dis mcd

HARLEN
----, --, --. Joseph b 1781,9,10; m Hannah
    ----- b 1782,10,26 (W)
        Ch: Sarah Ann b 1818, 3, 31
            Samuel   " 1820, 12, 15
            Joseph   " 1822, 2, 24
1839, 8, 22. Sarah Ann [Harlan] m John TRAGO,
    Jr. (H)

1817, 1, 14. Joseph [Harlan] & w, Hannah,
    rocf Kennet MM, Pa., dtd 1816,12,3
1828, 7, 30. Joseph [Harlon] rocf New Garden
    MM, dtd 1828,7,24 (H)
1828, 9, 24. Hannah [Harlon] recrq (H)
1828, 9, 24. Sarah Ann, Samuel & Joseph [Har-
    lon], ch Joseph & w recrq (H)
1840, 2, 19. Joseph gct Kennet MM, Pa. (H)
1841, 5, 19. Joseph [Harlan] rocf Kennett
    MM, Pa., dtd 1841,4,6 (H)
1843, 2, 22. Joseph [Harlan] dis mcd (H)
1843, 5, 24. Mary Ann [Harlan] (form Barber)
    dis mcd (H)

HARRIS
----, --, --. Jacob b 1779,10,19; m Mary -----
    b 1786,6,5 (H)
        Ch: John   b 1808, 10, 9
            Samuel   " 1810, 11, 25
            Mary Ann   " 1812, 12, 31
            Silas   " 1815, 2, 19

HARRIS, Jacob & Mary, continued
 Ch: Rachel   b 1817, 5, 12
   Rebecca " 1819, 9, 5
   Ellen   " 1821, 10, 28
   Joel   " 1824, 2, 17
   Wm.   " 1827, 3, 6 d 1837, 4, 2
   Jacob Ben-
    jamin " 1830, 2, 12
1819, 4, 6. Emily H. b (G)
1839, 1, 30. David F., s Joseph & Hepsibah,
 b 1780,8,17 d 1848,10,13 bur Salem; m 2nd
 Hannah WARRINGTON, dt Abraham & Rachel,
 Columbiana Co., O., b 1791,4,1 d 1865,5,4
 bur Salem (W)
1839, 11, 6. Mary Ann m Enos HILLES (H)
1842, 3, 30. Silas, s Jacob & Mary, Columbi-
 ana Co., O.; m at Salem, Ann HILLIS, dt
 Robert & Jane, Columbiana Co., O. (H)
----, --, --. Enoch & Emily (G)
 Ch: James A. b 1844, 10, 6
   Rebecca " 1848, 8, 13
   Enoch   " 1850, 11, 8
   Rees   " 1852, 11, 16
   Sarah   " 1855, 1, 1
   Mary   " 1857, 4, 22
   Ruthanna " 1859, 8, 7
   Linley   " 1864, 8, 4
1915, 10, 30. Marion, s C. E. & Alma J., Co-
 lumbiana Co., O.; m at home of Gertrude E.
 Richards, Jessie RICHARDS, dt Stephen B. &
 Gertrude E., Columbiana Co., O. (H)

1805, 10, 15. Isaiah rocf Coursound MM, N. C.,
 dtd 1804,7,28, endorsed by Concord MM,
 1805,9,24
1807, 3, 17. Sally recrq
1807, 3, 17. Anna, Chalkley, Carney & Nathan,
 ch Sally, recrq
1822, 6, 19. David F. rocf Creek MM, N. Y.,
 dtd 1819,6,18
1834, 5, 21. Jacob & w, Mary, & ch, Silas,
 Rachel, Rebecca, Ellen, Joel G., William &
 Jacob B. rocf Monallen MM, Pa., dtd 1834,4,
 24 (H)
1834, 5, 21. Mary Ann rocf Monallen MM, Pa.,
 dtd 1834,4,24 (H)
1836, 8, 24. Samuel rocf Providence MM, R. I.,
 dtd 1836,6,29
1837, 6, 21. Nathan & w, Hannah, & ch, Jane
 W., Samuel Westly, Anna Maria, Elizabeth,
 Rebecca & Jesse, rocf Monallin MM, Pa.,
 dtd 1837,5,17 (H)
1838, 2, 21. Samuel gct Upper Smithfield MM,
 R. I.
1838, 4, 25. Mary (form Trescott) dis mcd
1838, 7, 25. John dis mcd (H)
1839, 8, 21. Samuel con mcd (H)
1840, 3, 25. Esther C. rocf New Garden MM,
 dtd 1840,2,20 (H)
1845, 9, 23. Ruth Anna rocf Monallen MM, dtd
 1845,7,23 (H)
1847, 4, 21. Ruth Anna Trescott (form Harris)
 con mcd (H)

1850, 9, 25. Ann (form Hillis) dis mcd & jH
1862, 9, 25. Emily M. & ch, James A., Rebecca,
 Enoch, Reece, Sarah, Mary & Ruth Anna,
 rocf Short Creek MM
1862, 12, 25. Hannah W. dis joining separatists
 (W) of 1854
1865, 10, 26. James dis joining in military
 service

HARRISON
----, --, --. Mary Elizabeth, dt Benj. & Mary
 (Dixon), b 1844,7,1 d 1916,10,--

1862, 12, 25. Latham, Eliza, Benjamin, Mary,
 Mary Elizabeth, Lucina Ann, Matilda Ellen,
 John Franklin & Sabina Jane, dis joining
 separatists (W) of 1854
1866, 11, 22. William & w, Rebecca, & ch, Mary
 & William Henry, gct Spring Creek MM, Ia.
1866, 11, 22. Lydia M. gct Spring Creek MM,Ia.
1911, 9, 20. Mary Elizabeth rocf Middleton
 MM, O., dtd 1911,8,19 (W)
1933, 12, 30. Stella Clark gct Alliance MM

HARRY
1872, 11, 21. Sarah gct Clear Creek MM, Ill.
 (H)

HARSHMAN
1873, 10, 1. Mary M., dt Robert & Janet Auld,
 b (G)

1925, 3, 25. Mary M. recrq

HARTLEY
1843, 8, 23. Martha rocf Soleberry MM, Pa.,
 dtd 1843,4,4, endorsed by New Garden MM
 (H)
1843, 8, 23. Letitia & s, Henry, rocf Soleberry MM, Pa., dtd 1843,4,4, endorsed by
 New Garden MM
1843, 8, 23. Letitia, Jr. rocf Soleberry MM,
 Pa., dtd 1843,4,4, endorsed by New Garden
 MM
1843, 8, 23. William L. rocf Wrightstown MM,
 Pa., dtd 1843,4,5, endorsed by New Garden
 MM (H)
1844, 7, 24. Joseph [Hartly] rocf Makefield
 MM, Pa., dtd 1844,4,4 (H)

HARTZ
----, --, --. William A., s Alfred, b 1894,5,
 27; m ----- dt J. M. Young, b 1896,12,23
 (G)

1874, 6, 25. Alfred [Hart] recrq
1925, 3, 25. William Albert & w recrq

HATHAWAY
1824, 11, 24. Anna (form Varney) dis mcd

HAVEN
1923, 1, 24. Marion recrq

HAVILAND

----, --, --. Harry C., s Lindley & Anna, b
    1885,11,4; m Lucinda M. KNISELY, dt John
    W. & Sarah, b 1884,5,10 (G)
    Dt: Catharine
        Mae   b 1916, 3, 4

1870, 8, 10. Joseph & w, Lydia H., rocf Nine
    Partners MM, N. Y., dtd 1870,6,16
1877, 5, 9. Joseph gct Nine Partners MM,
    N. Y.
1917, 11, 21. Charles A., Ola G. & Alma V.
    relrq
1918, 8, 18. Alice relrq

HAWKS
1855, 9, 3. Wm. [Hawkes] d (G)
1857, 3, 5. Martha S. m John STANLEY

1855, 1, 25. William & w, Martha S., & dt,
    Lydia Maria, rocf Salem MM, Mass., dtd
    1855,1,11
1857, 4, 23. Lydia Maria gct Upper Spring-
    field MM
1870, 8, 25. Isaiah Jones recrq
1870, 8, 25. Elvira W. recrq
1873, 3, 20. Isaiah J. & w, Elvira W., gct
    Cedar Creek MM, Richmond, Va.

HAWLEY
1758, 2, 4. Hannah b (or 1759,3,-- (H)
1825, 2, 2. Benjamin, s Caleb & Hannah, Co-
    lumbiana Co., O., b 1790,7,20; m at Salem,
    Mary DAVIS, dt Samuel & Mary, Columbiana
    Co., O., b 1791,8,10 (H)
    Ch: Eliza   b 1825, 12, 28
        Sarah   " 1828, 2, 2
        Samuel D. " 1830, 5, 8
        Wm.   " 1833, 12, 24

1823, 4, 23. Jesse rocf Middleton MM, dtd
    1823,4,21
1823, 4, 23. Hannah, Sr. & Hannah, Jr. rocf
    Middleton MM, dtd 1823,4,21
1826, --, --. Elisha gct Marlborough MM
1826, --, --. Jesse gct Marlborough MM
1828, 7, 30. Benjamin & w, Mary, & dt, Eliza
    & Sarah, rocf New Garden MM, dtd 1828,7,24
1828, 7, 30. Hannah rocf New Garden MM, dtd
    1828,7,24 (H)
1828, 8, 20. Benjamin dis jH
1828, 8, 20. Hannah dis jH
1828, 8, 20. Mary dis jH
1835, 12, 23. Hannah gct Marlborough MM (H)
1844, 7, 24. Eliza dis jH
1846, 12, 23. Eliza Thomas (form Hawley) con
    mcd (H)
1848, 6, 21. Sarah dis jH
1887, 4, 21. Robert rocf Springdale MM, Ia.,
    dtd 1887,3,19

HAWORTH
1931, 4, 20. Bonnie Lou, dt Edgar & Thelma,

b (G)

1866, 1, 25. Mary E. (form Leach) con mcd
1866, 2, 22. Mary E. [Heaworth] (form Leach)
    gct Le Grand MM, Ia.
1923, 10, 24. Charles E. & w, Frances, & ch,
    Edgar G. & Henrietta, rocf Van Wert MM, O.
1925, 3, 25. Asenath rocf Van Wert MM, O.
1928, 8, 15. Rev. & fam gct Portsmouth MM
1928, 8, 15. Asenath gct Miami MM, Okla.

HAYES
1813, 10, 20. Mordecai, s Mordecai & Ann, Ches-
    ter Co., Pa.; m at Lexington, Esther LOGUE,
    dt Stephen & Hannah, Stark Co., O.
1855, 5, 2. Charles I., s Israel & Lydia
    (Lord), b 1828,4,8 d 1898,7,9 bur Friends
    Burying Ground, Salem; m at Salem, Debo-
    rah FAWCETT, dt Jehu & Abigail (Williams)
    b 1834,10,26 d 1868,10,30 bur Friends Bur.
    Gr., Salem, O. (W)
    Ch: Lydia
        Ellen   b 1856, 12, 18
        Mary   " 1858, 5, 30 d 1898, 5,30
        Lizetta " 1862, 1, 3 " 1902, 4,27
        Albert   " 1864, 5, 18
        Sarah   " 1865, 6, 13
        Deborah " 1868, 10, 23
    Charles I. m 2nd 1870,10,5 at Salem, Elina
    (Elma) FAWCETT, dt Levi & Mary (Johnson),
    b 1835,7,23 d 1915,8,25 (W)
----, --, --. Albert, s Chas. I. & Deborah
    (Fawcett), b 1864,5,18; m Myra D. BRANSON,
    dt David & Sarah (Holloway), b 1869,3,8
    (W)
    Ch: Wm.
        Donald   b 1894, 10, 10
        Lillian
        Rebecca " 1896, 6, 18
        Virginia " 1899, 10, 24 d 1917, 6, 2
        bur Friends Bur. Gr., Salem, O.
1880, 6, 2. Mary m Edwin COOKE (W)
1893, 10, 26. Deborah F. m Chas. D. CONROW (W)
1901, 6, 26. Edith m Alfred SHARPLESS (W)
1902, 8, 27. Sarah m Edward P. FAWCETT (W)

1813, 12, 14. Esther [Hays] gct Bradford MM,
    Pa.
1855, 3, 21. Charles I. [Hays] rocf Salem
    MM, N. J., dtd 1855,1,31 (W)
1862, 12, 25. Charles I., Deborah, Lydia El-
    len, Tazetta & Mary [Hays] dis joining
    separatists (W) of 1854
1891, 7, 22. Albert [Hays] gct Flushing MM,
    to m Myra D. Branson (W)
1892, 1, 20. Myra D. rocf Flushing MM, dtd
    1891,12,24 (W)
1915, 8, 25. Elma gct Birmingham MM, Pa. (W)

HAYHURST
----, --, --. Wm. b 1792,2,2; m Jane -----
    b 1792,8,26 (H)
    Ch: Lydia   b 1815, 7, 25

HAYHURST, Wm. & Jane, continued
    Ch: Susan   b 1817, 4, 4
        Bezabel   " 1819, 2, 2
        Elizabeth " 1821, 4, 10
        Thos. Math-
          er   " 1823, 12, 1
        Mary   " 1826, 2, 12
        Wm.   " 1828, 2, 28
        Sarah   " 1830, 5, 20
        Joseph   " 1833, 8, 11
        Ezra   " 1838, 6, 26
1838, 5, 3. Susan m Israel COURTNEY (H)

1823, 10, 22. William & w, Jane, & ch, Lydia,
    Susannah, Bezabel & Elizabeth, rocf Muncy
    MM, Pa., dtd 1823,8,20
1828, 11, 19. William & w, Jane, & ch, Lydia,
    Susan, Bazebel, Elizabeth, Thomas, Mary &
    William, mbrp transferred from Upper
    Springfield by rq
1838, 4, 25. Israel Cortney prcf New Garden MM,
    dtd ----,3,22, to m Susan Hayhurst (H)

HEACOCK
----, --, --. Nathan b 1783,4,16; m Dinah ----
    b 1781,10,24 (H)
    Ch: Amos D.   b 1808, 10, 27 d 1841,11,18
        Edwin   " 1811, 4, 19
        Jane D.   " 1812, 8, 12 d 1837, 1,29
        Asenath   " 1814, 6, 26
        Milton   " 1815, 12, 23
        Barton   " 1818, 1, 13
        Uriah An-
          trim   " 1819, 6, 14
        Elias H.   " 1821, 1, 6
        Enos   " 1822, 9, 5
        Josiah
          Wilson   " 1824, 7, 28
        Tacy   " 1827, 4, 22
1826, 3, 29. Martha m Wm. KENNETT
1832, 5, 3. Jane D. m Ezra BORTON (H)
1838, 9, 27. Milton, s Nathan & Dinah, Colum-
    biana Co., O., b 1815,12,23; m at West MH,
    Rebecca THOMAS, dt John & Rebecca, Columbi-
    anna Co., O., b 1820,9,1 (H)
    Ch: Sarah Jane b 1839, 11, 13
        Ann Eliza " 1841, 5, 23
1839, 11, 14. Burton [Haycock], s Nathan & Di-
    nah, Columbiana Co., O.; m at West MH, Ra-
    chel BARBER, dt Isaac & Ales, Columbiana
    Co., O. (H)
1841, 1, 28. Asenath m Nathan THOMAS (H)
1843, 3, 2. Uriah, s Nathan & Dinah, Colum-
    biana Co., O.; m at West MH, Sarah BARBER,
    dt Isaac & Alice, Columbiana Co., O. (H)
1843, 10, 5. Elias N., s Nathan & Dinah, Co-
    lumbiana Co., O.; m at West MH, Eliza
    THOMAS, dt John & Rebecca, Columbiana Co.,
    O. (H)

1812, 6, 16. Nathan & w, Hannah, & ch, Phebe
    & Joseph, rocf Westland MM, dtd 1811,10,26
1817, 1, 14. Nathan & w, Dinah, & ch, Amos

Dennis, Edwin, Jane Dennis, Asenath &
    Milton, rocf Munsey MM, dtd 1816,5,22
1817, 1, 14. Jane rocf Monsey MM, Pa., dtd
    1816,6,19
1820, 3, 22. Jane Dennis (form Heacock) dis
    mcd (with first cousin)
1823, 11, 19. Eunice recrq
1824, 5, 19. Martha rocf Richland MM, Pa.,
    dtd 1824,4,2
1826, 1, 25. Rosamond rocf Richland MM, Pa.,
    dtd 1825,12,2
1827, 7, 25. Miriam rocf Richland MM, dtd
    1827,6,1
1828, 9, 24. Nathan & w, Dinah, & ch, Asen-
    ath, Milton, Barton, Uriah A., Elias H.,
    Enos, Josiah W. & Tacy, recrq (H)
1828, 11, 19. Eunice dis disunity
1829, 2, 25. Amos D. mbrp transferred from
    Upper Springfield MM by rq (H)
1829, 2, 25. Edwin mbrp transferred from
    Upper Springfield MM by rq (H)
1829, 2, 25. Jane D., dt Nathan & Dinah,
    mbrp transferred from Upper Springfield
    by rq (H)
1831, 1, 19. Rosamond dis JH
1832, 4, 25. Ezra Borton prcf Marlborough
    MM, to m Jane D. Heacock (H)
1837, 8, 23. Hannah [Haycock] (form Barber)
    dis mcd (H)
1837, 3, 22. Edwin dis mcd (H)
1867, 7, 25. Tacy L. (form Johnson) con mou
    (H)

HEADLAND
----, --, --. Kenneth, s Elmer & Della, b
    1911,3,15; m Mamie JEFFERIES, dt Edwin &
    Lida, b 1914,10,13 (G)
l
1933, 6, 21. Kenneth recrq
1933, 6, 21. Mrs. recrq

HEADLEY
1846, 5, 27. Edward [Headly], s Hartis & Re-
    becca, Orleans Co., N. Y.; m at Salem,
    Hannah BONSALL, dt Edward & Rachel, Colum-
    biana Co., O.

----, --, --. David B. & Anna (G)
    Ch: Laura   b 1872, 2, 10
        Edith M.   " 1873, 5, 19
        James Roger" 1874, 9, 9
        Mary E.   " 1876, 7, 11
        Edward Her-
          bert   " 1878, 5, 13
1873, 10, 7. Edith M. d (G)

1846, 11, 25. Hannah W. [Hedley] gct Elba MM,
    N. Y.
1887, 1, 20. Anna dropped from mbrp

HEALD
----, --, --. Jane b 1802,11,15 d 1878,11,14
    (W)

HEALD, continued
1828, 3, 12. Mary b (W)
1844, 2, 3. John b (W)

1835, 11, 25. Mary, minor, recrq
1840, 1, 22. John recrq
1848, 9, 20. John Oliphant gct Middleton MM,
    to m Maria Heald
1849, 3, 21. Mary Bard (form Heald) dis mcd
1851, 3, 19. John gct Salem MM, Ia.
1856, 3, 20. Allen & w, Rebecca, gct Drift-
    wood MM, Ind.
1862, 12, 25. Thomas, Meriam, Lucina, Israel,
    Rebecca, Lindley, Mary Ann & Cynthia, dis
    joining separatists (W) of 1854
1862, 12, 25. Sinia S., Henry, Sarah Ellen
    & Jane dis joining separatists (W) of 1854
1862, 12, 25. William dis joining separatists
    (W) of 1854
1862, 12, 25. Sarah dis joining separatists (W)
    of 1854
1864, 5, 25. Jane rocf Middleton MM, dtd
    1864,3,19 (W)

HEESTAND
----, --, --. Milan, s Samuel & Sarah, b 1871,
    3,5 d 1928,7,12; m Martha J. MYERS, dt
    Eli & Barbara E., b 1870,2,25 (G)

HEFFNER
1885, 2, 6. Harry [Hoffner] recrq
1886, 10, 21. Harry dropped from mbrp

HEIM
1882, 12, 21. Grace recrq

HEMINGWAY
----, --, --. James b 1760,4,12; m Elizabeth
    ----- b 1760,3,17 (W)
    Ch: James, Jr. b 1801, 7, 23
        Abigail   " 1804, 10, 30

1818, 12, 23. James & w, Elizabeth, & ch,
    James & Abigail, rocf Mount Holly MM,
    N. J., dtd 1818,10,8
1823, 8, 20. James [Hemmingway] con mou
1824, 2, 25. Hope recrq
1834, 6, 25. Abigail [Hemmingway] rocf Cherry
    St. MM, Phila., Pa., dtd 1834,2,19 (H)
1863, 8, 20. Abigail gct Falls MM, Pa. (H)
1865, 2, 23. Abigail rocf Falls MM, Pa., dtd
    1865,1,7 (H)

HENDERSON
1919, 6, 26. Joshua E., s Joseph & Anna C.,
    Alberta, Canada; m at Salem, Edith M.
    SATTERTHWAIT, dt William D. & Ida A. (New-
    lin), b 1896,4,23 d 1923,12,6 bur Winona,
    O. (W)
    Ch: Anna Marie b 1920, 5, 24
        J. Edward " 1922, 9, 22
    Joshua m 2nd Ellen R. SATTERTHWAIT, dt
    William D. & Ida A. (Newlin), b 1901,5,28

    Ch: Ida Jean   b 1928, 8, 24
        Franklin
        David   " 1930, 12, 15

1889, 7, 24. Ruth C. (form Campbell) dis mcd
    (W)
1929, 3, 20. Ellen (form Satterthwait) con
    mcd (W)

HENDRICKS
1816, 2, 21. Mary m Samuel PAINTER
1889, 11, 18. Lucy May, dt Milo & Eliza Davi-
    son, b (G)

1815, 9, 12. Mary [Hendrix] rocf Redstone
    MM, dtd 1815,6,2
1820, 9, 20. Ann [Hendrix] rocf Providence
    MM, Pa., dtd 1820,7,25
1821, 2, 21. Ann Richardson (form Hendrix)
    dis mcd
1932, 12, 29. Lucy May recrq

HERBERT
----, --, --. Scott, s Wesley & Mary, b 1880,7,
    25; m Minnie BELL, dt James & Isabell, b
    1882,5,3 (G)
    Ch: Loren P. b 1906, 2, 27
----, --, --. James m Mary MERCER (G)
    Ch: Kenneth
        James   b 1913, 7, 31
        Joseph
        Scott   " 1915, 11, 25
----, --, --. Loren, s Scott & Minnie, b 1906,
    2,27; m Ruth -----
    Ch: Donna
        Jean   b 1930, 8, 20
        Norma Jane " 1933, 3, 7
----, --, --. Louise, dt Monroe Mercer, b

----, --, --. Wesley, s James, b 1858,6,11;
    m Mary A. PATTERSON, dt Isaac, b 1852,6,
    11 (G)
    Ch: Maude   b 1884, 1, 25
        Anna Mary " 1891, 3, 4
        Scott   " 1880, 7, 25

1920, 6, 23. Louise recrq
1927, 12, 21. Ruth Cross recrq
1932, 12, 29. James & Joseph Scott recrq

HERST
1914, 9, 25. Edna Gibson dropped from mbrp

HESTON
----, --, --. David & Ruth (W)
    Ch: James   b 1831, 12, 10
        Martha
        Jane   " 1835, 10, 20
        Joseph   " 1839, 8, 27
        Jefferson " 1841, 7, 6
        Mary
        Elizabeth " 1846, 6, 21

HESTON, continued
1912, 2, 21. Lavay recrq
1912, 2, 21. Mrs. recrq
1915, 11, 24. Chester recrq
1915, 11, 24. Clifford recrq
1917, 8, 15. Ruby May recrq
1920, 3, 24. Sue & s, Clifford & Chester,
     gct Alliance MM, O.
1927, 6, 22. Vallaise dropped from mbrp

HEWITT
1815, 11, 22. Susannah m Moses RHODES
----, --, --. ----- m Sarah ----- b 1811,7,6
     Ch: John   b 1836, 2, 5
         Mary Jane   " 1838, 2, 15
         Martha   " 1840, 4, 23
         Wm. F.   " 1842, 6, 30
         Daniel   " 1844, 11, 11

1814, 9, 13. Susanna [Hewett] rocf Redstone
     MM, dtd 1814,4,1
1845, 6, 20. David & w, Thirza, & ch, Samuel,
     John & James, rocf West MM, dtd 1845,5,1
     (H)
1846, 1, 21. Sarah [Hewit] & ch, John, Mary
     Jane, Martha, William T. & Daniel, rocf
     Centre MM, Pa., dtd 1845,12,17
1860, 1, 25. Mary Jane Baum (form Hewit) dis
     mcd (W)
1860, 2, 23. Mary Jane Baum (form Hewit) dis
     mcd
1860, 9, 20. Martha dis
1860, 11, 21. Martha [Hewit] dis (W)
1862, 12, 25. Sarah [Hewit] dis joining sepa-
     ratists (W) of 1854
1872, 7, 24. John [Hewit] dis disunity (W)
1873, 2, 19. Daniel dis serving as volun-
     teer in army (W)
1873, 4, 23. William dis serving as a volun-
     teer in army (W)
1883, 9, 20. Laura M. rocf New Garden MM, O.

HICKLEN
----, --, --. Samuel b 1777,3,25; m Lydia
     ----- b 1778,3,25 (W)
     Ch: Jane   b 1809, 3, 10
         Hannah   " 1811, 2, 6
1856, 9, 27. Mary Ann [Hicklin] m James JACK-
     SON

1808, 6, 14. Samuel & w, Lydia, rocf Center
     MM, Del., dtd 1808,4,4
1857, 1, 27. Mary Ann Jackson & dt, Sarah Ann
     Hicklen, gct Gilead MM, O.
1862, 12, 25. Samuel & Ruth [Hickland] dis
     joining separatists (W) of 1854

HILLERMAN
1850, 6, 19. William R. gct Cincinnati MM (H)

HILLIS
----, --, --. Robert b 1782,12,23; m Jane
     ----- b 1780,7,19 (H)

     Ch: Phebe   b 1808, 3, 26
         David L.   " 1812, 5, 11
         Jeremiah   " 1814, 9, 30 d 1819, 9,10
         Enos   " 1816, 12, 12
         Wm.   " 1819, 8, 16
         Ann   " 1821, 10, 29
----, --, --. Isaac b 1806,2,16; m Elizabeth
     ----- b 1813,2,15 (H)
     Ch: Jacob
         Davies   b 1835, 1, 10
         Jeremiah   " 1836, 11, 28
         Ruth L.   " 1839, 6, 20
1839, 11, 6. Enos [Hilles], s Robert & Jane,
     Columbiana Co., O.; m at Salem, Mary Ann
     HARRIS, dt Jacob & Mary, Columbiana Co.,
     O. (H)
----, --, --. Enos b 1816,12,12; m Mary Ann
     ----- b 1812,1,1 (H)
     Ch: Arthur T.   b 1842, 1, 12
1842, 3, 30. Ann m Silas HARRIS (H)

1836, 5, 25. Robert & w, Jane, & ch, Enos,
     William & Ann, rocf Fallowfilld MM, Pa.,
     dtd 1836,4,9 (H)
1837, 7, 19. Isaac & w, Elizabeth, & ch, Ja-
     cob Davis & Jeremiah, rocf Exeter MM, Pa.,
     dtd 1837,5,13 (H)
1837, 9, 20. Enos, William & Ann, ch Robert,
     rocf Fallowfield MM, dtd 1837,8,11
1838, 5, 23. Nathan [Hillas] & w, Sarah, &
     ch, Skipwith C., William, Robert & Samuel,
     rocf New Garden MM, Pa., dtd 1838,4,5 (H)
1840, 7, 22. Nathan & w, Sarah, & ch, Skip-
     with C., William, Robert, Samuel & Rachel
     Ann, gct Middleton MM (H)
1841, 5, 19. Enos dis mcd
1845, 6, 25. William gct West MM (H)
1845, 6, 25. Robert & w, Jane, gct West MM
     (H)
1850, 8, 21. William dis mcd
1850, 8, 21. Ann Harris (form Hillis) dis
     mcd & jH

HILLMAN
1834, 7, 23. Martha F. rocf Green St. MM,
     Phila., Pa., dtd 1834,3,20 (H)
1848, 11, 19. Martha relrq (H)

HINCHMAN
1818, 10, 28. Elizabeth m Barbee BLACKBURN

1818, 5, 12. Elizabeth recrq
1842, 6, 22. Rebecca T. (form Bradshaw) con
     mou (H)

HINES
1905, 8, 10. Zelma Irene, dt Harvey & Clara,
     b (G)

1925, 3, 25. Harvey Ellsworth, Clara E. &
     Zelma Irene recrq

HIPPLEY
1927, 5, 25. Ann Eliza dropped from mbrp

HIVELY
1887, 3, 20. Ann Eliza dropped from mbrp

HOBSON
1857, 9, 30. Thomas, s John & Belinda, Wash-
        ington Co., O.; m at Salem, Mary STANLEY,
        dt Andrew & Ruth, Columbiana Co., O. (W)

1840, 8, 19. Joseph rocf Smithfield MM, dtd
        1840,3,23
1842, 3, 23. Joseph gct Gillead MM
1853, 4, 20. Barkly Stratton gct Flushing
        MM, to m Hannah Hobson
1858, 2, 24. Mary S. gct Plymouth MM (W)

HODGEN
1890, 10, 29. Stephen, s Eli & Mary (Engle)
        b 1826,6,25 d 1910,9,15 bur Friends Bur.
        Gr., Salem, O.; m Rebecca SMITH, dt Henry
        & Betsy (Holloway) Briggs, b 1843,11,1
        d 1926,4,22 bur Friends Bur. Gr., Salem,
        O. (W)
1891, 5, 20. Stephen [Hodgin] rocf New Garden
        MM, dtd 1891,4,23 (W)

HOGE
1843, 4, 26. John C., s Absalom & Rachel,
        Belmont Co., O.; m at Salem, Rebecca BON-
        SALL, dt Edward & Rachel, Columbiana Co.,
        O.

1842, 7, 20. John Thomas Jr. gct Marlborough
        MM, to m Mary S. [Hoag] (H)
1843, 4, 19. Benjamin Battin gct Marlborough
        MM, to m Hannah G. [Hoag] (H)
1843, 10, 25. Rebecca P. gct Plainfield MM

HOILES
1890, 7, 26. Rachel b (W)

1822, 9, 25. Rachel recrq
1829, 10, 21. Rachel [Hiles] rocf Upper
        Springfield MM, dtd 1829,9,26
1832, 2, 22. Martha (form Pidgeon) dis mcd
1844, 9, 25. Rachel gct Marlborough MM

HOLDMAN
1842, 5, 25. Sarah (form Jenkins) dis mcd

HOLE
1793, 9, 22. Sarah b (W)
1794, 4, 3. Nathan b (W)
1819, 12, 8. Mahlon, s Jacob & Mary, Columbi-
        ana Co., O., b 1792,12,1; m at Salem, Ra-
        chel SCHOOLEY, dt Elisha & Rachel, Colum-
        biana Co., O., b 1794,7,17 (W)
        Ch: Charlotte b 1822, 4, 26
            Jared   " 1823, 11, 8
            Israel   " 1827, 4, 2
1825, 11, 4. Robert b (W)

----, --, --. James M. b 1822,6,14; m Hannah
        B. ----- b 1825,11,2 (W)
        Ch: Linneus C. b 1847, 5, 30
            Ruth Anna   " 1850, 9, 2
----, --, --. Willis m Elma GILBERT, dt Joshua
        & Deborah (Hutton), b 1869,7,20 (W)
        Ch: Maurice   b 1905, 7, 23

1820, 7, 19. Rachel gct New Garden MM
1826, 3, 22. Mahlon & w, Rachel, & ch, Char-
        lotte & Jared, rocf Sandy Spring MM, dtd
        1826,2,24
1828, 6, 25. Mahlon & w, Rachel, & ch, Char-
        lotte, Jared & Israel, gct Sandy Spring
        MM
1832, 4, 25. Mahlon & w, Rachel, & ch, Char-
        lotte, Jared, Israel, Mary & Elisha, rocf
        Sandy Spring MM, dtd 1832,3,23
1834, 4, 23. Mahlon & w, Rachel, & ch, Char-
        lotte, Jared, Israel, Mary, Elisha & Jacob,
        gct Sandy Spring MM
1847, 3, 24. James M. rocf Carmel MM, dtd
        1847,2,20
1847, 3, 24. Thomas B. rocf Middleton MM, dtd
        1847,3,11
1847, 3, 24. Hannah B. rocf Middleton MM, dtd
        1847,3,11
1851, 2, 19. Robert rocf Carmel MM, dtd 1851,
        1,18
1853, 3, 23. Robert dis mcd
1853, 12, 21. Nathan & w, Sarah, rocf Middle-
        ton MM, dtd 1853,12,8
1855, 6, 21. Jacob gct Driftwood MM, Ind.
1855, 6, 21. Benjamin gct Driftwood MM, Ind.
1855, 6, 21. Hannah gct Driftwood MM, Ind.
1856, 2, 21. Elon & ch, Burla Ann, Lydia, Da-
        vid & Ann, gct Driftwood MM, Ind.
1857, 3, 26. Samuel J. & w, Rebecca, & ch,
        Louisa, Emerson B. & Ruth-Anna, gct Gilead
        MM, O.
1858, 6, 23. Nathan & w, Sarah, rocf Upper
        Springfield MM (W)
1862, 2, 19. James M. & w, Hannah B., & ch,
        Linneas E. & Ruth Anna, gct Upper Spring-
        field MM (W)
1862, 12, 25. Nathan, Sarah, James, Hannah,
        Charles, Linnois C. & Ruth Anna dis join-
        ing separatists (W) of 1854
1863, 6, 25. Benjamin & w, Isabel, & dt, Myra
        H., rocf Grove MM, Ind., dtd 1863,6,4
1864, 6, 23. Benjamin & w, Isabel W., & dt,
        Myra H., gct Bridgeport MM, Ind.
1867, 7, 25. Jacob rocf Grove MM, Ind.
1868, 4, 23. Jacob con mcd
1870, 5, 26. Hannah rocf Bridgeport MM, Ind.,
        dtd 1870,5,5
1870, 10, 20. Susan gct Marietta MM, Ia. (H)
1872, 11, 6. Emerson B. rocf Gillied MM, dtd
        1872,10,15
1878, 2, 21. Emerson B. gct Alum Creek MM
1887, 12, 22. Mary (form Raley) rpd mcd; drop-
        ped by rq (H)
1888, 5, 24. Susie E. relrq

HOLE, continued
1918, 3, 20. Elma G. rocf New Garden MM, O.
     (W)
1918, 5, 22. Maurice, s Willis R. & Elma G.,
     recrq (W)

HOLLINGSWORTH
1859, 9, 28. Louis, s Samuel & Margaret, Ker-
     kuk Co., Ia.; m at Salem, Hannah C. FAW-
     CETT, dt Wm. F. & Elizabeth, Columbiana
     Co., O. (W)

1821, 8, 22. Christopher & w, Elizabeth, &
     ch, John Fares, Samuel, Sarah Ann, Charles,
     Christopher & Edward, rocf Plainfield MM,
     dtd 1821,3,22
1828, 10, 22. John dis mcd
1834, 3, 19. Christopher dis disunity
1834, 5, 21. Elizabeth dis disunity
1842, 9, 21. Harrison P. Gamble gct Pennsville
     MM, to m Phebe Hollingsworth
1849, 7, 25. Lewis, minor, rocf Middleton
     MM, dtd 1849,5,10
1850, 12, 25. Christopher dis mcd
1850, 12, 25. Edward dis mcd
1851, 1, 22. Mary W. Calender (form Hollings-
     worth) dis mcd
1862, 12, 25. Thomas dis joining separatists
     (W) of 1854
1862, 12, 25. Samuel, Margaret & Thomas dis
     joining separatists (W) of 1854

HOLLOWAY
----, --, --. Jesse b 1754,12,5 d 1846,11,11;
     m Sarah ----- b 1762,8,25 d 1840,2,12 (W)
     Ch: Hannah   b 1782, 7, 6
         Susannah   " 1784, 8, 20
         Joel   " 1886, 12, 29
         Aaron   " 1789, 3, 29
         Margaret   " 1791, 4, 21
         Eunice   " 1797, 10, 9
         David   " 1800, 11, 14
         Joshua   " 1806, 8, 24
1786, 12, 29. Joel b (H)
----, --, --. Amos b 1759,4,9; m Hephzibah
     ----- b 1770,1,15 (W)
     Ch: Phebe   b 1787, 1, 3
         Stephen   " 1789, 6, 13
         Rhoda   " 1791, 3, 25
         Job   " 1793, 5, 10
         Aaron   " 1795, 4, 16
         Huldah   " 1798, 8, 30
         Jason   " 1801, 1, 14
         Anna   " 1803, 4, 12
         Elizabeth   " 1805, 7, 13
         Margaret   " 1808, 2, 16
1792, 8, 28. Mary b (H)
1807, 6, 17. Susannah m Moses STANLEY
1812, 1, 1. Rhoda m Levi BURDEN
----, --, --. Aaron b 1789,3,29 d 1872,4,13;
     m Oliva ----- b 1792,1,15 d 1872,4,22 (W)
     Ch: Edwin   b 1813, 8, 27
         Imlah   " 1815, 11, 13

     Ch: Jesse   b 1818, 5, 4 d 1826, 8,17
         bur Salem
         Alice Ann   " 1821, 1, 17 " 1836, 7,23
         bur Salem
         Joseph   " 1823, 5, 9
         Sarah   " 1826, 3, 9
         Samuel   " 1829, 5, 7
         Daniel   " 1833, 10, 15
1821, 9, 26. Margaret m Martin BRANTINGHAM
1823, 11, 26. David, s Jesse & Sarah, Columbi-
     ana Co., O.; m at Salem, Rachel PIGEON, dt
     Wm. & Alice, Columbiana Co., O.
1836, 11, 30. Edwin, s Aaron & Olive, Columbi-
     ana Co., O., b 1813,8,27; m at Salem, Re-
     becca D. STRATTON, dt Joseph & Sarah, Co-
     lumbiana Co., O., b 1816,3,29 (W)
     Ch: Isaac   b 1838, 1, 19
         Rhoda E.   " 1839, 7, 15
         Jesse   " 1840, 8, 12
         Alice Ann   " 1843, 2, 13
         Sarah   " 1845, 4, 21
         Lindley   " 1847, 4, 28
         Joseph S.   " 1850, 11, 17
1840, 2, 25. Emily b (W)
1848, 9, 21. Jacob, s Jacob & Martha, Belmont
     Co., O.; m at Salem, Sarah FAWCETT, dt
     Jehu & Abigail, Columbiana Co., O.
1861, 3, 27. Sarah P. m Theophilus MORLAN (W)
1903, --, --. Edwin d (W)
----, --, --. Alfred H., s Cyrus D. & Esther
     (Emery), b 1889,8,23; m Edith Lydia KIRK,
     dt Nathan & Mary F., b 1892,2,24 (W)
     Ch: Carol
         Thelma   b 1917, 2, 20
         Lois
         Marjorie   " 1918, 4, 1
         Mabel Lyda " 1919, 10, 14
         Mildred
         Lydia   " 1919, 10, 14 d 1920, 2, 5
         bur Middleton, O.

1806, 4, 15. Amos & w, Hepsiba, & ch, Phebe,
     Stephen, Rhoda, Job, Aaron, Huldah, Jason,
     Anna & Elizabeth, rocf South River MM,
     Va., dtd 1805,8,10, endorsed by Middleton
     MM, 1806,2,8
1806, 6, 17. Jesse & w, Sarah, & ch, Joel,
     Aaron, Margaret, Eunice & David, rocf
     Crooked Run MM, Va., dtd 1805,5,4, en-
     dorsed by Middleton MM, 1806,6,14
1806, 6, 17. Hannah & Susannah, dt Jesse &
     Sarah, rocf Crooked Run MM, dtd 1805,5,4,
     endorsed by Middleton MM, 1806,5,14
1806, 9, 16. Hannah Rossell (form Holloway)
     dis mcd
1812, 9, 15. Aaron gct Middleton MM, to m
     Olive Mercer
1813, 1, 12. Olive [Holliway] rocf Middleton
     MM, dtd 1812,12,10
1813, 5, 11. Joel gct Wilmington MM, Del.
1814, 7, 12. Joel rocf Wilmington MM, Del.,
     dtd 1814,6,3
1816, 6, 11. Joel con mcd

HOLLOWAY, continued
1818, 12, 23. Mary recrq
1824, 5, 19. David & w, Rachel, gct Marl-
    borough MM
1829, 1, 21. Joel dis JH
1829, 1, 21. Mary dis JH
1829, 9, 23. Joel & w, Mary, gct New Garden
    MM (H)
1833, 12, 25. William Mather gct Marlborough
    MM, to m Hannah Holloway (H)
1838, 4, 25. Joshua dis mcd
1838, 5, 23. Susan (form Painter) dis mcd
1842, 2, 23. Joel & w, Mary, rocf New Garden
    MM, dtd 1841,12,23
1842, 12, 21. Joseph dis jas
1844, 11, 20. Lydia (form Scholfield) dis JH
1844, 11, 20. Imlah dis disunity
1845, 11, 19. Lydia (form Schofield) con mcd
    (H)
1846, 7, 22. Zadok French gct Flushing MM, to
    m Meriam Holloway
1848, 9, 20. Eunice gct Marlborough MM
1849, 1, 24. Sarah F. gct Flushing MM
1851, 5, 21. Jesse & Martha B., ch David & Ra-
    chel, rocf Marlborough MM, dtd 1851,4,29
1851, 5, 21. Samuel dis disunity
1851, 6, 25. Sarah dis disunity
1853, 2, 23. Lydia (form Davis) dis mcd
1853, 12, 21. Emily, minor, rocf Upper Spring-
    field MM, dtd 1853,11,26
1854, 2, 22. Jehu Fawcett gct Flushing MM,
    to m Deborah S. Holloway (W)
1854, 3, 22. Daniel dis mcd (W)
1855, 4, 26. Upper Springfield MM was given
    permission to rst Lydia D. in mbrp
1855, 8, 23. Eunice rocf Marlborough MM, dtd
    1855,7,31
1856, 2, 20. Jesse dis mcd (W)
1856, 2, 20. Sarah P. rocf Upper Springfield
    MM, dtd 1856,1,25 (W)
1860, 4, 25. Rhoda E. gct Upper Springfield
    MM (W)
1860, 5, 23. Edwin & w, Rebecca D., & ch,
    Jesse, Alice Ann, Sarah, Lindley T. & Jo-
    seph S., gct Upper Springfield MM (W)
1862, 2, 20. Edwin & w, Rebecca, & ch, Sarah,
    Lindley & Joseph, gct Upper Springfield
    MM, O.
1862, 12, 25. Aaron & Olive dis joining separa-
    tists (W) of 1854
1869, 12, 22. Emily gct Middleton MM (W)
1870, 5, 25. Isaac dis mcd (W)
1871, 2, 22. Martin B. gct Coal Creek MM, Ia.
    (W)
1871, 5, 24. Edwin & w, Rebecca D., & s, Jo-
    seph S., rocf Upper Springfield MM, dtd
    1871,4,21 (W)
1873, 12, 24. Edwin & w, Rebecca D., gct
    Upper Springfield MM (W)
1877, 10, 24. Joseph S. dis jas (W)
1915, 12, 22. A. Howard recrq (W)
1916, 3, 22. Alfred Howard gct Middleton MM,
    to m Edith L. Kirk (W)

1917, 2, 21. Edith Lydia K. rocf Middleton
    MM, O., dtd 1917,2,17 (W)
1921, 4, 20. A. Howard & w, Edith L., & ch,
    Carol Thelma, Lois Marjorie & Mabel Lyda,
    gct Middleton MM (W)
1924, 6, 23. Rhoda Ann & ch, Sarah Louise &
    Myra May, recrq
1926, 11, 23. Loda & ch relrq

HOLMES
1861, 7, 25. Elizabeth H. gct Prairie Grove
    MM, Ia. (H)
1861, 7, 25. Kersey C., minor, gct Prairie
    Grove MM, Ia. (H)

HOOPES
1843, 1, 4. Ann m Daniel BONSALL

1833, 7, 24. Lydia (form Gibbons) con mcd (H)
1833, 12, 25. Lydia G. [Hoops] gct Middleton
    MM (H)
1839, 3, 20. Ann & Ann, Jr. rocf Sadsbury MM,
    Pa., dtd 1838,10,3 (H)
1870, 10, 19. Annie (form Barber) dis mcd (W)
1914, 12, 23. Blanch Briggs gct Damascus MM

HORNER
----, --, --. Thomas F., s John & Lydia, b
    1804,10,2; m Mary Ann PARKER, dt Thomas &
    Rachel, b 1804,12,8 (W)
    Ch: Margaret
        Wilson   b 1829, 4, 26
        Amos F.   " 1830, 9, 14
        Esther   " 1832, 8, 28
1858, 5, 27. Esther B. m George STREET

1828, 7, 23. Thomas & w, Mary Ann, rocf
    Plainfield MM, dtd 1828,5,22
1854, 6, 21. Amos F. dis disunity (W)
1854, 7, 19. Margaret dis disunity (W)
1864, 7, 20. Thomas F. dis joining separatists
    of 1854 (W)
1864, 7, 20. Mary Ann dis joining separatists
    of 1854 (W)

HOUGH
1838, 7, 25. Anna Maria rocf Redstone MM, Pa.,
    dtd 1838,5,2
1840, 8, 19. Sarah Louisa rocf Redstone MM,
    dtd 1840,7,1
1843, 7, 19. Sarah Louiza gct Redstone MM
1844, 6, 19. Anna Maria dis joining Baptist
    Society

HOUSE
1851, 3, 19. Evaline (form Kennet) con mcd
    (H)
1853, 6, 23. Evaline gct Dear Creek MM (H)

HOUTS
1887, 4, 21. Eliza rocf East Goshen MM, dtd
    1887,4,16
1890, 6, 26. Eliza dropped from mbrp

HOWARD

1834, 2, 19. Sarah recrq (H)
1834, 6, 25. Sarah gct Sandy Spring MM, Md.
   (H)
1872, 9, 18. Thomas rocf Munsey MM

HOWEL

----, --, --. ----- m Elma ----- b 1800,1,7
   Ch: Annie E.   b 1842, 7, 23
       Luther J. " 1843, 3, 8

1830, 8, 25. Elma (form Cadwalader) dis mcd
1842, 7, 20. Mary recrq
1853, 10, 19. Alum Creek MM was given permission to rst Elma in mbrp
1856, 8, 21. Elma & ch, Anna Elma & Luther
   Jonah, rocf Alum Creek MM, dtd 1856,7,24
1868, 3, 26. Ana E. [Howell] relrq
1871, 9, 21. Elma gct Chicago MM

HUBERTY

1922, 11, 22. Mildred Greenfield recrq
1932, 6, 29. Mildred dropped from mbrp

HUGHES

1834, 7, 23. Paulina S. [Hughs] (form Brook)
   con mcd (H)
1842, 3, 23. Cert rec for Ellis [Hews] from
   Exetre MM, dtd 1841,8,25, endorsed back
   to that mtg
1882, 2, 8. Howard recrq
1886, 10, 21. Howard [Hues] dropped from mbrp

HUMPHREYS

1818, 1, 14. Mary [Humphrey] b (W)
1822, 10, 30. Sarah W. [Humphrey] (G)
1861, 5, 19. Sarah W. d (G)

1851, 12, 24. Mary rocf Phila. MM, dtd 1851,10,
   30
1851, 12, 24. Sarah W. rocf Phila. MM, dtd
   1851,10,30
1865, 6, 21. Mary [Humphries] dis joining
   separatists of 1854 (W)

HUNT

1804, 8, 29. Wm. b (W)
1808, 5, 25. Nathan, s Joshua & Esther, Columbiana Co., O., b 1784,4,12; m at Salem,
   Ann WARRINGTON, dt Abraham & Rachel, Co-
   lumbiana Co., O., b 1789,8,8 d 1823,2,15
   bur Salem (W)
   Ch: Joshua   b 1809, 1, 17 d 1809, 1,20
       Ira   " 1810, 3, 10
       Esther   " 1811, 6, 1
       Enoch   " 1813, 1, 30
       Caleb   " 1814, 9, 15
       Rachel   " 1816, 11, 6
       Priscilla " 1821, 6, 10
       Ann   " 1823, 1, 5
   Nathan m 2nd at Salem 1824,4,28, Rebecca
   SHARP, dt Robert & Martha, Columbiana Co.,
   O., b 1783,11,17

   Ch: Nathan   b 1825, 3, 2
----, --, --. Stacy b 1789,4,21 d 1878,1,31;
   m Rebecca ----- b 1794,2,14 d 1829,10,9
   bur Salem (H)
   Ch: George
       Dillwyn   b 1819, 3, 13
       Milton   " 1821, 3, 23 d 1851, 8,15
       Esther   " 1823, 7, 7
       Wm.   " 1825, 10, 8 " 1851, 7,26
   Hannah, wd of Stacy, b 1795,6,18
----, --, --. Elisha b 1779,10,7; m Mary -----
   b 1775,4,6 (W)
   Ch: Emmor   b 1826, 8, 13
1835, 4, 1. Caleb, s Nathan & Ann, Cayahoga
   Co., O.; m at Salem, Mary Ann SHARP, dt
   Joel & Rebecca, Cayahoga Co., O. (H)
1836, 8, 31. Esther m Thomas DARLINGTON
1842, 8, 1. Priscilla W. m Jonathan COFFEE
----, --, --. Ira & -----
   Ch: Asenath   b 1844, 3, 13
       Elizabeth " 1846, 10, --
       Priscilla " 1850, 8, --
----, --, --. Asenath b 1844,3,18 d 1903,6,10
   (W)
1844, 5, 29. Ann W. m Charles D. BASSETT
1847, 6, 2. Nathan, s Nathan & Rebecca, Co-
   lumbiana Co., O.; m at Salem, Phebe Jane
   BOONE, dt Isaac & Esther, Columbiana Co.,
   O. (H)
1847, 6, 24. Esther m Jehu D. RALEY (H)

1807, 10, 13. Nathan & Stacy rocf Redstone
   MM, dtd 1807,8,28
1808, 8, 16. William dis mcd
1811, 4, 16. Stacy gct Redstone MM
1813, 10, 12. Abigail gct Short Creek MM
1814, 1, 11. Seth gct Short Creek MM
1817, 7, 15. Nathan & w, Ann, & ch, Ira, Esther, Enoch, Caleb & Rachel, gct Marlborough MM
1822, 12, 25. Nathan & w, Ann, & ch, Ira, Esther, Enoch, Caleb, Rachel & Priscilla,
   rocf Providence MM, Pa., dtd 1822,10,22
1823, 6, 25. Esther, Enoch & Rachel, ch Nathan, gct Redstone MM
1827, 5, 23. Elisha & w, Mary, & s, Emmor,
   rocf Redstone MM, dtd 1827,4,4
1828, 10, 22. Rebecca dis jH
1829, 1, 29. Nathan dis jH
1830, 2, 24. Elisha dis disunity
1830, 2, 24. Mary dis disunity
1830, 5, 6. Enoch rocf Redstone MM, dtd
   1830,3,3
1830, 5, 6. Rachel, minor, rocf Redstone MM,
   dtd 1830,3,31
1830, 6, 23. Stacy & ch, George, Milton, Esther & William, rocf Providence MM, dtd
   1830,6,3
1830, 6, 23. Emmor dis joining Separatists
1830, 6, 23. Stacy & ch, George, Milton, William & Esther, mbrp transferred from Providence MM, Pa., by rq
1831, 1, 19. Stacy dis jH

HUNT, continued

1831, 7, 20. Elisha & w, Mary, gct Redstone
    MM (H)
1835, 7, 22. Hannah (form Mercer) dis mcd (H)
1835, 9, 23. Stacy dis mcd (H)
1836, 7, 20. Esther rocf Chester MM, N. J.,
    dtd 1836,6,14
1836, 8, 24. Rachel Eldridge (form Hunt) dis
    mcd
1836, 12, 21. Caleb dis mcd
1837, 4, 19. Enoch dis JH
1839, 1, 23. Ira gct Salem MM, Ia.
1844, 6, 19. Esther dis JH
1845, 4, 23. Nathan, Jr. dis disunity
1845, 5, 21. George dis disunity
1845, 8, 20. Milton dis disunity
1845, 10, 22. Hannah C. rocf Fallowfield MM,
    dtd 1845,9,13 (H)
1854, 6, 21. Asenith, Elizabeth & Priscilla,
    ch Ira, rocf Salem MM, Ia., dtd 1854,1,21
    (W)
1860, 8, 23. Martha Jane rocf Concord MM, dtd
    1860,6,20 (H)
1862, 12, 25. Priscilla & Elizabeth dis join-
    ing separatists (W) of 1854
1868, 5, 21. Asenath gct Ypsalanta MM, Mich.
1872, 10, 23. Asenath dis joining separatists
    of 1854 (W)
1873, 2, 19. Priscilla gct Chester MM, N. J.
    (W)
1876, 11, 22. Priscilla W. rocf Chester MM,
    N. J., dtd 1876,9,12 (W)

HUNTER

----, --, --. Orrin Alex, s Elmer & Barbara,
    b 1881,10,17; m Grace Ruhl, dt Edward &
    Anna, b 1891,2,8 (G)
    Ch: Virginia   b 1919, 1, 15
        Eileen
          Elizabeth " 1929, --, --

1929, 12, 26. Orin & w, Grace, & dt, Eileen,
    recrq

HURFORD

1841, 2, 24. Joel rocf London Grove MM, Pa.,
    dtd 1841,1,6 (H)

HUSSEY

1837, 11, 22. Lydia, w Richard, & ch, Emily
    C., Charlotte B., Alexander T. & Maria
    Louisa, rocf Nantucket MM, dtd 1837,4,27
1839, 2, 20. Emily C. Kelley (form Hussey)
    dis mcd
1839, 3, 20. Charlotte B. dis disunity
1839, 3, 20. Lydia C. dis disunity

HUSTES

1862, 12, 25. Job & Rebecca dis joining separa-
    tists (W) of 1854

HUTTON

1813, 4, 28. Wm., s John & Massey, Portage

Co., O.; m at Lexington, Hannah BURDEN,
    dt Job & Mary, Stark Co., O.
1849, 12, 14. Susan G. b (W)
----, --, --. Finley, s Joel W. & Ann (Mains),
    b 1839,12,11 d 1920,1,19 bur Friends Bur.
    Gr., Salem, O.; m Eliza G. ----- (W)
    Ch: Elma G.   b 1875, 5, 18
        Joel
          Willets " 1876, 10, 28
    Finley m 2nd Agnes V. McGREW, dt James B.
    & Margaret (Vail), b 1860,7,8 d 1925,10,
    16 bur Friends Bur. Gr., Salem, O.
    Ch: Rebecca S. b 1885, 12, 14
        Finley, Jr. " 1886, 10, 27
1905, 9, 21. Elma m Joseph L. CONRAD (W)
1909, 10, 6. Rebecca Savry m Arthur PERRY,
    Jr. (W)

1809, 6, 13. John & ch, William, Gulielma,
    James, Hannah, Mary, Sarah, John & Benja-
    min, rocf Middleton MM, dtd 1809,2,11
1813, 10, 12. Gulielma Strong (form Hutton)
    dis mcd
1832, 2, 22. John & w, Rachel, & ch, Samuel
    W. & Margaret Jane, rocf Carmel MM, dtd
    1831,11,19
1832, 7, 25. John & w, Rachel, & ch, Samuel
    W. & Margaret Jane, gct Middleton MM
1834, 7, 23. John rocf Middleton MM, dtd
    1834,7,10
1836, 7, 20. Mary Ann rocf New Garden MM,
    Pa., dtd 1836,5,5 (H)
1838, 1, 24. Mary Ann dis (H)
1877, 10, 24. Susan G. Penrose (form Hutton)
    dis mcd (W)
1892, 2, 24. Finley & w, Agnes V., & ch,
    Elma G., Joel W., Rebecca S., Jr. & Fin-
    ley, Jr. rocf New Garden MM, dtd 1892,1,21
    (W)
1906, 2, 21. Joel W. con mcd (W)
1921, 5, 25. Finley, Jr. dis mou & jas (W)

HYKES

1932, 6, 29. Velma Kelley dropped from mbrp

ICENHOUR

----, --, --. John & Mary
    Ch: Elizabeth b 1801, 3, 29
        Sarah   " 1803, 4, 2
        David   " 1805, 6, 12
        Hannah   " 1807, 9, 1
        Mary   " 1810, 6, 14
        Susannah " 1812, 12, 6
        Gulielma " 1815, 7, 16
        Ann   " 1817, 9, 5
        John E. " 1820, 11, 11

1806, 2, 11. Elizabeth, Sarah & David, ch
    John & Mary, recrq

ILER

1923, 2, 21. Roy & w, Pearl, & ch, Eldon,
    Mary, Helen, Harry & Nettie, rocf Damascus

ILER, continued
    MM

INGLEDUE
1929, 7, 9. Catharine d (G)

1915, 11, 24. Emma recrq
1916, 8, 16. Idella & Raymond recrq
1920, 6, 23. Nellie & Catharine recrq
1927, 6, 22. Raymond dropped from mbrp

INGLING
1843, 9, 22. Esther (form Davis) con mcd (H)

INGRAM
1842, 11, 30. Joseph, s Robert & Mary, Columbi-
    ana Co., O.; m at Salem, Martha KENNET, dt
    Wm. & Miriam Heacock, Columbiana Co., O.(H)
1843, 5, 30. Joseph, s Joseph & Mary, Columbi-
    ana Co., O.; m at home of Eli Thomas, Phəbe
    THOMAS, dt Eli & Elizabeth, Columbiana
    Co., O. (H)
1877, 12, 24. Josephine m Horace G. WELCH (H)
1892, 5, 20. Ruth, dt John & Anna Eliza Galla-
    ger, b (G)
----, --, --. Jesse & Matilda (G)
    Ch: Raymond   b 1894, 1, 3
        Charles O. " 1894, 1, 3
        Mary C.   " 1890, 3, 27

1920, 4, 21. Ruth recrq
1920, 6, 23. Vida recrq
1926, 2, 24. Jesse rocf Winona MM
1930, 5, 21. Charles & w, Vida, & ch, Ruth &
    Jane, relrq

INNIS
1800, 4, 29. Mary b (W)
1832, 5, 24. Mary m Aaron CHAPMAN

1829, 1, 21. Mary rocf Redstone MM, dtd 1828,
    12,31

IRY
1807, 3, 17. Hannah rocf Westland MM, dtd
    1807,1,24
1821, 10, 24. Elizabeth [Ira] (form Morelan)
    dis mou

JACKSON
1856, 9, 27. James, s Isaac & Ann, Crawford
    Co., O.; m at Salem, Mary Ann HICKLIN, dt
    Ephraim & Elizabeth Oliphant, Columbiana
    Co., O.

1806, 5, 13. Isaac & w, Ann, rocf Hopewell
    MM, dtd 1806,3,3
1808, 7, 12. Abel rocf Hopewell MM, dtd 1808,
    2,1
1851, 8, 20. Sarah C. rocf Fallowfield MM,
    Pa., dtd 1851,9,8 (H)
1853, 1, 20. Sarah C. Lamborn (form Jackson)
    con mcd (H)

1857, 1, 27. Mary Ann Jackson & dt, Sarah
    Ann Hicklen, gct Gilead MM, O.
1926, 11, 23. Ora relrq

JACOBS
----, --, --. Wm. R., s Richard & Amanda
    (Phillips), b 1855,4,19 d 1930,12,4 bur
    Damascus Friends Bur. Gr.; m Caroline W.
    WOOLMAN, dt Abner & Elvira (Hall), b 1864,
    4,29 d 1932,10,15 bur Damascus Friends
    Bur. Gr.

1917, 4, 25. William R. & w, Caroline W.,
    rocf New Garden MM, O., dtd 1917,3,22 (W)

JAMES
----, --, --. ----- m Martha ----- b 1778,4,
    14 d 1852,1,4 (W)
    Ch: Sarah   b 1813, 7, 28
        Rachel   " 1817, 8, 22
1828, 7, 13. Isaac, s Thos. & Sarah, Colum-
    biana Co., O.; m at Salem, Leah WEBB, dt
    Benjamin & Lydia Morris, Columbiana Co.,
    O.
1848, 11, 1. Sarah m Mifflin CADWALLADER

1806, 3, 11. John & w, Martha, & ch, Eliza-
    beth, Abel & Tacy, rocf Middleton MM, dtd
    1806,1,11
1828, 10, 22. Leah & ch, Peninah & Lydia Webb,
    gct Carmel MM
1833, 10, 23. Elizabeth M. rocf Robison MM,
    dtd 1833,5,9, endorsed by New Garden MM,
    1833,9,26
1840, 5, 20. Elizabeth M. gct Exeter MM, Pa.
    (H)
1842, 3, 23. Isaac H., minor, rocf Carmel
    MM, dtd 1842,2,19
1843, 7, 19. Edward Stratton gct Sandy Spring
    MM, to m Mary James
1843, 9, 20. Sarah rocf Sandy Spring MM, dtd
    1843,8,25
1844, 7, 24. Martha rocf Sandy Spring MM, dtd
    1844,3,22
1844, 8, 21. Rachel rocf Sandy Spring MM, dtd
    1844,6,21
1844, 9, 25. Isaac H. gct Carmel MM

JANNEY
1808, 4, 12. Amos [Jenny] rocf Goose Creek
    MM, Va., dtd 1807,10,26
1850, 2, 20. Jacob gct Cincinnati MM (H)
1850, 2, 20. Ellen gct Cincinnati MM (H)

JAVENS
1871, 4, 28. Mary Viola, dt Levi & Margaret
    Rambo, b (G)

1926, 1, 20. Mary Viola recrq

JEFFRIES
----, --, --. Clare, dt Edwin & Lydia, b (G)
1909, 10, 8. Wilma, dt Lee & Mary Bowker, b

JEFFRIES, continued
     (G)

1932, 12, 29. Claire Marion, Wilma, Billie &
     Raymond [Jefferies] recrq

JENKINS
----, --, --. Zachariah b 1778,11,7 d 1856,8,
     23; m Rhoda ----- b 1782,7,2 d 1864,3,29
     (W)
     Ch: John W.   b 1808, 9, 6
         Isaac   " 1813, 4, 13
         Zachariah
          Jr.   " 1817, 9, 9
         Sarah   " 1821, 6, 2
         Elizabeth " 1824, 11, 12
         James   " 1829, 1, 1
----, --, --. Edward b 1805,7,4; m Rhoda Eliza-
     beth ----- b 1810,8,15 (W)
     Ch: Hannah S. b 1832, 4, 26
         Joseph Ed-
          ward   " 1839, 8, 15
         Joshua   " 1842, 12, 20 d 1843, 2, 3
1857, 3, 5. Hannah S. m Samuel WILLIAMS
1863, 10, 23. Edward, a minister, d ae 59y

1824, 10, 20. Zachariah & w, Rhoda, rocf
     Little Egg Harbour MM, N. J., dtd 1824,9,9
1825, 2, 23. John W., Isaac, Zachariah & Sa-
     rah [Jinkings], ch Zachariah & Rhoda, rec-
     rq
1831, 5, 25. John dis mcd
1838, 5, 23. Edward & w, Rhoda Elizabeth, &
     dt, Hannah Sawyer, rocf Salem MM, Mass.,
     dtd 1838,4,12
1838, 11, 5. Edward & w, Rhoda Elizabeth, &
     dt, Hannah Sawyer, gct New Garden MM
1840, 4, 22. Zachariah dis mcd
1841, 10, 20. William rocf Berwick MM, Maine,
     dtd 1841,7,22
1842, 5, 25. Sarah Holdman (form Jenkins) dis
     mcd
1843, 4, 19. William [Jinkens] gct New Garden
     MM
1843, 11, 22. Edward & w, Rhoda Elisabeth, &
     ch, Hannah Sawyer & Joshua, rocf New Gar-
     den MM, dtd 1843,10,26
1864, 4, 21. Rhoda Elizabeth gct New Garden
     MM
1864, 11, 11. Rhoda Elizabeth dis joining sepa-
     ratists of 1854 (W)
1867, 8, 22. Joshua gct New Garden MM
1870, 6, 22. Joshua dis joining separatists
     of 1854 (W)

JESSUP
1889, 6, 25. James H., s Wm. T. & Mary A.
     (Brown), Hartford Co., N. C., b 1862,12,9
     d 1929,2,2 bur Hope Cemetery, Salem, O.;
     m Martha D. STRATTON, dt John M. & Rachel
     W. (Bonsall), b 1861,11,13 d 1933,12,2
     bur Hope Cemetery, Salem, O. (W)
     Ch: Myra S.   b 1890, 12, 10

     Ch: John
         William   b 1892, 12, 18
         Anna R.   " 1897, 7, 27 d 1920,11, 2
         bur Hope Cem., Salem, O.

1893, 7, 19. James H. recrq (W)

JEWELL
1882, 2, 8. Ann Eliza recrq

JOHN
1808, 10, 26. Amy m Aden MORLAN
1830, 6, 14. Samuel b (W)
1834, 7, 20. Abner b (W)
1834, 10, 23. Sarah m Abraham FARRINGTON (H)
1839, 12, 11. Levi b (W)
1844, 9, 12. Maribah b (W)

1806, 11, 11. Griffith & w, Sarah, & ch, Abner,
     Rachel, Benjamin, Sarah, Nathan & Abigail,
     rocf Sadsbury MM, dtd 1806,9,2
1806, 11, 11. Amy rocf Sadsbury MM, dtd 1806,
     9,2
1824, 11, 24. Sarah rocf Summerset MM, dtd
     1824,7,26
1829, 2, 25. Sarah mbrp transferred from Up-
     per Springfield MM by rq
1834, 10, 22. Abraham Farrington prcf New Gar-
     den MM, dtd 1834,9,25, to m Sarah John
     (H)

JOHNSON
----, --, --. Thos. b 1772,12,2; m Ann -----
     b 1768, 2,19 (W)
1808, 12, 8. Tacy b (H)
1809, 1, 25. John, s Elijah & Pherebe, Co-
     lumbiana Co., O., b 1783,2,24 d 1816,1,3
     bur Salem; m Hannah PENNOCK, dt Wm. &
     Mary, Stark Co., O., b 1781,5,17 d 1826,6,
     18 bur Salem (W)
     Ch: Mary   b 1810, 1, 10
         Elizabeth " 1813, 6, 13
         Juliann   " 1816, 2, 12
----, --, --. Wm., nm, m Sarah ----- b 1794,3,
     13 (W)
     Ch: Hannah   b 1815, 9, 11
         Martha   " 1818, 11, 28
1832, 11, 7. Robert, s Demcey & Mourning,
     Stark Co., O.; m at Salem, Milly STANLEY,
     dt Jonathan & Mary, Columbiana Co., O.
1835, 10, 15. Matilda b (H)
1837, 6, 28. Elizabeth m James STANLEY
1837, 11, 1. Hannah m Mark BONSALL
1840, 10, 28. Martha m Stacy COOKE, Jr.
1842, 11, 30. Julian H. m Jacob BRANSON
1844, 10, 30. John W., s Philip & Hannah, Co-
     lumbiana Co., O.; m at Salem, Ann FRENCH,
     dt Robert & Anna, Columbiana Co., O., b
     1816, 4, 12 d 1898,6,29
     Ch: Anna   b 1845, 9, 27
1871, 3, 2. Aley Anna, dt Hiram & Jennette
     Carle, b (G)
1875, 1, 23. Sarah d (W)

JOHNSON, continued

1806, 12, 16. John, Jr. rocf Western Branch MM, Va., dtd 1806,8,23

1806, 12, 16. Robert rocf Western Branch MM, Va., dtd 1806,8,23

1807, 12, 15. Robert gct Western Branch MM, Va.

1816, 4, 16. Thomas rst by rq

1816, 10, 15. Ann rocf Evesham MM, N. J., dtd 1816,8,9

1819, 8, 25. Exum rocf West Branch MM, dtd 1819,4,24

1821, 9, 19. Sarah rst by rq

1828, 12, 24. Thomas & w, Ann, gct Upper Springfield MM

1829, 4, 22. Mary gct Marlborough MM

1829, 4, 22. Elizabeth, minor, gct Marlborough MM

1831, 11, 23. Elizabeth gct Marlborough MM, dtd 1831,10,25

1833, 2, 20. Milly gct Marlborough MM

1835, 4, 22. Hannah & Martha recrq

1843, 4, 19. Sarah gct Sandy Spring MM

1849, 2, 20. Benjamin & w, Tacy, & ch, William L., Matilda Ann, Clayton F., Eli L. & Evan R., rocf Richland MM, dtd 1849,2,2

1852, 9, 23. Garretson & w, Lydia, & ch, Esther, Elisabeth & Nathan, rocf West Branch MM, Pa., dtd 1852,8,19 (H)

1854, 6, 21. John W. dis disunity

1859, 8, 24. Sarah rocf Sandy Spring MM, dtd 1859,6,25 (W)

1862, 12, 25. Ann & Anna dis joining separatists (W) of 1854

1863, 2, 25. Eliphalet & Anna gct Salem MM,O.

1863, 9, 23. Eliphalet & Anna rocf Ferrisburgh MM, Vt., dtd 1863,2,25

1867, 7, 25. Tacy L. Heacock (form Johnson) con mou (H)

1880, 7, 21. Anna Fawcett (form Johnson) dis mcd (W)

1885, 2, 26. William recrq

1910, 2, 23. Lida recrq

1917, 1, 24. James relrq

1926, 3, 24. Alcy Anna recrq

JONES

1749, 1, 15. Catlit b (W)

1770, 4, 7. Sarah b (W)

1805, 4, 24. Benjamin b (W)

1807, 10, 1. Catlit b (W)

----, --, --. Joseph b 1809,9,8 d 1809,12,14 bur Springfield (W)

1810, 10, 22. Joshua b (W)

1813, 7, 5. Caleb b (W)

1839, 11, 27. Hannah m Edward BONSALL

1806, 11, 11. Catlet & w, Sarah, & s, Benjamin, rocf Cedar Creek MM, Va., dtd 1806,9, 13

1815, 1, 17. Nancy rocf Middleton MM, dtd 1814,8,11

1830, 5, 6. Nancy dis disunity

1838, 12, 19. Hannah rocf Frankford MM, Pa.,

dtd 1838,11,27

1840, 5, 20. Elizabeth M. gct Exeter MM, Pa. (H)

1864, 2, 25. Elizabeth rocf Marlborough MM, dtd 1864,1,26

1879, 12, 25. Matthew Oliver gct Chicago MM

1911, 10, 25. Truman W. & w, Eithel, recrq

1913, 6, 25. Truman & w, Eathel, gct Beloit MM

KALE

1885, 2, 6. George & w, Elizabeth, recrq

1890, 6, 26. Elizabeth ----- (form Kale) dropped from mbrp

KARLIS

----, --, --. John m Mary Katherine REDMOND, dt Frank & Myrtle, b 1898,3,22 (G)
        Ch: George   b 1922, 5, 10
            Basil   " 1923, 7, 15
            Percy   " 1925, 11, 8
            Paul   " 1927, 5, 6
            Vivian   " 1928, 6, 18

1929, 12, 26. Mary & ch recrq

KAYLER

1912, 2, 21. Albert A. recrq

1915, 6, 23. Bell recrq

1917, 8, 15. Effie May [Kaylor] recrq

KELLEY

----, --, --. Edward A. m Olive BUTCHER, dt Ephraim & Hannah, b 1877,10,2 (G)
        Ch: Walter S.   b 1901, 4, 18
            Edwin C.   " 1909, 10, 1
            Herbert A. " 1914, 1, 8

1823, 6, 25. Rebecca gct Marlborough MM

1839, 2, 20. Emily C. (form Hussey) dis mcd

1869, 6, 24. Alfred D. & w, Abigail, & ch, Susan A. & Abbie H., rocf Greenwich MM, dtd 1869,5,16

1869, 6, 24. Mary Alice rocf Greenwich MM, dtd 1869,5,16

1888, 7, 26. Abbie H. rocf Dover MM, N. H., dtd 1888,7,11

1911, 12, 20. Walter S. [Kelly] rec in mbrp

1924, 1, 23. Hubert Austin & Elvin Chas. [Kelly] recrq

1924, 7, 23. Hilda & ch, Kenneth Ray, Donald Eugene & Agnes Belle, rocf Winona MM

1924, 7, 23. Ralph Earnest rocf Winona MM

1924, 7, 23. William A. & w, Samantha A., & ch, Thomas Russell, Velma Odessa & Hazel Leora, rocf Winona MM

1927, 6, 22. Ralph, Kenneth, Hilda, Agnes & Walter dropped from mbrp

1933, 1, 25. Mrs. Russell recrq

KELLOGG

1841, 9, 22. Cert rec for Wait Ann from Rochester MM, N. Y., dtd 1841,5,28, en-

KELLOGG, continued
       dorsed to Marlborough MM

KELTY
1881, 5, 11. James W. & w, Alvina B., recrq

KENNEDY
1878, 4, 24. Sibyl (form Trescott) dis mcd
    (W)

KENNETT
1783, 5, 16. Martha b (H)
1814, 9, 10. Ruth Ann b (H)
1820, 7, 13. Eveline b (H)
1826, 3, 29. Wm., s Kendall & Leah, Columbi-
    ana Co., O.; m at Salem, Martha HEACOCK,
    dt Wm. & Marian, Bucks Co., Pa.
1842, 11, 30. Martha m Joseph INGRAM (H)

1826, 5, 24. Martha gct New Garden MM
1833, 7, 24. Thomas [Kennett] dis disunity
1842, 6, 22. Martha, Evaline & Ruth Anna rocf
    New Garden MM, dtd 1842,5,26 (H)
1842, 11, 23. Joseph Ingram rocf New Garden
    MM, to m Martha Kennett (H)
1844, 3, 20. Ruth Ann Votaw (form Kennet)
    con mcd (H)
1851, 3, 19. Evaline House (form Kennet) con
    mcd (H)

KENT
1913, 8, 20. George E. & w, Eleanor G., & ch,
    Arther & Robert Howard, gct Mt. Gilead MM

KERSEY
1846, 9, 23. Ann rocf Birmingham MM, Pa., dtd
    1846,7,1
1847, 12, 22. Ann H. Pusey (form Kersey) dis
    mcd

KEYSER
----, --, --. Solomon, s Henry & Mary, b 1859,
    2,16; m Mary DOUGLAS, dt John & Eliza, b
    1855,7,31 (G)
    Ch: Ella   b 1914, 11, 25

KILLE
1823, 4, 3. Clayton, s Isaac & Martha, Stark
    Co., O.; m at Springfield, Rebecca COPPOCK
    dt Isaac & Eleanor, Columbiana Co., O.

KILLCRECE
1885, 2, 6. William H. & w, Sarah E., recrq
1885, 2, 6. Birdie L. recrq
1886, 10, 21. William H. & w & dt dropped from
    mbrp

KIMBERLY
----, --, --. Amos E. b 1793,6,22 d 1841,8,10;
    m Jane ----- b 1787,10,20 (W)
    Ch: John   b 1816, 12, 8 d 1817, 1,28
        bur Salem
      Samuel   " 1817, 11, 12

    Ch: Wm.   b 1819, 9, 29 d 1824, 8,24
        bur Salem
      Elizabeth " 1821, 8, 2 " 1825,10, 6
        bur Salem
1815, 11, 14. Amos E. gct Marlborough MM, to m
1816, 3, 12. Jane rocf Marlborough MM, dtd
    1816,1,17
1837, 5, 24. Samuel dis mcd
1842, 10, 19. Amos E. dis
1851, 7, 23. Salem MM, Ia. rq permission to
    rst Amos E. in mbrp (not granted)
1853, 5, 25. Salem MM, Ia. was given per-
    mission to rec Amos E. in mbrp

KING
----, --, --. Wm. m Priscilla HUNT, dt Ira &
    Hannah (Maxwell), b 1850,8,19 d 1929,5,30
    bur Cleveland, O.

1911, 12, 20. Dorris rec in mbrp
1911, 12, 20. Lottie rec in mbrp
1912, 2, 21. ----- (man) recrq

KINGSBERRY
1833, 9, 25. Abey Sally rocf Nine Partners
    MM, N. Y., dtd 1833,5,16 (H)

KINGSLEY
1895, 5, 7. Gladys, dt John & Lillian Shaf-
    fer, b (G)

1927, 6, 22. Gladys dropped from mbrp

KINSEY
1917, 8, 15. Isaac L. rocf Alliance MM, O.,
    dtd 1917,8,2
1917, 8, 15. Edith E. C. rocf Alliance MM,
    O., dtd 1917,8,2
1917, 8, 15. Wilma V. rocf Alliance MM, O.,
    dtd 1917,8,2
1922, 8, 30. Isaac & w & dt, Wilma, gct
    Portsmouth MM, Va.

KINTZ
1886, 1, 21. Edith H. con mcd (H)
1886, 5, 20. Edith H. (form Carpenter) gct
    Rochester MM, N. Y. (H)

KIRBY
1876, 2, 24. Abigail T. rocf Chesterfield MM,
    N. J., dtd 1876,2,8 (H)
1878, 3, 21. Abigail T. gct Chesterfield MM,
    N. J. (H)

KIRK
1913, 4, 30. Louis J., s Nathan & Mary M.,
    Columbiana Co., O.; m at Salem, Elizabeth
    Alice COPE, dt Albert M. & Phebe Y. (Ash-
    ton), b 1886,4,20 (W)
1930, 6, 7. Lydia d (G)

1809, 7, 11. Mary & ch, Charity, Timothy,

KIRK, continued
    Phebe, Sidwell & Elisha, rocf Short Creek
    MM, dtd 1809,5,23
1811, 5, 14. Cert rec for Joshua from Short
    Creek MM, dtd 1811,2,19, endorsed to New
    Garden MM
1811, 6, 11. Mary, w Joshua, & ch, Charity,
    Timothy, Phebe, Sidwell, Elisha & Joshua,
    gct New Garden MM
1824, 7, 21. Sidwell rocf New Garden MM, dtd
    1823,3,25
1834, 1, 22. Mary G. rocf Sandy Spring MM,
    dtd 1833,12,27
1834, 5, 21. Joshua rocf New Garden MM, dtd
    1834,3,20
1835, 1, 21. Joshua dis mcd
1835, 10, 21. William & w, Elizabeth, & ch,
    Ann Eliza, Susan Lindley & Comly, rocf
    New Garden MM, dtd 1835,8,20 (H)
1836, 1, 20. Ann Eliza & Susan, ch William &
    Elizabeth, rocf Sadsbury MM, Pa., dtd
    1835,12,8
1839, 7, 24. Mary gct Short Creek MM
1849, 3, 21. Ann Eliza dis jH
1849, 3, 21. Susan dis jH
1871, 4, 20. Elizabeth, Ann Eliza & Susan
    gct Prairie Grove MM, Ia. (H)
1913, 12, 24. Alice C. gct Middleton MM, O. (W)
1916, 3, 22. Alfred Howard Holloway gct Mid-
    dleton MM, to m Edith L. Kirk (W)
1916, 3, 22. Elizabeth Virginia rocf Guern-
    sey MM, O.
1916, 3, 22. Lydia Jane rocf Guernsey MM, O.
1923, 10, 24. Lydia gct Damascus MM
1928, 1, 25. Mrs. Lydia rocf Damascus MM, O.

KIRKBRIDE
1826, 6, 26. Nancy b (H)
1827, 9, 29. Ferdinand b (H)
1829, 9, 19. Mary b (H)
1830, 2, 5. Benjamin Franklin b (H)
1834, 11, 23. Watson b (H)
1837, 2, 17. James S. b (H)

1832, 9, 19. Sarah & ch, Nancy, Ferdinand,
    Mary & Benjamin Franklin, rocf Buckingham
    MM, Pa., dtd 1832,8,6 (H)

KITE
1837, 8, 23. Cert rec for Jehu Lord & w, Re-
    becca, & grandson, Jehu Lord Kite, from
    Stroudsburgh MM, Pa., dtd 1837,5,25, en-
    dorsed to Upper Springfield MM

KNIGHT
1868, 2, 20. Abel gct Kansas MM

KOLL
----, --, ---. Daniel b 1812,12,18; m Julia ----
    b 1810,5,26 d 1866,1,19 (W)
    Ch: Benj. C. b 1836, 5, 26
        Lydia " 1839, 8, 26
        Esther " 1841, 12, 11

    Ch: Joseph b 1844, 2, 24
        Wm. " 1845, 11, 28
        Mary " 1848, 2, 17 d 1875, 1, 5
        Charles " 1851, 9, 8
        Martha " 1853, 6, 10
1880, 5, 20. Lydia m Benjamin LIGHTFOOT (W)

1844, 6, 19. Daniel & w, Julia, & ch, Benja-
    min, Lydia Esther & Joseph, rocf Middleton
    MM, dtd 1844,5,9
1860, 5, 19. Lydia dis joining separatists (W)
1861, 7, 24. Benj. S. dis mcd (W)
1862, 1, 23. Benjamin S. dis mcd
1862, 12, 25. Daniel, Julia, Lydia, Esther,
    William, Mary, Charles, Martha & Joseph,
    dis joining separatists (W) of 1854
1865, 2, 22. Daniel dis disunity (W)
1865, 8, 23. Esther Tolerton (form Koll) dis
    mcd (W)
1868, 2, 19. Joseph dis mcd (W)
1868, 8, 19. Mary J. (form Fawcett) dis at-
    tending mtg set up contrary to discipline
    & mcd (W)
1869, 5, 19. Lydia dis disunity
1872, 8, 21. Lydia rst by rq
1875, 6, 23. William dis mcd (W)
1875, 11, 24. Charles dis disunity
1891, 10, 21. Martha K. Otis (form Koll) dis
    mcd & joining separatists of 1854 (W)

KUHNAMOND
1924, 1, 23. Anna Louise [Kucheremund] recrq
1932, 6, 29. ----- dropped from mbrp

KUHNS
----, --, --. Harrison m Willetta BOLES, dt
    George & Rebecca, b 1895,7,--
    Ch: Dorothy b 1913, 6, 30
        Elmer " 1915, 5, 12
        Vernon " 1917, 8, 9

1928, 8, 15. Willetta, Dorothy, Elmer & Ver-
    non recrq

KYNETT
----, --, --. Anna, dt Samuel & Sarah Hutchin-
    son, b 1845,9,16 d 1910,8,13

LACKEY
----, --, --. Thos. S. m Florence N. COPE, dt
    Louis & Hannah Y. (Hollingsworth), b 1862,
    7,6 (W)

1888, 7, 25. Florence N. (form Cope) dis mcd
    (W)

LADD
1831, 12, 21. Samuel Whitfield rocf Upper
    Springfield MM, dtd 1831,10,22
1834, 1, 22. Samuel Whitfield gct Upper
    Springfield MM

LAMB

1850, 9, 25. Mariah (form Garetson) dis mcd
     (H)

LAMBORN

----, --, --. Parmenas b 1766,8,4; m Hannah
     ----- b 1776,1,8 (W)
     Ch: Isaac   b 1800, 1, 22
         Miriam   " 1801, 12, 27
         Elizabeth " 1804, 1, 3
         Dinah   " 1806, 5, 26
         Anna   " 1808, 8, 25
         Wm.   " 1810, 11, 14
         Lydia   " 1813, 9, 14 (1813,9,13
         in H)
         Mary   " 1818, 2, 9
----, --, --. ----- m Ann ----- b 1780,4,12
     d 1855,11,19 (W)
     Ch: Clayton   b 1808, 8, 28
         Ann J.   " 1811, 11, 25
         Lydia   " 1819, 12, 1
         Hannah M. " 1832, 10, 31
         Levi L.   " 1827, 10, 10
----, --, --. Job [Lambourn] b 1799,8,16; m Es-
     ther ----- b 1803,1,20 (H)
     Ch: Philena   b 1823, 1, 23
         Thos. Ell-
         wood   " 1824, 7, 8
         Elizabeth " 1827, 4, 28
         Wm. C.   " 1829, 8, 6
         Susanna M. " 1832, 10, 31
         Edward H. " 1834, 10, 26
1823, 10, 2. Miriam m John BUCK
1829, 3, 31. Ann H. m Elijah WHINNERY (H)
1837, 11, 8. Ann J. m Samuel TEST, Jr.
1839, 5, 1. Clayton [Lambourn], s Townsend
     & Ann, Columbiana Co., O., b 1808,8,28
     d 1893,1,31; m at Salem, Hannah TEST. dt
     Isaac & Margaret, Columbiana Co., O., b
     1811,1,29 (W)
     Ch: Martha S. b 1840, 2, 14
         Lemuel T. " 1841, 2, 14 d 1921,12,27
         bur Friends Bur. Gr., Winona, O.
1843, 6, 29. Wm. W., s Parmenas & Hannah, Co-
     lumbiana Co., O.; m at West MH, Phebe
     REEVES dt Henry & Mary, Columbiana Co.,O.
     (H)

1812, 7, 14. Parmenes [Lamburn] & w, Hannah,
     & ch, Isaac, Miriam, Elizabeth, Dinah
     Anna & William, rocf Fairfax MM, Va., dtd
     1812,2,26, endorsed by New Garden MM,
     1812,6,18
1820, 9, 20. Isaac gct Alexandria MM
1821, 2, 21. Cert granted to Alexandria MM
     for Isaac [Lambern] returned
1821, 2, 21. Isaac [Lambern] gct Fairfax MM
1828, 11, 19. Dinah & Anna mbrp transferred
     from Upper Springfield MM by rq (H)
1832, 7, 25. Anna gct New Garden MM (H)
1837, 1, 25. Clayton [Lambern] rocf Bradford
     MM, Pa., dtd 1836,12,7
1837, 3, 22. Lydia, Hannah M. & Levi L., ch

Ann, rocf Bradford MM, Pa., dtd 1837,1,4
1837, 3, 22. Ann J. rocf Bradford MM, Pa.,
     dtd 1837,1,4
1837, 6, 21. Job & w, Esther (or Elizabeth),
     & ch, Philena, Thomas Elwood, Elizabeth,
     William C., Susannah M. & Edward H., rocf
     London Grove MM, dtd 1837,5,3 (H)
1837, 9, 20. Ann rocf Bradford MM, Pa., dtd
     1837,8,9
1837, 10, 25. Dinah gct New Garden MM (H)
1841, 7, 21. Clayton & w, Hannah, & ch, Mar-
     tha & Lemuel T., gct New Garden MM
1843, 5, 24. William rocf New Garden MM, dtd
     1843,3,23 (H)
1844, 7, 24. David rocf London Grove MM, Pa.,
     dtd 1844,4,10 (H)
1844, 9, 25. Hannah dis joining Baptist
     Society
1850, 7, 24. Levi L. dis mcd
1853, 1, 20. Sarah C. (form Jackson) con mcd
     (H)
1854, 7, 20. Sarah C. gct West MM (H)
1859, 2, 23. Lydia B. Clayton (form Lamborn)
     dis mcd (W)
1859, 4, 21. Lydia P. rst by rq (form a mbr
     of Sadsbury MM, Pa.; cert granted to
     Goshen MM, O. several yrs previous was
     lost)
1859, 6, 23. Job rocf West MM, dtd 1859,6,24
     (H)
1862, 5, 22. Job con mcd (H)
1862, 6, 26. Ann [Lamborne] recrq (H)
1867, 3, 21. Lydia W. rocf West MM, dtd 1867,
     1,25 (H)
1873, 9, 25. Jane B. gct Wapsinonoc MM, Ia.
     (H)
1917, 6, 20. Lemuel T. rocf New Garden MM,
     O., dtd 1917,5,24 (W)

LANDWERT

----, --, --. J. H., s John H. & Anna M., b
     1866,11,3; m Nancy J. ----- (G)
     Ch: Orville F. b 1910, 5, 16
1881, 5, 29. Adda Rose, dt Eliza & Thomas
     Lutton, b (G)

1913, 5, 21. J. H. released
1913, 5, 21. Henry [Landwerth] dis disunity
1916, 6, 21. Nancy dropped from mbrp
1925, 3, 25. Adda Rose [Landwer] recrq
1926, 4, 21. Mr. & Mrs. Henry [Landworth]
     relrq
1926, 4, 21. Adda Rose released
1932, 6, 29. Orville dropped from mbrp

LANGSTAFF

----, --, --. Rhoda b 1770,4,3 d 1882,8,1
1772, 10, 26. Thomas b
----, --, --. James b 1762,7,22; m Elizabeth
     ----- b 1776,9,21 (W)
----, --, --. Samuel b 1764,4,30; m Hannah
     ----- b 1778,9,6 (W)
     Ch: Samuel   b 1804, 4, 8

LANGSTAFF, Samuel & Hannah, continued
    Ch: Benjamin b 1806, 6, 5
        James   " 1808, 3, 2
        Thomas   " 1810, 2, 2
        John W.   " ----, 1, 4
        Mary   " 1815, 11, 30
        Elizabeth " 1818, 2, 3
        Evan   " 1820, 7, 25
1811, 4, 26. Thomas D. b
1829, 11, 26. Taylor F. b (W) (in care of Benjamin & Elizabeth D. Antrim)
1831, 1, 24. Drusilla b (W) (in care of Benjamin & Elizabeth D. Antrim)
1850, 6, 26. Priscilla m Zaccheus TEST
----, --, --. Robert William m E. Anetta BRANTINGHAM, dt Elisha K. & Mary A. (Masters), b 1893,8,16 d 1918,11,10 bur Friends South-Western Bur. Gr., Phila., Pa. (W)

1812, 12, 15. James & w, Elisabeth, & Elizabeth Dole, minor, rocf Maurices River MM, N. J., dtd 1812,10,2
1813, 8, 17. Samuel & w, Hannah, & ch, Samuel, Benjamin P., James, Thomas & John W., rocf Maurice River MM, N. J., dtd 1813,4,30
1813, 8, 17. Thomas & w, Rhoda, & s, Thomas D., rocf Maurice River MM, N. J., dtd 1813,4,30
1824, 8, 25. Thomas gct Flushing MM, to m Ann Farmer
1825, 5, 25. Ann & ch, Susannah, Tabitha, Joseph, Rachel & Thomas Farmer, rocf Flushing MM, dtd 1825,2,25
1828, 7, 30. James & w, Elizabeth, rocf New Garden MM, dtd 1828,7,24 (H)
1828, 8, 20. Elizabeth dis jH
1829, 4, 25. James, Jr. gct Smithfield MM
1829, 11, 25. James gct Smithfield MM
1832, 6, 20. Benjamin B. & w, Catharine, rocf Upper Springfield MM, dtd 1832,5,26
1833, 6, 19. Benjamin P. & w, Catharine, gct Marlborough MM
1835, 8, 19. Taylor F. & Drusilla, minors, rocf Upper Springfield MM, dtd 1835,7,25
1837, 6, 21. Thomas D. & w, Hannah, & ch, Rhoda, rocf Upper Springfield MM, dtd 1837,5,27
1839, 1, 23. Thomas B. & w, Hannah, & dt, Rhoda, gct Chesterfield MM
1854, 3, 22. Taylor F. gct Sandy Spring MM, to m Mary J. Miller (W)
1854, 6, 21. Taylor F. gct Red Cedar MM, Ia. (W)
1874, 2, 11. James & w, Sarah B., rocf Alliance MM, dtd 1873,12,30

LANNIN
1866, 6, 26. Hannah (form Stratton) con mcd (W)
1893, 7, 19. Hannah dis disunity (W)

LANTZ
----, --, --. Charles m Neva LEATHERBERRY,

dt Jacob & Rosa, b 1892,10,18 (G)
    Ch: Chas., Jr. b 1923, 4, 19
        Neta
        Charlotte " 1921, 11, 11

1932, 12, 29. Neva Edna, Neta Charlotte & Junior recrq

LAWRENCE
1843, 11, 22. Daniel Test gct Short Creek MM, to m Ann D. Lawrence
1855, 12, 19. Mary rocf Short Creek MM, dtd 1855,10,10 (W)
1884, 5, 25. Charles recrq

LAYMAN
1841, 11, 24. Meriam (form Wright) dis mcd (H)
1842, 5, 25. Miriam (form Wright) dis mcd

LEACH
1818, 11, 19. Rebecca b (H)

1858, 9, 23. Thomas & ch, Deborah Jane, John, Charles, Lewis & Ross, gct Red Cedar MM, Ia.
1860, 4, 26. Jane L. Hammond (form Leach) con mcd
1860, 9, 20. Cornelius [Leech] & w, Sarah, & ch, Sanford C., Thomas H., Alonzo H., Hannah Maria & Eleanor, gct Westland MM, Ia.
1862, 7, 24. Samuel Y. con mcd
1862, 11, 20. Samuel Y. gct Le Grand MM, Ia.
1865, 10, 26. Mary E. Hayworth (form Leach) con mcd
1866, 2, 22. Mary E. Heaworth (form Leach) gct Le Grand MM, Ia.
1881, 12, 21. Achsah E. (form Lupton) dis mcd & joining separatists of 1854 (W)
1885, 2, 6. James A. & w, Mary, recrq

LEAF
1885, 2, 26. Lula recrq
1888, 1, 26. Lula dropped from mbrp

LEBER
1911, 12, 20. Gertrude rec in mbrp

LEE
----, --, --. Josiah b 1799,1,14; m Hannah ----- b 1798,3,24 (W)
    Ch: Angaline   b 1819, 8, 7
        Joshua Boon" 1820, 11, 10
        Elmira Jane" 1822, 5, 14
        Rebecca J. " 1823, 9, 10
        Preston   " 1825, 6, 24 d 1846, 9,24
        Mary
        Elizabeth " 1826, 12, 19
        Martha
        Aleson   " 1828, 5, 17 " 1836, 7,27
        Hannah Boon" 1830, 7, 9
        Margaret
        Chrisman " 1832, 1, 15 " 1836, 9,13
        Anna M. " 1833, 4, 21

LEE, Josiah & Hannah, continued
  Ch: Lydia   b 1834, 11, 28
      Sarah Ellen" 1836, 12, 10
----, --, --. Jeremiah b 1787,9,11 d 1842,6,29;
  m Mary P. ----- b 1796,12,20 (H)
  Ch: Ephraim
        Penrose b 1834, 4, 20
        Thos. Par-
          vin   " 1836, 7, 26
----, --, --. Mordecai b 1811,7,14; m Amanda
  R. ----- b 1809,3,18 (W)
  Ch: Mary R.   b 1837, 12, 7
      Omar S.   " 1841, 9, 25
      Abet T.   " 1843, 12, 12
      Alvah W.   " 1845, 4, 13
      Elma E.   " 1847, 8, 8
1889, 12, --. Annie d (W)
1890, 8, --. Hannah M. d (W)

1840, 7, 22. Josiah & w, Hannah G., & ch,
  Angeline, Joshua Boone, Elmira-Jane, Rebecca, John Preston, Mary Elizabeth, Hannah Boone, Anna, Lydia Emma & Sarah Ellen,
  rocf Exeter MM, Pa., dtd 1840,6,24
1840, 9, 23. Jeremiah & w, Mary P., & ch,
  Ephraim Penrose & Thomas Parvin, rocf Exeter MM, dtd 1840,8,26
1841, 8, 25. Susannah (form Teetors) dis mcd
1845, 2, 19. Angelina Sharp (form Lee) con
  mcd
1846, 5, 20. Joshua Boone dis disunity
1847, 11, 24. Mary P. & ch, Ephraim Penrose &
  Thomas Parvin, gct Exeter MM, Pa. (H)
1851, 2, 19. Mary Boone (form Lee) dis mcd
  with first cousin
1851, 8, 20. Jesse & w, Margaret, rocf Exeter
  MM, Pa., dtd 1851,7,30
1852, 1, 21. Rebecca dis disunity
1852, 6, 23. Israel rocf Exeter MM, Pa., dtd
  1852,5,26
1854, 7, 20. Ruth Ann (form Garretson) dis
  mcd (H)
1854, 8, 23. Margaret E. gct Exeter MM, Pa.
  (W)
1856, 6, 25. Mordecai & w, Amanda R., & ch,
  Mary R., Omar S., Abel T., Alvah W. & Elma
  E., rocf London Grove MM, Pa., dtd 1856,6,
  5 (W)
1857, 3, 25. Henry M. rocf Exeter MM, Pa., dtd
  1857,2,25 (W)
1857, 10, 21. Hannah Boone (form Lee) dis mcd
  with first cousin (W)
1858, 6, 24. Hannah Boone (form Lee) con mcd
1861, 6, 19. Mordecai & w, Amanda R., & ch,
  Omar S., Abel T., Alva W. & Elma E., gct
  Upper Springfield MM (W)
1861, 6, 19. Mary R. gct Upper Springfield
  MM (W)
1872, 3, 20. Lydia Emma dis disunity (W)
1872, 9, 25. Sarah Ellen Shafer (form Lee)
  dis mcd (W)
1872, 10, 23. Israel dis mcd (W)
1873, 8, 20. Henry M. dis disunity (W)

LEVAN
1844, 4, 24. Sarah (form Garwood) dis mcd

LEWIS
1827, 2, 1. Henry J. b (W)
----, --, --. Charles, s Robert & Anna, b
  1860,11,8; m Lena SOBEHART, dt Andrew &
  Francis, b 1865,1,1 (G)
  Ch: Nicholas   b 1893, 9, 7
      Minnie   " 1892, 6, 19
      Mary   " 1895, 3, 20
      Nellie   " 1896, 8, 15
      Maude   "   d 1922, 7,12
-----, --, --. Nicholas, s Charles & Lena, b
  1893,9,7; m Florence NAYLOR, dt Harry &
  Marietta, b 1894,5,9 (G)
  Ch: Mary
       Esther   b 1924, 6, 18
      Robert
       Glenn   " 1929, 9, 11

1850, 2, 20. Henry J. rocf Phila. MM, dtd
  1850,1,24
1911, 12, 20. Mary, Minnie & Nellie rec in
  mbrp
1913, 1, 31. Mrs. Charlotte recrq
1915, 11, 24. Maud recrq
1916, 8, 16. Harry recrq
1918, 5, 22. Charlotte dropped from mbrp
1923, 1, 3. Florence Naylor rocf Beloit MM,
  O.
1927, 4, 20. Mildred & Harry gct Detroit MM
1932, 9, 21. Harry, Mildred, Ruth & Charles
  rocf Detroit Friends Church

LIGHTFOOT
----, --, --. Benjamin H., s David & Sarah,
  Phila. Co., Pa.; m at Salem, Lydia KOLL,
  dt Karl Daniel & Julia (Seebohm), b 1839,
  8,26 d 1926,7,29 bur Winona, O. (W)
  Ch: Ferris   b 1881, 9, 2 d 1907, 9, 4
  Lydia later m Elisha P. Steer 1911,8,24 (W)

1822, 5, 22. William rocf Plainfield MM, dtd
  1821,12,20, endorsed by New Garden MM,
  1822,4,25
1823, 8, 20. William gct Sandy Spring MM
1880, 8, 25. Lydia gct Phila. MM, Pa. (W)
1904, 6, 22. Ferris rocf Phila. MM, Pa., dtd
  1904,5,26 (W)
1905, 6, 22. Lydia K. rocf Phila. MM, Pa.,
  dtd 1904,5,26 (W)
1911, 10, 25. Ferris con mcd (W)

LILY
1871, 11, 23. Honor C. gct Gunpowder MM (H)

LIPPIATT
----, --, --. Charles A., s Jacob & Elanor, b
  1911,1,11; m Valda MOORE, dt Wilfred &
  Lucy (G)
  Ch: Frederick b 1930, 10, 25
      Katheryn

LIPPIATT, Charles A. & Valda, continued
    Ch: Eleanor b 1933, 5, 16

1933, 2, 22. Frederick [Lippiot] recrq

LIPSEY
1859, 7, 21. Sarah J. Armstrong (form Lipsey)
    con mcd
1862, 12, 25. John, Ann, Lemuel & Ann Eliza
    dis joining separatists (W) of 1854

LITTY
1911, 12, 20. Jean rec in mbrp
1911, 12, 20. John C. rec in mbrp
1924, 1, 23. Catharine Louise recrq

LIVEZEY
----, --, --. Jason d 1883,3,8 bur Abington
    MH, Pa.; m Eleanor ----- d 1882,9,21 bur
    Salem (H)

1880, 1, 22. Jason & w, Eleanor, rocf Abing-
    ton MM, Pa. (H)

LLEWELLYN
1903, 10, 22. Elisha m Rachel C. GILBERT, form
    w of James A., dt David & Rebecca B. (Hol-
    loway) Wickersham, b 1863,4,3 d 1922,11,
    17 bur East Springfield, Pa. (W)

1920, 12, 22. Rachel C. rocf Middleton MM (W)

LLOYD
1824, 2, 25. Pascal rocf Darby MM, Pa., dtd
    1823,9,30

LOCK
----, --, --. Philip [Locke], s John, b 1889,2,
    4 d 1918,5,22 (G)

1914, 9, 25. Laura, Philip & Lula May recrq
1918, 5, 22. Philip & Lula May dropped from
    mbrp
1918, 5, 22. Laura [Locke] relrq

LOGUE
1813, 10, 20. Esther m Mordecai HAYES

1812, 11, 17. Stephen & w, Hannah, & ch, Sa-
    rah, rocf Centre MM, Del., dtd 1812,9,7
1812, 11, 17. Samuel rocf Centre MM, Del.,
    dtd 1812,9,7
1813, 1, 12. Esther rocf Center MM, dtd 1812,
    9,7
1813, 2, 18. Elizabeth rocf Center MM, Del.,
    dtd 1812,9,7
1818, 12, 23. Sarah W. gct Marlborough MM
1845, 2, 19. Stephen, minor, rocf Marlborough
    MM, dtd 1845,1,28
1845, 12, 24. Stephen gct Sandy Spring MM

LONG
----, --, --. Ray m Iva D. SMITH, dt George

K. & Anna (Doudna), b 1900,3,22 (W)
----, --, --. Lewis Walker, s Ellett & Mary,
    b 1901,7,4; m Sylvia LIEBYER, dt Edward &
    Nancy, b 1904,2,16
    Ch: Lewis
          Ervin   b 1924, 5, 16
        Sylvia
          Jean   " 1931, 3, 20

1879, 6, 26. James recrq
1916, 8, 16. Thelma recrq
1826, 4, 21. Iva (form Smith) dis mcd (W)
1931, 3, 25. Lewis Walter & ch, Lewis & Syl-
    via Jean, recrq
1931, 3, 25. Sylvia recrq

LONGSHORE
1818, 2, 16. Mary b (H)

LORD
1837, 8, 23. Cert rec for Jehu & w, Rebecca,
    & grandson, Jehu Lord Kite, from Strouds-
    burgh MM, Pa., dtd 1837,5,25, endorsed to
    Upper Springfield MM
1837, 8, 23. Cert rec for Rebecca from
    Stroudsburgh MM, Pa., dtd 1837,5,25, en-
    dorsed to Upper Springfield MM

LORING
1813, 8, 25. Sarah b (G)
1861, 11, 7. Ann d (G)

LOSCHINSKY
1924, 1, 23. Joseph Wayne recrq

LOVETT
1914, 5, 21. Robert Pittfield, s Robert P. &
    Sarah A., Bucks Co., Pa., Columbiana Co.,
    O.; m at Salem, Caroline HOAGLAND BLACK-
    BURN, dt Wm. J. & Elizabeth (Coleman), b
    1889,7,25 (W)

1914, 11, 25. Caroline B. gct Falls MM, Pa.
    (W)

LUPTON
1816, 2, 9. Deborah Ann R. b
1817, 1, 21. Nathan, Jr. b
----, --, --. Gideon b 1795,5,16; m Susannah
    ----- b 1801,10,10 (W)
    Ch: Sarah   b 1820, 7, 30
        Margaret   " 1821, 9, 30
        Wm.   " 1823, 10, 31
1827, 6, 22. Martin, s Nathan & Margaret,
    Jefferson Co., O.; m at Salem, Lusina ROOD
    dt Jonathan & Clarissa, Columbiana Co., O.
1840, 5, 18. Mary Winston b (W)
----, --, --. David b 1830,11,24 d 1882,7,31;
    m Sarah ----- b 1830,6,13 d 1888,2,-- (W)
    Ch: Anna   b 1853, 2, 26
        Mary P.   " 1856, 8, 26
        Achsah E.   " 1859, 10, 15
        Drusilla S. " 1862, 4, 18

LUPTON, continued

1823, 11, 19. Gideon & w, Susannah, & ch, Sarah & Margaret, rocf Short Creek MM, dtd 1823,6,24

1827, 9, 19. Lucina gct Short Creek MM, O.

1828, 12, 24. Gideon & w, Susanna, & ch, Sarah, Margaret & William, gct Smithfield MM, O.

1840, 7, 22. Nathan, Jr. & w, Deborah Ann, rocf Short Creek MM, dtd 1840,6,23

1842, 1, 19. Nathan & w & dt, Mary Winston, gct Short Creek MM

1878, 1, 23. David & w, Sarah, & dt, Drusilla, rocf Plymouth MM, dtd 1878,9,17 (W)

1878, 2, 20. Anna, Mary P. & Achsah E. rocf Plymouth MM, dtd 1877,12,17 (W)

1878, 5, 23. Mary P. & Achsah Elizabeth rocf Short Creek MM, dtd 1878,3,21

1879, 6, 26. Anna rocf Short Creek MM, dtd 1879,5,22

1881, 12, 21. Drusilla S. Bumbaugh (form Lupton) dis mcd & joining separatists of 1854 (W)

1881, 12, 21. Achsah E. Leach (form Lupton) dis mcd & joining separatists of 1854 (W)

1883, 12, 19. Anna gct Cottonwood MM, Kans. (W)

1883, 12, 19. Mary P. gct New Garden MM, O. (W)

LYNCH

----, --, --. Joshua b 1778,5,17; m Rachel ----- b 1774,7,18 (W)
   Ch: Ann   b 1804, 7, 25
       Mary   " 1808, 5, 22 d 1811, 8,13
       Elizabeth " 1810, 1, 2
       Hannah   " 1811, 10, 17
       Joseph   " 1813, 11, 25

1806, 10, 14. Joshua & w, Rachel, & dt, Ann, rocf Greenwich MM, West Jersey, dtd 1806, 8,27

1810, 6, 12. Joshua & w, Rachel, & ch, Ann, Mary & Elizabeth, gct New Garden MM

1813, 10, 12. Joshua & w, Rachel, & ch, Ann, Elizabeth & Hannah, rocf New Garden MM, dtd 1813,9,26

1830, 10, 20. Benjamin Ball gct Upper Springfield MM, to m Hannah Lynch

LYON

1878, 12, 25. Matilda J. (form Watson) dis mcd (W)

McBRIDE

1808, 1, 21. Stephen, s Stephen & Hannah, Columbiana Co., O.; m at New Garden, Charity SANDERS, dt Mordecai & Margaret, Columbiana Co., O.

----, --, --. James b 1786,10,31; m Elizabeth ----- b 1796,12,1 (W)
   Ch: Benjamin b 1834, 2, 14
       Lydia   " 1835, 12, 27
       Rachel   " 1837, 12, 25

Ch: Abishai   b 1840, 12, 25

1806, 5, 13. Stephen & w, Hannah, & ch, James, Jeremiah, Evan, Mary, Hannah, Samuel, Andrew, Betty & Abraham, rocf Hopewell MM, dtd 1806,3,3

1807, 11, 17. Stephen, Jr. rocf Hopewell MM, dtd 1807,9,9

1808, 2, 16. John recrq

1844, 5, 22. Ann, Ruth & Hannah rocf Sandy Spring MM, dtd 1844,4,26

1847, 1, 20. Hannah gct Middleton MM

1848, 5, 24. Ann gct Short Creek MM

1850, 2, 20. Elizabeth & ch, Benjamin, Lydia, Rachel & Abisha, rocf Middleton MM, dtd 1850,1,10

1850, 2, 20. Grace rocf Middleton MM, dtd 1850,1,10

1850, 11, 20. James rocf Sandy Spring MM, dtd 1850,10,25

1855, 7, 25. James & w, Elizabeth, & s, Abishai, gct Middleton MM (W)

1857, 3, 25. Rachel dis joining Methodist Society (W)

1858, 2, 24. Benjamin dis mou (W)

1859, 6, 22. Grace gct Short Creek MM (W)

1859, 11, 23. Lydia dis joining Methodist Society (W)

1860, 6, 21. Lydia dis jas

1866, 3, 21. Ruth dis joining separatists of 1854 (W)

McCAMMON

----, --, --. Oscar L., s Sylvanus & Katharine, b 1893,10,7; m Edith L. KERNS, dt Orin & Minnie, b 1901,10,29 (G)

1932, 12, 29. Oscar L., Edith & Bueda recrq

McCAN

1806, 2, 11. Tacy [Mecan] rocf Short Creek MM, dtd 1805,10,19

1932, 6, 29. Alta dropped from mbrp

McCARTER

1882, 7, 30. Mary E. d (H)

McCLUER

1859, 10, 20. Lydia Cowgill (form McCluer) con mcd

McCLUGGAGE

1896, 7, 3. Gladys J., dt Joseph & Clara, b (G)

1924, 10, 22. Lawrence recrq

McCONNELL

1801, 5, 22. Anna [McConnel] b (G)

1862, 5, 22. Anna d (G)

1805, 12, 17. William rocf Darby MM, dtd 1805,5,13, endorsed by Middleton MM, 1805

McCONNELL, continued
  12,14
1858, 8, 26. Anna rocf Baltimore MM, dtd
  1858,7,15
1862, 12, 25. Edith, Mary Ann, Emaline, Emmet,
  Charles, Anabel & Laura [McConnol] dis
  joining separatists (W) of 1854

McCOWEN
1871, 7, 19. Mary Elizabeth (form Pinkham)
  dis mcd (W)

McCURDY
1851, 4, 23. Daniel gct Cherry St. MM, Phila.,
  Pa. (H)

McDONALD
1875, 8, 2. Kitty, dt Richard & Emily Elton,
  b (G)

McGAFFICK
1916, 8, 16. Emma A. recrq
1927, 6, 22. Emma [McGaffic] dropped from mbrp

McGHEE
1932, 6, 29. Grace dropped from mbrp

McGOWAN
1913, 1, 31. Eugene & w, Bertha, recrq

McGREW
1884, 4, 21. Rosanna d (W)
1888, 10, 26. Reece d (W)

1829, 8, 19. Finley rocf Monallen MM, dtd
  1829,7,22 (H)
1829, 8, 19. Finley rocf Monallen MM, dtd
  1829,7,22 (H)
1829, 10, 21. William rocf Monallen MM, dtd
  1829,7,22 (H)
1829, 10, 21. Rebecca [Megrue] rocf Monallen
  MM, dtd 1829,7,22 (H)
1829, 10, 21. Mary [Megrue] rocf Monallen MM
  (H)
1832, 8, 22. William dis mou (H)
1837, 1, 25. Mary Wright (form McGrew) con
  mcd (H)

McKINZIE
1853, 5, 26. Ada, dt John & Armintha Weaver,
  b (G)
----, --, --. Harry m Lizzie WOODWORTH, dt
  Joshua & Esther, b 1867,11,25 (G)
  Ch: Carl   b 1889, 10, 16 d 1913,12,24

1883, 8, 16. John & Harry recrq
1886, 10, 21. John [McKinsey] dropped from
  mbrp
1911, 12, 20. Russell rec in mbrp
1913, 12, 29. Karl [McKinsey] dropped from
  mbrp

McMILLEN
1845, 12, 24. Ruth Ann rocf Short Creek MM,
  dtd 1845,8,19
1846, 10, 21. Ruth Ann Bentley (form McMillan)
  dis mcd

McMULLEN
1910, 2, 23. Lulu recrq

McNEELY
1832, 7, 25. Abigail rocf Middleton MM, dtd
  1832,6,7
1833, 12, 25. Abigail gct Sandy Spring MM

McPHERSON
1910, 8, 17. Catharine & Sylvester gct First
  Friends Church, Alliance, O.

MACY
1764, 11, 25. Micajah b
1775, 4, 6. Sarah b
1795, 7, 1. John b
1802, 1, 4. Samuel b
1807, 10, 19. Anna b d 1878,7,6

1807, 9, 15. Micajah & w, Sarah, & ch, John
  & Samuel, rocf South River MM, Va., dtd
  1807,5,9
1849, 10, 24. Anna rocf Marlborough MM, dtd
  1849, 9, 25
1862, 12, 25. Anna dis joining separatists
  (W) of 1854

MAERKT
----, --, --. Frederick b 1817,4,23 d 1882,3,
  12 (an elder); m Emelia Caroline -----
  b 1814,1,28 d 1891,12,14 (W)
  Ch: Charlotte D.
              b 1839, 4, 22 d 1861,12, 7
    Wilhelmina " 1840, 9, 11
    Louisa   " 1845, 3, 7 " 1861,12,17
    Jane   " 1848, 1, 8
    Anna   " 1852, 3, 26
    Hannah G.   " 1854, 4, 28

1854, 4, 19. Frederick recrq (W)
1854, 6, 21. Emelia Caroline recrq (W)
1854, 9, 20. Charlotte D., Wilhelmina, Louisa,
  Jane, Anna & Hanna G., ch Frederick &
  Emelia Caroline, recrq (W)
1856, 4, 23. Frederick & w, Amelia Caroline,
  & ch, Charlotte D., Wilhelmina, Louiza,
  Jane, Anna & Hannah G., gct New Garden MM
1862, 2, 20. Frederick & w, Amelia, & ch,
  Wilhelmina, Hannah G., Jane & Anna, gct
  Redstone MM, Pa.
1866, 1, 24. Frederick & w, Amelia, & ch,
  Jane J., Ann & Hannah G., rocf Providence
  MM, Pa., dtd 1866,1,4 (W)
1866, 1, 24. Wilhelmina rocf Providence MM,
  dtd 1866,1,4 (W)
1867, 5, 22. Wilhelmina Boyed (form Maerkt)
  con mcd (W)

MAERKT, continued
1874, 1, 22. Jane J. Sim (form Maerkt) con
    mcd (W)
1881, 10, 19. Anna dis disunity (W)
1881, 10, 19. Hannah G. dis disunity (W)

MALMSBURY
----, --, --. Benjamin [Malmsburg] b 1779,5,6;
    m Jane ----- b 1780,4,22 (W)

1824, 4, 21. Benjamin recrq
1824, 4, 21. Jane rocf Burlington MM, N. J.,
    dtd 1824,3,1
1825, 5, 25. Elizabeth, James, Isaac, Rebecca,
    Hannah, Benjamin & Sarah V. [Malmsberry],
    ch Benjamin & Jane, recrq
1825, 5, 25. Jane [Malmsberry], Jr., dt Ben-
    jamin & Jane, recrq
1848, 5, 24. Sarah H. [Malmsberry] rocf New
    Garden MM, dtd 1848,4,20
1849, 4, 25. Sarah H. [Mallsbury] gct Upper
    Springfield MM

MALONE
1882, 5, 25. John Walter rocf Clear Creek MM
1882, 8, 23. Charles O. & s, Harrison, rocf
    Clear Creek MM, O.
1882, 8, 23. James S. rocf Clear Creek MM, O.
1882, 11, 8. Carrie H. recrq

MANKIN
1818, 3, 17. Charity (form Wright) dis

MANLEY
1927, 4, 20. Betty rocf Columbus MM

MAPLE
1910, 2, 23. L. F. recrq

MARIS
1825, 9, 28. Jonathan, s Joseph & Anne, Co-
    lumbiana Co., O.; m at Goshen, Thomason
    MORRIS, dt Joseph & Rachel, Columbiana
    Co., O.
1826, 7, 13. Barclay, s Jonathan & Thomison,
    b (G)

1853, 11, 23. Barkley rocf Upper Springfield
    MM, dtd 1853,10,22
1862, 12, 25. Lavina dis joining separatists
    (W) of 1854
1864, 11, 11. Barclay dis joining separatists
    of 1854 (W)
1874, 5, 6. Barclay gct Sandy Spring MM, to
    m Ann Pim
1874, 8, 5. Ann P. rocf Sandy Spring MM,
    dtd 1874,7,21
1877, 6, 21. Barclay & Ann P. gct East
    Goshen MM

MARSH
1806, 7, 15. Elias rocf Rahway & Plainfield
    MM, dtd 1806,1,16

1806, 10, 14. Elias, Samuel Davis Thomas
    Grissell & Joseph Pennock, ch Elias, recrq
1806, 10, 14. Lydia Fanny, Joseph, Samuel &
    Jane, ch Elias, recrq
1808, 4, 12. Lydia gct Miami MM
1814, 11, 15. Lydia Walton (form Marsh) con
    mcd
1859, 8, 25. Mary H. Stanley (form Marsh) con
    mcd
1876, 2, 24. Hannah gct Marietta MM, Ia. (H)
1884, 11, 20. Hannah gct Marietta MM, Ia. (H)

MARSHALL
1812, 12, 3. Joseph, s Wm. & Mary, Portage
    Co., O.; m at Marlborough, Mary WILEMAN,
    dt Abraham & Letitia, Stark Co., O.
1813, 4, 22. Benjamin, s Wm. & Mary, Portage
    Co., O.; m at Springfield, Ann CATTELL,
    dt James & Deborah, Columbiana Co., O.

1808, 7, 12. Joseph [Marshal] rocf Middleton
    MM, dtd 1808,4,9
1808, 7, 12. Sarah rocf Middleton MM, dtd
    1808,4,9
1808, 7, 12. Mary rocf Middleton MM, dtd 1808,
    4,9
1812, 7, 14. Benjamin [Marshal] recrq
1842, 9, 21. James C. rocf Middleton MM, dtd
    1842,9,15
1843, 2, 22. James C. gct Upper Springfield
    MM

MARTIN
1932, 6, 29. Vera Ritchy dropped from mbrp

MASTERS
----, --, --. Joseph, s Wm. & Naomi (Ball), b
    1839,12,6; m Esther STRATTON (W)
    Ch: Daniel S. b 1867, 4, 19
1875, 9, 2. Thos. Howard, s Burvin & Nar-
    cissa, Cayohoya Co., O.; m at Salem, Ma-
    tilda RASCHE, dt Jacob & Helena, Pa.
1877, 9, 5. Matilda m Jason Kirk MASTERS
----, --, --. Daniel S., s Joseph & Esther
    (Stratton), b 1867,4,19; m Hannah Mary
    HALL, dt Linton & Ann W. (Allmon), b 1863,
    3,25 (W)

1872, 11, 6. Thomas Howard rocf Muncy MM, dtd
    1872,9,18
1877, 5, 9. Matilda rocf Muncy MM, dtd 1877,
    4,11
1909, 7, 21. Daniel S. & w, Hannah M., rocf
    New Garden MM, O., dtd 1909,6,24 (W)
1910, 8, 24. Joseph rocf New Garden MM, dtd
    1910,7,21 (W)
1916, 12, 20. Joseph gct Phila. MM, Pa. (W)

MATHER
----, --, --. John b 1783,9,20; m Catharine
    ----- b 1782,6,7 (W)
    Ch: Samuel   b 1805, 7, 29
        Sarah   " 1807, 7, 9

MATHER, John & Catharine, continued
  Ch: Thomas b 1809, 2, 7
    Wm.   " 1811, 5, 1
    Daniel " 1813, 3, 19
    Jesse " 1815, 6, 2
    Ann   " 1817, 8, 30
    James " 1819, 12, 28 d 1832, 2, 8
    Lydia " 1822, 2, 4
    John Jr. " 1824, 10, 28
1823, 3, 28. Samuel, s John & Catharine, Co-
 lumbiana Co., O., b 1805,7,29; m at Salem,
 Lydia EVANS, dt Jonathan & Elizabeth, Co-
 lumbiana Co., O., b 1808,3,3 d 1845,8, 5
 (H)
  Ch: Sarah b 1828, 3, 24
    Hannah " 1829, 9, 19
1831, 11, 30. Thomas, s John & Catharine, Co-
 lumbiana Co., O.; m at Salem, Elizabeth
 WRIGHT, dt Joseph & Rebecca, Columbiana
 Co., O. (H)
  Ch: Benjamin B.b 1832, 9, 22
    Joseph
     Wright " 1834, 8, 14
    Alexander
     T. " 1836, 10, 21 d 1840, 5,14
    John " 1839, 2, 14 " 1839,11,13
    Maryann K. " 1840, 11, 16
    James
----, --, --. Daniel b 1813,3,19; m Rebecca
----- b 1818,11,27 (H)
  Ch: Alice Ann b 1839, 9, 19
    Catharine " 1842, 1, 11
1851, 2, 20. Thomas, s John & Catharine, Mahoning Co., O.; m at house of Samuel
 Richards, Huldah BROWN, dt Stephen & Hannah C., Susquehanna Co., Pa. (H)
1873, 10, 23. Mary Ann K. m Wm. NICKELS (H)

1823, 10, 22. John & w, Catharine, & ch, Samuel, Sarah, Thomas, William, Daniel,
 Jesse, Ann, James & Lydia, rocf Munsey MM,
 Pa., dtd 1823,8,20
1823, 10, 22. Lydia rocf Muncy MM, Pa., dtd
 1823,8,20
1828, 7, 30. John & w, Catharine, & ch, Sarah, Thomas, William, Daniel, Jesse, Ann,
 James, Lydia & John, rocf New Garden MM,
 dtd 1828,7,24 (H)
1828, 8, 20. John dis jH
1828, 8, 20. Catharine dis jH
1828, 10, 22. Samuel & Thomas dis jH
1828, 10, 22. Lydia dis jH
1829, 1, 21. Sarah dis jH
1830, 5, 6. William, Daniel, Jesse, Ann,
 James, Lydia & John, Jr., ch John & Catharine, gct Upper Springfield MM
1833, 4, 24. Sarah Street (form Mather) dis
 mcd (H)
1833, 5, 22. Isaac Street & Sarah Mather con
 mcd
1833, 12, 25. William gct Marlborough MM, to
 m Hannah Holloway (H)
1837, 7, 19. Samuel [Mathers] dis not attend-

ing mtg (H)
1839, 10, 23. Daniel dis military training (H)
1839, 12, 25. Daniel con mcd & attending military training (H)
1839, 12, 25. Rebecca [Mathers] (form Barber)
 con mcd (H)
1840, 3, 25. Jesse dis mcd (H)
1842, 10, 19. Ann Barber (form Mather) dis mcd
 (H)
1844, 6, 19. Lydia Stanley (form Mather) dis
 mcd (H)
1854, 3, 22. Red Cedar MM, Ia. was given permission to rec Lydia in mbrp (W)
1879, 12, 25. Charles L. relrq (H)

MATTHEW
1922, 12, 20. Mrs. Esther recrq

MATTOCK
1855, 2, 21. Richard B. Fawcett gct ND MM,
 Phila., Pa., to m Rebecca B. Mattock (W)

MAUL
1889, 6, 26. James E., s James E. & Margaret
 T., b 1863,3,25 d 1918,2,12; m at Salem,
 Hannah R. FAWCETT, dt Joseph & Mary R.,
 Columbiana Co., O., b 1866,2,15 (W)
  Ch: Esther b 1890, 7, 21

1845, 3, 19. Edward [Mall], minor, rocf Short
 Creek MM, dtd 1844,12,24
1847, 1, 20. Edward, minor, gct Short Creek
 MM
1889, 4, 24. James E. rocf Short Creek MM,
 dtd 1889,3,19 (W)
1894, 5, 23. James E. dis jas (W)
1894, 7, 25. Hannah R. dis jas (W)

MAYNARD
1885, 8, 20. Charles rocf Hanover MM, Mich.
1886, 10, 21. Charles dropped from mbrp

MEAD
1835, 7, 22. Hannah (form Wright) dis mcd
1836, 2, 24. Hannah (form Wright) dis mcd (H)
1839, 6, 19. Caroline (form Wright) con mou
 (H)
1853, 8, 25. Hannah recrq (H)

MEADER
1862, 12, 25. Almon, Susan & Webster dis joining separatists (W) of 1854

MENDENHALL
1831, 7, 20. George, minor, rocf Middleton MM,
 dtd 1831,6,9
1835, 5, 20. Committee appointed to give Pennel testimony of disownment issued by Concord MM, Pa., dtd 1835,4,30 (H)
1836, 10, 19. George [Mendinghall] dis jH

MERCER
----, --, --. Mary b 1796,10,12 d 1872,1,27(W)

MERCER, continued

1801, 10, 11. Rachel b

----, --, --. Phebe b 1809,3,20 d 1878,1,8 (W)

1824, 5, 26. Rachel m Joshua DAVIS

1831, 7, 27. Daniel, s Solomon & Olive, Columbiana Co., O.; m at Salem, Sarah SCHOOL-
EY, dt James & Lydia Pyle, Chester Co., Pa.

1913, 4, 25. Wm. S., s Daniel, d (G)

1811, 7, 16. Cert rec for Oloff from Kennet
MM, Pa., dtd 1811,5,7, endorsed to New Garden MM

1811, 8, 13. Cert rec for Daniel & w, Alice,
& ch, Rebecca, Mary, Hannah, Rachel, Solomon & Phebe, from Kennet MM, dtd 1811,5,7,
endorsed to Middleton MM

1812, 9, 15. Aaron Holloway gct Middleton MM,
to m Olive Mercer

1819, 5, 19. Rachel rocf Middleton MM, dtd
1819,3,22

1826, 2, 22. Mary rocf New Garden MM, dtd
1825,12,22

1830, 6, 23. Hannah rocf Providence MM, dtd
1830,6,3

1831, 1, 19. Hannah dis jH

1831, 2, 23. Hannah recrq (H)

1831, 9, 21. Sarah (form Schooley) & ch,
Emily Nicholas & Rachel Schooley, gct
Middleton, MM

1833, 5, 22. Phebe rocf Middleton MM, dtd
1833,5,9

1835, 7, 22. Hannah Hunt (form Mercer) dis
mcd (H)

1856, 11, 20. Anna rocf Middleton MM, dtd
1856,10,16 (H)

1862, 12, 25. Mary & Phebe dis joining separatists (W) of 1854

1914, 1, 21. Mrs. Ella & ch, Hazel & Arthur,
relrq

MEREDITH

1830, 3, 3. Mary M. [Meridith] m John VOTAW,
Jr.

1834, 1, 10. Sarah b (H)

1829, 3, 25. Mary E. rocf Uwchland MM, Pa.,
dtd 1828,12,4

1833, 4, 24. William & w, Sarah, & ch, Marga-
ret B., Simon C., Elizabeth R., William,
David C., John L., Sarah & Beulah, rocf
Uchlin MM, Pa., dtd 1833,3,4

1834, 1, 22. Cert rec for Margaret, Simon,
Elizabeth, William, David & John, ch William & Sarah, from Uwchlan MM, Pa., dtd
1833,10,10, endorsed to Upper Springfield
MM

1839, 10, 23. Margaret [Maredith] dis jas (H)

1844, 4, 24. Elizabeth Middleton (form Meredith) dis mcd (H)

METZGAR

1856, 12, 21. Miriam G. (form Painter) dis mcd
(W)

MICHENER

1811, 8, 25. Phebe H. b (H)

----, --, --. James b 1802,3,18; m Eliza ----
b 1801,4,18 d 1841,11,12 (H)
Ch: Thomas   b 1825, 11, 16
    Ann   " 1827, 1, 8
    Mary   " 1828, 7, 30
    Asenath   " 1830, 6, 18
    Wm. R.   " 1832, 7, 1
    Abraham   " 1835, 4, 20
    James   " 1838, 7, 2
    Eber   " 1840, 5, 6

1842, 12, 29. James, s Wm. & Ann, Columbiana
Co., O.; m at West MH, Sarah E. PEIRCE,
dt Isaac & Elizabeth, Columbiana Co., O.
(H)

1844, 4, 25. Ann E. m Enos COOK (H)

1826, 5, 24. James & w, Eliza, & s, Thomas,
rocf Sadsbury MM, Pa., dtd 1826,3,28

1827, 1, 24. James [Michener] & w, Eliza, &
s, Thomas, gct Upper Springfield MM

1828, 7, 30. James & w, Eliza, & ch, Thomas
& Ann, rocf New Garden MM, dtd 1828,7,24
(H)

1836, 8, 24. Phebe rocf New Garden MM, Pa.,
dtd 1836,7,7 (H)

MIDDLETON

1832, 8, 8. Hannah m Aaron FAWCETT

1834, 4, 30. Deborah m Abraham BONSALL

1845, 7, 3. Amelia R. m Alfred WRIGHT (H)

1817, 7, 13. Hudson, minor, rocf Middleton
MM, dtd 1817,6,14

1821, 5, 23. Hudson, Jr. gct Lees Creek MM,
O.

1825, 12, 21. Hannah rocf Sandy Spring MM, dtd
1825,11,25

1833, 6, 19. Deborah rocf Sandy Spring MM,
dtd 1833,5,24

1844, 4, 24. Elizabeth (form Meredith) dis
mcd (H)

MILBOURNE

1807, 4, 14. Sarah & ch, Samuel, Jonathan,
William, Jacob, Lott, Anna, David & Betsy,
rocf Middleton MM, dtd 1806,10,11

MILLER

----, --, --. Ann b 1775,11,5 d 1855,10,4

----, --, --. Moris b 1799,7,27 d 1883,11,18;
m ----- ----- (W)
Ch: Isaac V.   b 1826, 2, 29 d 1827,11,21
    Hannah
    Rebecca   " 1841, 11, 23 " 1857, 5,26

----, --, --. Robert b 1800,10,8 d 1895,8,18
(an elder); m Mary Hall   b 1812,1,11
d 1897,8,13 (an elder) (W)
Ch: Martha
    Hall   b 1849, 9, 1
    Sarah R.
    Hall   " 1851, 4, 4
    Ch of Mary by form m

MILLER, continued
1872, 8, 10. David d ae 79y (an elder)
1882, 8, 30. Elizabeth d ae 90y (an elder)

1807, 9, 15. Susannah (form Wilkins) con mcd
1831, 2, 23. Levi, Jr. gct New Garden MM, to
          m Mariah Pennington
1831, 11, 23. Levi, Jr. gct Sandy Spring MM
1842, 4, 20. Jonathan Stanley gct Redstone
          MM, to m Hannah Miller
1853, 5, 25. Emmor Fawcett gct Redstone MM,
          to m Lydia W. Miller
1854, 3, 22. Taylor F. Langstaff gct Sandy
          Spring MM, to m Mary J. Miller (W)
1865, 12, 21. David & w, Elizabeth, rocf Red
          Stone MM, dtd 1865,11,20
1865, 12, 21. Sabina & Rachel Jane rocf Red-
          stone MM, dtd 1865,11,20
1866, 11, 23. Ruth Anna Brooks (form Miller)
          dis mcd
1874, 1, 21. Robert & w, Mary H., rocf New
          Garden MM, dtd 1873,12,25 (W)
1885, 2, 6. Lizzie recrq

MILLIKIN
1813, 8, 17. John [Milligan] & w, Abigail, &
          ch, Ann, Clement, James, John, Joseph &
          William, rocf Westland MM, dtd 1813,3,27
1884, 12, 24. Mary (form Hancock) dis mcd (W)
1920, 3, 24. Earl & Martha [Milliken] rec in
          mbrp
1932, 6, 29. Earl & M----- [Milligan] dropped
          from mbrp

MILLS
1881, 1, 20. Rachel Allice (form Nickols) gct
          Marietta MM, Ia. (H)

MILNER
1809, 5, 18. Susannah rst in mbrp with per-
          mission of Fairfax MM, Va. (had been dis
          by that mtg for mcd
1864, 6, 23. Lydia B. (form Reeder) con mcd
          (H)

MINER
1812, 10, 23. Ellis b (W)

MITCHELL
1872, 5, 1. Joseph R., s Abel & Elizabeth,
          Baltimore Co., Md.; m at home of Sarah
          Ann Trago, Sarah E. TRAGO, dt John & Sarah,
          Columbiana Co., O. (H)

1817, 1, 24. Edith L. [Mitchel], dt Isabel
          Edith Steves, relrq

MONTAGUE
1887, 3, 20. George H. & w, Mary Ann, recrq
1890, 6, 26. Mary A. dropped from mbrp

MONTGOMERY
1814, 3, 18. Lydia b (H)

1839, 3, 20. Lydia (form Ball) con mou (H)
1910, 2, 23. J. J. & w recrq
1910, 2, 23. Clarence recrq

MOODY
1882, 8, 9. Jessie recrq

MOORE
1817, 1, 7. Sarah W. b (W)
----, --, --. Calvin C. b 1823,2,11 d 1865,7,
          14 (W)
----, --, --. Pemberton, s Moses & Mary (Kirk-
          wood), b 1841,3,27 d 1916,1,21 bur Friends
          Bur. Gr., Salem, O. (W)
1854, 2, 4. Walter T. b (W)
----, --, --. Harry E., s Clarkson & Mary E.
          (Harry), b 1866,6,13 d 1915,5,17 bur Da-
          mascus, O. (a minister); m Frances C.
          COOPER, dt Samuel & Sarah (Pennock), b
          1868,1,17 (W)
          Ch: Mary H.   b 1893, 8, 8; m Sheldon
               Smith
               Robert
               Barclay   " 1899, 1, 2
1914, 9, 17. Ralph Richard, s Wilfred & Lucy,
          b (G)
1923, 6, 27. Martha Frances m Allen J. HALL
          (W)
1926, 9, 1. Mary H. m Sheldon W. SMITH (W)

1808, 5, 17. William rocf Concord MM, dtd
          1808,3,24
1814, 1, 11. William gct Contentney MM, N.C.
1817, 5, 13. William dis
1851, 7, 23. Colvin C. rocf Sadsbury MM, Pa.,
          dtd 1851,7,8
1852, 4, 21. Calvin C. [More] gct Short
          Creek MM, to m Sarah Walter
1852, 10, 20. Sarah W. rocf Short Creek MM,
          dtd 1852,9,28
1862, 12, 25. Calvin, Sarah & Walter dis join-
          ing separatists (W) of 1854
1868, 3, 26. Sarah [More] rocf Green St. MM,
          Phila., Pa., dtd 1868,2,20 (H)
1868, 1, 22. Sarah W. & s, Walter T., gct
          Birmingham MM, Pa. (W)
1907, 5, 22. Harry E. & w, Frances C., & ch,
          Mary H. & Robert B., rocf New Garden MM,
          Pa., dtd 1907,5,8 (W)
1915, 4, 21. Pemberton rocf New Garden MM,
          Pa., dtd 1915,4,7 (W)
1920, 7, 21. Martha Frances, adopted dt Fran-
          ces C., recrq (W)
1933, 2, 22. Ralph Richard recrq

MORGAN
----, --, --. Wm. b 1804,5,25 d 1820,10,18 bur
          Salem

1809, 5, 18. Esther rst in mbrp with per-
          mission of Westland MM
1812, 7, 14. Esther gct New Garden MM
1815, 7, 11. Maria rocf New Garden MM, dtd

MORGAN, continued
     1815,5,18
1815, 7, 11. Esther Wright & ch, Matilda,
     William, Benjamin Townsend & Eliza Nailor
     Morgan, rocf New Garden MM, dtd 1815,6,15
1816, 5, 14. Maria gct New Garden MM
1816, 5, 14. Joseph Wright & w, Esther, & ch,
     Matilda, Benjamin Townsend & Eliza Nailer
     Morgan, gct New Garden MM
1864, 12, 22. Hannah & Edith gct Gunpowder MM,
     Md. (H)
1879, 8, 6. James H. rocf Caesars Creek MM,
     dtd 1879,6,26

MORLAN
----, --, --. Jonah [Moorelan] b 1779,3,16; m
     Mary ----- d 1815,7,24 (W)
     Ch: Elizabeth b 1802, 12, 6
         Huldah   " 1805, 11, 8
         Rhoda   " 1807, 10, 1
         Stephen   " 1809, 10, 20
         Joseph   " 1812, 9, 17
         Hiram   " 1814, 11, 25
         Huldah   " 1815, 11, 8
1808, 10, 26. Aden, s Stephen & Mary, Columbi-
     ana Co., O.; m at Sandy Spring, Amy JOHN,
     dt Griffith & Sarah, Columbiana Co., O.
1814, 1, 19. Isaac, s Stephen & Mary, Columbi-
     ana Co., O.; m at Salem, Martha WRIGHT, dt
     Joseph & Elizabeth, Columbiana Co., O.
----, --, --. Mordecai [Morelan] b 1793,5,14
     d 1880,1,28; m Eliza Ann ----- b 1801,1,
     26 d 1880,6,9 (W)
     Ch: Edwin D.   b 1822, 4, 18
         Lanora   " 1823, 10, 22
         Theophilus " 1826, 6, 16
         Roxany   " 1828, 1, 30
         Caroline " 1831, 8, 18
         Micajah   " 1833, 7, 29
         Newberry " 1835, 6, 3
         Elmira   " 1837, 3, 11
         Amelia   " 1839, 9, 20
         Albert M. " 1850, 10, 9
----, --, --. Theophilus b 1826,6,16; m Lydia
     F. ----- b 1827,12,2 d 1859,4,26 (W)
     Ch: Mary M.   b 1857, 8, 14
     Theophilus m 2nd 1861,8,27 at Salem, Sarah
     P. HOLLOWAY, dt David & Rachel, Columbiana
     Co., O. (W)-
     Ch: David M.   b 1862, 4, 8
         Anna   " 1865, 2, 21
         Charles P. " 1871, 8, 16
         Lewis T. " 1874, 8, 11
----, --, --. Micajah M. b 1833,7,29; m Anna
     ----- (W)
     Ch: Irene R.   b 1874, 2, 8
         Ida E.   " 1875, 11, 3
----, --, --. Louis T. m Eva D. COURTNEY, dt
     Joseph A. & Mary J. (Boyd), b 1866,8,23
     (W)
----, --, --. Charles P., s Theophilis & Sarah
     P. (Holloway), b 1871,8,16; m S. Ellen
     EDGERTON, dt Jesse & Semira (Stratton),

b 1875,9,30 (W)
Ch: Lawrence
    Lewis   b 1902, 11, 12
    Anna Mary " 1908, 1, 31
    Wilson
    Jesse   " 1910, 8, 28
    Elizabeth " 1913, 5, 23

1814, 5, 17. Martha [Morelan] gct Middleton
     MM
1817, 8, 12. Jonah [Moorlan] dis mcd
1818, 5, 12. Barzillai [Mooreland], minor,
     rocf Middleton MM, dtd 1818,4,15
1819, 7, 21. Stephen [Morelan], minor, gct
     New Garden MM
1821, 3, 21. Barzillai gct Middleton MM
1821, 5, 23. Elizabeth [Morelan] gct New Gar-
     den MM .
1821, 10, 24. Elizabeth Ira (form Morelan) dis
     mou
1822, 6, 19. Huldah [Moreland], minor, gct
     New Garden MM
1830, 7, 21. Rhoda [Moreland] dis JH
1831, 7, 20. Mordecai [Morelan] & w, Eliza
     Ann, & ch, Edwin, Lanora, Theopholis &
     Roxany, rocf Middleton MM, dtd 1831,7,7
1833, 9, 25. Lydia & Sarah [Moreland] rocf
     Carmel MM, dtd 1833,8,27
1834, 7, 23. Joseph gct New Garden MM
1834, 11, 19. Lydia [Mourland] gct Sandy
     Spring MM
1834, 12, 24. Sarah [Morland] gct Sandy Spring
     MM
1835, 8, 19. Hiram dis disunity
1836, 5, 25. Sarah gct Sandy Spring MM
1838, 3, 21. Mordecai [Mourland] & w, Eliza
     Ann, & ch, Edwin, Lanora, Theophilos, Rox-
     ana, Caroline, Micajah, Newberry & Elmira,
     gct Sandy Spring MM
1851, 9, 24. Theophilus rocf Middleton MM,
     dtd 1851,9,18
1852, 4, 21. Theophilus gct Upper Springfield
     MM, to m Sarah Atkinson
1852, 6, 23. Mordecai & w, Eliza Ann, & ch,
     Micajah, Newberry, Elmira, Amelia & Albert,
     rocf Middleton MM, dtd 1852,6,10
1854, 1, 25. Elmira Pyle (form Mourland) dis
     mcd
1856, 3, 19. Theophilus gct Upper Springfield
     MM, to m Lydia French (W)
1856, 7, 23. Lydia F. rocf Upper Springfield
     MM, dtd 1856,6,27 (W)
1859, 4, 20. Newbury dis mcd (W)
1859, 6, 22. Micajah dis mcd (W)
1861, 4, 21. Amelia E. dis jas (W)
1862, 12, 25. Alma Jane & John [Morland] dis
     joining separatists (W) of 1854
1862, 12, 25. Mordecia, Eliza Ann & Albert
     (Morland] dis joining separatists (W) of
     1854
1862, 12, 25. Theophilus, Sarah, Mary & David
     [Morland] dis joining separatists (W) of
     1854

MORLAN, continued

1863, 4, 22. Theophilos & w, Sarah, & ch,
      Mary M. & David H., gct Middleton MM (W)
1864, 3, 23. Micajah M. rst by rq (W)
1868, 2, 19. Anna M. recrq (W)
1872, 11, 20. Theophilus & w, Sarah P., & ch,
      Mary M., David H., Anna & Charles P., rocf
      Middleton MM, dtd 1872,11,16 (W)
1873, 6, 25. Amy Jane rocf Middleton MM, dtd
      1873,5,17 (W)
1874, 1, 21. Albert M. dis disunity (W)
1878, 2, 6. Mary I. Warrington (form Morlan)
      rocf Alliance MM, dtd 1877,12,25
1881, 9, 22. Edward recrq
1883, 5, 23. David H. gct Middleton MM (W)
1883, 6, 20. Micajah M. dis disunity (W)
1883, 9, 19. Theophilus & w, Sarah P., & ch,
      Charles P. & Louis T., gct Middleton MM
      (W)
1883, 9, 19. Mary F. gct Middleton MM (W)
1883, 9, 19. Anna gct Middleton MM (W)
1887, 1, 20. Edward dropped from mbrp
1909, 6, 23. Charles P. & w, S. Ellen, & ch,
      Lawrence L. & Anna Mary, rocf Middleton MM,
      O., dtd 1909,6,19
1910, 12, 21. Irene R. dis jas (W)
1914, 1, 21. Charles P. & w, S. Ellen, & ch,
      Lawrence L., Anna Mary, Wilson J. & Eliza-
      beth, gct Upper Springfield MM, O. (W)
1918, 7, 24. Eva D. rocf Middleton MM, O.,
      dtd 1918,7,20 (W)

MORRIS

----, --, --. Joseph b 1767,2,5 d 1825,3,17
      bur Goshen; m Rachel ----- b 1774,10,14 (W)
      Ch: Abraham   b 1793, 12, 21
          Sarah   " 1795, 11, 7
          John   " 1798, 5, 18
          Rebecca   " 1800, 4, 12
          Thomason   " 1802, 5, 21
          Joseph Jr. " 1804, 6, 23
          Rachel   " 1806, 9, 6
          Esther   " 1809, 3, 10
          Anthony   " 1811, 8, 22 d 1815,11, 6
          Caleb
            Shinn   " 1813, 12, 27
          Elizabeth " 1817, 5, 26
          Beulah W. " 1819, 11, 7
1794, 11, 14. Mary b (W)
----, --, --. Anthony b 1773,4,18 d 1825,5,18
      bur Springfield; m Hannah ----- b 1775,6,7
      (W)
      Ch: Barzillai b 1798, 5, 4
          Esther   " 1799, 8, 12
          Sarah   " 1801, 5, 31
          Thomas   " 1802, 12, 29 d 1809, 1,16
            bur Springfield
          Hannah   b 1804, 10, 17
          Joseph   " 1806, 12, 1
          Anthony   " 1809, 6, 13
          Elizabeth " 1809, 6, 13
          Mary   " 1811, .8, 12
          John   " 1813, 9, 2 d 1815, 4, 7

      Ch: Martha   b 1815, 6, 8 d 1815, 7,12
          Stephen   " 1818, 4, 14
1812, 2, 27. Susannah, dt Wm. & Susannah, b
      (W)
1813, 12, 2. Elizabeth I. b (W)
1814, 6, 20. Joshua, s Benjamin & Lydia, Co-
      lumbiana Co., O.; m at Springfield, Rachel
      COPPOCK, dt Samuel & Ellen, Columbiana
      Co., O.
1817, 11, 20. Sarah Ann b (W)
1820, 6, 22. Joseph b (W)
1821, 3, 1. Sarah m James B. BRUFF
1823, 4, 23. Isaiah b (W)
1823, 1, 2. Barzillai, s Anthony & Hannah,
      Columbiana Co., O.; m at Springfield, Sa-
      rah CREW, dt Obediah & Mary, Columbiana
      Co., O.
1823, 12, 31. Rebecca m Isaac STREET
1825, 9, 28. Thomason m Jonathan MARIS
1832, 3, 10. Albina b (H)
1846, 4, 29. Lydia m Joseph WILLIAMS
1857, 10, 29. Abraham, s Joseph & Rachel, Mor-
      row Co., O.; m at Salem, Mehetable J. COP-
      POCK, dt Joshua & Sibyl, Columbiana Co.,
      O.

1810, 3, 13. Sarah, dt Hannah, gct Abington
      MM, Pa.
1813, 4, 13. Sally gct Stillwater MM, O.
1814, 11, 15. William & w, Susannah, & ch,
      Benjamin, Ava, Mordecai, Jesse, Jonathan,
      Sarah, William, Susannah & Lydia, gct
      Stillwater MM
1817, 5, 13. Leah Webb (form Morris) dis mcd
1817, 9, 16. Mary gct Stillwater MM
1817, 9, 16. Nathan, minor, gct Stillwater MM
1818, 10, 21. Joshua & w, Rachel, & ch, Ellen
      & Samuel, gct Stillwater MM
1818, 10, 21. Lydia gct Stillwater MM
1819, 3, 24. Joseph Rhodes & ch, Harmon &
      Lydia, & Anna Morris, gct Short Creek MM
1820, 5, 24. Sarah rocf Frankford MM, dtd
      1820,4,28
1821, 12, 19. Joseph & w, Rachel, & ch, Jo-
      seph, Rachel, Esther, Caleb, Elizabeth &
      Beulah W., rocf Burlington MM, N. J., dtd
      1821,9,3, endorsed by Plainfield MM, 1821,
      11,22
1821, 12, 19. Abram rocf Burlington MM, N. J.,
      dtd 1821,9,3, endorsed by Plainfield MM,
      1821,11,22
1821, 12, 19. Sarah rocf Burlington MM, N. J.,
      dtd 1821,9,3, endorsed by Plainfield MM,
      1821,11,22
1821, 12, 19. John rocf Burlington MM, N. J.,
      dtd 1821,9,3, endorsed by Plainfield MM,
      1821,11,22
1821, 12, 19. Rebecca rocf Burlington MM, N.
      J., dtd 1821,9,3, endorsed by Plainfield
      MM, 1821,11,22
1822, 3, 20. Thomason rocf Salem MM, N. J.,
      dtd 1822,2,2
1822, 7, 24. Mary recrq

MORRIS, continued
1822, 10, 23. Sarah Ann & Joseph, ch Abram &
     Mary, recrq
1823, 10, 22. John dis disunity
1824, 4, 21. Sarah Smith (form Morris) dis
     mou
1829, 4, 22. Anthony dis disunity
1832, 10, 24. William Boulton gct Upper Spring-
     field MM, to m Mary Morris
1837, 4, 19. Stephen, a minor, rocf Upper
     Springfield MM, dtd 1837,3,25
1840, 10, 21. Stephen gct Upper Springfield
     MM
1841, 4, 21. Philip Evans gct Upper Spring-
     field MM, to m Esther Morris
1851, 1, 22. Elizabeth J. rocf Smithfield MM,
     dtd 1850,11,18
1858, 1, 21. Mahitable J. gct Gilead MM
1860, 2, 22. Elizabeth J. gct Phila. MM, Pa.
     (W)
1862, 12, 25. Elizabeth J. dis joining separa-
     tists (W) of 1854
1911, 12, 20. George rec in mbrp
1911, 12, 20. Fern rec in mbrp
1915, 3, 31. Harry B. relrq
1918, 5, 22. Mary S. relrq
1927, 6, 22. Grace dropped from mbrp

MORSE
1898, 4, 7. Kenneth, s Wm. H. Perry &
     Emma Jane (Lobb), b (W)

1921, 2, 23. Kenneth recrq (W)
1930, 6, 25. Kenneth gct Middleton MM, O. (W)

MOTESHAM
1910, 12, 21. Carrie Barley gct E. Goshen MM

MOTT
1920, 8, 26. Francis E., s James & Emma F.,
     O'Brian Co., Ia.; m Frances S. BINNS, dt
     Arthur H. & Tacie M. (Bundy), Cuyahoga
     Co., O., b 1899,6,6 (W)
     Ch: Mildred
          Elizabeth b 1921, 11, 10

1915, 7, 21. William L. Cope gct Springville
     MM, Ia., to m Rachel Tacy Mott (W)
1921, 11, 23. Frances B. & dt, Mildred Eliza-
     beth, gct Paulina MM, Ia. (W)

MOUNTS
1915, 12, 23. Beulah Haviland relrq

MULLETT
1912, 2, 21. Mrs. recrq

MURPHY
----, --, --. John b 1783,9,12; m Sarah -----
     b 1779,9,6 (H)

1825, 5, 25. Sarah rocf Fallowfield MM, Pa.,
     dtd 1825,8,11
1828, 10, 22. Sarah dis jH

1828, 12, 24. John recrq (H)

MYERS
1807, 12, 15. Elizabeth Burson (form Myers)
     dis mcd
1808, 9, 13. David dis mcd
1835, 3, 25. Pierce Garretson gct New Garden
     MM, to m Sarah H. Myers (H)
1844, 2, 17. Sarah & dt, Rebecca, Elizabeth,
     Sarah Ann & Eliza Jane, recrq (H)
1844, 4, 24. Israel, s Sarah, recrq (H)
1863, 4, 23. Samuel & w, Paulina, gct Green
     St. MM, Phila., Pa. (H)
1863, 4, 23. Jane V. gct Race St. MM, Phila.,
     Pa. (H)
1863, 4, 23. Julia A. gct Race St. MM, Phila.
     Pa. (H)

NAILOR
1819, 11, 7. Beulah [Naylor], dt Rachel Mor-
     ris, b (G)

1859, 3, 24. Beulah W. rocf Upper Springfield
     MM, dtd 1859,2,20
1865, 10, 26. Beulah [Nailer] gct Upper Spring-
     field MM

NARAMORE
1879, 9, 18. David, s John & Arna, Westmore-
     land Co., N. J.; m at Salem, Rebecca WAR-
     RINGTON, dt John A. & Rachel, Columbiana
     Co., O.

1879, 12, 25. Rebecca W. gct Westmorland MM,
     N. Y.

NEGUS
----, --, --. John b 1778,5,4; m Miriam -----
     b 1786,7,31 (G)
     Ch: John
          Wayte   b 1820, 5, 20
1845, 9, 22. Amasa Lipsey, s Bracken, b (G)
1848, 5, 31. Esther m Edward W. FAWCETT
1848, 12, 27. Elisha, s Shaidlock & Rachel,
     Cedar Co., Ia.; m at Salem, Elvira FAW-
     CETT, dt Jonathan & Mary, Columbiana Co.,
     O.
1857, 2, 8. Miriam, Jr. d (G)
1859, 3, 3. Mary M. m Israel OWEN

1823, 6, 25. Sarah, minor, rocf Providence
     MM, dtd 1823,5,20
1824, 6, 23. Sarah, minor, gct Providence MM,
     Pa.
1835, 6, 24. Septimus C. Sharpless gct Upper
     Springfield MM, to m Sarah Negus
1845, 6, 25. Miriam & dt, Esther, rocf Upper
     Springfield MM, dtd 1845,5,24
1850, 1, 23. Mary M. rocf Upper Springfield
     MM, dtd 1849,12,22
1850, 1, 23. Miriam, Jr. rocf Upper Spring-
     field MM, dtd 1849,12,22
1850, 2, 20. John W. rocf Upper Springfield

NEGUS, continued
    MM, dtd 1849,11,24
1850, 9, 25. Elvira gct Salem MM, Ia.
1854, 12, 21. John rocf Upper Springfield MM
1858, 6, 24. Amacy, minor, rocf Short Creek MM, dtd 1858,3,24
1862, 5, 22. Amasa L., minor, gct Short Creek MM
1864, 12, 22. John & w, Miriam, gct Springdale MM, Ia.
1865, 1, 25. John W. dis joining separatists of 1854 (W)
1869, 5, 19. Mary M. Owen (form Negus) dis joining separatists of 1854 (W)

NEILL
----, --, --. Moreton b 1811,9,4; m Hannah ---- b 1817,12,3 (W)
    Ch: Gula Elma b 1839, 7, 9
        Edith " 1842, 11, 13

1846, 1, 21. Morton & w, Ann, & ch, Gula-Elma & Edith, rocf Carmel MM, dtd 1845,6, 20
1848, 9, 20. Morton [Neal] & w, Ann, & ch, Guli-Elma & Edith, gct Carmel MM
1862, 12, 25. Merton, Ann, Gulielma E. & Edith [Neil] dis joining separatists (W) of 1854
1913, 1, 22. Emerson Conrad gct Middleton MM, to m Eva M. Neill (W)

NEWBURN
1839, 8, 21. Israel Barba gct Upper Springfield MM, to m Lydia Newburn

NEWPORT
1824, 1, 1. Nathan, s Aaron & Mary, Belmont Co., O.; m at Springfield, Elizabeth FAWCETT, dt Thomas & Sarah, Columbiana Co., O.

NICHOLSON
----, --, --. M. C., s George & Hannah, b 1844,3,31 d 1917,5,5 (G)

1919, 12, 24. Mrs. Mary relrq

NICKOLS
----, --, --. Mahlon b 1823,10,16; m Ruth Hannah ----- b 1829,6,21 (H)
    Ch: George S. b 1862, 4, 13
        John O. " 1867, 7, 4
        Robert H. " 1872, 9, 10
----, --, --. Jessee M. b 1850,5,8; m Lydia ----- b 1852,7,31 (H)
    Ch: Wilbur b 1873, 8, 20 d 1877,10,27
        Ruth " 1876, 8, 3
        Walter " 1878, 1, 2
1873, 10, 23. Wm. [Nickels], s Wm. & Mary, Columbiana Co., O.; m at Salem, Ann K. MATHER, dt Thomas & Elizabeth, Mahoning Co., O. (H)

1870, 4, 21. Jesse [Nichols] & ch, Charles, Mary C. & Virginia, gct Goose Creek MM, Va. (H)
1870, 4, 21. Edward [Nichols] gct Goose Creek MM, Va. (H)
1874, 8, 20. Lydia J. [Nichols] rocf Stillwater MM, dtd 1874,4,18 (H)
1875, 5, 20. Benjamin [Nichols] gct Marietta MM, Ia. (H)
1881, 1, 20. James H. gct Marietta MM, Ia. (H)
1881, 1, 20. Spencer I. gct Marietta MM, Ia. (H)
1881, 1, 20. William J. gct Marietta MM, Ia. (H)
1881, 1, 20. Triphena gct Marietta MM, Ia. (H)
1881, 1, 20. Rachel Allice Mills (form Nickols) gct Marietta MM, Ia. (H)

NICKOLA
1911, 12, 20. Lewis rec in mbrp

NICKUM
1840, 8, 19. Eliza T. (form Brown) con mcd (H)
1840, 10, 21. Ann Eliza P. (form Brook) con mou (H)

NIXON
1836, 3, 23. John Straughn gct Short Creek MM, to m Martha L. Nixon

NORTH
----, --, --. Jesse b 1810,5,30; m Elizabeth ----- b 1813,4,12 (W)
    Ch: Sarah b 1839, 10, 30
        Mary I. " 1841, 11, 8
        John " 1844, 3, 28
        Gustavus " 1846, 3, 2

1846, 6, 24. Jesse & w, Elizabeth, & ch, Sarah, Mary Jane, John & Gustavus, rocf Upper Springfield MM, dtd 1846,4,25
1847, 12, 22. Jessee & w, Elizabeth, & ch, Sarah, Mary Jane, John & Gustavis, gct Upper Springfield MM
1851, 9, 24. Jesse & w, Elizabeth, & ch, Sarah, Mary Jane, John & Gustavus, rocf Upper Springfield MM, dtd 1851,8,23
1853, 5, 25. Jesse & w, Elizabeth, & ch, Sarah, Mary Jane, John & Gustavus, gct New Garden MM

O'CONNELL
----, --, --. Charles m Grace WRIGLEY, dt J. L. & Ida, b 1882,4,8 (G)
    Ch: Lois b 1905, 10, 22
        Kenneth " 1921, 12, 12
        Thelma " 1910, 3, 29
        Nancy Jane " 1926, 7, 3

1916, 8, 16. Blanch Fay recrq

O'CONNELL, continued
1919, 9, 24. Lois recrq
1929, 4, 24. Kenneth recrq
1932, 2, 24. Thelma [O'Connel] recrq

ODEY
----, --, --. Ralph E., s Mrs. E. C. Burkhart,
     b 1889,4,12; m Irma B. HILL, dt J. C.,
     b 1904,12,2 (G)

1932, 12, 29. Ralph E., Irma Belle, Robert,
     Florence, Janice & Ralph, Jr. recrq

OGDEN
1826, 1, 1. Martha H. b (W)
1830, 6, 6. Anna M. b (W)
1845, 3, 26. Martha H. m John FRENCH
1848, 11, 1. Anna M. m Joseph BRUFF

1836, 12, 21. Anna Maria, minor, rocf Salem
     MM, N. J., dtd 1836,6,29
1836, 12, 21. Martha H., minor, rocf Salem
     MM, N. J., dtd 1836,11,2

OLIPHANT
----, --, --. Samuel b 1790,1,22 d 1849,4,7
     bur Salem; m Rachel ----- b 1793,7,16 (W)
     Ch: Wm. H.   b 1816, 5, 14
         Eliza   " 1817, 10, 8
         Ann   " 1820, 5, 7
         John   " 1822, 5, 26
         Rachel   " 1824, 4, 15
         Sarah   " 1826, 4, 19
         Israel   " 1828, 8, 20 d 1830, 7, 9
         Samuel H. " 1831, 5, 12
         Sinah   " 1833, 7, 29
         Lydia   " 1835, 12, 12
----, --, --. Ephraim & Elizabeth
     Ch: Sarah H.   b 1817, 3, 23
         Abner   " 1819, 9, 10
         Mahlon   " 1824, 11, 15
         Mary Ann   " 1827, 3, 13
         Lydia   " 1829, 6, 20 d 1834, 1,22
         Ruth   " 1833, 11, 23
         Israel   " 1836, 12, 15
         Jonathan   " 1830, 6, 11
     Ephraim 2m 2nd Sarah ----- b 1795,11,7
1840, 6, 25. Eliza m Wm. D. BRANSON
----, --, --. William H. b 1816,5,14; m Sina
     W. ----- b 1822,4,-- d 1847,8,29 bur Sa-
     lem (W) (William H., s of Samuel)
     William H. m 2nd Lydia BRUFF, dt James &
     Sarah, b 1822,1,26
     Ch: Anna Sina b 1855, 2, 22
         Sarah   " 1856, 2, 21 d 1856, 5, 3
         bur Salem
         William B. " 1861, 3, 9
----, --, --. John, s Samuel & Rachel, Mahon-
     ing Co., O., b 1822,5,20; m Maria K. -----
     b 1828,7,24 d 1859,1,24 bur Middleton (W)
     John m 2nd at Salem, 1860,12,26, Hannah P.
     WILLIAMS dt Daniel & Elizabeth, Mahoning
     Co. O. (W)

Ch: Elizabeth
        M.   b 1862, 1, 31
1922, 10, 26. John Howard, s Wm. D. & Ellazan
     H., Columbiana Co., O.; m at Salem, Alice
     Marie BLACKBURN, dt Wm. J. & Elizabeth
     (Coleman), b 1895,1,9 (W)

1829, 11, 25. Ephraim & w, Elizabeth, & ch,
     Sarah, Abner, Mahlon, Mary Ann & Lydia,
     rocf Middleton MM, dtd 1829,10,8
1830, 1, 20. Samuel [Olliphant], Jr. & w, Ra-
     chel, & ch, William H., Eliza, Ann, John,
     Sarah, Rachel & Israel, rocf Middleton MM,
     dtd 1830,1,7
1836, 6, 22. Sarah gct Middleton MM
1836, 6, 22. Ephraim & w, Elizabeth, & ch,
     Abner, Mahlon, Mary Ann & Ruth, gct Middle-
     ton MM
1837, 1, 25. Josiah Fawcett gct Middleton
     MM, to m Sarah Oliphant
1845, 4, 23. William H. gct Middleton MM, to
     m Sina Sidwell
1846, 2, 25. Sina W. rocf Middleton MM, dtd
     1846,12,11
1848, 9, 20. John gct Middleton MM, to m
     Maria Heald
1849, 2, 21. Maria H. rocf Middleton MM, dtd
     1849,2,8
1850, 6, 19. Rachel & ch, Samuel, Sina & Lyd-
     ia, gct Middleton MM
1850, 6, 19. Sarah gct Middleton MM
1850, 11, 20. Ann & Rachel gct Middleton MM
1851, 3, 19. William H. gct Upper Springfield
     MM, to m Lydia B. Bruff
1852, 4, 21. Lydia B. rocf Upper Springfield
     MM, dtd 1852,3,27
1852, 8, 25. Ephraim & w, Sarah, & ch, Israel
     & Jonathan, rocf Middleton MM, dtd 1852,7,
     8
1852, 10, 20. Ruth rocf Middleton MM, dtd
     1852,10,7
1857, 5, 21. Ephraim & w, Sarah, & s, Jona-
     than, gct Upper Springfield MM
1858, 10, 21. Ruth gct Upper Springfield MM
1862, 12, 25. John, Hannah, Phebe S. & Eliza-
     beth M. dis joining separatists (W) of
     1854
1862, 12, 25. Ann & Lydia dis joining separa-
     tists (W) of 1854
1863, 9, 23. Jonathan dis mcd (W)
1863, 10, 22. William H. [Olaphant] & w, Lyd-
     ia B., gct Red Cedar MM, Ia.
1863, 10, 22. Rachel gct Red Cedar MM, Ia.
1864, 5, 26. Israel con mcd
1864, 11, 23. Ruth & Sarah dis joining separa-
     tists of 1854 (W)
1865, 6, 21. John & w, Hannah P., & ch,
     Phebe S. & Elizabeth W., gct Hickory
     Grove MM, Ia. (W)
1865, 9, 20. Ephraim dis joining separatists
     of 1854 (W)
1868, 7, 22. William W. dis joining separa-
     tists of 1854 (W)

OLIPHANT, continued
1870, 8, 24. Anna Sina, dt William H. &
    Lydia B., gct Hickory Grove MM, Ia. (W)
1872, 4, 24. Israel dis mcd (W)
1923, 7, 25. Alice M. gct New Garden MM, O.
    (W)

OLIVER
1893, 11, 22. Elma F. [Olover] (form French)
    dis mcd & joining separatists of 1854 (W)
1910, 2, 23. Delilah H. recrq

OLMSTEAD
----, --, --. Anne b 1778,2,14 d 1854,9,11 (W)

1828, 7, 23. Anna, w William, rocf Oblong MM,
    N. Y., dtd 1827,1,15

OMAN
1835, 10, 1. Susan E., dt Judah & Susan
    Chase, b (G)

ORBAUGH
1864, 7, 21. Ruth Anna dis mcd

ORMSBY
1885, 4, 16. Blanch, dt Harry & Mary Morris,
    b (G)
----, --, --. James, s Wm. & Catharine, b
    1846,11,18 d 1918,10,3; m Malisa WINEINGER
    dt Jonathan, b 1855,1,18 d 1910,6,2 (G)
    Ch: Iva   b 1895, 6, 14 d 1914,11,25

1911, 2, 22. Blanch relrq
1911, 12, 20. Iva rec in mbrp
1914, 11, 25. Ivy dropped from mbrp
1915, 12, 23. Blanch recrq

OTIS
1891, 10, 21. Martha K. (form Koll) dis mcd
    & joining separatists of 1854

OTLIP
1862, 7, 25. Viola Mary, dt John & Catherine
    Middleton, b

1929, 4, 24. Viola recrq

OVINGTON
1856, 1, 29. Clara G. b (H)

1879, 8, 21. Clara G. con mcd (H)

OWEN
----, --, --. Joshua b 1760,4,1 d 1847,4,3; m
    Mary ----- b 1765,2,1 d 1843,3,16 (W)
1859, 3, 3. Israel, s Nathaniel & Phebe,
    Columbiana Co., O.; m at Salem, Mary M.
    NEGUS, dt John & Miriam, Columbiana Co.,O.
1884,1 7 14. Frances [Owens], dt Winfield &
    Elizabeth, b (G)

1822, 9, 25. Mary recrq

1823, 10, 22. Joshua recrq
1824, 3, 24. Sarah (form Dole) dis
1858, 6, 24. Israel rocf East Vasselborough
    MM, Maine, dtd 1858,5,19
1860, 2, 23. Israel & w, Mary, gct Drift-
    wood MM, Ind.
1860, 5, 19. Mary M. (form Negus) dis join-
    ing separatists of 1854 (W)

PAINTER
----, --, --. Jacob b 1766,8,21 d 1851,9,5;
    m Mary ----- b 1768,7,25 d 1818,9,7 (W)
    Ch: Joshua   b 1789, 12, 25 d 1793,11,11
        David   " 1792, 2, 4
        Samuel   " 1794, 3, 28
        Robert   " 1796, 8, 12
        Abigail   " 1798, 12, 21
        Joseph   " 1801, 6, 27
        Jacob   " 1804, 2, 1
        Mary   " 1806, 4, 15 d 1808,12, 1
        Susannah   " 1809, 10, 24
        Agnes E.   " 1812, 5, 19
    Jacob m 2nd Miriam ----- b 1779,4,10 d
    1851,8,28
    Ch: Mary Ann   b 1821, 12, 21
        Miriam   " 1821, 12, 21
1813, 10, 27. David, s Jacob & Mary, Columbi-
    ana Co., O., b 1792,2, 4 d 1866,8,5; m at
    Salem, Ann WEBB, dt John & Elizabeth, Co-
    lumbiana Co., O., b 1787,6,12 d 1867,5,6
    (W)
    Ch: Mary   b 1814, 11, 26
        Elizabeth " 1817, 6, 16
        Phebe E.   " 1819, 9, 3
        John H.   " 1819, 9, 3
        Martha W. " 1821, 6, 10
        Wm. M.   " 1823, 2, 6 d 1843,12,20
        Abraham   " 1827, 8, 15
1816, 2, 21. Samuel, s Jacob & Mary, Columbi-
    ana Co., O., b 1794,3,28; m at Salem, Mary
    HENDRICKS, dt Nathan & Mary, b 1793,12,27
    (W)
    Ch: Nathan   b 1816, 12, 21
        Lorenzo   " 1817, 12, 27
        Stephen   " 1820, 2, 9
        Seth   " 1822, 7, 4
        William   " 1823, 2, 6
        Louisa   " 1825, 10, 15 (1824,10,15
          in H)
        Lucinda   " 1827, 6, 1
        Lydia Ann " 1829, 11, 1
        Susannah   " 1834, 11, 3 d 1834,11,16
        Samuel H. " 1839, 2, 17
----, --, --. Joseph b 1801,6,27; m Rebecca
    ----- b 1800,7,12 (W)
    Ch: Thos.
        Price   b 1821, 5, 9 d 1844, 2,12
        Reuben G. " 1823, 3, 19
        Elwood   " 1833, 3, 23
        Sarah   " 1835, 1, 10
        Hannah E. " 1838, 7, 4
        Mary   " 1841, 4, 28
        Rachel Ann " 1847, 9, 21

PAINTER, continued

1837, 3, 29. Mary m Ross STRATTON

1839, 11, 27. Elizabeth m Elisha STRATTON

1842, 5, 4. John, s David & Ann, Columbiana
    Co., O., b 1819,9,3; m at Salem, Edith
    DEAN, dt James Harvey & Eleanor, Columbi-
    ana Co., O., b 1821,8,5 (W)
    Ch: Lewis   b 1843, 4, 23
        Wm. M.   " 1844, 2, 1

1844, 8, 28. Mary Ann m John PENNOCK

1847, 9, 29. Phebe E. m Stephen DEAN

1877, 3, 28. Reuben G., s Joseph & Rebecca,
    Columbiana Co., O.; m at Salem, Phebe FAW-
    CETT, dt Amos & Hannah, Columbiana Co., O.
    (W)

1880, 8, 26. Phebe F. m John P. GREWELL (W)

1814, 10, 11. Robert gct Short Creek MM

1817, 11, 11. Abigail Faulkner (form Painter)
    dis mcd

1820, 5, 24. Jacob gct New Garden MM, to m
    Miriam Richardson

1821, 2, 21. Miriam Painter & ch, Isaac G. &
    Elizabeth Richardson, rocf New Garden MM,
    dtd 1820,9,21

1821, 2, 21. Rebecca (form Griffith) dis mcd

1821, 3, 21. Joseph dis mcd

1828, 7, 30. Samuel & w, Mary, & ch, Lorenso,
    Stephen, Seth, Louiza & Lucinda, rocf New
    Gard en MM, dtd 1828,7,24 (H)

1828, 8, 20. Samuel dis jH

1828, 8, 20. Mary dis jH

1832, 7, 25. Rebecca rst by rq

1832, 8, 22. Agnes dis disunity

1833, 4, 24. Thomas & Reuben G., ch Joseph,
    recrq

1838, 5, 23. Susan Holloway (form Painter)
    dis mcd

1842, 4, 20. Stephen dis mcd

1843, 7, 19. Stephen con mcd (H)

1844, 3, 20. Louisa dis joining Baptist So-
    ciety

1845, 6, 25. Martha Teters (form Painter) dis
    mcd

1845, 8, 20. John H. & w, Edith, & ch gct
    Salem MM, Ia.

1845, 8, 20. Lucinda Grimacy (form Painter)
    dis mou

1845, 9, 23. Lucinda Grimmesy (form Painter)
    dis mou (H)

1845, 9, 23. Louiza Thomson (form Painter)
    con mou (H)

1846, 1, 21. Seth dis mcd

1852, 10, 20. Lorenzo dis mcd

1856, 6, 25. Reuben G. dis mcd (W)

1856, 12, 21. Miriam G. Metzgar (form Painter)
    dis mcd (W)

1857, 10, 21. Elwood dis mou (W)

1858, 4, 22. Elwood G. con mcd

1858, 4, 22. Reuben dis mcd

1860, 4, 25. Abraham dis mcd (W)

1860, 6, 20. Hannah E. Snyder (form Painter)
    dis mcd (W)

1861, 3, 21. Hannah Snider (form Painter)
    dis mcd

1862, 12, 25. Joseph, Rebecca, Sarah, Mary &
    Rachel dis joining separatists (W) of 1854

1862, 12, 25. David & Ann dis joining separa-
    tists (W) of 1854

1865, 5, 24. Joseph & w, Rebecca, & dt, Ra-
    chel Ann, gct Upper Springfield MM (W)

1865, 5, 24. Mary gct Upper Springfield MM
    (W)

1865, 6, 22. Lydia E. rocf Sandy Spring MM,
    dtd 1865,5,23

1867, 10, 23. Sarah Haines (form Painter) dis
    mcd (W)

1872, 12, 26. Jacob recrq

1874, 5, 20. Upper Springfield MM was given
    permission to rst Reuben G. in mbrp (W)

PALMER

1880, 3, 25. William Henry recrq

1886, 10, 21. William dropped from mbrp

1913, 10, 22. Myra Litty gct First Friends
    Church, Cleveland, O.

PANCOAST

1826, 8, 23. Mary gct Frankford MM, Pa.

PARKER

1867, 12, 26. Ann F. gct Alliance MM

PARKS

----, --, --. Lincoln S., s David & Asenath,
    b 1863,12,1; m Mary Ida KIRK, dt Wm. &
    Lydia, b 1867,9,24 (G)
    Ch: Bessie L. b 1892, 9, 6
        Martha E. " 1894, 9, 2
        Wm. K.   " 1906, 6, 6
        John L.   " 1910, 5, 23

1885, 10, 7. Mary, dt Clem & Lucy Williaman
    b (G)

1914, 12, 23. Mary Williman relrq

1928, 5, 23. Martha [Park] dropped from mbrp

PARRY

1847, 3, 31. Mary J. m Samuel FRENCH

1847, 2, 24. Mary J. rocf Chester MM, N. J.,
    dtd 1847,1,12

PARSONS

----, --, --. Harry, s Jabez & Susan, b 1881,
    1,25; m Nellie COPPOCK, dt Isaac & Phebe,
    b (G)

1911, 12, 20. Harry & w rec in mbrp

1917, 8, 15. Floyd Wesley, Doris Novene &
    Phebe Ellen recrq

1932, 6, 29. Floyd dropped from mbrp

PASSMORE

----, --, --. George b 1800,12,29; m Phebe H.
    ----- b 1794,12,23 (H)

PASSMORE, George & Phebe H., continued
    Ch: Hannah
        Ann   b 1825, 8, 10
        Joseph
        Harlan   " 1827, 9, 18
        Lindley   " 1829, 6, 26 d 1841, 9,30
        Pamela   " 1831, 2, 7
        Phebe   " 1833, 2, 2
        George   " 1834, 10, 24
        Mansel   " 1836, 8, 9

1839, 6, 19. George & w, Phebe H., & ch, Hannah Ann, Joseph Harlin, Lindley, Pamelia, Phebe, George & Mansel, rocf Fallowfield MM, Pa., dtd 1839,5,11 (H)
1885, 5, 21. John W. rocf Nottingham MM, Md. (H)
1885, 5, 21. Alice M. & ch, Elma, Edward S., Ellis P., Lincoln K. & Alice, Jr. recrq

PATTERSON
----, --, --. Lester John m Deborah STRATTON, dt Joseph R. & Anna Mary (Bundy), b 1905,5, 6 (W)
----, --, --. Randall & Dorothy (G)
    Ch: Dorothy
        Kuhns   b 1928, 8, 15
        Wayne
        Franklin " 1933, 6, 23

1933, 2, 22. Randall James recrq

PAULIN
1919, 6, 25. Mary relrq
1921, 4, 24. Mary recrq

PAXSON
1867, 10, 5. Effie J., dt Samuel & Sarah Jane Kaylor, b d 1925,4,4 (G)
----, --, --. Jessie D., s Charles & Isabelle, b 1868,2,17 d 1928,9,17; m Bessie PAXSON
    Ch: Jessie   [(G)
        Dallas   b 1928, 1, 27

1857, 11, 26. Maria [Paxon] rocf Deep Creek MM, dtd 1857,10,24 (H)
1859, 1, 20. Jacob [Paxon] rocf Abington MM, Pa., dtd 1858,11,29 (H)
1865, 11, 23. Jacob [Paxon] & w, Maria, gct Birmingham MM, Pa. (H)
1890, 6, 26. Jesse [Paxon] & w, Effie J., rocf Winona MM, dtd 1890,5,21
1927, 10, 19. Bessie [Paxson] & s, Dale, recrq

PEARSON
1845, 5, 21. Ann rocf Short Creek MM, dtd 1845,3,20 (H)
1882, 5, 25. Martha L. Taylor (form Pierson) rocf Marietta MM, Ia. (H)

PECK
1883, 2, 9. Charlotte E. recrq

PEDDRICK
1806, 5, 21. Philip, s Hugh & Elizabeth, Columbiana Co., O.; m at Salem, Judith TOWNSEND, dt Noah & Judith Smith, Columbiana Co., O.

1811, 12, 17. Philip [Pedrick] & w, Judith, & ch, Keturah & Jesse Townsend (ch of Judith), Catharine & Elizabeth Pedrick, gct Miami MM

PEIRPOINT
1807, 6, 11. Jonathan & w, Ann, & ch, William Obed & Benjamin, rocf Fairfax MM, Va., dtd 1807,3,28

PELO
----, --, --. Hervey m Essie HINES, dt James & Sarah, b 1885,5,8 (G)
    Ch: Dorothy E. b 1910, 10, 21
        Richard N. " 1912, 3, 22
        Ruth Janet " 1926, 7, 21

1923, 12, 19. Mrs. Essie recrq
1924, 1, 23. Dorothy Elizabeth, Richard Nelson & Ruth Janet recrq
1926, 7, 21. Mrs.& ch relrq

PENNINGTON
1831, 2, 23. Levi Miller, Jr. gct New Garden MM, to m Mariah Pennington

PENNOCK
1764, 7, 10. John b (H)
1777, 9, 29. Hannah b (H)
1809, 1, 25. Hannah m John H. JOHNSON
----, --, --. John b 1774,3,21 d 1837,4,9; m Sarah ----- b 1783,1,26 (W)
    Ch: Isaac   b 1811, 10, 31
        Samuel   " 1813, 5, 16
        Hannah   " 1815, 10, 10 d 1834,11,--
        Lydia   " 1818, 7, 1
        John   " 1820, 12, 29
        Sarah   " 1824, 9, 19
1812, 12, 3. Phebe m Matthew VAUGHAN
1844, 8, 28. John, s John & Sarah, Columbiana Co., O., b 1820,9,29; m at Salem, Mary Ann PAINTER, dt Jacob & Miriam, Columbiana Co., O., b 1821,12,21 (W)
    Ch: Elizabeth
        Ellen   b 1845, 9, 9
        Sarah   " 1849, 6, 1

1807, 7, 14. John rocf Goose Creek MM, Va., dtd 1807,3,5
1807, 7, 14. Mary, Jr. rocf Goose Creek MM, dtd 1807,3,5
1807, 11, 17. William & w, Mary, & ch, Hannah, Phebe, Jane & Moses, & gr ch (ch of s, John), William, Elizabeth & Alice, rocf Goose Creek MM, Va., dtd 1807,9,3
1809, 4, 11. Mary Clay (form Pennock) con mou
1811, 4, 16. Sarah rocf Middleton MM, dtd 1811,3,9

PENNOCK, continued
1818, 9, 23. William, Jr. dis mcd
1820, 2, 23. Elizabeth Gaskill (form Pennock) dis mcd
1820, 7, 19. John & w, Sarah, & ch, Isaac, Samuel, Hannah & Lydia, gct Marlborough MM
1827, 12, 19. John & w, Sarah, & ch, Isaac, Samuel, Hannah, Lydia, John & Sarah, roc dtd 1827,11,27
1832, 8, 22. Lydia dis
1837, 1, 25. Samuel dis disunity
1840, 8, 19. Isaac W. gct Marlborough MM
1841, 3, 14. Sarah Webb (form Pennock) dis mcd
1841, 4, 21. Ann E. rocf Marlborough MM, dtd 1840,12,29
1841, 8, 25. John, Jr. & w, Sidney, & ch, Elizabeth H., Morris C. & Rachel P., rocf New Garden MM, dtd 1841,7,27 (H)
1841, 12, 22. Elizabeth, dt John & Sydney, rocf New Garden MM, dtd 1841,10,21
1842, 5, 25. John & w, Hannah, rocf New Garden MM, dtd 1842,4,21 (H)
1842, 7, 20. Isaac & w, Ann, & s, James, gct Marlborough MM
1847, 12, 22. Elizabeth dis jH
1865, 7, 19. Sina F. (form Fawcett) dis mcd (W)

PENROSE
----, --, --. John F. m Susan G. HUTTON, dt Joel W. & Ann (Mains), b 1849,12,14 d 1925,1,9 bur Grandview Cemetery, Salem, O. (W)

1877, 10, 24. Susan G. (form Hutton) dis mcd (W)
1885, 5, 1. Esther rocf Winona MM, dtd 1885, 3,--
1913, 5, 21. Susan H. rst by rq (W)

PERKINS
1925, 11, 11. Lois E. d (G)

1808, 1, 12. Jonathan rocf Hopewell MM, dtd 1807,2,2
1810, 2, 13. Ann rocf Westland MM, dtd 1809, 5,27
1810, 12, 11. Ann gct Miami MM
1921, 10, 19. Lois E. recrq

PERRY
1847, 3, 31. Mary J. m Samuel FRENCH
1909, 10, 6. Arthur, Jr., s Arther & Emma Foster, Suffolk Co., Mass.; m at Salem, Rebecca Savry HUTTON, dt Finley & Agnes, Columbiana Co., O. (W)

1816, 7, 16. Rachel recrq
1824, 9, 22. Rachel dis disunity
1910, 6, 22. Rebecca Hutton gct South Kingstown MM, R. I. (W)

PETTIS
1854, 10, 8. Lucy, dt Daniel & Lucinda Haviland, b (G)

1912, 7, 24. Lucy relrq
1913, 7, 25. Lucy J. recrq

PETTIT
----, --, --. Hannah W. b 1791,10,22 d 1872,9, 12 (W)
----, --, --. Joseph E., s Daniel R. & Rebecca, b 1855,5,11; m Lydia STANLEY, dt Robert & Sarah, b 1856,11,26 (G)
     Ch: Anna
         Blanch   b 1890, 4, 29

1808, 2, 16. William & w, Mary, & ch, Benjamin, Elizabeth & William, rocf Catiwessy MM, dtd 1807,5,23, endorsed by Short Creek MM, 1807,9,19
1826, 8, 23. Bula Ann [Petit] rocf New Garden MM, dtd 1826,4,20
1828, 3, 19. Beulah Ann gct Carmel MM
1829, 11, 25. Elizabeth (form Schooley) dis mou
1834, 3, 19. Elnathan [Pettitt] rocf Sandy Spring MM, dtd 1834,3,21
1836, 10, 19. Elnathan gct Sandy Spring MM
1842, 1, 19. Rebecca W. (form Garretson) con mou (H)
1874, 12, 24. Jane R. rocf Short Creek MM, dtd 1874,11,26
1910, 9, 21. Joseph & w gct Damascus MM

PHILLIPS
1909, 6, 24. Brooke K., s Curtis & Bertha, b (G)
1931, 1, 3. R. W. d (G)

1924, 8, 10. Mr. & Mrs. R. W. recrq
1925, 3, 25. Brooks recrq
1932, 6, 29. Brook dropped from mbrp

PICKERING
1867, 7, 25. Margaret E. (form White) con mcd (H)
1871, 11, 23. Margaret E. gct Prairie Grove MM, Ia. (H)

PICKET
1862, 12, 25. Hannah, Phebe, Mary Ann & Reuben E. dis joining separatists (W) of 1854

PIERCE
1828, 10, 1. Rebecca [Peirce] m Isaac VOTAW, Jr.
1842, 12, 29. Sarah E. m James MICHENER (H)
1844, 4, 25. Isaac Newton [Peirce], s Isaac & Mercy, Columbiana Co., O.; m at house of John Garretson, Maria GARRETSON, dt John & Ann, Columbiana Co., O. (H)

1828, 5, 21. Rebecca recrq

PIERCE, continued

1841, 8, 25. Mercy L. & dt, Sarah E., rocf
MM in New York, dtd 1841,3,3 (H)
1846, 8, 19. Maria G. gct West MM (H)
1916, 8, 16. Masie recrq
1920, 3, 24. Marie gct Cleveland MM

PIGEON

----, --, --. Wm. [Pigion] b 1767,12,24 d 1835,
11,10 bur Salem; m Alice ----- b 1773,5,23
d 1809,4,2 bur Salem (W)
Ch: Mary   b 1797, 5, 13
    Rachel   " 1798, 7, 29
    Elizabeth   " 1799, 12, 19
    Benj.   " 1801, 6, 23
    Wm.   " 1804, 2, 16
    Martha   " 1807, 3, 18
Wm. m 2nd Mary ----- b 1776,2,4
1820, 3, 1. Elizabeth m Simon DIXON
1823, 11, 26. Rachel m David HOLLOWAY
1825, 10, 26. Mary m Edmund STANLEY

1826, 10, 25. Mary [Pidgeon] rocf New Garden
MM, dtd 1826,9,21
1828, 7, 23. Benjamin dis mcd
1829, 10, 21. William, Jr. gct Carmel MM
1830, 5, 6. Cert for William, Jr. returned
by Carmel MM, because of disunity
1830, 6, 23. William, Jr. dis mcd
1832, 2, 22. Martha Hoiles (form Pidgeon) dis
mcd

PIM

----, --, --. Willard b 1888,11,17; m Lena ----
(G)
Ch: Loren   b 1914, 3, 26
    Norman   " 1917, 4, 29
    Esther   " 1921, 2, 16
Willard m 2nd Blanche STRATTON, dt Charles
& Martha, b 1895,3,31

1874, 5, 6. Barclay Maris gct Sandy Spring
MM, to m Ann Pim
1886, 10, 21. Rhoda dropped from mbrp
1915, 10, 20. Lewis G. & w, Mary B., rocf
Tecumseh MM, Mich., dtd 1915,9,22
1919, 6, 25. Lewis G. & Mary B. gct Caesars
Creek MM, O.
1930, 12, 24. Blanche & ch recrq
1930, 12, 24. William rocf Alliance MM, O.

PINE

1810, 7, 17. Elizabeth rocf Haddonfield MM,
N. J., dtd 1810,4,19   •
1813, 2, 18. Elizabeth Field (form Pine) con
mcd

PINKHAM

----, --, --. Thomas, s Elijah & Abigail, b
1795,9,30; m Mary BEEDE, s Jonathan & Anna
Winslow Beede, b 1802,2,16 (G)
Ch: Mary
    Elizabeth b 1830, 1, 4

Ch: Thos. Ed-
    ward   b 1831, 11, 1
    Huldah
    Caroline   " 1833, 5, 10
    James Par-
    nel   " 1834, 11, 28
    Wm. Penn   " 1843, 9, 3
    Gilbert
    Latey   " 1843, 9, 9
1860, 9, 27. Wm. P., s Thomas & Mary, Columbiana Co., O.; m at Salem, Emma CURRY, dt
Cornelius & Hannah, Columbiana Co., O. (G)
Ch: Mary
    Cornelia b 1861, 7, 28
    Arthur Ed-
    ward   " 1862, 8, 31

1845, 4, 23. Thomas & w, Mary B., & ch, Mary
Elizabeth, Thomas Edward, Caroline H.,
James Parnell, William Penn & Gilbert Latey, rocf Redstone MM, dtd 1845,4,2
1860, 1, 26. James P. con mcd
1860, 6, 21. James P. gct Bloomington MM, Ia.
1861, 4, 25. Thomas Edward gct Upper Springfield MM, to m Mary Fuller
1861, 7, 25. Thomas Edward gct Short Creek MM
O.
1862, 11, 20. William P. & w, Emma C., & ch,
Mary, Cornelia & Arthur Edward, gct Short
Creek MM
1864, 2, 24. Thomas dis taking part in separation of 1854 (W)
1864, 4, 20. Mary B. dis joining separatists
of 1854 (W)
1865, 11, 23. Thomas & w, Mary B., gct Bloomington MM, Ia.
1867, 3, 21. Mary Elizabeth gct Bloomington
MM, Ia.
1869, 2, 24. James Parnell dis joining separatists of 1854 (W)
1869, 8, 26. Gilbert L. gct Bloomington MM,
Ia.
1869, 8, 26. Caroline H. gct Bloomington MM,
Ia.
1871, 6, 21. Huldah Caroline dis joining
separatists of 1854 (W)
1871, 7, 19. Mary Elizabeth McCowen (form
Pinkham) dis mcd (W)
1872, 4, 24. Gilbert L. dis joining separatists of 1854 (W)
1872, 4, 24. William P. dis joining separatists of 1854 (W)

PIPES

1910, 2, 23. George D. & w recrq

PIPPETT

1834, 2, 19. Susan R. (form Craft) dis mcd

PLATT

1865, 11, 2. Hiram, s Simeon & Sarah, Beaver
Co., Pa.; m at Salem, Hannah A. TRAGO, dt
John & Sarah Ann (H)

PLEASE
1906, 3, 21. Margret recrq (W)

POLLOCK
1851, 3, 19. Levina (form Stanley) dis mcd

POOL
1837, 4, 19. Jonas & w, Ann, & ch, Asenith &
    Priscilla, rocf Upper Springfield MM, dtd
    1837,3,27
1838, 6, 20. Jonas & w, Ann, & ch, Asenith &
    Priscilla, gct Carmel MM
1862, 12, 25. Jonas, Ann, Priscilla & Sarah
    Jane dis joining separatists (W) of 1854
1880, 2, 26. Otis recrq

POPE
1856, 3, 20. Alton & w, Theodate S., & ch,
    Ellen M., Edward C., John L. & Alfred, rocf
    Vasselborough MM, Maine, dtd 1856,2,20
1860, 5, 24. Alton & w, Theodate S., & s, Al-
    fred, gct Baltimore MM
1860, 5, 24. Ellen gct Baltimore MM
1865, 6, 22. Alton & w, Theodate S., rocf
    Sandy Spring MM, dtd 1865,5,23
1865, 6, 22. Ellen Maria & Alfred rocf Sandy
    Spring MM, dtd 1865,5,23
1868, 4, 23. Edward C. dis mcd
1868, 4, 23. John S. con mcd
1874, 8, 5. Francis E. & ch, Henry J., Ed-
    ward M., Herbert A. & Carlyle W., recrq
1876, 5, 25. Alfred A. relrq

POTTER
1838, 7, 25. Mary rocf Darby MM, dtd 1838,5,2

POUND
----, --, --. Thos. C. b 1812,12,22; m Susan I.
    ----- b 1819,8,29 (H)
    Ch: Wm. I.   b 1840, 9, 14

1839, 9, 25. Thomas C. rocf Marlborough MM,
    dtd 1839,7,27 (H)
1839, 10, 23. Thomas C. gct New Garden MM, to
    m Susan Ingram (H)
1840, 1, 20. Susan rocf New Garden MM, dtd
    1840,9,24 (H)

PRESTON
1870, 3, 24. Mary & dt, Deborah, recrq (H)

PRICE
----, --, --. Dorcas b 1830,8,27 d 1906,9,11
    bur Sewickley (W)
----, --, --. Isaac d 1877,6,7; m ----- (W)
    Ch: Mary Me-
        lissa   b 1841, 6, 19 d 1888,3,27

1836, 2, 24. Martha rocf Gunpowder MM, dtd
    1835,9,9 (H)
1870, 8, 25. William B. & w, Ellen F., & ch,
    William F. & Florence L., rocf Sandy
    Spring MM, dtd 1870,8,23

1870, 8, 25. Warrick & w, Beulah, & ch,
    Edith M., Laura Elizabeth & Beulah F.,
    rocf Sandy Spring MM, dtd 1870,8,23
1873, 9, 25. John F. & w, Rebecca W., & ch,
    Ferris W., Charles C., Hannah B. & Clara
    M., gct Phila. MM, Pa. (H)
1879, 6, 25. Dorcas recrq (W)
1881, 8, 10. Beulah R. & dt, Edith, relrq

PROUDFOOT
1882, 12, 21. Margaret recrq

PUSEY
1847, 12, 22. Ann H. (form Kersey) dis mcd

PYLE
1854, 1, 25. Elmira (form Mourland) dis mcd
1816, 1, 16. Israel Schooley gct Short Creek
    MM, to m Sarah Pyle

PYATT
1917, 7, 25. Leroy C. recrq
1917, 7, 25. Julia B. recrq

RAKESTRAW
----, --, --. Thomas b 1811,8,15; m Susan ----
    b 1806,8,8 (H)
    Ch: James   b 1836, 7, 13
        Wm.   " 1838, 7, 15
        Mary Ann   " 1840, 10, 12
        Eliza   " 1842, 4, 6

1824, 6, 23. Rebecca recrq
1824, 11, 24. Levi recrq
1825, 7, 20. Isaac, Hannah, Sarah, Benjamin
    H. M. & Haron B., ch Levi & Rebecca, rec-
    rq
1836, 3, 23. Thomas, Jr. & w, Susan, rocf
    Sadsbury MM, Pa., dtd 1835,11,4 (H)

RALEIGH
1852, 5, 19. Joshua W. Bonsall gct Sandy
    Spring MM, to m Elazan Raleigh

RALEY
----, --, --. Kersey b 1827,8,19; m Asenath
    ----- b 1830,4,17 (H)
1847, 6, 24. Jehu D., s Thomas & Ann, Colum-
    biana Co., O., b 1822,5,12; m at house of
    Stacy Hunt, Esther D. HUNT, dt Stacy &
    Rebecca, Columbiana Co., O., b 1823,7,7
    (H)
    Ch: Mary
        Emmor
        Wm.   b 1853, 5, 13
        Thomas   " 1856, 9, 10
        Ruth A.   " 1862, 3, 15
        Laura   " 1859, 3, 15
----, --, --. Milton b 1824,4,4; m Sarah -----
    b 1829,10,5 (W)
    Ch: Mary Ann b 1855, 12, 4
        Sarah
        Elizabeth " 1859, 6, 28

RALEY, Milton & Sarah, continued
    Ch: Abraham
        Lincoln b 1861, 3, 7 d 1862, 8,13
        Clara Ma-
        linda   " 1865, 10, 10
        Flora Bell " 1869, 11, 9

1841, 2, 24. Eliza, minor, rocf Sandy Spring
    MM, dtd 1840,12,27
1846, 12, 23. Eliza gct Sandy Spring MM
1848, 1, 19. Esther gct Carmel MM (H)
1887, 12, 22. Mary Hole (form Raley) rpd mcd;
    dropped from mbrp by rq (H)

RANDLES
1862, 12, 25. Esther & Isaac dis joining separ-
    atists (W) of 1854

RASCHE
----, --, --. Julius b 1833,5,17; m Elizabeth
    G. ----- b 1842,3,30 (W)
    Ch: Albert T. b 1864, 11, 9
        Charles   " 1867, 11, 4
        Deborah   " 1874, 7, 3
        Hellena
        Luella   " 1870, 4, 10
1875, 9, 2. Matilda m Thos. Howard MASTERS

1861, 1, 24. Julius rocf two months mtg of
    Pyrmont & Minden, dtd 1860,9,2
1861, 2, 20. Julius recrq (W)
1862, 3, 20. Julius gct Upper Springfield MM,
    O.
1862, 11, 19. Julius gct Upper Springfield MM,
    to m Eoizabeth G. Fawcett (W)
1863, 5, 20. Elizabeth G. rocf Upper Spring-
    field MM, dtd 1863,4,24 (W)
1870, 5, 11. Matilda [Rash] rocf Minden Two
    Months Mtg, dtd 1870,3,6

RAWLINGS
1826, 4, 26. Margaret m Joseph FISHER

1826, 1, 25. Margaret rocf Richland MM, Pa.,
    dtd 1825,12,2

RAWLS
1830, 8, 25. Burwell & w, Sarah, & ch, David,
    Mary Ann, Micajah, Michael, Jonathan, Wil-
    liam & Elizabeth, rocf Marlboro MM, dtd
    1830,6,29
1832, 8, 22. Berwell & w, Sarah, & ch, David,
    Mary Ann, Micajah, Michal, Jonathan, Wil-
    liam, Elizabeth & Esther, gct Sandy Spring
    MM

REAMS
1882, 12, 21. Mary recrq

REDD
1811, 2, 12. Isaac rocf Hopewell MM, dtd
    1810,1,1
1813, 7, 13. Isaac dis

REED
1805, 4, 17. Angelina b (W)
1807, 5, 22. Avelina b (W)
1816, 5, 22. Miliscent m Joshua STANLEY

1815, 10, 17. Rebecca & dt, Angelina & Avel-
    ina, recrq
1817, 7, 15. Rebecca Gaskill (form Reed) dis
1827, 4, 25. Angelina Hains (form Reed) dis
    mcd
1828, 4, 23. Avaline Gaskill (form Reed) dis
    mcd

REEDER
----, --, --. John b 1802,5,30 d 1870,5,7 (W)
----, --, --. Joseph b 1778,2,28 d 1866,7,18;
    m Hannah ----- b 1785,2,28 d 1840,9,24 (W)
    Joseph m 2nd Mary W. ----- b 1795,10,21
    d 1858,3,27
1808, 10, 26. Wm., s Thomas & Priscilla, Co-
    lumbiana Co., O.; m at Lexington, Deborah
    WILDMAN, dt Abraham & Letitia, Stark Co.,
    O.
----, --, --. James b 1796,9,3 d 1879,1,14; m
    Mary ----- b 1798,7,9 d 1885,4,23 (W)
    Ch: Eneas G. b 1820, 8, 15
        Hannah D. " 1822, 1, 10
        Esther F. " 1826, 5, 29
        Samuel   " 1827, 11, 10
        Benjamin N." 1830, 2, 12
        Ann Eliza " 1832, 12, 24
        Philena D. " 1837, 4, 24
        Eli D.   " 1841, 2, 12
----, --, --. Levi b 1805,9,18 d 1877,4,18; m
    Elizabeth ----- b 1805,10,4 (W)
    Ch: Benjamin b 1832, 7, 28
        Wm.   " 1836, 1, 21
        Lydia Ann " 1838, 3, 23 d 1843, 3,20
        Evan C.   " 1840, 9, 15
        Lewis   " 1846, 1, 18
1921, 1, 30. Caroline d (G)
1925, 4, 19. David d (G)

1806, 2, 11. Thomas [Reader] & w, Priscilla,
    & ch, Elizabeth & Priscilla, rocf South
    River MM, Va., dtd 1805,10,9, endorsed by
    Middleton MM, 1806,1,11
1806, 12, 16. Samuel [Reader] & w, Ann, & ch,
    William, Hannah, James, Mary, Samuel,
    John, -----, Ann & Levi, rocf Sadsbury MM,
    dtd 1806,9,2
1860, 7, 25. Joshua Stafford gct Sandy Spring
    MM, to m Esther F. Reeder (W)
1860, 7, 26. Joanna & Lydia B. rocf West MM,
    dtd 1860,4,27 (H)
1864, 6, 23. Lydia B. Milner (form Reeder)
    con mcd (H)
1917, 7, 25. David W. & Caroline recrq

REESE
1910, 2, 23. Lenius recrq

REEVES

1786, 8, 2. David b (W) (1796,8,2 in H)

----, --, --. Joshua [Reeve] b 1775,11,22 d
      1812,7,22 bur Salem; m Hannah ----- d
      1797,9,16 (W)
      Ch: Hannah   b 1797, 9, 16
      Joshua m 2nd Millisént ----- b 1781,1,16
      Ch: Benjamin   b 1801, 4, 9 d 1801, 4,10
          Samuel C. " 1803, 4, 6
          Ellen   " 1805, 3, 31
          Catharine " 1807, 7, 5
          Joshua   " 1809, 8, 13
          Job   " 1811, 6, 7 d 1811, 7, 1

1816, 10, 23. Hannah [Reeve] m Wm. SCHOOLEY

----, --, --. Abraham & Mary P. (H)
      Ch: Mansel P. b 1831, 11, 6
          Nathan   " 1832, 10, 23
          George   " 1834, 5, 18
          Phebe Ann " 1836, 12, 2
          Hannah   " 1838, 12, 21
          Mary Ellen " 1841, 5, 18

----, --, --. Joshua [Reeve] b 1809,8,13 d
      1869,3,17; m Elizabeth ----- b 1805,12,2(W)
      Ch: Job   b 1842, 7, 13 d 1890, 5,11

1843, 6, 29. Phebe m Wm. W. LAMBORN (H)

1808, 10, 11. Mary rocf Middleton MM, dtd 1808,
      6,11

1808, 11, 15. Mary gct Philadelphia MM, Pa.

1821, 10, 24. David rocf Mount Holly MM, N. J.,
      dtd 1821,8,9

1821, 11, 21. Samuel C. [Reeve] gct Planefield
      MM, O.

1824, 5, 19. Samuel C. [Reeve] rocf Still
      Water MM, dtd 1824,4,2

1828, 7, 30. David rocf New Garden MM, dtd
      1828,7,24 (H)

1828, 8, 20. David dis jH

1839, 6, 19. Abraham & w, Mary P., & ch, Man-
      sel P., Nathan, George, Phebe Ann & Han-
      nah, rocf Fallowfield MM, Pa., dtd 1839,5,
      11 (H)

1839, 7, 24. Lewis rocf Fallowfield MM, Pa.,
      dtd 1839,5,11 (H)

1839, 12, 25. George M. rocf Fallowfield MM,
      Pa., dtd 1839,10,12 (H)

1840, 7, 22. Daniel rocf Phila. MM held at
      Cherry St., dtd 1840,4,15 (H)

1841, 8, 25. William & Thomas, minors, rocf
      Fallowfield MM, Pa., dtd 1841,6,12

1843, 5, 24. :hebe recrq (H)

1843, 5, 24. Cert rec for Thomas [Reeve],
      minor, from Upper Springfield MM, dtd
      1843,4,22, endorsed to New Garden MM

1843, 6, 21. Phebe rocf Fallowfield MM, Pa.,
      dtd 1843,4,8 (H)

1843, 7, 19. Ann (form Barnaby) con mcd (H)

1865, 10, 25. Joshua & w, Elizabeth, rocf
      Plymouth MM, dtd 1865,9,23 (W)

1865, 10, 25. Job rocf Plymouth MM, dtd 1865,
      9,23 (W)

REGAL

----, --, --. Walter m Isabel DERR, dt Edgar

      & Lillian, b 1906,5,15 (G)
      Ch: Donna Jean b 1928, 8, 8
          Robert Lee " 1930, 1, 29
          Walter
          Dean   " 1931, 10, 29

1927, 8, 17. Walter recrq

RESSLER

1854, 7, 30. Carrie, dt Jacob & Druzilla Gor-
      don, b (G)

REYNOLDS

----, --, --. Samuel b 1806,1,16; m Hannah
      ----- b 1803,8,8 (W)
      Ch: Elizabeth
          Emily   b 1831, 12, 12
          Martha   " 1833, 4, 11
          Margaretta " 1839, 4, 12
          Mary Caro-
          line   " 1842, 2, 20

1806, 7, 5. Levi & w, Mary, & ch, Joel &
      Eliza, rocf Notingham MM, dtd 1805,10,12,
      endorsed by Short Creek MM, 1806,3,15

1835, 7, 22. Samuel & w, Hannah, & ch, Eliza-
      beth Emily & Martha, rocf New Garden MM,
      dtd 1835,6,25

1840, 5, 20. Samuel dis

1843, 1, 25. Hannah & ch, Elizabeth, Martha,
      Franklin, William, Margaretta & Mary Cor-
      nelia, gct Cincinnati MM

RHODES

1808, 10, 19. Mary m James CRAIG

1815, 11, 22. Moses, s Joseph & Martha, Colum-
      biana Co., O.; m at Salem, Susannah HEW-
      ITT, dt Jonathan & Ann, Fayette Co., Pa.

1818, 10, 28. Amy m John TIMBERLAKE

1806, 6, 17. Joseph & w, Martha, & ch, Amy,
      Moses & Harmon, rocf Goose Creek MM, Va.,
      dtd 1806,4,8

1808, 8, 16. Mary & Mary, Jr. recrq

1818, 8, 11. Joseph gct Short Creek MM, to m

1818, 12, 23. Moses & w, Susannah, & ch, Jo-
      seph & Martha, gct Miami MM

1818, 12, 23. Moses & w, Susannah, & ch, Jo-
      seph & Martha, gct Miami MM

1819, 3, 24. Joseph Rhodes & ch, Harmon &
      Lydia, & Anna Morris, gct Short Creek MM

1911, 12, 20. Mrs. George rec in mbrp

RICE

----, --, --. Francis C., s Edwin & Fanny, b
      1882,11,19; m Effie ALLEN, dt Ebenezer &
      Sarah J., b 1878,5,25 (G)
      Ch: Lester
          Allen   b 1911, 6, 19 d 1911, 6,26
          Hilda   " 1913, 5, 27

1836, 2, 24. Martha rocf Gunpowder MM, dtd
      1836,9,9 (?)

RICE, continued

1854, 2, 24. Martha dis (H)
1889, 7, 25. Deborah B. (form Trescott) gct East Goshen MM
1910, 2, 23. Francis recrq
1913, 10, 22. Francis & w, Ella, & dt, Hilda, gct Beloit MM
1918, 6, 19. Mrs. Verna relrq

RICH

1834, 8, 11. Francis B. b (W)
----, --, --. Joseph A., s David & Sophia, b 1872,1,17; m Clara B. STAMP, dt Wm. & Mary, b 1875,4,4 (G)
    Ch: J. Evert   b 1893, 12, 21
        Gladys J.   " 1896, 7, 3
        Frederick
        C.   " 1899, 3, 5
        Gordon
        Anderson   " 1907, 10, 17
----, --, --. Wm., s David & Sophia, b 1868, 1,15; m Maggie ----- (G)
    Ch: Grace   b 1896, 9, 1
        Gertrude   " 1897, 12, 7

1845, 4, 23. Francis B. recrq (a minor under care of Edward & Rachel Bonsall)
1865, 10, 25. Francis B. con mcd (W)
1866, 4, 25. Francis B. gct Hickory Grove MM, Ia. (W)
1911, 2, 22. Joseph relrq
1911, 3, 22. Will relrq
1912, 2, 21. Grace, Will & Gertrude recrq
1921, 9, 21. Clara B., Gladys & Frederick relrq
1923, 1, 3. Clara & Gladys recrq
1923, 5, 23. Mrs. Marie recrq
1924, 6, 23. Joseph recrq
1928, 5, 23. Everett dropped from mbrp
1929, 12, 26. Gordon gct La Juanta Heights MM

RICHARDS

----, --, --. Daniel b 1769,10,2; m ----- ----- (H)
    Ch: Elizabeth
        W.   b 1808, 4, 17
        Samuel   " 1801, 12, 14
----, --, --. Samuel b 1801,12,14; m Lydia B. ----- b 1814,12,1 (H)
    Ch: Charles
        Edward   b 1839, 2, 16 d 1840, 6, 4
        Stephen   " 1842, 3, 28
1915, 10, 30. Jessie m Marion HARRIS (H)

1840, 11, 25. Daniel & w, Lydia, & dt, Elizabeth W., rocf Friendsville MM, Pa., dtd 1840,9,3 (Lydia d before cert was rec) (H)
1840, 11, 25. Samuel & w, Lydia B., rocf Friendsville MM, Pa., dtd 1840,9,3 (H)
1844, 4, 24. Daniel gct Friendsville MM, Pa. (H)
1844, 4, 24. Elizabeth W. gct Friendsville MM, Pa. (H)

1862, 12, 25. Samuel dis joining separatists (W) of 1854
1881, 7, 21. Hannah R. Snode (form Richards) con mcd (H)

RICHARDSON

1824, 3, 9. Hannah b (H)

1808, 5, 17. Fielder & w, Miriam, & ch, Richard, Abram & Ann, rocf Fairfax MM, dtd 1807,4,25
1820, 5, 24. Jacob gct New Garden MM, to m Miriam Richardson
1821, 2, 21. Miriam & ch, Isaac G. & Elizabeth, rocf New Garden MM, dtd 1820,9,21
1821, 2, 21. Ann (form Hendrix) dis mcd
1833, 2, 7. Elizabeth Wisener (form Richardson) dis mou
1835, 9, 23. Isaac dis mcd

RICKS

1853, 5, 25. Cert rec for Margaret from Springborough MM, endorsed by Short Creek MM; returned by this mtg to Springborough MM since she had returned there to reside
1882, 12, 21. Angeline [Riks] recrq

RICHIE

----, --, --. William m Mary E. BARTON, dt James & Alice, b 1870,7,1 (G)
    Ch: Earl   b 1895, 9, 28

1882, 2, 8. Dora & Daniel W. recrq
1886, 10, 21. Dora [Richey] dropped from mbrp
1911, 12, 20. Earl rec in mbrp
1912, 2, 21. Mrs. [Ritchie] recrq
1916, 8, 16. Vera & Alta recrq
1924, 1, 23. Ida Mary [Ritchie] recrq
1932, 6, 29. Earl [Ritchey] dropped from mbrp

ROBBINS

1825, 3, 23. Mary rocf Middleton MM, dtd 1825,2,21

ROESSLER

1920, 3, 24. Carrie gct Alliance MM

ROGERS

1869, 5, 20. Eli H. con mcd
1870, 2, 9. Mary H. rocf Springborough MM, dtd 1869,12,21
1871, 11, 23. Eli H. & w, Mary H., & dt, Charlotte A., gct Springborough MM, O.

ROHER

----, --, --. Raymond, s W. D., b 1898,9,23; m Vera FORMAN, dt Wm. & Margaret, b 1899, 5,14 (G)
    Ch: Donald
        McKinley b 1919, 9, 1
        Raymond
        Paul   " 1926, 8, 3

ROHER, Raymond & Vera, continued
    Ch: George
          Wayne   b 1933, 6, 28

1929, 12, 26. Raymond & s recrq
1929, 12, 26. Vera roc

ROLLING
1874, 2, 26. Alfred G. recrq

ROOD
1807, 2, 17. Abigail, wd Jonathan, b (W)
----, --, --. Jonathan b 1764,10,10 d 1851,9,14
    m Clarissa ----- b 1787,9,14 (W)
    Ch: Luvina   b 1808, 8, 18
        Lucina   " 1808, 8, 18
        Ithamar   " 1810, 7, 22
        Emmor   " 1814, 2, 21
1827, 6, 22. Lusina m Martin LUPTON
1827, 12, 20. Lavina m Amos STEER
1845, 7, 30. Jonathan, s Roger & Betty, Car-
    roll Co., O.; m at Salem, Abigail STRATTON,
    dt Michael & Rhoda, Columbiana Co., O.
1853, 12, 28. Abigail m Christopher ALLEN

1824, 7, 21. Jonathan & w, Clarissa, & ch,
    Lavina, Lucina, Ithamar & Emmor, rocf Nine
    Partners MM, N. Y., dtd 1823,9,18
1828, 7, 23. Jonathan & w, Elizabeth, & ch,
    Ithamer & Emmor, gct Upper Springfield MM
1830, 7, 21. Jonathan & w, Clarissa, & ch,
    Emmor, rocf Upper Springfield MM, dtd
    1830,6,26
1834, 5, 21. Jonathan & w, Clarissa, & s, Em-
    mor, gct Upper Springfield MM
1841, 8, 25. Isaiah rocf Smithfield MM, dtd
    1841,6,21
1845, 9, 24. Abigail gct Sandy Spring MM
1853, 8, 24. Abigail rocf Sandy Spring MM,
    dtd 1853,6,24
1858, 12, 22. Jane L. (form Trescott) dis mcd
    (W)
1859, 7, 21. Jane L. (form Trescott) dis mcd

ROOSE
1861, 7, 24. Mary N. (form Barber) dis mcd
    (W)
1862, 12, 25. Mary [Rouse] dis joining separa-
    tists (W) of 1854

ROYER
1861, 1, 23. Unity (form Stanley) dis mcd (W)
1861, 11, 21. Unity [Royar] (form Stanley) dis
    mcd

RUMMELL
1880, 2, 26. J. H. & w, Elizabeth, recrq
1886, 10, 21. J. H. [Rummel] dropped from mbrp

RUSSELL
1877, 9, 5. Jason Kirk, s John & Eliza,
    Clearfield Co., Pa.;m at Cleveland, O.,
    Matilda M. MASTERS, dt Parvin & Deborah E.

1879, 6, 3. Frances C., dt Daniel & Rachel
    Courtney, b (G)

1806, 9, 16. Hannah [Rossell] (form Holloway)
    dis mcd
1856, 11, 19. Mary Ann (form Stanley) dis mcd
    (W)
1858, 4, 22. Mary Ann [Russel] (form Stanley)
    dis mcd
1893, 11, 22. Gibson Binns gct Short Creek MM,
    to m Martha Russell (W)

RUST
1910, 2, 23. Albert recrq

RUTTER
1917, 7, 25. Susan b (G)

1917, 7, 25. Susan recrq

RYSER
----, --, --. Earnest Lewis, s Earnest & Lena,
    b 1901,5,28; m Edith Louise RICE, dt Louis
    & Elsie, b 1905,9,20 (G)
    Ch: Paul
        Earnest   b 1928, 7, 29
        Carol
        Elsie   " 1929, 8, 23

1930, 3, 19. Ernest & w, Edith, & ch, Paul &
    Carol, recrq

SACKETT
1807, 3, 25. Lucinda m Robert THOMAS

1806, 12, 16. Lucinda, sister of Elizabeth
    Ball, recrq

SALTER
1873, 12, 25. Joseph & w, Hannah, & s, Arth-
    ur John, rocf Luton & Leighton MM, Eng-
    land, dtd 1873,10,10
1873, 12, 25. Frederick rocf Westminster &
    Longford MM, England, dtd 1873,11,6
1882, 11, 8. Joseph & w, Hannah, & ch, Arth-
    ur J. & Frederick, gct Adrian MM, Mich.

SAMS
1836, 11, 23. John, Jr. rocf Middleton MM, dtd
    1836,9,19
1840, 4, 22. John, Jr. gct Middleton MM
1910, 12, 21. Edith gct Beloit MM

SANDERS
1808, 1, 21. Charity m Stephen McBRIDE

SANTEE
1818, 6, 15. Sarah rocf Richland MM, dtd
    1818,4,3

SATTERTHWAITE
----, --, --. Richard b 1785,4,24 d 1834,7,25
    bur Salem; m Rebecca ----- b 1790,12,18

SATTERTHWAITE, Richard & Rebecca, continued
    d 1878,8,1 (H)
    Ch: John
        Wright   b 1813, 1, 22
        Barclay A. " 1814, 10, 7
        James M.   " 1818, 3, 22
        Caroline
        Wright   " 1820, 10, 16
        Joseph W.   " 1823, 11, 7
        Wm. T.   " 1826, 9, 25 d 1833, 4,25
        Isaac W.   " 1829, 3, 14
        Martha A.   " 1831, 9, 15 " 1862, 6,18
----, --, --. Rebecca G. b 1810,7,10 d 1884,12,
    6 (H)
----, --, --. David b 1793,4,25 d 1884,3,22; m
    Ruth ----- b 1798,7,13 d 1872,12,22 (W)
    Ch: Hutchen   b 1819, 1, 3
        Lydia Ann " 1821, 4, 29 d 1842, 11, 5
        Charles W. " 1833, 12, 31
        George T. " 1830, 10, 25
        Rachel   " 1838, 7, 21
        John   " 1840, 9, 29 d 1842, 9,11
----, --, --. John W. b 1813,1,22; m Sarah
    ----- b 1817,2,25 d 1849,2,10 (H)
    Ch: George   b 1842, 3, 3
1843, 8, 30. Isaac, s Jacob & Rebecca, Colum-
    biana Co., O., b 1818,11,1; m at Salem,
    Beulah TATUM, dt George & Beulah, Columbi-
    ana Co., O., b 1817,3,21 d 1845,2,21 (W)
    Ch: Wm.   b 1845, 3, 16 d 1845, 8, 8
1846, 4, 29. Hutchin, s David & Sarah, Colum-
    biana Co., O., b 1819,1,3 d 1907,2,19; m
    Lydia FAWCETT, dt David & Hannah, Columbi-
    ana Co., O., b 1822,11,3 d 1889,3,16 (W)
    Ch: David F.   b 1847, 1, 3
        Sarah   " 1850, 5, 21 d 1867,11,24
        bur New Garden
        Mary Ella b 1853, 4, 25 d 1898, 2, 6
        Edgar   " 1855, 9, 13
        Howard   " 1857, 5, 27 d 1933, 6,10
        bur Hope Cemetery, Salem, O.
        Hannah   b 1859, 12, 7 d 1930,11,14
        bur Hope Cemetery, Salem, O.
1853, 4, 27. Caroline F. m Evan BONSALL
----, --, --. Charles W. b 1833,12,31; m -----
    ----- (W)
    Ch: Franklin
        P.   b 1861, 2, 11
        Ann B.   " 1863, 8, 15
        Wm. D.   " 1866, 11, 8
        Isaac H.   " 1866, 11, 8
        Ruth C.   " 1871, 11, 11
----, --, --. George b 1836,10,25; m Sarah C.
    ----- b 1838,2,5 (W)
    Ch: Earnest H. b 1861, 1, 10
        Annie M.   " 1864, 1, 22
        Edward   " 1865, 5, 7
        Rowland   " 1866, 9, 14
1892, --, --. Ann d bur Westland, Pa.
----, --, --. William D., s Charles W. & Ada-
    line M. (Bye), b 1866,11,8; m Ida A. NEW-
    LIN, dt Wm. W. & Edith M. (Gilbert), b
    1868,4,10 d 1908,2,23 bur Friends Bur. Gr.,

    Winona, O. (W)
    Ch: Edith M.   b 1896, 4, 23
        Mary E.   " 1898, 8, 23
        Ellen R.   " 1901, 5, 28
        Ellis W.   " 1905, 1, 16
    William D. m 2nd Mabel C. CAMERON, dt Mil-
    ton & Beulah (Fogg), b 1880,12,23
    Ch: Elma
        Adaline   b 1918, 2, 20
        Cameron   " 1920, 7, 26
1919, 6, 26. Edith M. m Joshua E. HENDERSON
    (W)
1920, 4, 28. Mary E. m Russell B. HAMPTON (W)

1827, 6, 20. Richard & w, Rebecca, & ch,
    John W., Barkly A., James M., Caroline
    W., Joseph W. & William, rocf Green St.
    MM, Phila., Pa.
1828, 7, 30. Richard & ch, John W., Barkley
    A., James M., Caroline W., Joseph W. &
    William, rocf New Garden MM, dtd 1828,7,
    24 (H)
1828, 8, 20. Richard dis jH
1829, 2, 25. Rebecca dis jH
1835, 8, 19. David & w, Ruth, & ch, Hutchen,
    Lydia & Charles W., rocf Stillwater MM,
    dtd 1835,4,25
1836, 4, 20. John dis jH
1836, 5, 25. Barklay dis jH
1836, 9, 21. Sarah recrq (H)
1837, 1, 25. John con mou (H)
1842, 7, 20. Isaac rocf Chesterfield MM,
    N. J., dtd 1842,6,7
1847, 10, 20. Isaac H. [Satterthwaite] gct
    Chesterfield MM, N. J.
1852, 3, 25. John W. gct West MM, to m Re-
    becca Garretson (H)
1852, 7, 22. John W. & s, George, gct West
    MM (H)
1858, 3, 24. Charles W. dis mou (W)
1858, 5, 20. Martha Schilling (form Satter-
    thwait) dis mou (H)
1860, 10, 24. George S. gct New Garden MM, Pa.
    to m Sarah C. Conard (W)
1861, 4, 21. Sarah C. rocf New Garden MM,
    Pa., dtd 1861,3,6 (W)
1862, 12, 25. David, Ruth, Rachel, George &
    Charles dis joining separatists (W) of
    1854
1862, 12, 25. Hutchin, Lydia, David & Hannah
    dis joining separatists (W) of 1854
1865, 8, 24. John W. & w, Rebecca G., rocf
    West MM, dtd 1865,7,21 (H)
1866, 1, 24. Rachel S. French (form Satterth-
    wait) con mcd (W)
1866, 8, 22. Franklin P. & Hannah B., ch
    Charles, recrq (W)
1867, 2, 20. George T. & w, Sarah C., & ch,
    Earnest H., Annie M., Edward & Rowland
    T., gct New Garden MM, Pa. (W)
1872, 8, 21. William D., Isaac H. & Ruth C.,
    ch Charles W., recrq (W)
1873, 2, 19. Charles W. & ch, Franklin P.,

SATTERTHWAIT, continued
        Ann B., William D., Isaac H. & Ruth C.,
        gct·New Garden MM (W)
1875, 9, 22. David F. dis disunity (W)
1894, 7, 25. Edgar dis disunity (W)
1904, 3, 23. William D. & w, Ida A., & ch,
        Edith M., Mary E. & Ellen R., rocf New
        Garden MM, O., dtd 1904,2,25 (W)
1913, 7, 23. William D. gct Upper Springfield
        MM, to m Mabel H. Cameron (W)
1913, 11, 8. Mabel C. rocf Upper Springfield
        MM, O., dtd 1913,10,24 (W)
1929, 3, 20. Ellen Henderson (form Satterth-
        wait) con mcd (W)

SAVERY
1847, 2, 18. Rebecca H. b (W)

1876, 10, 25. Rebecca H. gct WD MM, Pa. (W)

SAWYER
1846, 1, 21. Rhoda P. rocf Farmington MM,
        N. Y., dtd 1845,9,25
1881, 10, 19. Sarah R. (form Hall) dis mcd (W)

SAXON
----, --, --. Betty b 1783,2,5 d 1837,2,12 (H)

1829, 7, 22. Betty recrq (H)

SAYERS
----, --, --. Robert, s William & Mary, b 1837,
        1,15 d 1910,6,12; m Anna KERN, dt Samuel &
        Jane, b 1850,5,13 d 1918,6,18 (H)

SCALE
1803, 4, 9. Mona b (W)

SCATTERGOOD
----, --, --. Samuel b 1813,2,19; m Mary C.
        ----- b 1812,7,15 (W)
        Ch: Edward   b 1837, 6, 29
            Sarah   " 1839, 4, 5 d 1846, 1,30
            Thomas   " 1841, 1, 22
            Susan   " 1842, 11, 13
            Joseph   " 1844, 8, 27
            Anna   " 1846, 7, 12
            Rebecca   " 1848, 5, 21
            David   " 1850, 6, 4
            Elizabeth " 1852, 12, 13 d 1853, 3,14

1841, 9, 22. Samuel & w, Mary C., & ch, Ed-
        ward, Sarah & Thomas, rocf ND MM, Phila.,
        Pa., dtd 1841,8,24
1854, 2, 22. Samuel & w, Mary, & ch, Edward,
        Sarah, Susan, Joseph, Anna, Rebecca & Da-
        vid, gct ND MM, Phila., Pa. (W)

SCHILLING
1858, 5, 20. Martha (form Satterthwait) dis
        mou (H)

SCHLECHER
1882, 9, 21. William A. recrq

SCHOLFIELD
1805, 11, 20. David, s David & Rachel, Colum-
        biana Co., O., b 1778,8,29; m at Salem,
        Rebecca DAVIS, dt Samuel & Mary, Columbi-
        ana Co., O., b 1784,5,25 (W)
        Ch: Samuel   b 1807, 1, 22
            Wm.   " 1809, 3, 7
            Rachel   "" 1811, 4, 21
            Joseph   " 1813, 3, 13 d 1815, 3, 7
             bur Salem
            Joshua   " 1816, 5, 2
            Mary   " 1818, 7, 24 d 1822, 3,12
            David   " 1820, 10, 5 " 1821, 8,23
            Rebecca   " 1820, 10, 5 " 1821, 4,27
            Rebecca   " 1822, 12, 12
            Lydia   " 1825, 8, 9
1829, 12, 2. Samuel, s David & Rebecca, Colum-
        biana Co., O.; m at Salem, Margaret TEET-
        ARS, dt John & Mary, Columbiana Co., O.
        (H)
----, --, --. Samuel b 1807,1,22; m Margaret
        ----- b 1808,6,27 (H)
        Ch: Mary   b 1830, 7, 20
            Elizabeth
            W.   " 1834, 7, 4
1838, 11, 28. Rachel m David BALL (H)
----, --, --. Joshua b 1816,5,2; m Margaret
        Ann ----- b 1818,8,1 (H)
        Ch: Joseph
            Clark   b 1840, 5, 6
            Robert
            Marcus   " 1841, 8, 30

1828, 7, 30. David & w, Rebecca, & dt, Ra-
        chel, rocf New Garden MM, dtd 1828,7,24 (H)
1828, 8, 20. Rebecca dis jH
1828, 11, 19. Samuel dis jH
1829, 6, 24. William dis jH
1830, 12, 22. Rachel dis jH
1838, 6, 20. Joshua dis jH
1839, 2, 20. Joshua gct Plainfield MM, to m
        Margaret Ann·Clark
1839, 9, 25. Margaret Ann rocf Plainfield MM,
        dtd 1839,7,18 (H)
1841, 11, 24. Margaret dis jas (H)
1841, 11, 24. Samuel dis jas
1843, 8, 23. Rebecca, Jr. dis joining Metho-
        dist Society
1844, 11, 20. Lydia Holloway (form Schol-
        field) dis jH
1845, 2, 19. Joshua & w, Margaret Ann, & ch,
        Joseph Clark, Robert Marcus, David & Re-
        becca Jane, gct Short Creek MM, O.
1845, 11, 19. Lydia Holloway (form Schofield)
        con mcd (H)
1851, 11, 19. Joshua & Margaret Ann, & ch,
        Joseph Clark, Robert Marcus, David, Re-
        becca Jane, William Davis, Samuel Silves-
        ter & Hugh Clark, rocf Short Creek MM, dtd
        1851,9,25 (H)

SCHOOLEY

----, --, --. Elisha b 1756,4,23 d 1838,6,19
  (an elder); m Rachel ----- b 1757,4,17
  d 1833,7,18 (an elder) (W)
  Ch: John   b 1780, 10, 11
    Mary   " 1782, 4, 5
    Sarah   " 1784, 10, 8
    Deborah   " 1787, 8, 29
    Israel   " 1791, 1, 16
    Wm.   " 1792, 8, 5
    Rachel   " 1794, 7, 17
    Elizabeth   " 1796, 9, 7
1781, 7, 9. Richard b (W)
1792, 8, 5. William b (W)
----, --, --. Hannah b 1797,9,16 d 1817,8,20
  bur Salem (W)
1817, 8, 11. Hannah R. b (W)
1816, 10, 23. Wm., s Elisha & Rachel, Columbiana Co., O.; m at Salem, Hannah REEVE, dt
  Joshua & Hannah
1819, 12, 8. Rachel m Mahlon HOLE
1820, 3, 29. Wm., s Elisha & Rachel, Columbiana Co., O.; m at Salem, Matilda ENGLAND,
  Columbiana Co., O.
1831, 7, 27. Sarah m Daniel MERCER

1807, 4, 14. John gct Middleton MM, to m
  Phebe Beason
1807, 11, 17. Phebe rocf Middleton MM, dtd
  1807,11,10
1816, 1, 16. Israel gct Short Creek MM, to m
  Sarah Pyle
1816, 7, 16. Sarah rocf Short Creek MM, dtd
  1816,5,21
1822, 3, 20. William dis jas
1822, 3, 20. Matilda dis jas
1829, 11, 25. Elizabeth Pettit (form Schooley)
  dis mou
1831, 8, 24. Anne Jane Wright (form Schooley)
  dis mcd
1831, 9, 21. Sarah Mercer (form Schooley) &
  ch, Emily Nicholas & Rachel Schooley, gct
  Middleton MM
1832, 9, 19. James gct Upper Springfield MM
1835, 7, 22. Henry [Scholey] dis disunity
1835, 11, 25. Hannah Durham (form Scholey) dis
  mcd & jas
1836, 3, 23. Elisha [Scholey], minor, gct
  Middleton MM
1836, 10, 19. Reuben dis mcd
1837, 9, 20. James rocf Upper Springfield MM,
  dtd 1837,8,24
1838, 12, 19. Elisha dis jas
1840, 1, 22. James gct Upper Springfield MM
1842, 1, 19. Dilworth, minor, gct Upper
  Springfield MM
1862, 12, 25. John & Phebe dis joining separatists (W) of 1854

SCOTT

----, --, --. Benjamin b 1799,3,13; m Ann
  ----- b 1791,11,24 (W)
  Ch: Mary Ann   b 1820, 12, 31

  Ch: Phebe H.   b 1822, 10, 10
    Prophet   " 1824, 5, 1
    Sarah   " 1825, 12, 19
    Elisabeth   " 1827, 11, 20
    Lydia   " 1829, 5, 15
    Joseph   " 1831, 5, 5

1812, 6, 16. Israel & w, Sarah, & ch, Mary &
  Phebe, rocf Middleton MM, dtd 1812,1,9
1816, 11, 12. Israel & w, Sarah, & ch, Mary,
  Phebe, Eli, Eliza, Ann & Job, gct Middleton MM
1823, 9, 24. William & w, Abigail, & ch, Hiram & Margaret, rocf Carmel MM, dtd 1823,
  7,30
1832, 8, 22. Benjamin dis disunity
1832, 10, 24. Ann & ch, Mary Ann, Phebe, Prophet, Sarah, Elizabeth, Lydia & Joseph,
  gct Upper Springfield MM

SCULLION

1912, 2, 21. Dessy [Schullin] recrq
1915, 11, 24. Harold recrq
1915, 11, 24. Cecil recrq

SEARS

1883, 2, 9. Elizabeth rocf Van Wert MM, O.

SEBRELL

----, --, --. Joseph b 1763,4,13; m Rebecca
  ----- b 1755,2,10 (W)
  Ch: Sally   b 1787, 6, 9
    Matthew   " 1791, 10, 4 d 1819, 7,22
    bur Salem
    Susannah   " 1794, 1, 25
    Joseph   " 1796, 4, 15
    Polly   " 1798, 7, 29
1796, 4, 15. Joseph, Jr. b (W)
1798, 7, 2. Mary b (W)
1807, 10, 24. Susannah d (W)
1816, 12, 25. Sarah m Thos. SHINN
1817, 2, 19. Joseph, s Joseph & Rebecca, Columbiana Co., O.; m at Salem, Mary SHINN,
  dt Thomas & Abigail, Columbiana Co., O.
1818, 2, 23. Abigail b (W)
1819, 2, 4. Matthew, s Joseph & Rebecca, Columbiana Co., O.; m at Springfield, Hannah
  CATTALL, dt James & Deborah, Columbiana
  Co., O.
1820, 6, 22. Matthew B. b (W)
1823, 8, 21. Rebecca J. b (W)

1807, 6, 11. Joseph [Sabrell] & w, Rebecca, &
  ch, Sally, Benjamin, Matthew, Susannah, Joseph & Polly, rocf Blackwater MM, Va., dtd
  1807,3,25
1811, 6, 11. Benjamin dis
1811, 6, 11. Sarah dis
1821, 12, 19. Marlborough MM was given permission to rec Benjamin & Sarah in mbrp
1824, 4, 21. Joseph & w, Rebecca, gct Marlborough MM
1824, 4, 21. Joseph, Jr. & w, Mary, & ch,

SEBRELL, continued
    Abigail G., Matthew B. & Rebecca J., gct
    Marlborough MM
1824, 4, 21. Mary gct Marlborough MM

SEGAR
1882, 8, 9. Catharine [Seiger] recrq
1882, 12, 21. Mary E. recrq

SEIGENTHALER
1914, 11, 25. Katharine dropped from mbrp

SERVEN
1910, 2, 23. J. W. recrq
1910, 2, 23. Sarah recrq

SHAFFER
1876, 3, 27. Lillian, dt Rhuben & Lydia Ann
    Sampsel, b (G)

1872, 9, 25. Sarah Ellen [Shafer] (form Lee)
    dis mcd (W)
1911, 12, 20. Gladys rec in mbrp
1933, 7, 19. Mrs. Clara recrq

SHALLENBERG
----, --, --. Walter, s Augustus & Faynetta,
    b 1896,6,30; m Grace DENKHOUS, dt Louis &
    Ella, b 1896,9,2 (G)
    Ch: Lowell   b 1918, 2, 4
        Robert   " 1919, 12, 20
        Marjorie " 1924, 6, 18
        Kenneth   " 1926, 2, 19

1929, 12, 26. Walter & w, Grace, & ch rocf Wi-
    nona MM

SHARP
----, --, --. Joel b 1779,8,13 d 1820,3,10 bur
    Salem, O.; m Rebecca ----- b 1783,11,17
    (W)
    Ch: Ruth   b 1802, 12, 12
        Martha   " 1805, 6, 3
        Thomas   " 1808, 2, 16
        Clayton   " 1811, 11, 18
        Mary Ann " 1814, 12, 4
        Simeon   " 1817, 5, 30
        Joel   " 1820, 2, 22
1824, 4, 28. Rebecca m Nathan HUNT
1825, 8, 31. Martha m Daniel BONSALL
1835, 4, 1. Mary Ann m Caleb HUNT (H)

1813, 5, 11. Joel & w, Rebecca, & ch, Ruth,
    Martha, Thomas & Clayton, recrq
1828, 10, 22. Ruth dis jH
1830, 3, 24. Thomas dis mcd
1831, 3, 23. Ruth gct Green St. MM, Phila.,
    Pa. (H)
1832, 12, 19. Ruth rocf Green St. MM, Phila.,
    Pa., dtd 1832,9,20 (H)
1833, 5, 22. Mary Ann dis jH
1836, 12, 21. Clayton dis mcd
1843, 2, 22. Simeon dis disunity

1845, 1, 22. Joel dis mcd
1845, 2, 19. Angelina (form Lee) con mcd
1851, 3, 19. Angelina dis disunity

SHARPLESS
1810, 1, 25. Sabina b (W)
1901, 6, 26. Alfred, s Zebedie & Anna P.,
    Chester Co., Pa.; m at Salem, Edith HAYES,
    dt Chas. I. & Elma, Columbiana Co., O.
    (W)

1834, 6, 25. Septimus C. rocf Middleton MM,
    dtd 1834,6,12
1835, 6, 24. Septimus C. gct Upper Spring-
    field MM, to m Sarah Negus
1835, 9, 23. Sarah rocf Upper Springfield MM,
    dtd 1835,8,22
1837, 5, 24. Septimus C. & w, Sarah, & ch,
    Isaac & John, gct Upper Springfield MM

SHARPNACK
----, --, --. Elizabeth M., dt Joseph Wright,
    b (G)

1882, 2, 8. Sarah recrq
1887, 3, 20. Sarah dropped from mbrp
1914, 8, 19. Sarah [Sharpnie] recrq
1918, 5, 22. Sarah dropped from mbrp
1932, 12, 29. Elizabeth M. recrq

SHAW
----, --, --. Levi b 1818,1,14; m Hannah -----
    b 1822,1,10 (W)
1851, 1, 10. Sarah Louiza b (W)

1808, 6, 14. Samuel & w, Sarah, & dt, Marga-
    ret, rocf Westland MM, dtd 1808,3,26
1832, 9, 19. James & w, Hannah, rocf Bucking-
    ham MM, dtd 1832,8,6 (H)
1835, 6, 24. John, minor, rocf New Garden MM,
    dtd 1835,6,23
1835, 7, 22. Abigail (form Branin) con mcd
    (H)
1838, 6, 20. Jonathan T. rocf Abington MM,
    Pa., dtd 1838,3,26
1838, 6, 20. Maria rocf Abington MM, dtd
    1838,3,26 (H)
1838, 6, 20. Rebecca A. rocf Abington MM,
    Pa., dtd 1838,3,26 (H)
1840, 3, 25. Rebecca Thomas (form Shaw) con
    mou (H)
1840, 10, 21. John gct Sandy Spring MM
1846, 12, 23. Maria gct Marlborough MM (H)
1856, 11, 20. Jonathan T. gct West MM (H)
1857, 3, 26. Jemima rocf West MM, dtd 1857,2,
    27 (H)
1862, 8, 20. Hiel rocf Middleton MM, dtd
    1862,8,16 (W)
1862, 12, 25. Samuel, Penina, Seth & Rebecca
    dis joining separatists (W) of 1854
1862, 12, 25. William, Hannah, Lindley, Mil-
    ton, William Wilson & Phebe Ellen, dis
    joining separatists (W) of 1854

SHAW, continued
1862, 12, 25. Hiel dis joining separatists (W) of 1854

SHEARMAN
1865, 6, 22. Thomas Stinson rocf Stratford-shire MM, held at Stoke upon Trent
1868, 9, 24. Thomas Stinson gct Pellham MM, Canada

SHIELL
1876, 12, 25. Andrew, s Robert & Euphemia, Wellan Co., Ontario; m at home of John W. Fawcett, Mary G. Fawcett, dt John W. & Emeline, Columbiana Co., O. (H)

SHINN
----, --, --. Thomas b 1772,2,14; m Abigail ----- d 1804,5,27 bur Salem (W)
    Thomas m 2nd Rebecca ----- b ----,2,20 d 1815,11,14 bur Salem (W)
    Ch: Mary   b 1798, 7, 2
        Joshua   " 1800, 11, 15
        James   " 1807, 9, 29
        Hannah   " 1809, 12, 22
        Hiram   " 1815, 10, 28 d 1819, 6,29
        Caleb   " 1819, 9, 23
        Susannah   " 1820, 7, 13
        Sally Ann   " 1822, 1, 6
----, --, --. John b 1791,3,19; m Sibilah ---- b 1795,12,25 (H)
    Ch: Joseph   b 1815, 12, 1
        Mary   " 1817, 5, 22
        Grace   " 1819, 2, 17 d 1819, 4, 1
        Elijah   " 1822, 8, 22
        John   " 1824, 11, 25
        Ann   " 1827, 9, 14
        Aaron   " 1830, 11, 11

1813, 9, 14. Thomas gct Mount Holly MM, N. J.
1813, 9, 14. Mary, minor dt Thomas, gct Mt. Holly MM, N. J.
1816, 6, 11. Mary Thompson (form Shinn) dis mcd
1816, 11, 12. Mary rocf Mt. Holly MM, N. J., dtd 1816,7,4
1824, 4, 21. Thomas & w, Sarah, & ch, James, Hannah, Caleb, Susannah S. & Sally Ann, gct Marlborough MM
1825, 5, 25. Joshua gct New Garden MM
1826, 5, 24. Cert rec for David & w, Susan, & ch, Charles, Rachel, Hannah & David R., from Frankford MM, Pa., dtd 1826,3,23, endorsed to Upper Springfield MM
1826, 7, 19. John & w, Sybella, & ch, Joseph, Mary, Elijah & John C., rocf Frankford MM, Pa., dtd 1826,4,27
1827, 5, 23. John & w, Sibillah, & ch, Joseph, Mary, Elijah & John C., gct Upper Springfield MM
1829, 6, 24. John & w, Sybella, & minor ch, Joseph, Mary, Elijah, John C. & Ann, mbrp transferred from Upper Springfield MM by rq

1831, 6, 22. Abraham rocf Mt. Holly MM, N.J., dtd 1831,5,5
1831, 6, 22. Grace rocf Burlington MM, N.J., dtd 1831,5,2 (H)
1856, 5, 22. John & w, Sabilla, rocf West MM, dtd 1856,4,25 (H)
1856, 5, 22. Abraham rocf West MM, dtd 1856,4, 25 (H)

SHIRKLER
1911, 12, 20. Earl rec in mbrp

SHISLER
----, --, --. Jesse L., s Jacob & Sarah, b 1874,10,5; m Olive ----- b 1876,3,30 d 1920,11,29 (G)
    Ch: Earle   b 1897, 1, 29
        Harold F.   " 1903, 7, 18
----, --, --. Sarah E., dt Richard & Lydia Beck, b 1835,10,14 d 1915,8,3 (G)

1912, 3, 10. Jesse relrq
1927, 1, 19. Earl relrq

SHOE
----, --, --. Herbert m Gertrude RICH, dt Wm. & Maggie, b 1897,12,7 (G)
    Ch: Mary Jane b 1918, 11, 28
        Robert Wm. " 1922, 10, 20
1881, 5, 26. Jacob recrq
1932, 12, 29. Mary Jane & Robert William recrq

SHORE
1796, 6, 27. Rachel b (H)

1828, 7, 30. Rachel rocf New Garden MM, dtd 1828,7,24 (H)

SHREEVE
----, --, --. Stacy b 1782,4,2; m Vashti ----- b 1782,5,5 (W)
    Ch: Wm.   b 1811, 6, 20
        Anna   " 1812, 9, 27
        Enoch   " 1814, 1, 22
        Joel   " 1815, 5, 4 d 1815,12,20
        Mary   " 1816, 8, 23
        Stacy   " 1818, 7, 22
        Vashti   " 1820, 5, 4
        Joshua   " 1821, 6, 17
        John   " 1824, 5, 4
1825, 6, 29. George W. [Shreve], s John & Abigail, Columbiana Co., O.; m at Salem, Martha FAWCETT, dt Richard & Eunice, Columbiana Co., O., b 1808,9,19 (W) (Geo. W. b 1798,1,30)
    Ch: Eunice   b 1826, 3, 27
        Mary Eliza " 1832, 5, 11
        David   " 1834, 8, 19
        Abigail   " 1839, 9, 21 d 1842, 9, 9
        Asenath   " 1845, 10, 27
1829, 5, 27. Elizabeth [Shreve] m Israel GASKILL (H)

SHREEVE, continued
1852, 3, 26. Eunice m Joshua WARRINGTON

1806, 12, 16. Stacey [Shreve] rocf Evesham MM,
        dtd 1806,6,6
1807, 10, 13. Vashti recrq
1822, 12, 25. Elisabeth rocf Haddonfield MM,
        N. J., dtd 1822,11,11
1823, 6, 25. Joseph rocf Providence MM, dtd
        1823,5,20
1823, 6, 25. Eliza [Shreeves], minor, rocf
        Providence MM, Pa., dtd 1823,5,20
1823, 6, 25. Mary rocf Providence MM, Pa.,
        dtd 1823,5,20
1823, 8, 1. George M. [Shreve] rocf Provi-
        dence MM, dtd 1823,6,24
1823, 11, 19. Solomon, minor, rocf Providence
        MM, dtd 1823,10,21
1824, 1, 21. Thomas C. rocf Providence MM,
        dtd 1823,12,23
1824, 7, 21. Benjamin R. rocf Providence MM,
        Pa., dtd 1824,5,25
1826, 6, 21. Benjamin R. gct Providence MM,
        Pa.
1827, 2, 21. George W. & w, Martha, & dt,
        Eunice, gct Upper Springfield MM
1827, 8, 22. Solomon [Shreve] gct Upper
        Springfield MM
1828, 8, 20. Thomas C. [Shreve] dis jH
1829, 4, 22. George W. [Shreve] & w, Martha,
        & dt, Eunice, rocf Upper Springfield MM,
        dtd 1829,3,28
1829, 6, 24. Benjamin R. [Shreve] dis mcd
1829, 11, 25. Elizabeth Gaskill (form Shreve)
        dis mcd & jH
1830, 1, 20. John [Shreve] rocf Providence
        MM, dtd 1829,11,9
1834, 12, 24. Mary & Eliza gct Marlborough MM
1841, 2, 24. John [Shreve] dis rec pension
        for his services as an officer in the Amer-
        ican Army in the Revolutionary War
1854, 11, 22. George W. [Shreve] & w, Martha,
        & ch, David & Asenith, gct Driftwood MM,
        Ind. (W)
1854, 11, 22. Mary Eliza [Shreve] gct Drift-
        wood MM, Ind. (W)
1855, 1, 25. George W. & w, Martha, & ch, Da-
        vid & Asenath, gct Driftwood MM, Ind.
1855, 1, 25. Mary Eliza gct Driftwood MM,
        Ind.
1860, 3, 21. Ann (form England) dis mcd (W)
1864, 2, 25. Mary rocf Marlborough MM, dtd
        1864,1,26

SHULTZ
1882, 2, 8. Rebecca recrq

SIDWELL
1845, 4, 23. William H. Oliphant gct Middle-
        ton MM, to m Sina Sidwell

SILVER
----, --, --. Adna B. b 1800,12,18; m Lydia

A. ----- b 1795,11,25 (H)
    Ch: Sarah A. b 1823, 11, 8
        Joseph   " 1828, 5, 3 d 1828, 6, 8
        (1828,7,7 in 0)
        Elizabeth b 1830, 6, 8
        Allen   " 1832, 1, 30
        Mary   " 1833, 6, 25

1827, 5, 23. Adnah B. [Silvin] & w, Lydia,
        & dt, Sarah, & Joseph P. Allen, an appren-
        tice, rocf Piles Grove MM, N. J., dtd
        1827,3,27
1828, 10, 22. Adna B. dis jH
1828, 10, 22. Lydia dis jH
1833, 3, 20. Sarah, minor dt Adna & Lydia,
        gct Upper Springfield MM
1836, 6, 22. Adney B. dis not attending mtg
1843, 7, 19. Sarah Davis (form Silvers) dis
        mcd (H)

SIM
1848, 1, 8. Jane J. b (W)

1874, 1, 22. Jane J. (form Maerkt) con mcd
        (W)
1904, 7, 20. Jane J. dis jas (W)

SLOCUM
1883, 10, 23. Ada, dt Harvey & Annie Watson,
        b (G)

1911, 12, 20. George & w rec in mbrp
1918, 5, 22. George & Ada dropped from mbrp

SMART
1857, 3, 4. Ruth m Wm. FISHER (W)

SMITH
1823, 3, 14. Susannah b (H)
1829, 10, 9. Abraham b (W)
1865, 5, 25. Wm. D., s Robert H. & Elizabeth,
        Belmont Co., O.; m at Salem, Hannah
        STREET, dt Samuel & Sarah, Columbiana
        Co., O. (W)
1880, 5, 20. John W., s William & Margaret,
        b (G)
1888, 5, 9. Lavina, dt Lindley E. & Anna C.,
        Haviland, b (G)
1890, 10, 29. Rebecca m Stephen HODGIN (W)
----, --, --. Geo. K. m Anna D. DOUDNA, dt
        Thomas & Rachel (Wood), b 1857,1,9 (W)
    Ch: Ethel C. b 1884, 2, 10
        Mary R.   " 1890, 6, 1
        Ella T.   " 1897, 4, 28
        Iva D.   " 1900, 3, 22
----, --, --. M. S., s Samuel & Catharine,
        b 1868,1,16; m Lavina STANLEY, dt Amos &
        Rachel, b 1870,12,10 d 1925,11,24 (G)
    Ch: L. Marlin b 1902, 6, 7
        Mildred   " 1904, 3, 10
1904, 8, 25. Ethel C. m Albert STARBUCK (W)
1906, --, --. Vera E. b (G)
----, --, --. Edgar & Minnie

SMITH, Edgar & Minnie, continued
    Ch: Carl L.   b 1923, 5, 21
      R. Frederick
             b 1911, 7, 3
      Harry L.   " 1916, 10, 27
1926, 9, 1. Sheldon W., s Joshua W. & Eva
    Irene, Linn Co., Ia.; m at Salem, Mary H.
    MOORE, dt Harry E. & Frances (Cooper),
    b 1893,8,8 (W)

1806, 2, 11. Samuel dis
1824, 4, 21. Sarah (form Morris) dis mou
1825, 10, 19. Sarah rst by rq
1843, 1, 25. Hannah B., dt Sarah, rocf Upper
    Springfield MM, dtd 1842,11,26
1853, 6, 22. Abraham rocf Upper Springfield
    MM, dtd 1853,4,23
1858, 10, 21. Hannah B. gct Upper Springfield
    MM
1860, 2, 23. Josiah B. & w, Elizabeth, & ch,
    Alvin, Eugene, Mildred, Horace, Matilda
    & Martha, rocf Buckingham MM, Pa., dtd
    1860,2,6 (H)
1866, 5, 23. Hannah S. gct Stillwater MM (W)
1879, 6, 26. Mary Ann recrq
1882, 2, 8. Harrison recrq
1885, 2, 26. Lyman recrq
1887, 4, 23. Alice rocf Short Creek MM, O.,
    dtd 1887,6,9 (H)
1887, 7, 20. Rebecca rocf Flushing MM, dtd
    1887,6,23 (W)
1902, 7, 23. Ethel C. rocf Flushing MM, dtd
    1902,6,26 (W)
1904, 3, 24. Anna D. & dt, Mary R., Ella T. &
    Iva D., rocf Flushing MM, dtd 1904,2,25 (W)
1911, 12, 20. Roy rec in mbrp
1915, 3, 31. John W. & w, Lovina, recrq
1916, 9, 20. Murray L. relrq
1918, 7, 24. John & Lovina relrq
1924, 1, 23. Edgar & w, Minnie, recrq
1924, 1, 23. Fred & Vera recrq
1926, 4, 21. Iva Long (form Smith) dis mcd
    (W)
1927, 5, 25. Mary H. gct Whittier MM, Ia. (W)

SNEDDON
----, --, --. William, s Charles & Janet, b
    1907,11,28; m Ruth Bernice MOORE, dt Wil-
    fred & Lucy, b 1911,11,8 (G)

1933, 2, 22. William & Ruth Bernice Moore rec-
    rq

SNODE
1841, 10, 20. Susannah (form Branin) con mou
    (H)
1881, 7, 21. Hannah R. (form Richards) con
    mcd (H)

SNYDER
1860, 6, 20. Hannah E. (form Painter) dis mcd
    (W)
1861, 3, 21. Hannah [Snider] (form Painter)

    dis mcd
1920, 9, 22. Mrs. C. L. relrq

SPECK
1871, 5, 24. Phebe S. (form White) dis mcd
    (W)

SPENCER
----, --, --. Robert b 1781,7,21; m Amy -----
    b 1782,11,25 d 1862,9,7 (W)

1823, 12, 24. Priscilla (form Stanley) dis
    mcd
1856, 1, 23. Robert & w, Amy, rocf Upper
    Springfield MM, dtd 1855,11,23 (W)

SPICKLER
1889, --, --. Lulu, dt James & Malisa Ormsby,
    b (G)

SPIKER
----, --, --. Fred, s Frederick & Margaret,
    b 1893,4,23; m Pearl E. A. RICHIE, dt
    Wm. & Mary, b 1894,2,20 (G)
    Ch: Florence
        Margaret b 1917, 1, 5

1913, 11, 19. Frederick [Spicker] recrq
1917, 7, 25. George & Mary recrq
1926, 3, 24. George dropped from mbrp

STACKHOUSE
1808, 8, 16. Benjamin con mou (form dis
    by Falls MM, Pa.)

STACKPOLE
1865, 10, 26. Mary D. rocf Vasselboro MM,
    Maine, dtd 1865,8,16

STAFFORD
----, --, --. Joshua b 1799,6,28 d 1876,1,28
    (W)

1846, 10, 21. Joshua recrq
1860, 7, 25. Joshua gct Sandy Spring MM, to
    m Esther F. Reeder (W)

STANLEY
----, --, --. Thomas b 1752,5,5 d 1823,2,28
    bur near his home at Springfield; m Unity
    ----- b 1760,8,31 (W)
    Ch: Moses   b 1781, 11, 15
        John   " 1783, 11, 2
        James   " 1787, 3, 10
        Joseph   " 1789, 2, 19
        Benjamin " 1791, 2, 10
        Judith   " 1793, 9, 28
        Abigail   " 1796, 10, 19
        Thomas C. " 1801, 12, 12
----, --, --. Littleberry b 1756,2,2 d 1821,
    8,8; m Agatha ----- b 1754,8,4 (W)
    Ch: Solomon   b 1787, 12, 26

STANLEY, Littleberry & Agatha, continued
    Ch: Martha   b 1789, 11, 8
----, --, --. Thos. b 1757,5,19; m Edith -----
    Thos. m 2nd Priscilla ----- b 1772,12,6(W)
    Ch: Milly   b 1791, 9, 7
        Edmund   " 1793, 2, 10
        John   " 1795, 9, 19
        Elijah   " 1796, 9, 8
        Frances   " 1798, 10, 1
        Isaac   " 1803, 3, 24
        Thos. Bin-
          ford   " 1805, 9, 5
        Sarah   " 1807, 11, 18
        Micajah   " 1810, 2, 11
        Henrietta " 1814, 4, 14
----, --, --. Waddy b 1759,6,26; m Rebecca
    ----- b 1775,6,29 (W)
    Ch: Samuel   b 1796, 4, 1
        Priscilla " 1798, 7, 15
        Lucy   " 1801, 4, 9
        Anne   " 1803, 6, 23
        Joel   " 1805, 11, 18
        Nancy   " 1808, 9, 25
        Thomas Crew" 1811, 5, 19
        Deborah   " 1814, 8, 12
        Waddy   " 1816, 9, 4
        Rebecca   " 1819, 2, 17
----, --, --. Ruth b 1798,11,9 d 1872,10,15
    (W)
----, --, --. Jonathan b 1776,6,12 d 1852,7,
    22 bur Salem (an elder); m Mary STRATTON
    b 1781,7,20 d 1857,10,16 (W)
    Ch: Andrew   b 1799, 11, 11
        Fleming   " 1802, 3, 8 d 1829, 8,10
          bur Salem
        Abraham   " 1804, 8, 30
        Milly   " 1808, 8, 25
        James   " 1810, 10, 19
        John   " 1813, 6, 19
        Jonathan " 1819, 4, 20
----, --, --. Joshua, s John & Milly, Columbi-
    ana Co., O., b 1774,7,15; m Rachel -----
    b 1778,9,13 d 1815,4,6 (W)
    Ch: Jordan   b 1799, 10, 4 d 1820, 8,13
        Maria   " 1800, 12, 1
        Matilda   " 1803, 11, 13
        Overton   " 1805, 3, 20
        Frederick " 1807, 1, 14
        Eliza   " 1808, 12, 2
        John   " 1811, 7, 7
        Elwood   " 1813, 10, 23
    Joshua m 2nd 1816,5,22 at Salem, Milis-
    cent REED, dt Job & Catharine, b 1791,1,16
    Ch: Job   b 1817, 3, 6 d 1817, 9,12
        Martin   " 1818, 8, 14
        Rachel   " 1820, 11, 17
        Jacob   " 1823, 6, 21
1807, 6, 17. Moses, s Thomas & Unity, Colum-
    biana Co., O., b 1781,11,15 d 1834,10,7
    bur Salem; m at Salem, Susannah HOLLOWAY,
    dt Jesse & Sarah, Columbiana Co., O., b
    1784,8,20 d 1866,12,17 bur Salem (W)
    Ch: Jesse Crew b 1808, 4, 2 d 1859, 7,17

    Ch: Thomas P. b 1809, 10, 2
        Esther   " 1811, 7, 23
        Isaiah   " 1813, 4, 8
        Jeremiah " 1815, 5, 20
        Catharine " 1817, 6, 21
        Moses   " 1819, 12, 6
        Susannah
          Jr.   " 1821, 9, 11
        Unity, Jr. " 1823, 8, 28
1809, 9, 21. John, s Thomas & Unity, Columbi-
    ana Co., O., b 1783,11,2; m at Springfield
    Mary Ann WOOLMAN, dt Samuel & Jane, Colum-
    biana Co., O., b 1792,9,20 d 1822,7,2 (W)
    Ch: Clotilda b 1811, 9, 16
        Deborah   " 1813, 9, 23
        Unity   " 1815, 8, 16 d 1819, 2,15
        Jane   " 1817, 4, 18
        Thomas   " 1818, 11, 20
        Samuel W. " 1818, 11, 20
        James   " 1821, 3, 3
1811, 7, 24. Garland, s James C. & Mary, Co-
    lumbiana Co., O., b 1790,2,12; m at Lex-
    ington, Sarah BURDEN, dt Job & Mary, Stark
    Co., O., b 1788,5,19 (W)
    Ch: Mary   b 1812, 7, 11
        Martha   " 1817, 8, 13
        Edith   " 1820, 4, 16
        Priscilla " 1822, 5, 1
1811, 12, 26. James, s Thomas & Unity, Colum-
    biana Co., O., b 1787,3,10 d 1820,9,11
    bur Springfield; m Rhoda COBBS, dt Pleas-
    ant & Amy, Columbiana Co., O., b 1790,9,
    30 (W)
    Ch: Milton   b 1812, 11, 5
        Amy   " 1815, 7, 30
        Robert   " 1817, 8, 15
        Judith C. " 1818, 11, 24
1812, 10, 14. Abram, s John & Milly, Columbi-
    ana Co., O.; m at Salem, Sarah BLACKBURN,
    dt David & Margaret, Columbiana Co., O.
1812, 10, 15. Milly m Joshua CREW
1812, 7, 2. Joseph, s Thomas & Unity, Colum-
    biana Co., O., b 1789,2,19; m at Spring-
    field, Abigail COBBS, dt Pleasant & Amy,
    Columbiana Co., O., b 1792,3,28 (W)
    Ch: Timothy b 1813, 6, 26
        Jennet   " 1814, 12, 8
        Ansalem   " 1817, 7, 13
        Joseph   " 1819, 6, 9
        Joanna   " 1821, 8, 23 d 1823, 8, 5
1813, 6, 24. Benjamin, s Thomas & Unity, Co-
    lumbiana Co., O., b 1791,2,10; m at
    Springfield, Elizabeth COBBS, dt Pleas-
    ant & Amy, Columbiana Co., O., b 1793,11,
    19 (W)
    Ch: Pleasant
        Thomas   b 1814, 5, 30
        Osborn   " 1815, 12, 19
        Ann   " 1818, 1, 1
        Unity C. " 1820, 1, 27
        Eliza Ter-
          rell   " 1821, 11, 2
        Meribah   " 1823, 4, 12

STANLEY, Benjamin & Elizabeth, continued
Ch: Amy   b 1825, 1, 4
1813, 6, 24. Solomon, s Littleberry & Agatha,
Columbiana Co., O., b 1787,12,28; m at
Springfield, Mary COBBS, dt Pleasant &
Amy, Columbiana Co., O., b 1789,3,18 (W)
Ch: Walter   b 1814, 5, 9
    Joanna   " 1815, 11, 21
    Amy   " 1817, 6, 20
    Littleberry " 1819, 1, 20
    Agatha   " 1821, 4, 25
    Tacy   " 1823, 2, 1
    Nathan   " 1825, 10, 4
1814, 1, 20. Judith m Jehu COPPOCK
1815, 9, 20. Elizabeth m David WILEY
----, --, --. James b 1792,9,15; m Rachel ----
b 1794,10,18 (W)
Ch: Israel   b 1816, 1, 18
    Jesse   " 1818, 5, 1
    James   " 1821, 3, 3
1818, 12, 3. Samuel, s Waldy & Rebecca, Columbiana Co., O.; m at Springfield, Sarah
CATTELL, dt James & Deborah, Columbiana
Co., O.
1819, 8, 30. Sarah Ann, dt Samuel & Sarah, b
(W)
1819, 5, 26. Frances m Isaac VOTAW
1819, 1, 28. Andrew, s Jonathan & Mary, Columbiana Co., O., b 1799,11,11 d 1833,5,5;
m at Springfield, Ruth COPPOCK, dt Samuel
& Ellen, Columbiana Co., O., b 1798,11,9
(W)
Ch: Jehu   b 1819, 11, 23 d 1821, 8,17
    bur Salem
    Rebecca   " 1821, 7, 15 " 1822, 9,29
    bur Salem
    Mary   " 1823, 4, 9
    Ellen   " 1824, 12, 20
    Abraham Jr." 1826, 7, 3
    Simeon   " 1828, 4, 23
    Milly   " 1830, 4, 3 d 1858, 1, 2
    Ann   " 1831, 10, 20
    Ruth   " 1833, 6, 20 " 1855, 3,31
----, --, --. Susannah b 1821,9,11 d 1882,5,6
(W)
1820, 3, 2. John, s Thomas & Edith, Columbiana Co., O., b 1795,9,19; m at Springfield
Abigail STANLEY, dt Thomas & Unity, Columbiana Co., O., b 1796,10,19 (W)
Ch: Edith   b 1822, 2, 18
    Thomas
    Gerard   " 1824, 6, 5
    Elihu B.   " 1826, 8, 24
    Josiah   " 1829, 3, 26
1822, 8, 29. Rhoda m James VAUGHAN
1823, 12, 4. Elijah, s Thomas & Edith, Columbiana Co., O.; m at Springfield, Uree WAL-
TON, dt Jesse & Ann, Columbiana Co., O.
1823, 1, 9. Lucy m James Simpson Cowgill
1823, 10, 13. John, s Thomas & Unity, Columbiana Co., O.; m at Springfield, Margaret
BLACKBURN, dt David & Margaret, Columbiana
Co., O.

1824, 4, 28. Maria m Warner ATKINSON
1825, 10, 26. Edmund, s Thomas & Edith, Columbiana Co., O.; m at Salem, Mary PIGEON, dt
Wm. & Alice, Columbiana Co., O.
----, --, --. William, s Binford & Mary, b
1829,9,19 d 1914,2,27 (G)
----, --, --. Ann b 1831,10,20 d 1886,12,21
(W)
1832, 11, 7. Milly m Robert JOHNSON
1827, 1, 31. Overton, s Joshua & Rachel, Columbiana Co., O., b 1805,3,20; m at Salem,
Mary STRATTON, dt David & Mary, Columbi-
ana Co., O., b 1809,3,5 (W)
Ch: Levina   b 1833, 2, 21
    Isaac   " 1828, 8, 13
    Mary Ann   " 1835, 8, 12
----, --, -. Phebe b 1833,11,13 d 1914,12,24
(G)
1837, 6, 28. James, s Jonathan & Mary, Co-
lumbiana Co., O., b 1810,10,19 d 1883,6,
25; m at Salem, Elizabeth JOHNSON, dt
John H. & Hannah, Columbiana Co., O. (W)
Ch: Andrew   b 1838, 6, 8
    John J.   " 1840, 4, 18
    Laura   " 1842, 9, 30
    George   " 1844, 9, 13
James m 2nd 1855,5,30 at Salem, Sarah AL-
LISON, dt George & Rebecca, Columbiana
Co., O., b 1811,4,4 d 1886,10,10 (W)
1843, 8, 17. Isaac E., s Jeremiah & Ann, b
(W)
----, --, --. Jefferson & Nora (G)
Ch: Harriet R. b 1894, 3, 10
    George   " 1898, 6, 15
----, --, --. Jonathan, Jr. b 1819,4,20; m
Hannah MILLER, dt David & Elizabeth, b
1817,12,17 (Jonathan was s Jonathan &
Mary) (W)
Ch: Mary
    Elizabeth b 1843, 12, 22 d 1846, 2,25
    David M.   " 1846, 6, 25 " 1847, 9, 4
    Eliza   " 1848, 7, 6
    Isabella   " 1855, 11, 3
    Abraham   " 1860, 2, 18
1844, 2, 2. Ann d bur Salem (W)
1846, 10, 28. Jeremiah, s Moses & Susannah,
Columbiana Co., O.; m at Salem, Martha
DAVEIS, dt Wm. & Anna, Columbiana Co., O.
1848, 5, 31. Ellen m Benjamin D. STRATTON
1849, 11, 28. Esther m Daniel GREEN
----, --, --. Jeremiah b 1815,5,20 d 1864,4,
11; m Almond ----- (W)
Ch: Almond   b 1850, 11, 29
    Ezra   " 1852, 10, 15
    Willis   " 1855, 4, 5
1857, 3, 5. John, s Thomas & Edith, Columbiana Co., O.; m at Salem, Martha HAWKS,
dt Edward & Phebe COBB, Columbiana Co.,O.
1857, 9, 30. Mary m Thomas HOBSON (W)
1865, 8, 14. Hannah M. d (G)
1867, 5, 29. Eliza m Wm. BONSALL (W)
1868, 10, 28. Catharine m Josiah FAWCETT (W)
1871, 2, 6. Amelia F., dt Jonathan & Amelia

STANLEY, continued
    F., b (G)
1871, 2, 10. Amelia F. d (G)
----, --, --. Roscoe R., s Mervin T. & Ger-
    trude (Pickett), b 1900,6,24; m Sina Emily
    HOLLOWAY, dt Cyrus D. & Esther (Emery), b
    1900,7,30 (W)
    Ch: Wilmer
            Wilid   b 1925, 2, 4
        Robert
            Clarence " 1927, 1, 31

1805, 12, 17. Thomas & w, Unity, & ch, James,
    Joseph, Benjamin, Judith, Abigail & Thom-
    as, rocf Cedar Creek MM, Va., dtd 1805,10,
    12, endorsed by Middleton MM, 1805,12,14
1805, 12, 17. John rocf Cedar Creek MM, Va.,
    dtd 1805,10,12, endorsed by Middleton MM,
    dtd 1805,12,14
1806, 5, 13. Moses rocf Cedar Creek MM, dtd
    1805,10,12, endorsed by Middleton MM, dtd
    1806,3,8
1806, 6, 17. Jonathan & w, Mary, & ch, An-
    drew, Fleming & Abraham, rocf Cedar Creek
    MM, dtd 1805,11,9, endorsed by Middleton
    MM, 1806,6,14
1806, 8, 12. James Crew & w, Mary, & ch, Gar-
    land, James, Nathaniel, Gerard, Elizabeth,
    Jesse, Littleberry & Lemuel, rocf Cedar
    Creek MM, Va., dtd 1806,6,14
1806, 11, 11. Waddy & w, Rebecca, & ch, Sam-
    uel, Priscilla, Lucy, Ann & Joel, rocf
    Cedar Creek MM, dtd 1806,9,13
1810, 6, 12. Solomon rocf Cedar Creek MM, Va.,
    dtd 1810,4,14
1810, 8, 14. Littleberry & w, Agatha, rocf
    Cedar Creek MM, Va., dtd 1810,4,14
1810, 11, 13. Joshua & w, Rachel, & ch, Jor-
    don, Maria, Matilda, Overton, Frederick &
    Eliza, rocf Cedar Creek MM, Va., dtd 1810,
    10,13
1812, 6, 16. Thomas & w, Priscilla, & ch,
    Milly, Edmund, John, Elijah, Fanny, Isaac,
    Thomas Benford, Sarah & Micajah, rocf
    Cedar Creek MM, Va., dtd 1812,4,11
1812, 9, 15. Abram rocf Cedar Creek MM, Va.,
    dtd 1812,7,11
1813, 1, 12. Nancy rocf Cedar Creek MM, Va.,
    dtd 1812,8,8
1813, 5, 11. Abram & w, Sarah, gct Cedar Creek
    MM, Va.
1814, 12, 13. James, Jr. gct Middleton MM, to
    m Rachel Cowgill
1815, 11, 14. Rachel rocf Middleton MM, dtd
    1815,11,9
1816, 11, 12. Nathaniel J. dis mou
1818, 1, 13. Edmund dis
1818, 1, 13. James C. & w, Mary, & ch, Jesse,
    Littleberry, Lemuel, Jonathan & Rhoda, gct
    Stillwater MM
1818, 5, 12. James, Jr. & w, Rachel, & ch,
    Israel & Jesse, gct Stillwater MM
1819, 4, 21. James, Jr. & w, Rachel, & ch,

Israel & Jesse, rocf Stillwater MM, dtd
    1819,1,23
1819, 12, 22. Nathaniel rst by rq
1820, 5, 24. Edmund rst by rq
1820, 7, 19. Nathaniel gct Carmel MM
1820, 11, 22. Samuel dis disunity
1820, 12 20. Lydia rocf Carmel MM, dtd 1820,
    12,16
1821, 12, 19. Allen & Joseph Hinchman, ch Na-
    thaniel, recrq
1822, 11, 20. Thomas C. gct New Garden MM, to
    m Leah Votaw
1823, 6, 25. Leah rocf New Garden MM, dtd
    1823,4,24
1823, 12, 24. Priscilla Spencer (form Stanley)
    dis mcd
1824, 8, 25. Elijah dis
1825, 1, 19. Garland & w, Sarah, & ch, Mary,
    Martha, Edith & Priscilla, gct Marlborough
    MM
1825, 6, 22. Anna Foughty (form Stanley) dis
    mcd
1829, 6, 24. Cert rec for Priscilla from
    Smithfield MM, dtd 1829,2,3, endorsed to
    Upper Springfield MM
1830, 5, 19. Overton & w, Mary, & s, Isaac,
    gct Upper Springfield MM
1830, 5, 19. Elisa gct Upper Springfield MM
1831, 6, 22. John & w, Abigail, & ch, Edith,
    Thomas, Jared, Elihu B. & Josiah, gct Up-
    per Springfield MM
1832, 8, 22. John H. gct Upper Springfield MM
1832, 10, 24. Milisent & ch, Martin, Rachel &
    Jacob, gct Marlborough MM
1832, 10, 24. Overton & w, Mary, & s, Isaac,
    rocf Upper Springfield MM, dtd 1832,6,23
1832, 11, 21. Elwood gct Upper Springfield MM
1833, 5, 22. Abraham gct Marlborough MM
1836, 10, 19. Thomas P. gct Marlborough MM, to
    m Hannah Grewell
1837, 3, 22. Thomas P. gct Upper Springfield
    MM
1837, 5, 24. Isaiah gct Upper Springfield MM,
    to m Nancy Crew
1837, 11, 22. James & w, Elizabeth, gct Upper
    Springfield MM
1838, 1, 24. Isaiah gct Upper Springfield MM
1838, 2, 21. John gct Redstone MM
1841, 7, 21. Frederick dis disunity
1842, 4, 20. Jonathan gct Redstone MM, to m
    Hannah Miller
1842, 8, 24. Hannah M. rocf Redstone MM, dtd
    1842,6,29
1842, 10, 19. Jeremiah gct Upper Springfield
    MM, to m Ann Elyson
1843, 4, 19. Ann rocf Upper Springfield MM,
    dtd 1843,3,25
1844, 6, 19. Lydia (form Mather) dis mcd (H)
1844, 7, 24. Moses dis mcd
1851, 3, 19. Levina Pollock (form Stanley)
    dis mcd
1851, 4, 23. Jesse Thomas gct Upper Spring-
    field MM, to m Joanna Stanley

STANLEY, continued

1851, 5, 21. Simon dis mcd
1853, 1, 19. Isaac dis mcd
1853, 6, 22. James & ch, Andrew, John J.,
    Laura, George & Eli, rocf Upper Spring-
    field MM, dtd 1853,5,28
1856, 11, 19. Mary Ann Russell (form Stanley)
    dis mcd (W)
1857, 4, 23. Martha gct Upper Springfield MM
1857, 5, 21. Abraham gct Upper Springfield
    MM, to m Isabel Stanley
1858, 4, 22 Mary Ann Russel (form Stanley)
    dis mcd
1858, 9, 23. Jeremiah & w, Martha, & ch,
    Isaac E., Almond, Ezra & Willis, gct
    Spring Creek MM, Ia.
1859, 8, 25. Mary H. (form Marsh) con mcd
1860, 4, 26. Mary H. gct Upper Springfield MM
1860, 6, 20. Overton & w, Mary, gct Upper
    Springfield MM (W)
1861, 1, 23. Unity Royer (form Stanley) dis
    mcd (W)
1861, 11, 21. Unity Royar (form Stanley) dis
    mcd
1862, 12, 25. James, Sarah, Andrew, John,
    Laura, George & Eli dis joining separatists
    (W) of 1854
1862, 12, 25. Overton & Mary dis joining sepa-
    ratists (W) of 1854
1862, 12, 25. Susan, Catharine & Susanna dis
    joining separatists (W) of 1854
1863, 7, 23. Abraham gct Bangor MM, Ia.
1864, 7, 20. Hannah M. dis joining separa-
    tists of 1854 (W)
1864, 8, 24. Jonathan dis joining separatists
    of 1854 (W)
1864, 12, 22. Laura gct Springdale MM, Ia.
1865, 1, 25. Andrew dis mou (W)
1866, 11, 23. Jonathan gct Alum Creek MM, to
    m Amelia F. Benedict
1867, 1, 23. John J. dis mou (W)
1867, 9, 26. Amelia F. rocf Alum Creek MM,
    dtd 1867,8,22
1869, 3, 24. Laura Bonsall (form Stanley) dis
    mcd (W)
1873, 3, 19. Abram dis mcd (W)
1874, 4, 22. George dis mcd (W)
1881, 5, 26. Eli recrq
1884, 3, 20. Cert rec for Benjamin from Damas-
    cus MM; returned because of obstruction
1886, 10, 21. Abraham dropped from mbrp
1888, 6, 20. Eli [Stanly] dis joining separa-
    tists of 1854 (W)
1888, 6, 21. Felicia A. rocf Alum Creek MM,
    dtd 1888,4,19
1888, 6, 21. Emerson L. & w, Laura F., & ch,
    Mary E. & Alfred W., rocf Damascus MM, dtd
    1888,5,26
1889, 1, 24. William P. & w, Eliza C., rocf
    Damascus MM, dtd 1888,12,22
1891, 11, 14. Jefferson rocf Grove MM, Ind.
1911, 12, 20. Harriet rec in mbrp
1914, 2, 25. Mabel Coy gct Damascus MM

1924, 7, 23. Roscoe R. rocf Mill Creek MM,
    Ind., dtd 1824,6,26 (W)
1924, 7, 23. Sina E. rocf Middleton MM, O.
    (W)

1929, 8, 24. Roscoe R. & w, Sina E., & ch,
    Wilmer W. & Robert C., gct New Garden MM,
    O. (W)

STANTON

----, --, --. James b 1767,11,20; m Mary
    ----- b 1770,7,6 (W)
    Ch: Hannah   b 1794, 12, 19
        John   " 1798, 12, 7
        Elijah   " 1802, 11, 26
        Susannah " 1805, 6, 16
        Amor   " 1810, 2, 1
----, --, --. Zacheus b 1779,11,6; m Sarah
    ----- b 1778,4,3 (W)
    Ch: Hannah   b 1804, 8, 14
        Thomas   " 1807, 5, 4
        Eli   " 1810, 4, 5
1816, 8, 21. Benjamin, s Benjamin & Abigail,
    Columbiana Co., O., b 1793,7,28 d 1861,2,
    27; m Martha M. TOWNSEND, dt Joseph &
    Sina, Columbiana Co., O., b 1794,4,18 (H)
    Ch: Rebecca   b 1819, 1, 8
        Laura   " 1820, 9, 20
        Oliver   " 1822, 7, 26
        Joseph   " 1824, 5, 30
        Caroline " 1826, 6, 28 (1826,7,28
        in O)
        David   " 1829, 6, 9
        Wm.   " 1832, 8, 28
        Dalton   " 1834, 8, 14
        Byron   " 1834, 8, 14
        Benj.
        Lundy   " 1839, 10, 19 d 1841, 2,12
1843, 7, 26. Laura m James BARNABY, Jr. (H)
1909, 7, 28. Elwood Dean Stanton, s Wm. &
    Jane D., Chester Co., Pa.; m at Salem,
    Esther Sidney FAWCETT, dt Thos. F. & Sid-
    ney A., Columbiana Co., O. (W)

1806, 3, 11. Aaron rocf South River MM, Va.,
    dtd 1805,11,9
1806, 6, 17. James & w, Mary, & ch, John,
    Elijah & Hannah, rocf Cain Creek MM, dtd
    1805,4,6, endorsed by Concord MM, 1805,
    11,19
1806, 6, 17. William & dt, Deborah, rocf
    South River MM, Va., dtd 1806,4,12
1806, 7, 15. Zaccheus & w, Sarah, & dt, Han-
    nah, rocf South River MM, dtd 1806,4,12
1810, 12, 11. Lydia recrq
1811, 3, 12. William, Alfred & Elizabeth, ch
    Aaron & Lydia, recrq
1811, 9, 17. James & w, Mary, & ch, Hannah,
    John, Elijah, Susannah & Amos, gct Miami
    MM
1812, 9, 15. Aaron & w, Lydia, & ch, William,

STANTON, continued

Alfred, Elizabeth & Elwood, gct White
Water MM

1816, 7, 16. Benjamin rocf Short Creek MM,
dtd 1816,6,18

1828, 7, 23. Benjamin dis JH

1828, 7, 30. Benjamin & w, Martha, & ch, Rebecca, Laura, Oliver, Joseph & Caroline,
rocf New Garden MM, dtd 1828,7,24 (H)

1828, 8, 20. Martha dis JH

1839, 8, 21. Laura dis JH

1839, 8, 21. Rebecca dis JH

1840, 6, 24. Rebecca Weaver (form Stanton)
dis mou (H)

1845, 9, 24. Caroline dis JH

1846, 6, 24. Joseph dis JH

1851, 8, 20. David gct Beaver Falls MM (H)

1910, 3, 23. Esther Sddney gct Phila. MM, Pa.
(W)

STAR

1910, 2, 23. Eva recrq

STARBUCK

1855, 10, 31. George, s George & Elizabeth,
Belmont Co., O.; m at Salem, Mary P. STRAT-
TON, dt David & Ann PAINTER (W)

----, --, --. Benjamin Franklin, s John & Sarah (Bundy), b 1855,7,21; m Anna M. LLEW-
ELLYN, dt Thomas & Martha (Hollingsworth),
b 1859,1,28 (W)

Ch: Mary T.   b 1898, 1, 11
    Emily   " 1899, 5, 4
    Jesse   " 1902, 4, 2

1904, 8, 25. Albert W., s Benjamin Franklin
& Sarah (Milhouse), b 1882,12,16; m at
Salem, Ethel C. SMITH, dt Geo. K. & Ann
(Doudna), b 1884,3,10 (W)

Ch: Dorothy
    Sarah   b 1905, 6, 2 d 1906, 8,2
    bur Friends Bur. Gr., Salem, O.
    Robert Geo. b 1906, 8, 15
    Lucile R. " 1907, 9, 30 " 1909, 6,23
    bur Friends Bur. Gr., Salem, O.
    Ralph John b 1908, 11, 26
    Lois Cathe-
    rine   " 1911, 5, 19 d 1912, 8,7
    bur Friends Bur. Gr., Salem, O.
    Carlton
    Franklin   b 1915, 8, 17 d 1918, 8,9
    bur Friends Bur. Gr., Salem, O.
    Donald Ed-
    ward   b 1916, 12, 28

1919, 6, 26. Martha m Herbert D. HALL (W)

----, --, --. Jesse, s Benjamin F. & Anna M.
(Llewellyn), b 1902,4,2; m Clara Esther
BEDELL, dt Albert J. & Anna Elizabeth
(Fisher), b 1900,8,22 (W)

Ch: Anna Mae   b 1925, 3, 25
    Ruth Emily " 1927, 3, 2
    Dorothy Jean

b 1930, 7, 14

1856, 3, 19. Mary P. & dt, Deborah Ann Stratton, gct Stillwater MM (W)

1906, 12, 19. Albert W. rocf Short Creek MM,
O., dtd 1906,11,20 (W)

1917, 8, 22. Benjamin F. & w, Anna L., & s,
Jesse, rocf Short Creek MM, O., dtd 1917,
7,24 (W)

1917, 8, 22. Martha, Mary T. & Emily rocf
Short Creek MM, O., dtd 1917,7,24 (W)

1924, 4, 23. Jesse R. gct Springville MM, Ia.
to m Clara Esther Bedell (W)

1926, 4, 21. Clara E. rocf Springville MM,
Ia. (W)

STEARNS

1868, 7, 23. Ann gct Spring Creek MM, Ia.

STEELE

1885, 2, 6. Carl S. & w, Olive M., recrq

1885, 2, 26. Maggie Edward & Ada L. recrq

STEER

1827, 12, 20. Amos, s Joseph & Grace, Jefferson Co., O.; m at Salem, Lavina ROOD, dt
Jonathan & Clarissa, Columbiana Co., O.

----, --, --. Joseph G. m Elmira T. FRENCH,
dt John & Martha H. (Ogden), b 1858,5,15
(W)

Dt: Anna B.   b 1890, 9, 27

1911, 8, 24. Elisha P., s Israel & Rebecca
(Bracken), Belmont Co., O., b 1850,6,2; m
Lydia LIGHTFOOT (form w of Benjamin H.
Lightfoot), dt Karl Daniel & Julia (See-
bohm) KOLL, b 1839,8,26 d 1926,7,29 bur
Winona, O. (W)

1828, 2, 20. Lavina gct Short Creek MM

1840, 6, 24. Isaac Trescott gct Adrian MM,
to m Jane M. Steer

1863, 7, 22. Elizabeth E. (form Barr) dis
mcd (W)

1885, 8, 19. Elmira T. gct Stillwater MM (W)

1912, 7, 24. Elisha B. rocf Short Creek MM,
O., dtd 1912,7,23 (W)

1916, 10, 25. Anna B. rocf Stillwater MM, O.,
dtd 1916,9,20 (W)

1916, 10, 25. Elmira T. rocf Stillwater MM,
O., dtd 1916,9,20 (W)

1929, 6, 17. Elisha B. gct New Garden MM, O.,
to m Hannah C. Fowler (W)

1929, 8, 21. Elisha B. gct New Garden MM, O.
(W)

STEEVES

----, --, --. Elmer T., s Alfred J. & Flora,
b 1885,1,27 d 1914,6,20; m Edith LINTON,
dt Hilles & Belle, b 1884,9,10 (G)

Dt: Isabelle
    E.   b 1912, 6, 8

1911, 3, 22. Edith [Stives] rocf Damascus MM

STEEVES, continued
1912, 2, 21. Elma T. [Steves] recrq
1917, 1, 24. Edith L. Mitchel, dt Isabel
Edith [Steves], relrq

STEVENS
1869, 6, 24. Moses C. rocf WD MM, Phila.,
Pa., dtd 1869,5,19
1871, 11, 8. Moses C. con mcd
1871, 11, 8. Sarah (form Cooper) con mcd
1876, 11, 8. Moses C. Stevens & w, Sarah M.,
& ch, Harry, Charley & Mary E. Cooper &
Martha D. Stevens, gct Damascus MM

STEWART
1826, 2, 19. Emeline [Steward], dt David
Holloway, b (G)
1850, 7, 27. Rachel [Steward], dt Joseph &
Emeline, b (G)

1853, 5, 25. Emeline & dt, Rachel P., rocf
Upper Springfield MM, dtd 1853,4,23
1869, 6, 24. Emeline H. & dt, Rachel P., gct
Damascus MM
1872, 8, 21. Emaline H. dis joining separatists of 1854 (W)
1873, 9, 24. Tamer (form Young) dis mcd (W)
1873, 12, 24. Rachel P. Woolman (form Stewart)
con mcd (W)

STIFFLER
1912, 2, 21. Mary Griffith recrq

STIVER
1890, 4, 29. Blanche Pettit, dt Joseph &
Lydia S., b (G)

STOCK
1862, 12, 25. Elza dis joining separatists
(W) of 1854

STOUT
1835, 10, 21. Samuel gct Upper Springfield
MM, to m Sarah Butler

STRAHL
1813, 6, 30. Mary m Israel Shreeve BRIGGS

1811, 6, 11. Mary rocf Stillwater MM, dtd
1811,3,26

STRATTON
----, --, --. Michael b 1766,1,6 d 1858,1,27;
m Rhoda ----- b 1768,4,8 d 1842,1,6 (W)
Ch: Josiah   b 1789, 2, 21 d 1846,10,15
    Charles   " 1790, 6, 5 " 1852,11,10
    Joseph   " 1792, 4, 15 " 1843, 2,10
    Joshua   " 1796, 6, 1 " 1826, 8,23
    Daniel   " 1797, 12, 8 " 1872, 2, 6
    Elizabeth " 1800, 1, .10 " 1866, 6, 7
    Aaron   " 1801, 10, 31 " 1885, 5,27
    Mary   " 1805, 9, 23 " 1876,10,23
    Abigail   " 1807, 2, 17 " 1876,12,18

Ch: Michael   b 1808, 8, 13 d 1843, 2, 1
    George   " 1809, 11, 27 " 1887, 3,27
----, --, --. Aaron, s Joshua & Elizabeth, b
1764,9,16 d 1820,3,2 bur Salem; m Jerusha
SMITH, dt Evi & Mary, b 1759,9,18 d 1821,
1,22 bur Salem (W)
Ch: Evi   b 1796, 6, 1 d 1841,10, 2
    Aaron   " 1799, 1, 2 " 1851, 3,17
----, --, --. David b 1782,6,6; m Mary -----
b 1787,10,19 (W)
Ch: Isaac   b 1807, 12, 12 d 1825, 6,27
    Mary Jr. " 1809, 3, 5
    John   " 1811, 4, 10 " 1822, 8, 5
    Hope   " 1813, 9, 30
    Elias   " 1816, 2, 10 " 1816, 5,20
    Lydia   " 1817, 11, 22
    Wm.   " 1820, 2, 14
----, --, --. Charles b 1790,6,5 d 1852,11,10
bur Salem; m Hannah ----- b 1789,8,11 d
1835,8,2 bur Salem (W)
Ch: Anna M.   b 1812, 7, 12 d 1817, 6, 6
      bur Salem
    Rhoda   " 1815, 8, 9
    James   " 1818, 5, 23
    Michael   " 1818, 5, 23 d 1818, 6, 8
      bur Salem
    Martha   " 1821, 12, 1
    John Mickle" 1827, 7, 2
1812, 9, 30. Joseph, s Michael & Rhoda, Columbiana Co., O.; m at Salem, Deborah
SCHOOLEY, dt Elisha & Rachel, Columbiana
Co., O.
----, --, --. Josiah b 1789,2,21; m Deborah
----- b 1787,8,29 (W)
Ch: Ross   b 1813, 9, 12
    Elisha   " 1814, 12, 15
    Ellen   " 1817, 1, 30
    Ann   " 1819, 2, 8
    Sarah B. " 1822, 3, 22
    Lydia   " 1826, 1, 3
    Charles Jr." 1828, 1, 29
1814, 5, 25. Joseph, s Michael & Rhoda, Columbiana Co., O., b 1792,4,15 d 1843,2,5;
m at Salem, Sarah TEST, dt Zacheus & Re-
becca, Columbiana Co., O., b 1793,3,26
(W)
Ch: Rebecca   b 1816, 3, 29
    Anna M.   " 1817, 9, 1
    Abi   " 1819, 10, 4
    Mark   " 1821, 10, 20
    Zaccheus " 1824, 5, 10
    Joseph Jr. " 1825, 12, 9
    Rhoda Jr. " 1827, 3, 7 d 1830,11, 5
    Michael T. " 1829, 1, 30
    Sarah   " 1830, 6, 13
    Isaac   " 1832, 7, 17
    Josiah   " 1833, 12, 22
----, --, --. Rhoda b 1815,8,9 d 1886,3,13 (W)
----, --, --. Joshua b 1796,6,1 d 1826,8,23
bur Salem; m Rachel ----- b 1792,8,28 d
1826,12,27 (W)
Ch: Sina   b 1820, 5, 27 d 1896, 3,20
    Edward   " 1822, 5, 20

STRATTON, Joshua & Rachel, continued
    Ch: Francis   b 1825, 4, 6 d 1842, 6,25
        Joshua Jr. " 1826, 12, 3 " 1842, 6,25
1821, 8, 21. Aaron, Jr., s Aaron & Jerusha,
    Columbiana Co., O., b 1799,1,2 d 1851,3,17;
    m at Salem, Hannah TOWNSEND, dt Joseph &
    Sina, Columbiana Co., O., b 1800,2,8 d 1877,
    12,16 (W)
    Ch: Lewis
        W. T.   b 1822, 7, 20 d 1827, 6, 7
        bur Salem
        Joel   " 1824, 1, 5
        Emily   " 1825, 11, 26 d 1902, 4, 1
        Edwin   " 1827, 10, 1 " 1831, 3,12
        Rachel   " 1829, 5, 31 " 1862, 6,24
        Martha   " 1831, 5, 12 " 1860,12, 9
        Rebecca   " 1833, 4, 21
        Lydia   " 1835, 3, 16 " 1860, 8,11
        Jerusha   " 1837, 9, 11
        Sina   " 1840, 6, 13 " 1901, 2,10
        Louisa   " 1842, 4, 5
        Joseph W. " 1845, 5, 10
----, --, --. Daniel, s Michael & Rhoda, b
    1797,12,8 d 1858,1,11; m Abigail BORTON,
    dt John & Hannah, b 1789,9,10 d 1858,1,11
    (W)
    Ch: Michael   b 1824, 3, 7
        Benj.
        Davis   " 1825, 6, 5
        John   " 1827, 1, 9 d 1842, 6,25
        Barclay   " 1829, 12, 23
        Esther   " 1833, 5, 19
1827, 1, 31. Mary m Overton STANLEY
----, --, --. Aaron b 1801,10,31 d 1885,5,29;
    m Unity CREW b 1807,9,7 d 1881,--,-- (W)
    Ch: Simeon   b 1828, 10, 3
        Rachel C.   " 1830, 6, 27 d 1909, 3,18
        bur Hope Cem., Salem, O.
        Eliza   b 1834, 1, 19 d 1917, 5, 2
        bur Hope Cem., Salem, O.
        Lewis   b 1836, 11, 21
        Evi   " 1841, 11, 3 d 1862,10, 9
        Francis   " 1844, 2, 14
1834, 5, 17. George, s Michael & Rhoda, Co-
    lumbiana Co., O.; m at Salem,
    Susannah EVINS, dt Jonathan & Elizabeth,
    Columbiana Co., O.
1836, 11, 30. Rebecca D. m Edwin HOLLOWAY
1837, 3, 29. Ross, s Jonah & Deborah, Colum-
    biana Co., O., b 1813,9,12 d 1848,7,31; m
    at Salem, Mary PAINTER, dt David & Ann,
    Columbiana Co., O., b 1814,11,26 (W)
    Ch: Deborah
        Ann   b 1840, 8, 11
        John E.   " 1844, 3, 18
        Wm. M.   " 1844, 3, 18 d 1844, 8,28
1839, 11, 27. Elisha, s Joseph & Deborah, Co-
    lumbiana Co., O., b 1825,12,15; m at Sa-
    lem, Elizabeth PAINTER, dt David & Ann,
    Columbiana Co., O., b 1817,6,16 (W)
    Ch: David P.   b 1840, 8, 22
        Martha E.   " 1842, 12, 6 d 1843, 2,18
        Wm.   " 1848, 11, 8

1840, 5, 27. Mary m Jacob BARBER
1840, 12, 2. Elizabeth m Barton DEAN
1842, 10, 26. Martha m Wm. DANIEL
1843, 3, 29. James, s Charles & Hannah, Co-
    lumbiana Co., O., b 1818,5,23 d 1901,1,4;
    m at Salem, Louisa DAVEES, dt Wm. & Anna,
    Columbiana Co., O., b 1823,10,4 d 1909,8,
    2 (W)
    Ch: Hannah   b 1844, 4, 18
        Martha   " 1846, 10, 22
        Wm. D.   " 1850, 5, 13
        Charles   " 1867, 9, 20
----, --, --. Edward, s John & Rachel (Town-
    send), b 1822,5,20 d 1911,2,5 bur Friends
    Bur. Gr., Salem, O. (an elder); m Mary
    ----- b 1815,1,1 (W)
    Ch: Semyra   b 1844, 5, 5
        Joshua   " 1847, 3, 2
    Edward m 2nd Mary H. RALEY, dt Asa & Asen-
    ath (Hirst), b 1834,9,15 d 1916,9,14 bur
    Friends Bur. Gr., Salem, O. (W)
    Ch: Alfred H.   b 1872, 12, 23
        Joseph H.   " 1874, 5, 2
        Edward F.   " 1876, 8, 4
        William W. " 1863, 11, 10 (adopted)
1845, 7, 30. Abigail m Jonathan ROOD
1848, 5, 31. Benjamin D., s Daniel & Abigail,
    Columbiana Co., O.; m at Salem, Ellen
    STANLEY, dt Andrew & Ruth, Columbiana Co.,
    O.
----, --, --. Michael, Jr., s Daniel, b 1824,
    3,7 d 1847,5,10; m Martha ----- b 1822,12,
    21 (W)
1853, 5, 4. John Mickle, s Charles & Han-
    nah, Columbiana Co., O., b 1827,7,2 d
    1907,4,15; m at Salem, Rachel W. BONSALL,
    dt Edward & Rachel (Warrington) b 1825,
    3,12 d 1913,7,14 bur Hope Cemetery, Salem,
    O. (W)
    Ch: Anna M.   b 1854, 4, 1 d 1860, 8, 3
        Martha D.   " 1861, 11, 13
        Ella B.   " 1864, 9, 2 " 1867, 8,20
----, --, --. Barclay b 1829,12,23; m Hannah
    H. ----- b 1827,12,1 (W)
    Ch: Joseph C.   b 1855, 10, 5
        Elizabeth B.
            b 1857, 3, 22
1855, 10, 31. Mary P. m George STARBUCK (W)
1857, 7, 1. Sina m Wilson HALL (W)
1884, 1, 10. Susannah d ae 70y (a minister)
1889, 6, 25. Martha D. m James H. JESSUP (W)
1889, 8, 22. Charles, s Benj. D. & Ellen,
    Belmont Co., O.; m at Salem, Mary FRENCH,
    dt David & Eliza M., Columbiana Co., O.(W)
----, --, --. Joseph R. b 1874,5,2; m Anna M.
    BUNDY, dt Edmund & Deborah M. (Jones); b
    1873,9,22 (W)
    Ch: Frances   b 1898, 8, 4 d 1898, 8,12
        Mary
        Eleanor   " 1900, 6, 27
        Paul E.   " 1901, 8, 13
        Deborah A. " 1905, 5, 6
        J. Russell " 1905, 5, 6

STRATTON, continued

----, --, --. Edward F., s Edward & Mary H.
(Raley), b 1876,8,4; m Clara FRAME, dt
Amasa & Rachel E. (Plummer), b 1875,1,13
(W)
        Ch: Frances
             Rachel   b 1903, 11, 15
             Alice Syl-
             vania   " 1908, 1, 15
1914, 8, 26. Dillwyn, s Barclay & Hannah H.,
Columbiana Co., O.; m at Salem, Ella Lil-
lian COOKE, dt Archibald G. & Bessie
(Brainard), b 1875,3,3 (W)
1922, 8, 20. Eleanor m Walter Arthur DEW (W)

1806, 7, 15. Aron [Straton] & w, Jerusha, &
ch, Evi & Aron, rocf Egg Harbor MM, N.J.,
dtd 1806,5,5
1807, 6, 11. Josiah rocf Haddonfield MM, New
Jersey, dtd 1806,12,8
1810, 6, 12. Michael & w, Rhoda, & ch, Charles, Joseph, Joshua, Daniel, Aaron, Michael, George, Elisabeth, Mary & Abigail,
rocf Haddonfield MM, N. J., dtd 1810,3,12
1812, 3, 17. Hannah rocf Haddonfield MM,
N. J., dtd 1812,1,13
1816, 10, 15. David & w, Mary, & ch, Isaac,
Mary, John & Hope, rocf Middleton MM, dtd
1816,7,15
1817, 7, 13. Daniel, minor, rocf Middleton
MM, dtd 1817,6,14
1819, 1, 17. Joshua gct Middleton MM, to m
1819, 5, 19. Rachel rocf Middleton MM, dtd
1819,4,19
1821, 7, 25. Daniel gct White Water MM, Ind.
1823, 3, 19. Daniel gct Evesham MM, N. J.
1823, 9, 24. Daniel & w, Abigail, rocf Upper
Evesham MM, N. J., dtd 1823,8,9
1827, 6, 20. Evi gct Middleton MM
1828, 8, 20. Unity rocf Upper Springfield
MM, dtd 1828,7,26
1829, 1, 21. Hannah F. rst by rq
1830, 10, 20. Sina, minor, gct Flushing MM
1832, 5, 23. Hope Burns (form Stratton) dis
mcd
1834, 5, 21. Aaron & w, Hannah, & ch, Joel,
Emly, Rachel, Martha & Rebecca, gct Upper
Springfield MM
1835, 6, 24. George & w, Susannah, gct Upper
Springfield MM
1836, 11, 23. Lydia Burns (form Stratton) dis
mcd
1837, 6, 21. Evi [Strattan] rocf Upper
Springfield MM, dtd 1837,5,27
1838, 11, 5. Sina rocf Flushing MM, dtd 1838,
4,26
1839, 3, 20. Joseph & w, Sarah, & ch, Mark,
Zacheus, Joseph, Michael T., Sarah, Isaac
& Josiah, gct New Garden MM
1839, 3, 20. Josiah & w, Deborah, & ch, Sarah, Lydia & Charles, gct New Garden MM
1839, 3, 20. Ellen & Ann gct New Garden MM
1839, 4, 24. Anna M. & Abi gct New Garden MM

1839, 6, 19. Elisha gct Sandy Spring MM
1839, 8, 21. Ross & w, Mary, gct Sandy Spring
MM
1840, 2, 19. Elizabeth gct Sandy Spring MM
1842, 12, 21. William dis mcd
1843, 4, 19. David dis disunity
1843, 7, 19. Edward gct Sandy Spring MM, to m
Mary James
1843, 8, 23. Ross & w, Mary P., & dt, Deborah
Ann, rocf Sandy Spring MM, dtd 1843,6,23
1843, 9, 20. Mary rocf Sandy Spring MM, dtd
1843,8,25
1843, 12, 20. Mary dis disunity
1846, 11, 25. Michael, Jr. gct Flushing MM, to
m Martha Williams
1847, 4, 21. Martha W. rocf Flushing MM, dtd
1847,2,25
1848, 7, 19. Martha W. gct Short Creek MM
1850, 7, 24. Elisha & w, Elizabeth, & ch, David P. & William, rocf Sandy Spring MM,
dtd 1850,5,24
1851, 5, 21. Elisha & w, Elizabeth, & ch, David P., William M. & Mary Ann, gct Salem
MM, Ia.
1853, 4, 20. Barkly gct Flushing MM, to m
Hannah Hobson
1853, 9, 21. Hannah H. rocf Flushing MM, dtd
1853,8,25
1854, 6, 21. Simon dis mou (W)
1857, 6, 24. Benjamin D. & w, Ellen, & ch,
Ruthanna, Abagail, John, Charles & Abraham, gct New Garden MM (W)
1859, 3, 23. Edward & w, Mary, & ch, Semira
& Joshua, gct Middleton MM (W)
1859, 6, 22. Barclay & w, Hannah H., & ch,
Joseph C. & Elizabeth B., gct New Garden
MM (W)
1861, 1, 24. Joel rocf Upper Springfield MM,
dtd 1860,11,24
1862, 3, 20. Barclay & w, Hannah, & ch, Joseph, Elizabeth & Dilwyn, gct New Garden
MM, O.
1862, 3, 20. Benjamin D. & w, Ellen, & ch,
Ruth-Ann, Abigail, John, Charles & Abram,
gct New Garden MM, O.
1862, 6, 25. Daniel gct New Garden MM (W)
1862, 6, 25. Esther gct New Garden MM (W)
1862, 12, 25. Aaron, Unity, Rachel, Lewis,
Eliza & Frances dis joining separatists
of 1854 (W)
1862, 12, 25. Ed, Mary, Samira & Joshua dis
joining separatists (W) of 1854
1862, 12, 25. James, Louisa, Hannah M., Martha D. & William D. dis joining separatists (W) of 1854
1862, 12, 25. John M., Rachel W., Martha &
Esther dis joining separatists (W) of 1854
1863, 3, 25. Lewis dis mcd (W)
1863, 5, 20. John E., minor, gct Stillwater
MM (W)
1866, 2, 21. Francis dis disunity (W)
1866, 6, 26. Hannah Lannin (form Stratton)
con mcd (W)

STRATTON, continued

1868, 7, 22. Martha D. Bonsall (form Stratton) dis mcd (W)

1874, 2, 11. Mary Jane rocf Damascus MM, dtd 1874,1,24

1874, 2, 25. Edward & w, Mary H., & s, Alfred, & William W. Stratton, a minor under their care, rocf Middleton MM, dtd 1874,1,17 (W)

1874, 5, 6. Charles H. rocf East Goshen MM, dtd 1874,4,18

1874, 12, 24. Joseph H. & w, Esther, & dt, Margaret, rocf East Goshen MM, dtd 1874,12,19

1877, 1, 24. William D. dis (W)

1877, 11, 22. Joseph & w, Esther T., & dt, Margaret, gct East Goshen MM

1882, 3, 23. Joseph H. & w, Esther T., & dt, Margaret L., rocf East Goshen MM

1882, 3, 23. Franklin & w, Philena, & ch, Oliver B. & Willis T., rocf East Goshen MM

1882, 8, 9. George & w, Susannah, rocf East Goshen MM, dtd 1882,7,15

1884, 3, 20. Amelia Falicia, dt Jonathan, gct Alum Creek MM

1884, 5, 25. Joseph H. & w, & dt, Maggie, gct East Goshen MM, O.

1885, 2, 6. Ella recrq

1886, 9, 22. William W. dis mcd (W)

1890, 4, 23. Mary F. gct Flushing MM, O. (W)

1890, 6, 26. Ella dropped from mbrp

1892, 10, 19. Charles dis mcd (W)

1897, 8, 25. Joseph R. gct Short Creek MM, to m Anna M. Bundy (W)

1898, 4, 20. Anna M. B. rocf Short Creek MM, dtd 1898,3,22 (W)

1900, 8, 22. New Garden MM was given permission to rst Charles W. in mbrp (W)

1902, 7, 23. Edward F. gct Stillwater MM, to m Clara E. Frame (W)

1903, 2, 25. Clara E. rocf Stillwater MM, O., dtd 1902,12,24 (W)

1913, 2, 19. Frank [Stratten] dropped from mbrp

1914, 5, 10. Oliver B. gct Friends Church, Kansas City, Mo.

1914, 12, 23. Ella Lilian (form Cooke) gct New Garden MM, O. (W)

1926, 1, 20. Alfred H. dis mcd & jas (W)

1932, 12, 25. Emma Julia recrq

1933, 1, 1. Herman, Doris, Dolores Jean & Robert Lee recrq

STRAUGHN

----, --, --. Mary [Strawn] b 1808,7,8 d 1885, 3,20 (W)

1810, 5, 23. Margaret [Straughen] m Isaac TEST

----, --, --. John [Straughan] b 1776,12,12 d 1858,3,11; m Martha L. ----- b 1791,2,10 (W)

----, --, --. Hannah [Strawn], dt Townsend & Ann Lambourn, b 1822,10,31 d 1915,12,24 (G)

1846, 10, 14. Lydia Jane [Strawn] b (W)

1808, 6, 14. Rebecca [Straughan] (form Barber) dis mcd

1810, 1, 16. Margaret [Straughan] recrq

1812, 6, 16. Jacob [Strawn] gct Richland MM, Pa.

1817, 7, 13. John [Strawn] recrq

1836, 3, 23. John gct Short Creek MM, to m Martha L. Nixon

1837, 10, 25. Martha L. [Straughan] rocf Short Creek MM, dtd 1837,7,18

1862, 12, 25. Martha dis joining separatists (W) of 1854

1867, 1, 23. Martha dis disunity (W)

1870, 5, 25. Mary R. [Strawn] rst by rq (W)

1873, 12, 24. Lydia J. [Strawn] (form Thomas) con mcd (W)

1880, 12, 22. Lydia J. dis jas (W)

1885, 2, 6. Hannah M. [Strawn] recrq

STREET

----, --, --. Zadock b 1751,10,28 d 1807,10, 28 bur Salem; m Eunice ----- b 1751,9,13 d 1828,8,25 (W)
    Ch: Wm.   b 1775, 11, 10 d 1788, 3, 3 bur Salem, N. J.
        Aaron   b 1778, 5, 4
        John   " 1782, 3, 14
        Ann   " 1784, 8, 17
        Lydia   " 1789, 1, 1 d 1805,11,24 bur in Pa. on road from Phila.

----, --, --. Aaron b 1778,5,4; m Mary ----- (W)
    Ch: Samuel
        Scotton   b 1800, 4, 18
        Isaac   " 1803, 1, 6
        John   " 1804, 11, 9
        Lydia   " 1806, 9, 2
        Eunice   " 1809, 1, 20

1807, 2, 25. Anna m Robert FRENCH

----, --, --. John b 1782,3,14; m Ann ----- b 1783,11,22 d 1861,8,31 bur Salem (W)
    Ch: Zadock   b 1809, 10, 12
        Samuel   " 1814, 4, 16
        John Jr.   " 1820, 3, 6

1823, 12, 31. Isaac, s Aaron & Mary, Columbiana Co., O.; m at Goshen, Rebecca MORRIS, dt Joseph & Rebecca, Columbiana Co., O.

1830, 5, 26. Lydia m John ELLYSON

----, --, --. Zadok, s John & Ann, b 1809,10, 12; m Sibyl TATUM, dt Beulah, b 1810,3,28 (W)
    Ch: Lewis   b 1833, 4, 2
        George   " 1834, 12, 22
        John W.   " 1837, 2, 24
        David   " 1838, 2, 24
        Ann Jr.   " 1840, 8, 7
        Samuel Jr. " 1842, 5, 30
        Joseph J. " 1844, 12, 12
        Zadok Jr. " 1848, 2, 20
        Charles   " 1850, 6, 8 d 1852, 8, 7
        Sibyl T.   " 1852, 7, 19

----, --, --. Samuel b 1814,4,18 d 1884,8,18; m Sarah ----- b 1809,6,20 d 1883,3,20 (an

STREET, Samuel & Sarah, continued
     (an elder) (W)
     Ch: Mary Ann b 1836, 9, 25 d 1840, 2, 3
         Ogden   " 1838, 10, 18
         Lydia B. " 1843, 8, 31 " 1844, 9, 6
         Hannah   " 1844, 2, 26 " 1883, 7, 3
         Webster   " 1846, 6, 8
         Sarah Jr. " 1849, 9, 30 " 1851, 9,23
         Samuel W. " 1854, 2, 13 " 1881, 9,22
1844, 1, 31. John, s John & Ann, Columbiana
     Co., O., b 1820,3,6 d 1887,1,11; m at Sa-
     lem, Martha COOK, dt Stacey & Martha, Co-
     lumbiana Co., O., b 1822,11,30 d 1895,8,29
     (W)
     Ch: Wm. J.   b 1848, 1, 2
1858, 5, 27. George, s Zadok & Sibyl, Colum-
     biana Co., O., b 1834,12,22; m at Salem,
     Esther HORNER, dt Thomas F. & Mary Ann,
     b 1832,8,28 (G)
1859, 9, 29. David, s Zadok & Sibyl, Columbi-
     ana Co., O., b 1838,2,23; m at Salem, Eu-
     nice FAWCETT, dt David & Hannah, b 1837,
     5,9 (G)
     Ch: Alfred
         Earnest   b 1860, 11, 11
         Clement F. " 1862, 7, 13
1859, 2, 25. Louis, s Zadok & Sibyl, Marion
     Co., Ind.; m at Salem, Sarah L. FAWCETT,
     dt David & Hannah, Columbiana Co., O.
1865, 5, 25. Hannah m Wm. D. SMITH (W)
1880, 8, --. Zadok d (G)

1806, 3, 11. Zadok & w, Unice, & dt, Lydia,
     rocf Salem MM, West Jersey, dtd 1805,10,
     28, endorsed by Redstone MM, 1811,1,31
1806, 3, 11. Anna rocf Salem MM, N. J., dtd
     1805,10,28, endorsed by Redstone MM, 1806,
     1,31
1806, 7, 15. John & w, Ann, rocf Salem MM,
     West Jersey, dtd 1805,12,30, endorsed by
     Redstone MM, 1806,5,30
1808, 10, 11. Mary & ch, Samuel, Isaac, John
     & Lydia, rocf Miami MM, dtd 1808,7,14
1815, 9, 12. Mary & dt, Eunice, gct Miami MM
1822, 5, 22. Samuel S. gct Miami MM
1827, 1, 24. John gct White Water MM, Ind.
1828, 2, 20. Lavina gct Short Creek MM
1828, 6, 25. Lydia gct Upper Springfield MM
1828, 12, 24. Isaac & w, Rebecca, & ch, Mary-
     ann, Rachel & Belinda, rocf Concord MM,
     dtd 1828,10,22 (H)
1830, 3, 24. Lydia rocf Upper Springfield
     MM, dtd 1830,2,27
1831, 12, 21. Zadok gct Upper Springfield MM,
     to m Sibyl Tatum
1832, 7, 25. Sibyl rocf Upper Springfield MM,
     dtd 1832,6,23
1833, 4, 24. Sarah (form Mather) dis mcd (H)
1833, 5, 22. Isaac & Sarah (Mather) con mcd
1836, 2, 24. Sarah rocf Upper Springfield
     MM, dtd 1836,1,23
1842, 10, 19. John dis
1855, 9, 20. Lewis gct Cincinnati MM

1856, 1, 24. Cert granted to Lewis 1855,9mo,
     returned with endorsement by Cincinnati
     MM, O.
1857, 9, 24. Lewis gct New York MM
1857, 12, 24. Cert granted for Lewis to New
     York MM, returned with information he had
     returned within limits of this mtg
1858, 5, 20. Lewis gct Fairfield MM, Ind.
1859, 1, 20. John W. dis mcd
1859, 3, 23. John W. dis mcd (W)
1859, 8, 25. Sarah T. gct Bridgeport MM
1861, 12, 25. Ogden dis disunity (W)
1862, 6, 25. Ogden dis joining in military
     operations of the country
1862, 12, 25. John, Martha & William J. dis
     joining separatists (W) of 1854
1862, 12, 25. Samuel, Sarah, Hannah, Webster
     & Samuel J. dis joining separatists (W)
     of 1854
1862, 12, 25. Zadok dis disunity
1863, 7, 23. Samuel T. dis mcd
1863, 11, 26. Zadok rst in mbrp (decision re-
     versed by QM)
1864, 3, 23. Zadok dis joining separatists
     of 1854 (W)
1864, 4, 20. Sibyl dis joining separatists
     of 1854 (W)
1864, 5, 25. Samuel S. dis mcd (W)
1864, 8, 24. George dis joining separatists
     of 1854 (W)
1864, 12, 21. David & Eunice F. dis joining
     separatists of 1854 (W)
1865, 6, 21. Esther dis joining separatists
     of 1854 (W)
1866, 3, 21. Sarah T. (form Fawcett) dis
     joining separatists of 1854 (W)
1866, 4, 25. Lewis dis joining separatists
     of 1854 (W)
1868, 2, 19. Ann dis jas (W)
1868, 7, 22. Joseph dis serving as a volun-
     teer in the army (W)
1868, 7, 23. Ann relrq
1870, 6, 23. Zadok relrq
1870, 8, 24. Webster dis mcd (W)
1871, 4, 19. Zadok, Jr. dis mcd (W)
1871, 12, 21. David & w, Eunice F., relrq
1872, 6, 19. William J. dis mcd (W)
1876, 6, 22. Ann recrq
1887, 9, 22. Louis & w, Sarah T., rocf
     Indianapolis MM, Ind., dtd 1887,8,17

STRETCH
----, --, --. Abner B. b 1807,4,3 d 1843,1,
     12; m Ann ----- b 1803,9,28 (H)
     Ch: Samuel   b 1831, 2, 23 d 1831, 8,19
         Charles   " 1832, 5, 5
         James L. " 1835, 2, 2
         Rebecca G. " 1837, 7, 30
         Anna   " 1839, 11, 25

1835, 12, 23. Abner & w, Ann, & ch, Charles &
     James L., rocf Salem MM, N. J., dtd 1835,
     9,30 (H)

STRETCH, continued
1846, 5, 20. Ann Dole (form Strech) dis mou
    (H)

STRONG
1813, 10, 13. Gulielma (form Hutton) dis mcd

STULLER
----, --, --. Henry, s James & Catherine, b
    1856,5,18 d 1912,10,2; m Jane SUGGET, dt
    Thomas & Mary Ann, b 1863,8,23 (G)

1913, 1, 31. Harry & w, Elizabeth, recrq
1913, 2, 19. Mrs. Henry dropped from mbrp

SUMNER
1862, 12, 25. Charles, Sarah Emma & Mary Eliza-
    beth dis joining separatists (W) of 1854

SWARTZ
1916, 2, 23. Vera White relrq

TABER
----, --, --. Moses b 1798,12,25; m Phebe P.
    ----- b 1803,4,7 (G)
    Ch: Charles R. b 1827, 11, 18
        Joel Oscar " 1829, 7, 6
        Lucy Ann   " 1831, 6, 17
        Mary P.   " 1841, 11, 18
        Franklin M. " 1843, 11, 6
1861, 5, 17. Phebe P. d (G)
1884, 7, --. Moses d

1858, 1, 21. Moses & w, Phebe P., & ch, Mary
    P. & Moses Franklin, rocf Vasselborough
    MM, Maine, dtd 1857,12,16
1858, 3, 25. Lucy Ann rocf Vasselborough MM,
    Maine, dtd 1857,12,16
1858, 3, 25. J. Oscar rocf Vasselborough MM,
    Maine, dtd 1858,1,20
1858, 3, 25. Charles R. rocf Vasselborough
    MM, Maine, dtd 1858,1,20
1859, 1, 20. Charles R. con mcd
1864, 6, 23. Lucy Ann Campbell (form Taber)
    con mcd
1866, 4, 26. J. Oscar dis disunity
1866, 4, 26. Charles R. dis disunity

TATUM
1823, 12, 7. David [Tatam] b (W)
1843, 8, 30. Beulah m Isaac H. SATTERTHWAIT

1831, 12, 21. Zadok Street gct Upper Spring-
    field MM, to m Sibyl Tatum
1843, 7, 19. Beulah rocf Woodbury MM, N. J.,
    dtd 1843,6,30
1845, 6, 25. David rocf Upper Springfield
    MM, dtd 1845,5,24
1849, 1, 27. David gct Salem MM, Ia.
1869, 2, 25. David & w, Hannah B., & s, Law-
    rence W., rocf Uxbridge MM, Mass., dtd
    1869,1,29
1875, 7, 21. Martha M. (form Fawcett) dis

mcd & jas (W)
1881, 2, 9. Jane recrq
1881, 5, 11. Harry recrq

TAYLOR
----, --, --. Isaac b 1790,7,31; m Hannah
    ----- b 1794,11,13 (W)
    Ch: David   b 1814, 5, 11
        Joshua " 1816, 3, 6
        Milton " 1818, 6, 4
        Jacob   " 1820, 4, 10
        John   " 1822, 2, 24
1815, 4, 18. Sarah M. b (H)
1826, 8, 25. Almoria b (H)
1849, 6, 9. Mattie L. b (H)
1865, 11, 30. Joseph, Stark Co., O.; m Fanny
    TRIP, Columbiana Co., O. at Salem (H)

1820, 6, 21. Isaac & w, Hannah, & ch, David,
    Joshua & Milton, rocf Fallowfield MM, Pa.,
    dtd 1820,1,7
1850, 4, 24. Cert rec for Grace Anna from
    Fallowfield MM, dtd 1850,3,13, endorsed to
    West MM (H)
1862, 12, 25. Amos dis joining separatists
    (W) of 1854
1862, 12, 25. Thomas & Sarah E. dis joining
    separatists (W) of 1854
1862, 12, 25. Joseph, Mary & Oliver dis join-
    ing separatists (W) of 1854
1866, 2, 22. Joseph rocf West MM, dtd 1866,1,
    26 (H)
1876, 10, 26. Fanny gct Green Plain MM (H)
1880, 5, 20. James & w, Tillie, recrq
1882, 5, 25. Martha L. (form Pierson) rocf
    Marietta MM, Ia. (H)
1882, 12, 21. Maggie recrq
1885, 2, 6. Ralph recrq
1886, 10, 21. Ralph dropped from mbrp

TENNIS
1881, 11, 9. Moses & w, Matilda, recrq

TERRELL
----, --, --. Lemuel & Rebecca
    Ch: Kitty
        Pleasant   b 1805, 3, 28
        Nancy
        Thomas   " 1807, 3, 10
        Robert
        Samuel   " 1809, 12, 12
        Nisa Linch " 1811, 10, 18
1878, 9, 19. Matthew d (G)

1806, 11, 11. Lemuel & w, Rebecca, & dt, Kitty
    Pleasant, rocf Cedar Creek MM, dtd 1806,9,
    13
1810, 8, 14. Thomas & w, Martha, & dt, Eliza,
    rocf Cedar Creek MM, Va., dtd 1810,4,14
1810, 8, 14. Lemuel [Terrol] dis disunity
1812, 11, 17. Rebecca, w Lemuel, & ch, Kitty
    Pleasant, Nancy Thomas, Robert Samuel &
    Nicy Lynch, gct Cedar Creek MM, Va.

TERRELL, continued
1871, 5, 10. Matthew & w, Hester G., rocf
    Short Creek MM, dtd 1871,4,20
1871, 5, 10. Lydia Jane rocf Short Creek MM,
    dtd 1871,4,20

TESMER
----, --, --. Emil G., s Gattlieb & Rose, b
    1891,8,1; m Lavern C. CAPEL, dt George, b
    1898,11,12 (G)
    Ch: Cathern L. b 1926, 2, 15
        Lois I.   " 1928, 6, 25
        Melvin Leroy   d 1926, 8,24

1923, 12, 19. La Vern Catharine & Melvin Leroy
    recrq
1924, 1, 23. Emil G. [Tesimer] recrq

TEST
----, --, --. Zaccheus b 1762,9,23 d 1820,2,2,
    bur Salem; m Rebecca ----- b 1758,--,--
    d 1798,4,14 bur Woodbury (W)
    Ch: Benjamin b 1783, 11, 7
        Isaac   " 1789, 6, 8
        Samuel   " 1791, 1, 3
        Sarah   " 1793, 3, 26
        Rebecca   " 1796, 4, 18
    Zaccheus m 2nd Hannah ----- b 1775,4,3
    d 1842,6,8
    Ch: Joseph   b 1801, 8, 28
        Elizabeth " 1805, 8, 17
        Mary   " 1808, 7, 8
        Zaccheus " 1809, 12, 18
        Lydia   " 1812, 4, 18 d 1812, 8,19
         bur Salem
        Edith   " 1815, 7, 19
----, --, --. Benjamin b 1783,11,7; m Mary
    ----- b 1782,4,5 (W)
    Ch: Rebecca   b 1806, 5, 21
        Elisha   " 1807, 8, 15
        Rachel   " 1809, 9, 5
        Hannah   " 1811, 6, 15
        Mary   " 1813, 5, 4
        Elizabeth " 1817, 8, 19
        Deborah   " 1822, 5, 10
        Benjamin " 1825, 5, 7
1810, 5, 23. Isaac, s Zacheus, Columbiana
    Co., O., b 1787,6,8; m at Salem, Margaret
    STRAUGHEN, dt Daniel, Bucks Co., Pa., b
    1791,2,14 (W)
    Ch: Hannah   b 1811, 1, 27
        Daniel   " 1812, 8, 8 d 1864,12,18
        Samuel   " 1815, 2, 9
        Rebecca   " 1817, 8, 20
        Zaccheus
         Jr.   " 1826, 5, 16
        David   " 1826, 5, 16
        Ann L.   " 1829, 7, 3
1814, 5, 25. Sarah m Joseph STRATTON
1815, 8, 13. Samuel, s Zacheus & Rebecca,
    Columbiana Co., O., b 1791,1,3; m at Sa-
    lem, Mary Ann BARBER, dt Isaac & Mary, Co-
    lumbiana Co., O., b 1798,6,29 (W)

    Ch: Elizabeth b 1816, 6, 9
        Ann   " 1818, 3, 25
        John   " 1820, 9, 7
        Jane   " 1823, 1, 12
        Isaac   " 1825, 12, 24
        Benjamin B." 1828, 2, 29
        Samuel   " 1832, 9, 1
        Lusina   " 1835, 3, 9
1825, 4, 27. Elizabeth R. m Wm. F. FAWCETT
1827, 12, 6. Rebecca D. m Benjamin VOTAW
1834, 8, 27. Edith m Richard B. FAWCETT
1837, 11, 8. Samuel, Jr., s Isaac & Marga-
    ret, Columbiana Co., O.; m at Salem, Ann
    J. LAMBORN, dt Townsend & Ann, Chester
    Co., Pa.
1839, 5, 1. Hannah m Clayton LAMBORN
----, --, --. Daniel b 1812,8,8 d 1864,12,18
    bur New Garden; m Ann D. ----- b 1812,12,
    31 (W)
    Ch: Albert B. b 1845, 1, 5
        Mary L.   " 1847, 2, 10
        John S.   " 1848, 6, 6
        Martha   " 1849, 10, 23
        Deborah   " 1856, 2, 17
1850, 6, 26. Zaccheus, Jr., s Isaac B. & Mar-
    garet, Columbiana Co., O., b 1826,5,16; m
    at Salem, Drusilla LANGSTAFF, dt Samuel
    Jr. & Tabitha, Mahoning Co., O., b 1831,
    1,24 (W)
1923, 8, 21. Daniel b (W)

1813, 6, 15. Sarah rocf Woodbury MM, N. J.,
    dtd 1813,4,8
1815, 12, 12. Rebecca rocf Piles Grove MM,
    N. J., dtd 1815,7,27
1816, 1, 16. Benjamin & w, Mary, & ch, Re-
    becca, Elisha, Rachel, Hannah & Mary, gct
    Short Creek MM
1816, 1, 16. Rebecca gct Short Creek MM
1823, 6, 25. Benjamin & w, Mary, & ch, Re-
    becca, Rachel, Hannah, Mary & Elizabeth,
    rocf Stillwater MM, dtd 1823,5,24
1823, 6, 25. Mary Jr. dis jas
1823, 8, 1. Joseph dis jas
1823, 11, 19. Zaccheus, minor, gct New Garden
    MM
1831, 8, 24. Benjamin dis
1833, 7, 24. Mary & ch, Elizabeth, Deborah
    & Benjamin, gct White Water MM, Ind.
1833, 7, 24. Rachel, Hannah & Mary gct White
    Water MM, Ind.
1839, 3, 20. Isaac B. & w, Margaret, & ch,
    Zacheus, David & Ann, gct New Garden MM
1839, 3, 20. Samuel & w, Mary, & ch, John,
    Jane, Isaac, Benjamin, Samuel & Lucina,
    gct New Garden MM
1839, 3, 20. Elizabeth & Ann gct New Garden
    MM
1839, 4, 24. Samuel, Jr. & w, Ann J., gct
    New Garden MM
1839, 4, 24. Rebecca gct New Garden MM
1843, 11, 22. Daniel gct Short Creek MM, to m
    Ann D. Lawrence

TEST, continued
1844, 2, 21. Daniel dis mcd
1845, 3, 19. Ann D. rocf Short Creek MM, dtd
      1844,10,22
1850, 6, 19. Benjamin B. rocf New Garden MM,
      dtd 1850,5,23
1851, 8, 20. Benjamin B. con mcd
1851, 11, 19. Zacheus rocf New Garden MM, dtd
      1851,10,23
1853, 7, 23. Benjamin B. gct New Garden MM
1856, 8, 20. Daniel rst by rq (W)
1857, 5, 20. Albert B., Mary L., John S.,
      Martha & Deborah, ch Daniel & Ann D.,
      recrq (W)
1861, 7, 24. Benjamin rocf New Garden MM, dtd
      1861,6,20 (W)
1862, 12, 25. Zackeus, Drusilla, Benjamin &
      Ann dis joining separatists (W) of 1854
1864, 7, 20. Zaccheus & w, Drusilla, & ch,
      Benjamin A., William Emily & Lemuel, gct
      New Garden MM (W)
1865, 2, 22. Ann D. & ch, Albert B., Mary L.,
      John S., Martha & Deborah, gct New Garden
      MM (W)
1866, 9, 19. Benjamin gct New Garden MM (W)

TETARS
----, --, --. John b 1864,12,12; m Mary -----
      b 1787,2,9 (W)
      Ch: Ann   b 1806, 5, 9
          Margaret   " 1808, 6, 27
          Mary Jr.   " 1811, 8, 5
          Elisha Jr. " 1814, 1, 11
          Jonathan   " 1816, 6, 10
          Rebecca   " 1818, 7, 11 d 1819, 7,26
          Susanna   " 1820, 7, 26
          Job   " 1822, 12, 9
          Martha   " 1825, 3, 26 d 1831, 6,16
          Jesse   " 1827, 9, 23
          Jane   " 1827, 9, 23
          John C.   " 1831, 10, 5
1829, 12, 2. Margaret [Teetars] m Samuel
      SCHOLFIELD (H)

1818, 2, 17. Mary [Teeters] recrq
1818, 12, 23. John [Teeters] & w, Mary, & ch,
      Ann, Margaret, Mary, Elisha, Jonathan &
      Rebecca, recrq
1827, 6, 20. Ann Blackburn (form Teetars) dis
      mcd
1828, 10, 22. John [Teetors] dis jH
1828, 10, 22. Margaret [Teeters] dis jH
1831, 2, 23. Mary [Teeters] Jr. dis disunity
1835, 9, 23. Elisha [Teetors] dis mcd
1838, 1, 24. Jonathan [Teetors] dis disunity
1841, 8, 25. Susannah Lee (form Teetors) dis
      mcd
1843, 2, 22. John [Teetors] rst by rq
1845, 6, 25. Job [Teetors] dis mcd
1845, 7, 23. Martha W. [Teetors] (form Paint-
      er) dis mcd
1846, 7, 22. Jane dis jas
1846, 12, 23. Martha [Teetars] dis jas

1850, 6, 19. John [Teeters] & w, Mary, & s,
      John, gct Marlborough MM

THEKSTINE
1881, 5, 26. Elizabeth recrq

THOMAS
1807, 3, 25. Robert, s Lewis & Susannah, Co-
      lumbiana Co., O.; m at Salem, Lucinda
      SACKETT, dt Samuel & Sarah, Columbiana
      Co., O.
----, --, --. Eli b 1785,12,31; m Elizabeth
      ----- b 1795,11,8 (H)
      Ch: Maria   b 1816, 3, 22
          Isral   " 1817, 9, 5
          Phebe   " 1819, 12, 13
          Sarah Ann " 1822, 2, 15
          Hammond   " 1824, 9, 10
          Hiram A. " 1826, 8, 23
          Joseph
            Franklin " 1829, 8, 19
          Charles C. " 1831, 10, 12 d 1832, 9,22
          Edwin   " 1833, 9, 3
          Rebecca
            Ellin   " 1835, 10, 29
          Mary Ada-
            line   " 1838, 7, 8 d 1839,10, 7
----, --, --. John b 1819,1,21 (H)
----, --, --. Abner b 1790,12,15; m Phebe
      ----- b 1798,6,17 (H)
      Ch: Wm. Mode b 1820, 7, 11
          Eleanor
            Mildred " 1822, 3, 14
          Esther   " 1824, 5, 13
          Isaac   " 1826, 6, 18
          Elmirah
            Jane   " 1828, 10, 24
          Reuben   " 1831, 5, 21
          Phebe Ann " 1833, 6, 23
          Allen
            Alexander
            Mode   " 1835, 10, 25
1824, 2, 13. Eliza b (H)
----, --, --. Jacob b 1790,12,31 d 1873,4,19;
      m Rebecca LEE b 1805,12,14 d 1890,12,9 (W)
      Ch: Mary E.   b 1832, 1, 11
          Catharine
            M.   " 1833, 12, 24 d 1917,11,28
          bur Hope Cem., Salem, O.
          Hannah C. b 1836, 9, 2 " 1912,10,28
          Jesse   " 1840, 8, 15 " 1851, 8, 8
          Priscilla " 1843, 1, 25
          Colvin
            Henry   " 1844, 11, 15
          Lydia Jane " 1846, 10, 14
          Sarah B.   " 1849, 3, 26 d 1911, 8,15
1837, 5, 31. Mary m Jehu FAWCETT
1838, 9, 27. Rebecca Jr. m Milton HEACOCK (H)
1841, 1, 28. Nathan, s John & Rebecca, Colum-
      biana Co., O., b 1813,5,15; m at West MH,
      Asenath HEACOCK, dt Nathan & Dinah, Colum-
      biana Co., O., b 1814,6,26 (H)
----, --, --. Elwood b 1814,5,15; m Buelah

THOMAS, Elwood & Buelah, continued
----- (G)
    Ch: Mary M. b 1841, 3, 1
       Levi S.   " 1843, 12, 13
       Samuel C. " 1846, 12, 12
       Robert P. " 1851, 5, 1
1843, 5, 30. Phebe m Joseph INGRAM (H)
1843, 10, 5. Eliza m Elias HEACOCK (H)

1806, 9, 16. John & w, Hannah, & s, Henry, rocf Short Creek MM, dtd 1806,8,16
1806, 9, 16. Nathaniel & w, Dorcas, & ch, Joseph, John, Abel & William, rocf Short Creek MM, dtd 1806,7,19
1806, 9, 16. Robert rocf Darby Creek MM, Pa., dtd 1806,7,3
1807, 5, 12. Robert & w, Lucinda, gct Concord MM
1808, 8, 16. Thomas French & w, Esther, & their apprentices, Moses Townsend & Patience Thomas, rocf Redstone MM, dtd 1808, 7,1
1815, 3, 14. Patience Carr (form Thomas) con mcd
1820, 4, 19. Temperance gct New Garden MM
1825, 7, 20. Sarah & ch, Kersey G., Joseph Garritson & Isaac Green, rocf Warrington MM, dtd 1824,1,22, endorsed by New Garden MM, 1825,4,21
1827, 2, 21. Sarah & ch, Kersey G., Joseph G., Isaac Green, Rebecca Ann & Eleanor Jane, gct Upper Springfield MM
1828, 7, 30. Abner & w, Phebe, & ch, Elenor, Milard, Esther & Isaac, rocf New Garden MM, dtd 1828,7,24 (H)
1828, 7, 30. Eli & w, Elizabeth, & ch, Mary L., Israel, Phebe, Sarah Ann, Hammond & Hiram A., rocf New Garden MM (H)
1830, 5, 19. Jonathan rocf York MM, Pa., dtd 1829,6,10, endorsed by New Garden MM, 1830, 3,25 (H)
1831, 4, 20. Kersey G., Joseph G., Isaac Green, Rebecca Ann, Eleanor-Jane & Oliver Able, ch John & Sarah, rocf Upper Springfield MM, dtd 1831,2,26
1834, 8, 20. Jacob & w, Rebecca, & ch, Mary E. & Catharine M., rocf Exeter MM, Pa., dtd 1834,6,25
1834, 4, 23. Mary rocf Exeter MM, Pa., dtd 1834,2,26
1837, 11, 15. Jonathan gct Carmel MM, to m Hannah Tompson (H)
1838, 1, 24. Hannah Jr. recrq (H)
1838, 1, 24. Rebecca Jr. recrq (H)
1838, 11, 21. Nathan recrq (H)
1840, 3, 25. Rebecca (form Shaw) con mou (H)
1840, 6, 24. Hannah T. rocf Carmel MM, dtd 1840,6,16 (H)
1840, 6, 24. Kersey G. dis mcd
1842, 3, 23. Eliza recrq (H)
1842, 3, 23. John Jr. recrq (H)
1842, 3, 23. Joseph G. dis disunity

1842, 4, 20. Rebecca S. gct Marlborough MM (H)
1842, 7, 20. John Jr. gct Marlborough MM, to m Mary S. Hoag (H)
1843, 2, 22. Mary S. rocf Marlborough MM, dtd 1842,12,24 (H)
1844, 4, 24. Nuton recrq (H)
1844, 12, 25. John gct Marlborough MM, O. (H)
1846, 3, 25. Isaac G. dis jH
1846, 12, 23. Eliza (form Hawley) con mcd (H)
1847, 3, 24. Rebecca Ann Greiner (form Thomas) dis mcd
1847, 7, 21. Maria L. Boon (form Thomas) con mcd (H)
1848, 6, 21. Jesse rocf Chesterfield MM, dtd 1848,4,15
1848, 6, 21. Eleanor Jane dis disunity
1849, 7, 25. Mercy L. rocf Plainfield MM, dtd 1849,5,17 (H)
1851, 4, 23. Jesse gct Upper Springfield MM, to m Joanna Stanley
1851, 11, 19. Jesse gct Upper Springfield MM
1852, 3, 24. Oliver A. dis disunity
1856, 7, 24. Almira Jane Davenport (form Thomas) dis mcd (H)
1856, 8, 21. Ellen dis (H)
1862, 12, 25. Jacob, Rebecca, Mary, Catharine, Hannah, Calvin, Lydia Jane & Sarah B. dis joining separatists (W) of 1854
1865, 4, 20. Hiram A. gct Wapsononock MM, Ia. (H)
1868, 5, 20. Calvin H. dis serving as a volunteer in the army (W)
1873, 12, 24. Lydia J. Strawn (form Thomas) con mcd (W)
1874, 6, 24. Mary E. Tolerton (form Thomas) con mcd (W)
1881, 11, 9. Elwood relrq
1883, 10, 24. Sarah B. Coates (form Thomas) con mcd (W)
1889, 7, 24. Priscilla dis jas (W)
1912, 2, 21. John recrq

THOMPSON
1829, 8, 26. Martha m Brinton DARLINGTON
----, --, --. Harry L., s Albert & Carrie, b 1899,11,24 (or 1901,11,24); m Ada L. FOX, dt Gus & Tillie, b 1907,7,2 (G)

1816, 6, 11. Mary (form Shinn) dis mcd
1817, 2, 11. Mary rst by rq
1828, 9, 24. Martha rocf Redstone MM, dtd 1828,9,3
1837, 11, 15. Jonathan gct Carmel MM, to m Hannah Tompson (H)
1845, 9, 23. Louiza [Thomson] (form Painter) con mou (H)
1881, 8, 10. Margaret recrq
1825, 3, 25. Harry Lee recrq
1933, 2, 22. Ada L. & Harry L. recrq
1933, 2, 22. Ellen Lee & Billie Howard, ch Mr. & Mrs. Thompson, recrq

THORNBURY
1890, 10, 23. William J. & w, Mary A., & ch,
      Rishie W. & Rhoda D., rocf Freeport MM,
      O., dtd 1890,9,27

THORP
1860, 7, 26. Thomas rocf Deerfield MM, dtd
      1860,6,6 (H)
1860, 7, 26. Maria rocf West MM, dtd 1860,4,
      27 (H)
1860, 7, 26. Thomas, Jr. rocf Deerfield MM
      (H)
1864, 8, 25. Thomas & w, Maria, gct Miami MM,
      O. (H)

TILLEY
1861, 1, 18. Elizabeth, dt Sarah & Thos. Hum-
      phries, b (G)

1930, 10, 20. Mrs. Elizabeth recrq

TIMBERLAKE
1818, 10, 28. John, Jr., s John & Mary, High-
      land Co., O.; m at Salem, Amy RHODES, dt
      Joseph & Martha, Columbiana Co., O.

1818, 12, 23. Amy gct Clear Creek MM

TITUS
1841, 9, 22. Cert rec for Benjamin & w, Mary,
      from Rochester MM, N. Y., dtd 1841,5,28,
      endorsed to Marlborough MM
1841, 10, 20. Israel D. rocf Norwich MM, dtd
      1841,6,9

TODD
1876, 2, 27. Harry S., s John & Josephine, b
      (G)
1905, 8, 1. Mabel Lillian, dt Frank & Ger-
      trude Glenn, b (G)

1932, 12, 29. Harry, Mabel, Robert & Richard
      recrq

TOLERTON
----, --, --. James b 1778,7,19 (1776,7,19 in
      H); m Frances ----- b 1778,4,18 (1776,4,
      20 in H) (W)
      Ch: Alexander b 1806, 6, 26
          Robert   " 1808, 6, 5
          Hill   " 1812, 1, 4
          Ann   " 1814, 4, 3
          Wm.   " 1817, 1, 5 d 1817, 2,15
----, --, --. Robert m Mary E. THOMAS, dt Ja-
      cob & Rebecca (Lee), b 1832,1,11 d 1917,6,
      21 bur Hope Cem., Salem, O. (W)

1812, 3, 17. James rocf Plymouth MM, dtd
      1812,1,18
1813, 7, 13. Alexander, Robert & Hill, ch
      James, recrq
1813, 8, 17. Frances con mou
1828, 7, 30. James & w, Frances, & dt, Ann,

rocf New Garden MM, dtd 1828,7,24 (H)
1828, 8, 20. Frances dis JH
1828, 9, 24. James dis JH
1828, 12, 24. Alexander dis Jas
1832, 8, 22. Ann dis JH
1832, 12, 19. Hill dis JH
1833, 7, 24. Robert [Tollerton] dis disunity
1837, 10, 25. James dis not attending mtg
1865, 8, 23. Esther (form Koll) dis mcd (W)
1874, 6, 24. Mary E. (form Thomas) con mcd
      (W)

TOMLINSON
1823, 12, 29. Comly b (H)

1883, 11, 22. Comly rocf Short Creek MM, dtd
      1883,10,11 (H)

TOOL
----, --, --. Isaac, s David & Marrella, b
      1877,10,13; m Alpha RUGGBY, dt Henry &
      Anna, b 1884,1,28 (G)
      Ch: C. Lamoine b 1904, 11, 29

TOWNSEND
1764, 7, 15. Sina b (W)
1806, 5, 21. Judith m Philip PEDDRICK
----, --, --. James b 1793,12,4; m Martha
      ----- b 1796,8,23 (H)
      Ch: Nathan H. b 1814, 1, 30
          Benjamin G." 1815, 11, 22
          Abel T.   " 1818, 4, 3 (1817,4,3
          in O)
          Mary Ann   " 1820, 8, 2
          Lydia P.   " 1823, 3, 7
          Abner Gil-
            bert   " 1825, 9, 2
          Evi S.   " 1827, 9, 12
1815, 9, 20. Talbot, s Francis & Rachel, Mer-
      cer Co., Pa.; m at Salem, Edith WARE, dt
      Asa & Elizabeth, Columbiana Co., O.
1816, 8, 21. Martha M. m Benjamin STANTON
1818, 2, 25. Lewis, s Joseph & Sina, Columbi-
      ana Co., O., b 1798,2,14; m at Salem, Ra-
      chel DAVIS, dt Samuel & Mary, Columbiana
      Co., O., b 1799,8,17 (W)
      Ch: Mary D. b 1819, 9, 4
          Eliza   " 1824, 4, 4
1821, 8, 21. Hannah m Aaron STRATTON
----, --, --. Jonathan & Ann (H)
      Ch: Moses   b 1823, 3, 11
          Smith   " 1824, 9, 14
          Wm.   " 1825, 11, 5
          Dillon   " 1827, 3, 20
          Martha   " 1828, 9, 5
          Joseph   " 1830, 7, 2
          Sarah   " 1832, 12, 1
          Samuel   " 1836, 4, 4
          Edith   " 1837, 12, 20
----, --, --. Francis b 1804,9,1; m Ann -----
      b 1808,12,10 (W)
      Ch: Emmor   b 1827, 11, 5
          Lewis   " 1829, 8, 30

TOWNSEND, continued

----, --, --. Aaron b 1794,2,14 d 1836,10,19; m Jemima ----- b 1806,3,25 (H)

 Ch: Comley b 1828, 3, 25
   James B. " 1829, 9, 20
   Charles " 1831, 2, 24
   Joseph " 1834, 4, 4
   Hannah " 1836, 1, 30

1862, 2, 19. Rachel d (G)

1876, 2, 27. Mary, dt Joseph & Mary, b (G)

1805, 12, 17. Judith & ch, Josiah, Caturah & Jesse, rocf Greenwich MM, West Jersey, dtd 1805,5,1, endorsed by Concord MM, 1805, 11,19

1807, 6, 11. Edith rocf Short Creek MM, dtd 1806,11,15

1808, 8, 16. Thomas French & w, Esther, & their apprentices, Moses Townsend & Patience Thomas, rocf Redstone MM, dtd 1808, 7,1

1809, 4, 11. Moses gct Redstone MM

1811, 10, 15. Josiah, minor, gct Byberry MM, Pa.

1811, 12, 17. Philip Pedrick & w, Judith, & ch, Keturah & Jesse Townsend (ch of Judith) Catharine & Elizabeth Pedrick, gct Miami MM

1813, 2, 18. Martha rocf Westland MM, dtd 1812,7,25

1814, 8, 16. Lewis rocf Hopewell MM, dtd 1814,5,5

1815, 12, 12. James recrq

1815, 12, 12. Edith gct Middleton MM

1816, 9, 17. Martha rst in mbrp (form dis by Redstone MM)

1816, 11, 12. Nathan & Benjamin Gilbert, ch James, recrq

1817, 7, 15. Sinah rocf Middleton MM, dtd 1817,7,14

1821, 6, 20. Hannah rocf Middleton MM, dtd 1821,6,18

1827, 4, 25. Ann rocf Upper Springfield MM, dtd 1827,3,24

1828, 1, 23. Hannah rocf Redstone MM, dtd 1827,10,31

1828, 7, 23. James dis jH

1828, 7, 23. Hannah dis disunity

1828, 7, 30. James & w, Martha, & ch, Nathan H., Benjamin G., Able F., Lydia P., Mary Ann Gilbert & Evi S., rocf New Garden MM, dtd 1828,7,24 (H)

1828, 8, 20. Francis J. dis jH

1828, 8, 20. Martha dis jH

1828, 11, 19. Sina dis jH

1830, 7, 21. Ann, w Francis, & ch, Emmor & Lewis, gct Carmel MM

1830, 11, 24. Francis I. & ch, Emmor & Lewis, gct Carmel MM (H)

1832, 12, 19. Jonathan & ch, Moses, Smith, William, Dillon, Martha & Joseph, rocf Buckingham MM, Pa., dtd 1832,9,1 (H)

1833, 11, 20. John & w, Rebecca, rocf Bucking-

ham MM, Pa., dtd 1833,9,2 (H)

1835, 1, 21. Aaron & ch, Cumly, James B., Charles & Joseph, recrq (H)

1835, 1, 21. Jemima, w Aaron, recrq (H)

1850, 6, 19. William rocf Upper Springfield MM, dtd 1850,5,25

1851, 6, 25. William dis disunity

1855, 11, 22. Celicia Gantz (form Townsend) con mcd

1860, 10, 25. Lewis & w, Rachel, rocf Upper Springfield MM, dtd 1860,9,22

1862, 1, 23. Tazette Walton (form Townsend) con mcd

1863, 1, 22. Lewis gct Upper Springfield MM, O.

1864, 6, 23. Hannah rocf West MM, dtd 1864, 3,24 (H)

1870, 4, 21. David gct Wapsinonock MM, Ia. (H)

1873, 12, 25. Rebecca W. gct WD MM, Phila., Pa.

1873, 11, 20. Mary B. gct Buckingham MM, Pa. (H)

TRAGO

----, --, --. ----- m Mary ----- b 1787,5,4 (H)

 Ch: John   b 1814, 5, 14

1839, 8, 22. John, Jr., s John & Mary, Columbiana Co., O.; m at West MH, Sarah Ann HARLAN, dt Joseph & Hannah, Columbiana Co., O. (H)

1865, 11, 2. Hannah A. m Hiram PLATT (H)

1872, 5, 1. Sarah E. m Joseph R. MITCHELL (H)

1824, 7, 21. Mary rocf Sadsbury MM, Pa., dtd 1824,3,2

1830, 8, 25. Mary mbrp transferred from Upper Springfield MM by rq (H)

1837, 11, 22. John Jr. recrq

1863, 4, 23. Sarah Ann & dt, Sarah Emily, rocf West MM, dtd 1863,2,27 (H)

1863, 4, 23. Hannah A. rocf West MM, dtd 1863,2,27 (H)

TRASK

1875, 12, 23. Ruth rocf Farmington MM, N. Y., dtd 1875,10,28

1883, 12, 20. John recrq

TRESCOTT

----, --, --. Samuel C. b 1787,4,12; m Sophia ----- b 1790,8,16 d 1845,10,26 (W)

 Ch: Clark b 1809, 11, 16
   Mary " 1812, 3, 5
   Isaac " 1814, 3, 22
   Jane " 1817, 2, 4

----, --, --. Isaac b 1814,3,22; m Jane ----- b 1819,4,13 (W)

 Ch: David b 1841, 4, 6
   Samuel C. " 1842, 12, 9
   Isaac L. " 1844, 12, 5

TRESCOTT, Isaac & Jane, continued
    Ch: Phebe Jane b 1846, 12, 15

1827, 5, 23. Samuel [Ressket] & w, Sophia, &
    ch, Clark, Mary, Isaac & Jane, rocf Nine
    Partners MM, N. Y.
1837, 5, 24. Clark & w, Ann, & ch, Sibyl &
    Sophia, gct Marlborough MM
1838, 4, 25. Mary Harris (form Trescott) dis
    mcd
1840, 6, 24. Isaac gct Adrian MM, to m Jane
    M. Steer
1841, 2, 24. Jane M. rocf Adrian MM, dtd
    1841,1,14
1847, 3, 24. Samuel C. dis mcd
1847, 4, 21. Ruth Anna (form Harris) con mcd
    (H)
1848, 2, 23. Jane M. dis disunity
1849, 3, 21. Syble, Sophia, Benjamin & Sam-
    uel, ch Clark, rocf Marlborough MM, dtd
    1849,1,30
1850, 1, 23. Jane M. dis jH
1850, 5, 22. Isaac dis disunity
1858, 12, 22. Jane L. Rood (form Trescott)
    dis mcd (W)
1859, 7, 21. Jane L. Rood (form Trescott) dis
    mcd
1864, 2, 24. David S. dis mcd (W)
1865, 4, 20. David dis mcd & performing mili-
    tary duty
1867, 8, 22. Phebe relrq
1869, 5, 20. Ella Cooper (form Trescott) dis
    mcd
1870, 3, 20. Phebe Jane Crew (form Trescott)
    dis mcd (W)
1871, 2, 22. Isaac L. dis serving as a volun-
    teer in the army (W)
1878, 4, 24. Sibyl Kennedy (form Trescott)
    dis mcd (W)
1885, 2, 26. Lola G. recrq
1887, 4, 21. Deborah B. recrq
1889, 7, 25. Deborah B. Rice (form Trescott)
    gct East Goshen MM

TRIPP
1865, 11, 30. Fanny m Joseph TAYLOR (H)

1833, 2, 7. William Penn rocf Marlborough MM,
    dtd 1832,12,25
1854, 5, 25. Samuel & w, Fanny, rocf Deer
    Creek MM, dtd 1854,4,22 (H)

TROTTER
1908, 5, 19. Clarence P., s Jesse & Ada, b
    (G)

1918, 11, 20. Mr. & Mrs. Jessie recrq
1924, 1, 23. Clarence Philip recrq

TUCKER
1909, 9, 23. Jesse R., s Jesse & Mary Ann,
    Bristol Co., Mass.; m at Salem, Elizabeth
    BLACKBURN, dt Thomas & Sarah, Columbia

Co., O. (W)

1910, 1, 19. Elizabeth B. gct Dartmouth MM,
    Mass. (W)

TULUS
1862, 12, 25. Jason, Hannah, Lindley M.,
    Richard, Elizabeth, Jane & Martha dis
    joining separatists (W) of 1854

TUTTLE
1865, 6, 22. Asa C. & w, Lydia, & ch, Harry
    Walter & Thomas S., rocf Sandy Spring MM,
    dtd 1865,5,23
1872, 3, 21. Asa C. & ch, Walter S. & Thomas
    E., gct Spring River MM, Kans.

TWITCHELL
----, --, --. Hannah b 1813,1,13 d 1905,3,6
    (W)

UNDERWOOD
1827, 1, 24. Willin & w, Sarah, & dt, Rachel,
    rocf Carmel MM, dtd 1826,12,16
1827, 1, 24. Mary rocf Carmel MM, dtd 1826,
    11,18
1827, 11, 21. Sarah & dt, Rachel, gct Middle-
    ton MM
1827, 11, 21. Mary gct Middleton MM
1827, 12, 19. Amos gct Middleton MM

VAIL
1851, 1, 20. Louis Willets b (W)
1880, 5, 26. Isaac N., s John & Abigail, Bel-
    mont Co., O.; m at Salem, Mary M. COPE,
    dt Dawsy & Sarah Ann, Columbiana Co., O.
    (W)

1880, 11, 24. Mary C. gct Stillwater MM (W)
1883, 4, 25. Lewis dis mcd (W)

VALENTINE
1857, 5, 20. Anna Maria rocf Kennet MM, Pa.,
    dtd 1857,5,5 (W)
1859, 4, 20. Anna Maria dis joining Metho-
    dist Society (W)

VAN FOSSAN
1926, 2, 24. Harry rocf Winona MM

VANSYOC
1883, 6, 17. Enoch d

1877, 5, 9. Enoch & w, Phebe C., & ch,
    Anna, Mary, Eldora, John Oliver, Enoch
    Willet & Phebe Eva, rocf Damascus MM, dtd
    1877,3,24

VARNEY
1822, 6, 19. Hannah & ch, William, Isaac &
    Abel, rocf Short Creek MM, dtd 1822,5,21
1822, 6, 19. Anna rocf Short Creek MM, dtd
    1822,5,21

VARNEY, continued
1824, 11, 24. Anna Hathaway (form Varney) dis
    mcd
1833, 2, 7. Hannah dis joining Camelites
1833, 2, 7. Isaac dis disunity

VAUGHN
1812, 12, 3. Matthew [Vaughan], s Matthew &
    Rebecca, Stark Co., O.; m at Marlborough,
    Phebe PENNOCK, dt Wm. & Mary, Stark Co.,
    O.
1822, 8, 29. James, s Matthew & Rebecca, Co-
    lumbiana Co., O., b 1780,1,11; m at
    Springfield, Rhoda STANLEY, dt Pleasant &
    Amy COBBS, Columbiana Co., O., b 1790,9,
    30 (W)
    Ch: Rebecca
        Terrell   b 1823, 6, 2
----, --, --. Wm., s John & Marcelles, b
    1886,8,28; m Margaret ZIMMERMAN, dt Homer
    & Elizabeth, b 1885,12,11 (G)
    Ch: Charles   b 1906, 8, 28

1807, 8, 11. Benjamin recrq
1808, 1, 12. Benjamin gct Wayneoak MM, Va.
1809, 5, 16. Matthew rocf Isle of Wight Co.,
    Va., dtd 1807,3,25
1819, 12, 22. Polly Maria [Vaughan] (form
    Blackburn) dis mcd
1822, 7, 24. James rocf Western Branch MM,
    Va., dtd 1822,6,22
1827, 6, 22. Charles & Margaret [Vaughan]
    dropped from mbrp

VENABLE
1821, 3, 21. Jane [Venabal] (form Barber)
    dis mcd
1837, 5, 24. Vincent [Vanabald] gct Penns-
    ville MM
1853, 5, 25. Cert rec for Vincent from Ches-
    terfield MM, dtd 1852,12,18, endorsed to
    Upper Springfield MM
1919, 8, 20. Mr. & Mrs. recrq
1921, 5, 25. Lewis & Bertha gct Calif.

VEON
1894, 9, 25. Sarah, dt John & Margaret Coch-
    ran, b (G)

1925, 3, 25. Sarah Jane recrq
1926, 6, 23. Mrs. relrq

VERNON
1852, 5, 20. Rachel (form Bailey) dis mcd (H)

VICKERS
1881, 11, 10. Susan A. [Vickors], dt Joseph &
    Roxiana, b (G)

1840, 5, 20. Elwood rocf Concord MM, dtd
    1839,12,25
1841, 11, 24. Thomas Elwood gct New Garden MM
    (H)

1913, 12, 29. Mrs. Susie relrq

VINCENT
1926, 12, 22. Olive recrq

VIRDEN
----, --, --. Thos. C., s Thomas & Rebecca, b
    1875,9,27; m Nancy SNOWDEN, dt Peter &
    Emily Ann, b 1868,3,31 (G)
    Ch: Ruth E.   b 1906, 6, 24
        Emily R. " 1908, 3, 8

1915, 1, 20. Thomas & w, Nancy, & ch, Ruth
    Elizabeth & Emily, relrq

VOTAW
1746, 7, 20. Ann b (W)
----, --, --. Isaac, Jr. b 1776,2,4; m Sarah
    ----- b 1778,2,24 (W)
    Ch: Phebe Y. b 1799, 11, 22
        Mary   " 1802, 9, 25
        Benjamin " 1804, 4, 15
        Jemima   " 1806, 2, 25
        Sarah Jr. " 1808, 2, 17
        David   " 1810, 7, 26
        Rachel   " 1814, 5, 17
        Matilda   " 1816, 7, 4
----, --, --. Joseph b 1779,5,9 d 1832,8,26;
    m Phebe ----- b 1779,7,5 (W)
    Ch: Benjamin b 1803, 6, 28
        Isaac   " 1805, 6, 8
        John   " 1807, 5, 20
        Ann   " 1810, 6, 13
        Joseph   " 1812, 8, 21
        Phebe   " 1817, 9, 11
        Charles   " 1819, 8, 9
        Hannah   " 1823, 7, 22
1817, 10, 12. Isaac d bur Goshen (W)
1819, 5, 26. Isaac, s Moses & Mary, Columbi-
    ana Co., O.; m at Goshen, Frances STANLEY,
    dt Thomas & Edith, Columbiana Co., O.
1822, 2, 28. Isaac, s Moses & Mary, Columbi-
    ana Co., O.; m at Springfield, Susanna
    WOOLMAN, dt Abner & Martha, Columbiana
    Co., O.
1823, 5, 7. Phebe G. m Edward COURTNEY
1827, 12, 6. Benjamin, s Joseph & Phebe, Co-
    lumbiana Co., O., b 1803,6,28; m at Salem,
    Rebecca D. TEST, dt Benjamin & Mary, Co-
    lumbiana Co., O., b 1806,5,21 d 1831,2,13
    (W)
    Ch: Hannah   b 1828, 10, 12
        Mary Ann " 1830, 6, 12
1828, 10, 1. Isaac, s Joseph & Phebe, Colum-
    biana Co., O., b 1805,6,20; m at Salem,
    Rebecca PEIRCE, dt Ganer & Martha, Va., b
    1809,10,22 (W)
    Ch: Martha   b 1829, 8, 30
        Joshua   " 1831, 11, 29
        Rachel   " 1833, 5, 17
        Joseph   " 1836, 2, 5
        Peirce   " 1838, 6, 22
1830, 3, 3. John, s Joseph & Phebe, Columbi-

VOTAW, John, continued
    biana Co., O., b 1807,5,20; m at Salem,
    Mary E. MERIDITH, dt John & Rachel, Ches-
    ter Co., Pa. (W)
    Ch: Wm.   b 1831, 12, 11
        Joseph   " 1832, 4, 22
        Adaline   " 1835, 5, 5
        Harriet   " 1837, 4, 22
        Robert   " 1838, 11, 15
1831, 12, 7. Ann m Abraham WALTON, Jr.
1852, 10, 27. Isaac B., s Thomas & Elizabeth,
    Mahoning Co., O.; m at Salem, Hannah BAR-
    BER, dt Abraham & Drusilla, Columbiana
    Co., O.
----, --, --. Geo. E. m Emma SMITH, dt Wm.
    Peter & Anna Mary (Stoffer), b 1879,10,
    22 (W)
----, --, --. Lawrence, s Curtis & Anna, b
    1889,10,12; m Millie KING, dt Curtis &
    Miranda, b 1891,12,2 (G)
    Ch: Roscoe   b 1912, 8, 20
        Melissa   " 1915, 9, 22
        Virgil   " 1918, 12, 12
        Warren   " 1921, 7, 1
        Wanda   " 1921, 7, 1
        Minnie   " 1923, 2, 6
        Martha   " 1924, 10, 18
        Lawrence
        Jr.   " 1928, 7, 12
        Gail Wal-
        ter   " 1931, 7, 31

1806, 6, 17. Isaac, Jr. & w, Sarah, & ch,
    Phebe, Mary B., Benjamin & Jemima, rocf
    Westland MM, dtd 1806,5,24
1806, 7, 15. Samuel rocf Westland MM, dtd
    1806,4,26
1807, 10, 13. Daniel rocf Westland MM, dtd
    1807,7,25
1807, 12, 15. Thomas dis mou
1811, 4, 16. Daniel gct Miami MM
1815, 2, 14. Samuel gct New Garden MM
1816, 12, 17. Jonathan gct Miami MM
1819, 7, 21. Frances gct New Garden MM
1822, 6, 19. Susannah gct New Garden MM
1822, 11, 20. Thomas C. Stanley gct New Garden
    MM, to m Leah Votaw
1824, 2, 25. Thomas rst by rq
1825, 6, 22. Elizabeth recrq

1832, 10, 24. Benjamin dis mcd
1832, 11, 21. Rachel (form Walton) dis mcd (H)
1834, 6, 25. Isaac & w, Rebecca, & ch, Mar-
    tha, Joshua W. & Rachel, gct Chester MM,
    Ind.
1835, 1, 21. Phebe & ch, Phebe, Charles &
    Hannah, gct Chester MM, Ind.
1835, 10, 21. Hannah & Mary Ann, ch Benjamin,
    gct Chester MM, Ind.
1836, 6, 22. Joseph gct New Garden MM, Ind.
1836, 10, 19. Phebe & ch, Phebe, Charles &

Hannah, rocf Chester MM, Ind., dtd 1836,
    6,22
1837, 8, 23. Phebe & dt, Hannah, gct Center
    MM, O.
1837, 8, 23. Phebe, Jr. gct Center MM, O.
1838, 2, 21. Isaac & w, Rebecca, & ch, Mar-
    tha, Joshua M., Rachel & Joseph, rocf Up-
    per Springfield MM, dtd 1837,9,23
1840, 4, 22. Isaac & w, Rebecca, & ch, Mar-
    tha, Rachel, Joseph & Pierce, gct Dover
    MM, Ind.
1841, 5, 19. John & w, Mary, & ch, William,
    Joseph, Adaline, Harriet & Robert, gct
    Back Creek MM, Ind.
1841, 5, 19. Charles gct Chester MM, Ind.
1844, 3, 20. Ruth Ann (form Kennet) con mcd
    (H)
1849, 8, 22. Mississinawa MM was given per-
    mission to rec Benjamin in mbrp
1854, 7, 19. Hannah G. gct Upper Springfield
    MM (W)
1904, 2, 24. Emma M. rocf New Garden MM, O.,
    dtd 1904,1,21 (W)
1929, 4, 24. Lawrence & Millie recrq

WACHSMITH
----, --, --. Leo, s Ed., b 1906,3,13; m Opal
    L. OESCH, dt Walter, b 1908,3,7 (G)
    Ch: Joyce E.   b 1928, 3, 24
        Bobby   " 1930, 10, 10 d 1932, 6,11

WAGNER
----, --, --. John, s Daniel & Louvina, b 1864,
    8,4; m Ella HARRIS, dt Jacob & Susan, b
    1865,3,18 (G)
    Ch: Harry   b 1892, 8, 15

1911, 12, 20. Harry rec in mbrp
1913, 12, 29. John & Ella relrq
1917, 2, 21. John T. recrq
1921, 3, 23. John relrq
1924, 4, 23. Henry & w, Flora, & ch, Bernice
    & Marie, gct Alliance MM

WAITMAN
1927, 4, 20. Hazel [Waitham] recrq
1927, 5, 25. Melbourne recrq
1928, 1, 25. Mr. & Mrs. [Waithman] relrq

WALKER
1876, 11, 23. Abel, s Joseph & Maria, Columbi-
    ana Co., O.; m at Salem, Hannah L. FRENCH,
    dt Samuel & Mary J., Columbiana Co., O.
    (W)
----, --, --. James m Amelia KEISTER, dt Dan-
    iel & Sarah, b 1844,2,19 d 1931,9,20 (G)
    Ch: Pearl   b 1887, 1, 2
----, --, --. Ralph, s Ralph & Mary, b 1895,
    10,26; m Ada Hermina WACHSMITH, dt Edward
    & Mary, b 1900,6,12 (G)
    Ch: Mary Ada   b 1916, 5, 27
        Ralph O.   " 1918, 6, 14
        Lloyd J.   " 1920, 5, 20

WALKER, Ralph & Ada, continued
      Ch: Naomi May b 1922, 6, 20

1813, 4, 13. Elisabeth recrq
1815, 4, 11. Elizabeth Webb (form Walker) dis
    mcd
1821, 5, 23. Tacy rocf Middleton MM, dtd 1820,
    12,18
1822, 3, 20. Tacy gct Middleton MM
1878, 5, 22. Hannah L. gct Flushing MM (W)
1929, 12, 26. Ralph & w, Ada, & ch recrq

WALLACE
1873, 6, 13. Bessie b (G)

1931, 11, 18. Mrs. Bessie recrq

WALLER
1926, 10, 20. Mrs. Mildred, w Rev. Harry, rel-
    rq

WALTER
1852, 4, 21. Calvin C. More gct Short Creek
    MM, to m Sarah Walter

WALTON
----, --, --. Jonathan b 1787,11,6; m Wilhel-
    mina K. M. ----- b 1788,2,14 (W)
      Ch: Lewis   b 1811, 3, 23
          Josiah   " 1814, 1, 20
          Nathan   " 1820, 1, 19
          Mary Ann   " 1822, 11, 25
----, --, --. Jesse b 1771,3,20; m Ann -----
    b 1779,5,11 (W)
      Ch: Tacy   b 1803, 1, 22
          Uree   " 1804, 10, 29
          Amos   " 1806, 8, 29
          Jehu   " 1808, 11, 21
          Lydia   " 1811, 4, 4
          Ann   " 1813, 8, 25
          Benjamin   " 1815, 8, 23
          Jonathan C." 1817, 11, 29
1820, 11, 2. Tacy m Joseph COBBS
1823, 12, 4. Uree m Elijah STANLEY
1831, 12, 7. Abraham, Jr., s Abraham & Mary,
    Columbiana Co., O.; m at Salem, Ann VOTAW,
    dt Joseph & Phebe, Columbiana Co., O., b
    1810,6,13 (W)
      Ch: Joseph V. b 1832, 7, 27 d 1834, 7,30
          Amos   " 1834, 11, 12
1884, 7, 12. Thornton d bur Grove Cemetery (H)

1806, 3, 11. Mary rocf Westland MM, dtd 1806,
    2,22
1806, 6, 17. Benjamin rocf Westland MM, dtd
    1805,9,28, endorsed by Middleton MM, 1806,
    4,12
1807, 5, 12. Bathsheba rocf Westland MM, dtd
    1807,3,28
1807, 5, 12. Martha rocf Westland MM, dtd
    1807,3,28
1814, 11, 15. Lydia (form Marsh) con mcd
1815, 11, 14. Lydia gct New Garden MM

1816, 11, 12. Jesse & w, Ann, & ch, Tacy,
    Urie, Amos, Jehu, Lydia, Ann & Benjamin,
    rocf Redstone MM, dtd 1816,10,23
1817, 6, 17. Jonathan & w, Wilhelmina Hen-
    rietta Maria, & ch, Lewis & Josiah, rocf
    Sadsbury MM, dtd 1817,5,6
1831, 3, 23. Abraham, Jr. rocf Middleton MM,
    dtd 1831,2,10
1831, 7, 20. Achsah rocf Middleton MM, dtd
    1831,6,9
1831, 12, 21. Rachel rocf Middleton MM, dtd
    1831,10,11 (H)
1832, 11, 21. Rachel Votaw (form Walton) dis
    mcd (H)
1835, 1, 21. Abraham & w, Ann, & s, Amos, gct
    Chester MM, Ind.
1837, 8, 23. Cert rec for Ann from Strouds-
    burgh MM, Pa., dtd 1837,5,25, endorsed to
    Upper Springfield MM
1841, 8, 25. James rocf Solebury MM, Pa.,
    dtd 1841,5,4
1843, 6, 21. James gct Soleberry MM, Pa. (H)
1862, 1, 23. Tazette (form Townsend) con mcd
1873, 12, 25. Virginia, minor, gct Alexandria
    MM, dtd 1873,8,7 (H)
1885, 3, 26. Rachel gct Green St. MM, Phila.,
    Pa. (H)
1887, 8, 25. Wilmer gct Wapsononock MM, Ia.
    (H)
1932, 6, 29. Katherine Litty dropped from
    mbrp

WANK
----, --, --. Lloyd Kenneth, s Wm. & Emma, b
    1903,4,15; m Edith Melvina CRAWFORD, dt
    Wm. & Lottie, b 1906,5,20 (G)
    Dt: Lois Ilene b 1930, 1, 28
----, --, --. Orlan Clyde, s Wm. & Emma, b
    1905,6,11; m Margaret Jane SIMMONS, dt
    Frank, b 1907,6,8 (G)
      Ch: Robert
          Eldine   b 1931, 1, 3
          Donald J. " 1932, 4, 21

1929, 12, 26. Orlin & w, Margaret, & dt recrq
1929, 12, 26. Edith & Lloyd recrq
1930, 7, 23. Mr. & Mrs. William recrq

WARD
1919, 12, 24. Mattie B. recrq
1920, 6, 23. Mabel C. & Mildred A. recrq

WARE
----, --, --. Asa b 1755,9,12 d 1833,4,12; m
    Elizabeth ----- b 1764,1,6 d 1839,3,25 (W)
      Ch: John   b 1798, 7, 9
          Amos   " 1800, 1, 15
          Asa Jr.   " 1801, 10, 27
          Mary Ann   " 1803, 2, 26
          Samuel   " 1806, 9, 4
1815, 9, 20. Edith m Talbot TOWNSEND
1825, 10, 27. Asa, s Asa & Elizabeth, Columbi-
    ana Co., O., b 1801,10,24 d 1866,3,3; m

WARE, Asa, continued
    at Salem, Eliza Ann CREW, dt Obediah &
    Mary, Columbiana Co., O., b 1805,12,18
    d 1833,3,1 (W)
    Ch: Joseph   b 1827, 2, 15
        Benjamin " 1827, 2, 15
        Talbot   " 1829, 6, 20
        Emmor   " 1831, 3, 19
        Joel   " 1833, 2, 19
    Asa m 2nd Abigail ----- b 1799,11,19 d
    1878,10,21 (W)

1810, 11, 13. Asa & w, Elizabeth, & ch, John,
    Amos, Asa, Mary Ann & Samuel, rocf Upper
    Springfield MM, N. J., dtd 1810,9,5
1814, 10, 11. Edith recrq
1816, 9, 17. Latitia rocf Darby MM, Pa., dtd
    1816,4,30, endorsed by Concord MM, 1816,5,
    14
1817, 7, 15. John gct ND MM, Phila., Pa.
1819, 11, 24. John rocf ND MM, Phila., Pa., dtd
    1819,10,26
1822, 2, 20. Sarah rocf New Garden MM, dtd
    1822,2,2
1823, 2, 19. Amos gct Frankfort MM, Pa.
1824, 1, 21. Mary Ann dis
1824, 9, 22. Amos rocf Frankford MM, Pa.,
    dtd 1824,8,25
1826, 12, 20. John & w, Sarah, & ch, Stephen
    & Samuel, gct Marlborough MM
1828, 10, 22. Asa dis jH
1829, 11, 25. Elizabeth dis jH
1837, 8, 23. Cert rec for Abigail from
    Frankford MM, Pa., dtd 1837,8,1, endorsed
    to Upper Springfield MM
1848, 10, 25. Benjamin F. dis mcd
1850, 7, 24. Joseph dis mcd
1851, 6, 25. Asa & w, Abigail, & ch, Emmor
    & Joel, gct Upper Springfield MM
1853, 12, 21. Asa & w, Abigail, rocf Upper
    Springfield MM, dtd 1853,11,26
1860, 2, 23. Talbert gct Driftwood MM, Ind.
1870, 12, 21. Talbot dis joining separatists
    of 1854 (W)

WARNER
1922, 2, 18. Margaret V., dt Scott & Anna, b
    (G)

1933, 1, 25. Virginia recrq

WARREN
1862, 12, 25. Joseph dis joining separatists
    (W) of 1854
1913, 1, 31. Esther recrq

WARRINGTON
----, --, --. Abraham b 1755,2,22 d 1843,10,
    19 bur Salem; m Rachel ----- b 1760,3,31
    d 1827,9,2 bur Salem (W)
    Ch: Joshua   b 1786, 2, 10
        Rachel   " 1787, 10, 30
        Ann   " 1789, 8, 8

    Ch: Hannah   b 1791, 4, 1
        Thomas   " 1793, 5, 3 d 1815, 5, 3
        bur Salem
        Priscilla " 1795, 8, 15
        Evan   " 1797, 7, 2 " 1815, 6,20
        bur Salem
        Joshua   " 1802, 7, 5 " 1823, 8, 9
        bur Salem
1806, 12, 25. Abraham, s John & Mary, Columbi-
    ana Co., O., b 1783,4,25; m at Springfield
    Keziah WOOLMAN, dt Samuel & Jane, Columbi-
    ana Co., O., b 1782,8,7 (W)
    Ch: Mary   b 1808, 6, 17
        Jane   " 1810, 1, 15
        Ruth   " 1811, 10, 23
        John R.   " 1814, 1, 1
        Sarah   " 1815, 8, 14
        Martha   " 1817, 2, 4
        Nathan   " 1819, 2, 11
        Thomas   " 1821, 4, 15
        Evan   " 1825, 11, 15
1807, 5, 14. Rachel m Edward BONSALL
1808, 5, 25. Ann m Nathan HUNT
1832, 8, 29. Priscilla m Wm. FISHER
1839, 1, 30. Hannah m David F. HARRIS
1852, 3, 26. Joshua, s Abraham & Keziah, Co-
    lumbiana Co., O.; m at Salem, Eunice
    SHREEVE, dt George & Martha, Columbiana
    Co., O.
1879, 9, 18. Rebecca m David NARAMORE
1932, 2, 6. Lizzie J. d (W)
----, --, --. Alfred E., s Gilbert & Josephine
    (Bundy), b 1904,4,26; m Lenna Mae STANLEY,
    dt John W. & Floy O. (Woodward), b 1905,5,
    3 (W)
    Ch: James A. b 1932, 9, 4

1805, 11, 12. Abraham & w, Rachel, & ch, Ra-
    chel, Ann, Hannah, Thomas, Priscilla, Evan
    & Joshua, rocf Chester MM, West New Jersey
    dtd 1805,9,10, endorsed by Middleton MM,
    1805,11,9
1806, 2, 11. Abraham, Jr. rocf Chester MM,
    West Jersey, dtd 1805,12,10, endorsed by
    Middleton MM, 1806,2,8
1818, 3, 17. Sarah rocf Chester MM, N. J.,
    dtd 1818,2,5
1856, 3, 20. Eunice, w Joshua, & ch, Abigail
    & Martha, gct Driftwood MM, Ind.
1862, 1, 23. Nathan & w, Mary, & ch, Lineus,
    Henry, Sarah Ann, Hannah, Irving & Wilson,
    gct Upper Springfield MM, O.
1874, 6, 25. John R. & w, Rachel, rocf Damas-
    cus MM, dtd 1874,5,23
1875, 6, 24. Rebecca [Warrington] rocf Damas-
    cus MM, dtd 1875,5,22
1878, 2, 6. Mary I. (form Morlan) rocf Al-
    liance MM, dtd 1877,12,25
1879, 12, 25. David rocf Damascus MM, dtd
    1879,11,22
1883, 12, 20. David & w, Mary, recrq
1884, 5, 25. John gct Westmorland MM, N. Y.
1886, 10, 21. Three ch of David dropped from

WARRINGTON, continued
  mbrp
1931, 3, 25. Alfred E. rocf Upper Springfield
  MM, O., dtd 1931,2,27 (W)
1931, 4, 22. Lenna Mae rocf Plainfield MM,
  Ind., dtd 1931,3,4 (W)

WASHBURN
1882, 2, 8. Rachel H. rocf Greenwich MM, O.,
  dtd 1882,1,12
1853, 9, 21. Lydia (form Dixon) dis mcd & jas

WATERWORTH
1830, 12, 1. Wm., s James & Margaret, Columbiana Co., O., b 1797,4mo; m at Salem, Elizabeth DAVIS, dt Samuel & Mary, Columbiana
  Co., O., b 1797,2,4 (H)

1830, 11, 24. William [Watterworth] prcf Carmel
  MM, dtd 1830,11,20, to m Elizabeth Davis
  (H)
1831, 8, 24. William rocf Carmel MM, dtd 1831,
  7,16 (H)
1849, 11, 22. Elizabeth Allen (form Waterworth)
  con mcd (H)

WATSON
1846, 5, 1. Matilda J. b (W)

1864, 12, 21. Matilda J. recrq (W)
1878, 12, 25. Matilda J. Lyon (form Watson)
  dis mcd (W)
1880, 2, 26. Rachel recrq (H)
1887, 11, 24. Rachel dis disunity (H)

WAXSMITH
1921, 5, 25. Mrs. Mary [Wacksmith] recrq
1930, 3, 19. Lee & w, Opal, & dt, Joise
  Elaine, recrq

WAY
1828, 7, 30. Ann rocf London Grove MM, dtd
  1827,6,6 (H)

WEAVER
1788, 4, 10. Gulielma b (W)
----, --, --. Walter, s Mervin & Ella, b
  1885,9,8 d 1933,--,-- (G)
1896, 7, 15. Lucinda M., dt Robert H. & Adaline Smith, b (G)
1911, 10, 4. Vera Bruella, dt Walter & Clara,
  b (G)

1826, 1, 25. Gulielma rocf Salem MM, N. J.,
  dtd 1825,11,30
1840, 6, 24. Rebecca (form Stanton) dis mou
  (H)
1923, 12, 19. Walter W., Lucinda M. & Vera
  Buella recrq
1929, 6, 19. Lucinda M. relrq

WEBB
----, --, --. Elizabeth b 1792,9mo d 1851,3,23

  (W)
1813, 10, 27. Ann m David PAINTER
----, --, --. ----- m Leah ----- b 1786,8,8 (W)
  Ch: Benina   b 1817, 10, 21
      Benjamin " 1820, 11, 24
      Lydia   " 1822, 11, 12
1828, 7, 13. Leah m Isaac JAMES

1807, 4, 14. Ann recrq
1815, 4, 11. Elizabeth (form Walker) dis mcd
1817, 5, 13. Leah (form Morris) dis mcd
1823, 3, 19. Elizabeth rst by rq
1825, 1, 19. Leah rst by rq
1826, 3, 22. Penina, Benjamin & Lydia, ch
  Leah, recrq
1828, 10, 22. Leah James & ch, Penina & Lydia
  Webb, gct Carmel MM
1829, 11, 25. Benjamin, minor, gct Upper
  Springfield MM
1834, 11, 19. Peninah, minor, rocf Upper
  Springfield MM, dtd 1834,10,20
1835, 7, 22. Peninah gct Duck Creek MM, Ind.
1841, 3, 14. Sarah (form Pennock) dis mcd

WEEKS
1815, 12, 11. Maria b (G)
1842, 8, 5. Emma B. b (H)

1858, 8, 26. Mariah G. rocf Vasselborough MM,
  dtd 1858,7,14
1887, 5, 26. Hannah J. dropped from mbrp

WEISNER
----, --, --. Elizabeth, dt Frederick & Margaret Forney, b 1836,8,29 d 1923,--,-- (G)

WEITSEL
1863, 1, 22. Elizabeth gct Le Grand MM, Ia.

WELCH
1877, 12, 24. Horace G., s John & Ann, Cedar
  Co., Ia.; m at residence of Joseph Ingram,
  Josephine INGRAM, dt Joseph & Phebe, Columbiana Co., O. (H)

1878, 10, 24. Josephine gct Wapsinonoc MM, Ia.
  (H)

WEST
1821, 3, 12. Joseph b (W)

1836, 1, 20. Hannah, Jesse, Lydia & Joseph,
  ch Joseph & Rebecca, rocf New Garden MM,
  Pa., dtd 1835,8,5
1836, 7, 20. Joseph & w, Rebecca, & ch, Hannah, Jesse, Lydia & Joseph, rocf New Garden MM, Pa., dtd 1836,5,5 (H)
1836, 7, 20. Sidney rocf New Garden MM, Pa.,
  dtd 1836,5,5 (H)
1837, 8, 23. Joseph dis disunity
1837, 10, 25. Hannah dis disunity
1837, 12, 20. Jesse dis disunity
1838, 8, 22. Rebecca & Sidney dis disunity (H)

WEST, continued
1840, 8, 19. Lydia dis disunity
1853, 4, 20. Joseph dis mcd
1933, 2, 22. Mr. & Mrs. Frank & s, Alsom, recrq
1933, 3, 22. Mr. & Mrs. Frank & s, Eldon, relrq

WHINNERY
1817, 2 13. Rachel b (H)
1818, 4, 23. Zimri [Whinery], s Wm. & Abigail,
Columbiana Co., O.; m at Springfield, Judith WRIGHT, dt Joseph & Elizabeth, Columbiana Co., O.
1819, 2, 1. James b (H)
1829, 3, 31. Elijah, Columbiana Co., O., m at
home of Ann H. Lamborn, Ann H. LAMBORN,
Columbiana Co., O. (H)
1851, 12, 6. Leona b (H)
1924, 12, 9. Ethel L. b (G)
1929, 8, 30. Leander d (G)

1806, 5, 13. Thomas & w, Lydia, rocf Warrington MM, dtd 1806,1,11
1806, 11, 11. William & w, Abigail, & ch, William, James, Jane, Zimri, Sarah & Abigail,
rocf Warrington MM, Pa., dtd 1806,5,10
1818, 6, 16. Judith gct New Garden MM
1829, 11, 25. John Jr. [Whinery] gct New Garden
MM
1846, 2, 25. David Brown gct New Garden MM,
to m Ann Whinery
1852, 2, 25. Eunice [Whinery] (form Davis)
dis mcd
1852, 7, 21. Newton [Whinery] rocf New Garden
MM, dtd 1852,6,24
1853, 4, 20. Mary [Whinery] (form Barber) con
mcd
1853, 9, 21. Mary B. [Whinery] gct Driftwood
MM, Ind.
1888, 2, 23. Leander [Whinery] & w, Mary V.,
& ch, Florence L. & William D., recrq
1891, 9, 24. Joseph H. & w, Edna, & ch, Luella, Fileta & Raymond E., rocf Winona MM,
dtd 1891,8,19
1907, 12, 25. Rhoda [Whinery] rocf New Garden
MM, O., dtd 1907,11,21 (W)
1909, 3, 24. Rhoda [Whinery] gct New Garden
MM, O. (W)
1912, 4, 24. Wilmer D. [Whinery] rocf Winona
MM, dtd 1912,1,29
1914, 6, 24. Helen recrq
1916, 5, 24. Helen relrq
1918, 5, 22. Wilmer dropped from mbrp
1921, 1, 19. Leander & Mary rocf Winona MM
1923, 6, 20. Joseph & w, Edna, rocf Columbus
MM, O.
1924, 3, 19. Joseph & w, Edna, gct Columbus
MM
1926, 7, 21. Joseph & Edna H. rocf Columbus
MM, O.

WHITACRE
----, --, --. Frank, s Chas. R. & Sarah G.,
b 1857,10,10; m Ella STANLEY, dt Enocy P.
& Phebe Vansyoc, b 1867,7,28 (G)
Ch: Alma J.   b 1887, 10, 31
    Ralph C.   " 1900, 5, 12
    Eva Marie   " 1907, 7, 16

1806, 2, 11. Thomas [Whiticar] rocf Westland
MM, dtd 1806,2,8
1807, 1, 13. Caleb & ch, Thornton, Achsah &
David, rocf Goose Creek MM, dtd 1806,10,27
1808, 8, 16. Caleb gct Westland MM, to m
Rebecca Bracken
1890, 6, 26. Ella [Whitakre] dropped from
mbrp
1910, 7, 20. Frank & w gct Pamona MM, Calif.
1917, 10, 24. Ralph & Eva [Whittacre] dropped
from mbrp

WHITE
1840, 4, 1. Nathan, s Robert L. & Ann, Stark
Co., O.; m at Salem, Prudence H. GIBSON,
dt Joseph & Esther, Harden Co., O.
----, --, --. George b 1798,10,14; m Elizabeth ----- b 1820,9,18 d 1854,11,25 bur
Salem (W)
Ch: Phebe   b 1841, 8, 24
    Lydia   " 1843, 3, 23 d 1854, 5,10
      bur Salem
    Moses   " 1846, 4, 28
    Dinah Ann   " 1848, 6, 15
    Esther Jane " 1852, 9, 29 d 1853, 4,15
      bur Salem
----, --, --. Asenith, dt Isaac & Hannah T.,
b 1840,11,3 d 1921,5,12 (G)
1894, 1, 9. Vera, dt Wm. & Isadora, b (G)

1807, 9, 15. Uriah & w Martha, & ch, Jesse,
Thomas, James, Isaac & Margaret, rocf
Westland MM, dtd 1807,2,28
1811, 9, 17. Ann rocf Redstone MM, Pa., dtd
1811,6,28
1817, 5, 13. Ann gct Plymouth MM
1840, 7, 22. Prudence G. gct Marlboro MM
1847, 9, 22. George & w, Elizabeth, & ch,
Phebe, Lydia & Moses, rocf Caesars Creek
MM, O., dtd 1847,8,26
1860, 8, 23. Isaac & w, Hannah, & ch, William Hambleton, Mary Adaline, Margaret
Elma & Asenith Arabella, rocf Concord
MM, dtd 1860,6,20
1860, 9, 20. Phebe S. dis jas
1864, 4, 20. George dis joining separatists
of 1854 (W)
1867, 7, 25. Margaret E. Pickering (form
White) con mcd (H)
1868, 8, 20. Dinah Ann Conn (form White)
con mcd & jas
1871, 2, 22. Dinah Ann Conn (form White) dis
mcd (W)
1871, 5, 24. Phebe S. Speck (form White) dis
mcd (W)

WHITE, continued
1871, 12, 20. Moses S. dis mcd (W)
1885, 2, 6. Harry H. & w, Lillie B., recrq
1886, 10, 21. Harry dropped from mbrp
1887, 2, 24. Lilly dropped from mbrp
1911, 5, 24. Asenath rocf Winona MM, dtd
    1911,7,19
1911, 12, 20. Vera rec in mbrp
1919, 11, 26. Mrs. Effie (White) Broomal rec-
    rq
1923, 10, 24. R. W. Broomall & w, Effie
    (White) & ch relrq

WHITTON
1874, 10, 25. Irene, dt Joseph & Mary Town-
    send, b (G)
1879, 4, 9. Bert, s Chas. & Margaret, b (G)

1910, 9, 21. Bert recrq

WICKERSHAM
1821, 12, 19. Thomas & w, Sarah, rocf Red-
    stone MM, dtd 1821,10,3
1824, 4, 21. Thomas, Sr. & w, Sarah, gct
    Redstone MM
1862, 12, 25. David, Rebecca & Abby F. dis
    joining separatists (W) of 1854
1862, 12, 25. Joel, Ann, Ruth Anna, Thomas,
    Maria & Phebe F. dis joining separatists
    (W) of 1854
1862, 12, 25. Phebe dis joining separatists
    (W) of 1854

WIERMAN
1847, 4, 27. Mary A. m Thomas E. GRISELL (H)

WIGGINS
1914, 11, 25. Dessie Kaiser dropped from mbrp

WILDMAN
1808, 10, 26. Deborah m Wm. REEDER
1812, 12, 3. Mary m Joseph MARSHALL

1806, 6, 17. Abraham [Wileman] & w, Lettitia,
    & ch, Jonah, Elizabeth, Amy, Deborah, Mah-
    lon, Mary, Sarah, Nancy & Jesse, rocf
    South River MM, Va., dtd 1805,9,14, en-
    dorsed by Concord MM, dtd 1805,12,24

WILEY
1815, 9, 20. David, s Joseph & Elizabeth,
    b 1785,2,2; m at Goshen, O., Elizabeth
    STANLEY, dt James & Mary, b 1797,12,15 (W)
    Ch: Sarah   b 1816, 8, 17
        Joseph   " 1818, 2, 1
        Mary   " 1820, 4, 16
        James   " 1822, 2, 9
        Cynthia   " 1824, 4, 12

1810, 7, 17. David [Wyley] rocf Middleton MM,
    dtd 1810,3,10
1818, 3, 17. David & w, Elizabeth, & ch, Sa-
    rah & Joseph, gct Stillwater MM

1821, 4, 25. David [Wyley] & w, Elizabeth, &
    ch, Sarah, Joseph & Mary, rocf Somerset
    MM, dtd 1821,3,26

WILHELM
1909, 4, 6. Chas. Herman, s Chas. & Anna, b
    (G)

1929, 12, 26. Charles recrq

WILKINS
1806, 11, 11. Joseph & w, Sarah, & ch, Daniel,
    Joseph, Sarah, Elizabeth, Tamson, William,
    John, Thomas & Hannah, rocf Middleton MM,
    dtd 1806,10,11
1807, 9, 15. Susannah Miller (form Wilkins)
    con mcd

WILLAMAN
1860, 6, 12. Martha, dt Joseph & Ellen, b (G)
1912, 4, 24. Frank, s C. D. & Lucy, b (G)

1911, 12, 20. Frank rec in mbrp
1924, 12, 17. Frank [Williaman] dropped from
    mbrp

WILLIAMS
1807, 2, 19. Benjamin, s Isaiah & Dinah, Co-
    lumbiana Co., O.; m at New Garden, Catha-
    rine BATTIN, dt Richard & Catharine, Co-
    lumbiana Co., O.
----, --, --. Casper & Hannah (W)
    Ch: Thomas   b 1820, 2, 23 d 1832, 3,26
        Charles   " 1825, 2, 1
        Mary   " 1828, 4, 25 d 1833, 3,15
        Samuel   " 1834, 9, 19
----, --, --. Daniel b 1794,6,23 d 1861,4,14;
    m Elizabeth ----- b 1800,2,16 (W)
    Ch: Hannah   b 1828, 2, 23
        Joseph   " 1830, 5, 12
        Jane   " 1832, 9, 12 d 1834, 6,23
        Frances Ann" 1834, 9, 9 " 1836, 1,30
        Lindley Mur-
          ray   b 1838, 9, 4
1834, 8, 21. Asa, s Richard & Sarah, Stark
    Co., O.; m at Salem, Edith CADWALADER, dt
    Jonas & Ann, Fayette Co., Pa.
----, --, --. John G. b 1811,7,18; m Mary B.
    ----- b 1816,6,26 (H)
    Ch: Ann
          Elizabeth b 1836, 9, 6
1846, 4, 29. Joseph, s Daniel & Mary, Columbi-
    ana Co., O.; m at Salem, Lydia MORRIS, dt
    Samuel & Sally, Columbiana Co., O.
1846, 12, 30. Catharine m Wm. DARLINGTON
1857, 3, 5. Samuel, s Casper & Hannah, Co-
    lumbiana Co., O.; m at Salem, Hannah S.
    JENKINS, dt Edward & Elizabeth, Columbiana
    Co., O.
1860, 12, 26. Hannah P. m John OLIPHANT (W)
----, --, --. Chas. S., s Obidah & Sarah, b
    1854,9,10; m Julia Ann SIPP, dt Michael &
    Hannah, b 1865,5,20 (G)

WILLIAMS, Chas. S. & Julia Ann, continued
    Ch: Loyd L.   b 1889, 5, 3
       Vernia L. " 1891, 8, 7

1807, 4, 14. Mary rocf Middleton MM, dtd
    1807.4.11
1808, 3, 16. Benjamin rocf Middleton MM, dtd
    1809,10,10
1829, 9, 23. Daniel & w, Elizabeth, & ch,
    Hannah, rocf Smithfield MM, dtd 1829,5,18
1830, 7, 21. Dearman gct Deerfield MM
1831, 9, 21. Ephraim rocf Stillwater MM, dtd
    1831,8,27
1832, 9, 19. Casper & w, Hannah, & ch, Thom-
    as, Charles & Mary, rocf Exeter MM, dtd
    1832,2,29, endorsed by Flushing MM, O.,
    dtd 1832,5,23 (H)
1832, 9, 19. Benjamin, minor, rocf Marlborough
    MM, dtd 1832,7,31
1832, 10, 24. Hannah & ch, Charles & Mary,
    rocf Exeter MM, Pa., dtd 1832,9,26
1834, 11, 19. Casper dis not attending mtg
1834, 11, 19. Edith gct Goshen MM, O.
1834, 11, 19. Ephraim gct Stillwater MM
1835, 4, 22. Hannah dis disunity (H)
1837, 5, 24. Daniel & w, Elizabeth, & ch,
    Hannah & Joseph, gct Short Creek MM
1837, 7, 19. John G. & w, Mary, & dt, Ann
    Elizabeth, rocf Sadsbury MM, Pa., dtd
    1837,4,5 (H)
1839, 2, 20. Casper & w, Hannah, & ch,
    Charles & Samuel, gct New Garden MM
1839, 5, 22. Daniel & w, Elizabeth, & ch,
    Hannah, Joseph & Lindley M., rocf Short
    Creek MM, dtd 1839,3,19
1840, 7, 22. Catharine rocf Bradford MM, Pa.,
    dtd 1840,6,3
1846, 11, 25. Lydia M. gct Flushing MM
1846, 11, 25. Michael Stratton, Jr. gct Flush-
    ing MM, to m Martha Williams
1851, 6, 25. Casper & s, Samuel, rocf New
    Garden MM, dtd 1851,4,24
1852, 9, 22. Casper gct Redstone MM, to m
    Phebe J. Allen
1853, 2, 23. Casper & s, Samuel, gct Sandy
    Spring MM
1857, 4, 23. Samuel rocf New Garden MM, dtd
    1857,4,22
1860, 7, 25. Samuel & w, Hannah, & s, Edward
    H., gct New Garden MM, O.
1862, 12, 25. Elizabeth, Joseph & Lindley M.
    dis joining separatists (W) of 1854
1864, 11, 11. Hannah S. dis joining separa-
    tists of 1854 (W)
1864, 11, 23. Lindley M. con mcd (W)
1865, 2, 22. Edith gct Hickory Grove MM, Ia.
    (W)
1865, 4, 19. Elizabeth gct Hickory Grove MM,
    Ia. (W)
1865, 5, 24. Joseph gct Hickory Grove MM, Ia.
    (W)
1865, 12, 25. Lindley M. gct Hickory Grove MM,
    Ia. (W)

1873, 2, 20. Lydia Jane gct Chicago MM
1885, 2, 6. Joseph J. & w, Ann E., recrq
1885, 2, 6. Lizzie recrq
1886, 10, 21. Joseph dropped from mbrp
1886, 10, 21. Lizzie dropped from mbrp
1887, 2, 24. Elizabeth dropped from mbrp
1911, 3, 22. Charles S. & w, Julia Ann, rocf
    Damascus MM
1911, 3, 22. Loyd L. rocf Damascus MM
1912, 1, 24. Verna Louise rocf Winona MM, O.
1917, 6, 20. Charles & w gct Emporia, Kans.
1927, 6, 22. W. W. dropped from mbrp

WILLIAMSON
1921, 10, 19. Virginia recrq

WILLMOTT
1865, 6, 22. Henry rocf Warwickshire MM,
    North England
1868, 9, 24. Henry gct Raysville MM, Ind.

WILSON
1852, 10, 21. Wm. C., s Israel & Catharine,
    Harrison Co., O.; m at Salem, Esther
    FAWCETT, dt Levi & Mary, Columbiana Co.,
    O.
1871, 2, 20. Tacy d (W)
1873, 9, 25. Benjamin, s Joseph & Eliza,
    Gurnsey Co., O.; m at Salem, Mary A.
    FRENCH, dt John & Martha H. (Ogden), b
    1853,9,14 d 1911,11,5 bur Friends Bur.
    Gr., Salem, O. (W)
    Ch: John
        French   b 1886, 4, 15
1887, 4, 9. Frank Earl, s Frank & Elizabeth,
    b (G)
1887, 5, 27. Clara, dt Richard & Martha Chap-
    pell, b (G)
1904, 3, 8. Kermit, s Warren & Blanch, b (G)

1827, 1, 24. Tacy rocf Richland MM, Pa., dtd
    1826,1,12
1853, 4, 20. Esther gct Flushing MM
1862, 12, 25. Tacy dis joining separatists (W)
    of 1854
1864, 12, 21. Matilda recrq (W)
1875, 10, 20. Mary A. gct Flushing MM (W)
1882, 12, 21. Frank recrq
1883, 8, 16. Joseph recrq
1886, 10, 21. Joseph [Willson] dropped from
    mbrp
1911, 6, 21. John French rocf Flushing MM,
    O., dtd 1911,5,25 (W)
1911, 6, 21. Mary A. rocf Flushing MM, O.,
    dtd 1911,5,25 (W)
1911, 12, 20. Frank Earl rec in mbrp
1915, 11, 24. Kermit recrq
1917, 2, 21. Clara & Earl relrq
1927, 6, 22. Kermit dropped from mbrp

WINDER
----, --, --. Benjamin b 1797,7,30 d 1885,3,
    16; m Abigail ----- b 1801,11,3 d 1839,9,

WINDER, Benjamin & Abigail, continued
    23 (W)
    Benjamin m 2nd Hannah ----- b 1820,6,28
    d 1862,11,17
    Benjamin m 3rd Sarah S. ----- b 1818,8,27
    d 1890,2,14 (W)
----, --, --. Joseph b 1805,10,12 d 1893,4,23;
    m Ephama ----- b 1803,6,14 d 1839,11,7 (W)
    Ch: Lydia Ann b 1829, 1, 18 d 1864,12,24
        Adah B.   " 1831, 6, 13
    Joseph m 2nd Lydia ----- b 1809,12,28
    Ch: Esther   b 1844, 1, 25
        David   " 1845, 12, 14
        Amy   " 1848, 10, 24 d 1880, 7,12
        Leonard   " 1850, 9, 21

1807, 10, 13. William & w, Adah, & ch, Rachel,
    Hannah, Ann, Mary, Benjamin, Eleanor, Adah
    & Joseph, recrq
1887, 7, 20. Sarah S. [Winders] rocf New Gar-
    den MM, dtd 1887,5,26 (W)

WINELAND
1891, 7, 28. Margaret L., dt C. M., b (G)

1921, 4, 20. C. M. & Bessie recrq

WINNER
1872, 4, 24. Ellis rocf Muncy MM, Pa., dtd
    1871,12,20 (W)
1880, 2, 25. Ellis dis disunity (W)

WISE
----, --, --. George C., s Geo. C. & Albertine,
    b 1871,6,27; m Katharine S. -----, dt Jo-
    seph & Cornelia, b 1877,2,13 (G)
    Ch: Miriam C. b 1897, 11, 14
        Ruth S.   " 1899, 10, 4

1914, 1, 21. George C. Jr. & w, Katharine S.,
    & ch, Miriam C. & Ruth S., rocf Baltimore
    MM
1915, 9, 22. George C. Jr. gct Emporia, Kans.

WISENER
1833, 2, 7. Elizabeth (form Richardson) dis
    mou
1912, 2, 21. Elizy J. [Wisner] recrq

WOLF
1883, 3, 15. Frederick [Wolfe], s Wm. &
    Richa, b (G)

1882, 2, 8. Nancy recrq
1887, 3, 20. Nancy dropped from mbrp

WOLFGANG
----, --, --. Henry E., s Warren & Clara, b
    1908,4,12; m Thelma L. WITHROW, dt Rae &
    Virginia, b 1911,7,10 (G)

1933, 1, 25. Mr. & Mrs. recrq

WOOD
1824, 5, 8. Isaiah b (W)

1848, 1, 19. Greenberry P. & w, Hannah, &
    ch, Alfred & Sarah, rocf Upper Spring-
    field MM, dtd 1847,11,27
1848, 9, 20. Greenberry P. & w, Hannah, &
    ch, Alfred & Sarah, gct Salem MM, Ia.
1852, 7, 21. Isaiah dis mcd
1862, 12, 25. John, Sylvanus, Triphina & Sa-
    rah dis joining separatists (W) of 1854

WOODBRIDGE
1872, 8, 7. Mary A. recrq
1874, 3, 26. Mary A. relrq

WOOLMAN
1751, 1, 4. Jane b (or 1750,10,22) (W)
----, --, --. Samuel b 1753,3,19 d 1814,12,24
    bur Springfield (W)
----, --, --. Abner b 1773,7,5; m Martha -----
    b 1774,9,26 (W)
    Ch: Susannah b 1804, 1, 31
        Anna   " 1806, 3, 12
        Joseph A. " 1808, 2, 15 d 1810,11, 9
        Thos. B. " 1809, 6, 26
        Sarah   " 1811, 11, 1
        Mary   " 1813, 10, 27
        Martha   " 1815, 6, 20
----, --, --. Samuel Jr. b 1776,12,20; m Re-
    becca ----- b 1781,6,29 (W)
    Ch: Thos.
        Tucker   b 1806, 4, 17
        Elizabeth " 1808, 2, 17
        Mary   " 1809, 8, 27
        Joel   " 1811, 2, 12
        Benjamin " 1813, 1, 1
        Samuel   " 1814, 8, 17
        Jane   " 1816, 8, 23
        Rebecca   " 1818, 12, 23
1806, 12, 25. Keziah m Abraham WARRINGTON
1809, 9, 21. Mary Ann m John STANLEY
----, --, --. Aaron T. b 1786,8,27; m Mary W.
    ----- b 1787,11,8 (W)
    Ch: Rebecca H. b 1817, 6, 14
        Enoch   " 1819, 2, 15
        Amy   " 1821, 4, 12
        Ellis   " 1822, 10, 4
        Abner   " 1824, 12, 8
1822, 2, 28. Susannah m Isaac VOTAW
1826, 1, 5. Ann m Lindsey COBBS
1908, 5, 27. Lewis A., s Abner & Elvirah,
    Columbiana Co., O.; m at Salem, Lydia A.
    COOPER, dt Samuel & Sarah P., Columbiana
    Co., O. (W)
1919, 3, 20. Edward J., s Abner & Elvirah
    H.; m at Salem, Mary C. DEWEES, dt Joseph
    P. & Belinda (Hobson) BINNS, b 1884,2,11
    (W)

1805, 12, 17. Samuel & w, Rebecca, rocf Bur-
    lington MM, N. J., dtd 1805,10,7, endors-
    ed by Middleton MM, 1805,11,9

WOOLMAN, continued •

1806, 6, 17. Keziah rocf Burlington MM, dtd
         1806,5,5

1806, 7, 15. Samuel & w, Jane, & ch, Aaron
         Aaronson, George & Mary Ann, rocf Burling-
         ton MM, dtd 1806,5,5

1811, 3, 12. Aaron Aaronson gct Abington MM,
         Pa.

1812, 6, 16. Samuel & w, Jane, gct Abington
         MM, Pa.

1814, 2, 15. Samuel & w, Jane, rocf Abbington
         MM, Pa., dtd 1813,12,27

1815, 4, 11. George gct Abington MM, Pa.

1817, 2, 11. Aaron Airison rocf Frankford MM,
         Pa., dtd 1816,12,27

1817, 2, 11. Mary W. rocf Chester MM, Pa.,
         dtd 1816,11,7

1817, 6, 17. Abner & w, Martha, & ch, Susan-
         nah, Anna, Thomas B., Sarah, Mary & Mar-
         tha, rocf Abington MM, dtd 1817,4,28

1821, 5, 23. Asher & w, Maria, rocf Burlington
         MM, N. J., dtd 1821,4,2

1873, 12, 24. Rachel P. (form Stewart) con mcd
         (W)

1875, 8, 26. Rachel P. gct Upper Springfield
         MM (W)

1908, 8, 19. Lydia A. gct Upper Springfield
         MM (W)

1920, 9, 22. Mary C. Woolman (form Dewees) &
         ch, Florence Martha, Margaret Hannah, Jo-
         seph Howard, James Ezra & Jesse Hall De-
         wees, gct New Garden MM (W)

1920, 11, 24. Clara Rosella, Thomas Arthur &
         Mildred Rebecca Dewees, ch Mary Dewees
         Woolman, gct Birmingham MM, Pa. (W)

WOODRUFF
1910, 2, 23. Hollie recrq

WOODWARD
1811, 11, 12. James & w, Lettice, & ch, John &
         William, rocf Fallowfield MM, dtd 1811,8,
         12

1812, 9, 15. Cert rec for James & fam endors-
         ed to New Garden MM

1890, 7, 24. William rocf Sandy Spring MM,
         dtd 1890,5,20

WOODWORTH
1881, 12, 22. Anna recrq
1882, 2, 8. Elisha recrq
1883, 8, 16. Mary E. & Lizzie E. recrq
1885, 2, 6. George M. recrq
1886, 10, 21. Elisha & Mary dropped from mbrp
1927, 4, 20. Esther recrq

WORRELL
1808, 9, 13. Jonathan & w, Elenor, & ch, Sa-
         rah, Benjamin, John, Nathaniel, George &
         Joseph, rocf Short Creek MM, dtd 1807,3,21

1810, 12, 11. Jonathan & w, Eleanor, & ch, Sa-
         rah, Benjamin, Nathaniel, George, Joseph &
         Elizabeth, gct Short Creek MM

WRAY
1886, 1, 21. Mary Emma (form Carpenter) con
         mcd (H)

1886, 5, 20. Mary Emma (form Carpenter) gct
         Rochester MM, N. Y. (H)

WRIGHT
1779, 1, 29. Sally b (W)

----, --, --. Martha b 1788,3,13 d 1875,12,2
         (W)

----, --, --. Joseph b 1777,12,22; m Rebecca
         ----- b 1782,8,26 (W)
         Ch: Lydia   b 1801, 8, 3 d 1842, 2,15
             John   " 1803, 7, 27
             Mary Ann   " 1805, 9, 27
             Caroline   " 1808, 4, 29
             Elizabeth " 1811, 8, 28
             Hannah   " 1814, 5, 6
             Miriam   " 1817, 9, 1
             Joseph
             Hicks   " 1820, 3, 25 d 1834, 8,23
             (1834,3,23 in H)

1814, 1, 19. Martha m Isaac MORLAN

1818, 4, 23. Judith m Zimri WHINERY

1831, 4, 16. Joseph d (W)

1831, 11, 30. Elizabeth m Thomas MATHER)H)

1845, 7, 3. Alfred, s John & Elizabeth, Co-
         lumbiana Co., O.; m at house of Joshua
         Middleton, Amelia R. MIDDLETON, dt Joshua
         & Gustavius, Trumble Co., O. (H)

1858, 4, 14. Phebe, dt William & Winifred, b
         (G)

----, --, --. Wm. m Rachel -----, dt Jonathan
         & Emma, b 1897,12,5 (G)
         Ch: Dorothy
             Eileen   b 1915, 6, 7
             Jeanne
             Louise   " 1918, 7, 10

1809, 12, 12. Rebecca & ch, Lydia, John, Mary
         Ann & Caroline, rocf Chesterfield MM, N.J.
         dtd 1809,8,8

1810, 2, 13. John dis mou

1812, 6, 16. Henry rocf Chesterfield MM, N.J.
         dtd 1811,8,6

1813, 3, 16. Benjamin dis disunity

1813, 6, 15. John rst in mbrp

1815, 2, 14. John gct New Garden MM

1815, 7, 11. Esther Wright & ch, Matilda,
         William, Benjamin Townsend & Eliza Nailor
         Morgan, rocf New Garden MM, dtd 1815,6,15

1816, 5, 14. Joseph Wright & w, Esther, & ch,
         Matilda, Benjamin Townsend & Eliza Nailer
         Morgan, gct New Garden MM

1817, 5, 13. Joseph rocf Chesterfield MM,
         N. J., dtd 1817,1,7

1818, 3, 17. Charity Mankin (form Wright) dis

1818, 4, 14. Elizabeth & Hannah, dt Rebecca,
         recrq

1820, 2, 23. Sally recrq

1823, 8, 1. Henry dis mcd

1824, 10, 20. John dis mcd

1828, 7, 30. Joseph & w, Rebecca, & ch, Lydia,

WRIGHT, continued
    Elizabeth, Hannah Miriam & Joseph, rocf
    New Garden MM (H) dtd 1828,7,24
1828, 8, 20. Joseph dis jH
1828, 8, 20. Rebecca & Lydia dis jH
1829, 1, 21. Mary Ann, Caroline & Elizabeth
    dis jH
1829, 11, 25. Joseph rocf New Garden MM, dtd
    1829,10,22
1831, 8, 24. Anne Jane (form Schooley) dis
    mcd
1832, 12, 19. Martha rocf ND MM, Phila., Pa.,
    dtd 1832,11,27
1835, 7, 22. Hannah Mead (form Wright) dis
    mcd
1836, 2, 24. Hannah Mead (form Wright) dis
    mcd (H)
1837, 1, 25. Mary (form McGrew) con mcd (H)
1839, 6, 19. Caroline Mead (form Wright) con
    mou (H)
1841, 11, 24. Meriam Layman (form Wright) dis
    mcd (H)
1842, 5, 25. Miriam Layman (form Wright) dis
    mcd
1843, 2, 22. Alfred rocf Green St. MM, Phila.,
    Pa., dtd 1843,1,19 (H)
1849, 11, 22. Anna & s, Isaac N., rocf Monal-
    len MM, dtd 1849,10,18 (H)
1849, 11, 22. Julia Amelia & Anna, Jr. rocf
    Monallen MM, dtd 1849,10,18 (H)
1850, 9, 25. Sally gct Upper Springfield MM
1855, 9, 20. Lydia H. rocf Deer Creek MM, dtd
    1855,8,25 (H)
1883, 8, 16. Phebe A. recrq
1927, 6, 22. Phebe dropped from mbrp
1932, 12, 25. Jeane Louise, Dorothy Ellen &
    Rachel Edith recrq

WUNDERLIN
1923, 5, 23. Mrs. Margaret recrq

YATES
----, --, --. John b 1809,1,1; m Asenath -----
    b 1814,4,24 d 1874,11,15 (W)
    Ch: Sylvanus b 1833, 2, 7
        Robert   " 1838, 1, 18
        Hesley   " 1840, 6, 25
        Emeline   " 1844, 11, 1
        Anna Mary " 1846, 12, 30
        Clara Jane " 1855, 7, 1

1805, 12, 17. Benjamin & w, Phebe, & ch, Mary,
    Jemima & Benjamin, rocf Westland MM, dtd
    1805,10,26
1807, 1, 13. James rocf Westland MM, dtd
    1806,1,25
1807, 11, 17. James dis mcd
1810, 10, 16. Barzillai French gct New Garden
    MM, to m Mary Yates

YEAGER
1886, 2, 10. Alice, dt Adolph & Henrietta, b
    (G)

1922, 8, 16. Alice gct Clark Ave. MM, Clev.

YENGLING
1893, 9, 26. Willard Lee, s Park, b (G)

1932, 12, 25. Willard Lee recrq

YOUNG
----, --, --. Ann b 1772,10,12 d 1861,11,7 (W)
1813, 8, 25. Sarah b (W)
----, --, --. Benjamin b 1792,9,27 d 1854,8,
    23; m ----- ----- (W)
    Ch: Thomas   b 1829, 6, 21
        Amos   " 1833, 8, 12
        Jane   " 1837, 3, 7
        Tamor   " 1839, 12, 6
        Benj. Jr. " 1844, 10, 11
1843, 6, 28. Thomas, s Joseph & Ann, Columbi-
    ana Co., O., b 1801,1,31; m at Salem, Ann
    B. BARBER, dt Abraham & Drucilla, Columbi-
    ana Co., O., b 1823,12,3 d 1862,9,9 (W)
    Ch: Drusilla b 1844, 4, 19
        Joseph E. " 1845, 11, 12
        Charles   " 1848, 5, 2 d 1853, 4, 2
        David   " 1850, 12, 10
        Ann Jr.   " 1854, 11, 2
        Mary
        Elizabeth " 1857, 8, 25
        Rachel Ella
1888, 3, 28. Annie B. m Clarkson FRENCH (W)
----, --, --. Wilmer m Mildred M. BINNS, dt
    Arthur H. & Tacie M., b 1901,4,14 (W)
    Ch: Daniel
        Test   b 1923, 8, 21
        Margaret
        Sylvia   " 1924, 12, 26

1822, 6, 19. Thomas rocf Carmel MM, dtd 1822,
    6,15
1834, 5, 21. Thomas gct Upper Springfield MM
1843, 5, 24. Thomas rocf Upper Springfield MM
    dtd 1843,4,22
1850, 2, 20. Benjamin & ch, Thomas, Amos,
    Jane, Tamer & Benjamin, rocf Sandy Spring
    MM, dtd 1849,11,23
1851, 2, 19. Ann rocf Upper Springfield MM,
    dtd 1851,1,25
1851, 2, 19. Sarah rocf Upper Springfield MM,
    dtd 1851,1,25
1862, 12, 24. Drusilla Cook (form Young) dis
    mcd (W)
1862, 12, 25. Jessee, Thomas, Benjamin, Tamer
    & James dis joining separatists (W) of
    1854
1862, 12, 25. Thomas, Joseph, Drusilla, David
    & Anna dis joining separatists (W) of 1854
1862, 12, 25. Elizabeth dis joining separa-
    tists (W) of 1854
1864, 11, 23. Thomas dis mcd (W)
1870, 5, 25. Sarah dis joining separatists of
    1854 (W)
1870, 8, 24. Joseph E., David, Anna & Mary
    Elizabeth, ch Thomas, gct Hickory Grove MM,

YOUNG, continued
   Ia. (W)
1872, 3, 20. Amos dis mcd (W)
1872, 12, 25. Benjamin dis mcd (W)
1872, 12, 25. Thomas, Jr. dis joining separa-
      tists of 1854 (W)
1873, 9, 24. Tamer Stewart (form Young) dis
      mcd (W)
1873, 11, 19. Jane Estabrook (form Young) dis
      mcd (W)
1878, 1, 23. Annie rocf Hickory Grove MM,
      Ia., dtd 1868,1,5 (W)
1928, 1, 25. Mildred Binns con mcd (W)
1929, 12, 18. William J. Blackburn, Jr. gct
      Springville MM, Ia., to m Ann Lorena Young
      (W)
1931, 10, 21. Mildred Binns & ch, Daniel Test,
      Margaret Sylvia & William Robert, gct West-
      town MM, Pa. (W)

YOUNGER
----, --, --. Aurelius, s Benjamin & Amanda,
      b -----,8,31 d 1929,4,27 (G)

      *   *   *   *   *   *   *

ALLEN
----, --, --. L. Ebbert, s Ebenezer & Sarah
      J., b 1881,12,8; m Carrie OYSTER, dt Sam-
      uel & Sarah J. (G)
      Ch: Mary Ruth b 1913, 11, 2
          Ray   " 1901, 5, 16
          Donald Wade

ENGLAND
1820, 3, 29. Matilda m Wm. SCHOOLEY
1837, 4, 26. Josiah, s Joseph & Hannah, Colum-
      biana Co., O.; m at Salem, Sarah BARBER,
      dt Abraham & Drusilla, Columbiana Co., O.

FARQUHAR
1848, 8, 24. Elizabeth rocf Middleton MM, Pa.,
      dtd 1847,10,8 (H)
1858, 9, 23. Elizabeth W. gct Middletown MM,
      Pa. (H)

FAWCETT
1843, 3, 29. Lydia m Charles L. COOK
1846, 4, 29. Lydia m Hutchen SATTERTHWAIT

GREWELL
1835, 1, 2. Phebe F. [Gruwell] b (W)

HALDERMAN
1855, 12, 23. Richard N. b (W)

INGRAM
1839, 10, 23. Thomas C. Pound gct New Garden
      MM, to m Susan Ingram (H)
1842, 11, 23. Joseph rocf New Garden MM, to m
      Martha Kennett (H)
1843, 6, 21. Joseph rocf New Garden MM, dtd

1928, 8, 15. Aurelius recrq

ZAME
1932, 6, 29. Mrs. Elma dropped from mbrp

ZELLEY
1884, 3, 26. Joseph Howard, s Enoch S. &
      Sarah B. (Ashead), Burlington Co., N.J.,
      b 1857,11,8; m at Salem, Edith FAWCETT,
      dt Richard B. & Edith M. (Test), b 1852,
      1,14 (W)
1887, 4, 5. Sarah Edith b (W)

1886, 4, 21. Joseph Howard rocf Eavesham MM,
      N. J., dtd 1886,4,10 (W)

ZOLLARS
1866, 11, 22. Elizabeth gct Spring Creek MM,
      Ia.

      *   *   *   *   *   *   *

1843,3,25 (H)

LAMBORN
1840, 12, 23. Joseph Ball gct New Garden MM,
      to m Elizabeth [Lamburn] (H)

LITTY
----, --, --. Herman P., s Frederick & Eliza-
      beth, b 1861,12,18; m Cordelia R. FINEY,
      dt Robert & Catharine, b 1862,1,11 (G)
      Ch: John   b 1895, 4, 1
          Jean   " 1901, 9, 6
          Myra E.   " 1892, .3, 17

MILLER
----, --, --. Catherine b 1802,12,25 d 1825,
      9,6(W)
----, --, --. Susannah H. b 1803,7,11 d 1865,
      2,2 (W)
----, --, --. Catherine b 1825,5,15 d 1825,6,
      24 (W)
1828, 8, 3. Samuel H. b (W)
1852, 9, 24. Deborah D. Hall, dt Mary H. Mil-
      ler, b (W)

MORRIS
1793, 12, 21. Abraham b (W)

OLIPHANT
1849, 9, 20. Phebe L., dt Wm. H. & Sina W.,
      b (W)

SCHOOLEY
----, --, --. John b 1780,10,11 d 1866,1,28;
      m Phebe ----- d 1870,2,22 (W)
      Ch: Ann   b 1808, 2, 20
          Reuben " 1809, 9, 27

SCHOOLEY, continued
      Ch: Henry B.   b 1812, 1, 11
          Elisha Jr. " 1814, 11, 29
1812, 9, 30. Deborah m Joseph STRATTON
----, --, --. Israel b 1791,1,16 bur 1826,3,26;
      m Sarah ----- (W)
      Ch: James   b 1816, 12, 18
          Lydia   " 1818, 2, 12 d 1818, 5, 3
            bur Salem
          Rachel   " 1819, 10, 15
          Elisha   " 1821, 12, 24
          Dilworth   " 1823, 10, 20
          Emily   " 1825, 12, 7

SMART
1855, 10, 24. Ruth rocf Flushing MM, dtd 1855,
      8,23 (W)

SHINN
1816, 12, 25. Thomas, s Caleb & Mary, Columbi-
      ana Co., O.; m at Salem, Sarah SEBRELL, dt
      Joseph & Rebecca, Columbiana Co., O.
1817, 2, 19. Mary m Joseph SEBRELL

STANLEY
1846, 12, 2. Eli, s James & Elizabeth, b

TEST
1850, 6, 26. Zaccheus Jr. & Drusilla (W)
      Ch: Margaret   b 1852, 11, 25 d 1860, 2, 8
          Benjamin A." 1855, 2, 14
          Wm.   " 1857, 4, 17
          Emily   " 1859, 5, 12
          Lemuel   " 1863, 1, 27

VOTAW
1929, 4, 24. Roscoe, Melissa, Virgil, War-
      ren, Wanda, Minnie, Martha and Lawrence
      Jr. recrq

ARNOLD
1866, 6, 14. Rachel recrq

BROWN
1888, 4, 11. Atlantic dis disunity

CREW
1880, 11, 10. Amy B. (late Doudna) dis mou

DOUDNA
1873, 7, 16. James & w, Louisa, & ch, Edwin,
    Amy & Thomas Exum, Linn, Ia., acknowledged
    mbr of this mtg
1874, 11, 11. Joseph & w, Mary V., rst
1878, 5, 15. Edwin J. dis disunity
1880, 11, 10. Amy B. Crew (late Doudna) dis mou
1883, 12, 12. Thomas E. dis disunity

FAWCETT
1867, 12, 11. Mary J. rmt Daniel Koll

HALL
1881, 6, 16. John G. rocf Hector MM, N. Y.
1882, 3, 15. John G. gct Hector MM, N. Y.

HALLOCK
1880, 10, 13. Sarah E. rocf Hector MM, N. Y.,
    dtd 1880,9,8
1882, 9, 13. Sarah E. [Halleck] gct Hector MM

HAMPTON
1873, 7, 16. Sarah, Linn, Iowa, acknowledged
    mbr of this mtg
1873, 7, 16. Wm. & w, Charity, & ch, Sarah
    G., Emlen, Daniel C., Lydia Ann, Mary
    Eliza, Lewis Pusey, John C., Amy R., Lou-
    isa & Zachariah, Linn, Ia., acknowledged
    mbr of this mtg
1880, 8, 18. Lydia A. gct Scipio MM, N. Y.

HOLLOWAY
1884, 4, 29. Elisha J. d (an elder)

1870, 8, 10. Elisha J. & w, Lydia S., attach-
    ed to this mtg by the General Mtg

HUSSEY
1881, 3, 16. Samuel B. & w, Rachel W., &
    minor ch, Edith L. & Charlotte M., rocf
    Hector MM, dtd 1881,9,2
1883. 4, 11. Samuel B. & w & ch gct Scipio MM

KITE
1865, 12, 14. John C. & w, Mary, rocf Fallsing-
    ton General Mtg, dtd 1865,12,6
1865, 12, 24. Mary rocf Fallsington General
    Mtg, dtd 1865,12,6

KOLL
1867, 12, 11. Daniel rmt Mary J. Fawcett
1871, 11, 15. Charles dis disunity
1871, 11, 15. Wm. dis disunity

SEARS
1877, 2, 14. Jane H. rocf Falls MM, dtd 1877,
    1,31

SIMONSON
1871, 11, 15. Jacob Severn recrq
1872, 2, 14. Jacob Severn rmt Knuedsine Tor-
    son
1883, 4, 11. Jacob S. dis disunity

TOLBOTT
1876, 11, 15. Joseph & w, Margaret, recrq

TORSON
1871, 11, 15. Knud Sina recrq
1872, 2, 14. Knuedsine rmt Jacob Severn Simon-
    son

VERNON
1874, 8, 12. Joseph recrq

NEW GARDEN MONTHLY MEETING

New Garden Monthly Meeting, located in Columbiana County, Ohio, was established by Salem Quarterly Meeting 10th Mo. 13, 1808. It was composed of New Garden and Sandy Springs Preparative Meetings. This meeting suffered from both the Hicksite and Wilburite separations. On 12th Mo. 26, 1884, the name was changed from New Garden to Winona Monthly Meeting. (The Conservative Meeting still bears the name of New Garden).

Among charter members were McBride, Reeder, Batton, Bailey, Galbreath, Davis, Harris, Votaw, Griffith, Pettit, Burson, Crew, and Winder.

RECORDS

ALLABACK
1887, 12, 21. Thornton & John [Alaback] recrq
    (G)
1889, 6, 19. John dropped from mbrp (G)
1889, 6, 19. Thornton & w, Ida, dropped from
    mbrp (G)

ALLEN
----, --, --. Christopher Sr., s Richard &
    Martha, b 1804,4,13; m Amelia BENNETT
    Ch: Christopher
                   b 1829, 9, 25
    Christopher m 2nd Abigail STRATTON, dt
    Michael & Rhoda, b 1807,2,17 d 1876,12,18
    Ch: Mary   b 1846, 1, 14

1818, 3, 19. Hannah rst on consent of West-
    land MM
1853, 5, 26. Christopher rocf Sandy Spring
    MM, O., dtd 1853,4,22
1853, 9, 22. Christopher & ch, Elizabeth B.,
    Ebinazar & Mary, rocf Sandy Spring MM, O.,
    dtd 1853,8,26
1853, 11, 24. Christopher gct Salem MM, to m
    Abigail Rood
1854, 3, 23. Abigail rocf Salem MM, dtd
    1854,3,22
1859, 9, 22. Amelia recrq
1862, 4, 24. Christopher Jr. con mcd
1861, 10, 24. Elizabeth B. rmt Geo. L. Brant-
    ingham
1861, 11, 21. Elizabeth rmt Nathan Whinery
1868, 6, 25. Ebenezar dis mcd
1885, 1, 21. Herbert recrq (G)
1887, 12, 21. Ebenezer & Sarah Jane recrq (G)
1888, 7, 26. Mary Stevenson (form Allen) con
    mcd
1893, 3, 22. Ebenezer & w, Jennie, gct Salem
    MM (G)

ANGUS
1841, 5, 20. Mary Ann (form Wickersham) dis
    mcd & jH
1845, 7, 24. Mary Ann (form Wickersham) con
    mcd (H)
ANTRIM   [MM
1818, 7, 16. John prc of clearness from Salem
1818, 8, 13. John rmt Hannah Davis (wd with ch)
1818, 11, 26. Hannah gct Salem MM

ARMSTRONG   [MM, dtd 1811,10,10
1811, 11, 14. James & w, Mary, rocf Middleton
1812, 8, 13. James prc of clearness from
    Middleton MM, to m Deborah Craig   [ch
1812, 10, 15. James rmt Deborah Craig (wd with
1817, 6, 19. John & fam gct Middleton MM
1818, 9, 24. Nathan Hole gct Middleton MM, to
    m Sarah Armstrong
ARNOLD
1820, 12, 21. Rachel dis mou
1831, 12, 22. Rachel rst at Sandy Spring MM,

O. on consent of this mtg
1865, 10, 26. Lydia Ann rocf Salem MM, dtd
    1865,9,20
1865, 12, 21. Lydia Ann rmt Jephtha Fawcett

ASHTON
1892, 1, 22. Wm. L. m Dorothy H. STRATTON

1873, 1, 23. Albert M. Cope gct Middleton
    MM, to m Phebe Y. Ashton
1892, 4, 21. Dorothy S. & s, Geo. W. Stratton
    gct Flushing MM

BAILEY
----, --, --. Jehu, s Edmund & Margaret, b
    1821,3,3 d 1903,4,18 bur Winona, O.; m
    Martha STEER
    Ch: Ruth   b 1847, 12, 16 d 1907, 2,13
        bur Winona, O.
1879, 10, 24. James E. m Sarah COPPOCK
----, --, --. James, s Jehu & Martha (Steer),
    b 1855,4,19 d 1914,9,17 bur Winona; m Sa-
    rah C. COPPOCK, dt Joshua & Jane (Hoyle),
    b 1853,11,12
    Ch: Edmund J. b 1882, 11, 28
1903, 8, 10. Rebecca B., w Oliver, dt Wilson
    J. & Mary C. (Hall) Steer, b
----, --, --. Edmund J., s James E. & Sara C.,
    b 1882,11,28; m Lydia CLENDENON, dt Ste-
    phen & Elizabeth (Branson), b 1878,8,20
    Ch: Howard Ed-
        mund   b 1913, 12, 7
1922, 12, 26. Oliver B. m Rebecca B. STEER

1816, 4, 18. Yarnell, minor s Joseph, gct
    Salem MM
1820, 12, 21. Yarnel rocf Salem MM, dtd 1820,
    10,25
1822, 7, 25. Thomas Galbreath gct Bradford MM
    Pa., to m Ann Bailey
1822, 12, 26. Jesse gct Salem MM
1825, 4, 21. Randal [Baley], minor, gct
    Middleton MM
1826, 10, 26. Yarnell gct Birmingham MM
1826, 10, 26. Pennock gct Birmingham MM
1828, 1, 24. Ezra rmt Elizabeth Bye
1828, 2, 21. Elizabeth gct Short Creek MM, O.
1828, 7, 24. Joseph & Elizabeth dis jH
1829, 2, 26. Randal rocf Middleton MM, dtd
    1829,2,12 (H)
1829, 4, 23. Hoopes dis jH
1829, 5, 21. Randel rmt Sarah Ann Beck (H)
1830, 7, 22. Hannah dis jH
1830, 11, 25. Hoops rmt Ann B. Paxson (H)
1837, 6, 22. Elizabeth gct Salem MM (H)
1837, 6, 22. Hannah, Rachel & Elizabeth Jr.
    gct Salem MM (H)
1837, 8, 24. Ann & two ch gct Salem MM (H)
1840, 3, 26. Rachel dis jH
1840, 3, 26. Elizabeth dis jH
1842, 7, 21. Mary Ann (form Kennet) con mou
    (H)
1842, 10, 20. Mary Ann gct Salem MM (H)

BAILEY, continued
1880, 12, 23. James E. rocf Somerset MM, dtd
   1880,11,25
1911, 7, 20. Edmund J. con mcd
1911, 9, 14. Lydia C. rst on consent of Coal
   Creek MM, Ia.
1924, 2, 21. Rebecca Steer gct Stillwater MM,
   O.

BAKER
1889, 1, 23. Mattie recrq (G)

BALL
1841, 1, 21. Joseph rmt Elizabeth Lamborn (H)
1841, 4, 22. Elizabeth L. gct Salem MM (H)

BARBER
----, --, --. Samuel, s Jacob & Mary Ann, b
   1826,3,30; m Ann TEST, dt Isaac B. & Mar-
   garet, b 1828,7,3 d 1859,7,8
   Ch: Hartwell   b 1851, 11, 22
       Isaac E.   " 1856, 9, 16
   Samuel m 2nd Elizabeth HALL d 1867,7,4
   Ch: Martha
       Ellen   b 1861, 3, 19
       Anna Mary " 1863, 4, 1
       Elizabeth " 1865, 5, 9
   Samuel m 3rd Angeline WHINERY, dt Joseph
   & Martha, b 1830,7,4 d 1873,4,26
   Ch: Joseph W. b 1870, 3, 31[dtd 1814,12,13
1814, 12, 15. Isaac prc of clearness from Salem
1815, 1, 19. Isaac rmt Alice Shore
1815, 2, 16. Alice gct Salem MM
1828, 5, 22. Isaac recrq (H)
1828, 7, 24. Isaac gct Salem MM (H)
1847, 8, 26. Sarah (form Randels) dis mcd
1850, 1, 24. Ann L. (form Test) con mcd
1850, 6, 20. Ann L. gct Salem MM
1859, 12, 22. Samuel & ch, Heartwell & Isaac
   Elwood, recrq
1860, 5, 24. Samuel gct Stillwater MM, O., to
   m Elizabeth Hall
1860, 11, 22. Elizabeth rocf Stillwater MM,
   O., dtd 1860,10,27
1868, 12, 24. Samuel rmt Angeline Whinery
1869, 3, 25. Hulda Jane (form Crew) dis mcd
1875, 10, 20. Samuel & ch, Martha E., Annie
   Mary & Elizabeth C., recrq (G)
1876, 6, 22. Samuel dis jG
1876, 10, 25. Samuel & ch, Martha E., Anna
   Mary & Elizabeth E., gct Adrian MM, Mich.
   (G)
1887, 2, 24. Isaac dis mcd
1887, 3, 24. Martha Ellen, Anna Mary &
   Elizabeth dis jG
1887, 7, 21. Hartwell dis jG

BARKER
----, --, --. Luther, s Ezra & Mary Ellen, b
   1871,10,5; m Martha Emma LAMBORN, dt
   Lemuel T. & Nancy C., b 1870,12,11 d 1900,
   12,24
   Ch: Lawrence

   LaRue   b 1896, 2, 14
   Ch: Larwell
       Lamborn   " 1898, 9, 7 d 1899, 7,23
       bur Winona, O.

1894, 5, 24. Luther rmt Emma Lamborn
1917, 5, 24. LaRue gct Salem MM
1917, 5, 24. M. Luther gct Salem MM

BARRETT
1815, 1, 19. Rachel, minor in care of Nathan
   & Mary Walton, rocf Westland MM, dtd 1814,
   12,1
1818, 4, 16. Rachel Tulloss (form Barret) rpd
   mcd (dis 1818,6,18)

BASHAW
1874, 9, 24. Lucretia P. (form Pettit) dis
   mcd & jas

BASSETT
1887, 12, 21. Phebe recrq (G)

BATTIN
1809, 1, 19. Miriam [Batten] & ch, Espy, Ann
   & Catherine, recrq
1809, 11, 16. Jonathan [Batten] rmt Priscilla
   Reeder
1814, 7, 14. John & w, Ann, & ch, Eli, Robert,
   Elizabeth, Lydia, John, Fanny, David, Ann,
   Joshua & Ezra, rocf Salem MM, dtd 1814,5,
   17
1815, 2, 16. Elizabeth rmt James McBride
1815, 8, 17. Eli gct Short Creek MM, O.
1816, 4, 18. Eli rmt Phebe Pennock
1816, 5, 16. Phebe gct Short Creek MM, O.
1818, 11, 26. Cert rec for Phebe & dt, Jane,
   from Short Creek MM, O., dtd 1818,8,18,
   endorsed to Middleton MM
1819, 7, 22. John Jr. gct Short Creek MM, O.
1820, 12, 21. Lydia rmt Wm. Reeder
1821, 3, 22. Margaret (form Walton) dis mcd
1821, 3, 22. James dis mcd
1825, 12, 22. Richard [Batten] rocf Sandy
   Spring MM, dtd 1825,11,21
1827, 7, 26. Richard gct Silver Creek MM,
   Ind.
1828, 6, 26. Fanny recrq (H)
1828, 8, 21. John & w, Ann, & s, Ezra, rocf
   Sandy Spring MM, O. (H)
1828, 8, 21. Ann Jr. recrq (H)
1828, 8, 21. Joshua recrq (H)
1828, 11, 20. Ann Jr. gct Concord MM (H)
1829, 9, 24. Ann Jr. rocf Concord MM, dtd
   1829,8,19 (H)
1831, 8, 25. Fanny rmt Samuel Tripp (H)
1840, 4, 23. Robert & w, Abigail, & five ch
   gct Salem MM (H)

BAUGHMAN
1888, 2, 22. Emanuel & Florence recrq (G)
1889, 6, 19. Emanuel & w, Emma, dropped from
   mbrp (G)

BAXTER
1815, 10, 19. Deborah rocf Saddsbury MM, Pa.,
    dtd 1815,7,4
1821, 5, 24. Deborah gct Sandy Spring MM

BEASON
1820, 4, 20. Sarah & ch, Henry, Rachel, Char-
    ity, Elisha, Jesse, Edward & John, rocf
    Short Creek MM, O., dtd 1819,11,23
1824, 7, 24. Rachel Harbough (form Beason)
    dis mou
1825, 6, 23. Henry com for military exercise;
    Carmel MM to treat with him; dis 1825,12,22

BECK
----, --, --. Prexton Sr. b 1756,3,4 d 1844,5,3
----, --, --. Sarah b 1760,12,24 d 1835,1,24
----, --, --. Preston b 1796,6,5 d 1873,9,13;
    m Mary ----- b 1795,7,16 d 1837,6,25
    Ch: Ann   b 1818, 11, 18
        Isaac   " 1820, 2, 11
        Ruth   " 1821, 11, 5
        John   " 1823, 11, 7 d 1850,10,20
        Nathan   " 1825, 10, 30
        Aaron   " 1828, 1, 18
        Mariah   " 1830, 3, 22
        Preston   " 1832, 7, 23 d 1855, 8, 6
        Zebulon   " 1836, 5, 14 " 1836, 5,14
----, --, --. Sarah b 1806,5,19 d 1875,1,29
----, --, --. John b 1801,5,12; m Adah -----
    b 1800,12,24
    Ch: Avine   b 1825, 5, 23
        Alfred H. " 1827, 4, 7
        Sarah   " 1828, 5, 24
        Luiza   " 1830, 4, 11
        William   " 1833, 3, 22
        Vanaga   " 1837, 2, 26
        Sylvester " 1841, 10, 11

1810, 6, 15. Paul con mou
1813, 4, 15. Rachel Ferrel (form Beck) dis
    mcd
1817, 2, 13. Mary Speck (form Beck) dis mcd
1818, 3, 19. Preston Jr. rmt Mary Votaw
1823, 4, 24. Sarah Hinchman (form Beck) con
    mcd
1823, 7, 2. John con mcd
1823, 8, 21. Richard dis mcd
1824, 2, 26. Paul dis mou
1824, 6, 24. Adah rocf Sandy Spring MM, O.,
    dtd 1824,4,23
1826, 8, 24. Jamima Davison (form Beck) dis
    mou
1828, 12, 25. Ruth dis jH
1829, 1, 22. Edward dis jH
1829, 3, 26. Elizabeth & Sarah Jr. dis jH
1829, 5, 21. Sarah Ann rmt Randel Bailey (H)
1833, 9, 26. Phebe B. Whinery (form Beck)
    con mcd (H)
1834, 9, 25. Phebe Whinery (form Beck) dis
    mou
1839, 9, 26. Esther Ruth Berry (form Beck)
    con mcd (H)
1841, 4, 22. Esther Berry (form Beck) dis mcd

1844, 8, 22. Preston dis mcd
1844, 8, 22. Sarah (form Sharp) dis mcd
1846, 8, 20. Sarah Righter (form Beck) dis
    mcd
1849, 1, 25. Albert dis mcd
1849, 3, 22. Elizabeth (form Randels) dis
    mcd
1849, 12, 20. John & w, Adah, & ch, Wm. I.,
    Venajah H. & Sylvester, gct Mississinewa
    MM, Ind.
1849, 12, 20. Luiza gct Mississinewa MM, Ind.
1850, 2, 21. Ervine P. dis mcd
1853, 10, 20. Mariah rmt Eli J. Walker
1856, 1, 24. Nathan dis mcd
1856, 3, 20. Isaac dis mcd
1865, 1, 26. Ann dis jG in 1854
1865, 1, 26. Ruth dis jG in 1854
1865, 3, 23. Aaron dis jG
1871, 10, 26. Preston rstrq
1871, 10, 26. Sarah rstrq

BEEDY
1826, 4, 20. Abraham rocf Upper Springfield
    MM, O., dtd 1826,3,26
1826, 11, 23. Abraham rmt Hannah Ward
1828, 11, 20. Hannah dis jH
1829, 1, 22. Abraham dis jH
1832, 3, 22. Abraham & fam gct Marlborough MM
    (H)

BENEDICT
1866, 3, 22. Penelope dis jG

BENNETT
1832, 6, 21. James & w, Hannah, rocf Kennett
    MM, Pa., dtd 1832,3,6 (H)
1832, 6, 21. Lea rocf Birmingham MM, dtd
    1832,3,3 (H)
1832, 6, 21. Rebecca rocf Kennett MM, Pa.,
    dtd 1832,3,6
1832, 6, 21. Hannah rocf Kennett MM, Pa.,
    dtd 1832,3,6 (H)
1835, 5, 21. Hannah J. Yates (form Bennett)
    dis mcd (H)
1835, 6, 25. Lea rmt Mary F. Dugdale (H)
1836, 3, 25. Lee & w, Mary, gct Greenplain MM
1837, 10, 26. Mary (form Dugdale) rpd mou
1839, 6, 20. Rebecca Burson (form Bennett)
    con mcd (H)
1841, 4, 22. Mary I. & ch, Elmina, & Ann
    Elisa, rocf Green Plain MM, dtd 1841,3,17
    (H)
1841, 5, 20. Mary (form Dugdale) dis mcd in
    Hicksite mtg
1843, 2, 23. Mary I. & two ch gct Green Plain
    MM (H)

BENNETT, continued
1848, 4, 23. Phebe (form Hoopes) dis mcd
1892, 5, 25. Lee S. & w, Isaletta, & ch,
     Lauretta D. & Samuel H., recrq (G)
1892, 7, 20. Phebe gct Damascus MM (G)
1897, 5, 19. Lee & w, Isaletta, & ch, Retta,
     Sammie & Paul, relrq (G)

BENTLEY
1828, 8, 21. Joseph E. & w, Anna, & ch, Gran-
     ville S., Franklin H., Maria, Thomas M.,
     Hannah B. & Deborah R., rocf Sandy Spring
     MM (H)
1839, 4, 25. Maria relrq (H)
1844, 10, 24. Hannah B. dis jas (H)
1844, 10, 24. Deborah B. dis jas (H)

BERRY
1839, 9, 26. Esther Ruth (form Beck) con mou
     (H)
1839, 10, 24. Esther Ruth gct Concord MM (H)
1841, 4, 22. Esther (form Beck) dis mcd

BIDDLE
1832, 11, 22. Rachel (form Votaw) dis mou

BINFORD
1851, 10, 23. Thomas Johnson gct Upper Spring-
     field MM, O., to m Martha Binford
1865, 5, 25. Elizabeth dis jG

BINNS
----, --, --. David m Lizzie A. SIDWELL, dt
     Israel & Rachel, b 1852,9,19
     Ch: Rachel S. b 1882, 2, 17
         Mary E.   " 1883, 1, 12
----, --, --. Edward T., s Joseph & Belinda,
     b 1875,7,13; m Esther L. BRACKEN b 1876,6,
     20
     Ch: Arthur W. M.
                  b 1896, 3, 22
         Clarence H. " 1898, 5, 16
         Joseph H.   " 1905, 6, 28
1903, 12, 25. Rachel S. m Ogden J. BRACKEN
----, --, --. John, s Joseph & Belinda (Hob-
     son), b 1881,6,2 d 1927,1,21 bur Winona;
     m Mary E. COPE, dt Albert & Phebe (Ashton)
     b 1881,12,19 d 1925,2,22
     Ch: Alice Re-
         becca   b 1906, 1, 16
         Esther
         Mary   " 1913, 3, 24
         Albert John" 1916, 6, 29
1926, 3, 26. Alice R. m Jesse K. LIVEZEY

1880, 4, 22. Walter Edgerton gct Short Creek
     MM, O., to m Mary H. Binns
1903, 10, 22. Lizzie, Rachel S. & Mary E.,
     rocf Short Creek MM, O., dtd 1903,10,20
1905, 6, 22. Edward T. & w, Esther L., & ch,
     Arthur W. M. & Clarence H., rocf Spring-
     ville MM, Ia., dtd 1905,6,17
1905, 7, 20. John A. rocf Short Creek MM, O.,

dtd 1905,6,20
1905, 7, 20. Mary, w John, rocf Salem MM, O.,
     dtd 1905,6,21
1907, 1, 24. Edward T. & w, Esther S., & ch,
     Arthur W. M., Clarence H. & Joseph H.,
     gct Philadelphia MM, Pa.
1908, 8, 20. John A. & dt, Edith Margaret,
     gct Short Creek MM, O.
1908, 9, 7. Mary E. Smith (form Binns) dis
     mcd & jas
1911, 3, 23. Lizzie A. gct Short Creek MM, O.
1921, 8, 25. John A. & w, Mary E., & ch,
     Alice Rebecca, Esther Mary & Albert John,
     rocf Salem MM

BLACKBURN
1819, 7, 22. Joseph Thomas gct Salem MM, to
     m Temperance Blackburn
1843, 4, 20. Thomas Whinery gct Springfield
     MM, O., to m Mary Blackburn
1846, 3, 26. Lewis W. Hoopes gct Upper
     Springfield MM, O., to m Sarah Ann Black-
     burn
1854, 3, 23. Robert Crew gct Upper Spring-
     field MM, O., to m Margaret Blackburn
1876, 9, 2-. Elizabeth B. (form Galbreath)
     con mcd (G)
1877, 8, 22. Elizabeth B. gct East Goshen MM
     (G)
1882, 4, 19. Elizabeth rocf East Goshen MM,
     dtd 1882,3,18 (G)
1922, 9, 21. Howard John Oliphant gct Salem
     MM, to m Alice Marie Blackburn

BLACKLEDGE
----, --, --. Joseph b 1776,1,13; m Rachel
     ----- b 1787,1,1
     Ch: Thomas G. b 1809, 1, 23
         Martha   " 1810, 2, 27 d 1819, 6,15
         Hiram   " 1811, 10, 9
         Mary   " 1813, 11, 24
         Charles D. " 1815, 11, 18
         Hannah   " 1818, 1, 16
         Ann W.   " 1819, 9, 6
         Joseph   " 1821, 6, 20
         Jason R. " 1824, 7, 19

1809, 7, 13. Joseph [Blacklidge] & w, Rachel,
     & s, Thomas, rocf Middleton MM, dtd 1809,
     5,13
1811, 6, 13. Robert & w, Ruth, & ch, Benja-
     min & Isaac, rocf New Garden MM, Pa., dtd
     1811,5,9
1811, 6, 13. David rocf New Garden MM, Pa.,
     dtd 1811,5,9
1811, 6, 13. Margaret rocf New Garden MM, Pa.
     dtd 1811,5,9
1815, 3, 16. David gc
1815, 4, 13. Margaret Yeats (form Blackledge)
     dis mcd
1816, 1, 18. Joseph & w, Rachel, & ch, Thom-
     as, Martha, Hiram & Mary, rocf Marl-
     borough MM, dtd 1815,9,13

BLACKLEDGE, continued
1824, 4, 22. Isaac dis mcd
1827, 10, 25. Mary rocf ND MM, dtd 1827,8,28
1830, 6, 24. Mary gct Salem MM
1833, 11, 21. Thomas G. gct Providence MM
1837, 9, 21. Hannah gct White River MM, Ind.
1837, 9, 21. Ann W. gct White River MM, Ind.
1837, 9, 21. Mary gct White River MM, Ind.
1837, 10, 26. Joseph & fam gct White River MM, Ind.
1837, 10, 26. Charles gct White River MM, Ind.
1838, 7, 26. Hiram dis mou

BLYTHE
1893, 4, 19. Frank & Charlie recrq (G)
1919, 12, 24. Lucy recrq (G)
1925, 8, 19. Lucy relrq (G)

BONER
1923, 2, 21. Magdalena recrq (G)

BOON
1828, 6, 26. Isaac & w, Esther, & ch, Thomas, Chalkley, James & Phebe Jane, rocf Monallin MM, dtd 1827,11,21 (H)
1828, 7, 24. Isaac & w, Esther, & ch, Thomas Chalkley, James & Phebe Jane, gct Salem MM (H)

BORTON
1900, 12, 19. Daniel & w, Emma C., & s, Daniel D., recrq (G)
1905, 7, 19. David & w, Emma C., & s, Daniel Davis, gct Alliance MM (G)

BOULTON
1824, 12, 23. Sarah rocf Salem MM, dtd 1824, 11,24
1828, 6, 26. Sarah [Bolton] gct Upper Springfield MM, O.
1831, 1, 20. Sarah (form Brown) con mcd
1842, 11, 24. Joseph rst at Salem MM on consent of this mtg
1851, 8, 21. Joseph [Boalton] & w, Sarah, gct Wabash MM, Ind.

BOWERS
1888, 7, 26. Clara M. (form Raley) dis mcd

BOWMAN
1812, 11, 19. Isaac & w, Ann, & ch, Joseph & Ann, rocf Short Creek MM, O., dtd 1812, 6,23
1862, 3, 20. Thomas rmt Ann Test
1862, 5, 22. Ann gct Plymouth MM
1885, 1, 21. Joshua Frank & Sarah C. recrq (G)
1885, 9, 23. Susannah recrq (G)
1886, 2, 24. Walter rocf Salem MM (G)
1888, 5, 24. Ann rocf Plymouth MM
1893, 1, 25. Walter dropped from mbrp (G)

BRACKIN
1903, 12, 25. Ogden J. [Bracken] m Rachel S.
BINNS
1906, 6, 10. Edith Margaret, dt Ogden J. & Rachel S., b

1908, 9, 7. Rachel S. & dt, Edith Margaret, gct Short Creek MM, O.

BRADWAY
----, --, --. Wm. F., s James C. & Mary Jane (Fogg), b 1859,11,11; m Rachel S. DEAN, dt Jonathan & Elizabeth (Brantingham), b 1854,3,13
    Ch: Elizabeth b 1884, 6, 7
        Anna   " 1886, 2, 8
----, --, --. James W., s Jas. C. & Mary J., b 1863,5,1; m Annie E. MEGRAIL, dt Alfred & Rebecca, b 1862,10,6 d 1912,12,26
    Ch: Herman W. b 1887, 11, 14
1905, 9, 15. Elizabeth m Alfred W. PATTEN

1882, 7, 20. Wm. recrq
1883, 1, 25. Wm. F. rmt Rachel S. Dean
1883, 5, 24. James L. W., s Mary Jane Gamble, rocf Salem MM, dtd 1883,4,25
1886, 2, 25. James W. rmt Annie A. McGrail
1912, 12, 26. James & w, Amy, gct Pasadena MM, Calif.
1913, 7, 24. Herman W. con mcd
1914, 3, 26. Anna rmt Lindley Ellis STeer
1917, 6, 21. Herman D. gct Pasadena MM, Calif.

BRANIN
1828, 5, 22. Ezra & w, Rachel, & ch, Abigail, Hannah, Susanna, Mahlon, Nathaniel & Rachel, recrq (H)
1828, 7, 24. Ezra [Brannin] & w, Rachel, & ch, Abigail, Hannah, Susanna, Mahlon, Nathaniel & Rachel, gct Salem MM (H)

BRANSON
1869, 9, 24. Joseph H. m Ruthanna Stratton

1870, 2, 24. Ruthanna S. gct Flushing MM, O.

BRANTINGHAM
----, --, --. Joseph, s Geo. & Phebe, b 1807, 1,27 d 1852,9,23 bur Stephenson Co., Ill.; m Lydia WHINERY, dt Robert & Phebe, b 1804,8,13 d 1841,10,19
    Ch: Rachel   b 1827, 10, 22 d 1901, 1,25 bur Winona, O.
        William   b 1829, 1, 6
        Alfred   " 1830, 8, 24 d 1904, 8,11 bur Winona, O.
        Elizabeth b 1833, 9, 27 d 1916, 4, 6 bur Winona, O.
        Cyrus   b 1836, 1, 27 d 1906, 7,30 bur Winona, O.
        George
        Lydia (?) b 1841, 8, 15
    Joseph m 2nd Anna M. STRATTON, dt Joseph &

BRANTINGHAM, continued

    Sara, b 1817,9,1 d 1897,1,28 bur Winona,
    O.
       Ch: Lydia   b 1848, 4, 22
           Sina   " 1850,   7, 24 d 1905,12, 9
           bur Toledo, O.
----, --, --. George m Hannah ----- d 1842,8,7
       Ch: Rebecca   b 1833, 3, 21
           James   " 1836, 4, 15
           Edward   " 1838, 2, 6
           Robert S.   " 1840, 6, 1
    George m 2nd Mariah -----
       Ch: David   b 1847, 1, 2
           Barkley   " 1849, 1, 6
----, --, --. William b 1829,1,6 d 1861,2,10;
    m Rhoda ----- b 1831,2,10
       Ch: James Her-
           vey   b 1851, 1, 23
           Joseph   " 1853, 2, 7
----, --, --. Alfred b 1830,8,24 d 1904,8,11
    bur Winona, O.; m Ann DEAN, dt Barton &
    Hannah, b 1833,9,24 d 1920,11,26
       Ch: Joshua   b 1852, 7, 4
           Elizabeth   " 1854, 12, 23 d 1929, 1, 8
            bur Winona, O.
           Hannah D.   b 1856, 10, 27
           William   " 1860, 1, 3
           Mary C.   " 1869, 7, 20
----, --, --. Joshua, s Alfred & Ann (Dean),
    b 1852,7,4; m Sarah GILBERT, dt Geo. &
    Hannah, b 1840,1,20 d 1884,3,21 bur Winona,
    O.;
    Joshua m 2nd Rachel K. KIRK, dt Elisha &
    Christianna (Hall), b 1846,11,2 d 1918,7,
    25 bur Winona
       Ch: Joseph C.   b 1887, 1, 10
           Wilson J.   " 1888, 8, 20
    Joshua m 3rd Mary Morlan KIRK, dt Theophil-
    us & Lydia T. Morlan, wd Nathan Kirk
----, --, --. George Lydia b 1841,8,15 d 1888,
    9,10 bur Cherokee Co., Kansas; m Elizabeth
    B. ALLEN, dt Christopher & Amelia, b 1841,
    9,19
       Ch: Allen C.   b 1862, 5, 15
           Charles   " 1867, 10, 24
           Sina   " 1872, 7, 6
----, --, --. Cyrus, s Jos. & Lydia, b 1836,
    1,27 d 1906,7,30 bur Winona, O.; m Sarah
    KIRK, dt Elisha & Rachel, b 1835,7,22 d
    1902,12,31
       Ch: Elisha H.   b 1871, 3, 22 d 1895, 7,21
            bur Winona, O.
           Alfred J.   b 1873, 10, 2
           Rachel E.   " 1876, 7, 18
----, --, --. William, s Alfred & Ann, b 1860,
    1,4; m Anna C. COPE, dt Edward Y. & Alice
    G., b 1861,4,3 d 1919,1,9 bur Winona, O.
       Ch: Alice A.   b 1881, 12, 25
           Elma   " 1889, 2, 22
----, --, --. Elisha, s Cyrus & Sara K., b
    1871,3,22 d 1895,7,21 bur Winona; m Mary
    A. MASTERS, dt Joseph & Esther, b 1870,8,
    25

       Ch: Emma An-
           netta   b 1893, 8, 16
           C. Wilmer   " 1894, 11, 28
1896, 10, 23. Mary C. m Daniel D. TEST
----, --, --. Joseph C., s Joshua & Rachel,
    b 1887,1,10; m Grace C. CRAWFORD, dt Thos.
    & Sara, b 1889,3,3
       Ch: G. Alford   b 1910, 3, 24
           Wilford T.   " 1911, 9, 11
           Esther   " 1914, 4, 11
           George   " 1916, 7, 5
----, --, --. Wilson J., s Joshua & Rachel K.
    (Kirk), b 1888,8,20; m Alice CRAWFORD, dt
    Thomas A. & Sara (Brantingham), b 1890,11,
    11
       Ch: Wilson
           Crawford   b 1918, 3, 8
           Joshua Clif-
           ford   b 1918, 3, 8
           Leslie Ray-
           mond   " 1921, 9, 7
           Jesse La-
           reau   " 1923, 12, 11 d 1927, 4,20
           bur Winona, O.

1824, 12, 23. George & w, Phebe, & ch, Joseph,
    Hannah, George & Sarah Hopper, rocf Salem
    MM, dtd 1824,11,24
1826, 11, 23. Joseph rmt Lydia Whinery
1828, 6, 26. George & w, Phebe, & ch, George
    & Sarah H., gct Upper Springfield MM, O.
1828, 6, 26. Hannah gct Upper Springfield MM,
    O.
1832, 4, 26. George Jr. rmt Hannah Shinn
1832, 11, 22. Joseph & w, Lydia, & ch gct
    Upper Springfield MM, O.
1833, 4, 25. George Jr. rocf Springfield MM,
    O., dtd 1833,1,31
1835, 11, 26. George & fam gct Upper Spring-
    field MM, O.
1836, 2, 25. Joseph & w, Lydia, & ch, Rachel,
    Alfred, Wm. & Elizabeth, rocf Upper
    Springfield MM, O.
1838, 8, 23. George & w, Hannah, & ch, Re-
    becca, James & Edward, rocf Upper Spring-
    field MM, O.
1843, 5, 25. Joseph rmt Anna M. Stratton
1845, 8, 21. Geo. rmt Polly Maria Vaughn
1847, 12, 23. Rachel rmt Joseph Stratton
1850, 3, 21. Wm. rmt Rhoda Dean
1851, 3, 20. Elizabeth rmt Jonathan Dean
1851, 3, 20. Wm. & w, Rhoda, & ch, James Har-
    vey, gct Salem MM, Ia.
1851, 4, 24. Rebecca gct Upper Springfield
    MM, O.
1851, 5, 22. Alfred gct Sandy Spring MM, O.,
    to m Ann Dean
1851, 10, 23. Ann rocf Sandy Spring MM, O.,
    dtd 1851,8,22
1852, 10, 21. Wm. & w, Rhoda, & s, James H.,
    rocf Salem MM, Ia., dtd 1852,3,17
1853, 1, 20. George & w, Polly Marie, & ch,
    Edward, David, Barclay & Phebe, gct

BRANTINGHAM, continued
Driftwood MM, Ind.
1853, 12, 22. Wm. & fam gct Driftwood MM, Ind.
1854, 3, 23. Alfred & fam gct Sandy Spring MM, O.
1855, 1, 24. Wm. & w, Lydia, & ch, James Hervey & Joseph, rec as mbr without cert from Driftwood MM, Ind. which fell into hands of Gurney Separatists (women's minutes give w's name as Rhoda)
1857, 6, 25. Alfred & w, Ann, & ch, Joshua, Elizabeth & Hannah D., rocf Sandy Spring MM, O., dtd 1857,5,23
1857, 6, 25. Anna M. Edgerton & ch, Lydia & Sina Brantingham, gct Somerset MM
1861, 10, 24. George L. rmt Elizabeth B. Allen
1863, 1, 23. Cyrus con mcd
1869, 8, 26. Sina rocf Coal Creek MM, Ia., dtd 1869,8,14
1869, 8, 26. Lydia rocf Coal Creek MM, Ia., dtd 1869,8,14
1870, 5, 26. Cyrus rmt Sarah Kirk
1871, 6, 22. Sina rmt Linnoeus Warrington
1871, 6, 22. Lydia rmt David Thomas
1874, 3, 26. James H. dis jG
1878, 12, 26. Joseph gct Springville MM, Ia., to m Mary Esther Hodgin
1879, 7, 24. Joseph gct Springville MM, Ia.
1879, 10, 24. Hannah D. rmt Abram Stratton
1880, 1, 22. Joshua rmt Sarah Gilbert
1880, 2, 24. William rmt Ann Cope
1882, 11, 23. Elizabeth rmt Joseph C. Stratton
1886, 3, 25. Joshua rmt Rachel Kirk
1888, 1, 26. Elizabeth gct Spring River MM, Ia. (G)
1888, 6, 21. Allen C. dis mcd
1889, 3, 21. Sina gct Spring River MM, Kans.
1889, 5, 23. Charles gct Spring River MM, Kans.
1890, 4, 24. Joseph & w, Mary Esther, & ch, Sarah R., Phebe & Wm. S., rocf Damorris MM, Kans., dtd 1890,4,9
1892, 6, 23. Joseph & w, Mary E., & ch, Sarah R., Phebe D. & Wm. S., gct Damorris MM, Kans.
1892, 9, 22. Elisha K. rmt Anna Masters
1897, 3, 24. James H. & w, Anna E., & s, James Arthur, gct Damascus MM (G)
1908, 12, 23. Ella Coppock gct East Goshen MM (G)
1910, 1, 20. Grace C. rocf Upper Springfield MM, O., dtd 1909,12,24
1910, 3, 24. Alace A. rmt Chas. Edward Crawford
1911, 8, 24. Mary & ch, E. Annetta & C. Wilmer, gct Salem MM
1911, 10, 26. Wilson J. gct Upper Springfield MM, O., to m Alice Crawford
1912, 2, 22. Alice C. rocf Upper Springfield MM, O., dtd 1912,1,26
1914, 5, 21. Elma rmt Barclay W. Stratton
1917, 1, 25. Alice dis jas
1917, 12, 20. Alice C. rst

1918, 1, 24. Rachel gct Philadelphia MM, Pa.
1918, 6, 20. Sina rmt Geo. G. Megrail
1918, 3, 21. Sina rocf Spring River MM, Kans.
1919, 10, 23. Joshua rmt Mary M. Kirk
1921, 1, 20. Wm. gct Arch St. MM, Phila.
1928, 1, 25. Wilson recrq (G)
1928, 10, 24. Wilson relrq (G)
1931, 3, 26. Alice (form Crawford) dis

BRIGGS
1819, 7, 22. John J. & w, Rebecca, rocf Salem MM, dtd 1819,7,21 (& ch, John J. & Rebecca [Ann,
1823, 2, 20. John dis mou
1825, 10, 19. Julia (form Griffith) con mou
1826, 9, 21. John J., minor, gct Salem MM
1829, 4, 23. Juliah dis jH

BROGAN
1835, 2, 26. Emma (form Wickersham) con mou (H)
1836, 6, 23. Rachel rocf Londongrove MM, Pa., dtd 1836,4,6 (H)

BROOMALL
1824, 2, 26. Elizabeth recrq
1824, 2, 26. Lydia recrq
1826, 1, 26. Hannah & Sarah recrq
1830, 2, 25. Phebe (form Brown) con mou
1831, 8, 25. Hannah gct Concord MM, Pa.
1832, 2, 23. Lydia Votaw (form Broomall) dis mcd
1834, 7, 24. Sarah T. gct Middleton MM
1835, 3, 26. Sarah gct Middleton MM (H)
1864, 11, 10. Phebe dis jG
1888, 2, 22. Rachel, Luella & Sheridan J. [Broomwell] recrq (G)
1897, 1, 20. Gertrude recrq (G)
1904, 9, 21. Pauline [Broomal] recrq (G)
1905, 3, 22. Lida recrq (G)
1911, 1, 25. Sheridan & w, Lida, & ch, Pauline, Raymond & Vernon, gct Salem MM (G)

BROWN
----, --, --. Jonathan, s Levi & Hannah b 1821 8,26 d 1906,6,3 bur Crestline, O.
1838, 8, 1. Harmon H., s Joshua & Ann, b
----, --, --. Enoch S., s Jeremiah & Deborah, b 1827,11,23; m Mary H. WALKER, b 1831,8,8 d 1909,2,23 bur Winona
Ch: Tamson W. b 1851, 10, 18 d 1868, 7,11 bur Winona
Deborah
Elizabeth b 1854, 11, 17
Charles L. " 1856, 10, 29
Wm. Weston " 1858, 8, 28
Edwin J. " 1860, 9, 6
Oliver R. " 1866, 11, 15

1816, 10, 17. Thomas & w, Elizabeth, & ch, Francis Foster (her s by form m), Samuel, Sarah, Margaret, Eleanor, Joshua, Timothy & Esther Brown, rocf Redstone MM, dtd 1816,4,24

BROWN, continued

1827, 6, 21. Jeremiah Jr. & w, Deborah, & ch, Sarah Ann & Abner, rocf Middleton MM, dtd 1827,5,10

1828, 3, 20. Prophet & w, Rachel, & ch, John S. & Jeremiah, rocf Middleton MM, dtd 1828,2,7

1828, 6, 26. Phebe rocf Middleton MM, dtd 1828,5,8

1828, 6, 26. Hannah rocf Middleton MM, dtd 1828,5,8

1828, 6, 26. Phebe Jr. rocf Middleton MM, dtd 1828,5,8

1828, 7, 24. Asa rocf Middleton MM, dtd 1828, 5,8

1829, 3, 26. Jeremiah dis jH

1829, 3, 26. Prophet & w, Rachel, dis jH

1829, 5, 21. Deborah dis jH

1825, 6, 25. Phebe (form Kirk) con mou (H)

1829, 7, 23. Phebe (form Kirk) dis mou & jH

1829, 9, 24. Phebe dis jH

1830, 2, 25. Phebe Broomall (form Brown) con mou

1830, 5, 20. Prophet & fam gct Middleton MM (H)

1830, 5, 20. Phebe gct Salem MM (H)

1830, 12, 23. Eleazer dis mcd

1831, 1, 20. Sarah Boulton (form Brown) con mcd

1832, 1, 26. Samuel dis mou

1832, 11, 22. Phebe rocf Salem MM, dtd 1832,7, 25 (H)

1833, 10, 24. Hannah rmt Jeremiah Coppock

1833, 11, 21. Timothy rmt Susannah Hoopes

1834, 7, 24. David Whinery gct Upper Spring-field MM, O., to m Sarah Brown

1837, 11, 23. Joshua gct Sandy Spring MM, O., to m Ann Holderman

1837, 7, 20. Prophet & w, Rachel, & ch, John S., Jeremiah, Sarah, Wm., Phebe Ann & Lydia, rocf Middleton MM, O., dtd 1836,12,8 (H)

1838, 4, 26. Ann rocf Sandy Spring MM, O., dtd 1838,3,23

1839, 12, 26. Phebe dis jas (H)

1840, 3, 26. Esther Ann dis disunity

1840, 10, 22. Joshua & fam gct Sandy Spring MM, O.

1842, 5, 26. Thomas dis disunity

1843, 5, 25. Sarah Ann dis jH

1843, 8, 24. Cert for minor ch of Prophet & Rachel granted to Marlborough MM, returned 1843,12,21; not in limits

1844, 8, 22. Timothy dis mcd

1844, 9, 26. Catharine Davis (form Brown) con mcd (H)

1845, 4, 24. Catharine gct Plainfield MM (H)

1846, 3, 26. David rmt Ann Whinery

1846, 5, 21. Ann gct Salem MM

1850, 9, 26. Enoch S. rmt Mary H. Walker

1851, 8, 21. Elizabeth gct Wabash MM, Ind.

1864, 10, 20. Phebe dis jG in 1854

1876, 6, 22. Deborah E. Mercer (form Brown)

dis mcd

1881, 11, 24. Wm. Weston dis mcd

1882, 1, 26. Edwin J. dis mcd

1883, 7, 25. Mary F. rocf Gilead MM, O. (G)

1884, 7, 24. Jonathan rocf Salem MM, dtd 1884,6,26

1885, 9, 24. Charles dis disunity

1887, 4, 20. Mary F. gct Gilead MM (G)

1888, 4, 26. Oliver R. dis mcd

1889, 10, 24. Enoch S. dis disunity

BRUCK

1825, 3, 24. William A. & w, Catharine, & ch, Elizabeth & Edwin, rocf Philadelphia MM, Pa., dtd 1825,1,27 endorsed by Salem MM, 1825,3,23

1828, 7, 24. Wm. A. dis jH

1829, 6, 25. Catherine dis jH

1835, 4, 23. Wm. A. & w, Katharine, & ch gct White Water MM, Ind. (H)

1841, 9, 23. Wm. A. & w, Catharone, & ch, Wm., Catharine, Ollita, Louisa & David Townsend, roc dtd 1841,7,28 (H)

BUCK

1820, 10, 26. George & w, Martha, & ch, Philip & Lewis Dawson, recrq

1823, 3, 20. John recrq

1823, 8, 21. John gct Salem MM, to m Miriam Lamborn

1823, 12, 25. Miriam rocf Salem MM, dtd 1823, 11,19

1825, 6, 23. Moses recrq

1826, 6, 22. John & w, Miriam, & ch, Nathan & Jonathan, gct Upper Springfield MM, O.

1829, 5, 21. George dis disunity

1830, 3, 25. Moses dis mou

BUNDY

----, --, --. Oliver W. m Sina SIDWELL, dt Israel & Rachel, b 1859,9,15
     Ch: Laurence G.
                 b 1883, 5, 30
       Chester M. " 1887, 8, 17 d 1889, 1,23
       bur Winona, O.

1882, 9, 21. Albert Cameron gct Short Creek MM, O., to m Elizabeth D. Bundy

1887, 12, 22. Sina H. & ch, Lawrence G. & Chester M., rocf Short Creek MM, O., dtd 1887,11,22

1891, 5, 21. Sina dis jas

1899, 11, 22. Maud relrq (G).

BURCHAL

1866, 1, 25. Sarah (form North) con mcd

1866, 8, 23. Sarah [Burchel] gct Springville MM, Ia.

BURSON

1809, 10, 19. David rocf Westland MM, dtd 1809 9,23

1809, 12, 14. David rmt Jane Whinery

BURSON, continued
1810, 9, 13. Silas rocf Westland MM, dtd 1810,3,24
1814, 9, 15. David & w gct Westland MM
1819, 10, 21. Hannah rst on consent of Goose Creek MM, Va.

1820, 11, 23. Hannah gct Short Creek MM
1823, 5, 22. John dis disunity
1824, 6, 24. Sarah Richy (form Burson) con mou
1826, 11, 23. Elizabeth rst on consent of Salem MM
1827, 7, 26. Sina & Margaret recrq
1829, 3, 26. Sinah Hinchman (form Burson) dis mcd
1829, 7, 23. Sinah Hinksman (form Burson) con mcd (H)
1829, 8, 20. Joseph dis jH
1830, 4, 22. Catherine & Ann dis disunity
1834, 11, 20. Margaret Malmsbury (form Burson) dis mcd
1839, 6, 20. Rebecca (form Bennett) con mou (H)
1853, 4, 21. Laney Ann (form Harris) con mcd
1887, 12, 21. David S. & Mary recrq (G)
1895, 1, 23. Mary relrq (G)

BURTON
1819, 12, 23. Elizabeth gct Clear Creek MM, O.

BUTLER
1820, 4, 20. Lawrence W. rmt Sarah Votaw
1820, 5, 25. Sarah gct Salem MM
1830, 8, 26. Lawrence W. & w, Sarah, & ch, Moses V., Hannah, Lewis, Joseph, Benjamin & Mary, rocf Sandy Spring MM, dtd 1830,7,23
1831, 6, 23. Lawrence W. & w, Sarah, & ch, Moses V., Hannah, Louis, Joseph, Benjamin & Mary, gct Upper Springfield MM, O.
1868, 12, 23. Ann V. gct Alliance MM (G)
1870, 12, 21. R. Elizabeth gct Damascus MM (G)

BUTZ
1897, 6, 23. Elizabeth recrq (G)

BYE
1816, 6, 13. Sarah rocf Middleton MM, dtd 1816,4,15
1826, 7, 20. Ann (form Jackson) dis mou
1826, 8, 24. Elizabeth recrq
1828, 1, 24. Elizabeth rmt Ezra Bailey

CADWALADER
1835, 1, 22. Rees rmt Sarah Johnson
1835, 3, 26. Sarah gct Stillwater MM, O.
1841, 10, 21. Howard rmt Margaret Johnson
1841, 12, 23. Margaret gct Salem MM

CAMERON
----, --, --. Josiah, s Alexander & Jane, d 1890,4,25 bur Winona; m Hannah ----- d 1883,3,27 bur Winona
Ch: William M. b 1837, 5, 4 d 1841, 9,28

Ch: Edward   b 1838, 10, 9
    Albert   " 1840, 12, 20
    Hirum   " 1843, 7, 12
    Sarah Jane " 1847, 4, 18
    Lydia Ann " 1849, 1, 5
    Louiza   " 1853, 7, 23
    Milton   " 1855, 11, 11 d 1889,11, 6
----, --, --. Milton, s Josiah & Hannah, b 1855,11,11; m Beulah FOGG, dt Edmin & Eliza A., b 1860,9,22
Ch: Mable   b 1880,12,23
1908, 10, 26. Clara Elizabeth, w Holland, dt Alfred A. & Elizabeth (Bradway) Patten, b

1833, 8, 22. Josiah recrq
1836, 7, 21. Josiah gct Middleton MM, to m Hannah Mendenhall
1837, 2, 23. Hannah rocf Middleton MM, dtd 1837,11,21
1867, 6, 20. Edwin dis mcd
1871, 10, 26. Albert dis disunity
1871, 10, 26. Ann Derr (form Cameron) dis mcd
1872, 11, 21. Sarah Jane Johnson (form Cameron) dis mcd
1873, 5, 22. Albert rst rq
1873, 6, 26. Hiram dis mcd
1879, 5, 22. Milton gct Upper Springfield MM, O., to m Bula Fogg
1879, 11, 20. Beulah rocf Springfield MM, O., dtd 1879,9,23
1882, 5, 25. Milton & w, Beulah, & dt, Mabel, gct Upper Springfield MM, O.
1882, 9, 21. Albert gct Short Creek MM, O., to m Elizabeth D. Bundy
1883, 9, 20. Albert gct Salem MM
1885, 1, 22. Louisa Ray (form Cameron) dis mcd

CAMP
1896, 12, 24. Phebe Jane (form Gambler) dis mcd

CARROLL
1809, 3, 16. Edward & w, Elizabeth, & ch, Debby, Thomas, Eliza & Ann, roc
1809, 3, 16. Joseph roc
1809, 3, 16. Edward Jr. roc
1809, 3, 16. Sally rocf Middleton MM, dtd 1809,1,14
1809, 3, 16. Margory rocf Middleton MM, dtd 1809,1,14
1810, 3, 15. Sally rmt James Whinery
1810, 5, 17. Joseph gct Abington MM, Pa.
1811, 5, 16. Margary rmt Wm. Whinery Jr.
1813, 10, 14. Joseph rocf ND MM, dtd 1813,3,23
1817, 4, 17. Thomas gct Short Creek MM, O.
1817, 10, 16. Joseph rmt Elizabeth Ellis
1817, 11, 13. Edward Jr. gct Middleton MM, to m Rachel Hamilton
1818, 4, 16. Rachel rocf Carmel MM, dtd 1818,2,21
1823, 6, 26. Thomas & w, Ann, rocf White Water MM, Ind., dtd 1823,2,15

CARROLL, continued

1824, 5, 20. Joseph & w, Elizabeth, gct Sandy Spring MM, O.

1824, 7, 24. Thomas & w, Ann, & s, Forester W. gct Plainfield MM

1827, 3, 22. Joseph & w, Elizabeth, & ch, Enos, Edward, Mary & John, & Emmet b since cert was granted, rocf Sandy Spring MM, dtd 1826,2,24

1828, 7, 24. Susannah rocf Providence MM, Pa., dtd 1828,11,31, end by Upper Springfield MM, O., 1828,6,28

1828, 10, 23. Edward Jr. dis jH

1829, 2, 26. Joseph dis jH

1829, 3, 26. Eliza dis jH

1829, 3, 26. Ann dis jH

1829, 3, 26. Elizabeth dis jH

1829, 4, 23. Rachel dis jH

1829, 5, 21. Phebe dis jH

1829, 9, 24. Elizabeth Jr. dis jH

1832, 10, 25. Deborah Randolf (form Carroll) con mou (H)

1833, 3, 21. Mary Ann & Wm., minor ch Edward, gct Carmel MM (H)

1833, 7, 25. Elizabeth gct Carmel MM (H)

1833, 11, 20. Eliza & Ann gct Carmel MM (H)

1837, 5, 4. Susannah gct Providence MM, Pa.

1838, 8, 23. Mary Ann, minor, gct Salem MM

1838, 10, 25. Elizabeth & fam gct Plainfield MM (H)

1838, 11, 22. Wm. gct Upper Springfield MM, O.

1839, 11, 24. Mary Shepperd (form Carroll) con mcd (H)

CARSON

1811, 5, 16. Jemima   con mcd

1811, 7, 18. Jemima gct Salem MM

CASKEY

1896, 11, 25. James R. & w recrq (G)

1897, 2, 24. Hollis recrq (G)

1901, 9, 25. Charles recrq (G)

1904, 9, 21. Vesta recrq (G)

1907, 4, 24. John, Harriet, Chas., Hollis & Vesta relrq (G)

CASS

1860, 1, 26. Mary Ann (form Hoopes) dis mcd

CASTOUGH

1902, 10, 22. B. F. recrq (G)

CATTELL

1882, 4, 19. Joseph & w, Eleanor, rocf East Goshen MM, dtd 1882,4,15 (G)

1906, 1, 24. Gertrude H. gct First Friends Church, Alliance, O. (G)

CHAMBERS

1810, 1, 18. James & w, Mary, & ch, Ann & Jane, rocf Short Creek MM, O., dtd 1809, 10,24

1814, 10, 13. Cert rec for Samuel & w, Deborah, & ch, John Robert Abigail Deborah Samuel Margaret Stacy & James, from Butternuts MM, N. Y., dtd 1814,4,5, endorsed to Plainfield MM, O.

1817, 4, 17. James & fam gct Plainfield MM

1819, 6, 24. James & w, Mary, & ch, Ann, Eleanor, Thomas, Elizabeth, James & Mary, rocf Plainfield MM, dtd 1819,4,22

1877, 9, 20. Benjamin S. dis jG

1877, 11, 22. James N. dis jG

1897, 10, 20. J. N. & w, Susanna, & dt, Laura May, recrq (G)

1898, 1, 19. Laura May rocf Sandy Spring MM, O. (G)

1911, 11, 22. James N. & w, T. Susanna, gct Damascus MM (G)

1911, 11, 22. Laura May gct Damascus MM (G)

CHARLTON

1825, 7, 21. Elizabeth (form Hoopes) dis mcd

CLARK

1823, 11, 20. John & w, Rachel, & ch, Rebecca, Martha, Thomas, Henry & William, rocf Muncy MM, dtd 1823,7,23, also Jane & John b before certificate was granted, but since their rem

1832, 6, 21. Martha gct Sandy Spring MM, O.

1832, 6, 21. Rebecca gct Sandy Spring MM, O.

1832, 7, 26. John & w, Rachel, & five ch gct Sandy Spring MM, O.

1887, 12, 21. Rosa recrq (G)

1889, 1, 23. Wilson recrq (G)

1889, 2, 20. Lillian H. rocf East Goshen MM, dtd 1889,2,16 (G)

1892, 3, 23. Robert recrq (G)

1894, 8, 22. Wilson & fam gct Salem MM (G)

1895, 5, 22. Robert gct Salem MM (G)

1897, 6, 23. Henrietta recrq (G)

CLEAVER

1842, 3, 24. Deborah (form Dutton) con mcd (H)

1845, 4, 24. Hiram T. rmt Anna Hanna (H)

CLEMSEN

1853, 9, 22. James L. & w, Triphemia, & dt, Allice, rocf Sandy Spring MM, O., dtd 1853,8,26

1857, 1, 22. James Lee & w, Tryphena, & ch, Eliza & Rosco, gct Upper Springfield MM, O.

COBBS

1825, 11, 24. Ansalem rmt Ann Coppock

1826, 4, 20. Ann gct Upper Springfield MM, O.

COBURN

1818, 7, 16. Benjamin & w, Abigail, & ch, Benjamin, Sarah, Hannah, Jacob & Elizabeth, rocf Little Britain MM, Pa., dtd 1818,4,11

1818, 7, 16. Abigail Jr. rocf Little Britain

COBURN, continued
  MM, Pa., dtd 1818,4,11
1818, 8, 13. John rocf Little Britain MM, dtd
  1818,4,11
1819, 6, 24. David rocf Little Britain MM,
  Pa., dtd 1819,1,9
1898, 10, 19. George & Ella [Cobourn] gct Sandy Spring MM (G)

COFFIN
1812, 10, 15. Charles & w, Mary, & s, Albert,
  rocf Nantucket MM, dtd 1812,7,29
1816, 4, 18. Cert rec for Phebe from ND MM
  dtd 1813,10,26 endorsed to Marlborough MM

COFFMAN
1917, 3, 22. Jesse N. Edgerton gct Stillwater
  MM, O., to m Minerva E. Coffman

COLBURN
1894, 5, 23. George & w, Ida E., rocf Salem
  MM (G)

COLBY
1912, 12, 25. Ray F. & Myrta recrq (G)
1921, 8, 17. Fam of Colby relrq (G)

COMLY
1821, 12, 20. Sarah (form Whinery) dis mcd
1839, 10, 24. Sarah rst at Short Creek MM, O.
  on consent of this mtg

CONRAD
----, --, --. Elwood B., s Lewis & Rebecca,
  b 1850,1,25; m Phebe B. DEAN, dt Jonathan
  & Elizabeth, b 1855,12,14
  Ch: Eunice H. b 1879, 7, 6
      Joseph   " 1880, 11, 26

1878, 4, 25. Elwood rocf Hickory Grove MM,
  Ia., dtd 1878,4,6
1878, 9, 26. Elwood B. rmt Phebe Dean
1882, 1, 26. Elwood B. & w, Phebe, & ch,
  Eunice & Joseph, gct Upper Springfield MM,
  O.

COOK
1887, 12, 21. Martha J. & Della recrq (G)
1900, 3, 21. Mattie J. relrq (G)
1914, 7, 23. Dillwyn Stratton gct Salem MM,
  to m Ella Lillian Cooke

COOPER
1812, 1, 16. Ann & ch, Susanna, Evan, Jane,
  Elizabeth, Phebe & Mary Ann, rocf Sadsbury MM, dtd 1811,9,3, endorsed by Middleton MM, 1811,12,12
1814, 11, 17. Joshua rocf Sadsbury MM, dtd 1814,
  10,4
1817, 5, 15. Joshua dis mou
1820, 4, 20. Susannah rmt Joseph Raley
1823, 11, 20. Elizabeth gct Sandy Spring MM, O.
1904, 4, 21. Harry E. rmt Ruth C. Satterth-

wait
1904, 11, 24. Ruth C. gct New Garden MM, Pa.

COPE
----, --, --. Edward Y., s Joseph & Rachel,
  b 1831,8,1 d 1896,9,13 bur Winona, O.; m
  Alice G. GILBERT, dt Geo. D. & Hannah,
  b 1835,3,3 d 1915,4,29 bur Winona, O. (an
  elder)
  Ch: Charles   b 1858, 8, 7
      Anna   " 1861, 4, 3 d 1917, 1, 9
      bur Winona, O.
----, --, --. Albert M., s Benjamin & Eliza-
  beth, b 1847,1,19; m Phebe Y. ASHTON, dt
  Barak & Jane, b 1853,5,16
  Ch: Elbert
      Lorin   b 1874, 4, 19
----, --, --. Alexander Logan m Rachel G.
  COPPOCK, dt Joshua & Jane, b 1851,10,8
  d 1926,12,17 bur Winona
  Ch: Seward
      Burton   b 1879, 8, 29
      Leedom
      Sharp   " 1882, 7, 11
      Alta Eliza-
      beth   " 1889, 3, 2
----, --, --. Charles, s Edward Y. & Alice G.,
  b 1858,8,7 d 1921,5,21 bur Winona; m Ra-
  chel E. EDGERTON, dt Joseph & Anna, b
  1862,5,2 d 1931,5,5
  Ch: Anna   b 1882, 10, 11
      Edward J. " 1884, 9, 26 d 1885, 7,28
      Ellen S. " 1887, 6, 1
1899, 9, 13. Sarah M., w Byron H., dt Walter
  & Mary H. (Binns) Edgerton, b
1914, 8, 21. Ellen S. m J. Wetherill HUTTON
1921, 9, 23. Byron H. m Sarah EDGERTON

1871, 12, 21. Edward Y. & w, Alice G., & ch,
  Charles & Anna, rocf Sewickley MM, dtd
  1871,10,28
1872, 6, 20. Albert M. rocf Hickory Grove
  MM, Ia., dtd 1872,6,1
1873, 1, 23. Albert M. gct Middleton MM, to
  m Phebe Y. Ashton
1873, 7, 24. Phebe Y. rocf Middleton MM, dtd
  1873,7,19
1876, 2, 24. Oliver rocf Middleton MM, dtd
  1876,1,15
1878, 10, 24. Albert M. & w, Phebe Y., & s,
  Elbert Lorain, gct Salem MM
1877, 11, 22. Rachel G. (form Coppock) con mcd
1880, 10, 21. Charles rmt Rachel Edgerton
1881, 2, 24. Ann rmt Wm. Brantingham
1893, 3, 22. Lester recrq (G)
1893, 4, 19. Frederick A. & w, Etta V., & dt,
  Inez A., rocf Smithfield MM (G)
1895, 4, 24. Frederick J. & fam gct Westland
  MM (G)
1897, 3, 25. Seward Burton, Leedom Sharp &
  Alta Elizabeth, ch A. L. & Rachel G.,
  recrq
1905, 10, 26. Anna rmt Dillwyn E. Hall

COPE, continued
1908, 12, 23. Lester recrq (G)
1910, 6, 23. Alta E. rmt Walter C. Stratton
1917, 2, 21. Lois recrq (G)
1924, 2, 21. Sarah M. gct Paulina MM, Ia.
1927, 7, 20. Lester, Earl & Clarence dropped
    from mbrp (G)
1933, 8, 24. Francis E. Price gct Middleton
    MM, O., to m Helen P. Cope

COPPOCK
----, --, --. Milley b 1802,9,21 d 1820,1,23
----, --, --. John b 1776,11,4 d 1854,5,12;
    m Catherine ----- b 1777,3,4 d 1871,3,5
    Ch: Lydia   b 1809, 4, 2
        Jeremiah   " 1810, 10, 23
        Joshua   " 1814, 1, 21
        David   " 1815, 10, 1
        Timothy   " 1805, 9, 14
        Mary   " 1812, 3, 23
-- -, --, --. Mary, w Jonathan, dt Enoch & Sa-
    rah Sharp, b 1813,12,24 d 1899,8,4 bur
    Winona, O.
----, --, --. Jeremiah b 1812,3,23 d 1885,4,16;
    m Hannah ----- d 1838,11,30
    Ch: Ezra   b 1834, 6, 25
        John   " 1837, 2, 14 d 1886, 1,31
----, --, --. Joshua, s John & Catherine, b
    1814,1,21 d 1899,2,5; m Jane HOYLE, dt
    John & Elizabeth, b 1817,3,2 d 1895,2,9
    (Joshua bur Winona)
    Ch: William G. b 1842, 2, 19
        Benjamin H." 1843, 10, 15
        Elizabeth " 1845, 10, 11 d 1857, 9,20
          bur Winona
        Samuel   b 1847, 1, 20
        Thomas   " 1850, 7, 15
        Rachel   " 1851, 10, 8
        Sarah   " 1853, 11, 12
        Joseph   " 1855, 10, 7
        Hannah   " 1858, 4, 5
        John S.   " 1861, 4, 1 d 1862, 4,16
          bur Winona
        Ruthanna   b 1863, 7, 7
----, --, --. Timothy b 1805,9,14; m Mahet-
    able -----
    Ch: Timothy   b 1845, 4, 30
----, --, --. David b 1815,10,1 d 1860,4,24;
    m Rebecca TEST, dt Isaac B. & Margaret,
    b 1817,9,8 d 1879,4,1 bur Winona
    Ch: Isaac T.   b 1849, 1, 10
        Samuel
        Jones   " 1852, 2, 5 d 1853, 8,24
        Margaret
        Ellen   " 1854, 1, 26
----, --, --. Benjamin H., s Joshua & Jane,
    b 1843,10,15; m Esther W. WINDER, dt Jo-
    seph & Lydia, b 1844,1,25
    Ch: Elmer B.   b 1866, 11, 26
        Lydda Ann " 1868, 4, 8
        Albert   " 1870, 2, 18
        Edith   " 1872, 7, 22
        David   " 1875, 7, 6 d 1878, 5, 1

bur Winona, O.
1879, 10, 24. Sarah m James E. BAILEY

1825, 11, 24. Ann rmt Ansalem Cobbs
1829, 9, 24. Lydia rmt Levi Heald
1831, 3, 24. Samuel gct Upper Springfield MM,
    O., to m Ann Lynch
1831, 5, 26. Samuel gct Upper Springfield
    MM, O.
1833, 3, 21. Jonathan rmt Sarah Crew
1833, 8, 22. Mary rmt Thomas Emmons Jr.
1833, 8, 22. Jonathan & w, Sarah, gct Upper
    Springfield MM, O.
1833, 10, 24. Jeremiah rmt Hannah Brown
1837, 9, 21. Jonathan & ch, Catharine, Ben-
    jamin & Ruthanna, rocf Upper Springfield
    MM, O., dtd 1837,8,26
1838, 6, 21. Jonathan rmt Mary Sharp
1838, 7, 26. Jonathan & fam gct Chesterfield
    MM
1840, 7, 23. Mary, Catharine & Ruth Anna,
    latter two minors, ch Jonathan, dec, rocf
    Chesterfield MM, dtd 1840,5,16
1840, 11, 26. Joshua gct Smithfield MM, O., to
    m Jane Hoyle
1841, 5, 20. Jane H. rocf Smithfield MM, dtd
    1841,5,7
1842, 6, 23. Jeremiah rmt Milley Crew
1843, 11, 23. Lydia, minor dt Samuel & Ann,
    rocf Upper Springfield MM, O., dtd 1843,
    7,22
1844, 3, 21. Timothy rmt Mehetable Jenkins
1845, 5, 22. Joseph L., minor, rocf Upper
    Springfield MM, O., dtd 1845,4,26
1847, 6, 24. David rmt Rebecca Test
1848, 5, 25. Mary gct Upper Springfield MM,O.
1850, 8, 22. Joseph L. & Lydia, minor ch
    James & Ann, gct Salem MM
1853, 8, 25. Mary rocf Upper Springfield MM,
    O., dtd 1853,6,25
1855, 9, 20. Catharine gct Plymouth MM
1857, 11, 26. Ruth Anna rmt Elias Crew
1859, 2, 24. John dis mcd
1859, 5, 26. Ezra gct Upper Springfield MM,
    O., to m Ruth Ann French
1860, 5, 24. Ann rocf Upper Springfield MM,
    O., dtd 1860,4,27
1862, 2, 20. Wm. G. gct Sandy Spring MM, O.,
    to m Abigail Deem
1862, 4, 24. Ezra & w, Ann, & ch, Hannah Le-
    vina, gct Salem MM
1862, 7, 24. Abigail rocf Sandy Spring MM, O.,
    dtd 1862,5,24
1863, 4, 23. Wm. G. & w, Abigail, gct Sandy
    Spring MM, O.
1865, 9, 21. Benjamin N. gct Sandy Spring
    MM, O., to m Esther Winder
1866, 7, 26. Catharine rocf Plymouth MM, dtd
    1866,6,18
1866, 10, 25. Benjamin H. gct Salem MM
1867, 7, 25. Benjamin H. & w, Esther, & s,
    Elmer B., rocf Salem MM, dtd 1867,6,19
1868, 7, 23. Rebecca rmt Job Warren

COPPOCK, continued

1871, 6, 22. Wm. G. & w, Abigail, & ch, Barton D., Elizabeth Jane & Harlen L., rocf Sandy Spring MM, O., dtd 1871,5,27

1871, 10, 26. Jeremiah gct Middleton MM, to m Rebecca Shaw

1872, 3, 23. Rebecca rocf Middleton MM, dtd 1872,4,20

1872, 9, 26. Samuel dis mcd

1874, 6, 25. Thomas dis mcd

1874, 9, 24. Isaac L. dis disunity

1877, 11, 22. Rachel G. Cope (form Coppock) con mcd

1879, 5, 21. Isaac T. recrq (G)

1880, 3, 24. William G. & w, Abigail D., & ch, Barton D., Elizabeth J. & Harlan L., gct Springville MM, Ia.

1883, 4, 26. Benjamin A. & w, Esther, & ch, Elmer, Lyddaann, Albert & Edith, gct Coal Creek MM, Ia.

1885, 1, 22. Joseph J. gct Hickory Grove MM, Ia., to m Rebecca Ellyson

1883, 9, 19. Isaac T. & w, Phebe, & ch gct East Goshen MM (G)

1884, 8, 21. Hannah rmt Edgar Warrington

1887, 4, 20. Ella recrq (G)

1887, 6, 23. Rebecca gct Middleton MM

1887, 12, 21. Lucinda & Ida S. recrq (G)

1889, 2, 21. Ruth Anna rmt Leonard Winder

1889, 3, 21. Margaret Ellen dis jG

1888, 11, 21. Isaac T. & w, Phebe, & ch, Ralph S., Homer J. & Ella Florence, rocf East Goshen MM, O., dtd 1888,10,20 (G)

1890, 4, 24. Joseph J. gct Hickory Grove MM, Ia.

1890, 11, 19. Lucy relrq (G)

1898, 2, 23. Ella M. gct Cleveland MM (G)

1899, 8, 23. Ella rocf Cleveland MM (G)

1899, 12, 20. Mrs. Lucinda recrq (G)

1902, 2, 19. Ralph gct Damascus MM (G)

1904, 12, 21. Homer J. gct Vasselborough MM, Maine (G)

COULSON

1811, 9, 19. Jehu & w, Jane, & ch, Jehu, David, Jabez, Rachel & Jesse, rocf Middleton MM, dtd 1811,9,12

1814, 5, 19. David rmt Elizabeth Reeder

1815, 4, 13. Uriah rocf Middleton MM, dtd 1815,4,6

1816, 11, 14. Uriah rmt Ann Winder

1817, 1, 16. Jehu Jr. dis attending a mcd

1818, 4, 16. Jehu & w, Jane, & ch, Rachel & Jesse, gct Carmel MM

1819, 1, 21. Jabez rmt Sarah Pim (wd with ch)

1883, 7, 26. John dis disunity

COURTNEY

1815, 1, 19. Martha gct Westland MM

1820, 12, 21. Martha rocf Westland MM, Pa., dtd 1820,7,27

1823, 3, 20. Edward gct Salem MM, to m Phebe Y. Votaw

1823, 9, 25. Edward gct Salem MM

1828, 8, 21. Ann dis jH

1829, 1, 22. Dozier dis jH

1829, 7, 23. Mary Ann dis jH

1829, 10, 22. Martha dis jH

1830, 1, 21. James dis jH

1830, 2, 25. Moses dis jH

1830, 4, 22. James dis disunity; decision reversed by QM 1831,1,20 (H)

1830, 4, 22. Hannah dis jH

1833, 11, 21. Israel dis jH

CRAIG

1809, 5, 18. James & Mary dis

1809, 5, 18. William, Elizabeth, Absolom, Jonathan & Lydia, ch Deborah, recrq

1809, 5, 18. Jane recrq

1809, 9, 14. James & Mary rstrq

1811, 11, 14. Jane rmt Samuel Milbourn

1812, 10, 15. Deborah rmt James Armstrong

1813, 5, 13. Wm. & Absalom gct Goose Creek MM, Va. (Loudon Co., Va.)

1813, 7, 15. Elizabeth gct Middleton MM

1813, 11, 18. Cert to Goose Creek MM, Va. for Absalom returned unused

1815, 10, 19. James dis

1815, 11, 16. Absalom dis disunity

1818, 6, 18. Jonathan gct Lick Creek MM, Ind.

1824, 5, 20. Eloner gct Middleton MM

CRAWFORD

----, --, --. Chas. Edward, s Thomas A. & Sara (Brantingham), b 1887,2,15; m Alice BRANTINGHAM, dt Wm. & Anna (Cope), b 1881, 12,25

Ch: Robert W.   b 1911, 7, 24
    Arthur B.   " 1914, 3, 8

1910, 3, 24. Charles Edwin rmt Alice A. Brantingham

1910, 9, 15. Alice A. gct Upper Springfield MM, O.

1914, 7, 23. Charles E. & w, Alice A., & ch, Robert W. & Arthur B., rocf Upper Springfield MM, O.

1915, 5, 20. Albert I. Steer gct Upper Springfield MM, O., to m Jessie Leah Crawford

1922, 12, 21. Charles E. & w, Alice H., & ch, Robert W. & Arthur B., gct Upper Springfield MM, O.

1931, 3, 26. Alice Brantingham (form Crawford) dis

CREW

----, --, --. Littleberry b 1762,12,18 d 1840, 9,12 ae 78 (an elder); m Hannah ----- b 1771,11,10 d 1853,3,10

Ch: James   b 1798, 9, 22
    Benjamin " 1799, 11, 16 d 1833,10, 4
    John   " 1801, 4, 30 d 1801,10,26
    Milley   " 1802, 9, 21
    Judith   " 1804, 8, 30 d 1853, 3, 8

CREW, Littleberry & Hannah, continued
    Ch: Sarah   b 1806, 6, 29 d 1837, 3,11
        Robert   " 1808, 11, 2 " 1817, 3,10
        Jonathan " 1810, 7, 2
        Martha   " 1812, 2, 6
        Abraham   " 1812, 2, 6
        Malcohm   " 1816, 5, 6 d 1856, 7,26
----, --, --. Abraham b 1812,2,6; m Jane -----
    b 1809,12,21 d 1891,10,21
    Ch: Robert   b 1831, 8, 22
        Phebe   " 1833, 11, 13
        Martha   " 1835, 8, 15 d 1852, 10,5
        Abigail   " 1838, 1, 19
        Mahlon   " 1840, 3, 7
        Nancy   " 1842, 1, 22
        William   " 1844, 12, 26
        Huldah Jane" 1847, 7, 20
        David   " 1850, 7, 14
----, --, --. Malcohm b 1816,5,6 d 1856,7,26;
    m Susanna ----- b 1818,3,24
    Ch: Jonathan b 1837, 7, 17 d 1837, 7,17
        David   " 1837, 7, 17 " 1837, 7,17
        Sarah   " 1838, 9, 2
        Joseph   " 1840, 9, 21
        Lewindy   " 1845, 6, 7
        Thomas   " 1847, 8, 24
        Matilda P. " 1850, 5, 16

1820, 5, 25. James gct White Water MM, Ind.
1822, 12, 26. Benjamin gct Darby Creek MM
1829, 11, 26. Martha rmt Joseph Whinery
1830, 11, 16. Abraham rmt Jane Whinery
1831, 7, 21. Jonathan gct Upper Springfield
    MM, O.
1833, 3, 21. Sarah rmt Jonathan Coppock
1834, 12, 25. Ruth (form Neal) dis mou
1836, 12, 22. Malcom rmt Susanna Whinery
1842, 6, 23. Milley rmt Jeremiah Coppock
1848, 11, 23. Judith gct Upper Springfield MM,
    O.
1852, 9, 23. Phebe rmt Enoch Vansyoc
1854, 3, 23. Robert gct Upper Springfield MM,
    O., to m Margaret Blackburn
1857, 11, 26. Elias rmt Ruth Anna Coppock
1858, 5, 20. Ruth Ann gct Plymouth MM
1862, 4, 24. Sarah Votaw (form Crew) dis mcd
1864, 6, 23. Joseph dis enlisting in military
    service
1864, 7, 21. Mahlon dis mcd
1865, 12, 21. Abram dis disunity
1867, 2, 21. Nancy dis disunity
1867, 7, 25. Jane dis disunity
1869, 3, 25. Hulda Jane Barber (form Crew)
    dis mcd
1870, 3, 24. Matilda M. Johnson (form Crew)
    dis disunity
1870, 3, 24. Lucinda Hoops (form Crew) dis
    mcd
1871, 3, 23. Abigail dis disunity
1871, 9, 21. Rebecca (form Whinery) dis
1881, 5, 26. David dis mcd
1882, 6, 21. Joseph & Phebe recrq (G)
1887, 12, 21. David & Emma recrq (G)

1892, 12, 21. Abigail recrq (G)
1901, 12, 25. Nellie recrq (G)
1907, 2, 20. David & w, Emma, & ch, Lena &
    Norma relrq (G)
1907, 2, 20. Nellie relrq (G)
1911, 9, 20. Joseph & w, Phebe, gct Damascus
    MM (G)

CULL
1892, 7, 20. Lucy recrq (G)
1893, 3, 22. Lucy gct Tecumseh MM, Mich. (G)

DAVIS
1809, 1, 19. Ellis gct Plymouth MM
1809, 7, 13. Ellis & w, Ann, rocf Plymouth
    MM, dtd 1809,6,17
1810, 12, 13. Phebe rmt Daniel Wilkins
1812, 10, 15. David recrq
1812, 12, 17. Eleanor recrq
1814, 1, 13. David rmt Rachel John
1816, 3, 14. Edith rocf Middleton MM, dtd
    1815,7,6
1817, 1, 16. Hannah rocf Marlsborough MM,
    dtd 1816,12,18
1817, 1, 16. Mary rocf Marlsborough MM, dtd
    1816,12,18
1818, 8, 13. Hannah rmt John Antrim
1818, 11, 26. Phebe (form Whitacre) con mou
1819, 8, 26. Lydia rocf Middleton MM, dtd
1819, 11, 25. Mary rmt James Reeder[1819,8,23
1819, 11, 25. Phebe gct Marlborough MM
1820, 6, 22. John & w, Lydia, & ch, James,
    Mary Ann, Hannah & Robert, recrq
1826, 5, 25. Ellis rmt Sarah Mendenhall
1828, 5, 22. Samuel recrq (H)
1828, 5, 22. Mary & dt, Elizabeth, recrq (H)
1828, 5, 22. Joshua & w, Rachel, & ch, Mary,
    recrq (H)
1828, 8, 21. Ellis dis jH
1828, 7, 24. Samuel & w, Mary, gct Salem MM
    (H)
1828, 7, 24. Elizabeth gct Salem MM (H)
1828, 7, 24. Joshua & w, Rachel, & dt, Mary,
    gct Salem MM (H)
1828, 12, 25. Rachel dis jH
1828, 12, 25. Sarah dis jH
1833, 1, 24. Amos & w, Anna, & ch, Nelson H.,
    Hahmah D. & Sarah F., rocf Roaring Creek
    MM, dtd 1832,9,12 (H)
1833, 1, 24. Elizabeth L. rocf Roaring Creek
    MM, dtd 1832,9,12 (H)
1833, 11, 20. Benjamin B. rmt Mary B. Ingram
    (H)
1833, 11, 20. Elizabeth L. rmt Thomas C. Pound [(H)
1834, 5, 22. Mary (form Ingram) dis mcd among
    H
1834, 6, 26. Benjamin dis jH
1836, 9, 22. Sarah & fam gct White Water MM,
    Ind (H)
1839, 7, 25. Catherine rocf Alexandria MM,
    D. C., dtd 1839,5,23 (H)
1839, 8, 23. Herophila rocf Alexandria MM,
    D. C., dtd 1839,5,18 (H)

DAVIS, continued
1839, 12, 26. Herophila rmt Elisha Fawcett (H)
1844, 9, 26. Catharine (form Brown) con mcd
               (H)
1897, 6, 23. Lillian recrq (G)

DAVISON
1826, 8, 24. Jamima (form Beck) dis mou

DEAN
----, --, --. James Hervey b 1799,4,14 d 1885,
               3,28; m Eleanor ----- b 1799,3,17
        Ch: Edith   b 1821, 8, 5
            Stephen   " 1822, 10, 21
            Hannah   " 1824, 5, 5
            Milton   " 1826, 6, 13 d 1850,10,29
            Mary Ann   " 1828, 5, 26
            Rhoda   " 1831, 2, 10
            William W. " 1833, 4, 26
----, --, --. Ephraim, s Barton & Hannah, b
               1827,2,13 d 1906,7,12 bur Winona, O.
----, --, --. Jonathan, s Barton & Hannah,
               b 1830,8,2 d 1911,1,24 bur Winona; m
               Elizabeth BRANTINGHAM, dt Joseph & Lydia,
               b 1833,9,27 d 1916,4,6 bur Winona, O.
        Ch: Francis   b 1852, 2, 15
            Rachel   " 1854, 3, 13
            Phebe W.   " 1855, 12, 14
            Joseph B. " 1858, 5, 23
            Sarah Ann " 1859, 11, 9
            Hannah C. " 1862, 11, 19
            Lydia B.   " 1864, 1, 4
            Edward   " 1868, 1, 18
            Martha   " 1869, 10, 20
----, --, --. Joshua S., s Barton & Elizabeth,
               b 1843,10,2; m Mary Ann HOBSON, b 1845,3,
               21
        Ch: Evaretta L.b 1876, 7, 20

1810, 4, 19. Hannah, w Jonathan, & ch, James,
               Henry, Eliza Barton & Caroline, rocf
               Scipio MM, N. Y., dtd 1810,2,15
1811, 4, 18. Jonathan R. rocf Scipio MM,
               N. Y., dtd 1811,2,11   [fine
1811, 12, 19. Jonathan R. dis paying muster
1815, 3, 16. Jonathan R. rst
1816, 3, 14. Amy, dt Jonathan R. recrq
1816, 6, 13. Polly (form Rogers)dis
1820, 10, 26. James Harvey rmt Eleanor Winder
1826, 5, 25. Barton rmt Hannah Jackson
1826, 9, 21. Hannah gct Sandy Spring MM, O.
1838, 2, 22. James H. & w, Eleanor, & ch,
               Edith, Stephen, Hannah, Milton, Maryann,
               Rhoda & William W., rocf Marlborough MM
1840, 2, 20. Stephen, minor, gct Smithfield
               MM
1842, 2, 24. Edith gct Salem MM
1842, 3, 24. Hannah rmt Mahlon Whinery
1845, 5, 22. Milton gct Smithfield MM
1848, 2, 25. Mary Ann rmt Lawrie Tatum
1848, 7, 20. Milton rocf Smithfield MM, dtd
               1848,4,17
1850, 3, 21. Rhoda rmt Wm. Brantingham

1851, 5, 22. Alfred Brantingham gct Sandy
               Spring MM, O., to m Ann Dean
1851, 3, 20. Jonathan rmt Elizabeth Brant-
               ingham
1851, 5, 22. Elizabeth D. gct Sandy Spring
               MM, O.
1853, 11, 24. Wm. W. dis mcd
1855, 7, 26. Jonathan & w, Elizabeth B.,
               & ch, Francis & Rachel, rocf Sandy Spring
               MM, O., dtd 1855,6,23
1862, 2, 20. Wm. G. Coppock gct Sandy Spring
               MM, O., to m Abigail Dean
1864, 7, 21. Eleanor dis jG in 1854
1864, 8, 25. Mary B. dis jG in 1854
1870, 12, 22. Barton & Ann rocf Sandy Spring
               MM, O., dtd 1870,11,26
1870, 12, 22. Joshua & w, Mary Ann, rocf
               Sandy Spring MM, O., dtd 1870,11,26
1870, 12, 26. Ephraim rocf Sandy Spring MM,
               O., dtd 1870,11,26
1874, 2, 26. Isaac dis jG
1874, 9, 24. Francis gct Plymouth MM, to m
               Penina Hollingsworth
1875, 2, 25. Penina rocf Plymouth MM, dtd
               1874,12,21
1875, 2, 24. Isaac & w, Sarah L., & ch, Mary
               A., Alice J. & Tazetta E., rocf Spring
               Creek MM, Ia., dtd 1875,3,6 (G)
1875, 11, 25. Francis & w, Penina gct Plymouth
               MM
1877, 3, 21. Isaac & w, Sarah L., & ch, Mary
               A., Alice J. & Tazetta E., gct New Sharon
               MM, Ia. (G)
1878, 9, 26. Phebe rmt Elwood B. Conrad
1880, 3, 25. Jonathan & w, Elizabeth, & ch,
               Hannah C., Lydia, Edward & Martha, gct
               Plymouth MM
1881, 2, 24. Ephraim gct Plymouth MM
1881, 3, 24. Joshua S. & w, Mary Ann, & ch,
               Evaretta Lydia, gct Plymouth MM, O.
1881, 7, 21. Joseph B. gct Hickory Grove MM,
               Ia.
1882, 5, 25. Sarah Ann gct Plymouth MM
1883, 1, 25. Rachel S. rmt Wm. F. Bradway
1884, 5, 22. Barton & Ann gct Springfield MM,
               Ia.
1889, 8, 22. Edward rocf Plymouth MM, dtd
               1889,7,22
1891, 1, 22. Jonathan & Elizabeth rocf Ply-
               mouth MM, dtd 1891,1,19
1892, 2, 25. Martha rocf Plymouth MM, dtd
               1892,1,18
1892, 11, 24. Martha rmt Andrew Zippernick

DENKHAUS
1902, 11, 22. Lewis & w, Ella, recrq (G)
1904, 9, 21. Vesta recrq (G)
1908, 12, 23. Lewis [Denkhouse] Jr. recrq (G)

DERR
1871, 10, 26. Ann (form Cameron) dis mcd
1887, 12, 21. James D. & Lydia A. recrq (G)
1888, 2, 22. Maud recrq (G)

DERR, continued
1888, 10, 24. M. F. [Dorr] recrq (G)
1894, 11, 21. Margaret F. relrq (G)
1902, 4, 23. Lillian D. gct Damascus MM (G)
1905, 4, 19. James relrq (G)
1905, 12, 20. Edgar & w, Lillian, & dt, Naomi,
       recrq (G)
1915, 4, 21. Naomi & Isabella, ch Edgar &
       Lillian, relrq (G)
1915, 8, 18. Edgar & Lillian relrq (G)
1916, 7, 19. Lamoine gct Salem MM (G)

DEWEESE
----, --, --. Griffith [Dewees], s Wm. &
       Debby, b 1831,4,11 d 1915,12,14 bur Salem,
       O.; m Ruth Anna MASTERS, dt Wm. & Naomi,
       b 1832,11,1 d 1915,8,12 bur Salem, O.
       Ch: Louisa M. b 1858, 8, 31
           Naomi   " 1862, 8, 14 d 1913,11,29
             bur Salem
           Charles W. b 1865, 4, 28
----, --, --. Charles W. [Dewees], s Griffith
       & Ruthanna (Masters), b 1865,4,28; m
       Mary R. GAMBLE, dt Samuel & Mary Jane
       (Fogg), b 1876,7,12
       Ch: Isaac E.   b 1905, 3, 30
           Martha Ruth" 1907, 2, 18
----, --, --. Jesse m Mary C. BINNS, dt Joseph
       & Balinda, b 1884,2,11
       Ch: Florence
           Martha   b 1905, 5, 31
           Mildred H. " 1909, 3, 2
           Margaret
           Hannah   " 1910, 9, 2
           Joseph
           Howard   " 1912, 1, 24
           James Ezra " 1914, 9, 24
           Jesse H.   " 1918, 2, 14

1891, 10, 22. Louise [Dewees] rocf Chester-
       field MM, dtd 1891,9,19
1891, 10, 22. Griffith & Ruthanna [Dewees]
       rocf Chesterfield MM, dtd 1891,8,15
1896, 3, 26. Naomi [Dewees] rocf Chester-
       field MM, dtd 1896,1,18
1896, 5, 21. Louisa rmt Richard Haworth
1904, 6, 23. Charles W. rmt Mary R. Gamble
1918, 2, 21. Charles W. & w, Mary G., & ch,
       Isaac Edwin & Martha Ruth, gct Upper
       Springfield MM, O.
1919, 2, 20. Edward J. Woolman gct Salem MM,
       to m Mary C. Deweese
1920, 10, 21. Mary C. Woolman & ch, Florence
       Martha, Margaret Hanna, Joseph Howard,
       James Ezra & Jesse Hall Deweese, rocf Sa-
       lem MM
1923, 8, 23. Margaret, minor, gct Birming-
       ham MM, Pa.
1924, 1, 24. Mildred H., minor, rocf Bir-
       mingham MM, Pa., dtd 1923,8,29
1925, 11, 26. Joseph H., minor s Mary Woolman,
       gct Birmingham MM, Pa.

DINGEE
1809, 2, 16. John rmt Bathsheba Walton
1809, 3, 16. Bathsheba gct Westland MM

DIXON
1818, 6, 18. Cert for Nathan & fam returned to
       Middleton MM, because of their rem back

DOBSON
1898, 8, 24. Anna (form Tomlinson) gct Lane
       MM, Mich. (G)

DONLEY
1908, 12, 23. Mary recrq (G)
1909, 1, 20. Edna & Howard recrq (G)
1914, 3, 25. Mary [Donally] relrq (G)

DOWNES
1844, 6, 20. Anna rocf Marlborough MM, dtd
       1844,4,20

DUGDALE
1828, 5, 22. John & w, Sarah B., & ch, Joseph,
       William, Mary, Thomas, Charles, Sally & Ra-
       chel, recrq on cert from Solesbury MM, dtd
       6th mo last to Salem MM (H)
1833, 6, 20. Wm. R., Mary, Thomas, Charles,
       Sarah & Rachel, ch John & Sarah, rocf Salem
       MM, dtd 1833,3,20
1833, 7, 25. Ruth rocf Redstone MM, dtd 1833,
       7,3 (H)
1833, 12, 26. Wm. R. rmt Ann Hillis (H)
1834, 4, 24. Wm. dis mou
1835, 6, 25. Mary F. rmt Lea Bennett (H)
1835, 10, 22. Joseph A. & w, Ruth, gct Green-
       plain MM, O. (H)
1836, 4, 21. John & w, Sarah, & six minor ch
       gct Greenplain MM (H)
1837, 1, 26. Wm. R. & w, Ann, & dt, Eveline,
       gct Green Plain MM (H)
1837, 10, 26. Mary Bennet (form Dugdale) rpd
       mou
1839, 5, 23. Thomas G., Charles R., Sarah,
       Rachel & Elizabeth, ch John, gct Green
       Plain MM, O.
1841, 5, 20. Mary Bennet (form Dugdale) dis
       mcd in H Mtg

DUNLAP
1898, 8, 24. Elizabeth (form Tomlinson) gct
       Lame MM, Mich (G)

DUTTON
1828, 7, 24. Joseph & w, Joanna, & ch, Maria,
       Sarah, Eliza, Phebe, Matilda, Deborah &
       David, also Edmund, Thomas, Henry & David
       Smith recrq (H)
1828, 8, 21. Elisha & Hannah recrq from
       Sandy Spring MM (H)
1834, 5, 22. Maria McBride (form Dutton) dis
       mcd (H)
1834, 10, 25. Eliza rmt Edmund Smith (H)
1835, 5, 21. Hannah rmt Wm. Hilles (H)

DUTTON, continued

1836, 4, 21. Sarah West (form Dutton) con
    mou (H)

1839, 9, 26. Sarah & s, John H. Mendinghall,
    rocf Short Creek MM, O., dtd 1839,7,26 (H)

1840, 3, 26. Phebe D. Windle (form Dutton)
    con mou (H)

1842. 3. 24. Deborah Cleaver (form Dutton)
    con mcd (H)

1884, 1, 23. Emma E. recrq (G)

EDGERTON

1857, 4, 24. Joseph m Anna M. Brantingham

----, --, --. Joseph b 1797,9,10 d 1865,10,30;
    m Anna M. STRATTON, b 1817,9,1 d 1897,1,28
    Ch: Walter   b 1858, 9, 21
        Sarah   " 1860, 8, 13
        Rachel   " 1862, 2, 5

----, --, --. Jesse, s Joseph & Charity, b
    1845,7,12; m Samira STRATTON, dt Edward &
    Mary, b 1844,5,5 d 1878,9,12 bur Coal
    Creek, Iowa
    Ch: Mary Ann   b 1866, 8, 15
        J. Howard " 1869, 3, 13
        Arthur   " 1871, 6, 6
        Wilson   " 1873, 6, 24
        Samira
        Ellen   " 1875, 9, 30

----, --, --. Walter, s Joseph & Anna M., b
    1858,9,21 d 1930,10,11 bur Winona; m Mary
    H. BINNS, dt David & Rebecca, b 1861,9,22
    d 1905,7,22 bur Winona
    Ch: Horace J. b 1881, 9, 15
        Rebecca
        Bertha   " 1883, 12, 28
        Anna Mabel " 1886, 3, 5
        Mildred Ra-
        chel   " 1889, 3, 16
        Wilford D. " 1891, 10, 16
        Jesse N.   " 1895, 12, 26
        Sara M.   " 1899, 9, 13
        James
        Charles   " 1902, 10, 26
    Walter m 2nd Beulah FOGG, dt Edwin &
    Eliza Ann, b 1860,9,22

----, --, --. Horace J., s Walter & Mary H.,
    b 1881,9,15; m Anna V. CAMERON, dt Milton
    & Beulah, b 1883,9,28
    Ch: Raymond
        Milton   b 1905, 12, 12

1911, 11, 24. Anna Mabel m Henry Alden HALL

----, --, --. Walter G., s Jesse & Susan G.,
    b 1884, 6,4; m Mary STRATTON, dt Joseph
    C. & Elizabeth B., b 1884,1,25
    Ch: Gilbert J. b 1914, 12, 23

1918, 7, 26. Mildred Rachel m Jesse Wilmer
    HALL

1921, 9, 22. Sarah m Byron H. COPE

----, --, --. Jesse N., s Walter & Mary H.,
    b 1895,12,26; m Minerva E. COFFMAN, dt
    James & Jane, b 1893,1,23 d 1931,2,3 bur
    Winona

----, --, --. James C., s Walter & Mary H.

(Binns), b 1902,10,26; m Esther Irene
NEWLIN
    Ch: Janice
        Mary   b 1929, 7, 11

1857, 6, 25. Anna M. & ch, Lydia & Sina
    Brantingham gct Somerset MM

1868, 9, 24. Anna M. & ch, Walter, Sarah &
    Rachel, rocf Coal Creek MM, Ia., dtd
    1868,9,12

1875, 1, 21. Jesse & w, Semira, & ch, Mary
    Anna, J. Howard & Arthur, rocf Middleton
    MM, dtd 1875,1,16

1880, 4, 22. Walter gct Short Creek MM, O.,
    to m Mary H. Binns

1880, 10, 21. Rachel rmt Charles Cope

1881, 1, 20. Mary H. rocf Short Creek MM,
    O., dtd 1880,12,21

1881, 7, 21. Walter & Mary H. gct Spring-
    ville MM, Ia.

1882, 2, 23. Jesse gct Salem MM, to m Susan
    Gilbert

1884, 1, 24. Jesse & ch, Mary Anna, J.
    Howard, Arthur H. & Semira Ellen, gct
    Middleton MM

1886, 7, 23. Annie M. & Sarah gct Short
    Creek MM, O.

1901, 7, 25. Walter & w, Mary H., & ch, Hor-
    ace J., Rebecca B., Anna M., Mildred R.,
    Wilford D., Jesse N. & Sara M., rocf Short
    Creek MM, O.

1905, 7, 20. Anna V. rocf Upper Springfield
    MM, O., dtd 1905,6,23

1908, 3, 28. Horace J. & w, Anna V., & s,
    Raymond, gct Upper Springfield MM, O.

1908, 4, 23. Beulah rocf Upper Springfield
    MM, O., dtd 1908,3,27

1909, 1, 21. Walter G. rmt Mary C. Stratton

1917, 3, 22. Jesse N. gct Stillwater MM, O.,
    to m Minerva E. Coffman

1919, 1, 23. Minerva E. rocf Stillwater MM,
    O., dtd 1918,12,25

1921, 2, 24. Wilfred dis mcd & jas

1925, 9, 24. James C. gct Plainfield MM, Ind.,
    to m Esther Irene Newlin

1926, 3, 25. R. Bertha rmt Edgar W. McGrew

1934, 1, 25. Jesse N. & Ethel N. Satterthwait
    declared intentions of m

EDWARDS

1838, 10, 25. Margaret rocf London Grove MM,
    dtd 1838,3,8

1841, 10, 21. Margaret gct Sandy Spring MM

1883, 7, 26. Mary Ann (form Raley) dis mcd

ELLIOTT

1817, 3, 13. Martha rocf Warrington MM, dtd
    1816,3,21

1817, 6, 19. Elizabeth rocf Middleton MM,
    dtd 1817,5,12

1840, 6, 25. Maria (form Heston) dis mou (H)

1850, 3, 21. Martha gct Goshen MM, O.

ELLIS
1811, 8, 15. Enos rocf Salem MM, dtd 1811,8, 13
1816, 5, 16. Gainer rmt Mercy Jackson
1817, 10, 16. Elizabeth rmt Joseph Carroll
1818, 1, 15. Enos dis disunity
1821, 11, 22. John Neal Jr. gct Sandy Spring MM, to m Mary M. Ellis
1824, 6, 24. Enos Jr. rpd mcd; dis 1825,1,20

ELLISON
1853, 12, 23. Sarah (form Votaw) dis mcd

1885, 1, 22. Joseph J. Coppock gct Hickory Grove MM, Ia., to m Rebecca[Ellyson]

EMBLY
1812, 6, 18. Richard rocf West Hartford MM, Conn., dtd 1812,1,8, endorsed by Concord MM, 1812,3,26
1812, 6, 18. Mariah, w Richard, rocf Chesterfield MM, N. J., dtd 1811,12,3, endorsed by Concord MM, 1812,3,26
1813, 5, 13. Richard [Emley] & w gct Chesterfield MM, N. J.

EMBREY
1817, 8, 14. John & fam gct Plainfield MM

EMMINGER
1910, 7, 20. Chas. H. & w, Lena, rocf Spiceland MM, Ind. (G)
1916, 5, 24. Herchel relrq (G)

EMMONS
1820, 10, 26. Elias & w & ch, Enos, Martin, Rebecca, Jonathan, Levi, Lydia & Susanna, recrq
1830, 11, 25. Thomas, minor, rocf Sandy Spring MM, O., dtd 1830,10,22
1833, 8, 22. Thomas Jr. rmt Mary Coppock
1834, 1, 23. Thomas Jr. & w, Mary, gct Sandy Spring MM, O.
1908, 12, 23. Wm. recrq (G)
1910, 2, 23. Will & w relrq (G)

ENGLAND
1834, 12, 25. Samuel & w, Hannah, & ch, Sarah Ann & Milton V., rocf Pipe Creek MM, dtd 1834,11,15 (H)
1842, 2, 24. Hannah & s gct Smithfield MM (H)
1842, 2, 24. Sarah Ann gct Smithfield MM (H)

ENLOWS
----, --, --. Samuel [Enloes] m Huldah ----- b 1832,8,19
          Ch: William S. b 1852, 1, 12

1844, 1, 25. Robert Whinery gct Marlborough MM, to m Susan Enlows
1851, 4, 24. Samuel rmt Huldah Whinery
1851, 11, 20. Samuel rocf Marlborough MM

ENTRIKIN
1833, 2, 21. Emmor & w, Susanna, & ch, Franklin Wayne & James Bennett, rocf Birmingham MM, dtd 1833,1,5 (H)

EWIN
1818, 11, 26. Samuel rocf Darby MM, dtd 1818, 1,27
1818, 12, 24. Samuel [Ewing] dis mcd

FAGAN
1818, 1, 15. Euphemy [Phegan] rocf Middleton MM, dtd 1817,12,15
1818, 3, 19. Harmon & w, Lydia, rocf Middleton MM, dtd 1817,11,10
1828, 9, 25. Harmon dis jH

FARMER
1809, 12, 14. Edith recrq
1819, 11, 25. Mary Jr. gct Stillwater MM
1820, 3, 23. Susanna gct Stillwater MM
1820, 11, 23. Ann & six ch gct Stillwater MM
1821, 10, 25. Kitura gct Flushing MM

FARRINGTON
1816, 5, 16. Abraham & w, Deborah, & ch, Moses, Judith, Jesse Kirk, Phebe, Bellion, John & Deborah, rocf Salem MM, dtd 1816,4, 16
1825, 11, 24. Moses rocf Sandy Spring MM, O., dtd 1825,4,22
1826, 11, 23. Moses rmt Armella Kirk
1829, 8, 20. Moses dis jH
1831, 10, 20. Moses & w, Armella, & ch gct Owl Creek MM (H)
1832, 2, 23. Armelia dis jH
1835, 8, 20. Sarah rocf Sandy Spring MM, O., dtd 1835,6,26
1835, 8, 20. Deborah rocf Sandy Spring MM, O., dtd 1835,6,26
1836, 1, 21. Sarah gct Burlington MM, N. J.
1836, 2, 25. Sarah rocf Salem MM, dtd 1835, 12,24 (H)
1836, 4, 21. Sarah gct Salem MM (H)
1839, 1, 24. Abraham & w, Sarah, rocf Salem MM, dtd 1838,9,25 (H)
1842, 7, 21. Mary & Sarah, minors, gct Gilead MM

FAWCETT
1839, 8, 23. Elisha rmt Herophila Davis (H)
1840, 5, 21. Herophila gct Plainfield MM (H)
1844, 7, 25. Emeline (form Griffith) dis mcd
1862, 6, 26. Sarah (form Negus) dis mcd
1865, 12, 21. Jephtha rmt Lydia Ann Arnold
1866, 7, 26. Lydia Ann gct Chesterfield MM

FERGUSON
1879, 5, 21. Wm. C. recrq (G)
1880, 5, 19. Wm. dis (G)

FERREL
1813, 4, 15. Rachel (form Beck) dis mcd

FERREL, continued
1817, 11, 13. Rachel rst
1824, 9, 23. Rachel [Fereel] dis jas

FINCH
1820, 6, 22. Hannah (form Williams) dis mcd

FISTLER
1893, 3, 22. Frank & w, May, & ch gct Tecum-
      seh MM, Mich. (G)

FLANNER
1878, 8, 21. Anna recrq (G)
1880, 4, 21. Anna E. relrq (G)

FOGG
1879, 5, 22. Milton Cameron gct Upper Spring-
      field MM, O., to m Bula Fogg

FOLGER
1815, 4, 13. Cert rec for Mahew & fam from
      Uwchland MM, Pa., dtd 1813,9,9, endorsed
      to Marlborough MM

FORSYTHE
1921, 8, 25. Chas. Walter Satterthwait gct
      Birmingham MM, Pa., to m Helen M. For-
      sythe

FOSTER
----, --, --. Millicent, w Wm., dt Wilson J.
      & Mary C. (Hall) Steer, b 1900,1,24
1923, 8, 15. Wm. O. m Millicent H. STEER

1816, 10, 17. Thomas Brown & w, Elizabeth, &
      ch, Francis Foster, her s by form m, &
      Samuel, Sarah, Margaret, Eleanor, Joshua,
      Timothy & Esther Brown, rocf Redstone MM,
      dtd 1816,4,24
1834, 5, 22. Francis dis mou
1885, 6, 26. Esther (form Stafford) dis mcd
1923, 12, 20. Millicent S. gct Nantucket MM

FOWLER
----, --, --. Edmund Smith m Mary MILES, dt
      Wm. & Mary P., b 1830,2,15 d 1915,10,28
      bur Winona
      Ch: Mary Sara b 1868, 8, 26
----, --, --. John S., s Caleb & Sarah S.,
      b 1832,8,22 d 1910,12,11 bur Winona (an
      elder) m Esther HUESTES, dt Isaac & Sa-
      rah, b 1845,6,27 d 1922,5,17 bur Winona
----, --, --. Orlando, s Edmund & Mary, b 1859,
      11,20 d 1914,3,28 bur Winona (an elder);
      m Hannah C. DEAN, dt Jonathan & Elizabeth,
      b 1862,11,19
      Ch: Edgar L.   b 1881, 11, 4
          Emerson J. " 1883, 5, 30 d 1889,11, 5
          Alfred Ir-
          ving   " 1888, 5, 21
          Mary E.   " 1892, 10, 23 d 1892,11,21
          bur Winona, O.
----, --, --. Alfred Irving, s Orland R. &

Hannah C., b 1888,5,2; m Emma E. MORRIS,
dt John W. & Susanna, b 1883,4,29
Ch: Dorothy
        Margaret b 1910, 9, 16
        Ruth E.   " 1913, 6, 16
        Esther
        Hanna   " 1922, 5, 25
1929, 6, 22. Hannah C. m Elisha B. STEER

1835, 7, 23. Samuel & w, Phebe, & ch gct
      Salem MM (H)
1889, 9, 26. Orland R. & w, Hannah C., & ch,
      Edgar L., Emmerson J. & Alfred Irving,
      rocf Plymouth MM, dtd 1889,8,19
1898, 3, 24. John S. & Esther rocf Birmingham
      MM, dtd 1898,3,2
1909, 10, 21. Mary M. rocf Chesterfield MM
1909, 10, 21. Sarah rocf Chesterfield MM
1910, 6, 23. Emma E. (Morris) rocf Westbranch
      MM, Ia., dtd 1910,6,11
1917, 6, 21. Mary Sara rmt Albert Warrington

FRENCH
1810, 11, 15. Barzillai rmt Mary Yeates
1811, 11, 17. Mary gct Salem MM
1859, 5, 26. Ezra Coppock gct Upper Spring-
      field MM, O., to m Ruth Ann French
1865, 5, 25. Mary dis jG

FRITCHMAN
----, --, --. ----- m Mary HUTTON, dt Joel &
      Ann, b 1837,6,25 d 1899,9,12
      Ch: Emerson B. b 1870, 3, 7
          Adison H. " 1872, 5, 31
          John H.   " 1872, 10, 2
          Mary H.   " 1875, 8, 23
      (h's name given Joseph Fritchman in
      another volume)

1878, 5, 23. Mary H. rstrq
1878, 10, 24. Emmerson B., Addison H., John
      & Mary, ch Mary H., recrq
1914, 8, 20. Mary F. Hole (form Fritchman)
      con mcd
1922, 12, 21. Mary F. Hole (form Fritchman)
      dis mcd & jas

FUGATE
1814, 3, 17. Elizabeth (form Williams) dis
      mcd

FULTS
1887, 12, 21. Emma recrq (G)
1899, 7, 19. Nettie recrq (G)

GACHEL
1819, 11, 25. Hannah rocf Little Britain MM,
      Pa., dtd 1819,9,11

GALBREATH
1817, 9, 18. Nathan gct Marlborough MM, to m
      Ruth Logue
1818, 3, 19. Ruth rocf Marlborough MM, dtd

GALBREATH, continued
   1818,2,18
1818, 12, 24. David rmt Sarah Paxton
1821, 12, 20. Sarah rmt Stephen Hambleton
1822, 7, 25. Thomas gct Bradford MM, Pa., to
   m Ann Bailey
1822, 11, 21. Ann rmt Moses Hambleton
1823, 3, 20. Wm. rmt Mary Rogers
1823, 5, 22. Ann, w Thomas, rocf Bradford MM,
   Pa., dtd 1823,1,8
1828, 7, 24. Nathan & Ruth dis jH
1828, 7, 24. Thomas dis jH
1828, 7, 24. Susanna dis jH
1828, 11, 20. Mary, Sarah & Ann dis jH
1829, 1, 22. Wm. dis jH
1829, 1, 22. David dis jH
1829, 7, 23. Hannah & Sarah dis jH
1836, 5, 26. Hannah rmt Samuel Jackson (H)
1837, 10, 26. Nathan Jr. dis jH
1839, 12, 26. Elizabeth P. rmt Thomas E.
   Vickers (H)
1841, 5, 20. Elizabeth Vickers (form Galbreath) dis mcd in Hicksite Mtg
1842, 12, 22. David L. dis disunity
1842, 12, 22. Matilda dis jH
1843, 1, 26. James H. dis jH
1845, 1, 23. Esther Ann Lukens (form Galbreath) dis mcd
1848, 1, 20. Francis C. [Galbraith] dis mcd
1854, 6, 22. James & w, Jane, & ch, Sarah
   Ann, Charity & Elizabeth, rocf Deep River
   MM, N. C., dtd 1854,4,6
1868, 4, 23. Elizabeth B. & Sarah Ann dis
   jG
1876, 9, 2-. Elizabeth Blackburn (form Galbreath) con mcd (G)
1886, 7, 21. Leah rocf Damascus MM, dtd
   1886,6,26 (G)
1887, 7, 20. Samuel & adopted s, Roland Galbreath, recrq (G)
1894, 2, 21. Amanda recrq (G)

GAMBLE
----, --, --. Harrison b 1815,5,12 in Ireland;
   m Phebe ----- b 1825,2,17 d 1866,7,15
   Ch: Samuel   b 1844, 3, 1
      Charles   " 1846, 3, 10
      Sarah   " 1848, 3, 15
      William   " 1850, 3, 4
      Martha Jane" 1852, 7, 20
      Elisha   " 1854, 11, 28
      Ruth Ellen " 1857, 2, 24
----, --, --. Charles, s Harrison & Phebe,
   b 1846,3,10 d 1893,4,23; m Martha HALL,.
   dt Robert & Mary, b 1849,9,1
----, --, --. Samuel, s Harrison & Phebe
   (Hollingsworth), b 1844,3,1 d 1921,5,14
   bur Winona; m Mary Jane FOGG, dt Ebeneezer
   & Jane (Young), b 1838,4,7 d 1917,12,18
   bur Winona, O.
   Ch: Charles W. b 1868, 10, 31
      Phebe Jane " 1870, 9, 3
      Edward Y.   " 1874, 10, 12

   Ch: Mary R.   b 1876, 7, 12
      Irena H.   " 1879, 8, 1
      Alvina H.   " 1882, 7, 8
      Homer S.   " 1884, 12, 31
----, --, --. Charles W., s Samuel & Mary
   Jane, b 1868,10,31 d 1929,2,17; m Rachel
   S. WHINERY, dt Nathan & Amelia, b 1870,7,
   13
   Ch: Altha E.   b 1892, 10, 11 d 1908, 2,19
      bur Winona, O.
      Ernest J. b 1894, 10, 5 " 1898, 2,19
      bur Winona, O.
      Arthur S. b 1896, 8, 22
      Emma L.   " 1899, 2, 9
      Amelia B. " 1901, 10, 23
      Edith M.   " 1904, 1, 9
      Albert L. " 1907, 8, 12
----, --, --. Homer S., s Samuel & Mary Jane
   (Fogg), b 1884,12,31; m Lena BOHNER, dt
   Edward & Magdalena (Miller), b 1881,12,23
   Ch: Wilford
      Edward   b 1909, 7, 9
      Carl Samuel" 1911, 1, 21
      George
      Alfred   " 1912, 10, 12
      Alice Lena " 1915, 12, 17
      Catharine
      Rebecca   " 1917, 8, 31
      Homer J.   " 1919, 7, 17
1921, 5, 27. Emma L. m Walter C. LIVEZEY
1926, 7, 17. Bertha Amelia m Emery C. HOLLO-
   WAY
1932, 4, 23. Edith May m Milford MOTT

1853, 5, 26. Harrison & w, Phebe, & ch, Samuel, Charles, Sarah, Wm. & Martha Jane,
   rocf Salem MM, dtd 1853,5,25
1858, 4, 22. Harrison & w, Phebe, & ch,
   Samuel, Charles, Sarah, William, Martha
   Jane, Elisha & Ruth Ellen, gct Middleton
   MM
1883, 5, 24. Samuel & w, Mary Jane, & ch,
   Charles W., Phebe Jane, Edward Y., Mary
   R., Irena H. & Alvina H. & her s, James
   L. W. Bradway, rocf Salem MM, dtd 1883,4,
   25
1891, 10, 22. Charles W. rmt Rachel S. Whinery
1896, 12, 24. Phebe Jane Camp (form Gamble)
   dis mcd
1897, 5, 22. Charles & Martha H. rocf Salem
   MM, dtd 1897,5,19
1904, 6, 23. Mary R. rmt Chas. W. Deweese
1905, 8, 24. Irena H. rmt Edwin G. Price
1912, 5, 23. Lena M. recrq
1912, 8, 22. Alvin H. con mcd
1913, 6, 26. Alvin H. gct Middleton MM
1914, 2, 26. Wilford E. & Carol S., minor ch
   Homer S. & Lena M., recrq
1915, 7, 22. Martha H. gct Salem MM
1917, 9, 20. Homer S. & w, Lena M., & ch,
   Wilford Edward, Carl Samuel, George Alfred & Alice Lena, also Catharine Rebecca,
   gct Upper Springfield MM, O.

GAMBLE, continued

1920, 12, 23. Homer S. & w, Lena M., & ch, Wilford E., Karl S., G. Alfred, Alice M., Kay Rebecca & Homer Jr., rocf Upper Springfield MM, O.

1925, 7, 23. Arthur con mcd

GANT

1865, 6, 22. Sarah Ann (form Harris) dis mcd

GARDNER

1896, 2, 19. Roza C. gct Salem MM (G)

GARRETSON

1821, 1, 25. George [Gareson] & w, Anne, & ch, Joseph, Jesse & Hiram, rocf Warrington MM, dtd 1820,11,23

1828, 9, 25. George & Ann dis jH

1830, 7, 22. Cert rec for John & w, Ann, & ch, Eli, Mariah, Sidney & Ann, from Warrington MM, dtd 1830,5,20, endorsed to Salem MM (H)

1830, 7, 22. Cert rec for Pierce from Warrington MM, dtd 1830,5,20, endorsed to Salem MM (H)

1830, 7, 22. Cert rec for Rebecca & Hannah, from Warrington MM, dtd 1830,5,20, endorsed to Salem MM (H)

1831, 5, 26. Jesse dis mcd & jH

1831, 8, 25. Joseph dis jH

1835, 4, 23. Pierce rmt Sarah H. Myres (H)

1842, 11, 24. Hiram dis mcd

GARRIGAS

1832, 11, 22. Margaret E. & ch, Helen, Deborah, Charles & Sally Ann, rocf Indian Spring MM, dtd 1832,8,8 (H)

1838, 7, 26. Helen M. [Garrigus] rmt Edwin C. Hall (H)

GARWOOD

----, --, --. John W. b 1827,7,8; m Asenath ----- b 1825,6,5
    Ch: Sylvanus P.b 1851, 9, 24
        Ann Eliza " 1853, 6, 20 d 1870, 4,11
        Elizabeth
        Jane   " 1854, 9, 22
        Lewis J.   " 1856, 9, 9
        Anna Pris-
        cilla   " 1861, 6, 18
        Joseph D. " 1865, 7, 6
        Rachel H. " 1867, 8, 12

1864, 8, 25. John & w, Asenath, & ch, Ann, Eliza, Elizabeth Jane, Lewis G. & Anna Priscilla, rocf Middleton MM, dtd 1864,8, 20

1871, 1, 26. John & w, Ascenith, & ch gct Salem MM

1876, 9, 21. John W. & w, Aseneth, & ch, Lewis J., Anna P., Joseph D. & Rachel K., rocf Salem MM, dtd 1876,9,20

1879, 7, 27. John & w, Asenath, & ch, Anna P.,

Joseph D. & Rachel H., gct Upper Springfield MM, O.

GASKELL

1828, 5, 22. Israel & s, Nathan Robert, recrq (H)

1828, 7, 24. Israel [Gaskill] & s, Nathan R., gct Salem MM (H)

GAUCHER

1832, 3, 23. Margaret (form White) dis (H)

GAUSE

1811, 8, 15. Ann R. (form More) con mcd

1812, 7, 16. Ann R. gct Salem MM

GEORGE

1830, 11, 16. Henry rmt Lydia Hoopes

1831, 2, 24. Lydia & ch, Esther & Joseph Leech Hoops, gct Carmel MM

GIBSON

1839, 5, 23. Mary recrq

1840, 6, 25. Martha recrq

1841, 3, 25. Martha gct Salem MM

1843, 9, 21. Mary rmt Allen Reynolds

GILBERT

----, --, --. George D., s Abner & Anna, b 1802,4,10 d 1872,3,25 bur Winona; m Hannah COPE, dt Joshua & Alice, b 1805,2,26 d 1882,11,2 bur Winona
    Ch: Ann Eliza b 1832, 8, 17 d 1886, 4,14
        bur Winona, O.
        Sara   b 1840, 1, 26 " 1884, 3,21
        bur Winona, O.
        Ellen   b 1851, 3, 31

----, --, --. Joshua, s Geo. D. & Hannah, b 1837,11,18; m Deborah HUTTON, dt Joel & Ann, b 1841,11,17 d 1883,9,19 bur Winona
    Ch: Wilmer H. b 1862, 7, 20
        Edwin D.   " 1864, 8, 23
        Elma   " 1868, 1, 1
        Rebecca   " 1876, 3, 2 d 1903,12, 9
        bur Winona, O.

1874, 5, 22. Ellen C. m Elisha B. STEER

1824, 6, 24. Tacy (form Heald) dis mou

1871, 5, 25. George & w, Hannah, & dt, Ellen C., rocf Sewickley MM, dtd 1871,5,2

1871, 8, 24. Ann Eliza & Sarah rocf Sewickley MM, dtd 1871,8,1

1872, 1, 25. Joshua & w, Deborah, & ch, Wilmer H., Edwin D. & Elma, rocf Sewickley MM Pa., dtd 1872,1,2

1875, 2, 25. Hannah & gr ch, Ellen B. & Ida A. Newlin, recrq

1880, 1, 22. Sarah rmt Joshua Brantingham

1882, 2, 23. Jesse Edgerton gct Salem MM, to m Susan Gilbert

1889, 5, 23. Wilmer H. dis mcd

1892, 8, 25. Elma G. Hole (form Gilbert) con mcd

GILLINGHAM
1819, 3, 25. Joseph rocf Indian Spring MM,
    Md., dtd 1818,12,18
1820, 6, 22. Joseph rpd mcd
1824, 1, 22. Joseph con mou
1829, 3, 26. Joseph dis jH

GILSON
1892, 12, 21. Grace recrq (G)
1898, 7, 20. Grace gct Cleveland MM (G)

GRAVEN
1818, 10, 22. Cert rec for Rebecca from ND MM
    dtd 1816,10,22, endorsed to Marlborough MM

GREEN
1814, 3, 17. Thomas rocf Plainfield MM, dtd
    1814,1,22
1816, 5, 16. Thomas gct Salem MM
1818, 1, 15. Lydia rocf Middleton MM, dtd
    1817,12,15

GREWELL
1845, 6, 26. John P. & w, Sarah, & ch, Caro-
    line S., Ann Eliza, Alice & Charles B.,
    rocf Upper Springfield MM, O., dtd 1845,
    5,24
1849, 8, 23. John P. & w, Sarah, & ch, Alice,
    Ann Eliza & Charles B., gct Upper Spring-
    field MM, O.
1873, 11, 19. Rhoda A. P. con mcd (G)
1874, 2, 24. Rhoda A. P. gct Oskaloosa MM,
    Ia. (G)

GRIFFITH
1816, 8, 15. Reuben & ch, Ann Moor, Rebecca,
    Elizabeth, Mary & Ketura, gct Short Creek
    MM, O.
1819, 4, 22. Wm. rocf Middleton MM, dtd 1819,
    3,22
1820, 2, 24. Oliver rocf Warrington MM, dtd
    1818,10,20
1820, 7, 20. Ann M. rocf Short Creek MM, O.,
    dtd 1820,3,23
1820, 8, 24. Cert rec for Rebecca from Short
    Creek MM, O., dtd 1820,5,23, endorsed to
    Salem MM
1821, 9, 20. Ann Reaps (form Griffith) dis
    mcd
1822, 1, 24. Wm. rmt Mary Votaw
1823, 6, 26. Julia rocf Saddsbury MM, dtd
    1822,4,18
1825, 10, 19. Julia Briggs (form Griffith) con
    mcd
1828, 8, 21. Wm. dis jH
1828, 9, 25. Mary dis jH
1829, 6, 25. Oliver dis disunity & mou
1830, 3, 25. Oliver con mcd (H)
1830, 12, 23. Mary H. rocf Warrington MM, dtd
    1830,9,23 (H)
1844, 7, 25. Emeline Fawcett (form Griffith)
    dis mcd
1853, 3, 24. Albert dis mcd

GRIMSHAW
1825, 4, 21. James (Jane on women's minutes)
    rocf Smithfield MM, dtd 1825,3,21
1826, 10, 26. Jane gct Smithfield MM

GRISSELL
1830, 1, 22. Margaret [Grissle] m Enos LEWIS
    (H)

1810, 11, 15. Joseph rpd mcd; dis 1811,1,11
1814, 6, 16. Samuel dis mcd
1815, 4, 13. Ann Wilson (form Grissell) dis
    mcd
1817, 1, 16. Thomas [Grissle] Jr. dis mcd
1819, 8, 26. Martha rmt Benjamin Johnson
1821, 7, 26. Thomas Jr. rstrq
1821, 12, 20. Almira, w Thomas Jr., & ch,
    William, Nathan & Benjamin, recrq
1822, 2, 21. Samuel rstrq
1824, 5, 20. Ann, w Samuel, & ch, Sabina,
    Martha, Amos, Hiram, Mariah & Sarah, recrq
1826, 3, 23. Thomas Jr. & w, Almira, & ch,
    William, Nathan, Benjamin, Joseph & Mar-
    tha, gct Alum Creek MM, O.
1827, 9, 20. Charles D. rmt Mary F. Smith
1829, 3, 26. Samuel & w, Ann, dis jH
1829, 4, 23. Hannah rmt Samuel Reynolds
1829, 7, 23. Margaret, Mary & Martha dis jH
1829, 9, 24. Charles D. dis jH
1834, 9, 25. Samuel & w, Ann, & minor ch gct
    White Water MM, Ind. (H)
1834, 9, 25. Sabina & Martha gct White Water
    MM, Ind. (H)
1836, 3, 24. Cert rec for Almira, & ch, Wm.,
    Nathan, Benjamin, Joseph, Martha, Miriam,
    Almira & Rachel, from Alum Creek MM, O.,
    dtd 1834,11,20, endorsed back to Alum
    Creek MM
1837, 6, 22. Minor ch of Samuel gc
1837, 6, 22. Subbina gct White Water MM, Ind.
1837, 9, 21. Martha gct White Water MM, Ind.
    (H)
1851, 1, 23. Caroline E. dis disunity

GROSSE
1895, 4, 24. Deborah relrq (G)

HAINS
1809, 7, 13. Mahlon [Haines] & w, Rachel, &
    ch, Enos & William, rocf Middleton MM, dtd
    1809,5,13
1814, 6, 16. Rachel [Haines] & ch gct Middle-
    ton MM
1823, 6, 26. Chalkley rocf Redstone MM, dtd
    1823,5,30
1823, 12, 25. Enos, minor, rocf Middleton MM,
    dtd 1823,11,17
1824, 1, 22. Chalkley rmt Sarah Morgan
1824, 4, 22. Chalkley [Haines] & w, Sarah,
    gct Marlborough MM
1824, 4, 22. Chalkley [Haines] & w, Sarah,
    gct Marlborough MM
1826, 11, 23. Enos, minor, gct Middleton MM

HAINS, continued
1827, 6, 21. Cert granted to Middleton for
      Enos returned, unused

HALDERMAN
1819, 4, 22. David & w & ch, Benjamin, Jacob,
      Elizabeth, Ann & Martha, recrq
1876, 6, 22. Anna H. Winder (form Halderman)
      con mcd
1877, 9, 20. Richard dis jG
1877, 10, 25. Tamar Susannah dis jG

HALL
----, --, --. James E., s John & Tacy, b 1829,
      3,28 d 1907,10,30 bur Winona, O.
----, --, --. Lindley, s David & Sara T.,
      b 1839,3,11 d 1915,7,1 bur Winona, O.; m
      Millicent BAILEY, dt Edmund & Margaret
      (Doudna), b 1839,8,15 d 1920,6,3 (an elder)
      Ch: Dilwyn E. b 1876, 8, 23 d 1919, 6,24
          bur Winona, O.
1891, 3, 27. Joseph m Olive H. OLIPHANT
----, --, --. Joseph, s Wm. & Mary (Thomas),
      b 1868,1,16; m Olive H. OLIPHANT, dt John
      & Hannah P. (Williams), b 1869,4,17
      Ch: Emily C.   b 1892, 12, 27
          Albert J. " 1896, 6, 1 d 1908, 2,17
            bur Winona, O.
          Lindley W. b 1898, 6, 25
----, --, --. Dilwyn E., s Lindley & Millicent
      (Bailey), b 1876,8,23 d 1919,6,24 bur
      Winona; m Anna C. COPE, dt Chas. & Rachel
      E., b 1882,10,11 d 1933,11,16 bur Winona
      Ch: Edith
            Rachel b 1907, 1, 25
          Bertha
            Millicent" 1908, 11, 11
          Clifford D.
                    b 1915, 4, 4
          Edna Vir-
            ginia   " 1917, 5, 14
----, --, --. Clifton P., s Lewis & Margaret
      Ann, b 1883,2,26; m Anna PICKETT, dt
      Phineas & Harriett, b 1882,12,25
      Ch: Luella L. b 1907, 6, 10
          Ethel Mar-
            garet   " 1911, 3, 24
          Leiis
          Clifton   " 1917, 6, 27
----, --, --. Barclay S., s Lewis & Margaret
      Ann, b 1884,10,4; m Mary CAMERON, dt Mil-
      ton & Beulah, b 1887,2,16
      Ch: Willard B. b 1910, 6, 13
          Beulah
            Margaret " 1912, 8, 10
----, --, --. Mildred Rachel, w Jesse W., dt
      Walter & Mary H. (Binns) Edgerton, b 1889,
      3,16
1911, 11, 24. Henry Alden m Anna Mabel EDGERTON
1913, 8, 23. Emily C. m Oliver F. SIDWELL
1918, 7, 26. Jesse Wilmer m Mildred Rachel
      EDGERTON
----, --, --. Lindley W., s Joseph & Olive,

b 1898,6,25; m Orpha J. PIKE, dt Alpheus
& Jane (Haworth), b 1899,8,7
Ch: Margaret
      Evalyn   b 1922, 9, 3
    Raymond
      Lindley   " 1924, 8, 7
    Mildred
      Olive   " 1927, 3, 17
    Beulah Mar-
      jorie   " 1932, 1, 23
1929, 8, 14. Luella L. m Robert Leland THOMAS

1819, 11, 25. Jane rocf Sadsbury MM, dtd
      1819,9,7
1824, 4, 22. Edward & ch, Sarah P., Wm. W.,
      Mary, Rachel & Mahlon, recrq
1829, 3, 26. Jane dis jH
1829, 6, 25. Edward dis jH
1833, 9, 26. Thomas V. & w, Phebe, & ch, Ed-
      win, Rufus, William, Alfred & Elizabeth,
      rocf Cherry St. MM, Phila., dtd 1833,4,17
      (H)
1833, 12, 26. Jane rmt Abraham Heston (H)
1838, 7, 26. Edwin C. rmt Helen M. Garrihus
      (H)
1840, 8, 20. Wm. dis jas
1840, 9, 24. Sarah P. dis jas
1841, 11, 25. Helen M. dis (H)
1841, 3, 25. George E., Albert P. & Edward,
      ch Edward, dec, gct Darby MM, Pa.
1841, 3, 25. Mary & Thomas H., ch Edward,
      dec, gct Uwchland MM, Pa.
1842, 6, 23. Rachel dis jH
1844, 9, 26. Lydia Taylor (form Hall) dis
      mou (H)
1852, 3, 25. Mahlon dis mcd
1860, 5, 24. Samuel Barber gct Stillwater MM,
      O., to m Elizabeth Hall
1865, 11, 23. Martha Hollingsworth & s, Joseph
      Hall, rocf Middleton MM, dtd 1865,11,18
1865, 11, 23. Mary rocf Middleton MM, dtd
      1865,11,18
1870, 12, 22. James E. rocf Short Creek MM,
      O., dtd 1870,11,22
1874, 3, 26. Martha, Sarah R. & Deborah D.
      gct Salem MM
1891, 8, 20. Olive H. gct Short Creek MM, O.
1895, 9, 25. Bertha, Nancy & Ella recrq (G)
1898, 2, 23. Ralph recrq (G)
1904, 1, 21. Lindley & Millicent rocf Short
      Creek MM, O., dtd 1903,12,22
1904, 10, 20. Joseph & w, Olive H., & ch,
      Emily C., Albert J. & Lindley W., rocf
      Short Creek MM, O., dtd 1904,9,20
1905, 10, 26. Dillwyn E. rmt Anna Cope
1910, 10, 20. Clifton P. & w, Anna, & dt,
      Lewella L., rocf Short Creek MM, O., dtd
      1910, 10, 18
1910, 10, 20. Barclay S. & w, Mary C., & s,
      Willard B., rocf Short Creek MM, O., dtd
      1910,10,18
1812, 4, 25. Anna Mabel gct Stillwater MM,O.

HALL, continued
1914, 2, 26. Barclay S. & w, Mary C., & ch, Willard B. & Beulah M., gct Upper Spring-field MM, O.
1918, 12, 26. Mildred R. gct Somerset MM, O.
1920, 8, 26. Lindley W. gct Plainfield MM, Ind., to m Orpha Pike
1921, 2, 24. Orpha J. rocf Plainfield MM, Ind., dtd 1921,2,21

HAMBLETON
1817, 11, 13. Edward Carroll Jr. gct Middleton MM, to m Rachel Hamilton

1820, 7, 20. Moses rocf Eden MM, dtd 1819,12, 1
1820, 8, 24. Stephen rocf Eden MM, dtd 1820, 5,31
1821, 3, 22. Mary rocf Kingwood MM, N. J., dtd 1821,1,11
1821, 12, 20. Stephen rmt Sarah Galbreath
1822, 7, 25. Mary gct Carmel MM
1822, 11, 21. Moses rmt Ann Galbreath
1825, 4, 21. Stephen & w, Sarah, & ch, Thomas Elwood & Isaac Herbert, gct Carmel MM
1826, 6, 22. Benjamin & w, Ann, & ch, Rachel, Osborn, Levi, Catherine H. & Joel G., rocf Carmel MM, dtd 1826,6,17
1827, 10, 25. Moses & w, Ann, & ch, Charles & Eliza, gct Carmel MM
1828, 6, 26. Cert for Moses [Hamilton] & fam returned, unused (H)
1828, 8, 21. Ann dis JH
1828, 8, 21. Benjamin dis JH
1829, 5, 21. Moses & w, Ann, & ch, Charles, Eliza & Susanna, gct Carmel MM (H)
1830, 11, 16. Moses & Ann [Hamilton] dis JH
1832, 7, 26. Moses & w, Ann, & ch, Charles, Eliza, Susannah & Hannah, rocf Carmel MM, dtd 1832,6,16 (H)
1834, 10, 23. Moses & w, Ann, & fam gct White Water MM, Ind. (H)
1839, 12, 26. Rachel dis JH
1840, 4, 23. Osborn dis JH
1845, 9, 25. Levi dis JH

HAMPTON
----, --, --. Clinton E. s Richard & Maria (Bailey), b 1864,10,21; m Sarah SMITH, dt Evan & Mary (Burgess), b 1859,9,30
    Ch: Alva Jesse b 1891, 10, 11
        Russel B. " 1896, 8, 25
----, --, --. Russell B., s Clinton E. & Sarah (Smith), b 1896,8,25; m Mary E. SATTERTH-WAIT, dt Wm. D. & Ida A. (Newlin), b 1898,8,23
    Ch: Elmer N.   b 1921, 1, 20
        William R. " 1922, 3, 20
----, --, --. Alva J. b 1891,10,11; m Ruth Amy PICKETT, dt Robert B. & Irene J. (Allen), b 1896,5,13
    Ch: Lura
        Louise   b 1922, 7, 12

1918, 5, 23. Clinton E. & w, Sarah, & ch, Alva Jesse & Russell B., rocf Hickory Grove MM, Ia.
1820, 3, 25. Russell B. gct Salem MM, to m Mary E. Satterthwait
1920, 7, 22. Mary E. rocf Salem MM
1920, 10, 21. Alva J. gct Mill Creek MM, Ind., to m Ruth Amy Pickett
1921, 4, 21. Clinton E. & w, Sarah, gct Fair-hope MM, Ala.
1922, 10, 26. Russel B. & w, Mary E:, & ch, Elmer N. & Wm. R., gct Fairhope MM, Ala.
1924, 1, 24. Alva J. & dt, Lura Louise, gct Mill Creek MM, Ind.
1926, 4, 26. Clinton E. & w, Sara, rocf Fair-hope MM, Ala., dtd 1926,3,17

HANNAH
1816, 7, 18. Hannah rocf Warrington MM, dtd 1816,3,21
1819, 6, 24. Benjamin [Hanna] & w, Rachel, & ch, Joshua, Leonard, Levi, Zelinda, Robert, Triphena, Rebecca & Thomas, rocf Salem MM, dtd 1819,5,19
1824, 8, 26. Thomas [Hanna] & w, Anna, rocf Carmel MM, dtd 1824,7,17
1826, 5, 25. Robert [Hanna] & w, Catharine, rocf Carmel MM, dtd 1826,4,15
1828, 7, 24. Zalinda Hosteter (form Hanna) dis mou
1828, 9, 25. Zalinda Hosteter (form Hanna) con mcd (H)
1828, 9, 25. Benjamin & Rachel [Hanna] dis JH
1828, 12, 25. Anna [Hanna] dis JH
1829, 12, 24. Joshua & Leonard dis JH
1830, 2, 25. Levi dis JH
1833, 9, 26. Tryphena rmt Samuel Nichols (H)
1834, 11, 20. Anne gct Middleton MM (H)
1836, 12, 22. Robert gct Sandy Spring MM, O.
1837, 10, 26. Robert dis mou
1837, 6, 22. Rebecca rmt Jesse Holms (H)
1838, 7, 26. Rebecca Holmes (form Hannah) dis mcd & JH
1838, 12, 20. Triphena Nichols (form Hanna) dis mcd in Hicksite Mtg
1845, 4, 24. Anna [Hanna] rmt Hiram T. Cleaver (H)

HARBOUGH
1824, 7, 24. Rachel (form Beason) dis mou

HARDESTY
1838, 11, 22. Hannah (form Hillerman) dis mcd

HARLEN
1819, 6, 24. Sarah (form Hoopes) dis mcd
1828, 7, 24. Joseph recrq (H)
1828, 7, 24. Joseph [Harlin] gct Salem MM(H)

HARMER
1870, 5, 26. Margaret Emma (form Lamborn) dis mcd

HARRIS

----, --, --. Carney b 1798,7,22 d 1857,7,15;
   m Rachel ----- b 1805,4,6 d 1889,12,7
     Ch: Jonathan   b 1824, 10, 14
         Robert   " 1827, 6, 2
         David   " 1830, 5, 9
         Sarah Ann " 1846, 6, 8
----, --, --. Robert Jr., s Carney & Rachel,
   b 1827,6,2 d 1910,7,26; m Jane TEST, dt
   Samuel & Mary Ann, b 1823,1,12 d 1904,10,4
     Ch: Mary   b 1852, 1, 7 d 1874,11, 4
       bur Winona
       Rachel   b 1853, 6, 12 d 1862, 1,23
       Martha   " 1855, 4, 15
       Emmor   " 1857, 5, 4
1855, 4, 15. Martha, dt Robert & Jane (Test),
   b
----, .--, --. David, s Carney & Rachel, b
   1830,5,9; m Lusina TEST, dt Samuel & Mary
   A., b 1835,3,9 d 1916,3,25 bur Winona
     Ch: Ann Eliza b 1860, 6, 30 d 1916,11, 2
       bur Winona
       Clara Jane b 1862, 9, 1 d 1889, 3,30
       David S.   " 1866, 3, 23

1819, 7, 22. Chalkley rmt Penelope Johnson
1820, 7, 20. Ann rmt James Randals
1824, 1, 22. Carney rmt Rachel Yates
1826, 4, 20. Nathan dis mou
1830, 5, 20. Chalkley dis disunity
1832, 3, 22. Robert rmt Sarah Yates
1832, 9, 20. Robert rocf Short Creek MM, O.,
   dtd 1832,8,21
1837, 5, 25. Benjamin dis mou
1840, 1, 23. Esther (form Thomas) con mou
   (H)
1840, 2, 20. Esther C. gct Salem MM (H)
1848, 4, 20. Jonathan dis mcd
1850, 9, 26. Robert rmt Jane Test
1853, 4, 21. Laney Ann Burson (form Harris)
   con mcd
1853, 9, 22. Leah gct Upper Springfield MM,O.
1853, 9, 22. Robert & fam gct Upper Springfield MM, O.
1859, 7, 21. David dis mcd
1859, 8, 25. Lusine (form Test) dis mcd
1865, 6, 22. Sarah Ann Gant (form Harris) dis
   mcd
1865, 6, 22. Penelopy dis jG
1869, 11, 25. Lucina rstrq
1870, 2, 24. Clara Jane, Ann Eliza & David
   S., ch Lucina, recrq
1880, 5, 20. Emmor dis mcd
1883, 3, 22. Anna E. rmt George G. McGrail
1887, 12, 21. Emmor & Josephine recrq (G)
1889, 11, 21. David E. dis mcd
1890, 7, 23. Orvilla recrq (G)
1893, 3, 22. John & Mary recrq (G)

HARRISON
1811, 8, 15. Elizabeth rocf Middleton MM, dtd
   1811,5,9
1811, 8, 15. Rachel rocf Middleton MM, dtd

   1811,5,9
1813, 5, 13. Rachel gct Middleton MM
1817, 1, 16. Elizabeth Whiteleather (form
   Harrison) dis mou

HART
1879, 5, 21. Gracie recrq (G)
1884, 6, 25. Grace A. gct East Goshen MM (G)

HARTLEY
----, --, --. Alfred, s Elwood & Alice
   (Blowers), b 1899,9,1; m Ethel Alice STAN-
   LEY, dt Wm. & Edith A. (Wiles), b 1898,11,
   9
     Ch: Dorothy
       Lucile   b 1928, 9, 8
       Wm. Elwood " 1930, 6, 9
       Edith Alice" 1932, 10, 10

1931, 11, 26. Alfred J. & ch, Dorothy Lucile
   & Wm. Elwood, rocf Stillwater MM, O., dtd
   1931,10,21
1932, 4, 21. Ethel rocf Stillwater MM, O.,
   dtd 1932,3,23

HARTSOUGH
1904, 1, 20. Maggie recrq (G)

HATCHER
1817, 7, 17. Thomas & w, Ruth, & ch, Hannah &
   James, rocf Middleton MM, dtd 1817,5,12
1819, 3, 25. Thomas & fam gct Middleton MM

HAVILAND
1877, 7, 23. Daniel & w, Lucinda B., & ch,
   Edgar, Edna & Chas., rocf Adrian MM, Mich.
   dtd 1877,7,12
1882, 3, 22. Daniel & w, Lucinda B., & ch,
   Chas., rocf Honey Creek MM, Ia. (G)
1883, 10, 24. Edgar relrq (G)
1887, 1, 19. Daniel & Lucinda B. rocf Hubbard MM, Ia. (G)
1887, 2, 23. Viola G. recrq (G)
1887, 3, 23. Chas. A. rocf Hubbard MM, Ia.
   (G)
1896, 10, 21. Charles & fam gct Raisen MM,
   Mich. (G)
1896, 10, 21. Lucinda gct Raisen MM, Mich.
   (G)

HAWLEY
1819, 6, 24. Caleb & w, Catharine, & s, Joseph, rocf Middleton MM, dtd 1819,5,17
1828, 5, 22. Hannah recrq (H)
1828, 5, 22. Benjamin & w, Mary, & ch, Eliza
   & Sarah, recrq (H)
1828, 7, 24. Hannah gct Salem MM (H)
1828, 7, 24. Benjamin & w, Mary, & ch, Eliza
   & Sarah, gct Salem MM (H)

HAWORTH
----, --, --. Richard, s Elwood & Matilda
   (Folger), b 1852,1,16 d 1927,7,10 bur

HAWORTH, Richard, continued
    Winona; m Ann B. SATTERTHWAIT, dt Chas. &
    Adaline (Bye), b 1863,8,15

1896, 5, 21. Richard rmt Louisa Deweese
1897, 5, 22. Louisa D. gct Spring River MM,
    Kans.
1912, 7, 25. Richard rmt Ann B. Satterthwait
1913, 1, 23. Richard rocf Spring River MM,
    Kans., dtd 1913,1,15

HAYCOCK
1826, 2, 23. Wm. Kennett gct Salem MM, to m
    Martha Haycock

HEALD
----, --, --. James b 1786,4,1 d 1842,11,20;
    m Mary ----- b 1783,10,13
    Ch: Levi   b 1808, 11, 27
        Wm. W.   " 1810, 6, 13
        Charles   " 1814, 2, 24
        Rebecca   " 1818, 5, 10
        Eliza   " 1820, 3, 12
        James   " 1822, 9, 18
        Mary   " 1822, 9, 18
        Lydia   " 1825, 9, 6
----, --, --. James b 1822,9,18; m Abi -----
    b 1819,10,4
    Ch: Joseph S. b 1848, 12, 25
        Mathew   " 1850, 6, 22
        Edwin T. " 1852, 3, 28
        Francis   " 1854, 4, 2
        Sarah L. " 1856, 3, 25 d 1856, 5,28
        Charles   " 1857, 3, 27
1898/99,3, 3. Leota, dt Henry & Lydia, b

1810, 8, 16. Thomas Shaw gct Middleton MM, to
    m Rachel Heald
1816, 4, 18. James & w, Mary, & ch, Levi,
    Wm. W. & Charles, rocf Middleton MM, dtd
    1816,2,12
1823, 1, 23. Tacy rocf Middleton MM, dtd
    1822,10,21
1824, 6, 24. Tacy Gilbert (form Heald) dis
    mou
1829, 9, 24. Levi rmt Lydia Coppock
1831, 9, 22. Levi & w, Lydia, & s, Samuel,
    gct Upper Springfield MM, O.
1838, 6, 21. Charles gct Short Creek MM, O.
1838, 7, 26. Wm. W. gct Chesterfield MM
1838, 12, 20. James & w, Mary, & ch, James,
    Mary & Lydia, gct Sandy Spring MM, O.
1839, 3, 21. Rebecca & Eliza gct Sandy Spring
    MM, O.
1845, 6, 26. Mark Stratton gct Sandy Spring
    MM, O., to m Mary Heald
1846, 4, 23. James rmt Abi Stratton
1846, 7, 23. Abi gct Sandy Spring MM, O.
1849, 12, 20. James & w, Abi, & ch, Joseph,
    rocf Sandy Spring MM, O., dtd 1849,11,23
1858, 3, 25. James & w, Abi, & ch, Joseph S.,
    Mathew, Edwin, Frances & Charles, gct
    Middleton MM

1912, 5, 23. Leota rocf Coal Creek MM, Ia.,
    dtd 1912,5,11
1913, 5, 22. Leota gct Coal Creek MM, Ia.

HEARTLEY
1838, 3, 22. James rmt Dinah Lamborn (H)

HESTON
1813, 9, 16. John & w, Elizabeth, & ch,
    Anna, Tacy, Rebecca, John, Zebulon, Han-
    nah, Amos, David & Elizabeth, rocf Short
    Creek MM, O., dtd 1813,4,20
1813, 10, 14. Sarah, w Titus, & dt, Euphrimia,
    rocf Westland MM, dtd 1813,2,22
1814, 12, 15. Euphemy Johnson (form Heston)
    dis mcd
1815, 12, 14. Abraham & w, Deborah, & ch, Ma-
    riah, Ann, Elizabeth & David, rocf West-
    land MM, dtd 1815,11,2
1829, 3, 26. Deborah dis jH
1829, 6, 25. Abraham dis jH
1833, 12, 26. Abraham rmt Jane Hall (H)
1837, 6, 22. Elizabeth Shaw (form Heston) dis
    mcd
1837, 6, 22. Elizabeth Shaw (form Heston) dis
    mcd (H)
1838, 7, 26. Mariah dis disunity
1840, 9, 24. Ann dis jH
1840, 6, 25. Maria Elliott (form Heston) dis
    mou (H)
1840, 10, 22. David dis mou
1841, 3, 25. Sarah dis disunity
1842, 8, 25. Mary dis jH

HEWITT
1879, 6, 25. Laura recrq (G)
1883, 9, 19. Laura gct Salem MM (G)

HEWLETT
1890, 9, 27. Malva L., w Fred, dt Linneus &
    Sina Warrington, b

1926, 1, 21. Melva W. (form Warrington) dis

HIATT
1910, 8, 25. George J. rmt Mary Elma Warring-
    ton
1911, 8, 24. Mary Elma W. gct Chesterfield MM

HILLERMAN
1820, 7, 20. Wm. & w & ch, Loranzo D., Joseph
    L., Wm. I., Ann S. H., Hannah I., John I.
    & Sarah, recrq
1828, 9, 25. William dis jH
1829, 4, 23. Hannah dis jH
1831, 8, 25. Joseph dis jH
1832, 8, 23. Ann Kirts (form Hillerman) dis
    jas & mou
1832, 11, 22. Ann Kirts (form Hillerman) dis
    mou & jas (H)
1835, 4, 23. Hannah J. dis jas (H)
1837, 10, 26. Lorenzo dis mcd
1838, 11, 22. Hannah Hardesty (form Hillerman)

HILLERMAN, continued
dis mou
1838, 10, 25. Ann dis jas (H)

HILLIS
1810, 8, 16. Hugh & w, Elizabeth, & ch, Rebecca, Sarah, Ann & Wm., rocf Westland MM,
dtd 1810,5,26
1828, 7, 24. Hugh & w, Elizabetn, dis jH
1828, 12, 25. Sarah rmt Daniel Votaw (H)
1829, 3, 26. Rebecca Irey (form Hillis) con
mou (H)
1829, 5, 21. Rebecca Irey (form Hillis) dis
mcd & jH
1829, 6, 25. Sarah Votaw (form Hillis) dis
mou & jH
1830, 7, 22. Ann [Hilles] dis jH
1831, 9, 22. Wm. dis jH
1833, 12, 26. Ann rmt Wm. R. Dugdale (H)
1835, 5, 21. Wm. [Hilles] rmt Hannah Dutton
(H)
1836, 10, 20. Elizabeth & dt, Martha, gct
White Water MM, Ind. (H)
1836, 10, 20. Mary gct White Water MM, Ind.
(H)
1836, 11, 24. Wm. [Hilles] & w, Hannah, gct
White Water MM, Ind. (H)
1837, 6, 22. Mary gct White Water MM, Ind.
1837, 6, 22. Martha gct White Water MM, Ind.
1838, 6, 21. Elihu dis jH

HINCHMAN
1823, 4, 24. Sarah (form Beck) con mcd
1827, 6, 21. Sarah rmt Nathan John
1829, 3, 26. Sinah (form Burson) dis mcd
1829, 7, 23. Sinah [Hinksman] (form Burson)
con mcd (H)

HINER
1897, 2, 24. Lillie recrq (H)
1897, 4, 21. Robert recrq (H)

HISLER
1830, 11, 16. Rhoda (form Stanley) dis mou

HOAG
1817, 7, 17. Elisha Wm. [Hoeg] & w, Lydia,
& ch, Joel, Joanna & Hervey, rocf Stroudsburg MM, dtd 1817,6,5, endorsed by Marlborough MM, dtd 1817,7,16
1828, 7, 24. Lydia dis jH
1828, 9, 25. Elisha Wm. dis jH
1830, 7, 22. Joanna dis jH
1830, 9, 23. Elisha & w, Lydia, & ch gct
Marlborough MM (H)
1830, 9, 23. Joanna gct Marlborough MM (H)
1831, 4, 21. Joel gct Marlborough MM (H)
1834, 3, 20. Minor ch of Elisha Wm. & Lydia
gct Marlborough MM
1834, 8, 21. Joel dis jH

HOBSON
----, --, --. Sarah Ann, dt Thomas & Unity,

b 1844,10,15 d 1909,8,27 bur Winona, O.
1850, 4, 26. Benjamin m Sarah Ann JOHNSON

1839, 12, 26. Thomas rmt Unity Johnson
1840, 5, 21. Unity gct Smithfield MM
1850, 7, 25. Sarah Ann gct Smithfield MM
1880, 8, 26. Sarah Ann rocf Short Creek MM,
O., dtd 1880,6,22
1902, 11, 22. Eber S. rocf Gilead MM, dtd
1902,10,14 (G)
1903, 6, 24. Eber S. gct Lupton MM (G)
1903, 10, 21. Thomas C. & w, Ann, & s, Wm.,
rocf Mt. Gilead MM, O., dtd 1903,10,20
(G)
1905, 11, 22. Thomas C. & w, Ann, & s, Wm.,
gct Gilead MM (G)
1906, 12, 20. Sara Ann rmt Joseph Masters

HODGIN
1878, 12, 26. Joseph Brantingham gct Spring-
vill MM, Ia., to m Mary Esther Hodgin
1890, 4, 24. Stephen rocf Damorria MM, Kans.,
dtd 1890,3,5
1890, 4, 24. Amy R. rocf Damorris MM, Kans.,
dtd 1890,3,5
1892, 1, 21. Amy R. gct Damorris MM, Kans.
1896, 10, 21. T. C. & w, Ida M., recrq (G)
1898, 6, 22. Thos. & w & ch, Berneice, gct
E. Richland MM (G)

HOLDERMAN
1837, 11, 23. Joshua Brown gct Sandy Spring
MM, O., to m Ann Holderman
1874, 10, 20. John dis jG

HOLE
1869, 7, 20. Elma G., w Willis, dt Joshua &
Deborah (Hutton) Gilbert, b
1875, 8, 23. Mary F., w Chas. M., dt Joseph
& Mary (Hutton) Fritchman, b

1818, 3, 19. Jonah recrq
1818, 5, 14. Jacob & w, Mary, & ch, Jacob,
Rebecca & Sophia, recrq
1818, 9, 24. Nathan gct Middleton MM, to m
Sarah Armstrong
1818, 12, 24. Mahlon recrq
1819, 2, 25. Sarah rocf Middleton MM, dtd
1818,12,21
1819, 5, 20. Levi Miller gct Carmel MM, to m
Ann Hole
1819, 10, 21. Mahlon gct Salem MM, to m Rachel
Schooley
1820, 1, 20. John & w, Catharine, & s, Lemuel
rocf Carmel MM, dtd 1819,5,15
1820, 3, 23. Mary recrq
1820, 8, 24. Rachel rocf Salem MM, dtd 1820,
7,19
1821, 8, 23. Jonah gct Flushing MM
1892, 8, 25. Elma G. (form Gilbert) con mcd
1897, 10, 20. J. M. & w, Ella, & dt, Gertrude,
recrq (G)
1898, 1, 19. Gertrude F. rocf Sandy Spring

HOLE, continued
    MM (G)
1914, 8, 20. Mary F. (form Fritchman) con mcd
1914, 10, --. Mellvin gct Alliance MM .(G)
1918, 3, 21. Elma G. gct Salem MM
1922, 12, 21. Mary F. (form Fritchman) dis mcd
    & jas

HOLLAND
1815, 1, 19. Samuel & w, Sarah, & ch, Wil-
    liam, Susannah, John, Catharine, Sarah &
    Hannah, rocf Middleton MM, dtd 1814,12,8

HOLLINGSWORTH
1865, 11, 23. Martha, minor s, Joseph Hall,
    rocf Middleton MM, dtd 1865,11,18
1869, 2, 25. Martha gct Upper Springfield MM,
    O.
1874, 9, 24. Francis Dean gct Plymouth MM, to
    m Penina Hollingsworth

HOLLOWAY
----, --, --. Alfred Howard, s Cyrus & Esther
    (Emery), b 1889,8,23; m Edith L. KIRK, dt
    Nathan & Mary (Morlan), b 1892,2,24
    Ch: Carol
        Thelma   b 1917, 2, 20 d 1927, 4,23
        bur Middleton
        Lois Mar-
        jorie   b 1918, 4, 1
        Mable Lyda " 1920, 10, 14
        Edgar Ber-
        tram   " 1922, 4, 3
        Warren
        Oliver   " 1923, 10, 14
----, --, --. Leland W., s Cyrus & Esther
    (Emery), b 1895,2,17; m Thelma Leah
    STANLEY, dt Mervin & Gertrude (Pickett),
    b 1899,1,4
    Ch: Lynn Alvin b 1924, 6, 13
        Leslie Mer-
        vin   " 1928, 4, 19
----, --, --. Emery C., s Cyrus & Esther
    (Emery), b 1899,3,10; m Amelia B. GAMBLE,
    dt Chas. W. & Rachel (Whinery), b 1901,10,
    23
    Ch: Esther Ra-
        chel   b 1927, 6, 21
        Albert
        Leland   " 1931, 12, 30
1926, 7, 17. Emery C. m Bertha Amelia GAMBLE

1830, 7, 22. Joel & w, Mary, rocf Salem MM,
    dtd 1829,9,23 (H)
1841, 12, 23. Joel & Mary gct Salem MM (H)
1923, 10, 25. A. Howard & w, Edith L., & ch,
    Carol T., Lois M., Mabel L., Edgar B. &
    Warren Oliver, rocf Middleton MM
1924, 2, 21. Lealand W. & Emery P. recrq
1924, 7, 24. Thelma Leah rocf Mill Creek MM,
    Ind., dtd 1924,6,26
1927, 5, 26. Wm. D. Oliphant gct West§Town
    MM, to m Anna M. B. Holloway

HOLMS
1837, 6, 22. Jesse rmt Rebecca Hanna (H)
1838, 7, 26. Rebecca (form Hannah) dis mcd &
    jH
1842, 7, 21. Jesse & w, Rebecca, & ch gct
    Plainfield MM (H)

HOOPS
----, --, --. Mary b 1768,12,28 d 1842,8,30
----, --, --. George b 1770,9,6 d 1841,3,26
----, --, --. James b 1772,10,5; m Susanna
    ----- b 1780,12,--
    Ch: Phebe   b 1799, 1, 18 d 1800, 7, 2
        Joseph
        Leech   " 1801, 2, 7 d 1824,11, 4
        Daniel   " 1803, 8, 3
        Thomas   " 1803, 8, 3
        John   " 1805, 10, 4 " 1821, 5,20
        James D.   " 1808, 5, 23 " 1810, 8,31
        Jacob   " 1810, 9, 4 " 1816, 2, 5
        Susanna   " 1812, 12, 17
        James   " 1815, 8, 4 " 1844, 3,19
        William   " 1817, 9, 26
        Robert   " 1819, 7, 22
        Rebecca   " 1821, 8, 3
        Abigail   " 1825, 11, 14
----, --, --. Thomas m Charity ----- d 1836,5,
    9
    Ch: Lewes   b 1824, 2, 7
        Susannah
        Leech   " 1825, 7, 27
        John J.   " 1827, 3, 3
        Lydia Ann " 1828, 12, 6
        Mary Ann   " 1834, 11, 4
----, --, --. Daniel b 1803,8,3 d 1883,7,21;
    m Mary Ann -----
    Ch: Thomas   b 1830, 5, 15 d 1833, 1, 8
        Elisha   " 1832, 5, 23
        Joseph L. " 1833, 12, 15
        Sarah   " 1835, 9, 25
        Garretson " 1837, 6, 7
        Emaline   " 1839, 4, 27
        James   " 1841, 4, 27 d 1842, 6,14
1838, 8, 18. Elisha d
----, --, --. James b 1815,8,4 d 1844,3,19;
    m Phebe ----- b 1814,7,5
    Ch: Arminta   bb 1841, 4, 10
        James   " 1844, 7, 24
----, --, --. William b 1817,9,26; m Elizabeth
    Jane ----- b 1818,8,2
    Ch: Lemuel   b 1845, 4, 11
        Ann   " 1847, 4, 26 d 1852, 9,21
        Abigail   " 1849, 11, 8
----, --, --. Lewis b 1824,2,7; m Sarah Ann

    Ch: Thomas
        Barby   b 1847, 11, 19
        John Henry " 1849, 1, 11 d 1852,10, 6
        Charity
        Elizabeth " 1850, 7, 10

1816, 11, 14. Susanna rocf Warrington MM, dtd
    1816,9,19

HOOPS, continued

1817, 4, 17. James rocf Londongrove MM, dtd
 1817,2,5

1817, 7, 17. Elisha & w, Mary, & ch, Sarah,
 Elizabeth, Mary Ann & Lydia, rocf Warrington MM, dtd 1817,4,23

1819, 6, 24. Sarah Harlen (form Hoops) dis mcd

1820, 2, 24. Thomas, Daniel, John, Susanna &
 James, ch James, recrq

1820, 3, 23. Joseph L. recrq

1821, 9, 20. Mary rocf Warrington MM, dtd
 1821,3,22

1822, 1, 24. Mary rmt Timothy Kirk

1822, 4, 25. Joseph L. rmt Lydia Votaw

1823, 3, 20. Thomas [Hoopes] rmt Charity Kirk

1825, 7, 21. Elizabeth Charlton (form Hoopes)
 dis mcd

1828, 12, 25. Daniel [Hoopes] rmt Mary Ann
 Hoopes

1828, 12, 25. Mary Ann [Hoopes] rmt Daniel
 Hoopes

1830, 11, 16. Lydia [Hoopes] rmt Henry George

1831, 2, 24. Lydia George & ch, Esther & Joseph Leech Hoops, gct Carmel MM

1832, 2, 23. Lydia Whitacre (form Hoopes) dis
 mcd

1833, 11, 21. Susannah [Hoopes] rmt Timothy
 Brown

1838, 12, 20. Thomas [Hoopes] dis disunity

1840, 5, 21. John [Hoopes] dis disunity

1840, 5, 21. James [Hoopes] Jr. rmt Phebe
 Yates

1840, 9, 24. George [Hoopes] rocf Bradford
 MM, dtd 1840,8,5

1841, 11, 25. Robert [Hoopes] dis mcd

1842, 6, 23. Susannah Leach [Hoopes] dis

1844, 4, 25. Wm. [Hoopes] rmt Elizabeth Jane
 Yates

1844, 7, 25. Abigail Yates (form Hoopes) dis
 mcd

1845, 5, 22. Rebecca Yates (form Hoopes) dis
 mcd

1846, 3, 26. Lewis W. [Hoopes] gct Upper
 Springfield MM, O., to m Sarah Ann Blackburn

1847, 8, 26. Sarah Ann [Hoopes] rocf Upper
 Springfield MM, O., dtd 1847,6,26

1848, 3, 23. Phebe Bennett (form Hoopes) dis
 mcd

1853, 8, 25. John [Hoopes] dis mcd

1854, 2, 23. Lydia Ann [Hoopes] dis disunity

1855, 3, 22. Elisha dis mcd

1859, 2, 24. Armintha Murrell (form Hoops)
 dis mcd

1860, 1, 26. Mary Ann Cass (form Hoopes) dis
 mcd

1860, 8, 23. Emelina Ullery (form Hoopes)
 dis mcd

1861, 6, 20. Joseph [Hoopes] dis mcd

1861, 10, 24. Sarah Randel (form Hoopes) dis
 mcd

1863, 1, 22. Garretson [Hoopes] dis mcd

1866, 8, 23. Elizabeth Jane [Hoopes] dis jG

1866, 12, 20. Mary Ann dis disunity

1867, 2, 21. Wm. & James dis disunity

1868, 6, 25. Lemuel dis mcd

1869, 10, 21. Abigail dis disunity

1870, 4, 21. Lucinda (form Crew) dis disunity

1882, 6, 21. Wm. & w, Lucinda C., & ch, Walter M., Albert J., Malcolm C., Maryetta &
 Garfield, recrq (G)

1883, 6, 21. Deborah (form Test) dis mcd

1887, 12, 21. James, Elizabeth & Alfaretta
 [Hoopes] recrq (G)

1887, 12, 21. Lemuel [Hoopes] recrq (G)

1887, 12, 21. Elizabeth C. [Hoopes] recrq (G)

1888, 2, 22. Arminta & Sarah J. [Hoopes]
 recrq (G)

1889, 10, 23. Wm. A. [Hoopes] & w, Lucinda, &
 ch, Walter, Albert J., Malcolm, Marietta &
 Linden, gct Damascus MM, O. (G)

1897, 5, 19. John & Annie M. recrq (G)

1917, 8, 15. Florence [Hoopes] recrq (G)

HOOVER

1840, 1, 23. Mary P. (form Paxson) con mou
 (H)

HORNE

1832, 6, 21. Wm. D. & w, Sarah, & ch, Eliza,
 Anne & Stephen, rocf Darby MM, Pa., dtd
 1831,11,29, endorsed by Carmel MM, 1832,
 4,21 (H)

1832, 6, 21. Hiram rocf Darby MM, Pa., dtd
 1831,11,29, endorsed by Carmel MM, 1832,4,
 21 (H)

1832, 12, 20. Wm. D. [Horn] & w, Sarah, & ch,
 Ann & Steven, gct Carmel MM (H)

1833, 8, 22. Eliza [Horn] gct Carmel MM, O.
 (H)

HOSTETER

1828, 7, 24. Zalinda (form Hanna) dis mou

1828, 9, 25. Zelinda (form Hanna) con mou (H)

HOYLE

----, --, --. Dorothy J., dt John & Dorothy
 Johnson, b 1813,6,21 d 1892,2,19 bur Winona

----, --, --. John, s John & Elizabeth, b
 1815,3,2 d 1904,3,22, bur Winona

1837, 10, 26. John Jr. rmt Dorothy Johnson

1838, 1, 25. Dorothy gct Smithfield MM

1840, 11, 26. Joshua Coppock gct Smithfield
 MM, O., to m Jane Hoyle

1851, 2, 20. Thomas & w, Hannah, & ch, Joseph Lindley & Wm. G., rocf Plainfield MM,
 dtd 1850,12,25

1857, 4, 26. Thomas & w, Hannah, & ch, Joseph
 Lindley & Wm. G., gct Plainfield MM

1880, 7, 22. John & Dorothy rocf Short Creek
 MM, O., dtd 1880,6,22

HUGHES

1811, 10, 17. Gideon [Hughs] & w, Rebecca, &

HUGHES, continued
      ch, Edith & Ellis, rocf Middleton MM, dtd
      1811,7,11
1829, 3, 26. Ellis, Edwin, Hannah, Moses &
      Gideon [Hughs], ch Rebecca, gct Stillwater
      MM, O. (H)
1829, 8, 20. Gideon dis jas (H)
1831, 10, 20. Gideon dis jas
1831, 10, 20. Ellis, Edwin & Moses gct Still-
      water MM, O.
1831, 11, 25. Hannah gct Springborough MM
1831, 12, 22. Gideon Jr. gct Springborough MM

HUNTLEY
1897, 10, 15. Margaret R., w Ralph T., dt Wil-
      son J. & Mary C. (Hall) Steer, b

1924, 1, 24. Margaret (form Steer) con mcd
1933, 4, 20. Margaret Steer dis

HUTTON
1844, 4, 20. Annie, dt Joel & Ann, b
----, --, --. Finley, s Joel & Ann, b 1839,
      12,11; m Eliza W. -----
      Ch: Elma G.   b 1875, 5, 18
          Joel A.   " 1876, 10, 27
      Finley m 2nd Agnes V. McGREW, dt James B.
      & Margaret V., b 1860,7,8
      Ch: Rebecca S. b 1885, 12, 14
          Finley   " 1886, 10, 27
1914, 8, 21. J. Wetherill m Ellen S. COPE

1872, 3, 23. Annie rocf Sewickley MM, dtd
      1872,4,30
1886, 1, 21. Anna gct ND MM
1886, 12, 23. Finley & w, Agnes V., & ch,
      Elma G., Joel W., Rebecca S. & Finley Jr.
      rocf ND MM, dtd 1886,11,23
1892, 1, 21. Finley & w, Agnes V., & ch,
      Elma G., Joel W., Rebecca S. & Finley Jr.
      gct Salem MM
1914, 11, 26. Ellen C. gct Stillwater MM, O.

IDDINGS
1814, 11, 17. Samuel recrq
1815, 1, 19. Hannah rocf Kennet MM, Pa., dtd
      1814,10,4
1815, 6, 15. Wm. Townsend & Elwood, ch Sam-
      uel & Hannah, recrq
1822, 6, 28. Samuel & fam gct Sandy Spring MM

INGLEDUE
1832, 3, 22. Mary (form Kirk) dis mou
1832, 4, 26. Mary (form Kirk) dis mou (H)

INGRAM
1823, 4, 24. Joseph & w, Mary, & ch, Robert
      & Hannah, William, Mary B., Joseph, Susan
      & Lydia, rocf Bradford MM, Pa., dtd 1822,
      12,4
1828, 9, 25. Joseph dis jH
1828, 11, 20. Mary dis jH
1833, 11, 20. Mary B. rmt Benjamin B. Davis (H)

1834, 5, 22. Mary Davis (form Ingram) dis
      mcd among H
1839, 9, 26. Joseph Jr. dis jH
1839, 11, 24. Susan rmt Thomas C. Pound (H)
1840, 2, 20. Susan Pound (form Ingram) dis
      mcd in H Mtg
1850, 11, 21. Albin dis mcd
1887, 12, 21. Wm. F., Jessie, Sarah E. &
      Lillie recrq (G)
1890, 4, 23. Frank & w relrq (G)
1912, 4, 24. Raymond, Chas. O. & Mary Caro-
      line, gct Salem MM (G)
1916, 9, 20. Jessie & Tillie dropped from
      mbrp (G)
1926, 2, 24. Jessie rocf Salem MM (G)

IREY
1815, 10, 19. Sarah recrq
1816, 2, 15. Sarah rmt Fisher Quaintance
1816, 5, 16. Martha (form Whitacre) dis mcd
      to first cousin
1821, 7, 26. Isaac & w, Margaret, & ch,
      Hiram & Jane, recrq
1824, 8, 26. Rachel (form Paxson) con mou
1825, 10, 20. Mary recrq
1828, 8, 21. Isaac dis jH
1829, 3, 26. Rebecca (form Hillis) con mou
      (H)
1829, 5, 21. Rebecca (form Hillis) dis mcd &
      jH
1829, 7, 23. Rebecca dis jH
1829, 8, 20. Margaret dis jH
1829, 11, 26. Hannah dis jH
1837, 5, 25. Rebecca gct White Water MM, Ind.
      (H)
1837, 5, 25. Rachel [Iry] gct White Water
      MM, Ind. (H)
1838, 9, 20. Rachel dis jH
1838, 11, 22. Ann [Iry] (form Williams) dis
      mcd
1843, 12, 21. Rebecca rocf Sandy Spring MM,
      O., dtd 1843,9,22
1915, 9, 22. Dawson recrq (G)

IRISH
1832, 11, 22. Wm. B. & w, Lydia, & ch, Frank-
      lin Elias H. & Dallas, rocf Middleton MM,
      O., dtd 1832,11,8 (H)
1833, 6, 20. Franklin, minor, rocf Redstone
      MM, dtd 1833,1,30

IRWIN
1859, 12, 10. Ida M. b

1870, 1, 20. Ida M. recrq
1893, 11, 23. Ida M. dis jas

JACKSON
----, --, --. Isaac b 1777,7,11; m Ann -----
      b 1785,1,24
      Ch: Grace   b 1807, 6, 21
          Hannah   " 1808, 11, 21
          Ruth   " 1810, 9, 12

JACKSON, Isaac & Ann, continued
    Ch: Mary B.   b 1812, 7, 26
        Josiah   " 1818, 11, 16
        Stephen   " 1817, 5, 31
        James   " 1819, 9, 20
        Isaac   " 1822, 9, 21
        Ann   " 1825, 4, 17
        Abraham M. " 1828, 4, 22

1810, 5, 17. Abel gct Fairfax MM, Va.
1815, 1, 19. Sarah, Mercy, Sidney & Ann rocf
    Westland MM, dtd 1814,2,1
1815, 8, 17. Isaac & w, Margaret, rocf West-
    land MM, dtd 1815,4,29
1815, 12, 14. Samuel, minor, rocf Westland
    MM, dtd 1815,11,2
1816, 5, 16. Mercy rmt Gainor Ellis
1823, 9, 25. Alice (form Stackhouse); consent
    given Sandy Spring MM, to rst
1826, 5, 25. Hannah rmt Barton Dean
1826, 7, 20. Ann Bye (form Jackson) dis mou
1829, 4, 23. Sidney dis jH
1829, 5, 21. Isaac Sr. dis jH
1829, 10, 22. Margaret dis jH
1830, 1, 21. Samuel dis jH
1832, 2, 23. Isaac & w, Ann, & ch gct Alum
    Creek MM, O.
1832, 2, 23. Grace gct Alum Creek MM, O.
1832, 10, 25. Ruth gct Alum Creek MM, O.
1833, 11, 21. Mary gct Alum Creek MM, O.
1836, 5, 26. Samuel rmt Hannah Galbreath (H)

JACOBS
----, --, --. Wm. R., s Richard & Amanda, b
    1855,4,19; m Caroline WOOLMAN, dt Abner &
    Elvira H., b 1864,4,29

1909, 6, 24. Wm. R. & w, Caroline W., rocf
    Upper Springfield MM, O., dtd 1909,5,21
1917, 3, 22. Wm. R. & w, Caroline W., gct
    Salem MM

JAGGERS
1885, 4, 22. Rachel recrq (G)

JAMES
1813, 5, 13. John & fam gct Middleton MM
1818, 12, 24. Thomas Reeder gct Short Creek MM,
    O., to m Hannah James
1819, 2, 25. John & w, Elizabeth, rocf Carmel
    MM, dtd 1818,11,21
1833, 9, 26. Elizabeth M. rocf Robeson MM,
    dtd 1833,5,9 (H)
1834, 9, 25. Nathan Shaw gct Carmel MM, to m
    Miriam James

JANNEY
1809, 10, 19. Amos gct Plainfield MM
1834, 7, 24. Jacob [Jenny] & w, Elizabeth, &
    ch, Henry, Elanor, Caroline, Edward &
    James Fenton, rocf Alexandria MM, D. C.,
    dtd 1834,6,19 (H)

1838, 10, 25. Hannah R. [Jenney] rocf Alexan-
    der MM, D. C., dtd 1838,9,20 (H)

JENKINS
----, --, --. Edward b 1805,7,4; m Rhoda E.
    ----- b 1810,2,4
    Ch: Hannah L. b 1831, 4, 26
        Joseph E.   " 1839, 8, 15 d 1843, 2, 3
        Joshua   " 1842, 12, 10
----, --, --. William & Lydia
    Ch: Joseph
        Edward   b 1849, 2, 28
        Elizabeth
        M.   " 1851, 11, 22

1838, 11, 22. Edward & w, Rhoda Elizabeth, &
    dt, Hannah Sawyer, rocf Salem MM
1843, 4, 20. William rocf Salem MM, dtd 1843,
    4,19
1843, 10, 26. Edward & fam gct Salem MM
1843, 11, 23. Joshua & w, Sibil, rocf Berwick
    MM, dtd 1843,10,19
1843, 11, 23. Mehetable rocf Berwick MM, dtd
    1843,10,19
1844, 3, 21. Mehetable rmt Timothy Coppock
1848, 3, 23. Wm. gct Redstone MM, to m Lydia
    Miller
1848, 6, 22. Lydia M. rocf Redstone MM, Pa.,
    dtd 1848,5,30
1852, 11, 25. Wm. & w, Lydia M., & ch, Joseph
    Edwin & Elizabeth M., gct Marlborough MM
1867, 10, 23. Joshua rocf Salem MM, dtd 1867,
    8,22 (G)
1882, 7, 20. Phebe Ellen (form Whinery) dis
    mcd
1871, 2, 22. John E. & w, Laura J., rocf
    Alliance MM, dtd 1871,1,31 (G)
1875, 2, 24. Joshua con mcd (G)
1885, 2, 25. Ella recrq (G)
1887, 12, 21. Reba recrq (G)
1894, 8, 22. Edith P. & Fansie L., recrq (G)
1897, 5, 19. Joshua & w, Ella, & ch, Edith
    P., Francine L. & Edward M., relrq (G)
1897, 8, 25. Reba E. gct Cleveland MM (G)

JOHN
1814, 1, 13. Rachel rmt David Davis
1815, 11, 16. Abner rmt Hannah Reeder
1816, 11, 14. Isaiah & w, Martha, rocf Centre
    MM, Pa., dtd 1816,3,16
1817, 11, 13. Benjamin rmt Hannah Winder
1821, 4, 26. Abraham Walton gct Westland MM,
    to m Ann John
1821, 10, 25. Ann Walton & dt, Mary John, rocf
    Westland MM, dtd 1821,8,23
1825, 6, 23. Isaiah dis
1825, 7, 21. Martha dis
1827, 6, 21. Nathan rmt Sarah Hinchman
1827, 8, 23. Sarah gct Sandy Spring MM, O.
183-, 9, 23. Henry Thomas gct Carmel MM, to m
    Sarah Johns (H)
1832, 6, 21. Isaiah & w, Martha, recrq (H)
1832, 10, 25. Mary Walton (form Johns) dis mou

JOHN, continued

1832, 11, 22. Mary Walton (form Johns) dis mou (H)

1835, 4, 23. Nathan rmt Sarah Thomas (H)

1837, 12, 21. Sarah (form Thomas) dis mcd in H Mtg

1839, 9, 26. Richard [Johns] & w, Betsey, & ch, Bulahann, Samuel, Susannah & Caleb Carlton, rocf Carmel MM, dtd 1839,6,15 (H)

JOHNSON

----, --, --. John b 1771,2,10 d 1857,4,6; m Dorothy ----- b 1776,6,27 d 1868,4,10

  Ch: Benjamin b 1797, 12, 15
     Sarah   " 1799, 10, 27
     Penelope " 1802, 2, 13
     Judith " 1804, 5, 9
     James   " 1807, 5, 28
     Deborah " 1809, 11, 8 d 1810, 7,13
     Unity   " 1811, 4, 11
     Mary   " 1811, 4, 11
     Dorothy " 1813, 6, 21

----, --, --. Benjamin b 1797,12,15; m Martha ----- b 1797,10,26

  Ch: Margaret b 1820, 6, 13
     John H. " 1821, 10, 29
     Sarah Ann " 1823, 11, 21
     Thomas   " 1825, 11, 17
     Mary   " 1827, 11, 11
     Elizabeth M.
            b 1830, 8, 1
     Benjamin " 1833, 1, 26
     Charles " 1835, 1, 11
     Joseph " 1837, 1, 2
     Martha G. " 1839, 7, 20

----, --, --. John d 1834,1,17; m Sarah -----
  Ch: Edward b 1821, 8, 15

----, --, --. James b 1807,5,28; m Sarah ----- b 1808,2,17

  Ch: Isaac   b 1832, 2, 4
     Penelope " 1833, 9, 26
     Rachel   " 1835, 16, 16(?)
     Mary V. " 1837, 1, 6
     Martha   " 1838, 9, 7
     Joseph H. " 1840, 6, 5
     William " 1841, 9, 15
     James   " 1844, 3, 26
     Franklin " 1846, 4, 23
     Sarah C. " 1848, 5, 23
     Anna
     Louisa   " 1854, 11, 12

1850, 4, 26. Sarah Ann m Benjamin HOBSON

1812, 7, 16. John & w, Dorothy, & ch, Benjamin, Sarah, Penelope, Judith, James, Unitis & Mary, rocf Cedar Creek MM, Va., dtd 1812,1,11

1814, 12, 15. Euphemy (form Heston) dis mcd

1819, 7, 22. Penelope rmt Chalkley Harris

1819, 8, 26. Benjamin rmt Martha Grissell

1823, 12, 25. Judith rmt James Votaw

1826, 5, 25. John & ch, David, Deborah & Edward, also Harriet Templeton, minor in

their care, recrq

1826, 5, 25. Sarah rst on consent of Westland MM

1830, 5, 20. David dis disunity

1831, 1, 20. James gct Upper Springfield MM, to m Sarah Votaw

1831, 5, 26. Sarah V. rocf Upper Springfield MM, dtd 1831,4,23

1835, 1, 22. Sarah rmt Rees Cadwalader

1837, 10, 26. Dorothy rmt John Hoyle Jr.

1839, 12, 26. Unity rmt Thomas Hobson

1841, 10, 21. Margaret rmt Howard Cadwalader

1844, 6, 20. James & w, Sarah, & fam gct Upper Springfield MM, O.

1844, 8, 22. Edward dis mcd

1845, 6, 26. James & w, Sarah V., & ch, Isaac, Penelope, Rachel, Mary V., Martha, Joseph H., William & James, rocf Upper Springfield MM, O., dtd 1845,5,24

1851, 10, 23. Thomas gct Upper Springfield MM, O., to m Martha Binford

1852, 6, 24. Thomas gct Upper Springfield MM, O.

1859, 2, 24. Charles dis mcd

1862, 11, 20. Martha dis disunity

1864, 4, 21. Benjamin & Joseph G. dis jG in 1854

1864, 6, 23. Sarah V. dis jG in 1854

1864, 6, 23. Mary Sr. dis jG in 1854

1864, 9, 22. James dis jG in 1854

1865, 3, 23. James Oliver dis jG in 1854

1865, 5, 11. Isaac W. & Wm. dis jG in 1854

1866, 1, 25. Mary V. dis jG

1866, 3, 22. Martha G. & Rachel dis jG

1867, 2, 21. Martha Walker (form Johnson) dis mcd

1867, 8, 21. Mary gct Honey Creek MM, Ind. (G)

1867, 9, 25. Martha G. gct Damascus MM (G)

1870, 3, 24. Matilda M. (form Crew) dis disunity

1870, 11, 23. Mary gct White Water MM, Ind. (G)

1872, 7, 24. Wm. H. con mcd (G)

1872, 11, 21. Sarah Jane (form Cameron) dis mcd

1873, 1, 23. Sarah C. dis jG

1874, 3, 26. Anna L. dis jG

1878, 1, 23. Benjamin gct Damascus MM (G)

1879, 8, 20. Joseph H. rocf Kokomo MM, dtd 1879,6,11 (G)

1880, 4, 21. Joseph H. relrq (G)

1881, 6, 22. Wm. P. gct Oskaloosa MM, Ia. (G)

1884, 1, 23. Joseph H. & Roxie F. recrq (G)

1884, 5, 21. Chas. dropped from mbrp (G)

1891, 11, 25. Anna Jane gct Oskaloosa MM, Ia. (G)

JONES

1814, 4, 14. Rachel rmt George Parker

1816, 2, 15. Joseph & fam gct Stillwater MM, O.

KAYLOR
1889, 4, 24. Effie rocf Hubbard MM, Ia. (G)

KELLEY
1832, 7, 26. Charity [Kelly] (form Beeson)
    dis mou
1833, 6, 20. Hannah [Killy] (form Whinery)
    dis mou
1919, 1, 22. Wm. A., Samantha Alverda, Ralph
    Ernest, Thomas Russell, Velma Odessa,
    Hazel Leora, Hilda Rose, Kenneth Ray,
    Donald Eugene & Agnes Bell recrq, form
    mbr at Valley MM (G)
1924, 6, 24. Wm. Alvaro & fam gct Salem MM(G)

KENNETT
1822, 5, 23. Wm. & ch, Kendall, Thomas, Davis,
    Ruthanna, Maryann, Wm. Lewis & Eveline,
    recrq
1822, 10, 24. Martha rocf Kennett MM, Pa., dtd
    1822,8,6
1826, 2, 23. Wm. gct Salem MM, to m Martha
    Haycock
1826, 7, 20. Martha rocf Salem MM, dtd 1826,
    5,24
1827, 2, 27. Thomas gc
1828, 11, 20. Martha dis jH
1829, 1, 22. Wm. dis jH
1829, 12, 26. Ruthanna, Maryann & Eveline dis
    jH
1840, 3, 26. Wm. L. dis disunity
1841, 2, 25. Kendal dis mcd
1842, 5, 26. Martha, Ruthanna & Evaline gct
    Salem MM (H)
1842, 7, 21. Mary Ann Bailey (form Kennet)
    con mou (H)

KERNS
1899, 1, 25. Minnie relrq (G)
1919, 3, 19. Maria recrq (G)

KING
1919, 1, 22. James J., Cora & Murry J. recrq;
    form mbr at Valley MM (G)
1927, 7, 20. J. J. & Cora dropped from mbrp
    (G)

KINGKADE
1866, 1, 25. Mary Jane (form North) con mcd
1866, 8, 23. Mary Jane gct Springville MM,Ia.

KIRCHGESENER
1907, 9, 25. John & w, Nellie M., & ch, El-
    vin E. & Myrtle M., recrq (G)
1907, 12, 25. Nellie recrq (G)
1909, 8, 25. John [Kerchgessner] relrq (G)
1910, 1, 19. Nellie & ch relrq (G)
1910, 7, 20. Nellie & ch, Elvin & Myrtle M.,
    rstrq (G)
1912, 12, 25. John recrq (G)
1916, 9, 20. Family of Kirchgessner dropped
    from mbrp (G)

KIRK
----, --, --. Timothy & Mary Ann
    Ch: Mary Ann   b 1822, 9, 13
        Phebe   " 1824, 7, 14
        Rhoda H.   " 1825, 10, 23
        Nathan   " 1827, 4, 1
        Catherine   " 1829, 6, 9
        William J. " 1832, 9, 22
1835, 7, 22. Sarah b
----, --, --. Elisha m Christianna HALL, dt
    John & Tacy, b 1812,9,17 d 1894,7,17 bur
    Winona
    Ch: Nathan   b 1844, 2, 16
        Rachel   " 1846, 11, 2 d 1918, 7,25
        bur Winona, O.
1857, 8, 14. Mary M., w Nathan, dt Theophilus
    & Lydia (French) Morlan, b

1811, 6, 13. Mary, w Joshua, & ch, Charity,
    Timothy, Phebe, Sidwell, Elizabeth &
    Joshua, rocf Salem MM, dtd 1811,6,11
1811, 8, 15. Joshua rocf Short Creek MM, O.,
    dtd 1811,2,19, endorsed by Salem MM, 1811,
    5,14
1814, 10, 13. Caleb & w, Sarah, & ch, Isaac,
    Mary, Amelia, John & Joseph, rocf Plymouth
    MM, dtd 1814,9,17
1815, 10, 19. Caleb & ch, Isaac, Mary, Ar-
    melia & John, gct Plymouth MM
1816, 9, 19. Caleb rocf Plymouth MM, dtd
    1816,8,19
1817, 1, 16. Caleb rmt Hannah McBride
1822, 1, 24. Timothy rmt Mary Hoops
1823, 3, 20. Charity rmt Thomas Hoopes
1824, 3, 25. Sidwell, minor, gct Salem MM
1826, 11, 23. Armella rmt Moses Farrington
1827, 6, 21. Mary gct Smithfield MM
1829, 6, 25. Phebe Brown (form Kirk) con mou
    (H)
1829, 7, 23. Phebe Brown (form Kirk) dis mou
    & jH
1829, 11, 26. Timothy dis jH
1830, 6, 24. Elisha dis mou
1832, 3, 22. Mary Ingledue (form Kirk) dis
    mou
1832, 4, 26. Mary Ingledew (form Kirk) dis
    mou (H)
1834, 3, 20. Joshua gct Salem MM
1834, 7, 25. Caleb & Hannah & fam gct Alum
    Creek MM, O.
1834, 10, 23. Isaac gct Sandy Spring MM, O.
1834, 10, 23. John gct Alum Creek MM, O.
1824, 11, 20. Wm. & Elizabeth & ch, Ann
    Eliza, Susan & Lindley, rocf Sadsbury MM,
    dtd 1834,10,8 (H)
1835, 8, 20. Wm. & w, Elizabeth, & fam gct
    Salem MM (H)
1838, 9, 20. Mary dis disunity
1864, 5, 26. Christiana & ch, Nathan & Ra-
    chel, rocf Short Creek MM, O., dtd 1864,
    4,19
1864, 5, 26. Sarah rocf Short Creek MM, O.
1865, 5, 25. Susan dis jG

KIRK, continued
1868, 6, 24. Joseph G. dis disunity (G)
1870, 5, 26. Sarah rmt Cyrus Brantingham
1876, 8, 23. Susan Windle (form Kirk) con mcd (G)
1886, 3, 25. Rachel rmt Joshua Brantingham
1886, 11, 25. Nathan gct Middleton MM, to m Mary F. Morland
1887, 6, 23. Nathan gct Middleton MM
1917, 3, 22. Mary M. gct Middleton MM
1919, 10, 23. Mary M. rmt Joshua Brantingham

KIRTS
1832, 8, 23. Ann (form Hillerman) dis jas & mou
1832, 11, 22. Ann (form Hillerman) dis jas & mou (H)

KITE
----, --, --. John L. b 1798,7,24 d 1878,11, 13; m Mary ----- (John L. bur Winona)
  Ch: Benjamin b 1820, 5, 10 d 1903, 9,13 bur Nantucket
      Mary   b 1838, 7, 21 " 1913, 8,27 bur Phila.

1872, 7, 25. Benjamin rocf Upper Springfield MM, O., dtd 1872,6,21
1874, 6, 26. Benjamin dis jas (G)
1877, 10, 25. John L. rocf ND MM
1878, 8, 22. Mary rocf ND MM, dtd 1878,7,23

LAMBORN
----, --, --. Clayton m Hannah ----- b 1811,1, 27 d 1889,6,17
  Ch: Martha   b 1840, 2, 14 d 1857, 2,24
      Lemuel T. " 1841, 2, 14
      Margaret
      Emma   " 1845, 1, 25
----, --, --. Lemuel F., s Clayton & Hannah, b 1841,2,14; m Nancy C. CREW, dt Abram & Jane, b 1842,1,22 d 1909,11,23
  Ch: Martha
      Emma   b 1870, 12, 11 d 1900,12,24 bur Winona, O.
      Clarence
      Larwell b 1885, 6, 16 " 1894, 4,14 bur Winono, O.

1812, 6, 18. Cert rec for Permanas [Lambourn] & w, Hannah, & ch, Isaac, Miriam, Elizabeth, Dinah, Anna & William, from Fairfield MM, Va., dtd 1812,2,26, endorsed to Salem MM
1823, 8, 21. John Buck gct Salem MM, to m Miriam Lamborn
1828, 7, 24. Parmenus & w, Hannah, & ch, Wm., Lydia & Mary, recrq (H)
1831, 4, 21. Elizabeth rocf Westland MM, dtd 1831,3,24 (H)
1832, 11, 22. Anna rocf Salem MM, dtd 1832,7, 25 (H)
1837, 11, 23. Dinah rocf Salem MM, dtd 1837,

10,25 (H)
1838, 3, 22. Dinah rmt James Heartley (H)
1841, 1, 21. Elizabeth rmt Joseph Ball (H)
1841, 7, 22. Clayton [Lambourn] & w, Hannah, & ch, Martha S. & Lemuel T., rocf Salem MM, dtd 1841,7,21
1843, 3, 23. Wm. W. gct Salem MM (H)
1866, 9, 20. Clayton dis jG
1869, 7, 22. Lemuel T. dis mcd
1870, 5, 26. Margaret Emma Harmer (form Lamborn) dis mcd
1870, 12, 22. Edith dis jG
1878, 11, 21. Clayton rstrq
1886, 2, 25. Lemuel T. & Nancy C. rstrq
1886, 7, 23. Martha Emma & Clarence Larwell, ch Lemuel & Nancy, recrq
1887, 12, 21. Debbie recrq (G)
1892, 8, 25. Deborah dis jG
1894, 5, 24. Emma rmt Luther Barker
1893, 3, 22. Albert recrq (G)
1917, 5, 24. Lemuel T. gct Salem MM

LANGSTAFF
1828, 5, 22. James & Elizabeth recrq (G)
1828, 7, 24. James & Elizabeth gct Salem MM (H)
1850, 5, 23. Zacheus Test gct Salem MM, to m Drusilla Langstaff

LAURENCE
1815, 10, 19. Margaret rocf Bradford MM, Pa., dtd 1815,8,9

LEEDS
1827, 5, 24. Vincent rocf ND MM, dtd 1826,11, 21
1828, 2, 21. Cert granted to White Water MM, Ind. for Vincent returned, unused, 1828, 10,23
1830, 1, 21. Cert granted to ND MM for Vincent returned, unused 1831,5,26
1831, 6, 23. Vincent gct White Water MM, Ind.

LEVERIDGE
1809, 10, 19. Sarah (form Sanders) rpd mcd; Stillwater MM to treat with her; dis 1810, [4,19

LEWIS
1830, 1, 22. Enos m Margaret GRISSLE (H)
1830, 9, 23. Enos rocf Sandy Spring MM, O., dtd 1830,4,22 (H)
1837, 9, 21. Enos & fam gct White Water MM, Ind. (H)
1888, 6, 28. David J. & w, Ella H. J., rocf Short Creek MM, O. (G)
1889, 6, 19. David J. dropped from mbrp (G)
1890, 6, 25. David J. & w, Ella J., gct Adrian MM, Mich. (G)

LIBER
1887, 12, 21. Martha recrq (G)
1888, 2, 22. Ida recrq (G)
1893, 7, 19. Ida relrq (G)

LIBER, continued
1897, 6, 23. Ida recrq (G)

LLEWELLYN
1882, 5, 26. Elisha, s Thomas & Martha, b
    1856,9,6; m Abigail STRATTON, dt Benjamin
    & Ellen, b 1850,12,25 d 1901,9,13 bur
    Winona, O.
    Ch: Charles B. b 1883, 5, 20
        Mabel E.   " 1889, 6, 12
        William F. " 1891, 4, 5
    Elisha m 2nd Rachel C. WICKERSHAM, dt Da-
    vid & Rebecca B., b 1863,4,3

1882, 11, 23. Abigail S. [Lewellyn] gct Penns-
    ville MM
1891, 11, 26. Elisha [Lewellyn] & w, Abigail
    S., & ch, Charles B., Mabel E. & Wm. T.,
    rocf Pennsville MM, dtd 1891,10,15
1901, 11, 21. Mabel E. [Lewellyn] gct ND MM
1904, 3, 24. Rachel C. rocf Middleton MM, dtd
    1904,3,19
1906, 5, 24. Elisha & w, Rachel C., gct
    Chesterfield MM

LIGHTFOOT
1822, 4, 25. Cert rec for Wm. from Plainfield
    MM, dtd 1821,12,20, endorsed to Salem MM

LINTON
1902, 9, 24. Clarence recrq (G)

LIPSEY
----, --, --. Edmund m Sarah H. ----- b 1814,
    2,17
    Ch: Lydia H.   b 1834, 7, 19
        Martha J.   " 1835, 8, 31
        Eli M.   " 1837, 2, 1
        Mary Ann   " 1838, 3, 16
        Ruth   " 1839, 5, 5
        Amy   " 1840, 9, 8
        Eliza   " 1842, 3, 9
        Abraham S. " 1843, 11, 23
        Lindley M. " 1846, 5, 16
        Wm. Miller " 1848, 10, 2
        Oliva C.   " 1850, 11, 7
1843, 4, 21. Edmund & w, Sarah, & ch, Lydia,
    Martha, Eli, Maryann, Ruth & Amy, rocf
    Short Creek MM, O., dtd 1842,1,18
1853, 5, 26. Edmund & w, Sarah, & ten minor
    ch gct Upper Springfield MM, O.
1853, 5, 26. Lydia gct Upper Springfield MM,
    O.

LIVEZEY
1921, 5, 27. Walter C., s Chas. & Elizabeth
    (Smith), b 1899,1,24; m Emma L. GAMBLE, dt
    Chas. & Rachel (Whinery), b 1899,2,9
    Ch: Lura Mildred
                    b 1922, 5, 15
        Margaret
        Rebecca   " 1923, 11, 1

Ch: ward   b 1925, 8, 27
    Glen
        Charles   " 1927, 3, 16
1926, 3, 26. Jesse K., s Chas. & Elizabeth,
    b 1901,1,31; m Alice Rebecca BINNS, dt
    John & Mary E. (Cope), b 1906,1,16
    Ch: Donald
        William b 1927, 1, 17
        Ralph
        Arthur   " 1928, 8, 13

1922, 6, 22. Walter C. rocf Stillwater MM,
    O., dtd 1822,5,24
1926, 1, 21. Jesse K. rocf Stillwater MM, O.,
    dtd 1925,12,23
1929, 7, 25. Jesse K. & w, Alice R., & ch,
    Donald Wm. & Ralph Arthur, gct Middleton
    MM

LOGUE
1817, 9, 18. Nathan Galbreath gct Marl-
    borough MM, to m Ruth Logue
1821, 9, 20. Sarah rocf Marlborough MM, dtd
    1821,7,23
1821, 11, 22. Sarah rmt John Ware

LONGSHORE
1841, 4, 22. Thomas Elwood rmt Hannah E.
    Myers (H)
1841, 8, 26. Hannah E. gct Middleton MM, Pa.
    (H)

LUKENS
1845, 1, 23. Esther Ann (form Galbreath)
    dis mcd

LUPTON
----, --, --. Henry b 1789,11,21 d 1869,12,
    14 bur Winona
----, --, --. Sarah, dt Zacheus & Rebecca
    Test, b 1793,3,26 d 1880,9,9
1851, 6, 27. Henry m Sarah STRATTON
1865, 8, 26. Mary, dt David & Sarah, b

1851, 8, 21. Sarah gct Short Creek MM, O.
1859, 5, 26. Henry & w, Sarah, rocf Sandy
    Spring MM, O., dtd 1859,4,29
1864, 2, 25. David & w, Sarah, & ch, Anna,
    Mary P., Axche Elizabeth & Drucila, rocf
    Sandy Spring MM, O., dtd 1863,12,22
1865, 2, 23. David & w, Sarah, & ch, Anna,
    Mary P., Achsah E. & Drusilla, gct Ply-
    mouth MM
1875, 3, 25. Isaac B. & Mary rocf Short
    Creek MM, O., dtd 1875,2,23
1882, 5, 25. Isaac B. gct Short Creek MM, O.
1884, 1, 24. Mary P. rocf Salem MM
1894, 12, 20. Mary gct Cottonwood MM, Kans.

LYNCH
1810, 7, 19. Joshua & w, Rachel, & ch, Ann,
    Mary & Elizabeth, from Salem MM, dtd 1810,
    6,12

LYNCH, continued
1813, 9, 16. Joshua & fam gct Salem MM
1831, 3, 24. Samuel Coppock gct Upper Spring-
        field MM, O., to m Ann Lynch

McBRIDE
1810, 1, 18. Mary rmt John Whinery
1813, 8, 19. Jeremiah rmt Elizabeth Votaw
1815, 1, 19. Evan rmt Jane Pennock
1815, 2, 16. James rmt Elizabeth Batton
1817, 1, 16. Hannah rmt Caleb Kirk
1820, 2, 24. Andrew gct Hopewell MM, Va.
1820, 7, 20. Samuel dis disunity
1827, 7, 26. Betsy rocf Sandy Spring MM, O.,
        dtd 1827,6,22
1827, 12, 20. Abraham rocf Sandy Spring MM, O.,
        dtd 1827,11,23
1828, 7, 24. Betsy gct Sandy Spring MM, O.
1828, 11, 20. Abraham gct Sandy Spring MM
1834, 5, 22. Maria (form Dutton) dis mcd
1888, 6, 21. Mary Pettit (form McBride) dis

McCARTNEY
1895, 9, 25. James E. & w, Mary S., recrq (G)
1898, 5, 25. James E. & w, Mary S., relrq (G)

McCARTY
1819, 2, 25. Job & w, Jane, & ch, Mary Ann,
        & Martha L. Walton, & Rachel, Thomas Hes-
        ton, James W., Oliver C., Joseph Paxton &
        Sara, rocf Muncy MM, dtd 1818,10,21
1827, 8, 23. Job & w, Jane, & ch, Rachel E.,
        Thomas H., Oliver C., Joseph P. & Sarah
        Elizabeth, gct Marlborough MM
1833, 3, 21. Job & fam gct Marlborough MM

McCLUGGAGE
1888, 2, 22. Enoch & w recrq (G)
1897, 1, 20. Eva recrq (G)

McGRAIL
----, --, --. Alfred & Rebecca
        Ch: George G. b 1859, 6, 27
            Mary Ann " 1862, 10, 6
----, --, --. George G. [Megrail], s Alfred &
        Rebecca (Gilbert), b 1859,6,27; m Ann
        Eliza HARRIS, b 1860,6,30 d 1916,11,2
        Ch: Alfred H. b 1884, 5, 27
            Irving T. " 1886, 8, 6
            Mary Agnes " 1894, 11, 25
        George G. m 2nd Sina BRANTINGHAM, dt Geo.
        L. & Elizabeth B. (Allen), b 1872,7,6

1872, 6, 20. Uriah Price & w, Rebecca, & ch,
        Elizabeth, Edwin G. & Francis Price, &
        George G. & Amy Ann McGrail, rocf Sewick-
        ley MM, dtd 1872,5,28
1883, 3, 22. George G. rmt Anna E. Harris
1886, 2, 25. Annie A. rmt James W. Bradway
1912, 1, 25. Alfred H. [Megrail] con mcd
1914, 2, 26. Irving T. [Megrail] con mcd
1914, 7, 23. Alfred H. [Megrail] gct WD MM
1918, 6, 20. George G. [Megrail] rmt Sina

BRANTINGHAM
1923, 3, 22. Mary A. [Megrail] dis jas

McGREW
----, --, --. Edgar W., s James A. & Mary H.
        (Smith); m Rebecca Bertha Edgerton, dt
        Walter & Mary H. (Binns), b 1883,12,28

1832, 10, 25. Mary [Magrew] (form Smith) dis
        mou (H)
1926, 3, 25. Edwar W. rmt Bertha Edgerton
1927, 3, 24. R. Bertha gct Springville MM, Ia.
1933, 4, 20. Edgar W. & w, R. Bertha, rocf
        Springville MM, Ia., dtd 1933,3,18

McLAUGHLIN
1919, 12, 24. Katie recrq (G)
1921, 10, 19. Earl recrq (G)
1927, 7, 20. Earl & w relrq (G)

McMILLIN
1865, 11, 23. Rebecca Ann dis jG

McNEALY
1811, 10, 17. George & ch, Robert, Sarah, Abi-
        gail, William, Lydia & Mary recrq
1817, 5, 15. Sarah gc
1819, 1, 21. Sarah rocf Westland MM, dtd
        1818,11,26
1820, 8, 24. Sarah Richards (form McNealy)
        dis mou
1828, 8, 21. George [McNeely] & w recrq (H)
1833, 5, 23. Rachel dis jH (H)

MACY
1814, 10, 13. Cert rec for Mathew from Nan-
        tucket MM of Northern District, dtd 1814,5,
        25, endorsed to Marlborough MM

MAERKT
1856, 4, 24. Frederick [Mark] & w, Amelia
        Caroline, & ch, Charlot, Williamina,
        Louisa, Jane, Anna & Hannah, rocf Salem
        MM, dtd 1856,4,23
1861, 3, 21. Frederick & w, Amelia, & ch gct
        Providence MM
1861, 3, 21. Charlotte D. gct Providence MM
1861, 3, 21. Wilhelmina gct Providence MM

MALMSBERRY
1830, 6, 24. John Whinery gct Upper Spring-
        field MM, to m Elizabeth Malmsberry
1831, 11, 25. Isaac rocf Upper Springfield MM,
        O., dtd 1831,9,24
1834, 11, 20. Margaret (form Burson) dis mcd
1834, 11, 20. Isaac dis mcd
1848, 4, 20. Sarah H. gct Salem MM

MARRIS
1874, 11, 26. Anna Pim dis jG

MARSH
1810, 7, 19. Elias rmt Edith Townsend
1811, 7, 18. Elias dis
1813, 7, 15. Elias rstrq
1814, 4, 14. Fanny rmt Joseph Underwood

1817, 10, 16. Jane rmt Joseph Scott
1822, 3, 21. Elias & w, Edith, & ch, Robert,
     Martha, Wm., Lydia & Jesse, gct Sandy
     Spring MM, O.
1823, 10, 25. Samuel dis mcd

MARTIN
1898, 5, 25. Edgar J. recrq (G)
1900, 8, 22. Edgar J. gct Cleveland MM (G)
1902, 1, 22. Edgar relrq (G)

MASTERS
----, --, --. Joseph, s Wm. & Naomi, b 1839,
     12,6; m Esther STRATTON, dt Daniel & Abi-
     gail, b 1833,5,19 d 1904,2,10 bur Winona,
     O.
     Ch: Daniel S. b 1867, 4, 19
         Anna   " 1869, 3, 18
         Mary A.   " 1870, 8, 25
         Isaac   " 1873, 11, 27 d 1897, 7,20
         bur Winona, O.
         Barclay D. b 1875, 12, 7 d 1890, 3,20
         bur Winona, O.
----, --, --. Daniel S., s Joseph & Esther,
     b 1867,4,19; m Hannah Mary HALL, dt Linton
     & Ann W., b 1863,3,25

1866, 6, 21. Joseph rmt Esther Stratton
1866, 8, 23. Esther gct Pennsville MM
1884, 7, 24. Joseph & w, Esther, & ch, Daniel
     S., Anna, Mary A., Isaac & Barclay D.,
     rocf Pennsville MM, dtd 1884,7,17
1892, 9, 22. Anna rmt Benj. F. Whitson
1892, 9, 22. Anna rmt Elisha K. Brantingham
1897, 12, 23. Hannah Mary rocf Middleton MM,
     dtd 1897,11,26
1906, 12, 20. Joseph rmt Sara Ann Hobson
1909, 6, 24. Daniel S. & Hannah M. gct Salem
     MM

MATHER
1828, 5, 22. John & w, Catharine, & ch, Sa-
     rah, Thomas, William, Daniel, Jesse, Anne,
     James, Lydia & John, recrq (H)
1828, 7, 24. John & w, Catharine, & ch, Sa-
     rah, Thomas, Wm., Daniel, Jesse, Ann,
     James, Lydia & John, gct Salem MM (H)

MATHEWS
1824, 4, 22. Rebecca rocf Gunpowder MM, dtd
     1824,2,4
1825, 1, 20. Rebecca gct Gunpowder MM
1832, 9, 20. Juli Ann recrq (H)
1837, 7, 20. Julia Ann Steffey (form Mathews)
                              [dis mou (H)
MENDENHALL
1809, 7, 13. Aaron & w, Lydia, & ch, William,
     Abigail & Hannah, rocf Bradford MM, dtd

1808,9,7, endorsed by Westland MM, 1809,
     2,25
1821, 11, 22. Joshua & w, Sarah, rocf Bradford
     MM, dtd 1821,10,3
1826, 5, 25. Sarah rmt Ellis Davis
1830, 2, 25. William dis jH
1831, 8, 25. Wm. rmt Rebecca Ward (H)
1834, 2, 20. Abigail rmt Jarrett PIM
1835, 4, 23. Sarah rocf Ewchland MM, Pa., dtd
     1834,3,3 (H)
1835, 9, 24. Sarah rmt Thomas Shaw (H)
1836, 7, 21. Josiah Cameron gct Middleton MM,
     to m Hannah Mendenhall
1837, 8, 24. Aaron & w gct Sandy Spring MM, O.
1837, 8, 24. Lydia gct Sandy Spring MM, O.
1837, 8, 24. Hannah gct Sandy Spring MM, O.
1837, 9, 21. Wm. & w, Rebecca, & ch gct White
     Water MM, Ind. (H)
1839, 9, 26. Sarah Dutton & s, John H. Men-
     dinghall, rocf Short Creek MM, O., dtd
     1839,7,26 (H)

MERCER
1810, 2, 15. Cert rec for Wm. & w, Charity,
     & ch, Martha, Mary, George, William, John
     & Daniel, rocf Sadsbury MM, dtd 1809,11,
     7, endorsed to Middleton MM
1811, 7, 18. Olive rocf Kennet MM, dtd 1811,
     5,7, endorsed by Salem MM, 1811,7,16
1812, 8, 13. Olive gct Middleton MM
1821, 9, 20. Solomon rocf Middleton MM, dtd
     1821,2,19
1821, 9, 20. Mary rocf Middleton MM, dtd
     1821,8,27
1825, 12, 22. Mary gct Salem MM
1827, 11, 22. Solomon gct Middleton MM
1876, 6, 22. Deborah E. (form Brown) dis mcd
1919, 12, 24. Pearl recrq (G)

MERRIL
1888, 1, 11. Sara Etta, w Ferrand S., dt
     Linneus & Sina (Brantingham) Warrington, b

1913, 10, 23. Saretta (form Warrington) con
     mcd

MICHINER
1828, 5, 22. James & w, Eliza, & ch, Thomas
     & Ann, recrq (G)
1828, 7, 24. James & w, Eliza, & ch, Thomas
     & Ann, gct Salem MM (H)

MIDDLETON
1819, 4, 22. Nathaniel & w, Dorothy, & ch,
     Sarah & Ira, rocf Middleton MM, dtd 1818,
     8,10
1819, 8, 26. Deborah & ch, Hannah, Mary,
     Lydia & Deborah, rocf Middleton MM, dtd
     1819,7,19

MILBOURN
1811, 10, 17. Jonathan rpd mcd; dis 1813,3,18
1811, 11, 14. Samuel rmt Jane Craig

MILBOURN, continued
1815, 1, 19. Jacob dis training with militia
1815, 1, 19. William dis training with mili-
    tia
                              [musters
1816, 9, 19. Samuel dis attending military
1816, 11, 14. Lot dis   "   "   "
1821, 2, 22. David dis training in militia

MILLER
1810, 12, 13. Susannah rocf Westland MM, dtd
    1810,9,22
1811, 5, 16. Levi & w, Deborah, & ch, Morris,
    Robert, Isaac, Hannah, Mary & Levi, also
    one b since named Sarah, rocf Westland MM,
    dtd 1811,1,26
1814, 12, 15. Susanna gct Fall Creek MM, O.
1819, 5, 20. Levi gct Carmel MM, to m Ann
    Hole
1819, 10, 21. Ann rocf Carmel MM, dtd 1819,9,
    18
1819, 10, 21. Sarah rocf Gwynedd MM, Pa., dtd
    1817,7,31, endorsed by Short Creek MM, O.,
    dtd 1819,9,21
1823, 11, 20. Maurice rmt Ann Votaw
1824, 1, 22. Ann gct Sandy Spring MM, O.
1830, 6, 24. Isaac rmt Martha Pennington
1830, 10, 21. Martha gct Sandy Spring MM, O.
1831, 3, 24. Levi Jr. rmt Mariah Pennington
1831, 8, 25. Moses Votaw gct Sandy Spring MM,
    O., to m Mary Miller
1832, 1, 26. Mariah gct Sandy Spring MM, O.
1834, 11, 20. Samuel rmt Charity Pennington
1835, 1, 22. Charity P. gct Sandy Spring MM,O.
1838, 3, 23. Wm. Jenkins gct Redstone MM, Pa.,
    to m Lydia Miller
1873, 12, 25. Robert & w, Mary H., gct Salem
    MM
1878, 5, 23. Morris gct Upper Springfield
    MM, O.
1923, 2, 21. Margareta recrq (G)

MONTCRIEF
1907, 6, 19. Thomas, Jennie & Mary recrq (G)
1927, 7, 20. Tom & Jennie dropped from mbrp
    (G)
1931, 2, 24. Thomas & Jennie relrq (G)

MORE
1811, 8, 15. Ann R. Gause (form More) con mcd

MORELAND
1808, 12, 15. Amy gct Middleton MM
1819, 7, 22. Stephen [Morlan], minor, rocf
    Salem MM, dtd 1819,7,21
1820, 5, 25. Mordecai [Morlan] rocf Carmel
    MM, dtd 1819,12,18
1822, 7, 25. Huldah rocf Salem MM, dtd 1822,
    6,19
1823, 7, 2. Huldah gct Middleton MM
1826, 12, 21. Stephen, minor, gct Middleton MM
1834, 12, 25. Cert rec for Joseph from Salem
    MM, dtd 1834,7,23, endorsed to Alum Creek
    MM, O.

1886, 11, 25. Nathan Kirk gct Middleton MM,
    to m Mary F. Morland

MORGAN
1812, 7, 16. Esther rocf Salem MM, dtd 1812,
    7,14
1812, 10, 15. Mariah, Matilda, Sarah, William,
    Benjamin Townsend Eliza Nailor & Lydia,
    ch of Esther, recrq
1814, 8, 18. Sarah gct Middleton MM [Wright
1815, 4, 13. Esther, wd with ch, rmt Joseph
1816, 6, 13. Mariah rocf Salem MM, dtd 1816,
    5,14
1816, 6, 13. Joseph Wright & w, Esther, & ch,
    Matilda, Benjamin Townsend & Eliza Nailor
    Morgan, rocf Salem MM, dtd 1816,5,14
1817, 7, 17. Sarah rocf Middleton MM, dtd
    1817,6,16
1818, 10, 22. Maria rmt Wm. Paxton
1819, 11, 25. Matilda rmt Robert Talbott
1823, 6, 26. John & w, Ann, & ch, Edith,
    Edward, Deborah, Ann Eliza & Rebecca
    Mathews, rocf Redstone MM, dtd 1823,6,4
1823, 7, 2. Hannah rocf Redstone MM
1824, 1, 22. Sarah rmt Chalkley Hains
1824, 4, 22. Mary rocf Redstone MM, dtd 1823,
    10,29
1825, 12, 22. Mary & Hannah gct Redstone MM
1826, 1, 26. John & w, Ann, & ch, Edith, Ed-
    ward, Deborah, Ann Eliza, Rebecca &
    Charles, gct Redstone MM
1830, 5, 20. Eliza N. dis jH
1830, 8, 26. George rocf Westland MM, dtd
    1830,7,21
1832, 3, 22. Eliza Ward (form Morgan) con
    mou (H)
1832, 6, 21. George gct Westland MM

MORRISON
1817, 10, 16. Elizabeth & s, Jonas, rocf Sads-
    bury MM, dtd 1817,8,5
1820, 12, 21. Elizabeth gct Alum Creek MM, O.
1822, 4, 25. Jonas rpd mcd; living within
    limits of Alum Creek MM; dis 1823,1,23
MORTON
1923, 1, 25. Anna M. (form Satterthwait) dis
    mcd

MOTT
1904, 1, 9. Edith M., w Milford, dt Chas.
    W. & Rachel (Whinery) Gamble, b
1932, 4, 23. Milford m Edith May Gamble

MURPHY
1833, 4, 25. Margaret rocf Exeter MM, dtd
    1832,12,26 (H)

MURRELL
1859, 2, 24. Armintha (form Hoops) dis mcd

MUFRY
1845, 11, 20. Anne T. (form Thomas) con mcd
    (H)

MYERS

1809, 10, 19. William dis disunity
1818, 10, 22. Jonathan recrq
1818, 10, 22. Mahala recrq
1819, 3, 25. Elizabeth rst on consent of Goose
  Creek MM, Va.
1833, 9, 26. Samuel [Myres] & w, Pauline, &
  ch, Mary, Hannah, Rachel, Wm., Julianna &
  Jane, rocf Alexandria MM, Dist. of Col.,
  dtd 1833,8,22 (H)
1833, 9, 26. Sarah H. [Myres] rocf Alexandria
  MM, D. C., dtd 1833,8,22 (H)
1835, 4, 23. Sarah H. rmt Pierce Garretson
  (H)
1839, 8, 23. Mary F. rmt Thomas Owen (H)
1841, 4, 22. Hannah E. rmt Thomas Elwood
  Longshore (H)
1890, 4, 23. Lillian recrq (G)
1912, 4, 24. Nancy Hall dropped from mbrp (G)

NEGUS

----, --, --. West b 1788,2,5; m Mary -----
  b 1796,8,3
    Ch: William   b 1823, 12, 20
        Eliza   " 1825, 9, 16
        Esther   " 1827, 11, 16
        David   " 1829, 12, 31
        Sarah   " 1832, 3, 27
        John
          Thompson " 1834, 6, 19
        Joseph   b 1837, 9, 5 d 1838, 3, 3
        Martha   " 1839, 1, 8
        Elma   " 1841, 7, 14 d 1842,10, 7
1870, 2, 2. Mary d ae 76 (an elder) (G)
1927, 1, 22. Wilson A. m Jesse Leah C. STEER

1827, 11, 22. West & w, Mary, & ch, Wm. &
  Eliza, rocf Providence MM, dtd 1827,11,1
1837, 8, 24. Isaac Walker gct Upper Springfield MM, O., to m Lydia Negus
1854, 10, 23. Eliza rmt John Watson
1858, 2, 28. Esther Tomlinson (form Negus)
  dis mcd
1858, 8, 26. John dis disunity
1862, 6, 26. Martha Tomlinson (form Negus)
  dis mcd
1862, 6, 26. Sarah Fawcett (form Negus) dis
  mcd
1862, 11, 20. Mary dis disunity
1863, 6, 25. Wm. dis mcd
1863, 8, 20. David dis enlisting in military
  service
1864, 4, 21. West dis jG in 1854
1869, 1, 21. Eliza Watson (form Negus) dis jG
1927, 8, 25. Jessie Leah C. gct Short Creek
  MM, O.

NEAL

----, --, --. John & Mary [Neill]
    Ch: Eliza   b 1823, 11, 25
        Mary Ann   " 1826, 7, 30
        William   " 1828, 11, 7
        Samuel

Ch: Thompson
                   b 1831, 3, 27 d 1839, 8,18
        Margaret   " 1833, 1, 12
        Ruth Ann   " 1835, 9, 12
        Elme   " 1837, 9, 15 " 1839, 8,19
        Martha   " 1840, 1, 19
1819, 5, 20. John & w, John, rocf Carmel MM,
  dtd 1819,4,17
1819, 5, 20. Ruth rocf Carmel MM, dtd 1819,
  4,17
1821, 11, 22. John Jr. gct Sandy Spring MM,
  to m Mary M. Ellis
1821, 12, 20. Samuel [Neil] rocf Carmel MM,
  dtd 1821,11,17
1822, 9, 26. Mary M. [Neil] rocf Sandy Spring
  MM, dtd 1822,3,22
1824, 8, 26. Samuel [Neil] gct Carmel MM
1834, 12, 25. Ruth Crew (form Neal) dis mou
1840, 4, 23. John [Neil] & fam gct Carmel MM
1877, 9, 20. Wm. dis mcd
1877, 10, 25. Anna Mary dis jG
1878, 3, 21. James E. dis jG

NEWLIN

----, --, --. William W. m Edith GILBERT
    Ch: Ellen B.   b 1866, 1, 22
        Ida A.   " 1868, 4, 10
1891, 12, 25. Ellen B. m Isaac C. ROGERS

1875, 2, 25. Hannah Gilbert & gr ch, Ellen
  B. & Ida A. Newlin, recrq
1893, 4, 20. Ida A. rmt Wm. D. Satterthwait
1925, 9, 24. James C. Edgerton gct Plainfield MM, Ind., to m Esther Irene Newlin

NICHOLS

1906, 7, 5. Julia Rachel, w Elwood K., dt
  Alfred W. & Elizabeth (Bradway) Patten, b

1833, 9, 26. Samuel rmt Tryphena Hannah (H)
1834, 10, 23. Tryphena [Nicholas] gct Middleton MM (H)
1838, 12, 20. Triphena (form Hanna) dis mcd
  in H Mtg
1928, 7, 26. Elwood K. rmt Julia R. Patten

NICHOLSON

1813, 6, 17. Richard rocf ND MM, dtd 1812,5,
  26 [to treat with him; dis 1813,12,16
1813, 6, 17. Richard rpd mcd; Redstone MM rq
1814, 9, 15. Cert rec for Jonathan [Nickle-
  son] & w, Polly, from Butternuts MM, N.Y.,
  dtd 1814,5,4, endorsed to Plainfield MM,O.

NORTH

1853, 5, 26. Jesse & w, Elizabeth, & ch, Sarah, Mary Jane, John & Gustavious, rocf
  Salem MM, dtd 1853,5,25
1866, 1, 25. Sarah Burchal (form North) con
  mcd
1866, 1, 25. Mary Jane Kingkade (form North)
  con mcd

NORTH, continued
1866, 12, 20. Jesse & fam gct Springville MM,
    Ia.
1866, 12, 20. John gct Springville MM, Ia.

OGDEN
1819, 5, 20. Stephen & w, Hannah, & s, Benja-
    min Barton, rocf Carmel MM, dtd 1819,3,20
1829, 5, 21. Hannah dis jH
1829, 9, 24. Stephen dis jH
1837, 10, 26. Benjamin dis mcd

OLIPHANT
----, --, --. John, s Samuel & Rachel, b
    1822,5,26 d 1898,2,9 bur Winona; m Hannah
    P. WILLIAMS, dt Daniel & Elizabeth, b
    1828,2,23 d 1912,3,17
    Ch: Elizabeth
            M.   b 1862, 1, 31 d 1916, 3, 3
         bur Winona, O.
         William D. b 1866, 10, 13
         Olive H.   " 1869, 4, 17
1891, 3, 27. Olive H. m Joseph HALL
----, --, --. Wm. D., s John & Hannah (Wil-
    liams), b 1866,10,13; m Ellazan HOLLOWAY,
    dt Asa G. & Hannah (Hogue), b 1871,5,31
    d 1924,2,5
    Ch: Howard
         John   b 1897, 2, 19
         Arthur G. " 1899, 3, 26
         Beulah H. " 1906, 7, 17
    Wm. m 2nd Anna B. HOLLOWAY, dt Jos. &
    Ruthanna (Stratton) BRANSON, b 1875,11,27
    d 1930,2,8 bur Winona, O.
----, --, --. Howard John, s Wm. D. & Ellazan
    (Holloway), b 1897,2,19; m Alice Marie
    BLACKBURN, dt Wm. J. & Elizabeth (Coleman)
    b 1895,1,9
    Ch: Beulah
         Ruth   b 1923, 12, 29
         Howard John
                    " 1925, 9, 19
----, --, --. Arthur, s Wm. D. & Ellazan, b
    1899,3,26; m Laura M. STRATTON, dt Dilwyn
    & Elizabeth, b 1900,11,30
    Ch: Virginia E.
                    b 1924, 5, 23
         Richard W. " 1927, 1, 19
         George
         Barclay   " 1933, 3, 5

1884, 5, 22. John & w, Hannah P., & ch, Wm.
    D. & Olive H., rocf Hickory Grove MM, Ia.
1887, 3, 24. Elizabeth M. rocf Hickory Grove
    MM, Ia., dtd 1887,4,2
1894, 6, 21. Elizabeth M. rmt Albert Warring-
    ton
1896, 4, 26. Ellazan Holloway rocf Flushing
    MM, dtd 1896,3,26
1922, 9, 21. Howard John gct Salem MM, to m
    Alice Marie Blackburn
1923, 8, 23. Alice M. rocf Salem MM
1923, 7, 26. Arthur G. rmt Laura M. Stratton

1927, 5, 26. Wm. D. gct West-town MM, to m
    Anna M. B. Holloway
1928, 1, 26. Anna B. H. rocf West-town MM,
    Pa.

O'ROURKE
1890, 7, 25. Thomas gct Pleasant Plain MM,
    Ia. (G)
1898, 11, 23. Thomas rocf Pleasant Plain MM,
    Ia. (G)

OSBORN
1881, 9, 22. Clara J. (form Yates) dis mcd
    & jas

OTIS
1899, 2, 13. Debora, w Carlton, dt Dillwyn &
    Elizabeth Stratton, b

OWEN
1839, 8, 23. Thomas rmt Mary F. Myers (H)

OYSTER
1898, 2, 23. Sarah J. recrq (G)

PACKER
1821, 2, 22. George rocf Carmel MM, dtd
    1821,1,20
1823, 10, 25. George gct Carmel MM
1830, 1, 21. Elizabeth (form Thomas) dis
    mcd & jH
1830, 6, 24. Elizabeth (form Thomas) con mou
    (H)

PAINTER   [with ch)
1820, 6, 22. Jacob rmt Miriam Richardson (wd
1820, 9, 21. Miriam & ch, Isaac G. & Eliza-
    beth Richardson, gct Salem MM
1828, 5, 22. Samuel & w, Mary, & ch, Lorenzo,
    Stephen, Seth, Louisa & Lucinda, recrq (H)
1828, 7, 24. Samuel & w, Mary, & ch, Lorenzo,
    Stephen, Seth, Louisa & Lucinda, gct Salem
    MM (H)
1834, 3, 20. Sarah (form Wilkins) dis mou
1834, 4, 24. Sarah (form Wilkings) dis mcd
    (H)

PAIRPOINT
1811, 8, 15. Jonathan dis
1813, 1, 14. Jonathan rstrq

PARKER
1814, 4, 14. George rmt Rachel Jones
1814, 7, 14. Cert granted to Stillwater MM
    for Rachel, returned, unused 1814,9,15
1815, 7, 13. George rocf Stillwater MM, dtd
    1815,4,25   [O.
1816, 1, 18. George & fam gct Stillwater MM,

PATTEN
1883, 8, 22. Wm. m Elizabeth C. PRICE
1905, 9, 15. Alfred, s Wm. & Elizabeth (Price)

PATTEN, continued
      b 1884,9,10; m Elizabeth BRADWAY, dt Wm.
   T. & Rachel S., b 1884,6,7
   Ch: Julia
         Rachel   b 1906, 7, 5
         Clara
         Elizabeth " 1908, 10, 26
         James Wm. " 1910, 1, 28
         Clarence
         Edgar   " 1913, 3, 24

1883, 9, 20. Elizabeth C. gct Springville MM,
   Ia.
1928, 7, 26. Julia R. rmt Elwood K. Nichols

PATRICK
1897, 5, 19. Minnie recrq (G)

PAXSON
1815, 10, 19. Jacob & w, Elizabeth, & ch, Sarah, Edward, Mary P., Ann & Matilda, rocf
   Saddsbury MM, Pa., dtd 1815,8,8
1818, 8, 13. Wm. [Paxton] rocf Saddsbury MM,
   dtd 1818,7,7
1818, 10, 22. Wm. [Paxton] rmt Maria Morgan
1818, 12, 24. Sarah [Paxton] rmt David Galbreath
1819, 2, 25. Lydia [Paxton] & ch, Martha M.,
   Jesse E., Amos, Mary N. & Benjamin W.,
   rocf Sadsbury MM, dtd 1818,12,8

1819, 11, 25. Joseph J. [Paxon] rocf Sadsbury
   MM, dtd 1819,9,7
1821, 2, 22. Joseph rpd mcd; dis 1822,3,21
1821, 6, 21. Lydia dis jas
1823, 6, 26. Benjamin & w, Jane, & dt, Rachel,
   rocf Sadsbury MM, dtd 1823,6,3
1823, 6, 26. Heston rocf Sadsbury MM, dtd
   1823,6,3
1824, 1, 22. Martha M. dis jas
1824, 3, 25. Heston C. dis jas
1824, 8, 26. Rachel Irey (form Paxson) con
   mou
1828, 11, 20. Elizabeth dis jH
1829, 1, 22. Jacob dis jH
1829, 3, 26. William dis jH
1829, 3, 26. Maria dis jH
1830, 2, 25. Mary P. & Ann B. dis jH
1830, 2, 25. Edward dis jH
1830, 11, 25. Ann B. rmt Hoops Bailey (H)
1840, 1, 23. Mary P. Hoover (form Paxson) con
   mou (H)
1840, 6, 25. Matilda dis jH

1840, 11, 26. Jacob C. dis mcd
1841, 5, 20. Matilda dis jH
1841, 7, 22. Jane E. dis jH
1842, 3, 24. Sarah dis jH
1842, 6, 23. Abigail rocf Sandy Spring MM,
   O., dtd 1842,4,22
1842, 7, 21. Sarah Taylor (form Paxson, dis
   mcd (H)
1847, 12, 23. Abigail gct White River MM,
   Ind.
1853, 3, 24. Esther [Paxton] dis
1887, 12, 21. Jessie D. recrq (G)
1890, 5, 21. Jesse & w, Effie J., gct Salem
   MM (G)

PELLOTT
1835, 10, 22. Joseph & w, Sarah, & dt, Mary,
   rocf Carmel MM, dtd 1835,8,15 (H)

PENNINGTON
----, --, --. Levi b 1784,6,20; m Mary -----
   b 1782,10,31
   Ch: Sarah B.   b 1809, 2, 18
       Martha   " 1810, 10, 15
       Maria   " 1812, 2, 18
       Charity P. " 1813, 11, 24
       Lydia   " 1816, 5, 7
       Hezekiah
         Bye   " 1818, 3, 14
       Mary Ann   " 1820, 6, 23
       William   " 1823, 1, 11 d 1823,11,26
       Frances B. " 1824, 11, 12

1814, 4, 14. Levi & w, Mary, & ch, Sarah,
   Martha & Maria, rocf Center MM, Pa., dtd
   1813,8,14
1830, 6, 24. Martha rmt Isaac Miller
1831, 3, 24. Mariah rmt Levi Miller Jr.
1834, 11, 20. Charity rmt Samuel Miller
1834, 12, 25. Levi & w, Mary, gct Sandy Spring
   MM, O.
1835, 3, 26. Sarah rocf Upper Springfield MM,
   O., dtd 1834,11,22
1835, 6, 25. Hezekiah B. gct Sandy Spring MM,
   O.
1835, 6, 25. Sarah gct Cincinnati MM

PENNOCK
1815, 1, 19. Jane rmt Evan McBride
1816, 4, 18. Phebe rmt Eli Battin
1820, 8, 24. Joshua dis disunity
1820, 8, 24. Rebecca dis mou
1831, 4, 21. John & w, Hannah, & dt, Sarah,
   rocf London Grove MM, Pa., dtd 1831,4,5
   (H)
1831, 4, 21. John Jr. & w, Sidney, & ch,
   Elizabeth & Morris E., rocf London Grove
   MM, Pa., dtd 1831,4,5 (H)
1833, 5, 23. Thomas & w, Rachel, & ch, John
   Pim, Lydia Maria, Elizabeth & Sarah S.,
   rocf London Grove MM, Pa., dtd 1833,5,8
   (H)
1834, 2, 20. John Pim & Lydia, ch Thomas &

PENNOCK, continued
    Rachel, rocf London Grove MM, Pa., dtd
    1833,8,8
1834, 3, 20. Elizabeth, minor dt John & Sidney, rocf London Grove MM, Pa., dtd 1832, 5,12
1834, 4, 24. Cert for Sarah from London Grove MM, Pa., not accepted
1841, 7, 22. Sidney & three ch gct Salem MM (H)
1841, 10, 21. Elizabeth, minor dt John & Sidney, gct Salem MM
1842, 4, 21. John & w, Hannah, gct Salem MM (H)
1843, 2, 23. John Pim & Lydia, minor ch Thos. & Rachel, gct Goshen MM
1843, 3, 23. Thosl & w, Rachel, & ch rqct Goshen MM (H)

PENROSE
1871, 1, 25. Thomas con mcd (G)
1872, 2, 21. Thomas gct Alliance MM (G)
1877, 1, 24. Mary gct Minneapolis MM, Minn. (G)
1885, 3, 25. Esther gct Salem MM (G)
1899, 1, 25. John relrq (G)

PERKINS
1809, 11, 16. Jonathan gct Plainfield MM

PETTIT
1811, 3, 14. Charles rocf Sadsbury MM, dtd 1810,10,2, endorsed by Middleton MM, 1811,1,12
1813, 3, 18. Andrew rocf Muncy MM, dtd 1812, 8,19
1816, 9, 19. Andrew rpd mcd; dis 1817,5,15
1824, 11, 25. Abigail (form Whinery) con mcd
1825, 7, 21. Abigail gct Sandy Spring MM, O.
1825, 12, 22. Buly Ann rocf Sandy Spring MM, O., dtd 1825,2,25
1826, 4, 20. Buly Ann gct Salem MM
1829, 11, 26. Deborah (form Whinery) dis mou
1832, 10, 25. Mary Jane gct Smithfield MM, O.
1874, 9, 24. Lucretia P. Bashaw (form Pettit) dis mcd & jas
1887, 12, 21. Paris recrq (G)
1888, 6, 21. Mary (form McBride) dis

PHILLIPS
1917, 11, 21. Joseph & w, Margaret, & dt, Emily, rocf Long Lake MM, dtd 1917,11,7 (G)
1922, 4, 19. Joseph & w, Margaret, & ch gct Damascus MM (G)

PICKETT
1920, 10, 21. Alva J. Hampton gct Mill Creek MM, Ind., to m Ruth Amy Pickett

PICKLE
1845, 7, 24. Mary dis mcd

PIDGEON
1826, 6, 22. William rmt Mary Randels
1826, 9, 21. Mary gct Salem MM

PIERCE
1812, 1, 16. Jane rocf Sadsbury MM, dtd 1811,9,3, endrosed by Middleton MM, dtd 1811,12,12
1826, 3, 23. Jonathan & w, Hannah, & ch, Wm. D., Erasmus, Darwin, Susan D., Edwin & Jacob, rocf Center MM, dtd 1826,2,7
1829, 2, 26. Jonathan dis jH
1829, 3, 26. Jonathan & w, Hannah D., & ch, Edwin & Jacob, gct Springborough MM (H)
1829, 4, 23. Susan D. gct Springborough MM (H)
1829, 4, 23. Hannah & Susan dis jH

PIERPONT
1826, 3, 23. Jonathan & fam gct Stillwater MM, O.
1826, 3, 23. William gct Stillwater MM, O.
1826, 3, 23. Obed gct Stillwater MM, O.
1826, 3, 23. Ann & ch, Benjamin, Elizabeth, John, Mary & Eli, gct Stillwater MM, O.

PIERSON
1814, 10, 13. Ann & ch, Alice, Susanna, Sarah & Ann, rocf Redstone MM, dtd 1814,7,1
1817, 5, 15. Ann & ch gct Plainfield MM

PIKE
1920, 8, 26. Lindley W. Hall gct Plainfield MM, Ind., to m Orpha Pike

PIM
1813, 1, 14. Nathan & w, Sarah, & ch, Garret, Isaac, Lydia & Enos, rocf Bradford MM, dtd 1812,11,4
1819, 1, 21. Sarah/rmt Jabez Coulson wd with ch
1834, 2, 20. Jarrett rmt Abigail Mendenhall
1834, 5, 22. Abigail gct Sandy Spring MM, O.
1874, 10, 20. Aden, Asa & Rachel dis jG
1884, 5, 22. Lewis G. dis disunity
1931, 2, 26. Blanch (form Stratton) dis

POLLARD
1895, 10, 22. Lucinda, w Francis J., dt Dillwyn & Elizabeth (Hall) Stratton, b
1919, 6, 27. Andrew, s John & Janet (Henderson), b 1894,7,12; m Emily WOOLMAN, dt Edward J. & Anna (Whinery), b 1897,7,21
    Ch: Edward
        John   b 1920, 4, 27
        Robert A. " 1922, 1, 31
        Anna Janet " 1923, 9, 17
1921, 8, 26. Francis Joseph m Lucinda STRATTON

1917, 8, 23. Andrew rocf Norwich MM, Canada, dtd 1917,8,8
1922, 2, 23. Lucinda S. gct Norwich MM, Can.
1932, 11, 24. Andrew & w, Emily, dis jas

POOL,

1826, 6, 22. Jonas & w, Ann, & dt, Asaneth, rocf Carmel MM, dtd 1826,6,17

1828, 7, 24. Jonas & w, Ann, & ch, Asenith & Priscilla, gct Carmel MM

POUND

1829, 8, 20. David & w, Ann, & ch, Thomas C., Sarah H., Benjamin H., Isabella, Elijah, Mary H. & Ann H., rocf Allum Creek MM, O., dtd 1829,1,29, also s, David, b since that dte; this cert was directed to Juneus MM, but that MM was discontinued, they were rec here (H)

1830, 3, 25. David & fam gct Marlborough MM (H)

1833, 11, 20. Thomas C. rmt Elizabeth L. Davis (H)

1833, 12, 26. Elizabeth L. gct Marlborough MM (H)

1839, 11, 24. Thomas C. rmt Susan Ingram (H)

1840, 2, 20. Susan (form Ingrain) dis mcd in H Mtg

1840, 3, 26. Angelina E. rocf Marlborough MM, dtd 1839,7,27 (H)

1840, 9, 24. Susan gct Salem MM (H)

POWELL

1885, 12, 24. Mary Ann dis jas

PRESTON

1908, 2, 17. Debora M., w Ralph C., dt Wilson J. & Mary C. (Hall) Steer, b

1810, 10, 18. Amos rocf South River MM, Va., dtd 1810,4,14

1811, 8, 15. Amos con mcd with Drusilla Reeve

PRICE

----, --, --. Uriah, s Isaac & Margaret, b 1823,5,5 d 1895,2,4 bur Winona; m ----- -----
  Ch: Theodore   b 1851, 8, 23
     Elizabeth " 1859, 4, 4
Uriah m 2nd Rebecca McGRAIL, wd Alfred, dt Geo. D. & Hannah GILBERT, b 1830,3,14 d 1912,4,1
  Ch: Edwin G. b 1868, 9, 25
     Francis   " 1872, 1, 27 d 1875, 2,13
     bur Winona, O.

1883, 6, 22. Wm. m Elizabeth C. PRICE

----, --, --. Edwin G., s Uriah & Rebecca (Gilbert), b 1868,9,25; m Irene H. GAMBLE, dt Samuel & Mary Jane (Fogg), b 1879,8,1
  Ch: Francis
     Edward   b 1906, 10, 22
     Rebecca
     Marie   " 1909, 10, 16

1871, 11, 23. Theodore recrq

1872, 6, 20. Uriah & w, Rebecca, & ch, Elizabeth, Edwin G. & Francis Price & George G. & Amy Ann McGrail, rocf Sewick-

ley MM, dtd 1872,5,28

1881, 2, 24. Theodore dis mcd

1905, 8, 24. Edwin G. rmt Irena H. Gamble

1933, 8, 24. Francis E. gct Middleton MM, O., to m Helen P. Cope

1934, 1, 25. Helen C. rocf Middleton MM, O., dtd 1934,1,20

PUSEY

1837, 11, 23. Wm. E. rocf London Grove MM, Pa.

1839, 10, 24. Wm. E. dis disunity

QUAINTANCE

1815, 7, 13. Eli & w, Betty, & ch, Joseph & Lewis Cary, rocf Plymouth MM, dtd 1815,4,15 15

1816, 2, 15. Fisher rmt Sarah Irey

1816, 3, 14. Sarah gct Plymouth MM

1818, 7, 16. Eli & fam gct Smithfield MM

RAKESTRAW

1842, 8, 23. Rebecca b

1823, 6, 26. Rebecca rocf Sadsbury MM, dtd 1823,4,17 .

1829, 5, 21. Margaret con mou

1839, 10, 24. Margaret dis

RALEY

1817, 8, 14. Joseph gct Short Creek MM, O.

1817, 8, 14. James, minor, gct Short Creek MM, O.

1819, 11, 25. Joseph rocf Short Creek MM, dtd 1819,9,21

1820, 4,20. Joseph rmt Susanna Cooper

1869, 9, 22. Ann gct Damascus MM (G)

1873, 11, 20. Milton dis disunity

1883, 7, 26. Mary Ann Edwards (form Raley) dis mcd

1887, 10, 22. Sarah Elizabeth Sanor (form Raley) dis mcd

1888, 7, 26. Clara M. Bowers (form Raley) dis mcd

1892, 10, 20. Flora B. Ward (form Raley) dis mcd

RANDELS

----, --, --. James d 1853,1,27; m Anna -----
  Ch: Sarah   b 1821, 10, 17
     Isaac   " 1823, 1, 13 d 1848, 5, 7
     Elizabeth " 1825, 6, 30
     Maria   " 1830, 4, 16

1816, 6, 13. Wm. [Randall] & w, Elizabeth, rocf Warrington MM, dtd 1816,3,21

1816, 6, 13. James [Randall] rocf Warrington MM, dtd 1816,3,21

1816, 6, 13. John [Randall] rocf Warrington MM, dtd 1816,3,21

1816, 6, 13. Isaac [Randall] rocf Warrington MM, dtd 1816,3,21

1816, 6, 13. Mary [Randall] rocf Warrington MM, dtd 1816,3,21

RANDELS, continued
1820, 7, 20. James [Randals] rmt Ann Harris
1825, 3, 24. John rpd mou; con mou 1825,8,25
1826, 6, 22. Mary rmt Wm. Pidgeon
1830, 6, 24. Isaac [Randals] con mou
1837, 10, 26. Isaac [Randles] dis disunity
1840, 5, 21. John dis disunity
1847, 8, 26. Sarah Barber (form Randels) dis
       mcd
1849, 3, 22. Elizabeth Beck (form Randels)
       dis mcd
1861, 10, 24. Sarah [Randel] (form Hoopes)
       dis mcd

RANDOLF
1832, 10, 25. Deborah (form Carroll) con mou
       (H)

RAY
1816, 4, 18. Cert rec for Marah & ch, Thomas
       B. & Mary, from ND MM, dtd 1813,11,2, en-
       dorsed to Marlborough MM
1885, 1, 22. Louisa (form Cameron) dis mcd

READ
1827, 2, 27. Betty, w Charles, & ch, Joseph,
       Thomas, Samuel, George, Isaac, Joel &
       William, rocf Baltimore MM for Western
       District, dtd 1826,11,10

REAPS
1821, 9, 20. Ann (form Griffith) dis mcd

REEDER
1809, 11, 26. Priscilla rmt Jonathan Batten
1814, 5, 19. Elizabeth rmt David Coulson
1815, 11, 16. Hannah rmt Abner John
1818, 12, 24. Thomas gct Short Creek MM, O.,
       to m Hannah James
1819, 5, 20. Hannah rocf Short Creek MM, O.,
       dtd 1819,3,23
1819, 11, 25. James rmt Mary Davis
1820, 12, 21. Wm. rmt Lydia Battin
1821, 1, 25. Mary Williams (form Reeder) con
       mcd
1822, 7, 25. Hannah dis for leaving h
1833, 11, 20. Alice [Reader] rocf Buckingham
       MM, dtd 1833,8,2 (H)
1874, 11, 26. Ann Eliza dis
1875, 6, 24. Samuel dis disunity
1884, 5, 22. Deborah Shaw (form Reader) dis
       mcd

REEVES
1828, 5, 22. David recrq (H)
1828, 7, 24. David gct Salem MM (H)
1843, 6, 22. Thomas, minor, rocf Upper Spring-
       field MM, O., dtd 1843,4,22, endorsed by
       Salem MM, 1843,5,24
1848, 4, 20. Thomas con mcd
1848, 8, 24. Thomas gct Upper Springfield MM,
       O.

REICHENBAUGH
1907, 9, 25. Frank & w, Myrtle, & ch,
       Clarence E. & Ray L., recrq (G)
1920, 10, 20. Frank & w, Myrtle, & ch, Clar-
       ence, Ray, Vera, Pearl & Glenn, gct
       Friends Church, Monroe, Ind. (G)

REYNOLDS
----, --, --. Levi d 1844,3,22; m Mary -----
       d 1841,8,8
       Ch: Joel   b 1801, 11, 7
           Eliza   " 1803, 11, 24 d 1848, 4, 9
           Samuel   " 1806, 1, 17
           Thomas   " 1808, 1, 21
           Allen   " 1810, 6, 12
           Tabitha   " 1814, 2, 2
           Levi   " 1816, 11, 27
----, --, --. Samuel b 1806,1,16; m Hannah
       ----- b 1803,8,8
       Ch: Ezra   b 1829, 12, 28
           Elizabeth
           Emily   " 1831, 12, 12
           Martha   " 1833, 4, 11
----, --, --. Allen b 1810,6,12; m Mary -----
       Ch: Martha H. b 1844, 4, 22

1809, 6, 15. Michael rocf Little Britain MM,
       Pa., dtd 1808,4,9, endorsed by Short Creek
       MM, 1809,5,25
1829, 4, 23. Samuel rmt Hannah Grissell
1831, 5, 26. Tamer rmt Lewis S. White
1835, 6, 25. Samuel & fam gct Salem MM
1838, 7, 26. Tabitha rmt Paul White
1841, 9, 23. Joel dis disunity
1843, 5, 25. Levi Jr. gct Marlborough MM
1843, 9, 21. Allen rmt Mary Gibson
1845, 11, 20. Levi rocf Marlborough MM
1846, 3, 26. Allen & w, Mary, & dt, Martha
       K., gct Upper Springfield MM, O.
1848, 1, 20. Levi dis mcd

RHODES
1865, 6, 22. Harmon rmt Elizabeth Test
1865, 10, 26. Elizabeth [Rhoades] gct Chester-
       field MM

RICHARDS
1820, 8, 24. Sarah (form McNealy) dis mou
1887, 12, 21. Phebe recrq (G)
1892, 6, 22. Phebe gct Salem MM (G)

RICHARDSON   [Painter
1820, 6, 22. Miriam, wd with ch, rmt Jacob
1820, 9, 21. Miriam Painter & ch, Isaac G. &
       Elizabeth Richardson, gct Salem MM
1820, 11, 23. Richard dis mcd   [25
1824, 6, 24. Abraham G. rpd mou; dis 1824,11,

RICHY
1824, 6, 24. Sarah (form Burson) con mou
1837, 8, 24. Sarah [Richey] dis disunity

RIGHTER
1846, 8, 20. Sarah (form Beck) dis mcd

ROCKWELL
----, --, --. Edwin C., s Franklin & Mariah
     (Knowls), b 1881,11,3; m Luella WHITE, dt
     Lindsey & Samira (Cox), b 1883,5,18
     Ch: Glenn
             Rudolph   b 1908, 5, 19
         Helen Lu-
             ella   " 1910, 7, 7
         Margaret
             Georgianna" 1913, 3, 19
         Carl Frank-
             lin   " 1915, 9, 4

1926, 10, 21. Edwin C. & w, Luella, & ch,
     Glen Rudolph, Helen Luella, Margaret
     Georgianna & Carl Franklin, rocf Plain-
     field MM, Ind., dtd 1926,9,29
1930, 2, 30. Edwin C. & w, Luella W., & ch,
     Helen L., Margaret G. & Carl F., gct Pasa-
     dena MM, Calif.
1930, 3, 20. Glenn R. gct Stillwater MM, O.

ROGERS
----, --, --. Isaac C., s Amos Austin & Martha
     Lipponcott (Collins), b 1869,6,20; m Ellen
     B. NEWLIN, dt Wm. W. & Edith (Gilbert) b
     1866,1,22
     Ch: Edith M.
1891, 12, 25. Isaac C. m Ellen B. NEWLIN

1814, 9, 15. Ruth & ch, Mary, Levi & Ann,
     rocf Westland MM, dtd 1814,4,23
1822, 7, 25. Mary recrq
1823, 3, 20. Mary rmt Wm. Galbreath
1927, 6, 23. Isaac C. & w, Ellen B., rocf
     Chester MM, N. J.
1927, 6, 23. Edith Marion rocf Chester MM,
     N. J.

ROOD
1853, 11, 24. Christopher Allen gct Salem MM,
     to m Abigail Rood

ROTCH
1812, 7, 16. Thomas & w, Charity, rocf West
     Hartford MM, Conn., dtd 1811,9,11, en-
     dorsed by Concord MM, O.

RUBLE
1912, 4, 24. Emma dropped from mbrp (G)

SANDERS
1809, 10, 19. Sarah Leveridge (form Sanders)
     rpd mou; Stillwater MM to treat with her;
1810, 11, 15. Benjamin dis mcd [dis 1810,4,19
1811, 1, 17. Sarah (form Wilkens) dis mcd
1812, 11, 19. Abisha dis mcd
1817, 9, 18. Levi dis attending musters

SANOR
1887, 10, 20. Sarah Elizabeth (form Raley)
     dis mcd
1898, 1, 23. Perry & Mary recrq (G)
1892, 5, 25. Mardie relrq (G)

SATTERTHWAIT
----, --, --. Chas. W., s David & Ruth (Coffee)
     b 1833,12,31 d 1922,7,13 bur Winona, O.;
     m Adaline BYE, dt Hezekiah & Ann, b 1827,
     1,12 d 1897,8,14
     Ch: Franklin P.b 1861, 2, 11
         Anna B.   " 1863, 8, 15
         William D." 1866, 11, 8
         Isaac H. " 1866, 11, 8
         Ruth C.   " 1871, 4, 11
----, --, --. Wm. D., s Chas. W. & Adaline, b
     1866,11,8; m Ida A. NEWLIN, dt Wm. &
     Edith, b 1868,4,10
     Ch: Infant dt b 1894, 1, 7 d 1894, 1, 7
         Edith M. " 1896, 4, 23
         Mary E.   " 1898, 8, 23
         Ellen Ruth" 1901, 5, 28
----, --, --. Isaac H., s Chas. W. & Adaline,
     b 1866,11,8; m Emily S. HALL, dt Lindley &
     Millicent (Bailey), b 1870,6,17
     Ch: Anna M.   b 1896, 8, 18
         Charles
             Walter " 1899, 4, 2
         Wilmer L. " 1900, 7, 6
         Esther A. " 1903, 10, 10
         Alfred S. " 1909, 1, 4
         Mildred E." 1913, 9, 26 d 1918,10,17
         bur Winona, O.
----, --, --. Charles Walter, s Isaac & Emily,
     b 1899,4,2; m Helen FORSYTHE, dt Henry &
     Anna (Hutton), b 1898,11,24
     Ch: Donald
             Henry   b 1923, 4, 25 d 1923, 5, 7
         Mildred
             Emily   " 1924, 8, 20
         Richard
             Isaac   " 1926, 1, 1
         Marjorie
             Ann   " 1932, 6, 12
----, --, --. Wilmer L., s Isaac & Emily, b
     1900,7,6; m Alice R. THOMAS
     Ch: Martha
             Marie   b 1933, 6, 12

1828, 5, 22. Richard & ch, John W., Barkley
     A., James M., Caroline W., Joseph W. &
     William, recrq (H)
1828, 7, 24. Richard & ch, John W., Barkley
     A., James M., Caroline W., Joseph W. &
     William, gct Salem MM (H)
1873, 3, 20. Charles W. & ch, Franklin P.,
     Ann B., Wm. D., Isaac H. & Ruth C., rocf
     Salem MM, dtd 1873,2,19
1874, 4, 23. Adaline M. recrq
1889, 6, 20. Franklin B. gct Spring River MM,
     Kans.
1893, 4, 20. Wm. D. rmt Ida A. Newlin

SATTERTHWAIT, continued
1895, 12, 26. Emily S. rocf Short Creek MM,
     O., dtd 1895,11,19
1904, 2, 25. Wm. D. & w, Ida A., & ch,
     Edith M., Mary E. & Ellen R., gct Salem
     MM
1904, 4, 21. Ruth C. rmt Harry E. Cooper
1912, 7, 25. Ann B. rmt Richard Haworth
1920, 3, 25. Russell B. Hampton gct Salem MM,
     to m Mary E. Satterthwait
1921, 8, 25. Charles Walter gct Birmingham
     MM, Pa., to m Helen M. Forsythe
1922, 1, 26. Helen Forsythe rocf Birmingham
     MM, Pa., dtd 1921,12,28
1923, 1, 25. Anna M. Morton (form Satterth-
     wait) dis mcd
1932, 5, 26. Wilmer L. gct Short Creek MM,
     O., to m Alice R. Thomas
1932, 4, 20. Charles Waller & w, Helen F., &
     ch, Mildred Emily, Richard Isaac, Harold
     Walter & Marjorie Ann, gct Birmingham MM
1934, 1, 25. Ethel N. & Jesse N. Edgerton
     declared intention of m

SAUL
1813, 12, 16. Joseph Wilkinson rocf Holen MM,
     Eng., dtd 1811,4,18, endorsed by Abington
     MM, 1813,4,26

SCATTERGOOD
1874, 4, 23. Alpheus recrq (G)

SCHISLER
1902, 7, 23. Sarah recrq (G)

SCHOFIELD
1828, 5, 22. David & w, Rebecca, & ch, Rachel,
     recrq (H)
1828, 7, 24. David & w, Rebecca, & ch, Rachel,
     gct Salem MM (H)

SCHOOLEY
1814, 5, 19. Henry & w, Margaret, & ch,
     Hannah & John, rocf Short Creek MM, O.,
     dtd 1813,11,23
1815, 2, 16. Richard rocf Goose Creek MM,
     Va., dtd 1814,9,5
1819, 10, 21. Mahlon Hole gct Salem MM, to m
     Rachel Schooley

SCHWICKLICK
1914, 8, 19. Mrs. Anna recrq (G)

SCOTT
----, --, --. Benjamin & Ann
     Ch: Mary Ann b 1820, 12, 31
         Phebe   " ----, 10,10
         Prophet B. " 1824, 5, 1
         Sarah   " 1825, 12, 19
         Elizabeth " 1827, 11, 20
         Lydia   " 1829, 5, 16
         Joseph   " 1831, 5, 9
         Hannah   " 1835, 9, 20

1817, 10, 16. Joseph rmt Jane Marsh
1819, 1, 21. Jane gct Carmel MM
1833, 9, 26. Ann & ch, Mary Ann, Phebe,
     Phophet B., Sarah, Elizabeth, Lydia & Jo-
     seph, rocf Upper Springfield MM, dtd
     1833,8,24
1838, 11, 22. Ann & ch, Maryann, Phebe, Pro-
     phet B., Sarah, Elizabeth, Lydia, Joseph &
     Hannah, gct Upper Springfield MM, O.

SCULLION
1912, 4, 24. Bertha Hall dropped from mbrp
     (G)

SHAFER
1836, 11, 24. Hannah (form Wilkins) dis mou
     (H)

SHALLENBERG
1917, 4, 20. Walter recrq (G)

SHARP
----, --, --. Enoch b 1769,2,10 d 1851,6,14;
     m Sarah ----- b 1771,5,24 d 1838,4,4

1836, 7, 21. Sarah Jr. rocf Upper Springfield
     MM, O., dtd 1836,6,25
1836, 7, 21. Mary rocf Upper Springfield MM,
     O., dtd 1836,6,25
1837, 3, 23. Enoch & w, Sarah, rocf Upper
     Springfield MM, O., dtd 1837,2,25
1838, 6, 21. Mary rmt Jonathan Coppock
1844, 8, 22. Sarah Beck (form Sharp) dis mcd

SHAW
----, --, --. William, s Thomas & Rachel, b
     1824,12,29; m Hannah HEALD, dt Wm. W. &
     Susanna, b 1826,12,16
     Ch: Lindley   b 1852, 5, 26
         Milton J.   " 1854, 9, 8
         Wm. Wilson " 1856, 10, 9
         Phebe Ellen" 1860, 2, 24
         Thomas H.   " 1862, 5, 29 d 1862, 7,24
         Charles   " 1864, 6, 4
         Susanna   " 1866, 8, 8

1810, 8, 16. Thomas gct Middleton MM, to m
     Rachel Heald
1811, 2, 14. Rachel rocf Middleton MM, dtd
     1811,2,9
1815, 8, 19. Margaret rmt Benjamin Vore
1816, 9, 19. Susanna rocf Westland MM, dtd
     1816,8,22
1818, 3, 19. Susanna gct Westland MM
1828, 8, 21. Thomas gct Westland MM, to m
     Ann Vanscoyoc
1829, 7, 23. Anna rocf Westland MM, dtd 1829,
     5,28
1830, 2, 25. Thomas dis jH
1831, 5, 26. Samuel gct Sandy Spring MM
1834, 9, 25. Nathan gct Carmel MM, to m
     Miriam James
1835, 1, 22. Nathan gct Upper Springfield MM,

SHAW, continued
O.

1835, 4, 23. John gct Salem MM
1835, 9, 24. Thomas rmt Sarah Mendenhall (H)
1837, 6, 22. Elizabeth (form Heston) dis mcd
1837, 6, 22. Elizabeth (form Heston) dis mcd (H)
1838, 11, 22. Abner gct Sandy Spring MM, O.
1838, 11, 22. Rebecca & Wm., minors, gct Sandy Spring MM, O.
1839, 8, 22. Thomas rst at Sandy Spring MM, O. on consent of this mtg
1871, 10, 26. Jeremiah Coppock gct Middleton MM, to m Rebecca Shaw
1872, 9, 26. Lindley, Milton, Wm. Wilson, Phebe Ellen, Charles & Susanna, ch Wm. & Hannah, rocf Middleton MM, dtd 1872,9,21
1873, 6, 26. Hannah rst on rq of Middleton MM
1873, 11, 20. Wm. rst on consent of Middleton MM
1875, 6, 24. Wm. & Hannah & ch gct Hickory Grove MM, Ia.
1875, 9, 23. Lindley gct Springville MM, Ia.
1882, 1, 26. Levi dis disunity
1884, 5, 22. Deborah (form Reader) dis mcd
1885, 12, 24. Hannah dis disunity

SHEPPERD
1839, 11, 24. Mary (form Carroll) con mcd (H)
1841, 4, 22. Mary [Shepherd] gct Fall Creek MM (H)

SHINN
1825, 6, 23. Joshua rocf Salem MM, dtd 1825, 5,25
1826, 5, 25. Joshua rmt Abigail Whinery
1829, 12, 24. Hannah rocf Marlborough MM, dtd 1829,9,29
1832, 4, 26. Hannah rmt George Brantingham Jr.
1832, 8, 23. Joshua & w, Abigail, gct Upper Springfield MM, O.

SHISLER
1912, 4, 24. Sarah E. gct Salem MM (G)

SHORE
1815, 1, 19. Alice rmt Isaac Barber
1815, 6, 15. James Jr. dis mcd
1828, 5, 22. Rachel recrq (H)
1828, 7, 24. Rachel gct Salem MM (H)

SIDWELL
1913, 8, 23. Oliver T., s Wilson T. & Isabel (Fogg), b 1889,7,5; m Emily HALL, dt Joseph & Olive (Oliphant), b 1892,12,27
   Ch: Floyd Hall b 1914, 10, 27
       J. Wilson   " 1916, 8, 1
       Florence
         Olive   " 1918, 10, 22
       Bertha Isa-
         bel   " 1921, 3, 27
       Harold Oli-

Ch: ver   b 1923, 2, 26

1916, 1, 20. Emily C. H. & s, Floyd Hall, gct Hickory Grove MM, Ia.
1917, 11, 22. Oliver F. & w, Emily C. H., & ch, Floyd H. & J. Wilson, rocf Hickory Grove MM, Ia.

SINCLAIR
1814, 7, 14. Elizabeth (form Wilkins) dis mcd
1817, 6, 19. George gct Fairfield MM, O.
1819, 7, 22. David & w & ch, Jacob, Hudson, Barton, Ruth & Levi, recrq (w's name Lucy)
1819, 7, 22. Matilda recrq

SKIMMER
1813, 6, 17. Alexander rocf West Hartford MM, Conn., dtd 1813,1,13

SMITH
1872, 7, 15. Anna Leora, w Albert, dt Linneus & Sina (Brantingham) Warrington, b
1879, 10, 22. Emma, dt Peter & Mary, b

1818, 1, 15. Benjamin rocf Westland MM, dtd 1817,12,25
1822, 4, 25. Rachel, Robert, Phebe, Mary & Abraham, ch Benjamin, recrq
1822, 4, 25. Deborah, w Benjamin, recrq
1826, 8, 24. Mary recrq
1827, 9, 20. Mary F. rmt Chas. D. Grissell
1828, 7, 24. Joseph Dutton & w, Joanna, & ch, Maria, Sarah, Eliza, Phebe, Matilda, Deborah & David, also Edmund, Thomas Henry & David Smith, recrq
1828, 8, 21. Benjamin dis jH
1828, 9, 25. Deborah dis jH
1830, 3, 25. Mary dis jH
1830, 4, 22. Rachel dis disunity
1830, 5, 20. Phebe dis jH
1832, 10, 25. Mary Magrew (form Smith) dis mou (H)
1833, 10, 24. Phebe Votaw (form Smith) con mcd (H)
1824, 10, 23. Edmund rmt Eliza Dutton (H)
1836, 2, 25. Phebe gct Middleton MM (H)
1837, 8, 24. Rachel Stiles (form Smith) dis mou (H)
1838, 7, 27. Abraham dis mou
1842, 8, 25. Ruth (form Whinery) dis mcd
1894, 2, 22. Emma recrq
1903, 4, 23. Emma Votaw (form Smith) con mcd
1908, 9, 7. Mary E. (form Binns) dis mcd & jas
1914, 7, 23. Mary E. rst at Short Creek MM, O., on consent of this mtg
1919, 1, 22. Clara V. recrq (form mbr at Valley MM) (G)
1925, 3, 26. Anna Leora (form Warrington) dis mcd & jas
1927, 7, 20. Clara dropped from mbrp (G)

SPECK
1817, 2, 13. Mary (form Beck) dis mcd

STACKHOUSE
1809, 7, 13. Alsa recrq
1811, 7, 18. Alse dis
1813, 2, 18. Martha recrq
1818, 1, 15. Tacy dis mou
1819, 2, 25. Hannah rocf Middleton MM, dtd
        1818.12,21
1823, 9, 25. Alice Jackson (form Stackhouse);
        consent given Sandy Spring MM, O., to rst

STAFFORD
1837, 7, 20. Mary rocf Gwyned MM, Pa., dtd
        1835,10,29 (H)
1885, 6, 26. Esther Foster (form Stafford)
        dis mcd

STAHL
1898, 3, 22. Lavina, w Lester, dt Andrew &
        Martha (Dean) Zeppernick, b

1927, 6, 23. Lavina (form Zappernick) dis

STANLEY
1891, 3, 27. Thomas E. m Martha TEST
----, --, --. Roscoe R., s Mervin & Gertrude
        (Pickett), b 1900,6,24; m Sina Emily
        HOLLOWAY, dt Cyrus & Esther (Emery), b
        1900,7,20
        Ch: Wilmer
                Wilid   b 1925, 2, 4
            Robert
                Clarence   " 1927, 1, 31
            Dorothy
                May   " 1932, 12, 4

1819, 4, 22. Isaac Votaw gct Salem MM, to m
        Frances Stanley
1821, 4, 26. James C. [Standley] & w, Mary,
        & ch, Littleberry, Samuel, Jonathan &
        Rhoda, rocf Somerset MM, dtd 1821,3,26
1822, 12, 26. Thomas C. rmt Leah Votaw
1823, 4, 24. Leah [Standley] gct Salem MM
1825, 3, 24. Littleberry rpd mou; dis 1825,8,
1826, 12, 21. Lemuel dis mou   [25
1830, 9, 23. James C. & fam gct Upper Spring-
        field MM
1830, 11, 16. Rhoda Hisler (form Stanley) dis
        mou
1874, 10, 21. Lydia Maria & dt, Martha W.,
        gct Adrian MM, Mich. (G)
1891, 9, 24. Martha S. gct Springville MM,Ia.
1929, 7, 25. Rosco R. & w, Sina E., & ch,
        Wilmer W. & Robert C., rocf Salem MM, dtd
        1929,7,24

STANTON
1828, 5, 22. Benjamin & w, Martha, & ch, Re-
        becca, Laura, Oliver, Joseph & Caroline,
        recrq (H)
1828, 7, 24. Benjamin & w, Martha, & ch, Re-
        becca, Laura, Oliver, Joseph & Caroline,
        gct Salem MM (H)

STEEL
1811, 11, 14. Mary (form Williams) dis mcd
1820, 10, 26. Mary con mcd
1822, 12, 26. Mary dis jas
1825, 7, 21. Elizabeth (form Williams) dis
        mcd

STEER
----, --, --. Elisha B., s Israel & Rebecca
        (Brackin), b 1850,6,2 d 1930,1,25; m Han-
        nah FOWLER b 1862,11,19
1874, 5, 22. Elisha B. m Ellen C. GILBERT
----, --, --. Wilson J., s Israel & Rebecca
        (Bracken), b 1859,10,3; m Mary C. HALL,
        dt Lindley & Millicent (Bailey), b 1868,
        4,25
        Ch: Lindley
                Ellis   b 1892, 1, 31
            Albert I.   " 1893, 6, 28 d 1919, 1, 4
            bur Winona, O.
            James W.   b 1895, 7, 7
            Margaret R." 1897, 10, 15
            Millicent
            H.   " 1900, 1, 24
            Rebecca B.   " 1903, 8, 10
            Deborah M.   " 1908, 2, 17
----, --, --. Lindley Ellis, s Wilson J. &
        Mary C. (Hall); m Anna BRADWAY, dt Wm. T.
        & Rachel (Dean), b 1886,2,8
----, --, --. Albert J., s Wilson J. & Mary C.
        b 1893,6,28 d 1919,1,4 bur Winona; m Jes-
        sie Leah CRAWFORD, dt Thomas A. & Sara
        (Brantingham), b 1895,1,16
1922, 12, 26. Rebecca B. m Oliver B. Bailey
1923, 8, 15. Millicent H. m Wm. O. FOSTER
1927, 1, 22. Jessie Leah C. m Wilson A. NEGUS
1929, 6, 22. Elisha B. m Hannah C. FOWLER

1874, 11, 26. Ellen G. gct Short Creek MM,O.
1906, 1, 25. Wilson J. & w, Mary A., & ch,
        Lindley Ellis, Albert J., James W., Mar-
        garet R., Millicent H. & Rebecca B., rocf
        Short Creek MM, O., dtd 1905,12,19
1914, 3, 26. Lindley Ellis rmt Anna Bradway
1915, 5, 20. Albert I. gct Upper Springfield
        MM, O., to m Jessie Leah Crawford
1915, 12, 23. Jessie Leah rocf Upper Spring-
        field MM, O.
1924, 1, 24. Margaret Huntley (form Steer)
        con mcd
1829, 8, 22. Elisha B. rocf Salem MM, dtd
        1829,8,21
1930, 1, 23. James W. dis jas & mcd
1933, 9, 21. L. Ellis & w, Anna B., gct Pasa-
        dena MM, Calif.

STEFFEY
1837, 7, 20. Julia Ann (form Mathews) dis
        mou (H)

STEVENSON
1888, 7, 26. Mary (form Allen) con mcd
1888, 11, 22. Mary A. gct Spring River MM,Ia.

STILES
1837, 8, 24. Rachel (form Smith) dis mou
    (H)

STRATTON
----, --, --. Joseph, s Michael & Rhoda,
    b 1792,4,15 d 1843,2,5; m Sara TEST, dt
    Zacheus & Rebecca, b 1793,3.26 d 1880,9,9
    bur Winona
    Ch: Rebecca D. b 1816, 3, 29
        Anna M.   " 1817, 9, 1 d 1897, 1,28
        bur Winona
        Abi   b 1819, 10, 4
        Mark   " 1821, 10, 2
        Zacheus   " 1824, 5, 10
        Joseph   " 1825, 12, 9 d 1892, 3, 8
        bur Winona
        Rhoda   b 1827, 3, 7 d 1830,11, 5
        bur Winona
        Michael   b 1829, 1, 30 " 1854,12,14
        bur Winona
        Sara   b 1830, 6, 13 " 1888, 2, 8
        bur Winona
        Isaac   b 1832, 7, 17 " 1852,12, 4
        bur Minnesota
        Josiah   b 1833, 12, 22
1797, 12, 8. Daniel b d 1872,2,6
----, --, --. Mark & Mary
    Ch: Charles H. b 1846, 4, 2
        Ann Eliza " 1847, 11, 25 d 1849, 2,17
        Franklin   " 1849, 12, 31
        Joseph
        Henry   " 1852, 4, 6
        Isaac   " 1854, 7, 14
1851, 6, 27. Sarah m Henry LUPTON
----, --, --. Benjamin D., s Daniel & Abigail,
    b 1825,6,5 d 1879,1,19 bur Winona; m Ellen
    STANLEY, dt Andrew & Ruth, b 1824,12,20
    Ch: Ruthanna b 1849, 4, 7
        Abigail   " 1850, 12, 25
        John T.   " 1852, 2, 11 d 1878, 9,28
        bur Winona,0.
        Charles   " 1854, 2, 25
        Abram   " 1857, 2, 24
        Mary Ellen " 1862, 5, 22
        Sina   " 1864, 5, 17
----, --, --. Barclay, s Daniel & Abigail,
    b 1829,12,22 d 1892,7,21 bur Winona; m
    Hannah H. HOBSON, dt Joseph & Ruth, b
    1826,12,1 d 1903,12,5 bur Winona
    Ch: Joseph C. b 1855, 10, 5 d 1928,12,31
        bur Winona, 0.
        Elizabeth
        B.   b 1857, 3, 23 d 1872, 6,14
        bur Winona, 0.
        Dilwyn   b 1861, 7, 2
----, --, --. Joseph, s Joseph & Sarah, b
    1825,12,9 d 1892,3,8 bur Winona, 0.; m
    Rachel BRANTINGHAM, dt Jos. & Lydia, b
    1827,10,22 d 1901,1,25 bur Winona, 0.
----, --, --. Josiah b 1833,12,22; m Eliza-
    beth ----- b 1833,3,6
    Ch: Sarah S.   b 1857, 5, 19 d 1861, 4,12

        Ch: Willobee   b 1859, 8, 29
            Allice Ann " 1862, 10, 2
1869, 9, 24. Ruthanna m Joseph H. BRANSON
----, --, --. John F., s Benjamin D. & Ellen,
    b 1852,2,11 d 1878,9,28; m Dorothy HOB-
    SON, dt Thomas & Unity, b 1847,5,14
    Ch: George W. b 1876, 9, 12
----, --, --. Abram, s Benj. D. & Ellen, b
    1857,2,24; m Hannah D. BRANTINGHAM, dt
    Alfred & Ann, b 1856,10,27
    Ch: Alice E.   b 1881, 4, 10
        John A.   " 1882, 8, 17
        Edith   " 1888, 7, 5
1882, 5, 26. Abigail m Elisha LEWELLYN
----, --, --. Joseph C., s Barclay & Hannah
    (Hobson), b 1855,10,5; m Elizabeth BRANT-
    INGHAM, dt Alfred & Ann (Dean), b 1854,
    12,23 d 1929,1,8 bur Winona, 0.
    Ch: Mary   b 1884, 1, 25
        Walter B. " 1885, 11, 17
----, --, --. Dilwyn, s Barclay & Hannah (Hob-
    son), b 1861,6,2; m Elizabeth HALL, dt
    Wm. & Mary, b 1863,8,14 d 1911,3,18 bur
    Ch: Barclay W. b 1893, 3, 10 [Winona
        Lucinda   " 1895, 10, 22
        Deborah   " 1899, 2, 13
        Laura M.   " 1900, 11, 30
        Rebecca H. " 1906, 10, 7 d 1907, 6,10
        bur Winona, 0.
    Dilwyn m 2nd Ella Lillian COOKE, dt Archi-
    bald & Bessie, b 1875,3,3 d 1924,6,19 bur
    Salem, 0.
----, --, --. Charles W., s James & Louisa
    (Davis), b 1867,9,20; m Martha J. WHINERY,
    dt Nathen & Amelia, b 1867,1,21 d 1929,9,
    23 bur Winona, 0.
    Ch: Blanch   b 1895, 3, 31; m Willard L.
        PIM
        Allen J.   " 1903, 1, 13
        Wilford H. " 1907, 6, 8
----, --, --. Walter B., s Joseph C. & Eliza-
    beth (Brant), b 1885,11,17; m Alta E.
    COPE, dt A. L. & Rachel G. (Coppock), b
    1889,3,2
    Ch: Esther H. b 1911, 10, 7
        Rachel
        Elizabeth " 1914, 7, 2
        Margaret
        Ann   " 1917, 11, 24
        William J. " 1925, 3, 25
----, --, --. Barclay W., s Dilwyn & Eliza-
    beth H. (Hall), b 1893,3,10; m Elma
    BRANTINGHAM, dt Wm. & Anna (Cope), b 1889,
    2,22
    Ch: Albert B. b 1916, 5, 7
        Anna
        Elizabeth " 1919, 8, 28
        Wm.
        Brantingham
                   b 1919, 5, 2 (?)
1921, 8, 26. Lucinda m Francis Joseph POL-
    LARD
1927, 5, 17. Isaac d (Pastor) (G)

STRATTON, continued

1839, 3, 21. Joseph & w, Sarah, & ch, Mark, Zacheus, Joseph, Michael T., Sarah, Isaac & Josiah, rocf Salem MM, dtd 1839,3,20

1839, 4, 25. Anna M. rocf Salem MM, dtd 1839, 4,24

1839, 4, 25. Abi rocf Salem MM, dtd 1839,4,24

1839, 4, 25. Cert rec for Eleanor from Salem MM, dtd 1839,3,20, endorsed to Sandy Spring MM, O.

1839, 4, 25. Cert rec for Ann from Salem MM, dtd 1839,3,20, endorsed to Sandy Spring MM, O.

1839, 4, 25. Cert rec for Josiah & w, Deborah & ch, Sarah, Lydia & Charles, from Salem MM, dtd 1839,3,20, endorsed to Sandy Spring MM, O.

1843, 5, 25. Anna M. rmt Joseph Brantingham

1845, 6, 26. Mark gct Sandy Spring MM, O., to m Mary Heald

1845, 11, 20. Mary H. rocf Sandy Spring MM, O., dtd 1845,10,24

1846, 4, 23. Abi rmt James Heald

1847, 12, 23. Joseph rmt Rachel Brantingham

1849, 8, 23. Zacheus dis mcd

1849, 11, 22. Michael dis disunity

1851, 8, 21. Sarah gct Short Creek MM, O.

1857, 6, 25. Benjamin D. & w, Ellen, & ch, Ruthann, Abigail, John T., Charles & Abram rocf Salem MM, dtd 1857,6,24

1859, 7, 21. Barclay & w, Hannah H., & ch, Joseph C. & Elizabeth B., rocf Salem MM, dtd 1859,6,22

1862, 6, 26. Daniel rocf Salem MM

1862, 6, 26. Esther rocf Salem MM, dtd 1862, 6,25

1863, 10, 22. Josiah & ch, Walloby & Alice Ann, gct Hickery Grove MM, Iowa

1865, 5, 25. Mark & Mary dis jG

1866, 6, 21. Esther rmt Joseph Masters

1870, 3, 24. Daniel gct Pennsville MM

1872, 1, 25. Charles dis mcd

1872, 3, 23. Joseph Henry dis jG

1873, 4, 24. Franklin dis jG

1873, 6, 26. Barclay & w, Hannah H., & ch, Joseph C. & Dilwyn, gct Short Creek MM,O.

1874, 10, 22. Barclay & w, Hannah H., & ch, Joseph C. & Dillwyn, rocf Short Creek MM, dtd 1874,10,20

1875, 7, 22. John F. gct Plymouth MM, to m Dorothy Hobson

1876, 2, 24. Barclay & w, Hannah H., & ch, Joseph C. & Dilwyn, gct Stillwater MM, O.

1876, 6, 22. Dorothy H. rocf Plymouth MM, dtd 1876,5,22

1879, 10, 23. Abram rmt Hannah D. Brantingham

1880, 3, 25. Josiah & w, Elizabeth, & ch, Willoughby, Alice Ann, Lucinda, Lydia, Annie & Elizabeth R., rocf Springville MM, dtd 1880,2,21

1880, 10, 21. Charles gct Flushing MM

1881, 6, 23. Barclay & w, Hannah, & s, Dilwyn, rocf Stillwater MM, O., dtd 1881,5,25

1881, 6, 23. Joseph C. rocf Stillwater MM,O., dtd 1881,5,25

1882, 11, 23. Joseph C. rmt Elizabeth Brantingham

1884, 1, 24. Josiah & w, Elizabeth B., & ch, Lydia, Annie & Elizabeth Rachel, gct Cottonwood MM, Kans.

1884, 1, 24. Alice Ann & Lucinda, gct Cottonwood MM

1884, 2, 21. Willoughby con mcd

1884, 4, 24. Willoughby gct Cottonwood MM, Kans.

1886, 2, 25. Barclay & w, Hannah H., gct Stillwater MM, O.

1889, 1, 24. Sina gct ND MM

1890, 6, 26. Barclay & w, Hannah H., rocf Stillwater MM, O., dtd 1890,5,21

1890, 7, 24. Abram & w, Hannah D., & ch, Alice E., John A. & Edith, gct Chester MM, Pa.

1892, 4, 21. Dorothy S. Ashton & s, Geo. W. Stratton, gct Flushing MM

1892, 12, 20. Elizabeth H. rocf Short Creek MM, O., dtd 1892,11,22

1893, 1, 26. Martha J. (form Whinery) dis mcd

1900, 7, 26. Martha rst

1901, 11, 21. Ellen & Mary E. gct ND MM

1902, 11, 20. Blanch, minor dt Chas. W. & Martha J., recrq

1909, 1, 21. Mary C. rmt Walter G. Edgerton

1910, 6, 23. Walter B. rmt Alta E. Cope

1911, 4, 20. Joseph C. & w, Elizabeth B., gct Stillwater MM, O.

1914, 5, 21. Barclay W. rmt Elma Brantingham

1914, 7, 23. Dillwyn gct Salem MM, to m Ella Lillian Cooke

1914, 8, 19. Emma Kelley recrq (G)

1914, 8, 20. Joseph C. & w, Elizabeth B., rocf Stillwater MM, O., dtd 1914,7,22

1914, 12, 24. Ella Lillian rocf Salem MM

1922, 9, 21. Dillwyn dis

1922, 12, 20. Isaac rocf Damascus MM (G)

1923, 7, 26. Laura M. rmt Arthur B. Oliphant

1924, 8, 21. Dillwyn rstrq

1925, 11, 26. Dillwyn gct Norwich MM, Can., to m Alice A. Waring

1925, 12, 24. Barcley W. & w, Elma B., & ch, Albert B., Anna Elizabeth & Wm. Brantingham, gct Chester MM

1927, 5, 26. Dillwyn gct Norwich MM, Canada

1930, 9, 25. Debora gct Chester MM, Pa.

1931, 2, 26. Blanch Pim (form Stratton) dis

STREET

1841, 4, 22. Lydia S. rocf Albany MM, N. Y., dtd 1841,2,2 (H).

TALBOTT

1819, 9, 23. Robert prc of clearness from Smithfield MM, dtd 1819,9,20

1819, 11, 25. Robert rmt Matilda Morgan [(G)

1884, 11, 19. Emily B. gct Short Creek MM,O.

TANNER
1893, 3, 22. Wm. Albert recrq (G)

TATUM
1848, 2, 25. Lawrie rmt Mary Ann Dean
1848, 4, 20. Mary Ann gct Salem MM

TAYLOR
1818, 6, 18. Keziah dis mou
1842, 7, 21. Sarah (form Paxson) dis mcd (H)
1844, 9, 26. Lydia (form Hall) dis mou (H)
1897, 1, 20. Jacob & Mary recrq (G)
1909, 8, 25. Jacob relrq (G)
1909, 11, 24. Mary relrq (G)
1912, 4, 24. Ida dropped from mbrp (G)

TEMPLE
1818, 6, 18. Martha dis mcd

TEMPLETON
1826, 5, 25. Harriot, minor in care of John
    Johnson, recrq
1839, 6, 20. Harriet Whinery (form Templeton)
    dis mcd

TERWILLINGER
1920, 5, 20. Amy (form Winder) dis mcd

TEST
----, --, --. Isaac B., s Zacheus & Rebecca,
    b 1787,6,8 d 1874,1,24; m Margaret -----
    b 1790,2,14 d 1845,8,9
    Ch: Hannah   b 1811, 1, 27 d 1889, 6,17
          bur Winona
        Daniel   b 1812, 8, 8
        Samuel   " 1815, 2, 9
        Rebecca   " 1817, 8, 21 d 1879, 4, 1
          bur Winona
        Zacheus   b 1826, 5, 16 ·
        David   " 1826, 5, 16 d 1868, 3,27
        Ann   " 1828, 7, 3
----, --, --. Samuel b 1791,1,3 d 1876,9,13;
    m Mary Ann ----- b 1798,6,29 d 1870,2,10
    Ch: Elizabeth b 1816, 6, 9
        Ann   " 1818, 3, 25 d 1890, 7,30
        John   " 1820, 7, 9 " 1842,10,16
        Jane   " 1823, 1, 12
        Isaac   " 1825, 12, 24
        Benjamin B." 1828, 2, 29
        Samuel   " 1832, 9, 1
        Lucina   " 1835, 3, 9
----, --, --. Daniel, s Isaac B. & Margaret, b
    1812,8,8 d 1864,12,18 bur Winona; m Ann D.
    LAWRENCE, dt Robert & Elizabeth, b 1811,12,
    31 d 1870,12,14
    Ch: Albert B. b 1845, 1, 5
        Mary L.   " 1847, 2, 10
        John S.   " 1848, 6, 6
        Martha   " 1849, 10, 23
        Deborah   " 1856, 2, 17
----, --, --. Zacheus, s Isaac B. & Margaret,
    b 1826,5,26; m Drusilla LANGSTAFF, dt
    Samuel & Tabitha, b 1831,1,22 d 1873,3,11

    Ch: Margaret   b 1852, 11, 25
        Benjamin   " 1855, 2, 14
        William   " 1857, 4, 17
        Emily   " 1859, 5, 12
        Lemuel   " 1863, 1, 27
        Elizabeth   " 1865, 4, 14
        Daniel   " 1867, 3, 28
        Sallie   " 1869, 5, 18
        Taylor F.   " 1873, 2, 27 d 1873,9,9
          bur Winona, O.
1875, 12, 4. Benjamin B. d
1876, 9, 18. Emmet D., s John S. & Martha
    (Whinery), b
1891, 3, 27. Martha m Thomas E. STANLEY
1896, 10, 23. Daniel D. m Mary C. BRANTINGHAM
----, --, --. Daniel D. m Mary BRANTINGHAM,
    dt Alfred & Ann, b 1869,7,20
    Ch: Alfred
          Langstaff b 1898, 10, 11
1929, 8, 14. Robert Leland m Luella L. HALL

1823, 11, 20. Zacheus, minor, rocf Salem MM,
    dtd 1823,11, 19
1827, 11, 22. Zacheus, minor, gct ND MM
1839, 3, 21. Isaac B. & w, Margaret, & ch,
    Zacheus, David & Ann, rocf Salem MM, dtd
    1839,3,20
1839, 3, 21. Samuel & w, Maryann, & ch, John,
    Jane, Isaac, Benjamin, Samuel & Lucina,
    rocf Salem MM, dtd 1839,3,20
1839, 3, 21. Elizabeth rocf Salem MM, dtd
    1839,3,20
1839, 3, 21. Ann rocf Salem MM, dtd 1839,3,
    20
1839, 4, 25. Samuel Jr. & w, Ann J., rocf
    Salem MM, dtd 1839,4,24
1839, 4, 25. Rebecca rocf Salem MM, dtd 1839,
    4,24
1847, 6, 24. Rebecca rmt David Coppock
1849, 6, 21. Isaac dis mcd
1850, 1, 24. Ann L. Barber (form Test) con
    mou
1850, 5, 23. Zacheus gct Salem MM, to m Dru-
    cilla Langstaff
1850, 6, 20. Benjamin gct Salem MM
1850, 9, 26. Jane rmt Robert Harris
1851, 10, 23. Zacheus gct Salem MM
1853, 8, 25. Benjamin rocf Salem MM, O., dtd
    1853,7,20
1858, 5, 20. Samuel Jr. & w, Anna J., gct
    Upper Springfield MM, O.
1858, 7, 22. Samuel Jr., s Samuel, dis dis-
    unity
1859, 8, 25. Lusine Harris (form Test) dis
    mcd
1861, 6, 20. Benjamin B. gct Salem MM
1862, 3, 20. Ann rmt Thomas Bowman
1864, 7, 21. Zacheus & w, Drusilla, & ch,
    Benjamin A., Wm., Emily & Lemuel, rocf
    Salem MM, dtd 1864,7,20
1865, 3, 23. Ann D. & ch, Albert B., Mary L.,
    John S., Martha & Deborah, rocf Salem MM,
    dtd 1865,2,22

TEST, continued
1865, 6, 22. Maria (form Randels) dis mcd
1865, 6, 22. Elizabeth rmt Harmon Rhodes
1867, 5, 23. Benjamin rocf Salem MM, dtd
    1866,9,19
1870, 2, 24. Albert B. dis mcd
1876, 8, 24. John S. dis mcd
1877, 1, 25. Martha Emily (form Whinery) dis
    mcd
1879, 7, 24. Wm. con mcd
1879, 8, 21. Zacheus gct Springville MM, Ia.,
    to m Mary B. Young
1880, 3, 25. Wm. gct Springville MM, Ia.
1880, 4, 22. Zacheus & ch, Lemuel, Elizabeth
    D., Daniel & Sallie, gct Springville MM,
    Ia.
1883, 3, 23. Emily C. gct Springville MM, Ia.
1883, 6, 21. Deborah Hoops (form Test) dis
    mcd
1883, 12, 20. Wm. gct Springville MM, Ia.
1905, 2, 23. Mary S. gct Springville MM, Ia.

THOMAS
1907, 6, 10. Luella, w Robert Leland, dt
    Clifton P. & Anna (Pickett) Hall, b

1819, 7, 22. Joseph gct Salem MM, to m Tem-
    perance Blackburn
1819, 10, 21. Joseph gct Salem MM
1820, 7, 20. Temperance rocf Salem MM, dtd
    1820,4,19
1821, 6, 21. Nathaniel & fam gct Somerset MM
1821, 6, 21. Dorcas & fam gct Somerset MM
1821, 9, 20. Joseph & fam gct Somerset MM
1822, 8, 22. Abel gct Somerset MM
1822, 12, 26. John rocf Warrington MM, dtd
    1822,6,19
1824, 1, 22. John, the younger, dis jas
1824, 3, 25. John Jr. dis disunity
1825, 4, 21. Cert rec for Sarah & ch, Kersey,
    Joseph & Isaac, from Warrington MM, dtd
    1825,1,22, endorsed to Salem MM
1826, 12, 21. David dis disunity
1828, 5, 22. Abner & w, Phebe, & ch, Wm.
    Mode, Eleanor, Mildred, Esther & Isaac,
    recrq (H)
1828, 5, 22. Eli & w, Elizabeth, & ch, Maria,
    Israel, Phebe, Sarahann, Hammond & Hiram,
    rocf Monallen MM, dtd 1828,1,22 (H)
1828, 7, 24. Abner & w, Phebe, & ch, Ellanor,
    Willard, Esther & Isaac, gct Salem MM (H)
1828, 7, 24. Eli & w, Elizabeth, & ch, Maria,
    Phebe, Sarah Ann, Hammond & Hiram, gct
    Salem MM (H)
1828, 9, 25. Hannah dis jH
1829, 1, 22. John dis jH
1830, 1, 21. Jacob & w, Margaret, & ch, Es-
    ther, Ellen R. & Rachel, rocf York MM, dtd
    1829,6,10 (H)
1830, 1, 21. Elizabeth Packer (form Thomas),
    dis mcd & jH
1830, 1, 21. Thomas, Abel, rocf York MM, dtd
    1829,6,10 (H)

1830, 1, 21. Henry dis jH
1830, 1, 21. Hannah rocf York MM, dtd 1829,
    6,10 (H)
1830, 2, 25. Ann dis jH
1830, 3, 25. Cert rec for Jonathan from York
    MM, dtd 1829,6,10, endorsed to Salem MM
    (H)
1830, 6, 24. Elizabeth Packer (form Thomas)
    con mou (H)
1830, 9, 23. Henry gct Carmel MM, to m
    Sarah Johns (H)
1831, 1, 20. Sarah rocf Carmel MM, dtd 1830,
    12,18(H)
1834, 1, 23. Isaac dis jH
1835, 4, 23. Sarah rmt Nathan Johns (H)
1837, 12, 21. Sarah John (form Thomas) dis
    mcd in H Mtg
1837, 11, 23. H. & her ch, Elizabeth & Jacob
    rocf Carmel MM, dtd 1837,10,21 (H)
1840, 1, 23. Esther Harris (form Thomas) con
    mou (H)
1841, 2, 25. Owen dis mcd
1843, 7, 20. Hannah dis
1845, 3, 20. Nathan, minor, rocf Upper Spring
    field MM, O., dtd 1845,1,25
1845, 11, 20. Anne T. Murry (form Thomas) con
    mcd (H)
1851, 4, 24. Nathan, minor, gct Upper Spring-
    field MM, O.
1867, 6, 20. Rebecca Ann (form Votaw) dis
    mcd
1867, 9, 25. Rebecca Ann (form Votaw) con
    mcd (G)
1871, 6, 22. David rmt Lydia Brantingham
1871, 10, 26. Lydia B. gct Short Creek MM, O.
1884, 1, 23. Elizabeth A. recrq (G)
1887, 12, 21. Walter & Edwin recrq (G)
1889, 10, 23. Rebecca dropped from mbrp (G)
1894, 2, 21. Franklin recrq (G)
1896, 12, 23. Ida recrq (G)
1907, 8, 21. Edwin relrq (G)
1910, 5, 25. Emma E. & ch, Alma & Paul, rocf
    Alliance MM (G)
1930, 7, 23. Elizabeth Houston recrq (G)
1931, 6, 25. Luella L. (Hall) gct Short Creek
    MM, O.

THORNBERRY
1897, 2, 24. Wm. J. & w, Mary A., & dt,
    Rhoda D., rocf Salem MM (G)

TOLERTON
1828, 5, 22. James recrq (H)
1828, 5, 22. Francis & dt, Ann, recrq (H)
1828, 7, 24. James & w, Frances, & dt, Ann,
    gct Salem MM (H)

TOMLINSON
1858, 2, 28. Esther (form Negus) dis mcd
1862, 6, 26. Martha (form Negus) dis mcd
1884, 6, 25. Eliza C. & ch, Anna, Elizabeth,
    Benjamin J. & Mary L., rocf Sandy Spring
    MM, O. (G)

TOMLINSON, continued

1891, 9, 23. Eliza C. & ch, Benjamin J. &
    Mary L., gct Ashley MM, O. (G)
1891, 9, 23. Anna & Elizabeth gct Ashley MM,
    O. (G)
1892, 12, 21. Eliza & ch, Benjamin J. & Mary
    S., rocf Ashley MM, O. (G)
1892, 12, 21. Anna rocf Ashley MM, O. (G)
1894, 10, 24. Lizzie rocf Ashley MM, dtd 1894,
    9,18 (G)
1895, 1, 23. Eliza & ch, Benjamin J. & Mary
    L., gct Lane MM, Mich. (G)
1898, 8, 24. Anna Dobson (form Tomlinson)
    gct Lane MM, Mich. (G)
1898, 8, 24. Elizabeth Dunlap (form Tomlinson)
    gct Lane MM, Mich. (G)

TOWNSEND

1810, 3, 15. Benjamin & w, Elizabeth, rocf
    Plymouth MM, dtd 1809,9,16
1810, 7, 19. Edith rmt Elias Marsh
1815, 7, 13. Elizabeth gct ED MM, Baltimore
1822, 10, 24. Mariah, Samuel, John Dixon, Mary,
    Caroline, Rachel, Elizabeth & Lydia, ch
    Isaac & Elizabeth, recrq
1822, 12, 26. Isaac & w rst on consent of
    Middleton MM (w's name Elizabeth)
1828, 5, 22. James & w, Martha, & ch, Nathan
    H., Benjamin G., Abel T., Mary Ann, Lydia
    B., A. Gilbert & Evi S., recrq (H)
1828, 7, 24. James & w, Martha, & ch, Nathan
    H., Benjamin G., Abel T., Mary Ann, Lydia,
    A. Gilbert & Evi S., gct Salem MM (H)
1828, 9, 25. Elizabeth dis jH
1829, 5, 21. Isaac dis jH
1829, 6, 25. Isaac & w, Elizabeth, & ch,
    Samuel, John, Mary, Caroline, Rachel,
    Elizabeth, Lydia & Rebecca, gct Middleton
    MM (H)
1829, 6, 25. Mariah gct Middleton MM (H)
1831, 12, 22. Isaac & w, Elizabeth, & ch,
    Samuel, Mary, Caroline, Rebecca, Eliza-
    beth, Rachel, Lydia & Isaac, rocf Middle-
    ton MM, dtd 1831,7,7 (H)
1842, 2, 24. Caroline dis jas (H)
1842, 12, 22. Mary & Elizabeth dis disunity (H)
1843, 4, 20. Rebecca dis disunity

TRIPP

1831, 8, 25. Samuel rmt Fanny Battin (H)
1831, 9, 22. Fanny gct Marlborough MM (H)
1832, 8, 23. Samuel & w, Fannie, & ch,
    George F., Stephen, Mary & Labon, rocf
    Marlborough MM, dtd 1832,6,28 (H)
1833, 4, 25. Fanny & ch, George F., Stephen,
    Mary & Laban, gct Marlborough MM (H)

TULLOSS

1818, 4, 16. Rachel (form Barret) rpd mcd
    (dis 1818,6,18)

ULLERY

1860, 8, 23. Emelina (form Hoopes) dis mcd
1899, 11, 22. Lewulla [Ulery] relrq (G)

UNDERWOOD

1814, 2, 17. Joseph rocf Middleton MM, dtd
    1814,2,10
1814, 4, 14. Joseph rmt Fanny Marsh
1814, 8, 18. Joseph & w, gct Middleton MM
1817, 7, 17. Joseph & w, Fanny, rocf Middle-
    ton MM, dtd 1817,6,16
1822, 4, 25. Joseph & w, Fanny & two ch gct
    Carmel MM

VAN FOSSEN

1887, 12, 21. Harry recrq (G)
1926, 2, 24. Harry [Vanfosson] gct Salem MM
    (G)

VANSYOC

1828, 8, 21. Thomas Shaw gct Westland MM, to
    m Ann [Vanscoyoc]
1852, 9, 23. Enoch rmt Phebe Crew
1854, 4, 20. Phebe gct Marlborough MM

VAUGHN

1845, 7, 24. Polly Maria rocf Upper Spring-
    field MM, O., dtd 1845,6,28
1845, 8, 21. Polly Maria [Vaughan] rmt Geo.
    Brantingham

VICKERS

1839, 12, 26. Thomas E. rmt Elizabeth P.
    Galbreath (H)
1841, 5, 20. Elizabeth (form Galbreath) dis
    mcd in H Mtg

VINCENT

1908, 12, 23. Harry recrq (G)
1927, 7, 20. Harry dropped from mbrp (G)

VORE

1815, 8, 17. Benjamin rmt Margaret Shaw
1815, 9, 14. Margaret gct Westland MM

VOTAW

----, --, --. James m Judith ----- b 1804,5,9
    Ch: Ruth   b 1824, 8, 19
        John   " 1826, 2, 17 d 1830, 8,27
        Chalkley   " 1828, 11, 7 " 1829, 2,23
        Dorothy   " 1830, 6, 6
        Sarah   " 1832, 10, 7
        Deborah   " 1834, 11, 28
        James   " 1837, 12, 29
        Martha   " 1841, 8, 9
----, --, --. Moses & Mary
    Ch: Joseph   b 1832, 9, 29
        Levi   " 1834, 5, 22 d 1854, 1, 9
        Rebecca Ann " 1835, 7, 29
        Robert   " 1837, 1, 17
        Morris   " 1838, 7, 10
        Elmore   " 1840, 8, 5

1813, 8, 19. Elizabeth rmt Jeremiah McBride
1815, 2, 16. Samuel rocf Salem MM, dtd
    1815,2,14
1818, 3, 19. Mary rmt Preston Beck Jr.

VOTAW, continued

1819, 4, 22.   Isaac gct Salem MM, to m Frances Stanley

1819, 7, 22.   Frances rocf Salem MM, dtd 1819,
7,21

1820, 4, 20.   Sarah rmt Lawrence W. Butler

1822, 1, 24.   Mary rmt Wm. Griffith

1822, 1, 24.   Isaac gct Salem MM, to m Susanna
Woolman

1822, 4, 25.   Lydia rmt Joseph L. Hoops

1822, 8, 22.   Susanna rocf Salem MM, dtd 1822,
6,19

1822, 12, 26. Leah rmt Thomas C. Stanley

1823, 3, 20.   Edward Courtney gct Salem MM, to
m Phebe Y. Votaw

1823, 11, 20. Ann rmt Maurice Miller

1823, 12, 25. James rmt Judith Johnson

1828, 9, 25.   Moses dis jH

1828, 9, 25.   Mary dis jH

1828, 11, 20. Daniel rmt Sarah Hillis (H)

1829, 1, 22.   Daniel dis mcd & jH

1829, 3, 26.   Isaac dis jH

1829, 4, 23.   Susannah dis jH

1829, 6, 25.   Sarah (form Hillis) dis mcd & jH

1830, 7, 22.   Aaron dis disunity

1831, 1, 20.   James Johnson gct Upper Springfield MM, to m Sarah Votaw

1831, 3, 24.   Quinby dis disunity

1831, 8, 25.   Moses gct Sandy Spring MM, O.,
to m Mary Miller

1832, 2, 23.   Mary rocf Sandy Spring MM, O.,
dtd 1832,1,27

1832, 2, 23.   Lydia (form Broomall) dis mcd

1833, 10, 24. Phebe (form Smith) con mcd (H)

1838, 10, 25. Sarah & fam gct White Water MM,
Ind. (H)

1838, 11, 22. Isaac gct White River MM, Ind.

1839, 5, 23.   Sarah gct White River MM, Ind.

1839, 5, 23.   John & w, Rebecca, gct White
River MM, Ind.

1839, 5, 23.   John E. gct White River MM, Ind.

1839, 11, 21. Jonas gct White River MM, Ind.

1842, 6, 23.   Alice Ann dis jH

1844, 6, 26.   Ruth gct White River MM, Ind.

1844, 10, 24. James & w, Judith, & ch, Dorothy, Sarah, Deborah, James & Martha, gct
White River MM, Ind.

1844, 10, 24. James & w, Judith, & ch, Dorothy, Sarah, Deborah, James & Martha, gct
White River MM, Ind.

1850, 9, 26.   Abner dis disunity

1851, 3, 20.   Mahlon dis disunity

1853, 12, 23. Sarah Ellison (form Votaw) dis
mcd

1862, 4, 24.   Sarah (form Crew) dis mcd

1865, 3, 23.   Moses dis jG in 1854

1867, 6, 20.   Rebecca Ann Thomas (form Votaw)
dis mcd

1867, 7, 25.   Elmore dis military service & mcd

1867, 7, 25.   Robert dis military service &
mcd

1867, 7, 25.   Levi dis mcd & military service

1867, 9, 25.   Rebecca Ann Thomas (form Votaw)

con mcd (G)

1869, 1, 20.   Elnore dis mcd (G)

1869, 1, 20.   Levi dis mcd (G)

1870, 11, 23. Moses con mcd (G)

1876, 10, 25. Tamer recrq (G)

1884, 7, 23.   Rachel rocf Damascus MM, dtd
1884,5,24 (G)

1886, 3, 24.   Rachel gct East Goshen MM (G)

1886, 7, 21.   Tamer relrq

1893, 4, 19.   Minnie, Leroy, Argus, Thomas Edgar & Lewis H., recrq (G)

1898, 4, 20.   Alice K. recrq (G)

1903, 4, 23.   Emma (form Smith) con mcd

1904, 1, 21.   Emma gct Salem MM

1917, 4, 20.   Rosella recrq (G)

1920, 12, 22. Louis H. & w, Rosella M., gct
Damascus MM (G)

WALKER

----, --, --. Lewis B., s Able & Mary, b 1804,
9,12 d 1892,1,18 bur Winona; m Tamson
HAINES, dt Eli & Ruth, b 1810,12,3 d 1892,
2,5

Ch: Eli J.   b 1829, 12, 3 d 1870, 6,16
    Mary   " 1831, 8, 8
    Ruth   " 1832, 11, 22 " 1864, 9, 3
    Lydia   " 1835, 1, 15 " 1838,12, 7
    Martha   " 1836, 11, 24 " 1837, 9,22
    Abel   " 1839, 9, 3
    Joseph
    Collins   " 1846, 8, 4 " 1870, 6,16

----, --, --. Willis J. b 1865,9,7 d 1884,4,17

1830, 8, 26.   Lewis B. & w, Tamzon, & s, Eli,
rocf Flushing MM, dtd 1830,5,20

1837, 5, 25.   Isaac rocf Flushing MM, dtd
1837,4,20

1837, 8, 24.   Isaac gct Upper Springfield MM,
O., to m Lydia Negus

1838, 2, 22.   Lydia rocf Upper Springfield MM,
O., dtd 1838,1,27

1839, 5, 23.   Isaac & w, Lydia, gct Upper
Springfield MM, O.

1850, 9, 26.   Mary H. rmt Enoch S. Brown

1853, 10, 20. Eli J. rmt Mariah Beck

1865, 3, 23.   Eli J. dis jG in 1854

1865, 10, 26. Maria dis jG

1867, 1, 24.   Abel dis mcd & jG

1867, 2, 21.   Martha (form Johnson) dis mcd

1881, 6, 22.   Abel & s, Willis, gct LeGrand
MM, Ia. (G)

1889, 10, 23. Ely J., Anna M., Emma T., Ruth
E. & Lewis P. dropped from mbrp (G)

1897, 2, 24.   Evelyn recrq (G)

1899, 1, 25.   Eva relrq (G)

1899, 4, 19.   Eva relrq (G)

WALLACE

1888, 2, 22.   William & Elizabeth E. recrq
(G)

1898, 2, 23.   Bertha recrq (G)

WALTON

1809, 2, 16. Bathsheba rmt John Dingee
1809, 11, 16. Martha gct Middleton MM
1814, 12, 15. Mary rocf WD MM, dtd 1814,5,18 endorsed by Westland MM 1814,9,29
1815, 1, 19. Nathan & w, Mary, & Rachel Barrett, minor in their care, rocf Westland MM, dtd 1814.12.1
1815, 4, 13. Edith, Bathsheba, Joseph Townsend, Jesse & Moses recrq of mother, Mary
1815, 6, 15. Margaret rocf Westland MM, dtd 1815,6,1
1815, 8, 17. Jonathan rocf Westland MM, dtd 1815,4,29
1815, 8, 17. Abraham Jr. rocf Westland MM, dtd 1815,4,29
1815, 8, 17. Abraham Sr. & w, Rachel, she having dec since cert was granted, rocf Westland MM, dtd 1815,4,29
1815, 12, 14. Lydia rocf Salem MM, dtd 1815, 11,14
1816, 2, 15. David rocf Westland MM, dtd 1815,11,2
1817, 7, 17. John rst on consent of Middleton MM
1819, 2, 25. Job McCarty & w, Jane, & ch, Mary Ann & Martha L. Walton, & Rachel, Thomas Heston, James W., Oliver C., Joseph Paxton & Sara, rocf Muncy MM, dtd 1818,10, 21
1821, 3, 22. Margaret Battin (form Walton) dis mcd
1821, 4, 26. Abraham gct Westland MM, to m Ann John
1821, 10, 25. Ann & dt, Mary John, rocf Westland MM, dtd 1821,8,23
1822, 12, 26. David dis jas
1823, 11, 20. John & w, Lydia, & ch, Martha, Lydia Ann & Joseph Marsh, gct Carmel MM
1824, 9, 23. Elizabeth rocf Muncy MM, dtd 1824,7,21
1824, 11, 25. Mary Ann rmt Joseph Watson
1825, 12, 22. Elizabeth gct Muncy MM
1825, 12, 22. Martha gct Marlborough MM
1829, 4, 23. Ann dis jH
1829, 6, 25. Abraham Jr. dis jH
1832, 10, 25. Mary (form Johns) dis mou
1832, 11, 22. Mary (form Johns) dis mou (H)
1837, 5, 25. Mary rocf Middleton MM, Pa., dtd 1837,5,5 (H)
1844, 8, 22. Elizabeth B. dis jas
1844, 8, 22. Rachel dis jas
1864, 6, 23. Joseph dis jG in 1854
1867, 1, 24. Rhoda dis jG
1879, 5, 21. Abel John, Mary Emily & Phebe A. recrq (G)

WARD

1822, 1, 24. Hannah & Rebecca recrq
1826, 11, 23. Hannah rmt Abraham Beedy
1828, 12, 25. Rebecca dis jH
1831, 8, 25. Rebecca rmt Wm. Mendenhall (H)
1832, 3, 22. Eliza (form Morgan) con mou (H)

1892, 10, 20. Flora B. (form Raley) dis mcd
1919, 12, 24. Mattie gct Salem MM (G)

WARE

1821, 11, 22. John rmt Sarah Logue
1822, 1, 24. Sarah gct Salem MM

WARING

1925, 11, 26. Dillwyn Stratton gct Norwich MM, Canada, to m Alice A. Warring

WARREN

1868, 7, 23. Job rmt Rebecca Coppock
1870, 4, 21. Job & s, Samuel, rocf Upper Springfield MM, O., dtd 1870,3,25
1870, 4, 21. Adaline rocf Upper Springfield MM, O., dtd 1870,3,25
1874, 9, 24. Samuel dis mcd
1877, 2, 22. Job dis
1884, 1, 23. Samuel S. & Mary A. recrq (G)

WARRINGTON

----, --, --. Linneus, s Nathan & Mary, b 1847,6,22 d 1908,3,9 bur at Toledo, O.; m Sina BRANTINGHAM, dt Joseph & Ann M., b 1850,7,24 d 1905,12,9 bur Toledo, O.
   Ch: Anna Leora b 1872, 7, 15
       Cyrus J.   " 1874, 5, 16
       Phebe Ellen" 1878, 3, 24
       Mary Elma " 1884, 4, 10
       Sara Etta " 1888, 1, 11
       Melva S.   " 1890, 9, 27
----, --, --. Albert, s Thomas & Lydia (Crew), b 1860,4,4 d 1929,6,23 bur Winona; m Elizabeth M. OLIPHANT, dt John & Hannah, b 1862,1,31 d 1916,3,3 bur Winona
   Ch: Edith L. b 1896, 6, 4 d 1897, 7,23 bur Winona, O.
       Charles   b 1899, 1, 29 d 1908, 2,16 bur Winona, O.
   Albert m 2nd Mary Sara FOWLER, dt Edmund & Mary (Miles), b 1868,8,26
----, --, --. Edith L., dt Albert & Elizabeth M., b 1896,6,4 d 1897,7,27 bur Winona, O.

1871, 6, 22. Linneous rmt Sina Brantingham
1871, 12, 21. Sina B. gct Coal Creek MM, Ia.
1884, 8, 21. Edgar rmt Hannah Coppock
1884, 11, 20. Hannah C. gct Upper Springfield MM, O.
1891, 8, 20. Anna Leora rocf Stillwater MM, O., dtd 1891,7,22
1891, 8, 20. Linneus & w, Sina B., & ch, Cyrus J., Phebe Ellen, Mary Elma, Saretta & Melva L., rocf Stillwater MM, O., dtd 1891,7,22
1894, 6, 21. Albert rmt Elizabeth M. Oliphant
1910, 8, 25. Mary Elma rmt Geo. J. Hiatt
1911, 8, 24. Mary gct Chesterfield MM
1913, 10, 23. Saretta Merril (form Warrington) con mcd
1917, 6, 21. Albert rmt Mary Sara Fowler
1925, 3, 26. Anna Leora Smith (form Warring-

WARRINGTON, continued
        ton) dis mcd & jas
1926, 1, 21. Melva W. Hewlett (form Warring-
        ton) dis

WATERS
1897, 6, 23. George recrq (G)

WATERWORTH
1827, 4, 26. Wm. recrq
1829, 5, 21. Wm. dis jH
1830, 8, 26. Wm. gct Carmel MM (H)

WATSON
1824, 11, 25. Joseph rmt Mary Ann Walton
1824, 12, 23. Mary Ann gct Marlborough MM
1854, 10, 23. John rmt Eliza Negus
1869, 1, 21. Eliza (form Negus) dis jG
1874, 4, 23. John M. dis disunity (G)
1874, 8, 17. Eliza T. & dt, Elma Caroline,
        gct Columbus MM (G)
1874, 8, 17. Phebe Eva & Anna Mary, sisters,
        gct Columbus MM (G)
1875, 11, 24. John M. rst at Columbus MM on
        consent of this mtg (G)
1887, 12, 21. Addie M. recrq (G)
1891, 11, 25. Addie M. gct Oskaloosa MM, Ia.
        (G)

WEST
1836, 4, 21. Sarah (form Dutton) con mou
        (H)

WHETTON
1889, 12, 25. George & w, Sarah Jane, relrq
        (G)
1890, 7, 25. Minnie gct Salem MM (G)

WHINERY
----, --, --. Robert d 1845,3, 0; m Phebe
        ----- d 1854,3,26
        Ch: Abigail   b 1802, 9, 20
            Phebe   " 1803, 9, 9
            Lydia   " 1804, 8, 13 d 1841,10,19
            Joseph   " 1806, 3, 14
            John   " 1807, 10, 8
            Jane   " 1809, 12, 21
            Thomas   " 1813, 2, 25
            David   " 1814, 4, 24
            Leech   " 1815, 8, 22 d 1833, 5, 3
            Susannah   " 1818, 3, 24
            Mahlon   " 1819, 11, 17
            Rebecca Ann" 1822, 10, 13
----, --, --. John & Mary
        Ch: Stephen   b 1811, 12, 26
            Josiah   " 1813, 6, 25 d 1823, 8,--
            Hannah   "" 1815, 6, 1
            Robert   " 1817, 4, 25
            Ann   " 1819, 3, 30
            Hiram   " 1821, 7, 26
            Evan   " 1823, 8, 14
            Ruth   " 1826, 1, 17
            Jeremiah

Ch: Hubbard   b 1828, 1, 28
    John E. H. " 1831, 6, 5
    Mary Jane " 1834, 3, 13
----, --, --. Joseph b 1806,3,14 d 1860,9,26;
        m Martha ----- b 1812,2,6 d 1881,11,27
        Ch: Angeline   b 1830, 7, 14
            Huldah   " 1832, 8, 19
            Phebe   " 1837, 1, 18 d 1837, 2, 5
            Joshua S. " 1839, 6, 11
            Abraham C. " 1841, 7, 27 d 1842, 7,22
            Rebecca   " 1843, 7, 14
            Joseph B. " 1846, 8, 21
            Susan   " 1849, 6, 4
            Sarah Jane " 1852, 3, 19 d 1873, 2, 1
            Martha
            Emily   " 1855, 8, 28
----, --, --. David, s Robert & Phebe, b
        1814,4,24 d 1888,3,10 bur Winona; m Sarah
        BROWN, dt Nathan & Amy, b 1813,9,9 d
        1904,4,16 bur Winona
        Ch: Almira   b 1835, 8, 21
            Nathan   " 1837, 6, 6
            John Leach " 1839, 7, 1 d 1849,10, 7
            Isaiah   " 1841, 6, 12
            William J. " 1843, 2, 27
            Robert B. " 1845, 3, 22
            David   " 1847, 3, 15
            Amy   " 1850, 8, 18
            Leander   " 1852, 10, 9
            Cyrus   " 1855, 8, 5
----, --, --. Thomas b 1813,2,25; m Mary B.
        ----- b 1823,5,4
        Ch: Zalinda   b 1843, 2, 4 d 1844, 4,25
            Emily B.   " 1845, 6, 14
            Charles
            Leech   " 1849, 12, 6
            Barby
            Dallis   " 1855, 1, 2
----, --, --. Mahlon b 1819,11,17; m Hannah
        ----- b 1824,5,5
        Ch: Charles   b 1843, 5, 10 d 1843, 6,11
            Elwood D. " 1845, 2, 1
            Edith   " 1848, 1, 30
            Phebe Ellen" 1852, 5, 11
            Rhoda   " 1855, 4, 24 d 1931, 4,12
            bur Winona, O.
            Oliver   b 1858, 1, 18
            Joseph H. " 1860, 11, 21
            Anna   " 1868, 1, 23
----, --, --. Robert b 1817,4,25; m Susan
        ----- d 1848,2,23
        Ch: Samuel   b 1845, 10, 20
            Susan   " 1847, 12, 29
1853, 7, 25. Thomas d
----, --, --. Nathan, s David & Sara, b 1837,
        6,6 d 1913,8,4 bur Winona; m Amelia ALLEN,
        dt Christopher & Amelia, b 1838,6,12 in
        England d 1922,11,17 bur Winona
        Ch: Willis   b 1863, 7, 29
            Martha J. " 1867, 1, 21
            Rachel S. " 1870, 7, 13

1809, 12, 14. Jane rmt David Burson

WHINERY, continued
1810, 1, 18. John rmt Mary McBride
1810, 3, 15. James rmt Sally Carroll
1811, 5, 16. Wm. Jr. rmt Margary Carroll
1818, 3, 19. Zimri gct Salem MM, to m Judith
             Wright
1818, 7, 16. Judith rocf Salem MM, dtd 1818,
             6,16
1821, 8, 23. Zimri dis disunity
1821, 12, 20. Sarah Comly (form Whinery) dis
             mcd
1822, 1, 24. John dis disunity
1822, 4, 25. Abigail gct Short Creek MM, O.
1824, 5, 20. Abigail rocf Short Creek MM, O.,
             dtd 1824,4,20
1824, 11, 25. Abigail Pettit (form Whinery)
             con mcd
1826, 5, 25. Abigail rmt Joshua Shinn
1826, 11, 23. Lydia rmt Joseph Brantingham
1827, 3, 22. John, minor, gct Salem MM
1828, 9, 25. Thomas dis jH
1828, 9, 25. Lydia dis jH
1828, 12, 25. Margery dis jH
1829, 1, 22. William dis jH
1829, 1, 22. James dis jH
1829, 7, 23. Jediah dis mou
1829, 11, 26. Joseph rmt Martha Crew
1829, 11, 26. Deborah Pettit (form Whinery)
             dis mou
1829, 12, 24. John Jr. rocf Salem MM, dtd
             1829,11,25
1830, 6, 24. John gct Upper Springfield MM,
             to m Elizabeth Malmsberry
1830, 11, 16. Jane rmt Abraham Crew
1830, 11, 25. Elizabeth rocf Upper Springfield
             MM, O., dtd 1830,10,23
1831, 8, 25. Holland & Vincent dis jH
1832, 7, 26. Jane Ann gct Center MM, O. (H)
1832, 7, 26. Thomas & w, Lydia, & ch gct Cen-
             ter MM, O. (H)
1833, 6, 20. Hannah Killy (form Whinery) dis
             mou
1833, 9, 26. Phebe (form Beck) con mcd (H)
1834, 1, 23. Phebe gct Centre MM, O. (H)
1834, 3, 20. John & w, Elizabeth, & fam gct
             Upper Springfield MM
1834, 3, 20. Jane Ann & Sarah, gct Centre
             MM, O.
1834, 3, 20. Minor ch of Thomas & Lydia gct
             Centre MM, O.
1834, 6, 26. Edward dis jH
1834, 6, 26. Joseph, s James, dis jH
1834, 7, 24. David gct Upper Springfield MM,
             O., to m Sarah Brown
1834, 9, 25. Phebe (form Beck) dis mou
1835, 2, 26. Sarah rocf Upper Springfield MM,
             O., dtd 1834,11,22
1835, 8, 20. Judith & ch gct Centre MM
1836, 12, 22. Susanna rmt Malcom Crew
1837, 10, 26. Zimri dis jH
1839, 6, 20. Harriet (form Templeton) dis mcd
1839, 7, 25. John C., s James, dis mcd
1839, 12, 26. John & w, Elizabeth, & ch, Eme-

line P., Phebe Jane, Sarah & Benjamin M.,
rocf Upper Springfield MM, O., dtd 1839,
9,28
1840, 3, 26. Elizabeth dis jH
1840, 9, 24. Isaac dis jH
1840, 9, 24. Abigail dis jH
1841, 1, 21. Jacob C. dis mcd
1842, 3, 24. Evan dis disunity
1842, 3, 24. John & fam gct Upper Spring-
             field MM, O.
1842, 3, 24. Mahlon rmt Hannah Dean
1842, 8, 25. Ruth Smith (form Whinery) dis
             mcd
1843, 4, 20. Thomas gct Springfield MM, O.,
             to m Mary Blackburn
1843, 9, 21. Mary B. rocf Upper Springfield
             MM, O., dtd 1843,6,24
1844, 1, 25. Robert gct Marlborough MM, to
             m Susan Enlows
1844, 6, 20. Stephen dis mcd
1844, 7, 25. Susannah rocf Marlborough MM,
             dtd 1844,5,28
1844, 8, 22. George dis jH
1845, 4, 24. Elijah dis jH
1846, 3, 26. Ann rmt David Brown
1850, 3, 21. Eliza Ann dis disunity
1850, 3, 21. Abigail dis disunity
1850, 12, 26. John E. dis mcd
1851, 2, 20. Jeremiah H. dis mcd
1851, 4, 24. Huldah rmt Samuel Enlows
1851, 7, 24. Hiram dis disunity
1852, 6, 24. Elwood dis disunity
1852, 6, 24. Newton gct Salem MM
1853, 1, 20. James dis mcd
1853, 2, 24. Robert con mcd
1853, 9, 22. Robert & ch gct Driftwood MM,
             Ind.
1861, 9, 26. Joshua S. dis disunity
1861, 11, 21. Nathan rmt Elizabeth Allen
1863, 7, 23. Mary Jane dis
1863, 8, 20. Wm. dis enlisting in military
             service
1864, 4, 21. Thomas dis jG in 1854
1864, 6, 23. Robert B. dis enlisting in
             military service
1864, 8, 25. Mary B. dis jG in 1854
1864, 11, 24. Isaiah dis disunity
1866, 9, 20. Mahlon dis jG
1866, 8, 23. David dis jG
1866, 8, 23. Sarah dis jG
1867, 7, 25. Hannah dis jG
1868, 4, 23. Almira dis jG
1868, 12, 24. Angeline rmt Samuel Barber
1871, 1, 26. Joseph B. dis mcd
1871, 8, 24. Emily B. dis jG
1871, 9, 21. Rebecca Crew (form Whinery) dis
1871, 12, 21. Charles dis jG
1872, 6, 20. Susan dis disunity
1874, 2, 24. Charles L. con mcd (G)
1874, 4, 23. Amy dis disunity
1874, 12, 24. Phebe dis jG
1875, 11, 24. Chas. L. gct Damascus MM (G)
1876, 11, 23. Elwood D. con mcd & jG

WHINERY, continued
1876, 12, 21. David Jr. dis mcd
1877, 1, 25. Martha Emily Test (form Whinery)
               dis mcd
1877, 1, 25. Elwood D. gct Short Creek MM, O.
1877, 6, 21. Barby Dallis dis jG
1878, 8, 21. Mary H. recrq (G)
1879, 5, 21. Wm. recrq (G)
1880, 2, 24. Joseph H. dis mcd
1880, 4, 21. Wm. J. & w, Mary H., relrq
1882, 3, 22. Edna B. gct Albion MM, Ia. (G)
1882, 4, 20. David rstrq
1882, 5, 24. Sarah Elsie & s, Harold Clifton,
               recrq (G)
1882, 6, 21. Isaiah & w, Harriet, & ch, Sam-
               uel D., Wesley & Lesley, recrq (G)
1882, 7, 20. Phebe Ellen Jenkins (form Whin-
               ery) dis mcd
1882, 10, 26. Leander dis mcd
1883, 12, 20. Phebe rstrq
1884, 1, 23. J. H. recrq (G)
1884, 4, 23. Edna H. rocf Albion MM, Ia. (G)
1884, 4, 23. Luella, dt Joseph W. & Edna H.,
               recrq (G)
1885, 1, 21. Margaret recrq (G)
1885, 11, 26. Sarah rstrq
1886, 9, 23. Willis dis mcd
1886, 9, 23. Anna recrq
1891, 8, 19. Joseph H. & w, Edna, & ch, Lu-
               ella, Phileta & Raymond, gct Salem MM, O.
               (G)
1891, 10, 22. Rachel S. rmt Charles W. Gamble
1893, 1, 26. Martha J. Stratton (form Whinery)
               dis mcd
1893, 11, 23. Anna rmt Edward J. Woolman
1895, 6, 19. Joseph H. & w, Edna, & ch roc
               (G)
1897, 2, 24. Luella recrq (G)
1897, 6, 23. Leander, Mary, Florence, Wilmer
               recrq (G)
1897, 10, 20. Leander & w, Mary, & ch, Flor-
               ence L. & Wilmer D., roc dtd 1897,7,21
               (G)
1898, 1, 19. Joseph H. & fam gct Rollan MM
               (G)
1901, 12, 25. Leora May & Anna E. recrq (G)
1903, 9, 23. Leora May gct East Goshen MM (G)
1905, 3, 22. Joseph H. & w, Edna, & ch,
               Fileta & Raymond, gct Salem MM (G)
1907, 9, 25. Joseph H. & w, Edna H., & ch,
               Fileta & Raymond, gct Dover MM, O.
1907, 11, 21. Rhoda gct Salem MM, O.
1909, 3, 25. Rhoda rocf Salem MM, dtd 1909,3,
               24
1912, 1, 24. Wilmer D. gct Salem MM (G)
1912, 4, 24. Isaiah & Byron dropped from mbrp
               (G)
1920, 10, 20. Leander & w, Mary, gct Damascus
               MM (G)
1927, 7, 20. Bertram dropped from mbrp (G)

WHITACRE
1809, 4, 13. Mary gct Middleton MM

1810, 11, 15. Mahlon dis paying muster fine
1811, 6, 13. John dis disunity
1812, 8, 13. Thomas dis attending muster in
1812, 10, 15. Achsa dis   [military line
1815, 4, 13. Caleb gct Westland MM
1816, 5, 16. Martha Irey (form Whitacre) dis
               mcd to first cousin
1818, 6, 18. Isaac dis mcd
1818, 11, 26. Phebe Davis (form Whitacre) con
               mou
1819, 1, 21. Lydia recrq
1819, 2, 25. Cornelius recrq
1820, 8, 24. Edward Jr. dis mcd
1821, 7, 26. Asahel dis jas
1821, 8, 23. Susanna recrq
1822, 5, 23. Edward dis disunity
1822, 5, 23. Martha dis disunity
1822, 6, 28. Hannah dis jas
1826, 12, 21. Anne gct Sandy Spring MM, O.
1827, 6, 21. Anna gct Sandy Spring MM,
               returned because she jas
1827k 9, 20. Anna dis jas
1827, 11, 22. Joseph dis jas
1829, 1, 22. Cornelius dis jH
1829, 9, 24. Susannah dis jH
1832, 2, 23. Lydia (form Hoopes) dis mcd
1837, 10, 26. Daniel dis mcd
1896, 12, 23. Frank & w, Eldora, rocf Salem MM
               (G)
1897, 3, 24. Mary recrq
1897, 6, 23. Rachel, Dora, Elbridge, Maud &
               Myra, recrq (G)
1898, 7, 20. Alma recrq (G)
1899, 3, 22. Frank & w, Ella, & dt, Alma, gct
               Salem MM (G)
1901, 11, 20. Mary [Whitticer] relrq (G)
1902, 12, 24. Frank rocf Salem MM, dtd 1902,
               11,19 (G)
1906, 9, 13. Frank & fam gct Salem MM (G)
1907, 9, 25. Mary recrq (G)
1908, 12, 23. Ray recrq (G)
1917, 10, 24. Dora gct Damascus MM (G)
1923, 2, 21. Dora rocf Damascus MM (G)
1925, 8, 19. Ray relrq (G)

WHITE
1816, 5, 16. Cert rec for Benjamin from
               Butternuts MM, N. Y., dtd 1814,5,4, en-
               dorsed to Plainfield MM
1821, 10, 25. Jesse dis mcd
1827, 9, 20. Isaac rpd mcd
1828, 12, 28. Isaac gct Concord MM (H)
1828, 12, 25. Martha & Margaret dis jH
1829, 2, 26. Uriah dis jH
1829, 3, 26. Uriah dis disunity (H)
1829, 5, 21. Thomas dis jH
1829, 7, 23. Isaac dis mcd
1830, 4, 22. James dis disunity
1831, 5, 26. Lewis S. rmt Tamer Reynolds
1831, 9, 22. Thamar gct Marlborough MM
1832, 2, 23. Margaret Gaucher (form White)
               dis
1835, 8, 20. Isaac & w, Hannah, & ch, Mar-

WHITE, continued
  tha Jane, David G. & Mary Adaline, rocf
  Concord MM, dtd 1835,3,25 (H)
1837, 10, 26. Isaac & w, Hannah, & ch gct Concord MM (H)
1838, 7, 26. Paul rmt Tabitha Reynolds
1838, 11, 22. Tabitha gct Marlborough MM
1845, 9, 25. Paul & w, Tabitha, & ch, John
  M. & Joseph W., rocf Marlborough MM, dtd
  1845,7,29
1846, 3, 26. Israel & w, Massey, & ch, Hannah
  & Miriam, rocf Marlborough MM, dtd 1846,3,3
1848, 1, 20. Israel & fam gct Upper Springfield MM, O.
1848, 2, 24. Paul & w, Tabitha, & ch, John,
  Joseph, Wm. & Eliza Ann, gct Marlborough
  MM
1893, 7, 19. Asenith recrq (G)
1911, 4, 19. Asenath gct Salem MM (G)

WHITELEATHER
1817, 1, 16. Elizabeth (form Harrison) dis
  mou
1873, 12, 24. Elizabeth recrq (G)
1893, 3, 22. Bye recrq (G)
1915, 1, 20. Bye gct Damascus MM (G)

WHITSON
1892, 9, 22. Benjamin F. rmt Anna Masters
1893, 8, 24. Ida M. gct Chester MM, Pa.

WHITTON
1885, 1, 21. George B. & Sarah J. recrq

WIBEL
1917, 9, 19. L. Everet gct Berlinville MM
  (G)

WICKERSHAM
1826, 3, 23. Ellis & w, Eliza, & ch, Lewis
  Morgan, Mary Ann, Lydia Elma & Eliza Emeline, rocf Carmel MM, dtd 1826,2,18
1828, 11, 20. Eliza dis jH
1829, 3, 26. Ellis dis jH
1831, 2, 24. Amos & w, Amy, & dt, Amy, rocf
  Kennet MM, dtd 1830,10,5 (H)
1835, 2, 26. Enna Brogan (form Wickersham)
  con mou (H)
1841, 12, 23. Ellis & w, Eliza, & five ch gct
  Marlborough MM (H)
1841, 3, 25. Lewis dis jH
1841, 5, 20. Mary Ann Angus (form Wickersham)
  dis mcd & jH
1841, 5, 20. Lydia Elma dis jH
1842, 8, 25. Elizabeth Emeline & Ellis T.,
  ch Ellis, gct Marlborough MM
1843, 3, 23. Lydia Elma gct Marlborough MM (H)
1845, 7, 24. Mary Ann Angus (form Wickersham)
  con mcd (H)

WILKINS
1810, 12, 13. Daniel rmt Phebe Davis
1811, 1, 17. Sarah Sanders (form Wilkens) dis

mcd
1812, 5, 14. Joseph Jr. dis attending a mcd
1814, 7, 14. Elizabeth Sinclair (form Wilkins) dis mcd
1814, 12, 15. Joseph & fam gct Fall Creek
  MM, O.
1822, 2, 21. Daniel dis training in militia
1822, 4, 25. Joseph Jr.; consent given Fairfield MM to rst
1828, 12, 25. Phebe dis jH
1831, 9, 22. Hannah dis jH
1834, 3, 20. Sarah Painter (form Wilkins) dis
  mou
1834, 4, 24. Sarah Pinter (form Wilkings) dis
  dis mcd (H)
1836, 10, 20. Mary dis jas (H)
1836, 11, 24. Hannah Shafer (form Wilkins)
  dis mou (H)
1837, 2, 23. Ann dis jas (H)

WILKINSON
1879, 5, 21. Calvert recrq (G)
1886, 3, 24. Calvert & s, George James, gct
  East Goshen MM (G)

WILLIAMS
----, --, --. Casper b 1790; m Hannah -----
  b 1793,--,-- d 1848,6,22
  Ch: Charles b 1825, 2, 1
    Samuel " 1834, 9, 19

1811, 5, 16. Tacy dis
1811, 11, 14. Mary Steel (form Williams) dis
  mcd
1812, 11, 19. Richard & w, Sarah, & ch, Elizabeth, Abigail, Dearman, Deborah, Asa &
  Mary, rocf Short Creek MM, O., dtd 1812,
  7,25
1814, 3, 17. Elizabeth Fugate (form Williams)
  dis mcd
1816, 2, 15. Abraham dis mou
1816, 5, 16. Martha gct New Garden MM, Pa.
1817, 5, 15. Martha gct New Garden MM, Pa.,
  returned endorsed by that mtg 1816,12,5
1817, 7, 17. Benjamin dis disunity
1820, 6, 22. Hannah Finch (form Williams) dis
  mcd
1821, 1, 25. Mary (form Reeder) con mou
1821, 3, 22. Mary gct Sandy Spring MM
1824, 6, 24. John dis mou
1825, 7, 21. Elizabeth Steel (form Williams)
  dis mcd
1834, 6, 24. Ann dis
1838, 11, 22. Ann Iry (form Williams) dis mcd
1839, 3, 21. Casper & w, Hannah, & ch,
  Charles & Samuel, rocf Salem MM, dtd 1839,
  2,20
1851, 4, 24. Casper & s, Samuel, gct Salem MM
1853, 9, 22. Charles gct Sandy Spring MM, O.
1874, 4, 23. Charles dis mcd (G)
1875, 6, 23. Phebe J. gct Columbus MM (G)
1875, 6, 23. Hannah S., w Samuel, & ch, Edward H., Chas. C., Walter T. & Arthur, gct

WILLIAMS, continued
  Columbus MM, O.
1876, 3, 23. Charles dis mcd & jG
1876, 9, 21. Samuel dis jG
1878, 1, 23. Samuel gct Columbus MM (G)
1908, 7, 22. Charles S. & w, Julia Ann, & dt,
  Verna Louise, rocf Milan MM
1908, 10, 23. Lloyd L. rocf Milan MM (G)
1909, 9, 22. Charles S. & w, Julia Ann, rocf
  Damascus MM (G)
1909, 9, 22. Lloyd L., s Chas. S. & Julia Ann,
  gct Damascus MM (G)
1911, 12, 20. Verna Louise gct Salem MM (G)

WILSON
1764, 10, 10. Dinah b d 1840,2,26
1850, 11, 4. Isaiah d

1815, 4, 13. Ann (form Grissle) dis mcd

WINDER
----, --, --. Joseph, s Wm. & Adah (Bradfield)
  b 1805,10,12 d 1893,4,23 bur Winona; m
  Lydia MORLAN, dt Adem & Amy J., b 1809,
  12,23 d 1906,2,16 bur Winona
----, --, --. Leonard, s Joseph & Lydia, b
  1850,9,21; m Ruthanna COPPOCK, dt Joshua
  & Jane, b 1863,9,7
  Ch: Joseph C. b 1889, 11, 28
    Amy J. " 1891, 1, 7
    John J. " 1893, 6, 3 d 1918, 2, 1
    bur Damascus
    Esther L. b 1896, 1, 18
    Mary Ida " 1897, 3, 9
    Alice Re-
    becca " 1900, 7, 20
    Dorothy
    Emily " 1903, 2, 6
    Anna Eliza-
    beth " 1906, 3, 30

1816, 11, 14. Ann rmt Uriah Coulson
1817, 11, 13. Hannah rmt Benjamin John
1820, 10, 26. Eleanor rmt James Harvey Dean
1828, 5, 22. Joseph rmt Efphema Yates
1828, 8, 21. Efphama gct Sandy Spring MM, O.
1830, 9, 23. Joseph & w, Efphame, & dt, Lydia
  Ann, rocf Sandy Spring MM, dtd 1830,5,21
1832, 10, 25. Joseph & w, Euphema, & ch gct
  Sandy Spring MM, O.
1834, 4, 24. John Yates gct Sandy Spring MM,
  O., to m Asenath Winder
1838, 9, 20. Leah (form Yates) dis mcd
1865, 9, 21. Benjamin Coppock gct Sandy Spring
  MM, O., to m Esther Winder
1876, 6, 22. Anna H. (form Halderman) con mcd
1876, 6, 22. David con mcd
1876, 10, 26. David gct Coal Creek MM, Ia.
1876, 12, 21. Anna H. & dt, Clara May, gct
  Coal Creek MM, Ia.
1887, 5, 26. Sarah S. gct Salem MM
1889, 2, 21. Leonard rmt Ruth Anna Coppock
1913, 8, 21. Leonard & w, Ruthanna C., & ch,

  Esther Lydia, Mary Ida, Alice Rebecca,
  Dorothy Emily & Anna Elizabeth, gct Upper
  Springfield MM, O.
1916, 10, 26. Joseph C. con mcd
1917, 6, 21. Joseph C. gct Stillwater MM, O.
1920, 5, 20. Amy Terwillinger (form Winder)
  dis mcd

WINDLE
1841, 3, 26. Phebe D. (form Dutton) con mou
1876, 8, 23. Susan (form Kirk) con mcd (G)
1879, 1, 22. Joseph J. recrq (G)
1908, 12, 23. Emma recrq (G)
1909, 11, 24. Emma gct Damascus MM (G)

WIREMAN
1830, 4, 22. Mary Alexander rocf Warrington
  MM, dtd 1829,12,22 (H)

WOODS
1819, 5, 20. Enos & w, Elizabeth, & ch, Matilda, James, Joseph, Jacob & Isabel,
  rocf Carmel MM, dtd 1819,3,20
1838, 6, 21. Hannah recrq (H)

WOODWARD
1812, 10, 15. James & w, Lettice, & ch, John
  & William, rocf Fallowfield MM, dtd 1811,
  8,12, endorsed by Salem MM, 1812,9,15
1818, 10, 22. John con mcd
1820, 2, 24. Wm. con mcd
1830, 1, 21. John dis jH
1830, 4, 22. Wm. dis disunity
1832, 11, 22. Susannah dis disunity
1885, 1, 21. Wm. recrq (G)
1887, 7, 20. Wm. rocf Sandy Spring MM, O. (H)

WOOLMAN
----, --, --. Edward J., s Abner & Alvira
  (Hall), b 1869,7,13; m Anna WHINERY, dt
  Mahlon & Hannah, b 1868,1,23
  Ch: Addison M. b 1894, 10, 3
    Emily " 1897, 7, 21
    Russell J. " 1904, 7, 7
    Edith " 1908, 2, 18 d 1922, 7,29
    bur Winona
    Jessie
    Anna b 1910, 3, 29
  Edward J. m 2nd Mary C. BINNS, dt Jos. &
  Belinda (Hobson), b 1884,2,11
1822, 1, 24. Isaac Votaw gct Salem MM, to m
  Susanna Woolman
1893, 11, 23. Edward J. rmt Anna Whinery
1919, 2, 20. Edward J. gct Salem MM, to m
  Mary C. Deweese
1919, 6, 27. Emily m Andrew Pollard
1920, 10, 21. Mary C. & ch, Florence Martha,
  Margaret Hanna, Joseph Howard, James Ezra & Jesse Hall Deweese, rocf Salem MM
1924, 12, 25. Addison M. con mcd

WRIGHT
1829, 2, 24. Esther d

WRIGHT, continued
1815, 2, 16. John rocf Salem MM, dtd 1815,2, 14
1815, 4, 13. Joseph rmt Esther Morgan (wd with ch)
1815, 6, 15. Esther & four ch gct Salem MM
1815, 11, 16. Hannah recrq
1816, 1, 18. Ann, Joseph & David, ch John, recrq
1816, 3, 14. John & fam gct Fairfield MM, O.
1816, 6, 13. Joseph & w, Esther, & ch, Matilda, Benjamin Townsend & Eliza Nailor Morgan, rocf Salem MM, dtd 1816,5,14
1818, 3, 19. Zimri Whinery gct Salem MM, to m Judith Wright
1828, 5, 22. Joseph & w, Rebecca, & ch, Lydia, Elizabeth, Hannah, Mirium & Joseph H., recrq (H)
1828, 7, 24. Joseph & w, Rebecca, & ch, Lydia, Elizabeth, Hannah, Mirium & Joseph gct Salem MM (H)
1829, 10, 22. Joseph gct Salem MM
1839, 4, 25. Justice & w, Betsy, & ch, Ann & Thomas, rocf Queemans MM, dtd 1839,1,23

YATES
----, --, --. ----- m Ann ----- b 1782,5,8 d 1868,9,17
   Ch: Effama   b 1803, 6, 14
       Rachel   " 1805, 4, 6
       Benjamin " 1807, 2, 19 d 1826,10,16
       John   " 1809, 1, 1
       Leah   " 1810, 11, 18
       Sarah   " 1812, 12, 1
       Phebe   " 1814, 7, 5
       Charles   " 1816, 4, 10
       Elizabeth
         Jane   " 1818, 8, 2

1810, 11, 15. Mary rmt Barzillai French
1815, 3, 16. Benjamin rpd mcd; dis 1815,7,13
1815, 4, 13. Margaret (form Blackledge) dis mcd
1823, 3, 20. Ann rst on consent of Westland MM
1823, 4, 24. Elphamy recrq
1823, 6, 26. Benjamin, John, Leah, Sarah, Phebe, Charles & Elizabeth Jane, ch Ann, recrq
1823, 7, 2. Rachel recrq
1824, 1, 22. Rachel rmt Carney Harris
1828, 5, 22. Efphema rmt Joseph Winder
1832, 3, 22. Sarah rmt Robert Harris
1834, 4, 24. John gct Sandy Spring MM, O., to m Asenath Winder
1835, 3, 26. John gct Sandy Spring MM, O.
1835, 5, 21. Hannah J. (form Bennett) dis mcd (H)
1838, 9, 20. Leah Winder (form Yates) dis mcd
1839, 4, 25. Charles dis disunity
1840, 5, 21. Phebe rmt James Hoopes Jr.
1844, 4, 25. Elizabeth Jane rmt Wm. Hoopes
1844, 7, 25. Abigail (form Hoopes) dis mcd

1845, 5, 22. Rebecca (form Hoopes) dis mcd
1879, 1, 23. Sylvanus rpd mcd
1881, 9, 22. Clara J. Osborn (form Yates) dis mcd & jas
1883, 9, 20. John dis disunity

ZEPPERNICK
----, --, --. Andrew, s Cary & Lavina, b 1869, 6,20; m Martha DEAN, dt Jonathan & Elizabeth, b 1869,10,20
   Ch: Jonathan D.b 1893, 9, 12
       Harmon E. " 1895, 4, 26
       Lavina   " 1898, 3, 22
       Francis A." 1903, 3, 23
       Marion C. " 1909, 10, 5

1892, 11, 24. Andrew rmt Martha Dean
1917, 9, 20. Jonathan D. dis jas
1919, 2, 20. Harmon C. dis jas & entering U. S. Army
1925, 3, 26. Francis A. dis joining Marines
1927, 6, 23. Lavina Stahl (form Zeppernick) dis

* * * * * * *

ARMSTRONG
1815, 6, 15. James co

BAILEY
1827, 12, 20. Ezra prc of clearness from Short Creek MM, dtd 1827,11,20

BATTIN
1814, 10, 13. Richard dis
1815, 7, 13. Richard rst by QM
1816, 2, 15. Eli prc of clearness from Short Creek MM, dtd 1815,11,21
1816, 6, 13. John appointed clerk
1817, 7, 17. John appointed clerk
1829, 6, 25. John appointed clerk (H)

BEASON
1826, 8, 24. Elisha, minor, gct Salem MM
1827, 3, 22. Elisha returned cert granted in 7th mo 1826, unused

BLACKLEDGE
1824, 4, 22. Isaac rpd mcd; Redstone MM asked to treat with him; dis 1825,2,24

BURSON
1815, 2, 15. Levi to be treated with for mcd (rq of Westland MM)
1819, 8, 26. Isaiah rq rst; rq returned to him 1820,1,20

BUTLER
1820, 3, 23. Lawrence prc of clearness from Salem MM, dtd 1820,3,22

CHAMBERS
1820, 10, 26. James co

COBBS
1825, 10, 20. Ansalem prc of clearness from Sa-
        lem MM

COBURN
1818, 4, 16. David rpd mcd (mbr of Little
        Brittain MM, Pa.)

COFFIN
1813, 12, 16. Charles co

COURTNEY
1816, 3, 14. Ann chosen elder
1831, 1, 20. Moses dis (H)

CRAIG
1812, 8, 13. James Armstrong prc of clearness
        from Middleton MM, to m Deborah Craig
1813, 1, 14. James appointed clerk
1815, 5, 18. James rqct Middleton MM, to m
        Rebecca Way (cert was not granted)

CREW
1809, 7, 13. Littlebery chosen elder

DAVIS
1819, 11, 25. Mary rmt James Reeder

DEAN
1818, 10, 22. Jonathan R. co
1826, 4, 20. Barton prc of clearness from Sa-
        lem MM, dtd 1826,3,24

DINGEE
1809, 1, 19. John prcf Westland MM, dtd 1808,
        12,24, to m Bathsheba Walton (a mtg was
        appointed for the following day to permit
        them to accomplish their m)

DUTTON
1828, 4, 23. Joseph co (H)

EMMINS
1817, 5, 15. Thomas co

ENLOWS
1854, 1, 26. Samuel & w, Huldah, & s, Wm.,
        gct Driftwood MM, Ind.

FAGAN
1828, 11, 20. Harman co (H)
1829, 1, 22. Harman chosen elder (H)
1830, 1, 21. Harman chosen elder (H)

FARRINGTON
1830, 3, 25. Moses co (H)

FRENCH
1810, 10, 18. Barzillia prc of clearness from
        Salem MM

GALBREATH
1810, 2, 15. Nathan appointed clerk

1811, 6, 13. Nathan appointed clerk
1815, 6, 15. Nathan co
1818, 8, 13. Nathan appointed clerk
1819, 10, 21. Nathan appointed clerk
1820, 12, 21. Nathan appointed clerk
1822, 2, 2. Nathan chosen elder
1822, 2, 2. Nathan appointed clerk
1823, 1, 23. Nathan appointed clerk
1824, 1, 22. Nathan appointed clerk
1824, 2, 26. Wm. co
1825, 4, 21. Nathan appointed clerk
1826, 5, 25. Nathan appointed clerk
1828, 8, 21. Thomas & William co (H)
1829, 1, 22. Ruth chosen elder (H)
1830, 2, 25. Ruth chosen elder (H)
1830, 6, 24. David appointed assistant clerk
        (H)
1831, 6, 23. David appointed assistant clerk
        (H)

GARRETSON
1830, 4, 22. George co (H)

GRIFFITH
1811, 9, 19. Elizabeth chosen elder
1812, 5, 14. Elizabeth chosen elder
1815, 6, 15. Reuben appointed assistant clerk
1825, 4, 21. Wm. appointed assistant clerk
1826, 5, 25. Wm. appointed assistant clerk
1828, 6, 26. William appointed assistant
        clerk (H)
1830, 6, 24. William appointed clerk (H)
1831, 6, 23. Wm. appointed clerk (H)

GRISSELL
1810, 6, 15. Thomas recommended a minister

HANNAH
1828, 6, 25. Benjamin appointed assistant
        clerk (H)

HARRIS
1829, 3, 20. Cert rec for David Jr. from
        Butternut MM, N. Y., dtd 1828,7,4, en-
        dorsed to Sandy Spring MM (H)

HEALD
1817, 7, 17. James appointed assistant clerk

HILLIS
1812, 4, 16. Hugh appointed assistant clerk
1818, 8, 13. Hugh [Hilles] appointed assist-
        ant clerk
1819, 12, 23. Hugh appointed assistant clerk
1820, 12, 21. Hugh appointed assistant clerk
1823, 1, 23. Hugh [Hilles] appointed assist-
        ant clerk
1823, 11, 20. Hugh [Hilles] co
1827, 5, 24. Hugh [Hilles] appointed clerk
1828, 6, 26. Hugh appointed clerk (H)

HOAG
1822, 2, 2. Elisha Wm. appointed assistant

HOAG, continued
    clerk

HOLE
1818, 5, 14. Nathan recrq

HUGHS
1815, 6, 15. Gideon appointed clerk

JOHN
1827, 5, 27. Nathan prc of clearness from
    Sandy Spring MM, dtd 1827,4,27
1832, 6, 21. Isaiah & w, Martha, recrq (H)

JOHNSON
1819, 8, 26. John co
1826, 10, 26. Dorothy chosen elder

LEWIS
1830, 1, 21. Enos prc of clearness from
    Short Creek MM (H)

LYNCH
1811, 6, 13. Joshua appointed assistant clerk

McBRIDE
1809, 9, 14. Ann recrq (ch, Hannah, Rachel &
    step s, name not given, recrq of Ann & h)

McNEELY
1810, 7, 19. George & w, Jane, rq mbrp for
    themselves & their ch (Jane was dis by
    Phila. MM; committee appointed to write
    to that mtg)
1811, 6, 13. Jane rocf Phila. MM, dtd 1811,4,
    22
1828, 8, 21. George & w, Jane, & ch, Rachel,
    recrq (H)

MARSH
1816, 7, 18. Joseph com for mcd & training
    in militia; dis 1816,11,14

MILLER
1813, 1, 14. Levi appointed assistant clerk
1823, 10, 25. Maurice prc of clearness from
    Sandy Spring MM

NEIL
1820, 10, 26. John co

PAINTER
1820, 5, 25. Jacob prc of clearness from Sa-
    lem MM, dtd 1820,5,24

PARKER
1814, 2, 17. George prc of clearness from
    Stillwater MM

PAXSON
1820, 8, 24. Isaiah rpd dis by Sadsbury MM

PEIRPOINT
1822, 2, 2. Ann chosen elder
1824, 1, 22. Wm. appointed assistant clerk

PENNINGTON
1818, 7, 16. Levi co

PENNOCK
1818, 10, 22. Joseph accepted as a minister

PETTIT
1811, 10, 17. Permela rq mbrp; her h joined
    her in rq for their ch; committee rpd
    1812,1,16, but their recommendation is not
    recorded

PIDGEON
1826, 5, 25. William prc of clearness from
    Salem MM, dtd 1826,5,24

PIM
1816, 6, 13. Nathan appointed assistant clerk

PRESTON
1811, 8, 15. Amos con mcd with Drusila Reeve

QUAINTANCE
1816, 1, 18. Fisher prc of clearness from
    Plymouth MM, dtd 1815,12,27

READ
1827, 12, 20. Charles com by Baltimore MM for
    Western District for non-payment of debt

REEDER
1818, 1, 15. Samuel chosen elder

REEVE
1811, 8, 15. Amos Preston con mcd with Dru-
    sila Reeve

REYNOLDS
1809, 8, 17. Michael rqct Eastland MM, Pa.

RILEY
1809, 7, 13. Ruth Sinclair (form Riley) rpd
    mcd

ROGERS
1814, 11, 17. Ruth & two of her ch transferred
    to Marlborough MM
1816, 6, 13. Polly Dean (form Rogers) dis
    (had been treated with by Marlborough MM)

SCHOOLEY
1813, 12, 16. Richard rpd mou

SCOTT
1817, 8, 14. Joseph prc of clearness from
    Middleton MM

SHINN
1827, 5, 24. Joshua appointed assistant

SHINN, continued
    clerk

SINCLAIR
1809, 7, 13. Ruth (form Riley) rpd mcd

STALCUP
1818, 1, 15. Rebecca rq rst (had been dis by
    Goose Creek MM; committee appointed 1818,
    4,16 to write that mtg for its approbation.
    Report made 1818,5,14, that she is dec)

STANLEY
1822, 11, 21. Thomas C. prc of clearness from
    Salem MM, dtd 1822,10,20

THOMAS
1818, 5, 14. John co
1821, 9, 20. Temperence gct Somersett MM

TOWNSEND
1810, 9, 13. Benjamin recommended a minister

TRIPP
1831, 7, 21. Samuel prc of clearness from
    Marlborough MM

VORE
1815, 7, 13. Benjamin prc of clearness from
    Westland MM

VOTAW
1815, 3, 16. Moses co

WALTON
1809, 1, 19. John prcf Westland MM, dtd 1808,
    12,24, to m Bathsheba Walton (a mtg was
    appointed for the following day to permit
    them to accomplish their m)

WARE
1815, 10, 19. Jane treated with on behalf of
    Goose Creek MM; dis recommended
1821, 10, 25. John prc of clearness from Salem
    MM, dtd 1821,10,24

WATSON
1824, 10, 21. Joseph prc of clearness from
    Marlborough MM, dtd 1824,9,25

WAY
1815, 5, 18. James Craig rqct Middleton MM,
    to m Rebecca Way (cert was not granted)

WHINERY
1830, 3, 25. James co (H)

WHITACRE
1829, 3, 25. Cornelius co (H)
1830, 4, 22. Cornelius co (H)

WRIGHT
1815, 3, 16. Joseph prc of clearness from Sa-
    lem MM

CARMEL MONTHLY MEETING

Carmel Monthly Meeting, located in Columbiana County, Ohio, was established by Salem Quarterly Meeting 12th Mo. 20, 1817. It was made up of Elkrun and Carmel Preparative Meetings. This monthly meeting was laid down 12th Mo. 16, 1854. It became a Hicksite Meeting, the records of which are in the Friends Historical Library at Swarthmore, Pennsylvania.

Among early families belonging to this meeting were Fisher, Hannah, Pellet, Peacock, Hole, Heald, Antrim, Morland, Paxson, Richards and Young.

RECORDS

ADDIS
1834, 1, 18. Martha (form Morlan) dis mou

AKIN
1838, 6, 16. Elizabeth (form Randles) dis mou

ALLMON
1840, 6, 25. Silas, s Thomas & Abigail, Colum-
    biana Co., O.; m in Carmel MH, Phebe Elma
    HEALD, dt Joseph & Ury B., Columbiana Co.,
    O.

1840, 9, 19. Phebe Elma gct Middleton MM

ANDERSON
1822, 3, 16. Deborah (form Boyce) dis mcd

ANTRIM
1820, 4, 15. Ann & ch, James, P. Daniel &
    Elizabeth, gct Derby Creek MM, O.

ARMSTRONG
----, --, --. Samuel d 1853,8,22; m Anna -----
    Ch: Mary Ann   b 1822, 12, 6
    Samuel m 2nd Elizabeth -----
    Ch: Martha   b 1830, 8, 8
        Thomas   " 1832, 2, 20
        Joshua   " 1832, 10, 26
        Nathan   " 1835, 8, 29
        Alice   " 1837, 2, 14
        Dorcas   " 1839, 1, 13
        Phebe B.   " 1842, 2, 22
        Ruth Anna   " 1844, 8, 27
        Edith   " 1846, 6, 15
        Sarah
        Emily   " 1850, 8, 21
1827, 11, 23. Nathan H. d 1876,2,7; m in Elk-
    run MH, Rebecca COPE, dt Israel & Eliza-
    beth, Columbiana Co., O.
    Ch: Joseph   b 1828, 8, 31
        Dawsey   " 1830, 8, 20
        Israel   " 1832, 9, 20
        Samuel   " 1835, 8, 20 d 1839, 9, 2
        Elma   " 1838, 6, 20
        Ruth   " 1841, 1, 26 d 1869, 4, 6
        Samuel   " 1843, 11, 7
        Rebecca   " 1847, 4, 10 " 1848, 4, 5
1841, 6, 24. Emily Jane m John MARSH (H)
1844, 4, 24. Mary m James McCONNEL
----, --, --. Dawsey m Sarah Emily BAKER d 1859
    10,1
    Ch: Allis Anna b 1856, 11, 7
        Oscar Al-
        len   " 1858, 2, 16 d 1863, 3,21
----, --, --. Israel & Sina
    Ch: William   b 1857, 9, 13 d 1863, 2,20
        Anne Eliza " 1859, 5, 28.
        Nathan El-
        mer   " 1861, 3, 31 d 1863, 3, 5
----, --, --. Samuel m Emmeline C. ----- d
    1871,12,10

Ch: Nathan
    Edgar   b 1868, 7, 9
    Alvine
    Isaac   " 1870, 3, 27 d 1872, 2, 4

1823, 9, 20. Nathan rocf Middleton MM, dtd
    1823,6,23
1829, 1, 17. Nathan & w, Rebecca, & ch, Jo-
    seph, gct Sandy Spring MM
1834, 2, 15. Samuel & w, Elizabeth, & ch,
    Mary Ann, Martha, Thomas & Joshua, rocf
    Middleton MM, dtd 1834,1,9
1835, 9, 19. Bennett, Emily, Jane, Mary Ann
    & Nathan, ch Bennett & Elizabeth, rocf
    Sandy Spring MM, dtd 1835,8,21
1836, 1, 16. Nathan H. & w, Rebecca, & ch,
    Joseph, Dawsey, Israel & Samuel, rocf
    Sandy Spring MM, dtd 1835,11,27
1842, 5, 21. Emily Jane Marsh (form Armstrong)
    dis mou
1844, 7, 20. Nathan, minor s Bennet, dec, gct
    Middleton MM
1844, 7, 20. Mary Ann gct Middleton MM
1844, 10, 19. Mary Ann gct Middleton MM
1852, 9, 18. Nathan Jr. rocf Middleton MM,
    dtd 1852,8,12
1853, 3, 19. Joseph gct Middleton MM, to m
    Sarah Oliphant
1854, 4, 15. Joseph gct Middleton MM
1854, 11, 18. Nathan H. Jr. dis mou

ASHFORD
1824, 3, 20. Deborah (form Vale) dis mou
1837, 9, 16. Sarah (form Neill) dis mou

ASHTON
----, --, --. Thomas d 1840,3,1; m Martha
    ----- d 1867,1,13
    Ch: Elizabeth b 1803, 3, 24
        Mary   " 1805, 3, 11
        Jacob   " 1807, 7, 22
        Eliza   " 1810, 1, 16
        Margaret   " 1812, 4, 15
        Wm. Marsh   " 1814, 5, 8
        Martha   " 1816, 8, 5
        Justin Ann " 1818, 7, 21
        Thomas   " 1820, 11, 12 d 1822, 6,11
        Rachel   " 1822, 10, 7
        Barak   " 1824, 7, 26
1834, 10, 23. Margaret m Chalkley PEASLEY
1844, 1, 24. Barak, s Thomas, dec, & Martha,
    Columbiana Co., O.; m in Elkrun MH, Jane
    LEECH, dt Wm. & Jane, dec, Columbiana Co.,
    O.
    Ch: Martha   b 1846, 5, 21
        William L. " 1848, 8, 3
        Richard S. " 1850, 9, 15
        Phebe   " 1852, 5, 15
        Eliza   " 1856, 1, 8
        Thomas S. " 1867, 1, 11 (adopted)
        Caty Long-
        shore   " 1871, 2, 5

ASHTON, continued
1819, 4, 17. Martha & ch, Mary, Jacob, Eliza,
     Margaret, William, Martha & Justine Ann,
     recrq. The father, Thomas, was dis by a
     distant MM

1819, 12, 18. Thomas rocf Richland MM, Pa., dtd
     1819,9,3
1825, 8, 20. Jacob F., minor, gct Middleton
     MM
1824, 3, 20. Mary rmt Jonathan Wood Jr.
1838, 11, 17. Martha Johnson (form Ashton) dis
     mou
1844, 4, 20. Eliza Stock (form Ashton) con mou
1846, 3, 21. Rachel Thomas (form Ashton) con
     mou
1854, 7, 15. William dis disunity

BAKER
1846, 7, 18. James M. Hole gct Middleton MM,
     to m Hannah Baker

BALL
1828, 4, 24. Samuel S., s Thomas & Elizabeth,
     Columbiana Co., O.; m in Carmel MH, Hannah
     P. HEACOCK, dt Jonathan & Sarah, Columbi-
     ana Co., O.

1830, 12, 18. Hannah dis JH
1831 7, 16. Hannah & dt, Sarahann, gct Salem
     MM (H)
1833, 5, 18. Sarah Ann, dt Samuel S. & Han-
     nah P., gct Salem MM

BARNABY
1843, 6, 17. Zilpah T. (form Thompson) con
     mcd (H)

BARNETT
1922, 8, 12. Asa & Flora rocf Urbana MM, O.
     (G)

BARRETT
1820, 3, 18. Elizabeth rocf Centre MM, Pa.,
     dtd 1819,1,15
1825, 10, 15. Elizabeth gct Center MM, O.
1829, 8, 15. Elizabeth rocf Center MM, O.,
     dtd 1829,3,18
1832, 7, 21. Elizabeth, w John, gct Center MM,
     O.

BARTON
1840, 6, 20. Frances (form Scott) dis mcd

BEANS
1821, 2, 17. Elizabeth (form Burns) dis mou
1824, 3, 20. Jane (form Byrns) dis mou

BEESON
1840, 1, 22. Richard H., s Richard & Ann, Co-
     lumbiana Co., O.; m in Elkrun MH, Rebecca
     HEALD, dt Nathan & Rachel, dec, Columbi-
     ana Co., O.

1837, 10, 21. Martha (form Smith) dis mcd
1840, 4, 18. Rebecca H. gct Middleton MM

BEIHARDS
1818, 10, 17. Esther appointed elder

BELL
1872, 5, 30. Martha d ae 85

1833, 5, 18. Sarah Ann, minor, gct Salem MM
1835, 3, 21. Maria (form McMillan) con mou
     (H)

BOGUE
1821, 6, 16. Joshua dis disunity

BONSALL
1836, 5, 21. Eliza (form Cowgill) dis mou

BOON
1824, 3, 20. Ann (form Tulloss) dis mou

BOOTH
1844, 7, 20. Susan (form Vale) dis mou

BORAM
1827, 10, 25. Frances m Charles MORLAN

1826, 9, 16. Aaron [Borum] & w, Elizabeth,
     & ch, Richard, Nathan, Elizabeth, Frances,
     Cassander & Mary, rocf Westland MM, dtd
     1826,8,24
1829, 5, 16. Elizabeth Underwood (form Boram)
     dis mcd & JH
1829, 10, 17. Elizabeth dis JH
1829, 12, 19. Aaron dis JH
1833, 8, 17. Cassandra [Borum] dis JH
1833, 9, 21. Mary Underwood (form Borum) dis
     JH
1834, 4, 19. Richard dis mcd (H)
1834, 7, 19. Nathan dis disunity (H)
1834, 7, 19. Cassandra Packer (form Boram)
     con mou (H)

BOWERMAN
1932, 11, 10. Harley & w, Florence, & s,
     Howard, rocf Newport News MM (G)

BOWMAN
1822, 7, 20. Margaret (form Neill) dis mou

BOYCE
1820, 8, 19. Cert for Joshua [Boys] granted
     to New Garden MM not accepted
1820, 9, 16. Robert dis attending military
     muster
1820, 12, 16. Cert for Joshua granted to New
     Garden MM, returned
1821, 6, 16. Joshua dis attending military
     muster
1822, 3, 16. Deborah Anderson (form Boyce)
     dis mcd

BOYCE, continued
1828, 7, 21. Isaac dis disunity
1829, 4, 16. John dis mou
1829, 6, 20. Joseph dis disunity
1830, 5, 15. Samuel dis mou

BRACKEN
1832, 2, 18. Mary (form Neill) dis mou

BRADFIELD
1819, 3, 20. Cynthia & ch, Mary, Samuel,
    Elias, Rachel, Jonas & Carey, gct Clear
    Creek MM, Highland Co., O.
1821, 6, 16. John dis

BRIDGE
1846, 10, 13. James M. Jr. d

BROWN
1820, 2, 24. Ann m Benjamin SCOTT

1818, 9, 19. Prophet rocf Redstone MM, Pa.,
    dtd 1818,3,25
1818, 9, 19. Phebe & Ann rocf Redstone MM,
    Pa., dtd 1818,4,22
1820, 5, 20. Phebe gct Middleton MM
1820, 6, 17. Prophet gct Middleton MM

BURDG
1836, 12, 22. Hannah m Benjamin WALTON

1836, 6, 18. Jacob [Burge] & w, Miriam, & ch,
    Lewis, Oliver & Mary, rocf Upper Spring-
    field MM
1836, 8, 20. William [Burge] & w, Martha, &
    s, Albert, rocf Upper Springfield MM, dtd
    1836,6,25
1836, 9, 17. Hannah [Burge] rocf Upper
    Springfield MM, dtd 1836,6,25
1838, 7, 21. Jacob & w, Miriam, & ch, Lewis,
    Oliver & Mary, gct Sandy Spring MM
1839, 6, 15. William & w, Martha, & ch, Al-
    bert & Hiram, gct Upper Springfield MM

BURROUGHS
1921, 8, 6. Laurence, Ethel & Blanch recrq
    (G)
1921, 11, 12. William, Clark & Hazel recrq (G)

BYLER
1926, 1, 9. Paul recrq (G)

BYRNS
1822, 3, 16. John dis mou
1824, 3, 20. Jane Beans (form Byrns) dis mou
1830, 2, 20. Mary dis jH

CAREY
1924, 6, 14. Kenneth rocf Goshen MM (G)
1929, 10, 2. Kenneth & Agnes gct Alum Creek
    MM (G)

CARROLL
1818, 2, 21. Rachel gct New Garden MM
1833, 8, 17. Mary Ann & William, minors, rocf
    New Garden MM, dtd 1833,7,25 (H)
1833, 8, 17. Elizabeth rocf New Garden MM,
    dtd 1833,7,25 (H)
1834, 2, 15. Eliza & Ann rocf New Garden
    MM, dtd 1833,11,21 (H)
1837, 12, 16. Ann Thomas (form Carroll) dis
    mcd (H)

CARTER
1818, 2, 21. Mary, w James, & ch, Chalkley
    T., Collin B., Olivia, Harpless H.,
    Stella, Milton P., Zelda & Omer D., recrq

CHAMBERS
1845, 4, 19. Joseph Neill gct Sandy Spring
    MM, to m Mary J. Chambers

CLARK
1844, 4, 20. Elizabeth & ch, Mary, Holdridge,
    Ezra, Sarah & Amza recrq
1853, 3, 19. Holdridge dis jas
1853, 7, 16. Mary dis jas
1853, 8, 20. Elizabeth Ann (form Morlan)
    dis mou
1854, 9, 16. Elizabeth & minor ch, Ezra, Sa-
    rah & Amza, gct Greenfield MM, Ind.

CLAY
1838, 7, 21. Jane (form Crawford) con mcd (H)

CLEAVER
1848, 12, 16. Elizabeth (form Pyle) dis mcd &
    jH

CLOVER
1850, 6, 15. Elizabeth (form Pyle) dis mcd &
    jH

COLLINS
1922, 4, 8. Leo & w, Mary, recrq (G)
1924, 6, 14. Leo & Mary dropped from mbrp
    (G)

COMFORT
1924, 2, 9. Ralph Harold gct Central City
    MM, Neb. (G)
1924, 9, 13. Fred & Effie Arms gct Alum Creek
    MM (G)

CONKLE
1836, 10, 15. Beulah (form Vale) dis mou

COOK
1844, 1, 20. Emily H. (form Hambleton) dis
    (H)
1844, 10, 19. Emily (form Hambleton) dis mou

COOPER
1829, 11, 26. Calvin, s Geo. & Susannah, both
    dec, Lancaster Co., Pa.; m in Carmel MH,

COOPER, Calvin, continued
    Elizabeth HOLE, dt Charles & Mary, both
    dec, Bedford Co., Va.
1830, 3, 20. Elizabeth gct Sandy Spring MM
1922, 4, 8. Harry & w, Anna, & ch, Eva &
    Dorothy, recrq (G)
1927, 10, 8. Dorothy relrq (G)
1931, 6, 3. Harry & Anna relrq (G)
1932, 3, 2. Harry, Anna & Forest recrq (G)

COPE
----, --, --. Israel d 1874,2,15; m Elizabeth
    ----- d 1863,3,19
    Ch: Ann   b 1817, 12, 23
        Joseph   " 1820, 6, 3
        Elizabeth
         Dixon   " 1822, 11, 14
         Israel   " 1825, 11, 16
        Susanna
         Hosmer   " 1829, 7, 14
        Samuel
         Neill   " 1833, 10, 2 d 1839, 8,17
1824, 9, 22. Mary m Samuel NEILL
1827, 11, 23. Rebecca m Nathan H. ARMSTRONG
1829, 1, 28. Lydia m James MARSH
1837, 12, 21. Ann m Morton NEILL
1841, 6, 24. Joseph, s Israel & Elizabeth,
    Columbiana Co., O., d 1879,6,11; m in Car-
    mel MH, Phebe HOLE, dt Nathan & Sarah, Co-
    lumbiana Co., O.
    Ch: Lycurgus b 1841, 11, 26
        Lucina   " 1843, 10, 1
        James   " 1845, 8, 11
        Oliver   " 1847, 6, 7
        Mary   " 1849, 3, 10
        Eliphas   " 1851, 6, 9
        Edith   " 1853, 6, 9
        Emor   " 1855, 3, 25
        Sarah Emily" 1857, 10, 3 d 1858, 8,28
1841, 8, 26. Nathan, s Joseph & Elizabeth,
    Columbiana Co., O.; m in Carmel MH, Jane
    HOLE, dt Nathan & Sarah, Columbiana Co.,O.
----, --, --. Israel Jr. & Sarah
    Ch: Harvey
         Cleaver b 1853, 11, 6 d 1855,12, 7
        Harvey D. " 1856, 10, 12
        Mariah El-
         ma   " 1858, 4, 20
        Ella La-
         vina   " 1862, 3, 13

1823, 1, 18. Elizabeth, w Israel, & ch, Mary,
    Rebecca, Lydia, Ruth, Eliza, Ann & Jo-
    seph, rocf Middleton MM, dtd 1822,8,19
1829, 8, 15. Elizabeth, w Israel, & ch, Ruth,
    Eliza, Ann, Joseph, Elizabeth & Israel,
    gct Middleton MM
1834, 2, 15. Elizabeth, w Israel, & ch, Ann,
    Joseph, Elizabeth, Israel, Susanna & Sam-
    uel, rocf Middleton MM, dtd 1834,1,9
1834, 9, 20. John F. rocf Middleton MM, dtd
    1834,9,18
1839, 6, 15. John F. gct Providence MM,

Fayette Co., Pa.
1840, 9, 19. John F. rocf Providence MM, dtd
    1840,7,2
1841, 12, 18. Jane H. gct Middleton MM
1842, 2, 19. Ethan Allen Hole gct Middleton
    MM, to m Mary V. Cope
1842, 5, 21. John F. gct Upper Springfield MM
1844, 7, 20. Elizabeth, w Israel, & ch,
    Elizabeth, Israel, Susanna, & gr dt, Mary
    Marsh, gct Middleton MM
1846, 11, 21. Elizabeth & dt, Elizabeth & Su-
    sanna, & gr dt, Mary Marsh, rocf Middle-
    ton MM, dtd 1846,11,12
1847, 1, 16. Israel Jr. rocf Middleton MM,
    dtd 1846,10,12
1850, 7, 20. Elizabeth & dt, Elizabeth D.,
    gct Middleton MM
1850, 7, 20. Susannah gct Middleton MM
1850, 11, 16. Israel con mcd
1853, 10, 15. Sarah recrq

COULSON
----, --, --. Uriah d 1840,8,2; m Ann -----
    Ch: Susanna b 1817, 12, 22
        William   " 1819, 4, 4 d 1843, 7,11
        Elwood   " 1821, 6, 18
        Jehu   " 1823, 8, 14
        Sewel   " 1825, 9, 18
        Benjamin " 1828, 2, 7
        Ada Jane " 1830, 9, 16
        Caroline " 1833, 3, 29
        Uriah   " 1835, 5, 23
        Seth   " 1838, 6, 2
1824, 4, 21. Jesse, s Jehu & Jane, Beaver
    Co., Pa.; m in Dry Run MH, Mary YOUNG, dt
    Joseph & Ann, Beaver Co., Pa.
    Ch: David   b 1827, 2, 18
1825, 12, 21. Rachel m Benj. M. YOUNG
1827, 2, 18. David, s Jesse & Mary, b
1818, 6, 20. Jehu & w, Jane, & ch, Rachel &
    Jesse, rocf Newgarden MM, dtd 1818,4,16
1822, 8, 17. Uriah & w, Ann, & ch, Susanna,
    William & Elwood, rocf Sandy Spring MM,
    O., dtd 1822,6,21
1832, 8, 18. Mary & ch, David & Jesse, gct
    Upper Springfield MM
1835, 2, 21. Jehu & w, Jane, gct Sandy Spring
    MM
1836, 8, 20. Jehu & w, Jane, rocf Sandy
    Spring MM, dtd 1836,6,24
1838, 6, 18. Jehu & w, Jane, gct Upper
    Springfield MM
1842, 1, 15. Wm. con mcd
1845, 12, 20. Elwood dis mou
1845, 12, 20. Sarah Culbertson (form Coulson)
    con mou
1849, 7, 21. Jehu dis mcd
1851, 3, 15. Sewell con mcd
1851, 9, 20. Sewell gct Goshen MM, Logan
    Co., O.
1852, 2, 21. Benjamin con mou
1852, 10, 16. Benjamin gct Goshen MM, Logan
    Co., O.

COULSON, continued
1853, 3, 19. Ada Lane gct Sandy Spring MM

COWGILL
----, --, --. James m Charlotte ----- d 1819,
   3,28
     Ch: Rachel   b 1794, 10, 18
        Abigail   " 1796, 10, 16
        John   " 1798, 8, 21
        James Simp-
         son   " 1801, 5, 24
        Joel   " 1803, 9, 6
        Lemuel
         Crew   " 1805, 12, 1
        Margaret " 1808, 2, 29
        Israel   " 1810, 5, 23
        Eliza   " 1813, 5, 2
        David   " 1815, 9, 15
        Lewis   " 1818, 7, 15
1819, 7, 22. John, s James & Charlotte, dec,
   Columbiana Co., O.; m in Carmel MH, Sarah
   SCOTT, dt Benjamin & Sarah, Columbiana Co.,
   O.
1820, 2, 23. Abigail m Wm. SCOTT
----, --, --. James d 1839,11,25; m Sarah

     Ch: Evan
        Thomas   b 1822, 6, 3
        Jonathan " 1824, 3, 25
        Charlotte " 1826, 6, 22
1836, 12, 21. Lewis, s James & Charlotte, dec,
   Columbiana Co., O.; m in Elkrun MH, Miriam
   HARRISON, dt Latham & Mary, Columbiana
   Co., O.
     Ch: James
        Williamson
         b 1837, 9, 21
        Mary Eliza-
         beth   " 1838, 12, 25
        Latham T. " 1840, 5, 12
        William H. " 1841, 9, 5 d 1842, 3,21
        Joel   " 1843, 1, 1

1819, 8, 21. John rmt Sarah Scott Jr.
1820, 5, 20. Caleb & w, Rachel, & ch, Henry,
   Elizabeth & Lydia, gct White Water MM,
   Ind.
1821, 7, 21. James rmt Sarah Elliott
1821, 8, 18. John dis
1821, 10, 20. Rebecca (form Fowler) con mou
1821, 10, 20. Joel con mcd
1822, 3, 16. Joel con mcd
1822, 3, 16. Rebecca con mcd
1822, 5, 18. James Simpson gct Salem MM
1823, 3, 15. Joel & w, Rebecca, gct Salem MM
1823, 5, 17. Sarah & minor ch, Charlotte &
   Joseph, gct Salem MM
1827, 4, 21. Lemuel Crene gct Fairfield MM,
   Morgan Co., Ind.
1829, 2, 21. Israel dis jH
1830, 7, 17. James dis jH
1832, 4, 21. Margaret Woolman (form Cowgill)
   dis mcd

1834, 5, 17. James rst
1836, 4, 16. David & Lewis dis disunity
1836, 10, 15. Lewis rst
1836, 5, 21. Eliza Bonsall (form Cowgill)
   dis mou
1837, 8, 19. Sarah (form Harrison) dis mou
1846, 1, 17. Charlotte dis jas
1846, 5, 16. Lewis & w, Mariam, & minor ch,
   James, Mary Elizabeth, Latham, Joel &
   John, gct Goshen MM, O.
1849, 6, 16. Evan dis mcd
1922, 11, 11. Agnes Jane recrq (G)

CRAMFORD
1826, 10, 21. Josiah dis disunity

CRAWFORD
1824, 5, 15. Abel Lee & Josiah, rocf Redstone MM, Pa., dtd 1824,2,4
1824, 6, 19. Abel Lee dis mcd
1824, 7, 17. Jane (form McMillen) dis mcd
1831, 2, 19. Jane & s, Thomas M., recrq (H)
1838, 7, 21. Jane Clay (form Crawford) con
   mcd (H)

CROCHET
1844, 6, 15. Mary (form McConnel) dis mou &
   jas (H)

CROZER
1848, 5, 24. Elizabeth m John HARRISON
1848, 9, 20. Jonathan, s Thos. & Sarah, Columbiana Co., O.; m in Elkrun MH, Phebe S.
   JAMES, dt Jesse, dec, & Elizabeth, Columbiana Co., O.

1841, 6, 19. Thomas & w, Sarah, & ch, James,
   Mary, Jonathan, Elizabeth, Reason, Susannah & Martha, rocf Middleton MM, dtd 1841,
   6,11
1844, 12, 21. James dis mcd
1852, 12, 18. Thomas & w, Sarah, & dt, Martha
   H., gct Salem MM, Ia.
1852, 12, 18. Mary B. gct Salem MM, Henry Co.,
   Ia.
1852, 12, 18. Reason gct Salem MM, Henry Co.,
   Ia.
1852, 12, 18. Jonathan & w, Phebe S., & s,
   Jesse Leroy, gct Salem MM, Henry Co., Ia.
1852, 12, 18. Susanna P. gct Salem MM, Henry
   Co., Ia.

CULBERTSON
1845, 12, 20. Susan (form Coulson) con mcd

DAVIS
1819, 1, 16. Joshua gct Westland MM, Pa.

DEVENNY
1824, 5, 15. Eliza recrq
1829, 3, 21. Eliza dis jH

DILLON
1824, 12, 18. James & w, Elizabeth, gct Middle-
         ton MM

DINGEE
----, --, --. Charles & Mary
    Ch: William   b 1824, 8, 18
        Samuel   " 1826, 1, 17
        John T.   " 1827, 8, 29
        Hannah   " 1829, 3, 12

1830, 6, 19. Charles & w, Mary, & ch, William,
         Samuel, John, & Hannah, rocf Westland MM,
         dtd 1830,4,21
1837, 1, 21. Charles & w, Mary, & ch, William,
         Samuel, John, Talbot, Hannah, Richard,
         Adaline & David, gct Marlborough MM

DIXSON
1818, 9, 19. Nathan & w, Lucretia, & ch, Mary
         Ann, Martha & John, rocf Middleton MM, dtd
         1818,7,25
1820, 9, 16. Nathan & w, Lucretia, & ch,
         Mary-ann, Martha, John & Joshua, gct
         Middleton MM
1843, 8, 19. Benjamin Harrison Jr. gct Marl-
         borough MM, to m Mary Dixon
1847, 4, 17. Latham Harrison gct Goshen MM,
         O., to m Elizabeth Dixon
1847, 6, 19. Cyrus [Dixon], s Elizabeth Har-
         rison, rocf Goshen MM, O., dtd 1847,5,17

DOWNING
1822, 12, 21. William & w, Beulah, & ch, Dan-
         iel, Rebecca & John, rocf Middleton MM,
         dtd 1822,11,18
1829, 1, 17. Beulah dis jas
1829, 2, 21. William dis jas
1831, 9, 17. Rebecca dis disunity
1832, 1, 21. Daniel dis disunity
1834, 10, 18. John gct Alum Creek MM

DRAPER
1924, 12, 13. Joshua dropped from mbrp (G)

DUTTON
1827, 2, 21. Joseph, s Francis & Lydia, Har-
         rison Co., O.; m in Elkrun MH, Joanna
         SMITH, dt Richard & Joanna Alter, both dec,
         late of Sussex Co., N. J.

1827, 5, 19. Joanna & ch, Phebe, Thomas, Hen-
         ry, Martha & David Smith gct Sandy Spring
         MM

EATON
1924, 12, 13. Olive dropped from mbrp (G)

EDMUNDSON
1820, 12, 21. Sarah m Thos. TAYLOR

1819, 3, 20. Jonathan dis mcd
1819, 7, 17. Phebe (form Vale) dis mcd

1820, 10, 21. Eli gct Middleton MM, to m
         Ruth Heald
1821, 1, 20. Ruth rocf Middleton MM, dtd
         1820,12,18
1822, 4, 20. John Jr., minor, gct Middleton
         MM
1822, 4, 20. Eli & w, Ruth, & dt, Phebe, gct
         Middleton MM
1823, 7, 30. John Jr. rocf Middleton MM, dtd
         1823,5,19
1825, 3, 19. Eli & w, Ruth, & ch, Phebe,
         John & Jonathan, rocf Middleton MM, dtd
         1825,2,21
1826, 2, 18. John Jr. dis disunity
1828, 5, 17. Maria Vale (form Edmundson) dis
         mcd
1829, 1, 17. Ann dis jH
1829, 3, 21. John dis jH
1829, 8, 15. Amos dis jH
1830, 5, 15. Eli & w, Ruth, & ch, Phebe,
         John, Jonathan Abner, Ann & Sarah, gct
         Middleton MM
1830, 5, 15. Ruth gct Middleton MM
1831, 9, 17. Amos con mcd (H)
1834, 2, 15. Nathan dis disunity
1837, 6, 17. Nathan dis disunity
1838, 11, 17. Hiram gct Middleton MM
1845, 12, 20. Franklin dis mou

ELLIOTT
1821, 2, 17. Sarah rst; dis by Pipecreek MM,
         Md.
1821, 7, 21. Sarah rmt James Cowgill
1821, 10, 20. Elizabeth, minor dt Sarah, rec-
         rq
1827, 3, 17. Lydia, minor, rocf Sandy Spring
         MM, dtd 1826,5,26
1834, 5, 17. Lydia McCall (form Elliott) dis
         mcd
1836, 7, 16. Elizabeth Hoops (form Elliott)
         dis mou

ELLIS
1844, 11, 16. Eliza (form Neill) dis mou

EMMINGER
1924, 10, 11. Charles H. & w, Lena M., rocf
         Rush Creek MM (G)

ENGLE
1841, 1, 21. Nathan, s Josiah, dec, & Mary,
         Columbiana Co., O.; m in Carmel MH, Catha-
         rine HOLE, dt Charles & Esther, Columbi-
         ana Co., O.

1841, 3, 20. Catharine gct Middleton MM

FAGAN
1832, 5, 19. Hannah (form Neill) dis mou

FARQUHAR
----, --, --. Benajah & Elizabeth
    Ch: Sarah   b 1821, 3, 24

FARQUHAR, Benajah & Elizabeth, continued
    Ch: Edward A.
        Rebecca

1819, 3, 20. Elizabeth rocf WD MM, dtd 1819,
    1,20
1819, 3, 20. Rebecca P., minor, rocf Frank-
    fort MM, dtd 1819,1,22
1822, 4, 20. Edward Andrews, minor, rocf
    Baltimore MM for W. Dist., dtd 1821,12,7
1828, 12, 20. Elizabeth & Rebecca dis jH
1833, 9, 21. Edward Andrews dis jH
1834, 6, 21. Elizabeth & dt, Sarah, gct Salem
    MM (H)
1834, 9, 20. Sarah, minor dt Benajah & Eliza-
    beth, gct Salem MM
1839, 3, 16. Rebecca gct Middleton MM, Pa.(H)
1840, 4, 18. Edward dis (H)

FARR
1852, 6, 19. Catharine (form Hole) dis mou

FERGUSON
1828, 8, 16. Ruth (form Stooksberry) dis mou
1833, 6, 15. Catharine (form Tulloss) dis
    mou

FIELD
1851, 3, 15. Sophia (form Kreugar) dis mcd

FISHER
----, --, --. Joseph d 1848,4,--; m Hannah
    ----- d 1823,5,12
    Ch: Sylvanus b 1797, 10, 8
        Rachel   " 1799, 5, 14
        William   " 1800, 11, 24
        Isaac   " 1802, 5, 18
        Amase   " 1803, 10, 12
        Anne
         Knight   " 1806, 4, 8
        Elias   " 1808, 1, 10
        Ruth   " 1811, 6, 29
        Sina   " 1813, 11, 16
        Asahel Ex-
         chanze   " 1820, 4, 5
    Joseph m 2nd Margaret -----
    Ch: Thomas
        Rollings b 1829, 8, 16

1818, 6, 20. Cert for Sylvanus granted to
    Salem MM, returned
1823, 10, 18. Sylvanus dis jas
1824, 10, 16. Elias, minor, gct Middleton MM
1826, 1, 21. Elias, minor, rocf Middleton MM,
    dtd 1825,12,19
1826, 4, 15. Joseph gct Salem MM, to m Marga-
    ret Rawlings
1826, 8, 19. Margaret rocf Salem MM
1828, 10, 18. Amasa dis disunity
1831, 5, 21. Joseph & w, Margaret, & ch, Asa-
    hel Exchange & Thomas Rawlings, gct Salem
    MM
1831, 9, 17. Isaac gct Miami MM

1831, 11, 19. Elias dis
1831, 11, 19. William gct Salem MM
1832, 1, 21. Anne K. gct Springfield MM, O.,
    Clinton Co.
1832, 12, 15. Sina Stickel (form Fisher) dis
    mou
1833, 3, 16. Ruth gct Springfield MM, O.

FITZ-RANDOLPH
1826, 4, 15. Edward gct Upper Springfield MM

FOWLER
1820, 5, 25. Caleb, s James & Mary, Columbi-
    ana Co., O.; m in Carmel MH, Mary RICHARDS
    dt Abijah & Hester, Columbiana Co., O.
1820, 8, 23. Lydia m Nathaniel J. STANLEY

1818, 8, 15. Mary, minor, s Samuel, rocf
    Pipe Creek MM, Md., dtd 1818,2,14, en-
    dorsed by Middleton MM 1818,8,10
1819, 1, 16. James com by Pipe Creek MM, Md.
    for not settling his outward affairs
1819, 11, 20. James dis by Pipe Creek MM, Md.
1820, 9, 16. Joseph rocf Pipe Creek MM, Md.,
    dtd 1820,5,13
1821, 7, 21. Caleb & w, Mary, gct Sandy
    Spring MM
1821, 7, 21. Mary & s, Samuel, gct Sandy
    Spring MM
1821, 10, 20. Joseph gct Salem MM
1821, 10, 20. Rebecca Cowgill (form Fowler)
    con mou

FROST
1924, 6, 14. Adelbert & Goldie dropped from
    mbrp (G)
1928, 5, 12. Thomas & James recrq (G)
1934, 4, 4. Ruth recrq (G)

GAMBLE
----, --, --. Harrison m Phebe ----- d 1866,7,
    8
    Ch: Joseph H. b 1859, 6, 21 d 1884, 2, 3
        Martha Jane" 1852, 5, 20 " 1858, 8,15
        Ruth Ellen " 1857, 2, 24 " 1858, 8, 9
        Martha El-
         len   " 1861, 8, 23 " 1864, 4,23

GEORGE
----, --, --. Henry m Thamer ----- d 1828 (or
    1824) 1,29
    Ch: Caleb   b 1815, 10, 14
        Mary   " 1816, 12, 22
        Rachel   " 1819, 5, 4
        Richard " 1822, 6, 30

1830, 10, 16. Henry gct Newgarden MM, to m
    Lydia Hoops
1831, 5, 21. Lydia, w Henry, & ch, Esther &
    Joseph Leech Hoops, rocf Newgarden MM,
    dtd 1831,2,24
1834, 12, 20. Henry & w, Lydia, & ch, Mary,
    Caleb, Rachel & Richard George, & Hesther

GEORGE, continued
    & Joseph Leech Hoops, gct Whitewater MM,
    Ind.

GRANT
1923, 3, 10. Frances Ford recrq (G)
1924, 12, 13. Archilla recrq (G)

GRIFFITH
1833, 8, 22. Eli R., s Israel & Lettitia,
    Washington Co., Pa.; m in Carmel MH, Mary
    Ann MARSH, dt James & Edith, Columbiana
    Co., O. (H)

1833, 10, 19. Mary Ann gct Westland MM (H)
1833, 12, 21. Milton Marsh gct Westland MM, to
    m Elizabeth Griffith (H)

GRIMSHAW
1827, 2, 17. Chas. Hambleton gct Smithfield
    to m Jane Grimshaw

GROSSCUP
1853, 6, 18. Louisa (form Morlan) dis mou

HAINES
----, --, --. Levi & Sarah
    Ch: Israel   b 1812, 11, 19
        Nathan   " 1814, 4, 3
        Lydia   " 1816, 4, 5
        Hannah   " 1818, 1, 30
        Hinchman   " 1820, 2, 9
        William   " 1821, 12, 22
        Levi A.   " 1826, 11, 16
        Mary   " 1824, 1, 27

1825, 10, 15. William, minor, gct Short Creek
    MM
1829, 4, 18. Levi & w, Sarah, & ch, Israel,
    Malon, Lydia, Hannah, Hinchman, William,
    Mary, Levi A. & Sarah Ann, gct Marlborough
    MM

HALL
----, --, --. Edward, s Wilson & Sina, b
    1858,11,22 d 1861,11,27

HAMBLETON
----, --, --. James & Martha
    Ch: Mary   b 1812, 5, 7
        Edward   " 1815, 1, 18
        Emlie   " 1818, 12, 16
        Lydia Ann   " 1821, 10, 28
        Franklin
----, --, --. Benjamin & Ann
    Ch: Rachel   b 1816, 10, 14
        Osborn   " 1818, 6, 13
        Levi   " 1820, 8, 4
1829, 3, 26. Sarah L. m Cornelius LEECH

1820, 6, 17. Hannah (form West) con mcd
1820, 12, 16. William rocf Flushing MM, O.,
    dtd 1820,7,21

1822, 8, 17. Mary rocf Newgarden MM, dtd
    1822,7,25
1826, 6, 17. Benjamin & w, Ann, & ch, Rachel,
    Osborn, Levi, Catharine H. & Joel G., gct
    Newgarden MM
1826, 7, 15. Mary gct Middleton MM
1826, 10, 21. Emaline, Lewis & George, ch
    Hannah, recrq
1827, 1, 20. Sarah & Mary recrq
1827, 2, 17. Charles gct Smithfield MM, to m
    Jane Grimshaw
1827, 5, 19. Jane rocf Smithfield MM, dtd
    1827,4,23
1828, 11, 15. James & William Jr. dis jH
1828, 12, 20. Mary Heacock (form Hambleton)
    dis mcd & jH
1829, 4, 18. Hannah, Sarah & Stephen dis jH
1829, 5, 16. Charles dis jH
1829, 8, 15. Martha dis jH
1829, 8, 15. Moses & w, Ann, & ch, Charles,
    Eliza & Susannah, rocf New Garden MM, dtd
    1829,5,21 (H)
1831, 4, 16. Jane dis jH
1832, 2, 18. Isaac P. rocf Kennett MM, Pa.,
    dtd 1831,11,8 (H)
1832, 6, 18. Moses & fam gct New Garden MM
    (H)
1836, 5, 21. Thomas Elwood, Isaac Herbert &
    Ruth Ann, ch Stephen, gct Hamburgh MM, N.Y.
1839, 8, 17. William & Isaac Howard, ch Han-
    nah, recrq (H)
1842, 5, 21. Emeline Morris (form Hambleton)
    dis jH & mou
1843, 8, 19. Isaac P. con mou (H)
1844, 10, 19. Emily Cook (form Hambleton) dis
    mou
1852, 7, 17. George W. dis mou
1852, 7, 17. Louis dis mou
1854, 5, 20. Frank rpd mcd
1854, 8, 19. Mary gct Driftwood MM, Ind.

HAMILTON
1825, 6, 18. Stephen & w, Sarah, & ch, Thom-
    as Elwood & Isaac Herbert, rocf Newgarden
    MM, dtd 1825,4,21

HANLEY
1829, 5, 16. Caleb & Catharine & ch, Joseph,
    Benjamin, Phebe-Ann, James, Latham & Ca-
    leb P., gct Marlborough MM

HANNAH
1818, 1, 22. Catharine m Hogn HOLE

1824, 7, 17. Thomas & w, Anne, gct New Gar-
    den MM
1826, 4, 15. Robert [Hana] & w, Catharine,
    antient friends, gct New Garden MM

HARRISON
1798, 10, 10. Thomas b
----, --, --. Latham & Mary
    Ch: Phebe   b 1810, 2, 25

HARRISON, Latham & Mary, continued
 Ch: Mary Ann b 1811, 12, 23
   Sarah " 1813, 10, 23
   Isaac " 1815, 11, 2
   Miriam " 1817, 12, 16
 Latham m 2nd Elizabeth ----- b 1799,12,19
 d 1864,6,1
 Ch: Elizabeth b 1820, 3, 3
   Benjamin " 1822, 1, 11
   Latham " 1824, 4, 19 d 1842, 9,18
   John   " 1826, 9, 12 " 1851, 7,21
   David " 1829, 1, 20
   Edward H. " 1831, 4, 24
   Mildred P. " 1833, 6, 18
1836, 2, 15. Mirium d ae 69
1836, 12, 21. Miriam m Lewis COWGILL
1842, 2, 27. Mary d ae 49 (an elder)
----, --, --. Benjamin b 1822,1,11; m Mary
 ----- b 1821,2,3
 Ch: Mary
   Elizabeth b 1844, 7, 1
   Lucinda
   Ann   " 1848, 12, 24
   Matilda
   Ellen " 1852, 5, 22
   John Frank-
   lin   " 1856, 9, 10
   Sabina Jane" 1859, 9, 6
1848, 5, 24. John, s Latham & Mary, dec, Co-
 lumbiana Co., O.; m in Elkrun MH, Eliza-
 beth CROZER, dt Thomas & Sarah, Columbiana
 Co., O.
1857, 5, 10. Thomas d

1825, 10, 15. Abel J. Pellett gct Short Creek
 MM, O., to m Unity Harrison
1828, 4, 19. Phebe Richards (form Harrison)
 dis mou
1831, 6, 18. Mary (form Siddall) dis mou
1833, 5, 18. Sarah (form Siddell) dis mou
1837, 6, 17. Isaac dis mou
1837, 8, 19. Sarah Cowgill (form Harrison)
 dis mou
1839, 3, 16. Mary Ann McArtor (form Harrison)
 dis mou
1843, 8, 19. Benjamin Jr. gct Marlborough
 MM, to m Mary Dixon
1844, 1, 20. Mary rocf Marlborough MM, dtd
 1843,11,28
1846, 3, 21. Benjamin & w, Mary, & dt, Mary
 Elizabeth, gct Goshen MM, O.
1847, 4, 17. Latham gct Goshen MM, to m
 Elizabeth Dixon
1847, 6, 19. Elizabeth & s, Cyrus Dixon, rocf
 Goshen MM, dtd 1847,5,17
1849, 8, 18. Elizabeth Whitzell (form Harrison) con mcd
1852, 12, 18. Elizabeth C. gct Salem MM, Henry
 Co., Ia.
1853, 1, 15. David dis mcd
1853, 7, 16. Mildred Montgomery (form Harrison) dis mcd
1854, 12, 16. Benjamin & w, Mary, & ch, Mary

Elizabeth, Lucinda Ann & Matilda Ellen,
 rocf Gilead MM, dtd 1854,11,21

HAWLEY
----, --, --. Caleb & Catharine
 Ch: Joseph b 1818, 6, 30
   Benjamin " 1820, 5, 20
   Phebe Ann " 1822, 9, 3
   James " 1825, 12, 10
   Latham " 1827, 10, 7
   Caleb P. " 1829, 2, 10
1847, 10, 21. Caleb, s Caleb, dec, & Hannah,
 Stark Co., O.; m in Carmel MH, Tacy HOLE,
 dt David & Anna, dec, Columbiana Co., O.

1824, 7, 17. Caleb & w, Catherine, & ch,
 Joseph, Benjamin & Phebe Ann, rocf White
 Water MM, Ind., dtd 1824,5,15
1829, 5, 16. Caleb & w, Catharine, & ch,
 Joseph, Benjamin, Phebe Ann, James,
 Latham & Caleb P., gct Marlborough MM
1847, 12, 18. Tacy gct Marlborough MM

HAYES
1833, 8, 17. Ruth (form Heald) dis mou

HEACOCK
----, --, --. Jacob & Susannah
 Ch: Isaac b 1808, 12, 8
   Ann   " 1810, 12, 25
   Sarah " 1813, 5, 18
   Elizabeth " 1815, 12, 17
   William " 1817, 9, 3
   John   " 1820, 10, 1
   James
1828, 4, 24. Hannah P. m Samuel S. BALL
1840, 12, 24. Jonathan N., s Jonathan & Sarah,
 Columbiana Co., O.; m in Carmel MH, Hannah
 H. MARSH, dt James & Edith, Columbiana Co.
 O. (H)
1858, 8, 22. Sarah, wd Jonathan, d

1818, 7, 20. Hannah, Jacob, Susanna & Jonathan, ch Sarah, recrq
1828, 12, 20. Jacob dis jH
1828, 12, 27. Mary (form Hambleton) dis mcd &
 jH
1829, 1, 17. Isaac dis mcd & jH
1829, 1, 17. Mary dis jH
1829, 6, 20. Isaac con mcd (H)
1829, 6, 20. Mary (form Hambleton) con mcd
 (H)
1829, 7, 18. Susannah & Ann dis jH
1832, 12, 15. Susanna Jr. dis jH
1833, 8, 17. Elizabeth dis jH
1833, 9, 21. Jacob Jr. dis jH
1838, 11, 17. Susan Hole (form Heacock) con
 mou (H)
1839, 5, 18. Jonathan Jr. & William dis disunity
1840, 10, 16. John dis mou (H)
1840, 11, 21. Jacob con mou (H)
1841, 10, 16. John dis mcd

HEACOCK, continued
1841, 7, 17. Mary Moore (form Heacock) con
    mcd (H)
1842, 2, 19. William dis mou (H)
1846, 10, 17. James D. con mou (H)
1847, 3, 20. James dis mcd

HEALD
----, --, --. Nathan d 1853,5,26; m Rachel
    ----- d 1823,11,14
    Ch: Anne   b 1799, 2, 4
        Jesse   " 1801, 1, 3
        Hannah   " 1802, 10, 22
        Sarah   " 1805, 2, 10
        Ruth   " 1806, 5, 19
        William   " 1808, 9, 13
        Rachel
         Smith   " 1810, 8, 30
        Lizzie
         Stokes   " 1812, 7, 22 d 1820,11,13
        Smith   " 1814, 6, 28
        Nathan H.   " 1817, 1, 21
        Rebecca   " 1818, 12, 2
        Thomas S.   " 1820, 8, 17 d 1821, 8,16
----, --, --. Joseph d 1847,9,6; m Ury Betsy

    Ch: Hiel   b 1817, 11, 1
        Penina   " 1819, 3, 1
        Phebe Elma   " 1821, 7, 18
        Betsy Hole   " 1823, 5, 12
        Elmira   " 1825, 8, 5
        Ann   " 1828, 1, 14 d 1829, 3, 4
        Nathan
         Hole   " 1828, 1, 14
        Jonah   " 1830, 2, 2 " 1854, 5,23
        Mary Ru-
         anna   " 1832, 1, 28 " 1847,12,30
        John   " 1833, 8, 24
        Ann   " 1836, 4, 23
        Abner   " 1837, 12, 5
        Martha
         Jane   " 1839, 4, 17
1821, 1, 24. Hannah m Jason TULLOSS
1838, 8, 23. Penina m Samuel SHAW
1840, 1, 22. Rebecca m Richard H. BEESON
1840, 6, 25. Phebe Elma m Silas ALLMON
1842, 7, 21. Israel, s Wm. & Sarah, dec,
    Columbiana Co., O.; m in Carmel MH, Re-
    becca HOLE, dt Charles & Esther, Columbi-
    ana Co., O.
1845, 10, 23. Betsy H. m Edwin HOLLINGSWORTH
----, --, --. James m Abi ----- d 1877 or 1879
    10,11
    Ch: Joseph S. b 1848, 12, 25
        Mathew   " 1850, 6, 22
        Edwin T.   " 1852, 3, 28
        Francis   " 1854, 4, 2 d 1870, 4,11
        Sarah L.   " 1856, 2, 25 " 1856, 5,27
        Charles   " 1857, 3, 27 " 1858,10, 7
        Louis J.   " 1859, 10, 30
1847, 9, 23. Elmira m Caleb MARSHALL
1849, 10, 24. Allen, s Israel & Lydia, dec,
    Columbiana Co., O.; m in Elkrun MH, Rebec-

ca NEILL, dt Samuel & Mary, Columbiana
    Co., O.
1854, 11, 23. Ann M. m Samuel N. HOBSON

1818, 6, 20. Joseph & w, Ury B., & s, Hiel,
    rocf Middleton MM, dtd 1818,6,16
1820, 10, 21. Eli Edmundson gct Middleton MM,
    to m Ruth Heald
1821, 11, 17. Thomas prcf Middleton MM, to m
    Miriam Marsh
1821, 12, 15. Thomas rmt Miriam Marsh
1821, 12, 15. Morlan Aden gct Middleton MM, to
    m Rebecca Heald
1822, 2, 16. Miriam gct Middleton MM
1828, 2, 16. William, minor, gct Middleton MM
1828, 3, 15. Jesse dis mou
1830, 3, 20. Wm. Jr. rocf Middleton MM, dtd
    1830,3,11
1832, 1, 21. William S. dis mou
1833, 8, 17. Ruth Hayes (form Heald) dis mou
1836, 12, 17. Rachel dis
1837, 3, 18. Nathan Jr. dis mou
1842, 9, 17. Rebecca gct Middleton MM
1842, 9, 17. Smith gct Chesterfield MM
1849, 6, 16. Nathan H. gct Gilead MM
1850, 6, 15. Rebecca gct Middleton MM

HENRY
1833, 11, 16. Sarah (form Pellett) dis mou

HEPBURN
1832, 1, 21. Thomas dis
1836, 5, 21. Nancy Ann (form Morris) dis mou
    with cousin

HIBBERN
1845, 5, 17. Thomas recrq (H)

HOBSON
1854, 11, 23. Samuel N., s John & Rebecca P.,
    Washington Co., O.; m in Carmel MH, Ann M.
    HEALD, dt Joseph & Ury B., Columbiana Co.,
    O. (Joseph, dec)

HOLE
----, --, --. David d 1854,2,10 ae 83y; m
    Anne -----
    Ch: Elon   b 1800, 11, 22
        Catharine " 1802, 12, 25
        Tace   " 1805, 2, 21
        Jesse   " 1808, 8, 15
        Tirzah   " 1810, 12, 4
        Mary   " 1813, 3, 28
        Narcissa   " 1816, 5, 11
        Ruth   " 1818, 10, 30
        Anna   " 1821,10, 20 d 1823, 8,19
----, --, --. Charles d 1854,5(or 6)23; m Es-
    ther ----- d 1849,12,6
    Ch: Thomas   b 1812, 1, 2
        Rebecca   " 1813, 11, 13
        Catharine " 1816, 1, 24
        Mary Ann   " 1818, 7, 3
        Benjamin   " 1820, 10, 25

HOLE, Charles & Esther, continued
　　Ch: Joseph　　b 1823, 7, 26
　　　　Robert　　" 1825, 11, 4
　　　　Jacob　　 " 1828, 7, 18
　　　　Hannah　　" 1832, 4, 10
1818, 1, 22. John, s Jacob & Mary, Columbi-
　　ano Co., O.; m in Carmel MH, Catharine
　　HANNAH, dt Robert & Catharine, Columbiana
　　Co., O.
1824, 8, 26. Catharine m Robert MILLER
1826, 11, 26. Elizabeth m Calvin COOPER
1828, 5, 21. Elon, s David & Anna, Columbiana
　　Co., O., b 1800,11,22; m in Elkrun MH, Beu-
　　lah Ann PETITT, dt Charles & Permelia, both
　　dec, Columbiana Co., O.
　　Ch: Charles　　b 1829, 7, 9
　　　　Catharine　" 1832, 1, 30
　　Elon m 2nd Mary ----- d 1849,1,17
　　Ch: Beulah Ann b 1838, 6, 12
　　　　Lydia　　　 " 1842, 2, 2
　　　　David　　　 " 1843, 11, 29
　　　　Anna　　　　" 1847, 8, 11
1841, 1, 21. Catharine m Nathan ENGLE
1841, 6, 24. Phebe m Joseph COPE
1841, 8, 26. Jane m Nathan COPE
1842, 7, 21. Rebecca m Israel HEALD
1844, 12, 26. Mary Ann m Aaron HEUSTIS
1846, 11, 26. Joseph, s Chas. & Esther, Colum-
　　biana Co., O.; m in home of Elizabeth
　　Pyle, Esther M. PYLE, dt Benjamin & Eliza-
　　beth, Columbiana Co., O. (H)
1847, 10, 21. Tacy m Caleb HAWLEY

1819, 5, 15. John & w, Catharine & s, Lemuel,
　　gct Newgarden MM
1819, 7, 17. Ann rmt Levi Miller
1822, 1, 28. Nathan recorded a minister
1832, 6, 16. Jesse dis disunity
1834, 6, 21. Elon gct Marlborough MM
1835, 7, 18. Tirzah Lodge (form Hole) dis mou
1837, 5, 20. Elon gct Westland MM, to m Mary
　　Garwood
1837, 9, 16. Mary, w Elon, rocf Westland MM
1838, 11, 17. Susan (form Heacock) con mou (H)
1839, 7, 20. Nathan & w, Sarah, & ch, Ethan,
　　James, Jane, Mary, Samuel & Sarah, rocf
　　Sandyspring MM, dtd 1839,6,21
1840, 1, 18. Phebe rocf Sandy Spring MM, dtd
　　1839,8,23
1840, 10, 17. Narcissa Humphrey (form Hole)
　　dis mcd
1841, 3, 20. Elon & w, Mary, & ch, Catharine
　　& Beulah Ann, gct Westland MM
1842, 2, 19. Ethan Allen gct Middleton MM; to
　　m Mary V. Cope
1842, 6, 18. Ruth dis
1843, 2, 18. Thomas dis mou
1843, 7, 15. Ethan Allen gct Middleton MM
1846, 7, 18. James M. gct Middleton MM, to m
　　Hannah Baker
1847, 3, 20. James M. gct Salem MM
1847, 4, 17. Joseph dis mcd
1847, 5, 15. Esther (form Pyle) dis mcd

1849, 9, 15. Samuel gct Middleton MM, to m
　　Rebecca Woods
1850, 6, 15. Samuel & Rebecca gct Middleton
　　MM
1851, 1, 18. Robert gct Salem MM
1851, 5, 17. Elon & ch, Beulah Ann, Lydia,
　　David & Anna, rocf Westland MM, dtd 1851,
　　4,23
1851, 5, 17. Catharine rocf Westland MM, dtd
　　1851,4,23
1851, 12, 20. Nathan & w, Sarah, gct Middle-
　　ton MM
1851, 12, 20. Sarah Jr. gct Middleton MM
1852, 6, 19. Catharine Farr (form Hole) dis
　　mou

HOLLINGSWORTH
1824, 5, 20. Samuel, s Er & Phebe, form dec,
　　Columbiana Co., O.; m in Carmel MH, Marga-
　　ret LEECH, dt William & Jane, Columbiana
　　Co., O.
1845, 10, 23. Edwin, s Elisha & Sarah, dec,
　　Morgan Co.; m in Carmel MH, Betsy H.
　　HEALD, dt Joseph & Ury B., Columbiana Co.,
　　O.

1823, 10, 18. Wm. Leech gct Middleton MM, to
　　m Phebe Hollingsworth
1824, 8, 21. Margaret gct Middleton MM
1831, 4, 16. Mahlon, minor, gct Middleton MM
1833, 8, 17. Ann dis jas
1839, 9, 21. Rachel (form James) dis mcd
1845, 12, 20. Betsy H. gct Chesterfield MM, O.

HOOPS
1830, 10, 16. George Henry gct Newgarden MM,
　　to m Lydia Hoops
1834, 12, 20. Jesther & Joseph, ch Lydia
　　George, gct Whitewater MM, Ind.
1836, 7, 16. Elizabeth (form Elliott) dis
　　mou

HORN
1831, 4, 21. Edward, s Wm. & Sarah, Columbi-
　　ana Co., O.; m in Carmel MH, Elizabeth
　　PELLETT, dt Francis & Mary, Columbiana
　　Co., O. (H)

1830, 2, 20. Edward [Horne] rocf Darby MM,
　　Pa., dtd 1829,12,29 (H)
1832, 4, 21. William [Horne] & w, Sarah, &
　　ch, Eliza, Ann & Stephen, rocf Darby MM,
　　Pa., dtd 1831,11,29, endorsed to New Gar-
　　den MM (H)
1832, 4, 21. Hiram [Horne] rocf Darby MM,
　　Pa., dtd 1831,11,29; endorsed to New Gar-
　　den MM (H)
1833, 2, 16. Wm. D. & w, Sarah, & ch, Ste-
　　phen & Ann, rocf New Garden MM, dtd 1832,
　　12,20 (H)
1833, 2, 16. Hiram rocf New Garden MM, dtd
　　1832,12,20 (H)

HORN, continued
1833, 6, 15. Edward & fam gct Marlborough MM
    (H)
1834, 2, 15. Eliza rocf New Garden MM, dtd
    1833,8,22 (H)
1838, 2, 17. Edward & w, Elizabeth, & ch,
    Vincent P., Philena, Lindley & Louisa,
    rocf Marlborough MM, dtd 1837,6,24 (H)

HUESTIS
----, --, --. Aaron d 1847,9,20; m Esther -----
    d 1860,3,1 ae 83
    Ch: Elizabeth b 1805, 12, 2
        Isaac   " 1810, 4, 3
        Rebecca   " 1812, 9, 22
        Moses   " 1815, 5, 1 d 1841, 8,22
        Aaron   " 1817, 8, 26
        Job   " 1819, 10, 3
1835, 5, 20. Elizabeth m Joshua REEVE
1844, 12, 26. Aaron, s Aaron & Esther, Colum-
    biana Co., O.; m in Carmel MH, Mary Ann
    HOLE, dt Charles & Esther, Columbiana Co.,
    O.
    Ch: Isadora   b 1845, 12, 15
        Samantha " 1847, 12, 3
        Moses   " 1849, 12, 20
        Emmer   " 1852, 4, 29

1837, 6, 17. Isaac gct Pennsville MM
1854, 2, 18. Aaron & w, Mary Ann, & ch, Isa-
    dora, Samantha, Moses & Emma, gct Drift-
    wood MM, Ind.

HUMPHREY
1840, 10, 17. Narcissa (form Hole) dis mcd
1927, 9, 10. Mary relrq (G)

HUNT
1847, 6, 19. Jehu D. Raley gct Salem MM, to
    m Esther Hunt (H)

HUTTON
1826, 9, 21. John, s John & Jane, dec; m in
    Carmel MH, Rachel WEST, dt George & Eliza-
    beth, Columbiana Co., O.

1820, 10, 21. John Jr. gct Marlborough MM
1823, 4, 19. John Jr. rocf Marlborough MM,
    dtd 1823,3,22
1825, 2, 19. John rocf Middleton MM, dtd
    1824,11,22
1830, 7, 17. John gct Middleton MM
1831, 11, 19. John Jr. & w, Rachel, & ch, Sam-
    uel W. & Margaret Jane, gct Salem MM

JAMES
----, --, --. Joseph & Ann
    Ch: Benjamin   b 1813, 6, 16
        Miriam   " 1814, 12, 23
        Sarah Ann " 1817, 3, 7
        Eliza Ann " 1817, 3, 7
        Joseph P. " 1819, 1, 25
        Allen   " 1820, 9, 29

    Ch: Isaac H.   b 1822, 8, 29
        William   " 1825, 4, 6
        Samuel   " 1826, 10, 10 d 1827,11,14
        Eli   " 1828, 8, 23
        Levi   " 1832, 1, 9
1824, 4, 21. Jesse, s Isaac & Sarah, Columbi-
    ana Co., O., d 1844,1,16; m in Elkrun MH,
    Elizabeth SMITH, dt Joseph & Joanna, Co-
    lumbiana Co., O.
    Ch: Jonathan   b 1825, 3, 15 d 1833, 3,17
        Joseph
          Smith   " 1827, 6, 11 " 1833, 3,19
        Phebe S.   " 1829, 6, 11
        Susannah   " 1832, 5, 26
        Lewis   " 1834, 8, 28
        Eliza S.   " 1837, 1, 9
        Smith   " 1839, 3, 18
        Mary Katha-
          rine   " 1842, 3, 16
        Aten Parker" 1842, 3, 16 d 1843, 2, 4
        Jesse   " 1844, 9, 7
1827, 4, 11. Sarah d ae 60 (an elder)
1834, 10, 22. Miriam m Nathan SHAW
1848, 9, 20. Phebe S. m Jonathan CROZER

1818, 11, 21. John, s Isaac, & w, Esther, gct
    Newgarden MM
1821, 4, 21. Isaac recommended as a minister
1822, 12, 21. David gct White Water MM, Ind.
1824, 7, 17. David & w, Mary, & dt, Ruthann,
    rocf White Water MM, Ind., dtd 1824,5,15
1825, 4, 16. Jesse & w, Elizabeth, & s, Jona-
    than, gct Sandy Spring MM
1827, 4, 21. David & w, Mary, & ch, Ruthann,
    Mary & Martha, gct Sandy Spring MM
1828, 3, 15. David & w, Mary, & ch, Ruthann
    & Mary, rocf Sandy Spring MM, dtd 1828,1,
    25
1828, 7, 21. Isaac gct Salem MM, to m Leah
    Webb
1828, 11, 15. Leah & ch, Peninah & Lydia Webb,
    rocf Salem MM, dtd 1828,10,23
1830, 3, 20. David & w, Mary, & ch, Ruth
    Ann, Mary & Levi, gct Whitewater MM, Ind.
1831, 4, 16. Peninnah, dt Leah, gct Upper
    Springfield MM
1832, 4, 21. Jesse & w, Elizabeth, & ch,
    Jonathan, Joseph D. & Phebe S., rocf San-
    dy Spring MM
1832, 7, 21. Isaac & w, Leah, gct White
    Water MM, Ind.
1834, 1, 18. Daniel, s Isaac, gct Duck Creek
    MM, Ind.
1834, 6, 16. John & w, Esther, rocf Marl-
    borough MM, dtd 1834,7,1
1835, 4, 18. Isaac P. gct Whitewater MM, Ind.
1838, 11, 17. Rachel W. rocf Upper Spring-
    field MM, dtd 1838,7,28 endorsed by
    Plainfield MM, 1838,10,24
1839, 9, 21. John & w, Esther, gct White-
    water MM, Ind.
1839, 9, 21. Rachel Hollingsworth (form
    James) dis mcd

JAMES, continued
1842, 2, 19. Joseph P. dis disunity
1842, 2, 19. Isaac H., minor, gct Salem MM
1842, 10, 15. Allen gct Clear Creek MM, High-
    land Co., O.
1845, 6, 21. Allen rocf Salem MM, Ia., dtd
    1844,4,20
1846, 5, 16. Joseph & w, Ann, & ch, Eli &
    Levi, gct Goshen MM, Logan Co., O.
1846, 6, 16. William gct Goshen MM, O.
1846, 5, 16. Eliza Ann & Sarah Ann gct Goshen
    MM, O.
1846, 5, 16. Isaac H. dis mcd
1848, 3, 18. Allen gct Goshen MM, O.
1853, 10, 15. Elizabeth & ch, Louis, Eliza A.,
    Smith, Mary Catharine & Jesse, gct Red
    Cedar MM, Ia.
1853, 10, 15. Susanna gct Red Cedar MM, Ia.
1854, 10, 21. Thomas Leech gct Red Cedar MM,
    Ia., to m Elizabeth James

JOHNSON
1838, 11, 17. Martha (form Ashton) dis mou

JOHNS
1830, 10, 21. Sarah m Henry THOMAS (H)
1830, 11, 25. Samuel, s Nathan & Rachel, Co-
    lumbiana Co., O.; m Phebe Ann MARSH, dt
    Jonathan & Phebe, Columbiana Co., O. (H)
1837, 4, 20. Nathan, Columbiana Co., O.; m in
    Carmel MH, Ann PHILLIPS, Columbiana Co.,O.
    (H)

1823, 6, 21. Elizabeth Simpkins (form Johns)
    dis mcd
1823, 8, 16. Mary rocf Deer Creek MM, Md.,
    dtd 1823,1,16
1828, 3, 15. Richard dis mou
1829, 3, 21. Samuel dis jH
1829, 6, 20. John dis jH
1829, 7, 18. Nathan & Rachel dis jH
1829, 10, 17. John dis mou (H)
1829, 10, 17. Sarah dis jH
1830, 3, 20. Richard recrq (H)
1830, 3, 20. Elizabeth & infant dt, Beula
    Ann, recrq (H)
1830, 12, 18. Phebe Ann (form Marsh) dis jH
1832, 7, 21. Cert for Richard & fam granted
    to Plainfield MM; returned 1832,9,15 un-
    used (H)
1835, 3, 21. Nathan Jr. gct Newgarden MM, to
    m Sarah Thomas (H)
1836, 7, 16. Nathan Jr. gct New Garden MM (H)
1837, 8, 19. Nathan Jr. dis mou & jH
1839, 6, 15. Richard T. & w, Betty, & ch,
    Beulah Ann, Samuel, Susannah & Caleb Car-
    rolton, gct Newgarden MM (H)

JONES
1832, 6, 18. Susannah & ch, Aquilla, Yearsley,
    Lydia Ann, Alcinda, Abner & Mary Ann, rocf
    Goose Creek MM, dtd 1832,3,15 (H)
1833, 8, 17. Susannah & ch, Lydia-ann, Alcin-

da, Abner, Mary Ann & Almira, gct Still-
    water MM (H)
1925, 12, 12. Nila Cleona recrq (G)

KAUFFMAN
1922, 3, 11. Nellie recrq (G)
1924, 6, 14. Nellie dropped from mbrp (G)

KENNEDY
1823, 7, 30. Eleanor (form Pellet) dis mou
1825, 1, 15. Mary (form Pellet) dis mou
1923, 4, 14. Bertha recrq (G)

KINSEY
1822, 5, 18. Sarah gct Middleton MM
1823, 11, 15. Sarah rocf Middleton MM, dtd
    1823,10,20

KITSELMAN
1928, 5, 12. Raymond recrq (G)

KRUGER
1842, 9, 17. Christian rocf two months mtg
    of Minden, dtd 1842,9,5, endorsed by
    Middleton MM, 1842,9,15
1844, 7, 20. Sophia recrq
1851, 3, 15. Sophia Field (form Kreugar) dis
    mcd

KUEHNEL
1931, 1, 7. Edward & w, Mary, & dt, Esther,
    rocf Cleveland MM (G)
1932, 10, 5. Edward & w, Mary, & dt, Esther
    Mae, gct Mt. Gilead MM (G)

KUNTZ
1924, 6, 14. Minnie dropped from mbrp (G)

LANE
1922, 8, 12. Lela relrq (G)

LANTZ
1924, 6, 14. Lillian dropped from mbrp (G)

LEECH
----, --, --. William b 1776,8,30 d 1865,1,1;
    m Jane ----- d 1821,6,3
    Ch: Rebecca   b 1801, 6, 4
        Phebe   " 1803, 3, 1
        Margaret   " 1804, 12, 8
        Cornelius " 1807, 2, 9
        Hannah   " 1809, 3, 11
        Sarah   " 1810, 12, 14
        Maria   " 1813, 7, 27
        Thomas   " 1815, 7, 28
        Jane Jr.   " 1821, 3, 1
    William m 2nd Phebe ----- d 1854,9,12
1824, 5, 20. Margaret m Samuel HOLLINGSWORTH
1829, 3, 26. Cornelius, s William & Jane,
    dec, Columbiana Co., O.; m in Carmel MH,
    Sarah L. HAMBLETON, dt Benjamin K. & Ra-
    chel, latter dec, Columbiana Co., O.
    Ch: Hambleton b 1830, 1, 5 d 1830, 9,16

LEECH, Cornelius & Sarah, continued
    Ch: Jane   b 1831, 9, 11
        Phebe Y.   " 1833, 5, 21
        Rachel   " 1834, 10, 16
        Samuel   " 1836, 12, 9
----, --, --. Thomas m Ellen ----- d 1853,4,17
    Ch: John   b 1840, 11, 5
        Deborah
        Jane   " 1842, 10, 20
        Charles   " 1844, 9, 16
        Lewis J.   " 1846, 8, 3
        Ross   " 1848, 8, 24
1844, 1, 24. Jane m Barak ASHTON

1819, 1, 16. Rebecca Sands (form Leech) dis
    mou
1823, 10, 18. Wm. gct Middleton MM, to m Phebe
    Hollingsworth
1824, 2, 21. Phebe & ch, Ann & Mahlon Hol-
    lingsworth, rocf Middleton MM, dtd 1824,1,
    19
1826, 10, 21. Hannah Young (form Leech) dis mou
1831, 3, 19. Sarah Sansherry (form Leech) dis
    mou
1831, 7, 16. Sarah Sansbury (form Leach) dis
    mou
1831, 11, 19. Maria Straight (form Leech) dis
    mou
1840, 1, 18. Thomas gct Sandyspring MM, to
    m Ellan Stratton
1840, 7, 18. Ellon rocf Sandy Spring MM, dtd
    1840,5,22
1852, 6, 19. Phebe Y. dis jas
1854, 10, 21. Thomas gct Red Cedar MM, Ia., to
    m Elizabeth James

LEWIS
1827, 9, 15. Amos gct Middleton MM
1823, 10, 18. Amos rocf York MM, dtd 1817,9,10
    endorsed by Center MM, Pa., 1823,4,19

LEWELLEN
1825, 10, 15. Rhoda (form Tullis) dis mou

LOCKWOOD
1924, 6, 14. Mary dropped from mbrp (G)
1926, 8, 14. Otis & Hazel gct Goshen MM (G)
1928, 4, 14. Hildred recrq (G)
1932, 11, 10. Herman gct Goshen MM (G)

LODGE
1825, 7, 18. Tirzah (form Hole) dis mou

LONGSHORE
1834, 12, 20. Ann (form McMillen) dis mou
1835, 3, 21. Ann (form McMillan) con mcd (H)
1843, 4, 15. Ann dis (H)
1850, 6, 15. Mary (form Raley) dis mcd

LUMM
1818, 4, 18. Jane (form Tullis) dis mcd

McARTHUR
1833, 4, 20. Milton dis jH

McARTOR
1829, 4, 23. Olivia W. m Jacob VALE (H)

1839, 1, 19. Achilles dis disunity
1839, 3, 16. Mary Ann (form Harrison) dis mou

McBRIDE
1846, 10, 17. Elizabeth & ch, Elihu, Grace,
    Benjamin, Lydia, Rachel & Abisha, gct
    Middleton MM
1844, 8, 17. Elizabeth & ch, Elihu, Grace,
    James, Benjamin, Lydia, Rachel & Abisha,
    rocf Sandy Spring MM, dtd 1844,4,26

McCALL
1834, 5, 17. Lydia (form Elliott) dis mcd

McCARTER
1824, 10, 10. Atchalus, s Mary, recrq
1827, 4, 21. Chalkley T. dis mcd
1827, 7, 21. Collin B. dis disunity
1827, 4, 21. Susannah (form Smith) dis mou
1829, 1, 17. Mary, Olivia & Stella dis jH

McCASKY
1844, 3, 16. Mary (form Randles) dis mou

McCLURE
----, --, --. Seth C. & Mary
    Ch: Joseph   b 1813, 4, 8
        Samuel   " 1815, 2, 19
        Louisa   " 1816, 12, 2
        Abel   " 1819, 11, 12
        Sina Ann   " 1821, 9, 12
        Lydia
        Seth
        Endley

1822, 7, 17. Joseph, Samuel, Louisa, Abel &
    Sinai Ann, minor ch Mary, recrq through
    Elkrun PM
1831, 1, 15. Lydia, Seth & Endly, ch Mary,
    recrq
1834, 10, 18. Samuel dis disunity
1836, 12, 17. Myra, minor dt Mary, recrq
1837, 8, 19. Mary & ch, Abel T., Sina Ann,
    Lydia, Seth Jr., Endley & Myra S., gct
    Middleton MM
1837, 8 19. Louisa gct Middleton MM
1837, 8, 19. Joseph gct Middleton MM

McCONNEL
----, --, --. Edward & Lydia [McConnell]
    Ch: Townsend b 1813, 4, 15
        Talbott   " 1815, 7, 4
        Orpha   " 1818, 2, 20
        James   " 1820, 8, 16
        Adaline   " 1823, 5, 15
        Nathan   " 1825, 12, 7
        Amos   " 1828, 1, 29

McCONNEL, continued

1844, 4, 24. James, s Edward & Lydia, Columbiana Co., O.; m in Elkrun MH, Mary ARMSTRONG
dt Samuel & Ann, dec, Columbiana Co., O.

1817, 12, 20. Daniel dis mou   [QM]
1826, 3, 18. Rachel Sr. dis disunity (rst by
1826, 7, 15. Sarah [McConnell] dis disunity;
rst by QM 1827,2,17
1828, 5, 17. Edward & w, Lydia, & ch, Townsend, Talbot, Orpha, James, Adaline, Nathan & Amos, gct Middleton MM
1829, 3, 21. Rachel [McConnell], w Jesse,
& ch, Eliza Ann, Mary, Harriett, Rachel,
Susan Jane, Nelson & Melissa, rocf Middleton MM, dtd 1829,3,12
1829, 9, 19. Ann, Sarah & Mary dis JH
1830, 8, 21. Rachel Jr. & Eliza Ann dis JH
1835, 11, 9. Mary Williamson (form McConnel)
dis mou
1836, 7, 16. Harriet Stooksberry (form McConnel) dis mcd
1840, 6, 20. Nelson dis jas
1841, 4, 17. Rachel Jr. & Sarah Jane dis jas
1843, 6, 17. Ann & Sarah dis jas (H)
1844, 6, 15. Mary Crocket (form McConnel)
dis mou & jas (H)
1844, 8, 17. Mary [McConnell] gct Chesterfield MM

McMILLEN

1824, 7, 17. Jane Crawford (form McMillen)
dis mcd
1829, 1, 17. Thomas, Maria & Jane dis JH
1829, 5, 16. Taylor dis jH
1834, 7, 19. Taylor [McMillin] con mcd (H)
1834, 12, 20. Ann Longshore (form McMillen)
dis mou
1835, 3, 21. Maria Bell (form McMillan) con
mou (H)
1837, 5, 20. Joseph H. dis jH
1839, 1, 19. Enos [McMillin] & w, Sarah W., &
ch, Uriah, Eliza Ann, John W. & Sarah Jane,
rocf Warrington MM, dtd 1838,10,17 (H)
1841, 8, 21. Eliza dis jH
1844, 4, 20. Joseph [McMillin] dis mou & jas
(H)

MARSH

1829, 1, 28. James, s Jonathan & Phebe, dec,
Columbiana Co., O.; m in Elkrun MH, Lydia
COPE, dt Israel & Elizabeth, Columbiana
Co., O.
    Ch: Eliza   b 1830, 2, 18
        Mary   " 1832, 2, 18
1830, 11, 25. Phebe Ann m Samuel JOHNS (H)
1831, 12, 22. Zillah m Isaac UNDERWOOD (H)
1833, 8, 22. Mary Ann m Eli R. GRIFFITH (H)
1840, 12, 24. Hannah H. m Jonathan N. HEACOCK
(H)
1841, 6, 24. John, s James & Edith, Columbiana Co., O.; m in Carmel MH, Emily Jane
ARMSTRONG, dt Bennet & Elizabeth, Columbi-

ana Co., O. (H)
1853, 3, 23. Eliza C. m Wm. B. STANLEY

1820, 8, 19. Jonathan gct Middleton MM, to m
Ann Wickersham
1821, 5, 19. Jonathan dis
1821, 7, 21. Phebe-ann & Sarah, minors, gct
Sandy Spring MM
1821, 11, 21. Thomas Heald prcf Middleton MM,
to m Miriam Marsh
1821, 12, 15. Miriam rmt Thomas Heald
1822, 1, 28. James & Ruth, minor ch Jonathan,
gct Newgarden MM
1825, 4, 16. Phebe Ann & Sarah, minors, rocf
Sandy Spring MM, dtd 1824,12,24
1829, 1, 17. James Jr. rocf Middleton MM, dtd
1829,1,8
1829, 1, 17. Amos, Edith, Zillah & Mary Ann
dis jH
1829, 2, 21. James dis jH
1829, 2, 21. Ruth rocf Middleton MM, dtd
1829,2,12
1829, 3, 21. Hannah dis jH
1830, 12, 18. Phebe Ann Johns (form Marsh)
dis jH
1831, 6, 18. Milton dis jH
1831, 8, 21. Sarah & Ruth dis jH
1832, 5, 19. James Jr. & w, Lydia, & ch,
Eliza & Mary, gct Sandy Spring MM
1833, 12, 21. Milton gct Westland MM, to m
Elizabeth Griffith (H)
1834, 4, 19. Eliza G. rocf Westland MM, dtd
1834,3,27 (H)
1834, 7, 19. Sarah Taylor (form Marsh) con
mcd (H)
1835, 11, 21. Ruth Thomas (form Marsh) dis mcd
(H)
1836, 1, 16. Eliza & Mary, ch James & Lydia,
rocf Sandy Spring MM, dtd 1835,11,27
1836, 7, 16. John dis jH
1837, 5, 20. Milton & w, Eliza, gct Westland
MM (H)
1839, 10, 19. Amos gct Short Creek MM, O.,
to m Rebecca Thomlinson (H)
1840, 2, 15. Rebecca T. rocf Short Creek MM,
O. (H)
1842, 1, 15. Elizabeth recrq (H)
1842, 5, 21. Emily Jane (form Armstrong) dis
mou
1844, 7, 20. Mary, gr dt Elizabeth Cope, gct
Middleton MM
1846, 11, 21. Mary, gr dt Elizabeth Cope, rocf
Middleton MM, dtd 1846,11,12
1850, 7, 20. Mary H. gct Middleton MM

MARSHALL

1847, 9, 23. Caleb, s John & Ann Mercy, dec,
Washington Co., O.; m in Carmel MH, Elmira HEALD, dt Joseph & Ury B., Columbiana Co., O.

1847, 11, 20. Elmyra [Marshal] gct Chesterfield MM, Athens Co., O.

MARTIN
----, --, --. Joseph R. m Sarah ----- d 1839,
    12,--
        Ch: Rebecca   b 1819, 12, 21
            John A.   " 1821, 10, 22
            Thomas   " 1824, 1, 21

1822, 7, 20. Sarah & ch, Rebecca & John Alex-
    ander, recrq
1822, 7, 17. Joseph R. rocf Chester MM, Pa.,
    dtd 1822,1,29
1829, 6, 20. Joseph R. dis jH
1830, 5, 15. Sarah dis jH
1831, 3, 19. Rebecca, John, Thomas & James,
    ch Joseph R., gct Middleton MM
1840, 2, 15. John Thomas & James, ch Joseph
    R. rocf Middleton MM, dtd 1839,8,8
1840, 2, 15. Rebecca rocf Middleton MM, dtd
    1839,8,8
1841, 1, 16. John, Thomas & James, ch Joseph
    R., gct Middleton MM
1841, 1, 16. Rebecca, dt Joseph R., gct
    Middleton MM

MEAD
1839, 4, 27. Rachel (form Pellett) con mcd (H)

MERCER
1824, 5, 15. Charity dis jas
1824, 8, 21. William dis jas
1825, 6, 18. Mary Ann dis jas
1825, 11, 19. William Jr. dis mou
1825, 11, 19. George dis mou
1828, 12, 20. Beulah dis jas
1829, 2, 21. John dis jas
1829, 4, 16. Daniel dis jas
1832, 10, 20. Charity Jr. dis jas
1834, 10, 18. Abraham, minor s Wm. & Charity,
    gct Allum Creek MM, O.; rem with parents
    into Wood Co., O.
1834, 10, 18. Lucretia dis disunity
1834, 10, 18. Caleb dis disunity

MILLER
1824, 8, 26. Robert, s Levi & Deborah, Colum-
    biana Co., O.; m in Carmel MH, Catharine
    HOLE, dt David & Anne, Columbiana Co., O.

1819, 6, 19. Levi prcf Newgarden MM, to m
    Ann Hole
1819, 7, 17. Levi rmt Ann Hole
1819, 9, 18. Ann gct Newgarden MM
1824, 11, 20. Catharine gct Sandy Spring MM
1927, 6, 11. Mary Elizabeth recrq (G)

MONTGOMERY
1853, 7, 16. Mildred (form Harrison) dis mcd

MOORE
1841, 7, 17. Mary (form Heacock) con mcd (H)

MORLAN
----, --, --. Jason & Mary

Ch: Mary   b 1800, 9, 25 d 1833, 5,14
    Charles   " 1803, 2, 24 " 1852,12,30
    Ann   " 1805, 1, 10
    Martha B.   " 1807, 11, 1
    William H. " 1814, 10, 25
----, --, --. Aden d 1857,5,28; m Amy -----
    d 1817,5,11
    Ch: Lydia   b 1809, 12, 28
        Sarah   " 1811, 11, 9
        Mary   " 1813, 10, 15
        Achsah   " 1816, 1, 7
        John   " 1817, 5, 11
    Aden m 2nd Rebecca ----- d 1862,12,9
    Ch: Stephen R. b 1824, 2, 12
        Amy Jane   " 1825, 12, 11
        Phebe   " 1828, 5, 30
        Armella   " 1830, 2, 9 d 1838,11, 8
1827, 10, 25. Charles, s Jason & Mary, Colum-
    biana Co., O., d 1852,12,30; m in Carmel
    MH, Frances BORAM, dt Aaron & Elizabeth,
    Columbiana Co., O.
    Ch: Rezin   b 1829, 6, 16
        Anjelina   " 1831, 11, 28
        Louisa   " 1833, 12, 21
        Amanda   " 1836, 3, 14
        Elizabeth
        Ann   " 1838, 6, 10
        Mary   " 1841, 2, 15
        Lemuel   " 1843, 10, 25
        Martha   " 1846, 6, 9
        James Hervy " 1849, 10, 7
----, --, --. Theopholus b 1826,6,26; m Lydia
    FRENCH b 1827,12,2 d 1859,4,26
    Ch: Mary M.   b 1857, 8, 14
    Theopholus m 3rd Sarah P. HOLLOWAY b 1830,
    8,23
    Ch: David H.   b 1862, 4, 8
        Anna   " 1865, 2, 21

1819, 12, 18. Mordecai gct New Garden MM
1821, 12, 15. Aden gct Middleton MM, to m
    Rebecca Heald
1822, 3, 16. Rebecca rocf Middleton MM, dtd
    1822,2,18
1824, 9, 18. Stephen recrq
1825, 7, 11. Elizabeth, w Stephen, recrq
1829, 3, 21. Emily & ch, Ann, Deborah, James,
    Elizabeth, Phebe, Nathan & Jonah, gct San-
    dy Spring MM
1829, 3, 21. Cert for Ruth granted to Sandy
    Spring MM not accepted
1829, 11, 21. Ruth & Ann dis disunity
1829, 11, 21. John dis mou
1830, 12, 18. Stephen [Morelan] dis disunity
1833, 2, 4. Elizabeth, w Stephen, & ch, Re-
    becca, DeLorma & Elizabeth Amanda, gct
    Marlborough MM
1833, 8, 17. Lydia & Sarah gct Salem MM
1834, 1, 18. Martha Addis (form Morlan) dis
    mou
1836, 9, 17. Mary (form Morlan) dis mou
1836, 9, 17. Mary Morlan (form Morlan) dis
    mou

MORLAN, continued

1838, 11, 17. William H. dis mcd
1839, 10, 19. Jason & w, Mary, gct Chester-
     field MM, O.
1839, 10, 19. Ann gct Chesterfield MM, O.
1842, 1, 15. Achsah Reeder (form Morlan) con
     mou
1847, 10, 16. Stephen R. dis mcd
1852, 7, 17. Phebe dis
1852, 10, 16. Angeline Woolem (form Morlan)
     dis mcd
1853, 6, 18. Louisa Grosscup (form Morlan)
     dis mou
1853, 8, 20. Elizabeth Ann Clark (form Mor-
     lan) dis mou

MORRIS

----, --, --. Isaiah & Mary
     Ch: Joseph   b 1804, 11, 3
         Lydia   " 1808, 6, 22
         John   " 1809, 12, 29
         David   " 1812, 4, 5
         Rachel   " 1813, 4, 14
         Sarah   " 1814, 12, 10
         Miriam   " 1816, 5, 17 d 1839, 7, 8
         Nancy Ann   " 1817, 11, 14
         Robert
          Barkley   " 1819, 6, 26 d 1882, 8, --
         Isaiah
          Pierce   " 1819, 6, 26
         Phebe
         Elizabeth
         Martha   d 1843,10,21
         Amasa
         Ruth   " 1838,10,--
1847, 10, 20. Joshua Jr., s Joshua & Rachel,
     dec, Washington Co., O.; m in Elkrun MH,
     Eliza Ann TULLOSS, dt Jason & Hannah, Co-
     lumbiana Co., O.

1829, 4, 18. Isiah & Joseph dis jH
1829, 5, 16. Lydia dis jH
1831, 6, 18. John dis mou
1831, 6, 18. Jonathan rocf Westland MM (H)
1831, 10, 15. Rachel & Mary dis jH
1832, 2, 18. David dis jH
1835, 6, 20. Sarah dis jH
1836, 5, 21. Nancy Ann Hepburn (form Morris)
     dis mou with cousin
1842, 5, 21. Emeline (form Hambleton) dis mou
     & jH
1842, 8, 20. Phebe Ward (form Morris) dis
     mou
1842, 12, 17. Emeline (form Hambleton) con
     mou (H)
1844, 8, 17. Elizabeth Pike (form Morris)
     dis mou
1844, 12, 21. Robert con mcd
1845, 1, 18. Sarah dis jas (H)
1848, 1, 15. Eliza Ann gct Chesterfield MM

MOSHER

1925, 10, 10. Robert rocf Gilead MM (G)

1925, 10, 10. Elsie Roane, w Robert, rocf
     Alliance MM (G)
1928, 8, 11. Robert, Elsie & Claude Nathan,
     gct Adrian City MM, Mich. (G)

MYERS

1922, 3, 11. Leona recrq (G)
1924, 12, 13. Lena dropped from mbrp (G)

NEILL

----, --, --. William [Neil] d 1842,9,30; m
     Susanna ----- d 1839,7,30
     Ch: Margaret   b 1801, 9, 3
         Samuel   " 1803, 4, 22
         John   " 1805, 1, 26
         William   " 1806, 12, 4
         Mary   " 1809, 3, 22
         Morton   " 1811, 9, 4
         Hannah   " 1814, 2, 17
         Joseph   " 1816, 8, 2
         Sara   " 1818, 11, 17
1824, 9, 22. Samuel, s Wm. & Susannah, Colum-
     biana Co., O.; m in Elkrun MH, Mary COPE,
     dt Israel & Elizabeth, Columbiana Co., O.
     Ch: Malissa
         Ann   b 1825, 9, 14
         Rebecca   " 1828, 10, 21
         Willits
         Allison   " 1830, 9, 2
         Elizabeth   " 1832, 8, 8
         Samuel Mor-
          ton   " 1834, 9, 13
         James Cope   " 1836, 9, 3
         Eliza   " 1838, 8, 1
         Mary Ann   " 1840, 4, 8
         Margaret
         Susan   " 1842, 5, 29
         John Had-
          ley   " 1844, 5, 13
1837, 12, 21. Morton, s Wm. & Susannah, Colum-
     biana Co., O.; m in Carmel MH, Ann COPE,
     dt Israel & Elizabeth, ColumbianaCo., O.,
     d 1884,12,29
     Ch: Guli Elma   b 1839, 7, 9
         Edith C.   " 1844, 11, 13 d 1871, 3, 1
1849, 10, 24. Rebecca m Allen HEALD

1818, 6, 20. John [Neil] & s, John, rocf
     Dunning Creek MM, dtd 1818,3,11
1818, 6, 20. Wm. [Neil] & w, Susannah, & ch,
     Margaret, Samuel, John, William, Mary,
     Morton, Hannah & Joseph, rocf Dunning
     Creek MM, dtd 1818,3,11
1818, 7, 18. Ruth rocf Dunnings Creek MM,
     dtd 1818,3,11
1819, 4, 17. John [Neil] & s, John, gct New-
     garden MM
1819, 4, 17. Ruth [Neil] gct Newgarden MM
1821, 11, 17. Samuel [Neil], minor, gct New-
     garden MM
1822, 7, 20. Margaret Bowman (form Neill) dis
     mou
1824, 9, 18. Samuel [Neil] rocf Newgarden

NEILL, continued
    MM, dtd 1824,8,26
1830, 4, 26. John Jr. dis disunity
1832, 2, 18. Mary Bracken (form Neill) dis mou
1832, 5, 19. Hannah Fagan (form Neill) dis
    mou
1837, 9, 16. Sarah Ashford (form Neill) dis
    mou
1840, 5, 16. John & w, Mary, & ch, Eliza,
    Mary, Ann, William, Margaret, Ruth Ann &
    Martha, rocf Newgarden MM, dtd 1840,4,23
1842, 5, 21. Justine Ann gct Sandyspring MM
1844, 11, 16. Eliza Ellis (form Neill) dis
    mou
1845, 4, 19. Joseph gct Sandy Spring MM, to
    m Mary J. Chambers
1845, 6, 21. Morton & fam gct Salem MM
1845, 10, 18. Joseph gct Sandy Spring MM
1845, 12, 20. Mary Ann dis
1845, 12, 20. Malissa Ann Richardson (form
    Neill) dis mcd
1848, 10, 21. Mortan & w, Ann, & ch, Gulielma
    & Eadith. rocf Salem MM, dtd 1848,9,20
1852, 4, 17. Mary dis disunity
1852, 9, 18. Samuel dis disunity
1852, 9, 18. Elizabeth Richards (form Neill)
    con mou
1853, 2, 19. Minor ch of Samuel gct Drift-
    wood MM, Ind.
1853, 2, 19. Willets A. gct Driftwood MM, Ind.
1854, 4, 15. William dis mou

NEELY
1927, 1, 8. Florence Christine & Mabel
    Easter recrq (G)

NICHOLS
1924, 6, 14. Edward & Willis dropped from
    mbrp (G)

OGDEN
1819, 3, 20. Stephen & w, Hannah, & s, Ben-
    jamin Bartram, gct Newgarden MM

OLIPHANT
1820, 1, 15. Ephraim & w, Elizabeth, & ch,
    Sarah H. & Abner, gct Middleton MM
1853, 3, 19. Joseph Armstrong gct Middleton
    MM, to m Sarah Oliphant

PACKER
1821, 1, 20. George gct Newgarden MM
1823, 11, 15. George rocf New Garden MM, dtd
    1823,10,23
1834, 7, 19. Cassandra (form Boram) con mou
    (H)

PEARSON
1833, 2, 4. Sarah (form Heacock) dis jH
1834, 1, 18. Sarah (form Heacock) con mou (H)
1834, 5, 17. Susannah, dt Sarah, recrq (H)
1839, 2, 16. Elizabeth (form Heacock) con
    mou (H)

1843, 6, 17. Sarah Ann & Almira, ch Sarah,
    recrq (H)

PEASLEY
1834, 10, 23. Chalkley, s Joseph & Amy, Marion
    Co., O.; m in Carmel MH, Margaret ASHTON,
    dt Thomas & Martha, Columbiana Co., O.

1834, 12, 20. Margaret gct Allum Creek MM, O.

PELLETT
----, --, --. Francis & Mary [Pellet]
    Ch: Eleanor   b 1800, 12, 4
        Abel John " 1803, 2, 20
        Mary   " 1804, 6, 14
        Elizabeth " 1805, 12, 2
        Ann   " 1808, 8, 19
        Joseph   " 1810, 3, 2
        Vincent   " 1811, 11, 7 d 1822, 8,22
        Rachel   " 1813, 10, 29
        Matilda   " 1815, 7, 27
        Lorenzo   " 1818, 11, 12
1831, 4, 21. Elizabeth m Edward HORN (H)

1823, 7, 30. Eleanor Kennedy (form Pellet)
    dis mou
1824, 4, 17. Elizabeth & Mary [Pellet], min-
    ors, rocf Sandy Spring MM, dtd 1824,3,26
1825, 1, 15. Mary Kennedy (form Pellett) dis
    mou
1825, 10, 15. Abel J. gct Short Creek MM, O.,
    to m Unity Harrison
1826, 5, 20. Francis dis disunity
1829, 2, 21. Francis recrq (H)
1830, 12, 18. Unity & ch, George, Sarah,
    Elisha & Salathiel, gct Marlborough MM
1831, 4, 16. Joseph gct Marlborough MM, to m
    Sarah Holloway (H)
1831, 9, 17. Sarah rocf Marlborough MM, dtd
    1831,7,23
1833, 11, 16. Sarah Henry (form Pellett) dis
    mou
1833, 12, 21. Rachel dis jas
1834, 1, 18. Matilda dis jH
1835, 8, 15. Joseph & fam gct New Garden MM
    (H)
1835, 8, 15. Sarah & dt, Mary, gct New Garden
    MM (H)
1839, 4, 27. Rachel Mead (form Pellett) con
    mcd (H)
1839, 7, 20. Lorenzo dis jH
1841, 2, 20. Unity & ch, George, Sarah,
    Elisha, Salathiel, Seth, Mary - Ellen &
    Harrison, rocf Marlborough MM, dtd 1840,
    2,25
1844, 1, 20. Anne (form Randles) dis mou
1844, 4, 20. Lorenzo [Pellette] rpd mcd;
    dropped from mbrp; moved away (H)
1844, 7, 20. Unity & ch, George, Sarah,
    Elisha, Salathiel, Mary -Eleanor, Seth,
    Harrison & Allen, gct Alum Creek MM
1846, 3, 21. Francis [Pellette] & w, Mary,
    & dt, Matilda, gct Honey Creek MM, Ind.(H)

PETTIT
1828, 5, 21. Beulah Ann [Petitt] m Elon HOLE

1826, 3, 18. Mary, an orphan, gct Middleton
    MM
1828, 4, 19. Beulah Ann rocf Salem MM, dtd
    1828,3,19
1828, 8, 16. Francis [Pettett] dis
1828, 11, 15. Elizabeth [Pettitt] dis jas
1828, 12, 20. Unity [Pettitt] rocf Short Creek
    MM, O., dtd 1828,9,18
1828, 12, 20. Abel J., Joseph, Mary & Ann dis
    jH
1829, 3, 21. Elizabeth dis jH
1831, 12, 17. Mary, minor, gct Sandy Spring MM
1837, 1, 21. Mary Jr. rocf Sandy Spring MM,
    dtd 1826,10,21
1838, 5, 19. Mary Simpkins (form Pettit) dis
    mou

PHILLIPS
1837, 4, 20. Ann m Nathan JOHNS (H)

1828, 3, 15. Elizabeth rocf Warrington MM,
    Pa., dtd 1827,12,19
1830, 4, 26. Elizabeth dis disunity
1837, 2, 18. Ann recrq (H)
1843, 11, 18. Jane, Deborah & Rebecca, ch
    Ann Johns, recrq (H)

PIDGEON
1830, 1, 16. Cert for William from Salem MM,
    not accepted for disunity

PIKE
1844, 8, 17. Elizabeth (form Morris) dis mou

POOL
1824, 9, 2. Jonas, s Israel & Jane, Beaver
    Co., Pa.; m in Carmel MH, Ann TULLOSS,
    dt Richard & Ann, Columbiana Co., O., d
    1864,3,18 (Jonas d 1881,3,5)
    Ch: Asenath   b 1825, 6, 5
        Priscilla " 1827, 2, 15
        Sarah Jane " 1839, 7, 16

1819, 10, 16. Jane & ch, Phineas, Jonas, Sarah
    & Albinah, rocf Goose Creek MM, Va., dtd
    1819,4,18
1819, 10, 16. Lydia rocf Goose Creek MM, Va.,
    dtd 1819,4,18
1824, 11, 20. Phineas dis mou
1826, 6, 17. Jonas & w, Ann, & dt, Ascenath,
    gct Newgarden MM
1828, 11, 15. Jonas & w, Ann, & ch, Asenath &
    Priscilla, rocf Newgarden MM, dtd 1828,7,
    24
1831, 3, 19. Jane, Lydia & Sarah gct Upper
    Springfield MM
1834, 2, 15. Jonas & w, Ann, & ch, Asenath &
    Priscilla, gct Upper Springfield MM
1838, 7, 21. Jonas & w, Ann, & ch, Asceneth
    & Priscilla, rocf Salem MM, dtd 1838,6,20

1844, 3, 16. Cert for Asenath H. granted to
    Upper Springfield MM, returned unused
    1844,4,20
1845, 6, 21. Jonas & w, Ann, & dt, Sarah
    Jane, gct Middleton MM
1845, 6, 21. Asenath H. & Priscilla H. gct
    Middleton MM

PYLE
1846, 11, 26. Esther M. m Joseph HOLE (H)

1827, 6, 16. Benjamin & w, Elizabeth, & ch,
    Aaron, Hannah, Mary, Henry, Elwood, Es-
    ther & Elizabeth S., rocf Chester MM, Pa.,
    dtd 1827,4,30
1829, 3, 21. Elizabeth dis jH
1833, 9, 21. Aaron dis jH
1833, 11, 16. Hannah dis jH
1836, 9, 18. Hannah Richie (form Pyle) con
    mou (H)
1839, 7, 20. Henry dis jH
1847, 3, 20. Ellwood dis mcd
1847, 4, 17. Louisa (form Vale) dis mcd
1847, 5, 15. Esther Hole (form Pyle) dis mcd
1847, 8, 21. Aaron con mou (H)
1847, 12, 18. Elwood con mou (H)
1848, 12, 16. Elizabeth Cleaver (form Pyle)
    dis mcd & jH
1850, 6, 15. Elizabeth Clover (form Pyle) dis
    mcd & jH

RALEY
1832, 11, 17. Thomas [Raily] & w, Ann, & ch,
    Mary, Phebe, Jehu Dexon & Kersey, rocf
    Westland MM, dtd 1832,9,27 (H)
1837, 11, 18. Mary, Rhoda, Jehu & John, ch
    Thomas, rocf Westland MM
1847, 6, 19. Jehu D. gct Salem MM, to m
    Esther HUNT (H)
1848, 3, 18. Jehu dis mcd
1850, 6, 15. Mary Longshore (form Raley) dis
    mcd
1854, 6, 17. Phebe Jackson (form Raley) dis
    mcd

RANDLES
----, --, --. William d 1838,4,3; m Esther

    Ch: Anna   b 1816, 8, 23
        Elizabeth " 1819, 4, 12
        William   " 1821, 7, 19
        Mary   " 1824, 1, 16
        John   " 1828, 3, 28
        Isaac   " 1833, 8, 22

1838, 6, 16. Elizabeth Akin (form Randles)
    dis mou
1844, 1, 20. Anne Pellett (form Randles)
    dis mou
1844, 3, 16. Mary McCasky (form Randles) dis
    mou
1851, 2, 15. William [Randels] dis mcd

RANDOLPH
1822, 8, 17. Edwin F. rocf Middleton MM, dtd
     1822,6,17
1826, 4, 15. Edward Fitts gct Upperspring-
     field MM

RAWLINGS
1826, 4, 15. Joseph Fisher gct Salem MM, to
     m Margaret Rawlings
1831, 5, 21. Asahel Exchange & Thomas, s Mar-
     garet Fisher, gct Salem MM

REED
1842, 4, 16. Joseph, George & Samuel, ch
     Charles, rocf Baltimore MM for Eastern &
     Western Dist., dtd 1842,3,10
1842, 6, 18. George [Reid] gct Westland MM,
     Washington Co., Pa.
1850, 6, 15. Samuel [Read] dis mcd

REEDER
1842, 1, 15. Achsah (form Morlan) con mou
1844, 12, 21. Achsah gct Middleton MM

REEVE
1835, 5, 20. Joshua, s Joshua & Melescent,
     form dec, Columbiana Co., O.; m in Elkrun
     MH, Elizabeth HUESTIS, dt Aaron & Esther,
     Columbiana Co., O.

1830, 6, 19. Benjamin [Reeves] & w, Ann, rocf
     Middleton MM, dtd 1830,5,11 (H)
1835, 12, 19. Elizabeth gct Pennsville MM,
     Morgan Co., O.

RICE
1931, 11, 4. Mary Elizabeth relrq (G)

RICHARDS
1820, 5, 25. Mary m Caleb FOWLER
1821, --, --. Samuel d 1867,2,27; m Rachel
     WALKER, d 1876,10,24
     Ch: Merrium   b 1822, 2, 20
         Elizabeth " 1824, 1, 22
         Esther   " 1826, 10, 14
         Joseph   " 1828, 8, 11 d 1850, 2,16
1855, 5, 22. Esther d

1821, 6, 16. Samuel rmt Rachel Walker
1823, 8, 16. Rowland dis jas
1823, 10, 18. Eli dis jas
1826, 6, 17. Tace (form Walker) dis mou
1828, 4, 19. Phebe (form Harrison) dis mou
1831, 2, 19. Abijah dis disunity
1841, 2, 20. Mary, minor, gr dt Latham & Mary
     Harrison, recrq
1851, 5, 17. Esther Jr. dis jas
1852, 9, 18. Elizabeth (form Neill) con mou
1853, 2, 19. Elizabeth D. gct Driftwood MM,
     Ind.
1853, 7, 16. Mary Welker (form Richards) dis
     mcd
1838, 3, 17. Martha (form Vale) dis mou

1842, 9, 17. Hannah rocf Westland MM, dtd
     1842,6,23 (H)
1845, 12, 20. Malissa Ann (form Neill) dis
     mcd

RICHIE
1836, 9, 18. Hannah (form Pyle) con mou (H)

RIDGWAY
1926, 1, 9. Silas recrq (G)

RIGG
1836, 7, 16. Hiram rocf Short Creek MM, O.,
     dtd 1836,7,21 (H)
1836, 7, 16. Sarah & ch, Jesse, Mary Ann &
     David M. L., rocf Short Creek MM, O., dtd
     1835,10,22 (H)
1836, 10, 15. Hiram & w, Sarah, & ch, Jesse,
     Mary Ann & David, gct Middleton MM (H)

RUSSELL
1922, 3, 11. Dolph & Myrtle recrq (G)
1927, 6, 11. Lela & Bertha Agnes recrq (G)

SAMMS
1823, 7, 30. John Jr. rocf Middleton MM, dtd
     1823,4,21
1825, 6, 18. John Jr. gct Middleton MM

SANDS
1819, 1, 16. Rebecca (form Leech) dis mou

SANSHERRY
1831, 3, 19. Sarah (form Leech) dis mou
1831, 7, 16. Sarah [Sansbury] (form Leech)
     dis mou

SCOTT
1819, 7, 22. Sarah m John COWGILL
1820, 2, 23. William, s Benjamin & Sarah, Co-
     lumbiana Co., O.; m in Elkrun MH, Abigail
     COWGILL, dt James & Charlotte, Columbiana
     Co., O.
1820, 2, 24. Benjamin Jr., s Benjamin & Sa-
     rah, Columbiana Co., O.; m in Carmel MH,
     Ann BROWN, dt Jeremiah & Phebe, Columbi-
     ana Co., O.

1819, 2, 20. Jane rocf New Garden MM, dtd
     1819,1,21
1819, 7, 17. Ann dis
1819, 8, 21. Sarah Jr. rmt John Cowgill
1820, 3, 18. Wm. rmt Abigail Cowgill
1820, 6, 17. Benjamin dis disunity
1820, 8, 19. Benj. appealed to QM for rights
     of mbrp; QM reversed the decision
1823, 7, 30. Wm. & w, Abigail, & ch, Hiram &
     Margaret, gct Salem MM
1823, 7, 30. Joseph dis disunity
1826, 4, 15. Benjamin Jr. & w, Ann, & ch,
     Mary Ann, Pheobe, Prophet B. & Sarah, gct
     Salem MM
1824, 10, 10. Jacob dis mou

SCOTT, continued
1826, 4, 15. Benjamin Jr. & w, Ann, & ch,
     Maryann, Phebe, Prophet B. & Sarah, gct
     Salem MM
1826, 10, 21. Benjamin dis disunity
1840, 6, 20. Frances Barton (form Scott) dis
     mcd
1840, 3, 20. Isaac dis mcd

SHARPLESS
1826, 11, 18. Samuel rocf Providence MM, dtd
     1826,7,26
1832, 5, 19. Samuel gct Providence MM, Fay-
     ette Co., Pa.
1832, 12, 15. Samuel re-issued gct Providence
     MM, Fayette Co., Pa.; original cert lost

SHAW
1834, 10, 22. Nathan, s Thomas & Rachel, dec,
     Columbiana Co., O.; m in Elkrun MH, Miriam
     JAMES, dt Joseph & Ann, Columbiana Co., O.
     Ch: Joseph
          Lindley b 1836, 2, 7 d 1840, 3,14
          Rachel H. " 1837, 6, 24
          Sarah Ann " 1839, 1, 23
1838, 8, 23. Samuel, s Thos. & Rachel, dec,
     Columbiana Co., O.; m in Carmel MH, Penina
     HEALD, dt Joseph & Ury B., Columbiana Co.,
     O.

1834, 12, 20. Mariam gct Upperspringfield MM
1837, 6, 17. Nathan & w, Miriam, & s, Joseph
     Lindley, rocf Upper Springfield MM, dtd
     1837,5,27
1838, 12, 15. Penia gct Middleton MM
1840, 1, 18. Nathan & Miriam, & ch, Joseph L.,
     Rachel H. & Sarah, gct Middleton MM
1838, 12, 15. Penina gct Middleton MM
1840, 1, 18. Nathan & w, Mirium, & ch, Jo-
     seph L., Rachel & Sarah Ann, gct Middle-
     ton MM
1840, 1, 18. Jonathan & fam gct Middleton MM

SIDDALL
1819, 8, 21. Atticus & w, Sarah, & s, David,
     gct White Water MM, Ind.
1822, 10, 19. Hannah dis jas
1829, 12, 19. Sarah dis jH
1830, 1, 16. Aden & John dis jH
1831, 6, 18. Mary Harrison (form Siddall) dis
     mou
1833, 5, 18. Sarah Harrison (form Siddell) dis
     mou
1836, 11, 19. Ann dis disunity

SIMPKINS
1823, 6, 21. Elizabeth (form Johns) dis mcd
1838, 5, 19. Mary (form Pettit) dis mou

SMITH
----, --, --. Joseph & Joana
     Ch: Sarah   b 1804, 8, 28
         Elizabeth   " 1806, 11, 11

     Ch: Susanna   b 1808, 12, 10
         Phebe   " 1810, 12, 25
         John   " 1812, 10, 7
         Edmund   " 1814, 11, 4
         Thomas   " 1816, 10, 21
         Henry
1824, 4, 21. Elizabeth m Jesse JAMES
1827, 2, 21. Joanna m Joseph DUTTON

1818, 6, 20. Joana & ch, Sarah, Elizabeth,
     Susanna, Phebe, John, Edmund & Thomas,
     recrq
1822, 11, 16. Henry & Martha, minor ch Joanna,
     recrq
1824, 3, 20. David, infant s Joana, recrq
1827, 7, 21. Susanna McCartor (form Smith)
     dis mcd
1828, 12, 27. Sarah gct Sandy Spring MM
1832, 2, 18. Martha rocf Sandy Spring MM,
     dtd 1832,1,27
1833, 5, 18. John dis jH
1835, 2, 21. Edward dis mou
1836, 5, 21. Samuel dis mou
1837, 10, 21. Martha Beeson (form Smith) dis
     mcd
1841, 10, 16. David rocf Sandy Spring MM, dtd
     1841,8,27
1842, 10, 15. David H. dis jas

STANLEY
1820, 8, 23. Nathaniel J., s James C. & Mary,
     Belmont Co., O.; m in Elkrun MH, Lydia
     FOWLER, dt James & Mary, Columbiana Co.,O.
1853, 3, 23. William B., s Thomas B. & Mary
     K., Columbiana Co., O.; m in Elkrun MH,
     Eliza MARSH, dt James & Lydia, both dec,
     Columbiana Co., O.

1820, 12, 16. Lyeia gct Salem MM
1853, 6, 18. Eliza C. gct Upper Springfield
     MM

STAPLETON
1831, 8, 20. Samuel dis jH

STICKEL
1832, 12, 15. Sina (form Fisher) dis mou

STOCK
1844, 4, 20. Eliza (form Ashton) con mou

STOCKDALE
1848, 11, 30. Amy d

1843, 9, 16. Amy rocf Westland MM, dtd 1843,
     7,26

STOKES
1820, 9, 16. Elizabeth, minor, recrq of
     grandmother, Rachel Smith

STOOKSBERRY
----. --, --. John & Sarah

STOOKSBERRY, John & Sarah, continued
    Ch: Susannah b 1806, 5, 10 d 1844, 6, 8
        Rachel   " 1808, 2, 2 " 1845, 5, 4
        Isaac   " 1809, 11, 2
        William   " 1811, 9, 2
        Henry   " 1813, 5, 26
        John   " 1815, 5, 27

1828, 8, 16. Ruth Ferguson (form Stooksberry)
    dis mou
1834, 10, 18. Isaac [Stooksbetty] dis disunity
1836, 6, 18. Henry dis mcd
1836, 7, 16. Harriet (form McConnel) dis mcd
1840, 4, 18. William dis mou

STRAIGHT
1831, 11, 19. Maria (form Leech) dis mou

STRATTON
1840, 1, 18. Thomas Leech gct Sandy Spring
    MM, to m Ellan Stratton

TAYLOR
1820, 12, 21. Thomas, s Joseph & Sarah, Colum-
    biana Co., O.; m in Carmel MH, Sarah ED-
    MUNDSON, dt John & Ann, Columbiana Co., O.

1821, 3, 17. Sarah gct Middleton MM
1834, 7, 19. Sarah (form Marsh) con mou (H)

THOMAS
1830, 10, 21. Henry, s John & Hannah, Columbi-
    anna Co., O.; m in Carmel MH, Sarah JOHNS,
    dt Nathan & Rachel, Columbiana Co., O.(H)
1837, 11, 20. Jonathan, s Jacob & Margaret, Co-
    lumbiana Co., O.; m in Carmel MH, Hannah
    THOMPSON, dt Farlin & Pleasy, Columbiana
    Co., O. (H)

1830, 12, 18. Sarah gct New Garden MM (H)
1832, 9, 15. Ann (form Heacock) dis mcd (H)
1834, 5, 17. Isaac rocf New Garden MM, dtd
    1834,2,20 (H)
1834, 8, 16. Ann & dt, Elizabeth, recrq (H)
1835, 11, 21. Ruth (form Marsh) dis mcd (H)
1837, 10, 21. Ann H. & ch, Elizabeth & Jacob,
    gct New Garden MM (H)
1837, 12, 16. Ann (form Carroll) dis mcd (H)
1840, 5, 16. Hannah T. gct Salem MM (H)
1846, 3, 21. Rachel (form Ashton) con mou
1922, 3, 11. Edward, Dorothy & Mildred recrq
    (G)
1924, 3, 8. Robert relrq (G)

THOMPSON
1837, 11, 20. Hannah m Jonathan THOMAS (H)

1829, 4, 18. Joseph dis jH
1831, 2, 19. Pleasy & ch, Hannah, Zilpha,
    Amsey, Zolda, John & Annis, recrq (H)
1843, 6, 17. Zilpah T. Barnaby (form Thomp-
    son) con mcd (H)

TOWNSEND
1830, 8, 21. Ann & ch, Emer & Lewis, rocf
    Salem MM, dtd 1830,7,21
1830, 12, 18. Francis & ch, Emmor & Lewis,
    rocf Salem MM, dtd 1830,11,24 (H)
1832, 5, 19. Ann & ch, Emmor, Lewis & Joseph,
    gct Middleton MM

TRACY
1922, 9, 9. Xemena recrq (G)
1924, 12, 13. Xermena dropped from mbrp (G)

TULLOSS
----, --, --. Richard [Tullis] d 1853,10,12
    ae 87; m Ann ----- d 1854,4,9 ae 84
    Ch: William   b 1796, 12, 15
        Jason   " 1798, 6, 1
        Ann   " 1800, 5, 1
        Jane   " 1802, 12, 5 d 1859,12,29
        Sarah   " 1805, 5, 18 d 1853, 5, 2
        Joseph   " 1807, 8, --
        Elizabeth " 1810, 1, -- d 1841, 5,28
        Catharine " 1812, 4, --
1821, 1, 24. Jason, s Richard & Ann, Columbi-
    ana Co., O., d 1885,10,26; m in Elkrun
    MH, Hannah HEALD, dt Nathan & Rachel, Co-
    lumbiana Co., O., d 1880,3,13
    Ch: Jonathan b 1821, 11, 6
        Eliza Ann " 1822, 12, 13
        Sarah Ann " 1824, 7, 17 d 1847, 9,29
        Nathan   " 1826, 3, 24
        Lewis   " 1828, 2, 3 " 1831, 3, 4
        Rachel   " 1830, 3, 24 " 1831, 3, 9
        Richard J. " 1834, 4, 3
        Lindley H. " 1836, 1, 19
        Smith   " 1838, 7, 9
        Jane   " 1840, 8, 13
        Martha A. " 1843, 2, 1
        Er H.   " 1846, 2, 22
1824, 9, 2. Ann m James POOL
1839, 1, 26. John [Tullis] d
1839, 2, 23. Sard [Tullis] d
1847, 10, 20. Eliza Ann m Joshua MORRIS, Jr.

1818, 4, 18. Jane Lumm (form Tullis) dis mou
1824, 3, 20. Ann Boon (form Tulloss) dis mou
1825, 10, 15. Rhoda Lewellen (form Tullis) dis
    mou
1830, 10, 16. Joseph [Tuloss] dis mou
1832, 6, 16. Jason [Tuloss] & w, Hannah, &
    ch, Jonathan, Eliza Ann, Sarah Ann & Na-
    than, gct Middleton MM
1833, 6, 15. Catharine Ferguson (form Tul-
    loss) dis mou
1833, 8, 17. Jason & w, Hannah, & ch, Jona-
    than, Eliza Ann, Sarah Ann & Nathan, rocf
    Middleton MM, dtd 1833,7,11
1834, 1, 18. William dis mou
1843, 5, 20. Jonathan dis mou
1847, 6, 19. Nathan dis mou
1854, 9, 16. Jane gct Middleton MM

UNDERWOOD
1831, 12, 22. Isaac, s Jephaniah & Rebecca,
    Columbiana Co., O.; m in Carmel MH, Zillah
    MARSH, dt James & Edith, Columbiana Co.,O.
    (H)

1818, 4, 18. Isaac rocf Center MM, Pa., dtd
    1818,1,17, endorsed by Middleton MM, 1818,
    3,16
1818, 4, 18. Rebecca & Mary rocf Center MM,
    Pa., dtd 1818,1,17, endorsed by Middleton
    MM, 1818,3,16
1818, 11, 21. Mary recrq
1820, 3, 18. Mary recrq
1822, 2, 16. Fanny & ch, Elias & Susanna,
    rocf New Garden MM, dtd 1822,2,2
1822, 8, 17. Joseph rocf Newgarden MM, dtd
    1822,4,25
1823, 5, 17. Joseph dis disunity
1824, 10, 10. Isaac, John, Zephaniah & Amos,
    ch Amos, recrq
1825, 2, 19. Willin Jr. gct Middleton MM
1825, 8, 20. Fanny & ch, Elias, Susanna &
    Amos, gct Middleton MM
1825, 10, 15. Rebecca & Mary gct Centre MM,O.
1826, 5, 20. Lewis, infant s Mary, recrq
1826, 5, 20. Mary & ch, Rebecca, Isaac, John,
    Zephaniah, Amos & Levi, gct Centre MM,O.
1826, 11, 18. Mary gct Salem MM
1826, 12, 16. William & w, Sarah, & dt, Ra-
    chel, gct Salem MM
1827, 3, 18. Amos gct Salem MM
1829, 3, 21. Deborah dis jH
1829, 5, 16. Hannah dis jH
1829, 5, 16. Elizabeth (form Boram) dis mcd
    & jH
1829, 8, 15. Rebecca & Mary rocf Center MM,
    O., dtd 1829,3,18
1830, 5, 15. Isaac dis jH
1832, 6, 16. Rebecca gct Center MM (H)
1832, 7, 21. Rebecca & Mary gct Centre MM,
    Clinton Co., O.
1833, 9, 21. Mary (form Borum) dis jH
1834, 2, 15. Mary (form Boram) con mou (H)
1843, 4, 15. Jesse Deborah, Elizabeth &
    Nathan, ch Mary, recrq (H)
1847, 4, 18. Isaac gct Centre MM, O. (H)

VALE
1829, 4, 23. Jacob, s John & Deborah, Colum-
    biana Co., O.; m in Carmel MH, Olivia W.
    McARTOR, dt James & Mary, Columbiana Co.,
    O. (H)
----, --, --. Eli & Ann P.
    Ch: Mary Ann   b 1815, 2, 7
        John Thomas" 1816, 9, 19
        Beulah   " 1818, 7, 8
        Martha H. " 1820, 5, 31
        Hiram P.   " 1822, 8, 7
        Susanna
        Eliza

1818, 2, 21. Phebe gct Westland MM, Pa.

1819, 7, 17. Phebe Edmunson (form Vale) dis
    mcd
1824, 3, 20. Jane Beans (form Vale) dis mcd
1824, 3, 20. Deborah Ashford (form Vale) dis
    mou
1828, 4, 19. John Jr. dis mcd
1828, 5, 17. Maria (form Edmundson) dis mcd
1828, 12, 20. Deborah, Anna, John dis jH
1829, 1, 17. Eli dis jH
1830, 3, 20. Caroline dis jH
1831, 4, 16. Jacob dis mou & jH
1833, 8, 17. Jacob dis disunity (H)
1835, 4, 18. Mary Ann dis jH
1836, 10, 15. Beulah Conkle (form Vale) dis
    mou
1837, 6, 17. Eli dis mou (H)
1838, 3, 17. Martha Richardson (form Vale)
    dis mou
1838, 4, 21. John T. dis mcd
1838, 12, 15. John T. dis mcd (H)
1844, 7, 20. Susan Booth (form Vale) dis
    mou
1845, 6, 21. Morton [Veil] & w, Ann, & minor
    ch, Guli Elma & Edith, gct Salem MM
1847, 4, 17. Louisa Pyle (form Vale) dis mcd

WALKER
1821, 6, 16. Rachel rmt Samuel Richards
1825, 1, 15. Tacy rocf Middleton MM, dtd
    1824,12,20
1826, 5, 20. Tace Richards (form Walker) dis
    mou

WALTON
1836, 12, 22. Benjamin, s Jesse & Ann, both
    dec, Columbiana Co., O.; m in Carmel MH,
    Hannah BURDG, dt Jacob & Miriam, Columbi-
    ana Co., O.

1824, 2, 21. John & w, Lydia, & ch, Martha,
    Lydia, Ann & Joseph, rocf New Garden MM,
    dtd 1823,11,20
1829, 8, 15. John & w, Lydia, & ch, Martha,
    Lydia, Ann, Joseph Elias & David, gct
    Sandy Spring MM
1837, 3, 18. Hannah gct Upper Springfield MM

WARD
1842, 8, 20. Phebe (form Morris) dis mou

WATERWORTH
1830, 10, 16. William rocf New Garden MM, dtd
    1830,8,26 (H)
1830, 11, 20. William gct Salem MM, to m
    Elizabeth Davis (H)
1831, 7, 16. William gct Salem MM (H)

WEBB
1828, 7, 21. Isaac James gct Salem MM, to m
    Leah Webb
1828, 11, 15. Peninah & Lydia, ch Leah James,
    rocf Salem MM, dtd 1828,10,23
1831, 4, 16. Peninah, minor, gct Upper

WEBB, continued
    Springfield MM
1834, 1, 18. Lydia, minor, gct Duck Creek MM,
    Ind.

WELKER
1853, 7, 16. Mary (form Richards) dis mcd

WELL
1834, 1, 18. Lydia, dt Leah James, gct Duck
    Creek MM, Ind.

WEST
1826, 9, 21. Rachel m John HUTTON
1850, 2, 5. Elizabeth d

1820, 4, 15. Stephen dis
1820, 6, 17. Hannah Hambleton (form West) con
    mcd
1830, 8, 21. Mary dis jH
1833, 6, 15. George dis mou

WHITACRE
1819, 8, 21. Rebecca [Whitecre] gct Blue
    River MM, Ind.
1819, 8, 21. Mary, infant dt Mary, recrq of
    mother
1819, 9, 18. Mary & minor ch, William, Eliza-
    beth, Rachel, Levi, Samuel, Joseph, Jona-
    than & Mary, gct Blue River MM, Ind.
1819, 10, 16. John gct Blue River MM, Ind.

WHITZELL
1849, 8, 18. Elizabeth (form Harrison) con
    mcd

WICKERSHAM
1820, 7, 15. Margaret & ch, Eliza Ann & Job,
    recrq
1820, 8, 19. Jonathan Marsh gct Middleton MM,
    to m Ann Wickersham
1826, 2, 18. Ellis & w, Eliza, & ch, Lewis
    Morgan, Mary-ann, Lydia-elma & Elizabeth
    Emeline, gct Newgarden MM
1826, 4, 15. Joseph & Margaret & ch, Eliza
    Ann, Joel, Phoebe, Thomas & Mary, gct
    Middleton MM

WILEY
----, --, --. William & Sarah
    Ch: Jane   b 1809, 1, 14
       William   " 1815, 1, 4

1819, 1, 16. Sarah & ch, Jane & Wm., recrq
1830, 12, 18. Jane dis jH
1835, 1, 17. William Jr. dis disunity

WILKINS
1924, 6, 14. Norma dropped from mbrp (G)

WILLIAMSON
1835, 11, 9. Mary (form McConnel) dis mou

WOODS
1819, 3, 20. Enos & w, Elizabeth, & ch, Ma-
    tilda, James, Joseph, ----- & Israel, gct
    Newgarden MM
1824, 3, 20. Jonathan [Wood] Jr. rmt Mary
    Ashton
1824, 5, 15. Mary [Wood] gct Allum Creek MM
1849, 9, 15. Samuel Hole gct Middleton MM, to
    m Rebecca Woods

WOOLEM
1852, 10, 16. Angeline (form Morlan) dis mcd

WOOLMAN
1832, 4, 21. Margaret (form Cowgill) dis mcd
1846, 6, 20. Margaret rst at Salem MM, Ia.
    by consent of this mtg

WRIGHT
1819, 2, 20. Nathan rocf Phila. MM, Pa., dtd
    1818,9,24
1819, 6, 19. Nathan gct Phila. MM, Pa.

YOUNG
=----, --, --. Joseph & Ann
    Ch: Thomas   b 1801, 1, 31
       Joseph   " 1803, 2, 3
       William   " 1805, 12, 13
       Jane   " 1808, 6, 9
       Daniel   " 1810, 11, 19
       Sarah   " 1813, 8, 25
1824, 4, 21. Mary m Jesse COULSON
1825, 12, 21. Benjamin M., s Joseph & Ann,
    Beaver Co., Pa.; m in Dry-Run MH, Rachel
    COULSON, dt Jehu & Jane, Beaver Co., Pa.
    Ch: Jesse   b 1827, 11, 7

1822, 4, 20. Thomas gct Salem MM
1822, 6, 15. Thomas gct Salem MM
1822, 10, 20. Phebe (form Leech) dis mou
1823, 12, 20. Mary recrq
1825, 7, 11. Benjamin Morgan recrq
1826, 10, 21. Hannah (form Leech) dis mou
1829, 5, 16. Benjamin M. & w, Rachel, & s,
    Jesse, gct Upper Springfield MM
1829, 6, 20. Jane gct Middleton MM
1829, 7, 18. Joseph & w, Ann, & ch, Daniel &
    Sarah, gct Middleton MM
1829, 7, 18. Ann gct Middleton MM
1829, 10, 17. Joseph Jr. gct Middleton MM
1831, 12, 17. William dis mou
1846, 3, 21. Susanna rocf Westland MM, Pa.,
    dtd 1845,11,27 (H)

ZIMMERMAN
1841, 9, 18. William, minor, rocf Chester-
    field MM, dtd 1841,8,21
1843, 5, 20. William, minor, gct Salem MM,
    Ia.

| *   *   *   *   *   *   * | *   *   *   *   *   *   * |

HOLE
1854, 6, 23. Charles d ae 71 (an elder)

JACKSON
1854, 6, 17. Phebe (form Raley) dis mcd

MARLBOROUGH MONTHLY MEETING

Marlborough Monthly Meeting, in Stark County, was opened 4th Mo. 29, 1828, as a Hicksite Monthly Meeting, and in 1848 the name was changed to Deer Creek Monthly Meeting. No
data is available on the history of this monthly meeting as it existed before the Separation in 1828.

RECORDS

AKEY
1848, 4, 22. Mary (form Hicklen) con mcd

ALLEN
1838, 12, 26. Sarah m Asa HAMLEN

1829, 10, 24. Phebe (form Scott) dis mcd
1838, 9, 22. Ann Near (form Allen) con mcd

AUSTIN
1831, 10, 27. James, Stark Co., O.; m at Marl-
        borough MH, Stark Co., O., Hannah HICKLEN

BATTIN
1843, 4, 26. Benjamin, s Robert & Abigail,
        Columbiana Co., O.; m in Deer Creek MH,
        Stark Co., O., Hannah G. HOAG, dt Elisha
        W. & Lydia Hoag, Portage Co., O.
1852, 9, 29. Ann m Aaron PACKER

1843, 7, 22. Hannah G. gct Salem MM
1849, 1, 27. Ann Sr. rocf Newgarden MM, dtd
        1848,12,21
1849, 4, 28. Ann Jr. rocf Newgarden MM, dtd
        1849,3,22
1852, 9, 25. Benjamin C. & w, Hannah, & ch,
        Lydia H. & John, rocf West MM, O., dtd
        1852,6,23
1854, 11, 25. Ann gct Short Creek MM, O.

BEEDY
1832, 6, 23. Abraham & w, Hannah, & ch, Eli,
        Amy & Olive Ann, rocf Newgarden MM, O.,
        dtd 1832,3,22

BISHOP
1838, 5, 26. William & w, Lydia, & ch, Thom-
        as, Mary, Sarah & Lydia, rocf Middleton
        MM, O., dtd 1838,4,12
1851, 12, 27. Mary Hawley (form Bishop) dis
        mcd

BORTON
1838, 3, 28. Ezra, s Samuel & Mercy, Portage
        Co., O.; m in Deer Creek MH, Stark Co., O.
        Ann BROWN, dt Joseph & Sarah, Stark Co.,O.

1832, 8, 25. Jane D. rocf Salem MM, dtd 1832,
        6,20
1846, 2, 28. Jane A., minor dt Ezra, gct
        Salem MM

BROOKE
1834, 11, 6. Edward, s Samuel & Sarah, Stark
        Co., O.; m in Marlborough MH, Stark Co.,
        O., Hannah LUKENS, dt Samuel & Elizabeth,
        Stark Co., O.
1835, 3, 5. Mary M. m Robert GRAVES

1832, 12, 22. Abraham & w, Elizabeth, & dt,
        Harriet, rocf Indian Spring MM, Md., dtd

1832,11,7
1832, 12, 22. Mary M. rocf Indian Spring MM,
        Md., dtd 1832,11,7
1832, 12, 22. Margaret rocf Indian Spring MM,
        Md., dtd 1832,11,7
1832, 12, 22. Samuel & w, Sarah, & s, James
        B., rocf Indian Spring MM, Md., dtd 1832,
        11,7
1832, 12, 22. William & w, Lydia S., rocf
        Indian Spring MM, Md., dtd 1832,11,7
1837, 10, 28. Abraham & w, Elizabeth, & ch,
        Henry & Caroline, gct Center MM, O.
1839, 3, 25. Samuel & w, Sarah, gct Center
        MM, O.
1839, 3, 25. Margaret gct Center MM, O.
1839, 5, 25. Hannah & ch, Alfred & Mary, gct
        Center MM, O.
1849, 4, 28. Lydia & ch, Samuel, Gilpin, Sa-
        rah & Lydia Maria, rocf Centre MM, O.,
        dtd 1848,10,19

BROWN
1830, 6, 30. Amy m Benjamin HUTTON
1838, 3, 28. Ann m Ezra BORTON
1845, 10, 29. Bathsheba m John THOMAS

1831, 12, 24. Ruth dis jas
1838, 2, 24. William & w, Lydia, & two ch
        gct Center MM, O.

BUCKMAN
1833, 3, 23. Lydia (form Holloway) dis mcd

BURDEN
1838, 12, 22. Mary Ann Cousins (form Burden)
        dis mcd
1833, 3, 23. Charlotte Burden (form Gray)
        con mcd

BURDSAL
1836, 5, 28. Cert rec for Andrew & ch from
        Goose Creek MM, Va., end to Center MM,O.
1836, 5, 28. Cert rec for Mary C. from Goose
        Creek MM, Va., end to Center MM, O.

CAMP
1831, 1, 22. Abigail (form Fosdick) dis mcd

COATES
1828, 8, 27. Ann G. m Thomas C. SREVE
1844, 2, 29. Esther R. m William C. RICHMOND

1837, 9, 23. Rachel Sreve (form Coates)
        con mcd
1845, 5, 24. Sarah Jane Ware (form Coats)
        dis mcd
1848, 7, 22. Margaret Garrigus (form Coates)
        dis mcd

COUSINS
1838, 12, 22. Mary Ann (form Burden) dis mcd
        & jas

DAVIS
1831, 10, 26. Benjamin, s Enos & Hannah, Por-
        tage Co., O.; m at Deer Creek MH, Stark
        Co., O., Catharine SLUYTER, dt Wm. K. &
        Sarah, Stark Co., O.

1830, 9, 25. Martha & Mary, minor ch Wm.,
        recrq
1838, 3, 24. Benjamin & w, Catharine, & three
        ch gct White Water MM, Ind.
1840, 4, 25. Cynthia Horton, minor in care of
        John & Rachel Horton, gct Short Creek MM,
        O.
1849, 9, 22. Mary (form Evans) con mcd

DILLON
1852, 3, 27. Elizabeth D. Mendenhall (form
        Dillon) con mcd

DIXON
1838, 6, 7. Newton, s John & Hannah, Colum-
        biana Co., O.; m in Marlborough MH, Eliza
        Ann SCOTT, dt Israel & Sarah, Stark Co.,O.

1838, 11, 24. Eliza Ann S. gct Middleton MM,O.

ELLIOTT
1846, 4, 30. Rachel m Abraham VANSYOC

1830, 10, 23. Susanna & ch, Edith, Ann & Agnes
        recrq

EVANS
1843, 8, 26. Mary (form Richmond) con mcd
1849, 9, 22. Mary Davis (form Evans) con mcd

FOLGER
1831, 5, 26. Sarah dis disunity

FOSDICK
1830, 1, 23. Tamar & dt, Abigail & Eliza,
        rocf New York MM, N. Y., dtd 1829,9,2
1831, 1, 22. Abigail Camp (form Fosdick) dis
        mcd

FOWLER
1834, 10, 25. Daniel S. & w, Hannah, & ch,
        Anna W. & Emily, rocf Buckingham MM, Pa.
1839, 2, 23. Miriam rocf Richland MM, Pa.,
        dtd 1838,11,2
1839, 4, 27. Miriam Ware (form Fowler) con
        mcd

GARRIGUS
1848, 7, 22. Margaret (form Coates) dis mcd

GRAVES
1835, 3, 5. Robert, s Jonathan & Ann, Stark
        Co., O.; m in Marlborough MH, Stark Co.,
        O., Mary M. BROOKS, dt Samuel & Sarah,
        Stark Co., O.

1837, 1, 28. Mary dis disunity

GRAY
1833, 3, 23. Charlotte (form Burden) con mcd
1839, 6, 22. Charlotte dis disunity

HADEN
1847, 4, 24. Maria B. Lewis (form Haden) con
        mcd

HAMLEN
1838, 12, 26. Asa, s Wm. & Hannah, Stark Co.,
        O.; m in Deer Creek MH, Stark Co., O.,
        Sarah ALLEN, dt James, Stark Co., O.

HANCE
1847, 4, 24. Sarah D. rocf Farmington MM,
        N. Y., dtd 1847,1,28
1847, 4, 24. Thomas rocf Farmington MM,
        N. Y., dtd 1847,1,28
1853, 6, 25. Evaline rocf Salem MM, dtd
        1853,6,23

HARDEN
1845, 7, 26. Maria recrq

HAWLEY
1836, 3, 26. Hannah rocf Salem MM
1851, 12, 27. Mary (Bishop) dis mcd

HAYHURST
1847, 12, 25. Hannah (form Mather) con mcd
1848, 7, 22. Hannah gct West MM, O.

HAZEN
1848, 10, 28. Elizabeth E. (form Wickersham)
        dis mcd
HEACOCK
1834, 10, 30. Phebe m Charles SHINN
1842, 12, 24. Sarah M. (form Sebrell) con mcd
HICKLEN
1828, 7, 20. Hannah m Joseph MARSHALL
1831, 10, 27. Hannah m James AUSTIN
1847, 5, 26. Ann m Newton THOMAS

1835, 7, 25. Dinah dis jas
1837, 12, 23. Thomason & dt, Jane, recrq
1844, 7, 27. Rebecca Scott (form Hicklen)
        dis mcd
1847, 11, 27. William & w, Thomason, & ch gct
        Newgarden MM
1848, 4, 22. Mary Akey (form Hicklen) con mcd
1855, 4, 28. Hannah H. con mcd

HICKMAN
1841, 7, 24. Lydia rocf Middleton MM, O.,
        dtd 1841,5,6

HOAG
1842, 7, 27. Mary S. m John THOMAS

HOAG, continued
1843, 4, 26. Hannah G. m Benjamin BATTIN
1855, 6, 27. Lydia m Joseph WRIGHT

1830, 11, 27. Lydia & dt, Mary & Hannah, rocf
       Newgarden MM, O., dtd 1830,9,23
1830, 11, 27. Joanna rocf Newgarden MM, O.,
       dtd 1830,9,23
1841, 2, 27. Joanna B. Jones (form Hoag) con
       mcd

HOLLOWAY
1831, 4, 25. Sarah [Holaway] m Joseph PELLETT
1834, 1, 2. Hannah m William MATHER

1833, 3, 23. Lydia Buckman (form Holloway)
       dis mcd
1837, 6, 24. Jason & five ch gct Milford MM,
       Ind.
1837, 6, 24. Esther Johnson (form Holloway)
       con mcd

HORNE
1833, 7, 27. Edward & w, Elizabeth P., & s,
       Vincent P., rocf Carmel MM, dtd 1833,6,15
1837, 6, 24. Edward & w, Elizabeth, & four
       ch gct Carmel MM

HORTON
1834, 9, 27. John & w, Rachel, & dt, Mary,
       rocf Westland MM, Pa., dtd 1834,8,28
1840, 4, 25. John & w, Rachel, & Cynthia Hor-
       ton Davis, a minor in their care, gct
       Short Creek MM, O.
1840, 4, 25. Mary J. gct Short Creek MM, O.

HUTTON
1830, 6, 30. Benjamin, s John & Massey,
       Portage Co., O.; m in Deer Creek MH, Stark
       Co., O., Amy BROWN, dt Joseph & Sarah,
       Stark Co., O.

1828, 12, 27. Lydia Queer (form Hutton) dis
       mcd

INGLEDUE
1837, 1, 28. Rachel rocf Middleton MM, O.,
       dtd 1836,7,7

JOHNSON
1837, 6, 24. Esther (form Holloway) con mcd

JONES
1841, 2, 27. Joanna B. (form Hoag) con mcd

LEWIS
1847, 4, 24. Maria B. (form Haden) con mcd

LOGUE
1817, 5, 22. Elizabeth m Mahlon WILEMAN

LUKENS
1834, 11, 6. Hannah m Edward BROOKE

1832, 12, 22. Elizabeth & dt, Mary & Susan,
       rocf Indian Spring MM, Md., dtd 1832,11,7
1832, 12, 22. Hannah rocf Indian Spring MM,
       Md., dtd 1832,11,7
1835, 10, 24. Mary relrq

McCALL
1830, 9, 25. Alice & dt, Elizabeth & Hannah,
       recrq
1830, 9, 25. Ruth recrq
1843, 11, 25. Hannah dis jas
1844, 1, 27. Elizabeth dis jas
1849, 4, 28. Josiah gct Deerfield MM, O.
1849, 9, 22. Alice & three ch gct Deerfield
       MM, O.

McGIR
1839, 10, 26. Alexander & w, Sarah, & ch gct
       Deerfield MM, O.
1841, 5, 27. Thomas [McGirr] & w, Ann, gct
       Deerfield MM, O.

MARSHALL
1828, 7, 20. Joseph, s Wm. & Mary, Portage
       Co., O.; m at Deer Creek MH, Stark Co.,
       O., Hannah HICKLEN, dt Joshua & Tamer,
       Portage Co., O.

1837, 8, 26. Sarah Rigg (form Marshall) dis
       mcd
1850, 10, 26. Hannah Sebrell (form Marshall)
       dis mcd

MATHER
1834, 1, 2. William, s John & Catherine,
       Columbiana Co., O.; m at Lexington MH,
       Hannah HOLLOWAY, dt Aaron & Sarah, Stark
       Co., O.

1847, 12, 25. Hannah Hayhurst (form Mather)
       con mcd

MENDENHALL
1852, 3, 27. Elizabeth D. (form Dillon) con
       mcd
1852, 12, 25. Elizabeth D. gct White Water
       MM, Ind.

MILLARD
1833, 11, 27. David B., s Wm. & Rebecca,
       Portage Co., O.; m in Deer Creek MH,
       Stark Co., O., Sarah H. POUND, dt David
       & Ann, Portage Co., O.
       David B. m 2nd 1841,5,27 in Marlborough
       MH, Stark Co., O., Mary SCOTT, dt Israel
       & Sarah, Stark Co., O.

1836, 7, 23. David B. & w, Sarah H., and two
       ch gct White Water MM, Ind.

MOORE
1845, 10, 25. Cert rec for Sarah & ch, Lydia
     Ann, David Richard, Mifflin Young, Samuel
     Spencer, Edward Thomas, Sarah Elizabeth &
     Elvira, rocf Centre MM, Pa., dtd 1845,7,9,
     end to Centre MM, O.

MORGAN
1847, 9, 25. Lewis & w, Elizabeth, & ch,
     Joshua, James & Susan, recrq

MORLAN
1837, 1, 28. Ann & ch, Amos, Rachel, Sally
     Ann, Lucy Ann & Huldah A., rocf Middle-
     town MM, O., dtd 1836,6,9
1840, 10, 28. Rachel Shafer (form Morlan) con
     mcd
1850, 7, 27. Lucy Winder (form Morlan) dis
     mcd

MURPHY
1833, 8, 24. Margaret rocf Exeter MM, Pa.,
     dtd 1832,12,26, end by Newgarden MM, 1833,
     4,26
1836, 7, 23. Margaret gct Exeter MM, Pa.

NEAR
1838, 9, 22. Ann (form Allen) con mou

PACKER
1852, 9, 29. Aaron, s Eli & Elizabeth, Jef-
     ferson Co., O.; m in Deer Creek MM, Stark
     Co., O., Ann BATTON, dt John & Ann, Colum-
     biana Co., O.

1852, 11, 27. Ann gct Short Creek MM, O.

PELLETT
1831, 4, 25. Joseph, s Francis & Mary, Colum-
     biana Co., O.; m at Lexington MH, Sarah
     HOLAWAY, dt Amos & Hepzabath, Stark Co.,
     O.

1831, 7, 23. Sarah gct Carmel MM, O.

POUND
1833, 11, 27. Sarah H. m David B. MILLARD

1830, 4, 24. Ann & dt, Sarah H., Isabella,
     Mary H. & Ann H., rocf Newgarden MM, O.,
     dtd 1830,3,25
1833, 3, 23. Asa & w, Mary, rocf Farmington
     MM, N. Y., dtd 1833,2,21
1834, 4, 26. Elizabeth L. rocf Newgarden MM
1836, 7, 23. David & w, Ann, & six ch gct
     White Water MM, Ind.
1839, 2, 27. Angeline E., minor, gct New-
     garden MM

PRICE
1846, 6, 30. Thomas, s Thomas & Mary, Stark
     Co., O.; m in the home of James Dillon,
     Elizabeth D. WILLIAMSON, dt Isaac &

Elizabeth, Columbiana Co., O.

1844, 5, 25. Cynthia M. (form Underwood) con
     mcd

QUEER
1828, 12, 27. Lydia (form Hutton) dis mcd

RICHMOND
1844, 2, 29. William C., s Daniel & Eliza,
     Stark Co., O.; m in the home of Isaac
     Coates, Esther R. COATES, dt Isaac & Mary,
     Stark Co., O.

1841, 9, 25. Chloe relrq
1843, 8, 26. Mary Evans (form Richmond) con
     mcd

RIGG
1837, 8, 26. Sarah (form Marshall) dis mcd

ROCKHILL
1830, 11, 27. Anna rst
1833, 3, 23. Elizabeth, Nathan & Margaret
     [Rockhills], ch Ellis & Anna, recrq

SCOTT
1838, 6, 7. Eliza Ann m Newton DIXON
1841, 5, 27. Mary m David B. MILLARD

1829, 10, 24. Phebe Allen (form Scott) dis
     mcd
1844, 7, 27. Rebecca (form Hicklen) dis mcd

SEBRELL
1842, 12, 24. Sarah M. Heacock (form Sebrell)
     con mcd
1850, 10, 26. Hannah Sebrell (form Marshall)
     dis mcd

SHAFER
1848, 10, 28. Rachel (form Morlan) con mcd

SHAW
1847, 4, 24. Maria rocf Salem MM, dtd 1846,
     12,23

SHINN
1834, 10, 30. Charles, s David & Hannah,
     Stark Co., O.; m at Marlborough MH, Phebe
     HEACOCK, dt Nathan & Hannah, Stark Co.,O.

1837, 5, 23. David & w, Susan, & three ch
     gct Westfield MM, O.
1837, 5, 23. Rachel gct Westfield MM, O.
1851, 7, 26. Charles & three ch gct Green
     Plain MM, O.

SLATER
1829, 6, 27. Catharine rocf Richland MM,
     Pa., dtd 1829,5,1
1829, 6, 27. Sarah & dt, Elizabeth, Lucinda
     & Lavina, rocf Richland MM, Pa., dtd

SLATER, continued
    1829,5,1

SLUYTER
1831, 10, 24. Henry, s Wm. K. & Sarah, Stark
    Co., O.; m at Kendal MH, Nancy SMITH, dt
    Francis & Mary, Stark Co., O.
1831, 10, 26. Catharine m Benjamin DAVIS

1844, 9, 28. Sarah Ann rocf Newgarden MM, dtd
    1844,4,25

SMITH
1831, 10, 24. Nancy m Henry SLUYTER

SREVE
1828, 8, 27. Thomas C., s John & Abigail,
    Ohio Co., O.; m at Deer Creek MH, Stark
    Co., O., Ann G. COATS, dt Isaac & Mary,
    Stark Co., O.

1837, 9, 23. Rachel (form Coates) con mcd

THOMAS
1842, 7, 27. John, s John & Rebecca, Colum-
    biana Co., O.; m in Deer Creek MH, Stark
    Co., O., Mary S. HOAG, dt Elisha & Lydia,
    Ohio Co., O.
    John m 2nd 1845,10,29 in Deer Creek MH,
    Stark Co., O., Bathsheba BROWN, dt Joseph
    & Sarah, Stark Co., O.
1847, 5, 26. Newton, s John & Rebecca,
    Portage Co., O.; m in Deer Creek MH, Stark
    Co., O., Ann HICKLEN, dt Joseph & Alice

1842, 5, 26. Rebecca S. rocf Salem MM, dtd
    1842,4,20
1842, 12, 24. Mary S. gct Salem MM
1843, 11, 25. Ruth dis jas
1847, 6, 26. Susanna recrq

TOWNSEND
1835, 6, 27. Nathan & w, Sarah, & ch, Lydia
    Ann & Thomas M., rocf Middleton MM, O.,
    dtd 1835,3,12
1837, 5, 27. Nathan & w, Sarah, & ch, Lydia
    Ann, Thomas M. & David W., gct Middleton
    MM, O.

TRIPP
1831, 12, 24. Fanny [Trip] rocf Newgarden MM,
    O., dtd 1831,9,22
1832, 6, 23. Samuel & w, Fannie, & ch,
    George F., Stephen, Mary & Laban, gct
    Newgarden MM
1833, 7, 27. Samuel & w, Fannie, & ch, George
    F., Stephen, Mary & Laban, rocf Newgarden
    MM, dtd 1833,3,25

UNDERWOOD
1833, 5, 25. Wilber & w, Rachel, & ch, Cyn-
    thia & Mary, rocf Middleton MM, O., dtd
    1833,3,7

1835, 4, 25. Sarah rocf Middleton MM, O.,
    dtd 1835,3,12
1844, 5, 25. Cynthia M. Price (form Under-
    wood) con mcd

VANSYOC
1846, 4, 30. Abraham, s Enoch & Lydia, Wash-
    ington Co., Pa.; m in Marlborough MH,
    Stark Co., O., Rachel ELLIOTT, dt Benja-
    min & Susanna, Stark Co., O.

1845, 5, 24. Aaron & w, Ruth, & ch, Isaac,
    Enoch, Jesse, Abraham, Sarah Jane, Amos,
    Harrison & Simeon, rocf Westland MM, Pa.,
    dtd 1844,6,27

WALTON
1844, 7, 27. Esther H. (form Wileman) dis
    mcd

WARE
1839, 4, 27. Miriam (form Fowler) con mcd
1845, 5, 24. Sarah Jane (form Coats) dis mcd

WICKERSHAM
1842, 5, 26. Ellis & w, Elizabeth, & ch,
    Elizabeth Emeline, Ellis Taylor, Thomas
    M., Joseph L. & William Quimby, rocf New
    Garden MM, dtd 1841,12,23
1843, 10, 28. Lydia Elma rocf Newgarden MM,
    dtd 1843,8,23
1848, 10, 28. Lydia E. (lma) Wood (form
    Wickersham) dis mcd
1848, 10, 28. Elizabeth E. (meline) Hazen
    (form Wickersham) dis mcd

WILEMAN
1817, 5, 22. Mahlon, s Abraham & Letitia,
    Stark Co., O.; m in Marlborough MH, Stark
    Co., O., Elizabeth LOGUE, dt Stephen &
    Hannah, Stark Co., O.

1844, 7, 27. Esther H. Walton (form Wileman)
    dis mcd
1846, 10, 24. Lydia & ch gct Plainfield MM

WILLIAMSON
1846, 6, 30. Elizabeth D. m Thomas PRICE

1836, 3, 26. Elizabeth L., niece of Eliza-
    beth Dillon, recrq

WINDER
1850, 7, 27. Lucy (form Morlan) dis mcd

WOOD
1848, 10, 28. Lydia E. (form Wickersham) dis
    mcd

WREN
1832, 12, 27. William, s Wm. & Lydia, Stark
    Co., O.; m in Marlborough MH, Sarah HEA-
    COCK, dt Nathan & Hannah, Stark Co., O.

WRIGHT
1855, 6, 27. Joseph, Mahoning Co., O.; m in
     Deer Creek MH, Stark Co., O., Lydia HOAG

SANDY SPRING MONTHLY MEETING

An indulged meeting for worship near Tuscarawas Path was opened on 4th Mo. 16, 1815.
This meeting was established as a Preparative Meeting 9th Mo. 15, 1818 and named Augusta
Meeting. Pursuant to the directions of Salem Monthly Meeting, a monthly meeting was opened
at Sandy Spring, Columbiana Co., Ohio, 12th Mo. 22, 1820, to be held alternately at Sandy
Spring and Augusta. John Battin served as the first clerk of this meeting with John Hole
as assistant.

Among the prominent members were Levi Miller, William Winder, Jonathan R. Dean, Jacob
Hole, John Battin, Thomas Emmons, Stephen McBride, David Halderman, Mahlon Hole, James
Chambers, George McNuly, Joseph Raley, Caleb Hawley, and Morris Miller.

The first couple married in this meeting were Mordicai Morlan and Elizabeth Ann Dean.
There is a record of twenty-eight marriages between 1820 and 1835.

RECORDS

ANGLEMIRE
1886, 9, --. Joseph d

ANTREM
1855, 9, 22. Hannah rocf Salem MM, dtd 1855,
    7,25 (W)

ARMSTRONG
----, --, --. James, s James & Ruth, Chester
    Co., Del., b 1788,2,22; m Mary HEALD, dt
    John & Phebe, Fayette Co., Pa., b 1789,2,
    10
    Ch: Phebe   b 1812, 4, 5
        Ruth   " 1814, 2, 19
        Titus   " 1816, 4, 5
        Martha   " 1818, 4, 26
        Hannah   " 1820, 6, 28
        John   " 1822, 10, 23 d 1824, 8,19
         bur Sandy Spring
        Rachel   b 1825, 4, 2
        Joseph   " 1828, 1, 15 d 1828,11,14
         bur Sandy Spring
        Sarah   b 1829, 10, 5
----, --, --. Nathan H., s James & Ruth, Ches-
    ter Co., Del., b 1802,2,24; m Rebecca
    COPE, dt Israel & Elizabeth, Columbiana
    Co., O., b 1809,7,26
    Ch: Joseph   b 1828, 8, 31
        Dawsey   " 1830, 8, 20
1854, 11, 29. Sarah m Milton RALEY (W)
1861, 2, 27. Hannah m Benj. WINDER (W)

1826, 8, 25. Deborah rocf Middleton MM, dtd
    1826,3,20
1826, 8, 25. Bennett & w, Elizabeth, & ch,
    James C., William, Bennett, Jane Emily &
    Mary Ann, rocf Middleton MM, dtd 1826,3,20
1829, 3, 27. Elizabeth dis jH
1829, 4, 24. Nathan & w, Rebecca, & s, Jo-
    seph, rocf Carmel MM, dtd 1829,1,17
1830, 9, 24. Deborah dis jas
1830, 12, 24. Ruth rmt David Heston
1831, 10, 21. Phebe Heston (form Armstrong)
    dis mou
1835, 11, 27. Nathan H. & fam gct Carmel MM
1857, 1, 24. Titus dis mou (W)

ARNOLD
----, --, --. Stephen (nm) & Rachel
    Ch: Typhena Be-
            linda   b 1821, 10, 5 in Trumble
            Co., O. (nm)
        Lydia Ann b 1824, 10, 16 in Columbi-
            ana Co., O.
        Asenath W. b 1827, 2, 4 in Portage
            Co., O.

1831, 12, 23. Rachel rst on consent of New
    Garden MM
1833, 4, 26. Tryphena Belinda, Lydia Ann &
    Asenath W., ch Rachel, recrq

1833, 7, 26. Lydia Ann, minor dt Rachel, gct
    Middleton MM
1838, 4, 27. Lydia Ann, minor, rocf Middle-
    ton MM, dtd 1837,12,18
1844, 11, 22. Asenath W. Hall (form Arnold)
    dis jas

ATKINSON
1821, 5, 25. Melinda recrq
1821, 11, 23. Malinda rmt John Reley

BASHAW
----, --, --. Lunsford m Lucretia P. PETTIT,
    dt Jesse K. & Charlotte, Columbiana Co.,
    O., b 1846,6,3
    Ch: Leon H.   b 1872, 12, 18
        Leslie D. " 1874, 12, 22
        R. Odell   " 1876, 10, 24
        Alzana M. " 1884, 1, 20
    The mother & last two ch rem to M. E. Ch,
    Union Chapel; the first two ch were re-
    leased by rq

BATTIN
----, --, --. Robert & Abigail
    Ch: Benjamin   b 1822, 9, 7
        Hannah   " 1824, 5, 3
1823, 2, 27. Catharine, w Richard, d ae 73y
    1m 16d bur Sandy spring
----, --, --. John, s John & Ann, Washington
    Co., Pa., Westland Mtg, b 1800,2,2; m Sa-
    rah D. HOWARD, dt John & Cherry, Short
    Creek Mtg, O., b 1804,1,21
    Ch: Elvira   b 1825, 3, 5 d 1843, 2, 7
         bur Sandy Spring
        Howard   b 1826, 7, 5
        Asa   " 1829, 3, 16
        William   " 1832, 6, 14
        Mary   " 1834, 6, 14
        Lucinda   " 1838, 12, 27
        Ruth Anna " 1840, 10, 15
    Ch b in Sandy Spring Mtg
1882, --, --. Phebe d

1821, 9, 22. Phebe & dt, Jane W., rocf
    Middleton MM, dtd 1821,5,24
1821, 10, 26. Epsey Sanders (form Battin) con
    mcd
1821, 11, 23. Robert rmt Abigail Cobourn Jr.
1822, 10, 25. Ann dis jas
1822, 12, 27. Miriam & Priscilla dis jas
1824, 3, 26. Catharine dis jas
1825, 2, 25. Sarah D. rocf Short Creek MM,
    O., dtd 1825,1,18
1825, 7, 22. Sarah D. dis
1826, 11, 24. David rmt Sarah Ann Reeder
1828, 1, 25. Sarah D. rst
1828, 12, 20. Sarah Ann dis jH
1829, 1, 21. Ann & Fannie dis jH
1829, 9, 25. Abigail dis jH
1829, 11, 27. Ann Jr. dis jH
1832, 5, 25. Mary & Betsy dis jas
1836, 12, 23. Minor ch of Robert gct Upper

BATTIN, continued
      Springfield MM
1839, 6, 21. Ann dis disunity
1863, 5, 23. John, Sarah & Ruthanna dis
      jG in 1854 (W)

BAXTER
1822, 2, 22. Deborah rocf New Garden MM, dtd
      1821,5,24
1829, 4, 24. Betsy (form Milbourn) dis mou

BECK
1823, 8, 4. Adah con mcd
1824, 4, 23. Adah gct New Garden MM

BENTLEY
1827, 1, 26. John E. & w, Anna, & ch, Gran-
      ville S., Franklin H., Maria, Thomas M.,
      Hannah & Deborah, rocf Indian Spring MM,
      Md., dtd 1826,12,6
1829, 5, 22. Ann dis jH
1840, 5, 22. Maria Garrigues (form Bentley)
      dis mcd
1843, 5, 26. Elizabeth G. rocf Marlborough
      MM, dtd 1843,2,28
1843, 9, 22. Hannah H. rocf Marlborough MM,
      dtd 1842,5,31

BETTIS
----, --, --. Harry b 1865,5,18; m Lottie
      ----- b 1868,2,23
      Ch: Bird   b 1886, 1, 11
          Leonard   " 1888, 8, 18
          Grace   " 1889, 6, 7
----, --, --. Manten m Evylin ----- d 1905,4,
      27

BLANSHON
 1820, 12, 22. Eleanor (form Davis) con mcd
1823, 11, 21. Eleanor [Blancheon] gc
1825, 9, 23. Eleanor rocf Gunpowder MM, Md.,
      dtd 1825,6,8
1832, 4, 27. Eleanor [Blancheon] dis jH

BOND
1854, 11, 24. Abigail (form Reeder) dis mcd
      (W)

BOWERSOCK
1838, 1, 26. Rebecca (form McBride) con mou

BRANTINGHAM
1857, 5, 23. Alfred & w, Ann, & ch, Joshua,
      Elizabeth & Hannah D., gct New Garden MM
      (W)

BRATTEN
1837, 6, 23. Susanna (form Emmons) dis mou

BRIGGS
1866, 9, 22. Benjamin Winder gct Stillwater
      MM, to m Sarah S. Briggs (W)

BROGAN
1814, 10, 10. Emma b
----, --, --. Charles M., s Morris & Mary,
      Columbiana Co., O., b 1868,4,26; m Jean-
      nette ORR, dt Parker & Mary, Columbiana
      Co. O., b 1873,8,29
      Ch: Virgil C. b 1896, 12, 15
          Alice   " 1898, 11, 23
          Wayne J.   " 1900, 8, 28
          Lillian
          Charles

BROWN
----, --, --. Joshua K., s Thos. & Elizabeth,
      b 1811,8,20; m Ann HOLDEMAN, dt David &
      Ann, b 1816,11,28
      Ch: Harman   b 1838, 10, 1 in New-
          garden Mtg
          David H.   b 1841, 1, 22 in Augusta
          Mtg

1826, 9, 22. Harvey & w, Jane, & ch, Eliza
      Updegraff & Abigail, rocf Salem MM, dtd
      1826,9,20
1832, 8, 24. Eliza Updegraff & Abigail, ch
      Harvey & Jane, gct Smithfield MM
1833, 4, 26. Jane dis jas
1837, 12, 22. Joshua rmt Ann Haldeman
1838, 3, 23. Ann gct New Garden MM
----, --, --. Joshua H. & w, Ann, & s, Harmon,
      rocf New Garden MM, dtd 1840,10,22

BURGE
1838, 7, 27. Jacob & w, Miriam, & ch, Lewis,
      Oliver & Mary, rocf Carmel MM, dtd 1838,
      7,21
1839, 5, 24. Jacob & fam gct Upper Spring-
      field MM

BUTLER
1822, 7, 26. Lawrence W. & w, Sarah, rocf
      Salem MM, dtd 1822,4,24
1830, 7, 23. Lawrence W. & w, Sarah, & ch
      gct New Garden MM

CARROLL
1824, 6, 25. Joseph & Elizabeth, & ch, Enos
      & Edward, rocf Newgarden MM, dtd 1824,5,20
1826, 2, 24. Joseph & w, Elizabeth, & four
      ch gct Newgarden MM

CHAMBERS
----, --, --. James, s Thos. & Jane, Lurgan
      Mtg, Ire., b 1782,3,-- d 1864,5,6 bur
      Sandy Spring; m Mary NICHOLSON, dt James
      & Jane, Richhill, Ire., b 1784,1,21 d
      1861,10,23 bur Augusta
      Ch: Ann   b 1807, 9, 28 in Ireland
          Jane   " 1809, 3, 21 in Augus-
          ta Mtg, Va.
          Eleanor   " 1810, 7, 31 "   "
          Thomas   " 1812, 4, 20 "   "
          Elizabeth " 1814, 3, 18 d 1865,2,11

CHAMBERS, James & Mary, continued
    Ch: bur Augusta
        James   b 1816, 1, 1
        Mary   " 1818, 2, 22 in Goshen
        Mtg, Belmont Co., bur at Augusta
        Samuel   b 1820, 6, 12 in Augusta
        Mtg
        William   " 1822, 5, 25 d 1842, 5,30
        Abigail   " 1826, 5, 30 " 1852, 7,30
----, --, --. James H., s James & Mary, b 1816,
    1,1 d 1891,4,22 bur Augusta; m Ann STANLEY
    dt Benjamin & Elizabeth, Upper Springfield
    Mtg, b 1818,1,1 d 1863,11,11 bur Augusta
    Ch: Mary Jane b 1839, 3, 3
        Elizabeth   " 1841, 1, 17 d 1842, 8, 7
        bur Augusta
        Sina Ann   b 1843, 3, 31
        William   " 1845, 8, 10 " 1865, 7, 6
        bur Augusta
        Eliza   b 1848, 4, 15
        Benjamin   " 1850, 12, 22
        James N.   " 1853, 3, 27
        -----   " 1856, 11, 20
        John   " 1859, 1, 31
        Sorena   " 1862, 3, 4
    James H. m 2nd Elizabeth S. ----- b 1818,7,
    20
----, --, --. Thomas, s Jas. & Mary, b 1812,
    4,20; m Elizabeth LEE, dt Samuel & Cynthia,
    b 1819,10,13
----, --, --. James N., s James H. & Ann, Car-
    roll Co., b 1853,3,27; m Tamar S. HALDE-
    MAN, dt David & Julia A., Carroll Co.,
    b 1858,4,25
    Ch: Laura May b 1879, 12, 5
-----, --,--. Elizabeth S. d ae 96

1826, 9, 22. Samuel rmt Tamar Winder
1827, 1, 26. Tamar gct Plainfield MM
1828, 11, 21. Ann rmt Jacob Hole Jr.
1838, 9, 21. Ann rocf Upper Springfield MM,
    dtd 1838,8,25
1863, 4, 25. James, Ann & Sinah Ann dis jG
    in 1854 (W)
1863, 4, 25. James, Eleanor, Elizabeth &
    Thomas dis jG in 1854 (W)

CLARK
1832, 9, 21. John & w, Rachel, & ch, Thomas,
    Henry, Wm., Jane & John rocf Newgarden
    MM, dtd 1832,7,26
1832, 9, 21. Martha & Rebecca rocf Newgarden
    MM, dtd 1832,6,21
1842, 7, 22. Rebecca Irey (form Clark) con
    mcd
1843, 11, 24. Rachel dis
1864, 11, 7. William dis mcd (W)
1870, 10, 22. Henry con mou (W)

CLEMSON
1855, 4, 28. James rocf Upper Springfield
    MM, dtd 1855,4,27 (W)
1855, 5, 26. Lydia rocf Upper Springfield

MM, dtd 1855,4,27 (W)
1855, 5, 26. Mary A. rocf Upper Springfield
    MM, dtd 1855,4,27 (W)
1861, 10, 26. Mary Ann Powell (form Clemson)
    con mou (W)
1866, 10, 27. Isaac T. rocf Upper Spring-
    field MM, dtd 1866,10,26 (W)
1866, 11, 24. Hannah Dutton (form Clemson)
    con mcd (W)
1873, 4, 26. Reuben [Clempson] gct Upper
    Springfield MM (W)

COBOURN
----, --, --. John, s Benjamin & Abigail, b
    1795,7,18; m Sarah JOHN, dt Griffith &
    Sarah, Sadsbury Mtg, Pa., b 1795,7,11
    Ch: Rachel   b 1823, 8, 6
        Ezra   " 1824, 9, 16 d 1857, 6,12
        bur Sandyspring
        Nathan   b 1826, 8, 4
        Joseph   " 1836, 7, 28 d 1856,12,20
----, --, --. Ezra & Thirza
    Ch: Sarah
        Elizabeth b 1851, 8, 22 d 1856, 6, 1
        John Alex-
        ander   " 1852, 11, 6
        Harvy Fow-
        ler   " 1855, 5, 4 d 1862,10, 3
        bur Sandyspring
        Joseph La-
        ron   b 1857, 4, 2
----, --, --. J. George, s Nathan & Harriett,
    b 1863,7,20 d 1938,--,-- in Whittier,
    Calif.; m Ella THOMAS, dt Valentine &
    Maria, b 1862,4,21 d 1938,--,-- in
    Whittier, Calif.

1821, 11, 23. Abigail Jr. rmt Robert Batten
1822, 11, 22. John [Coubourn] rmt Sarah John
    Jr.
1824, 5, 20. Sarah Packer (form Cobourn) con
    mou
1833, 6, 21. Elizabeth gct Upper Springfield
    MM
1856, 6, 28. Rachel dis (W)
1863, 1, 24. John & Nathan dis jG in 1854
    (W)
1863, 1, 24. Sarah [Coborn] dis jG in 1854
    (W)

COOPER
----, --, --. Calvin, s Geo. & Susannah, Sads-
    bury Mtg, Lancaster Co., Pa., b 1772,5,--;
    m Ann PIERCE, dt Gainer & Jane, Sadsbury
    Mtg, Pa., b 1773,5,5 d 1828,7,18 bur
    Sandyspring
    Ch: Susannah b 1796, 10, 18
        Gainer   " 1799, 5, 13 d 1801, 4, 4
        in Pa.
        Evan   " 1801, 7, 15
        Jane   " 1802, 10, 31
        Elizabeth " 1805, 10, 4
        Phebe   " 1808, 11, 10

COOPER, Calvin & Ann, continued
    Ch: Maryann   b 1810, 10, 21
        Rachel   " 1813, 8, 3 at Sandy-
          spring; all others b in Sadsbury Mtg

1823, 9, 26. Evan rmt Mary Middleton
1823, 12, 26. Elizabeth rocf New Garden MM,
    dtd 1823,11,20
1827, 5, 25. Elizabeth rmt Levi Reeder
1830, 3, 26. Elizabeth rocf Carmel MM, dtd
    1830,3,20
1830, 5, 21. Evan & w, Mary, & ch gct Upper
    Springfield
1831, 1, 21. Phebe Hayes (form Cooper) con mou
1831, 10, 21. Evan & w, Mary, & ch, William,
    Chalkley & Martha, rocf Upper Springfield
    MM, 1831,8,27
1844, 1, 26. Jane rmt Levi Penington
1857, 5, 23. Evan & w, Mary, & ch, Albert,
    Ann & Sarah, gct Stillwater MM (W)
1857, 5, 23. Hinchman gct Stillwater MM (W)
1857, 6, 27. Martha gct Stillwater MM (W)

COPE
1859, 6, 1. John A., s Isaac & Rachel, Stark
    Co., O.; m in Sandy Spring MH, Adah B.
    WINDER, dt Joseph & Efphama, Carroll Co.,
    O. (W)

1859, 7, 23. Ada B. gct Upper Springfield MM
    (W)
1870, 2, 26. Anna Mary (form Yates) con mcd
    (W)

COPPOCK
1862, 2, 26. Wm. G., s Joshua & Jane, Colum-
    biana Co., O.; m in Sandy Spring MH, Abi-
    gail DEAN, dt Barton & Elizabeth, Colum-
    biana Co., O. (W)
1865, 9, 24. Benjamin, s Joshua & Jane, Co-
    lumbiana Co., O.; m in Sandy Spring MH,
    Esther WINDER, dt Joseph & Lydia, Carroll
    Co., O. (W)

1862, 5, 24. Abigail gct New Garden MM (W)
1863, 4, 25. Wm. G. [Copic] & w, Abigail,
    rocf New Garden MM, dtd 1863,4,23 (W)
1866, 8, 25. Esther W. gct Salem MM (W)
1871, 5, 27. William G. [Copock] & w, Abi-
    gail, & ch, Barton D., Elizabeth Jane &
    Harlem L., gct New Garden MM (W)

CRAIG
1871, 4, 22. Emelina (form Yates) dis mcd (W)

CRAWFORD
1848, 8, 16. Tobias J., s Nathan & Lydia,
    Carroll Co., b

CREW
----, --, --. Obediah, s John & Margery, b
    1822,4,3; m Mary H. HALDEMAN, dt David &
    Ann, Augusta, b 1830,12,15

Ch: Anna M.   b 1863, 12, 21
    Emily F.   " 1867, 3, 29
    Mary Ellen " 1868, 9, 27
    Lauretta C." 1872, 7, 14
1863, 4, 25. Mary dis jG in 1854 (W)
----, --, --. Anna M. gct Goshen MM, O.
----, --, --. Emily F. glt M. E. Ch., Herring-
ton
----, --, --. Mary Ellen gct Goshen MM, O.

CROZIER
1823, 8, 4. Thomas & w, Sarah, & s, James,
    rocf Flushing MM, dtd 1823,6,27
1824, 11, 26. Thomas [Crozer] & fam gct
    Middleton MM

COULSON
----, --, --. David, s Jehu & Jane, b 1794,10,
    7; m Elizabeth REEDER, dt Thos. & Pris-
    cilla, b 1786,5,2 d 1841,4,26 bur Sandy-
    spring
    Ch: William   b 1815, 11, 13
        Jane   " 1817, 9, 6
        Amy   " 1819, 11, 30
        Jesse   " 1822, 1, 2
        Fanny   " 1824, 2, 29
        Mahlon   " 1826, 5, 10
        Sarah   " 1828, 8, 7
        Allen   " 1830, 7, 30 d 1839, 8,13
    bur Sandyspring
----, --, --. Jabez, s Jehu & Jane, Redstone
    Mtg, Fayette Co., Pa., b 1797,1,17 d 1886,
    2,14; m Sarah GARRETT, dt Joseph & Charity
    Goshen MM, Chester Co., Pa., b 1783,6,23
    d 1850,7,31 bur Augusta
    Ch: Rachel   b 1819, 10, 26
        Joseph   " 1822, 11, 4
        Benjamin   " 1825, 1, 22
        Pim   " 1827, 6, 8 d 1829, 7,28
        Ch b in Augusta Mtg
    Jabez m 2nd Abigail COULSON, dt Robert &
    Abigail REGESTER, b 1810,9,9 d 1904,3,30
    bur Augusta
    Ch: John   b 1854, 3, 11
----, --, --. Job, s Jabez & Anna, Mercer Co.,
    Pa., b 1799,9,14 d 1883,12,6 bur Augusta;
    m Ruth HOWARD, dt John & Cherry, Mount-
    pleasant, O., b 1807,1,16 d 1889,11,2
1843, 8, 9. Lydia, w David, d ae 33y 11m 18d
    bur at Augusta
----, --, --. John, s Jabez & Abigail, Colum-
    biana Co., O., b 1854,3,11; m Della M.

    Ch: Frank C.   b 1888, 1, 10
        Mary L.   " 1890, 6, 13
        Lizzie A.   " 1892, 12, 16
        Laura V.   " 1896, 9, 17
1888, 5, 28. Catharine, dt Godfrey Trogler,
    d ae 52y 1m 27d bur Augusta

1822, 6, 21. Ann & fam gc
1821, 11, 21. Job rmt Ruth Howard
1833, 3, 22. Elizabeth (form Reeder) dis mou

COULSON, continued

1835, 3, 27. Jehu & w, Jane, rocf Carmel MM, dtd 1835,2,21

1836, 6, 24. Jehu & w, Jane, gct Carmel MM

1840, 10, 23. Jehu & w, Jane, rocf Upper Springfield MM, dtd 1840,9,26

1842, 12, 23. David rmt Lydia Pimm

1843, 3, 24. Jane Merrick (form Coulson) dis mcd

1844, 3, 22. Amy Wolf (form Coulson) dis mcd

1844, 10, 25. Hannah C. (form Reeder) dis mcd

1856, 4, 26. Ann & s, Seth, rocf Middleton MM, dtd 1856,3,6 (W)

1862, 1, 25. Seth dis training in militia (W)

1863, 4, 25. Jabez & Abigail dis jG in 1854 (W)

1863, 4, 25. David dis jG in 1854 (W)

1863, 5, 23. Job & Ruth dis jG in 1854 (W)

1863, 5, 23. Benjamin & Lydia dis jG in 1854 (W)

1871, 10, 28. Margaret gct Plymouth MM (W)

COWGILL

1824, 5, 20. Joel & w, Rebecca, & s, Joseph, rocf Salem MM, dtd 1824,4,21

1830, 1, 22. Rebecca & ch, Joseph & Mary, gct Upper Springfield MM

1833, 2, 1. Rebecca & ch, Joseph, Mary, Armina Jane & Ruth, rocf Upper Springfield MM, dtd 1832,11,24

1837, 5, 26. Rebecca dis jas

DAVIS

----, --, --. John, s Samuel & Mary, Bucks Co., Pa.; m Lydia GILBERT, dt Joseph & Ann, Bucks Co., Pa., b 1782,7,26
   Ch: Jane   b 1812, 10, 13
       Mary   " 1815, 3, 25
       Hannah   " 1817, 5, 6
       Robert   " 1819, 12, 1
       Lydia   " 1822, 1, 10
       John   " 1827, 4, 27

----, --, --. David m Rachel JOHN, dt Griffith & Sarah, Chester Co., Pa., b 1791,10,28 d 1879,4,26 bur Augusta
   Ch: Hannah   b 1816, 7, 21
       David   " 1823, 2, 9
       Albert   " 1832, 1, 7

1820, 12, 22. Eleanor Blanshon (form Davis) con mcd

1823, 2, 21. Edith dis jas

1824, 2, 27. Lydia dis jas

1835, 6, 26. Mary Ann Trip (form Davis) dis mcd

1836, 10, 21. Jane Estep (form Davis) dis mou

1838, 12, 21. Hannah rmt Nathan Pim

1844, 12, 27. Lydia Price (form Davis) rpd mcd

1863, 6, 27. Rachel dis (W)

DEAN

----, --, --. James Hervy, s Jonathan & Han-

nah, Dutchess Co., N. Y., b 1799,4,11; m Eleanor WINDER, dt William & Aedah Frederick Co., Va., b 1799,3,17
   Ch: Edith   b 1821, 8, 5
       Stephen   " 1822, 10, 21
       Hannah   " 1824, 5, 5
       Milton   " 1826, 6, 13
       Mary Ann   " 1828, 5, 26
       Rhoda   " 1831, 2, 10
       William W. " 1833, 4, 26
   Ch all b mbr of Augusta PM

----, --, --. Barton, s Jonathan & Hannah, b 1803,8,26; m Hannah JACKSON, dt Isaac & Ann, Newgarden, O., b 1808,11,21 d 1838,12,3 bur Augusta
   Ch: Ephraim   b 1827, 2, 13
       David   " 1828, 8, 28
       Jonathan " 1830, 8, 20
       Isaac   " 1832, 6, 10
       Ann   " 1833, 9, 24
       Amos   " 1836, 2, 25 d 1836, 2,25
       bur Augusta
   Barton m 2nd Elizabeth STRATTON, dt Michael & Rhoda, Gloster Co., N. J., b 1800,1,10
   Ch: Abigail   b 1841, 11, 13
       Joshua S. " 1843, 10, 2

1862, 2, 26. Abigail m Wm. G. COPPICK (W)

1821, 6, 22. Elizaann rmt Mordecai Morlan

1826, 10, 27. Caroline S. rmt Davis Emmons

1826, 11, 24. Hannah rocf Newgarden MM, dtd 1826,9,21

1835, 2, 27. Mary Ann Rood (form Dean) dis mcd

1835, 3, 27. James Hervey & fam gct Marlborough MM

1837, 12, 22. Elwood rmt Elizabeth Emmons

1839, 9, 27. Elwood & w, Elizabeth, gct Chesterfield MM

1839, 11, 22. Hannah & Lavina gct Gilead MM

1841, 2, 26. Elizabeth rocf Salem MM, dtd 1841,2,24

1841, 10, 22. Amy gct Chesterfield MM

1855, 6, 23. Jonathan & w, Elizabeth B., & ch, Francis & Rachel S., gct New Garden MM (W)

1863, 4, 25. Barton dis jG in 1854 (W)

1866, 9, 22. Joshua S. gct Plymouth MM, to m Mary Ann Hobson (W)

1867, 8, 24. Mary Ann rocf Plymouth MM, dtd 1867,7,22 (W)

1867, 11, 23. Barton gct Hickory Grove MM, Ia., to m Ann Oliphant (W)

1868, 5, 23. Ann rocf Hickory Grove MM, Ia., dtd 1868,3,25 (W)

1870, 11, 26. Barton & w, Ann, gct New Garden MM (W)

1870, 11, 26. Ephraim gct New Garden MM (W)

1870, 11, 26. Joshua S. & w, Mary Ann, gct New Garden MM (W)

DUTTON

1821, 8, 24. Joseph & w, Mary, & ch, Elisha,
     Hannah, Maria, Sarah, Eliza, Phebe, Matil-
     da & Deborah, recrq
1827, 5, 25. Joanna & ch, Phebe, Thomas, Hen-
     ry, Martha & David Smith, rocf Carmel MM,
     dtd 1827,5,19
1829, 1, 21. Joanna dis jH
1830, 6, 25. Maria & Sarah dis jH
1831, 12, 23. Hannah dis jH
1833, 10, 25. Eliza dis jH
1838, 3, 23. Phebe dis jH
1838, 6, 22. Matilda & Deborah dis jH
1866, 11, 24. Hannah (form Clemson) con mcd
     (W)

EASTMAN
1857, 7, 25. Heneretta Whitacre (form East-
     man) dis mcd (W)

EDWARDS
1841, 12, 24. Margaret rocf New Garden MM, dtd
     1841,11,27
1843, 8, 25. Margaret dis jas

ELLIOTT
1822, 6, 21. Lydia, dt Sarah Cowgill, recrq
1826, 5, 26. Lydia, minor, gct Carmel MM

ELLIS
1821, 12, 21. Mary M. rmt John Neill Jr.
1828, 9, 26. Mary dis jH
1839, 4, 26. Mary Jr. dis jH
1839, 11, 22. Mary gct Falls Creek MM

EMMONS
----, --, --. Thomas, s Serenius & Rebecca,
     b 1781,10,11 d 1861,12,30; m Mary DAVIS,
     dt Isaac & Hannah, b 1781,4,23 d 1850,8,
     12
     Ch: Davis   b 1804, 1, 7 Frederick
          Co., Va.
         Rebecca   " 1805, 5, 26   "
         Cassandra " 1807, 1, 18 Beaver Co.,
          Pa., d 1828,11,30 bur Augusta
         Jacob   b 1808, 12, 23 New Garden
          Mtg, O.
         Thomas   " 1810, 11, 9 "   "
         Joseph   " 1812, 7, 31 Augusta Mtg
         Mary   " 1814, 6, 11 "   "
         Phebe   " 1816, 3, 7   "   "
         Elizabeth " 1818, 2, 2   "   "
         Cyrenius   " 1820, 8, 30 "   "
         Isaac   " 1824, 11, 20
----, --, --. Davis, s Thos. & Mary, Frederick
     Co., Md., b 1804,1,7 d 1828,10,12 bur
     Augusta; m Caroline S. DEAN, dt Jonathan
     & Hannah, Cipio MM, N. Y., b 1805,11,17
     Ch: Micajah   b 1827, 7, 19
         Davis   " 1829, 4, 14

1826, 10, 27. Davis rmt Caroline S. Dean
1829, 7, 24. Rebecca rmt Garrett Pim

1832, 7, 27. Caroline S. rmt Isaac Pim
1834, 2, 21. Thomas Jr. & w, Mary, rocf New
     Garden MM, dtd 1834,1,23
1837, 6, 23. Susanna Bratten (form Emmons)
     dis mou
1837, 7, 21. Thomas Jr. & w, Mary, & ch gct
     Pennsville MM
1837, 8, 25. Lydia dis jas
1837, 9, 22. Mary W. rocf Marlborough MM,
     dtd 1837,7,25
1837, 12, 22. Miriam dis disunity
1837, 12, 22. Elizabeth rmt Elwood Dean
1837, 12, 22. Phebe rmt Enos Pim
1840, 1, 24. Mary (form Smedley) dis mou
1844, 4, 26. Cyrenius rmt Sarah Stratton
1844, 12, 27. Meriam Wigine (form Emmons) rpd
     mcd & jas

ESTEP
1836, 10, 21. Jane (form Davis) dis mou

FARMER
----, --, --. John, s Wm. & Rebecca, N. C.,
     b 1776,12,12 d 1857,4,12 bur Salinesville;
     m Mary TAYLOR, dt Richard & Mary, S. C.,
     b 1780,1,1 d 1849,4,9 bur Salinesville
     Ch: William   b 1800, 10, 2 in Columbia
          Co., Ga.
         James   " 1802, 7, 19
         Rebecca   " 1805, 1, 3
         Mary   " 1807, 4, 11 in Columbi-
          ana Co., O.
         Keturah   b 1809, 4, 30
         John   " 1811, 7, 6 d 1831, 8,27
         Ann   " 1815, 7, 22
         Rhoda   " 1818, 3, 11
----, --, --. William, s John & Mary, Columbia
     Co., Ga., b 1800,10,2; m Mary PARKER, dt
     Isaac & Sarah, N. C., b 1793,12,25
     Ch: Sarah P.   b 1828, 2, 26 in Jeffer-
          son Co., O.
         Isaac P.   b 1829, 8, 22 "   "
         Mary C.   " 1831, 5, 3   "   "
         John W.   " 1833, 2, 16 "   "
         Jacob   " 1834, 10, 9 d 1836, 7,24
         Martha   " 1837, 5, 13 in Columbi-
          ana Co., O.
         Abby Ann   b 1839, 2, 3   "   "
----, --, --. James, s John & Mary, Columbia
     Co., Ga., b 1802,7,19; m Meriboh BUTLER,
     dt Benjamin & Hannah, Phila. Co., Pa.,
     b 1805,7,14
     Ch: Elihu   b 1836, 2, 18
         Beulah   " 1837, 8, 8
         Ellen   " 1839, 10, 3
         Lydia   " 1842, 4, 14
         Laura   " 1844, 3, 19 d 1859, 7,8
         Elizabeth " 1845, 12, 13
         James   " 1849, 7, 13 " 1852, 8,23

1830, 12, 20. Mary rmt Dearman Williams
1832, 5, 25. Kiturah rocf Flushing MM, dtd
     1832,4,26

FARMER, continued
1833, 9, 27. Rebecca rmt James Penrose
1835, 4, 24. Meriby rocf Upper Springfield
    MM, dtd 1835,1,24
1836, 5, 27. William & w, Mary, & ch, Sarah
    P., Isaac Parker, Mary Casander, John &
    Jacob, rocf Smithfield MM, dtd 1836,4,18
1837, 12, 22. Ann rmt William J. Parker
1840, 5, 22. Keturah Moore (form Farmer) con
    mou
1843, 6, 23. William & w, Mary, & six ch gct
    Short Creek MM, O.
1863, 5, 23. James & Meribah dis jG in 1854
    (W)

FARRINGTON
1825, 11, 25. Judith gct Smithfield MM
1826, 8, 25. Phebe rmt Samuel Fowler
1828, 12, 20. Judith rocf Smithfield MM, dtd
    1828,10,20
1834, 2, 21. Judith gct Marlborough MM
1835, 6, 26. Deborah & Sarah gct New Garden
    MM

FAWCETT
1839, 11, 22. Simeon rmt Deborah Miller
1840, 3, 27. Deborah M. gct Upper Spring-
    field MM

FOWLER
----, --, --. Caleb, s James & Mary, Pipe
    Creek MM, Frederick Co., Md., b 1792,3,31;
    m Mary RICHARDS, dt Abijah & Esther, Bed-
    ford Co., Va., Goose Creek MM, b 1800,6,
    11 d 1828,12,10 bur Sandyspring
    Ch: Milton
            Dewberry b 1822, 6, 24 Columbiana
            Co., O.
        Achsah Og-
            born   " 1824, 9, 3
    Caleb m 2nd Sarah SMITH, dt Joseph & Jo-
    anna, Frederick Co., Va., b 1804,8,28
    Ch: Gustavus
            Adolphus b 1831, 8, 8 d 1831, 8, 8
        John Smith " 1832, 8, 22
        Edmund Smith
                    b 1834, 4, 20
    All ch b in Sandyspring MM

1821, 8, 24. Caleb & w, Mary, rocf Carmel MM,
    dtd 1821,7,21
1821, 8, 24. Mary rocf Carmel MM, dtd 1821,
    7,21
1826, 8, 25. Samuel rmt Phebe Farrington
1830, 8, 27. Sarah (form Smith) con mou
1832, 11, 23. Phebe dis jH
1835, 4, 24. Mary gct Upper Springfield MM
1838, 7, 27. Caleb & w, Mary, & ch gct Ches-
    terfield MM

FOX
1840, 11, 27. Lydia (form Milbourn) dis mou

FRENCH
1857, 4, 29. David, s Barzillai & Mary, Co-
    lumbiana Co., O.; m in Sandyspring MH,
    Eliza MILLER, dt Morris & Ann, Columbi-
    ana Co., O. (W)

1857, 6, 27. Eliza gct Salem MM (W)

GARRIGUES
1836, 2, 26. Hellen, Deborah, Charles, Sally
    Ann, Elizabeth, William, Richard, Hannah
    & Mary Ann [Guarrigues] rocf Baltimore MM
    E. & W. Dist., dtd 1836,2,4
1839, 3, 22. Helen Hall (form Garrigues) dis
    mcd among Hicksites
1840, 5, 22. Maria (form Bentley) dis mcd
1842, 3, 25. Deborah [Garrigus] dis jH
1843, 6, 23. Sally Ann dis jH

GLOVER
1867, 12, 28. Amy (form John) con mcd (W)
1868, 8, 22. Ann gct Hickory Grove MM, Ia.

GREEN
1825, 5, 27. John rmt Mary Hole
1825, 6, 24. Mary gct Flushing MM

GREWELL
1834, 6, 27. John R. [Gruwell] rmt Sarah
    Miller
1834, 7, 25. Sarah [Gruwell] gct Marlborough
    MM
1839, 1, 25. John P. & w, Sarah, & ch, Debo-
    rah Ann, Caroline S. & Alice, rocf Upper
    Springfield MM, dtd 1838,12,22
1844, 7, 26. John P. & fam gct Upper Spring-
    field MM

GROSE
1870, 2, 26. Phebe (form John) dis mcd (W)

HALDEMAN
----, --, --. David [Halderman], s Abraham &
    Mary, Chester Co., Pa., b 1787,7,-- d
    1844,8,27; m Ann JOHNSON, dt Benjamin &
    Ann JOHNSON,   Chester
    Co., Pa., b 1783,10,12 d 1878,3,14 bur
    Augusta
    Ch: Benjamin b 1811, 10, 23
        Jacob   " 1813, 8, 9
        Elizabeth " 1814, 12, 2
        Ann   " 1816, 11, 28
        Martha   " 1818, 11, 30
        David   " 1820, 12, 30
        Abraham   " 1822, 2, 25 d 1822, 9, 7
         bur Augusta
        Susanna   b 1823, 8, 6
        Tamar   " 1825, 7, 15 " 1906, 2,17
         bur Augusta
        Joseph   b 1827, 5, 15
        Mary   " 1830, 12, 15
----, --, --. David Jr. b 1894,5,5 ae 73y 4m
    5d bur Augusta, Carroll Co., O.; m Anna

HALDEMAN, David Jr. & Anna, continued
  ----- d 1850,11,2 ae 26y 4m 17d bur Augusta
  Ch: John
        Leondo   b 1847, 3, 16
        Anna H.   " 1850, 10, 26
  David Jr. m 2nd Julia F. EASTMAN, dt Richard & Lovisa, b 1832,2,18
  Ch: Angelletta b 1854, 1, 21 d 1858, 1,25
        bur Augusta
        Richard A. b 1855, 12, 23
        Tamar S.   " 1858, 4, 25
        Lovisa E. " 1861, 6, 22
        Benjamin   " 1864, 10, 3
        Mary E.   " 1867, 11, 15 d 1873, 7,24
        bur Augusta
1877, 8, --. Julia F. d
----, --, --. Richard N., s David & Julia L.,
    Carroll Co., b 1855,12,23; m Philena
    BROGAN, dt Amos & Mary J., Columbiana Co.,
    O., b 1854,8,14

1832, 3, 23. David [Halderman] & fam gct
    Salem MM
1834, 5, 23. David [Halderman] & w, Ann, &
    ch, Ann, Martha, David, Susannah, Thomas,
    Joseph & Mary, rocf Salem MM, dtd 1834,4,
    23
1837, 12, 22. Ann rmt Joshua Brown
1838, 3, 23. David & fam gct Salem MM
1838, 3, 23. Martha gct Salem
1840, 4, 24. David [Halderman] & w, Ann,
    & ch, David, Susanna, Tamar, Joseph &
    Mary, rocf Salem MM, dtd 1840,4,22
1840, 4, 24. Martha [Halderman] rocf Salem
    MM, dtd 1840,4,22
1842, 4, 22. Jacob [Halderman] rmt Margery
    McBride
1842, 7, 22. Jacob [Halderman] & Margery gct
    Salem MM
1863, 4, 25. David & Guly dis jG in 1854 (W)
1863, 4, 25. Joseph & Esther dis jG in 1854
    (W)
1863, 4, 25. Ann & Tamer dis jG in 1854 (W)
----, --, --. Benjamin rem by letter to M. E.
    Ch., Mt. Zion
----, --, --. Richard & Philena rem to Mt.
    Zion M. E. Ch.

HALL
1834, 6, 27. Edwin C., Rufus M., William,
    Alfred & Elizabeth, minor ch Thomas, rocf
    Bradford MM, Pa., dtd 1834,6,4
1839, 3, 22. Helen (form Garrigues) dis mcd
    among Hicksites
1844, 11, 22. Asenath W. (form Arnold) dis jas
1867, 10, 26. Robert Miller gct Somerset MM,
    to m Mary Hall (W)
1869, 1, 23. Mary, Sarah R. & Deborah D., dt
    Mary Miller, rocf Somerset MM, dtd 1868,
    12,28

HAMMOND
----, --, --. Arthur W. b 1877,5,21; m Lillian
    ----- b 1879,1,15
  Ch: Lois Maria b 1905, 5, 8

HANNAH
1837, 7, 17. Robert d ae 84y & nearly 6m bur
    at Augusta MH

HARRELL
----, --, --. Thomas b 1827,8,25; m Caroline
    ----- b 1836,6,23
  Ch: Robert   b 1866, 6, 13
      David L. " 1870, 6, 13
      Edward J. " 1873, 8, 28
      Jason   " 1881, 9, 18 d 1903, 9, 3
      bur Augusta

----, --, --. Robert & David L. dropped from
    mbrp

HAWLEY
1821, 4, 27. Caleb & w, Catharine, & ch gct
    White Water MM, Ind.
1832, 12, 21. Mary Ann (form McBride) dis mou

HAYES
1831, 1, 21. Phebe (form Cooper) con mou
1844, 12, 27. James H., Mary Ann, Calvin C.,
    Eliza Jane, Elizabeth & Susan [Hays] minor
    ch Wm. & Phebe, recrq

HEALD
----, --, --. James, s Nathan & Rebecca, b
    1786,4,1 d 1842,11,20; m Mary ----- b
    1783,10,13
  Ch: Rebecca b 1818, 5, 16
      Eliza   " 1820, 3, 12
      James   " 1822, 9, 18
      Mary   " 1822, 9, 18
      Lydia   " 1825, 9, 6

1830, 10, 22. Nathan Jr. rmt Elizabeth Heston
1832, 6, 22. Nathan & w gct Middleton MM
1839, 1, 25. James & w, Mary, & ch, James,
    Mary & Lydia, rocf New Garden MM, dtd
    1838,12,20
1839, 4, 26. Eliza & Rebecca rocf New Garden
    MM, dtd 1839,3,21

HENRY
----, --, --. Josiah m Sarah J. CARMEN, dt
    John & Araminta, b 1839,11,25
  Ch: Rachel Ann b 1867, 9,16
      Marion Sylvester " 1869, 6, 29
      Mariah Evaline   " 1876, 7, 16

HESTON
----, --, --. David, s John & Elizabeth, b
    1808,9,28; m Ruth ARMSTRONG, dt James &
    Mary, Columbiana Co., O., b 1814,2,19

HESTON, David & Ruth, continued
 Ch: James b 1831, 12, 10
  Martha
   Jane " 1833, 10, 20
  Joseph " 1835, 8, 27
  Jefferson " 1838, 7, 6

1822, 12, 27. Hannah dis jas
1825, 9, 23. Ann Reeder (form Heston) con mcd
1830, 10, 22. Elizabeth rmt Nathan Heald Jr.
1830, 12, 24. David rmt Ruth Armstrong
1831, 10, 21. Phebe (form Armstrong) dis mou
1832, 1, 27. Rebecca Reeder (form Heston) dis
 mou
1858, 12, 25. Jefferson dis disunity (W)
1862, 1, 25. Joseph dis training with militia
 (W)

HOBSON
1866, 9, 22. Joshua S. Dean gct Plymouth MM,
 to m Mary Ann Hobson (W)

HOLE
----, --, --. John, s Jacob & Mary, b 1785,1,
 7 d 1868,2,3 bur Augusta; m Catharine
 HANNAH, dt Robert & Catharine, South
 River Mtg, Va., b 1794,11,25 d 1881,5,3
 bur Augusta
 Ch: Lemuel b 1818, 10, 27 in Carmel
  Mtg, O.
  Elias " 1820, 5, 4 Augusta PM
  Esther " 1822, 5, 7 d 1890, 8,30
  Anna " 1824, 6, 15
  Caleb " 1827, 3, 6
  Robert H. " 1829, 5, 16
  Mary " 1833, 4, 2
  Rachel " 1837, 8, 16 d 1929, 1,15
   Alliance, O.; m 1858,12,29 W. P. Rice
----, --, --. Nathan, s Jacob & Mary (nm) b
 1794,4,3; m Sarah ARMSTRONG, dt James &
 Ruth, Kennet MM, Dela., b 1793,9,22
 Ch: Phebe b 1819, 8, 23
  Ethan " 1820, 11, 17
  James " 1822, 6, 14
  Jane " 1824, 3, 31
  Mary " 1826, 1, 6
  Samuel " 1827, 8, 29
  ----- " 1827, 8, 29 d 1827, 8,31
   bur Augusta
  Jacob b 1829, 10, 23 " 1830, 1,18
   bur Augusta
  Joseph b 1830, 11, 20 " 1831, 2, 8
   bur Augusta
  Sarah b 1832, 9, 29
----, --, --. Mahlon, s Jacob & Mary, Loudoun
 Co., Va., b 1792,12,1 d 1871,3,13 bur
 Augusta; m Rachel SCHOOLY, dt Elisha &
 Rachel, Bedford Co., Va., b 1794,7,17 d
 1895,2,12 ae 100y 6m 25d
 Ch: Charlotte b 1822, 4, 26
  Jared " 1823, 11, 8 d 1850, 3,20
   bur Augusta
  Israel b 1827, 4, 2

  Ch: Mary b 1829, 3, 14
  Elisha " 1831, 5, 14 d 1837, 3,23
   bur Augusta
----, --, --. Jacob Jr., s Jacob & Mary, Bed-
 ford Co., Va., b 1802,3,11; m Ann CHAMBERS
 dt James & Mary, Ireland, b 1807,9,28
 Ch: William b 1829, 11, 14
  Jonah " 1831, 1, 22
  James " 1832, 12, 30
  Charles " 1834, 11, 23 d 1842, 8, 5
   bur Augusta
  Thomas b 1837, 2, 24 d 1842, 8, 3
   bur Augusta
  John b 1839, 6, 9 " 1842, 8, 4
   bur Augusta
  Joshua b 1841, 9, 21
  Mary Ellen " 1843, 6, 22
  Rebecca
   Jane " 1845, 12, 28
  Joseph " 1848, 8, 3
----, --, --. Lemuel, s John & Casharn, Colum-
 biana Co., O., b 1818,10,27 d 1865,1,20;
 m Unity C. STANLEY, dt Benjamin & Eliza-
 beth, Columbiana Co., O., b 1820,1,27
 Ch: Benjamin b 1841, 4, 12
  Gulaelma " 1842, 11, 26 d 1856, 6,18
   bur Augusta
  Leonard H. b 1844, 6, 23
  Catharine
   Elizabeth " 1846, 10, 5
  Eliza Anna " 1848, 12, 27
  John Frank-
   lin " 1852, 3, 19 d 1856,12,17
   bur Augusta
  Jacob Thos.b 1854, 3, 18
  Charles
   Stanley " 1856, 8, 11
  Esther Elma" 1858, 7, 31
  Lemuel Pen-
   rose " 1860, 11, 5
----, --, --. Caleb, s John & Catharine, b
 1827,3,6; m Sophia MILLER, dt Morris &
 Ann, b 1839,1,8
 Ch: Norman W. b 1869, 5, 23
  Anna L. " 1873, 6, 18
1877, 9, --. Mary d (a minister)
1882, 2, --. Caleb d (an elder)
----, --, --. J. Melville, s Robert & Lydia,
 b 1859,4,27; m Lovisa E. HALDEMAN, dt
 David & Julia F., Augusta, O., b 1861,6,22
 Ch: Gertrude F.b 1886, 3, 14
----, --, --. Leander H., s Robert & Lydia,
 Augusta Mtg, b 1854,12,6; m Ida M. COUL-
 SON, dt Lewis & Mariah, Kensington, O.
 b 1854,10,17
 Ch: Erwing Jay b 1888, 10, 14 Carroll Co.

1825, 5, 27. Mary rmt John Green
1826, 2, 24. Mahlon & w, Rachel, & two ch
 gct Salem MM
1828, 7, 25. Mahlon & w, Rachel, & ch,
 Charlotte, Jared & Israel, rocf Salem MM,

HOLE, continued
    dtd 1828,6,25
1828, 11, 21. Jacob Jr. rmt Ann Chambers
1832, 3, 23. Mahlon & fam gct Salem MM
1834, 5, 23. Mahlon & w, Rachel, & ch, Char-
    lotte, Jared, Israel, Mary, Elisha & Ja-
    cob, rocf Salem MM, dtd 1834,4,23
1839, 6, 21. Nathan & w, Sarah, & ch gct
    Carmel MM
1839, 8, 23. Phebe gct Carmel MM
1840, 9, 25. Unity C. rocf Upper Springfield
    MM, dtd 1840,8,22
1844, 11, 22. Charlotte rmt Jesse K. Pettit
1856, 6, 28. Mary Tritt (form Hole) dis mcd
    & jas (W)
1860, 4, 28. Sophia (form Miller) dis mcd
1863, 4, 25. Mahlon & Rachel dis jG in 1854
    (W)
1863, 4, 25. John & Catharine dis jG in 1854
    (W)
1863, 4, 25. Lemuel, Unity & Benjamin dis jG
    in 1854 (W)
1863, 4, 25. Robert & Lydia dis jG in 1854
    (W)
1863, 4, 25. Israel & Mary dis jG in 1854
    (W)
1863, 4, 25. Jacob dis jG in 1854 (W)
----, --, --. J. Melville & Lovisa E. dis
----, --, --. Leander H. & w, Ida M., & fam rem
    to Lane MM, Mich.

IREY
1829, 12, 25. Rachel (form McBride) dis jas
1842, 7, 22. Rebecca (form Clark) con mcd
1843, 9, 22. Rebecca gct New Garden MM

IDDINGS
1822, 7, 26. Samuel [Idings] & w, Hannah, &
    ch, William, Townsend, Elwood, Thomas,
    Elihu & Eliza, rocf Newgarden MM, dtd
    1822,6,20
1840, 6, 26. Eliza dis disunity

JACKSON
1823, 10, 24. Alice rst on consent of New-
    garden MM
1835, 1, 23. Jane (form Battin) dis mou
1833, 11, 27. Anna (form Stackhouse) dis mou

JAMES
----, --, --. Thomas d 1840,4,1 ae 66y 10d bur
    at Augusta; m Sarah -----
    Ch: John   b 1774, 3, 21 d 1840, 4, 1
        bur Augusta
----, --, --. Jesse, s Isaac & Sarah, Columbi-
    ana Co., O., b 1805,4,30; m Elizabeth
    SMITH, dt Joseph & Joanna, Beaver Co.,
    Pa., b 1806,11,11
    Ch: Jonathan b 1825, 3, 15
        Joseph
         Smith   " 1827, 6, 11
        Phebe S. " 1829, 6, 11
        Ch b in Sandyspring Mtg

1825, 4, 22. Jesse & w, Elizabeth, & s,
    Jonathan, rocf Carmel MM, dtd 1825,4,16
1827, 4, 27. David & w, Mary, & ch, Ruth
    Ann, Mary & Martha, rocf Carmel MM, dtd
    1827,4,21
1828, 1, 25. David & fam gct Carmel MM
1830, 2, 26. John & w, Esther, gct Marl-
    borough MM
1831, 12, 23. Jesse & fam gct Carmel MM
1839, 11, 22. John & w, Martha, & s, John,
    rocf Upper Springfield MM, dtd 1839,10,26
1839, 11, 22. Mary & Rachel rocf Upper Spring-
    field MM, dtd 1839,10,26
1841, 3, 26. Sarah rocf Middleton MM, dtd
    1841,1,7
1842, 3, 25. Hannah (form McBride) con mou
1843, 7, 21. Mary rmt Edward Stratton
1843, 8, 25. Sarah gct Salem MM
1844, 3, 22. Martha gct Salem MM
1844, 6, 21. Rachel gct Salem MM

JOHN
----, --, --. Abner, s Griffith & Sarah, b
    1789,5,17; m Hannah READER, dt Samuel &
    Ann, Bucks Co., b 1795,1,11
    Ch: Ann   b 1816, 9, 6
        William   " 1818, 9, 4 d 1833, 3,15
        bur Sandy Spring
        Amy   b 1821, 2, 27
        Sarah   " 1825, 5, 29 d 1833, 3,11
        Samuel   " 1830, 6, 14
        Abner   " 1834, 7, 20
----, --, --. Benjamin, s Griffith & Sarah,
    Chester Co., Pa., b 1793,9,25 d 1827,8,19
    bur Sandy Spring; m Hannah WINDER, dt
    William & Adah, Bucks Co., Pa., b 1791,10,
    Ch: Rebecca   b 1818, 7, 26   [22
        Griffith   " 1820, 4, 16
        William   " 1822, 5, 31
        Abner   " 1825, 12, 20
        Mary   " 1827, 2, 25
----, --, --. Nathan, s Griffith & Sarah, b
    1799,10,19 d 1895,4,10; m Sarah BECK, dt
    Preston & Sarah, b 1803,1,10 d 1889,9,4
    Ch: Benjamin   b 1828, 9, 24
        Abigail   " 1830, 8, 29
        Lewis   " 1833, 4, 26
        Phebe   " 1835, 2, 26
        Levi   " 1839, 12, 11
        Meribah   " 1844, 9, 12
        Austin   " 1847, 11, 24
1853, 7, 10. Sarah, mother of Nathan, d ae
    93y 9m 25d

1821, 11, 23. Abigail rmt Benjamin Winder
1822, 11, 22. Sarah Jr. rmt John Cobourn
1827, 10, 26. Sarah rocf Newgarden MM, dtd
    1827,8,23
1833, 7, 26. Hannah Pettit (form Johns)
    dis mou
1839, 5, 24. Ann rmt Joseph Reeder
1863, 1, 24. Nathan dis jG in 1854 (W)
1863, 1, 24. Sarah dis jG in 1854

JOHN, continued

1863, 1, 24. Merihab dis jG in 1854 (W)
1865, 12, 23. Hannah dis disunity (W)
1867, 12, 28. Amy Glover (form John) con mcd (W)
1870, 2, 26. Phebe Grose (form John) dis mcd (W)

JONSON

1843, 5, 26. Sarah [Johnson] rocf Salem MM, dtd 1843,4,17
1859, 6, 25. Sarah gct Salem MM (W)
1863, 7, 25. Eliza (form Reeder) dis mcd (W)

JONES

1836, 1, 22. Joshua rmt Rebecca Miller
1836, 6, 24. Rebecca gct Upper Springfield MM

KELLEY

1863, 4, 25. Elizabeth dis jG in 1854 (W)

KIRK

1832, 6, 22. Mary G. rocf Smithfield MM, dtd 1832,3,19
1833, 12, 27. Mary G. gct Salem MM

LADD

1837, 5, 26. Thirza (form Mires) dis mou

LANGSTAFF

1840, 6, 26. Lydia (form Penington) con mou
1842, 6, 24. Lydia gct Cincinnati MM

LEE

1855, 9, 14. Amanda H., dt Allen & Amanda, b

LEECH

1840, 2, 21. Thomas rmt Ellen Stratton
1840, 5, 22. Ellen gct Carmel MM

LOCKHARD

1834, 1, 24. Sarah (form McBride) dis mou

LYNCH

1843, 1, 27. Joshua rmt Jane McBride
1843, 1, 27. Jane rqct Upper Springfield MM

McBRIDE

----, --, --. Stephen, s James & Mary, b
1759,2,10; m Hannah SMITH, dt Jeremiah &
Betty, Frederick Co., Va., b 1761,3,31 d
1823,12,24 bur Sandy Spring
Ch: John   b 1781, 9, 6 Hopewell MM
    Frederick Co., Va.
    Stephen   b 1783, 6, 15   "   "
    Ann   " 1785, 1, 4   "   "
    James   " 1786, 10, 31 "   "
    Jeremiah   " 1788, 7, 8   "   "
    Evan   " 1790, 5, 15   "   "
    Mary   " 1792, 5, 12. "   "
    Hannah   " 1794, 5, 9   "   "
    Samuel   " 1795, 12, 27 "   "

Ch: Andrew   b 1797, 11, 8 Hopewell
    MM, Frederick Co., Va.
    Charity   b 1800, 9, -- d 1802, 4,--
    bur Back Creek
    Betty   b 1802, 10, 31 Hopewell
    MM, Frederick Co., Va.
    Abraham   b 1805, 12, 3   "
Stephen m 2nd 1831,--,-- Jane HOWEL, dt
Timothy & Jane Rebecca, Loudon Co., Va.
----, --, --. Jeremiah, s Stephen & Hannah,
b 1788,7,18; m Elizabeth VOTAW, dt Mose
& Mary, b 1794,6,14
Ch: Isaac V.   b 1812, 12, 1
    Moses   " 1814, 3, 23
    Gideon   " 1817, 3, 19
    Mary   " 1818, 10, 7
    Mahlon   " 1820, 9, 30 d 1822, 3,22
    bur Augusta
    Hannah S.   b 1822, 5, 21
    Rachel   " 1824, 3, 28
    John   " 1826, 3, 1
    Joshua   " 1828, 1, 24
    Ann   " 1830, 8, 17
----, --, --. Evan, s Stephen & Hannah, Hope-
well MM, Va., b 1790,5,15 d 1826,6,-- bur
Augusta; m Jane PENNOCK, dt Joseph & Han-
nah, Westland, Pa., b 1795,7,1
Ch: Margery   b 1815, 11, 18 Augusta
    Mtg
    Hannah   " 1817, 5, 10   "
    Rebecca   " 1819, 7, 11   "
    Mary   " 1821, 8, 9   "
    Joseph P.   " 1824, 3, 9   "
    Mildred R. " 1826, 7, 12   "
----, --, --. Joseph P., s Evan & Jane, Carroll Co., b 1824,3,9 d 1871,1,21; m Susanna HALDEMAN, dt David & Ann, Columbi-
anna Co., O., b 1823,8,6
Ch: Mary A.   b 1853, 7, 20
    Jesse B.   " 1857, 10, 21
    Jacob H.   " 1860, 8, 22
    Sidney J.   " 1862, 10, 10
    David E.   " 1868, 4, 15 d 1869, 2,18
    bur Augusta

1826, 3, 24. Charity dis jas
1826, 6, 23. Hannah dis jas
1827, 6, 27. Betsy gct Newgarden MM
1828, 3, 21. Ann & Margaret, dt Stephen, dis jas
1828, 7, 25. Betsy rocf New Garden MM, dtd 1828,7,24
1828, 11, 21. Betsy rmt Benjamin Stanton
1831, 10, 21. Jane rocf Upper Springfield MM, dtd 1831,8,27
1832, 12, 21. Mary Ann Hawley (form McBride) dis mou
1834, 1, 24. Sarah Lockhard (form McBride) dis mou
1834, 9, 28. James & fam gct Alum Creek MM
1834, 10, 24. Ann & ch gct Alum Creek MM
1834, 10, 24. Maria gct Alum Creek MM
1836, 10, 21. Hannah (form Schooley) dis mou

McBRIDE, continued
1836, 11, 25. Rebecca gct Alum Creek MM
1837, 5, 3. James & w, Elizabeth, & ch,
    Isaac, David, Jesse, James, Ann, Ruth,
    Hannah, Elihu, Grace, James, Elizabeth,
    Benjamin & Lydia, rocf Allum Creek MM, dtd
    1837,2,23
1838, 1, 26. Rebecca Bowersock (form McBride)
    con mou
1838, 3, 23. Mary Perdue (form McBride) dis
    mou
1838, 11, 23. Charity McDonald (form McBride)
    dis mou
1842, 4, 22. Margety rmt Jacob Halderman
1842, 3, 25. Hannah James (form McBride) con
    mou
1843, 1, 27. Jame rmt Joshua Lynch
1843, 11,24. Rachel gct Lick Creek MM
1843, 11, 24. Elizabeth & ch, John, Joshua,
    Ann, Isaac & Albert, gct Lick Creek MM
1844, 4, 26. Elizabeth & seven minor ch gct
    Carmel MM
1844, 4, 26. Ann, Ruth & Hannah gct Salem MM
1871, 11, 25. Isaac rst at Cole Creek MM, Ia.
    on consent of this mtg (W)
----, --, --. Mary A. gct Damascus MM, O.
----, --, --. Jesse B. glt M. E. Church

McCARTY
----, --, --. Elizabeth d

McDONALD
1838, 11, 23. Charity (form McBride) dis mou

McGOWEN
----, --, --. James b 1764,4,1 d 1839,7,24 bur
    Augusta

McLEAN
1897, 11, 19. Alexander d

McNELY
1827, 4, 27. Abigail [McNely] gct Middleton
    MM
1828, 9, 26. Jane dis jH
1829, 9, 25. Lydia [McNely] dis jH
1830, 9, 24. Mary [McNely] dis jas
1831, 10, 21. Rachel dis jas
1838, 11, 23. Abigail Paxton (form McNeely)
    con mou

MALONE
1840, 5, 22. Mary Ann (form Penington) con
    mou

MARSH
----, --, --. Elias, s Elias & Martha, Wood-
    bridge, East Jersey, b 1788,9,7; m Edith
    TOWNSEND dt Benjamin & Jemima, Washing-
    ton Co. Pa., b 1791,12,7
      Ch: Robert   b 1811, 2, 25 Newgarden
          MM, O.
          Martha   " 1812, 9, 5   "

      Ch: William   b 1816, 1, 25 Newgarden
          MM, O.
          Lydia   " 1818, 4, 5 Sandyspring
          MM, O.
          Jesse   " 1820, 10, 11 Newgarden
          MM, O.
          Sabina   " 1823, 9, 12 Sandyspring
          MM, O.
          Fanny   " 1827, 6, 13   "
          Joseph   " 1830, 5, 8   "

1821, 8, 24. Phebe Ann & Sarah, minors, rocf
    Carmel MM, dtd 1821,7,21
1822, 5, 24. Elias & w, Edith, & ch, Robert,
    Martha, William, Lydia & Jesse, rocf New-
    garden MM, dtd 1822,3,21
1824, 12, 24. Phebe Ann & Sarah gct Carmel MM
1832, 6, 22. James Jr. & w, Lydia, & ch,
    Eliza & Mary, rocf Carmel MM, dtd 1832,5,
    9
1834, 5, 23. Elias & fam gct Duck Creek MM,
    Ind.
1834, 5, 23. Martha gct Duck Creek MM, Ind.
1835, 8, 21. Minor ch of Elizabeth gct Car-
    mel MM
1835, 11, 27. Eliza & Mary gct Carmel MM

MENDENHALL
1837, 10, 27. Aaron & w, Lydia, rocf New Gar-
    den MM, dtd 1837,8,24

MERCER
1832, 12, 21. Ruth rocf Middleton MM, dtd
    1832,11,8
1844, 11, 22. Ruth Wise (form Mercer) rpd
    mcd

MERRICK
1843, 3, 24. Jane (form Coulson) dis mcd

MIDDLETON
1823, 9, 26. Mary rmt Evan Cooper
1825, 11, 25. Hannah gct Salem MM
1828, 7, 25. Lydia rmt Isaac Sharp
1830, 5, 21. Nathaniel & w, Dorothy, & ch gct
    Upper Springfield MM
1833, 5, 24. Deborah Jr. gct Salem MM

MILBOURN
1829, 4, 24. Betsy Baxter (form Milbourn)
    dis mou
1829, 8, 21. Jane dis disunity
1840, 11, 27. Lydia Fox (form Milbourn) dis
    mou

MILLER
----, --, --. Levi, s Robert, Bucks Co., Pa.,
    b 1774,6,20 d 1838,8,6 bur Sandyspring; m
    Deborah MORRIS, dt Isaac & Hannah, b 1777,
    9,9 d 1816,12,20 bur Sandyspring
      Ch: Morris   b 1799, 7, 27 Westland MM,
          Pa.
          Robert   " 1800, 10, 8   "   "

MILLER, Levi & Deborah, continued
```
    Ch: Isaac       b 1802,  3, 24
        Nathan      " 1804,  1, 20 d 1808, 3,20
          bur Westland, Pa.
        Hannah      b 1805,  9, 28 Westland MM
        Mary        " 1807,  2, 23    "      "
        Levi        " 1808, 11,  6    "      "
        Sarah       " 1811,  1, 15 Sandyspring
          MM, O.
        Samuel      " 1812,  9,  5    "
        Rebecca     " 1814, 10,  9    "
        Debby       " 1816, 10, 22    "
    Levi m 2nd Ann HOLE, dt Chas. & Mary, b
    1777,11,5
```
----, --, --. Robert, s Levi & Deborah, West-
    land Mtg, Pa., b 1800,10,8; m Catharine
    ----- d 1825,6,9 ae 22y 5m 15d bur Sandy-
    spring
```
    Ch: Catharine
        H.          b 1825,  5, 15 d 1825, 6,24
          bur Carmel
```
    Robert m 2nd Susannah NIGHT, dt Samuel &
    Sarah HOLLAND, Phila., Pa., b 1803,7,11
```
    Ch: Samuel
        Holland     b 1828,  8,  3
```
----, --, --. Isaac, s Levi & Deborah, b 1802,
    3,24; m Martha PENNINGTON, dt Levi & Mary,
    b 1810,10,15
```
    Ch: Mary Jane   b 1831, 12, 18
        Zadock      " 1834,  1, 20
        Deborah Ann " 1836,  9, 13
        Wilmer      " 1841,  6, 28
        Isaac New-
        ton         " 1846,  9, 25
```

1824, 3, 26. Ann rocf Newgarden MM, dtd 1824,
    1,22
1824, 12, 24. Catharine rocf Carmel MM, dtd
    1824,11,21
1827, 11, 23. Robert rmt Susanna K. Holland
1828, 6, 27. Hannah rmt Jacob Reeder
1830, 8, 27. Ann Jr. dis jH
1830, 10, 22. Martha rocf Newgarden MM, dtd
    1830,10,21
1831, 8, 26. Mary rmt Moses Votaw
1832, 3, 23. Maria rocf New Garden MM, dtd
    1832,1,26
1834, 6, 27. Sarah rmt John P. Gruwell
1835, 1, 23. Charity P. rocf New Garden MM,
    dtd 1835,1,22
1836, 1, 22. Rebecca rmt Joshua Jones
1839, 11, 22. Deborah rmt Simeon Fawcett
1839, 12, 27. Maria & ch gct Westland MM
1843, 10, 27. Maria P. & ch, William B.,
    Franklin, Hezikiah P., Mary Ann, James
    Madison, Mordecai & Francis P., rocf
    Westland MM, 1843,9,20
1856, 9, 27. Morris Jr. dis disunity (W)
1860, 2, 25. Oliver dis disunity (W)
1860, 4, 28. Sophia Hole (form Miller) dis
    mcd (W)
1860, 9, 22. Sarah Ann Morris (form Miller)
    dis mcd (W)

1863, 4, 25. Robert dis jG in 1854 (W)
1867, 10, 26. Robert gct Somerset MM, to m
    Mary Hall (W)
1869, 1, 23. Mary H. & dt, Mary, Sarah R. &
    Deborah D. Hall, the latter two minors,
    rocf Somerset MM, dtd 1868,12,28 (W)

MOORE
1840, 5, 22. Keturah (form Farmer) con mou
1841, 6, 25. Keturah [More] gct Upper Spring-
    field MM

MORLAN
1821, 6, 22. Mordecai rmt Elizann Dean
1822, 9, 22. Mordecai & w, Eliza Ann, gct
    Middleton MM
1829, 6, 26. Emily & ch, Ann, Deborah,
    James, Elizabeth, Phebe, Nathan & Jonah,
    prcf Carmel MM, dtd 1829,3,21; not accept-
    ed because she attended mcd
1830, 9, 24. Emily & Deborah dis jas
1835, 1, 23. Lydia rocf Salem MM, dtd 1835,
    12,24
1836, 6, 24. Sarah [Morelan] rocf Salem MM,
    dtd 1836,5,25
1838, 4, 27. Mordecai & w, Eliza Ann, & ch,
    Edwin, Louisa, Theophilus, Roxana, Caro-
    line, Micajah, Newberry & Elmira, rocf
    Salem MM, dtd 1838,3,21
1839, 7, 26. Sarah rmt Lewis Pim
1839, 11, 22. Mordecai & w, Eliza Ann, & ch
    gct Middleton MM
1842, 3, 25. Lydia rmt Joseph Winder
1842, 4, 22. Phebe Whitacre (form Morlan)
    dis mou & jas
1843, 12, 22. Elizabeth dis jas

MORRIS
1860, 9, 22. Sarah Ann (form Miller) dis
    mcd (W)

MORRISON
1826, 5, 26. Matilda (form Woods) dis mou

MYERS
1822, 8, 23. Cynthia, Thirza & Elizabeth, ch
    Jonathan, recrq
1823, 6, 27. Cynthia rmt Joseph Pennock
1837, 5, 26. Thirza Ladd (form Mires) dis
    mou
1844, 3, 22. Elizabeth Wells (form Myers)
    dis jas

NEILL
1821, 12, 21. John Jr. rmt Mary M. Ellis
1822, 3, 22. Mary M. gct New Garden MM
1842, 6, 24. Justine Ann [Neille] rocf Car-
    mel MM, dtd 1842,5,21
1863, 4, 25. Joseph & Mary [Neal] dis jG in
    1854 (W)

NOLING
----, --, --. Coyt -----

NOLING, continued
----, --, --. Lewis _____
1860, 10, 10. Mary A. b

OLIPHANT
1867, 11, 23. Barton Dean gct Hickory Grove MM,
    Ia., to m Ann Oliphant (W)

ORR
1867, 5, 3. Harriet M., dt Parker & Mary, E.
    Rochester, O., b

----, --, --. Harriet M. rem by letter to Mt.
    Zion M. E. Ch.

PACKER
1824, 5, 20. Sarah (form Cobourn) con mou
1829, 10, 23. Sarah gct Upper Springfield MM

PARKER
1837, 12, 22. William J. rmt Ann Farmer
1838, 4, 27. Ann gct Short Creek MM
1844, 2, 23. William J. & w, Ann, & ch,
    Claudius Galen & Joseph John, rocf Short
    Creek MM, O., dtd 1843,7,18

PAXTON
1838, 11, 23. Abigail (form McNeely) con mou
1842, 2, 25. Abigail rst
1842, 4, 22. Abigail gct New Garden MM

PENNINGTON
1835, 1, 23. Levi & w, Mary, & ch, Mary Ann
    & Frances, rocf New Garden MM, dtd 1834,
    12,25
1835, 4, 24. Lydia rocf New Garden MM, dtd
    1835,3,26
1840, 5, 22. Mary Ann Malone (form Pennington)
    con mou
1840, 6, 26. Lydia Langstaff (form Pennington)
    con mou
1841, 8, 27. Frances B. gct Cincinnati MM
1844, 1, 26. Levi [Penington] rmt Jane Cooper

PENNOCK
1823, 6, 27. Joseph rmt Cynthia Myers
1824, 4, 23. Dinah dis disunity
1829, 8, 21. Hannah Jr. dis disunity
1833, 5, 24. Ruth Sanders (form Pennock) dis
    mou
1837, 3, 24. Hannah gct White River MM, Ind.
1837, 3, 24. Cynthia & seven ch gct White
    River MM, Ind.
1841, 8, 27. Cynthia [Penock] & ch, Hannah,
    Elizabeth, Elin, Grace, Rebecca, David &
    Jonathan, rocf White River MM, dtd 1841,
    5,8
1844, 3, 22. Elizabeth dis jas

PENROSE
----, --, --. James, s Thos. & Sarah,. Catta-
    wisse Mtg, Pa., b 1803,7,2; m Rebecca
    FARMER, dt John & Mary, Newgarden Mtg, O.

b 1805,1,3 d 1855,8,8 bur Salinesville
    Ch: William   b 1834, 11, 7
        Mary   " 1836, 6, 30
        Sarah   " 1838, 7, 8
        Meribah   " 1840, 6, 3
        Thomas   " 1842, 5, 7
        Rhoda   " 1844, 2, 27

1833, 9, 27. James rmt Rebecca Farmer
1833, 10, 25. Rebecca gct Deerfield MM
1840, 1, 24. James & w, Rebecca, & ch, Wil-
    liam, Mary & Sarah, rocf Pennsville MM,
    dtd 1839,12,19
1863, 9, 26. Benjamin, John & William [Pen-
    ros] dis jG in 1854 (W)
1863, 10, 24. James, Esther, John & Mary dis
    jG in 1854 (W)

PERDUE
1838, 3, 23. Mary (form McBride) dis mou

PETTIT
----, --, --. William, s Wm. & Sarah, Buck-
    ingham MM, Bucks Co., Pa., b 1773,4,18
    d 1849,7,27 bur Sandyspring; m Mary
    PHIPPS, dt Benj. & Margaret, Euchland
    MM, Chester Co., Pa., b 1782,7,6 d 1843,
    1,25 bur Sandyspring
    Ch: Benjamin b 1800, 8, 30 d 1883, 2,27
        bur Hanover
        Elizabeth b 1803, 3, 22
        Sarah   " 1805, 9, 1 d 1805, 9,18
        bur Northumberland Co., Pa.
        William   b 1806, 10, 2 d 1853, 8,30
        bur Laurel Hill Cem., Philadelphia
        Joseph   b 1809, 6, 28
        Margaret   " 1811, 11, 16 d 1861,10,14
        bur Sandyspring
        Charity   b 1814, 9, 17 " 1887,11,18
        bur Mt. Union Cem., Alliance, O.; m
        ----- RICE
        Elnathan   b 1817, 3, 27
        Jesse Ker-
        sey   " 1819, 10, 24
        Milton   " 1822, 7, 14
----, --, --. Joseph, s Wm. & Mary, b 1809,6,
    28; m Hannah Z. HUSSY, dt Christopher &
    Lydia, b 1810,8,29
    Ch: Curtis H. b 1833, 9, 18
        William   " 1835, 12, 14
        Asahel H. " 1841, 7, 2
        Mary   " 1843, 10, 12
----, --, --. Jesse Kersey, s Wm. & Mary P.,
    b 1819,10,24 d 1902,5,3 bur Augusta; m
    Charlotte HOLE, dt Mahlon & Rachel, Colum-
    biana Co., O., b 1822,4,26 d 1894,7,14
    bur Augusta
    Ch: Lucretia M.b 1846, 6, 30
        Elmyra   " 1848, 8, 30 d 1863,10,13
        bur Augusta
        Jared H.   b 1851, 12, 18 " 1902, 5,14
        bur Augusta

PETTIT, continued
1822, 11, 22. Elizabeth rmt James Raley
1824, 1, 23. Martha dis jas
1824, 3, 26. Elizabeth, Sarah & Mary, minor
    ch Chas., dec, gct Carmel MM
1825, 2, 25. Beulah Ann gct Newgarden MM
1825, 8, 26. Abigail rocf Newgarden MM, dtd
    1825,7,21
1831, 12, 23. Mary, minor, rocf Carmel MM,
    dtd 1831,12,17
1833, 6, 21. Hannah G. rocf Short Creek MM,
    O., dtd 1833,5,21
1833, 7, 26. Hannah (form John) dis mou
1834, 7, 25. Hannah [Pettitt] rst
1835, 2, 27. Charity D. rmt Chas. H. Rice
1836, 10, 21. Mary Jr. gct Carmel MM
1840, 9, 25. Hannah G. rocf Short Creek MM,
    O., dtd 1840,7,21
1841, 6, 25. Elnathen & fam gct Short Creek
    MM, O.
1844, 10, 25. Hannah G. rocf Short Creek MM,
    dtd 1844,9,24
1844, 11, 22. Jesse K. rmt Charlotte Hole
1863, 4, 25. Cursey & Charlotte dis jG in
    1854 (W)
1863, 9, 26. Joseph, Hannah G. & Mary dis jG
    in 1854 (W)

PIM
----, --, --. Nathan, s Isaac & Hannah, Ches-
    ter Co., Pa., b 1783,3,31 d 1816,11,26
    bur Augusta; m Sarah GARRETT, dt Joseph &
    Charity, Chester Co., Pa., b 1783,6,23
    Ch: Garrett   b 1805, 10, 26 Bradford
         MM, Chester Co., Pa.
        Isaac   b 1807, 6, 21   "
        Lydia   " 1809, 8, 21   "
        Enos   " 1811, 11, 24   "
        Lewis   " 1814, 4, 14.   "
        Nathan   " 1816, 9, 3   "
----, --, --. Garrett, s Nathan & Sarah, Calne
    Mtg, Chester Co., Pa., b 1805,10,26 d
    1865,5,19 bur Augusta; m Rebecca EMMONS,
    dt Thos. & Mary, Frederick Co., Va., b
    1805,5,26 d 1832,7,27 bur Augusta
    Ch: Thomas   b 1830, 7, 11 d 1832, 7,30
         bur Augusta
        Israel   b 1831, 8, 26 " 1832, 7,27
         bur Augusta
    Garrett m 2nd Abigail MENDENHALL, dt Aaron
    & Lydia, Chester Co., Pa., b 1803,1,17 d
    1884,12,28 bur Augusta
    Ch: Aaron   b 1835, 1, 21
        Joseph   " 1837, 7, 15 d 1888, 3,11
         bur Augusta
        Sarah   b 1839, 9, 29
        Nathan   " 1842, 9, 15 " 1923 or
         1924
----, --, --. Isaac, s Nathan & Sarah, Brad-
    ford MM, Pa., b 1807,6,21 d 1861,3,31;
    m Caroline S. DEAN, dt Jonathan & Hannah,
    Cipio MM, N. Y., b 1805,11,17
    Ch: Harvy   b 1833, 10, 20

Ch: Hannah   b 1836, 7, 10
    Nathan   " 1838, 12, 1 d 1839, 7, 5
    bur Augusta
    Sarah   b 1841, 5, 28
    Eliza   " 1843, 3, 8
    Lydia   " 1845, 4, 26
    Mary   " 1847, 4, 17 d 1860, 3, 8
----, --,---. Eneas, s Nathan & Sarah, Augus-
    ta, b 1811,11,24 d 1863,3,19; m Phebe
    EMMONS, dt Thomas & Mary, b 1816,3,7
    Ch: Franklin b 1838, 9, 30
        Elizabeth " 1841, 2, 22
        Thomas   " 1843, 2, 16
        Benjamin " 1845, 4, 8
        John   " 1848, 1, 3
        Charles   " 1850, 7, 1
----, --, --. Nathan, s Nathan & Sarah, Augus-
    ta, b 1816,9,3 d 1885,5,10 bur Augusta;
    m Hannah DAVIS, dt David & Rachel, Augus-
    ta, b 1816,7,21 d 1901,3,4 bur Augusta
----, --, --. Lewis, s Nathan & Sarah, Augus-
    ta Mtg, b 1814,4,14 d 1887,5,16 bur Au-
    gusta; m Sarah MORELAND, dt Aden & Amy,
    Carmel Mtg, Columbiana Co., O., b 1811,11,
    9 d 1881,3,12 bur Augusta
    Ch: Amy   b 1844, 10, 24 d 1851, 4,20
         bur Augusta
        Ann   b 1846, 5, 20
        Asa   " 1848, 3, 21
        Jabez   " 1850, 3, 3 " 1851, 5, 5
         bur Augusta
        Rachel   b 1851, 11, 27
        Aden   " 1854, 3, 21
        Lewis G. " 1856, 12, 7
----, --, --. Nathan, s Garrett & Abigail, Au-
    gusta, b 1842,9,15; m Sina Ann CHAMBERS,
    dt James H. & Ann, Augusta, b 1843,3,31
    Ch: Allen   b 1871, 10, 3
        Laura   " 1877, 9, 16
----, --, --. Asa, s Lewis & Sarah, Augusta,
    b 1848,3,21; m Mary Ann SHREVE, dt Enoch
    & Elizabeth, b 1848,8,25
    Ch: Joseph G. b 1872, 10, 9
        Mary Vietta" 1875, 1, 5
        Alice E. " 1876, 3, 5
        Curtis Bin-
         ford   " 1879, 8, 5
        Sarah E. " 1881, 1, 18
        Walter A. " 1884, 12, 6
        Frederick
         C.   " 1889, 11, 14
----, --, --. Aden, s Lewis & Sarah, Carroll
    Co., b 1854,3,21; m Lauretta HALDEMAN, dt
    Joseph & Esther, Columbiana Co., O., b
    1851,9,1
    Ch: Bertice   b 1880, 1, 24
----, --, --. Allen J., s Nathan & Sina A., b
    1871,10,3; m Mary Isabell CRAWFORD, dt
    Wm. & Levina, b 1876,6,21
    Ch: Anna Ar-
         wilda   b 1900, 1, 1
        Warren
         Lewis   " 1905, 6, 23

PIM, continued
1905, 6, 23. Lewis Warren b

1829, 7, 24. Garrett rmt Rebecca Emmons
1832, 7, 27. Isaac rmt Caroline S. Emmons
1834, 5, 23. Abigail rocf New Garden MM, dtd
        1834,5,22
1837, 12, 22. Enos rmt Phebe Emmons
1838, 12, 21. Nathan rmt Hannah Davis
1839, 7, 26. Lewis rmt Sarah Morlan
1841, 6, 25. Isaac & fam gct Middleton MM
1842, 12, 23. Lydia [Pimm] rmt David Coulson
1862, 12, 27. Caroline S. rst (W)
1863, 4, 25. Garret & Abigail dis jG in 1854
        (W)
1863, 4, 25. Lewis & Sarah dis jG in 1854 (W)
1863, 4, 25. Nathan & Hannah dis jG in 1854
        (W)
1863, 6, 27. Phebe dis (W)
1867, 1, 26. Thomas dis mcd & military ser-
        vice (W)
----, --, --. Joseph G. gct East Goshen Mtg, O.
----, --, --. Mary Vietta gct Salem, Ore.
----, --, --. Alice E. gct Minerva, O.
----, --, --. Sarah E. gct Alliance, O.

POOLE
1831, 10, 21. Sarah rocf Upper Springfield
        MM, dtd 1831,8,27

POWELL
1861, 10, 26. Mary Ann (form Clemson) con mou
        (W)

PRESTON
1836, 3, 25. Sarah rocf ND MM, dtd 1835,12,22

PRICE
1844, 12, 27. Lydia (form Davis) rpd mcd

RALEY
1854, 11, 29. Milton, s John & Malinda, Colum-
        biana Co., O.; m in Sandy Spring MH, Sa-
        rah ARMSTRONG dt James & Mary, Columbi-
        ana Co., O. (W)

1821, 11, 23. John [Reley] rmt Malinda Atkin-
        son
1822, 5, 24. Robert [Reley] rmt Mary Walton
1822, 11, 22. James rmt Elizabeth Pettit
1840, 12, 25. Eliza, minor dt Joseph, gct Sa-
        lem MM
1863, 1, 24. John & James dis jG in 1854
        (W)
1864, 6, 25. Elijah dis mcd (W)
1864, 7, 23. Abigail (form John) dis mcd (W)
1864, 1, 24. Thirza dis jG in 1854 (W)

RAWLS
1832, 10, 26. Burwell & w, Sarah, & ch, David,
        Mary Ann, Micajah, Michel, Jonathan, Wil-
        liam, Elizabeth & Esther, rocf Salem MM,
        dtd 1832,8,22

1835, 11, 6. Burwell & fam gct Center MM, O.

REEDER
----, --, --. James, s Samuel & Ann, b 1796,9,
        3; m Mary DAVIS, dt Enos & Hannah, b 1798,
        7,9
        Ch: Eneas G.   b 1820, 8, 15
            Hannah D.   " 1822, 1, 10
            Esther F.   " 1826, 5, 29
            Samuel   " 1827, 11, 10
            Benjamin
              Newton   " 1830, 2, 12
            Ann Eliza   " 1832, 12, 24
            Philena
              Deberah   " 1837, 4, 24
            Eli D.   " 1841, 2, 12
----, --, --. Levi, s Samuel & Ann, Lancaster
        Co., Pa., b 1805,9,18; m Elizabeth COOPER,
        dt Calvin & Ann, Lancaster Co., Pa., b
        1805,10,4
        Ch: Alice
              Malone   b 1830, 7, 20
            Benjamin
              Franklin   " 1832, 7, 28
            William   " 1836, 1, 21
            Lydia Ann   " 1838, 3, 24 d 1843, 3,20
              bur Sandy Spring
            Evan Cooper
                         b 1840, 9, 15
----, --, --. Jesse, s W. & D., Columbiana
        Co., O., b 1812 d 1874,12,5; m Ruth E.
        BROGAN, dt C. & R., Chester Co., Pa., b
        1819,6,8 d 1903,9,23
        Ch: Eden   b 1844, 1, 29 (joined
              Presbyterian Ch., Hanover, O.)
1860, 8, 1. Esther T. m Joshua STAFFORD (W)

1825, 9, 23. Ann (form Heston) con mou
1826, 11, 24. Sarah Ann rmt David Battin
1827, 5, 25. Levi rmt Elizabeth Cooper
1828, 6, 27. Jacob rmt Hannah Miller
1829, 1, 21. Lydia dis jH
1832, 3, 23. Rebecca (form Heston) dis mou
1833, 3, 22. Elizabeth Coulson (form Reeder)
        dis mou
1839, 5, 24. Joseph rmt Ann John
1842, 7, 22. Joseph [Reader] rmt Mary Winder
1842, 9, 23. Ruth recrq
1844, 7, 26. Hannah D. rmt Levi Shaw
1844, 10, 25. Hannah C. Coulson (form Reeder)
        dis mcd
1854, 11, 24. Abigail Bond (form Reeder) dis
        mcd (W)
1856, 11, 22. Franklin dis mou (W)
1861, 3, 23. William dis mcd (W)
1861, 8, 24. Evan dis disunity (W)
1861, 9, 28. Maria Thorp (form Reeder) dis
        mou (W)
1863, 7, 25. Eliza Jonson (form Reeder) dis
        mcd (W)
1864, 6, 25. Jacob gct Hickory Grove MM, Ia.
        (W)
1864, 7, 23. Abigail (form Stanley) dis mcd

REEDER, continued
(W)
1865, 1, 28. Eli dis military training (W)
1865, 11, 25. Ruth dis disunity (W)
1865, 12, 23. Ann & ch, Alva, Wm. & Juliana Josephine gct Hickory Grove MM, Ia. (W)
1865, 12, 23. Jesse dis disunity (W)
1866, 4, 28. Hannah Elizabeth & Sarah Ann gct Hickory Grove MM, Ia. (W)
1867, 4, 27. Eden dis military service (W)

REGESTER
----, --, --. Robert, s Wm. & Abigail, Chester Co., Pa., b 1779,12,24 d 1838,8,6 bur Augusta; m Abigail RIGBY, dt Daniel & Abigail, Chester Co., Pa., b 1785,1,8 d 1869, 4,8 bur Augusta
CH: Ann   b 1807, 12, 1 d 1810, 9,20
    Abigail   " 1810, 9, 9
    William   " 1813, 7, 1
    Daniel   " 1815, 12, 6
    David   " 1818, 8, 29
    Aaron   " 1820, 11, 30
    Thomas   " 1823, 3, 1
    Robert   " 1825, 10, 2
    James
    Robetson " 1828, 1, 14

1823, 11, 21. Abigail, w Robert, & ch, Abigail, William, Daniel, David, Aaron & Thomas, recrq
1863, 4, 25. Abigail dis jG in 1854 (W)

RELEY
----, --, --. Robert, b 1759,8,12 d 1849,10,14 bur Sandyspring; m Sarah ----- b 1764,1,24 d 1819,6,16
CH: Joseph   b 1791, 1, 18 Washington Co., Pa.
    Ruth   " 1792, 12, 29   "
    John   " 1796, 11, 27   "
    James   " 1799, 3, 8   "
    Amos   " 1803, 8, 18 Beaver Co.,
    Thomas   " 1806, 2, 10   " [Pa.
Robert m 2nd Mary WALTON, form w of Abraham, b 1769,12,3 Bucks Co., Pa.; d 1841, 9,19 bur Sandyspring
----, --, --. Joseph, s Robert & Sarah, b 1791,1,18; m Susannah COPE, dt Calvin & Ann, Lancaster Co., Pa., b 1796,10,18 d 1828,8,10 bur Sandyspring
CH: Absalom   b 1822, 4, 12
    Jordan   " 1824, 3, 7
    Eliza   " 1826, 5, 13
    Aseneth   " 1828, 4, 7
    All ch b in Sandyspring
----, --, --. John m Malinda ----- d 1845,4,3 bur Sandy Spring; lived in Hanover Township, Columbiana Co., O.
CH: Milton   b 1824, 2, 2
    Rebecca   " 1827, 9, 23 d 1831, 3,23
    bur Sandy Spring
    Elijah   b 1830, 5, 28

Ch: Levi   b 1832, 9, 2 d 1836, 9,28
    bur Sandyspring
    Sarah   b 1834, 9, 25 " 1836, 3,26
    bur Sandyspring
    Robert   b 1837, 10, 23
    Mary   " 1840, 3, 21 " 1843, 3,11
    bur Sandyspring
    Esther   b 1842, 9, 16
----, --, --. James, s Robert & Sarah, Westland MM, Wash. Co., Pa., b 1799,3,18; m Elizabeth PETTIT, dt William & Mary, Northumberland Co., Pa., b 1803,3,22 d 1845,4,1 bur Sandy spring
Ch: Elazan   b 1824, 8, 19
    William
    Pettit   " 1825, 8, 16
    Robert
    Franklin " 1829, 2, 1
    James Jr. " 1834, 8, 20
    Mary   " 1836, 9, 16

RICE
----, --, --. Charles H., s Wm. & Elizabeth, Belmont Co., O., b 1811,11,25 d 1898,10,8 bur Alliance, O.; m Charity D. PETTIT, dt Wm. & Mary, Columbiana Co., O., b 1814,9, 17 d 1887,11,18
Ch: William P. b 1835, 11, 27 d 1891,12, 9
    bur Alliance

1835, 2, 27. Charles H. rmt Charity D. Pettit
1835, 5, 22. Charity D. gct Upper Springfield MM
1836, 8, 26. Charles H. & w, Charity D., & s, William, rocf Upper Springfield MM, dtd 1836,4,23
1863, 4, 25. Wm. & Rachel dis jG in 1854 (W)
1863, 9, 26. Charles & Charity D. dis jG in 1854 (W)

ROOD
----, --, --. Jonathan, s Roger & Betty, Litchfield Co., Conn., b 1784,10,10; m Clarissa ROBERTS, dt John & Abigail, Mass., b 1787, 9,14 d 1843,11,17 bur Augusta MH
Ch: Lucina   b 1808, 8, 18
    Lavina   " 1808, 8, 18 d 1828,11,26
    m ----- STEERS
    Ithamar   b 1810, 10, 22 " 1843, 9,25
    Emmor   " 1814, 4, 21

1835, 2, 27. Mary Ann (form Dean) dis mcd
1838, 7, 27. Jonathan & w, Clarissa, rocf Upper Springfield MM, dtd 1838,5,26

SANDERS
1821, 10, 26. Epsey (form Battin) con mcd
1823, 3, 21. Epsy dis jas
1824, 4, 23. Ann dis jas
1825, 12, 23. Catharine dis jas
1833, 5, 24. Ruth (form Pennock) dis mou

SCHOOLEY
----, --, --. Henry b 1785,3,17; m Margaret
    WESTON, dt John & Elizabeth, Bucks Co.,
    Pa., b 1794,7,22 d 1832,2,13 bur Sandy
    Spring
    Ch: Hannah   b 1811, 11, 22
        John   " 1813, 3, 9
        Reuben   " 1816, 5, 27
        Hervy   " 1818, 7, 29
        Archibald " 1820, 3, 7
        Lewis   " 1822, 12, 14
        David   " 1825, 8, 25
        Obed   " 1829, 7, 10
        Ch b in Sandy Spring Mtg

1822, 11, 22. Sarah rocf Fairfax MM, dtd 1822,
    5,29
1834, 4, 25. Rachel [Schooly] rocf Middleton
    MM, dtd 1834,4,10
1836, 10, 21. Hannah McBride (form Schooley)
    dis mou

SHARP
1828, 7, 25. Isaac rmt Lydia Middleton
1829, 1, 21. Lydia gct Upper Springfield MM
1836, 7, 22. Isaac & w, Lydia, & ch, Ann,
    Oliver, Eliza, Adaline & Hannah, rocf
    Upper Springfield MM dtd 1836,--,--
1841, 10, 22. Isaac & w, Lydia, & ch gct Ches-
    terfield MM

SHAW
1828, 4, 25. Matilda (form Sinclair) con mcd
1839, 1, 25. Rebecca & William, minor ch
    Thomas, rocf New Garden MM, dtd 1838,11,22
1844, 7, 26. Levi rmt Hannah D. Reeder
1870, 2, 26. Sarah Louisa dis (W)

SHORE
1829, 1, 21. Rachel dis JH
1831, 3, 25. Mary rocf Marlborough MM, dtd
    1830,11,30
1834, 6, 27. James & w, Mary, gct Marlborough
    MM

SHORT
----, --, --. Isabella b 1873,8,3 d 1902,3,15

SHREVE
1847, 1, 30. Binford S., s Enoch & Elizabeth,
    Alliance, O., b

SINCLAIR
1828, 4, 25. Matilda Shaw (form Sinclair) con
    mcd
1839, 3, 22. Ruth dis jas

SMEDLEY
----, --, --. Benjamin m Mary RIGBY, dt Dan-
    iel & Abigail, Chester Co., Pa., b 1791,
    11,29
    Ch: Susanna   b 1823, 1, 19 Augusta Mtg
        John   " 1824, 7, 28   "   "

1826, 9, 22. Mary & ch, Susanna & John, rec-
    rq
1840, 1, 24. Mary Emmons (form Smedley) dis
    mou

SMITH
1829, 2, 27. Sarah rocf Carmel MM, dtd 1828,
    12,27
1830, 8, 27. Sarah Fowler (form Smith) con
    mcd
1831, 11, 25. Phebe dis jH
1832, 1, 27. Martha, minor, gct Carmel MM

STACKHOUSE
1824, 2, 27. Anna recrq
1835, 11, 27. Anna Jackson (form Stackhouse)
    dis mou

STAFFORD
1860, 8, 1. Joshua, s Abraham & Content,
    Geauga Co., O.; m in Springfield MH, Es-
    ther T. REEDER, dt James & Mary, Carroll
    Co., O. (W)

STANLEY
1864, 7, 23. Abigail Reeder (form Stanly)
    dis mcd (W)
1865, 3, 25. Timothy dis disunity (W)
1865, 3, 25. Elizabeth dis jG in 1854 (W)

STANTON
1828, 11, 21. Benjamin rmt Betsy McBride
1830, 4, 29. Charles Osborn, Mahlon, Ruth,
    Thomas & Elias, ch Benjamin, rocf Short
    Creek MM, O., dtd 1830,3,23
1830, 9, 24. Benjamin & fam gct Newgarden MM

STRATTON
----, --, --. Elisha, s Josiah & Deborah,
    b 1814,12,15; m Elizabeth PAINTER, dt Da-
    vid & Ann, Salem Mtg, Columbiana Co., O.,
    b 1817,6,16
    Ch: David P.   b 1840, 8, 22
        Martha E. " 1842, 12, 6 d 1843, 2,18
        bur Augusta
----, --, --. Ross, s Josiah & Deborah, b 1813
    9,13; m Mary PAINTER, dt David & Ann, Co-
    lumbiana Co., O., b 1814,11,26
    Ch: Deborah Ann
              b 1840, 8, 11

1839, 4, 26. Josiah & w, Deborah, & ch, Sa-
    rah, Lydia & Charles, rocf Salem MM, dtd
    1839,3,20
1839, 4, 26. Ellen & Ann rocf Salem MM, dtd
    1839,3,20
1839, 8, 23. Ross & w, Mary, rocf Salem MM,
    dtd 1839,8,21
1840, 2, 21. Ellen rmt Thomas Leech
1840, 2, 21. Elizabeth rocf Salem MM, dtd
    1840,2,19
1843, 6, 23. Ross & w, Mary, & ch gct Salem
    MM

STRATTON, continued
1843, 7, 21. Edward rmt Mary James
1843, 8, 25. Mary gct Salem MM
1844, 4, 26. Sarah rmt Cyrenius Emmons

THOMAS
----, --, --. Valentine b 1831,4,5; m Maria
     ----- b 1831,6,9
     Ch: John C.
----, --, --. John C., s Valentine & Mariah;
     m Sarah J. CREW, dt Robert & Margaret
     Ch: Charles O.   released
         Myrtle

THORP
1861, 9, 28. Maria (form Reeder) dis mou (W)

TODD
1838, 3, 23. Mary (form Williams) dis mou

TOMLINSON
----, --, --. Joseph, s Jonathan & Phebe, Pa.,
     b 1843,9,27 d 1880,3,30; m Eliza CHAMBERS,
     dt James & Ann, Carroll Co., b 1848,4,15
     Ch: Anna   b 1871, 12, 5
         Elizabeth " 1873, 1, 30
         Benjamin J." 1875, 3, 16
         Mary   " 1877, 8, 5

TRIBBY
1842, 12, 23. John W. & w, Jane, & s, Lindley,
     rocf Short Creek MM, O., dtd 1842,9,20
1844, 8, 23. John W. & fam gct Short Creek
     MM

TRIPP
1833, 2, 1. George Fox Stephen Mary & Labon
     rocf Marlborough MM, dtd 1832,12,25
1833, 10, 25. Minor ch Samuel gct Marlborough
     MM
1835, 6, 26. Mary Ann [Trip] (form Davis)
     dis mcd

TRITT
1856, 6, 28. Mary (form Hole) dis jas & mcd
     (W)

VOTAW
1831, 8, 26. Moses rmt Mary Miller
1832, 1, 27. Mary gct Newgarden MM

WALTON
1822, 5, 24. Mary rmt Robert Reley
1822, 10, 25. Mary & dt, Bathsheba, dis jas
1822, 12, 27. Edith dis jas
1829, 10, 23. John & w, Lydia, & ch, Martha,
     Lydia Ann, Joseph, Elias & David, rocf
     Carmel MM, dtd 1829,8,15
1843, 8, 25. Lydia & dt, Martha & Lydia Ann,
     dis jas

WATSON
----, --, --. Luella rem by letter to M. E.

Ch.

WELLS
1844, 3, 22. Elizabeth (form Myres) dis jas

WHITACRE
1823, 1, 24. Lydia dis jas
1823, 1, 24. Phebe & dt, Gulielma, dis jas
1839, 6, 21. Sarah rocf Birmingham MM, dtd
     1839,1,2
1841, 8, 27. Sarah [Whitaker] gct Berming-
     ham MM, Pa.
1842, 4, 22. Phebe (form Morlan) dis mou &
     jas
1857, 7, 25. Heneretta (form Eastman) dis
     mcd (W)

WIGINE
1844, 12, 27. Meriam (form Emmons) rpd mcd &
     jas

WILLIAMS
----, --, --. Dearman, s Richard & Sarah,
     b 1804,10,12; m Mary FARMER, dt John &
     Mary, Columbiana Co., O., b 1807,4,11 d
     1851,10,4 bur Salinesville
     Ch: John F.   b 1831, 8, 17 Morgan Co.,O.
         Rebecca   " 1833, 10, 26   "   "   "
         Sarah   " 1835, 1, 29   "   "   "
         Benjamin   " 1837, 1, 17   "   "   "
         Keturah Ann" 1839, 9, 22   "   "   "
         Mary Eliza " 1842, 5, 20   "   "   "
         James   " 1845, 6, --
         Edwin Frank-
            lin   b 1849, 2, 3
1821, 4, 27. Mary rocf Newgarden MM, dtd
     1821,4,26
1822, 10, 25. Catharine dis jas
1823, 4, 25. Mary dis jas
1830, 12, 20. Dearman rmt Mary Farmer
1831, 2, 25. Mary F. gct Deerfield MM
1838, 3, 23. Mary Todd (form Williams) dis
     mou
1843, 9, 22. Dearman & w, Mary, & ch, John
     F., Rebecca, Sarah, Benjamin, Keturah
     Ann & Mary, rocf Pennsville MM, dtd
     1843,8,17

WHITELEATHER
----, --, --. Idella rem
----, --, --. Lawrence rem
----, --, --. Thelma Marrietta rem

WINDER
----, --, --. William, s Benjamin & Hannah,
     Bucks Co., Pa., b 1764,1,27 d 1829,2,--;
     m Adah BRADFORD, dt Joseph & Eleanor,
     Bucks Co., Pa., b 1770,7,9 d 1836,1,17
     bur Sandyspring
     Ch: Rachel   b 1790, 2, 21 in E. Jer-
             sey; m ----- ARNOLD
         Hannah   b 1791, 10, 22 in Bucks

WINDER, William & Adah, continued
    Co., Pa.
      Ch: Ann   b 1793, 8, 18 Frederick
          Co., Va.
         Mary   " 1795, 10, 21   "
         Benjamin " 1797, 7, 30   "   d
          ae 87
         Eleanor   " 1799, 3, 17   "   "
          ae 92
         Adah   " 1800, 12, 2   ".
         Susannah " 1802, 11, 26 Middleton
          Mtg, O., d 1804,10,-- bur Middleton
         Sarah   b 1804, 9, 27 d 1804,11,--
         Joseph   " 1805, 10, 12 Middleton
          Mtg, O., d ae 95
         Tamar   b 1808, 2, 3 Sandyspring
          Mtg
         William   " 1810, 4, 28   "
         Asenath " 1812, 4, 22   "
         Aaron   " 1814, 7, 24
1859, 6, 1. Adah B. m John A. COPE (W)
1861, 2, 27. Benjamin, s Wm. & Ada, Colum-
    biana Co., O.; m in Springfield MH, Han-
    nah ARMSTRONG, dt James & Mary, Columbi-
    ana Co., O. (W)
1865, 9, 24. Esther m Benjamin COPPOCK (W)
1881, 2, 7. Anna H. d

1821, 11, 23. Benjamin rmt Abigail John
1826, 9, 22. Tamar rmt Samuel Chambers
1828, 8, 22. Ephama rocf Newgarden MM, dtd
    1828,8,21
1830, 5, 21. Joseph & w, Efphama, & ch gct
    Newgarden MM
1832, 11, 23. Joseph & w, Efphama, & ch,
    Lydia Ann & Adah B., rocf New Garden MM,
    dtd 1832,10,25
1834, 5, 23. Asenath rmt John Yates
1842, 3, 25. Joseph rmt Lydia Morlan
1842, 7, 22. Mary rmt Joseph Reader
1863, 4, 25. Benjamin & Joseph dis jG in
    1854 (W)
1866, 9, 22. Benjamin gct Stillwater MM, to
    m Sarah S. Briggs (W)
1867, 1, 26. Sarah S. rocf Stillwater MM,
    dtd 1866,12,22 (W)

     *   *   *   *   *   *   *
ADAMSON
1823, 4, 25. Thomas & w, Elizabeth, & ch, Re-
    becca, Hannah, John W. & James, rocf Middle
    ton MM, dtd 1823,2,17
1829, 2, 27. Elizabeth & eight ch gct Middle-
    ton MM

HOLLAND
1827, 11, 23. Susannah K. rmt Robert Miller
1829, 4, 24. Catharine dis jH
1829, 6, 26. Sarah dis jH
1832, 10, 26. Sarah Jr. & Hannah dis jH

HOOPES
----, --, --. Edward, s Abner & Mary, b 1864,

WISE
1844, 11, 22. Ruth (form Mercer) rpd mcd

WOLF
1844, 3, 22. Amy (form Coulson) dis mcd

WOOD
----, --, --. Frederick S., s Nathan L. &
    M. H., Jefferson Co., O., b 1861,6,23;
    m Lorena CHAMBERS, dt James H. & Ann, Car-
    roll Co., b 1862,3,4
    Ch: Helen L. b 1891, 2, 5

1827, 11, 23. Enos & w, Elizabeth, & ch gct
    Middleton MM
----, --, --. Helen L. gct Alliance MM, O.
----, --, --. Frederick & Lorena rem to M. E.
    Ch., Alliance, O.

WOODWARD
1831, 12, 24. John b d 1904,4,4

WRIGHT
1863, 4, 25. Sarah dis jG in 1854 (W)

YATES
1834, 5, 23. John rmt Asenath Winder
1859, 7, 23. Robert dis (W)
1870, 2, 26. Anna Mary Cope (form Yates) con
    mcd (W)
1871, 4, 22. Emeline Craig (form Yates) dis
    mcd (W)

YOUNG
1844, 11, 22. Benjamin & w, Rachel, & ch,
    Jesse, Thomas, Amos, Jane & Tamar, rocf
    Upper Springfield MM, dtd 1844,10,26

     *   *   *   *   *   *   *
    2,18; m Anna L. BROGAN, dt Morris & Mary,
    Columbiana Co., O.
    Ch: Arthur   b 1892, 1, 26
       Myrtle M. " 1894, 3, 21
       Howard J. " 1895, 7, 13 d 1895, 8,26
        bur Mt. Zion
       Elsie   b 1896, 12, 12
       Helen   " 1898, 9, 18
       Clara   " 1901, 10, 16
       Oscar   " dead
1900, 9, 15. Cora d bur Mt. Zion

HOWARD
1827, 2, 23. Ruth rocf Short Creek MM, O.,
    dtd 1826,11,21
1828, 11, 21. Ruth rmt Job COULSON

MILLER
1857, 4, 29. Eliza m David FRENCH
1865, 2, 2. Susannah K. d ae 62 (an elder)

UPPER SPRINGFIELD MONTHLY MEETING

A meeting for worship was established at Upper Springfield (later Damascus) by Salem Quarterly Meeting in 1807 and a Preparative Meeting was granted in 1808. One of the first appointments was that of William Morris who was to act as housekeeper. He agreed to keep the house, furnish and cut the wood for the fires, etc., for the sum of six dollars a year, said amount to be paid in produce, eggs and butter.

In 1825 a monthly meeting was established by Salem Quarterly Meeting and it remained a part of Salem Quarterly Meeting until 1837 when a Quarterly Meeting named Upper Springfield was established, composed of Marlboro, Sandy Spring and Upper Springfield Monthly Meetings.

Friends began settling in this part of the state as early as 1800. Among these early settlers were Samuel Wohman, Thomas Stanley, Catlett Jones, Joshua Lynch, Anthony Morris, Naddy Stanley, Thomas French, Isaac Votaw, Samuel Hicklin, James Stanley, Zacheus Stanton, Amos Holloway, Lemmel Terrell, Pleasant Cobbs, Soloman Stanley, Stacey Shreve, Benjamin Butler, Sr., William Faucett, Robert Armstrong, Abraham Warrington, Littleburg Stanley, Barzilla French, Thomas Longstaff, James Cattell, Zachariah Ellyson, John Carson, Louis Townsend and Edmond Stanley.

During these early years, schools were maintained by each preparative meeting, held mostly in log houses with crude equipment. In a report made on education in 1839 for Upper Springfield Quarterly Meeting, monthly meetings reported the number of schools taught by members within the limits to be twenty-three and ten of these were under the direction of monthly and preparative meetings.

The first marriage accomplished by sanction of Upper Springfield Monthly Meeting was that of Basil Brook and Rachel Morris.

RECORDS

ABEL

1853, 9, 29. Wm., s Lyman & Sally, Leeds Co., Johnstown District, Canada, West, m in Springfield MH, Esther STANLEY, dt Benjamin & Elizabeth, Columbiana Co., O., b 1829,2,19

1854, 10, 28. Wm. rocf Leeds MM, dtd 1854,10, 12

1856, 3, 22. Wm. & w, Esther, gct Red Cedar MM, Ia.

ADAMSON

----, --, --. Thomas b 1790,10,29 d 1847,4,8 bur Springfield; m Elizabeth ----- b 1796, 9,7 d 1854,3,11 bur Springfield

Ch: Rebecca   b 1817, 9, 13
 Hannah   " 1818, 10, 28
 John   " 1820, 5, 23
 James   " 1822, 2, 24
 Samuel   " 1823, 11, 30
 Nathan   " 1825, 7, 5
 Lydia   " 1826, 11, 19
 Thomas   " 1828, 9, 26 d 1847, 4, 4
  bur Springfield
 Joseph   b 1831, 5, 3
 Ellis   " 1834, 7, 25

1846, 4, 29. John W., s Thomas & Elizabeth, Columbiana Co., O., b 1820,5,23; m in Goshen MH, Martha VOTAW, dt Thomas & Elizabeth, b 1820,1,21 d 1856,3,29 bur Goshen

Ch: Mary   b 1847, 6, 18
 Thomas   " 1848, 10, 20
 Ellis   " 1851, 4, 12
 Lydia   " 1853, 9, 13
 Elizabeth
 Ann   " 1854, 7, 26

1846, 10, 29. Nathan, s Thomas & Elizabeth, Columbiana Co., O., b 1825,7,5; m in Springfield MH, Amy J. STANLEY, dt Benjamin & Elizabeth, Columbiana Co., O., b 1825,1,4

Ch: Melvina   b 1848, 11, 22
 Elizabeth
 Rebecca   " 1850, 10, 26
 Hannah Ann   " 1854, 2, 26

1850, 5, 30. Samuel, s Thomas & Elizabeth, Columbiana Co., O., b 1823,11,30; m in Springfield MH, Lydia Ann COBBS, dt Joseph & Tacy, Columbiana Co., O., b 1833, 5,11

Ch: Marietta   b 1851, 10, 28

----, --, --. Joseph b 1831,5,3; m Jane H. ----- b 1838,5,27

Ch: William
 Lindley   b 1859, 7, 17
 Anna Mary   " 1862, 5, 17 d 1864, 3,31
  bur Damascus

1835, 8, 22. Thomas & w, Elizabeth, & ch, Re-

becca, Hannah, John W., Samuel, Nathan, Lydia, Thomas, Joseph & Ellis, rocf Middleton MM, dtd 1835,8,17

1836, 10, 22. Rebecca Woods (form Adamson) dis mcd

1848, 3, 25. Nathan dis

1852, 11, 27. James gct Salem MM, Ia.

1853, 6, 25. Samuel & w, Lydia Ann, & dt, Marietta, gct Driftwood MM, Ind.

1856, 9, 27. Amy Jane & ch, Malvina, Elizabeth, Rebecca, Hannah Ann & Benjamin Thomas, gct Western Plain MM, Ia.

1856, 10, 25. Joseph con mcd

1857, 4, 25. Jane (form Hoops) dis mcd

1858, 7, 24. Nathan rst at Honey Creek MM, Ia. on consent of this mtg

1863, 9, 25. John, Joseph & Ellis dis jG (W)

1863, 9, 25. Hannah & Lydia dis jG (W)

1863, 9, 25. Jane H. dis jG (W)

1863, 11, 28. John con mcd

1865, 6, 24. Joseph & w, Jane, & s, Wm. Lindley, gct South River MM, Ia.

1865, 12, 23. John W. & ch, Thomas, Ellis & Lydia V., gct New Sharon MM, Ia.

1865, 12, 23. Mary gct New Sharon MM, Ia.

1866, 12, 22. Elizabeth Ann, minor dt John, gct New Sharon MM, Ia.

1866, 12, 22. Hannah gct New Sherron MM, Ia.

1869, 6, 26. Ellis rpd mcd

1870, 2, 26. Ellis gct South River MM, Ia.

1871, 6, 24. Lydia gct South River MM, Ia.

AIKEN

----, --, --. Wm. m Judith Ann COBURN, dt Jacob & Ellen, b 1837,9,5 d 1921,1,4

Ch: Ella A.   b 1879, 11, 9

1896, 8, 22. Ellen C. recrq

1917, 12, 22. Ella (Aiken) Packer relrq

AILES

----, --, --. Austin M b 1859,5,12 d 1892,4,28 m Celina ----- b 1862,2,22 d 1905,5,15

Ch: Curtis
 Lionel   b 1885, 3, 1
 Eugene Els-
 worth   " 1888, 3, 20 d 1907, 7,21
 Marguerite
 M.   " 1892, 8, 6

1886, 1, 23. Dr. Austin M. & Celina recrq

1901, 2, 23. Curtis recrq

1912, 7, 27. Marguerite dropped from mbrp

1920, 3, 27. Curtis L. relrq

ALAZIER

1885, 2, 22. Mary, dt Mathew & Catharine Alesi, b

1899, 12, 23. Mary recrq

ALLEN

1826, 8, 29. David, s Isaac & Sarah, Columbi-

ALLEN, continued
    ana Co., O.; m in Springfield MH, Sarah K.
    ISENHOUR, dt John & Mary, Columbiana Co.,O.

1827, 1, 27. Sarah K. gct Middleton MM
1831, 6, 25. Hannah (form Icenhour) dis mou
1831, 6, 25. Susanna (form Icenhour) dis mou

ALLISON
1896, 4, 25. Desda (form Binford) recrq

ALLMAN
1848, 11, 2. Jesse, s William & Lydia, Stark
    Co., O.; m in Upper Springfield MH, Esther
    W. HAINES, dt Chalkley & Sarah E., Colum-
    biana Co., O.

1849, 2, 24. John P. gct Marlborough MM
1858, 5, 21. Medre [Alman] & w, Susanna, & s,
    Webster Allison, rocf Middleton MM, dtd
    1858,4,17 (W)
1860, 5, 25. Meader [Alman] & w, Susanna, &
    ch, Webster Alison & Luanna C., gct Middle-
    ton MM (W)

ALTER
1872, 12, 26. Mary Emma Kille, w Newton, b

1905, 6, 24. Emma Kille dropped from mbrp

ANDREWS
1807, 8, 27. Ann b
1811, 3, 3. Susanna b
1823, 11, 8. Richard b
----, --, --. John m Edna ----- b 1798,12,11
    Ch: Benjamin   b 1822, 2, 8
        Eleazer   " 1824, 2, 26
        John F.   " 1826, 2, 15
        William F.   " 1829, 1, 20
        Miriam   " 1831, 3, 6
        Sarah   " 1833, 4, 17
        Joseph But-
         ler   " 1835, 7, 16
        Martha   " 1837, 7, 23
        Joshua   " 1840, 5, 11
        Susanna   " 1840, 5, 11
----, --, --. Daniel b 1803,11,6; m 2nd Mary
    ----- b 1807,12,21
    Ch: Margaret   b 1830, 9, 3
        Elizabeth   " 1834, 3, 27
        Thomas El-
         wood   " 1835, 11, 10 d 1836, 9,21
         bur Springfield
        Isaac R.
        Sarah Crew b 1839, 11, 7
        William   " 1842, 10, 19
        James   " 1845, 6, 7
        Martha   " 1847, 4, 10
        Mary   " 1849, 9, 30
        Deborah   " 1853, 1, 5
        Hannah B.   " 1854, 3, 9
----, --, --. Samuel b 1806,2,20; m Eliza J.
    ----- b 1809,10,30

    Ch: John S.   b 1833; 2, 20
        Lindley   " 1836, 1, 5
1837, 7, 23. Mattie b
1837, 6, 5. Ann m Thos. CREW
1848, 7, 27. Benjamin C., s John & Edna, Jef-
    ferson Co., Ia.; m Springfield MH, Mary
    BRUFF, dt James B. & Sarah, Mahoning Co.,O.
1850, 8, 29. Elizabeth m Adna FOGG
1851, 4, 29. Margaret m John LLOYD
1829, 11, 28. Daniel gct Short Creek MM, O.,
    to m Mary Ratliff
1829, 12, 26. John & w, Edna & ch, Benjamin,
    Eleazer & John H., rocf Wayne-oak MM, Va.,
    dtd 1829,10,3
1830, 4, 30. Mary rocf Short Creek MM, O.,
    dtd 1830,3,23
1831, 4, 23. John dis
1835, 8, 22. Samuel A. & w, Eliza L., & s,
    John S., & brother, Richard Andrews, rocf
    Hartland MM, dtd 1835,5,21
1835, 8, 22. Richard with brother's fam rocf
    Hartland MM, dtd 1835,5,21
1837, 2, 25. Ann & Susanna rocf W. Branch
    MM, Va., dtd 1836,12,24
1838, 1, 27. Richard gct Hartland MM

1838, 4, 28. Samuel A. & w, Eliza, & ch,
    John S. & Lindley, gct Allum Creek MM
1841, 3, 27. Edna & ch, Benjamin C., Eleazer,
    John H., Wm. F., Miriam, Sarah, Martha &
    Susanna, gct Salem MM, Iowa.
1842, 12, 24. John rst at Salem MM on consent
    of this mtg
1843, 12, 23. Susanna Butler (form Andrews)
    con mcd to first cousin
1848, 12, 23. Mary gct Pleasant Plain MM, Ia.

1856, 11, 22. Daniel & w, Mary R., & ch,
    Isaac R., Sarah C., William James, Martha,
    Mary, Deborah & Hannah B., gct Western
    Plain MM, Ia.
1863, 9, 25. Daniel & Mary R. dis jG (W)
1871, 12, 23. Martha B. rocf Honey Creek MM,
    Ia., dtd 1871,11,11

ANDROS
1828, 3, 22. Daniel rocf Upper MM, Va., dtd
    1827,12,15

ANTRIM
----, --, --. Benjamin b 1801,9,25; m Eliza-
    beth ----- b 1806,5,6

1832, 6, 23. Elizabeth recrq
1832, 8, 25. Benjamin recrq
1834, 6, 28. Benjamin & w, Elizabeth, gct
    Salem MM

ARBUCKLE
1855, 12, 22. Sarah (form Whinery) dis mcd

ARMITAGE
1830, 1, 23. Phebe, minor, rocf Buckingham

ARMITGAE, continued
 MM, dtd 1829,12,7 end by Salem MM, 1830,
 1,20
1844, 7, 27. Rachel dis jH
1848, 9, 23. Phebe dis disunity

ARMSTRONG
----, --, --. Robert b 1764,3,3; m Ann -----
 b 1779,6,16 d 1826,8,27 bur Goshen
 Bh: William   b 1800, 7, 23
     James   " 1802, 11, 11
     John   " 1805, 9, 27
     Joel   " 1808, 8, 9
     Mary Ann   " 1811, 11, 12
     Lydia   " 1812, 11, 17
     Rebecca   " 1815, 7, 31
     Robert   " 1817, 12, 8
     Sarah   " 1820, 7, 31
----, --, --. Joel b 1808,8,9 d 1865,2,10 bur
 Goshen; m Mary Ann ----- b 1821,4,26
----, --, --. Lewis m Judith Ann ----- b 1853,
 1,2
 Ch: Micajah
     Russel   b 1886,4,2
     Olin L.   " 1894, 11, 22

1828, 5, 24. Robert dis
1829, 6, 27. Wm. con mou
1830, 4, 30. John dis mou
1834, 1, 25. James dis
1837, 8, 26. Mary Ann Clark (form Armstrong)
 dis mou
1837, 10, 28. Joel con mcd
1837, 11, 25. William dis disunity
1842, 12, 24. Rebecca Haines (form Armstrong)
 dis mcd
1843, 4, 22. Sarah P. dis disunity
1843, 8, 26. Robert dis disunity
1856, 6, 28. Mary Ann recrq
1863, 6, 26. Joel dis jG (W)
1865, 8, 25. Lucinda (form Cope) dis mcd (W)
1874, 11, 27. Lucinda C. rst at Middleton MM
 on consent of this mtg (W)
1906, 7, 28. Judith Ann & s, Russell & Olin
 J., rocf East Goshen MM

ASHTON
1876, 6, 15. Ida B., dt Jonathan K. & Emily
 (Holloway) Blackburn, b (W)

1913, 9, 26. Ida B. rocf Middleton MM, dtd
 1913,8,16 (W)
1921, 3, 25. Ida D. Halderman (form Ashton)
 dis mcd (W)

ATKINSON
----, --, --. Warner b 1797,7,9; m Maria -----
 b 1800,12,1
 Ch: Hannah   b 1825, 2, 19
     Rachel   " 1826, 10, 20
     Sarah   " 1830, 9, 22
     Mary   " 1832, 10, 6
     Eliza   " 1835, 8, 2

 Ch: Edith   b 1836, 5, 11
     Matilda   " 1838, 2, 23 d 1841,10,10
      bur Goshen
----, --, --. Henry, s Geo. & Elizabeth, b
 1838,4,17; m Rebecca PHILLIPS, dt Geo. W.
 & Rebecca, b 1844,10,2
 Ch: Jessie   b 1878, 6, 6
     Mary Alice " 1869, 8, 12 (sic)
1850, 3, 27. Rachel m David COULSON
1850, 11, 15. Sarah J. (Lupton), w Geo., b
1851, 5, 28. Mary m Jesse COULSON
1852, 4, 28. Sarah m Theophilus MORLAN
1854, 11, 2. Eliza m Isaac STEWARD
1861, 1, 30. Hannah m Isaac JACKSON Jr.
1898, 11, 27. Mabel L., w Lee W., dt Joseph E.
 & Lydia PETTIT, b

1858, 2, 26. Edith Bell (form Atkinson) dis
 mcd (W)
1858, 3, 27. Edith Bell (form Atkinson) dis
 mcd
1862, 10, 24. Mary (form Lee) dis mcd (W)
1863, 1, 24. Warner & Maria dis jW
1864, 2, 26. Warner gct Hickory Grove MM, Ia.
 (W)
1884, 11, 22. Rebecca recrq
1889, 4, 27. Henry & dt, Jessie, recrq
1893, 1, 28. Sarah rocf East Goshen MM
1894, 1, 27. Mary Alice recrq

BAILEY
1864, 6, 14. Oscar b
1868, 12, 3. George W., s George & Ann,
 Mahoning Co., O., b 1845,7,12; m in Damas-
 cus MH, Ruthetta BUTLER, dt John & Ann,
 Columbiana Co., O., b 1848,10,22 d 1882,
 2,18
 Ch: John L.   b 1870, 4, 12
     Anna E.   " 1871, 9, 17
     Laura May   " 1874, 8, 10
     Edward H.   " 1876, 9, 9
     Irvin C.   " 1880, 12, 25
     William J. " 1884, 6, 7
     Charles   " 1889, 4, 25
     Chester M. " 1889, 4, 25 d 1889, 6,30
 George W. m 2nd Unity SHREVE, dt John &
 Abigail, b 1849,7,17
----, --, --. Charles F., s Geo. & Ruthetta,
 b 1889,4,25; m Ethel SHREVE, dt Calvin &
 Anna M., b 1891,12,15
 Ch: Walter
     Rollen   b 1914, 5, 17
     Lois Marie " 1917, 6, 13
     Paul Ches-
      ter   " 1918, 11, 3

1871, 2, 25. George W. & s, John L., recrq
1886, 2, 27. Oscar recrq
1892, 12, 24. Oscar gct Salem MM
1904, 6, 25. Edward H. gct Whittier MM, Calif.
1905, 4, 22. Ervin G. relrq
1913, 8, 23. Ethel rocf Beloit MM
1915, 3, 27. Wm. J. relrq

BAILEY, continued
1919, 1, 25. Charles F. & fam gct East Goshen
    MM

BAKER
----, --, --. Jacob b 1827,5,10; m Phila A.
    ----- b 1828,3,13
    Ch: Clara E.   b 1853, 10, 13

1866, 6, 22. Eliza rocf Middleton MM, dtd
    1866,5,19 (W)
1867, 9, 28. Marietta S. (form Stanley) con
    mcd
1867, 11, 22. Marietta (form Stanley) dis mcd
    (W)
1876, 6, 23. Eliza gct Salem MM (W)
1886, 4, 24. Jacob & w, Phila A., & dt, Clara
    E., rocf Raisin MM, Mich.
1893, 12, 23. Jacob & fam gct Raison MM, Mich.

BAINARD
1863, 9, 25. Esther dis jG (W)

BALDWIN
1843, 7, 22. Merihab (form Morris) dis
1902, 3, 22. Anna E. gct Whittier MM, Calif.

BALL
1826, 11, 1. Joseph, s Nathan & Atlantic,
    Columbiana Co., O.; m in Goshen MH, Hannah
    BROOKE, dt James & Esther, Columbiana Co.,
    O.
1830, 11, 4. Benjamin, s Nathan & Atlantic,
    Columbiana Co., O.; m in Damascus MH,
    Hannah LYNCH, dt Joshua & Rachel, Colum-
    biana Co., O.
----, --, --. George & -----
    Ch: Helen   b 1899, 12, 11
        Nellie   " 1902, 8, 1

1826, 12, 23. Hannah P. gct Salem MM
1830, 12, 25. Hannah gct Salem MM, O.
1916, 1, 22. Helen & Nellie recrq
1929, 6, 27. Helen (Ball) Hawn dropped from
                                mbrp
BARBER
1839, 8, 29. Israel, s Abraham & Drusilla,
    Columbiana Co., O., b 1811,3,31; m in
    Springfield MH, Lydia NEWBURN, dt Jacob
    & Mary, Columbiana Co., O., b 1817,11,8
    Ch: Mary N.   b 1841, 2, 8
        Jacob   " 1842, 3, 30
        Benjamin " 1844, 7, 8
1852, 10, 21. Jane, dt David & Elizabeth
    TAYLOR, b

1835, 6, 27. Alice & ch, Joseph, Rebecca,
    Rachel, Mary, Sarah, Isaac, Edith, Bar-
    clay & Levi Arnold, rocf Salem MM, dtd
    1835,5,21
1835, 6, 27. Hannah rocf Salem MM, dtd 1835,
    5,21
1836, 8, 27. Hannah Heacock (form Barber) dis

mcd
1839, 3, 23. Rebecca Mather (form Barber) dis
    mcd
1840, 1, 25. Rachel Heacock (form Barber) dis
    mcd in Hicksite Mtg
1840, 2, 22. Israel rocf Salem MM, dtd 1840,
    2,19
1843, 1, 28. Mary Ann Harlan (form Barber)
    dis mcd
1844, 1, 27. Sarah Heacock (form Barber) dis
    mcd
1845, 7, 26. Joseph dis jH
1846, 9, 29. Israel & w, Lydia, & ch, Mary
    N., Jacob & Benjamin, gct Salem MM
1849, 8, 25. Edith Mathers (form Barber) dis
    mcd
1852, 9, 25. Isaac B. Votaw gct Salem MM, to
    m Hannah Barber
1853, 11, 26. Jennet (form Cobbs) dis mcd
1896, 1, 24. Isabel (form Fogg) con mcd (W)
1912, 11, 22. Isabell dis disunity (W)

BARDO
1894, 10, 19. Esther, dt James C. & Emma
    (Ellett) HOOPES, b

BARLEY
1886, 2, 26. Charles, s Benjamin W. & Rebecca
    J., b

1911, 1, 28. Charles rocf Salem MM
1918, 11, 23. Charles dropped from mbrp

BARRINGER
1837, 12, 23. Sarah (form Rakestraw) dis mcd

BASHAW
----, --, --. George b 1838,10,28 d 1894,2,12
    bur Damascus; m Catharine E. ----- b 1846,
    10,5 d 1929,8,14
    Ch: Lemuel R. b 1871, 5, 21
        Ottiwell W." 1873, 5, 3
        John Her-
          bert   " 1881, 8, 16
        Clyde
        Leonard   " 1887, 8, 2

1873, 8, 23. Catharine (form Hole) con mcd
1882, 8, 17. George & ch recrq
1909, 4, 24. Lemuel relrq
1928, 6, 28. Herbert relrq

BATES   [jG (W)
1863, 7, 24. Benjamin, Edward & Jesse J. dis
1863, 7, 24. Lydia J. dis jG (W)
1866, 8, 21. Sibyl (form Votaw) dis mcd (W)

BATTEN
1837, 1, 28. Benjamin & Hannah, minor ch
    Robert & Abigail, rocf Sandy Spring MM,
    dtd 1836,12,23
1844, 5, 25. Benjamin [Battin] dis mcd & jH

BATZLI
1895, 4, 24. Mabel, w David, dt John & Mary
Etta (Cobbs) SEACHRIST, b

BAUMAN
----, --, --. Elmer m Iva Ola GREENAWALT, dt
John S. & Luella J. (Shreve), b 1888,1,25
Ch: Ethel Irene
b 1912, 5, 18
Lester John
b 1915, 6, 5
Berdena Ella
b 1917, 3, 28
1920, 2, 28. Ethel Irene, Lester John & Berdena Ella, minor ch Iva, recrq

BAYARD
1861, 2, 20. Martha Isabella, dt Stephen &
Narcissa COLLINS, b

1896, 12, 26. Isabella C. recrq
1899, 8, 17. Isabella C. gct Salem MM

BECK
1877, 10, 31. Jonas M., s Isaac & Miliscent,
Mahoning Co., O.; m in residence of Edith
Hall, Abigail HALL, dt Jesse & Edith, Mahoning Co., O.
1884, 1, 19. Rosetta, dt Marion & Abigail, b
1878, 4, 27. Abigail H. gct Alliance MM
1904, 5, 28. Rosetta rocf Hartland MM, N. Y.
1906, 9, 22. Rosetta gct East Goshen MM

BEEDE
1826, 3, 25. Abraham gct New Garden MM

BEESON
1839, 9, 28. Joseph Lynch gct Middleton MM,
to m Rebecca Beason
1866, 11, 22. Hannah (form Binford) con mcd
1867, 5, 25. Hannah gct Bangor MM, Ia.

BELL
1890, 5, 5. Irvin G., s Wm. G. & Catharine,
b

1858, 2, 26. Edith (form Atkinson) dis mcd
(W)
1858, 3, 27. Edith (form Atkinson) dis mcd
1911, 2, 25. Irvin recrq
1915, 7, 24. Irven gct Valley MM

BENEDICT
1843, 8, 29. Henry, s Cyrus & Hannah, Jefferson Co., O., b 1821,3,1 d 1865,6,1; m in
Springfield MH, Eliza T. STANLEY, dt Benjamin & Elizabeth, Columbiana Co., O., b
1821,11,2
Ch: Rebecca C. b 1844, 8, 22 d 1874, 1, 9
bur Oskaloosa
Elizabeth
Ann b 1846, 5, 28
Hannah G. " 1848, 5, 12

Ch: Mary Jane b 1852, 3, 21
Joseph C. " 1857, 10, 2

1836, 1, 23. Aaron Chapman gct Allum Creek
MM, to m Martha Benedict
1844, 2, 24. Eliza T. [Benadict] gct Gilead
MM
1857, 4, 25. Henry & w, Eliza T., & ch, Rebecca C., Elizabeth Ann, Hannah G. & Mary
Jane, rocf White Lick MM, Ind., dtd 1857,
2,18
1868, 11, 28. Eliza Walton (form Benedict) con
mcd
1870, 4, 23. Mary Jane Roberts (form Benedict)
con mcd
1890, 12, 27. Joseph Cope relrq

BENNETT
----, --, --. Phebe, dt Robert & Ann YATES,
b 1814,7,5 d 1895,9,11 bur Damascus
----, --, --. L. S. [Bennitt] b 1853,6,28;
m Isabella E. KING, b 1858,7,22
Ch: T. Paul b 1894, 5, 23

1892, 9, 24. Phebe Y. rocf Winona MM
1908, 1, 25. L. S. & w, Isaleeta, & s, Paul,
recrq
1912, 7, 27. Ellen Cobbs [Benner] dropped
from mbrp
1920, 8, 19. Lee S. & Isaletta relrq
1923, 12, 27. F. Paul relrq

BEST
----, --, --. Hiram T., s Jacob & Sarah, b
1853,1,15; m Lydia Ann BATES, dt Geo. &
Harriett, b 1858,2,28
Ch: Addie
Catherine b 1891, 10, 4

1890, 1, 25. Hiram L. & Lydia Ann recrq
1897, 2, 22. Hiram & Lydia relrq

BINFORD
----, --, --. Aquilla b 1799,2,23 d 1864,9,
10 bur Springfield; m Miriam ----- b 1805,
11,23 d 1862,3,25 bur Springfield
Ch: Martha b 1826, 10, 3
William H. " 1829, 8, 1 d 1852, 6, 2
bur Sugar Plain
Jesse b 1832, 4, 20
John " 1834, 3, 20 d 1856,10,25
Benjamin " 1836, 4, 23
Hannah " 1839, 8, 6
Robert " 1842, 1, 1
Samuel " 1844, 6, 19
----, --, --. Joseph b 1803,4,24; m Margaret
----- b 1808,2,25 d 1866,7,20 bur Damascus
Ch: Samuel Al-
fred b 1829, 2, 13
Elizabeth " 1831, 5, 23
Peter " 1833, 4, 28
Joshua " 1835, 7, 4
Mary Ladd " 1837, 12, 13 d 1838, 7,16

BINFORD, Joseph & Margaret, continued
    bur Springfield
      Ch: Thaddeus b 1839, 5, 14
         Oliver   " 1841, 9, 20
         Joseph Bay-
           ley   " 1844, 5, 22
         Julia   " 1846, 5, 3
         Margaret
           Ann   " 1851, 1, 10
1833, 5, 30. Peter, Jr., s Peter & Martha,
    Columbiana Co., O., b 1807,8,19; m in
    Springfield MH, Maria WHITACRE, dt Caleb
    & Rebecca, b 1811,8,30
      Ch: Caleb   b 1834, 4, 22
         Elizabeth
           Ann   " 1836, 6, 18
         Michael   " 1838, 8, 5
         David   " 1840, 7, 12
         Sarah   " 1842, 7, 20
         Deborah   " 1844, 1, 28
1851, 10, 30. Martha m Thomas Johnson
1855, 8, 3. Peter, s Joseph & Margaret, Co-
    lumbiana Co., O., b 1833,4,28; m in Spring-
    field MH, Margaret STANLEY, dt Isaac &
    Elizabeth, Mahoning Co., O., b 1834,2,19
      Ch: Isaac
         Summer   b 1855, 2, 14
         Joseph
           Emerson " 1858, 12, 30 d 1864, 6,12
           bur Springfield
         Alfred L. b 1867, 12, 12
         Delbert   " 1869, 10, 29
1858, 10, 26. Elizabeth m Milton Hollingsworth
----, --, --. Samuel Alford b 1829,1,13 d
    1903,11,6; m Elizabeth MEADER, b 1830,8,1
    d 1912,6,16
      Ch: Albert
         Judson   b 1857, 8, 5
         Parker
           Willis   " 1858, 8, 10 d 1861, 6, 8
           bur Springfield
         Oliver
           Clarkson b 1861, 1, 8 " 1863, 8, 9
           bur Springfield
         Benjamin J.b 1863, 11, 5
         Martha   " 1865, 7, 27
         Howard A. " 1871, 4, 17
----, --, --. Joshua b 1835,7,4 d 1911,10,2;
    m Lucy ----- b 1846,4,22
      Ch: Philena
         Pearl   b 1871, 10, 8
         Oliver F. " 1881, 12, 3
----, --, --. Oliver b 1841,9,20; m Abigail
    ----- b 1846,8,22
      Ch: Earnest b 1871, 1, 8
1863, 11, 5. Benjamin J., s Samuel & Eliza-
    beth, b
1867, 12, 12. Alfred L., s Peter & Margaret, b
----, --, --. Delbert, s Peter & Margaret, b
    1869,10,29; m Adesda ALLISON, dt Philip
    & Mary J.. b 1879,4,1
      Ch: Allison J. b 1898, 12, 8
----, --, --. Oliver Florin, s Joshua & Lucy

    E., b 1881,12,3; m Gertrude BARNES
    Ch: Louelwin
1830, 6, 26. Aquilla & w, Mariam, & ch, Mar-
    tha & Wm. H., rocf Upper MM, Va., dtd
    1830,4,17
1830, 12, 25. Joseph & w, Margaret, & s, Sam-
    uel Alfred, rocf Wayne Oak MM, Va., dtd
    1830,11,6
1833, 8, 24. Maria gct Sugar River MM, Ind.
1837, 9, 23. Peter Jr. & w, Mariah, & ch,
    Caleb & Elizabeth, rocf Sugar River MM,
    Ind., dtd 1837,3,25
1844, 9, 28. Peter & fam gct Sugar River MM,
    Ind.
1856, 8, 23. Samuel Alfred gct New Garden MM,
    to m Elizabeth M. Johnson
1857, 4, 25. Elizabeth M. rocf New Garden MM
1862, 11, 21. Aquilla dis jG (W)
1863, 2, 27. Joseph dis jG (W)
1863, 2, 27. Margaret dis jG (W)
1863, 4, 24. Peter dis jG (W)
1863, 4, 24. Hannah dis jG (W)
1863, 4, 24. Margaret dis jG (W)
1863, 4, 24. Alfred dis jG (W)
1863, 9, 25. Benjamin dis jG (W)
1863, 9, 25. Jesse dis jG (W)
1863, 9, 25. Robert dis jG (W)
1863, 9, 25. Thaddeus dis jG (W)
1863, 9, 25. Joshua dis jG (W)
1863, 9, 25. Oliver dis jG (W)
1865, 7, 22. Jesse con mcd
1866, 1, 27. Jesse gct Bangor MM, Ia.
1866, 11, 23. Abigail (form Fawcett) dis mcd
    (W)
1866, 11, 24. Hannah Beeson (form Binford) con
    mcd
1867, 1, 26. Lucy E. (form Cobbs) con mcd
1867, 1, 26. Joshua con mcd
1867, 5, 25. Abbie T. (form Fawcett) con mcd
1867, 5, 25. Oliver dis mcd
1867, 11, 23. Joshua & w, Lucy E., gct Alli-
    ance MM
1867, 12, 28. Joshua (or Joseph) & dt, Marga-
    ret Ann, gct Alliance MM
1870, 12, 24. Amanda (form Ong) con mcd
1870, 12, 24. Joseph B. con mcd
1870, 12, 24. Thadeus dis mcd
1871, 1, 28. Benjamin con mcd
1871, 1, 28. Robert con mcd
1871, 4, 22. Samuel gct Bangor MM, Ia.
1871, 4, 22. Wm. gc
1872, 7, 22. Benjamin gct LeGrand MM, Ia.
1874, 7, 25. Robert gct Legrand MM, Ia.
1877, 5, 22. Joshua & w, Lucy, & dt, Salina
    Pearl, rocf Alliance MM, O.
1877, 7, 28. Oliver L. relrq
1877, 11, 24. Abigail F. relrq
1881, 1, 22. Joseph Barley & w, Amanda, & ch,
    Iva & Florence, gct Summit Grove MM, Ia.
1881, 1, 22. Isaac Summer gct Walnut Center
    MM
1884, 3, 22. Ernest F. gct Legrand MM, Ia.

BINFORD, continued
    (minor s Oliver L.)
1892, 11, 26. Albert J. relrq
1896, 4, 25. Desda Allison recrq
1904, 12, 24. Joshua & w, Lucy, & ch, Pearl &
    Oliver Florin, rocf Beloit MM, Mich.
1905, 9, 23. Gertrude Barnes recrq
1908, 8, 22. Benjamin J. relrq
1913, 3, 22. Peter rocf Beloit MM
1914, 4, 25. Peter & Judith gct Whittier MM,
    Calif.
1916, 1, 22. Lucy gct Salem MM
1916, 1, 22. Pearl gct Salem MM
1926, 1, 28. Lewellyn J., minor s O. F., rel-
    rq
1929, 10, 24. Oliver F. & w relrq

BINNS
1838, 3, 24. Nathan Cook gct Redstone MM, to
    m Ann H. Binns

BISHOP
1827, 11, 28. William, s Nicholas & Hannah,
    Columbiana Co., O.; m in Goshen MH, Lydia
    MATHER, dt Thomas & Lydia, Columbiana Co.,
    O.

1828, 4, 26. Lydia gct Middleton MM

BLACKBURN
----, --, --. David b 1769,9,14 d 1849,2,18
    bur Springfield; m Margaret ----- b 1761,
    6,31 d 1831,1,29 bur Springfield
    Ch: Elizabeth b 1789, 11, 20
----, --, --. Barbee b 1796,1,11 d 1878,5,31
    bur Damascus; m Elizabeth ----- b 1797,1,
    1 d 1847,4,12 bur Springfield
    Ch: Hannah   b 1819, 7, 25
        Sarah Ann " 1821, 7, 2
        Mary   " 1823, 5, 4
        Esther " 1825, 9, 13 d 1890, 2, 6
        Ruth   " 1827, 11, 23
        Margaret " 1830, 11, 1
        Elizabeth " 1832, 9, 4 d 1888, 4,29
          bur Damascus
        Henry   b 1834, 10, 12
        Martha " 1838, 5, 14 d 1858, 5,30
          bur Springfield
        James   b 1840, 3, 15 d 1840, 8,21
          bur Springfield
        Temperance b 1842, 5, 10
1826, 9, 28. James C., s David & Margaret,
    Columbiana Co., O., b 1804,12,5; m in
    Springfield MH, Rebecca CREW, dt Obadiah
    & Mary, Columbiana Co., O., b 1809,8,11
    d 1863,8,10 bur Goshen
    Ch: Isabella E.b 1829, 3, 27
        William H. " 1827, 7, 13 (sic)
        Judith A. " 1830, 11, 2
        Uree   " 1832, 8, 5
        Mary P. " 1835, 6, 29
        Maja W. " 1836, 6, 18
        Barbee " 1838, 2, 28

Ch: Elizabeth b 1840, 8, 9
    Lewis   " 1842, 5, 14
    Luesa   " 1844, 6, 26 d 1884, 2, 4
      bur Damascus
    Sarah Jane b 1849, 3, 30
    Martha H. " 1854, 7, 2
1828, 8, 28. Elizabeth m Asa GIBSON
1843, 4, 27. Mary m Thomas WHINERY
1846, 4, 22. Sarah Ann m Lewis W. HOOPES
1847, 4, 1. Ruth m Josiah COBBS
1848, 6, 8. Judith Ann m John M. STANLEY
1849, 5, 21. Wm. Henry, s James C. & Rebecca,
    Mahoning Co., O., b 1827,7,13; m in Spring-
    field MH, Elizabeth STANLEY, dt Joseph &
    Abigail, Columbiana Co., O., b 1828,4,11
    Ch: Joseph   b 1854, 4, 24
        Mary   " 1856, 7, 1
        Emma   " 1859, 3, 4
        Dora   " 1861, 8, 27 d 1863, 9,10
          bur Springfield
        James   b 1863, 8, 29
        Hannah M. " 1867, 11, 29
1853, 3, 31. Hannah m Thomas W. LOGUE
1853, 6, 2. Mary m George COBBS
1854, 3, 30. Margaret m Robert CREW
1862, 1, 2. Elizabeth m Thos. S. CATTELL
----, --, --. Jonathan K., s Wm. & Ann (Hew-
    itt), b 1841,7,18 d 1926,9,28 bur Damascus
    m Emily HOLLOWAY, dt David & Rachel (Pid-
    geon), b 1840,2,25 d 1923,11,25
    Ch: Arthur   b 1871, 3, 20
        Ida   " 1876, 6, 15
1888, 5, 18. Laura Susan, dt Thos. L. & Mary
    A. E. (Bricker) STANLEY, b (w Harry)
1896, 12, 19. Rolland, s Chas. & Sara C.
    (Hollingsworth) b
1897, 1, 30. Julia Etta, dt Cyrus L. & Sarah
    M. PEMBERTON, b

1839, 5, 25. James C. dis disunity
1851, 3, 22. Isabella Emily Cobbs (form
    Blackburn) dis mcd
1859, 6, 25. Uree Crouse (form Blackburn) dis
    mcd
1862, 2, 22. Barbee Jr. dis mcd
1862, 2, 22. Maro dis mcd
1862, 11, 21. Barbee dis jG (W)
1863, 4, 24. Esther dis jG (W)
1863, 4, 24. Elizabeth dis jG (W)
1863, 4, 24. Temperance dis jG (W)
1863, 6, 26. Wm. H. & Elizabeth dis jG (W)
1863, 9, 25. Henry H. dis jG (W)
1865, 6, 24. Temperance B. Wood (form Black-
    burn) con mcd
1869, 10, 23. Louisa McDonnold (form Black-
    burn) con mcd
1870, 3, 26. Sarah Jane Engle (form Black-
    burn) con mcd
1871, 4, 22. Henry H. con mcd
1876, 9, 23. Martha H. dis
1883, 11, 24. Henry H. gct Baltimore MM, Md.;
    returned 3-22 with objections
1884, 2, 23. Joseph gct Salem MM

BLACKBURN, continued
1884, 8, 23. Joseph H. dropped from mbrp
1899, 2, 25. Emma recrq
1911, 1, 28. James dropped from mbrp
1912, 5, 24. Jonathan K. & w, Emily H., & s,
    Arthur, rocf Middleton MM, dtd 1912,4,20
    (W)   [(W)
1924, 9, 26. Roland rmt Julia Etta Pemberton
1926, 12, 24. Rolland rocf Middleton MM, dtd
    1926,12,18 (W)

BLACKLEGE
1878, 3, 26. Joseph, s Charles & Hannah,
    Harrison Co., O.; m in residence of Sarah
    STANLEY, Rhoda STANLEY, dt Robert & Sarah

1878, 5, 25. Rhoda S. gct Salem MM, Ia.

BLUNT
1853, 1, 12. Mary b d 1894,5,27 bur Damascus

1882, 7, 22. Mary recrq

BOGLEMAN
1895, 5, 23. Ella Mae, dt Monroe & Rose
    THOMAS, b

1929, 8, 26. Ella [Bokelman] recrq

BOLTON
1833, 4, 27. Mary gct Salem MM

BOND
1866, 8, 25. Josiah Butler gct Cherry Grove
    MM, Ind., to m Elizabeth Bond

BONER
1862, 12, 27. Sarah (form Engle) dis mcd
1865, 8, 25. Sarah (form Engle) dis mcd (W)

BOOTH
1830, 4, 30. Lucinde (form Cobbs) dis mcd

BORTON
1871, 6, 7. Emma C., dt Isaac & Susan DAVIS,
    b

1832, 11, 24. Jane (form Heacock) dis mou in
    Hicksite mtg
1921, 12, 24. Emma rocf Alliance MM
1922, 11, 25. Emma gct Alliance MM
1927, 6, 23. George Ross dropped from mbrp

BOULTON
1827, 12, 27. Daniel, s James & Hannah, Colum-
    biana Co., O.; m in Springfield MH, Esther
    MORRIS, dt Anthony & Hannah, Columbiana
    Co., O.
1832, 11, 1. William, s James & Hannah, Co-
    lumbiana Co., O.; m in Springfield MH,
    Mary MORRIS, dt Anthony & Hannah, Colum-
    biana Co., O.

1828, 6, 28. Sarah rocf New Garden MM, dtd
    1828,6,26
1828, 9, 27. Esther gct Salem MM
1838, 5, 26. Sarah gct Salem MM

BOWMAN
----, --, --. Thomas b 1813,8,4; m Elizabeth
    ----- b 1814,10,24

1839, 9, 28. Thomas rocf Marlborough MM, dtd
    1839,6,25
1839, 9, 28. Elizabeth L. rocf Short Creek
    MM, O., dtd 1839,4,23
1847, 4, 24. Thomas & w, Elizabeth L., gct
    Marlborough MM
1855, 6, 22. Thomas & w, Elizabeth, & dt,
    Achsah, gct Plymouth MM
1869, 8, 28. Lucy (form Thomas) dis mcd

BOYLE
1850, 7, 10. Charity E., dt Lewis & Sarah
    Ann HOOPS, b (w Wm.)
1875, 10, 12. Lenora S. [Boile], dt Wm. &
    Charity, b
1878, 12, 24. Irene T., dt Robert R. & Mary J.
    b
1881, 4, 26. Lewis Homer, s Wm. & Elizabeth,
    b
1886, 2, 16. Otley V., s James T. & Elnora,b
1905, 5, 28. Myrtle Naomi, dt Otley & Olive
    (Denny) b

1875, 2, 27. Charity (form Hoops) con mcd
1896, 2, 22. Lenora S. recrq
1897, 1, 23. Irma recrq
1900, 2, 24. Lester & L. Homer [Boyles]
    recrq
1902, 1, 25. Otley recrq
1906, 4, 28. Lester W. rocf Beloit MM, Mich.
1911, 2, 25. Lester [Boyles] gct Beloit MM,
    O.
1918, 11, 23. Otley dropped from mbrp
1921, 10, 22. Myrtle recrq

BRACKEN
1836, 6, 25. Caleb & w, Mary, rocf Redstone
    MM, dtd 1836,6,1
1840, 4, 25. Caleb & w, Mary, gct Redstone MM

BRADSHAW
1840, 10, 24. Townsend rocf Buckingham MM,
    Pa., dtd 1840,10,5
1840, 10, 24. James, Wm. & Rebecca, minors,
    rocf Buckingham MM, Pa., dtd 1840,7,6 (ch
    James, dec)
1842, 3, 26. Rebecca T. Hinchman (form
    Bradshaw) dis mcd
1842, 9, 24. Townsend dis jH
1842, 9, 24. James dis jH
1843, 8, 26. Sarah (form Fogg) dis mcd
1848, 2, 26. Wm. dis mcd

BRAIN
1904, 5, 28. Cora gct Beloit MM

BRANNEN
1833, 4, 27. Susan, Malon, Nathaniel & Rachel [Brannin] ch Ezra & Rachel, rocf Salem MM, dtd 1833,3,20
1848, 3, 25. Susanna Snowd (form Brannen) dis mcd
1848, 3, 25. Rachel Enke (form Brannen) dis mcd
1848, 5, 27. Mahlon dis mcd

BRANTINGHAM
----, --, --. George b 1770,11,7; m Phebe ----- b 1773,6,7
    Ch: Hannah   b 1809, 3, 1
       George   " 1811, 12, 5
       Sarah   " 1814, 9, 14
----, --, --. Margaret b 1791,4,21 d 1884,5,29 bur Marlboro
----, --, --. Joseph b 1807,1,27; m Lydia ----- b 1804,8,13
    Ch: Rachel   b 1827, 10, 22
       William   " 1829, 1, 6
       Alfred   " 1830, 8, 28
----, --, --. John b 1822, 9, 27 d 1884,9,12 bur Marlborough; m Hannah ----- b 1832,11, 8 d 1899,7,3
    Ch: Angelina   b 1850, 12, 29
       Martin   " 1853, 1, 13 d 1875,11,3
         bur Marlboro
       Samuel   b 1855, 9, 10
       Sarah   " 1861, 9, 8
       Ellen C.   " 1867, 2, 5
       Esther   " 1867, 2, 5 d 1867, 4,26
1851, 10, 29. Rebecca m Gideon CREW
----, --, --. Samuel, s John & Hannah (Carr) b 1855,9,10; m Mary Anna ----- b 1858,5, 11 d 1904,8,5, bur Marlborough
    Ch: Martin   b 1881, 5, 10
       Isabel   " 1883, 9, 2
       John R.   " 1885, 2, 10
       Florence   " 1887, 2, 10
       Alfred W.   " 1888, 6, 30 d 1888, 8,26
       Mary   " 1890, 4, 8; m -----
         Steel
       Adna   " 1892, 3, 24
       Elsie   " 1893, 4, 12; m -----
         Vaughn
       Roselia   " 1894, 11, 10; m -----
         Winn
       Frank   " 1899, 2, 9
       Alma   " 1901, 1, 1
----, --, --. James H., s Wm. & Rhoda, b 1851, 1,2; m Anna E. WHITELEATHER, dt Joseph & Leah, b 1857,3,15
    Ch: James
       Arthur   b 1892, 1, 12
1906, 1, 27. Ellen m Henry B. LEEDS (W)
1828, 6, 28. George & w, Phebe, & ch, George & Sarah H., rocf New Garden MM, dtd 1828, 6,26

1828, 6, 28. Hannah rocf New Garden MM, dtd 1828, 6, 26
1832, 2, 25. George gct New Garden MM, to m Hannah Shinn
1833, 1, 31. Joseph & w, Lydia, & ch, Rachel, William & Alfred, rocf New Garden MM, dtd 1832,11,22
1833, 1, 31. George Jr. gct New Garden MM
1835, 12, 26. Joseph & w, Lydia, & ch, Rachel, William, Alfred & Elizabeth, gct New Garden MM
1835, 12, 26. George & w, Hannah, & ch, Rebecca, rocf New Garden MM, dtd 1835,11,26
1837, 7, 22. Sarah H. Malmsberry (form Brantingham) dis mcd
1838, 5, 26. George & w, Phebe, gct Salem MM
1838, 5, 26. Hannah C. gct Salem MM
1838, 6, 23. George Jr. & w, Hannah, & ch, Rebecca, James & Edward, gct New Garden MM
1851, 4, 26. Rebecca rocf New Garden MM, dtd 1851,4,24
1858, 11, 26. John & w, Hannah, & ch, Angelina, Martin & Samuel, acknowledged as mbr since they could not bring cert because of Ind. YM going with the Separatists (W)
1874, 9, 22. Angeline Gaskill (form Brantingham) dis mcd (W)
1881, 8, 26. Anna M. con mcd (W)
1882, 1, 27. Sarah rmt Thomas A. Crawford (W)
1897, 3, 27. James H. & w, Anna E., & s, James Arthur, rocf Winona MM
1900, 8, 15. James & w & s gct East Goshen MM
1909, 5, 21. Joseph C. rmt Grace Crawford (W)
1909, 12, 24. Grace C. gct New Garden MM (W)
1910, 1, 21. Charles E. Crawford gct New Garden MM, to m Alice A. Brantingham (W)
1911, 11, 24. Wilson rmt Alice Crawford (W)
1912, 1, 26. Alice (Crawford) gct New Garden MM (W)
1916, 5, 26. Martin dis jas (W)
1920, 4, 23. Isabella dis jas (W)
1920, 12, 24. Florence dis jas (W)
1926, 1, 22. Mary (Brantingham) Steel dropped from mbrp (W)
1926, 1, 22. Elsie (Brantingham) Vaughn dropped from mbrp (W)
1926, 1, 22. Roselia (Brantingham) Shinn dropped from mbrp (W)
1926, 1, 22. Alma (Brantingham) Hallman dropped from mbrp (W)
1932, 11, 25. John R. dropped from mbrp (W)
1932, 11, 25. Adna dropped from mbrp (W)
1932, 11,25. Frank dropped from mbrp (W)

BREMER
----, --, --. Edith b 1834,12,15 d 1865,4,9 bur Springfield

BRENNER
1861, 6, 22. Esther [Brener] (form Stanley) con mcd

BRENNER, continued
1867, 10, 25. Elmira (form Stanley) dis mcd
    (W)
1867, 12, 18. Elmira (form Stanley) con mcd
1870, 8, 27. Philip recrq

BRIGGS
1871, 6, 1. Wm. Jr., s Jonathan & Elizabeth,
    Mahaska Co., Ia.; m in Damascus MH, Mar-
    tha T. KIRK, dt Joel & Mary Ann, Mahoning
    Co., O.
----, --, --. Clayton Albert, s Jonathan &
    Mary E., b 1885,8,11; m Cora Alverda
    BOWER, dt Albert D. & Elizabeth J. (Wolf),
    b 1889,11,16
    Ch: Virgil
          Duane   b 1913, 10, 8
        Velma
          Loretta   " 1915, 6, 21
        Lena Bur-
          deen   " 1916, 9, 15

1870, 2, 26. Elizabeth C. (form Cattell) con
    mcd
1870, 9, 24. Elizabeth C. gct New Sharon MM,
    Ia.
1872, 4, 27. Martha T. gct New Sharon MM, Ia.
1926, 1, 28. Clayton Albert & w, Cora Al-
    meda, & ch, Virgil D., Velma L. & Leona
    B., recrq

BROGAN
1880, 3, 18. Bertha H. Thomas, w John, b

1896, 2, 22. Jeannet Orr gct Sandy Spring MM
1901, 5, 20. Bertha Thomas relrq

BROOKS
----, --, --. James & Esther
    Ch: Isaiah
          Boon   b 1800, 12, 30
        Basil   " 1803, 2, 6
        Hannah
          Pancoast " 1805, 9, 23
        Gerard   " 1808, 3, 16
        James Jr.   " 1810, 8, 6 d 1831, 3,12
        Ann Eliza
          Pleasant " 1813, 4, 5
        Pauline
          Snowden   " 1816, 7, 30
        Jane Grey   " 1819, 2, 10
----, --, --. Isaiah B. b 1800,12,30; m Debo-
    rah ----- b 1801,11,30
    Ch: Caroline   b 1825, 7, 10
        Mordecai   " 1827, 1, 2
1826, 5, 31. Basil [Brooke], s James & Hes-
    ter, Columbiana Co., O., b 1803,2,6; m in
    Goshen MH, Rachel MORRIS, dt Joseph & Ra-
    chel, Columbiana Co., O., b 1806,9,6
1826, 11, 1. Hannah P. [Brooke] m Joseph
    Ball

1828, 9, 27. Isaiah B. [Brock] dis JH

1828, 10, 25. James [Brook] dis JH
1828, 10, 25. Esther dis JH
1828, 11, 22. Basil [Brook] dis Jas
1829, 7, 25. Deborah [Brook] dis disunity
1829, 11, 28. Rachel [Brook] dis disunity
1830, 7, 24. Gerard [Brooke] dis disunity
1833, 4, 27. Ann Eliza P. [Brooke] dis dis-
    unity
1833, 4, 27. Lolina [Brooke] dis disunity
1840, 8, 22. Jane [Brook] dis JH
1843, 3, 25. Caroliné Thompson (form Brook)
    dis mcd
1849, 2, 24. Arnold, minor, gct Gilead MM
1849, 12, 22. Mordecai dis disunity
1853, 8, 27. Geo. Washington dis mcd
1853, 11, 26. Hester Shinn (form Brooks) dis
    mcd
1866, 12, 22. Benjamin Butler gct Gilead MM,
    to m Hannah Pauline Brooks

BROSIUS
----, --, --. Samuel b 1829,8,30; m Mariam
    ----- b 1833,9,2
.1837, 3, 2. Marium, dt Clayton & Charlotte
    CRISPIN, b
1874, 3, 1. Emma M., dt Samuel, b (adopted)

1843, 7, 22. Jane (form Stanley) dis mcd
1859, 1, 22. Jane A. rocf Goshen MM,
    dtd 1858,12,18
1868, 5, 23. Samuel & Miriam recrq
1890, 2, 22. Mariam rocf East Goshen MM
1893, 6, 25. Emma M. recrq
1899, 10, 28. Jane W. recrq
1900, 7, 28. Jane relrq

BROWN
1830, 4, 8. Abia W., s Samuel & Ann, Colum-
    biana Co., O., b 1799,10,18; m in Damascus
    MH, Abby CADWALADER, dt Asa & Jane, Jef-
    ferson Co., O.
    Ch: Ann R.   b 1831, 4, 13
        Jane C.   " 1832, 6, 5
1834, 7, 0. Sarah m David Whinery
1828, 3, 22. Abia W. rocf ND MM, dtd 1827,8,
    28
1831, 5, 28. Wm., minor, rocf Burlington MM,
    N. J., dtd 1831,5,2
1832, 6, 23. William gct ND MM
1833, 6, 22. Nathan & w, Amy, & dt, Almina,
    rocf Salem MM, dtd 1833,6,19
1833, 6, 22. David rocf Salem MM, dtd 1833,
    6,19
1833, 6, 22. Mary, Sarah & Atlantic rocf
    Salem MM, dtd 1833,5,22

1836, 10, 22. Mary Atlantic & Almira gct
    Salem MM
1836, 10, 22. David gct Salem MM
1836, 10, 22. Nathan & w, Amy, gct Salem MM
1838, 11, 24. Abby & ch, Amos R., Jane C. &
    Hannah H., gct Miami MM, O.
1838, 12, 22. Abiah W. gct Miami MM, O.

BROWN, continued
1842, 12, 24. Abby & ch, Ann Jane Hannah Mary
     & Abia Wm. gct Short Creek MM, O.

BRUFF
1848, 7, 27. Mary m Benjamin C. ANDREWS
1849, 3, 29. Hannah m Edward WILLIAMS
----, --, --. James B. b 1797,9,28 d 1865,3,
     20; m Sarah ----- b 1802,5,31
     Ch: Lydia B.   b 1822, 1, 26
         Hannah   " 1823, 8, 27
         Charles   " 1825, 2, 24 d 1835, 4,--
           bur Springfield
         Joseph   b 1827, 3, 6
         Mary   " 1829, 5, 3
         James
          Morris   " 1831, 2, 27 d 1834, 8,30
           bur Springfield
         Sarah   b 1834, 8, 4
         Esther   " 1835, 10, 9
         Henrietta " 1837, 3, 5 d 1837, 9, 5
           bur Springfield
         Elizabeth b 1838, 9, 14
         Adna Louisa" 1840, 4, 11 " 1872, 2,25
           bur Damascus
         Susan   b 1840, 4, 20 " 1842, 8, 24
           bur Springfield
----, --, --. Joseph b 1827,3,6; m Anna M.
     ----- b 1830,6,6 d 1887,7,4
     Ch: Charles   b 1851, 6, 28 d 1871,11, 8
         James B.   " 1853, 5, 29
         Martha H. " 1855, 8, 24 " 1860, 2,27
         Edward Og-
          den   " 1861, 4, 27 " 1862, 2,10
         Sarah   " 1866, 8, 18
         Joseph Car-
          roll   " 1871, 5, 6 " 1872, 2,11
1851, 3, 27. Lydia m Wm. H. OLIPHANT
1859, 8, 30. Sarah m Tristram COGGESHALL
1864, 10, 27. Elizabeth m Lindley M. KIRK
----, --, --. James B. b 1853,5,29; m Jessie
     H. -----
     Ch: Joseph
          Carroll   b 1884, 3, 1
         Anna Marie " 1885, 8, 6
         Beulah   " 1886, 6, 30
         James Rus-
          sell   " 1891, 5, 1
         Wm. Cort-
          land   " 1896, 12, 17

1848, 7, 23. Joseph gct Salem MM, to m Anna
     M. Ogdon
1849, 4, 28. Anna M. rocf Salem MM, dtd
     1849,2,21
1856, 4, 26. James B. rocf New York MM, dtd
     1856,3,5
1857, 2, 22. Sibyl (form Cobbs) dis mcd (W)
1858, 9, 25. Sibyl (form Cobbs) dis mcd
1858, 9, 25. James B. Jr. con mcd
1859, 4, 23. Sibyl (form Cobbs) dis mcd
1862, 11, 21. James B. dis jG (W)
1863, 2, 27. Sarah dis jG (W)

1863, 7, 24. Esther dis jG (W)
1863, 7, 24. Elizabeth dis jG (W)
1863, 7, 24. Anne M. dis jG (W)
1863, 7, 24. Anna Louisa dis jG (W)
1866, 8, 25. Joseph dis military service
1867, 12, 21. Joseph dis military service (W)
1877, 2, 24. Esther gct Springdale MM, Ia.
1886, 3, 27. Jessie F. rocf Falworth MM, Me.
1888, 5, 26. Sarah relrq
1904, 12, 24. James Carrol, Anna M. & Beulah
     gct Oskaloosa MM, Ia.
1906, 12, 22. James Russel, s James B. & Jes-
     sie H., gct Oskaloosa MM, Ia.
1912, 6, 22. James B. & w, Jessie H., & s,
     Wm. C. gct Chestnut Hill MM, Ia.

BRYAN
1827, 6, 27. Martha m Thomas FRENCH

1827, 4, 28. Martha rocf Eversham MM, N. Y.,
     dtd 1827,2,9

BUCHANAN
1870, 9, 23. Margaretta (form Cobbs) dis mcd

BUCK
1826, 7, 22. John & w, Merriam, & ch, Nathan
     & Jonathan, rocf New Garden MM, dtd 1826,
     6,22
1828, 12, 27. John dis disunity
1829, 1, 24. Merriam dis disunity

BUCKMAN
----, --, --. Harding b 1795,12,15 d 1878,3,5
     bur Springfieldp m Mercy ----- b 1796,6,1
     d 1863,9,28 (W)

1853, 8, 27. Harding & w, Mercy, rocf Falls
     MM, Pa., dtd 1853,4,7
1863, 1, 24. Harding & Mercy dis jW

BUFFUM
1860, 3, 24. Joseph Cattell gct Uxbridge MM,
     Mass. to m Eleanor Buffum

BUNDY
1863, 6, 27. Deborah M. (form Jones) con mcd
1864, 11, 26. Deborah M. gct Short Creek MM, O.
1873, 6, 27. Deborah M. gct Short Creek MM,
     O. (W)
1895, 10, 25. Olive R. Whinery (form Bundy)
     con mcd (W)
1898, 4, 22. Gilbert Warrington gct Short
     Creek MM, O., to m Josephine Bundy

BURDGE
----, --, --. Jacob [Burge] b 1783,1,28; m
     Miriam ----- b 1786,8,11
     Ch: William   b 1813, 11, 22
         Hannah   " 1815, 8, 11
         Lewis   " 1819, 4, 16
         Oliver   " 1821, 9, 28
         Mary   " 1824, 1, 7

BURDGE, continued

----, --, --. William [Burge] b 1813,11,22; m
    Martha ----- b 1816,2,13
    Ch: Albert   b 1836, 1, 3
        Hiram   " 1837, 12, 21
        Ezra   " 1840, 1, 11 d 1843, 4, 2
        bur Springfield
        Bracken   b 1842, 2, 28
        Samantha " 1844, 3, 1
        Miriam   " 1846, 10, 27
----, --, --. Lewis [Burge] b 1819,4,16; m Sa-
    rah ----- b 1823,2,21
    Ch: Philena   b 1844, 4, 26
        Ezra   " 1846, 1, 25
        John   " 1847, 11, 7
1843, 5, 31. Levi, s Jacob & Miriam, Colum-
    biana Co., O.; m in Goshen MH, Sarah
    MALMSBERRY, dt Benj. & Jane, Columbiana
    Co., O.
1846, 4, 29. Oliver, s Jacob & Miriam, Colum-
    biana Co., O., b 1821,9,28; m in Goshen
    MH, Jane M. HEMINGWAY, dt James & Hope,
    Mahoning Co., O., b 1824,4,30
    Ch: Martin   b 1847, 4, 22
        Almira   " 1849, 9, 16   [BERRY
1850, 5, 30. Mary [Burdg] m Benjamin MALMSBERR

1835, 4, 25. Jacob [Burdg] & w, Miriam, & ch,
    Lewis, Olover & Mary, rocf Providence MM,
    dtd 1835,4,22
1835, 4, 25. Hannah [Burdg] rocf Providence
    MM, dtd 1835,4,2
1835, 5, 23. Wm. [Burdg] & w, Martha, rocf
    Providence MM, dtd 1835,4,30
1836, 5, 28. Jacob & w, Miriam, & ch, Lewis,
    Oliver & Mary, gct Carmel MM
1836, 6, 25. Hannah gct Carmel MM
1836, 6, 25. Wm. & fam gct Carmel MM
1836, 11, 26. Benjamin Walton gct Carmel MM,
    to m Hannah [Burdg]
1839, 6, 22. Wm. [Burdg] & w, Martha, & ch,
    Albert & Hiram, rocf Carmel MM, dtd 1839,
    6,15
1839, 6, 22. Jacob [Burdg] & w, Miriam, & ch,
    Lewis, Olover & Mary, rocf Sandy Spring
    MM, dtd 1839,5,24
1851, 10, 25. Lewis & w, Sarah, & ch, Philena
    & John, gct Driftwood MM, Ind.
1851, 11, 22. William & w, Martha, & ch, Al-
    bert, Hiram, Braden, Samantha, Miriam &
    Lewis, gct Driftwood MM, Ind.
1852, 9, 25. Oliver & w, Jane, & ch, Martin
    & Almira, gct Driftwood MM, Ind.
1853, 7, 23. Jacob & Miriam gct Driftwood MM,
    Ind.

BURGER

1905, 9, 20. Mildred Leora, w Walter, dt
    Irving Leroy & Myrtle (Kelly) HOOPES, b

BUSH

1883, 5, 25. Anna Priscilla (form Garwood)
    dis mcd (W)

BUTLER

----, --, --. Benjamin b 1762,8,21 d 1828,8,8
    bur Springfield; m Hannah ----- b 1771,8,7
    d 1856,3,19 bur Springfield
    Ch: Lawrence
        W.   b 1797, 9, 15
        Eleanor   " 1799, 2, 1
        Hannah   " 1802, 1, 2
        John   " 1803, 6, 14
        Meribah   " 1805, 7, 14
        Ann   " 1807, 9, 22
        Sarah   " 1809, 6, 20
        Lydia   " 1811, 10, 7 d 1843, 2,25
        bur Springfield
        William   b 1814, 10, 5
----, --, --. Lawrence W. b 1797,9,15; m Sarah
    ----- b 1797,11,4
    Ch: Moses V. b 1822, 5, 10
        Hannah   " 1824, 3, 2
        Lewis   " 1825, 12, 3
        Joseph   " 1827, 10, 1
        Benjamin " 1827, 10, 1
        Mary   " 1829, 8, 16
        Eunice   " 1831, 6, 29
        John L.   " 1833, 9, 9
        Sarah   " 1835, 9, 19
        Merihab   " 1837, 5, 21 d 1843, 1, 7
        bur Goshen
----, --, --. Jehu b 1803,6,14; m Drusilla
    ----- b 1805,6,6 d 1830,8,10 bur Salem
    Ch: Asenath b 1826, 5, 29
        Esther   " 1828, 7, 8 d 1828, 9,26
        bur Salem
        Benjamin " 1830, 5, 29
    Jehu m 2nd Elizabeth ----- b 1808,7,1 d
    1865,3,5 bur Salem
    Ch: George   b 1836, 1, 25 d 1841, 9,30
        bur Salem
        Richard   " 1837, 8, 11 " 1841, 9, 3
        Drusilla " 1840, 9, 16 " 1865, 3,15
        Beulah   " 1842, 7, 6 " 1856, 3,24
        Josiah   " 1844, 10, 2
        Elizabeth T" 1846, 8, 23
        Lydia   " 1847, 12, 30
        Hannah   " 1849, 11, 9
    Jehu m 3rd Elizabeth ----- b 1810,2,4 d
    1880,4,28 bur Winona
----, --, --. Lydia, dt John & Elizabeth, b
    1825,9,13 d 1901,8,5
1834, 7, 2. John, s Benjamin & Hannah, Co-
    lumbiana Co., O., b 1803,6,14 d 1887,12,
    12; m in Goshen MH, Elizabeth TATUM, dt
    George & Beulah, Columbiana Co., O., b
    1808,7,1 d 1867,3,4
    Ch: Drusilla b 1840, 9, 16 d 1865, 3,15
        bur Goshen
        Josiah   " 1844, 10, 2
        Elizabeth " 1846, 8, 23
        Lydia   " 1847, 12, 30
        Hannah   " 1849, 11, 9
1834, 10, 1. Meribah m James FARMER
1835, 10, 28. Sarah m Samuel STREET
1847, 5, 27. John, s Daniel & Mary, Stark

BUTLER, continued

Co., O., b 1823,10,10 d 1900,1,1; m in Springfield MH, Ann COPPOCK, dt Jehu & Judith, Columbiana Co., O., b 1828,11,9 d 1903,10,16

Ch: Ruthetta   b 1848, 10, 22
    Jesse   " 1850, 10, 8
    Jehu   " 1853, 6, 29 d 1859, 2,22
    Willis   " 1856, 4, 13 " 1859, 3,28
    Micajah D. " 1859, 1, 29
    Irena Mary " 1861, 7, 29
    Judith Ella " 1864, 5, 19
    Anna T.   " 1868, 6, 16
    Emma Jane   " 1872, 4, 6

1849, 5, 2. Mary m Joshua STEER
1849, 8, 29. Hannah m David TATUM
1849, 10, 4. Joseph, s Lawrence W. & Sarah, Mahoning Co.,.O., b 1827,10,1; m in Springfield MH, Emily Jane STANLEY, dt Elijah & Uree, Mahoning Co., O., b 1830,5,11

Ch: Uree   b 1851, 5, 8 d 1852, 3,18
    Calvin   " 1852, 10, 25
    Olive   " 1854, 8, 9

----, --, --. Benjamin, s John & Drusilla, Mahoning Co., O., b 1830,5,29 d 1904,2,16; m in Goshen MH, Hannah STANLEY, dt Isaac & Elizabeth, Mahoning Co., O., b 1831,10,13 d 1865,11,8 bur Springfield

Ch: Esther   b 1850, 10, 5
    Asenath   " 1857, 10, 29

Benjamin m 2nd Hannah P. ----- b 1830,12, 20 d 1910,10,13

1851, 5, 28. Eunice m Flemming A. STANLEY
1852, 10, 11. John L., s Lawrence W. & Sarah, Mahoning Co., O., b 1833,9,9; m in Goshen MH, Sarah FRENCH, dt Thomas & Martha, Mahoning Co., O., b 1835,11,22

Ch: Thomas   b 1858, 10, 24
    Lawrence W. " 1860, 6, 24
    Merihab J. " 1867, 2, 26

----, --, --. Josiah b 1844,10,2; m Elizabeth ----- dt Benj. & Sarah BOND, b 1839,2,7

Ch: Franklin J. b 1867, 10, 9
    Mary E.   " 1869, 6, 5
    Emma L.   " 1874, 2, 20
    William H.   " 1876, 2, 29

1865, 3, 4. Elizabeth d ae 57 (a minister)
1868, 12, 3. Ruthetta m Geo. W. BAILEY
1870, 4, 28. Elizabeth T. m Caleb MARIS
1870, 10, 27. Hannah W. m Isaac LLOYD
1874, 1, 1. Jesse, s John, Mahoning Co., O., b 1850,10,8; m in Damascus MH, Samantha STANLEY, dt Israel & Uree C., b 1852,6,25 d 1885,11,14

Ch: Walter E. b 1875, 1, 21
    Myra   " 1879, 10, 26

----, --, --. Micajah D., s John & Ann, b 1859, 1,23; m Emma C. BROWN, dt Wm. & Elizabeth, b 1859,2,11
1880, 4, 28. R. Elizabeth d ae 70 bur Winona

1831, 6, 25. Lawrence W. & w, Sarah, & ch, Moses V., Hannah, Lewis, Joseph, Benjamin

& Mary, rocf New Garden MM, dtd 1831,6,23
1833, 7, 27. Ann gct Salem MM
1836, 11, 26. Clayton Kille gct Marlborough MM, to m Mary Butler
1837, 9, 23. Ellen rocf Salem MM, dtd 1837,8, 23
1842, 10, 22. John, minor, rocf Marlborough MM, dtd 1842,9,27
1842, 11, 26. Ellen (now Kimbrough) dis
1843, 12, 23. Susanna (form Andrews) con mcd to first cousin
1844, 6, 22. Susanna gct Walnut Ridge MM
1845, 4, 26. Moses N. gct Middleton MM, to m Emily Schooley
1845, 9, 27. Emily S. rocf Middleton MM, dtd 1845,8,7
1845, 12, 27. Hannah gct Sandy Spring MM
1845, 12, 27. Asenath Park (form Butler) dis mcd
1846, 5, 23. William dis mou
1848, 4, 22. Moses V. & w, Emily, & ch, Lindley S. & Sarah Louisa, gct Salem MM, Ia.
1850, 1, 26. Lewis dis jas

1850, 5, 25. Hannah rocf Sandy Spring MM, dtd 1850,4,26
1852, 5, 22. Joseph dis
1855, 2, 24. Sarah Thomas (form Butler) dis mcd
1857, 6, 27. Lawrence W. & w, Sarah, gct Marlborough MM
1858, 12, 25. Benjamin dis mcd
1859, 2, 26. Emily Jane & ch, Calvin & Olive, gct West Union MM, Ind.
1863, 1, 24. Elizabeth dis jW
1863, 3, 27. John Jr. dis jG (W)
1863, 3, 27. Ann dis jG (W)
1863, 4, 24. Benjamin & Hannah dis jG (W)
1863, 5, 22. John dis jG (W)
1863, 6, 26. John L. & Sarah dis jG (W)
1863, 8, 21. Lawrence W. & Sarah dis jG (W)
1866, 8, 25. Josiah gct Cherry Grove MM, Ind., to m Elizabeth Bond
1866, 12, 22. Benjamin gct Gilead MM, to m Hannah Pauline Brooks
1867, 2, 23. Elizabeth rocf Cherry Grove MM, Ind.
1867, 6, 22. Hannah rocf Gilead MM, dtd 1867, 5,14
1870, 8, 27. John gct New Garden MM, to m Elizabeth Jenkins
1870, 12, 24. Elizabeth J. rocf New Garden MM, dtd 1870,12,21
1872, 5, 24. Elizabeth Maris (form Butler) dis mcd (W)
1872, 6, 21. Lydia dis jG (W)
1885, 11, 28. Josiah & w, Elizabeth, & ch, Franklin J., Mary E., Emma L. & Wm. H., gct Barkley MM, Kans.

BUTLER, continued
1888, 1, 28. Jesse & s, Walter E., gct
     Whittier MM, Calif.
1888, 1, 28. Micajah D. gct Whittier MM,
     Calif.
1890, 9, 27. Mira gct Whittier MM, Calif.
1891, 3, 28. Lydia gct Barclay MM, Kans.
1891, 3, 28. Lydia gct Barclay MM, Kans.
1895, 10, 26. Lydia rocf Barclay MM, Kans.
1900, 7, 28. Micajah D. & w, Emma C., gct
     Salem MM
1906, 10, 27. Anna T. relrq
1910, 2, 26. J. Ella gct Raisin MM, Mich.

CADWALADER
1830, 4, 28. Abby m Abia W. BROWN
----, --, --. John J., s Mifflin & Sarah J.,
     b 1853,7,6; m Mary A. COPE, dt Amos & Ra-
     chel, b 1851,10,31 d 1912,4,30
     Ch: Edgar M.   b 1889, 1, 30

1827, 5, 26. William rocf Short Creek MM, O.,
     dtd 1827,2,20
1827, 5, 26. Harmon rocf Short Creek MM, O.,
     dtd 1827,2,20
1827, 5, 26. Mary rocf Short Creek MM, O.,
     dtd 1827,2,20
1830, 7, 24. William dis
1840, 7, 25. Howard [Cadwallader] rocf
     Stillwater MM, dtd 1840,6,27
1841, 8, 28. Howard gct New Garden MM, to m
     Margaret Johnson
1842, 1, 22. Howard gct Salem MM
1904, 6, 25. Edgar M. recrq
1907, 4, 27. John J. & w, Mary, recrq
1914, 2, 28. John dropped from mbrp
1915, 4, 24. Edgar [Cadwallader] gct Alliance
     MM

CADWELL
1862, 1, 25. Mariam (form Downs) dis mcd

CALLAHAN
1887, 7, 24. Dennis [Callihan], s Lote & Jes-
     sie, b

1902, 1, 25. Dennis recrq
1922, 9, 23. Dennis dropped from mbrp

CAMERON
----, --, --. Milton b 1855,11,11 d 1889,11,6
     bur Upper Springfield; m Bulah ----- b
     1860,9,20 (W)
     Ch: Mabel   b 1880, 12, 23
         Anna Viola " 1883, 9, 28
         Mary E.   " 1887, 2, 16
         Edith M.   " 1890, 2, 24
1907, 3, 26. Mary m Barclay S. HALL (W)

1879, 6, 27. Milton rmt Beulah Fogg (W)
1879, 9, 23. Beulah gct New Garden MM (W)
1882, 6, 23. Milton & w, Beulah, & dt, Mabel,
     rocf New Garden MM, dtd 1882,5,20 (W)

1905, 3, 24. Anna V. rmt Horace J. Edgerton
     (W)
1905, 6, 23. Anna V.(Cameron) Edgerton gct
     New Garden MM (W)
1907, 10, 25. Beulah rmt Walter Edgerton (W)
1912, 7, 27. Mabel Cobbs dropped from mbrp
     (W)
1913, 8, 22. Mabel H. rmt Wm. D. Satterth-
     wait (W)
1921, 12, 23. Edith M. Hadley (form Cameron)
     dis mcd (W)

CAREY
1838, 1, 27. Edmund rocf Salem MM, dtd 1838,
     1,24
1841, 4, 24. Edmund dis mcd

CARLSON
1863, 1, 24. Benjamin & w, Martha, & ch, Sa-
     rah Jane, dis jW

CARNE
1857, 11, 28. Mary Ann (form Lipsey) dis mcd

CARR
----, --, --. Samuel b 1787,3,24 d 1873,8,9
     bur Marlboro; m Patience ----- b 1797,2,3
     d 1891,4,13 (W)
----, --, --. Isaac b 1793,11,4 d 1873,6,3 bur
     Damascus; m Ann ----- b 1793,11,30 d 1859,
     8,27
     Ch: Samuel   b 1816, 12, 29 d 1835, 2,14
         bur Springfield
         George   b 1819, 7, 25
         Isaac R. " 1822, 11, 12
         Robert F. " 1827, 1, 18
         Thomas W. " 1830, 6, 30
         Elizabeth
         Ann   " 1833, 5, 2 d 1844, 1, 8
         Joseph   " 1836, 3, 9
----, --, --. Samuel m Patience ----- b 1797,
     2,3
     Ch: David   b 1821, 4, 4
         Francis
         Dean   " 1823, 12, 14
         Esther   " 1826, 8, 11
         Hannah   " 1832, 11, 9
1837, 9, 28. William, Jefferson Co., O., m
     in Springfield MH, Lydia POOL, dt Israel
     & Jane, Columbiana Co., O.
1847, 10, 28. Isaac R., s Isaac & Ann, Mahon-
     ing Co., O., b 1822,11,12 d 1900,5,18; m
     in Springfield MH, Isabella CREW, dt Oba-
     diah & Mary, b 1819,9,19 d 1898,12,25

1826, 6, 24. Isaac & w, Ann, & ch, Samuel,
     George & Isaac R., rocf Salem MM, dtd 1826
     6,21
1833, 12, 28. Caleb rst on consent of Redstone
     MM
1834, 6, 28. Caleb gct Burlington MM
1834, 12, 27. Patience, w Samuel, & ch, David,
     Francis D., Esther & Hannah, gct Marl-

CARR, continued
borough MM

1835, 9, 26. Orpha rocf Short Creek MM, O.,
dtd 1835,5,19 end by Smithfield MM, 1835,8,
17
1837, 5, 27. Orpha gct Sommerset MM
1837, 11, 25. Lydia gct Springfield MM
1841, 8, 28. Orpha rocf Pennsville MM, dtd
1841,6,25
1845, 7, 26. George dis mcd
1846, 6, 27. Orpha gct Goshen MM
1853, 10, 22. Isaac Ridgeway & w, Isabella,
gct Driftwood MM, Ind.
1855, 5, 25. Robert F. dis mcd (W)
1857, 1, 24. Robert F. dis mcd
1857, 11, 27. Thomas W. dis mcd (W)
1858, 6, 26. Thomas W. dis mcd
1858, 8, 28. Joseph M. dis jas
1860, 4, 26. Isaac rmt Rebecca Woolman (W)
1860, 4, 27. Joseph dis jas (W)
1863, 1, 24. Isaac dis jW
1863, 1, 24. Rebecca dis jW
1863, 7, 24. Francis & Jane dis jG (W)
1869, 12, 24. Samuel rocf ND MM (W)
1872, 10, 25. Sarah (form Holloway) dis mcd (W)

CARRINGTON

----, --, --. ----- m Keziah ----- b 1782,8,7
d 1857,3,27 bur Springfield (W)
Ch: Mary   b 1808, 6, 17 d 1882, 10,4
Martha   " 1817, 2, 4 " 1892, 2, 2
Thomas   " 1821, 4, 15 " 1867, 9, 5

CARROLL

1828, 6, 28. Susanna rocf Providence MM, Pa.,
dtd 1828,1,31; end to New Garden MM
1838, 12, 22. Wm., minor, rocf New Garden MM,
dtd 1831,11,22
1850, 5, 25. Wm. gct Cincinnati MM

CARSON

----, --, --. John b 1789,6,25 d 1860,6,29
bur Goshen; m Jemima ----- b 1787,7,27 d
1862,11,29 bur Goshen
Ch: William   b 1811, 1, 7
Phebe   " 1813, 6, 22 d 1837,11,26
bur Goshen
Benjamin Y." 1815, 3, 9
Sarah   " 1818, 4, 25
Alfred   " 1820, 12, 13 " 1822, 7,27
bur Goshen
John T.   " 1824, 9, 7
1839, 11, 28. William, s John & Jemima, Columbiana Co., O., b 1811,1,7; m in Springfield MH, Elizabeth MORRIS, d Anthony &
Hannah, Columbiana Co., O., b 1809,6,13
d 1843,8,29 bur Springfield
Ch: Alfred   b 1840, 12, 17 d 1841, 2,11
bur Springfield
Morris   b 1843, 8, 16
1844, 3, 28. Benjamin, s John & Jemima, Columbiana Co., O., b 1815,3,9; m in Springfield MH, Martha WOOLMAN, dt Abner & Mar-

tha, Columbiana Co., O., b 1815,6,20 d
1894,11,25 bur Damascus
Ch: Mary Ann   b 1846, 10, 7 d 1847, 9,29
Sarah Jane " 1847, 8, 31
Adaline   " 1850, 12, 15
Julia   " 1853, 10, 16 d 1895,11,21
bur Damascus
Benjamin
Franklin b 1858, 8, 6
1848, 4, 26. John T., s John & Jemima, Mahon-
ing Co., O., b 1824,9,7; m in Goshen MH,
Martha LUPTON, dt Martin & Lucina, Mahon-
ing Co., O., b 1828,5,11
Ch: Martin L. b 1849, 6, 26
1850, 1, 30. Sarah m Jonathan C. WALTON
----, --, --. Benjamin Franklin b 1858,8,6;
m Almira ----- b 1853,10,12 (W)
Ch: Luster   b 1883, 4, 29

1863, 5, 22. John L. & Martha L. dis jG (W)
1864, 5, 28. John T. & w, Martha L., & ch,
Martin, gct Springdale MM, Ia.
1870, 4, 22. Benjamin dis disunity (W)
1870, 8, 27. Charlotte & dt, Ella & Sarah
Eliza, recrq
1875, 4, 23. Sarah Jane Cattell (form Carson)
dis mcd (W)
1883, 8, 24. Benjamin Franklin con mcd (W)
1883, 9, 18. Almira (form Cope) con mcd (W)
1899, 6, 23. Almira dis disunity (W)
1899, 6, 23. Elmira dis (W)
1899, 8, 25. Benjamin F. dis disunity (W)
1901, 6, 21. Adeline Spencer (form Carson)
dis mcd & jas

CASSIDY

1895, 5, 25. Ann recrq
1905, 6, 24. Anna [Cassady] Etzrodt dropped
from mbrp

CATTELL

----, --, --. James b 1771,6,4 d 1860,4,10
bur Goshen; m Deborah ----- b 1774,1,13
d 1853,12,14 bur Goshen
Ch: Ann   b 1793, 9, 6
Hannah   " 1795, 11, 16 d 1819, 8,14
bur Salem
Elizabeth " 1797, 9, 17
Sarah   " 1899, 9, 19 d 1819,--,20
bur Springfield
Deborah   b 1801, 11, 30
Mary   " 1804, 6, 11
Isaac   " 1807, 1, 4 " 1807, 2, 2
bur Springfield
Joseph   b 1808, 3, 19
Ezra   " 1810, 6, 20
Esther   " 1813, 5, 27 d 1841, 3, 8
bur Goshen
James   b 1815, 8, 18
Martha   " 1818, 2, 25 " 1818, 3,10
bur Springfield
Lydia   b 1819, 5, 7
1790, 3, 12. Sarah, w Jonas, b d 1850,4,18

CATTELL, continued
   bur Springfield
1830, 10, 27. Joseph, s James & Deborah, Columbiana Co., O., b 1808,3,19; m in Goshen MH,
   Annar SHREVE, dt Stacy & Vashti, Columbiana Co., O., b 1812,9,27 d 1858,3,10 bur
   Goshen
   Ch: Emaline   b 1831, 7, 27
       Elizabeth   " 1833, 3, 1
       Lavina   " 1835, 3, 11 d 1852, 3,12
         bur Goshen
       Lewis   b 1837, 4, 22
       Martha   " 1839, 8, 25 d 1843, 2, 2
         bur Goshen
       Fayetta   b 1842, 11, 13
       Arvine   " 1845, 3, 5 " 1845, 8, 7
         bur Goshen
   Joseph m 2nd Eleanor ----- b 1820, 7, 7
1833, 5, 29. Ezra, s James & Deborah, Columbiana Co., O., b 1810,6,20; m in Goshen
   MH, Henrietta STANLEY, dt Thomas & Priscilla, Columbiana Co., O., b 1814,4,14
   Ch: Thomas S.   b 1834, 6, 17
       Isaac   " 1836, 9, 29
       Hannah   " 1839, 2, 1 d 1862, 3,20
         bur Springfield
       Esther   b 1841, 2, 25
       Clark   " 1844, 1, 8
       Binford T. " 1846, 7, 20
       Albert R.   " 1849, 4, 13
       Alzada   " 1853, 5, 18
       Ezraetta   " 1856, 12, 20
1839, 5, 29. Esther m Wm. SHREVE
1840, 1, 29. Lydia m Robert STANLEY
----, --, --. James Jr. b 1815,8,18; m Hannah
   W. ----- b 1842,1,7
   Ch: Julia Ann b 1841, 8, 10
1842, 3, 20. Jonathan W., s David & Margaret,
   Fayette Co., Pa.; m in Goshen MH, Deborah
   ELLYSON, dt Isaac & Elizabeth, Columbiana
   Co., O.
1843, 11, 1. Wm., s David & Margaret, Fayette
   Co., Pa., b 1822,1,7 d 1884,5,2 bur Damas-
   cus; m in Goshen MH, Mary ELLYSON, dt
   Isaac & Elizabeth, b 1818,4,13
   Ch: Albert   b 1847, 7, 20 d 1930, 6, 9
       Elmira   " 1849, 11, 25
       Sarah
       Elizabeth   " 1854, 6, 18 " 1865, 7,25
         bur Springfield
       Esthar Beu-
         lah   b 1858, 5, 28
----, --, --. Isaac b 1836,9,29; m Rebecca A.
   ----- b 1834,5,15 (Isaac, s Ezra & Henrietta; Rebecca, dt Edward & Sarah PETTIT)
1851, 5, 28. Emeline m Timothy COBBS
1857, 6, 23. Lydia H. P., dt Ezra & Ruthanna
   (Patterson), b
1860, 9, 27. Lewis, s Joseph & Annar, Mahoning Co., O., b 1837,4,22; m in Damascus
   MH, Amy T. KIRK, dt Joel & Mary Ann, Mahoning Co., O., b 1841,10,15
   Ch: Orlando J. b 1864, 2, 27

   Ch: Mary Leota b 1866, 1, 12
       Charles   " 1868, 9, 21
1862, 1, 2. Thomas S., s Ezra & Henrietta,
   Mahoning Co., O., b 1834,6,17; m in Damascus MH, Elizabeth BLACKBURN, dt James C.
   & Rebecca, Mahoning Co., O., b 1840,8,9
   Ch: Clara H.   b 1864, 4, 7
       Lanora B.   " 1868, 6, 2
1829, 4, 25. Sarah recrq
1840, 9, 26. James Jr. gct Redstone MM, to m
   Hannah W. Cattell
1840, 9, 26. James Jr. gct Redstone MM, to m
   Hannah W. Cattell
1841, 1, 23. Hannah W. rocf Redstone MM, dtd
   1840,12,2
1842, 6, 25. Jonathan W. rocf Redstone MM,
   dtd 1842,6,1
1843, 10, 28. James Jr. gct Redstone MM, to m
   Ann Darlington
1844, 3, 23. Mary gct Redstone MM
1844, 6, 22. James & dt, Julian, gct Salem MM
1848, 2, 26. Jonathan & w, Deborah, gct Salem
   MM, Ia.
1860, 3, 24. Joseph gct Uxbridge MM, Mass.,
   to m Eleanor Buffum
1860, 9, 22. Eleanor rocf Uxbridge MM, Mass.
1862, 7, 26. Esther Cobbs (form Cattell) dis
   mcd
1863, 5, 22. Joseph, Ezra & w, Henrietta dis
   jG (W)
1863, 6, 26. Thomas, Lewis & Elizabeth dis
   jG (W)
1863, 9, 25. Isaac dis jG (W)
1863, 10, 24. Isaac con mcd
1864, 9, 24. Wm. & w, Mary, & ch, Albert, Elmira, Sarah E. & Esther B., rocf Redstone
   MM, dtd 1864,8,3
1866, 4, 28. Mary gct Gilead MM
1866, 7, 27. Albert, Almina & Esther B.,
   minor ch Wm. & Mary, rocf Providence MM,
   Pa., dtd 1866,5,31 (W)
1869, 3, 27. Lewis & w, Amy T., & ch, Orlando Mary Leota & Charles, gct New Sharon
   MM, Ia.
1870, 2, 26. Elizabeth C. Briggs (form Cattell) con mcd
1870, 5, 28. Rebecca A. recrq
1871, 6, 24. Almina M. C. Stanley (form
   Cattell) con mcd
1873, 11, 27. Elmina M. Stanley (form Cattell)
   dis mcd (W)
1875, 4, 23. Sarah Jane (form Carson) dis mcd
   (W)
1877, 12, 21. Albert dis jG (W)
1881, 7, 23. Uree E. gct East Goshen MM, O.
1891, 4, 25. Thomas S. & Elizabeth rocf
   East Goshen MM   [MM
1891, 4, 25. Isaac & Rebecca rocf East Goshen

CHALFANT
1756, 4, 14. Ann b d 1845,9,14 bur Springfield

CHAMBERS

1810, 7, 31. Eleanor, dt James & Mary, b

1838, 5, 3. James H., s James & Mary, Carroll Co.; m in Springfield MH, Ann STANLEY, dt Benjamin & Elizabeth, Columbiana Co., O.

----, --, --. James N. b 1853,3,27; m Tamer Susanna HOLDERMAN b 1858,4,25
Ch: Laura May b 1879, 12, 5

----, --, --. Voluntine M. b 1856,10,20 d 1929, 1,12; m Carrie Luanna CLEAVER, dt J. A. & Sarah H., b 1860,3,1
Ch: William R. b 1882, 7, 3
    Cloyde
    Cleaver   " 1886, 6, 3
    Binford
    Vincent   " 1892, 2, 11
    Frederick
    James   " 1898, 10, 19
    Beatrice
    Myrtle   " 1906, 4, 12

----, --, --. Binford Vincent b 1892,2,11 d 1925,3,6; m Margaret PATTERSON, dt Oscar W. & Edith L. (Morris), b 1890,7,23
Ch: Richard   b 1921, 1, 19
    Curtis Allen
               b 1924, 9, 24

----, --, --. Frederick James, s Valentine, b 1898,10,19; m Nora PEEPLES, dt Harry L. & Margaret A., b 1902,9,17
Ch: Frederick b 1926, 8, 7
    Margaret   " 1930, 5, 19

1838, 8, 25. Ann gct Sandy Spring MM
1875, 2, 27. Ellenor rocf Sandy Spring MM
1911, 11, 25. James & w, T. Susanna, & dt, Laura May, rocf Winona MM
1915, 7, 24. Wm. relrq
1920, 9, 25. James gct Huntington Park MM, Calif.
1922, 11, 25. Margaret E. & s, Richard Vincent, rocf Mt. Pleasant MM
1926, 1, 28. Cloyde C. relrq
1927, 4, 28. Nora Alice recrq
1931, 3, 26. Frederick recrq

CHAPMAN

1835, 4, 25. Aaron rocf Marlborough MM, dtd 1835,3,31
1836, 1, 23. Aaron gct Allum Creek MM, to m Martha Benedict
1836, 3, 26. Aaron gct Allum Creek MM

CHILSON

1896, 2, 22. Anna W. relrq

CHRISTEN

1905, 5, 27. Mabel relrq

CLARK

1837, 8, 26. Mary Ann (form Armstrong) dis mou

CLEAVER

----, --, --. Isaac Allen, s Isaac, b 1835,2, 26; m Sarah L. -----, dt Jas. & Mary MAXWELL, b 1840,8,31
Ch: Carrie
    Louanna   b 1860, 3, 1
    Wm. Jeffer-
    son   " 1862, 3, 2
    Lena M.   " 1866, 9, 6

----, --, --. William J., s I. A. & Sarah, b 1862,3,2; m Evalyn GRINNELL, b 1862,11, 2
Ch: Carrie
    Marie   b 1886, 5, 14
    Allen Grin-
    nell   " 1890, 2, 16

1879, 5, 24. Isaac Allen & w, Sarah H., recrq
1881, 5, 28. Carrie L. recrq
1881, 5, 28. Wm. J. recrq
1882, 5, 22. Lena M. recrq
1895, 6, 22. Wm. J. & fam gct Pleasant Grove MM, Mich.
1901, 10, 26. J. Allen & Sarah H. gct Dublin MM, Ind.

CLEMPSON

----, --, --. Reuben b 1818,5,22 d 1903,12,27 bur Goshen (W)

----, --, --. James Lee b 1823,11,22 d 1903,5, 29 bur Springfield; m Alice A. ----- b 1852,12,23 d 1905,9,18 bur Springfield

----, --, --. James P. b 1849,3,3 d 1922,7,12; m Mary C. PENNOCK b 1847,9,9 d 1920,3,13

1856, 8, 10. Martha E., dt Joel & Clotilda STANLEY, b (w Rosco)
1877, 1, 20. Benjamin [Clemson], s Francis & Lydia, b

1851, 8, 23. James [Clemson] & w, Ann, & dt, Lydia Star, rocf Sandy Spring MM, dtd 1851,7,25
1851, 8, 23. John [Clemson] rocf Sandy Spring MM, dtd 1851,7,25
1851, 8, 23. Mary Ann [Clemson] rocf Sandy Spring MM, dtd 1851,7,25
1854, 7, 22. Joseph [Clemson] rocf Sandy Spring MM, dtd 1854,6,23
1854, 7, 22. Isaac [Clemson] rocf Sandy Spring MM, dtd 1854,6,23
1854, 7, 22. Wm. P. [Clemson] rocf Sandy Spring MM, dtd 1854,6,23
1855, 4, 27. James [Clemson] & w, Ann, gct Sandy Spring MM (W)
1855, 4, 27. Mary A. & Lydia [Clemson] gct Sandy Spring MM (W)
1857, 1, 23. James L. [Clemson] & w, Tryphena B., & ch, Alice & Roscoe, rocf New Garden MM, dtd 1857,1,22 (W)
1863, 1, 24. John dis jW
1863, 1, 24. Ann dis jW
1863, 1, 24. James C. dis jW
1863, 1, 24. Joseph dis jW

CLEMPSON, continued
1863, 1, 24. Lydia Star dis jW
1863, 1, 24. Isaac dis jW
1866, 10, 26. Isaac [Clemson] gct Sandy Spring
    MM (W)
1872, 3, 22. James L. & w, Tryphena B., & ch,
    Alice & Roscoe, gct Plymouth MM (W)
1873, 5, 23. Reuben rocf Sandy Spring MM (W)
1891, 8, 21. James Lee & dt, Alice, rocf
    Plymouth MM, O., dtd 1891,6,22 (W)
1894, 11, 23. Alice A. Welch (form Clempson)
    con mcd (W)
1899, 12, 23. Benjamin F. recrq
1909, 8, 19. Benjamin F. relrq
1913, 6, 28. James & Mary [Clemson] rocf
    Beloit MM

COBBS
----, --, --. Pleasant b 1760,11,5 d 1840,9,18
    bur Springfield; m Ann ----- b 1766,11,8
    d 1838,5,8 bur Springfield
    Ch: Thomas
            Ferrell   b 1786, 4, 21 d 1814, 4, 5
         Rebecca   " 1787, 10, 20
         Mary   " 1789, 3, 18
         Rhoda   " 1790, 9, 30
         Abigail   " 1792, 3, 28
         Elizabeth   " 1793, 11, 19
         Pleasant   " 1795, 12, 13
         Joseph   " 1797, 6, 21
         Ansalem   " 1799, 4, 16
         Amy   " 1800, 12, 23
         Joanna   " 1803, 6, 17
         Robert Venc-
            nor   b 1806, 2, 26
1806, 6, 14. Elizabeth b
1809, 4, 14. Mary A. b
----, --, --. Thomas T. & -----
    Ch: Lucinda   b 1811, 10, 13
        Agatha   " 1813, 9, 2
        Thomas T.   " 1815, 7, 13
----, --, --. Pleasant Jr. b 1795,12,13; m
    Elizabeth ----- b 1801,3,29 d 1833,6,16
    bur Springfield
    Ch: John   b 1820, 10, 8
        Mary Ann   " 1822, 5, 6
        Gideon   " 1824, 2, 8
        Terrel   " 1825, 12, 29 d 1832,12, 8
        Amos Eng-
            land   " 1827, 12, 15
        Amy   " 1830, 1, 10
----, --, --. Joseph b 1797,6,21 d 1861,3,25
    bur Springfield; m Tacy ----- b 1803,1,22
    d 1863,4,23
    Ch: Jesse   b 1821, 10, 13 d 1821,10,13.
            bur Springfield
        Uree   b 1823, 10, 8
        Josiah   " 1825, 9, 13
        Jonathan   " 1828, 2, 25
        Joseph T.   " 1830, 7, 16
        Lydia Ann   " 1832, 5, 11
        Sidney   " 1835, 3, 31
        Elijah   " 1837, 9, 4 d 1841, 2,20

    bur Springfield
    Ch: Mary   b 1840, 9, 25
----, --, --. Ansalem b 1799,6,16; m Lucy

    Ch: Edna   b 1824, 1, 14
Ansalem m 2nd Ann ----- b 1801,7,30 d 1842,
5,13 bur Springfield
    Ch: Timothy   b 1827, 4, 23
        John   " 1828, 5, 23
        Jehu   " 1829, 8, 26 d 1850, 8,24
          bur Iowa
        Emmor   " 1831, 1, 9
        Elihu   " 1832, 9, 27
        Ansalem
          Lynch   " 1833, 12, 7
        Henry   " 1836, 4, 4
        Joshua   " 1837, 11, 5
        Lucy Jane   " 1841, 2, 26
        Lydia Ann   " 1840, 2, 4
Ansalem m 3rd Grace ----- b 1807,6,21 d
1864,12,4 bur New Sharon, Iowa
----, --, --. Lindsey b 1804,3,3 d 1875,8,21
    bur Springfield; m Anna ----- b 1806,3,20
    d 1891,4,15 (an elder)
    Ch: Lydia   b 1826, 11, 6
        Charles   " 1828, 9, 30
        Amasa   " 1830, 7, 26
        Sybil   " 1832, 5, 9
        Caspar   " 1835, 5, 13
        Simeon   " 1838, 3, 2 d 1838, 3,19
          bur Springfield
        Henry W.   b 1839, 2, 2 d 1862, 9,14
          bur Rebel Land
        Ruthanna   b 1841, 9, 21
        Margaretta " 1844, 2, 9
        Thomas L.   " 1848, 3, 31
1829, 8, 27. Elizabeth m Isaac STANLEY
1830, 12, 1. Robert, s Pleasant & Ann, Colum-
    biana Co., O., b 1806,2,26 d 1876,3,13;
    m in Goshen MH, Mary VOTAW, dt Thomas &
    Elizabeth, Columbiana Co., O., b 1809,9,28
    d 1873,1,19
    Ch: George   b 1833, 1, 16
        Jennett   " 1835, 2, 1
        Sarah   " 1837, 1, 4
        Albert   " 1839, 5, 9
        Ann   " 1841, 7, 25
        Eli   " 1843, 11, 13
        Lucy   " 1846, 4, 22
        Mary Jane   " 1848, 10, 3 d 1857, 4,12
        Simeon   " 1851, 3, 2
    Robert m 2nd Elizabeth P. LANGSTAFF, dt
    Samuel & Hannah, b 1818,2,3
1832, 2, 2. Mary A. m Catlet JONES
1832, 3, 8. Joanna m Jonathan JOHNSON
1836, 9, 29. Thomas T., s Thomas T. & Martha,
    Columbiana Co., O., b 1815,7,13; m in
    Springfield MH, Sarah Ann MORRIS, dt Abra-
    ham & Mary, Columbiana Co., O., b 1817,11,
    20
    Ch: Hannah   b 1837, 9, 27
----, --, --. Thomas W. [Cobb], s Waddy & Mar-
    garet, b 1817,10,8; m Hannah C. BATTEN, dt

COBBS, Thomas W. & Hannah C., continued
    Robert & Abigail
1845, 5, 1. Uree m Israel STANLEY
1847, 4, 1. Josiah, s Joseph & Tacy, Colum-
    biana Co., O.; m in Springfield MH, Ruth
    BLACKBURN, dt Barbee & Elizabeth, Colum-
    biana Co., O.
1850, 5, 30. Lydia Ann m Samuel ADAMSON
1851, 5, 28. Timothy, s Ansalem & Ann, Mahon-
    ing Co., O., b 1827,4,23; m in Goshen MH,
    Emaline CATTELL, dt Joseph & Anner, Mahon-
    ing Co., O., b 1831,7,27
    Ch: Lavina   b 1854, 2, 10
        Elinor B. " 1856, 2, 4 d 1860,10,11
        Annar   " 1858, 3, 12
        Catherine " 1860, 7, 4
        Martin   " 1862, 9, 17
        Silas   " 1865, 10, 11
1851, 10, 30. John T., s Ansalem & Ann, Mahon-
    ing Co., O., b 1829,8,26; m in Springfield
    MH, Elizabeth Ann STANLEY, dt John & Mar-
    garet, b 1831,9,11 d 1864,6,20
    Ch: John   b 1852, 10, 19
        Mary Annah " 1855, 3, 28
        Isaac I.   " 1857, 6, 22
        Sarah Ann " 1860, 11, 11
        Ansalem " 1864, 2, 18 d 1864, 7, 3
        bur Springfield
1853, 6, 2. George, s Robert & Mary, Mahon-
    ing Co., O., b 1833,1,16 d 1819,4,22; m in
    Springfield MH, Mary BLACKBURN, dt James &
    Rebecca, Mahoning Co., O., b 1835,6,29 d
    1913,6,27
    Ch: Uree Ella b 1854, 6, 6
        Alvay J. " 1867, 8, 17
1855, 5, 3. Elihu, s Ansalem & Ann, Colum-
    biana Co., O., b 1832,9,27; m in Spring-
    field MH, Mary Ann STANLEY, dt Joel &
    Chlotilda, Columbiana Co., O., b 1835,1,21
    Ch: William
        Henry   b 1856, 2, 2
        Judith Ann " 1859, 7, 19
        Clotilda
        Jane   " 1862, 5, 5 d 1864, 9,16
        bur Goshen
        Alice   " 1865, 9, 2
        Joel A. " 1869, 5, 23
1856, 2, 2. Wm. Henry b
1858, 4, 29. Ansalem L., s Ansalem & Ann,
    Columbiana Co., O., b 1833,12,7 d 1873,5,6
    bur Damascus; m in Springfield MH, Unity
    STANLEY, dt John Sr. & Margaret, Columbi-
    ana Co., O., b 1837,5,12 d 1895,9,15
    Ch: Margaret
        Annah   b 1859, 7, 12
        John Emer-
        son   " 1861, 5, 21
        Thomas
        Jefferson " 1864, 2, 8
        Ginerva " 1868, 2, 14
        Marietta A." 1873, 9, 29
----, --, --. Joshua b 1837,11,5 d 1887,11,30;
    m Emily W. ----- b 1838,10,27 d 1886,1,28

bur Damascus
    Ch: Ella B.   b 1860, 9, 21
        Clark Ed-
        gar   " 1862, 4, 9
        Julia C. " 1864, 5, 25
        William J. " 1870, 2, 28
1891, 4, 15. Anna W. [Cobb] d ae 86 (an eld-
    er) (W)
----, --, --. Henry P. b 1836,4,4; m Anna S.
    ----- b 1842,2,1
    Ch: Ansalem Er-
        vin   b 1863, 4, 16
1863, 4, 2. Lucy Jane m Daniel T. ROGERS
1864, 4, 28. Lydia Ann m John B. STANLEY
----, --, --. Albert [Cobb] b 1839,5,9 d 1890,
    7,18; m Esther ----- b 1841,2,25
    Ch: Hannah M. b 1866, 2, 15
        Cora   " 1869, 5, 5
        Isidore " 1882, 4, 30
----, --, --. Thomas L., s Linsey & Anne, b
    1848,3,31 d 1920,5,4; m Rachel A. STRAD-
    LEY, dt David & Mary (Buckman), b 1849,1,
    29 d 1933,6,17
    Ch: Ruthanna b 1872, 3, 31
        Homer   " 1879, 7, 17
        Caroline " 1882, 1, 21
        Mabel   " 1884, 4, 21
        Ellen   " 1886, 2, 24
----, --, --. Simeon R. & Anna E.
    Ch: Minnie V. b 1876, 12, 11
        Laura C. " 1883, 2, 7
1883, 2, 7. Laura C., dt Simeon & Anna, b
----, --, --. John Emerson [Cobb], s Lynch
    & Unity (Stanley), b 1861,5,21; m Sarah
    Ellen BLACKBURN, dt Wm. S. & Margaret A.
    (Sheets), b 1861,11,29
    Ch: Ervine   b 1887, 2, 25
        Lida   " 1890, 10, 21
        Ansalem L. " 1891, 9, 11
        David Al-
        bert   " 1895, 1, 22
----, --, --. Thomas J., s Lynch & Unity, b
    1864,2,8; m Mary E. STANLEY, dt Eli & Re-
    becca, b 1859,7,28
    Ch: Herbert S. b 1889, 9, 24
        Laura May " 1891, 5, 2
        Clara   " 1892, 5, 12
        Isabella " 1897, 6, 27
        Rebecca " 1899, 4, 29
        Carl Thomas" 1902, 4, 15
----, --, --. Irven T., s John E. & Sarah E.,
    b 1887,2,25; m Ada B. CROSSLEY, dt Roscoe
    S. & Eliza (Hopston), b 1893,6,29
    Ch: Verla Lucile
            b 1916, 4, 4
        Virgil Lee " 1918, 5, 12
        Kenneth
        Wade   " 1924, 5, 17
        Lois June " 1933, 6, 10

1926, 2, 25. Eliza, Lucinda & Agatha, minors,
    gct Marlborough MM
1826, 5, 27. Ann rocf New Garden MM, dtd

COBBS, continued
    1826,4,20
1826, 11, 25. Edna, dt Ansalem, recrq
1827, 1, 27. Elizabeth & Mary [Cobb] recrq
1827, 5, 26. Lucinda & Agatha, minors, rocf
    Marlborough MM, dtd 1827,3,27
1830, 4, 30. Lucinde Booth (form Cobbs) dis
    mou
1832, 9, 22. Pleasant Jr. dis disunity
1839, 3, 23. Thomas T. & w, Sarah Ann, gct
    Gilead MM
1840, 8, 22. Mary Ann Oyster (form Cobbs)
    dis mcd
1840, 10, 24. John dis mou
1843, 9, 23. Ansalem [Cobb] gct Gilead MM, to
    m Grace Jackson
1844, 3, 23. Grace rocf Gilead MM, dtd 1844,
    1,23
1845, 3, 22. Edna Stanley (form Cobbs) dis
    mcd
1846, 11, 28. Gideon dis mcd
1847, 8, 28. Lydia Ladd (form Cobbs) dis mcd
1848, 11, 25. Amy Rakestraw (form Cobbs) dis
    mcd
1849, 5, 26. Amos [Cobb] dis disunity
1849, 5,26. Jonathan dis disunity
1849, 7, 28. Charles dis disunity
1849, 10, 27. Josiah & w, Ruth, & s, Jesse, gct
    Gilead MM
1851, 3, 22. Isabella Emily (form Blackburn)
    dis mcd
1853, 11, 26. Jennet Barber (form Cobbs) dis
    mcd
1854, 8, 26. Emmor dis mcd
1854, 10, 28. Sarah dis mcd
1856, 3, 22. Joseph T. gct Driftwood MM, Ind.
1856, 7, 26. Sidney Cook (form Cobbs) dis mcd
1856, 9, 27. Cidna C. Hook (form Cobbs) dis
    mcd
1857, 2, 22. Sibyl Bruff (form Cobbs) dis mcd
1857, 6, 27. Caspar dis mcd
1857, 7, 24. Caspar dis mcd (W)
1857, 10, 23. Amos dis disunity
1858, 9, 25. Sibyl Bruff (form Cobbs) dis mcd
1860, 6, 22. Emily (form Crew) dis mcd (W)
1860, 9, 22. Ann Naylor (form Cobbs) con mcd
1861, 2, 23. Joshua con mcd
1861, 4, 27. Emily (form Crew) con mcd
1862, 4, 26. Henry P. gct Short Creek MM, O.,
    to m Anne U. Ladd
1862, 7, 26. Esther (form Cattell) dis mcd
1862, 10, 25. Albert dis mcd
1863, 1, 24. Lindsey dis jW
1863, 1, 24. Anna W. dis jW
1863, 1, 24. Margaretta dis jW
1863, 1, 24. Ruthanna dis jW
1863, 1, 24. Thomas L. dis jW
1863, 2, 27. Anslem dis jG (W)
1863, 2, 27. Robert dis jG (W)
1863, 2, 27. Robert dis jG (W)
1863, 2, 27. Grace dis jG (W)
1863, 2, 27. Mary dis jG (W)
1863, 3, 27. Tacy dis jG (W)

1863, 3, 27. Mary Jr. dis jG (W)
1863, 4, 24. John dis jG (W)
1863, 4, 24. Henry dis jG (W)
1863, 4, 24. Ansalem L. dis jG (W)
1863, 4, 24. Joshua dis jG (W)
1863, 4, 24. Elizabeth Ann dis jG (W)
1863, 4, 24. Unity dis jG (W)
1863, 5, 22. Timothy dis jG (W)
1863, 5, 22. Elihu dis jG (W)
1863, 5, 22. Emmeline dis jG (W)
1863, 5, 22. Mary Ann dis jG (W)
1863, 6, 26. George & Mary dis jG (W)
1863, 6, 27. Annie L. rocf Short Creek MM, O.,
    dtd 1863,5,20
1863, 9, 25. Albert & Esther dis jG (W)
1864, 3, 26. Joshua dis disunity
1864, 11, 26. Henry P. & w, Ann L., & s, An-
    slem E., gct New Sharon MM, Ia.
1865, 6, 24. John T. & ch, Jehu, Isaac J.,
    Maryanna & Sarah Ann, gct New Sharon MM,
    Ia.
1865, 8, 25. Ruthanna Tomlinson (form Cobbs)
    dis mcd (W)
1865, 11, 25. Mary S. gct Grove MM, Ind.
1865, 11, 25. Anslum gct Bangor MM, Ia.
1866, 2, 24. Timothy & w, Emaline, & ch, La-
    vina, Anner, Catherine, Martin & Silas,
    gct New Sharon MM
1866, 8, 25. Eli dis military service
1867, 1, 25. Lucy E. Binford (form Cobbs)
    con mcd
1867, 2, 22. Eli dis mcd & military service
1870, 5, 28. Albert & w, Esther, recrq
1870, 9, 23. Margaretta Buchanan (form Cobbs)
    dis mcd (W)
1872, 6, 21. Thomas L. dis mcd (W)
1875, 6, 25. Elizabeth (form Langstaff) dis
    mcd & jG (W)
1873, 6, 28. Simeon R. [Cobb] con mcd
1874, 4, 25. Robert [Cobb] gct East Goshen
    MM, to m Elizabeth P. Langstaff
1875, 1, 23. Elizabeth P. rocf East Goshen
    MM
1880, 5, 22. Joshua recrq
1882, 5, 27. Wm. Henry rocf East Goshen MM
1886, 1, 23. Sarah Ellen recrq
1887, 3, 26. Thomas A. & Rachel A. recrq
1887, 9, 24. Mary E. rocf Grove MM, Ind.
1889, 4, 27. Thomas W. & Hannah C. recrq
1890, 5, 24. Wm. H. gct East Goshen MM
1892, 4, 23. Ella relrq
1892, 6, 25. Wm. J. gct New Sharon MM, Ia.
1893, 1, 28. Hannah C. gct Salem MM
1894, 1, 27. Ruthanna recrq
1897, 1, 23. Minnie & Laura recrq
1897, 12, 25. Homer recrq
1897, 12, 25. Caroline, Mabel & Ellen, ch
    Thos. L. & Rachel, recrq
1905, 2, 25. Caroline relrq
1911, 2, 25. Thomas & fam, Mary E., Herbert
    L., Laura, Clara, Isabella & Carl Thomas,
    gct Beloit MM
1912, 7, 27. Mabel(Cobbs) Cameron dropped

COBBS, continued
from mbrp
1912, 7, 27. Ellen (Cobbs) Benner dropped
from mbrp
1913, 1, 25. Homer dropped from mbrp
1916, 9, 23. Ada Bell rocf Beloit MM
1916, 10, 28. Verla Lucile, minor dt Irven
& Ada B., recrq
1922, 9, 23. Alva J. dropped from mbrp
1923, 2, 24. Albert gct Salem MM

COBURN
----, --, --. Benjamin b 1770,8,15 d 1850,10,
20 bur Springfield; m 2nd Abigail -----
b 1792,3,28 d 1873,10,16 bur Beloit
1835, 12, 13. Elizabeth m Timothy STANLEY
----, --, --. Jacob b 1810,1,3 d 1893,12,19;
m Ellen ----- b 1816,2,26 d 1859,4,21
Ch: Judith Ann b 1837, 9, 5
Unity " 1841, 12, 22 d 1842, 4, 1
Jacob m 2nd Martha Jane KILLE b 1835,8,31
1812, 4, 13. Elizabeth b
1835, 3, 5. Jacob [Cobourn], s Benjamin &
Abigail, Columbiana Co., O.; m in Smith-
field MM, Ellen COPPCOCK dt Jehu & Judith,
Columbiana Co., O.
1862, 1, 2. Jacob [Cobourn], s Benjamin &
Abigail, Columbiana Co., O.; m in Damascus
MH, Martha Jane KILLE, dt Edmund & Sarah
LIPSEY, Columbiana Co., O.

1833, 3, 23. Benjamin [Cobourn] rocf Sandy
Spring MM, dtd 1833,3,22
1833, 7, 27. Jacob [Cobourn] rocf Sandy
Spring MM, dtd 1833,7,26
1833, 9, 28. Elizabeth [Cobourn] rocf Sandy
Spring MM, dtd 1833,6,21
1863, 2, 27. Jacob dis jG (W)
1864, 2, 27. Chas. W. & Alfaretta K., ch Martha J., recrq
1877, 9, 22. Martha J. dis
1877, 10, 27. Jacob dis
1886, 2, 27. Jacob recrq

COCHRAN
1884, 7, 14. Maud, w Willard, dt Leander &
Elmina (Cattell) STANLEY, b

1931, 12, 24. Maud Stanley dropped from mbrp

COGGESHALL
1859, 8, 30. Tristram, s Edward & Sophia,
Wayne Co., Ind.; m in Springfield MH, Sarah BRUFF, dt James B. & Sarah, Mahoning
Co., O.

1860, 3, 24. Sarah B. [Coggshall] gct Dover
MM, Ind.

COLBURN
1832, 11, 1. Benjamin, s Jacob & Sarah, Columbiana Co., O.; m in Springfield MH, Abigail STANLEY, dt Pleasant & Amy COBBS,

Columbiana Co., O.

COLE
1909, 4, 24. Mary rocf Alliance MM, O.

CONRAD
----, --, --. Ellwood B. b 1850,1,25; m Phebe
DEAN b 1856,12,14 (W)
Ch: Eunice H. b 1879, 7, 6
Joseph " 1880, 11, 26
Rebecca E. " 1882, 6, 12
Samuel " 1884, 7, 6
Emerson " 1890, 11, 29
Mary Eliza-
beth " 1894, 3, 28
----, --, --. Emerson, s Ellwood B. & Phebe
W. (Dean), b 1890,11,29; m Eva W. NEILLE,
dt Dilwyn B. & Ella (Crawford), b 1892,3,
12 (W)
Ch: Nelson J. b 1914, 7, 23
Virginia
May " 1916, 6, 12
Wauneta " 1918, 6, 27

1882, 1, 27. Ellwood B. & w, Phebe W., & ch,
Eunice H. & Joseph, rocf New Garden MM,
dtd 1882,1,26 (W)
1903, 5, 22. Elwood B. & w, Phebe W., & ch,
Samuel, Emmerson & Mary, gct Salem MM (W)
1905, 9, 19. Joseph L. gct Salem MM, to m
Elma G. Hutton (W)
1914, 3, 27. Emerson rocf Salem MM, dtd
1914,3,25 (W)
1914, 3, 27. Eva N. rocf Middleton MM, dtd
1914,3,21 (W)
1914, 10, 23. Joseph dis mcd (W)
1914, 10, 23. Rebecca C. Dickey (form Conrad)
con mcd (W)
1923, 2, 23. Eunice Richardson (form Conrad)
dis mcd (W)

COOK
----, --, --. Albert b 1839,5,9; m Esther
----- b 1841,2,25
Ch: Hannah M. b 1866, 5, 15
Cora " 1869, 5, 5
Isidore E. " 1882, 4, 30

1837, 12, 23. Nathan rocf Short Creek MM, O.,
dtd 1837,10,24
1838, 3, 24. Nathan gct Redstone MM, to m
Ann H. Binns
1839, 1, 26. Ann H. rocf Redstone MM, dtd
1839,1,2
1839, 6, 22. Nathan & w, Ann, & s, Elisha,
gct Short Creek MM, O.
1844, 9, 28. Ann (form Michener) dis mcd
1856, 7, 26. Sidney (form Cobbs) dis mcd

COOPER
1859, 3, 22. Mary E., dt Samuel & Sarah
(Pennock), b d 1930,12,30 bur Damascus
(W)

COOPER, continued

1830, 8, 28. Evan & w, Mary, & ch, Wm.
  Chalkley & Martha, rocf Sandy Spring MM,
  dtd 1830,5,21

1831, 8, 27. Evan & w, Mary, & ch, Wm.,
  Chalkley & Martha, gct Sandy Spring MM

1876, 11, 25. Harry J., Chas. Eli & Mary
  Elizabeth, with Moses C. Stephens' fam,
  rocf Salem MM

1878, 11, 23. Harry J., Charles E. & Mary E.
  gct Greenfield MM, Ind. with Moses C.
  Stevens' fam

1908, 4, 24. Lewis A. Woolman gct Salem MM,
  to m Lydia A. Cooper (W)

1926, 1, 22. Mary E. rocf Salem MM, dtd
  1926,1,20 (W)

COPE

1819, 5, 8. Edith b

----, --, --. Isaac b 1804,12,23 d 1881,10,--
  bur Marlboro; m Rachel ----- b 1808,2,18
  d 1859,10,1 bur Marlboro (W)
    Ch: John A.   b 1829, 7, 12
        Cyrus   " 1838, 2, 3
        Lucinda   " 1841, 8, 10
        Sarah A.   " 1843, 9, 13
        Emaline   " 1846, 2, 14

1837, 4, 30. Caroline b (W)

1838, 12, 29. Emily b (W)

1843, 11, 2. Edith m Benjamin MALMSBERRY Jr.

1844, 11, 3. Mercy b d 1899,3,12 (W)

1850, 12, 27. Lydia b (W)

1853, 10, 12. Almira b (W)

----, --, --. John A., s Isaac & Rachel (Embree), b 1829,7,12 d 1925,3,2 bur Damascus;
  m Adah B. ----- b 1831,6,13 d 1901,3,27
  bur Springfield (W)
    Ch: Joseph W. b 1860, 4, 1
        Alvah   " 1861, 10, 13 d 1861,12, 1
          bur Marlboro
        Isaac   b 1863, 2, 6
        Jesse   " 1866, 7, 29
        Lydia   " 1870, 1, 4

----, --, --. James A. b 1842,10,14 d 1887,7,
  24; m Achsah ELLYSON, dt Robert & Mary
  (Hall) Ratcliff, b 1847,8,3 (W)
    Ch: Robert J. b 1867, 11, 16 d 1886, 3,31
        Ellen B.   " 1870, 9, 22 " 1893, 3,22
        Elizabeth
        M.   " 1874, 3, 1
        Marietta   " 1876, 6, 18
        Edwin   " 1882, 2, 7
        Drusilla   " 1882, 2, 7 d 1887, 4,30

1839, 5, 25. Hiram rocf Providence MM, dtd
  1839,5,2

1840, 4, 25. Edith rocf Providence MM, dtd
  1840,3,5

1842, 7, 23. John F. rocf Carmel MM, dtd
  1842,5,21

1846, 2, 28. John F. gct Chesterfield MM

1847, 1, 23. Hiram dis mcd

1859, 5, 27. John A. gct Sandy Spring MM, to

  m Adah B. Winder (W)

1859, 9, 23. Adah B. rocf Sandy Spring MM,
  dtd 1859,7,23 (W)

1865, 3, 24. John Henry, minor, rocf Westland
  MM, Pa., dtd 1865,2,22 (W)

1865, 8, 25. Lucinda Armstrong (form Cope)
  dis mcd (W)

1866, 2, 23. Emeline gct Middleton MM (W)

1867, 3, 22. James A. rmt Achsah Ellyson (W)

1868, 5, 22. Achsah H. gct Providence MM (W)

1870, 7, 22. Cyrus con mcd (W)

1870, 8, 26. Sarah Rice (form Cope) dis mcd
  (W)

1871, 4, 21. David Ellyson gct Middleton MM,
  to m Margaret Cope (W)

1872, 12, 27. Cyrus gct Hickory Grove MM, Ia.
  (W)

1875, 3, 25. James A. & w, Achsah, & ch, Robert J., Ellen B. & Elizabeth M., rocf
  Middleton MM (W)

1877, 10, 26. Caroline, Emily, Mercy, Lydia &
  Almira, rocf Salem MM, dtd 1877,9,19 (W)

1878, 6, 21. Lydia gct Hickory Grove MM, Ia.
  (W)

1883, 9, 18. Almira Carson (form Cope) con
  mcd (W)

1886, 2, 26. Isaac dis mcd (W)

1889, 2, 22. Joseph con mcd (W)

1889, 12, 27. Joseph W. gct Middleton MM (W)

1893, 9, 19. Jesse dis disunity (W)

1895, 6, 21. Caroline & Emily gct Pasadena
  MM, Calif. (W)

1907, 10, 25. Lydia dis disunity (W)

1923, 2, 23. Achsah H. gct Pasadena MM, Calif.
  (W)

COPPOCK

1786, 3, 24. Ellen b

1812, 9, 28. Joseph b

----, --, --. Samuel b 1787,8,12 d 1867,11,26
  bur Damascus; m Rebecca ----- b 1787,10,
  20 d 1862,12,23 bur Damascus
    Ch: Pleasant b 1815, 8, 14
        Samuel R. " 1821, 5, 28 d 1823,--, 9
        Rhoda   " 1822, 9, 16 " 1836, 7,24
          bur Springfield
        Isaac   b 1825, 3, 23
        Lucy   " 1827, 6, 5 " 1844, 5, 7
          bur Springfield

----, --, --. Jehu b 1791,2,10 d 1842,3,28 bur
  Springfield; m Judith ----- b 1793,9,28
  d 1861,9,18 bur Springfield
    Ch: Ellen   b 1816, 2, 26
        Unity   " 1818, 10, 26
        Abigail   " 1821, 7, 9
        Ruth   " 1825, 7, 25
        Ann   " 1828, 11, 9

----, --, --. Aaron b 1797,1,24; m Amy -----
  b 1800,12,23
    Ch: Thomas   b 1819, 10, 1
        James   " 1821, 4, 25
        Lindsey   " 1823, 10, 23
        Eli   " 1826, 2, 17 d 1836, 8,14

COPPOCK, Aaron & Amy, continued
   bur Springfield
     Ch: Margaret   b 1827, 12, 15 d 1828, 8,28
          bur Springfield
          Mary   b 1827, 12, 15
          Benjamin " 1830, 3, 18
          Rebecca   " 1831, 12, 29
          Jacob   " 1834, 1, 1
          Aaron   " 1837, 6, 29
          Henry   " 1839, 4, 15
1831, 3, 31. Samuel, s John & Catharine, Columbiana Co., O.; m in Damascus MH, Ann
   LYNCH, dt Joshua & Rachel, Columbiana Co.,
   O.
----, --, --. Samuel Jr. b 1803,11,29 d 1841,
   11,8 bur Springfield; m Ann ----- b 1804,
   7,25
     Ch: Levi   b 1832, 2, 25
        Maria   " 1833, 10, 31
        Edwin   " 1835, 6, 30
        Lydia   " 1836, 12, 5
        Barclay   " 1839, 1, 4
----, --, --. Jonathan b 1809,2,4; m Sarah
   ----- b 1806,6,29
     Ch: Catharine b 1833, 12, 22
        Benjamin " 1835, 4, 16
1835, 3, 5. Ellen m Jacob COBOURN
1837, 9, 28. Unity m Micajah STANLEY
1845, 10, 2. Ruth m Jonathan C. WALTON
1847, 5, 27. Ann m John BUTLER
1848, 6, 1. Abigail m John SHREVE
1851, 5, 29. Rebecca m Eli STANLEY
----, --, --. Pleasant b 1815,8,14; m Lydia E.
   ----- b 1819,2,13 d 1873,7,15
     Ch: Lydia Anna b 1857, 3, 2
        Mary Lou-
          isa   " 1859, 9, 6
        Sarah Elmy " 1861, 12, 13
----, --, --. Isaac b 1825,3,23; m Hannah E.
   B. ----- b 1838,3,9
     Ch: Laura   b 1859, 8, 17
----, --, --. Samuel, s Pleasant & Lydia,
   b 1847,1,7; m Anna BUCKMAN, dt Thos. &
   Susanna, b 1849,7,3
----, --, --. Isaac T. b 1849,1,10 d 1922,1,
   21; m Phebe A. ----- b 1857,6,2 d 1923,
   12,7
     Ch: Ralph S. b 1880, 3, 15
----, --, --. Benjamin S. b 1849,2,13; m
   Hannah E. ----- b 1838,3,4
----, --, --. Enos b 1853,8,1; m Sophia
   STAUFFER, b 1853,12,23
     Ch: Mary Viola b 1875, 8, 9 d 1892, 8,22
          bur Oakland, Calif.
          Hannah E. b 1878, 4, 6
----, --, --. Joseph J., s Joshua & Jane
   (Hoyle), b 1855,10,7; m Rebecca ELLYSON,
   dt Benj. & Abigail (Hemingway), b 1858,3,
   6 d 1927,10,16 (W)
1883, 2, 28. Hannah E. m John LODEN
1884, 5, 28. Pleasant, s Samuel & Rebecca,
   Mahoning Co., O.; m in residence of Chas.
   Naylor, Eliza Ann TAYLOR, dt Seth & Eunice

PENNOCK, b 1827,6,22
----, --, --. Ralph S. b 1880,3,15; m Laura
   HOBSON b 1883,7,8
     Ch: Mildred   b 1909, 4, 25
        Mabel   " 1910, 10, 31

1826, 5, 27. Joseph rocf Marlborough MM, dtd
   1826,4,25
1831, 5, 28. Samuel rocf New Garden MM, dtd
   1831,5,26
1833, 1, 31. Ellen gct Salem MM
1833, 8, 24. Jonathan & w, Sarah, rocf New
   Garden MM, dtd 1833,8,22
1834, 9, 27. Joseph dis mou
1837, 5, 27. Pleasant dis mcd
1837, 8, 26. Jonathan & ch, Catharine, Benjamin & Ruthanna, gct New Garden MM
1842, 2, 26. Aaron & w, Amy, & ch, James,
   Lindsey, Mary, Benjamin, Rebecca, Jacob,
   Aaron & Henry, gct Salem MM, Ia.
1842, 2, 26. Thomas gct Salem MM, Ia.
1843, 7, 22. Levi, minor, gct Gilead MM
1843, 7, 22. Barclay, minor, gct Salem MM
1843, 7, 22. Lydia, minor dt Ann, gct New
   Garden MM
1845, 4, 26. Joseph L., minor, gct New Garden
   MM
1845, 4, 26. Maria, minor, gct Salem MM
1845, 12, 27. Pleasant rst
1846, 4, 25. Ann gct Salem MM
1848, 7, 22. Mary rocf New Garden MM, dtd
   1848,5,25
1850, 7, 27. Rebecca rocf Salem MM, Ia., dtd
   1850,6,12
1850, 8, 24. Edwin, minor, gct Salem MM, Ia.
1853, 6, 25. Mary gct New Garden MM
1858, 3, 27. Isaac con mcd
1858, 4, 24. Lydia & dt, Lydianna, recrq
1859, 6, 24. Ezra rmt Ann French (W)
1860, 4, 27. Ann gct New Garden MM (W)
1863, 1, 24. Ann dis jW
1863, 2, 27. Pleasant dis jG (W)
1863, 4, 24. Isaac dis jG (W)
1866, 9, 22. Hannah E. B. & dt, Phebe Laura,
   recrq
1868, 4, 25. Benjamin & Hannah recrq
1868, 5, 22. Job Warren gct New Garden MM, to
   m Rebecca Coppock (W)
1869, 2, 27. Isaac relrq
1875, 6, 26. Benjamin J. gct West Port MM,
   Mass.
1875, 8, 28. Isaac rst
1876, 3, 25. Enos recrq
1876, 4, 22. Sophia & dt, Mary Viola, recrq
1877, 5, 26. Benjamin S. rocf Westport MM,
   Mass.
1877, 10, 27. Benjamin S. gct Maryville MM,
   Tenn.
1887, 1, 22. Enos & Sophia relrq
1889, 1, 26. Enos & Sophia recrq
1890, 1, 25. Samuel & Anna H. recrq
1893, 3, 25. Isaac relrq
1896, 2, 22. Enos & dt, Hannah Elizabeth, gct

COPPOCK, continued
    San Jose MM, Calif.
1902, 2, 22. Ralph S. rocf Winona MM
1905, 10, 28. Ralph S. gct Blue River MM, Ind.
1906, 9, 22. Laura Hobson gct Blue River MM,
    Ind.
1910, 1, 22. Laura (Coppock) Linton relrq
1910, 7, 23. Ralph S. & w, Laura H., & dt,
    Mildred, rocf Bloomingdale MM, Ind.
1910, 11, 26. Isaac T. & Phebe A. recrq
1924, 5, 22. Judith recrq
1924, 10, 23. Ralph & fam gct Alliance MM
1926, 12, 24. Joseph J. & w, Rebecca E., rocf
    West Branch MM, Ia., dtd 1926,12,11

CORNELL
1896, 10, 24. Isabella dropped from mbrp

CORSE
1839, 8, 1. Elizabeth m Albert FRENCH

1839, 5, 25. Elizabeth M. rocf Wilmington
    MM, dtd 1839,3,30

COSAND
----, --, --. Clarence, s John & Elma (Engle)
    b 1883,8,14; m Maggie Vietta PIM, dt
    Chas. & Emily (Bryan), b 1886,2,25
    Ch: Evelyn
        Lorene   b 1916, 1, 23
        Rendel
        Loren   " 1918, 3, 1
        Theda Lou-
        ise   " 1919, 5, 12

1913, 10, 25. Maggie (Pim) gct Lupton MM,
    Mich.
1915, 6, 26. Clarence & w, Maggie, rocf
    Lupton MM, Mich.

COULSON
1795, 3, 25. Mary b
1850, 3, 27. David, s Jesse & Mary, Colum-
    biana Co., O.; m in Goshen MH, Rachel
    ATKINSON, dt Warner & Mariah, Mahoning
    Co., O.
1851, 5, 28. Jesse, s Jesse & Mary, Henry
    Co., Ia.; m in Goshen MH, Mary ATKINSON,
    dt Warner & Maria, Mahoning Co., O.

1832, 9, 22. Mary & ch, David & Jesse, rocf
    Carmel MM, dtd 1832,8,18
1834, 9, 27. David & Jesse, minor ch Mary,
    gct Sandy Spring MM
1838, 6, 23. Jehu & w, Jane, rocf Carmel MM,
    dtd 1838,6,16
1840, 9, 26. Jehu & w, Jane, gct Sandy Spring
    MM
1843, 11, 25. David, minor, rocf Sandy Spring
    MM, dtd 1843,9,22
1846, 8, 22. David gct Salem MM
1850, 11, 23. Rachel gct Salem MM, Ia.
1852, 2, 28. Mary gct Salem MM, Ia.

COURTNEY
----, --, --. Edward b 1794,10,11; m Phebe Y.
    ----- b 1799,11,22
    Ch: Sarah   b 1824, 2, 7
        John   " 1825, 3, 7
        Ann   " 1826, 7, 8
1858, 11, 24. Laura, dt Voluntine & Mary STAN-
    LEY, b
----, --, --. Wm. M., s Monroe & Emily R.
    (Taylor), b 1864,7,29 d 1932,3,11 bur
    Salem, O.; m Alpha Nettie BATES, dt Henry
    & Mary Ann (Miller), b 1866,9,27

1828, 11, 22. Edward dis jH
1829, 7, 25. Phebe Y. dis jH
1844, 6, 22. Sarah dis disunity
1847, 5, 22. John dis disunity
1852, 2, 28. Ann Hambleton (form Courtney)
    dis mcd
1853, 8, 27. Isaac dis mcd
1864, 3, 26. Rebecca Emily (form Taylor) rpd
    mcd
1868, 2, 21. Emily (form Taylor) dis mcd (W)
1870, 11, 26. James Monroe & w, Emly Jane, &
    s, Wm. M., recrq
1891, 4, 25. Laura rocf East Goshen MM
1897, 11, 27. Anna recrq
1900, 9, 22. Homer recrq
1908, 3, 28. Margaret(Courtney)McArtor recrq
1929, 6, 27. Wm. & w, Nettie, rocf Salem MM

COWGILL
----, --, --. James Simpson b 1801,5,23; m
    Lucy ----- b 1801,3,9
    Ch: Rebecca   b 1824, 4, 10
        James   " 1828, 6, 25
        Josiah   " 1830, 10, 29
        Joshua   " 1834, 12, 27
        Eliza   " 1837, 7, 21

1830, 2, 27. Rebecca & ch, Joseph & Mary,
    rocf Sandy Spring MM, dtd 1830,1,22
1832, 11, 24. Rebecca & ch, Joseph, Mary Ar-
    mina, Jane & Ruth, gct Sandy Spring MM
1839, 8, 24. James S. & w, Lucy, & ch, Re-
    becca, James, Johnson & Eliza, gct Ches-
    terfield MM
1846, 5, 23. Rebecca (form Stanley) dis mcd

COX
1826, 11, 25. Thomas dis disunity

CRABBS
----, --, --. Alvion Abram [Crabbe] b 1863,12,
    25 d 1925,2,12; m Martha FRANCES, b 1866,
    10,13

1919, 12, 27. Albion & w, Martha, recrq
1925, 4, 23. Anna M. relrq

CRAFT
1828, 7, 13. Sarah, w John, dt John & Marga-
    ret STANLEY, b d 1887,6,28

CRAFT, continued
1863, 7, 25. Sarah (form Stanley) con mcd
1863, 9, 25. Sarah dis jG (W)

CRAWFORD
----, --, --. Thomas b 1858,11,29; m Sarah
    BRANTINGHAM, b 1861,9,8 d 1930,11,5 bur
    Damascus
    Ch: John B.   b 1882, 10, 6
        Charles
        Edward   " 1887, 2, 15
        Grace   " 1889, 3, 31
        Alice   " 1890, 11, 11
        Jesse Leah " 1895, 1, 16
        Margaret " 1899, 6, 7
        Alfred
        Thomas   " 1903, 5, 19
        Deborah " 1904, 10, 15
----, --, --. Charles Edward, s Thomas A. &
    Sarah (Brantingham), b 1887,2,15; m Alice
    A. BRANTINGHAM, dt Wm. & Anna (Cope), b 1881,
    12,25 (W)
    Ch: Robert W. b 1911, 7, 24
        Arthur B. " 1914, 3, 8
1915, 6, 18. Jessie Leah m Albert J. STEER
    (W)
1925, 11, 28. Deborah m Walter N. WHINERY (W)
1930, 11, 5. Sarah B. d ae 69 (an elder)
1933, 6, 9. Thomas d at Brisbane, Australia,
    ae 75 (a minister)

1881, 9, 20. Thomas A. recrq (W)
1882, 1, 27. Thomas A. rmt Sarah Brantingham
    (W)
1905, 1, 27. John B. gct Philadelphia MM (W)
1909, 5, 21. Grace rmt Joseph C. Brantingham
    (W)
1910, 1, 21. Charles E. gct New Garden MM, to
    m Alice A. Brantingham (W)
1910, 9, 20. Alice A. rocf New Garden MM, dtd
    1910,9,15 (W)
1911, 11, 24. Alice rmt Wilson Brantingham (W)
1914, 6, 26. Charles E. & w, Alice A., & ch,
    Robert W. & Arthur B., gct New Garden MM(W)
1922, 9, 22. Margaret rmt John Dewees Mott (W)
1923, 1, 26. Chas. E. & w, Alice A., & ch,
    Robert W. & Arthur B. rocf New Garden
    MM, dtd 1922,12,21 (W)
1932, 1, 22. Alfred T. dis jas (W)
1932, 5, 27. Thomas A. gct Brisbane MM,
    Australia (W)

CRISPIN
1778, 2, 21. Hannah b d 1857,7,10 bur Goshen

1831, 3, 26. Hannah [Crispen] gct Salem MM
1833, 6, 22. Hannah rocf Salem MM, dtd 1833,
    5,22
1835, 8, 22. Hannah gct Marlborough MM
1843, 11, 25. Hannah [Crispen] rocf Marlborough
    MM, dtd 1843,9,26

CROUSE
1859, 6, 25. Uree (form Blackburn) dis mcd

CREW
1775, 3, 25. Miriam b d 1844,8,23 bur Spring-
    field
----, --, --. Obadiah b 1767,3,31 d 1845,10,
    10 bur Springfield; m Mary ----- b 1776,1,
    11 d 1841,10,13 bur Springfield
    Ch: John   b 1800, 8, 31
        Sarah   " 1802, 4, 4
        Judith   " 1804, 1, 1
        Eliza Ann " 1805, 12, 18
        Unity   " 1807, 9, 7
        Rebecca   " 1809, 8, 11
        Mary   " 1811, 1, 13
        Clotilda   " 1812, 9, 20
        Rachel   " 1814, 6, 20
        Esther   " 1816, 3, 26
        Isabell   " 1819, 7, 19
1814, 6, 26. Rachel b d 1887,1,8 bur Spring-
    field
----, --, --. Joshua b 1782,2,8 d 1853,12,15
    bur Springfield; m Milley ----- b 1791,9,7
    Ch: Caroline b 1813, 8, 19
        Nancy   " 1815, 2, 5
        Thomas   " 1816, 9, 8
        Fleming   " 1818, 7, 20
----, --, --. John b 1800,8,3 d 1864,2,1 bur
    Springfield; m Margery ----- b 1800,10,30
    d 1891,6,3 (an elder)
    Ch: Eliza Ann b 1823, 11, 1
        Mary   " 1825, 2, 20 d 1862, 4, 1
        bur Springfield
        Gideon   b 1827, 2, 27
        Obadiah   " 1829, 4, 3
        Unity   " 1831, 4, 12 d 1838,11,30
        bur Springfield
        Esther   b 1833, 3, 8
        Lydia   " 1835, 4, 19
        Zachariah E.
                   b 1837, 9, 5 d 1864, 4, 1
        bur Damascus
        Emily Jane b 1840, 2, 1 " 1843, 1,31
        bur Springfield
        John P.   b 1842, 9, 27 " 1869, 7, 9
        bur Maryville, Mo.
        James R.   b 1850, 5, 29
1826, 9, 28. Rebecca m James C. BLACKBURN
1828, 1, 31. Unity m Aaron STRATTON, Jr.
1832, 5, 3. Jonathan, s Littleberry & Huldah,
    Columbiana Co., O., b 1810,7,2; m in
    Damascus MH, Mary WOOLMAN, dt Abner & Mar-
    tha, Columbiana Co., O., b 1813,10,27 d
    1894,12,4 bur Springfield
    Ch: Emmor   b 1833, 4, 1
        Clark   " 1834, 9, 8 d 1858,10, 8
        bur Springfield
        Elizabeth b 1836, 7, 23
        Emily   " 1838, 10, 27
        Benjamin   " 1840, 9, 25 d 1865, 5,20
        Alfred   " 1843, 1, 24 " 1843, 1,27
        bur Springfield

CREW, Jonathan & Mary, continued
    Ch: Harriet   b 1844, 2, 17 d 1876, 5,15
      bur Springfield
      Wm. Henry b 1846, 11, 6." 1871, 1,30
      bur Springfield
      Judith Ann b 1846, 11, 6 " 1859, 2, 8
      bur Springfield
      Mary Maria b 1849, 5, 7 " 1853, 1, 4
      Jonathan
      Antrim   " 1852, 9, 25
1833, 2, 27. Chlotilda m Lewis WALTER
1833, 5, 2. Caroline m Joseph YOUNG Jr.
1837, 6, 5. Thomas, s Joshua & Milly, Colum-
    biana Co., O.; m in Springfield MH, Ann
    ANDREWS, dt John & Sarah
1837, 6, 8. Nancy m Isaiah STANLEY
1847, 10, 28. Isabella m Isaac R. CARR
1848, 6, 1. Eliza Ann m Edmin FOGG
1850, 10, 3. Esther m Joseph HALDERMAN
----, --, --. Gideon b 1827,2,27; m Rebecca
    ----- b 1832,3,23 (W)
    Ch: Charles   b 1853, 7, 2
      Joseph B.   " 1854, 10, 6
      Hannah   " 1858, 1, 31
1846, 3, 5. Joseph, s Jacob & Rachel, Bel-
    mont Co., O.; m in Springfield MH, Esther
    FRENCH, dt William R. & Judith, Columbi-
    ana Co., O.
1848, 12, 24. Joseph Leander d
1851, 10, 29. Gideon, s John & Margery, b 1827,
    2,27; m in Goshen MH, Rebecca BRANTINGHAM,
    dt George & Hannah, Columbiana Co., O.
    Ch: Charles   b 1853, 6, 22
      Joseph B.   " 1854, 10, 6
1854, 3, 30. Robert, s Abram & Jane, Colum-
    biana Co., O., b 1831,8,22 d 1873,9,29
    bur Damascus; m in Upper Springfield MH,
    Margaret BLACKBURN, dt Barbee & Elizabeth,
    Columbiana Co., O., b 1830,11,1 d 1896,11,
    6 bur Winona
    Ch: Henry   b 1855, 1, 24
      Wilson   " 1858, 5, 24 d 1877, 9, 13
      bur Damascus
      Sarah Jane b 1859, 8, 1
      Abraham S. b 1863, 12, 17
      Esther   " 1867, 3, 20
----, --, --. Joseph b 1840,9,21; m Phebe
    TRESCOT b 1844,12,15
----, --, --. Mahlon b 1840,3,7 d 1896,3,8;
    m Phebe Ann HOOPES b 1845,4,18 d 1931,4,5
    Ch: Ida Mary   b 1866, 1, 18
      Edwin A.   " 1867, 6, 21
      Laura Jane " 1872, 9, 18 d 1873, 4, 8
      Orris David" 1876, 4, 24
      Carrol M.   " 1881, 4, 18
1869, 3, 4. Robert T., s Jesse B. & Eliza-
    beth H., Harrison Co., O.; m in Damascus
    MH, Anna E. HOLE, dt Lemuel & Unity C.,
    Mahoning Co., O.
1869, 5, 5. Cora Cobb, w Edwin A., b
----, --, --. ----- m Eliza Ann ----- b 1848,
    12,27
    Ch: Elizabeth b 1870, 1, 16

Ch: Charles Cor-
    win   b 1871, 12, 17
    Mary Catha-
    rine   " 1875, 10, 15
----, --, --. James H., s John & Margery
    (Ellyson), b 1850,5,29; m Elizabeth Annar
    ----- b 1851,4,19 d 1931,8,19 bur Washing-
    ton, D. C.
    Ch: Theresa
      Mary   b 1873, 1, 17
      Clara Alma " 1874, 11, 19
1877, 9, 13. Wilson d ae 19 bur Winona
----, --, --. Abram, s Robert & Margaret, b
    1863,12,17; m Idella S. ELLYSON b 1862,8,
    22 d 1922,2,22
    Ch: Allard H. b 1903, 10, 6
1903, 10, 6. Allard H., s Abram L. & Idella
    (Ellyson), b
----, --, --. Orris D., s Mahlon & Phebe Ann,
    b 1876,4,24; m Eva C. WOOD, dt James &
    Alice, b 1873,8,3 d 1922,9,14
    Ch: Linwood
      David   b 1910, 10, 10 d 1922, 9,14
1827, 10, 27. Merriam rocf Weynoak MM, Va.,
    dtd 1827,9,1
1831, 7, 23. Jonathan rocf New Garden MM,
    dtd 1831,7,21
1838, 3, 24. Esther Woolman (form Crew) dis
    mcd
1838, 6, 23. Thomas & w, Ann, gct Chester-
    field MM
1839, 5, 25. Fleming gct Chesterfield MM, to
    m Sarah Ann Patterson
1840, 4, 25. Fleming gct Chesterfield MM
1846, 10, 24. Esther gct Somerset MM
1848, 7, 22. Esther & s, Joseph Leander, rocf
    Somerset MM, dtd 1848,5,29
1848, 9, 23. Jonathan dis disunity
1849, 3, 24. Judith rocf New Garden MM, dtd
    1848,11,23
1851, 7, 27. Mary gct Center MM
1855, 4, 28. Margaret gct New Garden MM
1856, 1, 25. Esther Strawn (form Crew) dis
    mcd (W)
1856, 7, 26. Esther Straughn (form Crew) dis
    mcd
1857, 4, 25. Milly gct Chesterfield MM
1858, 6, 25. Lydia rmt Thomas Warrington (W)
1858, 9, 25. Emmor con mcd
1858, 10, 22. Emmor dis mcd (W)
1860, 6, 22. Emily Cobbs (form Crew) dis mcd
1860, · 7, 28. Robert & w, Margaret, & ch, Hen-
    ry, Wilson & Sarah Jane, rocf Marlborough
    MM
1861, 4, 27. Emily Cobbs (form Crew) con mcd
1863, 1, 24. John dis jW
1863, 1, 24. Margery dis jW
1863, 1, 24. Zechariah E. dis jW
1863, 1, 24. John P. dis jW
1863, 1, 24. James H. dis jW
1863, 1, 24. Wm. H. dis jW
1863, 1, 24. Harriet dis jW

CREW, continued

1863, 1, 24. Mary dis jW
1863, 1, 24. Elizabeth dis jW
1863, 2, 28. Gideon & fam gct Red Cedar MM, Ia.
1863, 9, 25. Obadiah & Rebecca dis jG (W)
1863, 9, 25. Gideon dis jG (W)
1864, 6, 25. Obadiah dis mcd
1865, 2, 24. Phebe Ann (form Hoopes) dis mcd (W)
1866, 9, 22. Emmor dis military service
1868, 9, 26. Mahlon & w, Phebe Ann, & ch, Ida Mary & Edwin A. recrq (Mahlon by consent of New Garden MM)
1869, 11, 26. Elizabeth Jones (form Crew) dis mcd (W)
1871, 1, 27. James H. dis mcd (W)
1871, 4, 21. Charles, Joseph & Hannah, ch Gideon & Rebecca, gct Hickory Grove MM, Ia. (W)
1871, 5, 26. James H. con mcd
1871, 8, 26. Elizabeth Anna (form Shreeve) con mcd
1875, 1, 22. Jonathan Antrim con mcd (W)
1874, 3, 28. Obadiah rst at Sandy Spring MM on consent of this mtg
1874, 6, 27. Anna M., minor, gct Sandy Spring MM
1879, 11, 22. Henry gct Salem MM
1884, 9, 23. Jonathan Antrim dis disunity (W)
1884, 4, 26. Emmor dropped from mbrp
1886, 3, 26. Margery d 1891,6,3 ae 91 (an elder) (W)
1898, 12, 23. Idella D. (form Ellyson) dis mcd (W)
1899, 11, 25. Eva C. recrq
1901, 2, 23. Idella recrq
1905, 1, 28. Carroll gct Alliance MM
1907, 5, 25. Orris D. & Eva gct Alliance MM
1911, 9, 26. Joseph & w, Phebe, rocf Winona MM, O.
1913, 3, 22. Clara Crew Jones relrq
1917, 11, 24. Oris D. & Eva C. rocf S. Cleveland MM
1920, 10, 23. Joseph & Phebe gct Whittier MM, Calif.

CROZIER

1920, 7, 10. Lillian Madeline, dt Ray & Helen (Robison), b

1933, 3, 23. Lillian recrq

CRUM

----, --, --. ----- m Almira B. PARK, dt David & Asenith, b 1849,12,13
    Ch: William
        Alton   b 1882, 12, 30
        Asenath
        Lorena   " 1892, 5, 25
----, --, --. Gibson b 1856,5,29; m Alpharetta ----- b 1858,2,7
    Ch: Daisy J.   b 1883, 7, 22

1893, 5, 17. Mary C., w Alton W., dt David H. & Jerusha (Hobday) Hull, b

1882, 4, 22. Almira recrq
1894, 3, 24. Wm. Alton & Asenath Lorane, ch Elmira, recrq
1906, 2, 24. Gilson & w, Alfaretta, & dt, Daisy, dropped from mbrp
1916, 4, 22. Lorena (Crum) Wirsching relrq
1930, 2, 27. Mary Catharine recrq

DALKHE

1914, 2, 28. Rose relrq

DALZELL

----, --, --. Otley V. m Alfaretta LOVEJOY, dt Wm. W. & Eliza Jane (White), b 1859,10,17
    Ch: George B. b 1889, 4, 23
        Isadora
        Pearl   " 1891, 1, 29
        Harry Leo " 1894, 5, 16
        Hazel   " 1896, 7, 25

1902, 2, 22. George B. recrq
1902, 5, 24. Alpharetta & dt, Isadore Pearl, recrq
1909, 4, 24. Alpharetta [Delzell] & ch, Harry & Hazel, recrq
1925, 6, 25. George [Delzell] dropped from mbrp

DARLINGTON

1843, 10, 28. James Jr. gct Redstone MM, to m Ann Darlington (James Cattell Jr.)

DAVIS

----, --, --. William b 1794,6,17 d 1829,2,17 m Anna ----- b 1797,10,23
    Ch: Martha   b 1815, 3, 4
        Samuel   " 1816, 7, 5
        Rebecca   " 1818, 4, 5
        Esther   " 1819, 9, 13
        Mary   " 1821, 12, 3
        Louisa   " 1823, 10, 4
        Eunice   " 1825, 8, 6
----, --, --. John H., s David L. & Catharine, b 1843,9,29; m Hannah S. BRYAN, dt Wm. & Mary, b 1828,7,23

1831, 2, 26. Anna & ch, Samuel, Esther, Louisa, Eunice & Lydia, gct Salem MM
1838, 11, 24. Samuel rocf Salem MM, dtd 1838, 11,21
1838, 11, 24. Anna & dt, Eunice & Lydia, rocf Salem MM, dtd 1838,11,21
1842, 4, 23. Samuel dis mcd
1842, 8, 27. Sarah (form Silver) dis mcd
1843, 5, 27. Anna & ch, Eunice & Lydia, gct Salem MM
189-, 1, 25. John H. & Hannah L. recrq
1892, 7, 23. John H. & Hannah L. dis

DAY
----, --, --. Walter E., s Mahlon & Ruth, b
    1875,3,29; m Agnes LAWSON, dt John & Mary,
    b 1873,11,10

1896, 9, 26. Walter E. rocf Poplar Ridge MM,
    Ind.
1896, 9, 26. Agnes recrq
1899, 4, 22. W. E. & fam gct Poplar Ridge MM,
    Ind.

DEAN
1853, 1, 22. Jonathan & w, Elizabeth, & s,
    Francis, rocf Sandy Spring MM, dtd 1852,
    12,24
1853, 12, 24. Jonathan & w, Elizabeth, & s,
    Francis, gct Sandy Spring MM

DERR
----, --, --. Edgar D., s James & Eliza, b
    1878,7,24; m Lillian DAVIS, dt Jonathan &
    Kennie, b 1882,3,3
    Ch: Naomi De-
        light   b 1904, 6, 16

1902, 4, 26. Lillian D. rocf Winona MM, O.
1902, 4, 26. Edgar D. recrq
1905, 3, 25. Edgar & w, Lillian, & dt, Naomi
    D., gct Winona MM, O.

DEVOL
----, --, --. George m Mary Isabella FRENCH
    b 1869,11,18
    Ch: Mary Eliza-
        beth   b 1902, 1, 13 d 1902, 8,15
        Charles
        Edward   " 1903, 10, 2
        Catharine
        Isabella   " 1906, 1, 30
        William Ez-
        ra   " 1909, 9, 7

1929, 6, 27. Charles, Catharine & Ezra drop-
    ped from mbrp at Allum Creek

DEWEES
----, --, --. Charles W., s Griffith & Ruth-
    anna (Masters), b 1865,4,28; m Mary R.
    GAMBLE, dt Samuel & Mary Jane (Fogg), b
    1876,7,12 (W)
    Ch: Isaac Ed-
        win   b 1905, 3, 30
        Martha Ruth" 1907, 2, 18; m Raymond
        M. EDGERTON
1930, 1, 25. Martha R. m Raymond M. EDGERTON
    (W)

1918, 3, 22. Charles W. & w, Mary G., & ch,
    Isaac Edwin & Martha, rocf New Garden MM
    (W)
1933, 6, 23. Charles & w, Mary, & s, Isaac
    E., gct Salem MM

DICKEY
1882, 6, 12. Rebecca, dt Elwood B. & Phebe W.
    Conrad, b (W)

1914, 10, 23. Rebecca C. (form Conrad) con
    mcd (W)
1921, 3, 25. Rebecca C. gct Pasadena MM,
    Calif. (W)

DICKENSON
1835, 5, 23. Deborah (form Stanley) dis mcd

DINGY
1850, 7, 27. John rocf Marlborough MM, dtd
    1850,5,28; returned 9-28 because of dis-
    unity
1859, 11, 25. Adaline [Dingee] gct Westland
    MM, Pa.

DITHRIDGE
1876, 12, 11. Minnie V. Cobbs, w Ed, b
1905, 6, 24. Minnie dropped from mbrp

DIXON
----, --, --. Samuel b 1790,5,11; m Hannah
    ----- b 1797,12,20 (W)
1857, 2, 26. Frances Conrad b

1843, 10, 28. Nathan Warrington gct Middleton
    MM, to m Mary Dixon
1857, 6, 26. Samuel & w, Hannah, rocf
    Middleton MM, dtd 1857,6,11 (W)
1862, 1, 25. Samuel & w, H----- rocf Salem
    MM, dtd 1862,1,23
1863, 1, 24. Samuel & w, Hannah, dis jW
1864, 4, 23. Samuel & w, Hannah, gct Penns-
    ville MM (W)
1879, 6, 28. Lydia dis
1897, 1, 23. Francis recrq
1905, 6, 24. Francis dropped from mbrp

DONNALLY
1898, 8, 29. Laura Edith [Donnalley] b

1920, 2, 28. Laura Edith recrq

DOUDNA
1842, 10, 22. Abner Fawcett gct Chesterfield
    MM, to m Martha Doudna

DOWNS
1846, 8, 22. Miriam & John, minors, rocf
    Marlborough MM, dtd 1846,7,28
1846, 8, 22. Samuel, minor, rocf Marlborough
    MM, dtd 1846,7,28
1861, 5, 22. John con mcd
1861, 10, 26. John gct Wabash MM, Ind.
1862, 1, 25. Mariam Cadwell (form Downs) dis
    mcd

EASTERLING
1895, 6, 21. Horace V. rmt Anna M. FOGG (W)

EDGERTON

1844, 5, 1. David, s James & Anna, Belmont
Co., O.; m in Goshen MH, Esther ELLYSON,
dt Robert & Hannah, Columbiana Co., O.

1851, 3, 24. Mary A. Foster, w Jesse, dt
Jeremiah & Mialma R. (Kenyon), b

----, --, --. Jesse, s Joseph & Charity (Doudna); m Susan G. ----- b 1842,3,3 (W)
Ch: Walter G. b 1884, 6, 4

1885, 9, 24. Edward Edgerton m Ellen FOGG (W)

----, --, --. Horace Joseph, s Walter & Mary
(Binns); m Anna Viola -----, dt Milton &
Beulah (Fogg) CAMERON, b 1883,9,28 (W)
Ch: Raymond
      Milton   b 1905, 12, 13
      Lucile Mary" 1911, 9, 6
      Virgil W. " 1913, 3, 13
      Sybil B.   " 1918, 5, 29
      Melva A.   " 1920, 6, 26

1924, 3, 11. Jesse d ae 79 (a minister)

1930, 1, 25. Raymond M. m Martha R. DEWEES (W)

1844, 7, 27. Esther gct Chesterfield MM

1886, 3, 26. Ellen Fogg gct Coal Creek MM,
Ia. (W)

1905, 3, 24. Horace J. rmt Anna V. Cameron
(W)

1905, 6, 23. Anna V. Cameron gct New Garden
MM (W)

1906, 5, 25. Jesse & w, Susan G., rocf Stillwater MM, dtd 1906,5,23 (W)

1906, 9, 18. Walter G. rocf Middleton MM (W)

1907, 10, 25. Walter rmt Beulah Cameron (W)

1908, 3, 27. Beulah gct New Garden MM (W)

1908, 3, 27. Horace J. & w, Anna V., & s,
Raymond Milton, rocf New Garden MM (W)

1908, 11, 27. Walter G. gct New Garden MM, to
m Mary C. Stratton (W)

1910, 7, 22. Jesse gct Short Creek MM, O., to
m Elizabeth A. McGrew (W)

1910, 10, 21. Elizabeth A. rocf Short Creek
MM, O. (W)

1910, 11, 25. Walter J. gct New Garden MM (W)

1916, 9, 22. Jesse gct South Kingston MM,
R. I., to m Mary J. Foster (W)

1917, 6, 22. Mary J. F. rocf South Kingston
MM, R. I., dtd 1917,3,28 (W)

1922, 1, 22. Horace J. & w, Anna V., & ch,
Raymond M., Lucile M., Virgil W., Sibyl
B. & Melva A., gct Holly Spring MM, N. C.

1927, 1, 21. Mary J. A. gct South Kingston MM
R. I. (W)

EDWARDS

----, --, -- Rees m Mary EVANS b 1855,3,2
Ch: Pauli   b 1870, 8, 17

1900, 3, 24. Mary & Pauli recrq

ELLERMAN

----, --, --. Theophilus b 1802,8,24; m Sarah
----- b 1804,9,26

1839, 6, 22. Theopolis & w, Sarah, rocf
Middleton MM, dtd 1839,6,6

1842, 4, 23. Theophilus [Ellerton] & w, Sarah, gct Burlington MM, N. J.

ELLIOTT

1830, 6, 30. John, s Joseph & Elizabeth,
Stark Co., O.; m in Goshen MH, Mary STAN-
LEY, dt Garland & Sarah, Columbiana Co., O.

1832, 12, 26. Samuel, s Joseph & Elizabeth,
Stark Co., O.; m in Goshen MH, Martha
STANLEY, dt Garland & Sarah, Columbiana
Co., O.

----, --, --. Elmer S. [Ellet], s John & Al-
mira (Card); m Irena M. BUTLER, dt John &
Ann (Coppock), b 1861,7,29
Ch: Effie   b 1885, 4, 9
    Curtis   " 1887, 9, 26

----, --, --. Curtis, s Elmer E. & Irena M.
(Butler), b 1887,9,26; m Louise M. URTON,
dt Chas. & Isabel (Howell), b 1888,11,25

1830, 8, 28. Mary gct Marlborough MM

1833, 3, 23. Martha gct Marlborough MM

1834, 10, 25. Samuel & w, Martha, & dt, Sarah,
rocf Marlborough MM, dtd 1834,8,26

1834, 12, 27. Samuel & w, Martha, & dt, Sarah,
gct Marlborough MM

1902, 1, 25. Effie & Curtis [Ellett] recrq

1910, 12, 24. Elmer E. [Ellett] recrq

1913, 12, 27. Louise [Ellett] rocf Wilmington
MM

ELLYSON

----, --, --. Zachariah b 1762,10,6 d 1837,3,7
bur Goshen; m Mary ----- b 1768,10,12 d
1844,4,23 bur Goshen
Ch: Isaac   b 1789, 8, 28
    Gideon   " 1791, 11, 21
    Zachariah " 1794, 4, 2
    Robert   " 1796, 4, 11
    William   " 1898, 10, 9
    Margery   " 1800, 10, 20
    Anna   " 1803, 6, 3
    John   " 1806, 2, 6
    Joseph   " 1807, 12, 21 d 1813,11,23
    Mary   " 1812, 9, 17

1797, 9, 17. Elizabeth b

----, --, --. Isaac b 1789,8,28 d 1842,12,18
bur Goshen; m Elizabeth ----- b 1797,9,17
Ch: Deborah b 1816, 5, 5
    Mary   " 1818, 9, 13
    Ann   " 1820, 7, 12
    Enoch   " 1822, 7, 26 d 1823, 3,20
    bur Goshen
    Joseph   " 1824, 1, 30
    Gideon   " 1826, 2, 1 d 1854, 2, 1
    bur Brownsville
    Ezra   b 1827, 12, 8
    Hannah   " 1830, 1, 22
    Daniel   " 1832, 6, 2
    Sarah   " 1834, 8, 8 d 1854, 1,22
    bur Redstone

ELLYSON, continued

----, --, --. Robert b 1796,4,11; m Hannah
----- b 1802,1,2 d 1841,3,28 bur Goshen
   Ch: Esther   b 1820, 3, 27
      Miriam   " 1821, 12, 7 d 1839,10,29
      Benjamin   " 1824, 1, 29
      Webster   " 1826, 3, 18
      Zadoc   " 1828, 4, 26
      Drusilla   " 1830, 8, 8
      Ellen B.   " 1833, 3, 7
      Hannah   " 1835, 11, 6
      Robert   " 1839, 4, 6 d 1925, 1,31
        bur Damascus
   Robert m 2nd Mary RATCLIFF b 1809,5,6 d
   1863,9,27 bur Goshen
   Ch: David   b 1845, 7, 28 d 1925, 4,25
        bur Damascus
      Achsah   b 1847, 8, 3
      Tace   " 1851, 3, 2
----, --, --. Phebe b 1824,8,12 d 1917,11,24
bur Middleton (W)
1827, 2, 28. Anna m Samuel C. REEVE
----, --, --. John b 1806,2,6; m Lydia -----
b 1806,9,2
   Ch: Isaac   b 1831, 2, 19
      Eunice S. " 1834, 12, 28
      Zechariah " 1837, 12, 31
1841, 4, 28. Mary, w Joseph, dt Joseph & Rebecca Painter, b
1842, 3, 30. Deborah m Jonathan CATTELL
1842, 10, 26. Ann m Jeremiah STANLEY
1843, 11, 1. Mary m Wm. CATTELL
1844, 5, 1. Esther m David EDGERTON
1846, 12, 2. Benjamin, s Robert & Hannah, Mahoning Co., O., b 1824,1,29; m in Goshen
MH, Abigail HEMINGWAY, dt James & Hope,
Mahoning Co., O., b 1827,7,27
   Ch: Alfred   b 1848, 8, 11
      James H.   " 1851, 8, 20
      Miriam   " 1850, 3, 17
      William B. " 1852, 12, 19
      Robert M. " 1854, 11, 26
      Hannah   " 1856, 9, 12
      Rebecca P. " 1858, 3, 6
      Fidelia   " 1859, 11, 9
1849, 3, 8. Drusilla m Edwin FOGG
----, --, --. Robert Jr. b 1839,4,26; m Eunice
----- b 1840,5,29 d 1900,9,24 bur Damascus
   Ch: Adella   b 1862, 8, 22
      Walter J. " 1865, 6, 21
      Charles   " 1870, 7, 21
1863, 9, 27. Mary d ae 55 (an elder) (W)
----, --, --. Joseph b 1824,1,30; m Mary -----
b 1841,4,28
   Ch: Edgar P. b 1869, 8, 4
      Laura   " 1873, 5, 9
----, --, --. David b 1845,7,28; m Margaret
COPE b 1842,3,4 d 1914,9,8 bur Springfield
(W)
----, --, --. Walter J., s Robert & Eunice
(Fawcett), b 1865,6,21; m Sarah H. MALMS-
BERRY, dt Geo. & Fazetta (Cattell), b 1867,
9.6

   Ch: Florence   b 1895, 7, 26
      Homer M.   " 1901, 11, 1
----, --, --. Charles b 1870,7,22; m Emma SID-
WELL, b 1871,2,9
   Ch: Gertrude
      Rachel   b 1900, 6, 28
      Clarence
      Fawcett   " 1908, 8, 7
----, --, --. Charles, s Robert & Eunice (Faw-
cett), b 1870,7,22; m Emma SIDWELL, dt
Israel & Rachel (Branson), b 1871,2,9
   Ch: Clarence
      Fawcett   b 1908, 8, 7
      Gertrude R." 1900, 6, 28 (W)
----, --, --. Homer b 1901,11,1; m Mary Alice
JACKSON b 1906,10,30
   Ch: Betty Jane b 1923, 11, 1
      Robert Klar" 1927, 3, 27
1925, 4, 25. David d ae 80 (an elder) (W)

1830, 4, 30. John [Ellison] gct Salem MM, to
m Lydia Street
1830, 12, 25. Lydia rocf Salem MM, dtd 1830,
11,24
1834, 10, 25. Mary Jr. dis disunity
1838, 12, 22. William gct Marlborough MM
1844, 6, 22. John & w, Lydia, & ch, Isaac,
Eunice, Zachariah & Mary, gct Salem MM, Ia.
1844, 5, 25. Robert gct Stillwater MM, to m
Mary Ratcliff
1844, 11, 23. Mary & s, Josiah E. Ratcliff, rocf
rocf Stillwater MM, dtd 1844,9,28
1851, 7, 26. Hannah Santee (form Ellyson) dis
mcd
1851, 12, 27. Daniel & Sarah, minor ch Elizabeth, gct Redstone MM
1851, 12, 27. Webster dis mcd
1855, 5, 26. Zadoc gct Red Cedar MM, Ia.
1855, 5, 26. Benjamin & w, Abigail, & ch, Alfred, Miriam, James & Wm. gct Red Cedar MM,
Ia.
1856, 1, 26. Hannah gct Salem MM, Ia.
1856, 10, 25. Elizabeth gct Redstone MM, Pa.
1858, 4, 24. Joseph dis disunity
1860, 4, 28. Ezra gct Redstone MM
1861, 8, 28. Robert Jr. gct Salem MM, to m
Eunice T. Fawcett (W)
1862, 6, 27. Eunice rocf Salem MM, dtd 1862,
6,25
1863, 1, 23. Benjamin & w, Abigail, & ch, Alfred, Miriam, James H., Wm. B., Robert M.,
Hannah, Rebecca P. & Fidelia, gct Hickory
Grove MM, Ia. (W)
1863, 1, 24. Robert dis jW
1863, 1, 24. Mary dis jW
1863, 1, 24. Ellen dis jW
1863, 1, 24. Robert Jr. dis jW
1863, 1, 24. Achsah dis jW
1863, 1, 24. David dis jW
1863, 1, 24. Tacy dis jW
1863, 7, 24. Samuel dis jG (W)
1864, 9, 24. Elizabeth rocf Redstone MM, dtd
   1864, 3, 8

ELLYSON, continued

1865, 5, 9. Robert gct Middleton MM, to m
    Phebe Wickersham (W)
1865, 9, 22. Phebe rocf Middleton MM, dtd
    1865,9,10 (W)
1867, 3, 22. Achsah rmt James A. Cope (W)
1867, 5, 24. Robert & w, Phebe, & dt, Tacy
    M., gct Middleton MM (W)
1868, 5, 22. Mary (form Painter) dis mcd (W)
1869, 5, 24. Ellen B. rmt Jehu L. Kite (W)
1871, 4, 21. David gct Middleton MM, to m
    Margaret Cope (W)
1871, 10, 27. Margaret rocf Middleton MM, dtd
    1871,9,16 (W)
1874, 2, 28. Mary recrq
1883, 10, 26. Phebe rocf Salem MM, dtd 1883,8,
    22 (W)
1885, 9, 22. Phebe gct Middleton MM (W)
1886, 2, 27. Joseph, Edgar P. & Laura recrq
1891, 7, 25. Edgar P. relrq
1891, 8, 22. Laura relrq
1892, 11, 26. Joseph & Mary gct Salem MM
1897, 1, 22. Walter J. dis mcd (W)
1898, 12, 23. Idella S. Crew (form Ellyson) dis
    mcd (W)
1899, 11, 25. Sarah A. rocf East Goshen MM
1899, 11, 25. Walter J. & dt, Florence, recrq
1901, 9, 24. Charles dis mcd (W)
1910, 4, 23. Charles & w, Emma S., & ch, Ger-
    trude, Rachel & Clarence Fawcett Ellyson,
    recrq
1929, 12, 26. Homer & w, Mary, & two ch gct
    Salem MM

EMMONS

1814, 6, 4. Mary b
1866, 5, 3. Mary m Benjamin STANLEY

1865, 9, 23. Mary rocf Spring Creek MM, Ia.,
    dtd 1865,8,26

ENGLE

1827, 8, 29. Charles, s Josiah & Mary, b 1801,
    12,23 d 1853,10,31 bur Goshen; m in Goshen
    MH, Jane MALMSBERRY, dt Benjamin & Jane,
    Columbiana Co., O., b 1806,11,27
    Ch: Eliza   b 1828, 4, 21
        Mary Jane   " 1831, 2, 29
        Isaac   " 1834, 7, 1 d 1834, 4, 5
          bur Goshen
        Sarah   b 1836, 12, 2
        Josiah   " 1838, 9, 10 d 1861,10,14
          bur Goshen
        Rebecca M. b 1840, 4, 29
        Lewis   " 1842, 6, 5 " 1843, 3,21
        Charles D. " 1847, 12, 3
----, --, --. Zimri b 1811,7,9; m Ann -----
    b 1811,3,14
    Ch: Mary   b 1834, 7, 30
        Rachel Ann " 1835, 10, 13
        Elizabeth   " 1837, 2, 23
        Richard B. " 1839, 1, 20
        Zimri   " 1840, 11, 12

    Ch: Ann   b 1844, 1, 15
        Louisa   " 1845, 12, 8 d 1845,12;17
        Lucina   " 1845, 12, 8
        Mercy   " 1847, 4, 28   [(W)
----, --, --. ----- m Jane ----- b 1807,11,27
    Ch: Josiah   b   d 1861,10,14
        Sarah   " 1836, 12, 2
        Rebecca   " 1840, 4, 29
        Josiah   " 1838, 9, 11
        Charles D. " 1846, 12, 3

1829, 4, 25. Charles rocf Middleton MM, dtd
    1829,3,12
1834, 2, 22. Zimri & w, Ann B., rocf Middle-
    ton MM, dtd 1834,2,9
1848, 1, 22. Eliza C. Meredith (form Engle)
    dis mcd
1850, 1, 26. Mary Jane Hutton (form Engle)
    dis mcd
1862, 12, 27. Sarah Boner (form Engle) dis mcd
1863, 1, 24. James dis jW
1863, 6, 26. Zimri & w, Ann, & ch, Mary & Ra-
    chel Ann, dis jG (W)
1863, 6, 27. Rebecca M. dis disunity
1863, 9, 25. Richard dis jG (W)
1864, 1, 24. Richard B. dis mcd, jas & mili-
    tary service
1865, 8, 25. Sarah Boner (form Engle) dis mcd
    (W)
1866, 8, 25. Zimri Jr. dis military service
1867, 1, 25. Rebecca Middleton (form Engle)
    dis mcd (W)
1870, 3, 26. Sarah Jane (form Blackburn) con
    mcd
1870, 7, 23. Sarah Jane (form Blackburn) dis
    mcd (?)

ENGLISH

1857, 4, 11. Mary E., w Joseph H., dt Jesse
    & Edith Hall, b
1858, 5, 10. Joseph H. b

1884, 9, 27. Joseph H. recrq
1890, 1, 25. Joseph & Mary H. dropped from
    mbrp

ENKE

1848, 3, 25. Rachel (form Brannen) dis mcd

ENLOWS

1863, 7, 24. Thomas dis jG (W)

ERICKSON

1892, 6, 25. Julia gct New Sharon MM, Ia.

ERWIN

----, --, --. Lester d 1925,11,7; m Marie

    Ch: Lawrence
        Francis
        Alfred Glen
        Mary Eliza-
          beth

ERWIN, continued
1925, 3, 26. Marie & ch, Lawrence Francis &
     Alfred Glen, rocf Beloit MM
1927, 10, 27. Marie & fam gc

ETZRODT
1905, 6, 24. Anna [Cassady] dropped from mbrp

EVANS
1841, 4, 28. Philip, s Jonathan & Elizabeth,
     Columbiana Co., O.; m in Goshen MH, Esther
     MORRIS, dt Joseph & Rachel, Columbiana Co.,
     O.

1841, 6, 26. Esther gct Salem MM

EVERSTINE
----, --, --. George Henry, s Chas. & Augusta
     (Nelson), b 1884,11,26; m Loma Pauline OTT
     Ch: Charles
          Hawkind   b 1820, 7, 30
          Geraldine " 1924, 8, 10
          Maxine   " 1924, 8, 10
          Genevieve " 1926, 1, 19

1931, 3, 26. George, Pauline, Charles,
     Geraldine & Genevieve, rocf Salem MM
1932, 10, 27. Pauline relrq

FALLACK
1844, 4, 27. Rebecca (form Lord) dis mcd

FARMER
----, --, --. ----- m Ann ----- b 1778,11,13
     Ch: Susannah b 1804, 9, 25
         Tabitha   " 1807, 2, 25
         Joseph   " 1809, 3, 26 d 1831, 7,12
         Rachel   " 1817, 7, 11
         Thomas   " 1819, 10, 4
     Ann Farmer m 2nd Thomas LANGSTAFF
1827, 7, 4. Tabitha m Samuel LANGSTAFF Jr.
1834, 10, 1. James, s John & Mary, Columbiana
     Co., O.; m in Goshen MH, Meribah BUTLER,
     dt Benjamin & Hannah, Columbiana Co., O.

1828, 6, 28. Susanna gct Flushing MM
1831, 6, 25. Jesse, minor, rocf Smithfield
     MM, dtd 1831,5,28
1832, 12, 22. Jesse, minor, gct Stillwater MM
1832, 12, 22. Jesse gct Stillwater MM; return-
     ed 1833,5,25
1833, 3, 23. Taylor gct Flushing MM
1833, 11, 23. Jesse dis mcd
1835, 1, 24. Merihab gct Sandy Spring MM
1836, 4, 23. Rachel gct Stillwater MM
1841, 1, 23. Thomas gct Sandy Spring MM

FAWCETT
----, --, --. William b 1784,1,8 d 1849,6,29
     ae 65 bur Springfield (an elder); m Abi-
     gail ----- b 1787,8,8 d 1855,1,12 bur
     Springfield
     Ch: Samuel S. b 1812, 10, 21

     Ch: Abner   b 1814, 9, 1
         Lucinda   " 1816, 2, 25 d 1838, 3,14
         bur Springfield
         Simeon   b 1817, 10, 19
         Jephthah " 1821, 7, 23
         Jason   " 1825, 8, 16 d 1848, 8,11
         bur Springfield
----, --, --. Samuel b 1812,10,21; m Jane ----
     b 1817,4,18 d 1840,12,9 bur Springfield
     Ch: Mary Ann b 1835, 7, 12
         George W. " 1837, 12, 17
----, --, --. Abner b 1814,9,1; m Elizabeth
     ----- b 1811,4,9
1834, 8, 28. Samuel S., s William & Abigail,
     Columbiana Co., O.; m in Springfield MH,
     Jane STANLEY, dt John & Mary Ann
----, --, --. Simeon b 1817,10,19; m Deborah
     ----- b 1816,10,22
     Ch: Lucinda   b 1840, 9, 17
         Elizabeth
          G.   " 1842, 3, 30
         Alvira   " 1844, 10, 19
         Abigail " 1846, 8, 22
         Anna   " 1848, 7, 13
         Edwin   " 1850, 3, 21
         Simeon   " 1856, 9, 30
         Deborah " 1860, 9, 22
         Walter   " 1865, 2, 11
----, --, --. Jephthah b 1821,7,23; m Rachel

     Ch: William
         Henry   b 1849, 9, 17

1838, 9, 28. Abner gct Redstone MM, to m
     Elizabeth Garwood
1838, 12, 22. Elizabeth G. rocf Redstone MM,
     dtd 1838,11,28
1839, 9, 28. Simeon gct Sandy Spring MM, to m
     Deborah Miller
1840, 4, 25. Deborah M. rocf Sandy Spring MM,
     dtd 1840,3,27
1842, 4, 23. Samuel S. dis mcd
1842, 10, 22. Abner gct Chesterfield MM, to m
     Martha Doudna
1843, 7, 22. Abner gct Chesterfield MM
1848, 10, 28. Jeptha gct Stillwater MM, to m
     Rachel Williams
1849, 9, 22. Rachel rocf Stillwater MM, dtd
     1849,7,28
1854, 10, 28. Jephthah & w, Rachel, & s, Wm.
     H., gct Vermillion MM, Ill.
1860, 11, 23. Lucinda Grove (form Fawcett) dis
     mcd (W)
1861, 8, 23. Robery Ellyson Jr. gct Salem MM,
     to m Eunice T. Fawcett (W)
1862, 12, 26. Elizabeth G. rmt Julius Rasche
     (W)
1862, 12, 27. Lucinda Grove (form Fawcett) dis
     mcd
1863, 1, 24. Simeon & w, Deborah, & ch,
     Elizabeth, Elvira, Anna, Abigail & Edwin,
     dis jW
1863, 11, 28. Mary Ann Whinery (form Fawcett)

FAWCETT, continued
    dis mcd
1866, 11, 23. Abigail Binford (form Fawcett)
    dis mcd (W)
1867, 5, 24. Deborah M. dis jG (W)
1867, 5, 25. Abbie T. Binford (form Fawcett)
    con mcd
1867, 12, 21. Simeon dis jG (W)
1869, 1, 22. Elvira & Anna dis jG (W)
1872, 8, 24. Alvira A. Jones (form Fawcett)
    dis mcd
1872, 11, 23. Anna F. Tomlinson (form Fawcett)
    con mcd
1872, 11, 23. Edwin con mcd
1873, 2, 22. Simeon & w, Deborah, & ch,
    Simeon, Deborah & Walter, gct Shawnee MM,
    Kans.
1873, 3, 22. Edwin gct Shawnee MM, Kans.
1877, 2, 23. Reuben G. Painter gct Salem MM,
    to m Phebe Fawcett (W)

FIELDS
1864, 1, 3. Elizabeth d ae 87

1827, 4, 28. Elizabeth rocf Salem MM, dtd
    1827,4,25

FINNEY
1910, 12, 24. Edward & Barbara recrq

FISHER
1859, 6, 25. Ruth (form Lipsey) dis mcd

FITTRO
1907, 1, 4. Pearl Anna, w Lawrence, dt
    Louis H. & Rosella (Briggs) Votaw, b

FOGG
----, --, -- Eleazer & -----
    Ch: Edmin   b 1823, 11, 2
        Edwin   " 1823, 11, 2
        Charles   " 1826, 3, 9
        Adna   " 1828, 6, 14
1848, 6, 1. Edmin, s Ebeneezer & Mary, Ma-
    honing Co., O., b 1823,11,2 d 1896,3,4 bur
    Springfield; m in Springfield MH, Eliza
    Ann CREW, dt John & Margery, Mahoning Co.,
    O., b 1823,11,1 d 1913,5,14
    Ch: Emily   b 1849, 2, 18 d 1865, 4,21
          bur Springfield
        Comly   b 1852, 1, 25
        Mary   " 1854, 11, 11
        Lindley   " 1857, 8, 9 d 1912,12, 4
          bur Springfield (W)
        Beulah   b 1860, 9, 20 (W)
        Anna   " 1860, 9, 20 (W)
        Elma   " 1866, 5, 16 d 1890, 3, 7
          (W)
1849, 3, 8. Edwin, s Ebeneezer & Mary, Mahon-
    ing Co., O., b 1823,11,2 d 1906,3,11 bur
    Damascus; m in Goshen MH, Drusilla ELLY-
    SON, dt Robert & Hannah, Mahoning Co., O.,
    b 1830,8,8 d 1911,11,25

    Ch: Robert E. b 1850, 5, 16
        Ebeneezer F." 1852, 3, 11
        Elmor W.   " 1854, 6, 17 d 1856, 1,29
          bur Goshen
        Charles   b 1857, 4, 25 d 1862,10,26
          bur Springfield (W)
        Edgar   b 1860, 3, 4 (W)
        Ellen   " 1860, 3, 4 (W)
        Hanna   " 1863, 2, 16 (W)
        Albert   " 1865, 4, 11 (W)
        Isabel   " 1867, 11, 1 (W)
        David   " 1871, 1, 2 (W)
1850, 8, 29. Adna, s Ebeneezer & Mary, Ma-
    honing Co., O., b 1828,6,14; m in Spring-
    field MH, Elizabeth ANDREWS, dt Daniel &
    Mary R., b 1834,3,27
    Ch: Edward B. b 1851, 10, 4
        Maryanna   " 1853, 11, 29
1885, 9, 24. Ellen m Edward EDGERTON (W)
----, --, --. Albert b 1865,4,11; m Clara D.
    MEAD b 1869,9,26
    Ch: Wm. Edwin b 1894, 6, 21
        Erma D.   " 1896, 6, 6

1832, 7, 28. Edwin, Edmund, Charles & Adnah,
    ch Ebeneezer, rocf Salem MM, N. J., dtd
    1832,5,30
1833, 4, 27. Hannah, Aaron, Josiah & Sarah,
    ch Elisha & Tacy, rocf Salem MM, dtd 1833,
    5,22
1836, 1, 28. Hannah dis jH
1837, 9, 23. Jane (form Young) dis mcd
1838, 12, 22. Aaron dis disunity
1843, 8, 26. Sarah Bradshaw (form Fogg) dis
    mcd
1844, 10, 26. Josiah dis disunity
1851, 5, 24. Charles rpd mcd in Iowa
1855, 2, 23. Adnah & w, Elizabeth, & ch, Ed-
    ward & Marianna, gct Pleasant Plain MM,
    Ia.
1863, 1, 24. Edmin & w, Eliza Ann, & dt,
    Emily, dis jW
1863, 1, 24. Edwin & w, Druzilla, dis jW
1863, 9, 25. Adna & Elizabeth dis jG (W)
1878, 6, 21. Robert gct Hickory Grove MM, Ia.
    (W)
1878, 6, 21. Ebeneazer gct Hickory Grove MM,
    Ia. (W)
1879, 6, 27. Beulah rmt Milton Cameron (W)
1884, 5, 23. Edgar gct Hickory Grove MM, Ia.
    (W)
1892, 6, 24. Albert dis mcd (W)
1892, 6, 24. Mary Pearson (form Fogg) dis
    mcd (W)
1893, 4, 21. Hannah Maris (form Fogg) dis mcd
    (W)
1895, 6, 21. Anna M. rmt Horace V. Easterling
    (W)
1896, 1, 24. Isabel Berber (form Fogg) con
    mcd (W)
1906, 7, 27. David dis mcd (W)
1910, 12, 24. Albert & w, Clara D., & ch, Wm.
    E. D. & Erma D., recrq (W)

FOGG, continued
1919, 6, 28. Albert, Clara & Erma gct First
      Friends Church, Pasadena, Calif.
1922, 10, 28. Wm. relrq

FOSTER
1916, 9, 22. Jesse Edgerton gct S. Kingston
      MM, N. J., to m Mary J. Foster (W)

FOTCH
1900, 2, 24. John & Louisa recrq
1900, 8, 15. John & Louisa gct East Goshen MM

FOUTS
----, --, --. Garrison Elsworth, s Hiram G. &
      Hannah (Crawford), b 1862,3,25 d 1933,2,27
      bur Salem, O.; m Mary ELTON, dt Thos. R. &
      Anna E., b 1862,1,8
         Ch: Roy Elton b 1884, 2, 20

1896, 11, 28. Garrison Ellsworth & w, Mary E.,
      & s, Leroy E., recrq
1904, 2, 27. Roy relrq
1918, 8, 15. Elizabeth relrq

FOWLER
1826, 8, 26. James gct Sandy Spring MM
1826, 10, 28. Joseph gct Sandy Spring MM
1835, 5, 23. Mary rocf Sandy Spring MM, dtd
      1835,4,24

FRANTZ
1843, 8, 26. Matilda (form Votaw) dis mcd
1844, 7, 27. Martha rst
1846, 10, 24. Matilda gct Goshen MM
1848, 3, 25. Matilda rocf Goshen MM, dtd
      1847,11,20

FREEMAN
----, --, --. George W. m Emma J. RICHARDS
      b 1849,6,13 d 1919,9,27
         Charles   b 1881, 10, 27
         Mary F.   " 1884, 8, 28
         Austin H.   " 1886, 10, 23
         Belle L.   " 1889, 4, 7

1899, 12, 23. Mary F., Austin H. & Bell L.
      recrq
1901, 9, 28. Emma J. recrq
1910, 12, 24. George & Charles recrq

FRENCH
----, --, --. Thomas [Friench] b 1773,1,13;
      m Esther ----- b 1780,3,28
----, --, --. James b 1773,3,13 d 1844,8,28
      bur Springfield; m Mary ----- b 1780,1,29
      d 1850,4,22 bur Springfield
         Ch: William R. b 1802, 6, 13
         Ann   " 1808, 12, 10
         James   " 1814, 5, 24
         Charles   " 1816, 9, 3 d 1821, 9,13
         Richard   " 1818, 10, 13
----, --, --. Elijah [Friench] b 1784,5,4 d

1810,4,8 bur Springfield; m Susanna -----
b 1787,8,7
   Ch: Thomas   b 1808, 1, 5
      Rebecca   " 1808, 1, 5
      Eliza Ann   " 1809, 10, 13
      Joseph C.   " 1810, 12, 26
      Mariah   " 1812, 9, 20 d 1813, 8, 5
      Elijah   " 1814, 10, 2
----, --, --. Barzillai b 1781,7,21 d 1858,1,6
      bur Springfield; m Mary G. ----- b 1785,3,
      17 d 1851,8,22 bur Springfield
   Ch: Elizabeth b 1811, 10, 30 d 1831, 1, 3
         bur Springfield
      Albert   b 1815, 7, 9
      Thomas   " 1816, 7, 21
      Robert   " 1817, 8, 2 d 1836,10,20
         bur Springfield
      Ezra   b 1820, 11, 22
      Martha   " 1822, 6, 9 d 1822, 8, 4
         bur Springfield
      David   b 1823, 11, 3
      Barzillai   " 1826, 2, 14
      Lydia   " 1827, 10, 2
----, --, --. Thomas b 1795,1,3 d 1846,3,24
      bur Goshen; m Elizabeth -----
   Ch: Allen T.   b 1818, 4, 2
      Joseph T.   " 1819, 8, 21
      James F.   " 1821, 6, 10
      William F.   " 1823, 3, 30
   Thomas m 2nd Martha ----- b 1802,1,8
   Ch: Haran   b 1828, 3, 13 d 1846, 1,26
         bur Goshen
      Elizabeth   " 1830, 5, 24
      Newton   " 1833, 2, 14
      Sarah   " 1835, 11, 22
      Martha   " 1838, 2, 24
      Thomas   " 1844, 3, 27
----, --, --. Wm. F. b 1823,3,30 d 1901,4,3
      bur Goshen (W)
1823, 11, 3. David b
----, --, --. Wm. Rogers b 1802,6,13 d 1869,
      8,14 bur Springfield; m Judith ----- b
      1804,1,1 d 1868,9,20 bur Upper Springfield
   Ch: Unity   b 1825, 2, 23
      Mary C.   " 1826, 10, 16
      Esther   " 1828, 7, 3
      Charles   " 1830, 9, 21
      John   " 1832, 7, 4
      Obadiah   " 1834, 10, 5
      Elizabeth   " 1837, 2, 12
      Ann   " 1839, 11, 19
      Judith   " 1842, 3, 2
      Wm. James   " 1847, 1, 6
1827, 6, 27. Thomas, s James & Sarah, Jeffer-
      son Co., O.; m in Goshen MH, Martha BRYAN,
      dt Haram & Charity
1827, 12, 2. Lydia b
1827, 1, 4. Ann m Francis J. TOWNSEND
1831, 9, 4. Deborah, w Wm., b
1839, 8, 1. Albert, s Barzillai & Mary, Co-
      lumbiana Co., O., b 1815,7,9; m in Spring-
      field MH, Elizabeth M. CORSE, dt James &
      Rebecca, Knox Co., Md., b 1807,3,25

FRENCH, Albert & Elizabeth, continued
    Ch: William
        Henry   b 1840, 10, 25
        Anna   " 1842, 5, 10
        Rebecca   " 1845, 9, 17
        Albert E. " 1850, 10, 12
1845, 5, 1. Unity m Samuel WOOLMAN
1846, 3, 5. Esther m Joseph CREW
1854, 8, 31. Elizabeth m Josiah C. RATCLIFF
1856, 10, 11. Sarah m John L. BUTLER
----, --, --. James F. b 1821,6,10; m Mary E.
    ----- b 1839,7,16
1851, 5, 1. Ezra, s Barzillai & Mary, Mahon-
    ing Co., O., b 1820,11,22; m in Spring-
    field MH, Ann W. STANLEY, dt Elijah & Uree
    Mahoning Co., O., b 1826,9,4 d 1861,8,20
    bur Springfield
    Ch: Eli   b 1853, 12, 17
    Ezra m 2nd Mary J. ----- b 1827,11,11
    Ch: Benjamin b 1866, 7, 11
        Mary Isa-
          bella   " 1869, 11, 18
----, --, --. Barzillar b 1826,2,14; m Deborah

    Ch: Edgar   b 1853, 8, 13
        Mary   " 1854, 8, 4
----, --, --. Benjamin, s Ezra & Mary, b 1866,
    7,11; m Alma HEWITT, dt James & Almira, b
    1869,4,9
    Ch: Albert
        Hewitt   b 1898, 7, 9
        Mary Almyra" 1901, 4, 16
        James
          Creighton " 1905, 8, 30

1827, 12, 22. Martha gct Smithfield MM
1830, 9, 25. Robert, minor, gct Salem MM
1833, 11, 23. Thomas & w, Martha, & ch, Allen,
    Joseph T., James, Wm. F., Haram, Eliza-
    beth & Newton, rocf Smithfield MM, dtd
    1833,6,17
1835, 7, 25. James Jr. gct Burlington MM,
    N. J.
1835, 8, 22. Thomas Y., minor, gct Salem MM
1837, 10, 28. Thomas Y. rocf Salem MM, dtd
    1837,10,25
1841, 2, 27. James dis disunity
1841, 5, 22. Thomas Y. gct Middleton MM
1844, 2, 24. Joseph T. dis mcd
1844, 11, 23. Richard gct Burlington MM
1851, 6, 28. Allen T. dis disunity
1847, 9, 25. Mary Jobes (form French) dis mcd
1852, 7, 24. Martha (form Gibson) dis mcd
1852, 8, 28. Barzillar Jr. gct Sandy Spring
    MM
1852, 10, 23. Charles dis mcd
1853, 3, 26. Newton dis disunity
1853, 9, 24. Deborah M. rocf Sandy Spring
    MM, dtd 1853,8,26
1855, 11, 23. Anna E., w James, & ch, Hannah
    Ann, Charles, Mary B., Emmergene L. &
    James G., rocf ND MM, dtd 1855,10,23 (W)
1856, 4, 25. Lydia rmt Theophulus Morlan (W)

1856, 4, 26. John dis mcd
1856, 4, 26. Martha Templin (form French)
    dis mcd
1856, 6, 28. Abel & w, Elizabeth M., & ch,
    Wm. Henry, Anna, Rebecca C. & Albert E.,
    gct Salem MM
1856, 7, 26. John dis mcd (W)
1856, 10, 25. Obadiah C. dis mcd
1856, 12, 26. Obadiah C. dis mcd (W)
1857, 3, 27. Barzillar Jr. & w, Deborah M., &
    ch, Edgar & Mary, gct Salem MM (W)
1857, 4, 24. David gct Sandy Spring MM, to m
    Eliza Miller (W)
1857, 7, 25. William F. dis mcd
1858, 12, 25. James con mcd
1859, 6, 24. Ann rmt Ezra COPPOCK
1860, 6, 23. Elizabeth T. dis jas
1863, 1, 24. Barzillar & w, Deborah, dis jW
1863, 1, 24. Wm. R. & w, Judith, & ch, Ju-
    dith Jr., Wm. J. & David, dis jW
1863, 2, 27. Ezra dis jG (W)
1863, 6, 26. Martha dis jG (W)
1863, 7, 24. Albert & Elizabeth M. dis jG
    (W)
1863, 8, 22. Ezra gct New Garden MM, to m
    Mary Johnson
1863, 9, 25. Wm. Henry dis jG (W)
1864, 1, 24. Mary J. rocf New Garden MM, dtd
    1864,1,20
1866, 7, 28. Deborah G. recrq
1866, 8, 25. Thomas Emmor dis military ser-
    vice
1866, 11, 23. Anna E. & ch, Emmorgene L. &
    Robert P., gct Evasham MM, N. J. (W)
1867, 6, 21. Wm. G. dis military service (W)
1869, 3, 26. Mary Jane (form Taylor) dis mcd
    (W)
1870, 1, 21. Judith Woodward (form French)
    dis mcd (W)
1870, 3, 26. Mary E. recrq
1870, 9, 24. Thomas E. recrq
1870, 9, 24. Emmor recrq
1875, 9, 25. Mary Jane (form Taylor) dis mcd
1878, 8, 23. Emma (form Vansyoc) con mcd (W)
1878, 11, 22. Emma gct Salem MM (W)
1901, 4, 27. Eli gct Salem MM
1907, 2, 23. Benjamin relrq
1910, 12, 24. Albert Hewett recrq
1910, 12, 24. Alma Hewett recrq
1910, 12, 24. Benjamin J. recrq
1910, 12, 24. James Creighton recrq
1910, 12, 24. Mary Almyra recrq

FULLER
1833, 3, 11. Mary b
1861, 5, 2. Mary m Thomas Edward PINKHAM

1859, 2, 26. Mary rocf Providence MM, R. I.

GALBREATH
1832, 4, 3. Britain C. b
1835, 6, 21. Leah, w Samuel, dt Robert &
    Sarah Harris, b

GALBREATH, continued

----, --, --. Brinton G. b 1852,4,3; m Martha
    J. ----- b 1854,1,9
      Ch: Oliver E. b 1875, 12, 15 d 1886, 8,24
        Albert S.   " 1880, 2, 15
        Enoch Rus-
          sell   " 1883, 4, 15
        Ida May   " 1885, 9, 3

1851, 2, 22. Rhoda [Galbraith] (form Stanley)
    dis mcd
1860, 7, 28. Leah (form Harris) con mcd
1863, 9, 25. Leah [Gailbreath] dis jG (W)
1870, 5, 28. Brinton recrq
1875, 5, 22. Brinton R. con mcd
1875, 2, 27. Martha (form Vansyoc) con mcd
1877, 1, 26. Martha (form Vansyoc) dis mcd
1886, 6, 26. Leah Y gct Winona MM
1890, 10, 25. Brinton & w, Martha J., relrq

GAMBLE

----, --, --. Morrison P. b 1815,5,1; m Phebe
    ----- b 1825,2,17
----, --, --. Homer S., s Samuel & Mary Jane
    (Fogg), b 1884,12,31; m Lena M. BOHNER, dt
    Edward & Magdalena (Miller), b 1881,12,23
      Ch: Wilfred E. b 1909, 7, 9   [(W)
        Karl S.   " 1911, 1, 21
        G. Alfred " 1912, 10, 12
        Alice M.   " 1915, 12, 17
        K. Rebecca " 1917, 8, 31
        Homer Jr. " 1919, 7, 17

1845, 6, 28. Harrison P. & w, Phebe, & s,
    Samuel, rocf Middleton MM, dtd 1845,6,12
1846, 5, 23. Harrison & w, Phebe, & ch, Sam-
    uel & Charles, gct Salem MM
1917, 10, 26. Homer S. & w, Lena M., & ch,
    Wilford Edward, Karl Samuel, Geo. Alfred,
    Alice Lena & Catharine Rebecca, rocf New
    Garden MM, dtd 1917,9,20 (W)
1920, 11, 26. Homer & w, Lena, & ch, Wilfred
    E., Carl S., G. Alfred, Alice M., K. Re-
    becca & Homer Jr., gct New Garden MM (W)

GANT
1840, 3, 29. Cassie (Dugan), w John, b

1906, 10, 27. Cassie dropped from mbrp

GARRIGUES
1862, 11, 21. Wm. dis jG (W)

GARWOOD

----, --, --. John W. b 1827,7,8; m Asenath H.
    ----- b 1825,6,5 (W)
      Ch: Annie Pris-
          cilla   b 1861, 6, 18
        Joseph D. " 1865, 7, 6
        Rachel H. " 1867, 8, 12

1836, 3, 26. Israel Negus gct Redstone MM, to
    m Lydia Garwood

1838, 9, 28. Abner Fawcett gct Redstone MM,
    to m Elizabeth Garwood
1839, 2, 22. John R. Warrington gct Redstone
    MM, to m Rachel Garwood
1879, 7, 25. John W. & w, Ascenath H., & ch,
    Anna P., Joseph D. & Rachel H., rocf New
    Garden MM, dtd 1879,7,24 (W)
1882, 6, 23. John W. & w, Asenath H., & two
    ch gct Middleton MM (W)
1883, 5, 25. Anna Priscilla Bush (form Gar-
    wood) dis mcd (W)

GASKILL
1874, 9, 22. Angeline (form Brantingham) dis
    mcd (W)

GAUNT
1891, 3, 28. Casse recrq

GIBBONS
1831, 5, 28. Hugh Judge, Edward, Isaac & Sam-
    uel, ch Samuel, rocf Sadsbury MM, Pa., dtd
    1831,4,1, end by Salem MM
1834, 6, 28. Hugh Judge, Isaac & Samuel, ch
    Samuel, gct Middleton MM
1834, 6, 28. Edward, minor, gct Middleton MM

GIBSON
1809, 11, 17. William b
----, --, --. Asa b 1794,6,12; m Mary -----
    b 1794,8,15
      Ch: Sarah   b 1821, 9, 21 d 1853, 3,15
        bur Goshen
        Letitia   b 1823, 3, 7
        Lydia S. " 1825, 8, 23
        Elizabeth " 1827, 3, 21
    Asa, s Joseph & Sarah, Columbiana Co., O.,
    b 1794,6,12; m 3rd in Springfield MH,
    Elizabeth BLACKBURN, dt David & Margaret,
    Columbiana Co., O., b 1789,11,20 d 1831,4,
    4
      Ch: Aaron   b 1831, 3, 4
1828, 11, 26. Samuel, s Joseph & Esther, Co-
    lumbiana Co., O., b 1807,2,21; m in Goshen
    MH, Ann VOTAW, dt Thomas & Elizabeth, Co-
    lumbiana Co., O., b 1811,2,16
      Ch: Elizabeth b 1830, 4, 21
        Esther   " 1832, 11, 9
        Hannah   " 1834, 12, 6
        Tamar S.   " 1836, 12, 12
        Sarah   " 1839, 2, 1
        Thomas V. " 1841, 2, 20
        John S.   " 1842, 12, 11
        Lucetta   " 1844, 10, 22
        Lydia Ann " 1846, 10, 31
        Tabitha
         Jane   " 1850, 6, 8
        Lucina L. " 1852, 5, 6
----, --, --. John b 1811,6,28; m Rebecca
    ----- b 1812,9,19 d 1857,1,12 bur Damas-
    cus
      Ch: Hannah M. b 1837, 5, 7
        Lydia S.   " 1841, 2, 8

GIBSON, John & Rebecca, continued
    Ch: Mary Ann   b 1843, 3,   4
        Amos E.   " 1844, 9, 15
        William S. " 1846, 8,   6
        John Edwin " 1849, 11, 28
        Ruth Anna " 1852, 2, 22
        Rebecca W. " 1855, 3, 29
----, --, --. Aaron b 1831,3,4; m Elizabeth
    ----- b 1833,9,4
    Ch: Mathew B. b 1859, 4,   5
        Joseph Wil-
           liam   " 1863, 3,   2
        Albion   " 1865, 7,   4
1864, 1, 2. Aaron d

1826, 6, 24. Samuel recrq
1828, 4, 26. William recrq
1830, 6, 26. Aaron roc dtd 1830,5,6
1833, 5, 25. Asa dis mou
1834, 2, 22. Wm. con mou
1834, 6, 28. William gct Marlborough MM
1841, 6, 26. Tacy (form Stanley) dis mcd
1845, 7, 26. Lydia Rogers (form Gibson) dis
    mcd
1845, 11, 22. Elizabeth dis jas
1846, 9, 29. Martha rocf Marlborough MM, dtd
    1846,6,20
1847, 12, 25. Elizabeth (form Gibson) dis mcd
1848, 8, 26. John & w, Rebecca, & ch, Hannah,
    Lydia S., Mary Ann, Amos E. & Wm. S., rocf
    Redstone MM, dtd 1848,8,2
1849, 12, 22. Sarah rocf Redstone MM, dtd
    1849,10,31
1852, 7, 24. Martha French (form Gibson) dis
    mcd
1853, 4, 23. Aaron dis
1854, 2, 25. Aaron gct White Water MM, Ind.
1854, 7, 22. Sarah gct Short Creek MM, O.
1855, 2, 24. Samuel & w, Anne, & ch, Esther,
    Hannah, Tamar, Sarah, Thomas V., John, Lu-
    cretta, Lydia Ann, Tabitha Jane & Lucina,
    gct Red Cedar MM, Ia.
1857, 8, 22. Aaron rst rq
1858, 4, 24. Aaron gct Marlborough MM, to m
    Elizabeth H. Sebrall
1858, 9, 25. Elizabeth rocf Marlborough MM
1861, 4, 27. Hannah Kelly (form Gibson) dis
    mcd
1861, 6, 22. Lydia S. gct Short Creek MM, O.
1861, 6, 22. Mary Ann gct Short Creek MM, O.
1861, 6, 22. Minor ch of John gct Short Creek
    MM, O.
1863, 3, 27. John dis jG (W)
1863, 8, 21. Elizabeth dis jG (W)
1874, 5, 23. Lydia rocf Short Creek MM, O.
1880, 3, 27. Lydia gct Columbus MM
1880, 4, 24. John gct Columbus MM
1880, 5, 22. George recrq
1886, 8, 19. Mary Ann gct Waveland MM, Ia.

GILBERT
----, --, --. Gurney, s John J. & Mary (Lamb),
    b 1876,6,28; m Elizabeth T. LLOYD, dt

Isaac & Hannah (Butler), b 1876,4,14
    Ch: Dorothy L. b 1902, 7, 4
        J. Wendell " 1905, 9, 15
----, --, --. John Wendell, s John Gurney &
    Elizabeth (Lloyd), b 1905,9,15; m Lula Mae
    STOUT, dt Lew Wallace & Ina A. (Reagan), b
    1907,10,30

1902, 1, 25. Eliza T. L. gct Hopewell MM, Ind.
1915, 11, 27. J. Gurney & w, Elizabeth Lloyd,
    & ch, Dorothy L. & J. Wendell, rocf Rich-
    mond MM
1922, 4, 22. Rhea Stanley relrq
1930, 3, 27. Lulu Mae Stout rocf New London
    MM, Ind.
1931, 5, 28. Wendell & Lulu Mae gct New Lon-
    don MM, Ind.

GILL
----, --, --. Wallace E., s Geo. & Louisa,
    b 1880,5,29; m Lottie W. COLE, dt Wm. W.
    & Jane, b 1881,3,31
    Ch: Ruth W.   b 1904, 9, 12
        Mildred L. " 1907, 5, 25

1909, 4, 24. Wallace E. & w, Lottie W., & ch,
    Ruth W. & Mildred L., rocf Alliance MM, O.
1910, 8, 18. Wallace E. & fam gct Los Angeles
    MM, Calif.

GILLESPIE
1919, 1, 25. Margaret McArtor relrq

GLOSSER
1897, 1, 23. August [Glosir] recrq
1905, 6, 24. August dropped from mbrp

GLOVER
1790, 8, 27. Mary b

1839, 7, 27. Mary gct Salem MM, Iowa

GODDARD
1906, 10, 17. Treva, dt Reuben & Elizabeth, b

1921, 10, 22. Treva recrq
1924, 8, 21. Treva gct Alliance MM

GOOD
1865, 2, 25. Rebecca, dt David & Hannah
    Mercer, b (w Wm.)

1891, 3, 28. Rebecca recrq
1905, 6, 24. Rebecca dropped from mbrp

GRAVES
1878, 1, 23. Clara L., dt Willis & Sarah, b

1900, 4, 28. Clara L. recrq

GREEN
1868, 1, 30. Jacob A., s John & Mary, Harri-
    son Co., O., b 1836,9,24 d 1925,7,17; m

GREEN, continued
    in Damascus MH, Martha G. JOHNSON, dt Ben-
    jamin & Martha, Columbiana Co., O., b 1839,
    7,20 d 1921,5,21
1871, 6, 1. Israel J., s Samuel & Ann, Harri-
    son Co., O.; m in Damascus MH, Almeda V.
    SNELLING, dt John D. & Michael E. L., Co-
    lumbiana Co., O.

1844, 4, 27. George Tatum Jr. gct Stillwater
    MM, to m Hannah Green
1868, 11, 28. Martha J. gct Flushing MM
1871, 5, 27. Israel J. rocf Gurnsey MM, dtd
    1871,4,22
1872, 8, 24. Almeda V. gct Flushing MM
1905, 11, 25. Jacob A. & w, Martha J., rocf
    Gurnsey MM, O.

GREENAMYER

----, --, --. Wm. H. b 1840,12,2; m Emma S.
    PETTIT, dt Daniel & Rebecca, b 1848,12,14
    d 1895,2,22
    Ch: Charles E. b 1876, 12, 30
        Mary M.   " 1878, 12, 20
        John D.   " 1881, 10, 21
        Clarence   " 1884, 8, 16
        Ira M.   " 1887, 2, 8
        Elsie L.   " 1891, 7, 5 d 1893, 6,10
        Rosco L.   " 1889, 7, 15 " 1892, 12,13

1881, 5, 28. Wm. H. & w, Emma, & ch, Charles
    & Mary Maud, recrq
1901, 7, 27. Maud, John & Clarence gct Alli-
    ance MM
1903, 3, 28. Wm. H. gct Los Angeles MM, Calif.
1903, 2, 28. Charles E. gct Los Angeles MM,
    Calif.
1912, 10, 26. Iva M. [Greenamyre] dropped from
    mbrp

GREENAWALT
----, --, --. John S. b 1857,3,22 d 1913,9,20
    m Mary -----
    Ch: Lewis
        Leon   b 1882, 7, 6
    John S. m 2nd Luella SHREVE, dt Evan &
    Meribah, b 1863,10,23
    Ch: Iva Ola   b 1888, 1, 25
        Theressa
        May   " 1889, 6, 15
        Effie
        Marie   " 1905, 6, 10

1897, 1, 23. John S. [Greenwalt] & ch, Lou-
    isa J., Iva Ola & Thressa Mary, recrq

GREENWOOD
1873, 2, 21. Martha (form Stanley) dis mcd
    (W)

GREWELL
----, --, --. John P. b 1810,5,19; m Sarah
    ----- b 1811,1,15
    Ch: Deborah
        Ann   b 1835, 5, 28 d 1842, 3, 9
        bur Guilford
        Caroline S.b 1836, 10, 17 " 1847,11,16
        bur Guilford
        Alice P. b 1838, 6, 1
        Ann Eliza " 1840, 12, 18
        Mary Jane " 1842, 5, 2 " 1844, 7,19
        bur Springfield
        Charles B. b 1843, 7, 16
        James C. " 1846, 6, 24 " 1846, 9, 2
        bur Guilford
        Sarah Ellenb 1850, 8, 30
    John P. m 2nd Phebe F. ----- b 1835,2,1
    (W)
1890, 6, 9. Alice P. [Gruwell] b
1835, 11, 25. John P. & w, Sarah, & dt, Debo-
    rah Ann, rocf Marlborough MM, dtd 1835,9,
    29
1838, 12, 22. John P. & w, Sarah, & ch, Debo-
    rah Ann, Caroline & Alice, gct Sandy
    Spring MM
1844, 8, 24. John P. & w, Sarah, & ch, Caro-
    line S., Alice, Ann Eliza & Charles B.,
    rocf Sandy Spring MM, dtd 1844,7,26
1845, 5, 24. John P. & w, Sarah, & ch, Caro-
    line S., Alice, Ann Eliza & Charles B.,
    gct New Garden MM
1849, 8, 25. John P. & w, Sarah, & ch, Alice
    P., Ann Eliza & Charles B., rocf New Gar-
    den MM, dtd 1849,8,23
1863, 2, 27. John P. [Gruwell] dis jG (W)
1863, 2, 27. Sarah dis jG (W)
1863, 9, 25. Alice P. [Gruwell] & Ann Eliza
    dis jG (W)
1864, 5, 28. John P. & w, Sarah, & dt, Sarah
    E., gct Marlborough MM
1865, 10, 28. Alice P. gct Alliance MM
1867, 10, 26. Ann Eliza gct Spring Creek MM,
    Ia.
1869, 6, 26. Charles B. gct Spring Creek MM,
    Ia.
1880, 1, 23. John P. [Gruwell] rst rq (W)
1880, 5, 21. John P. gct Salem MM (W)
1884, 6, 27. John P. [Gruwell] & w, Phebe F.,
    rocf Salem MM, dtd 1884,6,25
1888, 9, 18. John P. [Gruell] dis (W)
1889, 11, 23. Alice P. [Gruel] rocf Oskaloosa
    MM, Ia.
1905, 4, 21. Phebe F. [Gruwell] gct Salem MM

GRAY
----, --, --. Horrice B. [Grey] b 1860,7,9
    d 1899,7,5; m Abigail URMSON, dt Ralph &
    Abigail, b 1870,6,30
----, --, --. ----- [Grey] m Hannah G. -----

959

GRAY, continued
     b 1848,5,12
     Ch: Loren B.
1860, 7, 9. Howard B. b

1863, 5, 22. Nathan rocf Westland MM, Pa.,
     dtd 1863,3,25 (W)
1863, 5, 22. Ann rocf Westland MM, Pa., dtd
     1863,3,25 (W)

1879, 12, 27. Hannah & s, Loren B., gct Raisin
     MM, Mich.
1880, 6, 26. Howard B. recrq
1892, 11, 26. Howard B. dropped from mbrp
1894, 6, 23. Horace & w, Abigail, recrq
1897, 11, 27. Harry & w relrq
1899, 6, 24. Horace B. & w, Abigail L., recrq

GRICE
1905, 6, 24. Louisa Hall dropped from mbrp

GRIFFITH
----, --, --. William m Mary Ellen O'BRIEN, dt
     John, b 1868,5,24
     Ch: Anna
          Olive   b 1905, 3, 12
          Donald
          Otis   " 1908, 4, 21
          Myrtle   " 1911, 2, 23 d 1924, 9,19
1902, 11, 2. Phyllis Gaye, dt Wm. & Mary, b
----, --, --. Mahlon F., s Wm. & Mary Ellen,
     b 1896,7,20; m Hazel DALZELL, dt Otley V.
     & Alfretta (Lovejoy), b 1896,7,25
     Ch: Wayne B. b 1923, 3, 11
          Keith Otis " 1925, 5, 26
          Richard
          Kendall " 1929, 8, 19
          Donald Eu-
          gene   " 1929, 7, 21
          Mahlon
          Franklin " 1932, 9, 14
----, --, --. Gilbert B., s Wm. & Mary Ellen
     (O'Brien), b 1899,3,11; m Mabel Sarah
     BAILEY, b 1901,7,6
     Ch: Edra Jean b 1925, 9, 5
          Charlotte
          Ellen   " 1924, 2, 1
          Donald   " 1930, 4, 7
          Virginia
          Rose   " 1932, 3, 30

1921, 10, 22. Phillis recrq
1922, 4, 22. Mabel recrq
1922, 5, 27. Mary E., Mahlon Franklin & Anna
     Olive, rocf Mt. Pleasant MM
1922, 6, 24. S. Brenneman rocf Mt. Pleasant
     MM
1922, 10, 28. Donald & Myrtle recrq

GRIM
----, --, --. John, s John & Barbary, b 1828,
     10,18; m Mary A. SMITH, dt Wm. & Sarah,

b 1831, 7, 4
     Ch: Robert
          Grant   b 1865, 7, 5

1890, 1, 25. John & Mary A. recrq
1897, 1, 23. Grant recrq
1899, 8, 17. Dinah recrq
1900, 3, 23. Diana gct Salem MM

GRINNELL
1880, 9, 28. Jeremiah, s Sylvester & Rhoda,
     Blount Co., Tenn., b 1816,10,2; m in Da-
     mascus MH, Jane M. KILLE, dt Wm. & Rebecca
     b 1825,6,30
     Ch: (by Jeremiah's first w)
          Evalyn   b 1862, 11, 2

1881, 4, 23. Jeremiah rocf Friendsville MM,
     Tenn.
1882, 7, 22. M. Evalyn rocf Friendsville MM,
     Tenn.
1887, 12, 24. Jeremiah A. & w, Jane M., gct
     Pasadena MM, Calif.

GROVE
1860, 11, 23. Lucinda (form Fawcett) dis mcd
     (W)
1862, 12, 27. Lucinda (form Fawcett) dis mcd

GUINDON
1911, 9, 20. Joseph N., s Francis T. & Su-
     sanna H. (Battey), b 1890,9,11; m Zoa
     Caroline MILES, dt Carroll H. & Selma
     (Taber), b 1887,9,10 (W)
     Ch: Carroll
          Taber   b 1913, 1, 27
          George Al-
          bert   " 1914, 8, 31
          Frances
          Ruth   " 1919, 8, 11

1912, 3, 22. Zoa Miles gct Nantucket MM,
     Mass. (W)
1919, 2, 21. Joseph N. & w, Zoa, & ch, Car-
     roll & George, rocf Nantucket MM, R. I.,
     dtd 1919,1,30 (W)
1922, 4, 21. Joseph N. & w, Zoa, & ch, George
     A., Carroll T. & Frances, gct Fairhope
     MM, Ala. (W)

GYGER
1869, 10, 22. Elma (form Lee) dis mcd (W)

HAINES
----, --, --. Chalkley b 1803,7,8 d 1852,3,30
     bur Springfield; m Sarah E. ----- b 1802,2
     23
     Ch: Esther   b 1825, 3, 17
          Eliza Ann " 1828, 9, 27 d 1836,10, 7
          Joseph W. " 1830, 11, 10

HAINES, continued
    Ch: Lydia M.   b 1832, 11, 15 d 1844,11, 5
        Mary T.   " 1834, 8, 6 " 1834, 6, 8
        Maria P.   " 1834, 8, 6 " 1836, 9,27
        Benjamin L." 1834, 8, 6
        Eli J.   " 1837, 12, 2
        Robert M. " 1836, 12, 29
        Matilda T. " 1840, 7, 16
        Thomas C. " 1842, 4, 21
        James Oli-
          ver   " 1864, 3, 10
1848, 11, 2. Esther W. m Jesse ALLMAN
1851, 7, 8. Chalkley d ae 49 (an elder)

1833, 11, 23. Chalkley & w, Sarah, & ch, Es-
    ther, Eliza-Ann, Joseph W. & Lydia M.,
    rocf Redstone MM, dtd 1833,10,30
1842, 12, 24. Rebecca (form Armstrong) dis mcd
1855, 10, 27. Joseph N. gct Western Plain MM,
    Ia.
1856, 8, 23. Benjamin L. gct Westland MM, Ia.
1856, 12, 27. Sarah E. & ch, Eli Jess, Robert
    M., Matilda E., Thomas C. & James Oliver,
    gct Westland MM, Ia.
1863, 9, 25. Joseph dis jG (W)
1863, 9, 25. Benjamin dis jG (W)
1863, 9, 25. Sarah E. dis jG (W)
1869, 7, 24. Genevieve W. (form Jones) dis
    mcd
1870, 8, 27. Rebecca recrq

HALDERMAN
1850, 10, 3. Joseph, s David & Ann, b 1827,5,
    15 d 1917,12,6; m in Springfield MH, Es-
    ther CREW, dt John & Margery, Mahoning Co.,
    O., b 1833,3,8 d 1925,9,17
    Ch: Lauretta   b 1851, 9, 1
        Sarah B.   " 1853, 1, 24
        Josephine " 1854, 8, 31
        Edwin G.   " 1856, 9, 26
        Alonzo O. " 1858, 9, 15
        Oscar J.   " 1863, 5, 10
        David Elly-
          son   " 1868, 11, 10
        Anna   " 1877, --, --
1883, 8, 16. Mabel, dt Edwin & Maria, b
1904, 10, 26. Mary Gladys, dt Benj. & Chris-
    tina (Caskey), b

1851, 5, 24. Esther gct Sandy Spring MM
1862, 5, 24. Joseph & w, Esther, & ch, Lau-
    retta, Sarah B., Josephine, Edwin G. &
    Alonzo O., rocf Sandy Spring MM
1865, 6, 24. Joseph & w, Esther, & ch, Lo-
    retta, Sarah B., Josephine, Ervin G.,
    Alonzo & Osker, gct Sandy Spring MM
1867, 5, 25. Joseph & w, Esther, & ch, Lau-
    retta, Sarah B., Josephine, Edwin G.,
    Alonzo O. & Oscar J., rocf Sandy Spring
    MM, O., dtd 1867,5,21
1898, 2, 26. Mabel recrq
1906, 7, 28. Joseph & Esther rocf East Goshen
    MM

1909, 4, 24. Anna J. rocf East Goshen MM
1921, 3, 25. Ida D. (form Ashton) dis mcd (W)
1932, 4, 28. Mary Gladys recrq

HALL
180-, 5, 3. Rebecca (Stanley), w Charles, b
----, --, --. Achsah b 1816,8,5 d 1872,8,9 bur
    Springfield (W)
1851, 3, 27. Jesse, s John & Tacy, Mahoning
    Co., O., b 1818,12,31; m in Springfield
    MH, Edith STANLEY, dt John Jr. & Abigail,
    Mahoning Co., O., b 1822,2,18
    Ch: Abigail S. b 1853, 4, 29
        Ezra   " 1855, 3, 3 d 1857, 3,29
        Elma   " 1855, 3, 3 " 1902, 5,20
        Mary Ellen " 1857, 4, 11
        Louisa   " 1860, 9, 22
----, --, --. Tilman b 1831,5,18; m Mary Eliza
    ----- b 1837,1,22
    Ch: Alice Ann b 1856, 3, 30
        Charles
          Henry   " 1860, 4, 9
        Emmor Wm. " 1861, 10, 23
        Ira K.   " 1865, 5, 24
        George B. " 1868, 8, 2
1861, 12, 13. Sarah E. (Coppock), w Emmor W.,
    b
1877, 10, 31. Abigail m Jones M. BECK
----, --, --. Charles H., s Tilman & Mary, b
    1860,4,9; m Rebecca STANLEY, dt Robert &
    Sarah, b 1860,5,3
    Ch: Walter W. b 1885, 7, 30
----, --, --. Wilson M., s Linton & Ann W.
    (Allman); m Mary Anna Edgerton, dt Jesse
    & Semira (Stratton), b 1866,8,15 d 1929,4,
    8 bur Damascus (Wilson M. b 1868,1,4)
    Ch: Jessie M. b 1894, 6, 23
        Foster A. " 1896, 10, 17
        Wilford Lin-
          ton   b 1902, 2, 20
        Edward
          Stratton " 1907, 12, 6
        Marian Helen
              b 1911, 7, 24 (foster ch)
----, --, --. Edwin P. m Minnie Catharine
    LOHMAN
    Ch: Nellie
        Ruth   b 1906, 12, 15
        Henry Lee " 1908, 11, 2
1907, 3, 26. Barclay S. m Mary CAMERON (W)
1908, 7, 14. Helen S., w Donald, dt Homer C.
    & Clara H. (Stanley) Phillips, b
----, --, --. Charles W., s Linton & Anna W.
    (Allman), b 1871,5,5; m Nettie M. BURT,
    b 1874,3,26 (W)
    Ch: Mildred b 1909, 8, 8
1907, 3, 26. Barclay S., s Lewis & Margaret
    Ann (Benns); m Mary CAMERON, dt Milton
    & Beulah (Fogg), b 1887,2,16
    Ch: Willard B. b 1910, 6, 13
        Beulah M. " 1912, 8, 10
        Francis
          Lindley " 1915, 10, 14

HALL, Barclay S. & Mary, continued
    Ch: Albert Ed-
        win   b 1917, 10, 24
----, --, --. Edwin P., s Linton & Ann W. (All-
    man), b 1879,11,19; m Minnie Catharine
    LOHMAN, dt Peter & Susanna (Wenger), b
    1883,12,8 (W)
    Ch: Walter
        Linton   b 1910, 8, 3
        Ezra Ben-
        jamin   " 1911, 12, 2
        Oscar
        Charles   " 1913, 8, 20
        Harry Edwin" 1916, 3, 31
        Oliver
        Horace   " 1921, 8, 8
        Wilmer
        Jeremiah " 1923, 9, 18
        Elsie Vir-
        ginia   " 1926, 4, 18
1920, 9, 7. Foster Arthur, s Wilson M. &
    Mary Anna (Edgerton), b 1896,10,17; m
    Ruthanna HEALD, dt Delbert & Esther (Mott),
    b 1896,11,14 (W)
    Ch: Wilson
        Luther   b 1921, 7, 1
        Mary Es-
        ther   " 1923, 12, 3
        Elton Har-
        rold   " 1926, 9, 30
        Ardith
        Eleanore " 1932, 10, 10
----, --, --. Wilfred Linton, s Wilson M. &
    Mary Anna (Edgerton), b 1902,2,20; m Ethel
    PICKETT (W)
    Ch: Delbert
        Lester   b 1923, 5, 7
        Wilford
        Leland   " 1925, 3, 2
        Donald Lin-
        ton   " 1928, 1, 2

1851, 2, 22. Jesse rocf Short Creek MM, O.,
    dtd 1851,1,21
1856, 7, 26. Cynthia A. J. (form Jones) dis
    mcd
1860, 1, 27. Achsah rocf Sandy Spring MM, O.,
    dtd 1859,12,20 (W)
1863, 4, 24. Jesse & Edith dis jG (W)
1863, 5, 22. Abner Woolman gct Middleton MM,
    to m Elvira Hall (W)
1867, 2, 23. Tillman & w, Mary Eliza, & ch,
    Alice Ann, Charles Henry, Emmor Wm. & Ira
    K., rocf Short Creek MM, O.
1876, 3, 25. Jesse relrq
1884, 7, 26. Charles rocf East Goshen MM
1889, 1, 26. Sarah E. gct East Goshen MM
1901, 5, 20. Edith gct Earlham MM, Ia.
1904, 8, 18. Charles H. & w, Rebecca S., & s,
    Walter W., gct Washington MM, D. C.
1905, 6, 24. Louisa(Hall)Grice dropped from
    mbrp
1907, 3, 22. Wilson M. & w, Maryanna E., &

ch, Jessie M., Foster A. & Wilford Linton,
    rocf Middleton MM, dtd 1907,3,16 (W)
1907, 8, 23. Mary Cameron gct Short Creek
    MM, O. (W)
1911, 10, 27. Thomas C. Warrington gct Middle-
    ton MM, to m Sarah Mabel Hall
1914, 3, 27. Barclay S. & w, Mary C., & ch,
    Willard B. & Beulah M., rocf New Garden
    MM, dtd 1914,2,26
1918, 2, 22. Edwin P. & w, Minnie Catharine,
    & ch, Nellie Ruth, Henry Lee, Walter Lin-
    ton, Ezra Benjamin, Oscar Chas. & Harry
    Edwin, rocf Middleton MM, dtd 1918,2,16
    (W)
1921, 6, 24. Marian Hellen, minor in care of
    Wilson M. & Maryanna E., recrq (W)
1921, 8, 26. Barclay S. & Mary A. & ch, Wil-
    lard Barclay, Beulah Margaret, Francis
    Lindley & Albert Edwin, gct Pasadena MM,
    Calif. (W)
1921, 12, 23. Wilson Mifflin & w, Maryanna E.,
    & ch, Edward S. & Marian Helen, gct Still-
    water MM (W)
1922, 7, 21. Wilford L. gct Plainfield MM,
    Ind., to m Ethel Pickett (W)
1926, 9, 24. Wilson Mifflin & w, Mary Anna
    E., & ch, Edward S. & Marian Helen, rocf
    Stillwater MM, dtd 1926,8,25 (W)
1928, 1, 27. Wilford L. & ch, Delbert Les-
    ter, Wilford Leland & Donald Linton, gct
    Stillwater MM (W)
1928, 4, 27. Charles W. & w, Nettie M., & dt,
    Mildred, rocf Middleton MM (W)
1928, 6, 22. Edwin P. & w, Minnie C., & ch,
    Henry L., Walter L., Ezra B., Oscar C.,
    Harry E., Wilmer J. & Elsie V., gct Holly
    Spring MM, N. C.(W)
1928, 6, 22. Nellie R. gct Holly Spring MM,
    N. C. (W)
1930, 10, 24. W. Mifflin gct Stillwater MM, to
    m Marianna Foster (W)
1931, 2, 27. Marianna Foster rocf Stillwater
    MM, dtd 1931,7,22 (W)
1931, 9, 25. Edwin P. & w, Minnie C., & ch,
    Walter L., Ezra B., Oscar C., Harry E.,
    Wilmer J. & Elsie V., rocf Holly Spring
    MM, N. C., dtd 1931,8,8 (W)

HALLMAN
1926, 1, 22. Alma Brantingham dropped from
    mbrp (W)

HAMBLETON
1852, 2, 28. Ann (form Courtney) dis mcd

HAMLIN
1863, 8, 21. Stephen & Abigail dis jG (W)

HAMMIT
1829, 4, 25. Ellen (form Reeve) dis mou
1835, 4, 25. Ellen rst at Marlborough MM on
    consent of this mtg

HADLY

----, --, --. Herbert L. b 1884,2,13; m Mary
  E. McLAUGHLIN, b 1879,1,10
    Ch: Helen A.   b 1915, 1, 3
        Josephine A.
                    b 1920, 2, 18

1921, 10, 22. Herbert H. [Haldy] & fam rocf
  Adrian MM, Mich.
1921, 12, 23. Edith M. (form Cameron) dis mcd
  (W)
1927, 10, 27. Herbert [Haldy] & fam gct Van
  Wert MM, O.

HAMPTON

1851, 11, 27. Jason, s Thomas & Hannah, Morgan
  Co., O., b 1822,1,14 d 1861,5,12 bur
  Springfield; m in Springfield MH, Mary Ann
  WALTON, dt Jonathan & Maria, Columbiana
  Co., O., b 1822,11,25
    Ch: Louisa   b 1853, 9, 16

1853, 3, 26. Jason rocf Chesterfield MM, dtd
  1853,2,19
1863, 1, 24. Mary Ann dis jW
1874, 6, 26. Mary Ann & Eliza dis disunity
  (W)

HANK

----, --, --. Judith b 1751,5,9 d 1830,3,5
  bur Springfield

1835, 4, 25. Judith rocf Providence MM, dtd
  1835,4,2

HANNAY

1875, 3, 22. Mary, w Charles H., dt Hilles &
  Isabella (Coe) Linton), b

HARLAN

----, --, --. Joseph b 1781,9,10; m Hannah
  ----- b 1782,10,26
    Ch: Sarah Ann b 1818, 3, 31
        Samuel   " 1820, 12, 15
        Joseph   " 1822, 2, 24

1828, 6, 28. Joseph [Harlen] dis disunity
1828, 12, 27. Hannah [Harlin] dis jH
1837, 8, 26. Sarah Ann dis jH
1843, 1, 28. Mary Ann (form Barber) dis mcd
1844, 7, 27. Joseph Jr. dis jH
1845, 7, 26. Samuel dis jH

HARRIS

----k --, --. Robert b 1805,11,15 d 1878,9,6
  bur Damascus; m Sarah Y. ----- b 1812,12,1
  d 1878,11,23 bur Damascus
    Ch: Leah   b 1835, 6, 21
        Oliver   " 1837, 6, 7 d 1859, 3, 2
          bur Damascus
        Enoch R. b 1841, 8, 7 " 1877, 9,13
          bur Damascus
        Milison S. b 1843, 8, 3 " 1868,10,28

bur Damascus
    Ch: Lemuel   b 1845, 4, 24 d 1871, 7,25
        bur Damascus

1853, 12, 24. Robert & w, Sarah, & ch, Olover,
  Enoch, Milicent & Lemuel, rocf New Garden
  MM, dtd 1853,9,22
1853, 12, 24. Leah rocf New Garden MM, dtd
  1853,9,22
1860, 7, 28. Leah Galbreath (form Harris)
  con mcd
1863, 9, 25. Robert, Enoch & Millicent dis
  jG (W)

HARTLEY

----, --, --. Mary b 1795,9,25 d 1872,6,28

1867, 6, 22. Mary rocf Alliance MM, dtd
  1867,5,28

HARTZELL

1873, 9, 27. Mary Ellen (form Stanley) con
  mcd
1880, 12, 25. Mary Ellen relrq
1881, 1, 22. Mary Ellen rst rq
1884, 2, 23. Mary Ellen dropped from mbrp

HATHAWAY

----, --, --. Caleb b 1832,9,25; m Sarah D.
  ----- b 1839,1,7
    Ch: Alford C. b 1858, 9, 5
        Ida Eliza   " 1860, 1, 26 d 1870,12,11
          bur Damascus
        Edith Aliceb 1863, 5, 6
        Caspar
          Henry   " 1865, 2, 15 d 1888, 8,26
        Francis
          Herman   " 1867, 7, 20 " 1888, 9, 5
        Mary Eva   " 1870, 10, 23 " 1888, 8,31
        William A. " 1872, 7, 9
        Earnest   " 1877, 8, 15

1868, 8, 22. Caleb & w, Sarah, & ch, Alfred
  Caleb, Ida Eliza, Edith Alice, Caspar Henry & Francis Herman, rocf Greenwich MM,
  dtd 1868,7,10
1882, 10, 28. Alfred C. gct Hanover MM, Mich.
1891, 3, 28. Caleb & w, Sarah D., granted
  open letter
1891, 11, 28. Edith R. relrq
1895, 6, 22. Wm. A. & Ernest relrq

HAWKES

1828, 12, 28. Lydia Maria, dt Martha S. Stanley, b
1859, 3, 31. Lydia m Jehu STANLEY

1857, 1, 24. Joseph Stanley Jr. gct Salem
  MM, to m Martha S. Hawks
1857, 4, 25. Lydia Mariah [Hawks] rocf Salem
  MM

HAWLEY
1863, 7, 24. Benjamin & Mary dis jG (W)

HAWN
1929, 6, 27. Helen Ball dropped from mbrp

HAWORTH
----, --, --. Charles Edgar b 1884,4,13; m
     Frances Willard GREEN b 1888,3,15
       Ch: Edgar G.   b 1910, 5, 10
           Henrietta " 1915, 5, 16

1916, 1, 22. Charles & w, Frances, & ch,
     Edgar & Henrietta, rocf Alliance MM
1919, 1, 25. Charles & w, Frances, & ch gct
     E. Cleveland MM

HAYHURST
----, --, --. William b 1792,2,2; m Jane -----
     b 1792,8,26
       Ch: Lydia   b 1815, 7, 25
           Susan   " 1817, 4, 4
           Bazaleel   " 1819, 2, 2
           Elizabeth " 1821, 4, 10
           Thomas   " 1824, 12, 1
           Mary   " 1826, 2, 12
           William   " 1828, 2, 28

1828, 10, 25. Wm. dis jH
1828, 10, 25. Jane dis jH
1836, 6, 25. Lydia dis jH
1838, 3, 24. Susan dis jH
1840, 5, 23. Elizabeth dis
1843, 5, 27. Bazaleel dis jH
1844, 1, 27. Mary dis jH
1845, 8, 23. Thomas dis disunity
1850, 1, 26. Wm. Jr. dis disunity
1852, 8, 28. Mary Ann (form Taylor) dis mcd

HAYNAM
1868, 11, 28. Louisa G. (form Thomas) dis mcd

HEACOCK
----, --, --. Nathan b 1783,4,16; m Dinah -----
     b 1781,10,24
       Ch: Amos D.   b 1808, 10, 27
           Edwin   " 1811, 4, 19
           Jane D.   " 1812, 6, 12
           Asenath   " 1814, 6, 26
           Milton   " 1815, 12, 23
           Borton   " 1818, 1, 13
           Ariah A. " 1819, 6, 14
           Elias H. " 1821, 1, 6
           Enos   " 1822, 9, 5
           Josiah W. " 1824, 7, 28
           Tacy   " 1827, 4, 22
1883, 4, 6. Rachel, dt Clarkson & Elizabeth,
     b

1828, 10, 25. Nathan dis jH
1828, 12, 27. Dinah dis jH
1832, 11, 24. Jane Borton (form Heacock) dis
     mou in H

1833, 8, 24. Edwin dis jH
1833, 9, 28. Amos dis jH
1836, 4, 23. Asenath dis jH
1836, 8, 27. Hannah (form Barber) dis mcd
1838, 7, 28. Milton dis disunity
1840, 1, 25. Rachel (form Barber) dis mcd in
     H
1840, 2, 22. Barton dis mcd in H
1844, 1, 27. Sarah (form Barber) dis mcd
1844, 5, 25. Elias H. dis mcd & jH
1844, 7, 27. Enos dis jH
1868, 8, 21. John & w, Ann, & ch gct Hickory
     Grove MM, Ia. (W)
1900, 3, 24. Rachel recrq
1915, 11, 27. Laura gct Beloit MM

HEALD
1783, 10, 13. Mary b d 1867,3,15 bur Goshen
1818, 5, 16. Rebecca b
1825, 9, 6. Lydia b
----, --, --. Levi b 1808,11,27; m Lydia
     ----- b 1809,4,4
       Ch: Samuel   b 1830, 9, 18
           Lucina   " 1832, 4, 24
           Louisa   " 1835, 3, 11
1920, 9, 7. Ruth A. m Foster A. HALL (W)

1831, 10, 22. Levi & w, Lydia, & s, Samuel,
     rocf New Garden MM, dtd 1831,9,22
1836, 5, 28. Levi dis disunity
1837, 1, 28. Lydia & ch, Samuel, Lucina &
     Louisa, gct Pennsville MM
1858, 9, 25. Mary rocf Sandy Spring MM
1858, 9, 25. Rebecca rocf Sandy Spring MM
1858, 9, 25. Lydia rocf Sandy Spring MM
1867, 1, 26. Lucina rocf Chesterdield MM, dtd
     1866,12,26
1867, 2, 22. Lydia rocf Plymouth MM, dtd
     1866,12,17 (W)
1867, 11, 23. Lydia & Rebecca gct Kansas MM,
     Kans.
1920, 7, 23. Ruthanna rocf Coal Creek MM, dtd
     1920,7,10 (W)

HECKEL
1858, 2, 27. Sarah V. (form Stanley) dis mcd

HEESTON
----, --, --. Homer m Ada Odessa STANLEY, dt
     Leander & Elmina, b 1872,2,12 d 1929,3,12

HEMINGWAY
----, --, --. Elizabeth b 1757,3,17 d 1837,1,
     15 bur Springfield
----, --, --. James b 1801,7,23; m Hope -----
     b 1804,9,7
       Ch: Jane M.   b 1824, 4, 30
           Eleazer   " 1825, 11, 6
           Abigail   " 1827, 7, 27
           Isaac   " 1829, 11, 13
           Joseph   " 1831, 10, 12
           Elizabeth " 1834, 12, 28
           John   " 1836, 3, 3

HEMINGWAY, James & Hope, continued
    Ch: Sarah   b 1838, 4, 1
       James   " 1840, 7, 10
       Benjamin   " 1843, 2, 12
       David   " 1845, 8, 28
1846, 4, 29. Jane M. m Oliver BURDGE
1846, 12, 2. Abigail m Benjamin ELLYSON

1827, 10, 27. Abigail [Hemmingway] gct Phila.
    MM, Pa.
1828, 8, 23. James [Hemmingway] dis
1850, 11, 28. Eleazer dis mcd
1854, 4, 22. Isaac gct Red Cedar MM, Ia.
1854, 4, 22. Hope & ch, Elizabeth C., John W.,
    Sarah, James, Benjamin & David, gct Red
    Cedar MM, Ia.
1856, 4, 26. Joseph [Hemmingway] con mcd
1857, 2, 28. Joseph gct Driftwood MM, Ind.

HESTON
1899, 8, 29. Agnes, dt Homer & Odessa, b

1923, 2, 24. Agnes recrq
1928, 2, 23. Agnes (Heston) White relrq

HIBBARD
1851, 4, 26. Jehu R. rocf Goshen MM, Pa.,
    dtd 1851,8,29
1863, 10, 24. Jehu L. dis mcd

HICK
1905, 6, 24. Levena Naylor dropped from mbrp

HILES
1829, 9, 26. Rachel gct Salem MM

HINCHMAN
1842, 3, 26. Rebecca T. (form Bradshaw) dis
    mcd

HIVELY
1853, 9, 16. Louisa b
1860, 10, 19. Elmor, s George, b

1879, 8, 23. Louisa relrq
1880, 5, 22. Elmer recrq
1884, 4, 26. Emor dropped from mbrp

HOBBS
1843, 3, 29. Barnabas C., s William & Pris-
    cilla, Jefferson Co., O.; m in Goshen MH,
    Rebecca TATUM, dt George & Beulah, Colum-
    biana Co., O.
1843, 5, 27. Rebecca T. gct White Water MM,
    Ind.

HOBSON
----, --, --. ----- m Sarah Ann ----- b 1823,
    11,21 d 1888,1,29
    Ch: Edwin T.   b 1851, 4, 5
       Thomas
        Chalkley " 1853, 1, 24 d 1872, 7,24
        bur Damascus

    Ch: John A.   b 1859, 11, 6
----, --, --. Edwin T. b 1851,4,5 d 1897,2,11;
    m Esther -----, dt Osborn & Margaret STAN-
    LEY, b 1852,6,18
    Ch: Laura   b 1883, 7, 8
       Flora   " 1883, 7, 8
       Carl Edwin " 1888, 1, 21
       Lee Stanley" 1890, 12, 12 d 1894, 4,23
----, --, --. Carl Edwin b 1888,1,21; m Isa-
    dore Pearl DELZELL, dt Otley V. & Alfretta
    b 1891,1,29
    Ch: Elizabeth
       Ruth   b 1914, 11, 13
       Margaret
       Virginia " 1917, 10, 17
       Robert Le-
       land   " 1922, 9, 21

1864, 8, 27. Sarah Ann & ch, Edwin S., Thomas
    Chalkley & John A., rocf Smithfield MM,
    dtd 1864,6,20
1897, 10, 23. John A. dropped from mbrp

HODGIN
----, --, --. Elza, s John E. & Tamir D. (Ver-
    non), b 1867,9,28; m Sarah POLLARD, dt
    Geo. & Mary J. (Cohoe), b 1869,9,12 (W)
    Ch: Margery
       Alice   b 1916, 6, 3 (adopted)

1920, 4, 20. Elza & w, Sarah P., rocf Nor-
    wich MM, Canada, dtd 1920,4,14 (W)
1923, 2, 23. Margery Alice, adopted dt Elza
    & Sarah P., recrq (W)
1924, 11, 21. Elza & w, Sarah P., & dt, Mar-
    gery Alice, gct Whittier MM, Calif. (W)

HOGAN
1918, 11, 23. Ruthanna dropped from mbrp

HOGE
1847, 7, 24. James rocf Short Creek MM, O.,
    dtd 1847,3,23
1870, 1, 22. Sarah A. (form Jones) con mcd
1875, 10, 23. Sarah B. [Hogue] gct Short Creek
    MM, O.

HOILES
1760, 7, 26. Rachel b

HOLE
----, --, --. Nathan b 1794,4,3 d 1870,11,9
    bur Middleton; m Sarah ----- b 1793,9,22
    d 1870,2,20 ae 77 bur Carmel (an elder)
    (W)
1840, 3, 13. Lemuel, s John & Catherine,
    Carroll Co.; m in Springfield MH, Unity C.
    STANLEY, dt Benjamin & Elizabeth, Colum-
    biana Co., O., b 1820,1,27
    Ch: Catharine
       Elizabeth b 1846, 10, 5
       Eliza Ann " 1848, 12, 27
       Jacob T. " 1854, 3, 18

HOLE, Lemuel & Unity, continued
    Ch: Charles S. b 1856, 8, 11
        Esther El-
            ma   " 1858, 7, 31
        Lemuel
            Penrose " 1860, 11, 5 d 1904, 5, 1
    Unity m 2nd James RALEY, b 1799,8,3 d 1872,
    10,14 bur Damascus
----, --, --. James M. b 1822,6,14; m Hannah
    ----- b 1824,11,2 (W)
    Ch: Linneaus C. b 1847, 5, 30
        Ruthanna   " 1850, 9, 2
1853, 10, 27. Robert H., s John & Catharine,
    Carroll Co., O.; m in Damascus MH, Lydia
    H. LIPSEY, dt Edmund & Sarah, Mahoning Co.,
    O.
----, --, --. Israel P., s Mahlon & Rachel,
    b 1827,2,4 d 1857,4,28; m Mary MILLER, dt
    Morris & Ann, b 1831,7,29 d 1911,12,28
    Ch: Morris J. b 1861, 2, 3
1868, 7, 2. Unity C. m James RALEY
1869, 3, 4. Anna E. m Robert T. CREW
----, --, --. Caleb, s John & Catharine, b
    1827,3,6; m Sophia A. MILLER, dt Morris &
    Ann, b 1839,1,8
    Ch: Anna L.   b 1873, 6, 18
        Norman W. " 1879, 5, 23 d 1896, 3, 8
            bur Damascus
----, --, --. Charles S. b 1856,8,11; m Hannah
    W. ----- b 1860,1,16
    Ch: Edward S. b 1881, 3, 5
        Carle C.   " 1884, 7, 3
        Elizabeth " 1889, 10, 17
        Esther   " 1894, 10, 20
        William Rus-
            sell   b 1896, 5, 31

1840, 8, 22. Unity gct Sandy Spring MM
1854, 3, 23. Lydia H. gct Sandy Spring MM
1858, 6, 25. Nathan & w, Sarah, rocf Salem
    MM, dtd 1858,6,23 (W)
1862, 2, 21. James M. & w, Hannah B., & ch,
    Linnaeus E. & Ruth Anna, rocf Salem MM,
    dtd 1862,2,19
1866, 10, 27. Israel P. & w, Mary M., & ch,
    Mahlon W. & Morris J., gct Sandy Spring
    MM
1868, 4, 25. Unity C. & ch, Jacob Thomas,
    Chas. Stanley, Esther Elma & Lemuel Pen-
    rose, rocf Sandy Spring MM, dtd 1868,4,21
1868, 4, 25. Catharine & Eliza Ann rocf Sandy
    Spring MM, dtd 1868,4,21
1869, 1, 22. Linnaeus C. dis mcd (W)
1869, 8, 26. Rachel Ann (form Painter) dis·
    mcd (W)
1870, 6, 24. James M. dis disunity (W)
1874, 1, 23. Ruthanna Park (form Hole) dis
    mcd (W)
1873, 8, 23. Catherine E. Bashaw (form Hole)
    con mcd
1878, 7, 26. Hannah dis disunity (W)
1878, 4, 27. Israel P. & w, Mary, & s, Morris
    J.. rocf Sandy Spring MM

1884, 11, 22. Hannah W. rocf Westland MM, O.
1889, 12, 28. Caleb & w, Sophia, & ch, Norman
    W. & Anna S., rocf Sandy Spring MM
1901, 5, 20. Charles S. & w, Hannah W., & ch,
    Edward L., Carl C., Elizabeth Esther, Wm.
    Russell, gct Westland MM, O.
1906, 4, 28. Norman W. relrq
1915, 11, 27. Sophia M. gct West Whittier MM,
    Calif.

HOLLINGSWORTH
----, --, --. Martha b 1818,9,29 d 1892,5,21
    bur Upper Springfield (W)
1858, 10, 26. Milton, s Wm. & Mary, Tippecanoe
    Co., Ind.; m ih Springfield MH, Elizabeth
    BINFORD, dt Joseph & Margaret, Columbiana
    Co., O.

1859, 4, 23. Elizabeth B. gct Greenfield MM,
    Ind.
1863, 9, 25. Elizabeth dis jG (W)

HOLLOWAY
----, --, --. Edwin b 1813,8,27 d 1903,5,8
    bur Springfield; m Rebecca D. ----- b 1816.
    3,29 d 1884,11,14 bur Springfield
    Ch: Rhoda
            Elizabeth b 1839, 7, 15
        Jesse   " 1840, 12, 8
        Alice Ann " 1843, 2, 13
        Sarah T. " 1845, 4, 21
        Lindley   " 1847, 4, 28
        Joseph S. " 1850, 11, 17

1848, 5, 27. Joseph Steward gct Marlborough
    MM, to m Emeline Holloway
1851, 5, 24. Sarah rocf Marlborough MM, dtd
    1851,4,29
1851, 5, 24. Emily, minor, rocf Marlborough
    MM, dtd 1851,4,29
1853, 11, 26. Emily, minor, gct Salem MM
1854, 6, 24. Wm. E. rocf Marlborough MM, dtd
    1854,5,30
1854, 8, 26. David rocf Marlborough MM, dtd
    1854,7,25
1855, 4, 28. Lydia D. rst on consent of Salem
    MM
1855, 8,25. Wm. E. & w, Lydia D., gct Red
    Cedar MM, Ia.
1856, 1, 25. Sarah P. gct Salem MM (W)
1856, 3, 21. Rachel (form Middleton) dis mcd
    (W)
1860, 5, 25. Edwin & w, Rebecca D., & ch,
    Jesse, Alice Ann, Sarah T. Lindley & Jo-
    seph S., rocf Salem MM, dtd 1860,5,13 (W)
1860, 5, 25. Rhoda E. rocf Salem MM, dtd
    1860,4,25 (W)
1862, 3, 22. Edwin & w, Rebecca, & ch, Sarah,
    Lindley & Joseph, rocf Salem MM
1863, 1, 24. Edwin & w, Rebecca D., & ch,
    Sarah, Lindley & Joseph, dis jW
1863, 4, 24. Alice A. rmt Abner S. Woolman
    (W)

HOLLOWAY, continued
1866, 3, 23. David dis mcd (W)
1866, 3, 23. Rhoda Pim (form Holloway) dis mcd
    (W)
1868, 12, 25. Lindley M. dis mcd & jas (W)
1869, 2, 26. Martha rocf New Garden MM, dtd
    1869,2,25 (W)
1869, 10, 22. David rst at Coal Creek MM, Ia.
    on consent of this mtg (W)
1871, 4, 21. Edwin & w, Rebecca D., & s, Jo-
    seph, gct Salem MM (W)
1872, 10, 25. Sarah Carr (form Holloway) dis
    mcd (W)
1874, 1, 23. Edwin & w, Rebecca D., rocf Salem
    MM, dtd 1873,12,24 (W)
1887, 3, 25. Jesse dis mcd (W)
1906, 10, 26. Alice A. Woolman (form Holloway)
    dis mcd (W)

HOLLY
----, --, --. John B. b 1862,12,25; m Fanny
    O. ----- b 1869,6,13

1883, 7, 28. John dropped from mbrp
1884, 6, 26. Anna V. (form Vansyoc) dis mcd
    (W)
1886, 4, 24. John B. & Fannie O. recrq
1887, 10, 22. John B. & Fannie O. dropped
    from mbrp

HOLMES
1852, 12, 25. Emily (form Stratton) dis mcd

HOOK
1856, 9, 27. Cidna C. (form Cobbs) dis mcd

HOOPES
----, --, --. Phineas b 1811,--,-- d 1865,3,1;
    m Mary R. ----- b 1816,11,16 d 1866,1,16
    bur New Garden (W)
    Ch: William A. b 1843, 9, 13
        Phebe Ann " 1845, 4, 18
        Alfred   " 1847, 6, 22
        Marshal B. " 1849, 1, 22 d 1869,12,23
1846, 4, 2. Lewis W., s Thomas & Charity,
    Columbiana Co., O., b 1824,2,7 d 1896,1,5;
    m in Springfield MH, Sarah Ann BLACKBURN,
    dt Barbee & Elizabeth, Columbiana Co., O.,
    b 1821,7,2 d 1872,4,1 bur Damascus
    Ch: John Henry b 1849, 1, 11
        Charity
          Elizabeth " 1850, 7, 10
        James C.   " 1855, 9, 23
        Byron R.   " 1858, 5, 22
----, --, --. Wm. A. [Hoops] b 1843,9,13 d
    1916,12,16; m Lucinda C. ----- b 1845,6,7
    d 1919,3,6
    Ch: Walter M. b 1870, 1, 27 d 1913, 9,24
        Albert J. " 1874, 7, 20
        Malcolm C. " 1878, 9, 17
        Marietta   " 1880, 8, 20
        Lynden Roy " 1886, 9, 23
----, --, --. James C., s Lewis & Sarah Ann,

m Emma V. ELLETT, dt John & Elmira (Card),
    b 1858,11,12
    Ch: Lewis J.   b 1881, 8, 17
        Irving T. " 1883, 1, 9
        Russel E. " 1886, 2, 24
        Myra E.   " 1887, 10, 21
        Clarence B." 1889, 9, 16
        Wilmer J. " 1891, 1, 30
        Esther B. " 1894, 10, 19
----, --, --. Albert, s Wm. A. & Lucinda, b
    1874,7,20; m Viola ----- b 1877,1,31
    Ch: William
        Joseph   b 1902, 3, 9 d 1907, 1,11
        Elsie Grace" 1907,12, 5
----, --, --. Lewis J. b 1881,8,17 d 1925,9,29
    m Mary Emma KUNTZMAN dt Robert & Louisa
    (Berger), b 1878,2,22
    Ch: Carrie Lu-
          cile   b 1903, 1, 4
        Leslie Wil-
          lard   " 1906, 6, 12
        Pauline
          Elizabeth " 1909, 7, 25
        Letha Wil-
          helmina " 1910, 9, 6
        Doris Na-
          omi   " 1914, 6, 12
        Eva May   " 1913, 1, 13
----, --, --. Irving Leroy, s James C. & Emma
    (Ellett), b 1883,1,9; m Myrtle May KELLY,
    dt Wm. A. & Samantha (Benner), b 1887,4,8
    Ch: Arlan Wal-
          ter   b 1908, 10, 8
        Gladys
          Arwilda " 1913, 1, 27 m Leonard
          Cameron
        Wilma Marie" 1915, 7, 17
        Elsie Myra " 1918, 4, 13
        Wilford Carl
                   b 1921, 5, 23
        Raynor
          Harold   "" 1926, 10, 13
----, --, --. Wilmer J., s James & Emma (El-
    lett), b 1891,1,30; m Blanche BRIGGS, dt
    Jonathan & Mary (Shry), b 1891,4,14
    Ch: Wain   b 1919, 8, 22
        Floyd   " 1921, 12, 10
        Viola Mae " 1925, 6, 26
----, --, --. Clarence b 1889,9,16; m Vera V.
    LADD, dt Julian & Ida M. (Crew), b 1890,9,
    18
    Ch: Clarence
          Lee   b 1921, 6, 19
        Glen Eu-
          gene   " 1924, 9, 25
        Donald Ju-
          lian   " 1926, 3, 12
        Kenneth
          Earl   " 1928, 4, 15
----, --, --. Leslie Willard, s Louis J. &
    Mary (Kuntzman), b 1906,6,12; m Margaret
    EAGLETON, dt Clarence, b 1907,11,13
    Ch: Louis John b 1928, 5, 21

HOOPES, Leslie Willard & Margaret, continued
    Ch: Richard
        Wendell b 1933, 2, 2

1847, 6, 26. Sarah Ann gct New Garden MM
1853, 8, 27. Phineas & w, Mary R., & ch,
    Jane G., Wm. A., Phebe Ann, Alfred & Mar-
    shall B., rocf New Garden MM, Pa.
1855, 6, 23. Lewis W. [Hoops] & w, Sarah Ann,
    & ch, John Henry & Charity Elizabeth,
    rocf New Garden MM, dtd 1855,6,20
1847, 4, 25. Jane Adamson (form Hoops) dis
    mcd
1863, 1, 24. Phineas & w, Mary R., & ch, Wm.
    A., Phebe Abb, Alfred & Marshall B., dis
    jW
1865, 2, 24. Phebe Ann Crew (form Hoopes) dis
    mcd (W)
1869, 8, 26. Wm. A. dis mcd (W)
1873, 3, 21. Alfred [Hoops] dis mcd & jas (W)
1875, 2, 27. Charity Boyle (form Hoops) con
    mcd
1876, 4, 22. John Henry [Hoops] con mcd
1889, 11, 23. Wm. A. [Hoops] & w, Lucinda, &
    ch, Walter J., Malcolm, Marietta & Linden,
    rocf Winona MM
1898, 3, 26. Byron [Hoops] relrq
1899, 4, 22. Albert [Hoops] gct Poplar Ridge
    MM, Ind.
1901, 1, 26. Albert & Viola [Hoops] rocf Pop-
    lar Ridge MM, Ind.
1902, 2, 22. Emma V. [Hoops] recrq
1902, 2, 22. Myra E. [Hoops] recrq
1902, 2, 22. Esther B. [Hoops] recrq
1902, 2, 22. Clarence B. [Hoops] recrq
1902, 2, 22. J. Wilmer [Hoops] recrq
1902, 2, 22. Russell E. [Hoops] recrq
1902, 2, 22. Erving T. [Hoops] recrq
1902, 2, 22. Lewis J. [Hoops] recrq
1911, 11, 25. Albert & w, Viola, & dt relrq
1912, 2, 24. Albert & fam dropped from mbrp
1915, 1, 23. Blanch Briggs [Hoops] rocf Salem
    MM
1915, 3, 27. Myra & Irving Leroy, charter mbr
    at Valley MM, dropped from mbrp
1918, 11, 23. Malcolm & Roy Linden dropped from
    mbrp
1923, 3, 24. Mary Emma & ch, Eva May, Pauline
    Elizabeth, Leatha-Willie & Lester Willard,
    recrq
1933, 7, 27. Margaret Melba & ch, Louis John
    & Richard Wendell, recrq

HOPKINS
1893, 4, 22. Lydia Ann (form Coppick) gct
    Butternut MM, N. Y.
1927, 5, 26. Hazel Jones relrq

HOUCK
----, --, --. Mahlon, s Mahlon A. & Mary, b
    1858,1,21; m Lydia E. STANLEY, dt Little-
    berry & Hannah, b 1858,9,15
    Ch: Clara   b 1882, 11, 20

1890, 1, 25. Isabella, Camille & Mahlon
    recrq
1897, 4, 24. Clara [Houk] recrq

HOWELL
1898, 10, 22. Mary recrq
1898, 12, 24. David J. recrq

HOWLEY
1880, 5, 22. John recrq

HUESTIS
1835, 4, 25. Joshua Reeve gct Carmel MM, to
    m Elizabeth Huestis

HUNNICUTT
----, --, --. Hannah b 1777,5,8 d 1855,7,11
    bur Springfield

1830, 8, 28. Hannah rocf Upper MM, Va., dtd
    1830,5,22

HUNT
----, --, --. Benjamin b 1809,2,12; m Sarah
    ----- b 1817,4,25 d 1865,12,7 bur Goshen
    Ch: Marianna b 1839, 10, 17

1843, 11, 25. Benjamin & w, Sarah, & dt,
    Mariana, rocf London Grove MM, Pa., dtd
    1843,10,5
1857, 7, 25. Benjamin dis disunity
1858, 3, 27. Marianna Johnson (form Hunt)
    dis mcd

HURD
1876, 3, 21. Kate, dt Albert, b

1923, 9, 27. Kate recrq
1924, 1, 24. Kate relrq

HUSSEY
1834, 3, 22. William Pettit gct Short Creek
    MM, O., to m Jane R. Hussey

HUTTON
----, --, --. John & Rachel
    Ch: Samuel W. b 1827, 9, 14
        Margaret
        Jane   " 1830, 4, 21
        William H. " 1833, 8, 6

1834, 6, 28. John & w, Rachel, & ch, Samuel
    W., Margaret Jane & William, rocf Middle-
    ton MM, dtd 1834,6,12
1838, 8, 25. John & w, Rachel, & ch, Samuel
    W., Margaret & William H., gct Middleton
    MM
1844, 8, 24. Thomas Votaw Jr. gct Marlborough
    MM, to m Guli Elma Hutton
1850, 1, 26. Mary Jane (form Engle) dis mcd
1905, 9, 19. Joseph L. Conrad gct Salem MM,
    to m Elma G. Hutton (W)

ICENHOUR
----, --, --. John b 1775,--,-- d 1826,4,29
        bur Springfield; m Mary ----- b 1778,3,3
        Ch: Elizabeth b 1801, 3, 29
            Sarah   " 1803, 4, 2
            David   " 1805, 6, 12
            Hannah   " 1807, 9, 1
            Mary   " 1810, 6, 14
            Susanna   " 1812, 12, 6
            Gulielma   " 1815, 7, 16
            Ann   " 1817, 9, 5
            John E.   " 1820, 11, 11
1826, 8, 29. Sarah K. [Isenhour] m David
        ALLEN

1831, 6, 25. Hannah Allen (form Icenhour) dis
        mou
1831, 6, 25. Susanna Allen (form Icenhour)
        dis mou
1832, 8, 25. Mary & ch, Gulielma, Ann & John,
        gct Middleton MM
1832, 8, 25. Mary Jr. gct Middleton MM

ILER
1923, 1, 27. Roy & fam gct Salem MM

INGRAM
1889, 4, 13. Edith Josephine, dt Elmore J. &
        Mary I., b

1904, 6, 25. Edith Josephine recrq
1908, 3, 28. Edith relrq

IRVIN
1887, 2, 24. Mary Viola, dt Alexander C. &
        Rachel A., b
1886, 10, 23. Sibyl, dt O. C. & Jenny Clampet,
        b (w L. W.)

1913, 6, 28. May rocf Beloit MM
1925, 10, 22. Lester [Irwin] recrq
1928, 5, 25. May [Irvine] gct Whittier MM,
        Calif.

ISRAEL
----, --, --. Henry m Mary Ann HARTIE b 1838,
        4,13 d 1917,11,24
----, --, --. Rose Barber, dt Benj. & Jennet,
        b 1857,1,25; m -----
        Ch: Herbert   b 1889, 9, 16
1897, 5, 3. Blanche E., w Dewie C., dt Mi-
        cajah B. & Annie M. (Crew) STANLEY, b

1897, 1, 23. Rosa & s, Herbert, recrq
1902, 2, 22. Mary A. recrq
1929, 6, 27. Herbert dropped from mbrp

JACKSON
1861, 1, 30. Isaac Jr., s Isaac & Ann, Morrow
        Co., O.; m in Goshen MH, Hannah ATKINSON,
        dt Warner & Maria
----, --, --. Howard m Mary Jane ILER, dt
        Everett & Eliza (Harding)b 1860,8,20

Ch: Pearlee   b 1883, 4, 23
    Sylvester " 1885, 1, 28
----, --, --. Pearlee, s Howard & Mary Jane
    (Iler); m Lillian CROSS, dt Alonzo &
    Maude (Smith) b 1893,1,18
    Ch: Hazel   b 1911, 11, 12
        Elwood " 1913, 6, 15
        Verna   " 1914, 10, 29
        George " 1918, 9, 10
        Naomi
----, --, --. Sylvester, s Howard & Mary Jane
    (Iler), b 1885,1,28; m Edith Elnora WOODS
    dt James & Sarah (Way), b 1885,4,28
    Ch: Velma M.   b 1912, 10, 4
        James Syl-
        vester   " 1915, 4, 21

1843, 9, 23. Ansalem Cobb gct Gilead MM, to
        m Grace Jackson
1861, 3, 23. Hannah gct Gilead MM

JACOBS
----, --, --. Wm. R. b 1855,4,19; m Caroline
        W. ----- b 1864,4,29 (W)
        Ch: Barclay Ab-
            ner   b 1908, 11, 24 d 1909, 2,18

1907, 1, 25. Wm. R. rocf Abington MM, Pa.,
        dtd 1907,1,2 (W)
1907, 11, 22. Wm. R. rmt Caroline H. Woolman
        (W)
1909, 5, 21. Wm. R. & w, Caroline W., gct
        New Garden MM (W)

JAMES
----, --, --. John b 1774,3,21; m Martha --- -
        b 1778,4,14
        Ch: Tace   b 1805, 3, 16
            Mary   " 1815, 1, 1
            Rachel " 1817, 8, 22
            John   " 1821, 6, 18
----, --, --. Abel b 1802,12,19; m Hannah
        ----- b 1797,1,28
        Ch: Emaline   b 1828, 6, 10
            Phebe   " 1830, 8, 7
            Lydia Ann " 1832, 11, 29 d 1853,11,--
                      bur Goshen
            Samuel   " 1837, 10, 28
            Hannah   " 1841, 10, 28
----, --, --. Samuel b 1806,10,13 d 1869,1,27
        bur Goshen; m Lany ----- b 1798,10,27
----, .--, --. Dock Wheeler b 1876,10,5; m Jo-
        sephine Sarah HUDGINS b 1876,7,26

1832, 11, 24. John & w, Martha, & ch, Mary,
        Rachel & John, rocf Middleton MM, dtd
        1832,11,8
1832, 11, 24. Tacy rocf Middleton MM, dtd
        1832,11,8
1833, 5, 25. Abel & w, Hannah, & ch, Emaline,
        Phebe & Lydia Ann, rocf Middleton MM, dtd
        1833,4,11
1834, 6, 28. Tacy Ward (form James) dis mou

JAMES, continued
1834, 10, 25. Rachel rocf Short Creek MM, O., dtd 1834,4,22
1838, 7, 28. Rachel gct Plainfield MM
1839, 10, 26. John & w, Martha, & s, John, gct Sandy Spring MM
1839, 10, 26. Mary gct Sandy Spring MM
1839, 10, 26. Rachel gct Sandy Spring MM
1846, 9, 29. Abel dis disunity
1857, 12, 26. Phebe dis jas
1861, 7, 27. Hannah K. dis disunity
1862, 1, 25. Samuel H. dis disunity
1863, 1, 24. Emaline dis jW
1868, 7, 25. Samuel E. recrq on consent of Short Creek MM, O.
1868, 7, 25. Laney recrq on consent of Short Creek MM, O.
1920, 7, 24. J. W. & w, Josie, rocf Winston Salem MM, N. C.
1925, 12, 24. Josie relrq

JEHU
1931, 4, 23. Emeline recrq

JENKINS
1795, 8, 10. Lydia M. b
----, --, --. William b 1815,11,27; m Lydia ----- b 1823,6,14
  Ch: Elizabeth b 1851, 11, 22
      Esther F. " 1854, 7, 22
      William
      Miller " 1856, 4, 25
      John K. " 1862, 6, 4
      Mary E. " 1864, 8, 22
1858, 10, 27. Israel W., s Israel & Lydia, Jefferson Co., O., b 1835,11,2; m in Goshen MH, Alvina STANLEY, dt Micajah & Unity, Mahoning Co., O., b 1838,7,1
  Ch: Lydia Ann b 1861, 12, 17 d 1864, 8,21
      Willis " 1865, 2, 21
      Viola " 1867, 4, 30
      Cary E. " 1870, 3, 7
      Judith Ella " 1880, 9, 25
----, --, --. John, s Wm. & Lydia M., b 1862, 4,6; m Margaret L. KINSEY, dt Wm. & Mercy
  Ch: Bernice
      Kinsey b 1888, 10, 3 d 1889,11,25
      Lydia Mildred " 1890, 3, 3
      Anna Margaret " 1891, 7, 14
      Lloyd Miller " 1895, 8, 28
1859, 3, 26. Alvina S. gct Short Creek MM, O.
1861, 10, 26. Israel W. & w, Alvina, rocf Short Creek MM, O.
1863, 6, 26. Alvina dis jG (W)
1863, 7, 24. Wm. & Lydia dis jG (W)
1864, 5, 28. Wm. & w, Lydia, & ch, Joseph, Edward, Elizabeth M., Esther F., Wm. & John R., rocf Marlborough MM, dtd 1864,3,29

1865, 2, 25. Lydia M. rocf Short Creek MM, O., dtd 1865,2,22
1867, 1, 26. Wm. & w, Lydia M., & ch, Joseph E., Elizabeth M., Esther F., Wm. M., John K. & Mary E., gct Alliance MM
1870, 8, 27. John Butler gct New Garden MM, to m Elizabeth Jenkins
1883, 7, 28. Lydia M. rocf Alliance MM
1883, 7, 28. Mary rocf Alliance MM
1884, 7, 26. John rocf East Goshen MM
1885, 11, 28. Elizabeth M. rocf East Goshen MM
1886, 2, 27. William recrq
1887, 2, 26. Wm. & w, Lydia M., gct Modena MM, Calif.
1887, 9, 24. Elizabeth M. gct Modena MM, Calif.
1888, 12, 22. Margaret L. rocf Short Creek MM, O.
1890, 8, 23. Mary E. gct Modena MM, Calif.
1900, 2, 24. John K. & w, Margaret L., & ch, L. Mildred, A. Margaret & Lloyd M., relrq
1900, 8, 15. John K. & fam rst on rq
1900, 8, 15. John K. & fam gct East Goshen MM
1913, 4, 26. Esther H. relrq
1913, 10, 25. Ella rocf East Goshen MM
1919, 11, 22. Ella relrq

JOBES
1856, 9, 7. Sarah T. (Stanley), w Wm., b
1847, 9, 25. Mary (form French) dis mcd
1905, 6, 24. Sarah T. dropped from mbrp

JOHN
1777, 2, 8. Sarah b
1829, 3, 28. Sarah dis jH
1839, 2, 22. Wm. W., minor, rocf Sandy Spring MM, dtd 1839,1,25
1843, 3, 25. William dis
1865, 3, 25. Wm. W. rst at Springdale MM, Ia. on consent of this mtg

JOHNSON
----1 --, --. Thomas b 1772,12,2; m Ann ----- b 1768,2,19 d 1846,1,4 bur Springfield
1797, 12, 15. Benjamin b d 1888,2,7
1799, 9, 9. Elizabeth b d 1884,9,24 bur Damascus
1831, 1, 26. James, s John & Dorothy, Columbiana Co., O.; m in Goshen MH, Sarah VOTAW, dt Isaac & Sarah, Columbiana Co.,O.
1832, 3, 8. Jonathan, s Thomas & Ann, Columbiana Co., O., b 1802,6,20; m in Damascus MH, Joanna COBBS, dt Pleasant & Amy, Columbiana Co., O., b 1803,6,17
  Ch: Pleasant
      T. b 1832, 12, 10
      Amy Ann " 1834, 4, 4 d 1837,12,16 bur Springfield
      Thomas C. b 1836, 6, 4 " 1837, 5,11

JOHNSON, Jonathan & Joanna, continued
    bur Springfield
  Ch: Abigail b 1838, 2, 13
    Rebecca " 1839, 9, 6
    Eliza M. " 1840, 12, 27
    Joanna C. " 1844, 1, 23
1851, 10, 30. Thomas, s Benjamin & Martha,
 Columbiana Co., O., b 1825,11,17; m in
 Springfield MH, Martha BINFORD, dt Aquilla
 & Miriam, b 1826,10,3 d 1888,1,21
  Ch: William B. b 1854, 7, 21 d 1873, 4,24
    John H. " 1856, 2, 16
    Emma   " 1858, 2, 25
    Aquilla " 1859, 12, 19
1851, 11, 2. Charles F. b
1857, 10, 26. Wm. C., s Micajah T. & Edna,
 Harrison Co., O.; m in Springfield MH, Ju-
 dith C. STANLEY, dt John & Abigail, Mahon-
 ing Co., O.
----, --, --. Joseph G. b 1837,1,2; m Sarah P.
 ----- b 1838,7,8
  Ch: Rebecca b 1866, 3, 9
1868, 1, 30. Martha G. m Jacob A. GREEN
----, --, --. John H., s Thomas & Martha, b
 1856,2,16; m Alzada C. ----- b 1853,5,18
  Ch: Arthur C. b 1881, 6, 22
    Willis T. " 1883, 5, 16
    Vera M. " 1886, 7, 11
    Elva   " 1889, 5, 17
    Clark New-
     ton   " 1892, 1, 9

1828, 12, 27. Thomas & w, Ann, rocf Salem MM,
 dtd 1828,12,24
1831, 4, 23. Sarah N. gct New Garden MM
1831, 9, 24. Benjamin recrq
1841, 9, 25. Benjamin Jones gct Miami MM, to
 m Cynthia Ann Johnson
1844, 7, 27. James & w, Sarah N., & ch, Isaac,
 Penelope, Rachel, Mary V., Martha, Joseph
 H., William & James, rocf New Garden MM
1844, 9, 28. Thomas dis jas
1845, 5, 24. James & w, Sarah, & ch, Isaac
 Penelope, Rachel Mary V. Martha Joseph H.
 William & James, gct New Garden MM
1846, 4, 25. Joshua & w, Joanna, & ch,
 Pleasant T., Abigail, Rebecca, Eliza Mary
 & Joanna C., gct Gilead MM
1852, 6, 26. Thomas rocf New Garden MM, dtd
 1852,6,24
1856, 8, 23. Samuel Alfred Binford gct New.
 Garden MM, to m Elizabeth M. Johnson
1857, 12, 26. Judith C. gct Short Creek MM, O.
1858, 3, 27. Marianna H. (form Hunt) dis mcd
1863, 4, 24. Thomas dis jG (W)
1863, 4, 24. Martha dis jG (W)
1863, 7, 24. Jesse, Martha & Mary dis jG (W)
1863, 8, 22. Ezra French gct New Garden MM,
 to m Mary Johnson
1866, 2, 24. Missouri L. (form Jones) dis mcd
1867, 6, 22. Joseph G. & w, Sarah P., & dt,
 Rebecca, rocf New Garden MM, dtd 1867,6,19
1867, 9, 28. Martha G. rocf New Garden MM,

 dtd 1867,9,25
1870, 6, 25. Charles F. recrq
1874, 5, 23. Elizabeth rocf Westland MM
1878, 2, 23. Benjamin rocf New Garden MM
1882, 3, 25. Alzada rocf East Goshen MM
1885, 10, 24. Thomas dis
1886, 3, 27. Aquilla relrq
1901, 4, 27. John & fam gct Alliance MM

JONES
----, --, --. Catlett Sr. b 1749,1,15 d 1828,
 9,6 bur Springfield; m Sarah ----- b 1770,
 4,7 d 1837,8,2
  Ch: Ann   b 1804, 4, 8
    Benjamin " 1805, 4, 24
    Catlett " 1807, 10, 1
    Joseph " 1809, 9, 8 d 1809,12,14
    bur Springfield
    Joshua b 1810, 10, 22
    Caleb   " 1813, 7, 5
1809, 5, 12. Charles b (W)
1832, 2, 2. Catlet, s Catlet & Sarah, Columbiana Co., O., b 1807,10,1; m in Damascus MH, Mary A. COBBS, dt Waddy & Margaret, Columbiana Co., O., b 1809,4,14
  Ch: Cynthia
    Ann   b 1832, 9, 13
    Louiza Jane" 1836, 6, 8
    Lindley
    Murray " 1838, 4, 25
    Mary C. " 1840, 3, 2
    Missouri " 1842, 8, 1
    Claudius
    Galen   " 1844, 6, 13
    Ginevra " 1848, 6, 17
----, --, --. Joshua b 1810,10,22 d 1890,6,4
 bur Damascus; m Rebecca ----- b 1814,10,9
 d 1895,9,18 bur Damascus
  Ch: Sarah Ann b 1836, 12, 19
    Thomas El-
    wood   " 1839, 1, 8
    Deborah M. " 1840, 2, 5
    Emily   " 1841, 8, 18 d 1916,11,26
    William
    Catlett " 1843, 1, 17
    Levi Mil-
    ler   " 1844, 9, 21 d 1931, 8,25
    Elizabeth
    L.   " 1846, 8, 12
    Hannah " 1848, 7, 15 d 1866,12,26
    bur Damascus
    Oliver b 1850, 9, 3 d 1853, 9,11
    bur Springfield
    Benjamin
    Franklin b 1852, 3, 21 d 1853, 5,15
    bur Springfield
    Joshua By-
    ron   b 1855, 8, 3
----, --, --. Benjamin b 1805,4,24; m Cynthia
 A. ----- b 1817,4,13
  Ch: Sarah Crew b 1843, 9, 24
    Micajah
    Johnson " 1844, 8, 21

JONES, Benjamin & Cynthia A., continued
    Ch: Eliza S.   b 1846, 11, 29
        Rebecca
        Emily   " 1849, 3, 28
----, --, --. Joseph B., s Joshua & Rebecca,
    b 1855,8,3 d 1926,7,17; m Delphina T.
    STANLEY, dt Israel & Uree C., b 1856,5,10
    Ch: Russell
        Stanley   b 1881, 8, 18
        Murry J. " 1883, 7, 23
        Edward
        Everett   " 1885, 2, 24
        Irving By-
        ron   " 1893, 2, 18
----, --, --. J. Murray b 1883,7,23; m Iva M.
    DENNY, dt Michael W. & Rosetta K. (Camer-
    on), b 1882,11,16
    Ch: Hazel
        Marie   b 1907, 4, 19
        Effa Pearl " 1913, 9, 4
        Oren Edward" 1917, 11, 17
        Erman Irene" 1919, 10, 9
        Anna Lu-
        cile   " 1922, 10, 13
----, --, --. Edward Everett b 1885,2,24; m
    Nellie E. COFFMAN b 1885,2,22
    Ch: Roberta
        Eleanor   b 1914, 9, 18
----, --, --. Russell m Chloe Theodosia HARVEY
    dt Rowland & Elizabeth (Nicodemus), b 1897,
    9,11

1829, 1, 27. Hannah (form Morris) dis mcd
1835, 11, 28. Joshua gct Sandy Spring MM, to
    m Rebecca Miller
1836, 8, 27. Rebecca rocf Sandy Spring MM,
    dtd 1836,6,24
1841, 9, 25. Benjamin gct Miami MM, to m
    Cynthia Ann Johnson
1843, 3, 25. Cynthia A. rocf Miami MM, O.,
    dtd 1853,1,25
1844, 12, 28. Caleb dis mcd
1850, 5, 25. Benjamin & w, Cynthia, & ch, Sa-
    rah C., Micajah J., Eliza S. & Rebecca E.,
    gct Centre MM, O.
1851, 9, 27. Hannah gct Gilead MM
1856, 7, 26. Cynthia A. J. Hall (form Jones)
    dis mcd
1856, 8, 23. Henry D. dis disunity
1859, 6, 25. Mary C. Stanley (form Jones) con
    mcd
1861, 11, 23. Louiza J. Stanley (form Jones)
    dis mcd
1863, 2, 27. Cartlet dis jG (W)
1863, 2, 27. Joshua dis jG (W)
1863, 2, 27. Lindley M. dis jG (W)
1863, 2, 27. Mary A. dis jG (W)
1863, 2, 27. Rebecca dis jG (W)
1863, 6, 27. Deborah M. Bundy (form Jones)
    con mcd
1863, 9, 25. Elwood dis jG (W)
1863, 9, 25. Sarah Ann dis jG (W)
1863, 9, 25. Emily dis jG (W)

1864, 6, 25. Lindley dis mcd
1866, 2, 24. Missouri L. Johnson (form Jones)
    dis mcd
1866, 12, 22. Catlet & w, Mary, gct Alliance
    MM
1869, 7, 24. Genevieve Haines (form Jones)
    dis mcd
1869, 11, 26. Elizabeth (form Crew) dis mcd
    (W)
1870, 1, 22. Sarah A. Hoge (form Jones) con
    mcd
1871, 4, 22. Rebecca rocf Sandy Spring MM
1872, 2, 24. Thomas Elwood dis mcd
1872, 8, 24. Alvira A. (form Fawcett) dis
    mcd
1872, 11, 23. Galen C. dis mcd & jas
1873, 10, 25. Elizabeth L. Purviance (form
    Jones) con mcd
1877, 4, 27. Charles recrq (adopted s of Jehu
    L. Kite) (W)
1880, 4, 24. W. C. relrq
1889, 2, 22. Joseph Charles dis mcd (W)
1889, 10, 25. Joseph Charles rst (W)
1896, 9, 22. Joseph Charles dis (W)
1911, 9, 26. Nellie E. recrq
1911, 11, 25. Iva M. recrq
1911, 11, 25. Hazel Marie, dt Murray & Iva,
    recrq
1913, 3, 22. Clara Crew relrq
1915, 3, 27. J. Murray & w, Iva Mary, & ch,
    Hazel Marie & Effie Pearl, released to
    Valley MM as charter mbr
1916, 5, 27. Irving Byron relrq
1921, 10, 22. E. Everett & w & dt, Roberta,
    relrq
1925, 6, 25. Russell dropped from mbrp
1927, 5, 26. Hazel(Jones)Hopkins relrq
1930, 3, 27. Chloe Theodosia recrq

JORDAN
1839, 7, 27. Susan (form Shinn) dis mcd

JUDSON
1927, 5, 26. Laura Donelly relrq

KEEN
----, --, --. Samuel S., s Samuel & Sarah,
    b 1867,9,14 d 1907,6,27; m Mary E. MERCER,
    dt David & Hannah, b 1873,11,15
    Ch: Aquilla   b 1888, 7, 14
        Lester L. " 1894, 10, 15
        Berdetta C." 1898, 1, 5
        Homer   " 1901, 8, 24
        Esek Her-
        mon   " 1904, 1, 8

1848, 1, 22. Martha (form Townsend) dis mcd
1902, 1, 25. Samuel S. & w, Mary E., & ch,
    Aquilla P., Lester L., Berdetta C. &
    Homer A., recrq
1911, 1, 28. Mary E. & fam dropped from mbrp

KEER

----, --, --. Ercy C., s W. Rufus & Delilah;
    b 1877,8,3; m Maud S. FRANK, dt Daniel D.
    & Sarah C., b 1877,1,27
----, --, --. Neil Monroe, s John & Jeanette
    (Towns), b 1891,12,18; m Lela Leona ELTON,
    dt Joseph & Emily (Emmons), b 1887,8,11
    Ch: Eldon Bar-
            nard   b 1917, 11, 1
        Russell
        Neil   " 1920, 3, 6
        Clifford
        Baylis   " 1921, 7, 16
        Margaret
        Elizabeth " 1929, 1, 24

1901, 8, 15. Ercy C. & Maud S. recrq
1904, 9, 24. Ercy C. & Maud F. relrq
1933, 3, 23. Nil & w, Lela Leona, & ch, El-
    don, Russell, Clifford & Margaret, recrq

KENWORTHY

----, --, --. Truman S., s Isaac & Abigail,
    b 1863,3,17; m Mary Anna THOMAS, dt Peter
    L. & Mary, b 1867,9,17
    Ch: Helen   b 1890, 7, 8
        Mary   " 1892, 5, 31
        Richard P. " 1894, 4, 14
        Catharine " 1898, 1, 3
        Eunice E. " 1899, 10, 24
        Isabel   " 1902, 10, 3

1903, 1, 24. Truman C. & w, Marianna, & ch,
    Helen, Mary, Richard P., Catharine, Eunice
    & Isabel, rocf Oskaloosa MM, Ia.
1908, 11, 28. Truman C. & w, Marianna, & ch,
    Helen, Mary, Richard P., Catharine, Eunice
    Edna & Isabel, gct Spiceland MM, Ind.

KILLE

----, --, --. Clayton b 1773,5,18; m ----- ---
    --
    Ch: Mary   b 1805, 9, 27
        Isaac C.   " 1808, 3, 8
        Ann   " 1810, 6, 17
        Thomas   " 1813, 3, 18
        Jemima   " 1816, 6, 20
        Elizabeth " 1818, 7, 8
    Clayton m 2nd Rebecca ----- b 1784,2,23
    Ch: John   b 1825, 2, 10
        William   " 1826, 1, 25
        Ruth   " 1827, 4, 10 d 1881, 9,10
        bur Damascus
        Clayton   b 1828, 4, 5
1827, 10, 31. Mary m Thomas B. STANLEY
1841, 3, 3. Elizabeth m Enoch SHREVE
----, --, --. John b 1825,2,10 d 1874,4,12;
    m Jane ----- b 1825,6,30
1862, 1, 2. Martha Jane m Jacob COBOURN
----, --, --. ----- m Martha Jane ----- b 1835,
    8,31
    Ch: Charles W. b 1856, 10, 31
        Alpharetta " 1858, 2, 7

----, --, --. Isaac E. b 1840,3,8; m Eliza-
    beth P. ----- b 1841,2,22 d 1892,12,30
    Ch: Eli S.   b 1865, 3, 9
        Elmer B.   " 1867, 4, 9 d 1868,10, 7
        Omer   " 1870, 8, 8
        Mary Emma   " 1872, 12, 26
        Benjamin A. " 1876, 5, 8
        Seward J.   " 1880, 8, 17
        Anna M.   " 1882, 11, 28
1880, 9, 28. Jane M. m Jeremiah GRINNELL

1826, 5, 27. Clayton [Killie] & w, Rebecca,
    & ch, Isaac Clever, Ann, Thomas, Jemima,
    Elizabeth, John & William, rocf Marl-
    borough MM, dtd 1826,4,25
1826, 5, 27. Mary [Killie] rocf Marlborough
    MM, dtd 1826,4,25
1833, 4, 27. Ann Milligan (form Kille) dis
    mou
1833, 6, 22. Thomas, minor, gct Marlborough
    MM
1834, 10, 25. Isaac dis mcd
1835, 5, 23. Jemima Wright (form Kille) dis
    mcd
1836, 11, 26. Clayton gct Marlborough MM, to
    m Mary Butler
1837, 5, 27. Clayton & s, John & Wm., gct
    Marlborough MM
1856, 3, 22. Martha J. [Killee] (form Lipsey)
    dis mcd
1859, 4, 23. Ruth [Kelly] gct Marlborough MM
1861, 4, 27. Hannah [Kelly] (form Gibson) dis
    mcd
1861, 10, 26. Hannah [Kelly] rst by rq
1862, 9, 27. Isaac recrq
1863, 1, 24. Isaac E. gct Sandy Spring MM,
    to m Elizabeth Pim
1863, 4, 25. Isaac E. gct Marlborough MM
1863, 7, 24. John dis jG (W)
1864, 2, 27. Chas. W. & Alpharetta recrq
1864, 7, 23. Isaac E. & w, Elizabeth P..,
    rocf Marlborough MM
1865, 1, 28. John & w, Jane M., rocf Marl-
    borough MM, dtd 1864,12,27
1874, 9, 26. Ruth rocf Alliance MM
1884, 4, 26. Charles W. dropped from mbrp
1901, 5, 20. Anna M. gct Alliance MM
1905, 6, 24. Benjamin dropped from mbrp
1905, 6, 24. Leeward dropped from mbrp
1905, 6, 24. Eli dropped from mbrp
1905, 6, 24. Chas. Omar dropped from mbrp
1905, 6, 24. Emma Alter Kille dropped from
    mbrp
1929, 6, 27. Edith [Kelly] dropped from mbrp

KIMBERLY
1851, 5, 24. Ellen rst at Salem MM, Ia., on
    consent of this mtg

KING
1906, 5, 14. Frank L., s James W. & Lottie
    (Leonard), b

KING, continued
1929, 6, 27. Olive dropped from mbrp
1932, 4, 28. Frank L. recrq
1933, 4, 27. Frank dis

KINSEY
----, --, --. George B. b 1845,8,6 d 1918,10,
    14; m Annie E. PETTIT b 1847,3,4 d 1917,
    12,13
----, --, --. Isaac L., s Wm., b 1861,6,26;
    m Edith CATTELL, dt Ezra, b 1865,8,21

1865, 10, 28. Jared Stanley gct Short Creek
    MM, O., to m Margaret B. Kinsey
1913, 12, 27. George B. rocf East Goshen MM
1913, 12, 27. Anna recrq
1925, 9, 24. Isaac L. & w, Edith, rocf
    Portsmoth MM, Va.

KIRK
----, --, --. Joel b 1812, 6, 29 d 1887,11,
    22; m Mary Ann ----- b 1813,6,5
    Ch: Lindley M. b 1839, 9, 20
        Amy T.   " 1841, 10, 15
        Badok P.   " 1844, 1, 3
        Martha T. " 1846, 4, 17
        Chalkley H." 1848, 11, 20 d 1885,2,10
          bur Damascus
        Anna Mary b 1851, 6, 13
        Rachel K. " 1853, 11, 21
1847, 8, 31. Lydia, dt John & Mary Greenfield,
    b
1860, 9, 27. Amy T. m Levi CATTELL
1864, 10, 27. Lindley M., s Joel & Maryan,
    Mahoning Co., O., b 1839,9,20; m in Damas-
    cus MH, Elizabeth BRUFF, dt James B. &
    Sarah, Mahoning Co., O., b 1838,9,14
    Ch: Alice T.   b 1866, 9, 4
        Lurena T. " 1869, 7, 23
        Willard B. " 1870, 8, 27
----, --, --. Newton G., s Wm. & Elizabeth,
    b 1841,8,20; m Annyetta ----- b 1849,8,9
    Ch: Rollin W. b 1875, 5, 1
        Carroll E. " 1877, 7, 11
        Arthur G. " 1880, 1, 14
        Elizabeth
        May   " 1884, 5, 20

1858, 6, 26. Joel & w, Mary Ann, & ch, Lind-
    ley M., Amy T., Zadok, Chalkley H., Mar-
    tha, Anna Mary & Rachel, rocf Smithfield
    MM
1860, 1, 27. Elizabeth rocf Sandy Spring
    MM, O., dtd 1859,12,20 (W)
1872, 8, 24. Zadock P. gct New Sharon MM, Ia.
1873, 3, 22. Amyetta (form Shreeve) con mcd
1877, 1, 27. Lindley W. & w, Elizabeth B., &
    ch, Alice T., Lorena & Willard B., gct
    Springdale MM, Ia.
1880, 8, 27. Joel rst on consent of Short
    Creek MM, O. (W)
1880, 9, 25. Joel relrq
1881, 4, 23. Nuton & s, Arter G., Rolen W. &

Carel, recrq
1881, 7, 23. Anna M. relrq
1882, 7, 22. Rachel B. relrq
1889, 2, 23. Newton G. & w, Amyetta, & ch,
    Rollen W., Carrel Evan, Arthur G. & Eliza-
    beth Mary, gct Newburg MM
1927, 12, 22. Lydia gct Salem MM

KIRKBRIDE
----, --, --. Mahlon d 1925,10,25; m Mary
    Esther ----- d 1925,7,17

1851, 6, 28. Eliza Ann (form Morris) dis mcd
1869, 6, 26. Esther (form Votaw) dis mcd
1897, 5, 22. Roberta S. relrq
1912, 2, 24. Mahlon & Mary Esther rocf East
    Goshen MM

KITE
1820, 5, 10. Benjamin b
1842, 9, 28. Jehu L., s John & Mary, Colum-
    biana Co., O., b 1819,1,30 d 1889,11,3;
    m in Goshen MH, Charlotte STANLEY, dt
    James & Rachel, Columbiana Co., O., b
    1820,12,21 d 1866,2,14
1833, 3, 7. Ellen B b (W)

1837, 8, 26. Jehu Lord, grandson of Jehu
    Lord, rocf Stroudsborough MM, dtd 1837,5,
    25 end by Salem MM, 1837,8,23
1851, 3, 22. Benjamin rocf London Grove MM,
    dtd 1851,2,6
1863, 5, 22. Jehu L. & Charlotta dis jG (W)
1866, 1, 27. Benjamin gct New Garden MM
1867, 11, 22. Jehu L. rst rq (W)
1868, 10, 24. Jehu L. relrq
1869, 5, 24. Jehu L. rmt Ellen B. Elltson (W)
1872, 6, 21. Benjamin gct New Garden MM (W)
1895, 5, 24. Ellen B. gct Hickory Grove MM,
    Ia. (W)

LADD
----, --, --. ----- m Elizabeth ----- d 1850,
    4,20 bur Springfield
    Ch: Samuel
        Whitfield b 1806, 10, 8 d 1845, 8,10
          bur Springfield
        Elizabeth b 1814, 3, 8
        Joshua   " 1817, 1, 7
        Joseph   " 1820, 7, 12
1841, 12, 2. Elizabeth m Pleasant T. STANLEY
----, --, --. Joshua & Lydia
    Ch: Samuel W. b 1853, 5, 21
        Henry C. " 1856, 11, 26
        Howard J. " 1859, 5, 16 d 1929, 5, 8
1860, 1, 9. Edith G. Ladd, dt Abram & Mary
    GARWOOD, b
1867, 10, 15. Margaret Luella, dt Joseph &
    Francina, b
1878, 7, 23. Erba dt Wm. E. & Anna, b
----, --, --. Julian, s Joseph & Francina, b
    1860,1,25; m Ida M. CREW, dt Mahlon &
    Phebe (Hoopes), b 1866,1,18

LADD, Julian & Ida M., continued
    Ch: Vera Viola b 1890, 9, 18
        Leon Mahlon" 1895, 9, 14
        Ethel Fran-
          cine   " 1899, 6, 3
----, --, --. Charles, s Howard J. & Cherrie,
    b 1887,8,17; m Sibyl E. TOMLINSON, dt Or-
    land & Emily, b 1887,10,23
    Ch: Elizabeth b 1911, 8, 4
        Rollin C. " 1914, 11, 23

1830, 12, 25. Samuel Whitefield rocf Wayne Oak
    MM, Va., dtd 1830,11,6
1830, 12, 25. Elizabeth & ch, Elizabeth,
    Joshua & Joseph, rocf Wayne Oak MM, Va.,
    dtd 1830,11,6
1831, 10, 22. Samuel Whitfield gct Salem MM
1834, 1, 25. Samuel Whitfield rocf Salem MM,
    dtd 1834,1,22
1847, 7, 24. Joshua dis mcd
1847, 7, 24. Joseph dis mcd
1847, 8, 28. Lydia (form Cobbs) dis mcd
1862, 4, 26. Henry P. Cobbs gct Short Creek
    MM, O., to m Anne U. Ladd
1882, 3, 25. Henry C. recrq
1882, 6, 24. Margaret L. recrq
1886, 1, 23. Edith G. recrq
1886, 4, 24. Samuel W. & Howard J. recrq
1887, 3, 26. Julian recrq
1898, 12, 24. Erba recrq
1905, 3, 25. S. W. gct Alliance MM
1909, 7, 24. Sibyl E. rocf East Goshen MM
1909, 7, 24. Charles recrq
1915, 3, 27. Julian J. & w, Ida May, & ch,
    Vera Viola, Ethel Fransena & Mahlon Leon,
    released as charter mbr at Valley MM
1927, 6, 23. Mahlon dropped from mbrp

LAMBORN
----, --, --. Parmenas b 1776,8,4; m Hannah
    ----- b 1776,1,8
    Ch: Isaac   b 1800, 1, 22
        Miriam   " 1801, 12, 27
        Elizabeth " 1804, 1, 3
        Dinah   " 1806, 5, 26
        Anna   " 1808, 8, 25
        William   " 1810, 11, 14
        Lydia   " 1813, 9, 14
        Mary   " 1818, 2, 9
1843, 6, 1. Philena m Milton TAYLOR
----, --, --. Wm. C. b 1829,8,6; m Sarah C.
    ----- b 1830,10,16

1826, 3, 25. Elizabeth gct Westland MM
1828, 4, 26. Parmenas dis disunity
1828, 5, 24. Hannah dis disunity
1829, 2, 28. Dinah dis jH
1829, 2, 28. Anna dis jH
1833, 8, 24. William dis disunity
1835, 9, 26. Lydia dis jH
1835, 9, 26. Mary dis jH
1837, 10, 28. Philena, Thomas Elwood & Eliza-
    beth, ch John & Esther, rocf London Grove

MM, Pa., dtd 1837,7,6
1847, 5, 22. Elizabeth Morris (form Lamborn)
    rpd mcd
1848, 1, 22. Thomas Elwood dis disunity
1870, 4, 23. Wm. & w, Sarah, recrq
1871, 3, 25. Wm. C. & w, Sarah C., gct Alli-
    ance MM
1872, 6, 22. Wm. C. & w, Sarah C., rocf Alli-
    ance MM
1877, 2, 24. Wm. C. & w, Sarah C., gct Alli-
    ance MM

LANGSTAFF
----, --, --. Samuel Sr. b 1764,4,30 d 1852,
    11,25 bur Goshen; m Hannah ----- b 1778,9,
    6 d 1860,5,7 bur Goshen
    Ch: Samuel   b 1804, 4, 8
        Benjamin P." 1806, 6, 5
        James   " 1808, 3, 2
        Thomas   " 1810, 2, 2 d 1831, 4,27
        bur Goshen
        John W.   " 1812, 1, 4
        Mary   " 1815, 10, 30 " 1892,10,30
        bur Damascus
        Elizabeth b 1818, 2, 3
        Evan   " 1820, 7, 25
----, --, --. Thomas b 1772,10,26; m Rhoda
    ----- b 1770,4,3 d 1822,8,1 bur Goshen
    Ch: Thomas D. b 1811, 4, 26
    Thomas m 2nd Ann FARMER b 1778,11,13
1827, 7, 4. Samuel Jr., s Samuel & Hannah,
    Columbiana Co., O., b 1804,4,8 d 1831,5,29
    bur Goshen; m in Goshen MH, Tabitha FARMER
    dt Thomas & Ann, Columbiana Co., O., b
    1807,2,26 d 1831,6,18
    Ch: David R. b 1828, 6, 21
        Taylor F. " 1829, 11, 26
        Drusilla " 1831, 1, 24
1829, 10, 29. Benjamin P., s Samuel & Hannah,
    Columbiana Co., O.; m in Damascus MH, Cath-
    arine REEVE, dt Joshua & Miliscent, Colum-
    biana Co., O.
1836, 4, 28. Thomas D., s Thomas & Rhoda, Co-
    lumbiana Co., O.; m in Springfield MH,
    Hannah SMITH, dt Thomas & Nancy, Columbi-
    ana Co., O.
1847, 10, 27. Evan, s Samuel & Hannah, Mahon-
    ing Co., O., b 1820,7,25; m in Goshen MH,
    Mary D. TOWNSEND, dt Lewis & Rachel, Ma-
    honing Co., O., b 1819,9,4
    Ch: Ella   b 1850, 2, 4 d 1853, 2,28
        bur Goshen
        Edgar   b 1852, 1, 16
        Mira   " 1855, 11, 24
        Elmore   " 1858, 11, 10
        Lewis T. " 1861, 10, 6

1827, 6, 23. James Jr., minor, gct Salem MM
1832, 5, 26. Benjamin P. & w, Catharine, gct
    Salem MM
1832, 12, 22. John W. dis disunity
1833, 11, 23. Benjamin P. & w, Catharine,
    rocf Marlborough MM, dtd 1833,10,29

LANGSTAFF, continued

1835, 7, 25. Taylor & Drusilla, minors, gct
      Salem MM

1836, 4, 23. Benjamin P. & w, Catharine, &
      s, Laban, gct Marlborough MM

1836, 4, 23. Thomas & w, Ann, gct Stillwater
      MM

1836, 9, 24. Thomas D. & w, Hannah, gct
      Pennsville MM

1837, 5, 27. Thomas D. & w, Hannah, & dt,
      Rhoda, gct Salem MM

1837, 5, 8. Thomas D. & w rocf Pennsville
      MM, dtd 1837,2,16

1863, 5, 22. Evan & Mary D. dis jG (W)

1868, 3, 28. Evan & w, Mary D., & ch, Edgar,
      Sarah E., Mira H., Elmore & Lewis T., gct
      Alliance MM

1869, 7, 24. Evan & w, Mary D., & ch, Edgar,
      Sarah E., Mira H., Elmore & Louis T., rocf
      Alliance MM

1874, 4, 25. Robert Cobb gct East Goshen MM,
      to m Elizabeth P. Langstaff

1875, 6, 25. Elizabeth Cobbs (form Langstaff)
      dis mcd & jG (W)

LATTY

1858, 5, 22. Rebecca (form Stratton) dis mcd

LAW

1839, 5, 12. Wm., s Thomas & Agnes, b

1900, 2, 24. William recrq

LEE

----, --, --. Nathaniel b 1811,7,14 d 1863,2,
      12 bur Springfield; m Amanda R. -----
      b 1809,3,18 d 1881,5,24 bur Springfield(W)
      Ch: Mary R.   b 1837, 12, 7
          Omar S.   " 1841, 9, 25
          Abel T.   " 1843, 12, 12
          Alva W.   " 1845, 4, 13 d 1862, 2,17
            bur Springfield
          Elma E.   b 1847, 8, 8

1861, 6, 21. Mordica & w, Amanda R., & ch,
      Omer S., Abel T., Alva W. & Elma E., rocf
      Salem MM, dtd 1861,6,19 (W)

1861, 6, 21. Mary R. rocf Salem MM, dtd 1861,
      6,19 (W)

1862, 10, 24. Mary Atkinson (form Lee) dis mcd
      (W)

1867, 12, 21. Omar S. dis military service (W)

1869, 10, 22. Elma Gyger (form Lee) dis mcd (W)

LEEDS

1906, 1, 27. Henry B. m Ellen BRANTINGHAM (W)

1906, 9, 18. Ellen (Brantingham) gct Burling-
      ton MM, N. J. (W)

LEGGOT

1892, 7, 23. Mary Louisa Coppock·gct Butter-
      nut MM, N. Y.

LEWIS

1868, 2, 14. Ginerva, w Wm., dt Lynch & Unity
      COBBS, b

----, --, --. David b 1846,6,10; m Margaret
      Anna COBBS, dt Lynch & Unity, b 1859,7,12
      d 1908,12,30
      Ch: Elmer G.   b 1880, 10, 4
          David A.   " 1887, 4, 16 d 1887, 4,17
          Iva Jane   " 1890, 4, 12

1885, 3, 28. David & s, Elmer G., recrq

1910, 6, 25. David D. relrq

1918, 11, 23. Genevra dropped from mbrp

1922, 9, 23. Elmer dropped from mbrp

LINTON

1859, 8, 17. Laura (Coppock), w Albert, b

----, --, --. Hilles & Belle
      Ch: Mary E.   b 1875, 3, 22
          Grace   " 1877, 1, 18
          Edith   " 1884, 9, 10

----, --, --. Hillis Lawrence b 1878,10,3; m
      Effie Amelia McCLUGGAGE b 1884,3,6
      Ch: Lois Evan-
            geline   b 1914, 9, 26

1900, 9, 22. Mary E. & Grace recrq

1901, 9, 28. Edith recrq

1905, 3, 25. Grace(Linton) Mountz relrq

1910, 1, 22. Laura Coppock relrq

1922, 12, 23. Laurence & w, Effie A., & ch,
      Lois E., rocf Newport News MM

1925, 10, 22. Lawrence & fam gct Colorado
      Springs MM, Colorado

LIPPINCOTT

1870, 10, 22. Rebecca recrq

LIPSEY

----, --, --. Edmund b 1807,4,3 d 1896,10,9;
      m Sarah ----- b 1814,2,17 d 1885,12,6 bur
      Damascus
      Ch: Lydia H.   b 1834, 7, 19
          Martha Jane" 1835, 8, 31
          Eli M.   " 1837, 2, 1
          Mary Ann   " 1838, 3, 16
          Ruth   " 1839, 5, 5
          Amy   " 1840, 9, 8
          Eliza M.   " 1842, 3, 9
          Abraham   " 1843, 11, 23 d 1862, 2,14
            bur Springfield
          Lindley M. b 1846, 5, 16 " 1861, 7,29
            bur Springfield
          William M. b 1848, 10, 3 " 1880, 3,22
            bur Minneapolis
          Olivia O. b 1850, 11, 19 " 1873, 5,14
            bur Damascus
          Amasa   b 1853, 6, 15

1853, 10, 27. Lydia H. m Robert H. HOLE

1865, 8, 31. Amy m Francis TRUEBLOOD

1853, 6, 25. Edmund & w, Sarah, & ch, Martha
      T., Eli M., Mary Ann, Ruth, Amy, Eliza,

LIPSEY, continued
    Abraham S., Lindley M., Wm. Mikker &
    Oliva O., rocf New Garden MM, dtd 1853,5,26
1853, 6, 25. Lydia H. rocf New Garden MM, dtd
    1853,5,26
1856, 3, 22. Martha J., Killee (form Lipsey)
    dis mcd
1857, 11, 28. Mary Ann Carne (form Lipsey) dis
    mcd
1859, 6, 25. Ruth Fisher (form Lipsey) dis
    mcd
1863, 2, 27. Edmund [Lipsy] dis jG (W)
1863, 2, 27. Sarah dis jG (W)
1863, 4, 24. Eli M. dis jG (W)
1871, 4, 22. Eli M. con mcd
1884, 4, 26. Eli M. dropped from mbrp

LLOYD
1851, 4, 29. John, s Isaac & Ruth, Belmont
    Co., O.; m in Springfield MH, Margaret
    ANDREWS, dt Daniel & Mary, Columbiana Co.,
    O.
1870, 10, 27. Isaac, s Isaac & Ruth, b 1830,2,
    6 d 1901,5,6; m in Damascus MH, Hannah W.
    BUTLER, dt John & Elizabeth, Mahoning Co.,
    O., b 1849,11,9
    Ch: Elizabeth
           T.   b 1876, 4, 14
          Chester J. " 1883, 7, 4 d 1916, 6,12

1851, 6, 28. Margaret gct Short Creek MM, O.
1861, 1, 26. Jesse Jr. & w, Edith, & dt,
    Anna L., rocf Short Creek MM, O., dtd
    1860,8,22
1861, 7, 27. Jesse & w, Edith, & ch, Anna
    Laura & Mary Adah, gct Short Creek MM, O.
1872, 5, 25. Hannah W. gct Short Creek MM, O.
1872, 8, 23. Hannah dis jG (W)
1885, 12, 26. Isaac & w, Hannah, & ch, Eliza-
    beth T. & Chester I., rocf Short Creek
    MM, O.

LODEN
1883, 2, 28. John, s Benjamin & Betsy, Os-
    wego Co., N. Y.; m in residence of Pleas-
    ant Coppock, Hannah E. COPPOCK, dt Pleas-
    ant & Lydia E., Columbiana Co., O.

1883, 8, 16. Hannah E. C. [Lodon] gct Butter-
    nut MM, N. Y.

LOGUE
----, --, --. Mordecai m Mary B. ----- b 1824,
    6,15 d 1856,11,13 (W)
    Ch: Lester
        Kirkland b 1853, 7, 30
        Mary B.
1853, 3, 31. Thomas W., s Stephen & Sarah,
    Columbiana Co., O., b 1820,7,23; m in
    Smithfield MM, Hannah BLACKBURN, dt Bar-
    bee & Elizabeth, b 1819,7,25 d 1884,3,4
    bur Damascus
    Ch: Alvin   b 1854, 9, 13 d 1916, 7,27

Ch: Howard W. b 1857, 8, 16
    Martha   " 1858, 11, 22
----, --, --. Howard, s Thos. & Hannah
    (Blackburn), b 1857,8,16; m Louie STANLEY,
    dt Osborn & Margaret, b 1862,7,1 d 1926,
    12,31
    Ch: Charles Wil-
        lard   b 1889, 2, 20
        Homer   " 1891, 5, 18
        Frances S. " 1897, 4, 7

1849, 11, 24. Sarah W. rocf Marlborough MM,
    dtd 1849,8,28
1851, 11, 22. Mary rocf Marlborough MM, dtd
    1851,9,30
1852, 5, 22. Thomas rocf Marlborough MM, dtd
    1852,4,27
1863, 1, 24. Hannah dis jW
1863, 1, 24. Joseph dis jW
1865, 2, 24. Mary Smith (form Logue) dis mcd
    (W)
1865, 11, 24. Thomas W. dis disunity (W)
1880, 11, 26. Mary dis jas (W)
1927, 5, 26. Francis relrq

LORD
----, --, --. Jehu, b 1770,2,27 d 1851,7,25
    bur Springfield; m Rebecca ----- b 1764,
    5,16 d 1852,12,6 bur Springfield (Jehu was
    a minister)
    Ch: Ann   b 1803, 7, 12
        Rebecca S. " 1805, 7, 7

1837, 8, 26. Jehu & w, Rebecca, & grandson,
    Jehu Lord Kite, rocf Stroudsborough MM,
    dtd 1837,5,25 end by Salem MM 1837,8,23
1837, 8, 26. Rebecca Jr. rocf Stroudsborough
    MM, dtd 1837,5,25 end by Salem MM 1837, 8,
    23
1844, 4, 27. Rebecca Fallack (form Lord) dis
    mcd

LUPTON
----, --, --. Nathan b 1761,8,7 d 1852,9,30
    bur Goshen; m Margaret ----- b 1771,2,14
    d 1855,1,6 bur Goshen
    Ch: Lydia   b 1807, 1, 28
----, --, --. Martin b 1797,5,19 d 1817,4,11
    bur Goshen; m Lucina ----- b 1808,8,18
    Ch: Martha   b 1828, 5, 11
        Emmor   " 1831, 4, 8
        Jonathan " 1838, 1, 23
1840, 4, 1. Lydia R. m Isaac RAKESTRAW
1848, 4, 26. Martha m John T. CARSON
1851, 3, 26. Emmor, s Martin & Lucina, Mahon-
    ing Co., O., b 1831,4,8; m in Goshen MH,
    Rebecca B. RAKESTRAW, dt Levi & Rebecca,
    Mahoning Co., O., b 1831,11,15
    Ch: Haran   b 1852, 3, 3 d 1852, 9,19
        bur Goshen
        Martin L. b 1853, 3, 14
        Evaline   " 1854, 11, 12
        Sarah Jane " 1856, 11, 15

LUPTON, Emmor & Rebecca, continued
    Ch: Isaac B. b 1858, 4, 25
       Levi   " 1860, 8, 26
       Lucina   " 1863, 1, 14
1861, 3, 27. Lucina m Nathan UPDEGRAFF

1833, 6, 22. Martin & w, Lucina, & ch, Mar-
    tha & Emmor, rocf Sandy Spring MM, O.,
    dtd 1833,5,20
1838, 9, 28. Nathan & w, Margaret, rocf
    Short Creek MM, O., dtd 1838,7,24
1838, 9, 28. Lydia rocf Short Creek MM, O.,
    dtd 1838,7,24
1863, 8, 21. Emmor & Rebecca dis jG (W)
1865, 7, 22. Jonathan dis military service

LUTES
1861, 9, 27. Sarah (form Morris) dis mcd (W)
1863, 1, 24. Sarah (form Morris) dis mcd

LYNCH
----, --, --. Joshua b 1778,5,17 d 1849,12,26
    bur Springfield; m Rachel ----- b 1775,7,
    18 d 1841,4,12 bur Springfield
    Ch: Ann   b 1804, 7, 25
       Mary   " 1805, 5, 22 d 1811, 8,13
       Elizabeth " 1810, 1, 2 " 1841, 6, 4
        bur Springfield
       Hannah   b 1811, 10, 17
       Joseph   " 1813, 11, 25
1830, 11, 4. Hannah m Benjamin BALL
1831, 3, 21. Ann m Samuel COPPOCK
----, --, --. Joseph b 1813,11,25 d 1893,9,20;
    m Rebecca ----- b 1810,5,18 d 1892,12,5
    Ch: Ann   b 1840, 7, 15 d 1843, 3,24
        bur Springfield
       Rachel   b 1842, 1, 23 d 1865, 9,14
        bur Iowa
       Asenath   " 1848, 5, 25

1839, 9, 28. Joseph gct Muddleton MM, to m
    Rebecca Beason
1840, 1, 25. Rebecca rocf Middleton MM, dtd
    1840,1,9
1842, 11, 26. Joshua gct Sandy Spring MM, to
    m Jane McBride
1843, 3, 25. Jane rocf Sandy Spring MM, dtd
    1843,2,25
1847, 4, 24. Joseph & w, Rebecca, & dt, Rachel
    gct Middleton MM
1851, 5, 24. Joseph & w, Rebecca, & ch, Ra-
    chel & Asenath, rocf Middleton MM, dtd
    1851,5,8
1851, 6, 28. Jane gct Salem MM, Ia.
1871, 6, 23. Asenath Philips (form Lynch) dis
    mcd (W)

McARTOR
1883, 10, 15. Margaret Courtney [McArter], dt
    Colin & Etta, b

1908, 3, 28. Margaret Courtney recrq
1919, 1, 25. Margaret [McArtor] Gillespie

relrq

McBRIDE
1831, 6, 2. Stephen m in Upper Springfield
    MH, Jane POOL, Columbiana Co., O.

1831, 8, 27. Jane gct Sandy Spring MM
1842, 11, 26. Joshua Lynch gct Sandy Spring
    MM, to m Jane McBride
1846, 9, 29. Mildred R. rocf Sandy Spring
    MM, dtd 1846,8,21
1848, 4, 22. Joseph & w, Susanna, rocf Sandy
    Spring MM, dtd 1848,3,24
1849, 10, 27. Joseph P. & w, Susanna, gct
    Sandy Spring MM
1851, 6, 28. Mildred R. gct Salem MM, Ia.

McCANN
1908, 3, 28. Estella Stanley gct S. W. Bay
    MM, Wis.

McCLAIN
1900, 2, 24. Frederick F. recrq

McCREW
1863, 12, 21. Anne b

McCONNELL
1835, 6, 27. Edward & w, Lydia, & ch, Tol-
    bert, Orpha, James, Adaline, Nathan, Al-
    bert, Jonathan & Ruth, rocf Middleton MM,
    dtd 1835,6,22
1837, 6, 24. Orpha gct Pennsville MM
1837, 6, 24. Edward & w, Lydia, & ch, James,
    Adaline, Mahlon, Albert, Jonathan & Ruth,
    gct Pennsville MM
1839, 4, 27. Talbot gct Chesterfield MM

McDONALD
----, --, --. Duncan, s Chas. & Mary, b 1846,
    2,25 d 1914,6,1; m Mary A. BLACKBURN, dt
    Wm. H. & Elizabeth, b 1856,7,1
    Ch: Bertha
       Elizabeth b 1886, 9, 1
       Rachel M. " 1894, 5, 31 d 1923,11,28

1869, 10, 23. Louisa [McDonnold] (form Black-
    burn) con mcd
1895, 5, 25. Esther E. [McDonel] relrq
1896, 10, 24. Mary dropped from mbrp
1906, 11, 24. Duncan & w, Mary A., & ch, Ber-
    tha E. & Rachel, recrq

McDOWEL
1858, 7, 21. Esther E. (Hole), w John, b

McGIRR
1863, 7, 24. John & Mary dis jG (W)

McGREW
1910, 7, 22. Jesse Edgerton gct Short Creek
    MM, O., to m Elizabeth A. McGrew

McHELL
1873, 1, 21. Nora, dt Wm. & Dula Larbet, b

McLEAN
1873, 11, 14. Frederick C., s Samuel & Sarah, b

McPHERSON
----, --, --. Chase Roe, s Forest S. & Ida
    Jane (Mounts), b 1907,2,21; m Anna TALBOTT
    dt Wm. K. & Laura (Crew), b 1904,12,3
    Ch: Joseph
            David   b 1931, 5, 24
            Chase Tal-
            bott   " 1932, 11, 24

MADDER
1884, 4, 26. Dellie dropped from mbrp

MADDOX
1878, 7, 23. Erba Ladd, w Wilson H., dt Wm. E.
    & Annie R. (Willis), b

1908, 3, 28. Erba gct Short Creek MM, O.
1932, 4, 28. Erba rocf Short Creek MM, O.

MALMSBERRY
----, --m --. Benjamin b 1779,5,6 d 1854,6,3
    bur Goshen; m Jane ----- b 1780,4,22 d
    1853,3,20 bur Goshen
    Ch: Jane   b 1806, 11, 27
        Elizabeth   " 1810, 4, 28
        James   " 1812, 4, 23
        Isaac   " 1813, 12, 3
        Rebecca   " 1815, 10, 4
        Hannah   " 1817, 8, 2
        Benjamin   " 1819, 10, 6
        Sarah   " 1823, 2, 21
1842, 4, 27. Rebecca m James SCHOOLEY
1843, 5, 21. Sarah m Levi BURDG
1827, 8, 29. Jane m Charles ENGLE
1830, 7, 7. Elizabeth m John WHINERY Jr.
1843, 11, 2. Benjamin, s Benjamin & Jane, Co-
    lumbiana Co., O., b 1819,10,6; m in Spring-
    field MH, Edith COPE, dt Joshua & Alice,
    Fayette Co., Pa., b 1819,5,8 d 1846,12,12
    bur Springfield
    Ch: Emmor   b 1846, 12, 4
    Benjamin m 2nd Mary ----- b 1824,1,7
    Ch: Edith   b 1851, 6, 19
1847, 5, 26. Hannah m Stacy SHREVE
1850, 5, 30. Benjamin, s Benjamin & Jane, Ma-
    honing Co., O.; m in Springfield MH, Mary
    BURDG, dt Jacob & Miriam, Columbiana Co.,
    O.
1859, 5, 21. Sarah b (W)
----, --, --. George B. b 1841,3,23; m Fa-
    zetta C. ----- b 1842,11,13
    Ch: Arvine C. b 1864, 10, 15
        Sarah Anna " 1867, 9, 6

1831, 9, 24. Isaac, minor, gct New Garden MM
1835, 3, 28. James dis disunity

1837, 7, 22. Sarah H. (form Brantingham) dis
    mou
1842, 12, 24. Sarah H. rst by New Garden MM
    on consent of this mtg
1849, 4, 28. Sarah H. rocf Salem MM, dtd
    1849,4,25
1857, 1, 24. Benjamin & w, Mary, & ch, Emmor
    C., Edith, Adella & Adelza, gct Driftwood
    MM, Ind.
1863, 2, 28. Tazetta C. (form Cattell) con
    mcd
1863, 5, 23. George B. recrq

MALONE
1830, 9, 25. Wm. Pettet Jr. gct Buckingham
    MM, to m Sarah C. Malone

MARIS
----, --, --. Jonathan [Merrice], b 1800,9,2
    d 1864,1,25 bur Goshen; m Thomasson -----
    b 1802,5,21
    Ch: Barclay   b 1826, 7, 13
        Ann   " 1827, 9, 27 d 1889, 6,20
        Esther   " 1829, 8, 18 " 1903, 1, 3
        Joseph M. " 1833, 1, 26
        Isaac   " 1834, 7, 16
        Caleb   " 1836, 5, 12
        Abraham   " 1838, 5, 18
        Jesse   " 1840, 9, 4 d 1862, 6,27
        Job Sreve " 1844, 5, 26
        William   " 1847, 6, 22
----, --, --. Caleb, s Jonathan & Thomason,
    Mahoning Co., O., b 1836,5,12 d 1912,3,31;
    m Deborah ----- b 1839,4,24
    Ch: Anna Belva b 1862, 4, 22
        Louisa
        Thomasson " 1863, 12, 18
    Caleb m 2nd in Damascus MH, 1870,4,28,
    Elizabeth T. BUTLER, dt John & Elizabeth,
    Mahoning Co., O.
    Ch: Earnest J. b 1872, 1, 26
        Clare E.   " 1875, 1, 15
        Edward W. " 1876, 2, 13
        Beulah   " 1877, 7, 24
        Russell   " 1879, 2, 28
----, --, --. Abram b 1838,5,12 d 1929,1,3;
    m Sarah B. WILLIAMS, dt Edward & Hannah,
    b 1850,1,3
----, --, --. Ernest J., s Caleb & Elizabeth,
    b 1872,1,26; m Mary A. ----- b 1869,8,12
    Ch: Henry C. b 1897, 2, 9
        Paul B.   " 1901, 10, 6
        Hellen   " 1911, 11, 6
1928, 2, 13. Ann P., dt Lewis & Sarah Pim, b

1853, 10, 22. Barclay gct Salem MM
1860, 2, 25. Isaac gct Spring Grove MM, Kans.
1859, 11, 26. Isaac con mcd
1861, 3, 23. Caleb gct Smithfield MM, to m
    Deborah Watson
1861, 10, 26. Deborah rocf Smithfield MM, dtd
    1861,9,23
1863, 5, 22. Jonathan dis jG (W)

MARIS, continued
1863, 5, 22. Thomasson dis jG (W)
1863, 5, 22. Esther dis jG (W)
1863, 5, 22. Ann dis jG (W)
1863, 8, 21. Joseph & Abraham dis jG (W)
1863, 9, 25. Caleb dis jG (W)
1864, 8, 27. Caleb & w, Deborah, & ch, Anna
Belva & Luiza, gct Kansas MM, Kans.
1866, 8, 25. Caleb & ch, Anna Belva & Louisa
Thomasson, rocf Kansas MM, Kans., dtd 1866,
5,16
1867, 2, 23. Wm., minor, gct Kansas MM
1872, 5, 24. Elizabeth (form Butler) dis mcd
(W)
1880, 7, 24. Abraham [Merris] rocf Goshen MM
1893, 4; 21. Hannah (form Fogg) dis mcd (W)
1898, 12, 24. Sarah B. Williams recrq
1899, 6, 23. Sarah B. (form Williams) dis
mcd
1905, 4, 22. Deborah gct Sandwich MM, Mass.
1910, 11, 26. Ann P. rocf East Goshen MM
1913, 6, 28. Louiza T. gct Hesper MM, Kans.
1925, 6, 25. Earnest & fam dropped from mbrp
1930, 2, 27. Edward gct Whittier MM, Calif.

MEREDITH
1834, 1, 25. Margaret, Simon, Elizabeth,
William, David & John, ch Wm. & Sarah,
rocf Uwchland MM, dtd 1833,10,10, end by
Salem MM 1834,1,22
1837, 2, 25. Margaret dis disunity
1843, 5, 27. Elizabeth Middleton (form Meredith) dis mcd
1844, 7, 27. Simon dis mcd
1844, 8, 24. Mary Ann (form Middleton) dis
mcd
1838, 1, 22. Eliza C. (form Engle) dis mcd
1848, 2, 26. Wm. dis mcd
1851, 4, 26. David [Merridith] dis mcd

MARSH
1853, 2, 26. Wm. P. Stanley gct Carmel MM,
to m Eliza C. Marsh

MARSHALL
1816, 9, 8. James C. b

1835, 11, 25. James C., minor, rocf Marlborough
MM, dtd 1835,9,29
1840, 11, 28. James C. gct Middleton MM
1843, 4, 22. James C. rocf Salem MM, dtd
1843,2,22
1844, 9, 28. James C. dis jas

MASON
1853, 6, 25. Esther rocf Robeson MM, dtd
1852,12,10

MASTON
1807, 5, 14. Rachel b

1868, 8, 26. Rachel & gr dt, Rachel Pennock,
recrq

MASSEY
----, --, --. Israel b 1808,9,8; m Massey ----
b 1816,5,3
Ch: Hannah   b 1835, 4, 19
    Miriam   " 1838, 7, 3
    Elwood   " 1847, 4, 29
    Parker
    Louis   " 1850, 8, 21

MATHER
1827, 11, 28. Lydia m Wm. BISHOP

1830, 6, 26. William, Daniel, Jesse, Ann,
James, Lydia & John [Mathers], minor ch
John & Catherine, roc dtd 1830,5,6
1834, 4, 26. William dis mcd & jH
1834, 6, 28. Daniel dis jH
1838, 12, 22. Jesse dis disunity
1838, 12, 22. Ann dis jH
1839, 3, 23. Rebecca (form Barber) dis mcd
1841, 2, 26. Lydia dis disunity
1849, 8, 25. Edith [Mathers] (form Barber)
dis mcd
1861, 10, 26. Lydia B. (form Whinery) dis mcd

MATTOX
1895, 1, 26. Margaret gct Short Creek MM, O.

MEDCALF
1893, 9, 23. Anna M. recrq

MILIGAN
1827, 5, 26. John [Meligan], minor, rocf
Marlborough MM, dtd 1827,3,27
1828, 2, 23. Joseph, minor, rocf Marlborough
MM, dtd 1828,1,29
1828, 12, 27. John, minor, gct Marlborough MM
1831, 3, 26. Joseph gct Smithfield MM
1833, 4, 27. Ann [Milligan] (form Kille) dis
mcd

MERCER
----, --, --. ----- m Sarah KEEN, dt Samuel &
Jane, b 1862,10,14
Ch: Philip   b 1883, 2, 20
    Pearl   " 1886, 5, 20
----, --, --. Harvey, s David & Hannah, b
1869,7,3; m Laura CRUM, dt C. C. & L. C.,
b 1871,1,9

1891, 4, 25. Harvey S. & Laura B. recrq
1897, 1, 23. Sarah recrq
1897, 1, 23. Phillip A. & Pearl recrq
1900, 4, 28. Sarah J. & ch, Pearl L. &
Phillip A. relrq
1918, 11, 23. Harvey & w dropped from mbrp

MICHENER
----, --, --. James b 1802,3,18; m Eliza -----
b 1801,4,18
Ch: Thomas   b 1825, 11, 16
    Ann   " 1827, 1, 8

MICHENER, continued
1827, 1, 27. James & w, Eliza, & s, Thomas,
    rocf Salem MM, dtd 1827,1,24
1828, 9, 27. James dis jH
1828, 9, 27. Eliza dis jH
1844, 9, 28. Ann Cook (form Michener) dis mcd

MIDDLETON
----, --, --. Nathaniel b 1792,12,8 d 1847,5,3
    bur Goshen; m Dorothy ----- b 1798,5,2 d
    1865,1,27
    Ch: Sarah   b 1816, 10, 20 d 1858,10,20
        Ira   " 1818, 1, 17
        Levi   " 1819, 11, 29
        Mahlon   " 1821, 10, 18
        Mary Ann " 1824, 1, 27
        Isaac   " 1826, 7, 25
        Micajah   " 1828, 4, 13
        Deborah   " 1830, 8, 15 d 1848, 2,18
          bur Goshen
        Joel   " 1832, 9, 16
        Rachel   " 1834, 11, 12
        Lewis   " 1837, 6 , 20 d 1842, 4,13
        William   " 1841, 6, 12

1830, 7, 24. Nathaniel & w, Doratha, & ch,
    Sarah, Irey, Levi, Malon, Mary Ann & Isaac
    rocf Sandy Spring MM, dtd 1830,5,21
1839, 3, 23. Ira dis training with militia
1843, 5, 27. Elizabeth (form Meredith) dis
    mcd
1843, 6, 24. Mahlon dis mcd
1844, 8, 24. Mary Ann Meredith (form Middle-
    ton) dis mcd
1848, 11, 25. Isaac dis mcd
1849, 3, 24. Esther (form Thomas) dis mcd
1852, 12, 25. Joel dis mcd
1853, 5, 27. Levi Middleton dis mcd
1856, 3, 21. Rachel Holloway (form Middleton)
    dis mcd (W)
1867, 1, 25. Rebecca (form Engle) dis mcd (W)
1867, 2, 23. Wm. dis mcd & military service

MILES
1887, 9, 10. Zoa Caroline b (W)
----, --, --. Carroll H., s Geo. & Caroline
    (Worth), b 1861,9,19; m Selma P. TABER,
    dt Louis & Mary Ann (Hill), b 1859,10,6
    Ch: Inez M. A. b 1894, 5, 16
        Iona H.   " 1896, 1, 18
        Irene K.J. " 1897, 9, 30
        Elma F.   " 1905, 8, 26; m C. H.
        MILLER
1911, 9, 20. Zoa C. Miles m Joseph N. GUIN-
    DON (W)
----, --, --. Zalo George, s Carroll H. &
    Selma P. (Taber), b 1886,2,26; m Lydia
    GUINDON, s Francis & Susannah (Battey),
    b 1896,9,7 (W)
    Ch: Mary Iona b 1926, 10, 3
        Carroll
        Hogan   " 1929, 2, 4

1911, 6, 23. Zoa Caroline rocf Short Creek
    MM, O., dtd 1911,5,23 (W)
1911, 9, 26. Zalo rocf Short Creek MM, O.
1912, 1, 27. Carroll H., Selma, Inez M.,
    Iona H., Irene K. J. & Elma F., rocf
    Short Creek MM, O. (W)
1915, 3, 27. Carroll H. & Inez "as charter
    mbr of Valley MM dropped from mbrp"
1918, 6, 22. Carroll & Inez rocf Valley MM
1918, 11, 23. Carroll & w, Selma, & ch, Ines
    M. A., Irena Katy, Hannah & Alma T., gct
    East Goshen MM
1920, 1, 24. Zalo gct East Goshen MM
1924, 6, 26. Carroll & w, Selma, & dt, Elna,
    rocf East Goshen MM
1924, 9, 25. Zalo rocf East Goshen MM
1930, 6, 27. Zalo C. & w, Lydia G., & ch,
    Mary Iona & Carroll Hagen, rocf Fairhope
    MM, Ala., dtd 1930,5,14 (W)
1931, 12, 24. Zalo dropped from mbrp

MILIGAN
1810, 2, 15. John b

1833, 5, 25. Ann [Milegan] dis mcd
1883, 9, 18.' Jesse [Milligan] recrq (W)

MILLER
----, --, --. Morris b 1799,7,27 d 1883,11,18
    bur Sandy Spring (W)
----, --, --. Samuel m Charity P. ----- b
    1813,11,24
    Ch: James
        Harrison b 1837, 10, 19
        Lydia E. " 1840, 12, 16
        Sarah C. " 1844, 5, 14
        Martha Jane" 1848, 4, 2

1835, 11, 28. Joshua Jones gct Sandy Spring
    MM, to m Rebecca Miller
1839, 9, 28. Simeon Fawcett gct Sandy Spring
    MM, to m Deborah Miller
1851, 4, 26. Charley P. & ch, James H.,
    Lydia E., Sarah C. & Martha J., rocf Sandy
    Spring MM, dtd 1851,3,24
1854, 6, 24. Charity P. & ch, James Harrison,
    Lydia Elizabeth, Sarah Charity & Martha
    Jane, gct Newberry MM
1857, 4, 24. David French gct Sandy Spring
    MM, to m Eliza Miller (W)
1878, 6, 21. Morris rocf New Garden MM, dtd
    1878,5,23 (W)
1916, 1, 23. Wm. J. recrq
1927, 4, 28. Martha Louise, dt Cornelius &
    Elma Miles, recrq
1929, 6, 27. Wm. dropped from mbrp

MONROE
1868, 6, 27. Hannah (form Stanley) con mcd
1870, 9, 24. Hannah Spiel (form Monroe) dis
    mcd

MORLAN

----, --, --. Chas. P., s Theophilus & Sarah
    P. (Holloway),b 1871,8,16; m S. Ellen
    EDGERTON, dt Jesse & Semira (Stratton),
    b 1875,9,30 (W)
    Ch: Laurence
        Louis   b 1902, 11, 12
        Anna Mary   " 1908, 1, 31; m Lenley B.
        COX
        Wilson
        Jesse   " 1910, 8, 25
        Elizabeth   " 1913, 5, 23
1852, 4, 28. Theophilus, s Mordecai & Eliza
    Ann, Columbiana Co., O.; m in Goshen MH,
    Sarah ATKINSON, dt Warner & Maria, b 1830,
    9,22 d 1853,2,9 bur Goshen (Sarah, dt
    Warner & Maria)
1856, 4, 25. Theophulus rmt Lydia French (W)
1856, 6, 27. Lydia F. gct Salem MM (W)
1914, 1, 23. Charles P. & w, S. Ellen, & ch,
    Lawrence L., Anna Mary, Wilson J. &
    Elizabeth, rocf Salem MM, dtd 1914,1,21
    (W)

MOORE

----, --, --. Robert Barclay, s Harry & Fran-
    ces, b 1899,1,2; m Phyllis Gaye GRIFFITH,
    dt Wm. & Mary E. (O'Brien), b 1902,11,2
    Ch: James
        Robert   b 1927, 10, --
        Margaret
        Ann   " 1829, 12, 30
        Joseph
        Harry   " 1932, 7, 13

1841, 8, 28. Keturah rocf Sandy Spring MM,
    dtd 1841,6,25
1846, 4, 25. Keturah gct Sandy Spring MM
1901, 1, 26. Harley M. rocf Scranton MM, Ia.
1923, 1, 27. Robert B. recrq

MORRIS

----, --, --. Hannah b 1775,6,7 d 1858,4,11
    bur Salem
----, --, --. Joseph d 1825,3,17 ae 58 bur
    Goshen; m Rachel ----- b 1771,10,14 d
    1863,8,7 bur Goshen
    Ch: Abraham   b 1793, 12, 21
        Sarah   " 1795, 11, 7
        John   " 1798, 5, 18
        Rebecca   " 1800, 4, 12
        Thomesson   " 1802, 5, 21
        Joseph   " 1804, 6, 23 d 1898, 9, 6
        Rachel   " 1806, 9, 6
        Esther   " 1809, 3, 10
        Anthony   " 1811, 8, 22 " 1815,11, 6
        Caleb Shinn " 1813, 12, 27 " 1864, 1,20
          bur Goshen
        Elizabeth   " 1817, 5, 26
        Beulah W.   " 1819, 11, 7
----, --, --. Anthony b 1773,11,18 d 1825,5,18
    bur Springfield; m Hannah ----- b 1775,6,7
    d 1858,4,11 bur Salem

    Ch: Barzillai b 1798, 5, 4
        Esther   " 1799, 8, 12
        Sarah   " 1801, 5, 31
        Thomas   " 1802, 12, 29
        Hannah   " 1804, 10, 17
        Joseph   " 1806, 12, 1
        Anthony   " 1809, 6, 13
        Elizabeth " 1809, 6, 13
        Mary   " 1811, 8, 12
        John   " 1813, 9, 2
        Martha   " 1815, 6, 8
        Stephen   " 1818, 4, 14
----, --, --. Abraham b 1793,12,21; m Mary
    ----- b 1794,11,14
    Ch: Sarah Ann b 1817, 11, 20
        Joseph   " 1820, 6, 22
        Isaiah   " 1823, 4, 23
        Rachel   " 1826, 6, 14
        Mary   " 1831, 4, 7
        Rebecca   " 1838, 5, 2
1818, 4, 14. Stephen d
----, --, --. Barzillar b 1798,5,4 d 1861,12,
    26 bur Springfield; m Sarah ----- b 1802,
    4,4 d 1863,11,10 bur Springfield
    Ch: Meribah   b 1823, 12, 13
        Jane   " 1825, 4, 25
        James B.   " 1826, 6, 1
        John W.   " 1826, 6, 1
        Thomas F. " 1828, 9, 22
        Hannah   8 1831, 2, 7
        E. Ann   " 1832, 11, 13
        Sarah C.   " 1834, 12, 17
        Mary P.   " 1838, 1, 29
1826, 5, 31. Rachel m Basil BROOKE
1827, 12, 27. Esther m Daniel BOULTON
1828, 11, 27. Joseph C., s Joseph & Rachel,
    Columbiana Co., O., b 1804,6,23; m in
    Damascus MH, Jane WARRINGTON, dt Abraham
    & Keziah, Columbiana Co., O., b 1810,1,15
    Ch: Abraham W. b 1829, 12, 21
        Tabitha   " 1831, 12, 17
1832, 11, 1. Mary m Wm. BOULTON
1836, 9, 29. Sarah Ann m Thos. T. COBBS
1839, 11, 28. Elizabeth m Wm. CARSON
1841, 4, 28. Esther m Philip EVANS
----, 7, 15. Viola Chlotilda, w Benj. H., dt
    Thomas L. & Mary A. E. (Bricker) Stanley,
    b
1827, 4, 28. Anthony, minor, gct Salem MM
1828, 10, 25. Joseph dis
1829, 1, 27. Hannah Jones (form Morris) dis
    mcd
1837, 3, 25. Stephen, minor, gct Salem MM
1837, 5, 27. Joseph & w, Jane, & ch, Abraham
    W., Tabitha & John, gct Allum Creek MM
1839, 9, 28. Abraham & w, Mary, & ch, Joseph,
    Isaiah, Rachel, Mary & Rebecca, gct Gilead
    MM
1840, 10, 24. Stephen rocf Salem MM, dtd 1840,
    10,21
1843, 7, 22. Meribah Baldwin (form Morris)
    dis
1846, 10, 24. James B. dis mcd

MORRIS, continued
1847, 5, 22. Elizabeth (form Lamborn) rpd
    mcd
1847, 7, 24. John W. dis mcd
1849, 8, 25. Hannah Woodruff (form Morris)
    dis mcd
1851, 6, 28. Eliza Ann Kirkbride (form Morris)
    dis mcd
1852, 3, 27. Stephen gct Gilead MM
1853, 2, 26. Thomas dis disunity
1856, 4, 26. Stephen rocf Gilead MM, dtd
    1856,3,25
1858, 7, 23. Mary P. Townsend (form Morris)
    dis mcd (W)
1858, 7, 24. Mary P. Townsend (form Morris)
    dis mcd
1859, 4, 22. Stephen acknowledged a mbr
    "since he could not bring cert because of
    Ind. YM joining Separatists" (W)
1861, 9, 27. Sarah Lutes (form Morris) dis
    mcd (W)
1863, 1, 24. Sarah Lutes (form Morris) dis
    mcd
1863, 6, 26. Caleb & Elizabeth dis jG (W)
1867, 12, 28. Elizabeth gct Alliance MM
1882, 1, 27. Joseph C. recrq (W)

MORROUGH
1851, 2, 22. Rebecca (form Stanley) dis mcd

MOTT
----, --, --. Jesse D. m Margaret CRAWFORD,
    dt Thomas A. & Sarah, b 1899,6,7 d 1926,
    11,9 bur Damascus (W)

1922, 9, 22. John Dewees rmt Margaret Craw-
    ford (W)

MOUNTZ
1905, 3, 25. Grace Linton relrq

MUNSELL
1873, 1, 21. Nora, w Stanton, dt Wm. & De-
    light Jane (Giund) Tarbet, b

1926, 1, 28. Nora Michel [Munsall] recrq

MYERS
1880, 11, 27. Martha A. relrq
1900, 7, 28. Ida recrq

NAYLOR
1819, 11, 7. Beulah b
----, --, --. Chas. A. b 1836,10,29; m Ann
    ----- b 1841,7,25 d 1884,9,21 bur Damascus
    Ch: Sarah
        Lorena   b 1874, 6, 15
----, --, --. Harry S., s Joseph C. & Hannah,
    b 1866,8,20; m Marietta PARK, dt Silves-
    ter & Elizabeth, b 1871,4,3
    Ch: Roberta   b 1892, 4, 11
        Florence
        Elizabeth " 1894, 5, 9

Ch: Joseph
    Sylvester b 1895, 12, 23
    Celia Marie" 1899, 7, 12
    Rebecca
    Ethel   " 1892, 4, 11
    Roberta   " 1902, 6, 20
    Hannah
    Lloyd   " 1904, 6, 17
    Ida Lu-
    cille   " ----, --, --

1859, 2, 26. Beulah W. [Neilor] gct Salem MM
1860, 9, 22. Ann (form Cobbs) con mcd
1863, 9, 25. Ann dis jG (W)
1865, 10, 28. Beulah rocf Salem MM, dtd 1865,
    10,26
1867, 12, 28. Beulah gct Alliance MM
1870, 5, 28. Charles [Nailor] recrq
1892, 4, 23. H. S. recrq
1903, 9, 26. Ethel recrq
1905, 6, 24. Charles A. dropped from mbrp
1905, 6, 24. Levena (Naylor) Hick dropped
    from mbrp
1911, 2, 25. Harry S. & w, Marietta, & ch,
    Florence Elizabeth, Joseph Sylvester,
    Celia Marie, Rebecca Ethel, Roberta
    Asenath, Hannah Lloyd & Ida Lucile, gct
    Beloit MM

NEAL
1874, 7, 24. Sarahetta (form Woolman) dis
    mcd (W)

NEGUS
----, --, --. John b 1778,5,4; m Miriam -----
    b 1780,7,31
    Ch: Sarah   b 1807, 4, 23
        Israel   " 1812, 8, 13
        Lydia   " 1816, 4, 22
        Mary Martin" 1818, 5, 31
        John Wayts " 1820, 5, 20
        Isaac   " 1822, 6, 30
        Miriam   " 1824, 11, 7
        Esther   " 1828, 5, 21
----, --, --. Shaidlock b 1790,12,16; m Rachel
    ----- b 1795,5,2
    Ch: Caleb
        Bracken   b 1819, 12, 5
        Rebecca
        Miller   " 1821, 5, 24
        Sarah
        Smith   " 1823, 1, 5
        Elisha   " 1825, 1, 10
        Meria
        Whitacre " 1827, 3, 29
        Albert
        Burge   " 1829, 4, 3
        Ellwood   " 1831, 1, 3
        Esther
        Fawcett   " 1832, 12, 12
        Lovina   " 1834, 4, 12
1835, 7, 2. Sarah m Septimus C. SHARPLESS
----, --, --. Israel b 1812,8,13; m Lydia

NEGUS, Israel, continued
    GARWOOD b 1813,4,4 d 1843,1,24 bur Spring-
    field
    Ch: Jesse   b 1837, 1, 8
        Jason   " 1838, 3, 3
        Eliza Ann " 1839, 10, 6 d 1841, 2,26
        bur Springfield
        Oliver   b 1841, 11, 28 " 1842, 3,13
        bur Springfield
        Griffith b 1842, 12, 9 " 1843, 3,19
        bur Springfield
    Israel m 2nd Ruth WARRINGTON b 1811,10,23
    (Ruth was dt Abraham & Keziah, Columbiana
    Co., O., m 1845,2,27)
1837, 8, 31. Lydia m Isaac WALKER

1832, 8, 25. Shedlock & w, Rachel, & ch,
    Caleb Bracken, Rebecca Miller, Sarah
    Smith, Elisha, Marie Whitacre, Albert
    Purdy & Elwood, rocf Westland MM, dtd
    1832,5,23
1833, 11, 23. John & w, Mariam, & ch, Lydia,
    Mary M., John W., Isaac, Mariam & Esther,
    rocf Providence MM, dtd 1833,10,31
1833, 11, 23. Israel rocf Providence MM, dtd
    1833,10,31
1833, 11, 23. Sarah rocf Providence MM, dtd
    1833,10,31
1836, 3, 26. Israel gct Redstone MM, to m
    Lydia Garwood
1836, 6, 25. Lydia G. rocf Redstone MM, dtd
    1836,6,1
1842, 2, 26. Caleb B. gct Short Creek MM, O.
1843, 6, 24. Rebecca rocf Providence MM, dtd
    1843,3,2
1844, 2, 24. John dis
1845, 4, 26. Shaidlock dis
1845, 5, 24. Miriam & dt, Esther, gct Salem
    MM
1846, 6, 27. Sarah S. gct Short Creek MM, O.
1846, 6, 27. Isaac gct Salem MM, Iowa
1846, 8, 22. Rachel & ch, Albert, Elwood,
    Esther T. & Lavina, gct Salem MM, Ia.
1846, 8, 22. Rebecca M. gct Salem MM, Ia.
1846, 8, 22. Maria W. gct Salem MM, Ia.
1846, 8, 22. Elisha gct Salem MM, Ia.
1849, 11, 24. John W. gct Salem MM
1849, 12, 22. Mary M. gct Salem MM
1849, 12, 22. Miriam gct Salem MM
1850, 4, 27. Israel & w, Ruth, & ch, Jesse
    & Jason, gct Salem MM
1850, 6, 22. Shaidlock rst at Salem MM, Ia.,
    on consent of this mtg
1851, 8, 23. John rst rq
1854, 3, 23. John gct Salem MM
1900, 4, 28. Emily gct Springdale MM, Ia.

NEVIS
1880, 6, 26. Ann & Esther rocf Goshen MM

NEWBERN
----, --, --. Jacob b 1789,10,28 d 1845,12,
    30 bur Springfield; m Mary ----- b 1790,

11,8
    Ch: Lydia   b 1817, 11, 8
1839, 8, 29. Lydia [Newburn] m Israel BARBER
1837, 5, 27. Jacob [Newborn] & w, Mary, & dt,
    Lydia, rocf Westland MM, dtd 1837,4,26

NORTH
----, --, --. Jesse b 1810,5,30; m Elizabeth
    ----- b 1813,4,12
    Ch: Sarah   b 1839, 10, 30
        Mary Jane " 1841, 11, 8
        John   " 1844, 2, 28
        Gustavus   " 1846, 3, 2
1845, 6, 28. Jesse & w, Elizabeth, & ch,
    Mary Jane & John, rocf Middleton MM, dtd
    1845,6,12
1846, 4, 25. Jesse & w, Elizabeth, & ch,
    Sarah, Mary Jane, John & Gustavus, gct
    Salem MM
1848, 1, 22. Jesse & w, Elizabeth, & ch,
    Sarah, Mary Jane, John & Gustavus, rocf
    Salem MM, dtd 1848,1,19
1851, 8, 25. Jesse & w, Elizabeth, & ch, Sa-
    rah, Mary Jane, John & Gustavus, gct
    Salem MM

OGDEN
1848, 9, 23. Joseph Bruff gct Salem MM, to m
    Anna M. Ogdon

OLIPHANT
-----,--, --. Ephraim & -----
    Ch: Ruth   b 1833, 11, 23
        Jonathan   " 1839, 6, 11
    Ephraim m 2nd Sarah SMITH, dt Joseph &
    Rachel Morris, Mahoning Co., O., (Ephraim
    was s Samuel & Elizabeth, Columbiana Co.,
    O.)
1851, 3, 27. Wm. H., s Samuel & Rachel, Ma-
    honing Co., O.; m in Springfield MH,
    Lydia BRUFF dt James B. & Sarah, Mahon-
    ing Co., O.

1850, 9, 28. Sarah gct Middleton MM
1852, 3, 27. Lydia B. gct Salem MM
1857, 5, 23. Ephraim & w, Sarah, & s, Jona-
    than, rocf Salem MM
1858, 11, 27. Ruth rocf Salem MM, dtd 1858,10,
    21
1863, 12, 26. Jonathan dis mcd & military
    service
1866, 10, 27. Ephraim gct Gilead MM
1867, 8, 24. Ruth gct Gilead MM
1877, 5, 22. Israel gct Gilead MM

OLIVER
1830, 1, 23. Rachel, minor, rocf Buckingham
    MM, dtd 1829,12,7, end by Salem MM, 1830,
    1,20

ONG
----, --, --. Lewis b 1816,3,15; m Elmira

ONG, continued
    ----- b 1820,12,20
      Ch: Annie E. b 1847, 3, 22
          Amanda   " 1851, 3, 1
          William P. " 1853, 7, 7
          Lewis B.   " 1856, 7, 6
          Anderson C." 1858, 4, 12
          Delbert T. " 1861, 4, 24
1867, 8, 28. Joseph P., s Lewis & Elmyra,
    Jefferson Co., O., b 1840,7,17; m in Goshen
    MH, Rhoda S. STRATTON, dt George & Su-
    sanna, Mahoning Co., O., b 1844,9,20
      Ch: Effa
          Lorena   b 1868, 11, 11

1868, 7, 25. Lewis & w, Elmira, & ch, Amanda,
    William P., Lewis B., Anderson C. & Del-
    bert T., rocf Smithfield MM, dtd 1868,6,22
1868, 10, 24. Joseph rocf Smithfield MM, dtd
    1868,10,19
1870, 12, 24. Amanda Binford (form Ong) con
    mcd
1872, 9, 25. Lewis & w, Almira, & ch, Wm. P.,
    Lewis B., Anderson C. & Delbert, gct
    Smithfield MM

ORR
1894, 1, 27. Jeannett recrq

OWEN
1827, 8, 25. Jesse rocf Piles Grove MM, N.J.,
    dtd 1827,5,1
1829, 6, 27. Jesse gct Chester MM, N. J.
1869, 6, 25. Elisan (form Votaw) dis mcd (W)

OYSTER
1840, 8, 22. Mary Ann (form Cobbs) dis mcd
1853, 9, 24. Amy (form Stanley) dis mcd

PACKER
1879, 11, 9. Ella C., w Wm., dt ----- AIKEN,
    b

1917, 12, 22. Ella (Aiken) relrq

PAINTER
----, --, --. Joseph b 1801,6,27 d 1880,11,28
    bur Springfield; m Rebecca ----- b 1800,
    12,7 d 1887,9,26 bur Springfield (W)
      Ch: Mary   b 1841, 4, 28
          Rachel Ann " 1847, 9, 21
----, --, --. Reuben G. b 1823,3,19 d 1877,4,
    30 bur Upper Springfield; m ----- -----
      Ch: Mary Anna b 1858, 5, 11   [(W)
          Joseph
            Willis   " 1861, 1, 3
          Adna Grif-
            fith   " 1862, 3, 2
1862, 4, 22. Anna B., w Willis, b

1865, 6, 23. Joseph & w, Rebecca, & dt, Ra-
    chel Ann, rocf Salem MM, dtd 1865,5,21
    (W)

1865, 7, 21. Mary rocf Salem MM, dtd 1865,5,
    24 (W)
1868, 5, 22. Mary Ellyson (form Painter) dis
    mcd (W)
1869, 8, 26. Rachel Ann Hole (form Painter)
    dis mcd (W)
1874, 5, 22. Reuben G. rst on consent of Sa-
    lem MM (W)
1874, 10, 23. Mary Ann, Joseph Willis & Adna
    Griffith, ch Reuben G., recrq (W)
1877, 2, 23. Reuben G. gct Salem MM, to m
    Phebe Fawcett (W)
1886, 8, 27. Joseph Willets dis mcd (W)
1900, 2, 24. Anna B. relrq

PALMER
1836, 9, 24. Sarah (form Wiley) con mcd
1838, 8, 25. Sarah gct Marlborough MM
1839, 8, 24. Sarah rocf Marlborough MM, dtd
    1839,7,30
1844, 7, 27. Sarah dis jas

PARK
----, --, --. David b 1824,8,23; m Asenath
    ----- b 1826,5,29 d 1882,9,2 bur Damascus
      Ch: David
          James   b 1862, 3, 23
          Lewis Lin-
            coln   " 1863, 12, 1
          Asenath
            Lorena   " 1866, 10, 18
    David m 2nd Asenath WHINERY, dt John &
    Elizabeth, b 1835,5,24
1869, 12, 30. Sylvester G., s David & Asen-
    ath, Mahoning Co., O., b 1846,6,1 d 1911,
    9,18; m in Damascus MH, Elizabeth STAN-
    LEY, dt Robert & Lydia, Columbiana Co.,
    O., b 1848,5,2
      Ch: Marietta b 1871, 4, 3
          Florence   " 1872, 12, 13 d 1890, 7,29
          Roberts   " 1874, 12, 22
1855, 10, 20. Sarah Emily, w Sylvester, dt
    Elijah & Elizabeth (Grisell) BRYANT, b
1889, 9, 1. Bertha Elizabeth [Parks], w F.W.
    dt Duncan & Mary (Blackburn) McDONALD, b
1921, 2, 6. Lida Ridgway b

1845, 12, 27. Asenath (form Butler) dis mcd
1870, 2, 26. Sylvester G. recrq
1870, 4, 23. David & w, Asenath, & ch, Da-
    vid J., Lewis L. & Asenath L. recrq
1870, 7, 23. Sylvester G. & w, Elizabeth,
    gct Gideon MM
1872, 6, 22. Sylvester G. & w, Elizabeth, &
    dt, Marietta, rocf Gilead MM
1874, 1, 23. Ruthanna (form Hole) dis mcd (W)
1887, 3, 26. Sarah W. recrq
1888, 11, 24. Sarah dis
1893, 4, 22. David J. relrq
1903, 2, 28. Lewis Lincoln gct Salem MM, O.
1916, 3, 25. Lida Ridgway rocf Barclay MM,
    Kans.

PARKER
1870, 7, 23. Louisa recrq

PARTINGTON
----, --, --. ----- m Flora HOBSON b 1883,7,8
    Ch: John Edwin b 1907, 11, 13
        Lee Paul   " 1908, 10, 31

1910, 11, 26. Flora H. & s, John Edwin & Lee
    Paul, gct Scipio MM, N. Y.

PATTERSON
1839, 5, 25. Fleming Crew gct Chesterfield
    MM, to m Sarah Ann Patterson

PEARCE
----, --, --. Archelaus b 1827,1,27 d 1920,3,
    27
----, --, --. Thomas H., s Archiles & Martha,
    b 1862,4,12 d 1907,2,17; m Asenath L.
    PARK, dt David & Asenith, b 1866,10,18
    Ch: Leonard W. b 1890, 2, 12
        Willis Ray " 1894, 5, 24

1904, 6, 25. Archelaus recrq
1922, 3, 25. Ray relrq

PEARSON
1892, 6, 24. Mary (form Fogg) dis mcd

PEELLE
1881, 5, 30. Albert, s Thomas & Rachel,
    Guilford Co., N. C.; m in Damascus MH,
    Mary Ann STANLEY, dt John Jr. & Abigail,
    Columbiana Co., O.

1881, 7, 23. Mary Ann gct New Garden MM, N.C.

PEEPLES
----, --, --. James, s James & Dinah, b 1846,
    7,22 d 1905,5,18; m Lucinda PIPER, dt
    James & Margaret, b 1842,4,7 d 1918,6,23
1896, 8, 22. James R. & Lucinda [Peoples] rec-
                                              [rq
PEMBERTON
----, --, --. Cyrus L., s Lemuel & Mary (Elle-
    man), b 1863,5,15; m Sarah M. LAWRENCE,
    dt Stephen & Julia Ann (Cox) b 1865,12,16
    Ch: Theoline
        Vera   b 1906, 2, 4
        Albert
        Lindley   " 1889, 7, 9
----, --, --. Elmer Lemuel, s Cyrus L. & Sarah
    M. (Lawrence), b 1887,5,24; m Helen Mae
    GILBERT, dt John & Nellie (Sharp), b
    1890,2,19 (W)
    Ch: Elmer Lloyd
                   b 1909, 8, 23
        Mildred
        Muriel   " 1911, 6, 18
        Earl Othel " 1917, 12, 6
        Pearl Opal " 1917, 12, 6
----, --, --. Albert Lindley, s Cyrus L. &
    Sarah M., b 1889,7,9; m Louisa M. HAMPTON,

dt Clinton E. & Sarah (Smith) bur Damas-
cus (W)
Ch: Lawrence
    Lindley   b 1914, 10, 25
    Clarence
    Leland   " 1816, 3, 10
    Margareta
    J.   " 1918, 2, 24
    Irena M.   " 1919, 11, 14
Albert Lindley m 2nd Mary E. WARRINGTON,
dt Edgar & Hannah (Coppock), b 1887,6,1
Ch: Bertha H. b 1923, 5, 2
    Dorothy
    Mabel   " 1924, 6, 28
    Elma S.   " 1928, 7, 7

1917, 4, 27. Albert Lindley rocf Spring
    River MM, Kans., dtd 1917,4,11 (W)
1917, 4, 27. Louisa, w Albert L., & ch,
    Lawrence Lindley & Clarence Leland, rocf
    Hickory Grove MM, Ia., dtd 1917,4,7 (W)
1922, 4, 21. Albert Lindley rmt Mary Eliza-
    beth Warrington (W)
1924, 7, 25. Julia Etta rocf Spring River
    MM, Kans., dtd 1924,7,16 (W)
1924, 7, 25. Cyrus L. & w, Sarah, & dt, Vera
    Theoline, rocf Spring River MM, Kans.,
    dtd 1824,7,16 (W)
1924, 9, 26. Julia Etta rmt Roland Blackburn
    (W)
1926, 7, 23. Elmer Lemuel & ch, Elmer Lloyd,
    Mildred Muriel, Earl Othel & Pearl Opal,
    rocf Spring River MM, Kans., dtd 1926,7,14
    (W)
1930, 3, 21. Helen Mae recrq (W)

PENNINGTON
----, --, --. John, s Levi T. & Anna M.
    (Burnside), b 1846,10,14; m Rebecca
    KENYON, b 1845,12,12 (John d 1933,12,10)
    Ch: Deborah   b 1869, 2, 20

1910, 7, 23. John & w, Rebecca, & dt, Deborah
    rocf Berlinville MM, O.
1915, 9, 25. John & w, Rebecca, & dt, Deborah
    gct Columbus MM
1918, 9, 28. John & w, Rebecca, & dt, Deborah
    rocf Columbus MM

PENNOCK
1868, 8, 26. Rachel & gr mother, Rachel Mas-
    ton, recrq

PENROSE
----, --, --. James, s John, b 1882,4,12;
    m Edith INGRAM, dt Elmore, b 1889,4,13
    Ch: James   b 1911, 7, 12
        Richard
        Hawley   " 1914, 11, 26

1891, 2, 28. M. Josephine relrq
1922, 4, 22. Edith recrq
1922, 5, 27. James & ch, James Jr. & Richard

PENROSE, continued
    H. recrq

PERRY
----, --, --. Mahlon b 1856,3,10; m Ella M.
    ----- b 1858,7,26
      Ch: Fred J.   b 1880, 8, 27
         M. William " 1882, 4, 17
         Hermon L.   " 1884, 1, 25
         Esek H.   " 1885, 8, 29

1896, 11, 28. Wyatt M. & w, Ella M., & ch,
    Fred J., Wm., Herman & Esek, rocf West-
    field MM
1902, 10, 25. W. Mahlon & w, Ella, & ch, M.
    Wm., Hermon L. & Esek H., gct Central City
    MM, Neb.
1904, 4, 23. Fred J. & w, Beulah, relrq

PETTIT
----, --, --. William b 1806,10,2; m Jane
    ----- b 1812,1,8
      Ch: Elizabeth b 1835, 3, 20
----, --, --. William, s Daniel & Rebecca,
    b 1853,3,6 d 1911,10,24; m Mary A. KIRK-
    BRIDE, dt Joseph & Susanna (Halderman)
    McBRIDE, b 1852,7,20
1856, 11, 26. Lydia S. [Pettet], w Joseph E.,
    dt Robert & Sarah (Tatum) STANLEY, b
1865, 1, 22. Laura E., dt Daniel & Rebecca
    (Garrison), b
1877, 11, 1. Joseph E., s Daniel R. & Rebecca
    W., Mahoning Co., O., b 1855,5,11 d 1922,
    8,7; m in residence of Sarah STANLEY, dt
    Robert & Sarah, Mahoning Co., O., b 1856,
    11,26
      Ch: Mable L.   b 1878, 11, 27
         Arthur Clyde
                b 1880, 7, 1
         Anna
           Blanche   " 1890, 4, 29
----, --, --. Arthur Clyde b 1880,7,1; m Effie
    ELLET b 1885,4,9
      Ch: Mildred
          Elizabeth b 1906, 3, 15
         Doris
          Irene   " 1909, 2, 20

1830, 6, 26. Wm. [Pettet] rocf Baltimore MM,
    dtd 1830,5,6
1830, 9, 25. Wm. [Pettet] Jr. gct Buckingham
    MM, to m Sarah C. Malone
1834, 3, 22. William gct Short Creek MM, O.,
    to m Jane R. Hussey
1834, 12, 27. Charles H. Rice gct Sandy Spring
    MM, to m Charity D. Pettit
1835, 2, 28. Jane R. rocf Short Creek MM, O.,
    dtd 1834,12,23
1835, 9, 26. Wm. Jr. & w, Jane, & dt, Eliza-
    beth H., gct Redstone MM

1878, 6, 22. Joseph C. recrq
1881, 5, 28. Laura E. recrq
1890, 5, 24. Mary A. rocf Sandy Spring MM
1893, 4, 22. Wm. recrq
1897, 1, 23. Laura gct East Goshen MM
1906, 7, 28. Joseph & fam gct Salem MM, O.
1910, 9, 24. Joseph & Lydia S. rocf Salem MM,
    O.
1913, 12, 27. Laura rocf East Goshen MM
1920, 8, 19. Clyde & fam gct Beloit MM

PHILLIPS
1881, 4, 7. Nancy Laura, dt John E. & Sallie,
    b
----, --, --. Thomas W. b 1851,6,28; m Kathe-
    rine ----- b 1851,9,25
      Ch: Rebecca   b 1885, 5, 31
         Lizzie   " 1887, 1, 25
----, --, --. Alonzo C., s Elmore & Mary, b
    1864,12,25; m Hannah COBBS, dt Albert &
    Esther, b 1866,5,15
      Ch: Frank E.   b 1889, 2, 18
----, --, --. Joseph E. b 1871,9,13; m Marga-
    ret RILEY, b 1874,10,14
      Ch: Emily
          Margaret b 1911, 10, 22
----, --, --. Homer, s Albert & Luella (San-
    tee), b 1883,8,28; m Clara STANLEY, dt
    Jehu C. & Edith (Shreve), b 1884,12,21
      Ch: Helen   b 1908, 7, 14

1871, 6, 23. Asenath (form Lynch) dis mcd
    (W)
1887, 10, 22. Alonzo E. rocf Short Creek MM,
    O.
1897, 1, 23. Thomas W. [Phillis] & w, Catha
    rin, & ch, Rebecca & Elizabeth, recrq
1897, 2, 27. Nancy Laura recrq
1911, 11, 25. Rebecca relrq
1922, 4, 22. Joseph & w, Margaret, & dt,
    Emily, rocf Winona MM
1927, 4, 28. Joseph & w, Margaret, & dt,
    Emily, gct Alliance MM
1927, 10, 27. Homer C., Clara & Helen rocf
    Greenfield MM, Ind.

PHINNEY
1912, 6, 22. Edward & Barbary gct Yorba MM,
    Calif.

PICKETT
1922, 7, 21. Wilford L. Hall gct Plainfield
    MM, Ind., to m Ethel Pickett (W)

PIDGEON
1865, 10, 12. Anzanetta, dt John B. & Lydia A.
    STANLEY, b

PIERCE
1792, 2, 7. James b
1866, 10, 18. Asenath L. Park, w Harry, b

1902, 1, 25. Thomas H., Leonard W. & Willis

PIERCE, continued
    Ray, recrq

PIM

----, --, --. ----- m Phebe ----- b 1816,3,7
    d 1890,6,19 bur Damascus
    Ch: John   b 1848, 1, 3
        Charles " 1850, 7, 1
1843, 4, 7. Benjamin b
----, --, --. Charles b 1850,7,1 d 1920,3,27;
    m Sarah Emily ----- b 1855,10,20
    Ch: Lydia G. b 1884, 2, 8 d 1902, 5, 6
        Maggie
          Vietta   " 1886, 2, 25
        Willard
          Lorain   " 1888, 11, 17
----, --, --. Aden, s Lewis & Sarah, b 1854,3,
    21 d 1918,1,31; m Lauretta HALDERMAN, dt
    Joseph & Esther, b 1851,9,1
    Ch: Bertice   b 1880, 1, 24
----, --, --. Asa b 1848,3,21 d 1930,5,13; m
    Mary Anna SHREVE, dt Enoch & Elizabeth
    (Chambers), b 1848,8,25

1829, 6, 27. Enos [Pimm] rocf Sandy Spring
    MM, dtd 1829,7,26
1835, 3, 28. Enos [Pimm] gct Sandy Spring
    MM
1863, 1, 24. Isaac E. Kille gct Sandy Spring
    MM, to m Elizabeth Pim
1864, 6, 25. Phebe & ch, John & Charles, rocf
    Sandy Spring MM, dtd 1864,3,24
1866, 3, 23. Rhoda (form Holloway) dis mcd
    (W)
1868, 2, 21. Anne (form Taylor) dis mcd (W)
1868, 2, 22. Anna (form Taylor) dis mcd
1869, 6, 26. John gct Spring Creek MM, Ia.
1884, 2, 23. Sarah Emma rocf Columbus MM
1887, 4, 23. Benjamin relrq
1889, 6, 22. Aden & w, Lauretta, & s, Bertie,
    rocf Sandy Spring MM, O.
1901, 4, 27. Benjamin dropped from mbrp
1913, 10, 25. Maggie (Pim) Cosand gct Lupton
    MM, Mich.
1917, 12, 22. Asa & w, Mary Ann, rocf Lupton
    MM, Mich.
1919, 1, 25. Willard gct Alliance MM
1922, 9, 23. Bertice dropped from mbrp

PINKHAM
1861, 5, 2. Thomas Edward, s Thos. & Mary
    B., Columbiana Co., O.; m in Damscus MH,
    Mary FULLER, dt Edward J. & Anna C.,
    Cuyahoga Co., O.

1861, 8, 24. Mary Fuller gct Short Creek MM,
    O.

POLLARD
----, --, --. Wm. Henry, s George & Mary J.
    (Cohoe), b 1874,10,10; m Emma Leota HEALD
    dt Joseph S. & Elizabeth D. (Emmons), b
    1874,5,20 (W)

    Ch: Alice Eliza-
        beth   b 1905, 4, 9
        Martha
          Irene   " 1908, 2, 22
        Dorothy
          Sarah   " 1909, 12, 23
        Edith
          Caroline " 1913, 2, 6
        Ellen H.   " 1914, 10, 11
        Rachel S. " 1916, 8, 1

1917, 11, 23. Wm. Henry & w, Emma Leota, &
    ch, Alice Elizabeth, Martha Irena, Doro-
    thy Sarah, Edith Caroline, Ellen H. &
    Rachel L., rocf Norwich MM, Canada, dtd
    1917,11,14 (W)

POOL
----, --, --. Jonas b 1801,12,21; m Ann -----
    b 1800,5,10
    Ch: Asemath   b 1825, 6, 5
        Priscilla " 1827, 2, 16
1831, 6, 2. Jane m Stephen McBRIDE
1837, 9, 28. Lydia m William CARR

1831, 4, 23. Jane rocf Carmel MM, dtd 1831,3,
    19
1831, 4, 23. Sarah rocf Carmel MM, dtd 1831,
    3,19
1831, 4, 23. Lydia rocf Carmel JM, dtd 1831,
    3,19
1831, 8, 27. Sarah gct Sandy Pool MM
1834, 5, 24. Jonas & w, Ann, & ch, Asenath &
    Priscilla, rocf Carmel MM, dtd 1834,2,15
1837, 3, 25. Jonas & w, Ann, & ch, Asenath &
    Priscilla, gct Salem MM

POORMAN
1866, 4, 28. Rebecca A. (form Thomas) dis mcd

PORTER
1868, 8, 12. Maggie, dt Wm. & Nancy BARGER, b
1846, 2, --. Susan M. b

1895, 12, 28. Maggie recrq
1897, 2, 27. Susan M. recrq

PULLAM
----, --, --. Burley T. m Anna May BONDURANT,
    dt John & Cassie E. (Harding), b 1886,10,
    14
    Ch: Edith
        Marie   b 1922, 5, 12

1931, 3, 26. Anna May & Edith recrq

PURVIANCE
----, --, --. Wm. b 1816,11,19; m Sarah -----
    b 1817,1,7
    Ch: William   b 1848, 8, 7
1846, 8, 12. Elizabeth L. b
1848, 8, 7. Wm. S. b

PURVIANCE, continued
1867, 1, 26. Wm. & w, Sarah, & s, Wm., rocf
    Smithfield MM, dtd 1866,12,17
1873, 12, 27. Wm. S. con mcd
1873, 10, 25. Elizabeth L. (form Jones) con
    mcd
1878, 4, 27. Wm. & w, Sarah, gct Smithfield
    MM
1878, 4, 27. Wm. S. & w, Elizabeth L., gct
    Smithfield MM

RAKESTRAW
----, --, --. Levi b 1785,12,2; m Rebecca
    ----- b 1795,4,8
    Ch: Isaac   b 1812, 3, 13
        Hannah   " 1814, 2, 2
        Sarah   " 1816, 10, 18
        Benjamin   " 1818, 12, 19
        Haran B.   " 1821, 10, 2
        Jane M.   " 1825, 3, 18
        Elisha   " 1827, 9, 13
        Rebecca   " 1831, 11, 15
1840, 4, 1. Isaac, s Levi & Rebecca, Colum-
    biana Co., O., b 1812,3,13; m in Goshen
    MH, Lydia R. LUPTON, dt Nathan & Margaret,
    Columbiana Co., O., b 1807,1,28
    Ch: Joshua L. b 1842, 11, 24
        Nathan   " 1845, 12, 30
1851, 3, 26. Rebecca B. m Emmor LUPTON
1864, 6, 29. Joshua L., s Isaac & Lydia R.,
    Mahoning Co., O., b 1842,11,24; m in
    Goshen MH, Ellen STANLEY, dt Micajah &
    Unity, Mahoning Co., O., b 1840,4,1
    Ch: Orlin   b 1866, 7, 24
        Olive   " 1867, 9, 12
1868, 8, 26. Nathan, s Isaac & Lydia, Mahon-
    ing Co., O.; m in Goshen MH, Ruthanna
    STANLEY, dt Micajah & Unity, Mahoning Co.,
    O.
1832, 6, 23. Hannah dis
1837, 12, 23. Sarah Barringer (form Rakestraw)
    dis mcd
1840, 8, 22. Benjamin dis mcd
1845, 1, 25. Haram B. dis mcd
1848, 8, 26. Elisha dis mcd
1848, 11, 25. Amy (form Cobbs) dis mcd
1849, 9, 22. Jane Young (form Rakestraw) dis
    mou
1863, 5, 22. Isaac dis jG (W)
1863, 5, 22. Lydia dis jG (W)
1863, 8, 21. Levi & Rebecca dis jG (W)
1910, 8, 18. Mary gct Los Angeles MM, Calif.

RALEY
----, --, --. Ann b 1803,7,12 d 1875,4,2 bur
    Damascus
----, --, --. James b 1799,8,3 d 1872,10,14
    bur Damascus; m Unity HOLE b 1820,1,27
    d 1885,8,29
1868, 7, 2. James, s Robert & Sarah, Mahon-
    ing Co., O.; m in Damascus MH, Unity C.
    HOLE, dt Benjamin & Elizabeth STANLEY,
    Mahoning Co., O.

1834, 2, 27. Amos rocf Sandy Spring MM, dtd
    1834,12,26
1842, 9, 24. Amos [Raleigh] gct Salem MM, Ia.
1847, 3, 27. Dilworth Schooley gct Sandy
    Spring MM, to m Eliza Raley
1855, 7, 28. Ann [Reley] gct Sandy Spring MM
1868, 5, 23. James rocf Burlington MM, N.J.,
    dtd 1868,5,7
1869, 9, 25. Ann [Railey] rocf New Garden
    MM, dtd 1869,9,22
1880, 8, 19. Unity C. [Railey] gct Alliance
    MM
1882, 11, 25. Unity C. [Raleigh] rocf Alliance
    MM

RANDOLPH
----, --, --. Edward F. b 1788,8,10 d 1872,3,
    19 bur Damascus

1826, 5, 27. Edward Fitz rocf Carmel MM, dtd
    1826,4,15
1863, 3, 27. Edward F. dis jG (W)

RASCHE
1862, 4, 26. Julius rocf Salem MM
1862, 12, 26. Julius & Elizabeth G. Fawcett
    rm (W)
1863, 4, 24. Elizabeth G. gct Salem MM (W)

RATCLIFF
1854, 8, 31. Josiah C., s Josiah & Mary, Ma-
    honing Co., O., b 1833,7,7 d 1898,2,17; m
    in Springfield MH, Elizabeth FRENCH, dt
    Wm. & Judith, Columbiana Co., O., b 1837,
    2,12
    Ch: Hurford   b 1855, 7, 29
        Emmor   " 1857, 5, 14
        William R. " 1859, 5, 4
        Mary Ju-
          dith   " 1861, 4, 11
        Alice Ann " 1862, 6, 11

1829, 11, 28. Daniel Andrews gct Short Creek
    MM, O., to m Mary [Ratliff]
1844, 5, 25. Robert Ellyson gct Stillwater
    MM, to m Mary Ratcliff
1844, 11, 23. Josiah E. & mother, Mary Ellyson
    rocf Stillwater MM, dtd 1844,9,28
1855, 6, 23. Josiah & w, Elizabeth, gct Three
    Rivers MM, Ia.
1856, 10, 25. Josiah C. & w, Elizabeth, & s,
    Hulford, rocf Pleasant Plain MM, Ia.
1863, 1, 24. Josiah & w, Elizabeth, dis jW

REDMAN
----, --, --. Henry b 1814,9,28 d 1891,4,30;
    m Maria ----- b 1812,9,14 d 1888,1,19

1870, 5, 28. Henry & Maria recrq

REED
1874, 6, 25. Sarah Lavena Naylor b

REEDER
1852, 3, 4. Levi, s Joseph & Hannah, Henry
Co., Ia.; m in Springfield MH, Rachel P.
STANLEY, dt Joseph & Abigail, Columbiana
Co., O.
1860, 6, 28. Levi, s Joseph & Hannah, Henry
Co., Ia.; m in Springfield MH, Joanna
THOMAS, dt Jesse & Rebecca

1852, 4, 24. Rachel P. gct Salem MM, Ia.
1860, 9, 22. Joanna gct Salem MM, Ia.
1876, 2, 25. Achsah rocf Middleton MM, dtd
1876,2,19 (W)

REEVE
----, --, --. Joshua [Reve] b 1775,11,22; m
Milicent ----- b 1781,1,16
Ch: Hannah   b 1799, 9, 16
    Benjamin " 1801, 4, 9
    Samuel C. " 1803, 4, 6
    Ellen   " 1805, 3, 31
    Catherine " 1807, 7, 5
    Joshua   " 1809, 8, 13
    Job   " 1811, 6, 7
----, --, --. ----- m Mary ----- b 1785,7,17
d 1840,10,31 bur Springfield
Ch: Lewis   b 1816, 11, 12
    -----   " 1819, 2, 6
    Phebe   " 1821, 5, 5
    William   " 1823, 7, 4
    Thomas   " 1825, 7, 15
1827, 2, 28. Samuel C., s Joshua & Melescent,
Columbiana Co., O., b 1803,4,6; m in Goshen
MH, Anna ELLYSON, dt Zachariah & Mary, Columbiana Co., O., b 1803,6,3
Ch: Benjamin b 1827, 12, 5
    Mary   " 1831, 1, 10
    Millicent " 1832, 1, 28
1829, 10, 29. Catharine m Benjamin P. LANG-
STAFF

1829, 4, 25. Ellen Hammit (form Reeve) dis
mou
1832, 4, 28. Samuel C. & w, Anna, & ch,
Benjamin, Mary & Milicent, gct Marlborough
MM
1835, 4, 25. Joshua gct Carmel MM, to m
Elizabeth Huestis
1835, 11, 28. Joshua gct Pennville MM
1840, 3, 28. Mary & ch, William & Thomas,
rocf London Grove MM, dtd 1839,11,7
1840, 3, 28. Phebe rocf London Grove MM, dtd
1839,11,7
1840, 3, 28. Lewis rocf London Grove MM, dtd
1839,11,7
1841, 7, 24. Daniel rocf ND MM
1843, 3, 25. Phebe dis disunity
1843, 4, 22. Thomas, minor, gct Salem MM
1844, 5, 25. Lewis [Reeves] gct Mississinewa
MM, Ind.
1847, 7, 24. Dorcas Ann (form Thomas) con mcd
1848, 9, 23. Thomas [Reeves] rocf New Garden
MM, dtd 1848,8,24

1854, 11, 25. Thomas [Reeves] & w, Dorcas, &
dt, Amanda, gct Wabash MM, Ind.
1863, 7, 24. Ann dis jG (W)
1865, 1, 27. John [Reeves] dis mcd (W)
1871, 4, 21. Samuel C. [Reeves] gct Springville MM, Ia.

RELEY
1855, 5, 31. John, s Robert & Sarah, Columbiana Co., O.; m in Springfield MH, Ann
WALTON, dt Jehu & Rebecca LORD, Mahoning
Co., O.

REYNOLDS
----, --, --. Allen b 1810,11,10; m Mary -----
b 1818,1,29
Ch: Martha K. b 1844, 4, 22
    Sarah   " 1847, 6, 14
    Albert   " 1848, 1, 13

1846, 3, 28. Allen & w, Mary, & dt, Martha
H., rocf New Garden MM
1853, 3, 27. Allen & w, Mary, & ch, Martha,
Sarah, Albert, Samuel & Wm. G., gct Driftwood MM, Ind.

RHUL
1861, 7, 27. Eliza Jane (form Thomas) dis mcd

RICE
1834, 9, 27. Charles H. recrq
1834, 12, 27. Charles H. gct Sandy Spring MM,
to m Charity D. Pettit
1835, 6, 27. Charley D. rocf Sandy Spring MM,
dtd 1835,5,22
1836, 4, 23. Charles H. & w, Charity D., & s,
William, gct Sandy Spring MM
1870, 8, 26. Sarah (form Cope) dis mcd (W)

RICHARDSON
1879, 7, 6. Eunice H., dt Elwood B. & Phebe
W. (Dean) CONRAD, b (W)

1923, 2, 23. Eunice (form Conrad) dis mcd (W)

RINGLEY
1898, 2, 26. Elpha recrq

ROBBINS
1874, 1, 11. Ona Mae Byers b

1922, 11, 25. Iona Mae recrq

ROBERTS
1866, 4, 28. Rebecca A. (form Walton) dis mcd
1870, 4, 23. Mary Jane (form Benedict) con
mcd
1870, 6, 25. Mary Jane gct New Sharon MM, Ia.

ROGERS
1863, 4, 2. Daniel T., s Ansel & Louisa,
Crawford Co., O.; m in Springfield MH,
Lucy Jane COBBS, dt Ansalm & Ann, Columbi-

ROGERS, continued
    ana Co., O., b 1841,2,26

1845, 7, 26. Lydia (form Gibson) dis mcd
1859, 3, 26. Cert rec for Jonathan T. from
    Westland MM, end to Spiceland MM, Ind.
1864, 6, 25. Daniel T. rocf Gilead MM
1864, 11, 26. Daniel Y. & w, Lucy Jane, &
    infant ch gct New Sharon MM, Ia.

ROOD
1828, 7, 26. Jonathan & w, Clarissa, & ch,
    Ithamer & Emmor, rocf Salem MM, dtd 1828,
    7,23
1830, 6, 26. Jonathan & w & s, Emmor, gct
    Salem MM
1834, 6, 28. Jonathan & w, Clarissa, & s,
    Emmor, rocf Salem MM, dtd 1834,5,21
1835, 1, 24. Ithamer dis mcd
1838, 5, 26. Jonathan & w, Clarissa, gct
    Sandy Spring MM
1838, 9, 28. Emmor gct Allum Creek MM

RUGGLY
----, --, --. Henry & Anna
    Ch: Elpha
        Viola   b 1884, 1, 29
        Alva   " 1887, 11, 11
        Fay   " 1889, 9, 16

1900, 4, 28. Alva & Fay [Rugley], ch Henry,
    recrq
1925, 6, 25. Alva & Fay [Rugley] dropped from
    mbrp

RYON
1886, 6, 10. Fred L., s Geo. L. & Polly M.,
    Jackson Co., Mich.; m in residence of
    George SHRIVER, Olive A. SHRIVER, dt Geo.
    & Elizabeth, Columbiana Co., O.

1886, 8, 19. Olive A. gct Rollin MM, Mich.

SANDERS
1862, 10, 1. Wm. H. b
----, --, --. Henry W. b 1838,11,5; m Mary A.
    ----- b 1838,7,27
    Ch: Fanny M. b 1874, 3, 3

1884, 4, 26. Wm. H. recrq
1884, 4, 26. Martha B. gct Honey Creek MM, Ia.
1887, 8, 18. Henry W. & w, Mary A., recrq
1888, 6, 23. Wm. H. dis disunity
1889, 4, 27. Fannie May recrq

SANTEE
1830, 1, 22. Hannah, w Delorma, b
----, --, --. Silvester J., s Deloram & Hannah
    b 1858,2,21 d 1925,8,3; m Philena M. STAN-
    LEY, dt Wm. P. & Eliza, b 1855,11,3
    Ch: Mabel   b 1889, 9, 10 d 1898, 1, 3
        Earl Stan-
        ley   " 1893, 10, 31

----, --, --. Earl Stanley b 1893,10,31; m
    Helen WHINERY, dt Samuel D. & Olive (Bun-
    dy), b 1895,11,16
    Ch: Ralph
        Wendell   b 1921, 6, 21
        Margery
        Beth   " 1923, 2, 1
        Kenneth
        Lee   " 1924, 12, 19
        Esek Ir-
        ving   " 1926, 9, 13
        Herbert
        Earl   " 1929, 1, 22
        Dean Paul " 1933, 1, 17

1851, 7, 26. Hannah (form Ellyson) dis mcd
1869, 6, 26. Hannah recrq
1870, 7, 23. Leon B. recrq
1886, 5, 22. Sylvester J. rocf East Goshen MM
1918, 1, 26. Florence E. gct East Goshen MM
1919, 9, 27. Helen recrq

SATTERTHWAIT
1913, 8, 22. Wm. D. rmt Mabel H. Cameron (W)
1913, 10, 24. Mabel C. gct Salem MM (W)

SAVAGE
1856, 8, 20. Florence N., dt David & Caroline
    b

1894, 1, 27. Florence recrq

SCHOOLEY
1842, 4, 27. James, s Israel & Sarah, Colum-
    biana Co., O., b 1816,12,18; m in Goshen
    MH, Rebecca MALMSBERRY, dt Benjamin &
    Jane, Columbiana Co., O., b 1815,10,4
----, --, --. Dillworth b 1823,10,20; m Eliza

1832, 9, 22. James, minor, rocf Salem MM, dtd
    1832,9,19
1837, 8, 26. James gct Salem MM
1840, 1, 25. James rocf Salem MM, dtd 1840,1,
    22
1842, 1, 22. Dilworth rocf Salem MM, dtd 1842
    1,19
1845, 4, 26. Moses N. Butler gct Middleton MM
    to m Emily Schooley
1847, 3, 27. Dilworth gct Sandy Spring MM, to
    m Eliza Raley
1847, 4, 24. James & w, Rebecca, & s, Israel,
    gct Middleton MM
1847, 10, 23. Eliza rocf Sandy Spring MM, dtd
    1847,9,28
1852, 6, 26. Dilworth & w, Eliza, gct Salem
    MM, Ia.

SCOTT
----, --, --. Benjamin m Ann ----- b 1791,11,
    24
    Ch: Mary Ann   b 1820, 12, 31
        Phebe   " 1822, 10, 10

SCOTT, Benjamin & Ann, continued
    Ch: Prophet   b 1824, 5, 1
        Sarah   " 1825, 12, 19
        Elizabeth " 1827, 11, 20
        Lydia   " 1829, 5, 16
        Joseph   " 1831, 5, 9
        Hannah   " 1835, 9, 20
----, --, --. ----- m Abigail ----- b 1796,10, 16
    Ch: Hiram   b 1821, 5, 10
        Margaret " 1823, 5, 6
        Lewis   " 1824, 5, 17
        Lemuel
         Nelson   " 1826, 12, 26
        James Cow-
         gill   " 1829, 3, 25
        Rachel   " 1831, 7, 15
        Jehu   " 1833, 7, 17

1832, 11, 24. Ann & ch, Mary Ann, Phebe, Prophet B., Sarah, Elizabeth, Lydia & Joseph, rocf Salem MM, dtd 1832,10,24
1833, 8, 24. Ann & ch, Mary Ann, Phebe, Hannah, Prophet B., Sarah, Elizabeth, Lydia & Joseph, gct New Garden MM
1839, 1, 26. Ann & ch, Mary Ann, Phebe, Prophet B., Sarah, Elizabeth, Lydia, Joseph & Hannah, rocf New Garden MM, dtd 1838,11,22
1841, 7, 24. Mary Ann gct Marlborough MM
1841, 7, 24. Phebe gct Marlborough MM
1841, 7, 24. Ann gct Marlborough MM
1843, 1, 28. Hiram dis mcd
1850, 4, 27. Abigail & s, Jehu, gct Salem MM, Ia.
1850, 4, 27. Margaret gct Salem MM, Ia.
185-, 4, 27. Rachel gct Salem MM, Ia.
1850, 11, 23. Lewis gct Salem MM, Ia.
1850, 11, 23. James C. gct Salem MM, Ia.
1853, 6, 25. Lemuel N. dis mcd

SEACHRIST
----, --, --. John, s Jacob & Meribas, b 1870,11,24; m Marietta A. COBBS, dt Lynch & Unity, b 1873,9,29
    Ch: Effie
        Mable   b 1895, 4, 24

1899, 1, 28. John & dt, Effie Mabel, recrq

SEBRALL
1858, 4, 24. Aaron Gibson gct Marlborough MM, to m Elizabeth H. Sebrall
1863, 8, 21. Joseph & Mary dis jG (W)

SELLARS
1881, 1, 22. Drusilla gct Alliance MM

SHARP
----, --, --. Enoch b 1769,2,16; m Sarah ----- b 1771,5,24
    Ch: Sarah   b 1806, 5, 19
        Mary   " 1813, 12, 24

----, --, --. Isaac b 1803,3,5; m Lydia ----- b 1807,12,24
    Ch: Ann   b 1829, 6, 19
        Oliver   " 1830, 8, 10
        Eliza   " 1832, 3, 3

1828, 6, 28. Enoch & w, Sarah, & dt, Mary, rocf Middleton MM, dtd 1828,5,28
1828, 6, 28. Sarah rocf Middleton MM, dtd 1828,5,8
1829, 1, 24. Isaac & w, Lydia, rocf Sandy Spring MM, dtd 1828,11,21
1836, 5, 28. Isaac & w, Lydia, & ch, Ann, Oliver, Eliza, Adaline & Hannah, gct Sandy Spring MM
1836, 6, 25. Sarah Jr. gct New Garden MM
1836, 6, 25. Mary gct New Garden MM
1837, 2, 25. Enoch & w, Sarah, gct New Garden MM

SHARPLESS
1835, 7, 2. Septimus C., s Benjamin & Amy, Columbiana Co., O., b 1804,6,21; m in Smithfield MM, Sarah NEGUS, dt John & Miriam, Columbiana Co., O., b 1807,4,23
    Ch: Isaac   b 1836, 5, 2
        John   " 1837, 4, 2 d 1838, 8,14 bur Springfield
        Nathan   b 1838, 4, 11
        Lavina   " 1839, 7, 21
        Amy   " 1840, 11, 26
        Miriam   " 1841, 11, 29

1835, 8, 22. Sarah gct Salem MM
1837, 6, 24. Septimus C. & w, Sarah, & ch, Isaac & John, rocf Salem MM, dtd 1837,5,4
1842, 12, 24. Septimus C. & w, Sarah, & ch, Isaac Nathan Lavina Amy & Miriam, gct Middleton MM
1865, 5, 27. Sarah rocf Gilead MM, dtd 1865, 4,18
1865, 5, 27. Albert & w, Lydia, & s, Wm., rocf Gilead MM, dtd 1865,4,18
1855, 3, 24. Albert & w, Lydia H., & s, Wm., gct Springdale MM, Ia.
1866, 3, 24. Sarah gct Springdale MM, Ia.

SHAW
----, --, --. Nathan b 1811,6,17; m Miriam ----- b 1814,12,23

1835, 2, 28. Miriam rocf Carmel MM, dtd 1834,12,20
1835, 3, 28. Nathan rocf New Garden MM, dtd 1835,1,22
1837, 5, 27. Nathan & w, Miriam, gct Carmel MM

SHEEHAN
1884, 6, 26. Mary E. (form Vansyoc) dis mcd (W)

SHEETS
1898, 6, 25. Lottie rocf Salem MM

SHELDON
1900, 2, 24. W. F. recrq

SHINN
----, --, --. John b 1791,3,19; m Sybilla ----
     b 1793,12,25
     Ch: Joseph   b 1815, 12, 1
         Mary   " 1817, 5, 22
         Elijah   " 1822, 8, 22
         John C.   " 1824, 11, 25
         Ann   " 1827, 9, 14
----, --, --. Thomas b 1772,2,14 d 1851,9,21
     bur Goshen; m Sarah ----- b 1787,6,9
     Ch: Susan S.   b 1820, 7, 13
         Sally Ann   " 1822, 1, 6 d 1848,10, 3
           bur Goshen
         Joseph   b 1825, 4, 19
         Benjamin   " 1828, 5, 1
----, --, --. Joshua b 1800,11,13; m Abigail
     ----- b 1802,9,2
1853, 10, 26. Mary Ann m Amos STANLEY
1854, 11, 8. Joseph, s Thomas & Sarah, Mahon-
     ing Co., O., b 1825,4,19; m in Goshen MH,
     Mary STRATTON, dt George & Susanna, Mahon-
     ing Co., O., b 1836,11,17
     Ch: Susanna S. b 1855, 10, 29
         Byron   " 1857, 11, 23

1826, 5, 27. David & w, Susan, & ch, Charles,
     Rachel, Hannah & David R., rocf Frankfort
     MM, Pa., dtd 1826,3,23, endorsed by Salem
     MM
1826, 12, 23. David & w, Susanna, & ch,
     Charles, Rachel, Hannah & David R., gct
     Marlborough MM
1827, 6, 23. John & w, Sabilla, & ch, Joseph,
     Mary, Elijah & John C., rocf Salem MM, dtd
     1827,5,23
1828, 10, 25. John dis jH
1828, 10, 25. Sibbilla dis jH
1832, 2, 25. George Brantingham gct New Gar-
     den MM, to m Hannah Shinn
1832, 8, 25. Joshua & w, Abigail, rocf New
     Garden MM, dtd 1832,8,23
1837, 1, 28. Mary dis jH
1839, 2, 22. Thomas & w, Sally, & ch, Sally
     Ann, Joseph & Benjamin, rocf Marlborough
     MM, dtd 1838,12,25
1839, 2, 22. Susan rocf Marlborough MM, dtd
     1838,11,27
1839, 7, 27. Susan Jordan (form Shinn) dis
     mcd
1840, 9, 26. Joseph dis jH
1844, 9, 28. Elijah dis disunity
1847, 7, 24. John Jr. dis mcd
1847, 9, 25. Lydia (form Votaw) dis mcd
1849, 10, 27. Mary Ann & Wm. H., minors, rocf
     Marlborough MM, dtd 1849,9,28
1853, 11, 26. Hester (form Brooks) dis mcd
1854, 4, 22. Benjamin dis mcd & jas

1856, 3, 22. Wm. H. dis disunity
1861, 10, 26. Joseph & w, Mary, & ch, Susanna
     S., Byron & Sarah Elizabeth, gct Red
     Cedar MM, Ia.
1862, 1, 25. Sarah gct Red Cedar MM, Ia.
1863, 5, 22. Joshua & Abigail dis jG (W)
1863, 9, 25. Joseph & Mary dis jG (W)
1926, 1, 22. Roselia Brantingham dropped from
     mbrp (W)

SHOOK
----, --, --. Edward S., s Wm. A. & Laura
     (Delantes), b 1886,2,18; m Mary ALAZIER,
     dt Matt & Catharine (Vinkler) ALESI, b
     1885,2,22
     Ch: Curtis Ed-
           ward   b 1909, 8, 29
         Virginia
           Travers   " 1915, 11, 19

1904, 6, 25. Edward S. recrq
1931, 12, 24. Curtis & Virginia dropped from
     mbrp

SNELLING
1871, 6, 1. Almeda V. m Israel J. GREEN

SHREVE
----, --, --. Stacy [Sreve] b 1782,4,2 d 1854,
     8,10 bur Goshen; m Vashti ----- b 1782,5,5
     d 1865,1,28 bur Goshen
     Ch: William   b 1811, 6, 20
         Annie   " 1812, 9, 27
         Enoch   " 1814, 1, 22
         Joel   " 1815, 5, 4 d 1815,12,12
           bur Goshen
         Mary   " 1816, 8, 23
         Stacy   " 1818, 7, 22
         Vashti   " 1820, 5, 4 d 1842,12,31
           bur Goshen
         Joshua   " 1821, 6, 17
         Evan   " 1822, 11, 27
         John   " 1824, 5, 4
1830, 10, 27. Annar m Joseph CATTELL
1839, 5, 29. William, s Stacy & Vashti, Co-
     lumbiana Co., O.; m in Goshen MH, Esther
     CATTELL, dt James & Deborah, Columbiana
     Co., O.
1841, 3, 3. Enoch, s Stacy & Vashti, Colum
     biana Co., O.; m in Goshen MH, Elizabeth
     KILLE, dt Clayton & Elizabeth, Stark Co.,
     O.
1845, 5, 29. Evan, s Stacy & Vashti, Colum-
     biana Co., O., b 1822,11,2 d 1905,1,20;
     m in Springfield MH, Meribah STANLEY, dt
     Benjamin & Elizabeth, Columbiana Co., O.,
     b 1823,4,12 d 1900,5,15
     Ch: Vashti R.   b 1847, 1, 12
         Angetta   " 1849, 8, 9
         Elizabeth
           Annar   " 1851, 4, 19
         Osborn   " 1853, 7, 10
         Stacy B.   " 1856, 12, 26
         Benjamin   " 1860, 9, 9

SHREVE, Evan & Meribah, continued
    Ch: Luella J. b 1863, 10, 23
1847, 5, 26. Stacy, s Stacy & Vashti, Mahon-
    ing Co., O., b 1818,7,22; m in Goshen MH,
    Hannah MALMSBERRY, dt Benjamin & James,
    Mahoning Co., O., b 1817,8,2
    Ch: Edith   b 1849, 3, 8
        Philena   " 1850, 1, 22
1848, 6, 1. John, s Stacy & Vashti, Mahoning
    Co., O., b 1824,5,4 d 1901,2,12; m in
    Springfield MH, Abigail COPPOCK, dt Jehu
    & Judith, Columbiana Co., O., b 1821,7,9
    d 1849,10,12
    Ch: Unity   b 1849, 7, 17
    John m 2nd Lavina ----- b 1832,3,15
    Ch: Annar   b 1865, 3, 29
        Wilson
        Rosetta L. " 1873, 3, 3
1850, 5, 2. Joshua, s Stacy & Vashti, b
    1821,6,17; m in Springfield MH, Judith
    STANLEY, dt Joseph & Abigail, Columbiana
    Co., O., b 1826,5,12 d 1851,1,24 bur
    Goshen
    Ch: Joseph J. b 1851, 1, 7
    Joshua m 2nd 1856,3,26, Elizabeth STANLEY,
    dt Edmund & Mary, Mahoning Co., O.
    Ch: Alice   b 1857, 1, 4
        Edmund   " 1858, 5, 25
        Annar   " 1859, 12, 31 d 1860, 1,17
         bur Goshen
        Calvin   b 1861, 2, 6
        Charles " 1864, 7, 7
        Mary V. " 1866, 8, 6
1853, 3, 30. Lizzie S., dt Geo. & Elizabeth,
    b
1864, 4, 27. John, s Stacy & Vashti, Mahon-
    ing Co., O., b 1824,5,11; m in Goshen MH,
    Lavina STANLEY, dt Edmund & Mary, Mahon-
    ing Co., O., b 1832,3,15
    Ch: Rozetta L. b 1873, 3, 3
----, --. Oscar P. b 1853,7,10; m Eliza-
    beth S. ----- b 1853,3,30
    Ch: Jesse
        Moshein   b 1881, 12, 26
----, --, --. Edmund, s Joshua & Elizabeth,
    b 1858,5,25; m Clara H. CATTELL, dt Thomas
    & Elizabeth, b 1864,4,7
    Ch: Mable E. b 1886, 2, 6
        Curtis T. " 1890, 9, 30
----, --, --. Benjamin S., s Evan & Meriha,
    b 1860,9,9 d 1923,2,21; m Esther CREW, dt
    Robert & Mary, b 1867,3,20
    Ch: Leroy M. b 1890, 1, 7
        Merle C.   " 1899, 1, 26
----, --, --. Calvin b 1861,2,6; m Anna M.
    BECK b 1861,2,20
    Ch: Lucile A. b 1894, 3, 4
        Marie L. " 1898, 4, 10
----, --, --. Albert, s Joshua & Elizabeth,
    b 1874,7,26; m Clara ----- b 1874,5,13
    Ch: Harris   b 1900, 2, 13
        Mildred   " 1902, 8, 14
        Olive

    Ch: Elizabeth b 1904, 9, 16
----, --, --. Lewis J., s Joshua & Elizabeth,
    b 1872,1,28; m Emma J. BUTLER, dt John &
    Ann, b 1872,4,6
    Ch: Arnold L. b 1900, 4, 21
----, --, --. Charles H., s Joshua & Elizabeth
    b 1864,7,7; m Lonora B. CATTELL, dt Thos.
    & Elizabeth (Blackburn), b 1868,6,2
    Ch: Carrie
        Aletha   b 1909, 12, 24
----, --, --. Leroy M. b 1890,1,7; m Marilla L
    GEROW, dt Ellsworth & Mary (Johnston), b
    1889,3,9
    Ch: Clark G.   b 1910, 1, 25
        Merle C.   " 1899, 1, 26
----, --, --. Curtis, s Edmund & Clara (Cat-
    tell), b 1890,8,30; m Unity STANLEY, dt
    Thos. & Rebecca (VanFossen), b 1893,7,20
    Ch: Ruth   b 1912, 6, 5
        Glenn   " 1914, 12, 14
        Betty   " 1921, 1, 12
----, --, --. Merle C. b 1899,1,26; m Ger-
    trude ELLYSON, dt Chas. & Emma (Sidwell),
    b 1900,6,28
    Ch: Charlotte
        Louise   b 1922, 1, 12
        Janet Es-
        ther   " 1925, 12, 2
        Donald
        Merle   " 1930, 12, 11

1827, 2, 24. George W. & w, Martha, & dt,
    Eunice, rocf Salem MM, dtd 1827,2,21
1827, 8, 25. Solomon rocf Salem MM, dtd 1827,
    8,22
1829, 3, 28. George W. & w, Martha, & dt,
    Eunice, gct Salem MM
1836, 10, 22. Solomon gct Marlborough MM
1839, 12, 28. William & w, Esther, gct Marl-
    borough MM
1841, 9, 25. Enoch & w, Elizabeth, gct Marl-
    borough MM
1851, 2, 22. Joshua Warrington gct Salem MM,
    to m Unice Shreeve
1863, 3, 27. Evan [Sreve] dis jG (W)
1863, 3, 27. Meribah [Sreve] dis jG (W)
1863, 5, 22. Stacy & Hannah dis jG (W)
1863, 6, 26. Joshua & Elizabeth [Sreeve] dis
    jG (W)
1863, 6, 26. John & Mary [Sreeve] dis jG (W)
1863, 8, 21. Enoch & Elizabeth [Sreeve]
    dis JG (W)
1863, 8, 21. Wm. & Emily [Sreeve] dis jG (W)
1871, 8, 26. Elizabeth Anna Crew (form
    Shreeve) con mcd
1873, 3, 22. Amyetta Kirk (form Shreeve) con
    mcd
1873, 7, 26. Mary [Sreeve] rocf East Goshen
    MM
1873, 7, 26. Unity [Sreeve] rocf East Goshen
    MM
1880, 5, 22. Lizzie recrq
1891, 4, 25. Edmund & w, Clara, & ch, Mabel

SHREVE, continued
    E. & Curtis G., rocf East Goshen MM
1894, 5, 26. Osborn P. & w, Elizabeth S., & s, Jesse Moskin, relrq
1896, 12, 26. John & Lavina rocf East Goshen MM
1896, 12, 26. Rosetta rocf East Goshen MM
1898, 1, 22. Emma J. gct East Goshen MM
1898, 3, 26. Stacy B. relrq
1899, 10, 28. Lewis J. & Emma J. rocf East Goshen MM
1902, 3, 22. Lewis J. & w, Emma J., & s, Arnold L., gct East Goshen MM
1905, 8, 17. Albert & w, Clara, & ch, Harris, Mildred & Alice Elizabeth, rocf Alliance MM
1909, 12, 2. Morilla rocf Marlborough MM, N.Y.
1912, 1, 27. .Albert & w, Clara, gct Whittier MM, Calif.
1914, 7, 25. Calvin & w, Anna, & dt, Lucile & Marie, rocf Beloit MM
1917, 6, 23. Calvin & w, Anna Mary, & ch, Lucile & Marie, gct Beloit MM
1920, 4, 24. Rosa L. gct Whittier MM, Calif.
1921, 2, 26. Bertha Marie gct East Goshen MM
1925, 9, 24. Curtis & w, Unity, & ch, Ruth, Glen & Bettie, rocf East Goshen MM
1927, 12, 22. Charles, Nora & Aletha, rocf Beloit MM

SHRIVER
1861, 9, 20. Olivada A., dt Geo. & Elizabeth, b

1886, 6, 10. Olive A. m Fred L. RYON
1884, 5, 24. Olive A. [Shriner] recrq

SILVER
1833, 6, 22. Sarah, minor dt Adna & Lydia, rocf Salem MM, dtd 1833,3,20
1842, 8, 27. Sarah Davis (form Silver) dis mcd

SINGLEDECKER
1896, 12, 14. Pearl Diday [Sindledicker] b

1920, 1, 24. Pearl A. recrq
1925, 6, 25. Pearl dropped from mbrp
1927, 6, 23. Pearl dropped from mbrp

SLATER
1858, 1, 22. Tamer dis (W)

SMITH
----, --, --. Thomas b 1787,9,26; m Nancy ----- b 1792,1,6
    Ch: Hannah   b 1814, 10, 17
        Elizabeth " 1817, 2, 27
        Evan   " 1819, 5, 31
        Samuel   " 1829, 11, 11
        Rachel   " 1823, 12, 6
        James   " 1826, 3, 16
        Thomas   " 1832, 8, 9

----, --, --. ----- m Sarah ----- b 1795,10, 7 d 1865,3,26 bur Springfield
    Ch: James   b 1825, 8, 24
        John   " 1827, 8, 20
        Abraham   " 1829, 10, 9
        Hannah   " 1832, 3, 15 d 1862,12,30
Sarah m 2nd Ephraim OLIPHANT
1836, 4, 28. Hannah m Thos. D. LANGSTAFF
----, --, --. John P. b 1799,7,16; m Ann E. ----- b 1820,1,10 d 1847,8,5 bur Goshen
    Ch: Anna   b 1847, 6, 28 d 1847, 8,21 bur Mt. Pleasant
1850, 3, 27. Sarah m Ephraim OLIPHANT
1868, 9, 3. Wm. R., s John N. & Edith, Gurnsey Co., O.; m in Damascus MH, Rachel C. STANLEY, dt Joseph & Talitha, Columbiana Co., O.

1834, 4, 26. Thomas & w, Nancy, & ch, Elizabeth, Evan, Samuel, Rachel, James & Thomas rocf Somerset MM, dtd 1834,3,24
1834, 4, 26. Hannah rocf Somerset MM, dtd 1834,3,24
1834, 5, 24. James, John, Abraham & Hannah, ch Sarah, recrq
1836, 8, 27. Thomas & w, Nancy, & ch, Evan, Samuel, Rachel, James & Thomas, gct Pennsville MM
1836, 8, 27. Elizabeth gct Pennsville MM
1842, 11, 26. Hannah B., minor, gct Salem MM (dt Sarah)
1844, 8, 24. John E. gct Gilead MM
1845, 6, 28. James B. gct Gilead MM
1846, 6, 27. John P. & w, Ann, rocf Goshen MM, Pa., dtd 1846,5,28
1849, 2, 24. John P. gct Short Creek MM
1853, 4, 23. Abraham gct Salem MM
1855, 3, 24. John Steward gct Vermillion MM, Ill., to m Matilda Smith
1858, 11, 27. Hannah B. rocf Salem MM
1863, 5, 22. Christiana rocf Westland MM, Pa., dtd 1863,3,25 (W)
1864, 11, 25. Christiana gct Coal Creek MM, Ia. (W)
1865, 2, 24. Mary (form Logue) dis mcd (W)
1869, 3, 27. Rachel C. Stanley gct Flushing MM
1897, 1, 23. Drusilla S. gct Scotts Mills MM, Ore.
1900, 4, 28. M. Lena gct Ypsilanta MM, Mich.
1925, 9, 24. Wilma Kinsey & s, Theodorie, rocf Portsmouth MM, Va.
1926, 11, 25. Wilma Kinsey & s, Theodorie relrq
1927, 6, 23. Lemuel dropped from mbrp

SNELLING
----, --, --. John m Michael E. S. ----- b 1810,2,2 d 1879,5,12 bur Damascus
    Ch: Almeda V. b 1845, 3, 8
        Parmelia Jane " 1851, 2, 13

SNELLING, continued
1870, 6, 25. Michael rst rq
1870, 6, 25. Alemeda V. & Amelia J. recrq
1886, 3, 27. Pamelia J. granted an open
     letter

SNOAD
1848, 3, 25. Susanna [Snowd] (form Brannen)
     dis mcd
1879, 9, 24. Esther B. & Elizabeth C. recrq
1870, 9, 24. Sarah Ann & ch, Charles S. &
     Warren W. recrq

SOMERVILLE
1873, 1, 5. Mary, dt James & Susanna ROHSER,
     b

1897, 3, 27. Mary [Sommerville] recrq

SPENCER
----, --, --. Robert b 1781,7,21; m Amy -----
     b 1782,11,25 (W)

1855, 11, 23. Robert & w, Amy, gct Salem MM
     (W)
1901, 6, 21. Adeline (form Carson) dis mcd &
     jas (W)

SPIEL
1870, 9, 24. Hannah (form Monroe) dis mcd

STACY
----, --, --. Thomas L., s Martin L. & Susan
     (Piper), b 1881,1,28; m Edna ALEXANDER,
     dt Wilson & Minerva (Carroll), b 1880,9,27

1921, 11, 26. Thomas & Edna recrq

STANLEY
----, --, --. Nancy b 1765,4,23   d 1847,1,23
----, --, --. Thomas b 1752,5,5 d 1833,2,28;
     m Unity ----- b 1760,8,3 d 1851,8,18 ae
     91 bur Springfield
     Ch: Moses   b 1781, 11, 15
         John   " 1783, 11, 2
         James   " 1787, 3, 10
         Joseph   " 1789, 2, 19
         Benjamin " 1791, 2, 10
         Judith   " 1793, 9, 28
         Abigail " 1796, 10, 19
         Thomas   " 1801, 12, 12
----, --, --. Littleberry b 1756,2,2 d 1821,
     8,8 bur Springfield; m Agatha ----- b 1754,
     8,4 d 1828,11,4 bur Springfield
     Ch: Solomon b 1787, 12, 26
         Martha   " 1789, 11, 8
----, --, --. James C. d 1841,10,12 ae 72 bur
     Goshen; m Mary ----- d 1842,3,2 ae 69 bur
     Goshen
     Ch: Garland b 1790, 2, 12
         James   " 1792, 9, 15
         Nathaniel
           Jared " 1795, 3, 4

Ch: Elizabeth b 1797, 12, 15
    Jesse   " 1800, 5, 27
    Littleberry" 1803, 6, 17
    Lemuel   " 1805, 10, 4
    Sarah   " 1808, 6, 19
    Jonathan   " 1811, 1, 24
----, --, --. Waddy b 1759,5,26 d 1837,10,24
     bur Springfield; m Rebecca ----- b 1774,6,
     29 d 1846,7,11 bur Springfield
     Ch: Samuel   b 1796, 4, 1
         Priscilla " 1798, 7, 15
         Lucy   " 1801, 4, 9
         Anna   " 1803, 6, 23
         Joel   " 1805, 11, 18
         Nancy   " 1808, 9, 25 d 1881, 2, 4
         Thomas   " 1811, 5, 19
         Deborah   " 1814, 8, 12
         Rebecca   " 1819, 2, 17
         Waddy   " 1816, 9, 4
----, --, --. Thomas b 1757,5,19 d 1831,6,8
     bur Goshen; m 2nd Priscilla ----- d 1847,
     12,24
     Ch: Isaac   b 1803, 3, 24 d 1889,11,11
         Thomas
           Binford " 1805, 9, 5
         Sarah   " 1807, 11, 18
         Micajah " 1810, 2, 11
         Henrietta " 1814, 4, 14
----, --, --. John b 1783,11,2 d 1874,3,24 bur
     Damascus; m Mary Ann ----- b 1792,9,20 d
     1822,7,2 bur Springfield
     Ch: Chlotilda b 1811, 9, 16
         Deborah   " 1813, 9, 23 d 1821, 8, 8
           bur Springfield
         Unity   b 1815, 8, 16 " 1819, 2,15
           bur Springfield
         James   b 1817, 4, 18
         Thomas H. " 1818, 11, 20
         Samuel N. " 1818, 11, 20
         James   " 1821, 3, 3
John m 2nd Margaret ----- d 1881,9,24 bur
     Damascus
     Ch: Elisha   b 1824, 7, 1 d 1850, 1,20
           bur Springfield
         Mary Ann b 1826, 5, 18 " 1870, 9, 1
           bur Springfield
         Sarah   b 1828, 7, 13
         Elizabeth
           Ann   " 1831, 9, 11
         Esther   " 1834, 12, 15
         Unity   " 1837, 5, 12
         John B.   " 1841, 5, 20
----, --, --. Garland b 1791,7,12; m Sarah
     ----- b 1788,5,19
     Ch: Mary   b 1812, 7, 11
         Martha   " 1817, 8, 13
         Edith   " 1820, 4, 16
         Priscilla " 1822, 5, 1
----, --, --. James & -----
     Ch: Milton   b.1812, 11, 5
         Amy   " 1815, 7, 30
         Robert   " 1817, 8, 15
         Judith   " 1818, 11, 24

STANLEY, continued
----, --, --. Joseph b 1789,2,19 d 1830,3,28
    bur Springfield; m Abigail ----- b 1792,3,
    28
    Ch: Timothy   b 1813, 6, 26
        Janet   " 1814, 12, 8
        Ansalem   " 1817, 7, 13
        Joseph   " 1819, 6, 9
        Joanna   " 1821, 8, 23 d 1823, 8, 5
        Rachel   " 1823, 7, 20
        Judith   " 1826, 5, 12
        Elizabeth " 1828, 4, 11
1813, 10, 23. Ellwood b
----, --, --. Solomon b 1787,12,26 d 1855,10,
    7 bur Springfield; m Mary ----- b 1789,3,
    18 d 1836,4,17 bur Springfield
    Ch: Walter   b 1814, 5, 9
        Joanna   " 1815, 11, 21
        Amy   " 1817, 6, 20
        Littleberry" 1819, 1, 20
        Agatha   " 1821, 4, 25 d 1829, 9, 1
          bur Springfield
        Tace   b 1823, 2, 1
        Nathan   " 1825, 4, 10 d 1851, 5,22
          bur Springfield
        Rhoda   b 1827, 5, 28[bur Damascus
        Solomon   " 1829, 4, 8 d 1885, 4, 7
----, --, --. Benjamin b 1791,2,10 d 1868,10,3
    bur Damascus; m Elizabeth ----- b 1793,11,
    19 d 1862,8,20 bur Springfield
    Ch: Pleasant T.b 1814, 5, 30
        Osborn   " 1815, 12, 19
        Ann   " 1818, 1, 1
        Unity C.   " 1820, 1, 27
        Eliza T.   " 1821, 11, 2
        Merihab   " 1823, 4, 12
        Amy   " 1825, 1, 4
        Joanna B. " 1827, 1, 27
        Esther   " 1829, 2, 19
        Hannah   " 1831, 10, 9
        Benjamin C." 1834, 10, 30
    Benjamin m 2nd Mary E. STANLEY b 1814,6,4
----, --, --. James b 1792,9,15 d 1843,7,18
    bur Goshen; m Rachel ----- b 1794,10,18
    Ch: Israel   b 1816, 1, 18
        Jesse   " 1818, 5, 1
        Charlotte " 1820, 12, 21
        Talitha   " 1823, 4, 30
        James   " 1825, 9, 29
----, --, --. Nathaniel b 1795,3,4; m -----

    Ch: Allen   b 1817, 7, 8
        Joseph   " 1819, 5, 23
        Caleb   " 1821, 7, 18
    Nathaniel m 2nd Lydia ----- b 1795,2,25
    d 1855,8,16 bur Goshen
    Ch: Jonathan   b 1823, 9, 8
        Elihu   " 1824, 12, 31
        Nathan   " 1826, 10, 26
        Mary   " 1829, 4, 12
        Isaac   " 1833, 12, 3
        Sarah   " 1833, 12, 3
----, --, --. Samuel m Sarah ----- b 1799,9,19

d 1819,8,14 bur Springfield
    Ch: Sarah Ann b 1819, 8, 30 d 1837,11,14
          bur Springfield
    Samuel m 2ndElizabeth ----- b 1802,5,26
    Ch: Aaron   b 1821, 8, 7
        Jane   " 1823, 6, 20
        John Martin" 1825, 5, 30
        Lindsey   " 1828, 8, 7
        Lucy   " 1830, 6, 1
        Rebecca
        Tamson   " 1832, 10, 24
        Lucinda   " 1838, 1, 17
        Eliza   " 1840, 3, 14
----, --, --. John Jr. b 1795,9,19; m Abigail
    ----- b 1796,10,19 d 1852,8,23
    Ch: Edith   b 1822, 2, 18
        Thomas
        Jared   " 1824, 6, 5
        Elihu B.   " 1826, 8, 28
        Josiah   " 1829, 3, 26
        Unity Crew " 1833, 2, 12 d 1835, 6,10
        Judith C. " 1835, 12, 22
        Mary Ann   " 1839, 10, 1
    John m 2nd Martha S. ----- b 1804,9,5
----, --, --. Elijah b 1796,9,8 d 1836,1,9 bur
    Springfield; m Uree ----- b 1804,10,29 d
    1888,3,12
    Ch: Jehu   b 1824, 9, 5
        Ann   " 1826, 9, 4
        Eli   " 1828, 2, 24
        Emily   " 1830, 5, 11
        Isabel   " 1832, 2, 20
        Juliet   " 1834, 2, 8
        Elijah   " 1836, 1, 21
----, --, --. Thomas C. b 1801,12,12; m Leah
    ----- b 1801,7,17
    Ch: Lydia   b 1825, 8, 30
        Phebe   " 1827, 8, 25
        Rebecca
        Ann   " 1829, 6, 15
        Keturah   " 1832, 9, 23
        Maria   " 1834, 8, 27
        Cyrus   " 1836, 11, 22
----, --, --. Edmond b 1793,2,10 d 1843,7,3
    bur Goshen; m Mary ----- b 1797,5,13 d
    1866,6,15 bur Goshen
    Ch: Alice   b 1826, 9, 9 d 1842,12,17
          bur Goshen
        Elizabeth b 1828, 3, 15
        Amos   " 1829, 12, 3
        Lavina   " 1832, 3, 15
        Jared   " 1834, 6, 2
        Edmond Jr. " 1838, 7, 20 d 1841, 8,26
          bur Goshen
        Elijah
        Thomas   " 1841, 7, 2
1827, 10, 31. Thomas B., s Thomas & Priscilla,
    Columbiana Co., O., b 1805,9,5; m in Gosh-
    en MH, Mary KILLE, dt Clayton & Elizabeth,
    Columbiana Co., O., b 1805,9,27
    Ch: William P. b 1829, 9, 19
        Micajah C. " 1832, 2, 6
----, --, --. Martha S. b 1804,9,5 d 1895,5,

STANLEY, continued
  21
  Ch: Lydia
      Maria   b 1829, 12, 28 d 1914, 4,27
1829, 8, 27. Isaac, s Thomas & Priscilla, Columbiana Co., O., b 1803,3,24; m in Damascus MH, Elizabeth COBBS, dt Waddy & Margaret, Columbiana Co., O., b 1806,6,14 d 1881,
  8,15 bur Damascus
  Ch: Fleming A. b 1830, 9, 7
      Hannah   " 1831, 10, 13
      Valentine
        M.   " 1833, 1, 31
      Margaret C." 1834, 2, 19
      Asenath   " 1837, 7, 13 d 1866, 4, 2
      Isaac W.   " 1840, 6, 19 d 1864, 7,25
        bur Atlanta, Ga.
      Ezra   b 1846, 6, 18
1830, 6, 30. Mary m John ELIOT
----, --, --. Thomas B. b 1805,4,5 d 1891,2,26
  bur Upper Springfield; m Mary K. -----
  b 1805,11,27 d 1886,2,21 bur Upper Springfield   (W)
----, --, --. Overton b 1805,3,20; m Mary ----
  b 1811,3,5 d 1866,10,18 bur Springfield
  (W)
----, --, --. John b 1811,7,7 d 1881,12,14
  bur Springfield; m Sarah ----- b 1811,3,1
  d 1892,2,28 bur Springfield (W)
  Ch: Jordan   b 1833, 9, 24
      Lucina   " 1834, 12, 10
      Joshua   " 1839, 3, 6
      Martha   " 1841, 10, 3
      Charles   " 1851, 3, 10
1832, 9, 27. Joel, s Waddy & Rebecca, Columbiana Co., O., b 1805,11,18 d 1875,3,10
  bur Damascus; m in Damascus MH, Chlotilda
  STANLEY, dt John & Mary Ann, Columbiana
  Co., O., b 1811,9,16 d 1894,11,21
  Ch: Mary Ann   b 1835, 1, 21
      Evan G.   " 1837, 3, 11
      Eli   " 1839, 7, 15 d 1841, 9,15
        bur Springfield
      Eliza Jane b 1841, 11, 27 d 1864, 9,19
        bur Springfield
      Lewis   b 1844, 4, 29 " 1868, 3,21
        bur Damascus
      Almira   b 1846, 11, 19
      Thomas
        Lindley   " 1849, 2, 2
      Unity C.   " 1851, 8, 28 d 1869, 4, 6
        bur Damascus
      John Martinb 1854, 3, 14 d 1922, 6,24
        bur Damascus
      Martha Emily
                  b 1856, 8, 16
1832, 11, 1. Abigail m Benjamin COBOURN
1832, 11, 29. John H., s Joshua & Rachel, Columbiana Co., O., b 1811,7,7; m in Springfield MH, Sarah WOOLMAN, dt Abner & Martha, Columbiana Co., O., b 1811,3,1
  Ch: Jordan   b 1833, 9, 24
      Lucina   " 1834, 12, 10

Ch: Matilda   b 1837, 1, 25 d 1843, 2,14
      bur Springfield
    Joshua   b 1839, 3, 6
    Martha   " 1841, 10, 3
    Anna Maria ' 1848, 8, 26
    Charles   " ----, --, --
1832, 12, 26. Martha m Samuel ELLIOTT
1833, 5, 29. Henrietta m Ezra CATTELL
1833, 11, 27. Sarah m Thos. B. WOOLMAN
1834, 8, 28. Jane m Samuel S. FAWCETT
1835, 12, 13. Timothy, s Joseph & Abigail,
  Columbiana Co., O., b 1813,6,26; m in
  Springfield MH, Elizabeth COBURN, dt Benjamin & Abigail, b 1812,4,13
  Ch: Abigail K. b 1837, 2, 13
      Jennet   " 1838, 10, 27
      Walker   " 1842, 8, 27
      Ansalem
        Tillman   " 1845, 3, 31
      Edwin   " 1848, 7, 23
      Daniel   " 1840, 10, 5
----, --, --. Thomas P. b 1809,10,2 d 1838,9,
  23 bur Springfield; m Hannah G. ----- b
  1815,9,13
  Ch: Allice
        Ann   b 1837, 10, 3
      Thomasson
        P.   " 1838, 12, 5
1837, 6, 8. Isaiah, s Moses & Susanna, Co-
  lumbiana Co., O., b 1813,4,8; m in Smith-
  field MM, Nancy CREW, dt Joshua & Milly
  Ch: Milley
        Crew   b 1838, 7, 31
      Moses   " 1840, 7, 20
1837, 9, 28. Micajah, s Thomas & Priscilla,
  Columbiana Co., O., b 1810,2,11; m in
  Springfield MH, Unity COPPOCK, dt Jehu
  & Judith, Columbiana Co., O., b 1818,10,26
  Ch: Alvina   b 1838, 7, 1
      Ellen   " 1840, 4, 1
      Thomas   " 1841, 11, 8
      Jehu C.   " 1844, 2, 12
      Ruthanna   " 1847, 10, 10
      Binford   " 1851, 2, 22
      Judith Ann " 1853, 1, 2
      Micajah B. " 1855, 11, 3
----, --, --. Osborn b 1815,12,19 d 1879,2,26
  bur Damascus; m Margaret A. ----- b 1821,
  4,1 d 1878,9,21 bur Damascus
  Ch: Elizabeth
        Ann   b 1838, 2, 25
      Mary Ann   " 1843, 12, 11 d 1914, 4,21
      Nathan
        Harrison " 1846, 4, 21
      Benjamin
        Walker   " 1848, 6, 17
      Emmor   " 1850, 3, 4 d 1870, 9,30
        bur Damascus
      Esther   b 1852, 6, 18
      Margaret
        Anna   " 1859, 10, 20
      Missouri   " 1862, 7, 1
----, --, --. James b 1810,10,19; m Elizabeth

STANLEY, James & Elizabeth, continued
    J. b 1813,6,13 d 1847,6,19 bur Goshen
      Ch: Andrew   b 1838, 6, 8
         John J.   " 1840, 4, 18
         Laura   " 1842, 9, 30
         George   " 1844, 9, 29
         Eli   " 1846, 12, 2
1838, 5, 3. Ann m James H. CHAMBERS
1840, 1, 29. Robert, s James & Rhoda, Dela-
    ware Co., O.; m in Goshen MH, Lydia CAT-
    TELL, dt James & Deborah, Columbiana Co.,
    O.
1840, 4, 13. Unity C. m Lemuel HOLE
1841, 12, 2. Pleasant T., s Benj. & Eliza-
    beth, Columbiana Co., O., b 1814,5,30 d
    1879,3,25 bur Damascus; m in Smithfield
    MM, Elizabeth LADD, dt Samuel & Eliza-
    beth, b 1814,3,8
      Ch: Marietta   b 1842, 12, 18 d 1868, 3,11
          bur Chester, Pa.
         Leander   b 1846, 4, 12
         Oliver   " 1850, 8, 1 " 1850, 9, 5
          bur Springfield
         Jason L.   b 1851, 10, 6
1842, 9, 28. Charlotte m Jehu L. KITE
1842, 10, 26. Jeremiah, s Moses & Susanna,
    Columbiana Co., O.; m in Goshen MH, Ann
    ELLYSON, dt Isaac & Elizabeth, Columbiana
    Co., O.
1843, 8, 29. Eliza T. m Henry BENEDICT
1844, 6, 26. Joseph, s Joseph & Abigail, Co-
    lumbiana Co., O., b 1819,6,9; m in Goshen
    MH, Talitha STANLEY, dt James & Rachel,
    b 1823,4,30 d 1847,5,22 bur Goshen
      Ch: Franklin   b 1845, 4, 25
         Rachel   " 1846, 10, 19
    Joseph m 2nd 1851,5,1, Lydia WILLIAMS, dt
    Richard & Sarah, b 1816,5,2
      Ch: Edward   b 1853, 1, 10
         Sarah Ta-
          litha   " 1856, 9, 7
         Charles
          Joseph   " 1859, 5, 27 d 1878,1,13
          bur Damascus
1845, 1, 29. Littleberry, s Solomon & Mary,
    Columbiana Co., O., b 1819,1,20; m in
    Goshen MH, Hannah VOTAW, dt Thomas &
    Elizabeth, Columbiana Co., O., d 1824,10,
    4
      Ch: Henry G.   b 1846, 2, 4
         Levi   " 1848, 5, 9
         Mary Ellen " 1851, 11, 1
         Martha Ann " 1855, 8, 9
         Lydia E.   " 1858, 9, 15
         Tacy   " 1860, 9, 30 d 1863, 9,29
         Elwood   " 1863, 5, 2 " 1864, 9,17
         Adora   " 1864, 6, 21
1845, 5, 1. Israel, s James & Rachel, Colum-
    biana Co., O., b 1816,1,18 d 1882,2,25;
    m in Springfield MH, Uree COBBS, dt Jo-
    seph & Tacy, Columbiana Co., O., b 1823,
    10,8 d 1907,1,28
      Ch: Sidney   b 1847, 3, 29 d 1873, 5,13

      Ch: Wilson   b 1849, 11, 24
         Samantha   " 1852, 6, 25
         Delphina T." 1856, 5, 10
         Charlotte K.
                   b 1858, 10, 8
1845, 5, 29. Meribah m Evan SHREVE
----, --, --. Walter b 1814,5,9; m Mary Anne

      Ch: Jesse T.   b 1846, 9, 8 d 1846, 9,25
         bur Springfield
         Addison W. b 1848, 10, 15
         Eli T.   " 1850, 3, 24
         Philena Ann" 1852, 7, 27
----, --, --. Caleb b 1821,7,18; m Margaret
    ----- b 1822,4,1
      Ch: Louisa   b 1846, 7, 25
         Esther   " 1849, 4, 18
         Calvin   " 1851, 7, 13
         Lydia   " 1856, 2, 10 d 1861, 1, 6
          bur Goshen
         Casper   " 1860, 4, 30
1846, 10, 29. Amy J. m Nathan ADAMSON
----, --, --. Jesse b 1800,5,27; m Abigail
    ----- b 1803,10,21
      Ch: David   b 1848, 3, 17
----, --, --. Robert b 1817,8,15 d 1871,6,2
    bur Damascus; m ----- -----
      Ch: Elizabeth b 1848, 5, 2
         James   " 1854, 4, 24
    Robert m 2nd Sarah ----- b 1825,12,29
    d 1884,2,12 bur Damascus
      Ch: Lydia   b 1856, 11, 26
         Rhoda   " 1858, 4, 30
         Rebecca   " 1860, 5, 3
         Sibyl   " 1861, 8, 22
         George T. " 1863, 2, 22
         Drusilla   " 1865, 3, 11
         Sarah R.   " 1867, 1, 23
         Henrietta " 1870, 9, 7
1848, 6, 8. John B., s Samuel & Elizabeth,
    Columbiana Co., O.; m in Springfield MH,
    Judith Ann BLACKBURN, dt James C. & Re-
    becca, Mahoning Co., O.
----, --, --. Elihu B. b 1826,8,28; m Mary
    Emily ----- b 1827,6,1
      Ch: Julia
         Catharine b 1849, 12, 3
         Christopher
          J.   b 1851, 12, 25
         Olive Abi-
          gail   " 1854, 4, 1
         Peter Ladd " 1856, 9, 29
         Albert R. " 1859, 2, 19
         Anna M.   " 1859, 2, 19 d 1860,11,26
         Thomas El-
          wood   " 1863, 3, 23
1849, 5, 21. Elizabeth m Wm. Henry BLACKBURN
1849, 8, 29. Emily Jane m Joseph BUTLER
1850, 5, 2. Judith m Joshua SHREVE
1850, 10, 2. Hannah m Benjamin BUTLER
1851, 3, 27. Edith m Jesse HALL
1851, 5, 1. Ann W. m Ezra FRENCH
1851, 5, 1. Joanna B. m Jesse THOMAS

STANLEY, continued

----, --, --. John Martin b 1825,5,30; m Judith Ann ----- b 1830,11,2
   Ch: Lavina   b 1852, 1, 15

1851, 5, 28. Flemming A., s Isaac & Elizabeth, Mahoning Co., O., b 1830,9,7; m in Goshen MH, Eunice BUTLER, dt Lawrence W. & Sarah, Mahoning Co., O., b 1831,6,29
   Ch: Harriet   b 1852, 6, 8

1851, 5, 29. Eli, s Elijah & Uree, b 1828,2,24; m in Springfield MH, Rebecca COPPOCK, dt Aaron & Amy, b 1831,12,29
   Ch: Jefferson b 1852, 7, 27

1851, 10, 30. Elizabeth Ann m John T. COBBS

1852, 3, 4. Rachel P. m Levi REEDER

----, --, --. Jesse b 1818,5,1; m Rebecca C. ----- b 1819,7,10
   Ch: Byron   b.1853, 4, 29
      Jesse T.   " 1855, 7, 15
      Mary Anna " 1858, 1, 14
      Elmer E.   " 1861, 6, 30
      Martin   " 1863, 3, 23

1853, 9, 29. Esther m Wm. ABEL

1853, 10, 26. Amos, s Edmund & Mary, Mahoning Co., O., b 1829,12,3; m in Goshen MH, Mary Ann SHINN, dt James & Mary, b 1835,3,16 d 1867,3,10 bur Goshen
   Ch: Annie   b 1855, 4, 16 d 1855, 5, 3
      Theodore   " 1858, 8, 26
      Mary Viola " 1862, 3, 22 " 1863, 7,19
      bur Goshen

----, --, --. William P. b 1829,9,19; m Eliza C. ----- b 1830,2,11, dt. James & Lydia MARSH
   Ch: Emerson L. b 1854, 2, 19
      Philena M. " 1855, 11, 3
      Binford T. " 1861, 8, 8
      Edward M. " 1863, 11, 27

1855, 5, 3. Mary Ann m Elihu COBBS

1855, 8, 3. Margaret m Peter BINFORD

1856, 1, 30. Robert, s James & Rhoda, Morrow Co., O.; m in Goshen MH, Sarah TATUM, dt Geo. & Lydia, Mahoning Co., O.
   Ch: Sybil   b 1861, 8, 22
      George T.   " 1863, 2, 22
      Drusilla   " 1865, 3, 11
      Henrietta " 1870, 9, 7

1856, 3, 26. Eoizabeth m Joshua SHREVE

1857, 5, 28. Abram, s Andrew & Ruth, St. Louis, Mo.; m in Springfield MH, Isabella STANLEY, dt Elijah & Uree, Mahoning Co., O.
   Ch: Isabella b 1858, 4, 13 d 1897, 5,18

1857, 10, 26. Judith C. m Wm. C. JOHNSON

----, --, --. Voluntine b 1833,1,31; m Mary ----- b 1832,2,5
   Ch: Laura   b 1858, 11, 24
      Wilmer C.   " 1861, 8, 31

1858, 4, 29. Unity m Ansalem L. COBBS

1858, 10, 27. Alvina m Israel W. JENKINS

----, --, --. Benjamin C. b 1834,10,30; m Mary J. C. ----- b 1840,3,2 d 1872,5,22 bur Damascus

   Ch: Roscoe Irving
              b 1859, 9, 11
      Willard Lorain   b 1861, 3, 13
      Homer Raymond   " 1862, 12, 19
      Alberti Galen   " 1867, 11, 24
      Mary J.   " 1872, 5, 15 d 1872,12,22
      Ina M.   " 1872, 5, 15 " 1872,12,22

1859, 3, 31. Jehu, s Elijah & Uree, Mahoning Co., O., b 1824,9,5 d 1861,3,24; m in Springfield MH, Lydia Maria HAWKES, dt Wm. & Martha, Columbiana Co., O., b 1828,12,28
   Ch: Martha W. b 1860, 6, 29

1859, 4, 25. Laura F. Stanley, dt Abraham & Mary, b

1859, 4, 28. Evan G., s Joel & Chlotilda, Columbiana Co., O., b 1837,3,11; m in Springfield MH, Elizabeth Ann STANLEY, dt Osborn & Margaret, Columbiana Co., O., b 1838,2,25 d 1860,5,31 bur Springfield
   Ch: Alice   b 1860, 3, 9 d 1860, 8,31
      bur Springfield

1864, 4, 27. Lavina m John SHREVE

1864, 4, 28. John B., s John & Margaret, Columbiana Co., O., b 1841,5,20; m in Springfield MH, Lydia Ann COBBS, dt Ansalem & Ann, b 1840,2,4 d 1874,7,19 bur Damascus
   Ch: Anzanetta b 1865, 10, 12
      Esther Elma " 1868, 3, 2

1864, 6, 29. Ellen m Joshua L. RAKESTRAW

1866, 5, 3. Benjamin, s Thomas & Unity, Mahoning Co., O.; m in Damascus MH, Mary EMMONS, dt Thomas & Mary, Mahoning Co., O. b 1814,6,4

----, --, --. Jared b 1834,6,2; m Margaret B. KINSEY, b 1839,12,17
   Ch: Marietta   b 1867, 4, 8
      Sarah Elizabeth " 1869, 5, 19
      Charles E. " 1874, 4, 7

----, --, --. Joshua W. b 1839,3,6; m Mary E. ----- b 1840,10,17
   Ch: Girtrude b 1868, 7, 31

1868, 8, 26. Ruthanna m Nathan RAKESTRAW

1868, 9, 3. Rachel C. m Wm. R. SMITH

----, --, --. ----- m Mary H. ----- b 1832,7,5
   Ch: Emma E.   b 1870, 10, 30

1869, 12, 30. Elizabeth m Sylvester G. PARK

1870, 10, 26. Esther m Joseph Henry STRATTON

----, --, --. Elijah & Almyra
   Ch: Juliet   b 1871, 12, 12
      Clarence   " 1877, 10, 19
      Warren E.   " 1882, 2, 21

----, --, --. Leander M., s Pleasant & Elizabeth, b 1846,4,12; m Elmina CATTELL, dt Wm. & Mary, b 1849,11,25 d 1921,1,2
   Ch: Ada Odissa   b 1872, 2, 12
      Bessie Estella   " 1874, 7, 14
      Carl Van

STANLEY, continued
    Ch: Roy   b 1878, 8, 30
        Percy C.   " 1882, 9, 17
        Maud Le-
        mina   " 1884, 7, 16
        Wm. Cat-
        tell   " 1889, 6, 29
1874, 1, 1. Samantha m Jesse BUTLER
1874, 9, 12. Horace J., s Edward & Lillas
    Adell, b
----, --, --. Thomas Lindley, s Joel & Clo-
    tilda, b 1849,2,22 d 1929,6,29; m Mary
    A. C. BRICKER, dt Jason R. & Susan L.
    (Hoopes), b 1856,2,18
    Ch: Franklin C.
                     b 1875, 2, 23
        Viola C.   " 1877, 7, 15
        Ida   " 1880, 6, 15
        Arthur   " 1883, 5, 3
        Lesley J.   " 1886, 1, 3
        Laura S.   " 1889, 5, 18
        Charles
        Ray   " 1891, 9, 28
        Vera Fay   " 1894, 8, 6
        Lorin C.   " 1898, 5, 22
        Bertha Ma-
        rie   " 1900, 9, 15
----, --, --. Henry, s Littleberry & Hannah,
    b 1846,2,4; m Alice SHEETS, dt Alva & Ma-
    tilda, b 1849,10,22
    Ch: Levi   b 1875, 10, 8 d 1899,8,11
----, --, --. Nathan Harrison b 1846,4,21; m
    Lydia Melvina ----- b 1853,9,25
    Ch: Emmor F.   b 1876, 3, 11
        Bessie Anna" 1877, 9, 17
        Robert
        Leslie   " 1879, 10, 15
1877, 11, 1. Lydia m Joseph E. PETTIT
----, --, --. Emmerson L. b 1854,2,19; m Laura
    F. ----- b 1859,4,25
    Ch: Mary Eliza b 1878, 6, 25
        Alfred W. " 1886, 2, 2
1878, 3, 26. Rhoda m Joseph BLACKLEGE
1881, 2, 4. Nancy d ae 72 bur Damascus
1881, 9, 28. Mary Ann m Albert PEELE
----, --, --. Jehu, s Micajah & Unity, b 1844,
    2,12; m Edith SHREVE b 1849,3,8 d 1922,4,
    14
    Ch: Homer S.   b 1886, 1, 3
----, --, --. Micajah B., s Micajah & Unity,
    b 1855,11,3; m Annie Margery CREW, dt Oba-
    diah & Mary, b 1863,12,21
    Ch: Clyde M.   b 1889, 8, 23
        Harris O. " 1891, 1, 22
        Rhea M.   " 1894, 9, 1
        Blanche   " 1897, 5, 3
        Morris J. " 1800, 8, 31
1894, 8, 6. Vera Fay, w Ernest G., dt Thos.
    L. & Mary A. E. STANLEY, b
----, --, --. Charles, s Jared & Margaret B.
    (Kinsey), b 1873,4,7; m Mary Ellen CREW,
    dt Obadiah & Mary (Halderman), b 1868,9,27
----, --, --. Arthur, s Thos. & Mary (Bricker),

    b 1883,5,3; m Pearl WEAVER, dt David, b
    1880,1,4
    Ch: Merlin
        David   b 1903, 11, 16
        Mildred
        Elizabeth " 1911, 8, 20
----, --, --. Homer, s Jehu C. & Edith
    (Shreve), b 1886,1,3; m Amy WHINERY, dt
    Cyrus & Anna (Vanfossen), b 1887,5,3
    Ch: Allen F.   b 1909, 1, 16
----, --, --. Charles Ray b 1891,9,28; m Ma-
    bel Anna COY b 1892,12,5
    Ch: Wilma
        Louelva   b 1918, 2, 7
        Lois Aileen
                   b 1920, 9, 18
        Mabel Vo-
        netta   " 1924, 8, 3
----, --, --. Harris O., s Micajah B. & Annie
    M. (Crew), b 1891,1,22; m Bernice ITTNER,
    dt Godfrey & Emma (Seabury), b 1893,1,26
    Ch: Robert
        Wade   b 1920, 6, 30
        Eleanor   " 1822, 4, 13
        Paul Leland" 1825, 6, 14
----, --, --. Lorin C., s Thos. L. & Mary A.
    E. (Bricker), b 1898,5,22; m Helen Elvira
    MILES, dt John & Mabel (Snode), b 1901,4,1
    Ch: Bertha
        Mertis   b 1923, 2, 9
        Mary El-
        vira   " 1930, 2, 18

1826, 8, 26. Garland & w, Sarah, & ch, Mary,
    Martha, Edith & Priscilla, rocf Marlbor-
    ough MM, dtd 1826,7,25
1827, 4, 28. Elijah rst on consent of Salem
    MM
1829, 1, 24. Elizabeth, w Samuel, recrq
1829, 7, 25. Aaron, Jane, John Martin &
    Lindsey, ch Samuel, recrq
1829, 9, 26. Priscilla rocf Smithfield MM,
    dtd 1829,2,23, end by Salem MM 1829,7,22,
    end by this MM to Smithfield
1830, 5, 23. Overton & w, Mary, & s, Isaac,
    rocf Salem MM, dtd 1830,5,19
1830, 6, 26. Elizabeth roc dtd 1830,5,6
1830, 11, 27. James C. & w, Mary, & s, Jona-
    than, rocf New Garden MM, dtd 1830,9,23
1831, 7, 23. John Jr. & w, Abigail, & ch,
    Edith, Thomas, Geroo, Elihu B. & Josiah,
    rocf Salem MM, dtd 1831,6,22
1832, 6, 23. Overton & w, Mary, & s, Isaac,
    gct Salem MM
1832, 9, 22. John H. rocf Salem MM, dtd
    1832,8,22
1832, 10, 27. James & w, Rachel, & ch, Isra-
    el, Jesse, Charlotte, Talitha & James,
    gct White Water MM, Ind.
1832, 11, 24. Elwood rocf Salem MM, dtd 1832,
    11,21
1833, 2, 23. Nathaniel J. & w, Lydia, & ch,
    Joseph H., Caleb, Jonathan, Elihu; Nathan,

STANLEY, continued
Isaac N. & Sarah N., gct Marlborough MM
1833, 4, 27. James & fam gct White Water MM, Ind., now endorsed back to this mtg
1833, 10, 26. Jonathan gct Marlborough MM
1834, 3, 22. Thomas Jr. dis mcd
1834, 6, 28. Milicent & ch rocf Marlborough MM, dtd 1834,5,27
1835, 5, 23. Milicent & ch, Martin, Rachel & Jacob, gct White Water MM, Ind.
1835, 5, 23. Deborah Dickenson (form Stanley) dis mcd
1836, 8, 27. Jonathan rocf Marlborough MM, dtd 1836,7,26
1836, 8, 27. Jacob rocf Marlborough MM, dtd 1836,7,26
1836, 9, 24. Garland & w, Sarah, & ch, Edith & Priscilla, gct Marlborough MM
1836, 10, 22. Milton dis mcd
1837, 3, 25. Thomas P. rocf Salem MM, dtd 1837,3,22
1837, 6, 24. Jacob, minor, rocf Pennsville MM, dtd 1837,5,18
1837, 6, 24. Hannah G. rocf Marlborough MM, dtd 1837,2,28
1837, 7, 22. James C. & w, Mary, rocf Marlborough MM, dtd 1837,6,27
1837, 7, 22. Osborn dis mcd
1837, 8, 26. Jenet dis disunity
1837, 10, 28. Jonathan dis mcd
1837, 11, 25. James & w, Elizabeth, rocf Salem MM, dtd 1837,11,22
1838, 1, 27. Isaiah rocf Salem MM, dtd 1838,1,24
1839, 2, 22. Robert gct Gilead MM
1839, 8, 24. Judith gct Gilead MM
1839, 8, 24. Amy gct Gilead MM
1839, 12, 28. Thomas H. gct Short Creek MM, O.
1839, 12, 28. Samuel W. gct Short Creek MM, O.
1840, 4, 25. Lydia gct Gilead MM
1840, 5, 23. Thomas C. & w, Leah, & ch, Lydia, Phebe, Rebecca, Keturah, Maria, Cyrus & James B., gct White River MM
1840, 11, 28. Allen dis mcd
1841, 5, 22. Ansalem gct Salem MM, Ia.
1841, 6, 26. Tacy Gibson (form Stanley) dis mcd
1842, 9, 24. James gct Short Creek MM, O.
1842, 12, 24. Jacob dis disunity
1843, 1, 28. Jesse dis mcd
1843, 3, 25. Ann gct Salem MM
1843, 3, 25. Ann gct Salem MM
1843, 7, 22. Jane Brosius (form Stanley) dis mcd
1843, 7, 22. Waddy dis mcd
1843, 9, 23. Jesse rst on consent of Somerset MM
1843, 10, 28. Elwood dis disunity
1844, 1, 27. Samuel & fam gct Marlborough MM
1844, 4, 27. Abigail recrq
1844, 8, 24. Nathaniel & w, Lydia, & ch, Elihu, Nathan, Isaac & Sarah, rocf Marlborough MM, dtd 1844,7,30

1844, 8, 24. Aaron gct Marlborough MM
1844, 8, 24. Hannah G. dis mcd
1845, 2, 22. Isaiah & w, Nancy, & ch, Milley Crew, Moses & Edwin, gct Chesterfield MM
1845, 2, 22. James dis mcd
1845, 3, 22. Edna (form Cobbs) dis mcd
1845, 4, 26. Walter gct Chesterfield MM, to m Mary Ann Thomas
1845, 6, 28. Samuel & w, Elizabeth, & ch, John, Lindsey, Lucy, Rebecca, Lucinda & Eliza, rocf Marlborough MM, dtd 1845,5,27
1845, 9, 27. Mary Ann rocf Chesterfield MM
1846, 5, 23. Rebecca Cowgill (form Stanley) dis mcd
1848, 7, 22. Elihu B. gct Short Creek MM, to m Mary Emily Ladd [dtd 1849,2,20
1849, 3, 24. Mary Emily rocf Short Creek MM,
1849, 3, 24. Lindsey dis mcd
1849, 8, 25. Timothy & w, Elizabeth, & ch, Abigail H., Janet, Daniel Walker, Ansalem & Edwin W., gct Sandy Spring MM
1850, 4, 27. Caleb & w, Margaret, & ch, Louisa & Esther, rocf Marlborough MM, dtd 1850,3,26
1850, 11, 23. Osborn rst
1851, 2, 22. Rebecca Morrough (form Stanley) dis mcd
1851, 2, 22. Margaret recrq
1851, 2, 22. Rhoda Galbreath (form Stanley) dis mcd
1851, 5, 24. Elihu B. & w, Mary Emily, & dt, Julia C., gct Wabash MM, Ind.
1851, 12, 28. Jesse & w, Abigail, & s, David, gct Allum Creek MM
1852, 2, 28. Elizabeth Ann, Mary A., Nathan Harrison, Benjamin Walker, Emmor, ch Osborn, recrq
1852, 4, 24. Thomas Jared gct Wabash MM, Ind.
1853, 2, 26. Wm. P. gct Carmel MM, to m Eliza C. Marsh
1853, 5, 28. James & ch, Andrew, John J., Laura, George & Eli, gct Salem MM
1853, 6, 25. Josiah gct Wabash MM, Ind.
1853, 7, 23. Joseph & w, Lydia, & ch, Franklin, Rachel & Edward, gct Goshen MM
1853, 7, 23. Eliza C. rocf Carmel MM, dtd 1853,6,18
1853, 9, 24. Amy Oyster (form Stanley) dis mcd
1853, 10, 22. Samuel & w, Elizabeth, & dt, Lucinda & Eliza, gct Driftwood MM, Ind.
1854, 6, 24. Eli & w, Rebecca, & s, Jefferson, gct Driftwood MM, Ind.
1854, 7, 22. Alice Ann & Thomasson, minors, gct Red Cedar MM, Ia.
1854, 10, 28. Walter & w, Mary Ann, & ch, Adiso W., Eli T. & Philena, gct Pleasant Plain MM, Ia.
1855, 5, 26. Lucy gct Driftwood MM, Ind.
1856, 1, 26. Amos & w, Mary Ann, gct Driftwood MM, Ind.
1856, 3, 22. Sarah gct Gilead MM
1857, 1, 24. Joseph Jr. gct Salem MM, to m

STANLEY, continued
    Martha S. Hawks
1857, 4, 25. Martha S. rocf Salem MM
1857, 8, 22. Fleming A. & w, Eunice, & ch,
    Harriet, Josephine & Lena May, gct Marl-
    borough MM
1858, 1, 23. Nathaniel J. con mcd
1858, 1, 23. Elihu dis mcd
1858, 1, 23. Isaac V. dis mcd
1858, 2, 27. Sarah V. Heckel (form Stanley)
    dis mcd
1858, 5, 22. Amos & w, Mary Ann, rocf Drift-
    wood MM, Ind.
1858, 10, 23. Nathaniel J. gct Rollin MM, Mich.
1859, 1, 22. Valentine M. con mcd
1859, 3, 26. Jerdon dis mcd
1859, 4, 23. John M. & w, Judith Ann, & ch,
    Lavina, Mary & Rosanna, gct Driftwood MM,
    Ind.
1859, 6, 25. Mary C. (form Jones) con mcd
1859, 7, 23. Benjamin C. con mcd
1860, 5, 25. Jordan dis mcd (W)
1860, 5, 26. Mary H. rocf Salem MM
1860, 7, 27. Overton & w, Mary, rocf Salem
    MM, dtd 1860,6,20 (W)

1860, 7, 28. Elihu B. & w, Mary Smith, & ch,
    Julia E., Christopher J., Alice A., Peter
    L., Albert R. & Anna M., rocf Wabash MM,
    Ind., dtd 1860,5,12
1861, 6, 22. Esther Brener (form Stanley) con
    mcd
1861, 10, 26. Micajah C. dis mcd
1861, 11, 23. Louiza J. (form Jones) dis mcd
1862, 10, 25. Evan G. dis mcd
1862, 11, 21. Benjamin dis jG (W)
1862, 11, 21. John Jr. dis jG (W)
1862, 11, 21. Isaac dis jG (W)
1863, 1, 24. John A. dis jW
1863, 1, 24. Sarah dis jW
1863, 1, 24. Lucinda dis jW
1863, 1, 24. Martha dis jW
1863, 2, 27. John dis jG (W)
1863, 2, 27. Thomas B. dis jG (W)
1863, 2, 27. Elizabeth C. dis jG (W)
1863, 2, 27. Margaret dis jG (W)
1863, 2, 27. Mary K. dis jG (W)
1863, 3, 27. Joel dis jG (W)
1863, 3, 27. Pleasant T. dis jG (W)
1863, 3, 27. Osborn dis jG (W)
1863, 3, 27. Israel dis jG (W)
1863, 3, 27. Clotilda dis jG (W)
1863, 3, 27. Elizabeth dis jG (W)
1863, 3, 27. Uree dis jG (W)
1863, 3, 27. Margaret dis jG (W)
1863, 3, 27. Juliet dis jG (W)
1863, 3, 27. Uree C. dis jG (W)
1863, 4, 24. Wm. P. dis jG (W)
1863, 4, 24. Littleberry dis jG (W)
1863, 4, 24. Benjamin C. dis jG (W)
1863, 4, 24. Micajah C. dis jG (W)
1863, 4, 24. Mary dis jG (W)

1863, 4, 24. Louisa dis jG (W)
1863, 4, 24. Hannah dis jG (W)
1863, 4, 24. Eliza dis jG (W)
1863, 5, 22. Micajah dis jG (W)
1863, 5, 22. Unity dis jG (W)
1863, 5, 22. Mary P. dis jG (W)
1863, 5, 22. Lavina dis jG (W)
1863, 6, 26. Valentine dis jG (W)
1863, 7, 24. Hannah dis jG (W)
1863, 7, 24. Asenath dis jG (W)
1863, 7, 25. Sarah J. Craft (form Stanley)
    con mcd
1863, 8, 21. Flemming & Eunice dis jG (W)
1863, 8, 21. Amos & Mary Ann dis jG (W)
1863, 8, 21. Israel dis jG (W)
1863, 8, 21. Elijah T. dis jG (W)
1863, 9, 25. Solomon dis jG (W)
1863, 9, 25. Elijah dis jG (W)
1863, 9, 25. Evan dis jG (W)
1863, 9, 25. John dis jG (W)
1864, 5, 28. Benjamin C. dis disunity
1864, 6, 25. Solomon dis military service
1864, 12, 24. Lydia Maria & dt, Marthha W.,
    gct New Garden MM
1865, 3, 24. Joshua dis disunity & attending
    muster (W)
1865, 3, 25. Elihu B. & w, Mary Emily, & ch,
    Julia C., Christopher J., Olive A., Peter
    L., Albert R. & Thomas Elwood, gct Spring
    Creek MM, Ia.
1865, 10, 28. Joseph & w, Lydia, & ch, Rich-
    ard Edward, Sarah Talitha & Chas. Joseph,
    rocf Goshen MM, dtd 1865,10,21
1865, 10, 28. Rachel rocf Goshen MM, dtd 1865,
    10,21
1865, 10, 28. Jared gct Short Creek MM, to m
    Margaret B. Kinsey
1866, 6, 23. Margaret B. rocf Short Creek MM,
    O., dtd 1866,5,23
1867, 9, 28. Marietta S. Baker (form Stanley)
    con mcd
1867, 10, 25. Elmira Brenner (form Stanley)
    dis mcd (W)
1867, 11, 22. Marietta Baker (form Stanley)
    dis mcd (W)
1868, 3, 28. Elijah T. dis mcd
1868, 6, 27. Hannah Monroe (form Stanley)
    con mcd
1868, 7, 25. Byron, Jesse T., Mariana & El-
    more E., recrq
1868, 7, 25. Jesse recrq
1868, 7, 25. Rebecca recrq
1868, 9, 25. Lucina Webb (form Stanley) dis
    mcd (W)
1868, 11, 28. Robert & w, Sarah, & ch, James
    C., Lydia Rhoda, Rebecca, Sibyl, George
    T. Drusilla & Sarah R., rocf Gilead MM,
    dtd 1868,10,20
1868, 11, 28. Elizabeth rocf Gilead MM, dtd
    1868,10,20
1868, 12, 26. Jehu C. dis mcd
1870, 1, 21. Overton dis mcd (W)
1870, 3, 26. Martin recrq

STANLEY, continued

1870, 8, 27. Benjamin C. rst
1870, 12, 24. Henry G. dis jas & mcd
1871, 1, 28. Elijah con mcd
1871, 5, 27. Leander M. con mcd
1871, 6, 24. Almina M. C. (form Cattell) con mcd
1872, 6, 21. Leander M. dis mcd (W)
1872, 6, 22. Elijah gct Bangor MM, Ia.
1873, 5, 23. Martha Greenwood (form Stanley) dis mcd (W)
1873, 9, 27. Mary Ellen Hartzell (form Stanley) con mcd
1873, 11, 27. Elmina (form Cattell) dis mcd (W)
1873, 12, 27. Nathan con mcd
1873, 12, 27. Thomas S. con mcd
1874, 2, 28. Benjamin C. con mcd
1874, 2, 28. Lydia Melvina recrq
1874, 2, 28. Mary A. E. recrq
1874, 6, 27. Levi dis mcd
1876, 2, 26. John B. con mcd
1876, 6, 24. Ezra dis mcd
1876, 7, 22. Wilson J. dis mcd
1877, 5, 22. Mary Ann gct Short Creek MM, O.
1877, 9, 22. Lydia Marie & dt, Martha W., rocf Adrian MM, Mich., dtd 1877,8,9
1879, 10, 25. Juliet relrq
1880, 5, 21. Charles dis mcd & jas (W)
1880, 6, 26. Laura T. recrq
1880, 6, 26. Mary Ann rocf Short Creek MM, O.
1881, 5, 28. Joshua W. & w, Mary E., recrq
1881, 11, 26. Thomas B. relrq
1882, 6, 24. John B. & dt, Anzonetta & Esther Elma, gct Canaan MM, Kans.
1882, 1, 27. Thomas B. rst (W)
1882, 6, 24. Mary K. relrq
1882, 12, 22. Mary K. rst rq (W)
1884, 1, 26. Valentine M. rocf Sandy Spring MM
1884, 2, 23. Benjamin W. gct Salem MM; returned 3-22 dis disunity
1884, 3, 22. R. Edward dropped from mbrp
1884, 7, 26. Sarah R. gct Salem MM, Ia.
1884, 8, 23. Benjamin W. dropped from mbrp
1885, 7, 25. Juliet, Clarence & Waren E., ch Elijah & Almyra, rocf Albion MM, Ia.
1885, 10, 24. Nettie & Elma rocf Fruitland MM, Kans.
1886, 3, 27. Joseph & w, Lydia, gct Archer MM, Fla.
1886, 4, 24. Nathan H. dis
1886, 4, 24. George T. gct Barkley MM, Kans.
1886, 5, 22. Joshua & w & dt granted an open letter
1887, 4, 23. Benjamin C. & s, Albert G., gct Triumph MM, Neb.
1888, 5, 26. Emerson L. & w, Laura F., & ch, Mary E. & Alfred W., gct Salem MM
1888, 12, 22. Wm. P. & w, Eliza C., gct Salem MM
1889, 5, 25. Uree C. gct Whittier MM, Calif.
1889, 5, 25. Charlotte K. gct Whittier MM, Calif.
1889, 11, 23. Rebecca gct East Goshen MM
1890, 2, 22. Henry & w recrq
1890, 7, 26. Mary H. & dt, Emma C., rocf East Goshen MM
1891, 2, 28. Uree C. & Charlotte rocf Whittier MM, Calif.
1892, 7, 23. Benjamin G. relrq
1894, 1, 27. Mary H. & Emma C. gct Salem MM
1895, 11, 23. Melvina & ch, Emmor, Bessie Anna & Robert Leslie, dropped from mbrp
1895, 11, 23. Lydia Maria & Martha W. gct Cleveland MM
1896, 2, 22. Levi Jr. recrq
1899, 1, 28. Mary H. rocf Salem MM
1899, 1, 28. Emerson L. & w, Laura F., & s, Alfred W., rocf Salem MM
1901, 1, 26. Leander M. dropped from mbrp
1902, 5, 24. Juliet relrq
1902, 5, 24. Jason L. dropped from mbrp
1903, 2, 28. Roy gct Marshalltown MM, Ia. (cert was lost, never used)
1905, 1, 28. Roy C. relrq
1905, 6, 24. Warren & Clarence dropped from mbrp
1906, 6, 23. Micajah B. & w, Anna M., & ch, Clyde M., Harris O., Rea M., Blanche & Morris J., rocf East Goshen MM
1907, 2, 23. Sibyl gct Lupton MM, Mich.
1908, 3, 28. Estella(Stanley)McCann gct S. W. Bay MM, Wis.
1910, 5, 28. Edward M. relrq
1911, 11, 25. Jehu C. & Edith rocf East Goshen MM
1914, 3, 28. Mabel Coy rocf Salem MM
1914, 12, 26. Homer & w, Amy, & s, Allen, rocf East Goshen MM
1919, 11, 22. Mrs. Harris O. recrq
1920, 7, 24. Pearl & ch, Merlin D. & Mildred Elizabeth, recrq
1921, 11, 26. Helen rocf East Goshen MM
1922, 4, 22. Rhea (Stanley) Gilbert relrq
1923, 4, 28. Sibyl rocf Lupton MM, Mich.
1924, 10, 23. Charles & w, Mary Ellen, rocf East Goshen MM
1928, 5, 25. Alfred E. Warrington gct Plainfield MM, Ind., to m Lenna Mae Stanley (W)
1929, 7, 25. Charles Ray & fam relrq
1931, 12, 24. Maude (Stanley) Cochran dropped from mbrp

STARBUCK
1897, 4, 24. Florence Savage relrq

STARK
1855, 8, 28. Hannah H. (form Young) con mcd
1859, 9, 24. Hannah H. gct Bloomington MM, Ia.

STEEL
1926, 1, 22. Jary (Brantingham) dropped from mbrp

STEER,
1849, 5, 2. Joshua, s Amos & Lusine, Mahoning Co., O., b 1828,11,17; m in Goshen MH,
Mary BUTLER, dt Lawrence W. & Sarah, Mahoning Co., O., b 1829,8,10 d 1856,7,21
Ch: Amos   b 1850, 9, 27
    Mary   " 1853, 2, 28
    Moses   " 1855, 2, 11
----, --, --. Edwin M., s Nathan & Mary (Bran-
son), b 1869,3,6; m Sara Mildred COPE, dt
Isaac G. & Elizabeth (Dungan), b 1872,11,
27
Ch: Ralph C. b 1900, 8, 8
    Frank
    Isaac   " 1902, 1, 21
    Edwin Na-
    than   " 1903, 3, 30
    Mary Eliza-
    beth   " 1905, 6, 25
    Ellis D. " 1912, 8, 5
1915, 6, 18. Albert J. m Jessie Leah CRAWFORD
(W)
----, --, --. Ralph C., s Edwin & Sarah (Cope)
b 1900,8,8; m Nellie BALL, dt George &
Ada (Crawford), b 1899,12,11
Ch: Dorothy   b 1923, 4, 9
    Marjorie
    Jean   " 1924, 9, 20
    Helen
    Elizabeth " 1926, 11, 13
    Donald
    Ralph   " 1930, 2, 22
----, --, --. Frank Isaac, s Edwin & Sarah
(Cope), b 1902,1,21; m Lena Irena HOOPES,
dt Irving Leroy & Myrtle (Kelly), b 1907,
1,30
Ch: Irving M. b 1927, 9, 26
    Elizabeth
    Ann   " 1928, 12, 18
    Wilda June
    Lois Marie " 1931, 9, 27
----, --, --. Edwin N., s Edwin M. & Sarah
(Cope), b 1903,3,30; m Ana Caroline DEN-
TON, dt Geo. A. & Caroline (Haldi), b
1904,1,27
Ch: Elise
    Nadine   b 1928, 5, 16
    Edwin   " 1932, 12, 31

1848, 8, 26. Joshua, minor, rocf Short Creek
MM, dtd 1848,6,20
1851, 9, 27. Joshua R. & w, Mary, & ch, Amos,
gct Marlborough MM
1854, 6, 24. Joshua R. & w, Mary, & ch, Amos
& Meribah, rocf Marlborough MM, dtd 1854,
5,30
1863, 12, 26. Joshua R. con mcd
1864, 5, 28. Joshua R. & ch, Mary & Moses,
gct Springdale MM, Ia.
1907, 9, 28. Sarah M. recrq
1907, 9, 28. Edwin M. & ch, Ralph C., Frank
Isaac, Edward Nathan & Mary Elizabeth,
recrq

1915, 11, 26. Jessie Leah C. gct New Garden
MM (W)
1931, 3, 26. Anna Caroline & Elese Nadine
recrq

STEIN
1907, 8, 1. Freda E., dt Anna (Hersley), b
(W)

1922, 11, 24. Freda, minor in care of Lewis
A. & Lydia A. Woolman, recrq (W)

STEVENS
1876, 11, 25. Moses C. & w, Sarah M., & ch,
Harry J., Chas. Eli & Mary Elizabeth
Cooper, & Martha D. Stevens, rocf Salem
MM
1878, 11, 23. Moses C. & w, Sarah M., & ch,
Harry J. Cooper, Charles E. Cooper, Mary
E. Cooper & Martha D. Stevens, gct Green-
field MM, Ind.
1911, 2, 25. Edith gct Salem MM, O.

STEWARD
----, --, --. Aaron b 1778,11,11 d 1855,10,27
bur Goshen; m Massey ----- b 1792,8,12 d
1855,3,28 bur Goshen
Ch: Eliza P. b 1813, 9, 10
    Samuel   " 1817, 9, 15
    Joseph   " 1820, 4, 1
    John   " 1822, 11, 18
    William   " 1825, 9, 28
    Isaac   " 1829, 7, 3
    Aaron A. " 1834, 1, 31
----, --, --. Joseph b 1820,4,1 d 1850,8,24
bur Lexington; m Emaline ----- b 1826,2,
19 d 1875,1,25 bur Goshen
Ch: Calvin   b 1849, 3, 30 d 1851, 2,22
    bur Goshen
    Rachel   " 1850, 9, 23
----, --, --. John b 1822,11,18; m Matilda

1854, 11, 1. Isaac, s Aaron & Mercy, Mahoning
Co., O., b 1829,7,3; m in Goshen MH, Eliza
ATKINSON, dt Warner & Maria, Mahoning Co.,
O., b 1835,8,2
Ch: Mercy
    Mariah   b 1855, 12, 19

1828, 11, 22. Aaron & w, Massey, & ch, Eliza,
Samuel, Joseph, John & William, rocf
Middleton MM
1842, 1, 22. Samuel dis mcd
1848, 5, 27. Joseph gct Marlborough MM, to m
Emeline Holloway
1848, 10, 28. Emeline rocf Marlborough MM,
dtd 1848,9,26
1853, 4, 23. Emeline & dt, Rachel P., gct
Salem MM
1853, 7, 23. William [Stewart] gct Red Cedar
MM, Ia.
1855, 3, 24. John [Stewart] gct Vermillion
MM, Ill., to m Matilda Smith

STEWARD, continued

1856, 3, 22. Matilda rocf Vermillion MM,
    Ill., dtd 1856,1,5
1856, 10, 25. John & w, Matilda, gct Vermilion
    MM, Ill.
1860, 1, 27. Eliza P. Vernon (form Stuart)
    con mcd (W)
1861, 3, 23. Isaac [Stewart] & w, Eliza, &
    dt, Mercy Mariah, gct Red Cedar MM, Ia.
1863, 10, 24. Eliza P. Vernon (form Steward)
    dis mcd
1869, 4, 24. Aaron [Stewart] gct Union MM, Mo.
1869, 6, 26. Emaline H. & dt, Rachel P., rocf
    Salem MM
1876, 7, 22. Rachel Woolman (form Stewart)
    con mcd

STILLWELL

1859, 5, 27. Eliza (form Warren) dis mcd (W)

STRATTON

1796, 6, 1. Evi b
----, --, --. Aaron b 1799,2,1 d 1851,3,17
    bur Springfield; m Hannah ----- b 1800,8,
    2 d 1878,1,16 bur Jefferson Co., 0.
    Ch: Joel   b 1824, 1, 5
       Emily   " 1825, 11, 26
       Rachel   " 1829, 5, 31
       Martha   " 1831, 5, 12 d 1860,12, 9
       Rebecca " 1833, 4, 21
       Lydia   " 1835, 3, 16
       Jerusha " 1837, 9, 11
       Sina   " 1840, 6, 13
       Joseph
       Whittier " 1845, 10, 5
1828, 1, 31. Aaron Jr., s Michael & Rhoda,
    Columbiana Co., 0.; m in Springfield MH,
    Unity CREW, dt Obadiah & Mary, Columbiana
    Co., 0.
----, --, --. George b 1809,11,27; m Susanna
    ----- b 1814,6,16
    Ch: Mary   b 1836, 11, 7
       Elizabeth
       E.   " 1841, 10, 25 d 1856,4,11
       bur Goshen
       Rhoda   " 1844, 9, 20
       Esther   " 1847, 10, 29
       Ann Eliza " 1858, 3, 7
----, --, --. Mark b 1821,10,20; m Mary H.
    ----- b 1822,9,18
    Ch: Charles H. b 1846, 4, 2
       Franklin " 1849, 12, 30
       Joseph
       Henry   " 1852, 4, 6
       Isaac   " 1854, 7, 14
----, --, --. Isaac b 1854,7,14; m Mary HAL-
    DERMAN, b 1853,1,24
1854, 11, 8. Mary m Joseph SHINN
1867, 8, 28. Rhoda S. m Joseph P. ONG
1870, 10, 26. Joseph Henry, s Mark & Mary H.,
    Mahoning Co., 0.; m in Goshen MH, Esther
    STANLEY, dt Caleb & Margaret, Mahoning
    Co., 0.

1828, 8, 26. Unity gct Salem MM
1834, 6, 28. Abraham & w, Hannah, & ch, Joel,
    Emily, Rachel, Martha & Rebecca, rocf
    Salem MM, dtd 1834,5,21
1835, 6, 27. George & w, Susanna, rocf Salem
    MM, dtd 1835,6,24
1835, 12, 26. Evi rocf Middleton MM, dtd 1835,
    11,23
1837, 5, 27. Evi gct Salem MM
1852, 12, 25. Emily Holmes (form Stratton)
    dis mcd
1854, 12, 23. Joel con mcd
1858, 5, 22. Rebecca S. Latty (form Stratton)
    dis mcd
1858, 7, 24. Mark & w, Mary, & ch, Charles
    M., Franklin, Joseph Henry & Isaac, rocf
    New Garden MM
1860, 11, 24. Joel gct Salem MM
1863, 5, 22. George & Susanna dis jG (W)
1863, 9, 25. Hannah T. dis jG (W)
1868, 9, 25. Edith (form Townsend) dis mcd
    (W)
1871, 5, 27. Mary Jane (form Walton) con mcd
1874, 1, 24. Mary Jane gct Salem MM
1898, 9, 24. Esther T. recrq
1898, 9, 24. Joseph Henry recrq
1908, 11, 27. Walter G. Edgerton gct New Gar-
    den MM, to m Mary C. Stratton (W)
1919, 8, 23. Isaac & w, Sarah B., rocf East
    Goshen MM
1922, 11, 25. Isaac gct Winona MM

STRAWN

1856, 1, 25. Esther (form Crew) dis mcd (W)

STREET

1831, 12, 28. Zadok, s John & Ann, Columbi-
    ana Co., 0.; m in Goshen MH, Sibyl TATUM,
    dt George & Beulah, Columbiana Co., 0.
1835, 10, 28. Samuel, s John & Ann, Columbi-
    ana Co., 0.; m in Goshen MH, Sarah BUTLER
    dt Benjamin & Hannah, Columbiana Co., 0.

1826, 9, 23. Isaac & w, Rebecca, & ch, Mary
    Ann & Rachel, gct Concord MM
1828, 6, 28. Lydia rocf Salem MM, dtd 1828,
    6,25
1829, 11, 28. Mary Ann, Rachel & Balinda,
    minors, rocf Short Creek MM, 0., dtd
    1829,1,20
1830, 2, 27. Lydia gct Salem MM
1830, 4, 30. John Ellison gct Salem MM, to m
    Lydia Street
1832, 6, 23. Sibyl gct Salem MM
1836, 1, 23. Sarah gct Salem MM
1837, 9, 23. Aaron recrq
1837, 10, 28. Elizabeth recrq
1838, 3, 24. Aaron & w, Elizabeth, gct Ver-
    million MM, Ill.

STROUP

----, --, --. Lawrence m Lida COBBS, dt John
    E. & Sarah Ellen (Blackburn), b 1890,10,21

STROUP, continued
    Ch: Lester
        Wilson   b 1920, 2, 22

1923, 3, 24. Lester, minor s Lida, recrq

TALBOTT
----, --, --. Joseph, s Kinsey & Sarah, b
    1844,12,15; m Esther STANLEY, dt Robert &
    Lydia, b 1844,1,19
    Ch: Delbert R. b 1866, 12, 23
        Mary
          Elizabeth " 1872, 2, 27
        Caroline K." 1875, 6, 3 d 1877, 7, 9
          bur Damascus
        Sarah E.   b 1879, 1, 7
----, --, --. Wm. M., s Kinsey M. & Caroline
    E., b 1846,9,18 d 1914,1,23; m Mary E.

    Ch: Anna Alice b 1879, 7, 12
    Wm. M. m 2nd Emily B. WHINERY, dt Thomas
    & Mary B.
----, --, --. Wm. Kinsey, s Wm. M. & Mary C.,
    b 1873,7,30; m Laura CREW, dt J. Antram &
    Rachel A. (Kelley), b 1877,12,27
    Ch: William A. b 1903, 11, 21
        Anna M.   " 1904, 12, 3

1877, 6, 23. Joseph A. & fam rocf Gilead MM,
    dtd 1877,6,19
1889, 11, 23. Joseph & w, Esther, & ch, M.
    Elizabeth & Sarah E., gct Short Creek MM,
    O.
1891, 11, 28. Delbert R. relrq
1902, 3, 22. Wm. Jr. rocf Short Creek MM, O.
1906, 10, 27. Wm. M. & w, Emily B., rocf Short
    Creek MM, O.
1906, 10, 27. Anna A. rocf Scipio MM, N. Y.
1907, 12, 28. Laura A. & ch, Wm. A. & Anna M.,
    recrq
1914, 12, 26. Anna [Talbot] gct New York MM,
    N. Y.

TATUM
----, --, --. George b 1785,9,1 d 1852,5,10
    bur Red Cedar, Ia. (an elder); m Beulah

    Ch: Elizabeth b 1808, 7, 1
        Sebyl   " 1810, 3, 28
        George   " 1813, 3, 3
        Isaac   " 1814, 9, 2 d 1833, 1,19
          bur Goshen
        Rebecca   " 1819, 4, 11
    George m 2nd Lydia ----- b 1789,10,15 d
    1856,4,21 bur Goshen
    Ch: Hannah   b 1820, 8, 16
        Laurie   " 1822, 5, 22
        David   " 1823, 7, 12
        Sarah   " 1825, 12, 29
1831, 12, 28. Sibyl m Zadock Street
1837, 4, 2. Elizabeth m John BUTLER
1843, 3, 29. Rebecca m Barnabas C. HOBBS
1844, 2, 8. Hannah m Greenberry P. WOOD

1849, 8, 29. David, s George & Lydia, Cedar
    Co., Ia., b 1823,7,12; m in Goshen MH,
    Hannah BUTLER, dt Lawrence W. & Sarah,
    Mahoning Co., O., b 1824,3,2
1856, 1, 30. Sarah m Robert STANLEY

1831, 1, 22. George & w, Lydia, & ch, Sibyl,
    George, Isaac, Rebecca, Hannah, Laura,
    David & Sarah, rocf Woodbury MM, N. J.,
    dtd 1830,11,30
1834, 5, 24. Elizabeth rocf Woodbury MM,
    N. J., dtd 1834,4,1
1844, 4, 27. George Jr. gct Stillwater MM, to
    m Hannah Green
1844, 11, 23. Hannah rocf Stillwater MM, dtd
    1844,9,28
1845, 5, 24. David gct Salem MM
1845, 11, 22. Laurie gct Salem MM
1846, 2, 28. George Jr. & w, Hannah, gct Som-
    erset MM
1850, 3, 23. Hannah B. gct Salem MM, Ia.
1857, 11, 28. David & w, Hannah B., & s, Law-
    rence, rocf Red Cedar MM, Ia.
1858, 9, 25. David & w, Hannah B., & s, Law-
    rece, gct Plainfield MM, Ind.

TAYLOR
----, --, --. Isaac b 1790,7,31 d 1876,5,24
    bur Damascus; m Hannah ----- b 1794,11,13
    d 1866,9,10 bur Damascus
    Ch: David   b 1814, 5, 11
        Joshua   " 1816, 3, 6 d 1841,10,7
          bur Springfield
        Milton   b 1818, 6, 4
        Jacob   " 1820, 4, 10
        John   " 1822, 2, 24
        Mary Ann   " 1824, 5, 6
        Jesse   " 1827, 4, 15 d 1853, 2,21
          bur Springfield
        Oliver   b 1829, 3, 2
        Jehu Lloyd " 1831, 4, 23 d 1851, 2, 4
          bur Springfield
        Lydia   b 1833, 6, 7 " 1913,11,20
        Rebecca   " 1837, 4, 21
1814, 3, 22. Elizabeth (Votaw), b
1827, 6, 22. Eliza Ann b
1842, 3, 30. David, s Isaac & Hannah, Colum-
    biana Co., O., b 1814,5,11 d 1862,11,17;
    m in Goshen MH, Elizabeth VOTAW, dt Thom-
    as & Elizabeth, Columbiana Co., O., b
    1814,3,22
    Ch: Drusilla
        Anna   b 1844, 12, 8
        Garrett   " 1846, 11, 3 d 1881,12,14
        Jane   " 1852, 10, 21
        Isaac Jesse" 1854, 12, 28
1843, 6, 1. Milton, s Isaac & Hannah, Co-
    lumbiana Co., O., b 1818,6,4; m in Spring-
    field MH, Philena LAMBORN, dt Job & Es-
    ther
    Ch: Rebecca
        Emily   b 1844, 1, 16
        Anna   " 1846, 6, 15

TAYLOR, Milton & Philena, continued
    Ch: Mary Jane b 1850, 8, 8
1884, 5, 28. Eliza Ann m Pleasant COPPOCK

1846, 4, 25. John dis jas
1852, 8, 28. Mary Ann Hayhurst (form Taylor)
    dis mcd
1853, 4, 23. Oliver dis mcd
1854, 7, 22. Jacob dis mcd
1854, 8, 26. Rebecca dis
1855, 1, 27. Milton dis mcd
1863, 3, 27. Isaac & Hannah dis jG (W)
1863, 9, 25. Elizabeth & Lydia dis jG (W)
1864, 3, 26. Rebecca Emily Courtney (form
    Taylor) rpd mcd
1868, 2, 21. Emily Courtney (form Taylor)
    dis mcd
1868, 2, 21. Anne Pim (form Taylor) dis mcd
    (W)
1868, 2, 22. Anna Pim (form Taylor) dis mcd
1868, 6, 27. Eliza Ann recrq
1869, 3, 26. Mary Jane French (form Taylor)
    dis mcd (W)
1875, 9, 25. Mary Jane French (form Taylor)
    dis mcd
1880, 2, 28. Jesse relrq

TEETERS
1862, 11, 21. John dis jG (W)
1863, 9, 25. Mary dis jG (W)

TEMPLIN
1856, 4, 26. Martha (form French) dis mcd

TERRELL
----, --, --. Mathew b 1804,3,27; m Eliza-
    beth D. ----- b 1803,2,14
    Ch: Amos H.   b 1827, 12, 5
        Joseph   " 1829, 9, 25
        Elizabeth
        Ann   " 1832, 3, 6

1829, 2, 28. Mathew rocf Short Creek MM, O.,
    dtd 1828,7,5
1834, 2, 22. Nathan & w, Elizabeth D., & ch,
    Amor H., Joseph & Elizabeth Ann, gct
    Short Creek MM, O.

TEST
----, --, --. Samuel b 1815,2,9; m Ann -----
    b 1811,11,25

1858, 5, 21. Samuel Jr. & w, Ann J., rocf
    New Garden MM, dtd 1858,5,20 (W)
1866, 2, 24. Samuel & w, Ann J., rocf New
    Garden MM
1866, 9, 21. Samuel dis jG (W)
1867, 7, 26. Ann J. dis jG (W)
1873, 6, 28. Samuel & w, Ann J., gct Alli-
    ance MM

THOMAS
-----, --, --. ------ m Sarah ----- b 1797,5,24

Ch: Kersey G.   b 1818, 1, 25
    Joseph
      Garretson   " 1820, 3, 23
    Isaac Green " 1822, 4, 13
    Rebecca Ann " 1824, 4, 26
    Eleanor
      Jane   " 1826, 9, 9
----, --, --. Joseph b 1796,10,10; m Temper-
    ance -----
    Ch: Sarah   b 1820, 5, 25 d 1821, 8,18
       Margaret   " 1822, 4, 1
       Mary   " 1824, 1, 25
       Dorcas Ann " 1826, 3, 17
       David
        Blackburn " 1827, 11, 10
       John B   " 1829, 11, 13
       Esther   " 1832, 9, 5
       Joseph   " 1824, 7, 18
       Nathan   " 1836, 8, 11
       Hannah T.   " 1838, 9, 3 d 1857, 9, 4
1840, 12, 24. James M. b
----, --, --. Joseph b 1814,12,5 d 1865,8,23
    bur Springfield; m Mary J. ----- b 1821,12
    28
    Ch: Eliza
       Jane   b 1844, 4, 1
       Rebecca Ann" 1845, 5, 15
       Lucy P.   " 1848, 4, 10
       Louiza G.   " 1848, 4, 10
       Lileas
        Adell   " 1856, 7, 6
       Mary
        Elizabeth " 1861, 12, 17 d 1862, 9,20
        bur Springfield
1851, 5, 1. Jesse, s Jesse & Rebecca, Colum-
    biana Co., O., b 1828,7,28; m in Spring-
    field MH, Joanna B. STANLEY, dt Benjamin
    & Elizabeth, Columbiana Co., O., b 1827,
    1,27
    Ch: Benjamin
       Franklin b 1852, 5, 26
       Zadoc Wil-
        lis   " 1856, 5, 18
       Elma Lu-
        ella   " 1860, 11, 8
       Mary Eldora" 1863, 12, 12
1860, 6, 28. Joanna m Levi REEDER
----, --, --. ----- m Mary T. GREEN, dt John
    & Mary, b 1834,5,25
    Ch: Esther
       H.   b 1873, 1, 24
----, --, --. John, s Voluntine, b 1856,12,21;
    m Sarah Jane CREW, dt Robert & Margaret,
    b 1859,8,1
    Ch: Birtha H. b 1880, 3, 18
       Charles
        Oscar   " 1882, 5, 4
       Myrtle   " 1887, 8, 13
1884, 6, 7. Jennie, dt John & Lizzie, b
1899, 4, 1. Arthur Richard, s Daniel & Mar-
    garet, b

1827, 3, 24. Sarah & ch, Kersey G., Joseph

THOMAS, continued
   G., Isaac Green, Rebecca & Eleanor Jane,
   rocf Salem MM, dtd 1827,2,21
1827, 7, 28. Abner & w, Phebe, & ch, Wm.
   Mode, Eleanor Miller, Esther & Isaac,
   rocf Monallin MM, Pa., dtd 1827,10,19
1827, 4, 26. Abner dis disunity
1828, 5, 24. Phebe dis disunity
1828, 10, 25. Sarah dis jH
1831, 2, 26. Kersey G., Joseph G., Isaac
   Green, Rebecca Ann, Eleanor Jane & Oliver
   Abel, ch John & Sarah, gct Salem MM
1831, 8, 27. Joseph & w, Temperance, & ch,
   Margaret, Dorcas, Ann & David B., rocf
   Goshen MM, dtd 1831,2,19
1837, 8, 26. Joseph dis disunity
1839, 10, 26. Josiah Walton gct Chesterfield
   MM, to m Deborah Thomas
1841, 11, 27. Margaret gct Marlborough MM
1840, 11, 27. Mary, Dorcas, Ann, David Blackburn, Esther, Joseph, Nathan & Hannah,
   ch Joseph, gct Marlborough MM
1841, 9, 25. Eleanor dis jH
1842, 9, 24. William dis jH
1843, 6, 24. Harvey rocf Middleton MM, dtd
   1843,6,8
1845, 1, 25. Nathan, minor, gct New Garden
   MM
1844, 5, 25. Esther dis jH
1844, 12, 28. Dorcas Ann, David, Esther, Joseph, Nathan & Hannah, ch Joseph & Temperance, rocf Marlborough MM, dtd 1844,10,29
1845, 4, 26. Stanley gct Chesterfield MM, to
   m Mary Ann Thomas
1846, 5, 23. Harvey gct Sugar Plain MM, Ind.
1847, 7, 24. Dorcas Ann Reeve (form Thomas)
   con mcd
1849, 2, 24. Esther Middleton (form Thomas)
   dis mcd
1851, 5, 24. Nathan, minor, rocf New Garden
   MM, dtd 1851,4,24
1851, 11, 22. Joanna rocf Plymouth MM, dtd
   1851,10,20
1851, 12, 27. Jesse rocf Salem MM, dtd 1851,
   11,19
1852, 7, 24. David dis mou
1853, 12, 24. Joseph gct Wabash MM, Ind.
1854, 10, 28. Joanna gct Pleasant Plain MM,
   Ia.
1855, 2, 24. Sarah (form Butler) dis mcd
1856, 3, 22. Nathan, minor, gct Red Cedar
   MM, Ia.
1859, 1, 22. Joanna rocf Pleasant Plain MM,
   Ia., dtd 1858,12,11
1860, 1, 27. Mary (form White) dis mcd (W)
1860, 8, 25. Joseph & w, Mary G., & ch,
   Eliza Jane, Rebecca Ann, Lucy P., Louiza,
   G. & Liles Adell, rocf Chesterfield MM
1861, 7, 27. Eliza Jane Rhul (form Thomas)
   dis mcd
1863, 3, 27. Jesse dis jG (W)
1863, 3, 27. Joanna B. dis jG (W)
1865, 4, 22. Jesse & w, Joanna B., & ch, Ben-

jamin Franklin, Zadock Willis, Elma Luella & Mary Eldora, gct Spring Creek MM,
   Ia.
1866, 4, 28. Rebecca A. Poorman (form Thomas)
   dis mcd
1868, 11, 28. Louisa G. Haynam (form Thomas)
   dis mcd
1869, 8, 28. Lucy Bowman (form Thomas) dis
   mcd
1880, 5, 22. John recrq
1892, 8, 19. John & w dropped from mbrp
1898, 9, 24. Mabel recrq
1898, 12, 24. James F. & Margaret recrq
1898, 12, 24. Daniel & w & dt, Maggie, recrq
1901, 5, 20. Bertha(Thomas)Brogan relrq
1901, 5, 20. Charles Oscar & Myrtle, ch John
   C. & Sarah J., gct Sandy Spring MM
1906, 6, 23. Mary T. & Esther H. rocf Oskaloosa MM, Ia.
1914, 4, 25. Mary T. gct White Water MM, Ind.

THOMPSON
----, --, --. Elizabeth [Thomson] b 1798,6,10
   d 1850,10,23 bur Goshen
1894, 12, 6. Lula Esther, dt Bismark & Margaret, b
1899, 3, 31. Floyd, s J. B. & Maggie, b

1840, 12, 26. Elizabeth recrq
1843, 3, 25. Caroline (form Brook) dis mcd
1897, 11, 27. J. B. [Thomson] & Maggie recrq
1898, 3, 26. Rose recrq
1900, 2, 24. Lulu Esther recrq

TOMLINSON
----, --, --. Orlando C., s Allen & Martha,
   b 1860,9,8; m Emily J. CLAMPITT, dt Joel
   K. & Eliza, b 1863,9,11
      Ch: Sibyl   b 1887, 10, 23
          Myra   " 1889, 5, 19
          Wymond   " 1891, 8, 8

1865, 8, 25. Ruthanna (form Cobbs) dis mcd
   (W)
1872, 11, 23. Anna F. (form Fawcett) con mcd
1873, 4, 26. Anna F. gct Smithfield MM, N. C.
1905, 2, 25. Orlando C. & w, Emily, & ch,
   Sibyl, Myra & Wymond, rocf Short Creek MM,
   O.
1905, 12, 23. O. C. & fam gct East Goshen MM

TOOL
1902, 4, 26. Elpha Rugley gct Salem MM

TOWNSEND
----, --, --. Lewis b 1798,2,14 d 1867,11,7
   bur Goshen; m Rachel ----- b 1799,8,17
      Ch: Mary D.   b 1819, 9, 4
          Eliza   " 1824, 4, 4
          Seth   " 1826, 10, 18
          William D. " 1829, 9, 19
          John   " 1831, 12, 24
----, --, --. Jonathan m Ann ----- b 1796,7,20

TOWNSEND, continued
1870,11,30
Ch: Moses J. b 1823, 3, 11
    Smith   " 1824, 9, 14
    William   " 1825, 11, 5
    Dillon   " 1827, 3, 20
    Martha   " 1828, 9, 5
    Joseph   " 1830, 7, 2 d 1845,10,25
    Sarah   " 1832, 12, 1
    Samuel   " 1836, 4, 4
    Edith   " 1837, 12, 30
1827, 1, 4. Francis J., s Joseph & Sina, Co-
    lumbiana Co., O.; m in Springfield MH, Ann
    FRENCH, dt James & Mary, Columbiana Co., O.
    Ch: Sina   b 1835, 9, 22
        Arvine
1847, 10, 27. Mary D. m Evan LANGSTAFF
----, --, --. Henry H. b 1851,10,13; m Anne
    R. HUNT b 1862,1,8
    Ch: Helen
        Hunt   b 1888, 6, 22
----, --, --. Oscar, s Chas. L. & Anna D., b
    1894,4,9; m Georgianna DUTTON, dt Chas. &
    Anna (Dutton), b 1900,12,31

1827, 2, 24. Ann gct Salem MM
1832, 12, 22. Ann, w Jonathan, & ch, Moses,
    Smith Wm., Dillon, Martha & Joseph, rocf
    Buckingham MM, Pa., dtd 1832,11,5
1834, 2, 22. Ann, w Francis, & ch, Emmor,
    Lewis, Joseph & Ervine, rocf Middleton
    MM, dtd 1834,2,9
1837, 9, 23. Ann & ch, Emmor, Lewis, Joseph,
    Arvine & Sina, gct Cincinnati MM
1847, 9, 25. Smith dis mcd
1848, 1, 22. Martha Keen (form Townsend) dis
    mcd
1848, 11, 25. Moses dis mcd
1850, 5, 25. Wm. gct Salem MM
1853, 2, 26. Dillon dis disunity
1856, 9, 26. Prissilla (form Woolman) dis
    mcd (W)
1856, 10, 25. John dis mcd
1857, 2, 28. Wm. D. dis disunity
1857, 2, 28. Eliza dis disunity
1857, 2, 28. Priscilla (form Woolman) dis mcd
1858, 7, 23. Mary P. (form Morris) dis mcd
    (W)
1858, 7, 24. Mary P. (form Morris) dis mcd
1858, 11, 27. Seth dis mcd & jas
1860, 9, 22. Lewis & w, Rachel, gct Salem MM
1861, 7, 27. Sarah dis disunity
1861, 7, 27. Edith dis disunity
1862, 1, 25. Samuel dis disunity
1863, 1, 24. Lewis rocf Salem MM, dtd 1863,
    1,22
1863, 1, 24. Ann dis jW
1863, 5, 22. Lewis dis jG (W)
1868, 9, 25. Edith Stratton (form Townsend)
    dis mcd (W)
1868, 11, 27. Sarah dis disunity (W)
1887, 11, 26. Henry H. rocf Legrand MM, Ia.
1887, 11, 26. Ann R. rocf Oskaloosa MM, Ia.

1890, 1, 25. Henry H. & w, Anne R., & dt,
    Hellen, gct North Branch MM, Kans.
1913, 1, 25. Oscar recrq
1918, 1, 26. Oscar gct Beloit MM
1920, 1, 24. Georgiana recrq

TREGO
1787, 5, 4. Mary b

1830, 10, 23. Mary [Trago] dis jH

TRUEBLOOD
1865, 8, 31. Francis, s John & Louisa, Wash.
    Co., Ind.; m in Damascus MH, Amy LIPSEY,
    dt Edmund & Sarah, Mahoning Co., O.

1865, 11, 25. Amy L. gct Blue River MM, Ind.

UPDEGRAFF
1861, 3, 27. Nathan, s Nathan & Ann, Jeffer-
    son Co., O.; m in Goshen MH, Lucina LUP-
    TON, dt Jonathan & Clarissa ROOD, Mahon-
    ing Co., O.

1861, 5, 25. Lusina gct Short Creek MM, O.

VAIL
----, --, --. John b 1801,10,19; m Esther
    ----- b 1816,6,17
    Ch: Phebe   b 1835, 1, 5
        Orpha   " 1837, 2, 16
        Thomas
        Carr   " 1839, 4, 6 d 1844, 1, 4
        bur Springfield
        John Law-
        rence   b 1841, 10, 17
        William H."" 1843, 10, 31 " 1844, 1, 9
        bur Springfield
        Samuel   b 1844, 12, 30

1835, 7, 25. John & w, Esther, & dt, Phebe,
    rocf Short Creek MM, O., dtd 1835,6,23
1837, 5, 27. John & w, Esther, & ch, Phebe
    & Orpha, gct Sommerset MM
1841, 8, 28. John & w, Esther, & ch, Phebe,
    Orpha & Thomas Carr, rocf Pennsville MM,
    dtd 1841,7,15
1846, 2, 28. John dis jas
1846, 6, 27. Esther & ch, Phebe, Orpha, John
    Lawrence & Samuel, gct Goshen MM

VANFOSSEN
1862, 12, 16. Rebecca M., dt Jacob & Margaret,
    b

1879, 4, 26. Rebecca M. [Vanfessen] recrq

VANSYOC
----, --, --. Enoch P. [Vanscoyoc] b 1830,1,
    19; m Phebe C. ----- b 1833,11,13
    Ch: Martha J. b 1854, 1, 9
        Albert A.   " 1855, 9, 18
        Ruth Emma   " 1858, 9, 5

VANSYOC, continued
```
    Ch: Anna          b 1862, 11, 30
        Mary          " 1864,  4, 25
        Eldora        " 1867,  7, 28
        Oliver        " 1870,  8, 16
        Enoch Wil-
          lis         " 1872, 11, 24
        Amos Em-
          mett        " 1874,  5,  2 d 1874, 9,21
          bur Damascus
```
1864, 4, 23. Enoch P. dis disunity (W)
1867, 5, 24. Phebe dis disunity (W)
1868, 8, 26. Enoch & w, Phebe, & ch, Martha
    Jane, Albert A., Ruth Emma, Anna, Mary &
    Eldora, rocf Alliance MM
1875, 2, 27. Martha Galbreath (form Vansyoc)
    con mcd
1877, 1, 26. Martha Galbreath (form Vansyoc)
    dis mcd (W)
1877, 3, 24. Enoch & w, Phebe C., & ch, Anna
    Mary, Eldora, John Oliver, Enoch Willit &
    Phebe Eva, gct Salem MM
1884, 6, 27. Anna Holly (form Vansyoc) dis
    mcd (W)
1884, 6, 27. Mary E. Sheehan (form Vansyoc)
    dis mcd (W)

VAUGHN
```
----, --, --. James b 1780,1,11; m Rhoda
    ----- b 1790,9,30
    Ch: Rebecca F. b 1823,  6,  2
        Mary A.    " 1825,  1, 27
        Joanna     " 1826,  8, 25
        Rhoda      " 1828,  2, 19
        Unity      " 1829,  9, 11
        Joseph     " 1831,  9, 24
        Lindley J. " 1835,  5, 12
```
1826, 5, 27. Pollie Maria, minor, recrq
1839, 8, 24. James & w, Rhoda, & ch, Rebecca
    T. Mary Ann, Joana Rhoda, Unity, Joseph
    & Lindley James, gct Gilead MM
1845, 6, 28. Polly Maria gct New Garden MM
1926, 1, 22. Elsie (Brantingham) dropped from
    mbrp (W)

VENABLE
1853, 5, 28. Vincent rocf Chesterfield MM,
    dtd 1852,12,18, end by Salem MM, 1853,5,25
1858, 12, 25. Vincent gct Goshen MM

VERNON   [(W)
1860, 1, 27. Eliza P. (form Stuart) con mcd
1863, 10, 24. Eliza P. (form Steward) dis mcd

VOTAW
```
----, --, --. Isaac Sr. b 1744,1,29 d 1817,8,12
    bur Goshen; m Ann ----- b 1746,7,20
----, --, --. Isaac b 1776,2,4 d 1863,6,7 bur
    Goshen; m Sarah ----- b 1778,2,24 d 1866,
    3,3 bur Goshen
    Ch: Phebe     b 1799, 11, 22
```

```
    Ch: Mary       b 1802,  9, 25 d 1830, 9,24
        bur Goshen
        Benjamin   b 1804,  4, 15
        Jemima     " 1806,  2, 25 " 1881, 3,27
        bur Goshen
        Sarah      " 1808,  2, 17
        David      " 1810,  7, 26
        Rachel     " 1814,  5, 17
        Matilda    " 1816,  7,  4
----, --, --. Thomas b 1781,5,30; m Elizabeth
    ----- b 1788,4,4 d 1851,5,14
    Ch: George     b 1808,  6,  5 d 1831, 7, 3
        bur Goshen
        Mary       b 1809,  9, 28
        Ann        " 1811,  2, 16
        Elizabeth  " 1814,  3, 22
        Samuel     " 1816,  5, 16
        Esther     " 1818,  2,  2 d 1891, 9,16
        Martha     " 1820,  1, 21
        Thomas     " 1822, 11, 22
        Hannah     " 1824, 10, 14
        Isaac B.   " 1826, 11, 23
        Lydia      " 1830,  1, 18
----, --, --. Isaac Jr. b 1805,6,20; m Rebec-
    ca ----- b 1809,10,22
    Ch: Martha     b 1829,  8, 30
        Joshua W.  " 1831, 11, 29
        Rachel     " 1833,  5, 17
        Joseph     " 1836,  2,  5
```
1828, 11, 26. Ann m Samuel GIBSON
1830, 12, 1. Mary m Robert COBBS
1831, 1, 26. Sarah m James JOHNSON
1841, 9, 30. Samuel, s Thomas & Elizabeth,
    Columbiana Co., O., b 1816,5,16; m in
    Springfield MH, Sarah WARRINGTON, dt Abram
    & Keziah, b 1815,8,14 d 1889,3,2 bur
    Springfield
```
    Ch: Jane       b 1843,  3,  5
        Sybil      " 1845,  9, 21
        Eliza Ann  " 1850,  8,  5
```
1842, 3, 20. Elizabeth m David TAYLOR
```
----, --, --. Thomas Jr. b 1822,11,22; m
    Gulielma ----- b 1822,11,21
    Ch: Lindley
        George     b 1845,  4, 19
        Mary Esther" 1849, 10, 31
```
1845, 1, 29. Hannah m Littleberry STANLEY
1846, 4, 29. Martha m John W. ADAMSON
```
----, --, --. Isaac B. b 1826,11,23 d 1863,11,
    18 bur Goshen; m Hannah ----- b 1825,12,
    22
    Ch: James T.   b 1853, 12, 18
        Mary Emma  " 1856,  7, 13
        John A.    " 1860, 11,  1 d 1863, 4,14
        bur Goshen
----, --, --. Louis H. b 1876,6,2 d 1922,2,5;
    m Rosella M. BRIGGS, dt Jonathan & Mary
    E. (Shry), b 1897,12,7
    Ch: Pearl
        Anna       b 1907,  1,  4
        Clarence
        J.         " 1909,  6, 12
        Olive May  " 1913,  8, 28
```

VOTAW, continued

1829, 8, 22. Benjamin dis mou

1836, 3, 26. Isaac & w, Rebecca, & ch, Martha, Joshua & Rachel, rocf Chester MM, Ind., dtd 1835,11,18

1837, 9, 23. Isaac Jr. & w, Rebecca, & ch, Martha, Joshua W., Rachel & Joseph, gct Salem MM

1843, 8, 26. Matilda Frantz (form Votaw) dis mcd

1844, 8, 24. Thomas Jr. gct Marlborough MM, to m Guli Elma Hutton

1845, 1, 25. Gulielma rocf Marlborough MM, dtd 1844,12,31

1847, 9, 25. Lydia Shinn (form Votaw) dis mcd

1852, 9, 25. Isaac B. gct Salem MM, to m Hannah Barber

1853, 6, 25. Thomas Jr. & Guli Elma dis joining Spiritualists

1854, 9, 23. Hannah G. rocf Salem MM, dtd 1854, 7, 19

1863, 1, 24. Samuel & w, Sarah, & ch, Jane, Sybil & Eliza Ann, dis jW

1863, 6, 26. David & Jemima dis jG (G)

1863, 6, 26. Rachel dis jG (W)

1863, 8, 21. Isaac & Hannah dis jG (W)

1865, 6, 24. Lindley George dis mcd & military service

1865, 8, 26. David dis disunity   [(W)

1866, 8, 21. Sibyl Bates (form Votaw) dis mcd

1869, 6, 26. Esther Kirkbride (form Votaw) dis mcd

1869, 6, 25. Elisan Owen (form Votaw) dis mcd (W)

1882, 4, 22. James & Hannah rocf East Goshen MM

1884, 5, 25. Rachel gct Winona MM

1892, 11, 26. James dropped from mbrp

1921, 2, 26. Lewis & w, Rosella M., rocf Winona MM

1921, 2, 26. Pearl Anna, Clarence J. & Olive May, ch Lewis & Rosella, recrq

WALKER

1837, 8, 31. Isaac, s Abel & Mary, Columbiana Co., O., b 1809,8,2; m in Springfield MH, Lydia NEGUS, dt John & Mirium, Columbiana Co., O., b 1816,4,22
Ch: William   b 1841, 4, 5

1838, 1, 27. Lydia gct New Garden MM

1839, 7, 27. Isaac & w, Lydia, rocf New Garden MM, dtd 1839,5,23

1841, 10, 23. Isaac & w, Lydia N., & s, Wm., gct Flushing MM

WALTON

----, --, --. Jesse b 1771,3,20 d 1830,2,10 bur Springfield; m Ann ----- b 1779,5,11 d 1830,7,27 bur Springfield
Ch: Tace   b 1803, 1, 22
    Uree   " 1804, 10, 29
    Amos   " 1806, 8, 29 d 1823, 3, 2

bur Springfield
Ch: Jehu   b 1808, 11, 21 d 1837, 5, 5
    bur Springfield
    Lydia   b 1811, 4, 4
    Ann   " 1813, 8, 25
    Benjamin " 1815, 8, 23
    Jonathan " 1817, 11, 29

----, --, --. Jonathan b 1787,11,6 d 1854,5,3 bur Springfield; m Wilhelmina H. M. ----- b 1788,2,14
Ch: Lewis   b 1811, 3, 23
    Josiah   " 1814, 1, 20
    Nathan   " 1820, 1, 19
    Mary Ann " 1822, 11, 25
    Harriet
    Maria   " 1829, 10, 9 d ----,12,20
    bur Springfield

1833, 3, 27. Lewis, s Jonathan & Maria, Columbiana Co., O., b 1811,3,23 d 1841,8,3 bur Springfield; m in Springfield MH, Chlotilda CREW, dt Obadiah & Mary, Columbiana Co., O., b 1812,9,20
Ch: Emmor C. b 1834, 2, 3
    Harriett
    Emily   " 1839, 8, 13 d 1860, 3,14
    bur Springfield

1834, 5, 1. Ann m Daniel YOUNG

----, --, --. Benjamin b 1815,8,23; m Hannah ----- b 1815,8,11
Ch: Jesse   b 1837, 10, 22
    Anzonetta " 1841, 9, 27
    Amos   " 1844, 3, 28
    Eli   " 1846, 8, 12
    Leander   " 1849, 7, 24
    William   " 1852, 8, 18

----, --, --. Josiah, s Jonathan & Maria, b 1814,1,20; m Deborah ----- b 1817,3,21 d 1862,12,16 bur Springfield
Ch: Rebecca
    Ann   b 1840, 10, 9
    Mary Jane " 1844, 7, 16
    Anna Marie " 1850, 8, 23
    Jonathan   " 1854, 8, 7
Josiah m 2nd Eliza -----, dt Benj. & Elizabeth STANLEY, b 1821,11,2 d 1903,3,1

1845, 10, 2. Jonathan C., s Jesse & Anne, Columbiana Co., O., b 1817,11,29 d 1850, 8,31; m in Springfield MH, Ruth COPPOCK, dt Jehu & Judith, Columbiana Co., O., b 1825,7,25 d 1848,1,25
Ch: Marietta   b 1847, 8, 12
Jonathan m 2nd Sarah ----- b 1818,4,25

1850, 1, 30. Jonathan C., s Jesse & Ann, Columbiana Co., O.; m in Goshen MH, Sarah CARSON, dt John & Jemimah, Mahoning Co., O.

1851, 11, 27. Mary Ann m Jason HAMPTON

1855, 5, 31. Ann m John RELEY

1836, 11, 26. Benjamin gct Carmel MM, to m Hannah Burdg

1837, 5, 27. Hannah rocf Carmel MM

1837, 8, 26. Ann rocf Stroudsborough MM, dtd

WALTON, continued
    1837,5,25, end by Salem MM, 1837,8,23
1839, 10, 26. Josiah gct Chesterfield MM, to
    m Deborah Thomas
1840, 8, 22. Deborah C. rocf Chesterfield
    MM, dtd 1840,6,26
1845, 6, 28. Nathan dis mcd
1845, 7, 26. Eliza Ann (form Wickersham) dis
    mcd
1848, 6, 24. Josiah & w, Deborah, & ch, Re-
    becca Ann & Mary Jane, gct Chesterfield
    MM
1851, 12, 27. Josiah & w, Deborah, & ch, Re-
    becca Ann, Mary Jane & Mariah, rocf
    Plymouth MM, dtd 1851,10,20
1853, 9, 24. Benjamin & w, Hannah, & ch,
    Jesse, Anzonetta, Amos, Eli, Leander &
    William, gct Driftwood MM, Ind.
1854, 11, 25. Josiah & w, Deborah, & ch, Re-
    becca Ann, Mary Jane, Anna Maria & Jona-
    than Walton, gct Pleasant Plain MM, Ia.
1857, 6, 27. Emmer C. dis mcd
1858, 4, 24. Josiah & w, Deborah D., & ch,
    Rebecca Ann, Mary Jane, Anne Mariah,
    Jonathan T., rocf Pleasant Plain MM, Ia.
1860, 5, 26. Lydia gct Goshen MM
1862, 2, 22. Chlotilda dis disunity
1863, 5, 22. Sarah dis jG (W)
1864, 12, 24. Sarah gct Springdale MM, Ia.
1865, 3, 24. Clotilda dis disunity (W)
1866, 4, 28. Rebecca A. Roberts (form Walton)
    dis mcd
1868, 11, 28. Eliza (form Benedict) con mcd
1868, 11, 28. Josiah con mcd
1870, 12, 24. Anna dis
1871, 5, 27. Mary Jane Stratton (form Walton)
    con mcd
1883, 12, 22. Jonathan relrq

WARD ·
1834, 6, 28. Tacy (form James) dis mou

WARE
1827, 2, 15. Benjamin, s Asa & Eliza Ann, b
1831, 3, 19. Emmor b

1829, 9, 26. Samuel gct ND MM
1851, 7, 26. Asa & w, Abigail, & ch, Emmor
    & Joel, rocf Salem MM, dtd 1851,6,25
1853, 11, 26. Asa & w, Abigail, gct Salem MM
1860, 5, 25. Emmor dis mcd (W)
1862, 2, 22. Emmor dis mcd
1889, 4, 27. Benjamin recrq
1897, 10, 23. Benjamin dropped from mbrp

WARREN
1854, 10, 28. Phebe Jane (form Whinery) dis
    mcd
1859, 5, 27. Eliza Stilwell (form Warren)
    dis mcd (W)
1868, 5, 22. Job gct New Garden MM, to m
    Rebecca Coppock (W)
1870, 3, 25. Job & s, Samuel, gct New Garden

MM (W)
1870, 3, 25. Adaline gct New Garden MM (W)

WARRINGTON
----, --, --. Abraham b 1783,4,25 d 1841,5,3
    bur Springfield; m Keziah ----- b 1782,8,7
    d 1857,3,27 (an elder)
    Ch: Mary   b 1808, 6, 17
        Jane   " 1810, 1, 15
        Ruth   " 1811, 10, 23
        John R.   " 1814, 1, 1
        Sarah   " 1815, 8, 14
        Martha   " 1817, 2, 4
        Nathan   " 1819, 2, 11
        Thomas   " 1821, 4, 15
        Evan   " 1821, 4, 15
        Joshua   " 1824, 10, 15
1828, 11, 27. Jane m Joseph C. MORRIS
----, --, --. John R. b 1814,1,1; m Rachel
    ----- b 1806,12,22
    Ch: Rebecca   b 1840, 9, 4
        Abraham   " 1842, 10, 9
        Jesse   " 1864, 1, 20
        David   " 1848, 7, 29
        Charles   " 1851, 3, 23
1841, 9, 30. Sarah m Samuel VOTAW
----, --, --. Nathan b 1819,2,11; m Mary D.
    ----- b 1822,5,15 (W)
    Ch: Samuel D.   b 1844, 9, 24 d 1849, 5, 8
        Linneus   " 1847, 6, 22
        Henry   " 1849, 7, 31
        Sarah Ann   " 1852, 12, 4
        Hannah   " 1855, 4, 1
        Irving   " 1857, 7, 6
        Wilson   " 1860, 1, 11
        Mary   " 1863, 2, 20
1845, 2, 27. Ruth m Israel NEGUS
----, --, --. Thomas b 1821,4,15 d 1867,9,5
    bur Springfield; m Lydia ----- b 1835,4,
    19 d 1910,12,15 (W)
    Ch: Edgar   b 1859, 3, 19 d 1929, 1,20
            bur Damascus
        Albert   b 1860, 4, 4
        Gilbert   " 1864, 10, 4
        Elizabeth   " 1866, 4, 3 d 1867, 9, 5
            bur Springfield
----, --, --. Edgar b 1859,3,19 d 1929,1,20
    bur Damascus; m Hannah C. ----- b 1858,4,5
    dt Joshua & Jane (Hoyle) COPPOCK (W)
    Ch: Thomas C.   b 1885, 6, 28
        Mary E.   " 1887, 6, 1
----, --, --. Gilbert, s Thomas & Lydia (Crew)
    b 1864,10,4; m Josephine B. BUNDY, dt
    Edmund & Deborah M. (Jones) b 1869,1,12
    (W)
    Ch: Ruth   b 1902, 10, 15
        Alfred E.   " 1904, 4, 26
        Margery   " 1907, 3, 3; m Elvin
        C. COX
----, --, --. Thomas C., s Edgar & Hannah,
    b 1885,6,28; m Sarah Mable HALL, dt Abner
    I. & Anna (Morlan), b 1888,4,18 (W)
    Ch: Paul A.   b 1913, 1, 31

WARRINGTON, continued

     Ch: Lawrence E. b 1915, 5, 3
         Morris J. " 1918, 8, 5 d 1923, 3, 2
         Walter H. " 1921, 4, 10
         Clara Es-
           ther   " 1926, 2, 15

1839, 2, 22. John R. gct Redstone MM, to m Rachel Garwood
1839, 8, 24. Rachel rocf Redstone MM, dtd 1839,7,3
1843, 10, 28. Nathan gct Middleton MM, to m Mary Dixon
1844, 4, 27. Nathan gct Middleton MM
1851, 2, 22. Joshua gct Salem MM, to m Unice Shreeve
1854, 1, 28. Evan dis mcd
1855, 6, 23. Joshua gct Driftwood MM, Ind.
1857, 6, 26. Nathan & w, Mary, & ch, Linneaus, Henry, Sarah Ann & Hannah, rocf Middleton MM, dtd 1857,6,11 (W)
1858, 6, 25. Thomas rmt Lydia Crew (W)
1862, 1, 25. Nathan & w, Mary D., & ch, Leneus Henry, Sarah Ann, Hannah, Irving & Wilson, rocf Salem MM, dtd 1862,1,23
1863, 1, 24. Nathan & w, Mary D., & ch, Lineus & Henry, dis jW
1863, 1, 24. Lydia dis jW
1863, 1, 24. Mary dis jW
1863, 1, 24. Martha dis jW
1863, 1, 24. Thomas dis jW
1863, 3, 27. John R. & Rachel dis jG (W)
1863, 9, 25. Rebecca dis jG (W)
1864, 4, 23. Nathan & w, Mary, & ch, Lineus, Henry, Sarah Ann, Hannah, Erving, Wilson & Mary, gct Pennsville MM
1866, 10, 27. Abraham gct Spring Creek MM, Ia.
1874, 5, 23. John & w, Rachel, gct Salem MM
1875, 5, 22. Rebecca gct Salem MM
1879, 10, 25. Jesse relrq
1879, 10, 25. Charles relrq
1879, 11, 22. David gct Salem MM
1884, 6, 27. Edgar gct New Garden MM, to m Hannah Coppock (W)
1884, 12, 26. Hannah C. rocf New Garden MM, dtd 1884,11,20
1894, 4, 27. Albert gct New Garden MM, to m Elizabeth M. Oliphant (W)
1897, 2, 26. Albert gct New Garden MM (W)
1898, 4, 22. Gilbert gct Short Creek MM, O., to m Josephine Bundy (W)
1899, 4, 21. Josephine B. rocf Short Creek MM, O., dtd 1899,3,21 (W)
1911, 10, 27. Thomas C. gct Middleton MM, to m Sara Mabel Hall (W)
1912, 9, 24. Sara Mabel rocf Middleton MM, dtd 1912,9,21 (W)
1922, 4, 21. Mary Elizabeth rmt Albert Lindley Pemberton (W)
1928, 5, 25. Alfred E. gct Plainfield MM, Ind., to m Lenna Mae Stanley (W)

WATSON

----, --, --. ----- m Eliza ----- b 1820,3,12
    ChP James   b 1846, 6, 16
       William   " 1847, 9, 6
       Mary H.   " 1848, 10, 25
       Barkley See-
         bohm   b 1850, 2, 8
1873, 1, 17. Thressa M., w Mark A., dt James & Elizabeth Anna (Shreve) CREW, b

1861, 3, 23. Caleb Maris gct Smithfield MM, to m Deborah Watson
1862, 9, 27. Eliza & ch, James H., Wm. W., Mary H. & Barclay S., rocf Smithfield MM, dtd 1862,8,16
1870, 6, 25. Wm. gct Kansas MM, Kans.
1870, 7, 23. Eliza & s, Barclay Seebohm, gct Kansas MM, Kans.
1870, 8, 27. James H. gct Kansas MM, Kans.
1871, 3, 25. Barclay gct Kansas MM, Kans.
1871, 4, 22. Mary H. gct Kansas MM, Kans.
1872, 1, 27. Eliza gct Kansas MM, Kans.

WATTERS

----, --, --. Russell B. m Clara COBBS
    Ch: Genevieve
       Avon   b 1917, 2, 6
       Juanita
       Elaine   " 1920, 4, 11

1933, 1, 26. Genevieve Avon & Juanita Elaine recrq

WEAVER

1865, 6, 26. Cassio O. b d 1917,--,--

1895, 5, 25. David Cassia recrq

WEBB

1829, 11, 28. Benjamin, minor, rocf Salem MM, dtd 1829,11,25
1831, 5, 28. Penina, minor, rocf Carmel MM, dtd 1831,4,16
1833, 12, 28. Benjamin, minor, gct Duck Creek MM, Ind.
1834, 10, 25. Penina, minor, gct Salem MM
1868, 9, 25. Lucina (form Stanley) dis mcd (W)

WELCH

----, --, --. John m Margaret RIDDLEY, dt Geo. & Dorothy, b 1847,8,2
    Ch: Dora   b 1888, 5, 19

1894, 11, 23. Alice A. (form Clempson) con mcd (W)
1898, 3, 26. Margaret & dt, Dora, recrq
1900, 3, 23. Dora & Lizzie gct Salem MM
1900, 4, 28. Lizzie recrq

WELLS

1903, 4, 25. Clara E. gct Spencer MM, Ia.

WHEALDON
1847, 8, 28. Matilda Smith rocf Westland MM,
  dtd 1847,7,21
1854, 2, 25. Martha S. [Wheldon] gct New
  Garden MM; returned 8-26 for disunity
1854, 11, 25. Martha S. dis disunity

WHINERY
1830, 7, 7. John Jr., s Robert & Phebe, Columbiana Co., O., b 1807,10,8 d 1886,11,30
  bur Upper Springfield; m in Goshen MH,
  Elizabeth MALMSBERRY, dt Benjamin & Jane,
  Columbiana Co., O., b 1810,4,28
    Ch: Emaline P. b 1831, 9, 16
        Phebe Jane " 1833, 8, 9
        Sarah   " 1835, 5, 24
        Benjamin M." 1839, 6, 5
        Lydia B.   " 1841, 6, 17
1834, 7, 31. David, s Robert & Phebe, Columbiana Co., O.; m in Upper Springfield MH,
  Sarah BROWN, dt Nathan & Amy, Columbiana
  Co., O.
1843, 4, 27. Thomas, s Robert & Phebe, Columbiana Co., O.; m in Upper Springfield MH,
  Mary BLACKBURN, dt Barbee & Elizabeth,
  Columbiana Co., O.
----, --, --. Chas. Leech, s Thos. & Mary,
  b 1849,12,6 d 1913,3,8; m Lydia A. -----
  b 1847,10,6 d 1905,8,13
    Ch: Clara May b 1874, 5, 11
        Arthur
        Dallas   " 1878, 4, 15
----, --, --. Leander b 1852,10,9; m Mary B.
  ----- b 1853,12,17
    Ch: Florence S.
                  b 1883, 5, 12
        Wilmer D. " 1886, 3, 1
-----, --, --. Cyrus m Anna Margarete VANFOSSEN
  dt Jacob & Margarete (Sell), b 1864,11,6
  d 1933,9,27
----, --, --. Arthur D., s Chas. L. & Lydia
  A., b 1878,4,15 d 1927,1,22; m Ida M.
  CATTELL, dt Binford & Sarah J., b 1874,10,
  3
    Ch: James C. b 1902, 9, 5
        Orval H. " 1908, 6, 28
        Sarah
        Leota   " 1911, 12, 8
1904, 10, 15. Deborah, w Walter N., dt Thos.
  A. & Sarah CRAWFORD, b (W)
1925, 11, 28. Walter N. m Deborah CRAWFORD
  dt Thos. A. & Sarah, b 1904,10,15 (W)

1830, 10, 23. Elizabeth gct New Garden MM
1834, 3, 22. John & w, Elizabeth, & ch, Emaline & Phebe Jane, rocf New Garden MM, dtd
  1834,3,20
1834, 11, 22. Sarah gct New Garden MM
1839, 9, 28. John & w, Elizabeth, & ch,
  Amelia P., Phebe Jane, Sarah & Benjamin
  N., gct New Garden MM
1842, 4, 23. John & w, Elizabeth, & ch,
  Emeline P., Phebe Jane, Sarah, Benjamin

M. & Lydia B., rocf New Garden MM, dtd
  1842,3,24
1843, 6, 24. Mary B. gct New Garden MM
1854, 10, 28. Phebe Jane Warren (form Whinery)
  dis mcd
1855, 12, 22. Sarah Arbuckle (form Whinery)
  dis mcd
1861, 10, 26. Lydia B. Mather (form Whinery)
  dis mcd
1862, 1, 25. Emaline P. dis disunity
1862, 2, 22. Benjamin dis disunity
1863, 5, 22. John dis jG (W)
1863, 5, 22. Elizabeth dis jG (W)
1863, 6, 26. Emeline dis jG (W)
1863, 9, 25. Benjamin dis jG (W)
1863, 11, 28. Mary Ann (form Fawcett) dis mcd
1875, 2, 27. John rocf East Goshen MM
1875, 11, 27. Charles L. rocf New Garden MM
1882, 3, 25. Lydia Ann & ch, Clara May &
  Arthur Dallas, recrq
1882, 4, 22. John relrq
1882, 6, 23. John rst rq (W)
1895, 10, 25. Olive R. (form Bundy) con mcd
  (W)
1895, 4, 27. Leander & w, Mary V., & ch,
  Florence L. & Wilmer D., rocf Salem MM
1897, 8, 19. Leander & w, Mary V., & ch,
  Florence L. & Wilmer D., gct Winona MM
1903, 11, 28. Ida rocf East Goshen MM
1926, 4, 23. Deborah Crawford gct Short
  Creek MM, O. (W)
1929, 6, 27. Orvil & James dropped from mbrp
1932, 8, 18. Camille relrq
1933, 1, 26. Anne rocf East Goshen MM

WHITACRE
1833, 5, 30. Maria m Peter BINFORD, Jr.
1859, 2, 25. Dora, dt Caleb & Rachel, b
1911, 6,26. Herbert Martin [Whitcher], s
  H. B., b

1832, 8, 25. Maria rocf Westland MM, dtd
  1832,5,23
1917, 11, 24. Dora rocf Winona MM
1923, 1, 27. Dora [Whittacre] gct Winona MM

WHITE
----, --, --. ----- m Thamar ----- b 1808,1,
  21 (W)
    Ch: Joel   b 1832, 2, 9
        Mary   " 1833, 9, 10
        Eliza   " 1837, 10, 20
        Matilda " 1839, 11, 23
        Lewis K. " 1842, 2, 24
        Cyrus   " 1844, 2, 10
        Emaline " 1848, 6, 17
----, --, --. ----- m Henryette STANLEY, dt
  Robert & Sarah, b 1870,9,7
    Ch: Mildred
        Esther b 1894, 2, 24
        Everett
        Stanley " 1895, 2, 15

WHITE, continued

1848, 2, 26. Israel & Mercy, & ch, Hannah,
  Miriam & Edward, rocf New Garden MM, dtd
  1848, 1,20

1852, 5, 26. Israel & w, Mary, & ch, Hannah,
  Miriam, Edward & Lewis Parker, gct Marlborough MM

1860, 1, 27. Mary Thomas (form White) dis mcd
  (W)

1860, 1, 27. Matilda Wilaby (form White) dis
  mcd (W)

1861, 6, 21. Joel dis disunity (W)

1863, 7, 24. Eliza dis jG (W)

1866, 7, 27. Cyrus dis disunity (W)

1879, 2, 21. Emaline Wiles (form White) dis
  mcd (W)

1897, 12, 25. Henrietta S. gct Rich Square MM,
  Ind.; returned 1898,11,26 mistake in name
  of mtg

1898, 9, 24. Henrietta & ch, Mildred Esther
  & Everett Stanley, gct Hopewell MM, Ind.

1928, 2, 23. Agnes Heston relrq

WHITELEATHER

1902, 1, 7. Blanch Elizabeth, dt Winfred B.
  & Katharine, b

1916, 1, 22. Blanche E. recrq

WICKERSHAM

----, --, --. Joseph [Wickershaw] & Margaret
  Ch: Eliza Ann b 1817, 9, 15
      Thomas   " 1823, 5, 11
      Mary J.   " 1826, 2, 11
      Ellis   " 1828, 2, 11
      Cyrus   " 1830, 8, 11
      Hannah   " 1833, 4, 6
      Pierce   " 1837, 11, 8

1843, 3, 25. Joseph & w, Margaret, & ch,
  Thomas, Mary, Ellis, Cyrus, Hannah &
  Pearce, rocf Middleton MM, dtd 1843,2,12

1843, 3, 25. Eliza Ann rocf Middleton MM,
  dtd 1843,2,12

1845, 7, 26. Eliza Ann Walton (form Wickersham) dis mcd

1849, 5, 26. Joseph & w, Margaret, & ch,
  Cyrus, Hannah & Pierce, gct Goshen MM

1849, 5, 26. Thomas gct Goshen MM

1849, 6, 23. Mary gct Goshen MM

1849, 7, 28. Ellis dis disunity

1865, 5, 9. Robert Ellyson gct Middleton
  MM, to m Phebe Wickersham (W)

WILABY

1860, 1, 27. Matilda (form White) dis mcd (W)

WILES

1879, 2, 21. Emaline (form White) dis mcd (W)

WILEY

----, --, --. David b 1785,2,2; m Elizabeth
  ----- b 1797,12,15

Ch: Sarah   b 1816, 8, 7
    Joseph   " 1818, 2, 1
    Mary   " 1820, 4, 16
    James   " 1822, 2, 9
    Cynthia   " 1824, 4, 17
    Elizabeth " 1826, 2, 10
    William   " 1828, 5, 29
    Margery   " 1830, 3, 31
    Drusilla   " 1832, 11, 6

----, --, --. Joseph b 1818,2,1; m Abigail
  ----- b 1818,2,23
  Ch: Rebecca
      Ann   b 1842, 1, 23
      John   " 1843, 7, 30
      Sarah M. " 1845, 2, 27
      Avarilla " 1847, 4, 26

1836, 9, 24. Sarah Palmer (form Wiley) con
  mcd

1837, 2, 25. David & w, Elizabeth, & ch,
  Joseph, Mary, James, Cynthia, Elizabeth,
  William, Margery, Drusilla & Richard,
  gct Marlborough MM

1844, 9, 28. Joseph & w, Abigail G., rocf
  Marlborough MM, dtd 1844,8,27

1844, 9, 28. Joseph & w, Mary G., & ch,
  Rebecca Ann & John, rocf Marlborough MM,
  dtd 1844,8,27

1848, 2, 26. Joseph & w, Abigail G., & ch,
  John, Sarah & Averilla, gct Marlborough
  MM

1863, 8, 21. Joseph & Abigail dis jG (W)

WILLIAMS

----, --, --. Richard b 1770,11,28 d 1852,3,
  10

1811, 11, 25. Phebe J. b

1818, 9, 23. David b

1849, 3, 29. Edward, s Richard & Sarah, Mahoning Co., O., b 1821,2,5 d 1894,9,2 ae
  74 bur Springfield; m in Springfield MH,
  Hannah BRUFF, dt James B. & Sarah, Mahoning Co., O., b 1823,8,27 d 1882,10,11
  bur Upper Springfield
  Ch: Sarah B. b 1850, 1, 3

1851, 5, 1. Lydia m Joseph STANLEY

----, --, --. Walter Rollin, s Thos. C. & Es-
  ther (Benedict), b 1884,3,10; m Myrtle
  May HOSACK, b 1884,2,13
  Ch: Paul Paton b 1921, 3, 20
      John
      Pennington " 1922, 7, 30

1847, 6, 26. Rachel rocf Marlborough MM, dtd
  1846,3,3 end by Allum Creek MM, 1847,5,23

1847, 10, 23. Lydia rocf Marlborough MM, dtd
  1847,9,28

1847, 11, 27. Edward rocf Marlborough MM, dtd
  1847,10,26

1848, 10, 28. Jeptha Fawcett gct Stillwater
  MM, to m Rachel Williams

1859, 10, 22. David rocf Goshen MM

1863, 2, 27. Edward dis jG (W)

WILLIAMS, continued
1863, 2, 27. Hannah B. dis jG (W)
1872, 12, 28. David gct Bangor MM, Ia.
1881, 10, 22. Edward & w, Hannah, relrq
1882, 3, 24. Edward & Hannah rst rq (W)
1886, 4, 24. Phebe J. rocf Gilead MM
1887, 9, 24. Phebe J. gct Modena MM, Calif.
1889, 12, 28. Sarah B. relrq
1898, 12, 24. Sarah B. (now Maris) recrq
1899, 6, 23. Sarah B. Maris (form Williams)
     dis mcd (W)
1809, 10, 23. Charles S. & w, Julia Ann, & s,
     Lloyd L., rocf Winona MM, O.
1911, 2, 25. Charles S. & w, Julia Ann, & s,
     Lloyd, gct Salem MM, O.
1931, 12, 24. Walter & w, Myrtle, & ch, Paul
     & John, rocf Smithfield MM

WILLIS
1910, 7, 25. Pauline Elizabeth, w Raymond S.,
     dt Louis J. & Mary (Kuntzman) HOOPES, b

WILT
----, --, --. Robert R., s Frank & Elizabeth
     (Naylor), b 1895,11,8; m Elizabeth PAXTON,
     dt Wm. & Adella (King), b 1899,11,7
     Ch: Jane
         Elizabeth b 1922, 3, 5
         William
         Franklin " 1923, 3, 18
         Ruth Pax-
         ton " 1924, 4, 1

1925, 12, 24. Elizabeth & ch, Jane Elizabeth,
     Wm. Franklin & Ruth Paxton, recrq
1927, 3, 24. Robert recrq
1933, 5, 25. Robert & w, Elizabeth, & ch
     relrq

WINDER
----, --, --. Leonard, s Joseph & Lydia (Mor-
     lan), b 1850,9,21; m Ruth Anna COPPOCK,
     dt Joshua & Jane (Hoyle), b 1863,7,7 (W)
     Ch: Esther
         Lydia b 1896, 1, 18
         Mary Ida " 1897, 3, 9
         Alice Re-
         becca " 1900, 7, 20
         Dorothy
         Emily " 1903, 2, 6
         Ann Eliza-
         beth " 1906, 3, 30

1859, 5, 27. John A. Cope gct Sandy Spring
     MM, to m Adah B. Winder (W)
1913, 9, 26. Leonard & w, Ruthanna, & ch,
     Esther Lydia, Mary Ida, Alice Rebecca,
     Dorotha Emily & Anna Elizabeth, rocf New
     Garden MM, dtd 1913,8,21 (W)
1924, 3, 21. Dorothy Emily gct Chesterfield
     MM, N. J. (W)
1924, 7, 25. Esther L. gct Abington MM (W)
1924, 10, 24. Alice R. gct Burlington MM, N.J.

(W)
1925, 5, 22. Leonard & w, Ruth Anna, & dt,
     Anna Elizabeth, gct Chesterfield MM, N. J.
(W)
1926, 1, 22. Mary E. gct Chesterfield MM,
     N. J. (W)

WINDLE
1850, 4, 28. Emma Pettit, dt Geo. & Paris
     (Bennet), b (w Milton E.)
1874, 3, 1. Emma M., adopted dt Samuel
     Brosius, b
1885, 1, 19. Bertha M., dt Edwin D. & Amy, b

1902, 1, 25. Bertha M. recrq
1904, 11, 23. Bertha relrq
1909, 12, 30. Emma rocf Winona MM, O.

WISE
1869, 3, 27. Pusey recrq
1870, 8, 27. Hannah recrq
1901, 8, 15. Clara M. gct East Goshen MM

WIRSCHING
1916, 4, 22. Lorena Crum relrq

WOOD
1844, 2, 8. Greenberry P., s Pusey & Char-
     ity, Columbiana Co., O.; m in Goshen MH,
     Hannah TATUM, dt George & Lydia, Columbi-
     ana Co., O.
----, --, --. Jonathan [Woods] d 1863,11,25
     ae 32; m Mary -----
     Ch: Almira
----, --, --. Walter m Jessie ATKINSON, dt
     Henry & Rebecca, b 1878,6,6
     Ch: Katharine
         Virginia b 1906, 6, 26
1878, 2, 20. Grace [Woods], dt John F. & Jane
     M., b

1836, 10, 22. Rebecca [Woods] (form Adamson)
     dis mcd
1843, 6, 24. Greenberry P. rocf Smithfield
     MM, dtd 1843,5,22
1847, 11, 27. Greenberry P. & w, Hannah, & ch,
     Alfred & Sarah, gct Salem MM
1853, 2, 26. Lydia rocf Middleton MM, dtd
     1853,2,10
1861, 4, 27. Jonathan & w, Mary, & dt, La-
     mira, rocf Gilead MM
1864, 2, 24. Mary & dt, Lamira, gct Gilead MM
1865, 6, 24. Temperance (form Blackburn) con
     mcd
1866, 1, 27. Temperance B. gct Gilead MM
1873, 6, 28. Lydia relrq
1900, 2, 24. Grace [Woods] recrq
1909, 1, 23. Jesse Atkinson & dt, Katharine
     Virginia, gct Scipio MM, N. Y.

WOODRUFF
1849, 8, 25. Hannah (form Morris) dis mcd

WOODWARD
1870, 1, 21. Judith (form French) dis mcd (W)

WOODWORTH
1871, 12, 8. Charles, s Elisha & Anna, b

1891, 3, 28. Charles recrq
1895, 3, 23. Charles gct Salem MM

WOOLF
1912, 6, 22. Marietta dropped from mbrp

WOOLMAN
----, --, --. Samuel Sr. b 1753,3,19; m Jane
----- b 1751,1,11 d 1837,12,3 ae 87 bur
Springfield
----, --, --. Abner b 1773,7,5 d 1859,9,27;
m Martha ----- b 1774,9,26 d 1856,12,16
Ch: Susanna   b 1804, 1, 31
    Anna   " 1806, 3, 12
    Joseph J.   " 1808, 2, 15 d 1810,11, 9
    Thomas B.   " 1809, 6, 26
    Sarah   " 1811, 11, 1
    Mary   " 1813, 10, 27
    Martha   " 1815, 6, 20
----, --, --. Samuel Jr. b 1776,12,20 d 1851,2,
8 bur Springfield; m Rebecca ----- b 1781,
6,29 d 1860,9,8 bur Springfield
Ch: Thomas T.   b 1806, 4, 17 d 1828,12,29
    bur Springfield
    Elizabeth b 1808, 2, 17 " 1865, 3,10
    bur Springfield
    Mary   b 1809, 8, 29 " 1894,11,22
    bur Damascus
    Joel   b 1811, 2, 12
    Benjamin " 1813, 1, 1
    Samuel   " 1814, 8, 17
    Jane   " 1816, 8, 23 d 1880, 2,10
    bur Springfield
    Rebecca   b 1818, 12, 23 " 1871, 8, 3
    bur Springfield
----, --, --. Aaron A. b 1786,8,27 d 1853,3,27
bur Springfield; m Mary WARRINGTON, b 1787,
11,8 d 1867,10,-- bur Springfield
Ch: Rebecca H. b 1817, 6, 14 d 1876, 7,--
    Enoch   " 1819, 2, 15 " 1895, 3,11
    Amy   " 1821, 4, 12 " 1867, 1, 4
    bur Damascus
    Ellis   b 1822, 10, 4 " 1852,12,30
    bur Damascus
    Abner   b 1824, 12, 18
    Sarah   " 1827, 8, 1 " 1853, 9,12
    bur Springfield
    John   b 1831, 3, 16 " 1846, 2, 4
    bur Springfield
----, --, --. Asher b 1798,12,30; m Maria
----- b 1801,12,10 d 1831,2,10 bur Springfield
Ch: Allen   b 1821, 10, 8
    Abraham   " 1823, 4, 5
    Leah   " 1825, 2, 10
    Phebe   " 1826, 11, 18
    Ann   " 1829, 2, 3

Ch: Maria Tay-
    lor   b 1831, 1, 9
1832, 5, 3. Mary m Jonathan CREW
1832, 11, 29. Sarah m John H. STANLEY
1833, 11, 27. Thomas B., s Abner & Martha,
Columbiana Co., O., b 1809,6,26 d 1876,
4,24 bur Springfield; m in Goshen MH, Sarah STANLEY, dt Thomas & Priscilla, Columbiana Co., O., b 1807,11,18 d 1890,8,28
Ch: Priscilla b 1834, 9, 21
    Abner S. " 1837, 1, 24
    Martin   " 1839, 8, 9 " 1843, 1,21
    bur Springfield
    Micajah   b 1841, 10, 18
    Henry   " 1844, 7, 7
    Joseph   " 1847, 4, 29 d 1848, 8,11
    bur Springfield
    Sarahetta b 1849, 12, 23
1844, 3, 28. Martha m Benjamin CARSON
1845, 5, 1. Samuel, s Samuel & Rebecca, Columbiana Co., O., b 1814,8,17; m in Spring
field MH, Unity FRENCH, dt Wm. & Judith,
Columbiana Co., O., b 1825,2,23
Ch: Thomas T. b 1846, 5, 31
    Judith Ann " 1848, 4, 8
    Marietta " 1850, 3, 16
1851, 2, 9. Samuel d ae 75 (an elder)
----, --, --. Abner b 1824,12,8 d 1914,5,4
bur Upper Springfield; m Elvira H. -----
b 1838,5,20 d 1880,7,13 bur Upper Spring-
field (W)
Ch: Caroline b 1864, 4, 29
    Lewis A. " 1868, 1, 14
    Edward J. " 1869, 7, 13
----, --, --. Abner S. b 1837,1,24; m Alice
A. ----- b 1843,2,13 (W)
----,Ch: Alva   b 1865, 5, 11
    Thos.
    Leonard   " 1868, 6, 19
    Maryetta " 1870, 11, 21
----, --, --. Lewis A., s Abner & Elvira
(Hall), b 1868,1,14 d 1928,9,4; m Lydia
A. COOPER, dt Samuel & Sarah (Pennock),
b 1858,2,8 (W)
----, --, --. Henry, s Thomas & Sarah, b
1844,7,7; m Rachel STEWARD, dt Joseph &
Emaline, b 1850,9,23
Ch: Gertrude b 1874, 9, 10
    Bertha S. " 1876, 4, 18
    Wm. Henry " 1877, 12, 25
----, --, --. Edward J. b 1869,7,13; m -----
----- (W)
Ch: Addison N. b 1894, 10, 3

1826, 1, 28. Thomas T., minor, gct Frankfort
MM, Pa.
1828, 6, 28. Thomas T. rocf Frankfort MM,
Pa., dtd 1828,4,29
1831, 9, 24. Asher dis mou
1834, 8, 23. Joel gct Frankford MM, Pa.
1838, 1, 27. Benjamin dis mcd
1838, 3, 24. Esther (form Crew) dis mcd
1842, 2, 26. Asher & ch, Allen Abraham, Leah,

WOOLMAN, continued
    Phebe, Ann & Maria Taylor, gct Salem MM, Ia.
1844, 6, 22. Asher rst at Salem MM on consent of this mtg
1852, 8, 28. Enoch gct Marlborough MM
1853, 1, 22. Samuel & w, Unity, & ch, Thomas F., Judith Ann & Marietta, gct Driftwood MM, Ind.
1856, 9, 26. Priscilla Townsend (form Woolman) dis mcd (W)
1857, 2, 28. Priscilla Townsend (form Woolman) dis mcd
1860, 4, 26. Rebecca rmt Isaac Carr (W)
1863, 1, 24. Eliza dis jW
1863, 1, 24. Mary dis jW
1863, 1, 24. Rebecca dis jW
1863, 1, 24. Jane dis jW
1863, 1, 24. Mary dis jW
1863, 1, 24. Abner dis jW
1863, 1, 24. Amy dis jW
1863, 1, 24. Thomas B. & w, Sarah, & ch, Abner Jr., Micajah, Henry & Sarahetta, dis jW
1863, 4, 24. Abner S. rmt Alice A. Holloway (W)
1863, 5, 22. Abner gct Middleton MM, to m Elvira Hall (W)
1863, 9, 25. Elvira H. rocf Middleton MM, dtd 1863,9,19 (W)
1866, 8, 24. Micajah dis mcd (W)
1874, 7, 24. Sarahetta Neal (form Woolman) dis mcd (W)
1874, 8, 21. Henry dis mcd (W)
1875, 8, 27. Rachel R. rocf Salem MM, dtd 1875,8,25 (W)
1876, 7, 22. Rachel (form Stewart) con mcd
1876, 9, 23. Henry con mcd
1880, 1, 23. Rachel dis jG (W)
1893, 4, 22. Henry relrq
1894, 4, 27. Alva dis mcd (W)
1894, 7, 28. Rachel & ch relrq
1895, 1, 25. Edward J. gct New Garden MM (W)
1897, 1, 23. Mary recrq
1901, 1, 25. Mary Etta dis jas (W)
1906, 10, 26. Alice A. (form Holloway) dis mcd (W)
1906, 11, 23. Abner S. dis disunity (W)
1907, 11, 22. Caroline H. rmt Wm. R. Jacobs (W)
1908, 4, 24. Lewis A. gct Salem MM, to m Lydia A. Cooper (W)
1908, 8, 21. Lydia A. rocf Salem MM (W)

WREN
1827, 1, 27. Cert rec for Lydia & ch, Mary, Anna, William & Lydia, from Upper MM, Va., dtd 1827,9,16, end to Marlborough MM
1827, 1, 27. Cert rec for Elijah from Upper MM, Va., dtd 1826,9,16, end to Marlborough MM

WRIGHT
1861, 4, 21. Wm. H., s Nathan & Emeline, b
1835, 5, 23. Jemima (form Kille) dis mcd
1845, 8, 23. Jemima rst
1850, 9, 29. Sally rocf Salem MM, dtd 1850, 9,25
1852, 5, 22. Jemima gct Gilead MM
1865, 4, 22. John & w, Sarah P., & s, Joseph A., rocf Sandy Spring MM, dtd 1865,4,18
1865, 12, 23. John & w, Sarah P., & s, Joseph, gct Ypsilanti MM, Mich.
1897, 1, 23. Wm. H. recrq
1901, 4, 27. Wm. H. dropped from mbrp

WUTHRICK
1905, 6, 10. Effie Marie, dt John S. & Luella J. (Shreve) GREENAWALT, b (w Fred C.)

YATES
1913, 1, 25. Louisa recrq
----, --, --. Louisa (Flickinger), w Shelton, b 1847,12,31 d 1920,7,29

YOUNG
----, --, --. Joseph b 1762,11,23 d 1848,10,1 bur Goshen; m Ann ----- b 1771,12,10
  Ch: Benjamin
    M.   " 1792, 9, 27
    Mary   " 1795, 3, 25
    Ann   " 1798, 7, 7
    Thomas   " 1801, 1, 31
    Joseph   " 1803, 1, 3
    William   " 1805, 12, 13
    Jane   " 1808, 6, 9
    Daniel   " 1810, 11, 19
    Sarah   " 1813, 8, 25
----, --, --. Benjamin M. b 1792,9,27; m Rachel ----- b 1800,7,4
  Ch: Jesse   b 1826, 11, 7
    Thomas   " 1829, 6, 21
    Amos   " 1833, 8, 12
    Jane   " 1837, 3, 7
    Tamar   " 1839, 12, 6
1833, 5, 2. Joseph Jr., s Joseph & Ann, Columbiana Co., O., b 1803,1,3; m in Springfield MH, Caroline CREW, dt Joshua & Millie, Columbiana Co., O., b 1813,8,19
  Ch: Hannah H. b 1835, 6, 24
    Joshua C.   " 1837, 7, 17
    Thomas S.   " 1838, 12, 27 d 1843, 4,15 bur Goshen
    Sarah   " 1840, 7, 5
    Milley   " 1842, 1, 6 " 1843, 4,15 bur Goshen
    Caroline   " 1843, 12, 16
    Fleming   " 1848, 5, 3
    John J.   " 1850, 10, 31
    Narcisa   " 1855, 11, 1

YOUNG, continued

1834, 5, 1. Daniel, s Joseph & Ann, Columbiana Co., O., b 1810,11,19; m in Springfield MH, Ann WALTON, dt Jesse & Ann, Columbiana Co., O., b 1813,8,25
Ch: Lavina   b 1835, 4, 1
    Lydia   " 1837, 2, 11 d 1847,12,19
      bur Goshen
    Jehu W.   " 1838, 6, 11
    Henry   " 1840, 5, 9
    Edwin   " 1842, 5, 15 " 1847,12, 5
      bur Goshen
    Mary   " 1844, 3, 6
    David   " 1846, 9, 24
    Jesse   " 1848, 12, 18 d 1849, 2, 1
      bur Goshen

1829, 5, 23. Benjamin & w, Rachel, & s, Jesse,
rocf Carmel MM, dtd 1829,5,16
1832, 3, 24. Joseph rocf Middleton MM, dtd
1832,3,8
1832, 6, 23. Joseph & w, Ann, rocf Middleton
MM, dtd 1832,6,7
1832, 6, 23. Daniel rocf Middleton MM, dtd
1832,6,7
1832, 6, 23. Jane rocf Middleton MM, dtd
1832,6,7
1832, 6, 23. Sarah rocf Middleton MM, dtd
1832,6,7
1834, 6, 28. Thomas rocf Salem MM, dtd 1834,
5,21
1843, 4, 22. Thomas gct Salem MM
1844, 10, 26. Benjamin & w, Rachel, & ch,
Jesse, Thomas, Amos, Jane & Tamer, gct
Sandy Spring MM
1849, 9, 22. Jane (form Rakestraw) dis mcd
1850, 6, 22. Daniel & w, Ann, & ch, Lavina,
Jehu W., Henry, Mary C. & David, gct
Goshen MM
1851, 1, 25. Ann gct Salem MM

1851, 1, 25. Sarah gct Salem MM
1855, 8, 25. Hannah H. Stark (form Young)
con mcd
1859, 3, 26. Joseph & w, Caroline, & ch,
Caroline, Joseph M., Fleming C., John J.
& Narcissa, gct Red Cedar MM, Ia.
1859, 3, 26. Joshua C. gct Red Cedar MM, Ia.
1859, 3, 26. Sarah gct Red Cedar MM, Ia.
1863, 9, 25. Joseph & Caroline dis jG (W)

ZEITLER
1927, 6, 23. Edward, Ella, Walter & Edith
dropped from mbrp

ZUERCHER
-----, --,--. Harrison Wm. b 1888,10,23; m
Blanche Mae RICE b 1889,10,21
Ch: Harrison
      Raymond b 1923, 4, 28
    Loris Wil-
      liam   " 1925, 2, 11
    Corinne
    Mae

1923, 2, 24. Harrison & Blanch recrq
1928, 6, 28. Harrison & Blanche & ch relrq

    *   *   *   *   *   *   *

EDGERTON
----, --, --. Elizabeth A. b 1842,12,10 d
1914,2,6

FRENCH
1851, 6, 28. Allen T. dis disunity

KIRK
1871, 6, 1. Martha T. m Wm. BRIGG, Jr.

LEEPER
1838, 10, 15. Anna b

1900, 2, 24. Anna recrq

WEST MONTHLY MEETING

West Monthly Meeting, Mahoning County, Ohio, was established in 1845 as a result of a recommendation of a general conference of men and women Friends of Salem and New Garden Quarterly Meeting of the Society of Friends (Hicksite). This monthly meeting consisted of the membership of West and Berlin Preparative Meetings. These meetings were placed under the supervision of New Garden Quarterly Meeting and the Quarterly Meeting was to meet at West on the second day in 2nd and 8th months.

William W. Lamborn was the first clerk, John Trago was assistant clerk, and William Heahurst, James Barnaby, William Merideth and Isaac Barker were Overseers. Other charter members were George Passmore, Simon Merideth, Charles Armitage, Harper Brosius, Nathan Heacock, Ezra Brannin, Robert Battin, Hoops Bailey, Daniel Mather, Joel and Ellen Harris, Thomas Rakestraw, Daniel B. Reeves, Enos Hilles, Samuel Harris, Rachel Harris, Ann B. Reeves, Susan Rakestraw, Mary Ann Hilles, Nathan Thomas, John Shinn, Jacob Harris, Pierce Garretson, Jacob and Owen Thomas, Silas Harris, Stephen Barnaby, Joseph S. Hartley, Catherine Barnaby, Rachel W. Thomas, Zilpha Barnaby, Esther C. Harris, Mary F. and Hannah C. Thomas, Mary Harris, Lee, Ann and Rachel M. Barnaby, Phebe H. Passmore, Sarah Armitage, Sabilla Shinn, Abigail Battin, Sarah Ann Trego, Edward Courtney, Clarkson Barnaby, Samuel and James Hartley, John and Miriam Buck, Sarah W. Garretson, Margaret Thomas, Ann Harris, Phebe Courtney, Phebe G. Brosius, Dinah Heacock, Esther Brosius, Lydia Hayhurst, Milton Heacock, Robert Hilles, William Lillas, Dinah Hartley, Phebe R. Lamborn, Ann B. Reeves, Elen R. Thomas, Uriah A. Heacock.

The records of this monthly meeting are in the Friends Historical Library, Swarthmore College, Swarthmore, Pennsylvania

RECORDS

ARMITAGE

1850, 5, 30. Rachel m Levi COBB
1855, 12, 27. Charle d ae 61
1858, 6, 30. Henry D., s Charles & Jane,
Mahoning Co., O.; m in home of Daniel
Mather, Elma J. BARBER, dt Isaac & Alice,
Mahoning Co., O.
1858, 6, 30. Phebe m Samuel C. HARLAN
1865, 5, 16. Sarah d ae 72

1880, 12, 22. Henry D. gct Fallowfield MM,
Pa., to m Eliza Jane Wood
1884, 1, 23. Eliza Jane rocf Fallowfield MM,
Pa., dtd 1884,1,12
1904, 7, 5. Eliza Jane gct Fallowfield MM,
Pa.

ARNOLD

1922, --, --. Anna Mary d

BAILEY

----, --, --. Hoops & Anne
Ch: Edward P. b 1839, 2, 17
Wm. Penn " 1841, 1, 10
Oakley H. " 1843, 6, 14
Francis C. " 1845, 4, 6
1876, 1, 7. Rebecca, dt Barton & Rachel
HEACOCK, d
1896, 3, 11. Lucretia M. d ae 48
1918, 4, 11. Sidney Leona d bur West

1851, 3, 21. Hoops dis setting up mtg contrary to discipline
1860, 12, 21. Mary Emily Lamborn (form Bailey)
dis mcd
1905, 8, 23. Sidney Leona recrq

BARBER

----, --, --. Isaac d 1851,1,12 ae 58; m Alice

Ch: Isaac   d 1858, 6,16
ae 32
Barclay   " 1857, 3,12
ae 27
Melissa   b 1841, 1, 24
Clarkson   " 1842, 1, 18
1858, 6, 30. Elma J. m Henry D. ARMITAGE
1873, 10, 30. Elizabeth A. m Clarkson HEACOCK
1877, 4, 24. Ezekiel d
1885, 7, 19. Ann d

1849, 1, 26. Edith Mather (form Barber) con
mcd
1863, 6, 26. Ezekiel & w, Ann, & ch, Elizabeth A., William M., Sarah S., Mary Emma,
John E., Henry & Ruth Anna, recrq
1879, 1, 22. Samuel rmt Hannah Mather

BARNABY

-----, --, --. Stephen & Catherine
Ch: Howard   b 1833, 3, 14

Ch: Louisa   b 1835, 6, 11
Samuel P.   " 1836, 4, 18
Leonard   " 1840, 7, 10
Samantha   " 1842, 12, 12
Anna Jane   " 1847, 1, 18
1844, 8, 20. Emeline, dt Lee & Zilpah, b
1847, 3, 16. James d

1848, 10, 27. Rachel Hilles (form Barnaby)
dis mcd
1858, 11, 26. Lee & w, Zilpah, dis setting
up mtg contrary discipline; rst 1866,11,23
by YM
1858, 11, 26. T. Clarkson dis setting up mtg
contrary to discipline; rst by YM 1866,11,
23
1858, 11, 26. Stephen & w, Rachel dis setting
up mtg contrary to discipline; rst by YM
1866,11,23

BATTIN

----, --, --. Robert & Abigail
Ch: Benjamin   b 1822, 9, 4
Hannah C.   " 1824, 5, 3
Josiah   " 1827, 9, 17 d 1833, 4,29
bur Sandy Spring Orthodox Graveyard
Thomas   b 1829, 5, 20
Ann   " 1832, 10, 2
Elizabeth   " 1834, 9, 28 d 1837,10, 6
Amos   " 1837, 1, 10 " 1837,10.17
David   " 1838, 8, 24 " 1846, 2,18
Rachel   " 1841, 1, 6 " 1846, 2,21
----, --, --. Benjamin m Hannah G. ----- b
1824,4,4
Ch: Lydia H.   b 1845, 4, 30
John   " 1848, 5, 4
Joseph   " 1850, 8, 29
1851, 10, 14. Josiah d bur West
1879, 1, 1. Winslow L., s Franklin & Jane,
Colombiana Co., O.; m in home of John
Mather, Elva MATHER, dt John & Edith,
Stark Co., O., d 1909,1,13
1886, 2, 11. C. Sumner, s Samuel R. & Lydia
Ann, Clark Co., O.; m in home of John
Mather, Mary A. MATHER, dt John & Edith,
Stark Co., O.

1850, 9, 27. David, Sarah Ann, Samuel R. &
Franklin, rocf Sandy Spring PM
1852, 2, 27. Thomas con mcd
1852, 6, 25. Benjamin C. & w, Hannah G., &
ch, Lydia & John, gct Deer Creek MM
1860, 10, 26. Thomas con mcd
1860, 12, 21. Robert & w, Abigail, gct Salem
MM
1860, 12, 21. Hannah C. gct Salem MM
1860, 12, 21. Ann gct Salem MM
1866, 4, 27. Samuel R. mcd several yrs ago,
con mcd
1866, 5, 25. Samuel R. gct Short Creek MM,
O., to m Emily Tomlinson
1866, 10, 26. Samuel R. gct Salem MM
1887, 5, 25. Mary A. gct Green Plain MM, O.

BATTIN, continued
1913, 11, 2. Winslow L. & Edith Dell (Mather)
    con mcd

BERGEN
1891, 4, 1. Edith R. d

1886, 2, 24. Edith H. con mcd
1886, 3, 24. Edith H. gct Central MM, Chicago,
    Ill.

BETTS
1848, 1, 21. Mary (form Shinn) con mcd

BISHOP
1861, 12, 27. William & w, Lydia, gct Prairie
    Grove MM, Ia.
1862, 11, 21. Sarah B. (Hawley) (form Bishop)
    con mcd

BLACKBURN
1857, 9, 17. Benjamin H., s James & Eleanor,
    Wells Co., Ind.; m in West MH, Mahoning
    Co., O., Mary F. HAYHURST, dt Wm. & Jane,
    Mahoning Co., O.

1885, 9, 23. Mary S. gct Wapsinonock MM, Ia.

BORTON
1863, 3, 27. Ezra con mcd
1863, 3, 27. Sarah B. (form Haycock) con mcd
1847, 12, 25. Ezra gc
1878, 4, 24. Sarah B. & dt, Alice A., gct
    Battle Creek MM, Mich.

BOWERS
1870, 6, 1. Wm. Irving, s Samuel L. & Mary,
    Hocking Co., O.; m in home of Barton Hea-
    cock, Melissa HEACOCK, dt Barton & Rachel,
    Mahoning Co., O., b 1841,1,24 d 1890,10,18

BRADSHAW
1848, 9, 22. Townsend con mcd
1850, 4, 26. William dis mcd

BRANIN
1845, 3, 9. Nathaniel d ae 19

1845, 12, 26. Mahlon [Brannin] dis mcd
1847, 6, 25. Rachel (Enke) (form Branin) dis
    mcd

BROGAN
1850, 9, 27. Rachel & Emma rocf Sandy Spring
    PM

BROSIUS
----, --, --. Harper b 1799,1,15; m Phebe -----
    b 1807,3,22
    Ch: Edward
        Hicks   b 1827, 10, 29
        Samuel
        Getchel   " 1829, 8, 30 d 1913, 3,25

Ch: Amos
    Preston   b 1831, 12, 21
    Joseph   " 1833, 2, 13
    William   " 1835, 8, 21
    Enos   " 1837, 2, 26 d 1915, 6,24
    Harper   " 1839, 2, 27
    Chalkley   " 1840, 11, 13
    Mary   " 1842, 11, 23
    Henry   " 1845, 11, 16
----, --, --. Amos d 1887,4,7 bur Alliance;
    m Esther ----- d 1899,2,11 bur Alliance
    Ch: Adaline   b 1840, 6, 11
        Martin   " 1842, 8, 3 d 1843, 4, 3
        Arthur   " 1844, 7, 15 " 1844, 7,27
        Hannah   " 1846, 5, 30
1881, 12, 1. Alice d

1846, 7, 24. Phebe rocf Salem MM, dtd 1846,6,
    24
1857, 9, 25. Charles & w, Mary, & ch, David
    L., William H., Amos Preston, Dalton, Ar-
    vine & Laura Jane, rocf Salem MM, dtd
    1857,8,20
1858, 11, 26. Phebe dis setting up mtg; rst
    by YM 1866,11,23
1858, 11, 26. Amos dis setting up mtg; rst
    by YM 1866,11,23
1860, 7, 27. Samuel con mcd
1860, 7, 27. Amos P. dis mcd

BUCK
----, --, --. John d 1876,5,21; m Marium
    ----- d 1881,9,6 ae 80
    Ch: Nathan   b 1824, 8, 1
        Jonathan   " 1826, 1, 11 d 1831, 2, 1
        Josiah   " 1827, 12, 24
        Rebecca   " 1830, 9, 3 " 1833, 4, 3
        John W.   " 1834, 9, 20
        Mary Anna " 1840, 3, 8

1857, 7, 24. John W. con mcd

BUCKMAN
1920, 6, 13. Selina E., dt Letitia Cobbs, d

1918, 4, 7. Selma E. recrq

COOK
----, --, --. Enos d 1908,11,28; m Ann -----
    d 1913,1,31
    Ch: Eliza M. b 1845, 3, 20
        Leander   " 1846, 11, 10 d 1847, 1,23
        Howard B. " 1856, 3, 17
1862, 5, 1. Hannah Kemp m Henry Fox PICKER-
    ING

1845, 10, 24. Elizabeth Cobb (form Cooks)
    dis mcd
1848, 3, 24. Fransina Ladd (form Cook) dis
    mcd

COBB
1850, 5, 30. Levi, s Waddy & Margaret, Ma-

COBB, continued
    honing Co., O.; m in West MH, Rachel ARMI-
    TAGE, dt Chas. & Jane, Mahoning Co., O.,
    d 1913,3,5 ae 90
1908, 11, 28. Letitia d ae 84

1845, 10, 24. Elizabeth (form Cooks) dis mcd
1845, 11, 21. Letitia (form Hartley) con mcd

COFFE
1891, 12, 24. Tacy H. d

1853, 11, 25. Tacy [Coffee] (form Haycock) dis
    mcd

COOPER
1849, 4, 27. Edward & w, Hannah, & ch, Ra-
    chel, Henry & James, rocf Richland MM,
    Pa., dtd 1849,2,2
1852, 8, 27. Mahlon & w, Mary, & ch, Ann,
    Ruth & Edward, rocf Wrightstown MM, Pa.,
    dtd 1852,5,5
1857, 2, 27. Edward & w, Hannah, & ch, Ra-
    chel, Henry, James & Phebe Ann, gct Wood-
    bury MM, N. J.
1860, 3, 23. Mahlon & w, Mary, & ch, Annie,
    Ruth & Edward, gct Wakefield MM, Pa.

COPE
1847, 2, 25. Mary Ann con mcd
1850, 5, 24. Mary Ann gct Salem MM

COURTNEY
----, --, --. Israel & Susan
    Ch: William H. b 1840, 3, 29
        Thomas M. " 1842, 1, 3
        Edward   " 1844, 2, 18
        Jane Ann   " 1846, 6, 25
----, --, --. Edward & Phebe
    Ch: Phebe C. b 1840, 10, 6
        Ruth B.   " 1844, 2, 22
        Jeduthan   d 1855, 9,6

1848, 9, 22. Sarah Kelly (form Courtney) con
    mcd
1849, 11, 23. Mary Mathews (form Courtney) con
    mcd
1852, 6, 25. Isaac dis mcd
1852, 8, 27. John con mcd
1852, 11, 26. Ann Hamilton (form Courtney)
    con mcd
1858, 2, 26. Emeline Pennock (form Courtney)
    dis mcd

DUTTON
1878, 12, 14. Philena d ae 38
1903, 9, 3. Jennet d ae 58

1863, 6, 26. Philena (form Hartley) con mcd
1863, 7, 24. Ezra rocf Short Creek MM, O.,
    dtd 1863,6,9

ENKE
1847, 6, 25. Rachel (form Branin) dis mcd

FOGG
1845, 9, 26. Josiah dis mcd
1848, 10, 27. Hannah Kelty (form Fogg) dis mcd

GARRETSON
----, --, --. Pierce d 1876,6,--; m Sarah ----
    d 1889,11,--
    Ch: Franklin b 1836, 7, 27
        Samantha M." 1837, 12, 15 d 1838, 4,21
        Barclay   " 1839, 5, 10
        Newton   " 1844, 4, 7
        Marsena
        Mary   " 1848, 3, 14
----, --, --. Eli d 1904,4,24; m Sarah J. ----
    Ch: John   b 1845, 2, 19 d 1845, 8, 5
        Rebecca
        Elma   " 1846, 10, 18 " 1873, 5, 2
        Lucretia
        Mot   " 1848, 2, 28 " 1896, 3,11
1852, 4, 1. Rebecca m John W. SATTERTHWAIT

1846, 9, 25. Anne P. rocf Salem MM, dtd
    1846,8,19
1846, 9, 25. John & w, Anne, rocf Salem MM,
    dtd 1846,8,19
1846, 9, 25. Rebecca rocf Salem MM, dtd
    1846,8,19
1849, 10, 26. Ann P. rmt Thomas E. Lamborn
1851, 5, 23. Eli dis setting up mtg contrary
    to discipline
1858, 11, 26. Pierce dis setting up mtg con-
    trary to discipline; rst by YM 1866,11,23
1862, 2, 21. Eli recrq
1863, 7, 24. Jazer rocf Short Creek MM, O.,
    dtd 1863,6,9
1864, 10, 21. Eli & w, Sarah J., & ch, Rebec-
    ca E. & Lucretia M., gct Salem MM
1865, 4, 21. Jazer gct Short Creek MM, O.
1868, 7, 24. Jazer gct Short Creek MM, O.

GARRISON
1841, 7, 15. William d

GASKEL
1850, 9, 27. Pamela (form Passmore) con mcd

GREGG
1871, 5, 26. Hannah B. & s, Kenworthy, rocf
    Plainfield MM, O., dtd 1870,5,19

GRICE
1859, 11, 25. Elizabeth d

HAMBLETON
1852, 11, 26. Ann [Hamilton] (form Courtney)
    con mcd
1854, 6, 23. Hannah rocf Carmel MM, dtd
    1853,12,17
1854, 9, 22. William rocf Carmel MM, dtd
    1854,5,20

HARLAN
1854, 8, 27. Samuel C., s Joseph & Hannah,
      Columbiana Co., O.; m in West MH, Phebe
      ARMITAGE, dt Chas. & Jane, Mahoning Co.,
      O., d 1857,3,20 ae 27
1859, 8, 2. Joseph d
----, --, --. J. Comly m Martha W. WAY
      Ch: Inez   b 1878, 9, 1
          Sara   " 1880, 11, 9
          J. Way   " 1889, 6, 3
1887, 8, 7. Mary Ann, w Joseph, d
1910, 6, 6. Joseph d
1915, 5, 2. Hannah d

1847, 1, 22. Samuel C. con mcd
1851, 3, 21. Joseph con mcd
1856, 8, 22. Joseph & w, Mary, & ch, Emily,
      Edith & Hannah, recrq
1857, 1, 23. Wilson, minor s Samuel C., recrq
1859, 4, 22. Samuel C. con mcd
1859, 11, 25. Samuel C. & ch, Wilson B. &
      Phebe A., gct Maple Grove MM, Ind.
1877, 9, 19. J. Comly gct Kennet MM, Pa., to
      m Martha Way
1878, 1, 23. Martha Way rocf Kennett MM, Pa.,
      dtd 1877,12,4
1897, 1, 20. Inez relrq
1902, 4, 23. J. Comly relrq
1856, 8, 22. Joseph & w, Mary Ann, & ch,
      Comly, Edith & Hannah, recrq

HARRIS
----, --, --. Samuel d 1892,1,14; m Esther
      ----- d 1895,6,1 bur Mt. Union
      Ch: Margaret
          Ellen   b 1840, 8, 13
          Rebecca
          Mary   " 1844, 4, 15
----, --, --. Silas & Ann
      Ch: Phebe Jane b 1844, 6, 15
          Mary Ann   " 1848, 2, 28

1849, 9, 21. Ellin Townsend (form Harris)
      dis mcd
1858, 11, 26. Samuel & w, Esther, dis setting
      up mtg contrary discipline; rst by YM 1866,
      11,23
1858, 11, 26. Ann dis setting up mtg contrary
      to discipline; rst by YM 1866,11,23
1858, 11, 26. Joel & w, Louisa, dis setting
      up mtg contrary discipline; rst by YM
      1866,11,23

HARTLEY
----, --, --. James [Heartley] d 1898,3,28 ae
      84; m Dinah ----- d 1891,3,28
      Ch: Sarah Ann b 1839, 1, 27
          Philena   " 1840, 9, 29 d 1878,12,14
          Mary Emily " 1842, 6, 25
          Jennet   " 1844, 12, 18 " 1903, 9, 3
          Amos   " 1847, 6, 19
          Rebecca   " 1849, 8, 13
----, --, --. Joseph d 1908,11,14 ae 87; m

Sarah M. ----- d 1891,12,28 ae 69
      Ch: Deborah V. b 1846, 6, 27
          Richard
            Griffith " 1847, 10, 8 d 1919, 4,24
          Marietta   " 1853, 6, 23
1861, 3, 7. Letitia d
1883, 10, 25. Richard G., s Joseph S. & Sarah
      M., Columbiana Co., O., b 1847,10,8 d
      1919,4,24; m in home of Alfred Wright,
      Ella V. WRIGHT, dt Alfred & Amelia, Stark
      Co., O.

1845, 11, 21. Letitia Cobb (form Hartley) con
      mcd
1846, 3, 27. Joseph S. [Heartley] con mcd
1846, 4, 24. Sarah recrq
1847, 3, 26. James & w, Dinah, & ch, Sarah
      Anne, Philena, Mary Emily & Jennet, rocf
      Newgarden MM, dtd 1847,1,21
1847, 3, 26. Mahlon, minor, rocf Newgarden
      MM, dtd 1847,1,21
1853, 3, 25. Mahlon con mcd
1858, 3, 26. Sarah Ann Lamborn (form Hartley)
      dis mcd
1860, 12, 21. Mahlon dis jas
1863, 6, 26. Philena Dutton (form Hartley)
      con mcd

HAWLEY
1862, 11, 21. Sarah B. (form Bishop) con mcd
1862, 12, 26. Sarah B. gct Prairie Grove MM,
      Ia.

HAYHURST
1847, 9, 3. Ellis, s Bezaleel & Hannah, b
1857, 9, 10. Elizabeth M. m Charles WILCOX
1857, 9, 17. Mary F. m Benjamin H. BLACKBURN

1847, 3, 26. Bazileel con mcd
1848, 8, 25. Hannah rocf Marlborough MM, O.,
      dtd 1848,7,22
1851, 5, 23. William dis setting up mtg con-
      taary to discipline
1851, 5, 23. Thomas dis setting up mtg con-
      trary to discipline
1852, 7, 23. Lydia B. gct Short Creek MM, O.
1861, 12, 27. Jane & dt, Sarah, gct Prairie
      Grove MM, Ia.

HEACOCK
----, --, --. Nathan d 1866,6,28 bur West;
      m Dinah ----- d 1854,1,31 ae 73
      Ch: Amos D.   b 1808, 10, 27 d 1841,11,18
                      bur West
          Edwin   " 1811, 4, 19 " 1894,12,27
          James D.   " 1812, 8, 12 " 1837, 1,29
          Asenath   " 1814, 6, 26
          Milton   " 1815, 12, 23
          Barton   " 1818, 1, 13 " 1899, 5,10
          Uriah A.   " 1819, 6, 14 " 1854, 5,21
          Elias H.   " 1821, 1, 6 " 1851, 1,15
          Enos   " 1822, 9, 5 " 1902, 3,21
          Josiah W. " 1824, 7,28 " 1852, 1,17

HEACOCK, Nathan & Dinah, continued
    Ch: Tacy   b 1827, 4, 22
----, --, --. Milton, s Nathan & Dinah, Colum-
    biana Co., O., b 1815,12,23; m Rebecca

    Ch: Sarah Jane b 1839, 11, 13
        Ann Eliza " 1841, 5, 23
        Ephraim   " 1842, 11, 30
    Milton m 2nd 1846,3,5 in West MH, Ann
    PASSMORE, dt George & Phebe, Columbiana
    Co., O.
    Ch: Joseph
        Lindley   b 1846, 12, 26
        Josiah
        Wilson   " 1848, 5, 8 d 1852, 1,17
----, --, --. Barton b 1818,1,13 d 1899,5,10;
    m Rachel ----- d 1899,4,18
    Ch: Melissa   b 1841, 1, 24 d 1890,10,18
        Clarkson   " 1842, 1, 18
        Oliver   " 1844, 5, 7 " 1882, 3, 4
        Rebecca
        Jane   " 1846, 5, 9 " 1876, 1, 7
        Sarah Ann " 1847, 12, 17 " 1879, 3, 4
        Isaac   " 1849, 12, 11 " 1918, 1,13
        Wm. Antrim " 1852, 7, 2 " 1900, 7,22
        Alice B.   " 1855, 4, 2 " 1861, 5,26
        Elvira   " 1856, 4, 25 " 1884, 8, 2
        Edith R.   " 1864, 9, 29 " 1891, 4, 1
----, --, --. Uriah Antrim, s Nathan & Dinah,
    b 1819,6,14 d 1854,5,12; m Sarah -----
    Ch: Barclay   b 1044, 8, 16
        Edwin   " 1849, 3, 28
        Charles D. " 1851, 3, 2
        Emma A.   " 1854, 11, 17
1852, 9, 30. Enos, s Nathan & Dinah, Mahoning
    Co., O., þ 1822,9,5 d 1902,3,21 bur at
    Homestead; m in West MH, Ann TAYLOR, dt
    Jacob & Anne, Chester Co., Pa., d 1890,11,
    2 (or 3)
    Ch: Taylor   b 1854, 11, 11 d 1864, 9, 1
        Addie
        Nathan
----, --, --. T. Chalkley & Rachel M.
    Ch: Alverda J. b 1871, 1, 14
        Preston
        Emerson   " 1873, 2, 5 d 1875, 4,19
        Rebecca
        Leona   " 1875, 3, 19
        Edgar   " 1877, 3, 14 " 1877, 3,18
        Oscar Edi-
        son   " 1878, 9, 4
1871, 9, 27. Barclay Barber, s Uriah A. &
    Sarah, Mahoning Co., O., b 1844,8,16; m
    in house of Marquis O. Sluyter, Deborah E.
    SLUYTER, dt Marquis O. & Sarah Ann, Stark
    Co., O., b 1853,3,19
1871, 9, 27. Melissa m William Irvin BOWERS
1873, 10, 30. Clarkson, s Barton & Rachel,
    Stark Co., O., b 1842,1,18 d 1899,5,10;
    m in house of Ezekiel Barber, Elizabeth A.
    BARBER, dt Ezekiel & Ann, Columbiana Co.,
    O.
    Ch: Wm. Chan-

    ning   b 1877, 8, 16
    Ch: Clyde L. " 1880, 3, 29
        Rachel Ann " 1883, 4, 6
        Arthur G. " 1885, 9, 8
        Corin   " 1888, 6, 14
1880, 3, 13. Hannah d bur West
----, --, --. Nathan & Nancy L.
    Ch: Elizabeth
        Ann   b 1895, 2, 25 d 1906,12,15
        Clara Hazel" 1896, 4, 13
        Enos George" 1898, 2, 26
        Bertha
        Olive   " 1901, 8, 21
1895, 12, 27. Edwin d bur West

1853, 11, 25. Tacy Coffee (form Haycock) dis
    mcd
1857, 5, 22. Rachel [Haycock] & ch, Melissa,
    Clarkson Oliver, Rebecca L., Sarah A.,
    Isaac William, Alice & Elvira, gct Alum
    Creek MM, O.
1857, 12, 25. Barton [Haycock] gct Alum Creek
    MM, O.
1859, 7, 22. Barton & w, Rachel, & ch,
    Clarkson, Oliver, Rebecca Jane, Sarah
    Ann, Isaac, William Antrim, Alice & El-
    vira, rocf Alum Creek MM, O., dtd 1859,6,
    23
1859, 7, 22. Melissa rocf Alum Creek MM, O.,
    dtd 1859,6,23
1863, 3, 27. Sarah B. Borton (form Haycock)
    con mcd
1863, 6, 26. Nathan & w, Hannah, gct Prairie
    Grove MM, Ia.
1867, 5, 24. George W., adopted s Enos & w,
    recrq
1867, 8, 23. Edwin & w, Hannah, & s, Edgar,
    recrq
1874, 5, 22. Chalkley & two ch recrq
1888, 10, 24. Barclay & ch gct Race St. MM,
    Phila., Pa.
1889, 4, 24. Charles gct Race St. MM, Phila.,
    Pa.
1895, 7, 24. William A. rst
1895, 7, 24. Lula M. & Emma, ch Wm. A., recrq
1895, 8, 21. William A. gct Chippaqua MM,
    N. Y., to m Lucretia M. Robinson
1895, 8, 21. Nancy L. recrq
1895, 10, 23. Wm. A. & ch, Lulu M. & Emma R.,
    gct Race St. MM, Phila., Pa.
1909, 5, 19. Nancy L. relrq
1909, 11, 24. Clara, minor dt N. E., relrq

HENDRIX
1849, 5, 25. Joel rocf Monallin MM, dtd
    1847,11,17

HILLIS
----, --, --. Enos d 1894,12,19 bur Mt.
    Union; m Mary Ann ----- d 1890,2,23 bur
    Mt. Union
    Ch: Arthur T. b 1842, 1, 12 d 1917, 4,15
        bur Mt. Union

HILLIS, Enos & Mary Ann, continued
    Ch: Jane Mary b 1844, 1, 21
       Howard   " 1845, 10, 14

1845, 7, 25. Robert [Hillas] & w, Jane, rocf
    Salem MM, dtd 1845,6,25
1845, 7, 25. William [Hillas] rocf Salem MM,
    dtd 1845,6,25
1848, 10, 27. Rachel [Hilles] (form Barnaby)
    dis mcd
1848, 12, 22. William [Hillas] dis mcd
1858, 11, 26. Enos & w, Mary Ann dis setting
    up mtg contrary to discipline; rst by YM
    1866,11,23
1858, 11, 26. Robert & w, Jane, dis setting up
    mtg contrary to discipline; rst by YM
    1866,11,23

HOAG
1874, 7, 24. Joel gct Marietta MM, Ia.

KEEN
1849, 1, 26. Martha (form Townsend) con mcd

KELTY
1848, 10, 27. Hannah (form Fogg) dis mcd

KELLY
1848, 9, 22. Sarah (form Courtney) con mcd

KIRK
1872, 2, 24. Elmer Kirk d bur Deer Creek
1872, 3, 27. Matilda d bur Deer Creek

1860, 4, 27. Elmer & w, Matilda, rocf Smith-
    field MM, O., dtd 1860,3,5

KIRKBRIDE
----, --, --. Robert & Sarah
    Ch: Asher   b 1844, 1, 8
       Mahlon   " 1846, 2, 1

1848, 1, 21. Nancy Morris (form Kirkbride)
    dis mcd
1849, 9, 21. Mary Morris (form Kirkbride) dis
    mcd

LADD
1848, 3, 24. Fransina (form Cook) dis mcd

LAMBORN
----, --, --. William m Phebe ----- d 1892,2,
    11
    Ch: Amos P.   b 1844, 7, 22
       Parmenas   " 1846, 2, 22
       Joseph A. " 1851, 6, 29
       Mary   " 1848, 5, 13 d 1848, 8,21
1857, 5, 17. Esther d ae 53
1857, 7, 12. John F. d
1859, 1, 20. Job, s David & Elizabeth, Mahon-
    ing Co., O.; m in home of Lydia Pennington,
    Lydia PENNINGTON, dt Benjamin & Ann LIN-
    VILLE

1860, 5, 8. Sarah A. d ae 21
----, --, --. Franklin m Alice CAMPP
    Ch: Anna Lee
       Dora   b 1883, 5, 2
       Gladys Emma" 1886, 12, 23
       Raymond
       Ellwood   " 1899, 11, 12
1883, 1, 7. Ann d bur West
1903, 1, 19. Elwood d bur West

1847, 5, 21. Lydia rocf Newgarden MM, dtd
    1847,5,20
1847, 5, 21. Anna rocf Newgarden MM, dtd
    1847,5,20
1848, 1, 21. Parmenas & w, Hannah, rocf
    Newgarden MM, dtd 1847,12,23
1849, 10, 26. Thomas E. rmt Ann P. Garretson
1853, 11, 25. William C. con mcd
1854, 7, 21. Sarah C. rocf Salem MM, dtd
    1854,5,20
1858, 3, 26. Sarah Ann (form Hartley) dis
    mcd
1859, 6, 24. Job gct Salem MM
1860, 12, 21. Mary Emily (form Bailey) dis
    mcd
1861, 1, 25. Edward dis mcd
1864, 10, 21. William W. & w, Phebe R., & ch,
    Amos P., Parmenas & Joseph Allen, gct
    Wapsinnonock MM, Ia.
1867, 1, 25. Lydia W. gct Salem MM
1867, 10, 25. Sarah C. dis
1867, 11, 22. W. C. relrq
1904, 12, 21. Sarah A. recrq
1847, 2, 25. Elizabeth Morris (form Lamborn)
    dis mcd
1847, 4, 23. Elizabeth Morriss (form Lamborn)
    dis mcd

LEWIS
1879, 5, 21. Maria gct Wapsinonoc MM, Ia.
1879, 5, 21. Maria B. gct Wapsinonox MM, Ia.

LINTON
1893, 11, 12. William d bur West

1853, 1, 21. William rocf Wakefield MM, Pa.,
    dtd 1852,4,8
1853, 6, 24. Joseph W. rocf Middleton MM,
    Pa., dtd 1852,4,8
1856, 4, 25. Joseph gct Middleton MM, Pa.
1853, 1, 21. William rocf Marlborough MM,
    Pa., dtd 1852,4,8

LONGSHORE
1881, 4, 20. Maria P. gct Race St. MM,
    Phila., Pa.

MATHER
----, --, --. Daniel & Rebecca
    Ch: Alice Ann b 1839, 9, 19
       Catharine " 1842, 1, 11
       Rachel   " 1844, 1, 22
       Hannah   " 1848, 6, 6

MATHER, Daniel & Rebecca, continued
    Ch: Isaac   b 1852, 5, 6
----, --, --. John d 1919,12,27 ae 95; m Edith
----- d 1912,5, --
    Ch: Alice Man-
        dana   b 1849, 2, 24
        Sophia   " 1851, 1, 3
        Mary Ann " 1852, 11, 28
        Isaac El-
        wood   " 1854, 8, 5 d 1908, 3,29
        Thomas Lo-
        renzo   " 1856, 2, 1 " 1859, 5, 2
        Elva   " 1858, 10, 3 " 1909, 1,13
        Willis El-
        mer   " 1862, 7, 4
        Daniel E. " 1866, 4, 21
        Edith Dell " 1870, 10, 13
1855, 3, 2. John d ae 71
1865, 11, 14. Catherine d
1879, 1, 1. Elva m Winslow L. BATTIN
1886, 2, 11. Mary A. m C. Sumner BATTIN

1849, ·1, 26. Edith (form Barber) con mcd
1849, 1, 26. John Jr. con mcd
1879, 1, 22. Hannah rmt Samuel Barber
1880, 5, 19. Hannah retained mbrp by rq
1894, 3, 21. Hannah gct Topeka, Kans.
1882, 7, 19. Sophia Packer (form Mather) con
    mcd
1913, 11, 2. Edith Dell Battin (form Mather)
    con mcd

MATHEWS
1849, 11, 23. Mary (form Courtney) dis mcd

MEREDITH
1845, 9, 26. Simon C. dis mcd
1850, 2, 22. William Jr. dis mcd

MICHENER
1858, 11, 26. Phebe dis setting up mtg contrary
    to discipline; rst by YM 1866,11,23
1858, 11, 26. James & w, Sarah, dis setting up
    mtg contrary to discipline; rst by YM
    1866,11,23
1847, 8, 27. Mary Queer (form Mitchaner) dis
    mcd

MIRES
1853, 11, 25. Rebecca Taylor (form Mires) con
    mcd

MORRIS
1892, 4, 11. Ellen Morris d bur Mt. Union

1847, 4, 23. Elizabeth [Morriss] (form Lam-
    born) dis mcd
1847, 2, 25. Elizabeth (form Lamborn) dis mcd
1848, 1, 21. Nancy (form Kirkbride) dis mcd
1849, 9, 21. Mary (form Kirkbride) dis mcd

NEASE
1884, 8, 2. Elvira H. d

PACKER
1882, 7, 19. Sophia (form Mather) con mcd

PASSMORE
1846, 3, 5. Hannah Ann m Milton HEACOCK
1858, 9, 6. Manrel, s Geo. & Phebe, d

1850, 9, 27. Pamela Gaskel (form Passmore)
    con mcd

PENNINGTON
1859, 1, 20. Lydia m Job LAMBORN

PENNOCK
1858, 2, 26. Emeline (form Courtney) dis mcd

PICKERING
1862, 5, 1. Henry Fox, s Elijah & Rebecca,
    Belmont Co., O.; m in West MH, Mahoning
    Co., O., Hannah Kemp COOK, dt Caleb &
    Hannah, Columbiana Co., O.

1862, 10, 24. Hannah K. gct Plainfield MM
1862, 10, 24. Hannah Hartley gct Plainfield MM

PIERCE
1846, 9, 25. Maria G. rocf Salem MM, dtd
    1846,8,19
1869, 4, 25. Sidney Maria rocf Darby MM,
    Pa., dtd 1869,3,23

QUEER
1847, 8, 27. Mary (form Mitchaner) dis mcd

RAKESTRAW
----, --, --. Thomas & Susan
    Ch: Phebe   b 1844, 4, 12
        Henrietta " 1846, 12, 24

1858, 11, 26. Thomas dis setting up mtg con-
    trary to discipline; rst by YM 1866,11,23

REEDER
1859, 11, 26. Maria m Thomas THORP

1850, 9, 27. Alice rocf Sandy Spring PM
1850, 9, 27. William, Lydia, Maria, Joanna,
    David, Lydia Jr. & Rebecca, rocf Sandy
    Spring PM
1852, 11, 26. Alice gct Horsham MM, Pa.
1860, 4, 27. Joanna & Lydia B. [Reader] gct
    Salem MM

REEVES
1851, 8, 22. Abraham con mcd
1858, 11, 26. D. B. & w, Ann, dis setting up
    mtg contrary to discipline; rst by YM
    1866,11,23
1851, 8, 22. Grace Anna (form Taylor) con
    mcd

RICH
1856, 8, 22. William W. & w, Ellen D., rocf

RICH, continued
       Fishing Creek MM, Pa., dtd 1856,5,21
1867, 1, 25. Della Jane, minor, gct Fishing
       Creek MM, Pa.

ROBINSON
1895, 8, 21. William A. Heacock gct Chippaqua
       MM, N. Y., to m Lucretia M. Robinson

SATTERTHWAITE
1852, 4, 1. John W., s Richard & Rebecca,
       Columbiana Co., O.; m in West MH, Mahoning
       Co., O., Rebecca GARRETSON, dt John & Ann,
       Mahoning Co., O.

1852, 10, 22. John W. & s, George, rocf Salem
       MM, dtd 1852,7,22
1865, 7, 21. John W. & w, Rebecca G., gct
       Salem MM

SHAW
1845, 9, 7. Hannah d ae 64
1845, 12, 17. James d ae 74
1856, 11, 22. Jonathan T., s Joseph & Eliza-
       beth, Columbiana Co., O.; m in West MH,
       Mahoning Co., O., Jemima TOWNSEND, dt Adam
       & Mary KITCHEN, Bradford Co., Pa.

1857, 2, 27. Jemima gct Salem MM

SHINN
1847, 2, 26. Elijah con mcd
1848, 1, 21. Mary Betts (form Shinn) con mcd
1848, 12, 22. John C. dis mcd
1856, 4, 25. Abraham gct Salem MM
1856, 4, 25. John & Sabilla gct Salem MM

SLUYTER
----, --, --. Marcus (Marquis) m Sarah Ann
       ----- d 1892,10,15 bur Deer Creek
       Ch: Henrietta
           B.   b 1849, 12, 2 d 1850, 7,16
           Sarah Maria" 1851, 7, 29 " 1851,10,25
           Deborah
             Ellen   " 1853, 3, 19
           Sylvester C." 1856, 1, 11
           Anna Mary " 1858, 12, 12 " 1922, --,--
           Margaret
1871, 9, 27. Deborah E. m Barclay Barber
       HEACOCK

1863, 12, 25. William K. recrq
1896, 4, 22. Marcus O. & w, Rebecca (form.
       Taylor) con mcd

STARR
1865, 2, 22. Nehemiah Robert Hillas William
       Henry Elizabeth & Edwin Albert, minor ch
       James, rocf Exeter MM, Pa., dtd 1855,10,31
1856, 2, 22. Mary L. rocf Exeter MM, Pa.,
       dtd 1855,10,31
1856, 2, 22. Jane rocf Exeter MM, Pa., dtd
       1855,10,31

TAYLOR
----, --, --. Howard & Alice M.
       Ch: Edith S. b 1880, 8, 9 d 1917, 7,22
           Mary   " 1884, 5, 22

1850, 6, 21. Grace Anna rocf Fallowfield MM,
       Pa., dtd 1850,4,13, end by Salem MM, 1850,
       5,22
1850, 8, 23. Grace rocf Fallowfield MM, Pa.,
       dtd 1850,4,13
1851, 8, 22. Grace Anna Reeves (form Taylor)
       con mcd
1852, 8, 27. Ann rocf Fallowfield MM, Pa.,
       dtd 1852,8,7
1853, 11, 25. Rebecca (form Mires) con mcd
1865, 8, 25. Joseph recrq
1865, 10, 22. Joseph gct Salem MM, to m Fanny
       Tripp
1866, 1, 26. Joseph gct Salem MM
1896, 4, 22. Rebecca Sluyter (form Taylor)
       con mcd
1909, 5, 19. Mary relrq

THOMAS
----, --, --. Nathan & Asenath
       Ch: Angeline G.b 1843, 9, 15
           Mary S.   " 1845, 5, 8
           Chalkley   " 1847, 5, 28
           Tacy Jane " 1850, 12, 31
           Kersey   " 1856, 2, 18
----, --, --. Newton m Ann ----- d 1858,6,15
       Ch: Charles B. b 1848, 10, 17 d 1918, 3,15
             bur Alliance
           Joseph H. b 1852, 2, 3 " 1853, 7, 6
           Melissa
           Alice   " 1854, 8, 2
           Leonard   " 1857, 10, 24
       Newton m 2nd Mary -----
       Ch: Lewis
           Arvine
1845, 10, 24. Newton gct Marlborough MM
1858, 11, 26. Margaret dis setting up mtg con-
       trary to discipline; rst by YM 1866,11,23
1863, 6, 26. Angeline G. & Mary S. gct
       Prairie Grove MM, Ia.
1863, 6, 26. Nathan & w, Ascenath, & ch,
       Chalkley, Tacy Jane & Kersey, gct Prairie
       Grove MM, Ia.
1868, 12, 25. Owen gct White Water MM, Ind.
       (he was a mbr of New Garden MM which has
       gone down)
1871, 12, 22. Mary & s, Lewis, recrq
1872, 2, 23. Mary & s, Newton, recrq
1897, 1, 20. Newton & Mary gct Salem MM

THORP
1859, 11, 26. Thomas, s Thomas & Mary, Mor-
       gan Co., O.; m in West MH, Mahoning Co.,
       O., Maria REEDER, dt Wm. & Lydia, Colum-
       biana Co., O.

1860, 4, 27. Maria R. gct Salem MM

TOMBAUGH
1879, 5, 1. William, s Solomon & Ruth, Mahoning Co., O.; m in home of Enos HEACOCK, Addie J. HEACOCK, dt Enos & Ann, Mahoning Co., O.

TOMLINSON
1866, 5, 25. Samuel R. Battin gct Short Creek MM, O., to m Emily Tomlinson

TOWNSEND
1846, 4, 30. Rebecca d ae 80
1844, 8, 24. Jonathan d ae 48
1856, 11, 22. Jemima m Jonathan T. SHAW

1849, 1, 26. Martha Keen (form Townsend) con mcd
1849, 9, 21. Ellin (form Harris) dis mcd
1849, 11, 23. Moses dis mcd
1864, 3, 25. Hannah gct Salem MM

TRAGO
----, --, --. John b 1814,5,14 d 1859,6,26; m Sarah Ann HARLAN, dt Joseph & Hannah, b 1818,3,3
    Ch: Hannah A. b 1843, 5, 2
        Sarah E.   " 1846, 7, 27

1863, 2, 22. Sarah Ann & dt, Sarah, gct Salem MM
1863, 2, 22. Hannah A. gct Salem MM

TRIPP
1865, 10, 22. Joseph Taylor gct Salem MM, to m Fanny Tripp

VANSYOC
1864, 10, 21. Ruth & ch, Oliver, Lydia & Aaron Emlen, gct Prairie Grove MM, Ia.
1866, 4, 27. Harrison gct Prairie Grove MM, Ia.

WALTON
1858, 5, 21. Benjamin & w, Ellen T., rocf Fallowfield MM, Pa., dtd 1858,4,10
1864, 10, 21. Benjamin gct Fallowfield MM, Pa.

*   *   *   *   *   *   *

BORTON
1874, 12, 21. Ezra gc to MM in O.

HEACOCK
1870, 6, 1. Melissa m Wm. Irvin BOWERS
1879, 5, 1. Addis J. m Wm. TOMBOUGH

WAY
1877, 9, 19. J. Comly Harlan gct Kennet MM, Pa., to m Martha Way

WHINERY
1849, 5, 25. Zimri rmt Mary B. Williams

WILCOX
1857, 9, 10. Charles, s Clement & Catharine, Stark Co., O.; m in West MH, Mahoning Co., O., Elizabeth M. Hayhurst, dt Wm. & Jane, Mahoning Co., O.

WILEMAN
1861, 11, 5. Amy d

WILEY
1863, 2, 27. Esther gct Maple Grove MM, Ind.
1862, 4, 25. Esther Wren (form Wiley) rpd mcd

WILLIAMS
----, --, --. John G. d 1844,8,20 ae 44; m Mary -----
    Ch: Ann
        Elizabeth b 1836, 9, 6
        Margaretta " 1838, 9, 28
        Lucretia M." 1841, 7, 15
        Garrison " 1841, 7, 15 d 1841, 7,15

1849, 5, 25. Mary B. rmt Zimri Whinery

WOOD
                    Armitage
1880, 12, 22. Henry D./gct Fallowfield MM, Pa., to m Eliza Jane Wood

WRENN
1860, 7, 27. Eliza, Lemuel & Lindley, minor ch William, gct Maple Grove MM, Ind.
1860, 7, 27. Levi gct Maple Grove MM, Ind.
1862, 3, 21. Sarah gct Prairie Grove MM, Ia.
1862, 4, 25. Esther [Wren] (form Wiley) rpd mcd

WRIGHT
1883, 10, 25. Ella V. m Richard G. HARTLEY

*   *   *   *   *   *   *

HANCE
1860, 10, 26. Sarah D. gct Farmington MM

POUND
1860, 10, 26. Mary H. gct Farmington MM

REEVES
1845, 1, 21. Mary Anna, dt Daniel & Ann, b

TAYLOR
1852, 9, 30. Ann m Enos HEACOCK

EAST GOSHEN MONTHLY MEETING

    East Goshen Monthly Meeting was established by Damascus Quarterly Meeting in 1870. This meeting, located in Mahoning County at Goshen, met on the third seventh-day of each month.

RECORDS

ABBOTT
1894, 2, 17. Elizabeth K. relrq

AKIN
1875, 8, 17. Esther relrq

ALLEN
1924, 7, 16. A. Ward gct Salem MM

ARMSTRONG
1882, 3, 18. R. Lewis recrq
1906, 7, 21. Judith A. & ch, M. Russell &
     Olin J., gct Damascus MM

ATKINSON
1893, 1, 21. Sarah gct Damascus MM

BAILEY
1919, 2, 15. Chas. F. & w, Ethel S., & ch,
     Walter, Lois & Paul Chester, rocf Damascus
     MM
1921, 10, 12. Chas. & w, Ethel, & ch, Walter,
     Lois & Paul, gct Adrian MM, Mich.

BAIRD
1907, 1, 19. Frank recrq
1910, 11, 19. Ida recrq
1912, 1, 2. Frank dropped from mbrp for jas
1924, 9, 17. Mrs. Frank recrq
1930, 4, 17. Ida dropped from mbrp
1930, 4, 17. Lorena Mae recrq

BALDWIN
1891, 12, 19. Catharine recrq
1900, 9, 15. Alvin C. & w, Martha W., & ch,
     Everett G. & Mary M., rocf Muncy MM, Ind.
1901, 7, 20. Alvin C. & fam set off to Alli-
     ance MM

BARBER
1903, 1, 17. Albert B. recrq
1919, 6, 21. Lottie recrq
1923, 5, 16. Albert B. relrq

BARTHELOW
1891, 1, 17. John W. & w, Eva, recrq
1895, 6, 10. John [Barthlow] & w, Eva, relrq

BARTHOLEMEW
1929, 6, 12. Grace dropped from mbrp

BASSETT
1891, 12, 19. Joseph B. recrq

BATES
1889, 11, 16. Ira B. recrq
1891, 2, 21. Francis Rosalie recrq
1891, 2, 21. Nellie & Ora May recrq
1900, 10, 20. Annie dropped from mbrp

BEACH
1920, 1, 14. Inez recrq

BECK
1871, 4, 15. Milicent & ch, Jonas M., Ellen
     R., Anna Mary, Isaac E. & John W., rocf
     Alliance MM, dtd 1871,3,28
1877, 10, 20. Jonas M. gct Damascus MM, to m
     Abigail Hall
1878, 4, 20. Jonas M. gct Alliance MM
1880, 6, 19. Jonas M. & w, Abigail H., & s,
     Chas. H., rocf Alliance MM
1889, 2, 16. Isaac Edwin gct Upland MM, Ind.
1893, 9, 16. Ellen R. gct Kokomo MM, Ind.
1895, 5, 18. J. W. relrq
1897, 7, 17. Milicent gct Knightstown MM, Ind.
1898, 12, 17. Rosa, dt Marion, gct Hartland
     MM, N. Y.
1904, 10, 15. J. Marion & Hallie A. recrq
1904, 10, 15. Wesley F., Dwight M., Ada Mae
     & Earl W., ch Marion & Hallie, rocf Havi-
     land MM, N. Y.
1905, 12, 16. J. M. & Hallie A. & ch, Dwight
     M., Ada Mae, Earl W. & Agnes Rhoda, relrq
1906, 10, 20. Rosella rocf Damascus MM
1913, 6, 21. Rosetta relrq

BECKWITH
1928, 10, 17. Aletha Bradway relrq

BEDELL
1900, 1, 20. Rosella recrq
1905, 1, 21. Rosella relrq

BERGER
1908, 3, 21. Dessa recrq
1930, 4, 17. Dessie dropped from mbrp

BLACKBURN
1877, 9, 15. Elizabeth B. rocf New Garden
     MM, dtd 1877,8,22
1882, 3, 18. Elizabeth gct New Garden MM

BLOUNT
1890, 7, 19. George H. & w, Esther F., & ch,
     Charles Garfield, Bessie Melvina & Wm. J.,
     gct Earlham MM, Calif.

BONNER
1893, 1, 21. Sarah recrq
1906, 12, 15. Sadie recrq

BOOTH
1906, 12, 15. George C. recrq
1929, 6, 12. George dropped from mbrp

BOWMAN
1918, 3, 16. Lavada recrq

BRADSHAW
1900, 7, 21. Albert E. & Daisey recrq
1901, 7, 20. Albert E. & Daisy set off with
     Alliance MM

BRADSHAW, continued
1918, 3, 16. Theda recrq

BRADT
1931, 5, 14. ----- & fam relrq

BRADWAY
1906, 2, 17. Carl recrq
1929, 6, 12. Carl dropped from mbrp

BRANTINGHAM
1900, 9, 15. James & w, A. Elizabeth, & s,
     Arthur, rocf Damascus MM
1909, 1, 16. Ella C. rocf Winona MM
1909, 12, 19. James & w, Ella, & s, Arthur,
     gct Alliance MM

BRENNER
1898, 2, 19. Catharine E. recrq
1918, 5, 18. Catharine relrq

BROOM
1891, 12, 19. George J. recrq

BROSIUS
1876, 8, 19. Samuel G. dis disunity
1890, 1, 18. Marium gct Damascus MM
1892, 12, 17. Enos H. dis disunity
1894, 2, 17. W. O. relrq
1894, 2, 17. Colvin M. relrq
1894, 2, 17. Edgar E. relrq
1894, 2, 17. Emily relrq
1894, 2, 17. Jane W. relrq

BRUEY
1907, 1, 19. Alice recrq
1907, 1, 19. Alfred recrq
1911, 1, 12. August recrq
1920, 5, 12. Alfred & w, Mary Ann, relrq
1930, 4, 17. Helen Mae recrq
1930, 4, 17. Gladys Victoria recrq

BUCK
1906, 11, 17. May recrq
1908, 3, 21. Harry recrq

BUCKHOLDT
1933, 6, 21. Robert relrq

BURKEY
1897, 3, 20. Emanuel J. & Margaret recrq
1900, 10, 20. Emanuel & Margaret & ch dropped
     from mbrp
1907, 4, 20. Aaron & Jane recrq
1929, 6, 12. Emanuel & w, Margaret, & ch,
     Harry J. & Wm. H. dropped from mbrp

BURT
1926, 4, 14. Pearl recrq

BURTON
1929, 6, 12. Mary dropped from mbrp

BUTLER
1929, 3, 12. Ray dropped from mbrp
1929, 6, 12. Leuba & Verda dropped from mbrp

CARRIER
1907, 5, --. Janet recrq
1908, 3, 21. Florence & Myrtle recrq
1910, 3, 19. Jacob recrq
1930, 4, 17. Florence, Myrtle & Bertha
     dropped from mbrp

CASSADAY
1900, 10, 20. Hannah E. rocf Butternuts MM,
     N. Y.
1901, 7, 20. Hannah E., minister, set off
     to Alliance MM

CATTELL
1881, 8, 20. Erce Etta rocf Damascus MM, dtd
     1881,7,23
1882, 4, 15. Joseph & Eleanor gct New Garden
     MM
1890, 4, 19. Sarah J. & ch, Ida May, Howard
     B., Frank C., Sarah Lela & Homer E., rec-
     rq
1891, 4, 18. Thos. S. [Cattrell] & w, Eliza-
     beth, gct Damascus MM
1891, 4, 18. Isaac [Cattrell] & w, Rebecca
     C., gct Damascus MM
1895, 7, 20. Lewis & w, Ann, & ch, Anna May
     & Herman Clifford, rocf Douglas MM, Neb.
1899, 1, 21. Charles B. rocf Douglas MM, Neb.
1899, 1, 21. Euphemia & ch, Janet G., Flor-
     ence Amy & Katie May, rocf Douglas MM,
     Neb.
1901, 7, 20. Albert R. & w, Urie Etta, & ch,
     Ezra & Mays, rocf Lane MM, Mich.
1901, 7, 20. Charles B. set off with Alliance
     MM
1903, 6, 20. Howard gct Beloit MM
1905, 12, 16. Herman gct Alliance MM
1914, 8, 15. Homer gct Beloit MM, Mich.
1916, 5, 20. Euphemia (Cattell) Evans relrq
1924, 4, 16. Chas. & w, Leota, & ch, Lois,
     rocf Alliance MM
1929, 6, 12. Ezra dropped from mbrp

CLARK
1889, 2, 16. Lillian H. gct Winona MM, O.
1895, 7, 20. Clara H. gct Salem MM, O.

CLEMSON
1910, 12, 17. James & Mary J. gct Beloit MM,
     Mich.

CLOSE
1933, 9, 20. Thelma dropped from mbrp

COBBS
1874, 12, 19. Elizabeth P. gct Damascus MM
1882, 5, 20. Wm. H. [Cobb] gct Damascus MM
1890, 6, 21. Wm. H. [Cobb] rocf Damascus MM,
     dtd 1890,5,24

COBBS, continued
1890, 7, 19. Rosa J. [Cobb] & ch, Myrtle M.,
     Leslie R. & Bertha L., recrq
1892, 7, 16. May recrq
1895, 2, 16. Elihu & Mary Ann [Cobb] gct Sa-
     lem MM, O.
1898, 5, 24. Wm. Y. & w, Rosa J., & ch,
     Myrtle M., Leslie R. & Bertha S., gct Sa-
     lem MM, O.
1912, 1, 2. Joel relrq

COCHRAN
1907, 5, --. Susie recrq
1930, 4, 17. Susie dropped from mbrp
1930, 5, 14. Mary Elizabeth recrq

COPE
1900, 11, 17. F. Wood & w, Elizabeth, & s, Cor-
     nelius, rocf Smithfield MM
1901, 7, 20. F. Wood & w, Elizabeth, & s,
     Cornelius, set off with Alliance MM

COPPOCK
1906, 9, 15. Cora Wise gct Indianapolis MM,
     Ind.

COURTNEY
1891, 4, 18. Laura gct Damascus MM
1899, 2, 18. Alpha Nettie & ch, Pilema Pearl
     & Orlar James, recrq
1910, 3, 19. Fred & Ella recrq
1910, 5, 21. J. M. gct Salem MM
1910, 5, 21. Wm. & w, Nettie, gct Salem MM
1918, 10, 19. Ella recrq
1933, 6, 21. Etta relrq

COUSE
1881, 2, 19. Lois R. recrq
1890, 9, 20. Louisa Tibbals (form Couse) rel-
     rq

DAILEY
1931, 5, 14. Eva recrq

DARYMAN
19-8, 3, 21. Charles & Lydia recrq
1933, 9, 20. Charles & Lydia dropped from
     mbrp

DENNIS
1900, 9, 15. Lizzie rocf Lane (later Lupton
     MM) Mich.
1901, 7, 20. Lizzie set off with Alliance MM

DERR
1910, 9, 17. Leroy & Mary E. recrq
1929, 6, 12. Leroy & Mary dropped from mbrp

DETCHEAN
1909, 4, 17. Arthur & w, Louisa, recrq

DIVER
1931, 9, 16. Helen recrq

DOW
1933, 6, 21. Josephine relrq

DUNN
1889, 8, 17. Ada relrq
1898, 5, 24. Robert & Mary Ann dropped from
     mbrp
1900, 1, 20. Robert & Mary Ann recrq

EARLY
1901, 12, 21. Lizzie S. gct Alliance MM

EARNEST
1914, 11, 21. Ada recrq
1933, 9, 20. Ada & Pearl dropped from mbrp

EDINGER
1930, 6, 18. Park B. & Margaret recrq

ELLYSON
1899, 11, 18. Sarah A. gct Damascus MM
1929, 6, 12. Mary dropped from mbrp

EMBURY
1893, 3, 18. Herbert H. recrq

EMES
1891, 2, 21. Luther & w, Eliza J., recrq
1891, 2, 21. Lillian M. recrq

ENGLE
1871, 1, 21. Rachel A. Stanley (form Engle)
     con mcd
1874, 3, 21. Chas. D. & ch, Josiah L. &
     Emmor G., recrq
1898, 5, 24. Josiah relrq
1903, 6, 20. Emmer G. dropped from mbrp
1929, 6, 12. Emmor dropped from mbrp
1930, 11, 12. Leanore relrq

EVANS
1916, 5, 20. Euphemia Cattell relrq

FOTCH
1900, 9, 15. John E. & Louisa rocf Damascus
     MM
1911, 6, 17. John gct Beloit MM, Mich.

FREDERICK
1900, 2, 17. Amos & Nellie recrq
1910, 1, 15. Nellie [Fredrick] recrq
1931, 9, 16. Russell & Pearl dropped from
     mbrp

FREET
1902, 4, 19. Harry recrq
1913, 2, 15. Harry relrq

FRENCH
1871, 2, 18. Esther C. rocf Alliance MM,
     dtd 1871,1,31
1871, 8, 19. Mary dis jas
1881, 9, 17. Lewis G. & w, Ella, recrq

FRENCH, continued
1892, 2, 20. Enoch J., Albert N. & Caroline
    M., ch Thomas E., relrq

GANTZ
1929, 4, 17. Ella relrq

GARDNER
1930, 4, 17. Clarence Leon & Lizzie Mae & ch,
    Wanda Eileen, Walter Gerald & Merril
    Clair, recrq
1933, 6, 21. C. L. & Lizzie & ch, Merrill,
    Gerald & Wanda, relrq

GIBBONS
1917, 2, 17. Ethel M. relrq

GIBSON
1890, 8, 16. Albion M. gct Oak Run MM, Ia.
1891, 5, 16. Albion M. rocf Oak Run MM, Iowa,
    dtd 1891,4,11
1902, 3, 15. Albion M. gct Londonderry MM, O.
1904, 10, 15. J. W. relrq

GODWARD
1881, 3, 19. Martha Ann recrq
1900, 10, 20. Martha dropped from mbrp

GONGWER
1894, 4, 21. Alice relrq

GRIFFITH
1906, 10, 20. John & Mary recrq
1906, 11, 17. Maud & Verna recrq
1907, 5, --. Edna recrq
1910, 11, 19. Sophie recrq

HABERLAND
1905, 1, 21. Fred recrq

HAFFNER
1905, 2,18. Charles recrq

HAINES
1873, 12, 20. Rebecca gct Alliance MM, O.
1908, 3, 21. Mary A. recrq

HALDERMAN
1900, 1, 20. Oscar J. relrq
1906, 7, 21. Joseph & Esther [Holderman] gct
    Damascus MM, O.
1907, 9, 21. Alonzo recrq
1907, 9, 21. Delbert recrq
1907, 9, 21. Howard W. recrq
1909, 3, 20. Anna J. gct Damascus MM

HALDI
1900, 11, 17. Robert & Malissa recrq
1917, 10, 20. Robert relrq

HALL
1877, 10, 20. Jonas M. Beck gct Damascus MM,
    to m Abigail Hall

1889, 2, 16. Sarah Elma & dt, Estella May,
    rocf Damascus MM, dtd 1889,1,26
1889, 3, 16. Emmor W. & w, Sarah H., relrq
1891, 1, 17. Emmor W. & fam gct Newburgh MM,
    Oregon
1891, 7, 18. Mary E. recrq
1896, 12, 19. George B. relrq
1912, 8, 17. Christian & Laura recrq
1929, 10, 16. Laura dropped from mbrp

HAMMOND
1891, 2, 21. Wm. recrq
1891, 12, 19. David & Matilda recrq

HAUGHT
1925, 4, 15. Hazel relrq

HELD
1922, 6, 14. Stanton & Isabelle B. recrq
1933, 6, 21. S. W. relrq

HELSEL
1907, 4, 20. Peter & Mary recrq
1907, 4, 20. Jesse recrq

HILLTS
1891, 2, 21. John recrq
1891, 2, 21. James W. recrq
1891, 12, 19. Hannah Matilda [Hilts] recrq

HIVERLY
1920, 1, 14. Katie Miles relrq

HOLDEMAN
1893, 7, 15. Edwin G. dropped from mbrp

HOLE
1893, 2, 18. Leander & w, Ida M., & s, Er-
    win Jay Hole, rocf Sandy Spring MM, dtd
    1893,1,24

HOPKINS
1911, 8, 19. Lydia A. recrq (form mbr Morris
    MM, N. Y. now laid down)

HUFFORD
1900, 2, 17. Wilbur recrq

HUTCHINSON
1927, 10, 12. Billie rocf Urbana MM

IRVIN
1901, 12, 21. Mary V. recrq
1910, 12, 17. May V. gct Beloit MM
1912, 2, 17. Lillie recrq
1912, 2, 17. Reuben A. & Ella M. recrq
1929, 10, 16. R. A. & fam dropped from mbrp

JACKSON
1924, 4, 16. Anna & Anna Belle recrq
1924, 4, 16. Bertha recrq
1929, 10, 16. Bertha dropped from mbrp
1933, 6, 21. Anna Bell relrq

JACKSON, continued
1933, 6, 21. Anna (Jackson) Weingart relrq

JACOBS
1927, 10, 12. Omar & Nelva rocf Urband MM

JAMES
1882, 1, 21. John & w, Anna Lena, & dt, Anna
    Lizetta, recrq
1902, 1, 18. Anna Lena & ch, Mary L., Bertha
    G., Martha Ruth, Wm. T., Josiah Carr &
    Harriet Catharine, gct Alliance MM
1913, 3, 15. Mary recrq
1914, 8, 15. Samuel recrq
1925, 3, 18. Catharine recrq
1931, 5, 14. Gladys recrq

JEFFERSON
1889, 7, 20. Charles A. recrq

JENKINS
1900, 9, 15. John K. & w, Margaret S., & ch,
    S. Mildred, A. Margaret & Lloyd M., rocf
    Damascus MM
1901, 7, 20. John H. & fam set off with Alli-
    ance MM
1902, 11, 15. Willis H. recrq
1910, 11, 19. Pearl & Lottie recrq
1913, 9, 20. Ella gct Damascus MM
1914, 3, 21. Cora E. relrq
1920, 10, 13. Elsie recrq
1924, 9, 12. Ada & Elizabeth recrq
1930, 4, 17. Arthur & Wm. dropped from mbrp
1930, 4, 17. Ethel recrq
1933, 9, 20. Elsie dropped from mbrp

JOHNSON
1877, 12, 15. Joseph G. & w, Sarah P., & dt,
    Rebecca, gct Oscaloosa MM, Iowa
1880, 12, 18. Theresa & ch, Olin M. & Nora
    Rebecca, recrq
1882, 3, 18. Alzada gct Damascus MM
1892, 1, 16. Chas. F. & w, Tharessa G., & ch,
    Olin M. & Rebecca, relrq

JONES
1930, 4, 17. Sarah Jane recrq

KEAN
1910, 3, 19. David recrq

KIME
1913, 3, 15. Ray, Sarah & Bertha recrq

KING
1915, 5, 15. Leroy recrq
1929, 3, 12. Leroy dropped from mbrp

KINSEY
1873, 7, 19. Sarah B. rocf Short Creek MM,
    O., dtd 1873,5,22
1873, 7, 19. George B. rocf Short Creek MM,
    O., dtd 1873,5,22

1900, 10, 20. Wm. G. & Margaret L. rocf Short
    Creek MM, O.
1900, 10, 20. Edwards F., Anna R., Samuel A.
    & Mary E. rocf Short Creek MM, O.
1901, 7, 20. Wm. E. & w, Mercy L., & ch, Ed-
    ward F., Anne R., Samuel A. & Mary E.
    set off to Alliance MM
1913, 12, 20. Leo B. gct Damascus MM

KIRBY
1892, 2, 20. Edith relrq

KIRKBRIDE
1912, 2, 17. Mahlon & w gct Damascus MM

LADD
1909, 6, 19. Sibyl E. gct Damascus MM

LaFOUNTAIN
1892, 3, 19. Wallas recrq

LANGSTAFF
1872, 3, 16. Evan & w, Mary D., & ch, Edgar,
    Sarah Elma, Mira H., Elmore & Lewis T.,
    gct Allience MM
1875, 4, 17. Evan & ch, Elmor & Lewis T.,
    rocf Alliance MM, O., dtd 1875,1,26
1875, 4, 17. Edgar, Sarah, Elma & Mira H.,
    rocf Alliance MM, O., dtd 1875,1,26
1875, 11, 22. Even gc
1876, 3, 18. Sarah Elma & Mira H. gct Cotton-
    wood MM, Kans.
1876, 3, 18. Evan & s, Elmor & Lewis T. gct
    Cottonwood MM, Kans.
1876, 3, 18. Edgar gct Cottonwood MM, Kans.

LANTHROP
1893, 2, 18. Joseph recrq

LEAPER
1881, 3, 19. William, Ida & Emma recrq

LEE
1903, 3, 21. I. Gurney rocf Clear Creek MM, O.
1903, 10, 17. Ida Johnson rocf Mt. Pleasant
    MM
1930, 5, 14. Abbie relrq
1931, 2, 18. Bricely O. & Anna Jenette recrq

LEGGETT
1908, 7, 18. Wm. W. & w, Lizzie M., & dt,
    Ruth M., rocf Alliance MM
1909, 11, 20. W. H. & w, Lizzie, & dt, Ruth
    M., gct Beloit MM

LaGRANE
1931, 5, 14. Fred W. [LeGraen] recrq
1933, 9, 20. Fred dropped from mbrp

LINDLEY
1910, 10, 15. Paul B. & w, Mary B., & dt,
    Mary Esther, rocf Raisen MM, Mich.
1913, 10, 18. Paul B. & fam gct Hughesville

LINDLEY, continued
    MM, Pa.

LOCKHART
1930, 6, 18. Ralph & Verna & ch, Frederick &
    Phyllis, recrq

LOWE
1929, 6, 12. Harriet dropped from mbrp

LOY
1933, 5, 17. Mildred Mottishaw relrq

LUPTON
1900, 9, 15. Levi R. & w, Laura, rocf Lane MM
1901, 7, 20. Levi R., minister, & w, Laura,
    set off to Alliance MM

LYTLE
1891, 12, 19. Samuel & Cloista Adell recrq

McBRIDE
1933, 6, 21. Frances relrq

McCANLEY
1912, 12, 21. Nara recrq
1914, 1, 17. Nara gct Beloit MM, Mich.

McELDOWNY
1914, 4, 18. W. & s, Harry W., recrq
1924, 4, 16. Emma recrq
1929, 3, 12. Harry [McEldowney] dropped from
    mbrp
1931, 9, 16. Wm., Emma & Paul [McEldowney]
    dropped from mbrp

McGIRR
1892, 7, 16. Benjamin & Sarah relrq

McKINZIE
1881, 6, 18. John recrq

McLEAN
1902, 1, 18. Lela gct Beloit MM, Mich.

McMAHAN
1889, 5, 18. John [McMan] recrq
1900, 10, 20. John dropped from mbrp

McNEAL
1933, 6, 21. Lillian relrq

MALMSBERRY
1910, 12, 17. Edith M. recrq

MARIS
1893, 3, 5. Barclay d ae 66y 7m 20d (an elder)

1877, 7, 21. Barclay & w, Ann P., rocf Salem
    MM, dtd 1877,6,21
1880, 6, 19. Ann & Esther & niece, Deborah
    W., gct Damascus MM
1880, 6, 19. Abram gct Damascus MM

1903, 6, 20. Joseph P. dropped from mbrp
1910, 11, 19. Ann P. gct Damascus MM

MARTIG
1918, 3, 16. Elizabeth recrq
1929, 8, 14. Mrs. Caleb relrq

MATHERS
1927, 2, 16. Raymond Chas. recrq

MATTI
1919, 9, 19. Charles A. gct South China MM,
    Me.

MEASE
1898, 12, 17. Grace A. gct Salem MM

MEEK
1907, 1, 19. Mary roc
1930, 4, 17. Mary dropped from mbrp

MERCER
1927, 2, 16. Jesse Blaine recrq
1927, 2, 16. Mary Idella recrq
1927, 2, 16. Kenneth Eli recrq
1927, 2, 16. Agnes Deborah recrq
1927, 2, 16. Gladys Alberta recrq
1927, 2, 16. Wm. James recrq

MIDDLETON
1880, 11, 20. Chas. & w, Mary, recrq
1880, 11, 20. Elizabeth recrq
1889, 5, 18. Wm. & Rebecca recrq
1896, 9, 19. Eliza recrq
1900, 1, 20. Levi & Elizabeth recrq
1912, 2, 17. Rebecca gct Whittier MM, Calif.

MILES
1918, 3, 16. John & Mabel E. recrq
1918, 3, 16. Helen recrq
1918, 3, 16. Mildred recrq
1918, 3, 16. Oral recrq

1918, 12, 21. Carroll & w, Selma, & ch, Inez
    M. A., Irena Katy J., Alma F. & I. Han-
    nah Miles Thomas rocf Damascus MM
1920, 1, 14. Katie Miles Hiverly relrq
1920, 2, 18. Zalo G. rocf Damascus MM
1924, 6, 18. Carroll H. & w, Selma, & dt,
    Elma, gct Damascus MM, O.
1925, 4, 15. Ines gct F St. Friends Ch.,
    Oskaloosa, Ia.

MILLER
1926, 7, 14. Frances Willard recrq

MOCK
1891, 2, 21. Addison T. recrq

MORGAN
1919, 1, 18. Elizabeth S. gct Alliance MM

MORTON
1925, 3, 18. Myrtle recrq

MOTTISHAW
1924, 4, 16. Carrie recrq
1924, 4, 16. Mildred recrq
1924, 4, 16. Elizabeth recrq
1924, 4, 16. Opal recrq
1933, 5, 17. Mildred (Mottishaw) Loy relrq

MYERS
1897, 6, 19. Clark recrq
1909, 4, 17. Paul, s Clark & Mary, recrq
1924, 4, 16. Verna recrq
1924, 4, 16. Violet Mae & Frank Richard, ch
Paul & Verna, recrq

OAKLEY
1911, 12, 16. Berneice C. rocf Fairmount MM,
Ind., dtd 1911,11,15
1918, 9, 21. Bernice (Oakley) Riddle gct
Stanford MM, Ia.

ONG
1874, 8, 15. Joseph P. & w, Rhoda S., & ch,
Effie Lorena & George Lewis, gct Columbus
MM

ORMSBY
1900, 10, 20. Lizzie dropped from mbrp
1929, 6, 12. Elizabeth dropped from mbrp

OWEN
1878, 4, 20. Stacy & w, Elazan, & ch, Lillie
M., Rosa A., Effa A. & Harvey A., recrq

PATCHIN
1891, 2, 21. Lawson K. recrq
1891, 2, 21. Albert M. recrq

PENNOCK
1875, 9, 18. Mary J. rocf Alliance MM, O.,
dtd 1875,8,31

PERKINS
1891, 2, 21. Deverna & Pizarro recrq
1891, 2, 21. Clarissa recrq
1891, 2, 21. David recrq
1891, 2, 21. Glenn recrq
1891, 2, 21. Floid recrq

PETTIT
1893, 2, 18. Mordecai L. recrq
1897, 2, 20. Laura S. rocf Damascus MM
1913, 12, 20. Laura gct Damascus MM

PHILLIPS
1893, 5, 20. Clara S. & Anna E. recrq
1900, 3, 17. Walter J. [Philips] recrq
1900, 9, 15. Lena [Philips] recrq
1901, 7, 20. Emily & Lena set off to Alliance
MM
1901, 7, 20. Clara set off to Alliance MM

1902, 1, 18. Homer recrq
1902, 4, 19. Wilmer recrq
1903, 12, 19. Walter J. gct Beloit MM
1904, 4, 16. Luella B. recrq
1904, 4, 16. Edna M. recrq
1907, 4, 20. Thos. recrq
1907, 5, --. Sadie recrq
1908, 11, 17. Homer C. & w, Clara H., & dt,
Helen S., rocf Maple City MM, Mich.
1909, 3, 20. Jesse & Wendell, ch Louella,
recrq
1911, 4, 15. John recrq
1924, 4, 16. Helen Mae [Phillis] recrq
1927, 2, 16. Donald D. [Phillip] recrq
1927, 2, 16. Anna Lucile [Phillip] recrq
1927, 2, 16. Frances Zorada [Phillip] recrq
1927, 3, 16. Elsie & Evelyn rocf Beloit MM,
Mich.
1927, 3, 16. Robert James rocf Beloit MM
1930, 4, 17. Carrie dropped from mbrp
1930, 4, 17. Mary Evelyn recrq
1930, 4, 17. Dwight L., Dorothy Mae & Effie
Marie, recrq
1930, 4, 17. Lucy Mae [Phillis] recrq
1933, 6, 21. Wilmer, Edward, Marguerite &
Kathleen relrq

PHINNEY
1910, 5, 21. Lauren rocf Pleasant Valley MM
1918, 6, 15. Loren A. gct Harmony MM, S. D.

PIM
1878, 12, 27. Lawretta gct Sandy Spring MM, O.
1902, 2, 15. Joseph G. rocf Sandy Spring MM

POWELL
1921, 10, 12. Chester A. & w, Essie, & ch,
Ralph, Walter & Thomas, roc
1927, 10, 12. Chester A. & w, Essie, & s,
Walter & Thomas, gct Smithfield MM
1930, 11, 12. Thomas rocf Smithfield MM
1933, 6, 21. Ralph relrq

PRUDHOE
1889, 7, 20. Margaret recrq
1891, 3, 21. Margaret relrq

QUIGLEY
1891, 2, 21. Wm. R. & Caroline E. & Rhoda V.
recrq

RABER
1898, 1, 15. Gotleib & w, Maggie, recrq

RABLE
1900, 2, 17. John recrq

RAKESTRAW
1901, 7, 20. Lewis M., Mary E. & Lloyd M.
set off with Alliance MM

REEVE
1873, 6, 21. Joshua rocf Alliance MM, dtd

REEVE, continued
       1873,4,29
1873, 8, 16. Ellen J. recrq
1875, 9, 18. Ellen J. relrq

REYNOLDS
1933, 6, 21. Irene relrq

RICE
1889, 8, 17. Deborah B. rocf Salem MM, dtd
       1889,7,25

RIDDLE
1918, 9, 21. Bernice Oakley gct Stanford MM,
       Ia.

RUFENER
1905, 9, 16. Lena recrq
1909, 2, 20. Lena [Rufner] relrq

RUGG
1908, 1, 18. Leverett J. & w, Anna, & ch,
       Allen M., rocf Farmington MM, N. Y.
1910, 11, 19. Leverett J. & Anna B. & Allen
       M., gct Paonia MM, Colo.

SAMPSON
1908, 3, 21. Mary Ann recrq
1911, 1, 12. Wm. recrq
1914, 11, 21. Sarah recrq
1925, 8, 12. Sarah relrq
1930, 4, 17. Sarah dropped from mbrp

SANTEE
1874, 1, 17. Delorma & ch, Thomas W. & Mary
       E., recrq
1878, 9, 21. Evangeline recrq
1898, 5, 24. Thomas dropped from mbrp
1902, 2, 15. Gideon E. relrq
1906, 2, 17. Gideon E. recrq
1909, 2, 20. Wm. & Curtis, ch G. E., recrq
1910, 3, 19. Anna recrq
1918, 2, 16. Florence E. rocf Damascus MM

SCHORSTEN
1930, 4, 17. Walter & Esther Sarah recrq

SCOTT
1891, 2, 21. Thomas H. recrq
1891, 8, 18. Hariet recrq
1891, 8, 18. Clarence Delbert recrq
1891, 8, 18. Thomas Leron recrq
1891, 8, 18. Cloey Luella recrq

SEBRELL
1890, 10, 18. Huldah K. & Hannah C. recrq

SHREVE
1873, 7, 19. Mary gct Damascus MM
1873, 7, 19. Unity gct Damascus MM
1875, 3, 20. Wm. & w, Emily, rocf Alliance
       MM, O., dtd 1875,3,2
1881, 1, 15. Ezra D. & w, Abi Cecelia P.,

       & ch, Judson W. & Hazel B., recrq
1882, 4, 15. Joseph J. & w, Josephine H., &
       ch, Lorena J. & Leonard G., gct Spring-
       dale MM, Iowa
1891, 4, 18. Edmund & w, Clarah H., & ch,
       Mabel E. & Curtis T., gct Damascus MM
1896, 12, 19. John & Savina & Rosa gct Damas-
       cus MM
1898, 2, 19. Emma J. rocf Damascus MM
1899, 11, 18. Lewis J. & Emma J. gct Damascus
       MM
1901, 7, 20. Eli T. set off with Alliance MM
1901, 7, 20. Anna Virginia set off with Al-
       liance MM
1901, 7, 20. Olive B. set off with Alliance
       MM
1901, 7, 20. William H. set off with Alliance
       MM
1901, 7, 20. Arthur J. set off with Alliance
       MM
1901, 7, 20. Enoch C. set off with Alliance
       MM
1901, 8, 17. Calvin & w, Anna M., & ch, Del-
       bert B., Lena M., Ethel E., Lucile A. &
       Marie L., gct Beloit MM, Mich.
1902, 1, 18. Albert & s, Harris, gct Alliance
       MM
1902, 4, 19. Lewis J. & w, Emma J., & s,
       Arnold L., rocf Damascus MM
1909, 9, 18. Edmond & w, Clara, & dt, Mabel,
       rocf Beloit MM
1913, 11, 15. Lewis J. & fam gct Whittier MM,
       Calif.
1914, 1, 17. Edmund & w, Clara, & dt, Mabel,
       gct Beloit MM, Mich.
1914, 12, 19. Curtis & ch rocf Beloit MM,
       Mich.
1912, 3, 16. Bertha Marie rocf Damascus MM
1922, 12, 13. Chas. H. & w, Lenara, & dt,
       Aletha, gct Beloit MM, Mich.
1925, 9, 16. Curtis & w, Unity, & ch, Ruth,
       Glenn & Betty, gct Damascus MM

SICKLES
1933, 9, 20. Elizabeth dropped from mbrp

SIMS
1891, 12, 19. Catharine recrq

SMITH
1891, 12, 19. Catharine recrq
1900, 1, 20. Lavina gct Salem MM

SNYDER
1911, 4, 15. Earl [Snider] recrq
1924, 9, 12. Olive L. recrq
1930, 4, 17. Earle dropped from mbrp
1933, 9, 20. Olive dropped from mbrp

SNITCIFF
1925, 3, 18. Thelma recrq

SNODE
1874, 3, 21. Wm. recrq

SOPER
1891, 2, 21. Edmond recrq

SPELL
1913, 3, 15. August & Mary recrq

St. AUBIN
1891, 12, 19. Peter & Margaret recrq

STANLEY
1899, 9, 2. Micajah d ae 89y 7m 9d (an elder)

1871, 1, 21. Rachel A. (form Engle) con mcd
1872, 7, 20. Hannah Ann rocf Short Creek MM,
     O., dtd 1873,6,20
1873, 7, 19. Rachel Ann & ch, Theodore, La-
     vina & Mary Ann, gct Bloomington MM, Iowa
1874, 1, 17. Esther B. & ch, Emma, Vernon &
     Eli J., recrq
1877, 4, 21. Rhoda M. rocf Greenwich MM, dtd
     1877,4,12
1878, 5, 18. John C. & s recrq
1880, 12, 18. Sarah T. & s, Summer, recrq
1889, 11, 16. Casper relrq
1889, 12, 21. Rebecca rocf Damascus MM, dtd
     1889,11,23
1890, 1, 18. Calvin & w, Esther, recrq
1891, 8, 15. George T. & ch, Robert Miles &
     Bertha Elvira, rocf Barclay MM, Kans.
1892, 1, 16. Mary E. recrq
1897, 10, 16. Binford & Mary J. relrq
1900, 5, 19. Mary Ellen rocf Sandy Spring MM
1901, 12, 21. Elsie recrq
1906, 3, 17. Guy C. recrq
1906, 5, 19. Micajah B. & w, Anna M., & ch,
     Clyde M., Harris O., Rhea M., Blanche &
     Morris J., gct Damascus MM
1906, 11, 17. Annie recrq
1911, 11, 18. Jehu & Edith gct Damascus MM
1912, 2, 17. Helen recrq
1914, 12, 19. Homer gct Dmmascus MM
1914, 12, 19. Rebecca gct Beloit MM, Mich.
1918, 3, 16. Albert E. & Mary E. recrq
1918, 3, 16. Edna May recrq
1918, 3, 16. Gladys, dt Guy & Edna, recrq
1918, 3, 16. Albert E., s Vernon & Mary, rec-
     rq
1918, 5, 18. Lawrence, Cora E. & Eli G., ch
     Vernon, recrq
1921, 11, 16. Helen Miles gct Damascus MM
1922, 12, 13. May E. gct Alliance MM
1922, 12, 13. Anna May & dt, Cora L., gct
     Alliance MM
1924, 10, 15. Charley E. & Ella gct Damascus
     MM
1925, 8, 12. Mrs. Violet recrq
1927, 12, 14. Chester G. gct Rush Creek MM
1929, 3, 12. Raymond & Russell dropped from
     mbrp

STATTON
1897, 1, 16. Isaac & w, Sarah B., rocf Free-
     port MM

STOCKWELL
1901, 7, 20. Etta M. set off to Alliance MM

STRATTON
1874, 12, 19. Joseph Henry & w, Esther F., &
     ch, Margaret, gct Salem MM, O.
1877, 12, 15. Joseph H. & w, Esther T., & dt,
     Margaret, roc
1882, 3, 18. Franklin & w, Philena, & ch,
     Oliver B. & Willie T., gct Salem MM

1882, 3, 18. Joseph Henry & w, Esther F., &
     dt, Margaret L., gct Salem MM
1889, 5, 18. Esther F. & dt, Margaret L.,
     relrq
1899, 10, 21. Isaac & Sarah B. gct Columbus
     MM
1914, 1, 17. Isaac & w, Sarah B., rocf Ber-
     linville MM
1919, 8, 16. Isaac & w, Sarah B., gct Damas-
     cus MM

SULLIVAN
1925, 3, 18. Thomas recrq

SUTCLIFF
1930, 4, 17. Viola recrq
1930, 4, 17. Marian Elizabeth recrq

SWANSON
1910, 11, 19. John & Mary recrq
1930, 4, 17. John dropped from mbrp

TAYLOR
1902, 3, 15. Marietta relrq

TEST
1877, 1, 20. Samuel & w, Ann J., rocf Alli-
     ance MM, dtd 1876,12,26

THOMAS
1918, 11, 16. Harry K. & dt, Eleanor, recrq
1918, 12, 21. I. Hannah (Miles) rocf Damascus
     MM
1920, 4, 14. Isadore Cobbs rocf Beloit MM
1924, 4, 16. Esther recrq
1924, 4, 16. Harley A. recrq
1924, 4, 16. Eva May recrq

TIBBALS
1890, 9, 20. Louisa (form Couse) relrq

TODD
1880, 1, 17. Anna E. relrq

TOMLINSON
1906, 1, 20. O. C. & fam rocf Damascus MM
1909, 5, 15. Orlando C. & w, Emily J., & ch,
     Myra & Wymond, gct Goshen MM, O.

TOOL
1889, 4, 20. Levi P. recrq
1903, 12, 19. Walter recrq
1909, 1, 16. Walter & Hannah gct Beloit MM,
    Mich.
1923, 4, 18. Horner relrq
1929, 10, 16. Clarence dropped from mbrp

TOWNSEND
1927, 3, 16. Wm. Ivan recrq

UPDEGRAFF
1889, 9, 21. Lucina rocf Stewart MM, Ia.,
    dtd 1889,8,3

VOTAW
1882, 3, 18. Hannah gct Damascus MM
1882, 3, 18. James gct Damascus MM

WAGGONER
1900, 7, 21. Milton recrq
1901, 7, 20. Milton [Wagoner] set off with
    Alliance MM

WALKER
1892, 3, 19. Albert recrq
1893, 3, 18. Gardner recrq

WALPERT
1928, 4, 18. Hazel relrq

WALTERS
1930, 4, 17. Ellen Rose & Eileen Alice recrq
1931, 5, 14. A. J. & Nellie recrq
1933, 4, 19. Albert J. & fam relrq

WARD
1900, 9, 15. Elizabeth Wager rocf Cleveland
    MM
1901, 7, 20. Elizabeth Wager, minister, set
    off with Alliance MM

WEAVER
1881, 3, 19. Joseph M. & w, Margaret, recrq
1892, 10, 15. Joseph & w & ch relrq
1908, 3, 21. Emma recrq

WEINGART
1933, 6, 21. Anna Jackson relrq

WHINNERY
1875, 2, 20. John gct Damascus MM, O. .
1876, 9, 16. Susan E. rocf Grove MM, dtd
    1876,8,12
1881, 6, 18. Wm. J. & w, Mary H., & ch,
    Lillian H., Anna Mary & Clarah Amy, recrq
1890, 5, 17. Wm. J. dis disunity
1903, 1, 17. Cyrus & w, Anna, & dt, Amy, rec-
    rq
1903, 10, 17. Ida gct Damascus MM
1903, 10, 17. Leora May rocf Winona MM
1933, 1, 18. Anna gct Damascus MM

WHITELEATHER
1901, 3, 16. Lawrence & Idella rocf Sandy
    Spring MM
1906, 1, 20. Lawrence & Idella & dt, Thelma,
    gct Sandy Spring MM, O.

WHITNEY
1904, 6, 18. Ray relrq

WILEY
1929, 6, 12. Joseph dropped from mbrp

WILLIAMS
1908, 3, 21. Samuel J. recrq
1913, 3, 15. Margaret Ann recrq
1924, 4, 16. Alice Bertha recrq
1924, 4, 16. Dolores Nail recrq
1924, 4, 16. Jennie Gayle recrq
1924, 4, 16. John Earl recrq

WILLIS
1900, 10, 20. John S. & Emaline recrq
1901, 7, 20. John S. & Emaline set off to
    Alliance MM

WILSON
1907, 4, 20. Morgan & Lizzie recrq
1907, 4, 20. John recrq
1908, 3, 21. Isabel recrq
1911, 5, 20. Ralph recrq
1913, 3, 15. Isabel relrq
1930, 4, 17. Margaret Ann & John dropped
    from mbrp

WISE
1873, 12, 20. Margaret & ch, Franklin B., Han-
    nah Laura & Charles N., recrq
1900, 5, 19. Franklin B. relrq
1901, 8, 17. Clara M. rocf Damascus MM

WOODWARD
1906, 11, 17. Bessie recrq
1930, 4, 17. Bessie dropped from mbrp
1933, 9, 20. Oscar dropped from mbrp

WOODWORTH
1879, 6, 21. Philo H. & w, Maria B., & dt,
    Lizzie R., recrq
1882, 5, 20. Maria B. relrq

WOOLMAN
1878, 6, 15. Micajah & w, Mary Elizabeth, &
    ch, Charles H. & Jesse J., recrq
1909, 7, 17. Clyde, s Jesse & Minnie, recrq
1919, 3, 15. Minnie recrq
1921, 11, 16. Zella recrq

WRIGHT
1900, 10, 20. Joseph A. rocf Lane MM, Mich.
1901, 3, 16. Joseph A. relrq

YOUNG
1911, 4, 15. Fred W. recrq

YOUNG, continued
1930, 4, 17. Fred dropped from mbrp

DEERFIELD MONTHLY MEETING

        Deerfield Monthly Meeting, located in Morgan County, Ohio, was established 4th Mo. 21,
1827. The name was later changed to Pennsville Monthly Meeting.

        Among the families of charter members were Brown, Embry, Gilbert, Gifford, Griffith,
Hampton, Healy, Hodgen, King, Kennard, Millhouse, Mills, Patton, Pierpont, Pickett, Strahl,
Todd, Williams and Wood.

RECORDS

ALLEN

1838, 6, 14. Jonathan, John Mercer & Chincy A
Ann, ch David, rocf Middleton MM, dtd
1837,7,17

1838, 7, 19. Jonathan, John Mercer & Cynthia
Ann, ch David, gct Chesterfield MM

ARNOLD

1829, 12, 21. Joseph, s Wm. & Mary, Belmont
Co., O.; m in Blue Rock, Bethula HAMPTON,
dt John & Mary, Muskingum Co., O.

1830, 7, 15. Bethula gct Somerset MM

BAILEY

----, --, --. Jesse & Mary
    Ch: Rachel   b 1813, --, --
        David   " 1817, --, --

----, --, --. Henry & Mary
    Ch: Mary   b 1852, 1, 29
       Sarah V. " 1856, 9, 4

1854, 4, 20. James, s James & Abigail, Belmont Co., O.; m in Hopewell, Rhoda PATTEN,
dt John & Rebecca, Morgan Co., O.
    Ch: John Henry b 1855, 4, 29
       Lydia Jane " 1862, 9, 11

1855, 11, 22. Elizabeth m Amos VERNON

1837, 6, 15. Wm. & w, Sarah, & ch, Abigail
F. & Elizabeth, rocf Short Creek MM, dtd
1837, 5, 23

1837, 11, 16. Samuel & w, Harriet, & ch, Hannah & Burden, rocf Stillwater MM

1839, 2, 14. Uriah & w, Susannah, & ch,
Tabitha, David, Elwood & Robert, rocf
Stillwater MM, dtd 1839,1,26

1839, 6, 13. Uriah & w, Susanna, & ch, Tabitha, David, Elwood & Robert, gct Chesterfield MM

1842, 3, 17. Samuel & w, Harriet, & ch, Hannah, Borden & Harriet, gct Chesterfield
MM

1843, 8, 17. David dis mcd & jas

1846, 3, 19. Mary recrq

1846, 7, 16. Henry rst on consent of Somerset
MM

1846, 9, 17. Anna, Elizabeth, James, John &
George, ch Henry & Mary, recrq

1850, 2, 14. Jehu gct WD MM

1850, 6, 13. Anna Yocom (form Bailey) dis mcd

1854, 9, 14. James rocf Somerset MM, dtd
1854,5,29

1856, 8, 14. James & w, Rhoda, & s, John
Henry, gct Stillwater MM

1862, 4, 17. James & w, Rhoda, & ch, John
Henry, Rebecca Alice & Charles Addison,
rocf Chesterfield MM, dtd 1862,3,15

1862, 8, 14. John dis mcd

1865, 4, 13. James dis military service

1867, 3, 14. James [Bayley] & w, Rhoda, & ch,
John Hervey, Rebecca Alice & Lydia, gct

Springville MM, Ia.

1872, 7, 18. George dis mcd

1875, 2, 18. Henry & w, Mary, gct Coal Creek
MM, Ia.

1875, 2, 18. Mary gct Coal Creek MM, Ia.

1875, 2, 18. Sarah gct Coal Creek MM, Ia.

BAIN

1828, 8, 14. Elijah & s, John, rocf Somerset
MM, dtd 1828,6,30

1831, 9, 15. Anna & Martha [Bane], minors,
rocf Somerset MM, dtd 1831,9,25

1833, 3, 14. John [Bane] dis disunity

1834, 8, 14. Ann Simpson (form Bain) dis mcd

1836, 1, 14. Elijah [Bane] dis mcd

1840, 6, 18. Martha Bishop (form Bain) dis
mcd

1845, 7, 17. Lydia Ann [Boan] (form Metcalf)
rpd mcd

BALDERSON

1835, 7, 16. Sidney (form Harris) dis mcd

1847, 2, 18. Deborah rst

1853, 6, 16. Esther recrq

1855, 3, 15. Deborah gct Red Cedar MM, Ia.

1857, 3, 19. Deborah gct Stillwater MM

BALL

1836, 7, 30. Amos, s David & Juliann, b

1845, 1, 23. Ruth m Wm. KING

1847, 11, 25. Gaynor m Elwood BURGESS

1856, 1, 31. Alice Ann m Foster LIGHTFOOT

1857, 3, 26. Abigail m George W. MOTT

1878, 2, 9. Juliann d ae 78 bur Hopewell

1879, 3, 19. David d ae 81 bur Hopewell

1836, 6, 16. David & w, Julian, & ch, Gaynor,
Ruth, Alice Ann & Abigail, rocf Smithfield
MM, dtd 1836,2,22

BECK

1835, 6, 18. Jesse & w, Elizabeth, & ch, Rachel, Grace & Sarah, rocf Somerset MM,
dtd 1835,3,30

BEDELL

1862, 7, 17. Elizabeth con mcd

1862, 11, 13. Elizabeth gct Hickory Grove MM,
Ia.

BERRY

1860, 11, 15. Susanna (form Lightfoot) dis
mcd

BINGHAM

1833, 10, 17. Catharine (form Kennard) dis mcd

BISHOP

1840, 6, 18. Martha (form Bain) dis mcd

BLOWERS

1882, 4, 14. Jeptha D., s Andrew & Rebecca,
Belmont Co., O.; m in Hopewell, Eliza B.

BLOWERS, continued
    CREW, dt Edwin & Mary B., Morgan Co., O.

BONSALL
1863, 8, 13. Evan & w, Caroline, & ch, Wm.
    F., Richard S., Lewis H. & Rebecca Eva,
    rocf Salem MM, dtd 1863,7,22

BOSWELL
----, --, --. Jesse & Eliza
    Ch: Dempsey   b 1833, 12, 12
        Elizabeth " 1835, 11, --

1833, 5, 16. Eliza rocf Somerset MM, dtd
    1833,4,29
1834, 2, 13. Jesse rocf Milford MM, Ind.,
    dtd 1833,8,24
1834, 7, 17. Demsey & w, Mary, & dt, Phebe,
    rocf Milford MM, Ind., dtd 1834,5,24
1836, 5, 19. Wm. & Rachel & ch, Ruth, Eliza-
    beth, Rebecca, Isaac, Joseph, Milicent,
    Elihu & Wilson, rocf West Grove MM, Ind.,
    dtd 1836,4,9

BOWERS
1839, 12, 19. Lydia (form Haines) dis mcd

BRACKEN
1869, 3, 18. Asaph Wood gct Short Creek MM,
    to m Phebe Bracken

BRADY
1848, 8, 17. Ruthanna (form Eaves) dis mcd &
    jas

BREWER
1838, 10, 18. Sarah rst at Spiceland MM, Ind.
    on consent of this mtg

BRIGGS
1836, 3, 1. Lindley H., s Israel S. & Mary,
    b

1832, 6, 14. Israel S. & w, Mary, & ch, Es-
    ther, Ann, John S., Benjamin, Job & Wm.,
    rocf Flushing MM, dtd 1832,4,26
1871, 3, 16. David gct Coal Creek MM, Ia.

BROWN
1846, 4, 22. Isaac, s Josiah & Sarah, Mor-
    gan Co., O.; m in Pennsville, Elizabeth
    WORTHINGTON, dt Jacob & Elizabeth TAYLOR,
    Morgan Co., O.

1829, 1, 10. Benjamin dis jH
1829, 1, 10. Amy dis jH
1834, 10, 16. Abigail dis disunity
1835, 6, 18. Isaac & w, Mary, rocf Somerset
    MM, dtd 1835,4,27
1846, 6, 12. Elizabeth & dt, Eliza Ann
    Worthington, gct Chesterfield MM

BUNDY
----, --, --. William & Mary
    Ch: Abigail   b 1830, 8, 16
        Millicent " 1832, 11, 8
        Martha   " 1835, 1, 10 d 1835, 3,10
        bur Deerfield
        Mary   b 1835, 12, 29
        Sarah   " 1835, 12, 29
        Deborah   " 1838, 8, 19
        Benjamin " 1841, 3, 27
        Elizabeth " 1843, 4, 26
        William   " 1845, 8, 18
        Caleb   " 1848, 2, 17
----, --, --. Jonathan & Achsah
    Ch: Lydia   b 1833, 3, 9
        Penina   " 1835, 11, 28
1835, 4, 14. Samuel, s Exum & Sally, b
1836, 9, 21. Thomas, s Thomas & Millicent,
    Morgan Co., O.; m in Pennsville, Ruth
    WORRELL, dt Thomas & Esther, Morgan Co.,
    O.
    Ch: Asenath b 1841, 2, 7
        Emlen   " 1843, 10, 22
1836, 10, 15. Robert, s Elias & Elizabeth, b
1836, 10, 25. Robert, infant, d
1836, 12, 7. David, s Thomas & Millicent,
    Morgan Co., O.; m in Pennsville, Achsah
    GILBERT, dt Abel & Rebecca, Morgan Co., O.
    Ch: Joel   b 1839, 2, 12
1837, 3, 3. Sarah d ae 1 bur Pennsville
1853, 1, 30. William d ae 44 bur Pennsville
1857, 7, 29. Mary m John PATTEN

1830, 8, 19. Mary, Joseph, Townsend, Josiah,
    Bethia, Susanna, Nehemiah Matson & Ruth-
    anna, ch Moses & Ann, rocf Short Creek MM,
    dtd 1830,6,22
1830, 11, 18. Jonathan & w, Achsah, & ch, Mary,
    John & Sarah, rocf Somerset MM, dtd 1830,
    10,25
1830, 11, 18. Wm. & w, Mary, & dt, Abigail,
    rocf Somerset MM, dtd 1830,10,25
1833, 5, 16. Thomas & w, Millicent, & ch, Da-
    vid, Thomas, Penninah, Ruth, Lydia & Za-
    doc, rocf Somerset MM, dtd 1833,4,29
1834, 6, 19. Moses rocf Somerset MM, dtd
    1834,4,28
1834, 6, 19. Exum & w, Sally, & ch, Joseph,
    Josiah & Elizabeth, rocf Somerset MM, dtd
    1834,4,28
1836, 2, 18. Elias & w, Elizabeth, & dt, Ma-
    riah, rocf Stillwater MM, dtd 1836,1,23
1837, 3, 16. Nathan & w, Sarah, rocf Still-
    water MM, dtd 1837,2,25
1839, 7, 18. Thomas & w, Millicent, & s, Za-
    doc, gct Chesterfield MM
1839, 7, 18. Penina gct Chesterfield MM
1839, 7, 18. Ruth gct Chesterfield MM
1839, 7, 18. Lydia gct Chesterfield MM
1839, 7, 18. Benjamin gct Chesterfield MM
1839, 9, 18. Joseph Townsend dis disunity
1840, 5, 14. Thomas Jr. & w, Ruth, & dt,
    Hannah, rocf Chesterfield MM, dtd 1840,4,

BUNDY, continued
18
1841, 1, 14. David & w, Achsah, & s, Joel, gct Chesterfield MM

1841, 4, 15. Susanna Todd (form Bundy) dis mcd

1842, 5, 19. Josiah dis mcd

1842, 6, 16. Bethia Woodruff (form Bundy) dis mcd

1845, 7, 17. Lucinda Maxwell (form Bundy) dis mcd

1846, 7, 16. Thomas & w, Ruth, & ch, Hannah, Asenath & Emlen, gct Chesterfield MM

1847, 11, 18. Joseph Embree gct Chesterfield MM, to m Achsah Bundy

1848, 2, 17. Achsah Embree & s, Joel Bundy, rocf Chesterfield MM, dtd 1848,1,15

1852, 5, 13. Abigail Ward (form Bundy) con mcd

1851, 10, 16. Jonathan & w, Achsah, & ch, Penninah & Thomas, rocf Somerset MM, dtd 1851,8,28

1851, 10, 16. Lydia rocf Somerset MM, dtd 1851,8,28

1851, 10, 16. Sarah M. rocf Sandy Spring MM, dtd 1851,8,28

1853, 4, 19. Mary & ch, Mary H., Deborah, Elizabeth, William & Caleb, gct Pleasant Plain MM, Ia.

1853, 4, 19. Milicent gct Pleasant Plain MM, Ia.

1853, 7, 16. Sarah M. gct Salem MM, Ia.

1853, 7, 16. Lydia gct Salem MM, Ia.

1853, 8, 18. Jonathan & w, Achsah, & ch, Peninah & Thomas, gct Salem MM, Ia.

1853, 9, 15. Joseph Embree & w, Achsah, & ch, Ezra Embree, Joel Bundy & David Embree, gct Red Cedar MM, Ia.

BURGESS
1838, 5, 5. Margaret d ae 55 bur Pennsville
1841, 11, 24. Mary m Evan SMITH
1847, 11, 25. Elwood, s John & Margaret, Morgan Co., O.; m in Hopewell, Gaynor BALL, dt David & Juliann, Morgan Co., O.
  Ch: David   b 1849, 2, 5
      Caroline   " 1850, 9, 6 d 1876, 1, 4
        bur Pennsville
      Nathan   b 1852, 11, 9
      Mary Alice " 1855, 1, 3
      Amos   " 1858, 2, 5
      John P.   " 1860, 9, 29 d 1866, 5,22
        bur Pennsville
      Julia Ann   b 1863, 2, 25
      Sarah
        Abbie   " 1866, 1, 9
      Louis A.   " 1869, 2, 13 d 1870, 2,19
        bur Pennsville
----, --, --. Clarkson & Susan
  Ch: Joel   b 1848, 1, 28
      Charles   " 1850, 7, 24
      Lydia Ann   " 1863, 6, 26
1851, 2, 26. Joseph d ae 88 bur Pennsville

1854, 8, 24. Ann d ae 33 bur Pennsville
1854, 8, 24. Lydia Ann, infant, d bur Pennsville
1861, 12, 10. John Burgess d ae 76 bur Pennsville

1836, 6, 16. John & w, Margaret, & ch, Clarkson, Elwood, Mary, Ann Elizabeth & Sarah, rocf Smithfield MM, dtd 1836,5,23

1838, 9, 13. Joseph [Berges] rocf Smithfield MM, dtd 1838,7,23

1846, 7, 16. Sarah gct Spiceland MM, Ind.

1847, 3, 18. Clarkson gct Short Creek MM, to m Susan Willis

1847, 8, 19. Susan W. rocf Short Creek MM, dtd 1847,5,18

1855, 1, 18. Clarkson & w, Susan, & ch, Joel & Charles, gct Plymouth MM

1862, 2, 13. Willis rocf Plymouth MM, dtd 1862,1,20

1871, 3, 16. Daniel gct Coal Creek MM, Ia.

1877, 10, 18. Nathan gct Plymouth MM, to m Elizabeth L. Penrose

1878, 5, 16. Elizabeth P. rocf Plymouth MM, dtd 1878,4,22

1880, 4, 15. Nathan & w, Elizabeth, & dt, Mary Emma, gct Plymouth MM

1881, 1, 13. Elwood & w, Gaynor, & ch, Julia Ann & Sarah Abbie, gct Plymouth MM

1884, 1, 17. Mary Alice gct Plymouth MM

1887, 4, 14. Amos gct Plymouth MM

BUTLER
----, --, --. Caleb & Mary
  Ch: Bailey   b 1828, --, --
      John   " 1830, --, --
      Eli   " 1831, 10, 13
      Mary   " 1834, 10, 10
      Joel Caleb " 1837, 4, 30
1865, 11, 2. Mary d ae 75 bur Blue Rock Township

1831, 2, 17. Caleb dis disunity
1850, 2, 19. Bailey dis jas
1850, 2, 14. John dis jas
1850, 4, 18. Mary Jr. dis jas
1852, 4, 15. Asenath (form Clark) con mcd
1871, 3, 16. Asenath dis jas

CADWALADER
1836, 10, 15. Reece & w, Sarah, & ch, Edith T., Loyd D. & Isaac D., rocf Stillwater MM, dtd 1836,9,24

CALVERT
1849, 9, 13. Mary Ann (form Pierpont) dis mcd

CARR
1838, 6, 14. Orpha rocf Somerset MM, dtd 1838,5,28

1841, 7, 15. Orpha gct Upper Springfield MM

CARTER
1837, 2, 16. Richard rocf Short Creek MM,
     dtd 1836,12,26

CHAMBERS   [to m Mary Chambers
1843, 5, 18. Wm. Llewelyn gct Plainfield MM,

CHANY
1840, 11, 19. Mary Chany (form Harry) dis mcd

CLARK
1852, 4, 15. Asenath Butler (form Clark) con
     mcd

CLENDENON
1830, 11, 24. Maria m Thomas PENROSE
1834, 12, 20. Isaac [Clendenen] d ae 66 bur
     Pennsville
1857, 10, 21. Hannah d ae 90 bur Pennsville

1827, 6, 16. Isaac & w, Hannah, rocf Still-
     water MM, dtd 1827,5,26
1827, 6, 16. Maria rocf Stillwater MM, dtd
     1827,4,28
1829, 7, 16. Isaac Jr. rocf Stillwater MM,
     dtd 1829,6,27
1831, 2, 17. Isaac Jr. dis mcd
1864, 11, 17. Mary (form Harmer) con mcd
1879, 6, 19. Wm. I., Eliza B., Martha J. &
     Charles Francis, ch David & Mary, recrq
1887, 10, 13. Wm. dis jas
1891, 1, 15. Mary H. dis jas
1891, 1, 15. Eliza B. dis jas
1897, 1, 14. Martha Jane McCall (form Clen-
     denon) dis mcd & jas

COLE
1846, 11, 26. Sarah S. m Mahlon PATTON
1847, 2, 25. Wm. B., s Richard M. & Mary,
     Morgan Co., O.; m in Hopewell, Rachel
     PATTON, dt Wm. & Phebe, Morgan Co., O.
     Ch: Richard   b 1847, 12, 25
         Mary   " 1849, 10, 5

1830, 8, 19. Wm. Llewelyn gct London Grove
     MM, to m Mary B. Cole
1831, 1, 13. Mary B. Llewelyn & dt, Sarah S.
     Cole, rocf London Grove MM, Pa., dtd
     1830,12,11
1836, 7, 14. Sarah S., minor, gct Sadsbury
     MM, Pa.
1846, 9, 17. Sarah S. rocf Sadsbury MM, dtd
     1846,7,7
1846, 10, 15. Wm. B. rocf New Garden MM,
     Pa., dtd 1846,7,8
1851, 1, 16. Wm. B. & w, Rachel, & ch, Rich-
     ard & Mary, gct Richland MM

COLLING
1836, 2, 18. Ernest & w, Elizabeth, & ch,
     Ernest, John, Elizabeth, David, Mary,
     Daniel, rocf Winder MM, Germany, dtd
     1835,7,5, end by Short Creek MM 1836,1,19

CONN
1847, 6, 17. Naomi (form Mendenhall) dis mcd

COPE
1846, 8, 13. Ruth (form Wilson) dis mcd
1847, 3, 18. Abigail rocf Short Creek MM, dtd
     1846,11,24
1850, 2, 14. Abigail dis disunity

COOPER
1863, 7, 22. Ida Adella, dt Albert & Sina
     Ellen, b

1863, 3, 19. Sina Ellen (form Heald) con mcd

COPPOCK
1837, 6, 15. Mary rocf Somerset MM, dtd
     1837,5,29

CRAFT
1857, 12, 24. Jesse, s Samuel & Ann, Washing-
     ton Co., O.; m in Hopewell, Mary VERNON,
     dt James & Rhoda, Morgan Co., O.
1858, 6, 23. Samuel, s James & Mary, Washing-
     ton Co., O.; m in Pennsville, Sarah
     DEWEES, dt Thomas & Nancy SMITH, Morgan
     Co., O.
1881, 12, 30. Samuel d ae 82 bur Pennsville

1858, 6, 17. Mary & ch, Hannah & Rhoda Ann
     Vernon, gct Plymouth MM
1858, 9, 16. Sarah gct Plymouth MM
1878, 1, 17. Samuel & w, Sarah, rocf Ply-
     mouth MM, dtd 1877,12,17
1885, 3, 19. Sarah gct Somerset MM

CRAVEN
1832, 3, 15. Thompson & Mary Walker, ch Mary
     Craven, rocf Short Creek MM, dtd 1831,9,20

CREW
1856, 3, 20. Edwin, s James & Sarah, Belmont
     Co., O.; m in Hopewell, Mary B. DOUDNA,
     dt Henry & Matilda, Morgan Co., O.
     Ch: Charles
         Lewis   b 1857, 7, 7
         Eliza B.   " 1859, 10, 11
         Anne   " 1862, 7, 11
         John H   " 1864, 9, 1
1868, 10, 21. Fleming, s Joshua & Milley, Mor-
     gan Co., O.; m in Pennsville, Mary C.
     MICHENER, dt George & Rebecca
1882, 4, 14. Eliza B. m Jeptha D. BLOWERS

1836, 11, 17. Wm. & w, Mary, & ch, Delitha,
     Phariba & Elias, rocf Somerset MM, dtd
     1836,10,24
1858, 12, 16. Edwin rocf Somerset MM, dtd
     1858,11,29
1865, 8, 17. Edwin dis military service
1869, 3, 18. Mary L. gct Chesterfield MM

DANCE
1837, 5, 18. Sarah rocf Phila. MM, dtd 1837,
     1,26

DARNEL
1846, 5, 14. Phariby (form Gifford) con mcd
1864, 5, 19. Pharaba dis jas

DAVIS
1869, 10, 7. Priscilla d ae 81 bur Pennsville

1833, 8, 15. Priscilla rocf Concord MM, Pa.,
     dtd 1832,11,27
1872, 3, 11. Rebecca (form Dewees) dis mcd

DEAN
1843, 4, 13. Michael King gct Chesterfield
     MM, to m Lavina Dean

DENNIS
1835, 12, 17. Mary & Grace rocf Baltimore MM,
     W. Dist., dtd 1835,11,5
1836, 4, 14. Mary Embree (form Dennis) dis
     mcd

DEWEES
----, --, --. Thomas & Mary
     Ch: Lewis M.   b 1817, 12, 18
         Jonathan F." 1820, 1, 12
         Ann M.   " 1821, 9, 20
         Isaiah   " 1823, 10, 1
         Mary Lee   " 1825, 7, 19
         William H. " 1827, 3, 5
         Charles B. " 1830, 5, 6
         Greenbury P. 1832, 1, 10
         Sarah M.   b 1834, 7, 12
----, --, --. David B. & Rachel
     Ch: Thomas K. b 1829, 6, 1
         Hannah   " 1831, 10, 28
         Isaac   " 1834, 1, 3
----, --, --. William & Sarah
     Ch: Smith   b 1834, 10, 14
         Caleb   " 1836, 9, 24
         William   " 1840, 12, 11
         Joshua   " 1842, 12, 11
         Aaron   " 1844, 10, 6
         Elizabeth   " 1838, 9, 24
1834, 3, 28. Thomas d bur Deerfield
1834, 3, 30. Ellis d ae 5 bur Deerfield
1837, 3, 23. Sarah m James DOUDNA
----, --, --. Lewis M. m Sarah Ann ----- d
     1844,12,19 ae 22 bur Pennsville
     Ch: Margaret   b 1841, 2, 4
         Beason T.   " 1842, 9, 27
         George M.   " 1844, 12, 10
1843, 11, 13. Mary d ae 89 bur Pennsville
     Hicksite Bur Gr
1844, 11, 1. Mary H. d ae 48 bur Pennsville
1845, 6, 27. Wm. d ae 36 bur Hopewell
1848, 4, 25. Sarah, dt James & Ann, b
1849, 6, 12. Thomas d ae 69
1851, 12, 11. Lydia, dt Aaron & Mary, b
1852, 1, 22. Wm., s Wm. & Debby, Washington

Co., O.; m in Hopewell, Maria EMBREE, dt
Joseph & Rebecca, Morgan Co., O.
1852, 4, 22. Mary d ae 36 bur Pennsville
1852, 6, 7. Lydia, infant, d bur Pennsville
----, --, --. Jesse & Rebecca
     Ch: Nathan   b 1856, 5, 1
         Samuel   " 1861, 5, 25
         Thomas   " 1848,,10,12
         James   " 1850, 9, 7
1857, 5, 10. Jane d ae 70 bur Hopewell
1857, 10, 28. Griffith, s William & Debby,
     Washington Co., O.; m in Pennsville, Anna
     MASTERS, dt Wm. & Naomi, Morgan Co., O.
1858, 6, 23. Sarah m Samuel CRAFT
1864, 11, 12. Richard Stanton, s Aaron &
     Eunice, b
1866, 5, 30. Margaret Jane m Wm. FOULKE
1870, 8, 31. James E., s Jesse & Rebecca,
     Morgan Co., O.; m in Pennsville, Anna
     HARMER, dt Wm. & Rachel, Morgan Co., O.
     Ch: Mary Emma b 1874, 9, 2 d 1894, 1,13
         bur Pennsville
         Rachel M. b 1877, 4, 17
         Lemuel F. " 1883, 4, 1 " 1884, 9, 5
         bur Pennsville
         Edith   b 1887, 3, 15
1873, 4, 24. James W. d ae 85 bur Bridgewater
     O.
1876, 9, 12. Hannah H., dt Thomas & Martha, b
----, --, --. Nathan & Rebecca H.
     Ch: Roy H.   b 1879, 2, 28
         Loyd N.   " 1884, 12, 29 d 1885, 1, 1
         bur Zaneville, O.
         Amy T.   b 1887, 3, 1
1880, 8, 7. Rebecca d ae 57 bur Hopewell
1904, 10, 23. Anna d ae 92 bur Bridgewater, O.

1829, 9, 17. David B. rocf Short Creek MM,
     dtd 1829,8,18
1829, 10, 15. Rachel [Deweese] rocf Smithfield
     MM, dtd 1829,7,20
1833, 6, 1. Thomas L. & w, Mary H., & ch,
     Lewis M., Jonathan F., Ann M., Isaiah F.,
     Mary S., Wm. H., Charles B. & Greenberry
     P., rocf Short Creek MM, dtd 1833,4,23
1833, 8, 15. Guli Elma rocf Short Creek MM,
     dtd 1833,6,18
1833, 8, 15. Bula Emily rocf Short Creek MM,
     dtd 1833,6,18
1833, 8, 15. Ellis, Thomas Lee, Hannah
     Maria & Maryanna, ch Samuel & Hannah, rocf
     Short Creek MM, dtd 1833,5,21
1834, 4, 17. Thomas & w, Jane, & ch, Rebecca,
     Aaron, Jesse, Joseph, Hannah & Ellis, rocf
     Stillwater MM, dtd 1834,3,22
1834, 4, 17. Wm. & w, Sarah, & ch, James &
     Thomas, rocf Somerset MM, dtd 1834,2,24
1834, 4, 17. Guli Elma Lincoln (form Dewees)
     dis mcd
1836, 4, 14. Wm. & w, Debbie, & ch, Isaac,
     Cornelius, Wm., Deborah & Griffith, rocf
     Stillwater MM, dtd 1836,3,26
1836, 4, 14. Mary rocf Stillwater MM, dtd

DEWEES, continued
        1836,3,26
1836, 4, 14. Sarah rocf Stillwater MM, dtd
        1836,3,26
1836, 11, 17. Beulah Emily Harris (form
        Dewees)dis mcd
1837, 9, 14. Mary rocf Short Creek MM, dtd
        1837,6,20
1837, 12, 14. Aaron gct Somerset MM
1838, 7, 19. Ellis dis JH
1840, 4, 16. Rebecca gct Somerset MM
1840, 6, 18. Lewis M. con mcd
1840, 11, 19. Jonathan dis
1841, 8, 19. Sarah Ann rocf Chesterfield MM,
        dtd 1841,4,17
1844, 8, 15. Ann Linken (form Dewees) dis mcd
1845, 2, 13. Isaiah F. con mcd
1846, 1, 15. Thomas L. [Deweese] dis mcd
1846, 1, 15. Mary L. Harris (form Dewees) con
        mcd
1846, 7, 16. Lewis M. & ch, Rezin Thompson
        & George M., gct Chesterfield MM
1846, 12, 17. Anna recrq
1847, 2, 18. James rst on consent of Still-
        water MM
1847, 3, 18. Hannah Maria Ward (form Dewees)
        dis mcd & JH
1847, 4, 15. Isaiah F. dis disunity
1847, 5, 13. Mary Ann McCall (form Dewees)
        dis mcd & JH
1847, 5, 13. Wm. H., Charles B., Greenberry
        P. & Sarah M., ch Thos. L., gct Chester-
        field MM
1847, 6, 17. Jesse, Barak & Rebecca, ch
        James & Anna, recrq
1847, 10, 14. Jesse gct Somerset MM, to m
        Rebecca Edgerton
1847, 12, 16. Jonathan dis mcd
1848, 3, 16. Jesse & nephew, Joshua Dewees,
        gct Somerset MM
1848, 5, 18. Thomas Lee dis mcd
1848, 8, 17. Hannah dis disunity
1850, 11, 14. Sarah & ch, Elizabeth & Aaron,
        gct Chesterfield MM
1851, 8, 14. James Jr. gct Chesterfield MM
1851, 11, 13. Jesse & w, Rebecca, & ch, Thom-
        as & James, & nephew, Joshua Dewees, rocf
        Somerset MM, dtd 1851,10,27
1851, 11, 13. Aaron & w, Mary, & ch, Mathew
        W., Watson, Margaret Jane & Almeda, rocf
        Stillwater MM, dtd 1851,10,25
1852, 2, 15. Sarah & ch, Elizabeth & Aaron,
        rocf Chesterfield MM, dtd 1852,1,17
1852, 4, 15. Maria gct Chesterfield MM
1852, 5, 13. James & w, Milicent, rocf Ches-
        terfield MM, dtd 1853,4,17
1853, 9, 15. Aaron dis mcd
1853, 10, 13. James & w, Anna, & ch, Baruch,
        Rebecca & Sarah, gct Red Cedar MM, Ia.
1854, 7, 13. Jesse Jr. dis mcd
1855, 9, 13. Aaron rst
1855, 11, 15. Eunice recrq
1856, 1, 17. Elizabeth Duff (form Dewees)

        dis mcd
1857, 6, 18. James dis disunity
1858, 4, 15. Ruthanna gct Chesterfield MM
1859, 3, 17. Smith dis disunity
1861, 8, 15. Wm. gct Chesterfield MM
1861, 2, 14. James & w, Anna, "acknowledged
        mbr of this mtg, since their right was
        lost in the separation in 1854"
1866, 2, 15. Aaron Jr. gct Somerset MM
1866, 2, 15. Aaron Jr. gct Somerset MM
1868, 7, 16. Isaac, s Aaron P. & Eunice,
        recrq
1869, 9, 19. Joshua gct Somerset MM
1871, 4, 13. Watson W. gct Kennet MM, Pa.
1871, 5, 18. Aaron & w, Maranda, rocf Somer-
        set MM, dtd 1871,3,23
1871, 9, 14. Thomas gct Short Creek MM, to m
        Martha W. Hall
1871, 12, 14. Thomas gct Short Creek MM
1871, 7, 13. Almedia McGrew (form Dewees)
        con mcd
1872, 2, 15. Aaron & Maranda gct Somerset MM
1872, 3, 11. Rebecca Davis (form Dewees) dis
        mcd
1875, 10, 14. James E. & w, Anna, & dt, Mary
        Emma, gct Stillwater MM
1876, 2, 17. Aaron P. & w, Eunice, & s,
        Richard S., gct Kennet MM, Pa.
1876, 8, 17. Thomas & w, Martha W., & ch,
        Jesse H. & Ezra, rocf Short Creek MM, dtd
        1876,7,18
1874, 12, 14. Aaron & w, Miranda, rocf Somer-
        set MM, dtd 1870,10,26
1877, 9, 13. Nathan gct Chesterfield MM, to
        m Rebecca Huestis
1878, 4, 18. James E. & w, Anna, & ch, Mary
        E. & Rachel, rocf Stillwater MM, dtd 1878,
        2,20
1878, 4, 18. Rebecca H. rocf Chesterfield MM,
        dtd 1878,3,16
1883, 3, 15. Jesse gct Stillwater MM, to m
        Miriam P. Hall
1883, 8, 16. Miriam P. rocf Stillwater MM,
        dtd 1883,7,25
1884, 11, 13. Aaron P. & w, Eunice, gct Phila.
        MM
1886, 5, 13. Isaac gct Chester MM, Pa.
1887, 5, 19. Samuel dis mcd
1887, 12, 15. Nathan & w, Rebecca H., & ch,
        Roy H. & Amy F., gct Chesterfield MM
1890, 5, 15. Aaron & w, Miranda J., gct
        Somerset MM
1900, 6, 19. Thomas & w, Martha W., gct Still-
        water MM
1900, 6, 14. Jesse H. gct Stillwater MM
1903, 4, 16. Hannah H. gct Phila. MM, Pa.

DIXON
1864, 5, 19. Samuel & w, Hannah, rocf Upper
        Springfield MM

DOAN
1828, 1, 24. William, s Daniel & Mary, Mus-

DOAN, William, continued
    kingum Co., O.; m in Blue Rock, Asenath
    HAMPTON, dt John & Mary, Muskingum Co., O.
    Ch: John   b 1828, --, --
        Mary   " 1830, --, --

1830, 11, 18. Deborah & Mary dis jH
1831, 2, 17. Asenath dis
1831, 3, 17. Wm. dis jH

DOUDNA
----, --, --. Henry d 1892,6,12 ae 79 bur
    Pennsville; m Matilda ----- d 1892,11,11
    ae 82 bur Pennsville
    Ch: Mary B.   b 1836, 2, 16
        Hannah W. " 1838, 3, 22 d 1841,10, 8
        bur Chesterfield
1837, 3, 23. James, s Henry & Martha, Bel-
    mont Co., O.; m in Chesterfield, Sarah
    DEWEES, dt Wm. & Debe, Washington Co., O.
1841, 10, 21. Elisha, s John & Miriam Belmont
    Co., O.; m in Morgan, Mary PICKETT, dt
    Thomas & Rhoda, Morgan Co., O.
1856, 3, 20. Mary B. m Edwin CREW
----, --, --. Jesse & Louisa
    Ch: John C.   b 1882, 12, 11 d 1883, 8, 8
        bur Pennsville
        Mary E.   b 1885, 7, 24

1836, 6, 16. Joseph & w, Mary, & ch, Jeptha,
    Samuel & Joshua, rocf Stillwater MM, dtd
    1836,5,28
1837, 1, 19. Isaac & w, Martha, & ch, Deborah
    & Miriam, rocf Somerset MM, dtd 1836,11,28
1837, 5, 18. Henry & w, Martha, rocf Still-
    water MM, dtd 1837,4,22
1837, 5, 18. Martha Jr. rocf Stillwater MM,
    dtd 1837,4,22
1837, 5, 18. James rocf Stillwater MM, dtd
    1837,4,22
1837, 10, 19. Isaac & w, Martha, & ch, Deborah
    & Miriam, gct Somerset MM
1838, 4, 19. Henry & w, Matilda, & dt, Mary,
    rocf Short Creek MM, dtd 1837,10,24
1839, 5, 16. Martha Jr. gct Chesterfield MM
1839, 6, 13. Henry & w, Martha, gct Chester-
    field MM
1841, 12, 16. Mary P. gct Stillwater MM
1881, 9, 15. Jesse & w, Louisa P., & s, Wm.
    W., rocf Somerset MM, dtd 1881,6,23
1887, 3, 17. Jesse I. & w, Louisa P., & ch,
    Wm. W. & Mary E., gct Somerset MM

DRAKE
1832, 5, 17. Alse (form Healy) dis mcd

DUFF
1856, 1, 17. Elizabeth (form Dewees) dis mcd

EDGERTON
1852, 8, 26. John, s John & Zilpha, Morgan
    Co., O.; m in Hopewell, Martha EMBREE, dt
    Israel & Mary Ann, Morgan Co., O.

1837, 4, 15. Elizabeth m Albert LAMBERT

1835, 6, 18. John & w, Zilpha, & ch, Abigail,
    Elizabeth, James, Asenath, Richard, John &
    Sarah, rocf Stillwater MM, dtd 1835,4,25
1843, 1, 19. David rocf Somerset MM, dtd
    1842,10,24
1847, 10, 14. Jesse Dewees gct Somerset MM,
    to m Rebecca Edgerton
1853, 4, 19. Martha gct Chesterfield MM
1865, 8, 17. John Vernon gct Chesterfield
    MM, to m Elizabeth Edgerton

EDMONSON
----, --, --. Jonathan & Phebe
    Ch: Eli   b 1858, 6, 12
        Ruth   " 1860, 11, 4
        Louis   " 1863, 4, 13
1863, 6, 18. Franklin [Edmundson], s John &
    Ruth, b

EMBREE
----, --, --. Samuel & Hannah
    Ch: Lydia   b 1797, 2, 28
        Joseph   " 1798, 11, 25
        Phebe   " 1801, 5, 1
        John   " 1803, 8, 1
        James   " 1805, 9, 1
        Jesse   " 1808, 3, 2
        Israel   " 1810, 4, 17
        Isaac   " 1814, 3, 8
        Samuel   " 1816, 5, 15
----, --, --. Joseph & Rebeckah
    Ch: Maria   b 1825, 1, 20
        Matilda   " 1827, 8, 4 d 1847, 4,17
        Pearson   " 1829, 4, 23
        Eza (sic) " 1833, 9, 17
    Joseph m 2nd Achsah -----
    Ch: David   b 1848, 9, 9
1830, 4, 6. Wm., s John & Avy, b
1832, 8, 4. Ava d ae 30 bur Deerfield
----, --, --. Israel & Mary Ann
    Ch: Martha   b 1834, 11, 8
        Lindley H. " 1835, 11, 11
        Jephtha   " 1838, 2, 5
        Robert   " 1839, 7, 16
        Deborah   " 1840, 12, 26
        Samuel   " 1842, 9, 13
        Hannah   " 1844, 8, 4
        Eliza   " 1846, 4, 30
        Caroline   " 1849, 1, 1
        Merrick   " 1851, 2, 12
        Israel   " 1853, 3, 16
        Jesse   " 1855, 3, 14
        Mary Ellen " 1857, 7, 19 d 1859, 2, 9
        bur Hopewell
1836, 4, 20. James, s Samuel & Hannah, Morgan
    Co., O.; m in Pennsville, Grace T. WORTH-
    INGTON, dt Zenas & Ann
    Ch: Rebecca   b 1837, 1, 22
        Barclay   " 1838, 12, 16
        Reuben   " 1841, 7, 4 d 1856, 3,25
        bur Hopewell

EMBREE, continued
1837, 10, 15. Samuel d ae 65 bur Pennsville
1838, 3, 21. John, s Samuel & Hannah, Washington Co., O.; m in Pennsville, Hannah GREY, dt Robert & Mary WOOD, Morgan Co., O.
1845, 6, 1. James d ae 39 bur Hopewell
1845, 7, 12. Rebecca d ae 47 bur Hopewell
1846, 1, 11. Hannah d ae 72
1847, 6, 24. Grace T. m Samuel KING
1850, 11, 20. Samuel, s Samuel & Hannah, Morgan Co., O.; m in Pennsville, Sarah Ann SCOTT, dt John & Deborah, Morgan Co., O.
1851, 7, 10. Sarah Ann d ae 45 bur Pennsville
1852, 1, 22. Maria m Wm. DEWEES
1852, 8, 26. Martha m John EDGERTON
1871, 11, 2. Jesse d ae 63 bur Pennsville
1873, 5, 5. Hannah d ae 28 bur Hopewell

1829, 5, 14. John gct Somerset MM, to m Ava Morris
1829, 10, 15. Ava rocf Somerset MM, dtd 1829, 7,27
1832, 6, 14. James gct Cincinnati MM
1833, 5, 16. Israel gct Stillwater MM
1834, 2, 13. Israel & w, Mary Ann, rocf Stillwater MM, dtd 1834,1,25
1834, 4, 17. Isaac dis disunity
1834, 9, 18. James rocf Cincinnati MM, dtd 1834,7,17
1835, 10, 15. Jesse dis mcd
1836, 4, 14. Mary (form Dennis) dis mcd
1838, 5, 17. Wm., minor s John, gct Chesterfield MM
1838, 6, 14. Elizabeth (form Worthington) dis mcd
1838, 6, 14. Hannah Jr. & ch gct Chesterfield MM
1846, 1, 15. Wm., minor, rocf Chesterfield MM, dtd 1845,12,20
1847, 11, 18. Joseph gct Chesterfield MM, to m Achsah Bundy
1848, 2, 17. Achsah & s, Joel Bundy, rocf Chesterfield MM, dtd 1848,1,15
1850, 9, 19. Wm. dis jas
1852, 12, 16. Samuel gct Smithfield MM
1853, 8, 18. Samuel rocf Smithfield MM, dtd 1853,7,18
1853, 9, 15. Joseph & w, Achsah, & ch, Ezra Embree, Joel Bundy & David Embree, gct Red Cedar MM, Ia.
1860, 1, 19. Deborah Lambert (form Embree) dis mcd
1862, 3, 13. Barclay dis disunity
1863, 1, 15. Lindley con mcd
1864, 9, 15. Rebecca dis
1866, 9, 13. Israel dis jG
1866, 9, 13. Mary Ann dis jG
1868, 4, 16. Samuel gct Springville MM, Ia.
1868, 12, 17. Jeptha dis mcd
1868, 12, 17. Robert dis mcd
1869, 4, 15. Mary rst
1869, 4, 15. Jesse rst
1870, 2, 17. Samuel dis mcd & jG

1870, 7, 14. Rebecca rst
1870, 10, 13. Ella, dt Rebecca, recrq
1873, 8, 14. Caroline Shields (form Embree) dis mcd
1874, 12, 14. Samuel rst rq
1875, 6, 17. Rachel Norton (form Embree) dis mcd
1877, 5, 17. Lindley H. dis mcd
1877, 5, 17. Samuel gct Springville MM, Ia.
1879, 11, 13. Samuel rocf Chesterfield MM, dtd 1879,10,18
1881, 11, 24. Israel W. dis mcd
1890, 8, 14. Mary Ann rst at Chesterfield MM on consent of this mtg

EMMONS
1853, 3, 27. Elizabeth D., dt Micajah & Delitha, b

1837, 10, 19. Thomas Sr. & w, Mary, & ch, Elmira & Albert, rocf Sandy Spring MM, dtd 1837,7,21
1853, 1, 13. Micajah & w, Deletha, & s, Harry D., rocf Plymouth MM, dtd 1853,12, 20
1853, 9, 15. Micajah & w, Delitha, & ch, Harvey D. & Elizabeth, gct Plymouth MM

ENGLE
1837, 11, 22. John, s Caleb & Mercy, Athens Co., O.; m in Pennsville, Elizabeth THOMAS, dt Jesse & Rebecca, Morgan Co., O.

1834, 2, 13. Caleb & w, Sarah, & ch, Richard & John, rocf Stillwater MM, dtd 1834,1,25
1837, 4, 13. John & ch, Maria, Sarah & Ephraim, rocf Stillwater MM, dtd 1837,1,28
1838, 7, 19. John & w, Elizabeth, & ch, Mariah, Sarah B. & Ephraim W., gct Chesterfield MM

EVANS
1835, 7, 16. Amos, Sarah, Henrietta, Asher, Parker & William Jones, minor ch Evan & Mary, rocf Short Creek MM, dtd 1835,2,24
1836, 6, 16. Sarah dis jas
1838, 4, 19. Henrietta dis disunity
1838, 4, 19. Amos H. dis disunity
1841, 4, 15. John & Mary Ellen, ch Thomas, rocf Exeter MM, Pa., dtd 1840,11,25
1847, 2, 18. Wm. dis jas
1847, 4, 15. Asher P. dis jas
1850, 4, 18. John dis jas
1851, 11, 13. Mary Ellen Rose (form Evans) dis mcd

EVES
1837, 3, 16. Ruthanna, Susan & John, ch James & Susanna, rocf Somerset MM, dtd 1837,1,30
1848, 8, 17. Ruthanna Brady (form Eaves) dis mcd & jas
1848, 10, 19. Susan Hampton (form Eaves) dis

EVES, continued
  mcd

FARMER
1829, 4, 16. Naylor & w, Isabela, rocf Short
  Creek MM, dtd 1829,2,24
1830, 10, 14. Dearman Williams gct Sandy
  Spring MM, to m Mary Farmer
1860, 10, 20. Abel Gilbert gct Somerset MM, to
  m Armelia Farmer

FAWCETT
1838, 10, 24. Samuel, s Richard & Mary, Belmont Co., O.; m in Pennsville, Mary Ann
  HARMER, dt Amos & Elizabeth, Morgan Co.,O.
1877, 9, 19. Samuel, s Richard & Mary, Cedar
  Co., Ia.; m in Pennsville, Patience Gifford, dt Marvin & Abigail, Morgan Co., O.
1887, 9, 21. Samuel d ae 70 bur Pennsville

1835, 1, 15. Jonathan & w, Rebecca, & ch,
  Eli, Martha W., Armela, Sarah, Susannah &
  Maria, rocf Flushing MM, dtd 1834,12,25
1836, 1, 14. Jesse rocf Flushing MM, dtd 1835,
  10,22
1839, 2, 14. Mary Ann gct Stillwater MM
1838, 12, 13. Austin Simson gct Stillwater MM,
  to m Sibilay Fawcett
1878, 1, 17. Samuel rocf Hickory Grove MM,
  Ia., dtd 1877,12,1

FISHER
1836, 12, 3. Wm. & Sarah, minors, rocf Stillwater MM, O., dtd 1836,11,26

FOULKE
----, --, --. William & Eliza
  Ch: Lewis W. b 1830, 7, 23 d 1854, 11, 1
    bur Pennsville
    Mary   b 1832, 2, 25
    Sarah   " 1834, 2, 26 d 1834, 7,26
    bur Deerfield
    Martha   b 1834, 2, 26 " 1834, 7,16
    bur Deerfield
    Hannah   b 1835, 10, 25
    Jesse   " 1838, 7, 13
    Elizabeth " 1838, 7, 13 " 1840, 5,19
    William   " 1843, 1, 2
    Ann   " 1847, 9, 7
1837, 1, 23. Jesse R. d ae 25 bur Short Creek
1852, 9, 22. Mary m David SMITH
1860, 5, 2. William d ae 55 bur Pennsville
1866, 5, 30. Wm., s William & Eliza, Morgan
  Co., O.; m in Pennsville, Margaret Jane
  DEWEES, dt Aaron P. & Mary, Morgan Co.,O.
  Ch: Lucius W. b 1870, 11, 10 d 1871, 5, 7
    Edith W. "-1872, 8, 2
    Anne Elsie " 1882, 7, 16
    Robert W. " 1887, 4, 30
1868, 9, 15. Eliza d ae 62 bur Pennsville

1829, 11, 19. Eliza rocf Flushing MM, dtd
  1829,10,22

1832, 9, 13. Jesse R. rocf Flushing MM, dtd
  1832,6,21
1841, 10, 14. Joshua, Milton, Phebe & Mary, ch
  Thomas & Sarah, rocf Stillwater MM, dtd
  1841,9,25
1842, 12, 15. Joshua dis jas
1842, 12, 15. Milton dis jas
1844, 7, 18. Phebe dis jas
1844, 12, 19. Sarah rocf Short Creek MM, dtd
  1842,12,20, end by Alum Creek MM, 1844,10,
  24
1845, 6, 19. Sarah gct Alum Creek MM
1862, 12, 18. Hannah Smith (form Foulke) con
  mcd
1870, 8, 18. Jesse R. dis disunity
1881, 3, 17. Wm. dis disunity

FOWLER
1832, 12, 13. Theodate (form Todd) dis mcd

FRENCH
----, --, --. William & Mary
  Ch: Eli   b 1824, 10, --
    Otho   " 1827, --, --

1827, 6, 16. Mary & s, Eli, rocf Stillwater
  MM, dtd 1827,4,28
1829, 4, 16. Mary dis jas

GAMBLE
1842, 10, 19. Harrison P., s Samuel & Jane,
  Columbiana Co., O.; m in Pennsville, Phebe
  HOLLINGSWORTH, dt Elisha & Sarah, Morgan
  Co., O.

1843, 11, 16. Phebe gct Middleton MM

GARRETSON
----, --, --. Joel & Elizabeth
  Ch: William b 1829, 3, 18
    Sarah   " 1831, 4, 1
    Ruthanna " 1833, 4, 26
    John   " 1835, 4, 6
    Richard " 1837, 12, 9
1836, 8, 24. Anna m Abel GILBERT
1845, 6, 10. Beulah d ae 49 bur Pennsville

1830, 5, 13. Joel & w, Elizabeth, & s, Wm.,
  rocf Stillwater MM, dtd 1830,4,24
1835, 9, 17. Beulah & ch, Eliza, Emily, Daniel & Eli, rocf Smithfield MM, dtd 1835,
  5,18
1836, 4, 14. Anna rocf Stillwater MM, dtd
  1836,3,26
1839, 7, 18. Joel & w, Elizabeth, & ch, Wm.,
  Sarah, Ruthanna, John & Richard, gct
  Chesterfield MM
1848, 4, 13. David & Eli, ch Isaac & Beulah,
  gct Chesterfield MM
1848, 4, 13. Eliza gct Chesterfield MM
1848, 4, 13. Emily gct Chesterfield MM

GIBBONS

1869, 10, 16. James, s Homer & Martha, Bel-
        mont Co., O.; m in Pennsville, Lydia
        WORTHINGTON, dt Elisha & Sarah HOLLINGS-
        WORTH, Morgan Co., O.

1871, 6, 15. Lydia & ch, Zenas, Rheuben, Sa-
        rah Ann & Mary J. Worthington, gct Somer-
        set MM

GIFFORD

----, --, --. Alexander & Isabella
        Ch: Abel
            Michael
            Patience   b 1825, 12, 28
            Catharine   " 1827, 6, 20
            Hannah   " 1829, 2, 13
            Alexander M. 1830, 11, 20
            Levi   b 1832, 9, 13
----, --, --. Marvin d 1867,4,21 ae 77 bur
        Pennsville; m Abigail ----- d 1845,5,30
        ae 48 bur Pennsville
        Ch: Phariba   b 1824, 8, 16
            Levi   " 1826, 7, 31 d 1833, 3,12
                bur Deerfield
            Patience   b 1828, 6, 26
            Abigail Jr. " 1831, 1, 16 " 1857, 3,27
                bur Pennsville
            Jesse   b 1834, 3, 12
            Abraham   " 1835, 12, 30
            Temperance " 1838, 6, 28
            Clarkson   " 1834, 9, 6 d 1845, 9, 5
                bur Pennsville
1834, 1, 24. Levi d
1838, 2, 21. Emlen, s William & Sarah, Wash-
        ington Co., O.; m in Pennsville, Sarah Ann
        PENROSE, dt Thomas & Sarah, Morgan Co., O.
1877, 9, 19. Patience m Samuel FAWCETT

1828, 1, 19. Owen dis mcd
1833, 1, 17. Alexander M. dis jas
1833, 8, 15. Rebecca (form Worrell) dis mcd
1842, 3, 17. Abel, Michael K., Patience,
        Catharine, Hannah & Alexander M., gct
        White River MM, Ind.
1846, 5, 14. Phariby Darnel (form Gifford)
        con mcd
1861, 5, 16. Jesse dis mcd

GILBERT

----, --, --. Abel & Rebecca
        Ch: Ruth   b 1807, 10, 21
            Achsah   " 1809, 6, 26
            Rachel   " 1811, 12, 23
            Mary   " 1814, 5, 27
            Joel   " 1816, 10, 7
            Daniel Wm. " 1819, 8, 16
            Eli   " 1822, 10, 17
            Elizabeth   " 1826, 4, 21
            William H. " 1828, 2, 28
1828, 2, 28. Rebecca d ae 42 bur Deerfield
1828, 6, 15. Wm. H., infant, d bur Deerfield
1833, 1, 29. Elizabeth d ae 84 bur Deerfield

1831, 8, 24. Rachel m Wm. HARMER
----, --, --. Thomas & Edith
        Ch: Mary S.   b 1837, 5, 23
            Elizabeth
            H.   " 1840, 6, 20
1836, 8, 24. Abel, s Joel & Elizabeth, Mor-
        gan Co., O.; m in Pennsville, Anna GARRET-
        SON, dt John & Henrietta, Monroe Co., O.
        Ch: Rebecca   b 1837, 6, 17
            Abel Jr.   " 1839, 9, 5
1836, 12, 7. Achsah m David BUNDY
1838, 6, 20. Joel, s Abel & Rebecca, Morgan
        Co., O.; m in Pennsville, Elizabeth
        SMITH, dt Thomas & Mary, Morgan Co., O.
1838, 8, 22. Mary m Joseph PENROSE
1839, 2, 15. Joel d ae 92
1840, 8, 6. Daniel W. d ae 20 bur Pennsville
1871, 6, 21. Daniel W., s Joel & Elizabeth,
        Morgan Co., O.; m in Hopewell, Mary S.
        KING, dt Samuel & Grace T., Morgan Co.,O.
        Ch: Edgar K.   b 1872, 5, 10
            William J. " 1874, 8, 28
1890, 4, 18. Joel d ae 72 bur Pennsville

1829, 7, 16. Sarah dis jH
1831, 2, 17. Ruth Kirby (form Gilbert) dis
        mcd
1838, 9, 13. Thomas & fam rocf Short Creek
        MM, dtd 1833,5,22
1840, 12, 17. Abel & w, Anna, & ch, Eli,
        Elizabeth, Rebecca & Abel, gct Chester-
        field MM
1841, 7, 15. Joel & w, Elizabeth, & ch,
        Cynthia Ann & Rebecca, gct Chesterfield
        MM
1845, 9, 18. Thomas & w, Edith, & ch, Jona-
        than, Daniel A., Mary S., Elizabeth H. &
        Sarah Ann, gct Chesterfield MM
1851, 2, 13. Elizabeth R. rocf Chesterfield
        MM, dtd 1851,1,18
1857, 12, 19. Amos Ball gct Plymouth MM, to m
        Cynthia Ann Gilbert
1858, 2, 18. Abel, minor, rocf Somerset MM,
        dtd 1857,12,28
1860, 10, 20. Abel gct Somerset MM, to m Ar-
        melia Farmer
1861, 8, 15. Abel gct Plymouth MM
1861, 9, 19. Barclay Penrose gct Plymouth
        MM, to m Mary P. Gilbert
1871, 5, 18. Daniel W. rocf Plymouth MM, dtd
        1871,4,17
1871, 5, 18. Charles E. rocf Plymouth MM,
        dtd 1871,4,17
1873, 8, 14. Elizabeth S. rocf Plymouth MM,
        dtd 1873,7,21
1879, 3, 13. Charles dis mcd
1880, 6, 17. Sarah Ann (form King) dis mcd
1887, 5, 19. Joel rst on consent of Plymouth
        MM

GOODING

1833, 3, 20. William, s James & Margaret,
        Morgan Co., O.; m in Deerfield, Susannah

GOODING, continued
    MORRIS, dt Wm. & Susannah, Morgan Co., O.
      Ch: Sarah   b 1833, 11, 27
          Susanna   " 1834, 12, 7
          Richard   " 1838, 2, 4
          Anna   " 1841, 1, 17
          William   " 1842, 5, 18
          James   " 1844, 1, 12 d 1844, 8, 8
            bur Hopewell
          Joseph   b 1845, 6, 28
          Isaac   " 1847, 5, 29
          George   " 1850, 2, 5
          Ruth   " 1852, 4, 27
          Mahlon   " 1855, 6, 6 d 1855, 7,11
            bur Hopewell
1883, 2, 2. Wm. d ae 78 bur Pennsville
1893, 11, 12. Susanna d ae 80 bur Pennsville

1833, 2, 3. Wm. rocf Short Creek MM, dtd
    1832,12,18
1866, 9, 13. Joseph dis military service &
    jas
1868, 7, 16. Richard con mcd
1874, 9, 17. Richard gct Plymouth MM
1874, 9, 17. Richard gct Plymouth MM
1875, 8, 2. Isaac dis mcd & jas
1877, 9, 13. George dis disunity
1892, 2, 18. Richard rocf Plymouth MM

GREEN
1831, 1, 7. Rebecca d ae 40

1829, 8, 13. Rebecca (form Lawton) con mcd

GREGG
----, --, --. Caleb & Millicent
    Ch: Daniel   b 1834, 6, 14
        Elwood   " 1837, 2, 6
        Emer   " 1839, 4, 16
        Hannah   " 1841, 6, 26
        Caleb   " 1843, 8, 10
        Mary   " 1845, 9, 1
        Sarah M. " 1849, 8, 14
        Joseph   " 1852, 1, 15
1854, 7, 27. Mary d ae 86
1851, 9, 25. Martha m Daniel WILSON

1834, 2, 13. Caleb & w, Milicent, & ch, Hen-
    ry, Martha & Elijah W., rocf Stillwater
    MM, dtd 1834,1,25
1844, 1, 18. Mary rocf Plainfield MM, dtd
    1843,11,22
1850, 11, 14. Henry dis mcd
1853, 4, 19. Caleb & w, Milicent, & ch, Da-
    vid, Elwood, Emmer, Hannah, Caleb, Mary,
    Sarah M. & Joseph, gct Pleasant Plain MM,
    Ia.
1853, 4, 19. Elijah W. gct Pleasant Plain
    MM, Ia.

GRENAWAUGH
1869, 7, 15. Rachel (form Kirby) dis mcd

GREY
1838, 3, 21. Hannah m John EMBREE

1837, 6, 15. Hannah & ch, Mary, Elijah,
    Lemuel, Samuel & Jesse, rocf Short Creek
    MM, dtd 1837,4,18
1839, 12, 19. Martha Ann (form Lewis) dis mcd

GRIFFITH
----, --, --. Eli & Rachel
    Ch: Wm. Patten b 1819, 5, 16
        Collins   " 1825, 7, 14
        Benajah   " 1831, 7, 15 d 1831, 7,20
          bur Deerfield
1821, 12, 25. Vialetta L., dt Abraham & Mary,
    b
1838, 8, 22. Milton, s William & Sarah, Mor-
    gan Co., O.; m in Pennsville, Eleanor
    KIRBY, dt Thomas & Rebecca, Washington
    Co., O.
    Ch: Thomas   b 1839, 7, 6
        Samuel C.   " 1841, 1, 24
        Sarah Re-
          becca   " 1843, 1, 17 d 1845, 3,11
          bur Pennsville
        Addison   b 1844, 8, 12
        Theodore   " 1848, 11, 9
1845, 8, 20. Sarah Ann m Elisha HOLLINGSWORTH

1829, 6, 18. Newton, minor, rocf Short Creek
    MM, dtd 1829,4,21
1829, 6, 18. Elma, minor, rocf Short Creek
    MM, dtd 1829,3,24
1832, 9, 13. Abraham dis
1832, 9, 13. Mary dis
1834, 9, 18. Milton rocf Providence MM, Pa.,
    dtd 1834,8,28
1836, 12, 3. Charles, minor, rocf Short Creek
    MM, dtd 1836,10,18
1838, 6, 14. Charles, minor, gct Plainfield
    MM
1838, 10, 18. Sarah Ann gct Chesterhill MM
1843, 6, 15. Milton dis disunity
1844, 7, 18. Violetta King (form Griffith)
    dis mcd
1845, 7, 17. Sarah Ann & s, Edwin, rocf Ches-
    terfield MM, dtd 1845,5,7
1849, 2, 15. Milton dis disunity
1872, 12, 19. Edwin gct Plymouth MM
1882, 12, 14. Edwin rocf Plymouth MM, dtd
    1882,10,23

GRIMES
1828, 6, 21. Hannah rocf Stillwater MM, dtd
    1828,3,22
1830, 2, 18. Hannah dis jH

GRIST
1863, 3, 19. Deborah Jane (form Plummer) con
    mcd

HAINES
----, --, --. Isaac & Lydia

HAINES, continued
    Ch: Smith   b 1805, 4, 12
        Davis   " 1806, 8, 11
        Samuel   " 1808, 2, 20
        Milton   " 1810, 5, 22
        Hannah   " 1811, 10, 8
        Lydia Ann " 1813, 7, 8
        Mary   " 1815, 2, 6

1832, 11, 15. Smith dis mcd
1834, 7, 17. Samuel dis mcd
1839, 6, 13. Isaac & w, Lydia, gct Chester-
    field MM
1839, 6, 13. Mary gct Chesterfield MM
1839, 12, 19. Lydia Bowers (form Haines) dis
    mcd
1840, 5, 14. Hannah gct Chesterfield MM
1841, 10, 14. Milton dis mcd

HALIMAN
1856, 2, 14. Sarah Elizabeth (form Penrose)
    dis mcd

HALL
1838, 4, 19. Elisha, minor s Moses, rocf
    Somerset MM, dtd 1838,3,26
1838, 4, 19. Joseph rocf Somerset MM, dtd
    1838,3,26
1848, 10, 19. Joseph dis mcd & jH
1854, 7, 13. Elizabeth (form Millhouse) dis
    mcd
1866, 1, 18. Rebecca (form Richardson) dis
    mcd
1871, 9, 14. Thomas Dewees gct Short Creek
    MM, to m Martha W. Hall
1883, 3, 15. Jesse Dewees gct Stillwater MM,
    to m Miriam P. Hall
1893, 5, 18. Rebecca W. (form Richardson) rst
    rq

HAMBLETON
1827, 11, 17. Rachel, w John, rocf Little
    Brittain MM,Pa., dtd 1827,2,17, end by
    Stillwater MM, 1827,10,27
1829, 9, 17. Rachel dis jH

HAMMITT
1837, 4, 13. Ellen rocf Marlborough MM, 1836,
    11,29

HAMMOND
1843, 11, 22. Joseph, s John & Rachel, Jeffer-
    son Co., O.; m in Pennsville, Harriet
    PIDGEON, dt Amos & Ann, Morgan Co., O.

1844, 5, 16. Harriet gct Smithfield MM
1850, 4, 18. James C. rocf Short Creek MM,
    dtd 1850,3,19
1854, 4, 13. James gct White Water MM, Ind.

HAMPTON
----, --, --. Thomas & Hannah
    Ch: Cary

    Ch: Eunice
        Jason
        Amos   b 1826, 6, 6 d 1834, 1,22
        bur Blue Rock
----, --, --. Zachariah & Sarah
    Ch: William b 1826, 3, 14
        Ruth C.   " 1828, 1, 2
        Lydia   " 1830, 8, 14 d 1845, 6, 7
        Sarah G. " 1832, 5, 18
        Mary   " 1835, 2, 8
1827, 10, 24. Asa, s John & Mary, Muskingum
    Co., O.; m in Deerfield, Esther PATTERSON,
    dt Joseph & Mary
    Ch: Eli   b 1833, 5, 11
        James   " 1835, 1, 23
1828, 1, 24. Asenath m Wm. DOAN
1829, 12, 21. Bethula m Joseph ARNOLD
1829, 9, 23. Samuel B., s John & Mary, Mus-
    kingum Co., O.; m in Deerfield, Elizabeth
    PIERPONT, dt Jonathan & Ann, Morgan Co.,
    O.
    Ch: Ann P.   b 1830, 7, 1 d 1833, 2,28
        bur Deerfield
        Jonathan P.b 1832, 5, 31
        William S. " 1847, 2, 8
----, --, --. John & Mary
    Ch: Oliver b 1831, 3, 2
        Sarah   " 1832, 12, 2
        Robert   " 1835, 6, 13
1837, 7, 13. Mary d bur Pennsville

1829, 4, 16. Asa C. & w, Esther, & dt, Mar-
    tha, gct Somerset MM
1829, 12, 17. John Jr. gct Somerset MM
1830, 10, 14. John & w, Mary, & ch, Cary, gct
    Somerset MM
1830, 10, 14. Mary Ann gct Somerset MM
1833, 3, 14. Asa C. & w, Esther, & ch, Mar-
    tha, Joseph & Benjamin, rocf Somerset MM,
    dtd 1833,1,28
1834, 4, 17. Cary rocf Somerset MM, dtd 1834,
    3,24
1834, 6, 19. John & w, Mary, & ch, Olive &
    Sarah, rocf Somerset MM, dtd 1834,4,28
1835, 8, 13. John & w, Mary, & Levi Hampton,
    minor in their care, rocf Somerset MM,
    dtd 1835,7,27
1835, 8, 13. Cary dis
1838, 4, 19. Mary Ann gct Somerset MM
1838, 4, 19. John gct Somerset MM
1838, 6, 14. Levi, minor, gct Somerset MM
1840, 12, 17. John rocf Somerset MM, dtd
    1840,11,30
1847, 5, 13. Samuel B. & w, Elizabeth, & ch,
    Jonathan, Mary, Ann, Isaac & Richard, rocf
    Chesterfield MM, dtd 1847,2,20
1848, 10, 19. Susan (form Eaves) dis mcd
1849, 11, 15. James H. rocf Somerset MM, dtd
    1849,10,29
1851, 9, 18. Zachariah & w, Sarah, & dt,
    Mary Elma, gct Pleasant Plain MM, Ia.
1851, 9, 18. Samuel B. & w, Elizabeth, & ch,
    Jonathan P., Mary, Ann, Isaac, Richard B.

HAMPTON, continued
    & Wm. S., gct Pleasant Plain, Ia.
1851, 9, 18. Ruth gct Pleasant Plain MM, Ia.
1851, 9, 18. Sarah G. gct Pleasant Plain MM, Ia.
1851, 9, 18. Wm. gct Pleasant Plain MM, Ia.
1854, 4, 13. James Hiram rpd mcd

HANN
1842, 9, 15. Lydia (form Wood) dis mcd

HANSON
----, --, --. William & Joanna
    Ch: James   b 1842, 5, 28
        Elijah " 1844, 12, 9
        Malinda " 1847, 4, 8
        Isaac   " 1849, 9, 28

1845, 4, 17. Wm. & w, Joanna, & ch, James & Elijah, rocf Stillwater MM, dtd 1845,4,17
1859, 3, 17. Joanna & ch, James, Elijah, Malinda, Isaac, Cidney & William, gct Stillwater MM

HARLAN
1828, 4, 19. Hannah & ch, Gibbons, Samuel & Rebecca, gct Fallowfield MM, Pa.
1828, 4, 19. George W. gct Fallowfield MM, Pa.
1828, 4, 19. Humphrey M. gct Fallowfield MM, Pa.
1835, 7, 16. Samuel rocf Fallowfield JM, Pa., dtd 1835,4,10
1839, 11, 14. Samuel dis mcd

HARMER
----, --, --. Naylor d 1884,7,20 ae 79 bur Pennsville; m Isabella ----- d 1887,6,26 ae 80 bur Pennsville
    Ch: Elizabeth b 1829, 6, 6
        Chalkley " 1832, 9, 1
        Amos   " 1835, 3, 3
        Lydia Ann " 1837, 8, 22
        Edward T. " 1840, 3, 18
        Rebecca " 1842, 5, 8
        Martha M. " 1844, 12, 18
        George W. " 1848, 3, 15.
1831, 8, 24. Wm., s Amos & Elizabeth, Morgan Co., O.; m in Deerfield, Rachel GILBERT, dt Abel & Rebecca, Morgan Co., O.
    Ch: Elwood b 1832, 6, 20 d 1842, 1, 5 bur Pennsville
        Martha b 1834, 6, 7
        Daniel " 1836, 2, 20
        Lemuel " 1838, 9, 1
        Mary   " 1841, 12, 30
        Thomas " 1844, 4, 22
        Anna   " 1846, 7, 23

1835, 3, 1. Amos d ae 60 bur Pennsville
1836, 6, 27. Elwood d ae 20 bur Pennsville
1838, 10, 24. Mary Ann m Samuel Fawcett
1846, 2, 24. Elizabeth d ae 72

1850, 5, 16. George d ae 50
1854, 5, 24. Martha m Jason PENROSE
1859, 9, 4. Amos d ae 41 bur Pennsville
1870, 8, 31. Anna m James E. DEWEES
1892, 3, 16. William d ae 82 bur Pennsville
1900, 1, 19. Rachel d ae 88 bur Pennsville

1831, 6, 16. Wm. rocf Short Creek MM, dtd 1831,3,22
1834, 4, 17. Amos & w, Elizabeth, & ch, Elwood & Amos R., rocf Short Creek MM, dtd 1834,2,18
1834, 4, 17. George rocf Short Creek MM, dtd 1834,3,18
1834, 4, 17. Mary Ann rocf Short Creek MM, dtd 1834,2,18
1854, 5, 18. Chalkley dis mcd
1864, 11, 17. Lydia dis jas
1864, 11, 17. Martha dis jas
1864, 11, 17. Mary Clendenon (form Harmer) con mcd
1864, 11, 17. Amos dis mcd
1867, 2, 14. George dis jas
1867, 5, 16. Rebecca Harris (form Harmer) dis mcd
1867, 7, 18. Elizabeth dis jas
1868, 12, 17. Thomas dis mcd
1884, 7, 17. Lemuel J. dis disunity

HARRIS
1832, 5, 17. Sarah d ae 79 bur Deerfield
1846, 9, 5. Wm. D., s Jurdan & Mary L., b

1829, 1, 10. Richard Kenny gct Short Creek MM, to m Susanna Harris
1830, 8, 19. Sarah rocf Stillwater MM, dtd 1830,6,26
1832, 12, 13. Richard & w, Beulah, & ch, Jonathan, Sidney, Jordan P., Eli & Thomas, rocf Short Creek MM, dtd 1832,11,20
1833, 12, 19. Jonathan dis disunity
1835, 7, 16. Wm. rocf Short Creek MM, dtd 1835,3,24
1835, 7, 16. Sidney Balderson (form Harris) dis mcd
1835, 8, 13. Watson dis mcd
1836, 11, 17. Beula Emily (form Dewees) dis mcd
1843, 11, 16. Eli dis mcd
1846, 1, 15. Jordan con mcd
1846, 1, 15. Mary L. (form Dewees) con mcd
1846, 5, 14. Richard & w, Beulah, gct Chesterfield MM
1847, 4, 15. Mary L. dis disunity
1847, 5, 13. Jordan dis disunity
1848, 4, 13. Thomas dis mcd
1867, 5, 16. Rebecca (form Harmer) dis mcd

HARRY
1827, 6, 16. Wm. & w, Hannah, & ch, John, Rebecca, Absalom & Mary, rocf Stillwater MM, dtd 1827,5,26
1830, 8, 19. Wm. dis disunity

HARRY, continued
1832, 1, 19. John dis JH
1838, 9, 13. Rebecca dis disunity
1840, 11, 19. Mary Chany (form Harry) dis mcd
1848, 9, 14. Absalom dis

HEALD
1863, 12, 11. Sina S. d ae 59 bur Coal Creek,
     Ia.

1837, 2, 16. Lydia & ch, Samuel Lusina &
     Luiza, rocf Upper Springfield MM, dtd
     1837,1,28
1845, 9, 18. Edwin Hollingsworth gct Carmel
     MM, to m Betsey Heald
1862, 2, 13. Sina & ch, Sina Ellen & Wm.,
     rocf Middleton MM, dtd 1862,1,18
1862, 2, 13. Henry rocf Middleton MM, dtd
     1862,1,18
1863, 3, 19. Sina Ellen Cooper (form Heald)
     con mcd

HEALY
1835, 8, 9. Mary P. [Heeley] d

1828, 8, 14. Thomas dis disunity
1828, 12, 18. Sarah dis JH
1829, 5, 14. Lydia dis JH
1831, 4, 14. Wm. P. [Healey] dis JH
1832, 5, 17. Alse Drake (form Healy) dis mcd
1832, 6, 14. Hannah Picket (form Healy) dis
     mcd
1835, 11, 19. Mary P. rocf Collins MM, dtd
     1834,6,20

HIATT
----, --, --. Elijah & Anna
     Ch: Demsey   b 1826, 11, 12
         Jehu   " 1828, 12, 2
         Tamer   " 1834, 11, 30

1834, 6, 19. Elijah & w, Anna, & ch, Dempsey,
     Jehu & Joseph, rocf Milford MM, Ind., dtd
     1834,3,22
1837, 4, 13. Jesse & w, Ruthanna, & ch, Mary,
     Rachel, Elijah, rocf Clear Creek MM, dtd
     1837,2,21
1837, 4, 13. Susanna rocf Clear Creek MM, dtd
     1837,2,21
1837, 4, 13. Jehu & Tamer rocf Clear Creek
     MM, dtd 1837,2,21
1837, 11, 16. Cert rec for Jonathan & w,.Mary,
     & ch, Elisha, Lewis, Wm. & Martha, from
     Clear Creek MM, dtd 1837,9,19, end to
     Chesterfield MM

HICKERSON
1882, 7, 13. Lydia Jane (form King) dis mcd

HODGIN
1852, 3, 24. Stephen, s Eli & Mary, Belmont
     Co., O.; m in Pennsville, Sarah MILHOUSE,
     dt Daniel & Esther, Morgan Co., O.

Ch: Clarkson b 1853, 3, 20
    Wilson   " 1855, 10, 5
    Charles   " 1---, --, --

1827, 5, 19. John [Hodgen] dis disunity
1829, 3, 19. Prudence & ch, Nancy, William,
     Leah, Elias, Frances & Edwin C., gct
     Stillwater MM
1852, 8, 19. Sarah M. [Hodgins] gct Still-
     water MM
1853, 9, 15. Stephen & w, Sarah, & s, Clark-
     son, rocf Stillwater MM, dtd 1853,8,27
1859, 10, 13. Stephen & w, Sarah, & ch, Clark-
     son, Wilson & Charles, gct Plymouth MM

HOLOWAY
1861, 12, 31. Francis Elmer, s David & Ann, b

HOLCOMB
1889, 4, 18. Rachel (form Penrose) dis mcd &
     jas

HOLLINGSWORTH
1838, 2, 11. Anne, dt Elisha & Sarah, b
1839, 10, 21. Sarah d ae 37 bur Pennsville
     (a minister)
1842, 10, 19. Phebe m Harrison P. GAMBLER
1844, 9, 25. Ruth m Abraham PATTEN
1845, 8, 20. Elisha, s Phebe, Morgan Co., O.;
     m in Pennsville, Sarah Ann GRIFFITH, dt
     Thomas & Sarah PENROSE, Morgan Co., O.
     Ch: Emmor   b 1846, 10, 4
1847, 1, 20. Martha m Thos. LLEWELYN
----, --, --. Edwin & Betsey
     Ch: Joseph   b 1848, 5, 24 d 1863, 5,14
         bur Pennsville
         Sarah   b 1852, 2, 19
         Peninah   " 1854, 9, 13
1860, 10, 10. Luella, dt Louis & Hannah C., b
----, --, --. Emmor & Sarah
     Ch: Charles B. b 1868, 12, 19
         Grace E.   " 1881, 9, 30
1869, 8, 22. Elisha d ae 70 (an elder)
1869, 8, 27. Elisha d ae 70 bur Pennsville
1871, 1, 3. Sarah Ann d ae 57 bur Pennsville

1837, 6, 15. Elisha & w, Sarah, & ch, Edwin,
     Ruth, Phebe, Er, Martha, Wm., Lydia & Ezra
     rocf Middleton MM, dtd 1837,5,11
1845, 9, 18. Edwin gct Carmel MM, to m Betsey
     Heald
1846, 4, 16. Edwin gct Chesterfield MM
1848, 3, 16. Er dis mcd
1848, 6, 15. Edwin & w, Betsy, & dt, Ury,
     rocf Chesterfield MM, dtd 1848,3,18
1857, 1, 15. Edwin & w, Betsey, & ch, Ury,
     Sarah & Peninah, gct Plymouth MM
1857, 3, 19. Wm. gct Stillwater MM
1862, 12, 18. Anna Vaughn (form Hollingsworth)
     dis mcd
1867, 4, 18. Ezra dis mcd & military service
1867, 4, 18. Lydia Ann (form Plummer) con
     mcd

HOLLINGSWORTH, continued
1868, 6, 18. Emmor con mcd
1874, 9, 17. Emmor & w, Sarah, gct Plymouth
    MM
1883, 3, 15. Emmor & w, Sarah, & ch, Charles
    Daniel, Cynthia May & Grace Elizabeth, rocf
    Plymouth MM, dtd 1883,2,19
1888, 5, 17. Sarah dis jas
1888, 8, 16. Emmor dis jas
1896, 5, 14. Cynthia May dis jas
1896, 11, 19. Charles Daniel dis mcd

HOOPS
----, --, --. James & Elizabeth
    Ch: Sarahann   b 1822, 3, 5
        Nathan   " 1824, 3, 11
        John G.   " 1826, 11, 13
        Elizabeth " 1829, 4, 4
        Priscilla
        Thomas

1830, 3, 18. Elizabeth [Hoopes] Jr. & ch,
    Sarah Ann, Nathan, John & Elizabeth, rocf
    Short Creek MM, dtd 1830,2,28
1848, 7, 13. Mercy (form King) dis mcd & JH

HUESTIS
1837, 7, 13. Isaac rocf Carmel MM, dtd 1837,
    6,17
1877, 9, 13. Nathan Dewees gct Chesterfield
    MM, to m Rebecca Huestis

HUNNICUTT
1846, 4, 16. Cert rec for Wm. P. & w, Edna,
    & ch, Burwell & Margaret, from Dover MM,
    O., dtd 1846,3,19, end to Chesterfield MM

INGRAM
----, --, --. Robert & Hannah
    Ch: Harlan
        Mary
        Martha
        Ann

1831, 2, 17. Robert & Hannah dis disunity

ISRAEL
1846, 1, 15. Hannah (form Kirby) con mcd
1863, 5, 14. Hannah dis jG

JOHN
1836, 11, 17. Ann rocf Somerset MM, dtd 1836,
    10,24

JONES
1851, 2, 13. Elizabeth (form Stephens) dis
    mcd

KENNARD
----, --, --. Joseph & Hannah
    Ch: Joseph
        Walton   b 1826 (or 27)
        David   " 1829

1828, --, --. Joseph d
1833, 11, 8. Tacy d

1827, 9, 15. Catharine & dt, Elizabeth, rocf
    Short Creek MM, dtd 1827,7,24
1828, 2, 16. Elizabeth McVay (form Kennard)
    dis mcd
1829, 10, 15. Hannah dis jH
1830, 7, 15. Mary [Kenard], minor, gct
    Somerset MM
1831, 4, 14. Catherine dis jH
1832, 6, 14. Eli, minor, gct Somerset MM
1833, 10, 17. Catharine Bingham (form Kennard)
    dis mcd
1834, 8, 14. Esther Kinsey (form Kennard)
    dis mcd
1842, 7, 14. Eli, minor, rocf Somerset MM,
    dtd 1842,5,30
1845, 2, 13. Eli [Kenard] dis mcd
1848, 11, 16. Joseph dis mcd
1848, 11, 16. Wm. dis jH

KENNY
1855, 3, 24. Richard d ae 77 bur Pennsville
1856, 3, 3. Susanna d ae 73 bur Pennsville

1829, 1, 10. Richard gct Short Creek MM, to
    m Susanna Harris
1829, 7, 16. Richard gct Short Creek MM
1830, 8, 19. Richard & w, Susanna, rocf
    Stillwater MM, dtd 1830,6,26
1839, 10, 17. Richard & w, Susanna, gct Still-
    water MM
1840, 6, 18. Richard & w, Susanna, rocf
    Stillwater MM, dtd 1840,5,23

KING
----, --, --. Joseph & Mary
    Ch: Michael   b 1819, 9, 10
        Samuel   " 1821, 3, 29 d 1893,12, 7
            bur Hopewell
        William   b 1823, 3, 9
        Hannah   " 1825, 5, 27
        Ruth   " 1827, 11, 16
----, --, --. Samuel & Content
    Ch: Ann   b 1822, 8, 12 d 1834,11,11
            bur Deerfield
        Obed   b 1824, 12, 1
        Robert   " 1828, 5, 5
        Ezra   " 1832, 3, 3
        Rebecca   " 1835, 6, 29
        William   " 1838, 11, 19
        Deborah   " 1842, 8, 10
1826, --, --. Lewis, s James & Rebecca, b
----, --, --. Joseph & Mary
    Ch: Sarah   b 1838, 4, 2
        Mariam   " 1840, 6, 5
        Eliza   " 1842, 11, 24
----, --, --. Michael & Lavina
    Ch: Elizabeth b 1844, 1, 27
        Caroline   " 1845, 3, 8
        Alfred   " 1846, 10, 4
        Hannah   " 1849, 1, 5

KING, Michael & Lavina, continued
  Ch: Ellwood b 1851, 8, 11
1844, 5, 23. Samuel, s Joseph & Mary, Morgan
  Co., O.; m in Hopewell, Mary STUBS, dt
  Isaac & Elizabeth, Morgan Co., O.
1844, 11, 20. Mary d ae 22 bur Pennsville
1845, 1, 23. Wm., s Joseph & Mary, Morgan
  Co., O.; m in Hopewell, Ruth BALL, dt David & Juliann, Morgan Co., O.
  Ch: Julyann b 1846, 2, 20 d 1851, 5,28
       bur Pennsville
    Joseph b 1848, 1, 20
    Amos " 1850, 12, 25
----, --, --. Jacob & Sarah
  Ch: Martha T. b 1846, 1, 14
    Jephtha " 1848, 9, 14
1845, 9, 2. Mary d ae 45
1846, 5, 20. Hannay m Samuel SMITH
1847, 4, 21. Ruth m James SMITH
1847, 6, 24. Samuel, s Joseph & Mary, Morgan
  Co., O.; m in Hopewell, Grace T. EMBREE,
  dt Zenas & Ann WORTHINGTON
  Ch: Mary b 1848, 3, 31
    James W. " 1855, 9, 19
    Sarah Ann " 1857, 8, 5
    Lydia Jane " 1860, 8, 8
1853, --, --. Anna d ae 18 bur Pennsville
1871, 6, 1. Mary S. m Daniel W. GILBERT
1880, 1, 5. Joseph d ae 84 bur Pennsville
1885, 7, 13. Grace T. d ae 70 bur Hopewell
1893, 12, 7. Samuel d ae 72 bur Hopewell

1828, 7, 17. Hyram rocf Little Brittain MM,
  Pa., dtd 1828,4,19
1828, 11, 13. James dis disunity
1828, 12, 18. Michael dis jH
1828, 12, 18. Joseph dis jH
1828, 12, 18. Rebecca dis jH
1829, 1, 10. Catharine dis jH
1829, 3, 19. Sarah (form Worthington) dis mcd
1829, 3, 19. Jacob dis mcd
1829, 3, 19. Mary dis jH
1829, 7, 16. Hyram dis jH
1830, 4, 15. Hannah & Deborah dis jH
1830, 5, 13. Abel dis disunity
1837, 12, 14. Joseph rst rq
1838, 1, 18. Mary rst rq
1838, 11, 15. Sarah (form King) dis mcd
1838, 11, 15. Sarah King (form King) dis mcd
1840, 9, 17. Sarah recrq
1840, 9, 17. Jacob rst rq
1841, 5, 13. Cyrus, Eli & Lydia, ch Joseph &
  Mary, recrq
1841, 9, 16. Deborah (form Stevens) dis mcd
1842, 2, 17. James Jr. dis mcd
1842, 5, 19. Rebecca Livizey (form King)
  dis mcd
1842, 6, 16. Phebe Morris (form King) dis mcd
1843, 1, 19. Samuel dis disunity
1843, 4, 13. Michael gct Chesterfield MM, to
  m Lavina Dean
1843, 10, 19. Content & ch, Obed, Robert, Ezra, Rebecca, William & Deborah, gct Salem

  MM
1843, 11, 16. Lavina rocf Chesterfield MM, dtd
  1843,7,15
1844, 7, 18. Violetta (form Griffith) dis mcd
1846, 10, 15. Deerman, Grace, Anna & Phebe,
  ch Jacob & Sarah M., recrq
1848, 4, 13. Joseph gct Somerset MM, to m
  Anne Patterson
1848, 7, 13. Mercy Hoops (form King) dis mcd
  & jH
1848, 8, 17. Lewis dis jH
1848, 10, 19. Anna rocf Somerset MM, dtd
  1848,6,26
1849, 2, 15. Dearman W. dis disunity
1853, 4, 19. Michael & w, Lavina, & ch,
  Elizabeth, Caroline, Alfred, Hannah & Elwood, gct Salem MM, Ia.
1853, 4, 19. Samuel rst at Salem MM, Ia., on
  consent of this mtg
1854, 4, 13. Wm. & w, Ruth, & ch, Joseph,
  Amos & Mary Alice, gct Red Cedar MM, Ia.
1854, 4, 13. Cyrus dis mcd
1857, 3, 19. Jacob & w, Sarah, & ch, Jeptha
  & Martha, gct Stillwater MM
1857, 3, 19. Phebe gct Stillwater MM
1857, 10, 15. Grace Oxley (form King) dis mcd
1861, 8, 15. Sarah Yocom (form King) dis mcd
1880, 6, 17. Sarah Ann Gilbert (form King)
  dis mcd
1879, 12, 18. James W. con mcd
1860, 3, 18. Anna gct Somerset MM
1881, 1, 13. James dis disunity
1882, 7, 13. Lydia Jane Hickerson (form King)
  dis mcd

KINSEY
1834, 4, 15. Elizabeth d

1827, 7, 21. Benjamin & ch, Aaron & Abi,
  rocf Little Brittain, Pa., dtd 1827,3,17,
  end by Stillwater MM, 1827,6,23
1827, 7, 21. Martha rocf Goshen MM, Pa., dtd
  1827,5,2, end by Stillwater MM, 1827,6,23
1827, 7, 21. Tacy rocf Goshen MM, Pa., dtd
  1827,5,2, end by Stillwater MM, 1827,6,23
1829, 9, 17. Benjamin & Aaron dis jH
1829, 9, 17. Tacy & Martha dis jH
1831, 3, 17. Elizabeth, minor, rocf Nottingham & Little Britain MM, dtd 1831,2,11
1833, 10, 17. Abi dis jH
1834, 8, 14. Esther (form Kennard) dis mcd

KIRBY
----, --, --. Thomas & Rebecca
  Ch: Isaac b 1809, 12, 16
    Eleanor " 1814, 10, 23
    Elizabeth " 1816, 5, 24
    Rebecca Ann" 1818, 8, 8
    Hannah " 1820, 6, 15
    Ketturah " 1822, 2, 28
1837, 2, 3. Thomas d ae 66 bur Pennsville
1838, 8, 22. Eleanor m Milton GRIFFITH
----, --, --. Isaac & Elizabeth

KIRBY, Isaac & Elizabeth, continued
    Ch: Jonathan b 1840, 8, 3
       Rebecca   " 1844, 6, 16
       Eleanor   " 1846, 7, 10
       Sarah   " 1848, 7, 3
----, --, --. Samuel & Ruth
    Ch: Samuel Jr. b 1841, 1, 8
       Rachel   " 1844, 8, 22
       Sarah   " 1846, 9, 22
1846, 7, 11. Samuel d bur Pennsville
1858, 8, 26. Rebecca d ae 82 bur Pennsville

1829, 10, 15. Thomas & w, Rebecca, & ch,
    Eleanor, Elizabeth, Farquhar, Rebecca
    Ann, Hannah & Keturah, rocf Smithfield
    MM, dtd 1829,7,20
1829, 10, 15. Isaac rocf Smithfield MM, dtd
    1829,7,20
1831, 2, 17. Ruth (form Gilbert) dis mcd
1839, 9, 18. Isaac gct Chesterfield MM, to
    m Elizabeth Worral
1840, 3, 19. Samuel recrq
1840, 3, 19. Ruth rst rq
1840, 5, 14. Elizabeth rocf Chesterfield MM,
    dtd 1840,4,18
1846, 1, 15. Hannah Israel (form Kirby) con
    mcd
1851, 12, 18. Keturah McNickles (form Kirby)
    dis mcd
1856, 3, 13. Rebecca Ann McNichols (form
    Kirby) dis mcd
1863, 4, 16. Isaac dis jG
1863, 4, 16. Jonathan dis jG
1863, 4, 16. Elizabeth dis jG
1863, 4, 16. Rebecca dis jG
1866, 5, 17. Sarah Moore (form Kirby) dis
    mcd & jas
1869, 2, 18. Samuel dis mcd
1869, 7, 15. Rachel Grenawaugh (form Kirby)
    dis mcd

KITE
----, --, --. James R. m Ruth M. ----- d 1884,
    1,31 ae 47 bur Pennsville
    Ch: Lydia B. b 1868, 5, 9
       Mary M.   " 1874, 1, 11
       Annie S.   " 1877, 6, 12

1867, 12, 19. James R. rocf SD MM, dtd 1867,
    11,27
1868, 3, 19. Ruth rocf Stillwater MM, dtd
    1868,1,25
1885, 5, 14. James R. gct Phila. MM, Pa.
1885, 5, 14. Lydia B., Mary M. & Anna S.,
    minor ch James R., gct Frankfort MM, Pa.

LAMBERT
1837, 4, 15. Albert, s Albert & Sarah, Bel-
    mont Co., O.; m in Chesterfield, Eliza-
    beth EDGERTON, dt John & Zilpha, Athens
    Co., O.
1836, 5, 19. Elizabeth rocf Somerset MM, dtd
    1836,4,25

1860, 1, 19. Deborah (form Embree) dis mcd

LANE
1870, 8, 18. Deborah dis

LANGSTAFF
1837, 1, 19. Thomas D. & w, Hannah, rocf
    Upper Springfield MM, dtd 1836,9,24
1837, 2, 16. Thomas D. & w, Hannah, gct
    Upper Springfield MM

LAWTON
1829, 7, 16. James & w, Susanna, & ch, Jesse,
    Rebecca & Simeon, rocf Westland MM, dtd
    1829,2,18
1829, 7, 16. Jesse rpd mcd
1829, 8, 13. Rebecca Green (form Lawton) con
    mcd
1830, 7, 15. Jesse dis mcd
1837, 7, 13. James & w, Susanna, gct Flush-
    ing MM
1838, 10, 18. James & w, Susanna, rocf Flush-
    ing MM, dtd 1838,6,21

LEE
1835, 9, 17. Wm. Chandler rocf Exeter MM,
    Pa., dtd 1835,4,29
1835, 12, 17. Wm. Chandler dis mcd
1836, 9, 15. Samuel & w, Cynthia, & ch,
    James, Elizabeth Ann & Esther, rocf Exe-
    ter MM, Pa., dtd 1836,7,27

LEEK
1835, 1, 15. Philip W. & w, Elizabeth, & dt,
    Hannah Ann, rocf Flushing MM, dtd 1834,11,
    20

LEWIS
1836, 10, 27. Isaac, s. Lewis & Elisabeth, b

1836, 4, 14. Lewis & w, Eliza, & ch, Martha
    Ann, Susan H. & Wm. Henry, rocf Short
    Creek MM, dtd 1835,12,22
1839, 12, 19. Martha Ann Gray (form Lewis)
    dis mcd

LIGHTFOOT
----, --, --. Joseph & Rachel
    Ch: Susannah b 1838, 8, 19
1855, 3, 22. Rachel m Abner SPENCER
1856, 1, 31. Foster, s Joseph & Rachel, Mor-
    gan Co., O.; m in Hopewell, Alice Ann
    BALL, dt David & Julian, Morgan Co., O.
    Ch: William
       Joseph   b 1857, 3, 8
       Harriet   " 1860, 8, 28
       Julian   " 1862, 2, 22

1835, 7, 16. Joseph & w, Rachel, & ch, Sam-
    uel & Foster, rocf Short Creek MM, dtd
    1835,5,19
1837, 6, 15. Samuel & w, Rachel, rocf Uwch-
    lan MM, Pa.,dtd 1837,2,9

LIGHTFOOT, continued

1837, 6, 15. Hannah M. rocf Uwchlan MM, Pa.,
      dtd 1837,2,9
1839, 5, 16. Samuel & w, Rachel, gct Short
      Creek MM
1839, 5, 16. Hannah M. gct Short Creek MM
1842, 4, 14. Joseph & w, Rachel, & ch, Samuel,
      Foster & Susanna, gct Chesterfield MM
1843, 5, 18. Joseph & w, Rachel, & ch, Samuel,
      Foster & Susanna, rocf Chesterfield MM,
      dtd 1843,4,15
1844, 4, 18. John Penrose gct Short Creek MM,
      to m Hannah Lightfoot
1858, 7, 15. Samuel dis mcd
1860, 11, 15. Susanna Berry (form Lightfoot)
      dis mcd
1868, 2, 13. Foster & w, Alice Ann, & ch,
      Wm. L., Harriet B. & Juliann D., gct Coal
      Creek MM, Ia.
1876, 3, 16. Foster H. & w, Alice A., & ch,
      Wm. J., Harriet B. & Julian D., rocf Coal
      Creek MM, Ia.

LINCOLN

1834, 4, 17. Guli Elma (form Dewees) dis mcd
1844, 8, 15. Ann (form Dewees) dis mcd

LIVEZEY

----, --, --. John H. & Sarah
      Ch: Oliver   b 1818, 7, 27
          Hannah Ann   " 1820, 7, 21
          Jesse   " 1823, 8, 9
          Jeremiah   " 1826, 12, 17
          Lavina   " 1830, 2, 26

1831, 3, 17. Ezra rocf Notingham & Little
      Britain MM, dtd 1831,2,11
1836, 5, 19. Ezra dis disunity
1842, 5, 19. Rebecca (form King) dis mcd

LLEWELLYN

1829, 2, 18. John, s Wm. & Sarah, b
1829, 2, 19. Sarah d ae 36 bur Newton Twp.,
      Muskingum Co., O.
----, --, --. William m Mary B. ----- d 1835,
      8,2 ae 35 bur Pennsville
      Ch: Bailey   b 1831, 8, 31
          Hannah   " 1833, 4, 6
          James   " 1835, 7, 21 d 1857,10,19
1840, 11, 1. Ezra d ae 13 bur Pennsville
1847, 1, 20. Thomas, s William & Sarah, Mor-
      gan Co., O.; m in Pennwville, Martha HOL-
      LINGSWORTH, dt Elisha & Sarah, Morgan Co.,
      O.
      Ch: Eza(sic)   b 1848, 1, 22
          Amos   " 1849, 9, 14 d 1854, 8, 7
            bur Pennsville
          Sarah   b 1854, 2, 4
          Elisha   " 1856, 9, 6
          Anne   " 1859, 1, 28
          William   " 1868, 2, 18 d 1882,12,20
            bur Pennsville
1852, 8, 28. Bailey d ae 2 bur Pennsville

1870, 9, 17. Mary d ae 67 bur Hopewell
----, --, --. Elisha & Abigail S.
      Ch: -----   1883, 5, 20
          -----   1889, 6, 12
          -----   1891, 4, 5
1893, 2, 17. Anna m Benjamin F. STARBUCK

1829, 2, 19. Wm. & w, Sarah, & ch, Thomas,
      Joseph & Ezra, rocf Stillwater MM, dtd
      1829,1,24
1830, 8, 19. Wm. gct London Grove MM, to m
      Mary B. Cole
1831, 1, 13. Mary B. & dt, Sarah S. Cole,
      rocf London Grove MM, Pa., dtd 1830,12,11
1831, 6, 16. Rebecca (form Sidwell) dis mcd
1836, 7, 14. Hannah, minor, gct New Garden
      MM, Pa.
1843, 5, 18. Wm. gct Plainfield MM, to m
      Mary Chambers
1844, 1, 18. Mary rocf Plainfield MM, dtd
      1843,11,22
1849, 9, 13. Joseph dis mcd
1854, 6, 15. John gct Red Cedar MM, Ia.
1869, 11, 18. Ezra con mcd
1873, 6, 19. Daniel & Elizabeth, ch Ezra &
      Sarah, recrq
1882, 5, 18. Elisha gct New Garden MM, to m
      Abigail Stratton
1883, 1, 18. Abigail S. rocf New Garden MM,
      dtd 1882,11,23
1891, 10, 15. Elisha & w, Abigail S., & ch,
      Charles B., Mabel E. & Wm. T., gct New
      Garden MM
1898, 10, 13. Elizabeth McInturf (form Llewel-
      lyn) dis mcd

McCALL

1847, 5, 13. Mary Ann (form Dewees) dis mcd
      & jH
1897, 1, 14. Martha Jane (form Clendenon)
      dis mcd & jas

McCONNEL

1837, 7, 13. Edward & w, Lydia, & ch, James,
      Adaline, Nathan, Jonathan & Ruth, rocf
      Upper Springfield MM, dtd 1837,6,24
1837, 7, 13. Orpha rocf Upper Springfield MM,
      dtd 1837,6,24

McGREW

1862, 3, 9. Margaret d ae 44 bur Hopewell
1866, 5, 19. Samuel d ae 18 bur Hopewell
1869, 11, 19. Alva d ae 19 bur Hopewell
1873, 3, 19. Lydia V. m David SMITH

1851, 11, 13. Margaret V. rocf Plymouth MM,
      dtd 1851,10,20
1860, 3, 10. Samuel, Lemuel, Alva, Jasper
      C. & Deborah, ch James & Margaret, recrq
1865, 12, 14. Lydia V. rocf Providence MM,
      dtd 1865,11,30
1871, 7, 14. Almedia (form Dewees) con mcd
1872, 2, 15. Lemuel dis mcd

McGREW, continued
1873, 5, 15. Agnes & Elmer, ch Lydia V.
    Smith, recrq
1873, 9, 18. Deborah Jane Penrose (form Mc-
    Grew) dis mcd
1878, 4, 18. David Smith & w, Lydia V., & s,
    Elmer McGrew, gct Chesterfield MM
1880, 8, 19. Almedia dis disunity
1883, 5, 17. Agnes V. gct Chesterfield MM

McINTURF
1898, 10, 13. Elizabeth (form Llewellyn) dis
    mcd

McMAHAN
1832, 4, 19. Ann (form Todd) dis mcd

McNICHOLS
1851, 12, 18. Keturah [McNickles] (form Kirby)
    dis mcd
1856, 3, 13. Rebecca Ann (form Kirby) dis
    mcd

McVAY
1828, 2, 16. Elizabeth (form Kennard) dis mcd

MARIS
1847, 10, 20. Owen, s David & Sarah, Morgan
    Co., O.; m in Pennsville, Ann VANLAW, dt
    Zenas & Ann WORTHINGTON, Morgan Co., O.

1836, 12, 3. Owen & w, Rachel, & ch, Sarah
    J., Michael J., Mary Anna, Phebe B. &
    George J., rocf Short Creek MM, dtd 1836,
    10,18
1846, 3, 19. Mary rocf Smithfield MM, dtd
    1845,10,22; end by Somerset MM 1846,3,2
1848, 3, 16. Ann W. & s, Elisha Vanlaw, gct
    Chesterfield MM
1848, 4, 13. Cidney rocf Somerset MM, dtd
    1848,2,28
1848, 4, 13. Rachel rocf Somerset MM, dtd
    1848,2,28
1848, 4, 13. Phebe rocf Somerset MM, dtd
    1848,2,28
1849, 1, 18. Cidney gct Chesterfield MM
1849, 1, 18. Phebe gct Chesterfield MM
1849, 1, 18. Rachel gct Chesterfield MM
1858, 5, 13. Mary D. Starlen (form Maris)
    dis mcd

MARSH
1859, 1, 6. Lavina [Mash] d

1853, 9, 15. Lavina rocf Flushing MM, dtd
    1853,6,23

MARSHALL
1837, 12, 14. Cert rec for John & w, Anna
    Mercy, & ch, James, Caleb & Jesse, from
    Stillwater MM, dtd 1837,11,25, end to
    Chesterfield MM

MASSEY
1876, 10, 5. Wm. d ae 90

1859, 9, 15. Wm. rst on consent of Stillwater
    MM

MASTERS
----, --, --. William & Naomi
    Ch: David James   d 1833, 5, 19
            bur Deerfield
        Ruthann
        Isaac   b 1834, 8, 25 d 1863, 9,16
            bur Pennsville
        Joseph   b 1839, 12, 6
        Stephen   " 1842, 9, 4
1857, 4, 30. David, s Wm. & Naomi, Morgan
    Co., O.; m in Hopewell, Priscilla WORTH-
    INGTON, dt Wm. & Elizabeth, Morgan Co., O.
    Ch: William   b 1858, 7, 12
        Hannah   " 1861, 11, 23 d 1876, 3,15
            bur Pennsville
1857, 10, 28. Anna m Griffith DEWEES
----, --, --. Joseph & Esther
    Ch: Daniel   b 1867, 4, 19
        Anna   " 1869, 3, 18
        Mary A.   " 1870, 8, 28
        Isaac   " 1873, 11, 27
        Barclay D. " 1876, 12, 7
1883, 11, 13. Wm. d ae 82
1888, 8, 17. Priscilla d ae 64 bur Pennsville

1834, 2, 13. Wm. & Naomi & ch, David, James
    & Ruthann, rocf Smithfield MM, dtd 1833,4,
    22
1866, 5, 17. Joseph gct New Garden MM, to m
    Esther Stratton
1866, 9, 13. Esther rocf New Garden MM, dtd
    1866, 8, 23
1875, 1, 14. Stephen H. dis mcd
1884, 7, 17. Joseph & w, Esther, & ch, Dan-
    iel S., Anna, Mary A., Isaac & Barclay D.,
    gct New Garden MM

MAULE
1852, 12, 22. Edward, s Jesse & Sarah, Bel-
    mont Co., O.; m in Pennsville, Hannah
    PENROSE, dt John & Anna, Morgan Co., O.
    Ch: John P.   b 1853, 9, 15
        Sarah   " 1854, 12, 18
        Henry   " 1856, 9, 1
        James S.   " 1858, 5, 4
        Walter   " 1862, 11, 1

1853, 4, 19. Edward rocf Short Creek MM, dtd
    1853,3,22
1864, 6, 16. Edward dis military service

MAXSON
1829, 6, 18. Hannah dis JH

MAXWELL
1845, 7, 17. Lucinda (form Bundy) dis mcd

METCALF
----, --, --. Jesse & Asenath [Medcalf]
    Ch: Jesse   b 1838, 6, 3
        Susanna   " 1840, 10, 10
        Lewis   " 1843, 12, 12
        Joseph Mead" 1845, 12, 30 d 1863, 3, 8
1838, 7, 10. Stephen [Medcalf] d ae 8 bur
    Pennsville
1844, 9, 18. Lewis [Medcalf] d ae 9 bur Penns-
    ville
1850, 9, 5. Asenath d ae 45 bur Pennsville
1851, 3, 5. Susannah d ae 84 bur Hopewell
1854, 2, 24. Joshua Hudson d ae 25 bur Penns-
    ville
1855, 9, 24. Jesse, s Moses & Susannah, Mor-
    gan Co., O.; m in Hopewell, Hannah E.
    RICHERSON, dt Samuel & Agness VAILE
1856, 8, 29. Asenath G. d ae 20 bur Penns-
    ville

1836, 6, 16. Jesse [Medkiff] & w, Asenath, &
    ch, Oliver, Caroline, Joshua, Stephen,
    Adaline, Wm. & Asenath, rocf Plainfield
    MM, dtd 1836,5,25
1837, 9, 14. Joseph [Medkiff] & w, Matilda,
    rocf Short Creek MM, dtd 1837,6,20
1837, 9, 14. Susanna [Medkeff] rocf Short
    Creek MM, dtd 1837,3,21
1841, 4, 15. Abraham rst on consent of Somer-
    set MM
1841, 10, 14. John B. rocf Sommerset MM, dtd
    1841,9,27
1841, 10, 14. Jemima S., Elizabeth & Lydia
    Ann, ch Abraham & Hannah, rocf Somerset
    MM, dtd 1841,9,27
1843, 1, 19. Abraham dis jH
1843, 3, 16. John dis mcd
1843, 12, 14. Jemima Wickersham (form Metcalf)
    dis mcd
1844, 4, 18. Elizabeth Scott (form Metcalf)
    dis mcd
1845, 7, 17. Lydia Ann (form Metcalf) rpd mcd
1846, 2, 19. Joseph dis disunity
1849, 2, 15. Caroline Wood (form Metcalf)
    dis mcd
1849, 3, 15. Oliver G. dis disunity
1861, 10, 17. Wm. dis mcd
1862, 6, 19. Matilda dis disunity
1866, 12, 13. Hannah D. dis jG
1867, 1, 17. James dis jG
1880, 12, 16. Matilda rst at Stillwater MM on
    consent of this mtg
1881, 8, 18. Hannah D. rst at Stillwater MM
    on consent of this mtg

MENDENHALL
----, --, --. John & Hannah [Mendinghall]
    Ch: Lydiann   b 1839, 7, 3
        Martha   " 1842, 4, 15
        Thomas   " 1844, 12, 27 d 1846, 8,26
        Charles W.   " 1848, 8, 27

1830, 8, 19. Elizabeth, Isaac, Joseph, Lydia,

Edith, Rachel, Thirza & Naomi, ch Aaron &
    Deborah, rocf Short Creek MM, dtd 1830,6,
    22
1831, 7, 14. Elizabeth Thompson (form Men-
    denhall) dis mcd
1838, 5, 17. Lydia Wood (form Mendenhall)
    dis mcd
1838, 6, 14. Isaac rocf Middleton MM, dtd
    1837,7,17
1838, 10, 18. John & w, Hannah, & s, Wm.,
    rocf Middleton MM, dtd 1838,5,21
1842, 2, 17. Isaac B. dis mcd
1842, 2, 17. Joseph dis mcd
1842, 5, 19. Edith Thompson (form Mendenhall)
    dis mcd
1842, 5, 19. Rachel Moore (form Mendenhall)
    dis mcd
1843, 2, 16. Thirza dis jas
1847, 6, 17. Naomi Conn (form Mendenhall)
    dis mcd
1848, 6, 15. Isaac dis mcd
1853, 6, 8. John & w, Hannah, & ch, William,
    Lydia Ann, Martha & Charles, gct Alum
    Creek MM

MICHENER
1868, 10, 21. Mary C. m Fleming CREW

1842, 3, 17. Mary Ann, David, Wilson, Senoca
    & Wm., ch Jacob & Martha, rocf Short Creek
    MM, dtd 1842,1,18
1862, 1, 16. Mary [Michner] rocf Chesterfield
    MM, dtd 1861,11,16

MILHOUSE
----, --, --. Daniel & Esther
    Ch: William   b 1823, 8, 27
        Sarah   " 1828, 8, 14
        Elizabeth   " 1831, 5, 5
        Hannah   " 1833, 10, 31
        Mary   " 1836, 6, 18
        Isaac   " 1840, 6, 1
        Rebecca   " 1843, 4, 29
----, --, --. Robert m Martha ----- d 1845,4,
    7 ae 33 bur Pennsville
    Ch: Ruth   b 1836, 12, 1
        Anna   " 1838, 11, 9
        Lydia   " 1840, 7, 23
        Sarah Ann   " 1842, 7, 27 d 1845, 6,10
        bur Pennsville
    Robert m 2nd Rachel -----
    Ch: Martha   b 1848, 5, 17
        Mary   " 1851, 9, 23
        Sarah   " 1855, 7, 14
1847, 7, 22. Robert, s Robert & Sarah, Mor-
    gan Co., O.; m in Hopewell, Rachel STUBBS
    dt Samuel & Mary BARNES
1852, 3, 24. Sarah m Stephen HODGIN
----, --, --. William & Charity [Millhouse]
    Ch: Mary Eliza-
        beth   b 1857, 10, 11
        Esther   " 1859, 8, 12
1858, 10, 4. Esther d bur Pennsville (an
    elder)

MILHOUSE, continued

1858, 12, 22. Hannah [Millhouse] m Joseph
VERNON

1865, 11, 15. Daniel d ae 65 bur Pennsville

1871, 5, 20. Anna [Millhouse] m David
STEPHENS

1872, 6, 2. Mary d ae 20 bur Pennsville

1879, 8, 15. Sarah m Benjamin F. STARBUCK

1889, 2, 14. Lydia d ae 48 bur Pennsville

1894, 2, 2. Rachel d ae 73 bur Pennsville
(an elder)

1896, 2, 8. Robert d ae 84 bur Pennsville
(a minister)

1896, 12, 23. Martha [Millhouse] m Joseph
VAUGHN

1834, 6, 19. Robert [Millhouse] rocf Stillwater MM, dtd 1834,5,24

1836, 2, 18. Robert [Millhouse] gct Stillwater MM, to m Martha Sears

1836, 7, 14. Martha [Millhouse] rocf Stillwater MM, dtd 1836,6,25

1846, 5, 14. Thomas rocf Short Creek MM, dtd
1846,3,24

1847, 8, 19. Thomas [Millhouse] dis mcd

1854, 7, 13. Elizabeth Hall (form Millhouse)
dis mcd

1858, 4, 16. Charity [Millhouse] rst "without
the consent of Fairfield MM, Ind."

1862, 11, 13. Ruth [Millhouse] gct Stillwater
MM

1864, 11, 17. Isaac [Millhouse] con mcd

1866, 9, 13. Rachel [Millhouse] & ch, Sarah
Esther & Jane, recrq

1868, 9, 17. Mary gct Springville MM, Ia.

1868, 9, 17. Rebecca gct Springville MM, Ia.

1869, 4, 15. Wm. & w, Charity, & ch, Mary
Elizabeth & Sarah Esther, gct Springville
MM, Ia.

1871, 5, 18. Isaac C. & w, Rachel, & ch, Sarah Esther, Jane, Mary & Daniel, gct
Springville MM, Ia.

MILLER

----, --, --. Robert & Lydia
    Ch: Jesse   b 1820, 3, 21
        Newton   " 1821, 6, 25
        Milton   " 1824, 9, 19
        David   " 1826, 10, 1
        William " 1828, --, --
        Reuben   " 1830, --, --
        Rachel   " 1831, 9, --

1831, 11, 17. Lydia dis disunity
1845, 3, 13. Newton dis mcd
1845, 11, 13. Rachel (form Wilson) dis mcd
1851, 5, 15. Milton rpd mcd
1853, 1, 13. Rachel Packingham (form Miller)
dis mcd & jas

MILLS

----, --, --. Gideon & Edith
    Ch: Eli   b 1809, 5, 30

        Elisha   b 1810, 11, 1
        Esther   " 1812, 9, 5
        Lewis   " 1814, 7, 28
        Isaac   " 1817, 2, 20
        Hugh J. " 1818, 10, 28
        Reuben   " 1820, 11, 19
        Thomas W. " 1822, 12, 31
        Issachar " 1826, 7, 7 d 1832, 6, 2
          bur Deerfield
        Ezra   b 1830, 10, 31

1836, 8, 25. Thomas d

1833, 2, 3. Eli dis mcd

1833, 9, 19. Elisha dis jas

1836, 5, 19. Lewis dis mcd

1836, 8, 18. Gideon & w, Edith, & ch, Isaac,
Hugh J., Reuben, Thomas W. & Ezra, gct
Mississinewa MM

1826, 8, 18. Esther gct Mississinewa MM

1837, 3, 16. Cert for Gideon & fam granted
to Mississinewa MM, Ind., end back to
this mtg

1837, 3, 16. Cert for Esther also end back
to this mtg

1838, 11, 15. Isaac dis jas

1839, 8, 15. Gideon & w, Edith, & ch, Hugh,
Reuben & Ezra, gct Chesterfield MM

MILTON

1867, 9, 19. Rebecca rocf Plymouth MM, dtd
1867,7,22

MOON

1838, 2, 18. Esther gct Newbury MM, O.

MOORE

1829, 6, 18. Samuel, John, Edward, Martha &
Isabella, ch Wm. & Lydia, rocf Short Creek
MM, dtd 1829,5,19

1839, 3, 14. Samuel dis disunity

1840, 4, 16. John dis mcd

1841, 4, 15. Edward dis disunity

1842, 5, 19. Rachel (form Mendenhall) dis
mcd

1848, 8, 17. Isabella Patterson (form Moore)
dis mcd

1848, 10, 19. Martha dis jH

1866, 5, 17. Sarah (form Kirby) dis mcd & jas

MORRIS

----, --, --. William & Susanna
    Ch: Ava   b 1801, 9, 21
        Jonathan " 1807, 2, 1
        Susanna " 1812, 2, 23
        Lydia   " 1814, 5, 21
        Ruth   " 1818, 9, 22
        Rachel   " 1824, 1, 15

1830, 3, 24. Jonathan, s William & Susanna,
Morgan Co., O.; m in Deerfield, Theodate
VERNON, dt Amos & Mary
    Ch: Ruthanna V. b 1831, 1, 23

----, --, --. Nathan & Tacy
    Ch: Samuel   b 1833, 11, 14

MORRIS, Nathan & Tacy, continued
    Ch: Jonathan b 1835, 4, 23
        William P. " 1837, 2, 26
1833, 3, 20. Susannah m Wm. GOODING

1829, 5, 14. John Embree gct Somerset MM, to
    m Ava Morris
1829, 12, 17. Sarah rocf Sommerset MM, dtd
    1829,10,26
1830, 3, 18. Jonathan rocf Somerset MM, dtd
    1830,3,1
1830, 6, 17. Wm. & w, Susanna, & ch, Susanna,
    Lydia, Ruth & Rachel, rocf Somerset MM, dtd
    1830,4,26
1831, 6, 16. Sarah dis
1832, 4, 19. Jonathan & w, Theodate, & dt,
    Ruth Anna, gct Duck Creek MM, Ind.
1834, 4, 17. Lydia gct Duck Creek MM, Ind.
1834, 5, 15. Wm. & w, Susanna, & ch, Ruth &
    Rachel, gct Milford MM, Ind.
1836, 2, 18. Aaron & w, Phebe, & dt, Lydia,
    rocf Stillwater MM, dtd 1835,11,28
1836, 5, 19. Mordecai & w, Alice, & ch, Ed-
    win, David, Martin & Susanna, rocf Somer-
    set MM, dtd 1836,4,25
1836, 11, 17. Rebecca & Rachel, ch Joshua,
    rocf Somerset MM, dtd 1836,10,24
1836, 12, 3. Eleanor rocf Somerset MM, dtd
    1836,10,24
1837, 3, 16. Nathan & w, Tacy, & ch, Samuel &
    Jonathan, rocf Somerset MM, dtd 1837,2,27
1842, 6, 16. Phebe (form King) dis mcd

MOTT
1857, 3, 26. George W., s Wm. & Sarah, Athens
    Co., O.; m in Hopewell, Abigail BALL, dt
    David & Juliann, Morgan Co., O.

1857, 8, 13. Abigail B. gct Plymouth MM
1861, 11, 14. George W. & w, Abigail, & s,
    David C., rocf Plymouth MM, dtd 1861,10,21
1863, 5, 14. George W. & w, Abigail, & s,
    David C., gct Hickory Grove MM, Ia.
1864, 4, 14. Asher & w, Mary Elvira, rocf
    Plymouth MM, dtd 1864,3,21

NAYLOR
1841, 8, 27. Addison, s Abraham & Rachel, b
1857, 8, 19. Mary Jane m Isaac PENROSE

1829, 10, 15. Abigail [Nailor] rocf Smithfield
    MM, dtd 1829,9,21
1839, 8, 15. Abraham P. & w, Rachel Ann, &
    ch, Albert & Mary Jane, rocf Smithfield
    MM, dtd 1839,7,22
1841, 7, 15. Abigail dis jas
1845, 7, 17. Rachel Ann dis jas
1845, 9, 18. Abraham P. dis jas
1858, 9, 16. Mary Jane (form Penrose) dis mcd
1864, 9, 15. Addison Wood dis mcd

NEWSOM
1842, 5, 13. Susanna d ae 27 bur Pennsville

1842, 5, 24. Rachel [Newson] d ae 19 bur
    Pennsville

1835, 3, 19. Wm. rocf Stillwater MM, dtd
    1835,1,24
1841, 8, 19. Susanna [Newson] rocf Stillwater
    MM, dtd 1841,7,24
1841, 8, 19. Rachel rocf Stillwater MM, dtd
    1841,7,24

NORTON
1875, 6, 17. Rachel (form Embree) dis mcd

OBLINGER
1864, 5, 19. Hannah Townsend & ch, Stephen
    & Hannah, & niece, Sarah T. Oblinger,
    rocf Somerset MM, dtd 1864,4,25

OSBORN
1868, 5, 14. Martha (form Ratcliff) dis mcd

OXLEY
1857, 10, 15. Grace (form King) dis mcd

PACKINGHAM
1853, 1, 13. Rachel (form Miller) dis mcd &
    jas

PAINTER
1886, 4, 15. Rebecca Ann gct Springville MM,
    Ia.

PARSONS
1867, 9, 10. Gaynor d ae 91 bur Hopewell

1851, 6, 19. Gayner rocf Smithfield MM, dtd
    1851,4,21

PATTEN
----, --, --. John & Rebecca
    Ch: Abraham   b 1818, 1, 22
        Rachel   " 1819, 10, 11
        Rhoda   " 1822, 3, 16
        Joseph   " 1823, 7, 10
        Sarah   " 1825, 1, 24
        William   " 1827, 3, 3
        John Quincy" 1829, 7, 13 d 1853,10, 9
        Richard   " 1831, 10, 7
        Isaac   " 1834, 3, 28
        Rebecca   " 1837k 3, 9
----, --, --. William & Phebe
    Ch: Elihu H.   b 1818, 1, 18
        Hannah   " 1820, 6, 22
        Rachel   " 1822, 8, 17
        Mary   " 1824, 4, 1
        Mahlon   " 1826, 6, 10
        Jared   " 1828, 4, 16
        Merrick   " 1830, 3, 27
        Esther   " 1834, 1, 27
        Lydia   " 1836, 9, 22
1837, 11, 2. Rebecca d ae 43 bur Pennsville
1838, 5, 23. Elihu H., s William & Phebe,
    Morgan Co., O.; m in Pennsville, Eliza

PATTEN, Elihu H., continued
    Jane TALBOT, dt William & Ann, Morgan Co.,
    O.
    Ch: William   b 1839, 3, 8
        Phebe Ann " 1840, 11, 10
        Jesse   " 1842, 9, 10
1838, 7, 25. Hannah [Pattan] m Joseph TALBOTT
1839, 9, 27. Phebe d ae 3 bur Pennsville
1844, 3, 20. Rachel B. m David SEARS
1844, 9, 25. Abraham, s John & Rebecca, Mor-
    gan Co., O.; m in Pennsville, Ruth HOLLINGS
    WORTH, dt Elisha & Sarah, Morgan Co., O.
1845, 6, 6. Ruth d ae 21 bur Hopewell
1846, 10, 2. Abraham d ae 29 bur Hopewell
1846, 11, 26. Mahlon [Patton], s Wm. & Phebe,
    Morgan Co., O.; m in Hopewell, Sarah S.
    COLE, dt Richard & Mary B.
    Ch: George D. b 1847, 8, 10
        Wm. Bailey " 1849, 1, 22
1847, 2, 25. Rachel [Patton] m Wm. B. COLE
1849, 10, 3. William d ae 60
1854, 4, 20. Rhoda m James BAILEY
1854, 5, 24. Richard, s John & Rebecca, Mor-
    gan Co., O.; m in Pennsville, Lydia
    PIERPONT, dt Wm. & Matilda, Morgan Co., C.
    Ch: Mary Ellen b 1855, 3, 27
        Isaac   " 1864, 4, 3
1855, 5, 17. Rachel [Patton] d ae 56
1857, 7, 29. John, s Wm. & Rachel, Morgan
    Co., O.; m in Pennsville, Mary BUNDY, dt
    Mordica & Abigal PEEBLES, Morgan Co., O.
1863, 1, 2. John d ae 67 bur Pennsville (an
    elder)
1842, 12, 15. John gct Stillwater MM, to m
    Rachel Patterson
1843, 3, 16. Rachel rocf Stillwater MM, dtd
    1843,2,25
1844, 12, 19. Elihu H. & w, Eliza Jane, & ch,
    Wm., Phebe Ann & Jesse, gct Hopewell MM
1845, 6, 19. Sarah Talbott (form Patton) dis
    mcd
1847, 3, 18. Joseph dis mcd
1848, 12, 14. Wm. Jr. gct Hopewell MM, Ind.
1849, 5, 17. Joseph rst at Hopewell MM, Ind.
    on consent of this mtg
1850, 12, 19. Mahlon & w, Sarah S., & ch,
    George & Wm., gct Westfield MM, Ind.
1851, 1, 16. Lydia, minor, gct Richland MM
1851, 2, 13. Mary gct Richland MM, Ind.
1851, 3, 13. Merrick gct Richland MM, Ind.
1851, 3, 13. Esther gct Richland MM, Ind.
1852, 8, 19. Jared gct Richland MM, Ind.
1858, 1, 14. Isaac dis mcd
1858, 3, 18. Richard & w, Lydia, & ch, Mary-
    Ellen & Wm. John, gct Chesterfield MM
1863, 8, 13. Mary [Patton] & ch, Wm. & Caleb
    S., gct Hickory Grove MM, Ia.
1863, 11, 19. Richard [Patton] & w, Lydia, &
    ch, Mary Ellen, Wm., Eliza Jane & John,
    rocf Chesterfield MM, dtd 1863,8,15
1866, 3, 15. Richard & w, Lydia, & ch, Mary
    Ellen, William, Eliza Jane, John & Isaac,
    gct Springville MM, Ia.

PATTERSON
1827, 10, 24. Esther m Asa C. HAMPTON
----, --, --. Jeremiah & Elizabeth
    Ch: Mary   b 1833, 5, 5
        Ann   " 1835, 10, --
1827, 9, 15. Esther rocf Somerset MM, dtd
    1827,7,30
1828, 10, 16. Laban B. dis disunity
1828, 12, 18. Sarah dis JH
1833, 12, 19. Elizabeth & ch, Rachel, Sarah,
    Wm., Caleb, Jared, Robert, Silas, Isaac
    B. & Mary, rocf Somerset MM, dtd 1833,11,
    25
1835, 3, 19. Jeremiah rocf Somerset MM, dtd
    1835,3,2
1836, 11, 17. Jordan & w, Mary, & ch, James,
    Joseph, Sarah, Amos, Bheriba & Mary, rocf
    Short Creek MM, dtd 1836,4,19
1836, 11, 17. Arnold & w, Rachel, & ch, Sarah,
    Rebecca, Clark & Rachel, rocf Somerset
    MM, dtd 1836,10,24
1838, 2, 18. Sarah Worrall (form Patterson)
    dis mcd
1842, 12, 15. John Patten gct Stillwater MM,
    to m Rachel Patterson
1846, 10, 15. Elizabeth rocf Stillwater MM,
    dtd 1846,9,26
1848, 4, 13. Joseph King gct Somerset MM, to
    m Anne Patterson
1848, 8, 17. Lydia Ann gct Somerset MM
1848, 8, 17. Isabella (form Moore) dis mcd
1854, 1, 19. Elizabeth gct Stillwater MM

PEARSON
1832, 6, 13. William, s Jesse & Cynthia, b
1833, 10, 5. Jesse, s William & Catharine, b

1831, 5, 19. Wm. & w, Catharine, & ch, Ben-
    jamin, Enoch, Mary & David, rocf Flush-
    ing MM, dtd 1831,2,24
1831, 6, 16. Jesse & w, Cynthia, & ch, Thom-
    as, George & Mary Jane, rocf Flushing MM,
    dtd 1831,4,21
1854, 7, 13. Embree gct Red Cedar MM, Ia.

PEEBLES
1834, 2, 13. Susanna rocf Stillwater MM, dtd
    1834,1,25
1835, 1, 15. Burwell & w, Asenath, & ch,
    Chalkley & Daniel, rocf Stillwater MM, dtd
    1834,10,25
1835, 1, 15. Wm. rocf Stillwater MM, dtd
    1834,12,27
1837, 10, 19. Wm. gct Stillwater MM, to m
    Rachel E. Plummer
1837, 10, 19. Susanna L. gct Somerset MM
1838, 6, 14. Rachel T. rocf Stillwater MM,
    dtd 1838,4,28
1840, 2, 13. Wm. S. & w, Rachel, & ch, Eliza-
    beth, gct Chesterfield MM

PENNELL
1873, 12, 18. Wm. H., minor, recrq
1886, 11, 18. Wm. H. [Pennel] dis mcd & jas

PENROSE
1830, 11, 24. Thomas, s Thomas & Sarah, Morgan
    Co., O.; m in Deerfield, Maria CLENDENON,
    dt Isaac & Hannah, Morgan Co., O.
    Ch: Clarkson T.b 1831, 9, 22
        Osborn   " 1833, 11, 4
        Isaac   " 1836, 4, 1
----, --, --. John & Anna
    Ch: Sarah
        Elizabeth b 1832, 4, 16
        Hannah   " 1834, 8, 21
        Jacob   " 1836, 7, 25
        Thomas   " 1839, 11, 19
        John D.   " 1840, 9, 27
    John m 2nd Hannah -----
    Ch: Mary   b 1846, 10, 9
        Charles   " 1848, 12, 2
        Jane   " 1851, 11, 6
----, --, --. James & Rebecca
    Ch: William   b 1834, 7, 11
        Mary   " 1836, 6, 30
        Sarah   " 1838, 7, 8
----, --, --. Richard & Elizabeth
    Ch: Margaret b 1836, 7, 25
        Barclay   " 1841, 4, 8
        Hannah   " 1843, 10, 10
        Mary   " 1848, 7, 9
1838, 2, 21. Sarah Ann m Emlen GRIFFITH
1838, 8, 22. Joseph, s Thomas & Sarah, Morgan
    Co., O.; m in Pennsville, Mary GILBERT, dt
    Abel & Rebecca, Morgan Co., O.
    Ch: Elvira   b 1839, 10, 9
        Albert   " 1841, 2, 24
1840, 5, 5. Margaret d ae 3 bur Pensville
1840, 12, 12. Anna d bur Pennsville
1841, 9, 19. Mary d ae 27 bur Pennsville
1846, 5, 20. Joseph, s Thomas & Sarah, Mor-
    gan Co., O.; m in Pennsville, Mildred
    WORTHINGTON, dt Wm. & Elizabeth, Muskingum
    Co., O.
1848, 5, 28. Sarah d ae 72
1852, 12, 22. Hannah m Edward MAULE
1853, 1, 29. Thomas d ae 86 bur Pennsville
1854, 5, 24. Jason, s Richard & Ann Eliza-
    beth, Morgan Co., O.; m in Pennsville,
    Martha HARMER, dt Wm. & Rachel, Morgan
    Co., O.
    Ch: Charles   b 1855, 4, 5
        Rachel Ann " 1857, 11, 23
        William H. " 1861, 2, 2
        Hannah S.   " 1867, 4, 23
1855, 8, 22. Osborn, s Thomas & Maria, Mor-
    gan Co., O.; m in Pennsville, Susan A.
    WOOD, dt Joshua & Esther, Washington Co.,
    O.
1856, 5, 2. John d ae 49 bur Pennsville
1857, 8, 19. Isaac, s Thomas & Maria, Morgan
    Co., O.; m in Pennsville, Mary Jane NAY-
    LOR, dt Abraham P. & Rachel, Morgan Co.,O.

1860, 7, 22. Adaline M., dt Thomas & Susan H.
    b
1861, 1, 20. Adaline M. d bur Pennsville
    (infant)
----, --, --. Barclay & Mary P.
    Ch: Oliver J. b 1862, 6, 14
        Elizabeth
          S.   " 1866, 2, 17
        Mahlon   " 1869, 1, 29
1862, 5, 10. Susan H. d ae 21 bur Pennsville
1863, 3, 26. Alton W., s James & Margaret
    Ann, b
1866, 10, 8. Naomi d ae 35 bur Pennsville
1883, 4, 27. Richard d ae 81 bur Pennsville
    (an elder)
1884, 3, 24. Ann Elizabeth d ae 75
1884, 3, 29. A. Elizabeth d ae 76 (an elder)
1892, 5, 2. Joseph d ae 63 bur Pennsville
1868, 11, 21. Hannah S. m Lindley STEER

1830, 4, 15. Thomas & w, Sarah, & ch, Sarah
    Ann & Joseph, rocf Smithfield MM, dtd
    1830,3,22
1830, 4, 15. Thomas rocf Smithfield MM, dtd
    1829,10,19
1831, 10, 19. John & w, Anna, rocf Smithfield
    MM, dtd 1831,7,18
1832, 11, 15. James rocf Smithfield MM, dtd
    1832,7,23
1833, 6, 1. Ann Elizabeth recrq
1833, 8, 15. James gct Sandy Spring MM, to
    m Rebecca Farmer
1833, 9, 19. Richard rst on consent of Sandy
    Spring MM
1834, 3, 13. Rebecca rocf Sandy Spring MM,
    dtd 1833,10,25
1834, 3, 13. Joseph & Jason, ch Richard,
    recrq
1839, 12, 19. James & w, Rebecca, & ch, Wm.,
    Mary & Sarah, gct Sandy Spring MM
1843, 10, 19. Joseph gct Chesterfield MM
1844, 4, 18. John gct Short Creek MM, to m
    Hannah Lightfoot
1844, 9, 19. Hannah M. rocf Short Creek MM,
    dtd 1844,6,18
1846, 10, 15. Mary Eliza & Albert, ch Joseph,
    gct Chesterfield MM
1846, 11, 19. Mildred gct Chesterfield MM
1855, 1, 18. Joseph con mcd
1856, 2, 14. Sarah Elizabeth Haliman (form
    Penrose) dis mcd
1856, 7, 17. Susan A. gct Chesterfield MM
1858, 9, 16. Mary Jane Naylor (form Penrose)
    dis mcd
1859, 11, 17. Thomas con mcd
1860, 1, 19. Susan con mcd
1861, 2, 14. Naomi recrq
1861, 9, 19. Barclay gct Plymouth MM, to m
    Mary P. Gilbert
1862, 8, 14. John A. dis mcd
1862, 12, 18. James con mcd
1863, 4, 16. Joseph dis disunity
1863, 8, 13. Osborn dis disunity

PENROSE, continued

1862, 12, 18. Margaret Ann (form Smith) con mcd

1863, 11, 19. Isaac rst on consent of Chesterhill MM

1863, 12, 17. Mary Jane rst

1864, 4, 14. Thomas dis mcd & military service

1867, 9, 19. Mary P. rocf Plymouth MM, dtd 1867,7,22

1870, 2, 17. Susan A. dis jas

1870, 11, 17. Jane Simpson (form Penrose) dis mcd

1871, 3, 16. Mary P. Simpson (form Penrose) con mcd

1873, 2, 13. Barclay & w, Mary P., & ch, Oliver J., Elizabeth & Mahlon, gct Coal Creek MM, Iowa

1873, 9, 18. Deborah Jane (form McGrew) dis mcd

1874, 1, 15. Charles dis mcd

1874, 10, 16. Mary P. Santee (form Penrose) dis mcd

1877, 10, 18. Nathan Burgess gct Plymouth MM, to m Elizabeth L. Penrose

1879, 1, 16. Barclay & w, Mary P., & ch, Oliver J., Elizabeth S. & Mahlon, rocf Coalcreek MM, Ia., dtd 1878,12,11

1882, 1, 19. Joseph rst

1882, 1, 19. Mary H. & ch, Jesse & Ruth Ellen, recrq (w Joseph)

1882, 4, 13. Charles dis mcd

1884, 11, 13. Wm. dis disunity

1887, 5, 19. Elizabeth S. Yocum (form Penrose) dis mcd

1889, 4, 18. Rachel Holcomb (form Penrose) dis mcd & jas

1889, 11, 14. Hannah S. Smith (form Penrose) dis mcd & jas

1893, 3, 16. Oliver J. dis mcd

1901, 3, 14. Barclay & w, Mary P., gct Somerset MM

PETTIT

1829, 1, 10. John dis jH

PICKERING

1836, 4, 14. Elizabeth rocf Somerset MM, dtd 1835,11,30

PICKET

----, --, --. Thomas & Rhoda [Pickett]
    Ch: William   b 1820, 2, 17
        Mary   " 1821, 5, 5
    Thomas m 2nd Mary -----
    Ch: Martha   b 1827, 3, 8
        Henry   " 1828, 4, 10 d 1832, 2,19
          bur Deerfield
        Rachel   b 1829, 11, 4
        Hannah   " 1831, 6, 4
        James   " 1833, 7, 3 d 1837,10, 9
          bur Pennsville
        Joseph   b 1835, 4, 9 " 1835, 4,28
          bur Deerfield

    Ch: Sarah   b 1836, 7, 23
        Nathan   " 1838, 6, -- d 1840, 5,29
        Thomas   " 1840, 8, 9 " 1857, 2, 1
          bur Short Creek
        Matilda   b 1843, 8, 17

1840, 8, 19. Wm. [Pickett], s Thomas & Rhoda, Morgan Co., O.; m in Pennsville, Rebecca WORTHINGTON, dt Wm. & Elizabeth, Morgan Co., O.
    Ch: John   b 1842, 9, 18
        Mary   " 1843, 8, 31
        Jesse   " 1845, 12, 31 d 1849, 7,7
        Elizabeth " 1849, 7, 12
        Perley   " 1851, 2, 8
        Isaac   " 1853, 8, 12
        Louisa   " 1856, 1, 28
        Thomas   " 1859, 7, 8
        Sarah   " 1861, 2, 7
        Edward   " 1864, 9, 8
        Annie R. " 1867, 6, 9 d 1870, 2,25
          bur Hopewell

1841, 10, 21. Mary [Pickett] m Elisha DOUDNA

1845, 7, 15. Mary [Pickett] d ae 42 bur Hopewell

1846, 7, 14. Thomas [Pickett] d ae 49 bur Hopewell

1846, 11, 26. Rachel m Jesse WORTHINGTON

1873, 11, 15. Mary m Joseph John TABER

1879, 4, 18. Louisa D. m Wm. G. STEER

1829, 1, 10. James dis jH

1829, 4, 15. Hannah [Pickett], Jr. dis jH

1832, 5, 17. Moses dis mcd

1832, 6, 14. Hannah (form Healy) dis mcd

1833, 2, 3. Hannah dis jH

1859, 4, 14. Sarah gct Chesterfield MM

1860, 1, 19. Martha gct Chesterfield MM

1860, 1, 19. Hannah gct Chesterfield MM

1865, 1, 19. John dis military service

1871, 4, 13. Matilda Wood (form Picket) dis mcd

1873, 4, 17. Perley gct Stillwater MM, to m Rebecca Scofield

1874, 10, 15. Perley gct Stillwater MM

1879, 3, 13. Isaac dis mcd

1882, 11, 16. Thomas dis mcd

1883, 11, 15. Elizabeth gct Stillwater MM

1883, 11, 15. Wm. & w, Rebecca, & s, Edward, gct Stillwater MM

1904, 4, 14. Sarah M. gct Stillwater MM

PIDGEON

1853, 1, 3. John S., s Joseph & Elizabeth, b

1833, 4, 18. Amos & w, Ann, & ch, Harriet, Joseph & John, rocf Smithfield MM, dtd 1832,11,19

1843, 11, 22. Harriet m Joseph HAMMOND

1847, 2, 18. Joseph W. gct Chesterfield MM

1851, 5, 15. John dis mcd

1852, 2, 15. Joseph W. & w, Elizabeth, rocf Chesterfield MM, dtd 1852,1,17

1863, 4, 16. Joseph dis jG

PIDGEON, continued
1863, 5, 14. Ann & Elizabeth dis jG

PIERPONT
----, --, --. William & Matilda
    Ch: Maryann   b 1827, 10, 28
        Sarah Es-
          ther   " 1829, 10, 25 d 1833, 2,15
          bur Deerfield
        Elizabeth b 1832, 1, 29 " 1833, 2,22
          bur Deerfield
        Lydia   b 1834, 1, 13
        Rachel   " 1836, 5, 8 " 1857,11,16
          bur Pennsville
        Leah   b 1838, 5, 23 " 1839,10,28
          bur Pennsville
        Phebe   b 1840, 9, 20
        Delitha   " 1842, 12, 18 " 1860,10, 6
          bur Pennsville
        Obed   b 1844, 11, 23
        Edmund   " 1847, 5, 20
        Hannah   " 1850, 5, 14
1829, 9, 23. Elizabeth m Samuel B. HAMPTON
1850, 10, 20. Ann d ae 73 bur Pennsville
1851, 11, 13. Hannah d bur Pennsville
1854, 5, 24. Lydia m Richard Patten
1862, 10, 22. Phebe m Abner VERNON

1829, 10, 15. Obed dis jH
1831, 11, 17. Benjamin dis mcd
1832, 10, 18. Jonathan dis disunity
1836, 10, 15. John dis mcd
1837, 12, 14. Mary Wood (form Pierpont) dis
    mcd
1847, 6, 17. Eli dis mcd
1849, 9, 13. Mary Ann Calvert (form Pierpont)
    dis mcd
1865, 8, 17. Wm. & w, Matilda, & s, Edmund,
    gct Hickory Grove MM, Ia.
1866, 3, 15. Obed dis disunity
1873, 7, 17. Obed rst at Springville MM, Ia.,
    on consent of this mtg

PLUMMER
1835, 1, 25. Thomas d
1835, 11, 27. Mary, dt Abraham & Elizabeth, b
1837, 1, 25. Thomas, s Samuel & Margaret, Mor-
    gan Co., O.; m in Pennsville, Mary Ann
    SCOTT, dt John & Deborah, Morgan Co., O.,
    d 1887,5,25 ae 72 bur Pennsville
    Ch: John   b 1837, 9, 4
        Lydia Ann " 1839, 8, 31
        Deborah
          Jane   " 1843, 5, 26
        Joshua T. " 1845, 6, 18
        Susanna   " 1847, 7, 7 d 1847, 7,26
        Margaret B." 1849, 2, 27
        Robert S. " 1851, 7, 18 " 1854, 7,30
          bur Pennsville
        Granville W.
                  b 1854, 10, 12
        Mary   " 1857, 7, 16 d 1903, 9,16
        Ira   " 1860, 5, 29

1845, 3, 10. Joshua d ae 36 bur Pennsville
1852, 12, 30. Susanna d ae 40 bur Pennsville
1854, 3, 15. Richard d ae 50 bur Pennsville
1864, 9, 1. Thomas d ae 53 bur Pennsville
1865, 12, 17. Rebecca d ae 56 bur Pennsville

1829, 6, 18. Ann dis disunity
1834, 5, 15. Abraham & w, Elizabeth, & ch,
    Sarah, Talbott, Caspar, Rachel, Elizabeth,
    Ruthanna & Thomas, rocf Stillwater MM, dtd
    1834,4,26
1836, 11, 17. Richard rocf Smithfield MM, dtd
    1836,10,17
1836, 11, 17. Thomas rocf Smithfield MM, dtd
    1836,10,17
1836, 11, 17. Susanna W. rocf Smithfield MM,
    dtd 1836,10,17
1836, 12, 3. Joshua rocf Smithfield MM, dtd
    1836,7,18
1836, 12, 3. Rebecca rocf Smithfield MM, dtd
    1836,7,18
1863, 3, 19. Deborah Jane Grist (form Plum-
    mer) con mcd
1867, 4, 18. Lydia Ann Hollingsworth (form
    Plummer) con mcd
1875, 8, 2. Joshua con mcd
1879, 8, 14. Granville con mcd
1880, 10, 14. Granville dis
1886, 6, 17. Ira dis mcd

PURVIS
----, --, --. John [Purvies] d 1845,5,16 ae
    59; m Mary ----- d 1845,6,8 ae 49
    Ch: Jonathan b 1821, 10, 19 d 1844, 9,17
        Moses   " 1823, 5, 21
        Rachel   " 1825, 5, 9
        Levi   " 1827, 4, 7
        Sarah   " 1829, 7, 1
        Isaac   " 1829, 7, 1 d 1842, 2,22
          bur Pennsville
        Elijah   b 1833, 6, 28
        Ann   " 1836, 10, 11
        Mary   " 1838, 7, 16

1844, 8, 15. Moses [Pervis] dis disunity
1845, 3, 13. Emily Ann (form Scott) dis mcd
1847, 2, 18. Elijah & Mary [Pervis] gct
    Chesterfield MM (minors)
1847, 11, 18. Sarah [Pervis] gct West Grove MM
    Ind.
1847, 11, 18. Rachel [Pervis] gct White Water
    MM, Ind.
1853, 1, 13. Elijah rocf Plymouth MM, dtd
    1852,12,20
1857, 3, 19. Levi [Pervis] gct Stillwater MM
1857, 3, 19. Ann [Pervis], minor, gct Still-
    water MM

RAINEY
1872, 5, 16. Ella Louisa (form Scott) dis mcd

RANDEL
1842, 6, 17. Mary d ae 86 bur Pennsville

RATCLIFF

----, --, --. Benjamin & Martha
 Ch: Martha   b 1845, 11, 24
   Rachel M. " 1848, 7, 21 d 1853, 8,18
    bur Hopewell
   Maria   b 1850, 11, 4 " 1855, 6, 8
    bur Hopewell

1844, 12, 19. Benjamin B. [Ratliff] & w, Martha, & ch, Lemuel, Sarah Ann, Charles,
 Elizabeth & John, rocf Flushing MM, dtd
 1844,11,21
1857, 2, 19. Lemuel dis mcd
1857, 3, 19. Rebecca (form Stubbs) dis mcd
1857, 4, 16. Rebecca (form Stubbs) dis mcd
1863, 3, 19. Benjamin dis jG
1864, 7, 14. Martha dis jG
1865, 5, 18. Charles dis military service
1865, 5, 18. John dis military service
1868, 3, 19. Elizabeth dis disunity
1868, 5, 14. Martha Osborn (form Ratcliff)
 dis mcd

REEVE
1836, 2, 18. Joshua rocf Upper Springfield
 MM, dtd 1835,11,28
1836, 3, 17. Elizabeth rocf Carmel MM, dtd
 1835,12,19

REYNOLDS
1838, 9, 13. Mary Jane rocf Flushing MM, dtd
 1838,5,24
1841, 11, 18. Mary Jane dis jas

RHODES
1836, 4, 14. Harmon & w, Elizabeth, & ch,
 Rebecca, Martha, Wm. & Isaac, rocf Short
 Creek MM, dtd 1835,11,12

RICHARDSON
1855, 2, 22. Hannah D. [Richerson] m Jesse
 METCALF
1860, 4, 21. Lydia P. m Thomas WEBSTER

1828, 6, 21. Isaac & w, Ann, & ch, Ruth &
 Hannah, rocf Little Brittain MM, Pa., dtd
 1828,3,15
1828, 7, 17. Samuel & w, Rebecca, & ch, Mary,
 Samuel, Eliza, Martha, Ann & Joseph, rocf
 Little Brittain MM, Pa., dtd 1828,4,19
1828, 7, 17. Rebecca W. rocf Little Brittain
 MM, Pa., dtd 1828,4,19
1828, 7, 17. Margaret rocf Little Britain
 MM, Pa., dtd 1828,4,19
1828, 7, 17. Lydia rocf Little Brittain MM,
 Pa., dtd 1828,4,19
1829, 3, 19. Samuel Jr. dis jH
1829, 4, 16. Samuel dis jH
1829, 4, 16. Isaac & w, Ann, & ch, Ruth C. &
 Hannah, gct Green Plain MM
1829, 4, 16. Rebecca, Rebecca W. & Lydia dis
 jH
1829, 10, 15. Margaret dis jH

1830, 5, 13. Mary dis jH
1834, 7, 17. Eliza dis jH
1834, 11, 13. Martha dis jH
1844, 3, 14. Ann dis jH
1844, 5, 16. Joseph dis disunity
1850, 10, 17. Hannah D. rst on consent of
 Providence MM
1851, 3, 13. Lydia, Margaret & Rebecca, ch
 Hannah S., recrq
1866, 1, 18. Rebecca Hall (form Richardson)
 dis mcd
1893, 5, 18. Rebecca W. Hall (form Richardson
 rst rq

ROBINS
----, --, --. Elihu & Mary Ann
 Ch: Zachariah
   H.   b 1839, 12, 11
   William D. " 1842, 3, 4
   Asenath " 1843, 11, 23

1840, 6, 18. Elihu [Robbins] & w, Mary Ann,
 & s, Zacheriah, rocf Somerset MM, dtd
 1840,4,27
1846, 11, 19. Mary Ann & ch, Zachariah, Wm.
 & Asenath, gct Salem MM, Ia.
1847, 8, 19. Elihu [Robbins] dis disunity

ROMANS
----, --, --. Isaac & Mary
 Ch: Mary
   Ephraim   b 1814, --, --
   Ezra   " 1816, --, --
   Sarah Ann " 1818, --, --
   Amos   " 1820, --, --
   Hampton " 1823, --, --
   Abraham " 1827, --, --
   Elizabeth " 1831, 9, 30

ROSE
1851, 11, 13. Mary Ellen (form Evans) dis mcd

SANTEE
1874, 11, 16. Mary P. (form Penrose) dis mcd

SCOTT
----, --, --. John m Deborah ----- d 1866,12,
 24 ae 81 bur Pennsville
 Ch: Emily Ann b 1824, 5, 24
   Asenath " 1828, 2, 27
1837, 1, 25. Mary Ann m Thomas PLUMMER
1850, 11, 20. Sarah Ann m Samuel EMBREE

1832, 7, 19. Robert gct Stillwater MM
1841, 4, 15. Samuel dis disunity
1843, 8, 17. Emily Ann dis disunity
1844, 3, 14. Cyrus dis mcd
1844, 4, 18. Elizabeth (form Metcalf) dis mcd
1845, 3, 13. Emily Ann Purvis (form Scott)
 dis mcd
1848, 4, 13. Thomas dis mcd
1872, 5, 16. Ella Louisa Rainey (form Scott)
 dis mcd

SCOFIELD
1873, 4, 17. Perley Picket gct Stillwater MM,
   to m Rebecca Scofield

SEARS
1844, 3, 20. David, s Peter & Anna, Belmont
   Co., O.; m in Pennsville, Rachel B. PATTEN
   dt John & Rebecca, Morgan Co., O.

1836, 2, 18. Robert Millhouse gct Stillwater
   MM, to m Martha Sears
1844, 6, 13. Rachel gct Stillwater MM
1862, 9, 18. Peter & w, Pheriba, & ch, Mary
   B., Sarah D., Benjamin S. & Edwin W., rocf
   Stillwater MM, dtd 1862,6,28

SHIELDS
1873, 8, 14. Caroline (form Embree) dis mcd

SIDWELL
1831, 6, 16. Rebecca Llewelyn (form Sidwell)
   dis mcd
1832, 4, 19. Nathan dis disunity
1832, 4, 19. Rebecca dis disunity

SIMPSON
----, --, --. Austin & Sabilla
      Ch: John   b 1840, 5, 11
          Richard   " 1842, 6, 13

1834, 8, 14. Ann (form Bain) dis mcd
1838, 8, 16. Austin recrq
1838, 12, 13. Austin gct Stillwater MM, to m
   Sibilah Fawcett
1839, 3, 14. Sabbilla F. rocf Stillwater MM,
   dtd 1839,2,23
1842, 9, 15. Austin & w, Sibbilla, & ch, John
   & Richard, gct Chesterfield MM
1870, 11, 17. Jane (form Penrose) dis mcd
1871, 3, 16. Mary P. (form Penrose) con mcd

SMITH
1841, 11, 24. Evan, s Thomas & Mary, Morgan
   Co., O.; m in Pennsville, Mary BURGESS, dt
   John & Margaret, Morgan Co., O.
      Ch: Margaret
             Ann   b 1842, 8, 25
             Maria   " 1844, 3, 31
             Louisa   " 1846, 2, 20
             Caroline " 1848, 1, 30
             Joshua   " 1850, 10, 20
             Marion   " 1862, 6, 18
1838, 6, 20. Elizabeth m Joel GILBERT
1846, 5, 20. Samuel, s Thomas & Nancy, Morgan Co., O.; m in Pennsville, Hannah
   KING, dt Joseph & Mary, Morgan Co., O.
      Ch: Lusinda   b 1849, 2, 24 d 1849, 7,31
          Sarah Elsa " 1850, 12, 31
1846, 11, 15. Rebecca L. d ae 48
1847, 4, 21. James, s Thomas & Nancy, Morgan
   Co., O.; m in Pennsville, Ruth KING, dt
   Joseph & Mary, Morgan Co., O.
      Ch: William   b 1848, 5, 29

Ch: Caroline N.b 1852, 11, 9
    Charles
      Thomas   " 1857, 8, 5
1852, 9, 22. David, s William & Ann, Morgan
   Co., O.; m in Pennsville, Mary FOULKE, dt
   Wm. & Eliza, Morgan Co., O.
1868, 11, 28. Hannah F. d ae 32 bur Pennsville
1873, 3, 19. David, s William & Ann, Morgan
   Co., O.; m in Pennsville, Lydia V. McGREW
   dt Samuel & Elizabeth VAILE

1828, 7, 17. James & w, Ruth, & ch, Rebecca,
   Kersey, Mary & Joseph, rocf Little Brittain MM, Pa., dtd 1828,4,19
1828, 12, 18. James dis jH
1829, 1, 10. Ruth dis jH
1836, 4, 14. Joseph & w, Mary, rocf Stillwater MM, dtd 1836,3,26
1836, 9, 15. Thomas & w, Nancy, & ch, Evan,
   Samuel, Rachel, James & Thomas, rocf Upper
   Springfield MM, dtd 1836,8,27
1836, 8, 15. Elizabeth rocf Upper Springfield
   MM, dtd 1836,8,27
1836, 12, 3. Wm. & w, Ann, & ch, Mary David,
   Humphrey, Elihu & Lydia, rocf Stillwater
   MM, dtd 1836,11,26
1837, 5, 18. Thomas & w, Elizabeth, & s, Wm.,
   rocf Stillwater MM, dtd 1837,4,22
1837, 11, 16. Cert rec for Henry & w, Maria, &
   ch, Wm. & Henry Timmerman & John Frederick
   & Helene Smith, from Minden MM, Germany
   2 months mtg, dtd 1837,7,27, end to Chesterfield MM
1839, 6, 13. Levi & w, Rebecca, & ch, Lydia
   Ann, Samuel & Phebe, rocf Short Creek MM,
   dtd 1839,5,21
1842, 3, 17. Evan & w, Mary, gct Chesterfield MM
1843, 12, 14. Rebecca & Mary dis jH
1844, 2, 15. Kersey dis disunity
1845, 2, 13. Evan & w, Mary, & ch, Margaret
   Ann & Mary, rocf Chesterfield MM, dtd
   1845,1,8
1846, 9, 17. Samuel & w, Hannah, gct Chesterfield MM
1847, 6, 17. Levi dis disunity
1848, 5, 18. Thomas & w, Nancy, & s, Thomas,
   gct Chesterfield MM
1848, 6, 15. Samuel & w, Hannah, & dt, Mary,
   rocf Chesterfield MM, dtd 1848,3,18
1848, 7, 13. Rachel gct Chesterfield MM
1849, 8, 16. Joseph dis disunity
1850, 2, 14. Lydia Ann dis jas
1851, 1, 16. Evan & w, Mary, & ch, Margaret,
   Ann, Maria, Louisa, Caroline & Joshua,
   gct Plymouth MM
1851, 5, 15. Samuel & w, Hannah, & ch, Mary
   J. & Sarah Eliza, gct Chesterfield MM
1853, 1, 13. Mary F. gct Chesterfield MM
1855, 2, 15. Nancy rocf Plymouth MM, dtd
   1855,1,22
1855, 3, 15. James dis disunity
1855, 10, 18. Thomas rocf Chesterfield MM,

SMITH, continued
    dtd 1855,9,15
1858, 6, 17. Nancy gct Plymouth MM
1858, 2, 18. Thomas dis disunity
1862, 12, 18. Hannah (form Foulke) con mcd
1862, 12, 18. Margaret Ann Penrose (form Smith)
    con mcd
1864, 1, 14. David & s, Wm. F., rocf Chester-
    field MM, dtd 1863,12,19
1866, 11, 15. Wm. dis military service
1871, 4, 13. Charles, minor s James & Ruth,
    gct Hickory Grove MM, Ia.
1871, 8, 17. Ruth gct Hickory Grove MM, Ia.
1873, 4, 17. Caroline dis disunity
1873, 5, 15. Agnes & Elmer McGrew, ch Lydia
    V. Smith, recrq
1878, 4, 18. David & w, Lydia V., & s, Elmer
    McGrew, gct Chesterfield MM
1880, 12, 16. Wm. F. dis mcd
1889, 11, 14. Hannah S. (form Penrose) dis
    mcd & jas

SPENCER
1836, 11, 21. Ira, s Abner & Harriett, b
1855, 3, 22. Abner, Belmont Co., O.; m in
    Hopewell, Rachel LIGHTFOOT, Morgan Co., O.

1836, 4, 14. Abner & w, Harriet, & ch,
    Lydia & Asenath, rocf Plainfield MM, dtd
    1836,3,23
1839, 5, 16. Abner & w, Harriet, & ch, Lydia
    Ann, Asenath & Ira, gct Plainfield MM
1855, 7, 19. Abner & s, Ira L., rocf Plain-
    field MM, dtd 1855,6,20
1855, 7, 19. Asenath rocf Plainfield MM, dtd
    1855,6,20
1860, 12, 14. Abner dis
1862, 5, 15. Rachel dis disunity
1867, 2, 14. Asenath gct Hickory Grove MM,
    Ia.

STANLEY
1836, 10, 15. Jacob, minor, rocf Marlborough
    MM, dtd 1836,7,26, end by Upper Spring-
    field MM 1836,8,27
1837, 4, 13. Millicent & ch, Martin & Rachel,
    rocf Marlborough MM, dtd 1837,9,27
1837, 5, 18. Jacob, minor, gct Upper Spring-
    field MM

STANTON
1830, 6, 17. Richard rocf Short Creek MM,
    dtd 1830,3,23
1845, 6, 19. Richard dis jas

STARBUCK
1879, 8, 15. Benjamin F., s John & Sarah,
    Belmont Co., O.; m in Pennsville, Sarah
    MILHOUSE, dt Robert & Rachel, Morgan Co.,
    O.
1893, 2, 17. Benjamin F., s John & Sarah,
    Belmont Co., O.; m in Pennsville, Anna
    LLEWELYN, dt Thomas & Martha, Morgan Co.,O.

1879, 12, 18. Sarah M. gct Short Creek MM
1880, 2, 19. Sarah M. gct Short Creek MM
1893, 8, 17. Ann L. gct Short Creek MM

STARLEN
1858, 5, 13. Mary D. (form Maris) dis mcd

STEADMAN
1863, 12, 23. Daniel, s Jefferson & Hannah,
    Morgan Co., O.; m in Pennsville, Louisa
    D. STUBBS, dt John & Rachel, Morgan Co.,
    O.
    Ch: John   b 1867, 10, 27
        Arthur   " 1868, 3, 19
        Lewis Elmer " 1870, 12, 9
        James F.   " 1875, 1, 11

1863, 10, 15. Daniel recrq
1888, 11, 15. Daniel dis jas
1889, 2, 14. Louisa J. dis jas
1890, 6, 19. Arthur dis mcd & jas
1895, 7, 18. John S. dis jas

STEER
1868, 11, 21. Lindley, s Israel & Rebecca,
    Belmont Co., O.; m in Pennsville, Hannah
    S. PENROSE, dt Richard & Ann Elizabeth,
    Morgan Co., O.
1879, 4, 18. Wm. G., s James & Mary, Belmont
    Co., O.; m in Hopewell, Louisa D. PICKETT
    dt Wm. & Rebecca, Morgan Co., O.

1869, 3, 18. Hannah P. gct Short Creek MM,
1879, 12, 18. Louisa D. gct Stillwater MM

STEPHENS
----, --, --. David & Rebecca [Stephen]
    Ch: William D. b 1830, 7, 20
        Ann   " 1833, 3, 15
        Elizabeth " 1835, 6, 25
        Elwood   " 1837, 7, 20
        Lydia   " 1839, 10, 22
        Rachel D. " 1842, 1, 7
1852, 7, 5. Jonathan d ae 63 bur Pennsville
1857, 1, 9. Esther d ae 71 bur Pennsville
1865, 3, 15. David [Stephen] d ae 72 bur
    Pennsville
1871, 5, 20. David [Stephen], s Zachariah &
    Elizabeth, Guernsey Co., O.; m in Penns-
    ville, Anna MILLHOUSE, dt Robert & Martha,
    Morgan Co., O.
1873, 6, 25. Lydia T. [Stephen] d ae 33 bur
    Pennsville
1874, 6, 27. Rebecca [Stephen] d ae 73 bur
    Pennsville

1829, 9, 17. Jonathan & w, Esther, & ch,
    Samuel, Joseph, Amos L., Elizabeth &
    Isaac, rocf Short Creek MM, dtd 1829,8,18
1831, 1, 13. David & Rebecca S. rocf Rober-
    son MM, Pa., dtd 1829,7,8, end by Short
    Creek MM, 1829,9,22
1832, 12, 13. Samuel dis disunity

STEPHENS, continued
1837, 1, 19. Phebe [Stephen] & ch, Deborah,
     Josiah, Samuel, Rebecca, Anna D. & Wm. M.,
     rocf Short Creek MM, dtd 1836,11,22
1838, 3, 15. Joseph dis disunity
1839, 10, 17. Amos L. [Stevens] dis disunity
1841, 9, 16. Deborah King (form Stevens) dis
     mcd
1842, 8, 18. Isaac [Stevens] dis jas
1848, 8, 18. Samuel [Stevens] dis jH
1848, 8, 17. Rebecca [Stevens] dis jH
1848, 11, 16. Caroline (form Todd) dis mcd
1850, 3, 14. Ann dis disunity
1851, 2, 13. Elizabeth Jones (form Stephens)
     dis mcd
1863, 2, 19. Elwood dis mcd
1869, 8, 19. Elizabeth Vanfoson (form Stephens)
     dis mcd
1871, 12, 14. Anna M. gct Flushing MM

STRAHL
1843, 5, 29. Stephen [Strall] d ae 18 bur
     Pennsville

1828, 9, 18. Mary & ch, Osborh, Angelina,
     Stephen & Philip, gct Stillwater MM
1836, 1, 14. Elmer rocf Flushing MM, dtd
     1835,10,22
1839, 5, 16. Mary & ch, Osborn, Stephen,
     Philip, Rebecca Ann, Mary Jane & Sibella,
     rocf Stillwater MM, dtd 1839,4,27
1843, 9, 14. Mary & ch, Philip, Rebecca Ann,
     Mary Jane, Cibilla & Sarah Lee, gct Salem
     MM, Ia.
1843, 9, 14. Osborn gct Salem MM, Ia.

STRATTON
1872, 2, 6. Daniel d ae 74 bur New Garden, O.

1866, 5, 17. Joseph Masters gct New Garden
     MM, to m Esther Stratton
1870, 5, 19. Daniel rocf New Garden MM, dtd
     1870,3,24
1882, 5, 18. Elisha Llewellyn gct New Garden
     MM, to m Abigail Stratton

STUBBS
1832, 10, 24. Sarah Stubbs m Isaac Vernon
----, --, --. Isaac & Elizabeth
     Ch: Rebecca   b 1833, 11, 19
         Joseph   " 1836, 10, 24
----, --, --. William & Hannah
     Ch: Esther   b 1839, 5, 17 d 1839, 6,18
         bur Pennsville
         Thomas W. b 1840, 6, 14
         Samuel   " 1842, 4, 6
         William   " 1844, 8, 26
----, --, --. John & Rachel
     Ch: Maria   b 1841, 12, 6 d 1868,11,11
         bur Pennsville
         Asenath   b 1844, 5, 22 " 1845, 1,10
         bur Pennsville
1844, 5, 23. Mary m Samuel KING

1844, 11, 11. Wm. d ae 30 bur Pennsville
1844, 11, 28. Elizabeth d ae 24 bur Pennsville
1845, 6, 1. John d ae 27 bur Hopewell
1847, 7, 22. Rachel m Robert MILLHOUSE
1863, 12, 23. Louisa W. m Daniel STEADMAN

1832, 4, 19. Isaac & w, Elizabeth, & ch,
     Isaac, Henry & Margaret, rocf Stillwater
     MM, dtd 1832,3,24
1832, 4, 19. Sarah rocf Stillwater MM, dtd
     1832,3,24
1838, 9, 13. Hannah (form Worrall) dis mcd
1839, 3, 14. Hannah [Stubs] rst rq
1839, 3, 14. Wm. [Stubs] recrq
1840, 1, 16. Elizabeth [Stubs] Jr. recrq
1840, 3, 19. John [Stubs] recrq
1840, 3, 19. Rachel [Stubs] & dt, Luiza,
     recrq
1841, 8, 19. Mary recrq
1848, 5, 18. Isaac Jr. dis mcd
1852, 6, 17. Margaret Talbott (form Stubbs)
     dis mcd
1852, 8, 18. Henry dis disunity
1857, 3, 19. Rebecca Ratcliff (form Stubbs)
     dis mcd
1857, 4, 16. Rebecca Ratcliff (form Stubbs)
     dis mcd
1858, 1, 14. Joseph dis disunity
1864, 4, 14. Samuel dis enlisting in army
1864, 5, 19. Elizabeth dis jG
1864, 5, 19. Isaac dis jG
1875, 11, 18. Hannah gct Coal Creek MM, Ia.

TABER
1873, 11, 15. Joseph John, s Louis & Mary Ann,
     Jefferson Co., O.; m in Hopewell, Mary
     PICKET, dt Wm. & Rebecca, Morgan Co., O.

1874, 10, 15. Mary P. gct Short Creek MM

TALBOTT
----, --, --. Wm. A. & Ann
     Ch: Mary Ann b 1832, 10, 28
         Abner   " 1836, 12, 19
     Wm. A. m 2nd Sarah -----
     Ch: Lewis   b 1842, 10, 16
1838, 5, 23. Eliza Jane [Talbot] m Elihu H.
     PATTEN
1838, 7, 25. Joseph, s William & Ann, Morgan
     Co., O.; m in Pennsville, Hannah PATTAN,
     dt Wm. & Phebe, Morgan Co., O.
     Ch: Elisha H. b 1839, 8, 9
         Ann P.   " 1841, 6, 13
         Phebe   " 1843, 10, 18
1839, 4, 27. Ann d ae 43 bur Pennsville
1839, 11, 30. Kinsey d ae 14 bur Pennsville
1851, 12, 24. Mary Ann m Abner WILLIAMS

1832, 11, 15. Wm. A. & w, Ann, & ch, Joseph,
     Eliza Jane, John, Kinsey, Allen & Wm.,
     rocf Smithfield MM, dtd 1832,7,23
1836, 11, 17. Joseph F. & w, Margaret, rocf
     Smithfield MM, dtd 1836,7,18

TALBOTT, continued
1840, 6, 18. Wm. gct Chesterfield MM, to m
    Sarah Hammet
1840, 11, 19. Sarah R. [Talbot] rocf Chester-
    field MM, dtd 1840,9,19
1845, 1, 16. John dis mcd
1845, 6, 19. Sarah (form Patton) dis mcd
1846, 7, 16. Joseph dis disunity
1851, 2, 13. Hannah & ch, Elisha, Ann &
    Phebe, gct White Water MM, Ind.
1852, 5, 13. Allen dis disunity
1852, 5, 13. Margaret (form Stubbs) dis mcd
1852, 6, 17. Wm. Jr. dis mcd
1857, 3, 19. Wm. & w, Sarah, & ch, Abner &
    Louis, gct Stillwater MM

TANNER
1866, --, --. Lydia d

1847, 5, 13. Lydia rocf Stillwater MM, dtd
    1847,4,24

THOMAS
----, --, --. Jesse & Rebecca
    Ch: Elizabeth b 1810, 1, 1
        Sarah   " 1811, 4, 17
        Mary Ann   " 1813, 3, 7
        Joseph   " 1814, 12, 5
        Debora   " 1817, 3, 27
        Philena   " 1819, 10, 9
        Joanna   " 1822, 1, 23
        Jonathan H." 1824, 3, 25
        Eli   " 1826, 5, 19
        Jesse Jr. " 1828, 7, 28
        David   " 1831, 6, 26 d 1832, 4,11
----, --, --. Aaron & Sarah
    Ch: Jonathan b 1822, 8, 11
        Susan   " 1825, 12, 24
        John   " 1828, 2, 14
        Mary L.   " 1829, 12, 23
        Wm. J.   " 1832, 4, 22
        Elleanor   " 1835, 2, 9
1825, 6, 30. Jonathan H. d ae 1 bur Blue Rock
1837, 11, 22. Elizabeth m John ENGLE

1835, 7, 16. Aaron & w, Sarah, & ch, Jonathan
    Susanna, John, Mary & William, rocf Short
    Creek MM, dtd 1835,5,19
1839, 5, 16. Jesse & w, Rebecca, & ch, Jo-
    anna, Eli & Jesse, gct Chesterfield MM
1839, 5, 16. Sarah gct Chesterfield MM
1839, 5, 16. Mary Ann gct Chesterfield MM
1839, 5, 16. Deborah gct Chesterfield MM
1839, 5, 16. Filena gct Chesterfield MM

THOMPSON
1828, 10, 16. David rocf Short Creek MM, dtd
    1828,6,24
1828, 12, 18. Joseph M., Joshua & Esther,
    minors, rocf Short Creek MM, dtd 1828,1,22
1829, 3, 19. David dis jH
1830, 8, 19. Joseph M. dis mcd
1831, 2, 17. Samuel & w, Mary, rocf Short

Creek MM, dtd 1830,11,23
1831, 7, 14. Elizabeth (form Mendenhall) dis
    mcd
1832, 12, 13. Ann rocf Short Creek MM, dtd
    1832,10,23
1833, 5, 16. Joshua Jr. gct Short Creek MM
1833, 10, 17. Ann gct Short Creek MM
1833, 12, 19. Esther C. dis disunity

1842, 5, 19. Edith (form Mendenhall) dis mcd
1843, 1, 19. Mary Ann (form Wood) dis mcd

TIMMERMAN (or ZIMMERMAN)
1837, 11, 16. Cert rec for Henry & w, Maria,
    & ch, Wm. & Henry Timmerman & John Fred-
    erick & HeleneSmith, from Minden MM
    (2 months) Mtg, Germany, dtd 1837,7,27,
    end to Chesterfield MM

TODD
----, --, --. Robert & Sarah
    Ch: Ann   b 1814, 1, 12
        Theodate   " 1815, 10, 28
        Rebecca   " 1818, 6, 11
        Robert   " 1820, 8, 9
        Maranda   " 1822, 3, 28
        Sarah   " 1825, 6, 3
        Caroline E." 1827, 7, 7

1831, 4, 14. James dis disunity
1832, 4, 19. Ann McMahan (form Todd) dis mcd
1832, 5, 17. Sarah dis disunity
1832, 7, 19. Robert dis disunity
1832, 12, 13. Theodate Fowler (form Todd)
    dis mcd
1841, 3, 18. Robert Jr. dis mcd
1841, 4, 15. Susanna (form Bundy) dis mcd
1841, 5, 13. Marinda dis disunity
1848, 11, 16. Caroline Stephens (form Todd)
    dis mcd
1849, 10, 19. Sarah dis disunity

TOWNSEND
1831, 6, 16. Ruth & dt, Juli-Ann, rocf Still-
    water MM, dtd 1831,3,26
1837, 5, 18. Ruth gct Somerset MM
1837, 5, 18. Juliann gct Somerset MM
1864, 5, 19. Hannah & ch, Stephen & Hannah
    & niece, Sarah T. Oblinger, rocf Somerset
    MM, dtd 1864,4,25

TRIMBLE
----, --, --. John & Lydia
    Ch: Caleb
        Harlan   b 1819, 10, --
        Mary   " 1822, 2, --
        Edwards   " 1824, --, --
        Isaac   " 1828, --, --

1829, 5, 14. John dis disunity
1829, 5, 14. Lydia dis disunity
1840, 3, 19. Elisha dis mcd
1843, 8, 17. James dis mcd

TRIMBLE, continued
1843, 8, 17. Harlen dis mcd
1850, 2, 14. Mary dis jas
1850, 11, 14. Edward dis mcd

TYSON
1837, 9, 14. Oswald E. rocf ND MM, dtd
    1837,5,23
1844, 4, 18. Oswald E. dis mcd & jas

VAIL
1827, 8, 18. John T. Wells gct Plainfield MM,
    to m Esther Vail
1838, 6, 14. John & w, Esther, & ch, Phebe
    & Orpha, rocf Somerset MM, dtd 1838,5,28
1841, 7, 15. John & w, Esther, & ch, Phebe,
    Orpha & Thomas Carr, gct Upper Springfield
    MM

VANCE
1853, 10, 13. Sarah gct Phila. MM held at
    Mulberry St.

VANFOSON
1869, 8, 19. Elizabeth (form Stephens) dis mcd

VANHORN
1839, 6, 13. Elizabeth rocf Short Creek MM,
    dtd 1839,5,21
1842, 7, 14. Elizabeth gct Chesterfield MM

VANLAW
1838, 8, 22. Elisha, s John & Sarah, Wash-
    ington Co., O.; m in Pennsville, Anna
    WORTHINGTON, dt Zenas & Ann, Morgan Co.,
    O.
1847, 10, 20. Ann m Owen MARIS

1839, 1, 17. Anna W. gct Chesterfield MM
1840, 1, 16. Anna W. & s, Elisha, rocf Ches-
    terfield MM, dtd 1839,12,21
1848, 3, 16. Ann W. Maris & s, Elisha Van-
    law, gct Chesterfield MM

VAUGHN
1896, 12, 23. Joseph, s James & Rhoda, Morrow
    Co.; m in Pennsville, Martha MILHOUSE, dt
    Robert & Rachel, Morgan Co., O.

1862, 12, 18. Anna (form Hollingsworth) dis
    mcd
1895, 12, 19. Joseph & s, Arthur L., recrq

VENABLE
1837, 6, 15. Vincent rocf Salem MM, dtd
    1837,5,24

VERNON
----, --, --. James & Rhoda
    ChP Mary   b 1824, 3, 26
        Isaac   " 1826, 7, 6
        Benjamin " 1828, 2, 22
        Joseph   " 1830, 5, 22

Ch: Amos   b 1833, 5, 20
    Abner   " 1837, 1, 19
    John   " 1840, 3, 17
    Zilpha   " 1842, 9, 21
    Elisha   " 1845, 9, 3
1830, 3, 24. Theodate m Jonathan MORRIS
1832, 10, 24. Isaac, s Amos & Mary, Morgan
    Co., O.; m in Deerfield, Sarah STUBS, dt
    Isaac & Elizabeth, Morgan Co., O.
    Ch: Joseph   b 1833, 9, 5
        Rachel   " 1836, 6, 12
        Matilda   " 1838, 8, 21
        Elizabeth " 1841, 12, 11
        Henry   " 1846, 2, 25
        James   " 1849, 4, 9
        Asenath   " 1852, 10, 28
1847, 3, 25. Elisha, s Wm. & Peninah, Athens
    Co., O.; m in Hopewell, Mary VERNON, dt
    James & Rhoda, Morgan Co., O.
    Ch: Hannah   b 1850, 8, 22
        Rhoda Ann " 1853, 2, 23
1848, 3, 6. James d ae 47 bur Hopewell, O.
1854, 1, 27. Elisha d ae 27 bur Hopewell
1855, 11, 22. Amos, s James & Rhoda, Morgan
    Co., O.; m in Hopewell, Elizabeth BAILEY,
    dt Henry & Mary, Morgan Co., O.
    Ch: Angeline b 1857, 9, 10
        Lauretta
        Asenath   " 1858, 12, 29
        Mary Adal-
        aide   " 1860, 11, 12
        Anna Alwil-
        da   " 1863, 2, 22
        Agnes Mar-
        tilda   " 1863, 2, 22
        Lucy Jane " 1866, 2, 2
        Elizabeth
        Ellen   " 1867, 10, 25
1857, 12, 24. Mary m Jesse CRAFT
1858, 12, 22. Joseph, s James & Rhoda, Morgan
    Co., O.; m in Pennsville, Hannah MIL-
    HOUSE, dt Daniel & Esther, Morgan Co., O.
    Ch: Edith   b 1862, 7, 2
1862, 10, 22. Abner, s James & Rhoda, Morgan
    Co., O.; m in Pennsville, Phebe PIERPOINT
    dt Wm. & Matilda, Morgan Co., O.
1863, 7, 1. Phebe d ae 22 bur Pennsville

1828, 12, 18. Theodate rocf Flushing MM, dtd
    1828,7,25
1832, 10, 18. Isaac rocf Stillwater MM, dtd
    1832,9,22
1837, 9, 14. Amos & w, Jane, & ch, Robert,
    David & Mary, rocf Somerset MM, dtd 1837,
    6,26
1838, 4, 19. James & w, Roda, & ch, Mary,
    Isaac, Benjamin, Joseph, Amos & Abner,
    rocf Stillwater MM, dtd 1838,3,24
1847, 7, 15. Mary gct Chesterfield MM
1850, 6, 13. Elisha & w, Mary, & s, Denny,
    rocf Chesterfield MM, dtd 1850,3,16
1853, 12, 15. Isaac & w, Sarah, & ch, Rachel,
    Matilda, Elizabeth, Henry, James &

VERNON, continued
       Asenath, gct Vermillion MM, Ill.
1856, 3, 13. Isaac dis mcd
1858, 6, 17. Mary Craft & ch, Hannah & Rhoda
    Ann Vernon, gct Plymouth MM
1859, 6, 11. Benjamin dis mcd
1864, 4, 14. Amos dis military service
1865, 8, 17. John gct Chesterfield MM, to m
    Elizabeth Edgerton
1868, 1, 16. Rhoda dis jG
1868, 9, 17. Joseph & w, Hannah, & ch, Edith
    & Isaac, gct Springville MM, Ia.
1870, 4, 14. John gct Chesterfield MM
1870, 5, 19. Abner dis mcd

VORE
1829, 5, 14. Rebecca rocf Stillwater MM, dtd
    1829,3,28

WALKER
1832, 3, 15. Thompson & Mary, ch Mary Craven,
    rocf Short Creek MM, dtd 1831,9,20
1839, 8, 15. Thompson gct Chesterfield MM

WALTER
1866, 3, 18. Phebe d ae 77 bur Hopewell

1839, 8, 15. Phebe rocf Plainfield MM, dtd
    1839,7,24

WARD
1847, 3, 18. Hannah Maria (form Dewees) dis
    mcd & jH
1852, 5, 13. Abigail (form Bundy) con mcd
1853, 6, 8. Abigail gct Pleasant Plain MM,
    Ia.

WARRINGTON
1864, 5, 19. Nathan & w, Mary D., & ch,
    Linneus, Henry, Sarah Ann, Hannah, Irving,
    Wilson & Mary, rocf Upper Springfield MM,
    dtd 1864,4,22

WAY
1835, 12, 17. Benjamin & w, Abigail, & ch,
    John & Deborah, rocf Somerset MM, dtd
    1835,10,26
1836, 4, 14. Robert & w, Lydia, & ch, Milli-
    cent, Mary Ann, David & Sarah, rocf Somer-
    set MM, dtd 1836,3,28
1837, 1, 19. Sarah rocf Somerset MM, dtd
    1836,11,28
1864, 3, 17. Hannah & ch, Mary Jane, Charles
    Harvey, George Washington, Alfancy Marion
    & Iradora Ann, rocf Plymouth MM, dtd 1864,
    1,18

WEBSTER
1860, 4, 21. Thomas, s Thomas & Ann, Guernsey
    Co., O.; m in Pennsville, Lydia P.
    RICHARDSON, dt Samuel W. & Hannah, Morgan
    Co., O.

1838, 9, 13. Hannah & ch, Jesse, Isaac &
    Sarah, rocf Flushing MM, dtd 1838,5,24
1841, 4, 15. Isaac dis disunity
1842, 5, 19. Jesse dis jas
1843, 3, 16. Hannah dis disunity
1861, 6, 13. Lydia P. (form Richardson) gct
    Stillwater MM

WELLS
1827, 12, 31. William, s Levi & Ann, b
1828, 12, 10. Margaret, dt John & Esther, b

1827, 5, 19. Levi G. con mcd
1827, 8, 18. John T. gct Plainfield MM, to m
    Esther Vail
1827, 11, 17. Ann M. rocf Concord MM, dtd
    1827,10,24
1828, 1, 19. Esther rocf Concord MM, dtd
    1827,12,20
1828, 12, 18. Wm. & Margaret dis jH
1829, 1, 10. Levi J. dis jH
1829, 1, 10. Ann dis jH
1829, 5, 14. John T. & w, Esther, dis jH
1829, 6, 18. Wm., Levi, Moses, Jonathan,
    Elisha & Hannah, minors, rocf Short Creek
    MM, dtd 1829,5,19
1835, 4, 16. Levi dis disunity
1836, 3, 17. Wm. dis jH
1836, 8, 18. Moses, Jonathan, Elisha & Han-
    nah, ch Isaac & Susan, gct Short Creek MM
1848, 7, 13. Margaret dis disunity

WICKERSHAM
1843, 12, 14. Jemima (form Metcalf) dis mcd

WILDMAN
1837, 6, 15. Mary rocf Short Creek MM, dtd
    1837,5,23
1839, 2, 14. Mary gct Stillwater MM
1842, 6, 16. Mary rocf Chesterfield MM, dtd
    1842,3,19
1852, 3, 18. Mary gct Plymouth MM
1855, 4, 19. Mary rocf Plymouth MM, dtd
    1855,3,19
1867, 3, 14. Mary dis jG

WILEY
1834, 2, 13. Hannah rocf Smithfield MM, dtd
    1833,8,19
1836, 7, 14. Rebecca dis disunity
1838, 8, 16. Hannah dis jH
1868, 8, 13. Elizabeth dis jas

WILLIAMS
----, --, --. Wm. & Lydia
    Ch: Hannah C. b 1822, 9, 6
        David Mil-
        ton   " 1826, 10, 2
        Lindley M. " 1830, 8, 3
        Elwood T. " 1832, 11, 23
        Elizabeth " 1835, 5, 13
----, --, --. Deerman & Mary
    Ch: John F.   b 1831, 8, 17

WILLIAMS, Deerman & Mary, continued
    Ch: Rebecca   b 1833, 10, 26
        Sarah   " 1836, 1, 29
        Benjamin " 1837, 1, 17
        Keturah Ann" 1839, 9, 22
        Mary   " 1842, 5, 20
1836, 9, 26. Elizabeth Ann, dt Isaiah & Han-
    nah, b
1837, 3, 4. Elizabeth Ann, infant, d bur
    Chesterfield
1837, 6, 4. Hannah d bur Chesterfield
1851, 12, 24. Abner, s Job M. & Elizabeth,
    Washington Co., O.; m in Pennsville, Mary
    Ann TALBOTT, dt Wm. A. & Ann, Morgan Co.,
    O.

1827, 6, 16. Wm. & w, Lydia, & ch, Hannah C.
    & Daniel, rocf Somerset MM, dtd 1827,4,30
1829, 4, 16. Rebecca & ch, Miriam, Levi,
    Phebe & Deborah, gct Stillwater MM
1830, 8, 19. Dearman rocf Salem MM, dtd 1830,
    7,21
1830, 10, 14. Dearman gct Sandy Spring MM, to
    m Mary Farmer
1831, 5, 19. Mary F. rocf Sandy Spring MM,
    dtd 1831,2,25
1835, 6, 18. Rachel & Jane, ch David & Sarah,
    rocf Somerset MM, dtd 1835,5,25
1836, 10, 15. Isaiah & w, Hannah, & s, Elias,
    rocf Somerset MM, dtd 1836,8,29
1843, 8, 17. Dearman & w, Mary, & ch, John
    F., Rebecca, Sarah, Benjamin, Ketura Ann
    & Mary, gct Sandy Spring MM
1846, 9, 17. Wm. & w, Lydia, & ch, Daniel
    M., Lindley, Elwood & Elizabeth, rocf
    Chesterfield MM, dtd 1846,8,15
1847, 6, 17. Daniel M. dis jas
1848, 4, 13. Wm. & w, Lydia, & ch, Lindley,
    Elwood & Elizabeth, gct Stillwater MM
1851, 11, 13. Abner rocf Somerset MM, dtd
    1851,10,27
1852, 10, 14. Abner & w, Mary Ann, gct Somer-
    set MM

WILLIS
1847, 3, 18. Clarkson Burgess gct Short Creek
    MM, to m Susan Willis

WILSON
1851, 9, 25. Daniel, s Daniel & Mary, Morgan
    Co., O.; m in Hopewell, Martha GREGG, dt
    Caleb & Millicent, Morgan Co., O.

1828, 6, 21. Mary & ch, Margaret, Sarah,
    Mary, Daniel & Ruth, rocf Stillwater MM,
    dtd 1828,3,22
1831, 5, 19. Mary & ch, Margaret, Sarah,
    Mary, Rachel, Daniel, Ruth & William &
    one b since her removal, gct Short Creek
    MM
1843, 3, 16. Mary & ch, Daniel, Ruth, Wm.,
    Owen, Thomas & Catherine, rocf Somerset
    MM, dtd 1843,2,27

1845, 3, 13. Rachel rocf Somerset MM, dtd
    1844,3,25
1845, 11, 13. Rachel Miller (form Wilson) dis
    mcd
1846, 8, 13. Ruth Cope (form Wilson) dis mcd
1853, 4, 19. Daniel & w, Martha, & s, Caleb,
    gct Pleasant Plain MM, Ia.
1853, 6, 8. Owen dis mcd
1860, 3, 10. Thomas dis mcd

WOOD
----, --, --. ----- & Elizabeth
    Ch: Rebecca Ann
                    b 1840, 5, 23
        Franklin   " 1842, 3, 17
----, --, --. Elisha & Martha
    Ch: Mary   b 1850, 2, 11
        Elizabeth
        Ann   " 1852, 6, 26
        Martha   " 1854, 11, 19
1853, 10, 8. Margaret d ae 74 bur Pennsville
1854, 8, 3. Thomas d bur Pennsville
1854, 11, 20. Elisha d bur Hopewell
1855, 8, 24. Susan A. m Osborn PENROSE
1862, 10, 31. Martha d ae 46 bur Hopewell
1871, 9, 17. Jane d

1828, 12, 18. Joseph rocf Flushing MM, dtd
    1828,1,25
1828, 12, 18. Mary, w Robert, & ch, Thomas,
    Robert, Kester, Josiah & Mary Ann, rocf
    Short Creek MM, dtd 1828,10,25
1829, 5, 14. Israel & w, Elizabeth, & ch, Jo-
    seph, Wilson, Ann, John, Sarah & Daniel,
    gct Cincinnati MM
1829, 9, 17. Mary dis jH
1830, 8, 19. Rachel rocf Short Creek MM, dtd
    1830,6,22
1831, 3, 17. Rachel dis jH
1831, 7, 14. Thomas dis jH
1831, 7, 14. Robert Jr. dis
1835, 3, 19. Abraham & w, Jane, & ch, Mary
    Ann, Abraham, John, Nathan & Emmor, rocf
    Stillwater MM, dtd 1835,1,24
1836, 5, 19. Caleb & w, Lydia, & ch, Milton,
    Alfred, Maryann & Wm., rocf Smithfield MM,
    dtd 1836,12,21
1837, 12, 14. Mary (form Pierpont) dis mcd
1838, 4, 19. Josiah dis mcd
1838, 5, 17. Lydia (form Mendenhall) dis mcd
1838, 10, 18. Kester dis jH
1839, 8, 15. Joshua & w, Esther, & ch, Lydia,
    Addison, Wm., Gerard Hopkins, Thomas, Es-
    ther Mariah & Susan Amos, rocf Smithfield
    MM, dtd 1839,7,22
1840, 5, 14. John P. & w, Susanna, & dt,
    Elizabeth, rocf Smithfield MM, dtd 1840,3,
    23
1842, 9, 15. Joshua dis disunity
1842, 9, 15. Lydia Hann (form Wood) dis mcd
1843, 1, 19. Mary Ann Thompson (form Wood)
    dis mcd
1843, 8, 17. Elizabeth gct Chesterfield MM

WOOD, continued

1844, 1, 18. Lidia Ann rocf Smithfield MM,
      dtd 1843,10,23
1844, 7, 18. John P. & w, Susan, & dt, Eliza-
      beth P., gct Chesterfield MM
1844, 10, 17. Wm. rocf Flushing MM, dtd 1844,
      7,25, end by Chesterhill MM, 1844,9,21
1845, 10, 16. Lydia Ann gct Smithfield MM
1846, 12, 17. Mary Ann dis jas
1847, 1, 14. John dis mcd
1847, 9, 16. Elihu & w, Martha, & ch, Asaph &
      Robert, rocf Chesterfield MM, dtd 1847,8,
      21
1848, 8, 17. Elizabeth rocf Chesterfield MM,
      dtd 1848,6,17
1849, 1, 18. Joseph Addison dis mcd
1849, 2, 15. Caroline (form Metcalf) dis mcd
1849, 3, 15. Wm. M. dis mcd
1850, 6, 13. Wm. D. dis jas
1850, 11, 14. Nathan dis mcd
1850, 11, 14. Emmor dis mcd
1851, 11, 13. Margaret rocf Stillwater MM, dtd
      1851,10,25
1853, 4, 19. Gerard con mcd
1853, 9, 15. Gerard gct New Garden MM, Ind.
1869, 3, 18. Asaph gct Short Creek MM, to m
      Phebe Bracken
1870, 6, 16. Mary gct Coal Creek MM, Ia.
1870, 7, 14. Asaph gct Coal Creek MM, Ia.
1871, 4, 13. Matilda (form Picket) dis mcd
1872, 2, 15. Robert gct Coal Creek MM, Ia.
1872, 2, 15. Martha gct Coal Creek MM, Ia.
1877, 2, 15. Elizabeth Ann gct Coal Creek
      MM, Ia.
1884, 3, 13. Lydia Worthington (form Wood)
      con mcd
1886, 4, 15. Elizabeth gct Coal Creek MM, Ia.

WOODRUFF

1842, 6, 16. Bethiah (form Bundy) dis mcd

WORK

1837, 2, 16. Elizabeth (form Worrall) dis
      mcd

WORRALL

----, --, --. Benjamin & Priscilla
      Ch: Eleanor   b 1822, 3, 16
          Ann   " 1824, 6, 19
          Sarah   " 1827, 1, 27
          Elizabeth " 1829, 3, 4
          Susanna   " 1831, 10, 31
          Jonathan G." 1834, 2, 21
1833, 3, 20. Amos d ae 13 bur Deerfield
1836, 9, 21. Ruth m Thomas BUNDY
1842, 5, 13. Esther d ae 56 bur Pennsville

1828, 12, 18. Benjamin Sr. rocf Short Creek
      MM, dtd 1828,11,18
1828, 12, 18. Elizabeth rocf Short Creek MM,
      dtd 1828,8,19
1829, 6, 18. Esther [Worrell] & ch, Hannah,
      Ruth, Lydia, Elizabeth, Amos & Miriam,

rocf Short Creek MM, dtd 1829,5,19
1830, 6, 17. Jonathan [Worrell] & w, Eleanor,
      & ch, Rebecca, Mordecai & Isaac, rocf
      Short Creek MM, dtd 1828,5,20
1830, 10, 14. Benjamin [Worrell] & w, Pris-
      cilla, & ch, Eleanor, Ann, Sarah & Eliza-
      beth, rocf Short Creek MM, dtd 1830,7,20
1831, 6, 16. Jonathan [Worrell] dis disunity
1833, 6, 1. Benjamin [Worrell] dis disunity
1833, 8, 15. Rebecca Gifford (form Worrell)
      dis mcd
1837, 2, 16. Elizabeth Work (form Worrall)
      dis mcd
1837, 9, 14. Zebulon & w, Martha, & ch,
      John, Rebecca, Margaret, Mary, Zebulon,
      Elwood, Elizabeth & Martha, rocf Short
      Creek MM, dtd 1837,7,18
1837, 12, 14. Lydia dis jas
1838, 2, 18. Sarah (form Patterson) dis mcd
1838, 9, 13. Hannah Stubbs (form Worrall)
      dis mcd
1839, 4, 18. Miriam dis jas
1839, 9, 18. Isaac Kirby gct Chesterfield
      MM, to m Elizabeth Worral
1847, 5, 13. Jonathan rst rq
1847, 7, 15. Jonathan gct Chesterfield MM

WORTHINGTON

----, --, --. William & Elizabeth
      Ch: Mary   b 1819, 8, 11
          Rebecca   " 1821, 1, 19
          Mildreth   " 1822, 10, 11
          Priscilla " 1824, 3, 31
          Jesse   " 1825, 8, 28
          Eliza Ann " 1831, 2, 6
1830, 11, 6. Wm. d ae 37 bur Blue Rock
1832, 1, 18. Elma d ae 9 bur Deerfield
1836, 4, 20. Grace T. m James EMBREE
1838, 8, 22. Anna m Elisha VANLAW
1840, 8, 19. Rebecca m Wm. PICKETT
1846, 4, 22. Elizabeth m Isaac BROWN
1846, 5, 20. -ildred m Joseph PENROSE
1846, 11, 26. Jesse, s Wm. & Elizabeth, Mor-
      gan Co., O.; m in Hopewell, Rachel PICKET,
      dt Mary, Morgan Co., O.
      Ch: William   b 1847, 9, 31
          Mary   " 1849, 3, 30
----, --, --. Jacob & Lydia
      Ch: Zenas   b 1852, 10, 12
          Reuben E. " 1856, 4, 27
          Sarah Ann " 1859, 8, 6
          Mary   " 1862, 4, 24
1854, 6, 16. Ann d ae 70 bur Pennsville
1857, 4, 30. Priscilla m David MASTERS
1862, 5, 12. Jacob d ae 49 bur Pennsville
1869, 10, 16. Lydia m James GIBBONS

1828, 7, 17. Ann & ch, Elizabeth, Jacob &
      Elma, rocf Nottingham MM, dtd 1828,5,16
1828, 7, 17. Sarah rocf Nottingham MM, dtd
      1828,5,16
1829, 4, 16. Wm. & w, Elizabeth, & ch, Mary,
      Rebecca, Mildreth, Priscilla & Jesse,

WORTHINGTON, continued
    rocf Nottingham MM, Md., dtd 1828,6,13
1834, 7, 17. Zenas rocf Nottingham & Little
    Brittain MM, dtd 1834,3,7
1834, 12, 18. Grace T. rocf Frankfort MM,
    Pa., dtd 1834,8,26
1835, 12, 17. Anna rocf Frankfort MM, Pa., dtd
    1835,7,28
1838, 6, 14. Elizabeth Embree (form Worthing-
    ton) dis mcd
1840, 5, 14. Zenas dis mcd
1846, 6, 12. Elizabeth Brown & dt, Eliza Ann
    Worthington, gct Chesterfield MM
1850, 5, 16. Jesse & w, Rachel, & ch, Wm. &
    Mary, gct Chesterfield MM
1851, 11, 13. Lydia (form Hollingsworth) con
    mcd
1851, 11, 13. Jacob con mcd
1852, 9, 16. Mary gct Chesterfield MM
1871, 6, 15. Lydia Gibbons & ch, Zenas, Rheu-
    ben, Sarah Ann & Mary J. Worthington, gct
    Somerset MM
1884, 3, 13. Lydia (form Wood) con mcd
1885, 2, 19. Lydia S. gct Chesterfield MM

YOCOM
1868, 9, 12. Joshua [Yocum], s Thomas D. &
    Mary P., b

1850, 6, 13. Anna (form Bailey) dis mcd
1861, 8, 15. Sarah (form King) dis mcd
1864, 8, 18. Thomas D. recrq
1866, 5, 17. Thomas D. con mcd
1867, 8, 15. Edward, Thomas Austin, Sarah
    Ann & Rachel, ch Thos. D. & Mary Jane,
    recrq
1867, 9, 19. Mary Jane recrq
1871, 6, 15. Thomas D. & w, Mary Jane, & ch,
    Edward Thomas Austin Sarah Ann, Rachel &
    Joshua, gct Springville MM, Ia.
1887, 5, 19. Elizabeth S. [Yocum] (form Pen-
    rose) dis mcd

    *   *   *   *   *   *   *

HOLLINGSWORTH
1851, 11, 13. Lydia Worthington (form Hol-
    lingsworth) con mcd

THOMAS
1839, 2, 14. John gct Chesterfield MM

CHESTERFIELD MONTHLY MEETING

Chesterfield Monthly Meeting, located in Athens County, Ohio, was established by Stillwater Quarterly Meeting, 10th Mo. 21, 1837. This became one of the prominent Conservative Monthly Meetings. It was characterized by a division in 1865 known as the Maulites, named for the leader, but they eventually went back to the main body of Friends. The records of this meeting are kept at Chesterhill, Ohio.

Among the charter members of this monthly meeting were the families of Boswell, Patterson, Engel, Edgerton, Bundy, Pennrose, Morris, Livesey, Deweese, Beck, Hiatt, Doudna, Tallburt, Roman and Way.

RECORDS

ADAMS
1845, 1, 22. Hannah, dt John T. & Patience, b

1844, 1, 20. John T. & w, Patience, & ch,
Wm. G., Edward, Henrietta & John T., rocf
Somerset MM, O., dtd 1843,11,21
1847, 7, 17. Rachel rocf Somerset MM, O.,
dtd 1847,3,29

ALLEN
1838, 9, 15. Jonathan, John Mercer & Cynthy
Ann, ch David, rocf Pennsville MM, O., dtd
1838,7,19
1843, 8, 19. Cynthia Ann, minor, gct Middleton MM, O.

ARMSTRONG
1844, 3, 16. James McConnel gct Carmel MM, to
m Mary Armstrong

ARNOLD
1846, 2, 21. Elizabeth (form Kester) dis mcd
1865, 11, 18. Jephthah Fawcett gct New Garden
MM, to m Lydia Ann Arnold

ASKEW
1847, 10, 16. Cornelius Dewees gct Plainfield
MM, O., to m Rebecca W. Askew

ATKINSON
1848, 6, 17. Sarah rocf Buckingham MM, Pa.,
dtd 1848,1,5

BAILEY
----, --, --. William & Sarah
Ch: Abigail   b 1834, 7, 24
    Elizabeth   " 1836, 9, 5
    Mary   " 1838, 2, 24
    Thomas
     Flanner   " 1838, 2, 24
    Benjamin   " 1840, 3, 20
    George   " 1841, 7, 18
    Mahala   " 1844, 3, 12
    Nathan   " 1845, 6, 19
----, --, --. Samuel & Harriet
Ch: Hannah   b 1835, 2, 28
    Borden   " 1837, 3, 24
    Edward E.   " 1840, 8, 28
    Lavina   " 1843, 11, 22
    Lydia   " 1848, 5, 1
    Sarah   " 1851, 7, 5
----, --, --. Jesse & Nancy
Ch: Laban   b 1836, 10, 28
    Edwin   " 1839, 9, 28
    Maria   " 1841, 10, 27
    Mary Ann   " 1843, 7, 28
1840, 6, 7. Benjamin d (an infant)
1845, 1, 22. Joel, s Henry & Mary, Washington
Co., O.; m in Plymouth, Lydia McGIRR, dt
James & Sarah, Washington,Co., O.
Ch: James   b 1845, 11, 19

----, --, --. James & Rhoda
Ch: Charles A. b 1859, 10, 18
1838, 6, 16. Jesse & w, Nancy, & s, Laban,
rocf Somerset MM, O., dtd 1838,4,30
1839, 3, 16. Wm. dis disunity
1839, 7, 20. Uriah & w, Susanna, & ch, Tabitha, David Elwood & Robert, rocf Pennsville MM, O., dtd 1829,5,16
1842, 4, 16. Samuel & w, Harriet, & ch, Hannah, Borden & Edward, rocf Pennsville MM,
O., dtd 1842,3,17
1843, 11, 18. Elisha M. Wood gct Pennsville
MM, O., to m Martha Bailey
1844, 8, 17. Joel rocf Somerset MM, O., dtd
1844,6,24
1845, 5, 17. Uriah gct Stillwater MM, O.
1848, 3, 18. Jesse & w, Nancy, & ch, Laban,
Edwin, Maria, Maryann, Lindley & Lydia
Jane, gct Stillwater MM, O.
1850, 5, 18. Sarah & ch, Abigail, Elizabeth,
Mary, Thomas T. & George M., gct Somerset
MM, O.
1854, 1, 21. Mary Jane rocf Stillwater MM,
O., dtd 1853,11,26
1856, 2, 16. Samuel & w & ch, Burden, Edwin
C., Lavina, Talbert, Lydia & Sarah, gct
Plymouth MM
1857, 10, 17. Robert & Maryann, ch Uriah, gct
Plainfield MM
1857, 10, 17. Ellwood gct Plainfield MM
1857, 10, 17. Tabitha gct Plainfield MM
1858, 3, 20. Hannah gct Plymouth MM
1858, 7, 17. James & w, Rhoda, & ch, John
Henry & Rebecca Alice, rocf Stillwater
MM, O., dtd 1858,6,26
1858, 10, 16. Mary dis jas
1862, 3, 15. James & w, Rhoda, & ch, John
Henry, Rebecca Alice & Chas. Addison, gct
Pennsville MM, O.
1867, 6, 15. Margaret (form Worrall) dis mcd
1887, 11, 19. George John gct Somerset MM, O.,
to m Sina Bailey

BALEAU
1847, 8, 21. Phreeby (form Patterson) dis mcd
1851, 3, 15. Rebecca [Boileau] (form Boswell)
dis mcd

BALL
1840, 8, 15. James R. & w, Mary Ann, & ch,
Henry C. & Mary Cassander, rocf Short
Creek MM, O., dtd 1840,7,21

BARBER
1854, 9, 16. Margaret (form Hunnicutt) dis
mcd
1867, 2, 16. Margaret H. rst
1867, 7, 20. Benjamin rst on consent of
Flushing MM, O.
1872, 4, 20. Benjamin & w, Margaret H., gct
Coal Creek MM, Ia.

BARNES
1846, 8, 15. Sarah (form Worrall) dis mcd
1879, 3, 15. Sarah (form Dewees) con mcd
1897, 6, 19. Sarah dis jas

BARTLETT
1852, 12, 18. Mary Ann (form Pearson) dis mcd
1868, 9, 19. Mary H. (form Smith) dis mcd
1879, 7, 19. ˜Adaline (form Edgerton) dis mcd

BECK
1839, 2, 6. John Sr. d ae 73
1839, 10, 24. Rachel m Isaac WORRALL
1840, 8, 20. Grace m Joseph PATTERSON
1842, 6, 29. Rachel d ae 71

1838, 12, 15. John & w, Rachel, rocf Somerset
    MM, O., dtd 1838,11,26
1844, 9, 21. Sarah Hodgin (form Beck) dis mcd
1859, 10, 15. Jesse gct Stillwater MM, O.

BENDURE
1877, 5, 19. Miriam (form Dennis) dis mcd

BLOWERS
1911, 8, 19. Ethel Carter (form Blowers) con
    mcd

BOSWELL
----, --, --. Jesse & Eliza
    Ch: Demsey   b 1833, 12, 12
        Elizabeth " 1835, 11, 4
        Jeremiah P." 1837, 11, 20 d 1841, 7,22
        bur Chesterhill
1837, 11, 27. Ruth m Mordecai WORRALL
1840, 3, 26. Elizabeth m Oliver LIVEZEY
1841, 5, 8. Jesse d ae 32
1851, 9, 25. Milicent m James DEWEES
1852, 7, 23. Demsey d ae 68y
1861, 8, 23. Mary d ae 77
1868, 10, 18. Sarah B. m Henry N. HOXIE

1843, 1, 21. Phebe McDaniel (rorm Boswell) dis
    mcd
1846, 7, 18. Eliza Garretson (form Boswell)
    dis mcd
1850, 1, 19. Isaac dis mcd
1851, 3, 15. Rebecca Boileau (form Boswell)
    dis mcd
1852, 3, 20. Ellen recrq
1853, 6, 18. Joseph dis mcd
1853, 7, 16. Dempsey dis disunity
1853, 11, 19. Mary gct Plymouth MM
1853, 11, 19. Lavina (form Livezey) dis mcd
1856, 10, 18. Elihu dis disunity
1860, 5, 19. Mary rocf Plymouth MM, dtd 1860,
    3,19
1860, 9, 15. Elizabeth Mathews (form Boswell)
    dis mcd
1862, 3, 15. Wilson D. dis mcd
1862, 3, 15. Sarah B. (form Michener) con mcd
1862, 8, 16. Levi dis disunity
1863, 1, 17. Wm. dis jG

1863, 2, 21. Rachel & Ellen dis jG

BOWMAN
----, --, --. James m Elizabeth BAILEY
    Ch: Phebe   b 1843, 6, 20 d 1843, 7,16
        Isaac   " 1844, 8, 22
        Henry   " 1847, 5, 11
        Emmor   " 1849, 7, 18
----, --, --. Emmor, s James & Elizabeth
    (Bailey), b 1849,7,18; m Elizabeth S. VAN-
    LAW
    Ch: Charles P. b 1888, 2, 26
        Harvey   " 1892, 12, 8
1898, 9, 28. James Arthur d ae 15
1911, 4, 20. Elizabeth d
1928, 3, 9. Elizabeth L., w Emmor, d ae 76
    bur Chester Hill (an elder)
1932, 2, 25. Emmor d ae 82 bur Chester Hill

1843, 8, 19. James & w, Elizabeth, rocf
    Marlborough MM, dtd 1843,4,25
1870, 10, 15. Rachel B. (form Crew) con mcd
1879, 6, 21. Elizabeth L. (form Vanlaw) con
    mcd
1884, 7, 19. Elizabeth rocf Plymouth MM, dtd
    1884,6,23
1889, 7, 20. Emmor rst on consent of Plymouth
    MM
1889, 6, 15. Rachel dis
1889, 12, 21. John V., James A., Wm. F. &
    Chas., ch Emmor & Elizabeth, recrq
1905, 2, 18. John V. dis mcd
1908, 9, 19. Wm. T. dis mcd
1931, 2, 21. John V. rst

BRANSON
1844, 10, 24. Smith, s David & Lydia, Washing-
    ton Co., O.; m in Chesterfield, Eliza
    VANLAW, dt John & Sarah, Washington Co.,O.
    Ch: John D.   b 1845, 11, 6 d 1868, 5,28
        Lydia
        Elizabeth " 1853, 5, 26
        Eleanor   " 1856, 3, 19
1847, 10, 21. Lydia Jane m Abel W. BYE
1878, 11, 19. Elenor m Nehemiah WRIGHT
1892, 2, 20. Eliza d ae 68 bur Chesterfield

1841, 10, 16. John Vanlaw & w, Lydia, & ch,
    Smith & Lydia Jane Branson, & Eliza, Jane,
    Samuel C., Jesse, Thomas & Ann S. Vanlaw,
    rocf Plainfield MM, dtd 1841,9,22
1863, 1, 17. Smith dis disunity
1883, 1, 20. Lydia E. Larkin (form Branson)
    dis mcd

BRIGGS
1844, 1, 25. John S., s Israel S. & Mary,
    m in Chesterfield, Rachel PATTERSON, dt
    Jeremiah & Elizabeth, Athens Co., O.

1846, 2, 21. Ann Lambert (form Briggs) dis
    mcd
1846, 6, 20. Mary, w Israel, & ch, Job, Wm.

BRIGGS, continued
    & Lindley, gct Salem MM, Ia.
1846, 6, 20. Benjamin gct Salem MM, Ia.
1846, 7, 18. Esther gct Salem MM, Ia.
1847, 9, 18. Israel S. dis disunity
1848, 11, 18. Israel S. gct Salem MM, Ia.
1853, 2, 19. John & w, Rachel, & ch, Elvina
    Jane, Mary Elizabeth & Sarahann, gct East
    Grove MM, Ia.

BROKAW
1862, 10, 18. Mary (form Hoopes) dis mcd

BROWN
1842, 1, 26. Mary d ae 72
1863, 2, 31. Isaac d ae 84
1870, 12, 31. Elizabeth d ae 76

1838, 3, 17. John C. & w, Abigail, rocf Plain-
    field MM, dtd 1838,1,24
1845, 4, 19. John C. & w, Abigail, & ch, Phebe
    C., Joseph W., Abram & Mary Louisa, gct
    New Garden MM, Pa.
1846, 3, 21. Isaac gct Pennsville MM, O., to
    m Elizabeth Worthington
1846, 6, 20. Elizabeth & dt, Eliza Ann
    Worthington, rocf Pennsville MM, O.

BUNDY
----, --, --. Elias & Elizabeth R.
    Ch: Ezekiel   b 1836, 10, 24
        Stephen T. " 1839, 12, 22
        Isaac C.   " 1842, 7, 21
----, --, --. Nathan & Sarah
    Ch: Milton   b 1837, 10, 20
        Martha   " 1839, 5, 30
        W. Henry   " 1841, 3, 6
        Clarkson   " 1842, 11, 7
        Chalkley   " 1844, 12, 8
        Nathan   " 1846, 11, 16
----, --, --. Thomas & Ruth
    Ch: Hannah   b 1837, 12, 13
        Amos   " 1839, 9, 8 d 1839, 9, 9
        bur Chester Hill
1838, 9, 26. Esther, dt Eli & Sarah, b
1839, 4, 10. Eli d
1839, 7, 24. Moses d bur Chesterhill
1841, --, --. Asenath, dt Thomas & Ruth (Wor-
    rall), b
1842, 5, 24. Peninah d ae 25
1842, 7, 28. Elizabeth d ae 28
1842, 4, 18. Sarah m Eli HODGIN
----, --, --. Exum & Sally
    Ch: Peninah   b 1843, 7, 28
        Thomas
        Ruthanna   " 1845, 11, 30 d 1847,11,20
        David   " 1847, 11, 10
1844, 3, 17. David d ae 30 bur Southland
1845, 7, 22. Ruth d ae 26
1846, 9, 4. Nathan d ae 29
1847, 11, 25. Achsah m Joseph EMBREE
1849, 1, 25. Benjamin, s Thomas & Millicent,
    Washington Co., O.; m in Southland, Rachel

MORRIS, dt Joshua & Rachel, Washington
    Co., O.
1849, 7, 26. Zadok, s Thomas & Meliscent,
    Morgan Co., O.; m in Chesterfield, Rebecca
    WORRALL, dt Zebulon & Martha, Morgan Co.,
    O.
    Ch: Adaline W. b 1849, 5, 13
        Thomas El-
        wood   " 1856, 7, 12
1849, 11, 22. Elias, s Thomas & Millicent,
    Morgan Co., O.; m in Chesterfield, Rachel
    P. SMITH, dt Thomas & Nancy, Morgan Co.,
    O.
1850, 6, 23. Millicent d ae 68
1850, 8, 22. Lydia M. m James VERNON
----, --, --. William C. d 1860,4,29; m Edith
    L. ----- d 1860,10,14
    Ch: Henry   b 1853, 12, 22
        Ellen   " 1856, 3, 31
        Eli   " 1858, 4, 3
1861, 3, 1. Eli d
1891, 8, 27. Martha d ae 52 bur Chesterhill
1892, 7, 25. Sarah D. d ae 73 bur Chesterhill

1838, 10, 20. Eli & w, Sarah, & ch, Wm., Mary
    & Ruthanna, rocf Stillwater MM, O., dtd
    1838,9,22
1839, 8, 17. Thomas & w, Millicent, & s, Za-
    dock, rocf Pennsville MM, O., dtd 1839,7,
    18
1839, 8, 17. Benjamin rocf Pennsville MM, O.,
    dtd 1839,7,18
1839, 8, 17. Peninah, Ruth & Lydia rocf
    Pennsville MM, O., dtd 1839,7,18
1840, 4, 18. Thomas & w, Ruth, & dt, Hannah,
    gct Pennsville MM, O.
1840, 12, 19. Jonathan & w, Achsah, & ch, Mary,
    John, Sarah, Lydia, Peninah & Thomas, gct
    Somerset MM, O.
1841, 2, 20. David & w, Achsah, & s, Joel,
    rocf Pennsville MM, O., dtd 1841,1,14
1846, 7, 18. Thomas & w, Ruth, & ch, Hannah,
    Asenath & Emlen, rocf Pennsville MM, O.,
    dtd 1846,7,16
1848, 1, 15. Achsah Embree & s, Joel Bundy,
    gct Pennsville MM, O.
1853, 10, 15. Maria Patterson (form Bundy)
    dis mcd
1854, 3, 18. Thomas gct Plymouth MM
1855, 1, 20. Elias & w, Rachel P., & ch,
    Ezekiel, Stephen T. & Isaac C., gct
    Plymouth MM
1858, 4, 17. Wm. C. & w, Edith, & ch, Henry
    & Ellen, rocf Stillwater MM, O., dtd
    1858,2,27
1861, 3, 16. Wm. Henry dis military service
1861, 12, 21. Milton dis military service
1863, 11, 21. David B. Smith gct Plymouth MM,
    to m Hannah S. Bundy
1864, 4, 16. Ellen, minor, gct Stillwater MM,
    O.
1866, 10, 20. Zadock G. dis disunity
1866, 11, 17. Clarkson dis military service

BUNDY, continued
1868, 8, 15. Henry, minor, gct Stillwater MM, O.
1871, 3, 18. Nathan dis mcd
1871, 5, 20. Harriet (form Smith) dis mcd
1879, 9, 20. Jason Fawcett gct Stillwater MM, O., to m Mary E. Bundy
1882, 7, 15. Rebecca W. dis jas
1891, 7, 18. Adaline Penrose (form Bundy) dis mcd

BURGESS
1798, 12, 17. Mary d ae 17
----, --, --. Clarkson & Margaret
      Ch: Sarah Jane b 1866, 10, 26
          Emmor   " 1872, 4, 17 d 1872, 4,23
----, --, --. Nathan m Elizabeth PENROSE
      Ch: Albert
          Lewis   b 1882, 10, 18
          Adda Irma " 1886, 5, 12
----, --, --. Amos, s Elwood & Gaynor (Ball), b 1858,2,5; m Rachel Ann MORRIS, dt Martin & Elizabeth (James), b 1856,1,10
      Ch:Ethel Julia b 1884, 9, 22
         Elizabeth G." 1890, 12, 10
         Anna Mable " 1892, 1, 31
         Eunice Julia" 1898, 10, 4
1891, 7, 7. Clarkson d ae 74
----, --, --. Nathan, s Elwood & Gaynor (Ball), b 1852,9,11; m Elizabeth PENROSE
      Ch: Lloyd Pen-
              rose   b 1893,12,11
1922, 7, 2. Elizabeth, w Nathan, d bur Southland

1868, 9, 19. Margaret rst on consent of Plymouth MM
1868, 10, 17. Clarkson rst on consent of Plymouth MM
1871, 4, 15. Sarah Jane, dt Clarkson & Margaret, recrq
1905, 12, 16. Sarah Jane dis jas
1905, 12, 16. Sarah Abbie gct Spring River MM, Kans.

BURT
1900, 10, 8. Edith Hobson, dt Alden & Tacy (Hobson), b 1900,10,8

BYE
1821, 8, 6. Lydia Jane b (M)
----, --, --. Jonas & Martha
      Ch: Joseph   b 1843, 7, 17 d 1854,10,14
          Mary   " 1846, 8, 1
1845, 10, 23. Edward, s Jonas & Martha, Morgan Co., O.; m in Chesterfield, Mary T. SMITH, dt William & Ann, Morgan Co., O.
      Ch: Joseph
             Addison b 1846, 10, 12
             William S. " 1854, 11, 11
             Emily   " 1858, 9, 26
             Eliza   " 1863, 4, 21
             Walter E. " 1865, 11, 24

1847, 10, 21. Abel W., s Jonas & Martha, Morgan Co., O.; m in Chesterfield, Lydia Jane BRANSON, dt David & Lydia, Washington Co., O.
      Ch: Amy
            Elizabeth b 1849, 6, 23
1849, 6, 21. Samuel, s Jonas & Martha, Morgan Co., O.; m in Chesterfield, Emily TODD, dt Elisha & Sally, Morgan Co., O.
      Ch: Samuel K. b 1851, 9, 25
1851, 10, 23. Elizabeth m Joseph W. PIDGEON
1851, 1, 23. Samuel d ae 26
1853, 12, 13. Elisha d ae 27
1857, 10, 24. William d ae 20
----, --, --. Louis & Phebe
      Ch: Rebecca
            Louisa   b 1859, 10, 20
            Elisha J. " 1861, 12, 27
            Anna M.   " 1865, 6, 1
            Martha   " 1868, 8, 23
1860, 9, 5. Jonas d ae 66
1861, 10, 18. Emily H. d
1866, 9, 16. Mary d ae 41 bur Chesterhill
1868, 3, 26. Mary m Joseph S. FAWCETT
1872, 2, 21. Martha d ae 70
1894, 3, 3. Abel W. d ae 72 bur Chesterhill
1918, 10, 28. Lydia Jane d

1839, 11, 16. Jonas & w, Martha, & ch, Abel W., Edward Samuel Elisha Elizabeth Lewis & Wm., rocf Flushing MM, dtd 1839,10,24
1852, 9, 18. Emily T. & s, Samuel K., gct Three Rivers MM, Ia.
1858, 10, 16. Lewis W. gct Flushing MM, O., to m Phebe H. Williams
1859, 4, 16. Phebe H. rocf Flushing MM, O., dtd 1859,2,24
1865, 4, 15. Abel W. dis disunity
1866, 10, 20. Lydia Jane dis disunity
1868, 7, 18. Edward dis mcd
1869, 8, 19. Amy Elizabeth dis disunity (M)
1869, 8, 19. Lydia Jane dis disunity (M)
1869, 8, 21. Wm. S., Mary Eliza & Walter E., ch Edward, gct Hickory Grove MM, Ia.
1871, 11, 18. Joseph Addison dis military service
1876, 8, 19. Abel W. rst
1876, 8, 19. Lydia Jane rst
1878, 3, 16. Lewis W. & w, Lydia, & ch, Elisha J., Anna M. & Martha, gct Hickory Grove MM, Ia.
1878, 3, 16. Rebecca Louisa gct Hickory Grove MM, Ia.
1890, 1, 18. Amy Elizabeth Smith (form Bye) con mcd

CADWALADER
1840, 8, 15. Edith T. Rodman (form Cadwalader) dis mcd
1841, 5, 15. Sarah & s, Joseph, rocf Short Creek MM, O., dtd 1841,3,3
1841, 5, 15. Sarah Ann rocf Short Creek MM, O., dtd 1841,3,23

CADWALADER, continued
1842, 1, 15. Sarah Ann Patterson (form Cad-
     walader) con mcd
1842, 5, 21. Reese & w, Sarah, & ch, Lloyd
     D. & Isaac D., gct Salem MM
1844, 5, 18. Joseph con mcd
1852, 11, 20. Joseph dis mcd

CARTER
1843, 12, 29. Richard d ae 78 bur Plymouth

1839, 12, 21. Mary rocf Short Creek MM, O.,
     dtd 1839,10,22
1844, 10, 19. Mary Steel (form Carter) dis jas
1911, 8, 19. Ethel (form Blowers) con mcd
1929, 8, 17. Geo. A. Patterson gct Plainfield
     MM, Ind., to m Dortha B. Carter

CHAMBERS
1870, 4, 16. Elizabeth A. (form Lee) dis mcd

CHANDLER
1846, 11, 21. Mary (form Wood) dis mcd

CHOGWELL
1888, 4, 21. Mary (form Hiatt) dis mcd

CONROW
1866, 9, 28. Thomas W. m Mary J. HOBSON (M)

1867, 5, 23. Mary J. gct Harrisville MM, O.
     (M) (Harrisville was the Short Creek Branch
     of Maulites)

COOK
1889, 10, 19. Anna C. (form Lee) con mcd

COPE
1846, 5, 16. John F. rocf Upper Springfield
     MM, O., dtd 1846,5,24

COPPOCK
1839, 9, 2. Jonathan [Copick] d ae 32
1842, 8, 14. Mary [Copick] d ae 60 bur Ply-
     mouth

1838, 9, 15. Jonathan & w, Mary, & ch, Catha-
     rine, Benjamin & Ruth Ann, rocf New Garden
     MM, dtd 1838,7,26
1840, 5, 16. Mary gct New Garden MM
1840, 5, 16. Catharine & Ruthanna, minor ch
     Jonathan & Sarah, gct New Garden MM

COWGILL
----, --, --. James S. & Lucy
     Ch: Eliza   b 1837, 7, 21 d 1839, 8, 7
         Matilda   " 1840, 6, 7

1839, 8, 17. James Simpson & w, Lucy, & ch,
     Rebecca, James, Josiah Joshua & Eliza,
     rocf Upper Springfield MM, O., dtd 1839,
     8,24
1845, 10, 18. James S. & w, Lucy, & ch, James,

Josiah Joshua & Eliza, rocf Salem MM, Ia.
1845, 10, 18. Rebecca gct Salem MM, Ia.

CRAFT
1844, 6, 19. Rachel B. m Joseph S. HANSON
1860, 1, 1. Zilpha E. b (M)

1838, 12, 15. Samuel & w, Ann, & ch, James
     John Rachel Wm. & Jesse, rocf Somerset
     MM, O., dtd 1838,11,26
1849, 4, 21. John dis mcd
1850, 5, 18. James dis mcd
1867, 10, 24. Mary V. & four ch gct Harris-
     ville MM, O. (M)

CREW
----, --, --. William & Mary
     Ch: Rachel   b 1838, 4, 5
         Ezra   " 1840, 7, 9
         Jesse   " 1842, 8, 29
         Rebecca   " 1844, 7, 23
----, --, --. Thomas & Ann
     Ch: Sarah E.   b 1839, 4, 26 d 1839, 8, 5
         bur Chesterhill
         Caroline   b 1842, 9, 4 " 1847,10,19
         bur Chesterhill
         Joshua   b 1844, 10, 5
         John Flem-
         ing   b 1847, 8, 4
1838, 7, 8. Pheriba d ae 4 bur Chesterhill
----, --, --. Henry d 1884,3,3 ae 72 bur
     Chesterhill; m Edith ----- d 1887,4,27 bur
     Chesterhill (an elder)
     Ch: Elwood   b 1839, 9, 28
         Sarah   " 1841, 2, 24
         David   " 1843, 3, 22
         Rachel   " 1845, 10, 21
         Joseph   " 1848, 8, 4
         Amos   " 1851, 2, 12
         William   " 1852, 12, 13
         Charles   " 1855, 4, 22
         Lucy E.   " 1857, 11, 2
1839, 6, 20. Fleming, s Joshua & Milley, Co-
     lumbiana Co., O.; m in Chesterfield, Sarah
     Ann PATTERSON, dt Arnold & Rachel, Athens
     Co., O.
     Ch: Terrell   b 1846, 3, 5
         Thomas El-
         wood   " 1848, 5, 12 d 1848, 8,23
         William B. " 1852, 4, 11
         Johua   " 1857, 4, 17 (Joshua?)
         Mary L.   " 1860, 7, 4
     Fleming m 2nd Mary L. -----
     Ch: Charles
         Evans   b 1870, 4, 23
         George M. " 1873, 5, 2
         Henry Car-
         ton   " 1874, 10, 4 d 1875, 8,13
         Anna M.   " 1876, 6, 16
         Arthur
         Fleming   " 1878, 10, 6
----, --, --. John & Ann
     Ch: Miriam   b 1844, 4, 11

CREW, John & Ann, continued
    Ch: Rebecca   b 1845, 9, 29
1849, 2, 24. Terrell d ae 7 bur Chesterhill
1850, 10, 23. Delitha m Micajah EMMONS
1853, 11, 10. Amos d ae 1 bur Chesterhill
1857, 2, 11. Lucy E., dt Henry & Edith (Cad-
    wallader), b
1857, 4, 20. Joshua d
----, --, --. Robert & Susannah
    Ch: Eva   b 1859, 11, 14
       Rebecca " 1861, 12, 28
       Emma   " 1863, 5, 11
       Almedia " 1865, 2, 14
       Jephtha " 1866, 10, 14
----, --, --. Edwin, s James & Sarah (Bain),
    b 1832,7,27 d 1923,7,20 bur Pennsville; m
    Mary B. DOUDNA, dt Henry & Matilda (Bird),
    b 1836,2,16 d 1923,9,7
    Ch: Edwin   b 1864, 9, 1
1865, 1, 12. Rebecca d ae 3 bur Chesterhill
1867, 8, 28. Sarah d ae 48
1867, 12, 23. -----, ch David & Lydia, b
1893, 7, 28. Fleming d ae 75 bur Chesterhill
1899, 11, 27. Mary L. d ae 61 bur Chesterhill
1923, 7, 10. Edwin d ae 90 bur Pennsville
1923, 9, 7. Mary B. d ae 87 bur Pennsville

1838, 7, 21. Thomas & w, Ann, rocf Upper
    Springfield MM, O., dtd 1838,6,23
1839, 8, 17. Henry & w, Edith, & s, Ellwood,
    rocf Somerset MM, O., dtd 1839,7,29
1840, 2, 15. Thomas dis disunity
1840, 5, 16. Fleming rocf Upper Springfield
    MM, O., dtd 1840,4,25
1843, 4, 15. John gct Stillwater MM, O., to
    m Ann Doudna
1843, 8, 19. Ann rocf Stillwater MM, O., dtd
    1843,7,22
1850, 6, 15. John & w, Ann, & ch, Miriam, Re-
    becca, Abner & Osborn, gct Somerset MM, O.
1854, 12, 16. Jacob & w, Abigail F., & dt, Es-
    ther, rocf Somerset MM, O., dtd 1854,10,30
1858, 12, 18. Robert rocf Somerset MM, O.,
    dtd 1838,11,29
1859, 5, 21. Susanna (form Hiatt) con mcd
1859, 7, 16. Robert con mcd
1860, 4, 21. Ellwood dis mcd
1863, 2, 21. Ann dis jG
1864, 11, 19. Jacob dis jas
1865, 7, 15. Abigail F. dis jas
1866, 2, 17. David W. con mcd
1866, 6, 16. Lydia S. (form Smith) con mcd
1868, 1, 18. John Fleming dis disunity
1868, 7, 18. Charles, Esther & Sarah E., ch
    Jacob & Abigail, gct Springville MM, Ia.
1868, 9, 19. Fleming gct Pennsville MM, O.,
    to m Mary L. Michener
1869, 2, 20. Sarah L. Vernon (form Crew) dis
    mcd
1869, 4, 17. Mary L. rocf Pennsville MM, O.,
    dtd 1869,3,18
1869, 9, 18. Sarah Vernon (form Crew) dis mcd
1870, 2, 19. Martha (form Doudna) dis mcd

1870, 10, 15. Rachel B. Bowman (form Crew)
    con mcd
1872, 1, 20. Joseph dis
1873, 1, 18. Joshua F. dis jas
1877, 2, 17. Wm. B. dis mcd
1882, 12, 16. Mary L. Hodgin (form Crew) dis
    mcd
1885, 7, 18. Charles Henry dis mcd
1889, 11, 16. Charles E. con mcd
1901, 8, 17. George M. dis mcd
1902, 6, 21. Charles E. dis disunity
1903, 8, 15. Anna McLaughlin (form Crew) con
    mcd

DAVIS
----, --, --. Daniel d 1841,4,28 ae 27 bur
    Chesterhill; m Ann -----
    Ch: Martha   b 1838, 12, 29
       Daniel   " 1841, 3, 20
1858, 9, 10. Daniel d
1862, 4, 8. Daniel C. d
----, --, --. Jehu & Ruth P.
    Ch: Daniel C. b 1863, 4, 1
       Charles E. " 1863, 4, 1
       Lucinda M. " 1864, 10, 29
       Tacy Ann " 1867, 3, 10
       William C. " 1869, 1, 24
       Mary Eliza-
         beth   " 1871, 3, 15
       Daniel N. " 1873, 12, 25
       Phebe Emma " 1876, 6, 13
       Albert
         Arthur " 1880, 3, 11
       Eva Lurena " 1882, 11, 28

1838, 4, 21. Daniel & w, Ann, & s, John, rocf
    Clear Creek MM, O., dtd 1838,2,20
1858, 4, 17. Martha Lambert (form Davis) dis
    mcd
1883, 1, 20. Jehu & w, Ruth P., & ch, Chas.
    E., Tacy Ann, Wm. C., Mary Elizabeth, Dan-
    iel N., Phebe Emma, Arthur F. & Eva D.,
    gct Plymouth MM
1883, 2, 17. Lucinda M. gct Plymouth MM
1904, 9, 17. Emma dis
1904, 12, 17. Alice Reed (form Davis) dis mcd

DAWSON
1838, 10, 20. Joel & w, Sarah, & ch, Chalkley
    & Matilda, rocf Stillwater MM, O., dtd
    1838,9,22
1839, 10, 19. Joel & w, Sarah, & ch, Chalkley
    & Matilda, gct Stillwater MM

DEAN
1843, 4, 19. Lavina m Michael KING
1844, 4, 24. Amy m Jesse JOHN
1887, 3, 25. Elizabeth, w Ellwood, d ae 69
    bur Chesterhill (an elder)
1888, 8, 30. Elwood, s Jonathan R. & Hannah,
    Morgan Co., O.; m in Chesterfield, Edna
    PEEBLES, dt Burwell & Asenath, Morgan Co.,
    O.

DEAN, continued
1890, 6, 7. Elwood d ae 73 (a minister)
1910, 4, 15. Edna P. d ae 68

1839, 10, 19. Ellwood & w, Elizabeth, rocf
Sandy Spring MM, O., dtd 1839,9,27
1841, 8, 21. Hannah & s, Rowland, rocf Gilead
MM, dtd 1841,7,20
1841, 8, 21. Lavina rocf Gilead MM, dtd
1841,7,20
1841, 11, 20. Amy rocf Sandy Spring MM, O.,
dtd 1841,10,22
1847, 6, 19. Roland dis jas

DENNIS
1811, 11, 18. Grace b
1877, 4, 22. Grace d ae 65 bur Pennsville

1868, 12, 19. Miriam A., minor, roc
1877, 5, 19. Miriam Bendure (form Dennis) dis
mcd

DEWEES
----, --, --. Cornelius d 1901,3,14 ae 79;
m Rebecca ----- d 1901,2,22 ae 85
Ch: Martha   b 1846, 8, 6
    Clarissa   " 1850, 5, 19
    Mary H.   " 1852, 8, 8
    William   "" 1854, 6, 18
    Hannah A. " 1856, 4, 6
    Sarah   " 1858, 5, 6
1846, 7, 23. Anna Harmer, w James E., dt Wm.
& Rachel (Gilbert) Harmer, b
1848, 11, 23. Mary m Robert HALL
1849, 4, 7. Martha d bur Chesterhill (infant)
1850, 9, 7. James E., s Jesse & Rebecca
(Edgerton), b
1850, 1, 2. William Sr. d ae 67 bur Chesterhill
1851, 9, 25. James, s William & Sarah, Morgan Co., O.; m in Chesterfield, Milicent
BOSWELL, dt Wm. & Rachel, Morgan Co., O.
1852, 12, 20. Matilda, dt Wm. & Maria, b
----, --, --. Griffith & -----
Ch: Louisa   b 1858, 8, 31
    Robert H. " 1860, 6, 7
    Naomi B.   " 1862, 8, 14
    Charles W. " 1865, 4, 28
    Isaac E.   " 1866, 7, 29
1861, 9, 26. William, s William & Sarah, Morgan Co., O.; m in Chesterfield, Elizabeth
WORRALL, dt Zebulon & Martha, Morgan Co.,
O.
Ch: Martha W. b 1862, 8, 25
    Zebulon   " 1866, 7, 7
1871, 1, 23. Debby d ae 81 bur Chesterhill
1875, 7, 29. Anna Harmer d ae 79 bur Penns-
ville
1877, 9, 20. Nathan, s Jesse & Rebecca,
Morgan Co., O.; m in Chesterhill, Rebecca
HUSTIS, dt Isaac & Esther C., Morgan Co.,
O.

1840, 11, 21. Sarah Ann (form Hoopes) con mcd
1841, 4, 17. Sarah Ann gct Pennsville MM, O.
1844, 11, 16. Isaac gct Providence MM, Pa.,
to m Rebecca McGrew
1845, 3, 15. Isaac gct Providence MM
1845, 5, 17. David dis mcd
1846, 7, 18. Lewis M. & ch, Rezin Thomas &
George M., roc
1846, 10, 17. Thomas, Hannah, Isaac, Wm. &
Rebecca, ch David, gct Elk MM, O.
1847, 5, 15. Wm. H., Charles B., Greenbury P.
& Sarah M., ch Thomas, rocf Pennsville
MM, O., dtd 1847,5,13
1847, 6, 19. Lewis M. dis mcd
1847, 10, 16. Cornelius gct Plainfield MM, O.,
to m Rebecca W. Askew
1848, 3, 18. Rebecca W. rocf Plainfield MM,
dtd 1848,2,22
1849, 7, 21. Mary (form McGirr) dis mcd & jH
1850, 12, 21. Sarah & ch, Elizabeth & Aaron,
rocf Pennsville MM, O., dtd 1850,11,14
1851, 7, 19. James Jr. rocf Pennsville MM,
O., dtd 1851,8,14(?)
1851, 12, 20. Wm. gct Pennsville MM, O., to
m Maria Embree
1852, 1, 17. Sarah & ch, Elizabeth & Aaron,
gct Pennsville MM, O.
1852, 4, 17. James & w gct Pennsville MM, O.
1852, 6, 19. Maria rocf Pennsville MM, O.,
dtd 1852,4,15
1853, 10, 15. Wm. & w, Maria, & dt, Matilda,
gct Red Cedar MM, Ia.
1857, 9, 19. Griffith gct Pennsville MM, O.,
to m Ruthann Masters
1858, 6, 19. Ruthanna rocf Pennsville MM, O.,
dtd 1858,4,15
1861, 8, 17. Wm. rocf Pennsville MM, O., dtd
1861,8,15
1863, 5, 16. Wm. dis disunity
1870, 11, 19. Wm. H. dis mcd & military
service
1870, 12, 17. Greenberry dis mcd
1871, 1, 21. Charles B. dis mcd
1872, 9, 21. Sarah Johnson (form Dewees) rpd
mcd
1874, 9, 17. Clarissa R. Swayne (form Dewees)
dis mcd
1877, 12, 15. Mary H. Gibbons (form Dewees)
dis mcd
1878, 3, 16. Rebecca H. gct Pennsville MM, O.
1878, 4, 20. Deborah gct Salem MM, Q.
1879, 3, 15. Sarah Barnes (form Dewees) con
mcd
1884, 1, 19. Anna (form Edgerton) dis mcd
1887, 12, 17. Nathan & w, Rebecca H., & ch,
Roy H. & Amy T., rocf Pennsville MM, O.,
dtd 1887,12,15
1891, 8, 15. Griffith & w, Ruthanna, gct
New Garden MM
1891, 9, 19. Louisa gct New Garden MM
1896, 1, 18. Naomi gct New Garden MM
1897, 6, 19. Rebecca H. dis jas
1898, 4, 16. Nathan dis jas

DEWEES, continued
1899, 6, 17. Wm. rst at Somerset MM, O., on
    consent of this mtg
1903, 11, 21. Chas. W. gct New Garden MM
1905, 7, 15. Rachel Smith (form Dewees) con
    mcd
1905, 7, 15. Ezra dis mcd & jas
1906, 11, 17. Jesse & w, Mariam P., gct Still-
    water MM, O.
1913, 1, 18. Edith dis jas
1921, 2, 17. Amy T. gct Phila. MM, Arch St. &
    4th St.

DOAN
1857, 10, 17. Lydia (form Morris) con mcd
1866, 1, 20. Lydia M. gct Springville MM, Ia.

DODD
1845, 9, 15. Anna d ae 39
1845, 12, 13. Nathan d ae 53

1842, 3, 19. Nathan & w, Anne, & ch, Eunice,
    Ruth & Joseph Patterson, rocf Somerset MM,
    O., dtd 1842,2,28

DOUDNA
----, --, --. Joseph b 1806,7,2; m Mary V.
    ----- b 1813,5,7
    Ch: Jephtha   b 1831, 7, 16
        Samuel   " 1833, 6, 3
        Joshua   " 1835, 8, 25
        Lindley   " 1837, 7, 5
        Lydia   " 1839, 11, 15
        Sarah   " 1842, 8, 30 d 1843,10, 9
         bur Chesterhill
        Charles   b 1847, 3, 29
        Henry   " 1845, 1, 28
        Rebecca   " 1849, 4, 26 d 1849, 1,17
        Joseph W. " 1852, 11, 3
        John   " 1855, 3, 6
----, --, --. James & Sarah
    Ch: Ezra   b 1838, 5, 13 d 1838, 6, 3
        Deborah   " 1839, 6, 15 " 1839, 8,12
1839, 8, 7. Sarah, dt Wm. & Debby Dewees, d
    ae 23
1842, 11, 24. Martha Jr. m Abner FAWCETT
1843, 2, 23. James, s Henry & Martha, Athens
    Co., O.; m in Chesterfield, Louisa M. VAN-
    LAW, dt John & Sarah, Washington Co., O.
    Ch: John V.   b 1843, 11, 19
        Sarah   " 1845, 2, 22
        Martha   " 1846, 3, 14
        Eliza Ann " 1848, 6, 9
        Mary H.   " 1851, 1, 19
        Edwin   " 1853, 7, 10
        Thomas E. " 1859, 5, 5
1846, 1, 23. Henry d ae 74 bur Hopewell
----, --, --. John m Mary B. ----- d 1868,6,3
    ae 33
    Ch: Eli B.   b 1854, 3, 13
        Stephen   " 1855, 5, 22 d 1855, 9,12
        Clarissa " 1858, 1, 14
        Evaline   " 1859, 9, 10

        Ch: Charles   b 1864, 4, 10
            Walter   " 1868, 3, 1
----, --, --. Robert & Esther
    Ch: Sarah
        Rebecca   b 1858, 8, 2
        Mary Me-
        lissa   " 1862, 3, 19 d 1862, 5,27
1864, 10, 3. Esther d bur Chesterhill
1864, 1, 4. Esther d
1868, 7, 30. Robert d

1839, 7, 20. Henry & w, Martha, rocf Penns-
    ville MM, O., dtd 1839,5,16
1839, 7, 20. Martha rocf Pennsville MM, O.,
    dtd 1839,5,16
1843, 4, 15. John Crew gct Stillwater MM, O.,
    to m Ann Doudna
1853, 7, 16. John & w, Mary B., rocf Still-
    water MM, O., dtd 1853,4,23
1854, 7, 15. Joshua gct Somerset MM, O.
1857, 1, 17. Robert H. & w, Esther, rocf
    Stillwater MM, O., dtd 1856,9,27
1857, 1, 17. Jephtha dis mcd
1858, 5, 15. Samuel dis mcd
1863, 1, 17. John dis disunity
1864, 11, 19. Joseph dis disunity
1865, 6, 17. James dis disunity
1865, 6, 17. Louisa M. dis disunity
1866, 8, 18. Mary V. dis disunity
1867, 10, 19. Ann Eliza Dutton (form Doudna)
    dis mcd
1868, 4, 18. Mary H., Edwin, Amy & Thomas E.,
    ch James & Louiza M., gct Springville MM,
    Ia.
1869, 4, 17. John V. dis mcd & military ser-
    vice
1869, 7, 17. Lydia Worrall (form Doudna) dis
    mcd
1870, 2, 19. Martha Crew (form Doudna) dis
    mcd
1870, 3, 24. Lydia Worrall (form Doudna) dis
    mcd (M)
1871, 9, 16. Henry dis mcd & military ser-
    vice
1872, 6, 15. Joseph dis mcd
1872, 11, 16. Sarah Rebecca gct Springville
    MM, Ia.
1874, 6, 20. Lindley dis mcd
1874, 10, 17. Eva gct Hickory Grove MM, Ia.
1874, 12, 19. Eli B., Clarissa & Walter, ch
    John, gct Stillwater MM, O.
1874, 12, 19. Charles gct Springville MM, Ia.
1877, 2, 17. Charles dis mcd
1877, 8, 18. John S. dis mcd

DUNN
1869, 6, 19. Lucetta (form Worrall) dis mcd

DUTTON
1867, 10, 19. Ann Eliza (form Doudna) dis mcd

EDGERTON
1837, 8, 3. Mary, dt John & Zilpha, b

EDGERTON, continued

----, --, --. Abijah d 1847,8,28 ae 30; m
    Rhoda -----
    Ch: Tilman P. b 1838, 9, 12
       Joseph V. " 1840, 2, 29
       Chalkley   " 1843, 7, 4
       Lydia   " 1845, 12, 3

----, --, --. David & Esther
    Ch: Anne   b 1845, 3, 23
       James   " 1848, 3, 14
       Robert " 1850, 12, 19

----, --, --. James & Mary
    Ch: Elizabeth b 1848, 12, 20
       Lucinda   " 1851, 1, 3 d 1851,10,18
       Joseph   " 1852, 9, 4
       Emeline   " 1855, 2, 18
       Lemuel Addi-
         son   b 1859, 8, 2 " 1861, 7,24
       James E.   " 1862, 6, 11 " 1885, 8,20
       bur Chesterhill

1848, 4, 20. Richard, s John & Zilpah, Morgan
    Co., O.; m in Chesterfield, Tamar VERNON,
    dt William & Penninah, Athens Co., O.
    Ch: William   b 1849, 12, 9 d 1850,12,10
       Jebtha   " 1851, 12, 15
       Mary T.   " 1854, 3, 29
       Sarah P.   " 1857, 3, 23
       Clarkson J." 1859, 10, 25
       Ruth Ann   " 1862, 7, 8
       Edward R. " 1866, 10, 5 d 1868, 8,18
       Arthur J. " 1869, 1, 30

1848, 11, 23. Sarah m Joseph VERNON

----, --, --. John Jr. & Martha
    Ch: Emily A. b 1853, 5, 11
       Lindley   " 1854, 12, 16
       Thomas Jef-
         ferson   " 1857, 4, 17
       Adaline   " 1860, 2, 29
       Sarah   " 1863, 8, 19
       Oliver   " 1866, 9, 1
       Israel   " 1868, 3, 26
       Martha   " 1872, 3, 15
       Ellen   " 1874, 6, 24
       John H.   " 1878, 5, 5

1858, 3, 13. Zilpha d
1865, 8, 31. Elizabeth m John VERNON
1869, 1, 6. John d ae 73 bur Lecompton, Kans.

----, --, --. Thomas J., s John & Martha (Em-
    bree), b 1857,4,17; m Elma WORTHINGTON,
    dt Jesse & Rachel (Pickett), b 1867,8,26

1888, 3, 9. Tamor d ae 55 bur Chesterhill
1892, 1, 22. James d ae 68 bur Chesterhill
1899, 8, --. Richard d ae 72 bur Chesterhill
1906, 12, 22. Martha d ae 72 bur Chesterhill
1908, 12, 23. Mary d ae 77 bur Chesterhill
1911, 12, 30. John d ae 81 bur Chesterhill
1925, 9, 30. Thomas J. d ae 68 bur Chester-
    hill

1837, 11, 18. Abijah gct Stillwater MM, O., to
    m Rhoda Vernon
1838, 3, 17. Rhoda rocf Stillwater MM, O.,
    dtd 1838,1,27
1842, 5, 2

1842, 5, 21. Isaac Huestis gct Somerset MM, O.
    to m Sarah Edgerton
1843, 1, 21. David rocf Somerset MM, O., dtd
    1842,10,24, endorsed by Pennsville MM, O.,
    1843,1,19
1844, 4, 20. David gct Upper Springfield MM,
    O., to m Esther Ellyson
1844, 5, 18. Asenath Lambert (form Edgerton)
    dis mcd
1844, 10, 19. Esther rocf Upper Springfield
    MM, O., dtd 1844,7,27
1847, 12, 18. James con mcd
1849, 12, 15. Rhoda Hiatt (form Edgerton) dis
    mcd
1850, 1, 19. Mary & dt, Elizabeth, recrq
1851, 9, 20. David & w, Esther, & ch, Anna,
    James & Robert, gct Somerset MM, O.
1852, 7, 17. John Jr. gct Pennsville MM, O.,
    to m Martha Embree
1854, 4, 15. Martha rocf Pennsville MM, O.,
    dtd 1854,4,14
1857, 3, 21. Allen T. Lee gct Somerset MM,
    O., to m Mary Edgerton
1859, 1, 15. Mary Vernon (form Edgerton) dis
    mcd
1859, 2, 20. Tilman P. dis military service &
    mcd
1869, 6, 19. Emily A. Patterson (form Edger-
    ton) dis mcd
1871, 2, 18. Chalkley dis mcd
1874, 10, 17. Joseph V. dis military service
1874, 11, 21. Emaline E. Pierpoint (form
    Edgerton) dis mcd
1875, 5, 15. Joseph W. dis disunity
1876, 5, 20. Mary Z. Hanson (form Edgerton)
    dis mcd
1876, 7, 15. Almeda (form Hanson) dis mcd
1867, 8, 19. Jephthah dis mcd & jas
1879, 7, 19. Adaline Bartlett (form Edgerton)
    dis mcd
1879, 8, 16. Sarah E. Forward (form Edgerton)
    dis mcd
1879, 10, 18. Lindley H. gct Hickory Grove MM,
    Ia.
1883, 1, 20. Clarkson J. dis mcd
1883, 1, 20. Thomas con mcd
1884, 1, 9. Anna Dewees (form Edgerton) dis
    mcd
1890, 2, 15. Laura Stanton (form Edgerton)
    con mcd
1890, 9, 20. Oliver dis mcd
1893, 1, 21. Israel dis mcd
1894, 5, 19. Thomas con mcd
1894, 2, 17. Elma (form Worthington) con mcd
1896, 7, 18. Martha Zumbro (form Edgerton)
    dis mcd
1901, 9, 21. Ella M. Hopkins (form Edgerton)
    con mcd
1907, 6, 15. Lena May (form Hobson) con mcd
1907, 6, 15. John Harvey dis mcd
1908, 11, 21. Lena May gct West Branch MM, Ia.

ELLIOTT
1840, 6, 20. Isaac J. & w, Adaline, & ch,
     Simeon, Levi, Israel W. & Ira S., rocf
     Marlborough MM, dtd 1840,4,28
1841, 11, 20. Isaac dis jas
1841, 11, 20. Adaline dis jas
1848, 10, 21. Simeon dis disunity

ELLIS
1848, 6, 17. Mary (form Hampton) dis mcd &
     jas
1853, 12, 17. Mary Jane (form Pearson) dis mcd

ELLYSON
1844, 4, 20. David Edgerton gct Upper Spring-
     field MM, O., to m Esther Ellyson

EMBREE
----, --, --. John & Hannah
     Ch: Joseph   b 1838, 12, 27
         Sarah   " 1841, 2, 20
         Ruth   " 1843, 2, 13
         Cyrenus   " 1845, 5, 23
----, --, --. Israel b 1810,4,17; m Mary Ann
     ----- b 1812,11,10 (M)
     Ch: Hannah   b 1844, 8, 4
         Eliza   " 1846, 4, 30
         Caroline   " 1849, 1, 1
         Merrick   " 1851, 2, 12
         Israel W.   " 1853, 3, 16
         Jesse   " 1855, 3, 14
1847, 11, 25. Joseph, s Samuel & Hannah, Mor-
     gan Co., O.; m in Southland, Achsah
     BUNDY, dt Abel & Rebecca GILBERT

1838, 2, 17. John gct Pennsville MM, O., to
     m Hannah Gray
1838, 7, 21. Hannah Jr. & ch, Mary, Elijah,
     Lemuel, Samuel & Jesse Gray, rocf Penns-
     ville MM, O., dtd 1838,6,14
1838, 8, 18. John, minor s John, rocf Penns-
     ville MM, O., dtd 1838,5,17
1845, 10, 18. John & w, Hannah, & ch, Lemuel,
     Samuel & Jesse Gray, & Joseph, Sarah, Ruth
     & Cyrenius Embree, gct Salem MM, Ia.
1845, 12, 20. Wm. gct Pennsville MM, O.
1848, 1, 15. Achsah & s, Joel Bundy, gct
     Pennsville MM, O.
1851, 12, 20. Wm. Dewees gct Pennsville MM, O.,
     to m Maria Embree
1852, 7, 17. John Edgerton Jr. gct Penns-
     ville MM, O., to m Martha Embree
1868, 4, 23. Eliza Guy (form Embree) dis mcd
     (M)
1878, 12, 21. Samuel rocf Springville MM, Ia.,
     dtd 1878,11,16
1879, 10, 18. Samuel gct Pennsville MM, O.

EMMONS
----, --, --. Thomas & Mary
     Ch: Elmina   b 1834, 8, 28
         Albert   " 1835, 7, 13
         Elwood D.   " 1842, 1, 23

1850, 10, 23. Micajah, s Davis & Caroline S.,
     Washington Co., O.; m in Plymouth, Delitha
     CREW, dt Wm. & Mary, Washington Co., O.
     Ch: Ellwood
         Dean   b 1861, 2, 28
         Wilson R.   " 1863, 5, 18

1846, 12, 19. Micajah rocf Sandy Spring MM,
     O., dtd 1846,9,25
1860, 10, 20. Micajah & w, Delitha, & ch,
     Harry Davis, Elizabeth, Mary C., Caroline
     S., Lindley F. & Edwin C., rocf Plymouth
     MM, dtd 1860,8,20
1866, 3, 17. Micajah [Emmons] & w, Delitha,
     & ch, Harvey Davis, Elizabeth D., Mary C.,
     Caroline S., Lindley F., Edison C., El-
     wood D. & Wilson B., gct Springville MM,
     Ia.

ENGLE
----, --, --. Caleb & Sarah
     Ch: Samuel   b 1837, 11, 20
         Deborah
         Jane   " 1839, 8, 15
         Ezekiel   " 1843, 5, 9 d 1844,12,26
         bur Plymouth
         Rachel   b 1845, 8, 23
         Joseph   " 1848, 5, 9
1843, 12, 20. Maria m Eli GILBERT
1847, 5, 19. Sarah B. m Dewit C. WILSON
1862, 6, 26. Caleb, s Caleb & Mercy, Washing-
     ton Co., O.; m in Chesterfield, Mary
     WORTHINGTON, dt William & Elizabeth, Mor-
     gan Co., O.

1838, 9, 15. John & w, Elizabeth, & ch, Ma-
     riah, Sarah B. & Ephraim W., rocf Penns-
     ville MM, O., dtd 1838,7,19
1863, 4, 18. Mary gct Plymouth MM

EVES
1893, 11, 18. Amanda J. gct Hickory Grove MM,
     Ia.

FAIRCHILD
1844, 3, 16. Rebecca (form Vickers) dis mcd

FARQUAR
1874, 6, 20. Lucinda (form Fawcett) dis mcd

FAWCETT
----, --, --. Elijah & Sarah
     Ch: Louisa   b 1842, 8, 8
         Joseph   " 1849, 3, 29
         Joshua H.   " 1851, 2, 23 d 1880, 7, 3
1842, 11, 24. Abner, s Wm. & Abigail, Colum-
     biana Co., O.; m in Chesterfield, Martha
     DOUDNA Jr., dt Henry & Martha, Athens
     Co., O.
     Ch: Abigail   b 1843, 10, 8 d 1899, 4, 8
         bur Chesterhill
         Margaret   b 1845, 4, 8
         Lucinda   " 1847, 2, 2

FAWCETT, Abner & Martha, continued
    Ch: Jason   b 1848, 10, 28
----, --, --. Samuel & Maryann
    Ch: Rachel
        Thomas
        Elwood
        Richard   b 1848, 3, 21
1844, 12, 25. Lydia m Amos ROMAN
1847, 5, 14. Mary d
1851, 5, 25. Martha d
1851, 8, 21. Eli, s Richard & Deborah, Morgan
    Co., O.; m in Chesterfield, Mary HIATT,
    dt Jesse & Ruthanna, Morgan Co., O.
    Ch: Elwood   b 1852, 6, 8
        Charles H. " 1855, 11, 27
        Tacy Jane " 1857, 10, 9
1853, 11, 11. Jonathan d ae 67
1856, 3, 12. Jane d
1857, 3, 24. Debby d
1858, 11, 29. Rebecca d
1859, 3, 3. Tacy d
1863, 3, 5. Lindley M., s Elijah & Sarah,
    Morgan Co., O.; m in Chesterfield, Mary
    HUESTIS, dt Isaac & Sarah, Morgan Co., O.
    Ch: Willis T. b 1864, 5, 4
        Sarah Jo-
          sephine " 1865, 11, 4
        Marietta B." 1867, 7, 24
        Walter H. " 1869, 5, 12
        Arthur   " 1873, 3, 21
        Edith L.   " 1876, 4, 10
1863, 12, 31. Samuel G., s Elijah & Sarah,
    Morgan Co., O.; m in Chesterfield, Amanda
    J. SMITH, dt. William & Ann, Morgan Co., O.
    Ch: Howard   b 1866, 4, 20
        Ann M.   " 1869, 6, 27
        George E. " 1873, 4, 19
1866, 10, 1. Jebtha d
1866, 10, 19. Jephtha Ann, dt Jephtha & Lydia
    Ann, b
1868, 3, 26. Joseph S., s Elijah & Sarah,
    Morgan Co., O.; m in Chesterfield, Mary
    BYE, dt Jonas & Martha, Morgan Co., O.
    Ch: Estella   b 1871, 3, 24
        Martha B. " 1877, 10, 24
        Carlos J. " 1880, 12, 10
1871, 8, 22. Lydia Ann m Daniel WILLIAMS
1873, 9, 25. Elijah d ae 69 bur Chesterhill
1880, 4, 25. Sarah d ae 65
----, --, --. Jason, s Abner & Martha (Doudna)
    b 1848,10,28; m Mary E. -----, dt Chalk-
    ley Bundy, b 1859/60,--,3
    Ch: Clarence
        Edward   b 1882, 6, 21
        Clifford J." 1884, 1, 3
        Martha D. " 1888, 9, 13
1899, 1, 14. Samuel G. d ae 6 bur Chesterhill
----, --, --. Clifford J., s Jason & Mary E.
    (Bundy), b 1884,1,3; m Florence H. STEER,
    dt Elisha B. & Ellen (Gilbert), b 1886,7,
    18
    Ch: Clarence
        Arthur   b 1909, 2, 11

    Ch: Edward
        Gilbert   b 1911, 2, 28
        David Clif-
          ford   " 1915, 11, 19
        Richard
          Stanton " 1919, --, --
1909, 4, 23. Patience d ae 80 bur Pennsville
1926, 11, 29. Amanda d ae 84 bur Chesterhill

1838, 2, 17. Jesse [Fossett] dis mcd
1840, 11, 21. Amelia dis
1840, 12, 19. Samuel & w, Mary Ann, & ch, Ra-
    chel, rocf Stillwater MM, O., dtd 1840,10,
    28
1841, 4, 17. John & Mary rocf Somerset MM,
    O., dtd 1841,3,29
1841, 11, 20. Deborah & ch, Lydia, Eli, Jane
    & Deborah, rocf Stillwater MM, O., dtd
    1841,10,23
1841, 12, 18. Ruth rocf Stillwater MM, O.,
    dtd 1841,10,23
1842, 2, 19. Elijah & w, Sarah, & ch, Lind-
    ley & Samuel, rocf Plainfield MM, dtd 1841
    12,12
1842, 12, 17. Eli dis mcd
1843, 8, 19. Abner rocf Upper Springfield
    MM, O., dtd 1843,7,22
1846, 8, 15. Sarah McCann (form Fawcett) dis
    mcd
1849, 5, 19. John dis mcd
1852, 9, 18. Samuel & w, Maryann, & ch, Ra-
    chel, Thomas, Elwood, Richard, Amos & Jo-
    seph S., gct Three Rivers MM, Ia.
1856, 2, 16. Maria dis jas
1857, 7, 18. Deborah Keats (form Fawcett)
    dis mcd
1858, 9, 18. Susanah dis jas
1859, 7, 16. Sarah Ann (form Hiatt) dis mcd
1859, 7, 16. Eli S. dis mcd
1864, 7, 16. Abner dis disunity
1864, 9, 17. Martha dis disunity
1865, 6, 17. Lindley M. dis disunity
1865, 9, 16. Jephthah & s, Wm. H. rec (their
    rights were in Western YM with which this
    mtg did not correspond; they could not have
    cert)
1865, 11, 18. Jephthah gct New Garden MM, to
    m Lydia Ann Arnold
1866, 4, 21. Margaret F. Hague (form Fawcett)
    dis mcd
1866, 8, 18. Lydia Ann rocf New Garden MM,
    dtd 1866,7,26
1870, 3, 19. Wm. Henry dis mcd
1871, 11, 18. Lydia Ann Williams & dt, Jeptha-
    ann Fawcett, gct Flushing MM, O.
1872, 7, 20. Ellwood dis disunity
1874, 3, 21. Louisa M. Wood (form Fawcett)
    dis mcd
1874, 6, 20. Lucinda Farquhar (form Fawcett)
    dis mcd
1875, 5, 15. Charles H. dis jas
1875, 6, 19. Sarah W. (form Worthington) dis
    mcd

FAWCETT, continued
1879, 9, 20. Jason gct Stillwater MM, O., to
    m Mary E. Bundy
1880, 7, 17. Mary E. rocf Stillwater MM, O.,
    dtd 1880,6,23
1889, 11, 16. Lydia Jane (form Schofield) con
    mcd
1889, 11, 16. Willis T. con mcd
1890, 4, 19. Willis T. & w, Lydia Jane, & dt,
    Alice S., gct Hickory Grove MM, Ia.
1892, 10, 16. Mary B. dis jas
1893, 3, 18. Sarah J. dis jas
1893, 4, 15. Joseph S. dis jas
1894, 7, 21. Anne Schofield (form Fawcett)
    con mcd
1895, 8, 17. Howard S. dis mcd
1896, 11, 16. Walter H. dis jas
1897, 10, 16. Marietta Scott (form Fawcett)
    dis mcd
1898, 12, 17. Edith dis jas
1904, 6, 18. Clarence E. gct WD MM, Pa.
1907, 9, 21. Clifford J. gct Short Creek MM,
    O., to m Florence H. Steer
1907, 11, 16. George E. con mcd
1908, 12, 19. Mary H. gct Pasadenia MM, Calif.
1909, 1, 6. Florence S. rocf Short Creek MM,
    O., dtd 1908,12,22

FISHER
1841, 8, 21. Wm. & Sarah, minors, rocf Still-
    water MM, O., dtd 1841,6,26
1867, 3, 16. Sarah dis jas

FORWARD
1879, 8, 16. Sarah E. (form Edgerton) dis mcd

FOULKE
1852, 8, 21. David Smith gct Pennsville MM,
    O., to m Mary Foulke

FOWLER
----, --, --. Caleb & Sarah
    Ch: Milton D. b 1822, 6, 24
       Achsah O. " 1824, 9, 3
       John S.   " 1832, 8, 22
       Edmund S. " 1834, 4, 20 d 1908, 4,24
        bur Winona
       Lindley M. b 1838, 4, 21
       Chalkley T." 1840, 4, 21
       Elizabeth
        Z.   " 1844, 1, 19
1846, 10, 21. Achsah m Smith HEALD
1882, 6, 22. John S., s Caleb & Sarah, Mor-
    gan Co., O., b 1832,8,22; m in Chester-
    field, Esther HUESTIS, dt Isaac & Sarah,
    Morgan Co., O.

1838, 8, 18. Caleb & w, Sarah, & ch, Milton
    D., Achsah, John S., Edmund S. & Lindley
    M., rocf Sandy Spring MM, O., dtd 1838,7,
    27
1882, 10, 21. Esther gct Plymouth MM
1909, 9, 18. Mary M. & Sarah gct New Garden

MM

FROST
1876, 12, 16. Amy (form Smith) dis mcd

GARDNER
1917, 4, 9. Eliza J. d ae 51

1902, 12, 20. Eliza J. (form Worthington) con
    mcd

GARRETSON
----, --, --. Joel & Elizabeth
    Ch: William   b 1829, 3, 18
       Sarah   " 1831, 4, 1
       Ruthanna   " 1833, 4, 26
       John   " 1835, 4, 6
       Richard   " 1837, 12, 9
       Rachel   " 1840, 4, 14
       Susanna   " 1842, 6, 25 d 1843, 8,31
        bur Plymouth
       Mary   b 1844, 9, 24
1840, 10, 19. Joseph F. d ae 30

1839, 8, 17. Joel & w, Elizabeth, & ch, Wm.,
    Sarah, Ruthanna, John & Richard, rocf
    Pennsville MM, O., dtd 1839,7,18
1846, 7, 18. Eliza (form Boswell) dis mcd
1848, 5, 20. Emily roc dtd 1848,4,13
1848, 5, 20. Eliza roc dtd 1848,4,13
1848, 5, 20. David & Eli roc dtd 1848,4,13
1849, 8, 18. Sarah Pickering (form Garretson)
    dis mcd
1850, 5, 18. Emily Selby (form Garretson)
    dis mcd

GIBBONS
1877, 12, 15. Mary H. (form Dewees) dis mcd

GIDLEY
1842, 9, 17. Jesse Vernon gct Alum Creek MM,
    O., to m Patience Gidley

GIFFORD
1914, 1, 20. Temperance d ae 76 bur Penns-
    ville

GILBERT
----, --, --. Joel & Elizabeth
    Ch: Mary   b 1843, 1, 1
       Thomas
        Smith   " 1845, 2, 7
       Sarah   " 1846, 5, 9
       William   " 1848, 3, 8 d 1850, 4,19
        bur Southland
       Daniel W. b 1849, 11, 20
1843, 12, 20. Eli, s Abel & Rebecca, Washing-
    ton Co., O.; m in Plymouth, Maria ENGLE,
    dt John & Deborah, Washington Co., O.
    Ch: John   b 1845, 5, 21
1844, 3, 30. Abel d ae 63 bur Southland
----, --, --. Thomas & Edith
    Ch: Sarah Ann b 1845, 1, 29

GILBERT, Thomas & Edith, continued
      Ch: Eliza Jane b 1849, 4, 9
1845, 6, 26. Thomas Smith d ae 4 bur Southland
1849, 9, 4. Daniel A. d bur Southland

1841, 4, 17. Abel & w, Anna, & ch, Eli,
    Elizabeth, Rebecca & Abel, rocf Pennsville
    MM, O., dtd 1840,12,17
1841, 7, 17. Joel & w, Elizabeth, & ch, Cyn-
    thia Ann & Rebecca, rocf Pennsville MM,
    O., dtd 1841,7,15
1845, 9, 21. Thomas & w, Edith, & ch, Jona-
    than, Daniel G., Mary S., Elizabeth H. &
    Sarah Ann, rocf Pennsville MM, O., dtd
    1845,9,18
1848, 9, 16. Anna & ch, Rebecca & Abel, gct
    Somerset MM, O.
1849, 10, 20. Jonathan dis jas
1849, 10, 20. Edith dis jas
1849, 11, 17. Thomas dis jas
1851, 1, 18. Elizabeth R. gct Pennsville MM,
    O.

GOODWIN
1846, 4, 18. Ruthann (form Morris) dis mcd

GRAY
1838, 2, 17. John Embree gct Pennsville MM,
    O., to m Hannah Gray
1838, 7, 21. Hannah Embree Jr. & ch, Mary,
    Elijah, Lemuel, Samuel & Jesse Gray, rocf
    Pennsville MM, O., dtd 1838,6,14
1841, 4, 17. Mary Merrill (form Gray) dis mcd
1845, 10, 18. John Embree & w, Hannah, & ch,
    Lemuel, Samuel & Jesse Gray, & Joseph,
    Sarah, Ruth & Cyrenius Embree, gct Salem
    MM, Ia.
1847, 8, 21. Elijah dis disunity
1890, 3, 15. Amy (form Vanlaw) dis mcd

GREWELL
1866, 7, 17. John d ae 85

1846, 3, 21. John rst on consent of Flushing
    MM

GRIEST
----, --, --. Milton, s John & Asenath
    (Stubbs), b 1838,11,22 d 1918,12,2 bur
    Hopewell

1909, 1, 6. Milton recrq

GRIFFITH
1839, 5, 2. Edwin, s Emlen & Sarah Ann, b
----, --, --. Emlen d bur Chesterhill
1911, 2, 11. Edwin d ae 70

1838, 1, 20. Emlen gct Pennsville MM, O., to
    m Sarah Ann Penrose
1838, 11, 17. Sarah Ann rocf Pennsville MM, O.,
    dtd 1838,10,18
1842, 10, 15. Newton dis disunity

1842, 10, 15. Eli & w, Rachel, & s, Collins,
    gct White Water MM, Ind.
1843, 8, 19. Wm. P. dis mcd
1845, 5, 17. Sarahann & s, Edwin, gct Penns-
    ville MM, O.
1846, 5, 16. Elma White (form Griffith) dis
    mcd

GRIMSHAW
1861, 7, 20. Hannah d ae 66

1851, 11, 15. Hannah rocf Stillwater MM, O.,
    dtd 1851,10,25

GUY
1845, 9, 20. Charlotte (form Kabberman) con
    mcd
1868, 4, 23. Eliza (form Embree) dis mcd (M)

HAGUE
1860, 7, 21. Jane (form Patterson) dis mcd
1866, 4, 21. Margaret F. (form Fawcett) dis
    mcd

HAINES
1849, 8, 30. Hannah m Elijah HIATT
1859, 9, 3. Lydia d ae 83

1839, 7, 20. Isaac & w, Lydia, rocf Penns-
    ville MM, O., dtd 1839,6,13
1839, 7, 20. Mary rocf Pennsville MM, O.,
    dtd 1839,6,13
1840, 5, 16. Hannah rocf Pennsville MM, O.,
    dtd 1840,5,14

HALL
1848, 11, 23. Robert, s John & Tacy, Belmont
    Co., O.; m in Chesterfield, Mary DEWEES,
    dt Wm. & Debby, Washington Co., O.

1849, 2, 17. Mary gct Plainfield MM

HAMMITT
1840, 6, 24. Sarah R. m Wm. A. TALBOTT
1846, 8, 2. Ellen d ae 41 bur Walpole Co.,
    Ia.

1839, 8, 17. Sarah R. rocf Salem MM, N. J.,
    dtd 1839,6,26

HAMPTON
----, --, --. Samuel B. & Elizabeth
    Ch: Jonathan P. b 1832, 5, 31
        Mary   " 1836, 10, 15
        Ann   " 1838, 11, 5
        Isaac   " 1841, 2, 14
        Richard B. " 1844, 11, 2
1839, 4, 25. Cary, s Thomas & Hannah, Athens
    Co., O.; m in Chesterfield, Sarah WAY,
    dt David & Ann, Monroe Co., O.
    Ch: Benjamin W. b 1840, 2, 4 d 1842, 3,19
        bur Chesterhill
        Amos   b 1841, 5, 15

HAMPTON, Cary & Sarah, continued
    Ch: Thomas P. b 1842, 12, 31
        Elvira   " 1845, 5, 12
        David   " 1848, 3, 14
        Hannah Ann " 1850, 1, 31
1842, 9, 22. Eunice m Robert TODD
1843, 9, 19. Jesse, s Asa & Esther, b
1850, 4, 5. Hannah d ae 64 bur Chesterhill

1839, 10, 19. John & w, Mary, & ch, Oliver,
    Sarah, Robert & Lucinda, gct Somerset MM,
    O.
1847, 2, 20. Samuel B. & w, Elizabeth, & ch,
    Jonathan, Mary, Ann, Isaac & Richard, gct
    Pennsville MM, O.
1848, 6, 17. Mary Ellis (form Hampton) dis
    mcd & jas
1849, 7, 21. Asa C. dis disunity
1851, 11, 15. Jason gct Upper Springfield MM,
    O., to m Maryann Walton
1851, 12, 20. Esther & ch, Benjamin, Eli,
    James, Ruth, Phebe, Jesse & Bethula Ann,
    gct Pleasant Plain MM, Ia.
1851, 12, 20. Martha gct Pleasant Plain MM,
    Ia.
1853, 2, 19. Jason gct Upper Springfield MM,
    O.

HANSON
1843, 11, 22. Manoah, s Manoah & Rachel, Wash-
    ington Co., O.; m in Plymouth, Millicent
    WAY, dt Robert & Lydia, Washington Co., O.
    Ch: Lovisa   b 1844, 8, 10
        Phebe   " 1846, 4, 21
1844, 6, 19. Joseph S., s Elijah & Eliza,
    Washington Co., O.; m in Plymouth, Rachel
    B. CRAFT, dt Samuel & Ann, Washington Co.,
    O.

1843, 8, 19. Joseph S. rocf Stillwater MM,
    O., dtd 1843,7,22
1843, 8, 19. Manoah rocf Stillwater MM, O.,
    dtd 1843,7,22
1844, 5, 18. Edwin Morris gct Stillwater MM,
    O., to m Rachel Hanson
1848, 6, 17. Manoah & w, Milisant, & ch, Le-
    vica & Phebe, gct Stillwater MM, O.
1853, 2, 19. Robert & w, Prudence, & ch,
    Thomas Osborn, rocf Somerset MM, O., dtd
    1852,11,29 endorsed by Plymouth MM, 1853,
    1,17
1859, 8, 20. Robert dis jas
1864, 1, 16. Prudence dis jas
1873, 7, 19. Thomas dis jas
1876, 5, 20. Mary Z. (form Edgerton) dis mcd
1876, 7, 15. Almeda Edgerton (form Hanson)
    dis mcd
1878, 1, 19. Emma J. dis jas

HARRIS
1849, 11, 26. Beuly d bur Pennsville

1846, 5, 16. Richard & w, Beulah, rocf Penns-

ville MM, O.

HARRISON
1880, 3, 20. James Hiatt gct Plymouth MM, to
    m Mary E. Harrison

HEALD
1846, 10, 21. Smith, s Nathan & Rachel, Wash-
    ington Co., O.; m in Plymouth, Achsah
    FOWLER, dt Caleb & Mary, Washington Co.,O.
1850, 10, 23. Samuel, s Levi & Lydia, Washing-
    ton Co., O.; m in Plymouth, Jane HOBSON,
    dt Stephen & Lydia, Washington Co., O.

1838, 9, 15. Wm. W. rocf New Garden MM, dtd
    1838,7,26
1842, 1, 15. Wm. W. dis mcd
1842, 11, 19. Smith rocf Carmel MM, dtd 1842,
    9,17
1847, 8, 21. Caleb Marshall gct Carmel MM,
    to m Elmira Heald
1854, 1, 21. Mary rocf Somerset MM, O., dtd
    1853,12,26

HEMPY
1905, 7, 15. Elizabeth (form Vernon) dis mcd

HENRY
1840, 1, 18. Sarah (form Patterson) dis mcd

HERALD
1855, 3, 11. Mary d

HIATT
----, --, --. Jesse & Ruthanna
    Ch: Sarah Ann b 1837, 12, 20
        Susanna   " 1839, 11, 11
        Grace   " 1841, 7, 19
        Amos   " 1843, 8, 26
        Jesse   " 1846, 9, 8
        James   " 1848, 7, 18
1837, 7, 13. Jehu d ae 56 bur Chesterhill
----, --, --. Jonathan & Mary
    Ch: Deborah   b 1841, 12, 19
        Lydia Ann " 1846, 2, 27
1841, 6, 28. Rachel d ae 7 bur Chesterhill
1846, 3, 29. Dempsey d
1848, 10, 26. Susanna m Aaron MORRIS
1849, 3, 23. Jehu d
1849, 8, 25. Jonathan d
1849, 8, 30. Elijah, s Jehu & Tamar, Morgan
    Co., O.; m in Chesterfield, Hannah HAINES,
    dt Isaac & Lydia, Morgan Co., O.
    Ch: Isaac   b 1850, 5, 20
1851, 8, 21. Mary m Eli FAWCETT
1860, 5, 31. Elijah J., s Jesse & Ruth Anna,
    Morgan Co., O.; m in Chesterfield, Sibbil-
    la PEEBLES, dt Burwell & Asenath, Morgan
    Co., O.
    Ch: Mary F.   b 1861, 3, 7
        Asenath P. " 1864, 4, 15
        Rolin D.   " 1870, 6, 15
        Ruthanna " 1873, 2, 10

HIATT, continued
1872, 6, 24. Tamor d ae 91 bur Chesterhill
----, --, --. James & Mary E.
  Ch: Elwood b 1882, 9, 13
    George J. " 1884, 7, 14 (or Grace J.)
    Infant s " 1892, 7, 27 d 1892, 9,8
     bur Chesterhill
    James Rus-
     sell b 1896, 10, 17
1885, 10, 2. Jesse d ae 77 bur Chesterhill
1890, 5, 3. Sybilla d ae 70 bur Chesterhill
1896, 9, 11. Ruthanna d ae 89 bur Chesterhill
1897, 11, 10. Hannah d ae 86 bur Mt. Chelville,
Ia.
1905, 1, 31. Mary E. d ae 47 bur Chesterhill

1837, 11, 18. Jonathan & w, Mary, & ch,
Elisha, Lewis, Willson & Martha, rocf
Clear Creek MM, O., dtd 1837,9,19, endorsed by Pennsville MM, O., 1837,11,10
1847, 3, 20. Elisha gct Clear Creek MM, O.
1849, 11, 17. Wilson gct Fairfield MM, O.
1849, 11, 17. Lewis dis mcd
1849, 12, 15. Rhoda (form Edgerton) dis mcd
1849, 12, 15. Mary & ch, Martha, Deborah &
Lydia Ann, gct Clear Creek MM, O.
1852, 11, 20. Tamer Pearson (form Hiatt) con
mcd
1853, 2, 19. Joseph dis disunity
1859, 5, 21. Susanna Crew (form Hiatt) con
mcd
1859, 7, 16. Sarah Ann Fawcett (form Hiatt)
dis mcd
1861, 7, 20. Grace Smith (form Hiatt) con mcd
1865, 4, 15. Elijah dis disunity
1866, 3, 17. Amos dis disunity
1869, 4, 17. Jesse Jr. dis mcd
1880, 3, 20. James gct Plymouth MM, to m
Mary E. Harrison
1880, 12, 18. James gct Plymouth MM
1883, 12, 15. James & w, Mary E., & s, Elwood D., rocf Plymouth MM, dtd 1883,11,22
1888, 4, 21. Mary Chogwell (form Hiatt) dis
mcd
1889, 5, 18. Isaac rpd mcd
1892, 10, 16. Asenath Murphy (form Hiatt) dis
mcd
1898, 11, 19. Ruthanna Mercer (form Hiatt) dis
mcd
1899, 8, 19. Rollin R. con mcd
1908, 4, 18. Jesse L. rst
1910, 7, 16. George J. gct New Garden MM, to
m Mary Elma Warrington
1911, 9, 16. Mary Warrington rocf New Garden
MM

HIRST
1854, 9, 21. James, s Thomas & Ann, Morgan
Co., O.; m in Chesterfield, Rachel PLUM-
MER, dt Abram & Elizabeth, Morgan Co., O.
Ch: Elizabeth
   P. b 1855, 9, 12
1855, 10, 31. Rachel d

1847, 9, 18. Allen T. Lee gct Flushing MM,
O., to m Amanda Hirst
1850, 1, 19. Thomas rocf Somerset MM, O., dtd
1850,11,20(?)
1854, 4, 15. James P. rocf Plymouth MM, dtd
1854,1,23

HOBSON
1817, 4, 14. Phebe b (M)
1820, 9, 5. Belinda b (M)
1843, 3, 13. Mary J. b (M)
1850, 10, 23. Jane m Samuel HEALD
1859, 9, 1. Anne m Thomas E. VANLAW
1866, 9, 28. Mary J. m Thomas W. CONROW (M)
1890, 5, 3. Belinda d ae 70 bur Chesterhill
----, --, --. Thomas Alden m Tacy A. -----
dt Jehu & Ruth P. (Morris) Davis, b 1867,
10,3
  Ch: E. Gertrude
        b 1893, 2, 20
    Howard E. " 1895, 4, 6
    Edith " 1900, 8, 10
1899, 6, 8. Thomas d ae 86 bur Plymouth
1902, 11, 22. Eliza A. d ae 71 bur Plymouth
1906, 7, 18. Phebe d ae 89 bur Chesterhill
1907, 12, 17. Benjamin J. d ae 66 bur Plymouth

1841, 2, 20. John rocf Flushing MM, O., dtd
1840,11,26
1844, 11, 16. John gct Springfield MM, O.
1847, 12, 18. Stephen & w, Lydia, & ch, Jane,
Belinda, John, James, William & Mary Ann,
rocf Smithfield MM, dtd 1847,10,18
1852, 7, 17. Anna, Phebe & Belinda rocf
Smithfield MM, O., dtd 1852,6,21
1862, 3, 15. John Scofield gct Plymouth MM,
to m Belinda S. Hobson
1864, 9, 17. Phebe dis disunity
1864, 9, 17. Belinda F. dis disunity
1880, 4, 17. Phebe rst
1880, 4, 17. Belinda rst
1904, 6, 18. Wm. E. dis mcd
1907, 4, 20. Mary Lucile, adopted dt Wm. &
Elizabeth, recrq
1907, 6, 15. Lena May Edgerton (form Hobson)
con mcd
1907, 5, 18. Wm. & w, Elizabeth J., & dt,
Mary Lucile, gct West Branch MM, Ia.
1907, 6, 15. Stephen dis mcd & jas
1910, 2, 19. John A. gct Springville MM, Ia.
1912, 8, 17. John A. gct Springville MM, Ia.

HODGIN
1841, 7, 22. Wm., s John & Prudence, Athens
Co., O.; m in Chesterfield, Margaret
WORRALL, dt Zebulon & Martha, Athens Co.,
O.
  Ch: Martha b 1842, 7, 10
1842, 4, 18. Eli, s Stephen & Elizabeth,
Belmont Co., O.; m in Chesterfield, Sarah
BUNDY, dt Amos & Mary VERNON   [b
1858, 9, 20. Jesse D., s Daniel & Tamer Jane
1859, 3, 8. Mary Eliza, dt John & Tamer, b

HODGIN, continued

1839, 12, 21. Elias rocf Stillwater MM, O.,
        dtd 1839,11,23
1840, 3, 21. Prudence & ch, Francis & Edwin,
        rocf Stillwater MM, O., dtd 1840,1,25
1840, 10, 17. Wm. rocf Stillwater MM, O., dtd
        1840,7,25
1842, 5, 21. Elias dis disunity
1842, 6, 18. Sarah & ch, Wm., Mary, Ruthanna
        & Esther, gct Stillwater MM, O.
1844, 9, 21. Sarah (form Beck) dis mcd
1848, 2, 19. Frances Parker (form Hodgin) con
        mcd
1848, 6, 17. Wm. & w, Margaret, & ch, Martha
        & Hariet, gct Stillwater MM, O.
1848, 6, 17. Martha (form Rhodes) dis mcd
1857, 3, 21. John E. & w, Tamer, rocf Ply-
        mouth MM, dtd 1857,2,23
1857, 12, 19. Daniel & w, Tamer Jane, rocf
        Stillwater MM, O., dtd 1857,10,26
1859, 3, 19. Ann (form Vanlaw) dis mcd
1862, 12, 20. Prudence gct Stillwater MM, O.
1863, 2, 21. John E. & w, Tamer D., & dt,
        Mary Eliza, gct Hickory Grove MM, Ia.
1863, 2, 21. Daniel W. & w, Tamer Jane, &
        dt, Harriet, gct Hickory Grove MM, Ia.
1879, 3, 15. Lydia Jane (form Vanlaw) dis
        mcd
1882, 12, 16. Mary L. (form Crew) dis mcd

HOLLINGSWORTH

1846, 8, 29. Ury, dt Edmond & Betsy, b

1846, 4, 18. Edwin rocf Pennsville MM, O.,
        dtd 1846,4,16
1846, 4, 18. Betsy rocf Carmel MM, dtd
        1845,12,20
1848, 3, 18. Edwin & w, Betsy, & dt, Ury,
        gct Pennsville MM, O.
1863, 8, 15. Joseph S. Vanlaw gct Middleton
        MM, O., to m Margaret Hollingsworth
1906, 6, 16. Grace Llewellyn (form Hollings-
        worth) dis mcd & jas

HOLLOWAY

----, --, --. Elisha J. b 1819,3,15; m Lydia
        S.,----- b 1820,5,1
        Ch: Lucinda   b 1849, 5, 10
1855, 10, 6. Samuel E., s Elisha & Lydia, b
1852, 7, 23. Samuel G. d bur Chesterhill
1852, 8, 16. James d bur Chesterhill

1844, 1, 20. Dorothy & ch, Elisha, Cornelius
        B., Ann B., Samuel B., Elizabeth, Jacob
        & Sarah, rocf Flushing MM, O., dtd 1843,
        12,21
1844, 9, 21. Elisha J. & w, Lydia, & dt,
        Phebe Louisa, rocf Flushing MM, O., dtd
        1844,7,25
1846, 11, 21. Elisha J. & w, Lydia S., & dt,
        Phebe Louisa, gct Flushing MM, O.
1849, 12, 15. Elisha J. & w, Lydia, & ch,
        Phebe Louisa, Mary S. & Lucinda, rocf

Flushing MM, O., dtd 1849,10,25
1850, 8, 17. Elisha dis mcd
1852, 8, 21. Samuel G. & w, Mary, & ch,
        James, Wm., Asa & Ephraim, rocf Flushing
        MM, O., dtd 1852,6,24
1853, 2, 19. Mary & ch, Wm., Asa & Ephraim,
        gct Flushing MM, O.
1853, 4, 16. Cornelius dis mcd
1854, 10, 21. Samuel B. dis mcd
1854, 11, 18. Angeline (form Plummer) dis mcd
1855, 2, 17. Dorothy & ch, Elizabeth & Sarah
        Jane, gct Duck Creek MM, Ind.
1855, 2, 17. Ann B. gct Duck Creek MM, Ind.
1862, 8, 16. Elisha J. & w, Lydia, & dt, Lu-
        cinda, gct Plymouth MM
1862, 8, 16. Phebe Louisa gct Plymouth MM
1869, 10, 27. Lucinda Steel (form Holloway)
        dis mcd (M)

HOOPS

----, --, --. James & Elizabeth
        Ch: Priscilla b 1831, 9, 8
            Thomas   " 1834, 1, 16
            Joseph   " 1836, 4, 7
            Susanna   " 1836, 4, 7
            Samuel
            Lewis   " 1840, 3, 7 d 1841, 3,31
            Mary M.   " 1842, 4, 10
1838, 8, 19. Elizabeth Jr. d
1854, 9, 18. Susan d

1840, 11, 21. Sarah Ann Dewees (form Hoopes)
        con mcd
1845, 4, 19. Nathan dis mcd
1860, 7, 21. Thomas dis mcd
1861, 4, 20. Joseph [Hoopes] dis mcd
1862, 10, 18. Mary Brokaw (form Hoopes) dis
        mcd

HOPKINS

1874, 6, 24. Ella, dt John & Martha (Embree)
        Edgerton, b

1901, 9, 21. Ella M. (form Edgerton) con mcd

HORTON

1866, 7, 21. Phebe M. (form Maris) dis mcd

HOXIE

1869, 10, 18. Henry N., s Joseph & Mary,
        Barnstable Co., Mass.; m in Chesterfield,
        Sarah B. BOSWELL, dt George & Rebecca
        MICHENER

1872, 11, 16. Sarah B. gct Birmingham MM, Pa.

HUESTIS

1850, 9, 30. Sarah d ae 32 bur Chesterhill
1853, 3, 28. Thomas d
----, --, --. Isaac, s Aaron & Esther, Morgan
        Co., O.; m Sarah -----
        Ch: Mary   b 1843, 5, 30
            Esther   " 1845, 6, 27
            Jesse   " 1848, 6, 10

HUESTIS, Isaac & Sarah, continued
    Ch: Thomas   b 1850, 8, 2
    Isaac m 2nd 1853,4,21, Esther C. LEE, dt
    Samuel & Cynthia, Morgan Co., O.
    Ch: Sarah   b 1855, 3, 23
        Elizabeth " 1856, 10, 28
        Rebecca   " 1858, 2, 17
1863, 3, 5. Mary m Lindley FAWCETT
1871, 3, 23. Jesse, s Isaac & Sarah, Morgan
    Co., O.; m in Chesterfield, Amanda J. WOOD
    dt Caleb & Lydie
1872, 8, 8. Amanda Jane d ae 24
1877, 9, 20. Rebecca m Nathan DEWEES
1882, 6, 22. Esther m John S. FOWLER
1888, 10, 8. Isaac d ae 78 bur Chesterhill

1842, 5, 21. Isaac gct Somerset MM, O., to
    m Sarah Edgerton
1842, 8, 20. Sarah rocf Somerset MM, O., dtd
    1842,7,25
1878, 2, 16. Jesse con mcd
1897, 3, 20. Elizabeth Lambert (form Huestis)
    con mcd
1902, 2, 15. Esther C. gct Pasadena MM, Calif.
1905, 2, 18. Sarah gct Pasadena MM, Calif.

HUNNICUTT
1846, 7, 18. Wm. P. & w, Edna, & ch, Burwell
    & Margaret, rocf Dover MM, endorsed by
    Pennsville MM, O.
1846, 12, 19. Mary (form Parkins) dis mcd
1852, 2, 21. Burwell dis mcd & jas
1854, 9, 16. Margaret Barber (form Hunnicutt)
    dis mcd
1863, 2, 21. Edna dis jG
1871, 12, 16. Wm. P. dis jG

HUNTER
1844, 3, 16. Nancy (form McGirr) dis mcd

HUTTON
1880, 10, 25. Finley, s Joel W. & Ann, Phila-
    delphia, Pa.; m in Chesterfield, Agnes V.
    McGREW, dt James P. & Margaret, Morgan
    Co., O.

1884, 2, 16. Agnes V. gct ND MM, Pa.

JAMES
1847, 8, 25. Elizabeth m Martin MORRIS

1843, 6, 17. Sarah & ch, Samuel B., Rachel
    & Rebecca D., rocf Flushing MM, O., dtd
    1843,5,25
1843, 7, 15. Elizabeth rocf Flushing MM, O.,
    dtd 1843,5,25
1844, 5, 18. Rachel dis
1850, 6, 15. Rebecca dis jas

JOHN
1844, 4, 24. Jesse, s Wm. & Sarah, Athens
    Co., O., d 1861,3,15 ae 44 bur Chester-
    hill; m in Plymouth, Amy DEAN, dt Jonathan

& Hannah, Washington Co., O., d 1901,2,27
bur Chesterhill
    Ch: Hannah   b 1845, 7, 16 d 1872,12,13
        bur Chesterhill
        Sarah   b 1846, 12, 18
        William   " 1849, 11, 5 d 1874,10,13
        bur Chesterhill
        George   b 1854, 8, 15 " 1921, 7,16
        bur Chesterhill
        Harvey   b 1859, 9, 29
1860, 6, 16. Harry d bur Chesterhill
----, --, --. George m Sina ----- d 1898,12,2
    ae 38 bur Chesterfield
    Ch: Harvey   b 1888, 10, 19
        Edith   " 1890, 1, 11 d 1890, 8,10
        Alice   " 1892, 7, 13
1887, 11, 19. George gct Somerset MM, O., to
    m Sina Bailey
1888, 7, 21. Sina rocf Somerset MM, O., dtd
    1888,6,21
1915, 9, 19. Alice gct Lansdowne MM, Pa.
1915, 11, 8. Harvey dis disunity

JOHNSON
1844, 12, 21. Sarah (form McGirr) dis mcd
1872, 9, 21. Sarah (form Dewees) rpd mcd

JONES
1898, 12, 15. Thelma Elizabeth, w Lee, dt
    Amos & Sarah Louisa (Peebles) Rabberman, b

1888, 8, 18. Cora E. recrq
1895, 10, 19. Cora E. Rodgers (form Jones)
    dis mcd

KEATS
1857, 7, 18. Deborah (form Fawcett) dis mcd

KESTER
1839, 3, 16. Elizabeth, minor dt Wm. & Mary,
    rocf Stillwater MM, O., dtd 1839,2,23
1846, 2, 21. Elizabeth Arnold (form Kester)
    dis mcd

KING
1843, 4, 19. Michael, s Joseph & Mary, Morgan
    Co., O.; m in Plymouth, Lavina DEAN, dt
    Jonathan R. & Hannah, Washington Co., O.
1915, 3, 25. Lucinda d ae 91 bur Chesterhill

1838, 1, 20. Rachel (form Stanley) dis mcd
1843, 7, 15. Lavina gct Pennsville MM, O.
1910, 3, 19. Lucinda rst

KIRBY
1839, 9, 26. Isaac, s Thomas & Rebecca, Wash-
    ington Co., O.; m in Chesterfield, Eliza-
    beth WORRELL, dt Jonathan & Eleanor, Wash-
    ington Co., O.

1840, 4, 18. Elizabeth gct Pennsville MM, O.

KIRK
1914, 11, 24. Maria d ae 85

1900, 2, 17. Maria rocf Stillwater MM, O.

KOLLING
1845, 11, 15. Ernest [Kollings] & w, Elizabeth,
     & ch, John, Mary, Daniel, Hannah & Benja-
     min, gct Salem MM, Ia.
1846, 2, 21. Ernest Jr. gct Salem MM, Ia.
1846, 5, 16. Elizabeth Jr. gct Middleton MM

LAMBERT
----, --, --. Elizabeth b 1798,10,19 d 1885,
     1,15
----, --, --. Albert & Elizabeth
     Ch: Mary D.   b 1841, 6, 27
         Sarah C.   " 1843, 10, 1
         Zilpha   " 1845, 9, 23
         Asenath   " 1847, 7, 29

1837, 12, 16. Elizabeth gct Somerset MM
1840, 4, 18. Albert & w, Elizabeth, & ch, Ra-
     chel & John, rocf Somerset MM, O., dtd
     1840,3,30
1844, 5, 18. Asenath (form Edgerton) dis mcd
1846, 2, 21. Ann (form Briggs) dis mcd
1858, 4, 17. Martha (form Davis) dis mcd
1897, 3, 20. Elizabeth (form Huestis) con mcd
1910, 1, 15. Elizabeth H. dis disunity

LANGSTAFF
1839, 4, 21. Thomas D. & w, Hannah, & ch,
     Rodah & Ellnathan, rocf Salem MM, dtd
     1838,1,23
1839, 8, 17. Benjamin P. & w, Catherine, & s,
     Laben, rocf Marlborough MM, dtd 1839,5,28
1841, 3, 20. Thomas D. & w, Hannah, & ch,
     Rhoda, Elnathan & Wm., gct Stillwater MM,
     O.
1841, 7, 17. Benjamin P. & w, Catharine, & ch,
     Laban, gct Cincinnati MM, O.
1843, 6, 17. Thomas D. & w, Hannah, & ch,
     Rhoda, Elnathan, Wm. & Enoch, rocf Still-
     water MM, O., dtd 1843,4,22
1846, 3, 21. Thomas D. & w, Hannah, & ch,
     Rhoda, Elnathan, Wm., Enoch & Henry H.,
     gct Cincinnati MM, O.

LARKIN
1883, 1, 20. Lydia E. (form Branson) dis mcd

LEE
----, --, --. Allen & Amanda
     Ch: Anna C.   b 1849, 2, 7
         Thomas J. " 1851, 9, 14 d 1854,10,16
         Isaac W.   " 1854, 1, 3 " 1854, 8,25
         Amanda H. " 1855, 9, 14
1853, 4, 21. Esther C. m Isaac HUESTIS
1855, 10, 20. Amanda d bur Chesterhill
1862, 1, 28. Samuel d ae 73 bur Exeter, Pa.
1868, 7, 15. Cynthia d

1840, 4, 18. James dis mcd
1840, 9, 19. Allen Thomas rocf Exeter MM,
     dtd 1840,3,25
1847, 9, 18. Allen T. gct Flushing MM, O.,
     to m Amanda Hirst
1848, 9, 16. Amanda rocf Flushing MM, O., dtd
     1848,2,24
1857, 3, 21. Allen T. gct Somerset MM, O.,
     to m Mary Edgerton
1857, 9, 19. Mary E. rocf Somerset MM, O.,
     dtd 1857,7,27
1865, 12, 16. Thomas Allen & w, Mary E., &
     ch, Amanda H., Emma E., Lydia C. & Elma
     Elizabeth, gct Coal Creek MM, Ia.
1870, 4, 16. Elizabeth A. Chambers (form
     Lee) dis mcd
1889, 10, 19. Anna C. Cook (form Lee) con mcd

LEEKE
1800, 10, 2. Philip W. b
1802, 1, 28. Elizabeth D. b
1850, 5, 23. Hannah Ann m John VANLAW, Jr.

1864, 7, 16. Philip W. dis disunity
1864, 7, 16. Elizabeth dis disunity

LEWIS
1837, 4, 27. Halanah b (M)
----, --, --. Lewis m Eliza ----- d 1863,5,1
     ae 50 bur Chesterfield
     Ch: Sarah C.   b 1838, 9, 1
         John   " 1840, 9, 17 d 1863, 8, 3
         Chalkley   " 1842, 10, 8
         Asenath P. " 1845, 4, 2
         Elizabeth
          Ann   " 1847, 5, 29
         Hannah Ad-
          dah   " 1850, 6, 7
         Esther
          Lundy   " 1852, 8, 20
         Samuel S. " 1855, 10, 1
         Elwood   " 1858, 11, 13
1856, 11, 20. Wm., s Lewis & Eliza, Morgan
     Co., O.; m in Chesterfield, Helena RABBER-
     MAN, dt Henry & Caroline, Morgan Co., O.
     Ch: Mary De-
          litha   b 1857, 8, 27
         Caroline
          Eliza   " 1863, 9, 6
1857, 7, 12. Delitha, w Henry, d bur Chester-
     hill
1857, 8, 25. Mary D. b
1861, 4, 25. Susan H. m Jonathan MORRIS
1863, 4, 6. Caroline E. b
1874, 1, 16. Lewis d ae 83

1857, 1, 17. Tabitha (form Plummer) con mcd
1863, 2, 21. Sarah C. dis jas
1864, 2, 20. Asenath P. dis jas
1864, 10, 15. Elizabeth Ann dis jas
1866, 4, 21. Wm. H. dis disunity
1868, 3, 21. Isaac dis mcd
1869, 4, 17. Chalkley dis military service

LEWIS, continued
1873, 11, 15. Helena dis jas
1878, 5, 18. Samuel Jr. dis mcd

LIGHTFOOT
1842, 4, 16. Joseph & w, Rachel, & ch, Sam-
     uel, Foster & Susanna, rocf Pennsville MM,
     O., dtd 1842,4,14
1843, 4, 15. Joseph & w, Rachel, & ch, Sam-
     uel, Foster & Susanna, gct Pennsville MM,
     O.
1844, 9, 21. Rachel rocf Short Creek MM, O.,
     dtd 1844,6,18

LIVEZEY
1840, 3, 26. Oliver, s John H. & Sarah,
     Athens Co., O.; m in Chesterfield, Eliza-
     beth BOSWELL, dt Wm. & Rachel, Athens Co.,
     O.
----, --, --. Oliver d 1851,7,12 ae 32; m
     Asenath -----
     Ch: Sarah Jane b 1841, 8, 17
         William B. " 1843, 6, 11
1844, 3, 25. Hannah Ann m Daniel M. MOTT

1849, 12, 15. Jesse K. gct Somerset MM, O.,
     to m Elizabeth Patterson
1850, 4, 20. Jesse K. gct Somerset MM
1850, 5, 18. Oliver & w, Elizabeth, & ch,
     Sarah Jane & Wm. B., gct Alum Creek MM, O.
1851, 7, 19. Oliver & w, Elizabeth, & ch,
     Sarah Jane & Wm. B., rocf Alum Creek MM,O.
1853, 11, 19. Lavina Boswell (form Livezey)
     dis mcd
1863, 2, 21. Elizabeth dis jG
1863, 4, 18. Sarah Jane dis disunity
1865, 3, 18. Wm. B. dis disunity
1865, 5, 20. John H. & w, Sarah, gct Plymouth
     MM

LLEWELLYN
1831, 4, 7. Ezra d ae 53 bur Pennsville
1848, 1, 21. Ezra, s Thomas & Martha (Hol-
     lingsworth), b

1906, 4, 21. Daniel W. dis mcd
1906, 6, 16. Elisha & w, Rachel C., rocf
     New Garden MM, dtd 1906,5,24
1906, 6, 16. Grace (form Hollingsworth) dis
     mcd & jas
1914, 12, 17. Elisha & w, Rachel C., gct
     Middleton MM

LOOMIS
1843, 1, 21. Hannah (form Williams) con mcd
1848, 4, 15. Hannah dis disunity

LOUDEN
 1857, 7, 10. Elizabeth (form Vernon) con mcd
1858, 8, 21. Elizabeth [Liuthan] gct Plymouth
     MM

LUPTON
1846, 4, 27. Harvey, s Norris & Rebecca, b

1844, 8, 17. Norris & w, Rebecca, & ch, Jo-
     seph & Mary, rocf Somerset MM, O., dtd
     1844,6,24
1848, 12, 16. Norris & w, Rebecca, & ch, Jo-
     seph, Mary & Harvey, gct Somerset MM, O.

McCANN
1846, 8, 15. Sarah (form Fawcett) dis mcd

McCALL
1848, 1, 15. Mary rocf Westland MM, Pa.,
     dtd 1848,10,27

McCLURE
1844, 10, 19. Mathew Patterson gct Middleton
     MM, O., to m Louisa McClure

McCOLLOUGH
1849, 9, 13. Martha L., adopted dt Philip &
     E. Leeke, d

1840, 10, 17. Martha, minor, recrq

McCONNEL
1837, 12, 13. Ruth d ae 3 bur Plymouth
1839, 9, 12. Talbot d ae 24 bur Plymouth
1839, 9, 20. Orpha d ae 2 bur Plymouth
1845, 4, 14. Elmira, dt James & Mary, b
1847, 1, 20. Edward d ae 57 bur Plymouth
1847, 4, 21. Adaline m Eli THOMAS

1839, 5, 18. Talbert rocf Upper Springfield
     MM, dtd 1839,4,27
1844, 3, 16. James gct Carmel MM, to m Mary
     Armstrong
1844, 9, 21. Mary rocf Carmel MM, dtd 1844,
     8,17
1847, 7, 17. James & w, Mary, gct Pleasant
     Plain MM, Ia.
1847, 7, 17. Lydia & ch, Albert & Jonathan,
     gct Pleasant Plain MM, Ia.
1847, 7, 17. Nathan gct Pleasant Plain MM, Ia.

McDANIEL
1851, 6, 20. Phebe d ae 29

1843, 1, 21. Phebe (form Boswell) dis mcd
1844, 4, 20. Phebe rst

McGIRR
1845, 1, 22. Lydia m Joel BAILEY

1839, 12, 21. Arthur, Latitia, Jonah & Sarah
     Ann, ch Alexander & Sarah, rocf Marl-
     borough MM, dtd 1839,10,29
1840, 6, 20. James & w, Sarah, & ch, Lydia,
     John, Wm., James, Harpley & Henry, rocf
     Marlborough MM, dtd 1840,4,28
1840, 12, 19. Mary, Levi, Wm. & Mahlon rocf
     Marlborough MM, dtd 1840,9,29

McGIRR, continued
1842, 5, 21. Francis J., Nancy H., Sarah C., Alexcinder C. & Eliza Ann, ch Arthur & Elizabeth, rocf Somerset MM, O., dtd 1842,4,25
1844, 3, 16. Nancy Hunter (form McGirr) dis mcd
1844, 12, 21. Sarah Johnson (form McGirr) dis mcd
1849, 7, 21. Mary Dewees (form McGirr) dis mcd & jH
1850, 7, 20. John gct Marlborough MM
1851, 2, 15. Frances J. dis jH
1904, 9, 17. Walter J. dis disunity
1905, 9, 16. Mary M. Maley (form McGirr) con mcd
1906, 1, 20. Lewis H. dis jas

McGREW
1880, 10, 25. Agnes V. m Finley HUTTON

1844, 11, 16. Isaac Dewees gct Providence MM, Pa., to m Rebecca McGrew
1883, 5, 19. Agnes V. rocf Pennsville MM, O., dtd 1883,5,17
1890, 1, 18. Elmer E. dis mcd

McLAUGHLIN
1903, 8, 15. Anna (form Crew) con mcd

MALEY
1905, 9, 16. Mary M. (form McGirr) con mcd

MARIS
----, --, --. Owen & Rachel
   Ch: Rebecca   b 1837, 5, 6
       Clark T.   " 1839, 4, 17
       George   " 1841, 6, 17
1837, 4, 26. George d bur Chesterfield
1843, 4, 15. Rachel d ae 36 bur Chesterfield
1845, 10, 30. Amy S., wd J. Vanlaw, 2nd w Owen Maris, d ae 29 bur Chesterfield
1846, 10, 22. Sarah J. m Talbott PLUMMER
1857, 8, 20. Mary Anna m Clarkson T. PENROSE
1861, 9, 24. Anna W. d
1879, 8, 25. Sidney d ae 87 bur McConnelsville

1847, 9, 18. Owen gct Pennsville MM, O., to m Anna W. Vanlaw
1848, 3, 18. Anna W. & w, Elisha Vanlaw, rocf Pennsville MM, O., dtd 1848,3,16
1849, 1, 20. Cidney, Phebe & Rachel H. rocf Pennsville MM, O., dtd 1849,1,18
1851, 7, 19. Elizabeth (form Worrall) dis mcd
1864, 10, 15. Owen & ch, James E., Thomas Elwood, Rachel, Edward B. & Charles, gct Hickory Grove MM, Ia.
1866, 7, 21. Clark dis military service
1866, 7, 21. Phebe M. Horton (form Maris) dis mcd
1869, 1, 16. Mishael dis mcd
1869, 1, 16. George J. dis mcd

1885, 4, 18. Rachel gct Short Creek MM, O.

MARSHALL
1838, 2, 4. James Engle d ae 2 bur Plymouth
1840, 10, 23. Anna Mercy d ae 34 bur Plymouth
1842, 5, 25. John, s Samuel & Elizabeth, Washington Co., O.; m in Plymouth, Ann MORELAND, dt Jason & Mary, Washington Co., O.
   Ch: Martha   b 1845, 3, 5

1837, 12, 16. John & w, Anna Mercy, & ch, James, Caleb & Jesse, rocf Stillwater MM, O., dtd 1837,11,25, endorsed by Pennsville MM, O., 1837,12,14
1847, 8, 21. Caleb gct Carmel MM, to m Elmira Heald
1848, 4, 15. Elmira rocf Carmel MM, dtd 1847,11,20

MASTERS
1907, 4, 28. David d ae 78 bur Pennsville

1857, 9, 19. Griffith Dewees gct Pennsville MM, O., to m Ruthann Masters
1909, 2, 20. Wm. gct Stillwater MM, O.

MATHEWS
1860, 9, 15. Elizabeth (form Boswell) dis mcd

MAULE
1868, 3, 26. Edward & w, Hannah, & five ch recrq (M)

MERCER
1868, 9, 19. Emily (form Patterson) dis mcd
1898, 11, 19. Ruthanna B. (form Hiatt) dis mcd

MERRILL
1841, 4, 17. Mary (form Gray) dis mcd

METCALF
1802, 10, 11. Jehu b
1810, 7, 5. Hannah D. b

MICHENER
----, --, --. George & Rebecca
   Ch: Elizabeth F.
              b 1834, 9, 28 d 1836, 8,31
       Mary   " 1838, 5, 13
       William " 1840, 3, 4
       Anne   " 1842, 3, 8
       Joseph " 1844, 2, 8
       Sarah " 1845, 12, 8
       Peninah " 1847, 10, 8
       Amy   " 1849, 10, 12

1840, 8, 15. George & w, Rebecca, & ch, Mary & Wm., rocf Short Creek MM, O., dtd 1840, 5,19
1850, 6, 15. George & w, Rebecca, & ch, Mary, William, Anne, Joseph, Sarah, Penninah & Amy, gct Stillwater MM, O.

MICHENER, continued

1850, 11, 16. George & w, Rebecca, & ch, Mary,
     William, Anna, Joseph, Sarah, Peninah &
     Amy, rocf Stillwater MM, O., dtd 1850,10,
     26
1861, 11, 16. Mary gct Pennsville MM, O.
1862, 3, 15. Sarah B. Boswell (form Michener)
     con mcd
1863, 3, 21. George & w, Rebecca, & ch, Jo-
     seph, Penina & Amy E., gct Hickory Grove
     MM, Ia.
1867, 10, 19. Wm. F. con mcd
1868, 7, 18. Wm. F. gct Hickory Grove MM, Ia.
1868, 9, 19. Fleming Crew gct Pennsville MM,
     O., to m Mary L. Michener
1890, 9, 20. Peninah F. Worrall (form Michen-
     er) con mcd

MILLS
1842, 3, 18. Edith d ae 54 bur Plymouth

1839, 8, 17. Gideon & w, Edith, & ch, High,
     Reuben & Ezra, rocf Pennsville MM, O.,
     dtd 1839,8,15
1843, 12, 16. Reuben gct Newberry MM, O.
1845, 6, 21. Gideon dis mcd
1851, 2, 15. Ezra dis disunity

MONTGOMERY
----, --, --. Thomas & Sarahann
     Ch: Thomas   b 1849, 5, 20
         Amy   " 1851, 5, 2

1852, 2, 21. Thomas & w, Sarahann, & ch,
     Ruthann, Wm. H., Henry C., Jane, Mary &
     Joel, rocf Stillwater MM, O., dtd 1851,12,
     23
1852, 9, 18. Thomas & w, Sarahann, & ch,
     Ruthann, Wm. H., Henry C., Jane, Mary,
     Joel, Thomas & Amy, gct Three Rivers MM,
     Ia.

MOORE
1839, 7, 20. Eleanor (form Worrall) con mcd
1852, 2, 21. Susannah (form Worrall) dis mcd

MORLAND
1842, 5, 25. Ann m John MARSHALL
1846, 11, 20. Joshua, s Albert, b

1838, 6, 16. Albert [Morlan] rocf Middleton
     MM, O., dtd 1838,4,23
1839, 3, 16. Albert con mcd
1839, 7, 20. Rebecca [Moreland] (form Morris)
     con mcd
1839, 12, 21. Jason [Morlan] & w, Mary, rocf
     Carmel MM, dtd 1839,10,19
1839, 12, 21. Ann rocf Carmel MM, dtd 1839,10,
     19

MORREY
1865, 1, 21. Mary Jenkinson (form Wright) dis
     mcd

MORRIS
----, --, --. Mordecai & Alice
     Ch: Edwin   b 1824, 1, 1 d 1903, 3,25
         David   " 1825, 10, 1
         Martin   " 1828, 11, 17
         Robert   " 1831, 11, 7
         Susann   " 1835, 8, 13
         Rachel   " 1837, 11, 13
         Lydia   " 1841, 12, 1
----, --, --. Nathan d 1882,2,26 ae 74 bur
     Chesterfield; m Tacy ----- d 1901,8,6 ae
     95 bur Chesterfield
     Ch: Samuel   b 1833, 11, 14
         Jonathan " 1835, 4, 23
         William P. " 1837, 2, 26
         Eli   " 1839, 10, 28 d 1925,12,26
         bur Chesterfield
         Joseph   b 1841, 9, 18
         Ruty   " 1843, 8, 17
         Thomas   " 1849, 11, 21
         Phebe   " 1847, 10, 20
1836, 5, 28. Joel d bur Chesterfield
1842, 2, 17. Mordecai d ae 39 bur Plymouth
1844, 7, 24. Alice m Elias PICKERING
1846, 4, 13. Phebe d ae 37 bur Chesterfield
1847, 8, 25. Martin, s Mordecai & Alice,
     Washington Co., O.; m in Plymouth, Eliza-
     beth JAMES, dt Geo. & Sarah
1848, 10, 26. Aaron, s Samuel & Sally, Morgan
     Co., O.; m in Chesterfield, Susanna
     HIATT, dt Jehu & Tamar, Morgan Co., O.
     Ch: Amos W.   b 1845, 7, 21
         Phebe Ann " 1849, 9, 8
         Jehu H.   " 1851, 2, 23
         Sarah   " 1853, 4, 21
1849, 1, 25. Rachel m Benjamin BUNDY
1861, 4, 25. Jonathan, s Nathan & Tacy, Mor-
     gan Co., O.; m in Chesterfield, Susan H.
     LEWIS, dt Lewis & Eliza, Morgan Co., O.,
     d 1861,12,12 ae 68
1883, 11, 20. Samuel, s Nathan & Tacy, Morgan
     Co., O.; m in Chesterfield, Mary E. TODD,
     dt Robert & Eunis, Morgan Co., O.
     Ch: Oliver T. b 1886, 3, 26
         Robert N. " 1890, 1, 1 d 1901, 4,21
         bur Chesterhill
1899, 4, 16. Rachel H. d ae 77
1908, 1, 3. Samuel d ae 74
1922, 11, 18. Mary T. d ae 76 bur Akron, O.
1927, 10, 19. David Linneaus d ae 69 bur
     Bartlett, O.

1838, 10, 20. Theodate & ch, Ruthanna, Wm. W.
     & Benajah, rocf Milford MM, dtd 1838,6,23
1839, 6, 15. Theodate dis jas
1839, 7, 20. Rebecca Morland (form Morris)
     con mcd
1841, 7, 17. Benjamin dis mcd
1844, 5, 18. Edwin gct Stillwater MM, O., to
     m Rachel Hanson
1845, 3, 15. Rachel rocf Stillwater MM, O.,
     dtd 1845,2,22
1846, 4, 18. Ruthann Goodwin (form Morris)

MORRIS, continued
    dis mcd
1847, 9, 18. Joshua Jr. gct Carmel MM, to m
    Eliza Ann Tulloss
1847, 11, 20. David dis mcd
1848, 3, 18. Eliza M. rocf Carmel MM, dtd
    1848,1,15
1856, 2, 16. Rachel dis jas
1857, 10, 17. Lydia Doan (form Morris) con mcd
1858, 9, 18. Lydia dis jas
1861, 9, 21. Susanna Randolph (form Morris)
    dis mcd
1862, 12, 20. Wm. dis disunity
1864, 8, 20. Aaron & w, Susannah, & ch, Amos
    W., Phebe Ann, John H. & Sarah T., gct
    Hickory Grove MM, Ia.
1865, 6, 17. Mary gct Hickory Grove MM, Ia.
1867, 8, 17. David P. dis mcd & military ser-
    vice
1869, 2, 20. Joseph K. dis mcd
1869, 7, 17. Eli dis mcd
1870, 6, 18. Mary T. (form Rabberman) dis mcd
1870, 9, 22. Mary (form Rabberman) dis mcd
    (M)
1870, 10, 15. Jonathan dis military service
1874, 10, 17. Thomas Elwood dis jas
1876, 11, 18. Phebe dis jas
1909, 5, 15. Mary E. gct Springville MM, Ia.

MORRISON
1874, 8, 15. Ann (form Patterson) dis mcd

MOTT
1841, 5, 22. Wm., s Wm. & Sarah, b
1844, 3, 25. Daniel M., s Wm. & Sarah, Athens
    Co., O.; m in Chesterfield, Hannah Ann
    LIVEZEY, dt John H. & Sarah, Athens Co.,O.
----, --, --. Smith H. & Matilda Jane
    Ch: Clendenon b 1898, 7, 22 d 1898,10,17
        bur Chesterfield
        Mildred
        Carroll   b 1905, 4, 25

1839, 5, 18. Wm. & w, Sarah, & ch, Daniel M.,
    Mary, James E., Richard, Gershom, Asher,
    George W. & Eleanor, rocf Somerset MM, O.,
    dtd 1839,4,29
1847, 4, 17. Richard, minor, gct Stillwater
    MM, O.
1905, 2, 18. Sarah J. gct Pasadena MM, Calif.
1906, 5, 19. Smith H. & w, Matilda Jane, &
    ch, Eleanor, Amy, James, Frederick, Mar-
    jorie A. & Mildred C., gct West Branch
    MM, Ia.
1906, 5, 19. Achsah, Mary P. & Elizabeth gct
    West Branch MM, Ia.

MURPHY
1892, 10, 16. Asenath (form Hiatt) dis mcd

NAYLOR
1857, 7, 18. Isaac Penrose gct Pennsville MM,
    O., to m Mary Jane Naylor

PARKER
1842, 2, 7. Rhoda D. d ae 16 bur Plymouth
1840, 11, 25. Mary G. m Joseph THOMAS
1842, 2, 17. Rachel d ae 48 bur Plymouth
----, --, --. Isaac & Frances
    Ch: Anderson   b 1856, 5, 20
        Rebecca   " 1858, 12, 10 d 1876,12,27
        bur Chesterfield

1840, 10, 17. Mary G. rocf Stillwater MM, O.,
    dtd 1840,9,26
1841, 6, 19. George & w, Rachel, & ch, Ezra,
    Rhoda, Elisha, Isaac, Rachel Ann & Mar-
    tha, rocf Stillwater MM, O., dtd 1841,4,25
1841, 6, 19. Lindley rocf Stillwater MM, O.,
    dtd 1841,5,22
1841, 6, 19. Jacob rocf Stillwater MM, O.,
    dtd 1841,5,22
1846, 10, 17. Isaac Jr. rocf Short Creek MM,
    O., dtd 1846,8,18
1847, 7, 17. Jacob dis disunity
1847, 12, 18. Isaac con mcd
1848, 2, 19. Frances (form Hodgin) con mcd
1848, 4, 15. Ezra dis disunity
1848, 5, 20. Joseph rocf Short Creek MM, O.,
    dtd 1847,10,28
1849, 2, 17. Isaac Jr. dis disunity
1850, 6, 15. Elisha dis mcd
1857, 5, 16. Isaac dis disunity
1863, 2, 21. Frances dis jG
1867, 11, 28. Sarah (form Rabberman) dis mcd
    (M)
1869, 12, 18. Sarah (form Rabberman) dis mcd
1872, 10, 19. Sarah (form Rabberman) dis mcd
1877, 8, 18. Anderson J. dis mcd
1880, 1, 19. Lydia M. (form Williams) con mcd

PARKINS
1875, 6, 20. Jonathan d ae 91 bur Chester-
    field
1877, 8, 17. David d ae 92 bur Chesterfield
1878, 7, 28. Lydia d ae 87

1838, 3, 17. David & w, Lydia, & ch, Jacob,
    Levi, John, Mary, Sarah J. & David, rocf
    Flushing MM, O., dtd 1838,1,25
1838, 3, 17. Lucinda & Rachel rocf Flushing
    MM, O., dtd 1838,1,25
1845, 4, 19. Jacob dis disunity
1845, 5, 17. Levi dis mcd
1846, 12, 19. Mary Hunnicutt (form Parkins)
    dis mcd
1850, 5, 18. John dis mcd
1858, 9, 18. Sarah Jane dis jas
1861, 4, 20. David Jr. dis mcd
1873, 10, 18. Jonathan rocf Flushing MM, O.,
    dtd 1873,9,25

PARRY
1847, 6, 19. Miriam (form Williams) dis mcd

PATTEN
1844, 3, 15. Mahlon d bur Plymouth

PATTERSON

----, --, --. George Arnold b 1904,3,9; m
  Dortha Beulah CARTER
    Ch: Charles
          Carter   b 1833, 4, 28
1839, 6, 20. Sarah Ann m Fleming CREW
----, --, --. Jordan & Mary
    Ch: Jordan   b 1838, 1, 2 d 1844, 9,18
          bur Chesterfield
       Mary   b 1838, 1, 2 " 1844, 9,18
          bur Chesterfield
       Martha   b 1842, 8, 21 " 1842, 9, 5
1840, 8, 20. Joseph, s Jordan & Mary, Athens
  Co., O.; m in Chesterfield, Grace BECK,
  dt Jesse & Elizabeth, Athens Co., O.
    Ch: Mary G.   b 1841, 10, 25
1840, 12, 22. Emily, dt Ira & Mahala, d ae 14
  bur Chesterfield
1841, 11, 8. Grace d bur Chesterfield
----, --, --. William & Sarah Ann
    Ch: Joseph B. b 1842, 8, 28
       Sarah
          Elizabeth " 1845, 4, 19
       Rachel B. " 1848, 5, 19
1841, 9, 19. Rachel d ae 45 bur Chesterfield
1843, 5, 5. Ephamy d ae 56 bur Plymouth
1843, 9, 8. Eunice d ae 15 bur Chesterfield
----, --, --. Arnold & Lucinda
    Ch: Charles b 1844, 5, 16
       Lindley   " 1847, 4, 15 d 1851,12,27
          bur Chesterfield
       Emily   b 1850, 2, 20
       George
1844, 1, 25. Rachel m John S. BRIGGS
1847, 3, 10. Edna d ae 28 bur Chesterfield
1848, 8, 9. Phereby d ae 18 bur Chesterfield
1853, 8, 25. Rachel F. m Jesse VANLAW
1856, 4, 8. Mahala d ae 65 bur Chesterfield
1861, 5, 30. Ira, s Jeremiah & Faith, Morgan
  Co., O.; m in Chesterfield, Rebecca WIL-
  LIAMS, dt John & Sarah M.
    Ch: John
       William   b 1864, 5, 10
1865, 2, 2. Jordan d
1873, 7, 30. Ira d ae 79 bur Chesterfield
1885, 1, 14. Mary d ae 86 bur Chesterfield
----, --, --. Carl, s Chas. & Elizabeth Ann
  (Morris), b 1873,10,27; m Edith SCHOFIELD
  dt John & Belinda (Hobson), b 1871,7,30
    Ch: George
       Arnold   b 1904, 3, 9
       John Scho-
          field   " 1909, 2, 14
----, --, --. John Schofield b 1909,2,14; m
  Sarah TUCKER
    Ch: Elizabeth
       Ann   b 1932, 5, 15

1838, 10, 20. James dis mcd
1839, 5, 18. Achsah & ch, Francis E., Marmaduke, Priscilla, Thomas P., James, Catharine J., Abigail P. & John G., rocf Somerset MM, dtd 1839,3,25

1839, 5, 18. Sarah rocf Somerset MM, dtd
  1839,3,25
1840, 1, 18. Sarah Henry (form Patterson) dis
  mcd
1840, 3, 21. Ira & w, Mahala, & ch, Mathew
  T., Emly, Elwood, Pharaby, Rix & Thomas
  T., rocf Somerset MM, O., dtd 1840,2,24
1840, 3, 21. Edna rocf Somerset MM, O., dtd
  1840,2,24
1841, 11, 20. Wm. dis disunity
1842, 1, 15. Sarah Ann (form Cadwalader) con
  mcd
1842, 7, 16. Wm. con mcd
1842, 9, 17. Jeremiah dis disunity
1842, 11, 19. Arnold con mcd
1843, 6, 17. Francis E. dis mcd
1843, 11, 18. Caleb dis mcd
1843, 12, 16. Lucinda recrq
1844, 4, 20. Joseph dis mcd
1844, 4, 20. Sarah (form Plummer) dis mcd
1844, 8, 17. Rebecca Williams (form Patterson)
  dis mcd
1844, 10, 19. Amasa dis disunity
1844, 10, 19. Mathew gct Middleton MM, O., to
  m Louisa McClure
1845, 4, 19. Louisa rocf Middleton MM, dtd
  1845,2,6
1846, 11, 21. Marmaduke dis mcd
1847, 8, 21. Phreeby Baleau (form Patterson)
  dis mcd
1847, 9, 18. Amos dis disunity
1847, 12, 18. Robert dis disunity
1848, 2, 19. Jared dis disunity
1848, 3, 18. Priscilla dis disunity
1848, 3, 18. James dis disunity
1848, 8, 19. Sarah dis disunity
1849, 10, 20. John dis disunity
1849, 11, 17. Elwood gct Short Creek MM, O.
1849, 11, 17. Rix gct Short Creek MM, O.
1849, 12, 15. Jesse K. Livezey gct Sandy
  Spring MM, O., to m Elizabeth Patterson
1850, 7, 20. Thomas P. dis disunity
1851, 4, 19. Mary Swart (form Patterson) dis
  mcd
1851, 9, 20. Isaac dis disunity
1852, 3, 20. Elwood rocf Short Creek MM, O.,
  dtd 1852,7,22
1852, 3, 20. Rix rocf Short Creek MM, O.,
  dtd 1852,7,22
1853, 4, 16. Clark dis mcd
1853, 8, 20. Ruth Worrall (form Patterson)
  dis mcd
1853, 10, 15. Maria (form Bundy) dis mcd
1854, 5, 20. Elwood dis mcd
1855, 7, 21. Rix dis mcd
1859, 2, 19. Thomas T. dis mcd
1859, 3, 19. Susan (form Wood) dis mcd
1860, 7, 21. Jane Hague (form Patterson) dis
  mcd
1863, 1, 17. Arnold dis jG
1863, 2, 21. Lucinda dis jG
1863, 7, 18. Charles dis disunity
1863, 8, 15. Mary G. Shadle (form Patterson)

PATTERSON, continued
    dis mcd
1868, 9, 19. Emily Mercer (form Patterson)
    dis mcd
1869, 6, 19. Emily A. (form Edgerton) dis mcd
1874, 3, 21. George dis mcd & jas
1874, 8, 15. Ann Morrison (form Patterson)
    dis mcd
1876, 4, 15. Rebecca W. & s, John W., gct
    ND MM, Pa.
1897, 7, 17. Carl recrq
1897, 7, 17. Edith (form Schofield) con mcd
1929, 8, 17. Geo. A. gct Plainfield MM, Ind.,
    to m Dortha B. Carter
1931, 6, 20. John S. gct Dartmouth MM, Mass.,
    to m Sarah Tucker
1933, 2, 18. Dortha B. Carter rocf Plainfield
    MM, Ind., dtd 1933,2,1

PATTON
----, --, --. Richard & Lydia
    Ch: Eliza Jane b 1860, 1, 7
        John   " 1862, 1, 29

1838, 6, 16. Mahlon & w, Euphamy, rocf Still-
    water MM, O., dtd 1838,4,28
1858, 4, 17. Richard & w, Lydia, & ch, Mary-
    ellen & Wm. John, rocf Pennsville MM, O.,
    dtd 1858,3,18
1863, 8, 15. Richard & w, Lydia, & ch, Mary
    Ellin, Wm., Jane & John, gct Pennsville
    MM, O.

PEARSON
----, --, --. William m Catharine ----- d
    1846,7,7 ae 47 bur Chesterfield
    Ch: Benjamin   b 1817, 8, 19
        Stephen B. " 1819, 10, 3
        John   " 1821, 6, 24
        Enoch   " 1823, 9, 15
        Mary   " 1826, 9, 11
        David   " 1829, 10, 17
        Jesse   " 1833, 10, 5
        William   " 1835, 10, 11
        Amos   " 1840, 12, 17
        Smith   " 1843, 9, 7
----, --, --. Jesse & Cynthia
    Ch: Thomas   b 1824, 12, 7
        George   " 1826, 11, 16
        Mary Jane " 1829, 5, 13
        William
        Elizabeth S." 1835, 4, 7
        James   " 1837, 8, 21 d 1846, 2,22
        bur Chesterfield
        Hannah Ann b 1841, 10, 17 d 1853,10,--
1849, 9, 20. William, s Benjamin & Jane, Mor-
    gan Co., O.; m in Chesterfield, Rebecca
    SMITH, dt Stephen & Sibbilla TODD, Morgan
    Co., O.
1853, 8, 22. Anna Maria, dt David & Tamer, b

1843, 12, 16. Benjamin dis mcd
1850, 2, 15. George dis mcd

1851, 2, 15. Jane rocf Flushing MM, O., dtd
    1851,1,23
1851, 7, 19. Wm. & w, Rebecca H., & ch,
    Jesse, Wm., Amos & Smith Pearson, & Ell-
    wood, Hannah, Stephen & Phebe Smith, gct
    Spring Creek MM, Ia.
1852, 11, 20. Tamer (form Hiatt) con mcd
1852, 12, 18. Mary Ann Bartlett (form Pearson)
    dis mcd
1852, 12, 18. David con mcd
1853, 6, 18. Thomas dis mcd
1853, 10, 15. Jesse & w, Cynthia, gct Red
    Cedar MM, Ia.
1853, 10, 15. Jane gct Red Cedar MM, Ia.
1853, 10, 15. Elizabeth S. gct Red Cedar MM,
    Ia.
1853, 12, 17. Mary Jane Ellis (form Pearson)
    dis mcd
1854, 4, 15. Wm. dis mcd
1854, 10, 21. David & w, Anna Maria, gct
    Three Rivers MM, Ia.
1864, 5, 21. Anna (form Michener) dis mcd

PEEBLES
----, --, --. Burwell d 1884,1,24 ae 78; m
    Asenath ----- d 1885,9,8 ae 71
    Ch: Robert   b 1838, 5, 4 d 1878, 9,30
        bur Chesterfield
        William   b 1840, 8, 16 " 1858, 8, 6
        Edna   " 1842, 4, 12
        Stephen   " 1844, 9, 11
----, --, --. William & Rachel
    Ch: Elizabeth b 1838, 10, 27 d 1910, 4, 8
        bur Chesterfield
        Mordecai b 1840, 10, 9
        Martha   " 1842, 12, 18
        Rachel E. " 1845, 4, 18
        Deborah Jane
                  b 1848, 1, 6
        John W.   " 1850, 3, 12
        Amelia   " 1853, 3, 12
        Asenath   " 1856, 4, 22
        Josiah   " 1858, 8, 3
        Eli   " 1861, 7, 29
1853, 2, 1. Rachel d
1859, 10, 20. Robert, s Burwell & Asenath,
    Morgan Co., O.; m in Chesterfield, Eliza-
    beth H. THOMAS, dt Aaron & Sarah, Morgan
    Co., O.
    Ch: Sarah
        Louiza   b 1860, 10, 7
        William   " 1863, 11, 22
        Ruanna   " 1869, 10, 13
1860, 5, 31. Sibbilla m Elijah J. HIATT
1888, 8, 30. Edna m Elwood DEAN
1910, 4, 8. Elizabeth d ae 72 bur Chester-
    field

1340, 3, 21. Wm. S. & w, Rachel, & dt, Eliza-
    beth, rocf Pennsville MM, O., dtd 1840,2,
    13
1856, 1, 19. Chalkley dis mcd
1856, 1, 19. Daniel dis mcd

PEEBLES, continued
1856, 2, 16. Mary Ann (form Wood) dis mcd
1859, 7, 16. Elizabeth dis jas
1861, 9, 21. Martha dis jas
1862, 8, 16. Mordecai dis jas
1865, 4, 15. Wm. dis jas
1865, 5, 20. Deborah Jane dis jas
1865, 5, 20. Rachel dis jas
1867, 2, 16. Stephen dis mcd
1872, 4, 20. John dis jas
1877, 3, 21. Josiah dis mcd
1882, 8, 19. Eli dis jas
1898, 9, 17. Sarah L. Rabberman (form Peebles)
     con mcd
1902, 3, 15. Ruanna Schofield (form Peebles)
     con mcd
1902, 7, 19. Wm. A. dis mcd

PEITSMIRE
1868, 12, 8. Albertine d ae 33

1866, 1, 20. Albertine [Peitsmeyer] recrq

PENNOCK
1849, 6, 16. Cynthia & ch, David, Elon, Re-
     becca, Jonathan, Matilda & Jacob, rocf
     Sandy Spring MM, O., dtd 1847,11,22
1850, 1, 19. Cynthia dis jas
1850, 8, 17. Elon dis jas

PENROSE
----, --, --. Thomas & Mariah
     Ch: Clarkson T.
                 b 1831, 9, 22
         Osborn   " 1833, 10, 4
         Isaac   " 1836, 4, 1
         William W. " 1839, 4, 23
         James   " 1841, 10, 25
         Emlen   " 1844, 8, 22
         Hannah C. " 1851, 1, 14
1832, 4, 21. Jason, s Richard & Ann Elizabeth
     (Swicard), b
1857, 8, 20. Clarkson T., s Thomas & Maria,
     Morgan Co., O.; m in Chesterfield, Mary
     Anna MARIS, dt Owen & Rachel, Morgan Co.,
     O.
     Ch: Maria Ada b 1859, 2, 22
         Rachel Eva " 1859, 2, 22
1858, 3, 17. Hervey, s Isaac & Mary, b
1899, 2, 2. Mildred d ae 76
1912, 4, 15. Martha d ae 77 bur Pennsville
1922, 12, 7. Jason d ae 90 bur Pennsville

1838, 1, 20. Emlen Griffith gct Pennsville
     MM, O., to m Sarah Ann Penrose
1843, 11, 18. Joseph rocf Pennsville MM, O.,
     dtd 1843,10,19
1846, 4, 18. Joseph gct Pennsville MM, O.,
     to m Mildred Worthington
1846, 11, 21. Mildred rocf Pennsville MM, O.,
     dtd 1846,11,19
1855, 7, 21. Osborn gct Pennsville MM, O.,
     to m Susan A. Wood

1856, 10, 18. Susan H. rocf Pennsville MM, O.,
     to m Susan A. Wood
1857, 7, 18. Isaac gct Pennsville MM, O., to
     m Mary Jane Naylor
1858, 8, 21. Isaac dis
1863, 10, 17. Isaac rst at Pennsville MM, O.,
     on consent of this mtg
1891, 7, 18. Adaline W. (form Bundy) dis mcd

PERKINS
1843, 6, 17. Rachel Selby (form Perkins) dis
     mcd

PERVIS
1847, 2, 20. Elijah & Mary, minors, rocf
     Pennsville MM, O., dtd 1847,2,18

PHIPPS
1861, 2, 16. Rachel Emily (form Worrall) con
     mcd
1879, 4, 19. Rachel Emily dis disunity

PICKERING
1843, 5, 11. Elizabeth L. d ae 54 bur Ply-
     mouth
1844, 7, 24. Elias, s Jonathan & Sarah,
     Washington Co., O.; m in Plymouth, Alice
     MORRIS, dt David & Ann WAY, Monroe Co.,O.
     Ch: Evan   b 1847, 5, 29
         Mordecai " 1850, 3, 14
1887, 10, 7. Isaac d ae 79
1888, 3, 6. Armelia d ae 68

1840, 6, 20. Elias rst on consent of Plain-
     field MM
1849, 8, 18. Sarah (form Garretson) dis mcd
1853, 6, 17. Elias dis
1861, 8, 17. Alice dis jas
1870, 9, 17. Evan dis mcd
1873, 5, 17. Mordecai dis jas
1874, 8, 15. Isaac rst on consent of Short
     Creek MM, O.
1877, 3, 17. Armelia rst on consent of Flush-
     ing MM, O.

PICKET
1860, 3, 22. Hannah m Elihu SMITH
1870, 12, 1. Sarah m Elihu TODD

1860, 1, 21. Martha rocf Pennsville MM, O.,
     dtd 1860,1,19
1860, 1, 21. Hannah rocf Pennsville MM, O.,
     dtd 1860,1,19
1865, 12, 16. Martha dis jas

PIDGEON
1851, 10, 23. Joseph W., s Amos & Ann, Morgan
     Co., O.; m in Chesterfield, Elizabeth BLY,
     dt Jonas & Martha, Morgan Co., O.

1847, 2, 20. Joseph W. rocf Pennsville MM,
     O., dtd 1847,2,18
1852, 1, 17. Joseph W. & w, Elizabeth, gct

PIDGEON, continued
    Pennsville MM, O.

PIERPONT
1887, 10, 14. Rebecca d ae 47

1868, 4, 18. Rebecca L. (form Smith) con mcd
1874, 11, 21. Emaline E. (form Edgerton) dis
    mcd

PLUMLEY
1841, 10, 16. Elizabeth (form Way) dis mcd
1846, 2, 21. Rebecca (form Tribby) dis mcd

PLUMMER
1835, 6, 25. Thomas d
----, --, --. Abraham & Elizabeth
    Ch: Elizabeth b 1829, 9, 16
        Thomas   " 1835, 11, 27
        Kinsey   " 1837, 11, 20
        Amos   " 1839, 3, 28
        Abraham   " 1842, 1, 2
        Robert   " 1844, 7, 25
----, --, --. John & Rachel
    Ch: Isaac   b 1840, 4, 21
        Greenberry " 1844, 3, 23 d 1845, 3, 3
        bur Chesterfield
1842, 10, 20. Deborah m John WORRALL
1845, 9, 29. Axum d bur Chesterfield
1846, 10, 22. Talbott, s Abram & Elizabeth,
    Morgan Co., O.; m in Chesterfield, Sarah
    J. MARIS, dt Owen & Rachel, Morgan Co., O.
    Ch: Thomas C. b 1848, 3, 19
        Rachel A. " 1850, 7, 7 d 1853, 3,17
        Caspar M. " 1852, 2, 11
        Leroy   " 1855, 2, 2
        Mary E.   " 1861, 3, 23
        Nellie J. " 1864, 12, 12
1848, 8, 18. Rebecca d ae 15
1849, 2, 27. Margaret, dt Thos. & Mary Ann
    (Scott), b
1853, 8, 25. Ruth Ann m Elwood R. WORRALL
1854, 1, 22. Elizabeth d
1854, 9, 21. Rachel m James HIRST
1856, 8, 3. Elizabeth d
1865, 11, 21. John d
1870, 8, 24. Rachel d ae 70
1933, 5, 27. Margaret d

1839, 4, 21. John & w, Rachel, & ch, Deborah,
    Robert, Mary B., Wm., Exum, Tabitha, Re-
    becca, Angeline & John, rocf Stillwater
    MM, O., dtd 1839,3,23
1844, 4, 20. Sarah Patterson (form Plummer)
    dis mcd
1847, 1, 16. Robert dis mcd
1847, 7, 17. Mary dis
1850, 5, 18. Wm. dis mcd
1852, 6, 19. Caspar dis mcd
1854, 11, 18. Angeline Holloway (form Plum-
    mer) dis mcd
1857, 1, 17. Tabitha Lewis (form Plummer)
    con mcd

1864, 1, 16. Isaac dis disunity
1868, 7, 18. Abraham gct Springville MM, Ia.
1868, 9, 19. Talbert & w, Sarah, & ch, Thom-
    as C., Caspar M., Leroy, Mary E. & Nellie,
    gct Springville MM, Ia.
1871, 4, 15. John dis jas

PRICE
1839, 12, 21. Jesse rocf Marlborough MM, dtd
    1839,10,29
1839, 12, 21. Isaac, Sarah, John & Thomas,
    minor ch Thomas, rocf Marlborough MM, dtd
    1839,10,29
1840, 10, 17. Sarah dis jas
1842, 5, 21. Isaac dis mcd
1843, 5, 20. Jesse dis jas
1848, 2, 19. Thomas Jr. rpd mcd
1848, 3, 18. John dis disunity

PUCKET
1859, 6, 18. Sarah rocf Pennsville MM, O.,
    dtd 1859,4,14

RABBERMAN
----, --, --. Henry b 1799,5,14 d 1860,6,6;
    m Caroline ----- b 1809,11,11
    Ch: Hellen   b 1837, 4, 27
        Mary T.   " 1839, 6, 30
        Lewis W.   " 1842, 1, 11 d 1893, 8,21
        Jonathan H." 1844, 5, 9
        Sarah   " 1846, 5, 11
        Lydia   " 1849, 6, 14
        John E.   " 1851, 5, 27
        Amos   " 1853, 8, 22 d 1917, 2,24
        bur Chesterfield
1856, 11, 20. Helena m Wm. LEWIS
1860, 10, 7. Sarah Louisa, w Amos, dt Robert
    & Elizabeth H. (Thomas) Peebles, b
1898, 12, 15. Thelma S., dt Amos & Sarah Lou-
    isa, b

1841, 9, 18. Henry Sr., Henry Jr. & Char-
    lotte rocf Middleton MM, O., dtd 1841,6,10
1843, 5, 20. Henry & w, Caroline, & ch, He-
    lena, Mary & Lewis W., rocf Middleton MM,
    dtd 1842,10,6
1845, 9, 20. Charlotte Guy (form Rabberman)
    con mcd
1852, 8, 21. Henry con mcd
1864, 11, 19. Henry dis disunity
1866, 3, 17. Caroline dis disunity
1867, 11, 28. Sarah Parker (form Rabberman)
    dis mcd (M)
1868, 9, 19. Jonathan dis disunity
1869, 12, 18. Sarah Parker (form Rabberman)
    dis mcd
1870, 6, 18. Mary T. Morris (form Rabberman)
    dis mcd
1870, 9, 22. Mary Morris (form Rabberman)
    dis mcd (M)
1871, 4, 15. Lewis W. con mcd
1872, 4, 20. John dis disunity
1872, 10, 19. Sarah Parker (form Rabberman)

RABBERMAN, continued
    dis mcd
1873, 11, 15. Lydia dis disunity
1876, 5, 20. Henry D. dis mcd
1898, 9, 17. Sarah L. (form Peebles) con mcd
1899, 4, 15. Amos con mcd

RANDOLPH
1861, 9, 21. Susanna (form Morris) dis mcd

REED
1839, 11, 16. Mary [Read] rocf Flushing MM,
    dtd 1839,8,23
1841, 12, 18. Mary [Redd] gct Stillwater MM,O.
1843, 3, 18. Joseph, minor, rocf Darlington
    MM, Eng., dtd 1842,12,13
1904, 12, 17. Alice (form Davis) dis mcd

REEVE
----, --, --. Joshua & Elizabeth
    Ch: Latitia   b 1837, 6, 4 d 1842, 1,18
        Esther   " 1840, 4, 22 " 1842, 1,24
        bur Plymouth

RHODES
1843, 6, 21. Rebecca m James TRIBBY
1896, 6, 20. Elizabeth T. d ae 80 bur Ches-
    terfield
1898, 9, 29. Harmon d ae 96 bur Winona, O.
1916, 5, 10. Isaac d bur Bartlett, O.

1848, 6, 17. Martha Hodgin (form Rhodes) dis
    mcd
1865, 11, 18. Harmon rocf Plymouth MM, dtd
    1865,10,23
1866, 2, 17. Elizabeth rocf New Garden MM,
    dtd 1866,10,26

RICHARDSON
1843, 7, 25. Martha V. b

1911, 12, 16. Martha V. gct Stillwater MM, O.

ROBERTS
----, --, --. Aaron, s Aaron & Elizabeth, Mor-
    gan Co., O.; m Matilda -----
    Ch: Mary   b 1841, 6, 12 d 1865, 5, 4
        bur Iowa
        Hannah   " 1843, 6, 13 " 1854,10, 3
        Elizabeth " 1845, 9, 1
        Sarah   " 1848, 1, 9 " 1854, 4,27
        bur Iowa
        William   " 1853, 10, 1
    Aaron m 2nd 1856,10,30, in Chesterfield,
    Lydia ROMANS, dt Richard & Mary FAWCETT
    Ch: Matilda   b 1857, 12, 27 d 1865, 4,21
        bur Iowa
        Rachel T. " 1859, 5, 14
        Esther Anne   " 1865, 7, 5
        bur Iowa
1853, 10, 23. Matilda d ae 34 bur Chesterfield
1853, 10, 27. William d

1839, 11, 16. Matilda rocf Short Creek MM, O.,
    dtd 1839,7,23
1839, 11, 16. Aaron rocf Flushing MM, dtd
    1839,10,24
1865, 10, 21. Aaron & w, Lydia, & dt, Rachel
    J., gct Hickory Grove MM, Ia.
1865, 10, 21. Elizabeth gct Hickory Grove MM,
    Ia.

RODGERS
1895, 10, 19. Cora E. (form Jones) dis mcd

RODMAN
1840, 8, 15. Edith T. (form Cadwalader) dis
    mcd

ROMAN
1838, 9, 20. Ephraim, s Isaac & Mary, Athens
    Co., O.; m in Chesterfield, Ann JOHN
    Ch: Rachel   b 1839, 11, 21
        Isaac   " 1841, 4, 13
        Mary Jane " 1843, 5, 30
        Jesse   " 1845, 5, 23
        Amos   " 1849, 10, 5
1844, 12, 25. Amos, s Isaac & Mary, Athens
    Co., O.; m in Plymouth, Lydia FAWCETT, dt
    Richard & Mary
    Ch: Mary W.   b 1846, 3, 13
1847, 5, 14. Amos d
1849, 5, 26. Jesse d bur Plymouth
1856, 10, 30. Lydia m Aaron ROBERTS

1850, 8, 17. Hampton con mcd
1865, 10, 21. Mary W. gct Hickory Grove MM, Ia.

ROSS
1843, 5, 5. Margaret d ae 36 bur Chester-
    field

1840, 7, 18. Margaret rocf Somerset MM, O.,
    dtd 1840,4,27

SCHOFIELD
1804, 10, 20. Rachel G. b
----, --, --. John b 1828,12,28; m Belinda
    ----- b 1834,3,20
    Ch: Andrew   b 1863, 1, 22
        Lydia Jane " 1864, 9, 20
1863, 1, 23. Andrew, s John & Belinda (Hob-
    son), b
----, --, --. Stephen m Anna M. ----- d 1897,
    7,25 ae 26 bur Chesterfield
    Ch: Blanche
        Edith   b 1893, 9, 5
        Clarence I." 1896, 3, 1
1894, 9, 2. Issachar d ae 20 bur Chester-
    field
----, --, --. Andrew T. m Ruanna -----, dt
    Robert & Elizabeth (Thomas) Peebles, b
    1869,10,13
    Ch: John Robert
                 b 1901, 11, 19
        William S. " 1903, 12, 2

SCHOFIELD, continued
1924, 12, 19. Belinda H. d
1927, 2, 12. Stephen H. d bur Chester Hill

1853, 3, 19. Rachel & s, Issachar, rocf Ver-
    million MM, dtd 1852,11,6
1858, 7, 17. John rocf Flushing MM, O., dtd
    1858,7,22
1839, 2, 19. Issachar dis mcd
1862, 3, 15. John gct Plymouth MM, to m Be-
    linda S. Hobson
1862, 7, 19. Belinda H. rocf Plymouth MM,
    dtd 1862,6,23
1865, 4, 15. John dis disunity
1865, 8, 19. Rachel dis disunity
1865, 8, 19. Belinda H. dis disunity
1879, 8, 16. Belinda H. rst
1879, 9, 20. Rachel Ann, Stephen H., Edith
    M. & Isaachar, ch Belinda, recrq
1889, 11, 16. Lydia Jane Fawcett (form Scho-
    field) con mcd
1894, 7, 21. Stephen con mcd
1894, 7, 21. Anne (form Fawcett) con mcd
1896, 12, 19. Rachel Worthington (form Scho-
    field) con mcd
1897, 7, 17. Edith Patterson (form Schofield)
    con mcd
1902, 3, 15. Ruanna (form Peebles) con mcd
1903, 5, 16. Andrew con mcd

SCOTT
1897, 10, 16. Marietta (form Fawcett) dis mcd

SEARS
1837, 10, 3. Jane H. b
1859, 8, 10. Margaret d

1880, 1, 17. Jane H. rocf Stillwater MM, O.,
    dtd 1879,12,24
1893, 5, 20. Jane H. gct Coal Creek MM, Ia.

SELBY
1843, 6, 17. Rachel (form Perkins) dis mcd
1850, 5, 18. Emily (form Garretson) dis mcd

SHADLE
1863,, 8, 15. Mary G. (form Patterson) dis mcd

SHARP
1846, 4, 17. Mark, s Isaac & Lydia, b

1841, 11, 20. Isaac & w, Lydia, & ch, Ann,
    Oliver, Eliza, Adaline, Hannah, Emaline,
    Deborah & Dorothy, rocf Springfield MM,
    O., dtd 1841,10,22
1848, 1, 15. Ann dis
1848, 8, 19. Eliza dis
1849, 7, 21. Isaac dis disunity
1863, 6, 20. Isaac rst at Plymouth MM, on
    consent of this mtg

SHAW
1888, 9, 13. Martha D., w Walter, dt Jason &

Mary E. Fawcett, b

SHOTWELL
1842, 5, 21. Mary Ruth & Titus, ch Isaac &
    Hope, rocf Somerset MM, O., dtd 1842,4,25
1843, 7, 15. Mary Vickers (form Shotwell)
    dis mcd
1845, 6, 21. Ruth Vickers (form Shotwell) dis
    mcd

SIMPSON
1842, 9, 17. Austin & w, Sabilla, & ch, John
    & Richard, rocf Pennsville MM, O., dtd
    1842,9,15
1854, 6, 17. Austin E. & w, Sabilla, & ch,
    John, Richard, Rebecca, Jeptha E., Oliver,
    Mary & Wm. F., gct Red Cedar MM, Ia.

SMITH
----, --, --. Henry & Mary
    Ch: Helina   b 1834, 1, 28
        David   " 1836, 11, 6
        Maria   " 1839, 2, 10
        Lydia   " 1842, 4, 5
        Joseph   " 1845, 6, 6
----, --, --. Thomas & Elizabeth
    Ch: William H. b 1835, 6, 18
        Sarah   " 1837, 9, 13
        Stephen   " 1839, 8, 5
        Samuel   " 1841, 11, 4
        Eli   " 1843, 11, 3
        Asenath E. " 1845, 10, 9 d 1895,10,12
        bur Chesterfield
        Mary   b 1847, 10, 15
        Harriet   " 1850, 3, 3
        Amy   " 1852, 3, 21
        Lucinda   " 1853, 12, 16
----, --, --. Joseph & Mary
    Ch: Thomas P. F.
            b 1836, 9, 15 d 1837, 9,16
        Milton   " 1838, 11, 13 " 1861, 2,12
        Richard   " 1840, 1, 6
        David   " 1843, 2, 21
        Osborn   " 1845, 10, 9
        William A. " 1850, 2, 22 " 1851, 7,30
        Ruth F.   " 1851, 12, 31
        Lydia Jane " 1858, 4, 5
----, --, --. Hannah, w David B., dt Thos. &
    Ruth (Worrall) Bundy, b 1837,--,-- d 1918,
    4,22 bur Bartlett
----, --, --. Sarah Todd b 1837,9,13 d 1921,1,
    28 (dt Thos. K. & Eliza (Starbuck)
----, --, --. William & Ann
    Ch: Rebecca   b 1840, 8, 22
        Amanda Jane" 1842, 11, 19
        Wm. Silvan-
        us   " 1848, 8, 1 d 1918,11, 5
        bur Chester Hill
1840, 11, 23. Phebe, dt Wm. & Rebecca, b
1841, 7, 7. Wm. Jr. d ae 5 bur Chesterfield
1842, 3, 22. Wm. Sr. d ae 42
1842, 3, 4. Hannah d bur Chesterfield
1844, 4, 12. David d ae 68 bur Chesterfield

SMITH, continued

1845, 10, 23. Mary T. m Edward BYE
1848, 8, 7. Judith d ae 72 bur Chesterfield
1849, 5, 20. William d ae 47 bur Chesterfield
----, --, --. Amy Elizabeth, w Osborne, dt
        Abel & Lydia Jane (Bransen) Bye, b 1849,
        6,23
1849, 9, 20. Rebecca m Wm. PEARSON
1849, 11, 22. Rachel P. m Elias BUNDY
----, --, --. David & Mary
        Ch: William   b 1854, 6, 5
            Eliza   " 1856, 4, 21 d 1858, 8,13
1858, 10, 6. Mary F. d ae 26 bur Chesterfield
1860, 3, 22. Elihu, s William & Ann, Morgan
        Co., O.; m in Chesterfield, Hannah PICKETT
        dt Thomas & Mary, Morgan Co., O.
        Ch: William
              Thomas   b 1861, 4, 21
            Mary Elihu " 1862, 9, 9
1861, 9, 17. Lydia d ae 25
1862, 9, 15. Elihu d ae 29 bur Chesterfield
1863, 12, 3. Amanda J. m Samuel G. FAWCETT
1863, 12, 4. Mary d ae 64 bur Chesterfield
----, --, --. Stephen & Elizabeth
        Ch: Aaron
              Thomas   b 1875, 8, 13
            Wilfred B. " 1877, 11, 4
            Lindley M. " 1881, 9, 27
1890, 12, 12. Thomas K. d ae 77 bur Chester-
        field
1892, 3, 15. Ann d ae 83 bur Chesterfield
1901, 2, 11. Eliza d ae 84 bur Chesterfield
----, --, --. Aaron Thomas m Rachel DEWEES
        Ch: Marjorie
              Anna   b 1905, 5, 16
            Irving
              James   " 1907, 2, 27
            Ada Alber-
              ta   " 1909, 12, 2
            Oscar
              Stephen   " 1914, 4, 25
1908, 4, 26. David d ae 80 bur Chesterfield
1916, 8, 19. Hannah P. d
1918, 4, 22. Hannah d bur Southland
1922, 7, 27. Mary E. d bur Chesterfield
1926, 2, 28. Elizabeth Roberts, w Stephen,
        d ae 80
1931, 3, 17. Amy Elizabeth, w Osborn, d ae 81
        bur Chester Hill

1837, 11, 18. Henry & w, Maria, & ch, Wm. &
        Henry Zimmerman, & John Frederick & Helene
        Smith, rocf Minden MM, Germany, dtd 1837,
        7,27, endorsed by Pennsville MM, O., 1837,
        11,16
1840, 6, 20. William & w, Rebecca, & ch, Thom-
        as, Sibilla, Elisha, Mary Ann, Asenath,
        Elwood, Hannah, Wm. & Stephen, rocf Still-
        water MM, O., dtd 1840,5,23
1841, 12, 18. David & w, Judith, rocf Still-
        water MM, O., dtd 1841,11,27
1842, 4, 16. Evan & w, Mary, rocf Pennsville
        MM, O., dtd 1842,3,17

1842, 7, 16. Rebecca & ch, Thomas, Sibbilla,
        Elisha, Mary Ann, Asenath, Elwood, Hannah,
        Stephen & Phebe, gct Stillwater MM, O.
1845, 1, 18. Evan & w, Mary, & ch, Margaret
        Ann & Maria, gct Pennsville MM, O.
1846, 9, 19. Samuel & w, Hannah, rocf Penns-
        ville MM, O., dtd 1846,9,17
1848, 5, 20. Thomas & w, Nancy, & ch, Thomas,
        rocf Pennsville MM, O., dtd 1848,5,12
1848, 5, 20. Samuel & w, Hannah, & dt, Mary,
        gct Pennsville MM, O.
1848, 8, 19. Rachel P. rocf Pennsville MM,
        O., dtd 1848,7,13
1848, 10, 21. Rebecca & ch, Hannah, Stephen &
        Phebe, rocf Stillwater MM, O., dtd 1848,
        9,23
1850, 1, 19. Thomas rocf Stillwater MM, O.,
        dtd 1849,12,22
1851, 6, 21. Samuel & w, Hannah, & ch, Mary
        J. & Sarah Eliza, rocf Pennsville MM, O.,
        dtd 1851,5,15
1851, 7, 19. Henry dis disunity
1851, 7, 19. Wm. Pearson & w, Rebecca H., &
        ch, Jesse, Wm., Amos & Smith Pearson, &
        Ellwood, Hannah, Stephen & Phebe Smith,
        gct Spring Creek MM, Ia.
1852, 8, 21. David gct Pennsville MM, O., to
        m Mary Foulke
1853, 2, 19. Mary F. rocf Pennsville MM, O.,
        dtd 1853,1,13
1853, 6, 18. Samuel & w, Hannah, & ch, Mary
        J. & Sarah Eliza, gct Plymouth MM
1854, 2, 18. Nancy gct Plymouth MM
1854, 4, 15. Frederick gct Spring Creek MM,Ia
1855, 3, 17. Humphrey dis mcd
1855, 9, 15. Thomas gct Pennsville MM, O.
1861, 7, 20. Grace (form Hiatt) con mcd
1862, 9, 20. David dis mcd
1863, 8, 15. David rst
1863, 11, 21. David B. gct Plymouth MM, to m
        Hannah S. Bundy
1863, 12, 19. David & s, Wm. F., gct Plymouth
        MM
1864, 2, 20. Grace dis jas
1866, 6, 16. Lydia S. Crew (form Smith) con
        mcd
1866, 7, 21. Richard dis mcd
1866, 10, 20. Mary dis disunity
1866, 10, 20. Mary Ellen (form Worrall) dis
        mcd
1867, 1, 19. Henry dis disunity
1868, 4, 18. Rebecca L. Pierponnt (form
        Smith) con mcd
1868, 9, 19. Mary H. Bartlett (form Smith)
        dis mcd
1869, 3, 20. Samuel dis disunity
1869, 8, 21. David F. dis mcd
1870, 7, 16. Wm. S. con mcd
1870, 8, 20. David gct Plymouth MM
1871, 5, 20. Harriet Bundy (form Smith) dis
        mcd
1871, 8, 19. Joseph dis jG
1872, 5, 18. Osborn dis mcd

SMITH, continued
1873, 9, 20. Wm. H. dis mcd
1874, 6, 20. Stephen con mcd
1875, 11, 20. Eli dis mcd
1876, 12, 16. Amy Frost (form Smith) dis mcd
1877, 7, 21. Elizabeth R. rocf Hickory Grove
    MM, Ia., dtd 1877,7,7
1878, 4, 20. David & w, Lydia V., & s, Elmer
    McGrew, rocf Pennsville MM, O., dtd 1878,
    4,18
1878, 6, 15. Joseph Jr. dis mcd
1883, 9, 15. Lydia Jane dis jG
1890, 1, 18. Amy Elizabeth (form Bye) con
    mcd
1894, 7, 21. Wm. T. con mcd
1899, 8, 19. Mariam dis jas
1900, 10, 20. David B. dis disunity
1903, 1, 17. Wieford B. con mcd
1905, 2, 18. Aaron Thomas con mcd
1905, 7, 15. Rachel (form Dewees) con mcd
1910, 2, 19. John A. Hobson gct Springville
    MM, Ia., to m Mary R. Smith
1926, 6, 19. Aaron T. & w, Rachel R., & ch,
    Irving James, Ada Alberta, Oscar Stephen
    & Clinton Lindley, gct Short Creek MM, O.
1926, 6, 19. Marjorie Anna gct Short Creek
    MM, O.

STANLEY
----, --, --. Isaiah & Ann
    Ch: Milley Crew
                    b 1838, 7, 31
        Moses   " 1840, 7, 20
        Edwin   " 1844, 5, 2
        Susannah   " 1847, 7, 6
1845, 5, 21. Walter, s Solomon & Mary, Colum-
    biana Co., O.; m in Plymouth, Mary Ann
    THOMAS, dt Jesse & Rebecca, Washington
    Co., O.

1838, 1, 20. Martin dis jas
1838, 1, 20. Rachel King (form Stanley) dis
    mcd
1845, 3, 16. Isaiah & w, Nancy, & ch, Milley
    Crew, Moses & Edwin, rocf Upper Springfield
    MM, O., dtd 1845,2,22
1845, 7, 19. Mary Ann gct Upper Springfield
    MM, O.
1847, 5, 15. Milicent gct Cincinnati MM, O.
1849, 10, 20. Isaiah & w, Nancy, & ch, Milley
    Crew, Moses, Edwin & Susannah, gct Gilead
    MM

STANTON
----, --, --. Edmond & Sarah
    Ch: Ephraim   b 1841, 8, 2 d 1841, 8,14
        Rebecca   " 1842, 7, 5
1862, 8, 17. Laura, w E. E., dt John & Mar-
    tha (Embree) Edgerton, b
1923, 7, 8. Laura Edgerton d bur Nebraska

1840, 11, 21. Edmond & w, Sarah, rocf Still-
    water MM, O., dtd 1840,10,24

1845, 1, 18. Edmond & w, Sarah, & dt, Rebec-
    ca, gct Stillwater MM, O.
1890, 3, 15. Laura (form Edgerton) con mcd

STEEL
1844, 10, 19. Mary (form Carter) dis jas
1869, 10, 27. Lucinda (form Holloway) dis mcd
    (M)

STEER
1907, 9, 21. Clifford J. Fawcett gct Short
    Creek MM, O., to m Florence H. Steer

STEPHENS
1883, 11, 20. David [Stephen], s Zachariah &
    Elizabeth, Guernsey Co., O.; m in Ches-
    terfield, Sarah TODD, dt Robert & Eunice,
    Morgan Co., O.

1839, 11, 16. Elizabeth & ch, Francinah,
    Catharine, Silas & Sarah, rocf Short Creek
    MM, O., dtd 1839,6,18
1840, 9, 19. Samuel rocf Short Creek MM, O.,
    dtd 1840,8,18
1841, 1, 16. Elizabeth & ch, Catherine, Si-
    las & Sarah, gct Short Creek MM, O.
1844, 6, 15. Francina gct Flushing MM, O.
1844, 10, 19. Samuel gct Flushing MM, O.
1884, 2, 16. Sarah T. [Stevens] gct Flushing
    MM, O.

STRAHL
1869, 5, 4. Elmer [Strawl] d bur Plymouth

1848, 12, 16. Eleanor gct Salem MM, Ia.
1652, 6, 19. Elmer rocf Salem MM, Ia.

SWART
1851, 4, 19. Mary (form Patterson) dis mcd

SWAYNE
1874, 9, 17. Clarissa R. (form Dewees) dis
    mcd

TALBOTT
1801, 9, 29. Margaret b (M)
1804, 10, 26. Joseph F. b (M)
----, --, --. Joseph d 1890,1,12 ae 85 bur
    Chesterfield; m Margaret -----
    Ch: Jonathan   b 1839, 8, 4
        Lydia   " 1840, 9, 4 d 1845, 3, 2
        bur Chesterfield
        David   b 1842, 9, 15
1840, 6, 24. Wm. A., s Joseph & Mary, Morgan
    Co., O.; m in Plymouth, Sarah R. HAMMITT,
    dt Edward & Elizabeth

1840, 9, 19. Sarah M. [Talbert] gct Penns-
    ville MM, O.
1863, 5, 16. David dis disunity
1864, 5, 21. Jonathan dis disunity
1864, 8, 20. Joseph dis disunity
1865, 6, 17. Margaret dis disunity

TALBOTT, continued
1885, 11, 21. Joseph [Talbot] rst

THOMAS
1839, 11, 20. Deborah m Josiah WALTON
1840, 11, 25. Joseph, s Jesse & Rebecca, Washington Co., O.; m in Plymouth, Mary G. PARKER, dt Geo. & Rachel, Washington Co.,O.
1842, 2, 20. Jesse d ae 55 bur Plymouth
1842, 10, 2. John d ae 14
1844, 10, 23. Philena m Seth WILLIAMS
1845, 5, 21. Mary Ann m Walter STANLEY
1847, 4, 21. Eli, s Jesse & Rebecca, Washington Co., O.; m in Plymouth, Adeline McCONNELL, dt Edward M. & Lydia, Washington Co., O.
    Ch: Addison J. b 1848, 12, 3
1855, 10, 8. Sarah d ae 59 bur Chesterfield
1856, 9, 25. William, s Aaron & Sarah, Morgan Co., O.; m in Chesterfield, Martha WORRALL, dt Zebulon & Martha, Morgan Co., O.
    Ch: Isaac   b 1858, 1, 4
        Pearly   " 1862, 1, 4
        Hiram   " 1863, 12, 7
1859, 10, 20. Elizabeth H. m Robert PEEBLES
1910, 4, 23. Ellen d ae 75 bur Chester Hill

1839, 3, 16. Joseph rocf Pennsville MM, O., dtd 1839,2,14
1839, 7, 20. Jesse & w, Rebecca, & ch, Joanna, Eli & Jesse, rocf Pennsville MM, O., dtd 1839,5,16
1839, 7, 20. Sarah, Mary Ann, Deborah & Philena, rocf Pennsville MM, O., dtd 1839,5,16
1844, 12, 21. Jonathan dis mcd
1848, 4, 15. Jesse, minor, gct Salem MM, O.
1849, 4, 21. Eli & w, Adaline T., gct Pleasant Plain MM, Ia.
1854, 1, 21. Mary Worstell (form Thomas) dis mcd
1857, 1, 17. Susannah Worstel (form Thomas) dis mcd
1860, 7, 21. Aaron dis mcd
1863, 2, 21. Wm. dis disunity
1869, 8, 21. Martha dis jas
1878, 9, 21. Isaac dis mcd

THOMPSON
1860, 6, 12. Sarah Ann d

1839, 5, 18. Mary gct Flushing MM
1841, 4, 17. Samuel gct Flushing MM
1857, 6, 20. Sarah Ann [Thomson] rocf Plymouth MM, dtd 1857,5,18

THORP
1839, 4, 21. James & Jabes rocf Plainfield MM, dtd 1839,3,20
1839, 4, 21. Thomas, minor, rocf Plainfield MM, dtd 1839,3,20
1840, 11, 21. Jabez dis jH
1840, 11, 21. James dis jH

TODD
1838, 5, 30. Sibbilla d ae 62 bur Chesterfield
1842, 9, 22. Robert, s Stephen & Sibilla, Washington Co., O.; m in Chesterfield, Eunice HAMPTON, dt Thomas & Hannah, Morgan Co., O., d 1847,7,10 ae 28
    Ch: Sarah   b 1843, 7, 11
        Oliver " 1844, 9, 14
        Mary   " 1846, 7, 30
----, --, --. Elisha & Sally
    Ch: Mariah b 1843, 7, 17
        Tillman " 1846, --, --
1847, 3, 31. Stephen d ae 71
1849, 6, 21. Emily m Samuel BYE
1861, 7, 7. Robert d ae 64 bur Chesterfield
1870, 12, 1. Elihu, s Stephen & Sibbella, Morgan Co., O.; m in Chesterfield, Sarah PICKET, dt Thomas & Mary, Morgan Co., O.
    Ch: Thomas
        William b 1872, 9, 27 d 1872,10,18
        Lillian " 1874, 2, 4
1883, 11, 20. Sarah m David STEPHENS
1883, 11, 20. Mary E. m Samuel MORRIS
1883, 12, 30. William d ae 81 bur Chesterfield
1897, 2, 22. Mary H. d ae 84 bur Chesterfield
1903, 11, 21. Elihu d ae 86 bur Chesterfield
1917, 11, 7. Sarah d bur Chesterfield

1838, 6, 16. Stephen & w, Sibbilla, & s, Elihu, rocf Stillwater MM, O., dtd 1838,4,28
1838, 6, 16. Robert rocf Stillwater MM, O., dtd 1838,4,28
1839, 10, 19. Robert gct Stillwater MM, O.
1842, 2, 19. Robert rocf Stillwater MM, O., dtd 1842,1,22
1842, 4, 16. Elisha & w, Sallie, & ch, Emily, Shannon, Lydia, John, Lydia & Sabilla, rocf Stillwater MM, O., dtd 1842,3,26
1852, 9, 18. Lydia gct Three Rivers MM, Ia.
1852, 9, 18. Elisha & w, Sally, & ch, Shannon, John, Lindley, Sabilla, Maria & Tilman, gct Three Rivers MM, Ia.
1863, 9, 19. Robert & w, Mary, & ch, Oliver & Mary, gct Hickory Grove MM, Ia.
1869, 2, 20. Sarah gct Hickory Grove MM, Ia.
1872, 2, 17. Robert & w, Mary, rocf Hickory Grove MM, Ia., dtd 1872,1,6
1872, 2, 17. Sarah rocf Hickory Grove MM, Ia., dtd 1872,1,6
1872, 2, 17. Mary rocf Hickory Grove MM, Ia., dtd 1872,1,6
1880, 1, 17. Wm. rst on consent of Stillwater MM, O.

TRIBBY
1843, 6, 21. James, s John & Ann, Harrison Co., O.; m in Plymouth, Rebecca RHODES, dt Harmon & Elizabeth, Washington Co., O.

1846, 2, 21. Rebecca Plumley (form Tribby) dis mcd

TUCKER
1931, 6, 20. John S. Patterson gct Dartmouth
    MM, Mass., to m Sarah Tucker

TULLOSS
1847, 9, 18. Joshua Morris Jr. gct Carmel
    MM, to m Eliza Ann Tulloss

VAIL
1851, 4, 19. Jesse rocf Plainfield MM, dtd
    1850,12,25
1851, 7, 19. Cert for Jesse endorsed to
    Plymouth MM

VANHORN
1842, 8, 20. Elizabeth rocf Pennsville MM, O.

VANLAW
1799, 9, 30. Lydia b
----, --, --. Jephtha & Amy
    Ch: Sarah
        Louisa   b 1840, 3, 12
        Elizabeth
        L.   " 1842, 4, 11 d 1845,12,2
        bur Chesterfield
1842, 9, 23. Jephtha S. d ae 27 bur Chester-
    field
1843, 2, 23. Louisa M. m James DOUDNA
1844, 10, 24. Eliza m Smith BRANSON
1845, 10, 2. Amy S. m Owen MARIS

1848, 10, 24. David B. d
----, --, --. Thomas b 1819,1,5; m Amy -----
    b 1810,7,26 (M)
    Ch: Rebecca W. b 1850, 3, 22
        Lydia Jane " 1856, 10, 9
1850, 5, 23. John Jr., b 1826,2,27, s John &
    Sarah, Morgan Co., O.; m in Chesterfield,
    Hannah Ann LEEKE, dt Philip W. & Elizabeth,
    Morgan Co., O., b 1827,7,14
    Ch: Elizabeth L.
               b 1851, 4, 30
        Charles W. " 1864, 1, 3 d 1930,10,23
        bur Chesterfield
1853, 8, 25. Jesse, s John & Sarah, Morgan
    Co., O.; m in Chesterfield, Rachel F. PAT-
    TERSON, dt Arnold & Rachel, Morgan Co., O.
    Ch: George S. b 1854, 8, 6
1857, 5, 15. Amy B. d
1859, 9, 1. Thomas E., s Thomas & Ann, Mor-
    gan Co., O., d 1883,11,5 ae 64 bur Ches-
    terfield; m in Chesterfield, Anne HOBSON,
    dt John & Belinda
----, --, --. Joseph L. & Margaret H.
    Ch: Amy   b 1864, 11, 14
        Annie El-
        vyan   " 1869, 7, 11 d 1870,10,10
        bur Chesterfield
        Carlos T. b 1873, 6, 4
        Jesse M.   " 1882, 8, 8
1871, 9, 19. Rebecca W. m Wm. WRIGHT
1885, 4, 8. Martha D. ae 70 bur Chesterfield
1890, 5, 14. John d ae 64 bur Chesterfield

1903, 1, 17. Hannah Ann d ae 75 bur Chester-
    field

1838, 12, 15. Elisha rocf Plainfield MM, dtd
    1838,10,24
1839, 1, 19. Anna W. rocf Pennsville MM, O.,
    dtd 1839,1,17
1839, 6, 15. Jeptha & w, Amy, rocf Plainfield
    MM, dtd 1839,4,24
1839, 12, 21. Anna W. & s, Elisha, gct Penns-
    ville MM, O.
1841, 3, 20. Amy B. rocf Plainfield MM,
    dtd 1841,2,24
1841, 6, 19. Thomas E. rocf Flushing MM, O.,
    dtd 1841,3,25
1841, 10, 16. John & w, Lydia, & ch, Smith &
    Lydia Jane Branson, & Eliza, Jane, Samuel
    C., Jesse, Thomas & Ann S. Vanlaw, rocf
    Plainfield MM, dtd 1841,9,22
1841, 10, 16. Lucinda rocf Plainfield MM, dtd
    1841,9,22
1841, 10, 16. Louisa M. rocf Plainfield MM,
    dtd 1841,9,22
1845, 8, 16. Lucinda Williams (form Vanlaw)
    dis mcd
1847, 9, 18. Owen Maris gct Pennsville MM, O.
    to m Anna W. Vanlaw
1848, 3, 18. Anna W. Maris & s, Elisha Van-
    law, rocf Pennsville MM, O.. dtd 1848,3,16
1851, 2, 15. Samuel con mcd
1855, 10, 20. Samuel C. gct Plymouth MM
1856, 1, 19. Thomas dis mcd
1859, 3, 19. Ann Hodgin (form Vanlaw) dis mcd
1863, 8, 15. Joseph S. gct Middleton MM, O.,
    to m Margaret Hollingsworth
1864, 1, 16. Margaret H. rocf Middleton MM,
    dtd 1863,11,21
1864, 5, 21. John dis disunity
1864, 7, 16. Lydia dis disunity
1864, 7, 16. Ann H. dis disunity
1865, 3, 18. Thomas E. dis disunity
1865, 4, 15. Hannah Ann dis disunity
1866, 2, 17. John dis disunity
1870, 6, 18. Rachel dis jas
1870, 7, 16. Jesse dis jas & military service
1873, 9, 20. Joseph S. dis disunity
1877, 3, 17. John rst
1877, 4, 21. Hannahann rst
1879, 3, 15. Lydia Jane Hodgin (form Vanlaw)
    dis mcd
1879, 6, 21. Elizabeth L. Bowman (form Vanlaw)
    con mcd
1879, 7, 19. George S. dis jas
1880, 4, 17. Thomas E. rst
1880, 4, 17. Martha D. rst
1890, 3, 15. Margaret H. dis jas
1890, 3, 15. Amy Gray (form Vanlaw) dis mcd

VAUGHAN
1848, 5, 17. Martha M., w Joseph, dt Robert
    & Rachel (Barnes) Millhouse, b
1928, 10, 26. Martha Millhouse d ae 80 (an
    elder)

VAUGHN, continued
1909, 3, 20. Arthur L. dis mcd & jas

VENABLE
1852, 3, 20. Vincent con mcd
1852, 12, 18. Vincent gct Salem MM

VERNON
1830, 5, 22. Joseph b
----, --, --. Amos & Jane
    Ch: Robert   b 1833, 9, 24
        David   " 1835, 11, 14
        Mary   " 1837, 4, 1
        James   " 1839, 5, 10
        Mordecai " 1842, 10, 16
        William   " 1845, 8, 30
----, --, --. William & Peninah
    Ch: Asa   b 1840, 12, 6
        Enoch   " 1844, 5, 19
1842, 9, 21. Zilpha b
----, --, --. Eli & Eliza
    Ch: Jesse   b 1843, 3, 26
        Manoah   " 1847, 5, 4
        William T. " 1849, 11, 28
1843, 12, 15. Sarah, dt Jesse & Patience, b
1845, 9, 3. Elisha b
1848, 9, 15. Dempsey B. b
1848, 4, 20. Tamar m Richard EDGERTON
1848, 11, 23. Joseph, s William & Peninah,
    Athens Co., O.; m in Chesterfield, Sarah
    EDGERTON, dt John & Zilpah, Morgan Co., O.
    Ch: John   b 1849, 10, 12
        William H. " 1852, 2, 6
        Osborn   " 1854, 7, 23 d 1855,12,16
        bur Chesterfield
        Elwood   b 1856, 8, 5
1849, 11, 28. William d bur Chesterfield
1850, 8, 22. James, s James & Tamer, Morgan
    Co., O.; m in Chesterfield, Lydia M. BUNDY
    dt Thomas & Milicent, Morgan Co., O.
    Ch: Charles D. b 1851, 7, 14
        James L.   " 1853, 9, 21
1850, 8, 22. Hannah F. b
1853, 2, 23. Rhoda Ann b
1853, 9, 26. Lydia d bur Linn Co., Iowa
1857, 6, 12. Sarah d ae 24 bur Chesterfield
1863, 9, 16. Asa d
1863, 10, 9. Peninah d
1865, 8, 31. John, s James & Rhoda, Morgan
    Co., O.; m in Chesterfield, Elizabeth
    EDGERTON, dt James & Mary, Morgan Co., O.
    Ch: Evaline   b 1866, 8, 2
        Addison   " 1868, 12, 5
        James E.   " 1870, 10, 4

1837, 11, 18. Abijah Edgerton gct Stillwater
    MM, O., to m Rhoda Vernon
1838, 4, 21. Wm. & w, Pennina, & ch, Elijah,
    Elisha, Joseph, Tamar & Elizabeth, rocf
    Somerset MM, O., dtd 1838,3,26
1839, 12, 21. Jesse rocf Alum Creek MM, O.,
    dtd 1839,9,23
1840, 4, 18. James rocf Alum Creek MM, O.,

dtd 1840,3,26
1842, 9, 17. Jesse gct Alum Creek MM, O., to
    m Patience Gidley
1842, 10, 15. Eli & w, Elizabeth, & ch, Tamer,
    Rachel & Deborah, rocf Stillwater MM, O.,
    dtd 1842,8,27
1843, 4, 15. Patience rocf Alum Creek MM, O.,
    dtd 1842,12,22
1845, 11, 15. Jesse & w, Patience, & dt, Sa-
    rah, gct Alum Creek MM, O.
1847, 2, 20. Elisha gct Pennsville MM, O.,
    to m Mary Vernon
1847, 7, 17. Mary rocf Pennsville MM, O.,
    ddtd 1847,7,15
1848, 11, 18. Elijah con mcd
1850, 3, 16. Elisha & w, Mary, & s, Dempsey,
    gct Pennsville MM, O.
1852, 5, 15. Elijah dis jas
1857, 7, 10. Elizabeth Louden (form Vernon)
    con mcd
1859, 1, 15. Mary (form Edgerton) dis mcd
1859, 6, 18. Joseph dis mcd
1860, 3, 17. James dis mcd
1864, 4, 16. Chas. D. & James L., ch James,
    gct Hickory Grove MM, Ia.
1867, 10, 24. Joseph dis disunity (M)
1868, 2, 20. Sarah L. (form Crew) dis mcd
1869, 9, 18. Sarah (form Crew) dis mcd
1870, 3, 19. James rst
1870, 5, 21. John rocf Pennsville MM, O., dtd
    1870,4,14
1870, 12, 17. James gct Springville MM, Ia.
1872, 10, 19. John & w, Elizabeth, & ch, Eva-
    line, Addison & James E., gct Plymouth MM
1879, 10, 18. Elizabeth E. & ch, Evaline,
    Addison & James E. rocf Plymouth MM, dtd
    1879,9,22
1885, 7, 18. John E. dis mcd
1889, 5, 18. Wm. H. dis mcd
1900, 2, 17. Evaline Worthington (form Ver-
    non) dis mcd
1902, 1, 18. Addison dis mcd
1902, 1, 18. James E. dis mcd & jas
1905, 7, 15. Elizabeth Hempy (form Vernon)
    dis mcd

VICKERS
1842, 12, 17. Chalkley, Rebecca L., Jesse
    Elijah & Barclay, ch Thos. & Hannah, rocf
    Short Creek MM, O., dtd 1842,9,20
1843, 7, 15. Mary (form Shotwell) dis mcd
1844, 3, 16. Rebecca Fairchild (form Vickers)
    dis mcd
1845, 5, 17. Chalkley dis mcd
1845, 6, 21. Ruth (form Shotwell) dis mcd

WALKER
----, --, --. Isaac & Lydia
    Ch: William   b 1841, 4, 5
        Miriam   " 1843, 1, 25
        Israel   " 1844, 4, 15
        Eliza Ann " 1845, 12, 29
        Martha B. " 1847, 11, 10

WALKER, Isaac & Lydia, continued
        Ch: Sarah   b 1849, 10, 2
----, --, --. Thompson & Ruthanna
        Ch: Amanda   b 1842, 9, 5
            George   " 1845, 5, 18

1842, 12, 17. Thompson & w, Ruthanna, & dt,
    Amanda, rocf Short Creek MM, O., dtd
    1842,10,18
1843, 7, 15. Daniel & w, Jane, rocf Middle-
    ton MM, dtd 1843,5,11
1843, 7, 15. Tacy rocf Flushing MM, dtd
    1843,5,25
1845, 4, 19. Tacy Willis (form Walker) dis
    mcd
1846, 6, 20. Mary T. dis jas
1847, 2, 20. Isaac & w, Lydia, & ch, Wm.,
    Mariam J., Israel & Eliza Ann, rocf Flush-
    ing MM, O., dtd 1846,12,24
1865, 5, 20. Isaac & w, Lydia N., & ch, Mar-
    tha B. & Sarah, gct Hickory Grove MM, Ia.
1865, 5, 20. Wm. & Israel N. gct Hickory
    Grove MM, Ia.
1865, 5, 20. Miriam & Eliza Ann gct Hickory
    Grove MM, Ia.

WALTON
1839, 11, 20. Josiah, s Jonathan & Maria, Co-
    lumbiana Co., O.; m in Plymouth, Debora
    THOMAS, dt Jesse & Rebecca, Washington
    Co., O.
        Ch: Jesse   b 1849, 4, 11 d 1849, 8, 7
            bur Plymouth

1840, 6, 20. Deborah T. gct Upper Springfield
    MM, O.
1848, 7, 15. Josiah & w, Deborah, & ch, Re-
    becca Ann & Mary Jane, rocf Upper Spring-
    field MM, O., dtd 1848,6,24
1851, 11, 15. Jason Hampton gct Upper Spring-
    field MM, O., to m Maryann Walton

WARD
1891, 1, 17. Thomas & w, Abigail P., rocf
    Coal Creek MM, Ia., dtd 1891,1,10
1895, 4, 20. Thomas & w, Abigail P., gct Pasa-
    dena MM, Calif.

WATSON
1839, 7, 20. John & w, Mary Ann, & dt, Re-
    becca, rocf Smithfield MM
1842, 5, 21. Mary Ann & ch, Rebecca & Joseph,
    gct Springfield MM, O.
1850, 12, 21. John gct Springfield MM, O.

WAY
----, --, --. Benjamin & Abigail
        Ch: Ann   b 1836, 4, 30
            Samuel   " 1838, 6, 28
            Margaret " 1840, 3, 25 d 1842, 6,16
            bur Chesterfield
----, --, --. Robert & Lydia
        Ch: Margaret J.b 1839, 6, 26

        Ch: Milton   b 1842, 1, 13
            John B.   " 1845, 9, 13
1839, 4, 25. Sarah m Cary HAMPTON
1843, 11, 22. Millicent m Manoah HANSON
1849, 3, 21. John, s Benjamin & Jane, Washing-
    ton Co., O.; m in Plymouth, Hannah WOOD,
    dt Joseph & Mary, Washington Co., O.

1838, 1, 20. Elizabeth rocf Somerset MM, dtd
    1837,11,27
1841, 10, 16. Elizabeth Plumley (form Way) dis
    mcd
1850, 7, 20. David dis mcd

WEBSTER
1869, 8, 21. Ruth (form Worrall) dis mcd

WHITE
1846, 5, 16. Elma (form Griffith) dis mcd

WILEMAN
1841, 2, 20. Mary rocf Stillwater MM, O., dtd
    1841,1,23
1842, 3, 19. Mary gct Pennsville MM, O.

WILLIAMS
1844, 10, 23. Seth, s Job M. & Elizabeth,
    Washington Co., O.; m in Plymouth, Philena
    THOMAS, dt Jesse & Rebecca, Washington Co.
    O.
        Ch: Addison   b 1845, 7, 8
            Jesse
            Davis   " 1847, 7, 3
1850, 4, 14. Isaac, s Isaiah & Anna, b
1861, 5, 30. Rebecca m Ira PATTERSON
1871, 8, 22. Daniel, s Joseph & Mary, Belmont
    Co., O.; m in Chesterfield, Lydia Ann FAW-
    CETT, dt Stephen & Rachel ARNOLD
1879, 7, 31. Wm. C. d ae 69 bur Chesterfield

1837, 11, 18. Isaiah, & minor s, Elias, gct
    Stillwater MM, O.
1841, 4, 17. Rebecca & ch, Mariam, Levi,
    Phebe Deborah Jephthah Willet Eliza Penin-
    ah Preston & Isaac, rocf Stillwater MM,O.,
    dtd 1841,3,27
1841, 6, 19. Seth rocf Somerset MM, O., dtd
    1841,4,26
1843, 1, 21. Hannah Loomis (form Williams)
    con mcd
1844, 8, 17. Rebecca (form Patterson) dis mcd
1855, 8, 16. Lucinda (form Vanlaw) dis mcd
1846, 7, 18. Isaiah & w, Anna P., & ch, Elias,
    John P. & Nathan, rocf Stillwater MM, O.,
    dtd 1846,3,28
1846, 7, 18. Rebecca & ch, Deborah, Jephthat,
    Willet, Ezra, Peninah, Preston & Isaac,
    gct Stillwater MM, O.
1846, 7, 18. Phebe gct Stillwater MM, O.
1846, 8, 15. Wm. & w, Lydia, & ch, Daniel M.,
    Lindley, Elwood & Elizabeth, gct Penns-
    ville MM, O.
1846, 10, 17. Levi dis mcd

WILLIAMS, continued
1847, 6, 19. Mariam Parry (form Williams) dis
    mcd
1849, 4, 21. Seth dis disunity
1851, 2, 15. Rebecca rst
1858, 10, 16. Lewis W. Bye gct Flushing MM, O.
    to m Phebe H. Williams
1861, 4, 20. Rebecca rocf Frankfort MM, dtd
    1861,1,10
1863, 2, 21. Rebecca dis jG
1871, 11, 18. Lydia Ann & dt, Jephthann Faw-
    cett, gct Flushing MM, O.
1875, 3, 20. Wm. C. rocf Flushing MM, O., dtd
    1875,2,25
1875, 3, 20. Lydia M. rocf Flushing MM, O.,
    dtd 1875,2,25
1880, 1, 19. Lydia M. Parker (form Williams)
    con mcd

WILLIS
1845, 4, 19. Tacy (form Walker) dis mcd

WILMAN
1798, 10, 26. Mary b

WILLSON
1842, 3, 7. Harmon T., s Wm. & Sarah, b
1847, 5, 19. Dewit C., s William & Sarah,
    Washington Co., O.; m in Plymouth, Sarah
    B. ENGLE, dt John & Deborah, Washington
    Co., O.

1840, 10, 17. Joseph Isaac Hannah Nathan &
    Ann Elizabeth, ch Isaac & Elizabeth, rocf
    Stillwater MM, O., dtd 1840,9,26
1841, 2, 20. Wm. rocf Providence MM, Pa., dtd
    1840,12,31
1841, 4, 17. Joseph dis jas
1841, 7, 17. Sarah recrq
1842, 1, 15. Dewit C., Arthur H., Wm. F.,
    Abram P., George L., Robert A. & Jacob P.,
    ch Wm. & Sarah, recrq
1850, 8, 17. Wm. Finley dis disunity
1850, 10, 19. Wm. Finley rst

WOOD
----, --, --. Joseph & Mary
    Ch: Elisha   b 1820, 12, 8
        Rachel   " 1824, 5, 5
        Hannah   " 1826, 9, 1
        Robert   " 1827, 3, 12
        Mary   " 1829, 12, 1
        Joseph   " 1831, 3, 18
        Edna   " 1833, 1, 12
        Enoch   " 1834, 4, 2
        Nathan   " 1837, 1, 13
----, --, --. Caleb & Lydia
    Ch: Rebecca C. b 1836, 2, 29 d 1840, 1,21
        bur Chesterfield
        Lydia   b 1838, 3, 4 " 1840, 1,13
        bur Chesterfield
        Susan   b 1840, 8, 10
        George R. " 1842, 9, 8

Ch: Amanda Jane b 1847, 8, 22
1846, 7, 3. Robert, s Elisha & Martha, b
1849, 3, 21. Hannah m John WAY
1871, 3, 23. Amanda J. m Jesse HUESTIS

1840, 5, 16. Elisha recrq
1841, 12, 18. Mary rst on consent of Flushing
    MM
1843, 8, 19. Elizabeth rocf Pennsville MM,
    O., dtd 1843,7,17
1843, 11, 18. Elisha M. gct Somerset MM, O.,
    to m Martha Bailey
1844, 2, 17. Hannah recrq
1844, 4, 20. Martha rocf Somerset MM, O.,
    dtd 1844,1,29
1844, 7, 20. John P. & w, Susanna, & dt,
    Elizabeth P., rocf Pennsville MM, O., dtd
    1844,7,18
1844, 9, 21. Wm. rocf Flushing MM, O., dtd
    1844,7,25, endorsed to Pennsville MM
1846, 11, 21. Mary Chandler (form Wood) dis
    mcd
1847, 8, 21. Elisha & w, Martha, & ch, Asaph
    & Robert, gct Pennsville MM, O.
1848, 6, 17. Elizabeth gct Pennsville MM, O.
1848, 12, 16. Elizabeth P. gct Alum Creek MM,
    O.
1848, 12, 16. John P. & w, Susannah, gct Alum
    Creek MM, O.
1850, 2, 15. John Milton dis disunity
1655, 7, 21. Osborn Penrose gct Pennsville
    MM, O., to m Susan A. Wood
1856, 2, 16. Mary Ann Peebles (form Wood)
    dis mcd
1859, 3, 19. Susan Patterson (form Wood) dis
    mcd
1859, 6, 18. Wm. dis disunity
1863, 1, 17. Caleb dis jG
1863, 2, 21. Lydia dis jG
1866, 12, 15. George B. dis mcd
1870, 3, 19. Alfred dis mcd
1874, 3, 21. Louisa M. (form Fawcett) dis mcd

WOOLMAN
1847, 12, 16. George d bur Chesterfield

1839, 12, 21. George rocf Frankford MM, dtd
    1839,10,29

WOOTEN
1840, 3, 21. Rebecca rocf Somerset MM, O.,
    dtd 1840,2,24
1842, 2, 19. Rebecca gct Pennsville MM, O.

WORRALL
----, --, --. Benjamin m Prissilla ----- d
    1878,1,6 ae 74 bur Chesterfield
    Ch: Jonathan J.b 1834, 2, 21
        John   " 1836, 8, 7
        Mary   " 1839, 10, 7 d 1841,11,29
        bur Chesterfield
        Lucetta   b 1842, 4, 21
        Ruth   " 1844, 9, 29
        Joseph G.   " 1851, 3, 5

WORRALL, Benjamin & Prissilla, continued
    Ch: Rebecca   b 1847, 5, 30
       Aaron   " 1847, 5, 30
1837, 11, 23. Mordecai, s Jonathan & Eleanor,
    Washington Co., O.; m in Chesterfield,
    Ruth BOSWELL, dt Wm. & Rachel, Athens Co.,
    O.
    Ch: Rebecca B. b 1838, 10, 14
       Rachel   " 1840, 10, 18
       Mary E.   " 1842, 8, 23
       William   " 1851, 3, 2
       Elizabeth " 1855, 2, 23
1839, 9, 26. Elizabeth m Isaac KIRBY
1839, 10, 24. Isaac, s Jonathan & Eleanor,
    Washington Co., O.; m in Chesterfield,
    Rachel BECK, dt Jesse & Elizabeth, Athens
    Co., O.
    Ch: Jesse   b 1840, 11, 11 d 1859, 8,18
       William P. " 1844, 7, 2
       Eliza   " 1846, 8, 23
       Clarkson " 1857, 7, 6
       Sarah Ellen" 1862, 7, 8
----, --, --. Zebulon & Martha
    Ch: Alfred   b 1840, 10, 26
       Rachel
        Emily   " 1843, 4, 30
       Edward   " 1846, 1, 23
1841, 7, 22. Margaret m Wm. HODGIN
1842, 10, 20. John, s Zebulon & Martha, Athens
    Co., O.; m in Chesterfield, Deborah PLUM-
    MER, dt John & Rachel, Athens Co., O.
    Ch: Rebecca   b 1843, 7, 11
       Margaret " 1844, 12, 24
       Isaac   " 1847, 1, 10
1844, 5, 31. Mary d ae 17 bur Chesterfield
1846, 1, 14. Eleanor d ae 70 bur Chesterhill
1849, 7, 26. Rebecca m Zadok BUNDY
1853, 8, 25. Elwood R., s Zebulon & Martha,
    Morgan Co., O.; m in Chesterfield, Ruth
    Ann PLUMMER, dt Abram & Elizabeth, Morgan
    Co., O.
    Ch: Elizabeth
       P.   b 1854, 8, 17
1854, 6, 24. Jonathan d ae 83
1856, 9, 25. Martha m Wm. THOMAS
1861, 9, 26. Elizabeth m Wm. DEWEES
1863, 1, 24. Sarah d
1866, 7, 6. Zebulon d
1870, 1, 11. Benjamin d ae 7 bur Chesterfield
1872, 5, 6. Ruth F. Smith d ae 20 bur Ches-
    terfield
1887, 9, 18. Martha d ae 84 bur Chesterfield
1898, 10, 14. Peninah d ae 51 bur Chesterfield
1907, 2, 10. Ann d ae 82 bur Chesterfield
1932, 9, 17. Rebecca d ae 85 bur Chester Hill

1839, 7, 20. Eleanor Moore (form Worrall) con
    mcd
1846, 8, 15. Sarah Barnes (form Worrell) dis
    mcd
1847, 7, 17. Jonathan rocf Pennsville MM, O.,
    dtd 1847,7,15
1848, 2, 19. John dis disunity

1848, 11, 18. Deborah dis disunity
1849, 6, 16. Zebulon Jr. dis disunity
1851, 7, 19. Elizabeth Maris (form Worrall)
    dis mcd
1851, 9, 20. Sarah G. rocf Springfield MM,
    O., dtd 1851,8,18
1852, 2, 21. Susannah Moore (form Worrall)
    dis mcd
1853, 8, 20. Ruth (form Patterson) dis mcd
1856, 12, 20. Mordecai dis disunity
1858, 5, 15. John dis mcd
1861, 2, 16. Rachel Emily Phipps (form Wor-
    rall) con mcd
1861, 5, 18. Jonathan G. con mcd
1861, 10, 19. Elwood dis military service
1863, 2, 21. Ruth dis jG
1863, 5, 16. Ruthann dis jG
1864, 3, 19. Rebecca Wright (form Worrall)
    dis mcd
1865, 3, 18. Alfred dis disunity
1865, 4, 15. Isaac & w, Rachel E., & ch, Wm.
    P., Eliza, Joseph, Clarkson & Sarah Ellen,
    gct Hickory Grove MM, Ia.
1866, 10, 20. Mary Ellen Smith (form Worrall)
    dis mcd
1867, 6, 15. Margaret Bailey (form Worrall)
    dis mcd
1869, 6, 19. Lucetta Dunn (form Worrall) dis
    mcd
1869, 7, 17. Lydia (form Doudna) dis mcd
1869, 8, 21. Ruth Webster (form Worrall) dis
    mcd
1870, 3, 24. Lydia (form Doudna) dis mcd (M)
1871, 11, 18. Edward P. con mcd
1872, 3, 16. Wm. dis mcd
1874, 1, 17. Elizabeth P. dis disunity
1875, 4, 17. Edward P. dis mcd
1890, 9, 20. Peninah (form Michiner) con mcd
1892, 7, 16. Rebecca (form Worthington) dis
    mcd

WORSTELL
1913, 5, 19. Susan d ae 87 bur Chester Hill

1854, 1, 21. Mary (form Thomas) dis mcd
1857, 1, 17. Susannah [Worstel] (form Thom-
    as) dis mcd
1877, 12, 15. Lucinda (form Smith) dis mcd
1879, 9, 20. Susan rst

WORTHINGTON
----, --, --. Jesse m Rachel PICKETT
    Ch: Sarah   b 1851, 10, 20
       Louisa M. " 1852, 10, 9
       Elizabeth " 1854, 9, 23 d 1895, 1, 4
       bur Chesterfield
       Ann   b 1856, 8, 5 " 1861,10, 9
       Thomas
        Jefferson " 1858, 4, 8 " 1861,10, 9
       Rebecca P. " 1860, 1, 24
       Edwin T.   " 1861, 9, 29
       Amanda A. " 1863, 10, 22
       Eliza J.   " 1865, 9, 12

WORTHINGTON, Jesse & Rachel, continued
  Ch: Elma   b 1867, **8, 26**
    Frederick " 1869, 11, 3
    Walter " 1871, 6, 10 d 1900, 8, 6
    bur Chesterfield
1862, 6, 26. Mary m Caleb ENGLE
----, --, --. Edwin T. d 1912,3,15 ae 50 bur
  Chesterfield; m Rachel -----
  Ch: Grace B. b 1895, 11, 14
    Jesse J. " 1898, 8, 27
    Walter Guy " 1900, 11, 22 •
1892, 8, 25. Rachel d ae 62 bur Chesterfield
1912, 11, 20. Rachel Schofield d ae 46 bur
  Chester Hill
1922, 5, 3. Mary d ae 72 bur Chester Hill

1846, 3, 21. Isaac Brown gct Pennsville MM,
  O., to m Elizabeth Worthington
1846, 4, 18. Joseph Penrose gct Pennsville
  MM, O., to m Mildred Worthington
1846, 6, 20. Elizabeth Brown & dt, Eliza Ann
  Worthington, rocf Pennsville MM, O.
1850, 6, 15. Jesse & w, Rachel, & ch, Wm. &
  Mary, rocf Pennsville MM, O., dtd 1850,5,
  16
1852, 11, 20. Mary rocf Pennsville MM, O., dtd
  1852,9,16
1864, 10, 16. Jesse dis disunity
1872, 9, 21. Eliza A. gct Plymouth MM
1875, 6, 19. Sarah W. Fawcitt (form Worthington) dis mcd
1883, 9, 15. Wm. E. con mcd
1885, 3, 21. Lydia S. rocf Pennsville MM, O.,
  dtd 1885,2,19
1889, 1, 19. Wm. H. & w, Lydia S., gct Coal
  Creek MM, Ia.
1892, 7, 16. Rebecca Worrall (form Worthington) dis mcd
1894, 2, 17. Elma Edgerton (form Worthington)
  con mcd
1896, 12, 19. Edwin con mcd
1896, 12, 19. Rachel (form Schofield) con mcd
1900, 2, 17. Evaline (form Vernon) dis mcd
1902, 8, 16. Frederick con mcd
1902, 12, 20. Eliza J. Gardner (form Worthington) con mcd

  * * * * * * *

JOHN
1838, 9, 20. Ann m Ephraim ROMAN

MARIS
1845, 10, 2. Owen, s David & Sarah, Morgan .
  Co., O.; m in Chesterfield, Amy S. VANLAW,
  dt Joseph & Sarah SPENCER, d 1845,10,30

MORRIS
----, --, --. Aaron, s Samuel & Sally, Morgan

WRIGHT
----, --, --. John D. d 1884,11,13 ae 66 bur
  Chesterfield; m Hannah A. ----- d 1884,10,
  11 ae 71 bur Chesterfield
  Ch: Isaac A. b 1841, 3, 27
    Mary Jen-
    kinson " 1843, 11, 8
    William " 1847, 1, 17
    Nehemiah " 1849, 12, 25 d 1889, 4,2
    bur Chesterfield
    Ann   b 1851, 12, 6 " 1853,5,10
    bur St. Clairville
    Sherwood b 1854, 1, 24 " 1861,10,
    23 bur Chesterfield
1871, 9, 19. Wm., s John D. & Hannah, Morgan
  Co., O.; m in Chesterfield, Rebecca W.
  VANLAW, dt Thomas E. & Amy B.
  Ch: Mary Thomas b 1875, 7, 31
1878, 11, 19. Nehemiah, s John D. & Hannah A.,
  Morgan Co., O.; m in Chesterfield, Elenor
  BRANSON, dt Smith & Eliza, Morgan Co., O.
  Ch: Allison b 1881, 3, 28
    Mary L. " 1885, 12, 16

1845, 6, 21. John D. & w, Hannah, & ch,
  Isaac A. & Mary Jenkinson, rocf Plainfield
  MM, dtd 1845,5,21
1864, 3, 19. Rebecca (form Worrall) dis mcd
1865, 1, 21. Mary Jenkinson Morrey (form
  Wright) dis mcd
1868, 11, 21. Isaac A. dis mcd
1906, 3, 17. Rebecca W. dis jas

ZIMMERMAN
1837, 11, 18. Henry Smith & w, Maria, & ch,
  Wm. & Henry Zimmerman, & John Frederick &
  Helene Smith, rocf Minden MM, Germany,
  dtd 1837,7,2 endorsed by Pennsville MM,O.,
  1837,11,16
1841, 8, 21. Wm. gct Carmel MM
1845, 7, 19. Henry gct Salem MM, Ia.

ZUMBRO
1896, 7, 18. Martha (form Edgerton) dis mcd

  * * * * * * *

  Co., O.; m Phebe -----
  Ch: Joel   b 1836, 3, 18
    David " 1837, 6, 17
    Mary " 1839, 10, 28

WILLIAMS
1838, 12, 15. Rachel & Jane, ch David, gct
  Stillwater MM, O.

PLYMOUTH MONTHLY MEETING

    Plymouth Monthly Meeting, located in Washington County, Ohio, was established by Still-
water Quarterly Meeting, 11th Mo. 18, 1850. It consisted of Plymouth and Southland Preparative Meetings. For four years it was an Orthodox Meeting, but in 1854 it became a Wilbur
Meeting.

    Among the well-known families belonging to this meeting were Crew, Cope, Emmons, Hob-
son, Dean, Heald, McGirr, Rhoades, Wilson, Parker, Marshall, Engle, Morris, Willis, Bundy,
Gilbert, Pennrose, Garretson, Roman, Morland, Mott and Hampton.

RECORDS

ADAMS
----, --, --. John & Patience
    Ch: Sarah   b 1851, 9, 16
         Nathan   " 1854, --, --

1854, 9, 18. John dis disunity
1854, 11, 20. Rachel gct Somerset MM, O.

ARNOLD
1882, 1, 6. Rachel d ae 92

1872, 4, 22. Rachel rocf Salem MM, O., dtd
    1872,3,20

BAILEY
----, --, --. Joel d 1890,4,5 ae 68; m Lydia
    -----, dt James & Sarah McGIRR, d 1893,7,
    21 ae 70
    Ch: James   b 1845, 11, 13
         Henry
         Sarah   " 1851, 5, 9
         Tamar   " 1853, 8, 10 d 1863, 4, 1
         Jane F.   " 1859, 2, 18
         Marshall   " 1863, 3, 3
1857, 4, 26. Edward d
1857, 5, 9. Borden d
1863, 2, 16. Talbott d
1879, 1, 14. Harriett d
1882, 2, 21. Samuel d ae 82

1856, 2, 18. Samuel & w, Harriet, & ch, Bor-
    den, Edward, Levina, Talbott, Lydia & Sa-
    rah, rocf Chesterfield MM, dtd 1856,2,16
1856, 12, 22. James McGirr gct Somerset MM,
    O., to m Rachel Bailey
1858, 3, 22. Hannah rocf Chesterfield MM, dtd
    1858,3,20
1864, 1, 18. Lavina Driggs (form Bailey) dis
    mcd
1866, 7, 23. Ann rocf Somerset MM, O., dtd
    1866,3,26
1866, 7, 23. Margaret Burgess (form Bailey)
    dis mcd
1869, 4, 19. James dis mcd
1871, 9, 18. Sarah Johnson (form Bailey) dis
    mcd
1878, 8, 19. Ann Bell (form Bailey) dis mcd
1880, 11, 22. Henry dis mcd
1881, 3, 21. Jane F. McDaniels (form Bailey)
    dis mcd
1882, 5, 22. Jane F. McDonnald (form Bailey)
    dis mcd
1860, 2, 20. Hannah Wildman (form Bailey) dis
    mcd
1871, 9, 18. Lydia White (form Bailey) dis
    mcd
1873, 3, 17. Sarah Maria Noland (form Bailey)
    dis mcd
1876, 10, 23. Mary Ann Noland (form Bailey) dis
    mcd
1887, 12, 19. Marshall dis jas

BALL
1857, 12, 31. Amos P., s David & Julian, Mor-
    gan Co., O.; m in Southland MH, Cynthiann
    GILBERT, dt Joel & Elizabeth, Washington
    Co., O.

1857, 2, 23. George W. Mott gct Pennsville
    MM, O., to m Abigail Ball

BEAVER
1860, 3, 19. Rachel (form Garretson) dis mcd

BELL
1878, 8, 19. Ann (form Bailey) dis mcd

BENNETT
1876, 10, 23. Louisa (form Morris) dis mcd

BINNS
1874, 3, 26. Joseph P., s David & Rebecca,
    Jefferson Co., O.; m in Plymouth MH, Be-
    linda HOBSON, dt Thomas & Unity, Washing-
    ton Co., O.

1874, 8, 17. Belinda H. gct Short Creek MM,
    O.

BLACKBURN
1874, 9, 22. Charles, s Wm. & Ann, Columbi-
    ana Co., O.; m in Plymouth MH, Sarah
    HOLLINGSWORTH, dt Edwin & Betsy, Washing-
    ton Co., O.

1874, 12, 21. Sarah C. gct Middleton MM

BOSWELL
1853, 12, 19. Mary rocf Chesterfield MM, dtd
    1853,11,19
1860, 3, 19. Mary gct Chesterfield MM

BOUGHMAN
1878, 10, 21. Ury Etta (form Marshall) dis
    mcd

BOWMAN
----, --, --. James d 1880,7,14 ae 61; m
    Elizabeth ----- d 1860,5,14 ae 45
    Ch: Thomas I. b 1852, 4, 29
         Phebe   " 1843, 6, 20 d 1843, 7,16
         Isaac   " 1844, 8, 22 " 1863, 2,15
         Henry   " 1847, 5, 11
         Emmor   " 1849, 7, 18
1858, 2, 24. Achsah L., dt Thomas & E., d
1887, 3, 22. Thomas d ae 74

1855, 7, 23. Thomas & w, Elizabeth, & dt,
    Achsah L., rocf Upper Springfield MM, O.,
    dtd 1855,6,22
1862, 1, 20. Thomas gct Newgarden MM, O., to
    m Ann Test
1862, 6, 23. Ann rocf Newgarden MM, O., dtd
    1862,5,22
1868, 9, 21. Henry dis jas & military ser-

BOWMAN, continued
    vice
1874, 11, 23. Thomas I. con mcd
1876, 6, 19. Thos. I. dis jG
1876, 11, 20. Emmor dis
1884, 6, 23. Elizabeth gct Chesterfield MM
1888, 4, 23. Ann gct New Garden MM
1889, 7, 22. Emmor rst at Chesterfield MM

BRANSON
1873, 6, 23. John A. Hobson gct Flushing MM,
    O., to m Martha H. Branson

BRIGGS
1851, 8, 18. Esther rocf East Grove MM, Ia.,
    dtd 1851,6,19

BRILL
1889, 7, 22. · Esther (form Steadman) dis jas
    & mcd

BROWN
1870, 1, 3. Isaac, s Daniel & Mary Ann, d
    ae 92

1856, 2, 18. Isaac rocf Short Creek MM, O.,
    dtd 1856,1,22

BRUCE
1862, 4, 21. Martha Jane (form Heald) dis mcd

BUNDY
----, --, --. Benjamin d 1853,3,21 ae 41; m
    Rachel ----- d 1861,5,17 ae 38
      Ch: Esther   b 1850, 1, 21
          Lindley   " 1850, 1, 21
          Benjamin " 1853, 6, 30
1854, 10, 1. Thomas d ae 77
1863, 12, 3. Hannah S. m David R. SMITH
1884, 8, 17. Thomas d ae 69 (an elder)
1886, 3, 31. Ruth W. d ae 72

1853, 9, 19. Exum & w, Sally, & ch, Samuel,
    Sarah W., Peninah & David, gct Red Cedar
    MM, Ia.
1853, 9, 19. Josiah gct Red Cedar MM, Ia.
1853, 9, 19. Elizabeth gct Red Cedar MM, Ia.
1854,. 3, 20. Thomas rocf Chesterfield MM,
    dtd 1854,3,18
1854, 10, 23. Joseph gct Red Cedar MM, Ia.
1855, 1, 22. Elias & w, Rachel, & ch, Eze-
    kiel, Stephen T. & Isaac C., rocf Ches-
    terfield MM, dtd 1855,1,20
1856, 2, 18. Asher Mott gct Stillwater MM,
    O., to m Sarah Bundy
1856, 9, 22. Gershom Mott gct Stillwater MM,
    O., to m Ruthanna Bundy
1862, 9, 23. Ezekiel dis mcd
1862, 12, 22. Elias & Rachel dis jG
1867, 1, 21. Emlen dis mcd
1867, 4, 22. Stephen dis mcd & military ser-
    vice
1869, 2, 22. Isaac rpd mcd & military service

1890, 5, 19. Lucinda (form Davis) dis mcd

BURGESS
1858, 12, 25. Willis I., s Clarkson & Susan,b
1877, 10, 24. Nathan, s Elwood & Gaynor, Mor-
    gan Co., O.; m in Southland MH, Elizabeth
    PENROSE, dt Joseph & Mildred, Washington
    Co., O.
      Ch: Grace   b 1881, 3, 18
          Albert
          Louis   " 1882, 10, 18
          Ethel
          Julia   " 1884, 9, 22
          Adda Irma " 1886, 5, 12
          Lloyd Pen-
          rose   " 1893, 12, 11
1883, 3, 17. Elwood d ae 67
1884, 2, 19. Mary Alice m Lindley SHAW
1884, 12, 24. Julia A. m Richard HAWORTH
1889, 11, 28. Amos, s Ellwood & Gaynor,
    Athens Co., O.; m in Southland MH, Rachel
    A. MORRIS, dt Martin & Elizabeth, Washing-
    ton Co., O.
      Ch: Elizabeth
          J.   b 1890, 12, 10
          Anna Mable " 1892, 1, 31
          Emerson
          Elwood   " 1894, 11, 4

1855, 2, 17. Clarkson & w, Susan, & ch, Joel,
    & Chas., rocf Pennsville MM, dtd 1855,1,
    18
1862, 1, 20. Willis J., minor, gct Penns-
    ville MM
1862, 4, 21. Clarkson dis jG
1866, 7, 23. Margaret (form Bailey) dis mcd
1868, 8, 17. Clarkson & Margaret rst at
    Chesterfield MM
1876, 5, 22. Joel dis mcd
1878, 4, 22. Elizabeth P. gct Pennsville MM
1880, 5, 17. Nathan & w, Elizabeth P., &
    dt, Mary Emma, rocf Pennsville MM, dtd
    1880,4,16
1881, 2, 21. Elwood & w, Gaynor, & ch,
    Julia Ann & Sarah Abbie, rocf Pennsville
    MM, dtd 1881,1,13
1884, 1, 21. Mary Alice rocf Pennsville MM,
    dtd 1884,1,17
1885, 4, 20. Julia A. Haworth (form Burgess)
    gct Springriver MM, Kans.
1885, 4, 20. Mary Alice Shaw (form Burgess)
    gct Springville MM, Ia.
1887, 4, 18. Amos rocf Pennsville MM, dtd
    1887,4,14

BURNETT
1865, 11, 20. Eliza (form Garretson) dis mcd
    & jG

CLARK
1870, 4, 18. Matilda (form Pennock) dis mcd

CLEMSON
1891, 1, 31. Tryphena B. d ae 69

1872, 4, 22. James L. [Clempson] & w, Try-
    phena B., & ch, Alice & Rosco, rocf Upper
    Springfield MM
1877, 11, 19. Rosco dis mcd
1891, 6, 22. James L. & Alice [Clempson] gct
    Springfield MM

CLENDENON
1885, 7, 20. Smith H. Mott gct Coal Creek MM,
    Ia., to m Matilda Jane Clendenon

CONROW
1874, 4, 20. Mary rst at Flushing MM, O., on
    consent of this mtg

COOK
1887, 9, 19. Eliza Jane (form Penrose) con
    mcd

COOPER
1853, 4, 18. Thomas Hirst gct Sandy Spring
    MM, to m Mary Ann Cooper

COPE
1880, 11, 25. John d ae 75

COPPOCK
1855, 10, 22. Catharine [Coppoc] rocf Newgar-
    den MM, dtd 1855,9,20
1857, 9, 21. Elias Crew gct Newgarden MM, to
    m Ruthanna Coppock
1866, 6, 18. Catharine gct New Garden MM

CRAFT
1854, 5, 26. Ann d ae 54
----, --, --. Jesse & Mary
    Ch: Zilpha   b 1860, 1, 1
        Wm. Elisha " 1861, 12, 1

1857, 11, 23. Jesse gct Pennsville MM, O., to
    m Mary Vernon
1858, 5, 17. Samuel gct Pennsville MM, O., to
    m Sarah Dewees
1858, 8, 23. Mary & ch, Hannah & Rhoda Ann
    Vernon, rocf Pennsville MM, O., dtd 1858,
    6,17
1858, 10, 18. Sarah rocf Pennsville MM, O.,
    dtd 1858,9,16
1872, 2, 19. Mary Thompson (form Craft) dis
    mcd & jG
1877, 12, 17. Samuel & w, Sarah, gct Penns-
    ville MM, O.

CREW
----, --, --. William d 1867,7,7 ae 61; m Mary
    ----- d 1866,8,16 ae 56
    Ch: Charles   b 1849, 5, 13
        Phebe   " 1852, 5, 4 d 1853, 3,24
        Mary   " 1856, 4, 1 " 1870, 8,12
----, --, --. Elias & Ruthanna

Ch: William
    Allison   b 1858, 9, 15 d 1880,12, 5
Jonathan
    Clarance   " 1859, 8, 5
1857, 12, 2. Rachel m Albert EMMONS
1873, 12, 8. Sarah Jane, dt Martin & Eliza-
    beth MORRIS, d ae 24

1857, 9, 21. Elias gct Newgarden MM, to m
    Ruthanna Coppock
1858, 6, 21. Ruthanna rocf Newgarden MM, dtd
    1858,5,20
1866, 10, 22. Elias dis disunity
1867, 12, 23. Ezra dis disunity
1870, 4, 18. Jesse dis mcd
1872, 5, 20. Rebecca J. Lupton (form Crew)
    con mcd
1874, 4, 20. Charles dis mcd
1884, 4, 21. Jonathan Clarence dis mcd
1890, 5, 19. Ruthanna gct West Branch MM, Ia.

CROTHERS
1885, 7, 20. Rachel B. (form Morris) dis mcd

COULSON
1881, 11, 25. Margaret d ae 75

1871, 11, 20. Margaret rocf Sandy Spring MM,
    dtd 1871,10,28

DAVIS
----, --, --. Jehu d 1887,9,8 ae 60; m Ruth

    Ch: Eva Irene b 1882, 11, 28
        Alice   " 1885, 2, 28
        Clarence   " 1887, 7, 1
1891, 8, 27. Tacy Ann m Thomas Alden HOBSON

1883, 1, 23. Jehu H. & w, Ruth P., & ch,
    Charles E., Tacy Ann, Wm. C., Mary E.,
    Daniel N., Phebe E., Arthur T. & Eva L.,
    rocf Chesterfield MM, dtd 1883,1,20
1883, 3, 19. Lucinda M. rocf Chesterfield
    MM, dtd 1883,2,17
1890, 3, 17. Charles E. dis mcd
1890, 5, 19. Lucinda Bundy (form Davis) dis
    mcd

DEAMS
1881, 11, 21. Sarah Elizabeth (form Roman) dis
    mcd

DEAN
1866, 10, 24. John S., s Barten & Elizabeth,
    Columbiana Co., O.; m Mary Ann HOBSON, dt
    Stephen & Lydia, Washington,Co., O.
1874, 10, 1. Francis, s Jonathan & Elizabeth,
    Columbiana Co., O.; m in Plymouth MH,
    Penina HOLLINGSWORTH, dt Edwin & Betsy,
    Washington Co., O.
    Ch: Almeda B. b 1875, 10, 19
        Caroline   " 1879, 6, 11
        Ida J.   " 1883, 11, 26

DEAN, continued
1851, 10, 19. Hannah d ae 73
1881, 1, 27. . Hannah C. m Orlando R. FOWLER
1882, 8, 31. Sarah A. m Benj. J. HOBSON

1867, 7, 22. Mary Ann gct Sandy Spring MM
1874, 12, 21. Penina H. gct Newgarden MM
1875, 12, 20. Francis & w, Penina, rocf New-
     garden MM, dtd 1875,11,25
1877, 7, 23. Francis & w, Penina, & dt, Al-
     meda, gct Coal Creek MM, Ia.
1880, 4, 19. Jonathan & w, Elizabeth, & ch,
     Hannah C., Lydia, Edward & Martha, rocf
     Newgarden MM, dtd 1880,3,25
1880, 12, 20. Elwood & w, Elizabeth, gct Ches-
     terfield MM
1881, 3, 21. Ephraim rocf Newgarden MM, dtd
     1881,2,24
1881, 4, 18. Joshua S. & w, Mary Ann, & dt,
     Evaretta Lydia, rocf Newgarden MM, dtd
     1881,3,24
1882, 2, 20. Francis & w, Penina, & dt, Al-
     meda B. & Caroline, rocf Hickory Grove MM,
     Ia., dtd 1882,2,4
1882, 6, 19. Sarah Ann rocf Newgarden MM,
     dtd 1882,5,25
1884, 4, 21. Joshua S. & w, Mary Ann, & dt,
     Evaretta, gct Springville MM, Ia.
1885, 10, 19. Lydia gct Hickory Grove MM, Ia.
1889, 7, 22. Edward gct Newgarden MM
1890, 8, 18. Francis & w, Penina H., & ch,
     Almeda B., Caroline & Ida J., gct Hickory
     Grove MM, Ia.
1890, 12, 22. Jonathan & w, Elizabeth, gct
     Newgarden MM
1890, 12, 22. Ephraim gct Newgarden MM
1892, 1, 18. Martha gct Newgarden MM

DEWEES
1858, 5, 17. Samuel Craft gct Pennsville MM,
     O., to m Sarah Dewees

DONALDSON
1875, 2, 22. Alice (form Morris) dis mcd

DRIGGS
1864, 1, 18. Lavina (form Bailey) dis mcd

ELLIOT
1868, 10, 19. Milicent (form Hanson) dis mcd

ELLIS
1853, 6, 6. Rachel Ann (form Parker) dis mcd
1853, 9, 19. Rachel Ann (form Parks) dis mcd
1867, 6, 17. Rebecca Jane (form Hobson) dis
     mcd
1867, 7, 22. Rebecca Jane (form Hobson) dis
     mcd
1869, 2, 22. Ury (form Hollingsworth) dis
     mcd
1889, 9, 23. Ury & Elizabeth J. rocf Coal
     Creek MM, Ia., dtd 1889,8,10
1890, 9, 22. Harvey G., minor s Ury, recrq

1893, 5, 22. Elizabeth J. gct Springville MM,
     Ia.
1897, 6, 21. Ury Ellen & s, Harvey J., gct
     Springville MM, Ia.

EMBREE
1859, 3, 21. Ann (form Hirst) dis mcd
1872, 2, 19. Ann H. rst at Springville MM,
     Ia. with consent of this mtg

EMMONS
----, --, --. Micajah & Delitha
     Ch: Hervey D. b 1851, 11, 17
         Elizabeth
                D. " 1853, 3, 27
         Mary C.   " 1854, 11, 8
         Caroline
         Susan   " 1856, 3, 5
         Lindley   " 1857, 9, 23
         Edwin   " 1859, 1, 28
----, --, --.. Thomas & Mary
     Ch: John T.   b 1852, 10, 27
         Elwood D. " 1842, 1, 23 d 1862, 8, 7
1857, 12, 2. Albert, s Thos. & Mary, Washing-
     ton Co., O.; m in Plymouth MH, Rachel
     CREW, dt Wm. & Mary, Washington Co., O.
     Ch: Mary Ellen b 1859, 2, 8
         Orlin D.   " 1860, 5, 12
         Elwood D.   " 1862, 6, 5

1852, 12, 20. Micajah & w, Delitha, & s, Har-
     vey, gct Pennsville MM
1853, 11, 21. Micajah & w, Delitha, & ch,
     Harvey D., & Elizabeth, rocf Pennsville
     MM, dtd 1853,9,15
1860, 8, 21. Micajah & w, Delitha, & ch,
     Harvey Davis, Elizabeth D., Mary C.,
     Caroline S., Lindley & Edwin C., gct
     Chesterhill MM
1864, 10, 17. Thomas & w, Mary, & ch, John
     Thomas, gct Coal Creek MM, Ia.
1864, 10, 17. Albert & w, Rachel, & ch, Mary
     Ellen, Orlando & Elwood D., gct Coal
     Creek MM, Ia.
1864, 10, 17. Elmira gct Coal Creek MM, Ia.
1880, 7, 19. Gershom Mott gct Coal Creek MM,
     Ia., to m Elmira Emmons

ENGLE
----, --, --. Caleb d 1887,2,23 ae 79; m Sa-
     rah -----, dt Richard & Mary FANCETT,
     d 1860,12,10 ae 47
     Ch: Caleb W. b 1851, 7, 1
         Elwood   " 1855, 5, 1 d 1855, 9, 6
         Sarah
         Sabilla   " 1855,12,12
1854, 7, 26. John, s Caleb & Sarah, Washing-
     ton Co., O.; m in Plymouth MH, Louisa
     HEALD, dt Levi & Lydia, Washington Co.,O.
     Ch: Levi H. b 1855, 6, 9
         William   " 1858, 11, 10 d 1860, 8,10
1863, 7, 1. Sarah Elizabeth, dt Caleb &
     Mary, b

ENGLE, continued
1879, 2, 16. Mary S. d ae 60

1853, 6, 20. Ephraim W., minor, gct Still-
    water MM, O.
1855, 3, 19. Richard dis mcd
1862, 4, 21. Caleb gct Chesterfield MM, to m
    Mary T. Worthington
1863, 4, 20. Mary rocf Chesterfield MM, dtd
    1863,4,18
1863, 6, 22. John & dt, Philena W., gct
    Hickory Grove MM, Ia.
1863, 12, 21. Rachel gct Hickory Grove MM, Ia.
1865, 1, 23. Rebecca Penn (form Engle) dis
    mcd
1865, 2, 20. John & w, Louisa, & s, Levi H.,
    gct Hickory Grove MM, Ia.
1866, 8, 20. Deborah Jane dis jas
1867, 6, 17. Rachel Ann Worrell (form Engle)
    dis mcd & jG
1871, 7, 17. Caleb T. con mcd
1871, 8, 21. Samuel dis mcd
1871, 11, 20. Caleb T. gct Springville MM, Ia.
1880, 5, 17. Caleb gct Coal Creek MM, Ia.
1880, 10, 18. Hannah rocf Coal Creek MM, Ia.,
    dtd 1880,8,14
1883, 1, 22. Sarah E. Shaner (form Engle) con
    mcd
1886, 2, 22. Hannah dis disunity

FOWLER
1858, 4, 28. Lindley M., s Caleb & Sarah,
    Washington Co., O.; m in Plymouth MH, Be-
    linda H. HOBSON, dt John & Rebecca, Wash-
    ington Co., O.
    Ch: Addison I. b 1860, 1, 18
        Emilada   " 1861, 3, 21
        Mary Anna
            P.   " 1864, 1, 9
----, --, --. Edmund S. & Mary M.
    Ch: Orlando R. b 1859, 11, 20
        Eva Irene " 1860, 11, 23
        Mary Sarah " 1868, 8, 26
1861, 7, 21. Caleb d ae 69
1861, 11, 27. Chalkley T., s Caleb & Sarah,
    Washington Co., O.; m in Plymouth MH,
    Phebe HOBSON, dt John & Rebecca P., Wash-
    ington Co., O.
    Ch: Anne B.   b 1862, 9, 11 d 1864, 8,21
        Ella M.   " 1865, 7, 20
        Charles E." 1867, 2, 10
1877, 12, 26. Mary S. m John W. MORRIS
1881, 1, 9. Sarah d ae 76
1881, 1, 27. Orlando R., s Edmond & Mary M.,
    Washington Co., O., b 1859,11,20; m in
    Southland MH, Hannah C. DEAN, dt Jonathan
    & Elizabeth B., Washington Co., O.
    Ch: Edgar L.   b 1881, 11, 4
        Emmerson J." 1883, 5, 30
        Alfred Ir-
            ving   " 1883, 5, 21
1884, 2, 19. Eva Irene m Joshua W. SMITH

1859, 2, 21. Edmund S. con mcd
1864, 5, 23. Milton D. con mcd
1868, 9, 21. Lindley M. dis disunity
1868, 11, 23. Chalkley T. dis disunity
1869, 5, 17. Susanna J. recrq
1869, 5, 17. Susanna J. recrq
1877, 7, 23. Elizabeth Hobson (form Fowler)
    con mcd
1880, 2, 23. Phebe dis jas
1882, 10, 23. Esther rocf Chesterfield MM,
    dtd 1882,10,21
1884, 12, 22. Addison J. dis mcd
1887, 1, 17. Mary Ann Whalen (form Fowler)
    dis mcd
1887, 12, 19. Ella M. dis jas
1889, 7, 22. Emmolada Langtree (form Fowler)
    dis mcd
1889, 8, 19. Orlando R. & w, Hannah C., & ch,
    Edgar L., Emerson & Alfred, gct Newgarden
    MM
1892, 11, 18. John S. & w, Esther, gct Bir-
    mingham MM
1893, 9, 18. Charles E. dis mcd
1897, 4, 19. Milton D. & w, Susan J., gct
    Hickory Grove MM, Ia.

GILBERT
----, --, --. Joel, s Abel & Rebecca, Washing-
    ton Co., O.; m Elizabeth ----- d 1853,7,
    17 ae 37
    Ch: William   b 1848, 3, 8 d 1850, 4,19
        Daniel W. " 1849, 11, 20
        Charles E. " 1851, 10, 30
        Eli   " 1853, 6, 20 " 1853, 7, 8
    Joel m 2nd 1854,12,28 in Southland MH,
    Mary MOTT, dt Wm. & Sarah, Athens Co., O.,
    d 1859,10,19
    Ch: Elizabeth
            S.   b 1856, 6, 24
        Addison S. " 1857, 10, 1
        Rachel
            Eleanor " 1859, 10, 1 d 1861,11, 8
1857, 12, 31. Cynthiann m Amos P. BALL
1861, 8, 17. Ida Armela, dt Abel & Armela, b
1861, 9, 24. Mary P. m Barclay PENROSE
1861, 12, 22. Armelia, dt Taylor & Ann FARMER,
    d ae 21

1861, 8, 19. Abel rocf Pennsville MM, dtd
    1861,8,15
1861, 8, 19. Armela C. rocf Pennsville MM,
    dtd 1861,6,24
1862, 2, 17. Joel dis mcd
1864, 3, 21. Rebecca Melton (form Gilbert)
    con mcd
1867, 6, 17. Abel dis mcd & military service
1868, 7, 20. Sarah Hollingsworth (form Gil-
    bert) con mcd
1871, 4, 17. Daniel W. & Chas. E. gct Penns-
    ville MM
1873, 7, 21. Edith S. gct Pennsville MM
1873, 7, 21. Elizabeth S. gct Pennsville MM
1887, 4, 18. Joel rst at Pennsville MM

GILBERT, continued
1890, 10, 20. Addison rpd mcd

GOODING
1874, 9, 21. Richard rocf Pennsville MM, O.,
                dtd 1874,9,17
1892, 1, 18. Richard gct Pennsville MM

GRIFFITH
1873, 2, 17. Edwin rocf Pennsville MM, dtd
                1872,12,19
1882, 10, 23. Edwin gct Pennsville MM

GARRETSON
1852, 7, 13. Emily S., dt Joel & Elizabeth, b
1853, 3, 3. Mary d ae 8

1851, 12, 22. William dis mcd
1853, 1, 17. David dis disunity
1853, 10, 17. Ruthanna Way (form Garretson)
                dis mcd
1858, 5, 17. John dis mcd
1859, 10, 19. Joel & w, Elizabeth, & ch, Han-
                nah & Emily Sophia, gct Stillwater MM, O.
1860, 3, 19. Rachel Beaver (form Garretson)
                dis mcd
1860, 4, 23. Richard dis mcd
1862, 2, 17. Eli dis mcd
1865, 11, 20. Eliza Burnett (form Garretson)
                dis mcd & jG

HAMPTON
1854, 2, 15. Cary P. d
1854, 3, 10. David N. d
1859, 6, 30. Sarah d ae 45

1866, 4, 23. Thomas dis jas & military service
1866, 5, 21. Elvira & Hannah Ann gct Spring-
                ville MM, Ia.

HANSON
----, --, --. Joseph & Rachel
        Ch: John C.   b 1845, 4, 23
            Ann E.   " 1846, 8, 14
            Lydia   " 1848, 7, 13
1851, --, --. Lydia d
1880, 3, 24. Mary E. m James HIATT

1852, 5, 17. Joseph dis disunity
1853, 1, 17. Cert rec for Robert & w, Pru-
                dence, & s, Thomas Osborn, from Somerset
                MM, O., dtd 1852,11,29, end to Chester-
                field MM, O.
1855, 7, 23. Rachel & ch, John Clarkson, Ann
                Eliza, Wm. Lindley, Henry, Martha & Mary,
                gct Stillwater MM, O.
1859, 6, 20. Milicent & ch, Levisa W., Phebe
                J., Demsey B., John M., George T. & Mary
                E., rocf Stillwater MM, O., dtd 1859,5,28
1862, 4, 21. Levisa Stanton (form Hanson)
                dis mcd
1866, 3, 19. Phebe Jane Pierce (form Hanson)
                dis mcd

1868, 10, 19. Milicent Elliot (form Hanson)
                dis mcd
1872, 1, 23. Dempsey B. dis mcd & military
                service

HAWORTH
1884, 12, 24. Richard, s Elwood & Matilda,
                Cherokee Co., Kans.; m in Southland MH,
                Julia A. BURGESS, dt Elwood & Gaynor,
                Athens Co., O.

1885, 4, 20. Julia A. (form Burgess) gct
                Springriver MM, Kans.

HEALD
----, --, --. Smith d 1853,1,10 ae 38; m Ach-
                sah -----
                Ch: Martha   b 1847, 11, 8
                    Milton   " 1850, 1, 3
                    Ruthann   "" 1852, 2, 9 d 1883, 8,27
----, --, --. Samuel & Jane
                Ch: Alfred W. b 1851, 7, 2
                    Caroline L." 1853, 5, 9
                    Wilford
                     Lewis   " 1855, 11, 17
                    Evaline   " 1860, 10, 23
1854, 7, 26. Louisa m John ENGLE
1857, 12, 2. Mary Ann m John W. HOBSON
1858, 3, 31. Achsah m James E. MOTT
1860, 12, 12. Ury B. d ae 64

1854, 10, 23. Samuel N. Hobson gct Carmel MM,
                O., to m Anna M. Heald
1858, 8, 23. Mary B. & s, Abner J., rocf
                Middleton MM, dtd 1858,7,17
1858, 8, 23. Martha Jane rocf Middleton MM,
                dtd 1858,7,17
1861, 7, 22. Abner J. dis jas
1862, 4, 21. Martha Jane Bruce (form Heald)
                dis mcd
1863, 4, 20. Samuel dis disunity
1866, 12, 17. Lydia gct Springfield MM
1869, 2, 22. Lucina dis jG
1873, 2, 17. Alfred dis mcd
1876, 5, 22. Caroline S. West (form Heald)
                dis mcd
1877, 1, 22. Marietta gct Hickory Grove MM,
                Ia.
1879, 4, 21. Milton gct Hickory Grove MM, Ia.

HEYMAN
1867, 2, 18. Louisa (form Thomas) dis mcd

HIATT
1880, 3, 24. James, s Jesse & Ruthanna, Mor-
                gan Co., O.; m in Plymouth MH, Mary E.
                HANSON, dt Manoah & Millicent
                Ch: Elwood D. b 1882, 9, 13

1880, 12, 20. James rocf Chesterfield MM,
                dtd·1880,12,19
1883, 10, 22. James & w, Mary E., & s, El-
                wood D., gct Chesterfield MM

HIRST
1853, --, --. Thomas d 1868,3,9 ae 71; m Mary
Ann COOPER
Ch: Dillwyn G. b 1854, 9, 15 d 1854,10,10
    Calvin C. " 1854, 9, 15 " 1856, 1,18

1852, 3, 22. James & Ann rocf Short Creek MM,
O., dtd 1852,1,20
1853, 4, 18. Thomas gct Sandy Spring MM, to
m Mary Ann Cooper
1853, 8, 22. Mary Ann rocf Sandy Spring MM,
dtd 1853,6,24
1854, 1, 21. James R. gct Chesterfield MM, O.
1859, 3, 21. Ann Embree (form Hirst) dis mcd
1873, 7, 21. Mary Ann gct Middleton MM, O.

HOBSON
----, --, --. Samuel & Ann
Ch: Maryanne b 1855, 8, 22
    Adaliza   " 1857, 4, 22
1856, 3, 13. Unity d ae 44
1857, 12, 2. John W., s Stephen & Lydia,
Washington Co., O.; m in Plymouth MH, Mary
Ann HEALD, dt Levi & Lydia, Washington
Co., O., d 1871,10,20
1858, 4, 28. Belinda H. m Lindley M. FOWLER
1859, 1, 18. Linneaus D., s John W. & Mary, b
1861, 11, 27. Phebe W. m Chalkley T. FOWLER
1862, 3, 26. Belinda S. m John SCHOFIELD
1862, 9, 24. Benjamin J., s Thos. & Unity,
Washington Co., O.; m in Plymouth MH, Martha E. MARSHALL, dt John & Ann, Washington
Co., O., d 1881,2,1 ae 37
Ch: Emma   b 1864, 9, 7 d 1868, 8,14
    Thomas Al-
        den " 1868, 11, 12
    Arthur Brun-
        son" 1871, 3, 16
    William C. " 1874, 11, 10
Benjamin J. m 2nd 1882,8,31 in Southland
MH, Sarah A. DEAN, dt Jonathan & Elizabeth, Washington Co., O.
Ch: John A. b 1887, 8, 4
1864, 2, 26. Thomas C., s John & Rebecca, d
ae 20
1866, 10, 24. Mary Ann m John S. DEAN
1874, 3, 26. Belinda m Joseph P. BINNS
1875, 8, 24. Dorothy m John F. STRATTON
----, --, --. William & Elizabeth
Ch: George W. b 1886, 5, 15 d 1896, 8,26
1879, 11, 28. Mary S., dt Andrew & Ruth STAN-
LEY, d ae 57
1882, 7, 27. Thomas, s John & Belinda, Washington Co., O.; m in Southland MH, Eliza
A. WORTHINGTON, dt Wm. & Elizabeth, Washington Co., O.
1891, 8, 27. Thomas Alden, s Benjamin J. &
Martha, Washington Co., O.; m in Southland
MH, Tacy Ann DAVIS, dt Jehu & Ruth, Washington Co., O.
Ch: Emma
    Gertrude b 1893, 2, 20
    Howard

Emmerson   b 1895, 4, 6
1893, 3, 20. Rebecca, dt John NAYLOR, d ae 84
1893, 6, 30. Stephen, s John & Belinda, d
1893, 7, 7. Lydia, dt John & Jane MOTT, d ae
79
1893, 11, 5. John d ae 85

1852, 7, 19. Thomas & w, Unity, & ch, Benjamin J., Mary, Dorothy, John A. & Belinda,
rocf Smithfield MM, O., dtd 1852,4,19
1854, 10, 23. Samuel N. gct Carmel MM, O., to
m Anna M. Heald
1855, 3, 19. Anna M. rocf Middleton MM, O.,
dtd 1855,2,8
1857, 8, 17. Thomas gct Salem MM, to m Mary
Stanley
1858, 3, 22. Mary S. rocf Salem MM, dtd 1858,
2,21
1863, 8, 17. Samuel N. & w, Anna M., dis
disunity
1864, 11, 21. James dis mcd
1866, 8, 20. Mary J. dis jG
1867, 6, 17. Rebecca Jane Ellis (form Hobson)
dis mcd
1869, 4, 19. John W. dis disunity
1870, 12, 19. William dis mcd
1873, 6, 23. John A. gct Flushing MM, O., to
m Martha H. Branson
1873, 11, 17. Mary Ann Lovell (form Hobson)
dis mcd
1874, 2, 23. Marianna Lovel (form Hobson)
dis mcd
1874, 4, 20. John A. gct Flushing MM, O.
1877, 7, 23. Elizabeth J. (form Fowler) con
mcd
1877, 11, 19. Joseph G. dis mcd
1880, 10, 18. Adaliza Lovel (form Hobson) dis
mcd
1883, 8, 20. William rst rq
1887, 2, 21. Linneaus D. dis mcd
1891, 6, 22. Lena M. & Stephen J., ch Wm. &
Elizabeth, recrq

HODGINS
1855, 10, 31. John E., s Eli & Mary, Washington Co., O.; m Tamer D. VERNON, dt Eli &
Eliza, Athens Co., O.
1860, 3, 21. Charles d ae 1

1855, 7, 23. John E. rocf Stillwater MM, O.,
dtd 1855,4,24
1857, 2, 23. John E. & w, Tamer D., gct
Chesterfield MM
1860, 1, 23. Stephen [Hodgin] & w, Sarah, &
ch, Clarkson, Wilson & Charles, rocf
Pennsville MM, dtd 1859,10,13
1862, 7, 21. Stephen [Hodgin] & w, Sarah, &
ch, Clarkson, Wilson & Mary Esther, gct
Hickory Grove MM, Ia.

HOLLINGSWORTH
1865, 4, 15. Mary Ann, dt Edwin & Betsey, b
1874, 9, 22. Sarah m Charles BLACKBURN

HOLLINGSWORTH, continued
1874, 10, 1. Penina m Francis DEAN
----, --, --. Emmor & Sarah
    Ch: Cynthia
        May   b 1877, 3, 12
        Joel G.   d 1878, 3, 7
          ae 6
1887, 11, 22. Mary A. m Nathan THOMASSON

1857, 1, 19. Edwin & w, Betsey, & ch, Ury,
    Sarah & Pennina, rocf Pennsville MM, dtd
    1857,1,15
1868, 7, 20. Sarah (form Gilbert) con mcd
1869, 2, 22. Ury Ellis (form Hollingsworth)
    dis mcd
1874, 9, 21. Emmor & w, Sarah, & ch, Charles
    D. & Joel G., rocf Pennsville MM, dtd
    1874,9,17
1883, 2, 19. Emmor & w, Sarah, & ch, Charles
    D., Sintha M. & Grace E., gct Pennsville
    MM
1894, 3, 19. Edwin & w, Betsy H., gct Middle-
    ton MM

HOLLOWAY
1862, 8, 18. Elisha J. & w, Lydia, & dt, Lu-
    cinda, rocf Chesterfield MM, dtd 1862,8,
    16
1862, 8, 18. Phebe Louisa rocf Chesterfield
    MM, dtd 1862,8,16
1866, 1, 22. Elisha J. & Lydia J. dis jG
1867, 6, 17. Phebe Kirby (form Holloway) dis
    mcd
1869, 2, 22. Lucinda dis jas

HUTTON
1851, 6, 23. Joel W. & w, Ann, & ch, Adison,
    Mary, Findley, Deborah, Ann, Rebecca &
    Susan, rocf Providence MM, Pa., dtd 1851,
    5,1
1851, 12, 22. Joel W. & fam gct Providence MM,
    Pa.

JOHNSON
1871, 9, 18. Sarah (form Bailey) dis mcd

JONES
1893, 2, 10. Ruth, dt Joshua & Eliza Ann
    MORRIS, d

KIEHL
1868, 1, 20. Anna Maria (form Marshall) dis
    jas

KIRBY
1867, 6, 17. Phebe (form Holloway) dis mcd

LAMBERT
----, --, --. Albert & Elizabeth
    Ch: Albert   b 1850, 3, 10
        Elizabeth   " 1852, 3, 30
        Martha   " 1855, 3, 13
        Phebe   " 1857, 5, 23

        Ch: James D. b 1860, 9, 15
1854, 8, 30. Rachel E. m Robert VERNON

1858, 4, 19. John dis mcd
1860, 5, 21. Mary Sharp (form Lambert) dis
    mcd
1861, 12, 23. Sarah Vernon (form Lambert) dis
    mcd

LANGSTAFF
1852, 10, 12. Lindley T., s Thos. D. & Hannah
    L., b

1853, 1, 17. Thomas D. & w, Hannah, & ch,
    Rhoda, Elnathan, Wm., Enoch, Henry & El-
    len, rocf Cincinnati MM, O., dtd 1852,12,
    16
1854, 8, 21. Thomas D. & w, Hannah, & ch,
    Rhoda, Elnathan, William, Enoch, Henry
    H., Ellen M. & Lindley T., gct Red Cedar
    MM, Ia.

LANGTREE
1889, 7, 22. Emmolada (form Fowler) dis mcd

LIVEZEY
1864, 8, 21. John H. d ae 71
1870, 1, 27. Sarah d ae 77

1865, 5, 22. Sarah rocf Chesterfield MM, dtd
    1865,5,20

LOTHAM
1858, 7, 20. Elizabeth rocf Chesterfield MM,
    dtd 1858,8,21
1864, 1, 18. Elizabeth dis jas

LOVELL
1873, 11, 17. Mary Ann (form Hobson) dis mcd
1874, 2, 23. Marianna (form Hobson) dis mcd
1880, 10, 18. Adaliza (form Hobson) dis mcd

LUPTON
1851, 3, 17. James E. Mott gct Short Creek
    MM, O., to m Mary P. Lupton
1856, 5, 19. Isaac & w, Mary, rocf Somerset
    MM, dtd 1856,4,28
1856, 12, 22. David & w, Sarah, & ch, Anna &
    Mary P., rocf Short Creek MM, O., dtd
    1856,11,18
1860, 4, 23. David & w, Sarah, gct Short
    Creek MM, O.
1863, 1, 19. Isaac & w, Mary, gct Short
    Creek MM, O.
1865, 4, 17. David & w, Sarah, & ch, Anna,
    Mary P., Achsah & Drusilla, rocf Newgar-
    den MM, dtd 1865,2,23
1872, 5, 20. Rebecca J. (form Crew) con mcd
1873, 7, 21. Rebecca J. gct Springville MM,
    Ia.
1877, 12, 17. David & w, Sarah, & dt, Dru-
    silla, gct Salem MM
1877, 12, 17. Anna, Mary P. & Achsah C. gct

LUPTON, continued
    Salem MM

McDANIELS
1881, 3, 21. Jane F. (form Bailey) dis mcd

McDONNALD
1882, 5, 22. Jane F. (form Bailey) dis mcd

McGIRR
----, --, --. James d 1876,4,6 ae 90; m Rachel

    Ch: Jane F.   b 1858, 3, 13 d 1861, 3, 2
        Mary   " 1859, 4, 4
        Ann   " 1861, 3, 2 " 1864, 3,20
        Thomas El-
          wood   " 1862, 3, 9 d 1864,10, 5
        Lewis Henry" 1864, 5, 5
        Elizabeth   " 1865, 11, 3 " 1868, 3,17
        Walter J.   " 1873, 9, 3
1866, 6, 16. Sarah d ae 70

1851, 7, 21. Letitia Vickers (form McGirr)
    dis mcd
1851, 10, 20. Wm. H. dis mcd
1853, 2, 21. Jonah dis mcd
1853, 3, 21. Alexander dis mcd
1856, 12, 22. James gct Somerset MM, O., to m
    Rachel Bailey
1857, 9, 21. Rachel rocf Somerset MM, O., dtd
    1857,6,29
1867, 1, 21. Harpley con mcd
1868, 2, 17. Henry con mcd
1881, 8, 22. Harpley dis jas
1886, 3, 22. Henry dis jas

McGRAIL
1872, 3, 6. Sarah d ae 75

1871, 3, 20. Sarah rocf Sewickley MM, Pa.,
    dtd 1871,1,31

McGREW
1851, 5, 19. Margaret rocf Providence MM,
    Pa., dtd 1851,5,1
1851, 10, 20. Margaret gct Pennsville MM, O.

MARSHALL
----, --, --. Caleb & Elmira
    Ch: Anna M.   b 1848, 11, 25
        Maryetta   " 1855, 6, 28
1862, 1, 27. John d ae 74
1862, 9, 24. Martha E. m Benj. J. HOBSON
1885, 11, 17. Ann d ae 80

1856, 9, 22. Jesse dis mcd
1861, 8, 19. Caleb & Elmira dis jas
1868, 1, 20. Anna Maria Kiehl (form Marshall)
    dis jas
1878, 10, 21. Ury Etta Boughman (form Marshall)
    dis mcd

MELTON
1864, 3, 21. Rebecca (form Gilbert) con mcd
1867, 7, 22. Rebecca [Milton] gct Pennsville
    MM

MONROE
1858, 7, 19. Deborah (form Vernon) dis mcd &
    jas

MORELAN
1849, 3, 11. Mary [Moreland] d ae 80
1849, 11, 25. Jason [Moreland] d ae 77
1851, 12, 27. Rebecca d ae 31
1852, 1, 4. Joel d
1852, 3, 30. Robert [Moreland], s Albert &
    Rebecca, b
1857, 3, 6. Isaac d

1853, 6, 20. Albert [Morlan] dis mcd
1867, 10, 21. Caroline [Morland] dis disunity
1868, 8, 17. Martha Elizabeth [Morland] (form
    Naylor) dis mcd
1874, 7, 20. Robert [Morland] dis mcd

MORRIS
----, --, --. Edwin & Rachel
    Ch: Silas S.   b 1846, 10, 18
        Charles K.
        Lewis   " 1850, 5, 13
        Alice   " 1852, 6, 28
        John Web-
          ster   " 1854, 5, 10 d 1888, 9,13
        Edwin H.   " 1862, 6, 5
----, --, --. Joshua m Eliza Ann TULLOSS d
    1892,5,21 ae 70
    Ch: Hannah   b 1848, 8, 28
        Rebecca   " 1852, 11, 6 d 1874,10,28
        Maria   " 1855, 1, 30 " 1878, 9,22
        Emlen I.   " 1856, 10, 1
        Rachel   " 1857, 2, 16
        Lindley   " 1859, 8, 29
        Ruth Anna   " 1862, 3, 10 " 1893, 2,10
        Franklin   " 1865, 1, 28
        Err T.   " 1867, 1, 18
----, --, --. Martin & Elizabeth
    Ch: Sarah J.   b 1849, 10, 19 d 1873,12, 8
        Hannah
        Alice   " 1853, 7, 27 " 1854,10,11
        Rachel Ann " 1856, 10, 1
        David Lin-
          neaus   " 1858, 5, 2
----, --, --. Jesse & Mary Ellen
    Ch: Matilda P. b 1872, 9, 10
        Lizzie   " 1876, 5, 4
        Lydia S.   " 1876, 5, 4
        Daniel E.   " 1879, 7, 9
        Rachel   " 1881, 7, 16
1877, 12, 26. John W., s Edwin & Rachel, Wash-
    ington Co., O., d 1888,9,13 ae 34; m in
    Plymouth MH, Mary S. FOWLER, dt Caleb &
    Sarah, Washington Co., O.
    Ch: Ethel J.   b 1879, 6, 19 d 1879, 6,21
        Arthur

MORRIS, John W. & Mary S., continued
        Lewis   b 1880, 12, 20
    Ch: Emma Liz-
        zie   " 1883, 4, 29
        Clarence I.
        Everett C. " 1887, 6, 27
1888, 4, 20. Ruth d ae 92
1889, 11, 28. Rachel A. m Amos BURGESS

1857, 3, 23. Wm. Wright dis mcd
1859, 4, 18. Jesse, minor, recrq
1867, 1, 21. Joshua Jr. dis disunity
1867, 4, 22. Silas dis mcd & military service
1868, 11, 23. Benajah dis mcd & military ser-
    vice
1870, 1, 20. Mordecai dis military service
1871, 11, 20. Jesse gct Springville MM, Ia.,
    to m Mary Ellen Patten
1874, 8, 17. Ruth rst on consent of Short
    Creek MM, O.
1875, 2, 22. Alice Donaldson (form Morris)
    dis mcd
1876, 10, 23. Louisa (or Lavisa) Bennett
    (form Morris) dis mcd
1877, 8, 20. Charles K. dis mcd
1878, 1, 21. Mary Ella & ch, Matilda, Hannah
    Jane & Lydia, rocf Springville MM, Ia.,
    dtd 1877,12,15
1881, 4, 18. Emlen dis mcd & jas
1886, 8, 23. Benjamin F. dis disunity
1886, 10, 18. Lindley dis disunity
1893, 4, 17. Jesse J. & w, Ellen, & ch,
    Lydia P., Daniel M. & Rachel M., gct
    Springville MM, Ia.
1893, 4, 17. Matilda P. gct Springville MM,
    Ia.
1894, 7, 23. David Linneaus con mcd
1897, 4, 19. Mary Susanna & ch, Arthur
    Everett, Joseph Earl, Alice Unice, Edna
    V. & Edith, gct Springville MM, Ia.

MOTT
----, --, --. William & Sarah
    Ch: Daniel M.   d 1892, 6, 7
        ae 69
        Eleanor   " 1857, 4, 9
        ae 18
1854, 12, 28. Mary m Joel GILBERT
1855, 12, 9. Mary P. d ae 34
----, --, --. Gershom m Ruthanna ----- d 1878,
    5,14 ae 41
    Ch: Eli P.   b 1857, 8, 19 d 1870, 7,8
        Sarah   " 1861, 2, 28
        William C. " 1865, 3, 14
        Elenor   " 1868, 3, 28
        Esther   " 1870, 7, 8
1858, 3, 21. James E., s Wm. & Sarah, Athens
    Co., O., d 1867,11,20 ae 40; m in Plymouth
    MH, Achsah HEALD, dt Caleb & Mary FOWLER,
    Washington Co., O.
    Ch: Smith   b 1859, 1, 17
        John W.   " 1861, 5, 18
        George Her-
            vey " 1864, 1, 29

        vey   b 1864, 1, 29
        Ch: Mary S.   " 1866, 11, 17
1858, 3, 23. David C., s G. W. & Abigail, b
1858, 12, 30. Asher, s Wm. & Sarah, Athen Co.,
    O.; m in Southland MH, Mary Elvira PEN-
    ROSE, dt Joseph & Mary, Washington Co.,O.
1861, 2, 28. Sarah d ae 59
1870, 3, 1. William d ae 79
1870, 11, 13. William Jr. d ae 28
----, --, --. Smith H. & Matilda Jane
    Ch: Elizabeth b 1887, 11, 4
        Eleanor   " 1889, 9, 21
        Amy   " 1891, 8, 14
        Jas. Fred-
        erick   " 1893, 4, 9
        Marjarie A." 1895, 4, 1
1893, 8, 4. Hannah Ann, dt John LIVEZEY, d
    ae 73

1851, 3, 17. James E. gct Short Creek MM,
    O., to m Mary P. Lupton
1852, 4, 19. Mary P. rocf Short Creek MM, O.
1856, 2, 18. Asher gct Stillwater MM, O., to
    m Sarah Bundy
1856, 9, 22. Gershom gct Stillwater MM, O.,
    to m Ruthanna Bundy
1857, 2, 23. Ruthanna rocf Stillwater MM, O.,
    dtd 1857,1,24
1857, 2, 23. George W. gct Pennsville MM, O.,
    to m Abigail Ball
1857, 9, 21. Abigail B. rocf Pennsville MM,
    O., dtd 1857,8,13
1861, 10, 21. Geo. W. & w, Abigail, & s,
    Davis C., gct Pennsville MM, O.
1864, 3, 21. Asher & w, Elvira, gct Penns-
    ville MM, O.
1871, 5, 22. Sarah J., adopted dt Daniel M.
    & Hannah Ann, recrq
1879, 9, 22. Esther, minor, gct Coal Creek
    MM, Ia.
1880, 7, 19. Gershom gct Coal Creek MM, Ia.,
    to m Elmira Emmons
1881, 12, 19. Gershom & ch, William & Eleanor,
    gct Coal Creek MM, Ia.
1885, 7, 20. Smith H. gct Coal Creek MM, Ia.,
    to m Matilda Jane Clendenon
1886, 12, 20. Sarah J. gct Springville MM, Ia.
1886, 12, 20. Daniel M. & w, Hannah Ann, gct
    Springville MM, Ia.
1887, 9, 19. Sarah J. rocf Springville MM,
    Ia., dtd 1887,8,20
1887, 12, 19. Daniel M. & w, Hannah Ann, rocf
    Springville MM, Ia., dtd 1887,11,20
1887, 12, 19. Sarah J. rocf Springville MM,
    Ia., dtd 1887,11,20
1889, 1, 21. John W. dis mcd
1889, 9, 23. Martha Jane rocf Coal Creek MM,
    Ia., dtd 1889,8,--
1890, 1, 20. George Harvey rpd mcd

NAYLOR
----, --, --. John d 1895,1,25 ae 78; m Sarah
    ----- d 1856,10,9

NAYLOR, John & Sarah, continued
>   Ch: Ruthanna   b 1854, 12, 18 d 1855, 3,26
>   Narcissa   " 1856, 8, 15 " 1856, 9,24

1853, 6, 20. John & w, Sarah, & ch, David E.,
    Martha Elizabeth, George G. & Uriah C.,
    rocf Providence MM, Pa., dtd 1853,1,2
1868, 8, 17. Martha Elizabeth Morland (form
    Naylor) dis mcd
1872, 4, 22. George Gilbert dis mcd to first
    cousin
1872, 7, 22. John con mcd
1873, 8, 18. David dis mcd

NOLAND
1873, 3, 17. Sarah Maria (form Bailey) dis
    mcd
1876, 10, 23. Mary Ann (form Bailey) dis mcd

PATTEN
1871, 11, 20. Jesse Morris gct Springville
    MM, Ia., to m Mary Ellen Patten

PARKER
1853, 3, 21. Joseph dis mcd
1853, 6, 6. Rachel Ann Ellis (form Parker)
    dis mcd
1856, 2, 18. Martha dis disunity

PARKS
1853, 9, 19. Rachel Ann Ellis (form Parks)
    dis mcd

PENN
1864, 10, 17. Rebecca (form Engle) dis mcd
1865, 1, 23. Rebecca (form Engle) dis mcd

PENROSE
----, --, --. Joseph d 1894,11,25 ae 76; m
    Mildred -----
>   Ch: Sarah   b 1850, 2, 22 d 1858, 4,25
>   Lindley   " 1852, 5, 18
>   Elizabeth " 1854, 10, 24
>   John Adison" 1857, 9, 30
>   Eliza Jane " 1865, 2, 24
1858, 12, 30. Mary Elvira m Asher MOTT
1861, 9, 24. Barclay, s Richard & Ann Eliza-
    beth, Morgan Co., O.; m in Plymouth MH,
    Mary P. GILBERT, dt Joel & Elizabeth,
    Washington Co., O.
1877, 10, 24. Elizabeth L. m Nathan BURGESS

1851, 3, 17. Rebecca dis jas
1866, 12, 17. Joseph dis disunity; rst 1870,
    2,21
1867, 7, 22. Mary P. gct Pennsville MM, O.
1868, 6, 22. Wm. dis jas & military service
1880, 10, 18. Lindley dis mcd
1887, 9, 19. Eliza Jane Cook (form Penrose)
    con mcd
1887, 10, 17. John dis mcd

PIERCE
1866, 3, 19. Phebe Jane (form Hanson) dis
    mcd

POORMAN
1867, 2, 18. Rebecca Ann (form Thomas) dis
    mcd

PURVIS
1852, 12, 20. Elijah gct Pennsville MM, O.

REEVES
1865, 10, 23. Joshua & w, Elizabeth, gct
    Salem MM
1865, 10, 23. Job gct Salem MM

RHODES
----, --, --. Harmon m Elizabeth BROWN, dt
    Isaac & Elizabeth, d 1862,12,28 ae 59
>   Ch: Rebecca   b 1825, 1, 28
>   Martha   " 1828, 7, 29
>   William   " 1831, 7, 10 d 1838, 5,10
>   Isaac   " 1834, 6, 7
>   Joseph   " 1837, 7, 24

1862, 11, 17. Joseph dis mcd
1865, 4, 17. Harmon gct Newgarden MM, to m
    Elizabeth Test
1865, 10, 23. Harmon gct Chesterfield MM

ROMAN
----, --, --. Ephraim d 1880,8,21 ae 66; m
    Ann ----- d 1880,5,24 ae 66
>   Ch: Mary Jane   d 1864,12,19
>   ae 21
>   Jesse   " 1849, 5,26
>   ae 3
>   William   " 1850, 4,29
>   ae 3
>   Eli   b 1852, 1, 1
>   Elwood   " 1854, 2, 18
>   Sarah
>   Elizabeth " 1858, 9, 18
1854, 6, 2. Mary d

1855, 8, 20. Sarah Ann Thompson (form Roman)
    con mcd
1858, 5, 17. Abraham dis mcd
1862, 10, 20. Elizabeth dis jas
1863, 3, 23. Isaac dis military service
1881, 11, 21. Sarah Elizabeth Deams (form
    Roman) dis mcd
1882, 2, 20. Ellwood dis mcd
1889, 5, 20. Eli dis mcd
1867, 10, 21. Rachel Way (form Roman) dis mcd

RUHL
1863, 7, 20. Eliza Jane (form Thomas) dis mcd

SCHOFIELD
1862, 3, 26. John, s Andrew & Rachel J.,
    Morgan Co., O.; m in Plymouth MH, Belinda
    S. HOBSON, dt Stephen & Lydia, Washington

SCHOFIELD, John & Belinda, continued
    Co., O.

1862, 6, 23. Belinda H. [Scholfield] gct
    Chesterfield MM

SHANER
1896, 12, 1. Sarah E., dt Caleb & Mary ENGLE,
    d ae 33

1883, 1, 22. Sarah E. (form Engle) con mcd

SHARP
1853, 9, 2. Hannah d

1858, 9, 20. Adaline dis
1860, 4, 23. Oliver dis mcd
1860, 5, 21. Mary (form Lambert) dis mcd
1863, 6, 22. Isaac rst on consent of Chester-
    field MM
1865, 6, 19. Isaac & w, Lydia, & ch, Amos &
    Mark, gct Coal Creek MM, Ia.
1865, 7, 17. Emaline A., Deborah & Dorothy M.
    gct Coal Creek MM, Ia.
1867, 10, 21. Joel dis military service
1868, 2, 17. Joel dis military service

SHAW
1884, 2, 19. Lindley, s Wm. & Hannah H.,
    Linn Co., Ia.; m in Southland MH, Mary
    Alice BURGESS, dt Elwood & Gaynor P.,
    Athens Co., O.

1885, 4, 20. Mary Alice (form Burgess) gct
    Springville MM, Ia.

SMITH
----, --, --. Evan & Mary
    Ch: Thomas E. b 1852, 12, 16
        Burgess " 1855, 11, 9 d 1858, 5,19
        Sarah   " 1859, 9, 30
----, --, --. Samuel & Hannah
    Ch: Oliver
        Thomas   b 1855, 7, 13
        Sarah
        Eliza   "   d 1862, 1,14
         ae 4
        Elizabeth " 1860, 8, 12 " 1861, 6,12
1860, 3, 17. Nancy d ae 69
1863, 12, 3. David R., s Henry & Mary, Wash-
    ington Co., O.; m in Southland MH, Hannah
    BUNDY, dt Thos. & Ruth, Washington Co., O.
    Ch: Miriam W. b 1865, 10, 31
1884, 2, 19. Joshua W., s Samuel B. & Lydia
    Ann, Guernsey Co., O.; m in Plymouth MH,
    Eva Irene FOWLER, dt Edmund & Mary, Wash-
    ington Co., O.

1851, 2, 17. Evan & w, Mary, & ch, Margaret
    Ann, Maria, Louisa, Caroline & Joshua,
    rocf Pennsville MM, O., dtd 1851,1,16
1851, 9, 22. Thomas gct Spring Creek MM, Ia.
1853, 6, 20. Samuel & w, Hannah, & ch, Mary

J. & Sarah Eliza, rocf Chesterfield MM,
    dtd 1853,6,18
1854, 2, 20. Nancy rocf Chesterfield MM, dtd
    1854,2,18
1855, 1, 22. Nancy gct Pennsville MM, O.
1858, 8, 23. Nancy rocf Pennsville MM, O.,
    dtd 1858,6,17
1867, 4, 22. Hannah & ch, Oliver Thomas, Jo-
    seph Franklin, Lydia M. & Emma R., gct
    Coal Creek MM, Ia.
1867, 4, 22. Samuel dis disunity
1867, 4, 22. Mary J. gct Coal Creek MM, Ia.
1870, 8, 22. David rocf Chesterfield MM
1886, 1, 18. Eva Irene & dt, Mary R., gct
    Springville MM, Ia.

STANLEY
1857, 8, 17. Thomas Hobson gct Salem MM, to
    m Mary Stanley

STANTON
1862, 4, 21. Levisa (form Hanson) dis mcd

STEADMAN
1883, 8, 20. Esther H. recrq
1889, 7, 22. Esther Brill (form Steadman) dis
    jas & mcd

STRATTON
1875, 8, 24. John F., s Benj. D. & Ellen,
    Columbiana Co., O.; m in Plymouth MH,
    Dorothy HOBSON, dt Thomas & Unity, Wash-
    ington Co., O.

1876, 5, 22. Dorothy H. gct Newgarden MM

TEST
1862, 1, 20. Thomas Bowman gct New Garden
    MM, O., to m Ann Test
1865, 4, 17. Harmon/gct New Garden MM, to m
    Elizabeth TEST Rhodes

THOMAS
1850, 12, 20. Rebecca d ae 60

1851, 10, 20. Joanna gct Upper Springfield
    MM, O.
1855, 4, 23. Sarah gct Stillwater MM, O.
1863, 4, 20. Joseph & Mary dis jG
1863, 7, 20. Eliza Jane Ruhl (form Thomas)
    dis mcd
1864, 8, 22. Rachel rocf Middleton MM, O.,
    dtd 1864,7,16
1867, 2, 18. Louise Heyman (form Thomas)
    dis mcd
1867, 2, 18. Rebecca Ann Poorman (form
    Thomas) dis mcd

THOMASSON
1887, 11, 22. Nathan, s John & Eunice, Bel-
    mont Co., O.; m in Plymouth MH, Mary A.
    HOLLINGSWORTH, dt Edwin & Betsey, Wash-
    ington Co., O.

THOMASSON, Nathan & Mary A., continued
 Ch: Joseph
   Earl   b 1889, 10, 5
   Alice E. " 1890, 10, 4
   Edna P. " 1892, 4, 22
   Edith " 1895, 12, 7

1888, 3, 19. Mary A. gct Somerset MM, O.
1890, 1, 20. Nathan & w, Mary A., & ch, Arthur Everett & Joseph Earl, rocf Somerset MM, O., dtd 1889,12,26
1892, 4, 18. Nathan dis
1896, 9, 21. Nathan rst by Pasadena MM, Calif.
1896, 12, 21. Mary Ann & ch, Arthur Everett, Joseph Earl, Alice Unice, Edna V. & Edith, gct Pasadena MM, Calif.

THOMPSON
1855, 8, 20. Sarah Ann (form Roman) con mcd
1857, 5, 18. Sarah Ann dis mcd
1872, 2, 19. Mary (form Craft) dis mcd & jG
1872, 5, 20. Mary (form Craft) dis mcd & jG

TOWNSEND
1854, 10, 1. Joseph d

1851, 3, 17. Levi rocf Somerset MM, dtd 1850,12,30
1851, 3, 17. Joseph rocf Somerset MM, dtd 1850,12,30
1872, 11, 18. Hannah (form Vernon) dis mcd

VAILE
1851, 8, 18. Jesse rocf Plainfield MM, O., dtd 1850,12,25, end by Chesterfield MM, O.
1857, 7, 20. Jesse gct Plainfield MM, O.

VANLAW
1855, 10, 22. Samuel C. rocf Chesterfield MM, dtd 1855,10,20
1859, 6, 20. Samuel C. dis jas

VERNON
----, --, --. Amos d 1865,11,19 ae 61; m Jane WAY, dt David & Ann, d 1870,1,31 ae 55
 Ch: Elizabeth b 1849, 1, 29
   Benjamin " 1852, 3, 28
----, --, --. Eli & Eliza
 Ch: Emily Ann b 1855, 5, 6
   E. Alonzo " 1858, 4, 22
   Jesse " d 1862, 5, 1
    ae 19
1854, 8, 30. Robert, s Amos & Jane, Athens Co., O.; m in Plymouth MH, Rachel E. LAMBERT, dt Albert & Elizabeth, Washington Co., O.
 Ch: Charles D. b 1855, 8, 22
   Elizabeth
   Jane " 1858, 3, 18
   Emma Lucy " 1861, 5, 26
   Cynthia
   Alice " 1863, 2, 6 d 1863, 4,18
   John Albert" 1865, 8, 12

 Ch: George
   William b 1869, 5, 10
1855, 10, 31. Tamar E. m John E. HODGENS
1862, 3, 19. Deborah d ae 54

1856, 6, 23. Edna (form Wood) dis mcd
1857, 11, 23. Jesse Craft gct Pennsville MM, O., to m Mary Vernon
1858, 7, 19. Deborah Monroe (form Vernon) dis mcd & jas
1860, 4, 23. Deborah rocf Stillwater MM, O., dtd 1860,3,24
1861, 11, 18. James dis mcd
1861, 12, 23. Sarah (form Lambert) dis mcd
1862, 8, 18. David dis mcd
1865, 12, 23. Mary Wood (form Vernon) con mcd
1866, 5, 21. Rachel gct Springville MM, Ia.
1866, 5, 21. Eli & w, Eliza, & ch, Jane W., Manoah H., Wm. P., Emily N. & Iddo L., gct Springville MM, Ia.
1867, 5, 20. Mordecai dis mcd & military service
1868, 3, 23. Elizabeth dis disunity
1868, 7, 20. Wm. dis mcd & military service
1872, 10, 21. John & w, Elizabeth, & ch, Evaline, Addison & James E., rocf Chesterfield MM, dtd 1872,10,19
1872, 11, 18. Hannah Townsend (form Vernon) dis mcd
1873, 5, 19. Rhoda Ann dis disunity
1879, 9, 22. Elizabeth & ch, Evaline, Addison & James E., gct Chesterfield MM

VICKERS
1851, 5, 19. Elijah dis mcd & jH
1851, 7, 21. Letitia (form McGirr) dis mcd

WALKER
----, --, --. Thompson & Ruthanna
 Ch: Thomas H. b 1848, 2, 24
   Hannah H. " 1850, 1, 12

1863, 4, 20. Thompson & Ruthanna dis jG

WALTON
1851, 10, 20. Josiah & w, Deborah, & ch, Rebecca Ann, Mary Jane & Anna Mariah, gct Upper Springfield MM, O.

WAY
----, --, --. Benjamin d 1864,11,15 ae 83; m Abigail ----- d 1883,3,25 ae 86
 Ch: Deborah   d 1851, 7,23
   ae 16
   Samuel   " 1863, 3,26
   ae 24
----, --, --. John & Hannah
 Ch: Mary Jane b 1849, 12, 31
   Charles
   Harvey " 1851, 7, 27
   Ruthanna " 1852, 9, 25 d 1852, 9,28
   George
   Washing-

WAY, John & Hannah, continued
                ton   b 1853, 11, 12
        Ch: Alfancy   " 1855, 5, 3
            Marian
            Isadora
            Ann   " 1858, 9, 5
1859, 10, 1. Robert d
1870, 9, 13. Lydia, dt Dempsey & Mary BOSWELL,
        d ae 63

1851, 9, 22. John dis disunity
1852, 10, 20. Mary Ann Wood (form Way) dis mcd
1853, 10, 17. Ruthanna (form Garretson) dis
        mcd
1855, 3, 19. Sarah Wood (form Way) dis mcd
1858, 11, 22. Margaret J. dis jas
1863, 4, 20. Milton dis military service
1864, 1, 18. Hannah & ch, Mary Jane, Charles
        Harvey, George Washington, Alfoncy Marion
        & Isadora Ann, gct Pennsville MM, O.
1867, 10, 21. Rachel (form Roman) dis mcd
1868, 6, 22. John B. dis jas & military ser-
        vice
1873, 10, 20. Jacob dis mcd

WEST
1876, 5, 22. Caroline S. (form Heald) dis mcd

WHALEN
1887, 1, 17. Mary Ann (form Fowler) dis mcd

WHITE
1871, 9, 18. Lydia (form Bailey) dis mcd

WILDMAN
1852, 3, 22. Mary rocf Pennsville MM, dtd
        1852,3,18
1855, 3, 19. Mary gct Pennsville MM
1860, 2, 20. Hannah (form Bailey) dis mcd

WILLIAMS
----, --, --. Seth & Philena
        Ch: Henry   b 1850, 2, 19
            Charles M. " 1851, 11, 27
1852, 7, 30. James E., s Isaiah & Anna, b

        *   *   *   *   *   *   *

PENNOCK
1851, 3, 17. Rebecca dis jas
1857, 2, 23. David dis mcd

1854, 7, 17. Philena & ch, Joseph Addison,
        Jesse Davis, Wm. Henry, Charles Mortimer
        & James Ezra, gct Pleasant Plain MM, Ia.
1863, 5, 18. Isaiah & Anna dis jG

WILSON
----, --, --. Dewitt C. & Sarah
        Ch: Mary C.   b 1848, 4, 16
            Rebecca A. " 1851, 1, 25

1851, 7, 21. Margaret rocf Providence MM,
        Pa., dtd 1851,6,5
1855, 3, 19. Arthur H. dis mcd
1858, 12, 20. William Findley dis mcd
1859, 4, 18. Abraham P. dis mcd
1860, 10, 22. William dis disunity
1865, 3, 20. Dewitt Clinton & w, Sarah B.,
        & ch, Mary Clarissa & Rebecca Ann, gct
        Hickory Grove MM, Ia.
1865, 12, 18. Sarah & Rebecca Jane gct Spring-
        ville MM, Ia.

WOOD
1854, 3, 21. Enoch d ae 19

1852, 10, 20. Mary Ann (form Way) dis mcd
1855, 3, 19. Sarah (form Way) dis mcd
1856, 4, 24. Joseph Jr. dis mcd
1856, 6, 23. Edna Vernon (form Wood) dis mcd
1856, 12, 22. Mary dis disunity
1857, 6, 22. Joseph dis
1865, 12, 23. Mary (form Vernon) con mcd
1871, 11, 20. Mary dis jas

WORRELL
1867, 7, 17. Rachel Ann (form Engle) dis mcd
        & jG

WORTHINGTON
1882, 6, 27. Eliza A. m Thomas HOBSON

1862, 4, 21. Caleb Engle gct Chesterfield MM,
        to m Mary T. Worthington
1872, 10, 21. Eliza A. rocf Chesterfield MM,
        dtd 1872,9,21

        *   *   *   *   *   *   *

1870, 4, 18. Matilda Clark (form Pennock)
        dis mcd

ALUM CREEK MONTHLY MEETING

Alum Creek Monthly Meeting, located in Delaware County, Ohio, was established by Short Creek Quarterly Meeting, 10th Mo. 30, 1817. It was transferred to Miami Quarterly Meeting of Indiana Yearly Meeting 8th Mo. 11, 1821, and years later, was transferred back to Ohio Yearly Meeting.

Among the charter members were the Benedict, Dillingham, Mosher, Osborn, Townsend, Willet, Wood and Wright families.

RECORDS

ADAMS
1834, 6, 8. Margaret T. d bur Middlebury, O.

1833, 3, 21. Margaret T. & ch, Sydney & Lewis, recrq
1835, 6, 25. John T. rocf Hartland MM, N.Y., dtd 1834,12,18
1839, 11, 21. Lewis, ch in care of Griffith Lewis, gct Goshen MM
1840, 3, 26. Sidney L., minor, gct Goshen MM
1849, 1, 25. Sidney L. rocf Goshen MM, dtd 1848,10,21

ALDRICH
1887, 1, 20. Oscar & Emma recrq
1887, 2, 17. David recrq
1887, 2, 17. Elias recrq
1887, 2, 17. Orrington recrq
1888, 5, 17. Elias relrq
1890, 3, 20. Mary Early dropped from mbrp

ALEXANDER
1875, 4, 15. Susan recrq
1880, 12, 16. Susie dis

ALLEN
1820, 1, 25. Phebe (form Buck) dis mcd
1910, 5, 19. Lottie recrq

AMADON
1857, 6, 25. Ann E. recrq
1859, 3, 24. Ann E. relrq

AMICK
1887, 4, 21. Maggie recrq

AMSBAUGH
1887, 11, 17. Olie Osborn relrq

ANDREWS
1838, 6, 21. Samuel A. & w, Eliza L., & ch, John L. & Lindley, rocf Upper Springfield MM, O., dtd 1838,4,28
1910, 3, 17. Flete recrq
1925, 4, 16. Fleet W. & w & ch relrq

ARCHIBALD
1860, 7, 26. Agnes, minor, recrq

ARMSTRONG
1862, 9, 25. Uree Ann (form Lee) dis mcd (H)

ASHBROOK
1904, 7, 21. Frank & w & ch, Mary & Ernest, transferred from Ashley MM
1905, 7, 20. Frank relrq
1907, 7, 18. Mrs. Frank & ch, Mary & Ernest, dropped from mbrp

ASHTON
1824, 1, 29. Jonathan Wood Jr. gct Carmel MM, to m Mary Ashton
1834, 9, 25. Chalkley Peasley gct Carmel MM, to m Margaret Ashley

AUSTIN
1887, 11, 17. H. G. recrq
1890, 3, 20. H. J. dropped from mbrp

AYRES
----, --, --. Thomas & Mary
    Ch: Andrew F. b 1864, 9, 12
        John E.   " 1868, 8, 31
        -----   " 1870, 8, 1
        -----   " 1873, 7, 25

1841, 4, 22. Lydia (form Wood) dis mcd
1875, 4, 15. Thomas [Ayers] & ch, Andrew John & Josiah, recrq
1875, 4, 15. Mary, w Thomas, & dt, Belle, recrq
1878, 2, 14. Thomas [Ayers] relrq
1878, 4, 18. Mary relrq
1881, 7, 21. Ch of Thomas & Mary [Ayers] relrq
1890, 5, 22. Helen Stone [Ayers] dropped from mbrp

BABCOCK
1887, 3, 17. Wm. J. & Saphrona recrq
1892, 1, 21. William dropped from mbrp
1897, 11, 18. Sophoronia relrq

BAILEY
1854, 5, 26. Joshua, s Exum & Tabitha, Warren Co., O.; m in Alum Creek MH, Sarah E. WOOD, dt Daniel & Elizabeth, Morrow Co., O.
----, --, --. Harris m Almira P. ----- d 1901, 9,14 ae 27 bur Alum Creek
    Ch: Edith
        Irene   d 1901, 8, 9
        ae 1 bur Alum Creek

1854, 7, 27. Sarah E. gct Springboro MM
1865, 5, 18. George E. & w, Eliza Jane, recrq
1878, 1, 17. George E. & Eliza Jane gct Iowa Falls MM
1894, 4, 19. Tilton H. recrq
1897, 3, 18. George & w, Martha A., & ch, Alvah B., Harris W., Edgar P., Myrtle D. & Leroy C. recrq
1906, 6, 21. Laura L. recrq
1909, 2, 18. Leroy C. relrq
1911, 4, 20. Edgar & w, Laura relrq
1917, 2, 15. Irvin recrq
1919, 7, 17. Harry dropped from mbrp

BAKER
1839, 2, 21. Mary D. rocf Bradford MM, dtd 1839,1,8 (H)
1886, 3, 18. Thomas recrq

BALDWIN

----, --, --.   Charles, s Joseph & Sarah, b
    1864,1,11; m Emma K. -----
       Ch: Alfred
             Eugene   b 1889, 9, 25
             Herold   " 1896, 6, 22
1902, 1, 8. Lavina H. d bur Alum Creek

1882, 7, 20. Stephen & fam rocf Goshen MM;
    retained at his rq
1882, 9, 21. Wm. H. rocf Gilead MM, dtd 1882,
    8,15; retained at his rq
1884, 2, 18. Benjamin recrq
1886, 4, 15. Joseph C. & w, Sarah, & dt, Mar-
    tha M., & s, Charles B., rocf Goshen MM
1887, 2, 17. Chloe H. relrq
1887, 5, 19. Chloe relrq
1893, 2, 16. Charles B. relrq
1907, 11, 21. Charles R. relrq
1910, 3, 17. Gertie recrq
1911, 4, 20. Alfred relrq
1916, 6, 15. Gertie dropped from mbrp
1924, 2, 14. Bertha Hatton relrq

BALL
1824, 3, 4. Charity rocf Junius MM, N. Y.,
    dtd 1823,9,24

BARBER
1842, 7, 28. Phebe (form Benedict) dis mcd

BARCLAY
1860, 6, 21. Hannah (form Mosher) dis mcd (H)

BARNARD

----, --, --.   Seth & Huldah
       Ch: Obed W.   b 1817, 12, 1
           David   " 1820, 2, 17
           Abigail   " 1822, 6, 17
           Sarah   " 1823, 12, 31
           Mara R.   " 1827, 12, 13
           Phebe   " 1829, 1, 13
           Huldah H.   " 1831, 5, 26
           Ruth H.   " 1836, 2, 26 d 1838,10, 4
            bur Peru, O.
           William G. b 1837, 3, 28
           Thadeus   " 1839, 10, 1

1834, 9, 25. Seth & w, Huldah, & ch, Obed W.,
    David, Abigail, Sarah, Mary R., Phebe &
    Huldah H., rocf Ferrisburgh MM, Vt., dtd
    1834, 7, 2
1838, 11, 22. David dis disunity
1842, 4, 21. Obed W. dis disunity
1842, 9, 19. Sarah dis jas
1842, 11, 24. Abigail Burk (form Barnard) dis
    mcd
1843, 8, 24. Huldah & ch, Mara R., Phebe,
    Huldah H., Wm. G. & Thadeus, gct Vermillion
    MM, Ill.

BARNES
1848, 3, 1. Samuel H., s John & Rachel, Knox

Co., O.; m in Owl Creek, Sarah VORE, dt
Jesse & Ann, Knox Co., O.
   Ch: Anna
         Elvira   b 1849, 1, 20
         Griffith C. " 1850, 8, 3
         Joseph V.   " 1855, 9, 8

1844, 3, 28. Samuel rocf Ferrisburg MM, Vt.,
    dtd 1844,1,3
1844, 12, 26. Samuel H. recrq
1870, 2, 17. Samuel H. & w, Sarah, & ch,
    Griffith L., Anna E., Jesse W. & Rachel
    W., gct Springdale MM, Ia.

BARRET
1838, 11, 8. Merriet H. d ae 4m 15d bur
    Huron Co., O. (H)
----, --, --.   Geo. & Mahala (H)
       Ch: Calista   b 1840, 9, 16
           Mary L.   " 1842, 4, 17
1840, 2, 13. Sarah d ae 10y 11m 4d bur Dela-
    ware Co., O. (H)

1821, 11, 29. Elisha rocf Danby MM, dtd
    1821,5,10
1839, 8, 22. Geo. & w, Mahala, & ch, Mariah,
    Isaac, Sarah, Slocumb, Mahalah M. & John
    B., rocf Danby MM, Vt., dtd 1839,7,11 (H)
1843, 9, 21. Geo. & w, Mahalah, & ch, Maria,
    Isaac Slocum, Mahala M., John, Calista &
    Mary L., gct Miami MM, O. (H)

BARRINGTON
1838, 6, 29. George d bur Vicksburg, Miss.
1840, 5, 27. Thomas, s Thomas & Elizabeth,
    Knox Co., O.; m in Owl Creek, Elizabeth W.
    TOWNSEND, dt Thomas & Ruth, Knox Co., O.
       Ch: George   b 1841, 4, 8
           Ruth   " 1844, 6, 8
1840, 9, 30. Joseph, s Thomas & Elizabeth,
    Knox Co., O.; m in Owl Creek, Elizabeth
    SHARP, dt John & Elizabeth, Knox Co., O.
1840, 10, 31. Elizabeth d ae 66 bur Middle-
    berry, O.
1844, 12, 24. Thomas d ae 72 bur Middleberry,
    O.
1860, 5, 4. Hannah d ae 63 bur Middleberry,
    O.
1838, 3, 22. Thomas & w, Elizabeth, & dt,
    Hannah, rocf Stroudsburg MM, Pa., dtd
    1837,9,21
1838, 3, 22. Joseph rocf Stroudsburg MM, Pa.,
    dtd 1838,2,22
1838, 3, 22. George rocf Stroudsburg MM, Pa.,
    dtd 1838,2,22
1838, 3, 22. Thomas rocf Stroudsburg MM, Pa.,
    dtd 1838,2,22
1851, 2, 20. Mark dis disunity
1855, 8, 23. Thomas & w, Elizabeth W., gct
    Red Cedar MM, Ia.

BARTLETT
----, --, --.   James & Phebe Ann

BARTLETT, continued
  Ch: Ann B. b 1837, 1, 1
    Martha W. " 1838, 9, 23
    George
    James " 1842, 1, 3
----, --, --. Joseph m Ann P. ----- d 1843,4,4
  bur Greenwich, O.
  Ch: Lavinia b 1839, 7, 25
    Susan Jane " 1840, 11, 28
1844, 5, 20. Ellen B. b
1844, 11, 28. Joseph, s Nathan & Deliverance,
  Huron Co., O.; m in Greenwich, Elizabeth
  D. JENNY, dt John & Catherine
1846, 3, 1. Mary P. b

1838, 2, 22. Joseph & w, Ann P., & ch, Ellen
  B., Mary P., Henrietta, Alfred, Phebe Ann,
  Agnes & Emily, rocf Little Eggharbor MM,
  N. J., dtd 1837,11,9
1840, 1, 23. James & w, Phebe Ann, & ch, Ann
  B. & Martha W., rocf Little Eggharbor MM,
  N. J., dtd 1839,4,11

BARTON
1887, 2, 17. Alice recrq
1889, 8, 22. Emma recrq
1904, 7, 21. Emma transferred from Ashton MM
1904, 7, 21. Allice transferred from Ashley
  MM
1912, 5, 16. Alice dropped from mbrp

BASH
1887, 4, 21. Willie M. & Allie M. recrq

BEADLE
1818, 8, 27. Anna & s, David, rocf Junius MM,
  N. Y., dtd 1818,1,26
1830, 12, 30. David [Beedle] Jr. dis disunity

BEARD
1838, 3, 22. Hannah, w Nathan, & ch, John,
  Oliver, Maria, Charles & George, rocf
  Dartmouth MM, Mass., dtd 1837,5,24
1838, 4, 26. John dis mcd
1887, 3, 17. Webster recrq
1889, 11, 21. Webster dropped from mbrp

BEARDSLEY
1892, 3, 17. Covington S. & Esther recrq
1893, 5, 18. C. H. & fam dropped from mbrp

BECKWITH
1889, 2, 14. Rosa dropped from mbrp

BEEBE
1838, 2, 22. Nancy (form Dillingham) dis mcd

BELL
1844, 9, 26. Abraham & w & ch, Robert W.,
  Samuel Thos., Rachel Jemima, Rebecca Fur-
  nass, Richard, Philena & Sarah Melissa,
  rocf Nottingham MM, Md., dtd 1838,3,16 (H)
1887, 2, 17. Harry recrq

1896, 2, 20. Arthur recrq
1898, 5, 19. Arthur dropped from mbrp

BELT
1900, 3, 22. Green & John recrq
1900, 4, 19. Corddlia recrq
1904, 8, 18. Green & John dropped from mbrp

BENEDICT
----, --, --. Aaron d 1825,7,27 ae 56 bur
  Peru, O.; m Esther ----- d 1825,9,25 ae
  49 bur Peru, O.
  Ch: Sarah b 1794, 5, 31
    Elizabeth " 1798, 5, 29
    Aaron L. " 1804, 7, 13
    Esther L. " 1819, 6, 10
    Phebe " 1801, 12, 6 d 1804,11,15
    bur Peru, N. Y.
----, --,---. Cyrus d 1828,5,7 ae 53 bur Mor-
  vin, O.; m Hannah ----- d 1862,8,26 bur
  Alum Creek
  Ch: Anna b 1801, 2, 22 d 1829,12,29
    bur Alum Creek
    Sylvester b 1805, 6, 25
    Clarinda " 1807, 9, 21
    Nicholas " 1810, 1, 15
    Eli   " 1812, 2, 22
    Daniel " 1814, 3, 15
    Lewis " 1816, 5, 7 d 1831, 2,25
    bur Morvin, O.
    David b 1819, 1, 24
    Henry " 1821, 3, 1
    Cyrus " 1823, 3, 3
    Charles " 1826, 8, 29 d 1841,10, 9
    bur Cookstown, Pa.
----, --, --. William d 1843,3,17 ae 67 bur
  Peru, O.; m Alse ----- d 1840,6,30 ae 55
  bur Peru, O.
  Ch: Daniel b 1807, 3, 29
    Phebe " 1809, 8, 25
    Elizabeth " 1813, 11, 25
    Aaron " 1817, 1, 21
    Sarah " 1821, 6, 30
    Anna " 1823, 8, 29 d 1912,7,27
    bur Oregon
----, --, --. Aaron d 1816,7,25 ae 75 bur
  Peru, O.; m Elizabeth ----- d 1821,8,15
  ae 80 bur Peru, O.
  Ch: Sylvester d 1821, 4, 8
    bur Peru, O.
----, --, --. Aden S. d 1843,3,21 ae 47 bur
  Peru, O.; m Sarah ----- bur Winnieshiek,
  Ia.
  Ch: Harvey b 1820, 1, 28
    Cynthia " 1821, 8, 26
    Ann   " 1824, 9, 5
    Matilda " 1827, 3, 8
    Asa A. " 1834, 3, 18
    Albert S. " 1838, 7, 22
----, --, --. John & Amy
  Ch: Lydia b 1824, 3, 13 d 1845, 4,11
    bur Peru, O.
    Rachel b 1825, 12, 25

BENEDICT, John & Amy, continued
    Ch: Israel   b 1827, 10, 14
        Emeline   " 1829, 3, 21
        Huldah   " 1831, 1, 8 d 1852, 6,27
        bur Peru, O.
        Peter   b 1832, 7, 15 " 1834,12, 9
        bur Peru, O.
        Jemima   b 1834, 7, 29
        Phebe   " 1836, 6, 28 " 1848, 9,10
        bur Peru, O.
        Melissa   b 1841, 3, 27
        Cyrus S. " 1843, 8, 19
1826, 9, 10. Allen, s Sylvester & Martha, d
    bur Peru, O.
----, --, --. Ezra d 1845,2,26 ae 41 bur Peru,
    O.; m Ruth -----
    Ch: Henry   b 1828, 8, 5
        Esther   " 1830, 4, 10
        Phebe Ann " 1831, 9, 10
        Catherine " 1834, 1, 25 d 1834, 5,29
        bur Peru, O.
        Theodore b 1835, 6, 6
        Reuben   " 1837, 11, 25 d 1841,10,24
        bur Peru, O.
        Sarah Jane b 1841, 5, 14
        Robert   " 1843, 2, 15 " 1899,--,--
        Annis   " 1845, 5, 28
----, --, --. Silvester & Susanna
    Ch: Jonathan b 1830, 4, 3
        William   " 1833, 1, 10
        Eli   " 1835, 8, 5
        John L.   " 1838, 4, 15
----, --, --. Aaron L. d 1867,6,25 bur Peru,O.;
    m Phebe H. ----- d 1885,3,20 bur Peru, O.
    Ch: Amelia F. b 1831, 11, 27 d 1871, 2,10
        bur Peru, O.
        Livius A. b 1834, 2, 26
        Charity T. " 1835, 11, 23 " 1903, 7,22
        bur Peru, O.
        Laetitia b 1837, 7, 10 " 1837, 8,18
        bur Peru, O.
        Lydia S. b 1838, 6, 24 " 1874, 3,18
        bur Peru, O.
        Edward A. b 1841, 3, 23 " 1918, 10, 6
        bur Salem, O.
        Griffith
        Bowring   b 1843, 10, 3 " 1844, 3,16
        bur Peru, O.
        Griffith
        Grafton   b 1845, 10, 3
        Phebe Alice" 1849, 12, 13 " 1851, 7,23
        bur Peru, O.
        Agnes S. b 1854, 7,31 " 1921, 2, 8
        bur Alum Creek
1831, 10, 2. Anna d ae 67 bur Peru, O.
1836, 3, 3. Martha m Aaron CHAPMAN
----, --, --. Daniel, s Wm. & Alse, Delaware
    Co., O., d 1891,4,17; m Phebe D. -----
    d 1832,12,31 bur Peru, O.
    Ch: Moses   b 1830, 5,20 d 1835, 1,23
        bur Peru, O.
    Daniel m 2nd 1837,2,9 Grace MICHINER, dt
    Mordecai & Susanna, Marion Co., O., d

1855,3,23
    Ch: Deborah S. b 1837, 12, 7 d 1878, 4,17
        Phebe A.   " 1839, 8, 12
        Dorcas   " 1841, 1, 15 " 1858, 6, 8
        Lavina H. " 1843, 7, 31 " 1902, 1, 8
        Mordecai J." 1845, 6, 26
        William   " 1847, 10, 8 " 1850, 3,17
        Esther   " 1851, 1, 12
        Martha   " 1854, 7, 25 " 1855, 1,22
    Daniel m 3rd Rachel ----- d 1881,10,13 ae
    70
1839, 1, 31. Cynthia m Nathan GRISSELL
1841, 2, 4. Harvy, s Aden S. & Sarah, Dela-
    ware Co., O.; m in Greenwich, Lavina B.
    WORSHBURN, dt Benjamin & Huldah, Huron
    Co., O.
    Ch: Margaret
        Jane   b 1846, 9, 21 d 1847, 9,10
        bur Greenwich
        Orlando   b 1848, 7, 9 " 1851, 1,31
        bur Greenwich
        Aden S.   b 1851, 1, 29
        Susan Adel-
        aide Careyb 1845, 3, 29
        Sarah Eva-
        line   " 1857, 12, 15
1841, 11, 4. Wm., s Aaron & Elizabeth, Dela-
    ware Co., O.; m in Alum Creek MH, Polly
    SIMMONS, dt Edward & Katharine SPARGER
1844, 9, 24. Sarah M. m Loren GRAY
----, --, --. Mordecai J. b 1845,6,26 d 1927,
    5,10
----, --, --. Aaron d 1905,2,17 ae 88 bur
    Alum Creek; m Caroline ----- d 1860,11,8
    bur Peru, O.
    Ch: Adessa T. b 1848, 3, 30
        Linton W. " 1850, 1, 25
        Margaret
        Jane   " 1852, 1, 6 d 1855, 7,17
        bur Peru, O.
        Wiman H.C. b 1854, 1, 17 " 1855, 7,30
        bur Peru, O.
        Direxa H. b 1856, 7, 10
        Lester   " 1858, 8, 7
        William J. " 1861, 4, 19
        Frederick M.
              b 1863, 8, 23 d 1898,10,29
        bur Alum Creek
        Charles A. b 1866, 3, 13 " 1866, 3,26
        bur Peru, O.
    Aaron m 2nd Louisa -----
    Ch: Preston H. b 1870, 4, 10
----, --, --. Eliza b 1848,12,4 d 1920,2,27
1848, 4, 29. Ella W., dt Joel & Cynthia Wil-
    lets, b
1849, 3, 23. Rachel m Robert Styles
1849, 8, 13. Sarah m Jonah Hole
----, --, --. Israel & Sarah
    Ch: Elwood   b 1850, 9, 1
        Phebe El-
        len   " 1852, 12, 24
1849, 11, 29. Emelina m David O. MICHENER
1854, 3, 6. Reuben d ae 85 bur Peru, O.

BENEDICT, continued
1854, 4, 28. Ruth m Robert COMFORT
----, --, --. Theodore d 1892,12,24 bur Alum
     Creek; m Susan -----
     Ch: Ruth
          Millicent b 1858, 8, 25
          George
          Dilwin " 1860, 8, 1 d 1865, 8,31
          bur Peru
          William " 1863, 3, 28
          Mary   " 1866, 2, 11 " 1892, 6,15
          Reuben   " 1870, 9, 29[bur AlumCreek
1859, 1, 28. Esther m Levi COWGILL
----, --, --. Levius A. d 1908,8,16 ae 74 bur
     Alum Creek; m Penelope J. ----- d 1874,2,
     27 bur Peru
     Charles
          Bowring b 1861, 11, 24
          Greenleaf
          W.   " 1864, 1, 16
          Elbert L. " 1866, 3, 18
          Walter
          Levering " 1870, 8, 16
     Levius m 2nd Mary BINNS d 1884,2,19 bur
     Alum Creek
     Ch: Nellie
          Ruthamie b 1880, 8, 26
     Levius m 3rd Mary K. ----- d 1892,--,0-
     Levius m 4th Rachel J. P. -----
1865, 4, 27. Lydia L. m Joseph H. JOHNSON
1866, 12, 29. Amelia F. m Jonathan STANLEY
1867, 3, 4. Martha W., dt Thomas & Kate
     (Howard) Wood, b
1867, 10, 24. Edward A., s Aaron L. & Phebe
     N., Morrow Co., O.; m in Alum Creek MH,
     Susan HATHAWAY, dt Caleb & Rachel, Erie
     Co., O.
     Ch: Carlos
          Christie b 1868, 8, 1
          Mary   " 1873, 7, 29
1870, 10, 27. Adessa T. m Albert J. STEWARD
1872, 7, 29. Katharine d ae 77 bur Peru, O.
----, --, --. Mordecai J. & Eliza G.
     Ch: Almira P. b 1874, 9, 14 d 1901, 9,14
          bur Alum Creek
          Grace M.   b 1878, 4, 29
          Anna Billa " 1881, 5, 1
          Mary Elnora" 1889, 1, 16
1873, 11, 27. Esther m Thos. Clarkson WILLIAMS
1881, 10, 13. Rachel d ae 71
1892, 10, 20. S. Levering b (s Wm. H. & Fannie
     E.)
----, --, --. Preston H. & May
     Ch: Walter
          Pearl   b 1894, 5, 1
          Merrell " 1903, 12, 31 d 1905,--,--
          bur Alum Creek
----, --, --. Walter, s Lewis A. & Penelope
     (Johnson), b 1870,8,16; m Katie O. OSBORN,
     dt Geo. & Sarah (Wood), b 1875,9,8
     Ch: Ramona
          Leila   b 1894, 12, 6
          Elizabeth

          Penelope b 1896, 9, 19
     Ch: Willard   " 1898, 4, 5
          Ruth
          Catharine " 1902, 11, 10
          George
          Lewis   " 1906, 3, 18
          Charles
          Edward   " 1908, 3, 31
----, --,---. Reuben & Florence
     Ch: Hugh Conray
                    b 1896, 8, 18
          Rollin
          Gretchel " 1898, 5, 5
1923, 10, 18. Elizabeth Penelope m Ralph
     BORING

1819, 5, 27. Sarah (form Gidley) dis mcd
1819, 9, 30. Sarah rstrq
1819, 12, 30. John recrq
1921, 2, 1. Sylvester & ch, Cyrus, Allen,
     Gideon, Ira, Mary, William, Jane & Amos,
     recrq
1822, 2, 28. Anna Daniels (form Benedict)
     con mcd
1822, 6, 27. Anna recrq
1823, 1, 30. John rmt Amy Gidley
1823, 5, 29. Harvey & Cynthia, ch Sarah,
     recrq
1824, 4, 1. Ezra recrq
1824, 4, 29. Aden S. recrq
1825, 3, 31. Sylvester con mcd
1825, 4, 28. Elizabeth rmt Daniel Wood
1825, 6, 30. Clarinda Lingshore (form Bene-
     dict) con mcd
1827, 11, 1. Ezra rmt Ruth Gidley
1827, 12, 27. Aaron L. rmt Phebe H. Wing
1828, 7, 3. Gideon dis disunity
1828, 7, 31. Susannah recrq
1828, 10, 2. Daniel rmt Phebe Gidley Jr.
1828, 10, 2. Cyrus dis mcd
1829, 4, 30. Nicholas dis mcd
1830, 7, 29. Eli con mcd
1830, 9, 2. John dis disunity
1831, 6, 2. Ezra dis disunity
1831, 12, 30. Mary dis jas
1832, 4, 26. Reuben dis mcd
1832, 7, 26. Daniel dis mcd
1832, 11, 22. Hannah rmt Wm. Gidley
1835, 1, 22. William 2nd dis disunity
1835, 11, 26. Henry, minor, gct Smithfield MM,
     O.
1836, 1, 26. Elizabeth McClary (form Bene-
     dict) dis mcd
1836, 5, 26. Jane dis jas
1837, 6, 22. Cyrus, minor, gct Smithfield MM
1840, 1, 23. Cyrus rst
1841, 1, 28. Amos dis jas
1841, 1, 28. Charles, minor, gct Providence
     MM, Pa.
1842, 7, 28. Phebe Barber (form Benedict) dis
     mcd
1843, 1, 26. David con mcd
1843, 5, 23. David gct Vermillion MM, Ill.

BENEDICT, continued
1846, 2, 20. Cert rec for Cyrus & w, Hannah
        C., from Providence MM, Pa., dtd 1845,10,
        2, endorsed to Vermillion MM, Ill.
1847, 1, 28. Aaron con'mcd
1849, 11, 22. Reuben rst
1849, 12, 28. Israel con mcd
1850, 3, 28. Katharine recrq
1854, 4, 26. Harvey & w, Lavina, & s, Adin
        S., & adopted dt, Susan Adelaide Coney,
        rocf MississinewaMM, Ind., dtd 1854,2,15
1854, 8, 24. Amy & ch gct Driftwood MM, Ind.
1854, 8, 24. Jemima gct Driftwood MM, Ind.
1855, 8, 23. Henry gct Winneshiek MM, Ia.
1855, 11, 22. Israel & w, Sarah, & ch, El-
        wood & Phebe Ellen, gct Driftwood MM, Ind.
1856, 12, 25. Theodore H. dis mcd
1857, 10, 22. Henry O. rocf Winneshiek MM,
        Ia., dtd 1857,9,2
1859, 8, 25. Albert A. gct Winneshiek MM, Ia.
1860, 3, 22. Daniel gct Goshen MM, to m Ra-
        chel Stanley
1860, 6, 21. Harvey & w, Lovina B., & ch,
        Aden S., Sarah Evaline & adopted dt, Su-
        san Coney, gct Gilead MM
1860, 7, 26. Livius A. gct New Garden MM, O.,
        to m Penelope Johnson
1860, 11, 22. Rachel rocf Goshen MM, dtd
        1860,11,17
1861, 3, 28. Penelope J. rocf New Garden MM,
        dtd 1861,3,20
1861, 7, 18. Jane Comfort (form Benedict) con
        mcd
1861, 7, 18. Henry O. con mcd
1862, 4, 17. Israel & w, Sarah, & ch, Elwood
        & Phebe Ellen, rocf Grove MM, Ind., dtd
        1862,2,27
1863, 10, 22. Asa A. gct Winneshiek MM, Ia.
1864, 1, 21. Caroline A., w Aaron, & ch,
        Odessa T., Linton W., Direxa H., Lester
        Wm. & Frederick M., recrq
1864, 9, 15. Israel & w, Sarah, & ch, Elwood,
        Phebe Ellen & Leenora, gct Caesars Creek
        MM, O.
1868, 1, 16. Robert con mcd
1868, 5, 21. Robert gct Winneshiek MM, Ia.
1868, 7, 16. Phebe A. Doty (form Benedict)
        dis mcd
1869, 1, 21. Aaron gct Plainfield MM, Ind.,
        to m Louisa Meeker
1869, 5, 20. Louisa M. rocf Plainfield MM,
        Ind., dtd 1869,3,31
1871, 8, 17. Mordecai J. con mcd
1871, 9, 21. Phebe Ann gct Winneshiek MM,Ia.
1874, 4, 16. Eliza G. recrq
1874, 6, 18. G. Grafton gct Gilead MM, to m
        Ellen Willits
1875, 3, 18. Theodore & w, Susan, & ch, Mary,
        Wm. & Reuben, recrq
1875, 3, 18. Ruth Milicent recrq
1875, 7, 22. Ellen W. rocf Gilead MM
1877, 11, 15. Edward A. & w, Susan H., & ch,
        Carlos Christy & Mary, gct Salem MM

1879, 9, 18. Mary B. rocf Columbus MM, O.,
        dtd 1879,9,3
1882, 3, 16. Francis Marion recrq
1884, 2, 18. Laura E. recrq
1884, 7, 17. Linton W. & Francis M. dropped
        from mbrp
1884, 8, 21. Wm. J. dropped from mbrp
1885, 4, 16. Martha E. relrq
1885, 7, 16. Lester P. relrq
1885, 7, 16. Frederick M. relrq
1886, 8, 19. Mary R. rocf Rollin MM, Mich.,
        dtd 1886,7,31
1887, 12, 22. Annis O. relrq
1892, 5, 19. Fannie E. rocf Maryville MM,
        Tenn., dtd 1892,3,26
1893, 8, 17. Grafton & fam rocf Ashley MM
1893, 12, 21. N. Edgar & Martha E. recrq
1894, 3, 22. Katie O. recrq
1894, 6, 21. Rachel J. P. rocf Westfield MM,
        Ind.
1895, 5, 16. Florence A. recrq
1896, 7, 16. Cora dropped from mbrp
1899, 3, 16. Wm. H. & w, Fannie, & s, Lever-
        ing, gct Marysville MM, Tenn.
1902, 4, 17. Edgar N. gct Delphi MM
1904, 3, 17. N. Edgar rocf Delphi MM
1904, 3, 17. Ethel & Francis relrq
1905, 3, 16. N. Edgar relrq
1909, 4, 15. Rachel E. gct S. 8th St., Rich-
        mond, Ind.
1917, 4, 19. Reuben, Florence, Hugh, Rolland,
        Marie & Ruth Della dropped from mbrp
1922, 1, 19. Ella Heverlo recrq
1923, 12, 20. Walter A. relrq
1926, 11, 18. Eliza M. rocf Rush Creek MM, dtd
        1926,10,27

BENSCHOTER
1930, 7, 1. Ann (form Mullenix) dis mcd

BENSON
1917, 6, 21. Harry recrq

BERRY
1904, 7, 21. Sylvia transferred from Ashton
        MM
1912, 5, 16. Sylvia dropped from mbrp

BIGGS
1903, 3, 14. Dora, dt Martin & Bertha (Green)
        Sperry, b

BIRDSELL
1835, 10, 29. Ann M. m Benj. JENNY

1834, 10, 23. Ann M. rocf Marlborough MM,
        N. Y., dtd 1834,2,26
1834, 10, 23. Jane F. rocf Marlborough MM,
        N. Y., dtd 1834,2,26
1836, 8, 25. Zephaniah [Birdsall] & w, Anna,
        rocf Marlborough MM, N. Y., dtd 1836,8,24

BISEL
1881, 5, 19. Eliza Vore relrq

BLACKBURN
1850, 10, 24. Thomas rst on consent of Provi-
    dence MM
1870, 2, 17. Thomas gct Alliance MM, O.

BLACKMARR
----, --, --. Edwin & Ann [Blackmer]
    Ch: Byron D.
        Oliette   b 1846, 5, 22
        Melvin Lo-
        renzo   " 1850, 11, 6
1847, 7, 19. Rosina [Blackmer], dt Lorenzo
    & Ann, b

1842, 5, 26. Anna [Blackmore] (form Washburn)
    rpd mcd
1843, 6, 22. Edwin recrq
1849, 9, 24. Anna & ch, Byron D. & Oliette,
    rocf Greenwich MM, dtd 1849,7,20
1851, 7, 24. Anna & ch, Byron D., Oliette &
    Melvin Lorenzo, gct Mississinewa MM, Ind.
1851, 7, 24. Ann gct Mississinewa MM, Ind.
1855, 1, 25. Ann E. rocf Mississinewa MM,
    Ind., dtd 1854,12,13
1856, 4, 24. Rosina, dt Ann, recrq
1857, 12, 24. Ann E. & dt, Rosina F., gct
    Winneshiek MM, Ia.

BLAIR
1887, 3, 17. Luella rocf Gilead MM

BENBOW
1887, 4, 21. Stephen recrq

BOHAM
1887, 1, 20. Rosa recrq
1887, 1, 20. Tina recrq
1887, 2, 17. Maggie recrq
1887, 2, 17. Etta recrq
1887, 2, 17. Thomas recrq
1889, 2, 14. Thomas dropped from mbrp
1912, 5, 16. George dropped from mbrp

BOMBARGER
1907, 2, 14. Hazel Gertrude recrq
1912, 5, 16. Hazel [Bomberger] dropped from
    mbrp

BONSIER
1892, 7, 21. Mary W. dropped from mbrp

BOOTH
1920, 5, 20. Marion relrq

BORING
1923, 10, 18. Ralph m Elizabeth Penelope
    BENEDICT

1923, 12, 20. Elizabeth Benedict gct Lincoln
    MM, Va.

BOWERMAN
1917, 11, 15. Harley & w, Florence, recrq
1918, 3, 21. Maude recrq
1924, 10, 16. Harley & w, Florence M., & ch,
    Maude A. & Howard Roy, gct Rush Creek MM

BOWMAN
1887, 4, 21. Maud recrq

BRADLEY
1887, 2, 17. Flora recrq
1890, 2, 13. Gladys recrq

BRADRICK
1871, 9, 3. Elizabeth d ae 73 bur Middlebury
    O. (w Paul)

BRADY
1836, 6, 30. Charity m Daniel OSBORN

1827, 5, 23. Charity [Braidy] recrq

BRADSHAW
1891, 1, 22. Mahlon & Angelina relrq

BRODRICK
1848, 11, 1. Eliza m Joseph VORE
1853, 4, 6. Nancy m Daniel MOSHER

1846, 3, 26. Sarah recrq
1848, 3, 23. Eliza recrq
1852, 3, 25. Nancy recrq
1855, 2, 22. Rebecca recrq
1860, 4, 26. Paul recrq
1861, 11, 21. Paul [Broderick] gct Goshen MM,
    to m Elizabeth Elliott
1862, 6, 19. Paul con mcd
1862, 11, 20. Elizabeth rocf Goshen MM, dtd
    1862,10,18
1868, 4, 10. Rebecca Green (form Broderick)
    con mcd

BROWN
1860, 4, 26. Samuel P. rocf Goose Creek MM,
    Va., dtd 1860,1,12 (H)
1887, 3, 17. James, Laroy & Lizzie recrq
1887, 4, 21. Evaline recrq
1887, 4, 21. Nannie recrq
1891, 3, 19. Myrtle O. gct Greenwich MM

BRUDEHAN
1890, 3, 20. Mahlon & Angelina recrq

BRYANT
1861, 5, 23. Martha (form Purviance) dis mcd

BUCK
1823, 9, 19. Phebe, w Israel, d bur Peru, O.
    (ae 61)
----, --, --. Frank M. & Carrie S.
    Ch: Verda D.   d 1889, 4,--
        bur Alum Creek
        Virgil P. b 1883, 10, 25

BUCK, continued

1817, 11, 27. Andrew con mcd
1829, 1, 25. Phebe Allen (form Buck) dis mcd
1830, 1, 28. Andrew dis jas
1877, 5, 17. Francis M. recrq
1882, 4, 20. Serepta Caroline recrq
1886, 3, 18. Verda recrq
1886, 12, 16. Andrew recrq
1917, 4, 19. Maud recrq
1921, 4, 21. Dorothy recrq
1923, 3, 22. Rachel Marietta & Ralph Marion
    recrq
1923, 6, 21. Virgil relrq

BUNKER

----, --, --. Isaac m Mary ----- d 1845,7,25 ae
    64 bur Peru, O.
       Ch: Slocum H. b 1805, 10, 7
           David   " 1807, 6, 11 d 1824, 9,13
            bur Morvin
           John   " 1808, 10, 24
           Thomas   " 1811, 4, 14
           Peleg   " 1812, 12, 21
           Isaac Jr. " 1814, 10, 10
           Sylvia   " 1817, 5, 10
           Henry   " 1819, 8, 2
           Mehitable " 1821, 3, 15
           Joseph   " 1823, 5, 15 d 1841, 9,14
           Justin H. " 1827, 3, 3
           Hannah   " 1829, 2, 20
----, --, --. Peleg d 1825,8,18 bur Marvin;
    m Hannah -----
       Ch: Elihu   b 1807, 3, 29
           Lucy   " 1808, 5, 22
           Reuben   " 1810, 5, 1 d 1870, 1, 5
            bur Peru
           Isaac   " 1813, 8, 1
           Lydia   " 1815, 6, 3
           Mary   " 1816, 1, 15 d 1874, 6,23
            bur Peru
           Silas   " 1819, 1, 29
           Jethro   " 1821, 8, 21
           David   " 1824, 3, 15
----, --, --. Slocum & Matilda
       Ch: Jane   b 1827, 10, 23
           David   " 1830, 7, 3
           Alice
           Rachel
           Julia
1831, 1, 8. Mary D., dt Robert W. & Mira, b
1832, 10, 7. Rosanna, dt Isaac L. & Emilia, b
1845, 7, 25. Mary d ae 64 bur Peru, O.
----, --, --. Byron & Sophia
       Ch: Minerva b 1865, 5, 3
           Cora   " 1867, 3, 20
           Lida   " 1869, 1, 20
           Katie   " 1871, 12, 12
           Elmora   " 1875, 10, 12
           William R. " 1878, 1, 3
1873, 10, 7. Clyde, s Elwood & Alice (Sage),b
1874, 4, 7. Hattie, dt Sanford & Mary (Find-
    ley), b

1818, 3, 5. Slocum, John, David, Thomas,
    Peleg, Isaac & Sylvia, ch Isaac, recrq
1824, 12, 2. Jonathan & w, Comfort, & dt,
    Susan, rocf Farmington MM, N. Y., dtd
    1824,4,29
1824, 12, 2. Robert A. rocf Farmington MM,
    N. Y., dtd 1824,4,29
1824, 12, 2. Emeline rocf Farmington MM,
    N. Y., dtd 1824,4,29
1824, 12, 2. Sarah P. rocf Farmington MM,
    N. Y., dtd 1824,4,29
1825, 7, 28. Sarah P. rmt Asa Mosher, Jr.
1825, 12, 1. Emeline Meeker (form Bunker)
    dis mcd
1826, 6, 29. Mary, w Isaac, & ch, Henry, Me-
    hitable & Joseph, recrq
1826, 12, 28. Slocum rmt Matilda Wood
1827, 8, 29. Susanna C. rmt Peleg Mosher
1827, 11, 29. John dis disunity
1828, 8, 28. Elihu dis disunity
1828, 11, 27. Isaac dis jH
1828, 11, 27. Slocum dis jH
1829, 4, 2. Hannah & Matilda dis jH
1829, 10, 29. Robert rmt Mira Dillingham
1831, 12, 30. Reuben dis disunity
1833, 1, 24. Isaac S. dis mcd
1833, 3, 21. Mila (form Slyter) dis mcd
1833, 2, 21. Slocum dis disunity (H)
1833, 7, 25. Jonathan & w gct White River MM,
    Ind.
1833, 10, 24. Robert W. & w, Mira, & ch, Mary
    D. & Hannah R., gct White River MM, Ind.
1834, 4, 24. Elizabeth Jane con mcd
1834, 8, 4. Isaac Jr. dis disunity
1834, 8, 21. Peleg dis disunity
1834, 12, 25. Thomas dis disunity
1836, 12, 22. Milia (form Slyter) con mcd (H)
1838, 6, 21. Lucy Purvis (form Bunker) con
    mcd
1840, 7, 23. Jane gct Adrian MM, Mich.
1841, 4, 22. Matilda, w Slocum, & ch, Jane,
    David, Alice, Rachel & Julia, gct Battle-
    creek MM, Mich. (H)
1843, 1, 26. Hannah rst at Gilead MM on con-
    sent of this mtg
1844, 1, 25. Mehitable dis jas
1844, 1, 25. Hannah dis jas
1844, 8, 22. Henry dis disunity
1844, 8, 22. Justin dis jas
1848, 7, 20. Milia gct Fall Creek MM, Ind.(H)
1859, 1, 27. David rocf Gilead MM, dtd 1858,
    12,21
1863, 4, 16. Reuben rst at Gilead MM on con-
    sent of this mtg
1864, 1, 21. Jethro rst
1864, 4, 21. Nancy recrq
1864, 10, 20. Edwin M. rocf Goshen MM, dtd
    1864,9,17
1865, 8, 17. Elizabeth J. rst on consent of
    Gilead MM
1866, 12, 20. Reuben rocf Gilead MM, dtd 1866,
    12,18
1867, 6, 20. Edwin M. con mcd

BUNKER, continued
1867, 8, 22. Lucretia recrq
1867, 9, 19. Jethro gct Summerset MM, N. Y.
1868, 4, 16. Lindley H. recrq
1868, 5, 21. Edwin gct Gilead MM
1869, 4, 15. Elisha rst
1874, 8, 20. Eva recrq
1875, 3, 18. Byron recrq
1875, 3, 18. Sylvia & dt, Minerva, recrq
1877, 4, 19. Sanaford recrq
1877, 4, 19. Elwood recrq
1877, 4, 19. Alice M. recrq
1877, 11, 15. Elihu & Elizabeth gct Gilead MM
1878, 6, 20. Lindley H. relrq
1879, 7, 17. Mary recrq
1882, 3, 16. Elmer recrq
1882, 10, 19. David O. dis disunity
1884, 11, 20. Nancy relrq
1885, 3, 19. Clyde recrq
1889, 2, 14. Ella recrq
1890, 5, 22. Byron & Silvia relrq
1892, 3, 17. Hattie recrq
1894, 2, 15. Lulu recrq
1895, 3, 21. Lenora C. recrq
1896, 7, 16. Wm. R. dropped from mbrp
1896, 7, 16. Minnie dropped from mbrp
1896, 7, 16. May dropped from mbrp
1896, 7, 16. Eva Fay dropped from mbrp
1896, 7, 16. Elwood dropped from mbrp
1896, 7, 16. Alice dropped from mbrp
1901, 2, 14. Rose recrq
1918, 3, 21. Virgil recrq
1919, 11, 20. Dora James recrq

BURK
1842, 11, 24. Abigail (form Barnard) dis mcd
1848, 5, 25. Hannah [Burke] (form Smith) dis
    mcd

BUTLER
1835, 4, 30. Jane d (H)
1858, 4, 10. Hannah d bur Whitstone, O. (H)

1835, 5, 21. Barak & w, Hannah, & ch, Jona-
    than, Deborah & David, rocf Short Creek
    MM, O., dtd 1835,3,26 (H)
1835, 8, 20. Jane rocf Short Creek MM, O.,
    dtd 1835,3,26 (H)
1843, 9, 21. Deborah Wells (form Butler) dis
    mcd (H)
1844, 1, 25. David dis mcd (H)
1851, 4, 24. Jonathan dis mcd (H)

CACKER
1887, 2, 17. D. C. recrq
1889, 2, 14. David [Cackler] dropped from
    mbrp

CADWALADER
1923, 7, --. Rayburn m Ruth WINDSOR

1923, 8, 16. Ruth Windsor gct Wilmington MM,O.

CAITY
1887, 5, 19. John C. recrq

CAMP
1826, 12, 28. Sarah (form Shaw) dis mcd

CAMPBELL
1889, 2, 14. C. W. recrq

CAMPTON
1887, 2, 17. John R. & Maria recrq

CAMPFIELD
1847, 4, 22. Armelia (form Farrington) dis
    mcd (H)

CAREY
----, --, --. Benjamin & Rachel
    Ch: Benjamin L.b 1824, 11, 21
    (Rachel, w Benjamin, d 1825,9,5 ae 35 bur
    Bucyrus)
----, --, --. Abel & Susanna
    Ch: Martha   b 1827, 8, 8
        Barclay   " 1829, 5, 16
        Franklin   " 1832, 8, 29
        Nancy   " 1834, 9, 4
1930, 11, 6. Myron Leslie, s Kenneth & Ag-
    nes (Wilkins), b

1823, 6, 25. Lewis & w, Rachel & ch, Susan,
    Abel, William, Aaron, Edmund, Isabella,
    Sarah & George, rocf Smithfield MM, dtd
    1822,10,21
1824, 4, 29. Abel recrq
1825, 12, 1. Susan Merriman (form Cary) dis
    mcd
1827, 2, 1. Abel con mcd
1827, 5, 3. Susannah (form Kirk) con mcd
1831, 3, 3. Abel gct Salem MM
1832, 6, 21. Edmund, s Lewis, gct Salem MM
1837, 2, 23. Sarah Ann (form Kirk) dis mcd
1837, 6, 22. Aaron dis disunity
1929, 10, 17. Kenneth & Agnes rocf Mt. Carmel
    MM
1932, 10, 19. Kenneth & w, Agnes, & s, Myron,
    gct Newport News MM

CARNES
----, --, --. Harley F., s Albert & Mary C.,
    b 1895,2,28 d 1895,12,31 bur Peru, O.

1891, 4, 16. Albert I. & w, Mary C., & ch,
    Flora, Sylvester Monroe, Jennie & Cora J.,
    recrq
1895, 4, 18. Effie recrq
1898, 7, 21. Lenna recrq
1902, 6, 19. Albert relrq
1907, 7, 18. Monroe dropped from mbrp
1923, 3, 22. Luella Mae recrq
1923, 10, 24. Luella rmt John Sherman

CARPENTER
1829, 1, 29. Henry, Sarah, David & Adny,

CARPENTER, continued
    minors, rocf Plains MM, N. Y., dtd 1828,
    3,25
1830, 7, 1. Sarah Hyte (form Carpenter) dis
    mcd
1832, 10, 25. Robert & w, Elizabeth, & ch,
    Phebe, Sophia, Mary, Henry, Isaac, David,
    Eliza & Deborah Ann, rocf Plains MM, dtd
    1832,7,26
1833, 11, 21. Sarah Hite (form Carpenter) dis
    mcd
1834, 4, 24. Mary dis disunity
1834, 5, 22. Phebe Holiday (form Carpenter)
    dis mcd
1834, 8, 21. Mary dis disunity
1837, 2, 23. Henry dis disunity
1837, 7, 20. Isaac dis disunity
1842, 10, 27. Sophia Turner (form Carpenter)
    dis mcd
1843, 4, 27. David dis disunity
**1844, 11, 21. Testimonial against Eliza Ann
    Tinney (form Carpenter) dis disunity**
1879, 9, 18. Aaron recrq

CARTER
1857, 7, 23. James & w, Julia, & ch, Joel B.,
    Joseph, Henry, Elton C., Levi S. & John
    S., rocf Silllwater MM, O., dtd 1857,6,20
    (H)

CARTY
1907, 7, 18. John dropped from mbrp

CASE
1890, 1, 16. A. J. recrq
1890, 1, 16. G. W. recrq
1890, 1, 16. Etta recrq
1890, 1, 16. Sarah recrq
1890, 1, 16. Charles recrq

CATT
1929, 4, 18. George & w, Ella, recrq
1930, 2, 13. George & Ella relrq

CATTELL
1927, 10, 13. Catherine DeVol gct Sullivant
    Ave. MM, Columbus

CECIL
1887, 3, 17. Esther rocf Gilead MM
1887, 3, 17. Naomi rocf Gilead MM
1887, 3, 17. Mollie rocf Gilead MM

CHAMBERS
----, --, --. John m Mary Ann ----- d 1846,9,2
    ae 46 bur Middlebury
    Ch: Deborah   b 1824, 7, 1 d 1847,10,25
        Ann Eliza " 1828, 2, 27
        Sarah Jane " 1830, 2, 24 " 1846,10,9
        bur Middlebury   [bur Perry, O.
        Mary Ellen b 1834, 9,10 " 1837,11,26
        Lewis D. b 1840, 7, 10
    John, s Samuel & Deborah, Richland Co.,
    O.; m 2nd Rachel W. LEWIS, dt Jonathan

S. & Lavina WRIGHT, Harrison Co., O., d
    1858,5,6 ae 45 bur Middlebury(m 1848,2,2)
    Ch: Eunace   b 1849, 4, 8
----, --, --. James & Mary
    Ch: Samuel   b 1834, 2, 1
        Luke   " 1835, 11, 14 d 1839, 8,10
        bur Middlebury
        John   b 1837, 11, 18
        William T. " 1841, 5, 4
        Robert El-
        wood   " 1843, 8, 14
        Priscilla
        Elma   " 1852, 3, 25
        Elihu   " 1849, 6, 22
1861, 8, 28. John C., s James & Mary, Knox
    Co., O.; m in Owl Creek, Jane W. LEWIS,
    dt Jason & Rachel

1824, 3, 4. John & w, Mary Ann, rocf Plain-
    field MM, dtd 1823,12,25
1829, 12, 3. Samuel & w, Tamer, & ch, Mar-
    garet & Ann, rocf Stillwater MM, dtd
    1829,10,24
1832, 3, 29. Samuel & fam gct Stillwater MM
1834, 5, 22. James & w, Mary, & s, Samuel,
    rocf Stillwater MM, dtd 1834,3,22
1851, 10, 23. Ann Eliza Mires (form Chambers)
    dis mcd
1860, 7, 26. John & ch, Lewis D. & Eunice,
    gct Sandy Spring MM, O.
1862, 9, 18. Mary dis
1863, 3, 19. James & ch, Elihu, Priscilla E.,
    & David, gct Pleasant Hill MM
1864, 6, 16. John C. & Jane & s, Elmore L.,
    gct Springdale MM

CHAPMAN
1836, 3, 3. Aaron, s Aaron & Mary, Columbi-
    ana Co., O.; m in Alum Creek MH, Martha
    BENEDICT, dt Robert & Mary ALLEN
1870, 7, 17. Martha d ae 84 bur Peru, O.
1871, 2, 23. Aaron d ae 86 bur Peru, O.

1836, 4, 21. Aaron rocf Upper Springfield
    MM, O., dtd 1836,3,26
1837, 3, 23. Mary J. rocf Marlborough MM,
    dtd 1836,3,29
1877, 4, 19. Norton D. recrq
1883, 7, 19. Norton C. dropped from mbrp

CHAPPELL
----, --, --. Henry N. & Matilda B.
    Ch: Merritt
        Brown   b 1846, 11, 29
        Sarah Jane " 1848, 6, 18
        James
        Douglas " 1849, 12, 1
        Cynthia Ann" 1851, 1, 25

1849, 6, 22. Henry N. recrq
1849, 10, 26. Merritt Brown & Sarah Jane, ch
    Henry N. & Matilda B., recrq
1851, 7, 24. Henry N. & w, Matilda, & ch,

CHAPPELL, continued
    Merritt Brown, Sarah Jane, James Douglas &
    Cynthia Ann, gct Mississinewa MM, Grant
    Co., Ind.

CHASE
1839, 6, 20. Nehemiah & w, Mary, & ch, Han-
    nah, Eliza, Wm., Joseph, Benjamin & Geo.,
    rocf Troy MM, N. Y., dtd 1838,12,13 (H)
1859, 7, 21. Nehemiah & w, Mary, & s, Thomas,
    gct Prairie Grove MM, Ia. (H)
1878, 8, 22. Charles recrq
1883, 7, 19. Charles dropped from mbrp
1890, 5, 22. Charles rstrq
1892, 7, 21. Charles dropped from mbrp

CLARK
1884, 2, 18. Charles S. recrq
1885, 1, 22. Charles S. relrq

CLAYPOLE
1894, 12, 20. Nancy, dt Mark Pettet, b

1916, 6, 15. Lindy dropped from mbrp

CLIFTON
1884, 4, 17. Charles & Margaret recrq
1885, 3, 19. Charles K. relrq
1886, 3, 18. Charles R. recrq
1904, 7, 21. Charles K. transferred from
    Ashley MM
1912, 5, 16. Charles dropped from mbrp

COATS
1840, 1, 9. Preston d ae 34y 8m bur San-
    dusky, O.

----, --, --. Isaac & Sarah Ann
    Ch: Phebe   d 1839, 6,11
            bur Chester Co., Pa.
        Rebecca   b 1840, 10, 5
        Joshua
        Richards   " 1843, 4, 15
1843, 9, 7. Lydie m Jacob L. MITCHNER (H)

1839, 8, 22. Preston & w, Mary Ann, & ch,
    Isaac Preston, Amelia Baker & James Sea-
    more, rocf Fallowfield MM, Pa., dtd 1839,
    5,11 (H)
1839, 8, 22. Isaac & w, Sarah Ann, & dt,
    Phebe R., rocf Fallowfield MM, Pa., dtd
    1839,4,17 (H)
1841, 9, 23. Deborah & dt, Rachel, rocf
    Phila. MM, Pa., dtd 1841,6,16 (H)
1841, 9, 23. Rebecca rocf Phila. MM, Pa.,
    dtd 1841,6,16 (H)
1842, 8, 25. Hannah rocf Concord MM, dtd
    1842,6,22 (H)
1842, 8, 25. Lydia rocf Concord MM, dtd
    1842,6,22 (H)
1846, 4, 23. Deborah gct Cincinnati MM, O.(H)
1847, 1, 21. Rebecca gct Cincinnati MM,O.(H)
1851, 1, 23. Mary Ann Goss (form Coats) con

mcd (H)

COLFLESH
1890, 1, 16. James recrq
1890, 1, 16. J. C. recrq
1890, 1, 16. Emma recrq
1890, 1, 16. Samuel recrq

COLLINS
1819, 7, 1. Benjamin rocf Farmington MM,
    dtd 1817,2,20, endorsed by Short Creek
    MM, 1819,2,23
1824, 12, 30. Benjamin dis jas
1831, 6, 30. Abram Jr. rocf Collins MM, N.Y.
    dtd 1831,5,26

COMBA
1834, 10, --. Benjamin d bur Friends Bur Gr,
    Knox Co., O.
1844, 7, 29. Samuel C. d bur Owl Creek (H)

1828, 11, 27. Benjamin & w, Charity, & three
    ch rocf Plainfield MM, dtd 1827,11,22(H)
1831, 1, 20. Benjamin Jr. dis disunity (H)
1831, 9, 15. Rebecca dis (H)
1839, 9, 23. Rebecca R. rst (H)

COMFORT
1851, 3, 24. Rhoda d bur Middlebury
1851, 6, 12. Robert Sr. d ae 88 bur Middle-
    bury, O.
1853, 4, 28. Robert, s Robert & Mary, Knox
    Co., O.; m in Alum Creek MH, Ruth BENE-
    DICT dt Wm. & Phebe, Morrow Co., O.
1861, 2, 6. Mary d ae 91 bur Middlebury,O.
1864, 6, 4. Robert d ae 67 bur Drummer,
    Grove, Ill.
1874, 3, 26. Ruth m Daniel OSBORN

1839, 8, 22. Robert & w, Mary, rocf Hartland
    MM, N. Y., dtd 1839,3,21
1839, 8, 22. Robert Jr. & w, Rhoda, & ch,
    Sarah, Phebe, Stephen, Edwin M., Robert
    P., William, James H. & Ezra, rocf Hart-
    land MM, N. Y., dtd 1839,3,21
1850, 12, 26. Stephen D. dis mcd
1851, 2, 20. Edwin W. dis disunity
1854, 6, 22. William dis mcd
1854, 10, 26. Dorcas (form Earl) dis mcd
1857, 10, 22. Robert P. con mcd
1861, 5, 23. Ezra dis disunity
1861, 7, 18. Jane (form Benedict) con mcd
1861, 7, 18. James H. con mcd
1864, 5, 17. Robert P. gct Red Cedar MM, Ia.
1864, 5, 19. James H. & w, Sarah Jane, & ch,
    Ezra, gct Red Cedar MM, Ia.
1924, 10, 16. Fred & w, Effie Arms, rocf
    Carmel MM
1929, 9, 19. Fred & w, Effie Arns, gct E.
    Richland MM
1932, 12, 22. Fred & w, Effie Arms, rocf E.
    Richland MM

CONE
1836, 8, 25. Birthday rocf Scipio MM, dtd
     1836,8,17

CONEY
1854, 4, 26. Susan Adelaide, adopted dt Har-
     vey & Lavina Benedict, roct Mississinewa
     MM, Ind., dtd 1854,2,15
1860, 6, 21. Benedict & w, Lovina B., & ch,
     Aden S. & Sarah Evaline, & adopted dt, Su-
     san Coney, gct Gilead MM

CONSTANT
1833, 10, 24. Benona & w, Lydia, & ch, Jona-
     than, Samuel, Zephaniah, Charles, Edgar,
     Benona, rocf Marlborough MM, N. Y., dtd
     1833,2,27

COOK
1825, 1, 27. Jennette recrq
1866, 3, 18. Ellen recrq
1890, 3, 20. Ellen recrq

COOMER
1887, 2, 17. Emma recrq
1890, 2, 13. Edward recrq
1911, 2, 16. Elbert recrq
1916, 6, 15. Elbert dropped from mbrp

COPE
1907, 2, 14. Alverda recrq
1909, 1, 21. Stanley rocf Salem MM, O.
1910, 11, 17. Stanley gct Alliance MM

COPPOCK
1867, 7, 24. Timothy d bur Peru, O.

1859, 7, 28. Timothy [Coppic] rocf New Garden
     MM, O., dtd 1859,1,19

CORBIN
----, --, --. Grover D. m Ellen Rhoda PHILLIPS
     dt John & Amelia, b 1890,8,23
     Ch: Ludlow Vin-
            cent   b 1915, 2, 21
         Betty Ilene"   1918, 7, 23

1932, 4, 21. Ellen Rhoda, Betty Ilene & Lud-
     low Vincent, recrq

COREY
1892, 3, 17. Nicy Lavina recrq

COTANT
1845, 9, 22. Joseph H. rocf Abington MM, Pa.,
     dtd 1845,8,25
1845, 12, 25. Gideon B. rocf Abington MM, Pa.
     dtd 1845,8,25
1846, 9, 21. Charles rocf Abington MM, Pa.,
     dtd 1846,5,25
1847, 6, 25. Samuel con mcd
1848, 2, 25. Joseph con mcd
1848, 7, 27. Charles con mcd

----, --, --. Benona & Lydia
     Ch: Jonathan   b 1822, 4, 24
         Samuel   " 1823, 12, 18
         Zephaniah   " 1825, 11, 30
         Charles S. " 1827, 10, 18
         Edgar   " 1829, 9, 19
         Benona Jr. " 1831, 9, 25 d 1833, 6,23
          bur Greenwich, O.
         Ann Matil-
           da   b 1833, 9, 24
         Purdy H.   " 1836, 8, 8

COUNTERMAN
1887, 2, 17. James recrq
1887, 2, 17. William H. recrq
1889, 5, 16. James relrq
1889, 6, 20. Wm. relrq

COURTRIGHT
1887, 3, 17. Amos & Maggie recrq
1893, 5, 18. Amos dropped from mbrp
1894, 1, 18. Amos recrq
1897, 1, 21. Amos relrq

COVILL
1818, 1, 1. Micajah & w, Hannah, rocf Sara-
     toga MM, N. Y., dtd 1817,8,6, endorsed by
     Short Creek MM, O., 1817,11,18
1819, 5, 27. Micajah [Covil] & w, Hannah,
     gct Deruyter MM, N. Y.

COWGILL
1856, 7, 10. Direxa H., dt Aaron & Caroline
     D. Benedict, b
1859, 1, 28. Levi, s Thomas & Sarah, Cham-
     paign Co., O., d 1859,5,-- bur Carmel,
     Ill.; m Esther BENEDICT, dt Ezra & Ruth,
     Morrow Co., O., d 1873,12,31 ae 43 bur
     Peru, O.
     Ch: Levi Jr.   b 1859, 12, 13
1873, 12, 31. Esther d bur Peru, O. (wd Levi)
1914, 4, 18. Aborilla d ae 74
----, --, --. Roscoe L. & Alverda (Cope)
     Ch: Alice
         Amelia   b 1919, 6, 9
         V. Irene   " 1911, 1, 11

1859, 3, 24. Esther gct Goshen MM
1862, 12, 18. Esther & s rocf Goshen MM, dtd
     1862,10,18
1907, 7, 18. Roy dropped from mbrp
1909, 6, 17. Abarilla rocf Gilead MM
1914, 1, 22. Ruthanna recrq
1919, 5, 22. Ruthanna gct Wilmington MM,O.

COX
----, --, --. Isaac W. d 1903,--,-- ae 55 bur
     Ashley, O.; m Emma D. -----
     Ch: Elsie   b 1877, 8, 19
         Merlin Lee " 1888, 1, 21

1877, 6, 21. Isaac N. & w, Emma D., & dt,
     Angie Latona, rocf Richland MM, Ind., dtd

COX, continued
    1877,6,6
1904, 7, 21. Emma D., Elsie, Belle & Merlin
    transferred from Ashley MM
1906, 1, 18. Emma D. & ch, Elsie, Belle &
    Merlin, relrq

CRAMER
1890, 2, 13. Wilson recrq

CRATTY
1874, 8, 20. Hannah recrq
1877, 4, 19. Sarah Jane recrq

CRAVENS
1887, 2, 17. Melville recrq

CROOK
1894, 12, 15. Mary Elizabeth, dt Chas. E. &
    Direxa (Benedict) Wood, b

CRUICKSHANKS
1890, 1, 16. Nellie May recrq

CUNNINGHAM
1889, 2, 14. Harriett recrq

CURL
1887, 3, 17. W. H. & Ova rocf Gilead MM
1887, 3, 17. Curl rocf Gilead MM

CURREN
1923, 3, 22. Charles & w, Nancy, recrq

DALZELL
1880, 2, 19. Sarah Jane gct Greenwich MM

DANIELS
----, --, --. Ebenezer m Anna ----- d 1826,12,
    29 ae 24 bur Morvin, O.
    Ch: Maria   b 1824, 6, 25
        William   " 1826, 12, 22
    Ebenezer m 2nd Sarah -----
    Ch: Anna   b 1828, 12, 20
        John Chap-
        man   " 1835, 11, 6

1822, 2, 28. Anna (form Benedict) con mcd
1824, 5, 27. Ebeneezar C. recrq
1828, 3, 27. Ebeneezer C. rmt Sarah Michiner
1887, 4, 21. Amanda recrq

DARLING
1818, 7, 30. Rebecca (form Morton) dis mcd

DAVIDSON
1841, 11, 25. George & w, Hannah, & ch, Sarah
    Ann, Charlotte, Emery, Parker & Reece,
    rocf Short Creek MM, O., dtd 1841,9,19

DAVIS
1826, 2, 2. Hiram E., minor, rocf Stillwater
    MM, dtd 1825,11,26

1833, 6, 20. Mary rocf Queensburg MM, N. Y.,
    dtd 1833,5,29
1835, 6, 25. Mary Mosher (form Davis) con
    mcd

DEGOOD
1885, 3, 19. Elizabeth recrq

DENNIS
1842, 2, 23. Arad & s, Arad P., rocf Scipio
    MM, N. Y., dtd 1841,12,15 (H)
1887, 2, 17. Flora & Hattie recrq

1887, 2, 17. Frank recrq
1887, 2, 17. Sarah recrq
1887, 4, 21. Lottie recrq

DENTON
1887, 2, 17. Albert recrq
1889, 5, 16. Albert relrq

DeVOL
1909, 9, 7. Ezra, s George & Isabella, b
----, --, --. Charles, s George & Isabella
    (French), b 1903,10,2; m Leona VAN MATRE,
    dt Loren, b 1902,12,28
    Ch: Margaret
        Ruth   b 1930, 9, 26

1921, 4, 21. Ezra recrq
1921, 11, 17. Charles & Catherine recrq
1926, 7, 28. Charles rmt Leora Van Matre

DILLINGHAM
----, --, --. John d 1848,2,27 ae 74 bur
    Peru, O.; m Mary ----- d 1849,3,5 ae 75
    bur Peru, O.
    Ch: Micajah   b 1797, 1, 16
        Silvanus " 1798, 8, 20
        Sarah   " 1799, 9, 12
        James   " 1801, 6, 3
        Hiram   " 1803, 4, 2
        Mira   " 1809, 6, 30
        Hannah   " 1812, 4, 30
        Nancy   " 1816, 1, 12
----, --, --. Micajah d 1851,3,18 bur Peru,O.;
    m Elizabeth -----
    Ch: Richard   b 1823, 6, 18 d 1850, 6,30
        bur Nashville, Tenn.
        Deborah   b 1825, 7, 13 " 1846, 8,10
        bur Peru, O.
        Jane   b 1827, 8, 30
        Alfred   " 1829, 9, 8 " 1853,12,22
        bur Peru, O.
        Abigail   b 1831, 11, 18
        Edith   " 1836, 10, 18
        Mary   " 1833, 2, 11 " 1853, 3,30
        bur Peru, O.
        Sarah W. b 1839, 1, 7
        Elwood   " 1841, 9, 17
1853, 1, 28. Elizabeth m Exum JOHNSON

1822, 2, 28. Micajah gct Marlborough MM, to

DILLINGHAM, continued
    m Eliza Williams
1823, 1, 30. Elizabeth rocf Marlborough MM,
    dtd 1822,10,20
1824, 1, 29. Sylvanus dis mcd
1829, 10, 29. Mira rmt Robert Bunker
1830, 9, 2. John dis disunity
1830, 12, 30. Hiram dis disunity
1832, 3, 29. Sarah Kerr (form Dillingham) dis
    mcd
1833k 4, 25. James dis
1833, 6, 20. Hannah Smith (form Dillingham)
    con mcd
1838, 2, 22. Nancy Beebe (form Dillingham) dis
    mcd
1849, 4, 27. Jane Gains (form Dillingham) dis
    mcd
1851, 1, 23. Alfred con mcd
1854, 5, 25. Edith & Sarah, dt Elizabeth
    Johnson, gct Goshen MM
1856, 1, 24. Abigail gct Goshen MM
1875, 3, 18. Oliver D. recrq
1879, 2, 13. Mary J. recrq
1881, 8, 18. Oliver D. & w, Mary J., & dt,
    Cemantha Adelia, gct Spring Grove MM, Kans.
1887, 5, 19. Oliver D. & w, Mary J., & ch,
    Cementha Adelia, & Wilmie Abigail, rocf
    Springboro MM, Kans., dtd 1887,4,16

DODGE
1838, 2, 22. Judith recrq
1840, 3, 26. Judith gct White River MM, Ind.
1845, 7, 24. Judith gct Gilead MM

DONNAN
----, --, --. John W. & Anna
    Ch: Milo Clark b 1876, 10, 20 d 1877, 2,26
        bur Peru, O.
        Bessie
        Pearl   b 1878, 9, 15

1876, 2, 17. John [Donnen] recrq
1878, 5, 16. John W. [Donnen] & w, Annie,
    relrq

DOTY
1868, 7, 16. Phebe A. (form Benedict) dis mcd
1885, 3, 19. John recrq
1894, 4, 19. Thomas O. recrq
1899, 10, 19. Thomas dropped from mbrp

DOUGLAS
1836, 4, 21. Laura A. rocf Rochester MM,
    N. Y., dtd 1836,1,27
1837, 8, 24. Laura A. Rickard (form Douglas)
    dis mcd

DOWNING
1834, 11, 20. John, minor s Wm., rocf Carmel
    MM, dtd 1834,10,18
1837, 1, 26. Susanna (form Quanitance) con
    mcd

DRAY
1886, 12, 16. Hattie rocf Gilead MM, dtd
    1886,11,16
1892, 7, 21. Hattie dropped from mbrp

DUDLEY
1928, 5, 17. Edith Smith relrq

DURANT
1887, 2, 17. Mattie recrq
1887, 2, 17. L. L. recrq
1887, 2, 17. Clara recrq
1888, 3, 22. L. L., Mattie & Clara dropped
    from mbrp

DURKEE
1912, 5, 16. Stella Reid dropped from mbrp

DYE
1919, 5, 22. Archie recrq
1927, 4, 21. Delmar & w, Lucy M., & Eva L.,
    recrq
1930, 6, 19. Edna relrq
1930, 6, 19. Archie dis
1931, 1, 22. Eva relrq

DYER
1820, 11, 30. Brackett rocf Marlem MM, Mass.,
    dtd 1816,6,18, endorsed by Stillwater
    MM, O., 1820,5,27
1847, 10, 29. Brackett dis disunity

EARL
1818, 6, 29. Benjamin d bur Peru. O.
----, --, --. Aaron d 1877,5,22 bur Peru, O.;
    m Hannah ----- d 1860,11,19 "   "   "
    Ch: Franklin b 1823, 2, 1 d 1877, 9,--
        bur Bennington
        Benjamin b 1824, 10, 5
        Louisa H. " 1826, 8, 29 " 1860, 6, 3
        bur Peru
        William " 1828, 7, 6 " 1846, 4,30
        bur Peru
        Dorcas " 1830, 3, 31
        Phebe " 1830, 3, 31 " 1861, 1,26
        bur Peru
        Nathaniel " 1831, 10, 24 " 1909,--,--
        bur Alum Creek
        Anne b 1834, 3, 28 " 1834, 7,17
        bur Peru, O.
        Adaline b 1834, 3, 28 " 1834, 4,28
        bur Peru, O.
        Sarah b 1840, 7, 15 " 1840,10, 2
        Leno Or-
        lando " 1846, 1, 1
1823, 10, 27. Dorcas, w Benj., d bur Peru,O.
----, --, --. Franklin d 1877,9,12 bur Peru,
    O.; m Henrietta -----
    Ch: George
        Delano b 1861, 11, 8
        William
        Gidley " 1863, 1, 23
        Louisa " 1866, 12, 8

EARL, Franklin & Henrietta, continued
    Ch: Nancy Jane b 1870, 2, 11
----, --, --. Benjamin d 1892,2,17 bur Alum
    Creek; m Alvira -----
    Ch: Clara Lil-
        lian Alberta
            b 1869, 3, 1

1818, 1, 29. Hannah rmt Maurice Pleas
1821, 9, 27. Aaron rmt Hannah Gidley
1826, 6, 29. Anna Gaylord (form Earl) dis mcd
1854, 10, 26. Dorcas Comfort (form Earl) dis
    mcd
1859, 3, 24. Nathaniel dis mcd
1860, 7, 26. Franklin con mcd
1862, 9, 18. Benjamin con mcd
1864, 4, 21. Zeno dis disunity
1864, 6, 16. Elvira recrq
1865, 3, 16. Aaron con mcd
1868, 6, 18. Henrietta recrq
1877, 5, 17. Nathaniel & w, Anna, & ch,
    Lewis & Clayton Laselle, recrq
1884, 7, 17. Nathaniel & Anna dropped from
    mbrp
1887, 4, 21. Henry recrq
1887, 4, 21. Clara recrq
1888, 7, 19. Henry & Clara dropped from mbrp
1892, 7, 21. Lewis dropped from mbrp
1893, 5, 18. Clayton dropped from mbrp
1896, 7, 16. Alvin dropped from mbrp
1899, 10, 19. Clayton dropped from mbrp

EARLY
1881, 4, 21. John recrq
1882, 3, 16. Charlotte recrq
1883, 8, 16. John dis disunity
1884, 2, 18. John recrq
1885, 7, 16. John relrq
1885, 7, 16. Charlotte relrq
1886, 3, 18. Charlotte & Mary recrq
1891, 5, 21. John recrq
1892, 3, 17. Artie J. recrq
1893, 5, 18. John & fam dropped from mbrp

EARNSHAW
1829, 7, 2. George Sr. rocf Smithfield MM,
    dtd 1829,4,20
1829, 7, 2. George Jr. & w, Sarah, rocf
    Smithfield MM, dtd 1829,4,20

EDDY
----, --, --. John S. & Lydia
    Ch: Reuben   b 1824, 1, 20
        Ira G.   " 1825, 9, 4
        Joseph   " 1827, 9, 27
        Lucy Ann   " 1829, 10, 29
        Perlina   " 1831, 10, 14
        Ruth   " 1833, 12, 6
        John R.   " 1835, 12, 25
        Sherman G. " 1837, 12, 27
        Huldah R.   " 1842, 9, 15
        Allen W.   " 1847, 4, 20
1845, 2, 1. Experience d ae 78 bur Camden,O.

----, --, --. Allen W. m Lydia B. ----- d
    1879,10,16 ae 32 bur Peru, O.
    Ch: Anna M.   b 1872, 8, 10
        Laura A.   " 1874, 5, 4

1834, 5, 22. John L. & w, Lydia, & ch, Reuben,
    Ira G., Joseph, Lucy Ann, Perlina & Ruth,
    rocf Collins MM, N. Y., dtd 1834,3,27
1875, 1, 21. Allen rocf Salem MM
1875, 6, 17. Lydia & ch, Anna Mary & Laura
    Annette, recrq
1892, 1, 21. Allen W. & w, Mattie Osborne,
    relrq
1893, 12, 21. Laura & Annie relrq
1907, 7, 18. Willard dropped from mbrp

EDGINGTON
1887, 3, 17. Hannah [Egington] recrq
1887, 3, 17. Lillie [Egington] recrq
1888, 7, 19. Minnie, Hannah & Lillie dropped
    from mbrp

EETER
1887, 4, 21. Addie C. recrq

ELLIOTT
1835, 4, 30. Sarah M. m John WRIGHT (H)
1837, 1, 30. Eli d (H)
1844, 7, 31. Wm. H. d bur Knox Co., O. (H)
1854, 11, 25. John D., s Isaac & Ruth, Logan
    Co., O.; m in Owl Creek, Elizabeth WIL-
    LETS, dt Ellis & Rachel, Knox Co., O.
1885, 7, 22. Lawrence A., s Martin & Ellie, b

1831, 10, 20. Eli Willets gct Plainfield MM,
    to m Lamira Elliot (H)
1833, 3, 21. Eli & w, Margaret, & ch, Ann,
    Wm. & Mary, rocf Alexandria MM, D. C., dtd
    1833,1,24 (H)
1833, 3, 21. Upton rocf Alexandria MM, D. C.,
    dtd 1833,1,24 (H)
1833, 3, 21. Sarah & Elizabeth rocf Alexan-
    dria MM, D. C., dtd 1833,1,24 (H)
1835, 3, 26. Reuben rocf Alexandria MM, D. C.,
    dtd 1835,3,26 (H)
1835, 7, 23. Upton gct White Water MM, Ind.
    (H)
1836, 8, 21. Elizabeth Gibson (form Elliott)
    dis mcd (H)
1839, 10, 24. Ann Palmer (form Elliott) dis
    mcd (H)
1840, 6, 25. Reuben con mcd (H)
1855, 3, 22. Elizabeth gct Goshen MM
1859, 7, 21. Reuben gct Prairie Grove MM, Ia.
    (H)
1859, 10, 27. Eliza Elma (form Willets) dis
    mcd
1861, 11, 21. Paul Broderick gct Goshen MM,
    to m Elizabeth Elliott
1884, 2, 18. Martin & Ella M. recrq
1887, 4, 21. Jehu & Ettie recrq
1888, 8, 16. Jehu & Alvaretta relrq
1893, 4, 20. Martin & w, Ellen, relrq

ELLIOTT, continued
1894, 8, 15. **Martin & w, Ella, recrq**
1900, 5, 17. Martin & w, Ella, gct Gilead MM
1907, 7, 18. Jennie dropped from mbrp

EVANS
1891, 3, 19. Minnie M. recrq
1891, 3, 19. Dilla recrq
1891, 3, 19. Della recrq
1891, 3, 19. Mary recrq
1891, 3, 19. Anna recrq

EVERETT
1827, 5, 21. William rocf Farmington MM, N.Y.,
    dtd 1826,9,21
1829, 10, 1. Wm. dis disunity
1837, 4, 24. Hannah, w Wm., recrq (H)

FARGO
1887, 2, 17. John recrq
1889, 4, 18. John relrq

FARRER
1834, 12, 25. Sarah gct Springboro MM

FARQUHAR
----, --, --. Moses B. & Massie (or Mercy) (H)
    Ch: William H. b 1814, 3, 4
        Edwin   " 1818, 7, 15
        Ruth P.   " 1820, 12, 9
        Mary B.   " 1823, 12, 29
        Francis P. " 1826, 12, 17
        Sarah A.   " 1831, 7, 1

1823, 3, 27. Moses B. & w, Massey, & ch, Wm.,
    Edwin & Ruth, rocf Pipe Creek MM, dtd
    1822,12,24
1825, 9, 29. Susan (form Wright) dis mcd
1827, 5, 23. Moses dis disunity
1829, 1, 29. Joseph dis jH
1829, 3, 5. Massey dis jH
1835, 11, 26. Wm. H. dis jH
1839, 5, 23. Ruth dis disunity
1840, 6, 25. Edwin dis disunity

FARRINGTON
----, --, --. Moses & Amelia (H)
    Ch: William
        Penn   b 1833, 3, 20 d 1850, 9,16
        bur Sandusky, O.
        Caleb Kirk b 1834, 7, 15
        Hannah   " " 1836, 5, 11
        Joseph John" 1838, 6, 27
        Moses   " 1840, 6, 25 d 1840, 8,20
1852, 9, 1. Mary m Stephen MOSHER (H)
----, --, --. John & Sarah Jane (H)
    Ch: Jesse T. b 1865, 4, 16
        Eddy   " 1866, 9, 8 d 1866, 9, 8
        bur Bucyrus, O.
        Armelia
        Jane   b 1866, 9, 8
        Mary Fran-
        ces   " 1868, 3, 15

Ch: Tacie Emma b 1870, 2, 1
    Phebe
    Ellin   " 1873, 3, 24
    Clarene H. " 1877, 1, 1

1832, 9, 20. Moses & w, Armella, & ch, Mary,
    Sarah & Priscilla, rocf New Garden MM,
    dtd 1831,10,20 (H)
1847, 4, 22. Armelia Campfield (form Farring-
    ton) dis mcd (H)
1856, 3, 26. Caleb K. [Farington] gct Prairie
    Grove MM, Ia. (H)
1860, 5, 24. Hannah P. Hodgin (form Farring-
    ton) dis mcd (H)
1877, 2, 15. Joseph John & w, Sarah, & ch,
    Jesse T., Amelia Jane, Mary Frances, Tacy
    Emma, Phebe Ellen & baby not named, rocf
    Gilead MM
1879, 10, 16. Sarah & ch, Jesse T., Amelia
    Jane, Mary Frances, Tacy Emma, Phebe Ellen
    & Clarance, gct Gilead MM
1880, 4, 15. Joseph John gct Gilead MM

FAULKMAN
1904, 7, 21. Mrs. & Eva transferred from Ash-
    ley MM
1907, 7, 18. Mrs. & Eva dropped from mbrp

FAUST
1887, 3, 17. Ella recrq
1887, 3, 17. Dellie recrq
1887, 4, 21. Maud L. recrq
1887, 4, 21. Mirieth M. recrq
1887, 4, 21. Dellie recrq

FAWCETT
----, --, --. Josiah & Sarah T. (H)
    Ch: Sarah
        Eunice   b 1817, 12, 27
        Oliver
        Goldsmith " 1820, 8, 27
        William
        Taylor   " 1826, 12, 29
        Mary Ellen " 1831, 4, 18
        Phineas A. " 1834, 2, 3
        Alpheus
        Harrison " 1836, 9, 6
        Virginia E." 1839, 1, 3
        Ann Mariah " 1841, 6, 18
        Louisa
        Penelope " 1843, 11, 18
        Edward S. " 1845, 1, 18
1855, 8, 29. Wm. T., s Josiah & Sarah T.,
    Knox Co., O.; m in Owl Creek, Elizabeth P.
    WOOD, dt John P. & Susan, Knox Co., O.
1888, 2, 12. Jean S., s Milo & Flora, b

1834, 10, 25. Josiah & w, Sarah, & ch, Sarah,
    Eunice, Oliver G., Wm. F., Mary Ellen &
    Phenias Anderton, rocf Hopewell MM, dtd
    1834,7,10 (H)
1855, 6, 21. Wm. T. rocf Salem MM, O., dtd
    1855,5,24

FAWCETT, continued
1858, 9, 20. Wm. T. & w, Elizabeth W., gct
    Plainfield MM, Ind.
1887, 2, 17. Huldah [Faucett] recrq
1887, 2, 17. Milo [Faucett] recrq

FISH
1835, 4, 23. Cert rec for Elizabeth, Rachel
    B. & Eliza F., from Ferrisburg MM, Vt.,
    dtd 1833,7,31, endorsed to Goshen MM

FISHER
1887, 4, 21. Charles C. & Georgie recrq
1887, 4, 21. Malinda recrq
1887, 6, 16. Malinda, Dora, George & Charlie
    relrq

FISK
1887, 3, 17. Lida S. recrq

FLEMING
1888, 1, 19. Ida Underwood relrq
1897, 2, 18. Frank recrq
1898, 5,19. Frank dropped from mbrp

FORD
1896, 12, 17. Lewis A. & Lena recrq
1897, 2, 18. Bertie H. recrq
1902, 7, 17. Lewis, Lena & Bertie H. dropped
    from mbrp

FORRER
1827, 5, 3. Sarah (form Howard) con mcd
1834, 12, 25. Sarah gct Springboro MM

FOULKE
1829, 10, 1. John Lewis gct Flushing MM, to m
    Hannah Foulke
1844, 10, 24. Cert rec for Sarah from Short
    Creek MM, O., dtd 1842,12,20, endorsed to
    Pennsville MM
1845, 7, 24. Sarah rocf Pennsville MM, dtd
    1845,6,19

FOUST
1887, 2, 17. Perry recrq
1890, 9, 18. Perry relrq
1904, 7, 21. Mrs. O. K. transferred from Ash-
    ley MM
1907, 7, 18. Mrs. O. K. dropped from mbrp

FREY
1889, 1, 17. Mary recrq
1894, 3, 22. Mary gct Gilead MM

FROST
1830, 5, 2. Robert d ae 70 bur Greenwich,O.
1844, 9, 15. Mary d ae 81 bur Greenwich, O.

1825, 6, 30. Robert & w, Mary, rocf Plains
    MM, N. Y., dtd 1824,10,26
1825, 6, 30. Joshua rocf Plains MM, N. Y.,
    dtd 1824,10,26

1841, 6, 24. Joshua dis mcd

FURNAS
1853, 9, 23. Robert F., s Seth & Dinah, War-
    ren Co., O.; m in Whetstone MH, Bethiah
    MOSHER, dt Robert & Edith, Morrow Co., O.
    (H)

1854, 1, 26. Bethiah M. gct Miami MM, O. (H)

GAFFIELD
1893, 5, 18. Mattie dropped from mbrp

GAINES
1849, 4, 27. Jane (form Dillingham) dis mcd

GARDNER
1887, 9, 31. Henry E., s Wm. & Martha, b

1876, 11, 16. William [Gardiner] recrq
1886, 3, 18. Henry recrq
1886, 3, 18. Martha recrq
1887, 2, 17. Mary Ann recrq
1889, 3, 21. Alvin [Gardnier] recrq
1893, 5, 18. Henry & Martha [Gardiner] drop-
    ped from mbrp
1896, 7, 16. Alvin, Fanny & Forest dropped
    from mbrp
1897, 2, 18. Henry & Ora recrq
1899, 10, 19. Henry, Ora & Wm. dropped from
    mbrp
1904, 7, 21. Mary Ann [Gardiner] transferred
    from Ashley MM
1911, 6, 15. Ethel recrq
1914, 6, 18. Ethel relrq
1923, 3, 22. Cleo recrq

GAYLORD
1826, 6, 29. Anna (form Earl) dis mcd
1850, 7, 25. Anna rst
1850, 11, 21. Catharine, dt Eleazer & Anna,
    recrq

GEORGE
----, --, --. John & Mary (H)
    Ch: John   b 1822, 8, 6
        Abel   " 1825, 4, 13
        Vilinda " 1827, 4, 9
        William H. " 1829, 8, 9

1825, 4, 28. John S. & ch, Jesse, Abigail,
    Samuel, Mary Ann, John & Abel, recrq
1831, 4, 28. Abigail dis jas
1832, 5, 24. Mary dis jH
1833, 5, 23. Mary Ann dis jas
1833, 5, 23. Abigail dis jas
1834, 8, 4. Jesse dis disunity
1835, 4, 23. John S. dis disunity
1838, 2, 22. John, Able, Vilinda & Wm., ch
    John & Mary, gct Goshen MM
1838, 2, 22. John S. & w, Mary, & ch, John
    S., Abel, Valinda & Wm. H., gct Goshen MM
    (H)

GEORGE, continued

1839, 8, 22. John & w, Mary, & ch, John S.,
      Abel, Valinda & Wm. A., rocf Goshen MM,O.,
      dtd 1839,5,18 (H)

GIBSON

1828, 10, 2. Permelia (form Wright) dis mcd·
1836, 8, 21. Elizabeth (form Elliott) dis mcd
  (H)

GIDLEY

----, --, --. William d 1855,4,18 ae 75 bur
      Peru, O.; m Phebe ----- d 1831,8,18 ae 53
      bur Peru, O.
      Ch: Sarah   b 1800, 6, 2
          Hannah   " 1802, 1, 10
          Esther   " 1803, 9, 18
          Amy   " 1805, 8, 5
          Ruth   " 1807, 7, 3
          Phebe D.   " 1809, 9, 20
          William   " 1811, 10, 15
          Patience   " 1813, 10, 4
          Moses   " 1815, 11, 23
          Daniel A.   " 1818, 3, 26
          David   " 1820, 2, 28
      William m 2nd Hannah BENEDICT d 1862,8,27
      ae 77 bur Peru, O.
      Ch: Isaac   b 1825, 7, 22
----, --, --. William & Sarah
      Ch: Susan   b 1840, 8, 11 d 1846, 4,26
            bur Peru, O.
          Daniel D. b 1844, 3, 1
          Royal G.   " 1848, 9, 24
1842, 10, 28. Patience m Jesse VERNON
1844, 8, 29. Daniel, s William & Phebe, Dela-
      ware Co., O.; m in Greenwich, Deborah
      HICKOK, dt Harry & Hannah, Huron Co., O.
      Ch: Terresse P.b 1845, 8, 6
          Cecelia A.
          Victoria   " 1847, 3, 7 d 1849,10, 5
          bur Peru
          Ellen Ann   " 1850, 1, 11
          Griffith L." 1852, 7, 1
1855, 4, 21. William d ae 76 (an elder)
----, --, --. Dorwin & Ellin
      Ch: Elwood
          Chellis   b 1877, 2, 19
          Arthur
          Emmett   " 1878, 4, 10

          Clifton   " 1880, 1, 19

1818, 1, 1. William & w, Phebe, & ch, Sarah,
      Hannah, Esther, Amy, Ruth, Phebe, William,
      Patience & Moses, rocf Saratoga MM, N. Y.,
      dtd 1817,8,6, endorsed by Short Creek MM,
      O., 1817,11,18
1819, 5, 27. Sarah Benedict (form Gidley) dis
      mcd
1821, 9, 27. Hannah rmt Aaron Earl
1823, 1, 30. Amy rmt John Benedict
1824, 1, 1. Esther rmt Henry Osborn
1827, 11, 1. Ruth rmt Ezra Benedict

1828, 10, 2. Phebe Jr. rmt Daniel Benedict
1832, 11, 22. William rmt Hannah Benedict
1837, 1, 26. Moses dis disunity
1837, 2, 23. Wm. Jr. con mcd
1838, 7, 26. Wm. Jr. gct Goshen MM
1840, 12, 24. David dis jas
1843, 1, 26. Sarah recrq
1844, 10, 24. Susan, dt Wm. Jr. & Sarah, rec-
      rq
1847, 9, 20. Isaac gct Goshen MM
1854, 2, 23. Daniel A. & w, Deborah, & ch,
      Terressa & Ellen, gct Red Cedar MM, Ia.
1864, 4, 21. Wm. & w, Sarah, & ch, Daniel D.
      & Royal G., gct Adrian MM, Mich.
1876, 6, 15. Darwin & w, Ella P., rocf West-
      land MM
1880, 5, 20. Darwin & w, Ella P., & ch, El-
      wood Chellis, Arthur Emmett & Walter
      Clifton, gct Geneva MM, Kans.
1902, 6, 19. Elwood Chellis recrq
1902, 3, 19. Minnie recrq
1904, 7, 21. Chellis & fam relrq

GIFFORD

----, --, --. Joseph A. & Sylvia C.
      Ch: Giles J.   b 1825, 9, 23
          Lucy   " 1828, 4, 25 d 1829, 5,23
          bur N. Y. State
          Job J.   b 1831, 8, 21
          Charles   " 1833, 3, 17
          Obadiah   " 1835, 1, 15 d 1837, 9, 8
          bur Greenwich, O.
          Elizabeth b 1838, 12, 15
          Sylvia Ann b 1837, 5, 13
          Sarah Jane " 1842, 6, 1
          Joseph B.   " 1845, 4, 1
          Benjamin   " 1847, 10, 31
----, --, --. Humphrey & Jane
      Ch: Mary I.   b 1829, 11, 22
          Abraham   " 1831, 7, 3
          Sarah   " 1834, 11, 23
          Catherine D" 1836, 2, 19
          William
          Henry   " 1840, 9, 24
          Humphrey J." 1842, 10, 24
          Eliza Jane " 1845, 10, 9
1841, 1, 26. Ruth d bur Greenwich, O.

1831, 4, 28. Joseph A. & w, Sylvia C., & s,
      Giles T., rocf Collins MM, dtd 1830,11,25
1831, 12, 1. Humphrey rocf Collins MM, N.Y.,
      dtd 1831,9,29
1838, 4, 26. Ruth rocf Collins MM, N. Y., dtd
      1837,6,29
1839, 3, 21. Edward, David & Rufus rocf Col-
      lins MM, dtd 1838,12,27
1840, 1, 23. Micajah rocf Colins MM, N. J.,
      dtd 1839,12,26
1840, 9, 21. Abraham dis mcd
1840, 9, 21. Edward con mcd
1842, 1, 27. David dis mcd
1842, 1, 27. Rufus rpd mcd
1843, 8, 24. Micajah dis disunity

GIFFORD, continued
1848, 2, 25. Giles J. con mcd

GILCHRIST
1883, 4, 17. David d bur North Carolina

1871, 12, 21. David D. recrq
1889, 2, 14. Blanche L. recrq

GLENN
1888, 3, 22. Lizzie recrq

GOSS
1851, 1, 23. Mary Ann (form Coats) con mcd (H)

GRANT
1893, 5, 18. Lulu Worth dropped from mbrp
1900, 3, 22. Arthur & Luella Mae recrq
1901, 3, 21. Luella May relrq
1904, 8, 18. Arthur dropped from mbrp
1907, 1, 17. Asa & Alice recrq
1907, 3, 21. Mary recrq
1908, 1, 16. Stella Westbrook relrq
1913, 6, 19. Anna recrq
1916, 6, 15. Asa, Alice & May dropped from
    mbrp
1919, 5, 22. Arthur recrq
1924, 11, 20. Arthur relrq

GRAY
1844, 9, 24. Loren, s William & Lydia, Dela-
    ware Co., O., d 1863,4,4 bur Peru, O.; m
    in Alum Creek MH, Sarah M. BENEDICT, dt
    Wm. & Alse, Delaware Co., O., d 1883,3,5
    bur Peru, O.
    Ch: Lydia Jane b 1845, 7, 13 d 1893, 6,24
          bur Wabash, Ind.
        Gardner
          Bennett b 1846, 7, 12 " 1917, 12,--
          bur Pa.
        Edwin N.   " 1847, 10, 31 " 1848, 9,25
          bur Peru, O.
        William B. b 1849, 5, 7
        Adelbert W." 1851, 1, 24
        Eli Noble " 1854, 9, 7
        Edgar E.   " 1856, 3, 23 d 1902, 2, 5
          bur Bloomfield, O.
1862, 4, 24. Lydia Jane m Myron T. HARTLEY
----, --, --. Bennett & Lucinda
    Ch: Charles
          Loren   b 1867, 6, 13
        Cordelia
          Ellen   " 1867, 7, 15

1844, 6, 27. Loren recrq
1847, 11, 25. Loren dis disunity
1851, 1, 23. Loren recrq
1859, 3, 24. Loren & w, Sarah, & ch, Lydia
    Jane, Gardner Bennett, William B., Adel-
    bert W., Eli Noble & Edgar E., gct Spring
    Creek MM, Ia.
1860, 5, 24. Loren & w, Sarah, & ch, Lydia
    Jane, Gardner Bennet, William, Adelbert,

    Elizabeth & Edgar Emmet, rocf Spring
    Creek MM, Ia., dtd 1860,2,4
1867, 5, 16. Gardner Bennett con mcd
1867, 5, 16. Lucinda (form Romans) con mcd
1871, 3, 16. William con mcd
1877, 10, 18. Wm. B. gct Raisin MM, Mich.
1884, 7, 17. Noble dropped from mbrp
1886, 5, 20. Sarah Ellen relrq
1890, 3, 20. Loren [Grey] dropped from mbrp
1896, 7, 16. Adelbert dropped from mbrp
1896, 7, 16. Gardner B. dropped from mbrp
1896, 7, 16. Louisa Olive dropped from mbrp

GREEN
----, --, --. Frank L., s Uriah & Barbara
    (Games), b 1858,5,10; m Mary HATTEN
    Ch: Howard   b 1888, 10, 4
        Willis   " 1891, 2, 6
        Stanley   " 1894, 3, 30
1882, 12, 10. Lena Smith, dt Fred & Mary
    (Burgraff) Hack, b
1888, 8, 19. Jessie, dt Lewis & Keturah
    George, b
----, --, --. Stanley, s Frank K. & Mary
    (Hatten), b 1894,3,30; m Bertha MARTIN,
    dt Wm. & Loretta, b 1895,3,21
    Ch: Phillis
          Pauline b 1916, 9, 20
        Florence
          Marice   " 1921, 3, 6
1868, 4, 10. Rebecca (form Broderick) con mcd
1875, 3, 18. Noah recrq
1879, 4, 17. Noah gct Greenwich MM
1881, 7, 21. Rebecca relrq
1882, 1, 19. Noah rocf Greenwich MM, dtd
    1881,9,8
1883, 6, 21. Noah dis
1884, 7, 17. Delilah dropped from mbrp
1885, 3, 19. Noah recrq
1890, 2, 13. Noah dropped from mbrp
1907, 3, 21. Lillie R. recrq
1907, 5, 16. Howard recrq
1907, 5, 16. Mary recrq
1907, 6, 20. Willis, Stanley & Frances recrq
1914, 5, 21. Howard H. gct Gilead MM
1915, 8, 19. Stella recrq
1921, 7, 21. Bertha recrq
1928, 3, 22. Florence Marise & Phillis
    Pauline recrq
1928, 3, 22. Harry F. & w, LaVanchie, & ch,
    Mary Alice, Stella May, Ruth Lucile &
    Paul Franklin, gct Gilead MM
1928, 4, 17. Howard & w, Jessie, rocf Sulli-
    vant Ave. MM, Columbus MM
1929, 5, 16. F. K. recrq

GREGG
----, --, --. Eli & Martha
    Ch: Robert W. b 1815, 7, 17 d 1816, 3, 3
          bur Wayne, O.
        Rachel   b 1816, 10, 7
        Phebe   " 1819, 1, 11

GREGG, Eli & Martha, continued
    Ch: Mary W. b 1820, 12, 31 d 1821, 1,16
        Ann   " 1822, 3, 31
        Alma A.   " 1824, 5, 17
        William W." 1826, 7, 9

1821, 3, 29. Abel dis disunity
1822, 2, 28. David, Betty Ann, Jesse, Phebe &
    Nancy, ch Hannah, gct Flushing MM
1823, 7, 31. Hannah gct Flushing MM
1824, 12, 30. William gct Plainfield MM
1827, 5, 21. Phineas con mcd
1828, 7, 31. Tacy McVey (form Gregg) dis mcd
1829, 1, 29. Ann dis jH
1829, 1, 29. Martha dis jH
1829, 1, 29. Samuel dis jH
1829, 1, 29. Phineas dis jH
1829, 1, 29. Israel dis jH
1829, 1, 29. Asa dis jH
1829, 3, 5. Eli dis jH
1830, 4, 22. Israel dis attending a public
    ball (H)
1830, 5, 20. Asa dis attending a public ball
    (H)
1832, 8, 23. Eli & w, Martha, & ch, Rachel,
    Phebe, Ann, Alma A., Wm. W., Eli & Edgar,
    rocf Miami MM, O. (H)
1834, 6, 26. Phineas gct Goshen MM, O. (H)
1834, 10, 27. Rachel, Phebe, Ann, Alma J. &
    William, ch Eli & Martha, gct Miami MM,O.
1835, 12, 24. Rachel Redfern (form Gregg) dis
    mcd
1836, 10, 20. Samuel & w, Ann, gct Goshen MM,
    O. (H)
1842, 10, 20. Ann (form Wright) rpd mcd (H)

GREGORY
1837, 10, 28. Mary m Wm. W. SEYMOUR
1845, 6, 1. Selah d ae 75 bur Peru,O.

1833, 9, 26. Selah & s, James & Benjamin,
    rocf Ferrisburg MM, Vt., dtd 1833,7,31
1834, 8, 4. Lydia D. rocf Ferrisburg MM,
    Vt., dtd 1833,7,31
1839, 7, 25. Lydia D. gct Goshen MM
1842, 3, 24. James dis disunity
1859, 2, 24. Benjamin dis mcd
1912, 5, 16. Hazel Smith dropped from mbrp

GRIFFIN
1842, 6, 23. Philena (form Worshburn) dis mcd

GRIMIEL
1887, 3, 17. Belle recrq

GRINNEL
1839, 2, 11. Cert rec for Jeremiah from
    Starksborough MM, Vt., dtd 1838,11,30, en-
    dorsed to Gilead MM
1893, 5, 18. Belle [Grinnell] dropped from
    mbrp

GRISE
1873, 10, 16. Augusta recrq

GRISELL
----, --, --. Thomas m Almira ----- d 1843,3,
    5 ae 46 bur Peru, O.
    Ch: William   b 1817, 3, 27
        Nathan   " 1819, 1, 19
        Benjamin   " 1820, 9, 24
        Joseph   " 1822, 8, 4
        Martha   " 1825, 8, 2
        Mariam   " 1827, 11, 27
        Thomas Jr. " 1830, 5, 17 d 1830, 7,10
        Almira Jr. " 1830, 5, 17 d 1905,12,23
        bur Richmond, Ind.
        Rachel   b 1832, 3, 29
        Simeon   " 1839, 5, 10
1839, 1, 31. Nathan, s Thomas & Almira, Dela-
    ware Co., O.; m in Alum Creek MH, Cynthia
    BENEDICT, dt Aden S. & Sarah, Delaware
    Co., O.
    Ch: Lydia Ann b 1840, 1, 10
        Harvey   " 1841, 10, 12 d 1849,11, 7
1851, 1, 24. Cynthia m Ansel ROGERS
1864, 10, 6. Priscilla m Ansel ROGERS
----, --, --. Milo P. d 1868,4,13 bur Palmyra,
    Mich; m Martha Jane -----
    Ch: Mary   b 1868, 1, 20 d 1868, 6,21
1826, 9, 29. Thomas & w, Elmira, & ch, Wil-
    liam, Nathan, Benjamin, Joseph & Martha,
    rocf New Garden MM, dtd 1826,3,23
1828, 7, 3. Thomas & w, Elmira, & ch gct
    New Garden MM
1829, 12, 3. Thomas dis disunity
1834, 11, 20. Almira & ch, Wm., Nathan, Ben-
    jamin, Joseph, Martha, Miriam, Almira &
    Rachel, gct New Garden MM
1836, 6, 26. Cert rec for Almira & ch endors-
    ed back because they returned
1839, 6, 20. Wm. [Grissell] dis jas
1840, 1, 23. Priscilla [Grissell] (form Os-
    born) dis mcd
1843, 8, 24. Joseph dis jas
1846, 10, 23. Miriam dis disunity
1847, 5, 27. Thomas rst
1848, 2, 25. Benjamin [Grissell] dis mcd
1848, 10, 27. Thomas & s, Simeon, gct Gilead
    MM
1850, 9, 23. Martha & Rachel dis disunity
1851, 1, 23. Almira dis jas
1851, 4, 24. Lydia Ann gct Adrian MM, Mich.
    (with mother, Cynthia Rogers)
1864, 1, 21. Priscilla [Griswell] rst
1864, 2, 18. Milo P. [Grisell] recrq
1868, 1, 16. Milo con mcd
1868, 1, 16. Martha Jane (form Taber) con mcd
1868, 7, 16. Martha Jane gct Raisin MM, Mich.
1873, 6, 29. Ann rocf West Grove MM, Ind.,
    dtd 1873,5,10

GROVES
1887, 4, 21. Joseph & Alvira recrq

GUTHRIE
1889, 2, 14. Katie Sr. & Katie Jr. recrq
1896, 2, 20. Kate & Katharine B. gct Columbus
    MM

GUYER
1906, 8, 16. Olive E. rocf Pleasant Grove MM,
    Ill., dtd 1906,7,14
1908, 12, 17. Olive E. gct Elwood Friends Ch.,
    Ill.

HALL
1863, 10, 22. Harriett Ann (form Lee) dis mcd
    (H)
1878, 8, 22. Joseph S. recrq
1878, 8, 22. Clara J. recrq
1883, 7, 19. Joseph S. dropped from mbrp
1907, 12, 19. James recrq
1912, 5, 16. Lewis dropped from mbrp
1898, 12, 20. Clarabelle Osborn dropped from
    mbrp

HALLOCK
1856, 12, 17. Hannah d ae 72 bur Peru, O.

HAMMON
1850, 1, 24. Selemma recrq
1855, 5, 24. Selemma gct Red Cedar MM, Ia.
1887, 4, 21. Martha J. [Hammond] recrq

HANCE
1822, 1, 31. William recrq
1824, 12, 2. Cert for Benjamin & fam from
    Farmington MM, N. Y., dtd 1823,5,26, re-
    turned because of his return
1826, 6, 29. Thomas & w, Esther, & ch, Ben-
    jamin, Sarah, Abram & Thomas, rocf Farm-
    ington MM, N. Y., dtd 1826,1,26
1828, 5, 1. Thomas C. & w, Esther, & ch gct
    Farmington MM, N. Y.
1830, 1, 28. William dis jH
1839, 7, 25. Eliza rocf Farmington MM, N.Y.,
    dtd 1838,7,26

HANDLEY
1836, 6, 8. Elizabeth d ae 64 bur Peru, O.

1827, 6, 28. Elizabeth recrq on consent of
    Peru MM, N. Y.

HARE
1900, 6, 20. Ruth Esther, dt Walter L. &
    Kate (Osborn) Benedict, b

HARKNESS
1843, 12, 28. Jesse S. & w, Cynthia T., rocf
    Starksborough MM, Vt., dtd 1843,12,1
1874, 2, 19. Jesse S. & w, Cynthia T., gct
    Clear Creek MM, O.
1875, 2, 18. Jesse T. & Cynthia S. rocf Clear
    Creek MM

HARLAN
----, --, --. Caleb d 1867,12,4 ae 57 bur[(H)
    Gilead Twp., Morrow Co.; m Pamelia -----
    Ch: Lewis   d 1864, 10, 9
        ae 21y 25d bur Morrow Co.
1861, 5, 1. Edward, s Caleb & Pemela, Morrow
    Co., O.; m in Whetstone MH, Amy D. SPEN-
    CER, dt George & Eunice, Morrow Co., O.(H)
    Ch: William   b 1862, 9, 12 d 1863,10,12
        bur Whetstone, O.
        Manelva   b 1865, 2, 21

1857, 6, 25. Caleb & w, Parmelia, & ch, Ed-
    ward, Mary Jane, Lewis Oliver, Phebe Ann,
    Henry & John W., rocf Stillwater MM (H)
1860, 5, 24. Mary Jane Webster (form Harlan)
    con mcd (H)

HARP
1887, 2, 17. Lewis L. recrq
1887, 2, 17. Bertie recrq

HARRISON
1821, 11, 29. Rachel (form Howard) con mcd
1823, 3, 27. Rachel gct Somerset MM

HARSHBERGER
1887, 4, 21. Nora D. recrq
1888, 7, 19. Noara D. [Hartberger] dropped
    from mbrp

HARTLEY
1862, 4, 24. Myron T., s Edwin & Ruth M.,
    Morrow Co., O.; m in Alum Creek MH, Lydia
    Jane GRAY, dt Loren & Sarah, Morrow Co.,O.

1836, 4, 21. Elias dis mcd
1862, 9, 18. Lydia Jane gct Gilead MM

HATHAWAY
----, --, --. Caleb & Rachel
    Ch: Peter   b 1824, 8, 2
        Henry   " 1826, 8, 17
        Mary   " 1828, 9, 3 d 1829, 8,15
        bur Milan, O.
        Phebe R.   b 1830, 1, 13
        Caleb Jr.   " 1832, 9, 25
        Joshua   " 1835, 1, 8
        Israel   " 1838, 3, 20
        Susan   " 1840, 5, 16
        William   " 1844, 8, 23
1840, 5, 20. Wm. Penn, s Richmond & Phebe, b
1850, 5, 29. Henry, s Caleb & Rachel, Erie
    Co., O.; m in Owl Creek, Esther W.
    TOWNSEND, dt Thomas & Ruth, Knox Co., O.
1867, 10, 24. Susan m Edward A. BENEDICT

1823, 5, 1. Caleb rocf Radner MM, Pa., dtd
    1823,3,13
1823, 11, 27. Caleb rmt Rachel Wood Jr.
1824, 7, 29. Thomas W. rocf SD MM, dtd 1824,
    5,26
1826, 6, 29. Mary rocf SD MM, dtd 1825,8,24

HATHAWAY, continued

1826, 6, 29. Caleb & s, Peter, rocf SD MM,
     dtd 1825,8,24
1830, 7, 1. Thomas dis mcd
1832, 2, 2. Peter dis disunity
1832, 2, 2. Caleb dis disunity
1839, 7, 25. Richmond & w, Phebe B., & ch,
     Isaac N. & Samuel B., rocf Farmington MM,
     N. Y., dtd 1838,7,26
1841, 1, 28. Richmond & w, Phebe B., & ch,
     Isaac N., Samuel B. & Wm. Penn & ward,
     Seneca James Pickum, gct Farmington MM,
     N. Y.
1845, 6, 25. Caleb rst
1846, 2, 20. Peter rst
1846, 8, 28. Prudence Direxa recrq
1848, 2, 25. Elizabeth, dt Peter & Prudence
     D., recrq
1851, 1, 23. Esther W. gct Greenwich MM
1852, 10, 28. Samuel Levering gct Greenwich MM
     to m Phebe R. Hathaway
1861, 6, 20. Susan rocf Greenwich MM, dtd
     1861,6,14

HATTEN

1890, 9, 28. Walter, s Geo. W. & Rosa, d
     bur Alum Creek
----, --, --. Paul, s Harvey & Mary E. (Bartin)
     b 1898,3,4; m Imo SMITH, dt Lemuel J. &
     Lena (Hack), b 1904,3,15
     Ch: Harry Lloyd
                    b 1925, 7, 25
         Rosalene
          Mary   " 1928, 11, 4
         Elma Elnora" 1930, 8, 17
         Norma Jean " 1931, 12, 2
         Annie Marie" 1932, 7, 28

1875, 7, 22. Robert [Hatton] Jr. rocf Green
     Plain MM, O.
1875, 9, 16. Ellen recrq
1879, 4, 17. George, Marian & Chloe [Hatton]
     recrq
1879, 5, 22. Delilah recrq
1879, 6, 19. Sidney recrq
1879, 12, 18. Josephine recrq
1884, 3, 20. Robert & w, Josephine, & ch,
     Robert M. & Hugh W., gct Green Plain MM,O.
1884, 7, 17. George dropped from mbrp
1884, 7, 17. Marion dropped from mbrp
1884, 7, 17. Sidney dropped from mbrp
1884, 7, 17. Phebe dropped from mbrp
1889, 5, 16. George W. & w, Rosa, & ch, Ella
     G., Rilla B. & Willard E., recrq
1892, 7, 21. Ellen dropped from mbrp
1905, 11, 16. George
1911, 2, 16. Bertha [Hatton] recrq
1912, 5, 16. Willard [Hatton] dropped from
     mbrp
1918, 11, 21. George [Hatton] recrq
1919, 5, 22. Willard [Hatton] recrq
1919, 5, 22. Anna [Hatton] recrq
1921, 4, 21. Harvey, Mary, Paul, Lewis &

Frances [Hatton] recrq

1921, 4, 21. Clifton & Leora [Hatton) recrq
1923, 3, 22. Imo Martin [Hatton] recrq
1925, 2, 19. Willard [Hatton] & fam gct Colum-
     bus MM
1930, 8, 21. Nora Newell [Hatton] recrq

HAVILAND

----, --, --. Samuel P. & Lavina
     Ch: Samuel   b 1829, 3, 30
         William B. " 1830, 10, 10
         Alfred S.   " 1831, 12, 30
         Nelson Mor-
            ris   " 1835, 11, 21

1833, 4, 25. Samuel P. rocf Cornwall MM,
     N. Y., dtd 1833,7,28
1833, 4, 25. Lavinia, w Samuel P., & ch, Sam-
     uel, Wm. B. & Alfred S., rocf Marlborough
     MM, N. Y., dtd 1832,7,25

HEACOCK

1858, 2, 25. Barton & w, Rachel, & ch, Me-
     lissa, Clarkson, Oliver, Rebecca Jane,
     Sarah Anne, Isaac B., Wm. Antrim, Alice &
     Eliza, rocf West MM, dtd 1857,12,25 (H)
1859, 6, 23. Barton & w, Rachel, & ch,
     Clarkson, Oliver, Rebecca Jane, Sarah
     Ann, Isaac B., Wm. Antrim, Alice & Alvira,
     gct West MM (H)
1859, 6, 23. Malissa [Haycock] gct West MM,
     O. (H)
1859, 10, 20. Mary Ann dis disunity (H)
1895, 4, 18. Irving [Haycock] recrq

HEALD

1851, 2, 20. Harriet (form McGrew) dis mcd
1852, 1, 22. Sidwell rocf Middleton MM, dtd
     1852,1,8
1854, 6, 22. Sidwell gct Gilead MM
1878, 4, 18. Francis C. recrq
1878, 6, 20. Carrie recrq
1879, 3, 20. Carrie relrq
1883, 7, 19. Frank dropped from mbrp

HEALY

----, --, --. Joseph & Phebe [Heely]
     Ch: Abraham   b 1806, 4, 24
         Isaac   " 1808, 1, 31
         Elizabeth " 1810, 1, 16 d 1833,10, 5
         bur Greenwich, O.
         Jacob   b 1813, 6, 11
         Phebe S.   " 1815, 5, 27
----, --, --. Smith & Ann [Heeley]
     Ch: Edith Ann b 1832, 8, 6
         Elizabeth
           P.   " 1835, 11, 30
         Sarah Jane " 1840, 3, 15
         Huldah   " 1843, 7, 10
----, --, --. Abraham m Elizabeth ----- d
     1835,1,19 bur Greenwich, O.
     Ch: Mary Elizabeth
                    b 1835, --, --

HEALY, continued

1837, 4, 21. Jacob, s Joseph & Phebe, Huron
    Co., O.; m in Peru, Jemima WOOD, dt Phebe,
    Delaware Co., O.
        Ch: Phebe   b 1839, 12, 13
            Rachel   " 1842, 7, 9
            Caleb   " 1844, 12, 12
1837, 12, 27. Abram, s Joseph & Phebe, Huron
    Co., O.; m in Greenwich, Phebe C. WARREN,
    dt John & Hannah, Huron Co., O.
        Ch: John B.   b 1838, 12, 31
            Henry A.   " 1840, 2, 16
            Hannah Ma-
              ria   " 1843, 1, 8
            Smith Al-
              vin   " 1846, 4, 11
1845, 11, 12. Phebe d ae 73 bur Greenwich, O.

1834, 4, 24. Joseph & w, Phebe, & ch, Jacob
    & Phebe, rocf Coeymans MM, dtd 1834,1,23
1834, 6, 26. Smith & w, Anna, & dt, Edith
    Ann, rocf Caymans MM, N. Y., dtd 1833,10,
    24
1835, 10, 22. Abram rocf Coeymans MM, N. Y.,
    dtd 1835,7,23
1835, 10, 22. Elizabeth rocf Plains MM, N. Y.,
    dtd 1835,6,24
1847, 5, 27. Joseph dis mcd

HEDDINGTON
1890, 1, 16. Mamie recrq
1890, 1, 16. Clara recrq

HENRY
----, --, --. J. B. m Helen C. WESTBROOK, dt
    Albert & Annetta (Wood), b 1897,2,7
        Ch: Ruth Ellen b 1921, 3, 24
            Charles Ed-
              ward   " 1923, 4, 22
            Wilbur
              Ellis   " 1924, 12, 30

1914, 3, 19. Wm. & w, Frankie, & ch, Ralph
    Forest, rocf Gilead MM
1915, 8, 19. Stella Belle recrq
1915, 8, 19. Amos Neal recrq
1916, 9, 21. Paul recrq
1916, 11, 16. William & w, Frankie, & ch,
    Stella, Amos, Paul & Ralph, gct Gilead MM
1918, 11, 21. Jefferson recrq

HERENDEEN
1832k 4, 26. Nathan & w, Judith, & ch,
    Joshua, Nathan, Pennsylvania, Joseph, Wel-
    come, Anna, Huldah & Mary, rocf Farmington
    MM, N. Y., dtd 1832,2,23
1832, 7, 26. Elizabeth & Sarah rocf Farming-
    ton MM, N. Y., dtd 1832,3,24
1834, 3, 20. Nathan Jr. dis disunity
1836, 8, 25. Joshua dis mcd

HEVERLO
1889, 3, 21. Hattie A. recrq

1894, 3, 22. Hattie gct Ashley MM
1904, 7, 21. Ella N. transferred from Ashley
    MM
1916, 6, 15. Ella [Haverlo] dropped from
    mbrp

HIAT
1890, 1, 16. Mattie recrq
1893, 5, 18. Martha [Hyatt] dropped from
    mbrp

HICKMAN
1887, 3, 17. Thomas N. recrq

HICKOK
1844, 8, 29. Deborah m Daniel GIDLEY

1843, 4, 27. Deborah recrq

HICKSON
1889, 8, 22. Sarah [Hixon] recrq
1900, 3, 22. Willie recrq
1904, 7, 21. Sarah transferred from Ashton
    MM
1916, 5, 20. Wm. relrq
1916, 6, 15. Wm. dropped from mbrp

HINDERLONG
1907, 2, 14. Edna Pearl recrq
1909, 3, 18. Charles Ross recrq
1911, 1, 19. Charlie relrq
1915, 5, 20. Charles recrq
1916, 11, 16. Clara recrq
1928, 2, 16. Charley & w, Clara, & ch relrq

HOAG
1836, 3, 4. Ruth d ae 29 bur Peru, O.
1840, 4, 30. Jesse, s Jonathan & Phebe, Dela-
    ware Co., O.; m in Greenwich, Mary WATSON,
    dt Granger & Elizabeth, Huron Co., O.
        Ch: Ruth Tem-
              ple   b 1841, 6, 4 d 1841, 9,26
            Harriet
              Temple   " 1843, 1, 7

1833, 12, 26. Jesse & w, Ruth, rocf Ferris-
    burg MM, Vt., dtd 1833,10,30

HODGIN
1860, 5, 24. Hannah P. (form Farrington) dis
    mcd (H)

HOLE
1849, 9, 13. Jonah, s Jacob & Mary, Cham-
    paign Co., O.; m in Alum Creek MH, Sarah
    BENEDICT, dt Wm. & Phebe GIDLEY, Morrow
    Co., O.
1862, 10, 19. Jonah d ae 66 bur Peru, O.

1849, 11, 22. Sarah gct Goshen MM
1852, 4, 22. Jonathan & w, Sarah, rocf Goshen
    MM, dtd 1852,4,17
1855, 1, 25. Sophia rocf Sandy Spring MM, O.,

HOLE, continued
    dtd 1854,12,22
1860, 7, 26. Jonah & w, Sarah, gct Center MM,
    Pa.
1861, 8, 22. Jonah & w, Sarah, rocf Center
    MM, Pa., dtd 1861,8,17
1865, 11, 16. Sarah gct Winneshiek MM, Ia.
1874, 7, 16. Sophia gct Sandy Spring MM, O.
1878, 3, 21. Emmerson B. rocf Salem MM, dtd
    1878,2,21
1883, 7, 19. Emerson B. dropped from mbrp

HOLIDAY
1834, 5, 22. Phebe (form Carpenter) dis mcd

HOLLY
1889, 11, 21. J. B. recrq
1890, 1, 16. Fanny O. recrq
1891, 3, 19. John B. gct Hanover MM, Mich.

HOPPER
1887, 2, 17. Leroy recrq
1887, 3, 17. Lizzie recrq
1888, 3, 22. Emily recrq

HOUSTON
1888, 4, 19. Ellsworth dropped from mbrp

HOWARD
----, --, --. Horton b 1770,1,22 d 1833,8,14
    bur Columbus, O.; m Hannah ----- b 1774,2,
    24 d 1835,8,21 bur Columbus, O. (H)
    Ch: Ann   b 1811, 6, 11 d 1833, 8, 9
        bur Columbus, O.

1825, 8, 6. Hannah Jr. d bur Morvin

1820, 8, 31. Horton & w, Hannah, & ch, Sarah,
    Mary, Ann, Hannah & John, rocf Plainfield
    MM, dtd 1820,7,20
1820, 8, 31. Joseph rocf Plainfield MM, dtd
    1820,7,20
1820, 8, 31. Rachel rocf Plainfield MM, dtd
    1820,7,20
1821, 7, 5. Joseph gct Short Creek MM, O.,
    to m Pharaby Patterson
1821, 11, 29. Rachel Harrison (form Howard)
    con mcd
1827, 5, 3. Sarah Forrer (form Howard) con
    mcd
1828, 10, 2. Mary Little (form Howard) dis
    mcd
1829, 1, 1. Horton & w, Hannah, & dt, Ann,
    dis jH
1831, 6, 2. Joseph dis disunity
1872, 6, 20. John recrq
1884, 7, 17. John dropped from mbrp
1889, 3, 21. John recrq
1890, 2, 13. Lester recrq
1890, 4, 17. Mead recrq
1891, 4, 16. Arthur recrq
1893, 5, 18. Arthur dropped from mbrp

1893, 7, 20. Lucy & Henrietta recrq
1901, 1, 17. Lester E. relrq
1901, 3, 21. Lester E. recrq
1910, 5, 19. Lester E. relrq
1923, 3, 22. Lester Eugene & w, Alice, & ch,
    Alice Naomi, Chester Lester & Luther Fol-
    ger, recrq

HOWELL
----, --, --. George d 1872,3,2 bur Peru, O.;
    m Phebe Catherine -----
    Ch: William   b 1853, 9, 9
        Charlotte
        Ann   " 1859, 12, 21
        Mary Eliza " 1861, 10, 25
        George
        Francis " 1862, 12, 23

1855, 3, 22. Annie Elma & Luther Jonah, ch
    Elma, recrq
1855, 11, 22. George recrq
1855, 11, 22. Phebe recrq
1856, 1, 24. William, s Geo. & Phillie,
    recrq
1856, 7, 24. Elma & ch, Anna Elma & Luther
    Jonah, gct Salem MM
1876, 6, 15. William gct Goshen MM
1895, 3, 21. George F. relrq
1896, 1, 16. Wm. recrq
1897, 2, 18. Francis & Arthur recrq
1899, 8, 17. Francis E. relrq
1900, 5, 17. Grace M. relrq
1902, 1, 16. Arthur E. relrq
1903, 3, 19. Grace M. recrq
1920, 6, 17. Clarence recrq
1925, 7, 16. Clarence relrq
1929, 3, 21. Wm. gct Highland Ave. MM, Colum-
    bus
1932, 8, 18. Wm. rocf Highland Ave. MM, Colum
    bus

HUBBELL
1818, 8, 27. Hannah recrq
1821, 8, 30. Hannah McConahey (form Hubbell)
    dis mcd

HUDSON
1889, 2, 14. Maggie & Fannie recrq
1889, 7, 18. Mary M. recrq
1892, 1, 21. Mary E. & dt, Maggie & Fannie,
    relrq

HULL
1832, 10, 25. Solomon & w, Elizabeth, & ch,
    John, Rachel, Henry, Samuel & Martha, rocf
    Scipio MM, N. Y., dtd 1832,8,15
1835, 9, 24. Solomon & fam gct White Water
    MM, Ind.
1840, 2, 20. Ruth (form Slyter) dis mcd (H)

HURLEY
----, --, --. ----- & Harriet
    Ch: Durward b 1859, 6, 11 d 1880,9,21

HURLEY, continued
            bur Saginaw, Mich.
      Ch: Frank M.   b 1861, 8, 20
          Robert B. " 1863, 3, 22
1894,   8, 17. Durward, s Frank M. & Chattie, b

1865, 9, 21. Harriet rocf Plainfield MM, Ind.
1866, 11, 15. Durward O., Frank M. & Robert
      B., ch Harriett, recrq
1883, 7, 19. Frank M. dropped from mbrp
1884, 4, 17. Frank M. recrq
1887, 5, 19. Robert relrq
1896, 7, 16. Harriett recrq
1900, 4, 19. Frank M. & w, Chatta, & s, Der-
      ward, rocf Guernsey MM
1901, 7, 18. Frank M. relrq
1917, 4, 19. Durward dropped from mbrp

HURLOW
1927, 3, 17. Martha Adelia recrq

HURVIS
1891, 4, 16. Hannah E. rocf Westland MM, dtd
      1891,3,7

HUSTON
1887, 2, 17. Elsworth recrq

HYTE
1830, 7, 1. Sarah (form Carpenter) dis mcd
1833, 11, 21. Sarah [Hite] (form Carpenter)
      dis mcd

IRISH
1840, 8, 27. Israel & w, Esther, & ch,
      Lydia M., Rachel W., Israel Jr., Allen,
      Enoch, Joel T. & Samuel, rocf Peru MM,
      N. Y., dtd 1839,4,24
1842, 6, 23. Esther & ch, Israel A., Enoch,
      Joel S. & Samuel, gct Gilead MM
1842, 7, 28. Hannah Roby (form Irish) dis mcd
1842, 9, 19. Lydia dis disunity
1842, 10, 27. Israel dis
1851, 1, 23. Israel rst
1851, 4, 24. Israel gct Gilead MM

ISAACS
1897, 2, 18. Frank R. recrq
1904, 8, 18. Frank dropped from mbrp

JACKSON
1835, 4, 2. Mary m Joseph MORLAN

1832, 5, 24. Grace rocf New Garden MM, dtd
      1832,2,23
1832, 5, 24. Isaac & w, Ann, & ch, Josiah,
      Stephen, Isaac, James, Ann & Abraham, rocf
      New Garden MM, dtd 1832,2,23
1833, 1, 24. Ruth rocf New Garden MM, dtd
      1832,10,25
1834, 4, 24. Mary rocf New Garden MM, dtd
      1833,11,21
1834, 6, 26. Grace gct Goshen MM

1836, 3, 24. Grace rocf Goshen MM, dtd 1835,
      8,15
1838, 1, 25. Josiah gct Sandy Spring MM, O.
1907, 11, 21. Cora O. gct Gilead MM
1912, 7, 18. J. Wesley & w, Cora, & ch, Mar-
      garet & Wesley Elmore, rocf Gilead MM
1918, 11, 21. J. Wesley, Cora, Margaret &
      W. Elmore, gct Green Lead MM, Idaho

JAYCOX
1890, 1, 16. W. W. recrq
1890, 1, 16. Mrs. E. A. recrq

JEFFRIES
1832, 8, 23. Caleb & fam rocf Plainfield MM,
      dtd 1831,9,21 (H)

JENKINS
1887, 2, 17. Elmore L. recrq
1888, 6, 21. Elmer relrq

JENNINGS
1885, 3, 19. Lafayette recrq
1886, 10, 21. Lafayette dis

JENNY
1835, 10, 29. Benjamin, s John & Mary, Huron
      Co., O.; m in Greenwich, Ann M. BIRDSALL,
      dt Zephamiah & Anna
      Ch: Joannah   b 1836, 10, 10 d 1837, 1,10
          Anna S.   " 1839, 11, 13
          Nicholas D." 1841, 1, 18
1837, 6, 29. Mary G. m Benjamin WATSON
1844, 11, 28. Elizabeth D. m Joseph BARTLETT

1824, 7, 1. John & w, Catherine, & ch,
      Elizabeth Jane, Benjamin, Mary, Abraham,
      rocf Scipio MM, dtd 1823,10,--
1826, 12, 28. Eliza dis
1828, 5, 28. Elizabeth D. rstrq
1829, 10, 29. Benjamin dis disunity
1835, 7, 23. Benjamin rst
1839, 11, 21. Samuel & w, Sarah, & ch, Mary
      Ruth & Levi, rocf Danby MM, Vt., dtd 1836,
      1,7 (H)
1842, 8, 25. Abraham D. con mcd

JENT
1924, 2, 14. Sarah recrq

JOHNSON
----, --, --. John & Phila
      Ch: Seymour R. b 1833, 6, 23
          Abigail K. " 1835, 7, 3
          Sevier D.   " 1839, 7, 4
          Robert   " 1841, 7, 21
          Lucy   " 1847, 10, 1 d 1847,10,11
          bur Peru, O.
          Dorcas   b 1850, 5, 4
1853, 1, 28. Exum, s Elijah & Pheriba, Morrow
      Co., O.; m in Alum Creek MH, Elizabeth
      DILLINGHAM, dt Richard & Sarah WILLIAMS,
      Morrow Co., O.

JOHNSON, continued
1865, 4, 27. Joseph N., s James & Sarah V.,
     Morrow Co., O.; m in Alum Creek MH, Lydia
     L. BENEDICT, dt Aaron L.&Phebe H., Morrow
     Co., O.

1840, 9, 21. John recrq
1840, 11, 26. Phila recrq
1842, 4, 21. Seymour R., Abigail K. & Sevies
     D., ch John & Phila, recrq
1852, 12, 23. Exum & s, James & Charles O.,
     rocf Goshen MM
1854, 5, 25. Exum & w, Elizabeth, & ch,
     Edith Dillingham, Sarah Dillingham, James
     Johnson & Charles O. Johnson, gct Goshen MM
1858, 7, 22. John & w, Philia Ann, & ch,
     Robert & Dorcas O., gct Spring Creek MM,Ia.
1858, 7, 22. Seymour R. gct Spring Creek MM,
     Ia.
1858, 7, 22. Abigail K. gct Spring Creek MM,
     Ia.
1858, 7, 22. Leviah D. gct Spring Creek MM,
     Ia.
1860, 7, 26. Livius A. Benedict gct New Gar-
     den MM, O., to m Penelope Johnson
1862, 10, 16. Joseph H. rocf New Garden MM,
     dtd 1862,8,26
1870, 3, 17. Joseph H. & w, Lydia S., gct
     Kokomo MM, Ind.
1879, 7, 17. Edward Irvin rocf Kokomo MM,
     Ind., dtd 1879,6,11
1895, 12, 19. Edward I. relrq
1896, 7, 16. Clara L.A.E. Bailey dropped
     from mbrp
1896, 7, 16. Augusta Geise dropped from mbrp
1907, 9, 26. Anna recrq

JONES
1849, 3, 24. Amanda d bur Peru, O.

1875, 2, 18. Mary F. rocf Gilead MM
1875, 3, 18. Daniel recrq
1879, 4, 17. Amanda recrq
1884, 2, 18. Ernest recrq
1885, 3, 19. Nettie recrq
1886, 5, 20. Daniel dis
1887, 1, 20. Lizzie recrq
1887, 2, 17. Wesley recrq
1887, 2, 17. Addie recrq
1889, 2, 14. Alice recrq
1890, 3, 20. Nettie dropped from mbrp
1891, 3, 19. Loretta recrq
1893, 5, 18. Earnest dropped from mbrp
1901, 4, 18. Nellie Ruthanna B. relrq

JORDAN
1906, 7, 2. Dorothy [Jordon], dt Carrol R.
     & Daisy (Miller) Williams, b

1878, 8, 22. Enos recrq
1894, 11, 15. Compton recrq
1896, 7, 16. Compton dropped from mbrp

JUMP
1836, 12, 22. Eunice (form Slyter) con mcd
     (H)

KAUFMAN
1887, 5, 19. Olive E. recrq

KEEN
1823, 8, 10. Joseph d ae 65 bur Peru, O.

1887, 3, 17. Hattie recrq
1887, 4, 21. Ada recrq
1888, 7, 19. Ida & Hattie dropped from mbrp

KEENWICKER
1888, 7, 19. Katie dropped from mbrp

KEESE
----, --, --. John & Sarah
     Ch: Esther   b 1816, 5, 4 d 1833, 5, 7
          bur Centre, O.
          Oliver   b 1819, 8, 15
          Richard   " 1821, 9, 21
          Ann Eliza   " 1824, 12, 7
          Samuel T.   " 1827, 6, 2
----, --, --. Titus & Martha
     Ch: Lydia   b 1828, 4, 6
          Mary S.   " 1831, 10, 4
          Sarah Ann   " 1832, 12, 9
          Gula Elma   " 1839, 9, 21
----, --, --. Richard d 1874,8,11 bur Peru,O.;
     m Gulielma ----- d 1894,--,--
     Ch: Sarah
         Evelyn   b 1848, 10, 16
         Isaac
         Wilford   " 1850, 8, 24
         Samuel
         John   " 1852, 11, 26
         Willits
         Hansen   " 1855, 6, 4 d 1870, 4,19
          bur Peru, O.
         C. E. Le-
         nore   b 1857, 7, 14

1818, 4, 2. John rst on consent of Peru MM,
     N. Y.
1818, 5, 28. Esther, dt John & Sarah, recrq
1826, 11, 2. Titus rmt Martha Michiner
1827, 8, 29. Stephen R. con mcd
1829, 3, 5. Stephen R. dis disunity
1832, 7, 26. Stephen gct Miami MM, O. (H)
1850, 6, 27. Guli Elma gct Gilead MM
1865, 9, 21. Richard & w, Gulielma, & ch, Sa-
     rah Evelyn, Wilfred J., Samuel John, Wil-
     lots Hanson & C. E. Lenore, rocf Gilead MM
1873, 7, 17. Wilfred con mcd
1888, 2, 16. Gulielna & ch, Sarah Evalyn,
     Wilford I., Samuel John & Lenore, gct Pasa-
     dena MM, Calif.

KEHRWICKER
1887, 3, 17. Katie recrq
1891, 3, 19. S. E. recrq

KENNER
1887, 3, 17. Lydia rocf Gilead MM

KENNEY
1884, 4, 17. David [Kinney] recrq
1886, 2, 18. David dis
1887, 3, 17. Louisa & Johnnie recrq
1887, 3, 17. Bessie recrq
1889, 2, 14. Grace L. recrq

KERR
1832, 3, 29. Sarah (form Dillingham) dis mcd

KING
1842, 6, 23. Jane (form Reynolds) dis mcd
1876, 2, 17. Phebe Ann recrq

KINGMAN
1887, 2, 17. O. F. recrq
1888, 5, 17. O. F. relrq

KIRK
1819, 2, 3. Benjamin Jr., s Benjamin &
    Elizabeth, b
----, --, --. Timothy & Susanna
    Ch: Susanna   b 1825, 1, 1
1835, 9, 19. Edmund, s Caleb & Hannah, b
1846, 5, 23. Wm. Allen, s Wm. & Elizabeth,
    Cecil Co., Md.; m in Owl Creek MH, Lydia
    SPENCER, dt George & Eunice, Knox Co.,O.
    (H)

1818, 8, 27. Elizabeth & ch, Isaah, Rebecca,
    William & Sarah, recrq
1818, 12, 3. Benjamin rst on consent of Red-
    stone MM
1822, 8, 1. Benjamin & fam gct White Water
    MM, Ind.
1822, 8, 1. Isaiah gct White Water MM, Ind.
1823, 10, 23. Timothy & w, Susannah, & ch,
    Wm., Joseph, Sarah Ann, Rachel, Mary &
    Rebecca, rocf Smithfield MM, dtd 1823,9,
    22
1827, 5, 3. Susannah Carey (form Kirk) con
    mcd
1830, 7, 29. Wm. gct Plainfield MM
1831, 9, 29. Joseph gct Smithfield MM
1833, 6, 20. Timothy rmt Hannah Townsend
1833, 8, 22. Rachel dis jas
1834, 2, 20. Hannah gct Center MM
1835, 5, 21. Caleb & w, Hannah, & ch, Jo-
    seph, Samuel, Betsy, William, Howard A.,
    Rachel C., Stephen, Ann, Caleb L. & Sarah
    rocf New Garden MM, dtd 1834,9,25
1835, 5, 21. John rocf New Garden MM, dtd
    1834,10,23
1837, 2, 23. Sarah Ann Carey (form Kirk) dis
    mcd
1838, 1, 25. Joseph gct Sandy Spring MM, O.
1844, 9, 26. Roger & w & ch, Lewis T., Rue-
    ben Thos., Theodore J., Susannah Jemima,
    John K., Abraham B., Sarah Elizabeth &
    Grace Anna, rocf Nottingham MM, Md., dtd

1838,2,16 (H)
1844, 9, 26. John rocf Nottingham MM, Md.,
    dtd 1838,2,16 (H)
1846, 5, 21. Wm. Allen rocf Nottingham MM,
    Md., dtd 1846,4,17 (H)
1848, 3, 22. Wm. A. gct Nottingham MM, Md.
    (H)
1849, 11, 22. Eunice Elizabeth, dt Wm. R.,
    gct Nottingham MM, Md. (H)

KIRKPATRIC
1887, 4, 21. Fronie recrq

KNIFFIN
1826, 6, 29. Sarah rocf Scipio MM, N. Y.,
    dtd 1824,4,15

LANE
1887, 2, 17. Louis R. recrq

LANGDEN
1831, 9, 1. Lucinda (form Potter) con mcd

LAPHAM
1831, 6, 30. Joseph rocf Scipio MM, N. Y.,
    dtd 1826,11,10
1836, 5, 26. Robert A., Stephen, John P. &
    Elizabeth, ch Humphrey, rocf Scipio MM,
    N. Y., dtd 1836,2,17
1836, 5, 26. Phebe rocf Scipio MM, N. Y.,
    dtd 1836,2,17

LAYCORK
1851, 5, 22. Mary Ann (form Lee) con mcd (H)

LEE
1837, 12, 12. Harriett Ann b (H)
1839, 10, 14. Levi B. b (H)
1841, 10, 14. Rachel N. b (H)
1842, 8, 26. Jane b (H)   l (H)
1847, 7, 28. Nathan d ae 54 bur Whitstone,O.
----, 11, 15. John d b d 1852,9,29 ae 8y 10m
    bur Noble Co., O. (H)

1840, 11, 26. Nathan & w, Ury, & ch, Eliza-
    beth W., Isaac, Mary Ann, David Wilson,
    Thomas Boon, Ury Ann, Wm. Scarlot & Lucy
    Wilson, rocf Fallowfield MM, Pa., dtd
    1840,6,6 (H)
1849, 1, 25. Elizabeth dis disunity (H)
1851, 4, 24. Isaac con mcd (H)
1851, 5, 22. Mary Ann Laycork (form Lee) con
    mcd (H)
1856, 9, 24. John E. & w, Elizabeth B., & ch,
    Levi B., Rachel N., Sebela A., Martha E.,
    Eliza Jane & Phebe E., rocf Stillwater MM,
    O., dtd 1856,8,16 (H)
1856, 9, 24. Harriet Ann rocf Stillwater MM,
    O., dtd 1856,8,16 (H)
1857, 5, 21. Thomas B. dis mcd (H)
1859, 1, 20. David Wilson rpd mcd (H)
1860, 7, 26. Lucella Wilson Moody (form Lee)
    dis mcd (H)

LEE, continued

1862, 9, 25. Uree Ann Armstrong (form Lee)
 dis mcd (H)
1863, 10, 22. Harriett Ann Hall (form Lee)
 dis mcd (H)
1864, 2, 25. John E. & w, Elizabeth B., & ch,
 Sebela A., Martha E., Eliza J., Phebe E.
 & Sarah P., gct Stillwater MM, O. (H)
1864, 3, 24. Rachel N. gct White Water MM,
 Ind. (H)
1883, 4, 19. Mary W. gct Milan MM

LEGG

1892, 3, 17. Albert & Bertha recrq
1896, 7, 16. Albert & Martha dropped from
 mbrp
1899, 3, 16. Albert & Bertha recrq
1901, 5, 16. Albert & Bertha relrq

LESTER

1889, 6, 3. Bertha May, dt Wm. & Sarah
 Crawford, b

1838, 12, 20. Abel [Leister] & w, Margaret W.,
 & ch, Samuel, Sarah, Jeremiah, Wm. Howard
 Benj. Wm. & Mary Margaret, rocf Richland
 MM, Pa., dtd 1838,11,30 (H)
1851, 11, 20. Samuel V. con mcd (H)
1851, 11, 20. Mary C. (form Walters) con mcd
 (H)
1856, 11, 20. Abel & w, Margaret, & dt, Mary,
 gct White Water MM, Ind. (H)
1928, 4, 17. Bertha May Crawford recrq

LEONARD

1884, 2, 18. Lafayette recrq
1894, 3, 22. Lafayette dropped from mbrp
1900, 4, 19. Laffa recrq
1902, 6, 19. Lafe dropped from mbrp
1907, 2, 14. Lafayette recrq
1910, 5, 19. Lafayette dropped from mbrp

LEVAN

1890, 1, 16. C. O. & Lucina recrq

LEVERING

----, --, --. Thomas d 1857,6,11 ae 75 bur
 Peru, O.; m Rachel Ann -----
 Ch: Hannah b 1834, 4, 8 d 1838,10,27
  bur Peru, O.
  Susanna b 1835,12,28 d 1838,10,19
  bur Peru, O.
----, --, --. Griffith d 1873,9,25 bur Peru,O.;
 m Esther L. ----- d 1877,9,28 bur Peru, O.
 Ch: Mary
  Elizabeth b 1843, 11, 18
  Rachel
  Annette " 1846,12, 3 d 1915, 5, 9
  bur Washington, D. C.
  Lydia Fran-
  cine b 1849, 1, 31 " 1872, 3,23
  bur Peru, O.
  Elma Catha-

  rine b 1859, 5, 8
----, --, --. Samuel m Phebe ----- d 1915,9,--
 Ch: Rachel
  Ella b 1853, 9, 6
  Thomas
  Henry " 1855, 2, 5
  Mary Alice " 1856, 9, 23 d 1869, 6,14
  bur Peru
  Clara Ma-
  ria " 1859, 12, 9
  Laura Le-
  titia " 1861, 6, 24
  Susannah M." 1863, 3, 20 d 1887, 4,26
  bur Alum Creek
  Jennie Eva b 1864, 12, 7
  Fanny Es-
  ther " 1867, 1, 11
  Ralph
  Griffith " 1871, 3, 29
  George Can-
  by " 1875, 3, 27
1872, 8, 23. Rachel Annet m Clayton W. TOWN-
 SEND

1833, 4, 25. Thomas & ch, Griffith, Samuel &
 Susanna, rocf Baltimore MM, E. & W. Dist.,
 dtd 1833,3,7
1836, 4, 21. Rachel Ann rocf Baltimore MM,
 Md., dtd 1836,1,3
1839, 9, 23. Thomas & w, Rachel Ann, & s,
 Samuel, gct Philadelphia MM, Pa.
1839, 9, 23. Griffith gct Philadelphia MM,Pa.
1847, 3, 25. Griffith & w, Esther, & ch, Mary
 Elizabeth & Rachel Annette, rocf Nottingham & Little Britain MM, Pa., dtd 1847,1,8
1850, 2, 21. Thomas & w, Rachel Ann, & s, Sam
 uel, rocf Nottingham & Little Britain MM,
 Pa., dtd 1850,1,11
1852, 10, 28. Samuel gct Greenwich MM, to m
 Phebe R. Hathaway
1853, 2, 24. Phebe R. rocf Greenwich MM, dtd
 1853,1,21
1853, 3, 24. Thomas & w, Rachel Ann, gct W.
 Nottingham & Little Britain MM
1854, 2, 24. Thomas & w, Rachel Ann, rocf
 Nottingham & Little Britain MM, Md., dtd
 1854,1,6
1877, 9, 20. Arthur Rollin, minor, recrq
1881, 10, 20. Mary E. & Elma C. gct Marysville MM, Tenn.
1882, 1, 19. Thomas H. gct Marysville MM,
 Tenn.
1883, 6, 21. Samuel & w, Phebe R., & ch,
 Fanny Esther, Ralph Griffith & George
 Canby, gct Marysville MM, Tenn.
1883, 6, 21. Rachel Ann & Jannie gct Marysville MM, Tenn.
1889, 7, 18. Clara M. gct Maryville MM, Tenn.
1892, 1, 21. R. Ella gct Marysville MM, Tenn.
1897, 12, 16. R. Ella gct Colerain MM
1898, 1, 20. Cert for R. Ella to Colerain returned because she returned
1902, 8, 21. R. Ella gct Maryville MM, Tenn.

LEWIS
----, --, --. John d 1851,9,24 ae 79 bur
     Middleberry; m Hannah ----- d 1819,10,17
     ae 42 bur Knox Co., O.
     Ch: Elvira   b 1810, 9, 29
         Jason   " 1812, 9, 10
         John Jr. "   d 1818, 8, 4
           bur Wayne, O.
----, --, --. Adoni d 1850,8,16 bur Middle-
     berry, O.; m Rebecca ----- d 1855,10,20
     bur Middleberry, O.
     Ch: John W.   b 1829, 9, 15
         Elisha   " 1832, 4, 15 d 1860, 4,28
         Mary   " 1833, 5, 16 " 1861, --,--
           bur Middleberry, O.
         William   b 1835, 4, 2
         Lydia   " 1838, 4, 9 " 1838, 8,15
           bur Middleberry, O.
         Lemuel   b 1840, 5, 10 " 1850, 5,24
           bur Middleberry, O.
----, --, --. Jehu & Hannah
     Ch: Sarah   b 1830, 8, 28
         Rachel   " 1831, 11, 15 d 1854, 7, 3
           bur Middleberry
         Elizabeth b 1833, 3, 18
         Hannah   " 1834, 9, 9 " 1916, 2,12
           bur Middleberry ae 81
         William   b 1836, 8, 19
         Enoch   " 1838, 5, 5
         Jane   " 1840, 1, 19 " 1863, 7,19
         Jehu   " 1842, 1, 27 " 1857,11,14
           bur Middleberry
         Flemming B.b 1850, 6, 27 (adopted)
1834, 5, 1. Griffith, s John & Hannah, Knox
     Co., O.; m in Alum Creek MH, Anna WOOD,
     dt Daniel & Phebe
     Ch: Daniel W. b 1835, 10, 20
         Emeline   " 1838, 4, 4
1837, 8, 26. Jason, s John & Hannah, Knox
     Co., O.; m in Owl Creek, Rachel WRIGHT,
     dt Jonathan & Lavina, Knox Co., O.
     Ch: Adna   b 1838, 6, 19 d 1851, 8,20
           bur Middlebury, O.
         Jane   b 1839, 11, 23
1848, 2, 2. Rachel W. m John CHAMBERS
1850, 9, 13. Jane d ae 65 bur Middleberry,O.
1857, 11, 14. Jehu d ae 55 (an elder)
1861, 4, 3. Wm. F., s John & Hannah, Knox
     Co., O.; m in Owl Creek, Ruth TOWNSEND,
     dt Thomas & Ruth, Knox Co., O.
1861, 8, 28. Jane W. m John C. CHAMBERS

1821, 9, 27. John gct Flushing MM, to m Jane
     Roberts
1821, 9, 27. Adoni, s John, gct Flushing MM
1822, 3, 28. Jane rocf Flushing MM, dtd
     1822,2,22
1822, 6, 27. Rachel rmt Ellis Willets
1827, 9, 27. Cynthia rmt Joel Willets
1828, 10, 2. Adoni & Rebecca H. rocf Flushing
     MM, dtd 1828,8,22
1829, 10, 1. John gct Flushing MM, to m Han-
     nah Foulke

1830, 4, 29. Hannah rocf Flushing MM, dtd
     1830,2,25
1833, 10, 24. Almira rmt Reuben L. Roberts
1839, 4, 25. John & w, Jane, gct Goshen MM
1839, 4, 25. Jason & w, Rachel, & s, Adnah,
     gct Goshen MM
1839, 11, 21. Griffith & w, Anna, & ch, Daniel
     W. & Emlin & Lewis Adams, a ch in their
     care, gct Goshen MM
1843, 1, 26. John & w, Jane, rocf Goshen
     MM, dtd 1842,11,19
1856, 4, 24. Elisha dis mcd
1856, 4, 24. William dis mcd
1857, 1, 22. Elisha rst
1861, 5, 23. Wm. F. & w, Ruth T. gct Goshen
     MM
1865, 12, 21. Hannah & ch, Sarah Elizabeth,
     Hannah & Fleming B., gct Bangor MM, Ia.
1867, 7, 18. Enoch gct Bangor MM, Ia.
1867, 11, 29. Jehu gct Springfield MM, N. C.
1889, 2, 14. G. C. & Martha recrq

LEYFFER
1887, 1, 20. Minnie recrq

LIPSEY
1849, 8, 29. Wm. B., s John & Ann, Morrow
     Co., O.; m in Owl Creek, Hannah WILLETS,
     dt Ellis & Rachel, Columbiana Co., O.

1850, 2, 21. Hannah gct Gilead MM

LITTLE
1828, 10, 2. Mary (form Howard) dis mcd

LIVESEY
1850, 6, 27. Oliver & w, Elizabeth, & ch,
     Sarah Jane & Wm. B., rocf Chesterfield MM,
     dtd 1850,5,18
1851, 5, 22. Oliver & w, Elizabeth, & ch, Sa-
     rah Jane & Wm. B., gct Chesterfield MM

LONG
1882, 9, 21. Lewis recrq
1883, 6, 21. Lewis relrq

LONGDEN
1831, 9, 1. Lucinda (form Potter) con mcd

LONGSHORE
1825, 6, 30. Clarinda (form Benedict) con mcd
1840, 8, 27. Clarinda dis disunity

LOUDER
1887, 1, 20. Lawrence recrq

LOWTHER
1887, 2, 17. Sylvie recrq
1887, 2, 17. Jefferson recrq

LUKENS
----, --, --. Benjamin C., s Peter & Hannah,
     b 1839,8,8 d 1841,4,15 bur Owls Creek (H)

LUKENS, continued
1856, 11, 7. Peter d bur Owls Creek, Knox Co.,
     0. (H)

1838, 10, 25. Peter & w, Hannah, & ch, Mary
     Ann, Lydia, Joseph,Wm. & Martha Elizabeth,
     rocf Hopewell MM, Va., dtd 1838,7,5 (H)
1841, 10, 21. Mary Ann Palmer (form Lukins)
     con mcd (H)

LUMBART
1911, 6, 15. Hazel recrq
1916, 6, 15. Hazel [Lumbert] dropped from
     mbrp

McBRIDE
1835, 12, 27. Lydia, dt James & Elizabeth, b
1836, 4, 28. Maria m Lewis QUAINTANCE

1834, 12, 25. James & w, Elizabeth, & ch,
     Isaac, David, Ann, Jesse, Ruth, Hannah,
     Elihu, Grace, James, Elizabeth & Benjamin,
     rocf Sandy Spring MM, 0., dtd 1834,9,21
1834, 12, 25. Ann & ch, Joseph, Jeremiah &
     John, rocf Sandy Spring MM, 0., dtd 1834,
     10,24
1834, 12, 25. Maria rocf Sandy Spring MM, 0.,
     dtd 1834,10,24
1837, 2, 23. Rebecca rocf Sandy Spring MM,0.,
     dtd 1836,11,25
1837, 2, 23. James & w, Elizabeth, & ch,
     Isaac, David, Jesse, Ann, Ruth, Hannah,
     Elihu, Grace, James, Eliza, Benjamin &
     Lydia, gct Sandy Spring MM, 0.

McCLARY
1836, 1, 26. Elizabeth (form Benedict) dis
     mcd

McCLOUD
1895, 3, 21. Pearl B. & Lulu W. recrq
1895, 8, 22. Effa C. recrq
1898, 5, 19. Pearl & Lulu gct Columbus MM
1899, 2, 16. Effie relrq

McCONAHEY
1821, 8, 30. Hannah (form Hubbell) dis mcd

McCURDY
1904, 7, 21. Emma transferred from Ashley MM
1904, 7, 21. Emma relrq

McGREW
----, --, --. David Davis & Deborah
     Ch: Anderson H.
                b 1849, 2, 14
       Harriet C. " 1850, 9, 27
       Benjamin H." 1852, 12, 16
1851, 9, 27. James B. d bur Middleberry, 0.

1848, 6, 23. Jacob B. & w, Martha, & ch,
     Finley, Dorsey, James B. & Benjamin H.,
     rocf Smithfield MM, dtd 1848,4,17

1849, 6, 22. Deborah rocf Smithfield MM, dtd
     1849,5,22
1850, 4, 25. Harriet recrq
1850, 8, 22. David Davis recrq
1850, 11, 21. Anderson H., s Davis D. & Debo-
     rah, recrq
1851, 2, 20. Harriet Heald (form McGrew) dis
     mcd
1854, 5, 25. Finley con mcd
1856, 8, 28. David D. & w, Deborah, & ch,
     Anderson H., Caroline & Benjamin H., gct
     Westland MM, Ia.
1857, 6, 25. Findley gct Westland MM, Ia.
1859, 4, 21. Jacob B. & w, Martha, gct West-
     land MM, Ia.

McKENNY
1839, 12, 26. Louisa (form Spencer) dis mcd

McKINNIE
1890, 1, 16. W. H. & Gertie M. recrq

McLEAD
1887, 1, 20. Lena recrq
1887, 2, 17. Lammie recrq
189-, 2, 13. Amanda & Freddie recrq
1891, 2, 19. Amanda dropped from mbrp

McMICHAEL
1887, 1, 20. Hattie recrq
1887, 2, 17. Thomas recrq
1887, 2, 17. Jane recrq
1887, 2, 17. Ella recrq
1887, 2, 17. General recrq
1887, 2, 17. A. J. recrq
1889, 1, 17. A. J. relrq
1890, 9, 18. Ella relrq

McPEAK
1904, 7, 21. Tobias transferred from Ashley
     MM
1912, 5, 16. Tobias dropped from mbrp
1915, 2, 18. Ernest & Laura recrq
1921, 3, 17. Ernest & Laura dropped from
     mbrp

McVEY
1828, 7, 31. Tacy (form Gregg) dis disunity

McWHENNEY
1839, 7, 25. Louisa (form Spencer) con mcd
     (H)

McWHIRK
1887, 3, 17. Hattie recrq

MAIN
1887, 1, 20. Hannah recrq

MANVILLE
1887, 3, 17. Edwin recrq

MARTIN
1869, 1, 15. Phebe d bur Middleberry, O.
----, --, --. Sperry, s Wm. & Loretta (Ruggles)
     b 1872,11,22; m Bertha GREEN, dt Frank K.
     & Mary (Hatten), b 1880,5,15
       Ch: Harold   b 1906, 1, 7
----, --, --. Harold, s Sperry & Bertha (Green)
     b 1906,1,7; m Martha HERLOW
       Ch: Harold
           Eugene   b 1830, 1, 15

1884, 2, 18. Sarah F. recrq
1884, 4, 17. Phillip rocf Gilead MM, dtd
     1884,4,15
1889, 2, 14. Owcar, Lottie & Bessie L. recrq
1889, 2, 14. William & Emma recrq
1891, 1, 22. Philip gct Gilead MM
1891, 4, 16. Elizabeth recrq
1900, 10, 18. Lottie relrq
1902, 1, 16. Emma & Oscar relrq
1902, 7, 17. William dropped from mbrp
1904, 8, 18. Lenna dropped from mbrp
1910, 5, 19. Sperry Leroy & w, Bertha May, &
     dt, Dora, recrq
1917, 4, 19. Eugene recrq
1921, 3, 17. Eugene dropped from mbrp
1927, 3, 17. Harold Dwight recrq

MARVIN
1886, 3, 18. Isaac recrq
1896, 7, 16. Isaac dropped from mbrp

MATHEWS
1921, 3, 17. Lenna dropped from mbrp

MAYHUE
1842, 1, 27. Hannah (form Warren) dis mcd
     (living in the verge of Marlborough MM)

MEADER
1843, 2, 23. Cert rec for Gideon & w, Louisa,
     from Farnham MM, Lower Canada, dtd 1842,6,
     20, endorsed to Vermillion MM, Ill.
1843, 2, 23. Cert rec for James & w, Micca,
     & ch, Priscilla H., Lydia, Levi J. &
     Eunice N., from Farnham MM, Lower Canada,
     dtd 1842,6,20, endorsed to Vermillion MM,
     Ill.

MEEKER
----, --, --. Robert B. d 1906 bur Alum Creek;
     m Susan E. ----- d 1906,11,22 bur Alum
       Ch: Harriett H.b 1857, 3, 27   [Creek

1825, 12, 1. Emeline (form Bunker) dis mcd
1832, 5, 24. Elizabeth (form Michiner) dis mcd
1833, 7, 25. Emaline rst at White River MM,
     Ind. on consent of this mtg
1855, 1, 25. Rachel (form Mosher) dis mcd
     (H)
1855, 5, 24. Robert rocf Poplar Run MM, Ind.,
     dtd 1855,4,19
1860, 5, 24. Susan Elizabeth recrq
1862, 5, 22. Harriet H., dt Robert & Susan,

recrq
1869, 1, 21. Aaron Benedict gct Plainfield
     MM, Ind., to m Louisa Meeker
1902, 10, 16. Robert B. & Susan Elizabeth
     gct Cleveland MM

MELLINGER
1900, 4, 19. Rosetta recrq
1900, 4, 19. Clarence recrq
1907, 7, 18. Clarence [Millenger] dropped
     from mbrp
1903, 10, 22. Rose relrq

MENDENHALL
1853, 7, 28. John & w, Hannah, & ch, Wil-
     liam, Lydia Ann, Martha & Charles W.,
     rocf Pennsville MM, dtd 1853,6,8
1855, 8, 23. John & w, Hannah, & ch, Wil-
     liam, Lydia Ann, Martha & Charles, gct
     Short Creek MM, O.
1877, 4, 19. Parhaltha recrq
1884, 7, 17. Pernatha dropped from mbrp
1887, 3, 17. Fannie recrq
1889, 3, 21. Andrew & Jane recrq
1890, 12, 18. Andy dropped from mbrp
1892, 3, 17. Andy recrq
1893, 5, 18. Andrew dropped from mbrp
1902, 7, 17. Jane dropped from mbrp

MERCER
1835, 4, 23. Abraham, minor, rocf Carmel MM,
     O., dtd 1834,10,18

MERRIMAN
1825, 12, 1. Susan (form Cary) dis mcd
1891, 3, 19. Lucinda recrq

MICHINER
----, --, --. Mordecai d 1836,8,15 ae 54 bur
     Morvin; m Susanna ----- d 1834,5,4 ae 50
     bur Morvin
       Ch: Martha   b 1805, 9, 15
           Elizabeth " 1807, 10, 30
           Sarah   " 1810, 3, 22
           John   " 1812, 4, 18
           Grace   " 1813, 11, 28
           Ruth   " 1818, 10, 10
           Jane   " 1820, 7, 9
           Daniel   " 1822, 3, 18
           David O.   " 1825, 10, 23
1837, 2, 9. Grace m Daniel BENEDICT
1843, 9, 7. Jacob Lukens [Mitchener], s Wm.
     & Rachel, Marion Co., O.; m in Owl Creek
     MH, Lydia COATS, dt Seymour & Deborah,
     Richland Co., O. (H)
1849, 11, 29. David O. [Michener], s Mordecai
     & Susanna, Morrow Co., O.; m in Alum Creek
     MH, Emeline BENEDICT, dt John & Amy
----, --, --. Daniel & Emeline
       Ch: Edwin   b 1850, 8, 17

MICHINER, Daniel & Emeline, continued
 Ch: Enos P. b 1854, 11, 19 d 1915,10,21

1818, 7, 2. Mordecai recrq
1819, 9, 2. Susannah rocf New Garden MM,
 Pa., dtd 1819,6,10
1820, 4, 27. Martha, Elizabeth, Sarah, Grace
 & Ruth [Michener], ch Mordecai & Susannah,
 recrq
1826, 11, 2. Titus rmt Martha Michiner
1828, 3, 27. Sarah rmt Ebeneezer C. Daniels
1832, 5, 24. Elizabeth Meeker (form Michiner)
 dis mcd
1837, 4, 20. John gct Goshen MM, to m Susanna P. Pearson
1837, 7, 20. Susanna P. rocf Goshen MM, dtd
 1837,7,15
1843, 6, 22. Jacob L. [Mitchner] rocf Bradford MM, Pa., dtd 1843,3,7 (H)
1847, 1, 21. Jacob Lukens [Mitchner] & w,
 Lydian, gct Cincinnati MM, O. (H)
1848, 6, 23. David O. rocf Gilead MM, dtd
 1848,6,20
1855, 7, 26. David O. & w, Emeline, gct
 Driftwood MM, Ind.

MILES
1852, 4, 23. Lindley, s John & Rebecca,
 Miami Co., O.; m in Owl Creek, Lydia
 WILLETS, dt Ellis & Rachel, Knox Co., O.

1852, 8, 26. Lydia gct Union MM, O.
1857, 2, 19. Jehu Willets gct Wabash MM,
 Ind.. to m Mary J. Miles

MILLER
1885, 1, 22. Belle recrq
1887, 4, 21. Elma recrq
1887, 4, 21. Mary C. recrq
1891, 3, 19. Lewis recrq
1892, 7, 21. Belle dropped from mbrp
1932, 8, 18. Ruth Ellen, Ada, Virgil & Edna
 recrq
1932, 8, 18. Harvey & w, Florence, & ch,
 John & Robert, rocf Highland Ave. MM,
 Columbus

MILLS
1818, 8, 27. Cornelius & w, Matulda, rocf
 Junius MM, N. Y., dtd 1818,1,26
1820, 12, 28. Cornelius & fam gct Norwich
 MM, Upper Canada
1872, 9, 16. Helen G. recrq
1873, 8, 21. Helen G. gct Spring Dale MM, Ia.

MINNEAR
1923, 12, 20. George & Lydia rocf Columbus
 MM, dtd 1923,12,5
1925, 4, 16. George & Lydia gct Columbus MM,O.

MIRES
1851, 10, 23. Ann Eliza (form Chambers) dis mcd
1887, 4, 21. Harry [Meyers] recrq

MOODY
1860, 7, 26. Lucella Wilson (form Lee) dis
 mcd (H)

MOONEY
1888, 3, 22. Hattie recrq
1889, 12, 19. Hattie relrq

MOORE
1865, 6, 15. Hannah recrq
1868, 12, 17. Amanda (form Purviance) dis mcd
1878, 1, 17. Hannah gct Iowa Falls MM

MOREHOUSE
1887, 2, 17. William recrq

MORGAN
1839, 9, 23. Cert rec for Albina from Kennet
 MM, Pa., dtd 1838,6,5, endorsed to Gilead·
 MM

MORLAN
1835, 4, 2. Joseph, s Jonah & Mary, Colum-
 biana Co., O.; m in Sandusky, Mary JACK-
 SON, dt Isaac & Ann, Columbiana Co., O.
 Ch: Ann b 1836, 1, 6
   Ruth " 1838, 1, 13

1835, 2, 26. Joseph rocf Salem MM, dtd 1834,
 7,23, endorsed by New Garden MM, 1834,12,
 25

MORRIS
1837, 6, 22. Joseph & w, Jane, & ch, Abraham
 W., Tabitha & John, rocf Upper Springfield
 MM, O., dtd 1837,5,27

MORRISON
1855, 8, 30. Daniel d ae 70 bur Wms. Co., O.

1819, 9, 2. Daniel rocf Danby MM, Vt., dtd
 1818,5,7
1821, 2, 1. Elizabeth rocf New Garden MM,
 dtd 1820,12,21
1897, 7, 22. Wm. & Maggie recrq

MORTON
1818, 7, 30. Rebecca Darling (form Morton)
 dis mcd

MORSE
1923, 2, 15. Rilla dropped from mbrp

MOSES
1840, 11, 26. Nathan U. rocf Short Creek MM,
 O., dtd 1840,7,21

MOSHER
----, --, --. Asa b 1771,11,25 d 1843,3,4
 bur Marion Co., O.; m Bethia ----- b
 1771,7,23 d 1847,7,31 bur Marion Co.,O.
 (H)
 Ch: Peace b 1808, 4, 4

MOSHER, Asa & Bethia, continued
    Ch: Joseph   b 1809, 12, 26
        John   " 1812, 1, 7
----, --, --. Gershon & Ruth
    Ch: Seneca   b 1819, 5, 2
        Stephen   " 1821, 7, 6 d 1823,11,12
       bur Peru, O.
        Harriet   " 1823, 10, 1
        Perlina   " 1825, 4, 15
        Dennis   " 1827, 6, 27
        Cassander " 1830, 2, 15
        Manford   " 1832, 6, 11
----, -, --. Robert, s Asa & Bethiah, b
    1800,3,27; m Edith ----- b 1804,1,14 (H)
    Ch: Phebe   b 1823, 4, 8
        Gideon   " 1825, 3, 5
        Nathan N. " 1827, 2, 2
        Ruth   " 1829, 2, 9 d 1830, 8,22
       bur Marion Co., O.
        Bethiah   b 1831, 3, 3
        Rachel   " 1834, 1, 27
        Peace   " 1836, 9, 25
        Eunice   " 1838, 12, 27
        Edith Ann " 1841, 1, 24 d 1843, 3,27
       bur Marion Co., O.
        Calista   b 1843, 3, 6
        Cynthia W. " 1845, 9, 18
1828, 8, 6. Stephen b (H)
1828, 2, 14. Mary F. b (H)
----, --, --. Stephen, s Asa & Bethiah, b
    1806,9,22; m Ruth SMITH, dt Israel &
    Elizabeth, b 1806,2,26 (H)
    Ch: Elizabeth b 1829, 10, 8 d 1832, 5, 8
       bur Marion Co., O.
        Lemuel   b 1831, 5, 25 " 1832, 5, 2
       bur Marion Co., O.
        Elizabeth
        Jane   b 1833, 6, 2
        Hannah   " 1835, 7, 3
        Ruth   " 1837, 12, 1
        Henry   " 1840, 3, 27
        Mary S.   " 1842, 10, 7
        Esther Ann " 1845, 3, 15
        Lemuel Obe-
        diah   " 1847, 4, 28
        Elsy Beth-
        iah
----, --, --. Peleg, s Asa & Bethiah, b 1804,
    9,20; m Susannah C. BUNKER, dt Jonathan &
    Comfort, b 1809,5,21 (H)
    Ch: Peleg Jr. b 1834, 11, 20 d 1834,11,20
       bur Marion Co., O.
        John   b 1843, 1, 9
----, --, --. Asa, s Asa & Bethiah, b 1802,
    3,22; m Sarah P. BUNKER, dt Jonathan &
    Comfort, b 1805,7,29 (H)
    Ch: Stephen   b 1836, 8, 6
        Jonathan B." 1828, 10, 18
        Hannah   " 1830, 5, 18 d 1830, 5,18
       bur Marion Co., O.
        Thomas   b 1832, 6, 2 " 1847,10, 3
       bur Marion Co., O.
        Susannah B.b 1834, 11, 30

    Ch: Joseph   b 1836, 10, 5
        Elijah   " 1838, 9, 3
        Sarah An-
        gelina   " 1840, 6, 13
        Mary Ann " 1843, 10, 25
        Asa Obediah" 1847, 1, 5
1836, 12, 1. Joseph, s Asa & Bethiah, Marion
    Co., O.; m in Owl Creek MH, Beulah PITMAN,
    dt Levi & Elizabeth, Richland Co., O. (H)
1844, 3, 27. Phebe m Wm. F. SPENCER (H)
----, --, --. Daniel, s Gershom & Ruth, Mor-
    row Co., O., d 1866,8,15 bur Peru, O.; m
    Mary ----- d 1851,9,13 bur Peru, O.
    Ch: Elizabeth b 1846, 8, 10
        Mary Jr. " 1851, 8, 18
    Daniel m 2nd 1853,4,6 in Owl Creek MH,
    Nancy BRODRICK, dt Paul & Sarah, Richland
    Co., O.
    Ch: Sarah   b 1855, 10, 4 d 1860,12,19
       bur Peru, O.
1852, 9, 1. Stephen Jr., s Asa & Sarah T.,
    Morrow Co., O.; m in Whetstone MH, Mary
    FARRINGTON, dt Moses & Amelia, Crawford
    Co., O. (H)
1853, 6, 9. Lemuel b
1853, 9, 23. Bethiah m Robert F. FURNAS (H)
1855, 9, 25. Asa W. b

1818, 4, 2. Asa & w, Bethiah, & ch, Obediah,
    Ruth, Esther, Robert, Asa, Peleg, Stephen,
    Pearl, Joseph, John & Hannah, rocf Danby
    MM, dtd 1818,1,8
1818, 7, 2. Obediah dis mcd
1818, 12, 3. Gershon & w, Ruth, & ch, Joseph,
    Samuel, Daniel, David W., Guli Elma & Al-
    len, rocf Deruyter MM, N. Y., dtd 1818,1,
    21, endorsed by Short Creek MM 1818,11,24
1819, 9, 2. Esther rmt David Wood
1819, 9, 30. Ruth rmt Thomas Townsend
1822, 5, 30. Robert dis mcd
1823, 3, 27. Robert rstrq
1823, 5, 1. Edith recrq
1823, 8, 28. Asa dis disunity
1825, 7, 28. Asa Jr. rmt Sarah P. Bunker
1827, 8, 29. Peleg rmt Susanna C. Bunker
1828, 7, 3. Gershom & w, Ruth, & ch, Joseph,
    Samuel, Daniel, David W., Guli Elma, Allen
    Seneca, Harriet, Pauline & Dennis, rocf
    De Ruyter MM, N. Y., dtd 1828,4,30
1828, 10, 2. Stephen rmt Ruth Smith
1828, 11, 27. Joseph dis mcd
1829, 1, 29. Bethiah dis jH
1829, 1, 29. Edith dis jH
1829, 1, 29. Sarah T. dis jH
1829, 1, 29. Susan C. dis jH
1829, 1, 29. Peace dis jH
1829, 1, 29. Ruth dis jH
1829, 1, 29. Robert dis jH
1829, 1, 29. Peleg dis jH
1829, 1, 29. Asa Jr. dis jH
1829, 1, 29. Stephen dis jH
1829, 4, 2. Gershom dis jH
1830, 1, 28. Samuel dis mcd

MOSHER, continued
1831, 3, 3.   Daniel dis disunity
1831, 9, 29. Joseph dis disunity
1831, 9, 29. Guli Elma dis disunity
1832, 11, 22. David dis disunity
1832, 11, 22. Asa rstrq (H)
1835, 6, 25. Mary (form Davis) con mcd
1835, 12, 24. John dis jH
1837, 2, 23. Seneca dis disunity
1837, 2, 23. Allen dis disunity
1839, 12, 26. Ruth dis disunity
1840, 5, 23. Harriet dis disunity
1840, 5, 23. Paulina dis disunity
1844, 1, 25. John dis mcd (H)
1844, 6, 20. Peace Wright (form Mosher) con
    mcd (H)
1848, 4, 28. Cassander dis disunity
1848, 4, 28. Manford dis disunity
1849, 11, 22. Daniel rst
1851, 4, 24. Nathan N. dis mcd (H)
1851, 4, 24. Gideon dis mcd (H)
1855, 1, 25. Rachel Meeker (form Mosher) dis
    mcd (H)
1855, 11, 15. Jonathan B. gct Miami MM, to m
    (H)
1855, 6, 21. Elizabeth, dt Daniel & Eliza-
    beth, recrq
1859, 4, 21. Stephen & w, Ruth, & ch, Henry,
    Mary S., Esther Ann, Lemuel Obedia & Elsy
    Bethiah, gct Prairie Grove MM, Ia. (H)
1860, 3, 23. Jonathan B. gct Miami MM, O. (H)
1860, 6, 21. Hannah B. Barclay (form Mosher)
    dis mcd (H)
1860, 6, 21. Ruth Wilson (form Mosher) dis
    mcd (H)
1862, 5, 23. Beulah gct Springboro MM (H)
1863, 3, 26. Joseph dis disunity

MOTT
1837, 3, 23. Burger rocf Hector MM, N. Y.,
    dtd 1836,12,7

MUCKEY
1887, 4, 21. Oliver M. recrq

MULLENNIX
----, --, --. Moses d 1836,9,11 bur Huron
    Co., O.; m Priscilla ----- d 1835,7,5
    bur N. Y. State
    Ch: Rhoda   b 1824, 2, 8
        George F.   " 1826, 10, 12
        William   " 1830, 1, 31 d 1838, 8,11
           bur Huron, O.
1828, 9, 27. Gideon d ae 61 bur Ridgefield
1834, 1, 24. Gideon, s Moses & Priscilla,
    Huron Co., O.; m in Northen, Hannah WHITE,
    dt Joshua & Mercy, Marion Co., O.
    Ch: Moses   b 1836, 12, 28

1826, 6, 29. Gideon [Mullinix] & w, Rhoda,
    rocf Plains MM, N. Y., dtd 1826,2,21
1826, 6, 29. Moses & w, Priscilla, & ch,
    Aaron, Gideon, Samuel, Martha, Priscilla

& Thomas, rocf Plains MM, N. Y., dtd
    1826,2,21
1830, 7, 1.   Ann Benschoter (form Mullenix)
    dis mcd
1832, 4, 26. Anna VanVinshitter (form Mul-
    lenix) dis mcd
1833, 10, 24. Rhoda rmt Jonathan Wood
1842, 1, 27. Rhoda Tappin (form Mullenix)
    rpd mcd
1842, 6, 23. Priscilla dis
1842, 8, 25. Samuel dis mcd

NEIDIGH
1917, 4, 19. Ella dropped from mbrp

NEIL
1897, 2, 18. Justine d ae 78 bur Alum Creek

1847, 7, 22. Justin Ann [Neill] rocf Sandy
    Spring MM, O., dtd 1847,3,26, endorsed by
    Gilead MM, 1847,6,22
1851, 8, 28. Phebe Elma, Richard Thomas, Omar,
    William A. & Barak [Neale], ch Josiah &
    Justine A., recrq
1871, 10, 19. Omar O. [Neill] dis disunity
1881, 2, 17. Richard T. & Wm. relrq
1883, 7, 19. Barack dropped from mbrp
1885, 3, 19. Jonathan & Mary W. recrq
1892, 7, 21. Jonathan dropped from mbrp
1898, 5, 19. Elma dropped from mbrp

NEVILL
----, --, --. Greenwood & Rhoda
    Ch: 1864, 8, 24
                  1866, 9, 6
                  1868, 10, 15

1861, 6, 20. Benjamin & w, Rhoda E., rocf
    Gilead MM, dtd 1861,6,18
1869, 3, 18. Benjamin G. & w, Rhoda, & ch,
    Alfred, Mary Agnes & Sarah Elizabeth, gct
    Greenwich MM, O.

NEWVILLE
1887, 2, 17. Myrtle recrq
1888, 3, 22. Lorie recrq

NICHOLSON
1891, 2, 19. William & w, Lydia T., & ch,
    Jesse B. F. & Mary A. K., rocf Milan MM,
    dtd 1891,1,17
1904, 7, 21. Jesse & Hattie transferred from
    Ashley MM
1920, 4, 15. Jesse dropped from mbrp
1921, 3, 17. Hattie & ch dropped from mbrp

NICHOLS
1826, 4, 27. Tacy [Nickols] rocf Goose Creek
    MM, Va., dtd 1825,11,17
1831, 6, 30. Tacy dis jas
1847, 4, 23. Eliza, Lloyd, Eugene, Susan &
    Hortentia, rocf Plainfield MM, dtd 1846,
    10,29 (minor ch of Eli & Rachel)

NICHOLS, continued

1850, 1, 24. Athenissa [Nickles] gct Gilead MM

1856, 1, 24. Jacob [Nickols] rocf Goose Creek MM, Va., dtd 1855,11,15 (H)

NOBLE

1898, 7, 21. James A. & w, Mary M., & ch, Mary Blanche, James Arthur, Irene Elizabeth & Frank, roc

1901, 1, 17. James A. & w, Mary M., & ch, Mary Blanch, James Arthur, Irene Elizabeth & Frank & infant s not named, gct Van Wert MM, O.

1901, 7, 18. James A. & w, Mary, & ch, Blanche, Arthur, Irene, Frank & Ralph, gct Delphi MM

NUTT

1890, 1, 16. E. N. recrq

OLIVER

1877, 5, 30. Annis d ae 64 bur Peru, O.

1877, 4, 19. Anise recrq
1895, 8, 22. George & w, Esther V., recrq
1902, 2, 13. George C. & Esther relrq

OLMSTEAD

1896, 4, 16. Elmer C. recrq
1898, 5, 19. Elmer dropped from mbrp

OSBORN

----, --, --. David d 1849,11,14 ae 79 bur Peru, O.; m Anna ----- d 1848,1,15 ae 81 bur Peru, O.
    Ch: Daniel   b 1797, 12, 5 d 1881, 7,30 bur Peru, O.
        Azur   b 1800, 8, 31
        Henry   " 1802, 2, 26
        Dorcas   " 1804, 3, 17 d 1864,12, 5 bur Peru, O.
        David Jr. b 1806, 4, 25 " 1876, 4,24 bur Peru, O.
1872, 8, 29. Charity d ae 80 bur Peru, O.
1884, 10, 9. Susan d
----, --, --. Daniel d 1881,7,30 ae 84 bur Peru, O.; m Lydia ----- d 1823,10,2 ae 24 bur Peru, O.
    Ch: Priscilla b 1821, 3, 23 d 1893, 2,11 bur Alum Creek
    Daniel m 2nd Deborah ----- d 1834, 5,26 ae 27 bur Peru, O.
    Ch: Josephine b 1830, 8, 19 d 1898, 2,12
    Daniel m 3rd 1836,6,30 in Alum Creek MH, Charity BRADY, dt James & Sarah KNIFFIN, Huron Co., O., d 1872,8,29 ae 80 bur Peru, O.
    Daniel m 4d 1874,3,26 in Alum Creek MH, Ruth COMFORT, dt Wm. & Phebe GIDNEY, d 1894,8,25 ae 87 bur Peru, O.
1824, 10, 13. Charles, s Henry & Esther, d bur Peru, O.

1828, 6, 28. Henry d bur Peru, O.
1842, 12, 29. Esther m Thomas SHARP
----, --, --. David Jr. d 1876,4,24 bur Peru, O.; m Susan ----- d 1884,9,10 bur Peru,O.
    Ch: Edward W. b 1846, 9, 21 d 1913, 2,19 bur Alum Creek
        Mary   b 1848, 3, 25
        Anne   " 1850, 10, 21
        Sarah   " 1853, 6, 29
        Martha   " 1857, 3, 16
        Esther   " 1858, 11, 25 d 1906,--,-- bur Alum Creek
1850, 10, 21. Anna, dt David & Susan (Hobbs) b
1855, 10, 29. Elizabeth W., dt Thomas & Catherine (Howard) Wood, b
----, --, --. John & Minerva
    Ch: William
        Elmore   b 1856, 9, 27
        John D.   " 1860, 4, 26
        Alicutt P. " 1864, 11, 19
        Francine L." 1869, 11, 25
        Myrtle A. " 1871, 9, 1
----, --, --. Josephus d 1898,2,12 bur Stayton, Ore.; m Lydia Ann -----
    Ch: Henry Edwin   b 1857, 4, 25
1859, 12, 21. Charlotte A., dt Geo. & Phebe (Buck) Howell, b
1865, 11, 26. Lenore W., dt Daniel & Caroline (Starr), b
1870, 9, 15. Mary W. m Thos. C. WILLIAMS
----, --, --. Elmore & Laura
    Ch: Ethel   b 1883, 11, 25
        Cora J.   " 1886, 3, 1
        Alice   " 1888, 9, --
        Clarabelle " 1899, --, --
1889, 4, --. Merritt d bur Alum Creek

1819, 9, 30. Daniel rmt Lydia Wood
1824, 1, 1. Henry rmt Esther Gidley
1824, 1, 1. Azur dis mcd
1825, 6, 30. Desire rocf Salem MM, Mass., dtd 1825,1,13
1826, 2, 2. Desire rmt Jonathan Wood
1829, 4, 30. Daniel gct Marlborough MM, to m Deborah Williams
1830, 3, 4. Deborah rocf Marlborough MM, dtd 1829,7,28
1830, 12, 30. Esther & s, Charles, gct Goshen MM
1832, 4, 26. Esther & s, Charles, rocf Goshen MM, dtd 1832,2,17
1840, 1, 23. Priscilla Grissell (form Osborn) dis mcd
1844, 5, 23. David Jr. gct White Water MM, Ind., to m Susan Williams
1844, 11, 21. Susan rocf White Water MM, Ind., dtd 1844,9,25
1847, 8, 27. Charles gct Goshen MM
1852, 10, 28. Josephus con mcd
1854, 11, 23. Lydia Ann recrq
1863, 11, 19. Josephus F. & w, Lydia, & s, Edwin, gct Winneshiek MM, Ia.

OSBORN, continued

1867, 6, 20. Josephus & w, Lydia Ann, & s,
    Henry Edwin, rocf Winneshiek MM, Ia., dtd
    1867,5,18

1870, 2, 17. George A. & Mary A. recrq

1873, 12, 18. Josephus & w, Lydia Ann, & s,
    Henry Edwin, gct Winneshiek MM, Ia.

1874, 7, 16. John & Minerva recrq

1875, 3, 18. Oliett P., dt John & Minerva,
    recrq

1875, 5, 20. Edgar recrq

1876, 11, 16. Wm. Elmore recrq

1877, 8, 16. George A. relrq

1879, 3, 20. Edgar relrq

1879, 4, 17. Alice recrq

1884, 2, 18. Francene L. recrq

1884, 6, 19. Adelbert D. recrq

1885, 3, 19. Seth C. & John D. recrq

1889, 2, 14. Cecil V. recrq

1891, 4, 16. May recrq

1894, 1, 18. Dell D. & w, Millie R., gct
    Westland MM

1894, 5, 17. W. Herbert gct Westland MM

1895, 3, 21. Lenora W. relrq

1896, 7, 16. Cecil O. dropped from mbrp

1902, 7, 17. Seth & Hattie dropped from mbrp

1903, 11, 19. Lydia Ann rocf Marion MM, dtd
    1902,7,21

1907, 2, 14. Ernest Franklin recrq

1907, 3, 21. Ralph H. recrq

1911, 12, 21. Ralph H. relrq

1912, 1, 18. Hubert H. relrq

1912, 5, 16. Ernest dropped from mbrp

1914, 3, 19. John D. relrq

1916, 1, 20. Lottie relrq

1919, 5, 22. Lizzie recrq

1921, 4, 21. Della H. recrq

1922, 5, 18. Merritt J. relrq

1923, 3, 22. Grace Gertrude recrq

1925, 4, 16. Lenore rocf Cedar Ave. MM,
    Cleveland

1930, 5, 22. Grace [Osborne] dropped from
    mbrp

OSMOND

1892, 2, 18. Sarah recrq

1893, 9, 21. Sarah gct Portland MM, Ore.

1897, 5, 20. Sarah rocf Portland MM, Ore.

1899, 10, 19. Sarah gct Columbus MM

OVERMAN

1864, 5, 25. Nixon, s Eli & Elizabeth, Wash-
    ington Co., Ind.; m in Owl Creek, Mary
    WILLETS, dt Ellis & Rachel, Knox Co.,O.

1864, 11, 17. Mary W. gct Blue River MM, Ind.

OWEN

1841, 6, 24. Parvis W. dis mcd

1895, 2, 14. Phebe [Owens] relrq

PACKER

1830, 9, 10. Moses d ae 66 bur Middlebury,O.

PAGE

1878, 4, 18. Wm. R. recrq

1884, 7, 17. William dropped from mbrp

PALMER

1828, 1, 1. Elizabeth rocf Pipe Creek MM,
    dtd 1828,4,19 (H)

1829, 7, 30. Prudence rocf Pipe Creek MM,
    dtd 1829,3,15 (H)

1839, 10, 24. Ann (form Elliott) dis mcd (H)

1841, 10, 21. Mary Ann (form Lukins) con mcd
    (H)

1864, 2, 18. George A. dis military service

PARKER

1894, 6, 21. Fidelia rocf Westfield MM, Ind.

1903, 7, 16. Fidelia gct S. 8th St. MM,
    Richmond, Ind.

PARKINS

----, --, --. Isaac & Nancy (H)
    Ch: Sarah   b 1822, 8, 9
        Jesse   " 1823, 4, 30 d 1855, 6,23
        bur Whitestone, O.
        Jane   b 1825, 2, 11
        Louisa   b 1828, 10, 30 d 1855, 9,11
        bur Cardington
        Mary   b 1831, 10, 25 " 1831,10,25
        Hannah   " 1834, 2, 9
        Lydia   " 1836, 4, 7 " 1839, 3, 1
        bur Whetstone, O.
        Schooley   b 1838, 1, 31 " 1861,12,24
        bur Whetstone, O.

1838, 12, 20. Cert rec for Sarah, Jesse, Jane
    & Louisa, from Flushing MM, O., endorsed
    to Gilead MM

1845, 7, 29. Sarah Russel (form Parkins) con
    mcd (H)

1862, 3, 20. Schooley dis mcd (H)

1862, 12, 25. Jane dis disunity (H)

PARRY

1834, 4, 24. John rocf Pipe Creek MM, dtd
    1833,9,14 (H)

PARTHMORE

1890, 2, 13. Frederick recrq

1891, 11, 19. Sarah [Parthemore] recrq

1892, 7, 21. Fred dropped from mbrp

1895, 11, 21. Sarah [Parthemore] relrq

1900, 1, 22. Fred & Rose recrq

1907, 7, 18. Fred & Rose [Pathemore] dropped
    from mbrp

PAST

1887, 4, 21. Samuel & Lavina recrq

PATEE

1837, 2, 23. Mary rocf Scipio MM, N. Y.. dtd
    1837,1,18

PATTERSON

1821, 7, 5. Joseph Howard gct Short Creek

PATTERSON, continued
    MM, O., to m Pharaby Patterson

PEARSON
1837, 4, 20. John Michiner gct Goshen MM, to
    m Susanna P. Pearson
1852, 7, 22. Lewis Willets gct West Branch MM,
    to m Charity Pearson

PEASLEY
----, --, --. Joseph d 1835,8,21 ae 40 bur
    Morvin, O.; m Amy -----
      Ch: David   b 1825, 6, 30 d 1830,11, 6
         bur Morvin, O.
        Jane   b 1828, 6, 6
        Joseph Jr." 1830, 6, 20
        Amy Ann " 1833, 8, 19
1835, 8, 16. Wm., s Samuel & Betsy, b
----, --, --. Chalkley & Margaret
      Ch: Jacob A. b 1836, 4, 22
        Joseph
        John   " 1838, 4, 13

1823, 6, 25. Joseph & w, Amy, & ch, Chalkley,
    Jonathan W., Lydia, Micajah & Mary, rocf
    Peru MM, N. Y., dtd 1823,3,27
1834, 6, 26. Samuel & w, Betsy, & ch, Henry
    G., Enoch, Mary Jane, Phebe Ann & Charles
    L., rocf Peru MM, N. Y., dtd 1834,4,23
1834, 9, 25. Chalkley gct Carmel MM, to m
    Margaret Ashton
1835, 4, 23. Margaret rocf Carmel MM, O.,
    dtd 1834,12,20
1846, 6, 26. Samuel & w, Betsy, & ch, Phebe
    Ann, Charles L. & Samuel Wm., rocf Gilead
    MM, dtd 1846,5,26
1849, 4, 27. Samuel & w, Betsy, & ch, Charles
    & William, gct Gilead MM
1849, 4, 27. Phebe Ann gct Gilead MM

PECKHAM
1839, 7, 25. James S. rocf Farmington MM,
    N. Y., dtd 1838,7,26
1841, 2, 25. Seneca James [Peckum], ward of
    Richmond Hathaway, gct Farmington MM,N.Y.

PELLETT
1844, 9, 23. Unity [Pellet] & ch, George,
    Sarah, Elisha, Salathiel, Mary Elanor,
    Seth, Harrison & Allen, rocf Carmel MM,
    dtd 1844,7,20
1848, 10, 27. Uniay & ch, Elisha, Salathiel,
    Seth, Mary Ellen, Harrison, Allen & Albert,
    gct Goshen MM
1849, 12, 28. George gct Goshen MM

PENNINGTON
1835, 6, 25. Joseph & w, Sarah, & ch, Maria,
    Robert, Lewis, Edwin, Isaac, Sarah Ann,
    Barclay, William K. & Caroline, rocf
    Scipio MM, N. Y., dtd 1835,4,15

PENROSE
1841, 10, 21. Edwin & w, Mary, & ch, Lovina,
    Eliza Ann, Robert & Nathan Linville, rocf
    Plainfield MM, dtd 1841,9,16 (H)
1846, 5, 21. Edwin & w, Mary, & ch, Lavina,
    Eliza, Ann, Rachel, Nathan L. & Jesse, gct
    Clear Creek MM, Ill. (H)

PERKINS
1836, 3, 24. Isaac & w, Nancy, & ch, Sarah,
    Jesse, Jane Louisa & Hannah, rocf Flush-
    ing MM, dtd 1835,8,22 (H)

PERRY
1836, 11, 25. John d bur Knox Co., O. (H)

PETERS
1905, 12, 21. Frank recrq
1912, 5, 16. Frank dropped from mbrp

PETTIT
1914, 1, 22. Nancy recrq

PHILBROOK
1884, 4, 17. Wm. C. recrq

PHILLIPS
1887, 1, 20. Letta recrq
1887, 2, 17. Jenkins recrq
1887, 2, 17. Sarah A. recrq
1887, 2, 17. Benjamin recrq
1887, 2, 17. Julia recrq

PIERCE
1860, 7, 26. Ruth L. (form Wood) dis mcd (H)

PIERPONT
1855, 6, 21. Jonah & Sarah C. rocf Goose
    Creek MM, Va., dtd 1854,10,12 (H)

PIM
1862, 7, 17. John Wright gct Sandy Spring MM,
    to m Sarah Pim

PINDER
1887, 3, 17. George recrq
1887, 3, 17. Orley recrq
1887, 3, 17. Samuel recrq
1887, 3, 17. Ivah recrq
1887, 3, 17. John recrq
1887, 3, 17. Mary recrq
1893, 5, 18. Samuel, Laura S. & George
    dropped from mbrp
1893, 5, 18. Orley dropped from mbrp
1899, 10, 19. John & Mary dropped from mbrp

PITMAN
1835, 11, 11. Margaret V., dt Anthony & Marga-
    ret, b (H)
1836, 12, 1. Beulah m Joseph MOSHER (H)

1833, 1, 24. Anthony [Pittman] & w, Margaret,
    & ch, Rebecca, Esther, Elias & Eliza,

PITMAN, continued
    rocf Plainfield MM, dtd 1832,10,25 (H)
1833, 11, 21. Beulah [Pittman] rocf Plainfield
    MM, dtd 1833,7,25 (H)
1834, 5, 22. Rebecca, Esther, Elias & Eliza,
    ch Anthony & Margaret, rocf Short Creek
    MM, dtd 1834,1,21
1838, 1, 25. Anthony & w, Margaret, & ch, Re-
    becca, Esther, Eliza, Elias & Margaret V.,
    gct Miami MM, O. (H)
1840, 3, 26. Rebecca, Esther, Elias & Eliza,
    gct Green Plain MM

PLATT
1823, 3, 27. Benjamin rocf Oblong MM, N. Y.,
    dtd 1817,6,16, endorsed by Short Creek
    MM, O., 1823,1,21
1828, 10, 2. Benjamin con mcd
1829, 5, 28. Benjamin dis

PLEAS
----, --, --. Maurice & Hannah E. [Place]
    (Hannah d 1824,7,16 ae 25 bur Peru, O.)
    Ch: Isaac   b 1819, 3, 11
        Eliza   " 1821, 6, 20
        Benjamin   " 1824, 1, 1

1817, 10, 30. Maurice recrq
1818, 1, 29. Maurice rmt Hannah Earl
1818, 7, 30. Jane [Place] rmt John Smith
1821, 11, 29. Maurice & w, Hannah, & ch,
    Isaac & Eliza, gct White Water MM, Ind.
1823, 6, 25. Maurice & w, Hannah, & ch,
    Isaac & Eliza, rocf White Water MM, Ind.,
    dtd 1823,3,15
1823, 6, 25. Wm. rocf White Water MM, Ind.,
    dtd 1823,4,19
1825, 3, 31. Wm. [Place] gct White Water MM,
    Ind.
1825, 12, 29. Maurice gct White Water MM, Ind.
1830, 9, 16. Morris [Place] & ch, Isaac,
    Eliza & Benjamin, gct Green Plain MM, O.
    (H)

PLOGER
1887, 1, 20. Emma J. recrq
1887, 3, 17. Jehu H. recrq
1905, 12, 21. Emma & John Francis recrq
1912, 5, 16. Emma Ploger Sutmiller dropped
    from mbrp
1912, 5, 16. John Francis dropped from mbrp

POLLARD
1840, 6, 25. Warren W. & w, Ruth, rocf Ux-
    bridge MM, Mass., dtd 1840,1,31
1869, 12, 16. Warren W. con mcd
1874, 9, 17.· Warren W. gct Columbus MM, O.

POTTER
1835, 5, 11. Chloe d ae 63 bur Gilead, O.

1828, 5, 1. Chloe & dt, Lucinda, rocf Danby
    MM, Vt.

1831, 9, 1. Lucinda Langden (form Potter)
    con mcd

PORTER
1887, 1, 20. Eliza recrq

POUND
----, --, --. David & Ann
    Ch: Mary   b 1823, 9, 22
        Ann H.   " 1825, 12, 22

1822, 8, 1. Asa & w, Mary, rocf Junius MM,
    N. Y., dtd 1822,4,24
1822, 8, 1. David & w, Ann, & ch, Thomas
    C., Sarah H., Benjamin H., Isabella &
    Elijah, rocf Junius MM, N. Y., dtd 1822,
    4,22
1828, 11, 27. David dis jH
1829, 1, 29. Ann dis jH
1829, 1, 29. Asa & w, Margaret, gct Junius
    MM, N. Y. (H)
1829, 1, 29. David & w, Ann, & ch, Thos. C.,
    Sarah H., Benj. H., Isabella, Elijah,
    Mary H. & Ann H., gct Junius MM, N. Y.(H)
1832, 6, 21. Ch of David & Ann gc

POWELL
1929, 3, 21. Frances recrq

POWERS
1887, 2, 17. Arthur recrq
1904, 1, 21. Zeno Alvin recrq
1908, 2, 20. Zeno relrq

PRICE
1852, 2, 26. Warrick rocf Smithfield MM, O.,
    dtd 1851,12,26
1857, 1, 22. Warrick gct Smithfield MM, O.

PRIMER
1887, 2, 17. Ellen recrq

PURCEL
1839, 5, 2. Thos. V., s John & Mary, Fred-
    eric Co., Va.; m in Owl Creek MH, Nancy N.
    WALTERS, dt Mahlon & Elizabeth, Knox Co.,
    O. (H)
    Ch: Joseph Wm. b 1840, 4, 4
        Mahlon W. " 1843, 2, --

1837, 4, 24. John & w, Mary, & ch, Thomas V.,
    Lydia Ann, Priscilla H., Rosanna, John,
    Rebecca J. & Elias H., rocf Hopewell MM,
    dtd 1836,11,10 (H)
1837, 12, 21. John [Purcell] & w, Mary, & ch,
    Lydia Ann, Priscilla Hunt, Rosannah, John
    Beedle, Rebecca Anney & Elias Hix, gct
    Hopewell MM, Va. (H)
1838, 6, 21. Lucy (form Bunker) con mcd
1886, 11, 18. Hannah E. recrq
1887, 3, 17. Peleg recrq
1889, 6, 20. Hannah E. gct Westland MM
1904, 7, 21. Hannah transferred from Ashley MM

PURCEL, continued
1845, 8, 21. Thos. V. [Pursell] & w, Nancy
H., & ch, Joseph William & Mahlon W., gct
Hopewell MM, Va. (H)

PURINTON
----, --, --. John d 1837,1,10 bur Peru, O.;
m Philena -----
Ch: Caroline H.b 1831, 1, 2 d 1847, 3, 6
bur Peru, O.
Lydia G. b 1834, 11, 12 " 1838, 8,28
bur Peru, O.
John H. b 1836, 6, 12 " 1841, 8,27
bur Peru, O.

1833, 10, 24. John & w, Philena, & dt, Caroline
H., rocf Starksborough MM, Vt., dtd 1833,
8,2
1839, 5, 23. Philena dis disunity

PURVIANCE
----, --, --. Henry & Cynthia [Perviance]
Ch: Martha M. b 1841, 1, 28
Amanda " 1844, 7, 23
Joseph E. " 1846, 11, 2
William H. " 1852, 1, 16 d 1857, 5,11
bur Middlebury

1850, 12, 26. Henry S. rst on consent of Smithfield MM
1851, 6, 26. Cynthia recrq
1854, 4, 26. M. Amanda & Joseph Elwood, ch
Henry & Cynthia, recrq (Martha,Amanda)
1861, 5, 23. Martha Bryant (form Purviance)
dis mcd
1868, 12, 17. Amanda Moore (form Purviance)
dis mcd

QUAINTANCE
----, --, --. Eli & Betty
Ch: Martha b 1827, 1, 13 d 1835,10,30
bur Sandusky
Rachel b 1830, 9, 30
Caleb " 1832, 6, 17
Charles " 1834, 10, 4
----, --, --. Fisher & Sarah
Ch: George E. b 1831, 12, 3
Charles R. " 1831, 12, 5 (?)
Sarah Jane " 1834, 3, 23
1836, 4, 28. Lewis, s Eli & Betty, Crawford
Co., O.; m in Sandusky, Maria McBRIDE, dt
John & Ann, Crawford Co., O.
Ch: Rebecca
Ann b 1837, 3, 4

1825, 12, 29. Eli & w, Betty, & ch, Joseph,
Lewis Coy, Susannah, William, Edward
Courtney & Ann, rocf Smithfield MM, dtd
1825,9,19
1829, 7, 2. Joseph & w, Susannah, rocf

Smithfield MM, dtd 1829,4,20
1831, 1, 27. Fisher & w, Sarah, & ch, Ann,
Eli P., Irey, Susanna, Dawson & Joseph W.,
rocf Smithfield MM, dtd 1830,12,20
1831, 1, 27. William & w, Esther, & ch, Rebecca, Charlotte, Joseph & William, rocf
Smithfield MM, dtd 1830,12,20
1833, 1, 24. Joseph K. con mcd
1837, 1, 26. Susanna Downing (form Quaintance)
con mcd

RANDOLPH
1885, 3, 19. Nellie recrq
1885, 3, 19. Chattie recrq
1894, 2, 15. Guy D. recrq
1895, 2, 14. Guy D. relrq

RASEY
1911, 2, 16. Harrison recrq
1917, 4, 19. Harrison dropped from mbrp

RATHBURN
1911, 2, 16. Pearl recrq
1921, 3, 17. Pearl & w & ch dropped from
mbrp

REDFERN
1835, 12, 24. Rachel (form Gregg) dis mcd

REECE
1828, 11, 27. David Smith gct Cherry Grove
MM, Ind.,) to m Elizabeth Reece

REID
1879, 5, 22. Emma recrq
1879, 7, 17. Mary Jane recrq
1879, 8, 21. Jehu recrq
1882, 3, 16. Arnold recrq
1884, 2, 18. Eugene A. recrq
1885, 10, 22. John relrq
1891, 5, 21. Arnold S. relrq
1892, 11, 17. Martha B. relrq
1906, 3, 22. Stella Imo recrq
1912, 5, 16. Lula dropped from mbrp
1916, 5, 20. Effie relrq

RENZ
1891, 3, 19. Mary A. recrq
1891, 3, 19. Frederick recrq

RETTER
1887, 3, 17. Martha rocf Gilead MM

REXFORD
1842, 1, 27. Abigail (form Warren) dis mcd
(living in the verge of Marlborough MM)

REYNOLDS
1846, 6, 13. Phebe d ae 61 bur Berlin, O.

REYNOLDS, continued
1826, 6, 29. Daniel & w, Phebe, & ch, Isaac,
    Jane & Polly, rocf Plains MM, N. Y., dtd
    1826,2,21
1832, 2, 2. Isaac T. dis mcd
1842, 1, 27. Jane King (form Reynolds) dis
    mcd
1842, 6, 23. Polly Wetherbon (form Reynolds)
    dis mcd
1848, 10, 27. Daniel gct Gilead MM, to m
    Miriam Taber
1910, 10, 12. Clinton O. & w, Mary V., & ch,
    Lois Esther, Ruth Gladys & Alice Lucile,
    roc
1917, 9, 20. Clinton & w, Mary V., & ch,
    Lois Esther, Ruth Gladys, Alice Lucile &
    Elizabeth Marie, gct Fountain City MM,
    Ind.

RICHARDSON
1838, 1, 30. Rachel d bur Knox Co., O. (H)

1823, 5, 1. Rachel rocf Pipe Creek MM, dtd
    1822,12,14
1829, 3, 5. Rachel dis jH
1830, 3, 4. Eleanor dis jH
1859, 7, 21. Eleanor gct Prairie Grove MM,
    Ia. (H)

RICHMOND
----, --, --. Ernest, s Lester & Dora (Steck-
    neck), b 1894,3,9; m Lelia BENEDICT, dt
    Walter L & Kate (Osborn), b 1894,12,6

1911, 2, 16. Earnest recrq
1811, 3, 16. Bryan recrq
1918, 2, 14. Bryan relrq

RICKARD
1837, 8, 24. Laura A. (form Douglas) dis mcd

RIDENHOUR
1880, 8, 19. Julia Wollem relrq

RIDGEWAY
1850, 5, 1. Mary m John Q. SPENCER

1825, 3, 3. Joseph rocf Scipio MM, N. Y.,
    dtd 1824,8,19
1829, 1, 1. Joseph dis jH
1850, 3, 28. Mary rocf Flushing MM, dtd
    1850,2,21

RINEHART
1911, 6, 15. Marguerite recrq
1914, 6, 18. Margueritte relrq

RING
1824, 12, 2. Marian, w Enos, rocf Farmington
    MM, N. Y., dtd 1824,5,27
1824, 12, 2. Mary Ann & dt, Sally Ann, rocf
    Farmington MM, N. Y., dtd 1824,6,27
1833, 11, 21. Mary Ann & dt, Sally Ann, gct

White River MM, Ind.

RITTER
1890, 7, 17. Martha J. relrq

ROBB
1911, 2, 16. Theo recrq

ROBERTS
1823, 7, 15. Ann d ae 61 bur Wayne
----, --, --. Reuben S. & Elvira
    Ch: Griffith b 1834, 7, 20 d 1834, 9,7
        bur Morvin
        Charles   b 1835, 8, 5
        Elwood   " 1837, 8, 15 " 1838,10, 4
        bur Morvin

1821, 9, 27. John Lewis gct Flushing MM, to
    m Jane Roberts
1824, 10, 28. Isaiah dis disunity
1829, 1, 29. Henry dis jH
1831, 3, 3. Jonathan rmt Mary Smith
1831, 3, 31. Mary [Roberds] gct White Water
    MM, Ind.
1833, 5, 23. Reuben L. rocf Flushing MM, dtd
    1833,4,25
1833, 10, 24. Reuben L. rmt Almira Lewis
1891, 3, 19. Daisy recrq

ROBINSON
1887, 4, 21. Anna recrq

ROBY
1842, 7, 28. Hannah (form Irish) dis mcd
1887, 4, 21. Maud recrq
1893, 5, 18. Maud dropped from mbrp

ROGERS
1851, 1, 24. Ansel, s Thomas & Hannah, Lena-
    wee Co., Mich.; m in Alum Creek MH, Cyn-
    thia GRISELL, dt Aden S. & Sarah BENEDICT
1864, 10, 6. Ansel, s Thomas & Hannah, Morrow
    Co., O.; m in Alum Creek MH, Priscilla
    GRISELL, dt Daniel & Lydia OSBORN, Morrow
    Co., O.

1828, 7, 31. Thomas & w, Catherine, rocf
    Short Creek MM, dtd 1828,5,20
1829, 1, 29. Catharine dis jH
1829, 3, 5. Thomas dis jH
1851, 1, 23. Ansel rocf Adrian MM, Mich.,
    dtd 1851,1,9
1851, 4, 24. Ancel & w, Cynthia, & her dt,
    Lydia Ann Grisell, gct Adrian MM, Mich.
1864, 2, 18. Ansel & ch, Alonzo, Sarah
    Louisa & Arthur, rocf Gilead MM, dtd
    1864,2,16
1865, 2, 16. Ancel & w, Priscilla, & ch, Sa-
    rah & Arthur, gct Rasin MM, Mich.
1867, 5, 61. Alonzo relrq
1873 6, 19. Priscilla rocf West Grove MM,
    Ind., dtd 1873,5,10

ROMANS
1877, 12, 6.   Joseph d bur Philadelphia (s
    Sally)

1839, 10, 24.   Ephraim rocf Bradford MM, Pa.,
    dtd 1839,7,2 (H)
1858, 12, 23.   Sally & s, Joseph, rocf Gilead
    MM, dtd 1858,11,23
1861, 10, 17.   Lucinda recrq
1867, 5, 16.   Lucinda Gray (form Romans) con
    mcd

ROMICK
1873, 6, 19.   Lida G. rocf West Grove MM,
    Ind., dtd 1873,5,10
1893, 9, 21.   Lida G. gct Portland MM, Oregon
1897, 3, 18.   Lida G. rocf Portland MM, Oregon
1899, 10, 19.   Lida G. gct Columbus MM

ROOD
1839, 3, 21.   Emmore rocf Upper Springfield
    MM, O., dtd 1838,9,22
1840, 8, 27.   Emmor gct Sandy Spring MM, O.

ROSS
1887, 3, 17.   Milton & Mina recrq

ROWLAND
1883, 10, 19.   Ethel K., dt Wm. Elmore & Laura
    (Levering) Osborn, b

RUSSELL
1845, 7, 29.   Sarah [Russel] (form Parkins)
    con mcd (H)
1862, 12, 25.   Sarah dis disunity (H)
1884, 6, 19.   Phebe C. Howell gct West Branch
    MM

SAITER
1887, 3, 17.   Ella recrq

SAMS
1907, 1, 17.   Herbert J. recrq
1907, 1, 17.   Louisa M. recrq
1907, 1, 17.   Alpharetta recrq
1912, 5, 16.   Hubert, Louisa & Alpharetta
    dropped from mbrp

SANDS
1834, 9, 25.   Samuel rocf Baltimore MM, E. &
    W. Dist., dtd 1833,5,9

SANTEE
----, --, --.   David & Jane
    Ch: Washington b 1831, 5, 14
        Sarah L.   " 1833, 7, 14
        Ann H.   " 1835, 11, 27
        Mary   " 1838, 12, 26
        Isaac P.   " 1842, 8, 5
        Margaret
         Elizabeth " 1844, 11, 14
        Christopher
          C.   " 1847, 7, 5 d 1848,10, 6

    bur Peru, O.
    Ch: Looyde   b 1849, 9, 3
        Phebe Jane " 1852, 12, 23

1841, 2, 25.   David & w, Jane, & ch, Wash-
    ington, Sarah Ann & Mary, rocf Marlborough
    MM, dtd 1840,12,29
1854, 5, 25.   Washington dis mcd
1855, 6, 21.   David & w, Jane, & ch, Sarah
    L., Ann H., Mary, Isaac P., Margaret
    Elizabeth, Loyde & Phebe Jane, gct Spring
    Creek MM, Ia.

SCHNAPP
1926, 8, 19.   Allie Ross & w, Ella Sellars,
    recrq

SCHOLFIELD
----, --, --.   Andrew & Rachel
    Ch: Thomas   b 1827, 1, 4
        John   " 1828, 12, 28
        Margaret " 1831, 3, 18
        Issachar " 1833, 7, 16
        William   " 1835, 8, 6

1832, 3, 29.   Andrew [Schofield] & w, Rachel,
    & ch, Thomas, John & Margaret, rocf Still-
    water MM, dtd 1832,2,25
1843, 2, 23.   Andrew & w, Rachel, & ch,
    Thomas, John, Margaret, Isaachar & Wil-
    liam, gct Vermillion MM, Ill.

SCHOOLEY
1837, 1, 26.   Isaac & w, Sarah, rocf Flush-
    ing MM, dtd 1835,2,28 (H)
1859, 2, 24.   Elizabeth Jane con mcd (H)
1859, 12, 22.   Elizabeth Mosher gct Prairie
    Grove MM, Ia. (H)

SCOTT
1839, 10, 29.   Joseph, s Stephen & Sarah,
    Richland Co., O.; m in home of Abel
    Leister, Mary Ann VANSYKLE, dt Abraham &
    Hannah, Bucks Co., Pa. (H)
    Ch: Sarah   b 1840, 11, 12
        Isaac   " 1842, 7, 17
        Hannah   " 1844, 12, 12
        Stephen
        Elwood   " 1848, 1, 24

1840, 10, 21.   Isaac rocf Fairfax MM, Va., dtd
    1840,6,10 (H)
1862, 12, 25.   Joseph & w, Mary Ann, & ch,
    Isaac V., Hannah S. & Stephen E., gct
    White Water MM, Ind. (H)
1863, 3, 26.   Sarah T. gct White Water MM,
    Ind. (H)
1871, 1, 19.   Permelia recrq
1875, 4, 15.   Franklin recrq
1882, 3, 16.   Azar recrq
1884, 7, 17.   Azor & Frank dropped from mbrp
1887, 7, 21.   Pamelia relrq
1891, 3, 19.   Elnora, Albert M. & Fanny recrq

SEALY
1890, 2, 13. Robert recrq
1890, 3, 20. Albert S. recrq
1891, 3, 19. Caroline [Seely] recrq

SEYMOUR
1837, 10, 28. Wm. W., s Martin & Rhoda, Huron
        Co., O.; m in Alum Creek MH, Mary GREGORY,
        dt Selah & Mary, Delaware Co., O.
1838, 8, 23. Huldah d ae 68 bur Greenwich,O.
1839, 2, 17. Martin d ae 49 bur Greenwich,O.
1839, 8, 31. Mary d bur Peru, O.
1848, 1, 6. Anna A. m Harvey UNDERHILL

1834, 9, 25. Levi & w, Huldah, & s, Levi,
        rocf Galway MM, dtd 1834,8,8
1834, 9, 25. Martin & w, Rhoda, & ch, Silas,
        William, Manning, Edwin, Samuel & Ann,
        rocf Galway MM, dtd 1834,8,8
1839, 5, 23. Silas D. dis disunity
1845, 3, 27. William W. con mcd

SHAFFER
1891, 3, 19. George W. & Mary M. recrq
1898, 5, 19. N. Lavina Corie dropped from
        mbrp

SHARP
----, --, --. Thomas & Sarah
        Ch: Townsend b 1834, 4, 9
            Elizabeth " 1835, 5, 26
            Tacy   " 1837, 1, 15
1840, 5, 14. John d ae 86 bur Middlebury,O.
1840, 9, 30. Elizabeth m Joseph BARRINGTON
1842, 12, 29. Thomas, s John & Elizabeth,
        Marion Co., O.; m in Alum Creek MH, Esther
        OSBORN, dt Wm. & Phebe GIDLEY

1832, 12, 20. Thomas rocf Gunpowder MM, Md.,
        dtd 1832,11,7
1833, 2, 21. John rocf Deer Creek MM, Md.,
        dtd 1832,12,6
1833, 2, 21. Elizabeth rocf Deer Creek MM,
        Md., dtd 1832,12,6
1833, 5, 23. Thomas rmt Sarah Willets
1842, 2, 23. Esther gct Gilead MM

SHAW
1835, 4, 30. Elizabeth d ae 73 bur Westfield,
        O.

1818, 5, 28. Ruth recrq
1819, 5, 27. John & w, Elizabeth, & ch, Jo-
        seph & John, rocf Miami MM, O., dtd 1818,
        10,28
1819, 7, 1. Joseph con mcd
1840, 4, 27. Sylvia, gr dt John & Elizabeth,
        recrq
1826, 6, 1. John Jr. dis mcd
1826, 12, 28. Sarah Camp (form Shaw) dis mcd
1828, 7, 31. Silvia dis disunity
1829, 1, 1. Isaac M. dis disunity
1829, 7, 20. Joseph dis disunity

1832, 11, 22. Joseph, the 2nd, dis disunity
1885, 3, 19. Edward W. recrq
1885, 10, 22. Sarah Martin dropped from mbrp
1888, 6, 21. Jonathan recrq
1889, 2, 14. Isaacher recrq
1890, 3, 20. Edward W. dropped from mbrp
1895, 2, 14. George recrq
1896, 7, 16. I. A. dropped from mbrp
1907, 2, 14. Glenn Albert & Grace Mary recrq
1907, 7, 18. Glen A. & Grace M. dropped from
        mbrp

SHEPHERD
1843, 2, 23. Cert rec for Allen, Sewell,
        Sally Jane & Micca Sophia from Farnham
        MM, Lower Canada, dtd 1842,6,20, endorsed
        to Vermillion MM, Ill.

SHERMAN
1886, 3, 18. Newton recrq
1890, 3, 20. Newton dropped from mbrp
1900, 3, 22. Wesley, Eliza & Eva May recrq
1923, 3, 22. John Henry recrq
1923, 10, 24. John rmt Luella Carnes
1926, 7, 22. John & w, Luella, & ch dropped
        from mbrp

SHERWOOD
1917, 4, 19. Anna dropped from mbrp
1920, 5, 20. Jason & Anna recrq
1921, 3, 17. Jason relrq
1926, 12, 16. Jason H. & w, Anna H., & s, Ver-
        non Paul, gct Achilles MM, Va.

SHIELDS
1887, 3, 17. Payton B. & Mary J. recrq
1887, 3, 17. Donnie H. & Eddie P. recrq

SHOEMAKER
1887, 1, 20. Solomon & Hannah recrq
1887, 2, 17. James recrq
1889, 2, 14. Jerry recrq
1904, 7, 21. Solomon, Hannah & James trans-
        ferred from Ashley MM
1907, 7, 18. James dropped from mbrp
1926, 7, 22. Solomon dropped from mbrp

SHULTZ
1904, 1, 21. Wm. & Clara recrq
1907, 7, 18. Wm. & Mrs. dropped from mbrp

SIMMONS
1837, 1, 20. Ephraim d ae 68 bur Peru, O.
1841, 11, 4. Polly m Wm. BENEDICT

1829, 1, 1. Ephraim rocf Marlborough MM,
        dtd 1828,11,25
1829, 8, 27. Polly recrq

SIMPSON
1909, 3, 18. George O. & Lula May recrq

SINCLAIR
1819, 12, 2. Abijah rocf Plainfield MM, dtd
1819,7,28
1822, 8, 1. Albina gct Plainfield MM
1835, 11, 26. Elizabeth rocf Plainfield MM,
dtd 1835,6,18 (H)

SIPE
1885, 2, 19. Mary gct Gilead MM
1887, 4, 21. George recrq
1887, 4, 21. Nellie recrq
1907, 7, 18. Flora dropped from mbrp

SIVETER
1837, 12, 17. Samuel, s Thos. & Mary, b

1835, 12, 24. Thomas rocf Scipio MM, N. Y.,
dtd 1835,9,10
1837, 4, 20. Mary & Thomas, ch Thomas &
Lydia, recrq
1838, 4, 26. Lydia rst on consent of Warwickshire MM, North England
1838, 6, 21. Thomas & w, Lydia, & ch, Mary,
Thomas & Samuel, gct Scipio MM, N. Y.

SKELTON
1840, 8, 20. Geraldus dis mcd (H) (mbr Buckingham MM)

SLOAN
1871, 10, 18. Phebe P. (form Stanley) con mcd
1872, 2, 15. Phebe P. gct Spring Creek MM,
Ia.

SLYTER
----, --, --. Jacob b 1786,11,19; m Elizabeth
----- b 1890,12,8
Ch: Chalkley b 1811, 4, 26
Eunice " 1813, 1, 3
Milla " 1813, 11, 6
Ruth " 1817, 9, 29
Phebe " 1820, 1, 4
Amy " 1822, 2, 15
Elizabeth
Ann " 1824, 7, 4
Seth " 1826, 12, 1
Thomas " 1829, 9, 19
Horton H. " 1832, 5, 10

1818, 3, 5. Jacob & w, Elizabeth, & ch,
Chalkley, Eunice & Milla, rocf Peru MM,
N. Y., dtd 1817,9,25, endorsed by Short
Creek MM, O., 1818,2,24
1828, 10, 2. Jacob dis jH
1829, 1, 29. Elizabeth dis jH
1833, 3, 21. Mila Bunker (form Slyter) dis
mcd
1836, 12, 22. Eunice Jump (form Slyter) con
mcd (H)
1836, 12, 22. Milia Bunker (form Slyter) con
mcd (H)
1839, 7, 25. Jacob & w, Elizabeth, & ch,
Amy, Elizabeth Ann, Seth, Thomas & Horton

H., gct White Water MM, Ind. (H)
1840, 2, 20. Ruth Hull (form Slyter) dis mcd
(H)
1839, 7, 25. Phebe gct White Water MM, Ind.
(H)
1840, 4, 23. Chalkley gct White Water MM,
Ind. (H)

SMITH
----, --, --. Jirah & Airs
Ch: Sarah b 1802, 3, 19
Samuel " 1803, 1, 29
David " 1805, 5, 30
Abigail " 1807, 5, 15 d 1808, 3,24
bur Peru, N. Y.
Mary b 1810, 3, 26
Job " 1813, 4, 12
Anna " 1815, 7, 8
John " 1818, 3, 12
Phebe " 1820, 3, 30
----, --, --. Israel m Elzy ----- d 1831,6,16
ae 55 bur Morvin, O.
Ch: Isaac b 1802, 11, 23 d 1830, 4, 8
bur Morvin, O.
Ruth b 1811, 12, 10
Remington " 1811, 12, 10 " 1830, 4, 8
bur Morvin, O.
Henry b 1819, 10, 10 " 1830, 4, 8
bur Morvin, O.
Mary b 1815, 6, 13 " 1830, 9, 1
bur Morvin, O.
Esther b 1817, 3, 20
----, --, --. Willis R. & Ann
Ch: Alfred J. b 1814, 11, 25 d 1826, 9,23
bur Greenwich
Phebe K. b 1816, 10, 27
Daniel " 1819, 7, 3
Amelia " 1821, 6, 5
Williams " 1823, 6, 17
Sarah " 1825, 10, 23
Mary " 1829, 10, 3
Anne Maria " 1831, 12, 24
1831, 8, 22. Dale Martin, s Henry & Forest, b
----, --, --. Lemuel J. m Lena HACK
Ch: Henry b 1906, 9, 25
Isaac " 1909, 9, 29
Hazel " 1914, 7, 19
Clinton " 1917, 3, 28
Walter " 1919, 8, 19
Alice " 1924, 7, 10
Irvin Ed-
ward " 1926, 9, 3

1818, 7, 30. John rmt Jane Place
1818, 10, 1. Jane & ch, Jane & Martha N.
Place, gct White Water MM, Ind.
1825, 6, 30. Willis R. & w, Ann, & ch, Alfred I., Phebe K., Daniel, Amelia & Wm.
T., rocf Scipio MM, N. Y., dtd 1824,3,18
1825, 12, 1. Samuel dis mcd
1827, 11, 1. Israel & w, Elizabeth, & ch,
Israel, Ruth, Remington, Henry, Mary &
Esther, rocf Butternuts MM, dtd 1827,8,29

SMITH, continued

1828, 10, 2. Ruth rmt Stephen Mosher
1828, 11, 27. David gct Cherry Grove MM, Ind.,
               to m Elizabeth Reece
1829, 8, 27. Elizabeth rocf Cherry Grove MM,
               Ind., dtd 1829,7,15
1830, 4, 29. David dis
1830, 5, 27. Elizabeth & s gct Cherry Grove
               MM, Ind.
1830, 12, 30. Sarah gct Goshen MM
1831, 3, 3. Mary rmt Jonathan Roberts
1833, 6, 20. Hannah (form Dillingham) con mcd
1834, 4, 24. Hannah gct White River MM, Ind.
1835, 7, 23. Job gct Elk MM
1835, 12, 24. Jirah & w, Avis, & ch, John &
               Phebe, gct White Water MM, Ind.
1834, 12, 24. Anna gct White Water MM, Ind.
1837, 11, 23. Hannah & dt, Rosetta B., rocf
               White River MM, Ind., dtd 1837,10,18
1839, 6, 20. Joseph & w, Frances, recrq (H)
1848, 5, 25. Hannah Burke (form Smith) dis
               mcd
1857, 7, 23. Frances dis joining Spiritual-
               ists Society (H)
1876, 12, 21. Martha Baldwin gct Goshen MM
1884, 11, 20. Martha Baldwin relrq
1887, 2, 17. Elmore recrq
1887, 2, 17. James C. recrq
1887, 2, 17. Cassius recrq
1887, 2, 17. Henry recrq
1887, 2, 17. Charles recrq
1887, 3, 17. Freeman recrq
1887, 4, 21. Willie recrq
1889, 5, 16. Cassius relrq
1890, 5, 22. Elmore dropped from mbrp
1891, 3, 19. C. N. relrq
1893, 5, 18. Truman dropped from mbrp
1904, 7, 21. Elmer & w transferred from Ash-
               ley MM
1904, 7, 21. Maggie transferred from Ashley
               MM
1905, 12, 21. Chester recrq
1906, 1, 18. Warren recrq
1907, 9, 19. Carrie & Hazel recrq
1912, 5, 16. Warren, Elmer & Chester dropped
               from mbrp
1914, 11, 19. L. J. & Lena rocf Western MM
1921, 4, 21. Henry recrq
1921, 12, 22. Edith & Isaac recrq
1923, 3, 22. Imo recrq
1928, 1, 19. Forest Dudley recrq
1928, 3, 22. Ellen May recrq
1928, 5, 17. Ellen May recrq
1930, 6, 19. Ellen relrq

SPARKS
1896, 3, 19. George recrq
1901, 2, 14. George relrq

SPEAKMAN
1819, 5, 27. James rocf York MM, Pa., dtd
               1819,3,10

SPENCER

----, --, --. George & Eunice (H)
     Ch: Louisa   b 1818, 3, 31 d 1856, 9, 3
               bur Salem Methodist Bur. Gr., Knox
               Co.
         Athanissa   b 1819, 10, 20
         William F. " 1822, 2, 24
         Lydia   " 1823, 6, 10 d 1847, 1,23
               bur Sandusky, O.
         John   b 1825, 4, 10
         Ellwood   " 1827, 4, 9
         Eunice   " 1829, 4, 1 d 1849,11, 7
               bur Knox Co., O.
         Hannah Jane b 1831, 2, 26
         Geo. Clark-
           son   b 1835, 6, 12
         Amy Dru-
           silla   " 1840, 10, 26
         Hinson
           Clay   " 1844, 9, 30 d 1855, 9,15
               bur Knox Co., O.
1844, 3, 27. Wm. F., s George & Eunice, Knox
               Co., O.; m in Whetstone, Phebe MOSHER, dt
               Robert & Edith, Marion Co., O. (H)
     Ch: Edith Ann   b 1845, 3, 20
         Eunice Dru-
           silla   " 1846, 12, 29
         Lydia   " 1854, 6, 12
1846, 5, 23. Lydia m Wm. Allen KIRK (H)
1850, 5, 1. John Q., s George & Eunice,
               Knox Co., O.; m in Owl Creek, Mary RIDGE-
               WAY, dt Thomas & Elizabeth, Harrison Co.,
               O.
     Ch: George
           Thomas   b 1850, 2, 27 (?)
         Elwood
           Ridgeway " 1852, 9, 14
1861, 5, 1. Amy D. m Edward HARLAN (H)

1833, 4, 25. George & w, Eunice, & ch,
               Louisa, Althanissa, Wm. F., Lydia, John,
               Elwood, Eunice & Hannah Jane, rocf Plain-
               field MM, dtd 1833,3,21 (H)
1834, 2, 20. Louisa, Athanisa, William,
               Lydia, John, Elwood & Eunice, ch George &
               Eunice, rocf Stillwater MM, dtd 1833,9,28
1839, 6, 20. Louisa McWhenney (form Spencer)
               con mcd (H)
1839, 12, 26. Louisa McKenney (form Spencer)
               dis mcd
1841, 8, 26. Athenissa dis jH
1844, 8, 22. William dis disunity
1847, 12, 24. Hannah Jane, George Clarkson,
               Amy Drucilla & Huysen Clay recrq of
               guardian, Ellis Willets
1848, 3, 23. Athenissa rst
1852, 8, 26. Elwood gct Spring Creek MM, Ia.
1852, 10, 28. Hannah Jane White (form Spencer)
               dis mcd (living in verge of Plainfield MM)
1853, 10, 27. John D. & w, Mary, & ch, George
               T. & Elwood R., gct Spring Creek MM, Ia.
1856, 2, 21. Amy Drusilla gct Gilead MM
1856, 3, 27. George C. gct Spring Creek MM, Ia.

STANLEY

1866, 12, 29. Jonathan, s Jonathan & Mary,
Columbiana Co., O.; m in Alum Creek MH,
Amelia F. BENEDICT, dt Aaron L. & Phebe H.,
Morrow Co., O.

1851, 1, 23. Jesse & w, Abigail, & s, David,
rocf Upper Springfield MM, O., dtd 1850,
12,28
1857, 11, 26. Jesse & w, Abigail, & s, David,
gct Spring Creek MM, Ia.
1860, 3, 22. Daniel Benedict gct Goshen MM,
to m Rachel Stanley
1867, 8, 22. Amelia gct Salem MM
1871, 10, 18. Phebe P. Sloan (form Stanley)
con mcd
1881, 5, 19. Kate Gaylord relrq
1884, 4 17. Amelia Felicia rocf Salem MM,
O., dtd 1884,3,20
1888, 5, 17. Felicia A. gct Salem MM, O.

STARR
1840, 11, 26. Hannah U. rocf Short Creek MM,
O., dtd 1840,7,21

STEADMAN
1895, 3, 21. Ellen recrq
1899, 10, 19. Ellen [Stedman] dropped from
mbrp

STERNER
1887, 4, 21. Maud recrq
1888, 7, 19. Maud dropped from mbrp

STERRIT
1909, 4, 15. Francene relrq

STEWART
1825, 4, 26. Daniel, s Wm. & Patience, b
1870, 10, 27. Albert J. [Steward], s Robert &
Caroline, Morrow Co., O.; m Adessa T.
BENEDICT, dt Aaron & Caroline A., Morrow,
Co., O.
Ch: Caroline
Alberta   b 1871, 11, 4

1823, 2, 27. William rocf Junius MM, N. Y.,
dtd 1822,12,25
1825, 3, 31. Patience recrq
1827, 9, 27. Wm. H., Caroline Ann & George,
ch Wm. & Patience, recrq
1829, 1, 29. William dis jH
1832, 10, 25. Patience & ch gct Springborough
MM
1834, 9, 25. Wm. Jr. dis disunity
1871, 6, 15. Albert J. recrq
1877, 11, 15. Albert J. & w, Addessa T., &
dt, Caroline Alberta, gct Raisin MM, Mich.
1918, 5, 16. Adessa T. [Steward] rocf Raisin
MM, Mich., dtd 1918,4,17

STINER
1901, 3, 21. Erma recrq

STONE
1887, 2, 17. Helen recrq

STOUT
1887, 3, 17. Calvin, Rachel, Louisa & Wm.
recrq
1890, 10, 16. Calvin dis disunity
1893, 5, 18. Rachel C., Martha L. & Wm.
dropped from mbrp

STRATTON
1902, 2, 13. Isaac & w, Sarah, rocf Columbus
MM, dtd 1902,2,5
1910, 5, 19. Isaac & Sadie gct Berlinville
MM

STREET
1910, 5, 19. Charles Clifford recrq
1921, 3, 17. Clifford dropped from mbrp

STREETER
1887, 2, 17. Carrie recrq
1887, 2, 17. William recrq
1889, 12, 19. Wm. & Carrie relrq

STRUTHERS
1887, 8, 18. James C. P., Lenora Jane &
Flora May recrq
1892, 7, 21. J. C. P. [Strothers] dropped
from mbrp

STYLES
1849, 3, 23. Robert, s John & Ann, Lenawee
Co., Mich.; m in Alum Creek MH, Rachel
BENEDICT, dt John & Amy, Morrow Co., O.
Ch: Amy Ann   b 1850, 1, 21

1850, 2, 21. Robert [Stiles] rocf West Branch
MM, dtd ----,11,15
1850, 12, 26. Robert & w, Rachel, & dt, Amy
Ann, gct Smithfield MM, O.
1854, 2, 23. Robert & w, Rachel, & ch, Amy
Ann & Caroline, rocf Smithfield MM, dtd
1854,1,21
1854, 8, 24. Robert & w, Rachel, & ch, Amy
Ann & Caroline, gct Driftwood MM, Ind.

SUTMILLER
1912, 5, 16. Emma Ploger dropped from mbrp

SUTTON
1826, 3, 2. Phebe (form Washburn) con mcd
1834, 4, 24. Phebe dis disunity
1847, 8, 27. Mary (form Worshburn) dis mcd

SWAYNE
1834, 10, 25. Isaac B. rocf Hopewell MM, dtd
1834,7,10 (H)
1834, 11, 20. Maria rocf Hopewell MM, O., dtd
1834,10,7 (H)
1837, 7, 20. Isaac B. & w, Mariah, & dt,
Amanda Ann, gct Green Plain MM, O. (H)

TABER

----, --, --. Allen & Abigail
    Ch: George
        Martha Jane
        Mary Elizabeth
        Eliza Ann

1837, 5, 25. Thomas & w, Miriam, & ch, Wil-
    liam, Martha, Nathan, Freeman, Horace,
    Thomas Elwood & James, rocf Starksborough
    MM, Vt., dtd 1836,12,2
1837, 7, 20. Silas rocf Starksborough MM, Vt.,
    dtd 1837,6,30
1842, 8, 25. Nathan rocf Gilead MM, dtd
    1842,8,23
1844, 10, 24. Nathan gct Gilead MM
1848, 2, 25. Guli Elma M. rocf Farnham MM,
    Canada East, dtd 1847,11,22
1848, 10, 27. Daniel Reynolds gct Gilead MM,
    to m Miriam Taber
1853, 7, 28. Allen & w, Abigail, & ch,
    George, Martha Jane, Mary Elizabeth &
    Eliza Ann, rocf Butternuts MM,/dtd 1853,
    6,29   N.Y.,
1856, 1, 24. Sarah rocf Farnham MM, E. Canada,
    dtd 1855,9,24
1856, 1, 24. George M. rocf Farnham MM, E.
    Canada, dtd 1855,9,24
1856, 9, 22. Isaac rocf Farnham MM, E. Canada,
    dtd 1856,3,24
1863, 4, 16. George N. dis enlisting in army
1867, 4, 18. Allen & w, Abigail, & dt, Eliza
    Ann, gct New Sharon MM, Ia.
1868, 1, 16. Martha Jane Grissell (form
    Taber) con mcd
1870, 11, 17. George M. dis jas
1871, 2, 16. Mary Elizabeth gct Birch Lake
    MM, Mich.
1874, 2, 19. Isaac & w, Sarah, gct Clear
    Creek MM, O.
1875, 2, 18. Isaac & Sarah [Tabor] rocf Clear
    Creek MM, dtd 1875,1,9

TALBOTT

----, --, --. Allen & Mary
    Ch: Rebecca   b 1820, 9, 6
        Mary Farqu-
           har   " 1823, 9, 16
        John
           Roberts   " 1826, 10, 2
        Hannah
           Maria   " 1829, 10, 14
        Sarah   " 1831, 11, 18
        Joseph   " 1834, 4, 29
        Allen   " 1837, 4, 27

1830, 12, 30. Allen [Talbert] & w, Mary, & ch,
    Rebecca, Mary & John R., rocf Smithfield
    MM, dtd 1829,10,19

TAPPIN
1842, 1, 27. Rhoda (form Mullenix) rpd mcd

TAYLOR
1836, 2, 25. James rocf Longford MM, Eng.,
    dtd 1835,9,16
1837, 7, 20. James gct Albens MM, Eng.
1839, 6, 20. James rocf Longford MM, Eng.,
    dtd 1839,3,13
1840, 6, 25. James gct Scipio MM, N. Y.
1840, 6, 25. James gct Scipio MM, N. Y.
1841, 4, 22. Cert for James returned because
    of his return
1844, 5, 23. James gct Scipio MM, N. Y.
1853, 7, 21. Jonathan & w, Rebecca, rocf
    Goose Creek MM, Va., dtd 1853,5,12 (H)
1884, 4, 17. Jane recrq

TERRY
1823, 6, 25. Thomas & w, Sarah, & ch, David,
    Jeremiah, Jonathan & John B., rocf Fair-
    field MM, dtd 1823,5,31
1831, 6, 2. John P. dis mcd

THOMAS
1776, 3, 12. Ebenezar b d 1833,9,3 bur Colum-
    bus, O. (H)

1823, 10, 23. Ebeneezer & w, Mary Furman, &
    ch, James Christopher, Thomas, William,
    Ebeneezer, Mary Ann, Elizabeth, Huntington
    & George Henry, rocf Upper MM, Va., dtd
    1822,8,17
1829, 1, 1. Ebeneezer dis jH
1830, 10, 28. William dis mcd
1832, 11, 22. James dis disunity

THURSTON
1897, 2, 23. Vinal d bur Alum Creek
1902, 3, 28. Mary Jane d ae 81 bur Alum Creek

1855, 6, 21. Eliza rocf Whitelick MM, Ind.,
    dtd 1855,5,16
1858, 12, 23. Eliza gct Plainfield MM, Ind.
1879, 4, 17. Phebe, Vinal & Mary Jane recrq

TIPTON
----, --, --. David & Mary
    Ch: William K.
        Tacy Ann
        Luke
        Priscilla H.
        Phebe Jane b 1847, 4, 28

1847, 6, 26. David & w, Mary, & ch, Wm. K.,
    Tacy Ann, Luke & Priscilla H., rocf Somer-
    set MM, dtd 1847,5,24
1850, 10, 24. David & w, Mary, & ch, Wm. K.,
    Tacy Ann, Luke, Priscilla, Phebe Jane &
    Joseph Lindley, gct Somerset MM

THOMPSON
1887, 2, 17. James recrq
1887, 2, 17. Bernice recrq
1887, 2, 17. Lucy recrq
1887, 2, 17. E. W. H. recrq

TOWNSEND

----, --, --. Thomas d 1859,3,18 bur Middle-
berry; m Elizabeth ----- d 1817,10,5 bur
Wayne, O.
Ch: William   b 1809, 8, 14
    James   " 1811, 9, 13
    Hannah   " 1813, 12, 12
    Samuel   " 1816, 6, 2 d 1816, 10, 5
Thomas m 2nd Ruth ----- d 1848,1,15 bur
Middleberry
Ch: Elizabeth b 1820, 7, 27
    Bethiah M. " 1822, 7, 16 d 1854, 7,31
      bur Middleberry
    Asa M.   b 1824, 8, 10
    Rachel W. " 1826, 9, 16
    Esther   " 1829, 2, 27
    Mary   " 1831, 6, 22
    Thomas   " 1833, 11, 10
    Ruth   " 1836, 11, 20
    Letitia Ann" 1841, 1, 11
----, --, --. James & Susannah
  Ch: Israel
      Lewis   b 1830, 7, 19
      Jesse B.R. " 1841, 11, 12
      Timothy
      Westley " 1844, 4, 11
      William E. " 1851, 5, 18
1837, 7, 27. Wm., s Thomas & Elizabeth, Knox
Co., O.; m in Greenwich, Elizabeth WATSON,
dt Granger & Elizabeth, Huron Co., O.
Ch: Hannah W. b 1838, 4, 29 d 1838, 9,14
      bur Middlebury
    Joseph Wat-
      son   b 1839, 4, 29
    Lovisa   " 1841, 8, 1
    Mary Isa-
      bella   " 1843, 3, 16
    Charles   " 1846, 6, 25
    Ann Eliza-
      beth   " 1849, 2, 4
1840, 5, 27. Elizabeth W. m Thos. BARRINGTON
1843, 7, 26. Eli, s Levi & Mary, Logan Co.,
O.; m in Whetstone, O., Abigail WOOD, dt
David & Esther, Marion Co., O. (H)
----, --, -- Asa M. & Elizabeth G.
  Ch: Clayton W. b 1847, 11, 8 d 1880, 6,30
      Mary Ellen " 1849, 4, 24
      Henry H. " 1851, 10, 13
      Lydia W. " 1853, 12, 15 d 1864, 9, 1
        bur Middleberry
1850, 5, 29. Esther   W. m Henry HATHAWAY
1852, 4, 28. Rachel W. m Blackburn VORE
1861, 4, 3. Ruth m Wm. F. LEWIS
1872, 8, 23. Clayton W., s Asa M. & Eliza-
beth G., Knox Co., O.; m Rachel Annet
LEVERING, dt Griffith & Esther L., Morrow
Co., O.
Ch: Edith
      Elizabeth b 1873, 8, 7
    Griffith
      Levering " 1876, 3, 12 d 1876, 4, 4
        bur Peru
    Anna B.   " 1878, 7, 2

1819, 9, 30. Thomas rmt Ruth Mosher
1833, 6, 20. Hannah rmt Timothy Kirk
1835, 8, 20. James con mcd
1838, 3, 22. Susan recrq
1843, 11, 25. Abigail gct Goshen MM (H)
1846, 9, 21. Asa M. gct Gilead MM, to m
Elizabeth G. Wood
1847, 3, 25. Elizabeth G. rocf Gilead MM,
dtd 1847,2,23
1853, 1, 27. Wm. & w, Elizabeth, & ch gct
Salem MM, Ia.
1853, 11, 24. James & w, Susannah, & ch,
Israel L., Jesse B., Timothy W. & Wm. E.,
gct Red Cedar MM, Ia.
1861, 4, 25. Thomas gct Red Cedar MM, Ia.
1861, 4, 25. Mary & Letitia gct Red Cedar MM,
Ia.
1871, 10, 19. Asa M. & w, Elizabeth G., & ch,
Mary Ellen & Henry H., gct LeGrand MM,Ia.
1881, 10, 20. Annette R. L. & ch, Edith Elizabeth & Anne B., gct Marysville MM

TRAHERN
1831, 8, 25. Samuel rocf Goose Creek MM, Va.

TRAYER
1830, 9, 2. Parthenia recrq (H)
1858, 9, 22. Lydia Ann [Trayen] recrq
1867, 3, 21. Lydia Ann dis

TURNER
1842, 10, 27. Sophia (form Carpenter) dis mcd

TUTTLE
1867, 8, 22. Esther B. (form Wood) con mcd
1877, 9, 20. Esther B. gct Baltimore MM
1882, 12, 21. Esther B. rocf Baltimore MM, Md.
1885, 1, 22. Esther B. gct Chicago MM, Ill.

UHLICH
1906, 10, 18. Edith relrq

UNDERHILL
1848, 1, 6. Harvey, s Jacob & Rachel, Ash-
land Co., O.; m in Greenwich, Anna A. SEY-
MOUR, dt Martin & Rhoda C., Huron Co., O.

1845, 10, 23. Harvey recrq

UNDERWOOD
1824, 8, 25. Joseph Wilson gct Center MM, to
m Hannah Underwood
1884, 2, 18. Ida M., Wm. E. & John H. recrq
1884, 4, 17. Cemantha & Mary recrq
1885, 3, 19. Joseph recrq
1888, 6, 16. Wm. relrq
1895, 3, 21. Ida M. recrq
1898, 5, 19. Mary dis disunity
1899, 10, 19. ----- dropped from mbrp

VANAUSDEL
1911, 10, 19. Ida recrq
1913, 3, 20. Mrs. F. A. relrq

VANLAW
1833, 10, 24. Samuel & w, Lydia, & ch, Joseph
     P., Sarah P., Reason L. & Wm., rocf Plain-
     field MM, dtd 1833,5,23 (H)
1834, 2, 20. Joseph, Sarah & Reason, ch Sam-
     uel & Lydia, rocf Short Creek MM, O., dtd
     1833,9,28
1836, 11, 24. Samuel dis disunity (H)
1839, 2, 21. Joseph P., Sarah P., Reason L.,
     Wm. & Geo., ch Samuel & Lydia, gct Plain-
     field MM (H)
1842, 1, 27. Joseph, Sarah & Reason, ch Sam-
     uel, gct Plainfield MM, O.

VAN MATRE
1926, 4, 15. Leora recrq
1826, 7, 28. Leora rmt Charles DeVol

VANSICKLE
1839, 10, 29. Mary Ann [Vansykle]m Joseph
     Scott (H)

1910, 4, 6. Esther D., dt Chas. & Elnora
     (Benedict), b
1913, 6, 21. Walter Filmore, s Chas. & Elnora
     (Benedict), b

1838, 12, 20. Mary Ann rocf Richland MM, Pa.
     (H)
1900, 4, 19. Charley recrq
1923, 2, 15. Charles dropped from mbrp
1923, 2, 15. Elnora relrq

VAN VINSHITTER
1832, 4, 26. Anna (form Mullenix) dis mcd

VERNON
1835, 11, 27. James, s James & Tamar, Morrow
     Co., O.; m in Alum Creek MH, Rachel WOOD,
     dt Daniel & Phebe, Delaware Co., O.
1842, 10, 28. Jesse, s James & Tamar, Athens
     Co., O. m in Alum Creek MH, Patience GID-
     LEY, dt Wm. & Phebe, Delaware Co., O.
     Ch: Sarah   b 1843, 12, 15
         Rachel Ann" 1846, 9, 13
         Thomas   " 1848, 9, 18
         William G." 1851, 8, 17

1837, 3, 23. James rocf Somerset MM, dtd
     1837,2,29
1837, 10, 26. Jesse rocf Stillwater MM, O.,
     dtd 1837,7,22
1839, 9, 23. Jesse gct Chesterfield MM, O.
1840, 3, 26. James gct Chesterfield MM
1842, 12, 22. Patience gct Chesterfield MM
1846, 2, 20. Jesse & w, Patience, & dt, Sa-
     rah, rocf Chesterfield MM, dtd 1845,11,15
1853, 9, 19. Jesse & w, Patience, & ch, Sa-
     rah, Rachel Ann, Thomas L. & Wm. G., gct
     Red Cedar MM, Ia.

VINCENT
1887, 3, 17. Elizabeth recrq

VINING
1887, 3, 17. Hallet recrq
1890, 2, 13. Ella recrq
1894, 1, 18. Halet relrq
1904, 7, 21. Frank, Angie Kenneth transferred
     from Ashley MM
1904, 7, 21. Hal & w & ch, Emma & Maggie,
     transferred from Ashley MM
1904, 7, 21. Simeon transferred from Ashley
     MM
1911, 6, 15. Hazel recrq
1912, 5, 16. Frank dropped from mbrp
1912, 5, 16. Angie dropped from mbrp
1912, 5, 16. Kenneth dropped from mbrp
1912, 5, 16. Carl dropped from mbrp
1912, 5, 16. Simeon dropped from mbrp
1922, 4, 20. Harriet & dt, Maggie, Emma &
     Hazel relrq

VORE
----, --, --. Jesse m Ann ----- d 1863,11,26
     ae 70 bur Middlebury
     Ch: Lydia Jane b 1833, 8, 15
1848, 3, 1. Sarah m Samuel H. BARNES
1848, 11, 1. Joseph, s Jesse & Ann,   1863,
     4,28 bur Middlebury; m in Owl Cr
     Eliza BRADRICK, dt Paul & Sarah, Richland
     Co., O.
     Ch: Delilah
         Jane   b 1849, 8, 23 d 1862,10,24
         bur Middlebury
         Sarah Re-
         becca   b 1851, 4, 6 " 1877, 5, 8
         bur Middlebury
         Ann Maria b 1853, 5, 14 " 1862,10,25
         bur Middlebury
         Monroe
         Freeman   b 1856, 8, 25 " 1862,10,18
         bur Middlebury
         Malvina
         Amanda   b 1861, 1, 10
1852, 4, 28. Blackburn, s Jesse & Ann, Knox
     Co., O.; m in Owl Creek, Rachel W. TOWN-
     SEND, dt Thomas & Ruth, Knox Co., O.
----, --, --. Blackburn m Rachel W. ----- d
     1864,10,31 ae 38 bur Middleberry
     Ch: Ruth Ann b 1853, 3, 4
         Sarah
         Elizabeth " 1858, 4, 27
         Rachel   " 1864, 9, 20

1817, 11, 27. Isaac Jr. dis mcd
1822, 5, 30. Isaac dis disunity
1822, 5, 30. Mordecai dis disunity & train-
     ing with militia
1832, 6, 21. Jesse [Voar] & w, Ann, & ch,
     Susanna, Maria, Joseph, Sarah & Blackburn,
     rocf Smithfield MM, dtd 1831,8,22
1860, 5, 24. Joseph & w, Eliza, & ch, De-
     lilah Jane, Sarah R., Ann Maria, Monroe F.
     & Jesse T., gct White River MM, Ind.
1863, 4, 16. Joseph & w, Elizabeth, & ch,
     Delilah Jane, Sarah R., Ann Maria, Monroe

VORE, continued
    F., Jesse T. & Amanda Melvina, rocf White
    River MM, Ind.
1868, 4, 16. Blackburn con mcd
1870, 2, 17. Blackburn & ch, Ruthanna, Wil-
    liam T., Sarah E., Jesse W. & Rachel W.,
    gct Springdale MM, Ia.
1870, 2, 17. Jesse & dt, Susanna Maria &
    Lydia Jane, gct Springdale MM, Ia.
1881, 5, 19. Malvina relrq

WALLACE
1888, 3, 22. B. Proctor recrq
1888, 12, 20. Proctor relrq

WALTERS
----, --, --. Mahlon & Elizabeth (H)
    Ch: George W. b 1815, 6, 24
        William P. " 1818, 4, 6
        Nancy N. " 1820, 7, 8; m Thos. N.
          PURCELL
        Thomas H. " 1823, 3, 17
        Mary E. " 1826, 9, 22
        Lydia   " 1829, 4, 6
        John B. " 1831, 11, 6
        Sarah C. " 1838, 5, 24
1839, 5, 2. Nancy N. m Thos. V. PURCEL (H)
1843, 6, 29. Mary Elizabeth, dt Wm. & Lydia,
    b (H)

1834, 6, 26. Mahlon & w, Elizabeth, & ch,
    George W., Wm. P., Nancy N., Thomas H.,
    Mary Elizabeth, Lydia F. & John James,
    rocf Goose Creek MM, Va., dtd 1834,4,17
    (H)
1841, 10, 21. Wm. P. con mcd
1841, 10, 21. Lydia con mcd (H)
1851, 11, 20. Mary C. Lester (form Walters)
    con mcd (H)
1854, 9, 21. Thomas dis mcd (H)
1854, 9, 21. John dis mcd (H)

WARNER
1887, 4, 21. Jennie recrq
1888, 6, 21. John H. recrq

WARREN
1837, 12, 7. Phebe C. m Abram HEALY
1839, 11, 18. Phebe d bur Bronson, O.

1836, 12, 22. John & w, Hannah, & ch, John,
    Preserved & Nancy, rocf Farmington MM,
    dtd 1836,9,23
1836, 12, 22. Phebe C., Hannah, Abigail &
    Mary, rocf Farmington MM, dtd 1836,9,22
1840, 3, 26. Cert rec for Benjamin & fam from
    Muncy MM, Pa., endorsed to Gilead MM
1842, 3, 24. John Jr. dis mcd
1842, 1, 27. Abigail Rexford (form Warren)
    dis mcd
1842, 1, 27. Hannah Mayhue (form Warren)
    dis mcd
1842, 6, 23. John & w, Hannah, & ch, Pre-

    served & Nancy, gct Marlborough MM

WASHBURN
----, --, --. Henry m Mary ----- d 1826,5,12
    ae 31 bur Greenwich, O.
    Ch: Philena   b 1817, 6, 8
        Charles   " 1822, 2, 24
        Henry C.   " 1826, 5, 12
        Mary   " 1826, 5, 12
----, --, --. Benjamin d 1840,2,12 bur
    Greenwich; m Huldah ----- d 1840,9,3 bur
    Greenwich
    Ch: Ann   b 1822, 6, 1
        Levinia   " 1823, 10, 14
        Robert   " 1827, 3, 24
        Loisa   " 1830, 10, 15
1839, 1, 21. Philener d ae 67 bur Greenwich,
    O.
1840, 12, 3. Mary T. d bur Greenwich, O.
1841, 2, 4. Lavinia B. m Harvy BENEDICT

1823, 10, 23. Joseph [Washborn] & w, Philena,
    & ch, Joseph C., Phebe, James & William,
    rocf Plaines MM, N. Y., dtd 1822,9,24
1823, 10, 23. Henry [Washborn] & w, Mary, &
    ch, Philena & Charles A., rocf Plaines
    MM, N. Y., dtd 1823,9,24
1823, 10, 23. Benjamin [Washborn] & w, Hul-
    dah, & dt, Anna, rocf Plaines MM, N. Y.,
    dtd 1823,9,24
1826, 2, 2. Joseph Jr. dis mcd
1826, 3, 2. Phebe Sutton (form Washburn)
    con mcd
1828, 11, 27. Henry dis mcd
1830, 7, 1. James dis mcd
1833, 4, 25. Mary T. rocf Marlborough MM,
    N. Y., dtd 1832,7,25
1834, 5, 22. William dis disunity
1842, 6, 23. Philena Griffin (form Worshburn)
    dis mcd
1842, 5, 26. Anna Blackmore (form Washburn)
    rpd mcd
1842, 8, 25. Joseph dis mcd
1843, 2, 23. Charles dis mcd
1847, 8, 27. Mary Sutton (form Washburn) dis
    mcd
1848, 10, 27. Henry Craft dis disunity

WASHINGTON
1885, 3, 19. Henrietta recrq
1889, 2, 14. Henry recrq

WATKINS
1891, 3, 19. G. P. & Adille recrq

WATSON
1837, 6, 29. Benjamin, s Grainger & Eliza-
    beth, Huron Co., O.; m in Greenwich, Mary
    G. JENNY, dt John & Catharine, Huron Co.,
    O.
    Ch: John
        Grainger b 1838, 6, 29
        Elizabeth

WATSON, Benjamin & Mary, continued
    Ch: Catharine b 1842, 5, 9
1837, 7, 27. Elizabeth m Wm. TOWNSEND
1838, 11, 4. Grainger d ae 66 bur Greenwich,O.
1840, 4, 30. Mary m Jesse HOAG
1847, 8, 1. Elizabeth d ae 77 bur Greenwich,
    O.

1834, 6, 26. Granger & w, Elizabeth, rocf
    Scipio MM, N. Y., dtd 1834,4,16
1834, 6, 26. Benjamin rocf Scipio MM, N. Y.,
    dtd 1834,4,16
1834, 6, 26. Elizabeth rocf Scipio MM, N.Y.,
    dtd 1834,4,16
1837, 7, 20. Mary rocf Longford MM, Eng.,
    dtd 1836,10,12

WEBSTER
1860, 5, 24. Mary Jane (form Harlan) con mcd
    (H)

WEIR
1887, 11, 17. George [Wier] recrq
1888, 7, 19. George gct Columbus MM
1889, 1, 17. George rocf Columbus MM, dtd
    1889,1,2
1890, 6, 19. George & w, Martha H., gct
    Smithfield MM

WELCH
----, --, --. Theodore m Eva E. C. ----- d
    1899,--,--
    Ch: Frank
        Corbitt   b 1882, 1, 23

1877, 4, 19. Francis A. recrq
1877, 4, 19. Theodore recrq
1877, 4, 19. Eva E. C. recrq
1877, 4, 19. Samantha recrq
1884, 2, 18. Wm. Lyman recrq
1889, 2, 14. F. E. & Jessie recrq
1890, 5, 22. Theodore & Eva relrq
1892, 3, 17. Theodore M. recrq
1893, 2, 16. Eva recrq
1893, 5, 18. Emmerson dropped from mbrp
1894, 3, 22. Lyman dropped from mbrp
1896, 6, 18. Jessie E. relrq
1896, 7, 16. Tacy L. dropped from mbrp
1897, 2, 18. Roswell recrq
1897, 10, 21. Theodore K. & Eva relrq
1902, 7, 17. Frank C. dropped from mbrp
1907, 7, 18. Theodore dropped from mbrp
1907, 9, 26. Clara D. recrq
1912, 5, 16. Carrie Smith dropped from mbrp
1912, 5, 16. Clara D. dropped from mbrp

WELKER
1887, 2, 17. Charles recrq
1890, 5, 22. Charles dropped from mbrp

WELLS
1843, 9, 21. Deborah (form Butler) dis mcd
    (H)

1889, 3, 21. Eliza Ellen recrq

WERLIM
1887, 2, 17. Charles recrq

WESTBROOK
1862, 12, 22. Annetta, dt Daniel & Catherine
    (Starr), b
1895, 2, 4. Laurence L., s Albert & Annetta
    (Wood), b
----, --, --. Joy, s Albert & Annette (Wood),
    b 1886,8,31; m Gussie FLEMING, dt Harper,
    b 1887,5,23
    Ch: Kent   b 1912, 6, 28
        Albert
        Warren   " 1918, 12, 18
----, --, --. Huber m Pearl WINDSOR
    Ch: Daryl
        Richard   b 1923, 11, 21
        Ruth Anna " 1925, 11, 5
        Margaret " 1930, 10, 14

1879, 4, 17. Albert recrq
1891, 3, 19. Albert E. & Anna Etta relrq
1896, 10, 22. Albert E. & Etta W. recrq
1914, 2, 16. Lawrence recrq
1919, 4, 17. Gussie recrq
1921, 4, 21. Lawrence Kent recrq
1929, 7, 18. Rosa Theodosia recrq
1931, 1, 22. Theodosia relrq

WETHERBON
1842, 6, 23. Polly (form Reynolds) dis mcd

WHIPPLE
1897, 2, 18. W. Ernest & Pearl recrq
1902, 5, 22. Ernest & Pearl dropped from
    mbrp
1902, 7, 17. Clark dropped from mbrp

WHITE
1833, 10, 10. Henry d bur Morvin, O.
1834, 1, 24. Hannah m Gideon MULLENNIX

1819, 12, 2. Benjamin rocf Plainfield MM, dtd
    1819,7,28
1828, 7, 31. Joshua & w, Mercy, & ch, Edward
    Y., Hannah Y., Elias G. & Henry J., rocf
    Marlborough MM, N. Y., dtd 1828,5,21
1829, 1, 29. Benjamin dis jH
1832, 8, 23. Margaret recrq
1839, 7, 25. Benj. gct White Water MM, Ind.
    (H)
1840, 8, 20. Mary rocf Buckingham MM, Pa. (H)
1852, 10, 28. Hannah Jane (form Spencer) dis
    mcd (living in verge of Plainfield MM)

WILDMAN
1904, 3, 17. Wilbur recrq
1907, 7, 18. Wilbur dropped from mbrp
1916, 4, 20. Frank recrq
1924, 4, 17. Frank & fam relrq

WILKINSON
1887, 2, 17. Elmore & Clura recrq

WILLETS
----, --, --. Ellis d 1868,6,2 ae 69 bur Peru,
    O.; m Rachel -----
    Ch: Lewis   b 1823, 3, 16
        Elizabeth " 1824, 5, 22
        Hannah   " 1825, 6, 12
        Samuel C. " 1827, 1, 8 d 1831, 7, 8
        bur Middleberry
        Jehu   b 1828, 12, 26
        Joel   " 1828, 12, 26
        Lydia   " 1830, 12, 13
        Rebecca   " 1832, 11, 10 d 1858, 5,27
        bur Middleberry
        Ann   b 1834, 8, 8
        Rachel   " 1836, 1, 17
        Phebe   " 1838, 11, 26 d 1857, 9, 1
        bur Middleberry
        Mary   b 1840, 1, 11
        Ellis Jr. " 1841, 10, 8 " 1854,10,13
        bur Middleberry
        Joseph   b 1843, 5, 18
----, --, --. Joel & Cynthia [Willits]
    Ch: John   b 1828, 8, 7
        William   " 1831, 1, 9
        Samuel   " 1833, 4, 22
        Elvira   " 1835, 3, 29
        Deborah   " 1837, 4, 10
1831, 6, 17. Isaiah [Willits]d ae 36 bur
    Middlebury, O.
1831, 6, 23. Elizabeth [Willits] d ae 58 bur
    Middlebury, O.
----, --, --. Eli & Lemira [Willits] (H)
    Ch: Morton   b 1832, 11, 13
        John El-
        liott   " 1835, 6, 6
----, --, --. John M. [Willits] d 1843,9,24
    bur Freeport, O.; m Elizabeth P. -----
    d 1842,11,23 bur Middleberry
    Ch: David   b 1833, 6, 20
        Eliza Elma " 1837, 8, 10
1849, 8, 29. Hannah m Wm. B. LIPSEY
1852, 4, 23. Lydia m Lindley MILES
----, --, --. Lewis d 1874,6,20 bur Peru, O.;
    m Charity ----- d 1897,7,10 bur Peru, O.
    Ch: Martha   b 1853, 9, 26 d 1895, 6,
        15 bur Peru, O.
        Phebe Elma b 1857, 8, 3 " 1878, 2,13
        bur Peru, O.
1854, 11, 25. Elizabeth m John D. ELLIOTT
1855, 1, 27. Samira [Willits] d bur Middlebury,
    O.
----, --, --. Ezra & Margaret
    Ch: Charles   b 1855, 9, 9 d 1861, 4,16
        bur Middlebury
        Jesse   b 1857, 12, 18 " 1862,10, 7
        bur Middlebury
        Ellen   b 1860, 10, 30
        Milford   " 1862, 9, 18
1864 5, 25. Mary m Nixon OVERMAN

1822, 6, 27. Ellis rmt Rachel Lewis
1822, 8, 29. John gct Redstone MM
1823, 8, 28. Samuel dis disunity
1827, 9, 27. Joel rmt Cynthia Lewis
1829, 7, 2. Taylor dis mcd & jH
1829, 8, 27. Eli dis jH
1829, 9, 27. Taylor con mcd (H)
1831, 10, 20. Eli gct Plainfield MM, to m
    Lamira Elliot (H)
1832, 5, 24. John & w, Elizabeth, rocf Smith-
    field MM, dtd 1832,3,19
1833, 1, 24. Lamira rocf Plainfield MM (H)
1833, 5, 23. Sarah rmt Thomas SHARP
1835, 5, 21. Taylor gct Milton MM, Ind. (H)
1845, 6, 25. Eli rst
1845, 8, 28. Morton & John Eliot, ch Eli &
    Lamira, recrq
1852, 4, 22. Ammi & w, Maria, & ch, Milton
    & Mary H., rocf Smithfield MM, dtd 1852,
    3,22
1852, 7, 22. Lewis gct West Branch MM, to m
    Charity Pearson
1852, 10, 28. Charity rocf West Branch MM, dtd
    1852,10,14
1853, 3, 24. Ezra rocf Redstone MM, dtd 1853,
    3,2
1854, 1, 26. Lewis & w, Charity, & ch, Mar-
    tha, gct White Water MM, Ind.
1853, 7, 28. Rebecca rocf Redstone MM,Pa.,dtd
    1853,6,1
1855, 3, 22. Ezra con mcd
1855, 6, 21. Morton H. dis mcd
1855, 11, 22. John Elliott dis disunity
1855, 11, 22. David P. dis disunity
1856, 2, 21. Margaret rocf Smithfield MM,
    dtd 1855,10,22
1856, 3, 27. Lewis & w, Charity, & dt, Mar-
    tha Ellen, rocf White Water MM, Ind., dtd
    1856,2,27
1856, 4, 24. Eli dis mcd
1856, 4, 24. Joel gct Western Plain MM, Ia.
1856, 10, 23. Ammi & w, Maria, & ch, Milton,
    Mary H. & Oliver H., gct Westland MM, Ia.
1857, 2, 19. Jehu gct Wabash MM, Ind., to m
    Mary J. Miles
1857, 4, 23. Jehu gct Westland MM, Ia.
1859, 10, 27. Eliza Elma Elliott (form Wil-
    lets) dis mcd
1864, 7, 21. Ezra & w, Margaret, & ch, Ellen
    & Milford, gct LeGrand MM, Ia.
1864, 10, 20. Rebecca gct LeGrand MM, Ia.
1866, 4, 19. Ellis & w, Rachel, & ch, Anna &
    Rachel L., gct Milford MM, Ind.
1868, 5, 21. Ellis & w, Rachel, rocf Milford
    MM, Ind., dtd 1868,3,28
1874, 6, 18. G. Grafton Benedict gct Gilead
    MM, to m Ellen [Willits]
1877, 10, 18. Joseph C. gct Bangor MM, Ia.

WILLIAMS
1870, 9, 15. Thomas C., s Asa & Elizabeth,
    Champaign Co., O.; m in Alum Creek MH,
    Mary W. OSBORN, dt David & Susan, Morrow

WILLIAMS, Thomas C. & Mary W., continued
    Co., O.
      Ch: Laura B.   b 1874, 9, 14
         Robert C.   " 1877, 3, 5
         Arthur E.   " 1880, 3, 20
         Anna Ger-
           trude   " 1883, 1, 12
         Marjorie S." 1885, 12, 2
         Edith   " 1887, 3, 2
1873, 11, 23. Thomas Clarkson, s Obadiah H. &
    Sarah P., Hardin Co., O.; m in Alum Creek
    MH, Esther BENEDICT, dt Daniel & Grace,
    Morrow Co., O.

1822, 2, 28. Micajah Dillingham gct Marl-
    borough MM, to m Eliza Williams
1829, 4, 30. Daniel Osborn gct Marlborough
    MM, to m Deborah Williams
1837, 10, 26. Asa & w, Achsah P., rocf Goshen
    MM, dtd 1837,8,19
1838, 12, 20. Susan rocf Richland MM, Pa.,
    dtd 1838,11,30 (H)
1840, 1, 23. Asa dis disunity
1840, 8, 20. Isaac B. & w, Martha, & ch,
    Clayton N., Jeremiah, Chas. & Joseph, rocf
    Buckingham MM, Pa., dtd 1840,4,6 (H)
1844, 5, 23. David Osborn Jr. gct White Water
    MM, Ind., to m Susan Williams
1847, 5, 27. Cert rec for Richard from Marl-
    borough MM, dtd 1846,3,3, endorsed to
    Upper Springfield MM, O.
1848, 1, 27. Achsah dis
1872, 5, 16. Mary C. gct Goshen MM
1874, 8, 20. Esther B. gct Goshen MM
1876, 4, 20. Thomas & Mary & dt, Laura, rocf
    Gilead MM
1887, 4, 21. Susan M. recrq
1887, 4, 21. David recrq
1887, 4, 21. Mary E. recrq
1890, 1, 16. Robert recrq
1901, 3, 21. Edith P. recrq
1903, 8, 20. Edith P. & dt, Erma Stiner, relrq
1904, 10, 20. Laura B. relrq
1908, 5, 21. Arthur E. relrq
1909, 3, 18. Daisy M. recrq
1911, 2, 16. Dorothy Gladys, minor, recrq
1912, 3, 21. Marjory relrq
1920, 10, 21. Charles & w, Julia, rocf Em-
    poria MM, Kans.

WILLIS
1904, 7, 21. George transferred from Ashley
    MM

WILMETH
1890, 2, 13. Henry & Emily recrq

WILSON
1822, 1, 22. Samuel d ae 59 bur Wayne
----, --, --. Joseph & Hannah
    Ch: Samuel
        Willis   b 1826, 2, 18 d 1866, 5,24
        bur Knox Co., O. (d 1826,5,24 in O)

Ch: Willis S. b 1827, 3, 6
    Theodore F." 1829, 5, 20
    Deborah   " 1831, 8, 5
    Mary   " 1833, 12, 11
    Rachel W. " 1836, 4, 8 d 1839,10, 8
    bur Jay Co., Ind.
1828, 3, 14. Hannah d bur Middleberry
1839, 10, 28. Hannah d bur Jay Co., Ind.

1824, 8, 25. Joseph gct Center MM, to m
    Hannah Underwood
1825, 3, 31. Hannah rocf Center MM, dtd
    1824,12,18
1829, 1, 29. Hannah dis jH
1829, 1, 29. Joseph dis jH
1836, 11, 24. Eliza rocf Deerfield MM, O.,
    dtd 1836,9,14 (H)
1838, 5, 24. Joseph & dt, Mary, gct White
    Water MM, Ind. (H)
1840, 3, 26. Willis L., minor, gct White
    River MM, Ind.
1860, 6, 21. Ruth (form Mosher) dis mcd (H)
1884, 2, 18. Robert recrq
1891, 3, 19. Isaac J. & Ella A. recrq
1892, 7, 21. Robert B. dropped from mbrp

WINDHAM
1833, 4, 25. Mercy rocf Plainfield MM, dtd
    1833,1,24 (H)

WINDSOR
1923, 7, --. Ruth m Rayburn Cadwalader

1885, 3, 19. Charles T. recrq
1890, 3, 20. Charles L. dropped from mbrp
1901, 3, 21. Alvin E. recrq
1906, 2, 15. Wm. Arthur [Windson] & w, Bida
    Imo, recrq
1907, 7, 18. Will & Bida dropped from mbrp
1928, 5, 17. Alvin E., Myrta B., Ralph Leroy
    & Emma Louisa, relrq

WING
1824, 4, 1. Sarah & dt, Phebe H., rocf
    Stillwater MM, dtd 1823,12,27
1827, 12, 27. Phebe H. rmt Aaron L. Benedict
1829, 12, 3. Sarah dis jH

WINTERSTEIN
1886, 3, 18. Charles A. & Susan C. recrq
1887, 9, 15. Charles A. & w, Susan C., relrq
1893, 5, 18. Charles A. & Susan C. dropped
    from mbrp

WOLLAM
1875, 4, 15. Julia recrq

WOOD
----, --, --. Daniel d 1868,9,24 ae 79 bur
    Peru, O.; m Phebe ----- d 1822,7,28 bur
    Peru, O.
    Ch: Anna   b 1813, 3, 12
        Levi   " 1815, 1, 25 d 1893, 6,28

WOOD, Daniel & Phebe, continued
        bur Alum Creek
    Ch: Rachel   b 1817, 3, 26
        Jemima   " 1818, 12, 15
        Richard   " 1820, 10, 2 d 1895, 1, 6
        bur Woodbury, O.
        William   b 1822, 7, 21 " 1822, 9,--
        bur Peru, O.
    Daniel m 2nd Elizabeth ----- d 1871,1,2 ae
72 bur Peru, O.
    Ch: Sarah E.   b 1825, 4, 27
        George I.   " 1830, 8, 13
        Thomas E.   " 1832, 8, 11
        Samuel W.   " 1834, 12, 3 d 1837, 3,16
        bur ·Peru, O.
        Daniel H.   b 1838, 11, 15 " 18--, 9,24
        Esther B.   " 1840, 1, 24 " 1905, 8, 6
        bur Kokomo, Ind.
----, --, --. David, s Jonathan & Rachel, b
    1792,12,19 bur Rhode Island d 1847,7,7;
    m Esther MOSHER, dt Asa & Bethiah, b
    1798,3,31
    Ch: Asa M.   b 1820, 5, 16 d 1821, 9,13
        bur Marion Co., O.
        Abigail   b 1821, 8, 2
        Phebe B.   " 1822, 11, 22
        Joseph M.   " 1824, 7, 12
        Samuel H.   " 1825, 12, 30
        Jonathan   " 1828, 10, 12
        Hannah B.M." 1830, 7, 30 d 1832, 5, 8
        bur Marion Co., O.
        Stephen M. b 1832, 6, 10
        Asa M.   " 1834, 1, 2
        Ruth T.   " 1835, 10, 23
        David John " 1840, 3, 1
----, --, --. -Israel & Mary H.
    Ch: Priscilla   b 1821, 1, 19
        Elizabeth   " 1822, 7, 4
        Daniel T.   " 1824, 5, 3
        Frances T. " 1827, 10, 28
        Rachel   " 1825, 12, 8
        Sarah   " 1829, 5, 1
        Lydia   " 1830, 11, 17
        Jonathan B." 1823, 10, 4
        Rhoda E.   " 1836, 3, 8
        Eunáce   " 1837, 11, 14
1824, 9, 26. Rachel, w Jonathan, d ae 60 bur
    Morvin
----, --, --. Jonathan Jr. & Mary
    Ch: Thomas A.   b 1826, 12, 3
        Stephen   " 1829, 12, 2
        Rachel Ann " 1833, 7, 25
        Griffith L." 1835, 5, 29
        Lindley H. " 1837, 8, 28
----, --, --. Reuben & Anna
    Ch: William   b 1828, 9, 17
        Henry   " 1831, 11, 1
        Elizabeth   " 1833, 10, 1
        Peleg P.   " 1837, 1, 18
----, --, --. George J. b 1830,8,13 d 1918,4,17
1832, 7, 26. Desire d ae 70 bur Morvin, O.
1834, 5, 1. Anna m Griffith LEWIS
1835, 11, 27. Rachel m James VERNON

1837, 4, 21. Jemima m Jacob HEALY
1838, 5, 1. Jonathan d ae 77 bur Gilead, O.
1843, 7, 26. Abigail m Eli TOWNSEND (H)
----, --, --. Samuel & Priscilla
    Ch: Libius   b 1844, 2, 25
        Mary Fran-
        ces   " 1845, 11, 17
        Israel   " 1848, 3, 15
        Sarah Ellen" 1850, 4, 27
        Catharine   " 1852, 4, 20
        Martha
        Elizabeth   " 1855, 4, 20
1854, 5, 26. Sarah E. m Joshua BAILEY
1855, 8, 29. Elizabeth P. m Wm. T. FAWCETT
----, --, --. Charles d 1902,3,23 bur Alum
    Creek; m Direxa -----
    Ch: Arthur G.   b 1881, 6, 26 d 1885, 7,22
        bur Alum Creek
        George Al-
        bert   b 1885, 2, 13 " 1905, 2,24
        bur Alum Creek
        Oscar   b 1887, 3, 5
        Frederick   " 1889, 6, 23
        Eugene
        Mary
1898, 1, 8. Frances, dt Frank & Mary (Hatten)
    Green, b

1818, 3, 3. Jonathan & w, Rachel, & ch,
    Israel, Lydia, Jonathan, Reuben, Rachel &
    Matilda, rocf Peru MM, N. Y., dtd 1817,9,
    25, endorsed by Short Creek MM, O., 1818,2,
    24
1818, 8, 27. David rocf Peru MM, N. Y., dtd
    1818,7,23
1819, 9, 2. David rmt Esther Mosher
1819, 9, 30. Lydia rmt Daniel Osborn
1820, 3, 30. Israel C. dis mcd
1821, 3, 1. Israel rstrq
1823, 10, 23. Mary H. recrq
1823, 11, 27. Rachel Jr. rmt Caleb Hathaway
1824, 1, 29. Jonathan Jr. gct Carmel MM, to
    m Mary Ashton
1824, 8, 25. Mary rocf Carmel MM, dtd 1824,5,
    15
1825, 4, 28. Daniel rmt Elizabeth Benedict
1826, 2, 2. Jonathan rmt Desire Osborn
1826, 11, 2. Reuben con mcd
1826, 12, 28. Matilda rmt Slocum Bunker
1827, 9, 27. Anna recrq
1830, 5, 27. David dis disunity
1830, 5, 27. Esther dis disunity
1830, 7, 29. Priscilla & Elizabeth, ch Is-
    rael & Mary, recrq
1833, 10, 24. Jonathan rmt Rhoda Mullenix
1837, 7, 20. Lydia rocf LeRay MM, N. Y., dtd
    1837,6,8
1837, 10, 26. Jonathan & ch, Samuel, Eliza,
    Ruth R., Catherine, Amos & Benjamin, rocf
    Leray MM, N. Y., dtd 1837,9,7
1838, 9, 20. Martha rst on consent of LeRoy
    MM, N. Y.
1839, 2, 21. Robert & w, Tacy; & ch, Nancy,

WOOD, continued
    Kinsey & Mary Ellen, rocf Deerfield MM,
    O., dtd 1838,12,12 (H)
1839, 7, 25. Richard, minor, gct Goshen MM
1839, 12, 26. Eliza dis disunity
1839, 12, 26. Ruth dis disunity
1841, 4, 22. Lydia Ayers (form Wood) dis mcd
1841, 6, 24. Levi con mcd
1841, 10, 28. Martha dis
1842, 9, 19. Catharine dis jas
1842, 11, 24. Richard rocf Goshen MM, dtd
    1842,9,17
1842, 12, 22. Samuel gct Gilead MM, to m
    Priscilla H. Wood

1843, 8, 24. Richard dis jas
1844, 2, 22. Priscilla H. rocf Gilead MM,
    dtd 1843,11,21
1844, 6, 27. Martha rst
1845, 5, 23. Robert & w, Tacy, & ch, Kinsey,
    Mary Ellen, Thos. Clarkson & Lydia, gct
    Deerfield MM, O. (H)
1846, 9, 21. Asa M. Townsend gct Gilead MM,
    to m Elizabeth G. Wood
1849, 1, 25. John P. & w, Susannah, rocf
    Chesterfield MM, dtd 1848,12,16
1849, 1, 25. Elizabeth P. rocf Chesterfield
    MM, dtd 1848,12,16
1847, 7, 26. Amos dis disunity
1849, 7, 26. Benjamin dis disunity
1851, 8, 21. Elizabeth T. & ch, Mary T. &
    Esther N., recrq (H)
1852, 8, 26. Samuel dis disunity
1854, 9, 21. Stephen dis mcd (H)
1854, 11, 23. Thomas dis mcd
1856, 2, 21. Priscilla & ch, Libius, Mary
    Frances, Israel, Sarah Ellen, Catharine,
    Martha & Elizabeth, gct Gilead MM
1857, 6, 25. Asa M. dis mcd (H)
1858, 5, 27. John P. & w, Susan P., gct
    Plainfield MM, Ind.
1860, 1, 25. Joseph M. & w, Elizabeth, & ch,
    Mary T., Esther N. & Anna Cynthia, gct
    Prairie Grove MM, Ia. (H)
1860, 7, 26. Ruth L. Pierce (form Wood) dis
    mcd (H)
1860, 8, 23. Daniel H. dis mcd
1862, 5, 22. George J. con mcd
1865, 1, 19. Jonathan & w, Martha, gct Rollin
    MM, Mich.
1867, 8, 22. Esther B. Tuttle (form Wood) con
    mcd
1875, 1, 21. Charles recrq
1875, 3, 18. Mary B. recrq
1875, 4, 15. Thomas recrq
1875, 10, 21. Caroline A. & ch, Martha A.,
    Ann Etta & Lenora, recrq
1875, 10, 21. Daniel H. rst
1876, 1, 20. Catharine & ch, Martha T. &
    Mary W., recrq
1904, 7, 21. Thomas & Kate E. transferred
    from Ashley MM

1907, 1, 17. Grace F. recrq
1907, 5, 16. Daniel H. & w, Carrie, gct Co-
    lumbus MM
1910, 4, 21. Daniel H. & w, Carrie, rocf Co-
    lumbus MM
1913, 12, 18. Daniel H. & w, Carrie A., gct
    Columbus MM
1917, 4, 19. Fred dropped from mbrp
1823, 2, 15. Oscar dropped from mbrp
1926, 7, 22. Grace dropped from mbrp

WOOTING
1887, 3, 17. Martin recrq
1890, 2, 13. Martin [Wootring] relrq

WORLINE
1887, 3, 17. Ida B.

WORNSTAFF
1887, 2, 17. Mrs. M. L. recrq

WORTH
1834, 6, 26. Elma rocf Starksborough MM,
    Vt., dtd 1834,4,4
1885, 3, 19. Lula recrq
1893, 5, 18. Lula Worth Grant dropped from
    mbrp
1900, 4, 19. Sarah J. recrq
1904, 8, 18. Sarah dropped from mbrp

WRIGHT
----, --, --. Robert & Rachel
    Ch: Charles A. b 1811, 5, 15
    Robert m 2nd Sarah -----
    Ch: Sarah Ann b 1819, 12, 5
----, --,--. John m Ann ----- d 1833,6,21 bur
    Knox Co., O. (H)
    Ch: Isaac R. b 1824, 1, 14
        Rachel   " 1826, 8, 5
        Wm. Henry " 1827, 2, 11
        Edward R. " 1831, 8, 25
        George   "   d ae 3m bur
    Knox Co., O.
        Ann   " ae 5m bur
    Knox Co., O.
1829, 9, 30. Robert d ae 61y.1 m bur Friends
    Bur Gr., Knox Co., O. (H)
1835, 4, 30. John, s Robert & Rachel, Knox
    Co., O.; m in Owl Creek MH, Sarah M. EL-
    LIOTT, dt Eli & Margaret, Knox Co., O.(H)
1837, 8, 26. Rachel m Jason LEWIS
----, --, --. William W. & Peace (H)
    Ch: Wm. Mosher b 1844, 4, 11 d 1854, 6,23
        bur Owls Creek
        Hannah   b 1847, 4, 16 " 1848, 4,21
        bur Owls Creek
        Rachel   b 1846, 1, 19
        Joseph M. " 1849, 7, 13
1850, 3, 4. William d bur Owls Creek

1820, 4, 27. Robert rqc for s, Paxson
1821, 5, 28. William dis mcd
1822, 3, 28. Mary dis

WRIGHT   continued
1822, 3, 28. John con mcd
1825, 9, 29. Susan Farquhar (form Wright) dis mcd
1828, 10, 2. Pemelia Gibson (form Wright) dis mcd
1829, 1, 29. Sarah dis jH
1829, 1, 29. Robert dis jH
1829, 1, 29. John dis jH
1830, 6, 24. Ann & ch recrq (H)
1831, 4, 28. Charles A. dis jH
1835, 11, 26. Charles A. dis mcd (H)
1836, 5, 26. Rachel rocf Flushing MM, dtd 1836,11,26
1839, 6, 20. Sarah Ann gct Plainfield MM
1841, 10, 20. Sarah gct Plainfield MM (H)
1842, 10, 20. Ann Gregg (form Wright) rpd mcd (H)
1844, 6, 20. Peace (form Mosher) con mcd (H)
1844, 8, 22. William W. rst (H)
1849, 8, 24. Aaron rocf Flushing MM, dtd 1849,6,21
1854, 8, 24. Ann rocf Flushing MM, dtd 1854, 6,22
1858, 7, 22. Lovina H. & Mary recrq
1858, 6, 24. Elizabeth Jane recrq
1858, 11, 25. Lindley H. & John rocf Flushing MM, dtd 1858,9,25
1859, 4, 24. Wm. rst on consent of Flushing MM
1859, 7, 21. John & w, Sarah, & s, Charles, gct Prairie Grove MM, Ia. (H)
1859, 9, 19. Charles, adopted s Wm. & Ann, recrq
1862, 7, 17. John gct Sandy Spring MM, O., to m Sarah Pim
1863, 3, 19. John gct Agusta MM
1864, 6, 16. Wm. & w, Ann, & ch, Lavina, Mary & Elizabeth Jane, gct Ypsilanti MM, Mich.
1864, 12, 22. Aaron gct Ypsilanti MM, Mich.
1868, 1, 16. Lindley M. con mcd
1887, 1, 20. Myra recrq
1887, 2, 17. Henry recrq
1887, 5, 19. Charles recrq
1888, 3, 22. Jessie recrq
1892, 1, 21. Charles dropped from mbrp
1904, 7, 21. Henry, Palmyra & Jessie transferred from Ashley MM

        *   *   *   *   *   *   *

BARRINGTON
1852, 6, 24. Bethia M. (form Townsend) con mcd

BENEDICT
1842, 12, 22. Sarah chosen elder
1843, 1, 23. Anne Hide (form Benedict) con mcd
1843, 9, 18. Memorial signed for Phebe
1844, 9, 23. Ann Blackmore (form Benedict) con mcd
1845, 1, 23. Sarah Benedict & Dorcas Osborn appointed clerk & assistant clerk
1846, 6, 24. Matilda Chapel (form Benedict) con mcd

1850, 1, 24. Sarah Benedict (form Comfort) con mcd

BLACKMORE
1844, 9, 23. Ann (form Benedict) con mcd

CHAMBERS
1846, 7, 23. Deborah More (form Chambers) con mcd

CHAPEL
1846, 6, 24. Matilda (form Benedict) con mcd

CHAPMAN
1843, 4, 27. Martha chosen elder

COMFORT
1844, 8, 22. Phebe Martin (form Comfort) con mcd
1850, 1, 24. Sarah Benedict (form Comfort) con mcd

GIDLEY
1846, 3, 26. Hannah chosen elder
1854, 6, 22. Sarah recommended a minister

HAMMOND
1849, 2, 23. Deborah McGrew (form Hammond) con mcd (mbr Smithfield MM but living within our limits)

HIDE
1843, 1, 23. Anne (form Benedict) con mcd

HOLE
1852, 9, 20. Sarah chosen elder

HOWEL
1854, 1, 26. Elma rst in mbrp with consent of Salem MM (dis by Salem MM for mcd 1853,8,26)

KEESE
1848, 5, 25. Gulielma (form Taber) con mcd

LEWIS
1843, 1, 26. Rachel & ch, Adna & Jane, rocf Goshen, dtd 1842,11,19
1849, 4, 27. Hannah recommended a minister
1854, 8, 24. John W. dis mcd

McCULLY
1849, 6, 22. Louisa (form Washburn), mbr Greenwich MM, con mcd; Greenwich MM to be notified

McGREW
1849, 2, 23. Deborah (form Hammond) con mcd (mbr Smithfield MM but living within our limits)

MARTIN
1844, 8, 22. Phebe (form Comfort) con mcd

MORE
1846, 7, 23. Deborah (form Chambers) con mcd

NICHOLS
1849, 10, 26. Athanissa (form Spencer) con mcd

OSBORN
1845, 1, 23. Sarah Benedict & Dorcas Osborn appointed clerk & assistant clerk
1845, 2, 20. Dorcas appointed recorder
1851, 2, 20. Memorial signed for David
1851, 9, 22. Daniel chosen elder
1854, 1, 26. Dorcas chosen elder

PHILLIPS
1888, 6, 21. Jenkins, Sarah A., Benjamin & Julia dropped from mbrp
1888, 6, 21. Letta dropped from mbrp

SHEPHERD
1843, 1, 25. Margaret, mbr Farnham MM, rpd rem to Millwalky Co., Wis.

SMITH
1843, 3, 21. Willis R. recommended a minister

SPENCER
1849, 10, 26. Athanissa (form Spencer) con mcd

STANLEY
1853, 11, 24. Phebe P. recrq

TABER
1848, 5, 25. Gulielma Keese (form Taber) con mcd

TINNEY
1844, 11, 21. Testimonial against Eliza Ann Tinney (form Carpenter)

TOWNSEND
1852, 6, 24. Bethia M. Barrington (form Townsend) con mcd

WASHBURN
1849, 6, 22. Louisa McCully (form Washburn), mbr Greenwich MM, con mcd; Greenwich MM to be notified

WILLETS
1844, 3, 28. Lamira (or Almira) dis by Stillwater MM; rst 1844,7,25 with concurrence of Stillwater MM
1853, 6, 23. Charity [Willits] recommended a minister

WOOD
1853, 6, 23. Sarah E. recommended a minister

GILEAD MONTHLY MEETING

Gilead Monthly Meeting, located in Morrow County, Ohio, was established by Alum Creek Quarterly Meeting, 12th Mo. 18, 1838. This monthly meeting was made up of Northern, Weston, and Sandusky Preparative Meetings. Later Northern changed its name to Gilead.

When Greenwich Monthly Meeting was laid down in 1909, several members were transferred to Gilead and the same thing occurred when Weston Monthly Meeting was laid down in 1927.

RECORDS

ADAMS
1886, 3, 16. Louretta recrq
1904, 9, 13. Ova recrq
1923, 11, 13. Elizabeth & s, Virgil, recrq
1925, 10, 20. Lizzie & s, Virgil, relrq

ADELL
1864, 10, 28. Wm. T., s Jacob & Rachel T., Henry Co., Ia.; m in Gilead, Mary R. TABER dt Silas & Anna, Morrow Co., O.

1865, 1, 17. Mary R. dis disunity

ALLMON
1853, 1, 31. Mary Ruanna, dt Silas & Phebe, b

1847, 1, 26. Silas & w, Phebe Elma, & ch, Lucy Ann, Levi, James B., rocf Middleton MM, dtd 1846,12,10
1854, 12, 26. Phebe Ann dis joining Spiritualists
1855, 1, 23. Silas dis joining Spiritualists
1863, 5, 19. Lucy Ann Billmyer (form Allman) dis mcd
1867, 10, 15. Levi, James & Mary gct Legrand MM, Ia.

AMES
1875, 1, 21. Mary Amanda m Zeno KIRK

ANDERSON
----, --, --. Samuel A. & Liza A.
    Ch: Thomas   b 1840, 5, 10
        Mary Jane " 1842, 9, 19
        Deborah   " 1847, 7, 19
        Sarah M.   " 1849, 6, 11
        Lefy Anna " 1853, 7, 29

ANDREWS
1859, 6, 1. John L. d bur Gilead
1861, 9, 28. Mary Jane d bur Gilead
1862, 4, 17. Samuel A. d bur Gilead
1863, 9, 3. Sarah M. d bur Gilead

1839, 4, 23. Deborah recrq
1841, 1, 26. Joel rocf Elba MM, dtd 1840,12, 15
1841, 1, 26. Richard rocf Elba MM, dtd 1840, 12,15
1841, 1, 26. Wm. L. rocf Elba MM, dtd 1840, 10,13
1842, 10, 25. Wm. P. dis disunity
1844, 2, 20. Deborah Mosher (form Andrews) dis mcd
1844, 9, 21. Joel dis mcd
1844, 11, 19. Charlotte (form Quaintance) dis mcd
1845, 7, 22. Richard H. gct Cincinnati MM
1848, 10, 24. Martha (form Carey) dis disunity
1858, 3, 23. Thomas dis disunity
1863, 3, 17. Lindley M. dis mcd & joining

Spiritualists
1864, 7, 19. Deborah M. Roche (form Andrews) dis mcd

ASHBAUGH
1872, 10, 15. Orianna (form Taber) dis mcd

ATKINSON
1861, 1, 22. Isaac Jackson gct Upper Springfield MM, to m Hannah Atkinson

ATWATER
1860, 7, 24. Sarah E. rocf Hartland MM, N.Y., dtd 1860,7,19
1860, 10, 23. Sarah E. gct Ypsilanti MM, Mich.

AUKER
1886, 6, 15. Ella dropped from mbrp

AULT
1903, 1, 20. Charles recrq
1906, 2, 13. Mamie Bell recrq
1908, 9, 15. Charles & Lydia relrq
1923, 9, 18. Marion & w, Fernanda, & ch, Clarence, Noah & Paul, recrq
1927, 8, 16. M. F. relrq
1928, 3, 20. Fernanda relrq
1932, 6, 14. Noah dropped from mbrp

BALDWIN
1878, 3, 19. Wm. H. rocf Cherry Grove MM, Ind.
1882, 8, 15. Wm. H. gct Alum Creek MM, O.; cert returned 1882,11,14
1883, 2, 13. Wm. gct Goshen MM
1899, 5, 16. Benjamin & w, Jennie, recrq
1909, 3, 16. Bennie dropped from mbrp
1920, 5, 18. Louise recrq
1922, 3, 14. John Wesley & Dallas, recrq
1929, 4, 16. Jesse, John Wesley & Dallas dropped from mbrp

BALL
1909, 3, 16. Maria recrq

BARRY
1904, 1, 19. Laurence A., Hannah M., Hazel E. & Lottie Pearl, recrq
1911, 12, 19. E. E. & w recrq
1923, 5, 15. Hazel dropped from mbrp
1926, 1, 19. Lawrence relrq

BARTON
1923, 5, 15. Imo Shaw dropped from mbrp

BEAR
1878, 7, 16. David recrq

BEARD
1838, 6, 12. Mariah d bur Scipio

BENDING
1923, 5, 15. Lora dropped from mbrp

BENEDICT
1840, 6, 4. Esther L. m Griffith LEAVERING
1843, 7, 5. Eliza, dt Sylvester & Susanna, b
----, --, --. Henry & Eliza
    Ch: Rebecca C. b 1844, 8, 22
        Elizabeth " 1846, 5, 28
        Ann   " 1848, 5, 12
1846, 6, 9. Silvester d
1848, 11, 30. Susana m Thomas GRISELE
1850, 2, --. Jonathan G., s Sylvester & Su-
    sannah, Morrow Co.; m in Weston, Eliza-
    beth Ann WHITE, dt Wm. & Eliza Ann
    Ch: Cecelia   b 1851, 11, 24
        Florilia   " 1853, 1, 13
1856, 8, 20. Ruth d bur Weston
1874, 7, 23. Griffes Grafton, s Aaron D. &
    Phebe, Morrow Co.; m in Bucyrus, Ellen
    WILLETS, dt Joel & Cynthia, Morrow Co.

1839, 5, 21. Eli dis disunity
1840, 1, 21. Ruth, dt Sylvester & Susanna,
    recrq
1844, 3, 26. Henry rocf Smithfield MM, dtd
    1844,1,22
1844, 3, 26. Eliza T. rocf Upper Springfield
    MM, dtd 1844,2,24
1850, 4, 23. Henry & w, Eliza, & ch, Rebecca
    C., Elizabeth Ann & Hannah G., gct Goshen
    MM
1855, 2, 20. Eli dis disunity
1857, 6, 23. Jonathan S. & w, Elizabeth Ann,
    & ch, Cecilia, Flora, Martha E., gct West-
    ern Plain MM, Ia.
1869, 7, 24. Harvey & w, Lovina B., & ch,
    Aden S. & Sarah Evaline, & adopted dt,
    Susan Coney, rocf Alum Creek MM, dtd 1860,
    6,21
1860, 7, 24. Wm. G. dis mcd
1860, 7, 24. John dis mcd
1864, 6, 14. Harvey & w, Louisa, & ch, Adin
    L. & Sarah Eveline, gct Winneshiek MM, Ia.
1875, 5, 18. Ellen W. gct Alum Creek MM
1879, 3, 18. Levi recrq
1879, 6, 17. Ella May recrq
1884, 10, 14. Ella gct Salem MM
1886, 6, 15. Levi dropped from mbrp

BENNET
1865, 8, 15. Rebecca (form Hobson) dis mcd

BERRY
1929, 4, 16. Hanna M. dropped from mbrp

BIGGS
1885, 2, 17. Meaker J., Mary E. & Lula M.
    recrq
1893, 8, 15. M. J. & Lulu relrq

BLACKBURN
1883, 9, 18. Hannah gct Goshen MM

BLAIR
1882, 3, 14. Luella recrq

1887, 3, 15. Luella gct Alum Creek MM, O.
1887, 7, 19. David [Bair] dropped from mbrp

BLANEY
1929, 4, 16. Jesse dropped from mbrp

BORDERS
1933, 2, 14. Rossie recrq

BOULTON
1883, 11, 1. Wm. d bur Gilead
1884, 2, 5. Mary d ae 73 bur Gilead

1854, 1, 24. William & w, Mary, & ch, James
    & Charles, rocf Middleton MM, dtd 1854,1,
    12
1854, 1, 24. Elizabeth rocf Middleton MM,
    dtd 1854,1,12
1858, 9, 18. James [Bolton] dis disunity
1864, 8, 16. Charles dis military service

BRANTINGHAM
1892, 5, 17. Lizzie T. gct Indianapolis MM,
    Ind.

BREED
1872, 6, 22. Stephen, s Richard, Park Co.,
    Ind.; m in Gilead, Chloe Ann LANGDON, dt
    Wm. & Lucinda, Morrow Co.

1872, 7, 16. Chloe Ann gct Rocky Run MM, Ind.

BREESE
1840, 4, 21. Hannah B. (form Mosher) dis mcd
1865, 1, 17. Hannah [Brees] (form Wood) dis
    disunity
1913, 3, 18. Louisa P. [Breece] relrq

BREWER
1842, 8, 23. Joseph R. Quaintance gct Short
    Creek MM, to m Phebe Brewer

BREWSTER
1855, 6, 17. Cert rec for John O. & w, Han-
    nah A., from Butternut MM, N. Y., dtd
    1855,2,28, endorsed to Farmington MM, N.Y.

BROKAW
1910, 4, 19. Ethel recrq
1915, 5, 18. Ethel relrq

BROLLIER
1878, 1, 15. Mary & ch, Lewis Levi & C. W.,
    recrq
1892, 2, 16. W. Clennie recrq
1895, 5, 14. Lewis C. relrq
1906, 3, 20. Clennie W. [Broiler] & w, Myrtle
    recrq
1915, 2, 16. Candice recrq
1922, 2, 14. Mary recrq
1928, 2, 14. Dona recrq
1933, 8, 15. Mary (Brollier) Hoffmire drop-
    ped from mbrp

BROOKS
1866, 1, 23. Hannah P. m Benjamin Butler

1849, 3, 20. Arnold rocf Upper Springfield
    MM, dtd 1849,2,24
1849, 8, 21. Arnold dis disunity
1862, 4, 15. Hannah recrq

BROWN
1851, 9, 4. Jonathan, s Levi & Hannah, Mor-
    row Co.; m in Weston, Mary F. TALBOTT, dt
    Allen & Mary, Craw. Co.
    Ch: Thomas Lu-
            cius   b 1852, 10, 15
         Alfred   " 1854, 7, 17
         William
            Penn   " 1857, 5, 31
         Elizabeth
            T.   " 1861, 12, 4

1847, 11, 23. Jonathan rocf Starksborough MM,
    Vt., dtd 1847,1,10
1879, 1, 14. Charles & Harriett recrq
1879, 2, --. Melva relrq
1879, 4, 15. Jonathan relrq
1883, 6, 19. Mary F. gct New Garden MM
1885, 10, 20. Thomas L. relrq
1887, 5, 17. Susie recrq
1887, 6, 14. Mary F. rocf Winona MM
1887, 7, 19. W. P. dropped from mbrp
1889, 4, 16. Nancy (form Wheeler) relrq
1898, 12, 20. Bessie recrq
1900, 3, 20. Leslie recrq
1922, 3, 14. Blanch, Paul & Kenneth recrq
1923, 5, 15. Leslie dropped from mbrp
1927, 5, 17. Kenneth gct First Friends Ch.,
    Cleveland, O.

BRUNELL
1915, 9, 14. Perry & w, Nettie, & ch, Paul,
    Mildred & Cora recrq
1923, 5, 15. Perry, Nettie, Paul, Mildred &
    Carrie [Burnell] dropped from mbrp

BUNDY
1878, 3, 19. Esther M. relrq

BUNKER
----, --, --. Silas d 1883,7,17 bur Dardington;
    m Ann -----
    Ch: Marnilva   b 1848, 2, 14
         Lester P.   " 1849, 10, 16
         Isidore E. " 1853, 6, 16
1852, 12, 24. Hannah d ae 69 bur Howard Cem.
1872, 7, 4. Helen M. d bur Cardigon
1881, 12, 26. Elihu d ae 73 bur Cardington
1883, 2, 23. Elizabeth d ae 76 bur Cardington

1841, 11, 23. Lydia Purvis (form Bunker) dis
    mcd
1842, 3, 22. Silas con mcd
1842, 12, 20. Ann recrq
1843, 1, 24. Hannah rst on consent of Alum

Creek MM
1847, 10, 26. David con mcd
1849, 1, 23. Jethro dis mcd
1852, 9, 18. Henry, s Silas & Ann, recrq
1856, 8, 26. Elizabeth dis disunity
1858, 12, 21. David gct Alum Creek MM
1863, 5, 19. Reuben rst on consent of Alum
    Creek MM
1865, 9, 19. Elizabeth rst at Alum Creek MM
    on consent of this mtg
1866, 12, 18. Henry P. dis military service
1866, 12, 18. Reuben gct Alum Creek MM
1868, 7, 14. Edwin M. rocf Alum Creek MM,
    dtd 1868,5,21
1872, 2, 13. Lester P. relrq
1872, 6, 18. Hellen recrq
1874, 9, 15. Edwin M. con mcd
1875, 4, 13. Edwin M. gct Columbus MM
1877, 12, 18. Elihu & Elizabeth rocf Alum
    Creek MM, dtd 1877,11,15
1885, 3, 17. Lindley recrq
1886, 6, 15. Ann & dt, Nellie, gct Columbus
    MM
1887, 1, 18. Lindley H. relrq
1920, 7, 20. Lindley recrq

BURNS
1885, 2, 17. Phebe E. recrq
1888, 3, 20. Docy recrq
1889, 3, 19. Alfred & Sarah recrq
1893, 12, 19. Melissa recrq
1898, 12, 20. Dolphus D. recrq
1899, 9, 19. Malissa relrq
1900, 8, 14. Ola recrq
1909, 3, 16. Adolph dropped from mbrp
1923, 5, 15. Raymond dropped from mbrp

BURR
1924, 7, 14. Floretta Fay recrq

BUTLER
1866, 1, 23. Benjamin, s John & Drusilla,
    Mahoning Co.; m in Gilead, Hannah P.
    BROOKS, dt Isaiah B. & Deborah, Morrow Co.

1867, 5, 14. Hannah P. gct Damascus MM

CAMP
1841, 1, 26. Ruth (form Michinor) dis mcd

CARTER
1869, 10, 16. Joel d ae 63

1866, 7, 17. Joel recrq
1870, 12, 20. James & ch, James Edgar, Aldon
    W., Laura & Annetta, recrq
1871, 1, 17. Henry recrq
1875, 7, 20. Henry dis mcd
1881, 9, 13. James Edgar relrq
1887, 7, 19. Laura & Aldin W. dropped from
    mbrp

CAREY

1840, 8, 21.   Susannah [Cary] d ae 49 bur San-
      dusky
1841, 9, 30.   Sarah [Cary] d bur Bucyrus

1841, 9, 18.   Isabella dis jas
1842, 5, 24.   Abel dis mcd
1843, 4, 25.   Lewis dis
1845, 9, 20.   Benjamin L. dis disunity
1848, 10, 24.   Martha Andrews (form Carey) dis
      disunity

CASKEY

1905, 7, 18.   John F., Ida May & Mattie Pearl
      recrq

CASTO

1919, 2, 16.   Nella, Hazel & Wm. recrq
1930, 7, 15.   Hazel (Casto) Kreis dropped from
      mbrp
1932, 6, 14.   William dropped from mbrp

CATON

1900, 3, 20.   Florence recrq
1923, 5, 15.   Florence dropped from mbrp

CATTELL

1866, 6, 27.   Mary m Israel WOOD

1840, 1, 21.   Robert Stanley gct Upper Spring-
      field MM, to m Lydia Cattel
1866, 5, 15.   Mary rocf Upper Springfield MM,
      dtd 1866,4,28

CECIL

1882, 3, 14.   William, Naomi & Mary recrq
1885, 4, 14.   Esther Ann recrq
1887, 3, 15.   Naomi, Mollie & Esther gct Alum
      Creek MM, O.
1887, 7, 19.   Willie dropped from mbrp
1894, 4, 17.   Berdie & Daisy recrq
1927, 8, 16.   Naomi transferred from Weston
      MM, O.
1931, 7, 14.   Naomi dropped from mbrp

CHANCELLOR

1885, 2, 17.   Wm. & Alfred recrq
1889, 7, 16.   Wm. & Alfred dropped from mbrp

CHAPMAN

1855, 6, 7.   John, s Ellwood & Sarah Ann, b

1851, 12, 23.   Ellwood & w, Sarah Ann, & ch,
      Jane P. & Mary, rocf Middleton MM, O.,
      dtd 1851,10,9
1856, 4, 22.   Ellwood & w, Sarah Ann, & ch,
      Jane P., Mary W. & John, gct Driftwood MM,
      Ind.

CHILCOTE

1917, 2, 2.   Susan d ae 66

1878, 8, 20.   Viola & Mattie recrq

1885, 2, 17.   Denton recrq
1886, 2, 16.   Susan recrq
1886, 6, 15.   Mattie dropped from mbrp
1891, 2, 19.   Morgan T. recrq
1892, 2, 16.   Charles recrq
1896, 3, 17.   Luella recrq
1897, 2, 16.   Wm. B. recrq
1900, 3, 20.   Charley & Myrtle recrq
1914, 1, 20.   Laurie dropped from mbrp
1915, 2, 16.   Charles, Myrtle & Ruth dropped
      from mbrp
1920, 11, 16.   Roy & Voy relrq
1922, 3, 14.   Dorothy recrq
1922, 3, 14.   Morgan dropped from mbrp
1923, 5, 15.   Donald dropped from mbrp
1925, 1, 20.   Morgan recrq
1932, 12, 20.   Dorothy gct Short Creek MM, O.

CLARK

1908, 5, 19.   Laura relrq
1909, 3, 16.   Gertrude dropped from mbrp

CLEVENGER

1885, 5, 19.   Mahlon recrq
1887, 7, 19.   M. B. dropped from mbrp

COBBS

1839, 12, 21.   Belinda T., dt Thomas & Sarah,
      b
1840, 6, 18.   Thomas C. d bur Gilead
1843, 10, 26.   Ansalm, s Pleasant & Olmy, Co-
      lumbiana Co.; m in Sandusky, Grace JACK-
      SON, dt Isaac & Amelia, Crawford Co.
1848, 12, 28.   Sarahann m David HUNT
1852, 4, 19.   Cynthia, dt Josiah & Ruth, b
1861, 8, 28.   Hannah m David S. ELLIOTT

1839, 4, 23.   Thomas T. & w, Sarah Ann, & dt,
      Hannah, rocf Upper Springfield MM, dtd
      1839,3,23
1844, 1, 23.   Grace gct Upper Springfield MM
1849, 2, 20.   Sarahann Hunt & dt, Hannah &
      Balinda T. Cobbs gct Goshen MM
1849, 11, 20.   Josiah & w, Ruth, & s, Jesse,
      rocf Upper Springfield MM, dtd 1849,10,27
1850, 5, 21.   Josiah dis disunity
1854, 2, 21.   Ruth & ch, Jesse & Cynthia, gct
      Driftwood MM, Ind.
1856, 8, 26.   Hannah rocf Goshen MM, dtd 1856,
      8,16
1861, 7, 16.   Hannah rocf Honey Creek MM, Ia.,
      dtd 1861,5,21
1863, 3, 17.   Daniel T. Rogers gct Upper
      Springfield MM, to m Lucy Jane Cobb

CONANT

1928, 7, 17.   Marian U. & w, Frances, & dt,
      Virgie Marie, recrq
1929, 7, 16.   Lindora (Conant) Williamson rec-
      rq
1929, 7, 16.   Doris recrq

CONEY
1863, 4, 14. Susan A. dis

CONKLIN
1844, 3, 26. Maria (form Daniels) dis mcd
1909, 5, 18. Charles & Elsie transferred from
Greenwich MM
1923, 5, 15. Charles & Elsie dropped from
mbrp

CONLIN
1852, 2, 24. Hannah (form Keese) con mcd

CONNING
1932, 6, 14. Harold J. dropped from mbrp

COPE
1876, 6, 23. Eva May, dt Lycurgus & Eliza Ann,
b

1863, 5, 19. Eliza A. dis mcd
1871, 9, 19. Lycurgus & w & ch recrq
1879, 1, 14. Lycurgus & w, Eliza Ann, gct
Salem MM

COPPOCK
1843, 9, 16. Levi rocf Upper Springfield MM,
dtd 1843,7,22
1850, 2, 19. Levi, minor, gct Salem MM, O.
1857, 10, 20. Abraham Morris gct Salem MM, to
m Mehitable J. Coppock

CORWIN
1890, 4, 15. James & w recrq
1910, 5, 17. Mamie relrq

COTANT
1851, 4, 30. Zehamiah B., s Benoni & Lydia,
Huron Co.; m in Gilead, Rachel H. WOOD,
dt Israel & Mary H., Morrow Co.
Ch: Benoni
Leander   b 1855, 2, 11
1876, 5, 18. Edwin S., s Zephaniah B. & Rachel H., Morrow Co.; m in Gilead, Louisa
HOBSON, dt Joseph & Amy
1917, 7, 12. Gideon d ae 98

1851, 11, 25. Rachel H. gct Greenwich MM
1854, 7, 25. Zephamiah B. & w, Rachel, & ch,
Edwin S. & George W., rocf Greenwich MM,
dtd 1854,5,19
1859, 9, 17. Zephaniah & w, Rachel, & ch, Elwin S., George W. & Benoni L., gct Greenwich MM
1865, 5, 16. Zephaniah B. & w, Rachel, & ch,
Edwin P., George W., Benoni L. & Charles
Chester, rocf Greenwich MM
1876, 4, 17. Zephaniah & w, Rachel, & ch,
Benoni Leander & Charles Chester, gct
Winneshiek MM, Ia.
1876, 4, 18. Benoni gct Winneshiek MM, Ia.
1877, 6, 19. Elwel S. & w, Louisa H., gct
Ackworth MM, Ia.

1909, 5, 18. Gideon B., Eliza & Joseph [Cou-
tant] transferred from Greenwich MM
1918, 3, 15. Edwin [Coutant] & w, Louisa,
recrq

COWGILL
1909, 5, 18. Avarilla transferred from
Greenwich MM
1909, 5, 18. Abbarilla gct Alum Creek MM, O.

COX
1928, 7, 17. R. Paten & w, Alice J., & ch,
Virgil H., Lawrence P. & John Calvin, recrq

CROOK
1923, 5, 15. Mina Davis dropped from mbrp

CUMMINS
1922, 8, 15. W. T. & w relrq
1925, 2, 17. W. T. & w, Frances F., recrq
1929, 11, 19. W. T. & Frances relrq

CURL
1882, 3, 14. Willie & Ova recrq
1882, 4, 18. Wm. recrq
1887, 3, 15. Wm. H. gct Alum Creek MM
1887, 3, 15. Wm. Jr. gct Alum Creek MM
1887, 3, 15. Ora gct Alum Creek MM
1894, 4, 17. Alma recrq
1927, 8, 16. Mina & F. M. transferred from
Weston MM, O.

CURTIS
1887, 12, 12. Florence Gertrude, dt Emmet &
Elizabeth, b

1889, 7, 17. E. H. & M. E. relrq

DALL
1930, 7, 15. Robert recrq
1932, 6, 14. Robert dropped from mbrp

DANIELS
----, --, --. Lindley, s Ebenezer & Sarah,
b 1842,1,4 d 1842,9,14
1842, 1, 16. Sarah d

1843, 3, 20. Ebeneezer C. con mcd
1844, 3, 26. Maria Conklin (form Daniels)
dis mcd
1844, 4, 23. Ebenezer C. dis disunity
1845, 1, 21. Anna dis jas

DAVIS
1868, 3, 17. Sidney recrq
1882, 5, 16. Sidney G. & w, Mary B., relrq
1910, 4, 19. Glenn & Mina recrq
1929, 4, 16. Glen dropped from mbrp

DAY
1914, 10, 20. John recrq
1928, 7, 17. John Mahlon & w, Zephel Marie,

DAY, continued
& ch, Clarence Willard & Charles Roswell,
    recrq
1933, 7, 18. Mahlon & fam dropped from mbrp

DEAN
1839, 12, 24. Hannah & s, Rowland, rocf Sandy
    Spring MM, dtd 1839,11,22
1839, 12, 24. Lavina rocf Sandy Spring MM, dtd
    1839,11,22
1841, 5, 25. Lavina gct Chesterfield MM
1841, 5, 25. Hannah & s, Rowland, gct Ches-
    terfield MM

DENMAN
1892, 2, 16. Monroe, Sarah & Enola recrq
1899, 4, 18. Sarah relrq

DENZER
1906, 4, 17. Margaret relrq

DERBERT
1884, 4, 15. John H. recrq

DEXTER
1856, 2, 27. Wm. L., s Elijah & Christiana,
    Morrow Co.; m in Gilead, Elisa C. HEART-
    LEY, dt Jesse & Mary, Morrow Co.

1855, 12, 25. Wm. L. recrq
1865, 1, 17. Wm. L. & w, Eliza C., gct Green-
    field MM

DOBSON
1909, 3, 16. Ethel recrq

DODGE
1845, 12, 23. Judith rocf Alum Creek MM, dtd
    1845,2,24

DOTY
1884, 8, 7. Elias W. d

1878, 8, 20. Susie recrq
1878, 10, 15. Elias & s, Willie, recrq

DOWNING
1840, 6, 23. John dis

DREY
1879, 6, 17. Hattie recrq
1886, 11, 16. Hattie [Dray] gct Alum Creek MM

EARLE
1933, 5, 16. Mable A. Mosher relrq

EARNSHAW
1844, 5, 25. George d ae 91 bur Sandusky
1850, 9, 9. George d ae 59 bur Sandusky
1869, 11, 18. Sarah d ae 89 bur Bucyrus

ECCLES
1892, 2, 16. Mary recrq

1892, 3, 15. Wm. recrq

EDDY
1872, 7, 16. Joseph Jones gct Kingston MM,
    Canada, to m Mary Eddy

EDWARDS
----, --, --. Lemuel & Susanna
    Ch: Adaline   b 1841, 5, 19
        Willis   " 1843, 6, 28
1842, 12, 31. Willis d bur Sandusky
1843, 7, 3. Susan d

1841, 5, 25. Lemuel & w, Susannah, & ch,
    Cortland, Wellington, Caroline, Rachel,
    Willis & Volumna, rocf Hamburgh MM, dtd
    1841,2,24
1844, 7, 23. Lemuel dis mcd
1850, 6, 25. Cortland dis mcd
1852, 4, 20. Wellington dis mcd
1882, 7, 18. Willis dropped from mbrp
1885, 2, 17. Eliza recrq
1888, 3, 20. Minnie recrq

ELLIOTT
1861, 8, 28. David, s Elias & Martha, Grant
    Co., Ind.; m in Gilead, Hannah COBBS, dt
    Thomas & Sarahann, Morrow Co.
1872, 12, 25. Isaac Hamilton, s John D. &
    Ruth, Logan Co.; m in Gilead, Elizabeth
    T. HOBSON, dt Joseph & Amy P., Morrow Co.
    Ch: Amyetta   b 1873, 11, 21

1862, 3, 18. Hannah C. gct Back Creek MM
1874, 10, 20. Isaac H. rocf Goshen MM, dtd
    1874,9,19
1876, 2, 15. Isaac H. & w, Elizabeth, & ch,
    Amy Etta, gct Goshen MM
1878, 9, 17. Isaac H. & w, Elizabeth T., &
    s, Clarence H., rocf Goshen MM, dtd 1898,
    6,22
1880, 2, 17. Isaac Hamilton dis
1881, 3, 15. Elizabeth dis
1887, 7, 19. Clarence dropped from mbrp
1900, 7, 17. Martin & w, Ella, rocf Alum
    Creek MM

EMSWEILER
1897, 2, 16. John D. & Cora recrq

FARRINGTON
----, --, --. Joseph J. & Sarah J.
    Ch: Jesse T.   b 1865, 4, 16 d 1883, 8,26
        Amelia Jane" 1866, 9, 8
        Mary Fran-
           ces   " 1868, 3, 15
        Tacy Emma " 1870, 2, 1
        Phebe Ellen" 1873, 3, 24
        Ethel May " 1882, 4, 12

1843, 6, 20. Mary & Sarah [Farington], ch
    Moses & Armelia, rocf Newgarden MM, dtd
    1842,7,21

FARRINGTON, continued

1849, 11, 20. Sarah Hall (form Farrington) con
    mcd

1851, 7, 22. Priscilla recrq

1853, 2, 22. Mary Mosher (form Farrington)
    dis mou

1853, 11, 21. Priscillaann [Farungton] m
    John MORRIS

1862, 9, 16. Joseph John & w recrq

1877, 2, 10. Joseph John & fam gct Alum Creek
    MM

1879, 11, 18. Sarah & ch, Jesse T., Amelia
    Jane, Mary Frances, Tacy Emma, Phebe Ellen
    & Clarence, rocf Alum Creek MM, dtd 1879,
    10,16

1880, 5, 18. Joseph John rocf Alum Creek MM,
    dtd 1880,4,15

1884, 9, 16. J. J. & w, Sarah, & ch Eliza
    Hartley, relrq

FEIGHT

1882, 4, 18. Mariah recrq

FERGUSON

1931, 11, 17. Dwight H. recrq

1932, 10, 18. Dwight & Stella relrq

FIELDS

1871, 1, 12. Lefea d ae 81 bur Gilead

1861, 9, 17. Lefy rocf Elba MM, N. Y., dtd
    1861,8,13

FISHER

1843, 2, 21. Ann Eliza (form Keese) dis mcd

FRAME

1853, 4, 19. Ann (form Quaintance) rpd mcd

1854, 1, 24. Ann gct Red Cedar MM, Ia.

FRANCIS

1853, 1, 25. George W. & w, Mary Ann, & ch,
    Mary Taber, Joseph Parker & Elizabeth Aus-
    tin, rocf Dartmouth MM, dtd 1852,11,21

1854, 10, 24. George W. & w, Mary, & ch, Jo-
    seph Parker & Elizabeth Austin, gct New
    Bedford MM, Mass.

1854, 10, 24. Mary Taber gct New Bedford MM,
    Mass.

FRANKLAND

1858, 3, 23. Thomas Henry rocf Cheshire.MM,
    Eng., dtd 1858,1,7

1858, 11, 23. Thomas Henry gct Cheshire MM,
    Eng.

FRAZIER

1893, 3, 14. Kora S. & L. D. recrq

1894, 12, 18. Hyram & Lydia [Frazer] recrq

1900, 3, 20. Willis [Fraizer] recrq

FREY

1894, 4, 17. Mary rocf Alum Creek MM, dtd

    1894,3,22

1897, 12, 14. Mary [Fry] relrq

FRITZ

1888, 3, 20. Lonzo V. & Annis B. recrq

1889, 2, 12. Jane recrq

1889, 3, 19. Laur recrq

1889, 7, 16. Lonzo dropped from mbrp

1890, 10, 14. Matilda recrq

1891, 2, 9. Henry recrq

1900, 3, 20. Wm. & Ella recrq

1906, 2, 13. Pearl recrq

1909, 3, 16. Pearl dropped from mbrp

1924, 4, 15. Hazel recrq

1929, 4, 16. Hazel dropped from mbrp

1932, 3, 15. Annabelle & Kenneth M. recrq

FURBAY

1902, 8, 19. W. L. recrq

1910, 4, 19. Guy & Will recrq

1911, 6, 13. Walter R. recrq

1914, 10, 20. Francis recrq

1915, 11, 16. Guy & w, Frances, gct Gray MM

1917, 10, 16. Wm. relrq

1919, 10, 14. Leta Young rocf Columbus MM,O.

1921, 9, 13. Guy W. & w, Frances, rocf Melba
    MM, Idaho

1921, 9, 13. Guy & w, Frances, gct Mt.
    Pleasant MM, O.

1922, 10, 20. Elizabeth recrq

FURNACE

----, --, --. Isaac m Salista ----- d 1873,10,
    12
    Ch: Laura M. b 1872, 4, 22 d 1873, 9, 3

1870, 10, 18. Isaac & w, Calista, rocf Miami
    MM, dtd 1870,9,24

1886, 6, 15. Isaac dropped from mbrp

FURSTENBERGER

1927, 8, 16. Henry & Emma transferred from
    Weston MM, O.

1932, 6, 14. Henry & Emma dropped from mbrp

GARDNER

1844, 7, 23. Isaac Jackson Jr. gct Mill
    Creek to m Keturah Gardner

GATCHEL

1880, 5, 18. Wayne [Gatyell] recrq

1884, 3, 18. Laura L. recrq

1895, 7, 16. Wayne & Laura [Gatchal] dropped
    from mbrp

GEORGE

1889, 5, 14. Sarah recrq

1898, 12, 20. Tura recrq

1900, 3, 20. Lewis, Jesse, Charley & Walter
    recrq

1900, 3, 20. Rose & Patience recrq

1909, 3, 16. Rose dropped from mbrp

1910, 4, 19. Harry recrq

GEORGE, continued
1914, 4, 14. Mary recrq
1922, 3, 14. Harry relrq
1923, 5, 15. Sarah dropped from mbrp
1932, 3, 15. Donald recrq
1932, 3, 15. Walter dropped from mbrp

GIBBONS
1879, 2, 18. John recrq
1882, 7, 18. John dropped from mbrp
1887, 4, 19. John M. & w recrq
1893, 2, 14. Carlton recrq
1914, 4, 14. Helen [Gibbens] recrq
1916, 2, 15. Hartley & w relrq
1920, 3, 16. Willis Hartley & w, Leanna
        Pearl, & ch, Wm. Melville & Isabelle,
        recrq
1923, 10, 16. John dropped from mbrp
1931, 7, 14. Ray, Wm. & Iona Belle dropped
        from mbrp
1932, 6, 14. Helen dropped from mbrp

GIBBS
1881, 4, 19. Daniel recrq
1885, 2, 17. Kelly A. recrq
1893, 2, 14. Carlton recrq
1895, 7, 16. Carlton dropped from mbrp
1898, 12, 20. Carlton recrq
1920, 8, 17. Lydia recrq

GIDLEY
1874, 6, 24. Seth S., s Charles & Bathsheba,
        Crawford Co.; m in Gilead, Ruth OLEPHANT,
        dt Ephraim & Elizabeth, Morrow Co.
1873, 5, 22. Sarah Jane d bur Bucyrus

1869, 2, 16. Seth recrq
1876, 11, 14. Seth S. & w, Ruth O., & ch, Hi-
        bertus, gct Center MM, Ia.

GIFFORD
1909, 5, 18. Sarah transferred from Greenwich
        MM

GLASS
1878, 6, 18. Anna rocf Short Creek MM, dtd
        1878,5,23
1882, 5, 16. Logan recrq
1885, 3, 17. Logan L. dis
1885, 3, 17. Anna L. dis
1889, 12, 17. L. L. & Anna rst
1895, 1, 15. Logan L. dis
1895, 6, 18. Logan L. rst
1911, 10, 17. Logan L. dis

GOODMAN
1884, 10, 14. Thomas recrq
1890, 2, 11. Reece recrq
1890, 4, 15. Ella rocf Salem MM, dtd 1890,
        2,20
1892, 3, 15. Thomas & Viola relrq
1900, 3, 20. Carl M. & Clifton D. recrq
1910, 5, 17. Clifton relrq

GORDON
1878, 9, 17. George Washington recrq
1879, 1, 14. Charles recrq
1879, 1, 14. Minerva recrq
1888, 3, 20. Lillie & Lolly recrq

GREEN
1900, 3, 20. Blanche recrq
1914, 6, 16. Howard rocf Alum Creek MM
1915, 6, 15. Howard & w, Jessie E., gct Rais-
        in Center MM, Mich.
1928, 4, 17. Harry T. & w, La Vanchie May,
        & ch, Mary Alice, Stella Mae, Ruth Lucile
        & Paul Franklin, rocf Alum Creek MM, O.
1933, 1, 17. Harry & w, Vanchie, & ch, Ruth
        & Paul, gct Rush Creek MM

GRINNELL
1840, 12, 2. Jeremiah, s Sylvester & Rhoda,
        Del. Co., O.; m in Hilead, Martha TABOR,
        dt Thomas & Miriam, Marion Co., O.
        Ch: Edwin   b 1841, 11, 5
            Fordyce   " 1844, 4, 23
            Eliza Ellen" 1846, 5, 15
            Sylvester " 1850, 1, 12

1839, 3, 19. Jeremiah rocf Starksborough MM,
        dtd 1838,11,20, endorsed by Alum Creek
        MM, 1839,2,21
1850, 9, 21. Jeremiah [Grennell] & w, Martha,
        & ch, Edwin Fordis, Elisa Ellen & Sylves-
        ter, gct Salem MM, Ia.

GRISELE
1848, 11, 30. Thomas, s Thomas & Martha, Mor-
        row Co.; m in Weston, Susana BENEDICT, dt
        Jonathan & Ruth SHAW, Morrow Co.
        Ch: Thomas   b 1851, 10, 3
1876, 10, 5. Susannah [Grisell] d bur Weston

1848, 11, 21. Thomas [Grissel] & w, Simeon,
        rocf Alum Creek MM, dtd 1848,10,27
1875, 7, 20. Thomas [Grissell] dis mcd

HAINS
1875, 9, 3. Mary Ann d bur Gilead

1858, 10, 26. Mary Ann [Haines] rocf Elba MM,
        N. Y.

HALDY
1915, 11, 16. Arthur & Eliza rocf Short Creek
        MM, O.

HALL
1844, 9, 21. Mary (form Kirk) dis mcd
1849, 11, 20. Sarah (form Farrington) con mcd
1851, 7, 22. Sarah dis disunity
1894, 4, 17. Charley recrq
1909, 5, 18. George S. & Mary B. transferred
        from Greenwich MM
1923, 5, 15. George S. & Mary B. dropped from
        mbrp

HARDING
1907, 6, 18. Mary recrq

HARE
1909, 2, 16. Roy recrq
1916, 9, 16. Roy & Metta gct University MM,
    Kans.

HARLAN
1878, 4, 19. Oliver d bur Gilead
1879, 9, 10. Parnelia d bur Gilead

1861, 6, 18. Amy Drusilla (form Spencer) dis
1877, 4, 17. Amy & ch, Mornelvia & Mary L.,
    recrq
1877, 5, 15. Oliver & w, Elizabeth A., & dt,
    Laura, recrq
1878, 2, 12. Parmelia recrq
1889, 4, 16. Mornilva & Mary L. relrq

HARRISON
1852, 5, 21. Matilda Ellen, dt Benjamin &
    Mary, b

1850, 3, 26. Benjamin & w, Mary, & ch, Mary
    Elizabeth & Lucinda Ann, rocf Goshen MM,
    dtd 1850,2,16
1854, 11, 21. Benjamin & w, Mary, & ch, Mary
    Elizabeth, Lucinda Ann & Matilda Ellen,
    gct Carmel MM

HART
1930, 2, 11. Martha Hobson relrq

HARTLEY
----, --, --. Thomas m Huldah ----- d 1860,4,
    25 bur Gilead
    Ch: Reuben H. b 1855, 8, 1
        Levi Mead   " 1857, 7, 4
1861, 6,27. Thomas E., s Jesse & Mary, Mor-
    row Co.; m in Weston, Tabitha MORRIS, dt
    Joseph & Jane, Marion Co.
    Ch: William H. b 1862, 8, 17
----, --, --. Joseph & Marilla
    Ch: Albert L. b 1855, 10, 8
        Melva J.   " 1859, 9, 27
1856, 2, 27. Elisa C. [Heartley] m Wm. L. DEX-
    TER
1859, 2, 27. Mary d ae 72 bur Gilead
1859, 7, 27. Mary E. d ae 73 bur Gilead
1874, 8, 8. Joseph d bur Gilead

1852, 12, 21. Joseph & w, Merilla, & ch, Emma
    L. & Mary Ellen, rocf Hartland MM, N. Y.,
    dtd 1852,9,16
1854, 2, 21. Edwin M. & w, Ruth, rocf Elba
    MM, N. Y., dtd 1853,12,13
1854, 3, 21. Edwin & w, Ruth, & ch, Myron T.
    & Hannah J., recrq
1854, 8, 22. Jesse & w, Mary, rocf Hartland
    MM, N. Y., dtd 1854,7,20
1854, 8, 22. Jesse T. rocf Hartland MM, N.Y.,
    dtd 1854,6,15

1855, 4, 24. Thomas E. & w, Huldah H., & ch,
    Elmira Mianda, Walter Thomas & Sarah
    Eliza, rocf Hartland MM, dtd 1855,3,15
1855, 4, 24. Eliza rocf Hartland MM, N. Y.,
    dtd 1854,3,15
1860, 11, 20. Jesse gct Marlborough MM, to m
    Mary Kille
1861, 2, 19. Mary rocf Marlboro MM, dtd
    1861,1,29
1862, 4, 15. Myron T. gct Alum Creek MM, to
    m Lydia Jane Gray
1862, 11, 18. Lydia Jane rocf Alum Creek MM,
    dtd 1862,9,18
1864, 12, 20. Thomas & w, Tabitha, & ch, El-
    mira B., Walter T., Sarah Eliza, Reuben
    H., Levi Mead, Wm. Henry & Samuel, gct
    Red Cedar MM, Ia.
1865, 2, 14. Jesse & w, Mary, gct Marlborough
    MM
1866, 1, 16. Edwin A. & w, Ruth W., & dt,
    Hannah, gct Raisin MM, Mich.
1866, 12, 18. Myron B. & w, Lydia Jane, gct
    Raisin MM, Mich.
1870, 9, 13. Jesse G. gct Ferrisburgh MM,
    Vt., to m Eliza H. Meader
1870, 12, 20. Jesse T. gct Ferrisburgh MM, Vt.
1879, 2, --. Emma relrq
1884, 4, 15. Jesse T. & w, Eliza M., & ch,
    Mary E., Alice T. & Anna Maria, rocf Fair-
    field MM, Ind., dtd 1884,3,13
1885, 4, 14. Thomas E. & w, Tabitha, & ch,
    Jesse N. & Rachel J., roc
1885, 4, 14. Jesse N. gct New Garden MM, N.C.
1886, 4, 13. Marilla R. relrq
1889, 1, 15. A. L. relrq
1891, 3, 17. Philip rocf Alum Creek MM, dtd
    1891,1,22
1893, 9, 19. Alice T. relrq
1895, 6, 18. Ray relrq
1896, 4, 14. Anna relrq
1898, 7, 19. Mary E. relrq

HARTMAN
1883, 10, 16. Attie relrq

HAYDEN
1878, 8, 20. Dora recrq
1878, 9, 17. Hubert recrq
1879, 1, 14. George recrq
1886, 6, 15. George, Herbert & Dora dropped
    from mbrp

HAYS
1854, 6, 15. Calvin d bur Gilead
1863, 3, 15. Susan [Hayse] d bur Gilead

1847, 4, 20. Phebe & ch, James H., Maryann,
    Calvin C., Elizajane, Elizabeth & Susan,
    rocf Sandy Spring MM, dtd 1847,2,26
1850, 4, 20. James dis disunity
1858, 6, 22. Elizabeth Wood (form Hays) dis
    mcd
1888, 3, 20. Rosa & Maggie recrq

HAYS, continued

1896, 3, 17. Maggie (Hays) Patterson dropped from mbrp
1901, 1, 15. Rosa relrq

HEACOCK

1874, 4, 13. Preston, s Wm. & Eliza Ann, b
1884, 10, 24. Joseph d ae 87 bur Weston

1866, 4, 17. Joseph recrq
1867, 10, 15. Joseph con mcd
1868, 1, 14. Joseph gct Salem MM, Ia.; returned 4-14 because of non-residence
1871, 3, 14. Wm. S. & w & ch recrq
1880, 2, 17. W. S. relrq

HEALD

1848, 2, 21. Sarah d bur Gilead
1849, 4, 4. Joseph, s Wm. & Susannah, Morrow Co.; m in ----- Rachel MORRIS, dt Abraham & Mary, Morrow Co.
1849, 11, 1. Nathan, s Joseph & Ury, Morrow Co., O.; m in Weston, Mary S. KEESE, dt Titus & Martha W., Morrow Co., O.
    Ch: Sarah Ru-
            anna   b 1851, 9, 18
        John K.   " 1852, 10, 8
        William A. " 1854, 8, 24 d 1855, 7,15
            bur Weston
        Elma Alice " 1856, 2, 29
        Abner Titus" 1857, 10, 8
        Martha Elma
        Joseph E.
        Lydia Ann
1851, 7, 24. Hannah m Wm. SHAW
1853, 6, 19. Susanna d ae 58 bur Gilead
1858, 12, 3. Elma Alice d
1858, 12, 3. Sarah Roanna d
1863, 3, 6. Amy d bur Gilead
1867, 10, 13. Elizabeth d bur Gilead
1872, 11, 18. Susanna d ae 71 bur Gilead

1845, 1, 21. Wm. H. & w, Susannah, & ch, Joseph, Hannah, Rachel, Joel, Celina & Elizabeth, rocf Middleton MM, dtd 1844,12, 12
1845, 1, 21. Sarah rocf Middleton MM, dtd 1844,12,12
1845, 6, 24. Amy rocf Middleton MM, dtd 1845,5,18
1849, 7, 24. Nathan H. rocf Carmel MM, dtd 1849,6,16
1849, 9, 22. Joseph dis disunity
1850, 8, 20. Nathan H. dis disunity
1855, 2, 20. Wm. W. gct Cincinnati MM, to m Susanna Nevill
1855, 4, 24. Sidwell rocf Alum Creek MM, dtd 1854,6,22
1855, 7, 24. Susanna rocf Cincinnati MM, dtd 1855,5,17
1856, 11, 25. Harriet recrq
1856, 12, 23. Joel dis mcd
1858, 7, 20. Celina Morris (form Heald) dis

mcd
1858, 10, 26. Sidwell & w, Harriett, gct Westland MM, Ia.
1865, 6, 13. Mary & ch, Abner T., Joseph E. & Lydiann, gct New Sharon MM, Ia.
1875, 12, 14. Wm. W. gct Lyngrove MM, Iowa
1881, 2, 15. Dosie recrq
1923, 5, 15. Wm. dropped from mbrp

HEALEA

1900, 3, 20. Wm. recrq
1925, 3, 17. Nora Beheler recrq

HENRY

1910, 4, 19. Wm. & w, Frankie, recrq
1914, 3, 17. Wm. & w & s gct Alum Creek MM
1914, 4, 14. Wesley & Hazel recrq
1916, 12, 19. Wm. & w, Frankie, & ch, Stella, Ames, Paul & Ralph, rocf Alum Creek MM, O.
1928, 3, 20. Amos gct Adrian MM, Mich.
1930, 11, 18. Verda relrq

HERENDEEN

1842, 3, 24. Nathan [Herenden] d ae 59 bur Gilead

1839, 6, 18. Joseph [Herendeen] dis disunity
1839, 7, 23. Welcome dis disunity
1839, 7, 23. Sarah Kingman (form Herendeen) dis mcd
1839, 12, 24. Pennsylvania B. dis disunity
1842, 7, 26. Elizabeth (form Kirk) dis mcd
1846, 6, 23. Anna W. dis disunity
1846, 6, 23. Huldah H. dis disunity
1846, 6, 23. Mary S. P. dis disunity

HESKET

1895, 3, 19. N. W. & w recrq
1902, 3, 18. Norville W. & w, Alice, relrq

HICKLEN

1867, 10, 23. Sarah Ann [Hickland] m Francis C. STANLEY

1856, 9, 20. James Jackson gct Salem MM, O., to m Maryann Hicklen
1857, 2, 17. Mary Ann Jackson & dt, Sarah Ann Hicklen, rocf Salem MM, O., dtd 1857, 1,22

HICKMAN

1882, 10, 19. George Alfred Townsend, s Thomas & Jennie, b

1874, 12, 15. Thomas N. recrq
1876, 8, 15. Thomas N. dis
1882, 4, 18. T. N. & w, Jane, & ch, Halwin H., Leafy B., John M. & Robert F., recrq
1887, 3, 15. Thomas N. relrq
1895, 8, 20. Robert T. relrq
1912, 1, 16. T. S. relrq
1912, 11, 19. J. W. gct Spring Bank MM
1912, 12, 17. George dropped from mbrp

HICKMAN, continued
1913, 5, 20. Geo. & Pearl recrq
1914, 12, 15. Rhoda gct Hubbard MM, Ia.
1920, 6, 15. George & w, Pearl, gct Highland
    Ave. MM, Columbus, O.
1921, 9, 13. Pearl rocf Columbus MM
1922, 3, 14. Pearl relrq
1928, 2, 14. Rhoda recrq

HICKSON
1894, 4, 17. Will, Lucy & Grace recrq
1927, 8, 16. David & Hattie transferred from
    Weston MM, O.

HILDEBOLD
1900, 3, 20. Lenora recrq

HILDEBRAND
1913, 10, 14. Effie relrq

HINMAN
1848, 4, 25. Sarah Ann (form Penington) dis
    mcd

HOBSON
1842, 4, 27. Joseph, s Joseph & Rebecca, Ma-
    rion Co., O.; m in Gilead, Amy STANLEY, dt
    James & Rhoda, Columbiana Co., O.
    Ch: Rebecca T. b 1844, 8, 29
        Reuben   " 1845, 11, 5
        Rhoda Ann   " 1847, 3, 2
        Thomas C.   " 1848, 4, 1
        Elizabeth
          T.   " 1851, 7, 29
        Louisa   " 1854, 11, 16
1845, 8, 9. Rebecca T. d bur Gilead
1846, 9, 12. Reuben d bur Gilead
1855, 1, 28. Sylvester d bur Gilead
1872, 12, 25. Elizabeth m Isaac Hamilton
    ELLIOTT
1873, 5, 28. Thomas, s Joseph & Amy P., Mor-
    row Co.; m in Gilead, Ann JACKSON, dt
    Isaac & Keturah
    Ch: Joseph   b 1874, 1, 18
        Lilbwm (?) " 1875, 1, 27
        Eber   " 1878, 9, 13
        Charles   " 1882, 3, 17
1876, 5, 18. Louisa m Edwin S. COTANT

1842, 4, 19. Joseph rocf Salem MM, dtd 1842,
    3,23
1848, 3, 21. John & w, Mary E., & s, Benjamin,
    rocf Upper Springfield MM, dtd 1848,1,17
1854, 7, 25. Sarah B., Joseph C. & Rebecca
    T., ch John T. & Mary, recrq
1859, 10, 25. Joseph C., minor, gct Blue River
    MM, Ind.
1861, 3, 26. Sarah B. Perkins (form Hobson)
    dis mcd
1865, 8, 15. Rebecca Bennet (form Hobson) dis
    mcd
1867, 4, 16. John T. & w, Mary E., & ch,
    James E., Juliann D., Phebe V., Amy P.,

Mary Elizabeth, Unity Jane & Truman Ells-
    worth, gct Grove MM, Ind.
1868, 9, 15. Benjamin gct Grove MM
1902, 10, 14. Eber gct Winona MM
1903, 12, 20. Thomas C. & w, Ann, & s, Wm.,
    gct Winona MM
1905, 12, 19. J. J. gct Bellefountain Friends
    Ch, O.
1905, 12, 19. Thomas C. & w, Ann, & s, Wm.,
    roc
1910, 4, 19. Laura Levering recrq
1910, 6, 14. Eber S. & w, Hazel, rocf Rush
    Creek MM
1917, 8, 14. Lilburn & w relrq
1923, 7, 17. Charles dropped from mbrp
1923, 7, 17. Arthur dropped from mbrp
1923, 10, 16. Eber S. gct Shawnee MM, Okla.
1929, 1, 15. Charles relrq
1929, 7, 16. Virginia & ch, Ruth Aldine,
    Beverly Jean & Lewis Dale, recrq
1930, 2, 11. Martha (Hobson) Hart relrq
1930, 9, 16. Wm. relrq
1931, 4, 14. Anna relrq

HOFFMIRE
1850, 6, 25. Ann (form Kirk) dis mou
1852, 4, 20. Sarah M. dis mcd
1923, 5, 15. Mabel Smith dropped from mbrp
1933, 8, 15. Mary Brollier dropped from mbrp

HOLE
----, --, --. Samuel & Rebecca
    Ch: Charles b 1858, 4, 6
        Wm. F.   " 1860, 10, 4

1857, 4, 21. Samuel J. & w, Rebecca, & ch,
    Louisa, Emerson B. & Ruth Ann, rocf Salem
    MM, dtd 1857,3,26
1862, 7, 15. Samuel J. dis
1872, 10, 15. Emmerson B. gct Salem MM

HOLLAND
1885, 2, 17. Joseph & Sarah F. recrq
1932, 10, 18. Free W. recrq

HOLLER
1866, 11, 13. Lovina (form Quaintance) dis mcd

HOLLINGSWORTH
1882, 4, 18. Eda R. rocf Chesterfield MM, dtd
    1882,4,8
1886, 7, 20. Ida gct Chesterfield MM, O.

HOLSON
----, --, --. John & Mary Ann
    Ch: James   b 1849, 2, 13
        Juliann   " 1851, 4, 10
        Phebe V. " 1853, 4, 10
        Silvester " 1855, 1, 16
        Amy P.   " 1856, 2, 2
        Mary C.   " 1859, 2, 3
        Unity J. " 1860, 7, 17

HOPKINS
1882, 10, 17. Mary P. relrq

HOWARD
1927, 8, 16. Grace Hickson transferred from
    Weston MM, O.

HUDSON
1855, 4, 24. Rachel rocf Hartland MM, N. Y.,
    dtd 1854,3,15
1870, 9, 13. Rachel P. relrq

HUFF
1885, 4, 14. Mead recrq

HUGHES
1877, 5, 15. Wm. L. & w, Mary E., & ch, Wm.
    H., Margaret R., George T. & Stephen C.,
    recrq
1882, 8, 15. Wm. L. & fam gct Van Wert MM, O.

HULL
1897, 2, 16. Walter W. recrq
1900, 3, 20. Claud, Harriett, Gertrude &
    Retha recrq
1900, 3, 20. George, Mary & Arnold recrq
1919, 11, 18. Lizzie Shultz & niece, Iris
    Hull, recrq
1923, 5, 15. Gertrude & Retha dropped from
    mbrp
1923, 5, 15. Johnna dropped from mbrp
1925, 3, 17. Helen recrq
1929, 3, 19. Alice recrq
1930, 7, 15. Anna J. recrq

HUNT
1848, 12, 28. David, s Phineas & Elizabeth,
    Logan Co.; m in Gilead, Sarahann COBBS, dt
    Abraham & Mary MORRIS, Morrow Co.

1849, 2, 20. Sarahann & dt, Hannah & Balinda
    T. Cobbs, gct Goshen MM
1856, 8, 26. David & w, Sarahann, & dt, Be-
    linda, rocf Goshen MM, dtd 1856,8,16
1857, 2, 17. David & w, Sarahann, & dt, Han-
    nah. & Belinda T., gct Honey Creek MM, Ia.

IRISH
1842, 10, 25. Esther & ch, Israel A., Enoch,
    Joel S. & Samuel, rocf Alum Creek MM, dtd
    1842,6,23
1848, 7, 25. Stephen rst on consent of Peru
    MM, N. Y.
1851, 6, 24. Israel rocf Alum Creek MM, dtd
    1851,4,24
1852, 3, 23. Israel Allen con mcd
1852, 7, 20. Samuel gct White Water MM, Ind.,
    to m Avis Jane Roberts
1852, 8, 24. Enoch gct Salem MM, Ia.
1853, 6, 21. Samuel gct Dover MM, Ind.
1853, 12, 20. Stephen gct Red Cedar MM, Ia.
1854, 1, 24. Joel gct Red Cedar MM, Ia.
1855, 11, 20. Israel A. gct Red Cedar MM, Ia.

1856, 3, 25. Esther gct Red Cedar MM, Ia.

JACKSON
1841, 12, 2. James, s Isaac & Ann, Crawford
    Co., O.; m in Sandusky, Rebecca KIRK, dt
    Timothy & Susanna, Crawford Co., O.
    Ch: George E. b 1843, 9, 4
    James m 2nd Mary Ann OLIPHANT
    Ch: John H.   b 1857, 11, 15
        James Alvin" 1864, 11, 10
1843, 10, 26. Grace m Ansalm COBBS
1843, 11, 29. Stephen, s Isaac & Ann, Craw.
    Co.; m in Gilead, Elizabeth ROBERTS, Jr.,
    dt Aaron & Elizabeth, Belmont Co.
    Ch: Sarah Ann b 1844, 12, 26
        Mary   " 1846, 4, 19
        Beulah   " 1847, 10, 31
        Hannah   " 1850, 8, 18
        Elvira   " 1852, 1, 18
        Reuben   " 1853, 6, 5
        Ansalem   " 1855, 1, 15
        Jesse   " 1856, 12, 13
        James   " 1856, 12, 13
1845, 12, 4. Ann m John KIRK
----, --, --. Isaac & Keturah
    Ch: William   b 1846, 7, 20
        Irena   " 1848, 9, 9
    Isaac m 2nd Hannah ATKINSON
    Ch: Warner A. b 1861, 10, 29
        Edith Bell " 1864, 2, --
1850, 12, 25. Abraham, s Isaac & Ann, Craw.
    Co.; m in Weston, Lydia KEESE, dt Titus
    & Martha, Morrow Co.
    Ch: James
        Titus   b 1852, 6, 9
        Agis Isaac " 1853, 12, 8
        Grifith L. " 1855, 11, 10
1853, 6, 5. Mary d bur Sandusky
1854, 11, 16. Rebecca d bur Sandusky
1857, 10, 19. Jesse d bur Sandusky
1867, 1, 23. Isaac d ae 89 bur Gilead
1867, 6, 26. Stephen, s Isaac & Ann, Marshall
    Co., Ia.; m in Gilead, Francis T. WOOD,
    dt Israel & Mary, Morrow Co.
----, --, --. George & Mary
    Ch: Rebecca H. b 1872, 2, 24
        Milton P. " 1874, 4, 16
        J. Wesley " 1877, 5, 14
        F. Lesley " 1877, 5, 14
1873, 5, 28. Ann m Thomas HOBSON
1877, 5, 27. Ann d ae 92 bur Gilead
1894, 7, 19. Ruth d

1844, 7, 23. Isaac Jr. gct Mill Creek MM, to
    m Keturah Gardner
1844, 12, 24. Keturah rocf Mill Creek MM, dtd
    1844,11,12
1850, 9, 21. Isaac & w, Keturah, & ch, Wm. &
    Arena, gct Salem MM, Ia.
1856, 9, 20. Abraham & w, Lydia, & ch, James
    Titus, Agis Isaac & Griffith L., gct West-
    ern Plain MM, Ia.
1856, 9, 20. James gct Salem MM, O., to m

JACKSON, continued
Mary Ann Hicklen
1857, 2, 17. Mary Ann & dt, Sarah Ann Hicklen,
rocf Salem MM, O., dtd 1857,1,22
1858, 2, 23. Stephen & w, Elizabeth, & ch,
Sarah Ann, Beulah, Hannah, Elvira, Reuben,
Ansalem & James, gct Western Plain MM, Ia.
1860, 7, 24. Isaac & ch, Wm., Irena, Mary,
Ann & Chas., rocf Western Plain MM, Ia.,
dtd 1860,6,16
1861, 1, 22. Isaac gct Upper Springfield MM,
to m Hannah Atkinson
1861, 4, 23. Hannah rocf Upper Springfield
MM, dtd 1861,3,2
1865, 1, 17. Isaac & w, Hannah, & ch, Wm.,
Irena, Mary, Charles, Warner A. & Edith
B., gct Spring Creek MM, Ia.
1867, 9, 17. Francis T. gct Bangor MM
1870, 10, 18. George E. gct Short Creek MM, to
m Mary Pettett
1872, 2, 13. Mary C. rocf Short Creek MM, dtd
1872,1,25
1896, 12, 15. John H. relrq
1899, 4, 18. Mary C. relrq
1907, 12, 17. Cora O. roc
1909, 3, 16. J. A. dropped from mbrp
1911, 6, 13. Mary C. recrq
1911, 12, 19. Milton P. & Jay Dwight gct New
York MM, N. Y.
1912, 7, 16. J. W. & w, Cora, & ch, Margaret
& Wesley Elmon, gct Alum Creek MM
1917, 2, 13. Milton P. dropped from mbrp
1917, 2, 13. J. D. dropped from mbrp
1920, 8, 17. Mary C. relrq
1928, 8, 14. Lesley dis disunity

JAGGERS
1886, 2, 16. Nichodemus [Gagger] & w, Mary,
recrq
1896, 2, 18. N. H. relrq
1900, 3, 16. Mary dropped from mbrp
1914, 4, 14. Hazel recrq

JAMES
1924, 4, 15. Imo Wright recrq
1932, 4, 29. Imo dropped from mbrp

JOHNS
1900, 3, 20. Wm. recrq
1910, 4 19. Imo [John] recrq

JOHNSON
1846, 7, 8. Joanna C. d bur Gilead
1847, 3, 13. Silas [Jonson], s Jonathan & Joana, b
1853, 9, 17. Silas C. d bur Gilead
1855, 9, 3. Jonathan d bur Gilead
1863, 9, 26. Joanna d bur Gilead

1844, 3, 26. Susanna [Johnston] (form Warner)
dis mcd
1846, 7, 21. Jonathan & w, Joanna, & ch,
Pleasant, Abigail, Rebecca, Elizamary &

Joanna C., rocf Upper Springfield MM, dtd
1846,4,25
1858, 11, 23. Rebecca dis disunity
1861, 3, 26. Eliza Mary Woods (form Johnson)
con mcd
1861, 12, 17. Pleasant T. con mcd
1862, 5, 20. Elizabeth recrq
1862, 8, 19. Pleasant T. & w, Elizabeth, gct
Greenwich MM
1864, 8, 16. Abigail gct Spring Creek MM, Ia.
1910, 4, 19. Leona recrq
1923, 5, 15. Imo & Leona dropped from mbrp

JONES
1870, 12, 4. Hannah d bur Gilead
1874, 7, 5. Joseph d ae 71 bur Gilead

1851, 12, 23. Hannah rocf Upper Springfield
MM, dtd 1851,9,27
1865, 4, 18. Joseph recrq
1869, 1, 19. Mary rocf Rose Mount MM, Ia.,
dtd 1868,1,12
1872, 7, 16. Joseph gct Kingston MM, Canada,
to m Mary Eddy
1873, 8, 19. Mary E. rocf Kingston MM, Canada, dtd 1873,6,14
1874, 9, 15. Mary E. gct Kingston MM, Canada
1875, 1, 19. Mary T. gct Alum Creek MM
1892, 11, 15. Docie gct Pasadena MM, Calif.

JUMP
1843, 9, 16. Eunice (form Slyter) dis mcd

KEELER
1917, 11, 13. Carrie recrq

KEESE
1841, 6, 5. Oliver d bur Weston
1843, 1, 1. Sarah d bur Weston ae 48
----, --, --. Richard & Gulielma [Kees]
Ch: Sarah
Evelyn   b 1849, 10, 16
Isaac Wit-
ford   " 1850, 8, 24
Samuel John " 1852, 11, 26
Willets Han-
son   b 1855, 6, 14
Cynthia
Eliza Le-
nore   " 1857, 7, 14
1849, 1, 29. Titus d bur Westen
1849, 11, 1. Mary S. m Nathan HEALD
1850, 12, 25. Lydia m Abraham JACKSON
1860, 2, 12. John d ae 86 bur Weston

1843, 2, 21. Ann Eliza Fisher (form Keese)
dis mcd
1846, 9, 19. Samuel dis disunity
1848, 2, 22. Richard con mcd
1850, 8, 20. Gulielma A. rocf Alum Creek MM,
dtd 1850,6,27
1852, 2, 24. Hannah Conlin (form Keese) con
mcd

KEESE, continued
1856, 12, 23. Martha gct Western Plain MM, Ia.
1857, 1, 20. Guli Elma gct Western Plain MM,
    Ia.
1865, 8, 15. Richard & w, Gulia Elma, & ch,
    Sarah Evelyn, Wilfred J., Samuel John,
    Willits Hanson & C. E. Lenore, gct Alum
    Creek MM
1892, 11, 15. Mira recrq
1893, 6, 13. Eva recrq
1894, 3, 20. Nora recrq

KELLY
1890, 12, 16. Luly recrq

KENNER
1879, 3, 18. Emanuel & Emma recrq
1579, 4, 15. Wm. & Lydia recrq
1882, 3, 14. Augustus recrq
1885, 4, 14. Henry L. recrq
1887, 3, 15. Lydia gct Alum Creek MM
1887, 7, 19. Wm., Harry, Augustus, Emanuel &
    Emma dropped from mbrp

KENT
1913, 10, 14. George & w, Elinor G., & ch,
    Arthur & Robert Howard, rocf Salem MM
1915, 9, 14. George E. relrq
1916, 2, 15. Howard relrq of father, G. E.
    Kent
1916, 11, 14. Arthur relrq

KERR
1890, 9, 16. Rebecca T. relrq

KESTER
1919, 10, 14. Harry & w, Lena, recrq
1927, 8, 16. Mary transferred from Weston
    MM, O.
1927, 8, 16. Harrison transferred from Weston
    MM, O.
1930, 4, 15. Harrison & w, Mary, & ch gct
    Orange MM

KEY
1908, 4, 14. Lenora relrq

KIDNEY
1862, 4, 23. Helen A. m Chas. ROBERTS

1860, 11, 20. Aurilla recrq
1861, 9, 17. Helen A. recrq
1861, 12, 17. Aurilla gct Hartland MM, N. Y.
1864, 10, 18. Aurilla roc

KILLE
1860, 11, 20. Jesse Hartley gct Marlborough
    MM, to m Mary Kille

KING
1879, 2, 18. Ruth Anna recrq
1879, 9, 16. Alice recrq
1909, 3, 16. Elizabeth dropped from mbrp

KINGMAN
1839, 7, 23. Sarah (form Herendeen) dis mcd

KINNEY
1863, 12, 15. Louisa dis

KINSEY
1863, 3, 17. Louisa (form Warner) dis mcd

KIRK
1841, 12, 2. Rebecca m James JACKSON
1842, 6, 1. Hannah A. m Eli QUAINTANCE
1842, 8, 31. Wm. B., s Caleb & Hannah, Del.
    Co., O.; m in Gilead, Rebecca T. VAUGHN,
    dt James & Rhoda, Marion Co., O.
    Ch: James V.   b 1843, 8, 8
        Caleb   " 1846, 5, 18
        Hannah   " 1848, 9, 14
        Emmeline   " 1852, 9, 20
        Allice Ann " 1856, 7, 8
        Sarah S.   " 1859, 11, 27
        Amy E.   " 1862, 9, 28
1845, 10, 22. Rachel C. m Joseph ROBERTS
1845, 12, 4. John, s Caleb & Sarah, Del.
    Co.; m in Sandusky, Ann JACKSON, dt
    Isaac & Ann, Crawford Co.
    Ch: Sarah Ann b 1846, 10, 28
        Zeno   " 1848, 9, 9
        Lorenzo   " 1851, 1, 5
        Isaac   " 1854, 11, 21
        Joseph   " 1854, 11, 21
        Albert   " 1860, 9, 3
        Mary Elma " 1866, 9, 23
1847, 4, 6. Caleb d ae 70 bur Gilead
1869, 10, 4. Isaac d bur Gilead
1875, 1, 21. Zeno, s John & Ann, Crawford
    Co.; m in Gilead, Amanda AMES, dt Almon
    & Mary Jane, Crawford Co.

1842, 7, 26. Elizabeth Herendeen (form Kirk)
    dis mcd
1842, 7, 26. Susanna Rodgers (form Kirk) dis
    mcd
1843, 1, 24. Samuel dis mcd
1844, 9, 21. Mary Hall (form Kirk) dis mcd
1845, 3, 25. Stephen dis disunity
1848, 10, 24. Wm. B. dis disunity
1850, 6, 25. Ann Hoffmire (form Kirk) dis mou
1851, 8, 26. Caleb Lewis dis disunity
1854, 2, 21. Hannah & s, Edmund, gct Spring
    Creek MM, Ia.
1854, 4, 25. Rebecca & ch, James V., Caleb,
    Hannah & Emaline R., gct Spring Creek MM,
    Iowa
1858, 12, 21. Wm. B. rst
1859, 3, 22. Rebecca T. & ch, James V.,
    Caleb, Hannah, Rhoda Emaline, Alice Ann &
    Sarah, rocf Spring Creek MM, Ia., dtd
    1859,2,5
1859, 5, 24. Hannah & gr ch, Martha C., Ra-
    chel Elizabeth Roberts, rocf Spring Creek
    MM, Ia., dtd 1859,3,5
1864, 12, 20. Hannah & gr dt, Rachel Roberts,

KIRK, continued
    gct New Sharon MM, Ia.
1864, 12, 20. Wm. B. & w, Rebecca T., & ch, Ca-
    leb, Hannah Rhoda, Emaline, Alice Ann,
    Sara S. & Amy Etta, gct Newsharron MM, Ia.
1874, 8, 18. Lorenzo relrq
1876, 3, 14. Zeno relrq
1878, 7, 16. Joseph relrq
1895, 7, 16. Albert dropped from mbrp
1909, 3, 16. Sarah & Mary dropped from mbrp

KISLING
1879, 4, 15. Charles H. recrq
1880, 12, 14. Chas. H. relrq
1885, 2, 17. Charles H. & Lusetta recrq
1888, 4, 17. Charles & w, Lusetta, gct Van
    Wert MM, O.

KOCH
1882, 3, 14. James B. recrq

KREIS
1930, 7, 15. Hazel Casto dropped from mbrp

KUCHNEL
1932, 10, 18. Edward W. & w, Mary, & dt, Es-
    ther Mae, rocf Mt. Carmel MM

KUHN
1844, 8, 20. Maria (form Pennington) dis mcd

KUNTZ
1906, 8, 14. Catherine recrq

LANGDON
1872, 5, 22. Chloe Ann m Stephen BREED

1841, 5, 25. Chloe Ann, Mary P. & Samuel P.,
    ch Lucinda, recrq
1867, 1, 15. Chloe Ann gct Greenfield MM
1867, 6, 18. Samuel P. con mcd
1871, 12, 19. Chloe Ann rocf Greenfield MM,
    dtd 1871,11,18
1873, 3, 18. Samuel P. relrq

LAPHAM
1843, 9, 16. Stephen dis mcd
1882, 7, 18. Phebe, Joseph, John & Elizabeth
    [Lappum] dropped from mbrp

LAURENCE
1885, 2, 17. Phillip W. recrq
1895, 7, 16. Philip [Lawrence] dropped from
    mbrp

LAVELLE
1928, 7, 17. Alice recrq

LEAVERING
1840, 6, 4. Griffith, s Thomas & Rachel Ann,
    Cecil Co., Md.; m in Weston, Esther L.
    BENEDICT, dt Aaron & Esther, Del. Co., O.

1840, 7, 21. Esther L. gct Nottingham MM &
    Little Britain MM, Pa.

LEE
1907, 11, 19. I. G. & w, Ida J., & s, Walter,
    roc
1909, 5, 18. Mary W. transferred from Green-
    wich MM
1911, 9, 19. Almira relrq

LEWIS
1878, 8, 20. Willoughby recrq
1879, 1, 14. Charles recrq
1886, 2, 16. Clara recrq
1886, 6, 15. Willoughby dropped from mbrp
1893, 2, 14. Willaby recrq
1900, 3, 20. Ambrose & Jessie recrq
1909, 3, 16. Ambrose & Jessie dropped from
    mbrp
1914, 2, 16. Mary relrq

LIPSEY
----, --, --. Wm. & Hannah
    Ch: Oliver   b 1850, 9, 6
        Rachel Ann " 1853, 12, 7
        Seneca   " 1855, 6, 24
        Lucius   " 1857, 10, 17

1848, 10, 24. Wm. B. rocf Middleton MM, dtd
    1848,8,10
1849, 8, 21. Wm. B. gct Alum Creek MM, to m
    Hannah Willets
1850, 3, 26. Hannah W. rocf Alum Creek MM,
    dtd 1850,2,21
1859, 5, 24. Wm. B. & w, Hannah, & ch, Oliver
    J., Rachel Ann, Lenira H. & Lwien W., gct
    Blue River MM, Ind.

LONG
1906, 1, 16. Judith relrq
1909, 3, 16. Daisy dropped from mbrp

LOREIN
1914, 6, 16. Mamie relrq

LOTHREY
1911, 3, 14. Esther recrq

LUCAS
1882, 4, 18. Ruth relrq
1893, 3, 14. Ruth A. & Upton recrq
1896, 3, 17. Glen recrq
1900, 3, 20. Jesse recrq
1903, 10, 20. Jessie relrq

McBRIDE
1841, 9, 16. John d bur Sandusky
1842, 2, 5. Ann d bur Sandusky
1847, 3, 15. John d ae 65 bur Gilead

1839, 4, 23. Rebecca Sell (form McBride) dis
    mcd
1841, 4, 20. Joseph dis mcd

McBRIDE, continued
1843, 10, 24.   Jeremiah dis disunity

McCRACKEN
1909, 3, 16.   Ollie dropped from mbrp
1914, 5, 19.   Brice recrq
1929, 4, 16.   Brice dropped from mbrp
1932, 3, 15.   Lois Evelyn & Ward Endell recrq

McFEETERS
1882, 3, 14.   Mary recrq

McKIBBINS
1880, 4, 13.   Lydia relrq

McKINNEY
1877, 4, 17.   Melvin recrq

McPARK
1915, 9, 14.   Jessie & w, Artie, & ch, Ber-
     nisa, Gladys & Wilford, recrq

McPEEK
1893, 2, 14.   Elijah & Jane recrq
1929, 4, 16.   Jane & ch, Artie, Benisa,
     Gladyse & Wilford, dropped from mbrp
1929, 4, 16.   Jesse dropped from mbrp

McWHIRK
1920, 10, 19.   Printie recrq
1929, 11, 19.   Printie relrq

McWILLIAMS
1900, 3, 20.   Harry recrq
1923, 5, 15.   G. G. dropped from mbrp

MANN
1900, 3, 20.   Bessie recrq

MARKHAM
1904, 10, 18.   George & Roxa recrq
1923, 5, 15.   George & Roxy dropped from mbrp

MARTIN
1850, 1, 23.   Thomas rocf Middleton MM, dtd
     1849,12,6
1878, 6, 18.   Phillip & s, Wm., recrq
1879, 1, 14.   Ella recrq
1882, 3, 14.   R. R. recrq
1884, 4, 15.   Philip gct Alum Creek MM
1897, 2, 16.   John recrq
1923, 5, 15.   John dropped from mbrp

MASON
1893, 3, 14.   Aaron recrq
1895, 7, 16.   Aaron dropped from mbrp
1914, 5, 19.   Grant & ch, Florence, Pearl,
     Irene, Ketha, Keese & Royal, recrq
1922, 4, 18.   Ketha dropped from mbrp
1923, 8, 14.   Ketha recrq
1926, 7, 20.   Ketha dropped from mbrp
1931, 7, 14.   Irene dropped from mbrp

MATHEWS
1897, 2, 16.   Oliver recrq

MATTI
1923, 5, 15.   Charles A. & w, Elsie V., rocf
     China MM, Me.

MAXWELL
1927, 8, 16.   Nathan Miner transferred from
     Weston MM, O.
1932, 6, 14.   Minor dropped from mbrp

MEADER
1870, 9, 13.   Jesse G. Hartley gct Ferris-
     burgh MM, Vt., to m Eliza H. Meader

MEEKER
1853, 11, 22.   Benjamin rocf White Lick MM, dtd
     1853,10,12
1856, 1, 22.   Benjamin gct White Lick MM, Ind.
1871, 3, 14.   Benjamin & w, Rachel, & ch,
     Alpharetta, Edith Emaline, Phebe, Harriett
     Davis, Louisa, Robert, Gideon & Eunice,
     rocf Spring River MM
1873, 4, 15.   Benjamin & w, Rachel, & ch, Al-
     fretta, Edith, Emeline, Phebe, Harriett,
     Davis, Louisa, Robert, Eunice, Gideon &
     Alden, gct Spring River MM, Kans.
1922, 3, 14.   Arlington recrq
1924, 5, 20.   Nellie recrq
1929, 4, 16.   Arlington & Nellie dropped from
     mbrp

MENDENHALL
----, --, --.   Israel & Ann
     Ch: Evin
          Penock   b 1849, 9, 17
          Joseph   " 1852, 2, 11 d 1853, 8,16
          bur Weston
          Zenis R.

1848, 10, 24.   Israel & w, Ann, rocf Middleton
     MM, dtd 1848,10,12
1856, 9, 20.   Israel & w, Ann, & ch, Evon P. &
     Zenis R., gct Salem MM, Ia.

MERCER
1880, 7, 18.   Abraham dropped from mbrp

METTLER
1900, 3, 20.   Riley [Metler] recrq
1910, 6, 14.   J. R. relrq
1932, 4, 29.   Ola dropped from mbrp

MICHINOR
----, --, --.   John & Susanna
     Ch: Charles   b 1839, 7, 26
          Enoch   " 1841, 3, 8
          Esther   " 1842, 12, 31
          Rebecca Ann " 1844, 7, 16
          Henry P.   " 1846, 3, 9
          Martha   " 1847, 4, 27

MICHINOR, continued
1840, 12, 22. Daniel [Mitchiner] dis mcd
1841, 1, 26. Ruth Camp (form Michinor) dis mcd
1842, 7, 26. Daniel [Michoner] rst
1843, 6, 20. Jane Mills (form Michiner) dis
  mcd
1845, 3, 25. Daniel [Michiner] dis disunity
1848, 6, 20. David O. [Mitchiner] gct Alum
  Creek MM
1851, 4, 22. John & w, Susanna, & ch, Wm. P.,
  Chas. Enoch, Esther C., Rebecca Ann, Henry
  P. & Martha H., gct East Grove MM, Ia.

MILLER
1853, 5, 24. Rachel (form Quaintance) dis mcd

MILLIGAN
----, --, --. Jesse & Ruth
  Ch: Elizabeth
      Hannah   b 1848, 1, 8
      Mary Ann   " 1850, 7, 31
      Elvira   " 1852, 9, 18
      Tryphenia " 1855, 2, 3
      Alice   " 1860, 1, 22
      Sarah Ellen" 1863, 2, 21
1860, 5, 5. Abigail d ae 87 bur Weston
1871, 11, 22. Elvira m Reuben E. WOOD

1848, 2, 22. Jesse & w, Ruth, & ch, Rebecca
  Ann, Esther & Samuel, rocf Goshen MM, dtd
  1847,10,16
1856, 11, 25. Abigail rocf Marlborough MM, dtd
  1856,8,26
1883, 5, 15. Jessie relrq

MILLMYER
1863, 5, 19. Lucy Ann (form Allman) dis mcd

MILLS
1843, 6, 20. Jane (form Michiner) dis mcd
1885, 4, 14. Milton recrq
1887, 7, 19. Milton dropped from mbrp

MITCHELL
1900, 4, 17. Daisy recrq

MOORE
1894, 4, 17. Pearl recrq

MORGAN
1839, 10, 22. Albina rocf Kenett MM, Pa.,
  dtd 1838,6,5, endorsed by Alum Creek MM,
  1839,9,23

MORLAN
----, --, --. Joseph & Mary
  Ch: Mary
      Elizabeth b 1842, 12, 24
      Smith   " 1848, 4, 18
      Hulda   " 1848, 4, 18
      Martha   " 1850, 9, 8

1846, 2, 17. Joseph [Morland] dis disunity

1853, 8, 23. Mary & ch, Ruth, Mary Elizabeth,
  Huldah & Martha, gct Red Cedar MM, Ia.

MORRIS
----, --, --. Joseph & Jane
  Ch: Joshua   b 1838, 10, 9
      Keziah   " 1842, 7, 24
      Rachel   " 1845, 4, 20
      Joseph C. " 1849, 8, 18
1846, 9, 21. Joseph, s Abraham & Mary, Marion
  Co., O.; m in Gilead, Sarah S. WHITING, dt
  Thomas & Anna, Del. Co.
  Ch: Henryetta b 1847, 6, 27
      Calmers J. " 1857, 2, 7
1848, 1, 5. Isaiah, s Abraham & Mary, Marion Co.; m in Gilead, Mary Anne VAUGHN,
  dt James & Rhoda, Marion Co., O.
  Ch: Byran   b 1848, 10, 4
      Harriett
      Lucretia " 1850, 1, 20
1849, 4, 4. Rachel m Joseph HEALD
1850, 10, 30. Mary m Wm. WOODS
1853, 11, 21. John, s Joseph & Jane, Marion
  Co.; m in Gilead, Priscillaann FARUNGTON,
  dt Moses & Armilla, Crawford Co.
  Ch: Precilla
      Jane   b 1854, 11, 19
      Rachel Ann
      Samuel A.
1855, 11, 29. Rebecca d bur Gilead
1856, 7, 28. Mary d ae 61 bur Gilead
1882, 5, 20. Joseph C., s Calmer & Trifena, b
1884, 1, 29. Abraham d ae 91 bur Gilead
1885, 9, 8. Mehetable d ae 77 bur Gilead
1861, 6, 27. Tabitha m Thos. E. HARTLEY

1839, 10, 22. Abraham & w, Mary, & ch, Joseph,
  Isaiah, Rachel, Mary & Rebecca, rocf Upper Springfield MM, dtd 1839,8,28
1849, 7, 24. Isaiah dis disunity
1851, 9, 20. Mary Ann & ch, Byron & Harriett
  Lucretia, gct Salem MM, Ia.
1852, 6, 22. Stephen rocf Upper Springfield
  MM, dtd 1852,3,27
1855, 7, 25. John & w, Priscilla Ann, & dt,
  Hannah Jane, gct Red Cedar MM, Ia.
1856, 3, 25. Stephen gct Upper Springfield
  MM
1856, 11, 25. Abraham W. gct Bloomington MM,
  Ia.
1857, 10, 20. Abraham gct Salem MM, to m
  Mehitable J. Coppock
1858, 7, 20. Celina (form Heald) dis mcd
1858, 10, 26. Abraham & w, Mehitable J., gct
  Goshen MM
1859, 5, 24. Abraham & w, Mehitable J., rocf
  Goshen MM
1860, 12, 25. John & w, Sarah G., & ch, Priscilla Jane, Rachel Ann & Samuel A., rocf
  Red Cedar MM, Ia., dtd 1860,11,7
1861, 9, 17. John & w, Sarah G., & ch, Rachel
  Ann & Samuel A., gct Red Cedar MM, Ia.
1862, 5, 20. Joshua gct Red Cedar MM, Ia.

MORRIS, continued
1868, 10, 20. Keziah gct Springdale MM, Ia.
1873, 9, 16. Joseph C. relrq
1876, 5, 15. Kesiah rocf Springdale MM, Ia.,
    dtd 1876,4,22
1879, 12, 16. Joshua rocf Springdale MM, Ia.,
    dtd 1879,10,18
1881, 11, 15. Joseph relrq
1883, 10, 16. John P. & s, Albert, rocf Friends-
    ville MM, Tenn., dtd 1883,10,6
1885, 4, 14. Christian recrq
1886, 5, 18. Calmer J. relrq
1887, 6, 14. John & w, Christina, & s, Albert,
    gct Springdale MM, Ia.
1894, 5, 15. John P. & w, Christina, rocf
    West Branch MM, Ia.
1900, 3, 20. Calmer J. recrq
1907, 5, 14. Carl relrq
1922, 5, 16. Calmer & w, Tryphena, relrq

MORTON
1884, 4, 15. Lucinda recrq
1895, 7, 16. Lucinda, Clarence, R. R. &
    Florence, dropped from mbrp

MOSHER
----, --, --. Robert F. b 1848,9,4 d 1932,4,25
1907, 10, 13. Phebe A. d ae 58 (an elder)

1840, 4, 21. Hannah B. Breese (form Mosher)
    dis mcd
1844, 2, 20. Deborah (form Andrews) dis mcd
1848, 8, 22. Gideon dis jas
1848, 8, 22. Stephen dis disunity
1848, 8, 22. Nathan N. dis disunity
1852, 8, 24. Jonathan dis disunity
1853, 2, 22. Mary (form Farrington) dis mou
1862, 1, 14. Stephen & fam rst at South
    River on consent of this mtg
1897, 1, 19. Robert F., Phebe A., Ralph N.,
    Adaline, Henry H., Mary M., Samuel J. &
    Phebe A., recrq
1900, 12, 18. Minnie D. rocf Columbus MM, dtd
    1900,11,7
1909, 5, 18. Lulu recrq
1909, 11, 16. James recrq
1909, 12, 14. Flora & ch, Marie & Carl, recrq
1920, 3, 16. Chester recrq
1920, 11, 16. Chester relrq
1923, 2, 20. Flora dropped from mbrp
1923, 10, 16. H. H. & w, Minnie, gct Union MM
1924, 4, 15. James relrq
1925, 9, 15. Robert E. gct Carmel MM
1927, 12, 20. Edith & ch, Ralph Harlan, Ro-
    sellen & Robert Allen, ---------------
1928, 11, 13. Harlan gct Raisin Center MM,
    Mich.
1929, 2, 12. Mae Casey & dt, Mary Evelyn,
    rocf Shirley MM, Ind., dtd 1929,2,2
1931, 7, 14. Marie, Carl, Virgil, J. Raymond
    & Olive J. dropped from mbrp
1933, 5, 16. Mable A. (Mosher) Earle relrq

MOUCH
1929, 4, 16. Blanch Brown dropped from mbrp

MULLENIX
1838, 12, 17. Joshua W., s Gideon & Hannah, b

1839, 8, 20. Gideon [Mulenix] dis disunity

MYERS
1919, 2, 16. Frank & Augustus recrq
1927, 10, 18. Frank & w, Augusta, & dt,
    Elaine, relrq

NEAL
1847, 6, 22. Cert rec for Jusline Ann from
    Sandy Spring MM, endorsed to Alum Creek
    MM

NEVILL
1860, 8, 29. Benjamin G., s Joseph & Susanna,
    Morrow Co.; m in Gilead, Rhoda E. WOOD, dt
    Israel & Mary

1855, 2, 20. Wm. W. Heald gct Cincinnati MM,
    to m Susanna Nevill
1860, 3, 20. Benjamin Greenwood [Nevil] rocf
    Cincinnati MM, dtd 1860,2,16
1861, 6, 18. Benjamin G. [Nevil] & w, Rhoda
    E., gct Alum Creek MM

NEWSOM
1870, 2, 15. Esther W. (form Wood) dis mcd
1882, 4, 18. Bell recrq
1885, 6, 16. Rosabel relrq

NICHOLS
1850, 2, 19. Athenissa rocf Alum Creek MM,
    dtd 1850,1,24
1886, 6, 15. Rachel dropped from mbrp
1895, 7, 16. Athenessa [Nicols] dropped from
    mbrp

OCHER
1885, 2, 17. Ella recrq

O'DAY
1929, 4, 16. John C. dropped from mbrp

OLIPHANT
1873, 9, 6. Ephraim d ae 78 bur Gilead
1874, 6, 24. Ruth [Olephant] m Seth S. GIDLEY

1849, 9, 22. Abner rocf Middleton MM, dtd
    1849,7,12
1866, 11, 13. Ephraim rocf Upper Springfield
    MM, dtd 1866,10,27
1867, 9, 17. Ruth rocf Damascus MM, dtd 1867,
    8,24

1874, 8, 18. Lucretia & ch, John Wilton,
    Mary Letta & Lulu Bell, recrq
1877, 6, 19. Israel rocf Damascus MM, dtd
    1877,5,26

OLIPHANT, continued
1883, 12, 18. Lucretia relrq
1886, 6, 15. Wm. dropped from mbrp
1887, 7, 19. Israel dropped from mbrp

ONG
1913, 10, 14. Effie rocf Columbus MM
1923, 10, 16. Effie gct Union MM

OSBORN
1842, 12, 20. Thomas Sharp gct Alum Creek MM,
     to m Esther Osborn
1887, 7, 19. Mary Netta dropped from mbrp

OWENS
1879, 2, 18. Henry recrq
1882, 5, 16. Henry dis

PARKER
1925, 11, 17. Paul E. & w, Eulalia, & s, Paul
     Jr., rocf Oak Creek MM, Kans.

PARKINS
1843, 11, 21. Sarah dis jH
1850, 12, 24. Jesse dis disunity

PARKS
1871, 4, 3. Mary Etta, dt Sylvester &
     Elizabeth, b

1870, 8, 16. Sylvester G. & w, Elizabeth,
     rocf Damascus MM, dtd 1870,7,23
1872, 5, 14. Sylvester G. & w, Elizabeth, &
     ch, Marietta, gct Damascus MM

PATTERSON
1896, 3, 17. Maggie Hays dropped from mbrp
1898, 12, 20. Chas. A. & Julia E. recrq
1902, 2, 11. Charles & w relrq

PAXTON
1845, 6, 25. Rowland R., s Jacob & Sitnah,
     Logan Co., O.; m in Gilead, Phebe B. WOOD,
     dt David & Esther, Marion Co.

1846, 6, 23. Phebe B. gct Goshen MM

PEASLEY
1840, 2, 27. Henry G., s Samuel & Jane,
     Marion Co., O.; m in Sandusky, Ann
     QUAINTANCE, dt Fisher & Sarah, Crawford
     Co., O.
     Ch: Sarah Jane b 1841, 3, 25
         Narcissa   " 1843, 3, 3
         Irie   " 1847, 9, 16
         Charles
          Enoch   " 1850, 8, 20
         Minerva   " 1855, 9, 23
         Cynthia   " 1858, 12, 14
----, --, --. Chocley & Margaret
     Ch: Martha   b 1841, 3, 8
         Eliza L. " 1845, 5, 22
1845, 1, 8. Mary Jane m Nathan TABOR

1846, 4, 20. Sarah Jane d bur Gilead
----, --, --. Enoch & Sarah J.
     Ch: Pheby Jane b 1847, 9, 22
         Ann Eliza " 1849, 10, 24
1847, 8, 16. Jonathan d bur Gilead
1853, 10, 9. Joseph d bur Gilead
1853, 10, 13. Jane A. d bur Gilead
1839, 7, 23. Micajah dis disunity
1844, 8, 20. Amy dis disunity
1845, 4, 22. Enoch con mcd
1845, 9, 20. Mary dis disunity
1846, 5, 26. Samuel & w, Betsy, & ch, Rhoda
     Ann, Charles L. & Samuel Wm., gct Alum
     Creek MM
1847, 4, 20. Sarah Jane recrq
1849, 6, 19. Samuel & w, Betsy, & ch,
     Charles L. & Samuel Wm., rocf Alum Creek
     MM, dtd 1849,4,22
1849, 4, 19. Phebe Ann rocf Alum Creek MM,
     dtd 1849,4,22
1852, 6, 22. Watson H., s Enoch & Sarah,
     recrq
1853, 1, 25. Enoch & w, Sarah Jane, & ch,
     Watson H., Phebe Jane & Ann Eliza, gct
     Salem MM, Ia.
1853, 5, 24. Charles con mcd
1853, 8, 23. Samuel & w, Betsy, & s, Wm., gct
     Red Cedar MM, Ia.
1853, 8, 23. Phebe Ann gct Red Cedar MM, Ia.
1854, 5, 21. Charles gct Red Cedar MM, Ia.
1861, 7, 16. Martha P. Wright (form Peasley)
     dis mcd & jas
1863, 8, 18. Jacob A. dis mcd & jas
1863, 8, 18. John dis mcd & jas
1865, 10, 17. Eliza S. dis jas
1866, 8, 15. Narsissa Redman (form Peasley)
     dis mcd
1870, 8, 16. Chalkley relrq
1871, 1, 17. Margaret relrq
1882, 7, 18. Cynthia dropped from mbrp

PENNINGTON
1843, 9, 16. Robert dis mcd
1844, 8, 20. Maria Kuhn (form Pennington) dis
     mcd
1847, 4, 20. Lewis dis mcd
1847, 4, 20. Isaac dis mcd
1848, 4, 25. Sarah Hinman (form Penington)
     dis mcd
1882, 7, 18. Joseph, Sarah, Edwin, Barclay &
     Wm. dropped from mbrp

PERKINS
1838, 1, 22. Sarah, Jesse, Jane & Louisa,
     rocf Flushing MM, dtd 1838,1,25, endorsed
     by Alum Creek MM, 1838,12,25
1848, 8, 22. Jane & Louisa dis disunity
1861, 3, 26. Sarah B. (form Hobson) dis mcd

PERRIN
1894, 1, 16. Adelbert [Parrin] recrq
1895, 7, 16. Adelbert dropped from mbrp
1897, 2, 16. James recrq

PERRIN, continued
1906, 2, 13. Charles Earl & James Eber recrq
1929, 4, 16. Charles E. & James E. dropped
    from mbrp

PETERSON
1885, 4, 14. Bertha J. recrq

PETTETT
1870, 10, 18. George E. Jackson gct Short
    Creek MM, to m Mary Pettett
1878, 6, 18. Hannah rocf Short Creek MM, dtd
    1878,5,23

PIEFER
1926, 7, 20. Pearl dropped from mbrp

PIM
1890, 4, 15. Alice (form Wood) relrq

PIPES
1910, 6, 14. Lizzie relrq

PITTS
1930, 10, 14. Martha relrq

PLUMLEY
1880, 5, 18. Anna recrq
1882, 4, 18. Charles [Plumbley] recrq
1887, 7, 19. Charles, Anna & M. W. [Plumly]
    dropped from mbrp

POWELL
1896, 3, 17. Thomas recrq

PRIEST
1915, 2, 16. Jennie Lewis relrq

PRYOR
----, --, --. Smith & Rachel
    Ch: Tedford P. b 1882, 9, 26
        Clyde M.   " 1885, 3, 20
        Jennie
        Pearl   " 1888, 1, 28

PUGH
1861, 7, 16. Hannah rocf Cincinnati MM, dtd
    1861,5,16

PURVIS
1841, 11, 23. Lydia (form Bunker) dis mcd
1847, 10, 26. Lucy dis disunity
1877, 4, 17. Peleg & ch recrq
1885, 5, 19. William recrq
1886, 6, 15. Peleg B. & w, Hannah E., & dt,
    Viola, relrq
1887, 7, 19. Willie dropped from mbrp
1889, 4, 16. Annette C. relrq
1900, 3, 20. Edward [Pervis] recrq
1927, 8, 16. Peleg transferred from Weston
    MM, O.
1929, 11, 19. Peleg relrq

QUAINTANCE
----, --, --. Lewis C. & Mariah M.
    Ch: Rebecca
       Ann   b 1837, 5, 4
       Ephron Os-
       nam   " 1838, 5, 31
       Abraham
       Morris   " 1840, 4, 4
       Sarahann   " 1842, 8, 6
       Hannah L. " 1845, 2, 7
       Mary Cor-
       delia   " 1848, 8, 8
       Joseph Or-
       lando   " 1851, 10, 6
       Silas Lew-
       is   " 1853, 9, 17
1840, 2, 8. Rebecca Ann d bur Sandusky
1840, 2, 27. Ann m Henry G. PEASLEY
1840, 10, 8. Wm. d ae 57 bur Sandusky
1841, 9, 4. Eli d ae 54 bur Sandusky
1841, 10, 20. Susanna d bur Sandusky
1842, 6, 6. Eli, s Fisher & Sarah, Craw-
    ford Co., O.; m in Gilead, Hannah A. KIRK,
    dt Caleb & Hannah, Del. Co., O.
    Ch: Melvin   b 1843, 3, 17
       Sarah Ann   " 1844, 9, 8
       Livonia T. " 1847, 6, 30
       Fisher   " 1851, 5, 5
       Cintha Jane " 1853, 2, 6
       Rachel Emma
       Charles L. " 1859, 11, 15
       George L.   " 1862, 12, 14
----, --, --. Joseph & Phebe
    Ch: Grenbery P. b 1845, 1, 7
       Ellen L.   " 1848, 4, 26
       Israel W.   " 1850, 10, 8

1840, 12, 22. Wm. dis disunity
1841, 9, 18. Edward C. dis disunity
1841, 10, 26. Rebecca B. dis jas
1842, 8, 23. Joseph R. gct Short Creek MM,
    to m Phebe Brewer
1843, 4, 25. Betty dis
1843, 5, 23. Phebe rocf Short Creek MM, dtd
    1842,12,20
1844, 1, 23. Eli D., Lucy Ann, Lydia & Jo-
    seph, ch Joseph & Phebe, recrq
1844, 10, 22. Joseph D. dis disunity
1844, 10, 22. Wm. P. dis disunity
1844, 11, 19. Charlotte (form Quaintance)
    dis mcd
1851, 4, 22. Joseph & w, Phebe, & ch, Eli D.,
    Lucy Ann, Lydia R., Greenbury P., Elem S.
    & Israel W., gct Salem MM, Ia.
1851, 4, 22. Dawson dis mcd
1852, 7, 20. Caleb dis jas
1853, 4, 19. Ann Frame (form Quaintance) rpd
    mcd
1853, 5, 24. Rachel Miller (form Quaintance)
    dis mcd
1853, 6, 21. Joseph W. con mcd
1855, 10, 23. Chas. R. dis disunity
1855, 2, 19. Ira dis mcd

QUAINTANCE, continued
1856, 3, 25. Charles gct Spring Creek MM, Ia.
1857, 5, 26. Lewis & w, Maria, & ch, Ephron
     O., Abraham Morris, Saryann, Hannah Louisa,
     Joseph O., Silas Lewis & Rachel Angeline,
     gct Spring Creek MM, Ia.
1859, 3, 22. George E. dis mcd
1865, 3, 14. Melvin dis mcd
1866, 11, 13. Lovina Holler (form Quaintance)
     dis mcd
1874, 3, 17. Sarah Ann relrq
1874, 3, 17. Fisher relrq
1874, 3, 17. Cintha J. relrq
1887, 7, 19. G. L. & C. L. dropped from mbrp
1909, 3, 16. Joseph dropped from mbrp

QUEEN
1891, 2, 19. W. C. & w, Mary E., recrq
1909, 3, 16. Webb dropped from mbrp
1913, 3, 18. Estella relrq

RAHN
1921, 2, 15. Louis recrq

RANDOLPH
1885, 4, 14. Albert recrq
1887, 7, 19. Albert dropped from mbrp

REDMAN
1866, 8, 15. Narcissa (form Peasley) dis mcd

RETTER
1882, 3, 14. Martha S. recrq
1887, 3, 15. Martha L. gct Alum Creek MM, O.

REYNOLDS
1848, 11, 23. Daniel, s Daniel & Elizabeth,
     Erie Co.; m in Gilead, Miriam TABOR, dt
     W. Worth & Betty

1849, 1, 23. Miriam gct Greenwich MM

RHODABECK
1889, 3, 19. Daniel O. recrq

RICHARDSON
1858, 12, 21. Joseph recrq
1861, 3, 20. Joseph gct Norwich MM, Canada
     West

RIFES
1900, 3, 20. Lizzie recrq

RILEY
1893, 9, 19. Matilda A. recrq
1904, 5, 17. Matilda relrq
1909, 3, 16. Matilda dropped from mbrp

RINEHART
1885, 2, 17. James E. & Mary B. recrq
1895, 7, 16. Mary B. dropped from mbrp
1897, 1, 19. Thomas recrq
1898, 12, 20. Ethel recrq

1909, 5, 18. Floyd E. & w, Grace W., recrq

ROBERTS
1843, 11, 29. Elizabeth Jr. m Stephen JACSON
1845, 10, 22. Joseph, s Aaron & Elizabeth,
     Marion Co.; m in Gilead, Rachel C. KIRK,
     dt Caleb & Hannah, Del. Co.
     Ch: Martha K. b 1846, 10, 19
         Ann   " 1848, 3, 20
         Beulah   " 1849, 7, 6
         Francis   " 1851, 3, 6 d 1851, 3,14
           bur Gilead
         Leverson   " 1852, 2, 5
1862, 4, 23. Charles, s Reuben & Elvira,
     Marshall Co., Ia.; m in Gilead, Helen A.
     KIDNEY, dt George & Aurilla, Morrow Co.

1839, 7, 23. Silas Taber gct Plainfield MM,
     to m Anna Roberts
1842, 6, 21. Elizabeth rocf Plainfield MM,
     dtd 1842,5,25
1844, 4, 23. Joseph rocf Plainfield MM, dtd
     1844,3,20
1850, 6, 25. Joseph dis disunity
1852, 7, 20. Samuel Irish gct White Water MM,
     Ind., to m Avis Jane Roberts
1854, 2, 21. Rachel C. & ch, Martha Ann,
     Beulah & Leverson, gct Spring Creek MM, Ia.
1859, 5, 24. Hannah Kirk & gr ch, Martha C.,
     & Rachel Elizabeth Roberts, rocf Spring
     Creek MM, Ia., dtd 1859,3,5
1860, 5, 22. Charles gct Western Plain MM,
     Ia.
1862, 12, 16. Helen A. gct Bangor MM, Ia.
1864, 10, 18. Reuben L. & w, Elvira, & ch,
     Wm. Linneus, Aaron Reuben & Sarah Josepha,
     also John L. Roberts, Elizabeth Roberts,
     Hannah Roberts & Cynthia Roberts, gct
     Greenfield MM, Ind.
1864, 10, 18. Cert granted to Greenfield
     MM, Ind. returned at John's rq
1864, 12, 20. Hannah Kirk & gr dt, Rachel
     Roberts, gct New Sharon MM, Ia.
1867, 12, 17. John gct Chicago MM, Ill.
1929, 4, 16. Blanch dropped from mbrp

ROCHE
1864, 7, 19. Deborah M. (form Andrews) dis
     mcd

ROGERS
1863, 8, 10. Cynthia d bur Gilead
1863, 9, 22. Lucie Saphonia, dt Silas & Abo-
     lone, b

1840, 10, 20. Lydia [Rodgers] recrq
1842, 7, 26. Susanna [Rodgers] (form Kirk)
     dis mcd
1847, 1, 26. Lydia White (form Rogers) dis
     mcd
1862, 8, 19. Ansel & w, Cynthia, & ch, Alon-
     zo, Sarah & Arthur, rocf Kansas MM, dtd
     1862,7,9

ROGERS, continued
1862, 8, 19. Daniel T. rocf Kansas MM, dtd
    1862,7,9
1862, 12, 6. Silas R. & w, Abilona B., & ch,
    Nancy Celora & Emma Delesta, rocf Kansas
    MM, dtd 1862,3,12
1863, 3, 17. Daniel T. gct Upper Springfield
    MM, to m Lucy Jane Cobb
1864, 2, 16. Ansel & ch, Alonzo, Sarah Louisa
    & Arthur T., gct Alum Creek MM
1864, 5, 17. Daniel T. gct Upper Springfield
    MM
1866, 4, 17. Silas R. & w, Abaline, & ch,
    Handy, Celora & Emma Delista, gct Winne-
    shiek MM, Ia.

ROGGIE
1896, 3, 17. Henry recrq

ROMANS
1857, 3, 24. Joseph recrq
1858, 3, 23. Sally rst on consent of Flushing
    MM
1858, 11, 23. Sally & s, Joseph, gct Alum
    Creek MM

RUHLE
1907, 5, 14. Jeremiah C. recrq
1928, 11, 13. J. C. [Ruhl] relrq

SATER
1887, 3, 15. Ella gct Alum Creek MM, O.

SCHOOLEY
1849, 1, 23. Isaac E. rocf Flushing MM, dtd
    1849,11,25
1853, 10, 25. Isaac E. gct Red Cedar MM, Ia.

SCHORB
1889, 3, 19. Mary recrq

SCOTT
1910, 4, 19. Alvernon recrq

SELL
1839, 4, 23. Rebecca (form McBride) dis mcd

SELLARS
1909, 3, 16. Bertha dropped from mbrp

SHAFFER
1907, 5, 14. James & Mary recrq

SHARP
----, --, --. Thomas m Sarah WILLETS, d 1841,
    10,23 bur Weston
    Ch: Addison   b 1839, 6, 5
    Thomas m 2nd Esther GIDLEY
    Ch: Harvey   b 1846, 6, 20
----, --, --. John & Hannah
    Ch: Oliver   b 1842, 7, 1
        Kennard   " 1846, 11, 3 d 1850, 2, 8
        bur Weston

Ch: Mary Esther
            b 1849, 2, 2
1854, 1, 31. Hannah d bur Weston
----, --, --. Levi & Rebecca Ann
    Ch: Jesse K. b 1859, 8, 28 d 1862,10,15
        bur Weston
    Hannah
    Ida   " 1862, 8, 8
1863, 7, 23. Hervey d bur Gilead

1842, 9, 17. John & ch, Elizabeth, Levi &
    Joseph W., rocf Dear Creek MM, dtd 1842,7,
    7
1842, 9, 17. Hannah, w John, rocf Gunpowder
    MM, dtd 1842,7,6
1842, 12, 20. Thomas gct Alum Creek MM, to m
    Esther Osborn
1843, 4, 25. Esther rocf Alum Creek MM, dtd
    1843,2,23
1858, 4, 20. Levi B. con mcd
1860, 3, 20. Townsend con mcd
1863, 3, 17. Joseph W. dis mcd
1864, 2, 16. Addison dis mcd
1864, 10, 18. Thomas & w, Esther, & dt, Mary
    A. Gidley, gct Bloomington MM, Ia.
1865, 1, 17. Oliver dis jas
1871, 7, 18. Levi B. & w, Rebecca, & ch, Han-
    nah Ida, Samuel L. & Edward H., gct Le-
    grand MM, Iowa

SHARPLESS
1848, 2, 12. Ellen [Sharples] d bur Weston
1853, 12, 30. Wm. [Sharples], s Albert &
    Lydia, b

1855, 6, 24. Albert & w, Lydia, & ch, Benja-
    min, Ellen & Sarah, rocf Middleton MM, dtd
    1845,5,8
1858, 3, 23. Benjamin con mcd
1860, 3, 20. Benjamin & w, Deborah, & s, Del-
    bert, gct Westland MM, Ia.
1865, 4, 18. Sarah H. gct Upper Springfield
    MM
1865, 4, 18. Albert & w, Lydia, gct Upper
    Springfield MM

SHAW
1846, 6, 15. John d ae 85 bur on his farm
1851, 7, 24. Wm., s Thomas & Rachel, Colum-
    biana Co.; m in Gilead, Hannah HEALD, dt
    Wm. W. & Susanna, Morrow Co.
1853, 1, 21. Ruth d ae 66 bur on John Shaw
    farm

1851, 9, 20. Hannah gct Middleton MM
1879, 4, 15. Jonathan recrq
1911, 11, 14. Sylvester, Mary & Iva Marie,
    rocf Weston MM
1923, 5, 15. Sylvester & Mary dropped from
    mbrp

SHERMAN
1895, 1, 15. Ezra & Eliza recrq

SHERMAN, continued
1899, 5, 16. Madison recrq
1901, 1, 15. Ezra & w, Eliza, relrq
1901, 12, 17. Ezra & w, Eliza, recrq
1902, 2, 11. Madison relrq
1904, 1, 19. Ezra & w, Eliza, relrq
1912, 10, 15. Ezra & Eliza recrq
1916, 4, 18. Ezra gct First Friends Church,
    Cleveland, O.

SHIELDS
1896, 2, 18. Payton B., Mary J., Eddie P. &
    Donnie H. rocf Ashley MM
1903, 4, 14. Eva & Edith May recrq
1923, 7, 17. Edd dropped from mbrp
1931, 7, 14. Don & Eva dropped from mbrp

SHIPMAN
1916, 4, 18. Stella relrq

SHULTZ
1898, 1, 18. Lizzie gct Lupton MM, Mich.
1908, 3, 17. Lizzie recrq
1913, 7, 15. Lizzie gct Beloit MM
1919, 11, 18. Lizzie & niece, Iris Hull, recrq

SIPE
1885, 2, 17. Mahlon F. [Sipes] recrq
1885, 2, 17. Mary rocf Alum Creek MM
1893, 3, 14. Wm. & Lydia [Sipes] recrq
1895, 4, 16. Clarence & Gertie recrq
1898, 7, 19. Wm. & w, Lydia, relrq
1900, 3, 20. Clint recrq
1909, 3, 16. Clint dropped from mbrp
1909, 10, 19. Gertrude (Sipe) Stratton relrq
1914, 1, 20. Lloyd dropped from mbrp
1914, 4, 14. Lloyd recrq
1923, 5, 15. Clarence dropped from mbrp
1924, 5, 20. May B. recrq
1933, 10, 17. Mary E. dropped from mbrp

SLYTER
1843, 9, 16. Eunice Jump (form Slyter) dis
    mcd
1848, 12, 26. Chalkley [Sliter] gct Mississin-
    ewa MM, Ind.
1848, 12, 26. Seth [Sliter] gct Mississinewa
    MM, Ind.

SMITH
1844, 1, 20. Israel d ae 68 bur Gilead
1848, 8, 20. James B., s Charles & Sarah,
    Morrow Co.; m in Gilead, Sarah T. WOOD, dt
    Israel & Mary, Marion Co.
    Ch: Anzonetta b 1850, 5, 17 d 1874,10,25
        bur Gilead
        Gilbert   " 1852, 2, 27
        Alphoretta " 1853, 8, 11 d 1884, 9, 7
        bur Gilead
        Chas. Ferdi-
        nand   b 1855, 1, 17 " 1875, 9,12
        bur Gilead
        Oscar C.   b 1857, 2, 13 " 1863, 1, 2

    bur Gilead
1839, 6, 18. Esther dis jas
1845, 1, 21. John E., minor, rocf Upper
    Springfield MM, dtd 1844,9,28
1845, 6, 24. James B., minor, rocf Upper
    Springfield MM, dtd 1845,6,28
1845, 7, 22. John E. dis disunity
1847, 1, 26. Esther rst
1851, 2, 18. Esther gct East Grove MM, Ia.
1858, 3, 23. James P. dis disunity
1862, 4, 15. Sarah Jane recrq
1868, 10, 20. Sarah J. relrq
1882, 3, 14. Eber recrq
1884, 3, 18. Prior S. & w, Rachel, & s, Ted-
    ford P., rocf Friendsville MM, Tenn.
1886, 6, 15. Gilbert dropped from mbrp
1886, 6, 15. Eber dropped from mbrp
1890, 7, 15. Rachel & ch, Tedford, Clyde &
    Jennie P., gct Gosper MM, Neb.
1890, 6, 15. Pryor dropped from mbrp
1909, 5, 18. Willis, Bertha, Milton, Lawrence
    & Virgil transferred from Greenwich MM
1910, 4, 19. Mabel recrq
1923, 5, 15. Willis, Bertha, Milton, Laurena
    & Vergil dropped from mbrp

SPENCER
1856, 4, 22. Amy Drucetta rocf Alum Creek MM,
    dtd 1856,2,21
1861, 6, 18. Amy Drusilla Harlan (form Spen-
    cer) dis

STANLEY
1842, 4, 27. Amy m Joseph HOBSON
----, --, --. Robert & Lydia
    Ch: Esther   b 1844, 1, 19
        Mary C.   " 1845, 11, 28
        Elizabeth
        E.   " 1848, 5, 2
        Juliann   " 1851, 3, 21
Robert m 2nd Sarah TATUM
    Ch: James C.   b 1854, 4, 24
        Lydia   " 1856, 11, 26
        Rhoda   " 1858, 4, 30
        Rebecca   " 1860, 5, 3
        Sibyl   " 1861, 8, 22
        George T.   " 1863, 2, 22
        Drusilla   " 1865, 3, 11
        Sarah K.   " 1867, 1, 23
----, --, --. Isaiah m Nancy -----
    Ch: Caroline A. b 1853, 12, 1
        Joshua   " 1856, 5, 11
1866, 3, 28. Esther m Joseph A. TALBOTT
1854, 7, 7. Lydia d bur Gilead
1856, 5, 13. Joshua d bur Gilead
1857, 11, 18. Juliann d bur Gilead
1867, 10, 23. Francis C., s Milton & Elizabeth
    Morrow Co.; m in Gilead, Sarah A. HICKLAND
    dt John & Mary Ann, Columbiana Co.
    Ch: Mary Eliza-
        beth   b 1868, 7, 8
        John Milton " 1871, 6, 20

STANLEY, continued
          Ch: Sarah F.   b 1876, 6, 23

1839, 4, 23. Robert rocf Upper Springfield
      MM, dtd 1839,2,23
1839, 9, 21. Amy rocf Upper Springfield MM,
      dtd 1839,8,24
1839, 9, 21. Judith rocf Upper Springfield
      MM, dtd 1839,8,24
1840, 1, 21. Robert gct Upper Springfield MM,
      to m Lydia Cattel
1840, 5, 19. Lydia rocf Upper Springfield MM,
      dtd 1840,4,25
1842, 7, 26. Judith C. Whiting (form Stanley)
      dis mcd
1849, 11, 20. Isaiah & w, Nancy, & ch, Milley
      Crew, Moses, Edwin & Susanna, rocf Ches-
      terfield MM, dtd 1849,10,20
1856, 1, 22. Robert gct Upper Springfield MM,
      to m Sarah Tatum
1856, 4, 22. Sarah rocf Upper Springfield MM,
      dtd 1856,3,22
1857, 6, 23. Isaiah & w, Nancy, & ch, Moses,
      Edwin, Susanna & Caroline Ann, gct Red
      Cedar MM, Ia.
1857, 6, 23. Millie C. gct Red Cedar MM, Ia.
1867, 7, 16. Francis C. recrq
1868, 10, 20. Robert & w, Sarah, & ch, James
      G., Lydia, Rhoda, Rebecca, Sibyl, George
      T., Drusilla & Sarah R., gct Damascus MM
1868, 10, 20. Elizabeth gct Damascus MM
1896, 12, 15. F. C. & w gct Stuart MM, Ia.
1898, 7, 19. Sadie F. gct Earlham MM, Ia.
1930, 4, 15. Evangeline Mosher gct Rush Creek
      MM

STARNER
1852, 8, 24. Mary (form Warner) dis mcd

START
1874, 7, 14. Minerva relrq

ST CLAIR
1888, 12, 19. Hannah d bur Gilead

1851, 8, 26. Mary rocf Short Creek MM, dtd
      1851,5,20
1851, 11, 25. Mary Stiner (form St. Clair)
      con mcd
1875, 4, 13. Irwih M. recrq
1882, 8, 15. Erwin gct Legrand MM, Ia.
1885, 4, 14. Hannah, Wm. H., Hannah M., Harry
      B. & Bessie B., recrq
1894, 7, 17. Harry relrq
1895, 2, 12. W. H., Hannah & Bessie recrq
1895, 7, 16. Glen dropped from mbrp

STEWART
1933, 2, 14. Almer recrq

STINER
1851, 12, 25. Mary (form St. Clair) con mcd

STOCK
1893, 3, 14. Jessie M. recrq
1895, 7, 16. Jesse dropped from mbrp

STRATTON
1909, 10, 19. Gertrude Sipe relrq

STROTHERS
1900, 3, 20. James P. & Lenora J. recrq
1901, 3, 19. James [Struthers] & w, Jennie,
      relrq

TABER
1838, 12, 7. Lewis, s Thomas & Meriam, b
----, --, --. Silas & Ann [Tabor]
      Ch: Mary R.   b 1841, 4, 26
          Benjamin S." 1842, 8, 2
          Reuben   " 1845, 1, 20
          James C.   " 1847, 4, 28
          Phebe E.   " 1848, 11, 15
          Sarah Matil-
          da   " 1854, 1, 6
1843, 5, 13. Thomas d ae 46 bur Gilead
1845, 1, 8. Nathan [Tabor], s Thomas & Mi-
      rium, Marion Co.; m in Gilead, Mary Jane
      PEASLEY, dt Samuel & Susanna, Morrow Co.
      Ch: Lysander O.b 1846, 3, 15
          Susana W. L.
                     b 1849, 9, 11
          Amanda Ma-
          hina   " 1851, 11, 4
          Miriam Al-
          mina   " 1851, 11, 4
----, --, --. William & Sarah
      Ch: Walter   b 1847, 2, 4 d 1849,7,20
          bur Gilead
          Wm. Garret-
          son   b 1849, 7, 16
          Orianna M. " 1853, 2, 16
          Ida Ro-
          sella   " 1856, 10, 4 d 1862, 1,1
          bur Gilead
----, --, --. Benjamin & Phebe Jane
      Ch: Francis Wm.
                     b 1855, 3, 3
          Adelbert E." 1859, 1, 24

1839, 7, 23. Silas gct Plainfield MM, to m
      Anna Roberts
1840, 1, 21. Anna [Tabor] rocf Plainfield MM,
      O., dtd 1839,10,23

1842, 8, 23. Nathan gct Alum Creek MM
1844, 11, 19. Nathan rocf Alum Creek MM, dtd
      1844,10,24
1845, 9, 20. Wm. con mcd
1846, 1, 20. Sarah recrq
1848, 11, 21. Freeman dis mcd
1849, 11, 20. Horace dis mcd
1850, 8, 20. Lenion rocf Starksboro MM, dtd
      1849,11,30
1850, 10, 22. Leamon dis mcd

TABER, continued
1852, 3, 23. Nathan & w, Mary Jane, & ch,
Orson L., Susannah W. L., Amanda M. & Miranda A., gct Salem MM, Ia.
1853, 5, 24. Thomas Elwood gct Salem MM, Ia.
1854, 1, 24. Benjamin J. & w, Phebe Jane, &
ch, Ervin Guiotto & Julia, rocf Ferrisburgh MM, Vt., dtd 1853,11,20
1854, 9, 16. Zeno C. rocf Starksboro MM, Vt.,
dtd 1854,8,2
1856, 11, 25. Zeno C. gct Red Cedar MM, Ia.
1858, 1, 26. James dis mcd
1859, 4, 19. Benjamin J. & w, Phebe Jane, &
ch, Ervin Quiotto, Julia, Francis, Wm. &
Adelbert Eugene, gct Winneshiek MM, Ia.
1866, 7, 17. Silas [Tabor] & w, Anna, & s,
Benjamin, & ch, James C., Phebe & Sarah
Ann, gct Greenfield MM, Ind.
1866, 7, 17. Reuben [Tabor] gct Greenfield
MM, Ind.
1869, 10, 19. Wm. Lloyd Garrison dis mcd & jas
1872, 10, 15. Orianna Ashbaugh (form Taber)
dis mcd
1919, 11, 18. W. L. G. [Tabor] & w, Ollie,
recrq

TALBOTT
----, --, --. Allen d 1874,10,6 ae 84 bur
Crestline; m Mary ----- d 1887,11,30 ae 89
bur Crestline
Ch: Thomas   b 1839, 7, 4
Elizabeth " 1841, 6, 11
1850, 11, 9. Thomas d bur Sandusky
1850, 11, 19. Elizabeth d ae 93 bur Sandusky
1851, 9, 4. Mary F. m Jonathan BROWN
1866, 3, 28. Joseph A., s Kinsey M. & Caro-
line E., Jefferson Co.; m in Gilead, Es-
ther STANLEY, dt Robert & Lydia, Morrow
Co.
Ch: Adelbert R.b 1866, 12, 23
Mary
Elizabeth " 1872, 2, 27
Caroline
Kinsey   " 1875, 6, 3
1873, 3, 26. John R. d bur Crestline

1856, 5, 20. John [Talbot] dis mcd
1860, 2, 21. Joseph dis mcd
1865, 2, 14. Joseph rocf Smithfield MM, dtd
1864,12,19
1865, 3, 14. Alvin Jr. con mcd
1867, 11, 19. Joseph A. & w, Sarah, & ch, Delbert, gct Short Creek MM
1869, 9, 14. Joseph A. & w, Esther S., & s,
Adelbert R., rocf Short Creek MM, dtd
1869,7,22
1873, 2, 11. John R. recrq
1877, 6, 19. Joseph A. & w, Esther, & ch gct
Damascus MM
1900, 12, 18. Allen relrq

TATUM
1856, 1, 22. Robert Stanley gct Upper Spring-

field MM, to m Sarah Tatum

TAYLOR
1884, 12, 28. Joe d bur Kansas

1878, 8, 20. Jehu recrq
1878, 8, 20. Adin recrq
1878, 9, 17. Mary recrq
1886, 6, 15. Alice & Mary dropped from mbrp

TEAPLE
1847, 5, 25. Henry H. & w, Mary, & ch,
Thomas & Sarahann, rocf Smithfield MM,
dtd 1847,2,22
1853, 4, 19. Thomas dis disunity

TERRY
1882, 7, 18. Jeremiah & Ephraim dropped from
mbrp

THOMAS
1894, 3, 20. John recrq
1919, 10, 14. Alva recrq

TOWNSEND
1846, 10, 28. Asa M., s Thomas & Ruth, Knox
Co.; m in Gilead, Elizabeth G. WOOD, dt
Israel & Mary, Marion Co.

1847, 2, 2. Elizabeth gct Alum Creek MM

UNDERWOOD
1842, 7, 26. Martha (form Warner) dis mcd
1865, 6, 13. Martha recrq

VAUGHN
1842, 8, 31. Rebecca T. m Wm. B. KIRK
1847, 9, 1. Rhoda m Thomas A. WOOD
1848, 1, 5. Mary Anne m Isaiah MORRIS
1853, 8, 31. James W., s Mathew & Phebe,
Morrow Co.; m in Gilead, Rachel Ann WOOD
dt Jonathan & Mary, Morrow Co.
Ch: Edgar J.   b 1857, 8, 9
William P. " 1862, 4, 17
Mary Nettie" 1864, 1, 13
Walter
1855, 7, 6. Unity d bur Gilead
1859, 12, 12. James d ae 79 bur Gilead
1869, 11, 15. Phebe d ae 84 bur Gilead
1877, 7, 20. Rhoda d ae 86 bur Gilead
1878, 8, 29. Mathew d ae 93 bur Gilead

1839, 9, 21. James & w, Rhoda, & ch, Rebecca
T., Mary Ann, Joana, Rhoda, Unity, Joseph
& Lindley James, rocf Upper Springfield
MM, dtd 1839,8,24
1851, 12, 23. Matthew & w, Phebe, & s, James
rocf Marlborough MM, O.
1857, 8, 25. Lindley J. dis mcd
1858, 3, 23. Joseph dis disunity
1859, 1, 25. James W. dis disunity
1877, 4, 17. Lindley J. & w recrq
1878, 4, 16. Clinton C. recrq

VAUGHN, continued
1881, 3, 15. Elizabeth R. recrq
1885, 2, 17. Maggie & Mary recrq

1886, 6, 15. Herbert recrq
1888, 3, 20. Joanna & Louis recrq
1892, 2, 16. Rhoda recrq
1902, 2, 11. Clinton C. gct Lupton Friends
    Church, Mich.
1903, 1, 20. Arthur L. & w, Edith D., & dt,
    Anna Mary, recrq
1921, 8, 16. Herbert gct Lupton MM, Mich.
1923, 10, 16. Herbert rocf Lupton MM, Mich.

WAKEFIELD
1879, 8, 19. Joseph & w, Mary, & ch, Eber H.,
    Lydia A. & Jane S. C. W. K., rocf Wilming-
    ton MM, dtd 1879,7,18
1880, 9, 14. Joseph J. relrq
1882, 7, 18. Eber dropped from mbrp
1888, 5, 15. Mary gct New Hope MM, Ind.
1888, 5, 15. Jennie C. Weber (form Wakefield)
    gct New Hope MM, Ind.

WALKER
1883, 12, 31. Daniel d bur Gilead
1884, 5, 8. Thomas d

1857, 3, 24. Daniel & w, Jane, rocf Chester-
    field MM, dtd 1857,2,28
1867, 5, 14. Thomas & w, Elizabeth, & ch,
    Ruth Ann, Charlotte Jane & Joseph Daniel,
    recrq
1882, 3, 14. Lotta, Joseph & Elizabeth relrq
1882, 7, 18. Daniel relrq
1893, 9, 19. Olive E. recrq

WARNER
----, --, --. Benjamin & Mary
    Ch: Sarah   b 1831, 10, 9
        Harriott   " 1837, 1, 18
        Louisa   " 1839, 8, 5
1838, 6, 3. Sarah d bur Laternbersville
1845, 2, 1. Sarah, dt Joseph & Phebe, b
1862, 6, 18. Phebe d ae 63 bur Bucyrus
1871, 5, 8. Benjamin Sr. d bur Bucyrus

1840, 1, 21. Phebe & ch, Martha, Susanna,
    Benjamin & Mary, rocf Hamburg MM, N. Y.,
    dtd 1839,9,25
1840, 4, 21. Benjamin & w, Mary, & ch, Robert
    K., Sarah & Hariet, rocf Muncy MM, Pa.,
    dtd 1837,10,18, endorsed by Alum Creek MM,
    1840,3,26
1841, 3, 24. Joseph rocf Hamburgh MM, dtd
    1840,12,20
1842, 7, 26. Martha Underwood (form Warner)
    dis mcd
1844, 3, 26. Susanna Johnston (form Warner)
    dis mcd
1847, 4, 20. Robert Kirkbride dis mcd
1852, 8, 24. Mary Starner (form Warner) dis
    mcd

1853, 1, 25. Benjamin II con mcd
1863, 3, 17. Louisa Kinsey (form Warner) dis
    mcd
1880, 5, 18. Bell recrq
1880, 7, 20. Levina recrq
1882, 3, 14. John H. recrq
1882, 3, 14. Samuel H. recrq

1885, 2, 17. Ollie recrq
1895, 7, 16. John Samuel, Bill & Grace drop-
    ped from mbrp
1897, 2, 16. Wm. & Elizabeth recrq
1909, 3, 16. Benjamin dropped from mbrp
1923, 5, 15. Wm. & Elizabeth dropped from
    mbrp

WATERMAN
----, --, --. John m Mary ----- d 1884,9,5 bur
    Gilead
    Ch: Almina
        Jane   b 1842, 4, 11 d 1860,12,21
        bur Gilead
        Sarah Rebec-
        ca   b 1844, 1, 15
        George
        Caleb   " 1846, 2, 24
1841, 3, 23. John & w, Mary, rocf Short
    Creek MM, dtd 1841,1,19
1867, 9, 17. George dis disunity & military
    service

WEATHERBY
1879, 3, 18. Melville [Weatherly] recrq
1882, 7, 18. Mevlville dropped from mbrp
1888, 3, 20. Melville recrq
1895, 7, 16. Melville dropped from mbrp

WEBER
1888, 5, 15. Jennie C. (form Wakefield) gct
    New Hope MM, Ind.

WERTS
1895, 4, 16. Lola relrq

WHEELER
1884, 10, 14. Nancy R. recrq
1889, 4, 16. Nancy Brown (form Wheeler) rel-
    rq
1900, 3, 20. Wm. & Olga recrq
1903, 6, 16. Will relrq
1923, 5, 15. Olga dropped from mbrp

WHIPPLE
1911, 6, 13. Lyman recrq
1919, 6, 17. Lyman & w, Pearl, relrq
1923, 5, 15. Pearl dropped from mbrp

WHITE
1844, 9, 14. Joshua d ae 76 bur Gilead
1850, 2, --. Elizabeth Ann m Jonathan G.
    BENEDICT

1839, 2, 19. Edward dis mcd

WHITE, continued
1844, 8, 20. Elizabeth Ann recrq
1846, 6, 23. Elias G. con mcd
1847, 1, 26. Lydia (form Rogers) dis mcd
1847, 8, 24. Elias G. dis disunity
1894, 3, 20. Alice relrq
1920, 11, 16. Arthur R. & w recrq

WHITING
1846, 9, 21. Sarah S. m Joseph MORRIS

1842, 7, 26. Judith C. (form Stanley) dis mcd
1846, 2, 17. Sarah S. recrq

WILLIAMS
1874, 9, 14. Laura, dt Thomas & Mary, b

1874, 3, 17. Thomas & Mary rocf Westland MM,
      dtd 1874,2,22
1876, 3, 14. Thomas & w, Mary, & ch, Laura,
      gct Alum Creek MM
1879, 9, 16. Phebe J. rocf Columbus MM, dtd
      1879,9,3
1886, 4, 13. Phebe J. gct Damascus MM
1909, 5, 18. Susan transferred from Greenwich
      MM

WILLIAMSON
1929, 7, 16. Linora Conant recrq

WILLIS
1922, 2, 14. Forest rocf Alliance MM, & w,
      Erma, recrq
1922, 10, 17. Forest & w, Erma, gct Ypsilanti
      MM, Mich.

WILLETS   [d 1887,1,2 ae 81 bur Weston)
----, --, --. Joel & Cynthia [Willits](Cynthia
      Ch: Wendill P. b 1839, 10, 31
          Esther Ann"" 1841, 9, 1
          Clayton N. " 1845, 5, 6
          Sarah Ellen" 1848, 4, 29
1874, 7, 23. Ellen m Griffen Grafton BENEDICT

1844, 2, 20. Joel dis disunity
1849, 8, 21. Wm. B. Lipsey gct Alum Creek MM,
      to m Hannah Willets
1851, 8, 26. John dis disunity
1860, 4, 24. Samuel gct Westland MM, Ia.
1863, 4, 14. Wm. dis mcd
1867, 7, 16. Clayton dis mcd & military ser-
      vice
1881, 3, 15. Esther A. relrq

WILSON
1870, 2, 18. Ann d ae 80 bur Weston

1842, 3, 22. Ann rocf Stillwater MM, dtd
      1841,12,25

WINDER
1864, 3, 15. Eunice N. gct Goshen MM

WINNER
1864, 11, 15. Mary recrq
1865, 2, 14. Ellis rocf Muncy MM, Pa.
1866, 1, 16. Charles, Henry C., Andrew C.,
      Lemuel, Simon P. & Daniel W., ch Ellis &
      Mary, recrq
1868, 7, 14. Mary relrq
1868, 9, 15. Ellis dis
1882, 7, 18. Charles, Henry, Andrew, Lemuel,
      Simon & Daniel, dropped from mbrp

WISEMAN
1923, 5, 15. Lottie dropped from mbrp

WOOD
----, --, --. Israel d 1874,11,6 ae 78 bur
      Gilead; m Mary H. ----- d 1862,2,18 ae 61
      bur Gilead
      Ch: William H. b 1839, 9, 10
          Mary Bulah " 1844, 11, 26
----, --, --. Reuben & Anna
      Ch: David   b 1840, 10, 29
          Hannah   " 1843, 2, 2
          Sarahann   " 1844, 11, 20
          Esther   " 1847, 2, 4
1843, 2, 1. Samuel, s Jonathan & Martha,
      Del. Co.; m in Gilead, Priscilla H. WOOD,
      dt Israel & Mary, Marion Co.
1845, 6, 25. Phebe m Rowland R. PAXTON
1846, 10, 28. Elizabeth G. m Asa M. TOWNSEND
1847, 9, 1. Thomas A., s Jonathan & Mary,
      Marion Co.; m in Gilead, Rhoda VAUGHN, dt
      James & Rhoda, Marion Co., O.
      Ch: Rubin   b 1849, 6, 23
          Mariette   " 1853, 8, 15
          Louisa T. " 1857, 12, 11
          Harriett M." 1862, 10, 22
          Caroline T." 1867, 7, 3
1847, 12, 29. Lamira, dt Jonathan & Mary, b
----, --, --. Thomas b 1819,1,19 d 1883,7,17
1848, 2, 2. Reuben d bur Gilead
1848, 8, 30. Sarah T. m James B. SMITH
1849, 7, 28. Wm. K. d
----, --, --. ----- m Rebecca K. WRIGHT b
      1839,10,19 d 1932,9,28
1850, 10, 30. Wm., s Reuben & Anna, Morrow
      Co.; m in Gilead, Mary MORRIS, dt Abraham
      & Mary, Morrow Co.
      Ch: Orlando   b 1851, 12, 6
          Rebecca   " 1857, 11, 16
          Marietta   "   d 1862,10,28
          bur Gilead
1851, 4, 30. Rachel H. m Zephamiah COTANT
1852, 5, 2. Lydia O. d bur Gilead
1853, 8, 31. Rachel Ann m James W. VAUGHN
1853, 12, 25. David d bur Gilead
1860, 8, 29. Rhoda E. m Benjamin G. NEVILL
1862, 2, 22. Walter d bur Gilead
1862, 8, 25. Rebecca M. d bur Gilead
1863, 9, 10. Martha Elizabeth d bur Gilead
----, --, --. Stephen & Elvira
      Ch: Mary E.   b 1864, 5, 5
          Harry

WOOD, Stephen & Elvira, continued
     Ch: Morton b 1865, 5, 12
            Mary   " 1867, 10, 12
            Charles
            Sumner   " 1869, 4, 10
1866, 6, 27. Israel, s Jonathan & Rachel, Mor-
     row Co.; m in Gilead, Mary CATTELL, dt
     James & Deborah, Morrow Co.
1867, 6, 26. Frances T. m Stephen JACKSON
1871, 11, 22. Reuben E., s Thomas A. & Rhoda,
     Morrow Co.; m in Gilead, Elvira MILLIGAN,
     dt Jesse & Ruth, Morrow Co.
     Ch: Ruth Etta b 1872, 7, 2
          Rosa   " 1873, 10, 13
1873, 2, 8. Mary d bur Gilead
1878, 7, 18. Marie C. d bur Gilead
1928, 8, 17. Orlando d ae 77

1839, 11, 19. Rhoda M. gct Cornel MM, N. Y.
1843, 6, 20. Abigail dis disunity
1843, 11, 21. Priscilla H. gct Alum Creek MM
1845, 4, 22. Joseph dis mcd
1850, 11, 19. Samuel N. dis mcd
1850, 11, 19. Mary Ann (form Hays) con mcd
1850, 11, 19. Jonathan Jr. dis mcd
1854, 12, 26. Mary Ann dis joining Spiritual-
     ists
1854, 12, 26. Stephen con mcd
1856, 9, 20. Henry dis mcd
1857, 5, 26. Stephen & w, Elvira, gct Spring
     Creek MM, Ia.
1858, 4, 20. Peleg dis disunity
1858, 4, 20. Griffith dis disunity
1858, 6, 22. Elizabeth (form Hays) dis mcd
1860, 9, 22. Stephen & w, Elvira, & s, Walter,
     rocf Spring Creek MM, dtd 1860,9,1
1861, 3, 26. Jonathan & w, Mary, & dt, La-
     mira, gct Upper Springfield MM
1861, 3, 26. Eliza Mary (form Johnson) con
     mcd
1861, 6, 18. David John M. recrq
1861, 9, 17. David John M. & w, Eliza Mary, gct
     gct Spring Creek MM, Ia.
1862, 3, 18. Jonathan B. con mcd
1863, 4, 14. Stephen A. dis disunity
1863, 6, 16. Lindley H. dis disunity
1864, 2, 16. Libius gct Rollin MM, Mich.
1864, 2, 16. Mary & dt, Lamira, rocf Upper
     Springfield MM, dtd 1864,1,23
1865, 1, 17. Hannah Brees (form Wood) dis
     disunity
1865, 1, 17. Sarah Ann dis disunity
1866, 2, 12. Temperance B. rocf Upper Spring-
     field MM, dtd 1866,1,27
1867, 1, 15. Lamira relrq
1867, 9, 17. Frances T. gct Bangor MM
1870, 2, 15. Esther W. Newsom (form Wood)
     dis mcd
1871, 12, 19. Daniel T. gct Greenwich MM
1873, 6, 17. Daniel rocf Greenwich MM, dtd
     1873,5,15
1874, 6, 16. Priscilla H. & ch, Mary, Frances,
     Israel, Sarah Ellen & Catherine, gct

     Rollan MM, Mich.
1877, 3, 20. Rebecca R. recrq
1880, 7, 20. William relrq
1882, 4, 18. Elmer C. recrq
1882, 8, 15. Re & fam gct Legrand MM, Ia.
1882, 8, 15. Daniel gct Legrand MM, Ia.
1885, 4, 14. Griffith L. & w, Rachel H., &
     dt, Mary E., recrq
1885, 4, 14. Alice recrq
1890, 4, 15. Alice Pim (form Wood) relrq
1890, 7, 15. Alvira & Mary dropped from mbrp
1892, 7, 19. Anna E. rocf Columbus MM, dtd
     1892,4,5
1895, 7, 16. Harry & Charles dropped from
     mbrp
1903, 5, 19. Florence recrq
1907, 5, 14. Effie M. recrq
1908, 5, 19. Eliza Jane recrq
1909, 3, 16. Mary dropped from mbrp
1911, 6, 13. Furbay Eugene recrq
1921, 8, 16. Clarence relrq

WOOTEN
1911, 9, 19. A. E. & w, Lucretta, & ch,
     Nellie Ruth, Gilbert Gurney, Dillen
     Moody, Helen Pauline & Isam C., rocf
     Springdale MM, Ia.
1913, 12, 16. A. E. & w, Lucetta, & ch,
     Nellie Ruth, Gilbert Gurney, Dillon
     Moody, Helen Pauline & Isam C., gct
     Miami MM, O.

WORTHINGTON
1902, 8, 19. Robert recrq
1906, 8, 14. James recrq
1915, 3, 16. Robert relrq

WRIGHT
1855, 3, 18. Thomas K., s Benjamin & Jamima,
     b
1890, 9, 25. Elizabeth d bur Gilead

1852, 6, 22. Jemima rocf Upper Springfield
     MM, dtd 1852,5,22
1854, 2, 21. Elizabeth, Joel, John C. & Jo-
     seph, ch Benjamin & Jemima, recrq
1854, 3, 21. Benjamin recrq
1858, 5, 25. Charles & w, Mary, & ch, Fran-
     cis, Benjamin & Edward B., rocf Short
     Creek MM, dtd 1858,4,21
1858, 5, 25. Elizabeth rocf Short Creek MM,
     dtd 1858,4,21
1859, 8, 23. Charles & w, Mary, & ch, Benja-
     min & Edward B., gct Blue River MM, Ind.
1859, 8, 23. Frances gct Blue River MM, Ind.
1859, 8, 23. Elizabeth gct Blue River MM,
     Ind.
1861, 7, 16. Martha (form Peasley) dis mcd
     & jas
1867, 7, 16. Joel gct Lynn Grove MM, Ia.
1873, 9, 16. Joseph dis mcd
1886, 2, 16. Mary recrq
1892, 2, 16. Judah recrq

WRIGHT, continued
1894, 2, 13. Levi & w recrq
1897, 5, 18. Levi & w relrq

*   *   *   *   *   *   *

QUAINTANCE
1849, 9, 26. Mary C. d bur Gilead
1852, 5, 12. Hester d ae 65 bur Sandusky
1860, 7, 17. Joseph d ae 86 bur Sandusky
1866, 3, 22. Fisher d ae 72 bur Sandusky

YATES
1909, 5, 18. Belle transferred from Greenwich MM

*   *   *   *   *   *   *

1871, 11, 18. Sarah d ae 80 bur Bucyrus
1885, 3, 23. Hannah d bur Bucyrus
1885, 4, 16. Eli d bur Bucyrus

TABER
1840, 12, 2. Martha [Tabor] m Jeremiah GRIN-
              NELL
1848, 11, 23. Miriam [Tabor] m Daniel REYNOLDS

GREENWICH MONTHLY MEETING

    Greenwich Monthly Meeting, located in Morrow County, Ohio, was established 11th Mo.
17, 1848, and was laid down 5th Mo. 18, 1909.

    Charter members of the women's meeting were Jane Brown, Ann Smith, Lavina Haviland,
Direxa Hathaway, Elizabeth Carpenter, Ann Healy, Jemima Healy, Mary Hathaway, Rachel Hatha-
way, Roda Seymour, Phebe Ann Bartlett, Lydia Eddy, Eliza Bartlett, Lavina Benedict, Jane
Gifford. No record of members of the men's meeting is available.

RECORDS

ABELE
1881, 1, 13. Michael & Emma recrq

ADAMS
1875, 9, 9. Charles recrq
1877, 1, 11. Hetty recrq
1877, 2, 8. Loretta recrq

ALBERTSON
1885, 2, 12. Frank recrq
1887, 10, 13. Frank dropped from mbrp
1889, 1, 10. Frank recrq

ATYEA
1889, 1, 10. Vernor recrq

BAILEY
1878, 2, 7. Lucy recrq

BAKER
1889, 12, 12. Fred & w, Emma, recrq
1889, 12, 12. W. H. recrq
1889, 12, 12. George recrq
1891, 11, 12. Fred & w relrq

BALL
1878, 12, 17. Jane E. m Andrew UNDERHILL

1874, 8, 13. Jane E. recrq

BARBER
1885, 1, 15. Alonzo D., Frances L. & Alanson
D. recrq

BARTLETT
----, --, --. James & Phebe Ann
Ch: Ann B.   b 1837, 1, 1
Martha W.   " 1838, 9, 23 d 1877, 7, 5
George
James   " 1842, 1, 3
----, --, --. Joseph & Ann
Ch: Agnes   d 1860,10,30
McCollon
----, --, --. Joseph B. d 1892,7,19 ae 88; m
Ann P. ----- d 1843,4,14 ae 42
Ch: Ellen B.   d 1844, 5,20
ae 16
Mary P.   " 1846, 3, 1
ae 14
Elizabeth D.   " 1870, 8,30
ae 14

1877, 2, 8. Willets G. recrq
1877, 3, 15. Anna Mary recrq
1882, 10, 12. Alfred H. & w, Harriett G., &
ch, Annie O., Willets G. & Emma Laura,
gct Adrian MM, Mich.
1887, 7, 14. Alfred H. & Hattie G., & dt,
Emma, rocf Adrian MM, Mich., dtd 1887,6,23

BARTLOW
1878, 2, 7. Cora recrq
1878, 2, 7. George & Mina recrq

BARTO
1879, 12, 11. Alice C. recrq

BECKWITH
1885, 1, 15. Erwin G. & Abbie M. recrq

BELL
1885, 3, 12. D. S. & w, Clara, recrq
1899, 9, 14. Henry recrq
1902, 11, 13. David S. Bell gl for himself &
w, Clara

BEMIS
1881, 1, 13. Kitty recrq
1881, 1, 13. Daniel recrq

BENEDICT
----, --, --. Harvey & Lovina B.
Ch: Margaret J.
b 1846, 9, 21 d 1847, 9,10
Orlando   " 1848, 7, 9

1851, 8, 22. Harvey & Lavina gct Mississinewa
MM, Ind.

BICKLEY
1881, 1, 13. Mary E. & Mary recrq

BIRDSALL
1850, 11, 28. Ann d ae 80 bur Greenwich
1856, 1, 11. Zephaniah d ae 87 bur Greenwich

BIRGE
1880, 5, 13. Zelma & Frances recrq
1887, 2, 10. Zelma relrq

BLACKMARR
----, --, --. Edwin & Anna
Ch: Byron D.   b 1846, 5, 22
Olette   " 1849, 2, 9

1849, 7, 20. Ann & ch, Byron Deloss & Oliett,
gct Alum Creek MM, O.

BOALT
1851, 3, 21. Charlotte dis mcd

BRENEMAN
1878, 4, 11. John recrq
1881, 10, 13. John dis disunity

BROOKINS
1887, 7, 14. Ruth relrq

BROWN
1903, 5, 1. Jane F. d ae 93 bur Greenwich

1874, 5, 14. Ella recrq
1875, 3, 11. Samuel recrq

BRYANT
1885, 2, 12. Robert, Eli & S. J. recrq

BUTLER
1881, 1, 13. Elisha & Nancy recrq
1881, 3, 10. John & Cory recrq

CARPENTER
1861, 8, 6. Robert d
1865, 1, 23. Elizabeth d

1850, 2, 15. Deborah Ann dis disunity
1884, 11, 13. Ruth O. recrq
1884, 12, 18. Riley recrq
1887, 7, 14. Ruth dropped from mbrp

CARSON
1885, 2, 12. Maggie, Lizzie & Minnie recrq

CLARK
1877, 3, 15. Freeman recrq
1880, 3, 11. Mary J. recrq
1880, 4, 8. William recrq
1882, 2, 9. Freeman relrq

COBB
1884, 12, 18. James Jr. recrq

COLVIN
1878, 2, 7. George & Mina recrq

CONKLIN
1889, 12, 12. Charles recrq
1892, 2, 11. Charles & Elizabeth recrq

COOK
1881, 1, 13. Henry & Kate recrq
1881, 1, 13. Elmore & Hattie recrq
1881, 3, 10. Hannah recrq

COOPER
1884, 12, 18. William, Harriett, Florence & Katie recrq
1888, 1, 12. Wm. & Harriet relrq

COTANT
----, --, --. Benona & Lydia
  Ch: Jonathan b 1822, 4, 24
      Samuel " 1823, 12, 18
      Zephaniah " 1825, 11, 20
      Charles E. " 1827, 10, 18
      Edgar " 1829, 9, 19 d 1849, 6,17
      Benona " 1831, 9, 25 " 1833, 6,23
      Ann Malinda" 1833, 9, 24
      Purdy H. " 1836, 8, 8
----, --, --. Samuel & Hannah
  Ch: Clara
      Mariah b 1852, 5, 8
      Josephine
      L. " 1854, 7, 3
      Mary " 1857, 9, 14 d 1857,10, 9
1864, 3, 16. Isaac W. d bur Greenwich
1883, 11, 23. Mercy A. d ae 63 bur Greenwich

1883, 10, 24. Mary Jane [Coutant] d ae 57 bur Greenwich

1851, 10, 16. Hannah recrq
1851, 12, 19. Rachel H. rocf Gilead MM, dtd 1851,11,25
1854, 5, 19. Zephaniah & fam gct Gilead MM
1854, 8, 18. Matilda A. rmt Daniel B. Wood
1856, 4, 18. Benoni & fam gct Winneshiek MM
1857, 1, 16. Phebe rocf Abbington MM, Pa., dtd 1856,12,29
1857, 5, 22. Mercy Ann rocf Marlborough MM, N. Y., dtd 1857,3,25
1858, 5, 21. Samuel [Coutant] & fam gct Winnishiek MM, Iowa
1859, 10, 21. Zehainah B. [Coutant] & w, Rachel H., & ch, Elwin S., George W. & Benoni L., rocf Gilead MM, dtd 1859,9,17
1860, 3, 16. Mary E. (form Healy) con mcd
1860, 9, 21. Mary Elizabeth gct Winneshiek MM, Ia.
1861, 12, 13. Mary Jane recrq
1864, 11, 11. Ella G. & Edward H., ch Joseph H. & Mary J., recrq
1866, 4, 14. Zephamiah B. & w, Rachel H., & ch, Elwin S., George W., Benona L. & Charles Chester, gct Gilead MM
1880, 4, 8. Charles gc
1884, 12, 18. Clarence recrq
1885, 7, 9. Eliza rocf Short Creek MM, O., dtd 1885,6,24
1894, 12, 13. Clarence [Coutant] dropped from mbrp

COWGILL
1884, 6, 12. Eli & w, Abarilla, rocf Columbus MM, O., dtd 1884,6,4

COY
1891, 3, 12. Henry recrq

CRAIG
1888, 6, 15. Frank recrq

CREPPS
1877, 3, 15. Moses W. & Jenet recrq
1879, 7, 10. Elizabeth & Orpha recrq
1887, 8, 13. Michael & Jennet dropped from mbrp

CUBIT
1885, 2, 12. Robert & Elizabeth recrq

CULVER
1859, 9, 10. Martha (form Barlett) con mcd
1874, 12, 10. Martha W. relrq

CURRIER
1881, 1, 13. Harriett & Precepta recrq

CURTIS
1881, 3, 10. Ann recrq

DAILY
1881, 1, 13. Myra recrq

DALZELLE
1878, 2, 7. George & Ransom recrq
1880, 3, 11. Sarah Jane rocf Alum Creek MM, O.

DANIELS
1885, 11, 15. Mary E. recrq
1889, 4, 11. Louie recrq

DELANCY
1884, 11, 13. Calvin & Lucy A. recrq
1887, 4, 14. Calvin & w, Lucy, relrq

DILLS
1889, 12, 12. Mary recrq

DOOLITTLE
1864, 12, 16. Sylvia Ann (form Gifford) dis mcd

EDDY
----, --, --. John L. m Lydia ----- d 1863,11,
    8
    Ch: Reuben   b 1824, 1, 20
        Ira G.   " 1825, 9, 4
        Joseph   " 1827, 9, 27
        Lucy Ann   " 1829, 10, 29
        Perlina   " 1831, 10, 14
        Ruth   " 1833, 1, 6
        John R.   " 1835, 12, 25
        Sherman G. " 1837, 12, 27
        Huldah R. " 1842, 9, 15
        Allen W.   " 1847, 4, 20

1854, 11, 17. Paulina Jenny (form Eddy) con
    mcd
1860, 2, 17. Huldah McDaniel (form Eddy) con
    mcd
1860, 4, 20. Lucy Ann Mowray (form Eddy)
    rpd mcd
1865, 2, 10. John L. gct Kingston MM, Canada,
    to m Mary Ferris
1865, 9, 15. John L. gct Kingston MM, Canada
1872, 1, 11. O. W. rpd mcd
1872, 6, 13. Allen W. gct Salem MM
1877, 4, 12. Elizabeth recrq
1877, 6, 14. Thomas recrq
1879, 12, 11. Walter H. recrq
1880, 1, 15. Direxa recrq
1880, 2, 12. Thomas & w, Elizabeth, & ch,
    Clara E., Sarah Alice, Anna L. & Elsie E.,
    recrq
1882, 6, 8. Sherman dis

EDWARDS
1891, 4, 9. William recrq

EVERINGHAM
1878, 2, 7. John & Carrie recrq

FERRIS
1865, 2, 10. John L. Eddy gct Kingston MM,

Canada, to m Mary Ferris

FIDLER
1884, 11, 13. Eliza C. & Mary C. recrq
1887, 8, 13. Mary C. dropped from mbrp

FIRS
1886, 10, 14. Wesley & Ella relrq

FLETCHER
1881, 1, 13. Francis & Wm. recrq

FRANKLAND
1871, 1, 12. Thomas Henry rocf Hardshaw
    West MM, Eng., dtd 1870,11,24
1880, 4, 8. Thomas H. gc

FULSTOW
1872, 12, 26. Robert d ae 66 bur Greenwich

1864, 7, 15. Robert & Charity recrq
1895, 11, 10. John D. & Sarah recrq
1904, 11, 10. John & Sarah glt Congregational
GALAWAY   [Church at Plipler
1884, 12, 18. J. M. recrq
1885, 1, 15. Maggie & Thomas H. [Galloway]
    recrq

GATES
1885, 2, 12. Belle recrq

GIBSON
1867, 5, 10. Huldah (form Healy) dis mcd
1877, 1, 11. Jerome G. & Huldah recrq
1883, 2, 8. Carrie W. & Anna H. recrq
1884, 11, 13. Jennie recrq
1884, 12, 18. Sammy recrq
1887, 8, 13. Carrie Shoup (form Gibson) rel-
    rq
1893, 12, 14. Jerome & Huldah dropped from
    mbrp

GIDLEY
1873, 5, 15. Dorwin rocf Westland MM
1874, 3, 12. Dorwin gct Carmel MM

GIFFORD
----, --, --. Joseph A. & Sylvia
    Ch: Giles J.   b 1825, 9, 23
        Lucy   " 1828, 4, 25
        John J.   " 1831, 8, 21
        Charles   " 1833, 3, 17
        Obadiah   " 1835, 1, 15
        Elizabeth " 1835, 12, 15
        Sylvia Ann " 1837, 5, 31
        Sarah Jane " 1842, 6, 1
        Joseph B. " 1845, 4, 1
        Benjamin   " 1847, 10, 31
----, --, --. Humphrey & Jane
    Ch: Mary J.   b 1829, 11, 22
        Abraham   " 1831, 7, 3
        Sarah   " 1834, 11, 23
        Catharine " 1836, 2, 19

GIFFORD, Humphrey & Jane, continued
    Ch: William
        Henry   b 1840, 9, 24
        Humphrey
          Jr.   " 1842, 10, 14
        Eliza Jane " 1845, 10, 9

1852, 9, 17. Masy Smith (form Gifford) rpd
    mcd
1863, 7, 10. John J. dis mcd
1864, 12, 16. Sylvia Ann Doolittle (form Gif-
    ford) dis mcd
1865, 6, 9. Sylvia C. & ch, Joseph B. &
    Benjamin J., gct Cottonwood MM, Kans.
1880, 4, 8. Charles gc
1880, 4, 8. Abram, William H. & Kate gc
1880, 5, 13. Eliza J. relrq
1887, 8, 13. Humphrey dropped from mbrp

GLEASON
1874, 8, 13. Gad recrq
1875, 1, 14. Jane recrq
1880, 4, 8. Gad & Jane gc
1889, 1, 10. Joseph recrq

GOLDEN
1863, 2, 13. Mary (form Smith) con mcd
1880, 12, 9. Mary relrq

GORHAM
1884, 12, 18. Jennie recrq
1887, 7, 14. Jennie dropped from mbrp

GRABILL
1865, 7, 14. Annie S. J. (form Jenny) con
    mcd
1873, 5, 15. Annie S. J. relrq

GREEN
1879, 5, 15. Noah roc
1881, 9, 8. Noah gc
1889, 12, 12. Noah recrq

GREGG
1887, 7, 14. Emmett dropped from mbrp

GRIFFIN
1884, 12, 18. Claude & Amy J. recrq
1886, 12, 9. Amy relrq
1887, 7, 14. Claud dropped from mbrp
1892, 2, 11. Frank recrq

HALL
1884, 3, 13. Elizabeth Charity, Phebe &
    Franklin G. rocf Freeport MM, dtd 1884,1,
    26
1884, 12, 18. Charity & Fred recrq
1884, 12, 18. George F., Mary B. & C. E. recrq
1887, 7, 14. Fred dropped from mbrp
1892, 12, 15. Frank G. gct Short Creek MM, O.
1892, 12, 15. Charity gct Short Creek MM, O.
1897, 4, 8. Sarah, minister, & h, Josiah, &
    dt, Cora, rocf Freeport MM, dtd 1897,2,27

HAMMER
1881, 1, 13. John H. recrq

HARVEY
1885, 5, 7. David & Anna recrq
1887, 7, 14. David & Anna dropped from mbrp

HATHAWAY
----, --, --. Caleb d 1852,4,13; m Rachel

    Ch: Peter   b 1824, 8, 2
        Henry   " 1826, 8, 17
        Mary   " 1828, 9, 3 d 1829, 8,15
        Phebe R. " 1830, 1, 13
        Caleb Jr. " 1832, 9, 25
        Joshua   " 1835, 1, 8
        Israel   " 1838, 3, 20
        Susan   " 1840, 5, 16
        William   " 1844, 8, 23
    Caleb m 2nd Sarah -----
    Ch: Alfred
        Caleb   b 1858, 9, 5
        Ida Eliza " 1860, 1, 26
----, --, --. Henry d 1864,10,12 bur Milan;
    m Esther -----
    Ch: Edward   b 1852, 8, 17
        Thomas T. " 1855, 9, 24
        Mary Elma " 1858, 11, 14
        Charles H. " 1864, 5, 29
1861, 3, 28. Joshua d
1856, 3, 21. Samuel,, s Peter & Betsy, b

1849, 12, 21. Richmond & w, Phebe R., & ch,
    Isaac N., Samuel B., William P. & Alfred
    R., rocf Adrian MM, dtd 1849,8,9
1851, 3, 21. Esther W. rocf Alum Creek MM,
    dtd 1851,1,23
1851, 3, 21. Peter rmt Betsy Stevens
1851, 3, 21. Nancy Ann McCumber, adopted dt
    Peter & Prudence D. Hathaway, recrq
1852, 9, 17. Richmond & w, Phebe B., & ch,
    Isaac N., Samuel B., Wm. P. & Alfred R.,
    gct Farmington MM, N. Y.
1852, 12, 17. Phebe R. rmt Samuel Levering
1854, 6, 16. Rachel rmt James Washburn
1858, 12, 17. Elizabeth dis jas
1860, 5, 18. Peter Sr. dis
1861, 6, 14. Susan gct Alum Creek MM
1863, 5, 15. Sarah D. rocf Gilead MM, dtd
    1863,4,18
1866, 7, 13. Wm. E. gct Greenfield MM, Ind.
1868, 7, 10. Caleb & w, Sarah D., & ch, Ca-
    leb Alfred, Ida Eliza, Edith Alice, Cas-
    per Henry & Francis Herman, gct Damascus
    MM, O.
1874, 1, 15. Esther & ch, Thomas F., Mary
    Elma & Chas. Henry, gct Springdale MM, Ia.
1874, 1, 15. Edward gct Springdale MM, Ia.
1878, 3, 14. Peter Sr. recrq

HAVILAND
----, --, --. Samuel m Susan E. ----- d
    1863,11,5

HAVILAND, Samuel & Susan E., continued
  Ch: Wm. Edward b 1801, 9, 6
    Geo. Sam-
     uel   " 1803, 4, 6 d 1864, 3,31
----, --, --. Samuel P. d 1887,8,26; m Lavina
----- d 1891,7,17
  Ch: Samuel Jr. b 1829, 3, 30
    William B. " 1830, 10, 16 d 1881, 3,16
    Alfred S. " 1831, 12, 30
    Nelson Mer-
     rit   " 1835, 11, 21
----, --, --. Wm. B. d 1881,3,16; m Edith Ann

  Ch: Abbie Jane b 1861, 10, 13 d 1896,12,22
    Smith Sam-
     uel   " 1863, 2, 27 " 1863, 4,12
    John Case " 1864, 2, 22 " 1865, 7,22
    Walter Al
     fred   " 1870, 4, 1
    George W. " 1866, 1, 1

1860, 11, 16. Samuel rmt Susan E. Wood
1861, 4, 19. Edith A. (form Healy) con mcd
1862, 6, 13. Nelson Merritt con mcd
1863, 2, 13. Alfred S. con mcd
1880, 4, 8. N. M. & Samuel gc
1880, 4, 8. Alfred gc
1884, 12, 18. George W. recrq
1885, 3, 12. Abbie J. relrq

HAYNES
1881, 1, 13. Elizabeth & Hattie recrq
1885, 2, 12. Edward [Hayes] recrq

HEALY
----, --, --. Abraham & Elizabeth
  Ch: Mary Elizabeth
  Abraham m 2nd Phebe -----
  Ch: John B. b 1838, 12, 31
    Henry A. " 1840, 2, 16
    Hannah Ma-
     ria   " 1843, 1, 8
    Smith Al-
     vin   " 1846, 4, 11
    Warren A. " 1854, 7, 19
----, --, --. Jacob d 1864,8,17; m Jemima ----
  Ch: Phebe b 1839, 12, 13
    Rachel " 1842, 7, 9 d 1880,12,25
    Caleb " 1844, 12, 12
    Anna " 1852, 11, 6
----, --, --. Smith d 1864,9,13; m Ann -----
  Ch: Edith Ann b 1832, 8, 6
    Elizabeth
     P.   " 1835, 11, 30 d 1864, 9,22
    Sarah Jane " 1840, 3, 15 " 1862, 9,18
    Huldah " 1843, 7, 10

1860, 3, 16. Mary E. Cotant (form Healy) con
 mcd
1861, 4, 19. Edith A. Haviland (form Healy)
 con mcd
1865, 8, 11. Hannah M. Rexford (form Healy)
 dis mcd

1865, 10, 13. Alfred con mcd
1867, 5, 10. Huldah Gibson (form Healy) dis
 mcd
1868, 4, 10. Caleb relrq
1872, 4, 11. John B. con mcd
1877, 1, 11. Anna, Fannie & Sarah recrq
1880, 4, 8. Smith, Warren & Edwin gc
1883, 2, 8. Warren & Mary recrq
1884, 12, 18. Carrie recrq
1887, 8, 13. Mary dropped from mbrp
1892, 2, 11. Fanny relrq

HEILEKER
1881, 3, 10. George recrq

HENLY
1887, 8, 13. Warren dropped from mbrp

HICKSON
1892, 2, 11. Anna recrq

HILL
1854, 4, 21. Louisa rocf Center MM, dtd
   1853,10,14
1871, 10, 12. Louisa gct Wilmington MM, O.

HOAG
----, --, --. Jesse m Mary ----- d 1876,3,6 ae
  76
  Ch: Ruth
    Temple b 1841, 6, 4 d 1841, 9,26
    Harriett
    Temple " 1843, 1, 7

1869, 7, 15. Harriett Travis (form Hoag) dis
 mcd

HODGES
1881, 3, 10. John recrq

HOLE
1889, 4, 11. J. W. & Sophia recrq

HOPKINS
1884, 12, 18. Emma recrq

HOUGH
1885, 2, 19. Mariah & Sylvester recrq
1887, 12, 15. Catherine recrq
1888, 2, 9. Maria relrq

HUFFMAN
1892, 2, 11. Amos, Elizabeth & John recrq
1896, 2, 13. Amos & w & s, John, relrq

HUDELSON
1898, 6, 9. J. L. & w, Ester W., rolf Methodist Episcopal Church, Greenwich, O., dtd
   1898,5,14

IRONMONGER
1874, 12, 10. John recrq
1875, 7, 15. Harriet recrq

IRONMONGER, continued
1877, 6, 14. John relrq
1890, 1, 9. John recrq

JACKSON
1880, 3, 11. Chester A., Louis Irena & Henry
     Vroman, recrq
1880, 4, 8. Luly M. recrq
1881, 1, 13. Mary recrq

JENNY
----, --, --. Benjamin & Ann M.
     Ch: Joannah   b 1836, 10, 10 d 1837, 1,10
         Anna S.   " 1839, 11, 13 " 1912, 4, 4
         Nicholas D." 1841, 1, 18 " 1898, 2,16
1852, 3, 2. John d bur Greenwich

1854, 11, 17. Pauline (form Eddy) con mcd
1865, 7, 14. Anna S. J. Grabill (form Jenny)
     con mcd
1865, 10, 13. Nicholas D. dis mcd
1872, 7, 11. Rufus recrq
1875, 3, 11. Truman recrq
1878, 2, 7. Susan rocf White Water MM, Ind.,
     dtd 1877,7,25
1881, 5, 19. Rufus S. relrq
1884, 12, 18. Lee W. & Earl recrq
1894, 10, 11. Susan & fam relrq

JOHNSON
1862, 9, 12. Pleasant T. & w, Elizabeth, rocf
     Gilead MM, dtd 1862,8,--
1863, 2, 13. Orville C., s Pleasant & Eliza-
     beth, recrq
1864, 1, 15. Pleasant & w, Elizabeth, & s,
     Orville, gct Spring Creek MM, Ia.

KARNES
1878, 2, 7. Caroline & Rosa recrq

KELLY
1865, 3, 10. Alfred D. & w, Abigail, & ch,
     Mary Alice, Susan A. & Abby Hannah, rocf
     Dover MM, N. H.
1869, 5, 13. A. D. & w & ch, Susan A. & Abbe
     H., gc
1869, 5, 13. Mary Alice gc
1885, 2, 12. Annie C. recrq
1888, 2, 9. Anna relrq

KENEDY
1881, 1, 13. Bell recrq

KERN
1885, 2, 12. Jessie recrq

KEYSER
1889, 1, 10. Ella recrq
1889, 4, 11. Cley recrq

KING
1877, 3, 15. Hiram recrq

KNAPP
1883, 2, 8. Orlando recrq

KNIFFIN
1875, 3, 11. Daniel recrq
1875, 5, 13. Minda recrq
1876, 6, 8. Lucy A. recrq
1877, 10, 11. Lucy A. relrq
1881, 1, 13. Mary recrq
1882, 2, 9. Mary relrq
1883, 2, 8. Lula recrq
1883, 11, 8. Lucy A. recrq
1884, 12, 18. Alfred & Kittie recrq
1884, 12, 18. Dolly & Ida recrq
1889, 11, 14. Lulu relrq
1892, 11, 10. Kitty relrq
1893, 12, 14. Daniel relrq
1893, 12, 14. Lucy relrq

KNIGHT
1885, 2, 19. Clifford recrq

LACY
1880, 12, 9. Joseph H. recrq
1881, 1, 13. Elizabeth recrq

LEE
1898, 1, 15. Mollie rolf Milan MM, dtd 1898,
     1,15

LAUGHLIN
1881, 1, 13. Ranson F. & Sarah recrq

LEVERING
1852, 12, 17. Samuel rmt Phebe R. Hathaway
1853, 1, 21. Phebe R. gct Alum Creek MM, O.

LEWIS
1898, 6, 9. Margaret, gr dt J. L. & Ester
     HUDELSON, rolf Methodist Episcopal Ch.,
     Greenwich, O., dtd 1898,5,14

LLOYD
1883, 4, 12. Jesse & w, Edith, & ch, Albert
     H., Edward H., Henry B. & Josephine Floyd,
     rocf Short Creek MM, O., dtd 1883,3,21
1886, 6, 10. Jesse W. & four ch gct Short
     Creek MM, O.

LYONS
1895, 6, 13. Rebecca recrq

McCULLOCK
1885, 2, 12. Solomon & Sarah A. recrq
1887, 7, 14. Solomon & Sarah A. dropped from
     mbrp

McCULLOW
1857, 11, 20. Agnes (form Bartlett) con mcd

McCULLY
1860, 9, 21. Louisa gct Winneshiek MM, Ia.

McCUMBER
1851, 3, 21. Nancy Ann, adopted dt Peter &
      Prudence D. Hathaway, recrq
1864, 2, 12. Nancy A. dis

McDANIEL
1860, 2, 17. Huldah (form Eddy) con mcd

McLEAN
1885, 2, 19. Noah C. rocf Hanover MM, Mich.,
      dtd 1885,2,7
1891, 1, 15. Noah C. gct Delphi MM

McVEIGH
1881, 3, 10. Thomas recrq

MASON
1881, 1, 13. Maggie & Anna recrq
1881, 1, 13. William recrq

MATHEWS
1878, 2, 7. Emme or Sarah recrq

MEYERS
1880, 4, 8. Levi & Sarah Ann recrq
1881, 1, 13. John A. & Grace Ann [Myers] rec-
MOETET   [rq
1872, 3, 1. Rhoda C. d ae 84 bur Greenwich

MOLOCK
1885, 2, 19. Phebe Jane recrq
1885, 3, 12. Ella recrq

MOODY
1881, 1, 13. Catherine recrq

MOREHOUSE
1877, 10, 11. Noly recrq

MORRIS
1877, 6, 14. Mary recrq

MOTT
1874, 5, 4. Berger d ae 87 bur North Fair-
      field

1850, 12, 20. Burger rmt Rhoda C. Seymour

MOWRAY
1860, 4, 20. Lucy Ann (form Eddy) rpd mcd
1880, 4, 8. Lucy Ann [Mory] gc

MUTERSBAUGH
1885, 2, 12. J. A. recrq
1885, 2, 19. Dora recrq

NEVILL
1871, 10, 29. Ernest G., s G. B. & Rhoda, b

1869, 6, 10. Benjamin G. & w, Rhoda, & ch,

Alfred W., Mary Agnes & Sarah Elizabeth,
      rocf Alum Creek MM, O., dtd 1869,3,18
1872, 6, 13. Benjamin G. & w, Rhoda, & ch,
      Alfred W., Mary Agness, Sarah E. & Earnest
      G., gct LeGrand MM, Ia.

NICHOLAS
1877, 4, 12. Elmer & Evaline recrq
1881, 10, 13. Elmer [Nichols] dis disunity

NICKISON
1891, 3, 12. William & Alice recrq

NIVER
1859, 3, 18. Lavina H. dis mcd

ODELL
1874, 5, 14. Almira recrq
1877, 4, 12. Wesley recrq
1878, 11, 14. Wesley dis disunity
1887, 8, 13. Lettie & Almira dropped from
      mbrp

OLDS
1884, 12, 18. Maggie recrq

OSBORN
1856, 12, 19. Ann B. (form Bartlett) dis mcd

OTIS
1884, 12, 18. Theodore, Loretta, Elizabeth &
      Adelbert, recrq

PARKER
1878, 2, 7. Charles recrq
1887, 5, 12. Eva recrq

PEABODY
1885, 3, 7. Alma recrq
1894, 10, 11. Alma relrq

PENNINGTON
1873, 5, 15. Samuel Edwin & w, Maria, rocf
      Carmel MM (Westland MM on women's minutes)
      dtd 1873,3,20
1878, 2, 7. S. E. & Maria gct North Lewis-
      burgh MM

PERRY
1905, 5, 11. Jessie (Doyle) Perry & minor
      dt, Hazel Doyle, recrq

PETERS
1880, 12, 9. Eliza recrq
1881, 1, 13. Frank & Kate recrq
1881, 1, 13. Hugh recrq

PETTIT
1885, 2, 12. A. J. Jeneura & Allie R. recrq
1885, 2, 12. Wm. H. recrq
1887, 10, 13. William dropped from mbrp
1888, 5, 10. Andrew & Genevra relrq
1889, 1, 10. Wesley & Ellen & Cora recrq

PIERCE
1875, 3, 11. Lyman recrq

PLOW
1883, 2, 8. Samuel & Charity recrq

PUTNAM
1889, 4, 11. Marsella recrq

REED
1888, 9, 13. Daniel & Susanna recrq

REES
1891, 1, 15. Cordelia rocf Westfield MM, Ind.,
        dtd 1891,1,1
1891, 7, 9. Delia gct Raisin MM, Mich.

REXFORD
1865, 8, 11. Hannah (form Healy) dis mcd

REYNOLDS
1846, 6, 13. Phebe d ae 61 bur Berlen, O.
1862, 1, 16. Miriam d ae 62 bur Berlen, O.

1849, 4, 20. Miriam rocf Gilead MM, dtd
        1849,1,23
1863, 6, 12. Daniel con mcd

RICHARDSON
1879, 5, 15. Jane recrq
1884, 11, 13. Julia W. recrq
1886, 1, 14. J. W. dropped from mbrp

RICKARD
1878, 2, 7. Orange J. & Jennie T. recrq
1879, 9, 14. Isaac S. & Jane recrq

RIDER
1877, 10, 11. Arabella & ch, William, Freder-
        ick, Cora, George F. & Grace, rocf Corn-
        wall MM, dtd 1877,6,28
1877, 10, 11. Emma Louisa rocf Cornwell MM,
        dtd 1877,6,28
1877, 12, 13. John recrq
1880, 4, 8. Emma gc
1880, 4, 8. Arabella & ch, Wm., Fred, Cora
        & Grace, gc

RIFE
1884, 11, 13. Daisy M. recrq
1884, 12, 18. Abram recrq
1885, 1, 15. Abram Sr. & John recrq

ROBERTS
1881, 1, 13. Albert & Eugene recrq

RUSCO
1897, 12, 9. Charity (form Hall) relrq

RUSSELL
1885, 2, 12. Minta Belle & Orville D. recrq
1887, 10, 13. Belle relrq

SANDS
1881, 1, 13. Nancy recrq

SATTISON
1885, 2, 12. Harriet & Clara recrq
1887, 10, 13. Clara relrq

SEYMOUR
1850, 9, 18. Levi d bur Greenwich

1850, 12, 20. Rhoda C. rmt Burger Mott
1874, 4, 9. Susan A. recrq
1875, 3, 11. Manning recrq
1886, 11, 11. Ella E. recrq
1889, 12, 12. Edward C., Eliza & Robbie recrq
1890, 1, 9. Waldo W. recrq

SHEETS
1879, 9, 14. William recrq
1880, 1, 15. Elizabeth H. recrq

SHELDON
1884, 11, 13. Nora recrq

SHERWOOD
1877, 6, 14. Phebe recrq

SHIPMAN
1881, 3, 10. Eunice & Gussie recrq

SHOUP
1887, 8, 13. Carrie (form Gibson) relrq

SHOURDS
1849, 2, 16. Mahetable & ch, Charlotte & ·
        Ruth, rocf Scipio MM, dtd 1849,1,17
1850, 3, 22. Ruth Sutherland (form Shrouds)
        dis mcd

SINGER
1882, 2, 9. Rachel gct Bear Creek MM, Ia.
        (with fam of Andrew Underwood)

SMITH
----, --, --. Willis R. d 1871,3,11; m Ann
        ----- d 1874,2,24 ae 83
        Ch: Alfred J. b 1814, 11, 25 d 1826, 9,23
            Phebe K.   " 1816, 10, 27
            Daniel   " 1819, 7, 3
            Amelia   " 1821, 6, 5
            William   " 1823, 6, 17
            Sarah   " 1825, 10, 23
            Mary   " 1829, 10, 3
            Ann Maria " 1831, 12, 24

1852, 9, 17. Masy (form Gifford) rpd mcd
1856, 1, 18. Wm. recrq
1863, 2, 13. Mary Golden (form Smith) con
        mcd
1870, 3, 10. Sarah relrq
1874, 6, 11. Asenath recrq
1874, 7, 9. Sarah recrq
1874, 8, 13. Celia, Yana, Alva, Willis J.,

SMITH, continued
      Sylinda Ann & Garland, ch Wm. T. & Ase-
      nath, recrq
1874, 8, 13. Charity recrq
1880, 12, 9. Daniel, Amelia, Sarah & Annie
      relrq
1880, 12, 9. Wm. T. & ch, Alva, Willis, Si-
      linda, Charity, Celia & Yana relrq
1881, 1, 13. Asenath dis
1892, 2, 11. Willis recrq

SONNAFRANK
1892, 2, 11. Bertha recrq

SPRINGER
1877, 4, 12. Lovina recrq

STANLEY
1877, 4, 12. Rhoda M. gct Goshen MM

STEVENS
1851, 1, 17. Betsy recrq
1851, 3, 21. Betsy rmt Peter Hathaway

STEWERT
1885, 2, 19. David C. recrq

STONE
1891, 10, 15. Wm. & Jenny recrq

STOTTS
1889, 1, 10. J. R. recrq

STOUT
1884, 12, 18. Rachel & Etta recrq

STRIMPLE
1902, 8, 14. Nettie M. glt East Greenwich
      M. E. Ch.

SUTHERLAND
1850, 3, 22. Ruth (form Shrouds) dis mcd

SUTTON
1883, 2, 8. James recrq

SWEET
1878, 2, 7. William, Irene, Lettie & Amelia
      recrq
1878, 2, 7. Charles W. recrq

TAYLOR
1900, 4, 12. Estelle recrq

THOMAS
1885, 3, 12. Rachel E. recrq

THRALL
1892, 2, 11. Frank & Anna recrq

TRAVIS
1869, 7, 15. .Harriett (form Hoag) dis mcd
1884, 11, 13. Daisy recrq

1884, 12, 18. Charles recrq
1884, 12, 18. Sarah recrq

TROUP
1889, 4, 11. William & Susan recrq
1889, 12, 12. Frank & Maria recrq
1895, 9, 12. Hattie & Mary recrq
1895, 10, 10. Frank & w & ch, Mary & Hattie,
      gct Milan MM
1897, 8, 12. Frank & two minor dt rocf Milan
      MM

TUCKER
1885, 2, 19. John W. recrq

TURNER
1884, 12, 18. Flaves G. recrq
1887, 7, 14. Flavis dropped from mbrp
1887, 7, 14. Stanley dropped from mbrp

UNDERHILL
----, --, --. Harvey & Anna
      Ch: Mary E.   b 1848, 10, 20 d 1852, 5,14
          Rhoda M.   " 1851, 12, 26
          Lydia Ann   " 1850, 7, 28 " 1852, 6,25
          Rachel A.   " 1854, 1, 3
          Andrew
           Harvey   " 1856, 11, 3
          Emily D.   " 1857, 8, 10 " 1862,12,17
          John Eddy   " 1861, 4, 2
          Charles R. " 1862, 9, 11
          Emline A.   " 1865, 8, 25
          Perline A. " 1867, 7, 4
1879, 11, 8. George Calvin, s Andrew H. &
      Jennie, b
1878, 12, 17. Andrew m Jane E. BALL

1881, 4, 14. Harvey relrq
1882, 2, 9. Harvey & w, Anna, & ch, John E.,
      Charles R., Emeline A. & Perlina A., gct
      Bear Creek MM, Ia.
1882, 2, 9. Andrew H. & w, Jane E., & s,
      George Colvin, also Rachel Singer, gct
      Bear Creek MM, Ia.

VAN SICKLE
1877, 4, 12. Josie recrq

VINING
1880, 4, 8. Marion & Flora E. recrq

WAGNER
1875, 9, 9. Charles recrq
1883, 1, 11. Chas. & Anna [Waggoner] relrq
1885, 2, 12. Tommy [Waggoner] recrq
1886, 6, 10. Myrtle [Wagoner] recrq
1887, 10, 13. Mirtie [Waggoner] dropped from
      mbrp
1887, 12, 15. Rose [Waggoner] recrq

WALTON
1886, 5, 13. John & W, Emeline, recrq

WARD
1881, 1, 13. John, Sarah & Joseph recrq

WARREN
1858, 4, 24. John d ae 81 bur Menter, O.
1864, 12, 24. Hannah d bur Menter, O.

1851, 6, 20. John [Waren] & w, Hannah, rocf
    Marlborough MM, dtd 1851,5,27

WASHBURN
1860, 12, 20. Joseph d bur Greenwich
1881, 3, 16. James d ae 71

1854, 6, 16. James rmt Rachel Hathaway
1877, 7, 12. Zelia recrq
1882, 1, 12. Rachel gc; rem & settled within
    limits of Salem MM

WATSON
----, --, --. Benjamin & Mary G.
    Ch: John
        Granger   b 1838, 6, 29
        Elizabeth
        Catharine " 1842, 5, 9

1880, 4, 8. Benjamin, Mary, John & Elizabeth
    gc

WIER
1895, 1, 10. George & w, Martha, & ch, Denslow
    & Jessie, rocf Smithfield MM

WILCOX
1878, 2, 7. Benjamin, Jane & Deborah recrq

WILLIAMS
1867, 5, 10. Susan Jane (form Bartlett) con
    mcd
1872, 4, 11. Susan Jane recrq

        *   *   *   *   *   *   *

BARTLETT
1852, 5, 21. James & fam gct Little Egg Har-
    bor MM
1853, 12, 16. James & w, Phebe Ann, & ch,
    Ann B., Martha W. & George J., rocf Little
    Egg Harbor MM, dtd 1853,10,13
1853, 3, 18. Phebe Ann York (form Bartlett)
    con mcd
1856, 12, 19. Ann B. Osborn (form Bartlett)
    dis mcd
1857, 11, 20. Agnes McCullow (form Bartlett)

1872, 4, 11. Armett recrq
1883, 2, 8. Frank recrq
1904, 7, 14. Armett dis

WINDER
1876, 7, 13. Alice recrq

WILLIS
1884, 11, 13. George W. recrq
1885, 11, 15. George, Brown & Mary E. recrq
1887, 2, 10. Mary E. relrq

WITTER
1885, 2, 12. Grant D. recrq
1887, 10, 13. Grant dropped from mbrp

WOOD
1871, 8, 12. Sarah Ann d bur Greenwich

1854, 8, 18. Daniel B. rmt Matilda A. Coutant
1857, 8, 21. Sarah Ann rocf Marlborough MM,
    dtd 1857,6,24
1857, 8, 21. Susan E. rocf Marlborough MM,
    N. Y., dtd 1857,6,24
1860, 11, 16. Susan E. rmt Samuel Haviland
1860, 9, 21. Daniel B. & w, Matilda, & fam
    gct Winneshiek MM, Ia.
1865, 10, 13. Samuel A. con mcd
1866, 5, 11. Samuel A. gct Winneshiek MM, Ia.
1872, 2, 18. Daniel T. rocf Gilead MM, dtd
    1871,12,19
1873, 5, 15. Daniel gct Gilead MM, O.

WOOLEY
1884, 12, 18. Charles recrq
1884, 12, 18. George recrq

YORK
1853, 3, 18. Phebe Ann (form Bartlett) con
    mcd
1873, 3, 13. Phebe Ann relrq

        *   *   *   *   *   *   *

    con mcd
1859, 9, 11. Martha Culver (form Bartlett)
    con mcd
1867, 5, 10. Susan Jane Williams (form Bart-
    lett) con mcd
1866, 4, 10. Emily D. relrq
1868, 4, 10. Emilie relrq
1869, 6, 10. George relrq
1872, 4, 11. Harriet J. recrq
1874, 8, 13. Clara K. recrq
1874, 8, 13. George J. recrq

SEITY
1881, 1, 13. Susan recrq

BURDGE
1891, 3, 12. Albert recrq

COLUMBUS MONTHLY MEETING

        Columbus Monthly Meeting, Franklin Co., Ohio, was established by Short Creek Quarterly Meeting, 6th Mo. 3, 1874, and was transferred from Short Creek Quarterly Meeting to Alum Creek Quarterly Meeting 4th Mo. 7, 1875.

        After 12th Mo. 5, 1923, the records continue under the name of Highland Avenue Monthly Meeting with no comment as to reason for the change in name.

RECORDS

ABRAM
1913, 3, 5. Wm. & Edith recrq
1919, 3, 5. Wm. & May gct Long Lake MM, Ind.
1920, 3, 3. Harold H., Luzena & Roy recrq
1921, 5, 9. J. H. & Minnie recrq

ACKLEY
1918, 4, 3. Mary recrq
1919, 5, 7. Walter recrq
1921, 7, 6. Mary & Walter dropped from mbrp

ADAMS
1899, 3, 1. Bell recrq
1907, 12, 4. Belle dropped from mbrp

ADKINS
1900, 3, 7. Minnie recrq
1908, 6, 3. Anna dropped from mbrp

AGEN
1897, 3, 3. Mamie recrq
1897, 3, 3. Hattie recrq
1909, 7, 7. Mamie & Hattie dropped from mbrp

AISEL
1904, 6, 1. Winnie recrq
1911, 9, 6. Thomas dropped from mbrp

AKIN
1897, 3, 3. Lizzie recrq
1909, 7, 7. Albert & Lizzie dropped from
    mbrp

ALLEN
1920, 5, 5. Wm. H. A. [Allam] recrq
1922, 2, 2. Vida E. recrq

ALTHEN
1900, 11, 2. William dropped from mbrp

ANDERSON
1836, 9, 16. John, s Wm. & Mary (Cosand), b
1838, 2, 25. Rilla, dt James & Rachel (Vars-
    sey), b
1861, 11, 7. Mahala b
1863, 12, 23. James b
1897, 3, 15. Rilla, dt James & Rachel (Vars-
    sey), d

1904, 7, 6. John & Louisa recrq
1908, 6, 3. Geneva Kailer dropped from mbrp
1913, 7, 2. John & Louisa dropped from mbrp
1917, 7, 4. Eva relrq

ARTHUR
1913, 3, 5. W. A. & w recrq
1916, 12, 6. W. A. [Arthurs] relrq
1919, 5, 7. Mrs. Will dropped from mbrp

ASHER
1905, 3, 1. Theda A. recrq

1906, 2, 7. Elizabeth recrq
1907, 3, 6. Thomas recrq
1912, 1, 3. Lloyd F. recrq

ATHER
1909, 4, 7. Emma recrq

ATKINS
1905, 9, 6. Anna E. recrq
1909, 7, 7. Minnie dropped from mbrp

ATKINSON
1909, 7, 7. Anna E. dropped from mbrp

AYERS
1897, 7, 7. Anna & Sadie E. recrq
1906, 10, 3. Charles recrq
1909, 7, 7. Thomas dropped from mbrp
1909, 7, 7. Annie E. dropped from mbrp
1909, 7, 7. Sadie dropped from mbrp

BACKNYER
1897, 3, 3. Katie recrq

BAILEY
1904, 8, 3. Hester Harris gct Whittier MM,
    Calif.

BAIRD
1896, 3, 4. Lennard E. recrq
1911, 6, 7. L. E. & w & ch, Earl W., Ray
    H. & Warren, dropped from mbrp

BALL
1913, 10, 1. Phebe Faust gct Orange MM

BANSETER
1923, 5, 2. Anna M. recrq

BARBER
1900, 11, 2. Charles & Minnie recrq
1901, 12, 4. Carl recrq
1909, 7, 7. Minnie N. dropped from mbrp
1909, 10, 6. Annetta G. relrq

BARFELL
1898, 9, 7. Othias recrq
1901, 6, 5. Othias dropped from mbrp

BARKER
1909, 4, 7. Ola recrq
1912, 10, 2. Stella Conard relrq
1913, 3, 5. Della relrq
1913, 7, 2. Ola dropped from mbrp

BARRETT
1897, 10, 6. Mary gct Spencer MM, Iowa

BARRY
1908, 10, 7. H. E. & w, Jessie B., & ch,
    Hazel Bell & Esther Lenora, recrq

BATES
1906, 8, 1. W. G., Mary & Paul recrq
1908, 3, 4. Orville recrq
1908, 3, 4. Raymond recrq
1909, 10, 6. Paul relrq
1910, 11, 2. W. J. & w, J., gct Cleveland MM,
          O.

BAUMAN
1906, 4, 4. Walter recrq
1909, 7, 7. Walter dropped from mbrp

BEAMAN
1909, 7, 7. Grace dropped from mbrp

BEAVER
1898, 12, 7. Hazel recrq

BECKWITH
1899, 12, 6. Ellen Jane recrq
1901, 2, 6. Charles O. recrq
1901, 5, 7. Cybella C. recrq
1913, 7, 2. Charles O. & Cecelia C. dropped
          from mbrp

BELK
1896, 3, 4. Nettie recrq

BELLAMY
1909, 4, 7. Maude recrq
1909, 4, 7. Clarence recrq
1909, 4, 7. Sarah recrq
1909, 7, 7. Florence dropped from mbrp
1912, 10, 2. Maud dropped from mbrp

BELL
1905, 12, 6. Lena recrq
1908, 12, 6. Lena dropped from mbrp
1909, 7, 7. Nettie dropped from mbrp

BENNETT
1898, 6, 1. George dropped from mbrp
1904, 12, 7. S. F. recrq
1909, 7, 7. S. F. dropped from mbrp
1909, 7, 7. Mary dropped from mbrp
1914, 3, 4. Ellen recrq
1919, 3, 5. Ellen dropped from mbrp

BENSON
1869, 10, 25. Martha, dt Seth & Lucinda (An-
          thony) Kern, b
1870, 1, 18. Robert, s Josiah & Ruth (Osborn)
          b
1896, 6, 10. Catharine b
1896, 11, 23. William b
1902, 2, 13. Mary b

BERG
1909, 4, 7. Hazel recrq

BETTON
1897, 4, 17. Eliza & dt, Ella, recrq
1897, 5, 5. Mary [Belton] recrq

1898, 6, 1. Ella, Mary & Eliza dropped from
          mbrp

BINNS
1876, 4, 5. Lillie Aurelia, minor dt Amos &
          Rebecca, both dec, rocf White Water MM,
          Ind.
1876, 11, 1. Charles rocf White Water MM, Ind.
1899, 12, 6. Mary E. recrq
1909, 7, 7. Oliver H. & Chas. S. dropped
          from mbrp
1921, 11, 2. Charles S. recrq

BIRDSELL
1904, 2, 3. Lena & Edna recrq
1909, 7, 7. Byron F. dropped from mbrp
1909, 7, 7. Cole dropped from mbrp
1909, 7, 7. John dropped from mbrp
1909, 7, 7. Boswell dropped from mbrp
1909, 7, 7. William dropped from mbrp
1909, 7, 7. Edna dropped from mbrp

BLACK
1876, 4, 5. Lora Ella recrq

BLOSSER
1913, 5, 7. Mamie recrq
1922, 2, 2. Merle & Thelma recrq

BLOWERS
1903, 4, 1. Hosetta rocf Washington MM
1906, 12, 6. Etta dropped from mbrp

BONN
1899, 4, 5. John Wesley & Mary recrq
1900, 6, 6. John & w relrq

BONDEN
1908, 6, 3. Myrtle dropped from mbrp

BOOTH
1911, 4, 5. Daisy May recrq

BORDER
1916, 4, 5. Ray & Constance recrq
1923, 12, 5. Ray & w, Constance, relrq

BOSTWICK
1914, 3, 4. Harry & Bettie recrq
1916, 6, 7. Harry & Birdie dropped from
          mbrp

BOSWELL
1902, 3, 5. John recrq

BOWDEN
1906, 12, 6. Myrtle recrq

BOWEN
1910, 9, 6. Robert J. & w, Archie, recrq
1914, 9, 2. Robert & Addie dropped from
          mbrp

BOWER
1898, 5, 4. Mary relrq

BRADFORD
1896, 12, 2. Charles recrq
1906, 12, 6. Rena dropped from mbrp
1913, 7, 2. Charles dropped from mbrp

BRATT
1909, 7, 7. Frank recrq

BRAZIER
1916, 4, 5. Effie recrq

BREHM
1899, 2, 1. Rosa recrq
1909, 7, 7. Rosa dropped from mbrp

BRETZ
1897, 3, 3. Albert recrq
1909, 7, 7. George A. dropped from mbrp
1909, 7, 7. Albert dropped from mbrp

BRINDENSTEIN
1909, 7, 7. Amanda C. dropped from mbrp

BRINK
1919, 1, 1. Mrs. S. M. recrq

BROBECK
1909, 7, 7. Carrie E. & Joseph dropped from
    mbrp

BROCKELESBY
1908, 7, 1. Peter recrq
1912, 6, 5. Peter [Brocklesby] dropped from
    mbrp

BROILER
1896, 3, 4. Cyrus M. [Brollier] & w, Rosa,
    recrq
1898, 6, 1. S. N. [Broyler] dropped from
    mbrp
1898, 12, 7. Sadie [Brollier] recrq
1901, 2, 6. Rosa [Broller] recrq
1909, 7, 7. Cyrus & Rose dropped from mbrp
1909, 7, 7. Sadie dropped from mbrp
1909, 7, 7. Rosa dropped from mbrp

BROUGH
1909, 7, 7. James S. dropped from mbrp

BROWN
1907, 12, 4. Mrs. Wm. Henry [Browne] dropped
    from mbrp
1908, 10, 7. Walter W. & w, Nellie, & dt,
    Esther, rocf Raisin MM
1909, 7, 7. Hazel dropped from mbrp
1910, 9, 6. Walter H. & fam gct Pleasant
    Valley MM
1918, 12, 4. Benjamin recrq

BRUNER
1902, 7, 2. Henry recrq
1909, 7, 7. John dropped from mbrp

BUCKIEN
1909, 7, 7. Katie dropped from mbrp

BUCKMYER
1900, 11, 2. Anna dropped from mbrp

BUNKER
1875, 5, 5. Edwin M. rocf Gilead MM
1876, 4, 5. Mary A. recrq

BURG
1911, 9, 6. Hazel & Henry dropped from mbrp

BURKE
1904, 4, 6. Willice Melon recrq
1905, 4, 5. Effie M. recrq
1909, 7, 7. W. M. dropped from mbrp

BUSH
1912, 3, 6. Charles & Carrie recrq
1915, 7, 7. Charles & Carrie dropped from
    mbrp
1923, 11, 7. Aletha May recrq

BUTLER
1909, 7, 7. James dropped from mbrp
1911, 9, 6. Mrs. dropped from mbrp

CALENTINE
1904, 4, 6. Tivilie recrq
1909, 7, 7. Tivilia dropped from mbrp

CAPEROFF
1921, 3, 2. Doris relrq

CARL
1917, 2, 7. Rosalee M. & Margaret E. recrq
1920, 7, 7. Rosetta & Margaret dropped from
    mbrp

CARLISLE
1907, 8, 7. Charlotte recrq
1909, 10, 6. Charlotta relrq

CARNEY
1912, 12, 4. Andrew N. & w, Margaret E., &
    dt, Marguerite, recrq
1918, 2, 6. Andrew relrq

CARSON
1905, 2, 1. Frank recrq

CARTER
1913, 5, 7. May recrq
1918, 7, 3. May dropped from mbrp
CARTRIGHT
1842, 11, 13. Jonathan, s Jesse & Mary (Haley)
    b
1844, 3, 18. Hannah b

CARTRIGHT, continued
1869, 2, 10. Murray b
1872, 6, 14. Edward b

CHAFFIN
1901, 9, 1. A. M. & E. J. recrq
1909, 7, 7. A. & E. J. dropped from mbrp

CHAMBERS
1896, 3, 4. Wm. J. & w, Emma, recrq
1898, 12, 7. John C. rocf Upper MM, Va.
1898, 12, 7. Ethel recrq
1909, 7, 7. Wm. J. dropped from mbrp
1916, 3, 1. Emma dropped from mbrp

CHANEY
1907, 10, 2. W. T. [Channey] & w, Ida, recrq
1910, 2, 2. Cyrus C. & Maggie Alice, Inez &
    Herman, recrq
1912, 7, 3. Cyrus, Maggie, Alice, Inez &
    Herman L. gct West Fork MM, O.
1917, 10, 3. Cyrus & w, Margaret, & s, Her-
    mon, recrq

CHELLIS
1902, 1, 1. George W. recrq
1909, 7, 7. George W. [Chillis] dropped
    from mbrp

CLARK
1896, 3, 4. John recrq
1905, 2, 1. Scott recrq
1906, 9, 5. Wm. Mark recrq
1909, 4, 7. Minnie recrq
1909, 7, 7. John dropped from mbrp
1910, 6, 1. Ethel recrq
1911, 4, 5. Nancy E. & Edith recrq
1912, 10, 2. Minnie dropped from mbrp
1913, 3, 5. Jane recrq
1913, 3, 5. Bernice recrq
1913, 3, 5. H. D. recrq
1913, 7, 2. Wm. M. & Libbie dropped from
    mbrp
1916, 7, 5. W. D. dropped from mbrp
1918, 9, 4. Nancy dropped from mbrp
1922, 2, 2. Harry & w, Nellie B., & ch, Mar-
    jorie, Kenneth E., Lloyd J. & Floyd C.,
    rocf West Grove MM, Ind.
1922, 2, 2. Vera recrq

CLOUSER
1899, 2, 1. A. recrq

COATES
1905, 9, 6. Christopher Columbus & Amanda
    [Coats] recrq
1907, 6, 5. Christopher Columbus [Coats]
    dropped from mbrp
1909, 3, 3. Jemima P. [Coate] & s, Benjamin
    W., rocf West Branch MM
1909, 7, 7. Amanda dropped from mbrp
1913, 12, 3. Amanda & dt, Mary B. S. recrq
1914, 4, 1. Amanda & dt, Mary S., dropped

from mbrp
1915, 7, 7. Jemima J. gct Van Wert MM
1922, 11, 1. B. W. [Coate] relrq

COCKEREL
1901, 10, 2. Benjamin D. & Roulber N. recrq
1910, 12, 7. John [Cochrel] recrq
1921, 7, 6. Benjamin D. & Rose [Cochrel]
    dropped from mbrp

COFFIN
1913, 5, 7. Anna Haldy gct Adrian MM, Mich.

COLE
1899, 11, 1. Jennie recrq
1906, 9, 5. Byron F. recrq
1907, 2, 6. A. F. dropped from mbrp
1907, 6, 5. Jennie relrq

COLIER
1906, 2, 7. Amos recrq
1909, 7, 7. Elizabeth A. dropped from mbrp

COLLINS
1902, 9, 10. Joseph recrq
1904, 1, 6. Homer & w, Melvina, recrq
1904, 1, 6. Lufern recrq
1907, 7, 3. Ransom & Ella recrq
1909, 7, 7. Ranso, & Ella dropped from mbrp
1909, 7, 7. Joseph dropped from mbrp
1912, 6, 5. Homer & Melvina relrq

COMPTON
1899, 3, 1. C. H. recrq
1899, 4, 5. Irvin recrq
1911, 9, 6. Irvin dropped from mbrp

CONGER
1901, 6, 5. Lettie O. recrq

CONLEY
1919, 9, 3. Mrs. C. C. recrq
1919, 11, 5. Chas. C. rocf Cleveland MM, O.
1922, 2, 2. Jeanette & Paul Jones recrq

CONRAD
1917, 9, 28. Clarence d

1908, 4, 7. Stella recrq
1914, 3, 4. Clarence, Carrie, Hilda May,
    Curboy & Harry, recrq
1915, 4, 17. Goldie recrq
1923, 7, 4. Harry & w, Myrtle, & ch, Harold
    & Orabel, dropped from mbrp

COOPER
1911, 12, 6. Mabel recrq
1913, 5, 7. James F. recrq
1915, 4, 17. Carrie Laota & Elmer, recrq
1916, 7, 5. James & Effie dropped from mbrp
1918, 4, 3. Ardelia recrq
1919, 3, 5. Elmer dropped from mbrp
1921, 7, 6. Ardelia dropped from mbrp

COPE
1903, 10, 7. Frederick J. & w, Etta V., & ch,
          Inez A. & Lois M., rocf Salem MM
1907, 10, 2. Fred J. & w, Marietta V., & ch,
          Inez, gct Adrian MM, Mich.
1907, 10, 2. Louis M. gct Adrian MM, Mich.

CORBIN
1898, 6, 1. Thomas N. dropped from mbrp
1907, 4, 3. Ellen N. & ch, Bryce T. & Earl
          T., recrq
1909, 7, 7. Jerome & Norah B. [Corben]
          dropped from mbrp
1910, 3, 2. Ellen & ch, Bruce, Lafayette &
          Earl, dropped from mbrp

CORSEN
1916, 3, 2. Frank & Ella dropped from mbrp

COX
1896, 3, 4. J. B. & w, Mary, recrq
1909, 7, 7. Joseph B. & Mary dropped from
          mbrp

COWGILL
1876, 11, 1. John & Elenor roc
1901, 12, 4. Josephine recrq

CREW
1877, 1, 3. Mary H. rocf Westland MM, O.,
          dtd 1876,12,21

CRITES
1903, 3, 6. Francis H. recrq

CROMWELL
1912, 5, 1. Anna recrq

CROOKS
1908, 5, 6. Anna M. recrq
1914, 5, 6. Anna M. dropped from mbrp

CROSSEN
1913, 11, 5. Deane & Bess recrq

CURL
1901, 2, 6. Nancy E. recrq

CUSTARD
1905, 5, 3. J. W. [Custeard] recrq
1912, 10, 2. J. W. dropped from mbrp

CUTHBERTSON
1913, 3, 5. Alice recrq
1916, 3, 1. Alice dropped from mbrp

DAGUE
1913, 3, 5. Lester recrq

DAUGHERTY
1898, 12, 7. Jessie recrq
1909, 7, 7. Jessie dropped from mbrp
1909, 7, 7. Arda dropped from mbrp

DAVENPORT
1896, 3, 4. Clark & w, Lucy, recrq
1898, 6, 1. Charles dropped from mbrp
1898, 12, 7. Charles recrq
1898, 12, 7. Anna recrq
1903, 1, 7. Anna relrq
1905, 3, 1. Wm. & Armeda recrq
1906, 12, 6. Will dropped from mbrp
1909, 7, 7. Lucy dropped from mbrp
1911, 6, 7. Amelia dropped from mbrp

DAVIDSON
1898, 6, 1. Hiram dropped from mbrp
1900, 3, 7. Ethel recrq
1909, 7, 7. Martha & Mack dropped from
          mbrp
1909, 7, 7. Ethel dropped from mbrp

DAVIS
1922, 2, 2. Birta & Flora recrq

DAWSON
1922, 2, 2. John & w, Marie, recrq

DAY
1913, 3, 5. Edward E. recrq
1914, 5, 6. Edward E. dropped from mbrp

DAYMUDE
1905, 10, 4. Cora recrq

DEAN
1900, 11, 2. Addie dropped from mbrp

DEEMS
1910, 11, 2. Eliza P. relrq

DEITCHLE
1915, 1, 6. Clarence & Carl [Deitchel] rec-
          rq
1915, 2, 3. Lula recrq
1921, 7, 6. Lula dropped from mbrp

DENNISON
1897, 4, 17. Charles & w, Laura, & dt, Maris,
          recrq
1913, 7, 2. Maria dropped from mbrp
1916, 6, 7. Goldie dropped from mbrp

DESHLER
1897, 3, 3. George recrq
1900, 12, 5. George relrq
1905, 9, 6. George & w, Helen, recrq
1908, 2, 5. Geo. A. & w, Helen, & ch gct
          Goshen MM

DEVON
1896, 3, 4. Addie recrq

DIXON
1905, 9, 6. W. J. rocf Los Angeles MM,
          Calif.
1909, 12, 6. W. T. gct Cleveland MM, O.

DIXON, continued
1916, 4, 5. Bessie Marie recrq

DOLDER
1897, 3, 3. Lillie & Willie recrq
1909, 7, 7. Wm. dropped from mbrp
1914, 4, 1. Wm. A. & Bessie recrq
1916, 7, 5. Rolland Miller & Ruth Eldora,
    ch Will & Bertha, recrq

DONALDSON
1909, 7, 7. W. G. dropped from mbrp

DONLEY
1900, 11, 2. Jonathan dropped from mbrp

DONNELLY
1909, 7, 7. Mary R. dropped from mbrp

DONNIGAN
1900, 1, 3. Mattie recrq

DORRELY
1900, 8, 1. Ada recrq

DOTY
1896, 3, 4. Joseph A. & w, Maude, recrq
1900, 11, 2. Joseph dropped from mbrp
1909, 7, 7. Mollie & Maud dropped from mbrp
1916, 4, 5. Mabel relrq

DOYLE
1904, 3, 2. Bessie recrq
1909, 7, 7. Bessie dropped from mbrp
1909, 9, 8. Edward & Bessie recrq
1915, 7, 7. Edward & Bessie dropped from
    mbrp

DUMM
1916, 4, 5. Bert & w, Etta, recrq

DUNBAR
1918, 4, 3. Helen recrq

DUNN
1909, 7, 7. Florence recrq

DURR
1898, 12, 7. Leona recrq
1902, 3, 5. Leona relrq

DUTTON
1899, 2, 1. Hattie recrq

DYER
1916, 3, 1. Ethel dropped from mbrp

EARL
1903, 7, 1. Mrs. recrq
1907, 3, 6. Edith relrq

EDGERTON
1897, 10, 6. Frank A. [Edgington] recrq

1900, 4, 4. Frank relrq

ELFORD
1923, 11, 7. Luther Edgar & w, Delia, & ch,
    Byron & Virginia, rocf Clark Ave. MM,
    Cleveland

ELLIS
1904, 2, 3. Robert & dt, Kitty, rocf Chagrin
    Valley MM
1904, 5, 4. Kittie A. M. relrq

EMMONS
1902, 3, 5. Frank & Mary recrq
1909, 7, 7. Frank & Mary dropped from mbrp

ERLENWEIN
1922, 4, 5. Howard recrq

EVANS
1899, 3, 1. Frank & Hattie recrq
1900, 2, 7. Daniel & Anna recrq
1900, 3, 7. Mary recrq
1909, 7, 7. Jonathan dropped from mbrp
1909, 7, 7. Frank dropped from mbrp
1909, 7, 7. Hattie dropped from mbrp
1909, 7, 7. Mary dropped from mbrp
1913, 7, 2. Daniel & Anna dropped from mbrp

FABRION
1914, 3, 4. Gustave R. & Ellen recrq

FARMER
1915, 4, 7. Mrs. Minnie recrq
1915, 4, 7. Addie E. recrq
1919, 3, 5. Ada & Minnie dropped from mbrp

FAULKNER
1900, 12, 5. Mary relrq
1901, 5, 7. Lewis B. recrq

FAWCETT
1919, 12, 3. Myrl recrq

FETHEROLT
1910, 2, 2. Lillie recrq
1910, 2, 2. Cecil May recrq
1910, 2, 2. Beryl recrq
1910, 2, 2. Margaret recrq
1910, 2, 2. Lillie recrq
1910, 11, 2. Lulu [Fetheralt] & ch relrq
1910, 12, 7. Lillie [Fetheralt] & ch rst
1918, 4, 3. Cecile [Fetherhoff] recrq
1918, 7, 3. Marguerite [Featheroll] recrq

FEEN
1899, 2, 1. Calla recrq
1917, 3, 7. Joanna Marie recrq

FELLOWS
1905, 4, 5. Frederick E. recrq
1905, 10, 4. Augustus recrq
1906, 12, 6. A. M. dropped from mbrp

FELLOWS, continued
1907, 2, 6. F. E. dropped from mbrp

FERGASON
1909, 7, 7. Elmer dropped from mbrp

FETTERS
1900, 3, 7. Clyde recrq
1909, 7, 7. Mary A. dropped from mbrp
1909, 7, 7. Clyde dropped from mbrp

FISHER
1896, 3, 4. James H. & w, Etta Irena, & dt,
     Ora Viola, recrq
1904, 7, 6. Sarah recrq
1912, 7, 3. Sarah E. dropped from mbrp
1913, 7, 2. James H. & Ella dropped from
     mbrp
1916, 6, 7. Paul recrq

FLEMING
1897, 3, 3. Mary [Flemming] recrq
1897, 3, 3. Mrs. James [Flemming] recrq
1902, 1, 1. Viola & Josephine [Flemming]
     recrq
1904, 6, 1. Jennie [Flemming] recrq
1904, 6, 1. Joseph H. [Flemming] recrq
1907, 12, 4. Joseph dropped from mbrp
1908, 6, 3. Lena M. recrq
1909, 7, 7. Samuel dropped from mbrp
1909, 7, 7. Mary dropped from mbrp
1909, 7, 7. Mrs. Joseph dropped from mbrp
1910, 7, 6. Lena dropped from mbrp
1911, 6, 7. Viola dropped from mbrp
1913, 2, 5. Jennie relrq
1915, 3, 3. Viola relrq
1916, 3, 1. Josephine dropped from mbrp

FLETCHER
1900, 11, 2. Joseph, Elizabeth & Joseph W.
     dropped from mbrp

FOGG
1874, 10, 7. William & w, Eliza Mary, & dt,
     Hellen, recrq

FOLTZ
1912, 1, 3. Eugene C. recrq
1913, 7, 2. Eugene C. dropped from mbrp
1919, 5, 7. Gladys recrq

FORESTER
1913, 3, 5. Lillian recrq
1914, 4, 1. Anna & dt, Gertrude & Freda S.,
     relrq

FOSSMYER
1902, 2, 5. Omelia recrq
1909, 7, 7. Omelia dropped from mbrp

FOSTER
1902, 6, 4. Grace M. recrq
1902, 6, 4. Dewitt L. rocf East Bend MM,N.C.

1906, 5, 2. DeWitt & w, Grace, & ch, Paul &
     Carl, gct Orange MM

FOUST
1910, 4, 6. Martha & Louisa recrq

FRAZELL
1897, 3, 3. Mary recrq
1897, 3, 3. Joshua recrq
1898, 6, 1. Joshua dropped from mbrp
1900, 11, 2. Joshua dropped from mbrp

FRIEND
1909, 7, 7. Albert & Olive K. dropped from
     mbrp
1913, 3, 5. Earl J. & w, Ollie, & ch, May-
     nard, recrq

FRISTO
1902, 9, 10. Elma recrq
1902, 9, 10. Nellie recrq
1902, 9, 10. Dollie recrq
1919, 3, 5. Elmer dropped from mbrp

FUNSTON
1899, 3, 1. Atwood & Alice recrq
1909, 7, 7. Joseph E. dropped from mbrp
1909, 10, 6. Alice relrq
1911, 9, 6. Joseph dropped from mbrp

FURBAY
1919, 9, 3. Leta Young gct Mt. Gilead MM

GARISH
1907, 5, 1. Comrade recrq
1909, 11, 3. Conrad [Gerrish] dropped from
     mbrp

GARRIGUS
1906, 8, 1. A. L. & w, Lydia, & s, Samuel,
     recrq
1910, 4, 6. A. S. & w, Lydia, & s, Samuel
     Wayne, relrq

GEARY
1899, 2, 1. Elizabeth M. recrq
1901, 10, 2. Elizabeth dropped from mbrp
1909, 7, 7. Elizabeth [Garry] dropped from
     mbrp

GERREN
1898, 12, 7. Feba O. recrq
1909, 7, 7. C. Felba dropped from mbrp

GERRMINHARD
1896, 10, 7. Mathew & w, Ella, & ch, Lizzie,
     Harry, Gussie & Samuel, recrq

GIBSON
1906, 10, 3. Mable rocf Short Creek MM, O.,
     dtd 1906,9,19
1909, 7, 7. Mabel dropped from mbrp

GILL
1899, 7, 5.   Wallace relrq
1900, 3, 7.   Wallace recrq
1902, 11, 5. Lottie Winona Cole recrq
1906, 12, 6. George E. & Louisa dropped from
    mbrp

GILLEN
1913, 3, 5.   Elba, Floyd, Grace & Dorothy
    recrq
1913, 7, 2.   Ella, Floyd, Grace & Dorothy
    dropped from mbrp

GINDER
1910, 1, 5.   Mary recrq

GINTER
1921, 8, 3.   Nora Stebbins rocf Cleveland MM

GLICK
1910, 4, 6.   Bessie recrq
1910, 9, 6.   Sophia recrq
1920, 7, 7.   Mrs. & Bessie relrq

GOFF
1909, 7, 7.   James dropped from mbrp
1918, 10, 2. James J. [Gough] recrq

GOODING
1900, 12, 5. Neda & Bertha relrq
1900, 12, 5. Stanley & Esther relrq
1901, 5, 7.   Edith recrq
1912, 5, 1.   Edith relrq

GOODWIN
1909, 12, 1. Lena recrq
1915, 7, 7.   Lena dropped from mbrp

GRAFEUSTINE
1902, 9, 10. M. H. & Mabel recrq
1909, 7, 7.   M. H. & Mabel [Grofenstein]
    dropped from mbrp

GRAVES
1899, 4, 5.   Curtis recrq

GREBBS
1876, 12, 6. Frank rocf Dublin MM, Ireland

GREEN
1902, 12, 3. Francetta recrq
1904, 3, 2.   Phebe dropped from mbrp
1909, 7, 7.   Francis dropped from mbrp

GOODRING
1905, 4, 5.   Edith rocf Orange MM

GRAMBO
1913, 7, 2.   Catherine dropped from mbrp

GREGG
1905, 2, 1.   J. C. recrq
1911, 6, 7.   James M. [Greeg] dropped from

    mbrp

GROUSSER
1901, 11, 6. Emily Jane recrq
1902, 2, 5.   E. J. dropped from mbrp

GROVES
1896, 2, 5.   Lizzie recrq
1898, 12, 7. Annetta [Grove] recrq
1909, 7, 7.   Alexander dropped from mbrp
1909, 7, 7.   Curtis dropped from mbrp

GRUESSER
1909, 10, 6. Emily J. recrq
1910, 6, 1.   Emily J. relrq

GUMMINHART
1909, 7, 7.   George & Louisa, & Wm., Ella,
    Lizzie, Harry, Gussie & Samuel, dropped
    from mbrp

GUMP
1913, 12, 3. Florence E. rst

GUTHRIE
1896, 3, 4.   Katherine & Katie roc
1902, 4, 2.   Katherine relrq
1909, 7, 7.   Katie dropped from mbrp

HADLEY
1902, 1, 1.   Joseph C. & w, Adalade, rocf
    Goshen MM
1904, 7, 6.   Adalaide G. gct Goshen MM
1907, 7, 3.   Eva R. recrq

HAERING
1914, 12, 2. Anna recrq
1915, 4, 17. Clarence L. recrq

HAGUE
1909, 7, 7.   Henry W. dropped from mbrp
1910, 9, 6.   Susan relrq
1910, 9, 6.   R. E. relrq
1910, 9, 6.   Helen relrq
1910, 9, 6.   M. S. relrq
1910, 9, 6.   Joseph relrq

HAHN
1909, 7, 7.   Mary dropped from mbrp

HALDY
1913, 2, 5.   Arthur gct Short Creek MM, O.
1915, 1, 6.   Howard relrq

HALLWOOD
1899, 2, 1.   Henry recrq

HAM
1898, 6, 1.   James dropped from mbrp
1909, 7, 7.   Frankie dropped from mbrp

HAMER
1914, 12, 2. Don P., Ida & Carol recrq

HAMER, continued
1916, 4, 5. Victor recrq

HAMIGER
1909, 7, 7. Israel J. dropped from mbrp

HAMILTON
1917, 2, 7. Gale W. & Mabel recrq

HAMOND
1902, 9, 10. Lyda recrq
1909, 7, 7. Lida [Hammond] dropped from mbrp

HANDY
1918, 12, 4. Herbert A. rocf Newport News MM

HANNA
1896, 3, 4. Lucy recrq

HARDING
1908, 7, 1. Peter & Kate recrq

HARMON
1897, 3, 3. Hattie E. recrq
1909, 7, 7. Lucy dropped from mbrp
1909, 7, 7. Hattie dropped from mbrp
1909, 7, 7. Edward dropped from mbrp
1909, 7, 7. Mary dropped from mbrp
1909, 7, 7. Lucy dropped from mbrp

HARRINGTON
1909, 7, 7. Taylor & Celia dropped from mbrp

HARRIS
1875, 4, 7. Wm. H. & w, Mary H., & ch, Anna
    E. & Edith R., rocf Springborough MM, O.
1909, 7, 7. Anna E. dropped from mbrp
1912, 11, 6. Wm. H., Mary H., Jessie & Hen-
    rietta, gct Calif.
1916, 3, 1. J. Warren dropped from mbrp

HARRISON
1907, 2, 6. Macon dropped from mbrp

HARRON
1917, 2, 7. Edith recrq

HARTER
1861, 6, 20. William b
1863, 1, 14. Sarah b

HARTMAN
1897, 4, 17. Artie recrq
1897, 6, 2. Cyrus recrq
1900, 7, 4. Edna M. recrq
1906, 7, 4. Cyrus M. relrq
1909, 7, 7. Edna dropped from mbrp
1912, 1, 3. Cyril F. recrq

HARTWELL
1908, 10, 7. Herman & Anna recrq
1909, 3, 3. Olive Matilda & Evelyn Ione
    recrq

1914, 3, 4. Washington & Garabell Evangeline
    recrq
1915, 12, 1. Herman & w & ch relrq
1919, 5, 7. Herman, Anna, Eveline & Olive
    recrq
1923, 11, 7. Herman & w, Anna, & ch, Olive &
    Evelyn, relrq

HARTZEL
1897, 7, 7. Myra recrq
1900, 11, 2. Myra dropped from mbrp

HATTON
1913, 5, 7. Sarah recrq

HAUHEIL
1915, 2, 3. Lillie Jane & Nellie Margaret
    recrq

HAWKS
1913, 3, 5. Mary recrq

HEALD
1909, 7, 7. H. C. dropped from mbrp

HEARING
1901, 12, 4. Grace Gertrude & Raymond J.
    recrq

HEARTLEY
1876, 2, 2. Thomas recrq

HEATH
1902, 3, 5. Mary Ray relrq

HEISE
1911, 4, 5. Maud, Mary Elizabeth, Dorothy
    Oneida & Esther Ellen, recrq
1915, 2, 3. Frances Louise recrq
1921, 8, 3. Chris recrq
1922, 5, 3. Chris & Dorothy dropped from
    mbrp
1923, 1, 3. Maud relrq
1923, 5, 2. Mary E. relrq

HELENTHAL
1916, 10, 4. Raymond & w, Stella M., & s,
    Paul Raymond, dropped from mbrp
1921, 9, 7. Raymond & w, Stella M., & s,
    Paul Raymond, dropped from mbrp

HELZER
1919, 5, 7. William recrq

HENDRIX
1899, 11, 1. Sarah recrq

HENEGAR
1903, 10, 7. Israel I. recrq

HENRY
1915, 2, 3. Jennie recrq
1916, 6, 7. Jennie dropped from mbrp

HENSLEY
1902, 11, 5. Harry C. & w, Cora, recrq
1904, 6, 1. Florence recrq
1913, 7, 2. Florence [Hensle] dropped from mbrp
1916, 7, 5. H. C. [Henslee] & fam relrq
1922, 4, 5. Ruth recrq

HERRING
1909, 7, 7. Edith dropped from mbrp

HESSINGER
1902, 1, 1. J. Dudley recrq
1913, 7, 2. Dudley J., Minnie & Paul J. dropped from mbrp

HEWITT
1904, 7, 6. Ollie M. recrq

HICKMAN
1920, 7, 7. George & w, Pearl, rocf Gilead MM
1921, 8, 3. George relrq
1921, 8, 3. Pearl gct Gilead MM

HINES
1900, 1, 3. Maxwell recrq
1900, 2, 7. Jessie recrq
1900, 11, 2. Maxwell & Jessie dropped from mbrp

HISSMEYER
1900, 6, 6. Minnie recrq

HOAK
1917, 12, 5. Ena recrq

HOBSON
1906, 1, 3. Lillian Shaffer gct Bellfountain MM

HODGINS
1909, 9, 8. G. Arnold & Jennie recrq
1910, 3, 2. Daniel G. recrq
1910, 3, 2. Elsie F. recrq
1912, 6, 5. Arnold [Hodges] & w relrq
1914, 10, 7. Daniel G. [Hodgen] & w gct Short Creek MM, O.
1921, 1, 5. David G. & w & ch, Jonathan, Frances, Mendel, Daniel & Elsie, rocf Mt. Pleasant MM

HOELCHER
1914, 3, 4. Lucile recrq

HOFFHINE
1907, 8, 7. Cora recrq

HOLCOMB
1900, 2, 7. Henry & Daisy recrq
1901, 2, 6. Louis, Jennie, Donald, Jennetta & Elmira, recrq
1909, 7, 7. Henry dropped from mbrp

1909, 7, 7. Daisy dropped from mbrp
1909, 7, 7. Lewis dropped from mbrp
1909, 7, 7. Jennie dropped from mbrp
1909, 7, 7. Donald dropped from mbrp
1909, 7, 7. Jennetta dropped from mbrp
1909, 7, 7. Ellwood dropped from mbrp

HOLLISTER
1914, 3, 4. Laura recrq

HOLT
1906, 1, 3. Jennie relrq

HOLTON
1918, 7, 3. Sarah dropped from mbrp

HOMAN
1896, 3, 4. Edward H. & w, Mary, recrq

HOOPS
1904, 4, 6. Israel recrq

HORNBECK
1919, 6, 4. Josephine dropped from mbrp

HOVEY
1913, 12, 3. Roy C. recrq
1914, 4, 1. Ray C. dropped from mbrp

HUBBARD
1876, 4, 5. Thomas D. rocf Wabash MM, Ind.
1897, 10, 6. Wm. B. gct Cleveland MM, O.
1897, 10, 6. Penrose, Wm. G., John B. & Margaret R., gct Cleveland MM, O.
1899, 9, 6. Wm. J. & dt, Margaret R., rocf Cleveland MM, O.
1908, 1, 1. Melissa recrq
1908, 10, 7. W. G. & w, Melissa, gct Goldsboro MM

HUGHES
1917, 3, 7. Carrie recrq
1919, 6, 4. Carrie relrq

HUIN
1904, 6, 1. Ella recrq
1904, 6, 1. Laura recrq

HULM (or HUHN)
1909, 4, 7. Fred, Chloreta, David S., Ruth E., Lillian & Elben, recrq
1912, 10, 2. Lillian dropped from mbrp
1913, 7, 2. Ella dropped from mbrp
1913, 7, 2. Davis dropped from mbrp
1913, 7, 2. Edward dropped from mbrp
1913, 7, 2. Ruth E. dropped from mbrp

HUSSEY
1901, 4, 29. John C. d ae 67

HUTCHINSON
1917, 7, 4. Melva gct Cleveland MM
1919, 3, 5. Etta, Edith & Wilmer recrq

HUTCHINSON, continued
1922, 5, 3. Welmer & Etta dropped from mbrp
1923, 4, 4. Edith relrq

HYSELL
1907, 3, 6. Eugene recrq
1909, 7, 7. Eugene dropped from mbrp

INQUIRE
1907, 4, 3. Sylvester W. [Inguire] recrq
1907, 4, 3. Lafayette [Inguire] recrq
1913, 7, 2. Sylvester dropped from mbrp

ISEL
1903, 4, 1. Nicholas & w, Margaret, & ch,
    Winona & Ida, recrq
1907, 12, 4. Mr. & Minnie dropped from mbrp
1909, 4, 7. Daisy Viola recrq
1909, 7, 7. Nicholas dropped from mbrp
1909, 7, 7. Marguarite dropped from mbrp
1909, 7, 7. Wynona dropped from mbrp
1909, 7, 7. Ida dropped from mbrp
1909, 7, 7. Daisy Viola dropped from mbrp

JAMES
1918, 5, 1. David recrq
1919, 3, 5. Nettie recrq
1919, 7, 2. David relrq

JARED
1922, 7, 5. Chloa rocf Valley Mills MM, Ind.

JOHN
1914, 3, 4. Herman recrq
1920, 5, 5. Ernest H. recrq
1920, 5, 5. Nina recrq

JOHNSON
1876, 4, 5. Alfred rocf Kokomo MM, Ind.
1898, 6, 1. James E. dropped from mbrp
1898, 12, 7. Albert recrq
1899, 3, 1. Ella recrq
1904, 7, 6. Albert & Cora dis disunity
1914, 3, 4. Glen Edwin recrq

JONES
1875, 4, 7. Samuel H. & w, Mary T., & ch,
    Gulielma & Wm. Alfred, rocf Westland MM,O.
1875, 7, 7. Charles N. rocf China MM, Me.,
    dtd 1875,5,19
1876, 10, 4. Charles N. gct Goshen MM, O.
1906, 5, 2. Ellis E. & fam relrq
1911, 11, 1. Ellis A. & w, Minnie B., & ch,
    Esther E., Mary C., Lydia C., Ellis N.,
    John L. & Minnie A., recrq
1913, 12, 3. Victor W., Adilia H. & Ruth Na-
    omi, recrq
1915, 3, 3. Ruth dropped from mbrp
1921, 2, 2. Will E. & dt, Anna Ruth & Mary
    Edna, rocf Valley Mound MM
1922, 3, 1. Amy Howard recrq
1922, 7, 5. Victor relrq

JUNGKAIRTH
1904, 12, 7. Charles recrq

KALB
1913, 5, 7. Charles L. recrq

KAILER
1898, 12, 7. Geneva & Joseph V. [Kaler] recrq
1908, 6, 3. J. B. dropped from mbrp
1908, 6, 3. Geneva (Kailer) Anderson dropped
    from mbrp

KAUFMAN
1900, 4, 4. Olive E. & Ellis S. recrq
1900, 11, 2. Newton recrq
1904, 12, 7. Newton & w, Olive, & ch, Vilas
    Summer & Lola Lucinda -----
1906, 1, 3. A. N. & w, Olive, & dt, Lola L.,
    relrq
1906, 12, 6. Ellis dropped from mbrp
1906, 12, 7. Ellis & Vilas dropped from mbrp

KEESE
1905, 8, 2. Paul Dewitt, James Albert & Emma
    D., recrq

KEISTER
1896, 3, 4. William recrq

KENT
1897, 3, 3. Emma recrq
1897, 3, 3. Dora recrq
1898, 12, 7. Olive recrq
1909, 7, 7. Edward & Dora dropped from mbrp

KENWORTHY
1875, 4, 7. Rachel rocf Springborough MM,O.
1876, 12, 6. Amos & w, Phebe, & s, Charles,
    roc

KEPLER
1902, 1, 1. Wm. R. recrq
1905, 5, 3. Eva May recrq
1906, 12, 6. W. R. recrq

KERSHAW
1911, 8, 2. Florence A. rocf Boulder MM,
    Colo., dtd 1911,7,12
1913, 3, 5. Wm. & Mable recrq
1913, 5, 7. Mary A. & Paul recrq
1916, 9, 16. Will & w dropped from mbrp
1917, 5, 2. Mary A. relrq
1918, 7, 3. Paul dropped from mbrp

KIMBALL
1909, 7, 7. L. P. dropped from mbrp

KIMBROUGH
1912, 5, 1. J. Edward & w, Lizzie, rocf
    Ogden MM
1916, 6, 7. Edward J. & Elizabeth dropped
    from mbrp

KING
1918, 4, 5. Lydia M. d

1909, 9, 8. Lula recrq
1913, 11, 5. Leola gct Fairmount MM, Ind.
1917, 3, 7. Lydia M. recrq

KIPP
1899, 3, 1. Leonard & Nora recrq
1900, 3, 7. Cora recrq
1900, 4, 4. Ruth recrq
1901, 12, 4. Ethel recrq
1907, 12, 4. Leonard dropped from mbrp
1909, 7, 7. Cora, Cara & Ruth dropped from
     mbrp

KIRBY
1912, 3, 6. William rocf Cleveland MM, O.
1912, 7, 3. Alice M. rocf Smithfield MM
1915, 9, 1. Wm. & minor ch gct Alliance MM

KNIGHT
1909, 10, 6. Hilda recrq
1912, 6, 5. Hilda dropped from mbrp

KNOWLES
1922, 3, 1. Susan L. gct Rollin MM

KOLB
1915, 7, 7. Charles L. dropped from mbrp

KONKLE
1922, 2, 2. Edward recrq

KURTHOLZ
1896, 8, 1. Henry [Kurtzholt] & w, Ella, &
     s, Chas., recrq
1902, 12, 3. Emerson [Kurtzholz] recrq
1907, 10, 2. Chas. & Kitty gct Germantown MM
1912, 3, 6. Henry & Ella relrq
1916, 3, 1. Mary Binns dropped from mbrp

LANDUS
1909, 7, 7. Geo. W. & Emasett dropped from
     mbrp

LANGDON
1918, 8, 7. W. E. & w, Ethel, & s, Elmore,
     recrq
1923, 4, 4. Paul Russell recrq

LAUGHMAN
1910, 4, 6. Ella recrq
1918, 9, 4. Ella dropped from mbrp

LAWRENCE
1901, 1, 2. John recrq
1910, 9, 6. Martha Jane rocf White Water MM,
     Ind.

LEACH
1902, 9, 10. Wm. & Carra recrq
1906, 7, 4. Della recrq

1907, 8, 7. Wm. N. & Della, dropped from
     mbrp

LEE
1905, 12, 6. Gurney & w, Ida Johnson, & s,
     Walter Pinckham, rocf East Goshen MM
1906, 1, 3. Grace recrq
1908, 11, 6. Gurney J. & Walter gct Gilead
     MM

LEHMAN
1900, 12, 5. Sarah relrq

LeROY
1916, 12, 6. Franklin & w, Martha Pearl, &
     dt, Martha E., rocf Muncie MM, Ind.

LERVIS
1896, 3, 4. Mary recrq

LESLIE
1905, 8, 2. Rilla recrq

LEWIS
1909, 7, 7. Mary dropped from mbrp
1915, 4, 17. Viola Pearl recrq
1915, 4, 17. Johnson Perry Jr. recrq
1918, 9, 4. Marguerite dropped from mbrp

LIMES
1898, 7, 6. Sarah & Essie recrq
1909, 7, 7. Mabel dropped from mbrp

LINCOLN
1900, 10, 3. Elizabeth Hague relrq

LINDLEY
1918, 9, 4. Paul B. & w, Mary R., & ch,
     Mary Esther, Anna Lois, Margarett Pauline
     & Maurice Bertram, rocf Gray MM, Ind.
1923, 11, 7. Paul B. & fam gct Urbana MM

LINK
1899, 9, 6. Margaret recrq
1906, 9, 5. Catharine recrq
1914, 3, 4. Laura M., Albert J. & Lu Nettie
     M., recrq

LITTLE
1913, 5, 7. Minnie recrq
1914, 3, 4. George E. recrq
1920, 3, 3. George & Minnie dropped from
     mbrp

LOFFER
1916, 3, 1. Mary recrq

LONG
1896, 4, 1. Mrs. recrq

LOOMIS
1900, 1, 3. Clark S. & Margaret recrq
1909, 7, 7. Charles H. & Margaret dropped

LOOMIS, continued
   from mbrp

LOOP
1901, 1, 2. Lawrence & Manerva recrq
1904, 10, 5. John recrq

LOTT
1902, 5, 7. William recrq
1904, 2, 3. Mary recrq

LOUKS
1922, 2, 2. Marie recrq

LUCAS
1913, 3, 5. Sarah & Edith, recrq

McBRIDE
1897, 6, 2. John & w, Martha A., rocf Springfield MM, O.
1909, 7, 7. Martha dropped from mbrp
1913, 3, 5. Martha recrq
1916, 6, 7. Martha dropped from mbrp

McCANN
1899, 2, 1. Julia & Jennie recrq
1899, 2, 1. Mary recrq
1899, 2, 1. Josie recrq
1899, 2, 1. Martha Alberta recrq
1909, 7, 7. Julia, Jennie & Martha A. dropped from mbrp

McCARTY
1901, 1, 2. Lucy recrq

McCLANE
1909, 10, 6. Wm. H. recrq
1912, 6, 5. Wm. H. [McClain] dropped from
   mbrp

McCLOUD
1898, 7, 6. Pearl & Lulu rocf Alum Creek MM,
   O.
1922, 9, 6. Leona dropped from mbrp

McCORMICK
1923, 2, 7. Emmett & w rocf First Friends
   Church, Cleveland

McDANIEL
1916, 1, 5. Mary rocf Xenia MM

McELHANY
1919, 3, 5. Doris recrq

McFARLAND
1906, 2, 7. Guy & w, Blanche, recrq
1909, 4, 7. Dessie recrq
1910, 3, 2. Guy & Blanch dropped from mbrp
1912, 10, 2. John & Dessie dropped from mbrp

McGILL
1913, 5, 7. Grace recrq

1918, 7, 3. Grace dropped from mbrp

McGLINCHREY
1914, 4, 1. Thomas A. & Bell recrq

McGREW
1874, 8, 5. Jamima & dt, Elizabeth W. & Martha, roc
1875, 3, 3. Anna L., Josephine K. & Mary T.
   rocf Smithfield MM, O.
1875, 3, 3. William rocf Smithfield MM, O.

McGUINESS
1911, 8, 2. Hannah Isabel recrq
1918, 7, 3. Isabel [McGinnis] dropped from
   mbrp

McKINLEY
1898, 6, 1. Pete dropped from mbrp

McMACHEN
1909, 4, 7. John recrq

McPHERSON
1917, 12, 5. Charles Earle rocf Boulder MM,
   Colo.
1921, 9, 7. Earl gct Muncie MM, Ind.

MABE
1916, 11, 1. Malissa recrq
1917, 2, 7. James Isaac recrq
1917, 2, 7. Josephine recrq
1917, 2, 7. Nettie recrq
1919, 3, 5. James, Josephine & Nettie
   dropped from mbrp

MALOTT
1903, 4, 1. Hiram V. recrq
1905, 6, 7. Ida Lathem recrq
1909, 7, 7. Ida L. dropped from mbrp
1909, 7, 7. Hiram dropped from mbrp

MANKER
1912, 12, 4. Frank rocf West Fork MM, dtd
   1912,11,16

MARIDETH
1900, 1, 3. Sarah E. recrq
1907, 11, 6. Frank Stanley recrq

MARLOW
1907, 10, 2. Ada recrq
1908, 3, 4. Chas. F., Grace, Lamond & Chas.
   W. Jr. recrq
1913, 3, 5. Grace recrq
1918, 7, 3. Ada, Grace & Lamont dropped from
   mbrp
1918, 7, 3. Charles W. dropped from mbrp

MARSHALL
1919, 7, 2. John W. & Angeline recrq

MARTIN
1877, 3, 7. William recrq
1877, 7, 4. William gct Goshen MM

MASON
1919, 11, 5. Margaret recrq

MAXWELL
1913, 3, 5. William recrq
1913, 3, 5. Electa rocf Londonderry MM
1919, 5, 7. William dropped from mbrp
1919, 5, 7. Electra dropped from mbrp
1922, 2, 2. Electa & W. J. recrq

MERCER
1917, 10, 30. John d

1899, 3, 1. John & Mary recrq

MEREDITH
1909, 7, 7. Frank S. dropped from mbrp
1909, 7, 7. Elizabeth S. dropped from mbrp

MERION
1918, 4, 3. T. N. & Mamie recrq

MERRIMAN
1917, 2, 7. Kate recrq

MESSER
1906, 6, 6. John A. & Ella recrq
1910, 3, 2. John & w, Della, dropped from
    mbrp

MICHAELS
1896, 3, 4. Lillie recrq

MILLER
1874, 6, 3. Joseph H. & w, Rebecca G., rocf
    Springborough MM, O.
1896, 3, 4. John recrq
1898, 6, 1. John dropped from mbrp
1898, 6, 1. John N., Mary E. & Charles W.
    recrq
1907, 6, 5. Sarah & Willie dropped from
    mbrp
1909, 7, 7. Mary E. & Chas. W. dropped from
    mbrp
1917, 2, 7. Catherine recrq
1917, 2, 7. Harold recrq
1917, 5, 2. Edna E. recrq
1919, 3, 5. Edna & Harold dropped from mbrp
1920, 7, 7. Nellie May recrq

MINEHART
1898, 12, 7. Mabel & Effie recrq

MINNEVER
1910, 4, 6. A. D. recrq
1915, 5, 5. Lucius recrq
1923, 12, 5. George & w gct Alum Creek MM,O.

MITCHELL
1897, 3, 3. Lydia recrq
1900, 11, 2. Lida dropped from mbrp
1922, 4, 5. John recrq

MOCK
1904, 4, 6. Earl Frank recrq
1909, 12, 1. Charles E. gct Rollins MM, Mich.

MOLTEY
1905, 9, 6. Susan recrq

MONTGOMERY
1898, 2, 2. Joseph recrq
1900, 11, 2. Joseph dropped from mbrp

MOORE
1897, 12, 1. Harley M. rocf Scranton MM, Ia.
1898, 12, 7. Harley M. gct Scranton MM, Ia.
1902, 5, 7. Edith R. gct Beloit MM
1914, 3, 4. Anna recrq
1914, 4, 1. Virginia A. recrq
1918, 7, 3. Virginia dropped from mbrp

MORGAN
1922, 2, 2. Cecil recrq

MORRIS
1904, 6, 1. Ora recrq
1909, 7, 7. Ona dropped from mbrp
1909, 10, 6. Robert M. recrq
1915, 2, 3. Margaret recrq
1916, 5, 3. Robert M. relrq

MOSHER
1900, 11, 2. Minnie Ong gct Gilead MM
1909, 7, 7. Chas. F. recrq
1915, 2, 3. Mary recrq
1916, 6, 7. Mary [Mosier] dropped from mbrp

MOTLEY
1907, 6, 5. Susie dropped from mbrp

MOTT
1911, 1, 4. Elizabeth H. rocf Cleveland MM
1911, 9, 6. Elizabeth H. gct Tecumseh MM,
    Md.

MUGRAGE
1922, 1, 4. Girden H. recrq

MUNSEY
1896, 1, 1. Nathan & w dropped from mbrp

MURRAY
1896, 2, 5. Alfred recrq

MUTH
1906, 4, 4. Henry recrq
1906, 7, 4. Winona L. rocf Westland MM

MYERS
1898, 12, 7. Clara recrq
1899, 3, 1. Charles & Susanna recrq

MYERS, continued
1900, 3, 7. Clara recrq
1904, 12, 7. Clara dis disunity
1909, 4, 7. Charles & Mary recrq
1909, 7, 7. Clara dropped from mbrp
1909, 10, 6. Susan relrq
1911, 9, 6. Charles dropped from mbrp
1914, 3, 4. Esther recrq
1919, 3, 5. Dorothy recrq

NEFF
1899, 2, 1. Bert H. recrq
1900, 10, 3. Bert H. dropped from mbrp
1917, 2, 7. Ethel recrq
1921, 8, 3. Lucile recrq
1922, 5, 3. Lucile relrq

NEGLE
1921, 12, 7. Mary Jane recrq

NICHOLES
1904, 3, 2. Tacy N. recrq
1913, 5, 7. Mamie [Nichols] recrq
1916, 3, 1. Mamie [Nicholas] dropped from
     mbrp

NICHOLSON
1900, 2, 7. Lafayette relrq

NORRIS
1904, 6, 1. Lulu M. recrq
1909, 7, 7. Lula M. dropped from mbrp

NORTHSTEIN
1901, 12, 4. Elizabeth Miller recrq
1909, 7, 7. Mable, Clara & Edith dropped
     from mbrp

NOTSHIRE
1901, 2, 6. Mary E. & Della recrq
1901, 2, 6. Claude recrq
1901, 2, 6. Noble recrq
1901, 2, 6. Hevy recrq

NOTHSTINE
1910, 3, 2. Henry dropped from mbrp

NULL
1897, 4, 17. George & w, Emma, & ch, Clara,
     Amy & William, recrq
1898, 2, 2. George & w, Emma, & ch, Clara,
     Amy & William, relrq

ODENMALD
1905, 8, 2. Albert & Louisa recrq
1907, 6, 5. Albert & Louisa C. dropped from
     mbrp

OLDS
1904, 12, 7. Ella recrq
1909, 7, 7. George dropped from mbrp

ONG
1901, 1, 19. Elmira d ae 80

1874, 8, 5. Lewis & w, Elmira, & ch, Louis
     B., Anderson C. & Delbert T., roc
1874, 10, 7. Joseph & w, Rhoda, & ch, Effie
     Lourena & George Lewis, rocf East Goshen
     MM, O.
1899, 11, 1. Minnie R. recrq
1900, 11, 2. Lewis B. recrq
1906, 5, 2. Lindley recrq
1907, 6, 5. L. B. & w, Minnie, relrq
1909, 5, 5. Lonore relrq
1909, 7, 7. Anderson C. & Lewis B. dropped
     from mbrp
1911, 9, 6. W. P. & w, Lida D., & ch, Lind-
     ley, Florence & Gertrude, relrq
1913, 8, 6. Effie gct Gilead MM
1916, 7, 5. George dropped from mbrp
1922, 3, 1. George & Ethel recrq

OREILEY
1911, 4, 5. Clara B. recrq

ORMDORF
1909, 1, 6. Sarah Ann recrq
1909, 7, 7. Sarah Ann relrq

OSBORN
1896, 6, 13. Seth roc
1904, 10, 5. Grace & Gilbert Jr. recrq
1918, 4, 3. A. W. & Jennie recrq
1921, 6, 1. Grace relrq
1922, 7, 5. Frieda E. recrq
1923, 3, 7. Helen A. recrq

OSMOND
1899, 11, 1. Sarah rocf Alum Creek MM, O.
1903, 11, 4. Sarah gct Berlinville MM

OVERLY
1913, 7, 2. Clara B. recrq

OWENS
1914, 5, 6. Belle & dt, Myrtle, recrq

PACK
1908, 10, 7. Samuel recrq
1910, 9, 6. Samuel gct Fairmount MM, Ind.

PAINTER
1913, 5, 7. Lawrence recrq

PALES
1907, 12, 4. Harry dropped from mbrp

PARKER
1904, 6, 1. Lottie recrq
1908, 10, 7. Lotta relrq

PARTLOW
1917, 10, 26: Alta d

PARTLOW, continued
1916, 10, 4. Alta M. dropped from mbrp
1917, 2, 7. John W. recrq
1919, 3, 5. John dropped from mbrp

PATTERSON
1904, 12, 7. L. W. recrq
1906, 12, 6. J. W. dropped from mbrp
1909, 7, 7. George N. dropped from mbrp

PATTON
1922, 5, 3. Sally recrq

PAYNE
1921, 4, 6. Helen recrq

PELT
1904, 1, 6. Robert rocf Short Creek MM, O.,
    dtd 1903,11,25
1907, 12, 4. Robert rocf Beloit MM
1907, 12, 4. Annie M. rocf Beloit MM
1912, 12, 4. Robert & w, Anna, & dt, Elma,
    gct Rockford MM
1916, 4, 5. Robert & w, Anna, & dt, Mary
    Elma, rocf Sheridan MM, Ind.
1916, 12, 6. Robert & w, Anna W., relrq

PENNELL
1917, 2, 7. Howard Lewis recrq
1917, 2, 7. Mabel Marie recrq
1917, 2, 7. Louise Mabel recrq
1917, 2, 7. Malcolm Harold recrq
1918, 3, 6. Howard L. & fam relrq

PENNINGTON
1915, 10, 6. John & w, Rebecca, rocf Damascus
    MM
1918, 9, 4. John & w, Rebecca, & ch, Deborah,
    gct Damascus MM, O.

PERMAR
1907, 4, 3. Edwin H. recrq
1909, 7, 7. Edwin H. [Permat] dropped from
    mbrp

PERRY
1922, 2, 2. Fannie Reynolds recrq
1922, 2, 2. Gail Duane recrq
1922, 2, 2. Harold Kent Jr. recrq

PETERS
1899, 3, 1. Jonathan & Mary recrq
1902, 6, 4. John & Jane recrq
1909, 7, 7. John & Mary Jane dropped from
    mbrp

PETTIT
1876, 6, 7. Elnathan & w, Margaret H., & s,
    Elnathan, rocf Short Creek MM, O., dtd
    1876,4,20
1909, 7, 7. Elnathan dropped from mbrp

PHEIMEY
1901, 5, 7. Lucian M. recrq
1901, 5, 7. John A. recrq
1901, 5, 7. Eral G. recrq
1901, 5, 7. May E. recrq
1909, 7, 7. Earl G., Mary E. & Lucy M.
    dropped from mbrp

PHILLIPS
1904, 6, 1. Ella recrq
1909, 7, 7. Ella dropped from mbrp

PIERCE
1904, 3, 2. Phebe recrq
1906, 10, 3. Phebe relrq

PLEASANT
1909, 7, 7. C. E. & w dropped from mbrp

POLLARD
1874, 10, 7. Warren W. rocf Alum Creek MM,O.

POOLE
1906, 1, 3. Clara recrq
1909, 10, 6. Clara relrq

POULSON
1910, 3, 2. Albert & Mary Bell dropped from
    mbrp

POWELL
1913, 3, 5. Chester & Essie recrq
1921, 10, 5. Chester & Bessie gct MM in Da-
    mascus QM

POWELSON
1908, 9, 3. Mary Bell Parker recrq
1908, 9, 3. Albert A. recrq

PROUDFOOT
1905, 7, 5. Faith G. recrq
1907, 2, 6. Faith J. G. dropped from mbrp

PUTNAM
1915, 5, 5. Bessie recrq
1919, 5, 7. Howard dropped from mbrp

QUIMBY
1877, 4, 4. George A. & w, Jennie, recrq

RADER
1899, 3, 1. Clara E. recrq
1902, 6, 4. Clara recrq
1909, 7, 7. Charles dropped from mbrp
1909, 7, 7. Clara E. dropped from mbrp

RADIGON
1907, 3, 6. Frank recrq
1909, 7, 7. Frank dropped from mbrp

RAMEY
1913, 5, 7. George & Hester recrq
1916, 3, 1. George & Hester [Ramie] dropped

RAMEY, continued
    from mbrp

RANDALL
1917, 9, 5. Effie rocf Marshalltown MM
1918, 9, 4. Effie T. gct Minneapolis MM,
    Minn.

RAYBORN
1897, 6, 2. Samuel & w, Susanna, rocf
    Springfield MM, O.
1897, 6, 2. James W. [Rayburn] rocf Spring-
    field MM, O.
1909, 7, 7. James W. [Rayburne] dropped
    from mbrp

RAYMOND
1912, 10, 2. Esther dropped from mbrp

REAMS
1904, 7, 6. Wm. & w, Nettie, rocf Westland
    MM
1904, 8, 3. Rankin Carl, Chas. Cyrus & Wal-
    ter Oren, ch Wm. & Nettie, recrq
1905, 4, 5. Evangeline rocf Goshen MM
1913, 7, 2. Charles, Rankin & Walter dropped
    from mbrp
1918, 9, 4. W. J., Nettie & Catherine drop-
    ped from mbrp

REAVER
1919, 1, 1. Dorothy Rose recrq
1919, 1, 1. Ruth Silvia recrq
1919, 1, 1. Charles Russell recrq
1919, 1, 1. Stanley Hershel recrq
1919, 1, 1. Adam Alfred recrq
1919, 1, 1. John Pennington recrq

REDMOND
1911, 6, 7. John D. recrq
1913, 5, 7. Herbert & Margaret recrq
1918, 9, 4. Herbert & Margaret [Redwood]
    dropped from mbrp

REED
1897, 3, 3. Nettie recrq
1899, 3, 1. Ida recrq
1904, 7, 6. Mary rocf Westland MM
1905, 10, 4. Mary E. relrq
1906, 3, 7. Mary E. rst
1909, 7, 7. Ida dropped from mbrp
1909, 7, 7. Nettie dropped from mbrp
1912, 1, 3. Goldie recrq
1913, 7, 2. Golda dropped from mbrp

REEDY
1899, 2, 1. Sarah E. recrq

REESE
1912, 7, 3. James A. & Paul Dervit dropped
    from mbrp
1913, 7, 2. Emma dropped from mbrp

REEVES
1899, 8, 2. Viola recrq

RHOADES
1903, 10, 7. Joseph relrq
1905, 6, 7. Joseph rst

RICE
1914, 3, 4. Walter recrq
1914, 12, 2. Ellen & Mary recrq
1918, 4, 3. Ellen gct Seattle MM
1918, 9, 4. Walter dropped from mbrp
1919, 3, 5. Catherine dropped from mbrp

RICHARDSON
1909, 7, 7. Charles dropped from mbrp

RIGHTER
1909, 7, 7. Elizabeth dropped from mbrp

RITTENHOUSE
1896, 3, 4. Nora recrq
1896, 4, 1. Lola recrq
1909, 7, 7. Lula dropped from mbrp

ROACH
1900, 3, 7. Carrie recrq
1900, 3, 7. Pearl S. recrq
1900, 6, 6. Emma recrq
1900, 8, 1. Nellie & Earl recrq
1902, 1, 1. John P. & Mary recrq
1902, 3, 5. Melvina recrq
1909, 7, 7. Pearl S., Carrie, Emma, Nellie
    & Earl dropped from mbrp
1909, 7, 7. John P. dropped from mbrp
1909, 7, 7. Mary dropped from mbrp
1909, 7, 7. Melvina dropped from mbrp

ROBERTSON
1918, 4, 3. Edna recrq

ROBERTS
1919, 11, 5. Mary, Margaret D. & Selma recrq

ROBINSON
1899, 12, 6. Edith recrq

RODGERS
1902, 9, 10. Wm. A. recrq
1907, 12, 4. Wm. dropped from mbrp

ROE
1901, 6, 5. Lottie M. & Ethel B. recrq
1905, 3, 2. Madge recrq
1906, 4, 4. Ralph recrq
1908, 3, 4. Grace, Claude & Etta Luella
    recrq
1909, 1, 6. Clark relrq
1909, 7, 7. Ralph dropped from mbrp
1909, 7, 7. Claude dropped from mbrp
1909, 7, 7. Lottie M. dropped from mbrp
1909, 7, 7. Ethel B. dropped from mbrp
1914, 6, 3. Claud H. & w, Margaret, rocf

ROE, continued
    Raisin MM
1914, 10, 7. Claud & w, Margaret, relrq
1915, 5, 5. Grace gct Springfield MM, Ind.

ROESE
1915, 11, 3. Grace recrq

ROHR
1913, 12, 3. May recrq
1918, 7, 3. May dropped from mbrp

ROLLIER
1909, 7, 7. Sadie dropped from mbrp

ROMANS
1922, 9, 6. Viola D. recrq

ROMICK
1899, 11, 1. Lida M. rocf Alum Creek MM, O.
1903, 11, 4. Lida G. gct Berlinville MM

ROSE
1919, 2, 5. Grace relrq

ROSS
1914, 3, 4. William L. & Okey D. recrq

ROWLAND
1901, 2, 6. Ida recrq

RUDELL
1923, 9, 5. Edna recrq

RUDOLPH
1909, 12, 1. Rachel recrq
1915, 7, 7. Rachel dropped from mbrp

RUFFING
1904, 1, 6. Nicholas recrq
1904, 1, 6. Lillian recrq
1904, 1, 6. Catherine recrq
1913, 7, 2. Ella & Catherine dropped from
    mbrp
1916, 3, 1. Nicholas dropped from mbrp

RUHL
1906, 12, 6. Mae W. & s, Miller, recrq
1911, 6, 7. May dropped from mbrp

RUSH
1916, 4, 5. Albert T. & Emma recrq
1917, 2, 7. Nettie recrq
1919, 3, 5. Albert, Emma, Edna & Nellie
    dropped from mbrp

RUSSELL
1897, 3, 3. Ethel & Rebecca recrq
1909, 7, 7. Rebecca & Ethel dropped from
    mbrp

SALISBURY
1913, 11, 5. Mamie L. recrq

SANDERS
1910, 4, 6. Hezekiah H. & w, Martha E., &
    ch, Pearl, rocf S. Eighth St. MM, Rich-
    mond, Ind.

SANDUSKY
1919, 1, 1. Abe & w, Susanna, & ch, J. Gil-
    ford & Julia, rocf Huntington Park MM,
    Calif.

SCALES
1896, 3, 4. Albert & w, Sarah, recrq
1897, 7, 7. Fannie, Maud & Myrtle [Scoles]
    recrq
1898, 6, 1. Wm. W. dropped from mbrp
1897, 7, 7. Elmyra [Scoles] recrq

SCHLISM
1902, 2, 5. Frank dropped from mbrp
1902, 2, 5. Helen relrq

SCOLDS
1909, 7, 7. Susan B. dropped from mbrp
1909, 7, 7. Sarah dropped from mbrp
1909, 7, 7. Fannie dropped from mbrp
1909, 7, 7. Almira dropped from mbrp

SCOTT
1900, 12, 5. Sarah relrq

SCOTTEN
1913, 11, 5. Everett E. & w, Emma E., rocf
    Ypsilanta MM, Mich.
1918, 10, 2. Everett E. gct Wessington MM,
    S. D.

SCOVELL
1901, 1, 2. Francis & Bell recrq
1909, 7, 7. Francis & Bell dropped from
    mbrp

SEBRING
1906, 9, 5. Minnie recrq
1913, 7, 2. Minnie dropped from mbrp

SEEBERT
1897, 3, 3. Irvin D. recrq
1903, 2, 4. Irvine & w, Nora, relrq

SEIPEL
1911, 4, 5. Anna Belle recrq

SELF
1898, 1, 4. Ralph & w, Fannie Alice, recrq

SESSIONS
1913, 7, 2. Charles Marlow dropped from mbrp

SHAFER
1904, 2, 3. Lillian rocf Cleveland MM, O.
1914, 9, 2. C. W. gct Xenia MM, O.

SHANKS
1900, 7, 4. David L. recrq
1909, 7, 7. David L. dropped from mbrp

SHAVER
1911, 5, 3. Guy recrq
1911, 6, 7. Charles W. recrq
1911, 6, 7. Rebecca A. recrq
1911, 6, 7. Hazel D. recrq
1914, 3, 4. Carl recrq
1915, 7, 7. Carl dropped from mbrp
1922, 4, 5. Charles W. & Rebecca A. relrq

SHAW
1898, 12, 7. Constance recrq
1909, 7, 7. Constantine dropped from mbrp

SHEATS
1902, 6, 4. Leah & Jane recrq
1909, 7, 7. Lea & Jane dropped from mbrp
1914, 10, 7. Lucie relrq

SHERMAN
1906, 4, 4. Susan B. recrq
1914, 2, 4. Susie Buffington recrq
1915, 12, 1. Susie B. gct Adrian MM

SHERRY
1896, 3, 4. William recrq
1909, 7, 7. Wm. dropped from mbrp

SHIVEY
1910, 6, 1. Earl C. recrq
1910, 6, 1. Flossie E. recrq

SHOECRAFT
1899, 3, 1. Charlotte recrq
1909, 7, 7. Charlotte dropped from mbrp

SHOEMAKER
1911, 9, 6. Fay dropped from mbrp
1905, 8, 2. Margaret [Shumaker] recrq
1915, 7, 7. Margaret dropped from mbrp

SHOWALTER
1901, 6, 5. John R. recrq
1902, 1, 1. Sewart J. recrq
1903, 7, 1. John R. dropped from mbrp
1910, 2, 2. Margaret & Alberta recrq
1910, 4, 6. Fay recrq
1912, 6, 5. Marguirite & Alberta dropped
       from mbrp
1912, 7, 3. Stewart J. dropped from mbrp
1921, 12, 7. Emma & dt, Alberta Moss, recrq
1922, 5, 3. Stewart J. relrq
1922, 5, 3. Emma & ch, Alberta Moss dropped
       from mbrp

SHRADER
1916, 3, 1. William dropped from mbrp

SHRUM
1898, 6, 1. Washington dropped from mbrp

SIMPSON
1896, 3, 4. W. R. recrq
1896, 3, 4. Mable recrq
1909, 7, 7. W. R. & Mabel dropped from mbrp

SIMS
1900, 2, 7. Mable recrq

SINGER
1905, 4, 5. Cora recrq
1910, 3, 2. Cora relrq

SIPLE
1918, 7, 3. Ann Belle dropped from mbrp

SITES
1900, 7, 4. Clark E. recrq
1902, 1, 1. Rena recrq

SKIPPER
1905, 1, 4. Edward Leroy recrq
1906, 9, 5. Lillie recrq
1909, 4, 7. Archie C. & G Stockton recrq
1916, 3, 1. Archie dropped from mbrp

SLACK
1907, 4, 3. Edward L. & Virginia recrq
1909, 7, 7. Edward L. & Virginia D. dropped
       from mbrp

SLONE
1901, 5, 7. Bert A. recrq
1909, 7, 7. Jennie dropped from mbrp

SMALLWOOD
1896, 3, 4. Dellie recrq
1918, 7, 3. Henry L. dropped from mbrp

SMALLEY
1900, 1, 3. Benjamin F. [Smally] recrq
1900, 2, 7. Wm. & Anna recrq
1900, 2, 7. Mont & Maggie recrq
1900, 11, 2. Benjamin F. [Smally] dropped
       from mbrp
1900, 11, 2. Maggie & Symantha dropped from
       mbrp
1901, 2, 6. Nellie recrq
1901, 2, 6. Ira M. recrq
1901, 2, 6. Roy recrq
1901, 2, 6. Carley recrq
1901, 2, 6. Margaret recrq
1903, 7, 1. Nellie dropped from mbrp
1907, 6, 5. Anna, Carey & Roy dropped from
       mbrp
1907, 8, 7. Mont & Margaret [Smally] drop-
       ped from mbrp
1909, 7, 7. Clara dropped from mbrp

SMITH
1897, 1, 16. Walker & w, Cora L., & ch,

SMITH, continued
        Lamar, H. J., Sterling & Walker L., recrq
1899, 2, 1. Daniel, Leslie & Amanda recrq
1902, 7, 2. Harry recrq
1907, 12, 4. Harry, Amanda & Daniel dropped
        from mbrp
1908, 9, 3. Sarah Jane recrq
1909, 7, 7. Walker, Lanore & H. J. Sterling
        dropped from mbrp
1909, 7, 7. Leslie dropped from mbrp
1913, 5, 7. Carrie recrq
1919, 6, 4. Carrie relrq
1922, 3, 1. Max C. recrq

SNYDER
1902, 9, 10. Gurtie recrq
1909, 7, 7. Gustie dropped from mbrp
1919, 3, 5. Winfield S. recrq
1922, 5, 3. Winfield dropped from mbrp

SPAULDING
1909, 10, 6. John recrq
1910, 5, 4. John relrq

SPEPLEN
1902, 7, 2. L. E. rocf Banbary Point, Eng.

SPICER
1904, 12, 7. Ella recrq
1905, 8, 2. Ella recrq
1907, 7, 3. Earl recrq
1913, 7, 2. Pearl dropped from mbrp
1913, 7, 2. Ella dropped from mbrp

STALKER
1904, 1, 6. Charles rocf Westfield MM, Ind.
1904, 1, 6. Catherine Stephen recrq
1919, 2, 5. Herman & w, Esther, & dt, Mary
        Elizabeth, rocf Westfield MM, Ind.
1919, 10, 1. Herman & Esther gct Westfield
        MM, Ind.

STARR
1912, 5, 1. Elmer A. recrq
1913, 5, 7. Helen recrq
1913, 5, 7. Helen recrq
1918, 9, 4. Elmer dropped from mbrp

STEPHENSON
1902, 9, 10. Curtis S. & Adelia B. recrq
1909, 3, 3. Briner L. recrq
1912, 10, 2. James H. dropped from mbrp
1917, 7, 4. Marshall rocf Dublin MM, Ind.
1917, 12, 5. Marshall gct Spiceland MM, Ind.

STEWART
1898, 12, 7. Mary recrq
1909, 7, 7. Mary dropped from mbrp
1913, 3, 5. Matilda recrq
1914, 3, 4. Helen & Anna E. recrq
1914, 4, 1. Edna recrq   [from mbrp
1913, 7, 3. Edna, Leslie & Harold dropped
1922, 2, 2. Martha [Stuart] recrq

STOFFNER
1906, 8, 1. John recrq
1906, 10, 3. John dis

STOKES
1904, 2, 3. Lena recrq
1907, 12, 4. Lena dropped from mbrp

STONE
1908, 3, 4. Ruth recrq

STONEROCK
1899, 12, 6. Sarah & Mattie recrq

STOOPS
1905, 3, 1. Lucinda, Edna May & Luetrel
        recrq
1907, 11, 6. Cora recrq
1913, 3, 5. Cora Ethel relrq

STOUFFER
1917, 2, 7. May & Evelyn recrq
1919, 6, 4. Margaret & Evelin dropped from
        mbrp

STOUT
1921, 8, 3. Minnie recrq

STOWELL
1901, 10, 2. Francis & Bell dropped from
        mbrp

STOWTER
1910, 12, 7. Alma recrq

STRADER
1914, 3, 4. Wm. B. recrq

STRATTON
1899, 10, 4. Isaac & w, Sarah B., rocf East
        Goshen MM
1902, 2, 5. Isaac & w, Sarah, gct Alum
        Creek MM, O.
1907, 12, 4. James & w, Hattie, recrq
1918, 9, 4. James & Hettie dropped from
        mbrp

STROUP
1905, 3, 1. Charles F. rocf Cleveland MM
1909, 10, 6. Chas. & w, Mary, rocf Urbana MM
1910, 4, 6. Bertha recrq
1916, 12, 6. Chas. F. & w, Mary M., & ch, Sa-
        rah Pauline, Mary Esther & Samuel, relrq

STUKEY
1896, 3, 4. Ordie recrq
1909, 7, 7. Ordie dropped from mbrp

SWITZER
1913, 7, 2. Wm. & Viola dropped from mbrp

TANNAR
1899, 12, 6.   Rebecca & Rosa recrq

TATE
1900, 12, 5.   Serena relrq

TAYLOR
1913, 5, 7.   Inez recrq
1915, 7, 7.   Inez dropped from mbrp

TAYMOR
1909, 7, 7.   Mary dropped from mbrp
1909, 7, 7.   Rosa [Tamer] dropped from mbrp
1913, 11, 5.   Roy [Taynor] recrq

TEMPLE
1901, 7, 3.   Alexander W. & Sarah C. recrq

THOMAS
1897, 4, 17.   Sarah & ch, Grace, Ada, Mary,
    Bessie & Clyde, recrq
1898, 6, 1.   Sarah & Grace dropped from mbrp
1898, 6, 1.   Bessie dropped from mbrp
1898, 6, 1.   Mary dropped from mbrp
1898, 6, 1.   Clyde dropped from mbrp
1900, 12, 5.   Christina relrq
1903, 12, 2.   Herbert G. & w, Lizzie, & dt,
    Leona, recrq
1908, 6, 3.   Hubert & w dropped from mbrp
1917, 2, 7.   Lulu recrq

THOMPSON
1896, 3, 4.   Harrie recrq
1898, 6, 1.   Harry dropped from mbrp
1900, 12, 5.   Mattie & Katie relrq
1909, 7, 7.   Walter & Hattie dropped from
    mbrp
1913, 5, 7.   Alta R. recrq
1916, 4, 5.   Elda Margaret recrq
1916, 4, 5.   James Howard recrq
1917, 2, 7.   Elizabeth & Margaret recrq
1919, 3, 5.   Margaret dropped from mbrp

THRAILKILL
1904, 4, 6.   Ostra & Catherine Elizabeth
    recrq
1904, 10, 5.   Tolford recrq
1905, 1, 4.   Elsie E. recrq
1906, 12, 6.   Elsie dropped from mbrp
1909, 7, 7.   Ostra dropped from mbrp
1913, 3, 5.   Walter recrq

THROP
1900, 7, 4.   Sarah recrq
1909, 7, 7.   Sarah dropped from mbrp

TIPPIN
1906, 5, 2.   Hattie relrq

TIPTON
1900, 11, 2.   Albert dropped from mbrp

THOMPSON
1910, 4, 6.   Edgar recrq
1912, 10, 2.   Edgar dropped from mbrp
1919, 3, 5.   Elizabeth dropped from mbrp

THORTON
1923, 4, 4.   Laura B. recrq

TINKER
1918, 9, 4.   Glenn & Edith dropped from mbrp

TOMLINSON
1913, 3, 5.   Olive gct Bellfountaine MM, O.
1916, 9, 16.   Olive & s, Allen, rocf Belle-
    fountain MM

TOMPKINS
1903, .2, 4.   Mary recrq
1907, 12, 4.   Frank Bancroft recrq
1915, 7, 7.   Mary dropped from mbrp

TRESTO
1909, 4, 7.   Ida recrq

TRIMBLE
1917, 2, 7.   Audrey recrq

TROMICKER
1901, 12, 4.   Hilda recrq

TROTTER
1913, 7, 2.   Viola dropped from mbrp

TURNER
1898, 10, 5.   Margaret recrq
1899, 1, 4.   David recrq
1907, 6, 5.   David dropped from mbrp

TWEED
1909, 10, 6.   W. W. recrq
1910, 9, 6.   Wm. M. gct Cleveland MM, O.

TYLER
1920, 5, 5.   Bertha recrq

UNGER
1920, 7, 7.   Rose Marie recrq

VANCE
1897, 4, 17.   Emma recrq
1909, 7, 7.   Emma dropped from mbrp

VANFASSAN
1898, 10, 5.   Anna, Wilda & William recrq
1900, 11, 2.   Anna, Wm. & Wildie [Vantassen]
    dropped from mbrp
1909, 7, 7.   Anna & Wm. [Van Fossen] dropped
    from mbrp

VEYHL
1903, 11, 4.   Fred & w, Minnie, recrq
1906, 10, 3.   Minnie, dt Fred & Minnie, recrq

VOLTZ
1908, 7, 1. Lauretta recrq
1909, 7, 7. Loretta dropped from mbrp

WAGER
1897, 10, 6. Elizabeth gct Spencer MM, Iowa

WAGNER
1919, 3, 5. Charles dropped from mbrp

WALCUT
1898, 6, 1. Nathan dropped from mbrp
1918, 1, 2. Daisy Ethel recrq
1918, 1, 2. Eugene Wilford recrq
1918, 1, 2. Verna Alice recrq
1918, 1, 2. Ralph Lewis recrq
1918, 1, 2. Ethel Marie recrq

WALTERS
1905, 2, 1. Libbie & dt recrq
1909, 5, 5. Libbie & dt relrq

WARD
1910, 11, 2. Elizabeth W. rocf Beloit MM, O.
1912, 1, 3. Elizabeth gct Cleveland MM, O.
1913, 12, 3. Charles recrq
1916, 9, 16. Charles dropped from mbrp
1918, 7, 3. Florence dropped from mbrp
1918, 7, 3. Mary V. dropped from mbrp

WASHBURN
1899, 6, 7. Minerva recrq
1909, 7, 7. Manerva dropped from mbrp

WATKINS
1922, 2, 2. Wallace D. recrq

WATROUS
1922, 5, 3. Walter dropped from mbrp

WATSON
1869, 11, 3. William b
1868, 2, 27. Emily b

1874, 10, 7. Eliza T. & dt, Elma Caroline,
    rocf Newgarden MM, O.
1874, 10, 7. Phebe Eva rocf New Garden MM, O.
1874, 10, 7. Anna Mary rocf New Garden MM, O.
1875, 11, 3. John N. rst
1916, 4, 5. Walter recrq

WEBB
1909, 7, 7. Carrie E. dropped from mbrp

WEIGLE
1903, 2, 4. Charles F. & w recrq
1908, 1, 1. Chas. [Weigles] & ch gct Pasa-
    dena MM, Calif.

WELCH
1897, 5, 5. A. R. & Rachel recrq
1901, 3, 6. A. B. & w gct Short Creek MM, O.
1902, 6, 4. Abner & w, Rachel, & ch, Har-

vey B., Payton H., Lucy E. & Alice, rocf
    Short Creek MM, O.
1904, 12, 7. Abner & w, Rachel, & ch, Lucy
    E., Harvey R., Allen & Payton H. relrq
1906, 1, 3. Elizabeth recrq

WELLS
1917, 2, 7. Nellie recrq
1918, 2, 6. B. W. recrq

WEST
1917, 3, 7. R. E. & Josephine recrq
1917, 3, 7. Stephen Rosenkrants & w, Anna
    Marie, & ch, Stephen Eric, Ernest Fuller-
    ton, Louis Monroe, Ruth Elizabeth & Leota
    Josephine, recrq
1922, 5, 3. Stephen R. & w, Anna M., & ch,
    Erick, Ernest F., Lewis H., Ruth E. &
    Leota J. dropped from mbrp

WESTENHAVER
1904, 3, 2. Annie M. recrq
1904, 8, 3. Elizabeth recrq
1909, 7, 7. Elizabeth dropped from mbrp
1913, 3, 5. Cleveland & Margaret [Westen-
    hour] recrq
1913, 3, 5. W. P. [Westenhour] recrq
1919, 5, 7. Margaret dropped from mbrp
1919, 5, 7. Cleveland dropped from mbrp

WHEATLEY
1923, 9, 5. Ada R. recrq

WHINERY
1921, 4, 6. Joseph H. rocf Rollin MM, dtd
    1921,3,16
1921, 4, 6. Edna H. & Susan L. rocf Rollin
    MM, dtd 1931,3,16
1923, 6, 6. J. H. & w gct Salem MM

WHITE
1900, 7, 4. Margaret A. recrq
1909, 7, 7. Margaret A. dropped from mbrp

WILLARD
1900, 2, 7. Abraham recrq
1907, 6, 5. Abraham dropped from mbrp

WILLIAMS
1875, 8, 4. Hannah S. & ch, Edward H.,
    Charles C., Walter T. & Arthur, rocf New
    Garden MM, dtd 1875,6,23
1875, 8, 4. Phebe J. rocf New Garden MM,
    dtd 1875,6,23
1896, 6, 13. Tennison & w, Amelia, & ch,
    Earl & Ruth, recrq
1896, 11, 4. Tennison relrq
1897, 3, 3. Harriett recrq
1897, 4, 17. Amelia & ch relrq
1900, 12, 5. Chester relrq
1900, 12, 5. David relrq
1900, 12, 5. George relrq
1900, 12, 5. Sarah relrq

WILLIAMS, continued
1900, 12, 5. Geneva relrq
1900, 12, 5. Elmer relrq
1900, 12, 5. Latha relrq
1900, 12, 5. Lena relrq
1901, 5, 7. Audren recrq
1901, 5, 7. Velma recrq
1902, 6, 4. Mary recrq
1909, 7, 7. Edward R. dropped from mbrp
1909, 7, 7. Edward dropped from mbrp
1909, 7, 7. V.dropped from mbrp
1909, 7, 7. Mary dropped from mbrp
1921, 7, 6. Florence dropped from mbrp

WILLIAMSON
1896, 2, 5. Edith recrq
1899, 12, 6. Anna recrq
1902, 4, 2. Edith C. relrq
1902, 9, 10. Florence, Maud, Mattie A. & M.
   recrq
1909, 7, 7. Anna dropped from mbrp

WILLS
1919, 2, 5. Elmer rocf Watseka MM, Ill.

WILSON
1899, 2, 1. Hattie recrq
1900, 11, 2. Hattie dropped from mbrp
1910, 12, 7. Estella May recrq
1912, 6, 5. Henry M. recrq
1913, 7, 2. Stella dropped from mbrp
1919, 3, 5. Mary Alice & Mabel F. recrq
1920, 5, 5. Nora recrq

WINSLOW
1911, 5, 3. Lottie Holding rocf Fairmount
   MM, Ind., dtd 1911,4,12
1912, 7, 3. Lottie Holding dropped from mbrp
1913, 7, 2. Lottie H. dropped from mbrp

WOOD
1906, 11, 7. Amanda J. recrq
1907, 6, 5. Daniel H. & w, Carrie, rocf
   Alum Creek MM, O.
1908, 6, 3. Amanda J. relrq
1910, 4, 6. Daniel H. & w, Carrie, gct
   Alum Creek MM, O.
1914, 1, 7. Daniel H. & w, Carrie, rocf
   Alum Creek MM, O.
1916, 7, 5. Roxie Johnson rocf Cleveland MM

WORK
1913, 3, 5. Anna & s, Daniel, recrq

WORLEY
1921, 10, 5. Clarence M. recrq
1922, 3, 1. Mary Elizabeth recrq

WRIGHT
1875, 10, 6. Wm. John & w, Mary H., & ch,
   Elizabeth P., Benjamin H., Wm. Edwin &
   Percy English, rocf Norwich MM, Canada,
   dtd 1875,8,11
1900, 2, 7. Nettie recrq
1907, 3, 6. Bernard & Myrtle recrq
1907, 6, 5. Nettie dropped from mbrp
1909, 7, 7. Della S. dropped from mbrp
1909, 7, 7. Bernard dropped from mbrp
1909, 7, 7. Myrtle dropped from mbrp

WYMER
1898, 6, 1. Frank & Elizabeth dropped from
   mbrp
1909, 7, 7. Charles dropped from mbrp
1909, 7, 7. Edgar F. dropped from mbrp
1909, 7, 7. James dropped from mbrp

YATKINS
1842, 11, 3. Hiram b
1844, 3, 19. Sarah b
1864, 12, 18. William b
1868, 7, 25. Marcus b

YOST
1904, 4, 6. Myrtle G. recrq
1905, 3, 1. Wallice W. & Sarah M. recrq
1906, 12, 6. W. W., Sarah & Myrtle dropped
   from mbrp

YOUNG
1877, 7, 4. Elma Jones gct Westland MM, O.
1896, 5, 6. Christiana recrq
1897, 4, 17. Laura Bell & Arda Ray recrq
1898, 12, 7. Albert recrq
1903, 7, 1. Laura B. & Ada Ray dropped from
   mbrp
1907, 3, 1. Christina relrq
1907, 2, 6. Mary Cowgill dropped from mbrp
1907, 4, 3. James W. relrq
1908, 6, 3. Mary dropped from mbrp
1913, 3, 5. Merrill recrq

ZEIGLER
1913, 5, 7. Charles F. recrq
1918, 9, 4. Charles T. dropped from mbrp

ZIMMER
1913, 3, 5. Tacy recrq

GOSHEN (DARBY CREEK) MONTHLY MEETING

        Goshen Monthly Meeting, Logan Co., Ohio, is located about one mile east of Zanesfield,
Ohio. A number of the original members came from Jack Swamp and Rich Square Meetings in
North Carolina. From Jack Swamp came members of the Marmon, Reams, Crew, Taylor, Stanton
and Patterson families, and from Rich Square came the Outlands, Peeles and Browns. The
Paxsons, Pickrells, Stanleys, Williams, and Greens came from Mount Pleasant, Virginia. This
emigration, which made the early Friends group at Goshen, started in 1806, and other families located the following year.

        During the year 1807, the first religious service was held and the first meeting house
was built during the latter part of that year. The first name selected was Mad River, but
when the monthly meeting was established, the name was changed to Goshen, August 8, 1824.

        There was also another meeting not many miles away, on Darby Creek, called Darby Creek.
In 1810 meetings for worship were established by Miami Monthly Meeting. Darby became the
first monthly meeting in this section, the first monthly meeting being held December 21,
1811. This meeting was discontinued about 1825. The earlier importance given to Darby
Meeting was probably due to the influence of Thomas Antrim, a minister in that community.

        A serious division in Goshen Meeting occurred in October 1828 and the Separatists
built a little brick meeting house just east of Zanesfield. Among the families who join-
ed the Hicksite branch were Aaron Horton, Zacharias Brown, Jonathan and Nathaniel Thomas,
Joseph Curl, Benjamin Taylor, Isaac and Thomas Rea, Joseph Dickinson, Thomas James, Job
Antrim, William Knox, Caleb Austin, W. P. Hunt, Elizabeth Grubbs, Hezekiah Starbuck and
Edmund Marmon. Among the families who remained with the original group were the Marmons,
Reams, Outlands, Paxsons, Peeles, Pickrells, Stantons, Stanleys, Watkins, Elliotts, Stan-
fields and Allens.

        After the Separation, both factions held their meetings for a time at Goshen, each
claiming the right to the property and blaming the other for the Separation. The question
was finally settled by court action which decided that the property belonged to the original
Society.

        Under date of January 21, 1830, the Hicksite branch reported "We have purchased the
lot and built a house on it which we expect will be inclosed and ready for occupancy
shortly". This, no doubt, was the last meeting held at the original Goshen Meeting House
by the Hicksite branch. In carrying their meeting to their new home they also carried
the name Goshen. The separation was complete by 1830.

RECORDS

ADAMS
1877, 1, 20. John B. recrq
1882, 3, 18. John B. dis

ALLEN
1874, 3, 21. Walton & w, Harriet, & dt, Ida,
 recrq
1874, 4, 18. Caroline recrq
1874, 5, 23. Ida recrq
1875, 12, 18. Walton recrq
1879, 3, 22. Benjamin F. recrq
1882, 7, 22. Walton relrq
1883, 8, 18. ----- F. dropped from mbrp
1885, 7, 11. Walter recrq
1914, 2, 11. Myrtle gct Lupton MM

ALLMAN
1851, 5, 5. Ebenezer d bur Westland
1855, 2, 11. Margaret d bur Westland
1859, 7, 24. John d bur Westland

1884, 5, 10.) Thomas rocf Westland MM
1921, 4, 13. Jasper, Bessie, Dora, Earl & Margaret [Allmon] recrq
1927, 3, 9. Jasper & Bessie S. dropped from
 mbrp
1927, 3, 9. Earl dropped from mbrp

AMINE (?)
1879, 2, 15. John recrq

AMSPOKER
1884, 7, 12. Samuel & w, Margaret, rocf Westland MM

ANDA
1890, 4, 12. Daniel & Eliza recrq

ANDERSON
1877, 8, 18. Alden recrq
1877, 10, 20. Vena recrq

ANDREWS
1879, 2, 15. Samuel recrq

ANTRIM
1826, 1, 21. Lydia (form Lupton) con mcd
1838, 3, 17. Lydia Gilen (form Antrim) dis
 mou (H)

ARGO
1877, 8, 18. Smith recrq

ARRIHOOD
1877, 4, 21. Joseph recrq
1883, 5, 19. Josephine [Arahood] dropped from
 mbrp

ARTIS
1884, 2, 9. Frazier H. recrq

ASHER
1826, 9, 16. Deborah (form Rea) dis mcd

ATHA
1890, 3, 8. Washington & w, Sarah, recrq
1891, 2, 14. Sarah relrq

ATKINSON
----, --, --. Cephas d 1860,11,15 ae 70 bur
 Carmel; m Abigail -----
  Ch: Levi   b 1818, 12, 5
    Mills   " 1821, 3, 16
    Ruth   " 1822, 12, 23
    John   " 1824, 5, 9 d 1868, 7,17
    bur Carmel
    Joseph " 1826, 12, 14
    Jane   " 1829, 8, 23
    William " 1832, 2, 2
    Aaron " 1834, 10, 26
    Margaret " 1836, 5, 21
    Thomas " 1839, 9, 19

1865, 5, 20. Margaret Hunt (form Atkinson)
 con mcd
1867, 9, 21. Wm. dis mcd
1870, 7, 23. Thomas F. relrq

BAILEY
1875, 2, 20. George W. recrq
1875, 4, 17. Martha recrq

BAKER
1888, 6, 7. Charles recrq
1889, 1, 12. Charles dropped from mbrp

BALDWIN
----, --, --. Enos & Sarah
  Ch: Jesse   b 1805, 11, 5
    Lewis C. " 1816, 5, 13
----, --, --. William & Matilda
  Ch: Matilda b 1811, 12, 3
    Uriah " 1814, 3, 17
    Amanda " 1815, 11, 4
    Hannah " 1818, 3, 27
    Lemuel " 1820, 3, 17
    Enos   " 1822, 4, 13
    Mary   " 1826, 5, 13
    Sarah " 1826, 9, --
    William " 1830, 3, 23
1814, 9, 30. Uriah d bur Carmel
1818, 1, 5. Amanda d bur Carmel
1830, 1, 19. John, s Jesse & Jane, b
1831, 4, 12. Jesse d bur Kings Creek
1843, 12, 7. Jesse d bur Carmel
1857, 1, 6. Jane d bur Carmel
1863, 6, 5. Wm. d

1825, 12, 17. Sarah rmt John Marmon
1826, 3, 18. Jane (form Marmon) dis mcd
1874, 5, 23. Joseph & w, Sarah, recrq
1875, 2, 20. Stephen H. & w, Eleanor M., &
 ch, Ella M. & Chas. B., recrq
1875, 2, 20. Mary Emma recrq

BALDWIN, continued
1875, 2, 20. Martha M. recrq
1875, 2, 20. Charles P. recrq
1883, 3, 24. Wm. K. rocf Gilead MM
1885, 2, 14. Stephen relrq
1885, 4, 11. Wm. H. & w, Mary C., & dt, Edna
     M., relrq
1886, 3, 13. W. Clark & w, Maria, recrq
1886, 4, 10. Joseph & fam gct Alum Creek MM
1890, 2, 8. Thomas recrq
1891, 8, 8. Clark dropped from mbrp
1892, 6, 11. Wm. & Thomas relrq

BALLENGER
1828, 11, 20. Samuel dis (H)

1863, 2, 1. Abigail Pope (form Ballenger) dis
     mcd & jas
1885, 9, 12. Adaline rocf Westland MM
1887, 3, 12. Adaline relrq
1890, 3, 8. Mabel recrq
1891, 12, 12. Myrtle relrq

BARTLOW
1932, 12, 14. John L. & w & dt, Eldora, rocf
     Hughesville MM, Pa.

BATEMAN
----, --, --. John & Lida S.
     Ch: Susan S. b 1849, 10, 9 d 1850, 5,20
          bur Goshen
          Edward S. " 1851, 10, 12
          Oliver W. " 1854, 3, 17
          Caroline   " 1856, 9, 2
1849, 10, 6. Mary Anna d bur Goshen
1849, 4, 16. Mahlon d bur Bellfontain

1862, 5, 24. Mary Ann & Hannah gct Cincinnati
     MM

BEARLINE
1889, 5, 11. Amanda Salina recrq

BEECH
1825, 5, 21. Elizabeth rocf Harrisburgh MM,
     dtd 1822,10,30

BENEDICT
----, --, --. Henry & Eliza
     Ch: Mary Jane b 1852, 3, 21
          Esther   " 1854, 1, 17 d 1854, 2,11
          bur Goshen

1873, 10, 10. Thos. Clarkson Williams gct Alum
     Creek MM, O., to m Esther Benedict

BEIGHTLER
1891, 7, 11. Estie recrq

BENNET
1875, 2, 20. Abel P. recrq
1875, 2, 20. Nancy A. recrq
1875, 2, 20. Mary L. recrq

1875, 2, 20. Franklin L. recrq
1875, 2, 20. Esther Ann recrq
1883, 1, 20. Able dropped from mbrp

BENTON
1921, 4, 13. Samuel & Mary recrq
1924, 2, 13. Samuel gct Flat Branch MM

BERRY
1826, 9, 16. Mary rocf Short Creek MM, O.,
     dtd 1826,9,19
1891, 2, 14. Wm. & w, Anna, recrq
1893, 5, 15. Mancil recrq

BETTS
1884, 7, 12. Margaret & Dollie recrq
1886, 3, 13. Carrie recrq
1888, 6, 7. Grace recrq
1891, 7, 11. Bertie recrq
1891, 8, 8. Carrie dropped from mbrp

BICKNER
1878, 4, 20. Charles J. recrq
1878, 4, 20. Catharine E. recrq

BIGGS
1881, 2, 19. Jesse recrq

BISHOP
1873, 5, 24. Hannah Isabell & Chas. Sumner,
     ch Louisa, recrq

BIVAN
1847, 12, 14. Stacy d bur Lewisburg
1848, 4, 9. Ellen Jane, dt Stacy & Jane, b

BLACKBURN
1874, 5, 23. Miles recrq
1875, 10, 23. Miles O. rmt Hannah Wanzer
1877, 1, 20. Anna & Drell recrq
1880, 11, 20. Miles relrq
1883, 6, 23. Ella recrq
1883, 6, 23. Drell relrq
1883, 9, 22. Hannah rocf Gilead MM
1884, 2, 9. Addie recrq
1885, 2, 14. Hannah L. gct Barclay MM, Kans.
1887, 5, 14. Ella Vernon (form Blackburn)
     relrq

BLUE
1893, 6, 10. Cora D. & Wm. M. recrq

BOOL
1893, 1, 14. Everett recrq

BOONE
1890, 2, 8. Stella recrq

BORTON
1839, 8, 17. Mirriam, William, Elizabeth &
     Ira, ch Asa, rocf Green Plain MM, dtd
     1839,7,17 (H)
1842, 11, 19. Minor ch of Asa gct Spring-

BORTON, continued
      borough MM (H)

BRAKE
1879, 3, 22. Laura J. recrq
1883, 9, 22. John & Laura dropped from mbrp

BRIGGS
1883, 11, 17. Jessie dropped from mbrp

BRINTON
1872, 3, 23. Lydia A. recrq

BRISTLEY
1891, 6, 13. Harry recrq
1891, 6, 13. Phillip recrq
1891, 6, 13. Maud recrq
1891, 6, 13. Mary recrq

BRODERICK
1862, 5, 24. Elizabeth (form Elliott) con mcd
1862, 10, 9. Elizabeth gct Alum Creek MM, O.
1893, 9, 9. Samuel [Broadrick] & w, Nanie,
    rocf Westland MM
1894, 6, 9. Samuel [Brodrick] & w, Nancy,
    relrq

BROSIUS
1867, 1, 19. Jane A. gct Alliance MM

BROWN
1844, 6, 11. Susanna d bur Goshen
1865, 11, 23. Olive d bur Lewisburg
1866, 8, 31. Asa d bur Goshen

1825, 3, 19. Elizabeth Garwood (form Brown)
    con mcd
1826, 3, 18. Ruth Nicholson (form Brown) dis
    mcd
1826, 12, 16. Zacheus rmt Hannah Marmon
1830, 2, 25. Benjamin dis mou (H)
1830, 5, 20. Ira rmt Rebecca Rea (H)
1833, 6, 15. Joel & w, Mary, & ch rocf Hope-
    well MM, Va. (H)
1833, 6, 15. David & ch rocf Hopewell MM, Va.
1834, 9, 20. Elihu & dt, Hannah, rocf Little
    Fall MM, Md., dtd 1834,9,2 (H)
1834, 9, 20. Jehu rocf Little Fall MM, Md.,
    dtd 1834,9,2 (H)
1836, 1, 16. Asa gct Greenplain MM, to m
    Hannah B. Sand (H)
1836, 2, 20. James con mou (H)
1836, 4, 19. Mary Ann rmt John J. Michener (H)
1836, 11, 19. Ama rmt Joshua Scott (H)
1837, 5, 20. John rmt Susannah Michener (H)
1837, 5, 20. Elizabeth Ann recrq (H)
1839, 5, 18. Isaac con mou (H)
1839, 12, 21. Joseph dis disunity (H)
1840, 2, 15. Isaac dis disunity (H)
1845, 6, 21. Rebecca rmt Enoch Scott (H)
1862, 3, 22. Thomas recrq
1862, 4, 19. Hannah recrq
1864, 12, 24. Olive (form Ingham) con mcd

1866, 6, 23. Ruth (form Elliott) con mcd
1870, 5, 21. Ellen rmt John J. Coran
1873, 10, 10. Thos. S. rmt Mary Eliza Knight
1874, 6, 20. Emma recrq
1874, 9, 19. Laura recrq
1876, 1, 22. Adaline Julia recrq
1877, 1, 20. Omar & w, Mary, & ch, Frederick
    & Jesse, recrq
1877, 1, 20. Linden F. recrq
1877, 1, 20. Samuel recrq
1878, 7, 20. Omar & fam relrq
1878, 10, 19. Addie recrq
1879, 5, 24. Carrie M. recrq
1880, 11, 20. Thomas & w & ch relrq
1884, 7, 12. Jennie recrq
1888, 6, 7. Julia A. recrq
1890, 12, 13. Ruth relrq
1921, 4, 13. Charles recrq
1926, 11, 17. Charles dropped from mbrp

BUNDY
1880, 7, 24. Henry C. & w, Mary E., & ch,
    Wm. H., Nellie & Alise, rocf Walnut Ridge
    MM, Ind., dtd 1880,7,17
1884, 9, 13. Henry C. & fam gct Caesars Creek
    MM, O.

BUNKER
1862, 10, 22. Edwin M. recrq
1864, 9, 17. Edwin M. gct Allum Creek MM, O.

BURGHTLER
1890, 3, 8. Dell recrq

BURRES
1891, 9, 12. Josiah recrq

BUSH
1876, 11, 18. Matilda recrq

BUTLER
1853, 2, 12. Sarah [Buttlar] d bur Goshen

1874, 3, 21. Melissa recrq
1876, 3, 18. Alonzo recrq
1877, 1, 20. Oscar & Joseph recrq
1877, 12, 22. Sylvester recrq
1889, 4, 13. Sadie recrq
1891, 6, 13. F. O. & Attie recrq

BYRD
1884, 9, 13. James Clark & w, Susannah, rec-
    rq
1889, 4, 13. Ella recrq

CADWALADER
1876, 10, 21. Wm. F. & dt, Emma W., gct Os-
    caloosa MM, Ia.
1876, 10, 21. Lizzie T. & Morris W., ch Wm.
    J., gct Oscaloosa MM, Ia.

CAHILL
1888, 6, 7. Joshua recrq

CAHILL, continued
1889, 1, 12. Joshua dropped from mbrp
1890, 3, 8. J. E. recrq

CANBY
1833, 11, 16. Sarah recrq (H)
1840, 11, 21. Sarah rmt Benjamin Michener (H)

CAREY
1920, 10, 30. Charles & w, Alice, & ch,
     Florence, Milford, Marvin & Margaret Har-
     bin, rocf Urbana MM
1921, 4, 13. Kenneth recrq
1924, 5, 14. Kenneth gct Carmel MM
1925, 7, 8. Rev. Chas. J. gct Mt. Pleasant
     MM
1925, 7, 8. Jennie Peel gct Mt. Pleasant MM
1925, 7, 8. Marvin gct Mt. Pleasant MM

CARPENTER
1885, 5, 9. James recrq

CARPER
1877, 9, 22. Jacob Sr. recrq
1883, 8, 18. Jacob [Carfer] dropped from mbrp

CAVE
1884, 5, 10. Joseph recrq
1885, 3, 14. J. [Caves] & w relrq
1887, 2, 12. Joseph & w, Mary Jane, relrq

CAVIS
1878, 6, 22. Joseph recrq

CEAS
1879, 6, 21. Louis & w, Lenora, recrq

CHAMBERLAIN
1890, 4, 12. Cora recrq
1890, 7, 12. Jennie recrq
1891, 7, 11. George recrq

CHENY
1888, 3, 10. Isah recrq
1890, 10, 11. Isah dropped from mbrp

CHEEVER
1890, 2, 8. Henry & w, Ettie, recrq
1891, 6, 13. Henry & Etta [Chevee] relrq

CLAPSADLE
1889, 4, 13. Jesse recrq
1927, 2, 9. Harry & w, Nellie, recrq

CLARK
1852, 1, 20. Elizabeth d bur Goshen

1826, 3, 18. Robert rmt Elizabeth Vincent
1826, 5, 20. Elizabeth gct Greenplain MM
1835, 12, 19. Solomon & w, Ann, & ch, Joseph,
     Deborah & Curtis, rocf Stillwater MM, dtd
     1835,6,20 (H)
1836, 5, 21. Solomon & fam gct Stillwater MM,

O. (H)
1893, 1, 14. Orran recrq

CLAYTON
1890, 4, 12. Susan recrq
1892, 7, 9. Susan relrq

CLEMENS
1891, 9, 12. C. recrq

CLEVELAND
1877, 4, 21. Huldah A. recrq

CLINGAMAN
1885, 5, 9. William recrq
1888, 2, 11. Horatio [Clingamon] recrq
1889, 1, 12. Lucy recrq
1889, 6, 8. Harry [Clingamon] recrq

CLOW
1884, 2, 9. E. N. recrq
1884, 2, 16. Belle recrq

COCHRAN
1891, 2, 14. Hollis recrq

COLE
1868, 2, 22. Emily (form Townsend) con mcd
1875, 2, 20. John A. recrq
1876, 1, 22. Louiza recrq
1883, 1, 20. John A. & Louisa dropped from
     mbrp

COLLINS
1889, 4, 13. Elma recrq

COLYER
1825, 6, 18. Miriam Marmon (form Colyer) con
     mcd

COMINS
1883, 8, 18. Mary dropped from mbrp

CONNER
1914, 1, 21. Rev. & Mrs. recrq

CONOVER
1921, 4, 13. Margaret, Kathelene & Fremont
     recrq

COOKSEY
1931, 5, 13. Hobart & Martha Dunaway recrq

COONS
1876, 2, 19. Mary A. recrq

COOPER
1889, 4, 13. C. D. recrq

COOVER
1868, 9, 8. Maryvalen, dt Wm. & Elizabeth, b

1865, 11, 18. Elizabeth D. (form Watkins) con

COOVER, continued
    mcd
1866, 4, 21. Wm. B. recrq
1884, 2, 9. Melvin L. recrq
1887, 8, 13. Dora (form Corbet) rocf Westland
    MM
1892, 6, 11. Melvin relrq

CORAM
----, --, --. John J. & Ellen
    Ch: Olive C. b 1871, 3, 24 d 1871, 9, 2
        Arthur B. " 1872, 2, 14 " 1872,10, 5
        Mary   " 1874, 11, 20 " 1874,11,20
        Nellie   " 1874, 11, 20 " 1874,11,20

1869, 4, 17. John James rocf Young St. MM,
    Canada, dtd 1868,12,17
1870, 5, 21. John J. [Coran] rmt Ellen Brown
1870, 12, 24. Ellen [Cormn] recrq
1880, 11, 20. John J. [Corum] & w & ch relrq

CORBET
1887, 8, 13. Dora Coover (form Corbet) rocf
    Westland MM

CORWIN
1877, 4, 21. Jane recrq
1879, 5, 24. John & w, Emline, recrq
1885, 4, 11. Lida recrq
1885, 4, 11. Nancy recrq
1885, 4, 11. Cornie recrq
1885, 4, 11. Dora recrq
1886, 4, 10. John dropped from mbrp
1890, 2, 8. Rollie recrq
1890, 2, 8. Guy recrq
1890, 2, 8. Charlie recrq
1892, 6, 11. Rollie relrq
1892, 6, 11. Guy relrq
1892, 6, 11. Charlie relrq

COWGILL
----, --, --. Thomas d 1846,9,15 ae 69 bur
    Carmel; m Sarah ----- d 1855,5,14 bur Car-
    mel
    Ch: Ann   b 1800, 11, 27
        Henry   " 1802, 10, 30
        Susannah " 1804, 11, 1
        Thomas   " 1812, 6, 19
        Joseph   " 1814, 5, 15
        Levi   " 1816, 4, .8
        Lydia   " 1818, 2, 1
        John   " 1820, 1, 4
        Eli   " 1822, 5, 27
----, --, --. Henry & Anna
    Ch: Angelina b 1826, 12, 11
        Eliza   " 1828, 2, 29
        Electa   " 1828, 2, 29
        Sarah   " 1829, 10, 13
        Samuel   " 1831, 7, 31
        Susanna   " 1834, 11, 26
        Martha Ann " 1837, 4, 2 d 1864, 6, 1
        bur Goshen
        Thomas   " 1839, 7, 21

Ch: Mary Jane b 1842, 2, 7 d 1846,12,10
    bur Carmel
    Lydia   " 1843, 11, 12 " 1846,12, 7
    bur Carmel
    Cynthia   " 1846, 8, 13
----, --, --. Joseph & Marthy
    Ch: Mary Ann b ----, --, --
        Robert W. " 1840, 3, 20
        Sarah Ann " 1843, 1, 5
        Caroline " 1844, 11, 6
        Eli   " 1847, 10, 8
        Allen   " 1849, 11, 3
        Henry   " 1854, 10, 8
        Obedience " 1857, 2, 19
        Asa M.   " 1861, 2, 1
1848, 1, 11. John d ae 73 bur Lewisburgh
1851, 2, 6. Susannah d bur Carmel
----, --, --. Thomas & Matilda
    Ch: Sarah   b 1855, 5, 10
        John   " 1856, 5, 12
1859, 5, 6. Levi d bur Carmel
1859, 12, 13. Levi, s Levi & Hester, b
1867, 3, 9. Mary Ann d bur Goshen
1867, 4, 24. Carrie E., dt Samuel & Mary, b
1868, 6, 9. Carrie E. d bur Carmel
1868, 6, 18. Sarah d bur Carmel ae 88 (an
    Elder)
1869, 9, 12. Henry d ae 66 bur Goshen

1826, 3, 18. Henry rmt Anna Marmon
1862, 10, 22. Esther & s, Levi, gct Allum
    Creek MM, O.
1863, 2, 1. Robert dis military service
1865, 5, 20. Martha Morgan (form Cowgill) con
    mcd
1865, 9, 23. Joseph S. rmt Mary Ann Hicks
1866, 2, 17. Mary E. recrq
1869, 9, 18. John gct Smithfield MM, to m
    Eleanor H. Crew
1870, 3, 19. Eleanor H. rocf Smithfield MM,
    O., dtd 1869,12,20

COWINS
1879, 3, 22. Wm. recrq
1892, 6, 11. Wm. [Cowan] relrq

CREVISTON
1876, 2, 19. Larkin recrq
1878, 3, 23. Sarah recrq
1883, 1, 20. Joseph, Sarah & Esther A.
    dropped from mbrp
1886, 3, 13. Rufus recrq
1889, 4, 13. Huldah recrq
1890, 3, 8. Emma recrq
1891, 7, 11. Eveline recrq

CREW
1869, 9, 18. John Cowgill gct Smithfield MM,
    to m Eleanor H. Crew
1869, 9, 18. Deborah A. gct Honey Creek MM,
    Iowa
1871, 10, 21. Mary H. rocf Smithfield MM

CROCKETT
1933, 11, 12. Mr. & Mrs. rocf Urbana MM
1932, 10, 12. Archie & Ruth gct Pomona MM, N.C.

CROSS
1884, 2, 9. Mollie recrq

CROWDER
1890, 2, 8. Charles & w, Mary, recrq
1890, 2, 8. Cora recrq
1891, 2, 14. Louie recrq

CRUMRINE
1890, 3, ·8. Ema recrq

CUMMINS
1877, 4, 21. Mary recrq

CURL
----, --, --. Amos & Eliza
        Ch: Emily E. b 1852, 2, 15
            Oscar B.   " 1853, 9, 8
            Edward D. " 1855, 6, 26
            Morris A. " 1858, 8, 4
            David A.   " 1863, 12, 1
            Mary E.   " 1866, 5, 3
            Otis W.   " 1870, 1, 21
1874, 10, 28. Amos P. m Eliza J. INSKEEP

1825, 10, 15. Ann, minor, gct Springfield MM

1840, 6, 20. Elihu dis mou (H)
1841, 6, 20. Louiza relrq (H)
1863, 4, 18. Joseph recrq
1863, 6, 20. Catharine recrq
1863, 10, 24. Louisa rmt David Mather
1868, 2, 22. Rachel rocf Wabash MM, Ind., dtd
        1867,9,14
1868, 9, 19. Rachel gct Cedar Creek MM, Ia.
1874, 11, 21. Amos P. rmt Eliza Inskip
1875, 1, 23. Eliza & ch, Pearl Inskip, recrq
1884, 5, 10. Amos P. & w, Eliza, & ch, Oscar
        B., Morris, Marietta, Alvin & Otis, gct
        Mill Creek MM, Kans.

CUTLER
1873, 2, 15. Lydia relrq

DAVIS
1886, 3, 13. E. Columbus & w, Jane, recrq
1891, 8, 8. Effie recrq
1893, 5, 15. George R. & Lewis M. recrq

DAWSON
1884, 7, 12. James & w, Sarah K., & dt, Cor-
        die B., recrq
1889, 5, 11. George recrq
1889, 5, 11. Minnie Dell recrq
1891, 8, 8. James dropped from mbrp

DEAL
1877, 4, 21. John recrq

DELONG
1890, 2, 8. William & Cora recrq
1890, 12, 13. Wm. & Chora [Belong] relrq

DEMPSEY
1871, 3, 18. Aneliza recrq

DENMAN
1885, 5, 9. Chas. W. recrq

DENNIS
1890, 2, 8. Mary recrq
1891, 2, 14. William [Denis] recrq

DERFLINGER
1884, 4, 12. Mattie recrq
1884, 7, 12. Alex recrq
1884, 10, 11. Wm. recrq

DEVER
1836, 3, 19. Margaret (form Lupton) dis mou
        (H)

DEVINE
1921, 1, 12. Caroline relrq

DEWITT
1884, 2, 16. Chas. K. recrq
1884, 2, 16. Frankie recrq
1892, 6, 11. Marselles relrq

DICKINSON
----, --, --. Thomas & Mariah
        Ch: Eliza   b 1810, 11, 19
            Robert   " 1812, 3, 15
            Susanna   " 1813, 6, 16
            Joseph N. " 1816, 5, 27
            Margaret M." 1817, 9, 17
            Hannah   " 1818, 12, 28
            Martin M. " 1820, 2, 20
            Gardner L. " 1821, 10, 6 d 1832, 9,18
            bur Goshen
            Duncan M. " 1822, 12, 3
            Joshua M. " 1824, 2, 18
            Patsy   " 1825, 3, 25
            Anna   " 1826, 8, 15

1835, 7, 18. Lydia (form Starbuck) dis mou
        (H)
1839, 2, 16. Elizabeth rmt Samuel Gregg (H)
1863, 3, 21. Matilda (form Elliott) con mcd
1890, 4, 12. Andrew recrq

DILLE
1875, 2, 20. Cyrus recrq

DILLINGHAM
1866, 3, 24. Elwood dis mcd & military ser-
        vice

DIMERY
1877, 4, 21. Micajah recrq
1884, 2, 16. C. H. & Watson [Dimary] recrq

DOUGLAS
1872, 3, 23. Cyrus & w, Susan, recrq

DOWNING
1894, 4, 14. Calvin recrq

DOWNS
1835, 10, 17. Esther recrq (H)
1862, 7, 6. Esther recrq

DRAKE
1891, 7, 11. John, Lida & Eva recrq

DUNAWAY
1931, 5, 13. Eleanor recrq
1931, 5, 13. Anna Van Hyning recrq
1931, 5, 13. Gertrude King recrq
1932, 7, 13. George Edward recrq
1932, 7, 13. Charles E. recrq

DUNLAP
1869, 8, 21. George recrq
1870, 11, 19. Wm. & Susan recrq
1872, 4, 20. Volantine & Lucinda recrq
1872, 5, 18. Oliver F. & Sarah M. recrq
1877, 7, 21. Asa & Cary recrq
1884, 2, 9. Blanch recrq
1884k 2, 16. Lawrence recrq
1885, 5, 9. Iva F. recrq
1891, 5, 9. Oliver F. relrq
1892, 5, 14. Cary relrq
1919, 9, 10. Mrs. J. P. relrq

EASTON
1884, 2, 9. Melville & Isabell recrq

EATON
1883, 1, 20. John H. dropped from mbrp
1884, 2, 9. Samuel recrq
1892, 6, 11. Smmuel relrq
1892, 6, 11. Isabella relrq
1892, 6, 11. Melville relrq
1880, 2, 21. John A. recrq

EBERSOLE
1886, 4, 10. Clara A. dropped from mbrp

EDGERTON
1826, 7, 16. Mary & fam gct White Water MM,
    Ind.

EDMONDSON
1836, 8, 20. Stanton Scott gct Greenplain MM,
    to m Hester Edmondson (H)

ELLIOTT
1846, 11, 20. Mary d ae 46 bur Goshen
1849, 11, 21. Rebecca d bur Goshen
----, --, --. John m Ruth ----- d 1853,8,7 bur
    Goshen
    Ch: Isaac H. b 1851, 11, 17
        John   " 1855, 7, 23
        Alfred   " 1857, 6, 19

    Ch: Mary   b 1859, 2, 26
        Lydia   " 1860, 7, 6
1862, 6, 27. Lydia M. d
1852, 8, 9. John Hadley d bur Goshen
1853, 7, 18. Hezekiah W. d bur Goshen
1853, 10, 17. Moses d bur Goshen
----, --, --. George m Eliza Ann ----- d 1862,
    7,8 bur Goshen
    Ch: Liana   b 1854, 1, 20
        Elizabeth
        Ann   " 1858, 9, 22
1857, 6, 18. Rebecca d ae 65 bur Goshen
1859, 4, 4. Isaac d ae 70 bur Goshen
1861, 1, 20. John d ae 79 bur Goshen
1862, 7, 27. Elizabeth d bur Goshen

1862, 5, 24. Elizabeth Broderick (form El-
    liott) con mcd
1863, 3, 21. Matilda Dickinson (form Elliott)
    con mcd
1864, 12, 24. Garland rst
1865, 4, 3. Ann & ch, James Sheldon & John
    Richard, recrq
1865, 5, 20. Matilda Ann recrq
1866, 6, 23. Ruth Brown (form Elliott) con
    mcd
1866, 6, 23. Amos gct Bear Creek MM, Iowa
1871, 2, 18. Thos. & w, Caroline, & ch,
    Thomas, Isaac D., Zacheus Olien & Anna
    Vesta, recrq
1872, 5, 18. Matthew & w, Ellen Elizabeth, &
    ch, Mary Rosilla, Abraham Lincoln, Wm.
    Ennis & Thos. Olien, recrq
1872, 5, 18. Rebecca Olive, dt Matthew & El-
    len E., recrq
1872, 5, 18. Priscilla Jane, dt Matthew & El-
    len E., recrq
1872, 5, 18. Hannah recrq
1872, 11, 23. Isaac Hamilton gct Gilead MM,
    O., to m Elizabeth T. Hobson
1874, 6, 20. Wm. G. recrq
1874, 9, 19. Isaac Hamilton gct Gilead MM, O.
1875, 2, 20. Wilkison & w, Nancy, & ch, El-
    ba L., Emerson E., Dillan L. & Sitka, rec-
    rq
1875, 2, 20. John D. recrq
1876, 4, 20. Isaac Hamilton & w, Elizabeth
    T., & dt, Annette, gct Gilead MM, O.
1877, 1, 20. Mahlon & Chloe recrq
1878, 6, 22. Isaac H. & w, Elizabeth, & ch,
    Clarence, gct Gilead MM
1879, 3, 22. Benjamin A. & w, Nancy, recrq
1879, 3, 22. Hamon & w, Nancy, recrq
1879, 3, 22. Jehew relrq
1884, 2, 16. Joseph recrq
1884, 2, 16. Mary recrq
1885, 5, 9. Elba & Dillard dropped from
    mbrp
1886, 4, 10. Mather & fam gct Iowa
1887, 3, 12. Wilkinson & w, Nancy, dropped
    from mbrp
1887, 4, 9. John D. gct Paton MM, Ia.
1889, 12, 14. Joseph relrq

ELLIOTT, continued
1890, 2, 8. Abner & Mary recrq
1890, 5, 10. Sitka relrq
1890, 5, 10. Alacka dropped from mbrp
1892, 6, 11. Esther relrq
1892, 6, 11. Charles relrq
1892, 6, 11. Martha relrq
1892, 6, 11. James M. relrq
1916, 3, 23. Harold [Eleyet] recrq

ELLIS
1884, 5, 10. John Henry recrq
1884, 5, 10. Isaac recrq
1884, 5, 10. Mary recrq
1884, 5, 10. Sarah recrq
1884, 5, 10. Catherine recrq

EMBREE
1825, 4, 16. Esther & fam gct Greenplain MM,O.

EVERINGHAM
1877, 6, 23. Charles recrq
1877, 6, 23. Sophrona recrq
1877, 6, 23. Mary A. recrq

EVINS
1886, 3, 13. B. D. & w, Jennie, recrq

FARINGTON
1878, 4, 20. Theadore [Ferington] recrq
1879, 3, 22. Theodore [Pherington] relrq
1885, 5, 9. T. P. recrq
1887, 1, 8. Lizie [Ferington] (form Williams) gct Barclay MM, Kans.
1890, 5, 10. Lida (form Fowler) dropped from mbrp
1916, 4, 12. Theodore & Annie [Farrington] relrq

FARQUHAR
1837, 5, 20. James P. rocf Pipe Creek MM, dtd 1837,3,18 (H)
1837, 5, 20. Elizabeth rocf Smithfield MM, O., dtd 1837,2,21 (H)
1838, 12, 15. James & fam gct Smithfield MM (H)

FAWCETT
1838, 9, 15. Charles recrq (H)
1839, 5, 18. Charles con mou (H)
1866, 3, 24. Jackson recrq
1933, 1, 11. O. H. relrq
1867, 6, 22. Jane Luken (form Fawcet) con mcd

FELL
1867, 1, 16. Ann d ae 72 bur Lewisburg

FIELDS
1886, 3, 13. J. T. recrq
1889, 1, 12. J. T. dropped from mbrp

FISHER
1877, 6, 23. Clara & Emma recrq

1886, 3, 13. Jesse C. & w, Mary, recrq
1886, 4, 10. Clara & Emma dropped from mbrp
1891, 6, 13. Ora recrq
1891, 7, 11. David recrq

FLEMING
1877, 4, 21. George W. recrq

FOLK
1877, 4, 21. Catharine & Etta J. recrq

FONT
1884, 4, 12. Ida recrq

FORD
1885, 3, 14. Mary Jane & dt, Sarah L., recrq

FOREMAN
1883, 4, 21. Mary recrq
1884, 2, 9. Wm. B. recrq
1884, 2, 16. John recrq
1886, 4, 10. Mary dropped from mbrp
1888, 6, 7. Ann E. recrq
1889, 4, 13. Minnie & Mary recrq
1891, 6, 13. J. W. recrq
1891, 7, 11. Elroy recrq

FOSTER
1889, 4, 13. James recrq

FOUT
1876, 2, 19. Cyrus recrq
1883, 1, 20. Cyrus dropped from mbrp
1894, 4, 14. Susie recrq

FOWLER
1862, 9, 12. Charity d bur Goshen

1870, 6, 18. George recrq
1875, 2, 20. Elizabeth recrq
1875, 2, 20. John recrq
1875, 2, 20. David H. recrq
1875, 2, 20. Eliza J. recrq
1889, 5, 11. George gct Honey Creek MM
1890, 5, 10. Lida Farington (form Fowler) dropped from mbrp
1890, 12, 13. John dropped from mbrp
1891, 12, 12. David H. relrq

FRAZIER
1890, 2, 8. Arthur recrq
1892, 6, 11. Arthur relrq

FRENCH
1826, 2, 18. Eliza Ann rocf Salem MM, dtd 1825,12,21
1863, 8, 22. Lucetta Johnson (form French) dis mcd
1870, 6, 18. Pheraba French (form Watkins) dis mcd & jas
1873, 12, 20. Huldah Mills (form French) con mcd
1877, 1, 20. Pheraba recrq

FRILHER (or Welch)
1883, 8, 18. Eliza E. dropped from mbrp

FRY
1890, 5, 10. Elizabeth (form Paxton) dropped
    from mbrp

FULK
1879, 3, 22. Adam recrq
1891, 9, 12. Isa recrq

FURBAY
1926, 11, 17. Rev. James R. & w, Ethel, & dt,
    Caroline, rocf Short Creek MM, O.
1933, 11, 12. James R. & fam gct Columbus MM,
    O.

FURROW
1875, 2, 20. John recrq
1876, 2, 19. Clarissa recrq
1883, 1, 20. John & Clarissa dropped from mbrp

GALAWAY
1886, 3, 13. J. C. recrq

GALLENTINE
1876, 4, 20. Sydner recrq
1879, 6, 21. Sydner dis disunity
1883, 1, 20. Mary dropped from mbrp
1886, 8, 14. William & w, Hester, recrq

GARWOOD
1825, 3, 19. Elizabeth (form Brown) con mcd
1837, 5, 20. Elizabeth rocf Upper Evesham MM,
    N. J., dtd 1836,9,12 (H)
1884, 4, 12. James recrq
1885, 5, 9. Thomas & w, Cynthia Ann, recrq
1891, 4, 11. Orie recrq
1894, 4, 14. Cloak recrq

GATES
1884, 5, 10. Daniel recrq
1890, 4, 12. Jacob recrq
1890, 4, 12. Anna Bell recrq
1890, 4, 12. Daniel recrq
1890, 4, 12. Jennie recrq
1890, 4, 12. Joseph recrq

GAUSE
1842, 10, 15. Isaac Michener gct Miami MM, O.,
    to m Martha Gause (H)

GEARHEART
1883, 5, 19. John T., Charlotte, Belle & Mary
    recrq
1888, 5, 12. Leonard [Gearhart] rocf Westland
    MM

GEHO
1921, 4, 13. Marshall & Paul recrq
1926, 11, 17. Paul & Marshall dropped from
    mbrp

GEORGE
1838, 6, 16. John S. & w, Mary, & ch, John
    S., Abel, Valinda & William H., rocf Alum
    Creek MM, dtd 1838,2,22 (H)
1839, 5, 18. John & fam gct Alum Creek MM (H)

GIBSON
----, --, --. William d 1866,9,15 bur Lewis-
    burg; m Marthy -----
    Ch: Prudence   b 1836, 5, 25
        Margaret   " 1839, 4, 30
        Mary   " 1841, 6, 11
        Susanna   " 1844, 4, 26
        Esther   " 1846, 8, 13
        James   " 1849, 1, 20

GIDLEY
----, --, --. Isaac M. m Mary ----- d 1855,4,
    ----- bur Lewisburg
    Ch: Lorana L.   b 1848, 8, 21
        Semantha   " 1851, 10, 10
        Darwin   " 1853, 7, 3

1863, 3, 21. Darwin gct Allum Creek MM, O.

GIFFORD
1890, 5, 10. Wm. recrq

GILBERT
1878, 4, 20. Edward & w, Katy, recrq

GILEN
1838, 3, 17. Lydia (form Antrim) dis mou (H)

GLASSFORD
1887, 7, 9. Robert & w rocf Westland MM
1891, 11, 14. Robert & w, Martha M., relrq

GLENDENNING
1890, 3, 8. Stella recrq

GODFREY
1873, 9, 20. Wm. H. recrq
1878, 2, 16. Wm. gct Miami MM, O.

GOFF
1890, 3, 8. Emily & Nora recrq
1891, 6, 13. Etta & Eva recrq
1932, 8, 10. Wm. Dwight recrq

GORDON
1893, 1, 14. Otis D. recrq

GORSUCH
1862, 10, 22. Ann recrq

GRANT
1875, 2, 20. Asa T. recrq
1875, 2, 20. Jennie recrq

GRAFTON
1931, 2, 11. Florence Carey gct Mt. Pleasant
    MM

GRAVE
1845, 8, 10. Kersey rmt Lydia Michener (H)

GREEN
----, --, --. John & Mary
    Ch: Jacob   b 1833, 8, 7
        Reuben   " 1835, 4, 21
        Robert   " 1838, 8, 13
        Susanna   " 1840, 10, 10
        Abigail   " 1843, 11, 18
        Obedience
        W.   " 1845, 3, 7
        Benjamin   " 1847, 6, 17 d 1863, 8, 4
        bur Westland
        David   b 1853, 9, 10
        Flora El-
        len.   " 1856, 6, 20
        Delphina M." 1858, 9, 4
        Mary   " 1859, 12, 2
1855, 2, 15. Mary Emily, dt Jonathan & Rachel,
    b
----, --, --. Jesse & Alice
    Ch: Rachel
        Jane   b 1856, 1, 12 d 1860, 7, 7
        bur -----
        Delphina   " 1859, 9, 4
----, --, --. Jacob H. & Anna Maria
    Ch: Harriett
        Florence   b 1861, 10, 22
        Edith Lu-
        ella   " 1863, 12, 4
        Mary Ada   " 1866, 1, 19
        Evelyn
        Strand   " 1867, 11, 23
1865, 5, 29. Susanna d bur Goshen
1867, 2, 11. Achsah d bur Westland
1869, 10, 11. Albert R., s Elias & Deborah, b

1869, 1, 23. Elias rmt Deborah A. Watkins
1870, 4, 23. John P. gct Cincinnati MM
1871, 1, 21. Robert W. con mcd
1871, 8, 19. Wm. P. con mcd
1871, 12, 23. Jesse & w, Alice, & ch, Delfina
    M., gct Union MM, Mo.
1871, 12, 23. Wm. P. gct Union MM, Mo.
1871, 12, 23. Anna P. gct Union MM, Mo.
1871, 12, 23. Angaline P. gct Union MM, Mo.
1873, 9, 20. Eunice & dt, Clara, recrq
1880, 2, 21. Carrie (form Watkins) relrq
1888, 7, 14. Mary recrq
1890, 3, 8. Rebecca & Della recrq

GREGG
1835, 2, --. Phineas rocf Allum Creek MM, dtd
    1834,6,26 (H)
1837, 5, 20. Samuel & w, Ann, rocf Allum Creek
    MM, dtd 1836,10,20 (H)
1839, 2, 16. Samuel rmt Elizabeth Dickenson(H)

GREY
1864, 2, 20. Martha recrq
1891, 6, 13. Josie [Gray] recrq

GRIMES
1891, 4, 11. Uly S. & w, Clara, recrq
1891, 7, 11. Lenora recrq

GRIPLE
1843, 8, 19. Elizabeth (form Lupton) gct
    Camden MM, Ind. (H)

GRUBB
1867, 10, 19. Katharine Pellett (form Grubb)
    dis mcd & jas
1890, 2, 8. Nathan & dt, Etta, recrq
1890, 4, 12. J. M. recrq

GUILBERT
1864, 1, 23. Katurah (form Hiatt) dis mou

HAITHCOCK
1889, 4, 13. S. G. recrq

HAMILTON
1889, 9, 14. W. G. recrq
1891, 6, 13. Bertie recrq
1891, 6, 13. Sally recrq

HAMLIN
1851, 4, 15. Elizabeth J. d bur Goshen

HANGLIN
1888, 6, 7. John H. recrq

HANNAH
1877, 8, 18. William recrq
1886, 3, 13. William dropped from mbrp

HARBIN
1923, 7, 11. Margaret gc to Calif.

HARE
1885, 8, 8. Cordelia recrq

HARMES
1925, 3, 11. Maude recrq

HAROLD
1883, 4, 21. David & w & ch, Ora J., Rosco
    C., Albert H. & Anna W., rocf Richland MM
1884, 1, 12. David & fam gct Richland MM, Ind

HARRIMAH
1889, 6, 8. Mary [Harimon] recrq
1891, 6, 13. James recrq
1891, 7, 11. Amos recrq

HARRIS
1877, 8, 18. Oren recrq
1883, 1, 20. Orin dropped from mbrp
1893, 1, 14. Amarilla recrq

HARRISON

1848, 12, 24. Lucinda Ann, dt Benjamin & Mary, b

1862, 3, 22. Deborah D. (form Watkins) con mcd

1863, 5, 23. Elizabeth Ann con mcd

1870, 3, 19. Elizabeth Ann gct Lawrence MM, Kans.

1870, 5, 21. Wm. & w, Margaret, & ch, Wm. H. & Elenore E., recrq

1879, 3, 22. Elizabeth recrq

1879, 3, 22. Hosea recrq

1879, 5, 24. Wm. & w, Nancy, rocf Green Plain MM

1887, 8, 13. Hosea gct Kansas MM

1887, 8, 13. Wm. Henry & w, Nancy, gct Kansas MM

1890, 12, 13. Deborah & Margaret dropped from mbrp

HARTLEY

1836, 7, 16. Aaron & ch rocf Plainfield MM, dtd 1836,1,14 (H)

1839, 12, 21. Aaron con mou (H)

HATCHER

1826, 4, 15. Ruth (form Thomas) con mcd

1826, 9, 16. Hope dis mcd

1831, 5, 21. Joshua con mou (H)

1862, 5, 24. Samuel recrq

1863, 10, 24. Esther recrq

1865, 2, 18. Samuel & Esther gct Vermillion MM, Ill.

1876, 2, 19. Abigail recrq

HATHAWAY

1863, 4, 18. Sarah D. gct Greenwich MM

HAUGHN

1891, 7, 11. Willie recrq

HAYES

1875, 2, 20. Orange M. [Hays] & w, Rebecca A., & ch, Florence A., Caddy J., Wm. O., John W., Joseph H. & Samuel E., recrq

1877, 10, 20. Orange dis

1883, 1, 20. Orange [Hays] & fam dropped from mbrp

1884, 2, 16. John H. recrq

HEARY

1885, 5, 9. James C. & Carrie recrq

HEATH

1871, 7, 22. Malissa (form Reams) rpd mcd

1890, 3, 8. Ida & William recrq

HECKLEY

1893, 7, 8. John recrq

HEMINGER

1884, 5, 10. Joseph [Hemming] & w, Jane, rec-

rq

1890, 2, 8. Elmer [Hemmings] recrq

1891, 2, 14. Elwood recrq

1892, 4, 9. Emory [Hemminger] & w, Dora, recrq

1892, 11, 12. Emery G. & w, Dora, relrq

1894, 4, 14. Elmer & w, Mary relrq

HENNIN

1885, 4, 11. Opa & Ella recrq

HENRY

1885, 4, 11. Alexander recrq

1888, 12, 8. Alexander & dt gct Van Wert MM, O.

1917, 4, 11. Minnie Wynn relrq

1924, 2, 13. Sewell & Minnie recrq

HIATT

----, --, --. Isom & Mary
    Ch: Betsy   b 1816, 6, 20
        Eunice   " 1818, 12, 2
        Anna   " 1822, 5, 18

----, --, --. William & Rebecca
    Ch: Mary   b 1828, 8, 22 d 1839, 8,11
        bur Westland
        Nancy   b 1830, 2, 8
        Eli   " 1831, 11, 15
        Ira S.   " 1833, 7, 27
        Almeda   " 1835, 9, 19
        Zimri   " 1837, 5, 8

----, --, --. Samuel & Susanna
    Ch: Elliott   b 1831, 8, 19
        Sarah Ann   " 1832, 11, 4
        Ezra   " 1834, 2, 12 d 1834, 8,16
        bur Westland
        Sidneyann   b 1835, 7, 2
        Sinthann   " 1837, 1, 20
        Wm. Henry   " 1838, 4, 18
        Rachel   " 1839, 9, 9 d 1839,11,16
        bur Westland
        Enoch   b 1841, 9, 25

1826, 7, 16. Rebecca recrq

1862, 4, 19. Susannah W. [Hiat] gct Spring Creek MM

1864, 1, 23. Katurah Guilbert (form Hiatt) dis mcd

HICKS

1865, 9, 23. Mary Ann rmt Joseph S. Cowgill

HILDRETH

1889, 4, 13. Warren & Malinda recrq

HOBSON

1872, 11, 23. Isaac Hamilton Elliott gct Gilead MM, O., to m Elizabeth T. Hobson

HOCKET

1869, 5, 22. Wm. & ch, Newton, Jeremiah, Emma & Ulysses recrq

1879, 6, 21. David recrq

HOCKET, continued
1890, 12, 13. David dropped from mbrp

HOGE
1841, 9, 18. Sarah Ann [Hogue] rocf Goose
    Creek MM, dtd 1841,5,18 (H)
1878, 5, 18. John recrq
1885, 2, 14. John relrq
1892, 6, 11. Mary C. [Hoag] gct N. Y.

HOLDEN
1884, 7, 12. Rosa recrq
1891, 8, 8. Rose dropped from mbrp

HOLE
1843, 7, 18. Elizabeth d bur Lewisburg

HOLLAND
1889, 5, 11. Richard & w, Allice, recrq

HOOVER
1886, 3, 13. Thomas recrq

HOWARD
1886, 4, 10. Nathaniel dropped from mbrp
1880, 4, 17. Clark recrq

HOWELL
1893, 6, 10. Wm. & w, Lida, & ch, Frances &
    Arthur, rocf Centerhill MM, Kans.

HUMPHREY
1877, 8, 18. Daniel recrq
1879, 5, 24. Mary Jane [Umphrey], w David,
    recrq
1890, 3, 8. Stella [Humphreys] recrq

HUNT
----, --, --. Eleazar & Martha
    Ch: Ann   b 1815, 5, 13
        Allen   " 1817, 5, 13
        Elizabeth " 1821, 2, 28 d 1844, 3, 7
         bur Carmel
        Elias W.   " 1823, 10, 2
        Oliver G. " 1825, 10, 27
        Sarah Ellen" 1828, 4, 14
        Martha Ma-
         riah   " 1833, 5, 19
----, --, --. David & Sarah
    Ch: James   b 1825, 5, 15
        Henry M.   " 1829, 4, 20 d 1829, 5, 6
         bur Goshen
        Lorenzo   " 1828, 4, 24 " 1833, 7,17
         bur Goshen
        Lewellyn   " 1830, 6, 6
        Martha   " 1832, 2, 8
        Mary   " 1833, 12, 17
        Emily   " 1836, 5, 4
1847, 3, 18. James d bur Westland
1847, 5, 18. Sarah d bur Westland
1864, 11, 7. Abbie Mary, dt James & Margaret
    C., b

1825, 1, 15. Margery rmt James Marmon
1825, 5, 21. Wm. P. rmt Patsy Marmon
1825, 12, 17. David rmt Sarah Marmon Jr.
1828, 11, 20. Phineas recrq (H)
1865, 5, 20. Margaret (form Atkinson) con mcd
1865, 9, 23. Margaret gct Newberry MM, O.
1866, 6, 23. Elma B. gc
1868, 6, 20. David rmt Edith Williams
1868, 8, 22. Edith gct Honey Creek MM, Iowa
1868, 11, 21. James & w, Margaret, & dt, Abi-
    gail, rocf Newberry MM, O., dtd 1868,10,19

HURLEY
1911, 12, 14. Lenna recrq
1919, 8, 21. Raymond & w, Viola, & ch, Ken-
    neth, Pauline, Florence, Ruth Alma, Cleo
    May, Donald Hubert & Evaline Edith, roc

HURST
1869, 10, 23. Elizabeth J. gct Spring Creek
    MM, Ia.

HUTCHINSON
1881, 2, 19. Ferona relrq

HYLAND
1893, 1, 14. Austin recrq
1893, 1, 14. Oscar recrq
1893, 1, 14. Essie recrq

ILIFF
1894, 4, 14. Lucile recrq

INGHAM
1864, 12, 24. Olive Brown (form Ingham) con
    mcd

INSKIP
1874, 10, 28. Eliza J. [Inskeep] m Amos P.
    CURL

1874, 11, 21. Eliza rmt Amos P. Curl
1875, 1, 23. Pearl, s Eliza Curl, recrq
1884, 5, 10. Pearl gct Mill Creek MM, Kans.
    with fam of Amos P. Curl
1890, 3, 8. Coleman [Inskeep] & w, Miranda,
    recrq

IRVIN
1871, 11, 18. Minnie Jane recrq

JACKSON
1844, 8, 9. Hester d bur Carmel

1877, 5, 18. Chas. & Jane recrq
1931, 5, 13. Nelson recrq

JACOBS
1875, 4, 17. Viola recrq
1877, 7, 21. Albert recrq
1879, 2, 15. Jennie recrq
1879, 3, 22. Robert & w, Ruth Jane, recrq
1883, 5, 19. Isaac recrq

JACOBS, continued
1883, 11, 17. Viola dropped from mbrp
1884, 2, 9. Eva recrq
1884, 2, 16. Walter & Alta recrq
1886, 4, 10. J. R. & Eva dropped from mbrp
1887, 2, 12. Joshua R., Eva R. & Jennie relrq
1925, 3, 11. Walter recrq
1927, 3, 9. Walter dropped from mbrp
1931, 5, 13. Walter recrq
1933, 7, 12. Walter dropped from mbrp

JAMES
1851, 12, 27. Isaac Sr. d ae 88 bur Goshen
1862, 12, 18. Ann d ae 72 bur Goshen

1876, 3, 18. Allen recrq
1876, 4, 20. Allie Bell recrq

JENINGS
1889, 4, 13. Sarah recrq

JEWELL
1890, 3, 8. John & w, Nellie, recrq

JOHNSON
1836, 12, 29. John H. d bur Westland
1837, 3, 26. Lindley d bur Westland
----, --, --. Exum d 1870,9,16 ae 78 bur
    Goshen; m Alice -----
       Ch: James   b 1842, 2, 21
           Charles " 1844, 1, 6
1843, 11, 4. Gulielma d bur Goshen

----, --, --. William & Rebecca
    Ch: Lindley H. b 1844, 4, 10
        Alice Ann " 1846, 9, 1
        Mahalon   " 1848, 12, 29
1846, 7, 23. Able d bur Goshen
1846, 11, 17. May d bur Goshen
1847, 8, 1. Leander, s Elijah & Eliza, b
1848, 5, 26. Leander T. d bur Westland
1849, 2, 24. Mahlon P. d bur Westland
1849, 8, 13. Eliza Jane d bur Westland
1850, 3, 24. Rebecca W. d bur Westland
1850, 4, 24. William d bur Westland

1863, 7, 18. Lindley H. dis mcd & military
    service
1863, 8, 22. Lucetta (form French) dis mcd
1864, 3, 19. James gct Winnesheik MM, Ia.
1875, 4, 17. Wm. recrq
1875, 4, 17. Mary recrq
1879, 5, 24. Peter recrq
1884, 2, 9. Clara recrq
1886, 4, 10. Peter dropped from mbrp
1890, 3, 8. Thomas M. & w, Margaret, recrq
1894, 4, 14. Nelson recrq

JONES
1865, 6, 17. Rachel rst
1877, 1, 20. Chas. N. rocf Columbus MM, dtd
    1876,10,4
1877, 4 21. Alfred recrq

1877, 4, 21. Susannah recrq
1879, 3, 22. Charles relrq
1883, 8, 18. Susana dropped from mbrp
1890, 12, 13. Elizabeth dropped from mbrp
1894, 4, 14. Rebecca recrq
1894, 6, 9. Theodore & Kate rocf Westland
    MM

JORDAN
1884, 2, 9. Nellie recrq
1887, 4, 9. Willie relrq

JOSLYN
1877, 1, 20. Newton recrq

JULIAN
1877, 4, 21. James & John R. recrq

KENNEDY
1891, 8, 8. Estella dropped from mbrp
1886, 3, 13. Doratha Estella [Kenedy] recrq

KESTER
1838, 11, 17. Jonathan L. & w, Sarah, & ch,
    Elizabeth A. & Emmy Ann, rocf Rochester
    MM, dtd 1835,3,27 (H)

KIBER
1884, 5, 10. Martin recrq

KINCHN
----, --, --. Ortice & Tabitha
    Ch: Tabitha   b 1823, 11, 16
        Newsom   " 1825, 10, 23
        Catherine " 1827, 9, 23

KING
1885, 8, 8. Joshua recrq
1885, 8, 8. Florence E. recrq

KINNEY
1917, 7, 25. Lillian Wynn relrq
1925, 3, 11. Carl & Abie [Kenney] recrq
1927, 3, 9. Carl & Alice L. dropped from
    mbrp

KNIGHT
1869, 4, 17. Benjamin Ansell & w, Ann, & ch,
    Sarah Ann, Elizabeth Jane, Mary Eliza,
    George Harris, James Edwards, Clara Alice,
    Phebe Lucy, Wm. Benjamin & Edward Samuel,
    rocf Young St. MM, Canada, dtd 1868,12,17
1871, 2, 18. Zilpha (form Watkins) con mcd
1873, 5, 24. John recrq
1873, 10, 10. Mary Eliza rmt Thos. S. Brown
1875, 2, 20. Benjamin recrq
1877, 5, 18. Charles F. recrq
1877, 7, 21. Margaret recrq
1883, 5, 19. Charley dropped from mbrp
1884, 4, 12. Fannie recrq
1886, 4, 10. George & James E. dropped from
    mbrp
1892, 6, 11. Hamilton relrq

KOONS
1885, 5, 9. George recrq
1888, 6, 7. Arland & Orville recrq

KOUTSMAN
1879, 2, 15. Mary recrq

LAMBERT
1857, 8, 12. Sarah d bur Goshen

LANGRAVEN
1890, 2, 8. Charles & w, Nettie, recrq

LAPHAM
1831, 10, 15. Rachel & ch, William Hannah
    Logan & Amelia, recrq (H)

LAPORT
1884, 2, 16. Ziphaniah recrq
1884, 2, 16. Sarah J. recrq

LEE
1919, 11, 12. Eva, Albert & Anna gct Whittier
    MM, Calif.

LEMON
1865, 4, 3. Mary recrq
1878, 4, 20. Gulia recrq
1878, 4, 20. Gulia recrq

LEVAN
1927, 3, 9. Margaret Allman dropped from
    mbrp

LEWIS
----, --, --. Griffith & Anna
    Ch: Ester L.   b 1840, 3, 25
        Elvira   " 1842, 10, 27
        Jason   " 1845, 4, 29
        Phebe   " 1848, 10, 7
1840, 11, 13. Jane R., dt Jason & Rachel, b
1842, 1, 29. Jason d bur Lewisburg

1863, 12, 19. Wm. F. & w, Ruth, & ch gct
    Minneapolis MM, Minn.
1890, 3, 8. Anna recrq

LINE
1885, 1, 10. Charles E. recrq
1885, 4, 11. Susan rocf Elk MM
1890, 5, 10. Chas. E. & w, Susia V., & ch,
    Mary L., Harry C. & Lulu, gct Pleasant
    View MM, Kans.

LINSON
1890, 2, 8. Scott recrq
1892, 6, 11. Scott relrq

LINTON
1839, 6, 15. Rachel Starbuck (form Linton)
    dis mou (H)

LINVILLE
1847, 11, 20. Ann rocf Sadsbury MM, Pa., dtd
    1846,8,5 (H)
1868, 4, 18. Ann recrq
1868, 4, 18. Jacob H. recrq
1871, 7, 22. Eva, dt Benj. A. & Harriet
    Jane, recrq
1872, 2, 17. Quincey recrq

LIPINCOT
1890, 5, 10. Darwin recrq

LITLER
1818, 5, 9. Albert & Sarah recrq
1888, 2, 11. Sallie Manson (form Littler)
    relrq
1890, 1, 11. Harriet recrq
1891, 3, 14. Albert relrq

LITTLE
1837, 5, 20. Deborah (form Monroe) dis mou
    (H)
1878, 4, 20. James H. & Katy recrq (H)
1884, 2, 16. M. E. recrq (H)

LOCKER
1877, 4, 21. George recrq
1877, 4, 21. Ellen recrq
1877, 4, 21. Mariah R. recrq
1877, 4, 21. John F. recrq

LOCKWOOD
1890, 2, 8. Warren & w, Martha, recrq
1890, 9, 13. H. H. & w, Nancy, recrq
1892, 6, 11. Clara recrq
1893, 1, 14. Della recrq
1893, 1, 14. Carl P. recrq
1894, 6, 9. Carl relrq
1926, 8, 18. Otis B. & w, Hazel C., & ch,
    Ercile, Evelyn, Lloyd & Wendell, rocf
    Carmel MM
1926, 10, 13. John J. & w, Hattie, & ch,
    Alberta F., J. Mildred, David A., Chas.
    M., Alma L. & J. Joseph, rocf Flat Branch
    MM
1930, 4, 19. Mrs. Lewelleyn recrq
1932, 12, 14. Herman rocf Mt. Carmel MM

LONDEN
1884, 4, 12. Samuel recrq

LONG
1814, 6, 17. Bertha M., J. H., Robert C. &
    Barbara G. recrq

LOUDEN
1877, 4, 21. Mary recrq
1884, 2, 9. Lovis S. recrq
1889, 4, 13. Wm. A. & Lenora recrq

LOWER
1928, 11, 14. Rev. O. O. & w, Gertrude, rocf
    Selkirk MM

LOWER, continued
1930, 8, 13. O. O. & w, Gertrude May, gct
    Van Wert MM, O.

LUCKER
1884, 5, 10. George recrq

LUKEN
1867, 6, 22. Jane (form Fawcett) con mcd
1867, 11, 23. Jane F. gct Miami MM, O.

LUNDY
1835, 1, 17. Levi & w, Sarah T., rocf Hard-
    wick & Randolph MM, dtd 1834,8,1 (H)
1838, 11, 17. John & w, Elizabeth, & ch, Han-
    nah, Henry, Elizabeth, Abner, Willson,
    Mary Ann, Emma & Huldah, rocf Hardwick &
    Randolph MM, dtd 1838,4,2 (H)
1838, 11, 17. Aaron rocf Hardwick & Randolph
    MM, dtd 1837,5,4 (H)
1842, 6, 18. James recrq (H)
1842, 6, 18. Elizabeth C. recrq (H)
1843, 5, 20. Hannah gct Hardwick & Randolph
    MM, N. J. (H)

LUPTON
1826, 1, 21. Lydia Antrim (form Lupton) con
    mcd
1836, 4, 16. Margaret Dever (form Lupton) dis
    mou (H)
1842, 4, 16. Solomon & fam gct Camden MM,
    Ind. (H)
1843, 8, 19. Elizabeth Griple (form Lupton)
    gct Camden MM, Ind. (H)

McATEE
1866, 6, 23. Obedience (form Watkins) con
    mcd
1889, 4, 13. James C. recrq

McCALL
1875, 7, 24. Wm. & Lucy recrq

McCARGER
1913, 11, 12. Leslie E. rocf Mt. Hebron MM
1914, 9, 16. L. E. gct Bur Oak MM, Ia.

McCOLLOCK
1884, 7, 12. Bernice recrq

McCORMICK
1888, 5, 12. John & w, Ida, & s, Jacob Frank-
    lin, recrq

McCRARY
1890, 2, 8. Elma recrq

McELROY
1891, 2, 14. Mary & Bell recrq
1892, 3, 12. Samuel recrq

McFADEN
1885, 4, 11. Sopha recrq

McIBRAY
1890, 12, 13. John M. & Emily recrq

McKENNON
1883, 5, 19. Daniel & Ellen recrq

McLEAN
1879, 1, 18. Noah C. rocf Spicewood MM, Ind.,
    dtd 1879,1,9

MABERY
1875, 2, 20. Wm. C. recrq
1875, 2, 20. Thomas L. recrq
1876, 4, 22. Cordelia recrq
1876, 8, 19. Abednego recrq
1885, 5, 9. Abednigo & Thos. L. dropped
    from mbrp

MANSON
1888, 2, 11. Sallie (form Litler) relrq

MARMON
----, --, --. Martin m Susanna ----- d 1846,
    10,30 ae 69 bur Goshen
        Ch: James W.   b 1803, 1, 15
            Anna   " 1804, 12, 24
            Robert   " 1806, 5, 1
            Sarah   " 1807, 9, 26
            Hannah   " 1809, 10, 19
            Henry   " 1811, 1, 23
            Jesse   " 1812, 10, 16
            Mary   " 1814, 11, 28
            Samuel   " 1816, 8, 18
            Susana   " 1818, 3, 14
----, --, --. David & Susanna
        Ch: Jesse   b 1819, 8, 30
            Elmina   " 1822, 3, 7 d 1846,11,21
              bur Goshen
            Elvira   " 1822, 3, 7
            Caleb   " 1824, 10, 13
            Henry   " 1831, 8, 4
----, --, --. Martin & Margaret
        Ch: Solomon   b 1822, 10, 4
            Matilda   " 1824, 9, 25
            Carlile   " 1836, 12, 27
----, --, --. Joshua m Zilpah ----- d 1868,12,
    17 ae 62 bur Goshen
        Ch: Letitia   b 1824, 9, 25 d 1846, 3,18
              bur Goshen
            Gideon   " 1827, 5, 11 " 1847, 2,25
              bur Goshen
            Asa   " 1829, 7, 19
            Robert   " 1831, 12, 16 " 1850, 6, 2
              bur Goshen
            Jesse   " 1833, 12, 14
            Lanson C.   " 1836, 12, 17
            Peter   " 1838, 8, 9
            Asenath   " 1841, 6, 16 d 1843,10, 7
              bur Goshen
            Richmond   " 1843, 11, 13
            Stephen   " 1845, 12, 13 " 1846, 5,12
              bur Goshen
            Joshua   " 1847, 12, 22

MARMON, Joshua & Zilpah, continued
    Ch: Zilpah   b 1850, 11, 1 d 1862, 5, 9
        bur Goshen
----, --, --. James W. m Margery ----- d 1838,
    4,12 bur Goshen
    Ch: William   b 1826, 3, 8
        Isaiah   " 1827, 11, 18
        Ann   " 1830, 8, 4
        Martin   " 1833, 2, 22
        Harriett   " 1834, 5, 17
        Mary   " 1836, 4, 2
1830, 8, 11. Henry d bur Goshen
1831, 9, 10. Robert d bur Goshen
1833, 4, 30. Jesse d bur Goshen
1833, 6, 18. Samuel d ae 60 bur Goshen
----, --, --. Henry W. d 1884,1,18; m Eliza B.

    Ch: Louisa Ann b 1835, 10, 23
        John M.   " 1837, 7, 24
        Nancy Stan-
        ton   " 1838, 11, 15
        Joseph E. " 1842, 7, 25
1839, 10, 30. Susanna d bur Goshen
1841, 7, 18. Dorothy d bur Goshen
1843, 2, 3. Martin d ae 65 bur Goshen
1844, 9, 20. Peggy d bur Goshen
1844, 10, 28. Samuel d bur Goshen
1849, 8, 3. Hannah Ann d bur Goshen
1852, 3, 19. Jesse d bur Goshen
1852, 12, 10. John H., s Joseph & Jane P., b
1853, 9, 20. John H. d bur Goshen
1854, 9, 30. Martin d
1856, 9, 2. Susan d bur Goshen
1863, 11, 4. David d bur Goshen
1868, 11, 16. Sarah Ann d bur Goshen
1878, 12, 16. Jesse L. d
1904, 7, 25. Joseph Emmons d

1825, 1, 15. James rmt Margery Hunt
1825, 5, 21. Patsy rmt Wm. P. Hunt
1825, 6, 18. Miriam (form Colyer) con mcd
1825, 12, 17. John rmt Sarah Baldwin
1825, 12, 17. Sarah Jr. rmt David Hunt
1826, 3, 18. Anna rmt Henry Cowgill
1826, 3, 18. Jane Baldwin (form Marmon) dis
    mcd
1826, 12, 16. Hannah rmt Zacheus Brown
1828, 10, 18. Margaret rmt David Reams (H)
1864, 1, 23. Lanson dis
1867, 2, 16. Ann rocf White Water MM, Ind.
1869, 6, 19. Ann gct White Water MM, Ind.
1871, 1, 21. Ann rocf White Water MM, Ind.,
    dtd 1870,11,21
1873, 1, 18. Joshua gct Greenwood MM, Ia.
1874, 3, 21. Joseph & w, Melissa, & ch, Mary
    A., Annie E., John Milton, Bessie B.,
    James Frederick & Nathaniel C., recrq
1877, 1, 20. Laura recrq
1877, 4, 21. Caleb recrq
1878, 5, 18. Samuel Lewis recrq
1888, 2, 11. Anna Pearson (form Marmon) gct
    Hesper MM, Ia.
1889, 4, 13. Eva recrq

1894, 4, 14. Ida recrq
1927, 3, 9. Shirley dropped from mbrp
1832, 7, 13. Ruth Furgeson recrq

MARROTT
1865, 6, 17. Henry & w, Lucy Anna, & ch,
    Lucy Mary, Emily Clara, Edith Anna & Jane
    Moyce & Lucy Moyce, rocf Young St. MM,
    Canada, dtd 1865,5,18
1879, 6, 21. Henry [Marott] & w, Lucy Ann,
    & ch, Lucy Mary, Jennie Mayse, Harriet
    Bertha & Bessie Louise, gct Ash Grove MM,
    Ill.

MARTIN
1877, 7, 21. William rocf Columbus MM, dtd
    1877,7,4
1880, 8, 21. Wm. relrq
1881, 11, 19. Emma relrq

MATHER
1863, 10, 24. David rmt Louisa Curl
1863, 11, 21. Louisa A. gct Miami MM, O.

MAY
1877, 4, 21. Floy recrq
1892, 6, 11. Floy relrq

MECHEM
1844, 1, 20. John relrq (H)
1844, 2, 17. Elisha [Mechems] dis training
    with the militia (H)

MEDAL
1886, 4, 10. Kate (form Sharp) dropped from
    mbrp

MICHEL
1883, 5, 19. Stanley recrq

MICHENER
1832, 5, 19. Benjamin & w, Abigail, & ch,
    John Henry David Isaac & Edwin, rocf
    Short Creek MM, O., dtd 1832,4,26 (H)
1832, 6, 16. Levi rocf Short Creek MM, O.,
    dtd 1832,4,26 (H)
1835, 11, 21. John & w, Lydia, & ch, Elisha
    G. & Jonathan E., rocf Stillwater MM,
    dtd 1835,4,18 (H)
1836, 4, 16. John J. rmt Mary Ann Brown (H)
1837, 5, 20. Susanna rmt John Brown (H)
1839, 9, 21. Henry gct Green Plain MM, to m
    Lydia Warner (H)
1840, 11, 21. Benjamin rmt Sarah Canby (H)
1841, 11, 20. Lydia W. rocf Greenplain MM,
    dtd 1841,9,15 (H)
1842, 10, 15. Isaac gct Miami MM, O., to m
    Martha Gause (H)
1843, 4, 15. Martha P. rocf Miami MM, O.,
    dtd 1843,3,22 (H)
1844, 12, 21. Edwin rmt Eliza Smith (H)
1845, 8, 10. Lydia rmt Kersey Grave (H)

MIDDLESWORTH
1892, 3, 12. Andrew J. recrq

MILLER
----, --, --. John & Margaret
     Ch: Ellis   b 1817, 11, 28
         Rees   " 1819, 7, 25
         Emily   " 1822, 1, 28
         Lydia   " 1824, 6, 25
         David   " 1827, 7, 28
         Margaretta " 1831, 1, 19
1864, 7, 24. John d bur Carmel
1872, 8, 24. Cynthia (form Paxton) relrq
1875, 2, 20. Wm. H. P. recrq
1878, 3, 23. Leanna D. gct Raisen MM, Mich.
1879, 2, 15. Sarah recrq
1883, 1, 20. Wm. dropped from mbrp
1888, 6, 7. John & w recrq
1891, 8, 8. John & w dropped from mbrp
1892, 6, 11. Sarah relrq
1892, 6, 11. Leanna relrq
1892, 11, 12. Lloyd, Charlotte C. & Wm. H.
     recrq
1893, 1, 14. Edward & Janette recrq
1893, 1, 14. Milo recrq
1893, 1, 14. Louise recrq

MILLIGAN
----, --, --. Wm. & Elizabeth
     Ch: Rebecca Ann
                   b 1840, 12, 22
         Sarah Ann " 1843, 11, 4

MITCHEL
1877, 4, 21. M. & Rachel recrq

MOFFETT
1884, 4, 12. James [Moffitt] & w, Anna, recrq
1885, 2, 14. James & w, Anna, dropped from
     mbrp
1889, 9, 14. Clara recrq

MONROE
1837, 5, 20. Deborah Little (form Monroe) dis
     mou (H)
1837, 6, 17. John dis disunity
1841, 10, 16. Moses rmt Elizabeth Rea (H)

MOODY
1891, 6, 13. Davis & Eliza recrq
1891, 6, 13. Lora recrq
1891, 7, 11. Jane recrq

MOON
1885, 7, 11. John recrq

MORE
1877, 4, 21. Albert recrq
1883, 8, 18. Albert dropped from mbrp
1884, 4, 12. Mary recrq
1888, 6, 7. Jennie recrq
1891, 6, 13. C. A. & Mattie [Moore] recrq
1891, 8, 8. May [Moore] dropped from mbrp

1891, 9, 12. Gales recrq

MORGAN
1865, 5, 20. Martha (form Cowgill) con mcd
1873, 9, 20. John D. recrq
1877, 4, 21. Josiah [Morgen] recrq
1877, 9, 22. Amanda recrq
1883, 5, 19. Josiah dropped from mbrp
1921, 4, 13. John recrq
1926, 11, 17. John dropped from mbrp

MORTON
1877, 4, 21. Albert F. [Morten] recrq
1883, 8, 18. Albert dropped from mbrp

MOYCE
1865, 6, 17. Jane & Lucy rocf Young St. MM,
     Canada with fam of Henry Marrott

MURDOCK
1877, 6, 23. Jonathan H. recrq

MYERS
1825, 9, 17. Abigail [Mierse] rmt Gershon
     Perdue
1887, 4, 9. H. M. recrq
1891, 8, 8. Mary [Mires] dropped from mbrp
1891, 8, 8. H. M. [Mires] dropped from mbrp

MYRIC
1888, 6, 7. Mary recrq

NEELY
----, --, --. Levi & Rebecca
     Ch: Cassius M. b 1845, 10, 17 d 1854,11,30
            bur Westland
         Anna
         Edith   b 1847, 5, 23
         Mary Abi-
            gail   " 1849, 12, 22
         Lowis   " 1853, 5, 11
1852, 8, 9. Levi H. d bur Westland

1866, 9, 22. Anna Reams (form Neely) con mcd

NICHOLS
1877, 4, 21. John recrq
1877, 4, 21. Susannah recrq
1883, 7, 21. John [Nicholas] relrq

NICHOLSON
1826, 3, 18. Ruth (form Brown) dis mcd

NOBLE
1891, 8, 8. Stuart L. rocf Spiceland MM,Ind.

NORMAN
1875, 4, 17. Florence recrq

NORVILLE
1891, 2, 14. Jessie recrq

OSBORNE
----, --, --. Charles & Charlotte
    Ch: Thomas Hen-
        ry   b 1853, 8, 26
        Esther   " 1856, 8, 24

1825, 2, 19. Rebecca [Osborn] & h & ch gct
    Springfield MM, Ind.
1870, 9, 17. Thos. C. Williams gct Alum Creek
    MM, O., to m Mary W. [Osborn]

OUTLAND
----, --, --. Josiah m Keziah ----- d 1840,9,
    26 bur Goshen
    Ch: Peter   b 1818, 5, 16
        Mary   " 1819, 11, 14
        James   " 1821, 11, 18
        Matilda   " 1823, 6, 30
        Sarah   " 1823, 6, 30
        Joseph   " 1825, 8, 31
        Samuel   " 1827, 8, 12
        Ezra   " 1828, 12, 2
----, --, --. Jeremiah & Martha
    Ch: Cinthyann b 1830, 6, 26
        Jane   " 1832, 4, 27
        Sarah   " 1837, 6, 16
        Isaiah   " 1848, 7, 10
        Mary Eliza-
          beth   " 1855, 9, 19
----, --, --. William & Susanna
    Ch: Ann B.   b 1836, 1, 19
        Ellen   " 1839, 1, 1
        Lucinda   " 1841, 8, 16
        Elisha   " 1844, 7, 4
        Bennett   " 1849, 9, 5
----, --, --. Edmon & Rachel
    Ch: Amazetta   b 1836, 2, 17
        Henry   " 1837, 4, 16
        Melissa   " 1838, 8, 25 d 1840, 7,27
        bur Goshen
        Naomi   " 1840, 9, 18 " 1840,10,27
        bur Goshen
1880, 8, 23. Martha m Mathew SANDS

1833, 4, 20. Sarah Ann dis mou (H)
1863, 9, 19. Susan dis
1867, 11, 23. Henry recrq
1877, 4, 21. Edmond recrq
1884, 2, 16. J. Wesley recrq
1884, 10, 11. Margaret recrq
1885, 4, 11. Ezra & w, Hettie, & ch, Elisha
    & Bewel, recrq
1888, 6, 7. Charles recrq
1889, 4, 13. Emma E. recrq
1890, 2, 8. Oren & w, Pattie, recrq
1890, 2, 8. Cora recrq
1891, 10, 10. Charles relrq
1891, 11, 14. Nora rocf Springfield MM, O.,
    dtd 1891,7,18
1892, 10, 8. J. Wesley relrq
1894, 4, 14. Oliver recrq

OVERFIELD
1893, 1, 14. Jonathan & Martha recrq
1893, 6, 10. Samuel recrq

PAGE
1888, 3, 10. Henry & w, Dora, recrq

PAINTER
1884, 2, 9. Charley recrq

PARK
1916, 3, 23. James recrq
1922, 3, 15. James gct Ipsilanta MM, Mich.
1932, 7, 13. Henry E. recrq

PARKER
1878, 6, 22. Rebecca, Eva & Noah rocf Green
    Plain MM, O., dtd 1878,6,12
1880, 4, 17. Nathan & dt, Deborah H., rocf
    Union MM, Ind., dtd 1880,3,1
1881, 9, 17. Eva rqct Milan MM
1883, 7, 21. Noah relrq

PARMENTER
1889, 5, 11. Albert & w, Carrie, & ch, Bes-
    sie V. Gamble & Albert O., recrq

PATRICK
1889, 4, 13. Elmer & Minnie recrq
1926, 10, 13. Ettie rocf Flat Branch MM

PATTERSON
1827, 5, 7. Rhoda d bur Goshen
1839, 7, 2. David d ae 78 bur Goshen

PATTON
1893, 6, 10. Albert & Lilly recrq

PAXSON
----, --, --. Jacob & Sidney
    Ch: Reuben   b 1807, 10, 27
        Susannah   " 1812, 3, 21
        Sarah   " 1814, 7, 9
        John Town-
          send   " 1816, 12, 19
        Joel C.   " 1819, 3, 15
        Rowland   " 1821, 5, 5
        Milton   " 1827, 4, 18
        Mahlon   " 1830, 5, 6
----, --, -- John m Anna ----- d 1863,8,4
    Ch: Achsah   b 1813, 1, 6
        James   " 1814, 6, 20
        Camila   " 1816, 2, 10 d 1847, 1,13
        bur Westland
        Dilce   b 1820, 10, 10
        Reuben   " 1823, 2, 10
        John   " 1828, 4, 4
        William   " 1830, 8, 10
        Asaph   " 1833, 5, 2
----, --, --. Reuben & Sarah
    Ch: Rachel   b 1846, 1, 22
        Elias G.   " 1848, 1, 16
        James   " 1850, 2, 18

PAXSON, continued
----, --, --. Rolin & Phebe
  Ch: Esther Ann b 1849, 11, 13
   David " 1846, 7, 14
----, --, --. John & Amy Ellen
  Ch: Elizann b 1850, 8, 2
   Hannah
    Elizabeth " 1853, 10, 13 d 1853,11,24
    bur Westland
   Asaph El-
    wood b 1855, 11, 30
   Enos Eddy "" 1857, 10, 1
   Jesse G. " 1859, 7, 10
1854, 11, 13. Hannah Elizabeth d bur Westland
----, --, --. Asaph & Margaret L.
  Ch: Elroy b 1855, 7, 21 d 1856, 2, 9
    bur Westland
   James H. b 1858, 3, 16
   Jesse
    Leonides " 1860, 11, 8 d 1861, 2, 5
    bur Westland
   Elisas G. b 1862, 8, 7
1863, 8, 4. Anna d

1864, 5, 21. Reuben [Paxton] & w, Sarah, &
  ch, Rachel G., Elias G., James, John,
  Margaret Ann, Mary Jane, Jonathan G. &
  Ruth Alice, gct Fairfield MM, O.
1864, 8, 20. William gct Fairfield MM, O.
1866, 2, 17. Wm. [Paxton] & w, Ruth, & ch,
  Mary Ellen, Anna Elizabeth, Florence N. &
  Thos. W., rocf Fairfield MM, O., dtd 1866,
  1,20
1868, 5, 23. John [Paxon] gct Birch Lake MM,
  Mich.
1869, 7, 24. Wm. [Paxton] & w, Margaret, recrq
1869, 12, 18. Wm. [Paxton] & w, Margaret, gct
  Bangor MM, Ia.
1869, 12, 18. Wm. & w, Ruth, & ch, Mary E.,
  Anne Elizabeth, Florence N., Thomas T. &
  Israel, gct Bangor MM, Ia.
1869, 12, 18. Amy Ellen & ch, Eliza Ann,
  Aseph Elwood, Enos L., Eddy, Alice, Jesse,
  Charles & John Henry, gc
1870, 3, 19. Asaph [Paxton] & w & ch, James
  Hamilton, Elias G. & Nelson W., gct
  Center MM
1871, 3, 18. Wm. [Paxton] & w, Margaret, gct
  Birch Lake MM, Mich.
1872, 8, 24. Phebe B. [Paxton] relrq
1872, 8, 24. Esther A. Short (form Paxton)
  relrq
1872, 8, 24. Cynthia Miller (form Paxton)
  relrq
1875, 2, 20. Franklin recrq
1875, 2, 20. Milton & w, Hannah, & ch, Por-
  tius, Sarah & Princes, recrq
1876, 2, 19. Sidney H. & Elizabeth [Paxon]
  recrq
1890, 5, 10. Elizabeth Fry (form Paxton)
  dropped from mbrp

PEARSON
----, --, --. William & Catharine
  Ch: Susanna b 1817, 8, 4
   Achsah " 1819, 7, 27
   Ichabod " 1821, 10, 20 d 1821,11,17
    bur Westland
   Rebecca b 1825, 7, 20
   Lydia " 1822, 10, 17
   Henry " 1828, 6, 26
   Mary " 1831, 3, 15
   Sidney A. " 1833, 4, 12
   William " 1835, 7, 8
   Catherine " 1838, 12, 7.

1888, 2, 11. Anna (form Marmon) gct Hesper
  MM, Ia.
1893, 1, 14. Thomas, Ruanna & John [Pierson]
  recrq
1893, 1, 14. Annie [Pierson] recrq

PEELLE
----, --, --. Josiah & Melisa
  Ch: John
   Henry b 1850, 6, 3
   Anzonetta " 1852, 3, 14
   Benjamin W." 1853, 11, 19 d 1860,10,21
    bur Goshen
   Robert " 1855, 9, 10
   Caroline
    Elizabeth " 1858, 5, 28 d 1860, 3,21
    bur Goshen
   Joshua M. " 1861, 1, 22

1894, 4, 14. Mable [Peel] recrq
1927, 3, 9. Delpha O. dropped from mbrp

PELLET
----, --, --. George & Sarah
  Ch: Frances
   Evaline b 1854, 7, 23
   Emmett " 1855, 11, 13
   Laura " 1858, 5, 23

1867, 9, 28. Albert [Pellit] dis mcd & jas
1868, 2, 22. Catharine dis
1867, 10, 19. Katharine [Pellett] (form
  Grubb) dis mcd & jas

PEMBERTON
1922, 4, 12. Harry & Weltha recrq

PENNINGTON
1841, 9, 18. Lydia & dt, Lucretia M., rocf
  Sadsbury MM, dtd 1839,6,5 (H)
1869, 6, 19. Samuel C. rmt Maria Winder
1869, 7, 24. Samuel Edwin recrq
1871, 7, 22. Mary Anna & dt, Mary Elizabeth,
  recrq
1871, 7, 22. Benjamin A. recrq
1871, 7, 22. Samuel recrq
1871, 7, 22. Charles recrq

PENNOCK
1843, 8, 19. Thomas & w, Rachel, & ch, John
     Pim, Lydia Maria, Elizabeth, Sarah Savory
     & Thomas Elwood, rocf New Garden MM, dtd
     1843,5,25 (H)

PENSE
1888, 6, 7. W. H. & w, Abbie, recrq

PERDUE
1825, 9, 17. Gershon rmt Abigail Mierse
1825, 12, 17. Abigail gct Fairfield MM

PERKINS
1888, 3, 10. E. P. recrq

PHELPS
1893, 5, 15. Roy D. recrq
1894, 6, 9. Roy relrq

PICKRELL
----, --, --. William & Mary
     Ch: Isaiah   b 1831, 2, 27
         Sarah Jane   " 1833, 1, 5
         Ruth Ann   " 1835, 2, 11
         Martha   " 1837, 5, 10
----, --, --. Jacob & Rachel
     Ch: Asa   b 1834, 7, 13
         Lindley H.   " 1836, 12, 1
         William   " 1841, 4, 11
         Peter M.   " 1843, 2, 27
         Harlen   " 1845, 4, 24
         Henry Har-
         vey   " 1847, 5, 16
----, --, --. Mahlon & Rachel
     Ch: Henry   b 1834, 8, 1
         Hannah W.   " 1836, 8, 22
         Susannah W." 1840, 4, 10
         Esther W.   " 1842, 9, 12
1838, 4, 4. Catharine d ae 83 bur Westland
1843, 4, 24. Rachel d bur Westland
1847, 2, 15. Henry d bur Westland

PIERCE
1868, 3, 21. Hiram W. & w, Hannah M., & ch,
     Marion S., Elwood C., Ella P., Mary A. &
     Luretta A., recrq
1875, 2, 20. Flora recrq
1875, 6, 19. Hannah Verona recrq
1881, 3, 19. Florence relrq

PILES
1879, 3, 22. Zachariah recrq

PIPER
1877, 7, 21. Mary Jane recrq
1888, 5, 12. Emma recrq
1890, 2, 8. George recrq
1890, 2, 8. Effie recrq

POPE
1863, 2, 1. Abigail (form Ballenger) dis
     mcd & jas

1884, 2, 9. Mariah recrq

PORTER
1888, 7, 14. Sarah L. recrq

POTEE
1874, 3, 21. Jeremiah recrq
1874, 9, 19. Jeremiah rmt Sarah A. Sager
1877, 11, 17. Lewis & w, Susan, & ch, Frank,
     Ella, Srefna & Elben, recrq
1878, 2, 16. Claudius recrq
1884, 3, 8. Ruth recrq
1887, 6, 11. Claudious & w, Ema, & ch,
     Lindley P., Flora, Ruth & Fred, rqct Dale
     MM, Kans.
1888, 10, 13. Sattie relrq
1891, 2, 14. Eliza Ann gct Long Lake MM,
     Mich.
1891, 11, 14. Ruth relrq
1892, 6, 11. Frank relrq

PRICE
1893, 1, 14. Wm. G., Amanda & Edgar recrq
1917, 4, 11. Joseph R. recrq
1917, 7, 25. John W. recrq
1917, 7, 25. Voylet recrq
1917, 7, 25. Clark B. recrq
1917, 7, 25. Opal recrq
1917, 7, 25. Geo. Wm. recrq
1917, 7, 25. Paul Robert recrq
1919, 9, 24. Sylvia recrq
1920, 11, 12. Joseph K. gct Bellefontaine MM
1926, 11, 17. John, Violet, Opal, George,
     Robert & Jesse dropped from mbrp

PRIEST
1893, 6, 10. Gertie recrq

PYRIS
1890, 3, 8. Nellie recrq

RANDALL
1877, 6, 23. Nettie recrq
1877, 7, 21. Melissa recrq
1883, 9, 22. Henrietta Wooley dropped from
     mbrp
1884, 2, 9. C. E. recrq
1890, 2, 8. Charles E. recrq
1892, 6, 11. Nettie relrq

RATCLIFF
1865, 10, 9. Wm. R. rmt Sarah Esther Williams
1866, 6, 23. Sarah Esther gct Short Creek MM,
     O.
1878, 10, 19. Joseph rocf Deer Creek MM, Ind.,
     dtd 1878,10,10
1879, 12, 20. Joseph & w, Hannah Isabel, gct
     Deer Creek MM, Ind.

RAYER
1885, 8, 8. Mamie recrq

REA

1826, 9, 16. Deborah Asher (form Rea) dis mcd
1828, 11, 20. Isaiah [Reas] relrq (H)
1828, 11, 20. Thomas dis mou (H)
1830, 5, 20. Rebecca rmt Ira Brown (H)
1831, 5, 21. Lot dis mou (H)
1833, 7, 20. Isaac dis disunity (H)
1835, 2, --. Gains dis disunity (H)
1838, 10, 20. Isaac con mou (H)
1839, 6, 15. Levi con mou (H)
1841, 10, 16. Elizabeth rmt Moses Monroe

REAMES

----, --, --. Elijah & Sarah
        Ch: Elias   b 1826, 9, 14
            Unity   " 1829, 2, 13
            Charles   " 1830, 11, 13
            Martha   " 1834, 1, 18
----, --, --. Jesse & Rebecca
        Ch: Thomas   b 1828, 4, 19
            Eliza   " 1830, 6, 20
            Elijah   " 1832, 6, 2
            Robert   " 1834, 4, 23
            John   " 1836, 8, 22
            Charles   " 1838, 8, 20
            Hannah   " 1841, 6, 12
            Levi   " 1844, 4, 23 d 1862, 7,30
              bur Goshen
            Jesse   " 1846, 1, 27
            Esther   " 1848, 5, 8
            Joseph El-
              wood   " 1853, 4, 19
1846, 9, 5. Jesse d bur Goshen
1853, 4, 3. Jesse d bur Goshen
----, --, --. Hezekiah [Reams] m Elizabeth
    ----- d 1859,6,25 bur Goshen
      Ch: Able
          Thomas   b 1838, 9, 19
          Ezra   " 1840, 10, 29
          Robert M. " 1842, 5, 15
          Josiah F. " 1845, 1, 22
          Melissa   " 1847, 11, 12
1846, 9, 5. Jesse d bur Goshen
1853, 4, 3. Jesse d bur Goshen
1857, 3, 2. Matilda d bur Goshen

1826, 2, 18. Sarah [Reams] & dt, Rebecca,
    Hannah & Mary, rocf Fairfield MM, dtd
    1826,1,28
1828, 10, 18. David [Reams] rmt Margaret
    Marmon (H)
1865, 11, 18. Deborah Ann [Reams] (form Ricks)
    dis mcd
1866, 9, 22. Anna [Reams] (form Neely) con
    mcd
1867, 6, 22. Josiah [Reams] dis mcd
1871, 7, 22. Malissa Heath (form Reams) rpd
    mcd
1871, 8, 19. Mary Jane [Reams] (form Ricks)
    dis mcd
1874, 6, 20. Robert [Reams] & w, Rachel, &
    ch, Lutheria, Effie & Luther, recrq
1874, 6, 20. Jordan [Reams] recrq

1874, 8, 22. Perly A. [Reams] recrq
1876, 9, 23. Lydia M. [Reams] recrq
1877, 1, 20. William [Reams] recrq
1877, 4, 21. Hezekiah J. [Reams] recrq
1877, 4, 21. Ezra recrq
1877, 4, 21. Francis L. recrq
1877, 5, 19. Evangelina & Florence Maud, ch
    Ezra & Pearlie, recrq
1877, 6, 23. George C. recrq
1878, 3, 23. Julana M. & Mary C. recrq
1879, 3, 22. Sollomon P. [Reams] & w, Har-
    riet N., & ch, Roswell K. & Willie, recrq
1879, 3, 22. Caleb [Reams] & w, Mary J., &
    ch, Franklin, Harlie M., Virgil F. &
    Olive M., recrq
1879, 3, 22. Chas. H. [Reams] & s, Chas. W.,
    recrq
1879, 3, 22. Matilda [Reams] recrq
1879, 5, 24. Nancy Jane & Cora [Reams] recrq
1879, 6, 21. Wesley [Reams] recrq
1880, 4, 17. Orlando [Reams] recrq
1884, 2, 16. Clara [Reams] recrq
1886, 4, 10. Clara [Reams] dropped from mbrp
1891, 4, 11. Nelson & w, Ada, recrq
1892, 6, 11. William relrq
1892, 6, 11. Mary J. relrq
1892, 6, 11. Wm. M. relrq
1892, 6, 11. Oswell relrq
1892, 6, 11. Franklin relrq
1892, 6, 11. Harlyn relrq
1892, 6, 11. Virgil relrq
1892, 6, 11. Olive relrq
1892, 6, 11. Arthur relrq
1892, 6, 11. Luther relrq
1892, 6, 11. Effie relrq
1892, 6, 11. Lucretia relrq
1892, 6, 11. Caleb relrq
1892, 6, 11. Abel F. relrq
1894, 4, 14. Mary [Reams] recrq
1894, 4, 14. Willie [Reams] recrq
1915, 11, 10. George relrq
1921, 4, 13. Samuel [Reams] recrq
1921, 4, 13. Retta [Reams] recrq
1921, 4, 13. Jennie [Reams] recrq
1921, 4, 13. Glenn [Reams] recrq
1921, 4, 13. Robert [Reams] recrq
1922, 6, 14. Corena [Reams] relrq
1925, 3, 11. Mary recrq
1927, 3, 9. Robert L. dropped from mbrp
1930, 2, 12. Glenn gct Springfield MM
1933, 7, 12. Mary dropped from mbrp

REED

1877, 4, 21. Mary C. recrq
1877, 4, 21. Elizabeth recrq
1877, 4, 21. Martha recrq
1883, 8, 18. Mary C., Elizabeth & Martha
    [Reid] dropped from mbrp
1892, 7, 9. Edward [Reid] recrq

REEVE

1877, 5, 19. Lydia B. recrq
1878, 1, 19. Benjamin [Reaves] recrq

REEVE, continued
1889, 9, 14. Benjamin [Reeves] & w, Lydia,
     dropped from mbrp

REYMER
1884, 2, 16. James recrq
1884, 2, 16. Lydia recrq

RICE
1888, 7, 14. Sarah recrq
1892, 6, 11. Alfred relrq

RICHARDS
1889, 4, 13. George recrq

RICHARDSON
1885, 7, 11. Granville M. recrq
1886, 3, 13. Hattie recrq
1889, 9, 14. Eliza Ann recrq
1892, 4, 9. George rocf Westland MM

RICHWINE
1893, 6, 10. James M. & Clara L. recrq

RICKS
----, --, --. John & Maryann
     Ch: Richard J. b 1837, 10, 19
         William P. " 1839, 2, 22 d 1839, 3, 25
           bur Goshen
         James M.   " 1840, 3, 31
         Lydia Maria" 1842, 4, 4
         Alpherd   " 1844, 3, 19
         Deborah
           Ann   " 1846, 4, 12
         Mary Jane " 1847, 11, 4
1846, 7, 19. Robert [Rix] d bur Goshen
1867, 4, 10. Pheriba Green d bur Goshen

1863, 2, 1. James dis military service
1864, 1, 23. Mary Ann & ch, Alfred, Deborah
     Ann, Mary Jane, John H., Martha & Pheriba
     Ellen, rocf Honey Creek MM, dtd 1863,10,20
1865, 11, 18. Deborah Ann Reams (form Ricks)
     dis mcd
1868, 4, 18. Jane relrq
1871, 7, 22. James recrq
1871, 8, 19. Mary Jane Reams (form Ricks)
     dis mcd
1892, 6, 11. John M. relrq
1892, 6, 11. Martha relrq

RILEY
1893, 1, 14. Joseph & Mary recrq
1933, 3, 8. Thomas rocf Short Creek MM, O.

ROBERTS
1881, 10, 22. John dis disunity
1879, 2, 15. John recrq
1879, 2, 15. Trilla recrq
1892, 6, 11. Frilla relrq

ROBINSON
----, --, --. James d 1865,2,22 ae 90 bur

Westland; m Hannah ----- d 1839,3,12 bur
Carmel
     Ch: Joshua   b 1799, 2, 21
         Mary   " 1813, 9, 13
1833, 9, 1. Sallie d bur Westland

1835, 8, 20. Esther recrq
1825, 12, 17. Mahala, Martha & Maria, dt
     Joshua, rocf Fairfield MM, dtd 1825,10,29
1837, 6, 17. George dis mou
1885, 5, 9. M. C. recrq
1887, 10, 8. McClelan dropped from mbrp
1889, 6, 8. Laticia [Robison] recrq

ROUND
1878, 6, 22. Wm. E. & s, Wm. Gilbert, recrq

ROWAND
1892, 6, 11. Wm. & Gilbert W. relrq

ROWNE
1877, 4, 21. John W. & Hannah recrq

ROYER
1893, 1, 14. Mary E. relrq

RUDY
1877, 4, 21. Samuel recrq
1877, 6, 23. John recrq
1883, 5, 19. John dropped from mbrp
1883, 7, 21. Samuel relrq
1886, 4, 10. John dropped from mbrp
1891, 1, 10. Elizabeth relrq

RUMMERY
1925, 3, 11. Wm. & Ethel recrq
1932, 6, 8. Wm. & Ethel [Rumery] relrq

RUSSELL
1878, 9, 21. Wm. P. [Russel] recrq
1883, 5, 19. Josiah dropped from mbrp

SAGER
1871, 11, 18. Sarah A. recrq
1874, 9, 19. Sarah A. rmt Jeremiah Potee
1877, 4, 21. Martin B. & Nanny E. recrq

SANDS
1880, 8, 23. Mathew m Martha OUTLAND

1836, 1, 16. Asa Brown gct Greenplain MM, O.
     to m Hannah B. [Sand] (H)

SANDERSON
1889, 4, 13. George & Ellen recrq
1889, 4, 13. John, Ida & Manerva recrq

SANDGRAVES
1891, 6, 13. Charles G. relrq

SCHUTZER
1886, 3, 13. Mary A. recrq
1891, 7, 11. Mary & Verty [Schertzer] recrq

SCOTT
1830, 4, 22.   Joshua & w, Elizabeth, & ch,
      Enoch M., Elizabeth, Joshua & Benjamin S.,
      rocf Stillwater MM (H)
1830, 4, 22.   Stanton rocf Stillwater MM (H)
1831, 8, 20.   Job & w, Merihab, & ch, Lydia
      Lee Martha William David Evaline Jason &
      Elizabeth, rocf Stillwater MM, dtd 1831,4,
      16 (H)
1833, 10, 19. Meribah & ch gct Miami MM, O. (H)
1836, 4, 16.   David gct Miami MM, O. (H)
1836, 8, 20.   Stanton gct Greenplain MM, to m
      Hester Edmondson (H)
1836, 11, 19. Joshua rmt Amy Brown (H)
1837, 3, 18.   Esther rocf Greenplain MM, dtd
      1837,1,18 (H)
1837, 8, 19.   Joshua Jr. dis (H)   [(H)
1842, 4, 16.   Stanton & fam gct Camden MM, Ind.
1845, 6, 21.   Enoch M. rmt Rebecca Brown (H)
1874, 3, 21.   Rebecca recrq
1889, 4, 13.   Oma Grace & Ollie B. recrq
1891, 6, 13.   Maude & J. H. recrq
1891, 7, 11.   Alfred recrq

SEAMAN
1889, 12, 14. Henry & w, Jennie, & dt, Blanche,
      recrq

SEARS
----, --, --. John & Elizabeth
      Ch: Abner
            Winder   b 1839, 10, 15
            Sarah Jane " 1841, 7, 17
            Huldah   " 1843, 6, 5
            Samuel   " 1845, 4, 9
            Moses   " 1847, 7, 18
            Mary
            Elizabeth " 1850, 2, 30
1849, 11, 22. John G. d bur Lewisburg

1865, 6, 17.   Samuel & Moses dis
1866, 8, 18.   Elizabeth dis jas

SEATON
1891, 2, 14.   Jennie recrq
1893, 1, 14.   Maggie recrq

SEWELL
1891, 6, 13.   James recrq
1891, 6, 13.   Susan recrq
1891, 6, 13.   George recrq

SHAFFER
1889, 4, 13.   A. D. [Shafer] recrq
1890, 2, 8.   Frank recrq
1894, 4, 14.   Lillie recrq
1894, 4, 14.   Mary recrq
1894, 4, 14.   Louie recrq
1894, 4, 14.   Ettie recrq

SHARP
1877, 4, 21.   John W. recrq
1877, 7, 21.   Loduski recrq

1877, 7, 21.   Kate recrq
1877, 7, 21.   Phebe recrq
1877, 8, 18.   Aaron & Lizzie recrq

1886, 4, 10.   Kate. Medal (form Sharp) dropped
      from mbrp
1886, 4, 10.   Phebie Townsend (form Sharp)
      dropped from mbrp
1888, 3, 10.   Johnson recrq
1889, 1, 12.   Jonathan dropped from mbrp
1890, 3, 8.   William & w, Carrie, recrq
1890, 4, 12.   Louis recrq
1893, 1, 14.   J. C. & Evalena G. recrq
1893, 9, 9.   Wm. & Carrie relrq

SHAW
----, --, --. Nathan & Miriam
      Ch: Lewis   b 1847, 6, 23
          Eli   " 1850, 2, --
          Levi   " 1854, 12, 23

1890, 2, 8.   Webster recrq

SHAWVER
1885, 8, 8.   George recrq

SHELLEY
1891, 6, 13.   H. M. recrq

SHERTZER
1889, 4, 13.   Jesse & Ally recrq
1891, 6, 13.   John M. recrq

SHERWOOD
1888, 6, 7.   Hester recrq
1891, 6, 13.   Estie recrq
1891, 6, 13.   Samuel recrq

SHIRK
1884, 3, 8.   Eva & Orpha recrq
1888, 6, 7.   Almina recrq
1891, 8, 8.   Delpha recrq

SHOCKLEY
----, --, --. Richard & Susanna
      Ch: Catherine   b 1819, 4, 14
          Jacob   " 1821, 11, 5
          Reuben   " 1824, 7, 1
          Almedia   " 1827, 4, 20
          Sally   " 1829, 9, 10
          Nancy   " 1831, 11, 4
          Amos   " 1835, 8, 1

SHORT
1872, 8, 24.   Esther A. (form Paxton) relrq
1884, 2, 9.   G. J. recrq
1892, 6, 11.   G. F. relrq
1892, 6, 11.   J. W. & Phebe relrq
1921, 4, 13.   Chester recrq
1926, 11, 17. Chester dropped from mbrp

SIMONS
1877, 4, 21. Samuel S. recrq
1883, 8, 18. Samuel dropped from mbrp

SLATER
1884, 2, 16. Minnie recrq

SLATON
1869, 12, 18. Mary rocf Springdale MM, Ia.,
     dtd 1869,9,18

SLICER
1885, 8, 8. Sarah A. & Julia A. recrq
1885, 8, 8. Albert W. recrq
1885, 8, 8. George F. recrq
1885, 8, 8. Sallie E. recrq
1885, 8, 8. Minie recrq

SMITH
1844, 12, 21. Eliza rmt Edwin Michener (H)
1874, 11, 21. Martha Baldwin rocf Cherry Grove
     MM, Ind., dtd 1874,11,14
1876, 10, 21. Martha Baldwin gct Alum Creek
     MM, O.
1877, 4, 21. George W. recrq
1877, 6, 23. Franklin recrq
1879, 9, 20. Frank dis disunity
1884, 2, 16. James recrq
1884, 3, 8. Philip & w, Emma, recrq
1884, 3, 8. William recrq
1884, 5, 10. Amos & Sarah C. recrq
1887, 2, 12. William relrq
1889, 5, 11. Sarah Jane recrq
1890, 2, 8. Joseph & Lydia recrq
1891, 2, 14. William recrq
1891, 2, 14. Eveline recrq
1891, 2, 14. Jerry recrq
1891, 2, 14. Wat E. recrq
1891, 2, 14. Albert recrq
1892, 6, 11. Emily recrq
1893, 6, 10. William recrq
1894, 4, 14. Bessie recrq
1894, 6, 9. Dora rocf Westland MM
1916, 1, 19. Frank & Anna recrq

SOOT
1887, 12, 10. Julia recrq

SOUTHARD
1878, 5, 18. Louisa recrq
1886, 3, 13. John & w, Louiza dropped from
     mbrp

SPARKS
1893, 1, 14. Isaac recrq

SPAIN
1889, 4, 13. Elijah & w, Lizie, recrq

SPEECE
1884, 7, 12. Allie [Speese] recrq
1884, 7, 12. Maggie [Speese] recrq
1891, 7, 11. Joseph recrq

1891, 7, 11. George recrq
1891, 8, 8. Allie dropped from mbrp

SPRAGUE
1879, 12, 20. James & w, Hannah M., & dt,
     Grace, recrq
1888, 3, 10. Franklin & w, Anna, recrq

SPRY
1885, 8, 8. Emma T. recrq
1885, 8, 8. Samuel recrq
1891, 1, 10. Samuel & w, Emma, relrq
1891, 5, 9. Samuel & w rst

STAHL
1889, 4, 13. Ella & Wm. recrq
1930, 2, 12. Jennie Reames [Stall] gct
     Springfield MM

STAMETS
1891, 6, 13. Frankie recrq

STANDISH
1890, 2, 8. Thomson recrq

STANFIELD
----, --, --. Thomas m Margaret ----- d 1859,
     7,4 bur Goshen
     Ch: Lydia   b 1814, 11, 24
         Sarah   " 1817, 5, 21 d 1828, 6, 6
         bur Stanfields
         Mary   b 1818, 10, 2
         John   " 1820, 8, 10
         William   " 1822, 6, 26
         Thomas   " 1824, 8, 13
         Jesse   " 1826, 8, 31
         Naomi   " 1829, 8, 1
         Samuel   " 1832, 11, 23
         David   " 1836, 8, 11
1838, 11, 12. Thomas d bur Goshen

1884, 2, 16. John recrq

STANLEY
----, --, --. Elesar & Elizabeth
     Ch: Rhoda   b 1832, 3, 6
         James   " 1834, 5, 13
     Elesar m 2nd Judith -----
     Ch: Abner H.   b 1841, 1, 24
         Mary E.   " 1842, 12, 7
1852, 9, 10. Mary d bur Westland
1853, 3, 19. Achsah d bur Westland
----, --, --. Ira & Sarah
     Ch: Ruth   b 1838, 8, 4
         Richard   " 1840, 2, 1
         Alphard   " 1841, 8, 26
         Townsen   " 1843, 11, 2
         Milton P.   " 1846, 12, 26
         Angelina   " 1849, 1, 11
         Newton   " 1853, 1, 23
         Joseph   " 1856, 6, 30
1851, 10, 18. Sarah d ae 63 bur Goshen
1852, 9, 10. Mary d bur Westland

STANLEY, continued
1853, 3, 19. Achsah d bur Westland
1853, 10, 17. Caleb d bur Westland
----, --, --. Joseph & Lydia
        Ch: Sarah T.   b 1856, 9, 7
            Charles
            Joseph   " 1859, 5, 27

1865, 10, 21. Joseph & w, Lydia, & ch, Richard
        Edward, Sarah Talitha & Charles Joseph, gct
        Upper Springfield MM, O.
1867, 8, 24. Townsend P. con mcd & military
        service
1879, 7, 19. Gennetta gct Westland MM
1880, 4, 17. Eleazar & Judith gct Westland MM
1884, 7, 12. Margaret E. recrq
1890, 9, 13. Lucinda & Martha recrq
1925, 1, 14. Gillmore & Goldie recrq

STANNARD
1891, 6, 13. Mary recrq

STANTON
----, --, --. Benjamin & Betsy
        Ch: Hannah   b 1831, 3, 29
            Stephen   " 1832, 8, 20
            Mary   " 1834, 4, 29
            William   " 1836, 2, 9
            Sarah Ann " 1839, 2, 17
            Jane   " 1839, 12, 28
----, --, --. Daniel & Angeline
        Ch: Elizabeth
            Ann   b 1835, 5, 16
            John W.   " 1838, 10, 12
            James D.   " 1840, 9, 12
            Deborah W. " 1843, 11, 13
            Mary Ann   " 1846, 8, 2 d 1860,12, 2
            bur Goshen
            William T. " 1848, 11, 15
            Lydia   " 1851, 1, 15
1850, 12, 14. Nathan d bur Westland

1876, 4, 20. John gct Peace MM, Kans.
1892, 4, 9. Lydia relrq

STARBUCK
1827, 1, 20. Rebecca dis disunity
1829, 2, 26. Hezekiah con mou (H)
1829, 3, 26. Edith recrq (H)
1832, 11, 17. Joseph con mou (H)
1835, 7, 18. Lydia Dickenson (form Starbuck)
        dis mou (H)
1836, 12, 17. Heziah dis disunity (H)
1838, 11, 17. Joseph dis mou (H)
1839, 6, 15. Rachel (form Linton) dis mou (H)
1841, 2, 20. Edith gct Fall Creek MM (H)
1842, 2, 19. Sydney Ann relrq (H)

STRATTON
----, --, --. Jacob & Rebecca
        Ch: Hannah   b 1803, 9, 29
            Mary   " 1812, 6, 27
            Joseph   " 1820, 7, 3

            Ch: Susannah   b 1822, 9, 16
                Rebecca   " 1824, 3, 14
----, --, --. Joel & Rebecca
        Ch: Rachel   b 1814, 4, 7
            Naomi   " 1815, 5, 18
            Susanna   " 1817, 3, 9
            Rebecca   " 1819, 4, 5
            Joel   " 1821, 8, 19
            Elizabeth " 1828, 1, 12
            David   " 1818, 12, 25

1825, 9, 7. Sarah [Stratten] gct West Grove
        MM, Ind.
1827, 1, 20. Sarah Wrightman (form Stratten)
        con mcd
1870, 6, 18. Eliza Jane [Straton] (form Wat-
        kins) dis mcd & jas

STERLING
1893, 5, 15. Otto recrq
1893, 5, 15. Homer recrq
1893, 5, 15. Sarah recrq
1893, 5, 15. Samuel recrq

STILES
1894, 4, 14. Mary S. recrq

STORMES
1884, 7, 12. W. H. recrq
1891, 8, 8. Willie dropped from mbrp

STOUT
1888, 7, 14. Elizabeth recrq

STROUD
1863, 4, 18. Charles & Susan B. gct Miami MM,
        O.
1863, 4, 18. Evaline gct Miami MM, O.

STULTS
1888, 7, 14. Susan recrq

SUDETH
1879, 12, 20. Benjamin recrq

SUIT
1891, 11, 14. Julia relrq

SUMERSALT
1916, 10, 18. Cora Small relrq

SUTHARD
1877, 4, 21. John recrq

SWAGER
1884, 5, 10. Mattie recrq

SWAYNE
1843, 3, 18. Isaac P. & w, Maria, & dt, Aman-
        da, rocf Green Plain MM, dtd 1842,5,18 (H)

SWISHER
1872, 1, 20. Mary recrq

TABORN
1877, 5, 18. Samuel recrq
1883, 5, 19. Samuel dropped from mbrp

TALLMAN
1889, 4, 13. J. recrq

TAMPLIN
1890, 4, 12. Mary recrq

TAYLOR
1832, 9, 15. Benjamin S. dis mou (H)
1878, 8, 24. Carrie A. gct Elk MM, O.

TEMPLE
1889, 5, 11. George recrq
1891, 6, 13. Ida recrq
1891, 6, 13. John H. & Mariah recrq
1891, 6, 13. Emmett recrq

TERRELL
1871, 8, 19. Benazette Williams gct Salem MM,
    O., to m Lydia J. Terrell

THATCHER
1834, 1, 18. Joshua dis disunity (H)

THOMAS
1826, 2, 18. Dorcas & dt, Ruth, rocf Somerset
    MM, dtd 1824,11,29
1826, 2, 18. Temperance & dt, Margaret &
    Mary, rocf Somerset MM, dtd 1824,11,29
1826, 4, 15. Ruth Hatcher (form Thomas) con
    mcd
1830, 6, 19. Jonathan dis mou (H)
1866, 12, 22. Prudence recrq(H)
1866, 12, 22. James recrq (H)
1891, 2, 14. Elisha & w, Alma, recrq (H)
1891, 3, 14. Anna E. relrq (H)

THOMSON
1890, 3, 8. Sherman recrq
1891, 2, 14. Rebecca recrq
1927, 2, 9. Elisha & w, Alma, recrq

THORN
1825, 1, 15. Rachel & dt, Hannah, Esther &
    Sarah, rocf Caesars Creek MM, O., dtd
    1824,11,25
1825, 3, 19. Rachel & fam gct Greenplain MM,O.

THORNTON
1888, 6, 7. Nelson recrq
1889, 4, 13. Boyd & Letitia recrq
1890, 3, 8. Emeline recrq
1891, 6, 13. Harley recrq

THORP
1877, 3, 24. Emma recrq

TIMBERLAKE
1857, 8, 29. Rebecca Emily [Timberleek], dt
    John & Rachel, b

1862, 10, 22. Rachel dis jas

TITUS
1893, 5, 15. Arthur recrq

TOBY
1886, 3, 13. Alise relrq

TOWNSEND
----, --, --. Wm. W. & Emely
    Ch: Mary Ann   b 1849, 5, 19 d 1850, 8,24
        bur Lewisburg
        Jane Anna b 1851, 7, 23
        Esther   " 1852, 7, 17
        Rozilla   " 1853, 12, 12 d 1854,10, 3
        bur Lewisburg
        Watson   b 1855, 6, 28
        Philena   " 1855, 6, 28
1851, 7, 26. Esther H. d bur Lewisburg
1851, 9, 28. Frances Anna d bur Lewisburg
1857, 10, 5. Wm. M. d bur Lewisburg

1835, 5, 16. Levi & w, Mary, & ch, Elizabeth
    Eli William W. Joseph & Abner, rocf Still-
    water MM, dtd 1835,3,21 (H)
1843, 7, 15. Eli gct Allum Creek MM, O., to
    m Abigail Wood (H)
1844, 3, 16. Abigail rocf Allum Creek MM,
    O., dtd 1843,11,23 (H)
1844, 10, 19. Elizabeth rmt Joseph M. Wood (H)
1868, 2, 22. Emily Cole (form Townsend) con
    mcd
1868, 8, 22. Mary recrq
1868, 8, 22. Joseph recrq
1870, 6, 18. Adella May, Emma Frances, Ern-
    est Hartley, Florance Effie & Eliza May,
    ch Joseph & Mary, recrq
1872, 1, 20. Joseph recrq
1886, 4, 10. Phebie (form Sharp) dropped
    from mbrp
1890, 2, 8. Henryetta & Phebe recrq

TROUT
1893, 5, 15. Matilda & Abraham recrq
1893, 6, 10. John recrq

TURNER
1893, 3, 15. Bernice, Maria & Henderson rec-
    rq
1893, 3, 15. John recrq
1893, 3, 15. Jane recrq
1893, 3, 15. Adrian recrq

TYLER
1884, 3, 8. Maria recrq

UMPHREY
1886, 4, 10. Daniel dropped from mbrp

UNDERWOOD
1838, 3, 17. Mary & ch, Stephen & Sarah, rocf
    Middleton MM, dtd 1837,8,10 (H)

VALENTINE
1884, 2, 16. Joseph L. recrq

VANAUSDLE
1887, 10, 8. Elisha recrq
1888, 6, 7. Margaret recrq
1891, 7, 11. Frank & Amanda recrq

VAN BUSKIRK
1919, 9, 24. Lola [VanBuskirt] recrq
1921, 4, 13. Alonzo & Arnold recrq
1930, 6, 11. Arnold relrq

VANGORDON
1883, 5, 19. Lodusky Sharp dropped from mbrp

VAN HORN
1925, 6, 10. Catharine recrq

VAN HYNING
1922, 4, 12. James recrq
1931, 5, 13. Grover recrq
1931, 5, 13. Levitha Geho recrq
1931, 5, 13. Hazel Marie recrq
1933, 7, 12. Grover & Levitha dropped from
    mbrp

VENABLE
1863, 5, 23. Vincent dis

VERNON
1887, 5, 14. Ella (form Blackburn) relrq

VINCENT
1826, 3, 18. Elizabeth rmt Robert Clark

WADE
1884, 2, 16. Frank C. recrq
1884, 2, 16. James C. recrq
1891, 5, 9. James G. relrq

WAGGLE
1888, 6, 7. Mary recrq

WALKER
1863, 5, 23. Rebecca (form Watkins) dis mcd
1879, 3, 22. Archibald applied for mbrp thru
    Goshen PM but d before considered by mtg
1881, 6, 18. Susan Sr. recrq

WALLACE
1877, 7, 21. William recrq
1879, 9, 20. William dis disunity

WALTZER
1924, 2, 13. Edward & Mary recrq
1925, 3, 11. Floyd recrq
1933, 7, 12. Floyd dropped from mbrp

WANGER
----, --, -- Abram d 1867,6,19 bur Goshen;
    m Hannah -----
    Ch: Charles M. b 1857, 9, 7

    Ch: Edwin P. b 1863, 5, 3
1860, 11, 15. David d bur Goshen

1868, 3, 21. Michael & w, Lavina, & dt,
    Emily, gct Adrian MM, Mich.
1875, 10, 23. Hannah rmt Miles O. Blackburn
1889, 5, 11. E. P. relrq
1890, 5, 10. Chas. M. relrq

WARNER
1839, 9, 21. Henry Michener gct Green Plain
    MM, to m Lydia Warner (H)
1889, 4, 13. Benjamin & w, Ann, recrq
1889, 4, 13. Ettie recrq

WATKINS
----, --, --. Benjamin m Obedience ----- d
    1843,9,15 ae 53 bur Goshen
    Ch: Mary Ann   b 1814, 11, 28
        Robert   " 1816, 5, 26 d 1859, 5, 5
        bur Goshen
        Martha Ann " 1817, 9, 15
        Matilda Ann " 1819, 1, 25
        Melissa Ann " 1820, 10, 27
        Gulielma   " 1822, 8, 25
        Almeda   " 1824, 4, 18
        Benjamin   " 1826, 1, 16
        Ezekiel   " 1829, 8, 17
        Ezra   " 1832, 2, 29
----, --, --. Lemuel m Mary S. ----- d 1854,6,
    14 bur Goshen
    Ch: Eliza J.   b 1828, 11, 28
        John T.   " 1831, 9, 28
        Lucinda   " 1836, 7, 12
        Edwin   " 1834, 8, 8 d 1839, 8,18
        bur Goshen
        Anzonetta   " 1844, 1, 16
        Sarah Ann   " 1848, 12, 17
----, --, --. Bennet & Amelia
    Ch: Elma   b 1834, 1, 6
        Deborah D. " 1836, 11, 18
        Joseph H.   " 1839, 12, 25
        William D. " 1848, 14, 18 d 1849, 2,15
        bur Goshen
        Mary Eliza " 1850, 6, 16
        Jamima   " 1852, 10, 3
----, --, --. Iry m Lurana ----- d 1852,8,29
    bur Westland
    Ch: Uriah   b 1835, 1, 23
        Ruth Ann   " 1833, 6, 18
        John Elwood " 1838, 12, 18
----, --, --. James & Obedience
    Ch: Samuel M.   b 1835, 9, 6
        Martin M.   " 1836, 9, 24
        Rebecca   " 1842, 11, 14
        Sarah Ann   " 1844, 9, 11
        Susannah   " 1847, 11, 17
        Pheriba Ann " 1849, 10, 11
        Eliza Jane " 1851, 8, 2
        Edgar J.   " 1855, 3, 23
1835, 9, 17. Reuben d bur Goshen
----, --, --. William & Matilda
    Ch: Elizabeth b 1835, 11, 11

WATKINS, William & Matilda, continued
    Ch: Irven   b 1837, 12, 20 d 1867, 6,13
      bur Westland
      James   b 1840, 9, 5
      Uriah   " 1843, 8, 31 " 1850,12,27
      bur Westland
      Lindley   b 1847, 9, 15
      Phenehas   " 1852, 1, 14 " 1852, 8,28
      bur Westland
----, --, --. Robert J. & Lydia
    Ch: Thomas   b 1838, 1, 19
      Deborah Ann" 1840, 4, 6
      Mary   " 1841, 11, 10 d 1851, 9,25
      bur Goshen
      Louisa   " 1843, 8, 26
      John W.   " 1845, 10, 7
      Albert   " 1847, 10, 7 " 1852, 9, 9
      bur Goshen
      Elizabeth " 1852, 3, 30
      Henry C.   " 1850, 5, 2 " 1852, 8,26
      bur Goshen
      Robert   " 1854, 4, 26
      Sarah Eva-
      line   " 1856, 5, 30 " 1860,11,21
      bur Goshen
      Geo. Wash-
      ington   " 1858, 2, 23 " 1860,11,23
      bur Goshen
      Lydia Alice" 1860, 6, 26
      Edward
      Horace   " 1862, 8, 14
----, --, --. Robert & Hannah
    Ch: Obedience b 1840, 12, 14
      Nathan   " 1841, 2, 4
      Elizabeth
      B.   " 1843, 6, 8
      Zilpah   " 1844, 10, 25
      Martha   " 1846, 5, 22
      Mary   " 1847, 12, 6
      Enos   " 1849, 5, 8
      Susanna   " 1851, 11, 20
      Ann   " 1853, 8, 28
      David H.   " 1856, 1, 23 d 1861, 2,27
      bur Goshen
      Alida   " 1857, 10, 29
1846, 10, 26. Anzonetta Rebecca d bur Goshen
----, --, --. Joel & Margaret
    Ch: Mary Jane b 1847, 10, 2
      Ann Eliza " 1850, 2, 14
      Sarah Elma " 1852, 8, 18
1850, 4, 15. Sarah Ann d bur Goshen
----, --, --. John & Asenath
    Ch: Mary
      Asenath   b 1852, 12, 31
      Edwin Lan-
      son   " 1854, 5, 11
      Sarah Del-
      phina   " 1857, 6, 15
      Anna Jen-
      nette   " 1859, 8, 4
1853, 7, 20. Catharine Melissa d bur Goshen
1856, 1, 10. Delphina, dt Benjamin & Rachel,
    b

1856, 1, 19. Joel d bur Goshen
1856, 7, 24. Rachel C. d bur Westland
1861, 3, 18. Susanna A. d bur Goshen
1861, 4, 10. Delphina d bur Westland
1866, 8, 13. James d ae 80 bur Goshen

1862, 3, 22. Deborah D. Harrison (form Wat-
    kins) con mcd
1863, 5, 23. Rebecca Walker (form Watkins)
    dis mcd
1863, 6, 20. Susanna & ch, Lurena Jane & Sa-
    rah Ann, recrq
1865, 11, 18. Elizabeth D. Coover (form Wat-
    kins) con mcd
1866, 6, 23. Obedience McAtee (form Watkins)
    con mcd
1866, 9, 22. Mary Jane dis disunity
1867, 6, 22. Susanna A. gct Baltimore MM, Md.
1868, 3, 21. Matilda A. & Susanna dis jas
1868, 6, 20. James relrq
1869, 1, 23. Deborah A. rmt Elias Green
1870, 4, 23. Wm. & Matilda gct Lawrence MM,
    Kans.
1870, 6, 18. Pheraba A. French (form Watkins)
    dis mcd & jas
1870, 6, 18. Eliza Jane Straton (form Wat-
    kins) dis mcd & jas
1871, 2, 18. Zilpah Knight (form Watkins)
    con mcd
1872, 3, 23. Ezra & w, Angalina, & ch, Al-
    meda, Evie M., Christiana B. & Naomi A.
    J., recrq
1875, 10, 23. Eliza Jane recrq
1877, 5, 18. Caroline recrq
1878, 6, 22. Joseph & fam gct Gilead MM, O.
1880, 2, 21. Carrie Green (form Watkins)
    relrq
1889, 6, 8. Eliza relrq
1890, 5, 10. Mary dropped from mbrp
1892, 7, 9. David B. recrq
1894, 6, 9. Howard rocf Bush Creek MM
1927, 3, 9. Chas. dropped from mbrp
1927, 3, 9. Wilford dropped from mbrp
1927, 3, 9. Winona dropped from mbrp
1927, 3, 9. Floyd dropped from mbrp
1927, 3, 9. Ernest dropped from mbrp
1927, 3, 9. Thelma dropped from mbrp
1927, 3, 9. Bernice dropped from mbrp

WELCH
1877, 4, 21. Rachel recrq
1877, 4, 21. Milton recrq
1877, 4, 21. John F. recrq
1877, 4, 21. Matilda recrq
1877, 4, 21. Eliza E. recrq
1877, 9, 22. Howard G. recrq
1883, 11, 17. John T. & Eliza relrq

WELLS
1870, 11, 19. David & w, Hannah Louisa, & ch,
    Wm. Benjamin & Chas. Edward, recrq

1884, 3, 8. John recrq

WELLS, continued
1884, 3, 8.   Albert recrq
1884, 3, 8.   Nellie recrq
1884, 3, 8.   Daniel recrq
1884, 3, 8.   William recrq
1884, 4, 12. Mary recrq
1884, 9, 13. Nellie W. dropped from mbrp
1885, 5, 9.   Daniel & Abner dropped from mbrp
1885, 5, 9.   William dropped from mbrp

WELTY
1890, 3, 8.   J. Jerome recrq
1891, 11, 14. J. Jerome relrq

WHEELER
1921, 4, 13. Floyd recrq

WHITACHER
1869, 11, 20. Hannah gct Pleasant Plain MM,Ia.

WHITE
1870, 1, 22. Ruth Win (form White) con mcd
1877, 1, 20. Warren recrq

WICKERSHAM
1892, 6, 11. Rebecca relrq
1919, 9, 24. Thomas recrq
1933, 7, 12. Anice dropped from mbrp

WIGLE
1893, 5, 15. Elizabeth, Jessie & Harry recrq

WILGUS
1875, 4, 17. Thomas & Rachel E. recrq

WILKINSON
1877, 4, 21. Thomas M. recrq

WILLCOX
1891, 2, 14. John L. recrq

WILLGANS
1883, 1, 20. Thomas dropped from mbrp

WILLIAMS
----, --, --. Silas d 1843,6,11 ae 61 bur
     Westland; m Sarah -----
     Ch: Sarah   b 1806, 11, 17 d 1810,11,23
          bur Westland
         Mary   b 1808, 4, 21
         Ora   " 1810, 5, 3
         John   " 1812, 5, 14
         Penelope " 1815, 1, 13
         Rachel   " 1817, 2, 12
         Andrew   " 1819, 7, 7
         Hannah   " 1821, 7, 28
         George   " 1823, 11, 6
         Enoch   " 1826, 3, 5
----, --, --. Asa & Eadith
     Ch: Mifflin   b 1835, 8, 4 d 1867, 2,16
          bur Westland
         Elma   b 1837, 6, 4 " 1861, 7, 8
          bur Westland

Ch: Deborah   b 1839, 11, 29
    Sarah Es-
       ther   " 1841, 8, 1
    Benezet   " 1844, 11, 9
    Louah Cad-
      walader   " 1847, 9, 15

1864, 9, 17. William & Sidney rst
1865, 1, 21. Daniel T. recrq
1865, 2, 18. Sarah recrq
1865, 10, 9. Sarah Esther rmt Wm. R. Ratcliff
1867, 6, 22. Thomas rocf Plainfield MM, dtd
     1867,5,1
1868, 6, 20. Emma P. recrq
1868, 6, 20. Edith rmt David Hunt
1868, 8, 22. J. Cadwallader gct New Provi-
     dence MM, Iowa
1869, 9, 18. Deborah Ann gct Honey Creek MM,
     Ia.
1870, 5, 21. Jesse recrq
1870, 5, 21. Thos. Clarkson recrq
1870, 5, 21. Genetta recrq
1870, 5, 21. Esther Ann recrq
1870, 9, 17. Thos. C. gct Alum Creek MM, O.,
     to m Mary W. Osborn
1871, 8, 19. Benazette gct Salem MM, O., to
     m Lydia J. Terrell
1872, 6, 22. Mary O. rocf Alum Creek MM, dtd
     1872,5,15
1873, 10, 10. Thos. Clarkson gct Alum Creek MM
     O., to m Esther Benedict
1874, 9, 19. Esther B. rocf Alum Creek MM,O.,
     dtd 1874,8,20
1875, 2, 20. Mary S. & ch, Homer, Elmerton &
     Bertrand recrq
1875, 2, 20. Charles S. recrq
1875, 2, 20. Edward E. recrq
1875, 2, 20. Lydia recrq
1875, 2, 20. Wm. Clinton recrq
1875, 2, 20. Edward H. recrq
1875, 2, 20. Luvenia recrq
1875, 2, 20. Obie recrq
1875, 2, 20. Mahlon P. recrq
1875, 2, 20. Obediah recrq
1876, 2, 19. Mary Anne recrq
1876, 4, 22. John Alvin recrq
1877, 1, 20. Eugene recrq
1884, 3, 8.   Lizzie recrq
1884, 4, 12. Mattie recrq
1885, 4, 11. Emaretta rocf Elk MM
1885, 10, 10. Ida B. rocf Short Creek MM, O.
1887, 1, 8.   Lizie Ferington (form Williams)
     gct Barclay MM, Kans.
1887, 3, 12. Lott G. & w, Emma, dropped from
     mbrp
1888, 12, 8. Julia rocf Milan MM, dtd 1887,
     3,16
1892, 3, 12. Neola recrq
1892, 6, 11. Anzonetta relrq
1921, 4, 13. Huston recrq
1922, 8, 9.   Lena recrq
1924, 11, 12. Ella & Lavernen rocf Westland MM
1924, 11, 12. Asa recrq

WILLIAMS, continued
1925, 3, 11. Mrs. Samuel recrq
1927, 3, 9. Laverne dropped from mbrp

WILSON
1838, 11, 17. Elisha & w, Huldah, rocf Hard-
    wick & Randolph MM, dtd 1838,4,2 (H)
1840, 11, 21. Enoch & w, Christiana, rocf
    Hardwick & Randolph MM, dtd 1835,4,2 (H)
1864, 9, 17. Macy rst
1864, 10, 22. Wm. & ch, Floy Gennetta, Sarah
    Alvaretta, Thos. L., Charles H. & Ada
    Catharine, recrq
I890, 4, 12. Sherman recrq

WIN
1870, 1, 22. Ruth (form White) con mcd
1885, 1, 10. Florence gct Westland MM

WINDER
----, --, --. John & Sarah
    Ch: Eliza Jane b 1839, 2, 17
        John Elwood" 1842, 10, 5
1839, 12, 1. John, s Aaron & Phebe, b
----, --, --. Abner & Rebecca
    Ch: Ester Ann
        Samuel
          Charles   b 1840, 7, 21
        Joseph John" 1843, 1, 31
        Phinehas   " 1845, 10, 5
        Abner Web-
          ster   " 1848, 9, 2
        Susan   " 1850, 10, 6
----, --, --. James & Eliza
    Ch: Nancy A.   b 1842, 1, 22
        Hope   " 1843, 1, 26
        Charlott   " 1846, 6, 7
        Joseph A. " 1848, 8, 12
----, --, --. Thomas & Hannah
    Ch: Deborah   b 1843, 6, 17
        Senneca   " 1845, 5, 10
1842, 3, 14. Phebe d bur Lewisburg
1846, 7, 23. Abner d ae 65 bur Lewisburg
1846, 9, 3. Levi d bur Lewisburg
1846, 9, 5. Moses d bur Lewisburg
----, --, --. David & Marthy J.
    Ch: Harriet
        Jane   b 1848, 3, 16
        Charles
          Blish   " 1850, 2, 1
1849, 8, 22. Abner Webster d bur Lewisburg
1850, 12, 26. Abner d bur Lewisburgh
1853, 4, 16. Phinehas M. d bur Lewisburgh
----, --, --. Edward & Mary
    Ch: Deborah Ann
                   b 1855, 1, 30
        Sarah Es-
          ther   " 1857, 9, 21
        Olivia   " 1860, 12, 16
        Howard   " 1868, 6, 15
----, --, --. Abner & Eunice
    Ch: Clearance b 1864, 5, 29
        Anna May   " 1868, 3, 24

1864, 1, 3. Hope d ae 77 bur Lewisburg

1864, 4, 23. Eunice H. rocf Gilead MM, dtd
    1864,3,15
1865, 5, 20. Sewel gct Springfield MM, Kans.
1866, 5, 19. Mary Jane recrq
1869, 6, 19. Maria rmt Samuel C. Pennington
1870, 4, 23. Margaret L. recrq
1876, 2, 19. Alfred recrq

WINER
1889, 6, 8. Eva & Hittie recrq

WINKLEY
1880, 4, 17. Joel recrq
1882, 3, 18. Joel gct Westland MM

WINTERS
1878, 4, 20. John & w, Lucy, recrq
1878, 6, 22. Woot, Joseph R. & Nancy Ilo, ch
    John & Lucy, recrq
1886, 4, 10. Joseph dropped from mbrp
1886, 4, 10. John dropped from mbrp
1886, 4, 10. Lucy dropped from mbrp
1886, 4, 10. Nancy dropped from mbrp

WIREMAN
----, --, --. Thomas & -----
    Ch: Martha
        Jane   b 1825, 2, 27
        Charlotte " 1827, 4, 24
        John W.   " 1829, 3, 6
        Sidney Re-
          becca   " 1831, 2, 8
        Nicholas
        Alexander " 1834, 9, 14

WIRICK
1877, 1, 20. Caroline recrq
1883, 7, 21. Caroline relrq
1884, 2, 16. Annie May [Wiric] recrq
1884, 2, 16. Kate [Wiric] recrq
1892, 6, 11. Anna M. relrq

WISE
1883, 8, 18. Daniel & w, Ellen, recrq
1888, 2, 11. Daniel & w, Ellen, relrq

WITCRAFT
1890, 3, 8. James & w, Mary, recrq
1891, 6, 13. James H. relrq
1891, 7, 11. Amos recrq
1892, 3, 12. Mary relrq
1893, 9, 9. Amos relrq

WOLFORD
1893, 6, 10. Julia recrq
1893, 6, 10. Frank recrq

WOOD
1843, 7, 15. Eli Townsend gct Allum Creek
    MM, to m Abigail Wood (H)
1844, 10, 19. Joseph M. rmt Elizabeth Town-

WOOD, continued
        send (H)
1893, 5, 15. William recrq

WOODLAND
1887, 4, 9. Mary A. recrq
1888, 6, 7. Jasper recrq
1891, 7, 11. Lizzie recrq

WOOLEY
1877, 4, 21. Henrietta M. & Sarah E. recrq
1878, 5, 18. William recrq
1883, 9, 22. Sarah E. dropped from mbrp
1887, 8, 13. Finley dropped from mbrp
1888, 3, 10. John Albert recrq
1888, 8, 11. Wm. & w, Mary, gct Van Wert MM,O.
1890, 4, 12. Amos recrq

WREN
1877, 7, 21. John & Rebecca recrq
1879, 2, 15. Anna M. recrq
1883, 11, 17. John & Rebecca dropped from
        mbrp

WRIGHT
1875, 4, 17. Lawrence & Delphia recrq
1877, 4, 21. John W. recrq
1881, 2, 19. Delpha relrq
1883, 5, 19. Alberta recrq
1883, 7, 21. Etta relrq
1883, 11, 18. Alonzo dropped from mbrp
1886, 3, 13. Ida Rosella recrq
1887, 2, 12. John & w relrq
1891, 8, 8. Ida R. dropped from mbrp

WRIGHTMAN
1827, 1, 20. Sarah (form Stratten) con mcd

YOUNG
----, --, --. Edward & Elizabeth
    Ch: Thomas W. b 1854, 9, 6
        Rebecca Eva
                  b 1857, 6, 8
        Hannah M. " 1860, 1, 16
        Maria   " 1862, 5, 8
1855, 2, 6. Martin Clarkson, s Daniel &
        Rhoda, b
1858, 3, 13. Daniel d bur Goshen

1862, 10, 9. Jehu dis joining another socie-
        ty & military service
1862, 12, 20. Henry dis military service
1863, 9, 19. Edward C. & w, Elizabeth N., &
        ch, Thomas Winder, Rebecca Eva, Hannah
        M. & Maria, rocf New Garden MM, dtd
        1863,7,18
1877, 4, 21. Henry S. & Mary E. recrq
1883, 8, 18. Mary E. & Henry dropped from
        mbrp

ZIMMERMAN
1926, 3, 10. Floyd recrq
1927, 3, 9. Edward Sr. dropped from mbrp
1929, 4, 10. Edward & w, Iva McCoy, recrq

CLEVELAND MONTHLY MEETING

    Cleveland Monthly Meeting, Cuyahoga County, was established by Salem Quarterly Meeting, 4th Mo. 13, 1883.

    Among the charter members are the names of the following families: Terrell, Pettit, Pope, Tatum, Price, Malone, Farr, French, and Brown.

RECORDS

ABRAM
1924, 2, 13. Roy E. & w, Jean, & Harold, recrq
1926, 6, 23. Ben C. recrq
1928, 4, 18. Harold rocf Highland Ave. MM,
     Columbus, O.
1928, 4, 18. Roy E., Eugene & Minnie rocf
     Highland Ave. MM, Columbus, O.

ACKERMAN
1904, 9, 15. Irene T. & Chloe Olive recrq

ACKLEY
1894, 4, 19. Flora recrq

ADAMS
1895, 2, 14. L. B. & Eva recrq
1906, 5, 17. Elmira recrq
1913, 6, 18. L. B., Eva & Elvira dropped from
     mbrp

ADDINGTON
1928, 9, 12. Luther E. & w, Elsie A., & dt,
     Esther I., rocf Second Friends Ch.,
     Indianapolis, Ind.
1931, 11, 18. Luther E. & w, Elsie A., & dt,
     Esther J., gct Westfield MM, Ind.

AIKEN
1902, 9, 18. Algeroy F. recrq
1904, 10, 13. A. F. dropped from mbrp

AITKEN
1913, 6, 18. Geo. Russell & Sarah Mabel, ch
     Thelmo Ernestine & Beula Marie, recrq
1917, 12, 12. George & w, Sarah, & ch gct
     Second Friends Church, Cleveland, O.

ALBRIGHT
1915, 2, 17. Joseph C. recrq
1917, 9, 12. Florence (Lipp), w Joseph, recrq
1918, 7, 17. Carl & Florence gct Achilles
     MM, Va.
1926, 4, 14. Miss recrq
1927, 6, 8. Jos. dropped from mbrp

ALEXANDER
1889, 9, 19. Nellie recrq
1902, 2, 13. Wm. & w, Maud, recrq
1904, 1, 14. Chas. S. & Carrie, recrq
1915, 11, 17. Chas. & Carrie dropped from mbrp
1924, 11, 12. Gladys recrq

ALFRED
1885, 8, 12. Ella recrq
1895, 10, 17. Ella dropped from mbrp

ALLEN
1888, 6, 14. Rachel H. rocf White Water MM,
     Ind.
1892, 6, 16. Rachel relrq
1893, 2, 16. Chas. E. recrq

1893, 5, 19. Charles recrq
1895, 8, 15. Chas. E. relrq
1913, 10, 15. Rachel dropped from mbrp
1918, 7, 17. Emma Y. recrq
1919, 1, 15. Myrtle rocf Salem MM, O.
1921, 10, 12. Myrtle O. gct Second Friends
     Church, Cleveland, O.
1923, 3, 14. Myrtle O. rocf S. Cleveland MM,
     O.
1928, 4, 18. Jesse & Viola E. rocf Highland
     Ave. MM, Columbus, O.

ANDERSON
----, --, --. Frederick, s John & Caroline,
     b 1845,--,--; m Amanda MAXON b 1846,--,--
     d 1925,--,--

1904, 12, 15. Elizabeth rocf Oskaloosa MM, Ia.
1909, 8, 19. Elizabeth gct Pleasant Valley MM
1913, 3, 12. Frederick & w recrq
1913, 10, 15. Mrs. Anna recrq
1913, 12, 17. Mrs. Anna & Edith recrq
1915, 11, 15. Mrs. C. D. & Edith Marie, recrq
1922, 2, 15. Sarah dropped from mbrp
1923, 3, 14. Mrs. Fred recrq
1932, 1, 13. Mrs. Anna dropped from mbrp

APEL
1895, 2, 14. Lora recrq
1897, 6, 17. Conrad recrq
1903, 11, 19. Laura rmt J. Edward Hartsuck

ARMITAGE
1896, 11, 19. Anna recrq
1899, 9, 20. Anna rmt Walter H. Mendenhall

ARMSTRONG
1917, 12, 12. Marjorie Wistar relrq

ARNEY
1911, 1, 19. Thos. A. recrq
1911, 4, 13. Olive rocf Hartford MM, Ia.
1922, 2, 15. Thomas dropped from mbrp
1928, 11, 14. Olive dropped from mbrp

ARNOLD
1932, --, --. Samuel d

1911, 3, 16. Hattie recrq
1925, 4, 8. Samuel & Vanona recrq

ASHER
----, --, --. Myrtle, dt Wm. & Mary, b

1883, 7, 18. Willie recrq
1905, 2, 16. Wm. dropped from mbrp
1913, 3, 12. Myrtle recrq
1926, 2, 17. Harry & w & ch, Merrill &
     Donald, relrq

AUSTIN
1903, 12, 17. Chas. R. recrq

AUSTIN, continued
1913, 6, 18. Baby dropped from mbrp
1922, 6, 14. Chas. dropped from mbrp

AVERY
1915, 2, 17. Carrie G. recrq
1927, 5, 18. Carrie dropped from mbrp

BABCOCK
1901, 2, 14. Chas. recrq
1913, 2, 12. Chas. H. & Belle H. rocf Ports-
    mouth MM, Va.
1920, 6, 16. Chas. & w relrq

BAGSHAM
1927, 1, 12. Catharine relrq

BAILEY
1924, 11, 12. Alta recrq

BAIRD
1892, 9, 16. Esther recrq

BAKER
----, --, --. Thos. A.s Augustus & Elizabeth,
    b 1871,4,17; m Rachel ----- b 1871,4,11
    Ch: Olive May b 1899, 3, 16

1895, 4, 18. Thos. & Rachel recrq
1908, 10, 15. Katharine Nehrenst gct Everett
    MM, Wash.

BALDWIN
1902, 7, 17. Walter E., Ida B. & Henry N.
    recrq
1923, 6, 13. Ida & Walter recrq; they were
    form mbr at Pleasant Valley which was laid
    down

BALL
1909, 2, 18. Nettie rocf West Branch MM, O.,
    dtd 1909,1,9
1915, 12, 15. Nettie relrq

BALLARD
1902, 5, 15. Fred Wayne & w, Bessie Todhunter,
    rocf Wilmington MM, O., dtd 1902,5,10
1907, 12, 19. Anthony & w, Sarah, gct Fremont
    MM, O.
1932, 1, 13. Fred W. & w, Bessie T. & Willis
    dropped from mbrp

BALLOON
1885, 2, 18. Mary & Maria recrq

BARBER
1902, 8, 14. Lulu recrq
1902, 9, 18. Blanche recrq
1904, 7, 14. Lulu recrq
1927, 6, 8. Miriam L. dropped from mbrp

BARKER
1906, 11, 15. Claude L. rocf Newberg MM, Ore.

1907, 11, 14. Claud gct Hopewell MM, Ind.
1908, 9, 29. Claud L. rmt Katharine Nehrenst

BARKHOUS
1887, 6, 16. Frederick dropped from mbrp

BARRETT
1898, 11, 17. Mary rocf Spencer MM
1911, 12, 14. Madge recrq

BARTLETT
1923, 6, 13. Della recrq; form mbr at Pleas-
    ant Valley which was laid down
1931, 4, 15. Mrs. Della relrq

BASS
1903, 3, 24. Lizzie Lillian recrq
1907, 3, 14. Lizzie L. relrq

BASSETT
1884, 8, 13. Lillie recrq
1891, 5, 14. Franklin recrq
1892, 5, 19. Franklin relrq
1892, 11, 17. Minnie rocf Short Creek MM, O.
1901, 9, 19. Minnie gct Spiceland MM, Ind.
1913, 6, 18. Winifred recrq
1922, 12, 13. Winnifred relrq

BASTER
1913, 1, 15. Joseph C. & w, Birdie L., recrq
1921, 6, 22. Joseph & w, Birdie L., dropped
    from mbrp

BASTOCK
1927, 4, 13. Mrs. Ruth recrq
1933, 5, 17. Mrs. Ruth dropped from mbrp

BATES
1910, 12, 15. W. J. & Mary rocf Columbus MM,O.
1911, 5, 18. Paul & Raymond, s W. J. & Mary,
    recrq
1917, 3, 14. Mary relrq
1922, 2, 15. J. W., Paul & Raymond dropped
    from mbrp

BATTELS
1902, 4, 17. Clarence recrq

BATTIN
1918, 1, 16. Oscar rocf Haviland MM, Kans.
1924, 1, 16. Oscar L. gct University MM

BAYERD
1919, 2, 12. Belle gct Huntington Park MM,
    Calif.

BECKWITH
1899, 2, 16. Mary recrq
1899, 11, 16. John & Mrs. Minnie recrq
1903, 9, 17. J. A. relrq
1903, 9, 17. Mrs. Minnie relrq
1903, 9, 17. Mary relrq

BECKWITH, continued
1909, 9, 8. John A. & Minnie recrq
1911, 12, 14. Frank recrq

BELL
1884, 7, 16. Edith recrq
1885, 2, 18. Francis & Mary recrq
1894, 4, 19. Minerva J. recrq
1908, 2, 13. Francis & Mary dropped from mbrp
1908, 11, 19. Francis & w, Mary, rst & gct
    Haddonfield MM
1909, 5, 13. Francis & Mary cert returned by
    Haddonfield MM, N. J.
1913, 10, 15. Minerva J. dropped from mbrp
1914, 6, 17. Bertha B. recrq
1919, 11, 12. Bertha B. dropped from mbrp
1922, 6, 14. Francis & Mary dropped from mbrp

BELLOUT
1887, 8, 18. Marie dropped from mbrp

BELM
1905, 5, 18. Elfreda recrq
1927, 6, 8. Freda [Behm] dropped from mbrp

BENDA
1895, 1, 17. Barbara recrq
1896, 5, 14. Barbara [Bender] dropped from
    mbrp

BENARFA
1894, 8, 16. Julia recrq

BENNET
1889, 9, 19. May recrq

BERG
1914, 11, 18. Hazel L. recrq
1922, 2, 15. Hazel dropped from mbrp

BERNARD
1893, 9, 14. Joseph recrq
1895, 10, 17. Joseph dropped from mbrp

BENTSON
1933, 2, 15. Arvilla recrq

BERRY
1922, 2, 15. Anna McCann dropped from mbrp

BESCH
1917, 6, 6. Lester John recrq
1922, 2, 15. Lester dropped from mbrp

BETTS
1898, 5, 19. Agnes [Betz] recrq
1911, 1, 19. Leroy Lewis recrq
1927, 6, 8. LeRoy dropped from mbrp
1927, 6, 8. T. E. dropped from mbrp

BEVELLYMEN
1927, 10, 19. Mr. & Mrs. Arthur recrq

BIDDLE
1917, 1, 16. Grace gct S. Cleveland MM, O.

BIDGOOD
----, --, --. Wm., s J. W. & Anna J., b 1882,
    5,23; m Mae PHINNEY, dt L. P. & Ella, b
    1880,5,12
1929, --, --. Mrs. Anna J. d

1909, 11, 18. Wm. & w, May, & ch, Isabella,
    rocf Wilson Mills MM
1933, 2, 15. Wm. & w, Mae E., & ch, Paul W.,
    Geo. R. & Helen M., recrq

BIDLAKE
1902, 7, 17. George L., Sarah A. & Frank S.
    recrq

BINDER
1893, 2, 16. Aaron Chas. recrq
1895, 10, 17. Aaron dropped from mbrp

BINGER
1929, 9, 18. Lillian rocf West Park MM

BINKLEY
1913, 3, 12. Earl Wright & Florence Farrow
    recrq
1922, 2, 15. Earle & Florence [Binkley] drop-
    ped from mbrp

BISHOP
1909, 9, 8. Lydia recrq
1932, 12, 14. Willis C. recrq

BLACKBURN
1921, 3, 16. Dr. Elisha & w, Virginia L., &
    ch, Doris Margaret & John, rocf Salem MM,
    O.

BLATSCHER
1894, 1, 18. John recrq

BLOHM
1906, 7, 19. Chas. A. recrq
1907, 4, 18. Chas. N. dis

BOHNERT
1932, 12, 14. Albert recrq

BOLLAND
1903, 6, 18. Anthony F. & Sarah K. recrq

BOOTH
1922, 8, 16. Minora recrq

BOUEY
1885, 2, 18. Eva recrq

BOWEN
1916, 12, 13. Edward recrq
1927, 3, 16. Edward dropped from mbrp
1927, 12, 14. Emily relrq

BOWEN, continued
1932, 1, 13. Emily dropped from mbrp

BOYER
1883, 6, 13. Laura [Bowyer] recrq
1886, 1, 13. Herbert Mead recrq
1887, 12, 15. Nettie M. [Bonyer] recrq
1889, 4, 18. Nettie [Bowyers] relrq
1904, 5, 19. Laura dropped from mbrp

BOWER
1918, 3, 13. Milford & Emily, minors, recrq

BOYD
1924, 2, 13. John A. & w recrq

BRADSHAW
1919, 5, 14. Eliza J. & dt, Helen, recrq
1921, 10, 27. Eliza & Helen relrq

BRAINARD
1898, 3, 23. Geo. & Emma recrq

BRANTINGHAM
1912, 7, 18. M. P. recrq
1913, 9, 17. Martin gct Wilson MM
1914, 4, 18. Mary recrq
1922, 3, 15. Mary (now Steel) dropped from
        mbrp

BRAZIER
1894, 2, 15. Anna recrq

BRENNER
1893, 8, 17. Edward J. recrq
1927, 6, 8. Clarence & Harold dropped from
        mbrp

BREYLEY
1914, 6, 17. James & Rose recrq

BRIDABAUGH
1890, 5, 15. P. W. recrq

BRINK
1894, 1, 18. Daniel P. recrq

BRISTOL
1933, 5, 17. Mrs. George dropped from mbrp

BROOKER
----, --, --. Wm. L., s Wm. & Rizpah, b
      1871,5,5; m Grace E. MONEY, dt James &
      Caroline, b 1879,1,10

1914, 2, 18. Wm. L. & w, Grace E., & ch,
      Helen, Thelma & W. Malchom, recrq
1927, 2, 16. Helen relrq
1927, 4, 13. Thelma relrq

BROOKS
1910, 4, 14. A. E. & w & Lenora B. recrq
1912, 2, 15. E. A. & w relrq

1912, 7, 18. Walter T. & Garnet J. recrq
1913, 1, 15. Roger, minor, recrq
1918, 3, 13. Elizabeth rocf Mt. Pleasant MM
1919, 11, 12. Walter F. & Roger dropped from
        mbrp
1927, 6, 8. Garnet dropped from mbrp

BROTH
1902, 7, 17. Everet H. & Daisy E. recrq
1902, 7, 17. Amanda M. & Cora A. recrq

BROWN
1886, 1, 13. Susan recrq
1886, 1, 19. Emma rmt J. Walter Malone
1893, 7, 13. Leo R. recrq
1895, 12, 24. Wm. W. rmt Alice L. Jones
1896, 4, 15. Carrie rmt Curtin Russell
1897, 12, 16. Walter W. rocf Indianapolis MM,
        Ind.
1899, 3, 16. Walter gct Amo MM, Ind.
1899, 11, 16. Walter W. & w, Mellie Milner,
        rocf Amo MM, Ind., dtd 1899,10,21
1899, 12, 24. LeRoy dropped from mbrp
1900, 2, 15. Chas. M. & Eva J. recrq
1900, 10, 19. John S. recrq
1906, 11, 15. Eva J. relrq
1909, 8, 19. Ruby P. recrq
1914, 10, 14. Anna F. recrq
1914, 10, 14. Wm. H. dropped from mbrp
1916, 4, 12. Eleanor recrq
1922, 2, 15. Eleanor dropped from mbrp
1922, 2, 15. Chas. dropped from mbrp
1926, 8, 18. Milford E. relrq
1927, 6, 22. Kenneth rocf Gilead MM
1931, 1, 14. Mrs. Carrie L. & ch, Ray Wilber
        & Fern Louise, recrq
1932, 1, 13. Mrs. Anna dropped from mbrp
1932, 12, 10. V. Kenneth gct Berlinville MM,O.
1933, 11, 15. Lucile recrq

BRUCE
1917, 6, 20. Mrs. F. H. & dt, Treva, recrq

BRYANT
1887, 7, 14. Mary Ellen recrq
1895, 9, 19. Margaret gct Mt. Pleasant MM,O.

BUCHANAN
1903, 6, 18. Chas. rocf Alum Creek MM, O.,
        dtd 1903,1,--
1922, 6, 14. Chas. dropped from mbrp

BUCK
1918, 8, 14. James & w, Helen, & ch, Esther,
        roc
1919, 12, 15. James & w, Helen, & dt, Esther,
        relrq

BUENGER
1904, 9, 15. Lillian recrq

BUFFITT
1894, 1, 18. Wm. recrq

BUFFITT, continued
1895, 11, 14.   Wm. H. [Buffet] relrq

BURDGE
1885, 9, 16.   John & w, Sarah, recrq
1888, 3, 15.   Jno. & Sarah relrq

BURGY
1887, 12, 15.   Sophia Ann recrq
1894, 1, 18.   Cora recrq
1903, 6, 24.   Cora M. rmt Perry P. Cook

BURHAUS
1897, 5, 13.   Mary recrq

BURKHEAD
1901, 11, 14.   Jennette recrq
1904, 7, 14.   Jeanette gct San Diago MM, Calif.

BURNHAM
1894, 1, 18.   M. A. recrq
1895, 10, 17.   M. A. dropped from mbrp

BURRIDGE
1891, 12, 17.   Adelaide recrq

BURROWS
1910, 5, 19.   Ellen recrq
1933, 8, 10.   Florence Sybelia recrq
1933, 10, 18.   Blanche Beatrice recrq

BUSCHLEN
1899, 10, 18.   Tillie recrq

BUSH
1916, 6, 14.   Grace Kahl relrq

BUTLER
1924, 2, 27.   C. W., Celia & Mrs. Selma recrq

BUTTERY
1887, 2, 17.   Frank P. recrq
1893, 3, 16.   Frank relrq

BUTTERWORTH
1913, 3, 12.   Charlie recrq
1929, 4, 17.   Walter Weyner & Arthur recrq

CADDICK
1913, 11, 19.   Walter G. recrq
1914, 9, 16.   Mrs. Hallie recrq
1917, 6, 13.   Thos. Henry recrq
1927, 5, 18.   Walter dropped from mbrp
1927, 6, 8.   Hallie dropped from mbrp
1927, 6, 8.   Thos. Henry dropped from mbrp

CALLAHAN
1912, 6, 24.   James Wilson rmt Rose Elizabeth
        Keetch
1913, 2, 12.   Rose Keetch relrq

CAMP
1887, 3, 17.   Lydia recrq

CAMPBELL
1902, 2, 13.   Chas. & w recrq
1927, 5, 18.   John dropped from mbrp
1928, 11, 14.   Adelia dropped from mbrp
1933, 3, 15.   Mary Belle recrq

CARNEGIE
1895, 7, 18.   George recrq
1896, 9, 17.   Janet recrq
1902, 5, 15.   Elizabeth P. recrq

CARPENTER
1902, 1, 16.   Ella Cottrell dropped from mbrp
1929, 3, 13.   Chas. L. rocf Huntington Park
        MM, Calif.

CARTER
1912, 3, 14.   Almond recrq
1927, 5, 18.   Almond dropped from mbrp
1932, 1, 13.   Celia Shulte dropped from mbrp

CARTRIGHT
1924, 11, 12.   Harley recrq

CATTELL
1931, 9, 23.   Everett L. & w, Catharine, & s,
        David, rocf Springfield MM, O.
1932, 11, 16.   Winifred recrq

CAVAN
1912, 5, 16.   Jordan recrq
1919, 5, 14.   Dora J. relrq

CHAFFIN
1898, 11, 17.   Lydia recrq
1902, 4, 17.   Wm. recrq
1913, 10, 15.   Wm. & Lydia gc

CHAMBERLAIN
1893, 12, 14.   Mina E. recrq

CHANDLER
1895, 8, 15.   Matilda recrq
1911, 9, 14.   Lucy Long recrq
1914, 10, 14.   Lucy Long dropped from mbrp

CHAPMAN
1893, 2, 16.   Robert A. & w, Wilmina, recrq
1922, 6, 14.   Robert dropped from mbrp

CHAREK
1909, 3, 18.   Emma & Rose recrq
1915, 8, 18.   Emma & Rose dropped from mbrp

CHASE
1913, 3, 12.   Estelle recrq
1922, 2, 15.   Estelle dropped from mbrp

CHENOWETH
1923, 6, 13.   Francis & Mary recrq; form mbr
        at Pleasant Valley MM which was laid down
1925, 6, 17.   Francis & w, Mary, relrq

CHERRY
1905, 2, 16. May Belle recrq

CHILDS
1895, 5, 16. Elbert E. & Phoebe recrq

CHILCOTE
1924, 11, 12. Dorothy recrq

CHILSON
1898, 5, 19. Arthur rocf Indianapolis MM, Ind.
1906, .8, 16. Arthur B. gct University MM

CHOATE
1902, 12, 18. Calvin R. rocf Vermillion MM, Ill.
1905, 1, 26. Louie Haladay rocf East Branch
      MM, Ind.
1908, 11, 19. Calvin & w & two ch gct Kokomo
      MM, Ind.

CHRISTIAN
1898, 5, 19. Wm. recrq

CHURCHILL
1903, 8, 13. John & Lillian recrq
1904, 12, 15. Eva, dt John & Lillie, recrq
1914, 2, 18. Eva Anna & Bertha Emma recrq
1917, 7, 18. Eva relrq
1924, 2, 27. Mrs. A. M. recrq
1927, 5, 18. Mrs. John dropped from mbrp
1927, 6, 8. Bertha dropped from mbrp

CICINESE
1931, 9, 16. John recrq

CLARK
1886, 4, 14. John recrq
1895, 4, 18. Catharine & Ida Ellen recrq
1895, 10, 17. Walter dropped from mbrp
1898, 4, 14. Chas. & ch, A. Bertie, Catha-
      rine M. & E. Josephine, recrq
1902, 4, 17. Elmer & Lizzie recrq
1902, 7, 17. Wm. H. recrq
1902, 7, 17. Florence P. recrq
1903, 2, 4. Geo. W. recrq
1903, 10, 15. Nettie recrq
1913, 6, 18. Chas. & fam dropped from mbrp
1913, 10, 15. Grace Fulton dropped from mbrp
1914, 10, 14. Elgie M. recrq
1914, 11, 18. Glenn W. & Olen, minors, recrq
1917, 1, 17. Eleanor S. relrq
1918, 3, 13. Eleanor S. rst
1924, 5, 14. Elinor S. relrq
1924, 11, 12. Mary E. recrq
1927, 6, 8. Geo. W. dropped from mbrp
1927, 12, 14. Mary E. recrq
1928, 1, 2. Mary E. rmt Edward H. Kuehnel
1929, 9, 18. Mrs. May, Maud, James R., Geo.
      Wm. & John, recrq

CLAUSEN
1925, 4, 8. Eva recrq

CLIFF
1921, 2, 16. Mary E. recrq

CLISE
1913, 3, 19. Lulu Barker dropped from mbrp

CLIFFORD
1902, 11, 13. Pearl Edith recrq
1911, 1, 19. Amelia recrq

CLIFT
1931, 2, 18. Mrs. Mary relrq

CLINE
1928, 10, 17. Mrs. Mary & Miss Lula F. recrq
1928, 11, 14. Bertha W. [Klein] dropped from
      mbrp

CLOUGH
1887, 2, 17. Marion recrq

CLOUSEN
1924, 1, 16. Eva recrq

COE
1914, 6, 17. Celeste recrq

COFFIN
1912, 7, 18. Merrill rocf Denver MM
1912, 9, 26. Merrill gct Rasin Valley MM,
      Mich.
1917, 11, 14. Merrill & w, Anna, & s, Eugene,
      rocf Berlinville MM, O.

COFFMAN
1915, 11, 17. Muriel M. recrq
1922, 2, 15. Muriel M. dropped from mbrp

COLEMAN
1924, 11, 12. Chas. recrq
1924, 12, 17. John J. & w recrq
1931, 1, 14. John J. & w, Viola May, & ch,
      Milton & Eugene, recrq
1933, 4, 12. Elsie Bertha recrq

COLLINS
1923, 6, --. Byron C. rmt Ruth C. Russell
1932, 1, 13. Ruth Russell dropped from mbrp

COMPTON
1914, 5, 20. Elizabeth relrq
1914, 6, 11. Elizabeth Mather rmt J. Walter
      Malone Jr.

COMSTOCK
1901, 9, 19. Andrew J. & Elizabeth recrq
1904, 7, 14. Samuel F. recrq
1927, 6, 8. Andrew & Eliza dropped from
      mbrp

CONKLIN
1915, 4, 14. C. Leslie & w recrq
1927, 5, 18. Mrs. Leslie dropped from mbrp

CONLEY
1914, 2, 18. Charles C. recrq
1917, 11, 14. Irene relrq
1919, 9, 17. Chas. C. gct Columbus MM, O.

CONNELL
1913, 3, 12. Fred recrq
1919, 11, 12. Fred dropped from mbrp

CONVERSE
1902, 6, 19. Hattie recrq
1903, 8, 13. Fred Sumner recrq
1905, 9, 14. Fred S. relrq
1907, 9, 19. Hattie M. relrq

COOK
1874, 10, 13. Cora Burgy, dt Lorenzo & Bertha
    A., b

1885, 12, 16. Bertha H. recrq
1888, 8, 16. Bertha relrq
1903, 6, 24. Perry P. rmt Cora M. Burgy
1903, 12, 17. Perry P. recrq
1906, 4, 19. Mabel J. T. recrq
1907, 1, 17. Albert rocf McLouth MM, Kans.
1913, 10, 15. Mabel J. dropped from mbrp
1919, 11, 12. Albert dropped from mbrp
1922, 12, 13. Gertrude gct First Friends Ch,
    Portland, Oregon
1932, 5, 18. Fern Bishop & Ellis T. recrq
1933, 7, 12. Ellis T. & Fern Bishop gct Vilas
    MM, Colo.

COOKSON
1910, 4, 14. G. B. recrq
1910, 6, 16. Mrs. Irene recrq

COOLEY
1924, 3, 13. Clementine B. rocf Colona MM,
    Ind.

COPE
1888, 3, 15. Earnest rocf Smithfield MM
1912, 1, 18. Stanley rocf Alliance MM, O.
1912, 10, 17. S. J. relrq

COPPOCK
1898, 4, 14. Ella M. rocf Winona MM
1899, 7, 13. Ella gct Winona MM, O.

CORBIN
1924, 2, 27. Paul recrq

CORLETTE
1899, 2, 16. Mary L., Mina C. & Lillian S.
    [Corlett] recrq
1903, 10, 15. Claribel recrq
1903, 10, 15. Jessie recrq
1903, 10, 15. Mary M. recrq
1903, 10, 15. Hariet M. recrq
1903, 10, 15. Martha recrq
1922, 2, 15. Harriett [Corlitt] dropped from
    mbrp

1922, 2, 15. Mrs. Mary [Corlitt] dropped from
    mbrp
1922, 2, 15. Lillian S. [Corlitt] dropped
    from mbrp
1922, 2, 15. Claribel [Corlitt] dropped from
    mbrp
1922, 6, 14. Jessie dropped from mbrp
1922, 6, 14. Mona dropped from mbrp

CORNELL
1901, 6, 13. Alfred recrq

CORTLETTE
1908, 2, 13. Mamie L. gct Alliance MM, O.

COTTRELL
1885, 12, 16. Emma, Ellce & Stella recrq
1887, 2, 17. Josephine recrq
1902, 1, 16. Josephine dropped from mbrp
1915, 3, 17. Mrs. Mary recrq

COUCH
1918, 1, 16. Burton L. recrq
1927, 3, 16. Burton L. dropped from mbrp

COUSE
1900, 12, 25. Clem E. recrq
1903, 1, 20. Elsie recrq
1912, 4, 18. Mrs. recrq
1915, 6, 16. Glenn E. & w, Lillian, relrq
1927, 6, 8. Walter, Esther, Crew & Marie
    dropped from mbrp

COVERT
1902, 4, 17. James recrq
1902, 4, 17. Martin recrq
1902, 7, 17. David M. & Minnie recrq

COWLES
1887, 2, 17. Mary recrq
1913, 10, 15. Mary dropped from mbrp

COX
1929, 11, --. Homer L. d
1929, 7, 10. Homer Jr. b

1912, 6, 13. Carson W. & w, Vercia Pitts,
    rocf Rose Hill MM, Kans.
1922, 1, 18. Homer L. & w, Blanche G., & dt,
    Catharine Marcile, rocf First Friends
    Church, Portland, Ore.
1927, 2, 16. Levi F. rocf White Water MM,
    Ind.
1928, 9, 12. Mary Nichols rocf White Water
    MM, Ind.
1930, 6, 18. Mary Nichols gct Cherry Grove
    MM, Ind.
1931, 10, 14. Levi gct Randolph Co., Ind.

COYLE
1912, 11, 13. Mary Maud recrq
1922, 2, 15. Mary Maud dropped from mbrp

CRABOUGH
1898, 7, 14. Daniel recrq

CRAIG
1901, 10, 17. Frank rocf'White Water MM, Ind.;
     returned, unable to locate him

CRANE
1903, 6, 18. Herbert D. recrq
1904, 6, 16. H. D. relrq
1931, 3, 18. Elgin recrq
1932, 11, 16. Iyla G. recrq
1932, 12, 14. Audrey recrq

CRAUSE
1896, 5, 14. Mate dropped from mbrp

CRIDER
1918, 1, 16. Fred recrq
1921, 12, 14. Fred C. relrq

CROBOUGH
1915, 12, 15. Samuel Chester recrq
1916, 4, 20. Chester rmt Margaret Malone
1927, 6, 8. S. Chester, Margaret, S. Chester
     Jr. & Jean dropped from mbrp

CROMELL
1922, 2, 15. Bessie dropped from mbrp

CROOKS
1916, 11, 15. Laura B. recrq
1927, 9, 24. Laura B. gct Salem MM

CROCKETT
1914, 3, 18. Edith D. recrq
1914, 10, 14. Jane recrq
1916, 5, 17. Gladys recrq
1924, 12, 17. A. C. & Ruth recrq
1927, 5, 18. Walter dropped from mbrp
1927, 6, 8. Edith D. dropped from mbrp

CROSBY
1913, 3, 19. Marie Haliday relrq

CROSS
1915, 2, 17. Mrs. C. W. recrq
1916, 6, 14. Alice E. recrq
1922, 2, 15. Alice dropped from mbrp

CROWEL
1897, 3, 18. James & w, Elizabeth, recrq
1905, 11, 16. Bessie recrq
1932, 1, 13. Elvira dropped from mbrp
1932, 1, 13. Daniel dropped from mbrp
1932, 1, 13. John dropped from mbrp
1932, 1, 13. Walter dropped from mbrp
1932, 1, 13. Percy dropped from mbrp
1932, 1, 13. Arnold dropped from mbrp
1932, 1, 13. Erving dropped from mbrp

CRUNKILTON
1932, 11, 16. Margaret Anita recrq

CUBBEN
1914, 3, 18. Edward recrq

CUCKLER
1918, 2, 13. Harry A. & Samuel H. recrq
1922, 2, 15. Samuel & Harry dropped from
     mbrp

CULBERTSON
1909, 11, 18. L. P. & Mrs. recrq
1927, 6, 8. L. P. & Mildred dropped from
     mbrp

CULLY
1900, 2, 15. Lillian Gambier gct Pa.

CUMMINS
1885, 2, 18. Edwin & w, Alice, & ch, Robert
     & Fannie, recrq
1899, 10, 18. Robert dropped from mbrp

CUNNINGTON
1888, 12, 13. Joseph & w, Anna, rocf Des
     Moines MM, Ia., dtd 1888,11,7
1896, 2, 13. Joseph & Anna [Cummington]
     dropped from mbrp

CURRIE
1898, 8, 10. James A., s Robert & Mary,
     b 1874,4,25; m Maud FULLER, dt John &
     Sarah, b 1874,10,14
----, --, --. Chas. F. & -----
     Ch: Chas.
          Campbell b 1926, 9, 14
          Ruth Lois " 1927, 11, 24

1909, 6, 17. Maud recrq
1909, 7, 1. James A. recrq
1924, 12, 17. Chas. F. gct Willowick Village
1925, 1, 21. Alice recrq
1928, 4, 18. Chas. F. & w & ch, Chas. Camp-
     bell & Ruth Lois, recrq

CUTHBERTSON
1910, 7, 14. Alexander & w recrq
1917, 4, 18. Jennie relrq
1919, 4, 16. Alexander dropped from mbrp

DALL
1887, 12, 15. Emma Elizabeth recrq

DANALA
1903, 1, 20. Elizabeth recrq
1922, 2, 15. Elizabeth dropped from mbrp

DANIELS
1922, 10, 18. Lucy Farnum rocf Worcester MM,
     Mass.

DAY
1916, 4, 12. Ruth C. recrq
1927, 5, 18. Ruth C. dropped from mbrp

DEAN
1915, 7, 14. L. Earl rocf Huntington Park MM,
    Calif.
1916, 12, 13. Mamie C. [Deane] rocf Scott
    Mills MM, Ore.
1919, 12, 15. Wm. H. & w, L. Marion, rocf
    Paonia MM, Colo.
1920, 5, 12. L. Earle & Mamie C. gct Scotts
    Mills MM, Ore.
1927, 6, 8. J. Earl & Minnie C. dropped from
    mbrp

DECKER
1916, 4, 12. Alice recrq
1922, 2, 15. Alice dropped from mbrp

DeKONING
1921, 10, 27. Blanche R. rocf Lynn Grove MM,
    Ia.
1922, 10, 18. Jacob recrq

DeMARET
1924, 2, 27. Catharine (Bagshaw) recrq

DENHAM
1884, 4, 16. Anna [Dennam] recrq
1914, 2, 18. Mabel recrq
1922, 2, 15. Mabel dropped from mbrp

DENNIS
1893, 8, 17. Lizzie rocf Ypsilanta MM, Mich.
1897, 5, 13. Lizzie M. gct Lane MM, Mich.

DERBY
1912, 1, 18. Anna recrq

DERBYSHIRE
1896, 2, 13. Gurney G. rocf Ypsilanti MM,
    Mich.

DERRICK
1921, 6, 15. Robert Lincoln recrq
1921, 9, --. Robert rmt Ruth Kuehnel

DeSIMONI
1924, 1, 16. Louis recrq

DeVECHARY
1920, 3, 18. Vera Frew dropped from mbrp

DEVERT
1902, 5, 15. Frederick & Lottie F. recrq
1913, 10, 15. Fred E. & Lottie gc

DeVIE
1894, 8, 16. Jessie recrq

DeWITT
1910, 5, 19. Gloria recrq
1922, 6, 14. Gloria dropped from mbrp

DIFFORD
1904, 1, 14. Wm. & w, Mary, & s, Alfred, rocf

Scranton MM, Ia.
1906, 4, 19. Wm. B. gct Smithfield MM, O.
1906, 4, 19. Mary A. gct Smithfield MM, O.
1907, 10, 17. Alfred gct Colorado Springs MM

DIMMICK
1894, 3, 15. Sydney recrq

DIXON
1908, 1, 16. Bertha P. gct Los Angeles MM,
    Calif.
1908, 3, 19. Cert granted to Los Angeles,
    Calif. for Bertha P. & s, Wendall Pinkham,
    returned
1908, 9, 17. Bertha dropped from mbrp

DIVERS
1924, 2, 13. Bess M. recrq

DODZWEIT
1932, 12, 14. Siegfried recrq

DOHRMAN
1933, 11, 15. Mabel recrq

DOMAN
1887, 12, 15. Catharine recrq
1895, 10, 17. Catharine [Dolman] dropped from
    mbrp

DOWEN
1908, 6, 18. Gertrude Modros gct Pleasant
    Valley MM
1923, 6, 13. Gertie recrq; form mbr at
    Pleasant Valley which was laid down
1928, 3, 14. Mrs. Gertrude Modros relrq

DRAKE
1897, 4, 15. Emma Dall dropped from mbrp

DREMAN
1922, 8, 16. Edward W. & ch, Caroline, recrq

DREWS
1914, 4, 18. Mrs. Gus recrq
1915, 3, 17. Gus recrq
1922, 2, 15. Mrs. Gus dropped from mbrp

DUNHAM
1933, 4, 12. Jessie Myrtle recrq

DUTCHER
1913, 1, 15. Nellie rocf Adrian MM, Mich.

DUTY
1903, 1, 20. Charlotte M. recrq
1908, 11, 19. Charlott M. relrq

EBLE
1894, 10, 18. Nancy recrq

ECKHERT
1902, 1, 16. Stella Cottrell dropped from

ECKHERT, continued
     mbrp

EDWARDS
1885, 2, 18. Leonard recrq
1893, 8, 17. Octavius recrq
1894, 10, 18. Chas. R. recrq
1899, 7, 13. Nancy dropped from mbrp
1913, 10, 15. Leonard dropped from mbrp

EHMER
1898, 1, 13. Christian & w, Anna, & ch, Mar-
                tha & Teddy, recrq
1904, 6, 16. Christian dropped from mbrp
1913, 10, 15. Mrs. Anna & ch, Martha & Fred,
                dropped from mbrp

ELFORD
1915, 7, 14. Edgar & w & Virginia, recrq
1916, 8, 16. Edgar & w, Delia, & dt, Virgin-
                ia, gct Clark Ave. MM, Cleveland, O.

ELINGER
1924, 11, 12. Florence M. recrq

EMERICK
1913, 3, 12. Mrs. recrq
1932, 1, 13. Mrs. dropped from mbrp

ENDLE
1904, 5, 19. Catharine dropped from mbrp

ENGLE
1933, 11, 15. Edna Mae recrq

ENNIS
1888, 12, 13. Frank & w, Josephine, & ch,
                Forrest Clifford & Leota, rocf West Branch
                MM, O., dtd 1888,10,13
1899, 7, 13. Frank & fam dropped from mbrp

ERSKINE
1909, 6, 17. Geo. W. recrq

ESCOLME
1913, 3, 12. Edward recrq

ESHNER
1913, 12, 17. Jerome Earle recrq
1922, 2, 15. Jerome dropped from mbrp

ETHRIDGE
1887, 3, 17. Blanch recrq
1913, 3, 19. Blanch gct San Diago MM, Calif.

EWING
1919, 3, 12. C. P. recrq
1927, 6, 8. C. P. dropped from mbrp

EYERDAMS
1911, 1, 19. Anna Louisa recrq

FAHLSTROM
1926, 2, 17. Mrs. Viola recrq
1930, 9, 17. Mrs. Viola relrq
1931, 2, 18. Mrs. Viola rst
1933, 4, 12. Mrs. Viola relrq

FAIRCLOUGH
1908, 12, 17. Florence Louise & dt, Caroline
                F., recrq
1912, 6, 13. Margaret Elizabeth & dt Wm. &
                Caroline, recrq
1917, 6, 13. Wm. & Carrie relrq

FALOR
1924, 11, 12. Harold recrq

FARMER
1891, 5, 14. Memorial for James

FARNSWORTH
1889, 6, 13. Mary recrq

FARR
1904, 5, 19. Edwin & Abbie dropped from mbrp
1913, 10, 15. Mabel E., Wm. E. & Edwin W.
                dropped from mbrp

FARREN
1897, 9, 16. May recrq
1902, 5, 15. Mrs. M. J. recrq
1902, 5, 15. Allen B. & Frances J. recrq
1902, 5, 15. Hattie M. recrq
1902, 5, 15. Sadie E. recrq
1926, 12, 15. May rocf Second Friends Church,
                S. Cleveland, O.
1927, 6, 22. Robert Willard rocf Gilead MM

FARROR
1901, 3, 16. George & Belle recrq
1902, 5, 15. John D. & Nellie B. recrq

FAWCETT
1917, 9, 12. Clara rocf Salem MM
1921, 10, 12. Clara gct First Friends Church,
                Pasadena, Calif.

FAYLE
1896, 11, 19. Thomas dropped from mbrp

FEDERER
1915, 2, 17. Mrs. Mary recrq
1927, 5, 18. Mary dropped from mbrp

FELGER
1913, 10, 15. Mrs. F. recrq

FELLOWS
1914, 11, 18. J. L. recrq
1922, 3, 15. J. L. relrq

FERBISH
1894, 2, 15. Lorena recrq

FERGUSON

1890, --, --. Thos. m Edith THOMPSON, dt
    James

1914, 1, 14. Edith & ch, Blanch, recrq
1933, 5, 17. Mrs. Edith dropped from mbrp

FINGULIN

1915, 2, 17. Ferdinan J. & w, Anna, & ch,
    Josephine, Viola & Lilian, recrq
1927, 5, 18. Ferdinand dropped from mbrp

FISHER

1895, 3, 14. May recrq
1908, 12, 17. Cora rocf Milan MM
1913, 10, 15. Mary dropped from mbrp
1914, 3, 18. Cora gct Berlinville MM, O.
1924, 11, 12. Raynette recrq

FISTLER

1888, 5, 17. Delia [Fisthler] recrq
1889, 5, 16. Franklin recrq
1890, 6, 19. Edward A. recrq
1892, 1, 14. Emma & Clara recrq
1894, 1, 18. Anna recrq
1897, 4, 15. Edward dropped from mbrp
1913, 10, 15. Emma gc
1913, 10, 15. Anna (Fistler) Westenberg gc

FITKINS

1897, 1, 14. Susie Noris relrq

FITZGERALD

1911, 1, 19. James recrq

FLEMING

1915, 4, 14. Mrs. Myrtle recrq
1927, 6, 8. Mrs. Myrtle [Flemming] dropped
    from mbrp

FLETCHER

1885, 6, 17. George recrq
1888, 12, 13. Geo. relrq
1927, 6, 8. Geo. dropped from mbrp

FOOTE

1903, 10, 15. Minnie A. recrq
1921, 5, 18. Minnie relrq

FORD

1898, 6, 16. Mr. & Mrs. T. G. & Jefferson
    recrq
1902, 4, 17. Helen M. rocf New Sharon MM,
    Ia., dtd 1902,3,15
1903, 2, 4. Jefferson W. & w, Helen, & dt,
    Clara Guinness, gct Mt. Vernon MM, S.
    Dakota
1904, 6, 16. Jefferson W. & w, Helen, & dt,
    Clara Guinness, rocf High Point MM, Ia.
1909, 3, 18. Jefferson & w & dt, Clara G.,
    gct Glen Haven MM, Ia.
1929, 10, 16. Wm. Harrison recrq
1931, 3, 18. Wm. gct Second Friends Church,

Cleveland, O.

FORSYTHE

1885, 6, 17. Joseph W. recrq
1885, 10, 14. Joseph W. & Mary Louisa Penti-
    cost declared intentions of m
1902, 1, 16. Joseph, Mary & Josephine dropped
    from mbrp

FOSDICK

1902, 2, 13. Jerry, Nora & Ida recrq
1902, 2, 13. A. Leonard recrq
1902, 4, 17. Frank recrq
1922, 6, 14. Frank, Nora & Ida dropped from
    mbrp

FOSTER

----, --, --. Harry, s G. L. & Marietta, b

1900, 12, 25. Marietta recrq
1902, 7, 17. Alice E. recrq
1909, 12, 16. Harry A., minor, recrq
1911, 7, 13. Alice Adella recrq
1921, 5, 18. Flora recrq
1928, 4, 18. Mrs. Flora relrq

FOWLER

1888, 6, 14. Libbie relrq
1897, 9, 16. Chas. dropped from mbrp

FOX

1912, 2, 15. George T. recrq
1921, 7, 14. George relrq

FRANCIS

1895, 1, 17. Ethel recrq
1913, 10, 15. Ethel dropped from mbrp

FRANK

1915, 12, 15. Minnie Louise recrq
1927, 6, 8. Minnie Louise dropped from mbrp

FRANKLIN

1907, 9, 19. Eugene, minor, recrq

FRAZEE

1902, 5, 15. Wm. D. recrq
1902, 5, 15. Geo. W. recrq
1902, 5, 15. Mrs. Augusta recrq
1909, 8, 19. Thos. L. & w, Augusta, & s,
    George, roc
1911, 11, 16. Harry Albert recrq

FRAZER

1899, 7, 13. Thos. L. recrq
1932, 11, 16. Ruby recrq

FREER

1906, 12, 13. Willard recrq
1906, 12, 13. Wm. P. gct Second Friends Ch.,
    Chicago, Ill.
1907, 2, 14. Willard P.'s cert to Chicago
    returned

FREER, continued
1909, 6, 17. Martha recrq
1910, 5, 19. Vera Ruth recrq
1915, 4, 14. Martha dropped from mbrp
1922, 2, 15. Willard dropped from mbrp

FRENCH
1883, 5, 16. Anna relrq
1889, 1, 17. Anna recrq

FRISBIE
1893, 1, 19. Mrs. Flonna Johnston & dt, Es-
     ther Louise, recrq
1896, 3, 19. Arthur G. & w, Flonna, & ch
     relrq

FRISHER
1890, 4, 17. Arthur G. recrq

FRISTOE
1910, 6, 16. Walter W. & Minnie recrq
1919, 11, 12. Walter W. & Minnie dropped from
     mbrp
1927, 6, 8. Minnie [Fristre] dropped from
     mbrp

FROELICK
1924, 2, 27. Cordelia recrq

FRUDENBERG
1906, 2, 15. Amelia rocf Salem MM

FULLER
1897, 5, 13. Dean D. recrq
1904, 6, 16. Dean relrq
1914, 4, 18. Albert recrq
1927, 6, 8. Albert dropped from mbrp

FULTON
1901, 1, 17. Jno S. recrq
1903, 6, 18. John S. rocf San Jose MM, Calif.
1917, 2, 14. Robert H. recrq
1927, 6, 8. Robert dropped from mbrp

FUNSTON
1922, 10, 18. Geo. F. & Flora Welhoff recrq

FURBISH
1904, 10, 13. Mrs. dropped from mbrp

FURGESON
1902, 4, 17. Martin N., Mira F. & Mabel I.
     recrq

GAINES
1926, 3, 31. Mrs. Cora May recrq
1928, 9, 12. Mrs. Cora dropped from mbrp

GALLAGHER
----, --, --. W. F. & Matilda [Gallager]
     Ch: Hannah C. b 1902, 2, 24
         Frederick W.
                 b 1903, 9, 6

1895, 8, 15. Wm. F. recrq
1901, 10, 17. Matilda C. relrq
1913, 6, 18. Hannah, Fred & Sterling recrq
1932, 8, 17. Hannah C. [Gallager] relrq
1932, 12, 10. Hannah C. [Gallager] recrq

GAMBIER
1887, 12, 15. Lillian & Frank recrq
1907, 1, 17. Frank gct Philadelphia MM, Pa.
     (12th St. Mtg)

GAMO
1914, 11, 18. Mrs. Flora A. recrq
1927, 6, 8. Flora dropped from mbrp

GANTER
1907, 10, 17. Helena Franziska recrq
1927, 6, 8. Helena dropped from mbrp

GARDINER
1903, 10, 15. Roswell & w, Lenora, & s, Geo.,
     rocf Whittier MM, Calif.
1913, 10, 15. Roswell H. & w, Lenora, & s,
     Geo., dropped from mbrp
1930, 9, 17. Cola & Erma Marie, minors,
     rocf Rollin MM
1931, 10, 14. Cola & w, Erma, & ch, Donald,
     relrq

GASE
1922, 2, 15. Bertha dropped from mbrp
1927, 5, 18. Bertha dropped from mbrp

GASKILL
1884, 2, 13. Thos. W. & ch, Harrie T. &
     Jennie M., recrq
1927, 6, 8. Jennie dropped from mbrp

GATES
1911, 2, 16. Belle rocf Delphi MM
1918, 9, 18. Belle gct Berlinville MM, O.

GAUB
1914, 2, 18. Minnie & Anna recrq
1915, 2, 17. Minnie relrq

GAUZ
1927, 5, 18. Vera dropped from mbrp

GEE
1922, 2, 15. Ellen Dodge dropped from mbrp
1927, 6, 8. Susie dropped from mbrp

GELLETTE
1932, 12, 14. Mariam recrq

GENS
1922, 3, 15. Vera Pearl recrq

GERRARD
1887, 10, 23. Dora C. rmt Chas. A. Hinman

GIBSON
1920, 5, 12. Myrtle & Kenneth rocf Salem MM, O.
1927, 6, 8. Myrtle & Kenneth dropped from mbrp

GIEK
1915, 8, 18. Geo. & w, Nina Angie, recrq
1922, 2, 15. Geo. & Nina dropped from mbrp

GIFFHORN
1884, 4, 16. Belle rocf Clear Creek MM, O.
1904, 6, 16. Belle relrq

GILBERT
1886, 12, 16. Isabell recrq

GILLESPI
1901, 8, 15. Geo. G. recrq
1902, 6, 19. Edward J. [Gillespie] recrq
1919, 7, 16. Louise & s, Harlan Edward, recrq

GILMORE
1911, 1, 19. Grace E. recrq
1922, 2, 15. Grace dropped from mbrp

GINTER
1921, 6, 15. Nora Stebbins gct Columbus MM,O.

GIRRARD
1853, 4, 18. Doris recrq

GLEESON
1902, 2, 13. Chas. & w, Frances, & ch, Grace, recrq
1913, 3, 12. Wm. F. recrq
1918, 2, 13. Chas. D. & w, Frances, gct S. Cleveland MM, O.
1918, 2, 13. Arthur C., Alvah B. & Franklin G. gct Cleveland MM, O.
1922, 2, 15. Wm. dropped from mbrp

GLECKNOR
1912, 6, 13. Mary recrq

GLOVER
1914, 2, 18. Daniel recrq
1915, 12, 15. Mrs. Elsie recrq
1927, 5, 18. Elsie dropped from mbrp

GOODSON
1902, 1, 16. Jessie D. dropped from mbrp

GOODWIN
1901, 9, 27. Howard S. rmt Ethel M. Russell
1904, 4, 14. Ethel Russell gct Lansdown MM, Pa.

GORMAN
1913, 3, 12. Thomas B. & Jennie A. recrq

GRAHAM
1910, 2, 24. Mary E. Pollock & dt, Grace Pollock & Irene Graham, recrq

GRANGER
1923, 1, 17. Bert & w, Florence, recrq
1924, 10, 15. Herbert C. & w, Florence, & ch, Beryl, relrq

GRANT
1888, 6, 14. Margaret recrq
1906, 10, 18. Margaret dropped from mbrp

GRAVES
1893, 11, 16. E. Adelaide recrq
1893, 11, 16. Myra E. recrq
1893, 11, 16. Stella M. recrq
1893, 11, 16. Edith C. recrq
1893, 11, 16. May H. recrq
1899, 3, 16. Emeline rocf Goshen MM
1907, 12, 19. Myra E. & Stella M. gct Hebron MM, N. C.
1909, 9, 8. May H. recrq

GRAY
1886, 7, 14. Wm. & w, Jessie, recrq
1892, 5, 19. Jessie B. recrq

GREEN
1902, 5, 15. Ruby J. recrq
1919, 11, 12. Lizzie recrq
1924, 2, 13. Leslie gct Newport News MM, Va.

GREETHAM
1912, 3, 14. Eva recrq
1913, 7, 16. Eva relrq

GRIFFEN
1904, 2, 18. Ella relrq

GRIFFITH
1926, 11, 17. Edna recrq
1932, 1, 13. Edna dropped from mbrp
1933, 4, 13. Frank Lewis & Martha Gardner recrq

GRIGGSBY
1914, 3, 18. Wm. B. & w, Ethel Louise, recrq

GRIMM
1913, 6, 18. Grace dropped from mbrp
1918, 3, 13. Helen Marie, minor, recrq
1922, 8, 16. Harold Hartford recrq
1927, 6, 8. Helen Marie dropped from mbrp
1930, 4, 16. Harold gct Columbus MM, O.

GRINDLE
1889, 4, 20. H. S. m Ella GREENAMYER, dt Dt. S. & Fannie, b 1858,4,12

1913, 10, 15. H. S. & Ella recrq
1916, 5, 17. Gladys recrq
1932, 1, 13. Stewart dropped from mbrp

GROSDIDIER
1920, 11, 17. Alma Muetzel relrq
1922, 7, 12. Gertrude Henderson relrq
1924, 4, 16. Lloyd & w, Gertrude, & ch recrq

GROVES
1929, 9, 18. Lola Ruth rocf Urbana MM

GRUBB
1903, 1, 20. Mary Elizabeth rocf Mt. Pleasant
        MM, O.
1909, 9, 8. Mary E. recrq

GUEST
1898, 3, 23. W. C. recrq
1916, 6, 14. Edith relrq
1927, 6, 8. Wm. dropped from mbrp

GUY
1899, 3, 16. Iva recrq
1899, 8, 17. Wm. H. recrq
1900, 10, 19. Wm. H. relrq
1902, 5, 15. Myrtle V. recrq
1902, 5, 15. Wm. H. recrq

GUYER
1915, 2, 17. Ausley recrq
1915, 6, 16. Ausley E. gct Hutsonville MM,
        Ill.

GYMER
1887, 12, 15. Mahala recrq
1889, 3, 14. Emma recrq
1895, 10, 17. Mahala relrq

HACKENBERG
1898, 3, 23. Henry W. & Hannah recrq
1902, 5, 15. Guy & Roy recrq
1902, 11, 13. Hanna's d mentioned

HACKETT
1927, 6, 8. Josephine Johns dropped from
        mbrp

HADDAD
1929, 10, 16. Gertrude recrq
1933, 5, 17. Gertrude dropped from mbrp

HADLEY
1894, 5, 17. J. C. gct Providence MM
1896, 10, 15. Joseph C. & Adelaide gct Dover
        MM
1913, 12, 17. Edward J. & w, Bertha, & ch,
        Lois Irene, Eugene, Melvin, Earl & Doro-
        thy, recrq
1921, 2, 16. Bertha & six ch relrq
1923, 8, 15. Myrtle O. Allen gct Clark Ave.
        MM, Cleveland, O.

HADOX
1929, 2, 13. Evelyn recrq

HAGEMAN
1894, 4, 19. James C. recrq
1895, 4, 18. James gct Tecumseh MM, Mich.

HAIGHT
1885, 4, 15. Frank recrq
1887, 8, 18. Frank dropped from mbrp
1895, 10, 17. Francis dropped from mbrp

HAINES
1915, 11, 17. Charlotte C. recrq
1921, 2, 16. Mrs. Charlotte relrq
1927, 10, 19. Ralph A. recrq

HALDY
1924, 11, 12. Delia recrq

HALE
1911, 9, 14. Clara & dt, Caroline F., recrq

HALIDAY
1904, 6, 16. James & Maggie recrq
1906, 12, 13. Marie recrq
1922, 6, 14. James & Maggie [Halliday] dropped
        [from mbrp
HALL
1888, 12, 13. Henry rocf Des Moines MM, Ia.
1895, 9, 19. Harry gct Chicago MM; returned
        address unknown
1903, 12, 17. Geo. H. & w, Hannah, & ch, Al-
        fred Henry & Bertha Rosina, rocf Toronto,
        Can.
1905, 1, 26. George H. & w, Hannah, & ch,
        Alfred Henry & Bertha Rosina, gct Boulder
        MM, Colo.
1913, 7, 16. John G. & w, Martha, rocf Al-
        liance MM, O.
1917, 3, 14. Edith Kirk relrq
1918, 6, 12. John & Martha gct Alliance MM,O.
1920, 6, 16. Della Lucile recrq
1921, 2, 16. Clara Lucile gct Hughsville MM,
        Pa.
1924, 4, 16. Nellie recrq
1924, 4, 16. Etta B. recrq

HALLIDAY
1922, 6, 14. James & Maggie dropped from
        mbrp

HAMER
1933, 9, 13. Kathleen Patricia recrq

HAMILTON
1893, 5, 19. Roy recrq
1895, 10, 17. Roy dropped from mbrp

HAMM
1896, 4, 16. Minnie Price relrq

HANEY
1914, 2, 18.   Mary E. & ch, Wm. & James, recrq
1922, 2, 15.   Mary E., Wm. & James dropped
        from mbrp

HART
1919, 2, 12.   Jennie B. relrq

HARTLAND
1893, 5, 19.   Frank recrq
1896, 9, 17.   Frank [Harland] dropped from
        mbrp

HARLOW
1901, 2, 14.   Harriet V. recrq
1912, 3, 14.   Mary recrq
1926, 1, 13.   Harriet V. relrq
HARRINGTON
1893, 7, 13.   Louise Belle recrq
1906, 3, 15.   Geo. & Mary E. recrq
1922, 6, 14.   Mary dropped from mbrp

HARRIS
1902, 4, 17.   Mellie M. recrq

HARRISON
1924, 2, 13.   Ray E. & w recrq

HART
1906, 10, 18.   Harriet dropped from mbrp

HARTMAN
1906, 12, 13.   Geo. Elmore recrq
1907, 5, 16.   Geo. gct Ramona MM
1912, 6, 13.   Mrs. & dt, Mary, recrq
1914, 3, 18.   Mrs. Geo. & two ch relrq
1915, 11, 17.   Mrs. Emma A., Earle & Mary recrq
1920, 10, 13.   Emma A. & s, Earl, relrq

HARTSUCK
1903, 11, 19.   J. Edward rmt Laura Apel
1906, 8, 16.   Laura A. gct Grand River MM

HARVEY
1901, 9, 19.   Wm. H. & Lela M. recrq·

HASENPFLUG
----, --, --.   John A., s Geo. & Elizabeth,
        b 1869,5,5; m Sophia BURGY, dt John &
        Christiana, b 1872,4,10
            Ch: Leroy J.   b 1898, 1, 20
                Arthur W.
                George

1889, 5, 16.   John A. & Sarah S. recrq
1891, 2, 19.   Ezra recrq
1907, 1, 17.   Sarah E. relrq
1913, 6, 18.   Ezra dropped from mbrp
1932, 3, 23.   Mildred relrq

HASLEY
1915, 3, 17.   Laura rocf Searsboro MM, Iowa
1916, 10, 8.   Laura gct Sugar Creek MM, Iowa

HASSONG
1915, 11, 17.   Emma recrq

HASTINGS
1902, 2, 13.   Gertrude R. rocf White Water
        MM, Ind.
1906, 6, 14.   Gertrude R. dropped from mbrp

HAWKINS
1887, 7, 14.   Chas. & Elizabeth recrq

HAWORTH
1911, 1, 19.   Dayton D. & w, Emma, & ch,
        Orpha & Alma Gladys, rocf Hopewell MM,
        Ind.
1913, 3, 12.   Dayton D. & w, Emma G., & ch,
        Orpha B. & Alma Gladys, gct Hopewell
        MM, Ind.
1918, 2, 13.   Esther recrq
1922, 2, 15.   Esther dropped from mbrp

HAWTHORN
1913, 9, 17.   Ruby Brown relrq

HAY
1891, 11, 19.   Margaret recrq
1913, 10, 15.   Margaret O. [Hey] dropped from
        mbrp

HAYES
1902, 12, 18.   John L. recrq

HEGERLING
1902, 4, 17.   C. recrq
1919, 1, 15.   Christopher & Lottie gct Bell
        MM, Calif.

HEINN
1894, 12, 13.   Lydia A. recrq
1927, 6, 8.   Grace [Heine] dropped from mbrp

HEINTON
1902, 5, 15.   Arthur & w, Kate, recrq
1915, 9, 15.   Robert & Louisa K. dropped from
        mbrp
1922, 6, 14.   Arthur & Kate dropped from mbrp

HELLER
1933, 11, 15.   Rebecca recrq

HEMMETER
1899, 2, 16.   John G. recrq

HENDERSON
1859, 2, 24.   Catherine, w A-●---, dt Haus &
        Sofia Johansen, b

1899, 5, 25.   Andrew & Catharine recrq
1913, 7, 16.   Gertrude recrq

HENDERSON, continued
1920, 6, 16. Thos. C. & fam relrq

HENEKS
1924, 2, 13. E. B. & w recrq

HENITON
1902, 2, 13. Robert & w, Louisa, recrq
1915, 8, 18. Robert H. & Louise K. [Heinton]
    dropped from mbrp

HENLY
1900, 12, 25. Otto rocf Carthage MM, Ind.,
    dtd 1900,11,8
1905, 1, 26. Otto gct Back Creek MM, Ind.

HENNINGSEN
1899, 2, 16. Andrew C. [Hemingson] & w,
    Lizzie, & ch, Wm. F. & Esther Olina, recrq
1899, 2, 16. Chas. K. & Emma C. [Hemingson]
    recrq
1900, 10, 19. Chas. & fam dropped from mbrp
1900, 10, 19. Andrew dropped from mbrp

HENRY
1927, 11, 16. Ruby Wilson gct Raisin Valley MM

HENSON
1892, 3, 17. Alice recrq

HENWOOD
1898, 3, 23. Marshall & w, Anna, & ch, Willie,
    Jennie & Merritt, recrq
1932, 1, 13. Marshall, Jennie, Willie & Mer-
    ritt dropped from mbrp

HERMAN
----, --, --. Jacob, s Jacob & Margaret, b
    1877,12,22; m Anna APEL, dt Bernbord & Mar-
    garet, b 1887,3,19
1931, --, --. La Vern B.

1907, 2, 14. Jacob & Anna recrq
1913, 3, 12. Florence recrq

HERRIER
1930, 12, 17. Elinore Felger gct Springfield
    MM

HERRINGTON
1915, 2, 17. Mrs. Matilda recrq
1927, 5, 18. Matilda dropped from mbrp

HEWITT
1908, 11, 19. Bessie N. recrq

HEYDORN
1901, 10, 17. Ida Mabel recrq

HICKMAN
1932, 1, 13. Mrs. Eleanor Clark dropped from
    mbrp

HICKS
1890, 6, 19. George N. & w, Jennie, recrq
1904, 11, 17. Geo. M. & w, Jennie, & ch, Doro-
    thy Ellen & George Lawrence, gct Collins
    MM, N. Y.
1907, 5, 16. George & w, Jennie, & ch, Law-
    rence & George, rocf Collins MM, dtd 1907,
    4,25
1916, 4, 12. Geo. M. & w, Jennie, & s, Law-
    rence, rocf Raisin MM, dtd 1916,2,23
1927, 6, 8. Lawrence dropped from mbrp

HIGGINS
1902, 4, 17. Geo. E. recrq

HILBORN
1902, 7, 17. Paul A. recrq
1902, 7, 17. Howard P. recrq

HILGENECK
1915, 4, 14. Lucy relrq

HILLMAN
1894, 1, 18. W. H. recrq
1913, 10, 15. N. H. [Hilman] dropped from
    mbrp

HILTON
1892, 1, 14. Fred recrq
1895, 10, 17. Frederick dropped from mbrp

HINE
1913, 6, 18. Lydia dropped from mbrp
1932, 12, 14. Willis E. [Hines] recrq

HINKLE
1932, 11, 16. Olive recrq
1933, 11, 15. Olive recrq

HINMAN
----, --, --. Charles & Dora
    Ch: Phila F.   b 1889, 6, 9
        Chas. A.Jr." 1894, 11, 8
        Harold B.   " 1898, 4, 28
        Dorothy G. " 1900, 9, 25; m Lester
        BESCH
1874, 11, 14. Percy A., s M. S. & Thekla
    (Thompson), b 1874,11,14; m Annie NORTH-
    COTT

1886, 5, 12. Charles recrq
1887, 10, 23. Chas. A. rmt Dora C. Gerrard
1892, 3, 17. Percy recrq
1893, 12, 14. Fred recrq
1894, 1, 18. Frank recrq
1903, 2, 4. Fred C. relrq
1904, 6, 16. Seth W. recrq
1905, 2, 16. Frank T. relrq
1907, 6, 13. Seth W. & w, Ruby Green, relrq
1912, 12, 18. Seth & w, Ruby, recrq
1914, 10, 14. Seth & Ruby relrq
1927, 7, 13. Mrs. Cecil recrq

HIRSCH
1912, 1, 18. Annie recrq

HIRSCHMAN
1912, 2, 15. Florence Slade relrq
1913, 3, 12. August & w recrq
1927, 6, 8. Ruth dropped from mbrp
1927, 6, 8. Milburn dropped from mbrp

HITCHCOCK
1891, 6, 18. Emma recrq
1913, 6, 18. Eunice dropped from mbrp

HITSON
1904, 5, 19. Albert dis

HOATH
1905, 2, 16. Lydia May rocf Blue River MM

HOAR
1918, 8, 14. Mr. & Mrs. A. K. & dt, Virginia Ruth, recrq
1924, 1, 16. Mrs. James recrq
1926, 9, 15. Alfred & w, Mamie, & dt, Ruth, relrq

HODSON
1885, 2, 18. John G. & Anna recrq

HOFF
1900, 12, 25. Daniel rocf Fairfield MM, O., dtd 1894,11,12

HOFFMAN
1902, 7, 17. Susanna recrq
1915, 11, 17. Mrs. Annie C. & Bruce D. recrq
1921, 2, 16. Mrs. Anna & s, Bruce, relrq

HOLCOMB
1910, 5, 19. Jennie R. J. recrq
1918, 4, 17. Jennie R. dropped from mbrp

HOLE
1893, 9, 14. Edgar T. rocf Salem MM
1895, 3, 14. Wilmer D. rocf Salem MM
1897, 4, 14. Edgar T. rmt Adelaide M. Weider
1910, 10, 13. Edgar T. & w, Adelaide, & ch gct New York MM
1915, 4, 14. Wilmer dropped from mbrp

HOLLIDAY
1910, 1, 13. Clyde C. & w, Edith W., & ch, Clyde Wray, rocf Upland MM, Ind.
1910, 6, 16. Clyde C. & w, Edith W., gct Elba MM, N. Y.

HOLLOWAY
1913, 3, 12. Mrs. W. S. recrq

HOLMES
1895, 5, 16. Eva May [Holm] recrq
1915, 4, 14. Mrs. Louise [Holme] recrq
1922, 2, 15. Mrs. L. dropped from mbrp

1922, 2, 15. Bruce dropped from mbrp

HOMAN
1910, 5, 19. Mrs. J. F. recrq

HOOVER
1897, 2, 18. Mary E. & dt, Anna, recrq
1902, 6, 19. Anna K. rmt Wm. B. Hubbard
1905, 10, 19. Mary E. relrq

HORNER
1914, 3, 18. Samuel recrq
1914, 4, 18. Samuel H. recrq
1918, 4, 17. Samuel dropped from mbrp

HOSKINS
1903, 7, 12. Maud Milner rocf Fairfield MM, dtd 1903,6,20
1906, 11, 15. Joseph & Maud gct Clear Creek MM

HOTCHKISS
----, --, --. Willis, s H. C. & Elizabeth, b 1844,6,3; m Mathilda KOEHLER d 1931,9, 14
        Ch: Livingston b 1901, 12, 13

1893, 8, 17. Willis recrq
1897, 4, 15. Elizabeth recrq
1901, 1, 17. Matilda K. recrq
1902, 12, 18. Henry C. recrq
1903, 7, 12. Joseph J. rocf Vermillion MM, dtd 1903,7,4
1912, 5, 16. Martha recrq
1927, 6, 8. Martha dropped from mbrp

HOUSE
1914, 2, 18. Emma E. & s, Eugene E., recrq
1922, 3, 15. Eugene relrq
1932, 1, 13. Mrs. Emma dropped from mbrp

HOWARD
1904, 11, 17. Mrs. Effie rocf Short Creek MM
1913, 12, 17. Effa gct Los Angeles MM, Calif.

HOYT
----, --, --. Fred R. m Matilda L. LUTHER, dt James O. & Mary E., b 1850,4,25 d 1931,10, 16
1922, 9, --. Fred d

1884, 1, 16. Matilda recrq
1885, 4, 15. Ida recrq
1888, 5, 17. Ida H. dropped from mbrp
1922, 3, 15. Fred recrq

HUBBARD
1897, 5, 13. Chas. rocf Carmel MM, Kans.
1897, 11, 18. Wm. G. rocf Columbus MM, O.
1897, 11, 18. Penrose H. & w, Wm. B., John B. & Margaret, rocf Columbus MM, O.
1899, 5, 25. Wm. G. & dt, Margaret, gct Columbus MM, O.

HUBBARD, continued
1902, 6, 19. Wm. B. rmt Anna K. Hoover
1905, 9, 27. Chas. E. rmt Bessie L. D. Wistar
1907, 1, 17. Chas. & w, Bessie Wister, gct
    Chicago MM
1912, 6, 27. Wm. G. rocf Goldboro MM, N. C.
1919, 4, 16. Wm. B. & w, Hanna H., & s, Paul,
    relrq
1932, 1, 13. Mrs. M. M. dropped from mbrp

HUDSON
1911, 4, 13. Homer & w recrq
1927, 2, 16. Homer & w, Florence, relrq

HUFF
1916, 5, 17. John I. rocf Liberal MM, Kans.
1919, 3, 12. John I. gct Berkley MM, Calif.
1919, 9, 17. Daniel gct Muncie MM, Ind.

HUFFORD
1909, 12, 16. Belle Keetch relrq
1914, 2, 18. Mary recrq

HUMPHRIES
1888, 4, 19. May relrq

HUNT
1914, 4, 18. Sarah Ann recrq
1927, 5, 18. Sarah dropped from mbrp

HUSSONG
1922, 2, 15. Emma dropped from mbrp

HUTCHINSON
1917, 8, 15. Melva rocf Columbus MM

HUTSON
1913, 6, 18. Mabel dropped from mbrp

HYNES
1903, 5, 19. Fred C. recrq
1906, 8, 16. Fred dropped from mbrp

HYPES
1926, 4, 14. Myrtle & Martha recrq
1931, 9, 23. Myrtle & Martha gct Indianola MM,
    Ia.

INGLETON
1927, 6, 8. Lulu dropped from mbrp

INSKEEP
1922, 7, 12. Lewis M. recrq
1924, 11, 12. Lewis & Lily gct St. Clairaville
    MM, O.

INWOOD
1926, 10, 13. Hattie Marie recrq
1926, 12, 15. Lucile recrq

ISAMAR
1915, 12, 15. Rosa Fredricka recrq
1922, 3, 15. Rose dropped from mbrp

JACKSON
1895, 5, 16. George rocf Lancaster MM, Eng.
1897, 9, 16. Wm. S., Julia & Maude E. recrq
1898, 3, 23. Kela & Edward recrq
1908, 2, 13. Mary Burhaus dropped from mbrp

JACOBS
1902, 7, 17. James N. & Addie M. recrq
1918, 2, 13. Wm. Omar recrq
1919, 2, 12. Omar & w gct Urbana MM, O.

JAROSH
1888, 3, 15. Martha H. recrq
1905, 9, 14. Dr. Martha H. [Jarosch] relrq

JARRETT
----, --, --. Eva, dt Geo. & Laura, b 1887,9,
    30 d 1931,12,16

1899, 2, 16. Lillian Gertrude recrq
1904, 9, 15. Eva V. recrq
1932, 1, 13. Eva dropped from mbrp

JARVIS
1889, 1, 17. Sarah A. recrq
1889, 3, 14. Sarah A. & Olive recrq
1890, 6, 19. Sarah A. relrq
1891, 2, 19. Olive relrq

JAY
1904, 11, 17. Samuel rocf Adrian MM
1913, 6, 18. Emily dropped from mbrp
1915, 2, 17. Mrs. Samuel rst
1915, 2, 17. Mrs. Samuel relrq

JEFFERS
1922, 3, 15. Guy recrq
1922, 7, 20. Guy V. rmt Miriam May Lafferty
1924, 1, 16. Guy & Miriam gct Orange MM, O.
1929, 4, 17. Chas. recrq
1932, 3, 16. Edna Lois, dt Chas. & Myrtle,
    recrq

JENKINS
1897, 10, 14. Reba rocf Winona MM
1903, 10, 15. Reba gct Central City MM, Neb.
1909, 11, 18. John K. & w, Margaret L., & ch,
    L. Mildred, A. Margaret & Lloyd M., rocf
    Alva MM, Ind.
1911, 11, 16. John & w, Margaret, & ch, Marga-
    ret & Lloyd, gct Haviland MM, Kans.
1913, 11, 19. Mildred gct Wichita MM, Kans.

JENNINGS
1919, 9, 17. Alpheus & Leona rocf Alliance
    MM, O.
1927, 5, 18. Mr. & fam dropped from mbrp

JENSEN
1932, 11, 16. Pearl V. recrq

JIBERG
----, --, --. John & Amelia

JIBERG, continued
    Ch: Caroline   b 1892, 3, 28
        Blanche   " 1893, 10, 5

1909, 4, 15. Caroline & Blanche [Jirherg]
    recrq

JOB
1902, 5, 15. Bert recrq

JOHNS
1897, 4, 15. Florence & ch, Gertrude & Jose-
    phine, recrq
1900, 5, 17. Myrtle recrq

JOHNSON
----, --, --. Elwood & Lucy
    Ch: Lawrence b 1819, 11, 18
       Mildred A. " 1922, 12, 24

1902, 11, 13. Arthur & w recrq
1905, 10, 19. Elwood & w, Lucy, & ch, Mildred
    C., Lawrence & Clara Lucile, rocf Back
    Creek MM
1908, 11, 19. Arthur H. & w relrq
1909, 3, 18. Rosana & s, Freddie, rocf Salem
    MM, O.
1911, 9, 9. Mildred rmt Ralph Watterbury
1913, 2, 12. Lucy D. relrq
1915, 12, 15. Clarence Russell & Berneice
    Geraldine recrq
1916, 10, 18. Lucile relrq
1918, 5, 15. Frederick dropped from mbrp
1920, 6, 16. Elwood gct Spring Brook MM, Ore.
1921, 4, 7. Clarence & w gct Second Friends
    Church, Cleveland, O.
1928, 11, 14. Belle Cherry dropped from mbrp

JOLLY
1903, 10, 22. Joseph A., s Philip & Mary, b
    1880,9,1; m Edna BROOKE, dt Wm. & Rizpah,
    b 1876,12,22
    Ch: Ruth E.   b 1904, 10, 29

1914, 3, 18. Joseph A. & w, Edna, & dt, Ruth,
    recrq

JONES
----, --, --. John Elias b 1869,8,5 d 1920,--,
    --
1930, --, --. Celia B. d

1884, 8, 13. Robert A. recrq
1884, 9, 17. Alice L. & Ella F. recrq
1894, 1, 18. Daniel D. recrq
1895, 12, 24. Alice L. rmt Wm. W. Brown
1906, 3, 15. John recrq
1907, 2, 14. Laura W. recrq
1908, 12, 17. Grace Anderson recrq
1909, 10, 14. Elizabeth rocf Paoli MM, Ind.,
    dtd 1909,9,8; returned
1914, 2, 18. Joseph R. recrq
1914, 11, 18. Celia B. rocf Adrian MM, Mich.

1915, 4, 14. Agnes recrq
1916, 4, 12. Milton S. recrq
1920, 11, 17. Laura W. relrq
1922, 6, 14. Daniel dropped from mbrp
1927, 5, 18. Milton dropped from mbrp
1927, 5, 18. Joseph dropped from mbrp
1927, 6, 8. Agnes dropped from mbrp

JORDAN
1903, 9, 17. Matilda J. recrq

JUDSON
1897, 1, 13. Florence E. & Grace R. recrq
1908, 4, 16. Grace relrq
1927, 4, 13. Mrs. J. E. relrq

KAHL
1913, 7, 16. Olive recrq

KAINE
1904, 10, 13. Rose Stemple dropped from mbrp

KALBRUNER
1910, 6, 16. George recrq
1913, 3, 12. Mrs. May recrq
1913, 3, 12. Mrs. Ruth recrq
1913, 3, 12. Miss Emma recrq
1913, 10, 15. Howard recrq
1927, 6, 8. Geo. & May dropped from mbrp
1928, 9, 12. Howard dropped from mbrp

KAYLOR
1894, --, --. Maggie d

KECK
1924, 11, 12. Mrs. recrq

KEETCH
1911, --, --. Josephine, w George, d

1887, 7, 14. George recrq
1889, 3, 14. Josephine & ch, Daisy, Violet
    & Arabella, recrq
1897, 12, 16. Thos. recrq
1899, 8, 17. Thomas relrq
1901, 10, 17. Joey relrq
1912, 6, 24. Rose Elizabeth rmt James Wilson
    Callahan
1927, 5, 18. Geo. T. dropped from mbrp

KELLY
1886, 1, 13. Adaline recrq
1887, 8, 18. Adeline dropped from mbrp
1893, 12, 14. Neal recrq
1913, 6, 18. Neil dropped from mbrp

KELLER
1926, 5, 12. Edith rocf Ackworth MM, Ia.
1928, 11, 14. Edith gct Ackworth MM, Ia.
1932, 1, 13. Edith dropped from mbrp

KENNEDY
1874, 5, 23. Grace, dt Archie & Cornelia, b

KENNEDY, continued
1893, 11, 16. John recrq
1895, 10, 17. John dropped from mbrp
1899, 2, 16. Grace recrq
1915, 2, 17. Mrs. Jennie recrq
1927, 6, 8. Jennie dropped from mbrp

KEPKE
1907, 10, 17. Minnie E. roc

KESLER
1922, 3, 15. Bruce Harrison recrq
1932, 1, 13. Bruce, Florence & Herman dropped
     from mbrp

KEYSER
1902, 5, 15. Ira & Alta L. recrq

KIMBERLIN
1915, 11, 17. Elsie recrq
1919, 3, 12. Elsie gct Clark Ave. MM, Cleve-
     land, O.

KING
1894, 1, 18. Edith recrq
1895, 5, 16. Andrew M. recrq
1896, 2, 13. Estella relrq
1901, 10, 17. Ida W. recrq
1913, 6, 18. Everett W. dropped from mbrp
1926, 11, 17. Laura recrq

KIRBY
1908, 10, 15. Theodore, Jennie E. & Wm. rocf
     Lynn Grove MM, Iowa, dtd 1908,9,5
1912, 4, 18. Theodore & Jennie gct Marshall-
     town MM, Ia.

KIRK
1914, 3, 18. Edith C. rocf Guernsey MM

KERMISH
1924, 2, 27. F. W. & Elizabeth recrq

KIRSHAW
1913, 3, 12. Sidney recrq

KITCHEN
1912, 1, 18. Nellie V. rocf Lynn Grove MM
1916, 7, 12. Nellie B. gct Lynnville MM, Ia.

KITSON
1902, 2, 13. Albert, Lizzie, Elsie & Eva
     recrq
1913, 2, 12. Lizzie relrq
1922, 6, 14. Eva & Elsie dropped from mbrp

KITTEL
1915, 12, 15. Geo. W. recrq
1919, 9, 17. Geo. W. [Kittle] gct Bloomfield
     MM, Neb.

KITTERINGHAM
1894, 3, 15. Walter recrq

1894, 12, 13. Walter gct London MM, Eng.

KLAUSE
1927, 6, 22. Ralph C. recrq

KNIGHT
1891, 2, 19. Rachel rocf West Lake MM, Can.
1904, 6, 16. Rachel S. gct Woodford MM,
     Ontario, Can.

KLINE
1919, 9, 17. Bertha Walker rocf Londonderry
     MM

KNOX
1889, 4, 18. Wm. A. & Ella recrq
1904, 6, 16. Wm. & w, Ella, & ch, Ruth &
     Lois, dropped from mbrp

KOEPKE
1917, 6, 20. Chas. & Mabel recrq
1932, 1, 13. Chas. & Mabel dropped from mbrp

KOESTER
1884, 8, 13. Henry J. recrq
1904, 10, 13. Henry dropped from mbrp

KOHLER
1916, 5, 17. Fred A. recrq
1932, 11, 16. Henry recrq
KOLLAR
1886, 11, 4. M. L., s Joseph, b 1863,6,27;
     m Nellie GAMBLE, dt Robert & Mary, b
     1866,5,15

1913, 6, 18. M. L. & w, Nellie, recrq
1931, 1, 14. Harvey Willard & w, Isole, &
     dt, Flossie Lucile, recrq
1931, 1, 14. Lionel LeMar & w, Mabel Wraight,
     recrq
1933, 10, 18. Lionel & w, Mabel, & dt, Betty
     Lou, dropped from mbrp

KOON
1914, 2, 18. Harry S. & w, Arlie V., recrq
1920, 5, 12. Mr. & Mrs. H. S. relrq
1932, 12, 14. Harold [Kuhn] recrq

KRAMER
1904, 7, 14. Ellen & Dell recrq
1908, 11, 19. Dell gct S. Cleveland MM
1922, 10, 18. Florence M. recrq
1926, 3, 31. Florence M. gct North Branch
     MM, Kans.
1927, 6, 8. Ellen dropped from mbrp

KRAUSE
1894, 8, 16. Kate recrq

KREKEL
1913, 3, 19. Madge Barrett relrq

KREMER
1915, 2, 17.   Phares S. & w, Carrie T., & ch,
     Pearl, recrq
1927, 5, 18.   Pharez, Carrie & Pearl dropped
     from mbrp

KRIKANA
1925, 4, 8.   Frank recrq

KUELMEL
----, --, --.   Wm. E. b 1868,6,11 d 1905,2,16;
     m Mary APEL, dt Bernard & Gretchen, b
     1870,10,2
        Ch: Margaretta b 1900, 3, 14
            Ruth   " 1901, 10, 26; m Robert E.
            DERRICK
            Wm. Edward

1887, 4, 14.   Emma recrq
1895, 2, 14.   Wm. & Mary recrq
1904, 10, 13.   Wm. dropped from mbrp
1905, 2, 16.   William [Kuelmell] dropped from
     mbrp
1921, 9, --.   Ruth rmt Robert Derrick
1928, 1, 2.   Edward H. [Kuehnel] rmt Mary E.
     Clark
1930, 9, 18.   Earl Wm. rmt Faith Martin

KUMHALL
1914, 10, 14.   Anastasia recrq
1927, 6, 8.   Anastacia dropped from mbrp

LADDS
1889, 4, 18.   Edward & Nora recrq
1913, 10, 15.   Edward & Nora dropped from mbrp

LAFFERTY
1918, 11, 5.   Dora A. d

1911, 1, 19.   L. S. & w, Dora A., & ch, Edson
     Brice, Dean Dewitt, Marion May & Paul
     LeMoine, recrq
1919, 4, 16.   L. S. dropped from mbrp
1922, 7, 20.   Miriam May rmt Guy V. Jeffers
1932, 1, 13.   Edson B. & Dean D. dropped from
     mbrp
1932, 2, 17.   Paul & w, Lucile, & ch gct Mt.
     Pleasant MM

LAIRD
1933, 11, 15.   Catharine recrq

LAMB
1907, 12, 19.   Flossie [Lamm] recrq
1909, 2, 18.   Flossie [Lamm] gct White Water
     MM, Ind.
1914, 10, 14.   Carrie recrq
1915, 2, 17.   Clarence H. recrq
1922, 3, 15.   Clarence dropped from mbrp

LAMOREAUX
1923, 6, 13.   Clarinda recrq; form mbr at
     Pleasant Valley MM which was laid down

LAMPRECHT
1887, 4, 14.   Louisa recrq

LANE
1933, 3, 15.   Claude Lee & w, Orie Adella,
     recrq
1933, 5, 17.   Claude Lee & w, Orie Adella,
     relrq

LANGTHORNE
1932, 12, 14.   Francis recrq

LANGTON
1927, 5, 18.   Kitty dropped from mbrp

LAPHAM
1931, 1, 14.   Mabel Rose recrq
1932, 7, 13.   Mrs. Mabel gc

LARGE
1899, 10, 18.   Mrs. Minnie recrq
1913, 10, 15.   Minnie dropped from mbrp

LASH
1894, 1, 18.   Edward recrq
1904, 10, 13.   Edward dropped from mbrp

LASHBROOK
1915, 12, 15.   Mrs. C. recrq
1927, 5, 18.   Mrs. dropped from mbrp

LATIMER
1894, 11, 15.   Florence, May & Florence Jr.
     recrq
1905, 2, 16.   Florence dropped from mbrp

LAUGHTON
1914, 10, 14.   Kittie Cowley recrq

LAUX
1883, 3, 15.   Mrs. L. b

1917, 6, 13.   Mrs. L. recrq

LAW
1932, 3, 16.   Mary Rytha recrq

LAWRENCE
1924, 4, 16.   Ralph S. recrq
1928, 10, 17.   Ralph S. gct Courtland Ave. Ch.,
     Kokomo, Ind.

LEASER
1932, 1, 13.   Hattie Inwood gct Mt. Pleasant
     MM

LEBER
1920, 4, 14.   Lilla Christiana recrq

LEE
1890, 9, 18. Ellen Dodge & dt, Susie May,
     recrq

LEESE
1926, 3, 31. Mrs. Gertrude recrq
1932, 1, 13. Mrs. Gertrude dropped from mbrp

LEEWORTHY
1913, 3, 12. Bessie recrq

LEIRCK
1924, 7, 16. Sophronie E. recrq

LeNORMAN
1922, 10, 18. Cora rocf Union MM, N. C.

LESTER
----, --, --. Harry m Ellen SMITH, dt Joseph &
     Elizabeth, b 1852,6,10 d 1929,5,--

1917, 6, 6. Mrs. Ellen W. & Alice E. recrq

LEUSZLER
1913, 7, 16. Helen recrq
1927, 6, 8. Helen [Lenzler] dropped from
     mbrp

LEWIS
1895, 1, 17. A. H. & May recrq
1897, 9, 16. Arthur P. & Mary A. recrq
1912, 6, 13. Mary recrq
1913, 10, 15. Albert H. & Mary dropped from
     mbrp
1921, 6, 22. Mary E. dropped from mbrp

LIBEK
1918, 7, 17. Charles dropped from mbrp

LICKES
1905, 10, 19. Nellie A. recrq

LILLIE
1902, 7, 17. Jefferson J. & Lena H. recrq
1902, 7, 17. Daniel & Therisa recrq

LINDLEY
1900, 10, 19. Zilpha rocf Sand Creek MM, Ind.

LINDLOW
1908, 12, 17. Frank W. & Louise E. & ch,
     Frank W. & Frederick D., recrq
1919, 9, 17. Frank W. & w, Louise E., & ch
     relrq

LING
1917, 6, 13. Robert H. recrq
1917, 7, 18. Robert H. relrq

LINKS
1908, 7, 16. Margaret gct Columbus MM, O.

LISTON
1918, 9, 18. Raymond rocf Muncie MM, Ind.
1922, 3, 15. Raymond dropped from mbrp

LITTLE
1892, 9, 16. Jessie G. recrq
1892, 9, 16. George Henry rocf MM in England
1896, 12, 17. Geo. H. & w, Jessie, gct Cin-
     cinnati MM, O.

LOCKNER
1932, 3, 16. Minnie Luella recrq

LOCKWOOD
1885, 2, 18. Walter & w, Janette, & ch, Ber-
     nard & Wm., recrq
1895, 12, 19. Walter & w, Jennie, dis disunity
1913, 10, 15. Wm. dropped from mbrp
1916, 6, 14. Harrison recrq
1927, 5, 18. Harrison dropped from mbrp

LOGAN
1911, 1, 19. Margaret recrq

LOLLEFEON
1924, 11, 12. Alice L. recrq

LONG
1907, 9, 19. Bertha recrq
1909, 4, 15. Bertha relrq
1932, 4, 20. Maud Clark relrq

LORENSEN
1927, 5, 18. Mr. & Mrs. dropped from mbrp

LORRIMER
1893, 5, 19. Alexander D. recrq
1895, 10, 17. A. dropped from mbrp

LOUDERBACK
1924, 1, 16. Vivian recrq

LOVERING
1894, 2, 15. C. H. & May recrq
1898, 3, 23. C. H. & w, May, relrq

LOVITT
1896, 8, 13. Sarah A. & Addie M. recrq
1913, 10, 15. Addie M. [Lovett] dropped from
     mbrp

LOY
1932, 11, 16. Gladys recrq

LUICK
1922, 3, 15. Gordon dropped from mbrp

LUTTLE
1884, 4, 16. Daniel recrq

LUXFORD
1913, 3, 12. Miss Florence recrq
1913, 10, 15. Mrs. A. E. recrq

LUXFORD, continued
1927, 6, 8. Florence dropped from mbrp
1932, 1, 13. Mrs. A. E. dropped from mbrp

LYONS
1910, 4, 14. Joseph H. & w recrq
1910, 4, 14. Annie Campbell recrq
1927, 5, 18. Joseph dropped from mbrp

LYTLE
1928, 12, 12. Ruth dropped from mbrp

McBAINE
1902, 2, 13. Lewis d

1895, 4, 18. Louis [McBain] recrq

McCANN
1892, 4, 14. Anna recrq
1922, 2, 15. Anna (McCann) Berry dropped from
    mbrp
1928, 5, 16. Myrtle rocf Highland Ave. MM,
    Columbus, O.

McCARTHY
1902, 4, 17. Elizabeth M. P. rocf Des Moines
    MM, Ia.; returned on rq

McCARTY
1915, 8, 18. Mary Hufford gct Bristol MM

McCLEAN
1902, 5, 15. Clarence F. recrq
1904, 3, 17. Clarence G. gct Centre MM

McCLINTOCK
1902, 7, 17. Maud A. recrq
1917, 12, 12. Priscilla recrq
1919, 2, 12. Priscilla relrq
1923, 6, 13. Irwin recrq; form mbr at Pleasant
    Valley which was laid down

McCLOSKEY
1894, 2, 15. Will & w, Fannie, recrq
1896, 2, 13. Wm. dropped from mbrp

McCONHEY
1914, 3, 18. Thomas & w recrq

McCORMICK
1916, 4, 12. Emmett A. & Blanche L. recrq
1922, 12, 13. Emmett & w gct First Friends
    Ch., Columbus, O.

McCRORY
1921, 3, 16. Mabel Packard relrq

McCOUGHIE
1922, 3, 15. Thos. dropped from mbrp

McCUTCHEN
1902, 8, 14. Wm. Henry recrq
1904, 3, 17. Wm. H. relrq

1920, 12, 15. Janet K. recrq

McDOWELL
1913, 3, 12. Mrs. Sarah A., Lottie & Leona,
    recrq
1917, 4, 18. Sarah A., Lottie & Leona gct
    Huntington Park MM, Calif.

McFARLAND
1894, 1, 18. Sabra recrq
1894, 2, 15. Thos. recrq
1895, 10, 17. Charles dropped from mbrp
1897, 2, 18. Sabra relrq
1914, 3, 18. Mrs. Stella M. recrq
1922, 3, 15. Stella dropped from mbrp

McGEHAN
1906, 10, 18. Mary recrq

McGONIGAL
1885, 2, 18. Geo. H. & Olive recrq

McGUIRE
1902, 4, 17. Mary recrq

McKAY
1887, 8, 18. Jene [McKaye] gc
1913, 7, 16. Jean rocf S. Cleveland MM, O.
1922, 3, 15. Jean dropped from mbrp

McKEE
1898, 4, 14. Carrie dropped from mbrp

McKINNON
1898, 4, 17. Lottie rmt Wm. Williams
1900, 11, 28. John rmt Lela Shaeffer
1914, 7, 15. John & Agnes rocf South Cleve-
    land MM, O.
1915, 11, 17. Clyde H. recrq
1918, 2, 13. Lillian [McKennon] recrq
1920, 2, 16. Florence recrq
1923, 1, 17. Clyde H. & Lillian rocf Alliance
    MM, O.
1923, 3, 14. Mrs. Ruth recrq
1929, 9, 18. Geo. Yapple & Phylis Ileen,
    minors, recrq
1933, 5, 17. Clyde & w, Lillian, & dt,
    Elizabeth, relrq

McKENZIE
1913, 3, 12. James recrq
1914, 4, 18. Mabel recrq
1927, 6, 8. James & Mabel dropped from mbrp
1932, 1, 13. Mrs. dropped from mbrp

McKINLEY
----, --, --. Al m Lillie B. BUSCHLER, dt
    Christian & Mary, b 1877,4,20
1911, 3, 19. Grace, dt Albert & Matilda, b

1893, 7, 13. Frank recrq
1899, 10, 18. Albert Sidney recrq
1906, 6, 14. Frank & w, Anna, & three ch rel-
    rq

McKINLEY, continued
    rq
1914, 1, 14. Albert dropped from mbrp
1927, 6, 8. Vincent dropped from mbrp

McLEAN
1909, 12, 16. Noah C. & w, rocf Smithfield
    MM; dropped from mbrp for jas

McMILLAN
1904, 1, 14. Rachel recrq

McNEIL
1902, 2, 13. Ella Hastings rocf White Water
    MM, Ind.
1906, 6, 14. Ella H. dropped from mbrp

McNICKLE
1914, 4, 18. Rachel recrq

McPHERSON
1907, 1, 17. Jesse & w, Angeline R., & dt,
    Alice Myrtle, rocf Salem MM, Mass.

McVICKERS
1930, 2, 12. Myra Mae recrq
1932, 3, 16. Myra relrq

McWILLIAMS
1913, 10, 15. Rachel dropped from mbrp

McQUIGAN
1897, 4, 15. Mary Elizabeth recrq

MADRAS
1903, 2, 4. Gertrude L. recrq

MAGNER
1913, 1, 15. Wm., Adah & minor Carlton, recrq
1916, 11, 15. Wm. & Ada gct Kedron MM, Minn.

MAGRAGE
1924, 11, 12. Mrs. G. T. recrq

MAITLAND
1914, 9, 16. Georgia A. & John recrq
1922, 3, 15. Georgia & John dropped from mbrp

MALKEY
1922, 3, 15. Chas. & w, Elizabeth, & ch,
    Elizabeth & Carl, dropped from mbrp

MALLEE
1900, 3, 15. George recrq

MALONE
----, --, --. Walter J., s John & Mary Ann,
    b 1857,8,11; m Emma BROWN
    Ch: Carroll B. b 1886, 11, 25; m Alma
        EARLE
        Esther A. " 1890, 7, 31; m Ralph
        WATERBURY
1903, 1, 24. Mary Ann d ae 82

1886, 1, 19. J. Walter rmt Emma Brown
1886, 3, 17. John C. & w, Mary Ann, rocf
    Clear Creek MM, O.
1887, 3, 17. Sarah recrq
1887, 3, 17. Harry & Florence, ch Chas. O. &
    Sarah, recrq
1914, 6, 11. J. Walter Jr. rmt Elizabeth
    Mather Compton
1916, 4, 20. Margaret rmt Chester Crobough
1916, 4, 20. Ruth rmt Byron L. Osboroune
1917, 6, 6. Sarah relrq
1920, 2, 18. J. Walter relrq
1922, 3, 15. Lloyd S. & Earl dropped from
    mbrp
1922, 6, 14. Harrison dropped from mbrp
1923, 1, 17. Elizabeth relrq
1927, 6, 8. Franklin dropped from mbrp

MALTBIE
1912, --, --. Narcissa d

1896, 7, 16. Narcissa E. [Maltby] recrq
1907, 11, 14. Narcissa relrq
1909, 12, 16. Narcissa recrq

MANY
----, --, --. Cecelia, dt J. J. & J. L., b
    1853,--,-- d 1918,10,--

1914, 1, 14. Cecelia recrq

MARCHAND
1919, 6, 18. Laura & dt, Myrtle Estelle,
    recrq
1923, 12, 14. Myrtle Estell relrq

MARINE
1886, 7, 14. Orland recrq
1889, 7, 18. Orlando gct New York MM

MARSHALL
1924, 1, 16. Ruth recrq
1927, 2, 17. Ruth recrq

MARTIN
1904, 12, 28. Louis A., s Wm., b 1883,5,19;
    m Alvina ROSE, dt Wm. & Augusta, b 1885,
    4,3
    Ch: Ruth   d 1909, 4,--
        Faith   b 1910, 3, 22
1909, 10, 17. Clifford, s Frank & Pearl, b

1899, 2, 16. Lewis Arthur, Conrad M. & Frank
    Percy recrq
1900, 10, 19. Edgar rocf Winona MM
1900, 12, 25. Edgar's cert returned to Winona
    MM
1900, 12, 25. Frank recrq
1901, 3, 14. Caroline Emily recrq
1902, 4, 17. Eliz. Annie recrq
1904, 8, 18. Frank P. relrq
1904, 9, 15. Frank P. rst
1905, 1, 26. Frank P. & w relrq

MARTIN, continued
1906, 7, 19. Frank & Pearl E. recrq
1906, 12, 13. Gracia recrq
1907, 5, 16. Frank P. & Pearl Clifford relrq
1909, 11, 18. Frank & Pearl recrq
1910, 4, 14. Alvina Rose recrq
1913, 10, 13. Mary dropped from mbrp
1921, 7, 14. Frank & w, Pearl, gct Highland
    MM, O.
1923, 10, 17. Dorothy Parker gct Dayton MM, O.
1925, 3, 18. Frank P. & w, Pearl, & dt, Doro-
    thy, rocf Dayton MM, O.
1927, 6, 8. Conrad dropped from mbrp
1927, 10, 19. Frank P. & w, Pearl, & dt, Doro-
    thy, gct Fullerton MM, O.
1928, 11, 14. Gracia dropped from mbrp
1930, 4, 23. Pearl rocf Fullerton MM
1930, 9, 18. Faith rmt Earl Wm. Kuhlman

MARTINSON
1910, 6, 16. Otto & w, Anna, recrq
1912, 10, 17. Otto & w, Anna, gct Greenville
    MM, Ia.

MASTERMAN
1915, 2, 17. Earl E. recrq
1922, 3, 15. Earl dropped from mbrp

MATCHETT
1918, --, --. Harriett A. d

1901, 8, 15. Elizabeth Jane recrq
1914, 4, 18. G. H. & w & ch, Cecelia, Harold
    & Ruth, recrq
1914, 6, 17. Harriett A. recrq
1922, 12, 13. Ruth [Matchett] White relrq
1927, 6, 8. Alice dropped from mbrp
1928, 7, 18. Miss Betty relrq
1932, 1, 13. Harold dropped from mbrp
1932, 1, 13. George dropped from mbrp
1933, 5, 17. Jennie dropped from mbrp

MATHEWS
1914, 2, 18. Joseph C. recrq
1918, 5, 15. Joseph A. dropped from mbrp
1924, 2, 27. Mrs. E. recrq
1924, 3, 13. Mrs. Anna recrq

MATSON
1915, 11, 17. Nellie A. recrq

MAXWELL
1883, 12, 12. Lizzie N. recrq
1912, 3, 14. John J. recrq
1927, 6, 8. John J. dropped from mbrp

MAY
1924, 2, 27. Ada & Lewis recrq

MEAD
1887, 4, 14. Stella recrq
1895, 10, 17. Stella [Meade] gct Chicago MM,
    Ill.

MEEKER
1902, 11, 13. Robert B. & w rocf Alum Creek MM

MEESE
1922, 3, 15. Grace dropped from mbrp

MEGNARD
1927, 5, 18. Maurice dropped from mbrp

MEINGER
1913, 10, 15. Wm. recrq
1922, 3, 15. Wm. dropped from mbrp

MELBOURNE
1887, 3, 17. George W. recrq
1897, 4, 15. George & Elizabeth dropped from
    mbrp

MELLINGER
1910, 1, 13. Fred E. rocf First Friends Ch.,
    Alliance, O.
1912, 8, 15. Fred C. relrq
1927, 6, 8. Eva dropped from mbrp

MENDENHALL
1915, --, --. Elbert, s Estus & Lucile, d

1899, 9, 20. Walter H. rmt Anna Armitage
1899, 12, 24. Anna Armintage gct Greensboro
    MM, N. C.
1903, 3, 24. Omar & w, Miriam C., & s, War-
    ren Orestes, rocf Stanwood MM, Kans.
1903, 12, 17. Walter & w, Anna A., & ch, Chas.
    Berkenshaw & Deborah Miriam, rocf Greens-
    borough MM, N. C.
1904, 2, 18. Omar & w, Miriam, gct University
    MM, Wichita, Kans.
1911, 2, 16. Estus rocf Lynnville MM, Ia.
1912, 1, 18. Moses & w, Margaret, & dt,
    Clara Lucile, rocf Lynn Grove MM
1914, 2, 18. Lucile Williams recrq
1914, 10, 14. Moses T. & w, Margaret, & ch
    gct Raisin Valley MM
1924, 7, 22. Chas. Berkinshaw rmt Helen Mar-
    guerite Webb
1926, 7, 14. Helen Webb recrq
1931, 7, 15. Walter W. gct Greensboro MM, N.C.
1932, 4, 20. Berkinshaw & w, Helen, & dt gct
    Arch St. MM, Philadelphia, Pa.

MERTON
1895, 5, 16. Edward & w & ch, John, Lula,
    George, Tracy & Samuel, recrq
1895, 5, 16. Chas. C. & w, Anna, & ch, Anna
    May, Mabel, Maggie & Willis, recrq
1895, 6, 13. Eddie recrq
1896, 5, 14. C. E. [Murton] relrq
1897, 9, 16. Edward & w, Margaret, & ch,

MERTON, continued
    John, Lola, George, Tracy, Samuel & Eddie,
    dropped from mbrp

MESSER
1887, 2, 17. Lena recrq
1893, 2, 16. Lena relrq
1893, 10, 19. Lena recrq

MESSERSMITH
1931, 12, 16. Helen, minor, recrq

MICHOLS
1927, 5, 18. H. S. dropped from mbrp

MIGNARD
1903, 6, 18. Maurice recrq

MIGRANGE
1928, 9, 12. Girden & fam gct Sullivant Ave.
    MM, Columbus, O.

MILLER
1908, 11, 19. Carl gct Mt. Hebron MM, N. C.
1909, 6, 17. Carl & w, Minnie, rocf Mt.
    Hebron MM, N. C.
1909, 12, 16. Carl & Minnie G. gct Maple City
    MM, Mich.
1913, 6, 18. Margaret A. & Fred W. recrq
1913, 10, 15. Geo. J. dropped from mbrp
1914, 10, 14. Ada Tompt dropped from mbrp
1915, 4, 14. F. W. & w relrq
1922, 2, 15. Neoma dropped from mbrp
1922, 3, 15. John W. dropped from mbrp
1927, 5, 18. Herbert & fam dropped from mbrp

MILLIKENS
1901, 10, 17. Agnes recrq

MINER
1922, 8, 16. Nellie C. & Sterling C. recrq

MINSHALL
1909, 9, 8. Reese recrq
1913, 2, 12. R. M. recrq
1913, 10, 15. R. M. relrq

MITCHELL
1913, 10, 15. Alice Cummins d

1895, 1, 17. W. J. recrq
1906, 12, 13. Wm. dropped from mbrp
1919, 12, 15. Flora recrq
1932, 1, 13. Mrs. Flora dropped from mbrp

MOCK
1932, 12, 14. Marguerite Baird recrq

MOFFITT
1915, 3, 17. Mrs. Lela recrq
1922, 3, 15. Lela dropped from mbrp

MOLLE
1873, 7, 22. Arthur, s Chas. & Louisa, b
    1873,7,22; m Elsie HINSEN

MONGHIMAN
1904, 6, 16. Elizabeth May recrq
1913, 10, 15. May gc
1914, 6, 17. May's cert to Chicago MM re-
    turned on her rq

MONROE
1884, 7, 16. Henry J. & w, Hazel, recrq
1884, 9, 17. Maud & Berlie, ch Henry, recrq
1924, 2, 27. Mrs. Cora, Margaret E., Cora
    Georgia, Orrin & Gladys recrq
1924, 4, 16. Geo. W. recrq
1927, 10, 19. Georgia relrq
1930, 9, 17. Georgia recrq

MOORE
1911, 1, 19. Chester M. & w, Helen C., recrq
1911, 5, 18. Egtna(?) rocf Pleasant Valley
    MM
1922, 3, 15. Elma dropped from mbrp
1927, 6, 8. Helen dropped from mbrp

MORRIS
1890, 6, 19. Jennie recrq
1892, 12, 15. Susie recrq

MORSE
1933, 3, 15. Harold Edwin & w, Glennie Lu-
    cile, & s, Robert Wayne, recrq

MOSSIN
1894, 1, 18. Peter recrq
1927, 6, 8. Peter dropped from mbrp

MOTT
1905, 10, 19. Edward & w, Ada M., & ch,
    Elizabeth H., Chas. A., Bernard E. &
    Edith, rocf Tecumseh MM
1906, 5, 17. Chas. R. & w, Hannah H., rocf
    Tecumseh MM
1910, 12, 15. Elizabeth gct Columbus MM, O.
1916, 5, 17. Bernard gct S. Cleveland MM, O.
1920, 6, 23. Chas. R. gct Long Beach MM,
    Calif.
1920, 6, 23. Edward & w, Ada, & ch, Edith &
    Willard, gct Long Beach MM, Calif.

MOUGHIMAN
1928, 11, 14. May dropped from mbrp

MURPHEY
1893, 1, 19. Mamie recrq
1902, 1, 16. Mamie dropped from mbrp

MUETZEL
1916, 5, 17. Alma C. recrq

MUNGER
1920, 2, 18. Walter dropped from mbrp

MURGRAGE
1924, 2, 13. Girden F. recrq
1925, 4, 8. Mildred P. recrq

MURRAY
1893, 11, 16. Ella recrq
1897, 12, 16. Ella dropped from mbrp

MUSE
1909, 3, 18. Grace rocf Salem MM, O.

MYERS
1908, 6, 18. Claus B. & w, Gertrude Whitman,
    Margaret A. & dt, Anna, recrq (?)

NAGEL
1913, 3, 12. Adeline recrq
1922, 3, 15. Adeline dropped from mbrp

NASH
1910, 7, 14. Theron & w, Ellen, recrq
1914, 11, 18. Theron & w relrq

NEILL
1922, 11, --. Lizzie E. d

1891, 12, 17. Richard Webb rocf Cincinnati MM,
    O.
1893, 2, 16. Anna & Harriet [Neil] recrq
1904, 6, 16. R. W. [Neale] dropped from mbrp
1906, 10, 18. Harriett [Neil] dropped from
    mbrp
1910, 12, 15. Lizzie E. rocf Sandy Spring MM,
    O.
1922, 2, 15. Anna Mary recrq

NEFF
1901, 10, 17. Thos. H. & Mary recrq
1906, 4, 19. James recrq
1927, 6, 8. Grace dropped from mbrp

NEHRNST
1903, 3, 24. Catherine recrq
1908, 9, 29. Katharine [Nehrenst] rmt Claud
    L. Barker

NELSON
1926, 1, 14. Paul Gordon, s John E. & Amy W.,
    b

1893, 12, 14. Christina L. recrq
1903, 5, 18. Olive recrq
1904, 8, 18. John F. recrq
1911, 1, 19. Olive dropped from mbrp
1913, 10, 15. Christian L. dropped from mbrp
1918, 8, 14. John E. & w, Amy Wilhelmina,
    recrq

NETTNAY
1901, 3, 14. Madeline recrq

NICHOLS
1898, 3, 23. Martha recrq

1917, 6, 20. Mr. & Mrs. recrq
1927, 6, 8. Mrs. Ella dropped from mbrp

NIEMAN
1913, 10, 15. Harry H. recrq
1922, 3, 15. Harry dropped from mbrp
1927, 5, 18. Carl dropped from mbrp

NIGUE
1924, 3, 13. Fred recrq

NOEL
1932, 12, 14. Lida recrq

NORD
1933, 6, 14. Paul H. recrq

NORDER
1913, 3, 12. Miss Hanna A. recrq
1922, 3, 15. Hannah dropped from mbrp

NORMAN
1894, 2, 15. Chas. A. recrq
1895, 10, 17. Charles dropped from mbrp
1923, 12, 14. Cora Lee [Normand] gct High
    Point MM, N. C.
1928, 11, 14. Cora Lee dropped from mbrp

NORTHCOTT
1894, 5, 17. Anna W. recrq
1900, 5, 17. Mrs. Wm. [Northcote] recrq

NULLINGER
1914, 9, 16. Fred E. & w, Eva S., recrq

NUTLER
1906, 4, 19. Carl recrq

OALE
1894, 6, 14. Maria recrq

OATLEY
1912, 6, 13. Lloyd recrq
1912, 12, 18. Olga Smithson rocf Fairmount
    MM
1916, 4, 12. Lloyd & w, Ola, & ch gct Fair-
    mount MM, Ind.
1927, 6, 8. Vincent dropped from mbrp

OBERTHIER
1885, 12, 16. Magdalena [Oberthier] recrq
1886, 4, 14. John recrq
1891, 11, 19. Mrs. Lena recrq
1902, 9, 18. John & fam gct San Jose MM,
    Calif.

OBRION
1902, 4, 17. William recrq
1902, 4, 17. Ava recrq
1902, 4, 17. Anna recrq
1902, 4, 17. Jay recrq

OLDHAM
1914, 4, 18. Blanche recrq
1916, 10, 18. Blanch relrq

OLDS
1884, 4, 16. Orcetues(?) & w, Alice, rocf
    Chesterfield MM
1906, 11, 15. O. L. & w dropped from mbrp

OLSON
1922, 10, 18. John A. recrq
1923, 3, 14. Mrs. Mariah recrq

O'ROWRK
1899, 2, 16. Edna Cohen recrq
1899, 9, 14. Edna Cohen gct Pleasant Plain
    MM, Ia.

ORWIG
----, --, --. A. W. m Kate HUTCHINGS, dt B. R.
    & Susan, b 1844,9,13 d 1903,3,19

1898, 12, 15. Mrs. A. W. recrq

OSBORNE
1912, 4, 18. Mrs. recrq
1916, 4, 20. Byron L. rmt Ruth Malone
1919, 5, 14. Ruth, w Byron, gct Sedley MM,
    Va.
1919, 12, 15. Seth G. recrq
1920, 12, 15. Byron L. & w, Ruth M., & ch
    rocf Black Creek MM, Va.
1925, 3, 18. Mrs. Lenora gct Alum Creek MM, O.
1932, 11, 16. Owen recrq

OST
1916, 10, 18. Mae recrq

OTT
1919, 4, 16. Ira & w, Irene Z., recrq
1932, 1, 13. Ira & w, Irene, & ch, Ira W.,
    dropped from mbrp

OVERHOLT
1911, 9, 14. Florence relrq

OWENS
1915, 12, 15. Eliza Ann recrq
1927, 6, 8. Eliza Ann dropped from mbrp

OZANNE
1890, 1, 16. Mrs. Julian L. recrq
1894, 4, 19. Mrs. [Ozan] relrq

PACKARD
1894, 11, 15. Clara Bell recrq
1896, 2, 13. John & ch, Cora Bell & Ruth,
    recrq
1904, 3, 17. Duty recrq
1907, 2, 14. Jenny Duty relrq
1910, 7, 14. Jennie recrq
1921, 1, 12. Mrs. John (Belle) relrq
1927, 6, 8. John dropped from mbrp

1928, 11, 14. Ruth dropped from mbrp

PAGE
1912, 8, 15. Curtis H. & w rocf Portsmouth
    MM, Va.
1914, 8, 12. Curtis H. & w gct Ports Mouth
    MM, Va.

PAINTON
1893, 2, 16. Alfred T. recrq
1927, 6, 8. Alfred dropped from mbrp

PALMBLA
1914, 3, 18. Mrs. recrq

PALMER
1890, 8, 14. Minnie recrq
1910, 2, 24. Delbert E. recrq
1913, 11, 19. Myra Litty rocf Dry St. Friends
    Church, Salem, O.
1914, 11, 18. Delbert & Myra gct Vera, Okla.

PARKER
1884, 9, 17. Philip B. rocf Raysville MM,
    Ind.
1891, 6, 18. Lotta B. recrq
1891, 6, 18. Philip W. recrq
1891, 6, 18. Fred B. recrq
1914, 2, 18. Ruth E. recrq
1916, 1, 12. Ruth Edna relrq
1916, 5, 17. Dorothy recrq
1920, 1, 21. Chas. J. & w, Mary, recrq
1920, 2, 18. Lottie, Philip, Frank B. &
    Eunice, dropped from mbrp
1927, 6, 8. Chas. & Mary dropped from mbrp

PARMENTER
1893, 5, 19. Watt recrq
1895, 10, 17. Wat dropped from mbrp

PATTERSON
1894, 1, 18. Francis recrq
1897, 12, 16. Frances [Paterson] dropped from
    mbrp
1917, 4, 18. Laura relrq

PAUL
1909, 4, 15. Jennie Viola recrq
1915, 3, 25. Jennie rmt Dillwyn C. Wistar

PECK
1924, 11, 12. W. Prentice recrq
1931, 10, 14. Ethel recrq

PECKHAM
1901, 3, 14. Errol Devere recrq
1901, 11, 14. Errol D. gct Stanford MM, Ia.

PEDERSON
1924, 4, 16. Florence recrq

PEEL
1892, 11, 17. Joseph H. rocf New Garden MM,

PEEL, continued
    N. C.
1895, 6, 13. Joseph [Peele] gct Salem MM

PENROD
1914, 9, 16. Justin G. & w recrq
1915, 12, 15. Justus G. & w relrq

PENTECOST
1885, 6, 17. Mary Louise recrq
1885, 10, 14. Mary Louisa [Penticost] & Joseph
    W. Forsythe declared intentions of m

PEREGAY
1918, 12, 18. Marion Frances recrq
1919, 10, 15. Marion gct Elk MM

PERMAN
1919, 10, 15. Paul P. gct Pomona MM

PERRINE
1922, 4, 12. Mrs. Nettie recrq
1928, 11, 14. Mrs. dropped from mbrp

PETERS
1892, 12, 15. May A. recrq
1911, 2, 16. Chas. & w, Elnora Elizabeth,
    recrq
1914, 3, 18. Mrs. Elnora E. dropped from mbrp
1932, 1, 13. Mary A. dropped from mbrp

PETERSON
1887, 2, 17. Mary recrq
1914, 4, 18. Florence recrq
1922, 3, 15. Florence dropped from mbrp

PETRE
1933, 2, 15. Mildred G. recrq

PETTIT
1895, 11, 7. Jane R. d

PHELPS
1887, 2, 17. Wilber J. recrq
1913, 10, 15. Wilbur dropped from mbrp

PHILLIPS
1902, 12, 18. Wm. Hays & Elizabeth recrq
1904, 1, 14. Wm. & Elizabeth gct Maple City
    MM, Mich.
1905, 7, 27. W. Hayes & w rocf Maple City
    MM, Mich.
1933, 11, 15. Ellis recrq

PHINNEY
1921, 4, 7. Lucian & w & ch, Harold, Roslie
    & Steril, recrq
1922, 1, 18. Lucian & fam relrq

PIATT
1915, 11, 17. Lorenzo J. & Lillian E. recrq
1917, 7, 18. Lillian relrq
1927, 5, 18. Lorenzo J. dropped from mbrp

PICKETT
1904, 10, 13. Margaret dropped from mbrp

PICKRELL
1919, 3, 12. Carrie rocf Chicago MM, Ill.

PIERCE
1920, 5, 12. Marie rocf Salem MM, O.
1927, 6, 8. Marie dropped from mbrp

PIERSON
1902, 4, 17. Chas. W. & Orilla Lorain recrq
1904, 6, 16. Chas. W. & w, Orilla L., & ch,
    Roscoe, George & Ruth Irene, dropped from
    mbrp

PIKE
1902, 7, 17. Loren D. & Lucy M. recrq
1902, 7, 17. Howard M. recrq
1902, 7, 17. Zoe E. recrq
1902, 7, 17. Ralph M. recrq
1902, 7, 17. Carl N. recrq
1902, 7, 17. Earl D. recrq
1913, 1, 15. Mrs. Anna & dt, Myrtle, recrq
1913, 10, 15. Mrs. Anna & dt, Myrtle, relrq

PILOT
1897, 9, 16. Wm. recrq
1901, 4, 18. Wm. H. gct New Providence MM,
    Ia.
1931, 11, 18. Lucile rocf Second Friends Ch.,
    Cleveland, O.

PIM
1903, 6, 18. Lewis G. rocf Alliance MM, O.,
    dtd 1903,6,4
1903, 6, 18. Mary Barrett rocf Alliance MM,
    O., dtd 1903,6,4
1913, 10, 15. Lewis G. & w, Mary Barrett, gct
    Tecumseh MM
1913, 10, 15. Laura gc
1922, 3, 15. Eva E. gct Rush Creek MM

PINKHAM
1908, 3, 19. Wm. P. & w, Emma C., gct Al-
    liance MM, O.

PLUMMER
1896, 10, 15. Benjamin recrq
1915, 4, 14. Benj. dropped from mbrp

POLLOCK
1885, 6, 17. Willis C. & Mary Elizabeth rec-
    rq
1910, 2, 24. Mary E. & dt, Grace Pollock &
    Irene Graham, recrq
1925, 5, 13. Grace relrq

POND
1903, 1, 20. Wm. E. recrq
1907, 12, 19. Ralph recrq
1909, 10, 14. Ralph dropped from mbrp
1916, 11, 15. Mr. & Mrs. E. rocf Clark Ave.

POND, continued
      MM, Cleveland, O.

PONTIUS
1900, 3, 15. Grace recrq
1922, 3, 15. Grace dropped from mbrp

POPE
1885, 6, 22. Alton d
1887, 5, 28. Theodate d

1890, 6, 19. Francis E. relrq
1890, 6, 19. Herbert A. relrq
1890, 6, 19. Carl W. relrq
1890, 6, 19. Alfred S. relrq
1890, 6, 19. Walter S. relrq
1890, 6, 19. Arthur relrq
1890, 6, 19. Henry F. relrq
1896, 10, 15. John L. relrq

PORTER
1912, 3, 14. Mr. rocf White Water MM, Ind.
1914, 2, 18. Margaret E. recrq
1914, 3, 18. Lorene recrq
1914, 4, 18. Lorene recrq
1916, 4, 12. Martha Ellen recrq
1922, 3, 15. Martha E. dropped from mbrp
1927, 6, 8. Lorene dropped from mbrp

PORTIS
1915, 12, 15. Elbert gct Ypsilanta MM, Mich.

POWELL
1897, 7, 15. James G. recrq
1901, 10, 17. Jas. G. dropped from mbrp

PRATT
1878, --, --. Ada Marian, dt J. F. & Mariah, b

1917, 6, 13. Ada Marion recrq
1932, 12, 14. Ella recrq

PRESNALL
1913, 2, 12. H. F. & w, Grace, & dt, Callie
      Eugenia, recrq
1917, 11, 14. Howard F. & w & dt relrq

PRICE
1884, 12, 17. Carrie recrq
1886, 7, 14. Mary recrq
1888, 6, 14. Wm. T., Richard & Chas. Mattock,
      ch Eleanor R., recrq
1888, 6, 14. Eleanor R. recrq
1894, 6, 14. J. W. recrq
1895, 6, 13. John W. rmt Elizabeth Wittman
1897, 4, 15. Carrie dropped from mbrp
1897, 10, 14. Warwick dropped from mbrp
1899, 9, 14. John & Elizabeth relrq
1904, 10, 13. Wm. T. & Chas. dropped from mbrp
1904, 10, 13. Mrs. E. dropped from mbrp
1904, 10, 13. Benj. F. dropped from mbrp

PRINDLE
1908, 11, 19. Elmira gct New York MM

PROCTOR
1913, 3, 12. Wm. Jay recrq
1914, 3, 18. Minnie May recrq
1927, 5, 18. Minnie dropped from mbrp
1927, 6, 8. Roy dropped from mbrp

PROUDFOOT
1913, 10, 15. Margaret dropped from mbrp

PROUT
1895, 3, 2. Stephen d

1893, 1, 19. Stephen & w, Selina, & ch, Geo.
      Henry, Nellie, Selina J. & Stephen, recrq

PULS
1910, 7, 14. Faye recrq

QUICK
1914, 4, 18. Maud recrq
1915, 2, 17. Gordon P. recrq
1918, 5, 15. Maud dropped from mbrp

QUIGGINS
1895, 6, 5. Robert d

1887, 8, 18. Robt. N. recrq
1890, 4, 17. Robert K. gct Shawneetown MM
1893, 8, 17. Robert K. & w, Edna H., rocf
      Grand River MM
1895, 12, 19. Edna gct Afton MM, Ind.

RADIKE
1898, 3, 23. Minnie, Gustave & Robert A.
      recrq
1902, 5, 15. Walter O. recrq

RAIDABAUGH
1891, 10, 15. Peter gct Chicago MM, Ill.

RANDOLPH
1896, 10, 15. J. Farland recrq
1903, 5, 19. J. Farland & w, Emma G., gct
      Duck Creek MM, Ind.
1932, 11, 16. Mrs. Margaret Monroe relrq

RASEC
1922, 3, 15. Lucile dropped from mbrp

RASOR
1905, 3, 16. Lucy Marie recrq
1915, 4, 14. Lucy M. relrq

RAYMOND
1914, 2, 18. Florence recrq
1922, 3, 15. Florence dropped from mbrp

REAMS
1885, 10, 14. Mary I. gct N. Lewisburg MM

REECE
1929, 12, 18. Ruth recrq
1930, 4, 23. Ruth rocf Barclay MM, Kans.

REDDING
1913, 1, 15. James C. recrq
1915, 11, 17. J. C. relrq

REED
1894, 3, 15. J. T. recrq
1894, 7, 19. J. F. relrq
1911, 11, 16. Emily Fuller recrq

REININGER
1915, 7, 14. Wm. N. & w, Nevada, recrq
1922, 3, 15. Nevada dropped from mbrp

REISS
1883, 6, 13. Francis recrq
1895, 10, 17. Francis [Reise] dropped from
     mbrp

REMINGTON
1894, 1, 18. Mary recrq

RENSHAW
1903, 4, 23. Samuel recrq
1922, 6, 14. Samuel dropped from mbrp

REPPERT
1917, 6, 20. Clarence recrq
1921, 2, 16. Clarence relrq

REYNOLDS
1898, 12, 15. Clinton O. rocf Rosedale MM,
     Ore.
1899, 12, 24. Clinton O. gct Salem MM, Ore.
1913, 3, 12. J. W. recrq
1920, 10, 13. L. Herbert gct Sterling MM,
     Kans.
1922, 3, 15. J. W. & Sarah dropped from mbrp

RHINER
1889, 9, 19. Millie recrq
1895, 10, 17. Nellie dropped from mbrp

RIBLET
1922, 4, 12. Clyde recrq

RICE
1901, 3, 14. Benj. F. recrq

RICHARDSON
1926, 3, 31. George recrq
1933, 6, 17. George dropped from mbrp

RICHIE
1909, 6, 22. David R. rmt Edith Russell
1910, 2, 24. Edith Russell [Ritchie] gct
     Lansdowne MM, Pa.

RILEY
1900, 10, 19. Nettie Smalley recrq

1901, 1, 17. John rocf Hopewell MM, dtd 1901,
     1,5
1904, 12, 15. John & Nettie gct Colorado
     Springs MM

RINEHART
1922, 7, 12. Helen S. relrq
1927, 4, 13. H. Stanley & w, Helen S., recrq
1930, 2, 12. H. Stanley & Helen S. dropped
     from mbrp

RING
1902, 5, 15. Raymond H. recrq

ROBBINS
1916, 2, 16. Nellie O. rocf Fairmount MM,
     Ind.

ROBERSON
1898, 3, 23. Orland W. recrq

ROBERTS
1891, 3, 20. L. H. & w, Alice, rocf Paton
     MM, Iowa
1897, 1, 14. Thomas recrq
1902, 3, 13. Chas. D. recrq
1904, 2, 18. Eunice Worth rocf Greensborough
     MM
1905, 9, 14. Chas. D. & w, Eunice W., gct
     Greensboro MM
1907, 10, 17. Howard E. recrq
1914, 3, 18. Everet Olney recrq
1915, 2, 17. Raymond recrq
1917, 3, 14. Emmett O. relrq
1922, 3, 15. Raymond dropped from mbrp
1927, 5, 18. Raymond dropped from mbrp
1927, 6, 8. L. H. & Alice dropped from mbrp

ROBINSON
1887, 3, 17. Charles recrq
1895, 6, 13. Mrs. John recrq
1896, 4, 16. Chas. dropped from mbrp
1896, 7, 16. Emma dropped from mbrp
1911, 1, 19. Effie B. [Robison] recrq
1913, 11, 19. Mrs. Effie gct Clark Ave. MM,
     Cleveland, O.
1924, 1, 16. T. K. & w recrq
1925, 4, 8. Thomas Knox & w, Lillian, & ch
     recrq
1930, 4, 23. Thomas & w relrq

ROBSON
1889, 8, 15. Wm. D. rocf Hartlang (?) MM, dtd

ROBSON, continued
      1889,7,18

ROHLY
1933, 11, 15. (Sally) Ida recrq

ROOT
1923, 3, 14. Fred recrq
1927, 5, 18. Fred dropped from mbrp

ROSE
1920, 2, 18. Alice Lester relrq
1933, 11, 13. Letah recrq

ROWE
1886, 1, 13. Magdeline Leigh [Roe] recrq
1887, 9, 15. Madeline [Roe] relrq
1911, 10, 19. Margaret Logan [Roe] gct Newport
      News MM
1899, 2, 16. Effie May recrq
1900, 8, 16. Effie May dis disunity
1927, 10, 19. Frederick & Bertha rocf Second
      Friends Church, S. Cleveland, O.
1930, 3, 13. Fred & w relrq
1933, 4, 12. Frederick Geo. & Bertha Jane
      recrq

RUGG
1893, 2, 16. J. L. rocf Adrian MM, Mich.

RUGGAN
1893, 12, 14. L. W. relrq

RUPERT
1924, 3, 13. Wm. B. recrq
1924, 4, 16. Nora E. rocf Searsboro MM, Ia.

RUSSELL
1872, 6, 25. Theodore, s Theodore & Marie, b
      1846,10,28 d 1910,--,--; m Sarah STOKES

1884, 10, 15. Jason Kirk recrq
1896, 4, 15. Curtin rmt Carrie Brown
1901, 9, 27. Ethel M. rmt Howard S. Goodwin
1902, 1, 16. Sarah A. recrq
1903, 2, 24. Theodore A. & w recrq
1909, 4, 15. Walter T. relrq
1909, 6, 22. Edith rmt David R. Richie
1910, 4, 14. Ruth M. rmt James G. Vail
1913, 2, 26. Edwin rmt Elizabeth Stokes
1913, 9, 17. Florence recrq
1915, 11, 17. Mrs. Rose M. recrq
1915, 11, 17. Ruth & Margaret recrq
1916, 4, 12. M. N. recrq
1916, 12, 13. M. N. dropped from mbrp
1917, 6, 6. Edwin A. gct Richmond MM, Va.
1921, 4, 7. Parvin gct Lansdowne MM, Pa.
1922, 3, 15. Rose M. dropped from mbrp
1923, 6, --. Ruth C. rmt Byron C. Collins
1932, 1, 13. Margaret dropped from mbrp

RYBECKER
1929, 4, 17. Mrs. & ch, Thelma & Kenneth, gct

Second Friends Church, S. Cleveland MM, O.

RYCKMAN
1911, 2, 16. Rhoda Canada relrq

RYDER
1893, 12, 14. Eliza [Rider] recrq
1893, 12, ·14. Jas. L. [Rider] recrq
1920, 2, 18. James dropped from mbrp
1927, 6, 8. John dropped from mbrp
1927, 6, 8. Nelson dropped from mbrp
1927, 6, 8. Harvey dropped from mbrp
1927, 6, 8. Herbert dropped from mbrp
1927, 6, 8. Margaret dropped from mbrp

RYKES
1887, 8, 18. Mary N. recrq

SADLER
1922, 6, 14. Louise dropped from mbrp

SAFFLE
1884, 11, 12. Richard H. & w, Mary E., recrq
1885, 2, 18. Walter E. M. recrq

SALMEN
1895, 5, 16. Mrs. Maria [Sammons] recrq
1895, 6, 13. Ada & Mary Ann [Salmons] recrq
1914, 8, 12. Samuel [Salmon] relrq
1920, 1, 21. Michael & w, Wilhelmina, recrq
1921, 4, 7. Michael & w relrq

SANDERS
1913, 3, 12. G. M. recrq
1920, 2, 18. G. M. dropped from mbrp

SANFORD
1894, 5, 17. Harry W. & w, Nora, & dt,
      Birdie, recrq
1904, 10, 13. Mr. & w dropped from mbrp

SAUNDERS
1885, 2, 18. John recrq
1885, 5, 13. Joseph & Elizabeth recrq
1895, 10, 17. John dropped from mbrp
1903, 10, 15. Edgar J. [Sanders] gct Blue
      River MM, Ind.
1922, 3, 15. G. M. [Sanders] dropped from
      mbrp

SCHAAB
1918, 12, 18. Nicholas P. recrq

SCHLEGEL
1931, --, --. Benj. d

1899, 2, 16. Frank Martin & Nellie recrq
1900, 8, 16. Frank M. & Nellie [Schleigle]
      dis disunity
1915, 8, 18. Josephine recrq

SCHLEGEL, continued
1918, 4, 17. Josephine [Schlagle] & dt, Ruth
& Faith, gct Clark Ave. MM, Cleveland, O.
1922, 4, 12. Benj. & Josephine & ch rocf
Clark Ave. MM, Cleveland, O.

SCHLEICHER
1928, 11, 14. William dropped from mbrp

SCHLENTER
1922, 6, 14. Eliz. dropped from mbrp
1922, 6, 14. Nettie dropped from mbrp
1927, 6, 8. Christian dropped from mbrp

SCHLUETER
1909, 6, 17. Fred & Elizabeth recrq
1911, 12, 14. Fred J. relrq

SCHNEIDER
1899, 9, 6. Philip, s Geo. & Magdelena, b
1875,3,12; m Louisa WANNAMAKER

1898, 3, 23. Geo. recrq
1906, 3, 15. Philip recrq
1911, 1, 19. Mamie relrq
1914, 1, 14. Geo. relrq
1914, 2, 18. Norman relrq
1921, 2, 16. Louise recrq

SCHOOL
1922, 3, 15. Nicholas dropped from mbrp

SCHOPP
1915, 8, 18. Harry & w, Fern, recrq
1916, 3, 15. Harry & w gct Alliance MM
1916, 8, 16. Harry & w gct Alliance MM
1918, 7, 17. Harry & w, Lucy, dropped from
mbrp
1922, 3, 15. Louis dropped from mbrp

SCHRIBER
1927, 5, 18. Grace Oldham dropped from mbrp

SCHROEDER
1902, 4, 17. Martin [Schroter] recrq
1907, 10, 17. Caroline recrq

SCHULKINS
1914, 3, 18. Frank & w dropped from mbrp

SCHULTE
1887, 10, 13. Geo. dropped from mbrp
1909, 3, 18. Celia S. recrq
1927, 6, 8. Walter P. [Schultz] dropped from
mbrp

SCHWARTZ
1911, 1, 19. Paul Otto & w, Pearl, recrq

SEIGER
1894, --, --. Mary d

1887, 3, 17. Frederick [Seagar] recrq

1896, 3, 19. Frederick dropped from mbrp

SEBEK
1893, 5, 19. Chas. recrq

SEIGMAN
1904, 2, 18. Louise recrq

SELLERS
1890, 11, 13. Nellie recrq
1922, 6, 14. Nellie dropped from mbrp

SEMPLE
1889, 9, 19. Lincoln dropped from mbrp

SHAEFFER
1895, 4, 18. Lela recrq
1898, 3, 23. Mary A. recrq
1900, 11, 28. Lela rmt John McKinnon
1902, 5, 15. Irene L. [Schaeffer] recrq
1903, 2, 4. Lillian rocf Goshen MM, dtd
1903,1,9
1903, 12, 17. Lillian gct Columbus MM, O.
SHANCK
1887, 7, 21. H. K. m Alice D. SURFACE, dt
Jacob & Margaret, b 1857,3,1

1892, 4, 14. Alice C. [Shank] recrq
1904, 10, 13. Henry K. [Shank] recrq

SHAPS
1919, 6, 18. Lewis recrq

SHARSKI
1917, 12, 12. Mrs. Frances recrq
1927, 6, 8. Mrs. Frances dropped from mbrp

SHAW
1920, 6, 16. Mrs. A. A. & dt, Doris, recrq

SHEALEY
1904, 12, 15. Florence V. recrq

SHEFFIELD
1902, 7, 17. Henry W. recrq
1902, 7, 17. Otis B. recrq

SHEPARD
1913, 10, 15. Bert & Effie recrq
1920, 6, 16. Nellie recrq
1922, 3, 15. Bert & Effie dropped from mbrp

SHERMON
1902, 4, 17. Parley G. recrq
1902, 4, 17. Frank V. recrq
1902, 4, 17. Blanch O. recrq
1902, 4, 17. Richard C. recrq
1902, 4, 17. Melissa E. recrq
1902, 4, 17. Peleg & Lucretia S. recrq
1902, 4, 17. Lydia A. recrq
1902, 4, 17. Florence recrq
1902, 4, 17. Wm. G. recrq
1922, 8, 16. Mrs. Ruth & ch recrq

SHIMER
1887, 4, 28. Samuel m Hattie THOMAS, dt Wm.
        & Minerva, b 1865,9,14
        Ch: Olive May b 1891, 1, 9

1886, 7, 14. Samuel M. recrq

SHOPPART
1901, 1, 17. L. Merritt recrq
1932, 1, 13. Lynn M. & w, Violet Keetch, &
        ch, Douglas & Merret K., dropped from mbrp

SHORT
1909, 8, 19. Geo. A. & w, Luella, & ch, Mabel
        & Estella, rocf West Branch MM, O.
1912, 1, 18. Geo. A. & w, Luella, & dt,
        Stella & Mabel, gct Lupton MM

SHOWALTER
1915, 2, 17. Samuel F. & w, Bertha, & dt,
        Viola, recrq
1927, 5, 18. Mr. & Mrs. & ch dropped from
        mbrp

SHULTZ
1886, 2, 17. Geo. A. recrq
1914, 10, 14. Paul H. & w, Maggie, & ch,
        Richard & Walter P., recrq
1922, 8, 16. Paul & fam relrq

SHUMWAY
1932, 12, 14. Alice recrq

SIEMON
1885, 2, 18. Catharine recrq
1885, 8, 12. Lester [Simeon] recrq
1922, 6, 14.' Dr. Lester dropped from mbrp

SILVERTHORN
1895, 1, 17. Albert recrq
1904, 5, 19. Albert dropped 'from mbrp

SIMMONS
1903, 1, 20. Delmer recrq
1905, 4, 13. Delmar L. relrq
1907, 2, 14. Mellie relrq
1919, 12, 15. Grace Lillian recrq
1920, 12, 15. Grace L. relrq

SIMPSON
1904, 2, 18. Ada Price recrq
1917, 6, 6. Fred recrq
1922, 3, 15. Fred dropped from mbrp
1927, 6, 8. Ada Rice dropped from mbrp

SINGLETARY
1917, 6, 6. Florence Malone relrq

SIPHER
1904, 12, 15. Owen recrq
1907, 12, 19. Ruth relrq
1909, 7, 1. Ruth A. recrq
1927, 1, 12. Ruth relrq

SLADE
1909, 10, 14. Florence recrq
1923, 3, 14. Mrs. C. N. recrq
1928, 11, 14. Mrs. C. C. dropped from mbrp

SLADEK
1922, 10, 18. James recrq
1927, 5, 8. James dropped from mbrp

SLAYTON
1914, 2, 18. Ray Chas. & sister, Margaret,
        recrq
1920, 5, 12. Ray & w, Mary, & s gct Richmond
        MM, Va.
1922, 3, 15. Margaret dropped from mbrp

SMELTZER
1909, 8, 19. Harry C. recrq
1922, 3, 15. Harry [Smelger] dropped from
        mbrp

SMITH
1884, 6, 22. Viola E., dt Edward & Mary J.,
        b

1888, 3, 15. Albert recrq
1895, 10, 17. Anna Webster gct Wellington MM,
        Can.
1904, 6, 16. Viola E. recrq
1904, 7, 14. Wm. & fam gct Alliance MM, O.
1906, 11, 15. Wm. O. rocf Bear Creek MM, Ia.
1913, 3, 12. Howard & w, Ella, recrq
1915, 11, 17. Louise Piatt recrq
1915, 12, 15. H. E. recrq
1918, 7, 17. Albert dropped from mbrp
1920, 2, 18. Aletha L. relrq
1922, 3, 15. Louisa Piatt dropped from mbrp
1924, 11, 12. Ray recrq
1927, 5, 18. Henry dropped from mbrp
1932, 1, 13. Howard & w, Ella, dropped from
        mbrp

SMITHLY
1897, 10, 14. Wm. & w, Ida, recrq

SNEDEKER
1829, 10, 18. Sadie recrq

SNELL
1889, 1, 17. Sophia recrq

SNOBERGER
1922, 2, 15. Rachel dropped from mbrp

SNOWDEN
1924, 3, 13. Ruth L. recrq

SNYDER
1901, 2, 14. Mrs. Clayton relrq
1922, 8, 16. J. O. & w recrq
1922, 8, 16. Clover recrq

SOBERHART
1913, 2, 12.   E. A. & w recrq
1917, 4, 18.   E. A. [Sobehart] & w relrq
1927, 6, 8.   Baby [Sobiehardt] dropped from
    mbrp

SOLOMON
1924, 1, 16.   Caroline recrq

SOPER
1899, 2, 16.   Joy L. recrq

SORENSON
1914, 4, 18.   Harriett E. recrq
1916, 5, 17.   Ruth M. recrq

SOXTON
1920, 12, 15.   Susan M. recrq

SPAHLINGER
1898, 4, 14.   Geo. & w, Mary, recrq
1927, 6, 8.   George, Mary & Walter dropped
    from mbrp

SPEAR
1894, 1, 18.   M. C. & Fannie recrq
1922, 6, 14.   M. C. & Fannie dropped from mbrp
1931, 1, 14.   Joseph Russell & Doriene White
    recrq

SPEDDY
1890, 11, 13.   Mable recrq

SPEICHER
1917, 6, 13.   Katharine recrq
1919, 4, 16.   Katharine [Spiecher] relrq

SPENCER
1913, 3, 12.   Mr. & Mrs. recrq
1916, 1, 12.   Mr. & Mrs. Albert relrq

SPRING
1911, 2, 16.   Jesse O. recrq
1922, 3, 15.   Jesse O. dropped from mbrp
1924, 1, 16.   Wortha recrq

SPRUNGER
1933, 11, 15.   Marguerite L. recrq

STABBIKER
1932, 1, 13.   Mrs. dropped from mbrp

STABLER
1926, 9, 15.   Raymond relrq

STACKHOUSE
1933, 2, 15.   Oscar M. recrq

STALEY
1912, 1, 18.   Frank & w, Dora, recrq

STALKER
1932, 12, 14.   Elizabeth recrq

STAHLLEKER
1924, 11, 12.   Elsie recrq
1928, 9, 12.   Elsie [Stahleker] dropped from
    mbrp

STANLEY
1895, 12, 19.   Lydia Maria rocf Damascus MM
1895, 12, 19.   Martha W. rocf Damascus MM
1902, 9, 18.   Lydia Maria rocf Amboy MM, Ind.,
    dtd 1902,9,6
1913, 1, 15.   Frank & w recrq
1932, 1, 13.   Mrs. Mayme dropped from mbrp

STEBBINS
1917, 3, 14.   Nora May recrq
1921, 3, 16.   Nora gct Columbus MM, O.

STEELE
1924, 11, 12.   Fernie recrq

STEINBERGER
1928, 12, 12.   Ralph D. rocf Urbana MM
1930, 11, 12.   Ralph & Laura gct Selkirk MM,
    Mich.

STEMPLE
1897, 3, 18.   Rose recrq
1904, 10, 13.   Rose (Stemple) Kaine dropped
    from mbrp

STEVENS
1899, 3, 16.   Beatrice recrq
1901, 4, 18.   Minnie relrq
1908, 4, 16.   Theresa recrq
1921, 10, 12.   Theresa gct Whittier MM, Calif.

ST. GEORGE
1913, 12, 17.   Elwin A. recrq
1914, 11, 18.   Elvina A. dropped from mbrp

STITES
1924, 2, 13.   Minnie recrq

STOCKWELL
1899, 11, 16.   Etta recrq

STOKES
1913, 2, 26.   Elizabeth rmt Edwin Russell

STOLTZ
1885, 12, 23.   Geo. W. m Sarah WEST, dt Rev.
    H. T. & M. A., b 1870,12,21
        Ch: Rufus   b 1890, 11, 18

1918, 4, 17.   Rufus & w, Sarah, & dt, Eloise,
    recrq

STONE
1887, 3, 26.   Geraldine E. d

1885, 5, 13.   Frank & w, Geraldine, rocf
    Glens Falls MM
1885, 5, 13.   Leo, s Frank & w recrq

STONE, continued
1901, 3, 16. Frank & Susie relrq
1901, 11, 14. Leo dropped from mbrp

STRATTON
1924, 11, 12. R. J. recrq

STROUD
1893, 12, 14. Emma & Myrtle recrq
1901, 10, 17. Myrtle dropped from mbrp
1904, 10, 13. Mrs. dropped from mbrp

SUMMER
1883, 10, 17. John rocf Darlington MM, Eng.

SWEET
1883, 12, 12. Chas. W. rocf Short Creek MM,
    O., dtd 1883,11,21
1884, 9, 17. Wright J. recrq
1886, 11, 19. Charles T. relrq
1899, 2, 16. Ada D. recrq
1904, 10, 13. Wright dropped from mbrp
1922, 6, 14. Wright & Ada dropped from mbrp

TAGGART
1913, 11, 19. Ruth E. & Mary F. recrq
1922, 3, 15. Mary F. & Ruth dropped from mbrp

TATUM
1891, 8, 13. David & w, Hannah, gct Chicago
    MM, Ill.

TAYLOR
1894, 6, 14. W. S. recrq
1895, 8, 15. Wm. S. relrq
1904, 6, 16. Estella Helen recrq
1917, 6, 13. Walter Francis recrq
1920, 2, 18. Walter F. relrq
1922, 3, 15. Walter Francis dropped from mbrp
1927, 6, 8. Estelle dropped from mbrp
1928, 11, 14. Blanche Barker dropped from mbrp

TEGETHOFF
1885, 10, 14. Florence Ada & Carrie Sophia
    recrq
1901, 10, 17. Florence relrq

TENNEL
1926, 12, 15. Isabelle Bidgood

TERRELL
----, --, --. Hezekiah M., s Alice, b 1873,3,
    4; m Mabel WISTAR, dt Bart & May D., b
    1873,3,2

1883, 6, 13. Hester G. gct Chicago MM, Ill.
1886, 3, 17. Alice & s, Hezekiah, rocf Clear
    Creek MM, O.
1897, 4, 15. Arthur recrq
1924, 1, 16. Glenn L. recrq
1932, 1, 13. John dropped from mbrp
1932, 1, 13. Harrison dropped from mbrp
1932, 1, 13. Florence Russell & ch dropped

from mbrp
1932, 1, 13. Arthur dropped from mbrp

THOMAS
1886, 5, 12. Hattie recrq
1886, 7, 14. Rachel E. rocf Greenwich MM, dtd
    1886,6,10
1887, 9, 15. Nellie recrq
1887, 12, 15. Margaret recrq
1898, 2, 24. Margaret dropped from mbrp
1902, 12, 18. J. Horace recrq
1910, 3, 17. Nellie M. relrq
1911, 12, 14. Sadie Russell relrq
1913, 12, 17. Amelia recrq
1914, 10, 14. Annie E. recrq
1915, 11, 17. Edward A. recrq
1915, 11, 17. Mrs. Emma A. & dt, Elizabeth,
    recrq
1915, 11, 17. Irene E. recrq
1915, 11, 17. Chas. E. recrq
1918, 3, 13. Mr. & Mrs. & ch, Elizabeth &
    Charles, recrq
1919, 7, 16. Chester rocf Indianapolis MM,
    Ind.
1920, 1, 21. Hattie gct Clark Ave. MM,
    Cleveland, O.
1920, 5, 12. Mr. & Mrs. E. A. gct Clark Ave.
    MM, Cleveland, O.
1922, 1, 18. Chas., minor, dropped from mbrp
1922, 3, 15. Annie E. dropped from mbrp
1922, 6, 14. Rachel dropped from mbrp
1924, 7, 16. Chester H. relrq
1927, 5, 18. Annie E. recrq
1928, 11, 14. Irene dropped from mbrp
1928, 11, 14. Mr. & Mrs. dropped from mbrp
1931, 3, 25. Chas. & w, Zella, & dt, Vir-
    ginia, rocf Kokomo MM, Ind.
1931, 9, 23. Chas. E. & w, Zella, & dt,
    Virginia, gct Mooresville MM, Ind.

THOMPSON
1887, 5, 19. Anna recrq
1892, 8, 18. Sidney recrq
1906, 12, 13. Sydney dropped from mbrp
1915, 11, 17. Amelia recrq
1922, 3, 15. Amelia dropped from mbrp
1923, 6, 13. Marion Beck recrq
1929, 9, 18. James Howard recrq
1933, 4, 12. James Howard & Gladys Allen &
    ch recrq

THOOS
1910, 1, 26. Christopher m Margaret DOUGLAS,
    dt Matthew & Elizabeth, b 1875,3,27

1917, 6, 13. Christopher M. & Margaret M.
    recrq
1922, 3, 15. Christopher dropped from mbrp

THURSTON
1924, 11, 12. Ruth L. recrq

TINKER
1902, 4, 17. Willis L. recrq

TITUS
1896, 11, 19. Sarah P. & Henrietta rocf Water-
bury MM, N. Y.

TOLAND
1914, 2, 18. Charles & Mary recrq
1917, 6, 13. W. E. recrq
1922, 3, 15. W. E., Mary & Chas. dropped from
mbrp

TOME
1899, 4, 13. Sophia & dt, Ella, recrq
1906, 1, 25. Wilburt W. recrq
1916, 5, 17. Ethel M. recrq
1927, 5, 18. Ethel dropped from mbrp

TOMLINSON
1902, 4, 17. John R. & Ella E. recrq
1933, 11, 15. Earl J. & Alberta S. & dt, Lois
E. recrq

TOMPT
1909, 9, 8. Ada recrq

TORMOHLEN
1917, 8, 15. Fred H. & w, Susie J., & dt,
Ruth E. & Martha, recrq
1925, 9, 16. F. H. & w & dt, Ruth & Martha
Helen, relrq

TOWNSEND
1929, 4, 17. Oscar & fam gct Beloit MM

TRANER
1915, 2, 17. Mrs. John R. recrq

TRAVER
1902, 7, 17. Walter J. & Miranda M. recrq
1927, 6, 8. Mrs. John dropped from mbrp

TRAYER
1886, 7, 14. Lucretia recrq

TREADGOLD
1895, 4, 18. Alexander S. recrq
1922, 6, 14. Alexander dropped from mbrp

TRICK
1918, 9, 18. Arthur S. recrq
1925, 4, 8. Elvina recrq
1927, 4, 13. Arthur S. & w, Elvira, & dt,
Lois, relrq
1929, 4, 17. Lois, dt Arthur & Elvina, gct
Sullivant Ave. MM, Columbus, O.

TRIPP
1924, 2, 13. Mrs. Ora recrq

TROUT
1916, 11, 15. Ada M. & Elizabeth recrq

1918, 8, 14. Elizabeth & Adda gct Portsmouth
MM, R. I.

TROVER
1923, 6, 13. Maranda recrq; form mbr at
Pleasant Valley which was laid down

TROWBRIDGE
1922, 6, 14. Seymour dropped from mbrp
1903, 1, 20. Seymour recrq

TUCKER
1910, 10, 13. Mabel recrq
1911, 3, 16. John Wesley & w, Delania, rocf
Delphi MM, O.

TULGA
1924, 2, 13. Albert C. recrq

TUPPER
1909, 4, 15. Josephine recrq
1927, 6, 8. Josephine dropped from mbrp

TURNER
1902, 4, 17. Chas. & Melvina recrq
1919, 6, 18. Chas. & w recrq
1927, 6, 8. Chas. & w dropped from mbrp

TUTTLE
1887, 6, 16. Daniel dropped from mbrp
1889, 3, 14. Nancy recrq
1904, 10, 13. Mrs. Nancy dropped from mbrp

TWEED
1910, 11, 17. Wm. M. rocf Columbus MM, O.
1922, 6, 14. Wm. M. dropped from mbrp

UNDERHILL
1902, 4, 17. Elizabeth G. rocf New York MM,
dtd 1902,4,2
1904, 10, 13. Elizabeth gct Cornwall MM, N.Y.

UPSON
1903, 4, 23. Henrietta recrq

VAIL
1910, 4, 14. James G. rmt Ruth M. Russell
1911, 2, 11. Ruth Russell gct Chester MM, Pa.

VANN
1915, 11, 17. Bert recrq
1915, 12, 15. Mrs. Louise recrq
1928, 11, 14. Bert & Louise dropped from mbrp

WAGAR
1898, 11, 17. Elizabeth rocf Spencer MM

WAGNER
1895, 4, 18. Ida B. recrq
1928, 11, 14. Carlton dropped from mbrp

WAKELEE
1913, 3, 12. Frank Drew recrq

WAKELEE, continued
1922, 3, 15. Frank [Wakeley] dropped from
     mbrp

WALKA
1897, 7, 15. Chas. & w & ch, Elizabeth &
     Carl, recrq

WALLACE
1914, 6, 17. Marian Coe recrq
1932, 1, 13. Mrs. Coe dropped from mbrp

WALLER
1901, --, --. Charlotte d

1890, 9, 18. Charlotte P. recrq

WALTERS
1922, 11, 15. Mr. & Mrs. recrq
1924, 2, 27. Albert & Sophia recrq
1928, 12, 12. Albert dropped from mbrp
1932, 11, 16. Dorothy recrq

WALTHALL
1898, 2, 24. Frederick gct Denver MM

WARD
1912, 1, 18. Elizabeth rocf Cincinnati MM

WARDWELL
1916, 11, 15. Helen recrq

WARNER
1927, 4, 13. Elizabeth recrq

WARREN
1883, 6, 13. Mary recrq

WATURBURY
1883, 10, 16. Wm. H., s Ralph P. & Maria, b
     1851,1,17; m Nellie S. WETMORE, dt Henry
     & Eliza, b 1861,11,26
     Ch: Ralph H.   b 1884, 8, 7
1911, 9, 9. Ralph H., s Wm. H. & Nellie S.,
     b 1884,8,7; m Mildred JOHNSON
     Ch: Dorothy E. b 1912, 10, 26
           Kenneth L. " 1921, 8, 6

1892, 5, 19. Nellie Sylvia [Waterbury] rocf
     Chicago MM, Ill.
1898, 3, 23. Wm. H. [Waterbury] recrq
1905, 5, 18. Ralph H. [Waterbury] recrq
1907, 2, 14. Sylvia, dt Wm. H. & Nellie S.,
     recrq
1911, 9, 9. Ralph [Watterbury] rmt Mildred
     Johnson

WATKINS
1904, 1, 14. Hoadley A. & Mary recrq
1913, 10, 15. Francis E. & w, Alice, & ch,
     Lillian, Ruth & Stanley, recrq
1915, 2, 17. Francis & w gct Collins MM, N.Y.
1916, 11, 15. Mary E. relrq

1931, 6, 24. Joseph & Ruth rocf Clark Ave.
     MM, Cleveland, O.

WATSON
1898, 3, 23. Beatrice recrq
1922, 3, 15. Millie dropped from mbrp

WEBB
1924, 7, 22. Helen Marguerite rmt Chas. B.
     Mendenhall

WEBBER
1913, 3, 12. Mrs. Anna recrq

WEBSTER
1886, 7, 14. Anna recrq
1929, 8, 14. Doris Blackburn gct Phila. Orth.
     MM, Pa.

WEIDER
1894, 1, 18. Addie [Wieder] recrq
1897, 4, 14. Adelaide M. rmt Edgar T. Hole

WEIGEL
1897, 6, 17. Clifford recrq   [mbrp
1901, 10, 17. Clifford [Wiegel] dropped from

WEIL
1903, 6, 18. Harriett R. dropped from mbrp

WEILER
1906, 7, 19. Wm. Smith recrq
1927, 6, 8. Wm. dropped from mbrp

WEIR
1889, 5, 16. Absalom rocf Largan MM, dtd
     1886,12,15
1907, 1, 17. Absalom dropped from mbrp

WELLS
1904, 12, 15. Eva recrq
1924, 11, 12. Ruth L. recrq

WELTE
1912, 3, 14. Mabel F. recrq
1927, 6, 8. Mabel [Welti] dropped from mbrp

WERFIELD
1916, 5, 17. Elmer recrq
1922, 3, 15. Elmer dropped from mbrp

WESTENBERG
1903, 5, 19. John Clarence & dt, Dorothy
     Mildred, recrq
1907, 2, 14. Laura R. recrq
1907, 4, 18. J. C. relrq
1913, 10, 15. Anna Fistler gc
1927, 6, 8. Mabel dropped from mbrp

WESTPFOHL
1895, 8, 15. Theodore recrq
1922, 6, 14. Thomas, Minnie, Florence &
     Mildred [Westfahl] dropped from mbrp

WESTON
1908, 10, 15. Clarence D. rocf Watseka MM,
     Ill., dtd 1908,9,17
1918, 7, 17. Clarence dropped from mbrp

WETZEL
1914, 4, 18. Helen M. recrq
1917, 6, 6. Mrs. Margaret recrq
1921, 5, 18. Mrs. Margaret relrq

WHALLON
1892, 12, 15. Carrie Bell rocf Boston MM, Mass.
1908, 12, 17. Carrie B. relrq
1909, 2, 18. Bertha relrq

WHALEN
1887, 5, 19. Carrie B. recrq
1888, 4, 19. Carrie relrq; later joined Bos-
     ton MM
1892, 12, 15. Carrie Bell [Whallon] rocf Bos-
     ton MM, Mass.
1896, 7, 16. Bertha & Isabella [Whallin] rec-
     rq
1898, 5, 19. Sarah [Whallen] recrq
1901, 8, 15. Frankie A. [Whallon] recrq
1902, 1, 16. Eleanor S. [Whollan] recrq
1908,. 12, 17. Carrie B. [Whallon] relrq
1909, 2, 18. Bertha [Whallon] relrq

WHEATLEY
1922, 11, --. Miriam Anna d

1918, 12, 18. Mariam Anna recrq

WHEELER
1915, 2, 17. Wm. J. & w, Keziah, recrq
1923, 3, 14. Mrs. Emma recrq
1928, 9, 12. Mrs. E. dropped from mbrp

WHERRIT
1884, 3, 9. Bertha d

WHEVIT
1890, 3, 13. John S. relrq

WHIGAM
1914, 4, 18. Wm. C. recrq
1915, 11, 17. Wm. C. [Whigham] recrq

WHITE
1917, 6, 6. Eliza recrq
1919, 8, 13. Eliza recrq
1920, 2, 18. Eliza relrq
1922, 12, 13. Ruth Matchett relrq
1924, 11, 12. Merva recrq
1928, 11, 14. Mary dropped from mbrp
1928, 11, 14. Eliza dropped from mbrp

WHITLOCK
1902, 12, 18. Wm. E. recrq
1906, 4, 19. Wm. relrq

WHITSON
1929, 10, 16. Mrs. Clara E. recrq

1933, 5, 17. Mrs. Clara dropped from mbrp

WHITWORTH
1889, 4, 18. Martha E. recrq

WIBEL
1913, 10, 15. Evert & Emma [Wibal] recrq
1916, 4, 12. Everett & w, Emma, & three ch.
     gct Pleasant Valley MM
1931, 4, 15. Mrs. Emma recrq
1932, 12, 10. Mrs. Emma dropped from mbrp

WICKER
1932, 12, 14. Anna recrq

WICKERSHAM
1897, 9, 16. Amos recrq

WILEY
1927, 2, 16. May Latimer gct Piedmont MM,
     Ore.

WILKS
1918, 7, 17. Olga E. dropped from mbrp

WILLARD
1895, 10, 17. Frank & w, Ida, recrq
1897, 2, 18. Mrs. relrq

WILLETT
1924, 11, 12. Beatrice recrq

WILLIAMS
1895, 5, 16. Mrs. Jennie & Stella recrq
1897, 6, 17. Thomas recrq
1898, 3, 23. Wm. recrq
1898, 7, 14. Wm. rmt Lottie McKinnon
1904, 10, 13. Thomas dropped from mbrp
1914, 2, 18. Anna Martin relrq
1922, 8, 16. Elzey P. recrq
1932, 1, 13. Mrs. E. P. & fam dropped from
     mbrp

WILLIS
1906, 6, 14. Geo. W. rocf Alum Creek MM, O.
1907, 9, 19. Geo. W. relrq

WILMORE
1895, 2, 14. Luther G. rocf Emporia MM, Kans.
1927, 6, 8. Luther dropped from mbrp

WILSON
1926, 2, 17. Ruby rocf West Grove MM, Ind.,
     dtd 1925,12,24

WINANS
1897, 12, 16. Luella rocf Iowa Falls MM

WINEBRENNER
1918, 2, 13. Frank & w, Minnie, recrq
1918, 3, 13. Edgar, minor, recrq
1919, 9, 17. Rachel & Philbert, minors, rec-
     rq

WINEBRENNER, continued
1920, 11, 17. Mr. & Mrs. & ch, Edgar, Rachel &
     Philbert, relrq

WINES
1924, 2, 13. Bessie M. recrq

WINGER
1888, 4, 19. Anna relrq

WINKLER
1927, 2, 16. Helen recrq
1932, 1, 13. Helen dropped from mbrp

WINNER
1924, 2, 27. Arthur Jay recrq
1933, 5, 17. Mrs. Gladys dropped from mbrp

WINSLOW
1902, 12, 18. Alice Pearl rocf Walnut Ridge
     MM
1906, 1, 25. Pearl gct Lupton MM

WINTERS
1885, 12, 16. Wm. recrq
1895, 10, 17. W. dropped from mbrp

WISTAR
----, --, --. Bart b 1849,12,29 d 1920,--,--;
     m May DORLAN b 1852,7,5 d 1925,--,--
     Ch: Dillwyn   b 1883, 11, 14
         Charles E. " 1885, 4, 6
1915, 3, 21. Dillwyn, s Bart & May, b 1883,
     11,14; m Jennie PAUL, dt Wm. P. & Hattie,
     b 1887,3,25

1891, 4, 16. May Dorland & ch, Emma Mabel,
     John Dorland, B. Wyatt, Bessie Louisa,
     Mary Emeline, Dillwyn, Charles & Robert
     Warder, rocf West Lake MM, Ontario, Can.
1891, 6, 18. Bart rocf Minneapolis MM, Minn.,
     dtd 1891,4,9
1905, 9, 27. Bessie L. D. rmt Chas. C. Hub-
     bard
1915, 3, 25. Dillwyn C. rmt Jennie Paul
1919, 12, 15. Robert relrq
1927, 6, 8. Virtinia dropped from mbrp
1932, 1, 13. R. Wyatt dropped from mbrp

WITTMAN
1895, 2, 14. Elizabeth recrq
1895, 6, 13. Elizabeth rmt John W. Price
1914, 4, 18. Bertha recrq
1922, 3, 15. Bertha dropped from mbrp

WITTY
1895, 5, 16. May recrq
1895, 6, 13. Jennie recrq
1898, 3, 23. Charles recrq

WOLF
1917, 11, 14. Martha recrq
1927, 2, 16. Martha Helen relrq

WOLLAM
1912, 6, 13. Edgar & w rocf Denver MM
1923, 7, 18. Edgar A. & fam gct Union MM,
     Kans.

WOODS
1887, 3, 17. Maud recrq
1889, 10, 17. Lorana B. recrq
1891, 8, 13. Loreno M. relrq
1893, 2, 16. Maude relrq
1913, 3, 12. Josie recrq
1916, 6, 14. Roxy Johnson gct Columbus MM,O.
1922, 3, 15. Jessie dropped from mbrp
1926, 3, 17. Janet McCutcheon gct Raisin MM

WOODY
1902, 11, 13. J. Waldo rocf New Garden MM,N.C.
1918, 7, 17. Jessie dropped from mbrp

WORKMAN
1929, 4, 17. Oma Marie recrq

WRATLIALL
1890, 4, 17. Frederic A. rocf Lisburn MM,
     dtd 1890,3,13

WRIGHT
1889, --, --. Amos d

1884, 7, 16. Amos F. & w, Henrietta M., & ch,
     Silisia M. & Linnetta M., recrq
1893, 11, 16. Frank & Dora recrq
1894, 8, 16. Nora recrq
1901, 3, 14. Silisia & Linnetta dropped from
     mbrp
1903, 3, 24. Pearl W. recrq
1912, 4, 18. Frank Winsor relrq
1913, 11, 19. Mary recrq
1914, 3, 18. Dora & Pearl dropped from mbrp
1922, 6, 14. Nora dropped from mbrp
1933, 4, 12. Mary relrq

WYATT
1914, 11, 18. Geo. H. recrq
1915, 2, 17. Geo. & w relrq
1922, 3, 15. Geo. H. dropped from mbrp

WYMAN
1924, 3, 13. Ruby recrq

YACOUBI
1909, 2, 18. Martha Stanton gct Taonia MM,
     Colo.

YEAKLEY
1916, 4, 12. Florence Latiner relrq

YONKERMAN
1886, 12, 16. Annis recrq
1887, 12, 15. John recrq

YOUNG
1911, 1, 19. Samuel recrq

YOUNG, continued
1918, 7, 17. Samuel dropped from mbrp
1929, 9, 18. Sarah Bell rocf Belfast MM, Ire.
1933, 4, 12. Mary Elizabeth recrq

ZELLAN
1889, 4, 18. Anna recrq

        *   *   *   *   *   *   *

McKINNON
1895, 5, 16. Willie recrq
1895, 5, 16. John C. recrq
1895, 5, 16. Agnes recrq

MAXWELL
1887, --, --. Elizabeth m George MELBOURNE
                    d 1897,4,15;

ZELLERS
1895, 10, 17. Anna dropped from mbrp

ZIMMERMAN
1927, 6, 8. Cora Packard dropped from mbrp

ZIMMERS
1897, 6, 17. Mamie recrq

        *   *   *   *   *   *   *

1895, 5, 16. Jno. Jr. recrq
1895, 5, 16. Lottie recrq
1920, 2, 18. Clyde & Lillian & ch gct Alli-
                    ance MM, O.

MELBOURNE
1887, --, --. George m Elizabeth MAXWELL

ADRIAN MONTHLY MEETING

Adrian Monthly Meeting was set off from Farmington Monthly Meeting, New York, on 6th Mo. 28, 1831. All friends in southern Michigan belonged to this one monthly meeting until Raisin Monthly Meeting was set off from Adrian Monthly Meeting in 8th Mo. 1842. Raisin Preparative Meeting was a transplanted body of believers from Royalton, Niagara County, New York, who emigrated en masse to Michigan. Three of the leading families were those of Charles Haviland, Josuah Beaverman and Sylvanus Westgate.

After belonging to New York Yearly Meeting for all these years and realizing the distance and difficulty attending it, a delegation was appointed in 1868 to attend Ohio Yearly Meeting with the thought of attaching themselves to this body. They were welcomed by the Yearly Meeting and were joined to Ohio Yearly Meeting in 1869. The place of the monthly meeting was about three and a half miles from the city of Adrian, in Adrian Township, later known as Raisin Valley.

In 1849 these Friends appointed a committee to solicit funds for the establishment of a Friends School. The school was opened on 12th Mo. 10, 1850, and was incorporated under the name Raisin Valley Seminary. It continued in operation until 1908.

RECORDS

AKIN
1844, 1, 11. Elizabeth recrq

ALDRICH
1768, 11, 12. Amos b in R. I.
1769, 12, 11. Rhoda b Worcester, Mass.
1789, 11, 8. Sarah b Stafford, N. J.
1790, 8, 16. Savil [Aldrick] b Warwick, Mass.
1809, 6, 11. Cynthia C. b Farmington, Ontario
    Co., N. Y.
1809, 9, 2. Erastus b Carrington, Wayne Co.,
    N. Y.
1810, 9, 15. Huldah b Palmyra, Ontario, N.Y.
1812, 2, 16. Amadon b Palmyra, Ontario, N. Y.
1814, 8, 7. Lavina b Palmyra, Ontario, N. Y.
1815, 3, 8. Abigail b Providence, Saratoga
    Co., N. Y.
1816, 3, 27. Savile, Jun. b Palmyra, Ontario,
    N. Y.
1818, 4, 4. Mary b Palmyra, Ontario Co., N.Y.
1820, 1, 27. Rhoda b Palmyra, Ontario Co.,N.Y.
1821, 12, 10. Judah b Palmyra, Ontario Co.,N.Y.
1824, 4, 9. Cloe b Palmyra, Ontario Co., N.Y.
1827, 6, 22. Willis b Palmyra, Ontario Co.,N.Y.
1831, 8, 17. Mary P. b Macedon, Wayne Co.,N.Y.
1835, 10, 14. Stephen H. Raisin, Lenawe Co.,
    Mich., s Jabez & Mary, dec; m at Raisin,
    Abigail HAVILAND dt Ingerson & Alice, the
    form dec, Raisin, Lenawe Co., Mich.
1837, 1, 8. Anson H. b
1838, 12, 26. Mary, dt Morganzia & Chloe, b
    Fairfield, Lenawee Co., Mich.
1861, 4, --. Morgancy, Madison, d
1874, 9, 10. Sarah A. m Emury A. JONES
----, -- --. Jacob b Macedon, Wayne Co., N.Y.
----, --, --. Ledia b
----, --, --. Sarah b

----, --, --. Israel Hoag & w, Susanna, &
    adopted ch, Jacob & Mary P. Aldrich, rocf
    Farmington MM N. Y., dtd 1831,9,22
----, --, --. Amos [Adrich] & w, Rhoda, rocf
    Uxbridge MM, dtd 1833,4,26
----, --, --. Abraham rocf Farmington MM, dtd
    1834,5,22
----, --, --. Harris H., Stephen H., Samuel &
    Isaac, minor s Jabez, rocf Farmington MM,
    dtd 1834,7,24
----, --, --. Elisabeth, w Asa, & minor ch, De-
    sire, Lyman, Ruth, Stephen, Amos & Asa,
    rocf Farmington MM, dtd 1834,11,27
----, --, --. Morganzy & w, Cloe, rocf Farming-
    ton MM, dtd 1835,1,29
----, --, --. Merril rocf Collins MM, dtd
    1836,6,30
1837, 3, 9. Cynthia dis
1837, 4, 13. Freeman, Freelove & Alvah, s
    Merril, recrq of father
1837, 8, 10. Lyman A. dis mou
1839, 6, 13. Erastus dis joining other religi-
    ous societies in their mode of worship

1840, 10, 8. Rhoda Thornton (form Aldrich)
    dis mcd & neglecting attendance
1841, 1, 14. Merril con neglecting attendance
1842, 8, 11. Richard L. & minor ch, Asa W. &
    Amy S., rocf Elba MM, dtd 1842,7,19
1843, 7, 13. Harris H. dis mou
1844, 9, 12. Eliza dis neglecting attendance
    & jas
1859, 8, 11. Asa dis disunity
1861, 10, 10. Amy Harkness (form Aldrich) dis
1863, 8, 13. Bathsheba rocf Elba MM, N. Y.,
    dtd 1863,7,14
1866, 3, 8. Complaint rec from Elba MM
    against Benjamin endorsed to Rollin MM as
    he resides within limits of that mtg

ALLEN
1834, 9, 6. Elijah b Ypsilanti, Washtenaw
    Co., Mich.
1834, 9, 15. Elijah, Ypsilanti, Washtenaw
    Co., Mich., d
1840, 3, 26. Henry H., s Tristram & Eliza-
    beth L., b Tecumseh, Lenawee Co., Mich.
----, --, --. Tristram & Lucinda
    Ch: Albert   b 1842, 8, 29 Tecumseh,
        Lenawee Co., Mich.
        Anna Com-
        fort   b 1845, 7, 13, Tecumseh,
        Lenawee Co., Mich.

----, --, --. Elijah & w, Phebe W., & minor
    ch, Stephen G. & Mary W., rocf Butternuts
    MM held at Laurens, dtd 1834,4,30
----, --, --. Tristram rocf MM of Friends held
    in N. Y., dtd 1835,9,2
1840, 4, 9. Elizabeth L. recrq
1840, 5, 14. Eve rocf Butternuts MM, dtd 1840
    4,3
1840, 9, 10. Eve, w Lemuel, rocf Butternuts
    MM, N. Y.
1841, 1, 14. David, Susan, Frederick William,
    Cornelia L. & Mary Elizabeth, recrq of
    parents, Tristram & Elizabeth L.
1844, 11, 7. Tristram co
1847, 11, 11. Elizabeth L. co
1851, 12, 11. Tristram co
1852, 1, 8. Elizabeth L. co
1853, 1, 13. Elizabeth L. co
1855, 12, 13. Tristrum & w & minor ch gct
    Winashiek
1856, 9, 11. David dis
1860, 12, 13. David rst at Winashiek MM

ARNOLD
1839, 6, 3. Sarah, Seneca, Lenawee Co.,
    Mich., d ae about 48y

1839, 8, 8. Jacob dis mcd
1839, 9, 12. Sarah dis mou
1856, 11, 13. Henry dis mou

ASH
1811, 5, 30. Martha b Providence, Saratoga

ASH, continued
    Co., N. Y.
1837, 2, 3. Martha d

ATKINSON
1840, 2, 13. Elizabeth m Samuel SATTERTHWAITE

----, --, --. Elizabeth rocf Upper Springfield
    MM, dtd 1831,12,7

AYERS
----, --, --. Amy, w Job, & minor ch, Stephen,
    Elizabeth & David, rocf Farmington MM, dtd
    1836,12,22
----, --, --. John, s Job, rocf Farmington
    MM, dtd 1836,12,22
1837, 12, 14. John dis misconduct
1842, 2, 10. Stephen dis misconduct
1846, 4, 9. Elizabeth Noice (form Ayres) dis
    neglecting attendance
1846, 5, 14. David [Ayres] dis

AYLSWORTH
1797, 1, 16. Warner b Adams, Berkshire Co.,
    Mass.
1800, 6, 21. Abigail b Adams, Berkshire Co.,
    Mass.
1820, 11, 11. Belinda Louisa b Deerfield,
    Oneida Co., N. Y.
1823, 3, 26. Susan b Manchester, Ontario Co.,
    N. Y.
1825, 7, 5. Francis Marion b Manchester, On-
    tario Co., N. Y.
1827, 8, 18. Frebon Maria b Logan, Lenawee
    Co., Mich.
1831, 1, 23. Warner B. b Logan, Lenawee Co.,
    Mich.
1835, 10, 24. Gulielma b Rollin, Lenawee Co.,
    Mich.
1840, 11, 13. Edwin P. [Aylesworth], s Robert
    & Rosanna, b Adrian, Lenawee Co., Mich.

----, --, --. Abigail [Aylesworth], w Warner,
    rocf MM held at Adams for East Hoosack,
    dtd 1832,11,28
1839, 9, 12. Abigail & Susanna [Aylesworth]
    dis neglecting attendance
1839, 11, 7. Warner [Aylesworth] con neglect-
    ing attendance & attending mtg appointed
    & held by a mbr of our society contrary to
    our discipline
1847, 2, 11. Abigail [Ailsworth] rst
1863, 5, 14. Edwin [Aylesworth] relrq

BAILY
1850, 11, 7. Lydia (form Smith) dis misconduct
1879, 5, 8. Henry M. & Hellen C. recrq

BAKER
1767, 9, 4. Cynthia b Taunton, Bristol Co.,
    Mass.
1776, 11, 5. Moses b Swanzey, Bristol Co.,
    Mass.

1779, 4, 26. David b Adams, Berkshire Co.,
    Mass.
1791, 5, 13. Betsey b Worcester Co., Mass.
1798, 1, 17. John b Adams, Berkshire Co.,
    Mass.
1799, 6, 24. David W. b Palmyra, Ontario
    Co., N. Y.
1800, 12, 1. Polly b Montreal, Canada
1801, 2, 21. Orin b Palmyra, Ontario, N. Y.
1804, 8, 8. Elisabeth b
1806, 1, 17. Moses C. b Palmyra, Ontario Co.,
    N. Y.
1818, 3, 14. John S. b Macedon, Wayne Co.,
    N. Y.
1820, 12, 14. Sarah H. b Macedon, Wayne Co.,
    N. Y.
1821, 6, 30. Rufus b Palmyra, Ontario, N. Y.
1822, 12, 26. Isaac S. b Macedon, Wayne Co.,
    N. Y.
1823, 3, 19. Nathaniel b Macedon, Wayne Co.,
    N. Y.
1823, 6, 12. Mercey b Macedon, Wayne Co.,N.Y.
1825, 3, 26. Mary b Macedon, Wayne Co., N. Y.
1825, 3, 26. Sarah b Macedon, Wayne Co.,N.Y.
1827, 5, 10. Jacob b Peninton, Monroe Co.,
    N. Y.
1827, 7, 27. David S. b Macedon, Wayne Co.,
    N. Y.
1828, 4, 15. ----- b Macedon, Wayne Co.,N.Y.
1829, 6, 26. Esther P. b Macedon, Wayne Co.,
    N. Y.
1829, 9, 23. Henry b Peninton, Monroe Co.,
    N. Y.
1831, 9, 26. Lucy b Peninton, Monroe Co.,
    N. Y.
1831, 10, 16. Cynthia W. b Peninton, Monroe
    Co., N. Y.
----, --, --. John & Polley
    Ch: Lydia Ann b 1834, 2, 9 Lenawee
        Co., Mich.
        Cloe Jane " 1835, 7, 8, "
        Co., Mich.
        Horace L. " 1839, 3, 3 Fairfield,
        Lenawee Co., Mich.
1834, 8, 19. Mary b Palmyra, Lenawee Co.,
    Mich.
1836, 8, 28. Sarah Jane b Palmyra, Lenawee
    Co., Mich.
1837, 7, 30. Levi b Rollin, Lenawee Co.,Mich.
1838, 9, 23. Mary Ann, Fairfield, Lenawee
    Co., Mich., d
1838, 10, 7. Israel H. b Raisin, Lenawee Co.,
    Mich.
1840, 11, 2. David S., Adrian, Lenawee Co.,
    Mich., d
1844, 11, 1. Davis, s David & Esther, Raisin,
    Lenawee Co., Mich., d ae 65y 6m 5d

----, --, --. Cynthia rocf Farmington MM dtd
    1832,6,21 (rem ith h, Moses)
----, --, --. John & w, Polly, & minor ch, Ru-
    fus, Mercy, Sylvia & Cynthia, rocf Farm-
    ington MM, dtd 1832,6,21

BAKER, continued

----, --, --. Lucy rocf Farmington MM, dtd
    1832,6,21

----, --, --. ----- & minor ch, Nathaniel, Sa-
    rah & Mary, rocf Farmington MM, dtd 1832,6,
    21

----, --, --. Lydia, w Asa, & minor ch, Julia
    Ann, rocf Farmington MM, dtd 1832,6,21

----, --, --. David & w, Betsey, & minor ch,
    Mary A., John S., Sarah H., Isaac S., Da-
    vid S., Esther O. & Betsy's minor s, Ste-
    phen Hoag, rocf Farmington MM, dtd 1833,5,
    24

----, --, --. David W. & w, Elizabeth, & minor
    ch, Jacob, Henry & Lucy, rocf Farmington
    MM, dtd 1833,6,27

----, --, --. Moses rocf Farmington MM, dtd
    1833,11,21

1837, 3, 9. Aaron T. dis

1837, 3, 9. Benjamin dis mou by direction of
    Farmington MM

1837, 10, 12. Moses C. con misconduct

1838, 3, 8. John L. dis misconduct

1838, 7, 12. Nehemiah Colvin & w, Lydia, &
    adopted minor ch, Caroline S. Colvin &
    Thomas S. Baker, gct Salem MM, O.

1838, 9, 13. David W. co

1838, 10, 11. Benjamin rocf Rochester MM dtd
    1838,8,24

1838, 10, 11. Jesse rocf Rochester MM, dtd
    1838,8,24

---- --, --. Mary Ann rocf Rochester MM, dtd
    1838,8,25

1838, 12, 13. Moses con misconduct

1839, 9, 12. Mary & minor ch, Daniel I., Moses
    D., Mary Jane & William, rocf Rochester MM,
    dtd 1838,8,25

1840, 7, 9. Nehemiah Colvin & w, Lydia, &
    two adopted ch, Caroline C. Colvin & Thom-
    as Baker, rocf Salem MM, O.

1840, 9, 10. Betsey co

1840, 10, 8. David W. appointed an elder

1841, 9, 9. Betsy co of Adrian Mtg

1843, 1, 12. Benjamin J. dis mou

1843, 1, 12. Jesse dis mou

1845, 6, 1. Esther P. dis neglecting attend-
    ance & jas

1851, 4, 10. Lydia (form Hoag) con mou (Raisin
    MM notified)

BALL

1840, 4, 9. Eliza recrq

1840, 4, 9. Thaddeus I. recrq

1841, 1, 1. Lemuel, s Thadeus & Elvira, b
    Pitt, Washtenaw Co., Mich.

BARBER

1879, 6, 12. Hannah Mather rq mbrp

1880, 4, 8. Hannah M. relrq

1881, 2, 10. Hartwell rq mbrp

BARKER

1842, 8, 11. Caroline S. (form Styles) dis
    mou

BARNHART

----, --, --. Lydia, w Jacob, rocf Farmington
    MM, dtd 1834,1,23

BASSETT

1836, 9, 15. Nathan H., Raisin, Lenawe Co.,
    Mich., s Artemas & Sarah; m at Logan,
    Adelia WEBB, dt Ezekiel & Fanny, Raisin,
    Lenawe Co., Mich.

1837, 9, 10. William Judson b Adrian, Lene-
    wee Co., Mich.

1855, 8, 16. Francis, s Nathan, d ae 5y 8m
    26d

1858, 1, 24. Artamas, s William & Margery, d
    ae 76y

----, --, --. Margery rocf Starksboro MM, Vt.,
    dtd 1834,5,2

----, --, --. Nathan H. rocf Starksborough MM,
    Vt., dtd 1834,5,2

1838, 2, 8. Artemas rq mbrp; committee to
    contact Starksborough regarding cert

----, --, --. Artemas & w, Sarah, & minor ch,
    Sarah Jr. & David, rocf Starksborough MM,
    Vt., dtd 1838,6,29

1843, 4, 13. Sarah Webb (form Bassett) dis
    mcd

1862, 5, 8. David gct Ferrisburg MM, Vt.

BATTY

1851, 1, 16. Mary, Raisin, Lenawee Co., Mich.
    d ae 76y

1841, 11, 11. Mary [Battey] rocf Farmington
    MM, dtd 1841,6,24

BEAKMAN

1864, 6, 9. Rachel rocf Rollin MM, dtd 1864,
    4,12

BEAL

1806, 3, 24. William b Northfield, Ontario,
    N. Y.

1811, 12, 13. Rachel S. b Farmington, Ontario
    Co., N. Y.

1833, 3, 11. William James b Logan, Lenewee
    Co., Mich.

1835, 3, 8. Joseph Otis b Rollin, Lenawee
    Co., Mich.

1840, 4, 9. Ruth dis mou

1840, 8, 13. Susan (form Brownell) dis mou

1840, 10, 8. William co

1843, 11, 9. William co

1844, 7, 11. William appointed an elder

1849, 12, 13. William co

1851, 1, 9. Rachel co

BELL

----, --, --. Dorothy rocf Upper Springfield
     MM held at Mansfield, Burlington Co., N.J.,
     dtd 1836,11,9
1848, 10, 12. Ann Eliza (form Brownell) dis
     neglecting attendance, mcd & jas

BELSON
1834, 9, 18. William gct New York MM

BENNETT

----, --, --. Prince & w, Esther, & ch, Lucy,
     Stephen, Prince, Joseph, Mary & George,
     rocf Butternuts MM held at Laurens, dtd
     1831,8,31
1841, 6, 10. Joseph dis mou
1841, 6, 10. Prince Jr. dis mou

BETTS

----, --, --. Hurome rocf West Lake MM, Upper
     Canada, dtd 1834,4,17

BINNS
1835, 12, 11. Hannah, Rollin, Lenawee Co.,
     Mich., d
1836, 9, 23. James b
1839, 4, 11. Charles b Rollin, Lenawee Co.,
     Mich.
1841, 9, 12. Joseph H., s John & Sarah D.,
     b Woodstock, Lenawee Co., Mich.
1842, 12, 14. Joseph, Woodstock, Lenawe Co.,
     Mich., s James & Alice, both dec; m at
     Woodstock, Sarah C. LUPTON, dt Gideon &
     Susannah, Woodstock, Lenawe Co., Mich.
     Ch: Priscilla b 1843, 11, 4, Rollin,
          Lenewee Co., Mich.
        Susannah L.   d 1846,10,
          16 ae 1y 2m
1845, 3, 3. Richard T., s John & Sarah D.,
     b Woodstock, Lenawee Co., Mich.
1845, 8, 19. Susannah L. b

----, --, --. John & w, Sarah, & dt, Martha,
     minor, rocf Providence MM, Pa., dtd 1835,
     4,30
----, --, --. Wilson, Hannah & Daniel, ch
     James & Elizabeth, rocf Providence MM,
     Pa., dtd 1835,4,30
----, --, --. Joseph rocf Providence MM, Pa.,
     dtd 1835,8,27
1842, 9, 8. Sarah co
1843, 10, 12. Sarah co
1843, 11, 9. John co
1844, 8, 8. Wilson con mou
1844, 11, 7. John co
1845, 12, 11. John co
1847, 11, 11. Sarah co
1849, 12, 13. Sarah D. co

BIRDSALL
1816, 4, 1. William b Hartland
1819, 8, 17. Lewis W., s Joseph & Hannah, b
     Hartland, N. Y.

----, --, --. Jonathan b 1797,4,20, Stafford,
     N. J.; m Mary ----- b 1797,4,5 Gloucester,
     R. I., d 1847,5,5
     Ch: Alice Jane b 1820, 5, 5 in Hartland
        Phebe Ann
        Mary Elma " 1825, 7, 15
        Sarah M.
        Asael E.   " 1830, 11, 15
        Jonathan
1820, 6, 19. Sally, dt Joseph & Hannah, b
     Hartland, N. Y.
----, --, --. Joseph b 1791,11,17, Stafford,
     N. J., d 1845,12,23 ae 47y less 5d; m
     Nancy ----- b 1795,2,7, Hanover, Pa.
     Ch: Jesse   b 1825, 11, 24
        Gula Elma
        Diantha   " 1832, 1, 3
        Richard   " 1835, 5, 16
1845, 3, 25. Lindley, s Daniel & Mariah,
     Scipio, Hillsdale Co., Mich., d ae 1y 6m
1846, 12, 3. Lindley, s William B. & Anne,
     b Scipio, Hillsdale, Mich.
1871, 3, 15. Harriet M. m Daniel M. HAVILAND
1877, 12, 25. William J., Adrian, Lenawee
     Co., Mich., s James & Jane H.; m at Rai-
     sin, Josephine STANLY, dt Fleming A. &
     Eunice, Raisin, Lenawee Co., Mich.

----, --, --. Jonathan & fam rocf Hartland MM,
     N. Y., dtd 1835,8,20
1839, 11, 7. Jonathan & fam rqct Hartland MM
1845, 1, 9. Edward & w, Evelina, & minor s,
     David, rocf Farmington MM, dtd 1844,9,26
----, --, --. Lewis W. rocf Hartland MM, dtd
     1845,6,19
1845, 8, 14. Jesse, Jr., Gulielma, Diantha &
     Richard, minor ch Joseph, rocf Hartland
     MM, dtd 1845,5,19
1845, 9, 11. Sally rocf Hartland MM, dtd 1845
     6,19
1845, 10, 9. Daniel & w & minor s, Lindley,
     rocf Farmington MM, dtd 1845,3,27
1845, 12, 11. Wm. B. & w, Anna D., & minor s,
     Israel (or Isaac) rocf Farmington MM, dtd
     1845,4,24
1848, 12, 14. Evalina co
1849, 10, 11. Sally Pembleton (form Birdsall)
     dis mcd & neglecting attendance
1851, 1, 9. Evelina co
1851, 4, 10. Willis dis mcd
1852, 8, 12. Timothy & w, Mary, gct Farming-
     ton MM, N. Y.
1867, 7, 11. Maria D. & minor dt, Harriet,
     rocf Rollin MM, dtd 1867,6,15

BLANCHARD
1838, 1, 11. John & w, Clarissa, & s, Samuel,
     rocf Collins MM, dtd 1837,1,26

BORTON
1839, 3, 14. Job, John, Martha Ann & Samuel
     C., minor ch, Bethuel, dec, rocf Eavesham
     MM, dtd 1839,1,11

BOWERMAN

1769, 10, 22. Eunice b Rochester, Plymouth Co.,
    Mass.
1786, 8, 20. Joshua b Falmouth, Barnstable
    Co., Mass.
1792, 8, 3. Abigail b
1804, 8, 29. Margaret b Providence, Saratoga
    Co., N. Y.
1810, 3, 26. Alice b Providence, Saratoga
    Co., N. Y.
1811, 5, 9. Joseph b Providence, Saratoga
    Co., N. Y.
1811, 5, 10. Joseph b Providence, Saratoga
    Co., N. Y.
1811, 11, 27. Moses b Providence, Saratoga Co.,
    N. Y.
1812, 10, 15. Dorcas b Providence, Saratoga
    Co., N. Y.
1814, 2, 5. Samuel b Providence, Saratoga
    Co., N. Y.
1814, 4, 7. Alice b Providence, Saratoga
    Co., N. Y.
1815, 5, 22. Dorcas b Providence, Saratoga
    Co., N. Y.
1816, 3, 6. Abigail b Providence, Saratoga
    Co., N. Y.
1817, 11, 12. Esther b Ontario, Wayne Co., N.Y.
1819, 3, 22. Joshua C. b Ontario, Wayne Co.,
    N. Y.
----, --, --. Joshua & Abigail
    Ch: Abigail
        Esther
        Joshua C.
        Margaret
        John W.
        Moses   b 1824, 1, 11
1821, 1, 17. Margaret b
1822, 11, 25. John W. b
1824, 11, 1. Moses b Royalton, Niagara Co.,
    N. Y.
----, --, --. Joseph & Alice
    Ch: Adah Ann   b 1830, 10, 3
        Charles
1830, 10, 3. Ada Ann b Royalton, Niagara Co.,
    N. Y.
1831, 11, 9. Zilpha b Providence, Saratoga
    Co., N. Y.
1831, 11, 14. Eunice b Royalton, Niagara Co.,
    N. Y.
1831, 11, 20. Charles b Royalton, Niagara Co.,
    N. Y.
1833, 3, 7. Nancy b Royalton Niagara Co.,
    N. Y.
1833, 4, 9. Martha b Logan, Lenewee Co., Mich.
1834, 6, 22. Peleg H. b Raisin, Lenawee Co.,
    Mich.
1834, 9, 2. Eunice, Raisin, Lenawee Co.,
    Mich., d
1835, 6, 23. Amy W. b Raisin, Lenawee Co.,
    Mich.
1835, 9, 9. Eunice b Raisin, Lenawee Co.,
    Mich.
1836, 2, 16. George H. b Raisin, Lenawee Co.,

Mich.
1836, 8, 7. Jeremiah Westgate, Raisin, Lena-
    wee Co., Mich., s Jonathan & Dorcas, lat-
    ter dec; m Dorcas HAYNES, dt Joshua & Abi-
    gail BOWERMAN, Raisin, Lenawe Co., Mich.
1836, 9, 23. Margaret b
1837, 4, 3. Esther M. b Raisin, Lenewee
    Co., Mich.
1838, 1, 18. Joseph M. b Raisin, Lenawee
    Co., Mich.
1838, 4, 13. Charles, Raisin, Lenawee Co.,
    Mich., d ae 6y 4m 23d
1838, 6, 11. Moses b Raisin, Lenawee Co.,
    Mich.
1838, 8, 8. Jane b Raisin, Lenawee Co., Mich.
1838, 10, 20. Nancy, Raisin, Lenawee Co.,
    Mich., d ae 5y 7m 18d
1839, 10, 29. Isaac b Raisin, Lenawee Co.,
    Mich.
1840, 1, 5. Roselinda b Rollin, Lenawee
    Co., Mich.
1840, 11, 15. Elvira, dt Samuel & Zilpha, b
    Raisin, Lenawee Co., Mich.
1840, 11, 18. Margaret m John W. HAVILAND
1840, 11, 18. Joshua C., Raisin, Lenawe Co.,
    Mich., s Joshua & Abigail; m at Raisin,
    Pamilia WESTGATE, dt Jeremiah & Amy, the
    latter dec, Raisin, Lenawe Co., Mich.
1851, 2, 12. Joseph, Raisin, Lenawee Co.,
    Mich., s Joshua & Abigail; m at Raisin,
    Maria ODELL, dt Anson & Charlotte, Adrian,
    Lenawee Co., Mich.
1856, 9, 17. Joseph, Raisin, Lenawee Co.,
    Mich., s Joshua & Abigail, form dec; m at
    Raisin, Amy DILLINGHAM, dt James COLLINS
    & w, Sophia, latter dec, Macon, Lenawee
    Co., Mich.

----, --, --. Alice rocf Hartland MM dtd
    1832,5,1
----, --, --. Dorras (or Dorcas) rocf Hart-
    land MM, dtd 1832,5,1
----, --, --. Joshua & Abigail & minor ch,
    Alice, Abigail, Esther, Joshua C., Marga-
    ret, John W. & Moses, rocf Hartland MM
    held at Lockport, dtd 1832,5,1
----, --, --. Joseph & w, Alice, & minor ch,
    Abraham & Charles, rocf Hartland MM held
    at Lockport, dtd 1832,9,25
----, --, --. Moses & w, Zilpha, & minor dt,
    Eunice, rocf Hartland MM, dtd 1832,9,25
----, --, --. Margaret rocf Hartland MM held
    at Lockport, dtd 1833,4,30
----, --, --. Samuel & w, Dorcas, & minor dt,
    Nancy, rocf Hartland MM held at Lockport,
    dtd 1833,4,30
----, --, --. Unice rocf Hartland MM held at
    Lockport, dtd 1833,4,30
1839, 9, 12. Abigail co
1840, 9, 10. Abigail co
1842, 3, 10. Allice con misconduct
1844, 3, 14. Alice Vibber (form Bowerman)
    con mou (com by Raisin MM)

BOWERMAN, continued
1851, 2, 6. Joseph prcf Raisin MM, to m
1851, 5, 7. Maria & minor dt, Mary Odell, gct
    Raisin MM
1856, 8, 14. Joseph prcf Raisin MM, to m
1857, 3, 12. Amy & minor dt, Elizabeth Dilling-
    ham, gct Raisin MM
1865, 2, 9. Benjamin & w, Polly, rocf Roches-
    ter MM, dtd 1865,12,15
1866, 8, 9. Elijah rocf Rochester MM, dtd
    1866,7,27

BOWMAN
1837, 11, 8. Elisabeth F. b Rollin, Lenawee
    Co., Mich.
1839, 5, 24. Rachel b Raisin, Lenawee Co.,
    Mich.
1839, 7, 19. Isaac, Rollin, Lenawee Co.,
    Mich., d
----, --, --. Joseph & Elizabeth
    Ch: John
        Spencer   b 1842, 4, 8 Rollin, Lena-
            wee Co., Mich.
        William F. b 1844, 9, 22 "   "
            Co., Mich. d 1849,9,26 New Brighton,
            Pa.
        Thomas   b 1847, 11, 12 Rollin, Len-
            awee Co., Mich.

----, --, --. Joseph H. & w, Elizabeth S., rocf
    Marlborough MM, O., dtd 1836,6,28
1851, 1, 9. Phebe rq mbrp; mbr New Hartford
    MM, N. Y.; case dismissed from our minutes
1851, 6, 12. Joseph con mcd

BOYCE
1867, 1, 12. Knowles, Benjamin, Smyrna, Chenan-
    ga Co., N. Y., s Henry & Susan; m at Adrian
    Anna HUNTINGTON, Raisin, Lenawee Co., Mich.
    dt Benjamin BOYCE & w, Catharine, latter
    dec

BRAMAN
1835, 7, 15. Amos Wooster, Palmyra, Lenawe
    Co., Mich., s Sylvester & Mercy, both dec;
    m at Raisin, Lodema HOAG, dt Jesse & Mar-
    tha BRAMAN, the form dec, Palmyra, Lenawe
    Co., Mich.

1839, 11, 7. Samuel com by Elba MM; complaint
    returned as he did not reside within lim-
    its of this mtg
1840, 2, 6. Cert for Nancy [Brayman] & ch
    from Shelby MM, returned to Ill.

BRANSON
1840, 2, 6. Cert rec for Nancy & minor ch.
    Sylvanus, Alpheus, Hopy, Laura & Jesse,
    from Elba MM returned; not living within
    limits of mtg

BROOKS
1836, 4, 25. Mary, Lenawee Co., Mich., d

1839, 9, 12. Catharine (form McAuley) con mou

BROWER
1838, 11, 8. Ruth Ann dis

BROWNELL
1801, 8, 14. Thomas b Westport, Mass.
1802, 2, 14. Elisabeth b Adams, Berkshire,
    Mass.
1804, 8, 29. Phebe b Providence Co., R. I.
1806, 8, 12. Elijah b Westport, Bristol Co.,
    Mass.
1823, 3, 2. Susan b Adams, Berkshire Co.,
    Mass.
1825, 7, 2. Judith b Macedon, Wayne Co.,
    N. Y.
1827, 3, 13. William Aikens b Worcester Co.,
    Mass.
1829, 2, 14. Ann Eliza b Ann Arbor, Washtenaw
    Co., Mich.
1830, 12, 3. Mary b Ann Arbor, Washtenaw Co.,
    Mich.
1830, 12, 22. Walter E. b Logan, Lenawee Co.,
    Mich.
1833, 2, 9. Lindley M. b Logan, Lenawee Co.,
    Mich.
1833, 7, 9. Joseph S. b Logan, Lenewee Co.,
    Mich.
1833, 8, 30. Elisabeth, Logan, Lenawee Co.,
    Mich., d
1835, 3, 28. Charles Stuart b Logan, Lenawee
    Co., Mich.
----, --, --. Elijah & Phebe
    Ch: Franklin b 1838, 3, 14 Rollin, Lena-
            wee Co., Mich.
        Milton   b 1838, 3, 14 "   "
            Co., Mich.
1838, 3, 15. Sands, Rollin, Lenawe Co., Mich.,
    s Shadrack, dec, & Mary, Mass.; m at Rol-
    lin, Hannah M. STEER, dt David & Phebe,
    Rollin, Lenawe Co., Mich.
1839, 4, 1. James Russel b Rollin, Lenawee
    Co., Mich.
1840, 9, 14. Elizabeth Margarett, dt Elijah
    & Phebe, b Raisin, Lenawee Co., Mich.
1842, 4, 4. Phebe S. b Rollin, Lenawee Co.,
    Mich.
----, --, --. Elijah & Phebe
    Ch: William   d 1851, 6, 6
        ae 23y
        Walter   " 1851, 6,17
        ae 20y
        Lindley M.   " 1851, 7,11
        ae 18y
1853, 1, 2. Elijah, s Shadrack & Mary, Rai-
    sin, Lenawee Co., Mich., d ae 46y 4m
----, --, --. Sands b

----, --, --. Elijah & w, Phebe, & s, William
    Aikens Brownell, rocf Smithfield MM, R.I.,
    dtd 1831,7,28
1837, 9, 7. Sands rocf Smithfield MM, R. I.,
    dtd 1837,6,29

BROWNELL, continued

1839, 7, 11. Elijah con neglecting attendance, appointing and attending mtg contrary to discipline

1840, 4, 9. Phebe con misconduct

1840, 8, 13. Susan Beal (form Brownell) dis mou

1848, 9, 7. Eliza Bell (form Brownel) dis

1848, 10, 12. Ann Eliza Bell (form Brownell) dis neglecting attendance, mcd & jas

1851, 10, 9. Hannah M. appointed clerk

1852, 1, 8. Phebe co

1852, 11, 11. Hannah M. appointed clerk

1854, 5, 11. Sands & w, Hannah, & minor ch, James Russel, Phebe S., Roby Jane & David Sands, gct Red Cedar MM, Ia.

1855, 12, 13. Joseph gct Winashiek MM, Ia.

1856, 11, 15. Phebe & mihor s, Franklin, gct Winoshiek MM, Ia.

1857, 8, 13. Charles con misconduct

1857, 9, 15. Charles gct Winashiek MM, Ia.

1857, 11, 12. Laura Jane gct Winneshiek MM, Ia.

1861, 5, 9. Phebe [Brownel] rocf Winashiek MM, Ia.

1867, 4, 11. Phebe [Brownel] gct Chicago MM, Ill.

----, --, --. Thomas & w, Elizabeth, & ch, Susan, Judith, Ann Eliza & Mary, rocf East Hoosack MM held at Adams, Berkshire Co., Mass. (rem from East Hoosack MM with one ch about 10 yrs ago to Genesee after residing there a short time rem to this territory)

BUCHANAN

1846, 5, 14. Content K. (form Densmore) dis mou & neglecting attendance

BULLARD

1855, 10, 11. John Jr. recrq

BUNKER

----, --, --. Eliza, Ann, Cornelia, Mary Ann & Rebecca, dt Jethro, rocf Hudson MM, dtd 1833,8,2

----, --, --. Deborah, dt Jethro & Rebecca, rocf Hudson MM held in Chatham, dtd 1834,9, 24

BUSH

1881, 2, 10. Mary rq mbrp

CALKIN

1826, 10, 1. Sabrina R. b

1839, 3, 31. Darius C. s Jared & Susannah, b Rollin, Lenawee Co., Mich.

1837, 9, 7. Jared [Calken] & w, Susannah, & minor ch, Almeron B., Asa K., William A., Sabrina R., Ashley R. & Minerva P., rocf Hartland MM, dtd 1837,1,19

1840, 10, 8. Jared co

CAMBRON

----, --, --. Abigail, w William, rocf Farmington MM, dtd 1833,8,22

----, --, --. Hannah rocf Farmington MM, dtd 1833,10,24

1847, 12, 9. Esther (form Haviland) dis mou

1849, 2, 8. Hannah com neglecting attendance & jas; mbr Raisin MM; case dismissed from these minutes

CAMPBELL

1839, 10, 10. Maria rocf Norwich MM, dtd 1839, 9,12 (w Silas)

1845, 3, 13. Maria [Campbel] gct Norwich MM, Upper Canada

CARNEL

1845, 3, 13. Mariah, Jemimah McCauley, Diana McCauley & Elizabeth McCauley, gct Norwich MM, Canada

CARPENTER

1840, 3, 19. George W., Raisin, Lenawee Co., Mich., s William, dec, & Phebe; m at Adrian, Mary C. HARKNESS, dt David & Mary, Adrian, Lenawee Co., Mich.
   Ch: Elmyra   b 1841, 2, 10 Raisin, Lenawee Co., Mich.
       Malvinia   b 1846, 3, 23   "
                  Co., Mich.

----, --, --. Elihu & Anna
   Ch: Mary   d 1844, 4,15
       ae 22y 9m 20d
       Julianna   " 1847,11,11

1861, 2, 21. Anna d ae 61y 3m 17d

1864, 7, 29. Elihu d ae 66y 5m 6d

----, --, --. Nancy, w Isaiah, rocf Greenfield MM held at Providence, N. Y., dtd 1836,8,12

1839, 1, 10. Lucy dis

1839, 5, 9. Elihu & w, Anna, & ch, Mary, Julia-Ann & Stephen J., rocf Starksborough MM, dtd 1838,11,2

1840, 2, 6. Geo. W. rocf Collins MM, dtd 1839,12,26

1842, 9, 8. Anna co

1843, 10, 12. Anna co

1843, 11, 9. Elihu co

1846, 11, 12. Ann co

1851, 9, 11. George W. dis misconduct

1852, 8, 12. Stephen com for mou

1860, 5, 10. Elmira Osiola (form Carpenter) dis

CARR

1838, 10, 18. James, Woodstock, Lenawe Co., Mich., s William & Sarah, latter dec; m at Rollin, Phebe WEAVER, dt John H. & Lydia, Woodstock, Lenawe Co., Mich.

1841, 7, 3. Joshua, Woodstock, Lenewee Co., Mich., d

1841, 7, 3. Joshua, s James & Phebe, b Wood-

CARR, continued
    stock, Lenawee Co., Mich.
1841, 8, 16. Phebe, Woodstock, Lenawee Co.,
    Mich., d
1846, 10, 22. William, Woodstock, Lenawee Co.,
    Mich., d ae about 80y

1837, 7, 13. James & dt, Sarah, Elizabeth &
    Mary C., rocf Smithfield MM, O., dtd 1837,
    4,17
1840, 5, 14. William rocf Smithfield MM, O.,
    dtd 1840,3,23
1842, 3, 10. Lydia rocf Smithfield MM, O., dtd
    1841,12,20
1842, 7, 14. Elizabeth (form Griffith) dis mcd
1842, 8, 11. James dis m dec w's sister
1843, 4, 13. James con mcd
1843, 6, 8. Elizabeth con mcd
1843, 6, 8. James rst
1847, 5, 13. Sarah Wood (form Carr) con mou &
    mcd

CATON
----, --, --. Nehemiah Colvin & w, Lydia, &
    adopted ch, Thomas Baker & Margaret Caton,
    rocf Farmington MM, dtd 1836,8,25

CHANDLER
1866, 7, 12. Rachel H. S. rocf Birch Lake MM,
    dtd 1866,7,7

CHAPLIN
1841, 5, 13. Frances (or Chapman) recrq
1853 7, 14. Francis A. (or Chapman) dis ne-
    glecting attendance & being out of unity
    with friends

CHARLES
1878, 5, 9. William H. rocf Fairmont MM, dtd
    1878,4,17
1878, 11, 7. Lenora rocf Fairmount MM, dtd
    1878,10,16

CHASE
1800, 3, 10. Peter b Sutton, Worcester Co.,
    Mass.
1806, 3, 29. Levi H. b Providence, Saratoga
    Co., N. Y.
1808, 7, 19. Elisabeth b Eggharbour, Burling-
    ton Co., N. Y.
1827, 12, 26. Eliza b Royalton, Niagara Co.,
    N. Y.
1828, 9, 23. Mary Jane b Macedon, Wayne Co.,
    N. Y.
1829, 8, 20. Laura H. b Royalton, Niagara Co.,
    N. Y.
1830, 11, 29. Ichabod b Farmington, Oakland
    Co., Mich.
1830, 12, 8. Phebe b Royalton, Niagara Co.,
    N. Y.
1832, 5 12. Sally Ann b Royalton, Niagara
    Co., N. Y.
1833, 6, 30. Thomas C. b Oakland Co., Mich.

1833, 9, 30. Daniel H. b Logan, Lenawee Co.,
    Mich.
1835, 3, 4. Amazia b Raisin
1837, 1, 31. Emelia b Raisin, Lenewee Co.,
    Mich.
1838, 5, 12. Artemas b Raisin, Lenawee Co.,
    Mich.
1847, 3, 18. Hannah, Lenawee Co., Mich., d
    ae 56y 6m
1848, 7, 20. Nathan, Rome, Lenawee Co.,
    Mich., s Ebenezer & Sarah; m at Adrian,
    Sarah HOAG, dt Richard SHOTWELL & w,
    Mary, Raisin, Lenawee Co., Mich.
1858, 5, 30. Nathan, Raisin, d ae 68y 9m 26d

----, --, --. Levi H. & w, Anna, & minor ch,
    Eliza, Laura, Phebe & Sallann, rocf Hart-
    land MM held at Lockport, dtd 1832,9,25
----, --, --. Nathan rocf Farmington MM, dtd
    1834,11,27
1839, 9, 12. Levi H. dis neglecting attend-
    ance & attending mtg contrary to discip-
    line
1840, 3, 12. Anna dis neglecting mtg & attend-
    ing mtg set up contrary to discipline
1843, 6, 8. Hannah recrq
1848, 12, 14. Nathan co
1850, 2, 7. Cert rec for Cynthia Chase, w
    Wing, & minor dt, Anna & Allice, forwarded
    to Raisin MM; they desired to be mbr there
1851, 1, 9. Sarah co
1851, 12, 11. Nathan co
1853, 1, 13. Nathan co
1854, 1, 12. Nathan co
1855, 1, 11. Nathan co
1856, 2, 7. Nathan co
1857, 2, 5. Nathan co
1858, 4, 8. Nathan appointed an elder
1864, 4, 7. Sarah appointed an elder

CLARK
1862, 10, 10. Hezekiah, Carthage, Rush Co.,
    Ind., s John & Nancy; m at Adrian, Caro-
    line A. HOAG, dt John & Susan, Lenawee
    Co., Mich.

1839, 9, 12. Sarah (form McAuley) con mou
    (com by Norwich MM)
1862, 10, 9. Hezekiah prcf Walnut Ridge MM,
    Ind., dtd 1862,9,20, to m
1863, 4, 9. Caroline A. gct Walnut Ridge MM,
    Ind.

CLAYTON
1855, 8, 9. Cert rec for Eliza Ann endorsed
    to Raisin MM; resided within limits of
    that mtg

COFFIN
1838, 4, 12. Phebe (form Hight) dis

COGGSHELL
1854, 8, 10. Cert rec for Meribah endorsed to

COGGSHELL, continued
    Rollin MM; resided within limits of that
    mtg

COLE
1846, 7, 9. Darius Jr., s Darius & Mary Ann,
    b Rollin, Lenawee, Mich.
1846, 9, 23. Darius, Rollin, Lenawee Co.,
    Mich., d ae 36y

1843, 3, 9. Mary Ann recrq
1845, 12, 11. Darius recrq
1849, 7, 12. Mary Ann dis m dec h's brother

COLLIER
1850, 12, 12. Sarah (or Collar) (form Dilling-
    ham) dis mou (Raisin MM notified)

COLLINS
1841, 2, 12. Amy R. m Joseph DILLINGHAM
1852, 11, 17. Rachel m Israel HOAG
1856, 9, 17. Joseph Bowerman, Raisin, Lenawee
    Co., Mich., s Joshua & Abigail, form dec;
    m at Raisin, Amy DILLINGHAM, dt James COL-
    LINS & w, Sophia, latter dec, Macon, Lena-
    wee Co., Mich.
1860, 11, 10. James P., s James & Sophia, Ma-
    con, Lenawee Co., Mich., d ae 33y 2m 26d

----, --, --. Mary & Rachel, dt James, rocf
    Little Eggharbour MM, N. J., dtd 1832,8,9
----, --, --. James & minor ch, Isaac, Eli,
    Samuel, Lucy Ann, Martha & James, rocf
    Little Eggharbour MM, N. J., dtd 1832,8,9
----, --, --. Joseph rocf Little Eggharbour
    MM, N. J., dtd 1832,9,13
1842, 2, 10. Lucy Ann Gray (form Collins) con
    mou
1842, 4, 7. Joseph con mou & neglecting at-
    tendance
1842, 5, 12. Isaac con mou & neglecting at-
    tendance
1843, 5, 11. James dis mou
1847, 10, 14. Eli con mou, mcd & neglecting at-
    tendance
1847, 10, 14. Samuel con mcd, mou & neglecting
    attendance
1850, 11, 7. Martha Collins (late Collins) dis
    mcd
1853, 12, 8. Martha rec in mbrp
1854, 7, 13. Martha gct Little Eggharbour MM
1859, 4, 7. James P. con misconduct

COLVIN
1807, 2, 5. Elisabeth W. b Palmyra, Wayne
    Co., N. Y.

----, --, --. Elisabeth W., w Isaac, & minor
    dt, Phebe (or Phila) rocf Hartland MM, dtd
    1833,9,19
----, --, --. Nehemiah & w, Lydia, & adopted
    ch, Thomas Baker & Margaret Caton, rocf
    Farmington MM, dtd 1836,8,25

1838, 7, 12. Nehemiah & w, Lydia, & adopted
    minor ch, Caroline S. Colvin & Thomas S.
    Baker, gct Salem MM, O.
1840, 7, 9. Nehemiah & w, Lydia, & adopted
    ch, Caroline C. Colvin & Thomas L. Baker,
    rocf Salem MM, O., dtd 1840,5,20

COMFORT
1843, 5, 18. Mary m Joshua TAYLOR
1848, 10, 18. Elizabeth M. m Joseph C. SATTER-
    THWAITE
1852, 9, 29. Elwood, Raisin, Lenawee Co.,
    Mich., s Aaron & Ann; m at Tecumseh,
    Elizabeth P. SATTERTHWAITE, dt Samuel &
    Hannah, the latter dec, Tecumseh, Lenawee
    Co., Mich.
1854, 9, 20. Jane m Samuel M. SATTERTHWAIT
1861, 11, 14. Moses, Raisin, Lenawee Co.,
    Mich., s Aaron & Ann; m at Adrian, Sarah
    MOSHER, dt Thomas & Lucy, Raisin, Lenawee
    Co., Mich.
1862, 11, 27. Aaron d ae 71y 9m 19d
1884, 10, 16. S. Emlen, Lenawee Co., Mich., s
    Elwood & Elizabeth R., Lenawee Co., Mich.;
    m at Thomas G. Mead's, Olivia C. TENNANT,
    dt Alfred A. & Fannie L., Blisfield

1840, 6, 11. Aaron & w, Anna, & ch, Mary, El-
    wood, Elizabeth M., Jane, Jonathan J.,
    Aaron, Woolston & Moses, rocf Falls MM,
    Pa., dtd 1840,5,7
1842, 9, 8. Ann co
1843, 4, 13. Ann appointed to serve as clerk
    in place of Mary G. Stout who rq to be re-
    leased
1843, 8, 10. Joseph E. dis mou & mcd
1843, 9, 7. Ann appointed clerk
1843, 10, 12. Ann co
1843, 11, 9. Aaron co
1844, 9, 12. Ann appointed clerk
1844, 10, 10. Ann co
1844, 11, 7. Aaron co
1845, 10, 9. Ann co
1845, 10, 9. Ann appointed clerk
1845, 12, 11. Aaron co
1846, 10, 8. Ann appointed clerk
1846, 11, 12. Ann co
1846, 12, 10. Aaron co
1847, 12, 9. Aaron co
1848, 12, 14. Aaron co
1849, 12, 13. Aaron co
1849, 12, 13. Ann co
1851, 1, 9. Ann co
1852, 1, 8. Ann co
1853, 1, 13. Ann co
1854, 1, 12. Aaron co
1855, 1, 11. Aaron co
1856, 2, 7. Aaron co
1857, 2, 5. Aaron co
1858, 5, 13. Aaron co
1859, 5, 12. Aaron co
1859, 8, 11. Jonathan J. gct Gwyned MM, Pa.
1860, 6, 7. Aaron co

COMFORT, continued

1861, 6, 13. Aaron co
1862, 6, 12. Aaron co
1863, 1, 8. Elwood co
1863, 3, 12. Wolston gct Raisin MM, to m
1863, 6, 11. Elwood co
1864, 6, 9. Elwood co
1864, 7, 14. Martha V. rocf Raisin MM, dtd
        1864,6,8
1865, 6, 8. Ellwood co
1866, 6, 7. Elwood co
1866, 10, 11. Elwood appointed clerk
1867, 6, 13. Elwood co
1878, 11, 7. Elizabeth R. co

COMSTOCK

1764, 12, 31. Jared b Smithfield, Providence,
        R. I.
1768, 7, 27. Darius b in Smithfield, R. I.
1773, 7, 2. Susannah b Northbridge, Worces-
        ter, Mass.
1781, 8, 17. Sally b Adams, Berkshire Co.,
        Mass.
1782, 3, 20. Anna b Independence, Sussex Co.,
        N. J.
1794, 5, 27. Minerva (Jackson) b Palmyra, On-
        tario Co., N. Y.
1795, 10, 19. Milo b Palmyra, Ontario Co., N.Y.
1797, 9, 19. Peace b Cambridge, Washington
        Co., N. Y.
1799, 8, 23. Esther b Farmington, Ontario,
        N. Y.
1800, 3, 15. Sydney P. b Palmyra, Ontario Co.,
        N. Y.
1802, 2, 10. Nathan b Farmington, Ontario
        Co., N. Y.
1803, 12, 28. Mary Gray (Stout) b Palmyra,
        Wayne Co., N. Y.
1804, 1, 27. Roby b Palmyra, Ontario Co.,N.Y.
1805, 3, 21. Stephen B., s Nathan & Chloe, b
        Palmyra, N. Y.
1805, 5, 23. Samuel b Farmington, Ontario, N.
        Y.
1807, 2, 17. Anna b Farmington, Ontario Co.,
        N. Y.
1810, 11, 12. Mary (Brooks) b Palmyra, Ontario
        Co., N. Y.
1812, 3, 20. Angeline M. b Farmington, Ontario
        Co., N. Y.
1814, 5 16. Joseph Otis b Farmington, Ontario
        Co., N. Y.
1816, 1, 3. James M., s Nathan & Chloe, b
        Palmyra, N. Y.
1816, 7, 16. Edwin b Farmington, Ontario, N.Y.
1818, 9, 25. Joseph Elliot b Lockport, Niagara
        Co. N. Y.
1818, 11, 19. Isaac Hathaway b Farmington, On-
        tario, N. Y.
1820, 12, 11. Phebe b Lockport, Niagara Co.,
        N. Y.
1821, 2, 20. Phebe Bailey b Farmington, On-
        tario, N. Y.
1825, 2, 10. Phebe Ann b Lockporte, Niagara

Co., N. Y.
1825, 6, 25. Alma J. b Lockport, Niagara Co.,
        N. Y.
1826, 5, 2. Caroline b Farmington, Ontario
        Co., N. Y.
1829, 12, 11. Huldah Ann b Logan, Lenawee Co.,
        Mich.
1829, 4, 16. Darius b Logan, Lenawee Co.,
        Mich.
1831, 5, 3. Caleb O. b Logan, Lenawee Co.,
        Mich.
1833, 8, 24. Daniel J., s Nathan & Chloe, d
        in Monroe, Mich.
1834, 2, 14. Patience m Nathan POWER
1834, 9, 3. Jared, Logan, Lenawee Co., Mich.,
        d
1836, 1, 8. Edny b Rollin, Lenawee Co., Mich.
1839, 2, 13. Wm. J. b Raisin, Lenawee Co.,
        Mich.
1842, 11, 17. Elizabeth m Isaac STEER
1843, 3, 23. Milo, Raisin, Lenewee Co., Mich.,
        d
1845, 4, 27. Phebe Maria d
1845, 5, 16. Sidney, s Darius, Raisin, Lena-
        wee Co., Mich., d
1845, 6, 2. Darius, Raisin, Lenawee Co.,
        Mich., d
1848, 1, 11. Susannah, Raisin, Lenewee Co.,
        Mich., d
1852, 12, 18. Joseph H., s Jared & Catharine,
        Raisin, Lenawee Co., Mich., d ae 30y 7m 2d
1861, 9, 21. Nathan L., s Jared, Raisin, Lena-
        Wee Co., Mich, d
1862, 4, 13. Sally d ae 80y 8m 17d
1865, 7, 23. Jared d ae 72y 9m 6d
1866, 3, 23. Ann d ae 84y 2m 3d
1870, 2, 8. Rowene d ae 83y 4m 8d

----, --, --. Lydia rocf Butternuts MM held at
        Laurens, N. Y., dtd 1831,8,31
----, --, --. Jared & Susannah, & dt, Esther,
        rocf Hartland MM held at Lockport, dtd
        1833,4,30
----, --, --. Samuel rocf Hartland MM held at
        Lockport, dtd 1833,4,30
----, --, --. John T. & w, Rowena, & minor dt,
        Elizabeth, rocf Farmington MM, dtd 1834,5,
        22
----, --, --. Patience rocf Farmington MM, dtd
        1834,10,23
----, --, --. Jared & w, Catharine, & minor
        ch, Joseph H., Elisabeth, Abigail, Mary S.,
        Nathan F. & William W., rocf Hartland MM
        held at Elba, dtd 1835,11,19
1837, 5, 11. Darius appointed an elder
1838, 11, 8. James M. rocf Hartland MM, dtd
        1838,9,20
1838, 11, 8. Stephen B. rocf Hartland MM, dtd
        1838,9,20
1839, 10, 10. Anna P. & minor ch, Caroline A.
        & Huldah Ann, gct Farmington MM (w Nathan)
1840, 4, 9. Isaac dis military duty
1840, 9, 10. Roena C. co

COMSTOCK, continued
1840, 10, 8. Jared co
1841, 9, 9. Rowena B. co of Rollin Mtg
1842, 4, 7. Lydia rocf Butternuts MM
1842, 9, 8. Roena C. co
1843, 10, 12. Roene C. co
1844, 10, 10. Roene C. co
1844, 11, 7. John T. co
1845, 10, 9. Jared & w, Catherine, & minor ch,
    Abigail, Mary S., Nathan P., Albert V. &
    Charlotte F., gct Raisin MM
1845, 10, 9. Roena co
1845, 12, 11. John T. co
1846, 11, 12. Joseph O. dis neglecting attend-
    ance
1847, 5, 13. Phebe Ann Dean (form Comstock)
    dis mcd
1847, 8, 12. Rhoene com for disunity
1847, 12, 9. John T. co
1848, 3, 4. Almy Jane Enearl (form Comstock)
    dis
1849, 12, 13. Rowena C. co
1851, 1, 9. John T. co
1852, 6, 10. Jared & w, Catharine, & minor ch,
    Nathan, Albert V. & Charlotte F., rocf
    Raisin MM
1853, 1, 13. Aaron co
1853, 7, 14. Jared appointed an elder
1854, 1, 12. Jared co
1854, 4, 13. Catharine appointed an elder
1855, 1, 11. Jared co
1855, 8, 9. Zeno & w, Sally, rocf Scipio MM,
    dtd 1855,6,13
1856, 3, 13. Derius gct Winneshiek MM, Ia.
1856, 9, 11. Caleb dis mou
1858, 5, 13. Jared co
1859, 5, 12. Jared co
1860, 6, 7. Jared co
1861, 6, 13. Zeno co
1861, 8, 8. Perry J. resigned mbrp; enlisted
    in the U. S. Service
1861, 9, 12. Albert V. dis
1862, 6, 12. Zeno co
1863, 2, 5. Zeno appointed an elder
1863, 6, 11. Zeno co

CONE
1839, 9, 12. Alice dis mou

COOK
1846, 6, 11. Cynthia recrq

CORNELIUS
1879, 4, 10. Edward recrq
1879, 4, 10. Phebe A. recrq
1879, 5, 8. William H. & Cynthia T. recrq

CORNELL
----, --, --. Mary U., w Stephen, & minor s,
    Jacob, rocf Oswego MM held at Poughkeepsie,
    dtd 1834,3,19
1837, 10, 12. Job dis by Hartland MM
1838, 1, 11. Daniel & w, Anna, com by Collins

MM; living within limits of this mtg
1838, 4, 12. Daniel Jr. dis disunity
1839, 1, 10. Esther dis
1840, 5, 14. Cert for Daniel & w, Anna, & ch,
    Job, Asa, Daniel, Lydia, Phebe, Sarah,
    Benjamin, Stephen & Samuel, from Collins
    MM, not accepted; Job dis by Hartland MM;
    Daniel previously dis; Asa com for neglect-
    ing attendance; taking these things into
    consideration, the cert was returned with
    this information
1841, 3, 11. Daniel & w, Anna, & minor ch,
    Phebe, Sarah, Benjamin, Stephen B. & Sam-
    uel N., rocf Collins MM, dtd 1840,10,29
1843, 7, 13. Daniel dis
1844, 1, 11. Anna dis disunity
1844, 1, 11. Lydia Ann Craft (form Cornell)
    dis mou
1844, 1, 11. Phebe Parkerson (form Cornell)
    dis
1844, 1, 11. Sarah Parkerson (form Cornell)
    dis mou

CRAFT
1836, 12, 26. Orin b
1837, 3, 5. Job b
1842, 6, 15. John A., Raisin, Lenawe Co.,
    Mich., s Job & Ann; m at Ypsilanti, Es-
    ther M. GORTON, dt David & Hannah, Ypsil-
    anti, Wastenaw Co., Mich.

----, --, --. Eli rocf Little Eggharbour MM,
    N. J., dtd 1834,8,14
----, --, --. Job & w, Ann, & minor ch, John,
    Elizabeth, Samuel & Amy Ann, rocf Little
    Eggharbour MM, N. J., dtd 1834,8,14
----, --, --. Charlotte rocf Little Eggharbour
    MM, dtd 1836,11,10
1838, 9, 13. Job co
1839, 9, 12. Ann co
1840, 9, 10. Ann co
1844, 1, 11. Lydia Ann (form Cornell) dis mou

CRANE
1782, 8, 7. Charrity b Taunton, Mass.
1783, 3, 31. George b Northbridge, Mass.
1810, 11, 20. George L. b Palmyra, Wayne Co.,
    N. Y.
1812, 10, 29. Benjamin L. b Palmyra, Wayne Co.,
    N. Y.
1816, 12, 25. Calvin b Palmyra, Wayne Co.,N.Y.
1824, 2, 22. Clarissa P. b Palmyra, Wayne Co.,
    N. Y.
1837, 9, 29. Lucy b
1838, 7, 19. Benjamin L., Palmyra, Lenawe
    Co., Mich., s George & Charity; m in Ad-
    rian, Ann Eliza HOAG, dt Nathaniel P. &
    Isabel, Raisin, Lenawe Co., Mich.
1843, 4, 20. Deborah R. m Richard HARKNESS
1850, 3, 21. Amos R., Raisin, Lenawee Co.,
    Mich., s Elijah & Mary; m at Adrian, Jane
    GRANDY, dt Edmund & Dorcas, Raisin, Lena-
    wee Co., Mich.

CRANE, continued
1863, 6, 30. Mary d ae 77y 11m 24d
1864, 1, 30. Elijah d ae 73y 10m 17d
1870, 10, 30. Amos d ae 53y

----, --, --. George & w, Charity, & minor ch,
    Benjamin L., Calvin B. & Clarissa, rocf
    Farmington MM, dtd 1833,5,23
----, --, --. George Jr. rocf Farmington MM,
    dtd 1833,10,24
----, --, --. Leah rocf Farmington MM, dtd
    1835,10,22
1838, 4, 12. George appointed an elder
1838, 9, 13. George co
----, --, --. Mary, w Elijah, & minor ch, Wm.
    E., Deborah R. & Nathan S., rocf New York
    MM, dtd 1839,5,1
1839, 9, 12. George co
1839, 9, 12. Sarah retained mbrp
1840, 9, 10. Mary, w Elijah, & minor ch, Wil-
    liam E., Deborah R. & Nathan S., rocf New
    York MM, dtd 1839,5,1
1841, 9, 9. Amos R. rocf New York MM, dtd
    1840,5,1 (1839 in N. Y.)
1844, 11, 7. Mary appointed an elder
1845, 2, 6. William E. com by Adrian PM;
    complaint directed to New York MM as he
    resided within limits of that mtg
1845, 7, 10. Wm. E. rst by New York MM
1850, 3, 14. Nathan S. con mou
1851, 9, 11. Elijah rst
1856, 6, 12. Nathan dis neglecting attendance
1856, 9, 11. Amos R. & w, Jane D., & minor
    ch, Charles Henry & Dorcas Jane, gct Rol-
    lin MM
1864, 11, 10. Amos R. & w, Jane D., & minor
    ch, Charles Henry & Dorcas Jane, rocf
    Rollin MM, dtd 1864,10,15

CRAWFORD
----, --, --. Mary, w Ransom, rocf Farmington
    MM, dtd 1832,6,21

CROFT
1839, 9, 12. Job co

CURRIN
1857, 1, 8. Susannah (form West) dis

DAILY
1780, 3, 20. Elisabeth b Northbridge, Mass.

DARLINGTON
1836, 10, 20. Jesse, Rollin, Lenawe Co., Mich.,
    s Stephen & Rachel; m at Rollin, Susannah
    TALBOTT, dt John & Rachel, Rollin, Lenawe
    Co., Mich.   [d
1843, 1, 1. Jesse, Rollin, Lenewee Co.,Mich.,
1846, 11, 18. Israel, Woodstock, Lenawee Co.,
    Mich., s Stephen & Rachel, Luzerne, Fay-
    ette Co., Pa.; m in Woodstock, Anna Mc-
    DONALD, dt James & Jerusha, Smyrna, Chenan-
    go Co., N. Y.

----, --, --. Ann rocf Redstone MM, dtd 1836,
    3,2
----, --, --. Israel rocf Redstone MM, dtd
    1836,3,2
----, --, --. Jesse rocf Redstone MM, dtd
    1836,6,29
1841, 1, 14. Ann gct Redstone MM, Fayette
    Co., Pa.
1847, 3, 11. Susannah McDonald (form Darling-
    ton) con mcd
1847, 4, 8. Israel co
1847, 12, 9. Israel co

DEAN
1872, 3, 12. William, Raisin, Lenawee Co.,
    Mich. d ae 76y

----, --, --. Artemas rocf Farmington MM, dtd
    1845,5,22
1847, 4, 8. Artemas I. dis mcd
1847, 5, 13. Phebe Ann (form Comstock) dis
    mcd
1851, 3, 13. Cert rec for Abigail M. Dean
    from La Rae MM, dtd 1850,6,6, endorsed
    to Raisin MM, as she resided within the
    limits of that mtg
1864, 5, 12. William & w, Mary, rocf Farming-
    ton MM, N. Y., dtd 1864,4,28
1864, 11, 10. John rocf Farmington MM, dtd
    1864,9,22
1866, 11, 8. Wm. appointed an elder

DeCAW (or DECOU)
1840, 8, 13. Joseph rocf Chesterfield MM,
    N. J., dtd 1840,6,2

DENNIS
1845, 8, 14. Frances recrq
1846, 5, 14. Jacob dis mcd

DENSMORE
1837, 8, 10. Abial & w, Abigail, & ch, John
    W., Harriet F., Caroline T., Charles K.,
    Uriah H., Josiah F., Content K., Joshua
    D. & Moses F., rocf Sidney MM held at
    Fairfield, Maine, dtd 1837,5,18
1844, 2, 8. John W. con misconduct
1846, 3, 12. Content K. (form Densmore) dis
    mou & neglecting attendance
1849, 6, 7. Uriah H. dis disunity

DERBYSHIRE
1833, --, --. David S., Logan, Lenawee Co.,
    Mich., d
1833, --, --. Mary Jane d
1834, 9, 8. Isaac, Logan, Lenawee Co., Mich.
    d
1834, 12, 30. Lydia, Logan, Lenawee Co., Mich.
    d
1838, 8, 9. Zachariah com by Scipio MM
1843, 1, 12. Cynthia recrq
1844, 2, 8. Zechariah retained mbrp; Scipio

DERBYSHIRE, continued
   MM informed
1848, 5, 11. Rosanna Town (form Derbyshire)
   dis neglecting attendance & jas
----, --, --. Lydia S., w Isaac, & minor ch,
   David, Joseph, Rosanna, Aaron & Mary Jane,
   rocf Deruyter MM

DEWEY
1855, 2, 8. Mariah (form Smith) dis

DILLINGHAM
1838, 2, 1. Elizabeth b Raisin, Lenewee Co.,
   Mich.
1838, 12, 7. Elizabeth, Raisin, Lenawee Co.,
   Mich., d
1841, 2, 12. Joseph, Palmyra, Lenawe Co.,
   Mich., s Silvanus & Mary, dec; m at Macon,
   Amy R. COLLINS, dt James & Sophia, latter
   dec, Macon, Lenawe Co., Mich.
1856, 9, 17. Amy m Joseph BOWERMAN

----, --, --. Joseph & w, Elisabeth, & minor
   ch, Mary, Allen, Sarah, Meribah, Joseph W.
   & Philip, rocf Rochester MM held at Wheatland, dtd 1836,9,23
1850, 12, 12. Sarah Collier (or Collar) (form
   Dillingham) dis mou (Raisin MM notified)
1851, 8, 14. Amy & minor ch, James Albert &
   Elizabeth, rocf Raisin MM, dtd 1851,8,13
1857, 3, 12. Amy Bowerman, w Joseph, & minor
   dt, Elizabeth Dillingham, gct Raisin MM
1859, 8, 11. Allen rocf Raisin MM, dtd 1859,
   6,8

DOTY
1834, 7, 24. John Jay, Logan, Lenawe Co.,
   Mich., s John & Lydia; m at Logan, Amy
   LAING, dt Smith & Abby, Raisin, Lenawe
   Co., Mich.
1835, 4, 6. Amy, Logan, Lenawee Co., Mich.,d
1835, 8, 28. John S., Raisin, Lenawee Co.,
   Mich., d
1835, 11, 6. John, Raisin, Lenawee Co., Mich.,
   d
185-, 4, 5. John S. b Logan, Lenawee Co.,
   Mich.

----, --, --. John & w, Lydia, & minor ch,
   John Jay, David, Silas, Selinda, Sarah &
   Mary, rocf Farmington MM, dtd 1833,11,21
1837, 3, 9. Enos dis
1839, 1, 10. David dis neglecting attendance
1839, 1, 10. Silas dis neglecting attendance
1842, 3, 10. Sarah dis
1842, 8, 11. Celinda dis neglecting attendance
1842, 8, 11. Sarah dis neglecting attendance
1843, 1, 12. Lydia dis
1843, 2, 9. Lydia dis misconduct.
1846, 1, 8. Lydia rq rst; not granted 1846,
   6,11
1854, 4, 13. Mary dis

DUNN
1850, 7, 11. Lydia (form Marshall) dis mou

DYE
1863, 9, 10. Solomon [Die] rocf Rocksylvania
   MM, Ia., dtd 1863,8,20
1863, 10, 8. Solomon rqct Raisin MM, to m
1866, 2, 8. Solomon gct Raisin MM

EARL
1854, 8, 2. Mercy, Raisin, Lenawee Co.,
   Mich., d ae 85y

----, --, --. Mercy rocf Hartland MM, dtd
   1835,9,17

EDDY
----, --, --. Sarah rocf Hartland MM, dtd
   1835,9,17

ELDRID
1811, 4, 12. Phebe (form Hoag) b Starksborough, Addison Co., Vt.

1849, 1, 11. Phebe dis jas

ELLISON
----, --, --. Mary rocf Little Eggharbour MM,
   dtd 1839,4,11

ELMA
1842, 2, 19. Rachel, dt Jesse & Susanah, b
   Rollin, Lenawee Co., Mich.

EMERY
1881, 2, 10. Ida rq mbrp
1881, 2, 10. Jermain B. rq mbrp

ENEARL
1848, 3, 4. Almy Jane (form Comstock) dis

FANAK
1838, 7, 12. Thomas & w, Mary, & ch, John,
   Robert, Thomas, Jane, Ann & Hannah, rocf
   Scipio MM, dtd 1838,6,13

FARMER
----, --, --. Thomas & fam rocf Norwich MM,
   dtd 1834,9,10
1847, 1, 14. Thomas dis neglecting attendance
   & identifying himself with other profes-
   sors of religion

FARRAH
1839, 3, 26. Elizabeth b Raisin, Lenawee
   Co., Mich.
1839, 4, 12. Elizabeth, Raisin, Lenawee Co.,
   Mich., d

----, --, --. Thomas & w, Mary, & ch, John,
   Robert, Thomas, Jane, Ann & Hannah, rocf
   Scipio MM, dtd 1838,6,13
1841, 5, 13. Jane Patterson (form Farrah) con

FARRAH, continued
    mou

FERGUSON
1807, 11, 25. Cynthia W. b Palmyra, Ontario,
    N. Y.

FEWMAN
----, --, --. Mary W., w Chauncey, rocf Butter-
    nutts MM, N. Y., dtd 1834,7,2

FINCH
----, --, --. Rebecca, w Trip, & minor ch,
    Samuel R., Daniel W., Otis D., Reuben,
    Hannah & Eliza Ann, rocf Butternuts MM,
    dtd 1834,4,30
1840, 11, 12. Tripp rst; Butternuts MM noti-
    fied
1843, 4, 13. Tripp con misconduct
1844, 11, 7. Samuel con mou
1845, 4, 10. Trip dis misconduct

FORD
1799, 6, 30. Phebe b Plainfield, Mass.
----, --, --. Phebe rocf Farmington MM, dtd
    1833,6,27

FRASER
1845, 10, 9. Edy, w John, rocf Rochester MM,
    dtd 1844,8,23

FREEMAN
1881, 2, 10. Lewis rq mbrp

FRENCH
----, --, --. Terril & Hannah
    Ch: Elijah   b 1830, 2, 12
        Helen
1848, 12, 24. Hannah d ae about 45y

1839, 2, 7. John T. con misconduct
1840, 6, 11. Terril & w, Hannah, & ch, Eli-
    jah & Helen, rocf Hartland MM, dtd 1840,2,
    13

FULLER
----, --, --. Cyrus rocf Farmington MM, dtd
    1833,9,26
1858, 1, 13. Isabella (form Smith) dis

FURMAN
1836, 1, 15. Phebe W. b Ypsilanti, Washtenaw
    Co., Mich.

1839, 7, 11. Mary, w Chancy, rocf Butternuts
    MM, dtd 1839,5,1

GAGE
1837, 11, 9. Mary dis

GARDENER
1846, 8, 13. Diana dis neglecting attendance
    (com by Elba MM, N. Y.)

GIBBONS
1797, 3, 14. Joseph b Phila., Pa.
1807, 7, 4. Lydia H. b Palmyra, Wayne Co.,
    N. Y.
1842, 10, 8. Lydia H., Adrian, Lenewee Co.,
    Mich., d
1843, 11, 16. Joseph, Adrian, Lenawee Co.,
    Mich., s Joseph & Sarah, both dec; m
    at Adrian, Elizabeth P. HOAG, dt Jacob &
    Sarah, Raisin, Lenawee Co., Mich.
        Ch: Joseph H. b 1844, 8, 13 Raisin, Lena-
            wee Co., Mich.
1845, 6, 10. Elizabeth, dt Jacob & Sarah Hoag
    Lenawee Co., Mich., d
1851, 6, 13. Joseph, Raisin, Lenawee Co.,
    Mich., s Joseph & Sarah; m at Adrian,
    Phebe G. THORN, dt Webster & Ruth, Raisin,
    Lenawee Co., Mich.
1875, 8, 12. Phebe G. m Isaac THOMAS
----, --, --. Margaret, dt Thomas & Martha
    Taylor, Raisin, Lenawee Co., Mich., d

----, --, --. Joseph & w, Lydia H., rocf Short
    Creek MM, O., dtd 1832,10,23
1838, 9, 13. Joseph co
1839, 9, 12. Joseph co
1840, 10, 8. Joseph co
1841, 9, 9. Lydia H. appointed clerk
1842, 8, 11. Joseph appointed clerk
1842, 9, 8. Lydia H. appointed clerk
1843, 8, 10. Joseph appointed clerk
1844, 8, 8. Joseph appointed clerk
1845, 8, 14. Joseph appointed clerk
1846, 8, 13. Joseph gct Burlington MM, to m
    Margaret Taylor
1846, 8, 13. J. appointed clerk
----, --, --. Margaret, w Joseph, rocf MM in
    Burlington, N. J., dtd 1847,2,1
1847, 8, 12. Joseph appointed clerk
1847, 12, 9. Joseph co
1848, 8, 10. Joseph appointed clerk
1848, 10, 12. Margaret appointed clerk
1848, 12, 14. Joseph co
1849, 9, 13. Joseph appointed clerk
1849, 12, 13. Joseph co
1850, 9, 12. Joseph appointed clerk
1855, 4, 12. Joseph & w & minor s, Joseph H.,
    gct Red Cedar MM, Ia.
1862, 8, 14. Joseph & w, Phebe G., & minor s,
    Joseph H., rocf Winneshiek MM, Ia., dtd
    1862,5,31
1864, 10, 13. Joseph appointed clerk

GIDLEY
1867, 5, 9. Wm. appointed an elder
1867, 6, 13. Wm. co
1864, 6, 9. William & w, Sarah, & minor ch,
    Daniel D. & Royal G., rocf Alum Creek MM,
    O., dtd 1864,4,21
1880, 5, 13. William released from being an
    elder

GIFFORD
1838, 1, 11. Benoni, Cynthia, Eliza, Clarissa & Maria, minor ch Isaac, rocf Collins
MM, dtd 1837,3,30 (living with parents in
Batavia, Branch Co., Mich.)
1845, 7, 10. Rufus dis mou

GLAZIER
----, --, --. Robert B., Elizabeth C. & Mary,
ch Richard, rocf MM held in New York, dtd
1835,6,3

GLUN
1881, 2, 10. Frank B. rq mbrp

GORMAN
1839, 5, 9. Harriet F. con misconduct
1841, 5, 13. Harriet F. dis neglecting attendance

GORTON
1835, 10, 14. Richard, Ypsilanta, Washtenaw
Co., Mich., s David & Hannah; m at Adrian,
Martha HAVILAND, dt Charles & Esther, Raisin, Lenawee Co., Mich.
1836, 11, 6. Charles b
1838, 8, 20. Zilpha b Raisin, Lenawee Co.,
Mich.
1840, 2, 26. Richard, Raisin, Lenawee Co.,
Mich., d ae 33y 11m 4d
1840, 5, 6. Hannah, dt Richard, b Raisin,
Lenawee Co., Mich.
1841, 7, 14. Martha m Silas GRIPMAN
1842, 4, 13. Hannah E. m Jonathan WESTGATE
1842, 6, 15. Esther M. m John A. CRAFT

----, --, --. David & w, Hannah, & ch, Richard,
Polly, Olive, Edward, Abigail, Hannah &
Esther, rocf Butternuts MM held at Laurens,
dtd 1831,8,30
----, --, --. Job rocf Butternuts MM held at
Laurens, dtd 1831,8,31
1839, 9, 12. Eliza co
1839, 9, 12. Hannah co
1839, 9, 12. Job Jr. co
1840, 8, 13. Sarah, w Job, rocf Deruyter MM,
dtd 1840,7,29
1840, 9, 10. Eliza Ann co
1841, 9, 9. Ann Eliza co of Ypsilanti Mtg

GRANDY
1850, 3, 21. Jane m Amos R. CRANE
1856, 2, 2. Edmund, s Parke & Rheuhamah,
Raisin, Lenawee Co., Mich., d ae 73y 11m
2d
1858, 6, 21. Dorcas, Raisin, d ae 74y 9m 26d
1861, 9, 13. George, Adrian, Lenawee Co.,
Mich., s Edmund & Dorcas, both dec; m at
Adrian, Sarah L. HAVILAND, dt Daniel &
Phebe, latter dec, Raisin, Lenawee Co.,
Mich.
1863, 8, 6. Joseph, s Edmund & Dorcas, Raisin, Lenawee Co., Mich., d ae 31y 1m 12d

1867, 4, 27. Sarah L., dt Daniel & Phebe,
Raisin, Lenawee Co., Mich., d ae 24y 9m 2d

1848, 8, 10. Anna, George & Francis, minors,
rocf Farmington MM, dtd 1848,5,25
1848, 8, 10. Edmund & w, Dorcas, & minor ch,
Enos, Jane & Joseph, rocf Farmington MM,
dtd 1848,5,25
1848, 8, 10. Anna rocf Farmington MM
1850, 5, 31. Benjamin & minor s, James, gct
New Hartford MM
1850, 8, 8. Benjamin & minor s, James, rocf
New Hartford MM, dtd 1850,5,21, endorsed
by Raisin MM, 1850,8,7
1852, 7, 8. Benjamin & minor s, James, gct
Raisin MM
1853, 2, 10. Complaint rec for Francis M. for
mcd forwarded to Raisin MM as he resided
within limits of that mtg
1856, 6, 12. Enos con mou
1859, 10, 13. Cert rec for William returned
to New Hartford MM, N. Y. with information
he mcd; con mce 1860,1,12
1864, 11, 10. Enos gct South River MM, Ia.

GRAY
1842, 2, 10. Lucy Ann (form Collins) con mou

GREEN
1843, 1, 12. Elizabeth (form Hathaway) con
mcd
1879, 2, 6. Wm. K. recrq
1879, 3, 13. Edna recrq
1879, 5, 8. Alice C. recrq
1879, 5, 8. Jane M. recrq
1879, 5, 8. Jonathan H. recrq

GRIFFIN
----, --, --. Stephen & w, Rachel, & minor ch,
Daniel A., Stephen W., Joel T., Charles H.
& Abigail R., rocf Butter Nutts MM, dtd
1834,5,28
1839, 9, 12. Stephen co
1842, 7, 14. Joel T. rpd mou

GRIFFITH
1837, 7, 13. Elisabeth rocf Smithfield MM, O.,
dtd 1837,4,17
1842, 7, 14. Elizabeth (form Griffith) dis
mcd

GRIPMAN
1841, 7, 14. Silas, Raisin, Lenawe Co., Mich.
s Uriah & Phebe; m at Raisin, Martha GOR-
TON, dt Charles & Esther, Raisin, Lenawe
Co., Mich.

1840, 10, 8. Phebe Jr. rocf Leray MM, dtd
1839,12,5
1840, 10, 8. Silas rocf Leray MM, dtd 1839,
12,5
1840, 10, 8. Uriah & w, Phebe, rocf LeRay
MM, dtd 1840,8,6

GRISCOM
----, --, --. Edward rocf Hudson MM, dtd 1836,
    2,24
1843, 5, 11. Edward dis neglecting attendance

GRISEL
1851, 6, 12. Ansel Rogers & w, Cynthia, & min-
    or dt, Lydia Ann Grisel, rocf Alum Creek
    MM, O., dtd 1851,4,24

GUFFIN
1838, 9, 13. Stephen co

HAIGHT
1838, 1, 11. David H., Phebe, Levi, Hannah,
    Huldah & Lydia, ch Reuben & Keziah, rocf
    Collins MM, dtd 1837,1,26

HALLOCK
----, --, --. Lucy & minor ch, Aaron L.,
    Powell C. & Martha M., rocf Collins MM,
    dtd 1832,11,1
----, --, --. Mary M., Hannah J., Daniel P.,
    Monzo, Catherine & Jared C., minor ch
    Powell & Hannah, rocf Collins MM, dtd
    1832,11,1
1838, 1, 11. Aaron L., Powel C., Denajah &
    Martha M., ch Abel & Lucy, rocf Collins
    MM, dtd 1837,3,30

HAMILTON
----, --, --. Esther rocf Little Eggharbour
    MM, dtd 1834,8,14

HANSEN
1879, 11, 3. William recrq

HARKNESS
1834, 9, 25. David Jr., Logan, Lenawe Co.,
    Mich., s David & Ruth, dec; m at Logan,
    Sarah Maria LAING, dt Smith & Abby, Rai-
    sin, Lenawe Co., Mich.
1835, 10, 1. Ruth Amy b Raisin, Lenawee Co.,
    Mich.
1836, 4, 11. Ruth Amy, Palmyra, Lenawee Co.,
    Mich., d
1837, 1, 19. Gideon, Logan, Lenawe Co., Mich.,
    s David & Ruth, latter dec; m at Logan,
    Elizabeth UNDERWOOD, dt John & Catharine,
    Logan, Lenawe Co., Mich.
1838, 9, 29. David Smith, s D. A. Jr., b Rai-
    sin, Lenawee Co., Mich.
1840, 3, 19. Mary C. m George W. CARPENTER.
1840, 5, 12. John, s Gideon & Elizabeth, b
    Raisin, Lenawee Co., Mich.
1841, 3, 20. Abigail, dt David & Sarah Maria,
    b Raisin, Lenawee Co., Mich.
1842, 5, 12. Abbey Jane, Raisin, Lenewee
    Co., Mich., d
1843, 4, 20. Richard, Adrian, Lenawe Co.,
    Mich., s David & Mary; m at Adrian, Debo-
    rah R. CRANE, dt Elijah & Mary, Raisin,
    Lenawe Co., Mich.

1844, 4, 5. Charles, s G. & Elizabeth, b
    Mich.
1844, 4, 24. Mary C., dt Richard, b Adrian,
    Lenawee Co., Mich.
1845, 2, 25. David, s Adam & Thankful, Adrian
    Lenawee Co., Mich., d ae 65y 7m 19d
1845, 10, 22. Phebe, dt Richard & Deborah, b
    Adrian, Lenawee Co., Mich.
1847, 4, 14. John b
1848, 6, 15. Sarah, dt Richard & Deborah,
    Adrian, Lenawee Co., Mich., d ae 10m 17d
1850, 11, 28. Mary, Raisin, Lenawee Co., Mich.
    d ae 65y
1851, 1, 9. Mary's d rpd
1858, 2, 3. Sarah R., dt Richard & Deborah,
    Raisin, Lenawee Co., Mich., d ae 7y 9m 26d
1858, 2, 21. Deborah, dt Richard & Deborah,
    Raisin, Lenawee Co., Mich., d ae 8y 9m 26d
1864, 10, 9. Phebe, dt Richard & Deborah, [12d
    Raisin, Lenawee Co., Mich., d ae 18y 11m
1864, 10, 15. William, s Richard & Deborah,
    Raisin, Lenawee Co., Mich., d ae 18y 9m
    15d
1865, 8, 17. Mary C. m Vincent Wood
1879, 10, 20. David, Adrian, Lenawee Co.,
    Mich., s Richard & Deborah; m at Adrian,
    Flora E. MURPHY, Adrian, dt Caleb & Miran-
    da

----, --, --. David Jr. rocf Farmington MM,
    dtd 1833,11,21
----, --, --. Gideon rocf Peru MM, dtd 1834,
    4,25
----, --, --. David & w, Mary, & minor ch,
    William, Richard, Mary & Daniel W., rocf
    Peru MM, dtd 1835,2,18
1839, 8, 8. Mary appointed an elder
1846, 5, 14. Gideon dis neglecting attendance
1846, 6, 11. Wm. dis mou
1846, 10, 8. Daniel W. dis mou
1847, 11, 11. Mary co
1848, 12, 14. Mary co
1849, 11, 8. Deborah R. appointed clerk
1849, 12, 13. Mary co
1851, 1, 9. Richard co
1851, 9, 11. Richard appointed clerk
1853, 1, 13. Deborah R. co
1853, 9, 8. Richard appointed clerk
1855, 9, 13. Richard appointed clerk
1856, 8, 14. Sarah Maria Harris (form Hark-
    ness) dis
1856, 9, 11. Richard appointed clerk
1857, 9, 15. Richard appointed clerk
1858, 6, 10. Gideon con misconduct; rst at
    Rollin MM
1858, 10, 14. Richard appointed clerk
1859, 4, 7. Deborah R. appointed an elder
1859, 4, 7. Richard recommended a minister
1859, 10, 13. Richard appointed clerk
1860, 10, 11. Richard appointed clerk
1861, 10, 10. Amy (form Aldrich) dis
1861, 10, 10. Richard appointed clerk
1862, 10, 9. Richard appointed clerk

HARKNESS, continued
1863, 10, 8. Richard appointed clerk
----, --, --. Stephen & minor dt, Eva, rocf
    Elba MM, dtd 1869,7,13
1878, 11, 7. Deborah R. co

HARNED
----, --, --. Jonathan & minor ch, Edward,
    John & Nathan, rocf Norwich MM, dtd 1834,
    11,12

HARRIS
1856, 8, 14. Sarah Maria (form Harkness) dis

HARVEY
----, --, --. Polly rocf Farmington MM, dtd
    1833,9,26
----, --, --. Nancy, w Barzilla, rocf Farming-
    ton MM, dtd 1835,6,25
1839, 9, 12. Polly co
1840, 9, 10. Polly co
1841, 9, 9. Polly co of Palmyra Mtg

HASTINGS
1881, 2, 10. Charles R. rq mbrp

HATFIELD
1848, 9, 7. Stephen rocf Farmington MM, dtd
    1848,7,27, endorsed by Raisin MM 1848,9,6
1848, 11, 9. Stephen gct Farmington MM, N. Y.

HATHAWAY
----, --, --. James & w, Dorothy, & minor ch,
    Charity G., Elisabeth Ann & Orvel Payne
    Hathaway, rocf East Hoosick MM, dtd 1835,
    4,29
1840, 5, 14. Jane Willets (form Hathaway)
    dis mou
1841, 4, 8. Sylvester R. & minor ch, William,
    Isaac N., Alonzo H., Albert T., Phebe E.
    & Julia S., rocf Hartland MM, dtd 1841,3,
    18
1841, 7, 8. James com by Rollin PM for ne-
    glecting attendance
1843, 1, 12. Charity Sloan (form Hathaway)
    con mcd
1843, 1, 12. Elizabeth Green (form Hathaway)
    con mcd
1843, 4, 13. Richmond & Phebe B. & minor ch,
    Isaac N., Samuel B., William P. & Alfred
    R., rocf Farmington MM, dtd 1843,2,23
1849, 8, 9. Richmond & w, Phebe B., & minor
    ch, Isaac N., Samuel B., William P. & Al-
    fred R., gct Greenwich MM

HAVENS
1850, 7, 11. Lucy (form Marshall) dis mou

HAVILAND
1775, 9, 28. Esther b Ninepartner, Dutchess
    Co., N. Y.
1777, 9, 26. Charles b Fairfield, Fairfield
    Co., Conn.

1795, 7, 20. Susannah b Galway, Saratoga, N.Y.
1788, 12, 5. Alice b Pittstown, Ransalear
    Co., N. Y.
1796, 4, 7. James b Broadalben, Saratoga,
    N. Y.
1800, 12, 5. Charles b Hoosic, Ransalar Co.,
    N. Y.
1805, 12, 26. Isaac b Providence, Saratoga
    Co., N. Y.
1807, 9, 4. Wing b Providence, Saratoga
    Co., N. Y.
1808, 12, 20. Laura b Hitley, Leeds Co., Upper
    Canada
1811, 5, 30. Martha b
1812, 7, 28. Minerva b Providence, Saratoga
    Co., N. Y.
1813, 3, 26. Peleg C. b Providence, Saratoga
    Co., N. Y.
1814, 3, 16. Daniel b Providence, Saratoga
    Co., N. Y.
1815, 3, 8. Abigail b Providence, N. Y.
----, --, --. Ingerson (or Ingersoll) b 1785,
    8,11 Oblong, N. Y.; m Alice ----- b 1785,
    12,5 Pittstown, N. Y.
    Ch: Alice   b 1817, 9, 26 Providence,
          Saratoga Co., N. Y.
        Esther   b 1819, 7, 11
          Saratoga Co., N. Y.
        Deborah   b 1821, 3, 15 d 1824, 8,27
        Sarah D. " 1824, 11, 25
1817, 2, 15. Martha b Providence, Saratoga
    Co., N. Y.
1817, 9, 26. Alice b Providence, Saratoga
    Co., N. Y.
1819, 7, 11. Esther b Providence, Saratoga
    Co., N. Y.
----, --, --. Samuel, s Charles & Esther, b
    1798,11,17, Hoosack, Renssalaer Co., N.Y.;
    m Phebe ----- b 1802,3,25 Providence,
    Saratoga Co., N. Y.
    Ch: Isaac   b 1824, 6, 1 d 1826, 2,16
        Anna   " 1829,12, 5
        Leonard   " 1832, 1,11

1821, 4, 7. John W., s James & Susannah,
    b Royalton, Niagara Co., N. Y.
1822, 11, 14. Seneca b Royalton, Niagara Co.,
    N. Y.
1824, 11, 10. Philo, s James & Susannah, b
1824, 10, 6. Philo D. b Royalton, Niagara Co.,
    N. Y.
1826, 8, 20. Harvey S. b Royalton, Niagara
    Co., N. Y.
1826, 9, 30. Ira b Royalton, Niagara Co., N.Y.
1826, 12, 9. James Jun. b Royalton, Niagara
    Co., N. Y.
1828, 2, 5. Daniel S. b Royalton, Niagara
    Co., N. Y.
1828, 11, 5. Mary Ann b Royalton, Niagara
    Co., N. Y.
1829, 12, 5. Anna b Royalton, Niagara Co.,

HAVILAND, continued
    N. Y.
1830, 2, 3. Jane, dt Isaac & Minerva, d ae ly
    lm 14d
1830, 7, 6. Esther M. b Logan, Lenawee Co.,
    Mich.
1830, 7, 17. Zilpha Ann, dt Isaac & Minerva,
    b
1831, 1, 15. Jared C., s James & Susannah,
    b Royalton, Niagara Co., N. Y.
1831, 7, 15. Zilphana b Royalton, Niagara Co.,
    N. Y.
1832, 3, 13. Julia, dt Isaac & Minerva, b
    Royalton, Niagara Co., N. Y.
1832, 8, 14. Anna Chase b Logan, Lenawee Co.,
    Mich.
1832, 12, 28. Susanna C. b Royalton, Niagara
    Co., N. Y.
1834, 4, 15. Eli b Raisin, Lenawee Co., Mich.
1834, 8, 16. Ingersol, Raisin, Lenawee Co.,
    Mich., d
1834, 10, 16. Daniel, Raisin, Lenawe Co., Mich.,
    s Charles & Esther; m at Logan, Phebe
    Smith, dt Daniel & Asenath, Logan, Lenawe
    Co., Mich.
1835, 3, 23. Joseph B. b Raisin, Lenawee Co.,
    Mich.
1835, 10, 9. Nelson b
1835, 10, 14. Abigail m Stephen H. ALDRICH
1835, 10, 14. Martha m Richard GORTON
1836, 2, 1. Edith Maria b Raisin, Lenawee
    Co., Mich.
1837, 4, 17. Artemas C. b
1837, 5, 4. Laura Jane b
1837, 10, 19. Julina b Raisin, Lenawee Co.,
    Mich.
1837, 12, 19. Julia b Raisin, Lenewee Co.,
    Mich.
1839, 2, 16. Eunice S. b Raisin, Lenawee Co.,
    Mich.
1841, 1, 14. Chancy, s Isaac & Minerva, b
    Raisin, Lenawee Co., Mich.
1840, 1, 10. Esther, Raisin, Lenawee Co.,
    Mich., d ae 64y 3m 12d
1840, 5, 14. Memorial for Esther; b 28th of
    9th Mo 1775; dt Samuel & Alice Mosher; w
    Charles Haviland; d 10th of 1st Mo 1840
    ae 65y
1840, 5, 23. Mary b Raisin, Lenawee Co., Mich.
1840, 11, 18. John W., Raisin, Lenawee Co.,
    Mich., s James & Susannah; m at Raisin,
    Margaret BOWERMAN, dt Joshua & Abigail,
    Raisin, Lenawee Co., Mich.
1841, 5, 14. Charles, Raisin, Lenawe Co.,
    Mich., s James & Martha, both dec; m at
    Raisin, Sarah L. POWER, dt William Lawton
    & Abigail, Farmington, Oakland Co., Mich.
1842, 6, 15. Eli C., Raisin, Lenawe Co.,
    Mich., s John & Naomi, former dec; m at
    Raisin, Vicena POWER, dt Thomas Hawly &
    Elizabeth, his w, Seneca, Lenawe Co., Mich.
1845, 10, 16. Seneca, Raisin, Lenawe Co.,
    Mich., s James & Susannah; m at Adrian,

Mary S. HOAG, dt Jacob & Sarah, former
dec, Raisin, Lenawe Co., Mich.
1846, 1, 20. Eliza Jane b
1846, 2, 20. Eliza Jane, dt Seneca & Mary,
    b Raisin, Lenawee Co., Mich.
1861, 9, 13. Sarah L. m George GRANDY
1871, 3, 15. Daniel M., Raisin, Lenawee Co.,
    Mich., s Daniel & Lucinda B., Raisin,
    Lenawee Co., Mich.; m at house of James
    Birdsall, Harriet M. BIRDSELL, dt Daniel
    & Maria D., form dec, Adrian, Lenawee Co.,
    Mich.

----, --, --. Isaac & Minerva & minor ch,
    Zilpha Ann & Julia, rocf Hartland MM, held
    at Lockport, dtd 1832,5,1
----, --, --. Samuel & Phebe & minor ch, Ira,
    Anna & Leonard, rocf Hartland MM held at
    Lockport, dtd 1832,5,1
----, --, --. Abigail rocf Hartland MM, dtd
    1833,4,24
----, --, --. Charles & w, Esther, & ch,
    Daniel & Martha, rocf Hartland MM held at
    Lockport, dtd 1833,4,30
----, --, --. James & w, Susannah, & minor ch,
    John W., Seneca, Philo D., James, Mary
    Ann, Jared C. & Susannah C., rocf Hart-
    land MM held at Lockport, dtd 1833,4,30
----, --, --. Martha rocf Farmington MM, dtd
    1833,6,25
----, --, --. Asineth rocf Farmington MM, dtd
    1834,1,9
----, --, --. Ingersoll & w, Alice, & minor ch,
    Alice & Esther, rocf Hartland MM, dtd
    1834,4,24
----, --, --. Martha rocf Hartland, N. Y., dtd
    1834,4,24
----, --, --. Peleg C. rocf Hartland MM, dtd
    1834,4,24
----, --, --. Eli rocf Le Ray MM, dtd 1835,6,
    11
----, --, --. Naomy, w John, & minor ch, Ira,
    Naomi, Charles & Daniel, rocf Le Ray MM
    held at Indian River, dtd 1835,7,9
1838, 9, 13. Charles Jr. co
1838, 6, 7. Wing rocf Hartland MM, dtd 1838,
    3,15
1839, 5, 9. Laura dis
1839, 6, 13. Charles dis attending mtg held
    contrary to discipline
1840, 5, 14. Daniel dis neglecting attend-
    ance & attending mtg set up contrary to
    the good order of the society
1841, 6, 10. Charles I. dis mou
1841, 9, 9. Sarah co of Raisin Mtg
1841, 12, 9. Daniel con misconduct
1842, 2, 10. Ira dis disunity
1842, 6, 9. Daniel C. dis neglecting attend-
    ance
1845, 10, 9. Seneca prcf Raisin MM, dtd 1845,
    10,8, to m
1846, 6, 11. Mary S. dis
1846, 6, 11. Seneca dis

HAVILAND, continued
1847, 7, 8. Harvey dis mcd
1847, 8, 12. Huldah (form West or Test) dis
    mcd
1847, 12, 9. Esther Cambron (form Haviland)
    dis
1848, 5, 11. Mary S. rst
1850, 2, 7. Daniel S. dis jas
1851, 2, 6. Anne C. dis neglecting attendance
1851, 12, 11. Susan C. (form Haviland) con mou
    (Raisin MM informed)
1860, 8, 9. Daniel & w, Lucinda B., & minor
    ch, Sarah L., Phebe L., Daniel M., Lucy
    Jane, Lindley, Edgar & Edna, rocf Raisin
    MM held at Palmyra, dtd 1860,7,11
1861, 6, 13. Joseph B. dis
1862, 11, 13. Seneca recrq

HAWKINS
1847, 3, 24. James William, s John R. & Han-
    nah, b Rollin, Lenawee Co., Mich.

1843, 7, 13. John R. recrq
1843, 10, 12. Hannah T. rst
1845, 8, 14. Mary Ann, Rose Ann & John H.,
    recrq of parents, John R. & Hannah T.

HAWLY
1842, 6, 15. Eli C. Haviland, Raisin, Lenawe
    Co., Mich., s John & Naomi, form dec; m at
    Raisin, Vicena POWER, dt Thomas HAWLY &
    Elizabeth, his w, Seneca, Lenawe Co., Mich.

HAYNES
1836, 8, 7. Dorcas m Jeremiah WESTGATE

1834, 6, 19. Dorcas gct Hartland MM, N. Y.
1881, 2, 10. Morris [Haines] rq mbrp

HAYWARD
----, --, --. Roswell rocf Farmington MM, dtd
    1834,10,23
----, --, --. Elisabeth & ch, Roseann, Judith
    W., Stephen W. & Micajah, rocf Farmington
    MM, dtd 1834,10,23

HENLY
1876, 10, 18. William P., Carthage, Rush Co.,
    Ind., s Henry & Ruth, Carthage, Rush Co.,
    Ind.; m at Adrian, Ida STEER, dt Benjamin
    W. & Emily H., Adrian, Mich.

1877, 1, 11. Ida S. gct Carthage MM, Ind.

HEWITT
1844, 10, 16. Joseph, Woodstock, Lenawee Co.,
    Mich., s Abel & Rachel, dec; m at Wood-
    stock, Margaret LUPTON, dt Gideon & Su-
    sanna, Woodstock, Lenawee Co., Mich.
1846, 6, 27. Susannah L., dt Joseph D. &
    Margaret, b Woodstock, Lenawee Co., Mich.
1847, 10, 2. Susannah L., dt Joseph D. & Mar-
    garet K., Woodstock, Lenawee Co., Mich.,

d ae ly 3m 5d

1838, 4, 12. Martha rocf Providence MM, dtd
    1837,11,2
1844, 2, 8. Joseph rst

HIGHT
1838, 4, 12. Phebe (form Hight) dis

HILL
1854, 6, 8. Minerva (form Howel) dis

HITCHCOCK
1849, 4, 12. Jane (form West) dis mou & mcd

HOAG
1787, 3, 30. Lodema b Warrensburgh, N. Y.
1789, 5, 1. Isabella b Rochester, Stafford
    Co., N. H.
1791, 8, 12. Nathaniel P. b Clinton, Dutchess
    Co., N. Y.
1793, 8, 7. Susanna b Orange, Hampshire Co.,
    Mass.
1796, 4, 3. Hazael b Starksboro, Addison
    Co., Vt.
1797, 4, 19. Israel b Chatham, Columbia Co.,
    N. Y.
1799, 3, 5. Sarah b Mendon, Morris Co.,
    N. J.
1799, 8, 8. Jacob b Green Co., N. Y.
1802, 4, 27. Sarah b Peru, Clinton Co., N.Y.
1805, 5, 17. Amos b Starksborough, Addison
    Co., Vt.
1807, 5, 31. John b Starksboro, Addison Co.,
    Vt.
1809, 3, 2. Chalkley b Starksboro, Addison
    Co., Vt.
1810, 1, 4. Susan b Richmond, N. H.
1812, 3, 22. Jesse b Ontario, Ontario Co.,
    N. Y.
1816, 6, 12. Mary b Palmyra, Ontario Co.,
    N. Y.
----, --, --. Jackson b 1796,9,13; m Phebe
    ----- b 1796,2,15
    Ch: Anna   b 1819, 3, 25
        Anna   " 1825, 2, 10
        Hannah   " 1825, 2, 10
        Lorenzo
        Abel T.
        George   " 1830, 4, 30
1818, 12, 29. Ann Eliza b Peru, Clinton Co.,
    N. Y.
1820, 6, 30. William b Palmyra, Ontario Co.,
    N. Y.
1822, 2, 5. Elisabeth (Gibbons) b Elba,
    Genesse Co., N. Y.
1823, 3, 18. Persis b Williston, Chittenden
    Co., Vt.
1823, 9, 22. Jonathan b Peru, Clinton Co.,
    N. Y.
1825, 6, 3. Mary S. b Elba, Genesse Co.,
    N. Y.
1825, 11, 1. Martha Ann b Macedon, Wayne Co.,

HOAG, continued
   N. Y.

1825, 12, 8.   Emily b Starksborough, Addison Co., Vt.

1826, 1, 22.   John Milton b Peru, Clinton Co., N. Y.

1827, 12, 12.   Lodema b Macedon, Wayne Co., N.Y.

1827, 12, 14.   Sarah Jane b Peru, Clinton Co., N. Y.

1828, 1, 1.   Jacob S. b Elba, Genesse Co., N. Y.

1829, 8, 13.   Dorcas b Peru, Clinton Co., N.Y.

1831, 10, 21.   Amos, Farmington, Oakland Co., Mich., s Elisha, dec, & Dorcas; m at Adrian Emeline POWER, dt Ezekiel WEBB & w, Fanny, Farmington, Oakland Co., Mich.

1832, 8, 14.   Parley Ann b Logan, Lenawee Co., Mich.

1832, 10, 22.   Parley, Logan, Lenawee Co., Mich. d

1833, 2, 17.   Elihu b Tecumseh, Lenawee Co., Mich.

1833, 7, 20.   Elisabeth b Richland, Kalamazoo Co., Mich.

1834, 5, 7.   Catharine b Richland, Kalamazoo Co., Mich.

1834, 11, 3.   Emeline A. b

1835, 7, 15.   Lodema m Amos WOOSTER

1836, 4, 11.   Catharine b

1836, 8, 4.   Caroline b

1836, 9, 9.   Sarah Jane b Raisin, Lenewee Co., Mich.

1837, 8, 3.   Ann b Rollin, Lenawee Co., Mich.

1838, 6, 25.   John Gurney, s John & Susan, b Raisin, Lenawee Co., Mich.

1838, 7, 19.   Ann Eliza m Benjamin L. CRANE

1838, 12, 7.   Emeline, Raisin, Lenawee Co., Mich., d

1839, 10, 11.   Addison C. b Adrian, Lenawee Co., Mich.

1839, 12, 13.   Amy Ann b Raisin, Lenewee Co., Mich.

1841, 1, 10.   Cornelia Jane, dt Amos & Emeline, b Adrian, Lenawee Co., Mich.

1841, 3, 1.   Edward, s John & Susan, b Raisin, Lenawee Co., Mich.

1841, 4, 7.   John Gurney, Raisin, Lenawee Co., Mich., d

1842, 9, 28.   Emaline Amelia, dt Amos & Emaline, b Adrian, Lenawee Co., Mich.

1843, 1, 26.   Emeline Amelia, Adrian, Lenewee Co., Mich.

1843, 11, 16.   Elizabeth P. m Joseph GIBBONS

1844, 10, 9.   Amos Edgar, s Amos & Emeline, d

1845, 3, 5.   Nathaniel P., Raisin, Lenawee Co., Mich., d ae 52y 6m 23d

1845, 5, 15.   Stephen Z., Raisin, Lenawe Co., Mich., s Stephen & Mary, form dec; m at Adrian, Hannah LAING, dt Smith & Abbey, Raisin, Lenawe Co., Mich.

1845, 5, 16.   Jacob, Raisin, Lenawee Co., Mich., d

1845, 10, 16.   Mary S. m Seneca HAVILAND

1845, 11, 25.   Edwin Amos, s Amos & Emaline, b Adrian, Lenawee Co., Mich.

1846, 6, 10.   Ellen Maria, dt Stephen & Hannah b

1847, 4, 9.   Jacob Smitt, Rome, Lenawee Co., Mich., d

1848, 4, 19.   Mahlon, s Amos & Emeline, Adrian Lennawee Co., Mich., d ae 3m 6d

1848, 7, 20.   Sarah m Nathan CHASE

1848, 11, 16.   Emily m Benjamin W. sTEER

1849, 9, 20.   Sarah Jane m Greenberry P. STEER

1850, 6, 10.   Charlotte V., dt Amos & Emeline, Adrian, Lenawee Co., Mich., d ae 2m 10d

1852, 3, 28.   Mary M., dt Thomas & Hannah Mosher, Raisin, Lenawee Co., Mich., d ae 60y

1852, 11, 17.   Israel, Palmyra, Lenawee Co., Mich., s Jacob & Elizabeth, the latter dec; m at Tecumseh, Rachel COLLINS, dt James & Sophia, the latter dec, Macon, Lenawee Co., Mich.

1858, 6, 17.   Sarah Jane m Enoch D. STRONG

1859, 3, 27.   Isabel d ae 69y 9m 26d

1861, 1, 17.   Elizabeth m Isaac H. MOSHER

1862, 10, 10.   Caroline A. m Hezekiah CLARK

----, --, --.   Israel & w, Susanna, & adopted ch, Jacob & Mary P. Aldrich, rocf Farmington MM, N. Y., dtd 1831,9,22

----, --, --.   Hazael & w, Sarah, & ch, Persis, Emily & Darius, rocf Peru MM, dtd 1831,10,26

----, --, --.   Amos rocf Starksborough MM, Addison Co., Vt., dtd 1831,11,4

----, --, --.   William & w, Hannah, & ch, Percilla, Paulina & Chilian W., rocf Peru MM, dtd 1831,12,21

----, --, --.   Chalkley rocf Starksborough MM held at Lincoln, Vt., dtd 1832,1,6

----, --, --.   John & w, Susan, rocf Starksborough MM, Starksborough, Vt., dtd 1832,5,4

----, --, --.   Phebe rocf Starksboro MM, Vt., dtd 1832,5,4 (1830,9,-- left Starksboro to reside in Arcadia, Kalamazoo Co., Mich.)

----, --, --.   Nathaniel P. & w, Isabella, & ch, Ann Eliza, Jonathan, John Milton & Sarah Jane, rocf Peru MM, dtd 1832,8,22

----, --, --.   Martin W. rocf Farmington MM, dtd 1833,4,25

----, --, --.   David Baker & w, Betsey, & minor ch, Mary A., John S., Sarah H., Isaac S., David S., Esther O. & Betsy's minor s, Stephen Hoag, rocf Farmington MM, dtd 1833,5,24

----, --, --.   Jesse rocf Farmington MM, dtd 1833,6,27

----, --, --.   Lodema & minor ch, Mary, Elizabeth M., William, Martha Ann & Lodema S., rocf Farmington MM, dtd 1833,6,27

----, --, --.   Jackson & w, Phebe, & minor ch, Anna, Lorenzo, Hannah, Abel T. & George, rocf Hartland MM, dtd 1834,5,15

HOAG, continued

1838, 1, 11. William dis

1839, 1, 10. William dis neglecting attendance

1839, 2, 7. Socrates, George, Charles, Lydia Ann, Abigail & John Milton, minor ch Joseph Hoag, 2d, rocf Ferrisburg MM, dtd 1838,11,28

1839, 3, 14. Stephen dis neglecting attendance

1839, 9, 12. Israel co

1839, 9, 12. Susanna co

1840, 9, 10. Sarah co

1840, 9, 10. Susanna co

1840, 10, 8. Israel co

1841, 9, 9. Mary M. & minor s, Stephen Z., rocf Hartland MM, dtd 1841,7,15

1841, 9, 9. Sarah co of Adrian Mtg

1841, 9, 9. Susanna co of Raisin Mtg

1842, 2, 10. Joseph 2nd dis mcd; Ferrisburg MM, Monkton, Vermont, notified

1842, 9, 8. Sarah co

1842, 10, 13. George dis military service & joining Methodists

1842, 12, 8. Hannah Millet (form Hoag) dis mou

1843, 10, 12. Sarah co

1844, 10, 10. Sarah co

1844, 12, 12. Jonathan dis neglecting attendance

1845, 6, 12. Jesse con misconduct; clerk directed to forward information to Raisin MM where he resided; rst at Raisin MM 1845,12,11

1845, 10, 9. Sarah co

1849, 1, 11. Persis dis joining Shaker Society & neglecting attendance

1849, 10, 11. Abigail gct Raisin MM

1849, 10, 11. Socrates com by Adrian PM for mcd & neglecting attendance; complaint forwarded to Raisin MM as he resided within limits of that mtg

1849, 11, 8. John & w, Susan, & minor ch, Elihu, Caroline, Edward & Chester, gct Raisin MM

1851, 4, 10. Lydia Baker (form Hoag) con mou (Raisin MM notified)

1851, 12, 11. Susan C. (form Haviland) con mou (Raisin MM informed)

1852, 10, 14. Israel prcf Raisin MM, dtd 1852, 10,13, to m

1854, 5, 11. Rachel gct Raisin MM

1854, 12, 14. Susan & minor ch, Caroline, Edward & Chester, rocf Raisin MM, dtd 1854, 11,8

1855, 5, 10. Amos & w, Emeline, & minor ch, Addison, Cornelis, Jane, Edwin A. & Millard, gct Red Cedar MM, Ia.

1856, 6, 12. John Milton dis mcd

1863, 4, 9. Susan gct Walnut Ridge MM, Ind.

1864, 12, 8. Edward H. com for enlisting as a soldier & mcd; Walnut Ridge MM, Ind. rq to treat with him

1865, 3, 9. Edward H. dis enlisting as a soldier & mcd; complaint not forwarded to

Walnut Ridge MM, Ind.; he returned to reside within the limits of this mtg

1866, 2, 8. Chester J. con enlisting in the Army; MM in Indiana where he resided notified

1867, 3, 14. Chester J. gct Honey Creek MM, Ind.

1867, 5, 9. John recrq

1867, 5, 9. Susan E. rec in mbrp

1867, 8, 8. Mary B. & s, Jay, rocf Butternuts MM, N. Y.

----, --, --. Mary W. rocf Indianapolis MM, dtd 1870,5,21

HOLLINGSWORTH

1851, 11, 13. Salem MM, O. rq this mtg to inform Christopher Hollingsworth that he is dis

HOPKINS

1860, 8, 9. Horace com by Collins MM; not living within limits of this mtg

HOWDER

----, --, --. Adaline rocf Hartland MM held at Elba, dtd 1833,11,14

HOWELL

1783, 5, 15. Charlott b Warwick, Hampshire, Mass.

1810, 11, 11. Mariah G. (O'Dell) b Victor, Ontario, N. Y.

1813, 8, 6. Mary G. (Rowe) b Victor, Ontario Co., N. Y.

1815, 9, 25. Sally b Victor, Ontario Co., N. Y.

1817, 7, 4. Hannah S. b Victor, Ontario Co., N. Y.

1819, 5, 27. Benjamin G. b Victor, Ontario Co., N. Y.

1820, 11, 5. Jared R. b Victor, Ontario Co., N. Y.

1822, 8, 24. Lydia E. b Victor, Ontario Co., N. Y.

1825, 4, 7. Altha Ann b Victor, Ontario Co., N. Y.

1827, 3, 18. Mynerva C. b Victor, Ontario Co. N. Y.

1829, 4, 22. Hannah S., Logan, Lenawee Co., Mich., d

1835, 2, 23. Benjamin G., Logan, Lenawee Co., Mich., d

1845, 7, 29. Charlotte d

1839, 9, 12. Charlotte co

1845, 9, 11. Sally A. Vanaken (form Howell) dis neglecting attendance & mou

1851, 7, 10. Altheann Parks (form Howell) dis by Raisin MM for mou

HOXSIE

1783, 2, 13. John b Beekman, Dutchess Co., N. Y.

HOXSIE, continued

1786, 8, 4. Phebe b Westport, Worcester Co.,
     Mass.
1810, 8, 12. Lydia b Galway, Saratoga Co.,
     N. Y.
1813, 3, 26. Leonard S. b Galway, Saratoga
     Co., N. Y.
1815, 5, 6. Harris P. b Galway, Saratoga
     Co., N. Y.
1818, 8, 1. Ezra b Scipio, Cayuga Co., N. Y.
1820, 10, 4. Betsey b Cayuga Co., N. Y.
1823, 7, 20. Orrin, s John & Phebe, b Cayuga
     Co., N. Y.
1827, 3, 4. Jane, a+ John & Phebe, b Cayuga
     Co., N. Y.
1840, 1, 31. Martha, Woodstock, Lenawee Co.,
     Mich., d

----, --, --. John [Hoxsey] & w, Phebe, &
     minor ch, Leonard, S. Horrace, Ezra (or
     Eliza), Betsey, Orren & Jane, rocf Scipio
     MM, dtd 1833,8,14
----, --, --. Lydia [Hoxsey], dt John, rocf
     Scipio MM dtd 1833,8,14
----, --, --. Phebe [Hoxie] & dt, Abigail, rocf
     Scipio MM, dtd 1835,5,20
1838, 6, 7. Mary [Hoxie] (form Underwood)
     dis
1839, 6, 13. Martha con misconduct
1841, 1, 14. Horace S. con mou
1841, 1, 14. Lydia Kelly (form Hoxey) con mcd
1841, 5, 13. Betsey [Hoxey] dis neglecting
     attendance
1842, 2, 10. Ezra [Hoxie] dis neglecting at-
     tendance
1842, 11, 10. Lenard P. [Hoxie] recrq

HUNT

1838, 1, 11. Cert granted to Collins MM for
     Abigail, w Thomas, & dt, Hannah, returned;
     they resided near or at Rockriver, Ill.,
     within the limits of this mtg
1838, 1, 11. Mercy, w Daniel, & minor ch,
     Nehemiah, Lydia, Mary Ann, Gennett & Ben-
     jamin, rocf Collins MM, dtd 1837,1,26
1838, 11, 8. Julia M. con misconduct
1839, 6, 13. Julia M. dis
1841, 10, 14. Lydia E. con mou

HUNTINGTON

1867, 1, 12. Anna m Benjamin KNOWLES

1865, 11, 9. Anna & minor dt, Allice G., rocf
     Collins MM, dtd 1865,9,25
1867, 7, 11. Anna H. Knowles & minor dt,
     Alice G. Huntington, gct Smyrna MM, N. Y.

HUSSEY

----, --, --. Sarah E., w Erastus, & minor dt,
     Susan, rocf Scipio MM, dtd 1832,2,15

IVESON

1839, 1, 10. Anna, w John, & minor s, Benja-

min, rocf Westbury & Jericho MM, L. I.,
     dtd 1838,11,14
1840, 7, 9. James rq mbrp through Palmyra
     PM; rq returned

JACKSON

----, --, --. Jesse & minor ch, Hiram, Sally,
     Mercy, Mary, Harriet, Amos & Levi, rocf
     Hartland MM, dtd 1834,12,18
1838, 4, 12. Sally dis
1838, 10, 11. Isaac & w, Ruth, & adopted minor
     s, Isaac W. Jackson, rocf Farmington MM,
     dtd 1838,1,25
1878, 4, 11. Mary recrq
1878, 4, 11. William H. rec in mbrp

JOHNSON

1839, 5, 9. Caroline T. con misconduct
1841, 4, 8. Caroline T. dis
1841, 5, 13. Caroline T. dis neglecting at-
     tendance
1865, 9, 7. Theron A. rocf Winneshiek MM,
     Ia., dtd 1865,1,21

JONES

1806, 5, 11. Mary b Sandwich, Barnstable Co.,
     Mass.
1806, 7, 12. Silas b Sandwich, Barnstable
     Co., Mass.
1831, 6, 28. Martha M. b Baltimore, N. Y.
1833, 4, 17. Walter J. b Sympronius, Cayuga
     Co., N. Y.
1835, 5, 30. George b Sympronius, Cayuga Co.,
     N. Y.
1837, 7, 27. Mary Eliza b Raisin, Lenewee
     Co., Mich.
1840, 9, 19. Charles W., s Silas & Mary, b
     Raisin, Lenawee Co., Mich.
1874, 9, 10. Emury A., Raisin, Lenawee Co.,
     Mich., s Asa & Martha, Raisin; m at home
     of Richard Aldrich, Sarah A. ALDRICH, dt
     Richard & Bathsheba, Raisin, Lenawee Co.,
     Mich.

----, --, --. Silas & w, Mary, & minor ch,
     Martha M., Walter J., George & Wetherton,
     rocf Scipio MM, dtd 1835,11,18
1872, 2, 29. Asa rocf Collins MM, N. Y.

KELLY

1839, 8, 19. Deborah, Raisin, Lenawee Co.,
     Mich., d ae 35y 7m 13d
1841, 2, 6. Edwin, s Libnit & Lydia, b
     Raisin, Lenawee Co., Mich.
1844, 3, 3. Ellen, dt Zeno & Mary Ann, b
     Tecumseh, Lenawee Co., Mich.

----, --, --. Zeno rocf Sidney MM, Maine, dtd
     1836,8,18
----, --, --. Libni & w, Deborah, & minor ch,
     Benjamin, Content, Mary Jane, Rufus &
     John W., rocf Rochester MM, held at Wheat-
     land, dtd 1836,9,23

KELLY, continued
1839, 8, 8. John W. [Kelley] & w, Content,
    rocf Sidney MM held at Fairfield, Maine,
    dtd 1839,5,16
1840, 8, 13. Mary Ann recrq
1840, 9, 10. Sarah M. & Harriet F., minor ch
    Zeno & Mary Ann, recrq of parents
1841, 1, 14. Libni con mcd
1841, 1, 14. Lydia (form Hoxey) con mcd
1849, 3, 8. Zeno com

KEMPTON
1843, 1, 24. Caleb, s Aaron W. & Jane I., b
    Woodstock, Lenawee Co., Mich.

1838, 1, 11. Aaron W. rocf New-bedford MM, dtd
    1837,10,26
1842, 6, 9. Aaron W. con mou
1842, 10, 13. Jane T. recrq

KENEDY
1838, 12, 13. Mary Jane con misconduct

KENYON
1862, 8, 14. Cert rec for Phebe Ann, w In-
    crease, endorsed to Rollin MM

KERR
1881, 2, 10. Ortense rq mbrp

KNAPP
----, --, --. Anna, w Seth, rocf Farmington
    MM, dtd 1835,8,27

KNOWLES
1843, 2, 21. Henry, s Henry A. & Mary C.,
    b Woodstock, Lenawee Co., Mich.
1867, 1, 12. Benjamin, Smyrna, Chenango Co.,
    N. Y., s Henry & Susan; m at Adrian, Anna
    HUNTINGTON, Raisin, Lenawee Co., Mich.,
    dt Benjamin BOYCE & w, Catharine, latter
    dec
----, --, --. Henry A. & w, Mary C., & ch,
    Sheffield C. & Eliza D., rocf Smyrna MM
    held at Brookfield, N. Y., dtd 1836,4,5
1838, 9, 13. Henry A. co
1839, 9, 12. Henry A. co
1840, 10, 8. Henry A. co
1841, 7, 8. Cert for Murray returned to
    Ferrisburgh MM; mcd before cert was pre-
    sented here; Ferrisburgh MM rq this mtg
    to treat with him; con mce 1842,7,14
1841, 12, 9. Benjamin dis mcd
1843, 5, 11. Henry A. & fam rqct Raisin MM
1843, 6, 8. Henry A. & w, Mary C., & minor
    ch, Sheffield C., Eliza D. & Abram H.,
    gct Raisin MM
1844, 4, 11. Nathaniel rocf Farnham MM, dtd
    1843,10,23
1847, 10, 14. Abram rocf Smyrna MM held at
    Brookfield, dtd 1847,8,4
1850, 6, 13. Abram A. gct Raisin MM, to m
1851, 3, 13. Martha M., w Abram, rocf Raisin

MM, dtd 1851,9,9
1867, 1, 10. Benjamin prc to m
1867, 7, 11. Anna H. & minor dt, Alice G.
    Huntington, gct Smyrna MM, N. Y.

KOHR
1879, 4, 10. Maria A. & Amanda E. recrq

LAING
1793, 11, 18. Smith b Fairfield, Middlesex
    Co., N. J.
1795, 1, 25. Abby b Randolph, Morris Co.,
    N. J.
1815, 12, 3. Sarah Maria b Waterloo, Seneca
    Co., N. Y.
1817, 9, 25. Amy b Waterloo, Seneca Co.,N.Y.
1819, 8, 19. Phebe Ann b Elba, Gennesse Co.,
    N. Y.
1823, 3, 16. Hannah b Elba, Gennesse Co.,
    N. Y.
1825, 5, 9. Joseph Smith b Elba, Gennessee
    Co., N. Y.
1828, 8, 3. Mary S. b Elba, Gennesse Co.,
    N. Y.
1834, 3, 27. Benjamin P. b Raisin, Lenewee
    Co., Mich.
1834, 7, 24. Amy m John Jay DOTY
1834, 9, 25. Sarah Maria m David HARKNESS,Jr.
1836, 5, 13. Webster A. b
1838, 12, 7. Mary S., Raisin, Lenawee Co.,
    Mich., d
1841, 6, 17. Phebe Ann m Samuel LEEDS, Jr.
1845, 5, 15. Hannah m Stephen Z. HOAG

----, --, --. Smith & w, Abby, & minor ch, Sa-
    rah Maria, Phebe Ann, Amy, Hannah, Joseph
    Smith & Mary, rocf Hartland MM, dtd 1832,
    6,26
1834, 3, 27. Benjamin T. b
1839, 9, 12. Abbey co
1839, 9, 12. Smith co
1840, 10, 8. Smith co
1843, 11, 9. Smith co
1844, 10, 10. Abby co
1844, 11, 7. Smith co
1845, 10, 9. Abby co
1845, 12, 11. Smith co
1851, 5, 7. Joseph dis misconduct
1855, 11, 8. Benjamin dis mou
1857, 3, 12. Webster A. dis

LAMB
1848, 11, 9. Matilda (form Soule) dis mcd &
    neglecting attendance

LAMBERT
1813, 3, 17. Sarah b Saratoga, Saratoga Co.,
    N. Y.
----, --, --. John & w, Mary, rocf Farmington
    MM, dtd 1833,5,23
----, --, --. Sarah, w Ansel, rocf Rochester
    MM held at Wheatland, dtd 1833,9,27

LAPHAM

1776, 8, 2. Milly b Northbridge, Mass.
1782, 1, 28. Ethen b Northbridge, Mass.
1801, 8, 9. Lavina (Smith) b Palmyra, Ontario Co., N. Y.
1805, 1, 7. Norton P. b Palmyra, Ontario Co., N. Y.
1808, 2, 15. Cynthia b Palmyra, Ontario Co., N. Y.
1810, 4, 2. Huldah b Palmyra, Ontario Co., N. Y.
1814, 8, 16. Ethen A. b Palmyra, Ontario Co., N. Y.
1817, 12, 2. Luther b Palmyra, Ontario Co., N. Y.
1829, 8, 25. Huldah, Farmington, Oakland Co., Mich., d

----, --, --. Rachel R. & Darius, minor ch Eli & Rachel, rocf Collins MM, dtd 1832,11,1
1838, 9, 13. Stephen co
1838, 1, 11. Alfred, s Asa, rocf Collins MM, dtd 1837,3,30
1838, 1, 11. Hannah, dt Ezra & Deborah Southwick, rocf Collins MM, dtd 1837,3,30
----, --, --. James H. rocf Collins MM, dtd 1837,3,30
1838, 2, 8. Stephen & w, Margaret, & minor ch, David, Deborah B., Daniel, Abraham & Margaret P., rocf Collins MM, dtd 1837,6,29
1838, 4, 12. James R. dis mcd by Collins MM
1838, 7, 12. Ethan com by Adrian PM for neglecting attendance & jH
1839, 6, 13. Cynthia dis
1839, 6, 13. Milla dis
1839, 7, 11. Ethan A. dis neglecting attendance, jH & mou
1839, 9, 12. Stephen co
1840, 9, 10. Deborah dis
1840, 10, 8. David dis mou & neglecting attendance
1840, 10, 8. Deborah (form Lapham) dis mcd & neglecting attendance
1840, 10, 8. Luther dis mcd & neglecting attendance
1840, 10, 8. Stephen co
1841, 9, 9. Margaret co of Ypsilanti Mtg

LASSING

1840, 10, 8. Peter G. dis; Norwick Mtg, Upper Canada, notified

LAWRENCE

1838, 6, 1. Daniel rocf Marlborough MM held in Ulster Co., N. Y., dtd 1837,8,23

LAWSON

1840, 12, 10. Lydia (form Smith) con mcd

LAWTON

1760, 5, 26. Phila b Northbridge, Mass.
1839, 8, 3. Phila, Palmyra, Lenawee Co., Mich., d ae 79y 2m 7d

1841, 5, 14. Charles Haviland, Raisin, Lenawe Co., Mich., s James & Martha, both dec; m at Raisin, Sarah L. POWER, dt William LAWTON & Abigail, Farmington, Oakland Co., Mich.

----, --, --. Phila, w Wm., rocf Farmington MM dtd 1833,10,24

LEE

1837, 3, 9. Dorothy B. rocf Upper Springfield MM, N. J., held at Mansfield, 1836,11,9

LEEDS

1837, 10, 11. John C., Macon, Lenawee Co., Mich., d ae 2y 7m 28d
1840, 12, 26. Hannah, Macon, Lenawee Co., Mich., d ae 31y 11m 8d
1841, 6, 17. Samuel Jr., Raisin, Lenawe Co., Mich., s Samuel & Ruth; m at Adrian, Phebe Ann LAING, dt Smith & Abbey, Raisin, Lenawe Co., Mich.
1842, 6, 16. Henry, Raisin, Lenawe Co., Mich. s Samuel & Ruth; m at Adrian, Maria WEST, dt Jacob & Lana, Adrian, Lenawee Co., Mich.
----, --, --. Ann, dt Henry & Maria, b 1844,7,5, Raisin, Lenawe Co., Mich.; d 1844,9,24 ae 2m 19d
1878, 6, 27. Samuel, Adrian, Lenawee Co., Mich., s Samuel & Ruth; m at Adrian, Elizabeth WORTHINGTON, dt Jeremiah & Sarah WILLETS, Phila.

1838, 6, 7. Henry & w, Hannah, & s, Samuel, rocf Eggharbour MM, dtd 1838,5,7
1838, 6, 7. Samuel Jr. rocf Eggharbour MM, dtd 1838,5,7
1848, 2, 10. Samuel T. gct Chester MM, N. J.
1851, 2, 6. Henry & minor ch, Charles H. & William W., gct Chester MM, Burlington Co., N. J.

LEFEVRE

1860, 9, 13. Mary Ann rec in mbrp

LINCOLN

----, --, --. Luther Jr. rocf Swanzey MM held at Troy, dtd 1833,6,24

LOVEJOY

1843, 10, 12. Cert rec for Patty from Sidney MM held at Fairfield, dtd 1843,5,18, endorsed to Raisin MM

LUDINGTON

1845, 2, 6. Cert rec for Hannah from Rochester MM, endorsed to Raisin MM, as she resided within limits of that mtg

LUPTON

1838, 3, 19. Benjamin T. b Woodstock, Lenawee Co., Mich.

LUPTON, continued
1842, 12, 14. Sarah C. m Joseph BINNS
1844, 10, 16. Margaret m Joseph HEWITT
1843, 10, 12. Susanna co
1843, 11, 9. Gideon co
1844, 10, 10. Susanna co
1844, 11, 7. Gideon co
1845, 10, 9. Susanna co
1847, 8, 12. William C. con mou
1848, 12, 14. Gideon co

LUTHER
1879, 4, 10. Jennie M. recrq
1881, 2, 10. Charles rq mbrp

McAULEY
----, --, --. Wm. Henry rocf Norwich MM, dtd
    1839,6,12
1839, 8, 8. Diana rocf Norwich MM, dtd 1839,
    6,12
1839, 8, 8. Jemima & minor ch, John D. &
    Elizabeth, rocf Norwich MM, dtd 1839,6,12
1839, 9, 12. Catharine Brooks (form McAuley)
    con mou
1839, 9, 12. Sarah Clark (form McAuley) con
    mou (com by Norwich MM)
1839, 11, 7. William Henry [McCauley] rocf
    Norwich MM, Upper Canada, dtd 1839,6,12
1842, 12, 8. William Henry [McCauley] dis
    neglecting attendance
1845, 2, 6. John D. [McAuly] gct Norwich MM,
    Upper Canada
1845, 3, 13. Mariah Carnel, Jemimah [McCau-
    ley], Diana [McCauley] & Elizabeth[McCau-
    ley] gct Norwich MM, Canada

McCALLEY
1839, 1, 10. Catharine rocf Norwich MM, Upper
    Canada, dtd 1838,9,12

McDONALD
1846, 11, 18. Anna m Israel DARLINGTON

1838, 2, 8. Thomas rocf Smyrna MM, dtd 1837,
    11,7
1839, 10, 10. Thomas con neglecting attendance
1843, 4, 13. Thomas con misconduct
1844, 12, 12. Nathaniel & w, Sarah, & minor s,
    James, rocf Smyrna MM, dtd 1844,9,10
1845, 10, 9. Sarah co
1845, 12, 11. Nathaniel co
1846, 6, 11. Estes, minor, rocf Smyrna MM held
    at Brookfield, dtd 1846,4,8 (residing with
    brother, Thomas)
1846, 8, 13. Anna recrq; Smyrna MM, N. Y. in-
    formed
1846, 11, 12. Sarah co
1846, 12, 10. Nathaniel co
1846, 12, 10. Thomas con misconduct
1847, 3, 11. Susannah (form Darlington) con
    mcd
1847, 6, 10. Estus dis neglecting attendance
1847, 11, 11. Sarah co

1848, 12, 14. Sarah co
1849, 12, 13. Sarah co
1851, 1, 9. Sarah co
1851, 12, 11. Nathaniel co
1852, 1, 8. Sarah co
1853, 1, 13. Nathaniel co
1853, 1, 13. Sarah co
1854, 6, 8. Nathaniel & w, Sarah, & minor s,
    James, gct Red Cedar MM, Ia.

MACOMBER
1864, 9, 8. Richard R. & w, Sarah Jane, &
    minor ch, Mary Elizabeth, Albert & Edwin,
    rocf Farmington MM, dtd 1864,8,25
1864, 9, 8. William P. & w, Esther, & minor
    s, Elmer Elwood, rocf Farmington MM, dtd
    1864,8,25
1867, 8, 8. Wm. P. & w & minor ch, Elmor
    Elwood & George Refine, gct West Post MM,
    Mass.

MACY
1773, 9, 12. Obed b Nantucket, Mass.
1780, 4, 7. Lydia b Nantucket, Mass.
1813, 10, 23. Phebe Coffin b Nantucket, Mass.
1821, 9, 16. Eliza Gardner b Nantucket, Mass.
1848, 1, 10. Obed d

----, --, --. Obed & w, Lydia, & minor dt,
    Eliza, rocf Hartland MM held at Lockport,
    dtd 1833,4,30
----, --, --. Phebe C. rocf Hartland MM held
    at Lockport, dtd 1833,4,30
1838, 6, 7. Elisa dis
1840, 7, 9. Phebe dis neglecting attendance
    & jas

MARSHALL
1841, 6, 10. David & w, Hannah, & minor s,
    William, rocf Hartland MM, dtd 1840,7,16
1841, 6, 10. Harriet, dt David & Hannah, rocf
    Hartland MM, dtd 1840,7,16
1842, 8, 11. Hiram & w, Mary, & minor ch,
    Joel D., Lydia W., Lucy R. & Marshall,
    rocf Farmington MM, dtd 1841,9,23
1846, 2, 5. Hiram dis neglecting attendance
1846, 5, 14. Mary dis neglecting attendance &
    jas
1849, 6, 7. Hiram con misconduct
1849, 7, 12. Mary con misconduct
1850, 7, 11. Lucy Havens (form Marshall) dis
    mou
1850, 7, 11. Lydia Dunn (form Marshall) dis
    mou

MASON
1805, 3, 16. Mary b Adams, Berkshire Co.,
    Mass.

MASTERS
----, --, --. Thomas rocf Hartland MM, N. Y.,
    dtd 1833,8,27

MEAD

1875, 9, 9. Thomas G., Raisin, Lenawee Co.,
Mich., s Thomas W. & Sarah S., Lenawee
Co., Mich.; m at the residence of Townsend
I. Sutton, Elizabeth R. SUTTON dt Asa U.
& Sarah A., Lenawee Co., Mich.

MEASURE

1852, 2, 12. Sarah J. (form Smith) dis mou &
jas

MESSNER

----, --, --. George & w, Rebecca, & ch, Ann
& Ellen, rocf Darlington MM held at Stockton, dtd 1851,7,15
----, --, --. John rocf Grisbrough MM held at
Ayton, dtd 1851,7,14
1860, 4, 12. John gct Winneshiek MM, Ia.
1860, 4, 12. George gct Winneshiek MM, Ia.

MILLER

1840, 1, 23. Abigail, Quincy, Branch Co.,
Mich., d ae 38y 9m 4d

----, --, --. Abigail, w Timothy, rocf Scipio
MM, dtd 1836,12,14
1878, 6, 13. Leanna rocf Goshen MM, O.

MILLET

1842, 12, 8. Hannah (form Hoag) dis

MILLS

1877, 8, 28. Joseph J., Indianapolis, Marion
Co., Ind., s Abner & Hannah, Marion Co.,
Ind.; m at residence of Michael Wanzer,
Emily WANZER, dt Michael & Lavinia, Adrian,
Mich.

----, --, --. Hannah rocf Little Eggharbour
MM, dtd 1834,8,14

MOSHER

1806, 12, 26. Thomas b Washington, Dutchess
Co., N. Y.
1809, 11, 25. Lucy, dt Moses & Cynthia, b
Palmyra, Ontario Co., N. Y.
1835, 8, 31. Isaac b Lenawee, Lenewee Co.,
Mich.
1840, 7, 4. Sarah, dt Thomas & Lucy, b Madison, Lenawee Co., Mich.
1861, 1, 17. Isaac H., Raisin, Lenawee Co.,
Mich., s Thomas & Lucy; m at Adrian,
Elizabeth HOAG, dt Hazael & Sarah, Adrian,
Lenawee Co., Mich.
1861, 11, 14. Sarah m Moses COMFORT
1865, 1, 29. Lucy Ellen, dt Isaac & Elizabeth,
Raisin, Lenawee Co., Mich., d ae 3y 9m 6d

----, --, --. Ruth & minor ch, Loretta M., Ruth
Ann, Abial Jr., Elias H., Jonathan R. &
Thomas R.,rocf Rochester MM held at Wheat-
land, 1832,3,23
----, --, --. Thomas rocf Elba MM, dtd 1833,8,

27

----, --, --. Eliza Ann, minor dt Abial, rocf
Rochester MM held at Wheatland, dtd 1833,
9,27
1838, 7, 12. Abial T. Jr. com by Palmyra PM
for mcd, neglecting attendance & attending
a place of diversion
1838, 9, 13. Thomas co
1839, 9, 12. Lucy co
1839, 9, 12. Thomas co
1840, 4, 9. Abial T. dis mcd & neglecting
attendance
1840, 9, 10. Lucy co
1840, 10, 8. Thomas co
1841, 9, 9. Lucy co of Palmyra Mtg
1851, 12, 11. Thomas [Moshier] & w, Lucy, &
minor ch, Isaac & Sarah, rocf Raisin MM,
dtd 1851,12,10
1856, 2, 7. Thomas [Moshier] co
1857, 2, 5. Thomas co
1858, 5, 13. Thomas [Moshier] co
1859, 5, 12. Thomas [Moshier] co
1860, 6, 7. Thomas co
1863, 6, 11. Thomas co
1861, 6, 13. Thomas co
1862, 6, 12. Thomas [Moshier] co
1864, 6, 9. Thomas co
1865, 4, 13. Thomas & Lucy appointed elders
1865, 6, 8. Thomas co
1866, 6, 7. Thomas co
1880, 5, 13. Thomas released from being an
elder

MOTT

1838, 2, 8. Richard Jr. & w, Elizabeth, &
minor ch, Mary T. & Catharine T., rocf
New York MM, dtd 1837,11,1

MOWER

1851, 12, 11. George & w, Rebecca, & minorch,
Ann & Ellen, rocf Darlington MM held at
Stockton, Old England, dtd 1851,10,15
1851, 12, 11. John rocf Guisborough MM held at
Ayton, England, dtd 1851,7,14
1860, 4, 12. George & John gct Winnisheik MM,
Ia.
1860, 9, 13. Ellen gct Winnisheik MM, Ia.
1861, 9, 12. Ann Taber (form Mower) dis

MUNSON

1849, 6, 7. Lydia Jane (form West) dis mou
& mcd (Raisin MM notified)

MURPHY

1879, 10, 20. Flora E. m David HARKNESS

NOICE

1846, 4, 9. Elizabeth (form Ayres) dis neglecting attendance

ODELL

1851, 2, 12. Maria m Joseph BOWERMAN

ODELL, continued
1851, 5, 7. Maria & minor dt, Mary Odell,
gct Raisin MM (Maria Bowerman)

OSIOLA
1860, 5, 10. Elmira (form Carpenter) dis

PALMER
1789, 8, 16. Henry b Ninepartner, Dutchess
Co., N. Y.
1794, 9, 9. Lydia b Danby, Rutland Co., Vt.
1814 12, 12. Randall b Danby, Rutland Co.,
Vt.
1817, 1, 23. Emeline b Danby, Rutland Co.,
Vt.
1820, 1, 6. Henry Freleigh b Riga, Monroe
Co., N. Y.
1824, 1, 29. Stephen H. b Riga, Monroe Co.,
N. Y.
1826, 5, 15. Catharine b Riga, Monroe Co.,
N. Y.
1830, 3, 6. Harvey b Riga, Monroe Co., N. Y.

----, --, --. Henry & w, Lydia, & minor ch,
Randell, Emeline, Henry F., Stephen, Catherine & Harvey, rocf Rochester MM held at
Wheatland, dtd 1832,11,23
1843, 4, 13. Ephraim com by Hartland MM; complaint endorsed to Raisin MM as he resided within limits of that mtg
1843, 5, 11. Henry F. dis disunity
1847, 2, 11. Emeline Smith (form Palmer) con
mcd
1849, 11, 8. Henry & w, Lydia, & minor ch,
Catharine, Harvey & Louisa, gct Raisin MM
1857, 7, 9. Randal dis

PARKER
1837, 9, 7. Esther (form Power) dis
1841, 11, 11. Phebe (form Cornell) com by Rollin PM for mou

PARKERSON
1844, 1, 11. Sarah (form Cornell) dis mou
1844, 1, 11. Phebe (form Cornell) dis

PARKS
1851, 7, 10. Altheann (form Howell) dis by
Raisin MM for mou

PARMER
1853, 3, 10. Randal con mou

PATE
1879, 5, 8. Henry & Mary recrq

PATTERSON
1841, 5, 13. Jane (form Farrah) con mou

PEACOCK
1848, 4, 13. Jonathan rocf Raisin MM, dtd
1848,4,12

PEARSON
1870, 7, 15. Calvin W., Richmond, Wayne Co.,
Ind., s Isaac & Rachel, dec; m at house
of Joshua Taylor, Marthanna TAYLOR, dt
Joshua & Mary E., Tecumseh, Mich.

PEASLEY
1838, 7, 12. Abraham gct Bartholomew Co., Ind

PECKHAM
1842, 2, 10. Cert rec for Richard endorsed
to -----

PEMBLETON
1849, 10, 11. Sally (form Birdsall) dis mcd &
neglecting attendance

PENNINGTON
1778, 8, 23. John [Penington], s Israel &
Abigail, b Stafford, Monmouth Co., N. J.
1789, 1, 31. Hannah [Penington], dt John &
Mary Willetts, b Independence, Sussex
Co., N. J.
1808, 11, 17. Israel [Penington] b Perinton,
Monroe Co., N. Y.
1813, 4, 3. John [Penington] b Perinton,
Monroe Co., N. Y.
1816, 4, 26. Abigail [Penington] b Perinton,
Monroe Co., N. Y.
1820, 3, 4. Joseph [Penington] b Perinton,
Monroe Co., N. Y.
1822, 3, 26. Isaac [Penington] b Perinton,
Monroe Co., N. Y.
1827, 3, 16. Mary [Penington] b Perinton,
Monroe Co., N. Y.
1860, 12, 29. John [Penington] Macon, Lenawee
Co., Mich., d
1864, 3, 26. Hannah, Macon, Lenawee Co.,
Mich., d

----, --, --. Abigail rocf Farmington MM, dtd
1835,8,27
1840, 11, 12. John Jr. dis mou & neglecting
attendance
1840, 12, 10. John dis neglecting attendance
1842, 12, 8. Joseph dis joining Baptist Society
1844, 12, 12. Israel con mou
1847, 3, 11. Isaac con mou
1847, 4, 8. Mary (form Pennington) dis mou
1848, 10, 2. John rst
1850, 2, 7. Mary [Penington] recrq
1863, 1, 8. Israel co
1863, 6, 11. Israel co
1864, 6, 9. Israel co
1865, 6, 8. Israel co
1866, 6, 7. Israel co
1867, 6, 13. Israel co

POLLARD
1854, 5, 11. Cert rec for Samuel endorsed
to Rolin MM; he resided within limits of
that mtg

POWER

1771, 11, 14. Arthur b Adams, Berkshire Co., Mass.

1785, 8, 7. Sarah L. b Summerset, Berkshire Co., Mass.

1797, 3, 3. John b Farmington, Ontario Co., N. Y.

1798, 4, 21. Patience C. b Farmington, Ontario Co., N. Y.

1799, 1, 3. Ira b Farmington, Ontario Co., N. Y.

1800, 10, 6. Selinda b Farmington, Ontario Co., N. Y.

1801, 4, 19. Nathan b Farmington, Ontario Co., N. Y.

1803, 2, 2. Amy b Palmyra, Ontario Co., N.Y.

1803, 4, 20. Mary (Stuart) b Farmington, Ontario Co., N. Y.

1804, 3, 3. Vicena b Victor, Ontario Co., N. Y.

1805, 6, 4. Jared b Farmington, Ontario Co., N. Y.

1807, 7, 6. Samuel b Farmington, Ontario Co., N. Y.

1809, 11, 4. Bulah E. (Spencer) b Farmington, Ontario Co., N. Y.

1812, 1, 6. Abraham b Farmington, Ontario Co., N. Y.

1814, 4, 29. William b Farmington, Ontario Co., N. Y.

1816, 7, 20. Esther b Farmington, Ontario Co., N. Y.

1820, 11, 19. Deborah b Farmington, Ontario Co., N. Y.

1823, 11, 4. Duana b Farmington, Ontario Co., N. Y.

1825, 5, 24. Matilda b Farmington, Ontario Co., N. Y.

1825, 11, 15. Gideon b Farmington, Ontario Co., N. Y.

1826, 11, 30. Phebe M. b Farmington, Oakland Co., Mich.

1827, 1, 27. Arthur P. b Farmington, Ontario Co., N. Y.

1828, 1, 16. Lorenzo b Farmington, Oakland Co., Mich.

1828, 3, 5. Lorenzo, Farmington, Oakland Co., Mich., d

1828, 7, 21. John, Farmington, Oakland Co., Mich., d

1828, 10, 5. Ethen L. b Farmington, Ontario Co., N. Y.

1828, 11, 23. John Webb b Farmington, Oakland Co., Mich.

1829, 3, 13. Ira S. b Farmington, Oakland Co., Mich.

1830, 3, 31. Francis b Farmington, Oakland Co., Mich.

1830, 7, 30. Huldah A. b Farmington, Ontario Co., N. Y.

1831, 10, 21. Emeline m Amos HOAG

1831, 11, 20. George b Farmington, Oakland Co., Mich.

1832, 8, 2. Phebe M., Farmington, Oakland Co., Mich., d

1832, 8, 2. Salinda, Farmington, Oakland Co., Mich., d

1834, 2, 14. Nathan, Farmington, Oakland Co., Mich., s Arthur & Deborah, dec; m at Adrian, Patience COMSTOCK, dt Otis & Huldah, dec

1836, 8, 6. Arthur, Farmington, Oakland Co., Mich., d

1836, 9, 15. Otis C. b

1838, 1, 1. Mary Lavina b

1841, 5, 14. Sarah L. m Charles HAVILAND

1842, 6, 15. Vicena m Eli C. HAVILAND

1837, 9, 7. Esther Parker (form Power) dis

1838, 1, 11. Abraham L. dis mcd & neglecting attendance

1839, 6, 13. Amy dis

1839, 7, 11. Ira dis neglecting attendance & jH

1838, 9, 13. Nathan co

1839, 9, 13. Nathan co

1839, 9, 12. Patience C. co

1839, 9, 12. Sarah co

1840, 9, 10. Patience C. co

1840, 10, 8. Nathan co

1842, 7, 14. William com by Ypsilanti PM for neglecting attendance

1861, 1, 10. John W. dis

PRATT

1852, 1, 2. Charles, s Abijah & Elizabeth, Adrian, Lenawee Co., Mich., d ae 65y

1861, 12, 27. Betsy d

----, --, --. Charles & w, Betsey, & her minor s, Jacob Arnold, rocf Farmington MM, dtd 1834,1,21

RAMSDELL

1838, 11, 8. Thomas D. & w, Martha, & minor ch, Lydia Jane, Eliza Ann, Margaret, William D. & Elizabeth, rocf Farmington MM, dtd 1838,7,26

RAYMOND

----, --, --. Lucretia rocf Farmington MM, dtd 1834,5,22

1842, 10, 13. Albern H. rst

1847, 12, 9. Albern H. co

1848, 12, 14. Alburn H. co

1849, 12, 13. Alburn H. co

1851, 1, 9. Alburn H. co

1863, 7, 9. Catharine rocf Farmington MM, N. Y., dtd 1863,6,25

REEVES

1839, 4, 18. Rachel, Batavia, Branch Co., Mich., d ae 58y 3m 3d

1838, 4, 12. Rachel [Reeve] & ch, William, Mary & Coats rocf Farmington MM, dtd

REEVES, continued
  1836,10,27

REYNOLDS
1845, 6, 12. Mary rec in mbrp

RHOADS
1845, 7, 10. Abigail recrq

RICHARDSON
1847, 1, 14. Nathan dis mou & neglecting attendance

RIDER
1851, 3, 13. Jarvis M. & w, Mehetable, rocf
  Scipio MM, dtd 1851,2,12
1851, 9, 11. Jarvis M. & Mehettable T., gct
  Scipio MM

RING
1841, 2, 11. Joseph R. dis neglecting attendance

ROBERTS
----, --, --. Clarissa, Reuben, Asa, Ethen &
  Hannah, minor ch Elisha & Cynthia, rocf
  Collins MM, dtd 1832,11,1

ROBINSON
1841, 3, 11. Barnabas rocf Collins MM, dtd
  1840,10,29

ROGERS
1811, 4, 10. Louisa b Litchfield, Herkimer
  Co., N. Y.
1811, 4, 15. Ansel b Colerain, Franklin Co.,
  Mass.
1833, 3, 20. Silas R. b Cohocton, Steuben
  Co., N. Y.
1836, 6, 15. Nathan b Raisin, Lenawee Co.,
  Mich.
1844, 4, 22. Alonzo, s Ansel & Louiza, b
  Rollin, Lenawee Co., Mich.
1849, 8, 18. Louisa, Rollin, Lenewee Co.,
  Mich., d ae 38y 4m
1864, 6, 23. Asa Wing, West Gwillimburg, Sim-
  coe Co., Province of Canada, s Levi &
  Amelia; m at Adrian, Meriba WELLS, dt Russell & Eliza R., Raisin, Lenawee Co., Mich.

----, --, --. Ansell & w, Louisa, & minor s,
  Silas rocf Farmington MM, dtd 1835,11,26
1846, 11, 12. Loisa co
1847, 11, 11. Louisa co
1848, 12, 14. Louisa co
1851, 1, 9. Ansel gct Allum Creek MM, O.
1851, 6, 12. Ansel & w, Cynthia, & minor dt,
  Lydia Ann Grisel, rocf Alum Creek MM, O.,
  dtd 1851,4,24
1864, 7, 14. Asa W. prc to m
1864, 11, 10. Meriba gct Yonge St. MM, Canada

ROSS
1837, 4, 9. Milton b
1840, 11, 16. Jacob, s Wilber & Rachel, b
  Raisin, Lenawee Co., Mich.

----, --, --. Rachel, w Wilbur, & minor ch,
  Webster T., Rebecca B., Margaret H. & William D., rocf Hartland MM held at Elba,
  dtd 1836,5,19
1839, 7, 11. Wilber con misconduct; Hartland
  MM notified
1844, 9, 12. Wilber dis misconduct
1849, 8, 9. Albert recrq of mother, Rachel
1851, 3, 13. Rebecca dis misconduct
1858, 5, 13. Margaret gc
1858, 5, 13. Rachel & minor s, Albert, gct
  Rolin MM
1867, 3, 14. Milton dis enlisting in U. S.
  Army & mcd

SACKRIDER
----, --, --. Phebe rocf Norwich MM, Upper
  Canada, dtd 1834,10,8

SATTERTHWAITE
1790, 7, 2. Samuel b Chesterfield, Burlington Co., N. J.
1797, 2, 12. Hannah A. b Chesterfield, Burlington Co., N. J.
1801, 3, 17. Reuben b Chesterfield, Burlington Co., N. J.
1820, 1, 15. Sarah A. b Chesterfield, Burlington Co., N. J.
1821, 7, 17. Joseph C. b Chesterfield, Burlington Co., N. J.
1823, 2, 5. William b Chesterfield, Burlington Co., N. J.
1825, 1, 16. Caleb b Chesterfield, Burlington Co., N. J.
1827, 2, 21. Samuel M. b Chesterfield, Burlington Co., N. J.
1829, 7, 26. Elisabeth R. b Chesterfield,
  Burlington Co., N. J.
1831, 11, 14. Daniel b Tecumseh, Lenawee Co.,
  Mich.
1834, 1, 11. Hannah S., Tecumseh, Lenawee
  Co., Mich., d
1838, 8, 8. Reuben, Tecumseh, Lenawee Co.,
  Mich., d
1839, 8, 14. Caleb, Tecumseh, Lenawee Co.,
  Mich., d
1839, 11, 14. Sarah m Stephen TITUS
1840, 2, 13. Samuel, Tecumseh, Lenawee Co.,
  Mich., s Joseph & Elizabeth, both dec;
  m at Adrian, Elizabeth ATKINSON, dt Moses
  & Sarah, both dec
1847, 5, 19. Asa W. Sutton, Bedford, Calhoun
  Co., Mich. s Isaac & Sarah; m at Tecumseh, Sarah A. TITUS, dt Samuel SATTERTH-
  WAITE & Hannah, latter dec, Tecumseh,
  Lenawee Co., Mich.
1848, 10, 18. Joseph C., Tecumseh, Lenawee
  Co., Mich., s Samuel & Hannah, dec; m at

SATTERTHWAITE, continued
    Tecumseh, Elizabeth M. COMFORT, dt Aaron
    & Ann, Raisin, Lenawee Co., Mich.
1852, 9, 29. Elizabeth P. m Elwood COMFORT
1854, 9, 20. Samuel M., Tecumseh, Lenawee
    Co., Mich., s Samuel & Hannah, the latter
    dec; m at Tecumseh, Jane COMFORT, dt Aaron
    & Ann, Raisin, Lenawee Co., Mich.
1854, 11, 15. Mary E. m Nehemiah SUTTON
1862, 8, 21. Samuel d ae 72y 8m 19d
1870, 5, 28. Edward B., s Samuel M. & Jane
    C., Raisin, Lenawee Co., Mich., d ae 14y
    6m 19d

----, --, --. Samuel & w, Hannah, & minor ch,
    Sarah A., Joseph C., William, Caleb, Sam-
    uel M. & Elizabeth R., rocf Upper Spring-
    field MM, dtd 1831,12,7
----, --, --. Reuben rocf Upper Springfield
    MM, N. J., dtd 1832,12,5
1838, 9, 13. Samuel co
1839, 8, 8. Samuel appointed an elder
1845, 2, 6. Mary Elizabeth rec in mbrp
1845, 2, 6. Samuel & Elizabeth rq mbrp for
    their niece, Mary Elizabeth Satterthwaite
1848, 12, 14. Elizabeth co
1849, 1, 11. Elizabeth appointed an elder
1849, 12, 13. Elizabeth co
1851, 1, 9. Samuel co
1851, 11, 13. William gct Raisin MM, to m
1851, 12, 11. Samuel co
1853, 1, 13. Samuel co
1853, 8, 11. Mary Jane rocf Raisin MM, dtd
    1853,8,10
1854, 1, 12. Samuel co
1855, 1, 11. Samuel co
1855, 5, 11. William & w, Mary Jane, & dt,
    Deborah Celia, gct Raisin MM
1856, 2, 7. Samuel co
1857, 2, 5. Samuel co
1858, 5, 13. Samuel co
1859, 5, 12. Samuel co
1860, 6, 7. Samuel co
1860, 8, 9. Daniel gct Winneshiek MM, to m
1861, 6, 13. Samuel co
1862, 6, 12. Samuel co
1863, 11, 12. Cornelius J. rocf Winneshiek MM,
    Ia., dtd 1863,10,10
1863, 12, 10. Joseph C. con misconduct
1867, 2, 7. Daniel & w, Cornelia, & minor ch,
    Estella & Mary E., gct Scipio MM
1880, 11, 11. Jane C. appointed clerk

SCRADDER (or SCUDDER)
----, --, --. Julia Ann (form Utley) rocf
    Scipio MM, dtd 1833,4,17

SHAW
----, --, --. Richard b 1774,6,7; m Huldah
    ----- b 1785,7,8

----, --, --. Richard & w, Huldah, rocf Scipio
    MM, N. Y., dtd 1834,5,14

SHEPARD
1849, 9, 13. John rocf Pembroke MM, Mass.,
    dtd 1849,6,28
1852, 6, 10. John [Shepherd] con mou
1867, 6, 13. John [Shephard] gct Chicago
    MM, Ill.

SHERMAN
1816, 1, 7. Mary A. b Macedon, Wayne Co.,
    N. Y.
----, --, --. Lydia, dt Elisha J. & Sarah G.,
    b 1846,3,1 Tecumseh, Lenawee Co., Mich.;
    d 1846,3,13, Tecumseh, Lenawee Co., Mich.,
    ae 12d
1849, 1, 4. Elisha Y., Tecumseh, Lenewee
    Co., Mich., d

1846, 4, 9. Elisha J. & w, Sarah G., & minor
    dt, Edy R., rocf Salem MM held at Lynn,
    Mass. dtd 1845,11,7
1849, 10, 11. Sarah G. & minor dt, Edy R., gct
    Pembroke MM, Mass.

SHOTWELL
1848, 7, 20. Nathan Chase, Rome, Lenawee Co.,
    Mich., s Ebenezer & Sarah; m at Adrian,
    Sarah HOAG, dt Richard SHOTWELL & w, Mary,
    Raisin, Lenawee Co., Mich.

1878, 4, 11. Nathan & fam gc

SHUMWAY
1795, 2, 18. Josiah b Belsher, Hampshire Co.,
    Mass.
1798, 11, 12. Abigail b Montreal, Canada
1828, 2, 22. Nathan b Macedon, Wayne Co.,
    N. Y.

SLOAN
1843, 1, 12. Charity (form Hathaway) con mcd
1845, 7, 10. Mary T. recrq

SMITH
1785, 3, 12. Daniel b Harwick, Vt.
1787, 5, 19. Sene b Jamaica, Vt.
1808, 12, 20. Laura (Haviland) b Kitley, Leeds
    Upper Canada
1811, 3, 25. Harvey b Kitley, Leeds Co., Up-
    per Canada
1813, 8, 4. Ira b Kitley, Leeds Co., Upper
    Canada
1817, 4, 24. Phebe b Cambria, Niagara Co.,
    N. Y.
1819, 4, 6. Sala b Cambria, Niagara Co.,N.Y.
1826, 5, 27. Samuel b Lockport, Niagara Co.,
    N. Y.
1829, 6, 15. Otis b Logan, Lenawee Co., Mich
1832, 6, 27. Lydia b Logan, Lenawee Co., Mich.
1834, 10, 16. Phebe m Daniel HAVILAND
1838, 11, 14. Sarah Jane, Adrian, Lenawee
    Co., Mich., d
1838, 11, 22. William B., Adrian, Lenawee
    Co., Mich., d

SMITH, continued

1843, 8, 17. Ira, Adrian, Lenawee Co., Mich.,
s Daniel & Sene; m at Adrian, Elizabeth
WEST, dt Abraham & Mary, latter dec, Adrian, Lenawee Co., Mich.
   Ch: Daniel W. b 1844, 6, 5, Rollin,
        Lenawee Co., Mich.

1846, 12, 20. Lydia Ann, Rollin, Lenawee Co.,
Mich., d ae 5m 4d

1856, 12, 26. Lydia, dt Zopher & Phebe, Raisin
Lenawee Co., Mich., d ae 38y 3m

----, --, --. John R., Hannah, Asa, Mary & Sarah, minor ch John R. & Mary, rocf Collins
MM, dtd 1832,11,1

----, --, --. Phebe K. rocf Collins MM, dtd
1832,11,1

----, --, --. Peter B., minor s Peter, rocf
Farmington MM, dtd 1835,4,22

1838, 10, 11. William P. & w, Sarah, & minor
ch, William & Sarah, rocf Farmington MM,
dtd 1838,6,21

1839, 6, 13. Lavina dis

1839, 7, 11. Asenath dis

1839, 7, 11. Daniel dis holding mtg contrary
to discipline

1839, 8, 8. Sene dis neglecting attendance
& attending mtg held contrary to the order of our society

1839, 10, 10. Freelove rocf Hudson MM, dtd
1839,5,22

1840, 12, 10. Lydia Lawson (form Smith) con
mcd

1841, 2, 11. Sophia (form West) con mcd

1841, 3, 11. Cert for Job returned to Burlington MM, N. J. with information that he
mou & neglected mtg while here

1846, 9, 10. Harvey dis disunity

1846, 12, 10. Sala dis joining Methodist Society

1846, 12, 10. Samuel dis joining Methodist
Society

1847, 2, 11. Emeline (form Palmer) con mcd

1847, 4, 8. Mary (form Pennington) dis mou

1847, 4, 8. Mary dis

1848, 4, 13. Lydia A. & Isabella W. rocf
Farmington MM, dtd 1848,2,24

1848, 4, 13. Zopher & w, Phidelia, & minor
ch, Sarah Jane & Lucina F., rocf Farmington
MM, dtd 1848,2,24

1849, 9, 13. Charles A. con mcd & neglecting
attendance; Farmington MM informed

1850, 11, 7. Lydia (form Smith) dis misconduct

1851, 9, 11. Mariah, w Charles, rocf Farmington MM, N. Y., dtd 1851,4,24

1852, 2, 12. Sarah J. Measure (form Smith)
dis mou & jas

1853, 2, 10. William P. & w, Sarah, gct
Farmington MM, N. Y.

1855, 2, 8. Mariah Dewey (form Smith) dis

1858, 1, 13. Isabella Fuller (form Smith) dis

1859, 9, 8. Lucina F. dis

1862, 5, 8. Sarah gct Farmington MM, N. Y.

1879, 3, 13. Charles recrq

SMOLK

----, --, --. Mary, w Abraham, rocf Scipio MM,
dtd 1834,2,12 (rem to Kalamazoo)

SNYDER

1841, 11, 11. Abigail dis mou

SORBY

1852, 5, 13. Mary (form Talbott) dis by
Middleton MM for mou & jas

SOULE

1845, 7, 7. Mahala L. dt Benjamin & Mahala
C., b Rollins, Lenawee Co., Mich.

1840, 9, 10. George [Sowle] rocf Duanesburgh
MM, dtd 1836,6,24

1844, 12, 12. Benjamin & w, Mahala, & minor ch
Matilda, Sarah M., Benjamin C. & Mabel
E., rocf Farmington MM, dtd 1844,10,24

1846, 11, 12. Howland rocf Farmington MM, dtd
1846,10,22

1846, 12, 10. Benjamin co

1848, 11, 9. Matilda Lamb (form Soule) dis
mcd & neglecting attendance

1850, 3, 14. Joel rocf Butternuts MM, dtd
1849,8,1

SOUTHWICK

----, --, --. Smith A. rocf Collins MM, dtd
1837,3,30

1838, 1, 11. Hannah Lapham, dt Ezra & Deborah Southwick, rocf Collins MM, dtd 1837,
1,26

1838, 1, 11. Smith A. rpd mcd by Collins MM

----, --, --. Ezra & w, Deborah, & minor ch,
Elizabeth, Mary Jane & Laura, rocf Collins
MM, dtd 1838,12,27

1839, 3, 14. Ford & w, Deborah, a minor ch,
Elizabeth, Mary Jane & Laura, rocf Collins
MM, dtd 1838,12,27

1839, 12, 12. Abraham L. & w, Maria, & minor
s, Albert, rocf Collins MM, dtd 1839,9,26

SOUTHWORTH

1860, 7, 12. Abram L. rqct Collins MM, N. Y.

STANLY

1871, 9, 27. Gertrude, dt Fleming & Eunice,
Raisin, Lenawee Co., Mich., d

1877, 12, 25. Josephine m William J. BIRDSALL

1878, 11, 7. Eunice [Stanley] co

1879, 11, 13. Fleming A. & Eunice [Stanley]
appointed elders

STAPLES

1837, 11, 9. Jacob rocf East Hossack MM, dtd
1837,8,20

STEER

1838, 3, 15. Hannah M. m Sands BROWNELL
1838, 6, 7. David Quincey, s Joseph & Deb.,
   b Rollin, Lenawee Co., Mich.
1840, 7, 11. Jane M. m Isaac TRESCOTT
1842, 11, 17. Isaac, Rollin, Lenawe Co., Mich.,
   s David & Phebe; m at Adrian, Elizabeth
   COMSTOCK, dt Jared & Catharine, Adrian,
   Lenawe Co., Mich.
      Ch: Catharine b 1843, 8, 25 Rollin, Lena-
      wee Co., Mich.
1848, 11, 16. Benjamin W., Raisin, Lenawee Co.,
   Mich., s David & Phebe; m at Adrian, Emily
   HOAG, dt Hazael & Sarah B., the form dec,
   Adrian, Lenawee Co., Mich.
1849, 9, 20. Greenberry P., Raisin, Lenawee
   Co., Mich., s David & Phebe; m at Adrian,
   Sarah Jane HOAG, dt Nathaniel P. & Issa-
   bella, form dec, Raisin, Lenawee Co., Mich.
1862, 8, 28. Kinard d ae 8y 8m 19d
1868, 3, 2. Phebe d ae 83y 9m 2d
1876, 10, 18. Ida m William P. HENLY

----, --, --. David & w, Phebe, & minor ch,
   William M., Isaac, Benjamin W., Jane M.,
   Amos, Greenbury P. & Harriet, rocf Short
   Creek MM, O., dtd 1833,11,19
----, --, --. Hannah M. rocf Short Creek MM,
   O., dtd 1833,11,19
----, --, --. Joseph Jr. rocf Short Creek MM,
   O., dtd 1834,10,21
----, --, --. Deborah H. rocf Short Creek MM,
   dtd 1835,10,20
1838, 9, 13. David co
1839, 1, 10. William dis mcd
1839, 4, 11. Joseph & w, Deborah H., & minor
   ch, Elisha B. & David Quincy, gct Short
   Creek MM, O.
1839, 8, 8. David & w gct Mount Pleasant, O.
1839, 9, 12. David co
1839, 9, 12. Phebe co
1839, 10, 10. Phebe appointed an elder
1840, 9, 10. Phebe co
1840, 10, 8. David co
1844, 11, 7. David co
1845, 12, 11. David co
1846, 11, 12. Phebe co
1846, 12, 10. David co
1847, 11, 11. Phebe co
1847, 12, 9. David co
1848, 12, 14. David co
1848, 12, 14. Phebe co
1849, 12, 13. David co
1851, 1, 9. David co
1852, 10, 14. Amos R. com by Adrian PM for jas;
   complaint forwarded to Cincinnati MM as he
   resided within limits of that mtg
1853, 12, 8. Isaac & w, Elizabeth, & minor ch,
   Catherine, Jane & Joseph, rocf Rolin MM,
   dtd 1853,11,12
1855, 7, 12. David & w, Phebe, gct Red Cedar
   MM, Ia.
1855, 7, 12. Greenberry P. & w, Sarah Jane,

& minor dt, Isabel, gct Red Cedar MM, Ia.
1855, 7, 12. Harriet gct Red Cedar MM, Ia.
1862, 1, 9. David & w, Phebe, rocf Winasheik
   MM, Ia., dtd 1861,9,28

STODDARD

----, --, --. Rhoda, w Nathan, rocf Farmington
   MM, dtd 1835,8,27
1840, 9, 10. Zimrada (Rhoda) rocf Farmington
   MM, dtd 1840,5,20

STOUT

1839, 9, 12. Mary G. appointed clerk
1842, 11, 10. Mary G. appointed clerk in place
   of Lydia H. Gibbons, dec
1843, 4, 13. Ann Comfort appointed to serve
   as clerk in place of Mary G. Stout, who rq
   to be released
1843, 11, 9. Mary G. dis neglecting attendance & jas

STRETCH

1879, 5, 8. Alice recrq
1879, 5, 8. Anne recrq

STRICTH

1843, 5, 11. Cert rec for Jesse from Cheshire
   MM, Old England, dtd 1842,11,16, endorsed
   to Raisin MM

STRONG

1858, 6, 17. Enoch D., Rollin, Lenawee Co.,
   Mich., s Daniel & Mercy, dec; m at Adrian,
   Sarah Jane HOAG, dt Jacob & Sarah, form
   dec, Raisin, Lenawee Co., Mich.
1870, 10, 20. Anna Mary, dt Enoch D. & Sarah
   J., Raisin, Lenawee Co., Mich., d ae 2m
   28d

1844, 2, 8. Asa W. rocf Hartland MM, dtd
   1843,9,4
----, --, --. Enoch D. rocf Hartland MM, N.Y.,
   dtd 1843,9,14
1858, 10, 14. Sarah J. gct Rollin MM
1863, 12, 10. Enoch D. & w, Sarah Jane, rocf
   Rollin MM, dtd 1863,11,5
1864, 6, 9. Enoch D. co
1865, 6, 8. Enoch D. co
1866, 6, 7. Enoch D. co
1867, 6, 13. Enoch D. co

STYLES

----, --, --. Robert rocf Rochester MM held
   at Wheatland, dtd 1836,9,23
1840, 6, 11. Caroline recrq
1842, 8, 11. Caroline S. (form Styles) dis
   mou
1847, 8, 12. Robert gct Millford MM, Wayne
   Co., Ind.

SUTTON

1847, 5, 19. Asa W., Bedford, Calhoun Co.,
   Mich., s Isaac & Sarah; m at Tecumseh,

SUTTON, continued
    Sarah A. TITUS, dt Samuel SATTERTHWAITE &
    Hannah, latter dec, Tecumseh, Lenawee Co.,
    Mich.
1854, 11, 15. Nehemiah, Detroit, Wayne Co.,
    Mich., s Isaac & Sarah U., Bedford, Cal-
    houn Co., Mich.; m at Tecumseh, Mary E.
    SATTERTHWAIT, dt Reuben & Rachel, both
    dec, Tecumseh, Lenawee Co., Mich.
1871, 10, 29. Asa W., Raisin, Lenawee Co.,
    Mich., d
1872, 9, 8. Sarah W., Raisin, Lenawee Co.,
    Mich., d
1873, 1, 1. Hannah A. m Benjamin SWAN
1873, 12, 26. Sarah A., Raisin, Lenawee Co.,
    Mich., d
1874, 1, 26. Moses, Raisin, Lenawee Co.,
    Mich., d
1875, 9, 9. Elizabeth R. m Thomas G. MEAD

----, --, --. Sarah W., w Isaac, rocf Scipio
    MM, dtd 1838,3,14
1838, 6, 7. William, Edward, Moses, Aaron,
    David & Nehemiah M., ch Isaac & Sarah,
    rocf Scipio MM, dtd 1838,3,14
1842, 4, 7. Edward gct Dartmouth MM, Mass.
1846, 1, 8. Asa rocf Creek MM, Clinton, Dut-
    ches Co., N. Y., dtd 1845,7,18
1847, 10, 14. Sarah A. appointed clerk
1847, 11, 11. Aaron gct New York MM
1850, 11, 7. Sarah A. appointed clerk
1859, 12, 8. David gct Milford MM, Ind.
1862, 5, 8. David gct Milford MM, Wayne Co.,
    Ind.

SWAN
1873, 1, 1. Benjamin, Tecumseh, Lenawee Co.,
    Mich., s Frederick & Patience D.; m at
    home of Hannah A. Sutton in Raisin, Hannah
    A. SUTTON, dt Asa W. & Sarah A., Raisin,
    Lenawee Co., Mich.
1879, 8, 19. Lydia B. m Edwin TAYLOR

1879, 8, 14. Lydia B. rocf Salem MM, Mass.,
    dtd 1879,7,10

SWEET
1838, 6, 7. Hermes & ch, Daniel, Lucius &
    Lydia, rocf Queensbury MM, dtd 1838,2,28

SWEETLAND
1838, 1, 11. Experience rocf Collins MM, dtd
    1837,1,26 (living in Livonia, Wayne Co.,
    Mich.)

TABER
1861, 9, 12. Ann (form Mower) dis

TAGG
----, --, --. Susannah, w George, & ch, Mary,
    ae about 15, John 14, Wilmot 12, Eliza 9
    and George 6, rocf New York MM, dtd 1835,
    9,2

TALBOTT
1836, 10, 20. Susannah m Jesse DARLINGTON
----, --, --. Benjamin & Priscilla
    Ch: Chandler b 1842, 8, 12 Woodstock,
       Lenawee Co., Mich.
      William B. b 1845, 12, 28
       Lenawee Co., Mich. d 1847, 8,20 Wood-
       stock, Lenawee Co., Mich.
1848, 12, 3. Priscilla, dt William & Sarah,
    Woodstock, Lenewee Co., Mich., d ae 42y
    27d

----, --, --. Benjamin & w, Precilla, rocf
    Smithfield MM, O., dtd 1835,4,20
----, --, --. John & w, Rachel, & s, David B.,
    rocf Flushing MM, dtd 1835,6,25
----, --, --. Mary S. rocf Flushing MM, dtd
    1835,6,25
----, --, --. Susannah C. rocf Flushing MM,
    dtd 1835,6,25
1839, 10, 10. Benjamin I. & w, Priscilla, gct
    Middleton MM
1839, 12, 12. Cert granted to Middleton MM for
    Benjamin I. & w, Priscilla, returned; now
    living within limits of this mtg
1841, 9, 9. Rachel co of Rollin Mtg
1842, 9, 8. Rachel co
1843, 2, 9. Benjamin I. con misconduct
1848, 10, 2. David B. dis neglecting attend-
    ance
1850, 11, 7. Benjamin I. & minor s, Chandler,
    gct Pleasant Plain MM
1851, 1, 9. Rachel co
1852, 5, 13. Mary Sorby (form Talbott) dis
    mou & jas by Middleton MM

TANNER
1838, 5, 10. Tilden rocf Smyrna MM held at
    Brookfield, dtd 1838,4,3
1849, 12, 13. Tildon co
1851, 1, 9. Tildon co

TAYLOR
1843, 5, 18. Joshua, Tecumseh, Lenawee Co.,
    Mich., s Thomas & Martha; m at Adrian,
    Mary COMFORT, dt Aaron & Ann, Raisin, Len-
    awee Co., Mich.
    Ch: Edwin C. b 1844, 7, 23 Tecumseh,
       Lenawee Co., Mich.
1870, 7, 15. Marthanna m Calvin W. PEARSON
1879, 8, 19. Edwin, Wyandotte, Wyandotte
    Co., Kans., s Joshua & Mary, Raisin, Lena-
    wee Co., Mich.; m at Tecumseh, Lydia B.
    SWAN, dt Frederic & Patience D., New Sha-
    ron, Franklin Co., Maine
1840, 7, 9. Joshua rocf Burlington MM, N.J.
    dtd 1840,4,6
1846, 8, 13. Joseph Gibbons gct Burlington
    MM, to m Margaret Taylor
1878, 10, 10. Mary C. appointed clerk
1878, 11, 7. Mary C. co
1879, 10, 9. Mary C. appointed clerk
1880, 2, 12. Thomas E. relrq

TENNANT
1884, 10, 16. Olivia C. m S. Emlen COMFORT

TEST
1847, 7, 8. Huldah Haviland (form Test) dis

THAYER
----, --, --. Marcy & w, Amy, & minor ch, Caro-
    lina Matilda, Phebe C. & Wait Almina, rocf
    Hartland MM, dtd 1834,10,16

THOMAS
1837, 5, 26. John b
1875, 8, 12. Isaac, Short Crick, Harrison
    Co., O., s Peter & Mary, Harrison Co., O.;
    m at Adrian, Phebe G. GIBBONS, dt Webster
    & Ruth THORN, Raisin, Lenawee Co., Mich.

----, --, --. Nathan rocf Short Creek MM, O.,
    dtd 1835,3,24

THOMPSON
----, --, --. Elizabeth, w Jeremiah, rocf
    Farmington MM, dtd 1834,6,26

THORN
----, --, --. ----- m Ruth ----- b 1782,11,12,
    Washington, N. Y.
      Ch: Martin M. b 1818, 1, 26 Royalton
          Phebe G.   " 1820, 7, 6   "
1845, 5, 3. Ruth, Raisin, Lenawee Co., Mich.,
    d
1851, 6, 13. Phebe G. m Joseph GIBBONS
1851, 10, 7. Webster, Raisin, Lenawee Co.,
    Mich., d ae 81y
1875, 8, 12. Isaac Thomas, Short Crick, Har-
    rison Co., O., s Peter & Mary, Harrison
    Co., O.; m at Adrian, Phebe G. GIBBONS,
    dt Webster & Ruth THORN, Raisin, Lenawee
    Co., Mich.

----, --, --. Ruth & minor ch, Martin M. &
    Phebe G. rocf Hartland MM, dtd 1835,12,17
1839, 10, 10. Webster com by Hartland MM; con
    misconduct in Hartland MM, but referred to
    this mtg as he resided within limits of
    this mtg; acknowledgement accepted here
    1839,11,7
1850, 7, 11. Martin M. con misconduct
1852, 12, 9. Martin M. gct New York MM

THORNTON
1840, 10, 8. Rhoda (form Aldrich) dis mcd &
    neglecting attendance

TITUS
1838, 11, 3. Anna, Rollin, Lenawee Co., Mich.,
    d
1839, 11, 14. Stephen, Raisin, Lenawe Co.,
    Mich., s Samuel, dec, & Mary; m at Adrian,
    Sarah SATTERTHWAITE, dt Samuel & Hannah,
    dec, Tecumseh, Lenawe Co., Mich.
1841, 2, 3. Samuel S., Raisin, Lenawee Co.,

                                Mich., d
1842, 8, 8. Edmund, s Stephen & Sarah, b
    Raisin, Lenawee Co., Mich.
1842, 8, 22. Edmond, Raisin, Lenewee Co.,
    Mich., d
1844, 11, 29. Stephen, s Samuel & Mary, Raisin
    Lenawee Co., Mich., d ae 3ly 8m 2d
1845, 3, 5. Orson, s Isaac & Anna, Rollin,
    Lenawee Co., Mich., d in 29th yr
1845, 3, 22. Isaac, Rollin, Lenawee Co.,
    Mich., d in 55th yr
1847, 5, 19. Sarah A. m Asa W. SUTTON

----, --, --. Isaac & w, Anna, & minor ch, Or-
    sin, Nelson & James, rocf Hartland MM, dtd
    1833,6,25
----, --, --. Eliza T. rocf Farmington MM, dtd
    1833,6,25
1839, 9, 12. Stephen rocf Westbury & Jericho
    MM, N. Y., dtd 1839,8,14
1845, 3, 13. James dis disunity

TOWN
1848, 5, 11. Rosanna (form Derbyshire) dis
    neglecting attendance & jas

TOWNSEND
1844, 10, 10. Joseph T. rocf Middleton MM, dtd
    1843,8,10

TRAP
1842, 4, 7. Eliza's d rpd

TRESCOTT
1840, 7, 11. Isaac, Salem, Columbiana Co.,
    O., s Samuel C. & Sophia; m at Rollin,
    Jane M. STEER, dt David & Phebe, Rollin,
    Lenawe Co., Mich.

1841, 1, 14. Jane M., w Isaac, gct Salem MM,
    O.

TRUEBLOOD
----, --, --. Benjamin rocf Blue River MM,
    Washington Co., Ind., dtd 1870,9,10

TUCKER
1857, 1, 8. Daniel B. rocf Salem MM, Ia.,
    dtd 1856,9,17
1857, 7, 9. Daniel B. gct Salem MM, Ia.

TWITCHEL
----, --, --. Sarah rocf Ferrisburgh MM held
    at Monkton, dtd 1832,5,30

UNDERWOOD
1835, 10, 19. John H. b Lenawee, Washtenaw
    Co., Mich.
1837, 1, 19. Elizabeth m Gideon HARKNESS
1838, 10, 3. Cornelius M., Palmyra, Lenawee
    Co., Mich., d
----, --, --. James F. & Rachel
      Ch: Lydia Jane b 1840, 4, 9 Tecumseh,

UNDERWOOD, James F. & Rachel, continued
    Lenawee Co., Mich.
    Ch: Elizabeth
        R.   b 1842, 9, 3, Tecumseh,
    Lenawee Co., Mich.
        Ann Eliza b   Palmyra,
    Lenawee Co., Mich.

----, --, --. Elizabeth rocf Farmington MM,
    dtd 1833,9,26
----, --, --. John & w, Catherine, & minor ch,
    Edwin, Hannah P., Charles, George & Van-
    wyck, rocf Farmington MM, dtd 1833,9,26
----, --, --. Mary rocf Farmington MM, dtd
    1833,9,26
----, --, --. Edward & w, Anna C., & minor ch,
    Mary Ann, Thomas, Lydia & Cornelius M.,
    rocf Farmington MM, dtd 1836,10,24
1837, 5, 11. John recommended a minister
1837, 6, 8. John appointed clerk
1838, 6, 7. Mary Hoxie (form Underwood) dis
1838, 9, 13. Edward co
1839, 6, 13. John appointed clerk
1839, 9, 12. Anna C. co
1839, 9, 12. Edward co
1839, 12, 12. Rachel recrq
1840, 7, 9. John appointed clerk
1840, 9, 10. Anna C. co
1840, 9, 10. James F. rocf Farmington MM, dtd
    1840,7,23
1840, 10, 8. Edward co
1841, 4, 8. Catherine appointed an elder
1841, 9, 9. Anna C. co of Palmyra Mtg
1842, 5, 12. Edwin con mou
1843, 11, 9. James F. co
1851, 6, 12. Van Wyke con mou
1879, 10, 9. Sarah C. rocf Raisin MM, dtd
    1879,9,10

UPTON
1847, 9, 11. Adonijah d
1847, 10, 18. Freeborn d

1837, 7, 13. Samuel & w, Charlotte, & ch,
    Samuel S., Daniel, Harvey, Stephen, Ed-
    mund, John, James, Charlotte & Gulielma,
    rocf Oswego MM held at Poughkeepsie, 1836,
    12,14
1846, 10, 8. Adonijah & w, Freborn, rocf
    Scipio MM, dtd 1846,8,19

UTLEY
----, --, --. Julia Ann Scradder (or Scudder)
    (form Utley) rocf Scipio MM, dtd 1833,4,17

VAIL
1837, 9, 7. Charlotte dis
1838, 2, 8. Albert L. dis mcd; Rahway &
    Plainfield MM notified

VANAKEN
1845, 9, 11. Sally A. (form Howell) dis
    neglecting attendance & mou

VANDERBURGH
1839, 8, 8. Caroline rocf Norwich MM, dtd
    1839,6,12
1839, 8, 8. Clayman & w, Roxana, & minor ch,
    Isaac, William D., Ann Maria, Charlotte
    Jane & George Warren, rocf Norwich MM,
    dtd 1839,6,12
1840, 2, 6. Cert for John & Robert returned
    to Salem MM, Ia.

VANDUZER
1845, 4, 30. John d in 79th yr

1840, 2, 6. John & w, Margaret, rocf Farming-
    ton MM, dtd 1839,6,27

VAN VOORHIS
1837, 7, 13. Eleanor rocf Oswego MM held at
    Poughkeepsie, dtd 1836,12,14

VIBER
1839, 12, 12. Esther con mcd (com by Little
    Eggharbour MM)
1840, 7, 9. Esther rocf Little Eggharbour
    MM, N. J., dtd 1840,5,14
1844, 3, 14. Alice [Vibber] (form Bowerman)
    con mou (com by Raisin MM)

WALKER
1840, 5, 21. Benjamin G., Adrian, Lenawee
    Co., Mich., s Stephen & Lydia, the latter
    dec, b 1812,10,13 Butternuts, Oswego Co.,
    N. Y., d 1851,4,17 Tecumseh, Lenawee Co.,
    Mich., ae 38y 6m 4d; m at Adrian, Mary Ann
    WEST, dt Abraham & Mary, Adrian, Lenawee
    Co., Mich.
    Ch: Samuel G. b 1841, 6, 14 Tecumseh,
        Lenawee Co., Mich.
        Stephen A. b 1844, 3, 30   "
        Lenawee Co., Mich. d 1845,10,2 ae 1y
        6m 2d
        Caroline b Tecumseh, Lenawee Co.,
        Mich., 1845,9,2

1837, 5, 11. Benjamin G. rocf Hamburgh MM,
    dtd 1837,3,29
1853, 7, 14. Mary Ann dis neglecting attend-
    ance & being out of unity

WALTON
----, --, --. Joseph, Jacob Jr. & Timothy,
    rocf Scipio MM, dtd 1835,5,20 (residing
    in town of Salem, Washtenaw Co with
    parents; Joseph clear of m engagements;
    Jacob & Timothy in their minority)

WANZER
1877, 8, 28. Emily m Joseph J. MILLS

WARREN
1857, 1, --. Samuel, Fairfield, Lenawee Co.,
    Mich., d

WARREN, continued
----, --, --. Samuel & w, Lucinda, & minor ch,
    Allen & Austin A., rocf Farmington MM, dtd
    1834,5,22

WAUGH
----, --, --. David H., Phebe, Levi, Hannah,
    Huldah & Lydia, ch Reuben & Keziah, rocf
    Collins MM, N. Y., dtd 1837,1,26

WEAVER
1838, 10, 18. Phebe m James CARR

1838, 4, 12. John & w, Lydia, & minor ch,
    John W., Charles H. & Gilbert, rocf Hart-
    land MM, dtd 1838,2,2
1839, 9, 12. Lydia co
1840, 6, 11. Jane T., w Elisha F., rocf Hart-
    land MM, dtd 1840,1,23
1841, 5, 13. Elisha T. & minor s, William N.,
    rocf Bridgewater MM held at New Hartford,
    dtd 1841,4,22
1841, 11, 11. Elisha T. & w, Jane T., & minor
    ch, William N. & Sarah Ann, gct Elba MM
1842, 5, 12. John H. & w, Lydia, & minor ch,
    John W. & Charles, gct Farmington MM, N.Y.
1843, 12, 14. Gilbert gct Elba MM, N. Y.

WEBB
1782, 6, 29. Ezekiel b Shawangunk, Ulster
    Co., N. Y.
1791, 6, 22. Fanny b Stratford, Fairfield
    Co., Conn.
1809, 6, 10. Emeline (Hoag) b Hackensack,
    Bergen Co., N. J.
1810, 12, 10. Julia Maria b Hackensack, Bergen
    Co., N. J.
1812, 11, 4. Adelia b Hackensack, Bergen Co.,
    N. J.
1815, 5, 22. Nathan Hall b Phelps, Ontario
    Co., N. Y.
1818, 10, 9. Charlotte b Farmington, Ontario
    Co., N. Y.
1821, 2, 5. Ezekiel Deyo b Royalton, Niagara
    Co., N. Y.
1823, 3, 1. Catharine b Royalton, Niagara
    Co., N. Y.
1825, 2, 3. James Knap b Lockport, Niagara
    Co., N. Y.
1828, 1, 12. Edwin Lorenzo b Farmington, Oak-
    land Co., Mich.
1830, 3, 9. Fanny Louisa b Farmington, Oak-
    land Co., Mich.
1831, 10, 21. Amos Hoag, Farmington, Oakland
    Co., Mich., s Elisha, dec, & Dorcas; m at
    Adrian, Emeline POWER, dt Ezekiel WEBB &
    w, Fanny, Farmington, Oakland Co., Mich.
1833, 12, 28. Joseph Chittenden b Tecumseh,
    Lenawee Co., Mich.
1833, 12, 29. Joseph Chittenden, Tecumseh,
    Lenawee Co., Mich., d
1836, 9, 16. Adelia m Nathan H. BASSETT
1838, 4, 11. Nathan H., Raisin, Lenawee Co.,

Mich., d
1853, 8, 30. Fanny, Raisin, Lenawee Co.,
    Mich., d ae 63y

1837, 10, 12. Nathan H. rpd mou; d before case
    was settled
1839, 6, 13. Ezekiel dis attending mtg held
    contrary to discipline
1840, 2, 6. Catharine dis neglecting mtg &
    jas
1843, 2, 9. Ezekiel D. com by Adrian PM for
    mcd
1843, 4, 13. Sarah Webb (form Bassett) dis
    mcd
1843, 6, 8. Ezekiel D. dis mcd
1852, 8, 12. Edwin dis neglecting attendance

WEBSTER
1847, 3, 29. Joseph, Rollin, Lenawee Co.,
    Mich., d ae 33y 3m 6d

1837, 4, 13. William rocf Norwich MM, Upper
    Canada, dtd 1837,1,11
1846, 10, 8. Joseph rocf Farmington MM, dtd
    1844,3,28, endorsed by Norwich MM, Canada,
    dtd 1846,8,12

WEEKS
1871, 11, 15. Sarah Ann, Raisin, Lenawee Co.,
    Mich., d

1845, 5, 8. Susanna Wilson (form Weeks) con
    mcd (com by Elba MM; Elba MM informed)
----, --, --. Samantha rocf Indianapolis MM,
    dtd 1870,5,21

WELLS
1779, 7, 29. Mary b Smithfield, Providence
    Co., R. I.
1854, 4, 8. Eliza C., dt Russell & Eliza,
    Raisin, Lenawee Co., Mich., d ae 19y
1864, 6, 23. Meriba m Asa Wing ROGERS

----, --, --. Mary rocf Farmington MM, dtd
    1832,7,26
1851, 9, 11. Russel & w, Eliza, & minor ch,
    Russel Thomas, Eliza C., Sarah H., Meribah
    & Julia Ann, rocf Elba MM held at Shelba,
    dtd 1851,8,19
1880, 1, 8. Julia A. recrq

WERTZ
1839, 4, 1. Charles H. rpd mcd by Raisin PM

WEST
1787, 4, 4. Abraham b Stanford, Dutchess
    Co., N. Y.
1799, 3, 13. Anna b Charlton, Saratoga Co.,
    N. Y.
1816, 2, 27. Elisabeth b Hallowwell, Upper
    Canada
1817, 12, 11. Mary Ann b Elba, Genessee Co.,
    N. Y.

WEST, continued
1824, 9, 21. Elijah b Elba, Genessee Co.,
     N. Y.
1826, 12, 15. Tabathy Jane b Logan, Lenawee
     Co., Mich.
1828, 4, 23. Huldah b Logan, Lenawee Co.,
     Mich.
1830, 7, 28. George b Logan, Lenawee Co.,
     Mich.
1833, 5, 20. Susannah b Logan, Lenawee Co.,
     Mich.
1835, 3, 13. Cordelia b Logan, Lenawee Co.,
     Mich.
1838, 7, 2. Sarah b Adrian, Lenawee Co.,
     Mich.
1840, 5, 31. Mary Ann m Benjamin G. WALKER
1842, 6, 16. Maria m Henry LEEDS
1843, 8, 17. Elizabeth m Ira SMITH

1838, 5, 10. Maria rec in mbrp
1838, 9, 13. Abraham co
1839, 3, 14. Benedict & Mary rocf Collins
     MM, dtd 1838,12,27
1839, 9, 12. Abraham co
1840, 7, 9. Levi & w & ch, Nathaniel, Lydia,
     Jane, Ira, William W., David L., Levi &
     Ichabad, rocf Norwich MM, Upper Canada,
     dtd 1839,8,14
1841, 2, 11. Sophia (form West) con mcd
1842, 7, 14. Lana recrq
1847, 8, 12. Huldah (form West) dis mcd
1849, 4, 12. Jane Hitchcock (form West) dis
     mou & mcd
1849, 6, 7. Lydia Jane Munson (form West)
     dis mou & mcd (Raisin MM notified)
1850, 4, 11. Elijah F. dis mou
1855, 3, 8. George rqct Red Cedar MM, Ia.
1855, 4, 12. Abram & w, Anna, & minor ch,
     Sarah & Lydia Ann, gct Red Cedar MM
1855, 4, 12. Cordelia gc
1857, 1, 8. Susannah Currin (form West) dis

WESTGATE
1763, 10, 15. Jonathan b Tivertown, R. I.
1777, 6, 29. Fanny b Dutchess Co., N. Y.
1792, 12, 19. Jeremiah b Saratoga, Saratoga
     Co., N. Y.
1816, 11, 6. Charles H. b Providence, Sara-
     toga Co., N. Y.
----, --, --. Jeremiah m Amy ----- d 1826,4,
     11 ae 28y 6m 2d
     Ch: Charles H.
         Jeremiah
         Amy   b 1820, 8, 12
         Nancy   d 1824, 8,15
            ae 1y 5m 9d
         Pamelia   b 1825, 3, 28
         Amanda
----, --, --. Sylvanus b 1797,5,15 Providence,
     Saratoga Co.; m Esther ----- b 1802,3,2
     Providence, Saratoga Co.
     Ch: Esther   b 1818, 7, 7
         Jonathan   " 1819, 11, 18

Ch: Sylvanus W. b 1821, 4, 11
    Samuel   " 1822, 11, 19
    Henry G.   " 1824, 12, 18
    Fanny M.   " 1826, 3, 17
    Mary
    Wanton
    Austin   " 1830, 9, 19
1819, 3, 17. Jeremiah Jun. b Royalton, Niag-
     ara Co., N. Y.
1824, 12, 18. Henry G. b Royalton, Niagara
     Co., N. Y.
1827, 5, 25. Mary S. b Royalton, Niagara Co.,
     N. Y.
1828, 5, 27. Amanda b Royalton, Niagara Co.,
     N. Y.
1829, 3, 2. Wanton b Royalton, Niagara Co.,
     N. Y.
1833, 4, 18. William b Logan, Lenewee Co.,
     Mich.
1836, 8, 7. Jeremiah, Raisin, Lenewee Co.,
     Mich., s Jonathan & Dorcas, the latter
     dec; m Dorcas HAYNES, dt Joshua & Abigail
     BOWERMAN, Raisin, Lenawe Co., Mich.
1837, 4, 6. Jonathan, Raisin, Lenawee Co.,
     Mich., d
1837, 5, 3. Nelson b
1838, 12, 24. Orlando b Raisin, Lenawee Co.,
     Mich.
1840, 6, 18. Albert, s Jeremiah & Dorcas, b
     Raisin, Lenawee Co., Mich.
1840, 11, 18. Pamilia m Joshua C. BOWERMAN
1842, 4, 13. Jonathan, Raisin, Lenawe Co.,
     Mich., s Sylvanus & Esther; m at Ypsilan-
     ti, Hannah E. GORTON, dt David & Hannah,
     Ypsilanti, Washtenaw Co., Mich.

----, --, --. Jonathan & Fanny, rocf Hartland
     MM, dtd 1832,5,1
----, --, --. Sylvanus & w, Esther, & ch,
     Esther, Jonathan, Sylvanus, Samuel, Henry
     G., Fanny, Mary, Wanton & Austin, rocf
     Hartland MM held at Lockport, dtd 1832,1,5
----, --, --. Jeremiah & minor ch, Charles H.,
     Jeremiah, Amy, Pamelia & Amanda, rocf
     Hartland MM held at Lockport, dtd 1833,4,3
     (or 30)
1838, 6, 7. Jeremiah dis mcd
1839, 8, 8. Charles H. dis mou
1839, 9, 12. Sylvanus co

WHALLEY
1843, 5, 11. Cert rec for Amelia from Hard-
     west MM, Liverpool, Old England, endorsed
     to Raisin MM

WHITE
1763, 4, 27. Edith b in R. I.
1764, 9, 14. John b near London, England

----, --, --. John & w, Edith, rocf Hartland
     MM held at Lockport, dtd 1833,4,30
1838, 11, 8. Dorothea, Chalkley & Joel, minor
     ch Crawford, rocf Chesterfield MM, N. J.,

WHITE, continued
    dtd 1838,9,4

WILLIAMS
1841, 1, 8. Benjamin, s Richard & Abigail,
    b Ypsilanti, Washtenaw Co., Mich.

1840, 4, 9. Richard recrq

WILLITTS
1778, 7, 9. Richard [Willitt] b Stafford,
    Monmouth Co., N. J.
1792, 9, 6. Deliverance b Stafford, Monmouth
    Co., N. J.
1804, 9, 24. Stephen [Willitt] b Stafford,
    Monmouth Co., N. J.
1813, 5, 18. Desiah S. [Willitt] b Penington,
    Monroe Co., N. Y.
1818, 5, 4. Micajah b Penington, Monroe Co.,
    N. Y.
1820, 1, 29. Judith [Willitt] b Penington,
    Monroe Co., N. Y.
1878, 6, 27. Samuel Leeds, Adrian, Lenawee
    Co., Mich., s Samuel & Ruth; m at Adrian,
    Elizabeth WORTHINGTON, dt Jeremiah & Sarah
    WILLETS, Phila.

----, --, --. Micajah & w, Judith, rocf Farm-
    ington MM, dtd 1832,6,21
----, --, --. Richard rocf Farmington MM, dtd
    1833,7,25
----, --, --. Deliverance [Willits], w Richard,
    & minor ch, Micajah & Judith, rocf Hart-
    land MM, dtd 1834,12,18
----, --, --. Micajah [Willits] & w, Judith,
    rocf Farmington MM, dtd 1835,9,24
1838, 4, 12. Benjamin dis mou
1840, 5, 14. John recrq
1840, 8, 13. Jane [Willets] (form Hathaway)
    dis mou
1840, 9, 10. Deliverance [Willets] co
1840, 10, 8. Richard co
1841, 9, 9. Deliverance [Willet] co of Ypsil-
    anti Mtg
1848, 9, 7. John [Willits] con mou & mcd

WILSON
1842, 4, 7. Watty [Willson] con misconduct
1845, 5, 8. Susanna (form Weeks) con mcd
    (com by Elba MM; Elba MM informed)
----, --, --. William S. & w, Margaret, rocf
    Junius MM, N. Y., dtd 1845,3,26 (H)
1846, 2, 5. Azaliah rpd mcd; Farmington MM
    rq this mtg to treat with him as he re-
    sided within limits of this mtg; rem from
    limits of this mtg; complaint returned to
    Farmington
1849, 6, 7. Michael S. recrq
1853, 7, 14. Thomas & w, Lydia, rocf Raisin MM
1854, 7, 13. Thomas & w, Lydia, gct Raisin MM
1855, 7, 12. Michael dis
1879, 5, 8. Martin W. relrq

WING
1839, 9, 12. Alvira, w Walter, rocf Farmington
    MM, dtd 1839,4,25
1847, 7, 8. Elvira dis neglecting attendance
    & jas

WOOD
1865, 8, 17. Vincent, Rollin, Lenawee Co.,
    Mich., s Joseph & Angeline; m at Adrian,
    Mary C. HARKNESS, dt Richard & Deborah R.,
    Adrian, Lenawee Co., Mich.

1847, 5, 13. Sarah (form Carr) con mou & mcd
1865, 8, 10. Vincent prcf Rollin MM, to m
1866, 4, 12. Vincent rocf Rollin MM, dtd
    1866,2,10

WOOLCOTT
----, --, --. Lydia, w Jason, rocf Farmington
    MM, dtd 1836,8,25

WORCESTER
1771, 10, 6. Amos b Southberry, Litchfield
    Co., Vt.
1806, 7, 7. Eunice b Providence, Saratoga
    Co., N. Y.
1835, 7, 15. Amos [Wooster], Palmyra, Lena-
    we Co., Mich., s Sylvester & Mercy, both
    dec; m at Raisin, Lodema HOAG, dt Jesse &
    Martha BRAMAN, the form dec, Palmyra, Lena-
    wee Co., Mich.

----, --, --. Eunice [Worster] rocf Farmington
    MM, dtd 1834,10,23
----, --, --. Amos rocf Rochester MM held at
    Wheatland, dtd 1835,5,29
1838, 6, 7. Amos dis neglecting attendance
1840, 5, 14. Lodema [Wooster] dis neglecting
    attendance & disunity
1844, 7, 11. Lodema [Wooster] con misconduct;
    rst at Raisin MM as she resided within
    limits of that mtg

WORTHINGTON
1878, 6, 27. Elizabeth m Samuel LEEDS

YOUNG
----, --, --. Phebe R. rocf Marlborough MM
    held at Plattskill, dtd 1868,8,26

    *   *   *   *   *   *   *
CHASE
1807, 9, 23. Anna b Providence, Saratoga
    Co., N. Y.

Schlueter 1337
Schnapp 1183
Schneider 1337
Schogin 434
Schofield Schofield 108 272   314 350 434
    496 548 593 758 842 1076 1113 1114 1137
    1138 1183 (441 1109)
Scholes 548
School 1337
Schooley Schooly 17 57 71 108 167 273 314 350
    434 548 562 593 603 654 655 667 759 792
    793 842 859 916 990 1183 1222 (722 907)
Schopp 1337
Schorb 1222
Schorsten 1042
Schriber 1337
Schroeder 1337
Schulkins 1337
Schulte 1337
Schutzer 1292
Schwartz 1337
Schwicklick 842
Scolds 1262
Scott 57 132 159 273 314 350 434 435 496 548
    593 655 759 842 859 882 883 894 990 991
    1042 1075 1114 1183 1222 1262 1293 (466
    1074 1112)
Scotten 1262
Scovell 1262
Scudder 496
Scullion 759 842
Seachrist 991
Sealy 655 1184
Seaman Seamans 273 350 435 1293
Sears 273 435 436 496 548 593 759 794 1076 1114
    1293
Seaton 1293
Sebek 1337
Sebrell 759 760 894 991 1042
Sebring 1262
Seebert 1262
Seebohm 655
Seeds 273
Segar 760
Seigenthaler 760
Seiger 273 1337
Seigman 1337
Seipel 1262
Seity 1242
Selby 436 1114
Self 1262
Sellars Sellers 991 1222 1337
Sells Sell 273 1222
Selman Selmon 273 496
Semple 1337
Serven 760
Sessions 1262
Seward 549
Sewell 1293
Sexton 57 108 350
Seymour 1184 1231 1240
Shackleford 273
Shaddock 496

Shadle 1114
Shaffer Shafer Shaeffer Schaeffer 108 273 496
    655 760 842 894 1184 1222 1262 1293 1336
    1337
Shahl 159
Shallcross 274 314 350
Shallenberg 760 842
Shamblain 350
Shamel 549
Shanck 1337
Shane 496 655
Shaner 132 1138
Shankland 436
Shanks 1263
Shannon Shanon 274 496
Shaps 1337
Sharon 274 497
Sharp 57 108 132 159 274 350 436 497 549 655
    760 842 916 991 1114 1138 1184 1222 1293
    (613 680 985)
Sharpless 57 108 132 159 274 350 436 655 760
    883 991 1222 (122 613 639)
Sharpnack Sharpneck 57 760
Sharrack 436
Sharski 1337
Shaver 1263
Shaw 57 58 108 274 655 656 760 761 842 843
    883 894 916 991 1030 1114 1138 1184 1222
    1263 1293 1337
Shawver 1293
Shay 108
Shealey 1337
Shearon 108
Sheehan 991
Sheets Sheats 992 1240 1263 (939 1000)
Sheffield 1337
Sheldon 992 1240
Shelley 1293
Shepherd Shepperd Shepard 58 108 132 549 843
    1184 1198 1337
Shepler 274
Sherman Shearman 274 761 1184 1222 1223 1263
    1337
Sherrick 58
Sherry 1263
Shertzer 1293
Sherwood 1184 1240 1293
Sheward 436
Shields 274 1076 1184 1223
Shiell 761
Shiletto 497
Shimer 1338
Shinbron 656
Shinn 58 656 761 793 843 859 894 992 1021 1030
    (999)
Shipley 58 436
Shipman 656 1223 1240
Shirk 1293
Shirkler 761
Shisler 761 843
Shivey 1263
Shockley 1293
Shoe 761